BUTTERWORTHS
INTELLECTUAL PROPERTY LAW
HANDBOOK

BUTTERWORTHS INTELLECTUAL PROPERTY LAW HANDBOOK

Thirteenth edition

Consultant Editor
MICHAEL EDENBOROUGH
One of Her Majesty's Counsel

LexisNexis®

Members of the LexisNexis Group worldwide

United Kingdom	RELX (UK) Limited trading as LexisNexis, 1–3 Strand, London WC2N 5JR and 9–10 St Andrew Square, Edinburgh EH2 2AF
Australia	Reed International Books Australia Pty Ltd trading as LexisNexis, Chatswood, New South Wales
Austria	LexisNexis Verlag ARD Orac GmbH & Co KG, Vienna
Benelux	LexisNexis Benelux, Amsterdam
Canada	LexisNexis Canada, Markham, Ontario
China	LexisNexis China, Beijing and Shanghai
France	LexisNexis SA, Paris
Germany	LexisNexis GmbH, Dusseldorf
Hong Kong	LexisNexis Hong Kong, Hong Kong
India	LexisNexis India, New Delhi
Italy	Giuffrè Editore, Milan
Japan	LexisNexis Japan, Tokyo
Malaysia	Malayan Law Journal Sdn Bhd, Kuala Lumpur
New Zealand	LexisNexis New Zealand Ltd, Wellington
Singapore	LexisNexis Singapore, Singapore
South Africa	LexisNexis, Durban
USA	LexisNexis, Dayton, Ohio

Published by LexisNexis
This is a Butterworths title

A CIP Catalogue record for this book is available from the British Library.

ISBN for this volume: 978 1 4743 0703 1

Printed and bound by CPI Group (UK) Ltd, Croydon, CR0 4YY

Visit LexisNexis at www.lexisnexis.co.uk

PREFACE

For the first twelve editions of this Handbook, Professor Jeremy Phillips was the Consultant Editor. He has now retired from this and his other IP roles: most notably from being the senior Blogmeister of the IPKat weblog. His contribution to the development of this work from its very first edition in 1990 over the ensuing two and a half decades cannot be underestimated.

Since the last edition, the UK has notified the European Council of the UK's intention to leave the EU pursuant to Article 50 of the Treaty on European Union. The government has also published a White Paper that outlines the legislative changes that this might involve. While the details are not yet fixed, it is clear that change is afoot. In an attempt to ameliorate the difficulties associated with planning for change, this edition will include for the first time some proposed, as opposed to ratified, legislation in order to allow practitioners to advise upon prospective changes. Of course, proposed legislation might change before being ratified. However, with that caveat, it is still sometimes necessary to chart ahead into unsettled waters.

Domestically, the Intellectual Property (Unjustified Threats) Act 2017 changes the IP litigation landscape fundamentally, in particular with the safe-harbour provisions for professional advisors. It will be interesting to see if these provisions will be abused to the detriment of SMEs as has been forewarned by some, but ignored by others.

More communally, the arrival of the Unified Patents Courts will affect patent litigation across the 26 participating (current) Member States of the EU. How this will unfold and what will be the status of the UK after it has left the EU are all open questions.

Internationally, the implementation of the Trans-Pacific Partnership and the Transatlantic Trade and Investment Partnership, and in particular their investors-state dispute settlement provisions and their application to IP issues, seem for the moment to have stalled due to the lack of enthusiasm by some hitherto keen prospective partners. It awaits to be seen if these potential Partnerships will be re-negotiated to give rise to a more artful deal for some. Into this maelstrom, there might be added various bi-lateral trade arrangements, which are likely to have significant IP-related protocols annexed.

I would like to thank the publication team at LexisNexis for helping me to settle into the role of Consultant Editor. Without their professionalism, this edition would have been the poorer.

This Handbook follows the standard Butterworths Handbooks style, with amendments made by new legislation incorporated into the text of existing legislation. The NOTES which follow a provision detail the changes that have been made to the text and list any prospective amendments. In the text:

- an ellipsis (. . .) indicates that text has been repealed or revoked (or is outside the scope of this Handbook);
- square brackets denote text that has been inserted or substituted;
- italicised text is prospectively repealed or substituted, or repealed subject to savings.

This Handbook is up to date to 1 July 2017, however later changes have been incorporated where possible.

Michael Edenborough QC
Serle Court
6 July 2017

CONTENTS

PART 3 DESIGNS

PART 4 UNREGISTERED DESIGN RIGHT

PART 5 TRADE MARKS

PART 6 PLANT VARIETIES PROTECTION

PART 7 OTHER UK LEGISLATION

PART 9 INTERNATIONAL

ALPHABETICAL LIST OF CONTENTS

PATENTS ACT 1977

(1977 c 37)

ARRANGEMENT OF SECTIONS

PART I
NEW DOMESTIC LAW

Patentability

Employees' inventions

Contracts as to patented products, etc

Licences of right and compulsory licences

Use of patented inventions for services of the Crown

Infringement

Revocation of patents

Putting validity in issue

Opinions by Patent Office

General provisions as to amendment of patents and applications

PART II
PROVISIONS ABOUT INTERNATIONAL CONVENTIONS

European patents and patent applications

SCHEDULES

An Act to establish a new law of patents applicable to future patents and applications for patents; to amend the law of patents applicable to existing patents and applications for patents; to give effect to certain international conventions on patents; and for connected purposes

[29 July 1977]

NOTES

Modification: this Act is modified in its application to the Isle of Man, by the Patents (Isle of Man) Order 2013, SI 2013/2602, art 2, Schedule (as amended by SI 2016/559, SI 2017/162).

PART I
NEW DOMESTIC LAW

Patentability

[1.1]
1 Patentable inventions

(1) A patent may be granted only for an invention in respect of which the following conditions are satisfied, that is to say—
- (a) the invention is new;
- (b) it involves an inventive step;
- (c) it is capable of industrial application;
- (d) the grant of a patent for it is not excluded by subsections (2) and (3) [or section 4A] below;

and references in this Act to a patentable invention shall be construed accordingly.

(2) It is hereby declared that the following (among other things) are not inventions for the purposes of this Act, that is to say, anything which consists of—
- (a) a discovery, scientific theory or mathematical method;
- (b) a literary, dramatic, musical or artistic work or any other aesthetic creation whatsoever;
- (c) a scheme, rule or method for performing a mental act, playing a game or doing business, or a program for a computer;
- (d) the presentation of information;

but the foregoing provision shall prevent anything from being treated as an invention for the purposes of this Act only to the extent that a patent or application for a patent relates to that thing as such.

[(3) A patent shall not be granted for an invention the commercial exploitation of which would be contrary to public policy or morality.

(4) For the purposes of subsection (3) above exploitation shall not be regarded as contrary to public policy or morality only because it is prohibited by any law in force in the United Kingdom or any part of it.]

(5) The Secretary of State may by order vary the provisions of subsection (2) above for the purpose of maintaining them in conformity with developments in science and technology; and no such order shall be made unless a draft of the order has been laid before, and approved by resolution of, each House of Parliament.

NOTES

Sub-s (1): words in square brackets inserted by the Patents Act 2004, s 16(1), Sch 2, paras 1, 2.

Sub-ss (3), (4): substituted by the Patents Regulations 2000, SI 2000/2037, regs 2, 3, in relation to applications for patents made on or after 28 July 2000.

[1.2]

2 Novelty

(1) An invention shall be taken to be new if it does not form part of the state of the art.

(2) The state of the art in the case of an invention shall be taken to comprise all matter (whether a product, a process, information about either, or anything else) which has at any time before the priority date of that invention been made available to the public (whether in the United Kingdom or elsewhere) by written or oral description, by use or in any other way.

(3) The state of the art in the case of an invention to which an application for a patent or a patent relates shall be taken also to comprise matter contained in an application for another patent which was published on or after the priority date of that invention, if the following conditions are satisfied, that is to say—

(a) that matter was contained in the application for that other patent both as filed and as published; and

(b) the priority date of that matter is earlier than that of the invention.

(4) For the purposes of this section the disclosure of matter constituting an invention shall be disregarded in the case of a patent or an application for a patent if occurring later than the beginning of the period of six months immediately preceding the date of filing the application for the patent and either—

(a) the disclosure was due to, or made in consequence of, the matter having been obtained unlawfully or in breach of confidence by any person—

(i) from the inventor or from any other person to whom the matter was made available in confidence by the inventor or who obtained it from the inventor because he or the inventor believed that he was entitled to obtain it; or

(ii) from any other person to whom the matter was made available in confidence by any person mentioned in sub-paragraph (i) above or in this sub-paragraph or who obtained it from any person so mentioned because he or the person from whom he obtained it believed that he was entitled to obtain it;

(b) the disclosure was made in breach of confidence by any person who obtained the matter in confidence from the inventor or from any other person to whom it was made available, or who obtained it, from the inventor; or

(c) the disclosure was due to, or made in consequence of the inventor displaying the invention at an international exhibition and the applicant states, on filing the application, that the invention has been so displayed and also, within the prescribed period, files written evidence in support of the statement complying with any prescribed conditions.

(5) In this section references to the inventor include references to any proprietor of the invention for the time being.

(6) . . .

NOTES

Sub-s (6): repealed by the Patents Act 2004, s 16(1), (2), Sch 2, paras 1, 3, Sch 3.

[1.3]

3 Inventive step

An invention shall be taken to involve an inventive step if it is not obvious to a person skilled in the art, having regard to any matter which forms part of the state of the art by virtue only of section 2(2) above (and disregarding section 2(3) above).

[1.4]

4 Industrial application

(1) . . . an invention shall be taken to be capable of industrial application if it can be made or used in any kind of industry, including agriculture.

(2), (3) . . .

NOTES

Sub-s (1): words omitted repealed by the Patents Act 2004, s 16(1), (2), Sch 2, paras 1, 4(a), Sch 3.
Sub-ss (2), (3): repealed by the Patents Act 2004, s 16(1), (2), Sch 2, paras 1, 4(b), Sch 3.

[1.5]

[4A Methods of treatment or diagnosis

(1) A patent shall not be granted for the invention of—

(a) a method of treatment of the human or animal body by surgery or therapy, or

(b) a method of diagnosis practised on the human or animal body.

(2) Subsection (1) above does not apply to an invention consisting of a substance or composition for use in any such method.

(3) In the case of an invention consisting of a substance or composition for use in any such method, the fact that the substance or composition forms part of the state of the art shall not prevent the invention from being taken to be new if the use of the substance or composition in any such method does not form part of the state of the art.

(4) In the case of an invention consisting of a substance or composition for a specific use in any such method, the fact that the substance or composition forms part of the state of the art shall not prevent the invention from being taken to be new if that specific use does not form part of the state of the art.]

NOTES

Inserted by the Patents Act 2004, s 1.

[1.6]

5 Priority date

(1) For the purposes of this Act the priority date of an invention to which an application for a patent relates and also of any matter (whether or not the same as the invention) contained in any such application is, except as provided by the following provisions of this Act, the date of filing the application.

(2) If in or in connection with an application for a patent (the application in suit) a declaration is made, whether by the applicant or any predecessor in title of his, complying with the relevant requirements of rules and specifying one or more earlier relevant applications for the purposes of this section made by the applicant or a predecessor in title of his and [the application in suit has a date of filing during the period allowed under subsection (2A)(a) or (b) below], then—

- (a) if an invention to which the application in suit relates is supported by matter disclosed in the earlier relevant application or applications, the priority date of that invention shall instead of being the date of filing the application in suit be the date of filing the relevant application in which that matter was disclosed or, if it was disclosed in more than one relevant application, the earliest of them;
- (b) the priority date of any matter contained in the application in suit which was also disclosed in the earlier relevant application or applications shall be the date of filing the relevant application in which that matter was disclosed or, if it was disclosed in more than one relevant application, the earliest of them.

[(2A) The periods are—

- (a) the period of twelve months immediately following the date of filing of the earlier specified relevant application, or if there is more than one, of the earliest of them; and
- (b) where the comptroller has given permission under subsection (2B) below for a late declaration to be made under subsection (2) above, the period commencing immediately after the end of the period allowed under paragraph (a) above and ending at the end of the prescribed period.

(2B) The applicant may make a request to the comptroller for permission to make a late declaration under subsection (2) above.

(2C) The comptroller shall grant a request made under subsection (2B) above if, and only if—

- (a) the request complies with the relevant requirements of rules; and
- (b) the comptroller is satisfied that the applicant's failure to file the application in suit within the period allowed under subsection (2A)(a) above was unintentional.]

(3) Where an invention or other matter contained in the application in suit was also disclosed in two earlier relevant applications filed by the same applicant as in the case of the application in suit or a predecessor in title of his and the second of those relevant applications was specified in or in connection with the application in suit, the second of those relevant applications shall, so far as concerns that invention or matter, be disregarded unless—

- (a) it was filed in or in respect of the same country as the first; and
- (b) not later than the date of filing the second, the first (whether or not so specified) was unconditionally withdrawn, or was abandoned or refused, without—
  - (i) having been made available to the public (whether in the United Kingdom or elsewhere);
  - (ii) leaving any rights outstanding; and
  - (iii) having served to establish a priority date in relation to another application, wherever made.

(4) The foregoing provisions of this section shall apply for determining the priority date of an invention for which a patent has been granted as they apply for determining the priority date of an invention to which an application for that patent relates.

(5) In this section "relevant application" means any of the following applications which has a date of filing, namely—

- (a) an application for a patent under this Act;
- [(aa) an application in or for a country (other than the United Kingdom) which is a member of the World Trade Organisation for protection in respect of an invention which, in accordance with the law of that country or a treaty or international obligation to which it is a party, is equivalent to an application for a patent under this Act;]

(b) an application in or for a convention country (specified under section 90 below) for protection in respect of an invention or an application which, in accordance with the law of a convention country or a treaty or international convention to which a convention country is a party, is equivalent to [an application for a patent under this Act].

[(6) . . .]

NOTES

Sub-s (2): words in square brackets substituted by the Regulatory Reform (Patents) Order 2004, SI 2004/2357, arts 2, 3, subject to transitional provisions in arts 20, 21 thereof at **[1.248]**, **[1.249]**.

Sub-ss (2A)–(2C): inserted by SI 2004/2357, arts 2, 3, subject to transitional provisions in arts 20, 21 thereof at **[1.248]**, **[1.249]**.

Sub-s (5): para (aa) inserted and words in square brackets in para (b) substituted, by the Intellectual Property Act 2014, s 19, Schedule, para 1(1), (2).

Sub-s (6): added by the Patents and Trade Marks (World Trade Organisation) Regulations 1999, SI 1999/1899, reg 7(1); repealed by the Intellectual Property Act 2014, s 19, Schedule, para 1(1), (3).

[1.7]

6 Disclosure of matter, etc, between earlier and later applications

(1) It is hereby declared for the avoidance of doubt that where an application (the application in suit) is made for a patent and a declaration is made in accordance with section 5(2) above in or in connection with that application specifying an earlier relevant application, the application in suit and any patent granted in pursuance of it shall not be invalidated by reason only of relevant intervening acts.

(2) In this section—

"relevant application" has the same meaning as in section 5 above; and

"relevant intervening acts" means acts done in relation to matter disclosed in an earlier relevant application between the dates of the earlier relevant application and the application in suit, as for example, filing another application for the invention for which the earlier relevant application was made, making information available to the public about that invention or that matter or working that invention, but disregarding any application, or the disclosure to the public of matter contained in any application, which is itself to be disregarded for the purposes of section 5(3) above.

Right to apply for and obtain a patent and be mentioned as inventor

[1.8]

7 Right to apply for and obtain a patent

(1) Any person may make an application for a patent either alone or jointly with another.

(2) A patent for an invention may be granted—

(a) primarily to the inventor or joint inventors;

(b) in preference to the foregoing, to any person or persons who, by virtue of any enactment or rule of law, or any foreign law or treaty or international convention, or by virtue of an enforceable term of any agreement entered into with the inventor before the making of the invention, was or were at the time of the making of the invention entitled to the whole of the property in it (other than equitable interests) in the United Kingdom;

(c) in any event, to the successor or successors in title of any person or persons mentioned in paragraph (a) or (b) above or any person so mentioned and the successor or successors in title of another person so mentioned;

and to no other person.

(3) In this Act "inventor" in relation to an invention means the actual deviser of the invention and "joint inventor" shall be construed accordingly.

(4) Except so far as the contrary is established, a person who makes an application for a patent shall be taken to be the person who is entitled under subsection (2) above to be granted a patent and two or more persons who make such an application jointly shall be taken to be the persons so entitled.

[1.9]

8 Determination before grant of questions about entitlement to patents, etc

(1) At any time before a patent has been granted for an invention (whether or not an application has been made for it)—

(a) any person may refer to the comptroller the question whether he is entitled to be granted (alone or with any other persons) a patent for that invention or has or would have any right in or under any patent so granted or any application for such a patent; or

(b) any of two or more co-proprietors of an application for a patent for that invention may so refer the question whether any right in or under the application should be transferred or granted to any other person;

and the comptroller shall determine the question and may make such order as he thinks fit to give effect to the determination.

(2) Where a person refers a question relating to an invention under subsection (1)(a) above to the comptroller after an application for a patent for the invention has been filed and before a patent is granted in pursuance of the application, then, unless the application is refused or withdrawn before the reference is disposed of by the comptroller, the comptroller may, without prejudice to the generality of subsection (1) above and subject to subsection (6) below,—

(a) order that the application shall proceed in the name of that person, either solely or jointly with that of any other applicant, instead of in the name of the applicant or any specified applicant;

(b) where the reference was made by two or more persons, order that the application shall proceed in all their names jointly;

(c) refuse to grant a patent in pursuance of the application or order the application to be amended so as to exclude any of the matter in respect of which the question was referred;

(d) make an order transferring or granting any licence or other right in or under the application and give directions to any person for carrying out the provisions of any such order.

(3) Where a question is referred to the comptroller under subsection (1)(a) above and—

(a) the comptroller orders an application for a patent for the invention to which the question relates to be so amended;

(b) any such application is refused under subsection 2(c) above before the comptroller has disposed of the reference (whether the reference was made before or after the publication of the application); or

(c) any such application is refused under any other provision of this Act or is withdrawn before the comptroller has disposed of the reference [(whether the application is refused or withdrawn before or after its publication)];

the comptroller may order that any person by whom the reference was made may within the prescribed period make a new application for a patent for the whole or part of any matter comprised in the earlier application or, as the case may be, for all or any of the matter excluded from the earlier application, subject in either case to section 76 below, and in either case that, if such a new application is made, it shall be treated as having been filed on the date of filing the earlier application.

(4) Where a person refers a question under subsection (1)(b) above relating to an application, any order under subsection (1) above may contain directions to any person for transferring or granting any right in or under the application.

(5) If any person to whom directions have been given under subsection (2)(d) or (4) above fails to do anything necessary for carrying out any such directions within 14 days after the date of the directions, the comptroller may, on application made to him by any person in whose favour or on whose reference the directions were given, authorise him to do that thing on behalf of the person to whom the directions were given.

(6) Where on a reference under this section it is alleged that, by virtue of any transaction, instrument or event relating to an invention or an application for a patent, any person other than the inventor or the applicant for the patent has become entitled to be granted (whether alone or with any other persons) a patent for the invention or has or would have any right in or under any patent so granted or any application for any such patent, an order shall not be made under subsection (2)(a), (b) or (d) above on the reference unless notice of the reference is given to the applicant and any such person, except any of them who is a party to the reference.

(7) If it appears to the comptroller on a reference of a question under this section that the question involves matters which would more properly be determined by the court, he may decline to deal with it and, without prejudice to the court's jurisdiction to determine any such question and make a declaration, or any declaratory jurisdiction of the court in Scotland, the court shall have jurisdiction to do so.

(8) No directions shall be given under this section so as to affect the mutual rights or obligations of trustees or of the personal representatives of deceased persons, or their rights or obligations as such.

NOTES

Sub-s (3): words in square brackets substituted by the Patents Act 2004, s 6(1), subject to transitional provisions contained in the Patents Act 2004 (Commencement No 2 and Consequential, etc and Transitional Provisions) Order 2004, SI 2004/3205, art 9(1), (2) at **[1.254]**.

[1.10]

9 Determination after grant of questions referred before grant

If a question with respect to a patent or application is referred by any person to the comptroller under section 8 above, whether before or after the making of an application for the patent, and is not determined before the time when the application is first in order for a grant of a patent in pursuance of the application, that fact shall not prevent the grant of a patent, but on its grant that person shall be treated as having referred to the comptroller under section 37 below any question mentioned in that section which the comptroller thinks appropriate.

[1.11]

10 Handling of application by joint applicants

If any dispute arises between joint applicants for a patent whether or in what manner the application should be proceeded with, the comptroller may, on a request made by any of the parties, give such directions as he thinks fit for enabling the application to proceed in the name of one or more of the parties alone or for regulating the manner in which it shall be proceeded with, or for both those purposes, according as the case may require.

[1.12]

11 Effect of transfer of application under s 8 or 10

(1) Where an order is made or directions are given under section 8 or 10 above that an application for a patent shall proceed in the name of one or some of the original applicants (whether or not it is also to proceed in the name of some other person), any licences or other rights in or under the application shall, subject to the provisions of the order and any directions under either of those sections, continue in force and be treated as granted by the persons in whose name the application is to proceed.

(2) Where an order is made or directions are given under section 8 above that an application for a patent shall proceed in the name of one or more persons none of whom was an original applicant (on the ground that the original applicant or applicants was or were not entitled to be granted the patent), any licences or other rights in or under the application shall, subject to the provisions of the order and any directions under that section and subject to subsection (3) below, lapse on the registration of that person or those persons as the applicant or applicants or, where the application has not been published, on the making of the order.

(3) If before registration of a reference under section 8 above resulting in the making of any order mentioned in subsection (2) above—

- (a) the original applicant or any of the applicants, acting in good faith, worked the invention in question in the United Kingdom or made effective and serious preparations to do so; or
- (b) a licensee of the applicant, acting in good faith, worked the invention in the United Kingdom or made effective and serious preparations to do so;

that or those original applicant or applicants or the licensee shall, on making a request within the prescribed period to the person in whose name the application is to proceed, be entitled to be granted a licence (but not an exclusive licence) to continue working or, as the case may be, to work the invention.

[(3A) If, before registration of a reference under section 8 above resulting in the making of an order under subsection (3) of that section, the condition in subsection (3)(a) or (b) above is met, the original applicant or any of the applicants or the licensee shall, on making a request within the prescribed period to the new applicant, be entitled to be granted a licence (but not an exclusive licence) to continue working or, as the case may be, to work the invention so far as it is the subject of the new application.]

(4) [A licence under subsection (3) or (3A) above] shall be granted for a reasonable period and on reasonable terms.

(5) Where an order is made as mentioned in subsection (2) [or (3A)] above, the person in whose name the application is to proceed [or, as the case may be, who makes the new application] or any person claiming that he is entitled to be granted any such licence may refer to the comptroller the question whether the latter is so entitled and whether any such period is or terms are reasonable, and the comptroller shall determine the question and may, if he considers it appropriate, order the grant of such a licence.

NOTES

Sub-s (3A): inserted by the Patents Act 2004, s 6(2), subject to transitional provisions contained in the Patents Act 2004 (Commencement No 2 and Consequential, etc and Transitional Provisions) Order 2004, SI 2004/3205, art 9(1), (2) at **[1.254]**.

Sub-s (4): words in square brackets substituted by the Patents Act 2004, s 6(3), subject to transitional provisions contained in the Patents Act 2004 (Commencement No 2 and Consequential, etc and Transitional Provisions) Order 2004, SI 2004/3205, art 9(1), (2) at **[1.254]**.

Sub-s (5): words in square brackets inserted by the Patents Act 2004, s 6(4), subject to transitional provisions contained in the Patents Act 2004 (Commencement No 2 and Consequential, etc and Transitional Provisions) Order 2004, SI 2004/3205, art 9(1), (2) at **[1.254]**.

[1.13]

12 Determination of questions about entitlement to foreign and convention patents, etc

(1) At any time before a patent is granted for an invention in pursuance of an application made under the law of any country other than the United Kingdom or under any treaty or international convention (whether or not that application has been made)—

- (a) any person may refer to the comptroller the question whether he is entitled to be granted (alone or with any other persons) any such patent for that invention or has or would have any right in or under any such patent or an application for such a patent; or
- (b) any of two or more co-proprietors of an application for such a patent for that invention may so refer the question whether any right in or under the application should be transferred or granted to any other person;

and the comptroller shall determine the question so far as he is able to and may make such order as he thinks fit to give effect to the determination.

(2) If it appears to the comptroller on a reference of a question under this section that the question involves matters which would more properly be determined by the court, he may decline to deal with it and, without prejudice to the court's jurisdiction to determine any such question and make a declaration, or any declaratory jurisdiction of the court in Scotland, the court shall have jurisdiction to do so.

(3) Subsection (1) above, in its application to a European patent and an application for any such patent, shall have effect subject to section 82 below.

(4) Section 10 above, except so much of it as enables the comptroller to regulate the manner in which an application is to proceed, shall apply to disputes between joint applicants for any such patent as is mentioned in subsection (1) above as it applies to joint applicants for a patent under this Act.

(5) Section 11 above shall apply in relation to—

(a) any orders made under subsection (1) above and any directions given under section 10 above by virtue of subsection (4) above; and

(b) any orders made and directions given by the relevant convention court with respect to a question corresponding to any question which may be determined under subsection (1) above;

as it applies to orders made and directions given apart from this section under section 8 or 10 above.

(6) In the following cases, that is to say—

(a) where an application for a European patent (UK) is refused or withdrawn, or the designation of the United Kingdom in the application is withdrawn, [whether before or] after publication of the application but before a question relating to the right to the patent has been referred to the comptroller under subsection (1) above or before proceedings relating to that right have begun before the relevant convention court;

(b) where an application has been made for a European patent (UK) and on a reference under subsection (1) above or any such proceedings as are mentioned in paragraph (a) above the comptroller, the court or the relevant convention court determines by a final decision (whether before or after publication of the application) that a person other than the applicant has the right to the patent, but that person requests the European Patent Office that the application for the patent should be refused; or

(c) where an international application for a patent (UK) is withdrawn, or the designation of the United Kingdom in the application is withdrawn, whether before or after the making of any reference under subsection (1) above [or the] publication of the application;

the comptroller may order that any person (other than the applicant) appearing to him to be entitled to be granted a patent under this Act may within the prescribed period make an application for such a patent for the whole or part of any matter comprised in the earlier application (subject, however, to section 76 below) and that if the application for a patent under this Act is filed, it shall be treated as having been filed on the date of filing the earlier application.

(7) In this section—

(a) references to a patent and an application for a patent include respectively references to protection in respect of an invention and an application which, in accordance with the law of any country other than the United Kingdom or any treaty or international convention, is equivalent to an application for a patent or for such protection; and

(b) a decision shall be taken to be final for the purposes of this section when the time for appealing from it has expired without an appeal being brought or, where an appeal is brought, when it is finally disposed of.

NOTES

Sub-s (6): words in square brackets in para (a) inserted, and words in square brackets in para (c) substituted by the Patents Act 2004, s 16(1), Sch 2, paras 1, 5, subject to transitional provisions contained in the Patents Act 2004 (Commencement No 2 and Consequential, etc and Transitional Provisions) Order 2004, SI 2004/3205, art 9(1), (2) at **[1.254]**.

[1.14]

13 Mention of inventor

(1) The inventor or joint inventors of an invention shall have a right to be mentioned as such in any patent granted for the invention and shall also have a right to be so mentioned if possible in any published application for a patent for the invention and, if not so mentioned, a right to be so mentioned in accordance with rules in a prescribed document.

(2) Unless he has already given the Patent Office the information hereinafter mentioned, an applicant for a patent shall within the prescribed period file with the Patent Office a statement—

(a) identifying the person or persons whom he believes to be the inventor or inventors; and

(b) where the applicant is not the sole inventor or the applicants are not the joint inventors, indicating the derivation of his or their right to be granted the patent;

and, if he fails to do so, the application shall be taken to be withdrawn.

(3) Where a person has been mentioned as sole or joint inventor in pursuance of this section, any other person who alleges that the former ought not to have been so mentioned may at any time apply to the comptroller for a certificate to that effect, and the comptroller may issue such a certificate; and if he does so, he shall accordingly rectify any undistributed copies of the patent and of any documents prescribed for the purposes of subsection (1) above.

Applications

[1.15]

14 Making of application

(1) Every application for a patent—

(a) shall be made in the prescribed form and shall be filed at the Patent Office in the prescribed manner; . . .

(b) . . .

[(1A) Where an application for a patent is made, the fee prescribed for the purposes of this subsection ("the application fee") shall be paid not later than the end of the period prescribed for the purposes of section 15(10)(c) below.]

(2) Every application for a patent shall contain—

(a) a request for the grant of a patent;

(b) a specification containing a description of the invention, a claim or claims and any drawing referred to in the description or any claim; and

(c) an abstract;

but the foregoing provision shall not prevent an application being initiated by documents complying with section 15(1) below.

(3) The specification of an application shall disclose the invention in a manner which is clear enough and complete enough for the invention to be performed by a person skilled in the art.

(4) . . .

(5) The claim or claims shall—

(a) define the matter for which the applicant seeks protection;

(b) be clear and concise;

(c) be supported by the description; and

(d) relate to one invention or to a group of inventions which are so linked as to form a single inventive concept.

(6) Without prejudice to the generality of subsection (5)(d) above, rules may provide for treating two or more inventions as being so linked as to form a single inventive concept for the purposes of this Act.

(7) The purpose of the abstract is to give technical information and on publication it shall not form part of the state of the art by virtue of section 2(3) above, and the comptroller may determine whether the abstract adequately fulfils its purpose and, if it does not, may reframe it so that it does.

(8) . . .

(9) An application for a patent may be withdrawn at any time before the patent is granted and any withdrawal of such an application may not be revoked.

[(10) Subsection (9) above does not affect the power of the comptroller under section 117(1) below to correct an error or mistake in a withdrawal of an application for a patent.]

NOTES

Sub-s (1): words omitted repealed by the Regulatory Reform (Patents) Order 2004, SI 2004/2357, arts 2, 4(1), (2), subject to transitional provisions in arts 20, 21 thereof at **[1.248]**, **[1.249]**.

Sub-s (1A): inserted by SI 2004/2357, arts 2, 4(1), (3), subject to transitional provisions in arts 20, 21 thereof at **[1.248]**, **[1.249]**.

Sub-ss (4), (8): repealed by the Copyright, Designs and Patents Act 1988, s 303(2), Sch 8.

Sub-s (10): added by SI 2004/2357, arts 2, 4(1), (4).

Comptroller: ie, the Comptroller-General of Patents, Designs and Trade Marks. The functions of the Comptroller under sub-s (7) above and ss 19(2), 21(1) and 117 may be contracted out: see the Contracting Out (Functions in Relation to Applications for Patents) Order 2002, SI 2002/3052 at **[1.236]**.

Rules: the Patents Rules 2007, SI 2007/3291 at **[1.262]**.

[1.16]

[15 Date of filing application

(1) Subject to the following provisions of this Act, the date of filing an application for a patent shall be taken to be the earliest date on which documents filed at the Patent Office to initiate the application satisfy the following conditions—

(a) the documents indicate that a patent is sought;

(b) the documents identify the person applying for a patent or contain information sufficient to enable that person to be contacted by the Patent Office; and

(c) the documents contain either—

(i) something which is or appears to be a description of the invention for which a patent is sought; or

(ii) a reference, complying with the relevant requirements of rules, to an earlier relevant application made by the applicant or a predecessor in title of his.

(2) It is immaterial for the purposes of subsection (1)(c)(i) above—

(a) whether the thing is in, or is accompanied by a translation into, a language accepted by the Patent Office in accordance with rules;
(b) whether the thing otherwise complies with the other provisions of this Act and with any relevant rules.

(3) Where documents filed at the Patent Office to initiate an application for a patent satisfy one or more of the conditions specified in subsection (1) above, but do not satisfy all those conditions, the comptroller shall as soon as practicable after the filing of those documents notify the applicant of what else must be filed in order for the application to have a date of filing.

(4) Where documents filed at the Patent Office to initiate an application for a patent satisfy all the conditions specified in subsection (1) above, the comptroller shall as soon as practicable after the filing of the last of those documents notify the applicant of—
(a) the date of filing the application, and
(b) the requirements that must be complied with, and the periods within which they are required by this Act or rules to be complied with, if the application is not to be treated as having been withdrawn.

(5) Subsection (6) below applies where—
(a) an application has a date of filing by virtue of subsection (1) above;
(b) within the prescribed period the applicant files at the Patent Office—
(i) a drawing, or
(ii) part of the description of the invention for which a patent is sought, and
(c) that drawing or that part of the description was missing from the application at the date of filing.

(6) Unless the applicant withdraws the drawing or the part of the description filed under subsection (5)(b) above ("the missing part") before the end of the prescribed period—
(a) the missing part shall be treated as included in the application; and
(b) the date of filing the application shall be the date on which the missing part is filed at the Patent Office.

(7) Subsection (6)(b) above does not apply if—
(a) on or before the date which is the date of filing the application by virtue of subsection (1) above a declaration is made under section 5(2) above in or in connection with the application;
(b) the applicant makes a request for subsection (6)(b) above not to apply; and
(c) the request complies with the relevant requirements of rules and is made within the prescribed period.

(8) Subsections (6) and (7) above do not affect the power of the comptroller under section 117(1) below to correct an error or mistake.

(9) Where, after an application for a patent has been filed and before the patent is granted—
(a) a new application is filed by the original applicant or his successor in title in accordance with rules in respect of any part of the matter contained in the earlier application, and
(b) the conditions mentioned in subsection (1) above are satisfied in relation to the new application (without the new application contravening section 76 below),

the new application shall be treated as having, as its date of filing, the date of filing the earlier application.

(10) Where an application has a date of filing by virtue of this section, the application shall be treated as having been withdrawn if any of the following applies—
(a) the applicant fails to file at the Patent Office, before the end of the prescribed period, one or more claims and the abstract;
(b) where a reference to an earlier relevant application has been filed as mentioned in subsection (1)(c)(ii) above—
(i) the applicant fails to file at the Patent Office, before the end of the prescribed period, a description of the invention for which the patent is sought;
(ii) the applicant fails to file at the Patent Office, before the end of the prescribed period, a copy of the application referred to, complying with the relevant requirements of rules;
(c) the applicant fails to pay the application fee before the end of the prescribed period;
(d) the applicant fails, before the end of the prescribed period, to make a request for a search under section 17 below and pay the search fee.

(11) In this section "relevant application" has the meaning given by section 5(5) above.]

NOTES

Substituted, together with s 15A for original s 15, by the Regulatory Reform (Patents) Order 2004, SI 2004/2357, arts 2, 5, subject to transitional provisions in arts 20–22 thereof at **[1.248]–[1.250]**.

[1.17]

[15A Preliminary examination

(1) The comptroller shall refer an application for a patent to an examiner for a preliminary examination if—
(a) the application has a date of filing;
(b) the application has not been withdrawn or treated as withdrawn; and

(c) the application fee has been paid.

(2) On a preliminary examination of an application the examiner shall—

(a) determine whether the application complies with those requirements of this Act and the rules which are designated by the rules as formal requirements for the purposes of this Act; and

(b) determine whether any requirements under section 13(2) or 15(10) above remain to be complied with.

(3) The examiner shall report to the comptroller his determinations under subsection (2) above.

(4) If on the preliminary examination of an application it is found that—

(a) any drawing referred to in the application, or

(b) part of the description of the invention for which the patent is sought,

is missing from the application, then the examiner shall include this finding in his report under subsection (3) above.

(5) Subsections (6) to (8) below apply if a report is made to the comptroller under subsection (3) above that not all the formal requirements have been complied with.

(6) The comptroller shall specify a period during which the applicant shall have the opportunity—

(a) to make observations on the report, and

(b) to amend the application so as to comply with those requirements (subject to section 76 below).

(7) The comptroller may refuse the application if the applicant fails to amend the application as mentioned in subsection (6)(b) above before the end of the period specified by the comptroller under that subsection.

(8) Subsection (7) above does not apply if—

(a) the applicant makes observations as mentioned in subsection (6)(a) above before the end of the period specified by the comptroller under that subsection, and

(b) as a result of the observations, the comptroller is satisfied that the formal requirements have been complied with.

(9) If a report is made to the comptroller under subsection (3) above—

(a) that any requirement of section 13(2) or 15(10) above has not been complied with; or

(b) that a drawing or part of the description of the invention has been found to be missing,

then the comptroller shall notify the applicant accordingly.]

NOTES

Substituted as noted to s 15 at **[1.16]**.

[1.18]

16 Publication of application

(1) Subject to section 22 below [and to any prescribed restrictions], where an application has a date of filing, then, as soon as possible after the end of the prescribed period, the comptroller shall, unless the application is withdrawn or refused before preparations for its publication have been completed by the Patent Office, publish it as filed (including not only the original claims but also any amendments of those claims and new claims subsisting immediately before the completion of those preparations) and he may, if so requested by the applicant, publish it as aforesaid during that period, and in either event shall advertise the fact and date of its publication in the journal.

(2) The comptroller may omit from the specification of a published application for a patent any matter—

(a) which in his opinion disparages any person in a way likely to damage him, or

(b) the publication or exploitation of which would in his opinion be generally expected to encourage offensive, immoral or anti-social behaviour.

NOTES

Sub-s (1): words in square brackets inserted by the Patents Act 2004, s 16(1), Sch 2, paras 1, 6.

Examination and search

[1.19]

17 [Search]

[(1) The comptroller shall refer an application for a patent to an examiner for a search if, and only if—

(a) the comptroller has referred the application to an examiner for a preliminary examination under section 15A(1) above;

(b) the application has not been withdrawn or treated as withdrawn;

(c) before the end of the prescribed period—

(i) the applicant makes a request to the Patent Office in the prescribed form for a search; and

(ii) the fee prescribed for the search ("the search fee") is paid;

(d) the application includes—

(i) a description of the invention for which a patent is sought; and

(ii) one or more claims; and

(e) the description and each of the claims comply with the requirements of rules as to language.]

(2), (3) . . .

(4) Subject to subsections (5) and (6) below, on a search requested under this section, the examiner shall make such investigation as in his opinion is reasonably practicable and necessary for him to identify the documents which he thinks will be needed to decide, on a substantive examination under section 18 below, whether the invention for which a patent is sought is new and involves an inventive step.

(5) On any such search the examiner shall determine whether or not the search would serve any useful purpose on the application as for the time being constituted and—

(a) if he determines that it would serve such a purpose in relation to the whole or part of the application, he shall proceed to conduct the search so far as it would serve such a purpose and shall report on the results of the search to the comptroller; and

(b) if he determines that the search would not serve such a purpose in relation to the whole or part of the application, he shall report accordingly to the comptroller;

and in either event the applicant shall be informed of the examiner's report.

(6) If it appears to the examiner, either before or on conducting a search under this section, that an application relates to two or more inventions, but that they are not so linked as to form a single inventive concept, he shall initially only conduct a search in relation to the first invention specified in the claims of the application, but may proceed to conduct a search in relation to another invention so specified if the applicant pays the search fee in respect of the application so far as it relates to that other invention.

(7) After a search has been requested under this section for an application the comptroller may at any time refer the application to an examiner for a supplementary search, and [subsections (4) and (5) above] shall apply in relation to a supplementary search as [they apply] in relation to any other search under this section.

[(8) A reference for a supplementary search in consequence of—

(a) an amendment of the application made by the applicant under section 18(3) or 19(1) below, or

(b) a correction of the application, or of a document filed in connection with the application, under section 117 below,

shall be made only on payment of the prescribed fee, unless the comptroller directs otherwise.]

NOTES

Section heading: substituted by the Regulatory Reform (Patents) Order 2004, SI 2004/2357, arts 2, 6(1), (2), subject to transitional provisions in arts 20–22 thereof at **[1.248]–[1.250]**.

Sub-s (1): substituted by SI 2004/2357, arts 2, 6(1), (3), subject to transitional provisions in arts 20–22 thereof at **[1.248]–[1.250]**.

Sub-ss (2), (3): repealed by SI 2004/2357, arts 2, 6(1), (4), subject to transitional provisions in arts 20–22 thereof at **[1.248]–[1.250]**.

Sub-s (7): words in square brackets substituted by the Copyright, Designs and Patents Act 1988, s 295, Sch 5, para 3(2).

Sub-s (8): added by the Copyright, Designs and Patents Act 1988, s 295, Sch 5, para 3(3).

[1.20]

18 Substantive examination and grant or refusal of patent

(1) Where the conditions imposed by section 17(1) above for the comptroller to refer an application to an examiner for a . . . search are satisfied and at the time of the request under that subsection or within the prescribed period—

(a) a request is made by the applicant to the Patent Office in the prescribed form for a substantive examination; and

(b) the prescribed fee is paid for the examination;

the comptroller shall refer the application to an examiner for a substantive examination; and if no such request is made or the prescribed fee is not paid within that period, the application shall be treated as having been withdrawn at the end of that period.

[(1A) If the examiner forms the view that a supplementary search under section 17 above is required for which a fee is payable, he shall inform the comptroller, who may decide that the substantive examination should not proceed until the fee is paid; and if he so decides, then unless within such period as he may allow—

(a) the fee is paid, or

(b) the application is amended so as to render the supplementary search unnecessary,

he may refuse the application.]

(2) On a substantive examination of an application the examiner shall investigate, to such extent as he considers necessary in view of any examination [carried out under section 15A above] and search carried out under section 17 above, whether the application complies with the requirements of this Act and the rules and shall determine that question and report his determination to the comptroller.

(3) If the examiner reports that any of those requirements are not complied with, the comptroller shall give the applicant an opportunity within a specified period to make observations on the report and to amend the application so as to comply with those requirements (subject, however, to

section 76 below), and if the applicant fails to satisfy the comptroller that those requirements are complied with, or to amend the application so as to comply with them, the comptroller may refuse the application.

(4) If the examiner reports that the application, whether as originally filed or as amended in pursuance of [section 15A] above, this section or section 19 below, complies with those requirements at any time before the end of the prescribed period, the comptroller shall notify the applicant of that fact and, subject to subsection (5) and sections 19 and 22 below and on payment within the prescribed period of any fee prescribed for the grant, grant him a patent.

(5) Where two or more applications for a patent for the same invention having the same priority date are filed by the same applicant or his successor in title, the comptroller may on that ground refuse to grant a patent in pursuance of more than one of the applications.

NOTES

Sub-s (1): words omitted repealed by the Regulatory Reform (Patents) Order 2004, SI 2004/2357, arts 2, 7(1), (2), subject to transitional provisions in arts 20–22 thereof at **[1.248]–[1.250]**.

Sub-s (1A): inserted by the Copyright, Designs and Patents Act 1988, s 295, Sch 5, para 4.

Sub-s (2): words in square brackets inserted by SI 2004/2357, arts 2, 7(1), (3), subject to transitional provisions in arts 20–22 thereof at **[1.248]–[1.250]**.

Sub-s (4): words in square brackets substituted by SI 2004/2357, arts 2, 7(1), (4), subject to transitional provisions in arts 20–22 thereof at **[1.248]–[1.250]**.

[1.21]

19 General power to amend application before grant

(1) At any time before a patent is granted in pursuance of an application the applicant may, in accordance with the prescribed conditions and subject to section 76 below, amend the application of his own volition.

(2) The comptroller may, without an application being made to him for the purpose, amend the specification and abstract contained in an application for a patent so as to acknowledge a registered trade mark.

NOTES

Registered trade marks: the reference to a registered trade mark in sub-s (2) is to be construed as a reference to a registered trade mark within the meaning of the Trade Marks Act 1994; see s 106(1) of, and Sch 4, para 1 to, the 1994 Act.

Comptroller: see the note to s 14 at **[1.15]**.

[1.22]

20 Failure of application

(1) If it is not determined that an application for a patent complies before the end of the prescribed period with all the requirements of this Act and the rules, the application shall be treated as having been refused by the comptroller at the end of that period, and section 97 below shall apply accordingly.

(2) If at the end of that period an appeal to the court is pending in respect of the application or the time within which such an appeal could be brought has not expired, that period—

- (a) where such an appeal is pending, or is brought within the said time or before the expiration of any extension of that time granted (in the case of a first extension) on an application made within that time or (in the case of a subsequent extension) on an application made before the expiration of the last previous extension, shall be extended until such date as the court may determine;
- (b) where no such appeal is pending or is so brought, shall continue until the end of the said time or, if any extension of that time is so granted, until the expiration of the extension or last extension so granted.

[1.23]

[20A Reinstatement of applications

(1) Subsection (2) below applies where an application for a patent is refused, or is treated as having been refused or withdrawn, as a direct consequence of a failure by the applicant to comply with a requirement of this Act or rules within a period which is—

- (a) set out in this Act or rules, or
- (b) specified by the comptroller.

(2) Subject to subsection (3) below, the comptroller shall reinstate the application if, and only if—

- (a) the applicant requests him to do so;
- (b) the request complies with the relevant requirements of rules; and
- (c) he is satisfied that the failure to comply referred to in subsection (1) above was unintentional.

(3) The comptroller shall not reinstate the application if—

- (a) an extension remains available under this Act or rules for the period referred to in subsection (1) above; or
- (b) the period referred to in subsection (1) above is set out or specified—
  - (i) in relation to any proceedings before the comptroller;
  - (ii) for the purposes of section 5(2A)(b) above; or

(iii) for the purposes of a request under this section or section 117B below.

(4) Where the application was made by two or more persons jointly, a request under subsection (2) above may, with the leave of the comptroller, be made by one or more of those persons without joining the others.

(5) If the application has been published under section 16 above, then the comptroller shall publish notice of a request under subsection (2) above in the prescribed manner.

(6) The reinstatement of an application under this section shall be by order.

(7) If an application is reinstated under this section the applicant shall comply with the requirement referred to in subsection (1) above within the further period specified by the comptroller in the order reinstating the application.

(8) The further period specified under subsection (7) above shall not be less than two months.

(9) If the applicant fails to comply with subsection (7) above the application shall be treated as having been withdrawn on the expiry of the period specified under that subsection.]

NOTES

Inserted, together with s 20B, by the Regulatory Reform (Patents) Order 2004, SI 2004/2357, arts 2, 8.

[1.24]

[20B Effect of reinstatement under section 20A

(1) The effect of reinstatement under section 20A of an application for a patent is as follows.

(2) Anything done under or in relation to the application during the period between termination and reinstatement shall be treated as valid.

(3) If the application has been published under section 16 above before its termination anything done during that period which would have constituted an infringement of the rights conferred by publication of the application if the termination had not occurred shall be treated as an infringement of those rights—

(a) if done at a time when it was possible for the period referred to in section 20A(1) above to be extended, or

(b) if it was a continuation or repetition of an earlier act infringing those rights.

(4) If the application has been published under section 16 above before its termination and, after the termination and before publication of notice of the request for its reinstatement, a person—

(a) began in good faith to do an act which would have constituted an infringement of the rights conferred by publication of the application if the termination had not taken place, or

(b) made in good faith effective and serious preparations to do such an act,

he has the right to continue to do the act or, as the case may be, to do the act, notwithstanding the reinstatement of the application and the grant of the patent; but this right does not extend to granting a licence to another person to do the act.

[(4A) The right conferred by subsection (4) does not become exercisable until the end of the period during which a request may be made under this Act, or under the rules, for an extension of the period referred to in section 20A(1).]

(5) If the act was done, or the preparations were made, in the course of a business, the person entitled to the right conferred by subsection (4) above may—

(a) authorise the doing of that act by any partners of his for the time being in that business, and

(b) assign that right, or transmit it on death (or in the case of a body corporate on its dissolution), to any person who acquires that part of the business in the course of which the act was done or the preparations were made.

(6) Where a product is disposed of to another in exercise of a right conferred by subsection (4) or (5) above, that other and any person claiming through him may deal with the product in the same way as if it had been disposed of by the applicant.

[(6A) The above provisions apply in relation to the use of a patented invention for the services of the Crown as they apply in relation to infringement of the rights conferred by publication of the application for a patent (or, as the case may be, infringement of the patent).

"Patented invention" has the same meaning as in section 55 below.]

(7) In this section "termination", in relation to an application, means—

(a) the refusal of the application, or

(b) the application being treated as having been refused or withdrawn.]

NOTES

Inserted as noted to s 20A at **[1.23]**.

Sub-s (4A): inserted by the Intellectual Property Act 2014, s 19, Schedule, para 2.

Sub-s (6A): inserted by the Patents Act 2004, s 16(1), Sch 2, paras 1, 7.

[1.25]

21 Observations by third party on patentability

(1) Where an application for a patent has been published but a patent has not been granted to the applicant, any other person may make observations in writing to the comptroller on the question whether the invention is a patentable invention, stating reasons for the observations, and the comptroller shall consider the observations in accordance with rules.

(2) It is hereby declared that a person does not become a party to any proceedings under this Act before the comptroller by reason only that he makes observations under this section.

NOTES

Comptroller: see the note to s 14 at **[1.15]**.

Security and safety

[1.26]

22 Information prejudicial to [national security] or safety of public

(1) Where an application for a patent is filed in the Patent Office (whether under this Act or any treaty or international convention to which the United Kingdom is a party and whether before or after the appointed day) and it appears to the comptroller that the application contains information of a description notified to him by the Secretary of State as being information the publication of which might be prejudicial to [national security], the comptroller may give directions prohibiting or restricting the publication of that information or its communication to any specified person or description of persons.

(2) If it appears to the comptroller that any application so filed contains information the publication of which might be prejudicial to the safety of the public, he may give directions prohibiting or restricting the publication of that information or its communication to any specified person or description of persons until the end of a period not exceeding three months from the end of the period prescribed for the purposes of section 16 above.

(3) While directions are in force under this section with respect to an application—

(a) if the application is made under this Act, it may proceed to the stage where it is in order for the grant of a patent, but it shall not be published and that information shall not be so communicated and no patent shall be granted in pursuance of the application;

(b) if it is an application for a European patent, it shall not be sent to the European Patent Office; and

(c) if it is an international application for a patent, a copy of it shall not be sent to the International Bureau or any international searching authority appointed under the Patent Co-operation Treaty.

(4) Subsection (3)(b) above shall not prevent the comptroller from sending the European Patent Office any information which it is his duty to send that office under the European Patent Convention.

(5) Where the comptroller gives directions under this section with respect to any application, he shall give notice of the application and of the directions to the Secretary of State, and the following provisions shall then have effect—

(a) the Secretary of State shall, on receipt of the notice, consider whether the publication of the application or the publication or communication of the information in question would be prejudicial to [national security] or the safety of the public;

(b) if the Secretary of State determines under paragraph (a) above that the publication of the application or the publication or communication of that information would be prejudicial to the safety of the public, he shall notify the comptroller who shall continue his directions under subsection (2) above until they are revoked under paragraph (e) below;

(c) if the Secretary of State determines under paragraph (a) above that the publication of the application or the publication or communication of that information would be prejudicial to [national security] or the safety of the public, he shall (unless a notice under paragraph (d) below has previously been given by the Secretary of State to the comptroller) reconsider that question during the period of nine months from the date of filing the application and at least once in every subsequent period of twelve months;

(d) if on consideration of an application at any time it appears to the Secretary of State that the publication of the application or the publication or communication of the information contained in it would not, or would no longer, be prejudicial to [national security] or the safety of the public, he shall give notice to the comptroller to that effect; and

(e) on receipt of such a notice the comptroller shall revoke the directions and may, subject to such conditions (if any) as he thinks fit, extend the time for doing anything required or authorised to be done by or under this Act in connection with the application, whether or not that time has previously expired.

(6) The Secretary of State may do the following for the purpose of enabling him to decide the question referred to in subsection (5)(c) above—

(a) where the application contains information relating to the production or use of atomic energy or research into matters connected with such production or use, he may at any time do one or both of the following, that is to say,

[(i) inspect the application and any documents sent to the comptroller in connection with it;

(ii) authorise a government body with responsibility for the production of atomic energy or for research into matters connected with its production or use, or a person appointed by such a government body, to inspect the application and any documents sent to the comptroller in connection with it]; and

(b) in any other case, he may at any time after (or, with the applicant's consent, before) the end of the period prescribed for the purposes of section 16 above inspect the application and any such documents;

and where [a government body or a person appointed by a government body carries out an inspection which the body or person is authorised to carry out under paragraph (a) above, the body or (as the case may be) the person shall report on the inspection to the Secretary of State as soon as practicable.]

(7) Where directions have been given under this section in respect of an application for a patent for an invention and, before the directions are revoked, that prescribed period expires and the application is brought in order for the grant of a patent, then—

(a) if while the directions are in force the invention is worked by (or with the written authorisation of or to the order of) a government department, the provisions of sections 55 to 59 below shall apply as if—

(i) the working were use made by virtue of section 55;

(ii) the application had been published at the end of that period; and

(iii) a patent had been granted for the invention at the time the application is brought in order for the grant of a patent (taking the terms of the patent to be those of the application as it stood at the time it was so brought in order); and

(b) if it appears to the Secretary of State that the applicant for the patent has suffered hardship by reason of the continuance in force of the directions, the Secretary of State may, with the consent of the Treasury, make such payment (if any) by way of compensation to the applicant as appears to the Secretary of State and the Treasury to be reasonable having regard to the inventive merit and utility of the invention, the purpose for which it is designed and any other relevant circumstances.

(8) Where a patent is granted in pursuance of an application in respect of which directions have been given under this section, no renewal fees shall be payable in respect of any period during which those directions were in force.

(9) A person who fails to comply with any direction under this section shall be liable—

(a) on summary conviction, to a fine not exceeding [the prescribed sum]; or

(b) on conviction on indictment, to imprisonment for a term not exceeding two years or a fine, or both.

NOTES

Section heading, sub-ss (1), (5), (6): words in square brackets substituted by the Patents Act 2004, s 16(1), Sch 2, paras 1, 8.

Sub-s (9): words in square brackets substituted by virtue of the Magistrates' Courts Act 1980, s 32(2).

[1.27]

23 Restrictions on applications abroad by United Kingdom residents

(1) Subject to the following provisions of this section, no person resident in the United Kingdom shall, without written authority granted by the comptroller, file or cause to be filed outside the United Kingdom an application for a patent for an invention [if subsection (1A) below applies to that application,] unless—

(a) an application for a patent for the same invention has been filed in the Patent Office (whether before, on or after the appointed day) not less than six weeks before the application outside the United Kingdom; and

(b) either no directions have been given under section 22 above in relation to the application in the United Kingdom or all such directions have been revoked.

[(1A) This subsection applies to an application if—

(a) the application contains information which relates to military technology or for any other reason publication of the information might be prejudicial to national security; or

(b) the application contains information the publication of which might be prejudicial to the safety of the public.]

(2) Subsection (1) above does not apply to an application for a patent for an invention for which an application for a patent has first been filed (whether before or after the appointed day) in a country outside the United Kingdom by a person resident outside the United Kingdom.

(3) A person who files or causes to be filed an application for the grant of a patent in contravention of this section shall be liable—

(a) on summary conviction, to a fine not exceeding [the prescribed sum]; or

(b) on conviction on indictment, to imprisonment for a term not exceeding two years or a fine, or both.

[(3A) A person is liable under subsection (3) above only if—

(a) he knows that filing the application, or causing it to be filed, would contravene this section; or

(b) he is reckless as to whether filing the application, or causing it to be filed, would contravene this section.]

(4) In this section—

(a) any reference to an application for a patent includes a reference to an application for other protection for an invention;

(b) any reference to either kind of application is a reference to an application under this Act, under the law of any country other than the United Kingdom or under any treaty or international convention to which the United Kingdom is a party.

NOTES

Sub-s (1): words in square brackets inserted by the Patents Act 2004, s 7(1).
Sub-ss (1A), (3A): inserted by the Patents Act 2004, s 7(2), (3).
Sub-s (3): words in square brackets substituted by virtue of the Magistrates' Courts Act 1980, s 32(2).

Provisions as to patents after grant

[1.28]

24 Publication and certificate of grant

(1) As soon as practicable after a patent has been granted under this Act the comptroller shall publish in the journal a notice that it has been granted.
(2) The comptroller shall, as soon as practicable after he publishes a notice under subsection (1) above, send the proprietor of the patent a certificate in the prescribed form that the patent has been granted to the proprietor.
(3) The comptroller shall, at the same time as he publishes a notice under subsection (1) above in relation to a patent publish the specification of the patent, the names of the proprietor and (if different) the inventor and any other matters constituting or relating to the patent which in the comptroller's opinion it is desirable to publish.
[(4) Subsection (3) above shall not require the comptroller to identify as inventor a person who has waived his right to be mentioned as inventor in any patent granted for the invention.]

NOTES

Sub-s (4): added by the Patents Act 2004, s 16(1), Sch 2, paras 1, 9.

[1.29]

25 Term of patent

(1) A patent granted under this Act shall be treated for the purposes of the following provisions of this Act as having been granted, and shall take effect, on the date on which notice of its grant is published in the journal and, subject to subsection (3) below, shall continue in force until the end of the period of 20 years beginning with the date of filing the application for the patent or with such other date as may be prescribed.
(2) A rule prescribing any such other date under this section shall not be made unless a draft of the rule has been laid before, and approved by resolution of, each House of Parliament.
[(3) Where any renewal fee in respect of a patent is not paid by the end of the period prescribed for payment (the "prescribed period") the patent shall cease to have effect at the end of such day, in the final month of that period, as may be prescribed.]
(4) If during [the period ending with the sixth month after the month in which the prescribed period ends] the renewal fee and any prescribed additional fee are paid, the patent shall be treated for the purposes of this Act as if it had never expired, and accordingly—

(a) anything done under or in relation to it during that further period shall be valid;
(b) an act which would constitute an infringement of it if it had not expired shall constitute such an infringement; and
(c) an act which would constitute the use of the patented invention for the services of the Crown if the patent had not expired shall constitute that use.

(5) Rules shall include provision requiring the comptroller to notify the registered proprietor of a patent that a renewal fee has not been received from him in the Patent Office before the end of the prescribed period and before the framing of the notification.

NOTES

Sub-s (3): substituted by the Patents Act 2004, s 8(1).
Sub-s (4): words in square brackets substituted by the Patents Act 2004, s 8(2).
Rules: the Patents Rules 2007, SI 2007/3291 at **[1.262]**.

[1.30]

26 Patent not to be impugned for lack of unity

No person may in any proceeding object to a patent or to an amendment of a specification of a patent on the ground that the claims contained in the specification of the patent, as they stand or, as the case may be, as proposed to be amended, relate—

(a) to more than one invention, or
(b) to a group of inventions which are not so linked as to form a single inventive concept.

[1.31]

27 General power to amend specification after grant

(1) Subject to the following provisions of this section and to section 76 below, the comptroller may, on an application made by the proprietor of a patent, allow the specification of the patent to be amended subject to such conditions, if any, as he thinks fit.

(2) No such amendment shall be allowed under this section where there are pending before the court or the comptroller proceedings in which the validity of the patent may be put in issue.
(3) An amendment of a specification of a patent under this section shall have effect and be deemed always to have had effect from the grant of the patent.
(4) The comptroller may, without an application being made to him for the purpose, amend the specification of a patent so as to acknowledge a registered trade-mark.
(5) A person may give notice to the comptroller of his opposition to an application under this section by the proprietor of a patent, and if he does so the comptroller shall notify the proprietor and consider the opposition in deciding whether to grant the application.
[(6) In considering whether or not to allow an application under this section, the comptroller shall have regard to any relevant principles applicable under the European Patent Convention.]

NOTES

Sub-s (6): added by the Patents Act 2004, s 2(1).

Registered trade mark: the reference to a registered trade mark in sub-s (4) is to be construed as a reference to a registered trade mark within the meaning of the Trade Marks Act 1994; see s 106(1) of, and Sch 4, para 1 to, the 1994 Act.

[1.32]
28 Restoration of lapsed patents
[(1) Where a patent has ceased to have effect by reason of a failure to pay any renewal fee, an application for the restoration of the patent may be made to the comptroller within the prescribed period.
(1A) Rules prescribing that period may contain such transitional provisions and savings as appear to the Secretary of State to be necessary or expedient.]
(2) An application under this section may be made by the person who was the proprietor of the patent or by any other person who would have been entitled to the patent if it had not ceased to have effect; and where the patent was held by two or more persons jointly, the application may, with the leave of the comptroller, be made by one or more of them without joining the others.
[(2A) Notice of the application shall be published by the comptroller in the prescribed manner.]
[(3) If the comptroller is satisfied that the failure of the proprietor of the patent—
(a) to pay the renewal fee within the prescribed period; or
(b) to pay that fee and any prescribed additional fee [within the period ending with the sixth month after the month in which the prescribed period ended],
was unintentional, the comptroller shall by order restore the patent on payment of any unpaid renewal fee and any prescribed additional fee.]
(4) An order under this section may be made subject to such conditions as the comptroller thinks fit (including a condition requiring compliance with any provisions of the rules relating to registration which have not been complied with), and if the proprietor of the patent does not comply with any condition of such an order the comptroller may revoke the order and give such directions consequential on the revocation as he thinks fit.
(5)–(9) . . .

NOTES

Sub-ss (1), (1A): substituted, for original sub-s (1), by the Copyright, Designs and Patents Act 1988, s 295, Sch 5, para 6(2).

Sub-s (2A): inserted by the Copyright, Designs and Patents Act 1988, s 295, Sch 5, para 6(3).

Sub-s (3): substituted by the Regulatory Reform (Patents) Order 2004, SI 2004/2357, arts 2, 9, subject to savings in art 23 thereof at **[1.251]**; words in square brackets substituted by the Patents Act 2004, s 8(3).

Sub-ss (5)–(9): repealed by the Copyright, Designs and Patents Act 1988, ss 295, 303(2), Sch 5, para 6(5), Sch 8.

[1.33]
[28A Effect of order for restoration of patent
(1) The effect of an order for the restoration of a patent is as follows.
(2) Anything done under or in relation to the patent during the period between expiry and restoration shall be treated as valid.
(3) Anything done during that period which would have constituted an infringement if the patent had not expired shall be treated as an infringement—
(a) if done at a time when it was possible for the patent to be renewed under section 25(4), or
(b) if it was a continuation or repetition of an earlier infringing act.
(4) If after it was no longer possible for the patent to be so renewed, and before publication of notice of the application for restoration, a person—
(a) began in good faith to do an act which would have constituted an infringement of the patent if it had not expired, or
(b) made in good faith effective and serious preparations to do such an act,
he has the right to continue to do the act or, as the case may be, to do the act, notwithstanding the restoration of the patent; but this right does not extend to granting a licence to another person to do the act.
(5) If the act was done, or the preparations were made, in the course of a business, the person entitled to the right conferred by subsection (4) may—
(a) authorise the doing of that act by any partners of his for the time being in that business, and

(b) assign that right, or transmit it on death (or in the case of a body corporate on its dissolution), to any person who acquires that part of the business in the course of which the act was done or the preparations were made.

(6) Where a product is disposed of to another in exercise of the rights conferred by subsection (4) or (5), that other and any person claiming through him may deal with the product in the same way as if it had been disposed of by the registered proprietor of the patent.

(7) The above provisions apply in relation to the use of a patent for the services of the Crown as they apply in relation to infringement of the patent.]

NOTES

Inserted by the Copyright, Designs and Patents Act 1988, s 295, Sch 5, para 7.

[1.34]

29 Surrender of patents

(1) The proprietor of a patent may at any time by notice given to the comptroller offer to surrender his patent.

(2) A person may give notice to the comptroller of his opposition to the surrender of a patent under this section, and if he does so the comptroller shall notify the proprietor of the patent and determine the question.

(3) If the comptroller is satisfied that the patent may properly be surrendered, he may accept the offer and, as from the date when notice of his acceptance is published in the journal, the patent shall cease to have effect, but no action for infringement shall lie in respect of any act done before that date and no right to compensation shall accrue for any use of the patented invention before that date for the services of the Crown.

Property in patents and applications, and registration

[1.35]

30 Nature of, and transactions in, patents and applications for patents

(1) Any patent or application for a patent is personal property (without being a thing in action), and any patent or any such application and rights in or under it may be transferred, created or granted in accordance with subsections (2) to (7) below.

(2) Subject to section 36(3) below, any patent or any such application, or any right in it, may be assigned or mortgaged.

(3) Any patent or any such application or right shall vest by operation of law in the same way as any other personal property and may be vested by an assent of personal representatives.

(4) Subject to section 36(3) below, a licence may be granted under any patent or any such application for working the invention which is the subject of the patent or the application; and—

(a) to the extent that the licence so provides, a sub-licence may be granted under any such licence and any such licence or sub-licence may be assigned or mortgaged; and

(b) any such licence or sub-licence shall vest by operation of law in the same way as any other personal property and may be vested by an assent of personal representatives.

(5) Subsections (2) to (4) above shall have effect subject to the following provisions of this Act.

(6) Any of the following transactions, that is to say—

(a) any assignment or mortgage of a patent or any such application, or any right in a patent or any such application;

(b) any assent relating to any patent or any such application or right;

shall be void unless it is in writing and is signed by or on behalf of [the assignor or mortgagor] (or, in the case of an assent or other transaction by a personal representative, by or on behalf of the personal representative) . . .

[(6A) If a transaction mentioned in subsection (6) above is by a body corporate, references in that subsection to such a transaction being signed by or on behalf of the assignor or mortgagor shall be taken to include references to its being under the seal of the body corporate.]

(7) An assignment of a patent or any such application or a share in it, and an exclusive licence granted under any patent or any such application, may confer on the assignee or licensee the right of the assignor or licensor to bring proceedings by virtue of section 61 or 69 below for a previous infringement or to bring proceedings under section 58 below for a previous act.

NOTES

Sub-s (6): words in square brackets substituted and words omitted repealed by the Regulatory Reform (Patents) Order 2004, SI 2004/2357, arts 2, 10(1), (2).

Sub-s (6A): inserted by SI 2004/2357, arts 2, 10(1), (3).

[1.36]

31 Nature of, and transactions in, patents and applications for patents in Scotland

(1) Section 30 above shall not extend to Scotland, but instead the following provisions of this section shall apply there.

(2) Any patent or application for a patent, and any right in or under any patent or any such application, is incorporeal moveable property, and the provisions of the following subsections and of section 36(3) below shall apply to any grant of licences, assignations and securities in relation to such property.

(3) Any patent or any such application, or any right in it, may be assigned and security may be granted over a patent or any such application or right.
(4) A licence may be granted, under any patent or any application for a patent, for working the invention which is the subject of the patent or application.
(5) To the extent that any licence granted under subsection (4) above so provides, a sub-licence may be granted under any such licence and any such licence or sub-licence may be assigned and security granted over it.
(6) Any assignation or grant of security under this section may be carried out only by writing [subscribed in accordance with the Requirements of Writing (Scotland) Act 1995].
(7) Any assignation of a patent or application for a patent or a share in it, and an exclusive licence granted under any patent or any such application, may confer on the assignee or licensee the right of the assignor or licensor to bring proceedings by virtue of section 61 or 69 below for a previous infringement or to bring proceedings under section 58 below for a previous act.

NOTES

Sub-s (6): words in square brackets substituted by the Requirements of Writing (Scotland) Act 1995, s 14(1), Sch 4, para 49.

[1.37]

[32 Register of patents etc

(1) The comptroller shall maintain the register of patents, which shall comply with rules made by virtue of this section and shall be kept in accordance with such rules.
(2) Without prejudice to any other provision of this Act or rules, rules may make provision with respect to the following matters, including provision imposing requirements as to any of those matters—
(a) the registration of patents and of published applications for patents;
(b) the registration of transactions, instruments or events affecting rights in or under patents and applications;
[(ba) the entering on the register of notices concerning opinions issued, or to be issued, under section 74A below;]
(c) the furnishing to the comptroller of any prescribed documents or description of documents in connection with any matter which is required to be registered;
(d) the correction of errors in the register and in any documents filed at the Patent Office in connection with registration; and
(e) the publication and advertisement of anything done under this Act or rules in relation to the register.
(3) Notwithstanding anything in subsection (2)(b) above, no notice of any trust, whether express, implied or constructive, shall be entered in the register and the comptroller shall not be affected by any such notice.
(4) The register need not be kept in documentary form.
(5) Subject to rules, the public shall have a right to inspect the register at the Patent Office at all convenient times.
(6) Any person who applies for a certified copy of an entry in the register or a certified extract from the register shall be entitled to obtain such a copy or extract on payment of a fee prescribed in relation to certified copies and extracts; and rules may provide that any person who applies for an uncertified copy or extract shall be entitled to such a copy or extract on payment of a fee prescribed in relation to uncertified copies and extracts.
(7) Applications under subsection (6) above or rules made by virtue of that subsection shall be made in such manner as may be prescribed.
(8) In relation to any portion of the register kept otherwise than in documentary form—
(a) the right of inspection conferred by subsection (5) above is a right to inspect the material on the register; and
(b) the right to a copy or extract conferred by subsection (6) above or rules is a right to a copy or extract in a form in which it can be taken away and in which it is visible and legible.
(9) . . . the register shall be prima facie evidence of anything required or authorised by this Act or rules to be registered and in Scotland shall be sufficient evidence of any such thing.
(10) A certificate purporting to be signed by the comptroller and certifying that any entry which he is authorised by this Act or rules to make has or has not been made, or that any other thing which he is so authorised to do has or has not been done, shall be prima facie evidence, and in Scotland shall be evidence, of the matters so certified.
(11) Each of the following, that is to say—
(a) a copy of an entry in the register or an extract from the register which is supplied under subsection (6) above;
(b) a copy of any document kept in the Patent Office or an extract from any such document, any specification of a patent or any application for a patent which has been published,

which purports to be a certified copy or a certified extract shall . . . be admitted in evidence without further proof and without production of any original; and in Scotland such evidence shall be sufficient evidence.
(12) . . .

(13) In this section "certified copy" and "certified extract" mean a copy and extract certified by the comptroller and sealed with the seal of the Patent Office.

(14) In this Act, except so far as the context otherwise requires—

"register", as a noun, means the register of patents;

"register", as a verb, means, in relation to any thing, to register or register particulars, or enter notice, of that thing in the register and, in relation to a person, means to enter his name in the register;

and cognate expressions shall be construed accordingly.]

NOTES

Substituted by the Patents, Designs and Marks Act 1986, s 1, Sch 1, para 4.

Sub-s (2): para (ba) inserted by the Patents Act 2004, s 13(3).

Sub-ss (9), (11): words omitted repealed by the Criminal Justice Act 2003, s 332, Sch 37, Pt 6.

Sub-s (12): repealed by the Youth Justice and Criminal Evidence Act 1999, s 67(3), Sch 6.

Rules: the Patents Rules 2007, SI 2007/3291 at **[1.262]**.

[1.38]

33 Effect of registration, etc, on rights in patents

(1) Any person who claims to have acquired the property in a patent or application for a patent by virtue of any transaction, instrument or event to which this section applies shall be entitled as against any other person who claims to have acquired that property by virtue of an earlier transaction, instrument or event to which this section applies if, at the time of the later transaction, instrument or event—

(a) the earlier transaction, instrument or event was not registered, or

(b) in the case of any application which has not been published, notice of the earlier transaction, instrument or event had not been given to the comptroller, and

(c) in any case, the person claiming under the later transaction, instrument or event, did not know of the earlier transaction, instrument or event.

(2) Subsection (1) above shall apply equally to the case where any person claims to have acquired any right in or under a patent or application for a patent, by virtue of a transaction, instrument or event to which this section applies, and that right is incompatible with any such right acquired by virtue of an earlier transaction, instrument or event to which this section applies.

(3) This section applies to the following transactions, instruments and events—

(a) the assignment or assignation of a patent or application for a patent, or a right in it;

(b) the mortgage of a patent or application or the granting of security over it;

(c) the grant, assignment or assignation of a licence or sub-licence, or mortgage of a licence or sub-licence, under a patent or application;

(d) the death of the proprietor or one of the proprietors of any such patent or application or any person having a right in or under a patent or application and the vesting by an assent of personal representatives of a patent, application or any such right; and

(e) any order or directions of a court or other competent authority—

(i) transferring a patent or application or any right in or under it to any person; or

(ii) that an application should proceed in the name of any person;

and in either case the event by virtue of which the court or authority had power to make any such order or give any such directions.

(4) Where an application for the registration of a transaction, instrument or event has been made, but the transaction, instrument or event has not been registered, then, for the purposes of subsection (1)(a) above, registration of the application shall be treated as registration of the transaction, instrument or event.

[1.39]

34 Rectification of register

(1) The court may, on the application of any person aggrieved, order the register to be rectified by the making, or the variation or deletion, of any entry in it.

(2) In proceedings under this section the court may determine any question which it may be necessary or expedient to decide in connection with the rectification of the register.

(3) Rules of court may provide for the notification of any application under this section to the comptroller and for his appearance on the application and for giving effect to any order of the court on the application.

35 (*Repealed by the Patents, Designs and Marks Act 1986, s 3, Sch 3, Pt I.*)

[1.40]

36 Co-ownership of patents and applications for patents

(1) Where a patent is granted to two or more persons, each of them shall, subject to any agreement to the contrary, be entitled to an equal undivided share in the patent.

(2) Where two or more persons are proprietors of a patent, then, subject to the provisions of this section and subject to any agreement to the contrary—

(a) each of them shall be entitled, by himself or his agents, to do in respect of the invention concerned, for his own benefit and without the consent of or the need to account to the other or others, any act which would apart from this subsection and section 55 below, amount to an infringement of the patent concerned; and

(b) any such act shall not amount to an infringement of the patent concerned.

(3) Subject to the provisions of sections 8 and 12 above and section 37 below and to any agreement for the time being in force, where two or more persons are proprietors of a patent one of them shall not without the consent of the other or others[—

(a) amend the specification of the patent or apply for such an amendment to be allowed or for the patent to be revoked, or

(b)] grant a licence under the patent or assign or mortgage a share in the patent or in Scotland cause or permit security to be granted over it.

(4) Subject to the provisions of those sections, where two or more persons are proprietors of a patent, anyone else may supply one of those persons with the means, relating to an essential element of the invention, for putting the invention into effect, and the supply of those means by virtue of this subsection shall not amount to an infringement of the patent.

(5) Where a patented product is disposed of by any of two or more proprietors to any person, that person and any other person claiming through him shall be entitled to deal with the product in the same way as if it had been disposed of by a sole registered proprietor.

(6) Nothing in subsection (1) or (2) above shall affect the mutual rights or obligations of trustees or of the personal representatives of a deceased person, or their rights or obligations as such.

(7) The foregoing provisions of this section shall have effect in relation to an application for a patent which is filed as they have effect in relation to a patent and—

(a) references to a patent and a patent being granted shall accordingly include references respectively to any such application and to the application being filed; and

(b) the reference in subsection (5) above to a patented product shall be construed accordingly.

NOTES

Sub-s (3): words in square brackets inserted by the Patents Act 2004, s 9.

[1.41]

37 Determination of right to patent after grant

[(1) After a patent has been granted for an invention any person having or claiming a proprietary interest in or under the patent may refer to the comptroller the question—

(a) who is or are the true proprietor or proprietors of the patent,

(b) whether the patent should have been granted to the person or persons to whom it was granted, or

(c) whether any right in or under the patent should be transferred or granted to any other person or persons;

and the comptroller shall determine the question and make such order as he thinks fit to give effect to the determination.]

(2) Without prejudice to the generality of subsection (1) above, an order under that subsection may contain provision—

(a) directing that the person by whom the reference is made under that subsection shall be included (whether or not to the exclusion of any other person) among the persons registered as proprietors of the patent;

(b) directing the registration of a transaction, instrument or event by virtue of which that person has acquired any right in or under the patent;

(c) granting any licence or other right in or under the patent;

(d) directing the proprietor of the patent or any person having any right in or under the patent to do anything specified in the order as necessary to carry out the other provisions of the order.

(3) If any person to whom directions have been given under subsection (2)(d) above fails to do anything necessary for carrying out any such directions within 14 days after the date of the order containing the directions, the comptroller may, on application made to him by any person in whose favour or on whose reference the order containing the directions was made, authorise him to do that thing on behalf of the person to whom the directions were given.

(4) Where the comptroller finds on a reference under [this section] that the patent was granted to a person not entitled to be granted that patent (whether alone or with other persons) and on an application made under section 72 below makes an order on the ground for the conditional or unconditional revocation of the patent, the comptroller may order that the person by whom the application was made or his successor in title may, subject to section 76 below, make a new application for a patent—

(a) in the case of unconditional revocation, for the whole of the matter comprised in the specification of that patent; and

(b) in the case of conditional revocation, for the matter which in the opinion of the comptroller should be excluded from that specification by amendment under section 75 below;

and where such a new application is made, it shall be treated as having been filed on the date of filing the application for the patent to which the reference relates.

(5) On any such reference no order shall be made under this section transferring the patent to which the reference relates on the ground that the patent was granted to a person not so entitled, and no order shall be made under subsection (4) above on that ground, if the reference was made after [the second anniversary of] the date of the grant, unless it is shown that any person registered as a proprietor of the patent knew at the time of the grant or, as the case may be, of the transfer of the patent to him that he was not entitled to the patent.

(6) An order under this section shall not be so made as to affect the mutual rights or obligations of trustees or of the personal representatives of a deceased person, or their rights or obligations as such.

(7) Where a question is referred to the comptroller under [this section] an order shall not be made by virtue of subsection (2) or under subsection (4) above on the reference unless notice of the reference is given to all persons registered as proprietor of the patent or as having a right in or under the patent, except those who are parties to the reference.

(8) If it appears to the comptroller on a reference under [this section] that the question referred to him would more properly be determined by the court, he may decline to deal with it and, without prejudice to the court's jurisdiction to determine any such question and make a declaration, or any declaratory jurisdiction of the court in Scotland, the court shall have jurisdiction to do so.

(9) The court shall not in the exercise of any such declaratory jurisdiction determine a question whether a patent was granted to a person not entitled to be granted the patent if the proceedings in which the jurisdiction is invoked were commenced after [the second anniversary of] the date of the grant of the patent, unless it is shown that any person registered as a proprietor of the patent knew at the time of the grant or, as the case may be, of the transfer of the patent to him that he was not entitled to the patent.

NOTES

Sub-s (1): substituted by the Copyright, Designs and Patents Act 1988, s 295, Sch 5, para 9(2).

Sub-ss (4), (7), (8): words in square brackets substituted by the Copyright, Designs and Patents Act 1988, s 295, Sch 5, para 9(3).

Sub-ss (5), (9): words in square brackets substituted by the Intellectual Property Act 2014, s 19, Schedule, para 3(1)(a).

[1.42]

38 Effect of transfer of patent under s 37

(1) Where an order is made under section 37 above that a patent shall be transferred from any person or persons (the old proprietor or proprietors) to one or more persons (whether or not including an old proprietor), then, except in a case falling within subsection (2) below, any licences or other rights granted or created by the old proprietor or proprietors shall, subject to section 33 above and to the provisions of the order, continue in force and be treated as granted by the person or persons to whom the patent is ordered to be transferred (the new proprietor or proprietors).

(2) Where an order is so made that a patent shall be transferred from the old proprietor or proprietors to one or more persons none of whom was an old proprietor (on the ground that the patent was granted to a person not entitled to be granted the patent), any licences or other rights in or under the patent shall, subject to the provisions of the order and subsection (3) below, lapse on the registration of that person or those persons as the new proprietor or proprietors of the patent.

(3) Where an order is so made that a patent shall be transferred as mentioned in subsection (2) above or that a person other than an old proprietor may make a new application for a patent and before the reference of the question under that section resulting in the making of any such order is registered, the old proprietor or proprietors or a licensee of the patent, acting in good faith, worked the invention in question in the United Kingdom or made effective and serious preparations to do so, the old proprietor or proprietors or the licensee shall, on making a request to the new proprietor or proprietors [or, as the case may be, the new applicant] within the prescribed period, be entitled to be granted a licence (but not an exclusive licence) to continue working or, as the case may be, to work the invention, so far as it is the subject of the new application.

(4) Any such licence shall be granted for a reasonable period and on reasonable terms.

(5) The new proprietor or proprietors of the patent [or, as the case may be, the new applicant] or any person claiming that he is entitled to be granted any such licence may refer to the comptroller the question whether that person is so entitled and whether any such period is or terms are reasonable, and the comptroller shall determine the question and may, if he considers it appropriate, order the grant of such a licence.

NOTES

Sub-ss (3), (5): words in square brackets inserted by the Patents Act 2004, s 16(1), Sch 2, paras 1, 10.

Employees' inventions

[1.43]

39 Right to employees' inventions

(1) Notwithstanding anything in any rule of law, an invention made by an employee shall, as between him and his employer, be taken to belong to his employer for the purposes of this Act and all other purposes if—

(a) it was made in the course of the normal duties of the employee or in the course of duties falling outside his normal duties, but specifically assigned to him, and the circumstances in either case were such that an invention might reasonably be expected to result from the carrying out of his duties; or

(b) the invention was made in the course of the duties of the employee and, at the time of making the invention, because of the nature of his duties and the particular responsibilities arising from the nature of his duties he had a special obligation to further the interests of the employer's undertaking.

(2) Any other invention made by an employee shall, as between him and his employer, be taken for those purposes to belong to the employee.

[(3) Where by virtue of this section an invention belongs, as between him and his employer, to an employee, nothing done—

(a) by or on behalf of the employee or any person claiming under him for the purposes of pursuing an application for a patent, or

(b) by any person for the purpose of performing or working the invention,

shall be taken to infringe any copyright or design right to which, as between him and his employer, his employer is entitled in any model or document relating to the invention.]

NOTES

Sub-s (3): added by the Copyright, Designs and Patents Act 1988, s 295, Sch 5, para 11(1).

[1.44]

40 Compensation of employees for certain inventions

[(1) Where it appears to the court or the comptroller on an application made by an employee within the prescribed period that—

(a) the employee has made an invention belonging to the employer for which a patent has been granted,

(b) having regard among other things to the size and nature of the employer's undertaking, the invention or the patent for it (or the combination of both) is of outstanding benefit to the employer, and

(c) by reason of those facts it is just that the employee should be awarded compensation to be paid by the employer,

the court or the comptroller may award him such compensation of an amount determined under section 41 below.]

(2) Where it appears to the court or the comptroller on an application made by an employee within the prescribed period that—

(a) a patent has been granted for an invention made by and belonging to the employee;

(b) his rights in the invention, or in any patent or application for a patent for the invention, have since the appointed day been assigned to the employer or an exclusive licence under the patent or application has since the appointed day been granted to the employer;

(c) the benefit derived by the employee from the contract of assignment, assignation or grant or any ancillary contract ("the relevant contract") is inadequate in relation to the benefit derived by the employer from [the invention or the patent for it (or both)]; and

(d) by reason of those facts it is just that the employee should be awarded compensation to be paid by the employer in addition to the benefit derived from the relevant contract;

the court or the comptroller may award him such compensation of an amount determined under section 41 below.

(3) Subsections (1) and (2) above shall not apply to the invention of an employee where a relevant collective agreement provides for the payment of compensation in respect of inventions of the same description as that invention to employees of the same description as that employee.

(4) Subsection (2) above shall have effect notwithstanding anything in the relevant contract or any agreement applicable to the invention (other than any such collective agreement).

(5) If it appears to the comptroller on an application under this section that application involves matters which would more properly be determined by the court, he may decline to deal with it.

(6) In this section—

"the prescribed period", in relation to proceedings before the court, means the period prescribed by rules of court, and

"relevant collective agreement" means a collective agreement within the meaning of [the Trade Union and Labour Relations (Consolidation) Act 1992], made by or on behalf of a trade union to which the employee belongs, and by the employer or an employers' association to which the employer belongs which is in force at the time of the making of the invention.

(7) References in this section to an invention belonging to an employer or employee are references to it so belonging as between the employer and the employee.

NOTES

Sub-s (1): substituted by the Patents Act 2004, s 10(1), (8), in relation to an invention the patent for which is applied for on or after 1 January 2005.

Sub-s (2): words in square brackets in para (c) substituted by the Patents Act 2004, s 10(2), (8), in relation to an invention the patent for which is applied for on or after 1 January 2005.

Sub-s (6): words in square brackets in definition "relevant collective agreement" substituted by the Trade Union and Labour Relations (Consolidation) Act 1992, s 300(2), Sch 2, para 9.

[1.45]

41 Amount of compensation

[(1) An award of compensation to an employee under section 40(1) or (2) above shall be such as will secure for the employee a fair share (having regard to all the circumstances) of the benefit which the employer has derived, or may reasonably be expected to derive, from any of the following—

- (a) the invention in question;
- (b) the patent for the invention;
- (c) the assignment, assignation or grant of—
  - (i) the property or any right in the invention, or
  - (ii) the property in, or any right in or under, an application for the patent,

to a person connected with the employer.]

(2) For the purposes of subsection (1) above the amount of any benefit derived or expected to be derived by an employer from the assignment, assignation or grant of—

- (a) the property in, or any right in or under, a patent for the invention or an application for such a patent; or
- (b) the property or any right in the invention;

to a person connected with him shall be taken to be the amount which could reasonably be expected to be so derived by the employer if that person had not been connected with him.

(3) Where the Crown[, United Kingdom Research and Innovation] or a Research Council in its capacity as employer assigns or grants the property in, or any right in or under, an invention, patent or application for a patent to a body having among its functions that of developing or exploiting inventions resulting from public research and does so for no consideration or only a nominal consideration, any benefit derived from the invention, patent or application by that body shall be treated for the purposes of the foregoing provisions of this section as so derived by the Crown *or, as the case may be, Research Council.*

In this subsection "Research Council" means a body which is a Research Council for the purposes of the Science and Technology Act 1965 *[or the Arts and Humanities Research Council (as defined by section 1 of the Higher Education Act 2004)].*

(4) In determining the fair share of the benefit to be secured for an employee in respect of . . . an invention which has always belonged to an employer, the court or the comptroller shall, among other things, take the following matters into account, that is to say—

- (a) the nature of the employee's duties, his remuneration and the other advantages he derives or has derived from his employment or has derived in relation to the invention under this Act;
- (b) the effort and skill which the employee has devoted to making the invention;
- (c) the effort and skill which any other person has devoted to making the invention jointly with the employee concerned, and the advice and other assistance contributed by any other employee who is not a joint inventor of the invention; and
- (d) the contribution made by the employer to the making, developing and working of the invention by the provision of advice, facilities and other assistance, by the provision of opportunities and by his managerial and commercial skill and activities.

(5) In determining the fair share of the benefit to be secured for an employee in respect of . . . an invention which originally belonged to him, the court or the comptroller shall, among other things, take the following matters into account, that is to say—

- (a) any conditions in a licence or licences granted under this Act or otherwise in respect of the invention or the patent [for it];
- (b) the extent to which the invention was made jointly by the employee with any other person; and
- (c) the contribution made by the employer to the making, developing and working of the invention as mentioned in subsection (4)(d) above.

(6) Any order for the payment of compensation under section 40 above may be an order for the payment of a lump sum or for periodical payment, or both.

(7) Without prejudice to section 32 of the Interpretation Act 1889 (which provides that a statutory power may in general be exercised from time to time), the refusal of the court or the comptroller to make any such order on an application made by an employee under section 40 above shall not prevent a further application being made under that section by him or any successor in title of his.

(8) Where the court or the comptroller has made any such order, the court or he may on the application of either the employer or the employee vary or discharge it or suspend any provision of the order and revive any provision so suspended, and section 40(5) above shall apply to the application as it applies to an application under that section.

(9) In England and Wales any sums awarded by the comptroller under section 40 above shall, if [the county court] so orders, be recoverable [under section 85 of the County Courts Act 1984] or otherwise as if they were payable under an order of that court.

(10) In Scotland an order made under section 40 above by the comptroller for the payment of any sums may be enforced in like manner as [an extract registered decree arbitral bearing a warrant for execution issued by the sheriff court of any sheriffdom in Scotland.]

(11) In Northern Ireland an order made under section 40 above by the comptroller for the payment of any sums may be enforced as if it were a money judgment.

NOTES

Sub-s (1): substituted by the Patents Act 2004, s 10(3), (8), in relation to an invention the patent for which is applied for on or after 1 January 2005.

Sub-s (3): words in first pair of square brackets inserted, for the first words in italics there are substituted the words ", United Kingdom Research and Innovation or the Research Council (as the case may be)" and second words in italics (as inserted by the Higher Education Act 2004, s 49, Sch 6, para 5) repealed, by the Higher Education and Research Act 2017, s 122(2), Sch 12, para 13, as from a day to be appointed.

Sub-s (4): words omitted repealed by the Patents Act 2004, ss 10(4), (8), 16(2), Sch 3, in relation to an invention the patent for which is applied for on or after 1 January 2005.

Sub-s (5): words omitted repealed, and words in square brackets inserted by the Patents Act 2004, ss 10(4), (5), (8), 16(2), Sch 3, in relation to an invention the patent for which is applied for on or after 1 January 2005.

Sub-s (9): words in first pair of square brackets substituted by the Crime and Courts Act 2013, s 17, Sch 9, Pt 3, para 52(1)(b), (2); words in second pair of square brackets substituted by the Tribunals, Courts and Enforcement Act 2007, s 62(3), Sch 13, paras 39, 40.

Sub-s (10): words in square brackets substituted by the Patents Act 2004, s 16(1), Sch 2, paras 1, 11.

Interpretation Act 1889, s 32: repealed by the Interpretation Act 1978, s 25, Sch 3, and replaced by ss 12, 14 of, and Sch 2, para 3 to, that Act.

[1.46]

42 Enforceability of contracts relating to employees' inventions

(1) This section applies to any contract (whenever made) relating to inventions made by an employee, being a contract entered into by him—

(a) with the employer (alone or with another); or

(b) with some other person at the request of the employer or in pursuance of the employee's contract of employment.

(2) Any term in a contract to which this section applies which diminishes the employee's rights in inventions of any description made by him after the appointed day and the date of the contract, or in or under patents for those inventions or applications for such patents, shall be unenforceable against him to the extent that it diminishes his rights in an invention of that description so made, or in or under a patent for such an invention or an application for any such patent.

(3) Subsection (2) above shall not be construed as derogating from any duty of confidentiality owed to his employer by an employee by virtue of any rule of law of otherwise.

(4) This section applies to any arrangement made with a Crown employee by or on behalf of the Crown as his employer as it applies to any contract made between an employee and an employer other than the Crown, and for the purposes of this section "Crown employee" means a person employed under or for the purposes of a government department or any officer or body exercising on behalf of the Crown functions conferred by any enactment [or a person serving in the naval, military or air forces of the Crown].

NOTES

Sub-s (4): words in square brackets added with retrospective effect by the Armed Forces Act 1981, s 22(1), (2).

[1.47]

43 Supplementary

(1) Sections 39 to 42 above shall not apply to an invention made before the appointed day.

(2) Sections 39 to 42 above shall not apply to an invention made by an employee unless at the time he made the invention one of the following conditions was satisfied in his case, that is to say—

(a) he was mainly employed in the United Kingdom; or

(b) he was not mainly employed anywhere or his place of employment could not be determined, but his employer had a place of business in the United Kingdom to which the employee was attached, whether or not he was also attached elsewhere.

(3) In sections 39 to 42 above and this section, except so far as the context otherwise requires, references to the making of an invention by an employee are references to his making it alone or jointly with any other person, but do not include references to his merely contributing advice or other assistance in the making of an invention by another employee.

(4) Any references [in sections 39 to 42] above to a patent and to a patent being granted are respectively references to a patent or other protection and to its being granted whether under the law of the United Kingdom or the law in force in any other country or under any treaty or international convention.

(5) For the purposes of sections 40 and 41 above the benefit derived or expected to be derived by an employer from [an invention or patent] shall, where he dies before any award is made under section 40 above in respect of [it], include any benefit derived or expected to be derived from [it] by his personal representatives or by any person in whom it was vested by their assent.

[(5A) For the purposes of sections 40 and 41 above the benefit derived or expected to be derived by an employer from an invention shall not include any benefit derived or expected to be derived from the invention after the patent for it has expired or has been surrendered or revoked.]

(6) Where an employee dies before an award is made under section 40 above in respect of a patented invention made by him, his personal representatives or their successors in title may exercise his right to make or proceed with an application for compensation under subsection (1) or (2) of that section.

(7) In sections 40 and 41 above and this section "benefit" means benefit in money or money's worth.

(8) Section 533 of the Income and Corporation Taxes Act 1970 (definition of connected persons) shall apply for determining for the purposes of section 41(2) above whether one person is connected with another as it applies for determining that question for the purposes of the Tax Acts.

NOTES

Sub-s (4): words in square brackets substituted by the Copyright, Designs and Patents Act 1988, s 295, Sch 5, para 11(2).

Sub-s (5): words in square brackets substituted by the Patents Act 2004, s 10(6), (8), in relation to an invention the patent for which is applied for on or after 1 January 2005.

Sub-s (5A): inserted by the Patents Act 2004, s 10(7), (8), in relation to an invention the patent for which is applied for on or after 1 January 2005.

Income and Corporation Taxes Act 1970, s 533: repealed by the Income and Corporation Taxes Act 1988, s 844(4), Sch 31; see now s 839 of the 1988 Act.

Contracts as to patented products, etc

[1.48]

44 Avoidance of certain restrictive conditions

(1) Subject to the provisions of this section, any condition or term of a contract for the supply of a patented product or of a licence to work a patented invention, or of a contract relating to any such supply or licence, shall be void in so far as it purports—

- *(a) in the case of a contract for supply, to require the person supplied to acquire from the supplier, or his nominee, or prohibit him from acquiring from any specified person, or from acquiring except from the supplier or his nominee, anything other than the patented product;*
- *(b) in the case of a licence to work a patented invention, to require the licensee to acquire from the licensor or his nominee, or prohibit him from acquiring from any specified person, or from acquiring except from the licensor or his nominee, anything other than the product which is the patented invention or (if it is a process) other than any product obtained directly by means of the process or to which the process has been applied;*
- *(c) in either case, to prohibit the person supplied or licensee from using articles (whether patented products or not) which are not supplied by, or any patented process which does not belong to, the supplier or licensor, or his nominee, or to restrict the right of the person supplied or licensee to use any such articles or process.*

(2) Subsection (1) above applies to contracts and licences whether made or granted before or after the appointed day, but not to those made or granted before 1st January 1950.

(3) In proceedings against any person for infringement of a patent it shall be a defence to prove that at the time of the infringement there was in force a contract relating to the patent made by or with the consent of the plaintiff or pursuer or a licence under the patent granted by him or with his consent and containing in either case a condition or term void by virtue of this section.

(4) A condition or term of a contract or licence shall not be void by virtue of this section if—

- *(a) at the time of the making of the contract or granting of the licence the supplier or licensor was willing to supply the product, or grant a licence to work the invention, as the case may be, to the person supplied or licensee, on reasonable terms specified in the contract or licence and without any such condition or term as is mentioned in subsection (1) above; and*
- *(b) the person supplied or licensee is entitled under the contract or licence to relieve himself of his liability to observe the condition or term on giving to the other party three months' notice in writing and subject to payment to that other party of such compensation (being, in the case of a contract to supply, a lump sum or rent for the residue of the term of the contract and, in the case of a licence, a royalty for the residue of the term of the licence) as may be determined by an arbitrator or arbiter appointed by the Secretary of State.*

(5) If in any proceeding it is alleged that any condition or term of a contract or licence is void by virtue of this section it shall lie on the supplier or licensor to prove the matters set out in paragraph (a) of subsection (4) above.

(6) A condition or term of a contract or licence shall not be void by virtue of this section by reason only that it prohibits any person from selling goods other than those supplied by a specific person or, in the case of a contract for the hiring of or licence to use a patented product, that it reserves to the bailor (or in Scotland, hirer) or licensor, or his nominee, the right to supply such new parts of the patented product as may be required to put or keep it in repair.

NOTES

Repealed by the Competition Act 1998, ss 70, 74(3), Sch 14, Pt I, except in respect of any agreement made before 1 March 2000.

45 (*Repealed by the Competition Act 1998, ss 70, 74(3), Sch 14, Pt I.*)

Licences of right and compulsory licences

[1.49]

46 Patentee's application for entry in register that licences are available as of right

(1) At any time after the grant of a patent its proprietor may apply to the comptroller for an entry to be made in the register to the effect that licences under the patent are to be available as of right.

(2) Where such an application is made, the comptroller shall give notice of the application to any person registered as having a right in or under the patent and, if satisfied that the proprietor of the patent is not precluded by contract from granting licences under the patent, shall make that entry.

(3) Where such an entry is made in respect of a patent—

(a) any person shall, at any time after the entry is made, be entitled as of right to a licence under the patent on such terms as may be settled by agreement or, in default of agreement, by the comptroller on the application of the proprietor of the patent or the person requiring the licence;

(b) the comptroller may, on the application of the holder of any licence granted under the patent before the entry was made, order the licence to be exchanged for a licence of right on terms so settled;

(c) if in proceedings for infringement of the patent (otherwise than by the importation of any article [from a country which is not a member State of the European Economic Community]) the defendant or defender undertakes to take a licence on such terms, no injunction or interdict shall be granted against him and the amount (if any) recoverable against him by way of damages shall not exceed double the amount which would have been payable by him as licensee if such a licence on those terms had been granted before the earliest infringement;

[(d) if the expiry date in relation to a renewal fee falls after the date of the entry, that fee shall be half the fee which would be payable had the entry not been made.]

[(3A) An undertaking under subsection (3)(c) above may be given at any time before final order in the proceedings, without any admission of liability.]

[(3B) For the purposes of subsection (3)(d) above the expiry date in relation to a renewal fee is the day at the end of which, by virtue of section 25(3) above, the patent in question ceases to have effect if that fee is not paid.]

(4) The licensee under a licence of right may (unless, in the case of a licence the terms of which are settled by agreement, the licence otherwise expressly provides) request the proprietor of the patent to take proceedings to prevent any infringement of the patent; and if the proprietor refuses or neglects to do so within two months after being so requested, the licensee may institute proceedings for the infringement in his own name as if he were proprietor, making the proprietor a defendant or defender.

(5) A proprietor so added as defendant or defender shall not be liable for any costs or expenses unless he enters an appearance and takes part in the proceedings.

NOTES

Sub-s (3): words in square brackets in para (c) inserted by the Copyright, Designs and Patents Act 1988, s 295, Sch 5, para 12(2); para (d) substituted by the Patents Act 2004, s 8(4)(a).

Sub-s (3A): inserted by the Copyright, Designs and Patents Act 1988, s 295, Sch 5, para 12(3).

Sub-s (3B): inserted by the Patents Act 2004, s 8(4)(b).

[1.50]

47 Cancellation of entry made under s 46

(1) At any time after an entry has been made under section 46 above in respect of a patent, the proprietor of the patent may apply to the comptroller for cancellation of the entry.

(2) Where such an application is made and the balance paid of all renewal fees which would have been payable if the entry had not been made, the comptroller may cancel the entry, if satisfied that there is no existing licence under the patent or that all licensees under the patent consent to the application.

(3) Within the prescribed period after an entry has been made under section 46 above in respect of a patent, any person who claims that the proprietor of the patent is, and was at the time of the entry, precluded by a contract in which the claimant is interested from granting licences under the patent may apply to the comptroller for cancellation of the entry.

(4) Where the comptroller is satisfied, on an application under subsection (3) above, that the proprietor of the patent is and was so precluded, he shall cancel the entry; and the proprietor shall then be liable to pay, within a period specified by the comptroller, a sum equal to the balance of all renewal fees which would have been payable if the entry had not been made, and the patent shall cease to have effect at the expiration of that period if that sum is not so paid.

(5) Where an entry is cancelled under this section, the rights and liabilities of the proprietor of the patent shall afterwards be the same as if the entry had not been made.

(6) Where an application has been made under this section then—

(a) in the case of an application under subsection (1) above, any person, and

(b) in the case of an application under subsection (3) above, the proprietor of the patent,

may within the prescribed period give notice to the comptroller of opposition to the cancellation; and the comptroller shall, in considering the application, determine whether the opposition is justified.

[1.51]

[48 Compulsory licences: general

(1) At any time after the expiration of three years, or of such other period as may be prescribed, from the date of the grant of a patent, any person may apply to the comptroller on one or more of the relevant grounds—

(a) for a licence under the patent;

(b) for an entry to be made in the register to the effect that licences under the patent are to be available as of right; or

(c) where the applicant is a government department, for the grant to any person specified in the application of a licence under the patent.

(2) Subject to sections 48A and 48B below, if he is satisfied that any of the relevant grounds are established, the comptroller may—

(a) where the application is under subsection (1)(a) above, order the grant of a licence to the applicant on such terms as the comptroller thinks fit;

(b) where the application is under subsection (1)(b) above, make such an entry as is there mentioned;

(c) where the application is under subsection (1)(c) above, order the grant of a licence to the person specified in the application on such terms as the comptroller thinks fit.

(3) An application may be made under this section in respect of a patent even though the applicant is already the holder of a licence under the patent; and no person shall be estopped or barred from alleging any of the matters specified in the relevant grounds by reason of any admission made by him, whether in such a licence or otherwise, or by reason of his having accepted a licence.

(4) In this section "the relevant grounds" means—

(a) in the case of an application made in respect of a patent whose proprietor is a WTO proprietor, the grounds set out in section 48A(1) below;

(b) in any other case, the grounds set out in section 48B(1) below.

(5) A proprietor is a WTO proprietor for the purposes of this section and sections 48A, 48B, 50 and 52 below if—

(a) he is a national of, or is domiciled in, a country which is a member of the World Trade Organisation; or

(b) he has a real and effective industrial or commercial establishment in such a country.

(6) A rule prescribing any such other period under subsection (1) above shall not be made unless a draft of the rule has been laid before, and approved by resolution of, each House of Parliament.]

NOTES

Substituted by the Patents and Trade Marks (World Trade Organisation) Regulations 1999, SI 1999/1899, reg 3.

[1.52]

[48A Compulsory licences: WTO proprietors

(1) In the case of an application made under section 48 above in respect of a patent whose proprietor is a WTO proprietor, the relevant grounds are—

(a) where the patented invention is a product, that a demand in the United Kingdom for that product is not being met on reasonable terms;

(b) that by reason of the refusal of the proprietor of the patent concerned to grant a licence or licences on reasonable terms—

(i) the exploitation in the United Kingdom of any other patented invention which involves an important technical advance of considerable economic significance in relation to the invention for which the patent concerned was granted is prevented or hindered, or

(ii) the establishment or development of commercial or industrial activities in the United Kingdom is unfairly prejudiced;

(c) that by reason of conditions imposed by the proprietor of the patent concerned on the grant of licences under the patent, or on the disposal or use of the patented product or on the use of the patented process, the manufacture, use or disposal of materials not protected by the patent, or the establishment or development of commercial or industrial activities in the United Kingdom, is unfairly prejudiced.

(2) No order or entry shall be made under section 48 above in respect of a patent whose proprietor is a WTO proprietor unless—

(a) the applicant has made efforts to obtain a licence from the proprietor on reasonable commercial terms and conditions; and

(b) his efforts have not been successful within a reasonable period.

(3) No order or entry shall be so made if the patented invention is in the field of semi-conductor technology.

(4) No order or entry shall be made under section 48 above in respect of a patent on the ground mentioned in subsection (1)(b)(i) above unless the comptroller is satisfied that the proprietor of the patent for the other invention is able and willing to grant the proprietor of the patent concerned and his licensees a licence under the patent for the other invention on reasonable terms.

(5) A licence granted in pursuance of an order or entry so made shall not be assigned except to a person to whom the patent for the other invention is also assigned.

(6) A licence granted in pursuance of an order or entry made under section 48 above in respect of a patent whose proprietor is a WTO proprietor—

(a) shall not be exclusive;

(b) shall not be assigned except to a person to whom there is also assigned the part of the enterprise that enjoys the use of the patented invention, or the part of the goodwill that belongs to that part;

(c) shall be predominantly for the supply of the market in the United Kingdom;

(d) shall include conditions entitling the proprietor of the patent concerned to remuneration adequate in the circumstances of the case, taking into account the economic value of the licence; and

(e) shall be limited in scope and in duration to the purpose for which the licence was granted.]

NOTES

Inserted by the Patents and Trade Marks (World Trade Organisation) Regulations 1999, SI 1999/1899, reg 4.

[1.53]

[48B Compulsory licences: other cases

(1) In the case of an application made under section 48 above in respect of a patent whose proprietor is not a WTO proprietor, the relevant grounds are—

(a) where the patented invention is capable of being commercially worked in the United Kingdom, that it is not being so worked or is not being so worked to the fullest extent that is reasonably practicable;

(b) where the patented invention is a product, that a demand for the product in the United Kingdom—

(i) is not being met on reasonable terms, or

(ii) is being met to a substantial extent by importation from a country which is not a member State;

(c) where the patented invention is capable of being commercially worked in the United Kingdom, that it is being prevented or hindered from being so worked—

(i) where the invention is a product, by the importation of the product from a country which is not a member State,

(ii) where the invention is a process, by the importation from such a country of a product obtained directly by means of the process or to which the process has been applied;

(d) that by reason of the refusal of the proprietor of the patent to grant a licence or licences on reasonable terms—

(i) a market for the export of any patented product made in the United Kingdom is not being supplied, or

(ii) the working or efficient working in the United Kingdom of any other patented invention which makes a substantial contribution to the art is prevented or hindered, or

(iii) the establishment or development of commercial or industrial activities in the United Kingdom is unfairly prejudiced;

(e) that by reason of conditions imposed by the proprietor of the patent on the grant of licences under the patent, or on the disposal or use of the patented product or on the use of the patented process, the manufacture, use or disposal of materials not protected by the patent, or the establishment or development of commercial or industrial activities in the United Kingdom, is unfairly prejudiced.

(2) Where—

(a) an application is made on the ground that the patented invention is not being commercially worked in the United Kingdom or is not being so worked to the fullest extent that is reasonably practicable; and

(b) it appears to the comptroller that the time which has elapsed since the publication in the journal of a notice of the grant of the patent has for any reason been insufficient to enable the invention to be so worked,

he may by order adjourn the application for such period as will in his opinion give sufficient time for the invention to be so worked.

(3) No order or entry shall be made under section 48 above in respect of a patent on the ground mentioned in subsection (1)(a) above if—

(a) the patented invention is being commercially worked in a country which is a member State; and

(b) demand in the United Kingdom is being met by importation from that country.

(4) No entry shall be made in the register under section 48 above on the ground mentioned in subsection (1)(d)(i) above, and any licence granted under section 48 above on that ground shall contain such provisions as appear to the comptroller to be expedient for restricting the countries in which any product concerned may be disposed of or used by the licensee.

(5) No order or entry shall be made under section 48 above in respect of a patent on the ground mentioned in subsection (1)(d)(ii) above unless the comptroller is satisfied that the proprietor of the patent for the other invention is able and willing to grant to the proprietor of the patent concerned and his licensees a licence under the patent for the other invention on reasonable terms.]

NOTES

Inserted by the Patents and Trade Marks (World Trade Organisation) Regulations 1999, SI 1999/1899, reg 5.

[1.54]

49 Provisions about licences under s 48

(1) Where the comptroller is satisfied, on an application made under section 48 above in respect of a patent, that the manufacture, use or disposal of materials not protected by the patent is unfairly prejudiced by reason of conditions imposed by the proprietor of the patent on the grant of licences under the patent, or on the disposal or use of the patented product or the use of the patented process, he may (subject to the provisions of that section) order the grant of licences under the patent to such customers of the applicant as he thinks fit as well as to the applicant.

(2) Where an application under section 48 above is made in respect of a patent by a person who holds a licence under the patent, the comptroller—

(a) may, if he orders the grant of a licence to the applicant, order the existing licence to be cancelled, or

(b) may, instead of ordering the grant of a licence to the applicant, order the existing licence to be amended.

(3) . . .

(4) Section 46(4) and (5) above shall apply to a licence granted in pursuance of an order under section 48 above and to a licence granted by virtue of an entry under that section as it applies to a licence granted by virtue of an entry under section 46 above.

NOTES

Sub-s (3): repealed by the Copyright, Designs and Patents Act 1988, ss 295, 303(2), Sch 5, para 13, Sch 8.

[1.55]

50 Exercise of powers on applications under s 48

(1) The powers of the comptroller on an application under section 48 above in respect of a patent [whose proprietor is not a WTO proprietor] shall be exercised with a view to securing the following general purposes—

(a) that inventions which can be worked on a commercial scale in the United Kingdom and which should in the public interest be so worked shall be worked there without undue delay and to the fullest extent that is reasonably practicable;

(b) that the inventor or other person beneficially entitled to a patent shall receive reasonable remuneration having regard to the nature of the invention;

(c) that the interests of any person for the time being working or developing an invention in the United Kingdom under the protection of a patent shall not be unfairly prejudiced.

(2) Subject to subsection (1) above, the comptroller shall, in determining whether to make an order or entry in pursuance of [any application under section 48 above], take account of the following matters, that is to say—

(a) the nature of the invention, the time which has elapsed since the publication in the journal of a notice of the grant of the patent and the measures already taken by the proprietor of the patent or any licensee to make full use of the invention;

(b) the ability of any person to whom a licence would be granted under the order concerned to work the invention to the public advantage; and

(c) the risks to be undertaken by that person in providing capital and working the invention if the application for an order is granted,

but shall not be required to take account of matters subsequent to the making of the application.

NOTES

Sub-s (1): words in square brackets inserted by the Patents and Trade Marks (World Trade Organisation) Regulations 1999, SI 1999/1899, reg 7(2).

Sub-s (2): words in square brackets substituted by SI 1999/1899, reg 7(3).

[1.56]

[50A Powers exercisable following merger and market investigations

(1) Subsection (2) below applies where—

(a) section 41(2), 55(2), 66(6), 75(2), 83(2), 138(2), 147(2)[, 147A(2)] or 160(2) of, or paragraph 5(2) or 10(2) of Schedule 7 to, the Enterprise Act 2002 (powers to take remedial action following merger or market investigations) applies;

(b) the [Competition and Markets Authority] or (as the case may be) the Secretary of State considers that it would be appropriate to make an application under this section for the purpose of remedying, mitigating or preventing a matter which cannot be dealt with under the enactment concerned; and

(c) the matter concerned involves—

(i) conditions in licences granted under a patent by its proprietor restricting the use of the invention by the licensee or the right of the proprietor to grant other licences; or

(ii) a refusal by the proprietor of a patent to grant licences on reasonable terms.

(2) The [Competition and Markets Authority] or (as the case may be) the Secretary of State may apply to the comptroller to take action under this section.

(3) Before making an application the [Competition and Markets Authority] or (as the case may be) the Secretary of State shall publish, in such manner as it or he thinks appropriate, a notice describing the nature of the proposed application and shall consider any representations which may be made within 30 days of such publication by persons whose interests appear to it or him to be affected.

(4) The comptroller may, if it appears to him on an application under this section that the application is made in accordance with this section, by order cancel or modify any condition concerned of the kind mentioned in subsection (1)(c)(i) above or may, instead or in addition, make an entry in the register to the effect that licences under the patent are to be available as of right.

[(5) References in this section to the Competition and Markets Authority are references to a CMA group except where—

(a) section 75(2) of the Enterprise Act 2002 applies; or

(b) any other enactment mentioned in subsection (1)(a) above applies and the functions of the Competition and Markets Authority under that enactment are being performed by the CMA Board by virtue of section 34C(3) or 133A(2) of the Enterprise Act 2002.]

(6) References in section 35, 36, 47, 63, 134[, 141 or 141A] of the Enterprise Act 2002 (questions to be decided by the [Competition and Markets Authority] in its reports) to taking action under section 41(2), 55, 66, 138[, 147 or 147A] shall include references to taking action under subsection (2) above.

(7) Action taken by virtue of subsection (4) above in consequence of an application under subsection (2) above where an enactment mentioned in subsection (1)(a) above applies shall be treated, for the purposes of sections 91(3), 92(1)(a), 162(1) and 166(3) of the Enterprise Act 2002 (duties to register and keep under review enforcement orders etc), as if it were the making of an enforcement order (within the meaning of the Part concerned) under the relevant power in Part 3 or (as the case may be) 4 of that Act.

[(8) In subsection (5) "CMA Board" and "CMA group" have the same meaning as in Schedule 4 to the Enterprise and Regulatory Reform Act 2013.]]

NOTES

Inserted by the Enterprise Act 2002, s 278(1), Sch 25, para 8(1).

Sub-s (1): figure in square brackets in para (a) inserted and words in square brackets in para (b) substituted by the Enterprise and Regulatory Reform Act 2013 (Competition) (Consequential, Transitional and Saving Provisions) Order 2014, SI 2014/892, art 2, Sch 1, Pt 2, paras 31, 32(1)–(3).

Sub-ss (2), (3), (6): words in square brackets substituted by SI 2014/892, art 2, Sch 1, Pt 2, paras 31, 32(1), (3), (5).

Sub-s (5): substituted by SI 2014/892, art 2, Sch 1, Pt 2, paras 31, 32(1), (4).

Sub-s (7): figure in square brackets in para (a) inserted and words in square brackets in para (b) substituted by SI 2014/892, art 2, Sch 1, Pt 2, paras 31, 32(1), (2).

Sub-s (8): added by SI 2014/892, art 2, Sch 1, Pt 2, paras 31, 32(1), (6).

[1.57]

[51 Powers exercisable in consequence of report of [Competition and Markets Authority]

(1) Where a report of the [Competition and Markets Authority] has been laid before Parliament containing conclusions to the effect—

(a), (b) . . .

(c) on a competition reference, that a person was engaged in an anti-competitive practice which operated or may be expected to operate against the public interest, or

(d) on a reference under section 11 of the Competition Act 1980 (reference of public bodies and certain other persons), that a person is pursuing a course of conduct which operates against the public interest,

the appropriate Minister or Ministers may apply to the comptroller to take action under this section.

(2) Before making an application the appropriate Minister or Ministers shall publish, in such manner as he or they think appropriate, a notice describing the nature of the proposed application and shall consider any representations which may be made within 30 days of such publication by persons whose interests appear to him or them to be affected.

(3) If on an application under this section it appears to the comptroller that the matters specified in the [Competition and Markets Authority's report as being those which in the opinion of the Competition and Markets Authority] operate, or operated or may be expected to operate, against the public interest include—

(a) conditions in licences granted under a patent by its proprietor restricting the use of the invention by the licensee or the right of the proprietor to grant other licences, or

(b) a refusal by the proprietor of a patent to grant licences on reasonable terms
he may by order cancel or modify any such condition or may, instead or in addition, make an entry in the register to the effect that licences under the patent are to be available as of right.
(4) In this section "the appropriate Minister or Ministers" means the Minister or Ministers to whom the report of the [Competition and Markets Authority] was made.]

NOTES

Substituted by the Copyright, Designs and Patents Act 1988, s 295, Sch 5, para 14.

Section heading: words in square brackets substituted by the Enterprise and Regulatory Reform Act 2013 (Competition) (Consequential, Transitional and Saving Provisions) Order 2014, SI 2014/892, art 2, Sch 1, Pt 2, paras 31, 33(1), (5).

Sub-s (1): words in square brackets substituted by SI 2014/892, art 2, Sch 1, Pt 2, paras 31, 33(1), (2); paras (a), (b) repealed by the Enterprise Act 2002, s 278, Sch 25, para 8(1), (3), Sch 26.

Sub-ss (3), (4): words in square brackets substituted by SI 2014/892, art 2, Sch 1, Pt 2, paras 31, 33(1), (3), (4).

[1.58]

[52 Opposition, appeal and arbitration

(1) The proprietor of the patent concerned or any other person wishing to oppose an application under sections 48 to 51 above may, in accordance with rules, give to the comptroller notice of opposition; and the comptroller shall consider any opposition in deciding whether to grant the application.

(2) Where an order or entry has been made under section 48 above in respect of a patent whose proprietor is a WTO proprietor—

(a) the proprietor or any other person may, in accordance with rules, apply to the comptroller to have the order revoked or the entry cancelled on the grounds that the circumstances which led to the making of the order or entry have ceased to exist and are unlikely to recur;

(b) any person wishing to oppose an application under paragraph (a) above may, in accordance with rules, give to the comptroller notice of opposition; and

(c) the comptroller shall consider any opposition in deciding whether to grant the application.

(3) If it appears to the comptroller on an application under subsection (2)(a) above that the circumstances which led to the making of the order or entry have ceased to exist and are unlikely to recur, he may—

(a) revoke the order or cancel the entry; and

(b) terminate any licence granted to a person in pursuance of the order or entry subject to such terms and conditions as he thinks necessary for the protection of the legitimate interests of that person.

(4) Where an appeal is brought—

(a) from an order made by the comptroller in pursuance of an application under sections 48 to 51 above;

(b) from a decision of his to make an entry in the register in pursuance of such an application;

(c) from a revocation or cancellation made by him under subsection (3) above; or

(d) from a refusal of his to make such an order, entry, revocation or cancellation,

the Attorney General, the appropriate Law Officer within the meaning of section 4A of the Crown Suits (Scotland) Act 1857 or the Attorney General for Northern Ireland, or [such other person who has a right of audience] as any of them may appoint, shall be entitled to appear and be heard.

(5) Where an application under sections 48 to 51 above or subsection (2) above is opposed, and either—

(a) the parties consent, or

(b) the proceedings require a prolonged examination of documents or any scientific or local investigation which cannot in the opinion of the comptroller conveniently be made before him,

the comptroller may at any time order the whole proceedings, or any question or issue of fact arising in them, to be referred to an arbitrator or arbiter agreed on by the parties or, in default of agreement, appointed by the comptroller.

(6) Where the whole proceedings are so referred, unless the parties otherwise agree before the award of the arbitrator or arbiter is made, an appeal shall lie from the award to the court.

(7) Where a question or issue of fact is so referred, the arbitrator or arbiter shall report his findings to the comptroller.]

NOTES

Substituted by the Patents and Trade Marks (World Trade Organisation) Regulations 1999, SI 1999/1899, reg 6.

Sub-s (4): words in square brackets substituted by the Intellectual Property Act 2014, s 19, Schedule, para 4(1).

[1.59]

53 Compulsory licences; supplementary provisions

(1) . . .

(2) In any proceedings on an [application made under section 48 above in respect of a patent], any statement with respect to any activity in relation to the patented invention, or with respect to the grant or refusal of licences under the patent, contained in a report of the [Competition and Markets

Authority] laid before Parliament under Part VII of the Fair Trading Act 1973 [or section 17 of the Competition Act 1980] [or published under Part 3 or 4 of the Enterprise Act 2002] shall be prima facie evidence of the matters stated, and in Scotland shall be sufficient evidence of those matters.

(3) The comptroller may make an entry in the register under sections 48 to 51 above notwithstanding any contract which would have precluded the entry on the application of the proprietor of the patent under section 46 above.

(4) An entry made in the register under sections 48 to 51 above shall for all purposes have the same effect as an entry made under section 46 above.

(5) No order or entry shall be made in pursuance of an application under sections 48 to 51 above which would be at variance with any treaty or international convention to which the United Kingdom is a party.

NOTES

Sub-s (1): repealed by the Patents Act 2004, s 16(1), (2), Sch 2, paras 1, 12, Sch 3.

Sub-s (2): words in first pair of square brackets substituted and words in third pair of square brackets inserted, by the Copyright, Designs and Patents Act 1988, s 295, Sch 5, para 15; words in second pair of square brackets substituted by the Enterprise and Regulatory Reform Act 2013 (Competition) (Consequential, Transitional and Saving Provisions) Order 2014, SI 2014/892, art 2, Sch 1, Pt 2, paras 31, 34; words in fourth pair of square brackets inserted by the Enterprise Act 2002, s 278(1), Sch 25, para 8(1), (4).

Modification: the reference in sub-s (2) to Part 3 includes a reference to the Enterprise Act 2002 (Protection of Legitimate Interests) Order 2003; see the Enterprise Act 2003 (Protection of Legitimate Interests) Order 2003, SI 2003/1592, art 16, Sch 4, para 3(2).

Fair Trading Act 1973, Pt VII: s 81 repealed by the Enterprise Act 2002, s 278(2).

[1.60]

54 Special provisions where patented invention is being worked abroad

(1) Her Majesty may by Order in Council provide that the comptroller may not (otherwise than for purposes of the public interest) make an order or entry in respect of a patent in pursuance of an application under sections 48 to 51 above if the invention concerned is being commercially worked in any relevant country specified in the Order and demand in the United Kingdom for any patented product resulting from that working is being met by importation from that country.

(2) In subsection (1) above "relevant country" means a country other than a member state [or a member of the World Trade Organisation] whose law in the opinion of Her Majesty in Council incorporates or will incorporate provisions treating the working of an invention in, and importation from, the United Kingdom in a similar way to that in which the Order in Council would (if made) treat the working of an invention in, and importation from, that country.

NOTES

Sub-s (2): words in square brackets inserted by the Patents and Trade Marks (World Trade Organisation) Regulations 1999, SI 1999/1899, reg 7(4).

Use of patented inventions for services of the Crown

[1.61]

55 Use of patented inventions for services of the Crown

(1) Notwithstanding anything in this Act, any government department and any person authorised in writing by a government department may, for the services of the Crown and in accordance with this section, do any of the following acts in the United Kingdom in relation to a patented invention without the consent of the proprietor of the patent, that is to say—

(a) where the invention is a product, may—

(i) make, use, import or keep the product, or sell or offer to sell it where to do so would be incidental or ancillary to making, using, importing or keeping it; or

(ii) in any event, sell or offer to sell it for foreign defence purposes or for the production or supply of specified drugs and medicines, or dispose or offer to dispose of it (otherwise than by selling it) for any purpose whatever;

(b) where the invention is a process, may use it or do in relation to any product obtained directly by means of the process anything mentioned in paragraph (a) above;

(c) without prejudice to the foregoing, where the invention or any product obtained directly by means of the invention is a specified drug or medicine, may sell or offer to sell the drug or medicine;

(d) may supply or offer to supply to any person any of the means, relating to an essential element of the invention, for putting the invention into effect;

(e) may dispose or offer to dispose of anything which was made, used, imported or kept in the exercise of the powers conferred by this section and which is no longer required for the purpose for which it was made, used, imported or kept (as the case may be),

and anything done by virtue of this subsection shall not amount to an infringement of the patent concerned.

(2) Any act done in relation to an invention by virtue of this section is in the following provisions of this section referred to as use of the invention; and "use", in relation to an invention, in sections 56 to 58 below shall be construed accordingly.

(3) So far as the invention has before its priority date been duly recorded by or tried by or on behalf of a government department or the United Kingdom Atomic Energy Authority otherwise than in consequence of a relevant communication made in confidence, any use of the invention by virtue of this section may be made free of any royalty or other payment to the proprietor.

(4) So far as the invention has not been so recorded or tried, any use of it made by virtue of this section at any time either—

- (a) after the publication of the application for the patent for the invention; or
- (b) without prejudice to paragraph (a) above, in consequence of a relevant communication made after the priority date of the invention otherwise than in confidence;

shall be made on such terms as may be agreed either before or after the use by the government department and the proprietor of the patent with the approval of the Treasury or as may in default of agreement be determined by the court on a reference under section 58 below.

(5) Where an invention is used by virtue of this section at any time after publication of an application for a patent for the invention but before such a patent is granted, and the terms for its use agreed or determined as mentioned in subsection (4) above include terms as to payment for the use, then (notwithstanding anything in those terms) any such payment shall be recoverable only—

- (a) after such a patent is granted; and
- (b) if (apart from this section) the use would, if the patent had been granted on the date of the publication of the application, have infringed not only the patent but also the claims (as interpreted by the description and any drawings referred to in the description or claims) in the form in which they were contained in the application immediately before the preparations for its publication were completed by the Patent Office.

(6) The authority of a government department in respect of an invention may be given under this section either before or after the patent is granted and either before or after the use in respect of which the authority is given is made, and may be given to any person whether or not he is authorised directly or indirectly by the proprietor of the patent to do anything in relation to the invention.

(7) Where any use of an invention is made by or with the authority of a government department under this section, then, unless it appears to the department that it would be contrary to the public interest to do so, the department shall notify the proprietor of the patent as soon as practicable after the second of the following events, that is to say, the use is begun and the patent is granted, and furnish him with such information as to the extent of the use as he may from time to time require.

(8) A person acquiring anything disposed of in the exercise of powers conferred by this section, and any person claiming through him, may deal with it in the same manner as if the patent were held on behalf of the Crown.

(9) In this section "relevant communication", in relation to an invention, means a communication of the invention directly or indirectly by the proprietor of the patent or any person from whom he derives title.

(10) Subsection (4) above is without prejudice to any rule of law relating to the confidentiality of information.

(11) In the application of this section to Northern Ireland, the reference in subsection (4) above to the Treasury shall, where the government department referred to in that subsection is a department of the Government of Northern Ireland, be construed as a reference to the Department of Finance for Northern Ireland.

[1.62]

56 Interpretation, etc, of provisions about Crown use

(1) Any reference in section 55 above to a patented invention, in relation to any time, is a reference to an invention for which a patent has before that time been, or is subsequently, granted.

(2) In this Act, except so far as the context otherwise requires, "the services of the Crown" includes—

- (a) the supply of anything for foreign defence purposes;
- (b) the production or supply of specified drugs and medicines; and
- (c) such purposes relating to the production or use of atomic energy or research into matters connected therewith as the Secretary of State thinks necessary or expedient;

and "use for the services of the Crown" shall be construed accordingly.

(3) In section 55(1)(a) above and subsection (2)(a) above, references to a sale or supply of anything for foreign defence purposes are references to a sale or supply of the thing—

- (a) to the government of any country outside the United Kingdom, in pursuance of an agreement or arrangement between Her Majesty's Government in the United Kingdom and the government of that country, where the thing is required for the defence of that country or of any other country whose government is party to any agreement or arrangement with Her Majesty's Government in respect of defence matters; or
- (b) to the United Nations, or to the government of any country belonging to that organisation, in pursuance of an agreement or arrangement between Her Majesty's Government and that organisation or government, where the thing is required for any armed forces operating in pursuance of a resolution of that organisation or any organ of that organisation.

(4) For the purposes of section 55(1)(a) and (c) above and subsection (2)(b) above, specified drugs and medicines are drugs and medicines which are both—

(a) required for the [provision of—

[(ai) primary medical services [under [the National Health Service Act 2006, the National Health Service (Wales) Act 2006], Part 1 of the National Health Service (Scotland) Act 1978 or any corresponding provisions of the law in force in Northern Ireland or the Isle of Man] or primary dental services under [the National Health Service Act 2006, the National Health Service (Wales) Act 2006], or any corresponding provisions of the law in force in Northern Ireland or the Isle of Man, or]

(i) pharmaceutical services, general medical services or general dental services under [Chapter 1 of Part 7 of the National Health Service Act 2006 or Chapter 1 of Part 7 of the National Health Service (Wales) Act 2006] [(in the case of pharmaceutical services)], Part II of the National Health Service (Scotland) Act 1978 [(in the case of *pharmaceutical services or* general dental services)], or the corresponding provisions of the law in force in Northern Ireland or the Isle of Man, or

(ii) personal medical services or personal dental services provided in accordance with arrangements made under . . . section 17C of the 1978 Act [(in the case of personal dental services)], or the corresponding provisions of the law in force in Northern Ireland or the Isle of Man][, or

(iii) local pharmaceutical services provided under a pilot scheme established under [section 134 of the National Health Service Act 2006, or section 92 of the National Health Service (Wales) Act 2006] or an LPS scheme established under [Schedule 12 to the National Health Service Act 2006, or Schedule 7 to the National Health Service (Wales) Act 2006], or under any corresponding provision of the law in force in the Isle of Man], [or

(iiia) pharmaceutical care services under Part 1 of the National Health Service (Scotland) Act 1978,] and

(b) specified for the purposes of this subsection in regulations made by the Secretary of State.

NOTES

Sub-s (4)(a) is amended as follows:

Opening paragraph: words in square brackets substituted, together with paras (i), (ii), by the National Health Service (Primary Care) Act 1997, s 41(10), Sch 2, Pt I, para 2.

Para (ai): inserted by the Health and Social Care (Community Health and Standards) Act 2003, s 184, Sch 11, para 6(1), (2); words in first (outer) pair of square brackets inserted by the Primary Medical Services (Scotland) Act 2004 (Consequential Modifications) Order 2004, SI 2004/957, art 2, Schedule, para 2(a); words in second (inner) and third pairs of square brackets substituted by the National Health Service (Consequential Provisions) Act 2006, s 2, Sch 1, paras 57, 58(a).

Para (i): substituted as noted to the opening paragraph; words in first pair of square brackets substituted by the National Health Service (Consequential Provisions) Act 2006, s 2, Sch 1, paras 57, 58(b); words in second pair of square brackets inserted by the Health and Social Care (Community Health and Standards) Act 2003, s 184, Sch 11, para 6(1), (3); words in third pair of square brackets inserted by SI 2004/957, art 2, Schedule, para 2(b); words in italics repealed by the Smoking, Health and Social Care (Scotland) Act 2005 (Consequential Modifications) (England, Wales and Northern Ireland) Order 2006, SI 2006/1056, art 2, Schedule, Pt 1, para 2(a), as from the day on which the Smoking, Health and Social Care (Scotland) Act 2005, s 20 comes into force.

Para (ii): substituted as noted to the opening paragraph; words omitted repealed by the Health and Social Care (Community Health and Standards) Act 2003, ss 184, 196, Sch 11, para 6(1), (4), Sch 14, Pt 4; words in square brackets inserted by SI 2004/957, art 2, Schedule, para 2(c).

Para (iii): inserted, together with the word immediately preceding it, by the Health and Social Care Act 2001, s 67(1), Sch 5, Pt 1, para 4; words in square brackets substituted by the National Health Service (Consequential Provisions) Act 2006, s 2, Sch 1, paras 57, 58(c).

Para (iiia): inserted, together with the word immediately preceding it, except in relation to Scotland, by SI 2006/1056, art 2, Schedule, Pt 1, para 2(b), as from the day on which the Smoking, Health and Social Care (Scotland) Act 2005, s 20 comes into force.

[1.63]

57 Rights of third parties in respect of Crown use

(1) In relation to—

(a) any use made for the services of the Crown of an invention by a government department, or a person authorised by a government department, by virtue of section 55 above, or

(b) anything done for the services of the Crown to the order of a government department by the proprietor of a patent in respect of a patented invention or by the proprietor of an application in respect of an invention for which an application for a patent has been filed and is still pending,

the provisions of any licence, assignment, assignation or agreement to which this subsection applies shall be of no effect so far as those provisions restrict or regulate the working of the invention, or the use of any model, document or information relating to it, or provide for the making of payments in respect of, or calculated by reference to, such working or use; and the reproduction or publication of any model or document in connection with the said working or use shall not be deemed to be an infringement of any copyright [or design right] subsisting in the model or document [or of any topography right].

(2) Subsection (1) above applies to a licence, assignment, assignation or agreement which is made, whether before or after the appointed day, between (on the one hand) any person who is a proprietor of or an applicant for the patent, or anyone who derives title from any such person or from whom such person derives title, and (on the other hand) any person whatever other than a government department.

(3) Where an exclusive licence granted otherwise than for royalties or other benefits determined by reference to the working of the invention is in force under the patent or application concerned, then—

(a) in relation to anything done in respect of the invention which, but for the provisions of this section and section 55 above, would constitute an infringement of the rights of the licensee, subsection (4) of that section shall have effect as if for the reference to the proprietor of the patent there were substituted a reference to the licensee; and

(b) in relation to anything done in respect of the invention by the licensee by virtue of an authority given under that section, that section shall have effect as if the said subsection (4) were omitted.

(4) Subject to the provisions of subsection (3) above, where the patent, or the right to the grant of the patent, has been assigned to the proprietor of the patent or application in consideration of royalties or other benefits determined by reference to the working of the invention, then—

(a) in relation to any use of the invention by virtue of section 55 above, subsection (4) of that section shall have effect as if the reference to the proprietor of the patent included a reference to the assignor, and any sum payable by virtue of that subsection shall be divided between the proprietor of the patent or application and the assignor in such proportion as may be agreed on by them or as may in default of agreement be determined by the court on a reference under section 58 below; and

(b) in relation to any act done in respect of the invention for the services of the Crown by the proprietor of the patent or application to the order of a government department, section 55(4) above shall have effect as if that act were use made by virtue of an authority given under that section.

(5) Where section 55(4) above applies to any use of an invention and a person holds an exclusive licence under the patent or application concerned (other than such a licence as is mentioned in subsection (3) above) authorising him to work the invention, then subsections (7) and (8) below shall apply.

(6) In those subsections "the section 55(4)" payment means such payment (if any) as the proprietor of the patent or application and the department agree under section 55 above, or the court determines under section 58 below, should be made by the department to the proprietor in respect of the use of the invention.

(7) The licensee shall be entitled to recover from the proprietor of the patent or application such part (if any) of the section 55(4) payment as may be agreed on by them or as may in default of agreement be determined by the court under section 58 below to be just having regard to any expenditure incurred by the licensee—

(a) in developing the invention, or

(b) in making payments to the proprietor in consideration of the licence, other than royalties or other payments determined by reference to the use of the invention.

(8) Any agreement by the proprietor of the patent or application and the department under section 55(4) above as to the amount of the section 55(4) payment shall be of no effect unless the licensee consents to the agreement; and any determination by the court under section 55(4) above as to the amount of that payment shall be of no effect unless the licensee has been informed of the reference to the court and is given an opportunity to be heard.

(9) Where any models, documents or information relating to an invention are used in connection with any use of the invention which falls within subsection (1)(a) above, or with anything done in respect of the invention which falls within subsection (1)(b) above, subsection (4) of section 55 above shall (whether or not it applies to any such use of the invention) apply to the use of the models, documents or information as if for the reference in it to the proprietor of the patent there were substituted a reference to the person entitled to the benefit of any provision of an agreement which is rendered inoperative by this section in relation to that use; and in section 58 below the references to terms for the use of an invention shall be construed accordingly.

(10) Nothing in this section shall be construed as authorising the disclosure to a government department or any other person of any model, document or information to the use of which this section applies in contravention of any such licence, assignment, assignation or agreement as is mentioned in this section.

NOTES

Sub-s (1): words in first pair of square brackets inserted by the Copyright, Designs and Patents Act 1988, s 303(1), Sch 7, para 20; words in second pair of square brackets added by the Semiconductor Products (Protection of Topography) Regulations 1987, SI 1987/1497, reg 9(2), Sch 2, para 2.

[1.64]

[57A Compensation for loss of profit

(1) Where use is made of an invention for the services of the Crown, the government department concerned shall pay—

(a) to the proprietor of the patent, or

(b) if there is an exclusive licence in force in respect of the patent, to the exclusive licensee, compensation for any loss resulting from his not being awarded a contract to supply the patented product or, as the case may be, to perform the patented process or supply a thing made by means of the patented process.

(2) Compensation is payable only to the extent that such a contract could have been fulfilled from his existing manufacturing or other capacity; but is payable notwithstanding the existence of circumstances rendering him ineligible for the award of such a contract.

(3) In determining the loss, regard shall be had to the profit which would have been made on such a contract and to the extent to which any manufacturing or other capacity was under-used.

(4) No compensation is payable in respect of any failure to secure contracts to supply the patented product or, as the case may be, to perform the patented process or supply a thing made by means of the patented process, otherwise than for the services of the Crown.

(5) The amount payable shall, if not agreed between the proprietor or licensee and the government department concerned with the approval of the Treasury, be determined by the court on a reference under section 58, and is in addition to any amount payable under section 55 or 57.

(6) In this section "the government department concerned", in relation to any use of an invention for the services of the Crown, means the government department by whom or on whose authority the use was made.

(7) In the application of this section to Northern Ireland, the reference in subsection (5) above to the Treasury shall, where the government department concerned is a department of the Government of Northern Ireland, be construed as a reference to the Department of Finance and Personnel.]

NOTES

Inserted by the Copyright, Designs and Patents Act 1988, s 295, Sch 5, para 16(1), (4), in relation to any use of an invention for the services of the Crown after 1 August 1989, even if the terms for such use were settled before that date.

[1.65]

58 References of disputes as to Crown use

[(1) Any dispute as to—

(a) the exercise by a government department, or a person authorised by a government department, of the powers conferred by section 55 above,

(b) terms for the use of an invention for the services of the Crown under that section,

(c) the right of any person to receive any part of a payment made in pursuance of subsection (4) of that section, or

(d) the right of any person to receive a payment under section 57A,

may be referred to the court by either party to the dispute after a patent has been granted for the invention.]

(2) If in such proceedings any question arises whether an invention has been recorded or tried as mentioned in section 55 above, and the disclosure of any document recording the invention, or of any evidence of the trial thereof, would in the opinion of the department be prejudicial to the public interest, the disclosure may be made confidentially to [the other party's legal representative] or to an independent expert mutually agreed upon.

(3) In determining under this section any dispute between a government department and any person as to the terms for the use of an invention for the services of the Crown, the court shall have regard—

(a) to any benefit or compensation which that person or any person from whom he derives title may have received or may be entitled to receive directly or indirectly from any government department in respect of the invention in question;

(b) to whether that person or any person from whom he derives title has in the court's opinion without reasonable cause failed to comply with a request of the department to use the invention for the services of the Crown on reasonable terms.

(4) In determining whether or not to grant any relief [under subsection (1)(a), (b) or (c) above] and the nature and extent of the relief granted the court shall, subject to the following provisions of this section, apply the principles applied by the court immediately before the appointed day to the granting of relief under section 48 of the 1949 Act.

(5) On a reference under this section the court may refuse to grant relief by way of compensation in respect of the use of an invention for the services of the Crown during any further period specified under section 25(4) above, but before the payment of the renewal fee and any additional fee prescribed for the purposes of that section.

(6) Where an amendment of the specification of a patent has been allowed under any of the provisions of this Act, [or, in the case of a European patent (UK), has been allowed under any of the provisions in the Agreement on a Unified Patent Court,] the court shall not grant relief by way of compensation under this section in respect of any such use before the decision to allow the amendment unless the court is satisfied that[—

(a)] the specification of the patent as published was framed in good faith and with reasonable skill and knowledge [and

(b) the relief is sought in good faith].

(7) If the validity of a patent is put in issue in proceedings under this section and it is found that the patent is only partially valid, the court may, subject to subsection (8) below, grant relief to the proprietor of the patent in respect of that part of the patent which is found to be valid and to have been used for the services of the Crown.

(8) Where in any such proceedings it is found that a patent is only partially valid, the court shall not grant relief by way of compensation, costs or expenses except where the proprietor of the patent proves that[—

(a)] the specification of the patent was framed in good faith and with reasonable skill and knowledge, and

[(b) the relief is sought in good faith, and]

in that event the court may grant relief in respect of that part of the patent which is valid and has been so used, subject to the discretion of the court as to costs and expenses and as to the date from which compensation should be awarded.

(9) As a condition of any such relief the court may direct that the specification of the patent shall be amended to its satisfaction upon an application made for that purpose under section 75 below, and an application may be so made accordingly, whether or not all other issues in the proceedings have been determined.

[(9A) The court may also grant such relief in the case of a European patent (UK) on condition that the claims of the patent are limited to its satisfaction by the European Patent Office at the request of the proprietor.]

(10) In considering the amount of any compensation for the use of an invention for the services of the Crown after publication of an application for a patent for the invention and before such a patent is granted, the court shall consider whether or not it would have been reasonable to expect, from a consideration of the application as published under section 16 above, that a patent would be granted conferring on the proprietor of the patent protection for an act of the same description as that found to constitute that use, and if the court finds that it would not have been reasonable, it shall reduce the compensation to such amount as it thinks just.

(11) Where by virtue of a transaction, instrument or event to which section 33 above applies a person becomes the proprietor or one of the proprietors or an exclusive licensee of a patent (the new proprietor or licensee) and a government department or a person authorised by a government department subsequently makes use under section 55 above of the patented invention, the new proprietor or licensee shall not be entitled to any compensation under section 55(4) above (as it stands or as modified by section 57(3) above)[, or to any compensation under section 57A above,] in respect of a subsequent use of the invention before the transaction, instrument or event is registered unless—

(a) the transaction, instrument or event is registered within the period of six months beginning with its date; or

(b) the court is satisfied that it was not practicable to register the transaction, instrument or event before the end of that period and that it was registered as soon as practicable thereafter.

(12) In any proceedings under this section the court may at any time order the whole proceedings or any question or issue of fact arising in them to be referred, on such terms as the court may direct, to a Circuit judge discharging the functions of an official referee or an arbitrator in England and Wales or Northern Ireland, or to an arbiter in Scotland; and references to the court in the foregoing provisions of this section shall be construed accordingly.

(13) One of two or more joint proprietors of a patent or application for a patent may without the concurrence of the others refer a dispute to the court under this section, but shall not do so unless the others are made parties to the proceedings; but any of the others made a defendant or defender shall not be liable for any costs or expenses unless he enters an appearance and takes part in the proceedings.

NOTES

Sub-s (1): substituted by the Copyright, Designs and Patents Act 1988, s 295, Sch 5, para 16(2), (4), in relation to any use of an invention for the services of the Crown after 1 August 1989, even if the terms for such use were settled before that date.

Sub-s (2): words in square brackets substituted by the Intellectual Property Act 2014, s 19, Schedule, para 4(2).

Sub-s (4): words in square brackets substituted by the Copyright, Designs and Patents Act 1988, s 295, Sch 5, para 16(2), (4), in relation to any use of an invention for the services of the Crown after 1 August 1989, even if the terms for such use were settled before that date.

Sub-s (6): words in first pair of square brackets inserted by the Patents (European Patent with Unitary Effect and Unified Patent Court) Order 2016, SI 2016/388, art 2(1), (2), as from a day to be appointed (being the date of entry into force of the Agreement on a Unified Patent Court signed at Brussels on 19 February 2013) and subject to art 3 thereof which provides that any question whether an act done before SI 2016/388 comes into force infringes a patent is to be determined in accordance with the law relating to infringement in force at the time the act was done; words in second pair of square brackets inserted by the Patents Act 2004, s 2(2)(a).

Sub-s (8): words in square brackets inserted by the Patents Act 2004, s 2(2)(b).

Sub-s (9A): inserted by the Patents Act 2004, s 3(2).

Sub-s (11): words in square brackets inserted by the Copyright, Designs and Patents Act 1988, s 295, Sch 5, para 16(3), (4), in relation to any use of an invention for the services of the Crown after 1 August 1989, even if the terms for such use were settled before that date.

[1.66]

59 Special provisions as to Crown use during emergency

(1) During any period of emergency within the meaning of this section the powers exercisable in relation to an invention by a government department or a person authorised by a government department under section 55 above shall include power to use the invention for any purpose which appears to the department necessary or expedient—

(a) for the efficient prosecution of any war in which Her Majesty may be engaged;
(b) for the maintenance of supplies and services essential to the life of the community;
(c) for securing a sufficiency of supplies and services essential to the wellbeing of the community;
(d) for promoting the productivity of industry, commerce and agriculture;
(e) for fostering and directing exports and reducing imports, or imports of any classes, from all or any countries and for redressing the balance of trade;
(f) generally for ensuring that the whole resources of the community are available for use, and are used, in a manner best calculated to serve the interests of the community; or
(g) for assisting the relief of suffering and the restoration and distribution of essential supplies and services in any country or territory outside the United Kingdom which is in grave distress as the result of war;

and any reference in this Act to the services of the Crown shall, as respects any period of emergency, include a reference to those purposes.

(2) In this section the use of an invention includes, in addition to any act constituting such use by virtue of section 55 above, any act which would, apart from that section and this section, amount to an infringement of the patent concerned or, as the case may be, give rise to a right under section 69 below to bring proceedings in respect of the application concerned, and any reference in this Act to "use for the services of the Crown" shall, as respects any period of emergency, be construed accordingly.

(3) In this section "period of emergency" means any period beginning with such date as may be declared by Order in Council to be the commencement, and ending with such date as may be so declared to be the termination, of a period of emergency for the purposes of this section.

(4) A draft of an Order under this section shall not be submitted to Her Majesty unless it has been laid before, and approved by resolution of, each House of Parliament.

Infringement

[1.67]

60 Meaning of infringement

(1) Subject to the provisions of this section, a person infringes a patent for an invention if, but only if, while the patent is in force, he does any of the following things in the United Kingdom in relation to the invention without the consent of the proprietor of the patent, that is to say—

(a) where the invention is a product, he makes, disposes of, offers to dispose of, uses or imports the product or keeps it whether for disposal or otherwise;
(b) where the invention is a process, he uses the process or he offers it for use in the United Kingdom when he knows, or it is obvious to a reasonable person in the circumstances, that its use there without the consent of the proprietor would be an infringement of the patent;
(c) where the invention is a process, he disposes of, offers to dispose of, uses or imports any product obtained directly by means of that process or keeps any such product whether for disposal or otherwise.

(2) Subject to the following provisions of this section, a person (other than the proprietor of the patent) also infringes a patent for an invention if, while the patent is in force and without the consent of the proprietor, he supplies or offers to supply in the United Kingdom a person other than a licensee or other person entitled to work the invention with any of the means, relating to an essential element of the invention, for putting the invention into effect when he knows, or it is obvious to a reasonable person in the circumstances, that those means are suitable for putting, and are intended to put, the invention into effect in the United Kingdom.

(3) Subsection (2) above shall not apply to the supply or offer of a staple commercial product unless the supply or the offer is made for the purpose of inducing the person supplied or, as the case may be, the person to whom the offer is made to do an act which constitutes an infringement of the patent by virtue of subsection (1) above.

(4) . . .

(5) An act which, apart from this subsection, would constitute an infringement of a patent for an invention shall not do so if—

(a) it is done privately and for purposes which are not commercial;
(b) it is done for experimental purposes relating to the subject-matter of the invention;
(c) it consists of the extemporaneous preparation in a pharmacy of a medicine for an individual in accordance with a prescription given by a registered medical or dental practitioner or consists of dealing with a medicine so prepared;

(d) it consists of the use, exclusively for the needs of a relevant ship, of a product or process in the body of such a ship or in its machinery, tackle, apparatus or other accessories, in a case where the ship has temporarily or accidentally entered the internal or territorial waters of the United Kingdom;

(e) it consists of the use of a product or process in the body or operation of a relevant aircraft, hovercraft or vehicle which has temporarily or accidentally entered or is crossing the United Kingdom (including the air space above it and its territorial waters) or the use of accessories for such a relevant aircraft, hovercraft or vehicle;

(f) it consists of the use of an exempted aircraft which has lawfully entered or is lawfully crossing the United Kingdom as aforesaid or of the importation into the United Kingdom, or the use or storage there, of any part or accessory for such an aircraft;

[(g) it consists of the use by a farmer of the product of his harvest for propagation or multiplication by him on his own holding, where there has been a sale of plant propagating material to the farmer by the proprietor of the patent or with his consent for agricultural use;

(h) it consists of the use of an animal or animal reproductive material by a farmer for an agricultural purpose following a sale to the farmer, by the proprietor of the patent or with his consent, of breeding stock or other animal reproductive material which constitutes or contains the patented invention;]

[(i) it consists of—

(i) an act done in conducting a study, test or trial which is necessary for and is conducted with a view to the application of paragraphs 1 to 5 of article 13 of Directive 2001/82/EC or paragraphs 1 to 4 of article 10 of Directive 2001/83/EC, or

(ii) any other act which is required for the purpose of the application of those paragraphs];

[(j) it consists of a use referred to in Article 27(c) of the Agreement on a Unified Patent Court;

(k) subject to subsection (6H), it consists of an act or use referred to in Article 27(k) of the Agreement on a Unified Patent Court.]

(6) For the purposes of subsection (2) above a person who does an act in relation to an invention which is prevented only by virtue of paragraph (a), (b) or (c) of subsection (5) above from constituting an infringement of a patent for the invention shall not be treated as a person entitled to work the invention, but—

(a) the reference in that subsection to a person entitled to work an invention includes a reference to a person so entitled by virtue of section 55 above, and

(b) a person who by virtue of [section 20B(4) or (5) above or] [section 28A(4) or (5)] above or section 64 below [or section 117A(4) or (5) below] is entitled to do an act in relation to the invention without it constituting such an infringement shall, so far as concerns that act, be treated as a person entitled to work the invention.

[(6A) Schedule A1 contains—

(a) provisions restricting the circumstances in which subsection (5)(g) applies; and

(b) provisions which apply where an act would constitute an infringement of a patent but for subsection (5)(g).

(6B) For the purposes of subsection (5)(h), use for an agricultural purpose—

(a) includes making an animal or animal reproductive material available for the purposes of pursuing the farmer's agricultural activity; but

(b) does not include sale within the framework, or for the purposes, of a commercial reproduction activity.

(6C) In paragraphs (g) and (h) of subsection (5) "sale" includes any other form of commercialisation.]

[(6D) For the purposes of subsection (5)(b), anything done in or for the purposes of a medicinal product assessment which would otherwise constitute an infringement of a patent for an invention is to be regarded as done for experimental purposes relating to the subject-matter of the invention.

(6E) In subsection (6D), "medicinal product assessment" means any testing, course of testing or other activity undertaken with a view to providing data for any of the following purposes—

(a) obtaining or varying an authorisation to sell or supply, or offer to sell or supply, a medicinal product (whether in the United Kingdom or elsewhere);

(b) complying with any regulatory requirement imposed (whether in the United Kingdom or elsewhere) in relation to such an authorisation;

(c) enabling a government or public authority (whether in the United Kingdom or elsewhere), or a person (whether in the United Kingdom or elsewhere) with functions of—

(i) providing health care on behalf of such a government or public authority, or

(ii) providing advice to, or on behalf of, such a government or public authority about the provision of health care,

to carry out an assessment of suitability of a medicinal product for human use for the purpose of determining whether to use it, or recommend its use, in the provision of health care.

(6F) In subsection (6E) and this subsection—

"medicinal product" means a medicinal product for human use or a veterinary medicinal product;

"medicinal product for human use" has the meaning given by article 1 of Directive 2001/83/EC;
"veterinary medicinal product" has the meaning given by article 1 of Directive 2001/82/EC.

(6G) Nothing in subsections (6D) to (6F) is to be read as affecting the application of subsection (5)(b) in relation to any act of a kind not falling within subsection (6D).]

[(6H) Subsection 5(k) applies to an act or use in relation to a European patent (UK) or a European patent with unitary effect, but does not apply to an act or use in relation to a patent granted by the comptroller.]

(7) In this section—

"relevant ship" and "relevant aircraft, hovercraft or vehicle" mean respectively a ship and an aircraft, hovercraft or vehicle registered in, or belonging to, any country, other than the United Kingdom, which is a party to the Convention for the Protection of Industrial Property signed at Paris on 20th March 1883 [or which is a member of the World Trade Organisation]; and

"exempted aircraft" means an aircraft to which [section 89 of the Civil Aviation Act 1982] (aircraft exempted from seizure in respect of patent claims) applies;

["Directive 2001/82/EC" means Directive 2001/82/EC of the European Parliament and of the Council on the Community code relating to veterinary medicinal products as amended by [Directive 2004/28/EC] of the European Parliament and of the Council;

"Directive 2001/83/EC" means Directive 2001/83/EC of the European Parliament and of the Council on the Community code relating to medicinal products for human use, as amended by Directive 2002/98/EC of the European Parliament and of the Council, by Commission Directive 2003/63/EC and by Directives 2004/24/EC and 2004/27/EC of the European Parliament and of the Council.]

NOTES

Sub-s (4): repealed by the Patents Act 2004, s 16(1), (2), Sch 2, paras 1, 13, Sch 3.

Sub-s (5): paras (g), (h) added by the Patents Regulations 2000, SI 2000/2037, regs 2, 4(a), in relation to applications for patents made on or after 28 July 2000; para (i) added by the Medicines (Marketing Authorisations Etc) Amendment Regulations 2005, SI 2005/2759, reg 3(a); paras (j), (k) added by the Patents (European Patent with Unitary Effect and Unified Patent Court) Order 2016, SI 2016/388, art 2(1), (3), as from a day to be appointed (being the date of entry into force of the Agreement on a Unified Patent Court signed at Brussels on 19 February 2013) and subject to art 3 thereof which provides that any question whether an act done before SI 2016/388 comes into force infringes a patent is to be determined in accordance with the law relating to infringement in force at the time the act was done.

Sub-s (6): words in first and third pairs of square brackets inserted by the Regulatory Reform (Patents) Order 2004, SI 2004/2357, arts 2, 11; words in second pair of square brackets substituted by the Copyright, Designs and Patents Act 1988, s 295, Sch 5, para 8(a).

Sub-ss (6A)–(6C): inserted by SI 2000/2037, regs 2, 4(b), in relation to applications for patents made on or after 28 July 2000.

Sub-ss (6D)–(6G): inserted by the Legislative Reform (Patents) Order 2014, SI 2014/1997, art 2.

Sub-s (6H): inserted by SI 2016/388, art 2(1), (4), as from a day to be appointed (being the date of entry into force of the Agreement on a Unified Patent Court signed at Brussels on 19 February 2013) and subject to art 3 thereof which provides that any question whether an act done before SI 2016/388 comes into force infringes a patent is to be determined in accordance with the law relating to infringement in force at the time the act was done.

Sub-s (7): words in square brackets in definition "relevant ship" inserted by the Patents and Trade Marks (World Trade Organisation) Regulations 1999, SI 1999/1899, reg 7(5); words in square brackets in definition "exempted aircraft" substituted by the Civil Aviation Act 1982, s 109, Sch 15; definitions "Directive 2001/82/EC" and "Directive 2001/83/EC" added by SI 2005/2759, reg 3(b); words in square brackets in definition "Directive 2001/82/EC" substituted by the Intellectual Property Act 2014, s 19, Schedule, para 5.

[1.68]

61 Proceedings for infringement of patent

(1) Subject to the following provisions of this Part of this Act, civil proceedings may be brought in the court by the proprietor of a patent in respect of any act alleged to infringe the patent and (without prejudice to any other jurisdiction of the court) in those proceedings a claim may be made—

(a) for an injunction or interdict restraining the defendant or defender from any apprehended act of infringement;

(b) for an order for him to deliver up or destroy any patented product in relation to which the patent is infringed or any article in which that product is inextricably comprised;

(c) for damages in respect of the infringement;

(d) for an account of the profits derived by him from the infringement;

(e) for a declaration or declarator that the patent is valid and has been infringed by him.

(2) The court shall not, in respect of the same infringement, both award the proprietor of a patent damages and order that he shall be given an account of the profits.

(3) The proprietor of a patent and any other person may by agreement with each other refer to the comptroller the question whether that other person has infringed the patent and on the reference the proprietor of the patent may make any claim mentioned in subsection (1)(c) or (e) above.

(4) Except so far as the context requires, in the following provisions of this Act—

(a) any reference to proceedings for infringement and the bringing of such proceedings includes a reference to a reference under subsection (3) above and the making of such a reference;

(b) any reference to a [claimant] or pursuer includes a reference to the proprietor of the patent; and

(c) any reference to a defendant or defender includes a reference to any other party to the reference.

(5) If it appears to the comptroller on a reference under subsection (3) above that the question referred to him would more properly be determined by the court, he may decline to deal with it and the court shall have jurisdiction to determine the question as if the reference were proceedings brought in the court.

(6) Subject to the following provisions of this Part of this Act, in determining whether or not to grant any kind of relief claimed under this section and the extent of the relief granted the court or the comptroller shall apply the principles applied by the court in relation to that kind of relief immediately before the appointed day.

[(7) If the comptroller awards any sum by way of damages on a reference under subsection (3) above, then—

(a) in England and Wales, the sum shall be recoverable, if [the county court] so orders, [under section 85 of the County Courts Act 1984] or otherwise as if it were payable under an order of that court;

(b) in Scotland, payment of the sum may be enforced in like manner as an extract registered decree arbitral bearing a warrant for execution issued by the sheriff court of any sheriffdom in Scotland;

(c) in Northern Ireland, payment of the sum may be enforced as if it were a money judgment.]

NOTES

Sub-s (4): word in square brackets substituted by the Patents Act 2004, s 16(1), Sch 2, paras 1, 14.

Sub-s (7): added by the Patents Act 2004, s 11; in para (a) words in first pair of square brackets substituted by the Crime and Courts Act 2013, s 17, Sch 9, Pt 3, para 52(1)(b), (2) and words in second pair of square brackets substituted by the Tribunals, Courts and Enforcement Act 2007, s 62(3), Sch 13, paras 39, 41.

[1.69]

62 Restrictions on recovery of damages for infringement

(1) In proceedings for infringement of a patent damages shall not be awarded, and no order shall be made for an account of profits, against a defendant or defender who proves that at the date of the infringement he was not aware, and had no reasonable grounds for supposing, that the patent existed; and a person shall not be taken to have been so aware or to have had reasonable grounds for so supposing by reason only of the application to a product of the word "patent" or "patented", or any word or words expressing or implying that a patent has been obtained for the product, unless the number of the patent [or a relevant internet link] accompanied the word or words in question.

[(1A) The reference in subsection (1) to a relevant internet link is a reference to an address of a posting on the internet—

(a) which is accessible to the public free of charge, and

(b) which clearly associates the product with the number of the patent.]

(2) In proceedings for infringement of a patent the court or the comptroller may, if it or he thinks fit, refuse to award any damages or make any such order in respect of an infringement committed during [the further period specified in] section 25(4) above, but before the payment of the renewal fee and any additional fee prescribed for the purposes of that subsection.

(3) Where an amendment of the specification of a patent has been allowed under any of the provisions of this Act, [the court or the comptroller shall, when awarding damages or making an order for an account of profits in proceedings for an infringement of the patent committed before the decision to allow the amendment, take into account the following—

(a) whether at the date of infringement the defendant or defender knew, or had reasonable grounds to know, that he was infringing the patent;

(b) whether the specification of the patent as published was framed in good faith and with reasonable skill and knowledge;

(c) whether the proceedings are brought in good faith.]

NOTES

Sub-s (1): words in square brackets inserted by the Intellectual Property Act 2014, s 15(1), except in relation to the infringement of a patent referred to in sub-s (1) above where the infringement occurred before 1 October 2014.

Sub-s (1A): inserted by the Intellectual Property Act 2014, s 15(2), except in relation to the infringement of a patent referred to in sub-s (1) above where the infringement occurred before 1 October 2014.

Sub-s (2): words in square brackets substituted by the Patents Act 2004, s 16(1), Sch 2, paras 1, 15.

Sub-s (3): words in square brackets substituted by the Intellectual Property (Enforcement, etc) Regulations 2006, SI 2006/1028, reg 2(2), Sch 2, paras 1, 2.

[1.70]

63 Relief for infringement of partially valid patent

(1) If the validity of a patent is put in issue in proceedings for infringement of the patent and it is found that the patent is only partially valid, the court or the comptroller may, subject to subsection (2) below, grant relief in respect of that part of the patent which is found to be valid and infringed.

(2) Where in any such proceedings it is found that a patent is only partially valid, the court or the comptroller shall[, when awarding damages, costs or expenses or making an order for an account of profits, take into account the following—

(a) whether at the date of the infringement the defendant or defender knew, or had reasonable grounds to know, that he was infringing the patent;

(b) whether the specification of the patent was framed in good faith and with reasonable skill and knowledge;

(c) whether the proceedings are brought in good faith;

and any relief granted shall be subject to the discretion of the court or the comptroller as to costs or expenses and as to the date from which damages or an account should be reckoned.]

(3) As a condition of relief under this section the court or the comptroller may direct that the specification of the patent shall be amended to its or his satisfaction upon an application made for that purpose under section 75 below, and an application may be so made accordingly, whether or not all other issues in the proceedings have been determined.

[(4) The court or the comptroller may also grant relief under this section in the case of a European patent (UK) on condition that the claims of the patent are limited to its or his satisfaction by the European Patent Office at the request of the proprietor.]

NOTES

Sub-s (2): words in square brackets substituted by the Intellectual Property (Enforcement, etc) Regulations 2006, SI 2006/1028, reg 2(2), Sch 2, paras 1, 3.

Sub-s (4): added by the Patents Act 2004, s 3(1).

[1.71]

[64 Right to continue use begun before priority date

(1) Where a patent is granted for an invention, a person who in the United Kingdom before the priority date of the invention—

(a) does in good faith an act which would constitute an infringement of the patent if it were in force, or

(b) makes in good faith effective and serious preparations to do such an act,

has the right to continue to do the act or, as the case may be, to do the act, notwithstanding the grant of the patent; but this right does not extend to granting a licence to another person to do the act.

(2) If the act was done, or the preparations were made, in the course of a business, the person entitled to the right conferred by subsection (1) may—

(a) authorise the doing of that act by any partners of his for the time being in that business, and

(b) assign that right, or transmit it on death (or in the case of a body corporate on its dissolution), to any person who acquires that part of the business in the course of which the act was done or the preparations were made.

(3) Where a product is disposed of to another in exercise of the rights conferred by subsection (1) or (2), that other and any person claiming through him may deal with the product in the same way as if it had been disposed of by the registered proprietor of the patent.]

NOTES

Substituted by the Copyright, Designs and Patents Act 1988, s 295, Sch 5, para 17.

[1.72]

65 Certificate of contested validity of patent

(1) If in any proceedings before the court or the comptroller the validity of a patent to any extent is contested and that patent is found by the court or the comptroller to be wholly or partially valid, the court or the comptroller may certify the finding and the fact that the validity of the patent was so contested.

(2) Where a certificate is granted under this section, then, if in any subsequent proceedings before the court or the comptroller for infringement of the patent concerned or for revocation of the patent a final order or judgment or interlocutor is made or given in favour of the party relying on the validity of the patent as found in the earlier proceedings, that party shall, unless the court or the comptroller otherwise directs, be entitled to his costs or expenses as between solicitor and own client (other than the costs or expenses of any appeal in the subsequent proceedings).

[1.73]

66 Proceedings for infringement by a co-owner

(1) In the application of section 60 above to a patent of which there are two or more joint proprietors the reference to the proprietor shall be construed—

(a) in relation to any act, as a reference to that proprietor or those proprietors who, by virtue of section 36 above or any agreement referred to in that section, is or are entitled to do that act without its amounting to an infringement; and

(b) in relation to any consent, as a reference to that proprietor or those proprietors who, by virtue of section 36 above or any such agreement, is or are the proper person or persons to give the requisite consent.

(2) One of two or more joint proprietors of a patent may without the concurrence of the others bring proceedings in respect of an act alleged to infringe the patent, but shall not do so unless the others are made parties to the proceedings; but any of the others made a defendant or defender shall not be liable for any costs or expenses unless he enters an appearance and takes part in the proceedings.

[1.74]

67 Proceedings for infringement by exclusive licensee

(1) Subject to the provisions of this section, the holder of an exclusive licence under a patent shall have the same right as the proprietor of the patent to bring proceedings in respect of any infringement of the patent committed after the date of the licence; and references to the proprietor of the patent in the provisions of this Act relating to infringement shall be construed accordingly.

(2) In awarding damages or granting any other relief in any such proceedings the court or the comptroller shall take into consideration any loss suffered or likely to be suffered by the exclusive licensee as such as a result of the infringement, or, as the case may be, the profits derived from the infringement, so far as it constitutes an infringement of the rights of the exclusive licensee as such.

(3) In any proceedings taken by an exclusive licensee by virtue of this section the proprietor of the patent shall be made a party to the proceedings, but if made a defendant or defender shall not be liable for any costs or expenses unless he enters an appearance and takes part in the proceedings.

[1.75]

68 Effect of non-registration on infringement proceedings

Where by virtue of a transaction, instrument or event to which section 33 above applies a person becomes the proprietor or one of the proprietors or an exclusive licensee of a patent and the patent is subsequently infringed . . . before the transaction, instrument or event is registered[, in proceedings for such an infringement, the court or comptroller shall not award him costs or expenses] unless—

(a) the transaction, instrument or event is registered within the period of six months beginning with its date; or

(b) the court or the comptroller is satisfied that it was not practicable to register the transaction, instrument or event before the end of that period and that it was registered as soon as practicable thereafter.

NOTES

Words omitted repealed and words in square brackets inserted by the Intellectual Property (Enforcement, etc) Regulations 2006, SI 2006/1028, reg 2(2), (4), Sch 2, paras 1, 4, Sch 4.

[1.76]

69 Infringement of rights conferred by publication of application

(1) Where an application for a patent for an invention is published, then, subject to subsections (2) and (3) below, the applicant shall have, as from the publication and until the grant of the patent, the same right as he would have had, if the patent had been granted on the date of the publication of the application, to bring proceedings in the court or before the comptroller for damages in respect of any act which would have infringed the patent; and (subject to subsections (2) and (3) below) references in sections 60 to 62 and 66 to 68 above to a patent and the proprietor of a patent shall be respectively construed as including references to any such application and the applicant, and references to a patent being in force, being granted, being valid or existing shall be construed accordingly.

(2) The applicant shall be entitled to bring proceedings by virtue of this section in respect of any act only—

(a) after the patent has been granted; and

(b) if the act would, if the patent had been granted on the date of the publication of the application, have infringed not only the patent, but also the claims (as interpreted by the description and any drawings referred to in the description or claims) in the form in which they were contained in the application immediately before the preparations for its publication were completed by the Patent Office.

(3) Section 62(2) and (3) above shall not apply to an infringement of the rights conferred by this section, but in considering the amount of any damages for such an infringement, the court or the comptroller shall consider whether or not it would have been reasonable to expect, from a consideration of the application as published under section 16 above, that a patent would be granted conferring on the proprietor of the patent protection from an act of the same description as that found to infringe those rights, and if the court or the comptroller finds that it would not have been reasonable, it or he shall reduce the damages to such an amount as it or he thinks just.

[1.77]

70 Remedy for groundless threats of infringement proceedings

(1) Where a person (whether or not the proprietor of, or entitled to any right in, a patent) by circulars, advertisements or otherwise threatens another person with proceedings for any infringement of a patent, a person aggrieved by the threats (whether or not he is the person to whom the threats are made) may, subject to subsection (4) below, bring proceedings in the court against the person making the threats, claiming any relief mentioned in subsection (3) below.

[(2) In any such proceedings the claimant or pursuer shall, subject to subsection (2A) below, be entitled to the relief claimed if he proves that the threats were so made and satisfies the court that he is a person aggrieved by them.

(2A) If the defendant or defender proves that the acts in respect of which proceedings were threatened constitute or, if done, would constitute an infringement of a patent—

(a) the claimant or pursuer shall be entitled to the relief claimed only if he shows that the patent alleged to be infringed is invalid in a relevant respect;

(b) even if the claimant or pursuer does show that the patent is invalid in a relevant respect, he shall not be entitled to the relief claimed if the defendant or defender proves that at the time of making the threats he did not know, and had no reason to suspect, that the patent was invalid in that respect.]

(3) The said relief is—

(a) a declaration or declarator to the effect that the threats are unjustifiable;

(b) an injunction or interdict against the continuance of the threats; and

(c) damages in respect of any loss which the [claimant] or pursuer has sustained by the threats.

[(4) Proceedings may not be brought under this section for—

(a) a threat to bring proceedings for an infringement alleged to consist of making or importing a product for disposal or of using a process, or

(b) a threat, made to a person who has made or imported a product for disposal or used a process, to bring proceedings for an infringement alleged to consist of doing anything else in relation to that product or process.

(5) For the purposes of this section a person does not threaten another person with proceedings for infringement of a patent if he merely—

(a) provides factual information about the patent,

(b) makes enquiries of the other person for the sole purpose of discovering whether, or by whom, the patent has been infringed as mentioned in subsection (4)(a) above, or

(c) makes an assertion about the patent for the purpose of any enquiries so made.]

[(6) In proceedings under this section for threats made by one person (A) to another (B) in respect of an alleged infringement of a patent for an invention, it shall be a defence for A to prove that he used his best endeavours, without success, to discover—

(a) where the invention is a product, the identity of the person (if any) who made or (in the case of an imported product) imported it for disposal;

(b) where the invention is a process and the alleged infringement consists of offering it for use, the identity of a person who used the process;

(c) where the invention is a process and the alleged infringement is an act falling within section 60(1)(c) above, the identity of the person who used the process to produce the product in question;

and that he notified B accordingly, before or at the time of making the threats, identifying the endeavours used.]

NOTES

Section 70 is substituted (by new ss 70, 70A–70F and preceding heading) by the Intellectual Property (Unjustified Threats) Act 2017, s 1(1), (2), as from a day to be appointed, as follows (and in s 70F as set out below the words in square brackets are inserted by s 1(1), (3) of the 2017 Act, as from a day to be appointed)—

"Unjustified threats

70 Threats of infringement proceedings

(1) A communication contains a "threat of infringement proceedings" if a reasonable person in the position of a recipient would understand from the communication that—

(a) a patent exists, and

(b) a person intends to bring proceedings (whether in a court in the United Kingdom or elsewhere) against another person for infringement of the patent by—

(i) an act done in the United Kingdom, or

(ii) an act which, if done, would be done in the United Kingdom.

(2) References in this section and in section 70C to a "recipient" include, in the case of a communication directed to the public or a section of the public, references to a person to whom the communication is directed.

70A Actionable threats

(1) Subject to subsections (2) to (5), a threat of infringement proceedings made by any person is actionable by any person aggrieved by the threat.

(2) A threat of infringement proceedings is not actionable if the infringement is alleged to consist of—

(a) where the invention is a product, making a product for disposal or importing a product for disposal, or

(b) where the invention is a process, using a process.

(3) A threat of infringement proceedings is not actionable if the infringement is alleged to consist of an act which, if done, would constitute an infringement of a kind mentioned in subsection (2)(a) or (b).

(4) A threat of infringement proceedings is not actionable if the threat—

(a) is made to a person who has done, or intends to do, an act mentioned in subsection (2)(a) or (b) in relation to a product or process, and

(b) is a threat of proceedings for an infringement alleged to consist of doing anything else in relation to that product or process.

(5) A threat of infringement proceedings which is not an express threat is not actionable if it is contained in a permitted communication.

(6) In sections 70C and 70D "an actionable threat" means a threat of infringement proceedings that is actionable in accordance with this section.

70B Permitted communications

(1) For the purposes of section 70A(5), a communication containing a threat of infringement proceedings is a "permitted communication" if—

(a) the communication, so far as it contains information that relates to the threat, is made for a permitted purpose;

(b) all of the information that relates to the threat is information that—

(i) is necessary for that purpose (see subsection (5)(a) to (c) for some examples of necessary information), and

(ii) the person making the communication reasonably believes is true.

(2) Each of the following is a "permitted purpose"—

(a) giving notice that a patent exists;

(b) discovering whether, or by whom, a patent has been infringed by an act mentioned in section 70A(2)(a) or (b);

(c) giving notice that a person has a right in or under a patent, where another person's awareness of the right is relevant to any proceedings that may be brought in respect of the patent.

(3) The court may, having regard to the nature of the purposes listed in subsection (2)(a) to (c), treat any other purpose as a "permitted purpose" if it considers that it is in the interests of justice to do so.

(4) But the following may not be treated as a "permitted purpose"—

(a) requesting a person to cease doing, for commercial purposes, anything in relation to a product or process,

(b) requesting a person to deliver up or destroy a product, or

(c) requesting a person to give an undertaking relating to a product or process.

(5) If any of the following information is included in a communication made for a permitted purpose, it is information that is "necessary for that purpose" (see subsection (1)(b)(i))—

(a) a statement that a patent exists and is in force or that an application for a patent has been made;

(b) details of the patent, or of a right in or under the patent, which—

(i) are accurate in all material respects, and

(ii) are not misleading in any material respect; and

(c) information enabling the identification of the products or processes in respect of which it is alleged that acts infringing the patent have been carried out.

70C Remedies and defences

(1) Proceedings in respect of an actionable threat may be brought against the person who made the threat for—

(a) a declaration that the threat is unjustified;

(b) an injunction against the continuance of the threat;

(c) damages in respect of any loss sustained by the aggrieved person by reason of the threat.

(2) In the application of subsection (1) to Scotland—

(a) "declaration" means "declarator", and

(b) "injunction" means "interdict".

(3) It is a defence for the person who made the threat to show that the act in respect of which proceedings were threatened constitutes (or if done would constitute) an infringement of the patent.

(4) It is a defence for the person who made the threat to show—

(a) that, despite having taken reasonable steps, the person has not identified anyone who has done an act mentioned in section 70A(2)(a) or (b) in relation to the product or the use of a process which is the subject of the threat, and

(b) that the person notified the recipient, before or at the time of making the threat, of the steps taken.

70D Professional advisers

(1) Proceedings in respect of an actionable threat may not be brought against a professional adviser (or any person vicariously liable for the actions of that professional adviser) if the conditions in subsection (3) are met.

(2) In this section "professional adviser" means a person who, in relation to the making of the communication containing the threat—

(a) is acting in a professional capacity in providing legal services or the services of a trade mark attorney or a patent attorney, and

(b) is regulated in the provision of legal services, or the services of a trade mark attorney or a patent attorney, by one or more regulatory bodies (whether through membership of a regulatory body, the issue of a licence to practise or any other means).

(3) The conditions are that—

(a) in making the communication the professional adviser is acting on the instructions of another person, and

(b) when the communication is made the professional adviser identifies the person on whose instructions the adviser is acting.

(4) This section does not affect any liability of the person on whose instructions the professional adviser is acting.

(5) It is for a person asserting that subsection (1) applies to prove (if required) that at the material time—

(a) the person concerned was acting as a professional adviser, and

(b) the conditions in subsection (3) were met.

70E Supplementary: pending registration

(1) In sections 70 and 70B references to a patent include references to an application for a patent that has been published under section 16.

(2) Where the threat of infringement proceedings is made after an application has been published (but before grant) the reference in section 70C(3) to "the patent" is to be treated as a reference to the patent as granted in pursuance of that application.

70F Supplementary: proceedings for delivery up etc

In section 70(1)(b) the reference to proceedings for infringement of a patent includes a reference to proceedings for an order under section 61(1)(b) (order to deliver up or destroy patented products etc) [and proceedings in the Unified Patent Court for an order for delivery up made in accordance with articles 32(1)(c) and 62(3) of the Agreement on a Unified Patent Court.]".

Sub-ss (2), (2A): substituted for original sub-s (2) by the Patents Act 2004, s 12(1), (2), subject to transitional provisions contained in the Patents Act 2004 (Commencement No 2 and Consequential, etc and Transitional Provisions) Order 2004, SI 2004/3205, art 9(1), (3) at **[1.254]**.

Sub-s (3): word in square brackets substituted by the Patents Act 2004, s 16(1), Sch 2, paras 1, 17, subject to transitional provisions contained in SI 2004/3205, art 9(1), (3) at **[1.254]**.

Sub-ss (4), (5): substituted by the Patents Act 2004, s 12(1), (3), (4), subject to transitional provisions contained in SI 2004/3205, art 9(1), (3) at **[1.254]**.

Sub-s (6): added by the Patents Act 2004, s 12(1), (5), subject to transitional provisions contained in SI 2004/3205, art 9(1), (3) at **[1.254]**.

[Declaration or declarator as to non-infringement]

NOTES

Heading inserted by the Intellectual Property (Unjustified Threats) Act 2017, s 1(1), (4), as from a day to be appointed.

[1.78]

71 Declaration or declarator as to non-infringement

(1) Without prejudice to the court's jurisdiction to make a declaration or declarator apart from this section, a declaration or declarator that an act does not, or a proposed act would not, constitute an infringement of a patent may be made by the court or the comptroller in proceedings between the person doing or proposing to do the act and the proprietor of the patent, notwithstanding that no assertion to the contrary has been made by the proprietor, if it is shown—

(a) that that person has applied in writing to the proprietor for a written acknowledgment to the effect of the declaration or declarator claimed, and has furnished him with full particulars in writing of the act in question; and

(b) that the proprietor has refused or failed to give any such acknowledgment.

(2) Subject to section 72(5) below, a declaration made by the comptroller under this section shall have the same effect as a declaration or declarator by the court.

Revocation of patents

[1.79]

72 Power to revoke patents on application

(1) Subject to the following provisions of this Act, the court or the comptroller may . . . by order revoke a patent for an invention [on the application of any person (including the proprietor of the patent)] on (but only on) any of the following grounds, that is to say—

(a) the invention is not a patentable invention;

[(b) that the patent was granted to a person who was not entitled to be granted that patent;]

(c) the specification of the patent does not disclose the invention clearly enough and completely enough for it to be performed by a person skilled in the art;

(d) the matter disclosed in the specification of the patent extends beyond that disclosed in the application for the patent, as filed, or, if the patent was granted on a new application filed under section 8(3), 12 or 37(4) above or as mentioned in [section 15(9)] above, in the earlier application, as filed;

(e) the protection conferred by the patent has been extended by an amendment which should not have been allowed.

(2) An application for the revocation of a patent on the ground mentioned in subsection (1)(b) above—

(a) may only be made by a person found by the court in an action for a declaration or declarator, or found by the court or the comptroller on a reference under section 37 above, to be entitled to be granted that patent or to be granted a patent for part of the matter comprised in the specification of the patent sought to be revoked; and

(b) may not be made if that action was commenced or that reference was made after [the second anniversary of] the date of the grant of the patent sought to be revoked, unless it is shown that any person registered as a proprietor of the patent knew at the time of the grant or of the transfer of the patent to him that he was not entitled to the patent.

(3) . . .

(4) An order under this section may be an order for the unconditional revocation of the patent or, where the court or the comptroller determines that one of the grounds mentioned in subsection (1) above has been established, but only so as to invalidate the patent to a limited extent, an order that the patent should be revoked unless within a specified time the specification is amended . . . to the satisfaction of the court or the comptroller, as the case may be.

[(4A) The reference in subsection (4) above to the specification being amended is to its being amended under section 75 below and also, in the case of a European patent (UK), to its being amended under any provision of the European Patent Convention under which the claims of the patent may be limited by amendment at the request of the proprietor.]

(5) A decision of the comptroller or on appeal from the comptroller shall not estop any party to civil proceedings in which infringement of a patent is in issue from alleging invalidity of the patent on any of the grounds referred to in subsection (1) above, whether or not any of the issues involved were decided in the said decision.

(6) Where the comptroller refuses to grant an application made to him by any person under this section, no application (otherwise than by way of appeal or by way of putting validity in issue in proceedings for infringement) may be made to the court by that person under this section in relation to the patent concerned, without the leave of the court.

(7) Where the comptroller has not disposed of an application made to him under this section, the applicant may not apply to the court under this section in respect of the patent concerned unless either—

(a) the proprietor of the patent agrees that the applicant may so apply, or

(b) the comptroller certifies in writing that it appears to him that the question whether the patent should be revoked is one which would more properly be determined by the court.

NOTES

Sub-s (1): words omitted repealed, and words in first pair of square brackets inserted by the Patents Act 2004, s 16(1), (2), Sch 2, paras 1, 18, Sch 3; para (b) substituted by the Copyright, Designs and Patents Act 1988, s 295, Sch 5, para 18; words in square brackets in para (d) substituted by the Regulatory Reform (Patents) Order 2004, SI 2004/2357, arts 2, 12, subject to transitional provisions in arts 20, 21 thereof at **[1.248]**, **[1.249]**.

Sub-s (2): words in square brackets in para (b) substituted by the Intellectual Property Act 2014, s 19, Schedule, para 3(1)(b).

Sub-s (3): repealed by the Copyright, Designs and Patents Act 1988, s 303(2), Sch 8.

Sub-s (4): words omitted repealed by the Patents Act 2004, ss 4, 16(2), Sch 3.

Sub-s (4A): inserted by the Patents Act 2004, s 4.

[1.80]

73 Comptroller's power to revoke patents on his own initiative

(1) If it appears to the comptroller that an invention for which a patent has been granted formed part of the state of the art by virtue only of section 2(3) above, he may on his own initiative by order revoke the patent, but shall not do so without giving the proprietor of the patent an opportunity of making any observations and of amending the specification of the patent so as to exclude any matter which formed part of the state of the art as aforesaid without contravening section 76 below.

[(1A) Where the comptroller issues an opinion under section 74A that section 1(1)(a) or (b) is not satisfied in relation to an invention for which there is a patent, the comptroller may revoke the patent.

(1B) The power under subsection (1A) may not be exercised before—

(a) the end of the period in which the proprietor of the patent may apply under the rules (by virtue of section 74B) for a review of the opinion, or

(b) if the proprietor applies for a review, the decision on the review is made (or, if there is an appeal against that decision, the appeal is determined).

(1C) The comptroller shall not exercise the power under subsection (1A) without giving the proprietor of the patent an opportunity to make any observations and to amend the specification of the patent without contravening section 76.]

[(2) If it appears to the comptroller that a patent under this Act and a European patent (UK) have been granted for the same invention having the same priority date, and that the applications for the patents were filed by the same applicant or his successor in title, he shall give the proprietor of the patent under this Act an opportunity of making observations and of amending the specification of the patent, and if the proprietor fails to satisfy the comptroller that there are not two patents in respect of the same invention, or to amend the specification so as to prevent there being two patents in respect of the same invention, the comptroller shall revoke the patent.

(3) The comptroller shall not take action under subsection (2) above before—

(a) the end of the period for filing an opposition to the European patent (UK) under the European Patent Convention, or

(b) if later, the date on which opposition proceedings are finally disposed of;

and he shall not then take any action if the decision is not to maintain the European patent or if it is amended so that there are not two patents in respect of the same invention.

(4) The comptroller shall not take action under subsection (2) above if the European patent (UK) has been surrendered under section 29(1) above before the date on which by virtue of section 25(1) above the patent under this Act is to be treated as having been granted or, if proceedings for the surrender of the European patent (UK) have been begun before that date, until those proceedings are finally disposed of; and he shall not then take any action if the decision is to accept the surrender of the European patent.]

NOTES

Sub-ss (1A)–(1C): inserted by the Intellectual Property Act 2014, s 16(4), where a request for an opinion is made under s 74A(1) at **[1.82]** on or after 1 October 2014.

Sub-ss (2)–(4): substituted, for original sub-ss (2), (3), by the Copyright, Designs and Patents Act 1988, s 295, Sch 5, para 19.

Putting validity in issue

[1.81]

74 Proceedings in which validity of patent may be put in issue

(1) Subject to the following provisions of this section, the validity of a patent may be put in issue—

(a) by way of defence, in proceedings for infringement of the patent under section 61 above or proceedings under section 69 above for infringement of rights conferred by the publication of an application;

(b) in proceedings *under section 70* above;

(c) in proceedings in which a declaration in relation to the patent is sought under section 71 above;

(d) in proceedings before the court or the comptroller under section 72 above for the revocation of the patent;

(e) in proceedings under section 58 above.

(2) The validity of a patent may not be put in issue in any other proceedings and, in particular, no proceedings may be instituted (whether under this Act or otherwise) seeking only a declaration as to the validity or invalidity of a patent.

(3) The only grounds on which the validity of a patent may be put in issue (whether in proceedings for revocation under section 72 above or otherwise) are the grounds on which the patent may be revoked under that section.

(4) No determination shall be made in any proceedings mentioned in subsection (1) above on the validity of a patent which any person puts in issue on the ground mentioned in section 72(1)(b) above unless—

(a) it has been determined in entitlement proceedings commenced by that person or in the proceedings in which the validity of the patent is in issue that the patent should have been granted to him and not some other person; and

(b) except where it has been so determined in entitlement proceedings, the proceedings in which the validity of the patent is in issue are commenced [on or before the second anniversary of] the date of the grant of the patent or it is shown that any person registered as a proprietor of the patent knew at the time of the grant or of the transfer of the patent to him that he was not entitled to the patent.

(5) Where the validity of a patent is put in issue by way of defence or counterclaim the court or the comptroller shall, if it or he thinks it just to do so, give the defendant an opportunity to comply with the condition in subsection (4)(a) above.

(6) In subsection (4) above "entitlement proceedings", in relation to a patent, means a reference under [section 37(1) above] on the ground that the patent was granted to a person not entitled to it or proceedings for a declaration or declarator that it was so granted.

(7) Where proceedings with respect to a patent are pending in the court under any provision of this Act mentioned in subsection (1) above, no proceedings may be instituted without the leave of the court before the comptroller with respect to that patent under section 61(3), 69, 71 or 72 above.

(8) It is hereby declared that for the purposes of this Act the validity of a patent is not put in issue merely because[—

(a)] the comptroller is considering its validity in order to decide whether to revoke it under section 73 above [or

(b) its validity is being considered in connection with an opinion under section 74A below or a review of such an opinion.]

NOTES

Sub-s (1): for the words in italics there are substituted the words "in respect of an actionable threat under section 70A" by the Intellectual Property (Unjustified Threats) Act 2017, s 1(1), (5), as from a day to be appointed.

Sub-s (4): words in square brackets in para (b) substituted by the Intellectual Property Act 2014, s 19, Schedule, para 3(2).

Sub-s (6): words in square brackets substituted by the Copyright, Designs and Patents Act 1988, s 295, Sch 5, para 10.

Sub-s (8): words in square brackets inserted by the Patents Act 2004, s 13(2).

[Opinions by Patent Office

[1.82]

74A [Opinions on matters prescribed in the rules]

(1) The proprietor of a patent or any other person may request the comptroller to issue [an opinion on a prescribed matter in relation to the patent].

(2) Subsection (1) above applies even if the patent has expired or has been surrendered.

(3) The comptroller shall issue an opinion if requested to do so under subsection (1) above, but shall not do so—

(a) in such circumstances as may be prescribed, or

(b) if for any reason he considers it inappropriate in all the circumstances to do so.

(4) An opinion under this section shall not be binding for any purposes.

(5) An opinion under this section shall be prepared by an examiner.

(6) In relation to a decision of the comptroller whether to issue an opinion under this section—

(a) for the purposes of section 101 below, only the person making the request under subsection (1) above shall be regarded as a party to a proceeding before the comptroller; and

(b) no appeal shall lie at the instance of any other person.]

NOTES

Inserted, together with preceding heading and s 74B, by the Patents Act 2004, s 13(1).

Words in square brackets in section heading and sub-s (1) substituted by the Intellectual Property Act 2014, s 16(1).

[1.83]

[74B Reviews of opinions under section 74A

(1) Rules may make provision for a review before the comptroller, on an application by the proprietor or an exclusive licensee of the patent in question, of an opinion under section 74A above.

(2) The rules may, in particular—

(a) prescribe the circumstances in which, and the period within which, an application may be made;

(b) provide that, in prescribed circumstances, proceedings for a review may not be brought or continued where other proceedings have been brought;

(c) . . .

(d) provide for there to be a right of appeal against a decision made on a review only in prescribed cases.]

NOTES

Inserted as noted to s 74A at **[1.82]**.

Sub-s (2): para (c) repealed by the Intellectual Property Act 2014, s 16(2).

Rules: the Patents Rules 2007, SI 2007/3291 at **[1.262]**.

General provisions as to amendment of patents and applications

[1.84]

75 Amendment of patent in infringement or revocation proceedings

(1) In any proceedings before the court or the comptroller in which the validity of a patent [may be] put in issue the court or, as the case may be, the comptroller may, subject to section 76 below, allow the proprietor of the patent to amend the specification of the patent in such manner, and subject to such terms as to advertising the proposed amendment and as to costs, expenses or otherwise, as the court or comptroller thinks fit.

(2) A person may give notice to the court or the comptroller of his opposition to an amendment proposed by the proprietor of the patent under this section, and if he does so the court or the comptroller shall notify the proprietor and consider the opposition in deciding whether the amendment or any amendment should be allowed.

(3) An amendment of a specification of a patent under this section shall have effect and be deemed always to have had effect from the grant of the patent.

(4) Where an application for an order under this section is made to the court, the applicant shall notify the comptroller, who shall be entitled to appear and be heard and shall appear if so directed by the court.

[(5) In considering whether or not to allow an amendment proposed under this section, the court or the comptroller shall have regard to any relevant principles applicable under the European Patent Convention.]

NOTES

Sub-s (1): words in square brackets substituted for original word "is" by the Patents Act 2004, s 16(1), Sch 2, paras 1, 19, subject to transitional provisions contained in the Patents Act 2004 (Commencement No 2 and Consequential, etc and Transitional Provisions) Order 2004, SI 2004/3205, art 9(1), (4) at **[1.254]**.

Sub-s (5): added by the Patents Act 2004, s 2(5).

[1.85]

[76 Amendments of applications and patents not to include added matter

(1) An application for a patent which—

(a) is made in respect of matter disclosed in an earlier application, or in the specification of a patent which has been granted, and

(b) discloses additional matter, that is, matter extending beyond that disclosed in the earlier application, as filed, or the application for the patent, as filed,

may be filed under section 8(3), 12 or 37(4) above, or as mentioned in [section 15(9)] above, but shall not be allowed to proceed unless it is amended so as to exclude the additional matter.

[(1A) Where, in relation to an application for a patent—

(a) a reference to an earlier relevant application has been filed as mentioned in section 15(1)(c)(ii) above; and

(b) the description filed under section 15(10)(b)(i) above discloses additional matter, that is, matter extending beyond that disclosed in the earlier relevant application,

the application shall not be allowed to proceed unless it is amended so as to exclude the additional matter.]

(2) No amendment of an application for a patent shall be allowed under [section 15A(6)], 18(3) or 19(1) if it results in the application disclosing matter extending beyond that disclosed in the application as filed.

(3) No amendment of the specification of a patent shall be allowed under section 27(1), 73 or 75 if it—

(a) results in the specification disclosing additional matter, or

(b) extends the protection conferred by the patent.

[(4) In subsection (1A) above "relevant application" has the meaning given by section 5(5) above.]]

NOTES

Substituted by the Copyright, Designs and Patents Act 1988, s 295, Sch 5, para 20.

Sub-s (1): words in square brackets substituted by the Regulatory Reform (Patents) Order 2004, SI 2004/2357, arts 2, 13(1), (2), subject to transitional provisions in arts 20, 21 thereof at **[1.248]**, **[1.249]**.

Sub-ss (1A), (4): inserted and added respectively by SI 2004/2357, arts 2, 13(1), (3), (5) subject to transitional provisions in arts 20, 21 thereof at **[1.248]**, **[1.249]**.

Sub-s (2): words in square brackets substituted by SI 2004/2357, arts 2, 13(1), (4), subject to transitional provisions in arts 20, 21 thereof at **[1.248]**, **[1.249]**.

[1.86]

[76A Biotechnological inventions

(1) Any provision of, or made under, this Act is to have effect in relation to a patent or an application for a patent which concerns a biotechnological invention, subject to the provisions of Schedule A2.

(2) Nothing in this section or Schedule A2 is to be read as affecting the application of any provision in relation to any other kind of patent or application for a patent.]

NOTES

Inserted by the Patents Regulations 2000, SI 2000/2037, regs 2, 5, in relation to applications for patents made on or after 28 July 2000.

PART II
PROVISIONS ABOUT INTERNATIONAL CONVENTIONS

European patents and patent applications

[1.87]

77 Effect of European patent (UK)

(1) Subject to the provisions of this Act, a European patent (UK) shall, as from the publication of the mention of its grant in the European Patent Bulletin, be treated for the purposes of Parts I and III of this Act as if it were a patent under this Act granted in pursuance of an application made under this Act and as if notice of the grant of the patent had, on the date of that publication, been published under section 24 above in the journal; and—

(a) the proprietor of a European patent (UK) shall accordingly as respects the United Kingdom have the same rights and remedies, subject to the same conditions, as the proprietor of a patent under this Act;

(b) references in Parts I and III of this Act to a patent shall be construed accordingly; and

(c) any statement made and any certificate filed for the purposes of the provision of the convention corresponding to section 2(4)(c) above shall be respectively treated as a statement made and written evidence filed for the purposes of the said paragraph (c).

(2) Subsection (1) above shall not affect the operation in relation to a European patent (UK) of any provisions of the European Patent Convention relating to the amendment or revocation of such a patent in proceedings before the European Patent Office.

[(3) Where in the case of a European patent (UK)—

(a) proceedings for infringement, or proceedings under section 58 above, have been commenced before the court or the comptroller and have not been finally disposed of, and

(b) it is established in proceedings before the European Patent Office that the patent is only partially valid,

the provisions of section 63 or, as the case may be, of subsections (7) to (9) of section 58 apply as they apply to proceedings in which the validity of a patent is put in issue and in which it is found that the patent is only partially valid.]

[(4) Where a European patent (UK) is amended in accordance with the European Patent Convention [or the Agreement on a Unified Patent Court], the amendment shall have effect for the purposes of Parts I and III of this Act as if the specification of the patent had been amended under this Act; but subject to subsection (6)(b) below.

(4A) Where a European patent (UK) is revoked in accordance with the European Patent Convention [or the Agreement on a Unified Patent Court], the patent shall be treated for the purposes of Parts I and III of this Act as having been revoked under this Act.]

(5) Where—

(a) under the European Patent Convention [or the Agreement on a Unified Patent Court] a European patent (UK) is revoked for failure to observe a time limit and is subsequently restored [or is revoked by the Board of Appeal and is subsequently restored by the Enlarged Board of Appeal] [or is revoked and subsequently restored by the Unified Patent Court]; and

(b) between the revocation and publication of the fact that it has been restored a person begins in good faith to do an act which would, apart from section 55 above, constitute an infringement of the patent or makes in good faith effective and serious preparations to do such an act;

he shall have the rights conferred by [section 28A(4) and (5) above, and subsections (6) and (7) of that section shall apply accordingly.]

[(5A) Where, under the European Patent Convention [or the Agreement on a Unified Patent Court], a European patent (UK) is revoked and subsequently restored (including where it is revoked by the Board of Appeal and subsequently restored by the Enlarged Board of Appeal), any fee that would have been imposed in relation to the patent after the revocation but before the restoration is payable within the prescribed period following the restoration.]

(6)

(7) Where [such a translation is not filed], the patent shall be treated as always having been void.

(8) The comptroller shall publish any translation filed at the Patent Office under subsection (6) above.

(9) Subsection (6) above shall come into force on a day appointed for the purpose by rules and shall cease to have effect on a day so appointed, without prejudice, however, to the power to bring it into force again.

[(10) Subsection (1) does not apply and is to be treated as never having applied in respect of a European patent (UK) whose unitary effect is registered by the European Patent Office in the Register for unitary patent protection (see, in particular, the Unitary Patent Regulation).]

NOTES

Sub-s (3): substituted by the Copyright, Designs and Patents Act 1988, s 295, Sch 5, para 21(1), (2).

Sub-ss (4), (4A): substituted for original sub-s (4), by the Copyright, Designs and Patent Act 1988, s 295, Sch 5, para 21(1), (3); words in square brackets inserted by the Patents (European Patent with Unitary Effect and Unified Patent Court) Order 2016, SI 2016/388, art 2(1), (5)(a), as from a day to be appointed (being the date of entry into force of the Agreement on a Unified Patent Court signed at Brussels on 19 February 2013) and subject to art 3 thereof which provides that any question whether an act done before SI 2016/388 comes into force infringes a patent is to be determined in accordance with the law relating to infringement in force at the time the act was done.

Sub-s (5): words in first and third pairs of square brackets inserted by SI 2016/388, art 2(1), (5)(b), as from a day to be appointed (being the date of entry into force of the Agreement on a Unified Patent Court signed at Brussels on 19 February 2013) and subject to art 3 thereof which provides that any question whether an act done before SI 2016/388 comes into force infringes a patent is to be determined in accordance with the law relating to infringement in force at the time the act was done; words in second pair of square brackets inserted by the Patents Act 2004, s 5, Sch 1, paras 1, 2; words in fourth pair of square brackets substituted by the Copyright, Designs and Patents Act 1988, s 295, Sch 5, para 8(b).

Sub-s (5A): inserted by the Intellectual Property Act 2014, s 19, Schedule, para 6, in cases where, under the European Patent Convention, a European patent (UK) is restored on or after 1 October 2014; words in square brackets inserted by SI 2016/388, art 2(1), (5)(a), as from a day to be appointed (being the date of entry into force of the Agreement on a Unified Patent Court signed at Brussels on 19 February 2013) and subject to art 3 thereof which provides that any question whether an act done before SI 2016/388 comes into force infringes a patent is to be determined in accordance with the law relating to infringement in force at the time the act was done.

Sub-s (6): repealed by the Patents (Translations) Rules 2005, SI 2005/687, r 3.

Sub-s (7): words in square brackets substituted by the Copyright, Designs and Patents Act 1988, s 295, Sch 5, paras 8, 21(1), (5).

Sub-s (10): added by SI 2016/388, art 2(1), (5)(c), as from a day to be appointed (being the date of entry into force of the Agreement on a Unified Patent Court signed at Brussels on 19 February 2013) and subject to art 3 thereof which provides that any question whether an act done before SI 2016/388 comes into force infringes a patent is to be determined in accordance with the law relating to infringement in force at the time the act was done.

Rules: the Patents Rules 2007, SI 2007/3291 at **[1.262]**.

[1.88]

78 Effect of filing an application for a European patent (UK)

(1) Subject to the provisions of this Act, an application for a European patent (UK) having a date of filing under the European Patent Convention shall be treated for the purposes of the provisions of this Act to which this section applies as an application for a patent under this Act having that date as its date of filing and having the other incidents listed in subsection (3) below, but subject to the modifications mentioned in the following provisions of this section.

(2) This section applies to the following provisions of this Act—

section 2(3) and so much of section 14(7) as relates to section 2(3);

section 5;

section 6;

so much of section 13(3) as relates to an application for and issue of a certificate under that subsection;
sections 30 to 33;
section 36;
sections 55 to 69;
[sections 70 to 70F];
section 74, so far as relevant to any of the provisions mentioned above;
section 111; and
section 125.

(3) The incidents referred to in subsection (1) above in relation to an application for a European patent (UK) are as follows—

(a) any declaration of priority made in connection with the application under the European Patent Convention shall be treated for the purposes of this Act as a declaration made under section 5(2) above;

(b) where a period of time relevant to priority is extended under that convention, the period of twelve months [allowed under section 5(2A)(a)] above shall be so treated as altered correspondingly;

(c) where the date of filing an application is re-dated under that convention to a later date, that date shall be so treated as the date of filing the application;

(d) the application, if published in accordance with that convention, shall, subject to subsection (6) and section 79 below, be so treated as published under section 16 above;

(e) any designation of the inventor under that convention or any statement under it indicating the origin of the right to a European patent shall be treated for the purposes of section 13(3) above as a statement filed under section 13(2) above;

(f) registration of the application in the register of European patents shall be treated as registration under this Act.

(4) Rules under section 32 above may not impose any requirements as to the registration of applications for European patents (UK) but may provide for the registration of copies of entries relating to such applications in the European register of patents.

[(5) Subsections (1) to (3) above shall cease to apply to an application for a European patent (UK), except as mentioned in subsection (5A) below, if—

(a) the application is refused or withdrawn or deemed to be withdrawn, or

(b) the designation of the United Kingdom in the application is withdrawn or deemed to be withdrawn,

but shall apply again if the rights of the applicant are re-established under the European Patent Convention, as from their re-establishment.

(5A) The occurrence of any of the events mentioned in subsection (5)(a) or (b) shall not affect the continued operation of section 2(3) above in relation to matter contained in an application for a European patent (UK) which by virtue of that provision has become part of the state of the art as regards other inventions[; and the occurrence of any event mentioned in subsection (5)(b) shall not prevent matter contained in an application for a European patent (UK) becoming part of the state of the art by virtue of section 2(3) above as regards other inventions where the event occurs before the publication of that application.]]

[(6) Where, between subsections (1) to (3) above ceasing to apply to an application for a European patent (UK) and the re-establishment of the rights of the applicant, a person—

(a) begins in good faith to do an act which would constitute an infringement of the rights conferred by publication of the application if those subsections then applied, or

(b) makes in good faith effective and serious preparations to do such an act,

he shall have the right to continue to do the act or, as the case may be, to do the act, notwithstanding subsections (1) to (3) applying again and notwithstanding the grant of the patent.

(6A) Subsections (5) and (6) of section 20B above have effect for the purposes of subsection (6) above as they have effect for the purposes of that section and as if the references to subsection (4) of that section were references to subsection (6) above.

(6B) Subject to subsection (6A) above, the right conferred by subsection (6) above does not extend to granting a licence to another person to do the act in question.

(6C) Subsections (6) to (6B) above apply in relation to the use of a patented invention for the services of the Crown as they apply in relation to an infringement of the rights conferred by publication of the application (or, as the case may be, infringement of the patent).

"Patented invention" has the same meaning as in section 55 above.]

(7) While this subsection is in force, an application for a European patent (UK) published by the European Patent Office under the European Patent Convention in French or German shall be treated for the purposes of sections 55 and 69 above as published under section 16 above when a translation into English of the claims of the specification of the application has been filed at and published by the Patent Office and the prescribed fee has been paid, but an applicant—

(a) may recover a payment by virtue of section 55(5) above in respect of the use of the invention in question before publication of that translation; or

(b) may bring proceedings by virtue of section 69 above in respect of an act mentioned in that section which is done before publication of that translation;

if before that use or the doing of that act he has sent by post or delivered to the government department who made use or authorised the use of the invention, or, as the case may be, to the person alleged to have done the act, a translation into English of those claims.

(8) Subsection (7) above shall come into force on a day appointed for the purpose by rules and shall cease to have effect on a day so appointed, without prejudice, however, to the power to bring it into force again.

NOTES

Sub-s (2): words in square brackets inserted by the Intellectual Property (Unjustified Threats) Act 2017, s 1(1), (6), as from a day to be appointed.

Sub-s (3): words in square brackets substituted by the Regulatory Reform (Patents) Order 2004, SI 2004/2357, arts 2, 14, subject to transitional provisions in arts 20, 21 thereof at **[1.248]**, **[1.249]**.

Sub-s (5): substituted, together with sub-s (5A) for original sub-s (5), by the Copyright, Designs and Patents Act 1988, s 295, Sch 5, para 22.

Sub-s (5A): substituted as noted to sub-s (5); words in square brackets inserted by the Patents Act 2004, s 5, Sch 1, paras 1, 3(1), (2).

Sub-ss (6), (6A)–(6C): substituted for original sub-s (6) by the Patents Act 2004, s 5, Sch 1, paras 1, 3(1), (3).

[1.89]

79 Operation of s 78 in relation to certain European patent applications

(1) Subject to the following provisions of this section, section 78 above, in its operation in relation to an international application for a patent (UK) which is treated by virtue of the European Patent Convention as an application for a European patent (UK), shall have effect as if any reference in that section to anything done in relation to the application under the European Patent Convention included a reference to the corresponding thing done under the Patent Co-operation Treaty.

(2) Any such international application which is published under that treaty shall be treated for the purposes of section 2(3) above as published only when a copy of the application has been supplied to the European Patent Office in English, French or German and the relevant fee has been paid under that convention.

(3) Any such international application which is published under that treaty in a language other than English, French or German shall, subject to section 78(7) above, be treated for the purposes of sections 55 and 69 above as published only when it is re-published in English, French or German by the European Patent Office under that convention.

[1.90]

80 Authentic text of European patents and patent applications

(1) Subject to subsection (2) below, the text of a European patent or application for such a patent in the language of the proceedings, that is to say, the language in which proceedings relating to the patent or the application are to be conducted before the European Patent Office, shall be the authentic text for the purposes of any domestic proceedings, that is to say, any proceedings relating to the patent or application before the comptroller or the court.

(2) Where the language of the proceedings is French or German, a translation into English of the specification of the patent under section 77 above or of the claims of the application under section 78 above shall be treated as the authentic text for the purpose of any domestic proceedings, other than proceedings for the revocation of the patent, if the patent or application as translated into English confers protection which is narrower than that conferred by it in French or German.

(3) If any such translation results in a European patent or application conferring the narrower protection, the proprietor of or applicant for the patent may file a corrected translation with the Patent Office and, if he pays the prescribed fee within the prescribed period, the Patent Office shall publish it, but—

(a) any payment for any use of the invention which (apart from section 55 above) would have infringed the patent as correctly translated, but not as originally translated, or in the case of an application would have infringed it as aforesaid if the patent had been granted, shall not be recoverable under that section,

(b) the proprietor or applicant shall not be entitled to bring proceedings in respect of an act which infringed the patent as correctly translated, but not as originally translated, or in the case of an application would have infringed it as aforesaid if the patent had been granted,

unless before that use or the doing of the act the corrected translation has been published by the Patent Office or the proprietor or applicant has sent the corrected translation by post or delivered it to the government department who made use or authorised the use of the invention or, as the case may be, to the person alleged to have done that act.

[(4) Where a correction of a translation is published under subsection (3) above and before it is so published a person—

(a) begins in good faith to do an act which would not constitute an infringement of the patent as originally translated, or of the rights conferred by publication of the application as originally translated, but would do so under the amended translation, or

(b) makes in good faith effective and serious preparations to do such an act,

he shall have the right to continue to do the act or, as the case may be, to do the act, notwithstanding the publication of the corrected translation and notwithstanding the grant of the patent.

(5) Subsections (5) and (6) of section 28A above have effect for the purposes of subsection (4) above as they have effect for the purposes of that section and as if—

(a) the references to subsection (4) of that section were references to subsection (4) above;

(b) the reference to the registered proprietor of the patent included a reference to the applicant.

(6) Subject to subsection (5) above, the right conferred by subsection (4) above does not extend to granting a licence to another person to do the act in question.

(7) Subsections (4) to (6) above apply in relation to the use of a patented invention for the services of the Crown as they apply in relation to an infringement of the patent or of the rights conferred by the publication of the application.

"Patented invention" has the same meaning as in section 55 above.]

NOTES

Sub-ss (4)–(7): substituted for original sub-s (4) by the Patents Act 2004, s 5, Sch 1, paras 1, 4.

[1.91]

81 Conversion of European patent applications

(1) The comptroller may direct that on compliance with the relevant conditions mentioned in subsection (2) below an application for a European patent (UK) shall be treated as an application for a patent under this Act [where the application is deemed to be withdrawn under the provisions of the European Patent Convention relating to the time for forwarding applications to the European Patent Office].

(2) The relevant conditions referred to above are . . . —

(a) . . .

(b) [that]—

(i) the applicant requests the comptroller within the relevant prescribed period (where the application was filed with the Patent Office) to give a direction under this section, or

(ii) the central industrial property office of a country which is party to the convention, other than the United Kingdom, with which the application was filed transmits within the relevant prescribed period a request that the application should be converted into an application under this Act, together with a copy of the application; and

(c) [that] the applicant within the relevant prescribed period pays the [application fee] and if the application is in a language other than English, files a translation into English of the application and of any amendments previously made in accordance with the convention.

(3) Where an application for a European patent falls to be treated as an application for a patent under this Act by virtue of a direction under this section—

(a) the date which is the date of filing the application under the European Patent Convention shall be treated as its date of filing for the purposes of this Act, but if that date is re-dated under the convention to a later date, that later date shall be treated for those purposes as the date of filing the application;

(b) if the application satisfies a requirement of the convention corresponding to any of the requirements of this Act or rules designated as formal requirements, it shall be treated as satisfying that formal requirement;

(c) any document filed with the European Patent Office under any provision of the convention corresponding to any of the following provisions of this Act, that is to say, sections 2(4)(c), 5, 13(2) and 14, or any rule made for the purposes of any of those provisions, shall be treated as filed with the Patent Office under that provision or rule; and

(d) the comptroller shall refer the application for only so much of the examination and search required by sections [15A,] 17 and 18 above as he considers appropriate in view of any examination and search carried out under the convention, and those sections shall apply with any necessary modifications accordingly.

NOTES

Sub-s (1): words in square brackets substituted by the Patents Act 2004, s 5, Sch 1, paras 1, 5(1), (2).

Sub-s (2): words omitted repealed, and word in square brackets in para (b) and word in first pair of square brackets in para (c) substituted by the Patents Act 2004, ss 5, 16(2), Sch 1, paras 1, 5(1), (3), Sch 3; words in second pair of square brackets in para (c) substituted by the Regulatory Reform (Patents) Order 2004, SI 2004/2357, arts 2, 15(1), (2), subject to transitional provisions in art 21 thereof at **[1.249]**.

Sub-s (3): number in square brackets in para (d) inserted by SI 2004/2357, arts 2, 15(1), (3), subject to transitional provisions in art 21 thereof at **[1.249]**.

[1.92]

82 Jurisdiction to determine questions as to right to a patent

(1) The court shall not have jurisdiction to determine a question to which this section applies except in accordance with the following provisions of this section.

(2) Section 12 above shall not confer jurisdiction on the comptroller to determine a question to which this section applies except in accordance with the following provisions of this section.

(3) This section applies to a question arising before the grant of a European patent whether a person has a right to be granted a European patent, or a share in any such patent, and in this section "employer-employee question" means any such question between an employer and an employee, or their successors in title, arising out of an application for a European patent for an invention made by the employee.

(4) The court and the comptroller shall have jurisdiction to determine any question to which this section applies, other than an employer-employee question, if either of the following conditions is satisfied, that is to say—

(a) the applicant has his residence or principal place of business in the United Kingdom; or

(b) the other party claims that the patent should be granted to him and he has his residence or principal place of business in the United Kingdom and the applicant does not have his residence or principal place of business in any of the relevant contracting states;

and also if in either of those cases there is no written evidence that the parties have agreed to submit to the jurisdiction of the competent authority of a relevant contracting state other than the United Kingdom.

(5) The court and the comptroller shall have jurisdiction to determine an employer-employee question if either of the following conditions is satisfied, that is to say—

(a) the employee is mainly employed in the United Kingdom; or

(b) the employee is not mainly employed anywhere or his place of main employment cannot be determined, but the employer has a place of business in the United Kingdom to which the employee is attached (whether or not he is also attached elsewhere);

and also if in either of those cases there is no written evidence that the parties have agreed to submit to the jurisdiction of the competent authority of a relevant contracting state other than the United Kingdom or, where there is such evidence of such an agreement, if the [law applicable to] the contract of employment does not recognise the validity of the agreement.

(6) Without prejudice to subsections (2) to (5) above, the court and the comptroller shall have jurisdiction to determine any question to which this section applies if there is written evidence that the parties have agreed to submit to the jurisdiction of the court or the comptroller, as the case may be, and, in the case of an employer-employee question, the [law applicable to] the contract of employment recognises the validity of the agreement.

(7) If, after proceedings to determine a question to which this section applies have been brought before the competent authority of a relevant contracting state other than the United Kingdom, proceedings are begun before the court or a reference is made to the comptroller under section 12 above to determine that question, the court or the comptroller, as the case may be, shall stay or sist the proceedings before the court or the comptroller unless or until the competent authority of that other state either—

(a) determines to decline jurisdiction and no appeal lies from the determination or the time for appealing expires, or

(b) makes a determination which the court or the comptroller refuses to recognise under section 83 below.

(8) References in this section to the determination of a question include respectively references to—

(a) the making of a declaration or the grant of a declarator with respect to that question (in the case of the court); and

(b) the making of an order under section 12 above in relation to that question (in the case of the court or the comptroller).

(9) In this section and section 83 below "relevant contracting state" means a country which is a party to the European Patent Convention and has not exercised its right under the convention to exclude the application of the protocol to the convention known as the Protocol on Recognition.

NOTES

Sub-ss (5), (6): words in square brackets substituted by the Contracts (Applicable Law) Act 1990, s 5, Sch 4, para 3.

[1.93]

83 Effect of patent decisions of competent authorities of other states

(1) A determination of a question to which section 82 above applies by the competent authority of a relevant contracting state other than the United Kingdom shall, if no appeal lies from the determination or the time for appealing has expired, be recognised in the United Kingdom as if it had been made by the court or the comptroller unless the court or he refuses to recognise it under subsection (2) below.

(2) The court or the comptroller may refuse to recognise any such determination that the applicant for a European patent had no right to be granted the patent, or any share in it, if either—

(a) the applicant did not contest the proceedings in question because he was not notified of them at all or in the proper manner or was not notified of them in time for him to contest the proceedings; or

(b) the determination in the proceedings in question conflicts with the determination of the competent authority of any relevant contracting state in proceedings instituted earlier between the same parties as in the proceedings in question.

[1.94]

[83A European patent with unitary effect and Unified Patent Court

(1) Schedule A3 contains provision about the application of this Act in relation to the European patent with unitary effect.

(2) Schedule A4 contains provision about the jurisdiction of the Unified Patent Court in relation to the European patent (UK) and the European patent with unitary effect.]

NOTES

Commencement: see the note below.

Inserted by the Patents (European Patent with Unitary Effect and Unified Patent Court) Order 2016, SI 2016/388, art 2(1), (6), as from a day to be appointed (being the date of entry into force of the Agreement on a Unified Patent Court signed at Brussels on 19 February 2013) and subject to art 3 thereof which provides that any question whether an act done before SI 2016/388 comes into force infringes a patent is to be determined in accordance with the law relating to infringement in force at the time the act was done.

84–88 *(Ss 84, 85, 88 repealed by the Copyright, Designs and Patents Act 1988, ss 295, 303(2), Sch 5, para 23, Sch 8; ss 86, 87 repealed by the Patents Act 2004, ss 5, 16(2), Sch 1, paras 1, 6, Sch 3.)*

[Unified Patent Court

[1.95]

88A Implementation of Agreement on a Unified Patent Court

(1) The Secretary of State may by order make provision for giving effect in the United Kingdom to the provisions of the Agreement on a Unified Patent Court made in Brussels on 19 February 2013.

(2) An order under this section may, in particular, make provision—

(a) to confer jurisdiction on a court, remove jurisdiction from a court or vary the jurisdiction of a court;

(b) to require the payment of fees.

(3) An order under this section may also make provision for varying the application of specified provisions of this Act so that they correspond to provision made by the Agreement.

(4) An order under this section may—

(a) make provision which applies generally or in relation only to specified cases;

(b) make different provision for different cases.

(5) An order under this section may amend this Act or any other enactment.

(6) An order under this section may not be made unless a draft of the order has been laid before, and approved by resolution of, each House of Parliament.

(7) The meaning of "court" in this section is not limited by the definition of that expression in section 130(1).]

NOTES

Commencement: 1 October 2014.

Inserted, together with preceding cross-heading and s 88B, by the Intellectual Property Act 2014, s 17.

Orders: the Patents (European Patent with Unitary Effect and Unified Patent Court) Order 2016, SI 2016/388.

[1.96]

[88B Designation as international organisation of which UK is member

The Unified Patent Court is to be treated for the purposes of section 1 of the International Organisations Act 1968 (organisations of which the United Kingdom is a member) as an organisation to which that section applies.]

NOTES

Commencement: 1 October 2014.

Inserted as noted to s 88A at **[1.95]**.

International applications for patents

[1.97]

[89 Effect of international application for patent

(1) An international application for a patent (UK) for which a date of filing has been accorded under the Patent Co-operation Treaty shall, subject to—

section 89A (international and national phases of application), and

section 89B (adaptation of provisions in relation to international application),

be treated for the purposes of Parts I and III of this Act as an application for a patent under this Act.

(2) If the application, or the designation of the United Kingdom in it, is withdrawn or (except as mentioned in subsection (3)) deemed to be withdrawn under the Treaty, it shall be treated as withdrawn under this Act.

(3) An application shall not be treated as withdrawn under this Act if it, or the designation of the United Kingdom in it, is deemed to be withdrawn under the Treaty—

(a) because of an error or omission in an institution having functions under the Treaty, or

(b) because, owing to circumstances outside the applicant's control, a copy of the application was not received by the International Bureau before the end of the time limited for that purpose under the Treaty,

or in such other circumstances as may be prescribed.

(4) . . .

(5) If an international application for a patent which designates the United Kingdom is refused a filing date under the Treaty and the comptroller determines that the refusal was caused by an error or omission in an institution having functions under the Treaty, he may direct that the application shall be treated as an application under this Act, having such date of filing as he may direct.]

NOTES

Substituted, together with ss 89A, 89B for original s 89, by the Copyright, Designs and Patents Act 1988, s 295, Sch 5, para 25.

Sub-s (4): repealed by the Patents Act 2004, ss 5, 16(2), Sch 1, paras 1, 7, Sch 3.

[1.98]

[89A International and national phases of application

(1) The provisions of the Patent Co-operation Treaty relating to publication, search, examination and amendment, and not those of this Act, apply to an international application for a patent (UK) during the international phase of the application.

(2) The international phase of the application means the period from the filing of the application in accordance with the Treaty until the national phase of the application begins.

(3) The national phase of the application begins—

(a) when the prescribed period expires, provided any necessary translation of the application into English has been filed at the Patent Office and the prescribed fee has been paid by the applicant; or

(b) on the applicant expressly requesting the comptroller to proceed earlier with the national phase of the application, filing at the Patent Office—

(i) a copy of the application, if none has yet been sent to the Patent Office in accordance with the Treaty, and

(ii) any necessary translation of the application into English,

and paying the prescribed fee.

For this purpose a "copy of the application" includes a copy published in accordance with the Treaty in a language other than that in which it was originally filed.

(4) If the prescribed period expires without the conditions mentioned in subsection (3)(a) being satisfied, the application shall be taken to be withdrawn.

(5) Where during the international phase the application is amended in accordance with the Treaty, the amendment shall be treated as made under this Act if—

(a) when the prescribed period expires, any necessary translation of the amendment into English has been filed at the Patent Office, or

(b) where the applicant expressly requests the comptroller to proceed earlier with the national phase of the application, there is then filed at the Patent Office—

(i) a copy of the amendment, if none has yet been sent to the Patent Office in accordance with the Treaty, and

(ii) any necessary translation of the amendment into English;

otherwise the amendment shall be disregarded.

(6) The comptroller shall on payment of the prescribed fee publish any translation filed at the Patent Office under subsection (3) or (5) above.]

NOTES

Substituted as noted to s 89 at **[1.97]**.

[1.99]

[89B Adaptation of provisions in relation to international application

(1) Where an international application for a patent (UK) is accorded a filing date under the Patent Co-operation Treaty—

(a) that date, or if the application is re-dated under the Treaty to a later date that later date, shall be treated as the date of filing the application under this Act,

(b) any declaration of priority made under the Treaty shall be treated as made under section 5(2) above, and where in accordance with the Treaty any extra days are allowed, the period of 12 months [allowed under section 5(2A)(a) above] shall be treated as altered accordingly, and

(c) any statement of the name of the inventor under the Treaty shall be treated as a statement filed under section 13(2) above.

(2) If the application, not having been published under this Act, is published in accordance with the Treaty it shall be treated, for purposes other than those mentioned in subsection (3), as published under section 16 above when the [national phase of the application begins or, if later, when published in accordance with the Treaty].

(3) For the purposes of section 55 (use of invention for service of the Crown) and section 69 (infringement of rights conferred by publication) the application, not having been published under this Act, shall be treated as published under section 16 above—

(a) if it is published in accordance with the Treaty in English, on its being so published; and

(b) if it is so published in a language other than English—

(i) on the publication of a translation of the application in accordance with section 89A(6) above, or

(ii) on the service by the applicant of a translation into English of the specification of the application on the government department concerned or, as the case may be, on the person committing the infringing act.

The reference in paragraph (b)(ii) to the service of a translation on a government department or other person is to its being sent by post or delivered to that department or person.

(4) During the international phase of the application, section 8 above does not apply (determination of questions of entitlement in relation to application under this Act) and section 12 above (determination of entitlement in relation to foreign and convention patents) applies notwithstanding the application; but after the end of the international phase, section 8 applies and section 12 does not.

(5) When the national phase begins the comptroller shall refer the application for so much of the examination and search [under sections 15A,] 17 and 18 above as he considers appropriate in view of any examination or search carried out under the Treaty.]

NOTES

Substituted as noted to s 89 at **[1.97]**.

Sub-s (1): words in square brackets in para (b) substituted by the Regulatory Reform (Patents) Order 2004, SI 2004/2357, arts 2, 16(1), (2), subject to transitional provisions in art 22 thereof at **[1.250]**.

Sub-s (2): words in square brackets substituted by the Patents Act 2004, s 5, Sch 1, paras 1, 8, subject to transitional provisions in the Patents Act 2004 (Commencement No 2 and Consequential, etc and Transitional Provisions) Order 2004, SI 2004/3205, art 9(1), (5) at **[1.254]**.

Sub-s (5): words in square brackets substituted by SI 2004/2357, arts 2, 16(1), (3), subject to transitional provisions in art 22 thereof at **[1.250]**.

Convention countries

[1.100]

90 Orders in Council as to convention countries

(1) Her Majesty may with a view to the fulfilment of a treaty or international convention, arrangement or engagement, by Order in Council declare that any country specified in the Order is a convention country for the purposes of section 5 above.

(2) Her Majesty may by Order in Council direct that any of the Channel Islands, any colony . . . shall be taken to be a convention country for those purposes.

(3) For the purposes of subsection (1) above every colony, protectorate, and territory subject to the authority or under the suzerainty of another country, and every territory administered by another country under the trusteeship system of the United Nations shall be taken to be a country in the case of which a declaration may be made under that subsection.

NOTES

Sub-s (2): words omitted repealed by the Statute Law (Repeals) Act 1986.

Orders: the Patents (Convention Countries) Order 2007, SI 2007/276 at **[1.259]**.

Miscellaneous

[1.101]

91 Evidence of conventions and instruments under conventions

(1) Judicial notice shall be taken of the following, that is to say—

(a) the European Patent Convention, the Community Patent Convention[, the Agreement on a Unified Patent Court] and the Patent Co-operation Treaty (each of which is hereafter in this section referred to as the relevant convention);

(b) any bulletin, journal or gazette published under the relevant convention and the register of European [patents kept under the European Patent Convention]; and

(c) any decision of, or expression of opinion by, the relevant convention court on any question arising under or in connection with the relevant convention.

(2) Any document mentioned in subsection (1)(b) above shall be admissible as evidence of any instrument or other act thereby communicated of any convention institution.

(3) Evidence of any instrument issued under the relevant convention by any such institution, including any judgment or order of the relevant convention court, or of any document in the custody of any such institution or reproducing in legible form any information in such custody otherwise than in legible form, or any entry in or extract from such a document, may be given in any legal proceedings by production of a copy certified as a true copy by an official of that institution; and any document purporting to be such a copy shall be received in evidence without proof of the official position or handwriting of the person signing the certificate.

(4) Evidence of any such instrument may also be given in any legal proceedings—

(a) by production of a copy purporting to be printed by the Queen's Printer;

(b) where the instrument is in the custody of a government department, by production of a copy certified on behalf of the department to be a true copy by an officer of the department generally or specially authorised to do so;

and any document purporting to be such a copy as is mentioned in paragraph (b) above of an instrument in the custody of a department shall be received in evidence without proof of the official position or handwriting of the person signing the certificate, or of his authority to do so, or of the document being in the custody of the department.

(5) In any legal proceedings in Scotland evidence of any matter given in a manner authorised by this section shall be sufficient evidence of it.

(6) In this section—

"convention institution" means an institution established by or having functions under the relevant convention;

"relevant convention court" does not include a court of the United Kingdom or of any other country which is a party to the relevant convention [but does include the Unified Patent Court;] and

"legal proceedings", in relation to the United Kingdom, includes proceedings before the comptroller.

NOTES

Sub-s (1): words in square brackets in para (a) inserted by the Patents (European Patent with Unitary Effect and Unified Patent Court) Order 2016, SI 2016/388, art 2(1), (7)(a), as from a day to be appointed (being the date of entry into force of the Agreement on a Unified Patent Court signed at Brussels on 19 February 2013) and subject to art 3 thereof which provides that any question whether an act done before SI 2016/388 comes into force infringes a patent is to be determined in accordance with the law relating to infringement in force at the time the act was done; words in square brackets in para (b) substituted by the Patents Act 2004, s 16(1), Sch 2, paras 1, 20.

Sub-s (6): words in square brackets inserted by SI 2016/388, art 2(1), (7)(b), as from a day to be appointed (being the date of entry into force of the Agreement on a Unified Patent Court signed at Brussels on 19 February 2013) and subject to art 3 thereof which provides that any question whether an act done before SI 2016/388 comes into force infringes a patent is to be determined in accordance with the law relating to infringement in force at the time the act was done.

[1.102]

92 Obtaining evidence for proceedings under the European Patent Convention

(1) Section 1 to 3 of the Evidence (Proceedings in Other Jurisdictions) Act 1975 (provisions enabling United Kingdom courts to assist in obtaining evidence for foreign courts) shall apply for the purpose of proceedings before a relevant convention court under the European Patent Convention [or proceedings before the Unified Patent Court] as they apply for the purpose of civil proceedings in a court exercising jurisdiction in a country outside the United Kingdom.

(2) In the application of those sections by virtue of this section any reference to the High Court, the Court of Session or the High Court of Justice in Northern Ireland shall include a reference to the comptroller.

(3) Rules under this Act may include provision—

(a) as to the manner in which an application under section 1 of the said Act of 1975 is to be made to the comptroller for the purpose of proceedings before a relevant convention court under the European Patent Convention; and

(b) subject to the provisions of that Act, as to the circumstances in which an order can be made under section 2 of that Act on any such application.

(4) Rules of court and rules under this Act may provide for an officer of the European Patent Office to attend the hearing of an application under section 1 of that Act before the court or the comptroller, as the case may be, and examine the witnesses or request the court or comptroller to put specified questions to the witnesses.

(5) Section 1(4) of the Perjury Act 1911 and [Article 3(4) of the Perjury (Northern Ireland) Order 1979] (statements made for the purposes, among others, of judicial proceedings in a tribunal of a foreign state) shall apply in relation to proceedings before a relevant convention court under the European Patent Convention [or proceedings before the Unified Patent Court] as they apply to a judicial proceeding in a tribunal of a foreign state.

NOTES

Sub-s (1): words in square brackets inserted by the Patents (European Patent with Unitary Effect and Unified Patent Court) Order 2016, SI 2016/388, art 2(1), (8), as from a day to be appointed (being the date of entry into force of the Agreement on a Unified Patent Court signed at Brussels on 19 February 2013) and subject to art 3 thereof which provides that any question whether an act done before SI 2016/388 comes into force infringes a patent is to be determined in accordance with the law relating to infringement in force at the time the act was done.

Sub-s (5): words in first pair of square brackets substituted by the Perjury (Northern Ireland) Order 1979, SI 1979/1714, art 19(1), Sch 1, para 28; words in second pair of square brackets inserted by SI 2016/388, art 2(1), (8), as from a day to be appointed (being the date of entry into force of the Agreement on a Unified Patent Court signed at Brussels on 19 February 2013) and subject to art 3 thereof which provides that any question whether an act done before SI 2016/388 comes into force infringes a patent is to be determined in accordance with the law relating to infringement in force at the time the act was done.

Rules: the Patents Rules 2007, SI 2007/3291 at **[1.262]**.

[1.103]

93 Enforcement of orders for costs

If the European Patent Office orders the payment of costs in any proceedings before it—

(a) in England and Wales the costs shall, if [the county court] so orders, be recoverable [under section 85 of the County Courts Act 1984] or otherwise as if they were payable under an order of that court;

(b) In Scotland the order may be enforced in like manner as [an extract registered decree arbitral bearing a warrant for execution issued by the sheriff court of any sheriffdom in Scotland];

(c) in Northern Ireland the order may be enforced as if it were a money judgment.

NOTES

In para (a) words in first pair of square brackets substituted by the Crime and Courts Act 2013, s 17, Sch 9, Pt 3, para 52(1)(b), (2), and words in second pair of square brackets substituted by the Tribunals, Courts and Enforcement Act 2007, s 62(3), Sch 13, paras 39, 42.

In para (b) words in square brackets substituted by the Debtors (Scotland) Act 1987, s 108(1), Sch 6, para 20.

[1.104]

94 Communication of information to the European Patent Office, etc

It shall not be unlawful by virtue of any enactment to communicate the following information in pursuance of the European Patent Convention to the European Patent Office or the competent authority of any country which is party to the Convention, that is to say—

(a) information in the files of the court which, in accordance with rules of court, the court authorises to be so communicated;

(b) information in the files of the Patent Office which, in accordance with rules under this Act, the comptroller authorises to be so communicated.

[1.105]

95 Financial provisions

(1) There shall be paid out of moneys provided by Parliament any sums required by any Minister of the Crown or government department to meet any financial obligation of the United Kingdom under the European Patent Convention, . . . or the Patent Co-operation Treaty.

(2) Any sums received by any Minister of the Crown or government department in pursuance of [that convention] or that treaty shall be paid into the Consolidated Fund.

NOTES

Sub-s (1): words omitted repealed by the Patents Act 2004, s 16(1), (2), Sch 2, paras 1, 21(a), Sch 3.

Sub-s (2): words in square brackets substituted by the Patents Act 2004, s 16(1), Sch 2, paras 1, 21(b).

PART III
MISCELLANEOUS AND GENERAL

Legal proceedings

96 (*Repealed by the Senior Courts Act 1981, s 152(4), Sch 7.*)

[1.106]

97 Appeals from the comptroller

(1) Except as provided by subsection (4) below, an appeal shall lie to the Patents Court from any decision of the comptroller under this Act or rules except any of the following decisions, that is to say—

(a) a decision falling within section 14(7) above;

(b) a decision under section 16(2) above to omit matter from a specification;

(c) a decision to give directions under subsection (1) or (2) of section 22 above;

(d) a decision under rules which is excepted by rules from the right of appeal conferred by this section.

(2) For the purpose of hearing appeals under this section the Patents Court may consist of one or more judges of that court in accordance with directions given by [the Lord Chief Justice of England and Wales after consulting the Lord Chancellor]; . . .

(3) An appeal shall not lie to the Court of Appeal from a decision of the Patents Court on appeal from a decision of the comptroller under this Act or rules—

(a) except where the comptroller's decision was given under section 8, 12, 18, 20, 27, 37, 40, 61, 72, 73 or 75 above; or

(b) except where the ground of appeal is that the decision of the Patents Court is wrong in law;

but an appeal shall only lie to the Court of Appeal under this section if leave to appeal is given by the Patents Court or the Court of Appeal.

(4) An appeal shall lie to the Court of Session from any decision of the comptroller in proceedings which under rules are held in Scotland, except any decision mentioned in paragraphs (a) to (d) of subsection (1) above.

[(4) The Lord Chief Justice may nominate a judicial office holder (as defined in section 109(4) of the Constitutional Reform Act 2005) to exercise his functions under subsection (2).]

(5) An appeal shall not lie to the Inner House of the Court of Session from a decision of an Outer House judge on appeal from a decision of the comptroller under this Act or rules—

(a) except where the comptroller's decision was given under section 8, 12, 18, 20, 27, 37, 40, 61, 72, 73 or 75 above; or

(b) except where the ground of appeal is that the decision of the Outer House judge is wrong in law.

NOTES

Sub-s (2): words in square brackets substituted by the Constitutional Reform Act 2005, s 15(1), Sch 4, Pt 1, paras 90, 91(1), (2); words omitted repealed by the Senior Courts Act 1981, s 152(4), Sch 7.

Second sub-s (4): added by the Constitutional Reform Act 2005, s 15(1), Sch 4, Pt 1, paras 90, 91(1), (3).

[1.107]

98 Proceedings in Scotland

(1) In Scotland proceedings relating primarily to patents (other than proceedings before the comptroller) shall be competent in the Court of Session only, and any jurisdiction of the sheriff court relating to patents is hereby abolished except in relation to questions which are incidental to the issue in proceedings which are otherwise competent there.

(2) The remuneration of any assessor appointed to assist the court in proceedings under this Act in the Court of Session shall be determined by the Lord President of the Court of Session with the consent of the Minister for the Civil Service and shall be defrayed out of moneys provided by Parliament.

[1.108]

99 General powers of the court

The court may, for the purpose of determining any question in the exercise of its original or appellate jurisdiction under this Act or any treaty or international convention to which the United Kingdom is a party, make any order or exercise any other power which the comptroller could have made or exercised for the purpose of determining that question.

[1.109]

[99A Power of Patents Court to order report

(1) Rules of court shall make provision empowering the Patents Court in any proceedings before it under this Act, on or without the application of any party, to order the Patent Office to inquire into and report on any question of fact or opinion.

(2) Where the court makes such an order on the application of a party, the fee payable to the Patent Office shall be at such rate as may be determined in accordance with rules of court and shall be costs of the proceedings unless otherwise ordered by the court.

(3) Where the court makes such an order of its own motion, the fee payable to the Patent Office shall be at such rate as may be determined by the Lord Chancellor with the approval of the Treasury and shall be paid out of money provided by Parliament.]

NOTES

Inserted, together with s 99B, by the Copyright, Designs and Patents Act 1988, s 295, Sch 5, para 26.

[1.110]

[99B Power of Court of Session to order report

(1) In any proceedings before the Court of Session under this Act the court may, either of its own volition or on the application of any party, order the Patent Office to inquire into and report on any question of fact or opinion.

(2) Where the court makes an order under subsection (1) above of its own volition the fee payable to the Patent Office shall be at such rate as may be determined by the Lord President of the Court of Session with the consent of the Treasury and shall be defrayed out of moneys provided by Parliament.

(3) Where the court makes an order under subsection (1) above on the application of a party, the fee payable to the Patent Office shall be at such rate as may be provided for in rules of court and shall be treated as expenses in the cause.]

NOTES

Inserted as noted to s 99A at **[1.109]**.

[1.111]

100 Burden of proof in certain cases

(1) If the invention for which a patent is granted is a process for obtaining a new product, the same product produced by a person other than the proprietor of the patent or a licensee of his shall, unless the contrary is proved, be taken in any proceedings to have been obtained by that process.

(2) In considering whether a party has discharged the burden imposed upon him by this section, the court shall not require him to disclose any manufacturing or commercial secrets if it appears to the court that it would be unreasonable to do so.

[1.112]

101 Exercise of comptroller's discretionary powers

Without prejudice to any rule of law, the comptroller shall give any party to a proceeding before him an opportunity of being heard before exercising adversely to that party any discretion vested in the comptroller by this Act or rules.

[1.113]

[102 Right of audience, &c in proceedings before comptroller

(1) A party to proceedings before the comptroller under this Act, or under any treaty or international convention to which the United Kingdom is a party, may appear before the comptroller in person or be represented by any person whom he desires to represent him.

(2) No offence is committed under the enactments relating to the preparation of documents by persons not legally qualified by reason only of the preparation by any person of a document, other than an a deed, for use in such proceedings.

[(2A) For the purposes of subsection (2), as it has effect in relation to England and Wales, "the enactment relating to the preparation of documents by persons not qualified" means section 14 of the Legal Services Act 2007 (offence to carry on a reserved legal activity if not entitled) as it applies in relation to an activity which amounts to the carrying on of reserved instrument activities within the meaning of that Act.]

(3) Subsection (1) has effect subject to rules made under section 281 of the Copyright, Designs and Patents Act 1988 (power of comptroller to refuse to recognise certain agents).

(4) In its application to proceedings in relation to applications for, or otherwise in connection with, European patents, this section has effect subject to any restrictions imposed by or under the European Patent Convention.

[(5) Nothing in this section is to be taken to limit any entitlement to prepare deeds conferred on a registered patent attorney by virtue of the Legal Services Act 2007.]]

NOTES

Substituted, together with s 102A for original s 102, by the Copyright, Designs and Patents Act 1988, s 295, Sch 5, para 27.

Sub-s (2A): inserted by the Legal Services Act 2007, s 208(1), Sch 21, para 40(a).

Sub-s (5): added by the Courts and Legal Services Act 1990, s 125(3), Sch 18, para 20; substituted by the Legal Services Act 2007, s 208(1), Sch 21, para 40(b).

102A (*Substituted as noted to s 102 at* **[1.113]***; repealed by the Legal Services Act 2007, s 210, Sch 23, subject to transitional provisions in Sch 5, Pt 2, paras 6, 9(1), 15 thereto.*)

[1.114]

103 Extension of privilege for communications with solicitors relating to patent proceedings

(1) It is hereby declared that the rule of law which confers privilege from disclosure in legal proceedings in respect of communications made with a solicitor or a person acting on his behalf, or in relation to information obtained or supplied for submission to a solicitor or a person acting on his behalf, for the purpose of any pending or contemplated proceedings before a court in the United Kingdom extends to such communications so made for the purpose of any pending or contemplated—

(a) proceedings before the comptroller under this Act or any of the relevant conventions, or

(b) proceedings before the relevant convention court under any of those conventions.

(2) In this section—

"legal proceedings" includes proceedings before the comptroller;

the references to legal proceedings and pending or contemplated proceedings include references to applications for a patent or a European patent and to international applications for a patent; and

"the relevant conventions" means the European Patent Convention, . . . and the Patent Co-operation Treaty.

(3) This section shall not extend to Scotland.

NOTES

Sub-s (2): in definition "the relevant conventions" words omitted repealed by the Patents Act 2004, s 16(1), (2), Sch 2, paras 1, 22, Sch 3.

Solicitors: references to solicitors are modified so as to include references to: (a) recognised bodies within the meaning of the Administration of Justice Act 1985, s 9, by the Solicitors' Recognised Bodies Order 1991, SI 1991/2684, arts 3–5, Sch 1; and (b) a body which holds a licence issued by the Law Society which is in force under the Legal Services Act 2007, Pt 5, by the Legal Services Act 2007 (Designation as a Licensing Authority) (No 2) Order 2011, SI 2011/2866, art 8(1), (2), Sch 2.

104 (*Repealed by the Copyrights, Designs and Patents Act 1988, s 303(2), Sch 8.*)

[1.115]

105 Extension of privilege in Scotland for communications relating to patent proceedings

[(1)] It is hereby declared that in Scotland the rules of law which confer privilege from disclosure in legal proceedings in respect of communications, reports or other documents (by whomsoever made) made for the purpose of any pending or contemplated proceedings in a court in the United Kingdom extend to communications, reports or other documents made for the purpose of patent proceedings . . .

[(2) In this section—

"patent proceedings" means proceedings under this Act or any of the relevant conventions, before the court, the comptroller or the relevant convention court, whether contested or uncontested and including an application for a patent; and

"the relevant conventions" means the European Patent Convention, . . . and the Patent Co-operation Treaty.]

NOTES

Sub-s (1): numbered as such, and words omitted repealed, by the Copyright, Designs and Patents Act 1988, s 303(1), (2), Sch 7, para 21, Sch 8.

Sub-s (2): added by the Copyright, Designs and Patents Act 1988, s 303(2), Sch 7, para 21; words omitted from definition "the relevant conventions" repealed by the Patents Act 2004, s 16(1), (2), Sch 2, paras 1, 22, Sch 3.

[1.116]

106 Costs and expenses in proceedings before the Court . . .

(1) In [proceedings to which this section applies], the court, in determining whether to award costs or expenses to any party and what costs or expenses to award, shall have regard to all the relevant circumstances, including the financial position of the parties.

[(1A) This section applies to proceedings before the court (including proceedings on an appeal to the court) which are—

(a) proceedings under section 40;
(b) proceedings for infringement;
(c) proceedings *under section 70*; or
(d) proceedings on an application for a declaration or declarator under section 71.]

(2) If in any such proceedings the Patents Court directs that any costs of one party shall be paid by another party, the court may settle the amount of the costs by fixing a lump sum or may direct that the costs shall be taxed on a scale specified by the court, being a scale of costs prescribed by [rules of court].

NOTES

Section heading: words omitted repealed by the Patents Act 2004, s 16(2), Sch 3.

Sub-s (1): words in square brackets substituted by the Patents Act 2004, s 14(1), (2), (4), in relation to proceedings commenced on or after 1 January 2005.

Sub-s (1A): inserted by the Patents Act 2004, s 14(1), (3), (4), in relation to proceedings commenced on or after 1 January 2005; for the words in italics in para (c) there are substituted the words "in respect of an actionable threat under section 70A" by the Intellectual Property (Unjustified Threats) Act 2017, s 1(1), (7), as from a day to be appointed.

Sub-s (2): words in square brackets substituted by the Constitutional Reform Act 2005, s 59(5), Sch 11, Pt 4, para 23(1), (4).

[1.117]

107 Costs and expenses in proceedings before the comptroller

(1) The comptroller may, in proceedings before him under this Act, by order award to any party such costs or, in Scotland, such expenses as he may consider reasonable and direct how and by what parties they are to be paid.

(2) In England and Wales any costs awarded under this section shall, if [the county court] so orders, be recoverable [under section 85 of the County Courts Act 1984] or otherwise as if they were payable under an order of that court.

(3) In Scotland any order under this section for the payment of expenses may be enforced in like manner as [an extract registered decree arbitral bearing a warrant for execution issued by the sheriff court of any sheriffdom in Scotland].

[(4) The comptroller may make an order for security for costs or expenses against any party to proceedings before him under this Act if—

(a) the prescribed conditions are met, and
(b) he is satisfied that it is just to make the order, having regard to all the circumstances of the case;

and in default of the required security being given the comptroller may treat the reference, application or notice in question as abandoned.]

(5) In Northern Ireland any order under this section for the payment of costs may be enforced as if it were a money judgment.

NOTES

Sub-s (2): words in first pair of square brackets substituted by the Crime and Courts Act 2013, s 17, Sch 9, Pt 3, para 52(1)(b), (2); words in second pair of square brackets substituted by the Tribunals, Courts and Enforcement Act 2007, s 62(3), Sch 13, paras 39, 43.

Sub-s (3): words in square brackets substituted by the Debtors (Scotland) Act 1987, s 108(1), Sch 6, para 20.

Sub-s (4): substituted by the Patents Act 2004, s 15, in respect of proceedings commenced on or after 1 October 2005.

[1.118]

108 Licences granted by order of comptroller

Any order for the grant of a licence under section 11, 38, 48 or 49 above shall, without prejudice to any other method of enforcement, have effect as if it were a deed, executed by the proprietor of the patent and all other necessary parties, granting a licence in accordance with the order.

Offences

[1.119]

109 Falsification of register, etc

If a person makes or causes to be made a false entry in any register kept under this Act, or a writing falsely purporting to be a copy or reproduction of an entry in any such register, or produces or tenders or causes to be produced or tendered in evidence any such writing, knowing the entry or writing to be false, he shall be liable—

(a) on summary conviction, to a fine not exceeding [the prescribed sum],
(b) on conviction on indictment, to imprisonment for a term not exceeding two years or a fine, or both.

NOTES

Words in square brackets substituted by virtue of the Magistrates' Courts Act 1980, s 32(2).

[1.120]

110 Unauthorised claim of patent rights

(1) If a person falsely represents that anything disposed of by him for value is a patented product he shall, subject to the following provisions of this section, be liable on summary conviction to a fine not exceeding [level 3 on the standard scale].

(2) For the purposes of subsection (1) above a person who for value disposes of an article having stamped, engraved or impressed on it or otherwise applied to it the word "patent" or "patented" or anything expressing or implying that the article is a patented product, shall be taken to represent that the article is a patented product.

(3) Subsection (1) above does not apply where the representation is made in respect of a product after the patent for that product or, as the case may be, the process in question has expired or been revoked and before the end of a period which is reasonably sufficient to enable the accused to take steps to ensure that the representation is not made (or does not continue to be made).

(4) In proceedings for an offence under this section it shall be a defence for the accused to prove that he used due diligence to prevent the commission of the offence.

NOTES

Sub-s (1): maximum fine increased and converted to a level on the standard scale by the Criminal Justice Act 1982, ss 37, 38, 46.

[1.121]

111 Unauthorised claim that patent has been applied for

(1) If a person represents that a patent has been applied for in respect of any article disposed of for value by him and—

(a) no such application has been made, or
(b) any such application has been refused or withdrawn,

he shall, subject to the following provisions of this section, be liable on summary conviction to a fine not exceeding [level 3 on the standard scale].

(2) Subsection (1)(b) above does not apply where the representation is made (or continues to be made) before the expiry of a period which commences with the refusal or withdrawal and which is reasonably sufficient to enable the accused to take steps to ensure that the representation is not made (or does not continue to be made).

(3) For the purposes of subsection (1) above a person who for value disposes of an article having stamped, engraved or impressed on it or otherwise applied to it the words "patent applied for" or "patent pending", or anything expressing or implying that a patent has been applied for in respect of the article, shall be taken to represent that a patent has been applied for in respect of it.

(4) In any proceedings for an offence under this section it shall be a defence for the accused to prove that he used due diligence to prevent the commission of such an offence.

NOTES

Sub-s (1): maximum fine increased and converted to a level on the standard scale by the Criminal Justice Act 1982, ss 37, 38, 46.

[1.122]
112 Misuse of title "Patent Office"
If any person uses on his place of business, or on any document issued by him, or otherwise, the words "Patent Office" or any other words suggesting that his place of business is, or is officially connected with, the Patent Office, he shall be liable on summary conviction to a fine not exceeding [level 4 on the standard scale].

NOTES
Maximum fine increased and converted to a level on the standard scale by the Criminal Justice Act 1982, ss 37, 38, 46.

[1.123]
113 Offences by corporations
(1) Where an offence under this Act which has been committed by a body corporate is proved to have been committed with the consent or connivance of, or to be attributable to any neglect on the part of, a director, manager, secretary or other similar officer of the body corporate, or any person who was purporting to act in any such capacity, he, as well as the body corporate, shall be guilty of that offence and shall be liable to be proceeded against and punished accordingly.
(2) Where the affairs of a body corporate are managed by its members, subsection (1) above shall apply in relation to the acts and defaults of a member in connection with his functions of management as if he were a director of the body corporate.

114, 115 (*Repealed by the Copyrights, Designs and Patents Act 1988, s 303(2), Sch 8.*)

Immunity of department

[1.124]
116 Immunity of department as regards official acts
Neither the Secretary of State nor any officer of his—
(a) shall be taken to warrant the validity of any patent granted under this Act or any treaty or international convention to which the United Kingdom is a party; or
(b) shall incur any liability by reason of or in connection with any examination or investigation required or authorised by this Act or any such treaty or convention, or any report or other proceedings consequent on any such examination or investigation.

Administrative provisions

[1.125]
117 Correction of errors in patents and applications
(1) The comptroller may, subject to any provision of rules, correct any error of translation or transcription, clerical error or mistake in any specification of a patent or application for a patent or any document filed in connection with a patent or such an application.
(2) Where the comptroller is requested to correct such an error or mistake, any person may in accordance with rules give the comptroller notice of opposition to the request and the comptroller shall determine the matter.
[(3) Where the comptroller is requested to correct an error or mistake in a withdrawal of an application for a patent, and—
(a) the application was published under section 16 above; and
(b) details of the withdrawal were published by the comptroller;
the comptroller shall publish notice of such a request in the prescribed manner.
(4) Where the comptroller publishes a notice under subsection (3) above, the comptroller may only correct an error or mistake under subsection (1) above by order.]

NOTES
Sub-ss (3), (4): added by the Regulatory Reform (Patents) Order 2004, SI 2004/2357, arts 2, 17.
Comptroller: see the note to s 14 at **[1.15]**.

[1.126]
[117A Effect of resuscitating a withdrawn application under section 117
(1) Where—
(a) the comptroller is requested to correct an error or mistake in a withdrawal of an application for a patent; and
(b) an application has been resuscitated in accordance with that request,
the effect of that resuscitation is as follows.
(2) Anything done under or in relation to the application during the period between the application being withdrawn and its resuscitation shall be treated as valid.
(3) If the comptroller has published notice of the request as mentioned in section 117(3) above, anything done during that period which would have constituted an infringement of the rights conferred by publication of the application if the application had not been withdrawn shall be treated as an infringement of those rights if it was a continuation or repetition of an earlier act infringing those rights.
(4) If the comptroller has published notice of the request as mentioned in section 117(3) above and, after the withdrawal of the application and before publication of the notice, a person—

(a) began in good faith to do an act which would have constituted an infringement of the rights conferred by publication of the application if the withdrawal had not taken place, or

(b) made in good faith effective and serious preparations to do such an act,

he has the right to continue to do the act or, as the case may be, to do the act, notwithstanding the resuscitation of the application and the grant of the patent; but this right does not extend to granting a licence to another person to do the act.

(5) If the act was done, or the preparations were made, in the course of a business, the person entitled to the right conferred by subsection (4) above may—

(a) authorise the doing of that act by any partners of his for the time being in that business, and

(b) assign that right, or transmit it on death (or in the case of a body corporate on its dissolution), to any person who acquires that part of the business in the course of which the act was done or the preparations were made.

(6) Where a product is disposed of to another in exercise of a right conferred by subsection (4) or (5) above, that other and any person claiming through him may deal with the product in the same way as if it had been disposed of by the applicant.

[(7) The above provisions apply in relation to the use of a patented invention for the services of the Crown as they apply in relation to infringement of the rights conferred by publication of the application for a patent (or, as the case may be, infringement of the patent).

"Patented invention" has the same meaning as in section 55 above.]]

NOTES

Inserted, together with s 117B, by the Regulatory Reform (Patents) Order 2004, SI 2004/2357, arts 2, 18.

Sub-s (7): added by the Patents Act 2004, s 16(1), Sch 2, para 23.

[1.127]

[117B Extension of time limits specified by comptroller

(1) Subsection (2) below applies in relation to a period if it is specified by the comptroller in connection with an application for a patent, or a patent.

(2) Subject to subsections (4) and (5) below, the comptroller shall extend a period to which this subsection applies if—

(a) the applicant or the proprietor of the patent requests him to do so; and

(b) the request complies with the relevant requirements of rules.

(3) An extension of a period under subsection (2) above expires—

(a) at the end of the period prescribed for the purposes of this subsection, or

(b) if sooner, at the end of the period prescribed for the purposes of section 20 above.

(4) If a period has already been extended under subsection (2) above—

(a) that subsection does not apply in relation to it again;

(b) the comptroller may further extend the period subject to such conditions as he thinks fit.

(5) Subsection (2) above does not apply to a period specified in relation to proceedings before the comptroller.]

NOTES

Inserted as noted to s 117A at **[1.126]**.

[1.128]

118 Information about patent applications and patents, and inspection of documents

(1) After publication of an application for a patent in accordance with section 16 above the comptroller shall on a request being made to him in the prescribed manner and on payment of the prescribed fee (if any) give the person making the request such information, and permit him to inspect such documents, relating to the application or to any patent granted in pursuance of the application as may be specified in the request, subject, however, to any prescribed restrictions.

(2) Subject to the following provisions of this section, until an application for a patent is so published documents or information constituting or relating to the application shall not, without the consent of the applicant, be published or communicated to any person by the comptroller.

(3) Subsection (2) above shall not prevent the comptroller from—

(a) sending the European Patent Office information which it is his duty to send that office in accordance with any provision of the European Patent Convention;

[(aa) sending any patent office outside the United Kingdom such information about unpublished applications for patents as that office requests;] or

(b) publishing or communicating to others any prescribed bibliographic information about an unpublished application for a patent;

nor shall that subsection prevent the Secretary of State from inspecting or authorising the inspection of an application for a patent or any connected documents under [section 22(6) above].

[(3A) Information may not be sent to a patent office in reliance on subsection (3)(aa) otherwise than in accordance with the working arrangements that the comptroller has made for that purpose with that office.

(3B) Those arrangements must include provision for ensuring that the confidentiality of information of the kind referred to in subsection (3)(aa) sent by the comptroller to the patent office in question is protected.

(3C) The reference in subsection (3)(aa) to a patent office is to an organisation which carries out, in relation to patents, functions of the kind carried out at the Patent Office.]

(4) Where a person is notified that an application for a patent has been made, but not published in accordance with section 16 above, and that the applicant will, if the patent is granted, bring proceedings against that person in the event of his doing an act specified in the notification after the application is so published, that person may make a request under subsection (1) above, notwithstanding that the application has not been published, and that subsection shall apply accordingly.

(5) Where an application for a patent is filed, but not published, and a new application is filed in respect of any part of the subject-matter of the earlier application (either in accordance with rules or in pursuance of an order under section 8 above) and is published, any person may make a request under subsection (1) above relating to the earlier application and on payment of the prescribed fee the comptroller shall give him such information and permit him to inspect such documents as could have been given or inspected if the earlier application had been published.

NOTES

Sub-s (3): para (aa) inserted by the Intellectual Property Act 2014, s 18(1), in respect of an application for a patent whose date of filing is on or after 1 October 2014; final words in square brackets substituted by the Copyright, Designs and Patents Act 1988, s 295, Sch 5, para 28.

Sub-ss (3A)–(3C): inserted by the Intellectual Property Act 2014, s 18(2), (3), in respect of an application for a patent whose date of filing is on or after 1 October 2014.

118A *(Inserted by the Patents Act 1977 (Amendment) Regulations 2011, SI 2011/2059, reg 2 and repealed by the Copyright (Public Administration) Regulations 2014, SI 2014/1385, reg 3(1).)*

[1.129]

119 Service by post

Any notice required or authorised to be given by this Act or rules, and any application or other document so authorised or required to be made or filed, may be given, made or filed by post.

[1.130]

120 Hours of business and excluded days

(1) [The comptroller may give directions specifying] the hour at which the Patent Office shall be taken to be closed on any day for purposes of the transaction by the public of business under this Act or of any class of such business, [and the directions may specify] days as excluded days for any such purposes.

(2) Any business done under this Act on any day after the hour so specified in relation to business of that class, or on a day which is an excluded day in relation to business of that class, shall be taken to have been done on the next following day not being an excluded day; and where the time for doing anything under this Act expires on an excluded day that time shall be extended to the next following day not being an excluded day.

[(3) Directions under this section shall be published in the prescribed manner.]

NOTES

Sub-s (1): words in square brackets substituted by the Patents Act 2004, s 16(1), Sch 2, paras 1, 24(1), (2), subject to transitional provisions contained in the Patents Act 2004 (Commencement No 1 and Consequential and Transitional Provisions) Order 2004, SI 2004/2177, arts 6, 8 at **[1.244]**, **[1.246]**.

Sub-s (3): added by the Patents Act 2004, s 16(1), Sch 2, paras 1, 24(1), (3), subject to transitional provisions contained in SI 2004/2177, arts 6, 8 at **[1.244]**, **[1.246]**.

[1.131]

121 Comptroller's annual report

Before [1st December] in every [financial year] the comptroller shall cause to be laid before both Houses of Parliament a report with respect to the execution of this Act and the discharge of his functions under the European Patent Convention, . . . and the Patent Co-operation Treaty, and every such report shall include an account of all fees, salaries and allowances, and other money received and paid by him under this Act, [that convention] and that treaty during the previous [financial year].

NOTES

Words in square brackets substituted and words omitted repealed by the Patents Act 2004, s 16(1), (2), Sch 2, paras 1, 25, Sch 3.

Supplemental

[1.132]

122 Crown's right to sell forfeited articles

Nothing in this Act affects the right of the Crown or any person deriving title directly or indirectly from the Crown to dispose of or use articles forfeited under the laws relating to customs or excise.

[1.133]

123 Rules

(1) The Secretary of State may make such rules as he thinks expedient for regulating the business of the Patent Office in relation to patents and applications for patents (including European patents, applications for European patents and international applications for patents) and for regulating all matters placed by this Act under the direction or control of the comptroller; and in this Act, except so far as the context otherwise requires, "prescribed" means prescribed by rules and "rules" means rules made under this section.

(2) Without prejudice to the generality of subsection (1) above, rules may make provision—

(a) prescribing the form and contents of applications for patents and other documents which may be filed at the Patent Office and requiring copies to be furnished of any such documents;

(b) regulating the procedure to be followed in connection with any proceeding or other matter before the comptroller or the Patent Office and authorising the rectification of irregularities of procedure;

(c) requiring fees to be paid in connection with any such proceeding or matter or in connection with the provision of any service by the Patent Office and providing for the remission of fees in the prescribed circumstances;

(d) regulating the mode of giving evidence in any such proceeding and empowering the comptroller to compel the attendance of witnesses and the discovery of and production of documents;

(e) requiring the comptroller to advertise any proposed amendments of patents and any other prescribed matters, including any prescribed steps in any such proceeding;

(f) requiring the comptroller to hold proceedings in Scotland in such circumstances as may be specified in the rules where there is more than one party to proceedings under section 8, 12, 37, 40(1) or (2), 41(8), 61(3), 71 or 72 above;

(g) providing for the appointment of advisers to assist the comptroller in any proceeding before him;

(h) prescribing time limits for doing anything required to be done in connection with any such proceeding by this Act or the rules and providing for the alteration of any period of time specified in this Act or the rules;

[(i) giving effect to an inventor's rights to be mentioned conferred by section 13, and providing for an inventor's waiver of any such right to be subject to acceptance by the comptroller;]

(j) without prejudice to any other provision of this Act, requiring and regulating the translation of documents in connection with an application for a patent or a European patent or an international application for a patent and the filing and authentication of any such translations;

(k) . . .

(l) providing for the publication and sale of documents in the Patent Office and of information about such documents.

[(2A) The comptroller may set out in directions any forms the use of which is required by rules; and any such directions shall be published in the prescribed manner.]

(3) Rules may make different provision for different cases.

[(3A) It is hereby declared that rules—

(a) authorising the rectification of irregularities of procedure, or

(b) providing for the alteration of any period of time,

may authorise the comptroller to extend or further extend any period notwithstanding that the period has already expired.]

(4), (5) . . .

(6) Rules shall provide for the publication by the comptroller of a journal (in this Act referred to as "the journal") containing particulars of applications for and grants of patents, and of other proceedings under this Act.

(7) Rules shall require or authorise the comptroller to make arrangements for the publication of reports of cases relating to patents, trade marks [registered designs or design right] decided by him and of cases relating to patents (whether under this Act or otherwise), trade marks, registered designs[, copyright and design right] decided by any court or body (whether in the United Kingdom or elsewhere).

NOTES

Sub-s (2): para (i) substituted by the Patents Act 2004, s 16(1), Sch 2, paras 1, 26(1), (2); para (k) repealed by the Copyright, Designs and Patents Act 1988, s 303(2), Sch 8.

Sub-s (2A): inserted by the Patents Act 2004, s 16(1), Sch 2, paras 1, 26(1), (3), subject to transitional provisions contained in the Patents Act 2004 (Commencement No 1 and Consequential and Transitional Provisions) Order 2004, SI 2004/2177, arts 7, 8 at **[1.245]**, **[1.246]**.

Sub-s (3A): inserted by the Copyright, Designs and Patents Act 1988, s 295, Sch 5, para 29.

Sub-ss (4), (5): repealed by the Patents Act 2004, s 16(1), (2), Sch 2, paras 1, 26(1), (4), Sch 3 subject to transitional provisions contained in SI 2004/2177, arts 7, 8 at **[1.245]**, **[1.246]**.

Sub-s (7): words in square brackets substituted by the Copyright, Designs and Patents Act 1988, s 303(1), Sch 7, para 22.

Registered trade marks: the reference to a registered trade mark in sub-s (7) is be construed as a reference to a registered trade mark within the meaning of the Trade Marks Act 1994; see s 106(1) of, and Sch 4, para 1 to, the 1994 Act.

Rules: the Patents (Companies Re-registration) Rules 1982, SI 1982/297; the Patents, Trade Marks and Designs (Address For Service and Time Limits, etc) Rules 2006, SI 2006/760; the Patent Rules 2007, SI 2007/3291 at **[1.262]**; the Patents (Fees) Rules 2007, SI 2007/3292; the Patents, Trade Marks and Designs (Address for Service) Rules 2009, SI 2009/546.

In addition, the Patents Rules 1978, SI 1978/216, r 124 (as amended) have effect as if made under this section and have the effect of continuing in force certain provisions of the Patents Rules 1968, SI 1968/1389 in relation to existing patents and applications (as defined by s 127 at **[1.138]**).

[1.134]

124 Rules, regulations and orders; supplementary

(1) Any power conferred on the Secretary of State by this Act to make rules, regulations or orders shall be exercisable by statutory instrument.

(2) Any Order in Council and any statutory instrument containing an order, rules or regulations under this Act, other than an order or rule required to be laid before Parliament in draft or an order under section 132(5) below, shall be subject to annulment in pursuance of a resolution of either House of Parliament.

(3) Any order in Council or order under any provision of this Act may be varied or revoked by a subsequent order.

[1.135]

[124A Use of electronic communications

(1) The comptroller may [give] directions as to the form and manner in which documents to be delivered to the comptroller—

(a) in electronic form; or

(b) using electronic communications,

are to be delivered to him.

(2) A direction under subsection (1) may provide that in order for a document to be delivered in compliance with the direction it shall be accompanied by one or more additional documents specified in the direction.

(3) [Subject to subsections (14) and (15), if a document to which a direction under subsection (1) or (2)] applies is delivered to the comptroller in a form or manner which does not comply with the direction the comptroller may treat the document as not having been delivered.

(4) Subsection (5) applies in relation to a case where—

(a) a document is delivered using electronic communications, and

(b) there is a requirement for a fee to accompany the document.

(5) The comptroller may [give] directions specifying—

(a) how the fee shall be paid; [and]

(b) when the fee shall be deemed to have been paid.

(6) The comptroller may [give] directions specifying that a person who delivers a document to the comptroller in electronic form or using electronic communications cannot treat the document as having been delivered unless its delivery has been acknowledged.

(7) The comptroller may [give] directions specifying how a time of delivery is to be accorded to a document delivered to him in electronic form or using electronic communications.

(8) A direction under this section may be given—

(a) generally;

(b) in relation to a description of cases specified in the direction;

(c) in relation to a particular person or persons.

(9), (10) . . .

(11) A direction under this section may be varied or revoked by a subsequent direction under this section.

(12) . . .

[(13) The delivery using electronic communications to any person by the comptroller of any document is deemed to be effected, unless the comptroller has otherwise specified, by transmitting an electronic communication containing the document to an address provided or made available to the comptroller by that person as an address of his for the receipt of electronic communications; and unless the contrary is proved such delivery is deemed to be effected immediately upon the transmission of the communication.

(14) A requirement of this Act that something must be done in the prescribed manner is satisfied in the case of something that is done—

(a) using a document in electronic form, or

(b) using electronic communications,

only if the directions under this section that apply to the manner in which it is done are complied with.

(15) In the case of an application made as mentioned in subsection (14)(a) or (b) above, a reference in this Act to the application not having been made in compliance with rules or requirements of this Act includes a reference to its not having been made in compliance with any applicable directions under this section.

(16) This section applies—

(a) to delivery at, in, with or to the Patent Office as it applies to delivery to the comptroller; and

(b) to delivery by the Patent Office as it applies to delivery by the comptroller.]

NOTES

Inserted by the Patents Act 1977 (Electronic Communications) Order 2003, SI 2003/512, art 2.

Sub-ss (1), (3), (6), (7): words in square brackets substituted by the Registered Designs Act 1949 and Patents Act 1977 (Electronic Communications) Order 2006, SI 2006/1229, art 4(1)–(3), (5), (6).

Sub-s (5): word in first pair of square brackets substituted and word in second pair of square brackets inserted by SI 2006/1229, art 4(1), (4).

Sub-ss (9), (10), (12): repealed by SI 2006/1229, art 4(1), (7).

Sub-ss (13)–(16): substituted, for original sub-ss (13)–(15), by SI 2006/1229, art 4(1), (8).

[1.136]

125 Extent of invention

(1) For the purposes of this Act an invention for a patent for which an application has been made or for which a patent has been granted shall, unless the context otherwise requires, be taken to be that specified in a claim of the specification of the application or patent, as the case may be, as interpreted by the description and any drawings contained in that specification, and the extent of the protection conferred by a patent or application for a patent shall be determined accordingly.

(2) It is hereby declared for the avoidance of doubt that where more than one invention is specified in any such claim, each invention may have a different priority date under section 5 above.

(3) The Protocol on the Interpretation of Article 69 of the European Patent Convention (which Article contains a provision corresponding to subsection (1) above) shall, as for the time being in force, apply for the purposes of subsection (1) above as it applies for the purposes of that Article.

[1.137]

[125A Disclosure of invention by specification: availability of samples of [biological material]

(1) Provision may be made by rules prescribing the circumstances in which the specification of an application for a patent, or of a patent, for an invention which [involves the use of or concerns biological material] is to be treated as disclosing the invention in a manner which is clear enough and complete enough for the invention to be performed by a person skilled in the art.

(2) The rules may in particular require the applicant or patentee—

(a) to take such steps as may be prescribed for the purposes of making available to the public samples of the [biological material], and

(b) not to impose or maintain restrictions on the uses to which such samples may be put, except as may be prescribed.

(3) The rules may provide that, in such cases as may be prescribed, samples need only be made available to such persons or descriptions of persons as may be prescribed; and the rules may identify a description of persons by reference to whether the comptroller has given his certificate as to any matter.

(4) An application for revocation of the patent under section 72(1)(c) above may be made if any of the requirements of the rules cease to be complied with.]

NOTES

Inserted by the Copyright, Designs and Patents Act 1988, s 295, Sch 5, para 30.

Section heading, sub-ss (1), (2): words in square brackets substituted by the Patents Regulations 2000, SI 2000/2037, regs 2, 6, in relation to applications for patents made on or after 28 July 2000.

Rules: the Patents Rules 2007, SI 2007/3291 at **[1.262]**.

126 (*Repealed by the Finance Act 2000, s 156, Sch 40, Pt III, in relation to instruments executed on or after 28 March 2000.*)

[1.138]

127 Existing patents and applications

(1) No application for a patent may be made under the 1949 Act on or after the appointed day.

(2) Schedule 1 to this Act shall have effect for securing that certain provisions of the 1949 Act shall continue to apply on and after the appointed day to—

(a) a patent granted before that day;

(b) an application for a patent which is filed before that day, and which is accompanied by a complete specification or in respect of which a complete specification is filed before that day;

(c) a patent granted in pursuance of such an application.

(3) Schedule 2 to this Act shall have effect for securing that (subject to the provisions of that Schedule) certain provisions of this Act shall apply on and after the appointed day to any patent and application to which subsection (2) above relates, but, except as provided by the following provisions of this Act, this Act shall not apply to any such patent or application.

(4) An application for a patent which is made before the appointed day, but which does not comply with subsection (2)(b) above, shall be taken to have been abandoned immediately before that day, but, notwithstanding anything in section 5(3) above, the application may nevertheless

serve to establish a priority date in relation to a later application for a patent under this Act if the date of filing the abandoned application falls within the period of fifteen months immediately preceding the filing of the later application.

(5) Schedule 3 to this Act shall have effect for repealing certain provisions of the 1949 Act.

(6) The transitional provisions and savings in Schedule 4 to this Act shall have effect.

(7) In Schedules 1 to 4 to this Act "existing patent" means a patent mentioned in subsection (2)(a) and (c) above, "existing application" means an application mentioned in subsection (2)(b) above, and expressions used in the 1949 Act and those Schedules have the same meanings in those Schedules as in that Act.

NOTES

1949 Act: Patents Act 1949. Although much of the 1949 Act is repealed by this Act, it continues to apply to existing patents and applications (see sub-s (2) above).

[1.139]

128 Priorities between patents and applications under 1949 Act and this Act

(1) The following provisions of this section shall have effect for the purpose of resolving questions of priority arising between patents and applications for patents under the 1949 Act and patents and applications for patents under this Act.

(2) A complete specification under the 1949 Act shall be treated for the purposes of sections 2(3) and 5(2) above—

(a) if published under that Act, as a published application for a patent under this Act;

(b) if it has a date of filing under that Act, as an application for a patent under this Act which has a date of filing under this Act:

and in the said section 2(3), as it applies by virtue of this subsection in relation to any such specification, the words "both as filed and" shall be omitted.

(3) In section 8(1), (2) and (4) of the 1949 Act (search for anticipation by prior claim) the references to any claim of a complete specification, other than the applicant's, published and filed as mentioned in section 8(1) shall include references to any claim contained in an application made and published under this Act or in the specification of a patent granted under this Act, being a claim in respect of an invention having a priority date earlier than the date of filing the complete specification under the 1949 Act.

(4) In section 32(1)(a) of the 1949 Act (which specifies, as one of the grounds of revoking a patent, that the invention was claimed in a valid claim of earlier priority date contained in the complete specification of another patent), the reference to such a claim shall include a reference to a claim contained in the specification of a patent granted under this Act (a new claim) which satisfies the following conditions—

(a) the new claim must be in respect of an invention having an earlier priority date than that of the relevant claim of the complete specification of the patent sought to be revoked; and

(b) the patent containing the new claim must be wholly valid or be valid in those respects which have a bearing on that relevant claim.

(5) For the purposes of this section and the provisions of the 1949 Act mentioned in this section the date of filing an application for a patent under that Act and the priority date of a claim of a complete specification under that Act shall be determined in accordance with the provisions of that Act, and the priority date of an invention which is the subject of a patent or application for a patent under this Act shall be determined in accordance with the provisions of this Act.

NOTES

1949 Act: Patents Act 1949.

[1.140]

[128A EU compulsory licences

(1) In this Act an "EU compulsory licence" means a compulsory licence granted under Regulation (EC) No 816/2006 of the European Parliament and of the Council of 17 May 2006 on compulsory licensing of patents relating to the manufacture of pharmaceutical products for export to countries with public health problems(a) (referred to in this Act as "the Compulsory Licensing Regulation").

(2) In the application to EU compulsory licences of the provisions of this Act listed in subsection (3)—

(a) references to a licence under a patent,

(b) references to a right under a patent, and

(c) references to a proprietary interest under a patent, include an EU compulsory licence.

(3) The provisions referred to in subsection (2) are—

sections 32 and 33 (registration of patents etc);

section 37 (determination of right to patent after grant);

section 38 (effect of transfer etc of patent under section 37), apart from subsection (2) and subsections (3) to (5) so far as relating to subsection (2);

section 41 (amount of compensation);

section 46(2) (notice of application for entry that licences are available as of right);

section 57(1) and (2) (rights of third parties in respect of Crown use).

(4) In the following provisions references to this Act include the Compulsory Licensing Regulation—

sections 97 to 99B, 101 to 103, 105 and 107 (legal proceedings);
section 119 (service by post);
section 120 (hours of business and excluded days);
section 121 (comptroller's annual report);
section 123 (rules);
section 124A (use of electronic communications);
section 130(8) (disapplication of Part 1 of Arbitration Act 1996).

(5) In section 108 (licences granted by order of comptroller) the reference to a licence under section 11, 38, 48 or 49 includes an EU compulsory licence.

(6) References in this Act to the Compulsory Licensing Regulation are to that Regulation as amended from time to time.]

NOTES

Inserted, together with s 128B, by the Patents (Compulsory Licensing and Supplementary Protection Certificates) Regulations 2007, SI 2007/3293, reg 2(1), (2).

[1.141]

[128B Supplementary protection certificates

(1) Schedule 4A contains provision about the application of this Act in relation to supplementary protection certificates and other provision about such certificates.

(2) In this Act a "supplementary protection certificate" means a certificate issued under—

(a) [Regulation (EC) No 469/2009 of the European Parliament and of the Council of 6th May 2009 concerning the supplementary protection certificate for medicinal products], or
(b) Regulation (EC) No 1610/96 of the European Parliament and of the Council of 23 July 1996 concerning the creation of a supplementary protection certificate for plant protection products.]

NOTES

Inserted as noted to s 128A at **[1.140]**.

Sub-s (2): words in square brackets in para (a) substituted by the Patents (Supplementary Protection Certificates) Regulations 2014, SI 2014/2411, reg 2(1), (2).

[1.142]

129 Application of Act to Crown

This Act does not affect Her Majesty in her private capacity but, subject to that, it binds the Crown.

[1.143]

130 Interpretation

(1) In this Act, except so far as the context otherwise requires—

["Agreement on a Unified Patent Court" means the Agreement on a Unified Patent Court signed at Brussels on 19th February 2013;]

["application fee" means the fee prescribed for the purposes of section 14(1A) above;]

"application for a European patent (UK)" and [(subject to subsection (4A) below)] "international application for a patent (UK)" each mean an application of the relevant description which, on its date of filing, designates the United Kingdom;

"appointed day", in any provision of this Act, means the day appointed under section 132 below for the coming into operation of that provision;

["biological material" means any material containing genetic information and capable of reproducing itself or being reproduced in a biological system;

"biotechnological invention" means an invention which concerns a product consisting of or containing biological material or a process by means of which biological material is produced, processed or used;]

. . .

"comptroller" means the Comptroller-General of Patents, Designs and Trade Marks;

"Convention on International Exhibitions" means the Convention relating to International Exhibitions signed in Paris on 22nd November 1928, as amended or supplemented by any protocol to that convention which is for the time being in force;

"court" means—

[(a) as respects England and Wales, the High [Court;]]
(b) as respects Scotland, the Court of Session;
(c) as respects Northern Ireland, the High Court in Northern Ireland;

[or the Unified Patent Court, as respects the jurisdiction which it has by virtue of Schedule A4;]

"date of filing" means—

(a) in relation to an application for a patent made under this Act, the date which is the date of filing that application by virtue of section 15 above; and
(b) in relation to any other application, the date which, under the law of the country where the application was made or in accordance with the terms of a treaty or convention to which that country is a party, is to be treated as the date of filing that

application or is equivalent to the date of filing an application in that country (whatever the outcome of the application);

"designate" in relation to an application or a patent, means designate the country or countries (in pursuance of the European Patent Convention or the Patent Co-operation Treaty) in which protection is sought for the invention which is the subject of the application or patent [and includes a reference to a country being treated as designated in pursuance of the convention or treaty];

["electronic communication" has the same meaning as in the Electronic Communications Act 2000;]

"employee" means a person who works or (where the employment has ceased) worked under a contract of employment or in employment under or for the purposes of a government department [or a person who serves (or served) in the naval, military or air forces of the Crown];

"employer", in relation to an employee, means the person by whom the employee is or was employed;

"European Patent Convention" means the Convention on the Grant of European Patents, "European patent" means a patent granted under that convention, "European patent (UK)" means a European patent designating the United Kingdom, "European Patent Bulletin" means the bulletin of that name published under that convention, and "European Patent Office" means the office of that name established by that convention;

["European patent with unitary effect" has the same meaning as in Article 2 of the Unitary Patent Regulation;]

"exclusive licence" means a licence from the proprietor of or applicant for a patent conferring on the licensee, or on him and persons authorised by him, to the exclusion of all other persons (including the proprietor or applicant), any right in respect of the invention to which the patent or application relates, and "exclusive licensee" and "non-exclusive licence" shall be construed accordingly;

. . .

"formal requirements" means those requirements designated as such by rules made for the purposes of [section 15A] above;

"international application for a patent" means an application made under the Patent Co-operation Treaty;

"International Bureau" means the secretariat of the World Intellectual Property Organisation established by a convention signed at Stockholm on 14th July 1967;

"international exhibition" means an official or officially recognised international exhibition falling within the terms of the Convention on International Exhibitions or falling within the terms of any subsequent treaty or convention replacing that convention;

"inventor" has the meaning assigned to it by section 7 above;

"journal" has the meaning assigned to it by section 123(6) above;

"mortgage", when used as a noun, includes a charge for securing money or money's worth and, when used as a verb, shall be construed accordingly;

"1949 Act" means the Patents Act 1949;

"patent" means a patent under this Act;

. . .

"Patent Co-operation Treaty" means the treaty of that name signed at Washington on 19th June 1970;

"patented invention" means an invention for which a patent is granted and "patented process" shall be construed accordingly;

"patented product" means a product which is a patented invention or, in relation to a patented process, a product obtained directly by means of the process or to which the process has been applied;

"prescribed" and "rules" have the meanings assigned to them by section 123 above;

"priority date" means the date determined as such under section 5 above;

"published" means made available to the public (whether in the United Kingdom or elsewhere) and a document shall be taken to be published under any provision of this Act if it can be inspected as of right at any place in the United Kingdom by members of the public, whether on payment of a fee or not; and "republished" shall be construed accordingly;

"register" and cognate expressions have the meanings assigned to them by section 32 above;

"relevant convention court", in relation to any proceedings under the European Patent Convention, . . . or the Patent Co-operation Treaty, means that court or other body which under that convention or treaty has jurisdiction over those proceedings, including (where it has such jurisdiction) any department of the European Patent Office;

"right", in relation to any patent or application, includes an interest in the patent or application and, without prejudice to the foregoing, any reference to a right in a patent includes a reference to a share in the patent;

"search fee" means the fee prescribed for the purposes of [section 17(1) above];

"services of the Crown" and "use for the services of the Crown" have the meanings assigned to them by section 56(2) above, including, as respects any period of emergency within the meaning of section 59 above, the meanings assigned to them by the said section 59;

["Unified Patent Court" means the court established under the Agreement on a Unified Patent Court;]

["Unitary Patent Regulation" means Regulation (EU) No 1257/2012 of the European Parliament and of the Council of 17 December 2012 implementing enhanced cooperation in the area of the creation of unitary patent protection.]

(2) Rules may provide for stating in the journal that an exhibition falls within the definition of international exhibition in subsection (1) above and any such statement shall be conclusive evidence that the exhibition falls within that definition.

(3) For the purposes of this Act matter shall be taken to have been disclosed in any relevant application within the meaning of section 5 above or in the specification of a patent if it was either claimed or disclosed (otherwise than by way of disclaimer or acknowledgment of prior art) in that application or specification.

(4) References in this Act to an application for a patent, as filed, are references to such an application in the state it was on the date of filing.

[(4A) An international application for a patent is not, by reason of being treated by virtue of the European Patent Convention as an application for a European patent (UK), to be treated also as an international application for a patent (UK).]

(5) References in this Act to an application for a patent being published are references to its being published under section 16 above.

[(5A) References in this Act to the amendment of a patent or its specification (whether under this Act or by the European Patent Office) include, in particular, limitation of the claims (as interpreted by the description and any drawings referred to in the description or claims).]

(6) References in this Act to any of the following conventions, that is to say—

(a) The European Patent Convention;
(b) The Community Patent Convention;
(c) The Patent Co-operation Treaty;
[(d) The Agreement on a Unified Patent Court;]

are references to that convention or any other international convention or agreement replacing it, as amended or supplemented by any convention or international agreement (including in either case any protocol or annex), or in accordance with the terms of any such convention or agreement, and include references to any instrument made under any such convention or agreement.

(7) Whereas by a resolution made on the signature of the Community Patent Convention the governments of the member states of the European Economic Community resolved to adjust their laws relating to patents so as (among other things) to bring those laws into conformity with the corresponding provisions of the European Patent Convention, the Community Patent Convention and the Patent Co-operation Treaty, it is hereby declared that the following provisions of this Act, this is to say, sections 1(1) to (4), 2 to 6, 14(3), (5) and (6), 37(5), 54, 60, 69, 72(1) and (2), 74(4), 82, 83, . . . 100 and 125, are so framed as to have, as nearly as practicable, the same effects in the United Kingdom as the corresponding provisions of the European Patent Convention, the Community Patent Convention and the Patent Co-operation Treaty have in the territories to which those Conventions apply.

(8) [Nothing in any of sections 1 to 15 of and schedule 1 to the Arbitration (Scotland) Act 2010 or] [Part I of the Arbitration Act 1996] [applies] to any proceedings before the comptroller under this Act.

(9) Except so far as the context otherwise requires, any reference in this Act to any enactment shall be construed as a reference to that enactment as amended or extended by or under any other enactment, including this Act.

NOTES

Sub-s (1) is amended as follows:

definitions "Agreement on a Unified Patent Court", "European patent with unitary effect", "Unified Patent Court", "Unitary Patent Regulation" inserted by the Patents (European Patent with Unitary Effect and Unified Patent Court) Order 2016, SI 2016/388, art 2(1), (9)(a), as from a day to be appointed (being the date of entry into force of the Agreement on a Unified Patent Court signed at Brussels on 19 February 2013) and subject to art 3 thereof which provides that any question whether an act done before SI 2016/388 comes into force infringes a patent is to be determined in accordance with the law relating to infringement in force at the time the act was done;

definition "application fee" inserted and definition "filing fee" (omitted) repealed by the Regulatory Reform (Patents) Order 2004, SI 2004/2357, arts 2, 19, subject to transitional provisions in arts 20, 21 thereof at **[1.248]**, **[1.249]**;

words in square brackets in definition "application for a European patent (UK)" inserted by the Patents Act 2004, s 5, Sch 1, paras 1, 9(1), (2)(a);

definitions "biological material" and "biotechnological invention" inserted by the Patents Regulations 2000, SI 2000/2037, regs 2, 7, in relation to applications for patents made on or after 28 July 2000;

definition "Community patent" (omitted), word preceding it, and words omitted from definition "relevant convention court" repealed by the Patents Act 2004, s 16(1), (2), Sch 2, paras 1, 27, Sch 3;

in definition "court", para (a) substituted by the Copyright, Designs and Patents Act 1988, s 303(1), word in square brackets in that paragraph substituted by the Crime and Courts Act 2013, s 17, Sch 9, Pt 2, para 27, and words in final pair of square brackets inserted by SI 2016/388, art 2(1), (9)(b), as from a day to be appointed (being the date of entry into force of the Agreement on a Unified Patent Court signed at Brussels on 19 February 2013) and subject to art 3 thereof which provides that any question whether an act done before SI 2016/388 comes into force infringes a patent is to be determined in accordance with the law relating to infringement in force at the time the act was done;

in definition "designate" words in square brackets inserted by the Patents Act 2004, s 5, Sch 1, paras 1, 9(1), (2)(b);

definition "electronic communication" inserted by the Patents Act 1977 (Electronic Communications) Order 2003, SI 2003/512, art 3;

in definition "employee", words in square brackets added with retrospective effect by the Armed Forces Act 1981, s 22(1), (3);

in definition "formal requirements" words in square brackets substituted by the Intellectual Property (Enforcement, etc) Regulations 2006, SI 2006/1028, reg 2(2), Sch 2, paras 1, 5, except in relation to an application for a patent to which article 20, 21 or 22 of the Regulatory Reform (Patents) Order 2004 applies;

definition "patent agent" (omitted) repealed by the Copyright, Designs and Patents Act 1988, s 303(2), Sch 8;

in definition "search fee", words in square brackets substituted by the Copyright, Designs and Patents Act 1988, s 295, Sch 5, para 5.

Sub-s (4A): inserted by the Patents Act 2004, s 5, Sch 1, paras 1, 9(1), (3).

Sub-s (5A): inserted by the Patents Act 2004, s 5, Sch 1, paras 1, 9(1), (4).

Sub-s (6): para (d) inserted by SI 2016/388, art 2(1), (9)(c), as from a day to be appointed (being the date of entry into force of the Agreement on a Unified Patent Court signed at Brussels on 19 February 2013) and subject to art 3 thereof which provides that any question whether an act done before SI 2016/388 comes into force infringes a patent is to be determined in accordance with the law relating to infringement in force at the time the act was done.

Sub-s (7): words omitted repealed by the Copyright, Designs and Patents Act 1988, s 303(2), Sch 8.

Sub-s (8): words in first pair of square brackets inserted and word in third pair of square brackets substituted by the Arbitration (Scotland) Act 2010 (Consequential Amendments) Order 2010, SSI 2010/220, art 2, Schedule, para 5; words in second pair of square brackets substituted by the Arbitration Act 1996, s 107(1), Sch 3, para 33.

Rules: the Patents Rules 2007, SI 2007/3291 at **[1.262]**.

[1.144]

131 Northern Ireland

In the application of this Act to Northern Ireland—

(a) "enactment" includes an enactment of the Parliament of Northern Ireland and a Measure of the Northern Ireland Assembly;

(b) any reference to a government department includes a reference to a Department of the Government of Northern Ireland;

(c) any reference to the Crown includes a reference to the Crown in right of Her Majesty's Government in Northern Ireland;

(d) any reference to the [Companies Act 1985] includes a reference to the corresponding enactments in force in Northern Ireland; and

(e) . . .

[(f) any reference to a claimant includes a reference to a plaintiff.]

NOTES

Para (d): words in square brackets substituted by the Companies Consolidation (Consequential Provisions) Act 1985, s 30, Sch 2.

Para (e): repealed by the Arbitration Act 1996, s 107(2), Sch 4.

Para (f): added by the Patents Act 2004, s 16(1), Sch 2, paras 1, 28.

[1.145]

[131A Scotland

In the application of this Act to Scotland—

(a) "enactment" includes an enactment comprised in, or in an instrument made under, an Act of the Scottish Parliament;

(b) any reference to a government department includes a reference to any part of the Scottish Administration; and

(c) any reference to the Crown includes a reference to the Crown in right of the Scottish Administration.]

NOTES

Inserted by the Scotland Act 1998 (Consequential Modifications) (No 2) Order 1999, SI 1999/1820, art 4, Sch 2, Pt I.

[1.146]

132 Short title, extent, commencement, consequential amendments and repeals

(1) This Act may be cited as the Patents Act 1977.

(2) This Act shall extend to the Isle of Man, subject to any modifications contained in an Order made by Her Majesty in Council, and accordingly, subject to any such order, references in this Act to the United Kingdom shall be construed as including references to the Isle of Man.

(3) For the purposes of this Act the territorial waters of the United Kingdom shall be treated as part of the United Kingdom.

(4) This Act applies to acts done in an area designated by order under section 1(7) of the Continental Shelf Act 1964, [or specified by Order under [section 10(8) of the Petroleum Act 1998] in connection with any activity falling within [section 11(2)] of that Act], as it applies to acts done in the United Kingdom.

(5) This Act (except sections 77(6), (7) and (9), 78(7) and (8), this subsection and the repeal of section 41 of the 1949 Act) shall come into operation on such day as may be appointed by the Secretary of State by order, and different days may be appointed under this subsection for different purposes.

(6) The consequential amendments in Schedule 5 shall have effect.

(7) Subject to the provisions of Schedule 4 to this Act, the enactments specified in Schedule 6 to this Act (which include certain enactments which were spent before the passing of this Act) are hereby repealed to the extent specified in column 3 of that Schedule.

NOTES

Sub-s (4): words in first (outer) pair of square brackets substituted by the Oil and Gas (Enterprise) Act 1982, s 37, Sch 3, para 39; words in second and third (inner) pairs of square brackets substituted by the Petroleum Act 1998, s 50, Sch 4, para 14.

1949 Act: Patents Act 1949.

Orders: the Patents Act 1977 (Commencement No 1) Order 1977, SI 1977/2090; the Patents Act 1977 (Commencement No 2) Order 1978, SI 1978/586; the Patents (Isle of Man) Order 2013, SI 2013/2602.

SCHEDULES

[SCHEDULE A1
DEROGATION FROM PATENT PROTECTION IN RESPECT OF BIOTECHNOLOGICAL INVENTIONS

Section 60(5)(g)

Interpretation

[1.147]

1. In this Schedule—

"Council Regulation" means Council Regulation (EC) No 2100/94 of 27th July 1994 on Community plant variety rights;

"farmer's own holding" means any land which a farmer actually exploits for plant growing, whether as his property or otherwise managed under his own responsibility and on his own account;

"the gazette" means the gazette published under section 34 of the Plant Variety and Seeds Act 1964;

"protected material" means plant propagating material which incorporates material subject to a patent;

"relevant activity" means the use by a farmer of the product of his harvest for propagation or multiplication by him on his own holding, where the product of the harvest constitutes or contains protected material;

"relevant rights holder" means the proprietor of a patent to which protected material is subject;

"seed" includes seed potatoes;

"seed year" means the period from 1st July in one year to 30th June in the following year, both dates inclusive.

Specified species

2. Section 60(5)(g) applies only to varieties of the following plant species and groups—

Name	***Common Name***
Fodder plants	
Cicer arietinum L	Chickpea milkvetch
Lupinus luteus L	Yellow lupin
Medicago sativa L	Lucerne
Pisum sativum L (partim)	Field pea
Trifolium alexandrinum L	Berseem/Egyptian clover
Trifolium resupinatum L	Persian clover
Vicia faba	Field bean
Vicia sativa L	Common vetch
Cereals	
Avena sativa	Oats
Hordeum vulgare L	Barley
Oryza sativa L	Rice
Phalaris canariensis L	Canary grass
Secale cereale L	Rye
X Triticosecale Wittm	Triticale
Triticum aestivum L emend Fiori et Paol	Wheat
Triticum durum Desf	Durum wheat
Triticum spelta L	Spelt wheat
Potatoes	

Name	*Common Name*
Solanum tuberosum	Potatoes
Oil and fibre plants	
Brassica napus L (partim)	Swede rape
Brassica rapa L (partim)	Turnip rape
Linum usitatissimum	Linseed with the exclusion of flax

Liability to pay equitable remuneration

3. (1) If a farmer's use of protected material is authorised by section 60(5)(g), he shall, at the time of the use, become liable to pay the relevant rights holder equitable remuneration.

(2) That remuneration must be sensibly lower than the amount charged for the production of protected material of the same variety in the same area with the holder's authority.

(3) Remuneration is to be taken to be sensibly lower if it would be taken to be sensibly lower within the meaning of Article 14(3) fourth indent of the Council Regulation.

Exemption for small farmers

4. (1) Paragraph 3 does not apply to a farmer who is considered to be a small farmer for the purposes of Article 14(3) third indent of the Council Regulation.

(2) It is for a farmer who claims to be a small farmer to prove that he is such a farmer.

Information to be supplied by farmer

5. (1) At the request of a relevant rights holder ("H"), a farmer must tell H—

- (a) his name and address;
- (b) whether he has performed a relevant activity; and
- (c) if he has performed such an activity, the address of the holding on which he performed it.

(2) If the farmer has performed such an activity, he must tell H whether he is—

- (a) liable to pay remuneration as a result of paragraph 3; or
- (b) not liable because he is a small farmer.

(3) If the farmer has told H that he is liable to pay remuneration as a result of paragraph 3, he must tell H—

- (a) the amount of the protected material used;
- (b) whether the protected material has been processed for planting; and
- (c) if it has, the name and address of the person who processed it.

(4) The farmer must comply with sub-paragraphs (2) and (3) when complying with sub-paragraph (1).

(5) If the farmer has told H that he is liable to pay remuneration as a result of paragraph 3, he must (if H asks him to do so) tell H—

- (a) whether he used any protected material with the authority of H within the same seed year; and
- (b) if he did, the amount used and the name and address of the person who supplied it.

Information to be supplied by seed processor

6. (1) On the request of a relevant rights holder, a seed processor shall supply the following information—

- (a) the name and address of the seed processor;
- (b) the address of the seed processor's principal place of business; and
- (c) whether the seed processor has processed seed of a species specified in paragraph 2 above.

(2) If the seed processor has processed seed of a species specified in paragraph 2 above he shall also supply the following information with the information referred to in sub-paragraph (1)—

- (a) the name and address of the person for whom the processing was carried out;
- (b) the amount of seed resulting from the processing;
- (c) the date processing commenced;
- (d) the date processing was completed;
- (e) the place where processing was carried out.

Information to be supplied by relevant rights holder

7. On the request of a farmer or a seed processor a relevant rights holder shall supply the following information—

- (a) his name and address; and
- (b) the amount of royalty charged for certified seed of the lowest certification category for seed containing that protected material.

Period in respect of which inquiry may be made

8. A request may be made under paragraphs 5, 6 and 7 in respect of the current seed year and the three preceding seed years.

Restriction on movement for processing from the holding

9. No person shall remove or cause to be removed from a holding protected material in order to process it unless—

(a) he has the permission of the relevant rights holder in respect of that protected material;

(b) he has taken measures to ensure that the same protected material is returned from processing as is sent for processing and the processor has undertaken to him that the processor has taken measures to ensure that the same protected material is returned from processing as is sent for processing; or

(c) he has the protected material processed by a seed processor on the list of processors referred to in the gazette as being permitted to process seed away from a holding.

Confidentiality

10. (1) A person who obtains information pursuant to this Schedule shall owe an obligation of confidence in respect of the information to the person who supplied it.

(2) Sub-paragraph (1) shall not have effect to restrict disclosure of information—

(a) for the purposes of, or in connection with, establishing the amount to be paid to the holder of rights pursuant to paragraph 3 and obtaining payment of that amount,

(b) for the purposes of, or in connection with, establishing whether a patent has been infringed, or

(c) for the purposes of, or in connection with, any proceedings for the infringement of a patent.

Formalities

11. (1) A request for information under this Schedule, and any information given in response to such a request, must be in writing.

(2) Information requested under this Schedule must be given—

(a) within 28 days; or

(b) if the request specifies a longer period, within the specified period.

Remedies

12. (1) If, in response to a request under this Schedule, a person—

(a) knowingly fails to provide information which he is required by this Schedule to give, or

(b) refuses to provide any such information,

the court may order him to provide it.

(2) Sub-paragraph (1) does not affect any of the court's other powers to make orders.

(3) A person who knowingly provides false information in response to a request under this Schedule is liable in damages to the person who made the request.

(4) In any action for damages under sub-paragraph (3) the court must have regard, in particular to—

(a) how flagrant the defendant was in providing the false information, and

(b) any benefit which accrued to him as a result of his providing false information, and shall award such additional damages as the justice of the case may require.]

NOTES

Inserted by the Patents Regulations 2000, SI 2000/2037, regs 2, 8(1), in relation to applications for patents made on or after 28 July 2000.

[SCHEDULE A2
BIOTECHNOLOGICAL INVENTIONS

Section 76A

[1.148]

1. An invention shall not be considered unpatentable solely on the ground that it concerns—

(a) a product consisting of or containing biological material; or

(b) a process by which biological material is produced, processed or used.

2. Biological material which is isolated from its natural environment or produced by means of a technical process may be the subject of an invention even if it previously occurred in nature.

3. The following are not patentable inventions—

(a) the human body, at the various stages of its formation and development, and the simple discovery of one of its elements, including the sequence or partial sequence of a gene;

(b) processes for cloning human beings;

(c) processes for modifying the germ line genetic identity of human beings;

(d) uses of human embryos for industrial or commercial purposes;

(e) processes for modifying the genetic identity of animals which are likely to cause them suffering without any substantial medical benefit to man or animal, and also animals resulting from such processes;

(f) any variety of animal or plant or any essentially biological process for the production of animals or plants, not being a micro-biological or other technical process or the product of such a process.

4. Inventions which concern plants or animals may be patentable if the technical feasibility of the invention is not confined to a particular plant or animal variety.

5. An element isolated from the human body or otherwise produced by means of a technical process, including the sequence or partial sequence of a gene, may constitute a patentable invention, even if the structure of that element is identical to that of a natural element.

6. The industrial application of a sequence or partial sequence of a gene must be disclosed in the patent application as filed.

7. The protection conferred by a patent on a biological material possessing specific characteristics as a result of the invention shall extend to any biological material derived from that biological material through propagation or multiplication in an identical or divergent form and possessing those same characteristics.

8. The protection conferred by a patent on a process that enables a biological material to be produced possessing specific characteristics as a result of the invention shall extend to biological material directly obtained through that process and to any other biological material derived from the directly obtained biological material through propagation or multiplication in an identical or divergent form and possessing those same characteristics.

9. The protection conferred by a patent on a product containing or consisting of genetic information shall extend to all material, save as provided for in paragraph 3(a) above, in which the product is incorporated and in which the genetic information is contained and performs its function.

10. The protection referred to in paragraphs 7, 8 and 9 above shall not extend to biological material obtained from the propagation or multiplication of biological material placed on the market by the proprietor of the patent or with his consent, where the multiplication or propagation necessarily results from the application for which the biological material was marketed, provided that the material obtained is not subsequently used for other propagation or multiplication.

11. In this Schedule—

"essentially biological process" means a process for the production of animals and plants which consists entirely of natural phenomena such as crossing and selection;

"microbiological process" means any process involving or performed upon or resulting in microbiological material;

"plant variety" means a plant grouping within a single botanical taxon of the lowest known rank, which grouping can be:

(a) defined by the expression of the characteristics that results from a given genotype or combination of genotypes; and

(b) distinguished from any other plant grouping by the expression of at least one of the said characteristics; and

(c) considered as a unit with regard to its suitability for being propagated unchanged.]

NOTES

Inserted by the Patents Regulations 2000, SI 2000/2037, regs 2, 8(2), in relation to applications for patents made on or after 28 July 2000.

[SCHEDULE A3
EUROPEAN PATENT WITH UNITARY EFFECT

Meaning of "relevant statutory provisions"

[1.149]

1 In this Schedule "relevant statutory provisions" means—

(a) the provisions of this Act which, by virtue of paragraph 2, apply in relation to the European patent with unitary effect, and

(b) the other provisions of this Act which, by virtue of the Unitary Patent Regulation, are to be treated as applying in relation to the European patent with unitary effect (see, in particular, Article 7 of that Regulation).

Provisions applied by this Schedule to the European patent with unitary effect

2 The following provisions of this Act apply in relation to a European patent with unitary effect, subject to paragraphs 3 and 4—

section 48 (compulsory licences: general);

section 48A (compulsory licences: WTO proprietors);
section 48B (compulsory licences: other cases);
section 49 (provisions about licences under section 48);
section 50 (exercise of powers on applications under section 48);
section 50A (powers exercisable following merger and market investigations);
section 51 (powers exercisable in consequence of report of Competition and Markets Authority);
section 52 (opposition, appeal and arbitration);
section 53 (compulsory licences; supplementary provisions);
section 54 (special provisions where patented invention is being worked abroad);
section 55 (use of patented inventions for services of the Crown);
section 56 (interpretation, etc, of provisions about Crown use);
section 57 (rights of third parties in respect of Crown use);
section 57A (compensation for loss of profit);
section 58(1) to (6) and (9A) to (13) (references of disputes as to Crown use);
section 59 (special provisions as to Crown use during emergency);
section 60 (meaning of infringement);
section 64 (right to continue use begun before priority date);
[sections 70 to 70F (unjustified threats);]
section 73(2) to (4) (Comptroller's power to revoke patents on his own initiative);
section 74A (opinions on matters prescribed in the rules);
section 74B (reviews of opinions under section 74A);
section 76A (biotechnological inventions);
section 77(4) to (5A) (effect of European patent (UK));
section 80(1) (authentic text of European patents and patent applications);
sections 97 to 100 (legal proceedings) so far as they relate to proceedings which do not fall within the exclusive jurisdiction of the Unified Patent Court as set out in paragraph 1 of Schedule A4;
section 101 (exercise of comptroller's discretionary powers);
section 102 (right of audience, &c in proceedings before comptroller);
sections 103 (extension of privilege for communications with solicitors relating to patent proceedings) and 105 (extension of privilege in Scotland for communications relating to patent proceedings) so far as they relate to proceedings before the comptroller;
section 107 (costs and expenses in proceedings before the comptroller);
section 108 (licences granted by order of comptroller);
section 110 (unauthorised claim of patent rights);
section 116 (immunity of department as regards official acts);
section 118 (information about patent applications and patents, and inspection of documents);
section 123 (rules);
section 124 (rules, regulations and orders; supplementary);
section 125 (extent of invention);
section 128A (EU compulsory licences);
section 128B (supplementary protection certificates).

Manner of application of relevant statutory provisions

3 The relevant statutory provisions apply in relation to a European patent with unitary effect in the same way as they apply in relation to a European patent (UK).

Modifications of relevant statutory provisions

4 (1) In their application in relation to the European patent with unitary effect, the relevant statutory provisions which are referred to in this paragraph have effect subject to the modifications set out in this paragraph.

(2) In section 7(2)(b), the reference to the United Kingdom is a reference to any of the Participating Member States.

(3) In sections 30(7) and 31(7), references to proceedings by virtue of section 61 or 69 are references to equivalent proceedings in the Unified Patent Court.

(4) In sections 33(1)(a), 33(4), 37(2), 37(7), 38(2) and 38(3), the reference to registration is a reference to registration in the Register for unitary patent protection.

(5) In sections 48(1)(b), 48B(4), 50A(4), 51(3), 53(3), and 53(4), the reference to the register is a reference to the Register for unitary patent protection.

(6) In sections 48(2)(b), 50A(4), 51(3), 53(3), 53(4) and 53(5), the reference to making an entry is a reference to directing the making of an entry.

(7) In sections 48B(2)(b) and 50(2)(a), the reference to the journal is a reference to the European Patent Bulletin.

(8) In section 55(5)(b), the reference to the Patent Office is a reference to the European Patent Office.

(9) In section 59(2), the reference to section 69 includes a reference to Article 67 of the European Patent Convention.

(10) In section 60—

(a) in subsections (1), (2), and (5)(d), (e) and (f), the references to the United Kingdom are references to the territory of a Contracting Member State in which the European patent with unitary effect has effect;

(b) in subsection (7)—

(i) in the definition of "relevant ship" and "relevant aircraft, hovercraft or vehicle", the reference to the United Kingdom is a reference to a Contracting Member State in which the European patent with unitary effect has effect; and

(ii) in the definition of "exempted aircraft", the reference to an aircraft to which section 89 of the Civil Aviation Act 1982 applies is a reference to an aircraft other than an aircraft of a Contracting Member State in which the European patent with unitary effect has effect.

Interpretation

5 In this Schedule—

(a) "Contracting Member State" has the same meaning as in Article 2(c) of the Agreement on a Unified Patent Court; and

(b) the following expressions have the same meanings as in Article 2 of the Unitary Patent Regulation—

Participating Member State;

Register for unitary patent protection.]

NOTES

Commencement: see the note below.

Inserted by the Patents (European Patent with Unitary Effect and Unified Patent Court) Order 2016, SI 2016/388, art 2(1), (10), as from a day to be appointed (being the date of entry into force of the Agreement on a Unified Patent Court signed at Brussels on 19 February 2013) and subject to transitional provisions in art 3 thereof which provides that any question whether an act done before the date upon which SI 2016/388 comes into force infringes a patent is to be determined in accordance with the law relating to infringement in force at the time the act was done.

Para 2: entry in square brackets inserted by the Intellectual Property (Unjustified Threats) Act 2017, s 1(1), (8), as from a day to be appointed.

[SCHEDULE A4
THE UNIFIED PATENT COURT

Jurisdiction

[1.150]

1 The Unified Patent Court has exclusive jurisdiction in respect of an Article 32(1) action which relates to—

(a) a European patent with unitary effect, or

(b) a supplementary protection certificate for which the basic patent is a European patent with unitary effect,

(c) subject to paragraph 2—

(i) a European patent (UK), or

(ii) a supplementary protection certificate for which the basic patent is a European patent (UK).

Transitional provisions

2 (1) The transitional provisions in Article 83 apply in relation to an action referred to in Article 83(1).

(2) An opt out referred to in Article 83(3) may be exercised in accordance with that provision and any relevant Rules of Procedure.

(3) Such opt out may be withdrawn in accordance with Article 83(4) and any relevant Rules of Procedure.

(4) For the purposes of this paragraph, a reference to Article 83 is a reference to Article 83 of the Agreement on a Unified Patent Court.

Modifications of law applicable where UPC has jurisdiction

3 (1) In the case of an Article 32(1) action relating to—

(a) a European patent with unitary effect, or

(b) a European patent (UK),

the provisions of this Act listed in sub-paragraph (2) do not apply in relation to the action where the Unified Patent Court has jurisdiction in accordance with paragraph 1.

(2) The provisions referred to in sub-paragraph (1) are—

section 58(7) to (9) (references of disputes as to Crown use);
section 61 (proceedings for infringement of patent);
section 62 (restrictions on recovery of damages for infringement);
section 63 (relief for infringement of partially valid patent);
section 65 (certificate of contested validity of patent);
section 66 (proceedings for infringement by a co-owner);
section 67 (proceedings for infringement by exclusive licensee);
section 68 (effect of non-registration on infringement proceedings);
section 69 (infringement of rights conferred by publication of application);
section 71 (declaration or declarator as to non-infringement);
section 72 (power to revoke patents on application);
section 73(1) to (1C) (comptroller's power to revoke patents on his own initiative);
section 74 (proceedings in which validity of patent may be put in issue);
section 75 (amendment of patent in infringement or revocation proceedings);
section 77(3) (effect of European patent (UK)).

(3) In the case of an Article 32(1) action relating to a supplementary protection certificate for which the basic patent is—

(a) a European patent with unitary effect, or
(b) a European patent (UK),

the provisions of this Act listed in sub-paragraph (4) do not apply in relation to the action where the Unified Patent Court has jurisdiction in accordance with paragraph 1.

(4) The provisions referred to in sub-paragraph (3) are—

section 58(7) to (9) (references of disputes as to Crown use);
section 61 (proceedings for infringement of patent);
section 62 (restrictions on recovery of damages for infringement);
section 63 (relief for infringement of partially valid patent);
section 65 (certificate of contested validity of patent);
section 66 (proceedings for infringement by a co-owner);
section 67 (proceedings for infringement by exclusive licensee);
section 68 (effect of non-registration on infringement proceedings);
section 69 (infringement of rights conferred by publication of application);
section 71 (declaration or declarator as to non-infringement);
section 74 (proceedings in which validity of patent may be put in issue);
section 75 (amendment of a patent in infringement or revocation proceedings).

Enforcement

4 (1) For the purposes of enforcement of a decision or order of the Unified Patent Court—

(a) the decision or order has the same force and effect,
(b) proceedings for or with respect to enforcement of the decision or order may be taken, and
(c) the enforcing court, or in a relevant Northern Ireland case the Enforcement of Judgments Office, has the same powers in relation to the enforcement of the decision or order,

as if the decision or order had originally been made by the enforcing court.

(2) The enforcing court, or in a relevant Northern Ireland case the Enforcement of Judgments Office, may enforce a mediation settlement in the same manner as a judgment or order of the enforcing court.

(3) In this paragraph—

"enforcing court" means—

(a) as respects England and Wales, the High Court,
(b) as respects Scotland, the Court of Session, and
(c) as respects Northern Ireland, the High Court in Northern Ireland;

"mediation settlement" means a settlement reached through mediation using the facilities of the patent mediation and arbitration centre established under Article 35 of the Agreement on a Unified Patent Court;

"relevant Northern Ireland case" means a case where—

(a) the decision or order of the Unified Patent Court would, if it had been given by the High Court in Northern Ireland, or
(b) the mediation settlement would, if enforced in the same manner as a judgment or order of the High Court in Northern Ireland,

be enforced by the Enforcement of Judgments Office under the Judgments Enforcement (Northern Ireland) Order 1981.

Interpretation

5 In this Schedule—

(a) "Article 32(1) action" means an action listed in Article 32(1) of the Agreement on a Unified Patent Court;

(b) "basic patent" has the same meaning as in Article 1(c) of Regulation (EC) No 469/2009 of the European Parliament and of the Council of 6th May 2009 concerning the supplementary protection certificate for medicinal products; and

(c) "Rules of Procedure" has the same meaning as in the Agreement on a Unified Patent Court.]

NOTES

Commencement: see the note below.

Inserted by the Patents (European Patent with Unitary Effect and Unified Patent Court) Order 2016, SI 2016/388, art 2(1), (10), as from a day to be appointed (being the date of entry into force of the Agreement on a Unified Patent Court signed at Brussels on 19 February 2013) and subject to transitional provisions in art 3 thereof which provides that any question whether an act done before the date upon which SI 2016/388 comes into force infringes a patent is to be determined in accordance with the law relating to infringement in force at the time the act was done.

SCHEDULE 1
APPLICATION OF 1949 ACT TO EXISTING PATENTS AND APPLICATIONS

Section 127

[1.151]

1. (1) The provisions of the 1949 Act referred to in sub-paragraph (2) below shall continue to apply on and after the appointed day in relation to existing patents and applications (but not in relation to patents and applications for patents under this Act).

(2) The provisions are sections 1 to 10, 11(1) and (2), 12, 13, 15 to 17, 19 to 21, 22(1) to (3), 23 to 26, 28 to 33, 46 to 53, 55, 56, 59 to 67, 69, 76, 80, 87(2), 92(1), 96, 101, 102(1) and 103 to 107.

(3) Sub-paragraph (1) above shall have effect subject to the following provisions of this Schedule, paragraph 2(b) of Schedule 3 below and the provisions of Schedule 4 below.

2. . . .

3. (1) This paragraph and paragraph 4 below shall have effect with respect to the duration of existing patents after the appointed day, and in those paragraphs—

(a) "old existing patent" means an existing patent the date of which fell eleven years or more before the appointed day and also any patent of addition where the patent for the main invention is, or was at any time, an old existing patent by virtue of the foregoing provision;

(b) "new existing patent" means any existing patent not falling within paragraph (a) above; and

(c) any reference to the date of a patent shall, in relation to a patent of addition, be construed as a reference to the date of the patent for the main invention.

(2) Sections 23 to 25 of the 1949 Act (extension of patents on grounds of inadequate remuneration and war loss) shall not apply to a new existing patent.

(3) The period for which the term of an old existing patent may be extended under section 23 or 24 of that Act shall not exceed in the aggregate four years, except where an application for an order under the relevant section has been made before the appointed day and has not been disposed of before that day.

4. (1) The term of every new existing patent under section 22(3) of the 1949 Act shall be twenty instead of sixteen years from the date of the patent, but—

(a) the foregoing provision shall have effect subject to section 25(3) to (5) above; and

(b) on and after the end of the sixteenth year from that date a patent shall not be renewed under section 25(3) to (5) above except by or with the consent of the proprietor of the patent.

(2) Where the term of a new existing patent is extended by this paragraph,—

(a) any licence in force under the patent from immediately before the appointed day until the end of the sixteenth year from the date of the patent shall, together with any contract relating to the licence, continue in force so long as the patent remains in force (unless determined otherwise than in accordance with this sub-paragraph), but, if it is an exclusive licence, it shall after the end of that year be treated as a non-exclusive licence;

(b) notwithstanding the terms of the licence, the licensee shall not be required to make any payment to the proprietor for working the invention in question after the end of that year;

(c) every such patent shall after the end of that year be treated as endorsed under section 35 of the 1949 Act (licences of right)[, but subject to paragraph 4A below].

(3) Where the term of a new existing patent is extended by this paragraph and any government department or any person authorised by a government department—

(a) has before the appointed day, used the invention in question for the services of the Crown; and

(b) continues to so use it until the end of the sixteenth year from the date of the patent,

any such use of the invention by any government department or person so authorised, after the end of that year, may be made free of any payment to the proprietor of the patent.

(4) Without prejudice to any rule of law about the frustration of contracts, where any person suffers loss or is subjected to liability by reason of the extension of the term of a patent by this paragraph, the court may on the application of that person determine how and by whom the loss or liability is to be borne and make such order as it thinks fit to give effect to the determination.

(5) No order shall be made on an application under sub-paragraph (4) above which has the effect of imposing a liability on any person other than the applicant unless notification of the application is given to that person.

[4A. (1) If the proprietor of a patent for an invention which is a product files a declaration with the Patent Office in accordance with this paragraph, the licences to which persons are entitled by virtue of paragraph 4(2)(c) above shall not extend to a use of the product which is excepted by or under this paragraph.

(2) Pharmaceutical use is excepted, that is—
- (a) use as a medicinal product within the meaning of the Medicines Act 1968, and
- (b) the doing of any other act mentioned in section 60(1)(a) above with a view to such use.

(3) The Secretary of State may by order except such other uses as he thinks fit; and an order may—
- (a) specify as an excepted use any act mentioned in section 60(1)(a) above, and
- (b) make different provision with respect to acts done in different circumstances or for different purposes.

(4) For the purposes of this paragraph the question what uses are excepted, so far as that depends on—
- (a) orders under section 130 of the Medicines Act 1968 (meaning of "medicinal product"), or
- (b) orders under sub-paragraph (3) above,

shall be determined in relation to a patent at the beginning of the sixteenth year of the patent.

(5) A declaration under this paragraph shall be in the prescribed form and shall be filed in the prescribed manner and within the prescribed time limits.

(6) A declaration may not be filed—
- (a) in respect of a patent which has at the commencement of section 293 of the Copyright, Designs and Patents Act 1988 passed the end of its fifteenth year; or
- (b) if at the date of filing there is—
  - (i) an existing licence for any description of excepted use of the product, or
  - (ii) an outstanding application under section 46(3)(a) or (b) above for the settlement by the comptroller of the terms of a licence for any description of excepted use of the product,

  and, in either case, the licence took or is to take effect at or after the end of the sixteenth year of the patent.

(7) Where a declaration has been filed under this paragraph in respect of a patent—
- (a) section 46(3)(c) above (restriction of remedies for infringement where licences available as of right) does not apply to an infringement of the patent in so far as it consists of the excepted use of the product after the filing of the declaration; and
- (b) section 46(3)(d) above (abatement of renewal fee if licences available as of right) does not apply to the patent.]

[4B. (1) An application under section 46(3)(a) or (b) above for the settlement by the comptroller of the terms on which a person is entitled to a licence by virtue of paragraph 4(2)(c) above is ineffective if made before the beginning of the sixteenth year of the patent.

(2) This paragraph applies to applications made after the commencement of section 294 of the Copyright, Designs and Patents Act 1988 and to any application made before the commencement of that section in respect of a patent which has not at the commencement of that section passed the end of its fifteenth year.]

5. . . .

6. Notwithstanding anything in section 32(1)(j) of the 1949 Act (ground for revocation that patent was obtained on a false suggestion or representation), it shall not be a ground of revoking a patent under that subsection that the patent was obtained on a false suggestion or representation that a claim of the complete specification of the patent had a priority date earlier than the date of filing the application for the patent, but if it is shown—
- (a) on a petition under that section or an application under section 33 of that Act; or
- (b) by way of defence or on a counterclaim on an action for infringement; that such a suggestion or representation was falsely made, the priority date of the claim shall be taken to be the date of filing the application for that patent.

7, 8. . . .

NOTES

Paras 2, 5, 7, 8: amend the Patents Act 1949, ss 6, 26, 33, 101.

Para 4: words in square brackets in sub-para (2)(c) added by the Copyright, Designs and Patents Act 1988, s 293.

Paras 4A, 4B: inserted by the Copyright, Designs and Patents Act 1988, ss 293, 294.
1949 Act: Patents Act 1949.
Orders: the Patents (Licences of Right) (Exception of Pesticidal Use) Order 1989, SI 1989/1202.

SCHEDULE 2
APPLICATION OF THIS ACT TO EXISTING PATENTS AND APPLICATIONS

Section 127

[1.152]
1. (1) Without prejudice to those provisions of Schedule 4 below which apply (in certain circumstances) provisions of this Act in relation to existing patents and applications, the provisions of this Act referred to in sub-paragraph (2) below shall apply in relation to existing patents and applications on and after the appointed day subject to the following provisions of this Schedule and the provisions of Schedule 4 below.

(2) The provisions are sections 22, 23, 25(3) to (5), 28 to 36, 44 to 54, 86, . . . 98, 99, 101 to 105, 107 to 111, 113 to 116, 118(1) to (3), 119 to 124, 130 and 132(2), (3) and (4).

2. In those provisions as they apply by virtue of this Schedule—
(a) a reference to this Act includes a reference to the 1949 Act;
(b) a reference to a specified provision of this Act other than one of those provisions shall be construed as a reference to the corresponding provision of the 1949 Act (any provision of that Act being treated as corresponding to a provision of this Act if it was enacted for purposes which are the same as or similar to that provision of this Act);
(c) a reference to rules includes a reference to rules under the 1949 Act;
(d) references to a patent under this Act and to an application for such a patent include respectively a reference to an existing patent and application;
(e) references to the grant of a patent under this Act includes a reference to the sealing and grant of an existing patent;
(f) a reference to a patented product and to a patented invention include respectively a reference to a product and invention patented under an existing patent;
(g) references to a published application for a patent under this Act, and to publication of such an application, include respectively references to a complete specification which has been published under the 1949 Act and to publication of such a specification (and a reference to an application for a patent under this Act which has not been published shall be construed accordingly);
(h) a reference to the publication in the journal of a notice of the grant of a patent includes a reference to the date of an existing patent;
(i) a reference to the priority date of an invention includes a reference to the priority date of the relevant claim of the complete specification.

NOTES

Para 1: figures omitted from sub-para (2) repealed by the Senior Courts Act 1981, s 152(4), Sch 7.
1949 Act: Patents Act 1949.

SCHEDULE 3

(Sch 3 repeals the Registered Designs Act 1949, ss 14, 32(3), 41, 42, 71, 72.)

SCHEDULE 4
TRANSITIONAL PROVISIONS

Section 127

General

[1.153]
1. In so far as any instrument made or other thing done under any provision of the 1949 Act which is repealed by virtue of this Act could have been made or done under a corresponding provision of this Act, it shall not be invalidated by the repeals made by virtue of this Act but shall have effect as if made or done under that corresponding provision.

Use of patented invention for services of the Crown

2. (1) Any question whether—
(a) an act done before the appointed day by a government department or a person authorised in writing by a government department amounts to the use of an invention for the services of the Crown; or
(b) any payment falls to be made in respect of any such use (whether to a person entitled to apply for a patent for the invention, to the patentee or to an exclusive licensee);

shall be determined under sections 46 to 49 of that Act and those sections shall apply accordingly.

(2) Sections 55 to 59 above shall apply to an act so done on or after the appointed day in relation to an invention—

(a) for which an existing patent has been granted or an existing application for a patent has been made; or

(b) which was communicated before that day to a government department or any person authorised in writing by a government department by the proprietor of the patent or any person from whom he derives title;

and shall so apply subject to sub-paragraph (3) below, the modifications contained in paragraph 2 of Schedule 2 above and the further modification that section 55(5)(b) and 58(10) above shall not apply in relation to an existing application.

(3) Where an act is commenced before the appointed day and continues to be done on or after that day, then, if it would not amount to the use of an invention for the services of the Crown under the 1949 Act, its continuance on or after that day shall not amount to such use under this Act.

Infringement

3. (1) Any question whether an act done before the appointed day infringes an existing patent or the privileges or rights arising under a complete specification which has been published shall be determined in accordance with the law relating to infringement in force immediately before that day and, in addition to those provisions of the 1949 Act which continue to apply by virtue of Schedule 1 above, section 70 of that Act shall apply accordingly.

(2) Sections 60 to 71 above shall apply to an act done on or after the appointed day which infringes an existing patent or the privileges or rights arising under a complete specification which has been published (whether before, on or after the appointed day) as they apply to infringements of a patent under this Act or the rights conferred by an application for such a patent, and shall so apply subject to sub-paragraph (3) below, the modifications contained in paragraph 2 of Schedule 2 above and the further modification that section 69(2) and (3) above shall not apply in relation to an existing application.

(3) Where an act is commenced before the appointed day and continues to be done on or after that day, then, if it would not, under the law in force immediately before that day, amount to an infringement of an existing patent or the privileges or rights arising under a complete specification, its continuance on or after that day shall not amount to the infringement of that patent or those privileges or rights.

Notice of opposition

4. (1) Where notice of opposition to the grant of a patent has been given under section 14 of the 1949 Act before the appointed day, the following provisions shall apply—

(a) if issue has been joined on the notice before the appointed day, the opposition, any appeal from the comptroller's decision on it and any further appeal shall be prosecuted under the old law, but as if references in the 1949 Act and rules made under it to the Appeal Tribunal were references to the Patents Court;

(b) in any other case, the notice shall be taken to have abated immediately before the appointed day.

(2) Sub-paragraph (1)(a) above shall have effect subject to paragraph 12(2) below.

Secrecy

5. (1) Where directions given under section 18 of the 1949 Act in respect of an existing application (directions restricting publication of information about inventions) are in force immediately before the appointed day, they shall continue in force on and after that day and that section shall continue to apply accordingly.

(2) Where sub-paragraph (1) above does not apply in the case of an existing application section 18 of the 1949 Act shall not apply to the application but section 22 of this Act shall.

(3) Where the comptroller has before the appointed day served a notice under section 12 of the Atomic Energy Act 1946 (restrictions on publication of information about atomic energy etc) in respect of an existing application that section shall continue to apply to the application on and after that day; but where no such notice has been so served that section shall not apply to the application on and after that day.

Revocation

6. (1) Where before the appointed day an application has been made under section 33 of the 1949 Act for the revocation of a patent (the original application), the following provisions shall apply—

(a) if issue has been joined on the application before the appointed day, the application, any appeal from the comptroller's decision on it and any further appeal shall be prosecuted under the old law, but as if references in the 1949 Act and rules made under it to the Appeal Tribunal were references to the Patents Court;

(b) if issue has not been so joined, the original application shall be taken to be an application under section 33 of the 1949 Act for the revocation of the patent on whichever of the grounds referred to in section 32(1) of that Act corresponds (in the comptroller's opinion) to the ground on which the original application was made, or, if there is no ground which so corresponds, shall be taken to have abated immediately before the appointed day.

(2) Sub-paragraph (1)(a) above shall have effect subject to paragraph 11(3) below.

7. (1) This paragraph applies where an application has been made before the appointed day under section 42 of the 1949 Act for the revocation of a patent.

(2) Where the comptroller has made no order before that day for the revocation of the patent under that section, the application shall be taken to have abated immediately before that day.

(3) Where the comptroller has made such an order before that day, then, without prejudice to section 38 of the Interpretation Act 1889, section 42 shall continue to apply to the patent concerned on and after that day as if this Act had not been enacted.

Licences of right and compulsory licences

8. (1) Sections 35 to 41 and 43 to 45 of the 1949 Act shall continue to apply on and after the relevant day—

(a) to any endorsement or order made or licence granted under sections 35 to 41 which is in force immediately before that day; and

(b) to any application made before that day under sections 35 to 41.

(2) Any appeal from a decision or order of the comptroller instituted under sections 35 to 41 or 43 to 45 on or after the relevant day (and any further appeal) shall be prosecuted under the old law, but as if references in the 1949 Act and rules made under it to the Appeal Tribunal were references to the Patents Court.

(3) In this paragraph "the relevant day" means, in relation to section 41, the date of the passing of this Act and, in relation to sections 35 to 40 and 43 to 45, the appointed day.

Convention countries

9. (1) Without prejudice to paragraph 1 above, an Order in Council declaring any country to be a convention country for all purposes of the 1949 Act or for the purposes of section 1(2) of that Act and in force immediately before the appointed day shall be treated as an Order in Council under section 90 above declaring that country to be a convention country for the purposes of section 5 above.

(2) Where an Order in Council declaring any country to be a convention country for all purposes of the 1949 Act or for the purposes of section 70 of that Act is in force immediately before the appointed day, a vessel registered in that country (whether before, on or after that day) shall be treated for the purposes of section 60 above, as it applies by virtue of paragraph 3(2) above to an existing patent or existing application, as a relevant ship and an aircraft so registered and a land vehicle owned by a person ordinarily resident in that country shall be so treated respectively as a relevant aircraft and a relevant vehicle.

Appeal from court on certain petitions for revocation

10. Where the court has given judgment on a petition under section 32(1)(j) of the 1949 Act before the appointed day, any appeal from the judgment (whether instituted before, on or after that day) shall be continued or instituted and be disposed of under the old law.

Appeals from comptroller under continuing provisions of 1949 Act

11. (1) In this paragraph "the continuing 1949 Act provisions" means the provisions of the 1949 Act which continue to apply on and after the appointed day as mentioned in paragraph 1 of Schedule 1 above.

(2) This paragraph applies where—

(a) the comptroller gives a decision or direction (whether before or on or after the appointed day) under any of the continuing 1949 Act provisions, and

(b) an appeal lies under those provisions from the decision or direction; but this paragraph applies subject to the foregoing provisions of this Schedule.

(3) Where such an appeal has been instituted before the Appeal Tribunal before the appointed day, and the hearing of the appeal has begun but has not been completed before that day, the appeal (and any further appeal) shall be continued and disposed of under the old law.

(4) Where such an appeal has been so instituted, but the hearing of it has not begun before the appointed day, it shall be transferred by virtue of this sub-paragraph to the Patents Court on that day and the appeal (and any further appeal) shall be prosecuted under the old law, but as if references in the 1949 Act and rules made under it to the Appeal Tribunal were references to the Patents Court.

(5) Any such appeal instituted on or after the appointed day shall lie to the Patents Court or, where the proceedings appealed against were held in Scotland, the Court of Session; and accordingly, the reference to the Appeal Tribunal in section 31(2) of the 1949 Act shall be taken to include a reference to the Patents Court or (as the case may be) the Court of Session.

(6) Section 97(3) of this Act shall apply to any decision of the Patents Court on an appeal instituted on or after the appointed day from a decision or direction of the comptroller under any of the continuing 1949 Act provisions as it applies to a decision of that Court referred to in that subsection, except that for references to the sections mentioned in paragraph (a) of that subsection there shall be substituted references to sections 33, 55 and 56 of the 1949 Act.

Appeals from comptroller under repealed provisions of 1949 Act

12. (1) This paragraph applies where an appeal to the Appeal Tribunal has been instituted before the appointed day under any provision of the 1949 Act repealed by this Act.

(2) Where the hearing of such an appeal has begun but has not been completed before that day, the appeal (and any further appeal) shall be continued and disposed of under the old law.

(3) Where the hearing of such an appeal has not begun before that day, it shall be transferred by virtue of this sub-paragraph to the Patents Court on that day and the appeal (and any further appeal) shall be prosecuted under the old law, but as if references in the 1949 Act and rules made under it to the Appeal Tribunal were references to the Patents Court.

Appeals from Appeal Tribunal to Court of Appeal

13. Section 87(1) of the 1949 Act shall continue to apply on and after the appointed day to any decision of the Appeal Tribunal given before that day, and any appeal by virtue of this paragraph (and any further appeal) shall be prosecuted under the old law.

Rules

14. The power to make rules under section 123 of this Act shall include power to make rules for any purpose mentioned in section 94 of the 1949 Act.

Supplementary

15. Section 97(2) of this Act applies to—

(a) any appeal to the Patents Court by virtue of paragraph 4(1)(a), 6(1)(a), 8(2) or 11(5) above, and

(b) any appeal which is transferred to that Court by virtue of paragraph 11(4) or 12(3) above,

as it applies to an appeal under that section; and section 97 of this Act shall apply for the purposes of any such appeal instead of section 85 of the 1949 Act.

16. In this Schedule "the old law" means the 1949 Act, any rules made under it and any relevant rule of law as it was or they were immediately before the appointed day.

17. For the purposes of this Schedule—

(a) issue is joined on a notice of opposition to the grant of a patent under section 14 of the 1949 Act when the applicant for the patent files a counter-statement fully setting out the grounds on which the opposition is contested;

(b) issue is joined on an application for the revocation of a patent under section 33 of that Act when the patentee files a counter-statement fully setting out the grounds on which the application is contested.

18. (1) Nothing in the repeals made by this Act in section 23 and 24 of the 1949 Act shall have effect as respects any such application as is mentioned in paragraph 3(3) of Schedule 1 above.

(2) Nothing in the repeal by this Act of the Patents Act 1957 shall have effect as respects existing applications.

(3) Section 69 of the 1949 Act (which is not repealed by this Act) and section 70 of that Act (which continues to have effect for certain purposes by virtue of paragraph 3 above) shall apply as if section 68 of that Act has not been repealed by this Act and as if paragraph 9 above had not been enacted.

NOTES

1949 Act: Patents Act 1949.

Atomic Energy Act 1946, s 12: sub-ss (1)–(7) repealed by s 132(7) of, and Sch 6 to, this Act.

Interpretation Act 1889, s 38: repealed by the Interpretation Act 1978, s 25, Sch 3, and replaced by ss 16(1), 17(2)(a) of, and Sch 2, para 3 to, that Act.

[SCHEDULE 4A
SUPPLEMENTARY PROTECTION CERTIFICATES

References to patents etc

[1.154]

1. (1) In the application to supplementary protection certificates of the provisions of this Act listed in sub-paragraph (2)—

(a) references to a patent are to a supplementary protection certificate;

(b) references to an application or the applicant for a patent are to an application or the applicant—

(i) for a supplementary protection certificate, or
(ii) for an extension of the duration of a supplementary protection certificate;

(c) references to the proprietor of a patent are to the holder of a supplementary protection certificate;

(d) references to the specification of a patent are to the text of a supplementary protection certificate;

(e) references to a patented product or an invention (including a patented invention) are to a product for which a supplementary protection certificate has effect;

(f) references to a patent having expired or having been revoked are to a supplementary protection certificate having lapsed or having been declared invalid;

(g) references to proceedings for the revocation of a patent are to proceedings—
(i) for a decision that a supplementary protection certificate has lapsed, or
(ii) for a declaration that a supplementary protection certificate is invalid;

(h) references to the issue of the validity of a patent include the issue of whether a supplementary protection certificate has lapsed or is invalid.

(2) The provisions referred to in sub-paragraph (1) are—
section 14(1), (9) and (10) (making of application);
section 19(1) (general power to amend application before grant);
sections 20A and 20B (reinstatement of applications);
section 21 (observations by third party on patentability);
section 27 (general power to amend specification after grant);
section 29 (surrender of patents);
sections 30 to 36, 37(1) to (3) and (5) to (9) and 38 (property in patents and applications, and registration);
sections 39 to 59 (employees' inventions, licences of right and compulsory licences and use of patented inventions for services of the Crown);
sections 60 to 71 (infringement);
section 74(1) and (7) (proceedings in which validity of patent may be put in issue);
[sections 74A and 74B (opinions by the Patent Office);]
section 75 (amendment of patent in infringement or revocation proceedings);
sections 103 and 105 (privilege for communications relating to patent proceedings);
section 108 (licences granted by order of comptroller);
sections 110 and 111 (unauthorised claim of patent rights or that patent has been applied for);
section 116 (immunity of department as regards official acts);
sections 117 to 118 (administrative provisions);
section 123 (rules);
section 130 (interpretation).

2. (1) In the case of the provisions of this Act listed in sub-paragraph (2), paragraph 1 applies in relation to an application for a supplementary protection certificate only if the basic patent expires before the certificate is granted.

(2) The provisions referred to in sub-paragraph (1) are—
section 20B(3) to (6A) (effect of reinstatement under section 20A);
section 55(5) and (7) (use of patented inventions for services of the Crown);
section 58(10) (disputes as to Crown use);
section 69 (infringement of rights conferred by publication of application);
section 117A(3) to (7) (effect of resuscitating a withdrawn application under section 117).

References to this Act etc

3. (1) In the provisions of this Act listed in sub-paragraph (2)—

(a) references to this Act include the Medicinal Products Regulation and the Plant Protection Products Regulation, and

(b) references to a provision of this Act include any equivalent provision of the Medicinal Products Regulation and the Plant Protection Products Regulation.

(2) The provisions referred to in sub-paragraph (1) are—
sections 20A and 20B (reinstatement of applications);
section 21 (observations by third party on patentability);
section 69 (infringement of rights conferred by publication of application);
section 74(1) and (7) (proceedings in which validity of patent may be put in issue);
sections 97 to 99B, 101 to 103, 105 and 107 (legal proceedings);
section 116 (immunity of department as regards official acts);
sections 117 and 118 to 121 (administrative provisions);
section 122 (Crown's right to sell forfeited articles);
section 123 (rules);
section 124A (use of electronic communications);
section 130 (interpretation).

Other references

4. (1) In the application of section 21(1) (observations by third party on patentability) to supplementary protection certificates, the reference to the question whether the invention is a patentable invention is to the question whether the product is one for which a supplementary protection certificate may have effect.

(2) In the application of section 69(2) (conditions for infringement of rights conferred by publication of application) to supplementary protection certificates, the condition in paragraph (b) is that the act would, if the certificate had been granted on the date of the publication of the application, have infringed not only the certificate as granted but also the certificate for which the application was made.

Fees

5. A supplementary protection certificate does not take effect unless—

(a) the prescribed fee is paid before the end of the prescribed period, or

(b) the prescribed fee and any prescribed additional fee are paid before the end of the period of six months beginning immediately after the prescribed period.

Interpretation

6. (1) Expressions used in this Act that are defined in the Medicinal Products Regulation or the Plant Protection Products Regulation have the same meaning as in that Regulation.

(2) References in this Act to, or to a provision of, the Medicinal Products Regulation or the Plant Protection Products Regulation are to that Regulation or that provision as amended from time to time.

7. In this Act—

(a) "the Medicinal Products Regulation" means [Regulation (EC) No 469/2009 of the European Parliament and of the Council of 6th May 2009 concerning the supplementary protection certificate for medicinal products], and

(b) "the Plant Protection Products Regulation" means Regulation (EC) No 1610/96 of the European Parliament and of the Council of 23 July 1996 concerning the creation of a supplementary protection certificate for plant protection products.

[Transitional provision

8. (1) A reference (express or implied) in this Act to the Medicinal Products Regulation, or a provision of it, is to be read as being or (subject to context) including a reference to the old Regulation, or the corresponding provision of the old Regulation, in relation to times, circumstances or purposes in relation to which the old Regulation, or that provision, had effect.

(2) Other than in relation to times, circumstances or purposes referred to in subparagraph (1), anything done, or having effect as if done, under (or for the purposes of or in reliance on) the old Regulation or a provision of the old Regulation and in force or effective immediately before 1st October 2014 (the day on which the Patents (Supplementary Protection Certificates) Regulations 2014 came into force) has effect on or after that date for the purposes of this Act as if done under (or for the purpose of or in reliance on) the Medicinal Products Regulation or the corresponding provision of it.

(3) In this paragraph "the old Regulation" means Council Regulation (EEC) No 1768/92 of 18th June 1992 concerning the creation of a supplementary protection certificate for medicinal products.]]

NOTES

Inserted by the Patents (Compulsory Licensing and Supplementary Protection Certificates) Regulations 2007, SI 2007/3293, reg 2(1), (3).

Para 1: words in square brackets in sub-para (2) inserted by the Intellectual Property Act 2014, s 16(3).

Para 7: words in square brackets in sub-para (a) substituted by the Patents (Supplementary Protection Certificates) Regulations 2014, SI 2014/2411, reg 2(1), (3)(a).

Para 8: added by SI 2014/2411, reg 2(1), (3)(b).

SCHEDULES 5 AND 6

(*Schedules 5 and 6, in so far as unrepealed, contain amendments and repeals respectively.*)

CORPORATION TAX ACT 2010

(2010 c 4)

ARRANGEMENT OF SECTIONS

PART 8A
PROFITS ARISING FROM THE EXPLOITATION OF PATENTS ETC

CHAPTER 1
REDUCED CORPORATION TAX RATE FOR PROFITS FROM PATENTS ETC

CHAPTER 2
QUALIFYING COMPANIES

CHAPTER 2A
RELEVANT IP PROFITS: CASES MENTIONED IN SECTION 357A(6)

Steps for calculating relevant IP profits of a trade

Finance income

Relevant IP income

Excluded debits etc

Routine return figure

Marketing assets return figure

R&D fraction

Profits arising before grant of right

Small claims treatment

CHAPTER 2B
RELEVANT IP PROFITS: CASES MENTIONED IN SECTION 357A(7): INCOME FROM NEW IP

CHAPTER 3
RELEVANT IP PROFITS: CASES MENTIONED IN SECTION 357A(7): NO INCOME FROM NEW IP

Steps for calculating relevant IP profits of a trade

Total gross income of trade

Calculating profits of trade

Routine return figure

Election for small claims treatment

Marketing assets return figure

Profits arising before grant of right

CHAPTER 4
STREAMING

CHAPTER 5
RELEVANT IP LOSSES

CHAPTER 6
ANTI-AVOIDANCE

Licences conferring exclusive rights

Incorporation of qualifying items

Tax advantage schemes

CHAPTER 7
SUPPLEMENTARY

Elections under section 357A

An Act to restate, with minor changes, certain enactments relating to corporation tax and certain enactments relating to company distributions; and for connected purposes

[3 March 2010]

1–357 (*(Pts 1–8) Outside the scope of this work.*)

[PART 8A
PROFITS ARISING FROM THE EXPLOITATION OF PATENTS ETC

CHAPTER 1
REDUCED CORPORATION TAX RATE FOR PROFITS FROM PATENTS ETC

[1.155]

357A Election for special treatment of profits from patents etc

(1) A company may elect that any relevant IP profits of a trade of the company for an accounting period for which it is a qualifying company are chargeable at a lower rate of corporation tax.

(2) An election under subsection (1) is to be given effect by allowing a deduction to be made in calculating for corporation tax purposes the profits of the trade for the period.

(3) The amount of the deduction is—

$$RP \times \left(\frac{MR - IPR}{MR}\right)$$

where—

RP is the relevant IP profits of the trade of the company,

MR is the main rate of corporation tax, and

IPR is the special IP rate of corporation tax.

(4) The special IP rate of corporation tax is 10%.

(5) Chapter 2 specifies when a company is a qualifying company.

[(6) Chapter 2A makes provision for determining the relevant IP profits or relevant IP losses of a trade of a company for an accounting period in a case where—

(a) the accounting period begins on or after 1 July 2021, or

(b) the company is a new entrant (see subsection (11)).

(7) Chapters 2B, 3 and 4 make provision for determining the relevant IP profits or relevant IP losses of a trade of a company for an accounting period in various cases where—

(a) the accounting period begins before 1 July 2021, and

(b) the company is not a new entrant.]

(8) Chapter 5 makes provision in relation to the relevant IP losses of a trade.

(9) Chapter 6 contains anti-avoidance provisions.

(10) Chapter 7 contains supplementary provision.

[(11) A company is a "new entrant" for the purposes of this Part if—

(a) the first accounting period for which the company's election (or most recent election) under subsection (1) has effect begins on or after 1 July 2016, or

(b) the company elects to be treated as a new entrant for the purposes of this Part.]]

NOTES

Part 8A (originally ss 357A, 357B–357BE, 357C–357CQ, 357D–357DC, 357E–357EF, 357F–357FB, 357G–357GE) inserted by the Finance Act 2012, s 19, Sch 2, Pt 1, para 1(1), with effect in relation to accounting periods beginning on or after 1 April 2013 for which an election under s 357A has effect: see the Finance Act 2012, s 19, Sch 2, Pt 3, para 7; for transitional provisions see s 19, Sch 2, Pt 3, para 8 thereto.

Sub-ss (6), (7): substituted by the Finance Act 2016, s 64(1), (2)(a), (7), with effect in relation to accounting periods beginning on or after 1 July 2016.

Sub-s (11): added by the Finance Act 2016, s 64(1), (2)(b), (7), with in relation to accounting periods beginning on or after 1 July 2016.

[CHAPTER 2
QUALIFYING COMPANIES

[1.156]

357B Meaning of "qualifying company"

(1) A company is a qualifying company for an accounting period if—

(a) condition A or B is met, and

(b) in the case of a company that is a member of a group, condition C is met.

(2) Condition A is that, at any time during the accounting period, the company—

(a) holds any qualifying IP rights, or

(b) holds an exclusive licence in respect of any qualifying IP rights.

For the meaning of "exclusive licence", see section 357BA.

(3) Condition B is that—

(a) the company has held a qualifying IP right or an exclusive licence in respect of such a right,

(b) the company has received income in respect of an event which occurred in relation to the right or licence, or any part of which so occurred, at a time when—

(i) the company was a qualifying company, and

(ii) an election under [section 357A(1)] had effect in relation to it, and

(c) the income falls to be taxed in the accounting period.

(4) A right is a qualifying IP right for the purposes of this Part if—

(a) it is a right to which this Part applies (see section 357BB), and

(b) the company meets the development condition in relation to the right (see section 357BC).

(5) Condition C is that the company meets the active ownership condition for the accounting period (see section 357BE).]

NOTES

Inserted, together with chapter heading, as noted to s 357A at **[1.155]**.

Sub-s (3): words in square brackets in para (b)(ii) substituted by the Finance Act 2016, s 64(6), (7), Sch 9, paras 1, 2, with effect in relation to accounting periods beginning on or after 1 July 2016.

[1.157]

[357BA Meaning of "exclusive licence"

(1) In this Part "exclusive licence", in relation to a right ("the principal right"), means a licence which—

(a) is granted by the person who holds either the principal right or an exclusive licence in respect of the principal right ("the proprietor"), and

(b) confers on the person holding the licence ("the licence-holder"), or on the licence-holder and persons authorised by it, the rights in respect of the principal right that are listed in subsection (2).

(2) The rights are—

(a) one or more rights conferred to the exclusion of all other persons (including the proprietor) in one or more countries or territories, and

(b) the right—

(i) to bring proceedings without the consent of the proprietor or any other person in respect of any infringement of the rights within paragraph (a), or

(ii) to receive the whole or the greater part of any damages awarded in respect of any such infringement.

(3) Where the licence-holder has any right within subsection (2)(b) by virtue of any enactment or rule of law, the right is to be regarded for the purposes of this section as conferred by the licence.

(4) Where—

(a) a company ("C") that is a member of a group holds either a right to which this Part applies or an exclusive licence in respect of such a right, and
(b) C confers on another company that is a member of the group all of the rights held by C in respect of the invention,

that other company is to be treated for the purposes of this Part as holding an exclusive licence in respect of that right.

(5) For the purposes of subsection (4) it does not matter if the rights conferred by C do not include the right to enforce, assign or grant a licence of any of those rights.]

NOTES

Inserted as noted to s 357A at **[1.155]**.

[1.158]

[357BB Rights to which this Part applies

(1) This Part applies to the following rights—
(a) a patent granted under the Patents Act 1977,
(b) a patent granted under the European Patent Convention,
(c) a right of a specified description which corresponds to a right within paragraph (a) or (b) and is granted under the law of a specified EEA state,
(d) a supplementary protection certificate,
(e) any plant breeders' rights granted in accordance with Part 1 of the Plant Varieties Act 1997,
(f) any Community plant variety rights granted under Council Regulation (EC) No 2100/94.

(2) Where—
(a) directions are in force under section 22 of the Patents Act 1977 (information prejudicial to national security or safety of public) with respect to an application for a patent under that Act, and
(b) the person making the application has been notified under section 18(4) of that Act that the application complies with the requirements of the Act and the rules,

the person is to be treated for the purposes of this Part as if the person had been granted the patent under that Act.

(3) Where—
(a) a person holds a marketing authorisation in respect of a product in accordance with any EU legislation, and
(b) the product benefits from marketing protection (see subsection (4)) or data protection (see subsection (5)),

the person is to be treated for the purposes of this Part as having been granted a right to which this Part applies in respect of the product.

(4) For the purposes of this section a product benefits from marketing protection if—
(a) the product benefits from marketing protection by virtue of Article 14.11 of Regulation (EC) No 726/2004 of the European Parliament and of the Council of 31 March 2004 laying down Community procedures for the authorisation and supervision of medicinal products for human use, or
(b) any of the following prohibitions is in force—
(i) the prohibition on placing on the market a generic of the product imposed by Article 10.1 of Directive 2001/83/EC of the European Parliament and of the Council of 6 November 2001 on the Community code relating to medicinal products for human use,
(ii) the prohibition imposed by Article 8.1 of Regulation (EC) No 141/2000 of the European Parliament and of the Council of 16 December 1999 on orphan medicinal products, and
(iii) the prohibition on placing on the market a generic of the product imposed by Article 13.1 of Directive 2001/82/EC of the European Parliament and of the Council of 6 November 2001 on the Community code relating to veterinary medicinal products.

(5) For the purposes of this section a product benefits from data protection if—
(a) the product benefits from the data exclusivity conferred by Article 10.5 of Directive 2001/83/EC of the European Parliament and of the Council,
(b) the prohibition on referring to the results of tests or trials in relation to the product imposed by Article 74a of that Directive is in force, or
(c) data relating to the product benefits from data protection under Article 59 of Regulation (EC) No 1107/2009 of the European Parliament and of the Council of 21 October 2009 concerning the placing of plant protection products on the market.

(6) The reference to data in subsection (5)(c) does not include a study necessary for the renewal or review of a marketing authorisation granted in respect of the product in accordance with Regulation (EC) No 1107/2009.

(7) In this section—

"European Patent Convention" means the Convention on the Grant of European Patents,
"rules" means rules made under section 123 of the Patents Act 1977,
"specified" means specified in an order made by the Treasury, and
"supplementary protection certificate" means a certificate issued under—

(a) Council Regulation (EC) No 469/2009 of the European Parliament and of the Council of 6 May 2009 concerning the supplementary protection certificate for medicinal products, or

(b) Regulation (EC) No 1610/96 of the European Parliament and of the Council of 23 July 1996 concerning the creation of a supplementary protection certificate for plant protection products.

(8) The Treasury may by order—

(a) amend this section so as to make provision about the circumstances in which a product benefits from marketing or data protection for the purposes of this section;

(b) make such provision amending any reference in this section to EU legislation as appears to them appropriate in consequence of any EU legislation amending or replacing that EU legislation.

(9) An order made under this section may make any incidental, supplemental, consequential, transitional or saving provision, including provision amending or modifying this Part.]

NOTES

Inserted as noted to s 357A at **[1.155]**.

Orders: the Profits from Patents (EEA Rights) Order 2013, SI 2013/420.

[1.159]

[357BC The development condition

(1) A company meets the development condition in relation to a right if condition A, B, C or D is met.

Section 357BD (meaning of "qualifying development") applies for the purposes of this section.

(2) Condition A is that—

(a) the company has at any time carried out qualifying development in relation to the right, and

(b) the company has not ceased to be, or become, a controlled member of a group since that time.

(3) Condition B is that—

(a) the company has at any time carried out qualifying development in relation to the right,

(b) the company has ceased to be, or become, a controlled member of a group since that time,

(c) the company has, for a period of 12 months beginning with the day on which it ceased to be, or became, a controlled member of the group, performed activities of the same description as those that constituted the qualifying development, and

(d) the company remains a member of that group or (as the case may be) does not become a controlled member of any other group.

(4) Condition C is that—

(a) the company is a member of a group,

(b) another company that is or has been a member of the group has carried out qualifying development in relation to the right, and

(c) that other company was a member of the group at the time it carried out the qualifying development.

(5) Condition D is that—

(a) the company is a member of a group,

(b) another company that is or has been a member of the group has carried out qualifying development in relation to the right,

(c) that other company ("T") or, where another member of the group begins to carry on the trade which T carried on immediately before becoming a member of the group, either or both of those companies have, while carrying on that trade as a member of the group, performed activities of the same description as those that constituted the qualifying development, and

(d) those activities of those companies, taken together, have been performed for a period of 12 months beginning with the day on which T became a member of the group.

(6) For the purposes of conditions A and B, a company becomes a controlled member of a group at any time if—

(a) another company ("P") either becomes the holder of a major interest in the company, or begins to control the company, at that time, and

(b) immediately before that time the company was not associated with P or with any company associated with P immediately before that time.

(7) For the purposes of conditions A and B, a company ceases to be a controlled member of a group at any time if—

(a) every other company which immediately before that time held a major interest in, or controlled, the company ceases to do so, and

(b) as a result the company ceases to be associated with any of those companies.

(8) Where—

(a) a company ceases to be a controlled member of a group at any time, and

(b) at that time the company holds a major interest in, or controls, any other company,

that other company is to be treated for the purposes of conditions A and B as also having ceased to be a controlled member of the group at that time.

(9) In subsections (6) and (7) "associated" is to be read in accordance with section 357GD(3).

(10) The following provisions apply for the purposes of subsections (6) to (8)—

section 472 of CTA 2009 (meaning of "control"), and

sections 473 and 474 of CTA 2009 (meaning of "major interest").

(11) A company that meets the development condition in relation to a right by virtue of the performance of the activities mentioned in subsection (3) or (5) for the period of 12 months so mentioned is to be regarded as meeting that condition in relation to the right during that period (as well as at any other time when the company meets the condition).]

NOTES

Inserted as noted to s 357A at **[1.155]**.

[1.160]

[357BD Meaning of "qualifying development"

(1) A company carries out "qualifying development" in relation to a right if—

(a) it creates, or significantly contributes to the creation of, the invention, or

(b) it performs a significant amount of activity for the purposes of developing the invention or any item or process incorporating the invention.

(2) The reference in subsection (1)(b) to developing the invention includes developing ways in which the invention may be used or applied.

(3) For the purposes of section 357BC it does not matter whether the qualifying development was carried out before or after—

(a) the company, or

(b) where the company is a member of a group, any member of the group,

became the holder of the right or (as the case may be) an exclusive licence in respect of the right.]

NOTES

Inserted as noted to s 357A at **[1.155]**.

[1.161]

[357BE The active ownership condition

(1) A company meets the active ownership condition for an accounting period if all or almost all of the qualifying IP rights held by the company in that accounting period are rights in respect of which condition A or B is met.

(2) Condition A is that during the accounting period the company performs a significant amount of management activity in relation to the rights.

(3) In subsection (2) "management activity", in relation to any qualifying IP rights, means formulating plans and making decisions in relation to the development or exploitation of the rights.

(4) Condition B is that the company meets the development condition in relation to the rights by virtue of section 357BC(2) or (3).

(5) Any reference in this section to a qualifying IP right held by the company includes a reference to a qualifying IP right in respect of which the company holds an exclusive licence.]

NOTES

Inserted as noted to s 357A at **[1.155]**.

[CHAPTER 2A

RELEVANT IP PROFITS: CASES MENTIONED IN SECTION 357A(6)

Steps for calculating relevant IP profits of a trade

[1.162]

357BF Relevant IP profits

(1) This section applies for the purposes of determining the relevant IP profits of a trade of a company for an accounting period in a case where—

(a) the accounting period begins on or after 1 July 2021, or

(b) the company is a new entrant (see section 357A(11)).

(2) To determine the relevant IP profits—

Step 1

Take any amounts which are brought into account as credits in calculating the profits of the trade for the accounting period, other than any amounts of finance income (see section 357BG), and divide them into two "streams", amounts of relevant IP income (see sections 357BH to 357BHC) and amounts that are not amounts of relevant IP income.

The stream consisting of relevant IP income is "the relevant IP income stream"; the other stream is the "standard income stream".

Step 2

Divide the relevant IP income stream into "relevant IP income sub-streams" so that each sub-stream is—

(a) a sub-stream consisting of income properly attributable to a particular qualifying IP right (an "individual IP right sub-stream"),

(b) a sub-stream consisting of income properly attributable to a particular kind of IP item (a "product sub-stream"), or

(c) a sub-stream consisting of income properly attributable to a particular kind of IP process (a "process sub-stream").

See subsection (5) for the meaning of "IP item" and "IP process" and see subsections (6) and (7) for further provision in connection with product sub-streams and process sub-streams.

Step 3

Take any amounts which are brought into account as debits in calculating the profits of the trade for the accounting period, other than any excluded debits (see section 357BI), and allocate them on a just and reasonable basis between the standard income stream and each of the relevant IP income sub-streams.

Step 4

Deduct from each relevant IP income sub-stream—

(a) the amounts allocated to the sub-stream at Step 3, and

(b) the routine return figure for the sub-stream (see section 357BJ).

But see section 357BIA (which provides that certain amounts allocated to a relevant IP income sub-stream at Step 3 are not to be deducted from the sub-stream at this Step).

Step 5

Deduct from each relevant IP income sub-stream which is greater than nil following Step 4 the marketing assets return figure for the sub-stream (see section 357BK).

Step 6

Multiply the amount of each relevant IP income sub-stream (following the deductions required at Steps 4 and 5) by the R&D fraction for the sub-stream (see section 357BL).

Step 7

Add together the amounts of the relevant IP income sub-streams (following Step 6).

Step 8

If the company has made an election under section 357BM (which provides in certain circumstances for profits arising before the grant of a right to be treated as relevant IP profits), add to the amount given by Step 7 any amount determined in accordance with subsection (3) of that section.

(3) If the amount given by subsection (2) is greater than nil, that amount is the relevant IP profits of the trade for the accounting period.

(4) If the amount given by subsection (2) is less than nil, that amount is the relevant IP losses of the trade for the accounting period (see Chapter 5).

(5) In this section—

"IP item" means—

(a) an item in respect of which a qualifying IP right held by the company has been granted, or

(b) an item which incorporates one or more items within paragraph (a);

"IP process" means—

(a) a process in respect of which a qualifying IP right held by the company has been granted, or

(b) a process which incorporates one or more processes within paragraph (a).

(6) For the purposes of this section two or more IP items, or two or more IP processes, may be treated as being of a particular kind if they are intended to be, or are capable of being, used for the same or substantially the same purposes.

(7) Income may be allocated at Step 2 of subsection (2) to a product sub-stream or process sub-stream only if—

(a) it would not be reasonably practicable to apportion the income between individual IP right sub-streams, or

(b) it would be reasonably practicable to do that but doing so would result in it not being reasonably practicable to apply any of the remaining steps in subsection (2).

(8) Any reference in this section to a qualifying IP right held by the company includes a reference to a qualifying IP right in respect of which the company holds an exclusive licence.]

NOTES

Chapter 2A (ss 357BF–357BNC) and Chapter 2B (ss 357BO–BQ) inserted by the Finance Act 2016, s 64(1), (3), (7), with effect in relation to accounting periods beginning on or after 1 July 2016.

[Finance income

[1.163]

357BG Finance income

(1) For the purposes of this Part "finance income", in relation to a trade of a company, means—

(a) any credits which are treated as receipts of the trade by virtue of—

(i) section 297 of CTA 2009 (credits in respect of loan relationships), or

(ii) section 573 of CTA 2009 (credits in respect of derivative contracts),

(b) any amount which in accordance with generally accepted accounting practice falls to be recognised as arising from a financial asset, and
(c) any return, in relation to an amount, which—
(i) is produced for the company by an arrangement to which it is a party, and
(ii) is economically equivalent to interest.

(2) In subsection (1)—
"economically equivalent to interest" is to be construed in accordance with section 486B(2) and (3) of CTA 2009, and
"financial asset" means a financial asset as defined for the purposes of generally accepted accounting practice.

(3) For the purposes of subsection (1)(c), the amount of a return is the amount which by virtue of the return would, in calculating the company's chargeable profits, be treated under section 486B of CTA 2009 (disguised interest to be regarded as profit from loan relationship) as profit arising to the company from a loan relationship.
But, in calculating that profit for the purposes of this subsection, sections 486B(7) and 486C to 486E of that Act are to be ignored.]

NOTES

Inserted as noted to s 357BF at **[1.162]**.

[Relevant IP income

[1.164]
357BH Relevant IP income

(1) For the purposes of this Part "relevant IP income" means income falling within any of the Heads set out in—
(a) subsection (2) (sales income),
(b) subsection (6) (licence fees),
(c) subsection (7) (proceeds of sale etc),
(d) subsection (8) (damages for infringement), and
(e) subsection (9) (other compensation).
This is subject to section 357BHB (excluded income).

(2) Head 1 is income arising from the sale by the company of any of the following items—
(a) items in respect of which a qualifying IP right held by the company has been granted ("qualifying items");
(b) items incorporating one or more qualifying items;
(c) items that are wholly or mainly designed to be incorporated into items within paragraph (a) or (b).

(3) For the purposes of this Part an item and its packaging are not to be treated as a single item, unless the packaging performs a function that is essential for the use of the item for the purposes for which it is intended to be used.

(4) In subsection (3) "packaging", in relation to an item, means any form of container or other packaging used for the containment, protection, handling, delivery or presentation of the item, including by way of attaching the item to, or winding the item round, some other article.

(5) In a case where a qualifying item and an item that is designed to incorporate that item ("the parent item") are sold together as, or as part of, a single unit for a single price, the reference in subsection (2)(b) to an item incorporating a qualifying item includes a reference to the parent item.

(6) Head 2 is income consisting of any licence fee or royalty which the company receives under an agreement granting another person any of the following rights only—
(a) a right in respect of any qualifying IP right held by the company,
(b) any other right in respect of a qualifying item or process, and
(c) in the case of an agreement granting any right within paragraph (a) or (b), a right granted for the same purposes as those for which that right was granted.
In this subsection "qualifying process" means a process in respect of which a qualifying IP right held by the company has been granted.

(7) Head 3 is any income arising from the sale or other disposal of a qualifying IP right or an exclusive licence in respect of such a right.

(8) Head 4 is any amount received by the company in respect of an infringement, or alleged infringement, of a qualifying IP right held by the company at the time of the infringement or alleged infringement.

(9) Head 5 is any amount of damages, proceeds of insurance or other compensation, other than an amount in respect of an infringement or alleged infringement of a qualifying IP right, which is received by the company in respect of an event and—
(a) is paid in respect of any items that fell within subsection (2) at the time of that event, or
(b) represents a loss of income which would, if received by the company at the time of that event, have been relevant IP income.

(10) But income is not relevant IP income by virtue of subsection (8) or (9) unless the event in respect of which the income is received, or any part of that event, occurred at a time when—
(a) the company was a qualifying company, and
(b) an election under section 357A(1) had effect in relation to it.

(11) In a case where the whole of that event does not occur at such a time, subsection (8) or (9) (as the case may be) applies only to so much of the amount received by the company in respect of the event as on a just and reasonable apportionment is properly attributable to such a time.
(12) Any reference in this section to a qualifying IP right held by the company includes a reference to a qualifying IP right in respect of which the company holds an exclusive licence.]

NOTES

Inserted as noted to s 357BF at **[1.162]**.

[1.165]
[357BHA Notional royalty

(1) This section applies where—
  (a) a company holds a qualifying IP right or an exclusive licence in respect of a qualifying IP right,
  (b) the qualifying IP right falls within paragraph (a), (b) or (c) of section 357BB(1), and
  (c) the income of a trade of the company for an accounting period includes income ("IP-derived income") which—
    (i) arises from things done by the company that involve the exploitation by the company of the qualifying IP right, and
    (ii) is not relevant IP income, finance income or excluded income.

(2) The company may elect that the appropriate percentage of the IP-derived income is to be treated for the purposes of this Part as if it were relevant IP income.
(3) The "appropriate percentage" is the proportion of the IP-derived income which the company would pay another person ("P") for the right to exploit the qualifying IP right in the accounting period concerned if thc company were not otherwise able to exploit it.
(4) For the purposes of determining the appropriate percentage under this section, assume that—
  (a) the company and P are dealing at arm's length,
  (b) the company, or the company and persons authorised by it, will have the right to exploit the qualifying IP right to the exclusion of any other person (including P),
  (c) the company will have the same rights in relation to the qualifying IP right as it actually has,
  (d) the right to exploit the qualifying IP right is conferred on the relevant day,
  (e) the appropriate percentage is determined at the beginning of the accounting period concerned,
  (f) the appropriate percentage will apply for each succeeding accounting period for which the company will have the right to exploit the qualifying IP right, and
  (g) no income other than IP-derived income will arise from anything done by the company that involves the exploitation by the company of the qualifying IP right.

(5) In subsection (4)(d) "the relevant day" means—
  (a) the first day of the accounting period concerned, or
  (b) if later, the day on which the company first began to hold the qualifying IP right or licence.

(6) In determining the appropriate percentage, the company must act in accordance with—
  (a) Article 9 of the OECD Model Tax Convention, and
  (b) the OECD transfer pricing guidelines.

(7) In this section "excluded income" means any income falling within either of the Heads in section 357BHB.]

NOTES

Inserted as noted to s 357BF at **[1.162]**.

[1.166]
[357BHB Excluded income

(1) For the purposes of this Part income falling within either of the Heads set out in the following subsections is not relevant IP income—
  (a) subsection (2) (ring fence income),
  (b) subsection (3) (income attributable to non-exclusive licences).

(2) Head 1 is income arising from oil extraction activities or oil rights.
In this subsection "oil extraction activities" and "oil rights" have the same meaning as in Part 8 (see sections 272 and 273).
(3) Head 2 is income which on a just and reasonable apportionment is properly attributable to a licence (a "non-exclusive licence") held by the company which—
  (a) is a licence in respect of an item or process, but
  (b) is not an exclusive licence in respect of a qualifying IP right.

(4) In a case where—
  (a) a company holds an exclusive licence in respect of a qualifying IP right, and
  (b) the licence also confers on the company (or on the company and persons authorised by it) any right in respect of the invention otherwise than to the exclusion of all other persons,

the licence is to be treated for the purposes of this Part as if it were two separate licences, one an exclusive licence that does not confer any such rights, and the other a non-exclusive licence conferring those rights.]

NOTES

Inserted as noted to s 357BF at **[1.162]**.

[1.167]

[357BHC Mixed sources of income

(1) This section applies to any income that—

(a) is mixed income, or

(b) is paid under a mixed agreement.

(2) "Mixed income" means the proceeds of sale where an item falling within subsection (2) of section 357BH and an item not falling within that subsection are sold together as, or as part of, a single unit for a single price.

(3) A "mixed agreement" is an agreement providing for—

(a) one or more of the matters in paragraphs (a) to (c) of subsection (4), and

(b) one or more of the matters in paragraphs (d) to (g) of that subsection.

(4) The matters are—

(a) the sale of an item falling within section 357BH(2),

(b) the grant of any right falling within paragraph (a), (b) or (c) of section 357BH(6),

(c) a sale or disposal falling within section 357BH(7),

(d) the sale of any other item,

(e) the grant of any other right,

(f) any other sale or disposal,

(g) the provision of any services.

(5) So much of the income as on a just and reasonable apportionment is properly attributable to—

(a) the sale of an item falling within section 357BH(2),

(b) the grant of any right falling within paragraph (a), (b) or (c) of section 357BH(6), or

(c) a sale or disposal falling within section 357BH(7),

is to be regarded for the purposes of this Part as relevant IP income.

(6) But where the amount of income that on such an apportionment is properly attributable to any of the matters in paragraphs (d) to (g) of subsection (4) is a trivial proportion of the income to which this section applies, all of that income is to be regarded for the purposes of this Part as relevant IP income.]

NOTES

Inserted as noted to s 357BF at **[1.162]**.

[Excluded debits etc

[1.168]

357BI Excluded debits

For the purposes of this Part "excluded debits" means—

(a) the amount of any debits which are treated as expenses of a trade by virtue of—

(i) section 297 of CTA 2009 (debits in respect of loan relationships), or

(ii) section 573 of CTA 2009 (debits in respect of derivative contracts),

(b) the amount of any additional deduction for an accounting period obtained by a company under Part 13 of CTA 2009 for expenditure on research and development in relation to a trade,

(c) the amount of any additional deduction for an accounting period obtained by a company under Part 15A of CTA 2009 in respect of qualifying expenditure on a television programme,

(d) the amount of any additional deduction for an accounting period obtained by a company under Part 15B of CTA 2009 in respect of qualifying expenditure on a video game, and

(e) the amount of any additional deduction for an accounting period obtained by a company under Part 15C of CTA 2009 in respect of qualifying expenditure on a theatrical production.]

NOTES

Inserted as noted to s 357BF at **[1.162]**.

[1.169]

[357BIA Certain amounts not to be deducted from sub-streams at Step 4 of section 357BF

(1) This section applies where a company enters into an arrangement with a person under which—

(a) the person assigns to the company a qualifying IP right or grants or transfers to the company an exclusive licence in respect of a qualifying IP right, and

(b) the company makes to the person an income-related payment.

(2) A payment is an "income-related payment" for the purposes of subsection (1) if—

(a) the obligation to make the payment arises under the arrangement by reason of the amount of income the company has accrued which is properly attributable to the right or licence, or
(b) the amount of the payment is determined under the arrangement by reference to the amount of income the company has accrued which is so attributable.

(3) If the amount of the income-related payment is allocated to a relevant IP income sub-stream at Step 3 of section 357BF(2), the amount is not to be deducted from the sub-stream at Step 4 of section 357BF(2) unless the payment will not affect the R&D fraction for the sub-stream.]

NOTES

Inserted as noted to s 357BF at **[1.162]**.

[Routine return figure

[1.170]

357BJ Routine return figure

(1) This section applies for the purpose of calculating the routine return figure for a relevant IP income sub-stream established at Step 2 in section 357BF(2) in determining the relevant IP profits of a trade of a company for an accounting period.

(2) The routine return figure for the sub-stream is 10% of the aggregate of any routine deductions which—
(a) have been made by the company in calculating the profits of the trade for the accounting period, and
(b) have been allocated to the sub-stream at Step 3 in section 357BF(2).

For the meaning of "routine deductions", see sections 357BJA and 357BJB.

(3) In a case where—
(a) the company ("C") is a member of a group,
(b) another member of the group has incurred expenses on behalf of C,
(c) had they been incurred by C, C would have made a deduction in respect of the expenses in calculating the profits of the trade for the accounting period,
(d) the deduction would have been a routine deduction, and
(e) the deduction would have been allocated to the sub-stream at Step 3 in section 357BF(2),

C is to be treated for the purposes of subsection (2) as having made such a routine deduction and as having allocated the deduction to the sub-stream.

(4) Where expenses have been incurred by any member of the group on behalf of C and any other member of the group, subsection (3) applies in relation to so much of the amount of the expenses as on a just and reasonable apportionment may properly be regarded as incurred on behalf of C.]

NOTES

Inserted as noted to s 357BF at **[1.162]**.

[1.171]

[357BJA Routine deductions

(1) For the purposes of this Part, "routine deductions" means deductions falling within any of the Heads set out in—
(a) subsection (2) (capital allowances),
(b) subsection (3) (costs of premises),
(c) subsection (4) (personnel costs),
(d) subsection (5) (plant and machinery costs),
(e) subsection (6) (professional services), and
(f) subsection (7) (miscellaneous services).

This is subject to section 357BJB (deductions that are not routine deductions).

(2) Head 1 is any allowances under CAA 2001.

(3) Head 2 is any deductions made by the company in respect of any premises occupied by the company.

(4) Head 3 is any deductions made by the company in respect of—
(a) any director or employee of the company, or
(b) any externally provided workers.

(5) Head 4 is any deductions made by the company in respect of any plant or machinery used by the company.

(6) Head 5 is any deductions made by the company in respect of any of the following services—
(a) legal services, other than IP-related services;
(b) financial services, including—
 (i) insurance services, and
 (ii) valuation or actuarial services;
(c) services provided in connection with the administration or management of the company's directors and employees;
(d) any other consultancy services.

(7) Head 6 is any deductions made by the company in respect of any of the following services—
(a) the supply of water, fuel or power;
(b) telecommunications services;

(c) computing services, including computer software;
(d) postal services;
(e) the transportation of any items;
(f) the collection, removal and disposal of refuse.

(8) In this section—

"externally provided worker" has the same meaning as in Part 13 of CTA 2009 (see section 1128 of that Act),

"IP-related services" means services provided in connection with—

(a) any application for a right to which this Part applies, or
(b) any proceedings relating to the enforcement of any such right,

"premises" includes any land,

"telecommunications service" means any service that consists in the provision of access to, and of facilities for making use of, any telecommunication system (whether or not one provided by the person providing the service), and

"telecommunication system" means any system (including the apparatus comprised in it) which exists for the purpose of facilitating the transmission of communications by any means involving the use of electrical or electromagnetic energy.

(9) The Treasury may by regulations amend this section.]

NOTES

Inserted as noted to s 357BF at **[1.162]**.

[1.172]

[357BJB Deductions that are not routine deductions

(1) For the purposes of this Part a deduction is not a "routine deduction" if it falls within any of the Heads set out in—

(a) subsection (2) (loan relationships and derivative contracts),
(b) subsection (3) (R&D expenses),
(c) subsection (4) (capital allowances for R&D or patents),
(d) subsection (5) (R&D-related employee share acquisitions),
(e) subsection (8) (television production expenditure),
(f) subsection (9) (video games development expenditure).

(2) Head 1 is any debits which are treated as expenses of the trade by virtue of—

(a) section 297 of CTA 2009 (debits in respect of loan relationships), or
(b) section 573 of CTA 2009 (debits in respect of derivative contracts).

(3) Head 2 is—

(a) the amount of any expenditure on research and development in relation to the trade—
 (i) for which an additional deduction for the accounting period is obtained by the company under Part 13 of CTA 2009, or
 (ii) in respect of which the company is entitled to an R&D expenditure credit for the accounting period under Chapter 6A of Part 3 of CTA 2009, and
(b) where the company obtains an additional deduction as mentioned in paragraph (a)(i), the amount of that additional deduction.

(4) Head 3 is any allowances under—

(a) Part 6 of CAA 2001 (research and development allowances), or
(b) Part 8 of CAA 2001 (patent allowances).

(5) Head 4 is the appropriate proportion of any deductions allowed under Part 12 of CTA 2009 (relief for employee share acquisitions) in a case where—

(a) shares are acquired by an employee or another person because of the employee's employment by the company, and
(b) the employee is wholly or partly engaged directly and actively in relevant research and development (within the meaning of section 1042 of CTA 2009).

(6) In subsection (5) "the appropriate proportion", in relation to a deduction allowed in respect of an employee, is the proportion of the staffing costs in respect of the employee which are attributable to relevant research and development for the purposes of Part 13 of CTA 2009 (see section 1124 of that Act).

"Staffing costs" has the same meaning as in that Part (see section 1123 of that Act).

(7) Subsections (5) and (6) of section 1124 of CTA 2009 apply for the purposes of subsection (5)(b) as they apply for the purposes of that section.

(8) Head 5 is—

(a) the amount of any qualifying expenditure on a television programme for which an additional deduction for the accounting period is obtained by the company under Part 15A of CTA 2009, and
(b) the amount of that additional deduction.

(9) Head 6 is—

(a) the amount of any qualifying expenditure on a video game for which an additional deduction for the accounting period is obtained by the company under Part 15B of CTA 2009, and
(b) the amount of that additional deduction.

(10) The Treasury may by regulations amend this section.]

NOTES

Inserted as noted to s 357BF at **[1.162]**.

[Marketing assets return figure

[1.173]

357BK Marketing assets return figure]

(1) The marketing assets return figure for a relevant IP income sub-stream is—

NMR - AMR

where—

NMR is the notional marketing royalty in respect of the sub-stream (see section 357BKA), and AMR is the actual marketing royalty in respect of the sub-stream (see section 357BKB).

(2) Where—

(a) AMR is greater than NMR, or

(b) the difference between NMR and AMR is less than 10% of the amount of the relevant IP income sub-stream following the deductions required by Step 4 in section 357BF(2),

the marketing assets return figure for the sub-stream is nil.]

NOTES

Inserted as noted to s 357BF at **[1.162]**.

[1.174]

[357BKA Notional marketing royalty

(1) The notional marketing royalty in respect of a relevant IP income sub-stream is the appropriate percentage of the income allocated to that sub-stream at Step 2 in section 357BF(2).

(2) The "appropriate percentage" is the proportion of that income which the company would pay another person ("P") for the right to exploit the relevant marketing assets in the accounting period concerned if the company were not otherwise able to exploit them.

(3) For the purposes of this section a marketing asset is a "relevant marketing asset" in relation to a relevant IP income sub-stream if the sub-stream includes any income arising from things done by the company that involve the exploitation by the company of that marketing asset.

(4) For the purpose of determining the appropriate percentage under this section, assume that—

(a) the company and P are dealing at arm's length,

(b) the company, or the company and persons authorised by it, will have the right to exploit the relevant marketing assets to the exclusion of any other person (including P),

(c) the company will have the same rights in relation to the relevant marketing assets as it actually has,

(d) the right to exploit the relevant marketing assets is conferred on the relevant day,

(e) the appropriate percentage is determined at the beginning of the accounting period concerned,

(f) the appropriate percentage will apply for each succeeding accounting period for which the company will have the right to exploit the relevant marketing assets, and

(g) no income other than income within the relevant IP income sub-stream will arise from anything done by the company that involves the exploitation by the company of the relevant marketing assets.

(5) In subsection (4)(d) "the relevant day", in relation to a relevant marketing asset, means—

(a) the first day of the accounting period concerned, or

(b) if later, the day on which the company first acquired the relevant marketing asset or the right to exploit the asset.

(6) In determining the appropriate percentage, the company must act in accordance with—

(a) Article 9 of the OECD Model Tax Convention, and

(b) the OECD transfer pricing guidelines.

(7) In this section "marketing asset" means any of the following (whether or not capable of being transferred or assigned)—

(a) anything in respect of which proceedings for passing off could be brought, including a registered trade mark (within the meaning of the Trade Marks Act 1994),

(b) anything that corresponds to a marketing asset within paragraph (a) and is recognised under the law of a country or territory outside the United Kingdom,

(c) any signs or indications (so far as not falling within paragraph (a) or (b)) which may serve, in trade, to designate the geographical origin of goods or services, and

(d) any information which relates to customers or potential customers of the company, or any other member of a group of which the company is a member, and is intended to be used for marketing purposes.]

NOTES

Inserted as noted to s 357BF at **[1.162]**.

[1.175]

[357BKB Actual marketing royalty

(1) The actual marketing royalty for a relevant IP income sub-stream is the aggregate of any sums which—

(a) were paid by the company for the purposes of acquiring any relevant marketing assets or the right to exploit any such assets, and

(b) have been allocated to the sub-stream at Step 3 in section 357BF(2).

(2) In this section "relevant marketing asset" has the same meaning as in section 357BKA.]

NOTES

Inserted as noted to s 357BF at **[1.162]**.

[R&D fraction

[1.176]

357BL Introduction

[(1) Sections 357BLA to 357BLH apply for the purpose of determining the R&D fraction for a relevant IP income sub-stream established at Step 2 in section 357BF(2) in determining the relevant IP profits of a trade of a company for an accounting period.

(2) In sections 357BLA to 357BLH, references to "the sub-stream", "the trade", "the company" and "the accounting period" are to the relevant IP income sub-stream, the trade, the company and the accounting period referred to in subsection (1).]

NOTES

Inserted as noted to s 357BF at **[1.162]**.

[1.177]

[357BLA The R&D fraction

(1) The R&D fraction for the sub-stream is the lesser of 1 and—

((D + S1) x 1.3) / (D + S1 + S2 + A)

where—

D is the company's qualifying expenditure on relevant R&D undertaken in-house (see section 357BLB),

S1 is the company's qualifying expenditure on relevant R&D sub-contracted to unconnected persons (see section 357BLC),

S2 is the company's qualifying expenditure on relevant R&D sub-contracted to connected persons (see section 357BLD), and

A is the company's qualifying expenditure on the acquisition of relevant qualifying IP rights (see section 357BLE).

(2) This section is subject to section 357BLH (R&D fraction: increase for exceptional circumstances).]

NOTES

Inserted as noted to s 357BF at **[1.162]**.

[1.178]

[357BLB Qualifying expenditure on relevant R&D undertaken in-house

(1) In section 357BLA, the company's "qualifying expenditure on relevant R&D undertaken in-house" means the expenditure incurred by the company during the relevant period which meets conditions A and B.

(2) Condition A is that the expenditure is—

(a) incurred on staffing costs,

(b) incurred on software or consumable items,

(c) qualifying expenditure on externally provided workers, or

(d) incurred on relevant payments to the subjects of clinical trials.

(3) Condition B is that the expenditure is attributable to relevant research and development undertaken by the company itself.

(4) If an election made by the company under section 18A of CTA 2009 (election for exemption for profits or losses of company's foreign permanent establishments) applies to the relevant period, expenditure incurred by the company during the period which meets conditions A and B—

(a) is not "qualifying expenditure on relevant R&D undertaken in-house", but

(b) is "qualifying expenditure on relevant R&D sub-contracted to connected persons",

so far as it is expenditure brought into account in calculating a relevant profits amount, or a relevant losses amount, aggregated at section 18A(4)(a) or (b) of CTA 2009 in calculating the company's foreign permanent establishments amount for the period.

(5) In this section and sections 357BLC and 357BLD, "relevant research and development" means research and development (within the meaning of section 1138) which—

(a) in a case where the sub-stream is an individual IP right sub-stream, relates to the qualifying IP right to which the income in the sub-stream is attributable,

(b) in a case where the sub-stream is a product sub-stream, relates to a qualifying IP right granted in respect of any item—
(i) to which income in the sub-stream is attributable, or
(ii) which is incorporated in an item to which income in the sub-stream is attributable, or
(c) in a case where the sub-stream is a process sub-stream, relates to a qualifying IP right granted in respect of any process—
(i) to which income in the sub-stream is attributable, or
(ii) which is incorporated in a process to which income in the sub-stream is attributable.

(6) Research and development "relates" to a qualifying IP right for the purposes of subsection (5) if—
(a) it creates, or contributes to the creation of, the invention,
(b) it is undertaken for the purpose of developing the invention,
(c) it is undertaken for the purpose of developing ways in which the invention may be used or applied, or
(d) it is undertaken for the purpose of developing any item or process incorporating the invention.

(7) The following provisions of CTA 2009 apply for the purposes of this section—
(a) section 1123 (meaning of "staffing costs"),
(b) section 1124 (when staffing costs are attributable to relevant research and development),
(c) section 1125 (meaning of "software or consumable items"),
(d) sections 1126 to 1126B (when software or consumable items are attributable to relevant research and development),
(e) sections 1127 to 1131 (meaning of "qualifying expenditure on externally provided workers"),
(f) section 1132 (when qualifying expenditure on externally provided workers is attributable to relevant research and development), and
(g) section 1140 (meaning of "relevant payments to the subjects of clinical trials"),

and in the application of those provisions for the purposes of this section any reference to "relevant research and development" is to be read as a reference to relevant research and development within the meaning given by subsection (5).]

NOTES

Inserted as noted to s 357BF at **[1.162]**.

[1.179]

[357BLC Qualifying expenditure on relevant R&D sub-contracted to unconnected persons

(1) In section 357BLA, the company's "qualifying expenditure on relevant R&D sub-contracted to unconnected persons" means the expenditure incurred by the company during the relevant period in making payments within subsection (2).

(2) A payment is within this subsection if—
(a) it is made to a person in respect of relevant research and development contracted out by the company to the person, and
(b) the company and the person are not connected (within the meaning given by section 1122).

(3) If an election made by the company under section 18A of CTA 2009 (election for exemption for profits or losses of company's foreign permanent establishments) applies to the relevant period, expenditure incurred by the company during the period in making payments within subsection (2)—
(a) is not "qualifying expenditure on relevant R&D sub-contracted to unconnected persons", but
(b) is "qualifying expenditure on relevant R&D sub-contracted to connected persons",

so far as it is expenditure brought into account in calculating a relevant profits amount, or a relevant losses amount, aggregated at section 18A(4)(a) or (b) of CTA 2009 in calculating the company's foreign permanent establishments amount for the period.

(4) Where a payment is made to a person in respect of relevant research and development contracted out to the person and in respect of other matters, so much of the payment as is properly attributable to other matters is to be disregarded for the purposes of this section.]

NOTES

Inserted as noted to s 357BF at **[1.162]**.

[1.180]

[357BLD Qualifying expenditure on relevant R&D sub-contracted to connected persons

(1) In section 357BLA, the company's "qualifying expenditure on relevant R&D sub-contracted to connected persons" means the total of—
(a) any expenditure which is "qualifying expenditure on relevant R&D sub-contracted to connected persons" as a result of section 357BLB(4) or 357BLC(3) (certain expenditure attributed to company's foreign permanent establishments), and
(b) the expenditure incurred by the company during the relevant period in making payments within subsection (2).

(2) A payment is within this subsection if—

(a) it is made to a person in respect of relevant research and development contracted out by the company to the person, and

(b) the company and the person are connected (within the meaning given by section 1122).

(3) Where a payment is made to a person in respect of relevant research and development contracted out to the person and in respect of other matters, so much of the payment as is properly attributable to other matters is to be disregarded for the purposes of this section.]

NOTES

Inserted as noted to s 357BF at **[1.162]**.

[1.181]

[357BLE Qualifying expenditure on acquisition of relevant qualifying IP rights

(1) In section 357BLA, the company's "qualifying expenditure on the acquisition of relevant qualifying IP rights" means the expenditure incurred by the company in making during the relevant period payments within any of subsections (2), (3) and (4).

(2) A payment is within this subsection if it is made to a person in respect of the assignment by that person to the company of a relevant qualifying IP right.

(3) A payment is within this subsection if it is made to a person in respect of the grant or transfer by that person to the company of an exclusive licence in respect of a relevant qualifying IP right.

(4) A payment is within this subsection if—

(a) it is made to a person in respect of the disclosure by that person to the company of any item or process, and

(b) the company applies for and is granted a relevant qualifying IP right in respect of that item or process (or any item or process derived from it).

(5) Where the company has incurred expenditure in making a series of payments to a person in respect of a single assignment, grant, transfer or disclosure, each of the payments in the series is to be treated for the purposes of this section as having been made on the date on which the first payment in the series was made.

(6) "Relevant qualifying IP right" means—

(a) in a case where the sub-stream is an individual IP right sub-stream, the qualifying IP right to which the income in the sub-stream is attributable,

(b) in a case where the sub-stream is a product sub-stream, a qualifying IP right granted in respect of an item—

(i) to which income in the sub-stream is attributable, or

(ii) which is incorporated in an item to which income in the sub-stream is attributable, or

(c) in a case where the sub-stream is a process sub-stream, a qualifying IP right granted in respect of a process—

(i) to which income in the sub-stream is attributable, or

(ii) which is incorporated in a process to which income in the sub-stream is attributable.]

NOTES

Inserted as noted to s 357BF at **[1.162]**.

[1.182]

[357BLF Meaning of the "relevant period" etc

(1) Subsections (2) to (6) define "the relevant period" for the purposes of sections 357BLB to 357BLE.

(2) The "relevant period" is the period which—

(a) ends with the last day of the accounting period, and

(b) begins on the relevant day or such earlier day as the company may elect.

This is subject to subsection (6).

(3) The "relevant day" is 1 July 2013 in a case where—

(a) the accounting period begins before 1 July 2021, and

(b) the company is a new entrant (see section 357A(11)).

(4) The "relevant day" is 1 July 2016 in any other case.

(5) A day elected under subsection (2)(b) must not be more than 20 years before the last day of the accounting period.

(6) If the last day of the accounting period is, or is after, 1 July 2036 the "relevant period" is the period of 20 years ending with that day.

(7) Expenditure incurred by the company is to be treated for the purposes of sections 357BLB to 357BLD as incurred during the relevant period if (and only if) the expenditure is allowable as a deduction in calculating for corporation tax purposes the profits of the trade for an accounting period which falls, in whole or in part, within the relevant period.]

NOTES

Inserted as noted to s 357BF at **[1.162]**.

[1.183]
[357BLG Cases where the company is a new entrant with insufficient information about pre-enactment expenditure

(1) This section applies if—

(a) the accounting period begins before 1 July 2021 and the company is a new entrant (so that subsection (3) of section 357BLF applies), and

(b) the company has insufficient information about its expenditure in the period which begins with 1 July 2013 and ends with 30 June 2016 to be able to calculate the R&D fraction for the sub-stream.

(2) If the accounting period begins on or after 1 July 2019, the company may elect that, for the purposes of enabling it to determine the R&D fraction for the sub-stream, section 357BLF is to have effect as if in subsection (3) for "1 July 2013" there were substituted "1 July 2016".

(3) If the accounting period begins before 1 July 2019 the company may elect that, for the purposes of enabling it to determine the R&D fraction for the sub-stream, sections 357BL to 357BLE are to have effect as if—

(a) any reference in those sections to the relevant period were to the period of three years ending with the last day of the accounting period,

(b) in section 357BLB, for subsections (5) and (6) there were substituted—

"(5) In this section and sections 357BLC and 357BLD, "relevant research and development" means research and development (within the meaning of section 1138) which relates to the trade.", and

(c) in section 357BLE—

(i) in each of subsections (2), (3) and (4) the word "relevant" were omitted, and

(ii) subsection (6) were omitted.]

NOTES

Inserted as noted to s 357BF at **[1.162]**.

[1.184]
[357BLH R&D fraction: increase for exceptional circumstances

(1) The company may elect to increase the R&D fraction for the sub-stream by the amount mentioned in subsection (2) if (but for the increase)—

(a) it would not be less than 0.325, and

(b) it would, because of exceptional circumstances, be less than the value fraction for the sub-stream (see subsection (3)).

(2) The amount of the increase referred to in subsection (1) is the amount which is equal to the difference between the R&D fraction (before the increase) and the value fraction.

(3) The "value fraction" for the sub-stream is the fraction which, on a just and reasonable assessment, represents the proportion of the value of the relevant qualifying IP rights which is properly attributable to research and development undertaken at any time—

(a) by the company itself, or

(b) on behalf of the company by persons not connected with it.

(4) An election under subsection (1) is made by the company giving notice to an officer of Revenue and Customs.

(5) The notice must be given on or before the last day on which an amendment of the company's tax return for the accounting period could be made under paragraph 15 of Schedule 18 to FA 1998.

(6) In this section—

"relevant qualifying IP rights" has the same meaning as in section 357BLE, and

"research and development" has the meaning given by section 1138.

(7) Section 1122 (meaning of "connected" persons") applies for the purposes of this section.]

NOTES

Inserted as noted to s 357BF at **[1.162]**.

[Profits arising before grant of right

[1.185]
357BM Profits arising before grant of right

(1) This section applies where a company—

(a) holds a right mentioned in paragraph (a), (b) or (c) of section 357BB(1) (rights to which this Part applies) or an exclusive licence in respect of such a right, or

(b) would hold such a right or licence but for the fact that the company disposed of any rights in the invention or (as the case may be) the licence before the right was granted.

(2) The company may elect that, for the purposes of determining the relevant IP profits of a trade of the company for the accounting period in which the right is granted, there is to be added the amount determined in accordance with subsection (3) (the "additional amount").

(3) The additional amount is the difference between—

(a) the aggregate of the relevant IP profits of the trade for each relevant accounting period, and

(b) the aggregate of what the relevant IP profits of the trade for each relevant accounting period would have been if the right had been granted on the relevant day.

(4) For the purposes of determining the additional amount, the amount of any relevant IP profits to which section 357A does not apply by virtue of Chapter 5 (relevant IP losses) is to be disregarded.

(5) In this section "relevant accounting period" means—

(a) the accounting period of the company in which the right is granted, and
(b) any earlier accounting period of the company which meets the conditions in subsection (6).

(6) The conditions mentioned in subsection (5)(b) are—

(a) that it is an accounting period for which an election made by the company under section 357A(1) has effect,
(b) that it is an accounting period for which the company is a qualifying company, and
(c) that it ends on or after the relevant day.

(7) In this section "the relevant day" is the later of—

(a) the first day of the period of 6 years ending with the day on which the right is granted, and
(b) the day on which—
 (i) the application for the grant of the right was filed, or
 (ii) in the case of a company that holds an exclusive licence in respect of the right, the licence was granted.

(8) Where the company would be a qualifying company for an accounting period but for the fact that the right had not been granted at any time during that accounting period, the company is to be treated for the purposes of this section as if it were a qualifying company for that accounting period.

(9) Where the company would be a qualifying company for the accounting period in which the right was granted but for the fact that the company disposed of the rights or licence mentioned in subsection (1)(b) before the right was granted, the company is to be treated for the purposes of section 357A as if it were a qualifying company for that accounting period.]

NOTES

Inserted as noted to s 357BF at **[1.162]**.

[Small claims treatment

[1.186]

[357BN Small claims treatment

(1) This section applies where—

(a) a company carries on only one trade during an accounting period,
(b) section 357BF applies for the purposes of determining the relevant IP profits of the trade for the accounting period, and
(c) the qualifying residual profit of the trade for the accounting period does not exceed whichever is the greater of—
 (i) £1,000,000, and
 (ii) the relevant maximum for the accounting period.

(2) The company may make any of the following elections for the accounting period—

(a) a notional royalty election (see section 357BNA),
(b) a small claims figure election (see section 357BNB), and
(c) a global streaming election (see section 357BNC).

This is subject to subsections (3) and (4).

(3) The company may not make a notional royalty election, a small claims figure election or a global streaming election for the accounting period if—

(a) the qualifying residual profit of the trade for the accounting period exceeds £1,000,000,
(b) section 357BF applied for the purposes of determining the relevant IP profits of the trade for any previous accounting period beginning within the relevant 4-year period, and
(c) the company did not make a notional royalty election, a small claims figure election or (as the case may be) a global streaming election for that previous accounting period.

(4) The company may not make a small claims figure election for the accounting period if—

(a) the qualifying residual profit of the trade for the accounting period exceeds £1,000,000,
(b) section 357C or 357DA applied for the purposes of determining the relevant IP profits of the trade for any previous accounting period beginning within the relevant 4-year period, and
(c) the company did not make an election under section 357CL for small claims treatment for that previous accounting period.

(5) In subsections (3) and (4) "the relevant 4-year period" means the period of 4 years ending with the beginning of the accounting period mentioned in subsection (1)(a).

(6) For the purposes of this section, the "qualifying residual profit" of a trade of a company for an accounting period is the amount which (assuming the company did not make an election under this section) would be equal to the aggregate of the relevant IP income sub-streams established at Step 2 in section 357BF(2) in determining the relevant IP profits of the trade for the accounting period, following the deductions from those sub-streams required by Step 4 in section 357BF(2) (ignoring the amount of any sub-stream which is not greater than nil following those deductions).

(7) For the purposes of this section, the "relevant maximum" for an accounting period of a company is—

(a) in a case where no company is a related 51% group company of the company in the accounting period, £3,000,000;

(b) in a case where one or more companies are related 51% group companies of the company in the accounting period, the amount given by the formula—

£3,000,000 / (1 + N)

where N is the number of those related 51% group companies in relation to which an election under section 357A(1) has effect for the accounting period.

(8) For an accounting period of less than 12 months, the relevant maximum is proportionally reduced.]

NOTES

Inserted as noted to s 357BF at **[1.162]**.

[1.187]

[357BNA Notional royalty election

(1) Subsection (2) applies where a company has made a notional royalty election for an accounting period under section 357BN(2)(a).

(2) In its application for the purposes of determining the relevant IP profits of the trade of the company for the accounting period, section 357BHA (notional royalty) has effect as if—

(a) in subsection (2) for "the appropriate percentage" there were substituted "75%", and

(b) subsections (3) to (6) were omitted.]

NOTES

Inserted as noted to s 357BF at **[1.162]**.

[1.188]

[357BNB Small claims figure election

(1) Subsection (2) applies where a company has made a small claims figure election for an accounting period under section 357BN(2)(b).

(2) In its application for the purposes of determining the relevant IP profits of the trade of the company for the accounting period, section 357BF(2) (steps for calculating relevant IP profits) has effect as if in Step 5—

(a) for "marketing assets return figure" there was substituted "small claims figure", and

(b) for "(see section 357BK)" there was substituted "(see section 357BNB(3))".

(3) Subsections (4) to (9) apply for the purpose of calculating the small claims figure for a relevant IP income sub-stream established at Step 2 in section 357BF(2) in determining the relevant IP profits of a trade of a company for an accounting period.

(4) If 75% of the qualifying residual profit of the trade for the accounting period is lower than the small claims threshold, the small claims figure for the sub-stream is 25% of the amount of the sub-stream following Step 4 in section 357BF(2).

(5) If 75% of the qualifying residual profit of the trade for the accounting period is higher than the small claims threshold, the small claims figure for the sub-stream is the amount given by—

A - ((A / QRP) x SCT)

where—

A is the amount of the sub-stream following the deductions required by Step 4 in section 357BF(2),

QRP is the qualifying residual profit of the trade of the company for the accounting period, and

SCT is the small claims threshold.

(6) If no company is a related 51% group company of the company in the accounting period, the small claims threshold is £1,000,000.

(7) If one or more companies are related 51% group companies of the company in the accounting period, the small claims threshold is—

£1,000,000 / (1 + N)

where N is the number of those related 51% group companies in relation to which an election under section 357A(1) has effect for the accounting period.

(8) For an accounting period of less than 12 months, the small claims threshold is proportionately reduced.

(9) Subsection (6) of section 357BN (meaning of "qualifying residual profit") applies for the purposes of subsection (4) and (5) of this section.]

NOTES

Inserted as noted to s 357BF at **[1.162]**.

[1.189]

[357BNC Global streaming election

(1) Subsection (2) applies where a company has made a global streaming election for an accounting period under section 357BN(2)(c).

(2) In its application for the purpose of determining the relevant IP profits of the trade of the company for the accounting period, this Chapter has effect with the following modifications.

(3) In subsection (2) of section 357BF (relevant IP profits)—

(a) omit Step 2,

(b) in Step 3 for "each of the relevant IP income sub-streams" substitute "the relevant IP income stream",

(c) in Step 4—

(i) in the words before paragraph (a), for "each" substitute "the",

(ii) for "sub-stream", in each place it occurs, substitute "stream",

(d) in Step 5—

(i) at the beginning insert "If the relevant IP income stream is greater than nil following Step 4,",

(ii) for the words from "each" to "Step 4" substitute "the stream",

(iii) for "sub-stream", in the second place it occurs, substitute "stream",

(e) in Step 6—

(i) for "each relevant IP income sub-stream" substitute "the relevant IP income stream",

(ii) for "sub-stream", in the second place it occurs, substitute "stream",

(f) omit Step 7, and

(g) in Step 8 for "given by Step 7" substitute "of the relevant IP income stream following Step 6".

(4) In subsection (3) of that section for "given by" substitute "of the relevant IP income stream following the Steps in".

(5) In subsection (4) of that section for "given by" substitute "of the relevant IP income stream following the Steps in".

(6) Omit subsections (5) to (7) of that section.

(7) In section 357BIA(3) (certain amounts not to be deducted from sub-streams at Step 4 of section 357BF)—

(a) for "a relevant IP income sub-stream" substitute "the relevant IP income stream";

(b) for "sub-stream", in the second and third places it occurs, substitute "stream".

(8) In section 357BJ (routine return figure)—

(a) for "sub-stream", in each place it occurs, substitute "stream", and

(b) in subsection (1) for "Step 2" substitute "Step 1".

(9) In section 357BK (marketing asset return figure) for "sub-stream", in each place it occurs, substitute "stream".

(10) In section 357BKA (notional marketing royalty)—

(a) for "sub-stream", in each place it occurs, substitute "stream", and

(b) in subsection (1) for "Step 2" substitute "Step 1".

(11) In section 357BKB (actual marketing royalty) for "sub-stream", in each place it occurs, substitute "stream".

(12) In section 357BL (R&D fraction: introduction)—

(a) for "sub-stream" (in each place it occurs) substitute "stream", and

(b) in subsection (1) for "Step 2" substitute "Step 1".

(13) In section 357BLA(1) (R&D fraction) for "sub-stream" substitute "stream".

(14) In section 357BLB(5) (qualifying expenditure on relevant R&D undertaken in-house) for the words after "1138)" substitute "which relates to a qualifying IP right to which income in the stream is attributable".

(15) In section 357BLE(6) (qualifying expenditure on acquisition of relevant qualifying IP rights) for the words from "means" to the end substitute "means a qualifying IP right to which income in the stream is attributable".

(16) In section 357BLG (cases where the company is a new entrant with insufficient information about pre-enactment expenditure) for "sub-stream", in each place it occurs, substitute "stream".

(17) In section 357BLH (R&D fraction: increase for exceptional circumstances) for "sub-stream", in each place it occurs, substitute "stream".

(18) In section 357BNB (small claims figure election)—

(a) for "sub-stream", in each place it occurs, substitute "stream", and

(b) in subsection (3) for "Step 2" substitute "Step 1".]

NOTES

Inserted as noted to s 357BF at **[1.162]**.

[CHAPTER 2B
RELEVANT IP PROFITS: CASES MENTIONED IN SECTION 357A(7): INCOME FROM NEW IP

[1.190]
357BO Relevant IP profits

(1) Section 357BF applies, with the modifications set out in section 357BQ, for the purposes of determining the relevant IP profits of a trade of a company for an accounting period in a case where—

(a) the accounting period begins before 1 July 2021,
(b) the company is not a new entrant (see section 357A(11)), and
(c) any amount of relevant IP income brought into account as a credit in calculating the profits of the trade for the accounting period is properly attributable to a new qualifying IP right (see section 357BP).

(2) Where it is necessary for the purposes of section 357BF, as applied by this section, to determine the R&D fraction for a relevant IP income sub-stream, the company concerned is to be treated for the purposes of sections 357BLF and 357BLG as if it were a new entrant.

(3) Where section 357BF applies by reason of this section for the purposes of determining the relevant IP profits of a trade of a company for an accounting period, the company may not make a global streaming election for the accounting period under section 357BN(2)(c).]

NOTES

Inserted as noted to s 357BF at **[1.162]**.

[1.191]

[357BP Meaning of "new qualifying IP right" and "old qualifying IP right"

(1) This section applies for the purposes of this Part.

(2) "New qualifying IP right", in relation to a company, means a qualifying IP right which meets condition A, B or C.

(3) "Old qualifying IP right", in relation to a company, means a qualifying IP right which does not meet any of those conditions.

(4) Condition A is that the right was granted or issued to the company in response to an application filed on or after the relevant date.

(5) Condition B is that the right was assigned to the company on or after the relevant date.

(6) Condition C is that an exclusive licence in respect of the right was granted to the company on or after the relevant date.

(7) The "relevant date" for the purposes of subsections (4), (5) and (6) is 1 July 2016; but this is subject to subsection (8).

(8) The "relevant date" for the purposes of subsections (5) and (6) is 2 January 2016 if—
(a) the company and the person who assigned the right or granted the licence were connected at the time of the assignment or grant,
(b) the main purpose, or one of the main purposes, of the assignment of the right or the grant of the licence was the avoidance of a foreign tax,
(c) the person who assigned the right or granted the licence was not within the charge to corporation tax at the time of the assignment or grant, and
(d) the person who assigned the right or granted the licence was not liable at the time of the assignment or grant to a foreign tax which is designated for the purposes of this section by regulations made by the Treasury.

(9) Regulations may be made under subsection (8)(d) which designate a foreign tax only if it appears to the Treasury that the tax may be charged at a reduced rate under provisions of the law of the country or territory concerned which correspond to the provisions of this Part.

(10) Regulations may not be made under subsection (8)(d) after 31 December 2016.

(11) In this section "foreign tax" means a tax under the law of a country or territory outside the United Kingdom.

(12) Section 1122 (meaning of "connected" persons) applies for the purposes of this section.]

NOTES

Inserted as noted to s 357BF at **[1.162]**.

Regulations: the Corporation Tax Act 2010 (Profits Arising from the Exploitation of Patents) Foreign Taxes Designation Regulations 2016, SI 2016/1181.

[1.192]

[357BQ The modifications

(1) The modifications of section 357BF referred to in section 357BO(1) are as follows.

(2) Omit subsection (1).

(3) In subsection (2)—
(a) in Step 2—
(i) before paragraph (a) insert—
"(aa) a sub-stream consisting of income properly attributable to old qualifying IP rights ("an old IP rights sub-stream"),",
(ii) in paragraph (a) before "qualifying IP right" insert "new",
(iii) in the words after paragraph (c) for "and (7)" substitute "to (7E)",
(b) in Step 6, for "relevant IP income sub-stream" substitute "individual IP right sub-stream, each product sub-stream and each process sub-stream", and
(c) for Step 7 substitute—

"*Step 7*

Add together—
(a) the amount of any old IP rights sub-stream (following Steps 4 and 5), and

(b) the amount of each of the individual IP right sub-streams, each of the product sub-streams and each of the process sub-streams (following Step 6)."

(4) In subsection (7) for paragraph (a) substitute—

"(a) it would not be reasonably practicable to apportion the income between—

(i) individual IP rights sub-streams, or

(ii) individual IP rights sub-streams and an old IP rights sub-stream, or".

(5) After subsection (7) insert—

"(7A) Subsections (7B) to (7E) apply where—

(a) income which is properly attributable to an IP item or IP process may in accordance with subsection (7) be allocated at Step 2 of subsection (2) to a product sub-stream or process sub stream, and

(b) the IP item or IP process incorporates—

(i) at least one item or process in respect of which an old qualifying IP right held by the company has been granted, and

(ii) at least one item or process in respect of which a new qualifying IP right held by the company has been granted.

(7B) If—

(a) the value of the IP item or IP process is wholly or mainly attributable to the incorporation in it of the items or processes referred to in subsection (7A)(b)(i), or

(b) the old IP percentage for the IP item or IP process is 80% or more,

the income properly attributable to the IP item or IP process may be treated as if it were properly attributable to old qualifying IP rights only; and, accordingly, the income may be allocated at Step 2 of subsection (2) to an old qualifying IP rights sub-stream (rather than to a product sub-stream or process sub-stream).

(7C) If the old IP percentage for the IP item or IP process is less than 80% but not less than 20%, that percentage of the income which is properly attributable to the IP item or IP process may be treated as if it were properly attributable to old qualifying IP rights only; and, accordingly, that percentage of the income may be allocated at Step 2 of subsection (2) to an old IP rights sub-stream (and the remainder is to be allocated to a product sub-stream or process sub-stream).

(7D) Where by reason of subsection (7C) only part of the income properly attributable to the IP item or IP process is allocated to a product sub-stream or process sub-stream, the IP item or IP process is to be treated, in determining the R&D fraction for the sub-stream, as if it did not incorporate the items or processes referred to in subsection (7A)(b)(i).

(7E) For the purposes of subsection (7B) and (7C), the "old IP percentage" for an IP item or IP process is the percentage found by the following calculation—

(O / T) x 100

where—

O is the number of items or processes incorporated in the IP item or IP process in respect of which an old qualifying IP right held by the company has been granted, and

T is the number of items or processes incorporated in the IP item or IP process in respect of which an old or a new qualifying IP right held by the company has been granted.".]

NOTES

Inserted as noted to s 357BF at **[1.162]**.

[CHAPTER 3

RELEVANT IP PROFITS[: CASES MENTIONED IN SECTION 357A(7): NO INCOME FROM NEW IP]

Steps for calculating relevant IP profits of a trade

[1.193]

357C Relevant IP profits

[(A1) This section applies for the purposes of determining the relevant IP profits of a trade of a company for an accounting period in a case where—

(a) the accounting period began before 1 July 2021,

(b) the company is not a new entrant (see section 357A(11)), and

(c) none of the amounts of relevant IP income brought into account as credits in calculating the profits of the trade for the accounting period is properly attributable to a new qualifying IP right (see section 357BP).

But see also section 357D (alternative method of calculating relevant IP profits in such a case).]

(1) To determine the relevant IP profits . . . —

Step 1

Calculate the total gross income of the trade for the accounting period (see section 357CA).

Step 2

Calculate the percentage ("X%") given by the following formula—

$$\frac{RIPI}{TI} \times 100$$

where—

"RIPI" is so much of the total gross income of the trade for the accounting period as is relevant IP income (see sections [357BH to 357BHC]), and

"TI" is the total gross income of the trade for the accounting period.

Step 3

Calculate X% of the profits of the trade for the accounting period. If there are no such profits, calculate X% of the losses of the trade (expressed as a negative figure) for the accounting period.

In calculating the profits of the trade for the purposes of this step, make any adjustments required by section 357CG (and references in this step to the profits or losses of the trade are to be read subject to any such adjustments).

Step 4

Deduct from the amount given by Step 3 the routine return figure [in relation to the trade for the accounting period] (see section 357CI).

The amount given by this step is the "qualifying residual profit".

If the amount of the qualifying residual profit is not greater than nil, go to Step 7.

Step 5

If the company has [made an election under section 357CL] for small claims treatment, calculate the small claims amount in relation to the trade (see section 357CM).

If the company has not, go to Step 6.

Step 6

Deduct from the qualifying residual profit the marketing assets return figure [in relation to the trade for the accounting period] (see section 357CN).

Step 7

If the company has made an election under section 357CQ (which provides in certain circumstances for profits arising before the grant of a right to be treated as relevant IP profits), add to the amount given by Step 5 or 6 (or, if the amount of the qualifying residual profit was not greater than nil, Step 4) any amount determined in accordance with subsection (3) of that section.

(2) If the amount given by subsection (1) is greater than nil, that amount is the relevant IP profits of the trade for the accounting period.

(3) If the amount given by subsection (1) is less than nil, that amount is the relevant IP losses of the trade for the accounting period (see Chapter 5).]

NOTES

Inserted, together with preceding headings, as noted to s 357A at **[1.155]**.

Chapter heading: words ": Cases Mentioned in Section 357A(7): No Income from New IP" in square brackets inserted by the Finance Act 2016, s 64(6), (7), Sch 9, paras 1, 3, with effect in relation to accounting periods beginning on or after 1 July 2016.

Sub-s (A1): inserted by the Finance Act 2016, s 64(6), (7), Sch 9, paras 1, 4(1), (2), with effect in relation to accounting periods beginning on or after 1 July 2016.

Sub-s (1): words omitted repealed, words in square brackets in Steps 2, 5 substituted and words in square brackets in Steps 4, 6 inserted, by the Finance Act 2016, s 64(6), (7), Sch 9, paras 1, 4(1), (3).

[Total gross income of trade

[1.194]

357CA Total gross income of a trade

(1) For the purposes of this Part the "total gross income" of a trade of a company for an accounting period is the aggregate of the amounts falling within the Heads set out in—

(a) subsection (3) (revenue),

(b) subsection (5) (compensation),

(c) subsection (6) (adjustments),

(d) subsection (7) (proceeds from intangible fixed assets),

(e) subsection (8) (profits from patent rights).

(2) But the total gross income of the trade does not include any finance income (see [section 357BG]).

(3) Head 1 is any amounts which—

(a) in accordance with generally accepted accounting practice ("GAAP") are recognised as revenue in the company's profit and loss account or income statement for the accounting period, and

(b) are brought into account as credits in calculating the profits of the trade for the accounting period.

(4) Where the company does not draw up accounts for an accounting period in accordance with GAAP, the reference in subsection (3)(a) to any amounts which in accordance with GAAP are recognised as revenue in the company's profit and loss account or income statement for the accounting period is to be read as a reference to any amounts which would be so recognised if the company had drawn up such accounts for that accounting period.

(5) Head 2 is any amounts of damages, proceeds of insurance or other compensation (so far as not falling within Head 1) which are brought into account as credits in calculating the profits of the trade for the accounting period.

(6) Head 3 is any amounts (so far as not falling within Head 1) which are brought into account as receipts under section 181 of CTA 2009 (adjustment on change of basis) in calculating the profits of the trade for the accounting period.

(7) Head 4 is any amounts (so far as not falling within Head 1) which are brought into account as credits under Chapter 4 of Part 8 of CTA 2009 (realisation of intangible fixed assets) in calculating the profits of the trade for the accounting period.

(8) Head 5 is any profits from the sale by the company of the whole or part of any patent rights held for the purposes of the trade which are taxed under section 912 of CTA 2009 in the accounting period.]

NOTES

Inserted, together with preceding heading, as noted to s 357A at **[1.155]**.

Sub-s (2): words in square brackets substituted by the Finance Act 2016, s 64(6), (7), Sch 9, paras 1, 5, with effect in relation to accounting periods beginning on or after 1 July 2016.

357CB–357CF (*Inserted as noted to s 357A at* **[1.155]**; *Repealed by the Finance Act 2016, s 64(6), (7), Sch 9, paras 1, 6, with effect in relation to accounting periods beginning on or after 1 July 2016.*)

[Calculating profits of trade

[1.195]

357CG Adjustments in calculating profits of trade

(1) This section applies for the purposes of determining [under section 357C] the relevant IP profits of a trade of a company for an accounting period.

(2) In calculating the profits of the trade for the accounting period—

(a) there are to be added the amounts in subsection (3), and

(b) there are to be deducted the amounts in subsection (4).

(3) The amounts to be added are—

(a) the amount of any debits which are treated as expenses of the trade by virtue of—

(i) section 297 of CTA 2009 (debits in respect of loan relationships), or

(ii) section 573 of CTA 2009 (debits in respect of derivative contracts), . . .

(b) the amount of any additional deduction for the accounting period obtained by the company under Part 13 of CTA 2009 for expenditure on research and development in relation to the trade.

[(c) the amount of any additional deduction for the accounting period obtained by the company under Part 15A of CTA 2009 in respect of qualifying expenditure on a television programme, . . .

(d) the amount of any additional deduction for the accounting period obtained by the company under Part 15B of CTA 2009 in respect of qualifying expenditure on a video game][, and

(e) the amount of any additional deduction for the accounting period obtained by the company under Part 15C of CTA 2009 in respect of qualifying expenditure on a theatrical production].

(4) The amounts to be deducted are[—

(a) the amount of any R&D expenditure credits (within the meaning of Chapter 6A of Part 3 of CTA 2009) brought into account in calculating the profits of the trade for the accounting period, and

(b)] any amounts of finance income brought into account in calculating the profits of the trade for the accounting period.

(For the meaning of "finance income", see [section 357BG].)

(5) In a case where there is a shortfall in R&D expenditure in relation to the trade for a relevant accounting period (see section 357CH), the amount of R&D expenditure brought into account in calculating the profits of the trade for that accounting period is to be increased by the amount mentioned in section 357CH(2).

[(5A) In a case where—

(a) the company is—

(i) a television production company in relation to a television programme, or

(ii) a video games development company in relation to a video game, and

(b) there is a shortfall in qualifying expenditure in relation to the separate programme trade or (as the case may be) the separate video game trade for a relevant accounting period (see section 357CHA), the amount of qualifying expenditure brought into account in calculating the profits of the trade for that accounting period is to be increased by the amount mentioned in section 357CHA(2).]

(6) For the purposes of [subsections (5) and (5A)]—

"R&D expenditure" means expenditure on research and development in relation to the trade,

"relevant accounting period", in relation to a company, means—

(a) the first accounting period for which—

(i) the company is a qualifying company, and

(ii) an election under [section 357A(1)] has effect in relation to it, and

(b) each accounting period that begins before the end of the period of 4 years beginning with that accounting period, . . .

"research and development" means activities, other than oil and gas exploration and appraisal, that fall to be treated as research and development in accordance with generally accepted accounting practice.

["the separate programme trade", in relation to a television production company, has the same meaning as in Chapter 2 of Part 15A of CTA 2009 (see section 1216B),]

["the separate video game trade", in relation to a video games development company, has the same meaning as in Chapter 2 of Part 15B of CTA 2009 (see section 1217B),]

["television production company" has the same meaning as in Part 15A of CTA 2009 (see section 1216AE), . . .]

["theatrical production" has the same meaning as in Part 15C of CTA 2009 (see section 1217FA of that Act), and]

["video games development company" has the same meaning as in Part 15B of CTA 2009 (see section 1217AB)].]

NOTES

Inserted, together with preceding heading, as noted to s 357A at **[1.155]**.

Sub-s (1): words in square brackets inserted by the Finance Act 2016, s 64(6), (7), Sch 9, paras 1, 7(1), (2), with effect in relation to accounting periods beginning on or after 1 July 2016.

Sub-s (3): word omitted from para (a) repealed and paras (c), (d) inserted, by the Finance Act 2013, s 36(3), Sch 18, paras 17, 18(1), (2); word omitted from para (c) repealed and para (e) inserted together with word preceding it, by the Finance Act 2014, s 36, Sch 4, Pt 2, para 15(1), (2), in relation to accounting periods beginning on or after 1 September 2014.

Sub-s (4): words in first pair of square brackets inserted by the Finance Act 2013, s 35, Sch 15, Pt 2, paras 9, 10, in relation to expenditure incurred on or after 1 April 2013; words in second pair of square brackets substituted by the Finance Act 2016, s 64(6), (7), Sch 9, paras 1, 7(1), (3), with effect in relation to accounting periods beginning on or after 1 July 2016.

Sub-s (5A): inserted by the Finance Act 2013, s 36(3), Sch 18, paras 17, 18(1), (3).

Sub-s (6) is amended as follows:

words in first pair of square brackets substituted by the Finance Act 2013, s 36(3), Sch 18, paras 17, 18(1), (4)(a);

definition "qualifying expenditure" inserted by the Finance Act 2013, s 36(3), Sch 18, paras 17, 18(1), (4)(b), and in that definition word omitted from para (a) repealed and para (c) and word ", and" immediately preceding it inserted by the Finance Act 2014, s 36, Sch 4, Pt 2, para 15(1), (3)(a), with effect in relation to accounting periods beginning on or after 1 September 2014;

in definition "relevant accounting period" in para (a)(ii) words in square brackets substituted by the Finance Act 2016, s 64(6), (7), Sch 9, paras 1, 7(1), (4), with effect in relation to accounting periods beginning on or after 1 July 2016; word omitted from para (b) repealed by the Finance Act 2013, s 36(3), Sch 18, paras 17, 18(1), (4)(c);

definitions "the separate programme trade", "the separate video game trade", "television production company", "video games development company" inserted by the Finance Act 2013, s 36(3), Sch 18, paras 17, 18(1), (4)(d);

in definition "television production company" word omitted repealed by the Finance Act 2014, s 36, Sch 4, Pt 2, para 15(1), (3)(b), with effect in relation to accounting periods beginning on or after 1 September 2014;

definition "theatrical production" inserted by the Finance Act 2014, s 36, Sch 4, Pt 2, para 15(1), (3)(b), with effect in relation to accounting periods beginning on or after 1 September 2014.

[1.196]
[357CH Shortfall in R&D expenditure

(1) There is a shortfall in R&D expenditure in relation to a trade of a company for a relevant accounting period if the actual R&D expenditure of the trade for the accounting period (as adjusted under subsections (8) to (11)) is less than 75% of the average amount of R&D expenditure.

(2) The amount that is to be added to the actual R&D expenditure for the purposes of section 357CG(5) is an amount equal to the difference between—

(a) 75% of the average amount of R&D expenditure, and

(b) the actual R&D expenditure, as adjusted under subsections (8) to (11).

(3) In this section—

(a) the "actual R&D expenditure" of a trade of a company for an accounting period is the amount of R&D expenditure that (ignoring section 357CG(5)) is brought into account in calculating the profits of the trade for the accounting period, and

(b) "R&D expenditure" and "relevant accounting period" have the meaning given by section 357CG(6).

(4) The average amount of R&D expenditure is—

$$\frac{E}{N} \times 365$$

where—

E is the amount of R&D expenditure that—

(a) has been incurred by the company during the relevant period, and

(b) has been brought into account in calculating the profits of the trade for any accounting period ending before the first relevant accounting period, and

N is the number of days in the relevant period.

(5) The relevant period is the shorter of—

(a) the period of 4 years ending immediately before the first relevant accounting period, and

(b) the period beginning with the day on which the company begins to carry on the trade and ending immediately before the first relevant accounting period.

(6) For a relevant accounting period of less than 12 months, the average amount of R&D expenditure is proportionately reduced.

(7) Subsections (8) to (11) apply for the purposes of determining—

(a) whether there is a shortfall in R&D expenditure for a relevant accounting period, and

(b) if there is such a shortfall, the amount to be added by virtue of subsection (2).

(8) If the amount of the actual R&D expenditure for a relevant accounting period is greater than the average amount of R&D expenditure, the difference between the two amounts is to be added to the actual R&D expenditure for the next relevant accounting period.

(9) If—

(a) there is not a shortfall in R&D expenditure for a relevant accounting period, but

(b) in the absence of any additional amount, there would be a shortfall in R&D expenditure for that accounting period,

the remaining portion of the additional amount is to be added to the actual R&D expenditure for the next relevant accounting period.

(10) For the purposes of this section—

"additional amount", in relation to a relevant accounting period, means any amount added to the actual R&D expenditure for that accounting period by virtue of subsection (8), (9) or (11), and

"the remaining portion" of an additional amount is so much of that amount as exceeds the difference between—

(a) the actual R&D expenditure for the relevant accounting period in the absence of the additional amount, and

(b) 75% of the average amount of R&D expenditure.

(11) If—

(a) there is not a shortfall in R&D expenditure for a relevant accounting period, and

(b) there would not be a shortfall in R&D expenditure for that accounting period in the absence of any additional amount,

the additional amount is to be added to the actual R&D expenditure for the next relevant accounting period (in addition to any additional amount so added by virtue of subsection (8)).]

NOTES

Inserted as noted to s 357A at **[1.155]**.

[1.197]

[357CHA Shortfall in qualifying expenditure

(1) There is a shortfall in qualifying expenditure in relation to the separate programme trade of a television production company or (as the case may be) the separate video game trade of a video games development company for a relevant accounting period if the actual qualifying expenditure of the trade for the accounting period (as adjusted under subsections (8) to (11)) is less than 75% of the average amount of qualifying expenditure.

(2) The amount that is to be added to the actual qualifying expenditure for the purposes of section 357CG(5A) is an amount equal to the difference between—

(a) 75% of the average amount of qualifying expenditure, and

(b) the actual qualifying expenditure, as adjusted under subsections (8) to (11).

(3) In this section—

(a) the "actual qualifying expenditure" of a trade of a company for an accounting period is the amount of qualifying expenditure that (ignoring section 357CG(5A)) is brought into account in calculating the profits of the trade for the accounting period, and

(b) the following terms have the meaning given by section 357CG(6)—

"qualifying expenditure",

"relevant accounting period",

"the separate programme trade",

"the separate video game trade",

"television production company",

"video games development company".

(4) The average amount of qualifying expenditure is—

(E / N) × 365 where—

E is the amount of qualifying expenditure that—

(a) has been incurred by the company during the relevant period, and

(b) has been brought into account in calculating the profits of the trade for any accounting period ending before the first relevant accounting period, and

N is the number of days in the relevant period.

(5) The relevant period is the shorter of—

(a) the period of 4 years ending immediately before the first relevant accounting period, and

(b) the period beginning with the day on which the company begins to carry on the trade and ending immediately before the first relevant accounting period.

(6) For a relevant accounting period of less than 12 months, the average amount of qualifying expenditure is proportionately reduced.

(7) Subsections (8) to (11) apply for the purposes of determining—

(a) whether there is a shortfall in qualifying expenditure for a relevant accounting period, and

(b) if there is such a shortfall, the amount to be added by virtue of subsection (2).

(8) If the amount of the actual qualifying expenditure for a relevant accounting period is greater than the average amount of qualifying expenditure, the difference between the two amounts is to be added to the actual qualifying expenditure for the next relevant accounting period.

(9) If—

(a) there is not a shortfall in qualifying expenditure for a relevant accounting period, but

(b) in the absence of any additional amount, there would be a shortfall in qualifying expenditure for that accounting period,

the remaining portion of the additional amount is to be added to the actual qualifying expenditure for the next relevant accounting period.

(10) For the purposes of this section—

"additional amount", in relation to a relevant accounting period, means any amount added to the actual qualifying expenditure for that accounting period by virtue of subsection (8), (9) or (11), and

"the remaining portion" of an additional amount is so much of that amount as exceeds the difference between—

(a) the actual qualifying expenditure for the relevant accounting period in the absence of the additional amount, and

(b) 75% of the average amount of qualifying expenditure.

(11) If—

(a) there is not a shortfall in qualifying expenditure for a relevant accounting period, and

(b) there would not be a shortfall in qualifying expenditure for that accounting period in the absence of any additional amount,

the additional amount is to be added to the actual qualifying expenditure for the next relevant accounting period (in addition to any additional amount so added by virtue of subsection (8)).]

NOTES

Commencement: 19 July 2013 (for the purposes of television tax relief); 1 April 2014 (for the purposes of video games development tax relief).

Inserted by the Finance Act 2013, s 36(3), Sch 18, paras 17, 19.

[Routine return figure

[1.198]

357CI Routine return figure

(1) To determine the routine return figure in relation to a trade of a company for an accounting period—

Step 1

Take the aggregate of any routine deductions made by the company in calculating the profits of the trade for the accounting period.

For the meaning of "routine deductions", see [sections 357BJA and 357BJB].

Step 2

Multiply that amount by 0.1.

Step 3

Calculate X% of the amount given by Step 2.

"X%" is the percentage given by Step 2 in section 357C(1).

(2) In a case where—

(a) the company ("C") is a member of a group,

(b) another member of the group incurs expenses on behalf of C,

(c) had they been incurred by C, C would have made a deduction in respect of the expenses in calculating the profits of the trade for the accounting period, and

(d) the deduction would have been a routine deduction,

C is to be treated for the purposes of subsection (1) as having made such a routine deduction.

(3) Where expenses are incurred by any member of the group on behalf of C and any other member of the group, subsection (2) applies in relation to so much of the amount of the expenses as on a just and reasonable apportionment may properly be regarded as incurred on behalf of C.]

NOTES

Inserted, together with preceding heading, as noted to s 357A at **[1.155]**.

Sub-s (1): words in square brackets substituted by the Finance Act 2016, s 64(6), (7), Sch 9, paras 1, 8, with effect in relation to accounting periods beginning on or after 1 July 2016.

357CJ, 357CK (*Inserted as noted to s 357A at* **[1.155]**; *repealed by the Finance Act 2016, s 64(6), (7), Sch 9, paras 1, 9, with effect in relation to accounting periods beginning on or after 1 July 2016.*)

[Election for small claims treatment

[1.199]

357CL Companies eligible to elect for small claims treatment

(1) A company may [make an election under this section] for small claims treatment for an accounting period if condition A or B is met in relation to the accounting period.

(2) Condition A is that the aggregate of the amounts of qualifying residual profit of each trade of the company for the accounting period does not exceed £1,000,000.

(3) Condition B is that—

- (a) the aggregate of the amounts of qualifying residual profit of each trade of the company for the accounting period does not exceed the relevant maximum, and
- (b) the company did not take Step 6 in section 357C(1) or 357DA(1) for the purpose of calculating the relevant IP profits of any trade of the company for any previous accounting period beginning within the relevant 4-year period.

(4) In subsection (3)(b) "the relevant 4-year period" means the period of 4 years ending immediately before the accounting period mentioned in subsection (3)(a).

(5) If [no other company is a related 51% group company of the company] in the accounting period, the relevant maximum is £3,000,000.

(6) If [one or more other companies are related 51% group companies of the company,] in the accounting period, the relevant maximum is—

$$\frac{£3,000,000}{1+N}$$

where N is the number of [those related 51% group] companies in relation to which an election under [section 357A(1)] has effect for the accounting period.

(7) For an accounting period of less than 12 months, the relevant maximum is proportionately reduced.

(8) Any amount of qualifying residual profit of a trade of the company that is not greater than nil is to be disregarded for the purposes of this section.

(9) . . .]

NOTES

Inserted, together with preceding heading, as noted to s 357A at **[1.155]**.

Sub-s (1): words in square brackets substituted by the Finance Act 2016, s 64(6), (7), Sch 9, paras 1, 10(1), (2), with effect in relation to accounting periods beginning on or after 1 July 2016.

Sub-s (5): words in square brackets substituted by the Finance Act 2014, s 7, Sch 1, Pt 2, para 13(1), (2)(a), in relation to accounting periods beginning on or after 1 April 2015.

Sub-s (6): words in first and second pairs of square brackets substituted by the Finance Act 2014, s 7, Sch 1, Pt 2, para 13(1), (2)(b), in relation to accounting periods beginning on or after 1 April 2015; words in third pair of square brackets substituted by the Finance Act 2016, s 64(6), (7), Sch 9, paras 1, 10(1), (3), with effect in relation to accounting periods beginning on or after 1 July 2016.

Sub-s (9): repealed by the Finance Act 2014, s 7, Sch 1, Pt 2, para 13(1), (2)(c), in relation to accounting periods beginning on or after 1 April 2015.

[1.200]

[357CM Small claims amount

(1) This section applies where a company [makes an election under section 357CL] for small claims treatment for an accounting period.

(2) The small claims amount in relation to each trade of the company for the accounting period is—

- (a) if the amount in subsection (3) is lower than the small claims threshold, 75% of the qualifying residual profit of the trade for the accounting period;
- (b) in any other case, the amount given by—

$$\frac{SCT}{T}$$

where—

SCT is the small claims threshold, and

T is the number of trades of the company.

(3) The amount referred to in subsection (2)(a) is—

$$0.75 \times QRP$$

where QRP is the aggregate of the amounts of qualifying residual profit of each trade of the company for the accounting period (but see subsection (4)).
(4) Any amount of qualifying residual profit of a trade of the company that is not greater than nil is to be disregarded for the purposes of subsection (3).
(5) If [no other company is a related 51% group company of the company] in the accounting period, the small claims threshold is £1,000,000.
(6) If [one or more other companies are related 51% group companies of the company,] in the accounting period, the small claims threshold is—

$$\frac{£1,000,000}{1+N}$$

where N is the number of [those related 51% group] companies in relation to which an election under section 357A has effect for the accounting period.
(7) For an accounting period of less than 12 months, the small claims threshold is proportionately reduced.
(8) . . .]

NOTES

Inserted as noted to s 357A at **[1.155]**.

Sub-s (1): words in square brackets substituted by the Finance Act 2016, s 64(6), (7), Sch 9, paras 1, 11, with effect in relation to accounting periods beginning on or after 1 July 2016.

Sub-s (5): words in square brackets substituted by the Finance Act 2014, s 7, Sch 1, Pt 2, para 13(1), (3)(a), in relation to accounting periods beginning on or after 1 April 2015.

Sub-s (6): words in square brackets substituted by the Finance Act 2014, s 7, Sch 1, Pt 2, para 13(1), (3)(b), in relation to accounting periods beginning on or after 1 April 2015.

Sub-s (8): repealed by the Finance Act 2014, s 7, Sch 1, Pt 2, para 13(1), (3)(c), in relation to accounting periods beginning on or after 1 April 2015.

[Marketing assets return figure

[1.201]
357CN Marketing assets return figure
(1) The marketing assets return figure in relation to a trade of a company for an accounting period is—

$$NMR - AMR$$

where—
NMR is the notional marketing royalty in respect of the trade for the accounting period (see section 357CO), and
AMR is the actual marketing royalty in respect of the trade for the accounting period (see section 357CP).
(2) Where—
(a) AMR is greater than NMR, or
(b) the difference between NMR and AMR is less than 10% of the qualifying residual profit of the trade for the accounting period,
the marketing assets return figure is nil.]

NOTES

Inserted, together with preceding heading, as noted to s 357A at **[1.155]**.

[1.202]
[357CO Notional marketing royalty
(1) The notional marketing royalty in respect of a trade of a company for an accounting period is the appropriate percentage of the relevant IP income for that accounting period.
In this section "relevant IP income", in relation to a trade of a company for an accounting period, means so much of the total gross income of the trade for the accounting period as is relevant IP income.
(2) The "appropriate percentage" is the proportion of any relevant IP income for an accounting period which the company would pay another person ("P") for the right to exploit the relevant marketing assets in that accounting period if the company were not otherwise able to exploit them.
(3) For the purposes of this section a marketing asset is a "relevant marketing asset" in relation to an accounting period if the relevant IP income of the trade of the company for the accounting period includes any income arising from things done by the company that involve the exploitation by the company of that marketing asset.
(4) For the purposes of determining the appropriate percentage under this section, assume that—

(a) the company and P are dealing at arm's length,
(b) the company, or the company and persons authorised by it, will have the right to exploit the relevant marketing assets to the exclusion of any other person (including P),
(c) the company will have the same rights in relation to the relevant marketing assets as it actually has,
(d) the right to exploit the relevant marketing assets is conferred on the relevant day,
(e) the appropriate percentage for the accounting period is determined at the beginning of the accounting period,
(f) the appropriate percentage for the accounting period will apply for each succeeding accounting period for which the company will have the right to exploit the relevant marketing assets, and
(g) no income other than relevant IP income will arise from anything done by the company that involves the exploitation by the company of the relevant marketing assets.

(5) In subsection (4)(d) "the relevant day", in relation to a relevant marketing asset, means—
(a) the first day of the accounting period, or
(b) if later, the day on which the company first acquired the relevant marketing asset or the right to exploit the asset.

(6) In determining the appropriate percentage, the company must act in accordance with—
(a) Article 9 of the OECD Model Tax Convention, and
(b) the OECD transfer pricing guidelines.

(7) In this section "marketing asset" means any of the following (whether or not capable of being transferred or assigned)—
(a) anything in respect of which proceedings for passing off could be brought, including a registered trade mark (within the meaning of the Trade Marks Act 1994),
(b) anything that corresponds to a marketing asset within paragraph (a) and is recognised under the law of a country or territory outside the United Kingdom,
(c) any signs or indications (so far as not falling within paragraph (a) or (b)) which may serve, in trade, to designate the geographical origin of goods or services, and
(d) any information which relates to customers or potential customers of the company, or any other member of a group of which the company is a member, and is intended to be used for marketing purposes.]

NOTES

Inserted as noted to s 357A at **[1.155]**.

[1.203]
[357CP Actual marketing royalty

(1) The actual marketing royalty in respect of a trade of a company for an accounting period is X% of the aggregate of any sums which—
(a) were paid by the company for the purposes of acquiring any relevant marketing assets, or the right to exploit any such assets, and
(b) were brought into account as debits in calculating the profits of the trade for the accounting period.

(2) In this section—
"relevant marketing assets" has the same meaning as in section 357CO, and
"X%" is the percentage given by Step 2 in section 357C(1).]

NOTES

Inserted as noted to s 357A at **[1.155]**.

[Profits arising before grant of right

[1.204]
357CQ Profits arising before grant of right

[(1) This section applies where a company—
(a) holds a right mentioned in paragraph (a), (b) or (c) of section 357BB(1) (rights to which this Part applies) or an exclusive licence in respect of such a right, or
(b) would hold such a right or licence but for the fact that the company disposed of any rights in the invention or (as the case may be) the licence before the right was granted.

(2) The company may elect that, for the purposes of determining the relevant IP profits of a trade of the company for the accounting period in which the right is granted, there is to be added the amount determined in accordance with subsection (3) (the "additional amount").

(3) The additional amount is the difference between—
(a) the aggregate of the relevant IP profits of the trade for each relevant accounting period, and
(b) the aggregate of what the relevant IP profits of the trade for each relevant accounting period would have been if the right had been granted on the relevant day.

(4) For the purposes of determining the additional amount, the amount of any relevant IP profits to which section 357A does not apply by virtue of Chapter 5 (relevant IP losses) is to be disregarded.

(5) In this section "relevant accounting period" means—

(a) the accounting period of the company in which the right is granted, and
(b) any earlier accounting period of the company which meets the conditions in subsection (6).

(6) The conditions mentioned in subsection (5)(b) are—
(a) that it is an accounting period for which an election made by the company under section 357A has effect,
(b) that it is an accounting period for which the company is a qualifying company, and
(c) that it ends on or after the relevant day.

(7) In this section "the relevant day" is the later of—
(a) the first day of the period of 6 years ending with the day on which the right is granted, or
(b) the day on which—
(i) the application for the grant of the right was filed, or
(ii) in the case of a company that holds an exclusive licence in respect of the right, the licence was granted.

(8) Where the company would be a qualifying company for an accounting period but for the fact that the right had not been granted at any time during that accounting period, the company is to be treated for the purposes of this section as if it were a qualifying company for that accounting period.

(9) Where the company would be a qualifying company for the accounting period in which the right was granted but for the fact that the company disposed of the rights or licence mentioned in subsection (1)(b) before the right was granted, the company is to be treated for the purposes of section 357A as if it were a qualifying company for that accounting period.]

NOTES

Inserted, together with preceding heading, as noted to s 357A at **[1.155]**.

[CHAPTER 4
STREAMING

[1.205]
357D Alternative method of calculating relevant IP profits: "streaming"

(1) A company may elect to apply section 357DA (instead of section 357C) for the purposes of determining the relevant IP profits of any trade of the company for an accounting period [in a case where—
(a) the accounting period began before 1 July 2021,
(b) the company is not a new entrant (see section 357A(11)), and
(c) none of the amounts of relevant IP income brought into account as credits in calculating the profits of the trade for the accounting period is properly attributable to a new qualifying IP right (see section 357BP)].

(2) An election made under subsection (1) is known as a "streaming election".

(3) A streaming election has effect—
(a) for the accounting period for which it is made, and
(b) for each subsequent accounting period.

This is subject to section 357DB.

[(4) A company must apply section 357DA (instead of section 357C) for the purposes of determining the relevant IP profits of a trade of the company for an accounting period in a case mentioned in subsection (1) if any of the mandatory streaming conditions in section 357DC is met in relation to the trade for the period.]]

NOTES

Inserted, together with preceding heading, as noted to s 357A at **[1.155]**.

Sub-s (1): words in square brackets inserted by the Finance Act 2016, s 64(6), (7), Sch 9, paras 1, 12(1), (2), with effect in relation to accounting periods beginning on or after 1 July 2016.

Sub-s (4): substituted by the Finance Act 2016, s 64(6), (7), Sch 9, paras 1, 12(1), (3), with effect in relation to accounting periods beginning on or after 1 July 2016.

[1.206]
[357DA Relevant IP profits

(1) To determine the relevant IP profits of a trade of a company for an accounting period in accordance with this section—

Step 1

Take any amounts which are brought into account as credits in calculating the profits of the trade for the accounting period, other than any amounts of finance income (see [section 357BG]), and divide them into two "streams", amounts of relevant IP income (see [sections 357BH to 357BHC]) and amounts that are not amounts of relevant IP income.

The stream consisting of relevant IP income is "the relevant IP income stream".

Step 2

Take any amounts which are brought into account as debits in calculating the profits of the trade for the accounting period, other than any amounts referred to in section 357CG(3), and allocate them on a just and reasonable basis between the two streams.

(See also section 357CG(5).)

Step 3

Deduct from the relevant IP income stream the amounts allocated to that stream under Step 2.

Step 4

Deduct from the amount given by Step 3 the routine return figure [in relation to the trade for the accounting period] (see subsection (4)).

The amount given by this step is the "qualifying residual profit".

If the amount of the qualifying residual profit is not greater than nil, go to Step 7.

Step 5

If the company has [made an election under section 357CL] for small claims treatment, calculate the small claims amount in relation to the trade (see section 357CM).

If the company has not, go to Step 6.

Step 6

Deduct from the qualifying residual profit the marketing assets return figure [in relation to the trade for the accounting period] (see section 357CN and subsection (6)).

Step 7

If the company has made an election under section 357CQ (which provides in certain circumstances for profits arising before the grant of a right to be treated as relevant IP profits), add to the amount given by Step 5 or 6 (or, if the amount of the qualifying residual profit was not greater than nil, Step 4) any amount determined in accordance with subsection (3) of that section.

(2) If the amount given by subsection (1) is greater than nil, that amount is the relevant IP profits of the trade for the accounting period.

(3) If the amount given by subsection (1) is less than nil, that amount is the relevant IP losses of the trade for the accounting period (see Chapter 5).

(4) The routine return figure, in relation to a trade of a company for an accounting period, is 10% of the aggregate of any routine deductions which—

- (a) have been made by the company in calculating the profits of the trade for the accounting period, and
- (b) have been allocated to the relevant IP income stream under Step 2.

In this subsection "routine deductions" is to be read in accordance with [sections 357BJA and 357BJB].

(5) Subsections (2) and (3) of section 357CI have effect for the purposes of subsection (4) of this section as they have effect for the purposes of that section.

(6) For the purposes of determining the marketing assets return figure in Step 6, section 357CP (actual marketing royalty) has effect as if the reference to X% of the aggregate of any sums falling within subsection (1) of that section were a reference to the aggregate of any such sums which have been allocated to the relevant IP income stream under Step 2.]

NOTES

Inserted as noted to s 357A at **[1.155]**.

Sub-s (1): words in square brackets substituted or inserted by the Finance Act 2016, s 64(6), (7), Sch 9, paras 1, 13(1), (2), with effect in relation to accounting periods beginning on or after 1 July 2016.

Sub-s (4): words in square brackets substituted by the Finance Act 2016, s 64(6), Sch 9, paras 1, 13(1), (3), with effect in relation to accounting periods beginning on or after 1 July 2016.

[1.207]

[357DB Method of allocation

(1) In this section "method of allocation" means the method of allocating, for the purposes of Step 2 in section 357DA(1), the amounts mentioned in that step.

(2) A company that applies section 357DA for the purposes of determining the relevant IP profits of a trade of the company for an accounting period must use the same method of allocation in relation to the trade for that accounting period as it used in the last accounting period of the company for which it applied that section for the purposes of determining the relevant IP profits of the trade.

(3) But subsection (2) does not apply if there is a change of circumstances relating to the trade which makes the use of that method of allocation in relation to the trade for the accounting period inappropriate.

(4) In such a case, the company may—

- (a) use a different method of allocation in relation to the trade for the accounting period (and subsection (2) applies accordingly for subsequent accounting periods), or
- (b) elect not to apply section 357DA for the purposes of determining the relevant IP profits of the trade for the accounting period.

(5) Subsection (4)(b) does not prevent the company making a fresh streaming election in relation to the trade for any subsequent accounting period.]

NOTES

Inserted as noted to s 357A at **[1.155]**.

[1.208]

[357DC The mandatory streaming conditions

(1) Mandatory streaming condition A is met in relation to a trade of a company for an accounting period if—

(a) any amount brought into account as a credit in calculating the profits of the trade for the accounting period is not fully recognised as revenue for the accounting period, and

(b) the amount, or the aggregate of any such amounts, is substantial.

(2) An amount is a "substantial" amount for the purposes of this section if it is greater than—

(a) £2,000,000, or

(b) 20% of the total gross income of the trade for the accounting period,

whichever is the lower.

(3) But an amount is not a substantial amount for the purposes of this section if it does not exceed £50,000.

(4) The reference in subsection (1)(a) to an amount brought into account as a credit includes a reference to any amount brought into account by virtue of section 147 of TIOPA 2010 (basic transfer-pricing rule).

(5) Mandatory streaming condition B is met in relation to a trade of a company for an accounting period if the total gross income of the trade for the accounting period includes—

(a) relevant IP income, and

(b) a substantial amount of licensing income that is not relevant IP income.

(6) In subsection (5) "licensing income" means income consisting of any licence fee, royalty or other payment which the company has received under an agreement granting another person any right in respect of any intellectual property held by the company.

"Intellectual property" has the meaning given by section 712(3) of CTA 2009.

(7) Mandatory streaming condition C is met in relation to a trade of a company for an accounting period if the total gross income of the trade for the accounting period includes—

(a) income that is not relevant IP income, and

(b) a substantial amount of relevant Head 2 income.

(8) Income is "relevant Head 2 income" for the purposes of subsection (7) if—

(a) it is relevant IP income received under an agreement falling within subsection (6) of [section 357BH], and

(b) every qualifying IP right—

(i) in respect of which a right within paragraph (a) of that subsection is granted by the agreement, or

(ii) which is granted in respect of an invention in respect of which a right within paragraph (b) of that subsection is granted by the agreement,

is a right in respect of which the company holds an exclusive licence.

(9) In a case where—

(a) relevant IP income is received under an agreement falling within [section 357BH(6)], but

(b) the condition in paragraph (b) of subsection (8) above is not met,

so much of the relevant IP income as on a just and reasonable apportionment is attributable to any qualifying IP right falling within that paragraph is relevant Head 2 income for the purposes of subsection (7).]

NOTES

Inserted as noted to s 357A at **[1.155]**.

Sub-ss (8), (9): words in square brackets substituted by the Finance Act 2016, s 64(6), (7), Sch 9, paras 1, 14, with effect in relation to accounting periods beginning on or after 1 July 2016.

[CHAPTER 5
RELEVANT IP LOSSES

[1.209]

357E Company with relevant IP losses: set-off amount

Where a company would be entitled to make a deduction under section 357A(2) in calculating the profits of a trade of the company for an accounting period but for the fact that there are relevant IP losses of the trade for the accounting period, there is a "set-off amount" in relation to the trade of the company for the accounting period which is equal to the amount of the relevant IP losses.]

NOTES

Inserted, together with preceding heading, as noted to s 357A at **[1.155]**.

[1.210]

[357EA Effect of set-off amount on company with more than one trade

(1) This section applies where—

(a) there is a set-off amount in relation to a trade of a company for an accounting period, and

(b) the company carries on any other trade.

(2) The set-off amount is to be reduced (but not to below nil) by any relevant IP profits of that other trade for the accounting period.

(3) Section 357A does not apply in relation to so much of the amount of relevant IP profits of that other trade for the accounting period as is equal to the amount by which the set-off amount is reduced under subsection (2).]

NOTES

Inserted as noted to s 357A at **[1.155]**.

[1.211]

[357EB Allocation of set-off amount within a group

(1) This section applies where—

(a) there is a set-off amount in relation to a trade of a company for an accounting period,

(b) the company is a member of a group, and

(c) the set-off amount has not been reduced to nil by the operation of section 357EA(2).

(2) The set-off amount (or so much of it as remains after the operation of section 357EA(2)) is to be reduced (but not to below nil) by any relevant IP profits of a trade of a relevant group member for the relevant accounting period.

(3) For the purposes of this section—

(a) "relevant group member" means another member of the group that has made an election under [section 357A(1)] and is a qualifying company for the relevant accounting period, and

(b) "relevant accounting period", in relation to a company, means the accounting period of the company in or at the end of which the accounting period mentioned in subsection (1)(a) ends.

(4) Section 357A does not apply in relation to so much of the amount of relevant IP profits of the trade of the relevant group member for the relevant accounting period as is equal to the amount by which the set-off amount (or so much of it as remains after the operation of section 357EA(2)) is reduced under subsection (2).

(5) Where there is more than one relevant group member, the relevant group members may jointly determine the order in which subsection (2) is to apply to them.

(6) If no determination is made under subsection (5), subsection (2) is to apply first to the trade that has the greatest amount of relevant IP profits of any trade of any of the relevant group members for a relevant accounting period, then to the trade that has the second greatest amount of relevant IP profits of any of those trades for such a period, and so on.]

NOTES

Inserted as noted to s 357A at **[1.155]**.

Sub-s (3): in para (a) words in square brackets substituted by the Finance Act 2016, s 64(6), (7), Sch 9, paras 1, 15, with effect in relation to accounting periods beginning on or after 1 July 2016.

[1.212]

[357EC Carry-forward of set-off amount

(1) This section applies where—

(a) there is a set-off amount in relation to a trade of a company for an accounting period, and

(b) the set-off amount has not been reduced to nil by the operation of section 357EA(2) or 357EB(2).

(2) The set-off amount (or so much of it as remains after the operation of section 357EA(2) or 357EB(2)) is to be reduced (but not to below nil) by the amount of any relevant IP profits of the trade of the company for the current accounting period.

The "current accounting period" is the accounting period immediately following the accounting period mentioned in subsection (1)(a).

(3) Section 357A does not apply in relation to so much of the amount of relevant IP profits of the trade of the company for the current accounting period as is equal to the amount by which the set-off amount (or so much of it as remains after the operation of section 357EA(2) or 357EB(2)) is reduced under subsection (2).

(4) If any portion of the set-off amount remains after the operation of subsection (2), that portion ("the remaining portion") is to be treated as the set-off amount in relation to the trade of the company for the current accounting period (and the provisions of this Chapter apply accordingly).

(5) If there are relevant IP losses of the trade of the company for the current accounting period, the set-off amount in relation to the trade of the company for that accounting period is the aggregate of the remaining portion and an amount equal to the amount of those relevant IP losses (and the provisions of this Chapter apply accordingly).]

NOTES

Inserted as noted to s 357A at **[1.155]**.

[1.213]

[357ED Company ceasing to carry on trade, etc

(1) This section applies where—

(a) there is a set-off amount in relation to a trade of a company for an accounting period, and

(b) at any time in the accounting period immediately following that accounting period, the company meets any of the conditions in subsection (2).

(2) The conditions are—

(a) that the company ceases to carry on the trade,

(b) that the company ceases to be within the charge to corporation tax in respect of the trade, or

(c) that any election made by the company under [section 357A(1)] ceases to have effect.

(3) Sections 357EA to 357EC continue to have effect in relation to the set-off amount subject to the following provisions of this section.

(4) Section 357EB has effect as if—

(a) the reference in subsection (1)(b) to the company being a member of a group were a reference to the company having been a member of the group at the time referred to in subsection (1)(b) of this section,

(b) for subsection (2) there were substituted—

"(2) The set-off amount (or so much of it as remains after the operation of section 357EA(2)) is to become, or be added to, the set-off amount in relation to a trade of a relevant group member for the relevant accounting period.",

(c) subsection (4) were omitted,

(d) for the words after "determine" in subsection (5) there were substituted "the relevant group member to which subsection (2) is to apply", and

(e) for subsection (6) there were substituted—

"(6) If no determination is made under subsection (5), subsection (2) is to apply to the trade that has the greatest amount of relevant IP profits of any trade of any of the relevant group members for a relevant accounting period.

(7) If there is no relevant group member with any relevant IP profits of a trade for the relevant accounting period, subsection (2) is to apply to the trade that has the greatest set-off amount in relation to any trade of any of the relevant group members for a relevant accounting period."

(5) Sections 357EA to 357EC cease to have effect in relation to the set-off amount in relation to the trade of the company for an accounting period if—

(a) the company is not carrying on any other trade in that accounting period, and

(b) in the case of a company that was a member of a group at the time referred to in subsection (1)(b) of this section, none of the members of the group is a relevant group member (within the meaning of section 357EB).

(6) In such a case, the set-off amount (so far as remaining after the operation of those sections) is to be reduced to nil.]

NOTES

Inserted as noted to s 357A at **[1.155]**.

Sub-s (2): in para (c) words in square brackets substituted by the Finance Act 2016, s 64(6), (7), Sch 9, paras 1, 16, with effect in relation to accounting periods beginning on or after 1 July 2016.

[1.214]

[357EE Transfer of a trade between group members

(1) This section applies where—

(a) there is a set-off amount in relation to a trade of a company for an accounting period,

(b) the company is a member of a group,

(c) the company ceases to carry on the trade, and

(d) another company ("the transferee") that is a member of the group begins to carry on that trade.

(2) For the purposes of this Chapter an amount equal to the set-off amount is to become, or be added to, the set-off amount in relation to the trade of the transferee for the accounting period in which the transferee begins to carry on the trade.]

NOTES

Inserted as noted to s 357A at **[1.155]**.

[1.215]

[357EF Payments between group members in consequence of section 357EB

(1) This section applies if—

(a) there is a set-off amount in relation to a trade of a company for an accounting period,

(b) subsection (2) of section 357EB has effect in relation to a relevant group member for the relevant accounting period (within the meaning of that section),

(c) the company and the relevant group member have an agreement between them in relation to the relevant IP losses of the company, and

(d) as a result of the agreement the company makes a payment to the relevant group member that does not exceed the reduction in the relevant IP profits of the relevant group member arising under section 357EB(4).

(2) The payment—

(a) is not to be taken into account in determining the profits or losses of either company for corporation tax purposes, and

(b) is not for any purposes of the Corporation Tax Acts to be regarded as a distribution.

(3) In a case where section 357ED applies (company ceasing to carry on trade, etc), the reference in subsection (1)(d) to the reduction in the relevant IP profits of the relevant group member is to be read as a reference to the amount that becomes, or is added to, the set-off amount in relation to a trade of the relevant group member for the relevant accounting period under section 357EB(2).]

NOTES

Inserted as noted to s 357A at **[1.155]**.

[CHAPTER 6
ANTI-AVOIDANCE

Licences conferring exclusive rights

[1.216]

357F Licences conferring exclusive rights

A licence that confers any right in respect of a qualifying IP right to the exclusion of all other persons is not to be regarded as an exclusive licence if the main purpose, or one of the main purposes, of conferring the right is to secure that the licence is an exclusive licence for the purposes of this Part.]

NOTES

Inserted, together with preceding headings, as noted to s 357A at **[1.155]**.

[Incorporation of qualifying items

[1.217]

357FA Incorporation of qualifying items

(1) Income arising from the sale of any item that incorporates a qualifying item is not relevant IP income if the main purpose, or one of the main purposes, of incorporating the qualifying item is to secure that income arising from any such sale is relevant IP income.

(2) "Qualifying item" has the same meaning as in section [357BH(2)].]

NOTES

Inserted, together with preceding heading, as noted to s 357A at **[1.155]**.

Sub-s (2): reference in square brackets substituted by the Finance Act 2016, s 64(6), (7), Sch 9, paras 1, 17, with effect in relation to accounting periods beginning on or after 1 July 2016.

[Tax advantage schemes

[1.218]

357FB Tax advantage schemes

(1) This section applies where—

(a) a company is entitled to make a deduction under section 357A(2) in calculating the profits of a trade of the company for an accounting period,

(b) the company is or has at any time been a party to a scheme, and

(c) the main purpose, or one of the main purposes, of the company or, where the company is a member of a group, any member of the group in being a party to the scheme is (or was) to obtain the chance of securing a relevant tax advantage.

(2) There is a "relevant tax advantage" for the purposes of this section if—

(a) (apart from this section) there would be an increase in the amount of any deduction made under section 357A(2) in calculating the profits of a trade of the company or (as the case may be) any other member of the group for any accounting period, and

(b) the increase would arise from—

(i) the avoidance of the operation of any provision of this Part,

(ii) artificially inflating the amount of relevant IP income brought into account in calculating those profits (see subsection (3)), . . .

(iii) a mismatch between relevant IP income and expenditure (see subsection (4))[, or

(iv) an R&D fraction (see subsection (4A)) being greater than it would be but for the scheme].

(3) The reference in subsection (2)(b) to artificially inflating the amount of relevant IP income brought into account in calculating the profits mentioned in subsection (2)(a) is a reference to doing any of the following—

(a) bringing into account in calculating those profits an amount of relevant IP income that wholly or substantially corresponds to an increase in the amounts brought into account as debits in calculating those profits;

(b) bringing into account in calculating those profits an additional amount of relevant IP income that wholly or substantially corresponds to a decrease in the amount of income that is not relevant IP income which is brought into account in calculating those profits.

(4) For the purposes of this section there is a mismatch between relevant IP income and expenditure if—

(a) any relevant IP income brought into account in calculating the profits mentioned in subsection (2)(a) is attributable to any qualifying IP right or an exclusive licence in respect of any such right, and

(b) any expenditure incurred in relation to that right is brought into account in calculating the profits of a trade of the company or (as the case may be) any other member of the group for an accounting period for which an election under [section 357A(1)] did not have effect.

[(4A) The reference in subsection (2)(b)(iv) to an R&D fraction is a reference to such a fraction as is mentioned at Step 6 of section 357BF(2).]

(5) The amount of the deduction which may be made by the company for the accounting period mentioned in subsection (1)(a) is the amount that would secure that no relevant tax advantage arises (and may be nil).

(6) In this section "scheme" includes any scheme, arrangements or understanding of any kind whatever, whether or not legally enforceable, involving a single transaction or two or more transactions.]

NOTES

Inserted, together with preceding heading, as noted to s 357A at **[1.155]**.

Sub-s (2): word omitted from para (b)(ii) repealed para (b)(iv) and word ", or" immediately preceding it inserted, by the Finance Act 2016, s 64(1), (4)(a), (7), with effect in relation to accounting periods beginning on or after 1 July 2016.

Sub-s (4): in para (b) words in square brackets substituted by the Finance Act 2016, s 64(6), (7), Sch 9, paras 1, 18, with effect in relation to accounting periods beginning on or after 1 July 2016.

Sub-s (4A): inserted by the Finance Act 2016, s 64(1), (4)(b), (7), with effect in relation to accounting periods beginning on or after 1 July 2016.

[CHAPTER 7
SUPPLEMENTARY

Elections under section 357A

[1.219]

357G Making of election under [section 357A(1) or (11)(b)]

(1) An election made by a company under [section 357A(1) or (11)(b)] is made by giving notice to an officer of Revenue and Customs.

(2) The notice must specify the first accounting period of the company for which the election is to have effect.

(3) The notice must be given on or before the last day on which an amendment of the company's tax return for that accounting period could be made under paragraph 15 of Schedule 18 to FA 1998.

(4) The election has effect in relation to each trade carried on by the company.

(5) Subject to section 357GA, the election has effect for the accounting period specified in the notice and all subsequent accounting periods of the company.]

NOTES

Inserted, together with preceding headings, as noted to s 357A at **[1.155]**.

Section heading: words in square brackets substituted by the Finance Act 2016, s 64(6), (7), Sch 9, paras 1, 19(1), (2), with effect in relation to accounting periods beginning on or after 1 July 2016.

Sub-s (1): words in square brackets substituted by the Finance Act 2016, s 64(6), (7), Sch 9, paras 1, 19(1), (3), with effect in relation to accounting periods beginning on or after 1 July 2016.

[1.220]

[357GA Revocation of election made under [section 357A(1)]

(1) A company may revoke an election made by it under [section 357A(1)] by giving notice to an officer of Revenue and Customs.

(2) The notice must specify the first accounting period of the company for which the revocation is to have effect.

(3) The notice must be given on or before the last day on which an amendment of the company's tax return for that accounting period could be made under paragraph 15 of Schedule 18 to FA 1998.

(4) The revocation has effect in relation to the accounting period specified in the notice and all subsequent accounting periods of the company.

(5) An election made under [section 357A(1)]by a company that has given notice under this section does not have effect in relation to any accounting period of the company that begins before the end of the period of 5 years beginning with the day after the last day of the accounting period specified in the notice.]

NOTES

Inserted as noted to s 357A at **[1.155]**.

Section heading: words in square brackets substituted by the Finance Act 2016, s 64(6), (7), Sch 9, paras 1, 20(1), (2), with effect in relation to accounting periods beginning on or after 1 July 2016.

Sub-ss (1), (5): words in square brackets substituted by the Finance Act 2016, s 64(6), (7), Sch 9, paras 1, 20(1), (3), (4), with effect in relation to accounting periods beginning on or after 1 July 2016.

[Partnerships

[1.221]

357GB Application of this Part in relation to partnerships

(1) This section applies if a firm (within the meaning of CTA 2009) carries on a trade and any partner in the firm is a company within the charge to corporation tax.

Such a partner is referred to in this section as a "corporate partner".

(2) Subject to the following provisions of this section, this Part applies in relation to the firm as it applies in relation to a company.

(3) Any election under this Part—

(a) may be made or revoked not by the firm but instead by any one or more of the corporate partners (whether jointly or otherwise), and

(b) has effect in relation to each corporate partner making or revoking it as if made or revoked by the firm.

(4) Accordingly, any reference in section 357G(3) or 357GA(3) (time limit for making or revoking elections under section 357A) to the company making or revoking the election is to be read as a reference to the corporate partner so doing.

(5) Section 1261 of CTA 2009 (accounting periods of firms) applies for the purposes of this Part as it applies for the purposes of Part 17 of that Act.

(6) Section 357B (meaning of "qualifying company") has effect as if in subsection (1) the words "in the case of a company that is a member of a group" were omitted.

(7) For the purposes of this Part the firm meets the development condition in relation to a right to which this Part applies if—

(a) the firm has at any time carried out qualifying development in relation to the right, or

(b) there is a relevant corporate partner in the firm who meets the development condition in relation to the right.

(8) A "relevant corporate partner" is a corporate partner who is entitled to a share of at least 40% of the profits or losses of the firm for any accounting period of the firm.

(9) Section 357BD applies for the purposes of subsection (7)(a) of this section as it applies for the purposes of section 357BC.

(10) Section 357BE (active ownership condition) has effect as if the reference in subsection (4) to section 357BC(2) or (3) included a reference to subsection (7)(a) of this section.

(11) Sections [357BK, 357BKA,] 357CL and 357CM (election for small claims treatment) have effect as if—

(a) any reference to a company having one or more associated companies were a reference to any corporate partner in relation to which an election under section [357BK or] 357CL has effect having one or more associated companies, and

(b) any reference to a company having no associated company were a reference to each such corporate partner having no associated company.

(12) Subsection (13) applies where a corporate partner is a party to an arrangement at any time during an accounting period of the firm which produces for the corporate partner a return within [section 357BG(1)(c)].

(13) For the accounting period of the firm the corporate partner's share of a profit or loss of a trade carried on by the firm is determined for corporation tax purposes as if no election under section 357A had effect in relation to the trade.]

NOTES

Inserted, together with preceding heading, as noted to s 357A at **[1.155]**.

Sub-s (11): words in square brackets inserted by the Finance Act 2016, s 64(6), (7), Sch 9, paras 1, 21(1), (2), with effect in relation to accounting periods beginning on or after 1 July 2016.

Sub-s (12): words in square brackets substituted by the Finance Act 2016, s 64(6), (7), Sch 9, paras 1, 21(1), (3), with effect in relation to accounting periods beginning on or after 1 July 2016.

[Cost-sharing arrangements

[1.222]

357GC Application of this Part in relation to cost-sharing arrangements

[(1) This section applies where a company is a party to an arrangement under which—

(a) one of the parties to the arrangement holds a qualifying IP right or an exclusive licence in respect of such a right,

(b) each of the parties to the arrangement is required to contribute to the cost of, or perform activities for the purpose of, creating or developing the invention or any item or process incorporating the invention,

(c) under the arrangement each of those parties—

(i) is entitled to a share of any income attributable to the right or licence, or

(ii) has one or more rights in respect of the invention, and

(d) the amount of any income received by each of those parties is proportionate to its particIPation in the arrangement as described in paragraph (b).

(2) The company is to be treated for the purposes of this Part as if it held the qualifying IP right or (as the case may be) the exclusive licence in respect of the qualifying IP right.

(3) But this section does not apply where the arrangement produces for the company a return within [section 357BG(1)(c)].

(4) The reference in subsection (1)(b) to developing the invention includes developing ways in which the invention may be used or applied.]

NOTES

Inserted, together with preceding heading, as noted to s 357A at **[1.155]**.

Sub-s (3): words in square brackets substituted by the Finance Act 2016, s 64(6), (7), Sch 9, paras 1, 22, with effect in relation to accounting periods beginning on or after 1 July 2016.

[Transferred trades

[1.223]

357GCA Application of this Part in relation to transferred trades

(1) Where—

(a) a company ("the transferor") ceases to carry on a trade which involves the exploitation of a qualifying IP right ("the relevant qualifying IP right"),

(b) the transferor assigns the relevant qualifying IP right, or grants or transfers an exclusive licence in respect of it, to another company ("the transferee"), and

(c) the transferee begins to carry on the trade,

the following provisions apply in determining under this Part the relevant IP profits of the trade carried on by the transferee.

(2) The transferee is to be treated as not being a new entrant if—

(a) an election under section 357A(1) has effect in relation to the transferor on the date of the assignment, grant or transfer mentioned in subsection (1)(b) ("the transfer date"), and

(b) the first accounting period of the transferor for which that election had effect began before 1 July 2016.

(3) The relevant qualifying IP right is to be treated as being an old qualifying IP right in relation to the transferee if by reason of section 357BP it is an old qualifying IP right in relation to the transferor.

(4) Expenditure incurred prior to the transfer date by the transferor which is attributable to relevant research and development undertaken by the transferor is to be treated for the purposes of section 357BLB as if it is expenditure incurred by the transferee which is attributable to relevant research and development undertaken by the transferee.

(5) Expenditure incurred prior to the transfer date by the transferor in making a payment to a person in respect of relevant research and development contracted out by the transferor to that person is to be treated for the purposes of sections 357BLC and 357BLD as if it is expenditure incurred by the transferee in making a payment to that person in respect of relevant research and development contracted out by the transferee to that person.

(6) Expenditure incurred prior to the transfer date by the transferor in making a payment in connection with the relevant qualifying IP right which is within subsection (2), (3) or (4) of section 357BLE is to be treated for the purposes of that section as if it is expenditure incurred by the transferee in making a payment in connection with that right which is within one of those subsections.

(7) Expenditure incurred by the transferee in making a payment to the transferor in respect of the assignment, grant or transfer mentioned in subsection (1)(b) is to be ignored for the purposes of section 357BLE.

(8) In this section—

"trade" includes part of a trade, and

"relevant research and development" means research and development which relates to the relevant qualifying IP right.

(9) For the purposes of this section research and development "relates" to the relevant qualifying IP right if—

(a) it creates, or contributes to the creation of the invention,

(b) it is undertaken for the purpose of developing the invention,

(c) it is undertaken for the purpose of developing ways in which the invention may be used or applied, or

(d) it is undertaken for the purpose of developing any item or process incorporating the invention.]

NOTES

Inserted by the Finance Act 2016, s 64(1), (5), (7), with effect in relation to accounting periods beginning on or after 1 July 2016.

[Interpretation

[1.224]
357GD Meaning of "group"

(1) For the purposes of this Part a company ("company A") is a member of a group at any time if any other company is at that time associated with company A.
(2) The group consists of company A and each company in relation to which the condition in subsection (1) is met.
(3) For the purposes of this section a company ("company B") is associated with company A at a time ("the relevant time") if any of the following five conditions is met.
(4) The first condition is that the financial results of company A and company B, for a period that includes the relevant time, meet the consolidation condition.
(5) The second condition is that there is a connection between company A and company B for the accounting period of company A in which the relevant time falls.
(6) The third condition is that, at the relevant time, company A has a major interest in company B or company B has a major interest in company A.
(7) The fourth condition is that—
 (a) the financial results of company A and a third company, for a period that includes the relevant time, meet the consolidation condition, and
 (b) at the relevant time the third company has a major interest in company B.
(8) The fifth condition is that—
 (a) there is a connection between company A and a third company for the accounting period of company A in which the relevant time falls, and
 (b) at the relevant time the third company has a major interest in company B.
(9) In this section, the financial results of any two companies for any period meet "the consolidation condition" if—
 (a) they are required to be fully comprised in group accounts,
 (b) they would be required to be fully comprised in such accounts but for the application of an exemption, or
 (c) they are in fact fully comprised in such accounts.
(10) In subsection (9) "group accounts" means accounts prepared under—
 (a) section 399 of the Companies Act 2006, or
 (b) any corresponding provision of the law of a country or territory outside the United Kingdom.
(11) The following provisions apply for the purposes of this section—
 sections 466 to 471 of CTA 2009 (companies connected for accounting period), and
 sections 473 and 474 of CTA 2009 (meaning of "major interest").]

NOTES

Inserted, together with preceding heading, as noted to s 357A at **[1.155]**.

[1.225]
[357GE Other interpretation

(1) In this Part—
 "invention", in relation to a right to which this Part applies, means the item or process in respect of which the right is granted,
 "item" includes any substance,
 "the OECD Model Tax Convention" means—
  (a) the version of the Model Tax Convention on Income and on Capital published in July 2010 by the Organisation for Economic Co-operation and Development ("the OECD"), or
  (b) such other document approved and published by the OECD in place of that (or a later) version or in place of that Convention as is designated for the time being by order made by the Treasury,
 "the OECD transfer pricing guidelines" [has the same meaning as "the transfer pricing guidelines" in section 164 of TIOPA 2010],
 including, in either case, such material published by the OECD as part of (or by way of update or supplement to) the version or other document concerned as may be so designated, and
 ["payment" includes payment in money's worth.]
 . . .

[(1A) In Chapters 3 and 4 of this Part "qualifying residual profit" of a trade, in relation to any accounting period, is the amount obtained by the application of Steps 1 to 4 in section 357C or (as the case may be) section 357DA in relation to the trade for the accounting period.]
(2) Any reference in this Part to calculating the profits of a trade of a company for an accounting period is a reference to calculating those profits for corporation tax purposes (and any reference to the profits or losses of a trade of a company for an accounting period is to be read accordingly).]

NOTES

Inserted as noted to s 357A at **[1.155]**.

Sub-s (1): in definition "the OECD transfer pricing guidelines" words in square brackets substituted by the Finance Act 2016, s 75(2), (4), in relation to accounting periods beginning on or after 1 April 2016; definition "payment" inserted and definition "qualifying residual profit" (omitted) repealed, by the Finance Act 2016, s 64(6), (7), Sch 9, paras 1, 23(1), (2), with effect in relation to accounting periods beginning on or after 1 July 2016.

Sub-s (1A): inserted by the Finance Act 2016, s 64(6), (7), Sch 9, paras 1, 23(1), (3), with effect in relation to accounting periods beginning on or after 1 July 2016.

358–1117 *((Pts 9–21, 21A–21C, 22, 23) Outside the scope of this work.)*

PART 24
CORPORATION TAX ACTS DEFINITIONS ETC

CHAPTER 1
DEFINITIONS

[1.226]

1118 Introduction to Chapter

(1) This Chapter contains definitions for the purposes of the Corporation Tax Acts.

(2) Section 1119 lists the definitions and either sets them out in full or indicates where they are set out in full.

(3) The definitions set out in sections 1120, 1129, 1138 and 1139 apply only for the purposes of the provisions of the Corporation Tax Acts that apply them.

(4) The definitions set out in sections 1122 and 1124 apply only for the purposes of provisions of the Corporation Tax Acts—

(a) which apply them, or

(b) to which they are applied (see section 1316 of CTA 2009 and section 1176 of this Act).

(5) The other definitions apply for the purposes of the Corporation Tax Acts unless otherwise indicated (whether expressly or by implication).

[1.227]

1119 The definitions

The definitions referred to in section 1118(2) are—

"accounting date" means the date to which a company makes up its accounts,

"accounting period" is to be read in accordance with Chapter 2 of Part 2 of CTA 2009,

"Act" includes Northern Ireland legislation,

"allowable loss", in relation to corporation tax in respect of chargeable gains, has the same meaning as in TCGA 1992 (see section 288(1) of that Act),

"authorised unit trust" has the same meaning as in Chapter 2 of Part 13 (see sections 616 and 619),

"bank" is to be read in accordance with section 1120,

"basic rate" means the rate of income tax determined in pursuance of section 6(2) of ITA 2007,

"body of persons" means any body politic, corporate or collegiate and any company, fraternity, fellowship and society of persons whether corporate or not corporate,

"branch or agency" means any factorship, agency, receivership, branch or management,

"building society" means a building society within the meaning of the Building Societies Act 1986,

"capital allowance" means any allowance under CAA 2001,

"the Capital Allowances Act" means CAA 2001,

"the charge to corporation tax on income" has the same meaning as in CTA 2009 (see section 2(3) of that Act),

"chargeable gain" has the same meaning as in TCGA 1992,

"chargeable period" means an accounting period of a company or a tax year,

"chargeable profits", in relation to a non-UK resident company carrying on a trade in the United Kingdom through a permanent establishment, has the meaning given by section 19 of CTA 2009,

. . .

"close company" is to be read in accordance with Chapter 2 of Part 10 (see in particular section 439),

"company" has the meaning given by section 1121,

"connected", in relation to two persons being connected with one another, is to be read in accordance with sections 1122 and 1123,

"control", in relation to the control of a body corporate or a partnership, is to be read in accordance with section 1124,

"derivative contract" has the same meaning as in Part 7 of CTA 2009,

"distribution" has the meaning given by Chapters 2 to 5 of Part 23,

"farming" has the meaning given by section 1125,

"the financial year 2010" means the financial year beginning with April 2010 (and any corresponding expression in which a year is similarly mentioned is to be read in the same way),

"for accounting purposes" has the meaning given by section 1127(4),

"forestry" is to be read in accordance with section 1125,
"franked investment income" has the meaning given by section 1126,
"generally accepted accounting practice" has the meaning given by section 1127(1) and (3),
"grossing up" is to be read in accordance with section 1128,
"group relief" has the meaning given by section 97(2),
"hire-purchase agreement" is to be read in accordance with section 1129,
"income" includes anything to which the charge to corporation tax on income applies,
"international accounting standards" has the meaning given by section 1127(5),
"investment trust" has the meaning given by section 1158,
"loan relationship" has the same meaning as in Part 5 of CTA 2009,
"local authority" has the meaning given by section 1130,
"local authority association" has the meaning given by section 1131,
["main ring fence profits rate" has the meaning given by section 279A(4),]
"market gardening" has the meaning given by section 1125(5),
"non-UK resident" means not resident in the United Kingdom (and references to a non-UK resident are to a person not resident there),
"notice" means notice in writing,
"offshore installation" has the meaning given by sections 1132 and 1133,
"oil and gas exploration and appraisal" has the meaning given by section 1134,
"ordinary share capital", in relation to a company, means all the company's issued share capital (however described), other than capital the holders of which have a right to a dividend at a fixed rate but have no other right to share in the company's profits,
"overseas property business" has the meaning given by Chapter 2 of Part 4 of CTA 2009,
"period of account"—
- (a) in relation to a person, means any period for which the person draws up accounts, and
- (b) in relation to a trade or other business, means any period for which the accounts of the business are drawn up,

"permanent establishment", in relation to a company, is to be read in accordance with Chapter 2 of this Part,
"personal representatives", in relation to a person who has died, means—
- (a) in the United Kingdom, persons responsible for administering the estate of the deceased, and
- (b) in a territory outside the United Kingdom, those persons having functions under its law equivalent to those of administering the estate of the deceased,

"property investment LLP" has the meaning given by section 1135,
"qualifying charitable donation" has the same meaning as in Part 6 (see section 190),
"qualifying distribution" has the meaning given by section 1136,
"recognised stock exchange" has the meaning given by section 1137,

"registered pension scheme" has the meaning given by section 150(2) of FA 2004,
["registered society" means—
- (a) a registered society within the meaning of the Co-operative and Community Benefit Societies Act 2014,
- (b) a society registered or treated as registered under the Industrial and Provident Societies Act (Northern Ireland) 1969,
- (c) a society registered as a credit union under the Credit Unions (Northern Ireland) Order 1985 (SI 1985/1205 (NI 12)), or
- (d) an SCE formed in accordance with Council Regulation (EC) No 1435/2003 on the Statute for a European Cooperative Society,]

["related 51% group company" is to be read in accordance with section 279F,]
"research and development" is to be read in accordance with section 1138,
"retail prices index" means—
- (a) the general index of retail prices (for all items) published by the Statistics Board, or
- (b) if that index is not published for a relevant month, any substituted index or index figures published by that Board,

"scheme administrator", in relation to a pension scheme, has the meaning given by section 270 of FA 2004 (but see also sections 271 to 274 of that Act),
"settled property" (together with references to property comprised in a settlement) is to be read in accordance with section 466 of ITA 2007 (as a result of the application of that section for the purposes of the Corporation Tax Acts by section 1169 below),
"settlor" is to be read in accordance with sections 467 to 473 of ITA 2007 (as a result of the application of those sections for the purposes of the Corporation Tax Acts by section 1169 below),
"51% subsidiary", "75% subsidiary" and "90% subsidiary", in relation to bodies corporate, is to be read in accordance with Chapter 3 of this Part,
"tax", if neither income tax nor corporation tax is specified, means either of those taxes,
"tax advantage" has the meaning given by section 1139,
"tax credit" means a tax credit under section 1109,

"tax year" means a year for which income tax is charged (see section 4(2) of ITA 2007),
"the tax year 2010–11" means the tax year beginning on 6 April 2010 (and any corresponding expression in which two years are similarly mentioned is to be read in the same way),
"total profits", in relation to an accounting period of a company, is to be read in accordance with section 4(3) and (4),
"trade" includes any venture in the nature of trade,
["trade of dealing in or developing UK land", in relation to a non-UK resident company, has the meaning given by section 5B of CTA 2009,]
"tribunal" means the First-tier Tribunal or, where determined by or under Tribunal Procedure Rules, the Upper Tribunal,
"UK generally accepted accounting practice" has the meaning given by section 1127(2),
"UK property business" has the meaning given by Chapter 2 of Part 4 of CTA 2009,
"UK resident" means resident in the United Kingdom (and references to a UK resident are to a person resident there),
"unauthorised unit trust" has the meaning given by section 1140,
"unit holder" has the same meaning as in Chapter 2 of Part 13 (see sections 616 and 619),
"unit trust scheme" has the meaning given by section 237 of FISMA 2000,
"venture capital trust" and "VCT" have the same meaning as in Part 6 of ITA 2007,
"woodlands" has the meaning given by section 1125(4),
"year of assessment" means a tax year, and
"the year 2010–11" means the tax year 2010–11 (and any corresponding expression in which two years are similarly mentioned is to be read in the same way).

NOTES

Definition "charity" (omitted) repealed by the Finance Act 2010, s 30, Sch 6, Pt 2, para 27(1), (6).

Definition "main ring fence profits rate" inserted by the Finance Act 2014, s 7, Sch 1, Pt 2, para 16, with effect for the financial year 2015 and subsequent financial years.

Definition "registered industrial and provident society" (omitted) repealed by the Co-operative and Community Benefit Societies Act 2014, s 151(1), Sch 4, Pt 2, paras 155, 168(1), (2).

Definition "registered society" inserted by the Co-operative and Community Benefit Societies Act 2014, s 151(1), Sch 4, Pt 2, paras 155, 168(1), (3) (as amended by the Finance Act 2014, s 298, Sch 39, paras 2, 13).

Definition "related 51% group company" inserted by the Finance Act 2014, s 7, Sch 1, Pt 2, para 16, with effect for the financial year 2015 and subsequent financial years.

Definition "trade of dealing in or developing UK land" inserted by the Finance Act 2016, ss 76(11), 81(1), in relation to disposals on or after 5 July 2016.

1120 (*Outside the scope of this work.*)

[1.228]
1121 "Company"

(1) In the Corporation Tax Acts "company" means any body corporate or unincorporated association, but does not include a partnership, [a co-ownership scheme (as defined by section 235A of the Financial Services and Markets Act 2000),] a local authority or a local authority association.

(2) Subsection (1) needs to be read with section 617 (under which the trustees of an authorised unit trust are treated for certain purposes as a UK resident company).

NOTES

Sub-s (1): words in square brackets inserted by the Collective Investment in Transferable Securities (Contractual Scheme) Regulations 2013, SI 2013/1388, reg 5.

1122–1126 (*Outside the scope of this work.*)

[1.229]
1127 "Generally accepted accounting practice" and related expressions

(1) In the Corporation Tax Acts "generally accepted accounting practice" means UK generally accepted accounting practice.

This is subject to subsection (3).

(2) In the Corporation Tax Acts "UK generally accepted accounting practice"—

(a) means generally accepted accounting practice in relation to accounts of UK companies (other than IAS accounts) that are intended to give a true and fair view, and
(b) has the same meaning in relation to—
 (i) individuals,
 (ii) entities other than companies, and
 (iii) companies that are not UK companies,
 as it has in relation to UK companies.

(3) In relation to the affairs of a company or other entity that prepares IAS accounts, in the Corporation Tax Acts "generally accepted accounting practice" means generally accepted accounting practice in relation to IAS accounts.

(4) In the Corporation Tax Acts "for accounting purposes" means for the purposes of accounts drawn up in accordance with generally accepted accounting practice.

(5) In the Corporation Tax Acts "international accounting standards" has the same meaning as in Regulation (EC) No 1606/2002 of the European Parliament and the Council of 19 July 2002 on the application of international accounting standards.

(6) If the European Commission has in accordance with that Regulation adopted an international accounting standard with modifications, then as regards matters covered by that standard—

(a) generally accepted accounting practice with respect to IAS accounts is to be regarded as permitting the use of the standard either with or without modifications, and

(b) accounts prepared on either basis are to be regarded for the purposes of the Corporation Tax Acts as prepared in accordance with international accounting standards.

(7) In this section—

"IAS accounts" means accounts prepared in accordance with international accounting standards, and

"UK companies" means companies incorporated or formed under the law of a part of the United Kingdom.

1128–1137 (*Outside the scope of this work.*)

[1.230]
1138 "Research and development"

(1) This section has effect for the purposes of the provisions of the Corporation Tax Acts which apply this section.

(2) "Research and development" means activities that fall to be treated as research and development in accordance with generally accepted accounting practice. This is subject to subsections (3) and (4).

(3) Activities that are "research and development" for the purposes of section 1006 of ITA 2007 as a result of regulations under that section are "research and development" for the purposes of this section.

(4) Activities that are not "research and development" for the purposes of section 1006 of ITA 2007 as a result of regulations under that section are not "research and development" for the purposes of this section.

(5) Unless otherwise expressly provided, "research and development" does not include oil and gas exploration and appraisal.

[1.231]
1139 "Tax advantage"

(1) This section has effect for the purposes of the provisions of the Corporation Tax Acts which apply this section.

(2) "Tax advantage" means—

(a) a relief from tax or increased relief from tax,

(b) a repayment of tax or increased repayment of tax,

(c) the avoidance or reduction of a charge to tax or an assessment to tax, . . .

(d) the avoidance of a possible assessment to tax[, . . .

[(da) the avoidance or reduction of a charge or assessment to a charge under Part 9A of TIOPA 2010 (controlled foreign companies), . . .]

(e) the avoidance or reduction of a charge or assessment to the bank levy under Schedule 19 to FA 2011 (the bank levy)][; or

(f) the avoidance or reduction of a charge to diverted profits tax].

(3) For the purposes of subsection (2)(c) and (d) it does not matter whether the avoidance or reduction is effected—

(a) by receipts accruing in such a way that the recipient does not pay or bear tax on them, or

(b) by a deduction in calculating profits or gains.

[(3A) The avoidance or reduction of a charge or assessment to the bank levy as a result of arrangements to which paragraph 47 of Schedule 19 to FA 2011 (bank levy: anti-avoidance) applies is to be ignored for the purposes of subsection (2)(e) to the extent that it results from arrangements, or part of arrangements, to which any of paragraph 47(7) to (12) of that Schedule applies.]

(4) . . .

NOTES

Sub-s (2): word omitted from para (c) repealed and para (e) and word ", or" immediately preceding it inserted, by the Finance Act 2011, s 73, Sch 19, Pt 5, para 48(1), (2); word omitted from para (d) repealed and para (da) inserted, by the Finance Act 2012, s 180, Sch 20, Pt 3, paras 37, 40; word omitted from para (da) repealed and para (f) and word ", or" immediately preceding it inserted, by the Finance Act 2015, s 115(3), with effect in relation to accounting periods beginning on or after 1 April 2015.

Sub-s (3A): inserted by the Finance Act 2011, s 73, Sch 19, Pt 5, para 48(1), (3).

Sub-s (4): repealed by the Finance Act 2016, s 5(11), Sch 1, paras 28, 48, in relation to dividends paid or arising (or treated as paid), and other distributions made (or treated as made), in the tax year 2016-17 or at any later time (see the Finance Act 2016, s 5(11), Sch 1, para 73(1)).

1140–1173 (*Outside the scope of this work.*)

PART 25
DEFINITIONS FOR PURPOSES OF ACT AND FINAL PROVISIONS

Definitions for the purposes of Act

[1.232]
1174 Abbreviated references to Acts

In this Act—

"CAA 2001" means the Capital Allowances Act 2001,
"CTA 2009" means the Corporation Tax Act 2009,
"FA", followed by a year, means the Finance Act of that year,
"F(No 2)A", followed by a year, means the Finance (No 2) Act of that year,
"FISMA 2000" means the Financial Services and Markets Act 2000,
"ICTA" means the Income and Corporation Taxes Act 1988,
"ITA 2007" means the Income Tax Act 2007,
"ITEPA 2003" means the Income Tax (Earnings and Pensions) Act 2003,
"ITTOIA 2005" means the Income Tax (Trading and Other Income) Act 2005,
"TCGA 1992" means the Taxation of Chargeable Gains Act 1992,
"TIOPA 2010" means the Taxation (International and Other Provisions) Act 2010, and
"TMA 1970" means the Taxes Management Act 1970.

1175, 1176 (*Outside the scope of this work.*)

Final provisions

1177–1182 (*Outside the scope of this work.*)

[1.233]
1183 Extent

(1) This Act extends to England and Wales, Scotland and Northern Ireland (but see subsection (2)).

(2) An amendment, repeal or revocation contained in Schedule 1 or 3 has the same extent as the provision amended, repealed or revoked.

[1.234]
1184 Commencement

(1) This Act comes into force on 1 April 2010 and has effect—
- (a) for corporation tax purposes, for accounting periods ending on or after that day, and
- (b) for income tax and capital gains tax purposes, for the tax year 2010–11 and subsequent tax years.

(2) Subsection (1) does not apply to the following provisions (which therefore come into force on the day on which this Act is passed)—
- (a) section 1178,
- (b) section 1179,
- (c) section 1180(2) to (4),
- (d) section 1183,
- (e) this section, and
- (f) section 1185.

(3) Subsection (1) is subject to Schedule 2.

(4) The reference in subsection (1)(a) to corporation tax includes amounts due or chargeable as if they were corporation tax.

[1.235]
1185 Short title

This Act may be cited as the Corporation Tax Act 2010.

SCHEDULES 1–4

(*Outside the scope of this work.*)

CONTRACTING OUT (FUNCTIONS IN RELATION TO APPLICATIONS FOR PATENTS) ORDER 2002

(SI 2002/3052)

NOTES

Made: 11 December 2002.
Authority: Deregulation and Contracting Out Act 1994, ss 69, 77(1)(b), 79(5).
Commencement: 12 December 2002.

ARRANGEMENT OF ARTICLES

SCHEDULES

[1.236]
1 Citation, commencement and extent

(1) This Order may be cited as the Contracting Out (Functions in Relation to Applications for Patents) Order 2002.

(2) This Order shall come into force on the day after the day on which it is made.

(3) This Order extends to England, Wales, Scotland, Northern Ireland and the Isle of Man.

[1.237]
2 Interpretation

In this Order—

(a) "the comptroller" means the Comptroller-General of Patents, Designs and Trade Marks;
(b) "the Patents Act" means the Patents Act 1977; and
(c) "the Patents Rules" means the Patents Rules 1995.

[1.238]
3 Contracting out of functions of the comptroller in relation to applications for patents

Any function of the comptroller which relates to or is connected with applications for patents and which is listed in Schedule 1 to this Order may be exercised by, or by employees of, such person (if any) as may be authorised in that behalf by the comptroller—

(a) either wholly or to such extent as may be specified in the authorisation;
(b) either generally or in such cases or areas as may be so specified; and
(c) either unconditionally or subject to the fulfilment of such conditions as may be so specified.

[1.239]
4 Contracting out of functions of examiners in relation to patent examinations and searches

Any function of an examiner of the Patent Office which relates to or is connected with patent examinations and searches and which is listed in Schedule 2 to this Order may be exercised by, or by employees of, such person (if any) as may be authorised in that behalf by the comptroller—

(a) either wholly or to such extent as may be specified in the authorisation;
(b) either generally or in such cases or areas as may be so specified; and
(c) either unconditionally or subject to the fulfilment of such conditions as may be so specified.

[1.240]
5 Supplementary

Anything which is authorised or required by or under any provision or rule listed in Schedule 2 to this Order to be referred to an examiner of the Patent Office may be referred, wholly or partly, to such person (if any) as may be authorised by virtue of article 4 above.

SCHEDULES

SCHEDULE 1
FUNCTIONS OF THE COMPTROLLER ENABLED TO BE CONTRACTED OUT

Article 3

[1.241]

1. Functions conferred by or under any of the following provisions of the Patents Act:

(a) section 14(7) (consideration and reframing of abstract);
(b) section 19(2) (amendment of an application for a patent before grant);
(c) section 21(1) (consideration of observations by third parties on patentability); and
(d) section 117 (correction of errors) except insofar as it relates to correction of errors in any specification of a patent or any document filed in connection with a patent.

2. Functions conferred by or under any of the following provisions of the Patents Rules:
(a) rule 19(4) (publication of figures characterising the invention);
(b) rule 36(2) and (6) (amendment of application before grant); and
(c) rule 37 (observations on patentability).

SCHEDULE 2
FUNCTIONS OF EXAMINERS OF THE PATENT OFFICE ENABLED TO BE CONTRACTED OUT

Article 4

[1.242]
1. Functions conferred by or under any of the following provisions of the Patents Act:
(a) section 17 (other than subsection (2)) (preliminary examination and search); and
(b) section 18 (substantive examination).

2. Functions conferred by or under rule 37(3) of the Patents Rules (observations on patentability).

PATENTS ACT 2004 (COMMENCEMENT NO 1 AND CONSEQUENTIAL AND TRANSITIONAL PROVISIONS) ORDER 2004

(SI 2004/2177)

NOTES
Made: 20 August 2004.
Authority: Patents Act 2004, s 17(1), (4), (6).
Commencement: 22 September 2004.

[1.243]
1 Citation, commencement and interpretation of this Order
(1) This Order may be cited as the Patents Act 2004 (Commencement No 1 and Consequential and Transitional Provisions) Order 2004, and shall come into force on 22nd September 2004.
(2) In this Order—
"the 1977 Act" means the Patents Act 1977;
"the 2004 Act" means the Patents Act 2004;
"the Rules" means the Patents Rules 1995.

2–5 (*Art 2 provides for the commencement of the Patents Act 2004, Sch 2, paras 24, 26(1), (3), (4) (and s 16(1), (2) of that Act in so far as it relates to the amendments made by those paragraphs) on 22 September 2004; arts 3–5 revoked by the Patents Rules, SI 2007/3291, r 120(2), Sch 6.*)

[1.244]
6 Transitional provisions
(1) This article applies on the coming into force, in accordance with article 2, of the amendments to section 120 of the 1977 Act (and references to section 120 are to that section 120 as so amended).
(2) The comptroller shall be deemed to have given directions under section 120(1) (and to have published them in the prescribed manner) specifying the hours specified in rule 98 of the Rules (immediately before it was revoked by article 5) as the hours at which time the Patent Office is taken to be closed for the purposes of the transaction by the public of the business specified therein.
(3) The comptroller shall be deemed to have given directions under section 120(1) (and to have published them in the prescribed manner) specifying the days specified in rule 99 of the Rules (immediately before it was revoked by article 5) as excluded days for the purposes of the transaction by the public of the business specified therein.

[1.245]
7
(1) This article applies on the coming into force, in accordance with article 2, of the amendments to section 123 of the 1977 Act.
(2) The comptroller shall be deemed to have set out, in directions under section 123(2A) of that Act, those forms set out in Schedule 1 to the Rules (immediately before it was revoked by article 5) as the forms of which the use is required by the Rules (and to have published the directions in the prescribed manner).

[1.246]
8

The directions deemed to have been given, in accordance with article 6 or 7, shall continue in effect until they are revoked by directions given under section 120(1) or 123(2A) of the 1977 Act.

REGULATORY REFORM (PATENTS) ORDER 2004

(SI 2004/2357)

NOTES

Made: 22 September 2004.
Authority: Regulatory Reform Act 2001, s 1.
Commencement: 1 January 2005 (see art 1(2)).

[1.247]
1 Citation, commencement and extent

(1) This Order may be cited as the Regulatory Reform (Patents) Order 2004.

(2) This Order shall come into force on the first day of the fourth month following the month in which it is made.

(3) This Order extends to the United Kingdom and the Isle of Man.

2–19 (*Amend the Patents Act 1977 at* **[1.1]** *et seq; those amendments have been incorporated at the appropriate place in this work.*)

[1.248]
20 Transitional provisions

(1) This article applies to an application for a patent where—
- (a) it was initiated by documents containing the information mentioned in any of paragraphs (a) to (c) of section 15(1) of the Patents Act 1977 (as that section had effect immediately before the coming into force of this Order) being filed at the Patent Office;
- (b) those documents were filed before the coming into force of this Order.

(2) Where this article applies to an application—
- (a) the following provisions have effect in relation to it in the form they had immediately before the coming into force of this Order—sections 5, 14(1)(b), 15, 17, 18, 72, 76, 78 and 130(1) of the Patents Act 1977; and
- (b) the following provisions, which are inserted by this Order, have no effect—sections 14(1A) and 15A of that Act.

[1.249]
21

(1) This article applies to an application for a patent where—
- (a) it is treated as an application for a patent under the Patents Act 1977 by reason of a direction given under section 81(1) of that Act;
- (b) that direction was given before the coming into force of this Order.

(2) Where this article applies to an application—
- (a) the following provisions have effect in relation to it in the form they had immediately before the coming into force of this Order—sections 5, 14(1)(b), 15, 17, 18, 72, 76, 78, 81 and 130(1); and
- (b) the following provisions, which are inserted by this Order, have no effect—sections 14(1A) and 15A of that Act.

[1.250]
22

(1) This article applies to an international application for a patent (UK) which began the national phase before the coming into force of this Order.

(2) Where this article applies to an application—
- (a) the following provisions have effect in relation to it in the form they had immediately before the coming into force of this Order—sections 15, 17, 18 and 89B of the Patents Act 1977; and
- (b) the following provision, which is inserted by this Order, has no effect—section 15A of that Act.

(3) For the purposes of paragraph (1) the national phase shall be treated as beginning at the same time as it does under section 89A(3) of the Patents Act 1977.

(4) In this article—

"international application for a patent" means an application made under the Patent Co-operation Treaty;

"Patent Co-operation Treaty" has the same meaning as in the Patents Act 1977.

[1.251]
23

Regulation 9 shall not apply in respect of any patent which ceased to have effect, by reason of section 25(3) of the Patents Act 1977, before the coming into force of this Order.

PATENTS ACT 2004 (COMMENCEMENT NO 2 AND CONSEQUENTIAL, ETC AND TRANSITIONAL PROVISIONS) ORDER 2004

(SI 2004/3205)

NOTES

Made: 29 November 2004.
Authority: Patents Act 2004, s 17.
Commencement: 1 January 2005.

[1.252]
1 Citation, commencement and interpretation of this Order

(1) This Order may be cited as the Patents Act 2004 (Commencement No 2 and Consequential, etc and Transitional Provisions) Order 2004, and shall come into force on 1st January 2005.

(2) In this Order—
"the 1977 Act" means the Patents Act 1977;
"the 2004 Act" means the Patents Act 2004;
"the appointed day" means the day appointed by article 2;
"the Rules" means the Patents Rules 1995.

[1.253]
2 Commencement of the 2004 Act

1st January 2005 is the day appointed for the coming into force of the following provisions of the 2004 Act—

(a) section 5 (for the purposes of the provisions mentioned in sub-paragraphs (i) and (j) below);
(b) section 6;
(c) section 7;
(d) sections 10 to 12;
(e) section 14;
(f) section 16(1) (for the purposes of the provisions mentioned in sub-paragraph (k) below);
(g) section 16(2) (for the purposes of the entries in Schedule 3 relating to provisions brought into force by this article and to the amendment of section 106 of the 1977 Act);
(h) section 16(3);
(i) paragraphs 1, 6, 7 and 8, and paragraph 9(1), (2)(a) and (3), of Schedule 1;
(j) paragraph 9(2)(b) of Schedule 1 (for the purposes of the Patent Co-operation Treaty);
(k) paragraphs 1, 5, 8, 10 to 14, 16, 17, 19, 20 to 22, 25, 27 and 28 of Schedule 2.

3–8 (*Revoked by the Patents Rules 2007, SI 2007/3291, r 120(2), Sch 6.*)

[1.254]
9 Transitional provisions

(1) The following transitional provisions have effect notwithstanding the amendments to the 1977 Act made by the provisions brought into force by article 2, or the amendments to the Rules made by articles 4 and 5.

(2) . . .

(3) Where proceedings are brought under section 70 of the 1977 Act in respect of an alleged threat made before the appointed day, that section has effect in relation to that alleged threat as if the amendments to that section had not been made.

(4) Where proceedings are brought before the appointed day, section 75(1) of the 1977 Act has effect in relation to those proceedings as if the amendment to that subsection had not been made.

(5) Where the national phase (as defined by section 89A(3) of the 1977 Act) of an international application for a patent (UK) begins before the appointed day, section 89B(2) of that Act has effect in relation to that application as if the amendment to that subsection had not been made.

NOTES

Para (2): revoked by the Patents Rules 2007, SI 2007/3291, r 120(2), Sch 6.

PATENTS ACT 2004 (COMMENCEMENT NO 3 AND TRANSITIONAL PROVISIONS) ORDER 2005

(SI 2005/2471)

NOTES

Made: 5 September 2005.
Authority: Patents Act 2004, s 17.
Commencement: 1 October 2005.

[1.255]

1 Citation, commencement and interpretation of this Order

(1) This Order may be cited as the Patents Act 2004 (Commencement No 3 and Transitional Provisions) Order 2005 and shall come into force on 1st October 2005.

(2) In this Order—

"the 1977 Act" means the Patents Act 1977;

"the 2004 Act" means the Patents Act 2004;

"the appointed day" means the day appointed by article 2.

[1.256]

2 Commencement of the 2004 Act

1st October 2005 is the day appointed for the coming into force of the following provisions of the 2004 Act—

(a) section 8;
(b) section 9;
(c) section 13;
(d) section 15;
(e) section 16(1) (for the purposes of the provisions of Schedule 2 mentioned below);
(f) section 16(2) (for the purpose of the entry in Schedule 3 relating to the repeal made by paragraph 18 of Schedule 2);
(g) paragraphs 6, 9, 15, 18 and 26(2) of Schedule 2.

[1.257]

3 Transitional provisions

(1) Where the prescribed period in respect of a patent expires on or after the appointed day, section 25(3) of the 1977 Act as amended by section 8(1) of the 2004 Act shall have effect in respect of that patent.

(2) Where, in respect of a patent—

(a) the renewal fee is not paid by the end of the prescribed period, and
(b) that period expires before the appointed day, but
(c) the period of six months immediately following the end of the prescribed period does not expire before the appointed day,

the provisions mentioned in paragraph (3) shall have effect in respect of that patent.

(3) Those provisions are—

(a) section 25(4) of the 1977 Act as amended by section 8(2) of the 2004 Act;
(b) section 28(3) of the 1977 Act as amended by section 8(3) of the 2004 Act.

(4) In this article, "prescribed period" means the period prescribed by rule 39 of the Patents Rules 1995 as it stands immediately before the appointed day.

[1.258]

4

Section 15 of the 2004 Act shall apply in respect of proceedings commenced on or after the appointed day.

PATENTS (CONVENTION COUNTRIES) ORDER 2007

(SI 2007/276)

NOTES

Made: 7 February 2007.
Authority: Patents Act 1977, ss 90(1), 124(3).
Commencement: 6 April 2007.

[1.259]
1

(1) This Order may be cited as the Patents (Convention Countries) Order 2007 and shall come into force on 6th April 2007.

(2) The Patents (Convention Countries) Order 2006 is revoked.

[1.260]
2

(1) The countries specified in the Schedule are declared to be convention countries for the purposes of section 5 of the Patents Act 1977.

SCHEDULE
CONVENTION COUNTRIES

Article 2

[1.261]
Albania

Algeria

Andorra

Angola

Antigua and Barbuda

Argentina

Armenia

Australia

Austria

Azerbaijan

Bahamas

Bahrain

Bangladesh

Barbados

Belarus

Belgium

Belize

Benin

Bhutan

Bolivia

Bosnia and Herzegovina

Botswana

Brazil

Brunei Darussalam

Bulgaria

Burkina Faso

Burundi

Cambodia

Cameroon

Canada

[Cape Verde]

Central African Republic

Chad

Chile

China

Columbia

Comoros

Congo

Congo, Democratic Republic of the

Costa Rica

Cote d'Ivoire

Croatia

Cuba

Cyprus

Czech Republic

Denmark

Djibouti

Dominica

Dominican Republic

Ecuador

Egypt

El Salvador

Equatorial Guinea

Estonia

Faeroe Islands

Fiji

Finland

France (including Overseas Departments and Territories)

Gabon

Gambia

Georgia

Germany

Ghana

Greece

Grenada

Guatemala

Guinea

Guinea-Bissau

Guyana

Haiti

Holy See

Honduras

Hong Kong

Hungary

Iceland

India

Indonesia

Iran, Islamic Republic of

Iraq

Ireland

Israel

Italy

Jamaica

Japan

Jordan

Kazakhstan

Kenya

Korea, Democratic People's Republic of

Korea, Republic of

Kuwait

Kyrgyzstan

Lao People's Democratic Republic

Latvia

Lebanon

Lesotho

Liberia

Libyan Arab Jamahiriya

Liechtenstein

Lithuania

Luxembourg

Macao

Macedonia, Former Yugoslav Republic of

Madagascar

Malawi

Malaysia

Maldives

Mali

Malta

Mauritania

Mauritius

Mexico

Moldova, Republic of

Monaco

Mongolia

Montenegro

Morocco

Mozambique

Myanmar

Namibia

Nepal

Netherlands

Netherlands Antilles and Aruba

New Zealand (including the Cook Islands, Niue and Tokelau)

Nicaragua

Niger

Nigeria

Norway

Oman

Pakistan

Panama

Papua New Guinea

Paraguay

Peru

Philippines

Poland

Portugal

Qatar

Romania

Russian Federation

Rwanda

Saint Kitts and Nevis

Saint Lucia

Saint Vincent and the Grenadines

[Samoa]

San Marino

Sao Tome and Principe

Saudi Arabia

Senegal

Serbia

Seychelles

Sierra Leone

Singapore

Slovakia

Slovenia

Solomon Islands

South Africa

Spain

Sri Lanka

Sudan

Suriname

Swaziland

Sweden

Switzerland

Syrian Arab Republic

Taiwan

Tajikistan

Tanzania, United Republic of

Thailand

Togo

Tonga

Trinidad and Tobago

Tunisia

Turkey

Turkmenistan

Uganda

Ukraine

United Arab Emirates

United States of America (including Puerto Rico and all territories and possessions)

Uruguay

Uzbekistan

[Vanuatu]

Venezuela

Viet Nam

Yemen

Zambia

Zimbabwe

NOTES

Entry "Cape Verde" inserted by the Patents (Convention Countries) (Amendment) Order 2009, SI 2009/2746, art 2; entries "Samoa" and "Vanuatu" inserted by the Patents (Convention Countries) (Amendment) Order 2013, SI 2013/538, art 2.

PATENTS RULES 2007

(SI 2007/3291)

NOTES

Made: 19 November 2007.
Authority: Patents Act 1977, ss 14(6), 25(5), 32, 74B, 77(9), 92, 123, 125A and 130(2).
Commencement: 17 December 2007.

ARRANGEMENT OF RULES

PART 1
INTRODUCTORY

PART 2
APPLICATIONS FOR PATENTS

PART 3
GRANTED PATENTS

PART 4
THE REGISTER AND OTHER INFORMATION

The Register

Copies of documents and corrections in relation to the register

Requests for information or documents

PART 5
EUROPEAN PATENTS (UK)

Translations

Conversion requests

Obligations to other contracting parties to the European Patent Convention

PART 6
INTERNATIONAL APPLICATIONS

Interpretation

Filing at the Patent Office

Beginning the national phase, international exhibitions and altered prescribed periods

Translations

Application deemed withdrawn or filing date refused under the Patent Co-operation Treaty

PART 7
PROCEEDINGS HEARD BEFORE THE COMPTROLLER

Introductory

PART 1
INTRODUCTORY

[1.262]
1 Citation and commencement

These Rules may be cited as the Patents Rules 2007 and shall come into force on 17th December 2007.

[1.263]
2 General interpretation

(1) In these Rules—

"the Act" means the Patents Act 1977 and "section", unless the contrary intention appears, means a section of the Act;

"application number" includes file number;

"compliance date" means the last day of the compliance period;

"compliance period" means the period prescribed by rule 30;

"declared priority date" has the meaning given to it by rule 3(1);

"initiation date" means the date on which a new application was initiated by documents, mentioned in section 15(1), being filed at the Patent Office;

"new application" means a new application filed under section 8(3), 12(6) or 37(4) or as mentioned in section 15(9);

"no declared priority date" has the meaning given to it by rule 3(2);

"Patents Form" has the meaning given to it by rule 4(1);

"priority application" means an earlier relevant application specified in a declaration for the purposes of section 5(2);

"sequence" and "sequence listing" have the same meaning as they have under the Patent Co-operation Treaty;

"start date" means, in relation to rules 106(6)(a) and 116 on supplementary protection certificates, the first day following the day on which the basic patent expires; and

"termination" has the meaning given by section 20B(7) and "terminated" shall be construed accordingly.

(2) Where a period of time has been altered under rules 20(4), 71(7), 81 or 107 to 111, any reference in these Rules to the period of time shall be construed as a reference to the period as altered.

(3) For the purposes of these Rules a document is available to the comptroller where—

(a) it is in electronic storage (whether in the Patent Office or elsewhere) and he can access it by using electronic communications; or

(b) it is kept at the Patent Office,

and he has been furnished with sufficient information to obtain a copy of the document.

(4) But a document may be treated as unavailable to the comptroller where—

(a) its accuracy cannot be verified to his satisfaction; or

(b) he has to pay to access it.

[1.264]

3 The declared priority date

(1) For the purposes of these Rules the "declared priority date" is the date of filing of the earliest relevant application specified in a declaration made for the purposes of section 5(2) in, or in connection with, an application in suit.

(2) For the purposes of these Rules there is "no declared priority date" if—

(a) no declaration has been made for the purposes of section 5(2); or

(b) every declaration made has been withdrawn or disregarded before the end of the relevant period.

(3) For the purposes of paragraph (2)(b) the relevant period ends—

(a) in the case of an application which falls to be treated as an application for a patent under the Act by virtue of a direction under section 81, when that direction is given;

(b) in the case of an international application for a patent (UK), when the national phase of the application begins; or

(c) in any other case, when preparations for the application's publication have been completed by the Patent Office.

(4) In this rule references to declarations made for the purposes of section 5(2) include declarations treated as made for those purposes.

[1.265]

4 Forms and documents

(1) The forms of which the use is required by these Rules are those set out in directions under section 123(2A) and are referred to in these Rules as Patents Forms.

(2) Such a requirement to use a form is satisfied by the use of a form which is acceptable to the comptroller and contains the information required by the form as so set out.

(3) Such directions must be published in accordance with rule 117(c).

(4) Unless the comptroller otherwise directs, to file any form or other document under the Act or these Rules only one side of each sheet of paper must be used and the other side must remain blank.

(5) But where the information is delivered in electronic form or using electronic communications—

(a) a requirement under these Rules to use a form; and

(b) the requirements in paragraph (4),

do not apply.

(6) Where any form or other document is delivered to the comptroller in electronic form or using electronic communications, any requirement in these Rules for multiple copies of that form or document to be filed does not apply.

PART 2
APPLICATIONS FOR PATENTS

International exhibitions

[1.266]

5 International exhibitions

(1) The statement mentioned in section 2(4)(c) that an invention has been displayed at an international exhibition must be in writing.

(2) The prescribed period for the purposes of section 2(4)(c) is four months [beginning immediately after] the date of filing.

(3) But paragraphs (1) and (2) do not apply where rule 67(2) applies.

(4) The written evidence required by section 2(4)(c) must be in the form of—

(a) a certificate issued by the authority responsible for the international exhibition; and

(b) a statement, duly authenticated by that authority, identifying the invention as being the invention displayed at the exhibition.

(5) The certificate must include the opening date of the exhibition (or if later, the date on which the invention was first displayed).

(6) The comptroller may publish a statement in the journal that a particular exhibition falls within the definition of "international exhibition" in section 130(1) (interpretation).

NOTES

Para (2): words in square brackets substituted by the Patents (Amendment) Rules 2011, SI 2011/2052, rr 2, 3, Schedule, for transitional provisions see r 4 thereof.

Declarations of priority

[1.267]

6 Declaration of priority for the purposes of section 5(2) (priority date)

(1) Subject to paragraph (2) and rule 7(9), a declaration for the purposes of section 5(2) must be made at the time of filing the application for a patent.

(2) Subject to rule 7(9), a declaration for the purposes of section 5(2) may be made after the date of filing provided that—

(a) it is made on Patents Form 3;
(b) it is made before the end of the period of sixteen months beginning immediately following the date of filing of the earlier relevant application (or if there is more than one, the earliest of them) specified in that, or any earlier, declaration; and
(c) the condition in paragraph (3) is met.

(3) The condition is that—

(a) the applicant has not made a request under section 16(1) for publication of the application during the period prescribed for the purposes of that section; or
(b) any request made was withdrawn before preparations for the application's publication have been completed by the Patent Office.

(4) A declaration for the purposes of section 5(2) must specify—

(a) the date of filing of each earlier relevant application; and
(b) the country it was filed in or in respect of.

(5) In the case of a new application filed as mentioned in section 15(9), no declaration shall be made which has not also been made in, or in connection with, the earlier application.

[1.268]

7 Request to the comptroller for permission to make a late declaration under section 5(2B)

(1) The period prescribed for the purposes of section 5(2A)(b) is two months.

(2) Subject to paragraph (4), a request under section 5(2B) must be—

(a) made on Patents Form 3; and
(b) supported by evidence of why the application in suit was not filed before the end of the period allowed under section 5(2A)(a).

(3) Where that evidence does not accompany the request, the comptroller must specify a period within which the evidence must be filed.

(4) In relation to a new application, a request under section 5(2B) may be made in writing, instead of on Patents Form 3, and no evidence shall accompany it.

(5) Subject to paragraph (6) and rule 66(3), a request under section 5(2B) may only be made before the end of the period allowed under section 5(2A)(b).

(6) Where a new application is filed after the end of the period allowed under section 5(2A)(b), a request under section 5(2B) may be made on the initiation date.

(7) A request under section 5(2B) may only be made where—

(a) the condition in paragraph (8) is met; or
(b) the request is made in relation to an international application for a patent (UK).

(8) The condition is that—

(a) the applicant has not made a request under section 16(1) for publication of the application during the period prescribed for the purposes of that section; or
(b) any request made was withdrawn before preparations for the application's publication have been completed by the Patent Office.

(9) Where an applicant makes a request under section 5(2B), he must make the declaration for the purposes of section 5(2) at the same time as making that request.

[1.269]

8 Filing of priority documents to support a declaration under section 5(2)

(1) In respect of each priority application to which this paragraph applies the applicant must, before the end of the relevant period, furnish to the comptroller the application number of that application; otherwise the comptroller must disregard the declaration made for the purposes of section 5(2), in so far as it relates to the priority application.

(2) In respect of each priority application to which this paragraph applies the applicant must, before the end of the relevant period, furnish to the comptroller a copy of that application—

(a) duly certified by the authority with which it was filed; or
(b) otherwise verified to the satisfaction of the comptroller,

otherwise the comptroller must disregard the declaration made for the purposes of section 5(2), in so far as it relates to the priority application.

(3) Paragraph (1) applies to every priority application except where the application in suit is an international application for a patent (UK) and the application number of the priority application was indicated in compliance with the Patent Co-operation Treaty.

(4) Paragraph (2) applies to every priority application except where—

(a) the application in suit is an international application for a patent (UK) and a certified copy of the priority application was filed in compliance with the Patent Co-operation Treaty; or

(b) the priority application or a copy of the priority application is available to the comptroller.

(5) For the purposes of this rule the relevant period is sixteen months [beginning immediately after] the declared priority date, subject to rule 21.

NOTES

Para (5): words in square brackets substituted by the Patents (Amendment) Rules 2011, SI 2011/2052, rr 2, 3, Schedule, for transitional provisions see r 4 thereof.

[1.270]

9 Translation of priority documents

(1) The comptroller may direct the applicant to comply with the requirements of paragraph (4), if—

(a) a copy of the priority application has been—

(i) furnished in accordance with rule 8(2),

(ii) filed in compliance with the European Patent Convention,

(iii) filed in compliance with the Patent Co-operation Treaty, or

(iv) made by the comptroller in accordance with rule 112(2);

(b) that copy is in a language other than English or Welsh; and

(c) the matters disclosed in the priority application are relevant to the determination of whether or not an invention, to which the application in suit relates, is new or involves an inventive step.

(2) In his direction under paragraph (1), the comptroller shall specify a period within which the applicant must comply with the requirements of paragraph (4).

(3) But the comptroller shall not specify a period that ends after the grant of the patent.

(4) Where the comptroller has given a direction under paragraph (1), the applicant must, before the end of the period specified by the comptroller, file—

(a) an English translation of the priority application; or

(b) a declaration that the application in suit is a complete translation into English of the priority application,

otherwise the comptroller must disregard the declaration made for the purposes of section 5(2), in so far as it relates to the priority application.

Mention of the inventor

[1.271]

10 Mention of the inventor

(1) An inventor or joint inventor of an invention, if not mentioned in any published application for a patent, or in any patent granted, for the invention, must be mentioned in an addendum or an erratum to the application or patent.

(2) A person who alleges that any person ought to have been mentioned as the inventor or joint inventor of an invention may apply to the comptroller for that person to be so mentioned—

(a) in any patent granted for the invention; and

(b) if possible in any published application for a patent for the invention,

and, if not so mentioned, in the manner prescribed by paragraph (1).

(3) Subject to rules 21, 58(4), 59(3) and 68(2), the period prescribed for the purposes of section 13(2) is sixteen months [beginning immediately after]—

(a) where there is no declared priority date, the date of filing of the application; or

(b) where there is a declared priority date, that date.

(4) A statement filed under section 13(2) must be made on Patents Form 7.

NOTES

Para (3): words in square brackets substituted by the Patents (Amendment) Rules 2011, SI 2011/2052, rr 2, 3, Schedule, for transitional provisions see r 4 thereof.

[1.272]

11 Waiving the right to be mentioned

(1) The inventor may, before preparations for the application's publication have been completed by the Patent Office, apply to the comptroller in writing to waive his right—

(a) to have his name and address mentioned as those of the inventor; or

(b) to have his address mentioned as that of the inventor.

(2) An application by an inventor under paragraph (1)(a) must—

(a) include his reasons for making the application; and

(b) be accepted by the comptroller where the comptroller is satisfied by those reasons.

(3) An application by an inventor under paragraph (1)(b) must be accepted by the comptroller.

(4) Where the comptroller has accepted an inventor's application to make a waiver under this rule, the inventor may apply to the comptroller to end that waiver.

(5) The comptroller may, if he thinks fit, accept an application to end a waiver, and his acceptance may be made subject to such conditions as he may direct.

(6) An application under paragraph (1)(a) or (b) or under paragraph (4) may also be made by a person who is not the inventor, but who has been identified as such for the purposes of section 13(2).

(7) Where a person makes an application in reliance on paragraph (6), the reference in this rule to an application to waive his right to have his name and address (or his address) mentioned shall be construed as a reference to an application not to have his name and address (or his address) mentioned; and paragraphs (4) and (5) shall be construed accordingly.

Form and content of applications

[1.273]

12 Applications for the grant of patents under sections 14 and 15

(1) A request for the grant of a patent must be made on Patents Form 1.

(2) Where the documents filed at the Patent Office to initiate an application for a patent do not include the applicant's name and address, the comptroller shall notify the applicant that his name and address are required.

(3) Where the applicant has been so notified, he must, before the end of the period of two months [beginning immediately after] the date of the notification, file his name and address; otherwise the comptroller may refuse his application.

(4) The specification mentioned in section 14(2)(b) must be preceded by the title of the invention and must be set out in the following order—

(a) description;
(b) the claim or claims; and
(c) any drawing [or photograph] referred to in the description or any claim.

(5) But paragraph (4) does not apply where an application is delivered in electronic form or using electronic communications.

(6) The title of the invention must be short and indicate the matter to which the invention relates.

[(6A) The claim or claims must not rely in respect of the technical features of the invention on references to the description or any drawing or photograph unless the feature cannot otherwise be clearly and concisely defined in words, by a mathematical or chemical formula or by any other written means.]

(7) Where the specification includes drawings [or photographs], the description must include a list of drawings [and photographs] briefly describing each of them.

(8) Where—

(a) the documents filed at the Patent Office to initiate an application for a patent include something which is or appears to be a description of the invention in a language other than English or Welsh; and
(b) the applicant has not filed a translation into English or Welsh of that thing,

the comptroller shall notify the applicant that a translation is required.

(9) Where the applicant has been so notified, he must, before the end of the period of two months [beginning immediately after] the date of the notification, file a translation; otherwise the comptroller may refuse his application.

NOTES

Paras (3), (9): words in square brackets substituted by the Patents (Amendment) Rules 2011, SI 2011/2052, rr 2, 3, Schedule, for transitional provisions see r 4 thereof.

Para (4): words in square brackets inserted by the Patents (Amendment) (No 2) Rules 2016, SI 2016/892, rr 2, 3(a).

Para (6A): inserted by SI 2016/892, rr 2, 3(b), 17, except in relation to an application for a patent in respect of which the compliance period expired before 6 April 2017.

Para (7): words in square brackets inserted by SI 2016/892, rr 2, 3(c).

[1.274]

13 Biological material and sequence listings

(1) The provisions of Schedule 1 prescribe the circumstances in which the specification of an application for a patent, or of a patent, for an invention which involves the use of or concerns biological material is to be treated as disclosing the invention in a manner which is clear enough and complete enough for the invention to be performed by a person skilled in the art.

(2) Where the specification of an application for a patent discloses a sequence, it must include a sequence listing.

(3) Where an applicant has not provided a sequence listing on filing the application, the comptroller may specify a period within which the applicant must provide the sequence listing; and if it is not provided within this period, the comptroller may refuse the application.

(4) Where a sequence listing is provided after the date of filing the application, the listing must be accompanied by a declaration that it does not contain matter extending beyond the sequence disclosed in the application.

(5) The sequence listing must comply with any requirements and standards adopted under the Patent Co-operation Treaty for the presentation of sequence listings in patent applications.

(6) A sequence listing shall, if it is reasonably possible, be delivered to the comptroller in electronic form or using electronic communications, even where the application for the patent is not delivered in electronic form or using electronic communications.

(7) A sequence listing may be set out either in the description or at the end of the application, but if set out at the end of the application rule 12(4) shall not apply.

[1.275]
14 Size and presentation of application

(1) The contents of all documents (including annotations to drawings [and photographs]) contained in an application for a patent must be in English or Welsh.

(2) The requirements for the documents contained in an application for a patent (other than drawings [and photographs]) are set out in Parts 1 and 2 of Schedule 2.

(3) The requirements for a drawing [and a photograph] contained in an application are set out in Parts 1 and 3 of that Schedule.

(4) All documents contained in an application (including drawings [and photographs]) must comply with the requirements set out in Part 4 of that Schedule.

(5) Paragraphs (2) and (3) do not apply to an application, or a sequence listing contained in an application, which is delivered in electronic form or using electronic communications.

NOTES

Paras (1)–(4): words in square brackets inserted by the Patents (Amendment) (No 2) Rules 2016, SI 2016/892, rr 2, 4.

[1.276]
15 The abstract

(1) The abstract must start with a title for the invention.

(2) The abstract must contain a concise summary of the matter contained in the specification.

(3) That summary must include—
- (a) an indication of the technical field to which the invention belongs;
- (b) a technical explanation of the invention;
- (c) the principal use of the invention.

(4) Where the specification contains more than one drawing [or photograph], the abstract must include an indication of the drawing [or photograph] which should accompany the abstract when it is published.

(5) Where it appears to the comptroller that a drawing [or photograph] included in the specification better characterises the invention he shall publish it with the abstract.

(6) Where a feature of the invention included in the abstract is illustrated in a drawing [or photograph], the feature must be followed by the reference for that feature used in that drawing.

(7) The abstract must not contain any statement on the merits or value of the invention or its speculative application.

NOTES

Paras (4)–(6): words in square brackets inserted by the Patents (Amendment) (No 2) Rules 2016, SI 2016/892, rr 2, 5.

[1.277]
16 Single inventive concept

(1) For the purposes of the Act, two or more inventions shall be treated as being so linked as to form a single inventive concept where there exists between those inventions a technical relationship which involves one or more of the same or corresponding special technical features.

(2) In paragraph (1) "special technical features" means those technical features which define a contribution which each of the claimed inventions, considered as a whole, makes over the prior art.

[1.278]
17 References under section 15(1)(c)(ii)

(1) A reference made under section 15(1)(c)(ii) must include—
- (a) the date of filing of the earlier relevant application;
- (b) its application number; and
- (c) the country it was filed in or in respect of.

(2) Subject to paragraph (3), the copy of the application provided under section 15(10)(b)(ii) must—
- (a) be duly certified by the authority with which it was filed or otherwise verified to the satisfaction of the comptroller; and
- (b) where it is in a language other than English or Welsh, be accompanied by—
  - (i) a translation into English of that application, or

(ii) a declaration that the description filed under sub-paragraph (i) of section 15(10)(b) is a complete and accurate translation into English of the description contained in the application provided under sub-paragraph (ii) of that provision.

(3) Where the application or a copy of the application is available to the comptroller it shall, for the purposes of section 15(10)(b)(ii), be treated as having been filed in accordance with rules.

[1.279]
18 Missing parts

(1) The period prescribed for the purposes of section 15(5)(b) and (6) is the period beginning with the date of filing of the application for a patent and ending with the date of the preliminary examination.

(2) But where the applicant is notified under section 15A(9) that a drawing or part of the description of the invention has been found to be missing, the period prescribed for the purposes of section 15(5)(b) and (6) shall be the period of two months [beginning immediately after] the date of the notification.

(3) An applicant may only withdraw a missing part by giving written notice to the comptroller.

(4) A request made under section 15(7)(b) must—
- (a) be made in writing;
- (b) include sufficient information to identify where in the priority application the contents of the document filed under section 15(5)(b) were included; and
- (c) be made before the end of the period prescribed for the purpose of section 15(5)(b).

(5) Any request under section 15(7)(b) shall be considered never to have been made where—
- (a) the priority application does not contain every missing part filed under section 15(5); or
- (b) the applicant fails, before the end of the relevant period, to furnish to the comptroller copies of all earlier relevant applications—
  - (i) duly certified by the authority with which they were filed, or
  - (ii) otherwise verified to the satisfaction of the comptroller.

(6) But paragraph (5)(b) does not apply in respect of an earlier relevant application where that application or a copy of the application is available to the comptroller.

(7) For the purposes of paragraph 5(b) the relevant period is—
- (a) sixteen months [beginning immediately after] the declared priority date; or
- (b) if it expires earlier, the period of four months [beginning immediately after] the date on which the request was made under section 15(7)(b).

NOTES

Paras (2), (7): words in square brackets substituted by the Patents (Amendment) Rules 2011, SI 2011/2052, rr 2, 3, Schedule, for transitional provisions see r 4 thereof.

New applications

[1.280]
[19 New applications filed as mentioned in section 15(9)

(1) For the purposes of section 15(9) a new application may only be filed in accordance with this rule.

(2) A new application may be filed as mentioned in section 15(9) if—
- (a) the earlier application has not been terminated or withdrawn; and
- (b) the period ending three months before the compliance date of the earlier application has not expired.

(3) A new application must include a statement that it is filed as mentioned in section 15(9).]

NOTES

Commencement: 1 October 2016.

Substituted by the Patents (Amendment) (No 2) Rules 2016, SI 2016/892, rr 2, 6.

[1.281]
20 New applications under sections 8(3), 12(6) and 37(4)

(1) The period prescribed for filing a new application under section 8(3) or section 12(6) is the relevant period.

(2) A new application for a patent may be filed under section 37(4) before the end of the relevant period.

(3) For the purposes of this rule the relevant period is—
- (a) where the comptroller's decision to make an order under those provisions is not appealed, three months [beginning immediately after] the date on which the order was made; or
- (b) where that decision is appealed, three months [beginning immediately after] the date on which the appeal was finally disposed of.

(4) But the comptroller may, if he thinks fit, shorten the relevant period after giving the parties such notice and subject to such conditions as the comptroller may direct.

NOTES

Para (3): words in square brackets substituted by the Patents (Amendment) Rules 2011, SI 2011/2052, rr 2, 3, Schedule, for transitional provisions see r 4 thereof.

[1.282]

21 Extensions for new applications

(1) Where a new application is filed—

(a) the period prescribed for the purposes of section 13(2) is—

(i) two months [beginning immediately after] its initiation date, or

(ii) if it expires later, the period prescribed by rule 10(3); and

(b) the relevant period for the purposes of rule 8 is—

(i) two months [beginning immediately after] its initiation date, or

(ii) if it expires later, the period specified in rule 8(5),

and the reference in rule 10(3) to the date of filing of the application is a reference to the date of filing of the earlier application.

(2) But where the new application is filed less than six months before the compliance date—

(a) the period prescribed for the purposes of section 13(2) is the period ending with its initiation date; and

(b) the relevant period for the purposes of rule 8 is the period ending with its initiation date.

(3) The second requirement in Schedule 1 must be complied with—

(a) on the initiation date; or

(b) if it expires later, before the end of the relevant period specified in paragraph 3(3) of that Schedule.

NOTES

Para (1): words in square brackets substituted by the Patents (Amendment) Rules 2011, SI 2011/2052, rr 2, 3, Schedule, for transitional provisions see r 4 thereof.

Periods for filing contents of application

[1.283]

22 Periods prescribed for the purposes of sections 15(10) and 17(1)

(1) The period prescribed for the purposes of section 15(10)(a) and (b)(i) is the relevant period.

(2) Subject to rules 58(4), 59(3) and 68(3), the period prescribed for the purposes of section 15(10)(c) and (d) and section 17(1) is the relevant period.

(3) The period prescribed for the purpose of section 15(10)(b)(ii) is four months [beginning immediately after] the date of filing of the application.

(4) But paragraphs (1) to (3) do not apply to a new application.

(5) In relation to a new application—

(a) the period prescribed for the purposes of section 15(10)(a), (b)(i), (c) and (d) and section 17(1) is—

(i) two months [beginning immediately after] its initiation date, or

(ii) if it expires later, the relevant period; and

(b) the period prescribed for the purposes of section 15(10)(b)(ii) is—

(i) two months [beginning immediately after] its initiation date, or

(ii) if it expires later, the period of four months [beginning immediately after] the date of filing of the earlier application,

and the reference in paragraph (7) to the date of filing of the application is a reference to the date of filing of the earlier application.

(6) But where the new application is filed less than six months before the compliance date, the period prescribed for the purposes of section 15(10)(a) to (d) and section 17(1) is the period ending with its initiation date.

(7) For the purposes of this rule the relevant period is—

(a) where there is no declared priority date, twelve months [beginning immediately after] the date of filing of the application; or

(b) where there is a declared priority date—

(i) twelve months [beginning immediately after] the declared priority date, or

(ii) if it expires later, the period of two months [beginning immediately after] the date of filing of the application.

NOTES

Paras (3), (5), (7): words in square brackets substituted by the Patents (Amendment) Rules 2011, SI 2011/2052, rr 2, 3, Schedule, for transitional provisions see r 4 thereof.

Preliminary examination

[1.284]
23 Preliminary examination under section 15A

(1) On the preliminary examination under section 15A of an application the examiner shall determine whether the application complies with the requirements of rules 6 to 9.

(2) The examiner must report to the comptroller his determinations under paragraph (1), and the comptroller must notify the applicant accordingly.

[1.285]
24 Correcting a declaration made for the purposes of section 5(2)

(1) Where, on the preliminary examination under section 15A of an application, the examiner finds that a declaration made for the purposes of section 5(2) specifies a date of filing for an earlier relevant application—

(a) more than twelve months before the date of filing of the application in suit; or

(b) where the comptroller has given permission for a late declaration to be made under section 5(2), more than fourteen months before the date of filing of the application in suit,

he must report this finding to the comptroller, and the comptroller must notify the applicant accordingly.

(2) Where the comptroller has notified the applicant under paragraph (1), the applicant must, before the end of the period of two months [beginning immediately after] the date of that notification, provide the comptroller with a corrected date; otherwise the comptroller must disregard the declaration in so far as it relates to the earlier relevant application.

(3) In paragraph (2) "corrected date" means a date that would not have been reported by the examiner under paragraph (1).

NOTES

Para (2): words in square brackets substituted by the Patents (Amendment) Rules 2011, SI 2011/2052, rr 2, 3, Schedule, for transitional provisions see r 4 thereof.

[1.286]
25 Formal requirements

(1) Subject to paragraphs (2) and (3), the requirements of the following provisions of these Rules are formal requirements—

(a) rule 12(1) (application for a patent on Patents Form 1);

(b) rule 14(1) (application in English or Welsh);

(c) rule 14(2) and (3) (form of documents and drawings).

(2) Where an application is delivered in electronic form or using electronic communications, only the requirements of rule 14(1) are formal requirements.

(3) Where an international application for a patent (UK) was filed in accordance with the provisions of the patent co-operation treaty, the requirements mentioned in paragraph (1) shall be treated as complied with to the extent that the application complies with any corresponding provision of that treaty.

Publication of application

[1.287]
26 Publication of application

(1) The period prescribed for the purposes of section 16(1) is eighteen months [beginning immediately after]—

(a) where there is no declared priority date, the date of filing of the application; or

(b) where there is a declared priority date, that date.

(2) Where a person's application under rule 11(1)(a) or (b) has been accepted by the comptroller, the comptroller must ensure that the application for the patent as published does not mention that person's name and address as those of the person believed to be the inventor (or, as the case may be, that person's address as that of the person so believed).

NOTES

Para (1): words in square brackets substituted by the Patents (Amendment) Rules 2011, SI 2011/2052, rr 2, 3, Schedule, for transitional provisions see r 4 thereof.

Search and substantive examination

[1.288]
27 Search under section 17

(1) A request under section 17(1)(c)(i) for a search must be made on Patents Form 9A.

(2) The comptroller may, if he thinks fit, send to the applicant a copy of any document (or any part of it) referred to in the examiner's report made under section 17.

(3) Where an examiner conducts a search in relation to the first only of two or more inventions, in accordance with section 17(6), he must report this fact to the comptroller, and the comptroller must notify the applicant accordingly.

(4) The applicant must pay any search fee in relation to those inventions (other than the first) on or before the relevant date.

(5) The relevant date is the first day of the three month period ending with the compliance date of the application.

(6) The fee for a supplementary search under section 17(8), or a search under section 17(6), must be accompanied by Patents Form 9A.

[1.289]

28 Request for substantive examination under section 18

(1) A request under section 18 for a substantive examination of an application must be made on Patents Form 10.

(2) Subject to paragraphs (3) and (4) and rules 60 and 68(4), the period prescribed for the purposes of section 18(1) is six months [beginning immediately after] the date the application was published.

(3) Where the comptroller has given directions under section 22(1) or (2) in relation to information contained in the application, the period prescribed for the purposes of section 18(1) is the relevant period.

(4) Paragraphs (2) and (3) do not apply to a new application.

(5) In relation to a new application, the period prescribed for the purposes of section 18(1) is—

(a) two months [beginning immediately after] its initiation date; or

(b) if it expires later, the relevant period,

and the reference in paragraph (7) to the date of filing of the application is a reference to the date of filing of the earlier application.

(6) But where the new application is filed less than six months before the compliance date, the period prescribed for the purposes of section 18(1) is the period ending with its initiation date.

(7) For the purposes of this rule the relevant period is two years [beginning immediately after]—

(a) where there is no declared priority date, the date of filing of the application; or

(b) where there is a declared priority date, that date.

NOTES

Paras (2), (5), (7): words in square brackets substituted by the Patents (Amendment) Rules 2011, SI 2011/2052, rr 2, 3, Schedule, for transitional provisions see r 4 thereof.

[1.290]

29 Substantive examination reports

(1) Whenever the examiner reports to the comptroller under either section 18(3) or (4) on whether the application complies with the requirements of the Act and these Rules, the comptroller must send a copy of that report to the applicant.

(2) The comptroller may, if he thinks fit, send to the applicant a copy of any document (or any part of it) referred to in the examiner's report.

(3) For the purposes of rules 30 and 31—

(a) "first substantive examination report" means the first report sent to the applicant under paragraph (1); and

(b) "first observations report" means a report sent to the applicant under paragraph (1) which meets the condition in paragraph (4).

(4) The condition is that—

(a) a person has made observations to the comptroller under section 21(1) on the question whether the invention is a patentable invention;

(b) the examiner has reported to the comptroller, as a consequence of those observations, that the invention does not comply with the requirements of the Act or these Rules; and

(c) the comptroller has not previously sent to the applicant a report, relating to those observations, under paragraph (1).

[1.291]

30 Period for putting application in order

(1) The period prescribed for the purposes of sections 18(4) and 20(1) (failure of application) is the compliance period.

(2) For the purposes of paragraph (1), subject to paragraphs (3) and (4), the compliance period is—

(a) four years and six months [beginning immediately after]—

(i) where there is no declared priority date, the date of filing of the application, or

(ii) where there is a declared priority date, that date; or

(b) if it expires later, the period of twelve months [beginning immediately after] the date on which the first substantive examination report is sent to the applicant.

(3) Subject to paragraph (4), where a new application is filed the compliance period is—

(a) where it is filed under section 8(3), 12(6) or 37(4)—

(i) the period specified in paragraph (2) in relation to the earlier application, or

(ii) if it expires later, the period of eighteen months [beginning immediately after] the initiation date; and

(b) where it is filed as mentioned in section 15(9), the period specified in paragraph (2) in relation to the earlier application.

(4) Where the first observations report is sent to the applicant during the last three months of the period specified in paragraphs (2) or (3), the compliance period is three months [beginning immediately after] the date on which that report is sent.

NOTES

Paras (2)–(4): words in square brackets substituted by the Patents (Amendment) Rules 2011, SI 2011/2052, rr 2, 3, Schedule, for transitional provisions see r 4 thereof.

[1.292]

31 Amendment of application before grant

(1) A request to amend an application for a patent under section 19(1) must be made in writing.

(2) The conditions prescribed under section 19(1) are as follows.

(3) [Subject to rule 66A] the applicant may amend his application only within the period beginning with the date on which the applicant is informed of the examiner's report under section 17(5) and ending with the date on which the comptroller sends him the first substantive examination report.

(4) But after the end of this period, the applicant may—

(a) where the first substantive examination report states that his application complies with the requirements of the Act and these Rules, amend his application once before the end of the period of two months [beginning immediately after] the date on which that report was sent; or

(b) where the first substantive examination report states that his application does not comply with the requirements of the Act and these Rules—

(i) amend his application once at the same time as he makes his first observations on, or amendments to, his application under section 18(3), and

(ii) if the first substantive examination report is sent before preparations for the application's publication have been completed by the Patent Office, amend his application prior to any further amendment he may make under sub-paragraph (b)(i).

(5) However, the conditions in paragraphs (3) and (4) do not apply—

(a) where the comptroller consents to the amendment; or

(b) to an amendment of a request for the grant of a patent.

(6) Where the comptroller's consent is required, or the applicant wishes to amend the request for the grant of a patent, the applicant must include the reasons for the amendment.

NOTES

Para (3): words in square brackets inserted by the Patents (Amendment) (No 2) Rules 2016, SI 2016/892, rr 2, 7.

Para (4): words in square brackets substituted by the Patents (Amendment) Rules 2011, SI 2011/2052, rr 2, 3, Schedule, for transitional provisions see r 4 thereof.

[1.293]

32 Reinstatement of applications under section 20A

(1) A request under section 20A for the reinstatement of an application must be made before the end of the relevant period.

[(2) For this purpose the relevant period is twelve months beginning immediately after the date on which the application was terminated.]

(3) The request must be made on Patents Form 14.

(4) Where the comptroller is required to publish a notice under section 20A(5), it must be published in the journal.

(5) The applicant must file evidence in support of that request.

(6) Where that evidence does not accompany the request, the comptroller must specify a period within which the evidence must be filed.

(7) Where, on consideration of that evidence, the comptroller is not satisfied that a case for an order under section 20A has been made out, he must notify the applicant accordingly.

(8) The applicant may, before the end of the period of one month [beginning immediately after] the date of that notification, request to be heard by the comptroller.

(9) Where the applicant requests a hearing, the comptroller must give him an opportunity to be heard, after which the comptroller shall determine whether the request under section 20A shall be allowed or refused.

(10) Where the comptroller reinstates the application after a notice was published under paragraph (4), he must advertise in the journal the fact that he has reinstated the application.

(11) . . .

NOTES

Para (2): substituted by the Patents (Amendment) (No 2) Rules 2016, SI 2016/892, rr 2, 8(a).

Para (8): words in square brackets substituted by the Patents (Amendment) Rules 2011, SI 2011/2052, rr 2, 3, Schedule, for transitional provisions see r 4 thereof.

Para (11): revoked by SI 2016/892, rr 2, 8(b).

[1.294]

33 Observations by third parties on patentability

(1) The comptroller must send to the applicant a copy of any observations on patentability he receives under section 21.

(2) But paragraph (1) does not apply to any observation which, in the opinion of the comptroller, would—

- (a) disparage any person in a way likely to damage such person; or
- (b) be generally expected to encourage offensive, immoral or anti-social behaviour.

(3) The comptroller may, if he thinks fit, send to the applicant a copy of any document referred to in the observations.

(4) The comptroller must send to an examiner any observations on patentability.

(5) But paragraph (4) does not apply where the observations are received after the examiner has reported under section 18(4) that an application complies with the requirements of the Act and these Rules.

PART 3
GRANTED PATENTS

Certificate and amendment

[1.295]

34 Certificate of grant

The certificate of grant of a patent must be in a form which includes—

- (a) the name of the proprietor;
- (b) the date of filing of the application; and
- (c) the number of the patent.

[1.296]

35 Amendment of specification after grant

(1) An application by the proprietor of a patent for the specification of the patent to be amended must—

- (a) be made in writing;
- (b) identify the proposed amendment; and
- (c) state the reason for making the amendment.

(2) The application must, if it is reasonably possible, be delivered to the comptroller in electronic form or using electronic communications.

(3) The comptroller may, if he thinks fit, direct the proprietor to file a copy of the specification with the amendment applied for marked on it.

(4) Where the specification of a European patent (UK) was published in a language other than English, the proprietor must file a translation into English of the part of the specification which he is applying to amend and a translation of the amendment.

(5) The comptroller may, if he thinks fit, direct the proprietor to file a translation into English of the specification as published.

(6) Where the court or the comptroller allows the proprietor of a patent to amend the specification of the patent, the comptroller may direct him to file an amended specification which complies with the requirements of schedule 2.

Renewal

[1.297]

36 Renewal of patents: general

(1) In this rule and in rules 37 to 41—

"renewal date" has the meaning given in rules 37(2) to (4) and 38(3);

"renewal fee" means the fee prescribed in respect of a renewal date;

"renewal period" means the period prescribed by rule 37 or 38 for the payment of a renewal fee [unless a renewal fee is payable by virtue of section 77(5A), in which case in this rule and in rules 39 and 41 "renewal period" means the period in which the fee is payable under section 77(5A) and rule 41A].

(2) If the renewal fee is not paid before the end of the renewal period, the patent shall cease to have [effect—

(a) where the renewal fee is payable by virtue of section 77(5A), at the end of the final day of the renewal period;

(b) in any other case, at the end of the renewal date.]

(3) Patents Form 12 must be filed before the end of the renewal period.

(4) But where payment is made under section 25(4) or section 28(3), Patents Form 12 must accompany the renewal fee and the prescribed additional fee.

(5) On receipt of the renewal fee the comptroller must issue a certificate of payment.

NOTES

Para (1): words in square brackets in definition "renewal period" inserted by the Patents (Amendment) (No 2) Rules 2014, SI 2014/2401, rr 2, 4.

Para (2): words in square brackets substituted by SI 2014/2401, rr 2, 5.

[1.298]
37 Renewal of patents: first renewal

(1) This rule prescribes the period for the payment of a renewal fee in respect of the first renewal date.

(2) Subject to paragraphs (3) and (4)—

(a) the first renewal date is the fourth anniversary of the date of filing; and

(b) the renewal period is three months ending with the last day of the month in which that renewal date falls.

(3) Where a patent is granted under the Act during the period of three months ending with the fourth anniversary of the date of filing, or at any time after that anniversary—

(a) the first renewal date is the last day of the period of three months [beginning immediately after] the date on which the patent was granted; and

(b) the renewal period begins with the date on which the patent was granted and ends with the last day of the month in which that renewal date falls.

(4) Where the grant of a patent is mentioned in the European Patent Bulletin during the period of three months ending with the fourth anniversary of the date of filing, or at any time after that anniversary—

(a) the first renewal date is the later of—

(i) the last day of the period of three months [beginning immediately after] the date on which the grant of the patent was mentioned in the European Patent Bulletin (case A), or

(ii) the next anniversary of the date of filing to fall after the date on which the grant of the patent was so mentioned (case B); and

(b) the renewal period is—

(i) in case A, the period beginning with the date on which the grant of the patent was mentioned in the European Patent Bulletin and ending with the last day of the month in which the first renewal date falls, or

(ii) in case B, three months ending with the last day of the month in which the first renewal date falls.

NOTES

Paras (3), (4): words in square brackets substituted by the Patents (Amendment) Rules 2011, SI 2011/2052, rr 2, 3, Schedule, for transitional provisions see r 4 thereof.

[1.299]
38 Renewal of patents: subsequent renewals

(1) This rule prescribes the period for the payment of a renewal fee in respect of renewal dates subsequent to the first renewal date.

(2) The renewal period is three months ending with the last day of the month in which the renewal date falls.

(3) For those purposes—

(a) the second renewal date is the next anniversary of the date of filing to fall after the first renewal date; and

(b) each subsequent renewal date is the anniversary of the previous renewal date.

[1.300]
39 Renewal notice

(1) This rule applies where the renewal fee has not been received by the end of the renewal period.

[(2) If the renewal fee remains unpaid, the comptroller must send a renewal notice to the proprietor of the patent—

(a) where the renewal fee is payable by virtue of section 77(5A), before the end of the period of six weeks beginning immediately after the later of—

(i) the end of the renewal period, and

(ii) the date on which the comptroller receives notification of the restoration of the patent from the European Patent Office;

(b) in any other case, before the end of the period of six weeks beginning immediately after the end of the renewal period.]

(3) The comptroller must send the renewal notice to—

[(a) the last address specified by the proprietor on payment of a renewal fee (or to another address that has since been notified to him for that purpose by the proprietor); or]

(b) where such an address has not been so specified or notified, the address for service entered in the register.

(4) The renewal notice must remind the proprietor of the patent—

(a) that payment is overdue; and

(b) of the consequences of non-payment.

NOTES

Para (2): substituted by the Patents (Amendment) (No 2) Rules 2014, SI 2014/2401, rr 2, 6.

Para (3): sub-para (a) substituted by the Patents (Amendment) (No 2) Rules 2016, SI 2016/892, rr 2, 9.

[1.301]
40 Restoration of lapsed patents under section 28

(1) An application under section 28 for restoration of a patent may be made at any time before the end of the period ending with the thirteenth month after the month in which the period specified in section 25(4) ends.

(2) The application must be made on Patents Form 16.

(3) The notice of the application must be published in the journal.

(4) The applicant must file evidence in support of the application.

(5) If that evidence does not accompany the application, the comptroller must specify a period within which the evidence shall be filed.

(6) If, on consideration of that evidence, the comptroller is not satisfied that a case for an order under section 28 has been made out, he must notify the applicant accordingly.

(7) The applicant may, before the end of the period of one month [beginning immediately after] the date of that notification, request to be heard by the comptroller.

(8) If the applicant requests a hearing, the comptroller must give the applicant an opportunity to be heard before he determines whether to grant or refuse the application under section 28.

(9) Where the comptroller grants the application he must advertise the fact in the journal.

NOTES

Para (7): words in square brackets substituted by the Patents (Amendment) Rules 2011, SI 2011/2052, rr 2, 3, Schedule, for transitional provisions see r 4 thereof.

[1.302]
41 Notification of lapsed patent

(1) This rule applies where—

(a) a patent has ceased to have effect because a renewal fee has not been paid by the end of the renewal period; and

(b) the renewal fee and the prescribed additional fee have not been paid by the end of the period specified in section 25(4) ("the extended period").

(2) The comptroller must, before the end of the period of six weeks beginning immediately after the end of the extended period, send a notice to the proprietor of the patent—

(a) stating that the extended period has expired; and

(b) referring him to the provisions of section 28.

(3) The comptroller must send the notice to the address specified by rule 39(3).

[1.303]
[41A Payment of fees under section 77(5A) following restoration of a European patent (UK)

The prescribed period for the purposes of section 77(5A) is two months.]

NOTES

Commencement: 1 October 2014.
Inserted by the Patents (Amendment) (No 2) Rules 2014, SI 2014/2401, rr 2, 7.

Surrender and cancelling entry that licences available as of right

[1.304]
42 Surrender

The notice of an offer by a proprietor to surrender a patent must be in writing and include—

(a) a declaration that no action is pending before the court for infringement or revocation of the patent; or

(b) where such an action is pending, the particulars of the action.

[1.305]
43 Application for, and cancellation of, an entry that licences are available as of right

(1) An application under section 46(1) must be made on Patents Form 28.

(2) Where an entry is made in the register to the effect that licences under a patent are to be available as of right, the comptroller must advertise the entry in the journal.

(3) An application under section 47(1) for the cancellation of an entry made under section 46 must be made on Patents Form 30.

(4) The period prescribed for the purposes of section 47(3) is two months [beginning immediately after] the date on which the entry was made under section 46.

NOTES

Para (4): words in square brackets substituted by the Patents (Amendment) Rules 2011, SI 2011/2052, rr 2, 3, Schedule, for transitional provisions see r 4 thereof.

PART 4
THE REGISTER AND OTHER INFORMATION

The Register

[1.306]
44 Entries in the register

(1) When an application for a patent is published, the comptroller must enter each of the following matters in the register—

(a) the name of the applicant;
(b) the name and address of the person identified as the inventor;
(c) the address of the applicant and his address for service;
(d) the title of the invention;
(e) the date of filing of the application for a patent;
(f) the application number;
(g) where a declaration has been made for the purposes of section 5(2)—
  (i) the date of filing of each earlier relevant application specified in the declaration,
  (ii) its application number, and
  (iii) the country it was filed in or in respect of; and
(h) the date of the application's publication.

(2) But where a person's application under rule 11(1)(a) or (b) has been accepted by the comptroller, the comptroller may omit from the register his name and address (or, as the case may be, his address) as that of the person believed to be the inventor.

(3) Where an application for a patent has been published, the comptroller must enter each of the following matters in the register as soon as practicable after the event to which they relate—

(a) the date on which a request is made by an applicant for the substantive examination of his application;
(b) the date on which an application is terminated or withdrawn.

(4) When the patent is granted, the comptroller must enter each of the following matters in the register—

(a) the date on which the comptroller granted the patent;
(b) the name of the proprietor of the patent;
(c) where the address of the proprietor or his address for service was not entered in the register under paragraph (1), that address or address for service.

(5) In relation to a request for an opinion under section 74A, [other than in relation to a European patent with unitary effect,] the comptroller must enter each of the following matters in the register as soon as practicable after the event to which they relate—

(a) a notice that a request under section 74A(1) . . . has been received;
(b) a notice that such a request has been refused or withdrawn;
(c) a notice that an opinion has been issued.

(6) A notice of any transaction, instrument or event mentioned in section 32(2)(b) or 33(3) must be entered in the register as soon as practicable after it occurs (or, if later, when the application is published).

(7) The comptroller may, at any time, enter in the register such other particulars as he thinks fit.

NOTES

Para (5): words in square brackets inserted by the Patents (Amendment) Rules 2016, SI 2016/517, r 2(1), (2), as from a day to be appointed (being the date of entry into force of the Agreement on a Unified Patent Court, which is reproduced at **[1.1009]**); words omitted from sub-para (a) revoked by the Patents (Amendment) (No 2) Rules 2014, SI 2014/2401, rr 2, 9.

[1.307]

45 Advertisement in relation to register

The comptroller may publish or advertise such things done under the Act or these Rules in relation to the register as he thinks fit.

[1.308]

46 Copies of entries in, or extracts from, the register and certified facts

(1) An application under section 32(6) for a certified copy of an entry in the register, or a certified extract from the register, must be made on Patents Form 23.

(2) A person may apply on Patents Form 23 for an uncertified copy of an entry in the register or an uncertified extract from the register and, on payment of the prescribed fee, he shall be entitled to such a copy or extract.

(3) A person may apply on Patents Form 23 for a certificate which certifies that—
- (a) an entry has or has not been made in the register; or
- (b) something which the comptroller is authorised to do has or has not been done.

[1.309]

47 Registrations of transactions, instruments and events

(1) An application to register (or in the case of an application for a patent which has not been published, to give notice of) any transaction, instrument or event mentioned in section 32(2)(b) or 33(3) must—
- (a) be made on Patents Form 21; and
- (b) include evidence establishing the transaction, instrument or event.

(2) The comptroller may direct that such evidence as he may require in connection with the application shall be sent to him within such period as he may specify.

Copies of documents and corrections in relation to the register

[1.310]

48 Copies of documents

(1) A person may apply to the comptroller for a certified copy of any relevant document and, on payment of the prescribed fee, he shall be entitled to such a copy.

(2) A person may apply to the comptroller for an uncertified copy of any relevant document and, on payment of the prescribed fee, he shall be entitled to such a copy.

(3) But a person is not entitled to a copy of a relevant document where—
- (a) it is not available for inspection under section 118; or
- (b) making or providing such a copy would infringe copyright.

(4) For the purposes of this rule a relevant document is any of the following—
- (a) an application for a patent which has been published;
- (b) a specification of a patent;
- (c) any other document, or extract from any such document, kept at the Patent Office.

(5) An application under paragraph (1) or (2) must be made on Patents Form 23.

[1.311]

49 [Correction or change of name or address; correction of address for service]

(1) Any person may request that a correction be entered in the register or made to any application or other document filed at the Patent Office in respect of any of the following—
- (a) his name;
- (b) his address;
- (c) his address for service.

(2) A request under paragraph (1)(a) to correct a name must be made on Patents Form 20.

(3) Any other request under paragraph (1) must be made in writing.

(4) If the comptroller has reasonable doubts about whether he should make the correction—
- (a) he must inform the person making the request of the reason for his doubts; and
- (b) he may require that person to file evidence in support of the request.

(5) If the comptroller has no doubts (or no longer has doubts) about whether he should make the correction, he must enter the correction in the register or make it to the application or document.

[(6) For the purposes of this rule a request for a correction includes—
(a) a correction made for the purposes of section 117; and
(b) a change to any of the matters listed in paragraph (1)(a) or (b) in respect of an entry recorded in the register or made to any application or other document filed at the Patent Office.]

NOTES

Rule heading: substituted by the Patents (Amendment) (No 2) Rules 2016, SI 2016/892, rr 2, 10(a).
Para (6): substituted by SI 2016/892, rr 2, 10(b).

[1.312]

50 Request for correction of error

(1) Subject to rule 49, any person may request the correction of an error in the register or in any document filed at the Patent Office in connection with registration.

(2) The request must be—
(a) made in writing; and
(b) accompanied by sufficient information to identify the nature of the error and the correction requested.

(3) If the comptroller has reasonable doubts about whether there is an error—
(a) he shall inform the person making the request of the reason for his doubts; and
(b) he may require that person to furnish a written explanation of the nature of the error or evidence in support of the request.

(4) If the comptroller has no doubts (or no longer has doubts) about whether an error has been made he shall make such correction as he may agree with the proprietor of the patent (or, as the case may be, the applicant).

Requests for information or documents

[1.313]

51 Restrictions on inspection of documents

(1) For the purposes of section 118(1) the prescribed restrictions are those set out in paragraphs (2) and (3).

(2) No document may be inspected—
(a) where that document was prepared by the comptroller, an examiner or the Patent Office for internal use only;
(b) where the circumstances specified in section 118(4) exist, before the end of the period of 14 days [beginning immediately after] the date of the notification under rule 52(2);
(c) where that document is a request or application made under section 118 or rule 46(2), 48(2) or 54(1); or
(d) where that document includes matter—
(i) which in the comptroller's opinion disparages any person in a way likely to damage him, or
(ii) the inspection of which would in his opinion be generally expected to encourage offensive, immoral or anti-social behaviour.

(3) Unless in a particular case the comptroller otherwise directs, no document may be inspected—
(a) where that document was filed at the Patent Office in connection with an application under section 40(1) or (2) or 41(8);
(b) where that document is treated as a confidential document under rule 53;
(c) where—
(i) that document was prepared by the comptroller, an examiner or the Patent Office other than for internal use, and
(ii) it contains information which the comptroller considers should remain confidential;
(d) where that document relates to an international application for a patent and the International Bureau would not be permitted to allow access to that document under the Patent Co-operation Treaty; or
(e) where—
(i) the comptroller has accepted a person's application under rule 11(1)(a) or (b), and
(ii) that person's name and address can be identified from that document as those of the inventor or of the person believed to be the inventor (or, as the case may be, his address can be so identified).

(4) In this rule references to a document include part of a document.

NOTES

Para (2): words in square brackets substituted by the Patents (Amendment) Rules 2011, SI 2011/2052, rr 2, 3, Schedule, for transitional provisions see r 4 thereof.

[1.314]

52 Request for information where section 118(4) applies

(1) Where the circumstances specified in section 118(4) exist, a request under section 118(1) must be accompanied by evidence verifying their existence.

(2) The comptroller must notify the applicant for the patent of any request.

(3) The notification must be accompanied by a copy of the request and the accompanying evidence.

(4) The applicant may, before the end of the period of 14 days [beginning immediately after] the date of the notification, inform the comptroller that the circumstances specified in section 118(4) do not exist; otherwise the comptroller may treat him as accepting that those circumstances exist.

NOTES

Para (4): words in square brackets substituted by the Patents (Amendment) Rules 2011, SI 2011/2052, rr 2, 3, Schedule, for transitional provisions see r 4 thereof.

[1.315]

53 Confidential documents

(1) Where a person files a document at the Patent Office or sends it to an examiner or the comptroller, any person may request that the document be treated as a confidential document.

(2) The comptroller must refuse any request where it relates to—

(a) a Patents Form; or

(b) any document filed in connection with a request under section 74A.

(3) A request to treat a document as confidential must—

(a) be made before the end of the period of 14 days [beginning immediately after] the date on which the document was—

(i) filed at the Patent Office, or

(ii) received by the comptroller, an examiner or the Patent Office; and

(b) include reasons for the request.

(4) Where a request has been made under paragraph (1), the document must be treated as confidential until the comptroller refuses that request or gives a direction under paragraph (5).

(5) If it appears to the comptroller that there is good reason for the document to remain confidential, he may direct that the document shall be treated as a confidential document; otherwise he must refuse the request made under paragraph (1).

(6) But where the comptroller believes there is no longer a good reason for the direction under paragraph (5) to continue in force, he must revoke it.

(7) In this rule references to a document include part of a document.

NOTES

Para (3): words in square brackets substituted by the Patents (Amendment) Rules 2011, SI 2011/2052, rr 2, 3, Schedule, for transitional provisions see r 4 thereof.

[1.316]

54 Requests for certain information

(1) Where a person requests to be notified of a relevant event, he must use Patents Form 49.

(2) Where a person has made such a request, the comptroller must notify him that the relevant event has occurred as soon as practicable after the event.

(3) But the comptroller shall not give him information or permit him to inspect a document unless he would be entitled to such information or to inspect such a document under section 118.

(4) A request on Patents Form 49 must be for information regarding a single relevant event only.

(5) For the purposes of paragraph (1), in relation to an application for a patent, each of the following is a relevant event—

(a) an applicant requesting, or failing to request, a substantive examination before the end of the period prescribed for the purposes of section 18(1);

(b) the application being published;

(c) the notice of grant of the patent being published under section 24;

(d) the application being terminated or withdrawn.

(6) For the purposes of paragraph (1), in relation to a patent, each of the following is a relevant event—

(a) a request for an opinion under section 74A;

(b) the patent ceasing to have effect by reason of section 25(3);

(c) the renewal fee and any additional fee being paid during the period specified in section 25(4);

(d) an application being made for the restoration of the patent which has ceased to have effect.

(7) For the purposes of paragraph (1), in relation to a patent or an application for a patent, each of the following is a relevant event—

(a) an entry being made in the register;
(b) a document becoming available for inspection under section 118 (by reason of a prescribed restriction no longer applying to the document);
(c) an application to register a transaction, instrument or event being made under rule 47;
(d) a matter being published in the journal.

[1.317]
55 Bibliographic information about an unpublished application

For the purposes of section 118(3)(b) the following bibliographic information is prescribed—
(a) the name of the applicant;
(b) the title of the invention;
(c) the number of the application;
(d) the date of filing of the application;
(e) where a declaration has been made for the purposes of section 5(2)—
(i) the date of filing of each earlier relevant application specified in the declaration,
(ii) its application number, and
(iii) the country it was filed in or in respect of;
(f) where an application has been terminated or withdrawn, that information; and
(g) where a transaction, instrument or event mentioned in section 32(2)(b) or 33(3) is notified to the comptroller, that information.

PART 5
EUROPEAN PATENTS (UK)

Translations

[1.318]
56 Translations of European patents (UK)

(1) A translation into English of either—
(a) the specification of the European patent (UK), which is filed under section 77(6); or
(b) the claims of the specification of the application for a European patent (UK), which is filed under section 78(7),
must be accompanied by Patents Form 54.

(2) The translation must comply with the requirements set out in Parts 1 to 3 of Schedule 2.

(3) The translation and Patents Form 54 must be filed in duplicate.

(4) But paragraph (2) does not apply where a translation is delivered in electronic form or using electronic communications.

(5) Where the specification includes any drawings all annotations in French or German must be replaced with annotations in English.

(6) The period prescribed for the purposes of section 77(6)(a) is three months beginning with the date on which the grant of the patent was mentioned in the European Patent Bulletin.

(7) The period prescribed for the purposes of section 77(6)(b) is three months beginning with the date of publication, by the European Patent Office, of the specification as amended.

(8) No translation may be filed under section 77(6)(a) or (b) before the beginning of the period prescribed for the purposes of that provision.

(9) On a day appointed under section 77(9), section 77(6) and paragraphs (1)(a) and (5) to (8) of this rule shall cease to have effect.

(10) The day appointed for the purpose of paragraph (9) shall be the day of the coming into force of the Agreement on the application of Article 65 of the Convention on the Grant of European Patents made in London on 17th October 2000.

[1.319]
57 Corrected translations

(1) A corrected translation filed under section 80(3) must be accompanied by Patents Form 54.

(2) The corrected translation must comply with the requirements set out in Parts 1 to 3 of Schedule 2.

(3) Where the corrected translation includes any drawings all annotations in French or German must be replaced with annotations in English.

(4) The corrected translation and Patents Form 54 must be filed in duplicate.

(5) But paragraph (2) does not apply where a translation is delivered in electronic form or using electronic communications.

(6) The period prescribed for the purposes of section 80(3) for payment of the prescribed fee is 14 days [beginning immediately after] the day the corrected translation is filed.

NOTES

Para (6): words in square brackets substituted by the Patents (Amendment) Rules 2011, SI 2011/2052, rr 2, 3, Schedule, for transitional provisions see r 4 thereof.

Conversion requests

[1.320]

58 Procedure for making a conversion request under section 81(2)(b)(i)

(1) A request under section 81(2)(b)(i) must be—

(a) made in writing; and

(b) accompanied by a copy of the notification by the European Patent Office that the application has been deemed to be withdrawn.

(2) When making such a request, a person may also request the comptroller to send—

(a) a copy of his application for a European patent (UK); and

(b) a copy of the request,

to the central industrial property office of any contracting state designated in the application.

(3) The period prescribed for the purposes of section 81(2)(b)(i) is three months [beginning immediately after] the date of the notification mentioned in paragraph (1)(b).

(4) Where a request has been made under section 81(2)(b)(i), the period prescribed for the purposes of sections 13(2), 15(10)(d) and 81(2)(c) is two months [beginning immediately after] the date on which the comptroller received that request.

(5) In paragraph (2) "contracting state" means a country which is a party to the European Patent Convention.

NOTES

Paras (3), (4): words in square brackets substituted by the Patents (Amendment) Rules 2011, SI 2011/2052, rr 2, 3, Schedule, for transitional provisions see r 4 thereof.

[1.321]

59 Procedure for making a conversion request under section 81(2)(b)(ii)

(1) The period prescribed for the purposes of section 81(2)(b)(ii) is twenty months [beginning immediately after]—

(a) where there is no declared priority date, the date of filing of the application; or

(b) where there is a declared priority date, that date.

(2) Where a request, transmitted under section 81(2)(b)(ii), has been received by the comptroller, he must notify the applicant accordingly.

(3) Where a request has been transmitted under section 81(2)(b)(ii), the period prescribed for the purposes of sections 13(2), 15(10)(d) and 81(2)(c) is four months [beginning immediately after] the date of that notification.

NOTES

Paras (1), (3): words in square brackets substituted by the Patents (Amendment) Rules 2011, SI 2011/2052, rr 2, 3, Schedule, for transitional provisions see r 4 thereof.

[1.322]

60 Request for substantive examination following a direction under section 81

Where an application for a European patent (UK) falls to be treated as an application for a patent under the Act by virtue of a direction under section 81, the period prescribed for the purposes of section 18(1) is two years [beginning immediately after]—

(a) where there is no declared priority date, the date of filing of the application; or

(b) where there is a declared priority date, that date.

NOTES

Words in square brackets substituted by the Patents (Amendment) Rules 2011, SI 2011/2052, rr 2, 3, Schedule, for transitional provisions see r 4 thereof.

Obligations to other contracting parties to the European Patent Convention

[1.323]

61 Recognition of patent decision of competent authorities of other states

(1) Where in proceedings before the comptroller a person seeks recognition of a relevant determination, he must furnish to the comptroller a copy of the determination duly certified by the relevant official of the competent authority.

(2) In paragraph (1) "relevant determination" means the determination of a question to which section 82 applies by the competent authority of a relevant contracting state other than the United Kingdom.

[1.324]

62 Procedure for obtaining evidence for proceedings under the European Patent Convention

(1) An application to the comptroller for an order under the Evidence (Proceedings in Other Jurisdictions) Act 1975 as applied by section 92(1) must be—

(a) made in writing;

(b) supported by written evidence;

(c) accompanied by the request as a result of which the application is made, and where appropriate, a translation of the request into English; and
(d) accompanied by the prescribed fee.

(2) The application must be made without notice.

(3) The comptroller may permit an officer of the European Patent Office to attend the hearing and either—
(a) examine the witnesses; or
(b) request the comptroller to put specified questions to the witnesses.

[1.325]
63 Communication of information to the European Patent Office

The comptroller may authorise any information in the files of the Patent Office to be communicated to the European Patent Office or to a competent authority of any country which is a party to the European Patent Convention, except where that information cannot be communicated under section 118.

PART 6
INTERNATIONAL APPLICATIONS

Interpretation

[1.326]
64 Interpretation relating to international applications

In this Part the following have the same meaning as they have in the Patent Co-operation Treaty—
"competent receiving Office";
"International Preliminary Examination Report";
"International Preliminary Report on Patentability";
"International Search Report";
"International Searching Authority";
"receiving Office".

Filing at the Patent Office

[1.327]
65 Filing of international applications at the Patent Office

(1) An international application for a patent filed at the Patent Office as a competent receiving Office under the Patent Co-operation Treaty must [be filed in English or Welsh.]

(2) . . .

(3) Where the Patent Office was acting on behalf of the International Bureau as the receiving Office, the comptroller shall only transmit an international application for a patent filed at the Patent Office to the International Bureau and the International Searching Authority after the appropriate fee has been paid.

(4) A request under the treaty for a certified copy of an international application for a patent (including any corrections to that application) filed at the Patent Office as the competent receiving Office must be filed on Patents Form 23.

NOTES

Para (1): words in square brackets substituted by the Patents (Amendment) (No 2) Rules 2016, SI 2016/892, rr 2, 11(a).
Para (2): revoked by SI 2016/892, rr 2, 11(b).

Beginning the national phase, international exhibitions and altered prescribed periods

[1.328]
66 Beginning of national phase

(1) The prescribed period for the purposes of section 89A(3)(a) and (5)(a) is thirty one months [beginning immediately after]—
(a) where there is no declared priority date, the date of filing of the application;
(b) where there is a declared priority date, that date.

(2) But where the applicant has been notified under rule 69(5), the period prescribed for the purposes of section 89A(3)(a) and (5)(a) is three months [beginning immediately after] the date of the notification.

(3) Where an international application for a patent (UK) has begun the national phase, a request for permission to make a late declaration may be made under section 5(2B) before the end of the period of one month [beginning immediately after] the date the national phase of the application begins.

NOTES

Words in square brackets substituted by the Patents (Amendment) Rules 2011, SI 2011/2052, rr 2, 3, Schedule, for transitional provisions see r 4 thereof.

[1.329]

[66A Amendment of international application before grant

(1) This rule applies to an international application for a patent (UK) which has begun the national phase of the application.

(2) The period within which an applicant may amend his application under section 19(1) is as follows.

(3) Where during the international phase of the application, the International Searching Authority has sent to the applicant the International Search Report relating to the invention, the period within which the applicant may amend his application is the period beginning with the date on which the national phase of the application begins and ending with the date on which the comptroller sends the applicant the first substantive examination report.

(4) Where during the international phase of the application, the International Searching Authority has not sent to the applicant the International Search Report relating to the invention, the period during which the applicant may amend his application is the first to commence of—

(a) the period prescribed by rule 31(3); and

(b) the period beginning with the date on which the International Searching Authority sends the International Search Report to the applicant and ending with the date on which the comptroller sends the applicant the first substantive examination report.]

NOTES

Commencement: 1 October 2016.

Inserted by the Patents (Amendment) (No 2) Rules 2016, SI 2016/892, rr 2, 12.

[1.330]

67 International exhibitions

(1) Paragraph (2) applies where an applicant, on filing an international application for a patent (UK), states in writing to the receiving office that the invention has been displayed at an international exhibition.

(2) The prescribed period for the purposes of section 2(4)(c) is two months [beginning immediately after] the date on which the national phase begins.

NOTES

Para (2): words in square brackets substituted by the Patents (Amendment) Rules 2011, SI 2011/2052, rr 2, 3, Schedule, for transitional provisions see r 4 thereof.

[1.331]

68 Altered prescribed periods

(1) This rule applies to an international application for a patent (UK) which has begun the national phase of the application.

(2) The period prescribed for the purposes of section 13(2) is—

(a) the period prescribed by rule 10(3); or

(b) if it expires later, the period of two months [beginning immediately after] the date on which the national phase begins.

(3) The period prescribed for the purposes of sections 15(10)(c) and (d) and 17(1) is—

(a) the period prescribed by rule 22(2) and (7); or

(b) if it expires later, the period of two months [beginning immediately after] the date on which the national phase begins.

(4) The period prescribed for the purposes of section 18(1) is—

(a) thirty three months [beginning immediately after]—

(i) where there is no declared priority date, the date of filing of the application; or

(ii) where there is a declared priority date, that date; or

(b) if it expires later, the period of two months [beginning immediately after] the date on which the national phase begins.

NOTES

Paras (2)–(4): words in square brackets substituted by the Patents (Amendment) Rules 2011, SI 2011/2052, rr 2, 3, Schedule, for transitional provisions see r 4 thereof.

Translations

[1.332]

69 Necessary translations under section 89A(3) and (5)

(1) A translation is necessary for the purposes of section 89A(3) where any of the following are not in English—

(a) the international application for a patent (UK) as published in accordance with the Patent Co-operation Treaty;

(b) where the information mentioned in paragraph 3(2)(a) and (b) of Schedule 1 (biological material) has been provided, that information.

(2) Where the applicant expressly requests the comptroller to proceed with the national phase before the end of the period prescribed by rule 66(1), the translation must include the request and abstract.

(3) But paragraph (2) does not apply where a copy of the application, as published in accordance with the Patent Co-operation Treaty, is available to the comptroller.

(4) A translation of an amendment is necessary for the purposes of section 89A(5) where any amendment made to the application is not in English and has either been—

(a) published under the Patent Co-operation Treaty; or

(b) annexed to the International Preliminary Examination Report.

(5) At the end of the period prescribed by rule 66(1), the comptroller must notify the applicant that a necessary translation is missing if—

(a) a translation of the application has been filed, but a translation of the amendment has not been filed; or

(b) the information mentioned in paragraph 3(2)(a) and (b) of Schedule 1 (biological material) has been provided, but a translation of that information has not been filed,

and the prescribed fee has been paid.

[1.333]

70 Requirements of necessary translations

(1) This rule applies to translations which are necessary for the purposes of section 89A(3) and (5).

(2) Such a translation is necessary for only that part of the application which is in a language other than English.

(3) Where the application includes a drawing which is annotated, the translation shall include either—

(a) a copy of the original drawing where the original annotations have been replaced by annotations in English; or

(b) a new drawing with the annotations in English.

(4) Where a title has been established for the application by the International Searching Authority, the translation must include that title (and not any title which was included in the application as it was originally filed).

(5) Where—

(a) the description of the invention includes a sequence listing; and

(b) the listing complies with the relevant requirements of the Patent Co-operation Treaty,

the translation of the application may exclude a translation of the sequence listing.

(6) This rule applies to translations of amendments as it applies to translations of applications and accordingly references to "application" shall be construed as references to "amendment".

Application deemed withdrawn or filing date refused under the Patent Co-operation Treaty

[1.334]

71 Directions under section 89(3) and (5)

(1) The applicant may, before the end of the relevant period, make a written request to the comptroller to give a direction under section 89(5).

(2) The applicant may notify the comptroller that the circumstances mentioned in section 89(3) or rule 72 apply to his application.

(3) The request under paragraph (1) must be accompanied by—

(a) a statement of the reasons for the request; and

(b) the fee prescribed for the purposes of section 89A(3).

(4) The relevant period is two months [beginning immediately after] the date on which—

(a) the International Bureau; or

(b) the receiving Office,

notifies the applicant that his international application for a patent (UK) is refused a filing date under the Patent Co-operation Treaty.

(5) Where the applicant has made a request to the comptroller under paragraph (1), the comptroller may direct the applicant to furnish him with any document, information or evidence within such period as the comptroller may specify.

(6) Where the applicant fails, before the end of the period specified, to comply with a direction given under paragraph (5), the comptroller may treat him as having withdrawn his request.

(7) Where section 89(3) applies or a direction has been given under section 89(5) the comptroller may—

(a) alter any period of time (whether it has already expired or not) specified in the Act or listed in Parts 1 to 3 of Schedule 4; and

(b) amend any document kept at the Patent Office in relation to the application,

subject to such conditions as the comptroller may direct.

NOTES

Para (4): words in square brackets substituted by the Patents (Amendment) Rules 2011, SI 2011/2052, rr 2, 3, Schedule, for transitional provisions see r 4 thereof.

[1.335]
72 Circumstance prescribed for the purposes of section 89(3)

The other circumstance prescribed for the purposes of section 89(3) is where the comptroller determines that, in comparable circumstances in relation to an application under the Act (other than an international application for a patent (UK)), he would have exercised his powers under rule 107 or 108 to prevent the application being treated as withdrawn.

PART 7
PROCEEDINGS HEARD BEFORE THE COMPTROLLER

Introductory

[1.336]
73 Scope and interpretation

(1) This Part applies to the following proceedings heard before the comptroller—
- (a) applications, references and requests under the provisions mentioned in Part 1 of Schedule 3;
- (b) oppositions under the provisions mentioned in Part 2 of that Schedule.

(2) The rules listed in Part 4 of that Schedule apply to any proceedings heard before the comptroller under the Act.

(3) In this Part—

"claimant" means a person who starts proceedings or is treated as starting proceedings under rule 76(1);

"defendant" means a person who files a counter-statement under rule 77(6) or (8);

"statement of case" means the statement of grounds or the counter-statement and references to a statement of case include part of the statement of case;

"statement of grounds" means a statement filed by the claimant;

"statement of truth" means a statement that the person making the statement believes that the facts stated in a particular document are true; and

"witness statement" means a written statement signed by a person that contains the evidence which that person would be allowed to give orally.

[1.337]
74 Overriding objective

(1) The rules in this Part set out a procedural code with the overriding objective of enabling the comptroller to deal with cases justly.

(2) Dealing with a case justly includes, so far as is practicable—
- (a) ensuring that the parties are on an equal footing;
- (b) saving expense;
- (c) dealing with the case in ways which are proportionate—
  - (i) to the amount of money involved,
  - (ii) to the importance of the case,
  - (iii) to the complexity of the issues, and
  - (iv) to the financial position of each party;
- (d) ensuring that it is dealt with expeditiously and fairly; and
- (e) allotting to it an appropriate share of the resources available to the comptroller, while taking into account the need to allot resources to other cases.

(3) The comptroller shall seek to give effect to the overriding objective when he—
- (a) exercises any power given to him by this Part; or
- (b) interprets any rule in this Part.

(4) The parties are required to help the comptroller to further the overriding objective.

[1.338]
[75 Publication of notices

(1) Subject to paragraph (2) and rule 105(5) the comptroller must advertise in the journal any event to which it is possible to object under any of the provisions mentioned in Part 2 or 3 of Schedule 3.

(2) Where an amendment to the specification of a patent is proposed by the proprietor under section 75(1) the comptroller may, if he thinks fit, advertise in the journal the proposed amendment.]

NOTES

Commencement: 1 October 2016.

Substituted by the Patents (Amendment) (No 2) Rules 2016, SI 2016/892, rr 2, 13.

Conduct of hearings

[1.339]

76 Starting proceedings

(1) Proceedings are started when a person files in duplicate—

(a) the relevant form; and

(b) his statement of grounds.

(2) Any person may give notice of opposition—

(a) in the case of section 75(2), before the end of the period of two weeks [beginning immediately after] the date of the relevant notice; and

(b) in the case of any of the other provisions mentioned in Part 2 of Schedule 3, before the end of the period of four weeks [beginning immediately after] the date of the relevant notice.

(3) For the purposes of this rule and rule 77—

"relevant form" means—

(a) in relation to applications or requests under the provisions of the Medicinal Products Regulation or the Plant Protection Products Regulation mentioned in Part 1 of Schedule 3, Patents Form SP3;

(b) in relation to applications, references or requests under any other provision mentioned in Part 1 of that Schedule, Patents Form 2; and

(c) in relation to oppositions under the provisions mentioned in Part 2 of that Schedule, Patents Form 15; and

"relevant notice" means the advertisement in the journal mentioned in rule 75.

(4) A statement of grounds must—

(a) include a concise statement of the facts and grounds on which the claimant relies;

(b) in the case of rule 89(5), include the grounds of objection to the draft licence;

(c) where appropriate, include the period or terms of the licence which he believes are reasonable;

(d) specify the remedy which he seeks;

(e) where it accompanies an application under the Compulsory Licensing Regulation, include any information required by that Regulation;

(f) be verified by a statement of truth; and

(g) comply with the requirements of Part 1 of Schedule 2.

NOTES

Para (2): words in square brackets substituted by the Patents (Amendment) Rules 2011, SI 2011/2052, rr 2, 3, Schedule, for transitional provisions see r 4 thereof.

[1.340]

77 Notification of the parties

(1) The comptroller must notify the applicant for, or proprietor of, the patent which is the subject matter of the case that proceedings have started.

(2) In addition, the comptroller may notify any persons who appear to him to be likely to have an interest in the case that proceedings have started.

(3) But where a person mentioned in paragraph (1) or (2)—

(a) is the claimant; or

(b) has indicated in writing to the comptroller that he supports the claimant's case,

the comptroller has no duty to notify him.

(4) The comptroller must send the relevant form and the statement of grounds with the notification under paragraph (1) or (2).

(5) In that notification, the comptroller must specify a period within which the persons notified may file a counter-statement.

(6) Any counter-statement must be filed in duplicate before the end of the period specified under paragraph (5).

(7) But paragraphs (5) and (6) do not apply to an opposition under any of the provisions mentioned in Part 3 of Schedule 3.

(8) In such oppositions, any counter-statement must be filed in duplicate before the end of the period of four weeks [beginning immediately after] the date of the relevant notice.

(9) Where—

(a) a person was notified under paragraph (1) or (2); and

(b) that person fails to file a counter-statement under paragraph (6) or (8),

the comptroller shall treat him as supporting the claimant's case.

(10) The period prescribed for the purposes of giving notice to the comptroller under section 47(6) of opposition to cancellation of an entry made under section 46 that licences are available as of right is the period prescribed by paragraph (8).

NOTES

Para (8): words in square brackets substituted by the Patents (Amendment) Rules 2011, SI 2011/2052, rr 2, 3, Schedule, for transitional provisions see r 4 thereof.

[1.341]

78 The counter-statement

(1) Any counter-statement filed by the defendant must—

(a) state which of the allegations in the statement of grounds he denies;

(b) state which of the allegations he is unable to admit or deny, but which he requires the claimant to prove;

(c) state which of the allegations he admits;

(d) be verified by a statement of truth; and

(e) comply with the requirements of Part 1 of Schedule 2.

(2) Where the defendant denies an allegation—

(a) he must state his reasons for doing so; and

(b) if he intends to put forward a different version of events from that given by the claimant, he must state his own version.

(3) A defendant who fails to deal with an allegation in a counter-statement shall be taken to admit that allegation.

(4) But a defendant who—

(a) fails to deal with an allegation; but

(b) has set out in his counter-statement the nature of his case in relation to the issue to which the allegation is relevant,

shall be taken to require the allegation to be proved.

[1.342]

79 Copies of documents

(1) Where a relevant statement refers to any other document, a copy of that document must accompany the relevant statement.

(2) Where more than one copy of a relevant statement is filed, each copy of the statement must be accompanied by a copy of any document referred to in the statement.

(3) But paragraphs (1) and (2) do not apply where—

(a) the relevant statement is sent to the comptroller; and

(b) the document referred to in the relevant statement was published by the comptroller or is kept at the Patent Office.

(4) In this rule "relevant statement" means a witness statement, statement of case, affidavit or statutory declaration.

[1.343]

80 Evidence rounds and the hearing

(1) When the defendant files a counter-statement, the comptroller must as soon as practicable—

(a) send the counter-statement to the claimant; . . .

[(aa) specify the period within which the claimant must file Patents Form 4; and]

(b) specify the periods within which evidence may be filed by the claimant and the defendant.

[(1A) If the claimant wishes to continue the proceedings following receipt of the counter-statement, the claimant must file Patents Form 4.]

(2) The comptroller may, at any time he thinks fit, give leave to either party to file evidence upon such terms as he thinks fit.

(3) Under this rule, evidence shall only be considered to be filed when—

(a) it has been received by the comptroller; and

(b) it has been sent to all the other parties to the proceedings.

(4) The comptroller must then give the parties an opportunity to be heard.

(5) If any party requests to be heard, the comptroller must send to the parties notice of a date for the hearing.

(6) When the comptroller has decided the matter he must notify all the parties of his decision, including his reasons for making the decision.

NOTES

Para (1): word omitted from sub-para (a) revoked and sub-para (aa) inserted by the Patents and Patents and Trade Marks (Fees) (Amendment) Rules 2010, SI 2010/33, rr 2, 3, 15, except in relation to proceedings which started before 6 April 2010.

Para (1A): inserted by SI 2010/33, rr 2, 4, 15, except in relation to proceedings which started before 6 April 2010.

[1.344]
81 Alteration of time limits

(1) The comptroller may extend or shorten (or further extend or shorten) any period of time which has been specified under any provision of this Part.

(2) An extension may be granted under paragraph (1) notwithstanding the period of time specified has expired.

[1.345]
[81A Failure to file Patents Form 4

If the claimant fails to file Patents Form 4 within the period specified by the comptroller the claimant shall be deemed to have filed a request to withdraw from the proceedings.]

NOTES

Inserted by the Patents and Patents and Trade Marks (Fees) (Amendment) Rules 2010, SI 2010/33, rr 2, 5, 15, except in relation to proceedings which started before 6 April 2010.

[1.346]
82 General powers of the comptroller in relation to proceedings before him

(1) Except where the Act or these Rules otherwise provide, the comptroller may give such directions as to the management of the proceedings as he thinks fit, and in particular he may—

(a) require a document, information or evidence to be filed;
(b) require a translation of a specification of a patent or application or any other document which is not in English;
(c) require a party or a party's legal representative to attend a hearing;
(d) hold a hearing and receive evidence by telephone or by using any other method of direct oral communication;
(e) allow a statement of case to be amended;
(f) stay the whole, or any part, of the proceedings either generally or until a specified date or event;
(g) consolidate proceedings;
(h) direct that part of any proceedings be dealt with as separate proceedings; and
(i) direct that the parties attend a case management conference or pre-hearing review.

(2) The comptroller may control the evidence by giving directions as to—

(a) the issues on which he requires evidence;
(b) the nature of the evidence which he requires to decide those issues; and
(c) the way in which the evidence is to be placed before him,

and the comptroller may use his power under this paragraph to exclude evidence which would otherwise be admissible.

(3) When the comptroller gives directions under any provision of this Part, he may—

(a) make them subject to conditions; and
(b) specify the consequence of failure to comply with the directions or a condition.

[1.347]
83 Striking out a statement of case and summary judgment

(1) A party may apply to the comptroller for him to strike out a statement of case or to give summary judgment.

(2) If it appears to the comptroller that—

(a) the statement of case discloses no reasonable grounds for bringing or defending the claim;
(b) the statement of case is an abuse of process or is otherwise likely to obstruct the just disposal of the proceedings; or
(c) there has been a failure to comply with a section, a rule or a previous direction given by the comptroller,

he may strike out the statement of case.

(3) The comptroller may give summary judgment against a claimant or defendant on the whole of a case or on a particular issue if—

(a) he considers that—
  (i) that claimant has no real prospect of succeeding on the case or issue, or
  (ii) that defendant has no real prospect of successfully defending the case or issue; and
(b) there is no other compelling reason why the case or issue should be disposed of at a hearing.

[1.348]
84 Hearings in public

(1) Subject to paragraphs (3) and (4), any hearing before the comptroller in proceedings relating to an application for a patent, or a patent, shall be held in public.

(2) Any party to the proceedings may apply to the comptroller for a hearing to be held in private.

(3) The comptroller may grant an application under paragraph (2) where—

(a) he considers there is good reason for the hearing to be held in private; and
(b) all the parties to the proceedings have had an opportunity to be heard on the matter,
and where the application is granted the hearing must be held in private.

(4) Any hearing—
(a) of an application under paragraph (2); or
(b) relating to an application for a patent which has not been published,
shall be held in private.

(5) For the purposes of this rule a reference to a hearing includes any part of a hearing.

Miscellaneous

[1.349]
85 Security for costs or expenses

(1) The conditions prescribed for the purposes of making an order for security for costs under section 107(4) are that the party against whom the order is made—
(a) is resident outside the United Kingdom, but not resident in—
(i) a Brussels Contracting State,
(ii) a Lugano Contracting State, or
(iii) a Regulation State,
as defined in section 1(3) of the Civil Jurisdiction and Judgments Act 1982;
(b) is a company or other body (whether incorporated inside or outside the United Kingdom) and there is reason to believe that it will be unable to pay another party's costs if ordered to do so;
(c) has changed his address for service with a view to evading the consequences of the litigation;
(d) has furnished an incorrect address for service; or
(e) has taken steps in relation to his assets that would make it difficult to enforce an order for costs against him.

(2) In relation to proceedings in Scotland, references in this rule to costs are references to expenses.

[1.350]
86 Powers of comptroller to compel attendance of witnesses and production of documents

The comptroller shall have the powers of a judge of the High Court (in Scotland, the Court of Session) as regards—
(a) the attendance of witnesses; and
(b) the discovery and production of documents,
but he shall have no power to punish summarily for contempt.

[1.351]
87 Evidence in proceedings before the comptroller

(1) Subject to paragraphs (2) to (5), evidence filed under this Part may be given—
(a) by witness statement, statement of case, affidavit, statutory declaration; or
(b) in any other form which would be admissible as evidence in proceedings before the court.

(2) A witness statement or a statement of case may only be given in evidence if it includes a statement of truth.

(3) Evidence is to be by witness statement unless the comptroller directs or any enactment requires otherwise.

(4) A witness statement, affidavit or statutory declaration must comply with the requirements of Part 1 of Schedule 2, unless the comptroller otherwise directs.

(5) For the purposes of this Part a statement of truth must be dated and signed by—
(a) in the case of a witness statement, the person making the statement; and
(b) in any other case, the party or his legal representative.

[1.352]
88 Proceedings in Scotland

(1) Where there is more than one party to proceedings, a party to the proceedings may apply to the comptroller to hold proceedings in Scotland.

(2) An application made under paragraph (1) must be granted—
(a) where all the parties consent to the proceedings being held in Scotland; or
(b) where the comptroller considers it appropriate.

(3) A refusal of an application made under paragraph (1) is excepted from the right of appeal conferred by section 97.

[1.353]
89 Proceedings started under section 46(3) by a person other than the proprietor

(1) An application by a person other than the proprietor to the comptroller under section 46(3)(a) or (b) must be—

(a) made on Patents Form 2; and
(b) accompanied by two copies of the draft of the licence he proposes should be granted.

(2) The comptroller must notify the proprietor of the patent that an application has been made.

(3) The comptroller must send a copy of the draft licence with the notification.

(4) In the notification, the comptroller must specify a period within which the proprietor may file a statement of grounds.

(5) The proprietor must file a statement of grounds in accordance with rule 76(4); otherwise he shall be treated as supporting the applicant's case.

(6) Proceedings shall continue under this Part as if they had been started under rule 76(1) and for those purposes the proprietor shall be "the claimant" and the applicant shall be "the defendant".

[1.354]
90 Licences following entitlement proceedings

(1) The period prescribed for the purposes of section 11(3) and (3A) shall be two months [beginning immediately after]—
(a) where section 11 is applied by section 12(5), the date on which the order under section 12(1) was made; and
(b) in any other case, the date on which the order under section 8 was made.

(2) The period prescribed for the purposes of section 38(3) shall be two months [beginning immediately after] the date on which the order mentioned in section 38(2) was made.

NOTES

Words in square brackets substituted by the Patents (Amendment) Rules 2011, SI 2011/2052, rr 2, 3, Schedule, for transitional provisions see r 4 thereof.

[1.355]
91 Period prescribed for applications by employee for compensation

(1) The period prescribed for the purposes of section 40(1) and (2) shall be the period beginning with the date of grant of the patent and ending one year after the patent ceased to have effect.

(2) But if an application for restoration is made under section 28 and—
(a) the application is granted, the period prescribed under paragraph (1) shall continue as if the patent had remained continuously in effect; or
(b) the application is refused, the period prescribed for the purposes of section 40(1) and (2) shall be—
(i) the period prescribed under paragraph (1), or
(ii) if it expires later, the period of six months [beginning immediately after] the date on which the application was refused.

NOTES

Para (2): words in square brackets substituted by the Patents (Amendment) Rules 2011, SI 2011/2052, rr 2, 3, Schedule, for transitional provisions see r 4 thereof.

PART 8
OPINIONS

Interpretation

[1.356]
92 Interpretation

In this Part—
"request" means, unless the context otherwise requires, a request for an opinion under section 74A;
"requester" means the person who makes that request;
"patent in suit" means the patent to which that request relates;
"patent holder" means the proprietor of that patent and any exclusive licensee of the patent; and
"relevant proceedings" means proceedings (whether pending or concluded) before the comptroller, the court or the European Patent Office.

Request for opinion

[1.357]
93 Request for an opinion under section 74A

(1) A request must be made on Patents Form 17 and must be accompanied by a copy and a statement setting out fully—
(a) the question upon which an opinion is sought;
(b) the requester's submissions on that question; and
(c) any matters of fact which are requested to be taken into account.

(2) The statement must be accompanied by—

(a) the name and address of any persons, of whom the requester is aware, having an interest in that question; and
(b) particulars of any relevant proceedings of which the requester is aware which relate to the patent in suit and which may be relevant to that question.

(3) However, where the requester is acting as an agent in making the request, the persons referred to in paragraph (2)(a) do not include the person for whom the requester is so acting.

(4) The statement shall be accompanied by a copy of any evidence or other document (except a document which has been published by the comptroller or is kept at the Patent Office) which is referred to in the statement.

(5) Each such statement, evidence or other document must be provided in duplicate.

[(6) The prescribed matters for the purposes of section 74A(1) are as follows—
(a) whether a particular act constitutes, or (if done) would constitute, an infringement of the patent;
(b) whether, or to what extent, an invention for which the patent has been granted is not a patentable invention;
(c) whether the specification of the patent discloses the invention clearly enough and completely enough for it to be performed by a person skilled in the art;
(d) whether the matter disclosed in the specification of the patent extends beyond that disclosed in the application for the patent as filed or, if the patent was granted on a new application, in the earlier application as filed;
(e) whether the protection conferred by the patent has been extended by an amendment which should not have been allowed;
(f) whether a supplementary protection certificate is invalid under Article 15 of the Medicinal Products Regulation; and
(g) whether a supplementary protection certificate is invalid under Article 15 of the Plant Protection Products Regulation.]

NOTES

Para (6): added by the Patents (Amendment) (No 2) Rules 2014, SI 2014/2401, rr 2, 10.

[1.358]
94 Refusal or withdrawal of request

(1) The comptroller shall not issue an opinion if—
(a) the request appears to him to be frivolous or vexatious; or
(b) the question upon which the opinion is sought appears to him to have been sufficiently considered in any relevant proceedings.

(2) The comptroller shall not issue an opinion if the requester gives him notice in writing that the request is withdrawn.

(3) If the comptroller intends at any time—
(a) to refuse the request because the condition in paragraph (1)(a) or (b) is satisfied; or
(b) to refuse the request because, in accordance with section 74A(3)(b), he considers it inappropriate in all the circumstances to issue an opinion,

he shall notify the requester accordingly.

[1.359]
95 Notification and advertisement of request

(1) The comptroller must notify each of the following persons of the request (except where the person concerned is the requester)—
(a) the patent holder;
(b) any holder of a licence or sub-licence under the patent in suit which has been registered under rule 47 [or, in the case of a European patent with unitary effect, in the Register for unitary patent protection kept under the Unitary Patent Regulation];
(c) any person who has made a request in respect of the patent in suit under rule 54 regarding an opinion being requested under rule 93;
(d) any person who is specified under rule 93(2)(a).

(2) In addition, the comptroller may notify of the request any persons who appear to him to be likely to have an interest in the question upon which the opinion is sought.

(3) The comptroller must send a copy of the form and statement filed under rule 93(1) to each person so notified, together with a copy of such other documents filed under rule 93 as he thinks fit.

(4) The comptroller must advertise a request in such manner as he thinks fit.

(5) However, if the request is refused or withdrawn before a notification has been made under paragraph (1)—
(a) the patent holder alone must be notified of the request (and of the fact that it has been refused or withdrawn); and
(b) paragraphs (3) and (4) do not apply.

NOTES

Para (1): words in square brackets in sub-para (b) inserted by the Patents (Amendment) Rules 2016, SI 2016/517, r 2(1), (3), as from a day to be appointed (being the date of entry into force of the Agreement on a Unified Patent Court, which is reproduced at **[1.1009]**).

[1.360]

96 Submission of observations and observations in reply

(1) If the request has not been refused or withdrawn, any person may, before the end of the relevant period, file observations on any issue raised by the request.

(2) Such observations may include reasons why the comptroller should refuse the request.

(3) Any person who files observations under paragraph (1) must ensure that, before the end of the relevant period, a copy of those observations is received—

(a) where that person is not the patent holder, by the patent holder; and
(b) by the requester.

(4) A person to whom observations are sent under paragraph (3) may, during the period of two weeks beginning immediately after the end of the relevant period, file observations confined strictly to matters in reply.

(5) Any person who files observations under paragraph (4) must ensure that, within that period of two weeks, a copy of those observations is received—

(a) where that person is the requester, by the patent holder; and
(b) where that person is the patent holder, by the requester.

(6) If it is reasonably possible, the observations filed under this rule and the copies of such observations shall be delivered only in electronic form or using electronic communications.

(7) For the purposes of this rule, the relevant period is four weeks [beginning immediately after] the date of advertisement under rule 95(4).

NOTES

Para (7): words in square brackets substituted by the Patents (Amendment) Rules 2011, SI 2011/2052, rr 2, 3, Schedule, for transitional provisions see r 4 thereof.

[1.361]

97 Issue of the opinion

(1) After the end of the procedure under rule 96, the comptroller must refer the request to an examiner for the preparation of the opinion.

(2) The comptroller must issue the opinion that has been prepared by sending a copy to—

(a) the requester;
(b) the patent holder; and
(c) any other person who filed observations under rule 96(1).

Review of opinion

[1.362]

98 Review of opinion

(1) The patent holder may, before the end of the period of three months [beginning immediately after] the date on which the opinion is issued, apply to the comptroller for a review of the opinion.

(2) However, such proceedings for a review may not be brought (or if brought may not be continued) if the issue raised by the review has been decided in other relevant proceedings.

(3) The application must be made on Patents Form 2 and be accompanied by a copy and a statement in duplicate setting out the grounds on which the review is sought.

(4) The statement must contain particulars of any relevant proceedings of which the applicant is aware which may be relevant to the question whether the proceedings for a review may be brought or continued.

(5) The application may be made on the following grounds only—

(a) that the opinion wrongly concluded that the patent in suit was invalid, or was invalid to a limited extent; or
(b) that, by reason of its interpretation of the specification of the patent in suit, the opinion wrongly concluded that a particular act did not or would not constitute an infringement of the patent.

NOTES

Para (1): words in square brackets substituted by the Patents (Amendment) Rules 2011, SI 2011/2052, rr 2, 3, Schedule, for transitional provisions see r 4 thereof.

[1.363]
99 Procedure on review

(1) On receipt of the application, the comptroller must send a copy of the form and statement filed under rule 98 to—

(a) the requester (if different from the applicant); and
(b) any person who filed observations under rule 96.

(2) The comptroller must advertise the application in such manner as he thinks fit.

(3) Before the end of the relevant period, any person may file a statement in support of the application or a counter-statement contesting it (which in either case must be in duplicate), and on so doing shall become a party to the proceedings for a review.

(4) For the purposes of paragraph (3) the relevant period is—

(a) four weeks [beginning immediately after] the date on which the application is advertised under paragraph (2); or
(b) if it expires later, the period of two months [beginning immediately after] the date on which the opinion is issued under rule 97(2).

(5) The comptroller shall send to the other parties a copy of each statement or counter-statement filed under paragraph (3).

(6) The rules listed in Parts 4 and 5 of Schedule 3 shall apply to the proceedings for a review and for the purposes of rule 83(3)—

(a) a reference to "the claimant" is a reference to the applicant for a review; and
(b) a reference to "the defendant" is a reference to any other party.

NOTES

Para (4): words in square brackets substituted by the Patents (Amendment) Rules 2011, SI 2011/2052, rr 2, 3, Schedule, for transitional provisions see r 4 thereof.

[1.364]
100 Outcome of review

(1) On completion of the proceedings under rule 99 the comptroller shall either—

(a) set aside the opinion in whole or in part; or
(b) decide that no reason has been shown for the opinion to be set aside.

(2) A decision under paragraph (1)(a) or (b) shall not estop any party to any proceedings from raising any issue regarding the validity or the infringement of the patent.

(3) No appeal under section 97 shall lie from a decision to set aside the opinion under paragraph (1)(a), except where the appeal relates to a part of the opinion that is not set aside.

PART 9
MISCELLANEOUS

Agents and advisers

[1.365]
101 Agents

(1) Any act required or authorised by the Act or these Rules to be done by or to any person in connection with an application for a patent, or any procedure relating to a patent, may be done by or to an agent authorised by that person orally or in writing—

(a) where an agent is appointed when a person starts or joins any proceeding under the Act, once the comptroller has been notified of his appointment in writing; or
(b) where an agent is appointed after a person has started or joined any proceeding under the Act, once Patents Form 51 has been filed . . .

(2) Where an agent has been authorised under paragraph (1), the comptroller may, in any particular case, require the signature or presence of his principal.

NOTES

Para (1): words omitted revoked by the Patents (Amendment) (No 2) Rules 2016, SI 2016/892, rr 2, 14.

[1.366]
102 Appointing advisers

The comptroller may appoint an adviser to assist him in any proceeding before him and shall settle any question or instructions to be given to the adviser.

Address for service

[1.367]
103 Address for service

(1) For the purposes of any proceeding under the Act or these Rules, an address for service must be furnished by—

(a) an applicant for the grant of a patent;

(b) a person who makes any other application, reference or request or gives any notice of opposition under the Act; and

(c) any person opposing such an application, reference, request or notice.

(2) The proprietor of a patent, or any person who has registered any right in or under a patent or application, may furnish an address for service by notifying the comptroller.

(3) Where a person has furnished an address for service under paragraph (1) or (2), he may substitute a new address for service by notifying the comptroller.

[(4) An address for service furnished under this Rule shall be an address in the United Kingdom, another EEA state or the Channel Islands.]

NOTES

Para (4): substituted for original paras (4), (5) by the Patents, Trade Marks and Designs (Address for Service) Rules 2009, SI 2009/546, rr 8, 9.

[1.368]

104 Failure to furnish an address for service

(1) Where—

(a) a person has failed to furnish an address for service under rule 103(1); and

(b) the comptroller has sufficient information enabling him to contact that person,

the comptroller shall direct that person to furnish an address for service.

(2) Where a direction has been given under paragraph (1), the person directed shall, before the end of the period of two months [beginning immediately after] the date of the direction, furnish an address for service.

(3) Paragraph (4) applies where—

(a) a direction was given under paragraph (1) and the period prescribed by paragraph (2) has expired; or

(b) the comptroller had insufficient information to give a direction under paragraph (1),

and the person has failed to furnish an address for service.

(4) Where this paragraph applies—

(a) in the case of an applicant for the grant of a patent, the application shall be treated as withdrawn;

(b) in the case of a person mentioned in rule 103(1)(b), his application, reference, request or notice of opposition shall be treated as withdrawn; and

(c) in the case of a person mentioned in rule 103(1)(c), he shall be deemed to have withdrawn from the proceedings.

(5) In this rule an "address for service" means an address which complies with the requirements of rule 103(4) . . .

NOTES

Para (2): words in square brackets substituted by the Patents (Amendment) Rules 2011, SI 2011/2052, rr 2, 3, Schedule, for transitional provisions see r 4 thereof.

Para (5): words omitted revoked by the Patents, Trade Marks and Designs (Address for Service) Rules 2009, SI 2009/546, rr 8, 10.

Corrections and remission of fees

[1.369]

105 Correction of errors

(1) A request to the comptroller to correct an error or mistake under section 117 must be made in writing and identify the proposed correction.

(2) The comptroller may, if he thinks fit, require the person requesting a correction to produce a copy of the document indicating the correction.

(3) Where the request is to correct a specification of a patent or application, the request shall not be granted unless the correction is obvious (meaning that it is immediately evident that nothing else could have been intended in the original specification).

(4) But paragraph (3) does not apply where the error in the specification of the patent or application is connected to the delivery of the application in electronic form or using electronic communications.

(5) Where the comptroller determines that no person could reasonably object to the correction no advertisement shall be published under rule 75.

(6) Where the comptroller is required to publish a notice under section 117(3), it must be published in the journal.

(7) This rule does not apply to a correction of a name, address or address for service (which may be corrected under rule 49).

[1.370]

106 Remission of fees

(1) A person may apply to the comptroller for the remission of a fee.

(2) The comptroller may remit the whole or part of a search fee where—

(a) in relation to an international application for a patent (UK), a copy of the International Search Report (as defined in rule 64) for that application is available to the comptroller; or

(b) a new application for a patent is filed as mentioned in section 15(9) and, in connection with the earlier application, the applicant has already paid the search fee for the invention described in the new application.

(3) The comptroller may remit the whole or part of any fee where—

(a) a person has requested the comptroller or an examiner to do something in accordance with the Act or these Rules; and

(b) the request is withdrawn before it is carried out.

(4) The comptroller may remit the whole or part of the fee payable in respect of a request for an opinion under section 74A where he has refused the request.

(5) Where a supplementary protection certificate lapses or is declared invalid, the comptroller must remit any fee which has been paid in respect of the relevant period.

(6) In paragraph (5) "the relevant period" is the period—

(a) beginning with the next anniversary of the start date following the date the certificate lapsed or was declared invalid; and

(b) ending with the date the certificate would have expired but for its lapse or invalidity.

(7) Any decision of the comptroller under this rule is excepted from the right of appeal conferred by section 97.

[1.371]

107 Correction of irregularities

(1) Subject to paragraph (3), the comptroller may, if he thinks fit, authorise the rectification of any irregularity of procedure connected with any proceeding or other matter before the comptroller, an examiner or the Patent Office.

(2) Any rectification made under paragraph (1) shall be made—

(a) after giving the parties such notice; and

(b) subject to such conditions,

as the comptroller may direct.

(3) A period of time specified in the Act or listed in Parts 1 to 3 of Schedule 4 (whether it has already expired or not) may be extended under paragraph (1) if, and only if—

(a) the irregularity or prospective irregularity is attributable, wholly or in part, to a default, omission or other error by the comptroller, an examiner or the Patent Office; and

(b) it appears to the comptroller that the irregularity should be rectified.

Time limits and delays

[1.372]

108 Extension of time limits

(1) The comptroller may, if he thinks fit, extend or further extend any period of time prescribed by these Rules except a period prescribed by the provisions listed in Parts 1 and 2 of Schedule 4.

(2) The comptroller shall extend, by a period of two months, any period of time prescribed by the provisions listed in Part 2 of Schedule 4 where—

(a) a request is filed on Patents Form 52;

(b) no previous request has been made under this paragraph; and

(c) that request is filed before the end of the period of two months [beginning immediately after] the date on which the relevant period of time expired.

(3) The comptroller may, if he thinks fit, extend or further extend any period of time prescribed by the rules listed in Part 2 of Schedule 4 where—

(a) a request is filed on Patents Form 52; and

(b) the person making the request has furnished evidence supporting the grounds of the request, except where the comptroller otherwise directs.

(4) Each request under paragraph (2) or (3) for a period of time to be extended must be made on a separate form unless—

(a) each of those requests relate to the same patent or application for a patent; and

(b) the grant of each of those requests would result in the expiry of all the extended periods of time on the same date,

in which case those requests may be combined and made on a single form.

(5) Any extension made under paragraph (1) or (3) shall be made—

(a) after giving the parties such notice; and

(b) subject to such conditions,

as the comptroller may direct, except that a period of time prescribed by the rules listed in Part 3 of Schedule 4 may be extended (or further extended) for a period of two months only.

(6) An extension may be granted under paragraph (1) or (3) notwithstanding the period of time prescribed by the relevant rule has expired.

(7) But no extension may be granted in relation to the periods of time prescribed by the rules listed in Part 3 of Schedule 4 after the end of the period of two months beginning immediately after the period of time as prescribed (or previously extended) has expired.

NOTES

Para (2): words in square brackets substituted by the Patents (Amendment) Rules 2011, SI 2011/2052, rr 2, 3, Schedule, for transitional provisions see r 4 thereof.

[1.373]

109 Extension of time limits specified by comptroller

(1) A request under section 117B(2) must be—

(a) made in writing; and

(b) made before the end of the period prescribed by paragraph (2).

(2) The period prescribed for the purposes of section 117B(3) is two months beginning immediately after the expiry of the period to which section 117B(2) applies.

[1.374]

110 Interrupted days

(1) The comptroller may certify any day as an interrupted day where—

(a) there is an event or circumstance causing an interruption in the normal operation of the Patent Office; or

(b) there is a general interruption or subsequent dislocation in the postal services of the United Kingdom.

(2) Any certificate of the comptroller given under paragraph (1) shall be displayed in the Patent Office and advertised in the journal.

(3) The comptroller shall, where the time for doing anything under the Act expires on an interrupted day, extend that time to the next following day not being an interrupted day (or an excluded day).

(4) In this rule—

"excluded day" means a day specified as an excluded day in directions given under section 120; and

"interrupted day" means a day which has been certified as such under paragraph (1).

[1.375]

111 Delays in communication services

(1) The comptroller shall extend any period of time specified in the Act or these Rules where he is satisfied that the failure to do something under the Act or these Rules was wholly or mainly attributable to a delay in, or failure of, a communication service.

(2) Any extension under paragraph (1) shall be made—

(a) after giving the parties such notice; and

(b) subject to such conditions,

as the comptroller may direct.

(3) In this rule "communication service" means a service by which documents may be sent and delivered and includes post, electronic communications, and courier.

Copies available to the comptroller

[1.376]

112 Copies available to the comptroller

(1) This rule applies where an applicant is not required to file a copy of an application at the Patent Office because that application or a copy of that application is available to the comptroller.

(2) Where this rule applies the comptroller shall make a copy (or further copy) of that application and certify it accordingly.

Translations

[1.377]

113 Translations

(1) Where any document filed at the Patent Office, or sent to the comptroller, is in a language other than English or Welsh it must be accompanied by a translation into English of that document.

(2) But paragraph (1) does not apply to the following documents—

(a) where the documents filed to initiate an application for a patent include something which is or appears to be a description of the invention, the document containing that thing;

(b) a priority application;

(c) a copy of an application provided under section 15(10)(b)(ii);

(d) a copy of a specification of a European patent (UK) filed in connection with an application by the proprietor to amend the specification;

(e) a copy of an application for a European patent (UK) provided under section 81(2)(b)(ii);
(f) an international application for a patent (UK), where a translation of the application or an amendment to it is a necessary translation;
(g) a document referred to in paragraph (5).

(3) Where more than one copy of the document mentioned in paragraph (1) is filed or sent, a corresponding number of translations shall accompany it.

(4) Where a document to which paragraph (1) applies is not accompanied by a translation, the comptroller may, if he thinks fit, take no further action in relation to that document.

(5) In relation to an international application for a patent (UK), where any document which is in a language other than English or Welsh is—
(a) referred to in an International Search Report or International Preliminary Report on Patentability; or
(b) cited in an International Preliminary Examination Report,
and the relevant report is filed at the Patent Office, the comptroller may direct that a translation into English of that document be filed.

(6) Where a direction is given under paragraph (5) a translation of that document must be filed before the end of the period of two months [beginning immediately after] the date on which the direction is given; otherwise the comptroller may, if he thinks fit, take no further action in relation to the application.

(7) Subject to rule 82(1)(b), where a patent application or any document related to such application is filed at the Patent Office or sent to the comptroller in Welsh, and is not accompanied by a translation into English, the comptroller must obtain such a translation.

(8) In this rule a reference to a document includes a reference to a part of a document; and in paragraph (5) "International Preliminary Examination Report", "International Preliminary Report on Patentability" and "International Search Report" and have the same meaning as in rule 64.

NOTES

Para (6): words in square brackets substituted by the Patents (Amendment) Rules 2011, SI 2011/2052, rr 2, 3, Schedule, for transitional provisions see r 4 thereof.

[1.378]
114 Translations in proceedings in relation to a European patent (UK)

(1) Where—
(a) proceedings are started before the comptroller in relation to a European patent (UK); and
(b) the specification of that patent was published in French or German,
the person who starts those proceedings shall file at the Patent Office a translation into English of the specification.

(2) But paragraph (1) shall not apply where—
(a) a translation into English of the specification has been filed under section 77(6); or
(b) the comptroller directs that a translation is unnecessary.

(3) Where, in the course of such proceedings, leave is given to amend the specification of the patent, the proprietor shall file at the Patent Office a translation of the amendment into the language in which the specification of the patent was published.

(4) This rule applies to making a request for an opinion under section 74A as it applies to proceedings started before the comptroller.

[1.379]
115 Establishing the accuracy of translations

If the comptroller has reasonable doubts about the accuracy of any translation of a document that has been filed at the Patent Office by any person in accordance with the Act or these Rules—
(a) he shall notify that person of the reasons for his doubts; and
(b) he may require that person to furnish evidence to establish that the translation is accurate,
and where that person fails to furnish evidence the comptroller may, if he thinks fit, take no further action in relation to that document.

Supplementary Protection Certificates

[1.380]
116 Supplementary protection certificates

(1) An application for—
(a) a supplementary protection certificate shall be made on Patents Form SP1; and
(b) an extension of the duration of a supplementary protection certificate under Article 8 of the Medicinal Products Regulation shall be made on Patents Form SP4.

(2) The period prescribed for the purposes of paragraph 5(a) of Schedule 4A to the Act is—
(a) three months ending with the start date; or
(b) where the certificate is granted after the beginning of that period, three months [beginning immediately after] the date the supplementary protection certificate is granted.

(3) The comptroller must send a notice to the applicant for the certificate—
- (a) before the beginning of the period of two months immediately preceding the start date; or
- (b) where the certificate is granted as mentioned in paragraph (2)(b), on the date the certificate is granted.

(4) The notice must notify the applicant for the certificate of—
- (a) the fact that payment is required for the certificate to take effect;
- (b) the prescribed fee due;
- (c) the date before which payment must be made; and
- (d) the start date.

(5) The prescribed fee must be accompanied by Patents Form SP2; and once the certificate has taken effect no further fee may be paid to extend the term of the certificate unless an application for an extension of the duration of the certificate is made under the Medicinal Products Regulation.

(6) Where the prescribed fee is not paid before the end of the period prescribed for the purposes of paragraph 5(a) of Schedule 4A to the Act, the comptroller shall, before the end of the period of six weeks beginning immediately after the end of that prescribed period, and if the fee remains unpaid, send a notice to the applicant for the certificate.

(7) The notice shall remind the applicant for the certificate—
- (a) that payment is overdue; and
- (b) of the consequences of non-payment.

(8) The comptroller must send the notices under this rule to—
- (a) the applicant's address for service; and
- (b) the address to which a renewal notice would be sent to the proprietor of the basic patent under rule 39(3).

NOTES

Para (2): words in square brackets substituted by the Patents (Amendment) Rules 2011, SI 2011/2052, rr 2, 3, Schedule, for transitional provisions see r 4 thereof.

Publications

[1.381]
117 The journal

The comptroller must publish a journal containing—
- (a) particulars of applications for and grants of patents and of other proceedings under the Act;
- (b) any directions given under section 120(1) specifying hours of business or excluded days;
- (c) any directions under section 123(2A) setting out forms; and
- (d) any other information that the comptroller considers to be generally useful or important.

[1.382]
118 Reports of cases

The comptroller must make arrangements for the publication of—
- (a) reports of cases relating to patents, trade marks, registered designs or design right decided by him; and
- (b) reports of cases relating to patents (whether under the Act or otherwise), trade marks, registered designs, copyright and design right decided by any court or body (whether in the United Kingdom or elsewhere).

[1.383]
119 Publication and sale of documents

The comptroller may arrange for the publication and sale of copies of documents (in particular, specifications of patents and applications for patents) in the Patent Office.

Transitional provisions and revocations

[1.384]
120 Transitional provisions and revocations

(1) Schedule 5 (transitional provisions) shall have effect.

(2) The instruments set out in Schedule 6 (revocations) shall be revoked to the extent specified.

SCHEDULE 1
BIOLOGICAL MATERIAL

Rule 13(1)

Introductory

[1.385]

1. In this Schedule—

"authorisation certificate" means a certificate issued by the comptroller authorising a depositary institution to make available a sample of biological material;

"Budapest Treaty" means the Treaty on the International Recognition of the Deposit of Micro-organisms for the purposes of Patent Procedure signed at Budapest on 28th April 1977, as amended on 26th September 1980, and includes references to the regulations made under that Treaty;

"depositary institution" means an institution which—

(a) carries out the functions of receiving, accepting and storing biological material and the furnishing of samples of such biological material (whether generally or of a specific type); and

(b) conducts its affairs, in so far as they relate to the carrying out of those functions, in an objective and impartial manner;

"expert" means independent expert;

"first requirement" means the first requirement in paragraph 3;

"international depositary authority" means a depositary institution which has acquired the status of international depositary authority as provided in the Budapest Treaty; and

"second requirement" means the second requirement in paragraph 3.

Specification of an application for a patent, or of a patent, for an invention which involves the use of or concerns biological material

2. (1) This paragraph applies where the specification of an application for a patent, or of a patent, for an invention which involves the use of or concerns biological material does not disclose the invention in a manner which is clear enough and complete enough for the invention to be performed by a person skilled in the art.

(2) Where this paragraph applies, the specification is to be treated as disclosing the invention in a manner which is clear enough and complete enough for the invention to be performed by a person skilled in the art, if—

(a) the first requirement and the second requirement are satisfied; and

(b) the specification of the application as filed contains such relevant information as is available to the applicant on the characteristics of the biological material.

The first and second requirements

3. (1) The first requirement is that—

(a) on or before the date of filing of the application, the biological material has been deposited in a depositary institution; and

(b) that institution will be able to furnish subsequently a sample of the biological material.

(2) The second requirement is that before the end of the relevant period—

(a) the name of the depositary institution and the accession number of the deposit are included in the specification; and

(b) where the biological material was deposited by a person other than the applicant ("the depositor")—

(i) a statement is filed which identifies the name and address of the depositor, and

(ii) a statement by the depositor has been filed, which authorises the applicant to refer to the biological material in his application and irrevocably authorises the making available to the public of the biological material in accordance with this Schedule.

(3) The relevant period is the first to expire of—

(a) the period of sixteen months—

(i) where there is no declared priority date, [beginning immediately after] the date of filing of the application; or

(ii) where there is a declared priority date, [beginning immediately after] that date;

(b) where the applicant has made a request under section 16(1) to publish the application during the period prescribed for the purposes of that section, the period ending with the date of the request; or

(c) where the applicant was notified under rule 52(2), the period of one month [beginning immediately after] the date of the notification.

(4) Where—

(a) the application is filed with the European Patent Office and documents have been filed under the provisions of the European Patent Convention corresponding to sub-paragraph (2); or

(b) the application in suit is an international application for a patent (UK) and documents have been filed in accordance with the Patent Co-operation Treaty under the provisions of the Treaty corresponding to sub-paragraph (2),

the second requirement shall be treated as having been met.

(5) In this paragraph—

"accession number" means the number given to the deposit by a depositary institution;

"specification" means the specification of an application for a patent.

A request by a person for biological material to be made available

4. (1) This paragraph applies when paragraph 7 does not apply.

(2) Where an application for a patent has been published, any person may request the comptroller to issue an authorisation certificate.

(3) Where the application has not been published, a person who has been notified in accordance with section 118(4) may request the comptroller to issue an authorisation certificate.

(4) A request must be made on Patents Form 8.

(5) Where the biological material has been deposited at an international depositary authority, the request must be accompanied by the relevant form required by the Budapest Treaty.

(6) Where the comptroller grants the request, he must send copies of the request and the certificate (and any form required by the Budapest Treaty) to—

(a) the applicant for, or the proprietor of, the patent;
(b) the depositary institution; and
(c) the person making the request.

The undertaking

5. (1) A request made under paragraph 4 or 7 shall include an undertaking by the person making the request—

(a) not to make the biological material, or any material derived from it, available to any other person; and
(b) not to use the biological material, or any material derived from it, except for experimental purposes relating to the subject matter of the invention,

subject to the following sub-paragraphs.

(2) The applicant for, or the proprietor of, a patent may agree to limit the effect of the undertaking in a particular case.

(3) The undertaking shall cease to have effect—

(a) when the application for a patent is terminated or withdrawn (but it will continue to have effect if the application is reinstated or resuscitated); or
(b) when the patent ceases to have effect.

(4) Where a request is made—

(a) by a government department or any person authorised in writing by a government department; and
(b) for the purposes of using the patented invention for the services of the Crown,

no undertaking is required and any undertaking by the government department or the person so authorised shall not have effect.

(5) Where—

(a) a licence under the patent to which the undertaking relates is available as of right; or
(b) a compulsory licence in respect of the patent to which the undertaking relates has been granted,

any undertaking made shall have no effect to the extent necessary to give effect to any such licence.

Restriction of availability of biological material to experts

6. (1) Where the first or the second condition is met (except in relation to Crown use), paragraph 7 applies until the end of the relevant period.

(2) The first condition is—

(a) the applicant requests on Patents Form 8A that a sample of the biological material should only be made available to an expert; and
(b) that request is made before the preparations for the application's publication have been completed by the Patent Office.

(3) The second condition is that, in relation to an international application for a patent (UK), the applicant made a reference to the deposited biological material in accordance with the Patent Co-operation Treaty.

(4) Where the first condition is met, the comptroller shall, when he publishes the application, include a notice that the provisions of paragraph 7 apply.

(5) In paragraph 6(1) "the relevant period" is—

(a) where the patent is granted, the period ending with the date on which the patent was granted; and
(b) where the application is terminated or withdrawn, twenty years [beginning immediately after] the date of filing.

(6) Nothing in this or the following paragraph affects the rights under section 55 of any government department or any person authorised in writing by a government department.

Request for a sample to be made available to expert

7. (1) A request for a sample to be made available to an expert must be made on Patents Form 8 and must include details of the expert.

(2) Where the biological material has been deposited at an international depositary authority, the request must be accompanied by any form required by the Budapest Treaty.

(3) The comptroller must send a copy of Patents Form 8 to the applicant for the patent.

(4) Before the end of the period of one month [beginning immediately after] the date on which a copy of Patents Form 8 is sent by the comptroller, the applicant may give notice of his objection to the particular expert, and where he objects the comptroller shall determine the matter.

(5) Where—

(a) the applicant does not object to the sample being made available; or

(b) following an objection, the comptroller decides that the sample should be made available to the particular expert,

the comptroller must issue a certificate authorising the release of a sample to the expert.

(6) A copy of Patents Form 8 (and any form required by the Budapest Treaty) and any certificate issued under sub-paragraph (5) must be sent to—

(a) the applicant for the patent;

(b) the depository institution where the sample of the biological material is stored;

(c) the expert; and

(d) the person who made the request.

New deposits

8. (1) This paragraph applies where the first, second or third circumstance occurs.

(2) The first circumstance is that the biological material ceases to be available at the depositary institution because it is no longer viable.

(3) The second circumstance is that—

(a) the depositary institution is, for any other reason, unable to supply the biological material; or

(b) the place where the biological material is deposited is no longer a depositary institution for that type of material (whether temporarily or permanently).

(4) The third circumstance is that the biological material is transferred to a different depositary institution.

(5) The first requirement and the second requirement shall be treated as having been complied with throughout the relevant period, if and only if—

(a) where the first or second circumstance occurs—

(i) a new deposit of biological material is made at the relevant depositary before the end of the relevant period, and

(ii) that deposit is accompanied by a statement, signed by the person making the deposit, that the biological material deposited is the same as that originally deposited; and

(b) in all circumstances, the applicant or proprietor, before the end of the relevant period, applies to the comptroller to amend the specification of the application for the patent, or the patent, so that it meets the second requirement.

(6) For the purposes of paragraph (5) "the relevant period" is the period beginning when the first, second or third circumstance occurs and ending—

(a) three months after the date on which the depositor is notified by the depositary institution that the first, second or third circumstance occurred; or

(b) where it expires later, three months after the date on which that circumstance is advertised in the journal.

(7) The relevant depositary is—

(a) where only the first circumstance occurs, the depositary institution where the original deposit was made; or

(b) in any other case, any depositary institution.

NOTES

Paras 3, 6, 7: words in square brackets substituted by the Patents (Amendment) Rules 2011, SI 2011/2052, rr 2, 3, Schedule, for transitional provisions see r 4 thereof.

SCHEDULE 2
FORMAL AND OTHER REQUIREMENTS

Rule 14

PART 1
REQUIREMENTS: ALL DOCUMENTS

[1.386]

1. A4 matt white paper must be used.

2. A document in paper form must be free from tears, folds or similar damage and its contents must be suitable for reproduction.

3. Frames (lines surrounding matter) must not be used.

PART 2
REQUIREMENTS: DOCUMENTS (OTHER THAN DRAWINGS [AND PHOTOGRAPHS])

[1.387]

4. The pages of the description and claims must be numbered consecutively in a single series.

5. But where a sequence listing is set out at the end of the application, it must be numbered consecutively in a separate series.

6. Page numbers must be located at the top or bottom of the page (but not in the margin) in the centre.

7. The minimum margins in any document must be 20mm.

8. Each of the following—

(a) the request for the grant of a patent;
(b) the description;
(c) the claims;
(d) the abstract,

must begin on a new sheet of paper.

9. The abstract, description and claims must use at least 1.5 line spacing, except where they form part of a translation or a sequence listing.

10. The capital letters in any typeface or font used must be more than 2mm high.

NOTES

Part heading: words in square brackets inserted by the Patents (Amendment) (No 2) Rules 2016, SI 2016/892, rr 2, 15(1), (2).

PART 3
REQUIREMENTS: DRAWINGS [AND PHOTOGRAPHS]

[1.388]

11. There must be a margin around any drawing [or photograph] which must be at least—

(a) at the top and left side, 20mm;
(b) at the right side, 15mm; and
(c) at the bottom, 10mm.

12. All drawings [or photographs] must be numbered consecutively in a single series.

13. The drawings [or photographs] must begin on a new sheet of paper.

14. The pages containing the drawings [or photographs] must be numbered consecutively in a single series.

[15. Drawings must comprise black lines and may be shaded where the shading assists in representing the shape of a thing provided that it does not obscure other elements of the drawing.]

16. Drawings may include cross-hatching to illustrate the cross-sections of a thing.

17. Any scale or other reference for making measurement must be represented diagrammatically.

18. Any drawing [or photograph] must be produced in such manner that it would still be clear if it were reduced by linear reduction to two thirds of its original size.

19. A drawing [or photograph] must not be included in the description, the claims, the abstract or the request for the grant of a patent.

20. The capital letters in any typeface or font used in any drawing [or photograph] must be more than 3mm high.

[20A. Photographs must be black and white, clear and capable of direct reproduction.]

NOTES

Part heading: words in square brackets inserted by the Patents (Amendment) (No 2) Rules 2016, SI 2016/892, rr 2, 15(1), (2).
Paras 11–14, 18–20: words in square brackets inserted by SI 2016/892, rr 2, 15(1), (3)(a), (b).
Para 15: substituted by SI 2016/892, rr 2, 15(1), (3)(c).
Para 20A: inserted by SI 2016/892, rr 2, 15(1), (3)(d).

PART 4
OTHER REQUIREMENTS

[1.389]
21. References must only be included in the drawing [or photograph] where they are mentioned in either the description or the claims.

22. Tables of information may only be included in the claims if the comptroller agrees.

23. The terminology and any references used must be consistent throughout the application for a patent.

24. Where units of measurement used in the application are not standard international units of measurement, the equivalent standard international units of measurement must be provided, and where no international standard exists, units must be used which are generally accepted in the field.

25. Only technical terms, signs and symbols which are generally accepted in the field may be used.

NOTES

Para 21: words in square brackets inserted by the Patents (Amendment) (No 2) Rules 2016, SI 2016/892, rr 2, 15(1), (4).

SCHEDULE 3
PROCEEDINGS HEARD BEFORE THE COMPTROLLER

Rule 73

PART 1
APPLICATIONS, REFERENCES AND REQUESTS

[1.390]
Patents Act 1977

section 8(1) (reference regarding entitlement in relation to a patent under the Act)

section 10 (request for directions for handling a joint application)

section 11(5) (reference regarding entitlement to a licence to continue working after transfer of application)

section 12(1) (reference regarding entitlement in relation to a foreign or convention patent)

section 12(4) (reference involving joint applications on entitlement in relation to a foreign or convention patent)

section 13(3) (application to comptroller to remove person mentioned as inventor)

section 37(1) (determination of right to patent after grant)

section 38(5) (reference regarding entitlement to a licence to continue working after transfer of patent)

section 40 (application for compensation by an employee)

section 41(8) (application to vary order for compensation for certain inventions)

section 46(3) (application to settle terms of licence available as of right)

section 47(3) (application to cancel licence available as of right)

section 48(1) (application for a compulsory licence)

section 50A(2) (application following merger and market investigation)

section 51(1) (application by Minister following report of Competition Commission)

section 52(2)(a) (application to cancel compulsory licence)

section 61(3) (reference on question of infringement before the comptroller)

section 71 (declaration of non-infringement)

section 72 (application to revoke patent)

Patents Rules 2007

rule 10(2) (application to be mentioned as inventor)

rule 88(1) (application to hold proceedings in Scotland)

paragraph 7(4) of Schedule 1 (notice of objection to expert)

Compulsory Licensing Regulation

Article 5(c) of the Compulsory Licensing Regulation (application to terminate EU compulsory licence)

Article 6(1) of that Regulation (application for an EU compulsory licence)

Article 10(8) of that Regulation (application to access books and records)

Article 16(1), second paragraph, of that Regulation (application for a review of an EU compulsory licence)

Article 16(4) of that Regulation (application for modification of an EU compulsory licence)

Medicinal Products Regulation and Plant Protection Products Regulation

Article 14(d) of the Medicinal Products Regulation and the Plant Protection Products Regulation (request to review lapse of supplementary protection certificate)

Article 15 of those Regulations (application for declaration of invalidity of supplementary protection certificate)

Article 15a of the Medicinal Products Regulation (application for revocation of an extension of the duration of a supplementary protection certificate)

PART 2
OPPOSITIONS WHICH START PROCEEDINGS

[1.391]
Patents Act 1977

section 27(5) (opposition to amendment of specification after grant)

section 29(2) (opposition to surrender of patent)

section 47(6) (opposition to cancellation of licence available as of right), where the application was made by the proprietor of the patent

section 75(2) (opposition to amendment during infringement or revocation proceedings)

section 117(2) (opposition to correction of error in patents and applications)

PART 3
OPPOSITIONS AFTER PROCEEDINGS HAVE STARTED

[1.392]
Patents Act 1977

section 47(6) (opposition to cancellation of licence available as of right), where the application was made by a person other than the proprietor of the patent

section 52(1) (opposition to an application for compulsory licence or under section 50A or 51)

section 52(2)(b) (opposition to an application to cancel a compulsory licence)

PART 4
RULES WHICH APPLY TO ANY PROCEEDINGS HEARD BEFORE THE COMPTROLLER

[1.393]
Patents Rules 2007

rule 74 (overriding objective)

rule 79 (copies of documents)

rule 80(2) to (6) (evidence and the hearing)

rule 81 (alteration of time limits)

rule 82 (general powers of the comptroller in relation to proceedings before him)

rule 84 (hearings in public)

rule 87 (evidence in proceedings before the comptroller)

PART 5
RULES WHICH APPLY TO A REVIEW OF AN OPINION

[1.394]
Patents Rules 2007

rule 83 (striking out a statement of case and summary judgment)

rule 85 (security for costs or expenses)

rule 86 (powers of comptroller to compel attendance of witness and production of documents)

rule 88 (proceedings in Scotland)

SCHEDULE 4
EXTENSION OF TIME LIMITS

Rule 108

PART 1
PERIODS OF TIME THAT CANNOT BE EXTENDED

[1.395]
rule 6(2)(b) (declaration of priority for the purposes of section 5(2) made after the date of filing)

rule 7(1) (period for making a request to the comptroller for permission to make a late declaration of priority)

rule 32(1) (application to reinstate a terminated application)

rule 37 and 38 (renewal of patents)

rule 40(1) (application to restore a lapsed patent)

[rule 41A (payment of fees under section 77(5A) following restoration of a European patent (UK))]

rule 43(4) (application to cancel entry that licence available as of right)

rule 58(3) (request for a direction under section 81)

rule 59(1) (request from a foreign industrial property office for a direction under section 81)

rule 66(3) (period for making a request to the comptroller for permission to make a late declaration of priority in respect of an international application for a patent (UK))

rule 76(2) (notice of opposition), except in relation to an opposition under section 27(5) where there are pending before the court or the comptroller proceedings in which the validity of the patent is put in issue

rule 77(8) and (10) (opposition periods)

. . .

rule 109 (extension of time limits specified by comptroller)

rule 116(2) (fee for supplementary protection certificate)

paragraph 8(5) of Schedule 1 (new deposits of biological material)

NOTES

Entry relating to rule 41A inserted by the Patents (Amendment) (No 2) Rules 2014, SI 2014/2401, rr 2, 8.
Entry relating to rule 104(2) (omitted) revoked by the Patents (Amendment) (No 2) Rules 2016, SI 2016/892, rr 2, 16(a).

PART 2
PERIODS OF TIME THAT MAY BE EXTENDED UNDER RULE 108(2) OR 108(3)

[1.396]
rule 8(1) and (2) (filing of information and priority documents)

rule 10(3) (filing of statement of inventorship and the right to be granted a patent)

rule 18(1) (missing parts)

rule 21 (extensions for new applications)

rule 22(1), (2) and (5) (periods prescribed for the purposes of sections 15(10) and 17(1))

rule 28(2), (3) and (5) (request for substantive examination)

rule 30 (period for putting an application in order)

rule 56(6) and (7) (filing of a translation of European patent (UK) specifications)

rule 58(4) (request under section 81(2)(b)(i))

rule 59(3) (request under section 81(2)(b)(ii))

rule 60 (request for substantive examination following a direction under section 81)

rule 66(1) and (2) (international applications for patents: entry into national phase)

rule 68 (international applications for patents: altered prescribed periods)

[rule 104(2) (period for furnishing an address for service), in relation to an application for a patent]

paragraph 3(2) of Schedule 1 (filing of information in relation to the deposit of biological matter)

NOTES

Entry relating to rule 104(2) inserted by the Patents (Amendment) (No 2) Rules 2016, SI 2016/892, rr 2, 16(b).

PART 3
PERIODS OF TIME TO WHICH RULE 108(5) AND 108(7) RELATE

[1.397]

rule 10(3) (filing of statement of inventorship and the right to be granted a patent)

rule 12(3) and (9) (filing of name and address and translations)

rule 19 (new applications filed as mentioned in section 15(9))

rule 21(1)(a) and (2)(a) (extensions for new applications)

rule 22 (periods prescribed for the purposes of sections 15(10) and 17(1))

rule 28 (request for substantive examination)

rule 30 (period for putting application in order)

rule 58(4) (request under section 81(2)(b)(i))

rule 59(3) (request under section 81(2)(b)(ii))

rule 60 (request for substantive examination following a direction under section 81)

rule 66(1) and (2) (international applications for patents: entry into national phase)

rule 68 (international applications for patents: altered prescribed periods)

[rule 104(2) (period for furnishing an address for service), in relation to an application for a patent]

NOTES

Entry relating to rule 104(2) inserted by the Patents (Amendment) (No 2) Rules 2016, SI 2016/892, rr 2, 16(b).

SCHEDULE 5
TRANSITIONAL PROVISIONS

Rule 120(1)

Interpretation

[1.398]

1. In this Schedule, the "1995 Rules" means the Patents Rules 1995 as they had effect immediately prior to their revocation by these Rules.

Periods of time

2. Where, in relation to any proceedings under the Act, a period of time prescribed by the 1995 Rules for the purposes of a particular provision of the Act has not expired before the date on which these Rules come into force, that period continues to apply.

Proceedings before the comptroller

3. Proceedings before the comptroller which commenced before these Rules came into force shall continue in accordance with Part 7 of these Rules, subject to paragraph 2 of this Schedule.

Service by post

4. Any document sent to the comptroller by posting it in the United Kingdom before the day these Rules come into force shall be deemed to have been filed at the time when it would be delivered in the ordinary course of post.

Applications to which certain amendments made to the Act by the Regulatory Reform (Patents) Order 2004 do not apply

5. (1) This paragraph applies to an application for a patent to which article 20, 21 or 22 of the Regulatory Reform (Patents) Order 2004 applies.

(2) Any reference in these Rules to—

(a) section 15(9) of the Act is a reference to section 15(4) of the unamended Act;
(b) section 15(10)(a) of the Act is a reference to section 15(5)(a) of the unamended Act;
(c) section 15(10)(b) or (c) of the Act shall be disregarded;
(d) section 15(10)(d) of the Act is a reference to section 15(5)(b) of the unamended Act;
(e) section 15A of the Act is a reference to section 17(1) of the unamended Act;
(f) section 17(1)(c)(i) of the Act is a reference to section 17(1)(a) of the unamended Act; and
(g) Patents Form 9A is a reference to Patents Form 9.

(3) The following provisions do not apply—

rule 6(2) and (3) (declaration of priority made after date of filing);
rule 7 (permission to make late declaration under section 5(2B));
rule 12(2), (3), (8) and (9) (notifications of deficiencies in application);
rule 17 (references under section 15(1)(c)(ii));
rule 18 (missing parts);
rule 22(3) (prescribed period for the purpose of section 15(10)(b)(ii)).

(4) In this paragraph "unamended Act" means the Act as it had effect immediately before the Regulatory Reform (Patents) Order 2004 came into effect.

Security for costs

6. Rule 85 does not apply in respect of proceedings started before 1st October 2005.

Patent applications filed before 7th January 1991

7. (1) This paragraph applies to an application for a patent filed before 7th January 1991 and to a patent granted in pursuance of such application.

(2) Schedule 1 has effect with the following modifications.

(3) In paragraph 2, for the words "involves the use of or concerns biological material" substitute the words "requires for its performance the use of a micro-organism".

(4) In paragraph 5(3)(b), insert at the beginning the words "in the case of an undertaking given in accordance with paragraph 1(a)," and insert at the end the word "or" followed by:

> "(c) in the case of an undertaking given in accordance with paragraph (1)(b), when the patent is granted.".

(5) Any reference to "biological material"—

(a) in paragraphs 3(1)(a), 4, 5 and 8 is a reference to "culture of the micro-organism"; and
(b) other than in those provisions, is a reference to "micro-organism".

(6) For the purposes of paragraph 3(2) the relevant period is the period of two months [beginning immediately after] the date of filing of the application for a patent.

(7) The following provisions do not have effect—

paragraph 3(3) (defining relevant period);
paragraph 6 (restriction of availability of biological material to experts);
paragraph 7 (request for sample to be made available to expert).

Patent applications filed between 7th January 1991 and 27th July 2000

8. (1) This paragraph applies to an application for a patent filed during the period beginning with 7th January 1991 and ending with 27th July 2000 and to a patent granted in pursuance of such application.

(2) Schedule 1 to these Rules has effect with the following modifications.

(3) In paragraph 2, for the words "involves the use of or concerns biological material" substitute the words "requires for its performance the use of a micro-organism".

(4) In paragraph 5(3)(b), insert at the beginning the words "in the case of an undertaking given in accordance with paragraph 1(a)," and insert at the end the word "or" followed by:

> "(c) in the case of an undertaking given in accordance with paragraph (1)(b), when the patent is granted.".

(5) Any reference to "biological material"—

(a) in paragraphs 3(1)(a), 4, 5, 6(3), 7(2) and 8 is a reference to "culture of the micro-organism"; and
(b) other than in those provisions, is a reference to "micro-organism".

(6) Paragraph 2(2)(b) (requirement that application contains relevant information) does not have effect.

(7) In paragraph 6(5)(b), for the words from "the period of 20 years" to the end of that provision substitute "the period ending with the date on which the application was terminated or withdrawn".

(8) The specification of an application for a patent, or of a patent, must mention any international agreement under which the micro-organism is deposited.

Continued application of Patents Rules 1968 to existing patents

9. (1) This paragraph and paragraph 10 apply to existing patents and applications.

(2) Rules 4, 58 and 59 of the Patents Rules 1968 continue to apply.

Application of these Rules to existing patents and applications

10. (1) Rules 4, 10(2), 44 to 50, 73 to 88, 101, 103 to 105 and 107 apply to existing patents and applications.

(2) In those provisions as they apply by virtue of this paragraph, a reference to a specified provision of these Rules other than one of those provisions is a reference to the corresponding provision of the Patents Rules 1968 (any provision of those Rules being treated as corresponding to a provision of these Rules if it was made for purposes which are the same as or similar to that provision of these Rules).

Application of the 1995 Rules to sections 8 and 12

11. If before 1st January 2005 a question has been referred to the comptroller under section 8 or 12, in relation to that reference, sections 8, 11 and 12 have effect as if the amendments to those sections by the Patents Act 2004 had not been made and rules 9 and 13 of the 1995 Rules have effect as in force immediately before 1st January 2005.

NOTES

Para 7: words in square brackets substituted by the Patents (Amendment) Rules 2011, SI 2011/2052, rr 2, 3, Schedule, for transitional provisions see r 4 thereof.

SCHEDULE 6

(*Sch 6 contains revocations only.*)

PATENTS COUNTY COURT (FINANCIAL LIMITS) ORDER 2011

(SI 2011/1402)

NOTES

Made: 8 June 2011.

Authority: Copyright. Designs and Patents Act 1988, s 288(1).

Commencement: 14 June 2011.

[1.399]

1 Citation and commencement

(1) This Order may be cited as the Patents County Court (Financial Limits) Order 2011 and shall come into force on 14th June 2011.

NOTES

Patents county court: s 287 of the Copyright, Designs and Patents Act 1988 is repealed, as from 1 October 2013, by the Crime and Courts Act 2013, s 17, Sch 9, which provides for a unified county court.

[1.400]

2 Financial limits

(1) In relation to all proceedings within the special jurisdiction of a patents county court and in which a claim is made for damages or an account of profits, the amount or value of that claim shall not exceed £500,000.

(2) In determining the amount or value of a claim for the purpose of paragraph (1), a claim for—

(a) interest, other than interest payable under an agreement, or

(b) costs,

shall be disregarded.

NOTES

Patents county court: see note to art 1 at **[1.399]**.

[1.401]

3 Transitional provision

A patents county court has jurisdiction to hear and determine a claim for damages or an account of profits for an amount or value exceeding the limit imposed by article 2 where, before the coming into force of this Order—

(a) the claim has been made in a patents county court in proceedings within its special jurisdiction, or

(b) the High Court orders the proceedings in which the claim has been made to be transferred to the special jurisdiction of a patents county court, or

(c) an application has been made to the High Court for transfer of the proceedings in which the claim has been made to a patents county court and, after the coming into force of this Order, the High Court orders the transfer of the proceedings to the special jurisdiction of a patents county court.

NOTES

Patents county court: see note to art 1 at **[1.399]**.

DRAFT UNIFIED PATENT COURT (IMMUNITIES AND PRIVILEGES) ORDER 2017

2017 No XXX

NOTES

This is a draft item of legislation and has not yet been made as a UK Statutory Instrument.

This Order is made in exercise of the powers conferred by sections 1 and 5 of the International Organisations Act 1968 ("the Act").

A draft of this Order has been approved by resolution of each House of Parliament pursuant to section 10(1) of the Act.

Accordingly, Her Majesty is pleased, by and with the advice of Her Privy Council, to order as follows—

PART 1
GENERAL

[1.402]

1 Citation, commencement, extent and application

(1) This Order may be cited as the Unified Patent Court (Immunities and Privileges) Order 2017 and comes into force on the date on which the Protocol enters into force in accordance with Article 18 of the Protocol.

(2) The Order extends to the whole of the United Kingdom subject to paragraph (3).

(3) Article 9 extends to England and Wales and Northern Ireland only.

(4) In Scotland—

(a) articles 5, 6, 7, 11, 16, 17 and 18 do not apply in so far as they would, if included in an Act of the Scottish Parliament, be within the legislative competence of that Parliament;

(b) article 8 does not apply to devolved taxes or local taxes to fund local authority expenditure (within the meaning of the exceptions to Section A1 (fiscal, economic and monetary policy) of Part 2 of Schedule 5 to the Scotland Act 1998.

[1.403]

2 Interpretation

In this Order—

"the Agreement" means the Agreement on a Unified Patent Court done in Brussels on 19th February 2013;

"Committee" means any of the Administrative Committee, the Budget Committee and the Advisory Committee established under Article 11 of the Agreement;

"the Court" means the Unified Patent Court established under Article 1 of the Agreement;

"Deputy-Registrar" means the Deputy-Registrar appointed under Article 25 of the Statute;

"Judge" means a Judge of the Court;

"official activities" in relation to the Court means the activities that are necessary for the purposes and functions conferred upon it by the Agreement and the Statute;

"premises of the Court" means land and buildings made available to the Court by a State party to the Agreement in accordance with Article 37 of the Agreement and used for the official activities of the Court;

"the Presidium" means the Presidium referred to in Article 15 of the Statute;

"the Protocol" means the Protocol on Privileges and Immunities of the Unified Patent Court done in Brussels on 29th June 2016;
"Registrar" means the Registrar appointed under Article 22 of the Statute;
"Staff" means all personnel employed by the Court as officials and other servants of the Court except the Judges, Registrar and Deputy-Registrar;
"State Party" means a State party to the Protocol; and
"the Statute" means the Statute of the Court as set out in Annex I of the Agreement.

PART 2
THE COURT

[1.404]
3.

The Court is an organisation of which the United Kingdom and other sovereign Powers are members.

[1.405]
4.

The Court has the legal capacities of a body corporate.

PART 3
IMMUNITIES, PRIVILEGES, RELIEFS AND EXEMPTIONS OF THE COURT

[1.406]
5.

(1) Subject to paragraph (2), the Court has immunity from suit and legal process except to the extent that it expressly waives such immunity.

(2) The immunity of the Court under paragraph (1) does not apply in respect of—
- (a) any civil action brought against it—
  - (i) with respect to contractual liability brought by persons other than the Judges, Registrar, Deputy-Registrar or the Staff of the Court;
  - (ii) with respect to non-contractual liability except where the claim is based on the performance of the Court's jurisprudence; and
  - (iii) by a third party for damages resulting from an accident caused by a motor vehicle belonging to, or operated on behalf of, the Court; or
- (b) a motor traffic offence involving such a vehicle.

[1.407]
6.

The official archives of the Court have the like inviolability as is accorded in respect of the official archives of a diplomatic mission in accordance with the 1961 Convention Articles.

[1.408]
7.

(1) Subject to paragraph (2), the premises of the Court have the like inviolability as is accorded in respect of the premises of a diplomatic mission in accordance with the 1961 Convention Articles.

(2) The inviolability of the premises of the Court does not apply to the extent that the Secretary of State is responsible for premises which have been made available to the Court by the Secretary of State.

[1.409]
8.

Within the scope of its official activities, the Court is exempt from all direct taxation and enjoys the exemptions and reliefs set out in articles 9 to 14.

[1.410]
9.

The Court has the like relief from non-domestic rates on the premises of the Court as, in accordance with Article 23 of the 1961 Convention Articles, is accorded in respect of the premises of a diplomatic mission.

[1.411]
10.

The Court is exempt from duties (whether of customs or excise) and taxes on the importation of goods imported by or on behalf of the Court for its official use in the United Kingdom.

[1.412]
11.

The Court is exempt from prohibitions and restrictions on importation or exportation in the case of goods imported or exported by the Court for its official use.

[1.413]
12.

The Court has relief, under arrangements made by the Commissioners for Her Majesty's Revenue and Customs, by way of refund of duty (whether of customs or excise) paid on imported hydrocarbon oil (within the meaning of the Hydrocarbon Oil Duties Act 1979(a)) or value added tax paid on the importation of such oil which is bought in the United Kingdom and is used for its official purposes.

[1.414]
13.

The Court has relief under arrangements made by the Secretary of State, by way of refund of car tax paid on any vehicle used for its official purposes and value added tax paid on the supply of any goods or services which are supplied for its official purposes.

[1.415]
14.

The Court has relief by way of refund of insurance premium tax paid by the Court in exercise of its official activities.

[1.416]
15.

The exemptions and relief granted in articles 10, 12 and 13 are to be subject to compliance with such conditions as the Commissioners for Her Majesty's Revenue and Customs may prescribe for the protection of the Revenue.

PART 4
REPRESENTATIVES

[1.417]
16.

(1) Except in so far as in any particular case any immunity is waived by the Presidium of the Court, representatives of a State Party shall enjoy immunity from suit and legal process in respect of all acts performed by them while attending a meeting of a Committee in their official capacity.

(2) This article does not apply to a person who is a British citizen, British overseas territories citizen, British Overseas citizen, British National (Overseas) or any person who at the time of taking up their functions with the Court is a permanent resident of the United Kingdom.

PART 5
JUDGES, REGISTRAR AND DEPUTY-REGISTRAR

[1.418]
17.

(1) Except in so far as in any particular case any privilege or immunity is waived by the Presidium of the Court, the Judges, Registrar and Deputy-Registrar of the Court have the privileges and immunities in this article.

(2) They have immunity from suit and legal process.

(3) They are exempt from national taxes in respect of salaries, wages and emoluments paid to them by the Court (other than pensions and annuities) from the date on which the internal tax for the benefit of the Court on salaries, wages and emoluments is applied to them.

(4) They are exempt from duties (whether of customs or excise) and taxes on the importation of furniture and effects and the right to re-export free of duty on termination of their duties.

(5) They are exempt from duties (whether of customs or excise) and taxes on—

- (a) the importation of a motor car for personal use, acquired either in the country of their last residence or in the country of which they are nationals; and
- (b) the exportation of that motor car on termination of their duties,

subject to compliance with such conditions as the Commissioners for Her Majesty's Revenue and Customs may prescribe for the protection of the Revenue.

(6) From the date on which they are subject to a social security and health scheme established by the Court, with respect to services rendered for the Court, they are deemed to be excepted from any class of employment in respect of which contributions under enactments relating to social security (including enactments in force in Northern Ireland) are payable.

(7) In the event of the death of a Judge, Registrar or Deputy-Registrar, where their presence in the United Kingdom at that time is solely due to their capacity as a Judge, Registrar or Deputy-Registrar, they are exempt from estate duty leviable on death under the law of any part of the United Kingdom in respect of moveable property which is in the United Kingdom immediately before their death.

PART 6
THE STAFF

[1.419]
18.

(1) Except in so far as in any particular case any privilege or immunity is waived by the Presidium of the Court, the Staff of the Court have the privileges and immunities set out in this article.

(2) They have immunity from suit and legal process in respect of things done or omitted to be done in the course of the performance of official duties.

(3) They are exempt from national taxes in respect of salaries, wages and emoluments paid to them by the Court (other than pensions and annuities) from the date on which the internal tax for the benefit of the Court on salaries, wages and emoluments is applied to them.

(4) From the date on which they are subject to a social security and health scheme established by the Court, with respect to services rendered for the Court, they are deemed to be excepted from any class of employment in respect of which contributions under enactments relating to social security (including enactments in force in Northern Ireland) are payable.

(5) Paragraphs (3) and (4) do not apply to a person who is a British citizen, British overseas territories citizen, British Overseas citizen, British National (Overseas) or any person who at the time of taking up their functions with the Court is a permanent resident of the United Kingdom.

CONVENTION ON THE GRANT OF EUROPEAN PATENTS (EUROPEAN PATENT CONVENTION)

(Munich, 5 October 1973, as revised by the Act revising Article 63 EPC of 17 December 1991 and the Act revising the EPC of 29 November 2000)

[The Convention has been ratified by the United Kingdom]

NOTES

The original source of this Convention is the European Patent Office (EPO) website at www.epo.org.

See also Decision of the Administrative Council on transitional provisions under Art 7 at **[1.771]**.

PREAMBLE

THE CONTRACTING STATES,

Desiring to strengthen co-operation between the States of Europe in respect of the protection of inventions,

Desiring that such protection may be obtained in those States by a single procedure for the grant of patents and by the establishment of certain standard rules governing patents so granted,

Desiring, for this purpose, to conclude a Convention which establishes a European Patent Organisation and which constitutes a special agreement within the meaning of Article 19 of the Convention for the Protection of Industrial Property, signed in Paris on 20 March 1883 and last revised on 14 July 1967, and a regional patent treaty within the meaning of Article 45, paragraph 1, of the Patent Cooperation Treaty of 19 June 1970,

Have agreed on the following provisions—

PART I
GENERAL AND INSTITUTIONAL PROVISIONS

CHAPTER I
GENERAL PROVISIONS

[1.420]
Article 1
European law for the grant of patents

A system of law, common to the Contracting States, for the grant of patents for invention is established by this Convention.

[1.421]
Article 2
European patent

(1) Patents granted under this Convention shall be called European patents.

(2) The European patent shall, in each of the Contracting States for which it is granted, have the effect of and be subject to the same conditions as a national patent granted by that State, unless this Convention provides otherwise.

[1.422]
Article 3
Territorial effect

The grant of a European patent may be requested for one or more of the Contracting States.

[1.423]
Article 4
European Patent Organisation

(1) A European Patent Organisation, hereinafter referred to as the Organisation, is established by this Convention. It shall have administrative and financial autonomy.

(2) The organs of the Organisation shall be—

(a) the European Patent Office;

(b) the Administrative Council.

(3) The task of the Organisation shall be to grant European patents. This shall be carried out by the European Patent Office supervised by the Administrative Council.

[1.424]
Article 4a
Conference of ministers of the Contracting States

A conference of ministers of the Contracting States responsible for patent matters shall meet at least every five years to discuss issues pertaining to the Organisation and to the European patent system.

CHAPTER II
THE EUROPEAN PATENT ORGANISATION

[1.425]
Article 5
Legal status

(1) The Organisation shall have legal personality.

(2) In each of the Contracting States, the Organisation shall enjoy the most extensive legal capacity accorded to legal persons under the national law of that State; it may in particular acquire or dispose of movable and immovable property and may be a party to legal proceedings.

(3) The President of the European Patent Office shall represent the Organisation.

[1.426]
Article 6
Headquarters

(1) The Organisation shall have its headquarters in Munich.

(2) The European Patent Office shall be located in Munich. It shall have a branch at The Hague.

[1.427]
Article 7
Sub-offices of the European Patent Office

By decision of the Administrative Council, sub-offices of the European Patent Office may be created, if need be, for the purpose of information and liaison, in the Contracting States and with intergovernmental organisations in the field of industrial property, subject to the approval of the Contracting State or organisation concerned.

[1.428]
Article 8
Privileges and immunities

The Protocol on Privileges and Immunities annexed to this Convention shall define the conditions under which the Organisation, the members of the Administrative Council, the employees of the European Patent Office, and such other persons specified in that Protocol as take part in the work of the Organisation, shall enjoy, in each Contracting State, the privileges and immunities necessary for the performance of their duties.

[1.429]
Article 9
Liability

(1) The contractual liability of the Organisation shall be governed by the law applicable to the contract in question.

(2) The non-contractual liability of the Organisation in respect of any damage caused by it or by the employees of the European Patent Office in the performance of their duties shall be governed by the law of the Federal Republic of Germany. Where the damage is caused by the branch at The Hague or a sub-office or employees attached thereto, the law of the Contracting State in which such branch or sub-office is located shall apply.
(3) The personal liability of the employees of the European Patent Office towards the Organisation shall be governed by their Service Regulations or conditions of employment.
(4) The courts with jurisdiction to settle disputes under paragraphs 1 and 2 shall be—
(a) for disputes under paragraph 1, the courts of the Federal Republic of Germany, unless the contract concluded between the parties designates a court of another State;
(b) for disputes under paragraph 2, the courts of the Federal Republic of Germany, or of the State in which the branch or sub-office is located.

CHAPTER III
THE EUROPEAN PATENT OFFICE

[1.430]
Article 10
Management
(1) The European Patent Office shall be managed by the President, who shall be responsible for its activities to the Administrative Council.
(2) To this end, the President shall have in particular the following functions and powers—
(a) he shall take all necessary steps to ensure the functioning of the European Patent Office, including the adoption of internal administrative instructions and information to the public;
(b) unless this Convention provides otherwise, he shall prescribe which acts are to be performed at the European Patent Office in Munich and its branch at The Hague respectively;
(c) he may submit to the Administrative Council any proposal for amending this Convention, for general regulations, or for decisions which come within the competence of the Administrative Council;
(d) he shall prepare and implement the budget and any amending or supplementary budget;
(e) he shall submit a management report to the Administrative Council each year;
(f) he shall exercise supervisory authority over the staff;
(g) subject to Article 11, he shall appoint the employees and decide on their promotion;
(h) he shall exercise disciplinary authority over the employees other than those referred to in Article 11, and may propose disciplinary action to the Administrative Council with regard to employees referred to in Article 11, paragraphs 2 and 3;
(i) he may delegate his functions and powers.
(3) The President shall be assisted by a number of Vice-Presidents. If the President is absent or indisposed, one of the Vice-Presidents shall take his place in accordance with the procedure laid down by the Administrative Council.

[1.431]
Article 11
Appointment of senior employees
(1) The President of the European Patent Office shall be appointed by the Administrative Council.
(2) The Vice-Presidents shall be appointed by the Administrative Council after the President of the European Patent Office has been consulted.
(3) The members, including the Chairmen, of the Boards of Appeal and of the Enlarged Board of Appeal shall be appointed by the Administrative Council on a proposal from the President of the European Patent Office. They may be re-appointed by the Administrative Council after the President of the European Patent Office has been consulted.
(4) The Administrative Council shall exercise disciplinary authority over the employees referred to in paragraphs 1 to 3.
(5) The Administrative Council, after consulting the President of the European Patent Office, may also appoint as members of the Enlarged Board of Appeal legally qualified members of the national courts or quasi-judicial authorities of the Contracting States, who may continue their judicial activities at the national level. They shall be appointed for a term of three years and may be re-appointed.

[1.432]
Article 12
Duties of office
Employees of the European Patent Office shall be bound, even after the termination of their employment, neither to disclose nor to make use of information which by its nature is a professional secret.

[1.433]
Article 13
Disputes between the Organisation and the employees of the European Patent Office

(1) Employees and former employees of the European Patent Office or their successors in title may apply to the Administrative Tribunal of the International Labour Organisation in the case of disputes with the European Patent Organisation, in accordance with the Statute of the Tribunal and within the limits and subject to the conditions laid down in the Service Regulations for permanent employees or the Pension Scheme Regulations or arising from the conditions of employment of other employees.

(2) An appeal shall only be admissible if the person concerned has exhausted such other means of appeal as are available to him under the Service Regulations, the Pension Scheme Regulations or the conditions of employment.

[1.434]
Article 14
Languages of the European Patent Office, European patent applications and other documents

(1) The official languages of the European Patent Office shall be English, French and German.

(2) A European patent application shall be filed in one of the official languages or, if filed in any other language, translated into one of the official languages in accordance with the Implementing Regulations. Throughout the proceedings before the European Patent Office, such translation may be brought into conformity with the application as filed. If a required translation is not filed in due time, the application shall be deemed to be withdrawn.

(3) The official language of the European Patent Office in which the European patent application is filed or into which it is translated shall be used as the language of the proceedings in all proceedings before the European Patent Office, unless the Implementing Regulations provide otherwise.

(4) Natural or legal persons having their residence or principal place of business within a Contracting State having a language other than English, French or German as an official language, and nationals of that State who are resident abroad, may file documents which have to be filed within a time limit in an official language of that State. They shall, however, file a translation in an official language of the European Patent Office in accordance with the Implementing Regulations. If any document, other than those documents making up the European patent application, is not filed in the prescribed language, or if any required translation is not filed in due time, the document shall be deemed not to have been filed.

(5) European patent applications shall be published in the language of the proceedings.

(6) Specifications of European patents shall be published in the language of the proceedings and shall include a translation of the claims in the other two official languages of the European Patent Office.

(7) The following shall be published in the three official languages of the European Patent Office—

- (a) the European Patent Bulletin;
- (b) the Official Journal of the European Patent Office.

(8) Entries in the European Patent Register shall be made in the three official languages of the European Patent Office. In cases of doubt, the entry in the language of the proceedings shall be authentic.

[1.435]
Article 15
Departments entrusted with the procedure

To carry out the procedures laid down in this Convention, the following shall be set up within the European Patent Office—

- (a) a Receiving Section;
- (b) Search Divisions;
- (c) Examining Divisions;
- (d) Opposition Divisions;
- (e) a Legal Division;
- (f) Boards of Appeal;
- (g) an Enlarged Board of Appeal.

[1.436]
Article 16
Receiving Section

The Receiving Section shall be responsible for the examination on filing and the examination as to formal requirements of European patent applications.

[1.437]
Article 17
Search Divisions

The Search Divisions shall be responsible for drawing up European search reports.

[1.438]
Article 18
Examining Divisions

(1) The Examining Divisions shall be responsible for the examination of European patent applications.

(2) An Examining Division shall consist of three technically qualified examiners. However, before a decision is taken on a European patent application, its examination shall, as a general rule, be entrusted to one member of the Examining Division. Oral proceedings shall be before the Examining Division itself. If the Examining Division considers that the nature of the decision so requires, it shall be enlarged by the addition of a legally qualified examiner. In the event of parity of votes, the vote of the Chairman of the Examining Division shall be decisive.

[1.439]
Article 19
Opposition Divisions

(1) The Opposition Divisions shall be responsible for the examination of oppositions against any European patent.

(2) An Opposition Division shall consist of three technically qualified examiners, at least two of whom shall not have taken part in the proceedings for grant of the patent to which the opposition relates. An examiner who has taken part in the proceedings for the grant of the European patent may not be the Chairman. Before a decision is taken on the opposition, the Opposition Division may entrust the examination of the opposition to one of its members. Oral proceedings shall be before the Opposition Division itself. If the Opposition Division considers that the nature of the decision so requires, it shall be enlarged by the addition of a legally qualified examiner who shall not have taken part in the proceedings for grant of the patent. In the event of parity of votes, the vote of the Chairman of the Opposition Division shall be decisive.

[1.440]
Article 20
Legal Division

(1) The Legal Division shall be responsible for decisions in respect of entries in the Register of European Patents and in respect of registration on, and deletion from, the list of professional representatives.

(2) Decisions of the Legal Division shall be taken by one legally qualified member.

[1.441]
Article 21
Boards of Appeal

(1) The Boards of Appeal shall be responsible for the examination of appeals from decisions of the Receiving Section, the Examining Divisions and Opposition Divisions, and the Legal Division.

(2) For appeals from decisions of the Receiving Section or the Legal Division, a Board of Appeal shall consist of three legally qualified members.

(3) For appeals from a decision of an Examining Division, a Board of Appeal shall consist of—
  (a) two technically qualified members and one legally qualified member, when the decision concerns the refusal of a European patent application or the grant, limitation or revocation of a European patent, and was taken by an Examining Division consisting of less than four members;
  (b) three technically and two legally qualified members, when the decision was taken by an Examining Division consisting of four members, or when the Board of Appeal considers that the nature of the appeal so requires;
  (c) three legally qualified members in all other cases.

(4) For appeals from a decision of an Opposition Division, a Board of Appeal shall consist of—
  (a) two technically qualified members and one legally qualified member, when the decision was taken by an Opposition Division consisting of three members;
  (b) three technically and two legally qualified members, when the decision was taken by an Opposition Division consisting of four members, or when the Board of Appeal considers that the nature of the appeal so requires.

[1.442]
Article 22
Enlarged Board of Appeal

(1) The Enlarged Board of Appeal shall be responsible for—
  (a) deciding on points of law referred to it by Boards of Appeal under Article 112;
  (b) giving opinions on points of law referred to it by the President of the European Patent Office under Article 112;
  (c) deciding on petitions for review of decisions of the Boards of Appeal under Article 112a.

(2) In proceedings under paragraph 1(a) and (b), the Enlarged Board of Appeal shall consist of five legally and two technically qualified members. In proceedings under paragraph 1(c), the Enlarged Board of Appeal shall consist of three or five members as laid down in the Implementing Regulations. In all proceedings, a legally qualified member shall be the Chairman.

[1.443]
Article 23
Independence of the members of the Boards

(1) The members of the Enlarged Board of Appeal and of the Boards of Appeal shall be appointed for a term of five years and may not be removed from office during this term, except if there are serious grounds for such removal and if the Administrative Council, on a proposal from the Enlarged Board of Appeal, takes a decision to this effect. Notwithstanding sentence 1, the term of office of members of the Boards shall end if they resign or are retired in accordance with the Service Regulations for permanent employees of the European Patent Office.

(2) The members of the Boards may not be members of the Receiving Section, Examining Divisions, Opposition Divisions or Legal Division.

(3) In their decisions the members of the Boards shall not be bound by any instructions and shall comply only with the provisions of this Convention.

(4) The Rules of Procedure of the Boards of Appeal and the Enlarged Board of Appeal shall be adopted in accordance with the Implementing Regulations. They shall be subject to the approval of the Administrative Council.

[1.444]
Article 24
Exclusion and objection

(1) Members of the Boards of Appeal or of the Enlarged Board of Appeal may not take part in a case in which they have any personal interest, or if they have previously been involved as representatives of one of the parties, or if they participated in the decision under appeal.

(2) If, for one of the reasons mentioned in paragraph 1, or for any other reason, a member of a Board of Appeal or of the Enlarged Board of Appeal considers that he should not take part in any appeal, he shall inform the Board accordingly.

(3) Members of a Board of Appeal or of the Enlarged Board of Appeal may be objected to by any party for one of the reasons mentioned in paragraph 1, or if suspected of partiality. An objection shall not be admissible if, while being aware of a reason for objection, the party has taken a procedural step. An objection may not be based upon the nationality of members.

(4) The Boards of Appeal and the Enlarged Board of Appeal shall decide as to the action to be taken in the cases specified in paragraphs 2 and 3, without the participation of the member concerned. For the purposes of taking this decision the member objected to shall be replaced by his alternate.

[1.445]
Article 25
Technical opinion

At the request of the competent national court hearing an infringement or revocation action, the European Patent Office shall be obliged, on payment of an appropriate fee, to give a technical opinion concerning the European patent which is the subject of the action. The Examining Division shall be responsible for issuing such opinions.

CHAPTER IV
THE ADMINISTRATIVE COUNCIL

[1.446]
Article 26
Membership

(1) The Administrative Council shall be composed of the Representatives and the alternate Representatives of the Contracting States. Each Contracting State shall be entitled to appoint one Representative and one alternate Representative to the Administrative Council.

(2) The members of the Administrative Council may, in accordance with the Rules of Procedure of the Administrative Council, be assisted by advisers or experts.

[1.447]
Article 27
Chairmanship

(1) The Administrative Council shall elect a Chairman and a Deputy Chairman from among the Representatives and alternate Representatives of the Contracting States. The Deputy Chairman shall *ex officio* replace the Chairman if he is prevented from carrying out his duties.

(2) The terms of office of the Chairman and the Deputy Chairman shall be three years. They may be re-elected.

[1.448]
Article 28
Board

(1) When there are at least eight Contracting States, the Administrative Council may set up a Board composed of five of its members.

(2) The Chairman and the Deputy Chairman of the Administrative Council shall be members of the Board *ex officio*; the other three members shall be elected by the Administrative Council.
(3) The term of office of the members elected by the Administrative Council shall be three years. They may not be re-elected.
(4) The Board shall perform the duties assigned to it by the Administrative Council in accordance with the Rules of Procedure.

[1.449]
Article 29
Meetings
(1) Meetings of the Administrative Council shall be convened by its Chairman.
(2) The President of the European Patent Office shall take part in the deliberations of the Administrative Council.
(3) The Administrative Council shall hold an ordinary meeting once each year. In addition, it shall meet on the initiative of its Chairman or at the request of one-third of the Contracting States.
(4) The deliberations of the Administrative Council shall be based on an agenda, and shall be held in accordance with its Rules of Procedure.
(5) The provisional agenda shall contain any question whose inclusion is requested by any Contracting State in accordance with the Rules of Procedure.

[1.450]
Article 30
Attendance of observers
(1) The World Intellectual Property Organisation shall be represented at the meetings of the Administrative Council, in accordance with an agreement between the Organisation and the World Intellectual Property Organisation.
(2) Other intergovernmental organisations entrusted with carrying out international procedures in the field of patents, with which the Organisation has concluded an agreement, shall be represented at the meetings of the Administrative Council, in accordance with such agreement.
(3) Any other intergovernmental and international non-governmental organisations carrying out an activity of interest to the Organisation may be invited by the Administrative Council to be represented at its meetings during any discussion of matters of mutual interest.

[1.451]
Article 31
Languages of the Administrative Council
(1) The languages used in the deliberations of the Administrative Council shall be English, French and German.
(2) Documents submitted to the Administrative Council, and the minutes of its deliberations, shall be drawn up in the three languages specified in paragraph 1.

[1.452]
Article 32
Staff, premises and equipment
The European Patent Office shall place at the disposal of the Administrative Council, and of any committee established by it, such staff, premises and equipment as may be necessary for the performance of their duties.

[1.453]
Article 33
Competence of the Administrative Council in certain cases
(1) The Administrative Council shall be competent to amend—
(a) the time limits laid down in this Convention;
(b) Parts II to VIII and Part X of this Convention, to bring them into line with an international treaty relating to patents or European Community legislation relating to patents;
(c) the Implementing Regulations.
(2) The Administrative Council shall be competent, in conformity with this Convention, to adopt or amend—
(a) the Financial Regulations;
(b) the Service Regulations for permanent employees and the conditions of employment of other employees of the European Patent Office, the salary scales of the said permanent and other employees, and also the nature of any supplementary benefits and the rules for granting them;
(c) the Pension Scheme Regulations and any appropriate increases in existing pensions to correspond to increases in salaries;
(d) the Rules relating to Fees;
(e) its Rules of Procedure.
(3) Notwithstanding Article 18, paragraph 2, the Administrative Council shall be competent to decide, in the light of experience, that in certain categories of cases Examining Divisions shall consist of one technically qualified examiner only. Such decision may be rescinded.

(4) The Administrative Council shall be competent to authorise the President of the European Patent Office to negotiate and, subject to its approval, to conclude agreements on behalf of the European Patent Organisation with States, with intergovernmental organisations and with documentation centres set up on the basis of agreements with such organisations.

(5) The Administrative Council may not take a decision under paragraph 1(b)—

— concerning an international treaty, before its entry into force;

— concerning European Community legislation, before its entry into force or, where that legislation lays down a period for its implementation, before the expiry of that period.

[1.454]
Article 34
Voting rights

(1) The right to vote in the Administrative Council shall be restricted to the Contracting States.

(2) Each Contracting State shall have one vote, except where Article 36 applies.

[1.455]
Article 35
Voting rules

(1) The Administrative Council shall take its decisions, other than those referred to in paragraphs 2 and 3, by a simple majority of the Contracting States represented and voting.

(2) A majority of three quarters of the votes of the Contracting States represented and voting shall be required for the decisions which the Administrative Council is empowered to take under Article 7, Article 11, paragraph 1, Article 33, paragraphs 1(a) and (c), and 2 to 4, Article 39, paragraph 1, Article 40, paragraphs 2 and 4, Article 46, Article 134a, Article 149a, paragraph 2, Article 152, Article 153, paragraph 7, Article 166 and Article 172.

(3) Unanimity of the Contracting States voting shall be required for the decisions which the Administrative Council is empowered to take under Article 33, paragraph 1(b). The Administrative Council shall take such decisions only if all the Contracting States are represented. A decision taken on the basis of Article 33, paragraph 1(b), shall not take effect if a Contracting State declares, within twelve months of the date of the decision, that it does not wish to be bound by that decision.

(4) Abstentions shall not be considered as votes.

[1.456]
Article 36
Weighting of votes

(1) In respect of the adoption or amendment of the Rules relating to Fees and, if the financial contribution to be made by the Contracting States would thereby be increased, the adoption of the budget of the Organisation and of any amending or supplementary budget, any Contracting State may require, following a first ballot in which each Contracting State shall have one vote, and whatever the result of this ballot, that a second ballot be taken immediately, in which votes shall be given to the States in accordance with paragraph 2. The decision shall be determined by the result of this second ballot.

(2) The number of votes that each Contracting State shall have in the second ballot shall be calculated as follows—

(a) the percentage obtained for each Contracting State in respect of the scale for the special financial contributions, pursuant to Article 40, paragraphs 3 and 4, shall be multiplied by the number of Contracting States and divided by five;

(b) the number of votes thus given shall be rounded upwards to the next whole number;

(c) five additional votes shall be added to this number;

(d) nevertheless, no Contracting State shall have more than 30 votes.

CHAPTER V
FINANCIAL PROVISIONS

[1.457]
Article 37
Budgetary funding

The budget of the Organisation shall be financed—

(a) by the Organisation's own resources;

(b) by payments made by the Contracting States in respect of renewal fees for European patents levied in these States;

(c) where necessary, by special financial contributions made by the Contracting States;

(d) where appropriate, by the revenue provided for in Article 146;

(e) where appropriate, and for tangible assets only, by third-party borrowings secured on land or buildings;

(f) where appropriate, by third-party funding for specific projects.

[1.458]
Article 38
The Organisation's own resources

The Organisation's own resources shall comprise—

(a) all income from fees and other sources and also the reserves of the Organisation;
(b) the resources of the Pension Reserve Fund, which shall be treated as a special class of asset of the Organisation, designed to support the Organisation's pension scheme by providing the appropriate reserves.

[1.459]
Article 39
Payments by the Contracting States in respect of renewal fees for European patents

(1) Each Contracting State shall pay to the Organisation in respect of each renewal fee received for a European patent in that State an amount equal to a proportion of that fee, to be fixed by the Administrative Council; the proportion shall not exceed 75% and shall be the same for all Contracting States. However, if the said proportion corresponds to an amount which is less than a uniform minimum amount fixed by the Administrative Council, the Contracting State shall pay that minimum to the Organisation.
(2) Each Contracting State shall communicate to the Organisation such information as the Administrative Council considers to be necessary to determine the amount of these payments.
(3) The due dates for these payments shall be determined by the Administrative Council.
(4) If a payment is not remitted fully by the due date, the Contracting State shall pay interest from the due date on the amount remaining unpaid.

[1.460]
Article 40
Level of fees and payments—Special financial contributions

(1) The amounts of the fees referred to in Article 38 and the proportion referred to in Article 39 shall be fixed at such a level as to ensure that the revenue in respect thereof is sufficient for the budget of the Organisation to be balanced.
(2) However, if the Organisation is unable to balance its budget under the conditions laid down in paragraph 1, the Contracting States shall remit to the Organisation special financial contributions, the amount of which shall be determined by the Administrative Council for the accounting period in question.
(3) These special financial contributions shall be determined in respect of any Contracting State on the basis of the number of patent applications filed in the last year but one prior to that of entry into force of this Convention, and calculated in the following manner—

(a) one half in proportion to the number of patent applications filed in that Contracting State;
(b) one half in proportion to the second highest number of patent applications filed in the other Contracting States by natural or legal persons having their residence or principal place of business in that Contracting State.

However, the amounts to be contributed by States in which the number of patent applications filed exceeds 25,000 shall then be taken as a whole and a new scale drawn up in proportion to the total number of patent applications filed in these States.
(4) Where the scale position of any Contracting State cannot be established in accordance with paragraph 3, the Administrative Council shall, with the consent of that State, decide its scale position.
(5) Article 39, paragraphs 3 and 4, shall apply *mutatis mutandis* to the special financial contributions.
(6) The special financial contributions shall be repaid with interest at a rate which shall be the same for all Contracting States. Repayments shall be made in so far as it is possible to provide for this purpose in the budget; the amount thus provided shall be distributed among the Contracting States in accordance with the scale referred to in paragraphs 3 and 4.
(7) The special financial contributions remitted in any accounting period shall be repaid in full before any such contributions or parts thereof remitted in any subsequent accounting period are repaid.

[1.461]
Article 41
Advances

(1) At the request of the President of the European Patent Office, the Contracting States shall grant advances to the Organisation, on account of their payments and contributions, within the limit of the amount fixed by the Administrative Council. The amount of such advances shall be determined in proportion to the amounts due from the Contracting States for the accounting period in question.
(2) Article 39, paragraphs 3 and 4, shall apply *mutatis mutandis* to the advances.

[1.462]
Article 42
Budget

(1) The budget of the Organisation shall be balanced. It shall be drawn up in accordance with the generally accepted accounting principles laid down in the Financial Regulations. If necessary, there may be amending or supplementary budgets.

(2) The budget shall be drawn up in the unit of account fixed in the Financial Regulations.

[1.463]
Article 43
Authorisation for expenditure

(1) The expenditure entered in the budget shall be authorised for the duration of one accounting period, unless the Financial Regulations provide otherwise.

(2) In accordance with the Financial Regulations, any appropriations, other than those relating to staff costs, which are unexpended at the end of the accounting period may be carried forward, but not beyond the end of the following accounting period.

(3) Appropriations shall be set out under different headings according to type and purpose of the expenditure and subdivided, as far as necessary, in accordance with the Financial Regulations.

[1.464]
Article 44
Appropriations for unforeseeable expenditure

(1) The budget of the Organisation may contain appropriations for unforeseeable expenditure.

(2) The employment of these appropriations by the Organisation shall be subject to the prior approval of the Administrative Council.

[1.465]
Article 45
Accounting period

The accounting period shall commence on 1 January and end on 31 December.

[1.466]
Article 46
Preparation and adoption of the budget

(1) The President of the European Patent Office shall submit the draft budget to the Administrative Council no later than the date prescribed in the Financial Regulations.

(2) The budget and any amending or supplementary budget shall be adopted by the Administrative Council.

[1.467]
Article 47
Provisional budget

(1) If, at the beginning of the accounting period, the budget has not been adopted by the Administrative Council, expenditures may be effected on a monthly basis per heading or other division of the budget, in accordance with the Financial Regulations, up to one-twelfth of the budget appropriations for the preceding accounting period, provided that the appropriations thus made available to the President of the European Patent Office shall not exceed one-twelfth of those provided for in the draft budget.

(2) The Administrative Council may, subject to the observance of the other provisions laid down in paragraph 1, authorise expenditure in excess of one-twelfth of the appropriations.

(3) The payments referred to in Article 37(b), shall continue to be made, on a provisional basis, under the conditions determined under Article 39 for the year preceding that to which the draft budget relates.

(4) The Contracting States shall pay each month, on a provisional basis and in accordance with the scale referred to in Article 40, paragraphs 3 and 4, any special financial contributions necessary to ensure implementation of paragraphs 1 and 2. Article 39, paragraph 4, shall apply *mutatis mutandis* to these contributions.

[1.468]
Article 48
Budget implementation

(1) The President of the European Patent Office shall implement the budget and any amending or supplementary budget on his own responsibility and within the limits of the allocated appropriations.

(2) Within the budget, the President of the European Patent Office may, in accordance with the Financial Regulations, transfer funds between the various headings or sub-headings.

[1.469]
Article 49
Auditing of accounts

(1) The income and expenditure account and a balance sheet of the Organisation shall be examined by auditors whose independence is beyond doubt, appointed by the Administrative Council for a period of five years, which shall be renewable or extensible.

(2) The audit shall be based on vouchers and shall take place, if necessary, *in situ*. The audit shall ascertain whether all income has been received and all expenditure effected in a lawful and proper manner and whether the financial management is sound. The auditors shall draw up a report containing a signed audit opinion after the end of each accounting period.

(3) The President of the European Patent Office shall annually submit to the Administrative Council the accounts of the preceding accounting period in respect of the budget and the balance sheet showing the assets and liabilities of the Organisation together with the report of the auditors.

(4) The Administrative Council shall approve the annual accounts together with the report of the auditors and shall discharge the President of the European Patent Office in respect of the implementation of the budget.

[1.470]
Article 50
Financial Regulations

The Financial Regulations shall lay down in particular—

(a) the arrangements relating to the establishment and implementation of the budget and for the rendering and auditing of accounts;
(b) the method and procedure whereby the payments and contributions provided for in Article 37 and the advances provided for in Article 41 are to be made available to the Organisation by the Contracting States;
(c) the rules concerning the responsibilities of authorising and accounting officers and the arrangements for their supervision;
(d) the rates of interest provided for in Articles 39, 40 and 47;
(e) the method of calculating the contributions payable by virtue of Article 146;
(f) the composition of and duties to be assigned to a Budget and Finance Committee which should be set up by the Administrative Council;
(g) the generally accepted accounting principles on which the budget and the annual financial statements shall be based.

[1.471]
Article 51
Fees

(1) The European Patent Office may levy fees for any official task or procedure carried out under this Convention.

(2) Time limits for the payment of fees other than those fixed by this Convention shall be laid down in the Implementing Regulations.

(3) Where the Implementing Regulations provide that a fee shall be paid, they shall also lay down the legal consequences of failure to pay such fee in due time.

(4) The Rules relating to Fees shall determine in particular the amounts of the fees and the ways in which they are to be paid.

PART II
SUBSTANTIVE PATENT LAW

CHAPTER I
PATENTABILITY

[1.472]
Article 52
Patentable inventions

(1) European patents shall be granted for any inventions, in all fields of technology, provided that they are new, involve an inventive step and are susceptible of industrial application.

(2) The following in particular shall not be regarded as inventions within the meaning of paragraph 1—

(a) discoveries, scientific theories and mathematical methods;
(b) aesthetic creations;
(c) schemes, rules and methods for performing mental acts, playing games or doing business, and programs for computers;
(d) presentations of information.

(3) Paragraph 2 shall exclude the patentability of the subject-matter or activities referred to therein only to the extent to which a European patent application or European patent relates to such subject-matter or activities as such.

[1.473]
Article 53
Exceptions to patentability

European patents shall not be granted in respect of—

(a) inventions the commercial exploitation of which would be contrary to *ordre public* or morality; such exploitation shall not be deemed to be so contrary merely because it is prohibited by law or regulation in some or all of the Contracting States;

(b) plant or animal varieties or essentially biological processes for the production of plants or animals; this provision shall not apply to microbiological processes or the products thereof;

(c) methods for treatment of the human or animal body by surgery or therapy and diagnostic methods practised on the human or animal body; this provision shall not apply to products, in particular substances or compositions, for use in any of these methods.

[1.474]
Article 54
Novelty

(1) An invention shall be considered to be new if it does not form part of the state of the art.

(2) The state of the art shall be held to comprise everything made available to the public by means of a written or oral description, by use, or in any other way, before the date of filing of the European patent application.

(3) Additionally, the content of European patent applications as filed, the dates of filing of which are prior to the date referred to in paragraph 2 and which were published on or after that date, shall be considered as comprised in the state of the art.

(4) Paragraphs 2 and 3 shall not exclude the patentability of any substance or composition, comprised in the state of the art, for use in a method referred to in Article 53(c), provided that its use for any such method is not comprised in the state of the art.

(5) Paragraphs 2 and 3 shall also not exclude the patentability of any substance or composition referred to in paragraph 4 for any specific use in a method referred to in Article 53(c), provided that such use is not comprised in the state of the art.

[1.475]
Article 55
Non-prejudicial disclosures

(1) For the application of Article 54, a disclosure of the invention shall not be taken into consideration if it occurred no earlier than six months preceding the filing of the European patent application and if it was due to, or in consequence of—

(a) an evident abuse in relation to the applicant or his legal predecessor, or

(b) the fact that the applicant or his legal predecessor has displayed the invention at an official, or officially recognised, international exhibition falling within the terms of the Convention on international exhibitions signed at Paris on 22 November 1928 and last revised on 30 November 1972.

(2) In the case of paragraph 1(b), paragraph 1 shall apply only if the applicant states, when filing the European patent application, that the invention has been so displayed and files a supporting certificate within the time limit and under the conditions laid down in the Implementing Regulations.

[1.476]
Article 56
Inventive step

An invention shall be considered as involving an inventive step if, having regard to the state of the art, it is not obvious to a person skilled in the art. If the state of the art also includes documents within the meaning of Article 54, paragraph 3, these documents shall not be considered in deciding whether there has been an inventive step.

[1.477]
Article 57
Industrial application

An invention shall be considered as susceptible of industrial application if it can be made or used in any kind of industry, including agriculture.

CHAPTER II
PERSONS ENTITLED TO APPLY FOR AND OBTAIN A EUROPEAN PATENT—MENTION OF THE INVENTOR

[1.478]
Article 58
Entitlement to file a European patent application

A European patent application may be filed by any natural or legal person, or any body equivalent to a legal person by virtue of the law governing it.

[1.479]
Article 59
Multiple applicants

A European patent application may also be filed either by joint applicants or by two or more applicants designating different Contracting States.

[1.480]
Article 60
Right to a European patent

(1) The right to a European patent shall belong to the inventor or his successor in title. If the inventor is an employee the right to a European patent shall be determined in accordance with the law of the State in which the employee is mainly employed; if the State in which the employee is mainly employed cannot be determined, the law to be applied shall be that of the State in which the employer has the place of business to which the employee is attached.

(2) If two or more persons have made an invention independently of each other, the right to a European patent therefor shall belong to the person whose European patent application has the earliest date of filing, provided that this first application has been published.

(3) In proceedings before the European Patent Office, the applicant shall be deemed to be entitled to exercise the right to a European patent.

[1.481]
Article 61
European patent applications filed by non-entitled persons

(1) If by a final decision it is adjudged that a person other than the applicant is entitled to the grant of the European patent, that person may, in accordance with the Implementing Regulations—

(a) prosecute the European patent application as his own application in place of the applicant;
(b) file a new European patent application in respect of the same invention; or
(c) request that the European patent application be refused.

(2) Article 76, paragraph 1, shall apply *mutatis mutandis* to a new European patent application filed under paragraph 1(b).

[1.482]
Article 62
Right of the inventor to be mentioned

The inventor shall have the right, vis-à-vis the applicant for or proprietor of a European patent, to be mentioned as such before the European Patent Office.

CHAPTER III
EFFECTS OF THE EUROPEAN PATENT AND THE EUROPEAN PATENT APPLICATION

[1.483]
Article 63
Term of the European patent

(1) The term of the European patent shall be 20 years from the date of filing of the application.

(2) Nothing in the preceding paragraph shall limit the right of a Contracting State to extend the term of a European patent, or to grant corresponding protection which follows immediately on expiry of the term of the patent, under the same conditions as those applying to national patents—

(a) in order to take account of a state of war or similar emergency conditions affecting that State;
(b) if the subject-matter of the European patent is a product or a process for manufacturing a product or a use of a product which has to undergo an administrative authorisation procedure required by law before it can be put on the market in that State.

(3) Paragraph 2 shall apply *mutatis mutandis* to European patents granted jointly for a group of Contracting States in accordance with Article 142.

(4) A Contracting State which makes provision for extension of the term or corresponding protection under paragraph 2(b) may, in accordance with an agreement concluded with the Organisation, entrust to the European Patent Office tasks associated with implementation of the relevant provisions.

[1.484]
Article 64
Rights conferred by a European patent

(1) A European patent shall, subject to the provisions of paragraph 2, confer on its proprietor from the date on which the mention of its grant is published in the European Patent Bulletin, in each Contracting State in respect of which it is granted, the same rights as would be conferred by a national patent granted in that State.

(2) If the subject-matter of the European patent is a process, the protection conferred by the patent shall extend to the products directly obtained by such process.

(3) Any infringement of a European patent shall be dealt with by national law.

[1.485]
Article 65
Translation of the European patent

(1) Any Contracting State may, if the European patent as granted, amended or limited by the European Patent Office is not drawn up in one of its official languages, prescribe that the proprietor of the patent shall supply to its central industrial property office a translation of the patent as granted, amended or limited in one of its official languages at his option or, where that State has prescribed the use of one specific official language, in that language. The period for supplying the translation shall end three months after the date on which the mention of the grant, maintenance in amended form or limitation of the European patent is published in the European Patent Bulletin, unless the State concerned prescribes a longer period.

(2) Any Contracting State which has adopted provisions pursuant to paragraph 1 may prescribe that the proprietor of the patent must pay all or part of the costs of publication of such translation within a period laid down by that State.

(3) Any Contracting State may prescribe that in the event of failure to observe the provisions adopted in accordance with paragraphs 1 and 2, the European patent shall be deemed to be void *ab initio* in that State.

[1.486]
Article 66
Equivalence of European filing with national filing

A European patent application which has been accorded a date of filing shall, in the designated Contracting States, be equivalent to a regular national filing, where appropriate with the priority claimed for the European patent application.

[1.487]
Article 67
Rights conferred by a European patent application after publication

(1) A European patent application shall, from the date of its publication, provisionally confer upon the applicant the protection provided for by Article 64, in the Contracting States designated in the application.

(2) Any Contracting State may prescribe that a European patent application shall not confer such protection as is conferred by Article 64. However, the protection attached to the publication of the European patent application may not be less than that which the laws of the State concerned attach to the compulsory publication of unexamined national patent applications. In any event, each State shall ensure at least that, from the date of publication of a European patent application, the applicant can claim compensation reasonable in the circumstances from any person who has used the invention in that State in circumstances where that person would be liable under national law for infringement of a national patent.

(3) Any Contracting State which does not have as an official language the language of the proceedings may prescribe that provisional protection in accordance with paragraphs 1 and 2 above shall not be effective until such time as a translation of the claims in one of its official languages at the option of the applicant or, where that State has prescribed the use of one specific official language, in that language—

(a) has been made available to the public in the manner prescribed by national law, or
(b) has been communicated to the person using the invention in the said State.

(4) The European patent application shall be deemed never to have had the effects set out in paragraphs 1 and 2 when it has been withdrawn, deemed to be withdrawn or finally refused. The same shall apply in respect of the effects of the European patent application in a Contracting State the designation of which is withdrawn or deemed to be withdrawn.

[1.488]
Article 68
Effect of revocation or limitation of the European patent

The European patent application and the resulting European patent shall be deemed not to have had, from the outset, the effects specified in Articles 64 and 67, to the extent that the patent has been revoked or limited in opposition, limitation or revocation proceedings.

[1.489]
Article 69
Extent of protection

(1) The extent of the protection conferred by a European patent or a European patent application shall be determined by the claims. Nevertheless, the description and drawings shall be used to interpret the claims.

(2) For the period up to grant of the European patent, the extent of the protection conferred by the European patent application shall be determined by the claims contained in the application as published. However, the European patent as granted or as amended in opposition, limitation or revocation proceedings shall determine retroactively the protection conferred by the application, in so far as such protection is not thereby extended.

[1.490]
Article 70
Authentic text of a European patent application or European patent

(1) The text of a European patent application or a European patent in the language of the proceedings shall be the authentic text in any proceedings before the European Patent Office and in any Contracting State.

(2) If, however, the European patent application has been filed in a language which is not an official language of the European Patent Office, that text shall be the application as filed within the meaning of this Convention.

(3) Any Contracting State may provide that a translation into one of its official languages, as prescribed by it according to this Convention, shall in that State be regarded as authentic, except for revocation proceedings, in the event of the European patent application or European patent in the language of the translation conferring protection which is narrower than that conferred by it in the language of the proceedings.

(4) Any Contracting State which adopts a provision under paragraph 3—

(a) shall allow the applicant for or proprietor of the patent to file a corrected translation of the European patent application or European patent. Such corrected translation shall not have any legal effect until any conditions established by the Contracting State under Article 65, paragraph 2, or Article 67, paragraph 3, have been complied with;

(b) may prescribe that any person who, in that State, in good faith has used or has made effective and serious preparations for using an invention the use of which would not constitute infringement of the application or patent in the original translation, may, after the corrected translation takes effect, continue such use in the course of his business or for the needs thereof without payment.

CHAPTER IV
THE EUROPEAN PATENT APPLICATION AS AN OBJECT OF PROPERTY

[1.491]
Article 71
Transfer and constitution of rights

A European patent application may be transferred or give rise to rights for one or more of the designated Contracting States.

[1.492]
Article 72
Assignment

An assignment of a European patent application shall be made in writing and shall require the signature of the parties to the contract.

[1.493]
Article 73
Contractual licensing

A European patent application may be licensed in whole or in part for the whole or part of the territories of the designated Contracting States.

[1.494]
Article 74
Law applicable

Unless this Convention provides otherwise, the European patent application as an object of property shall, in each designated Contracting State and with effect for such State, be subject to the law applicable in that State to national patent applications.

PART III
THE EUROPEAN PATENT APPLICATION

CHAPTER I
FILING AND REQUIREMENTS OF THE EUROPEAN PATENT APPLICATION

[1.495]
Article 75
Filing of a European patent application

(1) A European patent application may be filed—

(a) with the European Patent Office, or

(b) if the law of a Contracting State so permits, and subject to Article 76, paragraph 1, with the central industrial property office or other competent authority of that State. Any application filed in this way shall have the same effect as if it had been filed on the same date with the European Patent Office.

(2) Paragraph 1 shall not preclude the application of legislative or regulatory provisions which, in any Contracting State—

(a) govern inventions which, owing to the nature of their subject-matter, may not be communicated abroad without the prior authorisation of the competent authorities of that State, or
(b) prescribe that any application is to be filed initially with a national authority, or make direct filing with another authority subject to prior authorisation.

[1.496]
Article 76
European divisional applications

(1) A European divisional application shall be filed directly with the European Patent Office in accordance with the Implementing Regulations. It may be filed only in respect of subject-matter which does not extend beyond the content of the earlier application as filed; in so far as this requirement is complied with, the divisional application shall be deemed to have been filed on the date of filing of the earlier application and shall enjoy any right of priority.
(2) All the Contracting States designated in the earlier application at the time of filing of a European divisional application shall be deemed to be designated in the divisional application.

[1.497]
Article 77
Forwarding of European patent applications

(1) The central industrial property office of a Contracting State shall forward to the European Patent Office any European patent application filed with it or any other competent authority in that State, in accordance with the Implementing Regulations.
(2) A European patent application the subject of which has been made secret shall not be forwarded to the European Patent Office.
(3) A European patent application not forwarded to the European Patent Office in due time shall be deemed to be withdrawn.

[1.498]
Article 78
Requirements of a European patent application

(1) A European patent application shall contain—
(a) a request for the grant of a European patent;
(b) a description of the invention;
(c) one or more claims;
(d) any drawings referred to in the description or the claims;
(e) an abstract,

and satisfy the requirements laid down in the Implementing Regulations.
(2) A European patent application shall be subject to the payment of the filing fee and the search fee. If the filing fee or the search fee is not paid in due time, the application shall be deemed to be withdrawn.

[1.499]
Article 79
Designation of Contracting States

(1) All the Contracting States party to this Convention at the time of filing of the European patent application shall be deemed to be designated in the request for grant of a European patent.
(2) The designation of a Contracting State may be subject to the payment of a designation fee.
(3) The designation of a Contracting State may be withdrawn at any time up to the grant of the European patent.

[1.500]
Article 80
Date of filing

The date of filing of a European patent application shall be the date on which the requirements laid down in the Implementing Regulations are fulfilled.

[1.501]
Article 81
Designation of the inventor

The European patent application shall designate the inventor. If the applicant is not the inventor or is not the sole inventor, the designation shall contain a statement indicating the origin of the right to the European patent.

[1.502]
Article 82
Unity of invention

The European patent application shall relate to one invention only or to a group of inventions so linked as to form a single general inventive concept.

[1.503]
Article 83
Disclosure of the invention
The European patent application shall disclose the invention in a manner sufficiently clear and complete for it to be carried out by a person skilled in the art.

[1.504]
Article 84
Claims
The claims shall define the matter for which protection is sought. They shall be clear and concise and be supported by the description.

[1.505]
Article 85
Abstract
The abstract shall serve the purpose of technical information only; it may not be taken into account for any other purpose, in particular for interpreting the scope of the protection sought or applying Article 54, paragraph 3.

[1.506]
Article 86
Renewal fees for the European patent application
(1) Renewal fees for the European patent application shall be paid to the European Patent Office in accordance with the Implementing Regulations. These fees shall be due in respect of the third year and each subsequent year, calculated from the date of filing of the application. If a renewal fee is not paid in due time, the application shall be deemed to be withdrawn.
(2) The obligation to pay renewal fees shall terminate with the payment of the renewal fee due in respect of the year in which the mention of the grant of the European patent is published in the European Patent Bulletin.

CHAPTER II
PRIORITY

[1.507]
Article 87
Priority right
(1) Any person who has duly filed, in or for
(a) any State party to the Paris Convention for the Protection of Industrial Property or
(b) any Member of the World Trade Organisation,
an application for a patent, a utility model or a utility certificate, or his successor in title, shall enjoy, for the purpose of filing a European patent application in respect of the same invention, a right of priority during a period of twelve months from the date of filing of the first application.
(2) Every filing that is equivalent to a regular national filing under the national law of the State where it was made or under bilateral or multilateral agreements, including this Convention, shall be recognised as giving rise to a right of priority.
(3) A regular national filing shall mean any filing that is sufficient to establish the date on which the application was filed, whatever the outcome of the application may be.
(4) A subsequent application in respect of the same subject-matter as a previous first application and filed in or for the same State shall be considered as the first application for the purposes of determining priority, provided that, at the date of filing the subsequent application, the previous application has been withdrawn, abandoned or refused, without being open to public inspection and without leaving any rights outstanding, and has not served as a basis for claiming a right of priority. The previous application may not thereafter serve as a basis for claiming a right of priority.
(5) If the first filing has been made with an industrial property authority which is not subject to the Paris Convention for the Protection of Industrial Property or the Agreement Establishing the World Trade Organisation, paragraphs 1 to 4 shall apply if that authority, according to a communication issued by the President of the European Patent Office, recognises that a first filing made with the European Patent Office gives rise to a right of priority under conditions and with effects equivalent to those laid down in the Paris Convention.

[1.508]
Article 88
Claiming priority
(1) An applicant desiring to take advantage of the priority of a previous application shall file a declaration of priority and any other document required, in accordance with the Implementing Regulations.
(2) Multiple priorities may be claimed in respect of a European patent application, notwithstanding the fact that they originated in different countries. Where appropriate, multiple priorities may be claimed for any one claim. Where multiple priorities are claimed, time limits which run from the date of priority shall run from the earliest date of priority.

(3) If one or more priorities are claimed in respect of a European patent application, the right of priority shall cover only those elements of the European patent application which are included in the application or applications whose priority is claimed.
(4) If certain elements of the invention for which priority is claimed do not appear among the claims formulated in the previous application, priority may nonetheless be granted, provided that the documents of the previous application as a whole specifically disclose such elements.

[1.509]
Article 89
Effect of priority right
The right of priority shall have the effect that the date of priority shall count as the date of filing of the European patent application for the purposes of Article 54, paragraphs 2 and 3, and Article 60, paragraph 2.

PART IV
PROCEDURE UP TO GRANT

[1.510]
Article 90
Examination on filing and examination as to formal requirements
(1) The European Patent Office shall examine, in accordance with the Implementing Regulations, whether the application satisfies the requirements for the accordance of a date of filing.
(2) If a date of filing cannot be accorded following the examination under paragraph 1, the application shall not be dealt with as a European patent application.
(3) If the European patent application has been accorded a date of filing, the European Patent Office shall examine, in accordance with the Implementing Regulations, whether the requirements in Articles 14, 78 and 81, and, where applicable, Article 88, paragraph 1, and Article 133, paragraph 2, as well as any other requirement laid down in the Implementing Regulations, have been satisfied.
(4) Where the European Patent Office in carrying out the examination under paragraphs 1 or 3 notes that there are deficiencies which may be corrected, it shall give the applicant an opportunity to correct them.
(5) If any deficiency noted in the examination under paragraph 3 is not corrected, the European patent application shall be refused unless a different legal consequence is provided for by this Convention. Where the deficiency concerns the right of priority, this right shall be lost for the application.

Article 91
Examination as to formal requirements
(Deleted)

[1.511]
Article 92
Drawing up of the European search report
The European Patent Office shall, in accordance with the Implementing Regulations, draw up and publish a European search report in respect of the European patent application on the basis of the claims, with due regard to the description and any drawings.

[1.512]
Article 93
Publication of the European patent application
(1) The European Patent Office shall publish the European patent application as soon as possible
 (a) after the expiry of a period of eighteen months from the date of filing or, if priority has been claimed, from the date of priority, or
 (b) at the request of the applicant, before the expiry of that period.
(2) The European patent application shall be published at the same time as the specification of the European patent when the decision to grant the patent becomes effective before the expiry of the period referred to in paragraph 1(a).

[1.513]
Article 94
Examination of the European patent application
(1) The European Patent Office shall, in accordance with the Implementing Regulations, examine on request whether the European patent application and the invention to which it relates meet the requirements of this Convention. The request shall not be deemed to be filed until the examination fee has been paid.
(2) If no request for examination has been made in due time, the application shall be deemed to be withdrawn.

(3) If the examination reveals that the application or the invention to which it relates does not meet the requirements of this Convention, the Examining Division shall invite the applicant, as often as necessary, to file his observations and, subject to Article 123, paragraph 1, to amend the application.
(4) If the applicant fails to reply in due time to any communication from the Examining Division, the application shall be deemed to be withdrawn.

Article 95
Extension of the period within which requests for examination may be filed
(Deleted)

Article 96
Examination of the European patent application
(Deleted)

[1.514]
Article 97
Grant or refusal
(1) If the Examining Division is of the opinion that the European patent application and the invention to which it relates meet the requirements of this Convention, it shall decide to grant a European patent, provided that the conditions laid down in the Implementing Regulations are fulfilled.
(2) If the Examining Division is of the opinion that the European patent application or the invention to which it relates does not meet the requirements of this Convention, it shall refuse the application unless this Convention provides for a different legal consequence.
(3) The decision to grant a European patent shall take effect on the date on which the mention of the grant is published in the European Patent Bulletin.

[1.515]
Article 98
Publication of the specification of the European patent
The European Patent Office shall publish the specification of the European patent as soon as possible after the mention of the grant of the European patent has been published in the European Patent Bulletin.

PART V
OPPOSITION AND LIMITATION PROCEDURE

[1.516]
Article 99
Opposition
(1) Within nine months of the publication of the mention of the grant of the European patent in the European Patent Bulletin, any person may give notice to the European Patent Office of opposition to that patent, in accordance with the Implementing Regulations. Notice of opposition shall not be deemed to have been filed until the opposition fee has been paid.
(2) The opposition shall apply to the European patent in all the Contracting States in which that patent has effect.
(3) Opponents shall be parties to the opposition proceedings as well as the proprietor of the patent.
(4) Where a person provides evidence that in a Contracting State, following a final decision, he has been entered in the patent register of such State instead of the previous proprietor, such person shall, at his request, replace the previous proprietor in respect of such State. Notwithstanding Article 118, the previous proprietor and the person making the request shall not be regarded as joint proprietors unless both so request.

[1.517]
Article 100
Grounds for opposition
Opposition may only be filed on the grounds that—
- (a) the subject-matter of the European patent is not patentable under Articles 52 to 57;
- (b) the European patent does not disclose the invention in a manner sufficiently clear and complete for it to be carried out by a person skilled in the art;
- (c) the subject-matter of the European patent extends beyond the content of the application as filed, or, if the patent was granted on a divisional application or on a new application filed under Article 61, beyond the content of the earlier application as filed.

[1.518]
Article 101
Examination of the opposition—Revocation or maintenance of the European patent

(1) If the opposition is admissible, the Opposition Division shall examine, in accordance with the Implementing Regulations, whether at least one ground for opposition under Article 100 prejudices the maintenance of the European patent. During this examination, the Opposition Division shall invite the parties, as often as necessary, to file observations on communications from another party or issued by itself.

(2) If the Opposition Division is of the opinion that at least one ground for opposition prejudices the maintenance of the European patent, it shall revoke the patent. Otherwise, it shall reject the opposition.

(3) If the Opposition Division is of the opinion that, taking into consideration the amendments made by the proprietor of the European patent during the opposition proceedings, the patent and the invention to which it relates

(a) meet the requirements of this Convention, it shall decide to maintain the patent as amended, provided that the conditions laid down in the Implementing Regulations are fulfilled;

(b) do not meet the requirements of this Convention, it shall revoke the patent.

Article 102
Revocation or maintenance of the European patent
(Deleted)

[1.519]
Article 103
Publication of a new specification of the European patent

If the European patent is maintained as amended under Article 101, paragraph 3(a), the European Patent Office shall publish a new specification of the European patent as soon as possible after the mention of the opposition decision has been published in the European Patent Bulletin.

[1.520]
Article 104
Costs

(1) Each party to the opposition proceedings shall bear the costs it has incurred, unless the Opposition Division, for reasons of equity, orders, in accordance with the Implementing Regulations, a different apportionment of costs.

(2) The procedure for fixing costs shall be laid down in the Implementing Regulations.

(3) Any final decision of the European Patent Office fixing the amount of costs shall be dealt with, for the purpose of enforcement in the Contracting States, in the same way as a final decision given by a civil court of the State in which enforcement is to take place. Verification of such decision shall be limited to its authenticity.

[1.521]
Article 105
Intervention of the assumed infringer

(1) Any third party may, in accordance with the Implementing Regulations, intervene in opposition proceedings after the opposition period has expired, if the third party proves that

(a) proceedings for infringement of the same patent have been instituted against him, or

(b) following a request of the proprietor of the patent to cease alleged infringement, the third party has instituted proceedings for a ruling that he is not infringing the patent.

(2) An admissible intervention shall be treated as an opposition.

[1.522]
Article 105a
Request for limitation or revocation

(1) At the request of the proprietor, the European patent may be revoked or be limited by an amendment of the claims. The request shall be filed with the European Patent Office in accordance with the Implementing Regulations. It shall not be deemed to have been filed until the limitation or revocation fee has been paid.

(2) The request may not be filed while opposition proceedings in respect of the European patent are pending.

[1.523]
Article 105b
Limitation or revocation of the European patent

(1) The European Patent Office shall examine whether the requirements laid down in the Implementing Regulations for limiting or revoking the European patent have been met.

(2) If the European Patent Office considers that the request for limitation or revocation of the European patent meets these requirements, it shall decide to limit or revoke the European patent in accordance with the Implementing Regulations. Otherwise, it shall reject the request.

(3) The decision to limit or revoke the European patent shall apply to the European patent in all the Contracting States in respect of which it has been granted. It shall take effect on the date on which the mention of the decision is published in the European Patent Bulletin.

[1.524]
Article 105c
Publication of the amended specification of the European patent
If the European patent is limited under Article 105b, paragraph 2, the European Patent Office shall publish the amended specification of the European patent as soon as possible after the mention of the limitation has been published in the European Patent Bulletin.

PART VI
APPEALS PROCEDURE

[1.525]
Article 106
Decisions subject to appeal
(1) An appeal shall lie from decisions of the Receiving Section, Examining Divisions, Opposition Divisions and the Legal Division. It shall have suspensive effect.
(2) A decision which does not terminate proceedings as regards one of the parties can only be appealed together with the final decision, unless the decision allows a separate appeal.
(3) The right to file an appeal against decisions relating to the apportionment or fixing of costs in opposition proceedings may be restricted in the Implementing Regulations.

[1.526]
Article 107
Persons entitled to appeal and to be parties to appeal proceedings
Any party to proceedings adversely affected by a decision may appeal. Any other parties to the proceedings shall be parties to the appeal proceedings as of right.

[1.527]
Article 108
Time limit and form
Notice of appeal shall be filed, in accordance with the Implementing Regulations, at the European Patent Office within two months of notification of the decision. Notice of appeal shall not be deemed to have been filed until the fee for appeal has been paid. Within four months of notification of the decision, a statement setting out the grounds of appeal shall be filed in accordance with the Implementing Regulations.

[1.528]
Article 109
Interlocutory revision
(1) If the department whose decision is contested considers the appeal to be admissible and well founded, it shall rectify its decision. This shall not apply where the appellant is opposed by another party to the proceedings.
(2) If the appeal is not allowed within three months of receipt of the statement of grounds, it shall be remitted to the Board of Appeal without delay, and without comment as to its merit.

[1.529]
Article 110
Examination of appeals
If the appeal is admissible, the Board of Appeal shall examine whether the appeal is allowable. The examination of the appeal shall be conducted in accordance with the Implementing Regulations.

[1.530]
Article 111
Decision in respect of appeals
(1) Following the examination as to the allowability of the appeal, the Board of Appeal shall decide on the appeal. The Board of Appeal may either exercise any power within the competence of the department which was responsible for the decision appealed or remit the case to that department for further prosecution.
(2) If the Board of Appeal remits the case for further prosecution to the department whose decision was appealed, that department shall be bound by the *ratio decidendi* of the Board of Appeal, in so far as the facts are the same. If the decision under appeal was taken by the Receiving Section, the Examining Division shall also be bound by the *ratio decidendi* of the Board of Appeal.

[1.531]
Article 112
Decision or opinion of the Enlarged Board of Appeal
(1) In order to ensure uniform application of the law, or if a point of law of fundamental importance arises—

(a) the Board of Appeal shall, during proceedings on a case and either of its own motion or following a request from a party to the appeal, refer any question to the Enlarged Board of Appeal if it considers that a decision is required for the above purposes. If the Board of Appeal rejects the request, it shall give the reasons in its final decision;
(b) the President of the European Patent Office may refer a point of law to the Enlarged Board of Appeal where two Boards of Appeal have given different decisions on that question.

(2) In the cases referred to in paragraph 1(a) the parties to the appeal proceedings shall be parties to the proceedings before the Enlarged Board of Appeal.

(3) The decision of the Enlarged Board of Appeal referred to in paragraph 1(a) shall be binding on the Board of Appeal in respect of the appeal in question.

[1.532]
Article 112a
Petition for review by the Enlarged Board of Appeal

(1) Any party to appeal proceedings adversely affected by the decision of the Board of Appeal may file a petition for review of the decision by the Enlarged Board of Appeal.

(2) The petition may only be filed on the grounds that—
(a) a member of the Board of Appeal took part in the decision in breach of Article 24, paragraph 1, or despite being excluded pursuant to a decision under Article 24, paragraph 4;
(b) the Board of Appeal included a person not appointed as a member of the Boards of Appeal;
(c) a fundamental violation of Article 113 occurred;
(d) any other fundamental procedural defect defined in the Implementing Regulations occurred in the appeal proceedings; or
(e) a criminal act established under the conditions laid down in the Implementing Regulations may have had an impact on the decision.

(3) The petition for review shall not have suspensive effect.

(4) The petition for review shall be filed in a reasoned statement, in accordance with the Implementing Regulations. If based on paragraph 2(a) to (d), the petition shall be filed within two months of notification of the decision of the Board of Appeal. If based on paragraph 2(e), the petition shall be filed within two months of the date on which the criminal act has been established and in any event no later than five years from notification of the decision of the Board of Appeal. The petition shall not be deemed to have been filed until after the prescribed fee has been paid.

(5) The Enlarged Board of Appeal shall examine the petition for review in accordance with the Implementing Regulations. If the petition is allowable, the Enlarged Board of Appeal shall set aside the decision and shall re-open proceedings before the Boards of Appeal in accordance with the Implementing Regulations.

(6) Any person who, in a designated Contracting State, has in good faith used or made effective and serious preparations for using an invention which is the subject of a published European patent application or a European patent in the period between the decision of the Board of Appeal and publication in thc European Patent Bulletin of the mention of the decision of the Enlarged Board of Appeal on the petition, may without payment continue such use in the course of his business or for the needs thereof.

PART VII
COMMON PROVISIONS

CHAPTER I
COMMON PROVISIONS GOVERNING PROCEDURE

[1.533]
Article 113
Right to be heard and basis of decisions

(1) The decisions of the European Patent Office may only be based on grounds or evidence on which the parties concerned have had an opportunity to present their comments.

(2) The European Patent Office shall examine, and decide upon, the European patent application or the European patent only in the text submitted to it, or agreed, by the applicant or the proprietor of the patent.

[1.534]
Article 114
Examination by the European Patent Office of its own motion

(1) In proceedings before it, the European Patent Office shall examine the facts of its own motion; it shall not be restricted in this examination to the facts, evidence and arguments provided by the parties and the relief sought.

(2) The European Patent Office may disregard facts or evidence which are not submitted in due time by the parties concerned.

[1.535]
Article 115
Observations by third parties

In proceedings before the European Patent Office, following the publication of the European patent application, any third party may, in accordance with the Implementing Regulations, present observations concerning the patentability of the invention to which the application or patent relates. That person shall not be a party to the proceedings.

[1.536]
Article 116
Oral proceedings

(1) Oral proceedings shall take place either at the instance of the European Patent Office if it considers this to be expedient or at the request of any party to the proceedings. However, the European Patent Office may reject a request for further oral proceedings before the same department where the parties and the subject of the proceedings are the same.
(2) Nevertheless, oral proceedings shall take place before the Receiving Section at the request of the applicant only where the Receiving Section considers this to be expedient or where it intends to refuse the European patent application.
(3) Oral proceedings before the Receiving Section, the Examining Divisions and the Legal Division shall not be public.
(4) Oral proceedings, including delivery of the decision, shall be public, as regards the Boards of Appeal and the Enlarged Board of Appeal, after publication of the European patent application, and also before the Opposition Divisions, in so far as the department before which the proceedings are taking place does not decide otherwise in cases where admission of the public could have serious and unjustified disadvantages, in particular for a party to the proceedings.

[1.537]
Article 117
Means and taking of evidence

(1) In proceedings before the European Patent Office the means of giving or obtaining evidence shall include the following—
  (a) hearing the parties;
  (b) requests for information;
  (c) production of documents;
  (d) hearing witnesses;
  (e) opinions by experts;
  (f) inspection;
  (g) sworn statements in writing.
(2) The procedure for taking such evidence shall be laid down in the Implementing Regulations.

[1.538]
Article 118
Unity of the European patent application or European patent

Where the applicants for or proprietors of a European patent are not the same in respect of different designated Contracting States, they shall be regarded as joint applicants or proprietors for the purposes of proceedings before the European Patent Office. The unity of the application or patent in these proceedings shall not be affected; in particular the text of the application or patent shall be uniform for all designated Contracting States, unless this Convention provides otherwise.

[1.539]
Article 119
Notification

Decisions, summonses, notices and communications shall be notified by the European Patent Office of its own motion in accordance with the Implementing Regulations. Notification may, where exceptional circumstances so require, be effected through the intermediary of the central industrial property offices of the Contracting States.

[1.540]
Article 120
Time limits

The Implementing Regulations shall specify—
  (a) the time limits which are to be observed in proceedings before the European Patent Office and are not fixed by this Convention;
  (b) the manner of computation of time limits and the conditions under which time limits may be extended;
  (c) the minima and maxima for time limits to be determined by the European Patent Office.

[1.541]
Article 121
Further processing of the European patent application

(1) If an applicant fails to observe a time limit vis-à-vis the European Patent Office, he may request further processing of the European patent application.

(2) The European Patent Office shall grant the request, provided that the requirements laid down in the Implementing Regulations are met. Otherwise, it shall reject the request.

(3) If the request is granted, the legal consequences of the failure to observe the time limit shall be deemed not to have ensued.

(4) Further processing shall be ruled out in respect of the time limits in Article 87, paragraph 1, Article 108 and Article 112a, paragraph 4, as well as the time limits for requesting further processing or re-establishment of rights. The Implementing Regulations may rule out further processing for other time limits.

[1.542]
Article 122
Re-establishment of rights

(1) An applicant for or proprietor of a European patent who, in spite of all due care required by the circumstances having been taken, was unable to observe a time limit vis-à-vis the European Patent Office shall have his rights re-established upon request if the non-observance of this time limit has the direct consequence of causing the refusal of the European patent application or of a request, or the deeming of the application to have been withdrawn, or the revocation of the European patent, or the loss of any other right or means of redress.

(2) The European Patent Office shall grant the request, provided that the conditions of paragraph 1 and any other requirements laid down in the Implementing Regulations are met. Otherwise, it shall reject the request.

(3) If the request is granted, the legal consequences of the failure to observe the time limit shall be deemed not to have ensued.

(4) Re-establishment of rights shall be ruled out in respect of the time limit for requesting re-establishment of rights. The Implementing Regulations may rule out re-establishment for other time limits.

(5) Any person who, in a designated Contracting State, has in good faith used or made effective and serious preparations for using an invention which is the subject of a published European patent application or a European patent in the period between the loss of rights referred to in paragraph 1 and publication in the European Patent Bulletin of the mention of re-establishment of those rights, may without payment continue such use in the course of his business or for the needs thereof.

(6) Nothing in this Article shall limit the right of a Contracting State to grant re-establishment of rights in respect of time limits provided for in this Convention and to be observed vis-à-vis the authorities of such State.

[1.543]
Article 123
Amendments

(1) The European patent application or European patent may be amended in proceedings before the European Patent Office, in accordance with the Implementing Regulations. In any event, the applicant shall be given at least one opportunity to amend the application of his own volition.

(2) The European patent application or European patent may not be amended in such a way that it contains subject-matter which extends beyond the content of the application as filed.

(3) The European patent may not be amended in such a way as to extend the protection it confers.

[1.544]
Article 124
Information on prior art

(1) The European Patent Office may, in accordance with the Implementing Regulations, invite the applicant to provide information on prior art taken into consideration in national or regional patent proceedings and concerning an invention to which the European patent application relates.

(2) If the applicant fails to reply in due time to an invitation under paragraph 1, the European patent application shall be deemed to be withdrawn.

[1.545]
Article 125
Reference to general principles

In the absence of procedural provisions in this Convention, the European Patent Office shall take into account the principles of procedural law generally recognised in the Contracting States.

Article 126
Termination of financial obligations

(Deleted)

CHAPTER II
INFORMATION TO THE PUBLIC OR TO OFFICIAL AUTHORITIES

[1.546]
Article 127
European Patent Register
The European Patent Office shall keep a European Patent Register, in which the particulars specified in the Implementing Regulations shall be recorded. No entry shall be made in the European Patent Register before the publication of the European patent application. The European Patent Register shall be open to public inspection.

[1.547]
Article 128
Inspection of files
(1) Files relating to European patent applications which have not yet been published shall not be made available for inspection without the consent of the applicant.
(2) Any person who can prove that the applicant has invoked the rights under the European patent application against him may obtain inspection of the files before the publication of that application and without the consent of the applicant.
(3) Where a European divisional application or a new European patent application filed under Article 61, paragraph 1, is published, any person may obtain inspection of the files of the earlier application before the publication of that application and without the consent of the applicant.
(4) After the publication of the European patent application, the files relating to the application and the resulting European patent may be inspected on request, subject to the restrictions laid down in the Implementing Regulations.
(5) Even before the publication of the European patent application, the European Patent Office may communicate to third parties or publish the particulars specified in the Implementing Regulations.

[1.548]
Article 129
Periodical publications
The European Patent Office shall periodically publish—
(a) a European Patent Bulletin containing the particulars the publication of which is prescribed by this Convention, the Implementing Regulations or the President of the European Patent Office;
(b) an Official Journal containing notices and information of a general character issued by the President of the European Patent Office, as well as any other information relevant to this Convention or its implementation.

[1.549]
Article 130
Exchange of information
(1) Unless this Convention or national laws provide otherwise, the European Patent Office and the central industrial property office of any Contracting State shall, on request, communicate to each other any useful information regarding European or national patent applications and patents and any proceedings concerning them.
(2) Paragraph 1 shall apply to the communication of information by virtue of working agreements between the European Patent Office and
(a) the central industrial property offices of other States;
(b) any intergovernmental organisation entrusted with the task of granting patents;
(c) any other organisation.
(3) Communications under paragraphs 1 and 2(a) and (b) shall not be subject to the restrictions laid down in Article 128. The Administrative Council may decide that communications under paragraph 2(c) shall not be subject to such restrictions, provided that the organisation concerned treats the information communicated as confidential until the European patent application has been published.

[1.550]
Article 131
Administrative and legal co-operation
(1) Unless this Convention or national laws provide otherwise, the European Patent Office and the courts or authorities of Contracting States shall on request give assistance to each other by communicating information or opening files for inspection. Where the European Patent Office makes files available for inspection by courts, Public Prosecutors' Offices or central industrial property offices, the inspection shall not be subject to the restrictions laid down in Article 128.
(2) At the request of the European Patent Office, the courts or other competent authorities of Contracting States shall undertake, on behalf of the Office and within the limits of their jurisdiction, any necessary enquiries or other legal measures.

[1.551]
Article 132
Exchange of publications

(1) The European Patent Office and the central industrial property offices of the Contracting States shall despatch to each other on request and for their own use one or more copies of their respective publications free of charge.

(2) The European Patent Office may conclude agreements relating to the exchange or supply of publications.

CHAPTER III
REPRESENTATION

[1.552]
Article 133
General principles of representation

(1) Subject to paragraph 2, no person shall be compelled to be represented by a professional representative in proceedings established by this Convention.

(2) Natural or legal persons not having their residence or principal place of business in a Contracting State shall be represented by a professional representative and act through him in all proceedings established by this Convention, other than in filing a European patent application; the Implementing Regulations may permit other exceptions.

(3) Natural or legal persons having their residence or principal place of business in a Contracting State may be represented in proceedings established by this Convention by an employee, who need not be a professional representative but who shall be authorised in accordance with the Implementing Regulations. The Implementing Regulations may provide whether and under what conditions an employee of a legal person may also represent other legal persons which have their principal place of business in a Contracting State and which have economic connections with the first legal person.

(4) The Implementing Regulations may lay down special provisions concerning the common representation of parties acting in common.

[1.553]
Article 134
Representation before the European Patent Office

(1) Representation of natural or legal persons in proceedings established by this Convention may only be undertaken by professional representatives whose names appear on a list maintained for this purpose by the European Patent Office.

(2) Any natural person who
- (a) is a national of a Contracting State,
- (b) has his place of business or employment in a Contracting State and
- (c) has passed the European qualifying examination

may be entered on the list of professional representatives.

(3) During a period of one year from the date on which the accession of a State to this Convention takes effect, entry on that list may also be requested by any natural person who
- (a) is a national of a Contracting State,
- (b) has his place of business or employment in the State having acceded to the Convention and
- (c) is entitled to represent natural or legal persons in patent matters before the central industrial property office of that State. Where such entitlement is not conditional upon the requirement of special professional qualifications, the person shall have regularly so acted in that State for at least five years.

(4) Entry shall be effected upon request, accompanied by certificates indicating that the conditions laid down in paragraph 2 or 3 are fulfilled.

(5) Persons whose names appear on the list of professional representatives shall be entitled to act in all proceedings established by this Convention.

(6) For the purpose of acting as a professional representative, any person whose name appears on the list of professional representatives shall be entitled to establish a place of business in any Contracting State in which proceedings established by this Convention may be conducted, having regard to the Protocol on Centralisation annexed to this Convention. The authorities of such State may remove that entitlement in individual cases only in application of legal provisions adopted for the purpose of protecting public security and law and order. Before such action is taken, the President of the European Patent Office shall be consulted.

(7) The President of the European Patent Office may grant exemption from—
- (a) the requirement of paragraphs 2(a) or 3(a) in special circumstances;
- (b) the requirement of paragraph 3(c), second sentence, if the applicant furnishes proof that he has acquired the requisite qualification in another way.

(8) Representation in proceedings established by this Convention may also be undertaken, in the same way as by a professional representative, by any legal practitioner qualified in a Contracting State and having his place of business in that State, to the extent that he is entitled in that State to act as a professional representative in patent matters. Paragraph 6 shall apply *mutatis mutandis*.

[1.554]
Article 134a
Institute of Professional Representatives before the European Patent Office

(1) The Administrative Council shall be competent to adopt and amend provisions governing—

- (a) the Institute of Professional Representatives before the European Patent Office, hereinafter referred to as the Institute;
- (b) the qualifications and training required of a person for admission to the European qualifying examination and the conduct of such examination;
- (c) the disciplinary power exercised by the Institute or the European Patent Office in respect of professional representatives;
- (d) the obligation of confidentiality on the professional representative and the privilege from disclosure in proceedings before the European Patent Office in respect of communications between a professional representative and his client or any other person.

(2) Any person entered on the list of professional representatives referred to in Article 134, paragraph 1, shall be a member of the Institute.

PART VIII
IMPACT ON NATIONAL LAW

CHAPTER I
CONVERSION INTO A NATIONAL PATENT APPLICATION

[1.555]
Article 135
Request for conversion

(1) The central industrial property office of a designated Contracting State shall, at the request of the applicant for or proprietor of a European patent, apply the procedure for the grant of a national patent in the following circumstances—

- (a) where the European patent application is deemed to be withdrawn under Article 77, paragraph 3;
- (b) in such other cases as are provided for by the national law, in which the European patent application is refused or withdrawn or deemed to be withdrawn, or the European patent is revoked under this Convention.

(2) In the case referred to in paragraph 1(a), the request for conversion shall be filed with the central industrial property office with which the European patent application has been filed. That office shall, subject to the provisions governing national security, transmit the request directly to the central industrial property offices of the Contracting States specified therein.

(3) In the cases referred to in paragraph 1(b), the request for conversion shall be submitted to the European Patent Office in accordance with the Implementing Regulations. It shall not be deemed to be filed until the conversion fee has been paid. The European Patent Office shall transmit the request to the central industrial property offices of the Contracting States specified therein.

(4) The effect of the European patent application referred to in Article 66 shall lapse if the request for conversion is not submitted in due time.

Article 136
Submission and transmission of the request
(Deleted)

[1.556]
Article 137
Formal requirements for conversion

(1) A European patent application transmitted in accordance with Article 135, paragraph 2 or 3, shall not be subjected to formal requirements of national law which are different from or additional to those provided for in this Convention.

(2) Any central industrial property office to which the European patent application is transmitted may require that the applicant shall, within a period of not less than two months—

- (a) pay the national application fee; and
- (b) file a translation of the original text of the European patent application in an official language of the State in question and, where appropriate, of the text as amended during proceedings before the European Patent Office which the applicant wishes to use as the basis for the national procedure.

CHAPTER II
REVOCATION AND PRIOR RIGHTS

[1.557]
Article 138
Revocation of European patents

(1) Subject to Article 139, a European patent may be revoked with effect for a Contracting State only on the grounds that—
- (a) the subject-matter of the European patent is not patentable under Articles 52 to 57;
- (b) the European patent does not disclose the invention in a manner sufficiently clear and complete for it to be carried out by a person skilled in the art;
- (c) the subject-matter of the European patent extends beyond the content of the application as filed or, if the patent was granted on a divisional application or on a new application filed under Article 61, beyond the content of the earlier application as filed;
- (d) the protection conferred by the European patent has been extended; or
- (e) the proprietor of the European patent is not entitled under Article 60, paragraph 1.

(2) If the grounds for revocation affect the European patent only in part, the patent shall be limited by a corresponding amendment of the claims and revoked in part.
(3) In proceedings before the competent court or authority relating to the validity of the European patent, the proprietor of the patent shall have the right to limit the patent by amending the claims. The patent as thus limited shall form the basis for the proceedings.

[1.558]
Article 139
Prior rights and rights arising on the same date

(1) In any designated Contracting State a European patent application and a European patent shall have with regard to a national patent application and a national patent the same prior right effect as a national patent application and a national patent.
(2) A national patent application and a national patent in a Contracting State shall have with regard to a European patent designating that Contracting State the same prior right effect as if the European patent were a national patent.
(3) Any Contracting State may prescribe whether and on what terms an invention disclosed in both a European patent application or patent and a national application or patent having the same date of filing or, where priority is claimed, the same date of priority, may be protected simultaneously by both applications or patents.

CHAPTER III
MISCELLANEOUS EFFECTS

[1.559]
Article 140
National utility models and utility certificates

Articles 66, 124, 135, 137 and 139 shall apply to utility models and utility certificates and to applications for utility models and utility certificates registered or deposited in the Contracting States whose laws make provision for such models or certificates.

[1.560]
Article 141
Renewal fees for European patents

(1) Renewal fees for a European patent may only be imposed for the years which follow that referred to in Article 86, paragraph 2.
(2) Any renewal fees falling due within two months of the publication in the European Patent Bulletin of the mention of the grant of the European patent shall be deemed to have been validly paid if they are paid within that period. Any additional fee provided for under national law shall not be charged.

PART IX
SPECIAL AGREEMENTS

[1.561]
Article 142
Unitary patents

(1) Any group of Contracting States, which has provided by a special agreement that a European patent granted for those States has a unitary character throughout their territories, may provide that a European patent may only be granted jointly in respect of all those States.
(2) Where any group of Contracting States has availed itself of the authorisation given in paragraph 1, the provisions of this Part shall apply.

[1.562]
Article 143
Special departments of the European Patent Office

(1) The group of Contracting States may give additional tasks to the European Patent Office.

(2) Special departments common to the Contracting States in the group may be set up within the European Patent Office in order to carry out the additional tasks. The President of the European Patent Office shall direct such special departments; Article 10, paragraphs 2 and 3, shall apply *mutatis mutandis*.

[1.563]
Article 144
Representation before special departments

The group of Contracting States may lay down special provisions to govern representation of parties before the departments referred to in Article 143, paragraph 2.

[1.564]
Article 145
Select committee of the Administrative Council

(1) The group of Contracting States may set up a select committee of the Administrative Council for the purpose of supervising the activities of the special departments set up under Article 143, paragraph 2; the European Patent Office shall place at its disposal such staff, premises and equipment as may be necessary for the performance of its duties. The President of the European Patent Office shall be responsible for the activities of the special departments to the select committee of the Administrative Council.

(2) The composition, powers and functions of the select committee shall be determined by the group of Contracting States.

[1.565]
Article 146
Cover for expenditure for carrying out special tasks

Where additional tasks have been given to the European Patent Office under Article 143, the group of Contracting States shall bear the expenses incurred by the Organisation in carrying out these tasks. Where special departments have been set up in the European Patent Office to carry out these additional tasks, the group shall bear the expenditure on staff, premises and equipment chargeable in respect of these departments. Article 39, paragraphs 3 and 4, Article 41 and Article 47 shall apply *mutatis mutandis*.

[1.566]
Article 147
Payments in respect of renewal fees for unitary patents

If the group of Contracting States has fixed a common scale of renewal fees in respect of European patents the proportion referred to in Article 39, paragraph 1, shall be calculated on the basis of the common scale; the minimum amount referred to in Article 39, paragraph 1, shall apply to the unitary patent. Article 39, paragraphs 3 and 4, shall apply *mutatis mutandis*.

[1.567]
Article 148
The European patent application as an object of property

(1) Article 74 shall apply unless the group of Contracting States has specified otherwise.

(2) The group of Contracting States may provide that a European patent application for which these Contracting States are designated may only be transferred, mortgaged or subjected to any legal means of execution in respect of all the Contracting States of the group and in accordance with the provisions of the special agreement.

[1.568]
Article 149
Joint designation

(1) The group of Contracting States may provide that these States may only be designated jointly, and that the designation of one or some only of such States shall be deemed to constitute the designation of all the States of the group.

(2) Where the European Patent Office acts as a designated Office under Article 153, paragraph 1, paragraph 1 shall apply if the applicant has indicated in the international application that he wishes to obtain a European patent for one or more of the designated States of the group. The same shall apply if the applicant designates in the international application one of the Contracting States in the group, whose national law provides that the designation of that State shall have the effect of the application being for a European patent.

[1.569]
Article 149a
Other agreements between the Contracting States

(1) Nothing in this Convention shall be construed as limiting the right of some or all of the Contracting States to conclude special agreements on any matters concerning European patent applications or European patents which under this Convention are subject to and governed by national law, such as, in particular

(a) an agreement establishing a European patent court common to the Contracting States party to it;
(b) an agreement establishing an entity common to the Contracting States party to it to deliver, at the request of national courts or quasi-judicial authorities, opinions on issues of European or harmonised national patent law;
(c) an agreement under which the Contracting States party to it dispense fully or in part with translations of European patents under Article 65;
(d) an agreement under which the Contracting States party to it provide that translations of European patents as required under Article 65 may be filed with, and published by, the European Patent Office.

(2) The Administrative Council shall be competent to decide that—

(a) the members of the Boards of Appeal or the Enlarged Board of Appeal may serve on a European patent court or a common entity and take part in proceedings before that court or entity in accordance with any such agreement;
(b) the European Patent Office shall provide a common entity with such support staff, premises and equipment as may be necessary for the performance of its duties, and the expenses incurred by that entity shall be borne fully or in part by the Organisation.

PART X
INTERNATIONAL APPLICATIONS UNDER THE PATENT CO-OPERATION TREATY—EURO-PCT APPLICATIONS

[1.570]
Article 150
Application of the Patent Co-operation Treaty

(1) The Patent Co-operation Treaty of 19 June 1970, hereinafter referred to as the PCT, shall be applied in accordance with the provisions of this Part.

(2) International applications filed under the PCT may be the subject of proceedings before the European Patent Office. In such proceedings, the provisions of the PCT and its Regulations shall be applied, supplemented by the provisions of this Convention. In case of conflict, the provisions of the PCT or its Regulations shall prevail.

[1.571]
Article 151
The European Patent Office as a receiving Office

The European Patent Office shall act as a receiving Office within the meaning of the PCT, in accordance with the Implementing Regulations. Article 75, paragraph 2, shall apply.

[1.572]
Article 152
The European Patent Office as an International Searching Authority or International Preliminary Examining Authority

The European Patent Office shall act as an International Searching Authority and International Preliminary Examining Authority within the meaning of the PCT, in accordance with an agreement between the Organisation and the International Bureau of the World Intellectual Property Organisation, for applicants who are residents or nationals of a State party to this Convention. This agreement may provide that the European Patent Office shall also act for other applicants.

[1.573]
Article 153
The European Patent Office as designated Office or elected Office

(1) The European Patent Office shall be

(a) a designated Office for any State party to this Convention in respect of which the PCT is in force, which is designated in the international application and for which the applicant wishes to obtain a European patent, and
(b) an elected Office, if the applicant has elected a State designated pursuant to letter (a).

(2) An international application for which the European Patent Office is a designated or elected Office, and which has been accorded an international date of filing, shall be equivalent to a regular European application (Euro-PCT application).

(3) The international publication of a Euro-PCT application in an official language of the European Patent Office shall take the place of the publication of the European patent application and shall be mentioned in the European Patent Bulletin.

(4) If the Euro-PCT application is published in another language, a translation into one of the official languages shall be filed with the European Patent Office, which shall publish it. Subject to Article 67, paragraph 3, the provisional protection under Article 67, paragraphs 1 and 2, shall be effective from the date of that publication.
(5) The Euro-PCT application shall be treated as a European patent application and shall be considered as comprised in the state of the art under Article 54, paragraph 3, if the conditions laid down in paragraph 3 or 4 and in the Implementing Regulations are fulfilled.
(6) The international search report drawn up in respect of a Euro-PCT application or the declaration replacing it, and their international publication, shall take the place of the European search report and the mention of its publication in the European Patent Bulletin.
(7) A supplementary European search report shall be drawn up in respect of any Euro-PCT application under paragraph 5. The Administrative Council may decide that the supplementary search report is to be dispensed with or that the search fee is to be reduced.

Article 154
The European Patent Office as an International Searching Authority
(Deleted)

Article 155
The European Patent Office as an International Preliminary Examining Authority
(Deleted)

Article 156
The European Patent Office as an elected Office
(Deleted)

Article 157
International search report
(Deleted)

Article 158
Publication of the international application and its supply to the European Patent Office
(Deleted)

PART XI
TRANSITIONAL PROVISIONS

(Deleted)

PART XII
FINAL PROVISIONS

[1.574]
Article 164
Implementing Regulations and Protocols
(1) The Implementing Regulations, the Protocol on Recognition, the Protocol on Privileges and Immunities, the Protocol on Centralisation, the Protocol on the Interpretation of Article 69 and the Protocol on Staff Complement shall be integral parts of this Convention.
(2) In case of conflict between the provisions of this Convention and those of the Implementing Regulations, the provisions of this Convention shall prevail.

[1.575]
Article 165
Signature—Ratification
(1) This Convention shall be open for signature until 5 April 1974 by the States which took part in the Inter-Governmental Conference for the setting up of a European System for the Grant of Patents or were informed of the holding of that conference and offered the option of taking part therein.
(2) This Convention shall be subject to ratification; instruments of ratification shall be deposited with the Government of the Federal Republic of Germany.

[1.576]
Article 166
Accession
(1) This Convention shall be open to accession by—
(a) the States referred to in Article 165, paragraph 1;
(b) any other European State at the invitation of the Administrative Council.

(2) Any State which has been a party to the Convention and has ceased to be so as a result of the application of Article 172, paragraph 4, may again become a party to the Convention by acceding to it.

(3) Instruments of accession shall be deposited with the Government of the Federal Republic of Germany.

Article 167
Reservations
(Deleted)

[1.577]
Article 168
Territorial field of application

(1) Any Contracting State may declare in its instrument of ratification or accession, or may inform the Government of the Federal Republic of Germany by written notification at any time thereafter, that this Convention shall be applicable to one or more of the territories for the external relations of which it is responsible. European patents granted for that Contracting State shall also have effect in the territories for which such a declaration has taken effect.

(2) If the declaration referred to in paragraph 1 is contained in the instrument of ratification or accession, it shall take effect on the same date as the ratification or accession; if the declaration is notified after the deposit of the instrument of ratification or accession, such notification shall take effect six months after the date of its receipt by the Government of the Federal Republic of Germany.

(3) Any Contracting State may at any time declare that the Convention shall cease to apply to some or to all of the territories in respect of which it has given notification pursuant to paragraph 1. Such declaration shall take effect one year after the date on which the Government of the Federal Republic of Germany received notification thereof.

[1.578]
Article 169
Entry into force

(1) This Convention shall enter into force three months after the deposit of the last instrument of ratification or accession by six States on whose territory the total number of patent applications filed in 1970 amounted to at least 180,000 for all the said States.

(2) Any ratification or accession after the entry into force of this Convention shall take effect on the first day of the third month after the deposit of the instrument of ratification or accession.

[1.579]
Article 170
Initial contribution

(1) Any State which ratifies or accedes to this Convention after its entry into force shall pay to the Organisation an initial contribution, which shall not be refunded.

(2) The initial contribution shall be 5% of an amount calculated by applying the percentage obtained for the State in question, on the date on which ratification or accession takes effect, in accordance with the scale provided for in Article 40, paragraphs 3 and 4, to the sum of the special financial contributions due from the other Contracting States in respect of the accounting periods preceding the date referred to above.

(3) In the event that special financial contributions were not required in respect of the accounting period immediately preceding the date referred to in paragraph 2, the scale of contributions referred to in that paragraph shall be the scale that would have been applicable to the State concerned in respect of the last year for which financial contributions were required.

[1.580]
Article 171
Duration of the Convention

The present Convention shall be of unlimited duration.

[1.581]
Article 172
Revision

(1) This Convention may be revised by a Conference of the Contracting States.

(2) The Conference shall be prepared and convened by the Administrative Council. The Conference shall not be validly constituted unless at least three-quarters of the Contracting States are represented at it. Adoption of the revised text shall require a majority of three-quarters of the Contracting States represented and voting at the Conference. Abstentions shall not be considered as votes.

(3) The revised text shall enter into force when it has been ratified or acceded to by the number of Contracting States specified by the Conference, and at the time specified by that Conference.

(4) Such States as have not ratified or acceded to the revised text of the Convention at the time of its entry into force shall cease to be parties to this Convention as from that time.

[1.582]
Article 173
Disputes between Contracting States

(1) Any dispute between Contracting States concerning the interpretation or application of the present Convention which is not settled by negotiation shall be submitted, at the request of one of the States concerned, to the Administrative Council, which shall endeavour to bring about agreement between the States concerned.

(2) If such agreement is not reached within six months from the date when the dispute was referred to the Administrative Council, any one of the States concerned may submit the dispute to the International Court of Justice for a binding decision.

[1.583]
Article 174
Denunciation

Any Contracting State may at any time denounce this Convention. Denunciation shall be notified to the Government of the Federal Republic of Germany. It shall take effect one year after the date of receipt of such notification.

[1.584]
Article 175
Preservation of acquired rights

(1) In the event of a State ceasing to be party to this Convention in accordance with Article 172, paragraph 4, or Article 174, rights already acquired pursuant to this Convention shall not be impaired.

(2) A European patent application which is pending when a designated State ceases to be party to the Convention shall be processed by the European Patent Office, as far as that State is concerned, as if the Convention in force thereafter were applicable to that State.

(3) Paragraph 2 shall apply to European patents in respect of which, on the date mentioned in that paragraph, an opposition is pending or the opposition period has not expired.

(4) Nothing in this Article shall affect the right of any State that has ceased to be a party to this Convention to treat any European patent in accordance with the text to which it was a party.

[1.585]
Article 176
Financial rights and obligations of former Contracting States

(1) Any State which has ceased to be a party to this Convention in accordance with Article 172, paragraph 4, or Article 174, shall have the special financial contributions which it has paid pursuant to Article 40, paragraph 2, refunded to it by the Organisation only at the time when and under the conditions whereby the Organisation refunds special financial contributions paid by other States during the same accounting period.

(2) The State referred to in paragraph 1 shall, even after ceasing to be a party to this Convention, continue to pay the proportion pursuant to Article 39 of renewal fees in respect of European patents remaining in force in that State, at the rate current on the date on which it ceased to be a party.

[1.586]
Article 177
Languages of the Convention

(1) This Convention, drawn up in a single original, in the English, French and German languages, shall be deposited in the archives of the Government of the Federal Republic of Germany, the three texts being equally authentic.

(2) The texts of this Convention drawn up in official languages of Contracting States other than those specified in paragraph 1 shall, if they have been approved by the Administrative Council, be considered as official texts. In the event of disagreement on the interpretation of the various texts, the texts referred to in paragraph 1 shall be authentic.

[1.587]
Article 178
Transmission and notifications

(1) The Government of the Federal Republic of Germany shall draw up certified true copies of this Convention and shall transmit them to the Governments of all signatory or acceding States.

(2) The Government of the Federal Republic of Germany shall notify to the Governments of the States referred to in paragraph 1—

- (a) the deposit of any instrument of ratification or accession;
- (b) any declaration or notification received pursuant to Article 168;
- (c) any denunciation received pursuant to Article 174 and the date on which such denunciation comes into force.

(3) The Government of the Federal Republic of Germany shall register this Convention with the Secretariat of the United Nations.

In witness whereof, the Plenipotentiaries authorised thereto, having presented their Full Powers, found to be in good and due form, have signed this Convention.

Done at Munich this fifth day of October one thousand nine hundred and seventy-three.

IMPLEMENTING REGULATIONS TO THE CONVENTION ON THE GRANT OF EUROPEAN PATENTS

NOTES

The original source of these Regulations is the European Patent Office (EPO) website at www.epo.org.

PART I
IMPLEMENTING REGULATIONS TO PART I OF THE CONVENTION

CHAPTER I
GENERAL PROVISIONS

[1.588]
Rule 1
Written proceedings

In written proceedings before the European Patent Office, the requirement to use the written form shall be satisfied if the content of the documents can be reproduced in a legible form on paper.

[1.589]
Rule 2[1]
Filing of and formal requirements for documents

(1) [2] In proceedings before the European Patent Office, documents may be filed by delivery by hand, by postal services or by means of electronic communication. The President of the European Patent Office shall lay down the details and conditions and, where appropriate, any special formal or technical requirements for the filing of documents. In particular, he may specify that confirmation must be supplied. If such confirmation is not supplied in due time, the European patent application shall be refused; documents filed subsequently shall be deemed not to have been received.

(2) Where the Convention provides that a document must be signed, the authenticity of the document may be confirmed by handwritten signature or other appropriate means the use of which has been permitted by the President of the European Patent Office. A document authenticated by such other means shall be deemed to meet the legal requirements of signature in the same way as a document bearing a handwritten signature which has been filed in paper form.

NOTES

1 See decisions of the President of the EPO, Special edition No. 3 OJ EPO 2007, A.3, A.5 and OJ EPO 2015, A91 and 2016, A21, as well as OJ EPO 2012, 348 (revoking in part by its Article 9 the decisions of the President of the EPO, OJ EPO 1999, 509 and 2000, 458). See decision of the President of the EPO, OJ EPO 2015, A26. See the decisions of the President of the EPO concerning the filing of documents using the EPO case management system (OJ EPO 2015, A27) or the EPO web-form filing service (OJ EPO 2014, A98). See also decision of the President of the EPO concerning the pilot project to introduce new means of electronic communication in EPO proceedings, OJ EPO 2015, A28.

2 Amended by decision of the Administrative Council CA/D 6/14 of 15.10.2014 (OJ EPO 2015, A17), entered into force on 01.04.2015. See notice from the EPO, OJ EPO 2015, A36.

[1.590]
Rule 3[3]
Language in written proceedings

(1) In written proceedings before the European Patent Office, any party may use any official language of the European Patent Office. The translation referred to in Article 14, paragraph 4, may be filed in any official language of the European Patent Office.

(2) Amendments to a European patent application or European patent shall be filed in the language of the proceedings.

(3) Documentary evidence and, in particular, publications may be filed in any language. The European Patent Office may, however, require that a translation in one of its official languages be filed, within a period to be specified. If a required translation is not filed in due time, the European Patent Office may disregard the document in question.

NOTES

3 See decision of the Enlarged Board of Appeal G 3/99 (Annex I).

[1.591]
Rule 4
Language in oral proceedings

(1) Any party to oral proceedings before the European Patent Office may use an official language of the European Patent Office other than the language of the proceedings, if such party gives notice to the European Patent Office at least one month before the date of such oral proceedings or provides for interpretation into the language of the proceedings. Any party may use an official language of a Contracting State, if he provides for interpretation into the language of the proceedings. The European Patent Office may permit derogations from these provisions.

(2) In the course of oral proceedings, employees of the European Patent Office may use an official language of the European Patent Office other than the language of the proceedings.

(3) Where evidence is taken, any party, witness or expert to be heard who is unable to express himself adequately in an official language of the European Patent Office or of a Contracting State may use another language. Where evidence is taken upon request of a party, parties, witnesses or experts expressing themselves in a language other than an official language of the European Patent Office shall be heard only if that party provides for interpretation into the language of the proceedings. The European Patent Office may, however, permit interpretation into one of its other official languages.

(4) If the parties and the European Patent Office agree, any language may be used.

(5) The European Patent Office shall, if necessary, provide at its own expense interpretation into the language of the proceedings, or, where appropriate, into its other official languages, unless such interpretation is the responsibility of one of the parties.

(6) Statements by employees of the European Patent Office, parties, witnesses or experts, made in an official language of the European Patent Office, shall be entered in the minutes in that language. Statements made in any other language shall be entered in the official language into which they are translated. Amendments to a European patent application or European patent shall be entered in the minutes in the language of the proceedings.

[1.592]
Rule 5
Certification of translations

Where the translation of a document is required, the European Patent Office may require that a certificate that the translation corresponds to the original text be filed within a period to be specified. If the certificate is not filed in due time, such document shall be deemed not to have been filed, unless otherwise provided.

[1.593]
Rule 6[4]
Filing of translations and reduction of fees

(1) A translation under Article 14, paragraph 2, shall be filed within two months of filing the European patent application.

(2) A translation under Article 14, paragraph 4, shall be filed within one month of filing the document. This shall also apply to requests under Article 105a. Where the document is a notice of opposition or appeal, or a statement of grounds of appeal, or a petition for review, the translation may be filed within the period for filing such a notice or statement or petition, if that period expires later.

(3) [5] Where a person referred to in Article 14, paragraph 4, files a European patent application or a request for examination in a language admitted in that provision, the filing fee or examination fee shall be reduced in accordance with the Rules relating to Fees.

(4) The reduction referred to in paragraph 3 shall be available for:

- (a) small and medium-sized enterprises;
- (b) natural persons; or
- (c) non-profit organisations, universities or public research organisations.

(5) For the purposes of paragraph 4(a), Commission recommendation 2003/361/EC of 6 May 2003 concerning the definition of micro, small and medium-sized enterprises as published in the Official Journal of the European Union L 124, p. 36 of 20 May 2003 shall apply.

(6) An applicant wishing to benefit from the fee reduction referred to in paragraph 3 shall declare himself to be an entity or a natural person within the meaning of paragraph 4. In case of reasonable doubt as to the veracity of such declaration, the Office may require evidence.

(7) In case of multiple applicants, each applicant shall be an entity or a natural person within the meaning of paragraph 4.

NOTES

4 Paragraph 3 amended and paragraphs 4-7 inserted by decision of the Administrative Council CA/D 19/13 of 13.12.2013 (OJ EPO 2014, A4), entered into force on 01.04.2014. See also notice from the EPO, OJ EPO 2014, A23.

5 See decision of the Enlarged Board of Appeal G 6/91 (Annex I)

[1.594]
Rule 7
Legal authenticity of the translation of the European patent application
Unless evidence is provided to the contrary, the European Patent Office shall assume, for the purpose of determining whether the subject matter of the European patent application or European patent extends beyond the content of the application as filed, that the translation filed under Article 14, paragraph 2, or Rule 40, paragraph 3, is in conformity with the original text of the application.

CHAPTER II
ORGANISATION OF THE EUROPEAN PATENT OFFICE

SECTION 1
GENERAL MATTERS

[1.595]
Rule 8
Patent classification
The European Patent Office shall use the classification referred to in Article 1 of the Strasbourg Agreement concerning the International Patent Classification of 24 March 1971, hereinafter referred to as the international classification.

[1.596]
Rule 9
Administrative structure of the European Patent Office
(1) The European Patent Office shall be divided administratively into Directorates-General, to which the departments specified in Article 15, and the services set up to deal with legal matters and the internal administration of the Office, shall be assigned.
(2) Each Directorate-General shall be directed by a Vice-President. The assignment of a Vice-President to a Directorate-General shall be decided by the Administrative Council, after the President of the European Patent Office has been consulted.

[1.597]
Rule 10
Responsibility of the Receiving Section and the Examining Division
(1) The Receiving Section shall be responsible for the examination on filing and the examination as to formal requirements of a European patent application up to the time when the Examining Division becomes responsible for the examination of the European patent application under Article 94, paragraph 1.
(2) Subject to paragraphs 3 and 4, the Examining Division shall be responsible for the examination of a European patent application under Article 94, paragraph 1, from the time when a request for examination is filed.
(3) If a request for examination is filed before the European search report has been transmitted to the applicant, the Examining Division shall, subject to paragraph 4, be responsible from the time when the European Patent Office receives the indication under Rule 70, paragraph 2.
(4) If a request for examination is filed before the European search report has been transmitted to the applicant, and if the applicant has waived the right under Rule 70, paragraph 2, the Examining Division shall be responsible from the time when the search report is transmitted to the applicant.

[1.598]
Rule 11[6]
Allocation of duties to the departments of first instance
(1) Technically qualified examiners acting as members of Search, Examining or Opposition Divisions shall be assigned to Directorates. The President of the European Patent Office shall allocate duties to these Directorates by reference to the international classification.
(2) [7] The President of the European Patent Office may allocate further duties to the Receiving Section, the Search, Examining and Opposition Divisions, and the Legal Division, in addition to the responsibilities vested in them under the Convention.
(3) [8] The President of the European Patent Office may entrust to employees who are not technically or legally qualified examiners the execution of duties falling to the Search, Examining or Opposition Divisions and involving no technical or legal difficulties.

NOTES

6 See opinion of the Enlarged Board of Appeal G 1/02 (Annex I).

7 See decision of the President of the EPO, OJ EPO 2013, 600.

8 See decisions of the President of the EPO, OJ EPO 2014, A6, OJ EPO 2015, A104 and notice from the EPO, OJ EPO 2014, A32.

SECTION 2

ORGANISATION OF THE BOARDS OF APPEAL AND THE ENLARGED BOARD OF APPEAL

[1.599]

Rule 12[9]

Presidium of the Boards of Appeal

(1) [10] The autonomous authority within the organisational unit comprising the Boards of Appeal (the "Presidium of the Boards of Appeal") shall consist of the Vice-President in charge of the Boards of Appeal, who shall act as chairman, and twelve members of the Boards of Appeal, six being Chairmen and six being other members.

(2) All members of the Presidium shall be elected by the Chairmen and members of the Boards of Appeal for two working years. If the full composition of the Presidium cannot be reached, the vacancies shall be filled by designating the most senior Chairmen and members.

(3) [11] The Presidium shall adopt the Rules of Procedure of the Boards of Appeal and the Rules of Procedure for the election and designation of its members. The Presidium shall further advise the Vice-President in charge of the Boards of Appeal with regard to matters concerning the functioning of the Boards of Appeal in general.

(4) [12] Before the beginning of each working year, the Presidium, extended to include all Chairmen, shall allocate duties to the Boards of Appeal. In the same composition, it shall decide on conflicts regarding the allocation of duties between two or more Boards of Appeal. The extended Presidium shall designate the regular and alternate members of the various Boards of Appeal. Any member of a Board of Appeal may be designated as a member of more than one Board of Appeal. These measures may, where necessary, be amended during the course of the working year in question.

(5) The Presidium may only take a decision if at least five of its members are present; these must include the Vice-President in charge of the Boards of Appeal or his deputy, and the Chairmen of two Boards of Appeal. Where the tasks mentioned in paragraph 4 are concerned, nine members must be present, including the Vice-President in charge of the Boards of Appeal or his deputy, and the Chairmen of three Boards of Appeal. Decisions shall be taken by a majority vote; in the event of parity of votes, the Chairman or his deputy shall have the casting vote. Abstentions shall not be considered as votes.

(6) The Administrative Council may allocate duties under Article 134a, paragraph 1(c), to the Boards of Appeal.

NOTES

9 See decision of the Enlarged Board of Appeal G 6/95 Annex I).

10 See the notice concerning the composition of the Presidium of the Boards of Appeal (supplementary publication 1, OJ EPO 2016, 1).

11 See the Rules of Procedure of the Boards of Appeal, last amendments approved by decision of the Administrative Council CA/D 35/07 of 25.10.2007 OJ EPO 2007, 536). See also the Decision of the Presidium of the Boards of Appeal dated 12.11.2007 concerning the transfer of functions to the Registrars of the Boards of Appeal (Supplement to OJ EPO 1/2008, 49).

12 See the business distribution schemes of the Boards of Appeal for the year 2016 (supplementary publication 1, OJ EPO 2016, 11 ff).

[1.600]

Rule 13[13]

Business distribution scheme for the Enlarged Board of Appeal and adoption of its Rules of Procedure

(1) [14] Before the beginning of each working year, the members of the Enlarged Board of Appeal appointed under Article 11, paragraph 3, shall designate the regular and alternate members of the Enlarged Board of Appeal in proceedings under Article 22, paragraph 1(a) and (b), and the regular and alternate members in proceedings under Article 22, paragraph 1(c).

(2) [15] The members of the Enlarged Board of Appeal appointed under Article 11, paragraph 3, shall adopt the Rules of Procedure of the Enlarged Board of Appeal.

(3) Decisions on matters mentioned in paragraphs 1 and 2 may only be taken if at least five members are present, including the Chairman of the Enlarged Board of Appeal or his deputy; in the event of parity of votes, the Chairman or his deputy shall have the casting vote. Abstentions shall not be considered as votes.

NOTES

13 See decision of the Enlarged Board of Appeal G 6/95 (Annex I).

14 See the business distribution scheme of the Enlarged Board of Appeal for the year 2016 (supplementary publication 1, OJ EPO 2016, 2 ff).

15 See the Rules of Procedure of the Enlarged Board of Appeal, last amendments approved by decision of the Administrative Council CA/D 3/15 of 25.03.2015 (OJ EPO 2015, A35). See also the Decision of the Enlarged Board of Appeal dated 12.11.2007 concerning the transfer of tasks to the Registry of the Enlarged Board of Appeal (Supplement to OJ EPO 1/2008, 34).

PART II
IMPLEMENTING REGULATIONS TO PART II OF THE CONVENTION

CHAPTER I
PROCEDURE WHERE THE APPLICANT IS NOT ENTITLED

[1.601]
Rule 14[16]
Stay of proceedings

(1) If a third party provides evidence that he has instituted proceedings against the applicant seeking a decision within the meaning of Article 61, paragraph 1, the proceedings for grant shall be stayed unless the third party communicates to the European Patent Office in writing his consent to the continuation of such proceedings. Such consent shall be irrevocable. However, proceedings for grant shall not be stayed before the publication of the European patent application.

(2) Where evidence is provided that a final decision within the meaning of Article 61, paragraph 1, has been taken, the European Patent Office shall inform the applicant and any other party that the proceedings for grant shall be resumed as from the date stated in the communication, unless a new European patent application under Article 61, paragraph 1(b), has been filed for all the designated Contracting States. If the decision is in favour of the third party, the proceedings may not be resumed earlier than three months after the decision has become final, unless the third party requests the resumption.

(3) Upon staying the proceedings for grant, or thereafter, the European Patent Office may set a date on which it intends to resume the proceedings for grant, regardless of the stage reached in the national proceedings instituted under paragraph 1. It shall communicate this date to the third party, the applicant and any other party. If no evidence has been provided by that date that a final decision has been taken, the European Patent Office may resume proceedings.

(4) All periods other than those for the payment of renewal fees, running at the date of the stay of proceedings, shall be interrupted by such stay. The time which has not yet elapsed shall begin to run from the date on which proceedings are resumed. However, the time still to run after such resumption shall not be less than two months.

NOTES

16 See decision of the President of the EPO, OJ EPO 2013, 600.

[1.602]
Rule 15[17]
Limitation on withdrawals

From the date on which a third party provides evidence that he has instituted national proceedings under Rule 14, paragraph 1, and up to the date on which the proceedings for grant are resumed, neither the European patent application nor the designation of any Contracting State may be withdrawn.

NOTES

17 See decision of the Enlarged Board of Appeal G 3/92 (Annex I).

[1.603]
Rule 16
Procedure under Article 61, paragraph 1

(1) A person entitled to the grant of a European patent may only avail himself of the remedies under Article 61, paragraph 1, if:

(a) he does so no later than three months after the decision recognising his entitlement has become final, and

(b) the European patent has not yet been granted.

(2) Such remedies shall only apply in respect of Contracting States designated in the European patent application in which the decision has been taken or recognised or must be recognised on the basis of the Protocol on Recognition.

[1.604]
Rule 17[18]
Filing of a new European patent applicationby the entitled person

(1) Where the person adjudged by a final decision to be entitled to the grant of the European patent files a new European patent application under Article 61, paragraph 1(b), the original application shall be deemed to be withdrawn on the date of filing the new application for the Contracting States designated therein in which the decision has been taken or recognised or must be recognised on the basis of the Protocol on Recognition.

(2) The filing fee and search fee shall be paid within one month of filing the new application. If the filing fee or search fee is not paid in due time, the application shall be deemed to be withdrawn.

(3) [19] The designation fee shall be paid within six months of the date on which the European Patent Bulletin mentions the publication of the European search report drawn up in respect of the new application. Rule 39, paragraphs 2 and 3, shall apply.

NOTES

18 See opinion of the Enlarged Board of Appeal G 4/98 (Annex I).

19 Amended by decision of the Administrative Council CA/D 4/08 of 21.10.2008 (OJ EPO 2008, 513), entered into force on 01.04.2009.

[1.605]
Rule 18[20]
Partial transfer of the right to the European patent

(1) If a final decision determines that a third party is entitled to the grant of a European patent in respect of only part of the subject-matter disclosed in the original European patent application, Article 61 and Rules 16 and 17 shall apply to such part.

(2) Where appropriate, the original European patent application shall contain, for the designated Contracting States in which the decision was taken or recognised or must be recognised on the basis of the Protocol on Recognition, claims, a description and drawings which are different from those for the other designated Contracting States.

NOTES

20 See decision of the Enlarged Board of Appeal G 3/92 (Annex I).

CHAPTER II
MENTION OF THE INVENTOR

[1.606]
Rule 19
Designation of the inventor

(1) The request for grant of a European patent shall contain the designation of the inventor. However, if the applicant is not the inventor or is not the sole inventor, the designation shall be filed in a separate document. The designation shall state the family name, given names and full address of the inventor, contain the statement referred to in Article 81 and bear the signature of the applicant or his representative.

(2) The European Patent Office shall not verify the accuracy of the designation of the inventor.

(3) If the applicant is not the inventor or is not the sole inventor, the European Patent Office shall communicate to the designated inventor the information in the document designating him and the following data:

(a) the number of the European patent application;
(b) the date of filing of the European patent application and, if priority has been claimed, the date, State and file number of the previous application;
(c) the name of the applicant;
(d) the title of the invention;
(e) the Contracting States designated.

(4) The applicant and the inventor may invoke neither the omission of the communication under paragraph 3 nor any errors contained therein.

[1.607]
Rule 20
Publication of the mention of the inventor

(1) The designated inventor shall be mentioned in the published European patent application and the European patent specification, unless he informs the European Patent Office in writing that he has waived his right to be thus mentioned.

(2) Paragraph 1 shall apply where a third party files with the European Patent Office a final decision determining that the applicant for or proprietor of a European patent is required to designate him as an inventor.

[1.608]
Rule 21[21]
Rectification of the designation of an inventor

(1) An incorrect designation of an inventor shall be rectified upon request and only with the consent of the wrongly designated person and, where such a request is filed by a third party, the consent of the applicant for or proprietor of the patent. Rule 19 shall apply mutatis mutandis.

(2) Where an incorrect designation of the inventor has been recorded in the European Patent Register or published in the European Patent Bulletin, its rectification or cancellation shall also be recorded or published therein.

NOTES

21 See decisions of the President of the EPO, OJ EPO 2013, 600; 2013, 601

CHAPTER III
REGISTRATION OF TRANSFERS, LICENCES AND OTHER RIGHTS

[1.609]
Rule 22[22]
Registration of transfers
(1) The transfer of a European patent application shall be recorded in the European Patent Register at the request of an interested party, upon production of documents providing evidence of such transfer.
(2) The request shall not be deemed to have been filed until an administrative fee has been paid. It may be rejected only if paragraph 1 has not been complied with.
(3) A transfer shall have effect vis-à-vis the European Patent Office only at the date when and to the extent that the documents referred to in paragraph 1 have been produced.

NOTES
[22] See decisions of the President of the EPO, OJ EPO 2013, 600; 2013, 601.

[1.610]
Rule 23[23]
Registration of licences and other rights
(1) Rule 22, paragraphs 1 and 2, shall apply mutatis mutandis to the registration of the grant or transfer of a licence, the establishment or transfer of a right in rem in respect of a European patent application and any legal means of execution affecting such an application.
(2) A registration under paragraph 1 shall be cancelled upon request, supported by documents providing evidence that the right has lapsed, or by the written consent of the proprietor of the right to the cancellation of the registration. Rule 22, paragraph 2, shall apply mutatis mutandis.

NOTES
[23] See decision of the President of the EPO, OJ EPO 2013, 600.

[1.611]
Rule 24[24]
Special entries for licence registrations
A licence in respect of a European patent application shall be recorded
(a) as an exclusive licence if the applicant and the licensee so request;
(b) as a sub-licence where it is granted by a licensee whose licence is recorded in the European Patent Register.

NOTES
[24] See decision of the President of the EPO, OJ EPO 2013, 600.

CHAPTER IV
CERTIFICATE OF EXHIBITION

[1.612]
Rule 25[25]
Certificate of exhibition
Within four months of filing the European patent application, the applicant shall file the certificate referred to in Article 55, paragraph 2, which:
(a) is issued at the exhibition by the authority responsible for the protection of industrial property at that exhibition;
(b) states that the invention was in fact displayed there;
(c) states the opening date of the exhibition and, where the invention was disclosed later than on that date, the date on which the invention was first disclosed; and
(d) is accompanied by an identification of the invention, duly authenticated by the above-mentioned authority.

NOTES
[25] See decisions of the Enlarged Board of Appeal G 3/98, G 2/99 (Annex I).

CHAPTER V
BIOTECHNOLOGICAL INVENTIONS

[1.613]
Rule 26[26]
General and definitions

(1) For European patent applications and patents concerning biotechnological inventions, the relevant provisions of the Convention shall be applied and interpreted in accordance with the provisions of this Chapter. Directive 98/44/EC of 6 July 1998[27] on the legal protection of biotechnological inventions shall be used as a supplementary means of interpretation.
(2) "Biotechnological inventions" are inventions which concern a product consisting of or containing biological material or a process by means of which biological material is produced, processed or used.
(3) "Biological material" means any material containing genetic information and capable of reproducing itself or being reproduced in a biological system.
(4) "Plant variety" means any plant grouping within a single botanical taxon of the lowest known rank, which grouping, irrespective of whether the conditions for the grant of a plant variety right are fully met, can be:
- (a) defined by the expression of the characteristics that results from a given genotype or combination of genotypes,
- (b) distinguished from any other plant grouping by the expression of at least one of the said characteristics, and
- (c) considered as a unit with regard to its suitability for being propagated unchanged.

(5) A process for the production of plants or animals is essentially biological if it consists entirely of natural phenomena such as crossing or selection.
(6) "Microbiological process" means any process involving or performed upon or resulting in microbiological material.

NOTES

[26] See decisions of the Enlarged Board of Appeal G 1/98, G 2/06, G 2/07, G 1/08 (Annex I). 27 See OJ EPO 1999, 101.
[27] See OJ EPO 1999, 101.

[1.614]
Rule 27
Patentable biotechnological inventions

Biotechnological inventions shall also be patentable if they concern:
- (a) biological material which is isolated from its natural environment or produced by means of a technical process even if it previously occurred in nature;
- (b) [28] plants or animals if the technical feasibility of the invention is not confined to a particular plant or animal variety;
- (c) [29] a microbiological or other technical process, or a product obtained by means of such a process other than a plant or animal variety.

NOTES

[28] See decisions of the Enlarged Board of Appeal G 2/12, G 2/13 (Annex I).
[29] See decisions of the Enlarged Board of Appeal G 2/07, G 1/08, G 2/12, G 2/13 (Annex I).

[1.615]
Rule 28
Exceptions to patentability

Under Article 53(a), European patents shall not be granted in respect of biotechnological inventions which, in particular, concern the following:
- (a) processes for cloning human beings;
- (b) processes for modifying the germ line genetic identity of human beings;
- (c) [30] uses of human embryos for industrial or commercial purposes;
- (d) processes for modifying the genetic identity of animals which are likely to cause them suffering without any substantial medical benefit to man or animal, and also animals resulting from such processes.

NOTES

[30] See decision of the Enlarged Board of Appeal G 2/06 (Annex I).

[1.616]
Rule 29
The human body and its elements

(1) The human body, at the various stages of its formation and development, and the simple discovery of one of its elements, including the sequence or partial sequence of a gene, cannot constitute patentable inventions.

(2) An element isolated from the human body or otherwise produced by means of a technical process, including the sequence or partial sequence of a gene, may constitute a patentable invention, even if the structure of that element is identical to that of a natural element.
(3) The industrial application of a sequence or a partial sequence of a gene must be disclosed in the patent application.

[1.617]
Rule 30[31]
Requirements of European patent applications relating to nucleotide and amino acid sequences
(1) If nucleotide or amino acid sequences are disclosed in the European patent application, the description shall contain a sequence listing conforming to the rules laid down by the President of the European Patent Office for the standardised representation of nucleotide and amino acid sequences.
(2) A sequence listing filed after the date of filing shall not form part of the description.
(3) Where the applicant has not filed a sequence listing complying with the requirements under paragraph 1 at the date of filing, the European Patent Office shall invite the applicant to furnish such a sequence listing and pay the late furnishing fee. If the applicant does not furnish the required sequence listing and pay the required late furnishing fee within a period of two months after such an invitation, the application shall be refused.

NOTES

31 See decision of the President of the EPO, OJ EPO 2011, 372 and the notice from the EPO, OJ EPO 2013, 542.

[1.618]
Rule 31[32] [33]
Deposit of biological material
(1) If an invention involves the use of or concerns biological material which is not available to the public and which cannot be described in the European patent application in such a manner as to enable the invention to be carried out by a person skilled in the art, the invention shall only be regarded as being disclosed as prescribed in Article 83 if:
(a) a sample of the biological material has been deposited with a recognised depositary institution on the same terms as those laid down in the Budapest Treaty on the International Recognition of the Deposit of Microorganisms for the Purposes of Patent Procedure of 28 April 1977 not later than the date of filing of the application;
(b) the application as filed gives such relevant information as is available to the applicant on the characteristics of the biological material;
(c) the depositary institution and the accession number of the deposited biological material are stated in the application, and
(d) where the biological material has been deposited by a person other than the applicant, the name and address of the depositor are stated in the application and a document is submitted to the European Patent Office providing evidence that the depositor has authorised the applicant to refer to the deposited biological material in the application and has given his unreserved and irrevocable consent to the deposited material being made available to the public in accordance with Rule 33.

(2) The information referred to in paragraph 1(c) and (d) may be submitted
(a) within sixteen months after the date of filing of the application or, if priority has been claimed, after the priority date, this period being deemed to have been observed if the information is communicated before completion of the technical preparations for publication of the European patent application;
(b) up to the date of submission of a request under Article 93, paragraph 1(b);
(c) within one month after the European Patent Office has communicated to the applicant that the right to inspect the files under Article 128, paragraph 2, exists.

The ruling period shall be the one which is the first to expire. The communication of this information shall be considered as constituting the unreserved and irrevocable consent of the applicant to the deposited biological material being made available to the public in accordance with Rule 33.

NOTES

32 See notice from the EPO concerning inventions which involve the use of or concern biological material (OJ EPO 2010, 498).

33 See decision of the Enlarged Board of Appeal G 2/93 (Annex I).

[1.619]
Rule 32[34]
Expert solution
(1) Until completion of the technical preparations for publication of the European patent application, the applicant may inform the European Patent Office that,

(a) until the publication of the mention of the grant of the European patent or, where applicable,

(b) for twenty years from the date of filing, if the application is refused or withdrawn or deemed to be withdrawn,

the availability referred to in Rule 33 shall be effected only by the issue of a sample to an expert nominated by the requester.

(2) The following may be nominated as an expert:

(a) any natural person, provided that the requester furnishes evidence, when filing the request, that the nomination has the approval of the applicant;

(b) any natural person recognised as an expert by the President of the European Patent Office.

The nomination shall be accompanied by a declaration from the expert vis-à-vis the applicant in which he enters into the undertaking given under Rule 33 until either the date on which the patent expires in all the designated States or, where the application is refused, withdrawn or deemed to be withdrawn, the date referred to in paragraph 1(b), the requester being regarded as a third party.

NOTES

34 See notice from the EPO concerning inventions which involve the use of or concern biological material (OJ EPO 2010, 498).

[1.620]
Rule 33[35]
Availability of biological material

(1) Biological material deposited in accordance with Rule 31 shall be available upon request to any person from the date of publication of the European patent application and to any person having the right to inspect the files under Article 128, paragraph 2, prior to that date. Subject to Rule 32, such availability shall be effected by the issue of a sample of the biological material to the person making the request (hereinafter referred to as "the requester").

(2) Said issue shall be made only if the requester has undertaken vis-à-vis the applicant for or proprietor of the patent not to make the biological material or any biological material derived therefrom available to any third party and to use that material for experimental purposes only, until such time as the patent application is refused or withdrawn or deemed to be withdrawn, or before the European patent has expired in all the designated States, unless the applicant for or proprietor of the patent expressly waives such an undertaking.

The undertaking to use the biological material for experimental purposes only shall not apply in so far as the requester is using that material under a compulsory licence. The term "compulsory licence" shall be construed as including ex officio licences and the right to use patented inventions in the public interest.

(3) For the purposes of paragraph 2, derived biological material shall mean any material which still exhibits those characteristics of the deposited material which are essential to carrying out the invention. The undertaking under paragraph 2 shall not impede any deposit of derived biological material necessary for the purpose of patent procedure.

(4) The request referred to in paragraph 1 shall be submitted to the European Patent Office on a form recognised by that Office. The European Patent Office shall certify on the form that a European patent application referring to the deposit of the biological material has been filed, and that the requester or the expert nominated by him under Rule 32 is entitled to the issue of a sample of that material. After grant of the European patent, the request shall also be submitted to the European Patent Office.

(5) The European Patent Office shall transmit a copy of the request, with the certification provided for in paragraph 4, to the depositary institution and to the applicant for or the proprietor of the patent.

(6) The European Patent Office shall publish in its Official Journal the list of depositary institutions and experts recognised for the purpose of Rules 31 to 34.

NOTES

35 See notice from the EPO concerning inventions which involve the use of or concern biological material (OJ EPO 2010, 498).

[1.621]
Rule 34[36]
New deposit of biological material

If biological material deposited in accordance with Rule 31 ceases to be available from the recognised depositary institution, an interruption in availability shall be deemed not to have occurred if a new deposit of that material is made with a recognised depositary institution on the same terms as those laid down in the Budapest Treaty on the International Recognition of the Deposit of Microorganisms for the Purposes of Patent Procedure of 28 April 1977, and if a copy of the receipt of the new deposit issued by the depositary institution is forwarded to the European Patent Office within four months of the date of the new deposit, stating the number of the European patent application or of the European patent.

NOTES

36 See notice from the EPO concerning inventions which involve the use of or concern biological material OJ EPO 2010, 498).

PART III
IMPLEMENTING REGULATIONS TO PART III OF THE CONVENTION

CHAPTER I
FILING OF THE EUROPEAN PATENT APPLICATION

[1.622]
Rule 35[37]
General provisions

(1) European patent applications may be filed in writing with the European Patent Office in Munich, The Hague or Berlin, or the authorities referred to in Article 75, paragraph 1(b).
(2) The authority with which the European patent application is filed shall mark the documents making up the application with the date of their receipt, and issue without delay a receipt to the applicant including at least the application number and the nature, number and date of receipt of the documents.
(3) If the European patent application is filed with an authority referred to in Article 75, paragraph 1(b), such authority shall without delay inform the European Patent Office of the receipt of the application, and, in particular, of the nature and date of receipt of the documents, the application number and any priority date claimed.
(4) Upon receipt of a European patent application forwarded by the central industrial property office of a Contracting State, the European Patent Office shall inform the applicant accordingly, indicating the date of its receipt.

NOTES

37 See decisions of the President of the EPO, Special edition No. 3, OJ EPO 2007, A.1., A.3., A.5., OJ EPO 2009, 182; and the decision of the President of the EPO, OJ EPO 2015, A26. See the decisions of the President of the EPO concerning the filing of documents using the EPO case management system (OJ EPO 2015, A27), the EPO web-form filing service (OJ EPO 2014, A98) or online filing (OJ 2015, A91 and 2016, A21).

[1.623]
Rule 36[38]
European divisional applications

(1) [39] [40] The applicant may file a divisional application relating to any pending earlier European patent application.
(2) [41] A divisional application shall be filed in the language of the proceedings for the earlier application. If the latter was not in an official language of the European Patent Office, the divisional application may be filed in the language of the earlier application; a translation into the language of the proceedings for the earlier application shall then be filed within two months of the filing of the divisional application. The divisional application shall be filed with the European Patent Office in Munich, The Hague or Berlin.
(3) The filing fee and search fee shall be paid within one month of filing the divisional application. If the filing fee or search fee is not paid in due time, the application shall be deemed to be withdrawn.
(4) [42] The designation fee shall be paid within six months of the date on which the European Patent Bulletin mentions the publication of the European search report drawn up in respect of the divisional application. Rule 39, paragraphs 2 and 3, shall apply.

NOTES

38 See decisions of the Enlarged Board of Appeal G 1/05, G 1/06, G 1/09 (Annex I).

39 Amended by decision of the Administrative Council CA/D 15/13 of 16.10.2013 (OJ EPO 2013, 501), entered into force on 01.04.2014.

40 See also notice from the EPO, OJ EPO 2014, A22 (Corr. OJ EPO 2014, A109).

41 Amended by decision of the Administrative Council CA/D 2/09 of 25.03.2009 (OJ EPO 2009, 296), entered into force on 01.04.2010.

42 Amended by decision of the Administrative Council CA/D 4/08 of 21.10.2008 (OJ EPO 2008, 513),entered into force on 01.04.2009.

[1.624]
Rulc 37
Forwarding of European patent applications

(1) The central industrial property office of Contracting State shall forward European patent applications to the European Patent Office in the shortest time compatible with its national law relating to the secrecy of inventions in the interests of the State, and shall take all appropriate steps to ensure such forwarding within:

(a) six weeks of filing, where the subject of the application is evidently not liable to secrecy under the national law; or

(b) four months of filing or, if priority has been claimed, fourteen months of the date of priority, where the application requires further examination as to its liability to secrecy.

(2) A European patent application not received by the European Patent Office within fourteen months of filing or, if priority has been claimed, of the date of priority, shall be deemed to be withdrawn. Any fees paid in respect of this application shall be refunded.

[1.625]
Rule 38[43]
Filing fee and search fee

(1) [44] The filing fee and search fee shall be paid within one month of filing the European patent application.

(2) The Rules relating to Fees may provide for an additional fee as part of the filing fee if the application comprises more than 35 pages.

(3) The additional fee referred to in paragraph 2 shall be paid within one month of filing the European patent application or one month of filing the first set of claims or one month of filing the certified copy referred to in Rule 40, paragraph 3, whichever period expires last.

(4) [45] The Rules relating to Fees may provide for an additional fee as part of the filing fee in the case of a divisional application filed in respect of any earlier application which is itself a divisional application.

NOTES

[43] Amended by decision of the Administrative Council CA/D 4/08 of 21.10.2008 (OJ EPO 2008, 513), entered into force on 01.04.2009.

[44] See notice from the EPO, OJ EPO 2014, A31.

[45] 45 Inserted by decision of the Administrative Council CA/D 15/13 of 16.10.2013 (OJ EPO 2013, 501), entered into force on 01.04.2014. See also notice from the EPO, OJ EPO 2014, A22 (Corr. OJ EPO 2014, A109).

[1.626]
Rule 39[46]
Designation fees

(1) The designation fee shall be paid within six months of the date on which the European Patent Bulletin mentions the publication of the European search report.

(2) [47] Where the designation fee is not paid in due time or the designations of all the Contracting States are withdrawn, the European patent application shall be deemed to be withdrawn.

(3) Without prcjudice to Rule 37, paragraph 2, second sentence, the designation fee shall not be refunded.

NOTES

[46] Amended by decision of the Administrative Council CA/D 4/08 of 21.10.2008 (OJ EPO 2008, 513), entered into force on 01.04.2009.

[47] See opinion of the Enlarged Board of Appeal G 4/98 (Annex I).

[1.627]
Rule 40[48]
Date of filing

(1) The date of filing of a European patent application shall be the date on which the documents filed by the applicant contain:

(a) an indication that a European patent is sought;

(b) information identifying the applicant or allowing the applicant to be contacted; and

(c) a description or reference to a previously filed application.

(2) A reference to a previously filed application under paragraph 1(c) shall state the filing date and number of that application and the Office with which it was filed. Such reference shall indicate that it replaces the description and any drawings.

(3) Where the application contains a reference under paragraph 2, a certified copy of the previously filed application shall be filed within two months of filing the application. Where the previously filed application is not in an official language of the European Patent Office, a translation thereof in one of these languages shall be filed within the same period. Rule 53, paragraph 2, shall apply mutatis mutandis.

NOTES

48 See decision/opinion of the Enlarged Board of Appeal G 2/95, G 4/98 (Annex I).

CHAPTER II
PROVISIONS GOVERNING THE APPLICATION

[1.628]
Rule 41[49]
Request for grant

(1) The request for grant of a European patent shall be filed on a form drawn up p by the European Patent Office.

(2) The request shall contain:

(a) a petition for the grant of a European patent;

(b) the title of the invention, which shall clearly and concisely state the technical designation of the invention and shall exclude all fancy names;

(c) [50] the name, address and nationality of the applicant and the State in which his residence or principal place of business is located. Names of natural persons shall be indicated by the person's family name, followed by his given names. Names of legal persons, as well as of bodies equivalent to legal persons under the law governing them, shall be indicated by their official designations. Addresses shall be indicated in accordance with applicable customary requirements for prompt postal delivery and shall comprise all the relevant administrative units, including the house number, if any. It is recommended that the fax and telephone numbers be indicated;

(d) if the applicant has appointed a representative, his name and the address of his place of business as prescribed in sub-paragraph (c);

(e) where appropriate, an indication that the application constitutes a divisional application and the number of the earlier European patent application;

(f) in cases covered by Article 61, paragraph 1(b), the number of the original European patent application;

(g) where applicable, a declaration claiming the priority of an earlier application and indicating the date on which and the country in or for which the earlier application was filed;

(h) the signature of the applicant or his representative;

(i) a list of the documents accompanying the request. This list shall also indicate the number of sheets of the description, claims, drawings and abstract filed with the request;

(j) the designation of the inventor, where the applicant is the inventor.

(3) If there is more than one applicant, the request shall preferably contain the appointment of one applicant or representative as common representative.

NOTES

49 The updated version of the form is regularly published on the EPO website.

50 See also decision of the Enlarged Board of Appeal G 3/99 (Annex I).

[1.629]
Rule 42[51]
Content of the description

(1) The description shall:

(a) specify the technical field to which the invention relates;

(b) indicate the background art which, as far as is known to the applicant, can be regarded as useful to understand the invention, draw up the European search report and examine the European patent application, and, preferably, cite the documents reflecting such art;

(c) disclose the invention, as claimed, in such terms that the technical problem, even if not expressly stated as such, and its solution can be understood, and state any advantageous effects of the invention with reference to the background art;

(d) briefly describe the figures in the drawings, if any;

(e) describe in detail at least one way of carrying out the invention claimed, using examples where appropriate and referring to the drawings, if any;

(f) indicate explicitly, when it is not obvious from the description or nature of the invention, the way in which the invention is industrially applicable.

(2) The description shall be presented in the manner and order specified in paragraph 1, unless, owing to the nature of the invention, a different presentation would afford a better understanding or be more concise.

NOTES

51 See decisions of the Enlarged Board of Appeal G 1/03, G 2/03 (Annex I).

[1.630]
Rule 43[52]
Form and content of claims

(1) The claims shall define the matter for which protection is sought in terms of the technical features of the invention. Wherever appropriate, claims shall contain:

(a) a statement indicating the designation of the subject-matter of the invention and those technical features which are necessary for the definition of the claimed subject-matter but which, in combination, form part of the prior art;

(b) a characterising portion, beginning with the expression "characterised in that" or "characterised by" and specifying the technical features for which, in combination with the features stated under sub-paragraph (a), protection is sought.

(2) Without prejudice to Article 82, a European patent application may contain more than one independent claim in the same category (product, process, apparatus or use) only if the subject-matter of the application involves one of the following:

(a) a plurality of interrelated products,

(b) different uses of a product or apparatus,

(c) alternative solutions to a particular problem, where it is inappropriate to cover these alternatives by a single claim.

(3) Any claim stating the essential features of an invention may be followed by one or more claims concerning particular embodiments of that invention.

(4) Any claim which includes all the features of any other claim (dependent claim) shall contain, if possible at the beginning, a reference to the other claim and then state the additional features. A dependent claim directly referring to another dependent claim shall also be admissible. All dependent claims referring back to a single previous claim, and all dependent claims referring back to several previous claims, shall be grouped together to the extent and in the most appropriate way possible.

(5) The number of claims shall be reasonable with regard to the nature of the invention claimed. The claims shall be numbered consecutively in Arabic numerals.

(6) Except where absolutely necessary, claims shall not rely on references to the description or drawings in specifying the technical features of the invention. In particular, they shall not contain such expressions as "as described in part . . . of the description", or "as illustrated in figure . . . of the drawings".

(7) Where the European patent application contains drawings including reference signs, the technical features specified in the claims shall preferably be followed by such reference signs relating to these features, placed in parentheses, if the intelligibility of the claim can thereby be increased. These reference signs shall not be construed as limiting the claim.

NOTES

52 See decisions of the Enlarged Board of Appeal G 2/03, G 1/04 (Annex I).

[1.631]
Rule 44
Unity of invention

(1) Where a group of inventions is claimed in a European patent application, the requirement of unity of invention under Article 82 shall be fulfilled only when there is a technical relationship among those inventions involving one or more of the same or corresponding special technical features. The expression "special technical features" shall mean those features which define a contribution which each of the claimed inventions considered as a whole makes over the prior art.

(2) The determination whether a group of inventions is so linked as to form a single general inventive concept shall be made without regard to whether the inventions are claimed in separate claims or as alternatives within a single claim.

[1.632]
Rule 45
Claims incurring fees

(1) [53] Any European patent application comprising more than fifteen claims shall, in respect of the sixteenth and each subsequent claim, incur payment of claims fees as laid down in the Rules relating to Fees.

(2) The claims fees shall be paid within one month of filing the first set of claims. If the claims fees have not been paid in due time, they may still be paid within one month of a communication concerning the failure to observe the time limit.

(3) If a claims fee is not paid in due time, the claim concerned shall be deemed to be abandoned.

NOTES

53 Amended by decision of the Administrative Council CA/D 2/08 of 06.03.2008 (OJ EPO 2008, 124),entered into force on 01.04.2008.

[1.633]
Rule 46
Form of the drawings

(1) On sheets containing drawings, the usable surface area shall not exceed 26.2 cm x 17 cm. The usable or used surface shall not be surrounded by frames. The minimum margins shall be as follows:

top	2.5	cm
left side	2.5	cm
right side	1.5	cm
bottom	1	cm

(2) Drawings shall be executed as follows:

(a) Drawings shall be executed without colourings in durable, black, sufficiently dense and dark, uniformly thick and well-defined lines and strokes.

(b) Cross-sections shall be indicated by hatching which should not impede the clear reading of the reference signs and leading lines.

(c) The scale of the drawings and their graphical execution shall be such that electronic or photographic reproduction with a linear reduction in size to two-thirds will allow all details to be distinguished without difficulty. If, exceptionally, the scale is given on a drawing, it shall be represented graphically.

(d) All numbers, letters, and reference signs appearing on the drawings shall be simple and clear. Brackets, circles or inverted commas shall not be used in association with numbers and letters.

(e) Generally, all lines in the drawings shall be drawn with the aid of drafting instruments.

(f) Elements of the same figure shall be proportional to one another, unless a difference in proportion is indispensable for the clarity of the figure.

(g) The height of the numbers and letters shall not be less than 0.32 cm. For the lettering of drawings, the Latin and, where customary, the Greek alphabets shall be used.

(h) The same sheet of drawings may contain several figures. Where figures drawn on two or more sheets are intended to form a single figure, the figures on the several sheets shall be so arranged that the whole figure can be assembled without concealing any part of the partial figures. The different figures shall be arranged without wasting space, preferably in an upright position, clearly separated from one another. Where the figures are not arranged in an upright position, they shall be presented sideways with the top of the figures at the left side of the sheet. The different figures shall be numbered consecutively in Arabic numerals, independently of the numbering of the sheets.

(i) Reference signs not mentioned in the description and claims shall not appear in the drawings, and vice versa. Reference signs to features shall be consistent throughout the application.

(j) The drawings shall not contain text matter. Where indispensable to understand the drawings, a few short keywords, such as "water", "steam", "open", "closed" or "section on AB", may be included. Any such keywords shall be placed in such a way that, if required, they can be replaced by their translations without interfering with any lines of the drawings.

(3) Flow sheets and diagrams shall be deemed to be drawings.

[1.634]
Rule 47
Form and content of the abstract

(1) The abstract shall indicate the title of the invention.

(2) The abstract shall contain a concise summary of the disclosure as contained in the description, the claims and any drawings. The summary shall indicate the technical field to which the invention pertains, and shall be drafted in a manner allowing the clear understanding of the technical problem, the gist of the solution of that problem through the invention, and the principal use or uses of the invention. The abstract shall, where applicable, contain the chemical formula which, among those contained in the application, best characterises the invention. It shall not contain statements on the alleged merits or value of the invention or on speculative applications thereof.

(3) The abstract shall preferably not contain more than one hundred and fifty words.

(4) If the European patent application contains drawings, the applicant shall indicate the figure or, exceptionally, the figures of the drawings which should be published with the abstract. The European Patent Office may decide to publish one or more other figures if it considers that they better characterise the invention. Each essential feature mentioned in the abstract and illustrated by a drawing shall be followed by a reference sign placed in parentheses.

(5) The abstract shall be drafted in such a manner as to constitute an efficient instrument for the purpose of searching in the particular technical field. In particular, it shall make it possible to assess whether consultation of the European patent application itself is necessary.

[1.635]
Rule 48
Prohibited matter

(1) The European patent application shall not contain:

(a) statements or other matter contrary to "ordre public" or morality;

(b) statements disparaging the products or processes of any third party or the merits or validity of the applications or patents of any such party. Mere comparisons with the prior art shall not be considered disparaging per se;

(c) any statement or other matter obviously irrelevant or unnecessary under the circumstances.

(2) If the application contains matter prohibited under paragraph 1(a), the European Patent Office may omit such matter from the application as published, indicating the place and number of words or drawings omitted.

(3) If the application contains statements referred to in paragraph 1(b), the European Patent Office may omit them from the application as published, indicating the place and number of words omitted. Upon request, the European Patent Office shall furnish a copy of the passages omitted.

[1.636]
Rule 49
General provisions governing the presentation of the application documents

(1) Any translation filed under Article 14, paragraph 2, or Rule 40, paragraph 3, shall be deemed to be a document making up the European patent application.

(2) The documents making up the application shall be presented so as to allow electronic and direct reproduction, in particular by scanning, photography, electrostatic processes, photo offset and microfilming, in an unlimited number of copies. All sheets shall be free from cracks, creases and folds. Only one side of the sheet shall be used.

(3) [54] The documents making up the application shall be on A4 paper (29.7 cm x 21 cm) which shall be pliable, strong, white, smooth, matt and durable. Subject to paragraph 9 and Rule 46, paragraph 2(h), each sheet shall be used with its short sides at the top and bottom (upright position).

(4) Each of the documents making up the application (request, description, claims, drawings and abstract) shall commence on a new sheet. The sheets shall be connected in such a way that they can easily be turned over, separated and joined together again.

(5) Subject to Rule 46, paragraph 1, the minimum margins shall be as follows:

top	2	cm
left side	2.5	cm
right side	2	cm
bottom	2	cm

The recommended maximum for the margins quoted above is as follows

top	4	cm
left side	4	cm
right side	3	cm
bottom	3	cm

(6) All the sheets contained in the application shall be numbered in consecutive Arabic numerals. These shall be centred at the top of the sheet, but not placed in the top margin.

(7) The lines of each sheet of the description and of the claims shall preferably be numbered in sets of five, the numbers appearing on the left side, to the right of the margin

(8) [55] The request for grant of a European patent, the description, the claims and the abstract shall be typed or printed. Only graphic symbols and characters and chemical or mathematical formulae may, if necessary, be drawn or written by hand. The typing shall be 1½ spaced. All text matter shall be in characters, the capital letters of which are not less than 0.21 cm high, and shall be in a dark, indelible colour.

(9) The request for grant of a European patent, the description, the claims and the abstract shall not contain drawings. The description, claims and abstract may contain chemical or mathematical formulae. The description and abstract may contain tables. The claims may contain tables only if their subject-matter makes the use of tables desirable. Tables and chemical or mathematical formulae may be placed sideways on the sheet if they cannot be presented satisfactorily in an upright position. Tables or chemical or mathematical formulae presented sideways shall be placed so that the tops of the tables or formulae are at the lefthand side of the sheet.

(10) [56] Values shall be expressed in units conforming to international standards, wherever appropriate in terms of the metric system using SI units. Any data not meeting this requirement shall also be expressed in units conforming to international standards. Only the technical terms, formulae, signs and symbols generally accepted in the field in question shall be used.

(11) The terminology and the signs shall be consistent throughout the European patent application.

(12) Each sheet shall be reasonably free from erasures and shall be free from alterations. Non-compliance with this rule may be authorised if the authenticity of the content is not impugned and the requirements for good reproduction are not thereby jeopardised.

NOTES

[54] Amended by decision of the Administrative Council CA/D 4/08 of 21.10.2008 (OJ EPO 2008, 513), entered into force on 01.04.2009.

[55] See notice from the EPO, OJ EPO 2013, 603.

[56] Amended by decision of the Administrative Council CA/D 4/08 of 21.10.2008 (OJ EPO 2008, 513), entered into force on 01.04.2009.

[1.637]
Rule 50[57]
Documents filed subsequently

(1) Rules 42, 43 and 46 to 49 shall apply to documents replacing documents making up the European patent application. Rule 49, paragraphs 2 to 12, shall also apply to the translation of the claims referred to in Rule 71.
(2) All documents other than those making up the application shall generally be typewritten or printed. There shall be a margin of about 2.5 cm on the left-hand side of each page.
(3) Documents filed after filing the application shall be signed, with the exception of annexed documents. If a document has not been signed, the European Patent Office shall invite the party concerned to do so within a time limit to be specified. If signed in due time, the document shall retain its original date of receipt; otherwise it shall be deemed not to have been filed.

NOTES

[57] See decision of the President of the EPO, Special edition No. 3, OJ EPO 2007, A.3; see notice from the EPO, OJ EPO 2013, 603. See decision of the Enlarged Board of Appeal G 3/99 (Annex I).

CHAPTER III
RENEWAL FEES

[1.638]
Rule 51
Payment of renewal fees

(1) [58] A renewal fee for the European patent application in respect of the coming year shall be due on the last day of the month containing the anniversary of the date of filing of the European patent application. Renewal fees may not be validly paid more than three months before they fall due.
(2) If a renewal fee is not paid in due time, the fee may still be paid within six months of the due date, provided that an additional fee is also paid within that period.
(3) Renewal fees already due in respect of an earlier application at the date on which a divisional application is filed shall also be paid for the divisional application and shall be due on its filing. These fees and any renewal fee due within four months of filing the divisional application may be paid within that period without an additional fee. Paragraph 2 shall apply.
(4) If a European patent application has been refused or deemed to be withdrawn as a result of non-observance of a time limit, and if the applicant's rights are re-established under Article 122, a renewal fee

(a) which would have fallen due under paragraph 1 in the period starting on the date on which the loss of rights occurred, up to and including the date of the notification of the decision re-establishing the rights, shall be due on that latter date.

This fee and any renewal fee due within four months from that latter date may still be paid within four months of that latter date without an additional fee. Paragraph 2 shall apply.

(b) which, on the date on which the loss of rights has occurred, was already due but the period provided for in paragraph 2 has not yet expired, may still be paid within six months from the date of the notification of the decision re-establishing the rights, provided that the additional fee pursuant to paragraph 2 is also paid within that period.

(5) If the Enlarged Board of Appeal re-opens proceedings before the Board of Appeal under Article 112a, paragraph 5, second sentence, a renewal fee

(a) which would have fallen due under paragraph 1 in the period starting on the date when the decision of the Board of Appeal subject to the petition for review was taken, up to and including the date of the notification of the decision of the Enlarged Board of Appeal re-opening proceedings before the Board of Appeal, shall be due on that latter date.

This fee and any renewal fee due within four months from that latter date may still be paid within four months of that latter date without an additional fee. Paragraph 2 shall apply.

(b) which, on the day on which the decision of the Board of Appeal was taken, was already due but the period provided for in paragraph 2 has not yet expired, may still be paid within six months from the date of the notification of the decision of the Enlarged Board of Appeal re-opening proceedings before the Board of Appeal, provided that the additional fee pursuant to paragraph 2 is also paid within that period.

(6) A renewal fee shall not be payable for a new European patent application filed under Article 61, paragraph 1(b), in respect of the year in which it was filed and any preceding year.

NOTES

[58] Amended by decision of the Administrative Council CA/D 4/08 of 21.10.2008 (OJ EPO 2008, 513), entered into force on 01.04.2009.

CHAPTER IV
PRIORITY

[1.639]
Rule 52
Declaration of priority

(1) The declaration of priority referred to in Article 88, paragraph 1, shall indicate the date of the previous filing, the State party to the Paris Convention or Member of the World Trade Organization in or for which it was made and the file number. In the case referred to in Article 87, paragraph 5, the first sentence shall apply mutatis mutandis.

(2) The declaration of priority shall preferably be made on filing the European patent application. It may still be made within sixteen months from the earliest priority date claimed.

(3) The applicant may correct the declaration of priority within sixteen months from the earliest priority date claimed, or, where the correction would cause a change in the earliest priority date claimed, within sixteen months from the corrected earliest priority date, whichever sixteen-month period expires first, provided that such a correction may be submitted until the expiry of four months from the date of filing accorded to the European patent application.

(4) However, a declaration of priority may not be made or corrected after a request under Article 93, paragraph 1(b), has been filed.

(5) The particulars of the declaration of priority shall appear in the published European patent application and the European patent specification.

[1.640]
Rule 53
Priority documents

(1) An applicant claiming priority shall file a copy of the previous application within sixteen months of the earliest priority date claimed. This copy and the date of filing of the previous application shall be certified as correct by the authority with which that application was filed.

(2) [59] The copy of the previous application shall be deemed to be duly filed if a copy of that application available to the European Patent Office is to be included in the file of the European patent application under the conditions determined by the President of the European Patent Office.

(3) [60] Where the previous application is not in an official language of the European Patent Office and the validity of the priority claim is relevant to the determination of the patentability of the invention concerned, the European Patent Office shall invite the applicant for or proprietor of the European patent to file a translation of that application into one of the official languages within a period to be specified. Alternatively, a declaration may be submitted that the European patent application is a complete translation of the previous application. Paragraph 2 shall apply mutatis mutandis. If a requested translation of a previous application is not filed in due time, the right of priority for the European patent application or for the European patent with respect to that application shall be lost. The applicant for or proprietor of the European patent shall be informed accordingly.

NOTES

[59] See decisions of the President of the EPO, Special edition No. 3 OJ EPO 2007, B.2 and OJ EPO 2012, 492.

[60] Amended by decision of the Administrative Council CA/D 7/12 of 27.06.2012 (OJ EPO 2012, 442), entered into force on 01.04.2013. See also notice from the EPO, OJ EPO 2013, 150.

[1.641]
Rule 54
Issuing priority documents

On request, the European Patent Office shall issue to the applicant a certified copy of the European patent application (priority document), under the conditions determined by the President of the European Patent Office, including the form of the priority document and the circumstances under which an administrative fee shall be paid.

PART IV
IMPLEMENTING REGULATIONS TO PART IV OF THE CONVENTION

CHAPTER I
EXAMINATION BY THE RECEIVING SECTION

[1.642]
Rule 55
Examination on filing

If the examination under Article 90, paragraph 1, reveals that the application fails to meet the requirements laid down in Rule 40, paragraph 1(a) or (c), paragraph 2 or paragraph 3, first sentence, the European Patent Office shall inform the applicant of any deficiencies and advise him that the application will not be dealt with as a European patent application unless such deficiencies are remedied within two months. If the applicant does this, he shall be informed of the date of filing accorded by the Office.

[1.643]
Rule 56
Missing parts of the description or missing drawings

(1) If the examination under Article 90, paragraph 1, reveals that parts of the description, or drawings referred to in the description or in the claims, appear to be missing, the European Patent Office shall invite the applicant to file the missing parts within two months. The applicant may not invoke the omission of such a communication.

(2) If missing parts of the description or missing drawings are filed later than the date of filing, but within two months of the date of filing or, if a communication is issued under paragraph 1, within two months of that communication, the application shall be re-dated to the date on which the missing parts of the description or missing drawings were filed. The European Patent Office shall inform the applicant accordingly.

(3) If the missing parts of the description or missing drawings are filed within the period under paragraph 2, and the application claims priority of an earlier application, the date of filing shall, provided that the missing parts of the description or the missing drawings are completely contained in the earlier application, remain the date on which the requirements laid down in Rule 40, paragraph 1, were fulfilled, where the applicant so requests and files, within the period under paragraph 2:

(a) a copy of the earlier application, unless such copy is available to the European Patent Office under Rule 53, paragraph 2;

(b) where the earlier application is not in an official language of the European Patent Office, a translation thereof in one of these languages, unless such copy is available to the European Patent Office under Rule 53, paragraph 3; and

(c) an indication as to where the missing parts of the description or the missing drawings are completely contained in the earlier application and, where applicable, in the translation thereof.

(4) If the applicant:

(a) fails to file the missing parts of the description or the missing drawings within the period under paragraph 1 or 2,

or

(b) withdraws under paragraph 6 any missing part of the description or missing drawing filed under paragraph 2,

any references referred to in paragraph 1 shall be deemed to be deleted, and any filing of the missing parts of the description or missing drawings shall be deemed not to have been made. The European Patent Office shall inform the applicant accordingly.

(5) If the applicant fails to comply with the requirements referred to in paragraph 3(a) to (c) within the period under paragraph 2, the application shall be re-dated to the date on which the missing parts of the description or missing drawings were filed. The European Patent Office shall inform the applicant accordingly.

(6) Within one month of the notification referred to in paragraph 2 or 5, last sentence, the applicant may withdraw the missing parts of the description or the missing drawings filed, in which case the re-dating shall be deemed not to have been made. The European Patent Office shall inform the applicant accordingly.

[1.644]
Rule 57
Examination as to formal requirements

If the European patent application has been accorded a date of filing, the European Patent Office shall examine, in accordance with Article 90, paragraph 3, whether:

(a) [61] a translation of the application required under Article 14, paragraph 2, under Rule 36, paragraph 2, second sentence, or under Rule 40, paragraph 3, second sentence, has been filed in due time;

(b) the request for grant of a European patent satisfies the requirements of Rule 41;

(c) the application contains one or more claims in accordance with Article 78, paragraph 1(c), or a reference to a previously filed application in accordance with Rule 40, paragraphs 1(c), 2 and 3, indicating that it replaces also the claims;
(d) the application contains an abstract in accordance with Article 78, paragraph 1(e);
(e) the filing fee and the search fee have been paid in accordance with Rule 17, paragraph 2, Rule 36, paragraph 3, or Rule 38;
(f) the designation of the inventor has been made in accordance with Rule 19, paragraph 1;
(g) where appropriate, the requirements laid down in Rules 52 and 53 concerning the claim to priority have been satisfied;
(h) where appropriate, the requirements of Article 133, paragraph 2, have been satisfied;
(i) the application meets the requirements laid down in Rule 46 and Rule 49, paragraphs 1 to 9 and 12;
(j) [62] the application meets the requirements laid down in Rule 30.

NOTES

61 Amended by decision of the Administrative Council CA/D 2/09 of 25.03.2009 (OJ EPO 2009, 296), entered into force on 01.04.2010.

62 Amended by decision of the Administrative Council CA/D 4/08 of 21.10.2008 (OJ EPO 2008, 513), entered into force on 01.04.2009.

[1.645]
Rule 58
Correction of deficiencies in the application documents

If the European patent application does not comply with the requirements of Rule 57(a) to (d), (h) and (i), the European Patent Office shall inform the applicant accordingly and invite him to correct the deficiencies noted within two months. The description, claims and drawings may be amended only to an extent sufficient to remedy such deficiencies.

[1.646]
Rule 59
Deficiencies in claiming priority

If the file number of the previous application under Rule 52, paragraph 1, or the copy of that application under Rule 53, paragraph 1, have not been filed in due time, the European Patent Office shall inform the applicant accordingly and invite him to file them within a period to be specified.

[1.647]
Rule 60
Subsequent designation of the inventor

(1) If the designation of the inventor has not been made in accordance with Rule 19, the European Patent Office shall inform the applicant that the European patent application will be refused unless the designation is made within sixteen months of the date of filing of the application or, if priority is claimed, of the date of priority, this period being deemed to have been observed if the information is communicated before completion of the technical preparations for the publication of the European patent application.

(2) Where, in a divisional application or a new application under Article 61, paragraph 1(b), the designation of the inventor has not been made in accordance with Rule 19, the European Patent Office shall invite the applicant to make the designation within a period to be specified.

CHAPTER II
EUROPEAN SEARCH REPORT

[1.648]
Rule 61[63]
Content of the European search report

(1) The European search report shall mention those documents, available to the European Patent Office at the time of drawing up the report, which may be taken into consideration in deciding whether the invention to which the European patent application relates is new and involves an inventive step.

(2) Each citation shall be referred to the claims to which it relates. Where appropriate, relevant parts of the documents cited shall be identified.

(3) The European search report shall distinguish between cited documents published before the date of priority claimed, between such date of priority and the date of filing, and on or after the date of filing.

(4) Any document which refers to an oral disclosure, a use or any other means of disclosure which took place before the date of filing of the European patent application shall be mentioned in the European search report, together with an indication of the date of publication, if any, of the document and the date of the non-written disclosure.

(5) The European search report shall be drawn up in the language of the proceedings.

(6) The European search report shall contain the classification of the subject-matter of the European patent application in accordance with the international classification.

NOTES

63 See information from the EPO concerning the Annex to the European search report (OJ EPO 1982, 448 ff; 1984, 381; 1999, 90) and OJ EPO 2015, A86: Pilot programme on search strategies.

[1.649]
Rule 62[64]
Extended European search report

(1) The European search report shall be accompanied by an opinion on whether the application and the invention to which it relates seem to meet the requirements of this Convention, unless a communication under Rule 71, paragraph 1 or 3, can be issued.

(2) The opinion under paragraph 1 shall not be published together with the search report.

NOTES

64 Inserted by decision of the Administrative Council of 09.12.2004 (OJ EPO 2005, 5), entered into force on 01.07.2005.

[1.650]
Rule 62a[65]
Applications containing a plurality of independent claims

(1) If the European Patent Office considers that the claims as filed do not comply with Rule 43, paragraph 2, it shall invite the applicant to indicate, within a period of two months, the claims complying with Rule 43, paragraph 2, on the basis of which the search is to be carried out. If the applicant fails to provide such an indication in due time, the search shall be carried out on the basis of the first claim in each category.

(2) The Examining Division shall invite the applicant to restrict the claims to the subjectmatter searched unless it finds that the objection under paragraph 1 was not justified.

NOTES

65 Inserted by decision of the Administrative Council CA/D 3/09 of 25.03.2009 (OJ EPO 2009, 299), entered into force on 01.04.2010.

[1.651]
Rule 63[66]
Incomplete search

(1) If the European Patent Office considers that the European patent application fails to such an extent to comply with this Convention that it is impossible to carry out a meaningful search regarding the state of the art on the basis of all or some of the subject-matter claimed, it shall invite the applicant to file, within a period of two months, a statement indicating the subject-matter to be searched.

(2) If the statement under paragraph 1 is not filed in due time, or if it is not sufficient to overcome the deficiency noted under paragraph 1, the European Patent Office shall either issue a reasoned declaration stating that the European patent application fails to such an extent to comply with this Convention that it is impossible to carry out a meaningful search regarding the state of the art on the basis of all or some of the subject-matter claimed or, as far as is practicable, draw up a partial search report. The reasoned declaration or the partial search report shall be considered, for the purposes of subsequent proceedings, as the European search report.

(3) When a partial search report has been drawn up, the Examining Division shall invite the applicant to restrict the claims to the subject- matter searched unless it finds that the objection under paragraph 1 was not justified.

NOTES

66 Amended by decision of the Administrative Council CA/D 3/09 of 25.03.2009 (OJ EPO 2009, 299), entered into force on 01.04.2010.

[1.652]
Rule 64[67]
European search report where the invention lacks unity

(1) [68] If the European Patent Office considers that the European patent application does not comply with the requirement of unity of invention, it shall draw up a partial search report on those parts of the application which relate to the invention, or the group of inventions within the meaning of Article 82, first mentioned in the claims. It shall inform the applicant that, for the European search report to cover the other inventions, a further search fee must be paid, in respect of each invention involved, within a period of two months. The European search report shall be drawn up for the parts of the application relating to inventions in respect of which search fees have been paid.

(2) [69] Any fee paid under paragraph 1 shall be refunded if, during the examination of the European patent application, the applicant requests a refund and the Examining Division finds that the communication under paragraph 1 was not justified.

NOTES

67 See opinion of the Enlarged Board of Appeal G 2/92 (Annex I).

68 Amended by decision of the Administrative Council CA/D 3/09 of 25.03.2009 (OJ EPO 2009, 299), entered into force on 01.04.2010.

69 See decision of the Enlarged Board of Appeal G 1/11 (Annex I).

[1.653]
Rule 65
Transmittal of the European search report
Immediately after it has been drawn up, the European search report shall be transmitted to the applicant together with copies of any cited documents.

[1.654]
Rule 66
Definitive content of the abstract
Upon drawing up the European search report, the European Patent Office shall determine the definitive content of the abstract and transmit it to the applicant together with the search report.

CHAPTER III
PUBLICATION OF THE EUROPEAN PATENT APPLICATION

[1.655]
Rule 67[70]
Technical preparations for publication
(1) The President of the European Patent Office shall determine when the technical preparations for publication of the European patent application are deemed to have been completed.
(2) The application shall not be published if it has been finally refused or withdrawn or is deemed to be withdrawn before the termination of the technical preparations for publication.

NOTES

70 See decision of the President of the EPO, Special edition No. 3, OJ EPO 2007, D.1.

[1.656]
Rule 68[71]
Form of the publication of European patent applications and European search reports
(1) The publication of the European patent application shall contain the description, the claims and any drawings as filed, and the abstract, or, if these documents making up the application were not filed in an official language of the European Patent Office, a translation in the language of the proceedings, and, in an annex, the European search report, where it is available before the termination of the technical preparations for publication. If the search report or the abstract is not published at the same time as the application, it shall be published separately.
(2) The President of the European Patent Office shall determine the form of the publication of the application and the data to be included. The same shall apply where the European search report and the abstract are published separately.
(3) The designated Contracting States shall be indicated in the published application.
(4) [72] If the claims were not filed on the date of filing of the application, this shall be indicated when the application is published. If, before the termination of the technical preparations for publication of the application, the claims have been amended under Rule 137, paragraph 2, the new or amended claims shall be included in the publication in addition to the claims as filed.

NOTES

71 See decisions of the President of the EPO, Special edition No. 3, OJ EPO 2007, D.3., D.4.

72 English version amended by decision of the Administrative Council CA/D 4/08 of 21.10.2008 (OJ EPO 2008, 513), entered into force on 01.04.2009.

[1.657]
Rule 69[73]
Information about publication
(1) The European Patent Office shall inform the applicant of the date on which the European Patent Bulletin mentions the publication of the European search report and shall draw his attention to Rule 70, paragraph 1, Article 94, paragraph 2, and Rule 70a, paragraph 1.
(2) If a date of publication is specified in the communication under paragraph 1 which is later than the actual date of publication, that later date shall be the decisive date as regards the periods referred to in Rule 70, paragraph 1, and Rule 70a, paragraph 1, unless the error is obvious.

NOTES

73 Amended by decision of the Administrative Council CA/D 3/09 of 25.03.2009 (OJ EPO 2009, 299), entered into force on 01.04.2010.

[1.658]
Rule 70
Request for examination

(1) [74] The applicant may request examination of the European patent application up to six months after the date on which the European Patent Bulletin mentions the publication of the European search report. The request may not be withdrawn.

(2) If the request for examination has been filed before the European search report has been transmitted to the applicant, the European Patent Office shall invite the applicant to indicate, within a period to be specified, whether he wishes to proceed further with the application, and shall give him the opportunity to comment on the search report and to amend, where appropriate, the description, claims and drawings.

(3) If the applicant fails to reply in due time to the invitation under paragraph 2, the application shall be deemed to be withdrawn

NOTES

74 See notice from the EPO, OJ EPO 2016, A20.

CHAPTER IV
EXAMINATION BY THE EXAMINING DIVISION

[1.659]
Rule 70a[75]
Response to the extended European search report

(1) In the opinion accompanying the European search report the European Patent Office shall give the applicant the opportunity to comment on the extended European search report and, where appropriate, invite him to correct any deficiencies noted in the opinion accompanying the European search report and to amend the description, claims and drawings within the period referred to in Rule 70, paragraph 1.

(2) In the case referred to in Rule 70, paragraph 2, or if a supplementary European search report is drawn up on a Euro-PCT application, the European Patent Office shall give the applicant the opportunity to comment on the extended European search report and, where appropriate, invite him to correct any deficiencies noted in the opinion accompanying the European search report and to amend the description, claims and drawings within the period specified for indicating whether he wishes to proceed further with the application.

(3) If the applicant neither complies with nor comments on an invitation in accordance with paragraph 1or 2, the application shall be deemed to be withdrawn

NOTES

75 Inserted by decision of the Administrative Council CA/D 3/09 of 25.03.2009 (OJ EPO 2009, 299), entered into force on 01.04.2010.

[1.660]
Rule 70b[76]
Request for a copy of search results

(1) Where the European Patent Office notes, at the time the Examining Division assumes responsibility, that a copy referred to in Rule 141, paragraph 1, has not been filed by the applicant and is not deemed to be duly filed under Rule 141, paragraph 2, it shall invite the applicant to file, within a period of two months, the copy or a statement that the results of the search referred to in Rule 141, paragraph 1, are not available to him.

(2) If the applicant fails to reply in due time to the invitation under paragraph 1, the European patent application shall be deemed to be withdrawn.

NOTES

76 Inserted by decision of the Administrative Council CA/D 18/09 of 28.10.2009 (OJ EPO 2009, 585), entered into force on 01.01.2011.

See notices from the EPO, OJ EPO 2010, 410 and 2015, A3.

[1.661]
Rule 71[77] [78] [79]
Examination procedure

(1) In any communication under Article 94, paragraph 3, the Examining Division shall, where appropriate, invite the applicant to correct any deficiencies noted and to amend the description, claims and drawings within a period to be specified.

(2) Any communication under Article 94, paragraph 3, shall contain a reasoned statement covering, where appropriate, all the grounds against the grant of the European patent.

(3) [80] Before the Examining Division decides to grant the European patent, it shall inform the applicant of the text in which it intends to grant it and of the related bibliographic data. In this communication the Examining Division shall invite the applicant to pay the fee for grant and publishing and to file a translation of the claims in the two official languages of the European Patent Office other than the language of the proceedings within four months.

(4) If the European patent application in the text intended for grant comprises more than fifteen claims, the Examining Division shall invite the applicant to pay claims fees in respect of the sixteenth and each subsequent claim within the period under paragraph 3 unless the said fees have already been paid under Rule 45 or Rule 162.

(5) If the applicant, within the period laid down in paragraph 3, pays the fees under paragraph 3 and, where applicable, paragraph 4 and files the translations under paragraph 3, he shall be deemed to have approved the text communicated to him under paragraph 3 and verified the bibliographic data.

(6) If the applicant, within the period under paragraph 3, requests reasoned amendments or corrections to the communicated text or keeps to the latest text submitted by him, the Examining Division shall issue a new communication under paragraph 3 if it gives its consent; otherwise it shall resume the examination proceedings.

(7) If the fee for grant and publishing or the claims fees are not paid in due time, or if the translations are not filed in due time, the European patent application shall be deemed to be withdrawn.

NOTES

77 See decisions of the Enlarged Board of Appeal G 10/93, G 1/02, G 1/10 (Annex I).

78 Paragraphs 3-7 amended, paragraphs 8-11 deleted and Rule 71a inserted by decision of the Administrative Council CA/D 2/10 of 26.10.2010 (OJ EPO 2010, 637), entered into force on 01.04.2012.

79 See the notice from the EPO, OJ EPO 2012, 52.

80 See notice from the EPO concerning the possibility to waive the right to a further communication under Rule 71(3) EPC, OJ EPO 2015, A52.

[1.662]
Rule 71a[81]
Conclusion of the grant procedure

(1) The decision to grant the European patent shall be issued if all fees have been paid, a translation of the claims in the two official languages of the European Patent Office other than the language of the proceedings has been filed and there is agreement as to the text to be granted. It shall state which text of the European patent application forms the basis for the decision.

(2) Until the decision to grant the European patent, the Examining Division may resume the examination proceedings at any time.

(3) If the designation fee becomes due after the communication under Rule 71, paragraph 3, the mention of the grant of the European patent shall not be published until the designation fee has been paid. The applicant shall be informed accordingly.

(4) If a renewal fee becomes due after the communication under Rule 71, paragraph 3, and before the next possible date for publication of the mention of the grant of the European patent, the mention shall not be published until the renewal fee has been paid. The applicant shall be informed accordingly.

(5) If, in response to an invitation under Rule 71, paragraph 3, the applicant has already paid the fee for grant and publishing or the claims fees, the paid amount shall be credited if a further such invitation is issued.

(6) If the European patent application is refused, withdrawn prior to notification of the decision on the grant of a European patent or, at that time, deemed to be withdrawn, the fee for grant and publishing shall be refunded.

NOTES

81 Inserted by decision of the Administrative Council CA/D 2/10 of 26.10.2010 (OJ EPO 2010, 637), entered into force on 01.04.2012. See the notice from the EPO, OJ EPO 2012, 52.

[1.663]
Rule 72
Grant of the European patent to different applicants

Where different persons are recorded in the European Patent Register as applicants in respect of different Contracting States, the European Patent Office shall grant the European patent for each Contracting State accordingly.

CHAPTER V
THE EUROPEAN PATENT SPECIFICATION

[1.664]
Rule 73[82]
Content and form of the specification

(1) The specification of the European patent shall include the description, the claims and any drawings. It shall also indicate the period for opposing the European patent.
(2) The President of the European Patent Office shall determine the form of the publication of the specification and the data to be included.
(3) The designated Contracting States shall be indicated in the specification.

NOTES

[82] See decisions of the President of the EPO, Special edition No. 3, OJ EPO 2007, D.3., D.4.

[1.665]
Rule 74[83]
Certificate for a European patent

As soon as the specification of the European patent has been published, the European Patent Office shall issue to the proprietor of the patent a certificate for a European patent. The President of the European Patent Office shall prescribe the content, form and means of communication of the certificate and determine the circumstances in which an administrative fee is payable.

NOTES

[83] See decision of the President of the EPO, OJ EPO 2013, 416 and the notice from the EPO, OJ EPO 2013, 418.

PART V
IMPLEMENTING REGULATIONS TO PART V OF THE CONVENTION

CHAPTER I
OPPOSITION PROCEDURE

[1.666]
Rule 75
Surrender or lapse of the patent

An opposition may be filed even if the European patent has been surrendered in all the designated Contracting States or has lapsed in all those States.

[1.667]
Rule 76[84]
Form and content of the opposition

(1) Notice of opposition shall be filed in a written reasoned statement.
(2) The notice of opposition shall contain:
  (a) particulars of the opponent as provided in Rule 41, paragraph 2(c);
  (b) the number of the European patent against which opposition is filed, the name of the proprietor of the patent and the title of the invention;
  (c) a statement of the extent to which the European patent is opposed and of the grounds on which the opposition is based, as well as an indication of the facts and evidence presented in support of these grounds;
  (d) if the opponent has appointed a representative, particulars as provided in Rule 41, paragraph 2(d).
(3) Part III of the Implementing Regulations shall apply mutatis mutandis to the notice of opposition.

NOTES

[84] See decisions of the Enlarged Board of Appeal G 9/91, G 10/91, G 1/95, G 7/95, G 4/97, G 3/99, G 1/04 (Annex I).

[1.668]
Rule 77[85]
Rejection of the opposition as inadmissible

(1) [86] If the Opposition Division notes that the notice of opposition does not comply with Article 99, paragraph 1, or Rule 76, paragraph 2(c), or does not sufficiently identify the patent against which opposition has been filed, it shall reject the opposition as inadmissible, unless these deficiencies have been remedied before expiry of the opposition period.
(2) If the Opposition Division notes that the notice of opposition does not comply with provisions other than those referred to in paragraph 1, it shall communicate this to the opponent and shall invite him to remedy the deficiencies noted within a period to be specified. If the deficiencies are not remedied in due time, the Opposition Division shall reject the opposition as inadmissible.

(3) The decision to reject an opposition as inadmissible shall be communicated to the proprietor of the patent, together with a copy of the notice of opposition.

NOTES

85 See decisions of the Enlarged Board of Appeal G 9/91, G 10/91, G 1/95, G 7/95, G 3/99, G 1/02 (Annex I).

86 English version amended by decision of the Administrative Council (CA/D 4/08) of 21.10.2008 (OJ EPO 2008, 513), entered into force on 01.04.2009.

[1.669]
Rule 78[87]
Procedure where the proprietor of the patent is not entitled

(1) If a third party provides evidence, during opposition proceedings or during the opposition period, that he has instituted proceedings against the proprietor of the European patent, seeking a decision within the meaning of Article 61, paragraph 1, opposition proceedings shall be stayed unless the third party communicates to the European Patent Office in writing his consent to the continuation of such proceedings. Such consent shall be irrevocable. However, proceedings shall not be stayed until the Opposition Division has deemed the opposition admissible. Rule 14, paragraphs 2 to 4, shall apply mutatis mutandis.
(2) Where a third party has, in accordance with Article 99, paragraph 4, replaced the previous proprietor for one or some of the designated Contracting States, the patent as maintained in opposition proceedings may, for these States, contain claims, a description and drawings different from those for the other designated States.

NOTES

87 See decision of the Enlarged Board of Appeal G 3/92 (Annex I).

[1.670]
Rule 79[88]
Preparation of the examination of the opposition

(1) The Opposition Division shall communicate the notice of opposition to the proprietor of the patent and shall give him the opportunity to file his observations and to amend, where appropriate, the description, claims and drawings within a period to be specified.
(2) If several notices of opposition have been filed, the Opposition Division shall communicate them to the other opponents at the same time as the communication under paragraph 1.
(3) The Opposition Division shall communicate any observations and amendments filed by the proprietor of the patent to the other parties, and shall invite them, if it considers this expedient, to reply within a period to be specified.
(4) In the case of an intervention under Article 105, the Opposition Division may dispense with the application of paragraphs 1 to 3.

NOTES

88 See opinion of the Enlarged Board of Appeal G 1/02 (Annex I).

[1.671]
Rule 80[89]
Amendment of the European patent

Without prejudice to Rule 138, the description, claims and drawings may be amended, provided that the amendments are occasioned by a ground for opposition under Article 100, even if that ground has not been invoked by the opponent.

[1.672]
Rule 81[90]
Examination of opposition

(1) [91] The Opposition Division shall examine those grounds for opposition which are invoked in the opponent's statement under Rule 76, paragraph 2(c). Grounds for opposition not invoked by the opponent may be examined by the Opposition Division of its own motion if they would prejudice the maintenance of the European patent.
(2) Communications under Article 101, paragraph 1, second sentence, and all replies thereto shall be sent to all parties. If the Opposition Division considers this expedient, it shall invite the parties to reply within a period to be specified.
(3) In any communication under Article 101, paragraph 1, second sentence, the proprietor of the European patent shall, where necessary, be given the opportunity to amend, where appropriate, the description, claims and drawings. Where necessary, the communication shall contain a reasoned statement covering the grounds against the maintenance of the European patent.

NOTES

90 See decisions of the Enlarged Board of Appeal G 9/92, G 1/99 (Annex I).

91 See the notice from the EPO concerning acceleration of opposition proceedings (OJ EPO 2008, 221).

[1.673]
Rule 82[92]
Maintenance of the European patent in amended form

(1) Before the Opposition Division decides to maintain the European patent as amended, it shall inform the parties of the text in which it intends to maintain the patent, and shall invite them to file their observations within two months if they disapprove of that text.

(2) [93] If a party disapproves of the text communicated by the Opposition Division, examination of the opposition may be continued. Otherwise, the Opposition Division shall, on expiry of the period under paragraph 1, invite the proprietor of the patent to pay the prescribed fee and to file a translation of any amended claims in the official languages of the European Patent Office other than the language of the proceedings, within a period of three months. Where, in oral proceedings, decisions under Article 106, paragraph 2, or Article 111, paragraph 2, have been based on documents not complying with Rule 49, paragraph 8, the proprietor of the patent shall be invited to file the amended text in a form compliant with Rule 49, paragraph 8, within the three-month period.

(3) If the acts required under paragraph 2 are not performed in due time, they may still be performed within two months of a communication concerning the failure to observe the time limit, provided that a surcharge is paid within this period. Otherwise, the patent shall be revoked.

(4) The decision to maintain the European patent as amended shall state which text of the patent forms the basis for the decision.

NOTES

[92] See decisions of the Enlarged Board of Appeal G 1/88, G 1/90 (Annex I).

[93] Amended by decision of the Administrative Council CA/D 9/15 of 14.10.2015 (OJ EPO 2015, A82), entered into force on 01.05.2016.

See notice from the EPO, OJ EPO 2016, A22.

[1.674]
Rule 83
Request for documents

Documents referred to by a party to opposition proceedings shall be filed together with the notice of opposition or the written submissions. If such documents are neither enclosed nor filed in due time upon invitation by the European Patent Office, it may decide not to take into account any arguments based on them.

[1.675]
Rule 84[94]
Continuation of the opposition proceedings by the European Patent Office of its own motion

(1) If the European patent has been surrendered in all the designated Contracting States or has lapsed in all those States, the opposition proceedings may be continued at the request of the opponent filed within two months of a communication from the European Patent Office informing him of the surrender or lapse.

(2) In the event of the death or legal incapacity of an opponent, the opposition proceedings may be continued by the European Patent Office of its own motion, even without the participation of the heirs or legal representatives. The same shall apply where the opposition is withdrawn.

NOTES

[94] See decisions of the Enlarged Board of Appeal G 4/88, G 7/91, G 8/91, G 8/93, G 3/99 (Annex I).

[1.676]
Rule 85
Transfer of the European patent

Rule 22 shall apply to any transfer of the European patent made during the opposition period or during opposition proceedings.

[1.677]
Rule 86[95]
Documents in opposition proceedings

Part III of the Implementing Regulations shall apply mutatis mutandis to documents filed in opposition proceedings.

NOTES

[95] See decision of the Enlarged Board of Appeal G 1/91 (Annex I).

[1.678]
Rule 87
Content and form of the new specification of the European patent

The new specification of the European patent shall include the description, claims and drawings as amended. Rule 73, paragraphs 2 and 3, and Rule 74 shall apply.

[1.679]
Rule 88
Costs

(1) The apportionment of costs shall be dealt with in the decision on the opposition. Such apportionment shall only take into consideration the expenses necessary to assure proper protection of the rights involved. The costs shall include the remuneration of the representatives of the parties.
(2) The Opposition Division shall, on request, fix the amount of costs to be paid under a final decision apportioning them. A bill of costs, with supporting evidence, shall be attached to the request. Costs may be fixed once their credibility is established.
(3) A request for a decision by the Opposition Division may be filed within one month of the communication on the fixing of costs under paragraph 2. The request shall be filed in writing and state the grounds on which it is based. It shall not be deemed to be filed until the prescribed fee has been paid.
(4) The Opposition Division shall decide on the request under paragraph 3 without oral proceedings.

[1.680]
Rule 89[96]
Intervention of the assumed infringer

(1) Notice of intervention shall be filed within three months of the date on which proceedings referred to in Article 105 are instituted.
(2) Notice of intervention shall be filed in a written reasoned statement; Rules 76 and 77 shall apply mutatis mutandis. The notice of intervention shall not be deemed to have been filed until the opposition fee has been paid.

NOTES

[96] See decisions of the Enlarged Board of Appeal G 4/91, G 1/94, G 2/04, G 3/04, G 1/05 (Annex I).

CHAPTER II
PROCEDURE FOR LIMITATION OR REVOCATION

[1.681]
Rule 90
Subject of proceedings

The subject of limitation or revocation proceedings under Article 105a shall be the European patent as granted or as amended in opposition or limitation proceedings before the European Patent Office.

[1.682]
Rule 91
Responsibility for proceedings

Decisions on requests for limitation or revocation of the European patent under Article 105a shall be taken by the Examining Division. Article 18, paragraph 2, shall apply mutatis mutandis.

[1.683]
Rule 92
Requirements of the request

(1) [97] The request for limitation or revocation of a European patent shall be filed in writing in one of the official languages of the European Patent Office. It may also be filed in an official language of a Contracting State, provided that a translation is filed in one of the official languages of the European Patent Office within the period specified in Rule 6, paragraph 2. Part III of the Implementing Regulations shall apply mutatis mutandis to documents filed in limitation or revocation proceedings.
(2) The request shall contain:
- (a) particulars of the proprietor of the European patent making the request (the requester) as provided in Rule 41, paragraph 2(c), and an indication of the Contracting States for which the requester is the proprietor of the patent;
- (b) the number of the patent whose limitation or revocation is requested, and a list of the Contracting States in which the patent has taken effect;
- (c) where appropriate, the names and addresses of the proprietors of the patent for those Contracting States in which the requester is not the proprietor of the patent, and evidence that the requester is entitled to act on their behalf in the proceedings;
- (d) where limitation of the patent is requested, the complete version of the amended claims and, as the case may be, of the amended description and drawings;
- (e) where the requester has appointed a representative, particulars as provided in Rule 41, paragraph 2(d).

[1.684]
Rule 93
Precedence of opposition proceedings

(1) The request for limitation or revocation shall be deemed not to have been filed if opposition proceedings in respect of the patent are pending at the time of filing the request.

(2) If, at the time of filing an opposition to a European patent, limitation proceedings in respect of that patent are pending, the Examining Division shall terminate the limitation proceedings and order the reimbursement of the limitation fee. The reimbursement shall also be ordered in respect of the fee referred to in Rule 95, paragraph 3, first sentence, if the requester has already paid this fee.

[1.685]
Rule 94
Rejection of the request as inadmissible

If the Examining Division finds that the request for limitation or revocation fails to comply with the requirements of Rule 92, it shall invite the requester to correct the deficiencies noted, within a period to be specified. If the deficiencies are not corrected in due time, the Examining Division shall reject the request as inadmissible.

[1.686]
Rule 95
Decision on the request

(1) If a request for revocation is admissible, the Examining Division shall revoke the patent and communicate this to the requester.

(2) If a request for limitation is admissible, the Examining Division shall examine whether the amended claims constitute a limitation vis-à-vis the claims as granted or amended in opposition or limitation proceedings and comply with Article 84 and Article 123, paragraphs 2 and 3. If the request does not comply with these requirements, the Examining Division shall give the requester one opportunity to correct any deficiencies noted, and to amend the claims and, where appropriate, the description and drawings, within a period to be specified.

(3) [98] If a request for limitation is allowable under paragraph 2, the Examining Division shall communicate this to the requester and invite him to pay the prescribed fee and to file a translation of the amended claims in the official languages of the European Patent Office other than the language of the proceedings, within a period of three months; Rule 82, paragraph 3, first sentence, shall apply mutatis mutandis. If the requester performs these acts in due time, the Examining Division shall limit the patent.

(4) If the requester does not respond in due time to the communication issued under paragraph 2, or if the request for limitation is not allowable, or if the requester fails to perform the acts required under paragraph 3 in due time, the Examining Division shall reject the request.

NOTES

[98] Amended by decision of the Administrative Council CA/D 2/10 of 26.10.2010 (OJ EPO 2010, 637), entered into force on 01.04.2012.

[1.687]
Rule 96
Content and form of the amended European patent specification

The amended European patent specification shall include the description, claims and drawings as amended. Rule 73, paragraphs 2 and 3, and Rule 74 shall apply.

PART VI
IMPLEMENTING REGULATIONS TO PART VI OF THE CONVENTION

CHAPTER I
APPEALS PROCEDURE

[1.688]
Rule 97[99]
Appeal against apportionment and fixing of costs

(1) The apportionment of costs of opposition proceedings cannot be the sole subject of an appeal.

(2) A decision fixing the amount of costs of opposition proceedings cannot be appealed unless the amount exceeds that of the fee for appeal.

NOTES

[99] See decision of the Enlarged Board of Appeal G 3/03 (Annex I).

[1.689]
Rule 98
Surrender or lapse of the patent
The decision of an Opposition Division may be appealed even if the European patent has been surrendered in all the designated Contracting States or has lapsed in all those States.

[1.690]
Rule 99[100]
Content of the notice of appeal and the statement of grounds
(1) The notice of appeal shall contain:
(a) the name and the address of the appellant as provided in Rule 41, paragraph 2(c);
(b) an indication of the decision impugned; and
(c) a request defining the subject of the appeal.
(2) In the statement of grounds of appeal the appellant shall indicate the reasons for setting aside the decision impugned, or the extent to which it is to be amended, and the facts and evidence on which the appeal is based.
(3) Part III of the Implementing Regulations shall apply mutatis mutandis to the notice of appeal, the statement of grounds and the documents filed in appeal proceedings.

NOTES
100 See decisions of the Enlarged Board of Appeal G 9/92, G 1/99, G 1/12 (Annex I).

[1.691]
Rule 100[101]
Examination of appeals
(1) [102] Unless otherwise provided, the provisions relating to proceedings before the department which has taken the decision impugned shall apply to appeal proceedings.
(2) In the examination of the appeal, the Board of Appeal shall invite the parties, as often as necessary, to file observations, within a period to be specified, on communications issued by itself or observations submitted by another party.
(3) If the applicant fails to reply in due time to an invitation under paragraph 2, the European patent application shall be deemed to be withdrawn, unless the decision impugned was taken by the Legal Division.

NOTES
101 See decisions of the Enlarged Board of Appeal G 7/91, G 8/91, G 9/91, G 10/91, G 9/92, G 8/93, G 10/93, G 6/95, G 1/99, G 3/99 (Annex I).
102 See the notice from the Vice-President DG 3 concerning acceleration of appeal proceedings (OJ EPO 2008, 220).

[1.692]
Rule 101[103]
Rejection of the appeal as inadmissible
(1) If the appeal does not comply with Articles 106 to 108, Rule 97 or Rule 99, paragraph 1(b) or (c) or paragraph 2, the Board of Appeal shall reject it as inadmissible, unless any deficiency has been remedied before the relevant period under Article 108 has expired.
(2) If the Board of Appeal notes that the appeal does not comply with Rule 99, paragraph 1(a), it shall communicate this to the appellant and shall invite him to remedy the deficiencies noted within a period to be specified. If the deficiencies are not remedied in due time, the Board of Appeal shall reject the appeal as inadmissible.

[1.693]
Rule 102[104]
Form of decision of the Board of Appeal
The decision shall be authenticated by the Chairman of the Board of Appeal and by the competent employee of the registry of the Board of Appeal, either by their signature or by any other appropriate means.[105] The decision shall contain:
(a) a statement that it was delivered by the Board of Appeal;
(b) the date when the decision was taken;
(c) the names of the Chairman and of the other members of the Board of Appeal taking part;
(d) the names of the parties and their representatives;
(e) the requests of the parties;
(f) a summary of the facts;
(g) the reasons;
(h) the order of the Board of Appeal, including, where appropriate, a decision on costs.

NOTES
104 See decision of the Enlarged Board of Appeal G 1/05 (Annex I).
105 See the notice from the Vice-President DG 3 (OJ EPO 2012, 14).

[1.694]
Rule 103[106] [107]
Reimbursement of appeal fees

(1) The appeal fee shall be reimbursed in full
- (a) in the event of interlocutory revision or where the Board of Appeal deems an appeal to be allowable, if such reimbursement is equitable by reason of a substantial procedural violation, or
- (b) if the appeal is withdrawn before the filing of the statement of grounds of appeal and before the period for filing that statement has expired.

(2) The appeal fee shall be reimbursed at 50% if the appeal is withdrawn after expiry of the period under paragraph 1(b), provided withdrawal occurs:
- (a) if a date for oral proceedings has been set, at least four weeks before that date;
- (b) if no date for oral proceedings has been set, and the Board of Appeal has issued a communication inviting the appellant to file observations, before expiry of the period set by the Board for filing observations;
- (c) in all other cases, before the decision is issued.

(3) The department whose decision is impugned shall order the reimbursement if it revises its decision and considers reimbursement equitable by reason of a substantial procedural violation. In all other cases, matters of reimbursement shall be decided by the Board of Appeal.

NOTES

[106] See decision of the Enlarged Board of Appeal G 3/03 (Annex I).

[107] Amended by decision of the Administrative Council CA/D 16/13 of 13.12.2013 (OJ EPO 2014, A3) entered into force on 01.04.2014.

CHAPTER II
PETITIONS FOR REVIEW BY THE ENLARGED BOARD OF APPEAL

[1.695]
Rule 104
Further fundamental procedural defects

A fundamental procedural defect under Article 112a, paragraph 2(d), may have occurred where the Board of Appeal,
- (a) contrary to Article 116, failed to arrange for the holding of oral proceedings requested by the petitioner, or
- (b) decided on the appeal without deciding on a request relevant to that decision.

[1.696]
Rule 105
Criminal acts

A petition for review may be based on Article 112a, paragraph 2(e), if a competent court or authority has finally established that the criminal act occurred; a conviction is not necessary.

[1.697]
Rule 106
Obligation to raise objections

A petition under Article 112a, paragraph 2(a) to (d), is only admissible where an objection in respect of the procedural defect was raised during the appeal proceedings and dismissed by the Board of Appeal, except where such objection could not be raised during the appeal proceedings.

[1.698]
Rule 107
Contents of the petition for review

(1) The petition shall contain:
- (a) the name and the address of the petitioner as provided in Rule 41, paragraph 2(c);
- (b) an indication of the decision to be reviewed.

(2) The petition shall indicate the reasons for setting aside the decision of the Board of Appeal, and the facts and evidence on which the petition is based.

(3) Part III of the Implementing Regulations shall apply mutatis mutandis to the petition for review and the documents filed in the proceedings.

[1.699]
Rule 108
Examination of the petition

(1) If the petition does not comply with Article 112a, paragraphs 1, 2 or 4, Rule 106 or Rule 107, paragraph 1(b) or 2, the Enlarged Board of Appeal shall reject it as inadmissible, unless any defect has been remedied before the relevant period under Article 112a, paragraph 4, expires.

(2) If the Enlarged Board of Appeal notes that the petition does not comply with Rule 107, paragraph 1(a), it shall communicate this to the petitioner and shall invite him to remedy the deficiencies noted within a period to be specified. If the deficiencies are not remedied in due time, the Enlarged Board of Appeal shall reject the petition as inadmissible.
(3) If the petition is allowable, the Enlarged Board of Appeal shall set aside the decision of the Board of Appeal and order the re-opening of the proceedings before the Board of Appeal responsible under Rule 12, paragraph 4. The Enlarged Board of Appeal may order that members of the Board of Appeal who participated in taking the decision set aside shall be replaced.

[1.700]
Rule 109
Procedure in dealing with petitions for review
(1) In proceedings under Article 112a, the provisions relating to proceedings before the Boards of Appeal shall apply, unless otherwise provided. Rule 115, paragraph 1, second sentence, Rule 118, paragraph 2, first sentence, and Rule 132, paragraph 2, shall not apply. The Enlarged Board of Appeal may specify a period deviating from Rule 4, paragraph 1, first sentence.
(2) The Enlarged Board of Appeal
(a) consisting of two legally qualified members and one technically qualified member shall examine all petitions for review and shall reject those which are clearly inadmissible or unallowable; such decision shall require unanimity;
(b) consisting of four legally qualified members and one technically qualified member shall decide on any petition not rejected under sub-paragraph (a).
(3) The Enlarged Board of Appeal composed according to paragraph 2(a) shall decide without the involvement of other parties and on the basis of the petition.

[1.701]
Rule 110
Reimbursement of the fee for petitions for review
The Enlarged Board of Appeal shall order the reimbursement of the fee for a petition for review if the proceedings before the Boards of Appeal are reopened.

PART VII
IMPLEMENTING REGULATIONS TO PART VII OF THE CONVENTION

CHAPTER I
DECISIONS AND COMMUNICATIONS OF THE EUROPEAN PATENT OFFICE

[1.702]
Rule 111[108]
Form of decisions
(1) Where oral proceedings are held before the European Patent Office, the decision may be given orally. The decision shall subsequently be put in writing and notified to the parties.
(2) Decisions of the European Patent Office which are open to appeal shall be reasoned and shall be accompanied by a communication pointing out the possibility of appeal and drawing the attention of the parties to Articles 106 to 108, the text of which shall be attached. The parties may not invoke the omission of the communication.

NOTES
108 See decision of the Enlarged Board of Appeal G 12/91 (Annex I).

[1.703]
Rule 112[109]
Noting of loss of rights
(1) If the European Patent Office notes that a loss of rights has occurred, without any decision concerning the refusal of the European patent application or the grant, revocation or maintenance of the European patent, or the taking of evidence, it shall communicate this to the party concerned.
(2) If the party concerned considers that the finding of the European Patent Office is inaccurate, it may, within two months of the communication under paragraph 1, apply for a decision on the matter. The European Patent Office shall take such decision only if it does not share the opinion of the party requesting it; otherwise, it shall inform that party.

NOTES
109 See decisions of the Enlarged Board of Appeal G 1/90, G 2/97, G 1/02 (Annex I).

[1.704]
Rule 113
Signature, name, seal
(1) Any decisions, summonses, notices and communications from the European Patent Office shall be signed by, and state the name of, the employee responsible.

(2) Where a document referred to in paragraph 1 is produced by the employee responsible using a computer, a seal may replace the signature. Where the document is produced automatically by a computer, the employee's name may also be dispensed with. The same shall apply to pre-printed notices and communications.

CHAPTER II
OBSERVATIONS BY THIRD PARTIES

[1.705]
Rule 114[110]
Observations by third parties

(1) Any observations by a third party shall be filed in writing in an official language of the European Patent Office and state the grounds on which they are based. Rule 3, paragraph 3, shall apply.
(2) Any such observations shall be communicated to the applicant for or proprietor of the patent, who may comment on them.

NOTES

110 See the decision of the President of the EPO and the notice from the EPO (OJ EPO 2011, 418, 420).

CHAPTER III
ORAL PROCEEDINGS AND TAKING OF EVIDENCE

[1.706]
Rule 115[111]
Summons to oral proceedings

(1) The parties shall be summoned to oral proceedings under Article 116, drawing their attention to paragraph 2 of this Rule. At least two months' notice of the summons shall be given, unless the parties agree to a shorter period.
(2) If a party duly summoned to oral proceedings before the European Patent Office does not appear as summoned, the proceedings may continue without that party.

NOTES

111 See decision/opinion of the Enlarged Board of Appeal G 6/95, G 4/92 (Annex I).

[1.707]
Rule 116[112]
Preparation of oral proceedings

(1) When issuing the summons, the European Patent Office shall draw attention to the points which in its opinion need to be discussed for the purposes of the decision to be taken. At the same time a final date for making written submissions in preparation for the oral proceedings shall be fixed. Rule 132 shall not apply. New facts and evidence presented after that date need not be considered, unless admitted on the grounds that the subject of the proceedings has changed.
(2) If the applicant or patent proprietor has been notified of the grounds prejudicing the grant or maintenance of the patent, he may be invited to submit, by the date specified in paragraph 1, second sentence, documents which meet the requirements of the Convention. Paragraph 1, third and fourth sentences, shall apply mutatis mutandis.

NOTES

112 See decision of the Enlarged Board of Appeal G 6/95 (Annex I).

[1.708]
Rule 117
Decision on taking of evidence

Where the European Patent Office considers it necessary to hear a party, witness or expert, or to carry out an inspection, it shall take a decision to this end, setting out the investigation which it intends to carry out, relevant facts to be proved and the date, time and place of the investigation. If the hearing of a witness or expert is requested by a party, the decision shall specify the period within which the requester must make known the name and address of any witness or expert concerned.

[1.709]
Rule 118
Summons to give evidence before the European Patent Office

(1) A summons to give evidence before the European Patent Office shall be issued to the parties, witnesses or experts concerned.
(2) At least two months' notice of a summons issued to a party, witness or expert to testify shall be given, unless they agree to a shorter period. The summons shall contain:

(a) an extract from the decision under Rule 117, indicating the date, time and place of the investigation ordered and stating the facts in respect of which parties, witnesses or experts are to be heard;
(b) the names of the parties and particulars of the rights which the witnesses or experts may invoke under Rule 122, paragraphs 2 to 4;
(c) an indication that the party, witness or expert may request to be heard by a competent court of his country of residence under Rule 120, and an invitation to inform the European Patent Office, within a period to be specified, whether he is prepared to appear before it.

[1.710]
Rule 119
Examination of evidence before the European Patent Office
(1) The Examining Division, Opposition Division or Board of Appeal may commission one of its members to examine the evidence adduced.
(2) Before a party, witness or expert may be heard, he shall be informed that the European Patent Office may request the competent court in the country of residence of the person concerned to re-examine his testimony under oath or in an equally binding form.
(3) The parties may attend an investigation and may put relevant questions to the testifying party, witness or expert.

[1.711]
Rule 120
Hearing by a competent national court
(1) A party, witness or expert who is summoned before the European Patent Office may request the latter to allow him to be heard by a competent court in his country of residence. If this is requested, or if no reply is received within the period specified in the summons, the European Patent Office may, in accordance with Article 131, paragraph 2, request the competent court to hear the person concerned.
(2) If a party, witness or expert has been heard by the European Patent Office, the latter may, if it considers it advisable for the testimony to be given under oath or in an equally binding form, issue a request under Article 131, paragraph 2, to the competent court in the country of residence of the person concerned to re-examine his testimony under such conditions.
(3) When the European Patent Office requests a competent court to take evidence, it may request the court to take the evidence under oath or in an equally binding form and to permit a member of the department concerned to attend the hearing and question the party, witness or expert, either through the intermediary of the court or directly.

[1.712]
Rule 121
Commissioning of experts
(1) The European Patent Office shall decide in what form the opinion of an expert whom it appoints shall be submitted.
(2) The terms of reference of the expert shall include:
(a) a precise description of his task;
(b) the period specified for the submission of his opinion;
(c) the names of the parties to the proceedings;
(d) particulars of the rights which he may invoke under Rule 122, paragraphs 2 to 4.
(3) A copy of any written opinion shall be submitted to the parties.
(4) The parties may object to an expert. The department of the European Patent Office concerned shall decide on the objection.

[1.713]
Rule 122
Costs of taking of evidence
(1) The taking of evidence by the European Patent Office may be made conditional upon deposit with it, by the party requesting the evidence to be taken, of an amount to be fixed by reference to an estimate of the costs.
(2) Witnesses or experts who are summoned by and appear before the European Patent Office shall be entitled to appropriate reimbursement of expenses for travel and subsistence. An advance for these expenses may be granted to them. This shall also apply to persons who appear before the European Patent Office without being summoned by it and are heard as witnesses or experts.
(3) Witnesses entitled to reimbursement under paragraph 2 shall also be entitled to appropriate compensation for loss of earnings, and experts to fees for their work. These payments shall be made to the witnesses and experts after they have fulfilled their duties or tasks.
(4) [113] The Administrative Council shall lay down the details implementing paragraphs 2 and 3. Any amounts due under these provisions shall be paid by the European Patent Office.

NOTES

113 See the Regulation of the Administrative Council of 21.10.1977 on compensation and fees payable to witnesses and experts (OJ EPO 1983, 102).

[1.714]
Rule 123
Conservation of evidence

(1) On request, the European Patent Office may, without delay, take measures to conserve evidence of facts liable to affect a decision which it may be called upon to take with regard to a European patent application or a European patent, where there is reason to fear that it might subsequently become more difficult or even impossible to take evidence. The date on which the measures are to be taken shall be communicated to the applicant for or proprietor of the patent in sufficient time to allow him to attend. He may ask relevant questions.

(2) The request shall contain:

(a) particulars of the requester as provided in Rule 41, paragraph 2(c);
(b) sufficient identification of the European patent application or European patent in question;
(c) an indication of the facts in respect of which evidence is to be taken;
(d) particulars of the means of giving or obtaining evidence;
(e) a statement establishing a prima facie case for fearing that it might subsequently become more difficult or impossible to take evidence.

(3) The request shall not be deemed to have been filed until the prescribed fee has been paid.

(4) The decision on the request and any resulting taking of evidence shall be incumbent upon the department of the European Patent Office which would have to take the decision liable to be affected by the facts to be established. The provisions with regard to the taking of evidence in proceedings before the European Patent Office shall apply.

[1.715]
Rule 124
Minutes of oral proceedings and of taking of evidence

(1) Minutes of oral proceedings and of the taking of evidence shall be drawn up, containing the essentials of the oral proceedings or of the taking of evidence, the relevant statements made by the parties, the testimony of the parties, witnesses or experts and the result of any inspection.

(2) The minutes of the testimony of a witness, expert or party shall be read out, submitted to him, so that he may examine them or, where they are recorded by technical means, played back to him, unless he waives this right. It shall be noted in the minutes that this formality has been carried out and that the person who gave the testimony approved the minutes. If his approval is not given, his objections shall be noted. It is not necessary to play back the minutes or to obtain approval of them if the testimony has been recorded verbatim and directly using technical means.

(3) [114] The minutes shall be authenticated by the employee responsible for drawing them up and by the employee who conducted the oral proceedings or taking of evidence, either by their signature or by any other appropriate means.

(4) The parties shall be provided with a copy of the minutes.

CHAPTER IV
NOTIFICATIONS

[1.716]
Rule 125[115]
General provisions

(1) The European Patent Office shall, as a matter of course, notify those concerned of decisions and summonses, and of any notice or other communication from which a time limit is reckoned, or of which those concerned must be notified under the Convention, or of which notification has been ordered by the President of the European Patent Office. Any notification to be made shall take the form of the original document, a copy thereof certified by or bearing the seal of the European Patent Office, a computer print-out bearing such seal or an electronic document containing such seal or otherwise certified. Copies of documents emanating from the parties themselves shall not require such certification.

(2) Notification shall be made:

(a) by postal services in accordance with Rule 126;
(b) by means of electronic communication in accordance with Rule 127;
(c) by delivery on the premises of the European Patent Office in accordance with Rule 128; or
(d) by public notice in accordance with Rule 129.

(3) Notification through the central industrial property office of a Contracting State shall be made in accordance with the law applicable to that office in national proceedings.

(4) Where a document has reached the addressee, if the European Patent Office is unable to prove that it has been duly notified, or if provisions relating to its notification have not been observed, the document shall be deemed to have been notified on the date established by the European Patent Office as the date of receipt.

[1.717]
Rule 126[116]
Notification by postal services
(1) [117] Decisions incurring a period for appeal or a petition for review, summonses and other such documents as determined by the President of the European Patent Office shall be notified by registered letter with advice of delivery or equivalent. All other notifications by postal services shall be by registered letter.[118]
(2) Where notification is effected in accordance with paragraph 1, the letter shall be deemed to be delivered to the addressee on the tenth day following its handover to the postal service provider, unless it has failed to reach the addressee or has reached him at a later date; in the event of any dispute, it shall be incumbent on the European Patent Office to establish that the letter has reached its destination or to establish the date on which the letter was delivered to the addressee, as the case may be.
(3) Notification in accordance with paragraph 1 shall be deemed to have been effected even if acceptance of the letter has been refused.
(4) To the extent that notification by postal services is not covered by paragraphs 1 to 3, the law of the State in which the notification is made shall apply.

NOTES
116 Amended by decision of the Administrative Council CA/D 6/14 of 15.10.2014 (OJ EPO 2015, A17), entered into force on 01.04.2015.
See notice from the EPO, OJ EPO 2015, A36.
117 See decision of the Enlarged Board of Appeal G 1/14 (Annex I).
118 See also the notice of the EPO concerning the use of an address for correspondence, OJ EPO 2014, A99.

[1.718]
Rule 127[119]
Notification by means of electronic communication
(1) Notification may be effected by means of electronic communication as determined by the President of the European Patent Office and under the conditions laid down by him.
(2) Where notification is effected by means of electronic communication, the electronic document shall be deemed to be delivered to the addressee on the tenth day following its transmission, unless it has failed to reach its destination or has reached its destination at a later date; in the event of any dispute, it shall be incumbent on the European Patent Office to establish that the electronic document has reached its destination or to establish the date on which it reached its destination, as the case may be.

NOTES
119 Amended by decision of the Administrative Council CA/D 6/14 of 15.10.2014 (OJ EPO 2015, A17), entered into force on 01.04.2015.
See notice from the EPO, OJ EPO 2015, A36.
See the decision of the President of the EPO concerning the pilot project to introduce new means of electronic communication in EPO proceedings, OJ EPO 2015, A28.

[1.719]
Rule 128
Notification by delivery by hand
Notification may be effected on the premises of the European Patent Office by delivery by hand of the document to the addressee, who shall on delivery acknowledge its receipt. Notification shall be deemed to have been effected even if the addressee refuses to accept the document or to acknowledge receipt thereof.

[1.720]
Rule 129
Public notification
(1) [120] If the address of the addressee cannot be established, or if notification in accordance with Rule 126, paragraph 1, has proved to be impossible even after a second attempt, notification shall be effected by public notice.
(2) [121] The President of the European Patent Office shall determine how the public notice is to be given and the beginning of the period of one month on expiry of which the document shall be deemed to have been notified.

NOTES
120 German version of paragraph 1, amended by decision of the Administrative Council CA/D 6/14 of 15.10.2014 (OJ EPO 2015, A17), entered into force on 01.04.2015.
121 See decision of the President of the EPO, Special edition No. 3, OJ EPO 2007, K.1.

[1.721]
Rule 130
Notification to representatives

(1) If a representative has been appointed, notifications shall be addressed to him.

(2) If several representatives have been appointed for a single party, notification to any one of them shall be sufficient.

(3) If several parties have a common representative, notification to the common representative shall be sufficient.

CHAPTER V
TIME LIMITS

[1.722]
Rule 131
Calculation of periods

(1) Periods shall be laid down in terms of full years, months, weeks or days.

(2) Computation shall start on the day following the day on which the relevant event occurred, the event being either a procedural step or the expiry of another period. Where the procedural step is a notification, the relevant event shall be the receipt of the document notified, unless otherwise provided.

(3) When a period is expressed as one year or a certain number of years, it shall expire in the relevant subsequent year in the month having the same name and on the day having the same number as the month and the day on which the said event occurred; if the relevant subsequent month has no day with the same number, the period shall expire on the last day of that month.

(4) When a period is expressed as one month or a certain number of months, it shall expire in the relevant subsequent month on the day which has the same number as the day on which the said event occurred; if the relevant subsequent month has no day with the same number, the period shall expire on the last day of that month.

(5) When a period is expressed as one week or a certain number of weeks, it shall expire in the relevant subsequent week on the day having the same name as the day on which the said event occurred.

[1.723]
Rule 132
Periods specified by the European Patent Office

(1) Where the Convention or these Implementing Regulations refer to "a period to be specified", this period shall be specified by the European Patent Office.

(2) Unless otherwise provided, a period specified by the European Patent Office shall be neither less than two months nor more than four months; in certain circumstances it may be up to six months. In special cases, the period may be extended upon request, presented before the expiry of such period.

[1.724]
Rule 133[122]
Late receipt of documents

(1) [123] A document received late at the European Patent Office shall be deemed to have been received in due time if it was delivered to a recognised postal service provider in due time before expiry of the period in accordance with the conditions laid down by the President of the European Patent Office, unless the document was received later than three months after expiry of the period.

(2) Paragraph 1 shall apply mutatis mutandis to any period where transactions are carried out with the competent authority in accordance with Article 75, paragraphs 1(b) or 2(b).

NOTES

[122] See decision of the President of the EPO, OJ EPO 2015, A29.

[123] Amended by decision of the Administrative Council CA/D 6/14 of 15.10.2014 (OJ EPO 2015, A17), entered into force on 01.04.2015.

[1.725]
Rule 134[124]
Extension of periods

(1) [125] If a period expires on a day on which one of the filing offices of the European Patent Office under Rule 35, paragraph 1, is not open for receipt of documents or on which, for reasons other than those referred to in paragraph 2, mail is not delivered there, the period shall extend to the first day thereafter on which all the filing offices are open for receipt of documents and on which mail is delivered. The first sentence shall apply mutatis mutandis if documents filed by one of the means of electronic communication permitted by the President of the European Patent Office under Rule 2, paragraph 1, cannot be received.

(2) If a period expires on a day on which there is a general dislocation in the delivery or transmission of mail in a Contracting State, the period shall extend to the first day following the end of the interval of dislocation for parties which are resident in the State concerned or have appointed representatives with a place of business in that State. Where the State concerned is the State in which the European Patent Office is located, this provision shall apply to all parties and their representatives. This paragraph shall apply mutatis mutandis to the period referred to in Rule 37, paragraph 2.
(3) Paragraphs 1 and 2 shall apply mutatis mutandis where acts are performed with the competent authority in accordance with Article 75, paragraphs 1(b) or 2(b).
(4) The date of commencement and the end of any dislocation under paragraph 2 shall be published by the European Patent Office.
(5) Without prejudice to paragraphs 1 to 4, a party concerned may produce evidence that on any of the ten days preceding the day of expiry of a period the delivery or transmission of mail was dislocated due to an exceptional occurrence such as a natural disaster, war, civil disorder, a general breakdown in any of the means of electronic communication permitted by the President of the European Patent Office under Rule 2, paragraph 1, or other like reasons affecting the locality where the party or his representative resides or has his place of business. If the evidence produced satisfies the European Patent Office, a document received late shall be deemed to have been received in due time, provided that the mailing or the transmission was effected at the latest on the fifth day after the end of the dislocation.

NOTES

[124] Paragraphs 1 and 5 amended by decision of the Administrative Council CA/D 6/14 of 15.10.2014 (OJ EPO 2015, A17), entered into force on 01.04.2015.

See notice from the EPO, OJ EPO 2015, A36.

[125] See the list of days in 2016 on which EPO filing offices and national patent authorities of the EPC contracting states are closed (OJ EPO 2016, A6).

[1.726]
Rule 135
Further processing

(1) Further processing under Article 121, paragraph 1, shall be requested by payment of the prescribed fee within two months of the communication concerning either the failure to observe a time limit or a loss of rights. The omitted act shall be completed within the period for making the request.
(2) [126] Further processing shall be ruled out in respect of the periods referred to in Article 121, paragraph 4, and of the periods under Rule 6, paragraph 1, Rule 16, paragraph 1(a), Rule 31, paragraph 2, Rule 36, paragraph 2, Rule 40, paragraph 3, Rule 51, paragraphs 2 to 5, Rule 52, paragraphs 2 and 3, Rules 55, 56, 58, 59, 62a, 63, 64, Rule 112, paragraph 2, and Rule 164, paragraphs 1 and 2.
(3) The department competent to decide on the omitted act shall decide on the request for further processing.

NOTES

[126] Amended by decision of the Administrative Council CA/D 17/13 of 16.10.2013 (OJ EPO 2013, 503), entered into force on 01.11.2014.

See also notice from the EPO, OJ EPO 2014, A70.

[1.727]
Rule 136
Re-establishment of rights

(1) Any request for re-establishment of rights under Article 122, paragraph 1, shall be filed in writing within two months of the removal of the cause of non-compliance with the period, but at the latest within one year of expiry of the unobserved time limit. However, a request for re-establishment of rights in respect of any of the periods specified in Article 87, paragraph 1, and in Article 112a, paragraph 4, shall be filed within two months of expiry of that period. The request for re-establishment of rights shall not be deemed to have been filed until the prescribed fee has been paid.
(2) The request shall state the grounds on which it is based and shall set out the facts on which it relies. The omitted act shall be completed within the relevant period for filing the request according to paragraph 1.
(3) Re-establishment of rights shall be ruled out in respect of any period for which further processing under Article 121 is available and in respect of the period for requesting re-establishment of rights.
(4) The department competent to decide on the omitted act shall decide on the request for re-establishment of rights.

CHAPTER VI
AMENDMENTS AND CORRECTIONS

[1.728]
Rule 137[127] [128]
Amendment of the European patent application
(1) Before receiving the European search report, the applicant may not amend the description, claims or drawings of a European patent application unless otherwise provided.
(2) Together with any comments, corrections or amendments made in response to communications by the European Patent Office under Rule 70a, paragraph 1 or 2, or Rule 161, paragraph 1, the applicant may amend the description, claims and drawings of his own volition.
(3) No further amendment may be made without the consent of the Examining Division.
(4) When filing any amendments referred to in paragraphs 1 to 3, the applicant shall identify them and indicate the basis for them in the application as filed. If the Examining Division notes a failure to meet either requirement, it may request the correction of this deficiency within a period of one month.
(5) Amended claims may not relate to unsearched subject-matter which does not combine with the originally claimed invention or group of inventions to form a single general inventive concept. Nor may they relate to subject-matter not searched in accordance with Rule 62a or Rule 63.

NOTES

127 See opinion/decision of the Enlarged Board of Appeal G 3/89, G 11/91 (Annex I).

128 Amended by decision of the Administrative Council CA/D 3/09 of 25.03.2009 (OJ EPO 2009, 299), entered into force on 01.04.2010.

[1.729]
Rule 138[129]
Different claims, description and drawings for different States
If the European Patent Office is informed of the existence of a prior right under Article 139, paragraph 2, the European patent application or European patent may, for such State or States, contain claims and, where appropriate, a description and drawings which are different from those for the other designated States.

NOTES

129 See decision of the Enlarged Board of Appeal G 1/99 (Annex I).

[1.730]
Rule 139[130]
Correction of errors in documents filed with the European Patent Office
Linguistic errors, errors of transcription and mistakes in any document filed with the European Patent Office may be corrected on request. However, if the request for such correction concerns the description, claims or drawings, the correction must be obvious in the sense that it is immediately evident that nothing else would have been intended than what is offered as the correction.

NOTES

130 See decisions of the Enlarged Board of Appeal G 3/89, G 11/91, G 2/95, G 1/12 (Annex I).

[1.731]
Rule 140[131]
Correction of errors in decisions
In decisions of the European Patent Office, only linguistic errors, errors of transcription and obvious mistakes may be corrected.

NOTES

131 See decisions of the Enlarged Board of Appeal G 8/95, G 1/10 (Annex I).

CHAPTER VII
INFORMATION ON PRIOR ART

[1.732]
Rule 141[132]
Information on prior art
(1) An applicant claiming priority within the meaning of Article 87 shall file a copy of the results of any search carried out by the authority with which the previous application was filed together with the European patent application, in the case of a Euro-PCT application on entry into the European phase, or without delay after such results have been made available to him.
(2) [133] The copy referred to in paragraph 1 shall be deemed to be duly filed if it is available to the European Patent Office and to be included in the file of the European patent application under the conditions determined by the President of the European Patent Office.

(3) Without prejudice to paragraphs 1 and 2, the European Patent Office may invite the applicant to provide, within a period of two months, information on prior art within the meaning of Article 124, paragraph 1.

NOTES

132 Amended by decision of the Administrative Council CA/D 18/09 of 28.10.2009 (OJ EPO 2009, 585), entered into force on 01.01.2011.

133 See decision of the President of the EPO of 05.10.2010 on the filing of copies of search results under Rule 141(1) EPC – utilisation scheme (OJ EPO 2010, 600) and decisions of the President of the EPO exempting applicants claiming the priority of a first filing made in Austria, Japan, the United Kingdom, the United States of America, the Republic of Korea, Denmark or in Spain from filing a copy of the search results under Rule 141(1) EPC – utilisation scheme (OJ EPO 2011, 62; OJ EPO 2012, 540; OJ EPO 2013, 216; OJ EPO 2015, A2, OJ EPO 2016, A18).

See also notices from the EPO, OJ EPO 2010, 410; OJ EPO 2016, A19.

CHAPTER VIII
INTERRUPTION OF PROCEEDINGS

[1.733]
Rule 142[134]
Interruption of proceedings

(1) Proceedings before the European Patent Office shall be interrupted:

(a) in the event of the death or legal incapacity of the applicant for or proprietor of a European patent or of the person authorised by national law to act on his behalf. To the extent that the above events do not affect the authorisation of a representative appointed under Article 134, proceedings shall be interrupted only on application by such representative;

(b) in the event of the applicant for or proprietor of a patent, as a result of some action taken against his property, being prevented by legal reasons from continuing the proceedings;

(c) in the event of the death or legal incapacity of the representative of an applicant for or proprietor of a patent, or of his being prevented for legal reasons resulting from action taken against his property from continuing the proceedings.

(2) When, in the cases referred to in paragraph 1(a) or (b), the European Patent Office has been informed of the identity of the person authorised to continue the proceedings, it shall notify such person and, where applicable, any third party, that the proceedings will be resumed as from a specified date.

(3) In the case referred to in paragraph 1(c), the proceedings shall be resumed when the European Patent Office has been informed of the appointment of a new representative of the applicant or when the Office has informed the other parties of the appointment of a new representative of the proprietor of the patent. If, three months after the beginning of the interruption of the proceedings, the European Patent Office has not been informed of the appointment of a new representative, it shall communicate to the applicant for or proprietor of the patent:

(a) where Article 133, paragraph 2, is applicable, that the European patent application will be deemed to be withdrawn or the European patent will be revoked if the information is not submitted within two months of this communication; or

(b) otherwise, that the proceedings will be resumed with the applicant for or proprietor of the patent as from the notification of this communication.

(4) Any periods, other than those for requesting examination and paying renewal fees, in force at the date of interruption of the proceedings, shall begin again as from the day on which the proceedings are resumed. If such date is less than two months before the end of the period within which the request for examination must be filed, such a request may be filed within two months of such date.

NOTES

134 See decision of the President of the EPO, OJ EPO 2013, 600.

CHAPTER IX
INFORMATION TO THE PUBLIC

[1.734]
Rule 143[135]
Entries in the European Patent Register

(1) The European Patent Register shall contain the following entries:

(a) number of the European patent application;
(b) date of filing of the application;
(c) title of the invention;
(d) classification symbols assigned to the application;
(e) the Contracting States designated;
(f) particulars of the applicant for or proprietor of the patent as provided in Rule 41, paragraph 2(c);

(g) family name, given names and address of the inventor designated by the applicant for or proprietor of the patent, unless he has waived his right to be mentioned under Rule 20, paragraph 1;
(h) particulars of the representative of the applicant for or proprietor of the patent as provided in Rule 41, paragraph 2(d); in the case of several representatives only the particulars of the representative first named, followed by the words "and others" and, in the case of an association referred to in Rule 152, paragraph 11, only the name and address of the association;
(i) priority data (date, State and file number of the previous application);
(j) in the event of a division of the application, the numbers of all the divisional applications;
(k) in the case of a divisional application or a new application under Article 61, paragraph 1(b), the information referred to in sub-paragraphs (a), (b) and (i) with regard to the earlier application;
(l) date of publication of the application and, where appropriate, date of the separate publication of the European search report;
(m) date of filing of the request for examination;
(n) date on which the application is refused, withdrawn or deemed to be withdrawn;
(o) date of publication of the mention of the grant of the European patent;
(p) date of lapse of the European patent in a Contracting State during the opposition period and, where appropriate, pending a final decision on opposition;
(q) date of filing opposition;
(r) date and purport of the decision on opposition;
(s) dates of stay and resumption of proceedings in the cases referred to in Rules 14 and 78;
(t) dates of interruption and resumption of proceedings in the case referred to in Rule 142;
(u) date of re-establishment of rights where an entry has been made under sub-paragraphs (n) or (r);
(v) the filing of a request for conversion under Article 135, paragraph 3;
(w) rights and transfer of such rights relating to an application or a European patent where these Implementing Regulations provide that they shall be recorded.
(x) date and purport of the decision on the request for limitation or revocation of the European patent;
(y) date and purport of the decision of the Enlarged Board of Appeal on the petition for review.

(2) [136] The President of the European Patent Office may decide that entries other than those referred to in paragraph 1 shall be made in the European Patent Register.

NOTES

135 See decision of the President of the EPO, OJ EPO 2013, 600; 2013, 601.

136 See decisions of the President of the EPO, OJ EPO 2014, A86.

[1.735]
Rule 144[137]
Parts of the file excluded from inspection

The parts of the file excluded from inspection under Article 128, paragraph 4, shall be:
(a) the documents relating to the exclusion of or objections to members of the Boards of Appeal or of the Enlarged Board of Appeal;
(b) draft decisions and notices, and all other documents, used for the preparation of decisions and notices, which are not communicated to the parties;
(c) the designation of the inventor, if he has waived his right to be mentioned under Rule 20, paragraph 1;
(d) any other document excluded from inspection by the President of the European Patent Office on the ground that such inspection would not serve the purpose of informing the public about the European patent application or the European patent.

NOTES

137 See decision of the President of the EPO, Special edition No. 3, OJ EPO 2007, J.3.

[1.736]
Rule 145[138]
Procedures for the inspection of files

(1) Inspection of the files of European patent applications and patents shall either be of the original document, or of copies thereof, or of technical means of storage if the files are stored in this way.

(2) The President of the European Patent Office shall determine all file-inspection arrangements, including the circumstances in which an administrative fee is payable.

NOTES

138 See decision of the President of the EPO, Special edition No. 3, OJ EPO 2007, J.2.

[1.737]
Rule 146
Communication of information contained in the files
Subject to the restrictions laid down in Article 128, paragraphs 1 to 4, and in Rule 144, the European Patent Office may, upon request, communicate information concerning any file relating to a European patent application or European patent, subject to the payment of an administrative fee. However, the European Patent Office may refer to the option of file inspection where it deems this to be appropriate in view of the quantity of information to be supplied.

[1.738]
Rule 147[139]
Constitution, maintenance and preservation of files
(1) The European Patent Office shall constitute, maintain and preserve files relating to all European patent applications and patents.
(1) [140] *The European Patent Office shall constitute, maintain and preserve files relating to all European patent applications and patents in electronic form.*
(2) The President of the European Patent Office shall determine the form in which these files shall be constituted, maintained and preserved.
(2) [141] *The President of the European Patent Office shall determine all necessary technical and administrative arrangements relating to the management of electronic files according to paragraph 1.*
(3) Documents incorporated in an electronic file shall be considered to be originals.
(3) [142] *Documents incorporated in an electronic file shall be considered to be originals. The initial paper version of such documents shall only be destroyed after expiry of at least five years. This preservation period starts at the end of the year in which the document was incorporated in the electronic file.*
(4) Any files shall be preserved for at least five years from the end of the year in which:
(a) the application is refused or withdrawn or is deemed to be withdrawn;
(b) the patent is revoked by the European Patent Office; or
(c) the patent or the corresponding protection under Article 63, paragraph 2, lapses in the last of the designated States.
(5) Without prejudice to paragraph 4, files relating to applications which have given rise to divisional applications under Article 76 or new applications under Article 61, paragraph 1(b), shall be preserved for at least the same period as the files relating to any one of these last applications. The same shall apply to files relating to any resulting European patents.

NOTES

139 See decision of the President of the EPO, Special edition No. 3, OJ EPO 2007, J.1.

See the decision of the President of the EPO concerning the pilot project to introduce new means of electronic communication in EPO, OJ EPO 2015, A28.

140 Rule 147, paragraphs 1-3, amended by decision of the Administrative Council CA/D 10/15 of 14.10.2015 (OJ EPO 2015, A83), will enter into force on 01.11.2016.

141 Rule 147, paragraphs 1-3, amended by decision of the Administrative Council CA/D 10/15 of 14.10.2015 (OJ EPO 2015, A83), will enter into force on 01.11.2016.

142 Rule 147, paragraphs 1-3, amended by decision of the Administrative Council CA/D 10/15 of 14.10.2015 (OJ EPO 2015, A83), will enter into force on 01.11.2016.

CHAPTER X
LEGAL AND ADMINISTRATIVE CO-OPERATION

[1.739]
Rule 148
Communications between the European Patent Office and the authorities of the Contracting States
(1) Communications between the European Patent Office and the central industrial property offices of the Contracting States which arise out of the application of this Convention shall be effected directly between these authorities. Communications between the European Patent Office and the courts or other authorities of the Contracting States may be effected through the intermediary of the said central industrial property offices.
(2) Expenditure in respect of communications under paragraph 1 shall be borne by the authority making the communications, which shall be exempt from fees.

[1.740]
Rule 149
Inspection of files by or via courts or authorities of the Contracting States
(1) Inspection of the files of European patent applications or of European patents by courts or authorities of the Contracting States shall be of the original documents or of copies thereof; Rule 145 shall not apply.

(2) Courts or Public Prosecutors' offices of the Contracting States may, in the course of their proceedings, communicate to third parties files or copies thereof transmitted to them by the European Patent Office. Such communications shall be effected in accordance with Article 128 and shall not be subject to any fee.
(3) The European Patent Office shall, when transmitting the files, draw attention to the restrictions which may, under Article 128, paragraphs 1 and 4, apply to file inspection by third parties.

[1.741]
Rule 150
Procedure for letters rogatory
(1) Each Contracting State shall designate a central authority to receive letters rogatory issued by the European Patent Office and to transmit them to the court or authority competent to execute them.
(2) The European Patent Office shall draw up letters rogatory in the language of the competent court or authority or shall attach to such letters rogatory a translation into that language.
(3) Subject to paragraphs 5 and 6, the competent court or authority shall apply national law as to the procedures to be followed in executing such requests and, in particular, as to the appropriate measures of compulsion.
(4) If the court or authority to which the letters rogatory are transmitted is not competent to execute them, the letters rogatory shall be sent forthwith to the central authority referred to in paragraph 1. That authority shall transmit the letters rogatory either to the competent court or authority in that State, or to the European Patent Office where no court or authority is competent in that State.
(5) The European Patent Office shall be informed of the time when, and the place where, the enquiry or other legal measure is to take place and shall inform the parties, witnesses and experts concerned.
(6) If so requested by the European Patent Office, the competent court or authority shall permit the attendance of members of the department concerned and allow them to question any person giving evidence either directly or through the competent court or authority.
(7) The execution of letters rogatory shall not give rise to any reimbursement of fees or costs of any nature. Nevertheless, the State in which letters rogatory are executed has the right to require the Organisation to reimburse any fees paid to experts or interpreters and the costs arising from the procedure under paragraph 6.
(8) If the law applied by the competent court or authority obliges the parties to secure evidence and the competent court or authority is not able itself to execute the letters rogatory, that court or authority may, with the consent of the European Patent Office, appoint a suitable person to do so. When seeking such consent, the competent court or authority shall indicate the approximate costs which would result from this procedure. If the European Patent Office gives its consent, the Organisation shall reimburse any costs incurred; otherwise, the Organisation shall not be liable for such costs.

CHAPTER XI
REPRESENTATION

[1.742]
Rule 151[143]
Appointment of a common representative
(1) If there is more than one applicant and the request for grant of a European patent does not name a common representative, the applicant first named in the request shall be deemed to be the common representative. However, if one of the applicants is obliged to appoint a professional representative, this representative shall be deemed to be the common representative, unless the applicant first named has appointed a professional representative. The same shall apply to third parties acting in common in filing a notice of opposition or intervention and to joint proprietors of a European patent.
(2) If the European patent application is transferred to more than one person, and such persons have not appointed a common representative, paragraph 1 shall apply mutatis mutandis. If such application is not possible, the European Patent Office shall invite such persons to appoint a common representative within a period to be specified. If this invitation is not complied with, the European Patent Office shall appoint the common representative.

NOTES
[143] See decision of the Enlarged Board of Appeal G 3/99 (Annex I).

[1.743]
Rule 152
Authorisations
(1) [144] The President of the European Patent Office shall determine the cases in which a signed authorisation shall be filed by representatives acting before the European Patent Office.

(2) Where a representative fails to file such an authorisation, the European Patent Office shall invite him to do so within a period to be specified. The authorisation may cover one or more European patent applications or European patents and shall be filed in the corresponding number of copies.
(3) Where the requirements of Article 133, paragraph 2, have not been satisfied, the same period shall be specified for the appointment of a representative and the filing of the authorisation.
(4) [145] A general authorisation may be filed enabling a representative to act in respect of all the patent transactions of a party. A single copy shall suffice.
(5) The President of the European Patent Office may determine the form and content of:
(a) an authorisation relating to the representation of persons under Article 133, paragraph 2;
(b) a general authorisation.
(6) If a required authorisation is not filed in due time, any procedural steps taken by the representative, other than the filing of a European patent application, shall be deemed not to have been taken, without prejudice to any other legal consequences provided for by this Convention.
(7) Paragraphs 2 and 4 shall apply to the withdrawal of an authorisation.
(8) A representative shall be deemed to be authorised until the termination of his authorisation has been communicated to the European Patent Office.
(9) Unless it expressly provides otherwise, an authorisation shall not terminate vis-à-vis the European Patent Office upon the death of the person who gave it.
(10) [146] If a party appoints several representatives, they may act either jointly or singly, notwithstanding any provisions to the contrary in the communication of their appointment or in the authorisation.
(11) [147] The authorisation of an association of representatives shall be deemed to be an authorisation of any representative who can provide evidence that he practises within that association.

NOTES

[144] See decision of the President of the EPO, Special edition No. 3 OJ EPO 2007, L.1. See also decision of the President of the EPO (OJ EPO 2012, 352).

[145] See decision of the President of the EPO, OJ EPO 2013, 600.

[146] See the notice from the EPO, OJ EPO 2013, 535, section II.

[147] See decision of the Administrative Council CA/D 9/13 of 16.10.2013, OJ EPO 2013, 500, and notice from the EPO, OJ EPO 2013, 535, section I.

See decision of the President of the EPO, OJ EPO, OJ EPO 2013, 600.

[1.744]
Rule 153
Attorney-client evidentiary privilege[148]
(1) [149] Where advice is sought from a professional representative in his capacity as such, all communications between the professional representative and his client or any other person, relating to that purpose and falling under Article 2 of the Regulation on discipline for professional representatives, are permanently privileged from disclosure in proceedings before the European Patent Office, unless such privilege is expressly waived by the client.
(2) Such privilege from disclosure shall apply, in particular, to any communication or document relating to:
(a) the assessment of the patentability of an invention;
(b) the preparation or prosecution of a European patent application;
(c) any opinion relating to the validity, scope of protection or infringement of a European patent or a European patent application.

NOTES

[148] Title amended by decision of the Administrative Council (CA/D 4/08) of 21.10.2008 (OJ EPO 2008, 513), entered into force on 01.04.2009.

[149] French version amended by decision of the Administrative Council CA/D 4/08 of 21.10.2008 (OJ EPO 2008, 513), entered into force on 01.04.2009.

[1.745]
Rule 154[150]
Amendment of the list of professional representatives
(1) The entry of a professional representative shall be deleted from the list of professional representatives if he so requests or if, despite repeated reminders, he fails to pay the annual subscription to the Institute before the end of September of the year for which the subscription is due.
(2) Without prejudice to any disciplinary measures taken under Article 134a, paragraph 1(c), the entry of a professional representative may be deleted ex officio only:
(a) in the event of his death or legal incapacity;
(b) where he is no longer a national of one of the Contracting States, unless he was granted an exemption under Article 134, paragraph 7(a);

(c) where he no longer has his place of business or employment within one of the Contracting States.

(3) Any person entered on the list of professional representatives under Article 134, paragraphs (2) or (3), whose entry has been deleted shall, upon request, be re-entered on that list if the conditions for deletion no longer exist.

NOTES

150 See decision of the President of the EPO, OJ EPO 2013, 600; and the notice from the EPO, OJ EPO 2015, A55.

PART VIII
IMPLEMENTING REGULATIONS TO PART VIII OF THE CONVENTION

[1.746]
Rule 155
Filing and transmission of the request for conversion

(1) The request for conversion referred to in Article 135, paragraph 1(a) or (b), shall be filed within three months of the withdrawal of the European patent application, or of the communication that the application is deemed to be withdrawn, or of the decision refusing the application or revoking the European patent. The effect of the European patent application under Article 66 shall lapse if the request is not filed in due time.

(2) When transmitting the request for conversion to the central industrial property offices of the Contracting States specified in the request, the central industrial property office concerned or the European Patent Office shall attach to the request a copy of the file relating to the European patent application or European patent.

(3) [151] Article 135, paragraph 4, shall apply if the request for conversion referred to in Article 135, paragraphs 1(a) and (2), is not transmitted before the expiry of a period of twenty months from the date of filing or, if priority has been claimed, the date of priority.

NOTES

151 English version amended by decision of the Administrative Council (CA/D 1/08) of 21.10.2008 (OJ EPO 2008, 513), entered into force on 01.04.2009.

[1.747]
Rule 156
Information to the public in the event of conversion

(1) The documents accompanying the request for conversion under Rule 155, paragraph 2, shall be made available to the public by the central industrial property office under the same conditions and to the same extent as documents relating to national proceedings.

(2) The printed specification of the national patent resulting from the conversion of a European patent application shall mention that application.

PART IX
IMPLEMENTING REGULATIONS TO PART X OF THE CONVENTION

[1.748]
Rule 157[152]
The European Patent Office as a receiving Office

(1) The European Patent Office shall be competent to act as a receiving Office within the meaning of the PCT if the applicant is a resident or national of a Contracting State to this Convention and to the PCT. Without prejudice to paragraph 3, if the applicant chooses the European Patent Office as a receiving Office, the international application shall be filed directly with the European Patent Office. Article 75, paragraph 2, shall apply mutatis mutandis.

(2) Where the European Patent Office acts as a receiving Office under the PCT, the international application shall be filed in English, French or German. The President of the European Patent Office may determine that the international application and any related item shall be filed in more than one copy.

(3) If an international application is filed with an authority of a Contracting State for transmittal to the European Patent Office as the receiving Office, the Contracting State shall ensure that the application reaches the European Patent Office not later than two weeks before the end of the thirteenth month from filing or, if priority is claimed, from the date of priority.

(4) The transmittal fee for the international application shall be paid within one month of filing the application.

NOTES

152 See the notices from the EPO concerning the procedure for acknowledging receipt of international applications filed in paper form, OJ EPO 2010, 642, and concerning the requirements to be observed when filing an international application with the EPO as a PCT receiving Office, OJ EPO 2014, A33; and the decision of the President of the EPO concerning the filing of international applications with the EPO acting as receiving Office using ePCT-Filing, OJ EPO 2014, A107.

[1.749]
Rule 158
The European Patent Office as an International Searching Authority or International Preliminary Examining Authority

(1) In the case of Article 17, paragraph 3(a) PCT, an additional international search fee shall be paid for each further invention for which an international search is to be carried out.

(2) In the case of Article 34, paragraph 3(a) PCT, an additional fee for international preliminary examination shall be paid for each further invention for which the international preliminary examination is to be carried out.

(3) [153] Where an additional fee has been paid under protest, the European Patent Office shall examine the protest in accordance with Rule 40.2(c) to (e) or Rule 68.3(c) to (e) PCT, subject to payment of the prescribed protest fee. Further details concerning the procedure shall be determined by the President of the European Patent Office.

NOTES

[153] See decision of the President of the EPO, OJ EPO 2015, A59 and the notice from the EPO, OJ EPO 2010, 322.

[1.750]
Rule 159[154]
The European Patent Office as a designated or elected Office – Requirements for entry into the European phase

(1) In respect of an international application under Article 153, the applicant shall perform the following acts within thirty-one months from the date of filing of the application or, if priority has been claimed, from the priority date:

(a) [155] supply, where applicable, the translation of the international application required under Article 153, paragraph 4;
(b) specify the application documents, as originally filed or as amended, on which the European grant procedure is to be based;
(c) pay the filing fee provided for in Article 78, paragraph 2;
(d) [156], [157] pay the designation fee if the period under Rule 39 has expired earlier;
(e) pay the search fee, where a supplementary European search report has to be drawn up;
(f) file the request for examination provided for in Article 94, if the period under Rule 70, paragraph 1, has expired earlier;
(g) pay the renewal fee in respect of the third year provided for in Article 86, paragraph 1, if the fee has fallen due earlier under Rule 51, paragraph 1;
(h) file, where applicable, the certificate of exhibition referred to in Article 55, paragraph 2, and Rule 25.

(2) The Examining Division shall be competent to take decisions of the European Patent Office under Article 25, paragraph 2(a) PCT.

NOTES

[154] See the notice from the EPO concerning the request for early processing (OJ EPO 2013, 156).

[155] See decision of the Enlarged Board of Appeal G 4/08 (Annex I).

[156] See opinion of the Enlarged Board of Appeal G 4/98 (Annex I).

[157] Amended by decision of the Administrative Council CA/D 4/08 of 21.10.2008 (OJ EPO 2008, 513), entered into force on 01.04.2009.

[1.751]
Rule 160[158]
Consequences of non-fulfilment of certain requirements

(1) If either the translation of the international application or the request for examination is not filed in due time, or if the filing fee, the search fee or the designation fee is not paid in due time, the European patent application shall be deemed to be withdrawn.

(2) [159] If the European Patent Office notes that the application is deemed to be withdrawn under paragraph 1, it shall communicate this to the applicant. Rule 112, paragraph 2, shall apply mutatis mutandis.

NOTES

[158] Amended by decision of the Administrative Council CA/D 4/08 of 21.10.2008 (OJ EPO 2008, 513), entered into force on 01.04.2009.

[159] See opinion of the Enlarged Board of Appeal G 4/98 (Annex I).

[1.752]
Rule 161[160]
Amendment of the application

(1) If the European Patent Office has acted as the International Searching Authority and, where a demand under Article 31 PCT was filed, also as the International Preliminary Examining Authority for a Euro-PCT application, it shall give the applicant the opportunity to comment on the written

opinion of the International Searching Authority or the International Preliminary Examination Report and, where appropriate, invite him to correct any deficiencies noted in the written opinion or in the International Preliminary Examination Report and to amend the description, claims and drawings within a period of six months from the respective communication. If the European Patent Office has drawn up a supplementary international search report, an invitation in accordance with the first sentence shall be issued in respect of the explanations given in accordance with Rule 45*bis*.7(e) PCT. If the applicant does not comply with or comment on an invitation in accordance with the first or second sentence, the application shall be deemed to be withdrawn.
(2) Where the European Patent Office draws up a supplementary European search report on a Euro-PCT application, the application may be amended once within a period of six months from a communication informing the applicant accordingly. The application as amended shall serve as the basis for the supplementary European search.

NOTES

[160] Amended by decision of the Administrative Council CA/D 12/10 of 26.10.2010 (OJ EPO 2010, 634), entered into force on 01.05.2011. See also the notice from the EPO, OJ EPO 2010, 406.

[1.753]
Rule 162[161]
Claims incurring fees

(1) If the application documents on which the European grant procedure is to be based comprise more than fifteen claims, claims fees shall be paid for the sixteenth and each subsequent claim as laid down in the Rules relating to Fees within the period under Rule 159, paragraph 1.
(2) If the claims fees are not paid in due time, they may still be paid within six months from a communication concerning the failure to observe the time limit. If within this period amended claims are filed, the claims fees due shall be computed on the basis of such amended claims.
(3) Any claims fees paid within the period under paragraph 1 and in excess of those due under paragraph 2, second sentence, shall be refunded.
(4) Where a claims fee is not paid in due time, the claim concerned shall be deemed to be abandoned.

NOTES

[161] Amended by decision of the Administrative Council CA/D 12/10 of 26.10.2010 (OJ EPO 2010, 634), entered into force on 01.05.2011.

[1.754]
Rule 163
Examination of certain formal requirements by the European Patent Office

(1) Where the designation of the inventor under Rule 19, paragraph 1, has not yet been made within the period under Rule 159, paragraph 1, the European Patent Office shall invite the applicant to make the designation within two months.
(2) [162] Where the priority of an earlier application is claimed and the file number of the previous application or the copy thereof provided for in Rule 52, paragraph 1, and Rule 53 have not yet been submitted within the period under Rule 159, paragraph 1, the European Patent Office shall invite the applicant to furnish that number or copy within two months. Rule 53, paragraph 2, shall apply.
(3) [163] Where, at the expiry of the period under Rule 159, paragraph 1, a sequence listing complying with the standard provided for in the Administrative Instructions under the PCT is not available to the European Patent Office, the applicant shall be invited to file a sequence listing complying with the rules laid down by the President of the European Patent Office within two months. Rule 30, paragraphs 2 and 3, shall apply mutatis mutandis.
(4) Where, at the expiry of the period under Rule 159, paragraph 1, the address, the nationality or the State in which his residence or principal place of business is located is missing in respect of any applicant, the European Patent Office shall invite the applicant to furnish these indications within two months.
(5) Where, at the expiry of the period under Rule 159, paragraph 1, the requirements of Article 133, paragraph 2, have not been satisfied, the European Patent Office shall invite the applicant to appoint a professional representative within two months.
(6) If the deficiencies noted under paragraphs 1, 4 or 5 are not corrected in due time, the European patent application shall be refused. If the deficiency noted under paragraph 2 is not corrected in due time, the right of priority shall be lost for the application.

NOTES

[162] Amended by decision of the Administrative Council CA/D 4/08 of 21.10.2008 (OJ EPO 2008, 513), entered into force on 01.04.2009. See also the decision of the President of the EPO on the filing of priority documents (OJ EPO 2012, 492).

[163] See decision of the President of the EPO, OJ EPO 2011, 372, and the notice from the EPO, OJ EPO 2013, 542.

[1.755]
Rule 164[164]
Unity of invention and further searches

(1) If the European Patent Office considers that the application documents which are to serve as the basis for the supplementary European search do not comply with the requirement of unity of invention, it shall:

(a) draw up a partial supplementary search report on those parts of the application which relate to the invention, or the group of inventions within the meaning of Article 82, first mentioned in the claims;

(b) inform the applicant that, for the supplementary European search report to cover the other inventions, a further search fee must be paid, in respect of each invention involved, within a period of two months; and

(c) draw up the supplementary European search report for the parts of the application relating to inventions in respect of which search fees have been paid.

(2) If the supplementary European search report is dispensed with and the Examining Division considers that in the application documents which are to serve as the basis for examination an invention, or a group of inventions within the meaning of Article 82, is claimed which was not searched by the European Patent Office in its capacity as International Searching Authority or Authority specified for supplementary international search, the Examining Division shall:

(a) inform the applicant that a search will be performed in respect of any such invention for which a search fee is paid within a period of two months;

(b) issue the results of any search performed in accordance with paragraph (a) together with:

- a communication under Article 94, paragraph 3, and Rule 71, paragraphs 1 and 2, in which it shall give the applicant the opportunity to comment on these results and to amend the description, claims and drawings, or
- a communication under Rule 71, paragraph 3,

and

(c) where appropriate, in the communication issued under paragraph (b), invite the applicant to limit the application to one invention, or group of inventions within the meaning of Article 82, for which a search report was drawn up by the European Patent Office in its capacity either as International Searching Authority or as Authority specified for supplementary international search, or for which a search was performed in accordance with the procedure under paragraph (a).

(3) In the procedure under paragraph 2(a), Rules 62a and 63 shall apply mutatis mutandis.

(4) Rule 62 and Rule 70, paragraph 2, shall not apply to the results of any search performed in accordance with paragraph 2.

(5) Any fee paid under paragraphs 1 or 2 shall be refunded if the applicant requests a refund and the Examining Division finds that the communication under paragraphs 1(b) or 2(a) was not justified.

NOTES

164 Amended by decision of the Administrative Council CA/D 17/13 of 16.10.2013 (OJ EPO 2013, 503), entered into force on 01.11.2014.

See also notice from the EPO, OJ EPO 2014, A70.

[1.756]
Rule 165
The Euro-PCT application as conflicting application under Article 54, paragraph 3

A Euro-PCT application shall be considered as comprised in the state of the art under Article 54, paragraph 3, if in addition to the conditions laid down in Article 153, paragraph 3 or 4, the filing fee under Rule 159, paragraph 1(c) has been paid.

PROTOCOL ON JURISDICTION AND THE RECOGNITION OF DECISIONS IN RESPECT OF THE RIGHT TO THE GRANT OF A EUROPEAN PATENT (PROTOCOL ON RECOGNITION)

NOTES

The original source of this Protocol is the European Patent Office (EPO) website at www.epo.org.

SECTION I
JURISDICTION

[1.757]

Article 1[1]

(1) The courts of the Contracting States shall, in accordance with Articles 2 to 6, have jurisdiction to decide claims, against the applicant, to the right to the grant of a European patent in respect of one or more of the Contracting States designated in the European patent application.

(2) For the purposes of this Protocol, the term "courts" shall include authorities which, under the national law of a Contracting State, have jurisdiction to decide the claims referred to in paragraph 1. Any Contracting State shall notify the European Patent Office of the identity of any authority on which such a jurisdiction is conferred, and the European Patent Office shall inform the other Contracting States accordingly.

(3) For the purposes of this Protocol, the term "Contracting State" refers to a Contracting State which has not excluded application of this Protocol pursuant to Article 167 of the Convention.

[1] See decision of the Enlarged Board of Appeal G 3/92 (Annex I).

Article 2

Subject to Articles 4 and 5, if an applicant for a European patent has his residence or principal place of business within one of the Contracting States, proceedings shall be brought against him in the courts of that Contracting State.

Article 3

Subject to Articles 4 and 5, if an applicant for a European patent has his residence or principal place of business outside the Contracting States, and if the party claiming the right to the grant of the European patent has his residence or principal place of business within one of the Contracting States, the courts of the latter State shall have exclusive jurisdiction.

Article 4

Subject to Article 5, if the subject-matter of a European patent application is the invention of an employee, the courts of the Contracting State, if any, whose law determines the right to the European patent pursuant to Article 60, paragraph 1, second sentence, of the Convention, shall have exclusive jurisdiction over proceedings between the employee and the employer.

Article 5

(1) If the parties to a dispute concerning the right to the grant of a European patent have concluded an agreement, either in writing or verbally with written confirmation, to the effect that a court or the courts of a particular Contracting State shall decide on such a dispute, the court or courts of that State shall have exclusive jurisdiction.

(2) However, if the parties are an employee and his employer, paragraph 1 shall only apply insofar as the national law governing the contract of employment allows the agreement in question.

Article 6

In cases where neither Articles 2 to 4 nor Article 5, paragraph 1, apply, the courts of the Federal Republic of Germany shall have exclusive jurisdiction.

Article 7

The courts of Contracting States before which claims referred to in Article 1 are brought shall of their own motion decide whether or not they have jurisdiction pursuant to Articles 2 to 6.

Article 8

(1) In the event of proceedings based on the same claim and between the same parties being brought before courts of different Contracting States, the court to which a later application is made shall of its own motion decline jurisdiction in favour of the court to which an earlier application was made.

(2) In the event of the jurisdiction of the court to which an earlier application is made being challenged, the court to which a later application is made shall stay the proceedings until the other court takes a final decision.

SECTION II
RECOGNITION

[1.758]
Article 9[2]
(1) Subject to the provisions of Article 11, paragraph 2, final decisions given in any Contracting State on the right to the grant of a European patent in respect of one or more of the Contracting States designated in the European patent application shall be recognised without requiring a special procedure in the other Contracting States.
(2) The jurisdiction of the court whose decision is to be recognised and the validity of such decision may not be reviewed.

2 See decision of the Enlarged Board of Appeal G 3/92 (Annex I).

Article 10
Article 9, paragraph 1, shall not be applicable where—
(a) an applicant for a European patent who has not contested a claim proves that the document initiating the proceedings was not notified to him regularly and sufficiently early for him to defend himself; or
(b) an applicant proves that the decision is incompatible with another decision given in a Contracting State in proceedings between the same parties which were started before those in which the decision to be recognised was given.

Article 11
(1) In relations between any Contracting States the Provisions of this Protocol shall prevail over any conflicting provisions of other agreements on jurisdiction or the recognition of judgements.
(2) This Protocol shall not affect the implementation of any agreement between a Contracting State and a State which is not bound by the Protocol.

PROTOCOL ON PRIVILEGES AND IMMUNITIES OF THE EUROPEAN PATENT ORGANISATION (PROTOCOL ON PRIVILEGES AND IMMUNITIES)

NOTES
The original source of this Protocol is the European Patent Office (EPO) website at www.epo.org.

[1.759]
Article 1
(1) The premises of the Organisation shall be inviolable.
(2) The authorities of the States in which the Organisation has its premises shall not enter those premises except with the consent of the President of the European Patent Office. Such consent shall be assumed in the case of fire or other disaster requiring prompt protective action.
(3) Service of process at the premises of the Organisation and of any other procedural instruments relating to a cause of action against the Organisation shall not constitute breach of inviolability.

Article 2
The archives of the Organisation and any documents belonging to or held by it shall be inviolable.

Article 3
(1) Within the scope of its official activities the Organisation shall have immunity from jurisdiction and execution, except—
(a) to the extent that the Organisation shall have expressly waived such immunity in a particular case;
(b) in the case of a civil action brought by a third party for damage resulting from an accident caused by a motor vehicle belonging to, or operated on behalf of, the Organisation, or in respect of a motor traffic offence involving such a vehicle;
(c) in respect of the enforcement of an arbitration award made under Article 23.
(2) The property and assets of the Organisation, wherever situated, shall be immune from any form of requisition, confiscation, expropriation and sequestration.
(3) The property and assets of the Organisation shall also be immune from any form of administrative or provisional judicial constraint, except insofar as may be temporarily necessary in connection with the prevention of, and investigation into, accidents involving motor vehicles belonging to or operated on behalf of the Organisation.
(4) The official activities of the Organisation shall, for the purposes of this Protocol, be such as are strictly necessary for its administrative and technical operation, as set out in the Convention.

Article 4

(1) Within the scope of its official activities the Organisation and its property and income shall be exempt from all direct taxes.

(2) Where substantial purchases for the exercise of its official activities, and in the price of which taxes or duties are included, are made by the Organisation, appropriate measures shall, whenever possible, be taken by the Contracting States to remit or reimburse to the Organisation the amount of such taxes or duties.

(3) No exemption shall be accorded in respect of duties and taxes which are no more than charges for public utility services.

Article 5

Goods imported or exported by the Organisation for the exercise of its official activities shall be exempt from duties and charges on import or export other than fees or taxes representing services rendered, and from all prohibitions and restrictions on import or export.

Article 6

No exemption shall be granted under Articles 4 and 5 in respect of goods purchased or imported for the personal benefit of the employees of the European Patent Office.

Article 7

(1) Goods belonging to the Organisation which have been acquired or imported under Article 4 or Article 5 shall not be sold or given away except in accordance with conditions laid down by the Contracting States which have granted the exemptions.

(2) The transfer of goods and provision of services between the various buildings of the Organisation shall be exempt from charges or restrictions of any kind; where appropriate, the Contracting States shall take all the necessary measures to remit or reimburse the amount of such charges or to lift such restrictions.

Article 8

The transmission of publications and other information material by or to the Organisation shall not be restricted in any way.

Article 9

The Contracting States shall accord the Organisation the currency exemptions which are necessary for the exercise of its official activities.

Article 10

(1) With regard to its official communications and the transfer of all its documents, the Organisation shall in each Contracting State enjoy the most favourable treatment accorded by that State to any other international organisation.

(2) No censorship shall be applied to official communications of the Organisation by whatever means of communication.

Article 11

The Contracting States shall take all appropriate measures to facilitate the entry, stay and departure of the employees of the European Patent Office.

Article 12

(1) Representatives of Contracting States, alternate Representatives and their advisers or experts, if any, shall enjoy, while attending meetings of the Administrative Council and of any body established by it, and in the course of their journeys to and from the place of meeting, the following privileges and immunities—

(a) immunity from arrest or detention and from seisure of their personal luggage, except when found committing, attempting to commit, or just having committed an offence;

(b) immunity from jurisdiction, even after the termination of their mission, in respect of acts, including words written and spoken, done by them in the exercise of their functions; this immunity shall not apply, however, in the case of a motor traffic offence committed by one of the persons referred to above, nor in the case of damage caused by a motor vehicle belonging to or driven by such a person;

(c) inviolability for all their official papers and documents;

(d) the right to use codes and to receive documents or correspondence by special courier or sealed bag;

(e) exemption for themselves and their spouses from all measures restricting entry and from aliens' registration formalities;

(f) the same facilities in the matter of currency and exchange control as are accorded to the representatives of foreign Governments on temporary official missions.

(2) Privileges and immunities are accorded to the persons referred to in paragraph 1, not for their personal advantage, but in order to ensure complete independence in the exercise of their functions in connection with the Organisation. Consequently, a Contracting State has the duty to waive the immunity in all cases where, in the opinion of that State, such immunity would impede the course of justice and where it can be waived without prejudicing the purposes for which it was accorded.

Article 13

(1) Subject to the provisions of Article 6, the President of the European Patent Office shall enjoy the privileges and immunities accorded to diplomatic agents under the Vienna Convention on Diplomatic Relations of 18 April 1961.

(2) However, immunity from jurisdiction shall not apply in the case of a motor traffic offence committed by the President of the European Patent Office or damage caused by a motor vehicle belonging to or driven by him.

Article 14

The employees of the European Patent Office—

(a) shall, even after their service has terminated, have immunity from jurisdiction in respect of acts, including words written and spoken, done in the exercise of their functions; this immunity shall not apply, however, in the case of a motor traffic offence committed by an employee of the European Patent Office, nor in the case of damage caused by a motor vehicle belonging to or driven by an employee;

(b) shall be exempt from all obligations in respect of military service;

(c) shall enjoy inviolability for all their official papers and documents;

(d) shall enjoy the same facilities as regards exemption from all measures restricting immigration and governing aliens' registration as are normally accorded to staff members of international organisations, as shall members of their families forming part of their household;

(e) shall enjoy the same privileges in respect of exchange regulations as are normally accorded to the staff members of international organisations;

(f) shall enjoy the same facilities as to repatriation as diplomatic agents in time of international crises, as shall the members of their families forming part of their household;

(g) shall have the right to import duty-free their furniture and personal effects at the time of first taking up their post in the State concerned and the right on the termination of their functions in that State to export free of duty their furniture and personal effects, subject to the conditions considered necessary by the Government of the State in whose territory the right is exercised and with the exception of property acquired in that State which is subject to an export prohibition therein.

Article 15[1]

Experts performing functions on behalf of, or carrying out missions for, the Organisation shall enjoy the following privileges and immunities, to the extent that they are necessary for the carrying out of their functions, including during journeys made in carrying out their functions and in the course of such missions—

(a) immunity from jurisdiction in respect of acts done by them in the exercise of their functions, including words written or spoken, except in the case of a motor traffic offence committed by an expert or in the case of damage caused by a motor vehicle belonging to or driven by him; experts shall continue to enjoy this immunity after they have ceased to be employed by the Organisation;

(b) inviolability for all their official papers and documents;

(c) the exchange facilities necessary for the transfer of their remuneration.

[1] See decision CA/D 31/08 of the Administrative Council of 10 December 2008 determining the members of the Institute of Professional Representatives before the European Patent Office to whom Article 15 of the Protocol on Privileges and Immunities of the European Patent Organisation applies (OJ EPO 2009, 28).

Article 16

(1) The persons referred to in Articles 13 and 14 shall be subject to a tax for the benefit of the Organisation on salaries and emoluments paid by the Organisation, subject to the conditions and rules laid down by the Administrative Council within a period of one year from the date of the entry into force of the Convention. From the date on which this tax is applied, such salaries and emoluments shall be exempt from national income tax. The Contracting States may, however, take into account the salaries and emoluments thus exempt when assessing the amount of tax to be applied to income from other sources.

(2) Paragraph 1 shall not apply to pensions and annuities paid by the Organisation to the former employees of the European Patent Office.

Article 17[2]

The Administrative Council shall decide the categories of employees to whom the provisions of Article 14, in whole or in part, and Article 16 shall apply and the categories of experts to whom the provisions of Article 15 shall apply. The names, titles and addresses of the employees and experts included in such categories shall be communicated from time to time to the Contracting States.

[2] See decision CA/D 31/08 of the Administrative Council of 10 December 2008 determining the members of the Institute of Professional Representatives before the European Patent Office to whom Article 15 of the Protocol on Privileges and Immunities of the European Patent Organisation applies (OJ EPO 2009, 28).

Article 18

In the event of the Organisation establishing its own social security scheme, the Organisation and the employees of the European Patent Office shall be exempt from all compulsory contributions to national social security schemes, subject to the agreements made with the Contracting States in accordance with the provisions of Article 25.

Article 19

(1) The privileges and immunities provided for in this Protocol are not designed to give to employees of the European Patent Office or experts performing functions for or on behalf of the Organisation personal advantage. They are provided solely to ensure, in all circumstances, the unimpeded functioning of the Organisation and the complete independence of the persons to whom they are accorded.

(2) The President of the European Patent Office has the duty to waive immunity where he considers that such immunity prevents the normal course of justice and that it is possible to dispense with such immunity without prejudicing the interests of the Organisation. The Administrative Council may waive immunity of the President for the same reasons.

Article 20

(1) The Organisation shall co-operate at all times with the competent authorities of the Contracting States in order to facilitate the proper administration of justice, to ensure the observance of police regulations and regulations concerning public health, labour inspection or other similar national legislation, and to prevent any abuse of the privileges, immunities and facilities provided for in this Protocol.

(2) The procedure of co-operation mentioned in paragraph 1 may be laid down in the complementary agreements referred to in Article 25.

Article 21

Each Contracting State retains the right to take all precautions necessary in the interests of its security.

Article 22

No Contracting State is obliged to extend the privileges and immunities referred to in Article 12, Article 13, Article 14, sub-paragraphs (b), (e) and (g) and Article 15, sub-paragraph (c) to—

(a) its own nationals;

(b) any person who at the time of taking up his functions with the Organisation has his permanent residence in that State and is not an employee of any other inter-governmental organisation whose staff is incorporated into the Organisation.

Article 23

(1) Any Contracting State may submit to an international arbitration tribunal any dispute concerning the Organisation or an employee of the European Patent Office or an expert performing functions for or on its behalf, insofar as the Organisation or the employees and experts have claimed a privilege or an immunity under this Protocol in circumstances where that immunity has not been waived.

(2) If a Contracting State intends to submit a dispute to arbitration, it shall notify the Chairman of the Administrative Council, who shall forthwith inform each Contracting State of such notification.

(3) The procedure laid down in paragraph 1 of this Article shall not apply to disputes between the Organisation and the employees or experts in respect of the Service Regulations or conditions of employment or, with regard to the employees, the Pension Scheme Regulations.

(4) No appeal shall lie against the award of the arbitration tribunal, which shall be final; it shall be binding on the parties. In case of dispute concerning the import or scope of the award, it shall be incumbent upon the arbitration tribunal to interpret it on request by either party.

Article 24

(1) The arbitration tribunal referred to in Article 23 shall consist of three members, one arbitrator nominated by the State or States party to the arbitration, one arbitrator nominated by the Administrative Council and a third arbitrator, who shall be the chairman, nominated by the said two arbitrators.

(2) The arbitrators shall be nominated from a panel comprising no more than six arbitrators appointed by each Contracting State and six arbitrators appointed by the Administrative Council. This panel shall be established as soon as possible after the Protocol enters into force and shall be revised each time this proves necessary.

(3) If, within three months from the date of the notification referred to in Article 23, paragraph 2, either party fails to make the nomination referred to in paragraph 1 above, the choice of the arbitrator shall, on request of the other party, be made by the President of the International Court of Justice from the persons included in the said panel. This shall also apply, when so requested by either party, if within one month from the date of appointment of the second arbitrator, the first two arbitrators are unable to agree on the nomination of the third arbitrator. However, if, in these two cases, the President of the International Court of Justice is prevented from making the choice, or if he is a national of one of the States parties to the dispute, the Vice-President of the International Court of Justice shall make the afore-mentioned appointments, provided that he himself is not a national of one of the States parties to the dispute; if such is the case, the member of the International Court of Justice who is not a national of one of the States parties to the dispute and who has been chosen by the President or Vice-President shall make the appointments. A national of the State applying for arbitration may not be chosen to fill the post of the arbitrator whose appointment devolves on the Administrative Council nor may a person included in the panel and appointed by the Administrative Council be chosen to fill the post of an arbitrator whose appointment devolves on the State which is the claimant. Nor may a person of either of these categories be chosen as chairman of the Tribunal.

(4) The arbitration tribunal shall draw up its own rules of procedure.

Article 25

The Organisation may, on a decision of the Administrative Council, conclude with one or more Contracting States complementary agreements to give effect to the provisions of this Protocol as regards such State or States, and other arrangements to ensure the efficient functioning of the Organisation and the safeguarding of its interests.

PROTOCOL ON THE CENTRALISATION OF THE EUROPEAN PATENT SYSTEM AND ON ITS INTRODUCTION (PROTOCOL ON CENTRALISATION)

as revised by the Act revising the EPC of 29 November 2000[1]

NOTES

The original source of this Protocol is the European Patent Office (EPO) website at www.epo.org.

[1] The new text of the Protocol adopted by the Administrative Council of the European Patent Organisation in its decision of 28 June 2001 (see OJ EPO 2001, Special edition No 4, p. 55) has become an integral part of the Revision Act of 29 November 2000 under Article 3(2), second sentence, of that Act.

SECTION I[2]

[1.760]

(1)

(a) Upon entry into force of the Convention, States parties thereto which are also members of the International Patent Institute set up by the Hague Agreement of 6 June 1947 shall take all necessary steps to ensure the transfer to the European Patent Office, no later than the date referred to in *Article 162, paragraph 1*, of the Convention, of all assets and liabilities and all staff members of the International Patent Institute. Such transfer shall be effected by an agreement between the International Patent Institute and the European Patent Organisation. The above States and the other States parties to the Convention shall take all necessary steps to ensure that that agreement shall be implemented no later than the date referred to in *Article 162, paragraph 1*, of the Convention. Upon implementation of the agreement, those Member States of the International Patent Institute which are also parties to the Convention further undertake to terminate their participation in the Hague Agreement.

(b) The States parties to the Convention shall take all necessary steps to ensure that all the assets and liabilities and all the staff members of the International Patent Institute are taken into the European Patent Office in accordance with the agreement referred to in subparagraph (a). After the implementation of that agreement the tasks incumbent upon the International Patent Institute at the date on which the Convention is opened for signature, and in particular those carried out vis-à-vis its Member States, whether or not they become parties to the Convention, and such tasks as it has undertaken at the time of the entry into force of the Convention to carry out vis-à-vis States which, at that date, are both members of the International Patent Institute and parties to the Convention, shall be assumed by the European Patent Office. In addition, the Administrative Council of the European Patent Organisation may allocate further duties in the field of searching to the European Patent Office.

(c) The above obligations shall also apply *mutatis mutandis* to the sub-office set up under the Hague Agreement under the conditions set out in the agreement between the International Patent Institute and the Government of the Contracting State concerned. This Government hereby undertakes to make a new agreement with the European Patent Organisation in place of the one already made with the International Patent Institute to harmonise the clauses concerning the organisation, operation and financing of the sub-office with the provisions of this Protocol.

(2) Subject to the provisions of Section III, the States parties to the Convention shall, on behalf of their central industrial property offices, renounce in favour of the European Patent Office any activities as International Searching Authorities under the Patent Co-operation Treaty as from the date referred to in Article 162, paragraph 1, of the Convention.

(3)

(a) A sub-office of the European Patent Office shall be set up in Berlin as from the date referred to in Article 162, paragraph 1, of the Convention. It shall operate under the direction of the branch at The Hague.

(b) The Administrative Council shall determine the duties to be allocated to the sub-office in Berlin in the light of general considerations and of the requirements of the European Patent Office.

(c) At least at the beginning of the period following the progressive expansion of the field of activity of the European Patent Office, the amount of work assigned to that sub-office shall be sufficient to enable the examining staff of the Berlin Annex of the German Patent Office, as it stands at the date on which the Convention is opened for signature, to be fully employed.

(d) The Federal Republic of Germany shall bear any additional costs incurred by the European Patent Organisation in setting up and maintaining the sub-office in Berlin.

2 Amended by the Act revising the European Patent Convention of 29.11.2000.

SECTION II

[1.761]
Subject to the provisions of Sections III and IV, the States parties to the Convention shall, on behalf of their central industrial property offices, renounce in favour of the European Patent Office any activities as International Preliminary Examining Authorities under the Patent Co-operation Treaty. This obligation shall apply only to the extent to which the European Patent Office may examine European patent applications in accordance with *Article 162, paragraph 2*, of the Convention and shall not apply until two years after the date on which the European Patent Office has begun examining activities in the areas of technology concerned, on the basis of a five-year plan which shall progressively extend the activities of the European Patent Office to all areas of technology and which may be amended only by decision of the Administrative Council. The procedures for implementing this obligation shall be determined by decision of the Administrative Council.

SECTION III

[1.762]
(1) The central industrial property office of any State party to the Convention in which the official language is not one of the official languages of the European Patent Office, shall be authorised to act as an International Searching Authority and as an International Preliminary Examining Authority under the Patent Co-operation Treaty. Such authorisation shall be subject to an undertaking by the State concerned to restrict such activities to international applications filed by nationals or residents of such State and by nationals or residents of States parties to the Convention which are adjacent to that State. The Administrative Council may decide to authorise the central industrial property office of any State party to the Convention to extend such activities to cover such international applications as may be filed by nationals or residents of any non-Contracting State having the same official language as the Contracting State in question and drawn up in that language.

(2) For the purpose of harmonising search activities under the Patent Co-operation Treaty within the framework of the European system for the grant of patents, co-operation shall be established between the European Patent Office and any central industrial property office authorised under this

Section. Such co-operation shall be based on a special agreement which may cover eg, search procedures and methods, qualifications required for the recruitment and training of examiners, guidelines for the exchange of search and other services between the offices as well as other measures needed to establish the required control and supervision.

SECTION IV

[1.763]

(1)

(a) For the purpose of facilitating the adaptation of the national patent offices of the States parties to the Convention to the European patent system, the Administrative Council may, if it considers it desirable, and subject to the conditions set out below, entrust the central industrial property offices of such of those States in which it is possible to conduct the proceedings in one of the official languages of the European Patent Office with tasks concerning the examination of European patent applications drawn up in that language which, pursuant to Article 18, paragraph 2, of the Convention, shall, as a general rule, be entrusted to a member of the Examining Division. Such tasks shall be carried out within the framework of the proceedings for grant laid down in the Convention; decisions on such applications shall be taken by the Examining Division composed in accordance with Article 18, paragraph 2.

(b) Tasks entrusted under sub-paragraph (a) shall not be in respect of more than 40% of the total number of European patent applications filed; tasks entrusted to any one State shall not be in respect of more than one-third of the total number of European patent applications filed. These tasks shall be entrusted for a period of 15 years from the opening of the European Patent Office and shall be reduced progressively (in principle by 20% a year) to zero during the last 5 years of the period.

(c) The Administrative Council shall decide, while taking into account the provisions of sub-paragraph (b), upon the nature, origin and number of the European patent applications in respect of which examining tasks may be entrusted to the central industrial property office of each of the Contracting States mentioned above.

(d) The above implementing procedures shall be set out in a special agreement between the central industrial property office of the Contracting State concerned and the European Patent Organisation.

(e) An office with which such a special agreement has been concluded may act as an International Preliminary Examining Authority under the Patent Co-operation Treaty, until the expiry of the period of 15 years.

(2)

(a) If the Administrative Council considers that it is compatible with the proper functioning of the European Patent Office, and in order to alleviate the difficulties which may arise for certain Contracting States from the application of Section I, paragraph 2, it may entrust searching in respect of European patent applications to the central industrial property offices of those States in which the official language is one of the official languages of the European Patent Office, provided that these offices possess the necessary qualifications for appointment as an International Searching Authority in accordance with the conditions laid down in the Patent Co-operation Treaty.

(b) In carrying out such work, undertaken under the responsibility of the European Patent Office, the central industrial property offices concerned shall adhere to the guidelines applicable to the drawing up of the European search report.

(c) The provisions of paragraph 1(b), second sentence, and sub-paragraph (d) of this Section shall apply to this paragraph.

SECTION V

[1.764]

(1) The sub-office referred to in Section I, paragraph 1(c), shall be authorised to carry out searches, among the documentation which is at its disposal and which is in the official language of the State in which the sub-office is located, in respect of European patent applications filed by nationals and residents of that State. This authorisation shall be on the understanding that the procedure for the grant of European patents will not be delayed and that additional costs will not be incurred for the European Patent Organisation.

(2) The sub-office referred to in paragraph 1 shall be authorised to carry out, at the option of an applicant for a European patent and at his expense, a search on his patent application among the documentation referred to in paragraph 1. This authorisation shall be effective until the search provided for in Article 92 of the Convention has been extended, in accordance with Section VI, to cover such documentation and shall be on the understanding that the procedure for the grant of European patents will not be delayed.

(3) The Administrative Council may also extend the authorisations provided for in paragraphs 1 and 2, under the conditions of those paragraphs, to the central industrial property office of a Contracting State which does not have as an official language one of the official languages of the European Patent Office.

SECTION VI

[1.765]
The search provided for in Article 92 of the Convention shall, in principle, be extended, in respect of all European patent applications, to published patents, published patent applications and other relevant documents of Contracting States not included in the search documentation of the European Patent Office on the date referred to in *Article 162, paragraph 1*, of the Convention. The extent, conditions and timing of any such extension shall be determined by the Administrative Council on the basis of a study concerning particularly the technical and financial aspects.

SECTION VII

[1.766]
The provisions of this Protocol shall prevail over any contradictory provisions of the Convention.

SECTION VIII

[1.767]
The decisions of the Administrative Council provided for in this Protocol shall require a three-quarters majority (Article 35, paragraph 2, of the Convention). The provisions governing the weighting of votes (Article 36 of the Convention) shall apply.

PROTOCOL ON THE INTERPRETATION OF ARTICLE 69 OF THE CONVENTION

as revised by the Act revising the EPC of 29 November 2000[1]

NOTES
The original source of this Protocol is the European Patent Office (EPO) website at www.epo.org.

1 The new text of the Protocol adopted by the Administrative Council of the European Patent Organisation in its decision of 28 June 2001 (see OJ EPO 2001, Special edition No 4, p. 55) has become an integral part of the Revision Act of 29 November 2000 under Article 3(2), second sentence, of that Act.

[1.768]
Article 1
General principles
Article 69 should not be interpreted as meaning that the extent of the protection conferred by a European patent is to be understood as that defined by the strict, literal meaning of the wording used in the claims, the description and drawings being employed only for the purpose of resolving an ambiguity found in the claims. Nor should it be taken to mean that the claims serve only as a guideline and that the actual protection conferred may extend to what, from a consideration of the description and drawings by a person skilled in the art, the patent proprietor has contemplated. On the contrary, it is to be interpreted as defining a position between these extremes which combines a fair protection for the patent proprietor with a reasonable degree of legal certainty for third parties.

[1.769]
Article 2
Equivalents
For the purpose of determining the extent of protection conferred by a European patent, due account shall be taken of any element which is equivalent to an element specified in the claims.

PROTOCOL ON THE STAFF COMPLEMENT OF THE EUROPEAN PATENT OFFICE AT THE HAGUE (PROTOCOL ON STAFF COMPLEMENT)

of 29 November 2000[1]

NOTES
The original source of this Protocol is the European Patent Office (EPO) website at www.epo.org.

[1.770]
The European Patent Organisation shall ensure that the proportion of European Patent Office posts assigned to the duty station at The Hague as defined under the 2000 establishment plan and table of posts remains substantially unchanged. Any change in the number of posts assigned to the duty station at The Hague resulting in a deviation of more than ten per cent of that proportion, which proves necessary for the proper functioning of the European Patent Office, shall be subject to a decision by the Administrative Council of the Organisation on a proposal from the President of the European Patent Office after consultation with the Governments of the Federal Republic of Germany and the Kingdom of the Netherlands.[2]

[1] The new text of the Protocol adopted by the Administrative Council of the European Patent Organisation in its decision of 28 June 2001 (see OJ EPO 2001, Special edition No 4, p 55) has become an integral part of the Revision Act of 29 November 2000 under Article 3(2), second sentence, of that Act.

[2] Annexed to the European Patent Convention as an integral part thereof by the Act revising the European Patent Convention of 29.11.2000.

DECISION OF THE ADMINISTRATIVE COUNCIL

of 28 June 2001

on the transitional provisions under Article 7 of the Act revising the European Patent Convention of 29 November 2000

NOTES
The original source of this Decision is the European Patent Office (EPO) website at www.epo.org.

THE ADMINISTRATIVE COUNCIL OF THE EUROPEAN PATENT ORGANISATION,

Having regard to Article 7, paragraph 2, of the Act revising the European Patent Convention of 29 November 2000 ("Revision Act"),

On a proposal from the President of the European Patent Office, Having regard to the opinion of the Committee on Patent Law,

HAS DECIDED AS FOLLOWS:

[1.771]
Article 1
In accordance with Article 7, paragraph 1, second sentence, of the Revision Act, the following transitional provisions shall apply to the amended and new provisions of the European Patent Convention specified below:

1.
Articles 14(3) to (6), 51, 52, 53, 54(3) and (4), 61, 67, 68 and 69, the Protocol on the Interpretation of Article 69, and Articles 70, 86, 88, 90, 92, 93, 94, 97, 98, 106, 108, 110, 115, 117, 119, 120, 123, 124, 127, 128, 129, 133, 135, 137 and 141 shall apply to European patent applications pending at the time of their entry into force and to European patents already granted at that time. However, Article 54(4) of the version of the Convention in force before that time shall continue to apply to these applications and patents.

2.
Articles 65, 99, 101, 103, 104, 105, 105a-c and 138 shall apply to European patents already granted at the time of their entry into force and to European patents granted in respect of European patent applications pending at that time.

3.
Article 54(5) shall apply to European patent applications pending at the time of its entry into force, in so far as a decision on the grant of the patent has not yet been taken.

4.
Article 112a shall apply to decisions of the Boards of Appeal taken as from the date of its entry into force.

5.
Articles 121 and 122 shall apply to European patent applications pending at the time of their entry into force and to European patents already granted at that time, in so far as the time limits for requesting further processing or re-establishment of rights have not yet expired at that time.

6.
Articles 150 to 153 shall apply to international applications pending at the time of their entry into force. However, Articles 154(3) and 155(3) of the version of the Convention in force before that time shall continue to apply to these applications.

[1.772]
Article 2
This decision shall enter into force upon the entry into force of the revised text of the Convention in accordance with Article 8 of the Revision Act.
Done at Munich, 28 June 2001

PATENT CO-OPERATION TREATY (PCT)

(Done at Washington on June 19, 1970, amended on September 28, 1979, modified on February 3, 1984, and October 3, 2001)

(as in force from April 1, 2002)

NOTES
The original source for this Treaty is the World Intellectual Property Organisation (WIPO).

INTRODUCTORY PROVISIONS

[1.773]
Article 1
Establishment of a Union
(1) The States party to this Treaty (hereinafter called "the Contracting States") constitute a Union for co-operation in the filing, searching, and examination, of applications for the protection of inventions, and for rendering special technical services. The Union shall be known as the International Patent Co-operation Union.
(2) No provision of this Treaty shall be interpreted as diminishing the rights under the Paris Convention for the Protection of Industrial Property of any national or resident of any country party to that Convention.

[1.774]
Article 2
Definitions
For the purposes of this Treaty and the Regulations and unless expressly stated otherwise—

(i) "application" means an application for the protection of an invention; references to an "application" shall be construed as references to applications for patents for inventions, inventors' certificates, utility certificates, utility models, patents or certificates of addition, inventors' certificates of addition, and utility certificates of addition;
(ii) references to a "patent" shall be construed as references to patents for inventions, inventors' certificates, utility certificates, utility models, patents or certificates of addition, inventors' certificates of addition, and utility certificates of addition;
(iii) "national patent" means a patent granted by a national authority;
(iv) "regional patent" means a patent granted by a national or an intergovernmental authority having the power to grant patents effective in more than one State;
(v) "regional application" means an application for a regional patent;
(vi) references to a "national application" shall be construed as references to applications for national patents and regional patents, other than applications filed under this Treaty;
(vii) "international application" means an application filed under this Treaty;
(viii) references to an "application" shall be construed as references to international applications and national applications;
(ix) references to a "patent" shall be construed as references to national patents and regional patents;
(x) references to "national law" shall be construed as references to the national law of a Contracting State or, where a regional application or a regional patent is involved, to the treaty providing for the filing of regional applications or the granting of regional patents;
(xi) "priority date," for the purposes of computing time limits, means—
   (a) where the international application contains a priority claim under Article 8, the filing date of the application whose priority is so claimed;
   (b) where the international application contains several priority claims under Article 8, the filing date of the earliest application whose priority is so claimed;
   (c) where the international application does not contain any priority claim under Article 8, the international filing date of such application;
(xii) "national Office" means the government authority of a Contracting State entrusted with the granting of patents; references to a "national Office" shall be construed as referring also to

any intergovernmental authority which several States have entrusted with the task of granting regional patents, provided that at least one of those States is a Contracting State, and provided that the said States have authorised that authority to assume the obligations and exercise the powers which this Treaty and the Regulations provide for in respect of national Offices;

(xiii) "designated Office" means the national Office of or acting for the State designated by the applicant under Chapter I of this Treaty;

(xiv) "elected Office" means the national Office of or acting for the State elected by the applicant under Chapter II of this Treaty;

(xv) "receiving Office" means the national Office or the intergovernmental organisation with which the international application has been filed;

(xvi) "Union" means the International Patent Co-operation Union;

(xvii) "Assembly" means the Assembly of the Union;

(xviii) "Organisation" means the World Intellectual Property Organisation;

(xix) "International Bureau" means the International Bureau of the Organisation and, as long as it subsists, the United International Bureaux for the Protection of Intellectual Property (BIRPI);

(xx) "Director General" means the Director General of the Organisation and, as long as BIRPI subsists, the Director of BIRPI.

CHAPTER I
INTERNATIONAL APPLICATION AND INTERNATIONAL SEARCH

[1.775]
Article 3
The International Application

(1) Applications for the protection of inventions in any of the Contracting States may be filed as international applications under this Treaty.

(2) An international application shall contain, as specified in this Treaty and the Regulations, a request, a description, one or more claims, one or more drawings (where required), and an abstract.

(3) The abstract merely serves the purpose of technical information and cannot be taken into account for any other purpose, particularly not for the purpose of interpreting the scope of the protection sought.

(4) The international application shall—

(i) be in a prescribed language;

(ii) comply with the prescribed physical requirements;

(iii) comply with the prescribed requirement of unity of invention;

(iv) be subject to the payment of the prescribed fees.

[1.776]
Article 4
The Request

(1) The request shall contain—

(i) a petition to the effect that the international application be processed according to this Treaty;

(ii) the designation of the Contracting State or States in which protection for the invention is desired on the basis of the international application ("designated States"); if for any designated State a regional patent is available and the applicant wishes to obtain a regional patent rather than a national patent, the request shall so indicate; if, under a treaty concerning a regional patent, the applicant cannot limit his application to certain of the States party to that treaty, designation of one of those States and the indication of the wish to obtain the regional patent shall be treated as designation of all the States party to that treaty; if, under the national law of the designated State, the designation of that State has the effect of an application for a regional patent, the designation of the said State shall be treated as an indication of the wish to obtain the regional patent;

(iii) the name of and other prescribed data concerning the applicant and the agent (if any);

(iv) the title of the invention;

(v) the name of and other prescribed data concerning the inventor where the national law of at least one of the designated States requires that these indications be furnished at the time of filing a national application.

Otherwise, the said indications may be furnished either in the request or in separate notices addressed to each designated Office whose national law requires the furnishing of the said indications but allows that they be furnished at a time later than that of the filing of a national application.

(2) Every designation shall be subject to the payment of the prescribed fee within the prescribed time limit.

(3) Unless the applicant asks for any of the other kinds of protection referred to in Article 43, designation shall mean that the desired protection consists of the grant of a patent by or for the designated State. For the purposes of this paragraph, Article 2(ii) shall not apply.

(4) Failure to indicate in the request the name and other prescribed data concerning the inventor shall have no consequence in any designated State whose national law requires the furnishing of the said indications but allows that they be furnished at a time later than that of the filing of a national application. Failure to furnish the said indications in a separate notice shall have no consequence in any designated State whose national law does not require the furnishing of the said indications.

[1.777]
Article 5
The Description
The description shall disclose the invention in a manner sufficiently clear and complete for the invention to be carried out by a person skilled in the art.

[1.778]
Article 6
The Claims
The claim or claims shall define the matter for which protection is sought. Claims shall be clear and concise. They shall be fully supported by the description.

[1.779]
Article 7
The Drawings
(1) Subject to the provisions of paragraph (2)(ii), drawings shall be required when they are necessary for the understanding of the invention.
(2) Where, without being necessary for the understanding of the invention, the nature of the invention admits of illustration by drawings—
- (i) the applicant may include such drawings in the international application when filed,
- (ii) any designated Office may require that the applicant file such drawings with it within the prescribed time limit.

[1.780]
Article 8
Claiming Priority
(1) The international application may contain a declaration, as prescribed in the Regulations, claiming the priority of one or more earlier applications filed in or for any country party to the Paris Convention for the Protection of Industrial Property.
(2)
- (a) Subject to the provisions of sub-paragraph (b), the conditions for, and the effect of, any priority claim declared under paragraph (1) shall be as provided in Article 4 of the Stockholm Act of the Paris Convention for the Protection of Industrial Property.
- (b) The international application for which the priority of one or more earlier applications filed in or for a Contracting State is claimed may contain the designation of that State. Where, in the international application, the priority of one or more national applications filed in or for a designated State is claimed, or where the priority of an international application having designated only one State is claimed, the conditions for, and the effect of, the priority claim in that State shall be governed by the national law of that State.

[1.781]
Article 9
The Applicant
(1) Any resident or national of a Contracting State may file an international application.
(2) The Assembly may decide to allow the residents and the nationals of any country party to the Paris Convention for the Protection of Industrial Property which is not party to this Treaty to file international applications.
(3) The concepts of residence and nationality, and the application of those concepts in cases where there are several applicants or where the applicants are not the same for all the designated States, are defined in the Regulations.

[1.782]
Article 10
The Receiving Office
The international application shall be filed with the prescribed receiving Office, which will check and process it as provided in this Treaty and the Regulations.

[1.783]
Article 11
Filing Date and Effects of the International Application
(1) The receiving Office shall accord as the international filing date the date of receipt of the international application, provided that that Office has found that, at the time of receipt—
- (i) the applicant does not obviously lack, for reasons of residence or nationality, the right to file an international application with the receiving Office,

(ii) the international application is in the prescribed language,
(iii) the international application contains at least the following elements—
(a) an indication that it is intended as an international application,
(b) the designation of at least one Contracting State,
(c) the name of the applicant, as prescribed,
(d) a part which on the face of it appears to be a description,
(e) a part which on the face of it appears to be a claim or claims.

(2)
(a) If the receiving Office finds that the international application did not, at the time of receipt, fulfil the requirements listed in paragraph (1), it shall, as provided in the Regulations, invite the applicant to file the required correction.
(b) If the applicant complies with the invitation, as provided in the Regulations, the receiving Office shall accord as the international filing date the date of receipt of the required correction.

(3) Subject to Article 64(4), any international application fulfilling the requirements listed in items (i) to (iii) of paragraph (1) and accorded an international filing date shall have the effect of a regular national application in each designated State as of the international filing date, which date shall be considered to be the actual filing date in each designated State.
(4) Any international application fulfilling the requirements listed in items (i) to (iii) of paragraph (1) shall be equivalent to a regular national filing within the meaning of the Paris Convention for the Protection of Industrial Property.

[1.784]
Article 12
Transmittal of the International Application to the International Bureau and the International Searching Authority
(1) One copy of the international application shall be kept by the receiving Office ("home copy"), one copy ("record copy") shall be transmitted to the International Bureau, and another copy ("search copy") shall be transmitted to the competent International Searching Authority referred to in Article 16, as provided in the Regulations.
(2) The record copy shall be considered the true copy of the international application.
(3) The international application shall be considered withdrawn if the record copy has not been received by the International Bureau within the prescribed time limit.

[1.785]
Article 13
Availability of Copy of the International Application to Designated Offices
(1) Any designated Office may ask the International Bureau to transmit to it a copy of the international application prior to the communication provided for in Article 20, and the International Bureau shall transmit such copy to the designated Office as soon as possible after the expiration of one year from the priority date.
(2)
(a) The applicant may, at any time, transmit a copy of his international application to any designated Office.
(b) The applicant may, at any time, ask the International Bureau to transmit a copy of his international application to any designated Office, and the International Bureau shall transmit such copy to the designated Office as soon as possible.
(c) Any national Office may notify the International Bureau that it does not wish to receive copies as provided for in sub-paragraph (b), in which case that sub-paragraph shall not be applicable in respect of that Office.

[1.786]
Article 14
Certain Defects in the International Application
(1)
(a) The receiving Office shall check whether the international application contains any of the following defects, that is to say—
(i) it is not signed as provided in the Regulations;
(ii) it does not contain the prescribed indications concerning the applicant;
(iii) it does not contain a title;
(iv) it does not contain an abstract;
(v) it does not comply to the extent provided in the Regulations with the prescribed physical requirements.
(b) If the receiving Office finds any of the said defects, it shall invite the applicant to correct the international application within the prescribed time limit, failing which that application shall be considered withdrawn and the receiving Office shall so declare.

(2) If the international application refers to drawings which, in fact, are not included in that application, the receiving Office shall notify the applicant accordingly and he may furnish them within the prescribed time limit and, if he does, the international filing date shall be the date on which the drawings are received by the receiving Office. Otherwise, any reference to the said drawings shall be considered non-existent.

(3)

(a) If the receiving Office finds that, within the prescribed time limits, the fees prescribed under Article 3(4)(iv) have not been paid, or no fee prescribed under Article 4(2) has been paid in respect of any of the designated States, the international application shall be considered withdrawn and the receiving Office shall so declare.

(b) If the receiving Office finds that the fee prescribed under Article 4(2) has been paid in respect of one or more (but less than all) designated States within the prescribed time limit, the designation of those States in respect of which it has not been paid within the prescribed time limit shall be considered withdrawn and the receiving Office shall so declare.

(4) If, after having accorded an international filing date to the international application, the receiving Office finds, within the prescribed time limit, that any of the requirements listed in items (i) to (iii) of Article 11(1) was not complied with at that date, the said application shall be considered withdrawn and the receiving Office shall so declare.

[1.787]
Article 15
The International Search

(1) Each international application shall be the subject of international search.

(2) The objective of the international search is to discover relevant prior art.

(3) International search shall be made on the basis of the claims, with due regard to the description and the drawings (if any).

(4) The International Searching Authority referred to in Article 16 shall endeavour to discover as much of the relevant prior art as its facilities permit, and shall, in any case, consult the documentation specified in the Regulations.

(5)

(a) If the national law of the Contracting State so permits, the applicant who files a national application with the national Office of or acting for such State may, subject to the conditions provided for in such law, request that a search similar to an international search ("international-type search") be carried out on such application.

(b) If the national law of the Contracting State so permits, the national Office of or acting for such State may subject any national application filed with it to an international-type search.

(c) The international-type search shall be carried out by the International Searching Authority referred to in Article 16 which would be competent for an international search if the national application were an international application and were filed with the Office referred to in sub-paragraphs (a) and (b). If the national application is in a language which the International Searching Authority considers it is not equipped to handle, the international-type search shall be carried out on a translation prepared by the applicant in a language prescribed for international applications and which the International Searching Authority has undertaken to accept for international applications. The national application and the translation, when required, shall be presented in the form prescribed for international applications.

[1.788]
Article 16
The International Searching Authority

(1) International search shall be carried out by an International Searching Authority, which may be either a national Office or an intergovernmental organisation, such as the International Patent Institute, whose tasks include the establishing of documentary search reports on prior art with respect to inventions which are the subject of applications.

(2) If, pending the establishment of a single International Searching Authority, there are several International Searching Authorities, each receiving Office shall, in accordance with the provisions of the applicable agreement referred to in paragraph (3)(b), specify the International Searching Authority or Authorities competent for the searching of international applications filed with such Office.

(3)

(a) International Searching Authorities shall be appointed by the Assembly. Any national Office and any intergovernmental organisation satisfying the requirements referred to in sub-paragraph (c) may be appointed as International Searching Authority.

(b) Appointment shall be conditional on the consent of the national Office or intergovernmental organisation to be appointed and the conclusion of an agreement, subject to approval by the Assembly, between such Office or organisation and the

International Bureau. The agreement shall specify the rights and obligations of the parties, in particular, the formal undertaking by the said Office or organisation to apply and observe all the common rules of international search.

(c) The Regulations prescribe the minimum requirements, particularly as to manpower and documentation, which any Office or organisation must satisfy before it can be appointed and must continue to satisfy while it remains appointed.

(d) Appointment shall be for a fixed period of time and may be extended for further periods.

(e) Before the Assembly makes a decision on the appointment of any national Office or intergovernmental organisation, or on the extension of its appointment, or before it allows any such appointment to lapse, the Assembly shall hear the interested Office or organisation and seek the advice of the Committee for Technical Co-operation referred to in Article 56 once that Committee has been established.

[1.789]
Article 17
Procedure Before the International Searching Authority

(1) Procedure before the International Searching Authority shall be governed by the provisions of this Treaty, the Regulations, and the agreement which the International Bureau shall conclude, subject to this Treaty and the Regulations, with the said Authority.

(2)

(a) If the International Searching Authority considers

(i) that the international application relates to a subject matter which the International Searching Authority is not required, under the Regulations, to search, and in the particular case decides not to search, or

(ii) that the description, the claims, or the drawings, fail to comply with the prescribed requirements to such an extent that a meaningful search could not be carried out,

the said Authority shall so declare and shall notify the applicant and the International Bureau that no international search report will be established.

(b) If any of the situations referred to in sub-paragraph (a) is found to exist in connection with certain claims only, the international search report shall so indicate in respect of such claims, whereas, for the other claims, the said report shall be established as provided in Article 18.

(3)

(a) If the International Searching Authority considers that the international application does not comply with the requirement of unity of invention as set forth in the Regulations, it shall invite the applicant to pay additional fees. The International Searching Authority shall establish the international search report on those parts of the international application which relate to the invention first mentioned in the claims ("main invention") and, provided the required additional fees have been paid within the prescribed time limit, on those parts of the international application which relate to inventions in respect of which the said fees were paid.

(b) The national law of any designated State may provide that, where the national Office of that State finds the invitation, referred to in sub-paragraph (a), of the International Searching Authority justified and where the applicant has not paid all additional fees, those parts of the international application which consequently have not been searched shall, as far as effects in that State are concerned, be considered withdrawn unless a special fee is paid by the applicant to the national Office of that State.

[1.790]
Article 18
The International Search Report

(1) The international search report shall be established within the prescribed time limit and in the prescribed form.

(2) The international search report shall, as soon as it has been established, be transmitted by the International Searching Authority to the applicant and the International Bureau.

(3) The international search report or the declaration referred to in Article 17(2)(a) shall be translated as provided in the Regulations. The translations shall be prepared by or under the responsibility of the International Bureau.

[1.791]
Article 19
Amendment of the Claims Before the International Bureau

(1) The applicant shall, after having received the international search report, be entitled to one opportunity to amend the claims of the international application by filing amendments with the International Bureau within the prescribed time limit. He may, at the same time, file a brief statement, as provided in the Regulations, explaining the amendments and indicating any impact that such amendments might have on the description and the drawings.

(2) The amendments shall not go beyond the disclosure in the international application as filed.

(3) If the national law of any designated State permits amendments to go beyond the said disclosure, failure to comply with paragraph (2) shall have no consequence in that State.

[1.792]
Article 20
Communication to Designated Offices

(1)

(a) The international application, together with the international search report (including any indication referred to in Article 17(2)(b)) or the declaration referred to in Article 17(2)(a), shall be communicated to each designated Office, as provided in the Regulations, unless the designated Office waives such requirement in its entirety or in part.

(b) The communication shall include the translation (as prescribed) of the said report or declaration.

(2) If the claims have been amended by virtue of Article 19(1), the communication shall either contain the full text of the claims both as filed and as amended or shall contain the full text of the claims as filed and specify the amendments, and shall include the statement, if any, referred to in Article 19(1).

(3) At the request of the designated Office or the applicant, the International Searching Authority shall send to the said Office or the applicant, respectively, copies of the documents cited in the international search report, as provided in the Regulations.

[1.793]
Article 21
International Publication

(1) The International Bureau shall publish international applications.

(2)

(a) Subject to the exceptions provided for in sub-paragraph (b) and in Article 64(3), the international publication of the international application shall be effected promptly after the expiration of 18 months from the priority date of that application.

(b) The applicant may ask the International Bureau to publish his international application any time before the expiration of the time limit referred to in sub-paragraph (a). The International Bureau shall proceed accordingly, as provided in the Regulations.

(3) The international search report or the declaration referred to in Article 17(2)(a) shall be published as prescribed in the Regulations.

(4) The language and form of the international publication and other details are governed by the Regulations.

(5) There shall be no international publication if the international application is withdrawn or is considered withdrawn before the technical preparations for publication have been completed.

(6) If the international application contains expressions or drawings which, in the opinion of the International Bureau, are contrary to morality or public order, or if, in its opinion, the international application contains disparaging statements as defined in the Regulations, it may omit such expressions, drawings, and statements, from its publications, indicating the place and number of words or drawings omitted, and furnishing, upon request, individual copies of the passages omitted.

[1.794]
Article 22
Copy, Translation, and Fee, to Designated Offices

(1) The applicant shall furnish a copy of the international application (unless the communication provided for in Article 20 has already taken place) and a translation thereof (as prescribed), and pay the national fee (if any), to each designated Office not later than at the expiration of 30 months[1] from the priority date. Where the national law of the designated State requires the indication of the name of and other prescribed data concerning the inventor but allows that these indications be furnished at a time later than that of the filing of a national application, the applicant shall, unless they were contained in the request, furnish the said indications to the national Office of or acting for the State not later than at the expiration of 30[1] months from the priority date.

(2) Where the International Searching Authority makes a declaration, under Article 17(2)(a), that no international search report will be established, the time limit for performing the acts referred to in paragraph (1) of this Article shall be the same as that provided for in paragraph (1).

(3) Any national law may, for performing the acts referred to in paragraphs (1) or (2), fix time limits which expire later than the time limit provided for in those paragraphs.

NOTES

[1] The 30-month time limit, as in force from April 1, 2002, does not apply in respect of any designated Office which has notified the International Bureau of incompatibility with the national law applied by that Office. The 20-month time limit, as in force until March 31, 2002, continues to apply after that date in respect of any such designated Office for as long as Article 22(1), as modified, continues not to be compatible with the applicable national law. Notifications concerning any such incompatibility and any withdrawals of such notifications are published in the Gazette.

[1.795]
Article 23
Delaying of National Procedure

(1) No designated Office shall process or examine the international application prior to the expiration of the applicable time limit under Article 22.

(2) Notwithstanding the provisions of paragraph (1), any designated Office may, on the express request of the applicant, process or examine the international application at any time.

[1.796]
Article 24
Possible Loss of Effect in Designated States

(1) Subject, in case (ii) below, to the provisions of Article 25, the effect of the international application provided for in Article 11(3) shall cease in any designated State with the same consequences as the withdrawal of any national application in that State—

(i) if the applicant withdraws his international application or the designation of that State;

(ii) if the international application is considered withdrawn by virtue of Articles 12(3), 14(1)(b), 14(3)(a), or 14(4), or if the designation of that State is considered withdrawn by virtue of Article 14(3)(b);

(iii) if the applicant fails to perform the acts referred to in Article 22 within the applicable time limit.

(2) Notwithstanding the provisions of paragraph (1), any designated Office may maintain the effect provided for in Article 11(3) even where such effect is not required to be maintained by virtue of Article 25(2).

[1.797]
Article 25
Review by Designated Offices

(1)

(a) Where the receiving Office has refused to accord an international filing date or has declared that the international application is considered withdrawn, or where the International Bureau has made a finding under Article 12(3), the International Bureau shall promptly send, at the request of the applicant, copies of any document in the file to any of the designated Offices named by the applicant.

(b) Where the receiving Office has declared that the designation of any given State is considered withdrawn, the International Bureau shall promptly send, at the request of the applicant, copies of any document in the file to the national Office of such State.

(c) The request under sub-paragraphs (a) or (b) shall be presented within the prescribed time limit.

(2)

(a) Subject to the provisions of sub-paragraph (b), each designated Office shall, provided that the national fee (if any) has been paid and the appropriate translation (as prescribed) has been furnished within the prescribed time limit, decide whether the refusal, declaration, or finding, referred to in paragraph (1) was justified under the provisions of this Treaty and the Regulations, and, if it finds that the refusal or declaration was the result of an error or omission on the part of the receiving Office or that the finding was the result of an error or omission on the part of the International Bureau, it shall, as far as effects in the State of the designated Office are concerned, treat the international application as if such error or omission had not occurred.

(b) Where the record copy has reached the International Bureau after the expiration of the time limit prescribed under Article 12(3) on account of any error or omission on the part of the applicant, the provisions of sub-paragraph (a) shall apply only under the circumstances referred to in Article 48(2).

[1.798]
Article 26
Opportunity to Correct Before Designated Offices

No designated Office shall reject an international application on the grounds of non-compliance with the requirements of this Treaty and the Regulations without first giving the applicant the opportunity to correct the said application to the extent and according to the procedure provided by the national law for the same or comparable situations in respect of national applications.

[1.799]
Article 27
National Requirements

(1) No national law shall require compliance with requirements relating to the form or contents of the international application different from or additional to those which are provided for in this Treaty and the Regulations.

(2) The provisions of paragraph (1) neither affect the application of the provisions of Article 7(2) nor preclude any national law from requiring, once the processing of the international application has started in the designated Office, the furnishing—

(i) when the applicant is a legal entity, of the name of an officer entitled to represent such legal entity,
(ii) of documents not part of the international application but which constitute proof of allegations or statements made in that application, including the confirmation of the international application by the signature of the applicant when that application, as filed, was signed by his representative or agent.

(3) Where the applicant, for the purposes of any designated State, is not qualified according to the national law of that State to file a national application because he is not the inventor, the international application may be rejected by the designated Office.

(4) Where the national law provides, in respect of the form or contents of national applications, for requirements which, from the viewpoint of applicants, are more favourable than the requirements provided for by this Treaty and the Regulations in respect of international applications, the national Office, the courts and any other competent organs of or acting for the designated State may apply the former requirements, instead of the latter requirements, to international applications, except where the applicant insists that the requirements provided for by this Treaty and the Regulations be applied to his international application.

(5) Nothing in this Treaty and the Regulations is intended to be construed as prescribing anything that would limit the freedom of each Contracting State to prescribe such substantive conditions of patentability as it desires. In particular, any provision in this Treaty and the Regulations concerning the definition of prior art is exclusively for the purposes of the international procedure and, consequently, any Contracting State is free to apply, when determining the patentability of an invention claimed in an international application, the criteria of its national law in respect of prior art and other conditions of patentability not constituting requirements as to the form and contents of applications.

(6) The national law may require that the applicant furnish evidence in respect of any substantive condition of patentability prescribed by such law.

(7) Any receiving Office or, once the processing of the international application has started in the designated Office, that Office may apply the national law as far as it relates to any requirement that the applicant be represented by an agent having the right to represent applicants before the said Office and/or that the applicant have an address in the designated State for the purpose of receiving notifications.

(8) Nothing in this Treaty and the Regulations is intended to be construed as limiting the freedom of any Contracting State to apply measures deemed necessary for the preservation of its national security or to limit, for the protection of the general economic interests of that State, the right of its own residents or nationals to file international applications.

[1.800]
Article 28
Amendment of the Claims, the Description, and the Drawings, Before Designated Offices

(1) The applicant shall be given the opportunity to amend the claims, the description, and the drawings, before each designated Office within the prescribed time limit. No designated Office shall grant a patent, or refuse the grant of a patent, before such time limit has expired except with the express consent of the applicant.

(2) The amendments shall not go beyond the disclosure in the international application as filed unless the national law of the designated State permits them to go beyond the said disclosure.

(3) The amendments shall be in accordance with the national law of the designated State in all respects not provided for in this Treaty and the Regulations.

(4) Where the designated Office requires a translation of the international application, the amendments shall be in the language of the translation.

[1.801]
Article 29
Effects of the International Publication

(1) As far as the protection of any rights of the applicant in a designated State is concerned, the effects, in that State, of the international publication of an international application shall, subject to the provisions of paragraphs (2) to (4), be the same as those which the national law of the designated State provides for the compulsory national publication of unexamined national applications as such.

(2) If the language in which the international publication has been effected is different from the language in which publications under the national law are effected in the designated State, the said national law may provide that the effects provided for in paragraph (1) shall be applicable only from such time as—
(i) a translation into the latter language has been published as provided by the national law, or
(ii) a translation into the latter language has been made available to the public, by laying open for public inspection as provided by the national law, or
(iii) a translation into the latter language has been transmitted by the applicant to the actual or prospective unauthorised user of the invention claimed in the international application, or
(iv) both the acts described in (i) and (iii), or both the acts described in (ii) and (iii), have taken place.

(3) The national law of any designated State may provide that, where the international publication has been effected, on the request of the applicant, before the expiration of 18 months from the priority date, the effects provided for in paragraph (1) shall be applicable only from the expiration of 18 months from the priority date.
(4) The national law of any designated State may provide that the effects provided for in paragraph (1) shall be applicable only from the date on which a copy of the international application as published under Article 21 has been received in the national Office of or acting for such State. The said Office shall publish the date of receipt in its gazette as soon as possible.

[1.802]
Article 30
Confidential Nature of the International Application

(1)
- (a) Subject to the provisions of sub-paragraph (b), the International Bureau and the International Searching Authorities shall not allow access by any person or authority to the international application before the international publication of that application, unless requested or authorised by the applicant.
- (b) The provisions of sub-paragraph (a) shall not apply to any transmittal to the competent International Searching Authority, to transmittals provided for under Article 13, and to communications provided for under Article 20.

(2)
- (a) No national Office shall allow access to the international application by third parties, unless requested or authorised by the applicant, before the earliest of the following dates—
  - (i) date of the international publication of the international application,
  - (ii) date of the receipt of the communication of the international application under Article 20,
  - (iii) date of the receipt of a copy of the international application under Article 22.
- (b) The provisions of sub-paragraph (a) shall not prevent any national Office from informing third parties that it has been designated, or from publishing that fact. Such information or publication may, however, contain only the following data: identification of the receiving Office, name of the applicant, international filing date, international application number, and title of the invention.
- (c) The provisions of sub-paragraph (a) shall not prevent any designated Office from allowing access to the international application for the purposes of the judicial authorities.

(3) The provisions of paragraph (2)(a) shall apply to any receiving Office except as far as transmittals provided for under Article 12(1) are concerned.
(4) For the purposes of this Article, the term "access" covers any means by which third parties may acquire cognizance, including individual communication and general publication, provided, however, that no national Office shall generally publish an international application or its translation before the international publication or, if international publication has not taken place by the expiration of 20 months from the priority date, before the expiration of 20 months from the said priority date.

CHAPTER II
INTERNATIONAL PRELIMINARY EXAMINATION

[1.803]
Article 31
Demand for International Preliminary Examination

(1) On the demand of the applicant, his international application shall be the subject of an international preliminary examination as provided in the following provisions and the Regulations.
(2)
- (a) Any applicant who is a resident or national, as defined in the Regulations, of a Contracting State bound by Chapter II, and whose international application has been filed with the receiving Office of or acting for such State, may make a demand for international preliminary examination.
- (b) The Assembly may decide to allow persons entitled to file international applications to make a demand for international preliminary examination even if they are residents or nationals of a State not party to this Treaty or not bound by Chapter II.

(3) The demand for international preliminary examination shall be made separately from the international application. The demand shall contain the prescribed particulars and shall be in the prescribed language and form.
(4)
- (a) The demand shall indicate the Contracting State or States in which the applicant intends to use the results of the international preliminary examination ("elected States"). Additional Contracting States may be elected later. Election may relate only to Contracting States already designated under Article 4.

(b) Applicants referred to in paragraph (2)(a) may elect any Contracting State bound by Chapter II. Applicants referred to in paragraph (2)(b) may elect only such Contracting States bound by Chapter II as have declared that they are prepared to be elected by such applicants.

(5) The demand shall be subject to the payment of the prescribed fees within the prescribed time limit.

(6)

(a) The demand shall be submitted to the competent International Preliminary Examining Authority referred to in Article 32.

(b) Any later election shall be submitted to the International Bureau.

(7) Each elected Office shall be notified of its election.

[1.804]
Article 32
The International Preliminary Examining Authority

(1) International preliminary examination shall be carried out by the International Preliminary Examining Authority.

(2) In the case of demands referred to in Article 31(2)(a), the receiving Office, and, in the case of demands referred to in Article 31(2)(b), the Assembly, shall, in accordance with the applicable agreement between the interested International Preliminary Examining Authority or Authorities and the International Bureau, specify the International Preliminary Examining Authority or Authorities competent for the preliminary examination.

(3) The provisions of Article 16(3) shall apply, *mutatis mutandis*, in respect of International Preliminary Examining Authorities.

[1.805]
Article 33
The International Preliminary Examination

(1) The objective of the international preliminary examination is to formulate a preliminary and non-binding opinion on the questions whether the claimed invention appears to be novel, to involve an inventive step (to be non-obvious), and to be industrially applicable.

(2) For the purposes of the international preliminary examination, a claimed invention shall be considered novel if it is not anticipated by the prior art as defined in the Regulations.

(3) For the purposes of the international preliminary examination, a claimed invention shall be considered to involve an inventive step if, having regard to the prior art as defined in the Regulations, it is not, at the prescribed relevant date, obvious to a person skilled in the art.

(4) For the purposes of the international preliminary examination, a claimed invention shall be considered industrially applicable if, according to its nature, it can be made or used (in the technological sense) in any kind of industry. "Industry" shall be understood in its broadest sense, as in the Paris Convention for the Protection of Industrial Property.

(5) The criteria described above merely serve the purposes of international preliminary examination. Any Contracting State may apply additional or different criteria for the purpose of deciding whether, in that State, the claimed invention is patentable or not.

(6) The international preliminary examination shall take into consideration all the documents cited in the international search report. It may take into consideration any additional documents considered to be relevant in the particular case.

[1.806]
Article 34
Procedure Before the International Preliminary Examining Authority

(1) Procedure before the International Preliminary Examining Authority shall be governed by the provisions of this Treaty, the Regulations, and the agreement which the International Bureau shall conclude, subject to this Treaty and the Regulations, with the said Authority.

(2)

(a) The applicant shall have a right to communicate orally and in writing with the International Preliminary Examining Authority.

(b) The applicant shall have a right to amend the claims, the description, and the drawings, in the prescribed manner and within the prescribed time limit, before the international preliminary examination report is established. The amendment shall not go beyond the disclosure in the international application as filed.

(c) The applicant shall receive at least one written opinion from the International Preliminary Examining Authority unless such Authority considers that all of the following conditions are fulfilled—

(i) the invention satisfies the criteria set forth in Article 33(1),

(ii) the international application complies with the requirements of this Treaty and the Regulations in so far as checked by that Authority,

(iii) no observations are intended to be made under Article 35(2), last sentence.

(d) The applicant may respond to the written opinion.

(3)

(a) If the International Preliminary Examining Authority considers that the international application does not comply with the requirement of unity of invention as set forth in the Regulations, it may invite the applicant, at his option, to restrict the claims so as to comply with the requirement or to pay additional fees.

(b) The national law of any elected State may provide that, where the applicant chooses to restrict the claims under sub-paragraph (a), those parts of the international application which, as a consequence of the restriction, are not to be the subject of international preliminary examination shall, as far as effects in that State are concerned, be considered withdrawn unless a special fee is paid by the applicant to the national Office of that State.

(c) If the applicant does not comply with the invitation referred to in sub-paragraph (a) within the prescribed time limit, the International Preliminary Examining Authority shall establish an international preliminary examination report on those parts of the international application which relate to what appears to be the main invention and shall indicate the relevant facts in the said report. The national law of any elected State may provide that, where its national Office finds the invitation of the International Preliminary Examining Authority justified, those parts of the international application which do not relate to the main invention shall, as far as effects in that State are concerned, be considered withdrawn unless a special fee is paid by the applicant to that Office.

(4)

(a) If the International Preliminary Examining Authority considers

(i) that the international application relates to a subject matter on which the International Preliminary Examining Authority is not required, under the Regulations, to carry out an international preliminary examination, and in the particular case decides not to carry out such examination, or

(ii) that the description, the claims, or the drawings, are so unclear, or the claims are so inadequately supported by the description, that no meaningful opinion can be formed on the novelty, inventive step (non-obviousness), or industrial applicability, of the claimed invention,

the said Authority shall not go into the questions referred to in Article 33(1) and shall inform the applicant of this opinion and the reasons therefor.

(b) If any of the situations referred to in sub-paragraph (a) is found to exist in, or in connection with, certain claims only, the provisions of that sub-paragraph shall apply only to the said claims.

[1.807]
Article 35
The International Preliminary Examination Report

(1) The international preliminary examination report shall be established within the prescribed time limit and in the prescribed form.

(2) The international preliminary examination report shall not contain any statement on the question whether the claimed invention is or seems to be patentable or unpatentable according to any national law. It shall state, subject to the provisions of paragraph (3), in relation to each claim, whether the claim appears to satisfy the criteria of novelty, inventive step (non-obviousness), and industrial applicability, as defined for the purposes of the international preliminary examination in Article 33(1) to (4). The statement shall be accompanied by the citation of the documents believed to support the stated conclusion with such explanations as the circumstances of the case may require. The statement shall also be accompanied by such other observations as the Regulations provide for.

(3)

(a) If, at the time of establishing the international preliminary examination report, the International Preliminary Examining Authority considers that any of the situations referred to in Article 34(4)(a) exists, that report shall state this opinion and the reasons therefor. It shall not contain any statement as provided in paragraph (2).

(b) If a situation under Article 34(4)(b) is found to exist, the international preliminary examination report shall, in relation to the claims in question, contain the statement as provided in sub-paragraph (a), whereas, in relation to the other claims, it shall contain the statement as provided in paragraph (2).

[1.808]
Article 36
Transmittal, Translation, and Communication, of the International Preliminary Examination Report

(1) The international preliminary examination report, together with the prescribed annexes, shall be transmitted to the applicant and to the International Bureau.

(2)

(a) The international preliminary examination report and its annexes shall be translated into the prescribed languages.

(b) Any translation of the said report shall be prepared by or under the responsibility of the International Bureau, whereas any translation of the said annexes shall be prepared by the applicant.

(3)

(a) The international preliminary examination report, together with its translation (as prescribed) and its annexes (in the original language), shall be communicated by the International Bureau to each elected Office.

(b) The prescribed translation of the annexes shall be transmitted within the prescribed time limit by the applicant to the elected Offices.

(4) The provisions of Article 20(3) shall apply, *mutatis mutandis*, to copies of any document which is cited in the international preliminary examination report and which was not cited in the international search report.

[1.809]
Article 37
Withdrawal of Demand or Election

(1) The applicant may withdraw any or all elections.

(2) If the election of all elected States is withdrawn, the demand shall be considered withdrawn.

(3)

(a) Any withdrawal shall be notified to the International Bureau.

(b) The elected Offices concerned and the International Preliminary Examining Authority concerned shall be notified accordingly by the International Bureau.

(4)

(a) Subject to the provisions of sub-paragraph (b), withdrawal of the demand or of the election of a Contracting State shall, unless the national law of that State provides otherwise, be considered to be withdrawal of the international application as far as that State is concerned.

(b) Withdrawal of the demand or of the election shall not be considered to be withdrawal of the international application if such withdrawal is effected prior to the expiration of the applicable time limit under Article 22; however, any Contracting State may provide in its national law that the aforesaid shall apply only if its national Office has received, within the said time limit, a copy of the international application, together with a translation (as prescribed), and the national fee.

[1.810]
Article 38
Confidential Nature of the International Preliminary Examination

(1) Neither the International Bureau nor the International Preliminary Examining Authority shall, unless requested or authorised by the applicant, allow access within the meaning, and with the proviso, of Article 30(4) to the file of the international preliminary examination by any person or authority at any time, except by the elected Offices once the international preliminary examination report has been established.

(2) Subject to the provisions of paragraph (1) and Articles 36(1) and (3) and 37(3)(b), neither the International Bureau nor the International Preliminary Examining Authority shall, unless requested or authorised by the applicant, give information on the issuance or non-issuance of an international preliminary examination report and on the withdrawal or non-withdrawal of the demand or of any election.

[1.811]
Article 39
Copy, Translation, and Fee, to Elected Offices

(1)

(a) If the election of any Contracting State has been effected prior to the expiration of the 19th month from the priority date, the provisions of Article 22 shall not apply to such State and the applicant shall furnish a copy of the international application (unless the communication under Article 20 has already taken place) and a translation thereof (as prescribed), and pay the national fee (if any), to each elected Office not later than at the expiration of 30 months from the priority date.

(b) Any national law may, for performing the acts referred to in sub-paragraph (a), fix time limits which expire later than the time limit provided for in that sub-paragraph.

(2) The effect provided for in Article 11(3) shall cease in the elected State with the same consequences as the withdrawal of any national application in that State if the applicant fails to perform the acts referred to in paragraph (1)(a) within the time limit applicable under paragraph (1)(a) or (b).

(3) Any elected Office may maintain the effect provided for in Article 11(3) even where the applicant does not comply with the requirements provided for in paragraph (1)(a) or (b).

[1.812]
Article 40
Delaying of National Examination and Other Processing

(1) If the election of any Contracting State has been effected prior to the expiration of the 19th month from the priority date, the provisions of Article 23 shall not apply to such State and the national Office of or acting for that State shall not proceed, subject to the provisions of paragraph (2), to the examination and other processing of the international application prior to the expiration of the applicable time limit under Article 39.

(2) Notwithstanding the provisions of paragraph (1), any elected Office may, on the express request of the applicant, proceed to the examination and other processing of the international application at any time.

[1.813]
Article 41
Amendment of the Claims, the Description, and the Drawings, Before Elected Offices

(1) The applicant shall be given the opportunity to amend the claims, the description, and the drawings, before each elected Office within the prescribed time limit. No elected Office shall grant a patent, or refuse the grant of a patent, before such time limit has expired, except with the express consent of the applicant.

(2) The amendments shall not go beyond the disclosure in the international application as filed, unless the national law of the elected State permits them to go beyond the said disclosure.

(3) The amendments shall be in accordance with the national law of the elected State in all respects not provided for in this Treaty and the Regulations.

(4) Where an elected Office requires a translation of the international application, the amendments shall be in the language of the translation.

[1.814]
Article 42
Results of National Examination in Elected Offices

No elected Office receiving the international preliminary examination report may require that the applicant furnish copies, or information on the contents, of any papers connected with the examination relating to the same international application in any other elected Office.

CHAPTER III
COMMON PROVISIONS

[1.815]
Article 43
Seeking Certain Kinds of Protection

In respect of any designated or elected State whose law provides for the grant of inventors' certificates, utility certificates, utility models, patents or certificates of addition, inventors' certificates of addition, or utility certificates of addition, the applicant may indicate, as prescribed in the Regulations, that his international application is for the grant, as far as that State is concerned, of an inventor's certificate, a utility certificate, or a utility model, rather than a patent, or that it is for the grant of a patent or certificate of addition, an inventor's certificate of addition, or a utility certificate of addition, and the ensuing effect shall be governed by the applicant's choice. For the purposes of this Article and any Rule thereunder, Article 2(ii) shall not apply.

[1.816]
Article 44
Seeking Two Kinds of Protection

In respect of any designated or elected State whose law permits an application, while being for the grant of a patent or one of the other kinds of protection referred to in Article 43, to be also for the grant of another of the said kinds of protection, the applicant may indicate, as prescribed in the Regulations, the two kinds of protection he is seeking, and the ensuing effect shall be governed by the applicant's indications. For the purposes of this Article, Article 2(ii) shall not apply.

[1.817]
Article 45
Regional Patent Treaties

(1) Any treaty providing for the grant of regional patents ("regional patent treaty"), and giving to all persons who, according to Article 9, are entitled to file international applications the right to file applications for such patents, may provide that international applications designating or electing a State party to both the regional patent treaty and the present Treaty may be filed as applications for such patents.

(2) The national law of the said designated or elected State may provide that any designation or election of such State in the international application shall have the effect of an indication of the wish to obtain a regional patent under the regional patent treaty.

[1.818]
Article 46
Incorrect Translation of the International Application

If, because of an incorrect translation of the international application, the scope of any patent granted on that application exceeds the scope of the international application in its original language, the competent authorities of the Contracting State concerned may accordingly and retroactively limit the scope of the patent, and declare it null and void to the extent that its scope has exceeded the scope of the international application in its original language.

[1.819]
Article 47
Time Limits

(1) The details for computing time limits referred to in this Treaty are governed by the Regulations.

(2)

(a) All time limits fixed in Chapters I and II of this Treaty may, outside any revision under Article 60, be modified by a decision of the Contracting States.

(b) Such decisions shall be made in the Assembly or through voting by correspondence and must be unanimous.

(c) The details of the procedure are governed by the Regulations.

[1.820]
Article 48
Delay in Meeting Certain Time Limits

(1) Where any time limit fixed in this Treaty or the Regulations is not met because of interruption in the mail service or unavoidable loss or delay in the mail, the time limit shall be deemed to be met in the cases and subject to the proof and other conditions prescribed in the Regulations.

(2)

(a) Any Contracting State shall, as far as that State is concerned, excuse, for reasons admitted under its national law, any delay in meeting any time limit.

(b) Any Contracting State may, as far as that State is concerned, excuse, for reasons other than those referred to in sub-paragraph (a), any delay in meeting any time limit.

[1.821]
Article 49
Right to Practise Before International Authorities

Any attorney, patent agent, or other person, having the right to practise before the national Office with which the international application was filed, shall be entitled to practise before the International Bureau and the competent International Searching Authority and competent International Preliminary Examining Authority in respect of that application.

CHAPTER IV
TECHNICAL SERVICES

[1.822]
Article 50
Patent Information Services

(1) The International Bureau may furnish services by providing technical and any other pertinent information available to it on the basis of published documents, primarily patents and published applications (referred to in this Article as "the information services").

(2) The International Bureau may provide these information services either directly or through one or more International Searching Authorities or other national or international specialised institutions, with which the International Bureau may reach agreement.

(3) The information services shall be operated in a way particularly facilitating the acquisition by Contracting States which are developing countries of technical knowledge and technology, including available published know-how.

(4) The information services shall be available to Governments of Contracting States and their nationals and residents. The Assembly may decide to make these services available also to others.

(5)

(a) Any service to Governments of Contracting States shall be furnished at cost, provided that, when the Government is that of a Contracting State which is a developing country, the service shall be furnished below cost if the difference can be covered from profit made on services furnished to others than Governments of Contracting States or from the sources referred to in Article 51(4).

(b) The cost referred to in sub-paragraph (a) is to be understood as cost over and above costs normally incident to the performance of the services of a national Office or the obligations of an International Searching Authority.

(6) The details concerning the implementation of the provisions of this Article shall be governed by decisions of the Assembly and, within the limits to be fixed by the Assembly, such working groups as the Assembly may set up for that purpose.

(7) The Assembly shall, when it considers it necessary, recommend methods of providing financing supplementary to those referred to in paragraph (5).

[1.823]
Article 51
Technical Assistance

(1) The Assembly shall establish a Committee for Technical Assistance (referred to in this Article as "the Committee").

(2)

(a) The members of the Committee shall be elected among the Contracting States, with due regard to the representation of developing countries.

(b) The Director General shall, on his own initiative or at the request of the Committee, invite representatives of intergovernmental organisations concerned with technical assistance to developing countries to participate in the work of the Committee.

(3)

(a) The task of the Committee shall be to organise and supervise technical assistance for Contracting States which are developing countries in developing their patent systems individually or on a regional basis.

(b) The technical assistance shall comprise, among other things, the training of specialists, the loaning of experts, and the supply of equipment both for demonstration and for operational purposes.

(4) The International Bureau shall seek to enter into agreements, on the one hand, with international financing organisations and intergovernmental organisations, particularly the United Nations, the agencies of the United Nations, and the Specialised Agencies connected with the United Nations concerned with technical assistance, and, on the other hand, with the Governments of the States receiving the technical assistance, for the financing of projects pursuant to this Article.

(5) The details concerning the implementation of the provisions of this Article shall be governed by decisions of the Assembly and, within the limits to be fixed by the Assembly, such working groups as the Assembly may set up for that purpose.

[1.824]
Article 52
Relations with Other Provisions of the Treaty

Nothing in this Chapter shall affect the financial provisions contained in any other Chapter of this Treaty. Such provisions are not applicable to the present Chapter or to its implementation.

CHAPTER V
ADMINISTRATIVE PROVISIONS

[1.825]
Article 53
Assembly

(1)

(a) The Assembly shall, subject to Article 57(8), consist of the Contracting States.

(b) The Government of each Contracting State shall be represented by one delegate, who may be assisted by alternate delegates, advisors, and experts.

(2)

(a) The Assembly shall—

(i) deal with all matters concerning the maintenance and development of the Union and the implementation of this Treaty;

(ii) perform such tasks as are specifically assigned to it under other provisions of this Treaty;

(iii) give directions to the International Bureau concerning the preparation for revision conferences;

(iv) review and approve the reports and activities of the Director General concerning the Union, and give him all necessary instructions concerning matters within the competence of the Union;

(v) review and approve the reports and activities of the Executive Committee established under paragraph (9), and give instructions to such Committee;

(vi) determine the programme and adopt the triennial[1] budget of the Union, and approve its final accounts;

(vii) adopt the financial regulations of the Union;

(viii) establish such committees and working groups as it deems appropriate to achieve the objectives of the Union;

(ix) determine which States other than Contracting States and, subject to the provisions of paragraph (8), which intergovernmental and international non-governmental organisations shall be admitted to its meetings as observers;

(x) take any other appropriate action designed to further the objectives of the Union and perform such other functions as are appropriate under this Treaty.

(b) With respect to matters which are of interest also to other Unions administered by the Organisation, the Assembly shall make its decisions after having heard the advice of the Co-ordination Committee of the Organisation.

(3) A delegate may represent, and vote in the name of, one State only.

(4) Each Contracting State shall have one vote.

(5)

(a) One-half of the Contracting States shall constitute a quorum.

(b) In the absence of the quorum, the Assembly may make decisions but, with the exception of decisions concerning its own procedure, all such decisions shall take effect only if the quorum and the required majority are attained through voting by correspondence as provided in the Regulations.

(6)

(a) Subject to the provisions of Articles 47(2)(b), 58(2)(b), 58(3) and 61(2)(b), the decisions of the Assembly shall require two-thirds of the votes cast.

(b) Abstentions shall not be considered as votes.

(7) In connection with matters of exclusive interest to States bound by Chapter II, any reference to Contracting States in paragraphs (4), (5), and (6), shall be considered as applying only to States bound by Chapter II.

(8) Any intergovernmental organisation appointed as International Searching or Preliminary Examining Authority shall be admitted as observer to the Assembly.

(9) When the number of Contracting States exceeds forty, the Assembly shall establish an Executive Committee. Any reference to the Executive Committee in this Treaty and the Regulations shall be construed as references to such Committee once it has been established.

(10) Until the Executive Committee has been established, the Assembly shall approve, within the limits of the programme and triennial[1] budget, the annual programmes and budgets prepared by the Director General.

(11)

(a) The Assembly shall meet in every second calendar year in ordinary session upon convocation by the Director General and, in the absence of exceptional circumstances, during the same period and at the same place as the General Assembly of the Organisation.

(b) The Assembly shall meet in extraordinary session upon convocation by the Director General, at the request of the Executive Committee, or at the request of one-fourth of the Contracting States.

(12) The Assembly shall adopt its own rules of procedure.

NOTES

[1] Since 1980, the programme and budget of the Union have been biennial.

[1.826]
Article 54
Executive Committee

(1) When the Assembly has established an Executive Committee, that Committee shall be subject to the provisions set forth hereinafter.

(2)

(a) The Executive Committee shall, subject to Article 57(8), consist of States elected by the Assembly from among States members of the Assembly.

(b) The Government of each State member of the Executive Committee shall be represented by one delegate, who may be assisted by alternate delegates, advisors, and experts.

(3) The number of States members of the Executive Committee shall correspond to one-fourth of the number of States members of the Assembly. In establishing the number of seats to be filled, remainders after division by four shall be disregarded.

(4) In electing the members of the Executive Committee, the Assembly shall have due regard to an equitable geographical distribution.

(5)

(a) Each member of the Executive Committee shall serve from the close of the session of the Assembly which elected it to the close of the next ordinary session of the Assembly.

(b) Members of the Executive Committee may be re-elected but only up to a maximum of two-thirds of such members.

(c) The Assembly shall establish the details of the rules governing the election and possible re-election of the members of the Executive Committee.

(6)

(a) The Executive Committee shall—

(i) prepare the draft agenda of the Assembly;

(ii) submit proposals to the Assembly in respect of the draft programme and biennial budget of the Union prepared by the Director General;

(iii) *(deleted)*

(iv) submit, with appropriate comments, to the Assembly the periodical reports of the Director General and the yearly audit reports on the accounts;

(v) take all necessary measures to ensure the execution of the programme of the Union by the Director General, in accordance with the decisions of the Assembly and having regard to circumstances arising between two ordinary sessions of the Assembly;

(vi) perform such other functions as are allocated to it under this Treaty.

(b) With respect to matters which are of interest also to other Unions administered by the Organisation, the Executive Committee shall make its decisions after having heard the advice of the Co-ordination Committee of the Organisation.

(7)

(a) The Executive Committee shall meet once a year in ordinary session upon convocation by the Director General, preferably during the same period and at the same place as the Co-ordination Committee of the Organisation.

(b) The Executive Committee shall meet in extraordinary session upon convocation by the Director General, either on his own initiative or at the request of its Chairman or one-fourth of its members.

(8)

(a) Each State member of the Executive Committee shall have one vote.

(b) One-half of the members of the Executive Committee shall constitute a quorum.

(c) Decisions shall be made by a simple majority of the votes cast.

(d) Abstentions shall not be considered as votes.

(e) A delegate may represent, and vote in the name of, one State only.

(9) Contracting States not members of the Executive Committee shall be admitted to its meetings as observers, as well as any intergovernmental organisation appointed as International Searching or Preliminary Examining Authority.

(10) The Executive Committee shall adopt its own rules of procedure.

[1.827]
Article 55
International Bureau

(1) Administrative tasks concerning the Union shall be performed by the International Bureau.

(2) The International Bureau shall provide the secretariat of the various organs of the Union.

(3) The Director General shall be the chief executive of the Union and shall represent the Union.

(4) The International Bureau shall publish a Gazette and other publications provided for by the Regulations or required by the Assembly.

(5) The Regulations shall specify the services that national Offices shall perform in order to assist the International Bureau and the International Searching and Preliminary Examining Authorities in carrying out their tasks under this Treaty.

(6) The Director General and any staff member designated by him shall participate, without the right to vote, in all meetings of the Assembly, the Executive Committee and any other committee or working group established under this Treaty or the Regulations. The Director General, or a staff member designated by him, shall be *ex officio* secretary of these bodies.

(7)

(a) The International Bureau shall, in accordance with the directions of the Assembly and in co-operation with the Executive Committee, make the preparations for the revision conferences.

(b) The International Bureau may consult with intergovernmental and international non-governmental organisations concerning preparations for revision conferences.

(c) The Director General and persons designated by him shall take part, without the right to vote, in the discussions at revision conferences.

(8) The International Bureau shall carry out any other tasks assigned to it.

[1.828]
Article 56
Committee for Technical Co-operation

(1) The Assembly shall establish a Committee for Technical Co-operation (referred to in this Article as "the Committee").

(2)

(a) The Assembly shall determine the composition of the Committee and appoint its members, with due regard to an equitable representation of developing countries.

(b) The International Searching and Preliminary Examining Authorities shall be *ex officio* members of the Committee. In the case where such an Authority is the national Office of a Contracting State, that State shall not be additionally represented on the Committee.

(c) If the number of Contracting States so allows, the total number of members of the Committee shall be more than double the number of *ex officio* members.

(d) The Director General shall, on his own initiative or at the request of the Committee, invite representatives of interested organisations to participate in discussions of interest to them.

(3) The aim of the Committee shall be to contribute, by advice and recommendations—

(i) to the constant improvement of the services provided for under this Treaty,

(ii) to the securing, so long as there are several International Searching Authorities and several International Preliminary Examining Authorities, of the maximum degree of uniformity in their documentation and working methods and the maximum degree of uniformly high quality in their reports, and
(iii) on the initiative of the Assembly or the Executive Committee, to the solution of the technical problems specifically involved in the establishment of a single International Searching Authority.

(4) Any Contracting State and any interested international organisation may approach the Committee in writing on questions which fall within the competence of the Committee.

(5) The Committee may address its advice and recommendations to the Director General or, through him, to the Assembly, the Executive Committee, all or some of the International Searching and Preliminary Examining Authorities, and all or some of the receiving Offices.

(6)
(a) In any case, the Director General shall transmit to the Executive Committee the texts of all the advice and recommendations of the Committee. He may comment on such texts.
(b) The Executive Committee may express its views on any advice, recommendation, or other activity of the Committee, and may invite the Committee to study and report on questions falling within its competence. The Executive Committee may submit to the Assembly, with appropriate comments, the advice, recommendations and report of the Committee.

(7) Until the Executive Committee has been established, references in paragraph (6) to the Executive Committee shall be construed as references to the Assembly.

(8) The details of the procedure of the Committee shall be governed by the decisions of the Assembly.

[1.829]
Article 57
Finances

(1)
(a) The Union shall have a budget.
(b) The budget of the Union shall include the income and expenses proper to the Union and its contribution to the budget of expenses common to the Unions administered by the Organisation.
(c) Expenses not attributable exclusively to the Union but also to one or more other Unions administered by the Organisation shall be considered as expenses common to the Unions. The share of the Union in such common expenses shall be in proportion to the interest the Union has in them.

(2) The budget of the Union shall be established with due regard to the requirements of co-ordination with the budgets of the other Unions administered by the Organisation.

(3) Subject to the provisions of paragraph (5), the budget of the Union shall be financed from the following sources—
(i) fees and charges due for services rendered by the International Bureau in relation to the Union;
(ii) sale of, or royalties on, the publications of the International Bureau concerning the Union;
(iii) gifts, bequests, and subventions;
(iv) rents, interests, and other miscellaneous income.

(4) The amounts of fees and charges due to the International Bureau and the prices of its publications shall be so fixed that they should, under normal circumstances, be sufficient to cover all the expenses of the International Bureau connected with the administration of this Treaty.

(5)
(a) Should any financial year close with a deficit, the Contracting States shall, subject to the provisions of sub-paragraphs (b) and (c), pay contributions to cover such deficit.
(b) The amount of the contribution of each Contracting State shall be decided by the Assembly with due regard to the number of international applications which has emanated from each of them in the relevant year.
(c) If other means of provisionally covering any deficit or any part thereof are secured, the Assembly may decide that such deficit be carried forward and that the Contracting States should not be asked to pay contributions.
(d) If the financial situation of the Union so permits, the Assembly may decide that any contributions paid under sub-paragraph (a) be reimbursed to the Contracting States which have paid them.
(e) A Contracting State which has not paid, within two years of the due date as established by the Assembly, its contribution under sub-paragraph (b) may not exercise its right to vote in any of the organs of the Union. However, any organ of the Union may allow such a State to continue to exercise its right to vote in that organ so long as it is satisfied that the delay in payment is due to exceptional and unavoidable circumstances.

(6) If the budget is not adopted before the beginning of a new financial period, it shall be at the same level as the budget of the previous year, as provided in the financial regulations.

(7)

(7)

(a) The Union shall have a working capital fund which shall be constituted by a single payment made by each Contracting State. If the fund becomes insufficient, the Assembly shall arrange to increase it. If part of the fund is no longer needed, it shall be reimbursed.
(b) The amount of the initial payment of each Contracting State to the said fund or of its participation in the increase thereof shall be decided by the Assembly on the basis of principles similar to those provided for under paragraph (5)(b).
(c) The terms of payment shall be fixed by the Assembly on the proposal of the Director General and after it has heard the advice of the Co-ordination Committee of the Organisation.
(d) Any reimbursement shall be proportionate to the amounts paid by each Contracting State, taking into account the dates at which they were paid.

(8)

(a) In the headquarters agreement concluded with the State on the territory of which the Organisation has its headquarters, it shall be provided that, whenever the working capital fund is insufficient, such State shall grant advances. The amount of these advances and the conditions on which they are granted shall be the subject of separate agreements, in each case, between such State and the Organisation. As long as it remains under the obligation to grant advances, such State shall have an *ex officio* seat in the Assembly and on the Executive Committee.
(b) The State referred to in sub-paragraph (a) and the Organisation shall each have the right to denounce the obligation to grant advances, by written notification. Denunciation shall take effect three years after the end of the year in which it has been notified.

(9) The auditing of the accounts shall be effected by one or more of the Contracting States or by external auditors, as provided in the financial regulations. They shall be designated, with their agreement, by the Assembly.

[1.830]
Article 58
Regulations

(1) The Regulations annexed to this Treaty provide Rules—
(i) concerning matters in respect of which this Treaty expressly refers to the Regulations or expressly provides that they are or shall be prescribed,
(ii) concerning any administrative requirements, matters, or procedures,
(iii) concerning any details useful in the implementation of the provisions of this Treaty.

(2)

(a) The Assembly may amend the Regulations.
(b) Subject to the provisions of paragraph (3), amendments shall require three-fourths of the votes cast.

(3)

(a) The Regulations specify the Rules which may be amended
(i) only by unanimous consent, or
(ii) only if none of the Contracting States whose national Office acts as an International Searching or Preliminary Examining Authority dissents, and, where such Authority is an intergovernmental organisation, if the Contracting State member of that organisation authorised for that purpose by the other member States within the competent body of such organisation does not dissent.
(b) Exclusion, for the future, of any such Rules from the applicable requirement shall require the fulfilment of the conditions referred to in sub-paragraph (a)(i) or (a)(ii), respectively.
(c) Inclusion, for the future, of any Rule in one or the other of the requirements referred to in sub-paragraph (a) shall require unanimous consent.

(4) The Regulations provide for the establishment, under the control of the Assembly, of Administrative Instructions by the Director General.

(5) In the case of conflict between the provisions of the Treaty and those of the Regulations, the provisions of the Treaty shall prevail.

CHAPTER VI
DISPUTES

[1.831]
Article 59
Disputes

Subject to Article 64(5), any dispute between two or more Contracting States concerning the interpretation or application of this Treaty or the Regulations, not settled by negotiation, may, by any one of the States concerned, be brought before the International Court of Justice by application in conformity with the Statute of the Court, unless the States concerned agree on some other method of settlement. The Contracting State bringing the dispute before the Court shall inform the International Bureau; the International Bureau shall bring the matter to the attention of the other Contracting States.

CHAPTER VII
REVISION AND AMENDMENT

[1.832]
Article 60
Revision of the Treaty

(1) This Treaty may be revised from time to time by a special conference of the Contracting States.

(2) The convocation of any revision conference shall be decided by the Assembly.

(3) Any intergovernmental organisation appointed as International Searching or Preliminary Examining Authority shall be admitted as observer to any revision conference.

(4) Articles 53(5), (9) and (11), 54, 55(4) to (8), 56, and 57, may be amended either by a revision conference or according to the provisions of Article 61.

[1.833]
Article 61
Amendment of Certain Provisions of the Treaty

(1)
- (a) Proposals for the amendment of Articles 53(5), (9) and (11), 54, 55(4) to (8), 56, and 57, may be initiated by any State member of the Assembly, by the Executive Committee, or by the Director General.
- (b) Such proposals shall be communicated by the Director General to the Contracting States at least six months in advance of their consideration by the Assembly.

(2)
- (a) Amendments to the Articles referred to in paragraph (1) shall be adopted by the Assembly.
- (b) Adoption shall require three-fourths of the votes cast.

(3)
- (a) Any amendment to the Articles referred to in paragraph (1) shall enter into force one month after written notifications of acceptance, effected in accordance with their respective constitutional processes, have been received by the Director General from three-fourths of the States members of the Assembly at the time it adopted the amendment.
- (b) Any amendment to the said Articles thus accepted shall bind all the States which are members of the Assembly at the time the amendment enters into force, provided that any amendment increasing the financial obligations of the Contracting States shall bind only those States which have notified their acceptance of such amendment.
- (c) Any amendment accepted in accordance with the provisions of sub-paragraph (a) shall bind all States which become members of the Assembly after the date on which the amendment entered into force in accordance with the provisions of sub-paragraph (a).

CHAPTER VIII
FINAL PROVISIONS

[1.834]
Article 62
Becoming Party to the Treaty

(1) Any State member of the International Union for the Protection of Industrial Property may become party to this Treaty by—
- (i) signature followed by the deposit of an instrument of ratification, or
- (ii) deposit of an instrument of accession.

(2) Instruments of ratification or accession shall be deposited with the Director General.

(3) The provisions of Article 24 of the Stockholm Act of the Paris Convention for the Protection of Industrial Property shall apply to this Treaty.

(4) Paragraph (3) shall in no way be understood as implying the recognition or tacit acceptance by a Contracting State of the factual situation concerning a territory to which this Treaty is made applicable by another Contracting State by virtue of the said paragraph.

[1.835]
Article 63
Entry into Force of the Treaty

(1)
- (a) Subject to the provisions of paragraph (3), this Treaty shall enter into force three months after eight States have deposited their instruments of ratification or accession, provided that at least four of those States each fulfil any of the following conditions—
  - (i) the number of applications filed in the State has exceeded 40,000 according to the most recent annual statistics published by the International Bureau,
  - (ii) the nationals or residents of the State have filed at least 1,000 applications in one foreign country according to the most recent annual statistics published by the International Bureau,

(iii) the national Office of the State has received at least 10,000 applications from nationals or residents of foreign countries according to the most recent annual statistics published by the International Bureau.

(b) For the purposes of this paragraph, the term "applications" does not include applications for utility models.

(2) Subject to the provisions of paragraph (3), any State which does not become party to this Treaty upon entry into force under paragraph (1) shall become bound by this Treaty three months after the date on which such State has deposited its instrument of ratification or accession.

(3) The provisions of Chapter II and the corresponding provisions of the Regulations annexed to this Treaty shall become applicable, however, only on the date on which three States each of which fulfil at least one of the three requirements specified in paragraph (1) have become party to this Treaty without declaring, as provided in Article 64(1), that they do not intend to be bound by the provisions of Chapter II. That date shall not, however, be prior to that of the initial entry into force under paragraph (1).

[1.836]
Article 64
Reservations

(1)

(a) Any State may declare that it shall not be bound by the provisions of Chapter II.

(b) States making a declaration under sub-paragraph (a) shall not be bound by the provisions of Chapter II and the corresponding provisions of the Regulations.

(2)

(a) Any State not having made a declaration under paragraph (1)(a) may declare that—

(i) it shall not be bound by the provisions of Article 39(1) with respect to the furnishing of a copy of the international application and a translation thereof (as prescribed),

(ii) the obligation to delay national processing, as provided for under Article 40, shall not prevent publication, by or through its national Office, of the international application or a translation thereof, it being understood, however, that it is not exempted from the limitations provided for in Articles 30 and 38.

(b) States making such a declaration shall be bound accordingly.

(3)

(a) Any State may declare that, as far as it is concerned, international publication of international applications is not required.

(b) Where, at the expiration of 18 months from the priority date, the international application contains the designation only of such States as have made declarations under sub-paragraph (a), the international application shall not be published by virtue of Article 21(2).

(c) Where the provisions of sub-paragraph (b) apply, the international application shall nevertheless be published by the International Bureau—

(i) at the request of the applicant, as provided in the Regulations,

(ii) when a national application or a patent based on the international application is published by or on behalf of the national Office of any designated State having made a declaration under sub-paragraph (a), promptly after such publication but not before the expiration of 18 months from the priority date.

(4)

(a) Any State whose national law provides for prior art effect of its patents as from a date before publication, but does not equate for prior art purposes the priority date claimed under the Paris Convention for the Protection of Industrial Property to the actual filing date in that State, may declare that the filing outside that State of an international application designating that State is not equated to an actual filing in that State for prior art purposes.

(b) Any State making a declaration under sub-paragraph (a) shall to that extent not be bound by the provisions of Article 11(3).

(c) Any State making a declaration under sub-paragraph (a) shall, at the same time, state in writing the date from which, and the conditions under which, the prior art effect of any international application designating that State becomes effective in that State. This statement may be modified at any time by notification addressed to the Director General.

(5) Each State may declare that it does not consider itself bound by Article 59. With regard to any dispute between any Contracting State having made such a declaration and any other Contracting State, the provisions of Article 59 shall not apply.

(6)

(a) Any declaration made under this Article shall be made in writing. It may be made at the time of signing this Treaty, at the time of depositing the instrument of ratification or accession, or, except in the case referred to in paragraph (5), at any later time by notification addressed to the Director General. In the case of the said notification, the declaration shall take effect six months after the day on which the Director General has received the notification, and shall not affect international applications filed prior to the expiration of the said six-month period.

(b) Any declaration made under this Article may be withdrawn at any time by notification addressed to the Director General. Such withdrawal shall take effect three months after the day on which the Director General has received the notification and, in the case of the withdrawal of a declaration made under paragraph (3), shall not affect international applications filed prior to the expiration of the said three-month period.

(7) No reservations to this Treaty other than the reservations under paragraphs (1) to (5) are permitted.

NOTES

Information received by the International Bureau concerning reservations made under Article 64(1) to (5) is published in the Gazette and on the WIPO website at: www.wipo.int.

[1.837]
Article 65
Gradual Application

(1) If the agreement with any International Searching or Preliminary Examining Authority provides, transitionally, for limits on the number or kind of international applications that such Authority undertakes to process, the Assembly shall adopt the measures necessary for the gradual application of this Treaty and the Regulations in respect of given categories of international applications. This provision shall also apply to requests for an international-type search under Article 15(5).

(2) The Assembly shall fix the dates from which, subject to the provision of paragraph (1), international applications may be filed and demands for international preliminary examination may be submitted. Such dates shall not be later than six months after this Treaty has entered into force according to the provisions of Article 63(1), or after Chapter II has become applicable under Article 63(3), respectively.

[1.838]
Article 66
Denunciation

(1) Any Contracting State may denounce this Treaty by notification addressed to the Director General.

(2) Denunciation shall take effect six months after receipt of the said notification by the Director General. It shall not affect the effects of the international application in the denouncing State if the international application was filed, and, where the denouncing State has been elected, the election was made, prior to the expiration of the said six-month period.

[1.839]
Article 67
Signature and Languages

(1)
- (a) This Treaty shall be signed in a single original in the English and French languages, both texts being equally authentic.
- (b) Official texts shall be established by the Director General, after consultation with the interested Governments, in the German, Japanese, Portuguese, Russian and Spanish languages, and such other languages as the Assembly may designate.

(2) This Treaty shall remain open for signature at Washington until December 31, 1970.

[1.840]
Article 68
Depositary Functions

(1) The original of this Treaty, when no longer open for signature, shall be deposited with the Director General.

(2) The Director General shall transmit two copies, certified by him, of this Treaty and the Regulations annexed hereto to the Governments of all States party to the Paris Convention for the Protection of Industrial Property and, on request, to the Government of any other State.

(3) The Director General shall register this Treaty with the Secretariat of the United Nations.

(4) The Director General shall transmit two copies, certified by him, of any amendment to this Treaty and the Regulations to the Governments of all Contracting States and, on request, to the Government of any other State.

[1.841]
Article 69
Notifications

The Director General shall notify the Governments of all States party to the Paris Convention for the Protection of Industrial Property of—
- (i) signatures under Article 62,
- (ii) deposits of instruments of ratification or accession under Article 62,
- (iii) the date of entry into force of this Treaty and the date from which Chapter II is applicable in accordance with Article 63(3),
- (iv) any declarations made under Article 64(1) to (5),
- (v) withdrawals of any declarations made under Article 64(6)(b),

(vi) denunciations received under Article 66, and
(vii) any declarations made under Article 31(4).

REGULATIONS UNDER THE PATENT COOPERATION TREATY

(as in force from July 1, 2017)

(Adopted on June 19, 1970, and amended on April 14, 1978, October 3, 1978, May 1, 1979, June 16, 1980, September 26, 1980, July 3, 1981, September 10, 1982, October 4, 1983, February 3, 1984, September 28, 1984, October 1, 1985, July 12, 1991, October 2, 1991, September 29, 1992, September 29, 1993, October 3, 1995, October 1, 1997, September 15, 1998, September 29, 1999, March 17, 2000, October 3, 2000, October 3, 2001, October 1, 2002, October 1, 2003, October 5, 2004, October 5, 2005, October 3, 2006, November 12, 2007, May 15, 2008, September 29, 2008, October 1, 2009, September 29, 2010, October 5, 2011, October 9, 2012, October 2, 2013, September 30, 2014, October 14, 2015 and October 11, 2016.)

NOTES

The original source for these Regulations is the World Intellectual Property Organisation (WIPO).

PART A
INTRODUCTORY RULES

[1.842]
Rule 1
Abbreviated Expressions

1.1 *Meaning of Abbreviated Expressions*

(a) In these Regulations, the word "Treaty" means the Patent Cooperation Treaty.
(b) In these Regulations, the words "Chapter" and "Article" refer to the specified Chapter or Article of the Treaty.

[1.843]
Rule 2
Interpretation of Certain Words

2.1 *"Applicant"*

Whenever the word "applicant" is used, it shall be construed as meaning also the agent or other representative of the applicant, except where the contrary clearly follows from the wording or the nature of the provision, or the context in which the word is used, such as, in particular, where the provision refers to the residence or nationality of the applicant.

2.2 *"Agent"*

Whenever the word "agent" is used, it shall be construed as meaning an agent appointed under Rule 90.1, unless the contrary clearly follows from the wording or the nature of the provision, or the context in which the word is used.

2.2*bis* *"Common Representative"*

Whenever the expression "common representative" is used, it shall be construed as meaning an applicant appointed as, or considered to be, the common representative under Rule 90.2.

2.3 *"Signature"*

Whenever the word "signature" is used, it shall be understood that, if the national law applied by the receiving Office or the competent International Searching or Preliminary Examining Authority requires the use of a seal instead of a signature, the word, for the purposes of that Office or Authority, shall mean seal.

2.4 *"Priority Period"*

(a) Whenever the term "priority period" is used in relation to a priority claim, it shall be construed as meaning the period of 12 months from the filing date of the earlier application whose priority is so claimed. The day of filing of the earlier application shall not be included in that period.
(b) Rule 80.5 shall apply *mutatis mutandis* to the priority period.

PART B
RULES CONCERNING CHAPTER I OF THE TREATY

[1.844]
Rule 3
The Request (Form)

3.1 *Form of Request*

The request shall be made on a printed form or be presented as a computer print-out.

3.2 *Availability of Forms*

Copies of the printed form shall be furnished free of charge to the applicants by the receiving Office, or, if the receiving Office so desires, by the International Bureau.

3.3 *Check List*

(a) The request shall contain a list indicating:

(i) the total number of sheets constituting the international application and the number of the sheets of each element of the international application: request, description (separately indicating the number of sheets of any sequence listing part of the description), claims, drawings, abstract;

(ii) where applicable, that the international application as filed is accompanied by a power of attorney (i.e., a document appointing an agent or a common representative), a copy of a general power of attorney, a priority document, a sequence listing in electronic form, a document relating to the payment of fees, or any other document (to be specified in the check list);

(iii) the number of that figure of the drawings which the applicant suggests should accompany the abstract when the abstract is published; in exceptional cases, the applicant may suggest more than one figure.

(b) The list shall be completed by the applicant, failing which the receiving Office shall make the necessary indications, except that the number referred to in paragraph (a)(iii) shall not be indicated by the receiving Office.

3.4 *Particulars*

Subject to Rule 3.3, particulars of the printed request form and of a request presented as a computer print-out shall be prescribed by the Administrative Instructions.

[1.845]
Rule 4
The Request (Contents)

4.1 *Mandatory and Optional Contents; Signature*

(a) The request shall contain:

(i) a petition,

(ii) the title of the invention,

(iii) indications concerning the applicant and the agent, if there is an agent,

(iv) indications concerning the inventor where the national law of at least one of the designated States requires that the name of the inventor be furnished at the time of filing a national application.

(b) The request shall, where applicable, contain:

(i) a priority claim,

(ii) indications relating to an earlier search as provided in Rules 4.12(i) and 12*bis*.1(c) and (f),

(iii) a reference to a parent application or parent patent,

(iv) an indication of the applicant's choice of competent International Searching Authority.

(c) The request may contain:

(i) indications concerning the inventor where the national law of none of the designated States requires that the name of the inventor be furnished at the time of filing a national application,

(ii) a request to the receiving Office to prepare and transmit the priority document to the International Bureau where the application whose priority is claimed was filed with the national Office or intergovernmental authority which is the receiving Office,

(iii) declarations as provided in Rule 4.17,

(iv) a statement as provided in Rule 4.18,

(v) a request for restoration of the right of priority,

(vi) a statement as provided in Rule 4.12(ii).

(d) The request shall be signed.

4.2 *The Petition*

The petition shall be to the following effect and shall preferably be worded as follows: "The undersigned requests that the present international application be processed according to the Patent Cooperation Treaty."

4.3 *Title of the Invention*

The title of the invention shall be short (preferably from two to seven words when in English or translated into English) and precise.

4.4 *Names and Addresses*

(a) Names of natural persons shall be indicated by the person's family name and given name(s), the family name being indicated before the given name(s).

(b) Names of legal entities shall be indicated by their full, official designations.

(c) Addresses shall be indicated in such a way as to satisfy the customary requirements for prompt postal delivery at the indicated address and, in any case, shall consist of all the relevant administrative units up to, and including, the house number, if any. Where the national law of the designated State does not require the indication of the house number, failure to indicate such number shall have no effect in that State. In order to allow rapid communication with the applicant, it is recommended to indicate any teleprinter address, telephone and facsimile machine numbers, or corresponding data for other like means of communication, of the applicant or, where applicable, the agent or the common representative.

(d) For each applicant, inventor, or agent, only one address may be indicated, except that, if no agent has been appointed to represent the applicant, or all of them if more than one, the applicant or, if there is more than one applicant, the common representative, may indicate, in addition to any other address given in the request, an address to which notifications shall be sent.

4.5 *The Applicant*

(a) The request shall indicate:

(i) the name,

(ii) the address, and

(iii) the nationality and residence

of the applicant or, if there are several applicants, of each of them.

(b) The applicant's nationality shall be indicated by the name of the State of which he is a national.

(c) The applicant's residence shall be indicated by the name of the State of which he is a resident.

(d) The request may, for different designated States, indicate different applicants. In such a case, the request shall indicate the applicant or applicants for each designated State or group of designated States.

(e) Where the applicant is registered with the national Office that is acting as receiving Office, the request may indicate the number or other indication under which the applicant is so registered.

4.6 *The Inventor*

(a) Where Rule 4.1(a)(iv) or (c)(i) applies, the request shall indicate the name and address of the inventor or, if there are several inventors, of each of them.

(b) If the applicant is the inventor, the request, in lieu of the indication under paragraph (a), shall contain a statement to that effect.

(c) The request may, for different designated States, indicate different persons as inventors where, in this respect, the requirements of the national laws of the designated States are not the same. In such a case, the request shall contain a separate statement for each designated State or group of States in which a particular person, or the same person, is to be considered the inventor, or in which particular persons, or the same persons, are to be considered the inventors.

4.7 *The Agent*

(a) If an agent is appointed, the request shall so indicate, and shall state the agent's name and address.

(b) Where the agent is registered with the national Office that is acting as receiving Office, the request may indicate the number or other indication under which the agent is so registered.

4.8 *Common Representative*

If a common representative is appointed, the request shall so indicate.

4.9 *Designation of States; Kinds of Protection; National and Regional Patents*

(a) The filing of a request shall constitute:

(i) the designation of all Contracting States that are bound by the Treaty on the international filing date;

(ii) an indication that the international application is, in respect of each designated State to which Article 43 or 44 applies, for the grant of every kind of protection which is available by way of the designation of that State;

(iii) an indication that the international application is, in respect of each designated State to which Article 45(1) applies, for the grant of a regional patent and also, unless Article 45(2) applies, a national patent.

(b) Notwithstanding paragraph (a)(i), if, on October 5, 2005, the national law of a Contracting State provides that the filing of an international application which contains the designation of that State and claims the priority of an earlier national application having effect in that State shall have the result that the earlier national application ceases to have effect with the same consequences as the withdrawal of the earlier national application, any request in which the priority of an earlier national application filed in that State is claimed may contain an indication that the designation of that State is not made, provided that the designated Office notifies the International Bureau by January 5, 2006, that this paragraph shall apply in respect of designations of that State and that the notification is still in force on the international filing date. The information received shall be promptly published by the International Bureau in the Gazette.

4.10 *Priority Claim*

(a) Any declaration referred to in Article 8(1) ("priority claim") may claim the priority of one or more earlier applications filed either in or for any country party to the Paris Convention for the Protection of Industrial Property or in or for any Member of the World Trade Organization that is not party to that Convention. Any priority claim shall be made in the request; it shall consist of a statement to the effect that the priority of an earlier application is claimed and shall indicate:

(i) the date on which the earlier application was filed;

(ii) the number of the earlier application;

(iii) where the earlier application is a national application, the country party to the Paris Convention for the Protection of Industrial Property or the Member of the World Trade Organization that is not party to that Convention in which it was filed;

(iv) where the earlier application is a regional application, the authority entrusted with the granting of regional patents under the applicable regional patent treaty;

(v) where the earlier application is an international application, the receiving Office with which it was filed.

(b) In addition to any indication required under paragraph (a)(iv) or (v):

(i) where the earlier application is a regional application or an international application, the priority claim may indicate one or more countries party to the Paris Convention for the Protection of Industrial Property for which that earlier application was filed;

(ii) where the earlier application is a regional application and at least one of the countries party to the regional patent treaty is neither party to the Paris Convention for the Protection of Industrial Property nor a Member of the World Trade Organization, the priority claim shall indicate at least one country party to that Convention or one Member of that Organization for which that earlier application was filed.

(c) For the purposes of paragraphs (a) and (b), Article 2(vi) shall not apply.

(d) *[Deleted]*

4.11 *Reference to Continuation or Continuation-in-Part, or Parent Application or Grant*

(a) If:

(i) the applicant intends to make an indication under Rule 49*bis*.1(a) or (b) of the wish that the international application be treated, in any designated State, as an application for a patent of addition, certificate of addition, inventor's certificate of addition or utility certificate of addition; or

(ii) the applicant intends to make an indication under Rule 49*bis*.1(d) of the wish that the international application be treated, in any designated State, as an application for a continuation or a continuation-in-part of an earlier application;

the request shall so indicate and shall indicate the relevant parent application or parent patent or other parent grant.

(b) The inclusion in the request of an indication under paragraph (a) shall have no effect on the operation of Rule 4.9.

4.12 *Taking into Account Results of Earlier Search*

If the applicant wishes the International Searching Authority to take into account, in carrying out the international search, the results of an earlier international, international-type or national search carried out by the same or another International Searching Authority or by a national Office ("earlier search"):

(i) the request shall so indicate and shall specify the Authority or Office concerned and the application in respect of which the earlier search was carried out;

(ii) the request may, where applicable, contain a statement to the effect that the international application is the same, or substantially the same, as the application in respect of which the earlier search was carried out, or that the international application is the same, or substantially the same, as that earlier application except that it is filed in a different language.

4.13 and 4.14 *[Deleted]*

4.14*bis* *Choice of International Searching Authority*

If two or more International Searching Authorities are competent for the searching of the international application, the applicant shall indicate his choice of International Searching Authority in the request.

4.15 *Signature*

The request shall be signed by the applicant or, if there is more than one applicant, by all of them.

4.16 *Transliteration or Translation of Certain Words*

(a) Where any name or address is written in characters other than those of the Latin alphabet, the same shall also be indicated in characters of the Latin alphabet either as a mere transliteration or through translation into English. The applicant shall decide which words will be merely transliterated and which words will be so translated.

(b) The name of any country written in characters other than those of the Latin alphabet shall also be indicated in English.

4.17 *Declarations Relating to National Requirements Referred to in Rule 51bis.1(a)(i) to (v)*

The request may, for the purposes of the national law applicable in one or more designated States, contain one or more of the following declarations, worded as prescribed by the Administrative Instructions:

(i) a declaration as to the identity of the inventor, as referred to in Rule 51*bis*.1(a)(i);

(ii) a declaration as to the applicant's entitlement, as at the international filing date, to apply for and be granted a patent, as referred to in Rule 51*bis*.1(a)(ii);

(iii) a declaration as to the applicant's entitlement, as at the international filing date, to claim priority of the earlier application, as referred to in Rule 51*bis*.1(a)(iii);

(iv) a declaration of inventorship, as referred to in Rule 51*bis*.1(a)(iv), which shall be signed as prescribed by the Administrative Instructions;

(v) a declaration as to non-prejudicial disclosures or exceptions to lack of novelty, as referred to in Rule 51*bis*.1(a)(v).

4.18 *Statement of Incorporation by Reference*

Where the international application, on the date on which one or more elements referred to in Article 11(1)(iii) were first received by the receiving Office, claims the priority of an earlier application, the request may contain a statement that, where an element of the international application referred to in Article 11(1)(iii)(d) or (e) or a part of the description, claims or drawings referred to in Rule 20.5(a) is not otherwise contained in the international application but is completely contained in the earlier application, that element or part is, subject to confirmation under Rule 20.6, incorporated by reference in the international application for the purposes of Rule 20.6. Such a statement, if not contained in the request on that date, may be added to the request if, and only if, it was otherwise contained in, or submitted with, the international application on that date.

4.19 *Additional Matter*

(a) The request shall contain no matter other than that specified in Rules 4.1 to 4.18, provided that the Administrative Instructions may permit, but cannot make mandatory, the inclusion in the request of any additional matter specified in the Administrative Instructions.

(b) If the request contains matter other than that specified in Rules 4.1 to 4.18 or permitted under paragraph (a) by the Administrative Instructions, the receiving Office shall *ex officio* delete the additional matter.

[1.846]
Rule 5
The Description

5.1 *Manner of the Description*

(a) The description shall first state the title of the invention as appearing in the request and shall:

(i) specify the technical field to which the invention relates;

(ii) indicate the background art which, as far as known to the applicant, can be regarded as useful for the understanding, searching and examination of the invention, and, preferably, cite the documents reflecting such art;

(iii) disclose the invention, as claimed, in such terms that the technical problem (even if not expressly stated as such) and its solution can be understood, and state the advantageous effects, if any, of the invention with reference to the background art;

(iv) briefly describe the figures in the drawings, if any;

(v) set forth at least the best mode contemplated by the applicant for carrying out the invention claimed; this shall be done in terms of examples, where appropriate, and with reference to the drawings, if any; where the national law of the designated State does not require the description of the best mode but is satisfied with the description of any mode (whether it is the best contemplated or not), failure to describe the best mode contemplated shall have no effect in that State;

(vi) indicate explicitly, when it is not obvious from the description or nature of the invention, the way in which the invention is capable of exploitation in industry and the way in which it can be made and used, or, if it can only be used, the way in which it can be used; the term "industry" is to be understood in its broadest sense as in the Paris Convention for the Protection of Industrial Property.

(b) The manner and order specified in paragraph (a) shall be followed except when, because of the nature of the invention, a different manner or a different order would result in a better understanding and a more economic presentation.

(c) Subject to the provisions of paragraph (b), each of the parts referred to in paragraph (a) shall preferably be preceded by an appropriate heading as suggested in the Administrative Instructions.

5.2 *Nucleotide and/or Amino Acid Sequence Disclosure*

(a) Where the international application contains disclosure of one or more nucleotide and/or amino acid sequences, the description shall contain a sequence listing complying with the standard provided for in the Administrative Instructions and presented as a separate part of the description in accordance with that standard.

(b) Where the sequence listing part of the description contains any free text as defined in the standard provided for in the Administrative Instructions, that free text shall also appear in the main part of the description in the language thereof.

[1.847]
Rule 6
The Claims

6.1 *Number and Numbering of Claims*

(a) The number of the claims shall be reasonable in consideration of the nature of the invention claimed.

(b) If there are several claims, they shall be numbered consecutively in Arabic numerals.

(c) The method of numbering in the case of the amendment of claims shall be governed by the Administrative Instructions.

6.2 *References to Other Parts of the International Application*

(a) Claims shall not, except where absolutely necessary, rely, in respect of the technical features of the invention, on references to the description or drawings. In particular, they shall not rely on such references as: "as described in part . . . of the description," or "as illustrated in figure . . . of the drawings."

(b) Where the international application contains drawings, the technical features mentioned in the claims shall preferably be followed by the reference signs relating to such features. When used, the reference signs shall preferably be placed between parentheses. If inclusion of reference signs does not particularly facilitate quicker understanding of a claim, it should not be made. Reference signs may be removed by a designated Office for the purposes of publication by such Office.

6.3 *Manner of Claiming*

(a) The definition of the matter for which protection is sought shall be in terms of the technical features of the invention.

(b) Whenever appropriate, claims shall contain:

(i) a statement indicating those technical features of the invention which are necessary for the definition of the claimed subject matter but which, in combination, are part of the prior art,

(ii) a characterizing portion – preceded by the words "characterized in that," "characterized by," "wherein the improvement comprises," or any other words to the same effect – stating concisely the technical features which, in combination with the features stated under (i), it is desired to protect.

(c) Where the national law of the designated State does not require the manner of claiming provided for in paragraph (b), failure to use that manner of claiming shall have no effect in that State provided the manner of claiming actually used satisfies the national law of that State.

6.4 *Dependent Claims*

(a) Any claim which includes all the features of one or more other claims (claim in dependent form, hereinafter referred to as "dependent claim") shall do so by a reference, if possible at the beginning, to the other claim or claims and shall then state the additional features claimed. Any dependent claim which refers to more than one other claim ("multiple dependent claim") shall refer to such claims in the alternative only. Multiple dependent claims shall not serve as a basis for any other multiple dependent claim. Where the national law of the national Office acting as International Searching Authority does not allow multiple dependent claims to be drafted in a manner different from that provided for in the preceding two sentences, failure to use that manner of claiming may result in an indication under Article 17(2)(b) in the international search report. Failure to use the said manner of claiming shall have no effect in a designated State if the manner of claiming actually used satisfies the national law of that State.

(b) Any dependent claim shall be construed as including all the limitations contained in the claim to which it refers or, if the dependent claim is a multiple dependent claim, all the limitations contained in the particular claim in relation to which it is considered.

(c) All dependent claims referring back to a single previous claim, and all dependent claims referring back to several previous claims, shall be grouped together to the extent and in the most practical way possible.

6.5 *Utility Models*

Any designated State in which the grant of a utility model is sought on the basis of an international application may, instead of Rules 6.1 to 6.4, apply in respect of the matters regulated in those Rules the provisions of its national law concerning utility models once the processing of the international application has started in that State, provided that the applicant shall be allowed at least two months from the expiration of the time limit applicable under Article 22 to adapt his application to the requirements of the said provisions of the national law.

[1.848]
Rule 7
The Drawings

7.1 *Flow Sheets and Diagrams*

Flow sheets and diagrams are considered drawings.

7.2 *Time Limit*

The time limit referred to in Article 7(2)(ii) shall be reasonable under the circumstances of the case and shall, in no case, be shorter than two months from the date of the written invitation requiring the filing of drawings or additional drawings under the said provision.

[1.849]
Rule 8
The Abstract

8.1 *Contents and Form of the Abstract*

(a) The abstract shall consist of the following:

(i) a summary of the disclosure as contained in the description, the claims, and any drawings; the summary shall indicate the technical field to which the invention pertains and shall be drafted in a way which allows the clear understanding of the technical problem, the gist of the solution of that problem through the invention, and the principal use or uses of the invention;

(ii) where applicable, the chemical formula which, among all the formulae contained in the international application, best characterizes the invention.

(b) The abstract shall be as concise as the disclosure permits (preferably 50 to 150 words if it is in English or when translated into English).

(c) The abstract shall not contain statements on the alleged merits or value of the claimed invention or on its speculative application.

(d) Each main technical feature mentioned in the abstract and illustrated by a drawing in the international application shall bc followed by a reference sign, placed between parentheses.

8.2 *Figure*

(a) If the applicant fails to make the indication referred to in Rule 3.3(a)(iii), or if the International Searching Authority finds that a figurc or figures other than that figure or those figures suggested by the applicant would, among all the figures of all the drawings, better characterize the invention, it shall, subject to paragraph (b), indicate the figure or figures which should accompany the abstract when the latter is published by the International Bureau. In such case, the abstract shall be accompanied by the figure or figures so indicated by the International Searching Authority. Otherwise, the abstract shall, subject to paragraph (b), be accompanied by the figure or figures suggested by the applicant.

(b) If the International Searching Authority finds that none of the figures of the drawings is useful for the understanding of the abstract, it shall notify the International Bureau accordingly. In such case, the abstract, when published by the International Bureau, shall not be accompanied by any figure of the drawings even where the applicant has made a suggestion under Rule 3.3(a)(iii).

8.3 *Guiding Principles in Drafting*

The abstract shall be so drafted that it can efficiently serve as a scanning tool for purposes of searching in the particular art, especially by assisting the scientist, engineer or researcher in formulating an opinion on whether there is a need for consulting the international application itself.

[1.850]
Rulc 9
Expressions, Etc, Not to Be Used

9.1 *Definition*

The international application shall not contain:

(i) expressions or drawings contrary to morality;

(ii) expressions or drawings contrary to public order;

(iii) statements disparaging the products or processes of any particular person other than the applicant, or the merits or validity of applications or patents of any such person (mere comparisons with the prior art shall not be considered disparaging *per se*);

(iv) any statement or other matter obviously irrelevant or unnecessary under the circumstances.

9.2 *Noting of Lack of Compliance*

The receiving Office, the International Searching Authority, the Authority specified for supplementary search and the International Bureau may note lack of compliance with the prescriptions of Rule 9.1 and may suggest to the applicant that he voluntarily correct his international application accordingly, in which case the receiving Office, the competent International Searching Authority, the competent Authority specified for supplementary search and the International Bureau, as applicable, shall be informed of the suggestion.

9.3 *Reference to Article 21(6)*

"Disparaging statements," referred to in Article 21(6), shall have the meaning as defined in Rule 9.1(iii).

[1.851]
Rule 10
Terminology and Signs

10.1 *Terminology and Signs*

(a) Units of weights and measures shall be expressed in terms of the metric system, or also expressed in such terms if first expressed in terms of a different system.
(b) Temperatures shall be expressed in degrees Celsius, or also expressed in degrees Celsius, if first expressed in a different manner.
(c) *[Deleted]*
(d) For indications of heat, energy, light, sound, and magnetism, as well as for mathematical formulae and electrical units, the rules of international practice shall be observed; for chemical formulae, the symbols, atomic weights, and molecular formulae, in general use, shall be employed.
(e) In general, only such technical terms, signs and symbols should be used as are generally accepted in the art.
(f) When the international application or its translation is in Chinese, English or Japanese, the beginning of any decimal fraction shall be marked by a period, whereas, when the international application or its translation is in a language other than Chinese, English or Japanese, it shall be marked by a comma.

10.2 *Consistency*

The terminology and the signs shall be consistent throughout the international application.

[1.852]
Rule 11
Physical Requirements of the International Application

11.1 *Number of Copies*

(a) Subject to the provisions of paragraph (b), the international application and each of the documents referred to in the check list (Rule 3.3(a)(ii)) shall be filed in one copy.
(b) Any receiving Office may require that the international application and any of the documents referred to in the check list (Rule 3.3(a)(ii)), except the receipt for the fees paid or the check for the payment of the fees, be filed in two or three copies. In that case, the receiving Office shall be responsible for verifying the identity of the second and the third copies with the record copy.

11.2 *Fitness for Reproduction*

(a) All elements of the international application (i.e., the request, the description, the claims, the drawings, and the abstract) shall be so presented as to admit of direct reproduction by photography, electrostatic processes, photo offset, and microfilming, in any number of copies.
(b) All sheets shall be free from creases and cracks; they shall not be folded.
(c) Only one side of each sheet shall be used.
(d) Subject to Rule 11.10(d) and Rule 11.13(j), each sheet shall be used in an upright position (i.e., the short sides at the top and bottom).

11.3 *Material to Be Used*

All elements of the international application shall be on paper which shall be flexible, strong, white, smooth, non-shiny, and durable.

11.4 *Separate Sheets, Etc.*

(a) Each element (request, description, claims, drawings, abstract) of the international application shall commence on a new sheet.
(b) All sheets of the international application shall be so connected that they can be easily turned when consulted, and easily separated and joined again if they have been separated for reproduction purposes.

11.5 *Size of Sheets*

The size of the sheets shall be A4 (29.7 cm x 21 cm). However, any receiving Office may accept international applications on sheets of other sizes provided that the record copy, as transmitted to the International Bureau, and, if the competent International Searching Authority so desires, the search copy, shall be of A4 size.

11.6 *Margins*

(a) The minimum margins of the sheets containing the description, the claims, and the abstract, shall be as follows:
   – top: 2 cm
   – left side: 2.5 cm
   – right side: 2 cm
   – bottom: 2 cm.
(b) The recommended maximum, for the margins provided for in paragraph (a), is as follows:
   – top: 4 cm
   – left side: 4 cm
   – right side: 3 cm
   – bottom: 3 cm.
(c) On sheets containing drawings, the surface usable shall not exceed 26.2 cm x 17.0 cm. The sheets shall not contain frames around the usable or used surface. The minimum margins shall be as follows:
   – top: 2.5 cm
   – left side: 2.5 cm

(a) – right side: 1.5 cm
– bottom: 1 cm.

(d) The margins referred to in paragraphs (a) to (c) apply to A4-size sheets, so that, even if the receiving Office accepts other sizes, the A4-size record copy and, when so required, the A4-size search copy shall leave the aforesaid margins.

(e) Subject to paragraph (f) and to Rule 11.8(b), the margins of the international application, when submitted, must be completely blank.

(f) The top margin may contain in the left-hand corner an indication of the applicant's file reference, provided that the reference appears within 1.5 cm from the top of the sheet. The number of characters in the applicant's file reference shall not exceed the maximum fixed by the Administrative Instructions.

11.7 *Numbering of Sheets*

(a) All the sheets contained in the international application shall be numbered in consecutive Arabic numerals.

(b) The numbers shall be centered at the top or bottom of the sheet, but shall not be placed in the margin.

11.8 *Numbering of Lines*

(a) It is strongly recommended to number every fifth line of each sheet of the description, and of each sheet of claims.

(b) The numbers should appear in the right half of the left margin.

11.9 *Writing of Text Matter*

(a) The request, the description, the claims and the abstract shall be typed or printed.

(b) Only graphic symbols and characters, chemical or mathematical formulae, and certain characters in the Chinese or Japanese language may, when necessary, be written by hand or drawn.

(c) The typing shall be 1½-spaced.

(d) All text matter shall be in characters the capital letters of which are not less than 0.28 cm high, and shall be in a dark, indelible color, satisfying the requirements specified in Rule 11.2, provided that any text matter in the request may be in characters the capital letters of which are not less than 0.21 cm high.

(e) As far as the spacing of the typing and the size of the characters are concerned, paragraphs (c) and (d) shall not apply to texts in the Chinese or Japanese language.

11.10 *Drawings, Formulae, and Tables, in Text Matter*

(a) The request, the description, the claims and the abstract shall not contain drawings.

(b) The description, the claims and the abstract may contain chemical or mathematical formulae.

(c) The description and the abstract may contain tables; any claim may contain tables only if the subject matter of the claim makes the use of tables desirable.

(d) Tables and chemical or mathematical formulae may be placed sideways on the sheet if they cannot be presented satisfactorily in an upright position thereon; sheets on which tables or chemical or mathematical formulae are presented sideways shall be so presented that the tops of the tables or formulae are at the left side of the sheet.

11.11 *Words in Drawings*

(a) The drawings shall not contain text matter, except a single word or words, when absolutely indispensable, such as "water," "steam," "open," "closed," "section on AB," and, in the case of electric circuits and block schematic or flow sheet diagrams, a few short catchwords indispensable for understanding.

(b) Any words used shall be so placed that, if translated, they may be pasted over without interfering with any lines of the drawings.

11.12 *Alterations, Etc.*

Each sheet shall be reasonably free from erasures and shall be free from alterations, overwritings, and interlineations. Non-compliance with this Rule may be authorized if the authenticity of the content is not in question and the requirements for good reproduction are not in jeopardy.

11.13 *Special Requirements for Drawings*

(a) Drawings shall be executed in durable, black, sufficiently dense and dark, uniformly thick and well-defined, lines and strokes without colorings.

(b) Cross-sections shall be indicated by oblique hatching which should not impede the clear reading of the reference signs and leading lines.

(c) The scale of the drawings and the distinctness of their graphical execution shall be such that a photographic reproduction with a linear reduction in size to two-thirds would enable all details to be distinguished without difficulty.

(d) When, in exceptional cases, the scale is given on a drawing, it shall be represented graphically.

(e) All numbers, letters and reference lines, appearing on the drawings, shall be simple and clear. Brackets, circles or inverted commas shall not be used in association with numbers and letters.

(f) All lines in the drawings shall, ordinarily, be drawn with the aid of drafting instruments.

(g) Each element of each figure shall be in proper proportion to each of the other elements in the figure, except where the use of a different proportion is indispensable for the clarity of the figure.

(h) The height of the numbers and letters shall not be less than 0.32 cm. For the lettering of drawings, the Latin and, where customary, the Greek alphabets shall be used.

(i) The same sheet of drawings may contain several figures. Where figures on two or more sheets form in effect a single complete figure, the figures on the several sheets shall be so arranged that the complete figure can be assembled without concealing any part of any of the figures appearing on the various sheets.

(j) The different figures shall be arranged on a sheet or sheets without wasting space, preferably in an upright position, clearly separated from one another. Where the figures are not arranged in an upright position, they shall be presented sideways with the top of the figures at the left side of the sheet.

(k) The different figures shall be numbered in Arabic numerals consecutively and independently of the numbering of the sheets.

(l) Reference signs not mentioned in the description shall not appear in the drawings, and vice versa.

(m) The same features, when denoted by reference signs, shall, throughout the international application, be denoted by the same signs.

(n) If the drawings contain a large number of reference signs, it is strongly recommended to attach a separate sheet listing all reference signs and the features denoted by them.

11.14 *Later Documents*

Rules 10, and 11.1 to 11.13, also apply to any document – for example, replacement sheets, amended claims, translations – submitted after the filing of the international application.

[1.853]

Rule 12

Language of the International Application and Translations for the Purposes of International Search and International Publication

12.1 *Languages Accepted for the Filing of International Applications*

(a) An international application shall be filed in any language which the receiving Office accepts for that purpose.

(b) Each receiving Office shall, for the filing of international applications, accept at least one language which is both:

(i) a language accepted by the International Searching Authority, or, if applicable, by at least one of the International Searching Authorities, competent for the international searching of international applications filed with that receiving Office, and

(ii) a language of publication.

(c) Notwithstanding paragraph (a), the request shall be filed in any language of publication which the receiving Office accepts for the purposes of this paragraph.

(d) Notwithstanding paragraph (a), any text matter contained in the sequence listing part of the description referred to in Rule 5.2(a) shall be presented in accordance with the standard provided for in the Administrative Instructions.

12.1*bis* *Language of Elements and Parts Furnished under Rule 20.3, 20.5 or 20.6*

An element referred to in Article 11(1)(iii)(d) or (e) furnished by the applicant under Rule 20.3(b) or 20.6(a) and a part of the description, claims or drawings furnished by the applicant under Rule 20.5(b) or 20.6(a) shall be in the language of the international application as filed or, where a translation of the application is required under Rule 12.3(a) or 12.4(a), in both the language of the application as filed and the language of that translation.

12.1*ter* *Language of Indications Furnished under Rule 13bis.4*

Any indication in relation to deposited biological material furnished under Rule 13*bis*.4 shall be in the language in which the international application is filed, provided that, where a translation of the international application is required under Rule 12.3(a) or 12.4(a), any such indication shall be furnished in both the language in which the application is filed and the language of that translation.

12.2 *Language of Changes in the International Application*

(a) Any amendment of the international application shall, subject to Rules 46.3 and 55.3, be in the language in which the application is filed.

(b) Any rectification under Rule 91.1 of an obvious mistake in the international application shall be in the language in which the application is filed, provided that:

(i) where a translation of the international application is required under Rule 12.3(a), 12.4(a) or 55.2(a), rectifications referred to in Rule 91.1(b)(ii) and (iii) shall be filed in both the language of the application and the language of that translation;

(ii) where a translation of the request is required under Rule 26.3*ter* (c), rectifications referred to in Rule 91.1(b)(i) need only be filed in the language of that translation.

(c) Any correction under Rule 26 of a defect in the international application shall be in the language in which the international application is filed. Any correction under Rule 26 of a defect in a translation of the international application furnished under Rule 12.3 or 12.4, any correction under Rule 55.2(c) of a defect in a translation furnished under Rule 55.2(a), or any correction of a defect in a translation of the request furnished under Rule 26.3*ter* (c), shall be in the language of the translation.

12.3 *Translation for the Purposes of International Search*

(a) Where the language in which the international application is filed is not accepted by the International Searching Authority that is to carry out the international search, the applicant shall, within one month from the date of receipt of the international application by the receiving Office, furnish to that Office a translation of the international application into a language which is all of the following:

(i) a language accepted by that Authority, and

(ii) a language of publication, and

(iii) a language accepted by the receiving Office under Rule 12.1(a), unless the international application is filed in a language of publication.

(b) Paragraph (a) shall not apply to the request nor to any sequence listing part of the description.

(c) Where, by the time the receiving Office sends to the applicant the notification under Rule 20.2(c), the applicant has not furnished a translation required under paragraph (a), the receiving Office shall, preferably together with that notification, invite the applicant:

(i) to furnish the required translation within the time limit under paragraph (a);

(ii) in the event that the required translation is not furnished within the time limit under paragraph (a), to furnish it and to pay, where applicable, the late furnishing fee referred to in paragraph (e), within one month from the date of the invitation or two months from the date of receipt of the international application by the receiving Office, whichever expires later.

(d) Where the receiving Office has sent to the applicant an invitation under paragraph (c) and the applicant has not, within the applicable time limit under paragraph (c)(ii), furnished the required translation and paid any required late furnishing fee, the international application shall be considered withdrawn and the receiving Office shall so declare. Any translation and any payment received by the receiving Office before that Office makes the declaration under the previous sentence and before the expiration of 15 months from the priority date shall be considered to have been received before the expiration of that time limit.

(e) The furnishing of a translation after the expiration of the time limit under paragraph (a) may be subjected by the receiving Office to the payment to it, for its own benefit, of a late furnishing fee equal to 25% of the international filing fee referred to in item 1 of the Schedule of Fees, not taking into account any fee for each sheet of the international application in excess of 30 sheets.

12.4 *Translation for the Purposes of International Publication*

(a) Where the language in which the international application is filed is not a language of publication and no translation is required under Rule 12.3(a), the applicant shall, within 14 months from the priority date, furnish to the receiving Office a translation of the international application into any language of publication which the receiving Office accepts for the purposes of this paragraph.

(b) Paragraph (a) shall not apply to the request nor to any sequence listing part of the description.

(c) Where the applicant has not, within the time limit referred to in paragraph (a), furnished a translation required under that paragraph, the receiving Office shall invite the applicant to furnish the required translation, and to pay, where applicable, the late furnishing fee required under paragraph (e), within 16 months from the priority date. Any translation received by the receiving Office before that Office sends the invitation under the previous sentence shall be considered to have been received before the expiration of the time limit under paragraph (a).

(d) Where the applicant has not, within the time limit under paragraph (c), furnished the required translation and paid any required late furnishing fee, the international application shall be considered withdrawn and the receiving Office shall so declare. Any translation and any payment received by the receiving Office before that Office makes the declaration under the previous sentence and before the expiration of 17 months from the priority date shall be considered to have been received before the expiration of that time limit.

(e) The furnishing of a translation after the expiration of the time limit under paragraph (a) may be subjected by the receiving Office to the payment to it, for its own benefit, of a late furnishing fee equal to 25% of the international filing fee referred to in item 1 of the Schedule of Fees, not taking into account any fee for each sheet of the international application in excess of 30 sheets.

[1.854]

Rule 12*bis*

Submission by the Applicant of Documents Relating to Earlier Search

12*bis*.1 *Furnishing by the Applicant of Documents Related to Earlier Search in Case of Request under Rule 4.12*

(a) Where the applicant has, under Rule 4.12, requested the International Searching Authority to take into account the results of an earlier search carried out by the same or another International Searching Authority or by a national Office, the applicant shall, subject to paragraphs (b) to (d), submit to the receiving Office, together with the international application, a copy of the results of the earlier search, in whatever form (for example, in the form of a search report, a listing of cited prior art or an examination report) they are presented by the Authority or Office concerned.

(b) Where the earlier search was carried out by the same Office as that which is acting as the receiving Office, the applicant may, instead of submitting the copy referred to in paragraph (a), indicate the wish that the receiving Office prepare and transmit it to the International Searching Authority. Such request shall be made in the request and may be subjected by the receiving Office to the payment to it, for its own benefit, of a fee.

(c) Where the earlier search was carried out by the same International Searching Authority, or by the same Office as that which is acting as the International Searching Authority, no copy referred to in paragraph (a) shall be required to be submitted under that paragraph.

(d) Where a copy referred to in paragraph (a) is available to the receiving Office or the International Searching Authority in a form and manner acceptable to it, for example, from a digital library, and the applicant so indicates in the request, no copy shall be required to be submitted under that paragraph.

12*bis*.2 *Invitation by the International Searching Authority to Furnish Documents Related to Earlier Search in Case of Request under Rule 4.12*

(a) The International Searching Authority may, subject to paragraphs (b) and (c), invite the applicant to furnish to it, within a time limit which shall be reasonable under the circumstances:

(i) a copy of the earlier application concerned;

(ii) where the earlier application is in a language which is not accepted by the International Searching Authority, a translation of the earlier application into a language which is accepted by that Authority;

(iii) where the results of the earlier search are in a language which is not accepted by the International Searching Authority, a translation of those results into a language which is accepted by that Authority;

(iv) a copy of any document cited in the results of the earlier search.

(b) Where the earlier search was carried out by the same International Searching Authority, or by the same Office as that which is acting as the International Searching Authority, or where a copy or translation referred to in paragraph (a) is available to the International Searching Authority in a form and manner acceptable to it, for example, from a digital library, or in the form of the priority document, no copy or translation referred to in paragraph (a) shall be required to be submitted under that paragraph.

(c) Where the request contains a statement under Rule 4.12(ii) to the effect that the international application is the same, or substantially the same, as the application in respect of which the earlier search was carried out, or that the international application is the same, or substantially the same, as that earlier application except that it is filed in a different language, no copy or translation referred to in paragraphs (a)(i) and (ii) shall be required to be submitted under those paragraphs.

[1.855]

Rule 13
Unity of Invention

13.1 *Requirement*

The international application shall relate to one invention only or to a group of inventions so linked as to form a single general inventive concept ("requirement of unity of invention").

13.2 *Circumstances in Which the Requirement of Unity of Invention Is to Be Considered Fulfilled*

Where a group of inventions is claimed in one and the same international application, the requirement of unity of invention referred to in Rule 13.1 shall be fulfilled only when there is a technical relationship among those inventions involving one or more of the same or corresponding special technical features. The expression "special technical features" shall mean those technical features that define a contribution which each of the claimed inventions, considered as a whole, makes over the prior art.

13.3 *Determination of Unity of Invention Not Affected by Manner of Claiming*

The determination whether a group of inventions is so linked as to form a single general inventive concept shall be made without regard to whether the inventions are claimed in separate claims or as alternatives within a single claim.

13.4 *Dependent Claims*

Subject to Rule 13.1, it shall be permitted to include in the same international application a reasonable number of dependent claims, claiming specific forms of the invention claimed in an independent claim, even where the features of any dependent claim could be considered as constituting in themselves an invention.

13.5 *Utility Models*

Any designated State in which the grant of a utility model is sought on the basis of an international application may, instead of Rules 13.1 to 13.4, apply in respect of the matters regulated in those Rules the provisions of its national law concerning utility models once the processing of the international application has started in that State, provided that the applicant shall be allowed at least two months from the expiration of the time limit applicable under Article 22 to adapt his application to the requirements of the said provisions of the national law.

[1.856]
Rule 13*bis*
Inventions Relating to Biological Material

13*bis*.1 *Definition*

For the purposes of this Rule, "reference to deposited biological material" means particulars given in an international application with respect to the deposit of biological material with a depositary institution or to the biological material so deposited.

13*bis*.2 *References (General)*

Any reference to deposited biological material shall be made in accordance with this Rule and, if so made, shall be considered as satisfying the requirements of the national law of each designated State.

13*bis*.3 *References: Contents; Failure to Include Reference or Indication*

(a) A reference to deposited biological material shall indicate:
   (i) the name and the address of the depositary institution with which the deposit was made;
   (ii) the date of deposit of the biological material with that institution;
   (iii) the accession number given to the deposit by that institution; and
   (iv) any additional matter of which the International Bureau has been notified pursuant to Rule 13*bis*.7(a)(i), provided that the requirement to indicate that matter was published in the Gazette in accordance with Rule 13*bis*.7(c) at least two months before the filing of the international application.

(b) Failure to include a reference to deposited biological material or failure to include, in a reference to deposited biological material, an indication in accordance with paragraph (a), shall have no consequence in any designated State whose national law does not require such reference or such indication in a national application.

13*bis*.4 *References: Time Limit for Furnishing Indications*

(a) Subject to paragraphs (b) and (c), if any of the indications referred to in Rule 13*bis*.3(a) is not included in a reference to deposited biological material in the international application as filed but is furnished to the International Bureau:
   (i) within 16 months from the priority date, the indication shall be considered by any designated Office to have been furnished in time;
   (ii) after the expiration of 16 months from the priority date, the indication shall be considered by any designated Office to have been furnished on the last day of that time limit if it reaches the International Bureau before the technical preparations for international publication have been completed.

(b) If the national law applicable by a designated Office so requires in respect of national applications, that Office may require that any of the indications referred to in Rule 13*bis*.3(a) be furnished earlier than 16 months from the priority date, provided that the International Bureau has been notified of such requirement pursuant to Rule 13*bis*.7(a)(ii) and has published such requirement in the Gazette in accordance with Rule 13*bis*.7(c) at least two months before the filing of the international application.

(c) Where the applicant makes a request for early publication under Article 21(2)(b), any designated Office may consider any indication not furnished before the technical preparations for international publication have been completed as not having been furnished in time.

(d) The International Bureau shall notify the applicant of the date on which it received any indication furnished under paragraph (a), and:
   (i) if the indication was received before the technical preparations for international publication have been completed, publish the indication furnished under paragraph (a), and an indication of the date of receipt, together with the international application;
   (ii) if the indication was received after the technical preparations for international publication have been completed, notify that date and the relevant data from the indication to the designated Offices.

13*bis*.5 *References and Indications for the Purposes of One or More Designated States; Different Deposits for Different Designated States; Deposits with Depositary Institutions Other than Those Notified*

(a) A reference to deposited biological material shall be considered to be made for the purposes of all designated States, unless it is expressly made for the purposes of certain of the designated States only; the same applies to the indications included in the reference.

(b) References to different deposits of the biological material may be made for different designated States.

(c) Any designated Office may disregard a deposit made with a depositary institution other than one notified by it under Rule 13*bis*.7(b).

13*bis*.6 *Furnishing of Samples*

Pursuant to Articles 23 and 40, no furnishing of samples of the deposited biological material to which a reference is made in an international application shall, except with the authorization of the applicant, take place before the expiration of the applicable time limits after which national processing may start under the said Articles. However, where the applicant performs the acts referred to in Articles 22 or 39 after international publication but before the expiration of the said time limits, the furnishing of samples of the deposited biological material may take place, once the said acts have been performed. Notwithstanding the previous provision, the furnishing of samples of the deposited biological material may take place under the national law applicable by any designated Office as soon as, under that law, the international publication has the effects of the compulsory national publication of an unexamined national application.

13*bis*.7 *National Requirements: Notification and Publication*

(a) Any national Office may notify the International Bureau of any requirement of the national law:

(i) that any matter specified in the notification, in addition to those referred to in Rule 13*bis*.3(a)(i), (ii) and (iii), is required to be included in a reference to deposited biological material in a national application;

(ii) that one or more of the indications referred to in Rule 13*bis*.3(a) are required to be included in a national application as filed or are required to be furnished at a time specified in the notification which is earlier than 16 months from the priority date.

(b) Each national Office shall notify the International Bureau of the depositary institutions with which the national law permits deposits of biological materials to be made for the purposes of patent procedure before that Office or, if the national law does not provide for or permit such deposits, of that fact.

(c) The International Bureau shall promptly publish in the Gazette requirements notified to it under paragraph (a) and information notified to it under paragraph (b).

[1.857]

Rule 13*ter*

Nucleotide and/or Amino Acid Sequence Listings

13*ter*.1 *Procedure before the International Searching Authority*

(a) Where the international application contains disclosure of one or more nucleotide and/or amino acid sequences, the International Searching Authority may invite the applicant to furnish to it, for the purposes of the international search, a sequence listing in electronic form complying with the standard provided for in the Administrative Instructions, unless such listing in electronic form is already available to it in a form and manner acceptable to it, and to pay to it, where applicable, the late furnishing fee referred to in paragraph (c), within a time limit fixed in the invitation.

(b) Where at least part of the international application is filed on paper and the International Searching Authority finds that the description does not comply with Rule 5.2(a), it may invite the applicant to furnish, for the purposes of the international search, a sequence listing in paper form complying with the standard provided for in the Administrative Instructions, unless such listing in paper form is already available to it in a form and manner acceptable to it, whether or not the furnishing of a sequence listing in electronic form is invited under paragraph (a), and to pay, where applicable, the late furnishing fee referred to in paragraph (c), within a time limit fixed in the invitation.

(c) The furnishing of a sequence listing in response to an invitation under paragraph (a) or (b) may be subjected by the International Searching Authority to the payment to it, for its own benefit, of a late furnishing fee whose amount shall be determined by the International Searching Authority but shall not exceed 25% of the international filing fee referred to in item 1 of the Schedule of Fees, not taking into account any fee for each sheet of the international application in excess of 30 sheets, provided that a late furnishing fee may be required under either paragraph (a) or (b) but not both.

(d) If the applicant does not, within the time limit fixed in the invitation under paragraph (a) or (b), furnish the required sequence listing and pay any required late furnishing fee, the International Searching Authority shall only be required to search the international application to the extent that a meaningful search can be carried out without the sequence listing.

(e) Any sequence listing not contained in the international application as filed, whether furnished in response to an invitation under paragraph (a) or (b) or otherwise, shall not form part of the international application, but this paragraph shall not prevent the applicant from amending the description in relation to a sequence listing pursuant to Article 34(2)(b).

(f) Where the International Searching Authority finds that the description does not comply with Rule 5.2(b), it shall invite the applicant to submit the required correction. Rule 26.4 shall apply *mutatis mutandis* to any correction offered by the applicant. The International Searching Authority shall transmit the correction to the receiving Office and to the International Bureau.

13*ter*.2 *Procedure before the International Preliminary Examining Authority*
Rule 13*ter*.1 shall apply *mutatis mutandis* to the procedure before the International Preliminary Examining Authority.
13*ter*.3 *Sequence Listing for Designated Office*
No designated Office shall require the applicant to furnish to it a sequence listing other than a sequence listing complying with the standard provided for in the Administrative Instructions.

[1.858]
Rule 14
The Transmittal Fee
14.1 *The Transmittal Fee*
(a) Any receiving Office may require that the applicant pay a fee to it, for its own benefit, for receiving the international application, transmitting copies to the International Bureau and the competent International Searching Authority, and performing all the other tasks which it must perform in connection with the international application in its capacity of receiving Office ("transmittal fee").
(b) The amount of the transmittal fee, if any, shall be fixed by the receiving Office.
(c) The transmittal fee shall be paid within one month from the date of receipt of the international application. The amount payable shall be the amount applicable on that date of receipt.

[1.859]
Rule 15
The International Filing Fee
15.1 *The International Filing Fee*
Each international application shall be subject to the payment of a fee for the benefit of the International Bureau ("international filing fee") to be collected by the receiving Office.
15.2 *Amount*
(a) The amount of the international filing fee is as set out in the Schedule of Fees.
(b) The international filing fee shall be payable in the currency or one of the currencies prescribed by the receiving Office ("prescribed currency").
(c) Where the prescribed currency is the Swiss franc, the receiving Office shall promptly transfer the said fee to the International Bureau in Swiss francs.
(d) Where the prescribed currency is a currency other than the Swiss franc and that currency:
(i) is freely convertible into Swiss francs, the Director General shall establish, for each receiving Office which prescribes such a currency for the payment of the international filing fee, an equivalent amount of that fee in the prescribed currency according to directives given by the Assembly, and the amount in that currency shall promptly be transferred by the receiving Office to the International Bureau;
(ii) is not freely convertible into Swiss francs, the receiving Office shall be responsible for the conversion of the international filing fee from the prescribed currency into Swiss francs and shall promptly transfer that fee in Swiss francs, in the amount set out in the Schedule of Fees, to the International Bureau. Alternatively, if the receiving Office so wishes, it may convert the international filing fee from the prescribed currency into euros or US dollars and promptly transfer the equivalent amount of that fee in euros or US dollars, as established by the Director General according to directives given by the Assembly as referred to in item (i), to the International Bureau.
15.3 *Time Limit for Payment; Amount Payable*
The international filing fee shall be paid to the receiving Office within one month from the date of receipt of the international application. The amount payable shall be the amount applicable on that date of receipt.
15.4 *Refund*
The receiving Office shall refund the international filing fee to the applicant:
(i) if the determination under Article 11(1) is negative,
(ii) if, before the transmittal of the record copy to the International Bureau, the international application is withdrawn or considered withdrawn, or
(iii) if, due to prescriptions concerning national security, the international application is not treated as such.

[1.860]
Rule 16
The Search Fee
16.1 *Right to Ask for a Fee*
(a) Each International Searching Authority may require that the applicant pay a fee ("search fee") for its own benefit for carrying out the international search and for performing all other tasks entrusted to International Searching Authorities by the Treaty and these Regulations.

(b) The search fee shall be collected by the receiving Office. The said fee shall be payable in the currency prescribed by that Office ("prescribed currency").

(c) Where the prescribed currency is the currency in which the International Searching Authority has fixed the said fee ("fixed currency"), the receiving Office shall promptly transfer the said fee to that Authority in that currency.

(d) Where the prescribed currency is not the fixed currency and that currency:

(i) is freely convertible into the fixed currency, the Director General shall establish, for each receiving Office which prescribes such a currency for the payment of the search fee, an equivalent amount of that fee in the prescribed currency according to directives given by the Assembly, and the amount in that currency shall promptly be transferred by the receiving Office to the International Searching Authority;

(ii) is not freely convertible into the fixed currency, the receiving Office shall be responsible for the conversion of the search fee from the prescribed currency into the fixed currency and shall promptly transfer that fee in the fixed currency, in the amount fixed by the International Searching Authority, to the International Searching Authority.

(e) Where, in respect of the payment of the search fee in a prescribed currency, other than the fixed currency, the amount actually received under paragraph (d)(i) of this Rule by the International Searching Authority in the prescribed currency is, when converted by it into the fixed currency, less than that fixed by it, the difference will be paid to the International Searching Authority by the International Bureau, whereas, if the amount actually received is more, the difference will belong to the International Bureau.

(f) As to the time limit for payment of the search fee and the amount payable, the provisions of Rule 15.3 relating to the international filing fee shall apply *mutatis mutandis*.

16.2 *Refund*

The receiving Office shall refund the search fee to the applicant:

(i) if the determination under Article 11(1) is negative,

(ii) if, before the transmittal of the search copy to the International Searching Authority, the international application is withdrawn or considered withdrawn, or

(iii) if, due to prescriptions concerning national security, the international application is not treated as such.

16.3 *Partial Refund*

Where the International Searching Authority takes into account, under Rule 41.1, the results of an earlier search in carrying out the international search, that Authority shall refund the search fee paid in connection with the international application to the extent and under the conditions provided for in the agreement under Article 16(3)(b).

[1.861]
Rule 16*bis*
Extension of Time Limits for Payment of Fees

16*bis*.1 *Invitation by the Receiving Office*

(a) Where, by the time they are due under Rules 14.1(c), 15.3 and 16.1(f), the receiving Office finds that no fees were paid to it, or that the amount paid to it is insufficient to cover the transmittal fee, the international filing fee and the search fee, the receiving Office shall, subject to paragraph (d), invite the applicant to pay to it the amount required to cover those fees, together with, where applicable, the late payment fee under Rule 16*bis*.2, within a time limit of one month from the date of the invitation.

(b) *[Deleted]*

(c) Where the receiving Office has sent to the applicant an invitation under paragraph (a) and the applicant has not, within the time limit referred to in that paragraph, paid in full the amount due, including, where applicable, the late payment fee under Rule 16*bis*.2, the receiving Office shall, subject to paragraph (e):

(i) make the applicable declaration under Article 14(3), and

(ii) proceed as provided in Rule 29.

(d) Any payment received by the receiving Office before that Office sends the invitation under paragraph (a) shall be considered to have been received before the expiration of the time limit under Rule 14.1(c), 15.3 or 16.1(f), as the case may be.

(e) Any payment received by the receiving Office before that Office makes the applicable declaration under Article 14(3) shall be considered to have been received before the expiration of the time limit referred to in paragraph (a).

16*bis*.2 *Late Payment Fee*

(a) The payment of fees in response to an invitation under Rule 16*bis*.1(a) may be subjected by the receiving Office to the payment to it, for its own benefit, of a late payment fee. The amount of that fee shall be:

(i) 50% of the amount of unpaid fees which is specified in the invitation, or,

(ii) if the amount calculated under item (i) is less than the transmittal fee, an amount equal to the transmittal fee.

(b) The amount of the late payment fee shall not, however, exceed the amount of 50% of the international filing fee referred to in item 1 of the Schedule of Fees, not taking into account any fee for each sheet of the international application in excess of 30 sheets.

[1.862]
Rule 17
The Priority Document

17.1 *Obligation to Submit Copy of Earlier National or International Application*

(a) Where the priority of an earlier national or international application is claimed under Article 8, a copy of that earlier application, certified by the authority with which it was filed ("the priority document"), shall, unless that priority document has already been filed with the receiving Office together with the international application in which the priority claim is made, and subject to paragraphs (b) and (b-*bis*), be submitted by the applicant to the International Bureau or to the receiving Office not later than 16 months after the priority date, provided that any copy of the said earlier application which is received by the International Bureau after the expiration of that time limit shall be considered to have been received by that Bureau on the last day of that time limit if it reaches it before the date of international publication of the international application.

(b) Where the priority document is issued by the receiving Office, the applicant may, instead of submitting the priority document, request the receiving Office to prepare and transmit the priority document to the International Bureau. Such request shall be made not later than 16 months after the priority date and may be subjected by the receiving Office to the payment of a fee.

(b-*bis*) Where the priority document is, in accordance with the Administrative Instructions, made available to the International Bureau from a digital library prior to the date of international publication of the international application, the applicant may, instead of submitting the priority document, request the International Bureau, prior to the date of international publication, to obtain the priority document from such digital library.

(c) If the requirements of none of the three preceding paragraphs are complied with, any designated Office may, subject to paragraph (d), disregard the priority claim, provided that no designated Office shall disregard the priority claim before giving the applicant an opportunity to furnish the priority document within a time limit which shall be reasonable under the circumstances.

(d) No designated Office shall disregard the priority claim under paragraph (c) if the earlier application referred to in paragraph (a) was filed with it in its capacity as national Office or if the priority document is, in accordance with the Administrative Instructions, available to it from a digital library.

17.2 *Availability of Copies*

(a) Where the applicant has complied with Rule 17.1(a), (b) or (b-*bis*), the International Bureau shall, at the specific request of the designated Office, promptly but not prior to the international publication of the international application, furnish a copy of the priority document to that Office. No such Office shall ask the applicant himself to furnish it with a copy. The applicant shall not be required to furnish a translation to the designated Office before the expiration of the applicable time limit under Article 22. Where the applicant makes an express request to the designated Office under Article 23(2) prior to the international publication of the international application, the International Bureau shall, at the specific request of the designated Office, furnish a copy of the priority document to that Office promptly after receiving it.

(b) The International Bureau shall not make copies of the priority document available to the public prior to the international publication of the international application.

(c) Where the international application has been published under Article 21, the International Bureau shall furnish a copy of the priority document to any person upon request and subject to reimbursement of the cost unless, prior to that publication:

(i) the international application was withdrawn,

(ii) the relevant priority claim was withdrawn or considered, under Rule 26*bis*.2(b), not to have been made.

[1.863]
Rule 18
The Applicant

18.1 *Residence and Nationality*

(a) Subject to the provisions of paragraphs (b) and (c), the question whether an applicant is a resident or national of the Contracting State of which he claims to be a resident or national shall depend on the national law of that State and shall be decided by the receiving Office.

(b) In any case,

(i) possession of a real and effective industrial or commercial establishment in a Contracting State shall be considered residence in that State, and

(ii) a legal entity constituted according to the national law of a Contracting State shall be considered a national of that State.

(c) Where the international application is filed with the International Bureau as receiving Office, the International Bureau shall, in the circumstances specified in the Administrative Instructions, request the national Office of, or acting for, the Contracting State concerned to decide the question referred to in paragraph (a). The International Bureau shall inform the applicant of any such request. The applicant shall have an opportunity to submit arguments directly to the national Office. The national Office shall decide the said question promptly.

18.2 *[Deleted]*

18.3 *Two or More Applicants*

If there are two or more applicants, the right to file an international application shall exist if at least one of them is entitled to file an international application according to Article 9.

18.4 *Information on Requirements under National Law as to Applicants*

(a) and (b) *[Deleted]*

(c) The International Bureau shall, from time to time, publish information on the various national laws in respect of the question who is qualified (inventor, successor in title of the inventor, owner of the invention, or other) to file a national application and shall accompany such information by a warning that the effect of the international application in any designated State may depend on whether the person designated in the international application as applicant for the purposes of that State is a person who, under the national law of that State, is qualified to file a national application.

[1.864]

Rule 19

The Competent Receiving Office

19.1 *Where to File*

(a) Subject to the provisions of paragraph (b), the international application shall be filed, at the option of the applicant,

(i) with the national Office of or acting for the Contracting State of which the applicant is a resident,

(ii) with the national Office of or acting for the Contracting State of which the applicant is a national, or

(iii) irrespective of the Contracting State of which the applicant is a resident or national, with the International Bureau.

(b) Any Contracting State may agree with another Contracting State or any intergovernmental organization that the national Office of the latter State or the intergovernmental organization shall, for all or some purposes, act instead of the national Office of the former State as receiving Office for applicants who are residents or nationals of that former State. Notwithstanding such agreement, the national Office of the former State shall be considered the competent receiving Office for the purposes of Article 15(5).

(c) In connection with any decision made under Article 9(2), the Assembly shall appoint the national Office or the intergovernmental organization which will act as receiving Office for applications of residents or nationals of States specified by the Assembly. Such appointment shall require the previous consent of the said national Office or intergovernmental organization.

19.2 *Two or More Applicants*

If there are two or more applicants:

(i) the requirements of Rule 19.1 shall be considered to be met if the national Office with which the international application is filed is the national Office of or acting for a Contracting State of which at least one of the applicants is a resident or national;

(ii) the international application may be filed with the International Bureau under Rule 19.1(a)(iii) if at least one of the applicants is a resident or national of a Contracting State.

19.3 *Publication of Fact of Delegation of Duties of Receiving Office*

(a) Any agreement referred to in Rule 19.1(b) shall be promptly notified to the International Bureau by the Contracting State which delegates the duties of the receiving Office to the national Office of or acting for another Contracting State or an intergovernmental organization.

(b) The International Bureau shall, promptly upon receipt, publish the notification in the Gazette.

19.4 *Transmittal to the International Bureau as Receiving Office*

(a) Where an international application is filed with a national Office which acts as a receiving Office under the Treaty but

(i) that national Office is not competent under Rule 19.1 or 19.2 to receive that international application, or

(ii) that international application is not in a language accepted under Rule 12.1(a) by that national Office but is in a language accepted under that Rule by the International Bureau as receiving Office, or

(iii) that national Office and the International Bureau agree, for any reason other than those specified under items (i) and (ii), and with the authorization of the applicant, that the procedure under this Rule should apply, that international application shall, subject to paragraph (b), be considered to have been received by that Office on behalf of the International Bureau as receiving Office under Rule 19.1(a)(iii).

(b) Where, pursuant to paragraph (a), an international application is received by a national Office on behalf of the International Bureau as receiving Office under Rule 19.1(a)(iii), that national Office shall, unless prescriptions concerning national security prevent the international application from being so transmitted, promptly transmit it to the International Bureau. Such transmittal may be subjected by the national Office to the payment of a fee, for its own benefit, equal to the transmittal fee charged by that Office under Rule 14. The international application so transmitted shall be considered to have been received by the International Bureau as receiving Office under Rule 19.1(a)(iii) on the date of receipt of the international application by that national Office.

(c) For the purposes of Rules 14.1(c), 15.3 and 16.1(f), where the international application was transmitted to the International Bureau under paragraph (b), the date of receipt of the international application shall be considered to be the date on which the international application was actually received by the International Bureau. For the purposes of this paragraph, the last sentence of paragraph (b) shall not apply.

[1.865]
Rule 20
International Filing Date

20.1 *Determination under Article 11(1)*

(a) Promptly after receipt of the papers purporting to be an international application, the receiving Office shall determine whether the papers fulfill the requirements of Article 11(1).

(b) For the purposes of Article 11(1)(iii)(c), it shall be sufficient to indicate the name of the applicant in a way which allows the identity of the applicant to be established even if the name is misspelled, the given names are not fully indicated, or, in the case of legal entities, the indication of the name is abbreviated or incomplete.

(c) For the purposes of Article 11(1)(ii), it shall be sufficient that the part which appears to be a description (other than any sequence listing part thereof) and the part which appears to be a claim or claims be in a language accepted by the receiving Office under Rule 12.1(a).

(d) If, on October 1, 1997, paragraph (c) is not compatible with the national law applied by the receiving Office, paragraph (c) shall not apply to that receiving Office for as long as it continues not to be compatible with that law, provided that the said Office informs the International Bureau accordingly by December 31, 1997. The information received shall be promptly published by the International Bureau in the Gazette.

20.2 *Positive Determination under Article 11(1)*

(a) If the receiving Office determines that, at the time of receipt of the papers purporting to be an international application, the requirements of Article 11(1) were fulfilled, the receiving Office shall accord as the international filing date the date of receipt of the international application.

(b) The receiving Office shall stamp the request of the international application which it has accorded an international filing date as prescribed by the Administrative Instructions. The copy whose request has been so stamped shall be the record copy of the international application.

(c) The receiving Office shall promptly notify the applicant of the international application number and the international filing date. At the same time, it shall send to the International Bureau a copy of the notification sent to the applicant, except where it has already sent, or is sending at the same time, the record copy to the International Bureau under Rule 22.1(a).

20.3 *Defects under Article 11(1)*

(a) Where, in determining whether the papers purporting to be an international application fulfill the requirements of Article 11(1), the receiving Office finds that any of the requirements of Article 11(1) are not, or appear not to be fulfilled, it shall promptly invite the applicant, at the applicant's option:

(i) to furnish the required correction under Article 11(2); or

(ii) where the requirements concerned are those relating to an element referred to in Article 11(1)(iii)(d) or (e), to confirm in accordance with Rule 20.6(a) that the element is incorporated by reference under Rule 4.18;

and to make observations, if any, within the applicable time limit under Rule 20.7. If that time limit expires after the expiration of 12 months from the filing date of any application whose priority is claimed, the receiving Office shall call that circumstance to the attention of the applicant.

(b) Where, following an invitation under paragraph (a) or otherwise:

(i) the applicant furnishes to the receiving Office the required correction under Article 11(2) after the date of receipt of the purported international application but on a later date falling within the applicable time limit under Rule 20.7, the receiving Office shall accord that later date as the international filing date and proceed as provided in Rule 20.2(b) and (c);

(ii) an element referred to in Article 11(1)(iii)(d) or (e) is, under Rule 20.6(b), considered to have been contained in the international application on the date on which one or more elements referred to in Article 11(1)(iii) were first received by the receiving Office, the receiving Office shall accord as the international filing date the date on which all of the requirements of Article 11(1) are fulfilled and proceed as provided in Rule 20.2(b) and (c).

(c) If the receiving Office later discovers, or on the basis of the applicant's reply realizes, that it has erred in issuing an invitation under paragraph (a) since the requirements of Article 11(1) were fulfilled when the papers were received, it shall proceed as provided in Rule 20.2.

20.4 *Negative Determination under Article 11(1)*

If the receiving Office does not receive, within the applicable time limit under Rule 20.7, a correction or confirmation referred to in Rule 20.3(a), or if a correction or confirmation has been received but the application still does not fulfill the requirements of Article 11(1), the receiving Office shall:

(i) promptly notify the applicant that the application is not and will not be treated as an international application and shall indicate the reasons therefor;

(ii) notify the International Bureau that the number it has marked on the papers will not be used as an international application number;

(iii) keep the papers constituting the purported international application and any correspondence relating thereto as provided in Rule 93.1; and

(iv) send a copy of the said papers to the International Bureau where, pursuant to a request by the applicant under Article 25(1), the International Bureau needs such a copy and specially asks for it.

20.5 *Missing Parts*

(a) Where, in determining whether the papers purporting to be an international application fulfill the requirements of Article 11(1), the receiving Office finds that a part of the description, claims or drawings is or appears to be missing, including the case where all of the drawings are or appear to be missing but not including the case where an entire element referred to in Article 11(1)(iii)(d) or (e) is or appears to be missing, it shall promptly invite the applicant, at the applicant's option:

(i) to complete the purported international application by furnishing the missing part; or

(ii) to confirm, in accordance with Rule 20.6(a), that the part was incorporated by reference under Rule 4.18;

and to make observations, if any, within the applicable time limit under Rule 20.7. If that time limit expires after the expiration of 12 months from the filing date of any application whose priority is claimed, the receiving Office shall call that circumstance to the attention of the applicant.

(b) Where, following an invitation under paragraph (a) or otherwise, the applicant furnishes to the receiving Office, on or before the date on which all of the requirements of Article 11(1) are fulfilled but within the applicable time limit under Rule 20.7, a missing part referred to in paragraph (a) so as to complete the international application, that part shall be included in the application and the receiving Office shall accord as the international filing date the date on which all of the requirements of Article 11(1) are fulfilled and proceed as provided in Rule 20.2(b) and (c).

(c) Where, following an invitation under paragraph (a) or otherwise, the applicant furnishes to the receiving Office, after the date on which all of the requirements of Article 11(1) were fulfilled but within the applicable time limit under Rule 20.7, a missing part referred to in paragraph (a) so as to complete the international application, that part shall be included in the application, and the receiving Office shall correct the international filing date to the date on which the receiving Office received that part, notify the applicant accordingly and proceed as provided for in the Administrative Instructions.

(d) Where, following an invitation under paragraph (a) or otherwise, a part referred to in paragraph (a) is, under Rule 20.6(b), considered to have been contained in the purported international application on the date on which one or more elements referred to in Article 11(1)(iii) were first received by the receiving Office, the receiving Office shall accord as the international filing date the date on which all of the requirements of Article 11(1) are fulfilled and proceed as provided in Rule 20.2(b) and (c).

(e) Where the international filing date has been corrected under paragraph (c), the applicant may, in a notice submitted to the receiving Office within one month from the date of the notification under paragraph (c), request that the missing part concerned be disregarded, in which case the missing part shall be considered not to have been furnished and the correction of the international filing date under that paragraph shall be considered not to have been made, and the receiving Office shall proceed as provided for in the Administrative Instructions.

20.6 *Confirmation of Incorporation by Reference of Elements and Parts*

(a) The applicant may submit to the receiving Office, within the applicable time limit under Rule 20.7, a written notice confirming that an element or part is incorporated by reference in the international application under Rule 4.18, accompanied by:

(i) a sheet or sheets embodying the entire element as contained in the earlier application or embodying the part concerned;

(ii) where the applicant has not already complied with Rule 17.1(a), (b) or (b-*bis*) in relation to the priority document, a copy of the earlier application as filed;

(iii) where the earlier application is not in the language in which the international application is filed, a translation of the earlier application into that language or, where a translation of the international application is required under Rule 12.3(a) or 12.4(a), a translation of the earlier application into both the language in which the international application is filed and the language of that translation; and

(iv) in the case of a part of the description, claims or drawings, an indication as to where that part is contained in the earlier application and, where applicable, in any translation referred to in item (iii).

(b) Where the receiving Office finds that the requirements of Rule 4.18 and paragraph (a) have been complied with and that the element or part referred to in paragraph (a) is completely contained in the earlier application concerned, that element or part shall be considered to have been contained in the purported international application on the date on which one or more elements referred to in Article 11(1)(iii) were first received by the receiving Office.

(c) Where the receiving Office finds that a requirement under Rule 4.18 or paragraph (a) has not been complied with or that the element or part referred to in paragraph (a) is not completely contained in the earlier application concerned, the receiving Office shall proceed as provided for in Rule 20.3(b)(i), 20.5(b) or 20.5(c), as the case may be.

20.7 *Time Limit*

(a) The applicable time limit referred to in Rules 20.3(a) and (b), 20.4, 20.5(a), (b) and (c), and 20.6(a) shall be:

(i) where an invitation under Rule 20.3(a) or 20.5(a), as applicable, was sent to the applicant, two months from the date of the invitation;

(ii) where no such invitation was sent to the applicant, two months from the date on which one or more elements referred to in Article 11(1)(iii) were first received by the receiving Office.

(b) Where neither a correction under Article 11(2) nor a notice under Rule 20.6(a) confirming the incorporation by reference of an element referred to in Article 11(1)(iii)(d) or (e) is received by the receiving Office prior to the expiration of the applicable time limit under paragraph (a), any such correction or notice received by that Office after the expiration of that time limit but before it sends a notification to the applicant under Rule 20.4(i) shall be considered to have been received within that time limit.

20.8 *Incompatibility with National Laws*

(a) If, on October 5, 2005, any of Rules 20.3(a)(ii) and (b)(ii), 20.5(a)(ii) and (d), and 20.6 are not compatible with the national law applied by the receiving Office, the Rules concerned shall not apply to an international application filed with that receiving Office for as long as they continue not to be compatible with that law, provided that the said Office informs the International Bureau accordingly by April 5, 2006. The information received shall be promptly published by the International Bureau in the Gazette.

(a-*bis*) Where a missing element or part cannot be incorporated by reference in the international application under Rules 4.18 and 20.6 because of the operation of paragraph (a) of this Rule, the receiving Office shall proceed as provided for in Rule 20.3(b)(i), 20.5(b) or 20.5(c), as the case may be. Where the receiving Office proceeds as provided for in Rule 20.5(c), the applicant may proceed as provided for in Rule 20.5(e).

(b) If, on October 5, 2005, any of Rules 20.3(a)(ii) and (b)(ii), 20.5(a)(ii) and (d), and 20.6 are not compatible with the national law applied by the designated Office, the Rules concerned shall not apply in respect of that Office in relation to an international application in respect of which the acts referred to in Article 22 have been performed before that Office for as long as they continue not to be compatible with that law, provided that the said Office informs the International Bureau accordingly by April 5, 2006. The information received shall be promptly published by the International Bureau in the Gazette.

(c) Where an element or part is considered to have been incorporated by reference in the international application by virtue of a finding of the receiving Office under Rule 20.6(b), but that incorporation by reference does not apply to the international application for the purposes of the procedure before a designated Office because of the operation of paragraph (b) of this Rule, the designated Office may treat the application as if the international filing date had been accorded under Rule 20.3(b)(i) or 20.5(b), or corrected under Rule 20.5(c), as the case may be, provided that Rule 82*ter*.1(c) and (d) shall apply *mutatis mutandis*.

[1.866]
Rule 21
Preparation of Copies

21.1 *Responsibility of the Receiving Office*

(a) Where the international application is required to be filed in one copy, the receiving Office shall be responsible for preparing the home copy and the search copy required under Article 12(1).

(b) Where the international application is required to be filed in two copies, the receiving Office shall be responsible for preparing the home copy.

(c) If the international application is filed in less than the number of copies required under Rule 11.1(b), the receiving Office shall be responsible for the prompt preparation of the number of copies required, and shall have the right to fix a fee for performing that task and to collect such fee from the applicant.

21.2 *Certified Copy for the Applicant*

Against payment of a fee, the receiving Office shall furnish to the applicant, on request, certified copies of the international application as filed and of any corrections thereto.

[1.867]
Rule 22
Transmittal of the Record Copy and Translation

22.1 *Procedure*

(a) If the determination under Article 11(1) is positive, and unless prescriptions concerning national security prevent the international application from being treated as such, the receiving Office shall transmit the record copy to the International Bureau. Such transmittal shall be effected promptly after receipt of the international application or, if a check to preserve national security must be performed, as soon as the necessary clearance has been obtained. In any case, the receiving Office shall transmit the record copy in time for it to reach the International Bureau by the expiration of the 13th month from the priority date. If the transmittal is effected by mail, the receiving Office shall mail the record copy not later than five days prior to the expiration of the 13th month from the priority date.

(b) If the International Bureau has received a copy of the notification under Rule 20.2(c) but is not, by the expiration of 13 months from the priority date, in possession of the record copy, it shall remind the receiving Office that it should transmit the record copy to the International Bureau promptly.

(c) If the International Bureau has received a copy of the notification under Rule 20.2(c) but is not, by the expiration of 14 months from the priority date, in possession of the record copy, it shall notify the applicant and the receiving Office accordingly.

(d) After the expiration of 14 months from the priority date, the applicant may request the receiving Office to certify a copy of his international application as being identical with the international application as filed and may transmit such certified copy to the International Bureau.

(e) Any certification under paragraph (d) shall be free of charge and may be refused only on any of the following grounds:

(i) the copy which the receiving Office has been requested to certify is not identical with the international application as filed;

(ii) prescriptions concerning national security prevent the international application from being treated as such;

(iii) the receiving Office has already transmitted the record copy to the International Bureau and that Bureau has informed the receiving Office that it has received the record copy.

(f) Unless the International Bureau has received the record copy, or until it receives the record copy, the copy certified under paragraph (e) and received by the International Bureau shall be considered to be the record copy.

(g) If, by the expiration of the time limit applicable under Article 22, the applicant has performed the acts referred to in that Article but the designated Office has not been informed by the International Bureau of the receipt of the record copy, the designated Office shall inform the International Bureau. If the International Bureau is not in possession of the record copy, it shall promptly notify the applicant and the receiving Office unless it has already notified them under paragraph (c).

(h) Where the international application is to be published in the language of a translation furnished under Rule 12.3 or 12.4, that translation shall be transmitted by the receiving Office to the International Bureau together with the record copy under paragraph (a) or, if the receiving Office has already transmitted the record copy to the International Bureau under that paragraph, promptly after receipt of the translation.

22.2 *[Deleted]*

22.3 *Time Limit under Article 12(3)*

The time limit referred to in Article 12(3) shall be three months from the date of the notification sent by the International Bureau to the applicant under Rule 22.1(c) or (g).

[1.868]
Rule 23
Transmittal of the Search Copy, Translation and Sequence Listing

23.1 *Procedure*

(a) Where no translation of the international application is required under Rule 12.3(a), the search copy shall be transmitted by the receiving Office to the International Searching Authority at the latest on the same day as the record copy is transmitted to the International Bureau unless no search fee has been paid. In the latter case, it shall be transmitted promptly after payment of the search fee.

(b) Where a translation of the international application is furnished under Rule 12.3, a copy of that translation and of the request, which together shall be considered to be the search copy under Article 12(1), shall be transmitted by the receiving Office to the International Searching Authority, unless no search fee has been paid. In the latter case, a copy of the said translation and of the request shall be transmitted promptly after payment of the search fee.

(c) Any sequence listing in electronic form which is furnished for the purposes of Rule 13*ter* but submitted to the receiving Office instead of the International Searching Authority shall be promptly transmitted by that Office to that Authority.

[1.869]
Rule 23*bis*
Transmittal of Documents Relating to Earlier Search or Classification

23*bis*.1 *Transmittal of Documents Relating to Earlier Search in Case of Request under Rule 4.12*

(a) The receiving Office shall transmit to the International Searching Authority, together with the search copy, any copy referred to in Rule 12*bis*.1(a) related to an earlier search in respect of which the applicant has made a request under Rule 4.12, provided that any such copy:

(i) has been submitted by the applicant to the receiving Office together with the international application;

(ii) has been requested by the applicant to be prepared and transmitted by the receiving Office to that Authority; or

(iii) is available to the receiving Office in a form and manner acceptable to it, for example, from a digital library, in accordance with Rule 12*bis*.1(d).

(b) If it is not included in the copy of the results of the earlier search referred to in Rule 12bis.1(a), the receiving Office shall also transmit to the International Searching Authority, together with the search copy, a copy of the results of any earlier classification effected by that Office, if already available.

23*bis*.2 *Transmittal of Documents Relating to Earlier Search or Classification for the Purposes of Rule 41.2*

(a) For the purposes of Rule 41.2, where the international application claims the priority of one or more earlier applications filed with the same Office as that which is acting as the receiving Office and that Office has carried out an earlier search in respect of such an earlier application or has classified such earlier application, the receiving Office shall, subject to Article 30(2)(a) as applicable by virtue of Article 30(3) and paragraphs (b), (d) and (e), transmit to the International Searching Authority, together with the search copy, a copy of the results of any such earlier search, in whatever form (for example, in the form of a search report, a listing of cited prior art or an examination report) they are available to the Office, and a copy of the results of any such earlier classification effected by the Office, if already available. The receiving Office may, subject to Article 30(2)(a) as applicable by virtue of Article 30(3), also transmit to the International Searching Authority any further documents relating to such an earlier search which it considers useful to that Authority for the purposes of carrying out the international search.[1]

(b) Notwithstanding paragraph (a), a receiving Office may notify the International Bureau by April 14, 2016 that it may, on request of the applicant submitted together with the international application, decide not to transmit the results of an earlier search to the International Searching Authority. The International Bureau shall publish any notification under this provision in the Gazette.

(c) At the option of the receiving Office, paragraph (a) shall apply mutatis mutandis where the international application claims the priority of one or more earlier applications filed with an Office different from the one which is acting as the receiving Office and that Office has carried out an earlier search in respect of such an earlier application or has classified such earlier application, and the results of any such earlier search or classification are available to the receiving Office in a form and manner acceptable to it, for example, from a digital library.

(d) Paragraphs (a) and (c) shall not apply where the earlier search was carried out by the same International Searching Authority or by the same Office as that which is acting as the International Searching Authority, or where the receiving Office is aware that a copy of the earlier search or classification results is available to the International Searching Authority in a form and manner acceptable to it, for example, from a digital library.

(e) To the extent that, on October 14, 2015, the transmission of the copies referred to in paragraph (a), or the transmission of such copies in a particular form, such as those referred to in paragraph (a), without the authorization by the applicant is not compatible with the national law applied by the receiving Office, that paragraph shall not apply to the transmission of such copies, or to the transmission of such copies in the particular form concerned, in respect of any international application filed with that receiving Office for as long as such transmission without the authorization by the applicant continues not to be compatible with that law, provided that the said Office informs the International Bureau accordingly by April 14, 2016. The information received shall be promptly published by the International Bureau in the Gazette.

NOTES

1 Editorial note: Rule 23*bis*.2(a) as set out above applies to any international application whose international filing date is on or after July 1, 2017. Rule 23*bis*.2(a) previously read as follows: "For the purposes of Rule 41.2, where the international application claims the priority of one or more earlier applications filed with the same Office as that which is acting as the receiving Office and that Office has carried out an earlier search in respect of such an earlier application or has classified such earlier application, the receiving Office shall, subject to paragraphs (b), (d) and (e), transmit to the International Searching Authority, together with the search copy, a copy of the results of any such earlier search, in whatever form (for example, in the form of a search report, a listing of cited prior art or an examination report) they are available to the Office, and a copy of the results of any such earlier classification effected by the Office, if already available. The receiving Office may also transmit to the International Searching Authority any further documents relating to such an earlier search which it considers useful to that Authority for the purposes of carrying out the international search.".

[1.870]
Rule 24
Receipt of the Record Copy by the International Bureau

24.1 *[Deleted]*

24.2 *Notification of Receipt of the Record Copy*

(a) The International Bureau shall promptly notify:
- (i) the applicant,
- (ii) the receiving Office, and
- (iii) the International Searching Authority (unless it has informed the International Bureau that it wishes not to be so notified),

of the fact and the date of receipt of the record copy. The notification shall identify the international application by its number, the international filing date and the name of the applicant, and shall indicate the filing date of any earlier application whose priority is claimed. The notification sent to the applicant shall also contain a list of the designated Offices and, in the case of a designated Office which is responsible for granting regional patents, of the Contracting States designated for such regional patent.

(b) *[Deleted]*

(c) If the record copy is received after the expiration of the time limit fixed in Rule 22.3, the International Bureau shall promptly notify the applicant, the receiving Office, and the International Searching Authority, accordingly.

[1.871]
Rule 25
Receipt of the Search Copy by the International Searching Authority

25.1 *Notification of Receipt of the Search Copy*

The International Searching Authority shall promptly notify the International Bureau, the applicant, and – unless the International Searching Authority is the same as the receiving Office – the receiving Office, of the fact and the date of receipt of the search copy.

[1.872]
Rule 26
Checking by, and Correcting before, the Receiving Office of Certain Elements of the International Application

26.1 *Invitation under Article 14(1)(b) to Correct*

The receiving Office shall issue the invitation to correct provided for in Article 14(1)(b) as soon as possible, preferably within one month from the receipt of the international application. In the invitation, the receiving Office shall invite the applicant to furnish the required correction, and give the applicant the opportunity to make observations, within the time limit under Rule 26.2.

26.2 *Time Limit for Correction*

The time limit referred to in Rule 26.1 shall be two months from the date of the invitation to correct. It may be extended by the receiving Office at any time before a decision is taken.

26.2*bis* *Checking of Requirements under Article 14(1)(a)(i) and (ii)*

(a) For the purposes of Article 14(1)(a)(i), if there is more than one applicant, it shall be sufficient that the request be signed by one of them.

(b) For the purposes of Article 14(1)(a)(ii), if there is more than one applicant, it shall be sufficient that the indications required under Rule 4.5(a)(ii) and (iii) be provided in respect of one of them who is entitled according to Rule 19.1 to file the international application with the receiving Office.

26.3 *Checking of Physical Requirements under Article 14(1)(a)(v)*

(a) Where the international application is filed in a language of publication, the receiving Office shall check:

(i) the international application for compliance with the physical requirements referred to in Rule 11 only to the extent that compliance therewith is necessary for the purpose of reasonably uniform international publication;

(ii) any translation furnished under Rule 12.3 for compliance with the physical requirements referred to in Rule 11 to the extent that compliance therewith is necessary for the purpose of satisfactory reproduction.

(b) Where the international application is filed in a language which is not a language of publication, the receiving Office shall check:

(i) the international application for compliance with the physical requirements referred to in Rule 11 only to the extent that compliance therewith is necessary for the purpose of satisfactory reproduction;

(ii) any translation furnished under Rule 12.3 or 12.4 and the drawings for compliance with the physical requirements referred to in Rule 11 to the extent that compliance therewith is necessary for the purpose of reasonably uniform international publication.

26.3*bis* *Invitation under Article 14(1)(b) to Correct Defects under Rule 11*

The receiving Office shall not be required to issue the invitation under Article 14(1)(b) to correct a defect under Rule 11 where the physical requirements referred to in that Rule are complied with to the extent required under Rule 26.3.

26.3*ter* *Invitation to Correct Defects under Article 3(4)(i)*

(a) Where the abstract or any text matter of the drawings is filed in a language which is different from the language of the description and the claims, the receiving Office shall, unless

(i) a translation of the international application is required under Rule 12.3(a), or

(ii) the abstract or the text matter of the drawings is in the language in which the international application is to be published,

invite the applicant to furnish a translation of the abstract or the text matter of the drawings into the language in which the international application is to be published. Rules 26.1, 26.2, 26.3, 26.3*bis*, 26.5 and 29.1 shall apply *mutatis mutandis*.

(b) If, on October 1, 1997, paragraph (a) is not compatible with the national law applied by the receiving Office, paragraph (a) shall not apply to that receiving Office for as long as it continues not to be compatible with that law, provided that the said Office informs the International Bureau accordingly by December 31, 1997. The information received shall be promptly published by the International Bureau in the Gazette.

(c) Where the request does not comply with Rule 12.1(c), the receiving Office shall invite the applicant to file a translation so as to comply with that Rule. Rules 3, 26.1, 26.2, 26.5 and 29.1 shall apply *mutatis mutandis*.

(d) If, on October 1, 1997, paragraph (c) is not compatible with the national law applied by the receiving Office, paragraph (c) shall not apply to that receiving Office for as long as it continues not to be compatible with that law, provided that the said Office informs the International Bureau accordingly by December 31, 1997. The information received shall be promptly published by the International Bureau in the Gazette.

26.4 *Procedure*

A correction of the request offered to the receiving Office may be stated in a letter addressed to that Office if the correction is of such a nature that it can be transferred from the letter to the request without adversely affecting the clarity and the direct reproducibility of the sheet on to which the correction is to be transferred; otherwise, and in the case of a correction of any element of the international application other than the request, the applicant shall be required to submit a replacement sheet embodying the correction and the letter accompanying the replacement sheet shall draw attention to the differences between the replaced sheet and the replacement sheet.

26.5 *Decision of the Receiving Office*

The receiving Office shall decide whether the applicant has submitted the correction within the applicable time limit under Rule 26.2, and, if the correction has been submitted within that time limit, whether the international application so corrected is or is not to be considered withdrawn, provided that no international application shall be considered withdrawn for lack of compliance with the physical requirements referred to in Rule 11 if it complies with those requirements to the extent necessary for the purpose of reasonably uniform international publication.

[1.873]

Rule 26*bis*

Correction or Addition of Priority Claim

26*bis*.1 *Correction or Addition of Priority Claim*

(a) The applicant may correct a priority claim or add a priority claim to the request by a notice submitted to the receiving Office or the International Bureau within a time limit of 16 months from the priority date or, where the correction or addition would cause a change in the priority date, 16 months from the priority date as so changed, whichever 16-month period expires first, provided that such a notice may be submitted until the expiration of four months from the international filing date. The correction of a priority claim may include the addition of any indication referred to in Rule 4.10.

(b) Any notice referred to in paragraph (a) received by the receiving Office or the International Bureau after the applicant has made a request for early publication under Article 21(2)(b) shall be considered not to have been submitted, unless that request is withdrawn before the technical preparations for international publication have been completed.

(c) Where the correction or addition of a priority claim causes a change in the priority date, any time limit which is computed from the previously applicable priority date and which has not already expired shall be computed from the priority date as so changed.

26*bis*.2 *Defects in Priority Claims*

(a) Where the receiving Office or, if the receiving Office fails to do so, the International Bureau, finds in relation to a priority claim:

(i) that the international application has an international filing date which is later than the date on which the priority period expired and that a request for restoration of the right of priority under Rule 26*bis*.3 has not been submitted;

(ii) that the priority claim does not comply with the requirements of Rule 4.10; or

(iii) that any indication in the priority claim is inconsistent with the corresponding indication appearing in the priority document;

the receiving Office or the International Bureau, as the case may be, shall invite the applicant to correct the priority claim. In the case referred to in item (i), where the international filing date is within two months from the date on which the priority period expired, the receiving Office or the International Bureau, as the case may be, shall also notify the applicant of the possibility of submitting a request for the restoration of the right of priority in accordance with Rule 26*bis*.3, unless the receiving Office has notified the International Bureau under Rule 26*bis*.3(j) of the incompatibility of Rule 26*bis*.3(a) to (i) with the national law applied by that Office.

(b) If the applicant does not, before the expiration of the time limit under Rule 26*bis*.1(a), submit a notice correcting the priority claim, that priority claim shall, subject to paragraph (c), for the purposes of the procedure under the Treaty, be considered not to have been made ("considered void") and the receiving Office or the International Bureau, as the case may be, shall so declare and shall inform the applicant accordingly. Any notice correcting the priority claim which is received before the receiving Office or the International Bureau, as the case may be, so declares and not later than one month after the expiration of that time limit shall be considered to have been received before the expiration of that time limit.

(c) A priority claim shall not be considered void only because:

(i) the indication of the number of the earlier application referred to in Rule 4.10(a)(ii) is missing;

(ii) an indication in the priority claim is inconsistent with the corresponding indication appearing in the priority document; or

(iii) the international application has an international filing date which is later than the date on which the priority period expired, provided that the international filing date is within the period of two months from that date.

(d) Where the receiving Office or the International Bureau has made a declaration under paragraph (b) or where the priority claim has not been considered void only because paragraph (c) applies, the International Bureau shall publish, together with the international application, information concerning the priority claim as prescribed by the Administrative Instructions, as well as any information submitted by the applicant concerning such priority claim which is received by the International Bureau prior to the completion of the technical preparations for international publication. Such information shall be included in the communication under Article 20 where the international application is not published by virtue of Article 64(3).

(e) Where the applicant wishes to correct or add a priority claim but the time limit under Rule 26*bis*.1 has expired, the applicant may, prior to the expiration of 30 months from the priority date and subject to the payment of a special fee whose amount shall be fixed in the Administrative Instructions, request the International Bureau to publish information concerning the matter, and the International Bureau shall promptly publish such information.

26*bis*.3 *Restoration of Right of Priority by Receiving Office*

(a) Where the international application has an international filing date which is later than the date on which the priority period expired but within the period of two months from that date, the receiving Office shall, on the request of the applicant, and subject to paragraphs (b) to (g) of this Rule, restore the right of priority if the Office finds that a criterion applied by it ("criterion for restoration") is satisfied, namely, that the failure to file the international application within the priority period:

(i) occurred in spite of due care required by the circumstances having been taken; or

(ii) was unintentional.

Each receiving Office shall apply at least one of those criteria and may apply both of them.

(b) A request under paragraph (a) shall:

(i) be filed with the receiving Office within the time limit applicable under paragraph (e);

(ii) state the reasons for the failure to file the international application within the priority period; and

(iii) preferably be accompanied by any declaration or other evidence required under paragraph (f).

(c) Where a priority claim in respect of the earlier application is not contained in the international application, the applicant shall submit, within the time limit applicable under paragraph (e), a notice under Rule 26*bis*.1(a) adding the priority claim.

(d) The submission of a request under paragraph (a) may be subjected by the receiving Office to the payment to it, for its own benefit, of a fee for requesting restoration, payable within the time limit applicable under paragraph (e). The amount of that fee, if any, shall be fixed by the receiving Office. The time limit for payment of the fee may be extended, at the option of the receiving Office, for a period of up to two months from the expiration of the time limit applicable under paragraph (e).

(e) The time limit referred to in paragraphs (b)(i), (c) and (d) shall be two months from the date on which the priority period expired, provided that, where the applicant makes a request for early publication under Article 21(2)(b), any request under paragraph (a) or any notice referred to in paragraph (c) submitted, or any fee referred to in paragraph (d) paid, after the technical preparations for international publication have been completed shall be considered as not having been submitted or paid in time.

(f) The receiving Office may require that a declaration or other evidence in support of the statement of reasons referred to in paragraph (b)(ii) be filed with it within a time limit which shall be reasonable under the circumstances.

(g) The receiving Office shall not refuse, totally or in part, a request under paragraph (a) without giving the applicant the opportunity to make observations on the intended refusal within a time limit which shall be reasonable under the circumstances. Such notice of intended refusal by the receiving Office may be sent to the applicant together with any invitation to file a declaration or other evidence under paragraph (f).

(h) The receiving Office shall promptly:

(i) notify the International Bureau of the receipt of a request under paragraph (a);

(ii) make a decision upon the request;

(iii) notify the applicant and the International Bureau of its decision and the criterion for restoration upon which the decision was based;

(iv) subject to paragraph (h-*bis*), transmit to the International Bureau all documents received from the applicant relating to the request under paragraph (a) (including a copy of the request itself, any statement of reasons referred to in paragraph (b)(ii) and any declaration or other evidence referred to in paragraph (f)).

(h-*bis*) The receiving Office shall, upon a reasoned request by the applicant or on its own decision, not transmit documents or parts thereof received in relation to the request under paragraph (a), if it finds that:

(i) this document or part thereof does not obviously serve the purpose of informing the public about the international application;

(ii) publication or public access to any such document or part thereof would clearly prejudice the personal or economic interests of any person; and

(iii) there is no prevailing public interest to have access to that document or part thereof.

Where the receiving Office decides not to transmit documents or parts thereof to the International Bureau, it shall notify the International Bureau accordingly.

(i) Each receiving Office shall inform the International Bureau of which of the criteria for restoration it applies and of any subsequent changes in that respect. The International Bureau shall promptly publish such information in the Gazette.

(j) If, on October 5, 2005, paragraphs (a) to (i) are not compatible with the national law applied by the receiving Office, those paragraphs shall not apply in respect of that Office for as long as they continue not to be compatible with that law, provided that the said Office informs the International Bureau accordingly by April 5, 2006. The information received shall be promptly published by the International Bureau in the Gazette.

[1.874]
Rule 26*ter*
Correction or Addition of Declarations under Rule 4.17

26*ter*. 1 *Correction or Addition of Declarations*

The applicant may correct or add to the request any declaration referred to in Rule 4.17 by a notice submitted to the International Bureau within a time limit of 16 months from the priority date, provided that any notice which is received by the International Bureau after the expiration of that time limit shall be considered to have been received on the last day of that time limit if it reaches it before the technical preparations for international publication have been completed.

26*ter*.2 *Processing of Declarations*

(a) Where the receiving Office or the International Bureau finds that any declaration referred to in Rule 4.17 is not worded as required or, in the case of the declaration of inventorship referred to in Rule 4.17(iv), is not signed as required, the receiving Office or the International Bureau, as the case may be, may invite the applicant to correct the declaration within a time limit of 16 months from the priority date.

(b) Where the International Bureau receives any declaration or correction under Rule 26*ter*.1 after the expiration of the time limit under Rule 26*ter*.1, the International Bureau shall notify the applicant accordingly and shall proceed as provided for in the Administrative Instructions.

[1.875]
Rule 27
Lack of Payment of Fees

27.1 *Fees*

(a) For the purposes of Article 14(3)(a), "fees prescribed under Article 3(4)(iv)" means: the transmittal fee (Rule 14), the international filing fee (Rule 15.1), the search fee (Rule 16), and, where required, the late payment fee (Rule 16*bis*.2).

(b) For the purposes of Article 14(3)(a) and (b), "the fee prescribed under Article 4(2)" means the international filing fee (Rule 15.1) and, where required, the late payment fee (Rule 16*bis*.2).

[1.876]
Rule 28
Defects Noted by the International Bureau

28.1 *Note on Certain Defects*

(a) If, in the opinion of the International Bureau, the international application contains any of the defects referred to in Article 14(1)(a)(i), (ii) or (v), the International Bureau shall bring such defects to the attention of the receiving Office.

(b) The receiving Office shall, unless it disagrees with the said opinion, proceed as provided in Article 14(1)(b) and Rule 26.

[1.877]
Rule 29
International Applications Considered Withdrawn

29.1 *Finding by Receiving Office*

If the receiving Office declares, under Article 14(1)(b) and Rule 26.5 (failure to correct certain defects), or under Article 14(3)(a) (failure to pay the prescribed fees under Rule 27.1(a)), or under Article 14(4) (later finding of non-compliance with the requirements listed in items (i) to (iii) of Article 11(1)), or under Rule 12.3(d) or 12.4(d) (failure to furnish a required translation or, where applicable, to pay a late furnishing fee), or under Rule 92.4(g)(i) (failure to furnish the original of a document), that the international application is considered withdrawn:

(i) the receiving Office shall transmit the record copy (unless already transmitted), and any correction offered by the applicant, to the International Bureau;

(ii) the receiving Office shall promptly notify both the applicant and the International Bureau of the said declaration, and the International Bureau shall in turn notify each designated Office which has already been notified of its designation;

(iii) the receiving Office shall not transmit the search copy as provided in Rule 23, or, if such copy has already been transmitted, it shall notify the International Searching Authority of the said declaration;

(iv) the International Bureau shall not be required to notify the applicant of the receipt of the record copy;

(v) no international publication of the international application shall be effected if the notification of the said declaration transmitted by the receiving Office reaches the International Bureau before the technical preparations for international publication have been completed.

29.2 *[Deleted]*

29.3 *Calling Certain Facts to the Attention of the Receiving Office*

If the International Bureau or the International Searching Authority considers that the receiving Office should make a finding under Article 14(4), it shall call the relevant facts to the attention of the receiving Office.

29.4 *Notification of Intent to Make Declaration under Article 14(4)*

(a) Before the receiving Office issues any declaration under Article 14(4), it shall notify the applicant of its intent to issue such declaration and the reasons therefor. The applicant may, if he disagrees with the tentative finding of the receiving Office, submit arguments to that effect within two months from the date of the notification.

(b) Where the receiving Office intends to issue a declaration under Article 14(4) in respect of an element mentioned in Article 11(1)(iii)(d) or (e), the receiving Office shall, in the notification referred to in paragraph (a) of this Rule, invite the applicant to confirm in accordance with Rule 20.6(a) that the element is incorporated by reference under Rule 4.18. For the purposes of Rule 20.7(a)(i), the invitation sent to the applicant under this paragraph shall be considered to be an invitation under Rule 20.3(a)(ii).

(c) Paragraph (b) shall not apply where the receiving Office has informed the International Bureau in accordance with Rule 20.8(a) of the incompatibility of Rules 20.3(a)(ii) and (b)(ii) and 20.6 with the national law applied by that Office.

[1.878]
Rule 30
Time Limit under Article 14(4)

30.1 *Time Limit*

The time limit referred to in Article 14(4) shall be four months from the international filing date.

[1.879]
Rule 31
Copies Required under Article 13

31.1 *Request for Copies*

(a) Requests under Article 13(1) may relate to all, some kinds of, or individual international applications in which the national Office making the request is designated. Requests for all or some kinds of such international applications must be renewed for each year by means of a notification addressed by that Office before November 30 of the preceding year to the International Bureau.

(b) Requests under Article 13(2)(b) shall be subject to the payment of a fee covering the cost of preparing and mailing the copy.

31.2 *Preparation of Copies*

The preparation of copies required under Article 13 shall be the responsibility of the International Bureau.

[1.880]
Rule 32
Extension of Effects of International Application to Certain Successor States

32.1 *Extension of International Application to Successor State*

(a) The effects of any international application whose international filing date falls in the period defined in paragraph (b) are extended to a State ("the successor State") whose territory was, before the independence of that State, part of the territory of a Contracting State designated in the international application which subsequently ceased to exist ("the predecessor State"), provided that the successor State has become a Contracting State through the deposit, with the Director General, of a declaration of continuation the effect of which is that the Treaty is applied by the successor State.

(b) The period referred to in paragraph (a) starts on the day following the last day of the existence of the predecessor State and ends two months after the date on which the declaration referred to in paragraph (a) was notified by the Director General to the Governments of the States party to the Paris Convention for the Protection of Industrial Property. However, where the date of independence of the successor State is earlier than the date of the day following the last day of the existence of the predecessor State, the successor State may declare that the said period starts on the date of its independence; such a declaration shall be made together with the declaration referred to in paragraph (a) and shall specify the date of independence.

(c) Information on any international application whose filing date falls within the applicable period under paragraph (b) and whose effect is extended to the successor State shall be published by the International Bureau in the Gazette.

32.2 *Effects of Extension to Successor State*

(a) Where the effects of the international application are extended to the successor State in accordance with Rule 32.1,

(i) the successor State shall be considered as having been designated in the international application, and

(ii) the applicable time limit under Article 22 or 39(1) in relation to that State shall be extended until the expiration of at least six months from the date of the publication of the information under Rule 32.1(c).

(b) The successor State may fix a time limit which expires later than that provided in paragraph (a)(ii). The International Bureau shall publish information on such time limits in the Gazette.

[1.881]
Rule 33
Relevant Prior Art for the International Search

33.1 *Relevant Prior Art for the International Search*

(a) For the purposes of Article 15(2), relevant prior art shall consist of everything which has been made available to the public anywhere in the world by means of written disclosure (including drawings and other illustrations) and which is capable of being of assistance in determining that the claimed invention is or is not new and that it does or does not involve an inventive step (i.e., that it is or is not obvious), provided that the making available to the public occurred prior to the international filing date.

(b) When any written disclosure refers to an oral disclosure, use, exhibition, or other means whereby the contents of the written disclosure were made available to the public, and such making available to the public occurred on a date prior to the international filing date, the international search report shall separately mention that fact and the date on which it occurred if the making available to the public of the written disclosure occurred on a date which is the same as, or later than, the international filing date.

(c) Any published application or any patent whose publication date is the same as, or later than, but whose filing date, or, where applicable, claimed priority date, is earlier than the international filing date of the international application searched, and which would constitute relevant prior art for the purposes of Article 15(2) had it been published prior to the international filing date, shall be specially mentioned in the international search report.

33.2 *Fields to Be Covered by the International Search*

(a) The international search shall cover all those technical fields, and shall be carried out on the basis of all those search files, which may contain material pertinent to the invention.

(b) Consequently, not only shall the art in which the invention is classifiable be searched but also analogous arts regardless of where classified.

(c) The question what arts are, in any given case, to be regarded as analogous shall be considered in the light of what appears to be the necessary essential function or use of the invention and not only the specific functions expressly indicated in the international application.

(d) The international search shall embrace all subject matter that is generally recognized as equivalent to the subject matter of the claimed invention for all or certain of its features, even though, in its specifics, the invention as described in the international application is different.

33.3 *Orientation of the International Search*

(a) International search shall be made on the basis of the claims, with due regard to the description and the drawings (if any) and with particular emphasis on the inventive concept towards which the claims are directed.

(b) In so far as possible and reasonable, the international search shall cover the entire subject matter to which the claims are directed or to which they might reasonably be expected to be directed after they have been amended.

[1.882]
Rule 34
Minimum Documentation

34.1 *Definition*

(a) The definitions contained in Article 2(i) and (ii) shall not apply for the purposes of this Rule.

(b) The documentation referred to in Article 15(4) ("minimum documentation") shall consist of:

(i) the "national patent documents" as specified in paragraph (c),

(ii) the published international (PCT) applications, the published regional applications for patents and inventors' certificates, and the published regional patents and inventors' certificates,

(iii) such other published items of non-patent literature as the International Searching Authorities shall agree upon and which shall be published in a list by the International Bureau when agreed upon for the first time and whenever changed.

(c) Subject to paragraphs (d) and (e), the "national patent documents" shall be the following:

(i) the patents issued in and after 1920 by France, the former *Reichspatentamt* of Germany, Japan, the former Soviet Union, Switzerland (in the French and German languages only), the United Kingdom, and the United States of America,

(ii) the patents issued by the Federal Republic of Germany, the People's Republic of China, the Republic of Korea and the Russian Federation,

(iii) the patent applications, if any, published in and after 1920 in the countries referred to in items (i) and (ii),

(iv) the inventors' certificates issued by the former Soviet Union,

(v) the utility certificates issued by, and the published applications for utility certificates of, France,

(vi) such patents issued by, and such patent applications published in, any other country after 1920 as are in the English, French, German or Spanish language and in which no priority is claimed, provided that the national Office of the interested country sorts out these documents and places them at the disposal of each International Searching Authority.

(d) Where an application is republished once (for example, an *Offenlegungsschrift* as an *Auslegeschrift*) or more than once, no International Searching Authority shall be obliged to keep all versions in its documentation; consequently, each such Authority shall be entitled not to keep more than one version. Furthermore, where an application is granted and is issued in the form of a patent or a utility certificate (France), no International Searching Authority shall be obliged to keep both the application and the patent or utility certificate (France) in its documentation; consequently, each such Authority shall be entitled to keep either the application only or the patent or utility certificate (France) only.

(e) Any International Searching Authority whose official language, or one of whose official languages, is not Chinese, Japanese, Korean, Russian or Spanish is entitled not to include in its documentation those patent documents of the People's Republic of China, Japan, the Republic of Korea, the Russian Federation and the former Soviet Union as well as those patent documents in the Spanish language, respectively, for which no abstracts in the English language are generally available. English abstracts becoming generally available after the date of entry into force of these Regulations shall require the inclusion of the patent documents to which the abstracts refer no later than six months after such abstracts become generally available. In case of the interruption of abstracting services in English in technical fields in which English abstracts were formerly generally available, the Assembly shall take appropriate measures to provide for the prompt restoration of such services in the said fields.

(f) For the purposes of this Rule, applications which have only been laid open for public inspection are not considered published applications.

[1.883]
Rule 35
The Competent International Searching Authority

35.1 *When Only One International Searching Authority Is Competent*

Each receiving Office shall, in accordance with the terms of the applicable agreement referred to in Article 16(3)(b), inform the International Bureau which International Searching Authority is competent for the searching of the international applications filed with it, and the International Bureau shall promptly publish such information.

35.2 *When Several International Searching Authorities Are Competent*

(a) Any receiving Office may, in accordance with the terms of the applicable agreement referred to in Article 16(3)(b), specify several International Searching Authorities:

(i) by declaring all of them competent for any international application filed with it, and leaving the choice to the applicant, or

(ii) by declaring one or more competent for certain kinds of international applications filed with it, and declaring one or more others competent for other kinds of international applications filed with it, provided that, for those kinds of international applications for which several International Searching Authorities are declared to be competent, the choice shall be left to the applicant.

(b) Any receiving Office availing itself of the faculty provided in paragraph (a) shall promptly inform the International Bureau, and the International Bureau shall promptly publish such information.

35.3 *When the International Bureau Is Receiving Office under Rule 19.1(a)(iii)*

(a) Where the international application is filed with the International Bureau as receiving Office under Rule 19.1(a)(iii), an International Searching Authority shall be competent for the searching of that international application if it would have been competent had that international application been filed with a receiving Office competent under Rule 19.1(a)(i) or (ii), (b) or (c) or Rule 19.2(i).

(b) Where two or more International Searching Authorities are competent under paragraph (a), the choice shall be left to the applicant.

(c) Rules 35.1 and 35.2 shall not apply to the International Bureau as receiving Office under Rule 19.1(a)(iii).

[1.884]
Rule 36
Minimum Requirements for International Searching Authorities

36.1 *Definition of Minimum Requirements*

The minimum requirements referred to in Article 16(3)(c) shall be the following:

(i) the national Office or intergovernmental organization must have at least 100 full-time employees with sufficient technical qualifications to carry out searches;

(ii) that Office or organization must have in its possession, or have access to, at least the minimum documentation referred to in Rule 34, properly arranged for search purposes, on paper, in microform or stored on electronic media;
(iii) that Office or organization must have a staff which is capable of searching the required technical fields and which has the language facilities to understand at least those languages in which the minimum documentation referred to in Rule 34 is written or is translated;
(iv) that Office or organization must have in place a quality management system and internal review arrangements in accordance with the common rules of international search;
(v) that Office or organization must hold an appointment as an International Preliminary Examining Authority.

[1.885]
Rule 37
Missing or Defective Title

37.1 *Lack of Title*

If the international application does not contain a title and the receiving Office has notified the International Searching Authority that it has invited the applicant to correct such defect, the International Searching Authority shall proceed with the international search unless and until it receives notification that the said application is considered withdrawn.

37.2 *Establishment of Title*

If the international application does not contain a title and the International Searching Authority has not received a notification from the receiving Office to the effect that the applicant has been invited to furnish a title, or if the said Authority finds that the title does not comply with Rule 4.3, it shall itself establish a title. Such title shall be established in the language in which the international application is to be published or, if a translation into another language was transmitted under Rule 23.1(b) and the International Searching Authority so wishes, in the language of that translation.

[1.886]
Rule 38
Missing or Defective Abstract

38.1 *Lack of Abstract*

If the international application does not contain an abstract and the receiving Office has notified the International Searching Authority that it has invited the applicant to correct such defect, the International Searching Authority shall proceed with the international search unless and until it receives notification that the said application is considered withdrawn.

38.2 *Establishment of Abstract*

If the international application does not contain an abstract and the International Searching Authority has not received a notification from the receiving Office to the effect that the applicant has been invited to furnish an abstract, or if the said Authority finds that the abstract does not comply with Rule 8, it shall itself establish an abstract. Such abstract shall be established in the language in which the international application is to be published or, if a translation into another language was transmitted under Rule 23.1(b) and the International Searching Authority so wishes, in the language of that translation.

38.3 *Modification of Abstract*

The applicant may, until the expiration of one month from the date of mailing of the international search report, submit to the International Searching Authority:
(i) proposed modifications of the abstract; or
(ii) where the abstract has been established by the Authority, proposed modifications of, or comments on, that abstract, or both modifications and comments;

and the Authority shall decide whether to modify the abstract accordingly. Where the Authority modifies the abstract, it shall notify the modification to the International Bureau.

[1.887]
Rule 39
Subject Matter under Article 17(2)(a)(i)

39.1 *Definition*

No International Searching Authority shall be required to search an international application if, and to the extent to which, its subject matter is any of the following:
(i) scientific and mathematical theories,
(ii) plant or animal varieties or essentially biological processes for the production of plants and animals, other than microbiological processes and the products of such processes,
(iii) schemes, rules or methods of doing business, performing purely mental acts or playing games,
(iv) methods for treatment of the human or animal body by surgery or therapy, as well as diagnostic methods,
(v) mere presentations of information,
(vi) computer programs to the extent that the International Searching Authority is not equipped to search prior art concerning such programs.

[1.888]
Rule 40
Lack of Unity of Invention (International Search)

40.1 *Invitation to Pay Additional Fees; Time Limit*

The invitation to pay additional fees provided for in Article 17(3)(a) shall:

(i) specify the reasons for which the international application is not considered as complying with the requirement of unity of invention;

(ii) invite the applicant to pay the additional fees within one month from the date of the invitation, and indicate the amount of those fees to be paid; and

(iii) invite the applicant to pay, where applicable, the protest fee referred to in Rule 40.2(e) within one month from the date of the invitation, and indicate the amount to be paid.

40.2 *Additional Fees*

(a) The amount of the additional fees due for searching under Article 17(3)(a) shall be determined by the competent International Searching Authority.

(b) The additional fees due for searching under Article 17(3)(a) shall be payable direct to the International Searching Authority.

(c) Any applicant may pay the additional fees under protest, that is, accompanied by a reasoned statement to the effect that the international application complies with the requirement of unity of invention or that the amount of the required additional fees is excessive. Such protest shall be examined by a review body constituted in the framework of the International Searching Authority, which, to the extent that it finds the protest justified, shall order the total or partial reimbursement to the applicant of the additional fees. On the request of the applicant, the text of both the protest and the decision thereon shall be notified to the designated Offices together with the international search report. The applicant shall submit any translation thereof with the furnishing of the translation of the international application required under Article 22.

(d) The membership of the review body referred to in paragraph (c) may include, but shall not be limited to, the person who made the decision which is the subject of the protest.

(e) The examination of a protest referred to in paragraph (c) may be subjected by the International Searching Authority to the payment to it, for its own benefit, of a protest fee. Where the applicant has not, within the time limit under Rule 40.1(iii), paid any required protest fee, the protest shall be considered not to have been made and the International Searching Authority shall so declare. The protest fee shall be refunded to the applicant where the review body referred to in paragraph (c) finds that the protest was entirely justified.

[1.889]
Rule 41
Taking into Account Results of Earlier Search and Classification

41.1 *Taking into Account Results of Earlier Search in Case of a Request under Rule 4.12*

Where the applicant has, under Rule 4.12, requested the International Searching Authority to take into account the results of an earlier search and has complied with Rule 12*bis*.1 and:

(i) the earlier search was carried out by the same International Searching Authority, or by the same Office as that which is acting as the International Searching Authority, the International Searching Authority shall, to the extent possible, take those results into account in carrying out the international search;

(ii) the earlier search was carried out by another International Searching Authority, or by an Office other than that which is acting as the International Searching Authority, the International Searching Authority may take those results into account in carrying out the international search.

41.2 *Taking into Account Results of Earlier Search and Classification in Other Cases*

(a) Where the international application claims the priority of one or more earlier applications in respect of which an earlier search has been carried out by the same International Searching Authority, or by the same Office as that which is acting as the International Searching Authority, the International Searching Authority shall, to the extent possible, take the results of any such earlier search into account in carrying out the international search.

(a) Where the receiving Office has transmitted to the International Searching Authority a copy of the results of any earlier search or of any earlier classification under Rule 23bis.2(a) or (b), or where such a copy is available to the International Searching Authority in a form and manner acceptable to it, for example, from a digital library, the International Searching Authority may take those results into account in carrying out the international search.

[1.890]
Rule 42
Time Limit for International Search

42.1 *Time Limit for International Search*

The time limit for establishing the international search report or the declaration referred to in Article 17(2)(a) shall be three months from the receipt of the search copy by the International Searching Authority, or nine months from the priority date, whichever time limit expires later.

[1.891]
Rule 43
The International Search Report

43.1 *Identifications*

The international search report shall identify the International Searching Authority which established it by indicating the name of such Authority, and the international application by indicating the international application number, the name of the applicant, and the international filing date.

43.2 *Dates*

The international search report shall be dated and shall indicate the date on which the international search was actually completed. It shall also indicate the filing date of any earlier application whose priority is claimed or, if the priority of more than one earlier application is claimed, the filing date of the earliest among them.

43.3 *Classification*

(a) The international search report shall contain the classification of the subject matter at least according to the International Patent Classification.

(b) Such classification shall be effected by the International Searching Authority.

43.4 *Language*

Every international search report and any declaration made under Article 17(2)(a) shall be in the language in which the international application to which it relates is to be published, provided that:

(i) if a translation of the international application into another language was transmitted under Rule 23.1(b) and the International Searching Authority so wishes, the international search report and any declaration made under Article 17(2)(a) may be in the language of that translation;

(ii) if the international application is to be published in the language of a translation furnished under Rule 12.4 which is not accepted by the International Searching Authority and that Authority so wishes, the international search report and any declaration made under Article 17(2)(a) may be in a language which is both a language accepted by that Authority and a language of publication referred to in Rule 48.3(a).

43.5 *Citations*

(a) The international search report shall contain the citations of the documents considered to be relevant.

(b) The method of identifying any cited document shall be regulated by the Administrative Instructions.

(c) Citations of particular relevance shall be specially indicated.

(d) Citations which are not relevant to all the claims shall be cited in relation to the claim or claims to which they are relevant.

(e) If only certain passages of the cited document are relevant or particularly relevant, they shall be identified, for example, by indicating the page, the column, or the lines, where the passage appears. If the entire document is relevant but some passages are of particular relevance, such passages shall be identified unless such identification is not practicable.

43.6 *Fields Searched*

(a) The international search report shall list the classification identification of the fields searched. If that identification is effected on the basis of a classification other than the International Patent Classification, the International Searching Authority shall publish the classification used.

(b) If the international search extended to patents, inventors' certificates, utility certificates, utility models, patents or certificates of addition, inventors' certificates of addition, utility certificates of addition, or published applications for any of those kinds of protection, of States, periods, or languages, not included in the minimum documentation as defined in Rule 34, the international search report shall, when practicable, identify the kinds of documents, the States, the periods, and the languages to which it extended. For the purposes of this paragraph, Article 2(ii) shall not apply.

(c) If the international search was based on, or was extended to, any electronic data base, the international search report may indicate the name of the data base and, where considered useful to others and practicable, the search terms used.

43.6*bis* *Consideration of Rectifications of Obvious Mistakes*

(a) A rectification of an obvious mistake that is authorized under Rule 91.1 shall, subject to paragraph (b), be taken into account by the International Searching Authority for the purposes of the international search and the international search report shall so indicate.

(b) A rectification of an obvious mistake need not be taken into account by the International Searching Authority for the purposes of the international search if it is authorized by or notified to that Authority, as applicable, after it has begun to draw up the international search report, in which case the report shall, if possible, so indicate, failing which the International Searching Authority shall notify the International Bureau accordingly and the International Bureau shall proceed as provided for in the Administrative Instructions.

43.7 *Remarks Concerning Unity of Invention*

If the applicant paid additional fees for the international search, the international search report shall so indicate. Furthermore, where the international search was made on the main invention only or on less than all the inventions (Article 17(3)(a)), the international search report shall indicate what parts of the international application were and what parts were not searched.

43.8 *Authorized Officer*

The international search report shall indicate the name of the officer of the International Searching Authority responsible for that report.

43.9 *Additional Matter*

The international search report shall contain no matter other than that specified in Rules 33.1(b) and (c), 43.1 to 43.3, 43.5 to 43.8, and 44.2, and the indication referred to in Article 17(2)(b), provided that the Administrative Instructions may permit the inclusion in the international search report of any additional matter specified in the Administrative Instructions. The international search report shall not contain, and the Administrative Instructions shall not permit the inclusion of, any expressions of opinion, reasoning, arguments, or explanations.

43.10 *Form*

The physical requirements as to the form of the international search report shall be prescribed by the Administrative Instructions.

[1.892]
Rule 43*bis*
Written Opinion of the International Searching Authority

43*bis*.1 *Written Opinion*

(a) Subject to Rule 69.1(b-*bis*), the International Searching Authority shall, at the same time as it establishes the international search report or the declaration referred to in Article 17(2)(a), establish a written opinion as to:
  (i) whether the claimed invention appears to be novel, to involve an inventive step (to be non-obvious), and to be industrially applicable;
  (ii) whether the international application complies with the requirements of the Treaty and these Regulations in so far as checked by the International Searching Authority.

  The written opinion shall also be accompanied by such other observations as these Regulations provide for.

(b) For the purposes of establishing the written opinion, Articles 33(2) to (6) and 35(2) and (3) and Rules 43.4, 43.6*bis*, 64, 65, 66.1(e), 66.7, 67, 70.2(b) and (d), 70.3, 70.4(ii), 70.5(a), 70.6 to 70.10, 70.12, 70.14 and 70.15(a) shall apply *mutatis mutandis*.

(c) The written opinion shall contain a notification informing the applicant that, if a demand for international preliminary examination is made, the written opinion shall, under Rule 66.1*bis* (a) but subject to Rule 66.1*bis* (b), be considered to be a written opinion of the International Preliminary Examining Authority for the purposes of Rule 66.2(a), in which case the applicant is invited to submit to that Authority, before the expiration of the time limit under Rule 54*bis*.1(a), a written reply together, where appropriate, with amendments.

[1.893]
Rule 44
Transmittal of the International Search Report, Written Opinion, Etc.

44.1 *Copies of Report or Declaration and Written Opinion*

The International Searching Authority shall, on the same day, transmit one copy of the international search report or of the declaration referred to in Article 17(2)(a), and one copy of the written opinion established under Rule 43*bis*.1 to the International Bureau and one copy to the applicant.

44.2 *Title or Abstract*

The international search report shall either state that the International Searching Authority approves the title and the abstract as submitted by the applicant or be accompanied by the text of the title and/ or abstract as established by the International Searching Authority under Rules 37 and 38.

44.3 *Copies of Cited Documents*

(a) The request referred to in Article 20(3) may be presented any time during seven years from the international filing date of the international application to which the international search report relates.

(b) The International Searching Authority may require that the party (applicant or designated Office) presenting the request pay to it the cost of preparing and mailing the copies. The level of the cost of preparing copies shall be provided for in the agreements referred to in Article 16(3)(b) between the International Searching Authorities and the International Bureau.

(c) *[Deleted]*

(d) Any International Searching Authority may perform the obligations referred to in paragraphs (a) and (b) through another agency responsible to it.

[1.894]
Rule 44*bis*
International Preliminary Report on Patentability by the International Searching Authority

44*bis*.1 *Issuance of Report; Transmittal to the Applicant*

(a) Unless an international preliminary examination report has been or is to be established, the International Bureau shall issue a report on behalf of the International Searching Authority (in this Rule referred to as "the report") as to the matters referred to in Rule 43*bis*.1(a). The report shall have the same contents as the written opinion established under Rule 43*bis*.1.

(b) The report shall bear the title "international preliminary report on patentability (Chapter I of the Patent Cooperation Treaty)" together with an indication that it is issued under this Rule by the International Bureau on behalf of the International Searching Authority.

(c) The International Bureau shall promptly transmit one copy of the report issued under paragraph (a) to the applicant.

44*bis*.2 *Communication to Designated Offices*

(a) Where a report has been issued under Rule 44*bis*.1, the International Bureau shall communicate it to each designated Office in accordance with Rule 93*bis*.1 but not before the expiration of 30 months from the priority date.

(b) Where the applicant makes an express request to a designated Office under Article 23(2), the International Bureau shall communicate a copy of the written opinion established by the International Searching Authority under Rule 43*bis*.1 to that Office promptly upon the request of that Office or of the applicant.

44*bis*.3 *Translation for Designated Offices*

(a) Any designated State may, where a report has been issued under Rule 44*bis*.1 in a language other than the official language, or one of the official languages, of its national Office, require a translation of the report into English. Any such requirement shall be notified to the International Bureau, which shall promptly publish it in the Gazette.

(b) If a translation is required under paragraph (a), it shall be prepared by or under the responsibility of the International Bureau.

(c) The International Bureau shall transmit a copy of the translation to any interested designated Office and to the applicant at the same time as it communicates the report to that Office.

(d) In the case referred to in Rule 44*bis*.2(b), the written opinion established under Rule 43*bis*.1 shall, upon request of the designated Office concerned, be translated into English by or under the responsibility of the International Bureau. The International Bureau shall transmit a copy of the translation to the designated Office concerned within two months from the date of receipt of the request for translation, and shall at the same time transmit a copy to the applicant.

44*bis*.4 *Observations on the Translation*

The applicant may make written observations as to the correctness of the translation referred to in Rule 44*bis*.3(b) or (d) and shall send a copy of the observations to each of the interested designated Offices and to the International Bureau.

[1.895]
Rule 45
Translation of the International Search Report

45.1 *Languages*

International search reports and declarations referred to in Article 17(2)(a) shall, when not in English, be translated into English.

[1.896]
Rule 45*bis*
Supplementary International Searches

45*bis*.1 *Supplementary Search Request*

(a) The applicant may, at any time prior to the expiration of 22 months[1] from the priority date, request that a supplementary international search be carried out in respect of the international application by an International Searching Authority that is competent to do so under Rule 45*bis*.9. Such requests may be made in respect of more than one such Authority.

(b) A request under paragraph (a) ("supplementary search request") shall be submitted to the International Bureau and shall indicate:

(i) the name and address of the applicant and of the agent (if any), the title of the invention, the international filing date and the international application number;

(ii) the International Searching Authority that is requested to carry out the supplementary international search ("Authority specified for supplementary search"); and

(iii) where the international application was filed in a language which is not accepted by that Authority, whether any translation furnished to the receiving Office under Rule 12.3 or 12.4 is to form the basis of the supplementary international search.

(c) The supplementary search request shall, where applicable, be accompanied by:

(i) where neither the language in which the international application was filed nor that in which a translation (if any) has been furnished under Rule 12.3 or 12.4 is accepted by the Authority specified for supplementary search, a translation of the international application into a language which is accepted by that Authority;

(ii) preferably, a copy of a sequence listing in electronic form complying with the standard provided for in the Administrative Instructions, if required by the Authority specified for supplementary search.

(d) Where the International Searching Authority has found that the international application does not comply with the requirement of unity of invention, the supplementary search request may contain an indication of the wish of the applicant to restrict the supplementary international search to one of the inventions as identified by the International Searching Authority other than the main invention referred to in Article 17(3)(a).

(e) The supplementary search request shall be considered not to have been submitted, and the International Bureau shall so declare:

(i) if it is received after the expiration of the time limit referred to in paragraph (a); or

(ii) if the Authority specified for supplementary search has not stated, in the applicable agreement under Article 16(3)(b), its preparedness to carry out such searches or is not competent to do so under Rule 45*bis*.9(b).

NOTES

1 Editorial note: the words "22 months" are substituted for previous words "19 months" as from July 1, 2017, and shall apply to any international application, irrespective of its international filing date, in respect of which the time limit for filing a request for supplementary international search under Rule 45bis.1(a) as in force until June 30, 2017, has not yet expired on July 1, 2017.

45*bis*.2 *Supplementary Search Handling Fee*

(a) The supplementary search request shall be subject to the payment of a fee for the benefit of the International Bureau ("supplementary search handling fee") as set out in the Schedule of Fees.

(b) The supplementary search handling fee shall be paid in the currency in which the fee is set out in the Schedule of Fees or in any other currency prescribed by the International Bureau. The amount in such other currency shall be the equivalent, in round figures, as established by the International Bureau, of the amount as set out in the Schedule of Fees, and shall be published in the Gazette.

(c) The supplementary search handling fee shall be paid to the International Bureau within one month from the date of receipt of the supplementary search request. The amount payable shall be the amount applicable on the date of payment.

(d) The International Bureau shall refund the supplementary search handling fee to the applicant if, before the documents referred to in Rule 45*bis*.4(e)(i) to (iv) are transmitted to the Authority specified for supplementary search, the international application is withdrawn or considered withdrawn, or the supplementary search request is withdrawn or is considered not to have been submitted under Rule 45*bis*.1(e).

45*bis*.3 *Supplementary Search Fee*

(a) Each International Searching Authority carrying out supplementary international searches may require that the applicant pay a fee ("supplementary search fee") for its own benefit for carrying out such a search.

(b) The supplementary search fee shall be collected by the International Bureau. Rules 16.1(b) to (e) shall apply *mutatis mutandis*.

(c) As to the time limit for payment of the supplementary search fee and the amount payable, the provisions of Rule 45*bis*.2(c) shall apply *mutatis mutandis*.

(d) The International Bureau shall refund the supplementary search fee to the applicant if, before the documents referred to in Rule 45*bis*.4(e)(i) to (iv) are transmitted to the Authority specified for supplementary search, the international application is withdrawn or considered withdrawn, or the supplementary search request is withdrawn or is considered not to have been submitted under Rules 45*bis*.1(e) or 45*bis*.4(d).

(e) The Authority specified for supplementary search shall, to the extent and under the conditions provided for in the applicable agreement under Article 16(3)(b), refund the supplementary search fee if, before it has started the supplementary international search in accordance with Rule 45*bis*.5(a), the supplementary search request is considered not to have been submitted under Rule 45*bis*.5(g).

45*bis*.4 *Checking of Supplementary Search Request; Correction of Defects; Late Payment of Fees; Transmittal to Authority Specified for Supplementary Search*

(a) Promptly after receipt of a supplementary search request, the International Bureau shall check whether it complies with the requirements of Rule 45*bis*.1(b) and (c)(i) and shall invite the applicant to correct any defects within a time limit of one month from the date of the invitation.

(b) Where, by the time they are due under Rules 45*bis*.2(c) and 45*bis*.3(c), the International Bureau finds that the supplementary search handling fee and the supplementary search fee have not been paid in full, it shall invite the applicant to pay to it the amount required to cover those fees, together with the late payment fee under paragraph (c), within a time limit of one month from the date of the invitation.

(c) The payment of fees in response to an invitation under paragraph (b) shall be subject to the payment to the International Bureau, for its own benefit, of a late payment fee whose amount shall be 50% of the supplementary search handling fee.

(d) If the applicant does not furnish the required correction or does not pay the amount in full of the fees due, including the late payment fee, before the expiration of the time limit applicable under paragraph (a) or (b), respectively, the supplementary search request shall be considered not to have been submitted and the International Bureau shall so declare and shall inform the applicant accordingly.

(e) On finding that the requirements of Rule 45*bis*.1(b) and (c)(i), 45*bis*.2(c) and 45*bis*.3(c) have been complied with, the International Bureau shall promptly, but not before the date of receipt by it of the international search report or the expiration of 17 months from the priority date, whichever occurs first, transmit to the Authority specified for supplementary search a copy of each of the following:

(i) the supplementary search request;

(ii) the international application;

(iii) any sequence listing furnished under Rule 45*bis*.1(c)(ii); and

(iv) any translation furnished under Rule 12.3, 12.4 or 45*bis*.1(c)(i) which is to be used as the basis of the supplementary international search;

and, at the same time, or promptly after their later receipt by the International Bureau:

(v) the international search report and the written opinion established under Rule 43*bis*.1;

(vi) any invitation by the International Searching Authority to pay additional fees referred to in Article 17(3)(a); and

(vii) any protest by the applicant under Rule 40.2(c) and the decision thereon by the review body constituted in the framework of the International Searching Authority.

(f) Upon request of the Authority specified for supplementary search, the written opinion referred to in paragraph (e)(v) shall, when not in English or in a language accepted by that Authority, be translated into English by or under the responsibility of the International Bureau. The International Bureau shall transmit a copy of the translation to that Authority within two months from the date of receipt of the request for translation, and shall at the same time transmit a copy to the applicant.

45*bis*.5 *Start, Basis and Scope of Supplementary International Search*

(a) The Authority specified for supplementary search shall start the supplementary international search promptly after receipt of the documents specified in Rule 45*bis*.4(e)(i) to (iv), provided that the Authority may, at its option, delay the start of the search until it has also received the documents specified in Rule 45*bis*.4(e)(v) or until the expiration of 22 months from the priority date, whichever occurs first.

(b) The supplementary international search shall be carried out on the basis of the international application as filed or of a translation referred to in Rule 45*bis*.1(b)(iii) or 45*bis*.1(c)(i), taking due account of the international search report and the written opinion established under Rule 43*bis*.1 where they are available to the Authority specified for supplementary search before it starts the search. Where the supplementary search request contains an indication under Rule 45*bis*. 1(d), the supplementary international search may be restricted to the invention specified by the applicant under Rule 45*bis*.1(d) and those parts of the international application which relate to that invention.

(c) For the purposes of the supplementary international search, Article 17(2) and Rules 13*ter*.1, 33 and 39 shall apply *mutatis mutandis*.

(d) Where the international search report is available to the Authority specified for supplementary search before it starts the search under paragraph (a), that Authority may exclude from the supplementary search any claims which were not the subject of the international search.

(e) Where the International Searching Authority has made the declaration referred to in Article 17(2)(a) and that declaration is available to the Authority specified for supplementary search before it starts the search under paragraph (a), that Authority may decide not to establish a supplementary international search report, in which case it shall so declare and promptly notify the applicant and the International Bureau accordingly.

(f) The supplementary international search shall cover at least the documentation indicated for that purpose in the applicable agreement under Article 16(3)(b).

(g) If the Authority specified for supplementary search finds that carrying out the search is entirely excluded by a limitation or condition referred to in Rule 45*bis*.9(a), other than a limitation under Article 17(2) as applicable by virtue of Rule 45*bis*.5(c), the supplementary search request shall be considered not to have been submitted, and the Authority shall so declare and shall promptly notify the applicant and the International Bureau accordingly.

(h) The Authority specified for supplementary search may, in accordance with a limitation or condition referred to in Rule 45*bis*.9(a), decide to restrict the search to certain claims only, in which case the supplementary international search report shall so indicate.

45*bis*.6 *Unity of Invention*

(a) If the Authority specified for supplementary search finds that the international application does not comply with the requirement of unity of invention, it shall:

(i) establish the supplementary international search report on those parts of the international application which relate to the invention first mentioned in the claims ("main invention");

(ii) notify the applicant of its opinion that the international application does not comply with the requirement of unity of invention and specify the reasons for that opinion; and

(iii) inform the applicant of the possibility of requesting, within the time limit referred to in paragraph (c), a review of the opinion.

(b) In considering whether the international application complies with the requirement of unity of invention, the Authority shall take due account of any documents received by it under Rule 45*bis*.4(e)(vi) and (vii) before it starts the supplementary international search.

(c) The applicant may, within one month from the date of the notification under paragraph (a)(ii), request the Authority to review the opinion referred to in paragraph (a). The request for review may be subjected by the Authority to the payment to it, for its own benefit, of a review fee whose amount shall be fixed by it.

(d) If the applicant, within the time limit under paragraph (c), requests a review of the opinion by the Authority and pays any required review fee, the opinion shall be reviewed by the Authority. The review shall not be carried out only by the person who made the decision which is the subject of the review. Where the Authority:

(i) finds that the opinion was entirely justified, it shall notify the applicant accordingly;

(ii) finds that the opinion was partially unjustified but still considers that the international application does not comply with the requirement of unity of invention, it shall notify the applicant accordingly and, where necessary, proceed as provided for in paragraph (a)(i);

(iii) finds that the opinion was entirely unjustified, it shall notify the applicant accordingly, establish the supplementary international search report on all parts of the international application and refund the review fee to the applicant.

(e) On the request of the applicant, the text of both the request for review and the decision thereon shall be communicated to the designated Offices together with the supplementary international search report. The applicant shall submit any translation thereof with the furnishing of the translation of the international application required under Article 22.

(f) Paragraphs (a) to (e) shall apply *mutatis mutandis* where the Authority specified for supplementary search decides to restrict the supplementary international search in accordance with the second sentence of Rule 45*bis*.5(b) or with Rule 45*bis*.5(h), provided that any reference in the said paragraphs to the "international application" shall be construed as a reference to those parts of the international application which relate to the invention specified by the applicant under Rule 45*bis*.1(d) or which relate to the claims and those parts of the international application for which the Authority will carry out a supplementary international search, respectively.

45*bis*.7 *Supplementary International Search Report*

(a) The Authority specified for supplementary search shall, within 28 months from the priority date, establish the supplementary international search report, or make the declaration referred to in Article 17(2)(a) as applicable by virtue of Rule 45*bis*.5(c) that no supplementary international search report will be established.

(b) Every supplementary international search report, any declaration referred to in Article 17(2)(a) as applicable by virtue of Rule 45*bis*.5(c) and any declaration under Rule 45*bis*.5(e) shall be in a language of publication.

(c) For the purposes of establishing the supplementary international search report, Rules 43.1, 43.2, 43.5, 43.6, 43.6*bis*, 43.8 and 43.10 shall, subject to paragraphs (d) and (e), apply *mutatis mutandis*. Rule 43.9 shall apply *mutatis mutandis*, except that the references therein to Rules 43.3, 43.7 and 44.2 shall be considered non-existent. Article 20(3) and Rule 44.3 shall apply *mutatis mutandis*.

(d) The supplementary international search report need not contain the citation of any document cited in the international search report, except where the document needs to be cited in conjunction with other documents that were not cited in the international search report.

(e) The supplementary international search report may contain explanations:

(i) with regard to the citations of the documents considered to be relevant;

(ii) with regard to the scope of the supplementary international search.

45*bis*.8 *Transmittal and Effect of the Supplementary International Search Report*

(a) The Authority specified for supplementary search shall, on the same day, transmit one copy of the supplementary international search report or the declaration that no supplementary international search report shall be established, as applicable, to the International Bureau and one copy to the applicant.

(b) Subject to paragraph (c), Article 20(1) and Rules 45.1, 47.1(d) and 70.7(a) shall apply as if the supplementary international search report were part of the international search report.

(c) A supplementary international search report need not be taken into account by the International Preliminary Examining Authority for the purposes of a written opinion or the international preliminary examination report if it is received by that Authority after it has begun to draw up that opinion or report.

45*bis*.9 *International Searching Authorities Competent to Carry Out Supplementary International Search*

(a) An International Searching Authority shall be competent to carry out supplementary international searches if its preparedness to do so is stated in the applicable agreement under Article 16(3)(b), subject to any limitations and conditions set out in that agreement.

(b) The International Searching Authority carrying out the international search under Article 16(1) in respect of an international application shall not be competent to carry out a supplementary international search in respect of that application.

(c) The limitations referred to in paragraph (a) may, for example, include limitations as to the subject matter for which supplementary international searches will be carried out, other than limitations under Article 17(2) as applicable by virtue of Rule 45*bis*.5(c), limitations as to the total number of supplementary international searches which will be carried out in a given period, and limitations to the effect that the supplementary international searches will not extend to any claim beyond a certain number of claims.

[1.897]
Rule 46
Amendment of Claims before the International Bureau

46.1 *Time Limit*

The time limit referred to in Article 19 shall be two months from the date of transmittal of the international search report to the International Bureau and to the applicant by the International Searching Authority or 16 months from the priority date, whichever time limit expires later, provided that any amendment made under Article 19 which is received by the International Bureau after the expiration of the applicable time limit shall be considered to have been received by that Bureau on the last day of that time limit if it reaches it before the technical preparations for international publication have been completed.

46.2 *Where to File*

Amendments made under Article 19 shall be filed directly with the International Bureau.

46.3 *Language of Amendments*

If the international application has been filed in a language other than the language in which it is published, any amendment made under Article 19 shall be in the language of publication.

46.4 *Statement*

(a) The statement referred to in Article 19(1) shall be in the language in which the international application is published and shall not exceed 500 words if in the English language or if translated into that language. The statement shall be identified as such by a heading, preferably by using the words "Statement under Article 19(1)" or their equivalent in the language of the statement.

(b) The statement shall contain no disparaging comments on the international search report or the relevance of citations contained in that report. Reference to citations, relevant to a given claim, contained in the international search report may be made only in connection with an amendment of that claim.

46.5 *Form of Amendments*

(a) The applicant, when making amendments under Article 19, shall be required to submit a replacement sheet or sheets containing a complete set of claims in replacement of all the claims originally filed.

(b) The replacement sheet or sheets shall be accompanied by a letter which:
   (i) shall identify the claims which, on account of the amendments, differ from the claims originally filed, and shall draw attention to the differences between the claims originally filed and the claims as amended;
   (ii) shall identify the claims originally filed which, on account of the amendments, are cancelled;
   (iii) shall indicate the basis for the amendments in the application as filed.

[1.898]
Rule 47
Communication to Designated Offices

47.1 *Procedure*

(a) The communication provided for in Article 20 shall be effected by the International Bureau to each designated Office in accordance with Rule 93*bis*.1 but, subject to Rule 47.4, not prior to the international publication of the international application.

(a-*bis*) The International Bureau shall notify each designated Office, in accordance with Rule 93*bis*.1, of the fact and date of receipt of the record copy and of the fact and date of receipt of any priority document.

(b) Any amendment received by the International Bureau within the time limit under Rule 46.1 which was not included in the communication provided for in Article 20 shall be communicated promptly to the designated Offices by the International Bureau, and the latter shall notify the applicant accordingly.

(c) The International Bureau shall, promptly after the expiration of 28 months from the priority date, send a notice to the applicant indicating:

(i) the designated Offices which have requested that the communication provided for in Article 20 be effected under Rule 93*bis*.1 and the date of such communication to those Offices; and

(ii) the designated Offices which have not requested that the communication provided for in Article 20 be effected under Rule 93*bis*.1.

(c-*bis*) The notice referred to in paragraph (c) shall be accepted by designated Offices:

(i) in the case of a designated Office referred to in paragraph (c)(i), as conclusive evidence that the communication provided for in Article 20 was effected on the date specified in the notice;

(ii) in the case of a designated Office referred to in paragraph (c)(ii), as conclusive evidence that the Contracting State for which that Office acts as designated Office does not require the furnishing, under Article 22, by the applicant of a copy of the international application.

(d) Each designated Office shall, when it so requires, receive the international search reports and the declarations referred to in Article 17(2)(a) also in the translation referred to in Rule 45.1.

(e) Where any designated Office has not, before the expiration of 28 months from the priority date, requested the International Bureau to effect the communication provided for in Article 20 in accordance with Rule 93*bis*.1, the Contracting State for which that Office acts as designated Office shall be considered to have notified the International Bureau, under Rule 49.1(a-*bis*), that it does not require the furnishing, under Article 22, by the applicant of a copy of the international application.

47.2 *Copies*

The copies required for communication shall be prepared by the International Bureau. Further details concerning the copies required for communication may be provided for in the Administrative Instructions.

47.3 *Languages*

(a) The international application communicated under Article 20 shall be in the language in which it is published.

(b) Where the language in which the international application is published is different from the language in which it was filed, the International Bureau shall furnish to any designated Office, upon the request of that Office, a copy of that application in the language in which it was filed.

47.4 *Express Request under Article 23(2) prior to International Publication*

Where the applicant makes an express request to a designated Office under Article 23(2) prior to the international publication of the international application, the International Bureau shall, upon request of the applicant or the designated Office, promptly effect the communication provided for in Article 20 to that Office.

NOTES

Rule 47.1(c) and (e) shall apply to any international application whose international filing date is on or after January 1, 2004 and in respect of a designated Office which has made a notification under paragraph (2) of the decisions of the Assembly set out in Annex IV of document PCT/A/30/7 (to the effect that the modification of the time limit fixed in Article 22(1) was not compatible with the national law applied by that Office on October 3, 2001), and which has not withdrawn that notification under paragraph (3) of those decisions, as though the reference in each of Rule 47.1(c) and (e) to "28 months" was a reference to "19 months," with the consequence that two notifications under Rule 47.1(c) shall, if applicable, be sent in respect of such an application.

Information received by the International Bureau concerning any such incompatibility is published in the Gazette and on the WIPO website at: www.wipo.int.

[1.899]

Rule 48

International Publication

48.1 *Form and Means*

The form in which and the means by which international applications are published shall be governed by the Administrative Instructions.

48.2 *Contents*

(a) The publication of the international application shall contain:

(i) a standardized front page;
(ii) the description;
(iii) the claims;
(iv) the drawings, if any;
(v) subject to paragraph (g), the international search report or the declaration under Article 17(2)(a);
(vi) any statement filed under Article 19(1), unless the International Bureau finds that the statement does not comply with the provisions of Rule 46.4;
(vii) where the request for publication under Rule 91.3(d) was received by the International Bureau before the completion of the technical preparations for international publication, any request for rectification of an obvious mistake, any reasons and any comments referred to in Rule 91.3(d);
(viii) the indications in relation to deposited biological material furnished under Rule 13*bis* separately from the description, together with an indication of the date on which the International Bureau received such indications;
(ix) any information concerning a priority claim referred to in Rule 26*bis*.2(d);
(x) any declaration referred to in Rule 4.17, and any correction thereof under Rule 26*ter*.1, which was received by the International Bureau before the expiration of the time limit under Rule 26*ter*.1;
(xi) any information concerning a request under Rule 26*bis*.3 for restoration of the right of priority and the decision of the receiving Office upon such request, including information as to the criterion for restoration upon which the decision was based.

(b) Subject to paragraph (c), the front page shall include:
(i) data taken from the request sheet and such other data as are prescribed by the Administrative Instructions;
(ii) a figure or figures where the international application contains drawings, unless Rule 8.2(b) applies;
(iii) the abstract; if the abstract is both in English and in another language, the English text shall appear first;
(iv) where applicable, an indication that the request contains a declaration referred to in Rule 4.17 which was received by the International Bureau before the expiration of the time limit under Rule 26*ter*.1;
(v) where the international filing date has been accorded by the receiving Office under Rule 20.3(b)(ii) or 20.5(d) on the basis of the incorporation by reference under Rules 4.18 and 20.6 of an element or part, an indication to that effect, together with an indication as to whether the applicant, for the purposes of Rule 20.6(a)(ii), relied on compliance with Rule 17.1(a), (b) or (b-*bis*) in relation to the priority document or on a separately submitted copy of the earlier application concerned;
(vi) where applicable, an indication that the published international application contains information under Rule 26*bis*.2(d);
(vii) where applicable, an indication that the published international application contains information concerning a request under Rule 26*bis*.3 for restoration of the right of priority and the decision of the receiving Office upon such request;
(viii) [deleted].

(c) Where a declaration under Article 17(2)(a) has issued, the front page shall conspicuously refer to that fact and need include neither a drawing nor an abstract.

(d) The figure or figures referred to in paragraph (b)(ii) shall be selected as provided in Rule 8.2. Reproduction of such figure or figures on the front page may be in a reduced form.

(e) If there is not enough room on the front page for the totality of the abstract referred to in paragraph (b)(iii), the said abstract shall appear on the back of the front page. The same shall apply to the translation of the abstract when such translation is required to be published under Rule 48.3(c).

(f) If the claims have been amended under Article 19, the publication of the international application shall contain the full text of the claims both as filed and as amended. Any statement referred to in Article 19(1) shall be included as well, unless the International Bureau finds that the statement does not comply with the provisions of Rule 46.4. The date of receipt of the amended claims by the International Bureau shall be indicated.

(g) If, at the time of the completion of the technical preparations for international publication, the international search report is not yet available, the front page shall contain an indication to the effect that that report was not available and that the international search report (when it becomes available) will be separately published together with a revised front page.

(h) If, at the time of the completion of the technical preparations for international publication, the time limit for amending the claims under Article 19 has not expired, the front page shall refer to that fact and indicate that, should the claims be amended under Article 19, then, promptly after receipt by the International Bureau of such amendments within the time limit under Rule 46.1, the full text of the claims as amended will be published together with a revised front page. If a statement under Article 19(1) has been filed, that statement shall be published as well, unless the International Bureau finds that the statement does not comply with the provisions of Rule 46.4.

(i) If the authorization by the receiving Office, the International Searching Authority or the International Bureau of a rectification of an obvious mistake in the international application under Rule 91.1 is received by or, where applicable, given by the International Bureau after completion of the technical preparations for international publication, a statement reflecting all the rectifications shall be published, together with the sheets containing the rectifications, or the replacement sheets and the letter furnished under Rule 91.2, as the case may be, and the front page shall be republished.

(j) If, at the time of completion of the technical preparations for international publication, a request under Rule 26*bis*.3 for restoration of the right of priority is still pending, the published international application shall contain, in place of the decision by the receiving Office upon that request, an indication to the effect that such decision was not available and that the decision, when it becomes available, will be separately published.

(k) If a request for publication under Rule 91.3(d) was received by the International Bureau after the completion of the technical preparations for international publication, the request for rectification, any reasons and any comments referred to in that Rule shall be promptly published after the receipt of such request for publication, and the front page shall be republished;

(l) The International Bureau shall, upon a reasoned request by the applicant received by the International Bureau prior to the completion of the technical preparations for international publication, omit from publication any information, if it finds that:

(i) this information does not obviously serve the purpose of informing the public about the international application;

(ii) publication of such information would clearly prejudice the personal or economic interests of any person; and

(iii) there is no prevailing public interest to have access to that information.

Rule 26.4 shall apply *mutatis mutandis* as to the manner in which the applicant shall present the information which is the subject of a request made under this paragraph.

(m) Where the receiving Office, the International Searching Authority, the Authority specified for supplementary search or the International Bureau notes any information meeting the criteria set out under paragraph (l), that Office, Authority or Bureau may suggest to the applicant to request the omission from international publication in accordance with paragraph (l).

(n) Where the International Bureau has omitted information from international publication in accordance with paragraph (l) and that information is also contained in the file of the international application held by the receiving Office, the International Searching Authority, the Authority specified for supplementary search or the International Preliminary Examining Authority, the International Bureau shall promptly notify that Office and Authority accordingly.

48.3 *Languages of Publication*

(a) If the international application is filed in Arabic, Chinese, English, French, German, Japanese, Korean, Portuguese, Russian or Spanish ("languages of publication"), that application shall be published in the language in which it was filed.

(b) If the international application is not filed in a language of publication and a translation into a language of publication has been furnished under Rule 12.3 or 12.4, that application shall be published in the language of that translation.

(c) If the international application is published in a language other than English, the international search report to the extent that it is published under Rule 48.2(a)(v), or the declaration referred to in Article 17(2)(a), the title of the invention, the abstract and any text matter pertaining to the figure or figures accompanying the abstract shall be published both in that language and in English. The translations, if not furnished by the applicant under Rule 12.3, shall be prepared under the responsibility of the International Bureau.

48.4 *Earlier Publication on the Applicant's Request*

(a) Where the applicant asks for publication under Articles 21(2)(b) and 64(3)(c)(i) and the international search report, or the declaration referred to in Article 17(2)(a), is not yet available for publication together with the international application, the International Bureau shall collect a special publication fee whose amount shall be fixed in the Administrative Instructions.

(b) Publication under Articles 21(2)(b) and 64(3)(c)(i) shall be effected by the International Bureau promptly after the applicant has asked for it and, where a special fee is due under paragraph (a), after receipt of such fee.

48.5 *Notification of National Publication*

Where the publication of the international application by the International Bureau is governed by Article 64(3)(c)(ii), the national Office concerned shall, promptly after effecting the national publication referred to in the said provision, notify the International Bureau of the fact of such national publication.

48.6 *Announcing of Certain Facts*

(a) If any notification under Rule 29.1(ii) reaches the International Bureau at a time later than that at which it was able to prevent the international publication of the international application, the International Bureau shall promptly publish a notice in the Gazette reproducing the essence of such notification.

(b) *[Deleted]*

(c) If the international application, the designation of any designated State or the priority claim is withdrawn under Rule 90*bis* after the technical preparations for international publication have been completed, notice of the withdrawal shall be published in the Gazette.

[1.900]

Rule 49

Copy, Translation and Fee under Article 22

49.1 *Notification*

(a) Any Contracting State requiring the furnishing of a translation or the payment of a national fee, or both, under Article 22, shall notify the International Bureau of:

(i) the languages from which and the language into which it requires translation,

(ii) the amount of the national fee.

(a-*bis*) Any Contracting State not requiring the furnishing, under Article 22, by the applicant of a copy of the international application (even though the communication of the copy of the international application by the International Bureau under Rule 47 has not taken place by the expiration of the time limit applicable under Article 22) shall notify the International Bureau accordingly.

(a-*ter*) Any Contracting State which, pursuant to Article 24(2), maintains, if it is a designated State, the effect provided for in Article 11(3) even though a copy of the international application is not furnished by the applicant by the expiration of the time limit applicable under Article 22 shall notify the International Bureau accordingly.

(b) Any notification received by the International Bureau under paragraphs (a), (a-*bis*) or (a-*ter*) shall be promptly published by the International Bureau in the Gazette.

(c) If the requirements under paragraph (a) change later, such changes shall be notified by the Contracting State to the International Bureau and that Bureau shall promptly publish the notification in the Gazette. If the change means that translation is required into a language which, before the change, was not required, such change shall be effective only with respect to international applications filed later than two months after the publication of the notification in the Gazette. Otherwise, the effective date of any change shall be determined by the Contracting State.

49.2 *Languages*

The language into which translation may be required must be an official language of the designated Office. If there are several of such languages, no translation may be required if the international application is in one of them. If there are several official languages and a translation must be furnished, the applicant may choose any of those languages. Notwithstanding the foregoing provisions of this paragraph, if there are several official languages but the national law prescribes the use of one such language for foreigners, a translation into that language may be required.

49.3 *Statements under Article 19; Indications under Rule 13bis.4*

For the purposes of Article 22 and the present Rule, any statement made under Article 19(1) and any indication furnished under Rule 13*bis*.4 shall, subject to Rule 49.5(c) and (h), be considered part of the international application.

49.4 *Use of National Form*

No applicant shall be required to use a national form when performing the acts referred to in Article 22.

49.5 *Contents of and Physical Requirements for the Translation*

(a) For the purposes of Article 22, the translation of the international application shall contain the description (subject to paragraph (a-*bis*)), the claims, any text matter of the drawings and the abstract. If required by the designated Office, the translation shall also, subject to paragraphs (b), (c-*bis*) and (e),

(i) contain the request,

(ii) if the claims have been amended under Article 19, contain both the claims as filed and the claims as amended (the claims as amended shall be furnished in the form of a translation of the complete set of claims furnished under Rule 46.5(a) in replacement of all the claims originally filed), and

(iii) be accompanied by a copy of the drawings.

(a-*bis*) No designated Office shall require the applicant to furnish to it a translation of any text matter contained in the sequence listing part of the description if such sequence listing part complies with Rule 12.1(d) and if the description complies with Rule 5.2(b).

(b) Any designated Office requiring the furnishing of a translation of the request shall furnish copies of the request form in the language of the translation free of charge to the applicants. The form and contents of the request form in the language of the translation shall not be different from those of the request under Rules 3 and 4; in particular, the request form in the language of the translation shall not ask for any information that is not in the request as filed. The use of the request form in the language of the translation shall be optional.

(c) Where the applicant did not furnish a translation of any statement made under Article 19(1), the designated Office may disregard such statement.

(c-*bis*) Where the applicant furnishes, to a designated Office which requires under paragraph (a)(ii) a translation of both the claims as filed and the claims as amended, only one of the required two translations, the designated Office may disregard the claims of which a translation has not been furnished or invite the applicant to furnish the missing translation within a time limit which shall be reasonable under the circumstances and shall be fixed in the invitation. Where the designated Office chooses to invite the applicant to furnish the missing translation and the latter is not furnished within the time limit fixed in the invitation, the designated Office may disregard those claims of which a translation has not been furnished or consider the international application withdrawn.

(d) If any drawing contains text matter, the translation of that text matter shall be furnished either in the form of a copy of the original drawing with the translation pasted on the original text matter or in the form of a drawing executed anew.

(e) Any designated Office requiring under paragraph (a) the furnishing of a copy of the drawings shall, where the applicant failed to furnish such copy within the time limit applicable under Article 22, invite the applicant to furnish such copy within a time limit which shall be reasonable under the circumstances and shall be fixed in the invitation.

(f) The expression "Fig." does not require translation into any language.

(g) Where any copy of the drawings or any drawing executed anew which has been furnished under paragraph (d) or (e) does not comply with the physical requirements referred to in Rule 11, the designated Office may invite the applicant to correct the defect within a time limit which shall be reasonable under the circumstances and shall be fixed in the invitation.

(h) Where the applicant did not furnish a translation of the abstract or of any indication furnished under Rule 13*bis*.4, the designated Office shall invite the applicant to furnish such translation, if it deems it to be necessary, within a time limit which shall be reasonable under the circumstances and shall be fixed in the invitation.

(i) Information on any requirement and practice of designated Offices under the second sentence of paragraph (a) shall be published by the International Bureau in the Gazette.

(j) No designated Office shall require that the translation of the international application comply with physical requirements other than those prescribed for the international application as filed.

(k) Where a title has been established by the International Searching Authority pursuant to Rule 37.2, the translation shall contain the title as established by that Authority.

(l) If, on July 12, 1991, paragraph (c-*bis*) or paragraph (k) is not compatible with the national law applied by the designated Office, the paragraph concerned shall not apply to that designated Office for as long as it continues not to be compatible with that law, provided that the said Office informs the International Bureau accordingly by December 31, 1991. The information received shall be promptly published by the International Bureau in the Gazette.

49.6 *Reinstatement of Rights after Failure to Perform the Acts Referred to in Article 22*

(a) Where the effect of the international application provided for in Article 11(3) has ceased because the applicant failed to perform the acts referred to in Article 22 within the applicable time limit, the designated Office shall, upon request of the applicant, and subject to paragraphs (b) to (e) of this Rule, reinstate the rights of the applicant with respect to that international application if it finds that any delay in meeting that time limit was unintentional or, at the option of the designated Office, that the failure to meet that time limit occurred in spite of due care required by the circumstances having been taken.

(b) The request under paragraph (a) shall be submitted to the designated Office, and the acts referred to in Article 22 shall be performed, within whichever of the following periods expires first:

(i) two months from the date of removal of the cause of the failure to meet the applicable time limit under Article 22; or

(ii) 12 months from the date of the expiration of the applicable time limit under Article 22;

provided that the applicant may submit the request at any later time if so permitted by the national law applicable by the designated Office.

(c) The request under paragraph (a) shall state the reasons for the failure to comply with the applicable time limit under Article 22.

(d) The national law applicable by the designated Office may require:

(i) that a fee be paid in respect of a request under paragraph (a);

(ii) that a declaration or other evidence in support of the reasons referred to in paragraph (c) be filed.

(e) The designated Office shall not refuse a request under paragraph (a) without giving the applicant the opportunity to make observations on the intended refusal within a time limit which shall be reasonable under the circumstances.

(f) If, on October 1, 2002, paragraphs (a) to (e) are not compatible with the national law applied by the designated Office, those paragraphs shall not apply in respect of that designated Office for as long as they continue not to be compatible with that law, provided that the said Office informs the International Bureau accordingly by January 1, 2003. The information received shall be promptly published by the International Bureau in the Gazette.

NOTES

Paragraphs (a) to (e) of Rule 49.6 do not apply to any international application whose international filing date is before January 1, 2003, provided that:

(i) those paragraphs shall, subject to item (iii), apply to any international application whose international filing date is before January 1, 2003, and in respect of which the applicable time limit under Article 22 expires on or after January 1, 2003;

(ii) to the extent that those paragraphs are applicable by virtue of Rule 76.5, the latter Rule shall, subject to item (iii), apply to any international application whose international filing date is before January 1, 2003, and in respect of which the applicable time limit under Article 39(1) expires on or after January 1, 2003;

(iii) where a designated Office has informed the International Bureau under paragraph (f) of Rule 49.6 that paragraphs (a) to (e) of that Rule are not compatible with the national law applied by that Office, items (i) and (ii) of this paragraph shall apply in respect of that Office except that each reference in those items to the date January 1, 2003, shall be read as a reference to the date of entry into force of Rule 49.6(a) to (e) in respect of that Office.

Information received by the International Bureau concerning any such incompatibility is published in the Gazette and on the WIPO website at: www.wipo.int.

[1.901]

Rule 49*bis*

Indications as to Protection Sought for Purposes of National Processing

49*bis*.1 *Choice of Certain Kinds of Protection*

(a) If the applicant wishes the international application to be treated, in a designated State in respect of which Article 43 applies, as an application not for the grant of a patent but for the grant of another kind of protection referred to in that Article, the applicant, when performing the acts referred to in Article 22, shall so indicate to the designated Office.

(b) If the applicant wishes the international application to be treated, in a designated State in respect of which Article 44 applies, as an application for the grant of more than one kind of protection referred to in Article 43, the applicant, when performing the acts referred to in Article 22, shall so indicate to the designated Office and shall indicate, if applicable, which kind of protection is sought primarily and which kind is sought subsidiarily.

(c) In the cases referred to in paragraphs (a) and (b), if the applicant wishes the international application to be treated, in a designated State, as an application for a patent of addition, certificate of addition, inventor's certificate of addition or utility certificate of addition, the applicant, when performing the acts referred to in Article 22, shall indicate the relevant parent application, parent patent or other parent grant.

(d) If the applicant wishes the international application to be treated, in a designated State, as an application for a continuation or a continuation-in-part of an earlier application, the applicant, when performing the acts referred to in Article 22, shall so indicate to the designated Office and shall indicate the relevant parent application.

(e) Where no express indication under paragraph (a) is made by the applicant when performing the acts referred to in Article 22 but the national fee referred to in Article 22 paid by the applicant corresponds to the national fee for a particular kind of protection, the payment of that fee shall be considered to be an indication of the wish of the applicant that the international application is to be treated as an application for that kind of protection and the designated Office shall inform the applicant accordingly.

49*bis*.2 *Time of Furnishing Indications*

(a) No designated Office shall require the applicant to furnish, before performing the acts referred to in Article 22, any indication referred to in Rule 49*bis*.1 or, where applicable, any indication as to whether the applicant seeks the grant of a national patent or a regional patent.

(b) The applicant may, if so permitted by the national law applicable by the designated Office concerned, furnish such indication or, if applicable, convert from one kind of protection to another, at any later time.

[1.902]

Rule 49*ter*

Effect of Restoration of Right of Priority by Receiving Office; Restoration of Right of Priority by Designated Office

49*ter*.1 *Effect of Restoration of Right of Priority by Receiving Office*

(a) Where the receiving Office has restored a right of priority under Rule 26*bis*.3 based on a finding by it that the failure to file the international application within the priority period occurred in spite of due care required by the circumstances having been taken, that restoration shall, subject to paragraph (c), be effective in each designated State.

(b) Where the receiving Office has restored a right of priority under Rule 26*bis*.3 based on a finding by it that the failure to file the international application within the priority period was unintentional, that restoration shall, subject to paragraph (c), be effective in any designated State whose applicable national law provides for restoration of the right of priority based on that criterion or on a criterion which, from the viewpoint of applicants, is more favorable than that criterion.

(c) A decision by the receiving Office to restore a right of priority under Rule 26*bis*.3 shall not be effective in a designated State where the designated Office, a court or any other competent organ of or acting for that designated State finds that a requirement under Rule 26*bis*.3(a), (b)(i) or (c) was not complied with, taking into account the reasons stated in the request submitted to the receiving Office under Rule 26*bis*.3(a) and any declaration or other evidence filed with the receiving Office under Rule 26*bis*.3(b)(iii).

(d) A designated Office shall not review the decision of the receiving Office unless it may reasonably doubt that a requirement referred to in paragraph (c) was complied with, in which case the designated Office shall notify the applicant accordingly, indicating the reasons for that doubt and giving the applicant an opportunity to make observations within a reasonable time limit.

(e) No designated State shall be bound by a decision of the receiving Office refusing a request under Rule 26*bis*.3 for restoration of the right of priority.

(f) Where the receiving Office has refused a request for the restoration of the right of priority, any designated Office may consider that request to be a request for restoration submitted to that designated Office under Rule 49*ter*.2(a) within the time limit under that Rule.

(g) If, on October 5, 2005, paragraphs (a) to (d) are not compatible with the national law applied by the designated Office, those paragraphs shall not apply in respect of that Office for as long as they continue not to be compatible with that law, provided that the said Office informs the International Bureau accordingly by April 5, 2006. The information received shall be promptly published by the International Bureau in the Gazette.

49*ter*.2 *Restoration of Right of Priority by Designated Office*

(a) Where the international application claims the priority of an earlier application and has an international filing date which is later than the date on which the priority period expired but within the period of two months from that date, the designated Office shall, on the request of the applicant in accordance with paragraph (b), restore the right of priority if the Office finds that a criterion applied by it ("criterion for restoration") is satisfied, namely, that the failure to file the international application within the priority period:

(i) occurred in spite of due care required by the circumstances having been taken; or

(ii) was unintentional.

Each designated Office shall apply at least one of those criteria and may apply both of them.

(b) A request under paragraph (a) shall:

(i) be filed with the designated Office within a time limit of one month from the applicable time limit under Article 22 or, where the applicant makes an express request to the designated Office under Article 23(2), within a time limit of one month from the date of receipt of that request by the designated Office;

(ii) state the reasons for the failure to file the international application within the priority period and preferably be accompanied by any declaration or other evidence required under paragraph (c); and

(iii) be accompanied by any fee for requesting restoration required under paragraph (d).

(c) The designated Office may require that a declaration or other evidence in support of the statement of reasons referred to in paragraph (b)(ii) be filed with it within a time limit which shall be reasonable under the circumstances.

(d) The submission of a request under paragraph (a) may be subjected by the designated Office to the payment to it, for its own benefit, of a fee for requesting restoration.

(e) The designated Office shall not refuse, totally or in part, a request under paragraph (a) without giving the applicant the opportunity to make observations on the intended refusal within a time limit which shall be reasonable under the circumstances. Such notice of intended refusal may be sent by the designated Office to the applicant together with any invitation to file a declaration or other evidence under paragraph (c).

(f) Where the national law applicable by the designated Office provides, in respect of the restoration of the right of priority, for requirements which, from the viewpoint of applicants, are more favorable than the requirements provided for under paragraphs (a) and (b), the designated Office may, when determining the right of priority, apply the requirements under the applicable national law instead of the requirements under those paragraphs.

(g) Each designated Office shall inform the International Bureau of which of the criteria for restoration it applies, of the requirements, where applicable, of the national law applicable in accordance with paragraph (f), and of any subsequent changes in that respect. The International Bureau shall promptly publish such information in the Gazette.

(h) If, on October 5, 2005, paragraphs (a) to (g) are not compatible with the national law applied by the designated Office, those paragraphs shall not apply in respect of that Office for as long as they continue not to be compatible with that law, provided that the said Office informs the International Bureau accordingly by April 5, 2006. The information received shall be promptly published by the International Bureau in the Gazette.

NOTES

Rule 49*ter*.2 as in force from April 1, 2007, shall not apply to international applications whose international filing date is before April 1, 2007, but it shall apply to international applications whose international filing date is before April 1, 2007, and in respect of which the acts referred to in Article 22(1) are performed on or after April 1, 2007.

[1.903]

Rule 50

Faculty under Article 22(3)

50.1 *Exercise of Faculty*

(a) Any Contracting State allowing a time limit expiring later than the time limits provided for in Article 22(1) or (2) shall notify the International Bureau of the time limits so fixed.

(b) Any notification received by the International Bureau under paragraph (a) shall be promptly published by the International Bureau in the Gazette.

(c) Notifications concerning the shortening of the previously fixed time limit shall be effective in relation to international applications filed after the expiration of three months computed from the date on which the notification was published by the International Bureau.

(d) Notifications concerning the lengthening of the previously fixed time limit shall become effective upon publication by the International Bureau in the Gazette in respect of international applications pending at the time or filed after the date of such publication, or, if the Contracting State effecting the notification fixes some later date, as from the latter date.

[1.904]

Rule 51

Review by Designated Offices

51.1 *Time Limit for Presenting the Request to Send Copies*

The time limit referred to in Article 25(1)(c) shall be two months computed from the date of the notification sent to the applicant under Rule 20.4(i), 24.2(c) or 29.1(ii).

51.2 *Copy of the Notification*

Where the applicant, after having received a negative determination under Article 11(1), requests the International Bureau, under Article 25(1), to send copies of the file of the purported international application to any of the named Offices he has attempted to designate, he shall attach to his request a copy of the notification referred to in Rule 20.4(i).

51.3 *Time Limit for Paying National Fee and Furnishing Translation*

The time limit referred to in Article 25(2)(a) shall expire at the same time as the time limit prescribed in Rule 51.1.

[1.905]

Rule 51*bis*

Certain National Requirements Allowed under Article 27

51*bis*.1 *Certain National Requirements Allowed*

(a) Subject to Rule 51*bis*.2, the national law applicable by the designated Office may, in accordance with Article 27, require the applicant to furnish, in particular:

(i) any document relating to the identity of the inventor,

(ii) any document relating to the applicant's entitlement to apply for or be granted a patent,

(iii) any document containing any proof of the applicant's entitlement to claim priority of an earlier application where the applicant is not the applicant who filed the earlier application or where the applicant's name has changed since the date on which the earlier application was filed,

(iv) where the international application designates a State whose national law requires, on October 9, 2012, the furnishing of an oath or declaration of inventorship, any document containing an oath or declaration of inventorship,

(v) any evidence concerning non-prejudicial disclosures or exceptions to lack of novelty, such as disclosures resulting from abuse, disclosures at certain exhibitions and disclosures by the applicant during a certain period of time;

(vi) the confirmation of the international application by the signature of any applicant for the designated State who has not signed the request;

(vii) any missing indication required under Rule 4.5(a)(ii) and (iii) in respect of any applicant for the designated State.

(b) The national law applicable by the designated Office may, in accordance with Article 27(7), require that
(i) the applicant be represented by an agent having the right to represent applicants before that Office and/or have an address in the designated State for the purpose of receiving notifications,
(ii) the agent, if any, representing the applicant be duly appointed by the applicant.
(c) The national law applicable by the designated Office may, in accordance with Article 27(1), require that the international application, the translation thereof or any document relating thereto be furnished in more than one copy.
(d) The national law applicable by the designated Office may, in accordance with Article 27(2)(ii), require that the translation of the international application furnished by the applicant under Article 22 be:
(i) verified by the applicant or the person having translated the international application in a statement to the effect that, to the best of his knowledge, the translation is complete and faithful;
(ii) certified by a public authority or sworn translator, but only where the designated Office may reasonably doubt the accuracy of the translation.
(e) The national law applicable by the designated Office may, in accordance with Article 27, require the applicant to furnish a translation of the priority document, provided that such a translation may only be required:
(i) where the validity of the priority claim is relevant to the determination of whether the invention concerned is patentable; or
(ii) where the international filing date has been accorded by the receiving Office under Rule 20.3(b)(ii) or 20.5(d) on the basis of the incorporation by reference under Rules 4.18 and 20.6 of an element or part, for the purposes of determining under Rule 82*ter*.1(b) whether that element or part is completely contained in the priority document concerned, in which case the national law applicable by the designated Office may also require the applicant to furnish, in the case of a part of the description, claims or drawings, an indication as to where that part is contained in the translation of the priority document.
(f) *[Deleted]*

51*bis*. 2 *Certain Circumstances in Which Documents or Evidence May Not Be Required*

The designated Office shall not, unless it may reasonably doubt the veracity of the indications or declaration concerned, require any document or evidence:
(i) relating to the identity of the inventor (Rule 51*bis*.1(a)(i)) (other than a document containing an oath or declaration of inventorship (Rule 51*bis*.1(a)(iv)), if indications concerning the inventor, in accordance with Rule 4.6, are contained in the request or if a declaration as to the identity of the inventor, in accordance with Rule 4.17(i), is contained in the request or is submitted directly to the designated Office;
(ii) relating to the applicant's entitlement, as at the international filing date, to apply for and be granted a patent (Rule 51*bis*.1(a)(ii)), if a declaration as to that matter, in accordance with Rule 4.17(ii), is contained in the request or is submitted directly to the designated Office;
(iii) relating to the applicant's entitlement, as at the international filing date, to claim priority of an earlier application (Rule 51*bis*.1(a)(iii)), if a declaration as to that matter, in accordance with Rule 4.17(iii), is contained in the request or is submitted directly to the designated Office;
(iv) containing an oath or declaration of inventorship (Rule 51*bis*.1(a)(iv)), if a declaration of inventorship, in accordance with Rule 4.17(iv), is contained in the request or is submitted directly to the designated Office.

51*bis*.3 *Opportunity to Comply with National Requirements*

(a) Where any of the requirements referred to in Rule 51*bis*.1(a)(i) to (iv) and (c) to (e), or any other requirement of the national law applicable by the designated Office which that Office may apply in accordance with Article 27(1) or (2), is not already fulfilled during the same period within which the requirements under Article 22 must be complied with, the designated Office shall invite the applicant to comply with the requirement within a time limit which shall not be less than two months from the date of the invitation. Each designated Office may require that the applicant pay a fee for complying with national requirements in response to the invitation.
(b) Where any requirement of the national law applicable by the designated Office which that Office may apply in accordance with Article 27(6) or (7) is not already fulfilled during the same period within which the requirements under Article 22 must be complied with, the applicant shall have an opportunity to comply with the requirement after the expiration of that period.
(c) If, on March 17, 2000, paragraph (a) is not compatible with the national law applied by the designated Office in relation to the time limit referred to in that paragraph, the said paragraph shall not apply in respect of that Office in relation to that time limit for as long

as the said paragraph continues not to be compatible with that law, provided that the said Office informs the International Bureau accordingly by November 30, 2000. The information received shall be promptly published by the International Bureau in the Gazette.

NOTES

Rule 51*bis*.1 as in force from April 1, 2007, shall apply to international applications whose international filing date is on or after April 1, 2007, but it shall not apply to international applications in respect of which one or more elements referred to in Article 11(1)(iii) were first received by the receiving Office before April 1, 2007.

[1.906]
Rule 52
Amendment of the Claims, the Description, and the Drawings, before Designated Offices

52.1 *Time Limit*

(a) In any designated State in which processing or examination starts without special request, the applicant shall, if he so wishes, exercise the right under Article 28 within one month from the fulfillment of the requirements under Article 22, provided that, if the communication under Rule 47.1 has not been effected by the expiration of the time limit applicable under Article 22, he shall exercise the said right not later than four months after such expiration date. In either case, the applicant may exercise the said right at any later time if so permitted by the national law of the said State.

(b) In any designated State in which the national law provides that examination starts only on special request, the time limit within or the time at which the applicant may exercise the right under Article 28 shall be the same as that provided by the national law for the filing of amendments in the case of the examination, on special request, of national applications, provided that such time limit shall not expire prior to, or such time shall not come before, the expiration of the time limit applicable under paragraph (a).

PART C
RULES CONCERNING CHAPTER II OF THE TREATY

[1.907]
Rule 53
The Demand

53.1 *Form*

(a) The demand shall be made on a printed form or be presented as a computer print-out. The particulars of the printed form and of a demand presented as a computer print-out shall be prescribed by the Administrative Instructions.

(b) Copies of printed demand forms shall be furnished free of charge by the receiving Office or by the International Preliminary Examining Authority.

53.2 *Contents*

(a) The demand shall contain:
   (i) a petition,
   (ii) indications concerning the applicant and the agent if there is an agent,
   (iii) indications concerning the international application to which it relates,
   (iv) where applicable, a statement concerning amendments.

(b) The demand shall be signed.

53.3 *The Petition*

The petition shall be to the following effect and shall preferably be worded as follows: "Demand under Article 31 of the Patent Cooperation Treaty: The undersigned requests that the international application specified below be the subject of international preliminary examination according to the Patent Cooperation Treaty."

53.4 *The Applicant*

As to the indications concerning the applicant, Rules 4.4 and 4.16 shall apply, and Rule 4.5 shall apply *mutatis mutandis.*

53.5 *Agent or Common Representative*

If an agent or common representative is appointed, the demand shall so indicate. Rules 4.4 and 4.16 shall apply, and Rule 4.7 shall apply *mutatis mutandis.*

53.6 *Identification of the International Application*

The international application shall be identified by the name and address of the applicant, the title of the invention, the international filing date (if known to the applicant) and the international application number or, where such number is not known to the applicant, the name of the receiving Office with which the international application was filed.

53.7 *Election of States*

The filing of a demand shall constitute the election of all Contracting States which are designated and are bound by Chapter II of the Treaty.

53.8 *Signature*

The demand shall be signed by the applicant or, if there is more than one applicant, by all applicants making the demand.

53.9 *Statement Concerning Amendments*

(a) If amendments under Article 19 have been made, the statement concerning amendments shall indicate whether, for the purposes of the international preliminary examination, the applicant wishes those amendments:

(i) to be taken into account, in which case a copy of the amendments and of the letter required under Rule 46.5(b) shall preferably be submitted with the demand; or

(ii) to be considered as reversed by an amendment under Article 34.

(b) If no amendments under Article 19 have been made and the time limit for filing such amendments has not expired, the statement may indicate that, should the International Preliminary Examining Authority wish to start the international preliminary examination at the same time as the international search in accordance with Rule 69.1(b), the applicant wishes the start of the international preliminary examination to be postponed in accordance with Rule 69.1(d).

(c) If any amendments under Article 34 are submitted with the demand, the statement shall so indicate.

[1.908]
Rule 54
The Applicant Entitled to Make a Demand

54.1 *Residence and Nationality*

(a) Subject to the provisions of paragraph (b), the residence or nationality of the applicant shall, for the purposes of Article 31(2), be determined according to Rule 18.1(a) and (b).

(b) The International Preliminary Examining Authority shall, in the circumstances specified in the Administrative Instructions, request the receiving Office or, where the international application was filed with the International Bureau as receiving Office, the national Office of, or acting for, the Contracting State concerned to decide the question whether the applicant is a resident or national of the Contracting State of which he claims to be a resident or national. The International Preliminary Examining Authority shall inform the applicant of any such request. The applicant shall have an opportunity to submit arguments directly to the Office concerned. The Office concerned shall decide the said question promptly.

54.2 *Right to Make a Demand*

The right to make a demand under Article 31(2) shall exist if the applicant making the demand or, if there are two or more applicants, at least one of them is a resident or national of a Contracting State bound by Chapter II and the international application has been filed with a receiving Office of or acting for a Contracting State bound by Chapter II.

54.3 *International Applications Filed with the International Bureau as Receiving Office*

Where the international application is filed with the International Bureau as receiving Office under Rule 19.1(a)(iii), the International Bureau shall, for the purposes of Article 31(2)(a), be considered to be acting for the Contracting State of which the applicant is a resident or national.

54.4 *Applicant Not Entitled to Make a Demand*

If the applicant does not have the right to make a demand or, in the case of two or more applicants, if none of them has the right to make a demand under Rule 54.2, the demand shall be considered not to have been submitted.

[1.909]
Rule 54*bis*
Time Limit for Making a Demand

54*bis*.1 *Time Limit for Making a Demand*

(a) A demand may be made at any time prior to the expiration of whichever of the following periods expires later:

(i) three months from the date of transmittal to the applicant of the international search report or the declaration referred to in Article 17(2)(a), and of the written opinion established under Rule 43*bis*.1; or

(ii) 22 months from the priority date.

(b) Any demand made after the expiration of the time limit applicable under paragraph (a) shall be considered as if it had not been submitted and the International Preliminary Examining Authority shall so declare.

[1.910]
Rule 55
Languages (International Preliminary Examination)

55.1 *Language of Demand*

The demand shall be in the language of the international application or, if the international application has been filed in a language other than the language in which it is published, in the language of publication. However, if a translation of the international application is required under Rule 55.2, the demand shall be in the language of that translation.

55.2 *Translation of International Application*

(a) Where neither the language in which the international application is filed nor the language in which the international application is published is accepted by the International Preliminary Examining Authority that is to carry out the international preliminary examination, the applicant shall, subject to paragraph (b), furnish with the demand a translation of the international application into a language which is both:
(i) a language accepted by that Authority, and
(ii) a language of publication.

(a-*bis*) A translation of the international application into a language referred to in paragraph (a) shall include any element referred to in Article 11(1)(iii)(d) or (e) furnished by the applicant under Rule 20.3(b) or 20.6(a) and any part of the description, claims or drawings furnished by the applicant under Rule 20.5(b) or 20.6(a) which is considered to have been contained in the international application under Rule 20.6(b).

(a-*ter*) The International Preliminary Examining Authority shall check any translation furnished under paragraph (a) for compliance with the physical requirements referred to in Rule 11 to the extent that compliance therewith is necessary for the purposes of the international preliminary examination.

(b) Where a translation of the international application into a language referred to in paragraph (a) was transmitted to the International Searching Authority under Rule 23.1(b) and the International Preliminary Examining Authority is part of the same national Office or intergovernmental organization as the International Searching Authority, the applicant need not furnish a translation under paragraph (a). In such a case, unless the applicant furnishes a translation under paragraph (a), the international preliminary examination shall be carried out on the basis of the translation transmitted under Rule 23.1(b).

(c) If a requirement referred to in paragraphs (a), (a-*bis*) and (a-*ter*) is not complied with and paragraph (b) does not apply, the International Preliminary Examining Authority shall invite the applicant to furnish the required translation or the required correction, as the case may be, within a time limit which shall be reasonable under the circumstances. That time limit shall not be less than one month from the date of the invitation. It may be extended by the International Preliminary Examining Authority at any time before a decision is taken.

(d) If the applicant complies with the invitation within the time limit under paragraph (c), the said requirement shall be considered to have been complied with. If the applicant fails to do so, the demand shall be considered not to have been submitted and the International Preliminary Examining Authority shall so declare.

55.3 *Language and Translation of Amendments and Letters*

(a) Subject to paragraph (b), if the international application has been filed in a language other than the language in which it is published, any amendment under Article 34, as well as any letter referred to in Rule 66.8(a), Rule 66.8(b) and Rule 46.5(b) as applicable by virtue of Rule 66.8(c), shall be submitted in the language of publication.

(b) Where a translation of the international application is required under Rule 55.2:
(i) any amendment and any letter referred to in paragraph (a); and
(ii) any amendment under Article 19 which is to be taken into account under Rule 66.1(c) or (d) and any letter referred to in Rule 46.5(b);

shall be in the language of that translation. Where such amendments or letters have been or are submitted in another language, a translation shall also be submitted.

(c) If an amendment or letter is not submitted in a language as required under paragraph (a) or (b), the International Preliminary Examining Authority shall invite the applicant to submit the amendment or letter in the required language within a time limit which shall be reasonable under the circumstances. That time limit shall not be less than one month from the date of the invitation. It may be extended by the International Preliminary Examining Authority at any time before a decision is taken.

(d) If the applicant fails to comply, within the time limit under paragraph (c), with the invitation to furnish an amendment in the required language, the amendment shall not be taken into account for the purposes of the international preliminary examination. If the applicant fails to comply, within the time limit under paragraph (c), with the invitation to furnish a letter referred to in paragraph (a) in the required language, the amendment concerned need not be taken into account for the purposes of the international preliminary examination.

Rule 56
[Deleted]

[1.911]
Rule 57
The Handling Fee
57.1 *Requirement to Pay*

Each demand for international preliminary examination shall be subject to the payment of a fee for the benefit of the International Bureau ("handling fee") to be collected by the International Preliminary Examining Authority to which the demand is submitted.

57.2 *Amount*

(a) The amount of the handling fee is as set out in the Schedule of Fees.

(b) The handling fee shall be payable in the currency or one of the currencies prescribed by the International Preliminary Examining Authority ("prescribed currency").

(c) Where the prescribed currency is the Swiss franc, the Authority shall promptly transfer the said fee to the International Bureau in Swiss francs.

(d) Where the prescribed currency is a currency other than the Swiss franc and that currency:

(i) is freely convertible into Swiss francs, the Director General shall establish, for each Authority which prescribes such a currency for the payment of the handling fee, an equivalent amount of that fee in the prescribed currency according to directives given by the Assembly, and the amount in that currency shall promptly be transferred by the Authority to the International Bureau;

(ii) is not freely convertible into Swiss francs, the Authority shall be responsible for the conversion of the handling fee from the prescribed currency into Swiss francs and shall promptly transfer that fee in Swiss francs, in the amount set out in the Schedule of Fees, to the International Bureau. Alternatively, if the Authority so wishes, it may convert the handling fee from the prescribed currency into euros or US dollars and promptly transfer the equivalent amount of that fee in euros or US dollars, as established by the Director General according to directives given by the Assembly as referred to in item (i), to the International Bureau.

57.3 *Time Limit for Payment; Amount Payable*

(a) Subject to paragraphs (b) and (c), the handling fee shall be paid within one month from the date on which the demand was submitted or 22 months from the priority date, whichever expires later.

(b) Subject to paragraph (c), where the demand was transmitted to the International Preliminary Examining Authority under Rule 59.3, the handling fee shall be paid within one month from the date of receipt by that Authority or 22 months from the priority date, whichever expires later.

(c) Where, in accordance with Rule 69.1(b), the International Preliminary Examining Authority wishes to start the international preliminary examination at the same time as the international search, that Authority shall invite the applicant to pay the handling fee within one month from the date of the invitation.

(d) The amount of the handling fee payable shall be the amount applicable on the date of payment.

57.4 *Refund*

The International Preliminary Examining Authority shall refund the handling fee to the applicant:

(i) if the demand is withdrawn before the demand has been sent by that Authority to the International Bureau, or

(ii) if the demand is considered, under Rule 54.4 or 54*bis*.1(b), not to have been submitted.

[1.912]
Rule 58
The Preliminary Examination Fee

58.1 *Right to Ask for a Fee*

(a) Each International Preliminary Examining Authority may require that the applicant pay a fee ("preliminary examination fee") for its own benefit for carrying out the international preliminary examination and for performing all other tasks entrusted to International Preliminary Examining Authorities under the Treaty and these Regulations.

(b) The amount of the preliminary examination fee, if any, shall be fixed by the International Preliminary Examining Authority. As to the time limit for payment of the preliminary examination fee and the amount payable, the provisions of Rule 57.3 relating to the handling fee shall apply *mutatis mutandis*.

(c) The preliminary examination fee shall be payable directly to the International Preliminary Examining Authority. Where that Authority is a national Office, it shall be payable in the currency prescribed by that Office, and where the Authority is an intergovernmental organization, it shall be payable in the currency of the State in which the intergovernmental organization is located or in any other currency which is freely convertible into the currency of the said State.

58.2 *[Deleted]*

58.3 *Refund*

The International Preliminary Examining Authorities shall inform the International Bureau of the extent, if any, to which, and the conditions, if any, under which, they will refund any amount paid as a preliminary examination fee where the demand is considered as if it had not been submitted, and the International Bureau shall promptly publish such information.

[1.913]
Rule 58*bis*
Extension of Time Limits for Payment of Fees

58*bis*.1 *Invitation by the International Preliminary Examining Authority*

(a) Where the International Preliminary Examining Authority finds:

(i) that the amount paid to it is insufficient to cover the handling fee and the preliminary examination fee; or

(ii) by the time they are due under Rules 57.3 and 58.1(b), that no fees were paid to it;

the Authority shall invite the applicant to pay to it the amount required to cover those fees, together with, where applicable, the late payment fee under Rule 58*bis*.2, within a time limit of one month from the date of the invitation.

(b) Where the International Preliminary Examining Authority has sent an invitation under paragraph (a) and the applicant has not, within the time limit referred to in that paragraph, paid in full the amount due, including, where applicable, the late payment fee under Rule 58*bis*.2, the demand shall, subject to paragraph (c), be considered as if it had not been submitted and the International Preliminary Examining Authority shall so declare.

(c) Any payment received by the International Preliminary Examining Authority before that Authority sends the invitation under paragraph (a) shall be considered to have been received before the expiration of the time limit under Rule 57.3 or 58.1(b), as the case may be.

(d) Any payment received by the International Preliminary Examining Authority before that Authority proceeds under paragraph (b) shall be considered to have been received before the expiration of the time limit under paragraph (a).

58*bis*.2 *Late Payment Fee*

(a) The payment of fees in response to an invitation under Rule 58*bis*.1(a) may be subjected by the International Preliminary Examining Authority to the payment to it, for its own benefit, of a late payment fee. The amount of that fee shall be:

(i) 50% of the amount of unpaid fees which is specified in the invitation, or,

(ii) if the amount calculated under item (i) is less than the handling fee, an amount equal to the handling fee.

(b) The amount of the late payment fee shall not, however, exceed double the amount of the handling fee.

[1.914]
Rule 59
The Competent International Preliminary Examining Authority

59.1 *Demands under Article 31(2)(a)*

(a) For demands made under Article 31(2)(a), each receiving Office of or acting for a Contracting State bound by the provisions of Chapter II shall, in accordance with the terms of the applicable agreement referred to in Article 32(2) and (3), inform the International Bureau which International Preliminary Examining Authority is or which International Preliminary Examining Authorities are competent for the international preliminary examination of international applications filed with it. The International Bureau shall promptly publish such information. Where several International Preliminary Examining Authorities are competent, the provisions of Rule 35.2 shall apply *mutatis mutandis*.

(b) Where the international application was filed with the International Bureau as receiving Office under Rule 19.1(a)(iii), Rule 35.3(a) and (b) shall apply *mutatis mutandis*. Paragraph (a) of this Rule shall not apply to the International Bureau as receiving Office under Rule 19.1(a)(iii).

59.2 *Demands under Article 31(2)(b)*

As to demands made under Article 31(2)(b), the Assembly, in specifying the International Preliminary Examining Authority competent for international applications filed with a national Office which is an International Preliminary Examining Authority, shall give preference to that Authority; if the national Office is not an International Preliminary Examining Authority, the Assembly shall give preference to the International Preliminary Examining Authority recommended by that Office.

59.3 *Transmittal of the Demand to the Competent International Preliminary Examining Authority*

(a) If the demand is submitted to a receiving Office, an International Searching Authority, or an International Preliminary Examining Authority which is not competent for the international preliminary examination of the international application, that Office or Authority shall mark the date of receipt on the demand and, unless it decides to proceed under paragraph (f), transmit the demand promptly to the International Bureau.

(b) If the demand is submitted to the International Bureau, the International Bureau shall mark the date of receipt on the demand.

(c) Where the demand is transmitted to the International Bureau under paragraph (a) or submitted to it under paragraph (b), the International Bureau shall promptly:

(i) if there is only one competent International Preliminary Examining Authority, transmit the demand to that Authority and inform the applicant accordingly, or

(ii) if two or more International Preliminary Examining Authorities are competent, invite the applicant to indicate, within the time limit applicable under Rule 54*bis*.1(a) or 15 days from the date of the invitation, whichever is later, the competent International Preliminary Examining Authority to which the demand should be transmitted.

(d) Where an indication is furnished as required under paragraph (c)(ii), the International Bureau shall promptly transmit the demand to the competent International Preliminary Examining Authority indicated by the applicant. Where no indication is so furnished, the demand shall be considered not to have been submitted and the International Bureau shall so declare.

(e) Where the demand is transmitted to a competent International Preliminary Examining Authority under paragraph (c), it shall be considered to have been received on behalf of that Authority on the date marked on it under paragraph (a) or (b), as applicable, and the demand so transmitted shall be considered to have been received by that Authority on that date.

(f) Where an Office or Authority to which the demand is submitted under paragraph (a) decides to transmit that demand directly to the competent International Preliminary Examining Authority, paragraphs (c) to (e) shall apply *mutatis mutandis*.

[1.915]
Rule 60
Certain Defects in the Demand

60.1 *Defects in the Demand*

(a) Subject to paragraphs (a-*bis*) and (a-*ter*), if the demand does not comply with the requirements specified in Rules 53.1, 53.2(a)(i) to (iii), 53.2(b), 53.3 to 53.8 and 55.1, the International Preliminary Examining Authority shall invite the applicant to correct the defects within a time limit which shall be reasonable under the circumstances. That time limit shall not be less than one month from the date of the invitation. It may be extended by the International Preliminary Examining Authority at any time before a decision is taken.

(a-*bis*) For the purposes of Rule 53.4, if there are two or more applicants, it shall be sufficient that the indications referred to in Rule 4.5(a)(ii) and (iii) be provided in respect of one of them who has the right according to Rule 54.2 to make a demand.

(a-*ter*) For the purposes of Rule 53.8, if there are two or more applicants, it shall be sufficient that the demand be signed by one of them.

(b) If the applicant complies with the invitation within the time limit under paragraph (a), the demand shall be considered as if it had been received on the actual filing date, provided that the demand as submitted permitted the international application to be identified; otherwise, the demand shall be considered as if it had been received on the date on which the International Preliminary Examining Authority receives the correction.

(c) If the applicant does not comply with the invitation within the time limit under paragraph (a), the demand shall be considered as if it had not been submitted and the International Preliminary Examining Authority shall so declare.

(d) *[Deleted]*

(e) If the defect is noticed by the International Bureau, it shall bring the defect to the attention of the International Preliminary Examining Authority, which shall then proceed as provided in paragraphs (a) to (c).

(f) If the demand does not contain a statement concerning amendments, the International Preliminary Examining Authority shall proceed as provided for in Rules 66.1 and 69.1(a) or (b).

(g) Where the statement concerning amendments contains an indication that amendments under Article 34 are submitted with the demand (Rule 53.9(c)) but no such amendments are, in fact, submitted, the International Preliminary Examining Authority shall invite the applicant to submit the amendments within a time limit fixed in the invitation and shall proceed as provided for in Rule 69.1(e).

[1.916]
Rule 61
Notification of the Demand and Elections

61.1 *Notification to the International Bureau and the Applicant*

(a) The International Preliminary Examining Authority shall indicate on the demand the date of receipt or, where applicable, the date referred to in Rule 60.1(b). The International Preliminary Examining Authority shall promptly either send the demand to the International Bureau and keep a copy in its files or send a copy to the International Bureau and keep the demand in its files.

(b) The International Preliminary Examining Authority shall promptly notify the applicant of the date of receipt of the demand. Where the demand has been considered under Rules 54.4, 55.2(d), 58*bis*.1(b) or 60.1(c) as if it had not been submitted, the International Preliminary Examining Authority shall notify the applicant and the International Bureau accordingly.

61.2 *Notification to the Elected Offices*

(a) The notification provided for in Article 31(7) shall be effected by the International Bureau.

(b) The notification shall indicate the number and filing date of the international application, the name of the applicant, the filing date of the application whose priority is claimed (where priority is claimed) and the date of receipt by the International Preliminary Examining Authority of the demand.

(c) The notification shall be sent to the elected Office together with the communication provided for in Article 20. Elections effected after such communication shall be notified promptly after they have been made.

(d) Where the applicant makes an express request to an elected Office under Article 40(2) prior to the international publication of the international application, the International Bureau shall, upon request of the applicant or the elected Office, promptly effect the communication provided for in Article 20 to that Office.

61.3 *Information for the Applicant*

The International Bureau shall inform the applicant in writing of the notification referred to in Rule 61.2 and of the elected Offices notified under Article 31(7).

61.4 *Publication in the Gazette*

The International Bureau shall, promptly after the filing of the demand but not before the international publication of the international application, publish in the Gazette information on the demand and the elected States concerned, as provided in the Administrative Instructions.

[1.917]

Rule 62

Copy of the Written Opinion by the International Searching Authority and of Amendments under Article 19 for the International Preliminary Examining Authority

62.1 *Copy of Written Opinion by International Searching Authority and of Amendments Made before the Demand Is Filed*

Upon receipt of a demand, or a copy thereof, from the International Preliminary Examining Authority, the International Bureau shall promptly transmit to that Authority:

(i) a copy of the written opinion established under Rule 43*bis*.1, unless the national Office or intergovernmental organization that acted as International Searching Authority is also acting as International Preliminary Examining Authority; and

(ii) a copy of any amendment under Article 19, any statement referred to in that Article, and the letter required under Rule 46.5(b), unless that Authority has indicated that it has already received such a copy.

62.2 *Amendments Made after the Demand Is Filed*

If, at the time of filing any amendments under Article 19, a demand has already been submitted, the applicant shall preferably, at the same time as he files the amendments with the International Bureau, also file with the International Preliminary Examining Authority a copy of such amendments, any statement referred to in that Article and the letter required under Rule 46.5(b). In any case, the International Bureau shall promptly transmit a copy of such amendments, statement and letter to that Authority.

[1.918]

Rule 62*bis*

Translation for the International Preliminary Examining Authority of the Written Opinion of the International Searching Authority

62*bis*.1 *Translation and Observations*

(a) Upon request of the International Preliminary Examining Authority, the written opinion established under Rule 43*bis*.1 shall, when not in English or in a language accepted by that Authority, be translated into English by or under the responsibility of the International Bureau.

(b) The International Bureau shall transmit a copy of the translation to the International Preliminary Examining Authority within two months from the date of receipt of the request for translation, and shall at the same time transmit a copy to the applicant.

(c) The applicant may make written observations as to the correctness of the translation and shall send a copy of the observations to the International Preliminary Examining Authority and to the International Bureau.

[1.919]

Rule 63

Minimum Requirements for International Preliminary Examining Authorities

63.1 *Definition of Minimum Requirements*

The minimum requirements referred to in Article 32(3) shall be the following:

(i) the national Office or intergovernmental organization must have at least 100 full-time employees with sufficient technical qualifications to carry out examinations;

(ii) that Office or organization must have at its ready disposal at least the minimum documentation referred to in Rule 34, properly arranged for examination purposes;

(iii) that Office or organization must have a staff which is capable of examining in the required technical fields and which has the language facilities to understand at least those languages in which the minimum documentation referred to in Rule 34 is written or is translated;
(iv) that Office or organization must have in place a quality management system and internal review arrangements in accordance with the common rules of international preliminary examination;
(v) that Office or organization must hold an appointment as an International Searching Authority.

[1.920]
Rule 64
Prior Art for International Preliminary Examination
64.1 *Prior Art*
(a) For the purposes of Article 33(2) and (3), everything made available to the public anywhere in the world by means of written disclosure (including drawings and other illustrations) shall be considered prior art provided that such making available occurred prior to the relevant date.
(b) For the purposes of paragraph (a), the relevant date shall be:
(i) subject to items (ii) and (iii), the international filing date of the international application under international preliminary examination;
(ii) where the international application under international preliminary examination claims the priority of an earlier application and has an international filing date which is within the priority period, the filing date of such earlier application, unless the International Preliminary Examining Authority considers that the priority claim is not valid;
(iii) where the international application under international preliminary examination claims the priority of an earlier application and has an international filing date which is later than the date on which the priority period expired but within the period of two months from that date, the filing date of such earlier application, unless the International Preliminary Examining Authority considers that the priority claim is not valid for reasons other than the fact that the international application has an international filing date which is later than the date on which the priority period expired.

64.2 *Non-Written Disclosures*
In cases where the making available to the public occurred by means of an oral disclosure, use, exhibition or other non-written means ("non-written disclosure") before the relevant date as defined in Rule 64.1(b) and the date of such non-written disclosure is indicated in a written disclosure which has been made available to the public on a date which is the same as, or later than, the relevant date, the non-written disclosure shall not be considered part of the prior art for the purposes of Article 33(2) and (3). Nevertheless, the international preliminary examination report shall call attention to such non-written disclosure in the manner provided for in Rule 70.9.

64.3 *Certain Published Documents*
In cases where any application or any patent which would constitute prior art for the purposes of Article 33(2) and (3) had it been published prior to the relevant date referred to in Rule 64.1 was published on a date which is the same as, or later than, the relevant date but was filed earlier than the relevant date or claimed the priority of an earlier application which had been filed prior to the relevant date, such published application or patent shall not be considered part of the prior art for the purposes of Article 33(2) and (3). Nevertheless, the international preliminary examination report shall call attention to such application or patent in the manner provided for in Rule 70.10.

[1.921]
Rule 65
Inventive Step or Non-Obviousness
65.1 *Approach to Prior Art*
For the purposes of Article 33(3), the international preliminary examination shall take into consideration the relation of any particular claim to the prior art as a whole. It shall take into consideration the claim's relation not only to individual documents or parts thereof taken separately but also its relation to combinations of such documents or parts of documents, where such combinations are obvious to a person skilled in the art.

65.2 *Relevant Date*
For the purposes of Article 33(3), the relevant date for the consideration of inventive step (non-obviousness) is the date prescribed in Rule 64.1.

[1.922]
Rule 66
Procedure before the International Preliminary Examining Authority
66.1 *Basis of the International Preliminary Examination*
(a) Subject to paragraphs (b) to (d), the international preliminary examination shall be based on the international application as filed.

(b) The applicant may submit amendments under Article 34 at the time of filing the demand or, subject to Rule 66.4*bis*, until the international preliminary examination report is established.

(c) Any amendments under Article 19 made before the demand was filed shall be taken into account for the purposes of the international preliminary examination unless superseded, or considered as reversed, by an amendment under Article 34.

(d) Any amendments under Article 19 made after the demand was filed and any amendments under Article 34 submitted to the International Preliminary Examining Authority shall, subject to Rule 66.4*bis*, be taken into account for the purposes of the international preliminary examination.

(d-*bis*) A rectification of an obvious mistake that is authorized under Rule 91.1 shall, subject to Rule 66.4*bis*, be taken into account by the International Preliminary Examining Authority for the purposes of the international preliminary examination.

(e) Claims relating to inventions in respect of which no international search report has been established need not be the subject of international preliminary examination.

66.1*bis* *Written Opinion of the International Searching Authority*

(a) Subject to paragraph (b), the written opinion established by the International Searching Authority under Rule 43*bis*.1 shall be considered to be a written opinion of the International Preliminary Examining Authority for the purposes of Rule 66.2(a).

(b) An International Preliminary Examining Authority may notify the International Bureau that paragraph (a) shall not apply to the procedure before it in respect of written opinions established under Rule 43*bis*.1 by the International Searching Authority or Authorities specified in the notification, provided that such a notification shall not apply to cases where the national Office or intergovernmental organization that acted as International Searching Authority is also acting as International Preliminary Examining Authority. The International Bureau shall promptly publish any such notification in the Gazette.

(c) Where the written opinion established by the International Searching Authority under Rule 43*bis*.1 is not, by virtue of a notification under paragraph (b), considered to be a written opinion of the International Preliminary Examining Authority for the purposes of Rule 66.2(a), the International Preliminary Examining Authority shall notify the applicant accordingly in writing.

(d) A written opinion established by the International Searching Authority under Rule 43*bis*.1 which is not, by virtue of a notification under paragraph (b), considered to be a written opinion of the International Preliminary Examining Authority for the purposes of Rule 66.2(a) shall nevertheless be taken into account by the International Preliminary Examining Authority in proceeding under Rule 66.2(a).

66.1*ter* *Top-up searches*

The International Preliminary Examining Authority shall conduct a search ("top-up search") to discover documents referred to in Rule 64 which have been published or have become available to the said Authority for search subsequent to the date on which the international search report was established, unless it considers that such a search would serve no useful purpose. If the Authority finds that any of the situations referred to in Article 34(3) or (4) or Rule 66.1(e) exists, the top-up search shall cover only those parts of the international application that are the subject of international preliminary examination.

66.2 *Written Opinion of the International Preliminary Examining Authority*

(a) If the International Preliminary Examining Authority

(i) considers that any of the situations referred to in Article 34(4) exists,

(ii) considers that the international preliminary examination report should be negative in respect of any of the claims because the invention claimed therein does not appear to be novel, does not appear to involve an inventive step (does not appear to be non-obvious), or does not appear to be industrially applicable,

(iii) notices that there is some defect in the form or contents of the international application under the Treaty or these Regulations,

(iv) considers that any amendment goes beyond the disclosure in the international application as filed,

(v) wishes to accompany the international preliminary examination report by observations on the clarity of the claims, the description, and the drawings, or the question whether the claims are fully supported by the description,

(vi) considers that a claim relates to an invention in respect of which no international search report has been established and has decided not to carry out the international preliminary examination in respect of that claim, or

(vii) considers that a nucleotide and/or amino acid sequence listing is not available to it in such a form that a meaningful international preliminary examination can be carried out,

the said Authority shall notify the applicant accordingly in writing. Where the national law of the national Office acting as International Preliminary Examining Authority does not allow multiple dependent claims to be drafted in a manner different from that provided for in the second and third sentences of Rule 6.4(a), the International Preliminary Examining

Authority may, in case of failure to use that manner of claiming, apply Article 34(4)(b). In such case, it shall notify the applicant accordingly in writing.

(b) The notification shall fully state the reasons for the opinion of the International Preliminary Examining Authority.

(c) The notification shall invite the applicant to submit a written reply together, where appropriate, with amendments.

(d) The notification shall fix a time limit for the reply. The time limit shall be reasonable under the circumstances. It shall normally be two months after the date of notification. In no case shall it be shorter than one month after the said date. It shall be at least two months after the said date where the international search report is transmitted at the same time as the notification. It shall, subject to paragraph (e), not be more than three months after the said date.

(e) The time limit for replying to the notification may be extended if the applicant so requests before its expiration.

66.3 *Formal Response to the International Preliminary Examining Authority*

(a) The applicant may respond to the invitation referred to in Rule 66.2(c) of the International Preliminary Examining Authority by making amendments or – if he disagrees with the opinion of that Authority – by submitting arguments, as the case may be, or do both.

(b) Any response shall be submitted directly to the International Preliminary Examining Authority.

66.4 *Additional Opportunity for Submitting Amendments or Arguments*

(a) If the International Preliminary Examining Authority wishes to issue one or more additional written opinions, it may do so, and Rules 66.2 and 66.3 shall apply.

(b) On the request of the applicant, the International Preliminary Examining Authority may give him one or more additional opportunities to submit amendments or arguments.

66.4*bis* *Consideration of Amendments, Arguments and Rectifications of Obvious Mistakes*

Amendments, arguments and rectifications of obvious mistakes need not be taken into account by the International Preliminary Examining Authority for the purposes of a written opinion or the international preliminary examination report if they are received by, authorized by or notified to that Authority, as applicable, after it has begun to draw up that opinion or report.

66.5 *Amendment*

Any change, other than the rectification of an obvious mistake, in the claims, the description, or the drawings, including cancellation of claims, omission of passages in the description, or omission of certain drawings, shall be considered an amendment.

66.6 *Informal Communications with the Applicant*

The International Preliminary Examining Authority may, at any time, communicate informally, over the telephone, in writing, or through personal interviews, with the applicant. The said Authority shall, at its discretion, decide whether it wishes to grant more than one personal interview if so requested by the applicant, or whether it wishes to reply to any informal written communication from the applicant.

66.7 *Copy and Translation of Earlier Application Whose Priority Is Claimed*

(a) If the International Preliminary Examining Authority needs a copy of the earlier application whose priority is claimed in the international application, the International Bureau shall, on request, promptly furnish such copy. If that copy is not furnished to the International Preliminary Examining Authority because the applicant failed to comply with the requirements of Rule 17.1, and if that earlier application was not filed with that Authority in its capacity as a national Office or the priority document is not available to that Authority from a digital library in accordance with the Administrative Instructions, the international preliminary examination report may be established as if the priority had not been claimed.

(b) If the application whose priority is claimed in the international application is in a language other than the language or one of the languages of the International Preliminary Examining Authority, that Authority may, where the validity of the priority claim is relevant for the formulation of the opinion referred to in Article 33(1), invite the applicant to furnish a translation in the said language or one of the said languages within two months from the date of the invitation. If the translation is not furnished within that time limit, the international preliminary examination report may be established as if the priority had not been claimed.

66.8 *Form of Amendments*

(a) Subject to paragraph (b), when amending the description or the drawings, the applicant shall be required to submit a replacement sheet for every sheet of the international application which, on account of an amendment, differs from the sheet previously filed. The replacement sheet or sheets shall be accompanied by a letter which shall draw attention to the differences between the replaced sheets and the replacement sheets, shall indicate the basis for the amendment in the application as filed and shall preferably also explain the reasons for the amendment.

(b) Where the amendment consists in the deletion of passages or in minor alterations or additions, the replacement sheet referred to in paragraph (a) may be a copy of the relevant sheet of the international application containing the alterations or additions, provided that the clarity and direct reproducibility of that sheet are not adversely affected. To the extent that any amendment results in the cancellation of an entire sheet, that amendment shall be communicated in a letter which shall preferably also explain the reasons for the amendment.

(c) When amending the claims, Rule 46.5 shall apply *mutatis mutandis*. The set of claims submitted under Rule 46.5 as applicable by virtue of this paragraph shall replace all the claims originally filed or previously amended under Articles 19 or 34, as the case may be.

[1.923]
Rule 67
Subject Matter under Article 34(4)(a)(i)

67.1 *Definition*

No International Preliminary Examining Authority shall be required to carry out an international preliminary examination on an international application if, and to the extent to which, its subject matter is any of the following:

(i) scientific and mathematical theories,
(ii) plant or animal varieties or essentially biological processes for the production of plants and animals, other than microbiological processes and the products of such processes,
(iii) schemes, rules or methods of doing business, performing purely mental acts or playing games,
(iv) methods for treatment of the human or animal body by surgery or therapy, as well as diagnostic methods,
(v) mere presentations of information,
(vi) computer programs to the extent that the International Preliminary Examining Authority is not equipped to carry out an international preliminary examination concerning such programs.

[1.924]
Rule 68
Lack of Unity of Invention (International Preliminary Examination)

68.1 *No Invitation to Restrict or Pay*

Where the International Preliminary Examining Authority finds that the requirement of unity of invention is not complied with and chooses not to invite the applicant to restrict the claims or to pay additional fees, it shall proceed with the international preliminary examination, subject to Article 34(4)(b) and Rule 66.1(e), in respect of the entire international application, but shall indicate, in any written opinion and in the international preliminary examination report, that it considers that the requirement of unity of invention is not fulfilled and it shall specify the reasons therefor.

68.2 *Invitation to Restrict or Pay*

Where the International Preliminary Examining Authority finds that the requirement of unity of invention is not complied with and chooses to invite the applicant, at his option, to restrict the claims or to pay additional fees, the invitation shall:

(i) specify at least one possibility of restriction which, in the opinion of the International Preliminary Examining Authority, would be in compliance with the applicable requirement;
(ii) specify the reasons for which the international application is not considered as complying with the requirement of unity of invention;
(iii) invite the applicant to comply with the invitation within one month from the date of the invitation;
(iv) indicate the amount of the required additional fees to be paid in case the applicant so chooses; and
(v) invite the applicant to pay, where applicable, the protest fee referred to in Rule 68.3(e) within one month from the date of the invitation, and indicate the amount to be paid.

68.3 *Additional Fees*

(a) The amount of the additional fees due for international preliminary examination under Article 34(3)(a) shall be determined by the competent International Preliminary Examining Authority.

(b) The additional fees due for international preliminary examination under Article 34(3)(a) shall be payable direct to the International Preliminary Examining Authority.

(c) Any applicant may pay the additional fees under protest, that is, accompanied by a reasoned statement to the effect that the international application complies with the requirement of unity of invention or that the amount of the required additional fees is excessive. Such protest shall be examined by a review body constituted in the framework of the International Preliminary Examining Authority which, to the extent that it finds the protest justified, shall order the total or partial reimbursement to the applicant of the additional fees. On the request of the applicant, the text of both the protest and the decision thereon shall be notified to the elected Offices as an annex to the international preliminary examination report.

(d) The membership of the review body referred to in paragraph (c) may include, but shall not be limited to, the person who made the decision which is the subject of the protest.

(e) The examination of a protest referred to in paragraph (c) may be subjected by the International Preliminary Examining Authority to the payment to it, for its own benefit, of a protest fee. Where the applicant has not, within the time limit under Rule 68.2(v), paid any required protest fee, the protest shall be considered not to have been made and the International Preliminary Examining Authority shall so declare. The protest fee shall be refunded to the applicant where the review body referred to in paragraph (c) finds that the protest was entirely justified.

68.4 *Procedure in the Case of Insufficient Restriction of the Claims*

If the applicant restricts the claims but not sufficiently to comply with the requirement of unity of invention, the International Preliminary Examining Authority shall proceed as provided in Article 34(3)(c).

68.5 *Main Invention*

In case of doubt which invention is the main invention for the purposes of Article 34(3)(c), the invention first mentioned in the claims shall be considered the main invention.

[1.925]

Rule 69

Start of and Time Limit for International Preliminary Examination

69.1 *Start of International Preliminary Examination*

(a) Subject to paragraphs (b) to (e), the International Preliminary Examining Authority shall start the international preliminary examination when it is in possession of all of the following:

(i) the demand;

(ii) the amount due (in full) for the handling fee and the preliminary examination fee, including, where applicable, the late payment fee under Rule 58*bis*.2; and

(iii) either the international search report or the declaration by the International Searching Authority under Article 17(2)(a) that no international search report will be established, and the written opinion established under Rule 43*bis*.1;

provided that the International Preliminary Examining Authority shall not start the international preliminary examination before the expiration of the applicable time limit under Rule 54*bis*.1(a) unless the applicant expressly requests an earlier start.

(b) If the national Office or intergovernmental organization that acts as International Searching Authority also acts as International Preliminary Examining Authority, the international preliminary examination may, if that national Office or intergovernmental organization so wishes and subject to paragraphs (d) and (e), start at the same time as the international search.

(b-*bis*) Where, in accordance with paragraph (b), the national Office or intergovernmental organization that acts as both International Searching Authority and International Preliminary Examining Authority wishes to start the international preliminary examination at the same time as the international search and considers that all of the conditions referred to in Article 34(2)(c)(i) to (iii) are fulfilled, that national Office or intergovernmental organization need not, in its capacity as International Searching Authority, establish a written opinion under Rule 43*bis*.1.

(c) Where the statement concerning amendments contains an indication that amendments under Article 19 are to be taken into account (Rule 53.9(a)(i)), the International Preliminary Examining Authority shall not start the international preliminary examination before it has received a copy of the amendments concerned.

(d) Where the statement concerning amendments contains an indication that the start of the international preliminary examination is to be postponed (Rule 53.9(b)), the International Preliminary Examining Authority shall not start the international preliminary examination before whichever of the following occurs first:

(i) it has received a copy of any amendments made under Article 19;

(ii) it has received a notice from the applicant that he does not wish to make amendments under Article 19; or

(iii) the expiration of the applicable time limit under Rule 46.1.

(e) Where the statement concerning amendments contains an indication that amendments under Article 34 are submitted with the demand (Rule 53.9(c)) but no such amendments are, in fact, submitted, the International Preliminary Examining Authority shall not start the international preliminary examination before it has received the amendments or before the time limit fixed in the invitation referred to in Rule 60.1(g) has expired, whichever occurs first.

69.2 *Time Limit for International Preliminary Examination*

The time limit for establishing the international preliminary examination report shall be whichever of the following periods expires last:

(i) 28 months from the priority date; or

(ii) six months from the time provided under Rule 69.1 for the start of the international preliminary examination; or

(iii) six months from the date of receipt by the International Preliminary Examining Authority of the translation furnished under Rule 55.2.

[1.926]
Rule 70
International Preliminary Report on Patentability by the International Preliminary Examining Authority (International Preliminary Examination Report)

70.1 *Definition*
For the purposes of this Rule, "report" shall mean international preliminary examination report.

70.2 *Basis of the Report*
- (a) If the claims have been amended, the report shall issue on the claims as amended.
- (b) If, pursuant to Rule 66.7(a) or (b), the report is established as if the priority had not been claimed, the report shall so indicate.
- (c) If the International Preliminary Examining Authority considers that any amendment goes beyond the disclosure in the international application as filed, the report shall be established as if such amendment had not been made, and the report shall so indicate. It shall also indicate the reasons why it considers that the amendment goes beyond the said disclosure.
- (c-*bis*) If the claims, description or drawings have been amended but the replacement sheet or sheets were not accompanied by a letter indicating the basis for the amendment in the application as filed, as required under Rule 46.5(b)(iii), Rule 46.5(b)(iii) being applicable by virtue of Rule 66.8(c), or Rule 66.8(a), as applicable, the report may be established as if the amendment had not been made, in which case the report shall so indicate.
- (d) Where claims relate to inventions in respect of which no international search report has been established and have therefore not been the subject of international preliminary examination, the international preliminary examination report shall so indicate.
- (e) If a rectification of an obvious mistake is taken into account under Rule 66.1, the report shall so indicate. If a rectification of an obvious mistake is not taken into account pursuant to Rule 66.4*bis*, the report shall, if possible, so indicate, failing which the International Preliminary Examining Authority shall notify the International Bureau accordingly and the International Bureau shall proceed as provided for in the Administrative Instructions.
- (f) The report shall indicate the date on which a top-up search under Rule 66.1*ter* was made, or else state that no top-up search was made.

70.3 *Identifications*
The report shall identify the International Preliminary Examining Authority which established it by indicating the name of such Authority, and the
international application by indicating the international application number, the name of the applicant, and the international filing date.

70.4 *Dates*
The report shall indicate:
- (i) the date on which the demand was submitted, and
- (ii) the date of the report; that date shall be the date on which the report is completed.

70.5 *Classification*
- (a) The report shall repeat the classification given under Rule 43.3 if the International Preliminary Examining Authority agrees with such classification.
- (b) Otherwise, the International Preliminary Examining Authority shall indicate in the report the classification, at least according to the International Patent Classification, which it considers correct.

70.6 *Statement under Article 35(2)*
- (a) The statement referred to in Article 35(2) shall consist of the words "YES" or "NO," or their equivalent in the language of the report, or some appropriate sign provided for in the Administrative Instructions, and shall be accompanied by the citations, explanations and observations, if any, referred to in the last sentence of Article 35(2).
- (b) If any of the three criteria referred to in Article 35(2) (that is, novelty, inventive step (non-obviousness), industrial applicability) is not satisfied, the statement shall be negative. If, in such a case, any of the criteria, taken separately, is satisfied, the report shall specify the criterion or criteria so satisfied.

70.7 *Citations under Article 35(2)*
- (a) The report shall cite the documents considered to be relevant for supporting the statements made under Article 35(2), whether or not such documents are cited in the international search report. Documents cited in the international search report need only be cited in the report when they are considered by the International Preliminary Examining Authority to be relevant.
- (b) The provisions of Rule 43.5(b) and (e) shall apply also to the report.

70.8 *Explanations under Article 35(2)*
The Administrative Instructions shall contain guidelines for cases in which the explanations referred to in Article 35(2) should or should not be given and the form of such explanations. Such guidelines shall be based on the following principles:
- (i) explanations shall be given whenever the statement in relation to any claim is negative;

(ii) explanations shall be given whenever the statement is positive unless the reason for citing any document is easy to imagine on the basis of consultation of the cited document;

(iii) generally, explanations shall be given if the case provided for in the last sentence of Rule 70.6(b) obtains.

70.9 *Non-Written Disclosures*

Any non-written disclosure referred to in the report by virtue of Rule 64.2 shall be mentioned by indicating its kind, the date on which the written disclosure referring to the non-written disclosure was made available to the public, and the date on which the non-written disclosure occurred in public.

70.10 *Certain Published Documents*

Any published application or any patent referred to in the report by virtue of Rule 64.3 shall be mentioned as such and shall be accompanied by an indication of its date of publication, of its filing date, and its claimed priority date (if any). In respect of the priority date of any such document, the report may indicate that, in the opinion of the International Preliminary Examining Authority, such date has not been validly claimed.

70.11 *Mention of Amendments*

If, before the International Preliminary Examining Authority, amendments have been made, this fact shall be indicated in the report. Where any amendment has resulted in the cancellation of an entire sheet, this fact shall also be specified in the report.

70.12 *Mention of Certain Defects and Other Matters*

If the International Preliminary Examining Authority considers that, at the time it prepares the report:

(i) the international application contains any of the defects referred to in Rule 66.2(a)(iii), it shall include this opinion and the reasons therefor in the report;

(ii) the international application calls for any of the observations referred to in Rule 66.2(a)(v), it may include this opinion in the report and, if it does, it shall also indicate in the report the reasons for such opinion;

(iii) any of the situations referred to in Article 34(4) exists, it shall state this opinion and the reasons therefor in the report;

(iv) a nucleotide and/or amino acid sequence listing is not available to it in such a form that a meaningful international preliminary examination can be carried out, it shall so state in the report.

70.13 *Remarks Concerning Unity of Invention*

If the applicant paid additional fees for the international preliminary examination, or if the international application or the international preliminary examination was restricted under Article 34(3), the report shall so indicate. Furthermore, where the international preliminary examination was carried out on restricted claims (Article 34(3)(a)), or on the main invention only (Article 34(3)(c)), the report shall indicate what parts of the international application were and what parts were not the subject of international preliminary examination. The report shall contain the indications provided for in Rule 68.1, where the International Preliminary Examining Authority chose not to invite the applicant to restrict the claims or to pay additional fees.

70.14 *Authorized Officer*

The report shall indicate the name of the officer of the International Preliminary Examining Authority responsible for that report.

70.15 *Form; Title*

(a) The physical requirements as to the form of the report shall be prescribed by the Administrative Instructions.

(b) The report shall bear the title "international preliminary report on patentability (Chapter II of the Patent Cooperation Treaty)" together with an indication that it is the international preliminary examination report established by the International Preliminary Examining Authority.

70.16 *Annexes to the Report*

(a) The following replacement sheets and letters shall be annexed to the report:

(i) each replacement sheet under Rule 66.8 containing amendments under Article 34 and each letter under Rule 66.8(a), Rule 66.8(b) and Rule 46.5(b) as applicable by virtue of Rule 66.8(c);

(ii) each replacement sheet under Rule 46.5 containing amendments under Article 19 and each letter under Rule 46.5; and

(iii) each replacement sheet under Rule 26.4 as applicable by virtue of Rule 91.2 containing a rectification of an obvious mistake authorized by that Authority under Rule 91.1(b)(iii) and each letter under Rule 26.4 as applicable by virtue of Rule 91.2;

unless any such replacement sheet has been superseded or considered reversed by a later replacement sheet or an amendment resulting in the cancellation of an entire sheet under Rule 66.8(b); and

(iv) where the report contains an indication referred to in Rule 70.2(e), any sheet and letter relating to a rectification of an obvious mistake which is not taken into account pursuant to Rule 66.4*bis*.

(b) Notwithstanding paragraph (a), each superseded or reversed replacement sheet referred to in that paragraph and any letter referred to in that paragraph relating to such superseded or reversed sheet shall also be annexed to the report where:
- (i) the International Preliminary Examining Authority considers that the relevant superseding or reversing amendment goes beyond the disclosure in the international application as filed and the report contains an indication referred to in Rule 70.2(c);
- (ii) the relevant superseding or reversing amendment was not accompanied by a letter indicating the basis for the amendment in the application as filed and the report is established as if the amendment had not been made and contains an indication referred to in Rule 70.2(c-*bis*).

In such a case, the superseded or reversed replacement sheet shall be marked as provided by the Administrative Instructions.

70.17 *Languages of the Report and the Annexes*

The report and any annex shall be in the language in which the international application to which they relate is published, or, if the international preliminary examination is carried out, pursuant to Rule 55.2, on the basis of a translation of the international application, in the language of that translation.

[1.927]

Rule 71

Transmittal of the International Preliminary Examination Report

71.1 *Recipients*

The International Preliminary Examining Authority shall, on the same day, transmit one copy of the international preliminary examination report and its annexes, if any, to the International Bureau, and one copy to the applicant.

71.2 *Copies of Cited Documents*

(a) The request under Article 36(4) may be presented any time during seven years from the international filing date of the international application to which the report relates.

(b) The International Preliminary Examining Authority may require that the party (applicant or elected Office) presenting the request pay to it the cost of preparing and mailing the copies. The level of the cost of preparing copies shall be provided for in the agreements referred to in Article 32(2) between the International Preliminary Examining Authorities and the International Bureau.

(c) *[Deleted]*

(d) Any International Preliminary Examining Authority may perform the obligations referred to in paragraphs (a) and (b) through another agency responsible to it.

[1.928]

Rule 72

Translation of the International Preliminary Examination Report and of the Written Opinion of the International Searching Authority

72.1 *Languages*

(a) Any elected State may require that the international preliminary examination report, established in any language other than the official language, or one of the official languages, of its national Office, be translated into English.

(b) Any such requirement shall be notified to the International Bureau, which shall promptly publish it in the Gazette.

72.2 *Copy of Translation for the Applicant*

The International Bureau shall transmit a copy of the translation referred to in Rule 72.1(a) of the international preliminary examination report to the applicant at the same time as it communicates such translation to the interested elected Office or Offices.

72.2*bis* *Translation of the Written Opinion of the International Searching Authority Established under Rule 43bis.1*

In the case referred to in Rule 73.2(b)(ii), the written opinion established by the International Searching Authority under Rule 43*bis*.1 shall, upon request of the elected Office concerned, be translated into English by or under the responsibility of the International Bureau. The International Bureau shall transmit a copy of the translation to the elected Office concerned within two months from the date of receipt of the request for translation, and shall at the same time transmit a copy to the applicant.

72.3 *Observations on the Translation*

The applicant may make written observations as to the correctness of the translation of the international preliminary examination report or of the written opinion established by the International Searching Authority under Rule 43*bis*.1 and shall send a copy of the observations to each of the interested elected Offices and to the International Bureau.

[1.929]
Rule 73
Communication of the International Preliminary Examination Report or the Written Opinion of the International Searching Authority

73.1 *Preparation of Copies*

The International Bureau shall prepare the copies of the documents to be communicated under Article 36(3)(a).

73.2 *Communication to Elected Offices*

(a) The International Bureau shall effect the communication provided for in Article 36(3)(a) to each elected Office in accordance with Rule 93*bis*.1 but not before the expiration of 30 months from the priority date.

(b) Where the applicant makes an express request to an elected Office under Article 40(2), the International Bureau shall, upon the request of that Office or of the applicant,

(i) if the international preliminary examination report has already been transmitted to the International Bureau under Rule 71.1, promptly effect the communication provided for in Article 36(3)(a) to that Office;

(ii) if the international preliminary examination report has not been transmitted to the International Bureau under Rule 71.1, promptly communicate a copy of the written opinion established by the International Searching Authority under Rule 43*bis*.1 to that Office.

(c) Where the applicant has withdrawn the demand or any or all elections, the communication provided for in paragraph (a) shall nevertheless be effected, if the International Bureau has received the international preliminary examination report, to the elected Office or Offices affected by the withdrawal.

[1.930]
Rule 74
Translations of Annexes of the International Preliminary Examination Report and Transmittal Thereof

74.1 *Contents of Translation and Time Limit for Transmittal Thereof*

(a) Where the furnishing of a translation of the international application is required by the elected Office under Article 39(1), the applicant shall, within the time limit applicable under Article 39(1), transmit a translation of any replacement sheet referred to in Rule 70.16 which is annexed to the international preliminary examination report, unless such sheet is in the language of the required translation of the international application. The same time limit shall apply where the furnishing of a translation of the international application to the elected Office must, because of a declaration made under Article 64(2)(a)(i), be effected within the time limit applicable under Article 22.

(b) Where the furnishing under Article 39(1) of a translation of the international application is not required by the elected Office, that Office may require the applicant to furnish, within the time limit applicable under that Article, a translation into the language in which the international application was published of any replacement sheet referred to in Rule 70.16 which is annexed to the international preliminary examination report and is not in that language.

Rule 75
[Deleted]

[1.931]
Rule 76
Translation of Priority Document; Application of Certain Rules to Procedures before Elected Offices

76.1, 76.2 and 76.3 *[Deleted]*

76.4 *Time Limit for Translation of Priority Document*

The applicant shall not be required to furnish to any elected Office a translation of the priority document before the expiration of the applicable time limit under Article 39.

76.5 *Application of Certain Rules to Procedures before Elected Offices*

Rules 13*ter*.3, 20.8(c), 22.1(g), 47.1, 49, 49*bis*, 49*ter* and 51*bis* shall apply, provided that:

(i) any reference in the said Rules to the designated Office or to the designated State shall be construed as a reference to the elected Office or to the elected State, respectively;

(ii) any reference in the said Rules to Article 22, Article 23(2) or Article 24(2) shall be construed as a reference to Article 39(1), Article 40(2) or Article 39(3), respectively;

(iii) the words "international applications filed" in Rule 49.1(c) shall be replaced by the words "a demand submitted;"

(iv) for the purposes of Article 39(1), where an international preliminary examination report has been established, a translation of any amendment under Article 19 shall only be required if that amendment is annexed to that report;

(v) the reference in Rule 47.1(a) to Rule 47.4 shall be construed as a reference to Rule 61.2(d).

[1.932]
Rule 77
Faculty under Article 39(1)(b)

77.1 *Exercise of Faculty*

(a) Any Contracting State allowing a time limit expiring later than the time limit provided for in Article 39(1)(a) shall notify the International Bureau of the time limit so fixed.

(b) Any notification received by the International Bureau under paragraph (a) shall be promptly published by the International Bureau in the Gazette.

(c) Notifications concerning the shortening of the previously fixed time limit shall be effective in relation to demands submitted after the expiration of three months computed from the date on which the notification was published by the International Bureau.

(d) Notifications concerning the lengthening of the previously fixed time limit shall become effective upon publication by the International Bureau in the Gazette in respect of demands pending at the time or submitted after the date of such publication, or, if the Contracting State effecting the notification fixes some later date, as from the latter date.

[1.933]
Rule 78
Amendment of the Claims, the Description, and the Drawings, before Elected Offices

78.1 *Time Limit*

(a) The applicant shall, if he so wishes, exercise the right under Article 41 to amend the claims, the description and the drawings, before the elected Office concerned within one month from the fulfillment of the requirements under Article 39(1)(a), provided that, if the transmittal of the international preliminary examination report under Article 36(1) has not taken place by the expiration of the time limit applicable under Article 39, he shall exercise the said right not later than four months after such expiration date. In either case, the applicant may exercise the said right at any later time if so permitted by the national law of the said State.

(b) In any elected State in which the national law provides that examination starts only on special request, the national law may provide that the time limit within or the time at which the applicant may exercise the right under Article 41 shall be the same as that provided by the national law for the filing of amendments in the case of the examination, on special request, of national applications, provided that such time limit shall not expire prior to, or such time shall not come before, the expiration of the time limit applicable under paragraph (a).

78.2 *[Deleted]*

78.3 *Utility Models*

The provisions of Rules 6.5 and 13.5 shall apply, *mutatis mutandis*, before elected Offices. If the election was made before the expiration of the 19th month from the priority date, the reference to the time limit applicable under Article 22 is replaced by a reference to the time limit applicable under Article 39.

PART D
RULES CONCERNING CHAPTER III OF THE TREATY

[1.934]
Rule 79
Calendar

79.1 *Expressing Dates*

Applicants, national Offices, receiving Offices, International Searching and Preliminary Examining Authorities, and the International Bureau, shall, for the purposes of the Treaty and the Regulations, express any date in terms of the Christian era and the Gregorian calendar, or, if they use other eras and calendars, they shall also express any date in terms of the Christian era and the Gregorian calendar.

[1.935]
Rule 80
Computation of Time Limits

80.1 *Periods Expressed in Years*

When a period is expressed as one year or a certain number of years, computation shall start on the day following the day on which the relevant event occurred, and the period shall expire in the relevant subsequent year in the month having the same name and on the day having the same number as the month and the day on which the said event occurred, provided that if the relevant subsequent month has no day with the same number the period shall expire on the last day of that month.

80.2 *Periods Expressed in Months*

When a period is expressed as one month or a certain number of months, computation shall start on the day following the day on which the relevant event occurred, and the period shall expire in the relevant subsequent month on the day which has the same number as the day on which the said event occurred, provided that if the relevant subsequent month has no day with the same number the period shall expire on the last day of that month.

80.3 *Periods Expressed in Days*

When a period is expressed as a certain number of days, computation shall start on the day following the day on which the relevant event occurred, and the period shall expire on the day on which the last day of the count has been reached.

80.4 *Local Dates*

(a) The date which is taken into consideration as the starting date of the computation of any period shall be the date which prevails in the locality at the time when the relevant event occurred.

(b) The date on which any period expires shall be the date which prevails in the locality in which the required document must be filed or the required fee must be paid.

80.5 *Expiration on a Non-Working Day or Official Holiday*

If the expiration of any period during which any document or fee must reach a national Office or intergovernmental organization falls on a day:

(i) on which such Office or organization is not open to the public for the purposes of the transaction of official business;

(ii) on which ordinary mail is not delivered in the locality in which such Office or organization is situated;

(iii) which, where such Office or organization is situated in more than one locality, is an official holiday in at least one of the localities in which such Office or organization is situated, and in circumstances where the national law applicable by that Office or organization provides, in respect of national applications, that, in such a case, such period shall expire on a subsequent day; or

(iv) which, where such Office is the government authority of a Contracting State entrusted with the granting of patents, is an official holiday in part of that Contracting State, and in circumstances where the national law applicable by that Office provides, in respect of national applications, that, in such a case, such period shall expire on a subsequent day;

the period shall expire on the next subsequent day on which none of the said four circumstances exists.

80.6 *Date of Documents*

Where a period starts on the day of the date of a document or letter emanating from a national Office or intergovernmental organization, any interested party may prove that the said document or letter was mailed on a day later than the date it bears, in which case the date of actual mailing shall, for the purposes of computing the period, be considered to be the date on which the period starts. Irrespective of the date on which such a document or letter was mailed, if the applicant offers to the national Office or intergovernmental organization evidence which satisfies the national Office or intergovernmental organization that the document or letter was received more than seven days after the date it bears, the national Office or intergovernmental organization shall treat the period starting from the date of the document or letter as expiring later by an additional number of days which is equal to the number of days which the document or letter was received later than seven days after the date it bears.

80.7 *End of Working Day*

(a) A period expiring on a given day shall expire at the moment the national Office or intergovernmental organization with which the document must be filed or to which the fee must be paid closes for business on that day.

(b) Any Office or organization may depart from the provisions of paragraph (a) up to midnight on the relevant day.

[1.936]

Rule 81

Modification of Time Limits Fixed in the Treaty

81.1 *Proposal*

(a) Any Contracting State or the Director General may propose a modification under Article 47(2).

(b) Proposals made by a Contracting State shall be presented to the Director General.

81.2 *Decision by the Assembly*

(a) When the proposal is made to the Assembly, its text shall be sent by the Director General to all Contracting States at least two months in advance of that session of the Assembly whose agenda includes the proposal.

(b) During the discussion of the proposal in the Assembly, the proposal may be amended or consequential amendments proposed.

(c) The proposal shall be considered adopted if none of the Contracting States present at the time of voting votes against the proposal.

81.3 *Voting by Correspondence*

(a) When voting by correspondence is chosen, the proposal shall be included in a written communication from the Director General to the Contracting States, inviting them to express their vote in writing.

(b) The invitation shall fix the time limit within which the reply containing the vote expressed in writing must reach the International Bureau. That time limit shall not be less than three months from the date of the invitation.

(c) Replies must be either positive or negative. Proposals for amendments or mere observations shall not be regarded as votes.

(d) The proposal shall be considered adopted if none of the Contracting States opposes the amendment and if at least one-half of the Contracting States express either approval or indifference or abstention.

[1.937]
Rule 82
Irregularities in the Mail Service

82.1 *Delay or Loss in Mail*

(a) Any interested party may offer evidence that he has mailed the document or letter five days prior to the expiration of the time limit. Except in cases where surface mail normally arrives at its destination within two days of mailing, or where no airmail service is available, such evidence may be offered only if the mailing was by airmail. In any case, evidence may be offered only if the mailing was by mail registered by the postal authorities.

(b) If the mailing, in accordance with paragraph (a), of a document or letter is proven to the satisfaction of the national Office or intergovernmental organization which is the addressee, delay in arrival shall be excused, or, if the document or letter is lost in the mail, substitution for it of a new copy shall be permitted, provided that the interested party proves to the satisfaction of the said Office or organization that the document or letter offered in substitution is identical with the document or letter lost.

(c) In the cases provided for in paragraph (b), evidence of mailing within the prescribed time limit, and, where the document or letter was lost, the substitute document or letter as well as the evidence concerning its identity with the document or letter lost shall be submitted within one month after the date on which the interested party noticed – or with due diligence should have noticed – the delay or the loss, and in no case later than six months after the expiration of the time limit applicable in the given case.

(d) Any national Office or intergovernmental organization which has notified the International Bureau that it will do so shall, where a delivery service other than the postal authorities is used to mail a document or letter, apply the provisions of paragraphs (a) to (c) as if the delivery service was a postal authority. In such a case, the last sentence of paragraph (a) shall not apply but evidence may be offered only if details of the mailing were recorded by the delivery service at the time of mailing. The notification may contain an indication that it applies only to mailings using specified delivery services or delivery services which satisfy specified criteria. The International Bureau shall publish the information so notified in the Gazette.

(e) Any national Office or intergovernmental organization may proceed under paragraph (d):
   (i) even if, where applicable, the delivery service used was not one of those specified, or did not satisfy the criteria specified, in the relevant notification under paragraph (d), or
   (ii) even if that Office or organization has not sent to the International Bureau a notification under paragraph (d).

[1.938]
Rule 82*bis*
Excuse by the Designated or Elected State of Delays in Meeting Certain Time Limits

82*bis*.1 *Meaning of "Time Limit" in Article 48(2)*

The reference to "any time limit" in Article 48(2) shall be construed as comprising a reference:
   (i) to any time limit fixed in the Treaty or these Regulations;
   (ii) to any time limit fixed by the receiving Office, the International Searching Authority, the International Preliminary Examining Authority or the International Bureau or applicable by the receiving Office under its national law;
   (iii) to any time limit fixed by, or in the national law applicable by, the designated or elected Office, for the performance of any act by the applicant before that Office.

82*bis*.2 *Reinstatement of Rights and Other Provisions to Which Article 48(2) Applies*

The provisions of the national law which is referred to in Article 48(2) concerning the excusing, by the designated or elected State, of any delay in meeting any time limit are those provisions which provide for reinstatement of rights, restoration, *restitutio in integrum* or further processing in spite of non-compliance with a time limit, and any other provision providing for the extension of time limits or for excusing delays in meeting time limits.

[1.939]
Rule 82*ter*
Rectification of Errors Made by the Receiving Office or by the International Bureau

82*ter*.1 *Errors Concerning the International Filing Date and the Priority Claim*

(a) If the applicant proves to the satisfaction of any designated or elected Office that the international filing date is incorrect due to an error made by the receiving Office or that the priority claim has been erroneously considered void by the receiving Office or the International Bureau, and if the error is an error such that, had it been made by the designated or elected Office itself, that Office would rectify it under the national law or national practice, the said Office shall rectify the error and shall treat the international application as if it had been accorded the rectified international filing date or as if the priority claim had not been considered void.

(b) Where the international filing date has been accorded by the receiving Office under Rule 20.3(b)(ii) or 20.5(d) on the basis of the incorporation by reference under Rules 4.18 and 20.6 of an element or part but the designated or elected Office finds that:

(i) the applicant has not complied with Rule 17.1(a), (b) or (b-*bis*) in relation to the priority document;

(ii) a requirement under Rule 4.18, 20.6(a)(i) or 51*bis*.1(e)(ii) has not been complied with; or

(iii) the element or part is not completely contained in the priority document concerned;

the designated or elected Office may, subject to paragraph (c), treat the international application as if the international filing date had been accorded under Rule 20.3(b)(i) or 20.5(b), or corrected under Rule 20.5(c), as applicable, provided that Rule 17.1(c) shall apply *mutatis mutandis*.

(c) The designated or elected Office shall not treat the international application under paragraph (b) as if the international filing date had been accorded under Rule 20.3(b)(i) or 20.5(b), or corrected under Rule 20.5(c), without giving the applicant the opportunity to make observations on the intended treatment, or to make a request under paragraph (d), within a time limit which shall be reasonable under the circumstances.

(d) Where the designated or elected Office, in accordance with paragraph (c), has notified the applicant that it intends to treat the international application as if the international filing date had been corrected under Rule 20.5(c), the applicant may, in a notice submitted to that Office within the time limit referred to in paragraph (c), request that the missing part concerned be disregarded for the purposes of national processing before that Office, in which case that part shall be considered not to have been furnished and that Office shall not treat the international application as if the international filing date had been corrected.

[1.940]
Rule 82*quater*
Excuse of Delay in Meeting Time Limits

82*quater*.1 *Excuse of Delay in Meeting Time Limits*

(a) Any interested party may offer evidence that a time limit fixed in the Regulations for performing an action before the receiving Office, the International Searching Authority, the Authority specified for supplementary search, the International Preliminary Examining Authority or the International Bureau was not met due to war, revolution, civil disorder, strike, natural calamity, a general unavailability of electronic communications services or other like reason in the locality where the interested party resides, has his place of business or is staying, and that the relevant action was taken as soon as reasonably possible.

(b) Any such evidence shall be addressed to the Office, Authority or the International Bureau, as the case may be, not later than six months after the expiration of the time limit applicable in the given case. If such circumstances are proven to the satisfaction of the addressee, delay in meeting the time limit shall be excused.

(c) The excuse of a delay need not be taken into account by any designated or elected Office before which the applicant, at the time the decision to excuse the delay is taken, has already performed the acts referred to in Article 22 or Article 39.

[1.941]
Rule 83
Right to Practice before International Authorities

83.1 *Proof of Right*

The International Bureau, the competent International Searching Authority, and the competent International Preliminary Examining Authority, may require the production of proof of the right to practice referred to in Article 49.

83.1*bis* *Where the International Bureau Is the Receiving Office*

(a) Any person who has the right to practice before the national Office of, or acting for, a Contracting State of which the applicant or, if there are two or more applicants, any of the applicants is a resident or national shall be entitled to practice in respect of the international application before the International Bureau in its capacity as receiving Office under Rule 19.1(a)(iii).

(b) Any person having the right to practice before the International Bureau in its capacity as receiving Office in respect of an international application shall be entitled to practice in respect of that application before the International Bureau in any other capacity and before the competent International Searching Authority and competent International Preliminary Examining Authority.

83.2 *Information*

(a) The national Office or the intergovernmental organization which the interested person is alleged to have a right to practice before shall, upon request, inform the International Bureau, the competent International Searching Authority, or the competent International Preliminary Examining Authority, whether such person has the right to practice before it.

(b) Such information shall be binding upon the International Bureau, the International Searching Authority, or the International Preliminary Examining Authority, as the case may be.

PART E
RULES CONCERNING CHAPTER V OF THE TREATY

[1.942]
Rule 84
Expenses of Delegations

84.1 *Expenses Borne by Governments*

The expenses of each Delegation participating in any organ established by or under the Treaty shall be borne by the Government which has appointed it.

[1.943]
Rule 85
Absence of Quorum in the Assembly

85.1 *Voting by Correspondence*

In the case provided for in Article 53(5)(b), the International Bureau shall communicate the decisions of the Assembly (other than those concerning the Assembly's own procedure) to the Contracting States which were not represented and shall invite them to express in writing their vote or abstention within a period of three months from the date of the communication. If, at the expiration of that period, the number of Contracting States having thus expressed their vote or abstention attains the number of Contracting States which was lacking for attaining the quorum in the session itself, such decisions shall take effect provided that at the same time the required majority still obtains.

[1.944]
Rule 86
The Gazette

86.1 *Contents*

The Gazette referred to in Article 55(4) shall contain:

(i) for each published international application, the data specified by the Administrative Instructions taken from the front page of the publication of the international application, the drawing (if any) appearing on the said front page, and the abstract;

(ii) the schedule of all fees payable to the receiving Offices, the International Bureau, and the International Searching and Preliminary Examining Authorities;

(iii) notices the publication of which is required under the Treaty or these Regulations;

(iv) information concerning events at the designated and elected Offices notified to the International Bureau under Rule 95.1 in relation to published international applications;

(v) any other useful information prescribed by the Administrative Instructions, provided access to such information is not prohibited under the Treaty or these Regulations.

86.2 *Languages; Form and Means of Publication; Timing*

(a) The Gazette shall be published in English and French at the same time. The translations shall be ensured by the International Bureau in English and French.

(b) The Assembly may order the publication of the Gazette in languages other than those referred to in paragraph (a).

(c) The form in which and the means by which the Gazette is published shall be governed by the Administrative Instructions.

(d) The International Bureau shall ensure that, for each published international application, the information referred to in Rule 86.1(i) is published in the Gazette on, or as soon as possible after, the date of publication of the international application.

86.3 *Frequency*

The frequency of publication of the Gazette shall be determined by the Director General.

86.4 *Sale*

The subscription and other sale prices of the Gazette shall be determined by the Director General.

86.5 *Title*

The title of the Gazette shall be determined by the Director General.

86.6 *Further Details*

Further details concerning the Gazette may be provided for in the Administrative Instructions.

[1.945]
Rule 87
Communication of Publications
87.1 *Communication of Publications on Request*
The International Bureau shall communicate, free of charge, every published international application, the Gazette and any other publication of general interest published by the International Bureau in connection with the Treaty or these Regulations, to International Searching Authorities, International Preliminary Examining Authorities and national Offices upon request by the Authority or Office concerned. Further details concerning the form in which and the means by which publications are communicated shall be governed by the Administrative Instructions.

[1.946]
Rule 88
Amendment of the Regulations
88.1 *Requirement of Unanimity*
Amendment of the following provisions of these Regulations shall require that no State having the right to vote in the Assembly vote against the proposed amendment:

(i) Rule 14.1 (Transmittal Fee),
(ii) *[deleted]*
(iii) Rule 22.3 (Time Limit under Article 12(3)),
(iv) Rule 33 (Relevant Prior Art for International Search),
(v) Rule 64 (Prior Art for International Preliminary Examination),
(vi) Rule 81 (Modification of Time Limits Fixed in the Treaty),
(vii) the present paragraph (i.e., Rule 88.1).

88.2 *[Deleted]*
88.3 *Requirement of Absence of Opposition by Certain States*
Amendment of the following provisions of these Regulations shall require that no State referred to in Article 58(3)(a)(ii) and having the right to vote in the Assembly vote against the proposed amendment:

(i) Rule 34 (Minimum Documentation),
(ii) Rule 39 (Subject Matter under Article 17(2)(a)(i)),
(iii) Rule 67 (Subject Matter under Article 34(4)(a)(i)),
(iv) the present paragraph (i.e., Rule 88.3).

88.4 *Procedure*
Any proposal for amending a provision referred to in Rules 88.1 or 88.3 shall, if the proposal is to be decided upon in the Assembly, be communicated to all Contracting States at least two months prior to the opening of that session of the Assembly which is called upon to make a decision on the proposal.

[1.947]
Rule 89
Administrative Instructions
89.1 *Scope*

(a) The Administrative Instructions shall contain provisions:
  (i) concerning matters in respect of which these Regulations expressly refer to such Instructions,
  (ii) concerning any details in respect of the application of these Regulations.
(b) The Administrative Instructions shall not be in conflict with the provisions of the Treaty, these Regulations, or any agreement concluded by the International Bureau with an International Searching Authority, or an International Preliminary Examining Authority.

89.2 *Source*

(a) The Administrative Instructions shall be drawn up and promulgated by the Director General after consultation with the receiving Offices and the International Searching and Preliminary Examining Authorities.
(b) They may be modified by the Director General after consultation with the Offices or Authorities which have a direct interest in the proposed modification.
(c) The Assembly may invite the Director General to modify the Administrative Instructions, and the Director General shall proceed accordingly.

89.3 *Publication and Entry into Force*

(a) The Administrative Instructions and any modification thereof shall be published in the Gazette.
(b) Each publication shall specify the date on which the published provisions come into effect. The dates may be different for different provisions, provided that no provision may be declared effective prior to its publication in the Gazette.

PART F
RULES CONCERNING SEVERAL CHAPTERS OF THE TREATY

[1.948]
Rule 89*bis*
Filing, Processing and Communication of International Applications and Other Documents in Electronic Form or by Electronic Means

89*bis*.1 *International Applications*

(a) International applications may, subject to paragraphs (b) to (e), be filed and processed in electronic form or by electronic means, in accordance with the Administrative Instructions, provided that any receiving Office shall permit the filing of international applications on paper.

(b) These Regulations shall apply *mutatis mutandis* to international applications filed in electronic form or by electronic means, subject to any special provisions of the Administrative Instructions.

(c) The Administrative Instructions shall set out the provisions and requirements in relation to the filing and processing of international applications filed, in whole or in part, in electronic form or by electronic means, including but not limited to, provisions and requirements in relation to acknowledgment of receipt, procedures relating to the according of an international filing date, physical requirements and the consequences of non-compliance with those requirements, signature of documents, means of authentication of documents and of the identity of parties communicating with Offices and authorities, and the operation of Article 12 in relation to the home copy, the record copy and the search copy, and may contain different provisions and requirements in relation to international applications filed in different languages.

(d) No national Office or intergovernmental organization shall be obliged to receive or process international applications filed in electronic form or by electronic means unless it has notified the International Bureau that it is prepared to do so in compliance with the applicable provisions of the Administrative Instructions. The International Bureau shall publish the information so notified in the Gazette.

(e) No receiving Office which has given the International Bureau a notification under paragraph (d) may refuse to process an international application filed in electronic form or by electronic means which complies with the applicable requirements under the Administrative Instructions.

89*bis*.2 *Other Documents*

Rule 89*bis*.1 shall apply *mutatis mutandis* to other documents and correspondence relating to international applications.

89*bis*.3 *Communication between Offices*

Where the Treaty, these Regulations or the Administrative Instructions provide for the communication, notification or transmittal ("communication") of an international application, notification, communication, correspondence or other document by one national Office or intergovernmental organization to another, such communication may, where so agreed by both the sender and the receiver, be effected in electronic form or by electronic means.

[1.949]
Rule 89*ter*
Copies in Electronic Form of Documents Filed on Paper

89*ter*.1 *Copies in Electronic Form of Documents Filed on Paper*

Any national Office or intergovernmental organization may provide that, where an international application or other document relating to an international application is filed on paper, a copy thereof in electronic form, in accordance with the Administrative Instructions, may be furnished by the applicant.

[1.950]
Rule 90
Agents and Common Representatives

90.1 *Appointment as Agent*

(a) A person having the right to practice before the national Office with which the international application is filed or, where the international application is filed with the International Bureau, having the right to practice in respect of the international application before the International Bureau as receiving Office may be appointed by the applicant as his agent to represent him before the receiving Office, the International Bureau, the International Searching Authority, any Authority specified for supplementary search and the International Preliminary Examining Authority.

(b) A person having the right to practice before the national Office or intergovernmental organization which acts as the International Searching Authority may be appointed by the applicant as his agent to represent him specifically before that Authority.

(b-*bis*) A person having the right to practice before the national Office or intergovernmental organization which acts as the Authority specified for supplementary search may be appointed by the applicant as his agent to represent him specifically before that Authority.

(c) A person having the right to practice before the national Office or intergovernmental organization which acts as the International Preliminary Examining Authority may be appointed by the applicant as his agent to represent him specifically before that Authority.

(d) An agent appointed under paragraph (a) may, unless otherwise indicated in the document appointing him, appoint one or more sub-agents to represent the applicant as the applicant's agent:

(i) before the receiving Office, the International Bureau, the International Searching Authority, any Authority specified for supplementary search and the International Preliminary Examining Authority, provided that any person so appointed as sub-agent has the right to practice before the national Office with which the international application was filed or to practice in respect of the international application before the International Bureau as receiving Office, as the case may be;

(ii) specifically before the International Searching Authority, any Authority specified for supplementary search or the International Preliminary Examining Authority, provided that any person so appointed as sub-agent has the right to practice before the national Office or intergovernmental organization which acts as the International Searching Authority, the Authority specified for supplementary search or the International Preliminary Examining Authority, as the case may be.

90.2 *Common Representative*

(a) Where there are two or more applicants and the applicants have not appointed an agent representing all of them (a "common agent") under Rule 90.1(a), one of the applicants who is entitled to file an international application according to Article 9 may be appointed by the other applicants as their common representative.

(b) Where there are two or more applicants and all the applicants have not appointed a common agent under Rule 90.1(a) or a common representative under paragraph (a), the applicant first named in the request who is entitled according to Rule 19.1 to file an international application with the receiving Office shall be considered to be the common representative of all the applicants.

90.3 *Effects of Acts by or in Relation to Agents and Common Representatives*

(a) Any act by or in relation to an agent shall have the effect of an act by or in relation to the applicant or applicants concerned.

(b) If there are two or more agents representing the same applicant or applicants, any act by or in relation to any of those agents shall have the effect of an act by or in relation to the said applicant or applicants.

(c) Subject to Rule 90*bis*.5, second sentence, any act by or in relation to a common representative or his agent shall have the effect of an act by or in relation to all the applicants.

90.4 *Manner of Appointment of Agent or Common Representative*

(a) The appointment of an agent shall be effected by the applicant signing the request, the demand or a separate power of attorney. Where there are two or more applicants, the appointment of a common agent or common representative shall be effected by each applicant signing, at his choice, the request, the demand or a separate power of attorney.

(b) Subject to Rule 90.5, a separate power of attorney shall be submitted to either the receiving Office or the International Bureau, provided that, where a power of attorney appoints an agent under Rule 90.1(b), (b-*bis*), (c) or (d)(ii), it shall be submitted to the International Searching Authority, the Authority specified for supplementary search or the International Preliminary Examining Authority, as the case may be.

(c) If the separate power of attorney is not signed, or if the required separate power of attorney is missing, or if the indication of the name or address of the appointed person does not comply with Rule 4.4, the power of attorney shall be considered non-existent unless the defect is corrected.

(d) Subject to paragraph (e), any receiving Office, any International Searching Authority, any Authority competent to carry out supplementary searches, any International Preliminary Examining Authority and the International Bureau may waive the requirement under paragraph (b) that a separate power of attorney be submitted to it, in which case paragraph (c) shall not apply.

(e) Where the agent or the common representative submits any notice of withdrawal referred to in Rules 90*bis*.1 to 90*bis*.4, the requirement under paragraph (b) for a separate power of attorney shall not be waived under paragraph (d).

90.5 *General Power of Attorney*

(a) Appointment of an agent in relation to a particular international application may be effected by referring in the request, the demand or a separate notice to an existing separate power of attorney appointing that agent to represent the applicant in relation to any international application which may be filed by that applicant (i.e., a "general power of attorney"), provided that:

(i) the general power of attorney has been deposited in accordance with paragraph (b), and
(ii) a copy of it is attached to the request, the demand or the separate notice, as the case may be; that copy need not be signed.

(b) The general power of attorney shall be deposited with the receiving Office, provided that, where it appoints an agent under Rule 90.1(b), (b-*bis*), (c) or (d)(ii), it shall be deposited with the International Searching Authority, the Authority specified for supplementary search or the International Preliminary Examining Authority, as the case may be.

(c) Any receiving Office, any International Searching Authority, any Authority competent to carry out supplementary searches and any International Preliminary Examining Authority may waive the requirement under paragraph (a)(ii) that a copy of the general power of attorney is attached to the request, the demand or the separate notice, as the case may be.

(d) Notwithstanding paragraph (c), where the agent submits any notice of withdrawal referred to in Rules 90*bis*.1 to 90*bis*.4 to the receiving Office, the Authority specified for supplementary search, the International Preliminary Examining Authority or the International Bureau, as the case may be, a copy of the general power of attorney shall be submitted to that Office, Authority or Bureau.

90.6 *Revocation and Renunciation*

(a) Any appointment of an agent or common representative may be revoked by the persons who made the appointment or by their successors in title, in which case any appointment of a sub-agent under Rule 90.1(d) by that agent shall also be considered as revoked. Any appointment of a sub-agent under Rule 90.1(d) may also be revoked by the applicant concerned.

(b) The appointment of an agent under Rule 90.1(a) shall, unless otherwise indicated, have the effect of revoking any earlier appointment of an agent made under that Rule.

(c) The appointment of a common representative shall, unless otherwise indicated, have the effect of revoking any earlier appointment of a common representative.

(d) An agent or a common representative may renounce his appointment by a notification signed by him.

(e) Rule 90.4(b) and (c) shall apply, *mutatis mutandis*, to a document containing a revocation or renunciation under this Rule.

[1.951]
Rule 90*bis*
Withdrawals

90*bis*.1 *Withdrawal of the International Application*

(a) The applicant may withdraw the international application at any time prior to the expiration of 30 months from the priority date.

(b) Withdrawal shall be effective on receipt of a notice addressed by the applicant, at his option, to the International Bureau, to the receiving Office or, where Article 39(1) applies, to the International Preliminary Examining Authority.

(c) No international publication of the international application shall be effected if the notice of withdrawal sent by the applicant or transmitted by the receiving Office or the International Preliminary Examining Authority reaches the International Bureau before the technical preparations for international publication have been completed.

90*bis*.2 *Withdrawal of Designations*

(a) The applicant may withdraw the designation of any designated State at any time prior to the expiration of 30 months from the priority date. Withdrawal of the designation of a State which has been elected shall entail withdrawal of the corresponding election under Rule 90*bis*.4.

(b) Where a State has been designated for the purpose of obtaining both a national patent and a regional patent, withdrawal of the designation of that State shall be taken to mean withdrawal of only the designation for the purpose of obtaining a national patent, except where otherwise indicated.

(c) Withdrawal of the designations of all designated States shall be treated as withdrawal of the international application under Rule 90*bis*.1.

(d) Withdrawal shall be effective on receipt of a notice addressed by the applicant, at his option, to the International Bureau, to the receiving Office or, where Article 39(1) applies, to the International Preliminary Examining Authority.

(e) No international publication of the designation shall be effected if the notice of withdrawal sent by the applicant or transmitted by the receiving Office or the International Preliminary Examining Authority reaches the International Bureau before the technical preparations for international publication have been completed.

90*bis*.3 *Withdrawal of Priority Claims*

(a) The applicant may withdraw a priority claim, made in the international application under Article 8(1), at any time prior to the expiration of 30 months from the priority date.

(b) Where the international application contains more than one priority claim, the applicant may exercise the right provided for in paragraph (a) in respect of one or more or all of the priority claims.

(c) Withdrawal shall be effective on receipt of a notice addressed by the applicant, at his option, to the International Bureau, to the receiving Office or, where Article 39(1) applies, to the International Preliminary Examining Authority.

(d) Where the withdrawal of a priority claim causes a change in the priority date, any time limit which is computed from the original priority date and which has not already expired shall, subject to paragraph (e), be computed from the priority date resulting from that change.

(e) In the case of the time limit referred to in Article 21(2)(a), the International Bureau may nevertheless proceed with the international publication on the basis of the said time limit as computed from the original priority date if the notice of withdrawal sent by the applicant or transmitted by the receiving Office or the International Preliminary Examining Authority reaches the International Bureau after the completion of the technical preparations for international publication.

90*bis*.3*bis* *Withdrawal of Supplementary Search Request*

(a) The applicant may withdraw a supplementary search request at any time prior to the date of transmittal to the applicant and to the International Bureau, under Rule 45*bis*.8(a), of the supplementary international search report or the declaration that no such report will be established.

(b) Withdrawal shall be effective on receipt, within the time limit under paragraph (a), of a notice addressed by the applicant, at his option, to the Authority specified for supplementary search or to the International Bureau, provided that, where the notice does not reach the Authority specified for supplementary search in sufficient time to prevent the transmittal of the report or declaration referred to in paragraph (a), the communication of that report or declaration under Article 20(1), as applicable by virtue of Rule 45*bis*.8(b), shall nevertheless be effected.

90*bis*.4 *Withdrawal of the Demand, or of Elections*

(a) The applicant may withdraw the demand or any or all elections at any time prior to the expiration of 30 months from the priority date.

(b) Withdrawal shall be effective upon receipt of a notice addressed by the applicant to the International Bureau.

(c) If the notice of withdrawal is submitted by the applicant to the International Preliminary Examining Authority, that Authority shall mark the date of receipt on the notice and transmit it promptly to the International Bureau. The notice shall be considered to have been submitted to the International Bureau on the date marked.

90*bis*.5 *Signature*

Any notice of withdrawal referred to in Rules 90*bis*.1 to 90*bis*.4 shall be signed by the applicant or, if there are two or more applicants, by all of them. An applicant who is considered to be the common representative under Rule 90.2(b) shall not be entitled to sign such a notice on behalf of the other applicants.

90*bis*.6 *Effect of Withdrawal*

(a) Withdrawal under Rule 90*bis* of the international application, any designation, any priority claim, the demand or any election shall have no effect in any designated or elected Office where the processing or examination of the international application has already started under Article 23(2) or Article 40(2).

(b) Where the international application is withdrawn under Rule 90*bis*.1, the international processing of the international application shall be discontinued.

(b-*bis*) Where a supplementary search request is withdrawn under Rule 90*bis*.3*bis*, the supplementary international search by the Authority concerned shall be discontinued.

(c) Where the demand or all elections are withdrawn under Rule 90*bis*.4, the processing of the international application by the International Preliminary Examining Authority shall be discontinued.

90*bis*.7 *Faculty under Article 37(4)(b)*

(a) Any Contracting State whose national law provides for what is described in the second part of Article 37(4)(b) shall notify the International Bureau in writing.

(b) The notification referred to in paragraph (a) shall be promptly published by the International Bureau in the Gazette, and shall have effect in respect of international applications filed more than one month after the date of such publication.

[1.952]

Rule 91

Rectification of Obvious Mistakes in the International Application and Other Documents

91.1 *Rectification of Obvious Mistakes*

(a) An obvious mistake in the international application or another document submitted by the applicant may be rectified in accordance with this Rule if the applicant so requests.

(b) The rectification of a mistake shall be subject to authorization by the "competent authority", that is to say:

(i) in the case of a mistake in the request part of the international application or in a correction thereof – by the receiving Office;

(ii) in the case of a mistake in the description, claims or drawings or in a correction thereof, unless the International Preliminary Examining Authority is competent under item (iii) – by the International Searching Authority;

(iii) in the case of a mistake in the description, claims or drawings or in a correction thereof, or in an amendment under Article 19 or 34, where a demand for international preliminary examination has been made and has not been withdrawn and the date on which international preliminary examination shall start in accordance with Rule 69.1 has passed – by the International Preliminary Examining Authority;

(iv) in the case of a mistake in a document not referred to in items (i) to (iii) submitted to the receiving Office, the International Searching Authority, the International Preliminary Examining Authority or the International Bureau, other than a mistake in the abstract or in an amendment under Article 19 – by that Office, Authority or Bureau, as the case may be.

(c) The competent authority shall authorize the rectification under this Rule of a mistake if, and only if, it is obvious to the competent authority that, as at the applicable date under paragraph (f), something else was intended than what appears in the document concerned and that nothing else could have been intended than the proposed rectification.

(d) In the case of a mistake in the description, claims or drawings or in a correction or amendment thereof, the competent authority shall, for the purposes of paragraph (c), only take into account the contents of the description, claims and drawings and, where applicable, the correction or amendment concerned.

(e) In the case of a mistake in the request part of the international application or a correction thereof, or in a document referred to in paragraph (b)(iv), the competent authority shall, for the purposes of paragraph (c), only take into account the contents of the international application itself and, where applicable, the correction concerned, or the document referred to in paragraph (b)(iv), together with any other document submitted with the request, correction or document, as the case may be, any priority document in respect of the international application that is available to the authority in accordance with the Administrative Instructions, and any other document contained in the authority's international application file at the applicable date under paragraph (f).

(f) The applicable date for the purposes of paragraphs (c) and (e) shall be:

(i) in the case of a mistake in a part of the international application as filed – the international filing date;

(ii) in the case of a mistake in a document other than the international application as filed, including a mistake in a correction or an amendment of the international application – the date on which the document was submitted.

(g) A mistake shall not be rectifiable under this Rule if:

(i) the mistake lies in the omission of one or more entire elements of the international application referred to in Article 3(2) or one or more entire sheets of the international application;

(ii) the mistake is in the abstract;

(iii) the mistake is in an amendment under Article 19, unless the International Preliminary Examining Authority is competent to authorize the rectification of such mistake under paragraph (b)(iii); or

(iv) the mistake is in a priority claim or in a notice correcting or adding a priority claim under Rule 26*bis*.1(a), where the rectification of the mistake would cause a change in the priority date;

provided that this paragraph shall not affect the operation of Rules 20.4, 20.5, 26*bis* and 38.3.

(h) Where the receiving Office, the International Searching Authority, the International Preliminary Examining Authority or the International Bureau discovers what appears to be a rectifiable obvious mistake in the international application or another document, it may invite the applicant to request rectification under this Rule.

91.2 *Requests for Rectification*

A request for rectification under Rule 91.1 shall be submitted to the competent authority within 26 months from the priority date. It shall specify the mistake to be rectified and the proposed rectification, and may, at the option of the applicant, contain a brief explanation. Rule 26.4 shall apply *mutatis mutandis* as to the manner in which the proposed rectification shall be indicated.

91.3 *Authorization and Effect of Rectifications*

(a) The competent authority shall promptly decide whether to authorize or refuse to authorize a rectification under Rule 91.1 and shall promptly notify the applicant and the International Bureau of the authorization or refusal and, in the case of refusal, of the reasons therefor. The International Bureau shall proceed as provided for in the Administrative Instructions, including, as required, notifying the receiving Office, the International Searching Authority, the International Preliminary Examining Authority and the designated and elected Offices of the authorization or refusal.

(b) Where the rectification of an obvious mistake has been authorized under Rule 91.1, the document concerned shall be rectified in accordance with the Administrative Instructions.

(c) Where the rectification of an obvious mistake has been authorized, it shall be effective:
   (i) in the case of a mistake in the international application as filed, from the international filing date;
   (ii) in the case of a mistake in a document other than the international application as filed, including a mistake in a correction or an amendment of the international application, from the date on which that document was submitted.

(d) Where the competent authority refuses to authorize a rectification under Rule 91.1, the International Bureau shall, upon request submitted to it by the applicant within two months from the date of the refusal, and subject to the payment of a special fee whose amount shall be fixed in the Administrative Instructions, publish the request for rectification, the reasons for refusal by the authority and any further brief comments that may be submitted by the applicant, if possible together with the international application. A copy of the request, reasons and comments (if any) shall if possible be included in the communication under Article 20 where the international application is not published by virtue of Article 64(3).

(e) The rectification of an obvious mistake need not be taken into account by any designated Office in which the processing or examination of the international application has already started prior to the date on which that Office is notified under Rule 91.3(a) of the authorization of the rectification by the competent authority.

(f) A designated Office may disregard a rectification that was authorized under Rule 91.1 only if it finds that it would not have authorized the rectification under Rule 91.1 if it had been the competent authority, provided that no designated Office shall disregard any rectification that was authorized under Rule 91.1 without giving the applicant the opportunity to make observations, within a time limit which shall be reasonable under the circumstances, on the Office's intention to disregard the rectification.

[1.953]
Rule 92
Correspondence

92.1 *Need for Letter and for Signature*

(a) Any paper submitted by the applicant in the course of the international procedure provided for in the Treaty and these Regulations, other than the international application itself, shall, if not itself in the form of a letter, be accompanied by a letter identifying the international application to which it relates. The letter shall be signed by the applicant.

(b) If the requirements provided for in paragraph (a) are not complied with, the applicant shall be informed as to the non-compliance and invited to remedy the omission within a time limit fixed in the invitation. The time limit so fixed shall be reasonable in the circumstances; even where the time limit so fixed expires later than the time limit applying to the furnishing of the paper (or even if the latter time limit has already expired), it shall not be less than 10 days and not more than one month from the mailing of the invitation. If the omission is remedied within the time limit fixed in the invitation, the omission shall be disregarded; otherwise, the applicant shall be informed that the paper has been disregarded.

(c) Where non-compliance with the requirements provided for in paragraph (a) has been overlooked and the paper taken into account in the international procedure, the non-compliance shall be disregarded.

92.2 *Languages*

(a) Subject to Rules 55.1 and 55.3 and to paragraph (b) of this Rule, any letter or document submitted by the applicant to the International Searching Authority or the International Preliminary Examining Authority shall be in the same language as the international application to which it relates. However, where a translation of the international application has been transmitted under Rule 23.1(b) or furnished under Rule 55.2, the language of such translation shall be used.

(b) Any letter from the applicant to the International Searching Authority or the International Preliminary Examining Authority may be in a language other than that of the international application, provided the said Authority authorizes the use of such language.

(c) *[Deleted]*

(d) Any letter from the applicant to the International Bureau shall be in English, French or any other language of publication as may be permitted by the Administrative Instructions.

(e) Any letter or notification from the International Bureau to the applicant or to any national Office shall be in English or French.

92.3 *Mailings by National Offices and Intergovernmental Organizations*

Any document or letter emanating from or transmitted by a national Office or an intergovernmental organization and constituting an event from the date of which any time limit under the Treaty or these Regulations commences to run shall be sent by air mail, provided that surface mail may be used instead of air mail in cases where surface mail normally arrives at its destination within two days from mailing or where air mail service is not available.

92.4 *Use of Telegraph, Teleprinter, Facsimile Machine, Etc.*

(a) A document making up the international application, and any later document or correspondence relating thereto, may, notwithstanding the provisions of Rules 11.14 and 92.1(a), but subject to paragraph (h), be transmitted, to the extent feasible, by telegraph, teleprinter, facsimile machine or other like means of communication resulting in the filing of a printed or written document.

(b) A signature appearing on a document transmitted by facsimile machine shall be recognized for the purposes of the Treaty and these Regulations as a proper signature.

(c) Where the applicant has attempted to transmit a document by any of the means referred to in paragraph (a) but part or all of the received document is illegible or part of the document is not received, the document shall be treated as not having been received to the extent that the received document is illegible or that the attempted transmission failed. The national Office or intergovernmental organization shall promptly notify the applicant accordingly.

(d) Any national Office or intergovernmental organization may require that the original of any document transmitted by any of the means referred to in paragraph (a) and an accompanying letter identifying that earlier transmission be furnished within 14 days from the date of the transmission, provided that such requirement has been notified to the International Bureau and the International Bureau has published information thereon in the Gazette. The notification shall specify whether such requirement concerns all or only certain kinds of documents.

(e) Where the applicant fails to furnish the original of a document as required under paragraph (d), the national Office or intergovernmental organization concerned may, depending on the kind of document transmitted and having regard to Rules 11 and 26.3,

(i) waive the requirement under paragraph (d), or

(ii) invite the applicant to furnish, within a time limit which shall be reasonable under the circumstances and shall be fixed in the invitation, the original of the document transmitted,

provided that, where the document transmitted contains defects, or shows that the original contains defects, in respect of which the national Office or intergovernmental organization may issue an invitation to correct, that Office or organization may issue such an invitation in addition to, or instead of, proceeding under item (i) or (ii).

(f) Where the furnishing of the original of a document is not required under paragraph (d) but the national Office or intergovernmental organization considers it necessary to receive the original of the said document, it may issue an invitation as provided for under paragraph (e)(ii).

(g) If the applicant fails to comply with an invitation under paragraph (e)(ii) or (f):

(i) where the document concerned is the international application, the latter shall be considered withdrawn and the receiving Office shall so declare;

(ii) where the document concerned is a document subsequent to the international application, the document shall be considered as not having been submitted.

(h) No national Office or intergovernmental organization shall be obliged to receive any document submitted by a means referred to in paragraph (a) unless it has notified the International Bureau that it is prepared to receive such a document by that means and the International Bureau has published information thereon in the Gazette.

[1.954]
Rule 92*bis*
Recording of Changes in Certain Indications in the Request or the Demand

92*bis*.1 *Recording of Changes by the International Bureau*

(a) The International Bureau shall, on the request of the applicant or the receiving Office, record changes in the following indications appearing in the request or demand:

(i) person, name, residence, nationality or address of the applicant,

(ii) person, name or address of the agent, the common representative or the inventor.

(b) The International Bureau shall not record the requested change if the request for recording is received by it after the expiration of 30 months from the priority date.

[1.955]
Rule 93
Keeping of Records and Files

93.1 *The Receiving Office*

Each receiving Office shall keep the records relating to each international application or purported international application, including the home copy, for at least 10 years from the international filing date or, where no international filing date is accorded, from the date of receipt.

93.2 *The International Bureau*

(a) The International Bureau shall keep the file, including the record copy, of any international application for at least 30 years from the date of receipt of the record copy.

(b) The basic records of the International Bureau shall be kept indefinitely.

93.3 *The International Searching and Preliminary Examining Authorities*

Each International Searching Authority and each International Preliminary Examining Authority shall keep the file of each international application it receives for at least 10 years from the international filing date.

93.4 *Reproductions*

For the purposes of this Rule, records, copies and files may be kept as photographic, electronic or other reproductions, provided that the reproductions are such that the obligations to keep records, copies and files under Rules 93.1 to 93.3 are met.

[1.956]
Rule 93*bis*
Manner of Communication of Documents

93*bis*.1 *Communication on Request; Communication via Digital Library*

(a) Where the Treaty, these Regulations or the Administrative Instructions provide for the communication, notification or transmittal ("communication") of an international application, notification, communication, correspondence or other document ("document") by the International Bureau to any designated or elected Office, such communication shall be effected only upon request by the Office concerned and at the time specified by that Office. Such request may be made in relation to individually specified documents or a specified class or classes of documents.

(b) A communication under paragraph (a) shall, where so agreed by the International Bureau and the designated or elected Office concerned, be considered to be effected at the time when the International Bureau makes the document available to that Office in electronic form in a digital library, in accordance with the Administrative Instructions, from which that Office is entitled to retrieve that document.

[1.957]
Rule 94
Access to Files

94.1 *Access to the File Held by the International Bureau*

(a) At the request of the applicant or any person authorized by the applicant, the International Bureau shall furnish, subject to reimbursement of the cost of the service, copies of any document contained in its file.

(b) The International Bureau shall, at the request of any person but not before the international publication of the international application and subject to Article 38 and paragraphs (d) to (g), furnish copies of any document contained in its file. The furnishing of copies may be subject to reimbursement of the cost of the service.

(c) The International Bureau shall, if so requested by an elected Office, furnish copies of the international preliminary examination report under paragraph (b) on behalf of that Office. The International Bureau shall promptly publish details of any such request in the Gazette.

(d) The International Bureau shall not provide access to any information contained in its file which has been omitted from publication under Rule 48.2(l) and to any document contained in its file relating to a request under that Rule.

(e) Upon a reasoned request by the applicant, the International Bureau shall not provide access to any information contained in its file and to any document contained in its file relating to such a request, if it finds that:

(i) this information does not obviously serve the purpose of informing the public about the international application;

(ii) public access to such information would clearly prejudice the personal or economic interests of any person; and

(iii) there is no prevailing public interest to have access to that information.

Rule 26.4 shall apply mutatis mutandis as to the manner in which the applicant shall present the information which is the subject of a request made under this paragraph.

(f) Where the International Bureau has omitted information from public access in accordance with paragraphs (d) or (e), and that information is also contained in the file of the international application held by the receiving Office, the International Searching Authority, the Authority specified for supplementary search or the International Preliminary Examining Authority, the International Bureau shall promptly notify that Office and Authority accordingly.

(g) The International Bureau shall not provide access to any document contained in its file which was prepared solely for internal use by the International Bureau.

94.1*bis* *Access to the File Held by the Receiving Office*

(a) At the request of the applicant or any person authorized by the applicant, the receiving Office may provide access to any document contained in its file. The furnishing of copies of documents may be subject to reimbursement of the cost of the service.

(b) The receiving Office may, at the request of any person, but not before the international publication of the international application and subject to paragraph (c), provide access to any document contained in its file. The furnishing of copies of documents may be subject to reimbursement of the cost of the service.

(c) The receiving Office shall not provide access under paragraph (b) to any information in respect of which it has been notified by the International Bureau that the information has been omitted from publication in accordance with Rule 48.2(l) or from public access in accordance with Rule 94.1(d) or (e).

94.1*ter* *Access to the File Held by the International Searching Authority*

(a) At the request of the applicant or any person authorized by the applicant, the International Searching Authority may provide access to any document contained in its file. The furnishing of copies of documents may be subject to reimbursement of the cost of the service.

(b) The International Searching Authority may, at the request of any person, but not before the international publication of the international application and subject to paragraph (c), provide access to any document contained in its file. The furnishing of copies of documents may be subject to reimbursement of the cost of the service.

(c) The International Searching Authority shall not provide access under paragraph (b) to any information in respect of which it has been notified by the International Bureau that the information has been omitted from publication in accordance with Rule 48.2(l) or from public access in accordance with Rule 94.1(d) or (e).

(d) Paragraphs (a) to (c) shall apply *mutatis mutandis* to the Authority specified for supplementary search.

94.2 *Access to the File Held by the International Preliminary Examining Authority*

(a) At the request of the applicant or any person authorized by the applicant, the International Preliminary Examining Authority shall provide access to any document contained in its file. The furnishing of copies of documents may be subject to reimbursement of the cost of the service.

(b) At the request of any elected Office, but not before the establishment of the international preliminary examination report and subject to paragraph (c), the International Preliminary Examining Authority shall provide access to any document contained in its file. The furnishing of copies of documents may be subject to reimbursement of the cost of the service.

(c) The International Preliminary Examining Authority shall not provide access under paragraph (b) to any information in respect of which it has been notified by the International Bureau that the information has been omitted from publication in accordance with Rule 48.2(l) or from public access in accordance with Rule 94.1(d) or (e).

94.2*bis* *Access to the File Held by the Designated Office*

If the national law applicable by any designated Office allows access by third parties to the file of a national application, that Office may allow access to any documents relating to the international application, contained in its file, to the same extent as provided by the national law for access to the file of a national application, but not before the earliest of the dates specified in Article 30(2)(a). The furnishing of copies of documents may be subject to reimbursement of the cost of the service.

94.3 *Access to the File Held by the Elected Office*

If the national law applicable by any elected Office allows access by third parties to the file of a national application, that Office may allow access to any documents relating to the international application, including any document relating to the international preliminary examination, contained in its file, to the same extent as provided by the national law for access to the file of a national application, but not before the earliest of the dates specified in Article 30(2)(a). The furnishing of copies of documents may be subject to reimbursement of the cost of the service.

NOTES

Rule 94 as in force from July 1, 1998, applies only in respect of international applications filed on or after that date. Rule 94 as in force until June 30, 1998, continues to apply after that date in respect of international applications filed until that date. The text of Rule 94 as in force until June 30, 1998, is reproduced below:

> **"Rule 94 Furnishing of Copies by the International Bureau and the International Preliminary Examining Authority**
>
> 94.1 *Obligation to Furnish*
>
> At the request of the applicant or any person authorised by the applicant, the International Bureau and the International Preliminary Examining Authority shall furnish, subject to reimbursement of the cost of the service, copies of any document contained in the file of the applicant's international application or purported international application.".

Rule 94.1(c) as in force from January 1, 2004, applies to international applications filed on or after that date. Rule 94.1(c) also applies to the furnishing on or after January 1, 2004, of copies of the international preliminary examination report in respect of any international application, whether the international filing date of the application is before, on or after January 1, 2004.

Information concerning which elected Offices have requested the International Bureau to furnish copies of international preliminary examination reports on their behalf is also published on the WIPO website at: www.wipo.int.

[1.958]

Rule 95

Information and Translations from Designated and Elected Offices

95.1 *Information Concerning Events at the Designated and Elected Offices*

Any designated or elected Office shall notify the International Bureau of the following information concerning an international application within two months, or as soon as reasonably possible thereafter, of the occurrence of any of the following events:

(i) following the performance by the applicant of the acts referred to in Article 22 or Article 39, the date of performance of those acts and any national application number which has been assigned to the international application;

(ii) where the designated or elected Office explicitly publishes the international application under its national law or practice, the number and date of that national publication;

(iii) where a patent is granted, the date of grant of the patent and, where the designated or elected Office explicitly publishes the international application in the form in which it is granted under its national law, the number and date of that national publication.

95.2 *Furnishing of Copies of Translations*

(a) At the request of the International Bureau, any designated or elected Office shall provide it with a copy of the translation of the international application furnished by the applicant to that Office.

(b) The International Bureau may, upon request and subject to reimbursement of the cost, furnish to any person copies of the translations received under paragraph (a).

[1.959]
Rule 96
The Schedule of Fees

96.1 *Schedule of Fees Annexed to Regulations*

The amounts of the fees referred to in Rules 15, 45*bis*.2 and 57 shall be expressed in Swiss currency. They shall be specified in the Schedule of Fees which is annexed to these Regulations and forms an integral part thereof.

SCHEDULE OF FEES

[1.960]

Fees		**Amounts**
1.	International filing fee: (Rule 15.2)	1,330 Swiss francs plus
		15 Swiss francs for each sheet of the international application in excess of 30 sheets
2.	Supplementary search handling fee: (Rule 45*bis*.2)	200 Swiss francs
3.	Handling fee: (Rule 57.2)	200 Swiss francs
Reductions		
4.	The international filing fee is reduced by the following amount if the international application is, as provided for in the Administrative Instructions, filed:	
	(a) in electronic form, the request not being in character coded format:	100 Swiss francs
	(b) in electronic form, the request being in character coded format:	200 Swiss francs
	(c) in electronic form, the request, description, claims and abstract being in character coded format:	300 Swiss francs

5. The international filing fee under item 1 (where applicable, as reduced under item 4), the supplementary search handling fee under item 2 and the handling fee under item 3 are reduced by 90% if the international application is filed by:

(a) an applicant who is a natural person and who is a national of and resides in a State that is listed as being a State whose per capita gross domestic product is below US$ 25,000 (according to the most recent 10-year average per capita gross domestic product figures at constant 2005 US$ values published by the United Nations), and whose nationals and residents who are natural persons have filed less than 10 international applications per year (per million population) or less than 50 international applications per year (in absolute numbers) according to the most recent five-year average yearly filing figures published by the International Bureau; or

Fees	Amounts

(b) an applicant, whether a natural person or not, who is a national of and resides in a State that is listed as being classified by the United Nations as a least developed country;

provided that, if there are several applicants, each must satisfy the criteria set out in either sub-item (a) or (b). The lists of States referred to in sub-items (a) and (b)[1] shall be updated by the Director General at least every five years according to directives given by the Assembly. The criteria set out in sub-items (a) and (b) shall be reviewed by the Assembly at least every five years.

[1] *Editor's Note:* The first lists of States were published in the Gazette of February 12, 2015, page 32 (see www.wipo.int/pct/en/official_notices/index.html).

PATENT LAW TREATY

(Done at Geneva on June 1, 2000)

NOTES

The original source for this Treaty is the World Intellectual Property Organisation (WIPO).

[1.961]
Article 1
Abbreviated Expressions

For the purposes of this Treaty, unless expressly stated otherwise—

(i) "Office" means the authority of a Contracting Party entrusted with the granting of patents or with other matters covered by this Treaty;
(ii) "application" means an application for the grant of a patent, as referred to in Article 3;
(iii) "patent" means a patent as referred to in Article 3;
(iv) references to a "person" shall be construed as including, in particular, a natural person and a legal entity;
(v) "communication" means any application, or any request, declaration, document, correspondence or other information relating to an application or patent, whether relating to a procedure under this Treaty or not, which is filed with the Office;
(vi) "records of the Office" means the collection of information maintained by the Office, relating to and including the applications filed with, and the patents granted by, that Office or another authority with effect for the Contracting Party concerned, irrespective of the medium in which such information is maintained;
(vii) "recordation" means any act of including information in the records of the Office;
(viii) "applicant" means the person whom the records of the Office show, pursuant to the applicable law, as the person who is applying for the patent, or as another person who is filing or prosecuting the application;
(ix) "owner" means the person whom the records of the Office show as the owner of the patent;
(x) "representative" means a representative under the applicable law;
(xi) "signature" means any means of self-identification;
(xii) "a language accepted by the Office" means any one language accepted by the Office for the relevant procedure before the Office;
(xiii) "translation" means a translation into a language or, where appropriate, a transliteration into an alphabet or character set, accepted by the Office;
(xiv) "procedure before the Office" means any procedure in proceedings before the Office with respect to an application or patent;
(xv) except where the context indicates otherwise, words in the singular include the plural, and *vice versa*, and masculine personal pronouns include the feminine;
(xvi) "Paris Convention" means the Paris Convention for the Protection of Industrial Property, signed on March 20, 1883, as revised and amended;
(xvii) "Patent Co-operation Treaty" means the Patent Co-operation Treaty, signed on June 19, 1970, together with the Regulations and the Administrative Instructions under that Treaty, as revised, amended and modified;
(xviii) "Contracting Party" means any State or intergovernmental organisation that is party to this Treaty;
(xix) "applicable law" means, where the Contracting Party is a State, the law of that State and, where the Contracting Party is an intergovernmental organisation, the legal enactments under which that intergovernmental organisation operates;
(xx) "instrument of ratification" shall be construed as including instruments of acceptance or approval;
(xxi) "Organisation" means the World Intellectual Property Organisation;
(xxii) "International Bureau" means the International Bureau of the Organisation;

(xxiii) "Director General" means the Director General of the Organisation.

[1.962]
Article 2
General Principles

(1) [*More Favourable Requirements*] A Contracting Party shall be free to provide for requirements which, from the viewpoint of applicants and owners, are more favourable than the requirements referred to in this Treaty and the Regulations, other than Article 5.

(2) [*No Regulation of Substantive Patent Law*] Nothing in this Treaty or the Regulations is intended to be construed as prescribing anything that would limit the freedom of a Contracting Party to prescribe such requirements of the applicable substantive law relating to patents as it desires.

[1.963]
Article 3
Applications and Patents to Which the Treaty Applies

(1) [*Applications*]

(a) The provisions of this Treaty and the Regulations shall apply to national and regional applications for patents for invention and for patents of addition, which are filed with or for the Office of a Contracting Party, and which are—

(i) types of applications permitted to be filed as international applications under the Patent Co-operation Treaty;

(ii) divisional applications of the types of applications referred to in item (i), for patents for invention or for patents of addition, as referred to in Article 4G(1) or (2) of the Paris Convention.

(b) Subject to the provisions of the Patent Co-operation Treaty, the provisions of this Treaty and the Regulations shall apply to international applications, for patents for invention and for patents of addition, under the Patent Co-operation Treaty—

(i) in respect of the time limits applicable under Articles 22 and 39(1) of the Patent Co-operation Treaty in the Office of a Contracting Party;

(ii) in respect of any procedure commenced on or after the date on which processing or examination of the international application may start under Article 23 or 40 of that Treaty.

(2) [*Patents*] The provisions of this Treaty and the Regulations shall apply to national and regional patents for invention, and to national and regional patents of addition, which have been granted with effect for a Contracting Party.

[1.964]
Article 4
Security Exception

Nothing in this Treaty and the Regulations shall limit the freedom of a Contracting Party to take any action it deems necessary for the preservation of essential security interests.

[1.965]
Article 5
Filing Date

(1) [*Elements of Application*]

(a) Except as otherwise prescribed in the Regulations, and subject to paragraphs (2) to (8), a Contracting Party shall provide that the filing date of an application shall be the date on which its Office has received all of the following elements, filed, at the option of the applicant, on paper or as otherwise permitted by the Office for the purposes of the filing date—

(i) an express or implicit indication to the effect that the elements are intended to be an application;

(ii) indications allowing the identity of the applicant to be established or allowing the applicant to be contacted by the Office;

(iii) a part which on the face of it appears to be a description.

(b) A Contracting Party may, for the purposes of the filing date, accept a drawing as the element referred to in subparagraph (a)(iii).

(c) For the purposes of the filing date, a Contracting Party may require both information allowing the identity of the applicant to be established and information allowing the applicant to be contacted by the Office, or it may accept evidence allowing the identity of the applicant to be established or allowing the applicant to be contacted by the Office, as the element referred to in subparagraph (a)(ii).

(2) [*Language*]

(a) A Contracting Party may require that the indications referred to in paragraph (1)(a)(i) and (ii) be in a language accepted by the Office.

(b) The part referred to in paragraph (1)(a)(iii) may, for the purposes of the filing date, be filed in any language.

(3) [*Notification*] Where the application does not comply with one or more of the requirements applied by the Contracting Party under paragraphs (1) and (2), the Office shall, as soon as practicable, notify the applicant, giving the opportunity to comply with any such requirement, and to make observations, within the time limit prescribed in the Regulations.

(4) [*Subsequent Compliance with Requirements*]

(a) Where one or more of the requirements applied by the Contracting Party under paragraphs (1) and (2) are not complied with in the application as initially filed, the filing date shall, subject to subparagraph (b) and paragraph (6), be the date on which all of the requirements applied by the Contracting Party under paragraphs (1) and (2) are subsequently complied with.

(b) A Contracting Party may provide that, where one or more of the requirements referred to in subparagraph (a) are not complied with within the time limit prescribed in the Regulations, the application shall be deemed not to have been filed. Where the application is deemed not to have been filed, the Office shall notify the applicant accordingly, indicating the reasons therefor.

(5) [*Notification Concerning Missing Part of Description or Drawing*] Where, in establishing the filing date, the Office finds that a part of the description appears to be missing from the application, or that the application refers to a drawing which appears to be missing from the application, the Office shall promptly notify the applicant accordingly.

(6) [*Filing Date Where Missing Part of Description or Drawing is Filed*]

(a) Where a missing part of the description or a missing drawing is filed with the Office within the time limit prescribed in the Regulations, that part of the description or drawing shall be included in the application, and, subject to subparagraphs (b) and (c), the filing date shall be the date on which the Office has received that part of the description or that drawing, or the date on which all of the requirements applied by the Contracting Party under paragraphs (1) and (2) are complied with, whichever is later.

(b) Where the missing part of the description or the missing drawing is filed under subparagraph (a) to rectify its omission from an application which, at the date on which one or more elements referred to in paragraph (1)(a) were first received by the Office, claims the priority of an earlier application, the filing date shall, upon the request of the applicant filed within a time limit prescribed in the Regulations, and subject to the requirements prescribed in the Regulations, be the date on which all the requirements applied by the Contracting Party under paragraphs (1) and (2) are complied with.

(c) Where the missing part of the description or the missing drawing filed under subparagraph (a) is withdrawn within a time limit fixed by the Contracting Party, the filing date shall be the date on which the requirements applied by the Contracting Party under paragraphs (1) and (2) are complied with.

(7) [*Replacing Description and Drawings by Reference to a Previously Filed Application*]

(a) Subject to the requirements prescribed in the Regulations, a reference, made upon the filing of the application, in a language accepted by the Office, to a previously filed application shall, for the purposes of the filing date of the application, replace the description and any drawings.

(b) Where the requirements referred to in subparagraph (a) are not complied with, the application may be deemed not to have been filed. Where the application is deemed not to have been filed, the Office shall notify the applicant accordingly, indicating the reasons therefor.

(8) [*Exceptions*] Nothing in this Article shall limit—

(i) the right of an applicant under Article 4G(1) or (2) of the Paris Convention to preserve, as the date of a divisional application referred to in that Article, the date of the initial application referred to in that Article and the benefit of the right of priority, if any;

(ii) the freedom of a Contracting Party to apply any requirements necessary to accord the benefit of the filing date of an earlier application to an application of any type prescribed in the Regulations.

[1.966]

Article 6

Application

(1) [*Form or Contents of Application*] Except where otherwise provided for by this Treaty, no Contracting Party shall require compliance with any requirement relating to the form or contents of an application different from or additional to—

(i) the requirements relating to form or contents which are provided for in respect of international applications under the Patent Co-operation Treaty;

(ii) the requirements relating to form or contents compliance with which, under the Patent Co-operation Treaty, may be required by the Office of, or acting for, any State party to that Treaty once the processing or examination of an international application, as referred to in Article 23 or 40 of the said Treaty, has started;

(iii) any further requirements prescribed in the Regulations.

(2) [*Request Form*]

(a) A Contracting Party may require that the contents of an application which correspond to the contents of the request of an international application under the Patent Co-operation Treaty be presented on a request Form prescribed by that Contracting Party. A Contracting Party may also require that any further contents allowed under paragraph (1)(ii) or prescribed in the Regulations pursuant to paragraph (1)(iii) be contained in that request Form.

(b) Notwithstanding subparagraph (a), and subject to Article 8(1), a Contracting Party shall accept the presentation of the contents referred to in subparagraph (a) on a request Form provided for in the Regulations.

(3) [*Translation*] A Contracting Party may require a translation of any part of the application that is not in a language accepted by its Office. A Contracting Party may also require a translation of the parts of the application, as prescribed in the Regulations, that are in a language accepted by the Office, into any other languages accepted by that Office.

(4) [*Fees*] A Contracting Party may require that fees be paid in respect of the application. A Contracting Party may apply the provisions of the Patent Co-operation Treaty relating to payment of application fees.

(5) [*Priority Document*] Where the priority of an earlier application is claimed, a Contracting Party may require that a copy of the earlier application, and a translation where the earlier application is not in a language accepted by the Office, be filed in accordance with the requirements prescribed in the Regulations.

(6) [*Evidence*] A Contracting Party may require that evidence in respect of any matter referred to in paragraph (1) or (2) or in a declaration of priority, or any translation referred to in paragraph (3) or (5), be filed with its Office in the course of the processing of the application only where that Office may reasonably doubt the veracity of that matter or the accuracy of that translation.

(7) [*Notification*] Where one or more of the requirements applied by the Contracting Party under paragraphs (1) to (6) are not complied with, the Office shall notify the applicant, giving the opportunity to comply with any such requirement, and to make observations, within the time limit prescribed in the Regulations.

(8) [*Non-Compliance with Requirements*]

(a) Where one or more of the requirements applied by the Contracting Party under paragraphs (1) to (6) are not complied with within the time limit prescribed in the Regulations, the Contracting Party may, subject to subparagraph (b) and Articles 5 and 10, apply such sanction as is provided for in its law.

(b) Where any requirement applied by the Contracting Party under paragraph (1), (5) or (6) in respect of a priority claim is not complied with within the time limit prescribed in the Regulations, the priority claim may, subject to Article 13, be deemed non-existent. Subject to Article 5(7)(b), no other sanctions may be applied.

[1.967]
Article 7
Representation

(1) [*Representatives*]

(a) A Contracting Party may require that a representative appointed for the purposes of any procedure before the Office—

(i) have the right, under the applicable law, to practise before the Office in respect of applications and patents;

(ii) provide, as his address, an address on a territory prescribed by the Contracting Party.

(b) Subject to subparagraph (c), an act, with respect to any procedure before the Office, by or in relation to a representative who complies with the requirements applied by the Contracting Party under subparagraph (a), shall have the effect of an act by or in relation to the applicant, owner or other interested person who appointed that representative.

(c) A Contracting Party may provide that, in the case of an oath or declaration or the revocation of a power of attorney, the signature of a representative shall not have the effect of the signature of the applicant, owner or other interested person who appointed that representative.

(2) [*Mandatory Representation*]

(a) A Contracting Party may require that an applicant, owner or other interested person appoint a representative for the purposes of any procedure before the Office, except that an assignee of an application, an applicant, owner or other interested person may act himself before the Office for the following procedures—

(i) the filing of an application for the purposes of the filing date;

(ii) the mere payment of a fee;

(iii) any other procedure as prescribed in the Regulations;

(iv) the issue of a receipt or notification by the Office in respect of any procedure referred to in items (i) to (iii).

(b) A maintenance fee may be paid by any person.

(3) [*Appointment of Representative*] A Contracting Party shall accept that the appointment of the representative be filed with the Office in a manner prescribed in the Regulations.

(4) [*Prohibition of Other Requirements*] No Contracting Party may require that formal requirements other than those referred to in paragraphs (1) to (3) be complied with in respect of the matters dealt with in those paragraphs, except where otherwise provided for by this Treaty or prescribed in the Regulations.

(5) [*Notification*] Where one or more of the requirements applied by the Contracting Party under paragraphs (1) to (3) are not complied with, the Office shall notify the assignee of the application, applicant, owner or other interested person, giving the opportunity to comply with any such requirement, and to make observations, within the time limit prescribed in the Regulations.

(6) [*Non-Compliance with Requirements*] Where one or more of the requirements applied by the Contracting Party under paragraphs (1) to (3) are not complied with within the time limit prescribed in the Regulations, the Contracting Party may apply such sanction as is provided for in its law.

[1.968]
Article 8
Communications; Addresses

(1) [*Form and Means of Transmittal of Communications*]

(a) Except for the establishment of a filing date under Article 5(1), and subject to Article 6(1), the Regulations shall, subject to subparagraphs (b) to (d), set out the requirements which a Contracting Party shall be permitted to apply as regards the form and means of transmittal of communications.

(b) No Contracting Party shall be obliged to accept the filing of communications other than on paper.

(c) No Contracting Party shall be obliged to exclude the filing of communications on paper.

(d) A Contracting Party shall accept the filing of communications on paper for the purpose of complying with a time limit.

(2) [*Language of Communications*] A Contracting Party may, except where otherwise provided for by this Treaty or the Regulations, require that a communication be in a language accepted by the Office.

(3) [*Model International Forms*] Notwithstanding paragraph (1)(a), and subject to paragraph (1)(b) and Article 6(2)(b), a Contracting Party shall accept the presentation of the contents of a communication on a Form which corresponds to a Model International Form in respect of such a communication provided for in the Regulations, if any.

(4) [*Signature of Communications*]

(a) Where a Contracting Party requires a signature for the purposes of any communication, that Contracting Party shall accept any signature that complies with the requirements prescribed in the Regulations.

(b) No Contracting Party may require the attestation, notarisation, authentication, legalisation or other certification of any signature which is communicated to its Office, except in respect of any quasi-judicial proceedings or as prescribed in the Regulations.

(c) Subject to subparagraph (b), a Contracting Party may require that evidence be filed with the Office only where the Office may reasonably doubt the authenticity of any signature.

(5) [*Indications in Communications*] A Contracting Party may require that any communication contain one or more indications prescribed in the Regulations.

(6) [*Address for Correspondence, Address for Legal Service and Other Address*] A Contracting Party may, subject to any provisions prescribed in the Regulations, require that an applicant, owner or other interested person indicate in any communication—

(i) an address for correspondence;
(ii) an address for legal service;
(iii) any other address provided for in the Regulations.

(7) [*Notification*] Where one or more of the requirements applied by the Contracting Party under paragraphs (1) to (6) are not complied with in respect of communications, the Office shall notify the applicant, owner or other interested person, giving the opportunity to comply with any such requirement, and to make observations, within the time limit prescribed in the Regulations.

(8) [*Non-Compliance with Requirements*] Where one or more of the requirements applied by the Contracting Party under paragraphs (1) to (6) are not complied with within the time limit prescribed in the Regulations, the Contracting Party may, subject to Articles 5 and 10 and to any exceptions prescribed in the Regulations, apply such sanction as is provided for in its law.

[1.969]
Article 9
Notifications

(1) [*Sufficient Notification*] Any notification under this Treaty or the Regulations which is sent by the Office to an address for correspondence or address for legal service indicated under Article 8(6), or any other address provided for in the Regulations for the purpose of this provision, and which complies with the provisions with respect to that notification, shall constitute a sufficient notification for the purposes of this Treaty and the Regulations.

(2) [*If Indications Allowing Contact Were Not Filed*] Nothing in this Treaty and in the Regulations shall oblige a Contracting Party to send a notification to an applicant, owner or other interested person, if indications allowing that applicant, owner or other interested person to be contacted have not been filed with the Office.
(3) [*Failure to Notify*] Subject to Article 10(1), where an Office does not notify an applicant, owner or other interested person of a failure to comply with any requirement under this Treaty or the Regulations, that absence of notification does not relieve that applicant, owner or other interested person of the obligation to comply with that requirement.

[1.970]
Article 10
Validity of Patent; Revocation
(1) [*Validity of Patent Not Affected by Non-Compliance with Certain Formal Requirements*] Non-compliance with one or more of the formal requirements referred to in Articles 6(1), (2), (4) and (5) and 8(1) to (4) with respect to an application may not be a ground for revocation or invalidation of a patent, either totally or in part, except where the non-compliance with the formal requirement occurred as a result of a fraudulent intention.
(2) [*Opportunity to Make Observations, Amendments or Corrections in Case of Intended Revocation or Invalidation*] A patent may not be revoked or invalidated, either totally or in part, without the owner being given the opportunity to make observations on the intended revocation or invalidation, and to make amendments and corrections where permitted under the applicable law, within a reasonable time limit.
(3) [*No Obligation for Special Procedures*] Paragraphs (1) and (2) do not create any obligation to put in place judicial procedures for the enforcement of patent rights distinct from those for the enforcement of law in general.

[1.971]
Article 11
Relief in Respect of Time Limits
(1) [*Extension of Time Limits*] A Contracting Party may provide for the extension, for the period prescribed in the Regulations, of a time limit fixed by the Office for an action in a procedure before the Office in respect of an application or a patent, if a request to that effect is made to the Office in accordance with the requirements prescribed in the Regulations, and the request is filed, at the option of the Contracting Party—
(i) prior to the expiration of the time limit; or
(ii) after the expiration of the time limit, and within the time limit prescribed in the Regulations.
(2) [*Continued Processing*] Where an applicant or owner has failed to comply with a time limit fixed by the Office of a Contracting Party for an action in a procedure before the Office in respect of an application or a patent, and that Contracting Party does not provide for extension of a time limit under paragraph (1)(ii), the Contracting Party shall provide for continued processing with respect to the application or patent and, if necessary, reinstatement of the rights of the applicant or owner with respect to that application or patent, if—
(i) a request to that effect is made to the Office in accordance with the requirements prescribed in the Regulations;
(ii) the request is filed, and all of the requirements in respect of which the time limit for the action concerned applied are complied with, within the time limit prescribed in the Regulations.
(3) [*Exceptions*] No Contracting Party shall be required to provide for the relief referred to in paragraph (1) or (2) with respect to the exceptions prescribed in the Regulations.
(4) [*Fees*] A Contracting Party may require that a fee be paid in respect of a request under paragraph (1) or (2).
(5) [*Prohibition of Other Requirements*] No Contracting Party may require that requirements other than those referred to in paragraphs (1) to (4) be complied with in respect of the relief provided for under paragraph (1) or (2), except where otherwise provided for by this Treaty or prescribed in the Regulations.
(6) [*Opportunity to Make Observations in Case of Intended Refusal*] A request under paragraph (1) or (2) may not be refused without the applicant or owner being given the opportunity to make observations on the intended refusal within a reasonable time limit.

[1.972]
Article 12
Reinstatement of Rights After a Finding of Due Care or Unintentionality by the Office
(1) [*Request*] A Contracting Party shall provide that, where an applicant or owner has failed to comply with a time limit for an action in a procedure before the Office, and that failure has the direct consequence of causing a loss of rights with respect to an application or patent, the Office shall reinstate the rights of the applicant or owner with respect to the application or patent concerned, if—

(i) a request to that effect is made to the Office in accordance with the requirements prescribed in the Regulations;
(ii) the request is filed, and all of the requirements in respect of which the time limit for the said action applied are complied with, within the time limit prescribed in the Regulations;
(iii) the request states the reasons for the failure to comply with the time limit; and
(iv) the Office finds that the failure to comply with the time limit occurred in spite of due care required by the circumstances having been taken or, at the option of the Contracting Party, that any delay was unintentional.

(2) [*Exceptions*] No Contracting Party shall be required to provide for the reinstatement of rights under paragraph (1) with respect to the exceptions prescribed in the Regulations.
(3) [*Fees*] A Contracting Party may require that a fee be paid in respect of a request under paragraph (1).
(4) [*Evidence*] A Contracting Party may require that a declaration or other evidence in support of the reasons referred to in paragraph (1)(iii) be filed with the Office within a time limit fixed by the Office.
(5) [*Opportunity to Make Observations in Case of Intended Refusal*] A request under paragraph (1) may not be refused, totally or in part, without the requesting party being given the opportunity to make observations on the intended refusal within a reasonable time limit.

[1.973]
Article 13
Correction or Addition of Priority Claim; Restoration of Priority Right

(1) [*Correction or Addition of Priority Claim*] Except where otherwise prescribed in the Regulations, a Contracting Party shall provide for the correction or addition of a priority claim with respect to an application ("the subsequent application"), if—
(i) a request to that effect is made to the Office in accordance with the requirements prescribed in the Regulations;
(ii) the request is filed within the time limit prescribed in the Regulations; and
(iii) the filing date of the subsequent application is not later than the date of the expiration of the priority period calculated from the filing date of the earliest application whose priority is claimed.

(2) [*Delayed Filing of the Subsequent Application*] Taking into consideration Article 15, a Contracting Party shall provide that, where an application ("the subsequent application") which claims or could have claimed the priority of an earlier application has a filing date which is later than the date on which the priority period expired, but within the time limit prescribed in the Regulations, the Office shall restore the right of priority, if—
(i) a request to that effect is made to the Office in accordance with the requirements prescribed in the Regulations;
(ii) the request is filed within the time limit prescribed in the Regulations;
(iii) the request states the reasons for the failure to comply with the priority period; and
(iv) the Office finds that the failure to file the subsequent application within the priority period occurred in spite of due care required by the circumstances having been taken or, at the option of the Contracting Party, was unintentional.

(3) [*Failure to File a Copy of Earlier Application*] A Contracting Party shall provide that, where a copy of an earlier application required under Article 6(5) is not filed with the Office within the time limit prescribed in the Regulations pursuant to Article 6, the Office shall restore the right of priority, if—
(i) a request to that effect is made to the Office in accordance with the requirements prescribed in the Regulations;
(ii) the request is filed within the time limit for filing the copy of the earlier application prescribed in the Regulations pursuant to Article 6(5);
(iii) the Office finds that the request for the copy to be provided had been filed with the Office with which the earlier application was filed, within the time limit prescribed in the Regulations; and
(iv) a copy of the earlier application is filed within the time limit prescribed in the Regulations.

(4) [*Fees*] A Contracting Party may require that a fee be paid in respect of a request under paragraphs (1) to (3).
(5) [*Evidence*] A Contracting Party may require that a declaration or other evidence in support of the reasons referred to in paragraph (2)(iii) be filed with the Office within a time limit fixed by the Office.
(6) [*Opportunity to Make Observations in Case of Intended Refusal*] A request under paragraphs (1) to (3) may not be refused, totally or in part, without the requesting party being given the opportunity to make observations on the intended refusal within a reasonable time limit.

[1.974]
Article 14
Regulations

(1) [*Content*]
(a) The Regulations annexed to this Treaty provide rules concerning—

(i) matters which this Treaty expressly provides are to be "prescribed in the Regulations";
(ii) details useful in the implementation of the provisions of this Treaty;
(iii) administrative requirements, matters or procedures.

(b) The Regulations also provide rules concerning the formal requirements which a Contracting Party shall be permitted to apply in respect of requests for—
(i) recordation of change in name or address;
(ii) recordation of change in applicant or owner;
(iii) recordation of a licence or a security interest;
(iv) correction of a mistake.

(c) The Regulations also provide for the establishment of Model International Forms, and for the establishment of a request Form for the purposes of Article 6(2)(b), by the Assembly, with the assistance of the International Bureau.

(2) [*Amending the Regulations*] Subject to paragraph (3), any amendment of the Regulations shall require three-fourths of the votes cast.

(3) [*Requirement of Unanimity*]
(a) The Regulations may specify provisions of the Regulations which may be amended only by unanimity.
(b) Any amendment of the Regulations resulting in the addition of provisions to, or the deletion of provisions from, the provisions specified in the Regulations pursuant to subparagraph (a) shall require unanimity.
(c) In determining whether unanimity is attained, only votes actually cast shall be taken into consideration. Abstentions shall not be considered as votes.

(4) [*Conflict Between the Treaty and the Regulations*] In the case of conflict between the provisions of this Treaty and those of the Regulations, the former shall prevail.

[1.975]
Article 15
Relation to the Paris Convention

(1) [*Obligation to Comply with the Paris Convention*] Each Contracting Party shall comply with the provisions of the Paris Convention which concern patents.

(2) [*Obligations and Rights Under the Paris Convention*]
(a) Nothing in this Treaty shall derogate from obligations that Contracting Parties have to each other under the Paris Convention.
(b) Nothing in this Treaty shall derogate from rights that applicants and owners enjoy under the Paris Convention.

[1.976]
Article 16
Effect of Revisions, Amendments and Modifications of the Patent Co-operation Treaty

(1) [*Applicability of Revisions, Amendments and Modifications of the Patent Co-operation Treaty*] Subject to paragraph (2), any revision, amendment or modification of the Patent Co-operation Treaty made after June 2, 2000, which is consistent with the Articles of this Treaty, shall apply for the purposes of this Treaty and the Regulations if the Assembly so decides, in the particular case, by three-fourths of the votes cast.

(2) [*Non-Applicability of Transitional Provisions of the Patent Co-operation Treaty*] Any provision of the Patent Co-operation Treaty, by virtue of which a revised, amended or modified provision of that Treaty does not apply to a State party to it, or to the Office of or acting for such a State, for as long as the latter provision is incompatible with the law applied by that State or Office, shall not apply for the purposes of this Treaty and the Regulations.

[1.977]
Article 17
Assembly

(1) [*Composition*]
(a) The Contracting Parties shall have an Assembly.
(b) Each Contracting Party shall be represented in the Assembly by one delegate, who may be assisted by alternate delegates, advisors and experts. Each delegate may represent only one Contracting Party.

(2) [*Tasks*] The Assembly shall—
(i) deal with matters concerning the maintenance and development of this Treaty and the application and operation of this Treaty;
(ii) establish Model International Forms, and the request Form, referred to in Article 14(1)(c), with the assistance of the International Bureau;
(iii) amend the Regulations;
(iv) determine the conditions for the date of application of each Model International Form, and the request Form, referred to in item (ii), and each amendment referred to in item (iii);
(v) decide, pursuant to Article 16(1), whether any revision, amendment or modification of the Patent Co-operation Treaty shall apply for the purposes of this Treaty and the Regulations;

(vi) perform such other functions as are appropriate under this Treaty.

(3) [*Quorum*]

(a) One-half of the members of the Assembly which are States shall constitute a quorum.

(b) Notwithstanding subparagraph (a), if, in any session, the number of the members of the Assembly which are States and are represented is less than one-half but equal to or more than one-third of the members of the Assembly which are States, the Assembly may make decisions but, with the exception of decisions concerning its own procedure, all such decisions shall take effect only if the conditions set forth hereinafter are fulfilled. The International Bureau shall communicate the said decisions to the members of the Assembly which are States and were not represented and shall invite them to express in writing their vote or abstention within a period of three months from the date of the communication. If, at the expiration of this period, the number of such members having thus expressed their vote or abstention attains the number of the members which was lacking for attaining the quorum in the session itself, such decisions shall take effect, provided that at the same time the required majority still obtains.

(4) [*Taking Decisions in the Assembly*]

(a) The Assembly shall endeavour to take its decisions by consensus.

(b) Where a decision cannot be arrived at by consensus, the matter at issue shall be decided by voting. In such a case—

(i) each Contracting Party that is a State shall have one vote and shall vote only in its own name; and

(ii) any Contracting Party that is an intergovernmental organisation may participate in the vote, in place of its Member States, with a number of votes equal to the number of its Member States which are party to this Treaty. No such intergovernmental organisation shall participate in the vote if any one of its Member States exercises its right to vote and *vice versa*. In addition, no such intergovernmental organisation shall participate in the vote if any one of its Member States party to this Treaty is a Member State of another such intergovernmental organisation and that other intergovernmental organisation participates in that vote.

(5) [*Majorities*]

(a) Subject to Articles 14(2) and (3), 16(1) and 19(3), the decisions of the Assembly shall require two-thirds of the votes cast.

(b) In determining whether the required majority is attained, only votes actually cast shall be taken into consideration. Abstentions shall not be considered as votes.

(6) [*Sessions*] The Assembly shall meet in ordinary session once every two years upon convocation by the Director General.

(7) [*Rules of Procedure*] The Assembly shall establish its own rules of procedure, including rules for the convocation of extraordinary sessions.

[1.978]
Article 18
International Bureau

(1) [*Administrative Tasks*]

(a) The International Bureau shall perform the administrative tasks concerning this Treaty.

(b) In particular, the International Bureau shall prepare the meetings and provide the secretariat of the Assembly and of such committees of experts and working groups as may be established by the Assembly.

(2) [*Meetings Other than Sessions of the Assembly*] The Director General shall convene any committee and working group established by the Assembly.

(3) [*Role of the International Bureau in the Assembly and Other Meetings*]

(a) The Director General and persons designated by the Director General shall participate, without the right to vote, in all meetings of the Assembly, the committees and working groups established by the Assembly.

(b) The Director General or a staff member designated by the Director General shall be ex officio secretary of the Assembly, and of the committees and working groups referred to in subparagraph (a).

(4) [*Conferences*]

(a) The International Bureau shall, in accordance with the directions of the Assembly, make the preparations for any revision conferences.

(b) The International Bureau may consult with member States of the Organisation, intergovernmental organisations and international and national non-governmental organisations concerning the said preparations.

(c) The Director General and persons designated by the Director General shall take part, without the right to vote, in the discussions at revision conferences.

(5) [*Other Tasks*] The International Bureau shall carry out any other tasks assigned to it in relation to this Treaty.

[1.979]
Article 19
Revisions

(1) [*Revision of the Treaty*] Subject to paragraph (2), this Treaty may be revised by a conference of the Contracting Parties. The convocation of any revision conference shall be decided by the Assembly.

(2) [*Revision or Amendment of Certain Provisions of the Treaty*] Article 17(2) and (6) may be amended either by a revision conference, or by the Assembly according to the provisions of paragraph (3).

(3) [*Amendment by the Assembly of Certain Provisions of the Treaty*]

(a) Proposals for the amendment by the Assembly of Article 17(2) and (6) may be initiated by any Contracting Party or by the Director General. Such proposals shall be communicated by the Director General to the Contracting Parties at least six months in advance of their consideration by the Assembly.

(b) Adoption of any amendment to the provisions referred to in subparagraph (a) shall require three-fourths of the votes cast.

(c) Any amendment to the provisions referred to in subparagraph (a) shall enter into force one month after written notifications of acceptance, effected in accordance with their respective constitutional processes, have been received by the Director General from three-fourths of the Contracting Parties which were members of the Assembly at the time the Assembly adopted the amendment. Any amendment to the said provisions thus accepted shall bind all the Contracting Parties at the time the amendment enters into force, and States and intergovernmental organisations which become Contracting Parties at a subsequent date.

[1.980]
Article 20
Becoming Party to the Treaty

(1) [*States*] Any State which is party to the Paris Convention or which is a member of the Organisation, and in respect of which patents may be granted, either through the State's own Office or through the Office of another State or intergovernmental organisation, may become party to this Treaty.

(2) [*Intergovernmental Organisations*] Any intergovernmental organisation may become party to this Treaty if at least one member State of that intergovernmental organisation is party to the Paris Convention or a member of the Organisation, and the intergovernmental organisation declares that it has been duly authorised, in accordance with its internal procedures, to become party to this Treaty, and declares that—

(i) it is competent to grant patents with effect for its member States; or

(ii) it is competent in respect of, and has its own legislation binding on all its member States concerning, matters covered by this Treaty, and it has, or has charged, a regional Office for the purpose of granting patents with effect in its territory in accordance with that legislation.

Subject to paragraph (3), any such declaration shall be made at the time of the deposit of the instrument of ratification or accession.

(3) [*Regional Patent Organisations*] The European Patent Organisation, the Eurasian Patent Organisation and the African Regional Industrial Property Organisation, having made the declaration referred to in paragraph (2)(i) or (ii) in the Diplomatic Conference that has adopted this Treaty, may become party to this Treaty as an intergovernmental organisation, if it declares, at the time of the deposit of the instrument of ratification or accession that it has been duly authorised, in accordance with its internal procedures, to become party to this Treaty.

(4) [*Ratification or Accession*] Any State or intergovernmental organisation satisfying the requirements in paragraph (1), (2) or (3) may deposit—

(i) an instrument of ratification if it has signed this Treaty; or

(ii) an instrument of accession if it has not signed this Treaty.

[1.981]
Article 21
Entry into Force; Effective Dates of Ratifications and Accessions

(1) [*Entry into Force of this Treaty*] This Treaty shall enter into force three months after ten instruments of ratification or accession by States have been deposited with the Director General.

(2) [*Effective Dates of Ratifications and Accessions*] This Treaty shall bind—

(i) the ten States referred to in paragraph (1), from the date on which this Treaty has entered into force;

(ii) each other State, from the expiration of three months after the date on which the State has deposited its instrument of ratification or accession with the Director General, or from any later date indicated in that instrument, but no later than six months after the date of such deposit;

(iii) each of the European Patent Organisation, the Eurasian Patent Organisation and the African Regional Industrial Property Organisation, from the expiration of three months after the deposit of its instrument of ratification or accession, or from any later date indicated in that instrument, but no later than six months after the date of such deposit, if such instrument has been deposited after the entry into force of this Treaty according to paragraph (1), or three months after the entry into force of this Treaty if such instrument has been deposited before the entry into force of this Treaty;

(iv) any other intergovernmental organisation that is eligible to become party to this Treaty, from the expiration of three months after the deposit of its instrument of ratification or accession, or from any later date indicated in that instrument, but no later than six months after the date of such deposit.

[1.982]
Article 22
Application of the Treaty to Existing Applications and Patents

(1) [*Principle*] Subject to paragraph (2), a Contracting Party shall apply the provisions of this Treaty and the Regulations, other than Articles 5 and 6(1) and (2) and related Regulations, to applications which are pending, and to patents which are in force, on the date on which this Treaty binds that Contracting Party under Article 21.

(2) [*Procedures*] No Contracting Party shall be obliged to apply the provisions of this Treaty and the Regulations to any procedure in proceedings with respect to applications and patents referred to in paragraph (1), if such procedure commenced before the date on which this Treaty binds that Contracting Party under Article 21.

[1.983]
Article 23
Reservations

(1) [*Reservation*] Any State or intergovernmental organisation may declare through a reservation that the provisions of Article 6(1) shall not apply to any requirement relating to unity of invention applicable under the Patent Co-operation Treaty to an international application.

(2) [*Modalities*] Any reservation under paragraph (1) shall be made in a declaration accompanying the instrument of ratification of, or accession to, this Treaty of the State or intergovernmental organisation making the reservation.

(3) [*Withdrawal*] Any reservation under paragraph (1) may be withdrawn at any time.

(4) [*Prohibition of Other Reservations*] No reservation to this Treaty other than the reservation allowed under paragraph (1) shall be permitted.

[1.984]
Article 24
Denunciation of the Treaty

(1) [*Notification*] Any Contracting Party may denounce this Treaty by notification addressed to the Director General.

(2) [*Effective Date*] Any denunciation shall take effect one year from the date on which the Director General has received the notification or at any later date indicated in the notification. It shall not affect the application of this Treaty to any application pending or any patent in force in respect of the denouncing Contracting Party at the time of the coming into effect of the denunciation.

[1.985]
Article 25
Languages of the Treaty

(1) [*Authentic Texts*] This Treaty is signed in a single original in the English, Arabic, Chinese, French, Russian and Spanish languages, all texts being equally and exclusively authentic.

(2) [*Official Texts*] An official text in any language other than those referred to in paragraph (1) shall be established by the Director General, after consultation with the interested parties. For the purposes of this paragraph, interested party means any State which is party to the Treaty, or is eligible to become party to the Treaty under Article 20(1), whose official language, or one of whose official languages, is involved, and the European Patent Organisation, the Eurasian Patent Organisation and the African Regional Industrial Property Organisation and any other intergovernmental organisation that is party to the Treaty, or may become party to the Treaty, if one of its official languages is involved.

(3) [*Authentic Texts to Prevail*] In case of differences of opinion on interpretation between authentic and official texts, the authentic texts shall prevail.

[1.986]
Article 26
Signature of the Treaty

The Treaty shall remain open for signature by any State that is eligible for becoming party to the Treaty under Article 20(1) and by the European Patent Organisation, the Eurasian Patent Organisation and the African Regional Industrial Property Organisation at the headquarters of the Organisation for one year after its adoption.

[1.987]
Article 27
Depositary; Registration

(1) [*Depositary*] The Director General is the depositary of this Treaty.

(2) [*Registration*] The Director General shall register this Treaty with the Secretariat of the United Nations.

AGREED STATEMENTS BY THE DIPLOMATIC CONFERENCE REGARDING THE PATENT LAW TREATY

(*Not reproduced in this work.*)

REGULATIONS UNDER THE PATENT LAW TREATY

(Done at Geneva on June 1, 2000. As in force from January 1, 2006)

NOTES

The original source for these Regulations is the World Intellectual Property Organisation (WIPO).

[1.988]
Rule 1
Abbreviated Expressions

(1) [*"Treaty"; "Article"*]

(a) In these Regulations, the word "Treaty" means the Patent Law Treaty.

(b) In these Regulations, the word "Article" refers to the specified Article of the Treaty.

(2) [*Abbreviated Expressions Defined in the Treaty*] The abbreviated expressions defined in Article 1 for the purposes of the Treaty shall have the same meaning for the purposes of the Regulations.

[1.989]
Rule 2
Details Concerning Filing Date Under Article 5

(1) [*Time Limits Under Article 5(3) and (4)(b)*] Subject to paragraph (2), the time limits referred to in Article 5(3) and (4)(b) shall be not less than two months from the date of the notification referred to in Article 5(3).

(2) [*Exception to Time Limit Under Article 5(4)(b)*] Where a notification under Article 5(3) has not been made because indications allowing the applicant to be contacted by the Office have not been filed, the time limit referred to in Article 5(4)(b) shall be not less than two months from the date on which one or more elements referred to in Article 5(1)(a) were first received by the Office.

(3) [*Time Limits Under Article 5(6)(a) and (b)*] The time limits referred to in Article 5(6)(a) and (b) shall be—

(i) where a notification has been made under Article 5(5), not less than two months from the date of the notification;

(ii) where a notification has not been made, not less than two months from the date on which one or more elements referred to in Article 5(1)(a) were first received by the Office.

(4) [*Requirements Under Article 5(6)(b)*] Any Contracting Party may, subject to Rule 4(3), require that, for the filing date to be determined under Article 5(6)(b)—

(i) a copy of the earlier application be filed within the time limit applicable under paragraph (3);

(ii) a copy of the earlier application, and the date of filing of the earlier application, certified as correct by the Office with which the earlier application was filed, be filed upon invitation by the Office, within a time limit which shall be not less than four months from the date of that invitation, or the time limit applicable under Rule 4(1), whichever expires earlier;

(iii) where the earlier application is not in a language accepted by the Office, a translation of the earlier application be filed within the time limit applicable under paragraph (3);

(iv) the missing part of the description or missing drawing be completely contained in the earlier application;

(v) the application, at the date on which one or more elements referred to in Article 5(1)(a) were first received by the Office, contained an indication that the contents of the earlier application were incorporated by reference in the application;

(vi) an indication be filed within the time limit applicable under paragraph (3) as to where, in the earlier application or in the translation referred to in item (iii), the missing part of the description or the missing drawing is contained.

(5) [*Requirements Under Article 5(7)(a)*]

(a) The reference to the previously filed application referred to in Article 5(7)(a) shall indicate that, for the purposes of the filing date, the description and any drawings are replaced by the reference to the previously filed application; the reference shall also indicate the number of that application, and the Office with which that application was filed. A Contracting Party may require that the reference also indicate the filing date of the previously filed application.

(b) A Contracting Party may, subject to Rule 4(3), require that—

(i) a copy of the previously filed application and, where the previously filed application is not in a language accepted by the Office, a translation of that previously filed application, be filed with the Office within a time limit which shall be not less than two months from the date on which the application containing the reference referred to in Article 5(7)(a) was received by the Office;

(ii) a certified copy of the previously filed application be filed with the Office within a time limit which shall be not less than four months from the date of the receipt of the application containing the reference referred to in Article 5(7)(a).

(c) A Contracting Party may require that the reference referred to in Article 5(7)(a) be to a previously filed application that had been filed by the applicant or his predecessor or successor in title.

(6) [*Exceptions Under Article 5(8)(ii)*] The types of applications referred to in Article 5(8)(ii) shall be—

(i) divisional applications;

(ii) applications for continuation or continuation-in-part;

(iii) applications by new applicants determined to be entitled to an invention contained in an earlier application.

[1.990]
Rule 3
Details Concerning the Application under Article 6(1), (2) and (3)

(1) [*Further Requirements under Article 6(1)(iii)*]

(a) A Contracting Party may require that an applicant who wishes an application to be treated as a divisional application under Rule 2(6)(i) indicate:

(i) that he wishes the application to be so treated;

(ii) the number and filing date of the application from which the application is divided.

(b) A Contracting Party may require that an applicant who wishes an application to be treated as an application under Rule 2(6)(iii) indicate:

(i) that he wishes the application to be so treated;

(ii) the number and filing date of the earlier application.

(c) A Contracting Party may require that an applicant who wishes an application to be treated as an application for a patent of addition indicate:

(i) that he wishes the application to be so treated;

(ii) the number and filing date of the parent application.

(d) A Contracting Party may require that an applicant who wishes an application to be treated as an application for the continuation or the continuation-in-part of an earlier application indicate:

(i) that he wishes the application to be so treated;

(ii) the number and filing date of the earlier application.

(e) Where a Contracting Party is an intergovernmental organisation, it may require that an applicant indicate:

(i) a petition that the applicant wishes to obtain a regional patent;

(ii) the member States of that intergovernmental organisation in which protection for the invention is sought.

(2) [*Request Form under Article 6(2)(b)*] A Contracting Party shall accept the presentation of the contents referred to in Article 6(2)(a)—

(i) on a request Form, if that request Form corresponds to the Patent Co-operation Treaty request Form with any modifications under Rule 20(2);

(ii) on a Patent Co-operation Treaty request Form, if that request Form is accompanied by an indication to the effect that the applicant wishes the application to be treated as a national or regional application, in which case the request Form shall be deemed to incorporate the modifications referred to in item (i);

(iii) on a Patent Co-operation Treaty request Form which contains an indication to the effect that the applicant wishes the application to be treated as a national or regional application, if such a request Form is available under the Patent Co-operation Treaty.

(3) [*Requirement Under Article 6(3)*] A Contracting Party may require, under Article 6(3), a translation of the title, claims and abstract of an application that is in a language accepted by the Office, into any other languages accepted by that Office.

[1.991]
Rule 4
Availability of Earlier Application Under Article 6(5) and Rule 2(4) or of Previously Filed Application Under Rule 2(5)(b)

(1) [*Copy of Earlier Application Under Article 6(5)*] Subject to paragraph (3), a Contracting Party may require that a copy of the earlier application referred to in Article 6(5) be filed with the Office within a time limit which shall be not less than 16 months from the filing date of that earlier application or, where there is more than one such earlier application, from the earliest filing date of those earlier applications.

(2) [*Certification*] Subject to paragraph (3), a Contracting Party may require that the copy referred to in paragraph (1) and the date of filing of the earlier application be certified as correct by the Office with which the earlier application was filed.

(3) [*Availability of Earlier Application or of Previously Filed Application*] No Contracting Party shall require the filing of a copy or a certified copy of the earlier application or a certification of the filing date, as referred to in paragraphs (1) and (2), and Rule 2(4), or a copy or a certified copy of the previously filed application as referred to in Rule 2(5)(b), where the earlier application or the previously filed application was filed with its Office, or is available to that Office from a digital library which is accepted by the Office for that purpose.

(4) [*Translation*] Where the earlier application is not in a language accepted by the Office and the validity of the priority claim is relevant to the determination of whether the invention concerned is patentable, the Contracting Party may require that a translation of the earlier application referred to in paragraph (1) be filed by the applicant, upon invitation by the Office or other competent authority, within a time limit which shall be not less than two months from the date of that invitation, and not less than the time limit, if any, applied under that paragraph.

[1.992]
Rule 5
Evidence Under Articles 6(6) and 8(4)(c) and Rules 7(4), 15(4), 16(6), 17(6) and 18(4)

Where the Office notifies the applicant, owner or other person that evidence is required under Article 6(6) or 8(4)(c), or Rule 7(4), 15(4), 16(6), 17(6) or 18(4), the notification shall state the reason of the Office for doubting the veracity of the matter, indication or signature, or the accuracy of the translation, as the case may be.

[1.993]
Rule 6
Time Limits Concerning the Application Under Article 6(7) and (8)

(1) [*Time Limits Under Article 6(7) and (8)*] Subject to paragraphs (2) and (3), the time limits referred to in Article 6(7) and (8) shall be not less than two months from the date of the notification referred to in Article 6(7).

(2) [*Exception to Time Limit Under Article 6(8)*] Subject to paragraph (3), where a notification under Article 6(7) has not been made because indications allowing the applicant to be contacted by the Office have not been filed, the time limit referred to in Article 6(8) shall be not less than three months from the date on which one or more of the elements referred to in Article 5(1)(a) were first received by the Office.

(3) [*Time Limits Under Article 6(7) and (8) Relating to Payment of Application Fee in Accordance with the Patent Co-operation Treaty*] Where any fees required to be paid under Article 6(4) in respect of the filing of the application are not paid, a Contracting Party may, under Article 6(7) and (8), apply time limits for payment, including late payment, which are the same as those applicable under the Patent Co-operation Treaty in relation to the international filing fee.

[1.994]
Rule 7
Details Concerning Representation Under Article 7

(1) [*Other Procedures Under Article 7(2)(a)(iii)*] The other procedures referred to in Article 7(2)(a)(iii) for which a Contracting Party may not require appointment of a representative are—

(i) the filing of a copy of an earlier application under Rule 2(4);
(ii) the filing of a copy of a previously filed application under Rule 2(5)(b).

(2) [*Appointment of Representative Under Article 7(3)*]

(a) A Contracting Party shall accept that the appointment of a representative be filed with the Office in—
 (i) a separate communication (hereinafter referred to as a "power of attorney") signed by the applicant, owner or other interested person and indicating the name and address of the representative; or, at the applicant's option,
 (ii) the request Form referred to in Article 6(2), signed by the applicant.

(b) A single power of attorney shall be sufficient even where it relates to more than one application or patent of the same person, or to one or more applications and one or more patents of the same person, provided that all applications and patents concerned are identified in the single power of attorney. A single power of attorney shall also be sufficient even where it relates, subject to any exception indicated by the appointing person, to all existing and future applications or patents of that person. The Office may require that, where that single power of attorney is filed on paper or as otherwise permitted by the Office, a separate copy thereof be filed for each application and patent to which it relates.

(3) [*Translation of Power of Attorney*] A Contracting Party may require that, if a power of attorney is not in a language accepted by the Office, it be accompanied by a translation.

(4) [*Evidence*] A Contracting Party may require that evidence be filed with the Office only where the Office may reasonably doubt the veracity of any indication contained in any communication referred to in paragraph (2)(a).

(5) [*Time Limits Under Article 7(5) and (6)*] Subject to paragraph (6), the time limits referred to in Article 7(5) and (6) shall be not less than two months from the date of the notification referred to in Article 7(5).

(6) [*Exception to Time Limit Under Article 7(6)*] Where a notification referred to in Article 7(5) has not been made because indications allowing the applicant, owner or other interested person to be contacted by the Office have not been filed, the time limit referred to in Article 7(6) shall be not less than three months from the date on which the procedure referred to in Article 7(5) was commenced.

[1.995]
Rule 8
Filing of Communications Under Article 8(1)

(1) [*Communications Filed on Paper*]

(a) After June 2, 2005, any Contracting Party may, subject to Articles 5(1) and 8(1)(d), exclude the filing of communications on paper or may continue to permit the filing of communications on paper. Until that date, all Contracting Parties shall permit the filing of communications on paper.

(b) Subject to Article 8(3) and subparagraph (c), a Contracting Party may prescribe the requirements relating to the form of communications on paper.

(c) Where a Contracting Party permits the filing of communications on paper, the Office shall permit the filing of communications on paper in accordance with the requirements under the Patent Co-operation Treaty relating to the form of communications on paper.

(d) Notwithstanding subparagraph (a), where the receiving or processing of a communication on paper, due to its character or its size, is deemed not practicable, a Contracting Party may require the filing of that communication in another form or by other means of transmittal.

(2) [*Communications Filed in Electronic Form or by Electronic Means of Transmittal*]

(a) Where a Contracting Party permits the filing of communications in electronic form or by electronic means of transmittal with its Office in a particular language, including the filing of communications by telegraph, teleprinter, telefacsimile or other like means of transmittal, and there are requirements applicable to that Contracting Party under the Patent Co-operation Treaty in relation to communications filed in electronic form or by electronic means of transmittal in that language, the Office shall permit the filing of communications in electronic form or by electronic means of transmittal in the said language in accordance with those requirements.

(b) A Contracting Party which permits the filing of communications in electronic form or by electronic means of transmittal with its Office shall notify the International Bureau of the requirements under its applicable law relating to such filing. Any such notification shall be published by the International Bureau in the language in which it is notified and in the languages in which authentic and official texts of the Treaty are established under Article 25.

(c) Where, under subparagraph (a), a Contracting Party permits the filing of communications by telegraph, teleprinter, telefacsimile or other like means of transmittal, it may require that the original of any document which was transmitted by such means of transmittal, accompanied by a letter identifying that earlier transmission, be filed on paper with the Office within a time limit which shall be not less than one month from the date of the transmission.

(3) [*Copies, Filed in Electronic Form or by Electronic Means of Transmittal, of Communications Filed on Paper*]

(a) Where a Contracting Party permits the filing of a copy, in electronic form or by electronic means of transmittal, of a communication filed on paper in a language accepted by the Office, and there are requirements applicable to that Contracting Party under the Patent Co-operation Treaty in relation to the filing of such copies of communications, the Office shall permit the filing of copies of communications in electronic form or by electronic means of transmittal, in accordance with those requirements.

(b) Paragraph (2)(b) shall apply, *mutatis mutandis*, to copies, in electronic form or by electronic means of transmittal, of communications filed on paper.

[1.996]
Rule 9
Details Concerning the Signature Under Article 8(4)

(1) [*Indications Accompanying Signature*] A Contracting Party may require that the signature of the natural person who signs be accompanied by—

(i) an indication in letters of the family or principal name and the given or secondary name or names of that person or, at the option of that person, of the name or names customarily used by the said person;

(ii) an indication of the capacity in which that person signed, where such capacity is not obvious from reading the communication.

(2) [*Date of Signing*] A Contracting Party may require that a signature be accompanied by an indication of the date on which the signing was effected. Where that indication is required but is not supplied, the date on which the signing is deemed to have been effected shall be the date on which the communication bearing the signature was received by the Office or, if the Contracting Party so permits, a date earlier than the latter date.

(3) [*Signature of Communication on Paper*] Where a communication to the Office of a Contracting Party is on paper and a signature is required, that Contracting Party—

(i) shall, subject to item (iii), accept a handwritten signature;

(ii) may permit, instead of a handwritten signature, the use of other forms of signature, such as a printed or stamped signature, or the use of a seal or of a bar-coded label;

(iii) may, where the natural person who signs the communication is a national of the Contracting Party and such person's address is on its territory, or where the legal entity on behalf of which the communication is signed is organised under its law and has either a domicile or a real and effective industrial or commercial establishment on its territory, require that a seal be used instead of a handwritten signature.

(4) [*Signature of Communications Filed in Electronic Form or by Electronic Means of Transmittal Resulting in Graphic Representation*] Where a Contracting Party permits the filing of communications in electronic form or by electronic means of transmittal, it shall consider such a communication signed if a graphic representation of a signature accepted by that Contracting Party under paragraph (3) appears on that communication as received by the Office of that Contracting Party.

(5) [*Signature of Communications Filed in Electronic Form Not Resulting in Graphic Representation of Signature*]

(a) Where a Contracting Party permits the filing of communications in electronic form, and a graphic representation of a signature accepted by that Contracting Party under paragraph (3) does not appear on such a communication as received by the Office of that Contracting Party, the Contracting Party may require that the communication be signed using a signature in electronic form as prescribed by that Contracting Party.

(b) Notwithstanding subparagraph (a), where a Contracting Party permits the filing of communications in electronic form in a particular language, and there are requirements applicable to that Contracting Party under the Patent Co-operation Treaty in relation to signatures in electronic form of communications filed in electronic form in that language which do not result in a graphic representation of the signature, the Office of that Contracting Party shall accept a signature in electronic form in accordance with those requirements.

(c) Rule 8(2)(b) shall apply *mutatis mutandis*.

(6) [*Exception to Certification of Signature Under Article 8(4)(b)*] A Contracting Party may require that any signature referred to in paragraph (5) be confirmed by a process for certifying signatures in electronic form specified by that Contracting Party.

[1.997]
Rule 10
Details Concerning Indications Under Article 8(5), (6) and (8)

(1) [*Indications Under Article 8(5)*]

(a) A Contracting Party may require that any communication—

(i) indicate the name and address of the applicant, owner or other interested person;

(ii) indicate the number of the application or patent to which it relates;

(iii) contain, where the applicant, owner or other interested person is registered with the Office, the number or other indication under which he is so registered.

(b) A Contracting Party may require that any communication by a representative for the purposes of a procedure before the Office contain—

(i) the name and address of the representative;

(ii) a reference to the power of attorney, or other communication in which the appointment of that representative is or was effected, on the basis of which the said representative acts;

(iii) where the representative is registered with the Office, the number or other indication under which he is registered.

(2) [*Address for Correspondence and Address for Legal Service*] A Contracting Party may require that the address for correspondence referred to in Article 8(6)(i) and the address for legal service referred to in Article 8(6)(ii) be on a territory prescribed by that Contracting Party.

(3) [*Address Where No Representative is Appointed*] Where no representative is appointed and an applicant, owner or other interested person has provided, as his address, an address on a territory prescribed by the Contracting Party under paragraph (2), that Contracting Party shall consider that address to be the address for correspondence referred to in Article 8(6)(i) or the address for legal service referred to in Article 8(6)(ii), as required by the Contracting Party, unless that applicant, owner or other interested person expressly indicates another such address under Article 8(6).

(4) [*Address Where Representative is Appointed*] Where a representative is appointed, a Contracting Party shall consider the address of that representative to be the address for correspondence referred to in Article 8(6)(i) or the address for legal service referred to in Article 8(6)(ii), as required by the Contracting Party, unless that applicant, owner or other interested person expressly indicates another such address under Article 8(6).

(5) [*Sanctions for Non-Compliance with Requirements Under Article 8(8)*] No Contracting Party may provide for the refusal of an application for failure to comply with any requirement to file a registration number or other indication under paragraph (1)(a)(iii) and (b)(iii).

[1.998]
Rule 11
Time Limits Concerning Communications Under Article 8(7) and (8)

(1) [*Time Limits Under Article 8(7) and (8)*] Subject to paragraph (2), the time limits referred to in Article 8(7) and (8) shall be not less than two months from the date of the notification referred to in Article 8(7).

(2) [*Exception to Time Limit Under Article 8(8)*] Where a notification under Article 8(7) has not been made because indications allowing the applicant, owner or other interested person to be contacted by the Office have not been filed, the time limit referred to in Article 8(8) shall be not less than three months from the date on which the communication referred to in Article 8(7) was received by the Office.

[1.999]
Rule 12
Details Concerning Relief in Respect of Time Limits Under Article 11

(1) [*Requirements Under Article 11(1)*]

(a) A Contracting Party may require that a request referred to in Article 11(1)—

(i) be signed by the applicant or owner;

(ii) contain an indication to the effect that extension of a time limit is requested, and an identification of the time limit in question.

(b) Where a request for extension of a time limit is filed after the expiration of the time limit, a Contracting Party may require that all of the requirements in respect of which the time limit for the action concerned applied be complied with at the same time as the request is filed.

(2) [*Period and Time Limit Under Article 11(1)*]

(a) The period of extension of a time limit referred to in Article 11(1) shall be not less than two months from the date of the expiration of the unextended time limit.

(b) The time limit referred to in Article 11(1)(ii) shall expire not earlier than two months from the date of the expiration of the unextended time limit.

(3) [*Requirements Under Article 11(2)(i)*] A Contracting Party may require that a request referred to in Article 11(2)—

(i) be signed by the applicant or owner;

(ii) contain an indication to the effect that relief in respect of non-compliance with a time limit is requested, and an identification of the time limit in question.

(4) [*Time Limit for Filing a Request Under Article 11(2)(ii)*] The time limit referred to in Article 11(2)(ii) shall expire not earlier than two months after a notification by the Office that the applicant or owner did not comply with the time limit fixed by the Office.

(5) [*Exceptions Under Article 11(3)*]

(a) No Contracting Party shall be required under Article 11(1) or (2) to grant—

(i) a second, or any subsequent, relief in respect of a time limit for which relief has already been granted under Article 11(1) or (2);

(ii) relief for filing a request for relief under Article 11(1) or (2) or a request for reinstatement under Article 12(1);

(iii) relief in respect of a time limit for the payment of maintenance fees;

(iv) relief in respect of a time limit referred to in Article 13(1), (2) or (3);

(v) relief in respect of a time limit for an action before a board of appeal or other review body constituted in the framework of the Office;

(vi) relief in respect of a time limit for an action in *inter partes* proceedings.

(b) No Contracting Party which provides a maximum time limit for compliance with all of the requirements of a procedure before the Office shall be required under Article 11(1) or (2) to grant relief in respect of a time limit for an action in that procedure in respect of any of those requirements beyond that maximum time limit.

[1.1000]
Rule 13
Details Concerning Reinstatement of Rights After a Finding of Due Care or Unintentionality by the Office Under Article 12

(1) [*Requirements Under Article 12(1)(i)*] A Contracting Party may require that a request referred to in Article 12(1)(i) be signed by the applicant or owner.

(2) [*Time Limit Under Article 12(1)(ii)*] The time limit for making a request, and for complying with the requirements, under Article 12(1)(ii), shall be the earlier to expire of the following—

(i) not less than two months from the date of the removal of the cause of failure to comply with the time limit for the action in question;

(ii) not less than 12 months from the date of expiration of the time limit for the action in question, or, where a request relates to non-payment of a maintenance fee, not less than 12 months from the date of expiration of the period of grace provided under Article 5*bis* of the Paris Convention.

(3) [*Exceptions Under Article 12(2)*] The exceptions referred to in Article 12(2) are failure to comply with a time limit—

(i) for an action before a board of appeal or other review body constituted in the framework of the Office;

(ii) for making a request for relief under Article 11(1) or (2) or a request for reinstatement under Article 12(1);

(iii) referred to in Article 13(1), (2) or (3);

(iv) for an action in *inter partes* proceedings.

[1.1001]
Rule 14
Details Concerning Correction or Addition of Priority Claim and Restoration of Priority Right Under Article 13

(1) [*Exception Under Article 13(1)*] No Contracting Party shall be obliged to provide for the correction or addition of a priority claim under Article 13(1), where the request referred to in Article 13(1)(i) is received after the applicant has made a request for early publication or for expedited or accelerated processing, unless that request for early publication or for expedited or accelerated processing is withdrawn before the technical preparations for publication of the application have been completed.

(2) [*Requirements Under Article 13(1)(i)*] A Contracting Party may require that a request referred to in Article 13(1)(i) be signed by the applicant.

(3) [*Time Limit Under Article 13(1)(ii)*] The time limit referred to in Article 13(1)(ii) shall be not less than the time limit applicable under the Patent Co-operation Treaty to an international application for the submission of a priority claim after the filing of an international application.

(4) [*Time Limits Under Article 13(2)*]

(a) The time limit referred to in Article 13(2), introductory part, shall expire not less than two months from the date on which the priority period expired.

(b) The time limit referred to in Article 13(2)(ii) shall be the time limit applied under subparagraph (a), or the time that any technical preparations for publication of the subsequent application have been completed, whichever expires earlier.

(5) [*Requirements Under Article 13(2)(i)*] A Contracting Party may require that a request referred to in Article 13(2)(i)—

(i) be signed by the applicant; and

(ii) be accompanied, where the application did not claim the priority of the earlier application, by the priority claim.

(6) [*Requirements Under Article 13(3)*]

(a) A Contracting Party may require that a request referred to in Article 13(3)(i)—

(i) be signed by the applicant; and

(ii) indicate the Office to which the request for a copy of the earlier application had been made and the date of that request.

(b) A Contracting Party may require that—

(i) a declaration or other evidence in support of the request referred to in Article 13(3) be filed with the Office within a time limit fixed by the Office;

(ii) the copy of the earlier application referred to in Article 13(3)(iv) be filed with the Office within a time limit which shall be not less than one month from the date on which the applicant is provided with that copy by the Office with which the earlier application was filed.

(7) [*Time Limit Under Article 13(3)(iii)*] The time limit referred to in Article 13(3)(iii) shall expire two months before the expiration of the time limit prescribed in Rule 4(1).

[1.1002]
Rule 15
Request for Recordation of Change in Name or Address

(1) [*Request*] Where there is no change in the person of the applicant or owner but there is a change in his name or address, a Contracting Party shall accept that a request for recordation of the change be made in a communication signed by the applicant or owner and containing the following indications—

- (i) an indication to the effect that recordation of a change in name or address is requested;
- (ii) the number of the application or patent concerned;
- (iii) the change to be recorded;
- (iv) the name and address of the applicant or the owner prior to the change.

(2) [*Fees*] A Contracting Party may require that a fee be paid in respect of a request referred to in paragraph (1).

(3) [*Single Request*]

- (a) A single request shall be sufficient even where the change relates to both the name and address of the applicant or the owner.
- (b) A single request shall be sufficient even where the change relates to more than one application or patent of the same person, or to one or more applications and one or more patents of the same person, provided that the numbers of all applications and patents concerned are indicated in the request. A Contracting Party may require that, where that single request is filed on paper or as otherwise permitted by the Office, a separate copy thereof be filed for each application and patent to which it relates.

(4) [*Evidence*] A Contracting Party may require that evidence be filed with the Office only where the Office may reasonably doubt the veracity of any indication contained in the request.

(5) [*Prohibition of Other Requirements*] No Contracting Party may require that formal requirements other than those referred to in paragraphs (1) to (4) be complied with in respect of the request referred to in paragraph (1), except where otherwise provided for by the Treaty or prescribed in these Regulations. In particular, the filing of any certificate concerning the change may not be required.

(6) [*Notification*] Where one or more of the requirements applied by the Contracting Party under paragraphs (1) to (4) are not complied with, the Office shall notify the applicant or owner, giving the opportunity to comply with any such requirement, and to make observations, within not less than two months from the date of the notification.

(7) [*Non-Compliance with Requirements*]

- (a) Where one or more of the requirements applied by the Contracting Party under paragraphs (1) to (4) are not complied with within the time limit under subparagraph (b), the Contracting Party may provide that the request shall be refused, but no more severe sanction may be applied.
- (b) The time limit referred to in subparagraph (a) shall be—
  - (i) subject to item (ii), not less than two months from the date of the notification;
  - (ii) where indications allowing the Office to contact the person who made the request referred to in paragraph (1) have not been filed, not less than three months from the date on which that request was received by the Office.

(8) [*Change in the Name or Address of the Representative, or in the Address for Correspondence or Address for Legal Service*] Paragraphs (1) to (7) shall apply, *mutatis mutandis*, to any change in the name or address of the representative, and to any change relating to the address for correspondence or address for legal service.

[1.1003]
Rule 16
Request for Recordation of Change in Applicant or Owner

(1) [*Request for Recordation of a Change in Applicant or Owner*]

- (a) Where there is a change in the person of the applicant or owner, a Contracting Party shall accept that a request for recordation of the change be made in a communication signed by the applicant or owner, or by the new applicant or new owner, and containing the following indications—
  - (i) an indication to the effect that a recordation of change in applicant or owner is requested;
  - (ii) the number of the application or patent concerned;
  - (iii) the name and address of the applicant or owner;
  - (iv) the name and address of the new applicant or new owner;
  - (v) the date of the change in the person of the applicant or owner;
  - (vi) the name of a State of which the new applicant or new owner is a national if he is the national of any State, the name of a State in which the new applicant or new owner has his domicile, if any, and the name of a State in which the new applicant or new owner has a real and effective industrial or commercial establishment, if any;
  - (vii) the basis for the change requested.
- (b) A Contracting Party may require that the request contain—
  - (i) a statement that the information contained in the request is true and correct;

(ii) information relating to any government interest by that Contracting Party.

(2) [*Documentation of the Basis of the Change in Applicant or Owner*]

(a) Where the change in applicant or owner results from a contract, a Contracting Party may require that the request include information relating to the registration of the contract, where registration is compulsory under the applicable law, and that it be accompanied, at the option of the requesting party, by one of the following—

(i) a copy of the contract, which copy may be required to be certified, at the option of the requesting party, by a notary public or any other competent public authority or, where permitted under the applicable law, by a representative having the right to practise before the Office, as being in conformity with the original contract;

(ii) an extract of the contract showing the change, which extract may be required to be certified, at the option of the requesting party, by a notary public or any other competent public authority or, where permitted under the applicable law, by a representative having the right to practise before the Office, as being a true extract of the contract;

(iii) an uncertified certificate of transfer of ownership by contract drawn up with the content as prescribed in the Model International Form in respect of a certificate of transfer and signed by both the applicant and the new applicant, or by both the owner and the new owner.

(b) Where the change in applicant or owner results from a merger, or from the reorganisation or division of a legal entity, a Contracting Party may require that the request be accompanied by a copy of a document, which document originates from a competent authority and evidences the merger, or the reorganisation or division of the legal entity, and any attribution of rights involved, such as a copy of an extract from a register of commerce. A Contracting Party may also require that the copy be certified, at the option of the requesting party, by the authority which issued the document or by a notary public or any other competent public authority or, where permitted under the applicable law, by a representative having the right to practise before the Office, as being in conformity with the original document.

(c) Where the change in applicant or owner does not result from a contract, a merger, or the reorganisation or division of a legal entity, but results from another ground, for example, by operation of law or a court decision, a Contracting Party may require that the request be accompanied by a copy of a document evidencing the change. A Contracting Party may also require that the copy be certified as being in conformity with the original document, at the option of the requesting party, by the authority which issued the document or by a notary public or any other competent public authority or, where permitted under the applicable law, by a representative having the right to practise before the Office.

(d) Where the change is in the person of one or more but not all of several co-applicants or co-owners, a Contracting Party may require that evidence of the consent to the change of any co-applicant or co-owner in respect of whom there is no change be provided to the Office.

(3) [*Translation*] A Contracting Party may require a translation of any document filed under paragraph (2) that is not in a language accepted by the Office.

(4) [*Fees*] A Contracting Party may require that a fee be paid in respect of a request referred to in paragraph (1).

(5) [*Single Request*] A single request shall be sufficient even where the change relates to more than one application or patent of the same person, or to one or more applications and one or more patents of the same person, provided that the change in applicant or owner is the same for all applications and patents concerned, and the numbers of all applications and patents concerned are indicated in the request. A Contracting Party may require that, where that single request is filed on paper or as otherwise permitted by the Office, a separate copy thereof be filed for each application and patent to which it relates.

(6) [*Evidence*] A Contracting Party may require that evidence, or further evidence in the case of paragraph (2), be filed with the Office only where that Office may reasonably doubt the veracity of any indication contained in the request or in any document referred to in the present Rule, or the accuracy of any translation referred to in paragraph (3).

(7) [*Prohibition of Other Requirements*] No Contracting Party may require that formal requirements other than those referred to in paragraphs (1) to (6) be complied with in respect of the request referred to in this Rule, except where otherwise provided for by the Treaty or prescribed in these Regulations.

(8) [*Notification; Non-Compliance with Requirements*] Rule 15(6) and (7) shall apply, *mutatis mutandis*, where one or more of the requirements applied under paragraphs (1) to (5) are not complied with, or where evidence, or further evidence, is required under paragraph (6).

(9) [*Exclusion with Respect to Inventorship*] A Contracting Party may exclude the application of this Rule in respect of changes in inventorship. What constitutes inventorship shall be determined under the applicable law.

[1.1004]
Rule 17
Request for Recordation of a Licence or a Security Interest

(1) [*Request for Recordation of a Licence*]

(a) Where a licence in respect of an application or patent may be recorded under the applicable law, the Contracting Party shall accept that a request for recordation of that licence be made in a communication signed by the licensor or the licensee and containing the following indications—

(i) an indication to the effect that a recordation of a licence is requested;
(ii) the number of the application or patent concerned;
(iii) the name and address of the licensor;
(iv) the name and address of the licensee;
(v) an indication of whether the licence is an exclusive licence or a nonexclusive licence;
(vi) the name of a State of which the licensee is a national if he is the national of any State, the name of a State in which the licensee has his domicile, if any, and the name of a State in which the licensee has a real and effective industrial or commercial establishment, if any.

(b) A Contracting Party may require that the request contain—

(i) a statement that the information contained in the request is true and correct;
(ii) information relating to any government interest by that Contracting Party;
(iii) information relating to the registration of the licence, where registration is compulsory under the applicable law;
(iv) the date of the licence and its duration.

(2) [*Documentation of the Basis of the Licence*]

(a) Where the licence is a freely concluded agreement, a Contracting Party may require that the request be accompanied, at the option of the requesting party, by one of the following—

(i) a copy of the agreement, which copy may be required to be certified, at the option of the requesting party, by a notary public or any other competent public authority or, where permitted under the applicable law, by a representative having the right to practise before the Office, as being in conformity with the original agreement;
(ii) an extract of the agreement consisting of those portions of that agreement which show the rights licensed and their extent, which extract may be required to be certified, at the option of the requesting party, by a notary public or any other competent public authority or, where permitted under the applicable law, by a representative having the right to practise before the Office, as being a true extract of the agreement.

(b) A Contracting Party may require, where the licence is a freely concluded agreement, that any applicant, owner, exclusive licensee, co-applicant, co-owner or co-exclusive licensee who is not party to that agreement give his consent to the recordation of the agreement in a communication to the Office.

(c) Where the licence is not a freely concluded agreement, for example, it results from operation of law or a court decision, a Contracting Party may require that the request be accompanied by a copy of a document evidencing the licence. A Contracting Party may also require that the copy be certified as being in conformity with the original document, at the option of the requesting party, by the authority which issued the document or by a notary public or any other competent public authority or, where permitted under the applicable law, by a representative having the right to practise before the Office.

(3) [*Translation*] A Contracting Party may require a translation of any document filed under paragraph (2) that is not in a language accepted by the Office.

(4) [*Fees*] A Contracting Party may require that a fee be paid in respect of a request referred to in paragraph (1).

(5) [*Single Request*] Rule 16(5) shall apply, *mutatis mutandis*, to requests for recordation of a licence.

(6) [*Evidence*] Rule 16(6) shall apply, *mutatis mutandis*, to requests for recordation of a licence.

(7) [*Prohibition of Other Requirements*] No Contracting Party may require that formal requirements other than those referred to in paragraphs (1) to (6) be complied with in respect of the request referred to in paragraph (1), except where otherwise provided for by the Treaty or prescribed in these Regulations.

(8) [*Notification; Non-Compliance with Requirements*] Rule 15(6) and (7) shall apply, *mutatis mutandis*, where one or more of the requirements applied under paragraphs (1) to (5) are not complied with, or where evidence, or further evidence, is required under paragraph (6).

(9) [*Request for Recordation of a Security Interest or Cancellation of the Recordation of a Licence or a Security Interest*] Paragraphs (1) to (8) shall apply, *mutatis mutandis*, to requests for—

(i) recordation of a security interest in respect of an application or patent;
(ii) cancellation of the recordation of a licence or a security interest in respect of an application or patent.

[1.1005]
Rule 18
Request for Correction of a Mistake

(1) [*Request*]

(a) Where an application, a patent or any request communicated to the Office in respect of an application or a patent contains a mistake, not related to search or substantive examination, which is correctable by the Office under the applicable law, the Office shall accept that a request for correction of that mistake in the records and publications of the Office be made in a communication to the Office signed by the applicant or owner and containing the following indications—

(i) an indication to the effect that a correction of mistake is requested;
(ii) the number of the application or patent concerned;
(iii) the mistake to be corrected;
(iv) the correction to be made;
(v) the name and address of the requesting party.

(b) A Contracting Party may require that the request be accompanied by a replacement part or part incorporating the correction or, where paragraph (3) applies, by such a replacement part or part incorporating the correction for each application and patent to which the request relates.

(c) A Contracting Party may require that the request be subject to a declaration by the requesting party stating that the mistake was made in good faith.

(d) A Contracting Party may require that the request be subject to a declaration by the requesting party stating that the said request was made without undue delay or, at the option of the Contracting Party, that it was made without intentional delay, following the discovery of the mistake.

(2) [*Fees*]

(a) Subject to subparagraph (b), a Contracting Party may require that a fee be paid in respect of a request under paragraph (1).

(b) The Office shall correct its own mistakes, *ex officio* or upon request, for no fee.

(3) [*Single Request*] Rule 16(5) shall apply, *mutatis mutandis*, to requests for correction of a mistake, provided that the mistake and the requested correction are the same for all applications and patents concerned.

(4) [*Evidence*] A Contracting Party may only require that evidence in support of the request be filed with the Office where the Office may reasonably doubt that the alleged mistake is in fact a mistake, or where it may reasonably doubt the veracity of any matter contained in, or of any document filed in connection with, the request for correction of a mistake.

(5) [*Prohibition of Other Requirements*] No Contracting Party may require that formal requirements other than those referred to in paragraphs (1) to (4) be complied with in respect of the request referred to in paragraph (1), except where otherwise provided for by the Treaty or prescribed in these Regulations.

(6) [*Notification; Non-Compliance with Requirements*] Rule 15(6) and (7) shall apply, *mutatis mutandis*, where one or more of the requirements applied under paragraphs (1) to (3) are not complied with, or where evidence is required under paragraph (4).

(7) [*Exclusions*]

(a) A Contracting Party may exclude the application of this Rule in respect of changes in inventorship. What constitutes inventorship shall be determined under the applicable law.

(b) A Contracting Party may exclude the application of this Rule in respect of any mistake which must be corrected in that Contracting Party under a procedure for reissue of the patent.

[1.1006]
Rule 19
Manner of Identification of an Application Without its Application Number

(1) [*Manner of Identification*] Where it is required that an application be identified by its application number, but such a number has not yet been issued or is not known to the person concerned or his representative, the application shall be considered identified if one of the following is supplied, at that person's option—

(i) a provisional number for the application, if any, given by the Office;
(ii) a copy of the request part of the application along with the date on which the application was sent to the Office;
(iii) a reference number given to the application by the applicant or his representative and indicated in the application, along with the name and address of the applicant, the title of the invention and the date on which the application was sent to the Office.

(2) [*Prohibition of Other Requirements*] No Contracting Party may require that identification means other than those referred to in paragraph (1) be supplied in order for an application to be identified where its application number has not yet been issued or is not known to the person concerned or his representative.

[1.1007]
Rule 20
Establishment of Model International Forms

(1) [*Model International Forms*] The Assembly shall, under Article 14(1)(c), establish Model International Forms, in each of the languages referred to in Article 25(1), in respect of—
- (i) a power of attorney;
- (ii) a request for recordation of change in name or address;
- (iii) a request for recordation of change in applicant or owner;
- (iv) a certificate of transfer;
- (v) a request for recordation, or cancellation of recordation, of a licence;
- (vi) a request for recordation, or cancellation of recordation, of a security interest;
- (vii) a request for correction of a mistake.

(2) [*Modifications Referred to in Rule 3(2)(i)*] The Assembly shall establish the modifications of the Patent Co-operation Treaty request Form referred to in Rule 3(2)(i).

(3) [*Proposals by the International Bureau*] The International Bureau shall present proposals to the Assembly concerning—
- (i) the establishment of Model International Forms referred to in paragraph (1);
- (ii) the modifications of the Patent Co-operation Treaty request Form referred to in paragraph (2).

[1.1008]
Rule 21
Requirement of Unanimity Under Article 14(3)

Establishment or amendment of the following Rules shall require unanimity—
- (i) any Rules under Article 5(1)(a);
- (ii) any Rules under Article 6(1)(iii);
- (iii) any Rules under Article 6(3);
- (iv) any Rules under Article 7(2)(a)(iii);
- (v) Rule 8(1)(a);
- (vi) the present Rule.

AGREED STATEMENTS BY THE DIPLOMATIC CONFERENCE REGARDING THE PATENT LAW TREATY AND THE REGULATIONS UNDER THE PATENT LAW TREATY

(*Not reproduced in this work.*)

AGREEMENT ON A UNIFIED PATENT COURT

(Brussels, 19 February 2013)

NOTES

This Agreement was published in the Official Journal at OJ C175, 20.6.2013, p 1.

The Agreement was signed by 25 EU Member States on 19 February 2013. It will need to be ratified by at least 13 states, including France, Germany and the United Kingdom to enter into force. As at 1 July 2017 it had been ratified by Austria, Belgium, Bulgaria, Denmark, Finland, France, Italy, Luxembourg, Malta, Netherlands, Portugal and Sweden.

See further the Unified Patent Court website at www.unified-patent-court.org/.

THE CONTRACTING MEMBER STATES,

CONSIDERING that cooperation amongst the Member States of the European Union in the field of patents contributes significantly to the integration process in Europe, in particular to the establishment of an internal market within the European Union characterised by the free movement of goods and services and the creation of a system ensuring that competition in the internal market is not distorted;

CONSIDERING that the fragmented market for patents and the significant variations between national court systems are detrimental for innovation, in particular for small and medium sized enterprises which have difficulties to enforce their patents and to defend themselves against unfounded claims and claims relating to patents which should be revoked;

CONSIDERING that the European Patent Convention ("EPC") which has been ratified by all Member States of the European Union provides for a single procedure for granting European patents by the European Patent Office;

CONSIDERING that by virtue of Regulation (EU) No 1257/2012,[1] patent proprietors can request unitary effect of their European patents so as to obtain unitary patent protection in the Member States of the European Union participating in the enhanced cooperation;

WISHING to improve the enforcement of patents and the defence against unfounded claims and patents which should be revoked and to enhance legal certainty by setting up a Unified Patent Court for litigation relating to the infringement and validity of patents;

CONSIDERING that the Unified Patent Court should be devised to ensure expeditious and high quality decisions, striking a fair balance between the interests of right holders and other parties and taking into account the need for proportionality and flexibility;

CONSIDERING that the Unified Patent Court should be a court common to the Contracting Member States and thus part of their judicial system, with exclusive competence in respect of European patents with unitary effect and European patents granted under the provisions of the EPC;

CONSIDERING that the Court of Justice of the European Union is to ensure the uniformity of the Union legal order and the primacy of European Union law;

RECALLING the obligations of the Contracting Member States under the Treaty on European Union (TEU) and the Treaty on the Functioning of the European Union (TFEU), including the obligation of sincere cooperation as set out in Article 4(3) TEU and the obligation to ensure through the Unified Patent Court the full application of, and respect for, Union law in their respective territories and the judicial protection of an individual's rights under that law;

CONSIDERING that, as any national court, the Unified Patent Court must respect and apply Union law and, in collaboration with the Court of Justice of the European Union as guardian of Union law, ensure its correct application and uniform interpretation; the Unified Patent Court must in particular cooperate with the Court of Justice of the European Union in properly interpreting Union law by relying on the latter's case law and by requesting preliminary rulings in accordance with Article 267 TFEU;

CONSIDERING that the Contracting Member States should, in line with the case law of the Court of Justice of the European Union on non-contractual liability, be liable for damages caused by infringements of Union law by the Unified Patent Court, including the failure to request preliminary rulings from the Court of Justice of the European Union;

CONSIDERING that infringements of Union law by the Unified Patent Court, including the failure to request preliminary rulings from the Court of Justice of the European Union, are directly attributable to the Contracting Member States and infringement proceedings can therefore be brought under Article 258, 259 and 260 TFEU against any Contracting Member State to ensure the respect of the primacy and proper application of Union law;

RECALLING the primacy of Union law, which includes the TEU, the TFEU, the Charter of Fundamental Rights of the European Union, the general principles of Union law as developed by the Court of Justice of the European Union, and in particular the right to an effective remedy before a tribunal and a fair and public hearing within a reasonable time by an independent and impartial tribunal, the case law of the Court of Justice of the European Union and secondary Union law;

CONSIDERING that this Agreement should be open to accession by any Member State of the European Union; Member States which have decided not to participate in the enhanced cooperation in the area of the creation of unitary patent protection may participate in this Agreement in respect of European patents granted for their respective territory;

CONSIDERING that this Agreement should enter into force on 1 January 2014 or on the first day of the fourth month after the 13th deposit, provided that the Contracting Member States that will have deposited their instruments of ratification or accession include the three States in which the highest number of European patents was in force in the year preceding the year in which the signature of the Agreement takes place, or on the first day of the fourth month after the date of entry into force of the amendments to Regulation (EU) No 1215/2012[2] concerning its relationship with this Agreement, whichever is the latest,

NOTES

1 Regulation (EU) No 1257/2012 of the European Parliament and of the Council of 17 December 2012 implementing enhanced cooperation in the area of the creation of unitary patent protection (OJ L361, 31.12.2012, p 1) including any subsequent amendments.

2 Regulation (EU) No 1215/2012 of the European Parliament and of the Council of 12 December 2012 on jurisdiction and the recognition and enforcement of judgments in civil and commercial matters (OJ L351, 20.12.2012, p 1) including any subsequent amendments.

HAVE AGREED AS FOLLOWS:

PART I
GENERAL AND INSTITUTIONAL PROVISIONS

CHAPTER I
GENERAL PROVISIONS

[1.1009]
Article 1
Unified Patent Court

A Unified Patent Court for the settlement of disputes relating to European patents and European patents with unitary effect is hereby established.

The Unified Patent Court shall be a court common to the Contracting Member States and thus subject to the same obligations under Union law as any national court of the Contracting Member States.

[1.1010]
Article 2
Definitions

For the purposes of this Agreement:

(a) "Court" means the Unified Patent Court created by this Agreement.
(b) "Member State" means a Member State of the European Union.
(c) "Contracting Member State" means a Member State party to this Agreement.
(d) "EPC" means the Convention on the Grant of European Patents of 5 October 1973, including any subsequent amendments.
(e) "European patent" means a patent granted under the provisions of the EPC, which does not benefit from unitary effect by virtue of Regulation (EU) No 1257/2012.
(f) "European patent with unitary effect" means a patent granted under the provisions of the EPC which benefits from unitary effect by virtue of Regulation (EU) No 1257/2012.
(g) "Patent" means a European patent and/or a European patent with unitary effect.
(h) "Supplementary protection certificate" means a supplementary protection certificate granted under Regulation (EC) No 469/2009[1] or under Regulation (EC) No 1610/96.[2]
(i) "Statute" means the Statute of the Court as set out in Annex I, which shall be an integral part of this Agreement.
(j) "Rules of Procedure" means the Rules of Procedure of the Court, as established in accordance with Article 41.

NOTES

1 Regulation (EC) No 469/2009 of the European Parliament and of the Council of 6 May 2009 concerning the supplementary protection certificate for medicinal products, (OJ L152, 16.6.2009, p 1) including any subsequent amendments.

2 Regulation (EC) No 1610/96 of the European Parliament and of the Council of 23 July 1996 concerning the creation of a supplementary certificate for plant protection products, (OJ L198, 8.8.1996, p 30) including any subsequent amendments.

[1.1011]
Article 3
Scope of application

This Agreement shall apply to any:

(a) European patent with unitary effect;
(b) supplementary protection certificate issued for a product protected by a patent;
(c) European patent which has not yet lapsed at the date of entry into force of this Agreement or was granted after that date, without prejudice to Article 83; and
(d) European patent application which is pending at the date of entry into force of this Agreement or which is filed after that date, without prejudice to Article 83.

[1.1012]
Article 4
Legal status

(1) The Court shall have legal personality in each Contracting Member State and shall enjoy the most extensive legal capacity accorded to legal persons under the national law of that State.
(2) The Court shall be represented by the President of the Court of Appeal who shall be elected in accordance with the Statute.

[1.1013]
Article 5
Liability

(1) The contractual liability of the Court shall be governed by the law applicable to the contract in question in accordance with Regulation (EC) No. 593/2008[1] (Rome I), where applicable, or failing that in accordance with the law of the Member State of the court seized.
(2) The non-contractual liability of the Court in respect of any damage caused by it or its staff in the performance of their duties, to the extent that it is not a civil and commercial matter within the meaning of Regulation (EC) No. 864/20071[2] (Rome II), shall be governed by the law of the Contracting Member State in which the damage occurred. This provision is without prejudice to the application of Article 22.
(3) The court with jurisdiction to settle disputes under paragraph 2 shall be a court of the Contracting Member State in which the damage occurred.

NOTES

1 Regulation (EC) No 593/2008 of the European Parliament and of the Council of 17 June 2008 on the law applicable to contractual obligations (Rome I) (OJ L177, 4.7.2008, p 6) including any subsequent amendments.

2 Regulation (EC) No 864/2007 of the European Parliament and of the Council of 11 July 2007 on the law applicable to non-contractual obligations (Rome II) (OJ L199, 31.7.2007, p 40) including any subsequent amendments.

CHAPTER II
INSTITUTIONAL PROVISIONS

[1.1014]
Article 6
The Court

(1) The Court shall comprise a Court of First Instance, a Court of Appeal and a Registry.
(2) The Court shall perform the functions assigned to it by this Agreement.

[1.1015]
Article 7
The Court of First Instance

(1) The Court of First Instance shall comprise a central division as well as local and regional divisions.
(2) The central division shall have its seat in Paris, with sections in London and Munich. The cases before the central division shall be distributed in accordance with Annex II, which shall form an integral part of this Agreement.
(3) A local division shall be set up in a Contracting Member State upon its request in accordance with the Statute. A Contracting Member State hosting a local division shall designate its seat.
(4) An additional local division shall be set up in a Contracting Member State upon its request for every one hundred patent cases per calendar year that have been commenced in that Contracting Member State during three successive years prior to or subsequent to the date of entry into force of this Agreement. The number of local divisions in one Contracting Member State shall not exceed four.
(5) A regional division shall be set up for two or more Contracting Member States, upon their request in accordance with the Statute. Such Contracting Member States shall designate the seat of the division concerned. The regional division may hear cases in multiple locations.

[1.1016]
Article 8
Composition of the panels of the Court of First Instance

(1) Any panel of the Court of First Instance shall have a multinational composition. Without prejudice to paragraph 5 of this Article and to Article 33(3)(a), it shall sit in a composition of three judges.
(2) Any panel of a local division in a Contracting Member State where, during a period of three successive years prior or subsequent to the entry into force of this Agreement, less than fifty patent cases per calendar year on average have been commenced shall sit in a composition of one legally qualified judge who is a national of the Contracting Member State hosting the local division concerned and two legally qualified judges who are not nationals of the Contracting Member State concerned and are allocated from the Pool of Judges in accordance with Article 18(3) on a case by case basis.
(3) Notwithstanding paragraph 2, any panel of a local division in a Contracting Member State where, during a period of three successive years prior or subsequent to the entry into force of this Agreement, fifty or more patent cases per calendar year on average have been commenced, shall sit in a composition of two legally qualified judges who are nationals of the Contracting Member State hosting the local division concerned and one legally qualified judge who is not a national of the Contracting Member State concerned allocated from the Pool of Judges in accordance with Article 18(3). Such third judge shall serve at the local division on a long term basis, where this is necessary for the efficient functioning of divisions with a high work load.
(4) Any panel of a regional division shall sit in a composition of two legally qualified judges chosen from a regional list of judges, who shall be nationals of the Contracting Member States concerned, and one legally qualified judge who shall not be a national of the Contracting Member States concerned and who shall be allocated from the Pool of Judges in accordance with Article 18(3).
(5) Upon request by one of the parties, any panel of a local or regional division shall request the President of the Court of First Instance to allocate from the Pool of Judges in accordance with Article 18(3) an additional technically qualified judge with qualifications and experience in the field of technology concerned. Moreover, any panel of a local or regional division may, after having heard the parties, submit such request on its own initiative, where it deems this appropriate.
In cases where such a technically qualified judge is allocated, no further technically qualified judge may be allocated under Article 33(3)(a).
(6) Any panel of the central division shall sit in a composition of two legally qualified judges who are nationals of different Contracting Member States and one technically qualified judge allocated from the Pool of Judges in accordance with Article 18(3) with qualifications and experience in the field of technology concerned. However, any panel of the central division dealing with actions under Article 32(1)(i) shall sit in a composition of three legally qualified judges who are nationals of different Contracting Member States.
(7) Notwithstanding paragraphs 1 to 6 and in accordance with the Rules of Procedure, parties may agree to have their case heard by a single legally qualified judge.

(8) Any panel of the Court of First Instance shall be chaired by a legally qualified judge.

[1.1017]
Article 9
The Court of Appeal

(1) Any panel of the Court of Appeal shall sit in a multinational composition of five judges. It shall sit in a composition of three legally qualified judges who are nationals of different Contracting Member States and two technically qualified judges with qualifications and experience in the field of technology concerned. Those technically qualified judges shall be assigned to the panel by the President of the Court of Appeal from the pool of judges in accordance with Article 18.
(2) Notwithstanding paragraph 1, a panel dealing with actions under Article 32(1)(i) shall sit in a composition of three legally qualified judges who are nationals of different Contracting Member States.
(3) Any panel of the Court of Appeal shall be chaired by a legally qualified judge.
(4) The panels of the Court of Appeal shall be set up in accordance with the Statute.
(5) The Court of Appeal shall have its seat in Luxembourg.

[1.1018]
Article 10
The Registry

(1) A Registry shall be set up at the seat of the Court of Appeal. It shall be managed by the Registrar and perform the functions assigned to it in accordance with the Statute. Subject to conditions set out in this Agreement and the Rules of Procedure, the register kept by the Registry shall be public.
(2) Sub-registries shall be set up at all divisions of the Court of First Instance.
(3) The Registry shall keep records of all cases before the Court. Upon filing, the sub-registry concerned shall notify every case to the Registry.
(4) The Court shall appoint the Registrar in accordance with Article 22 of the Statute and lay down the rules governing the Registrar's service.

[1.1019]
Article 11
Committees

An Administrative Committee, a Budget Committee and an Advisory Committee shall be set up in order to ensure the effective implementation and operation of this Agreement. They shall in particular exercise the duties foreseen by this Agreement and the Statute.

[1.1020]
Article 12
The Administrative Committee

(1) The Administrative Committee shall be composed of one representative of each Contracting Member State. The European Commission shall be represented at the meetings of the Administrative Committee as observer.
(2) Each Contracting Member State shall have one vote.
(3) The Administrative Committee shall adopt its decisions by a majority of three quarters of the Contracting Member States represented and voting, except where this Agreement or the Statute provides otherwise.
(4) The Administrative Committee shall adopt its rules of procedure.
(5) The Administrative Committee shall elect a chairperson from among its members for a term of three years. That term shall be renewable.

[1.1021]
Article 13
The Budget Committee

(1) The Budget Committee shall be composed of one representative of each Contracting Member State.
(2) Each Contracting Member State shall have one vote.
(3) The Budget Committee shall take its decisions by a simple majority of the representatives of the Contracting Member States. However, a majority of three-quarters of the representatives of Contracting Member States shall be required for the adoption of the budget.
(4) The Budget Committee shall adopt its rules of procedure.
(5) The Budget Committee shall elect a chairperson from among its members for a term of three years. That term shall be renewable.

[1.1022]
Article 14
The Advisory Committee

(1) The Advisory Committee shall:
  (a) assist the Administrative Committee in the preparation of the appointment of judges of the Court;

(b) make proposals to the Presidium referred to in Article 15 of the Statute on the guidelines for the training framework for judges referred to in Article 19; and

(c) deliver opinions to the Administrative Committee concerning the requirements for qualifications referred to in Article 48(2).

(2) The Advisory Committee shall comprise patent judges and practitioners in patent law and patent litigation with the highest recognised competence. They shall be appointed, in accordance with the procedure laid down in the Statute, for a term of six years. That term shall be renewable.

(3) The composition of the Advisory Committee shall ensure a broad range of relevant expertise and the representation of each of the Contracting Member States. The members of the Advisory Committee shall be completely independent in the performance of their duties and shall not be bound by any instructions.

(4) The Advisory Committee shall adopt its rules of procedure.

(5) The Advisory Committee shall elect a chairperson from among its members for a term of three years. That term shall be renewable.

CHAPTER III
JUDGES OF THE COURT

[1.1023]
Article 15
Eligibility criteria for the appointment of judges

(1) The Court shall comprise both legally qualified judges and technically qualified judges. Judges shall ensure the highest standards of competence and shall have proven experience in the field of patent litigation.

(2) Legally qualified judges shall possess the qualifications required for appointment to judicial offices in a Contracting Member State.

(3) Technically qualified judges shall have a university degree and proven expertise in a field of technology. They shall also have proven knowledge of civil law and procedure relevant in patent litigation.

[1.1024]
Article 16
Appointment procedure

(1) The Advisory Committee shall establish a list of the most suitable candidates to be appointed as judges of the Court, in accordance with the Statute.

(2) On the basis of that list, the Administrative Committee shall appoint the judges of the Court acting by common accord.

(3) The implementing provisions for the appointment of judges are set out in the Statute.

[1.1025]
Article 17
Judicial independence and impartiality

(1) The Court, its judges and the Registrar shall enjoy judicial independence. In the performance of their duties, the judges shall not be bound by any instructions.

(2) Legally qualified judges, as well as technically qualified judges who are full-time judges of the Court, may not engage in any other occupation, whether gainful or not, unless an exception is granted by the Administrative Committee.

(3) Notwithstanding paragraph 2, the exercise of the office of judges shall not exclude the exercise of other judicial functions at national level.

(4) The exercise of the office of technically qualified judges who are part-time judges of the Court shall not exclude the exercise of other functions provided there is no conflict of interest.

(5) In case of a conflict of interest, the judge concerned shall not take part in proceedings. Rules governing conflicts of interest are set out in the Statute.

[1.1026]
Article 18
Pool of Judges

(1) A Pool of Judges shall be established in accordance with the Statute.

(2) The Pool of Judges shall be composed of all legally qualified judges and technically qualified judges from the Court of First Instance who are full-time or part-time judges of the Court. The Pool of Judges shall include at least one technically qualified judge per field of technology with the relevant qualifications and experience. The technically qualified judges from the Pool of Judges shall also be available to the Court of Appeal.

(3) Where so provided by this Agreement or the Statute, the judges from the Pool of Judges shall be allocated to the division concerned by the President of the Court of First Instance. The allocation of judges shall be based on their legal or technical expertise, linguistic skills and relevant experience. The allocation of judges shall guarantee the same high quality of work and the same high level of legal and technical expertise in all panels of the Court of First Instance.

[1.1027]
Article 19
Training framework

(1) A training framework for judges, the details of which are set out in the Statute, shall be set up in order to improve and increase available patent litigation expertise and to ensure a broad geographic distribution of such specific knowledge and experience. The facilities for that framework shall be situated in Budapest.

(2) The training framework shall in particular focus on:

(a) internships in national patent courts or divisions of the Court of First Instance hearing a substantial number of patent litigation cases;
(b) improvement of linguistic skills;
(c) technical aspects of patent law;
(d) the dissemination of knowledge and experience in civil procedure for technically qualified judges;
(e) the preparation of candidate-judges.

(3) The training framework shall provide for continuous training. Regular meetings shall be organised between all judges of the Court in order to discuss developments in patent law and to ensure the consistency of the Court's case law.

CHAPTER IV
THE PRIMACY OF UNION LAW, LIABILITY AND RESPONSIBILITY OF THE CONTRACTING MEMBER STATES

[1.1028]
Article 20
Primacy of and respect for Union law

The Court shall apply Union law in its entirety and shall respect its primacy.

[1.1029]
Article 21
Requests for preliminary rulings

As a court common to the Contracting Member States and as part of their judicial system, the Court shall cooperate with the Court of Justice of the European Union to ensure the correct application and uniform interpretation of Union law, as any national court, in accordance with Article 267 TFEU in particular. Decisions of the Court of Justice of the European Union shall be binding on the Court.

[1.1030]
Article 22
Liability for damage caused by infringements of Union law

(1) The Contracting Member States are jointly and severally liable for damage resulting from an infringement of Union law by the Court of Appeal, in accordance with Union law concerning non-contractual liability of Member States for damage caused by their national courts breaching Union law.

(2) An action for such damages shall be brought against the Contracting Member State where the claimant has its residence or principal place of business or, in the absence of residence or principal place of business, place of business, before the competent authority of that Contracting Member State. Where the claimant does not have its residence, or principal place of business or, in the absence of residence or principal place of business, place of business in a Contracting Member State, the claimant may bring such an action against the Contracting Member State where the Court of Appeal has its seat, before the competent authority of that Contracting Member State. The competent authority shall apply the *lex fori*, with the exception of its private international law, to all questions not regulated by Union law or by this Agreement. The claimant shall be entitled to obtain the entire amount of damages awarded by the competent authority from the Contracting Member State against which the action was brought.

(3) The Contracting Member State that has paid damages is entitled to obtain proportional contribution, established in accordance with the method laid down in Article 37(3) and (4), from the other Contracting Member States. The detailed rules governing the Contracting Member States' contribution under this paragraph shall be determined by the Administrative Committee.

[1.1031]
Article 23
Responsibility of the Contracting Member States

Actions of the Court are directly attributable to each Contracting Member State individually, including for the purposes of Articles 258, 259 and 260 TFEU, and to all Contracting Member States collectively.

CHAPTER V
SOURCES OF LAW AND SUBSTANTIVE LAW

[1.1032]
Article 24
Sources of law

(1) In full compliance with Article 20, when hearing a case brought before it under this Agreement, the Court shall base its decisions on:

(a) Union law, including Regulation (EU) No 1257/2012 and Regulation (EU) No 1260/2012;[1]
(b) this Agreement;
(c) the EPC;
(d) other international agreements applicable to patents and binding on all the Contracting Member States; and
(e) national law.

(2) To the extent that the Court shall base its decisions on national law, including where relevant the law of non-contracting States, the applicable law shall be determined:

(a) by directly applicable provisions of Union law containing private international law rules, or
(b) in the absence of directly applicable provisions of Union law or where the latter do not apply, by international instruments containing private international law rules; or
(c) in the absence of provisions referred to in points (a) and (b), by national provisions on private international law as determined by the Court.

(3) The law of non-contracting States shall apply when designated by application of the rules referred to in paragraph 2, in particular in relation to Articles 25 to 28, 54, 55, 64, 68 and 72.

NOTES

[1] Council Regulation (EU) No 1260/2012 of 17 December 2012 implementing enhanced cooperation in the area of the creation of unitary patent protection with regard to the applicable translation arrangements (OJ L361, 31.12.2012, p 89) including any subsequent amendments.

[1.1033]
Article 25
Right to prevent the direct use of the invention

A patent shall confer on its proprietor the right to prevent any third party not having the proprietor's consent from the following:

(a) making, offering, placing on the market or using a product which is the subject matter of the patent, or importing or storing the product for those purposes;
(b) using a process which is the subject matter of the patent or, where the third party knows, or should have known, that the use of the process is prohibited without the consent of the patent proprietor, offering the process for use within the territory of the Contracting Member States in which that patent has effect;
(c) offering, placing on the market, using, or importing or storing for those purposes a product obtained directly by a process which is the subject matter of the patent.

[1.1034]
Article 26
Right to prevent the indirect use of the invention

(1) A patent shall confer on its proprietor the right to prevent any third party not having the proprietor's consent from supplying or offering to supply, within the territory of the Contracting Member States in which that patent has effect, any person other than a party entitled to exploit the patented invention, with means, relating to an essential element of that invention, for putting it into effect therein, when the third party knows, or should have known, that those means are suitable and intended for putting that invention into effect.

(2) Paragraph 1 shall not apply when the means are staple commercial products, except where the third party induces the person supplied to perform any of the acts prohibited by Article 25.

(3) Persons performing the acts referred to in Article 27(a) to (e) shall not be considered to be parties entitled to exploit the invention within the meaning of paragraph 1.

[1.1035]
Article 27
Limitations of the effects of a patent

The rights conferred by a patent shall not extend to any of the following:

(a) acts done privately and for non-commercial purposes;
(b) acts done for experimental purposes relating to the subject matter of the patented invention;
(c) the use of biological material for the purpose of breeding, or discovering and developing other plant varieties;
(d) the acts allowed pursuant to Article 13(6) of Directive 2001/82/EC[1] or Article 10(6) of Directive 2001/83/EC[2] in respect of any patent covering the product within the meaning of either of those Directives;
(e) the extemporaneous preparation by a pharmacy, for individual cases, of a medicine in accordance with a medical prescription or acts concerning the medicine so prepared;

(f) the use of the patented invention on board vessels of countries of the International Union for the Protection of Industrial Property (Paris Union) or members of the World Trade Organisation, other than those Contracting Member States in which that patent has effect, in the body of such vessel, in the machinery, tackle, gear and other accessories, when such vessels temporarily or accidentally enter the waters of a Contracting Member State in which that patent has effect, provided that the invention is used there exclusively for the needs of the vessel;

(h) the acts specified in Article 27 of the Convention on International Civil Aviation of 7 December 1944,[3] where these acts concern the aircraft of a country party to that Convention other than a Contracting Member State in which that patent has effect;

(i) the use by a farmer of the product of his harvest for propagation or multiplication by him on his own holding, provided that the plant propagating material was sold or otherwise commercialised to the farmer by or with the consent of the patent proprietor for agricultural use. The extent and the conditions for this use correspond to those under Article 14 of Regulation (EC) No. 2100/94;[4]

(j) the use by a farmer of protected livestock for an agricultural purpose, provided that the breeding stock or other animal reproductive material were sold or otherwise commercialised to the farmer by or with the consent of the patent proprietor. Such use includes making the animal or other animal reproductive material available for the purposes of pursuing the farmer's agricultural activity, but not the sale thereof within the framework of, or for the purpose of, a commercial reproductive activity;

(k) the acts and the use of the obtained information as allowed under Articles 5 and 6 of Directive 2009/24/EC,[5] in particular, by its provisions on decompilation and interoperability; and

(l) the acts allowed pursuant to Article 10 of Directive 98/44/EC.[6]

NOTES

[1] Directive 2001/82/EC of the European Parliament and of the Council of 6 November 2001 on the Community code relating to veterinary medicinal products (OJ L311, 28.11.2001, p 1) including any subsequent amendments.

[2] Directive 2001/83/EC of the European Parliament and of the Council of 6 November 2001 on the Community code relating to medicinal products for human use (OJ L311, 28.11.2001, p 67) including any subsequent amendments. (g) the use of the patented invention in the construction or operation of aircraft or land vehicles or other means of transport of countries of the International Union for the Protection of Industrial Property (Paris Union) or members of the World Trade Organisation, other than those Contracting Member States in which that patent has effect, or of accessories to such aircraft or land vehicles, when these temporarily or accidentally enter the territory of a Contracting Member State in which that patent has effect;

[3] International Civil Aviation Organization (ICAO), "Chicago Convention", Document 7300/9 (9th edition, 2006)

[4] Council Regulation (EC) No 2100/94 of 27 July 1994 on Community plant variety rights (OJEC L227, 1.9.1994, p 1) including any subsequent amendments.

[5] Directive 2009/24/EC of the European Parliament and of the Council of 23 April 2009 on the legal protection of computer programs (OJ L111, 05/05/2009, p 16) including any subsequent amendments.

[6] Directive 98/44/EC of the European Parliament and of the Council of 6 July 1998 on the legal protection of biotechnological inventions (OJ L213, 30.7.1998, p 13) including any subsequent amendments.

[1.1036]
Article 28
Right based on prior use of the invention

Any person, who, if a national patent had been granted in respect of an invention, would have had, in a Contracting Member State, a right based on prior use of that invention or a right of personal possession of that invention, shall enjoy, in that Contracting Member State, the same rights in respect of a patent for the same invention.

[1.1037]
Article 29
Exhaustion of the rights conferred by a European patent

The rights conferred by a European patent shall not extend to acts concerning a product covered by that patent after that product has been placed on the market in the Union by, or with the consent of, the patent proprietor, unless there are legitimate grounds for the patent proprietor to oppose further commercialisation of the product.

[1.1038]
Article 30
Effects of supplementary protection certificates

A supplementary protection certificate shall confer the same rights as conferred by the patent and shall be subject to the same limitations and the same obligations.

CHAPTER VI
INTERNATIONAL JURISDICTION AND COMPETENCE

[1.1039]
Article 31
International jurisdiction

The international jurisdiction of the Court shall be established in accordance with Regulation (EU) No 1215/2012 or, where applicable, on the basis of the Convention on jurisdiction and the recognition and enforcement of judgments in civil and commercial matters (Lugano Convention).[1]

NOTES

[1] Convention on jurisdiction and the recognition and enforcement of judgments in civil and commercial matters, done at Lugano on 30 October 2007, including any subsequent amendments.

[1.1040]
Article 32
Competence of the Court

(1) The Court shall have exclusive competence in respect of:

(a) actions for actual or threatened infringements of patents and supplementary protection certificates and related defences, including counterclaims concerning licences;
(b) actions for declarations of non-infringement of patents and supplementary protection certificates;
(c) actions for provisional and protective measures and injunctions;
(d) actions for revocation of patents and for declaration of invalidity of supplementary protection certificates;
(e) counterclaims for revocation of patents and for declaration of invalidity of supplementary protection certificates;
(f) actions for damages or compensation derived from the provisional protection conferred by a published European patent application;
(g) actions relating to the use of the invention prior to the granting of the patent or to the right based on prior use of the invention;
(h) actions for compensation for licences on the basis of Article 8 of Regulation (EU) No 1257/2012; and
(i) actions concerning decisions of the European Patent Office in carrying out the tasks referred to in Article 9 of Regulation (EU) No 1257/2012.

(2) The national courts of the Contracting Member States shall remain competent for actions relating to patents and supplementary protection certificates which do not come within the exclusive competence of the Court.

[1.1041]
Article 33
Competence of the divisions of the Court of First Instance

(1) Without prejudice to paragraph 6 of this Article, actions referred to in Article 32(1)(a), (c), (f) and (g) shall be brought before:

(a) the local division hosted by the Contracting Member State where the actual or threatened infringement has occurred or may occur, or the regional division in which that Contracting Member State participates; or
(b) the local division hosted by the Contracting Member State where the defendant or, in the case of multiple defendants, one of the defendants has its residence, or principal place of business, or in the absence of residence or principal place of business, its place of business, or the regional division in which that Contracting Member State participates. An action may be brought against multiple defendants only where the defendants have a commercial relationship and where the action relates to the same alleged infringement.

Actions referred to in Article 32(1)(h) shall be brought before the local or regional division in accordance with point (b) of the first subparagraph.

Actions against defendants having their residence, or principal place of business or, in the absence of residence or principal place of business, their place of business, outside the territory of the Contracting Member States shall be brought before the local or regional division in accordance with point (a) of the first subparagraph or before the central division.

If the Contracting Member State concerned does not host a local division and does not participate in a regional division, actions shall be brought before the central division.

(2) If an action referred to in Article 32(1)(a), (c), (f), (g) or (h) is pending before a division of the Court of First Instance, any action referred to in Article 32(1)(a), (c), (f), (g) or (h) between the same parties on the same patent may not be brought before any other division.

If an action referred to in Article 32(1)(a) is pending before a regional division and the infringement has occurred in the territories of three or more regional divisions, the regional division concerned shall, at the request of the defendant, refer the case to the central division.

In case an action between the same parties on the same patent is brought before several different divisions, the division first seized shall be competent for the whole case and any division seized later shall declare the action inadmissible in accordance with the Rules of Procedure.

(3) A counterclaim for revocation as referred to in Article 32(1)(e) may be brought in the case of an action for infringement as referred to in Article 32(1)(a). The local or regional division concerned shall, after having heard the parties, have the discretion either to:

(a) proceed with both the action for infringement and with the counterclaim for revocation and request the President of the Court of First Instance to allocate from the Pool of Judges in accordance with Article 18(3) a technically qualified judge with qualifications and experience in the field of technology concerned.

(b) refer the counterclaim for revocation for decision to the central division and suspend or proceed with the action for infringement; or

(c) with the agreement of the parties, refer the case for decision to the central division.

(4) Actions referred to in Article 32(1)(b) and (d) shall be brought before the central division. If, however, an action for infringement as referred to in Article 32(1)(a) between the same parties relating to the same patent has been brought before a local or a regional division, these actions may only be brought before the same local or regional division.

(5) If an action for revocation as referred to in Article 32(1)(d) is pending before the central division, an action for infringement as referred to in Article 32(1)(a) between the same parties relating to the same patent may be brought before any division in accordance with paragraph 1 of this Article or before the central division. The local or regional division concerned shall have the discretion to proceed in accordance with paragraph 3 of this Article.

(6) An action for declaration of non-infringement as referred to in Article 32(1)(b) pending before the central division shall be stayed once an infringement action as referred to in Article 32(1)(a) between the same parties or between the holder of an exclusive licence and the party requesting a declaration of non-infringement relating to the same patent is brought before a local or regional division within three months of the date on which the action was initiated before the central division.

(7) Parties may agree to bring actions referred to in Article 32(1)(a) to (h) before the division of their choice, including the central division.

(8) Actions referred to in Article 32(1)(d) and (e) can be brought without the applicant having to file notice of opposition with the European Patent Office.

(9) Actions referred to in Article 32(1)(i) shall be brought before the central division.

(10) A party shall inform the Court of any pending revocation, limitation or opposition proceedings before the European Patent Office, and of any request for accelerated processing before the European Patent Office. The Court may stay its proceedings when a rapid decision may be expected from the European Patent Office.

[1.1042]
Article 34
Territorial scope of decisions

Decisions of the Court shall cover, in the case of a European patent, the territory of those Contracting Member States for which the European patent has effect.

CHAPTER VII
PATENT MEDIATION AND ARBITRATION

[1.1043]
Article 35
Patent mediation and arbitration centre

(1) A patent mediation and arbitration centre ("the Centre") is hereby established. It shall have its seats in Ljubljana and Lisbon.

(2) The Centre shall provide facilities for mediation and arbitration of patent disputes falling within the scope of this Agreement. Article 82 shall apply mutatis mutandis to any settlement reached through the use of the facilities of the Centre, including through mediation. However, a patent may not be revoked or limited in mediation or arbitration proceedings.

(3) The Centre shall establish Mediation and Arbitration Rules.

(4) The Centre shall draw up a list of mediators and arbitrators to assist the parties in the settlement of their dispute.

PART II
FINANCIAL PROVISIONS

[1.1044]
Article 36
Budget of the Court

(1) The budget of the Court shall be financed by the Court's own financial revenues and, at least in the transitional period referred to in Article 83 as necessary, by contributions from the Contracting Member States. The budget shall be balanced.

(2) The Court's own financial revenues shall comprise court fees and other revenues.
(3) Court fees shall be fixed by the Administrative Committee. They shall consist of a fixed fee, combined with a value-based fee above a pre-defined ceiling. The Court fees shall be fixed at such a level as to ensure a right balance between the principle of fair access to justice, in particular for small and medium-sized enterprises, micro-entities, natural persons, non-profit organisations, universities and public research organisations and an adequate contribution of the parties for the costs incurred by the Court, recognising the economic benefits to the parties involved, and the objective of a self-financing Court with balanced finances. The level of the Court fees shall be reviewed periodically by the Administrative Committee. Targeted support measures for small and medium-sized enterprises and micro entities may be considered.
(4) If the Court is unable to balance its budget out of its own resources, the Contracting Member States shall remit to it special financial contributions.

[1.1045]
Article 37
Financing of the Court
(1) The operating costs of the Court shall be covered by the budget of the Court, in accordance with the Statute. Contracting Member States setting up a local division shall provide the facilities necessary for that purpose. Contracting Member States sharing a regional division shall provide jointly the facilities necessary for that purpose.
Contracting Member States hosting the central division, its sections or the Court of Appeal shall provide the facilities necessary for that purpose. During an initial transitional period of seven years starting from the date of the entry into force of this Agreement, the Contracting Member States concerned shall also provide administrative support staff, without prejudice to the Statute of that staff.
(2) On the date of entry into force of this Agreement, the Contracting Member States shall provide the initial financial contributions necessary for the setting up of the Court.
(3) During the initial transitional period of seven years, starting from the date of the entry into force of this Agreement, the contribution by each Contracting Member State having ratified or acceded to the Agreement before the entry into force thereof shall be calculated on the basis of the number of European patents having effect in the territory of that State on the date of entry into force of this Agreement and the number of European patents with respect to which actions for infringement or for revocation have been brought before the national courts of that State in the three years preceding entry into force of this Agreement.
During the same initial transitional period of seven years, for Member States which ratify, or accede to, this Agreement after the entry into force thereof, the contributions shall be calculated on the basis of the number of European patents having effect in the territory of the ratifying or acceding Member State on the date of the ratification or accession and the number of European patents with respect to which actions for infringement or for revocation have been brought before the national courts of the ratifying or acceding Member State in the three years preceding the ratification or accession.
(4) After the end of the initial transitional period of seven years, by which the Court is expected to have become self-financing, should contributions by the Contracting Member States become necessary, they shall be determined in accordance with the scale for the distribution of annual renewal fees for European patents with unitary effect applicable at the time the contribution becomes necessary.

[1.1046]
Article 38
Financing of the training framework for judges
The training framework for judges shall be financed by the budget of the Court.

[1.1047]
Article 39
Financing of the Centre
The operating costs of the Centre shall be financed by the budget of the Court.

PART III
ORGANISATION AND PROCEDURAL PROVISIONS

CHAPTER I
GENERAL PROVISIONS

[1.1048]
Article 40
Statute
(1) The Statute shall lay down the details of the organisation and functioning of the Court.

(2) The Statute is annexed to this Agreement. The Statute may be amended by decision of the Administrative Committee, on the basis of a proposal of the Court or a proposal of a Contracting Member State after consultation with the Court. However, such amendments shall not contradict or alter this Agreement.

(3) The Statute shall guarantee that the functioning of the Court is organised in the most efficient and cost-effective manner and shall ensure equitable access to justice.

[1.1049]
Article 41
Rules of Procedure

(1) The Rules of Procedure shall lay down the details of the proceedings before the Court. They shall comply with this Agreement and the Statute.

(2) The Rules of Procedure shall be adopted by the Administrative Committee on the basis of broad consultations with stakeholders. The prior opinion of the European Commission on the compatibility of the Rules of Procedure with Union law shall be requested.

The Rules of Procedure may be amended by a decision of the Administrative Committee, on the basis of a proposal from the Court and after consultation with the European Commission. However, such amendments shall not contradict or alter this Agreement or the Statute.

(3) The Rules of Procedure shall guarantee that the decisions of the Court are of the highest quality and that proceedings are organised in the most efficient and cost effective manner. They shall ensure a fair balance between the legitimate interests of all parties. They shall provide for the required level of discretion of judges without impairing the predictability of proceedings for the parties.

[1.1050]
Article 42
Proportionality and fairness

(1) The Court shall deal with litigation in ways which are proportionate to the importance and complexity thereof.

(2) The Court shall ensure that the rules, procedures and remedies provided for in this Agreement and in the Statute are used in a fair and equitable manner and do not distort competition.

[1.1051]
Article 43
Case management

The Court shall actively manage the cases before it in accordance with the Rules of Procedure without impairing the freedom of the parties to determine the subject-matter of, and the supporting evidence for, their case.

[1.1052]
Article 44
Electronic procedures

The Court shall make best use of electronic procedures, such as the electronic filing of submissions of the parties and stating of evidence in electronic form, as well as video conferencing, in accordance with the Rules of Procedure.

[1.1053]
Article 45
Public proceedings

The proceedings shall be open to the public unless the Court decides to make them confidential, to the extent necessary, in the interest of one of the parties or other affected persons, or in the general interest of justice or public order.

[1.1054]
Article 46
Legal capacity

Any natural or legal person, or any body equivalent to a legal person entitled to initiate proceedings in accordance with its national law, shall have the capacity to be a party to the proceedings before the Court.

[1.1055]
Article 47
Parties

(1) The patent proprietor shall be entitled to bring actions before the Court.

(2) Unless the licensing agreement provides otherwise, the holder of an exclusive licence in respect of a patent shall be entitled to bring actions before the Court under the same circumstances as the patent proprietor, provided that the patent proprietor is given prior notice.

(3) The holder of a non-exclusive licence shall not be entitled to bring actions before the Court, unless the patent proprietor is given prior notice and in so far as expressly permitted by the licence agreement.

(4) In actions brought by a licence holder, the patent proprietor shall be entitled to join the action before the Court.

(5) The validity of a patent cannot be contested in an action for infringement brought by the holder of a licence where the patent proprietor does not take part in the proceedings. The party in an action for infringement wanting to contest the validity of a patent shall have to bring actions against the patent proprietor.

(6) Any other natural or legal person, or any body entitled to bring actions in accordance with its national law, who is concerned by a patent, may bring actions in accordance with the Rules of Procedure.

(7) Any natural or legal person, or any body entitled to bring actions in accordance with its national law and who is affected by a decision of the European Patent Office in carrying out the tasks referred to in Article 9 of Regulation (EU) No 1257/2012 is entitled to bring actions under Article 32(1)(i).

[1.1056]
Article 48
Representation

(1) Parties shall be represented by lawyers authorised to practise before a court of a Contracting Member State.

(2) Parties may alternatively be represented by European Patent Attorneys who are entitled to act as professional representatives before the European Patent Office pursuant to Article 134 of the EPC and who have appropriate qualifications such as a European Patent Litigation Certificate.

(3) The requirements for qualifications pursuant to paragraph 2 shall be established by the Administrative Committee. A list of European Patent Attorneys entitled to represent parties before the Court shall be kept by the Registrar.

(4) Representatives of the parties may be assisted by patent attorneys, who shall be allowed to speak at hearings of the Court in accordance with the Rules of Procedure.

(5) Representatives of the parties shall enjoy the rights and immunities necessary for the independent exercise of their duties, including the privilege from disclosure in proceedings before the Court in respect of communications between a representative and the party or any other person, under the conditions laid down in the Rules of Procedure, unless such privilege is expressly waived by the party concerned.

(6) Representatives of the parties shall be obliged not to misrepresent cases or facts before the Court either knowingly or with good reasons to know.

(7) Representation in accordance with paragraphs 1 and 2 of this Article shall not be required in proceedings under Article 32(1)(i).

CHAPTER II
LANGUAGE OF PROCEEDINGS

[1.1057]
Article 49
Language of proceedings at the Court of First Instance

(1) The language of proceedings before any local or regional division shall be an official European Union language which is the official language or one of the official languages of the Contracting Member State hosting the relevant division, or the official language(s) designated by Contracting Member States sharing a regional division.

(2) Notwithstanding paragraph 1, Contracting Member States may designate one or more of the official languages of the European Patent Office as the language of proceedings of their local or regional division.

(3) The parties may agree on the use of the language in which the patent was granted as the language of proceedings, subject to approval by the competent panel. If the panel does not approve their choice, the parties may request that the case be referred to the central division.

(4) With the agreement of the parties the competent panel may, on grounds of convenience and fairness, decide on the use of the language in which the patent was granted as the language of proceedings.

(5) At the request of one of the parties and after having heard the other parties and the competent panel, the President of the Court of First Instance may, on grounds of fairness and taking into account all relevant circumstances, including the position of parties, in particular the position of the defendant, decide on the use of the language in which the patent was granted as language of proceedings. In this case the President of the Court of First Instance shall assess the need for specific translation and interpretation arrangements.

(6) The language of proceedings at the central division shall be the language in which the patent concerned was granted.

[1.1058]
Article 50
Language of proceedings at the Court of Appeal

(1) The language of proceedings before the Court of Appeal shall be the language of proceedings before the Court of First Instance.

(2) Notwithstanding paragraph 1 the parties may agree on the use of the language in which the patent was granted as the language of proceedings.

(3) In exceptional cases and to the extent deemed appropriate, the Court of Appeal may decide on another official language of a Contracting Member State as the language of proceedings for the whole or part of the proceedings, subject to agreement by the parties.

[1.1059]
Article 51
Other language arrangements

(1) Any panel of the Court of First Instance and the Court of Appeal may, to the extent deemed appropriate, dispense with translation requirements.

(2) At the request of one of the parties, and to the extent deemed appropriate, any division of the Court of First Instance and the Court of Appeal shall provide interpretation facilities to assist the parties concerned at oral proceedings.

(3) Notwithstanding Article 49(6), in cases where an action for infringement is brought before the central division, a defendant having its residence, principal place of business or place of business in a Member State shall have the right to obtain, upon request, translations of relevant documents in the language of the Member State of residence, principal place of business or, in the absence of residence or principal place of business, place of business, in the following circumstances:

(a) jurisdiction is entrusted to the central division in accordance with Article 33(1) third or fourth subparagraph, and

(b) the language of proceedings at the central division is a language which is not an official language of the Member State where the defendant has its residence, principal place of business or, in the absence of residence or principal place of business, place of business, and

(c) the defendant does not have proper knowledge of the language of the proceedings.

CHAPTER III
PROCEEDINGS BEFORE THE COURT

[1.1060]
Article 52
Written, interim and oral procedures

(1) The proceedings before the Court shall consist of a written, an interim and an oral procedure, in accordance with the Rules of Procedure. All procedures shall be organized in a flexible and balanced manner.

(2) In the interim procedure, after the written procedure and if appropriate, the judge acting as Rapporteur, subject to a mandate of the full panel, shall be responsible for convening an interim hearing. That judge shall in particular explore with the parties the possibility for a settlement, including through mediation, and/or arbitration, by using the facilities of the Centre referred to in Article 35.

(3) The oral procedure shall give parties the opportunity to explain properly their arguments. The Court may, with the agreement of the parties, dispense with the oral hearing.

[1.1061]
Article 53
Means of evidence

(1) In proceedings before the Court, the means of giving or obtaining evidence shall include in particular the following:

(a) hearing the parties;

(b) requests for information;

(c) production of documents;

(d) hearing witnesses;

(e) opinions by experts;

(f) inspection;

(g) comparative tests or experiments;

(h) sworn statements in writing (affidavits).

(2) The Rules of Procedure shall govern the procedure for taking such evidence. Questioning of witnesses and experts shall be under the control of the Court and be limited to what is necessary.

[1.1062]
Article 54
Burden of proof

Without prejudice to Article 24(2) and (3), the burden of the proof of facts shall be on the party relying on those facts.

[1.1063]
Article 55
Reversal of burden of proof
(1) Without prejudice to Article 24(2) and (3), if the subject-matter of a patent is a process for obtaining a new product, the identical product when produced without the consent of the patent proprietor shall, in the absence of proof to the contrary, be deemed to have been obtained by the patented process.
(2) The principle set out in paragraph 1 shall also apply where there is a substantial likelihood that the identical product was made by the patented process and the patent proprietor has been unable, despite reasonable efforts, to determine the process actually used for such identical product.
(3) In the adduction of proof to the contrary, the legitimate interests of the defendant in protecting its manufacturing and trade secrets shall be taken into account.

CHAPTER IV
POWERS OF THE COURT

[1.1064]
Article 56
The general powers of the Court
(1) The Court may impose such measures, procedures and remedies as are laid down in this Agreement and may make its orders subject to conditions, in accordance with the Rules of Procedure.
(2) The Court shall take due account of the interest of the parties and shall, before making an order, give any party the opportunity to be heard, unless this is incompatible with the effective enforcement of such order.

[1.1065]
Article 57
Court experts
(1) Without prejudice to the possibility for the parties to produce expert evidence, the Court may at any time appoint court experts in order to provide expertise for specific aspects of the case. The Court shall provide such expert with all information necessary for the provision of the expert advice.
(2) To this end, an indicative list of experts shall be drawn up by the Court in accordance with the Rules of Procedure. That list shall be kept by the Registrar.
(3) The court experts shall guarantee independence and impartiality. Rules governing conflicts of interest applicable to judges set out in Article 7 of the Statute shall by analogy apply to court experts.
(4) Expert advice given to the Court by court experts shall be made available to the parties which shall have the possibility to comment on it.

[1.1066]
Article 58
Protection of confidential information
To protect the trade secrets, personal data or other confidential information of a party to the proceedings or of a third party, or to prevent an abuse of evidence, the Court may order that the collection and use of evidence in proceedings before it be restricted or prohibited or that access to such evidence be restricted to specific persons.

[1.1067]
Article 59
Order to produce evidence
(1) At the request of a party which has presented reasonably available evidence sufficient to support its claims and has, in substantiating those claims, specified evidence which lies in the control of the opposing party or a third party, the Court may order the opposing party or a third party to present such evidence, subject to the protection of confidential information. Such order shall not result in an obligation of self-incrimination.
(2) At the request of a party the Court may order, under the same conditions as specified in paragraph 1, the communication of banking, financial or commercial documents under the control of the opposing party, subject to the protection of confidential information.

[1.1068]
Article 60
Order to preserve evidence and to inspect premises
(1) At the request of the applicant which has presented reasonably available evidence to support the claim that the patent has been infringed or is about to be infringed the Court may, even before the commencement of proceedings on the merits of the case, order prompt and effective provisional measures to preserve relevant evidence in respect of the alleged infringement, subject to the protection of confidential information.

(2) Such measures may include the detailed description, with or without the taking of samples, or the physical seizure of the infringing products, and, in appropriate cases, the materials and implements used in the production and/or distribution of those products and the documents relating thereto.
(3) The Court may, even before the commencement of proceedings on the merits of the case, at the request of the applicant who has presented evidence to support the claim that the patent has been infringed or is about to be infringed, order the inspection of premises. Such inspection of premises shall be conducted by a person appointed by the Court in accordance with the Rules of Procedure.
(4) At the inspection of the premises the applicant shall not be present itself but may be represented by an independent professional practitioner whose name has to be specified in the Court's order.
(5) Measures shall be ordered, if necessary without the other party having been heard, in particular where any delay is likely to cause irreparable harm to the proprietor of the patent, or where there is a demonstrable risk of evidence being destroyed.
(6) Where measures to preserve evidence or inspect premises are ordered without the other party in the case having been heard, the parties affected shall be given notice, without delay and at the latest immediately after the execution of the measures. A review, including a right to be heard, shall take place upon request of the parties affected with a view to deciding, within a reasonable period after the notification of the measures, whether the measures are to be modified, revoked or confirmed.
(7) The measures to preserve evidence may be subject to the lodging by the applicant of adequate security or an equivalent assurance intended to ensure compensation for any prejudice suffered by the defendant as provided for in paragraph 9.
(8) The Court shall ensure that the measures to preserve evidence are revoked or otherwise cease to have effect, at the defendant's request, without prejudice to the damages which may be claimed, if the applicant does not bring, within a period not exceeding 31 calendar days or 20 working days, whichever is the longer, action leading to a decision on the merits of the case before the Court.
(9) Where the measures to preserve evidence are revoked, or where they lapse due to any act or omission by the applicant, or where it is subsequently found that there has been no infringement or threat of infringement of the patent, the Court may order the applicant, at the defendant's request, to provide the defendant with appropriate compensation for any damage suffered as a result of those measures.

[1.1069]
Article 61
Freezing orders
(1) At the request of the applicant which has presented reasonably available evidence to support the claim that the patent has been infringed or is about to be infringed the Court may, even before the commencement of proceedings on the merits of the case, order a party not to remove from its jurisdiction any assets located therein, or not to deal in any assets, whether located within its jurisdiction or not.
(2) Article 60(5) to (9) shall apply by analogy to the measures referred to in this Article.

[1.1070]
Article 62
Provisional and protective measures
(1) The Court may, by way of order, grant injunctions against an alleged infringer or against an intermediary whose services are used by the alleged infringer, intended to prevent any imminent infringement, to prohibit, on a provisional basis and subject, where appropriate, to a recurring penalty payment, the continuation of the alleged infringement or to make such continuation subject to the lodging of guarantees intended to ensure the compensation of the right holder.
(2) The Court shall have the discretion to weigh up the interests of the parties and in particular to take into account the potential harm for either of the parties resulting from the granting or the refusal of the injunction.
(3) The Court may also order the seizure or delivery up of the products suspected of infringing a patent so as to prevent their entry into, or movement, within the channels of commerce. If the applicant demonstrates circumstances likely to endanger the recovery of damages, the Court may order the precautionary seizure of the movable and immovable property of the alleged infringer, including the blocking of the bank accounts and of other assets of the alleged infringer.
(4) The Court may, in respect of the measures referred to in paragraphs 1 and 3, require the applicant to provide any reasonable evidence in order to satisfy itself with a sufficient degree of certainty that the applicant is the right holder and that the applicant's right is being infringed, or that such infringement is imminent.
(5) Article 60(5) to (9) shall apply by analogy to the measures referred to in this Article.

[1.1071]
Article 63
Permanent injunctions

(1) Where a decision is taken finding an infringement of a patent, the Court may grant an injunction against the infringer aimed at prohibiting the continuation of the infringement. The Court may also grant such injunction against an intermediary whose services are being used by a third party to infringe a patent.

(2) Where appropriate, non-compliance with the injunction referred to in paragraph 1 shall be subject to a recurring penalty payment payable to the Court.

[1.1072]
Article 64
Corrective measures in infringement proceedings

(1) Without prejudice to any damages due to the injured party by reason of the infringement, and without compensation of any sort, the Court may order, at the request of the applicant, that appropriate measures be taken with regard to products found to be infringing a patent and, in appropriate cases, with regard to materials and implements principally used in the creation or manufacture of those products.

(2) Such measures shall include:
- (a) a declaration of infringement;
- (b) recalling the products from the channels of commerce;
- (c) depriving the product of its infringing property;
- (d) definitively removing the products from the channels of commerce; or
- (e) the destruction of the products and/or of the materials and implements concerned.

(3) The Court shall order that those measures be carried out at the expense of the infringer, unless particular reasons are invoked for not doing so.

(4) In considering a request for corrective measures pursuant to this Article, the Court shall take into account the need for proportionality between the seriousness of the infringement and the remedies to be ordered, the willingness of the infringer to convert the materials into a non-infringing state, as well as the interests of third parties.

[1.1073]
Article 65
Decision on the validity of a patent

(1) The Court shall decide on the validity of a patent on the basis of an action for revocation or a counterclaim for revocation.

(2) The Court may revoke a patent, either entirely or partly, only on the grounds referred to in Articles 138(1) and 139(2) of the EPC.

(3) Without prejudice to Article 138(3) of the EPC, if the grounds for revocation affect the patent only in part, the patent shall be limited by a corresponding amendment of the claims and revoked in part.

(4) To the extent that a patent has been revoked it shall be deemed not to have had, from the outset, the effects specified in Articles 64 and 67 of the EPC.

(5) Where the Court, in a final decision, revokes a patent, either entirely or partly, it shall send a copy of the decision to the European Patent Office and, with respect to a European patent, to the national patent office of any Contracting Member State concerned.

[1.1074]
Article 66
Powers of the Court concerning decisions of the European Patent Office

(1) In actions brought under Article 32(1)(i), the Court may exercise any power entrusted on the European Patent Office in accordance with Article 9 of Regulation (EU) No 1257/2012, including the rectification of the Register for unitary patent protection.

(2) In actions brought under Article 32(1)(i) the parties shall, by way of derogation from Article 69, bear their own costs.

[1.1075]
Article 67
Power to order the communication of information

(1) The Court may, in response to a justified and proportionate request of the applicant and in accordance with the Rules of Procedure, order an infringer to inform the applicant of:
- (a) the origin and distribution channels of the infringing products or processes;
- (b) the quantities produced, manufactured, delivered, received or ordered, as well as the price obtained for the infringing products; and
- (c) the identity of any third person involved in the production or distribution of the infringing products or in the use of the infringing process.

(2) The Court may, in accordance with the Rules of Procedure, also order any third party who:
- (a) was found in the possession of the infringing products on a commercial scale or to be using an infringing process on a commercial scale;
- (b) was found to be providing on a commercial scale services used in infringing activities; or

(c) was indicated by the person referred to in points (a) or (b) as being involved in the production, manufacture or distribution of the infringing products or processes or in the provision of the services,

to provide the applicant with the information referred to in paragraph 1.

[1.1076]
Article 68
Award of damages

(1) The Court shall, at the request of the injured party, order the infringer who knowingly, or with reasonable grounds to know, engaged in a patent infringing activity, to pay the injured party damages appropriate to the harm actually suffered by that party as a result of the infringement.
(2) The injured party shall, to the extent possible, be placed in the position it would have been in if no infringement had taken place. The infringer shall not benefit from the infringement. However, damages shall not be punitive.
(3) When the Court sets the damages:

(a) it shall take into account all appropriate aspects, such as the negative economic consequences, including lost profits, which the injured party has suffered, any unfair profits made by the infringer and, in appropriate cases, elements other than economic factors, such as the moral prejudice caused to the injured party by the infringement; or

(b) as an alternative to point (a), it may, in appropriate cases, set the damages as a lump sum on the basis of elements such as at least the amount of the royalties or fees which would have been due if the infringer had requested authorisation to use the patent in question.

(4) Where the infringer did not knowingly, or with reasonable grounds to know, engage in the infringing activity, the Court may order the recovery of profits or the payment of compensation.

[1.1077]
Article 69
Legal costs

(1) Reasonable and proportionate legal costs and other expenses incurred by the successful party shall, as a general rule, be borne by the unsuccessful party, unless equity requires otherwise, up to a ceiling set in accordance with the Rules of Procedure.
(2) Where a party succeeds only in part or in exceptional circumstances, the Court may order that costs be apportioned equitably or that the parties bear their own costs.
(3) A party should bear any unnecessary costs it has caused the Court or another party.
(4) At the request of the defendant, the Court may order the applicant to provide adequate security for the legal costs and other expenses incurred by the defendant which the applicant may be liable to bear, in particular in the cases referred to in Articles 59 to 62.

[1.1078]
Article 70
Court fees

(1) Parties to proceedings before the Court shall pay court fees.
(2) Court fees shall be paid in advance, unless the Rules of Procedure provide otherwise. Any party which has not paid a prescribed court fee may be excluded from further participation in the proceedings.

[1.1079]
Article 71
Legal aid

(1) A party who is a natural person and who is unable to meet the costs of the proceedings, either wholly or in part, may at any time apply for legal aid. The conditions for granting of legal aid shall be laid down in the Rules of Procedure.
(2) The Court shall decide whether legal aid should be granted in full or in part, or whether it should be refused, in accordance with the Rules of Procedure. (3) On a proposal from the Court, the Administrative Committee shall set the level of legal aid and the rules on bearing the costs thereof.

[1.1080]
Article 72

Period of limitation Without prejudice to Article 24(2) and (3), actions relating to all forms of financial compensation may not be brought more than five years after the date on which the applicant became aware, or had reasonable grounds to become aware, of the last fact justifying the action.

CHAPTER V
APPEALS

[1.1081]
Article 73
Appeal

(1) An appeal against a decision of the Court of First Instance may be brought before the Court of Appeal by any party which has been unsuccessful, in whole or in part, in its submissions, within two months of the date of the notification of the decision.

(2) An appeal against an order of the Court of First Instance may be brought before the Court of Appeal by any party which has been unsuccessful, in whole or in part, in its submissions:

- (a) for the orders referred to in Articles 49(5), 59 to 62 and 67 within 15 calendar days of the notification of the order to the applicant;
- (b) for other orders than the orders referred to in point (a):
  - (i) together with the appeal against the decision, or
  - (ii) where the Court grants leave to appeal, within 15 days of the notification of the Court's decision to that effect.

(3) The appeal against a decision or an order of the Court of First Instance may be based on points of law and matters of fact.

(4) New facts and new evidence may only be introduced in accordance with the Rules of Procedure and where the submission thereof by the party concerned could not reasonably have been expected during proceedings before the Court of First Instance.

[1.1082]
Article 74
Effects of an appeal

(1) An appeal shall not have suspensive effect unless the Court of Appeal decides otherwise at the motivated request of one of the parties. The Rules of Procedure shall guarantee that such a decision is taken without delay.

(2) Notwithstanding paragraph 1, an appeal against a decision on actions or counterclaims for revocation and on actions based on Article 32(1)(i) shall always have suspensive effect.

(3) An appeal against an order referred to in Articles 49(5), 59 to 62 or 67 shall not prevent the continuation of the main proceedings. However, the Court of First Instance shall not give a decision in the main proceedings before the decision of the Court of Appeal concerning an appealed order has been given.

[1.1083]
Article 75
Decision on appeal and referral back

(1) If an appeal pursuant to Article 73 is well-founded, the Court of Appeal shall revoke the decision of the Court of First Instance and give a final decision. The Court of Appeal may in exceptional cases and in accordance with the Rules of Procedure refer the case back to the Court of First Instance for decision.

(2) Where a case is referred back to the Court of First Instance pursuant to paragraph 1, the Court of First Instance shall be bound by the decision of the Court of Appeal on points of law.

CHAPTER VI
DECISIONS

[1.1084]
Article 76
Basis for decisions and right to be heard

(1) The Court shall decide in accordance with the requests submitted by the parties and shall not award more than is requested.

(2) Decisions on the merits may only be based on grounds, facts and evidence, which were submitted by the parties or introduced into the procedure by an order of the Court and on which the parties have had an opportunity to present their comments.

(3) The Court shall evaluate evidence freely and independently.

[1.1085]
Article 77
Formal requirements

(1) Decisions and orders of the Court shall be reasoned and shall be given in writing in accordance with the Rules of Procedure.

(2) Decisions and orders of the Court shall be delivered in the language of proceedings.

[1.1086]
Article 78
Decisions of the Court and dissenting opinions

(1) Decisions and orders of the Court shall be taken by a majority of the panel, in accordance with the Statute. In case of equal votes, the vote of the presiding judge shall prevail.
(2) In exceptional circumstances, any judge of the panel may express a dissenting opinion separately from the decision of the Court.

[1.1087]
Article 79
Settlement

The parties may, at any time in the course of proceedings, conclude their case by way of settlement, which shall be confirmed by a decision of the Court. A patent may not be revoked or limited by way of settlement.

[1.1088]
Article 80
Publication of decisions

The Court may order, at the request of the applicant and at the expense of the infringer, appropriate measures for the dissemination of information concerning the Court's decision, including displaying the decision and publishing it in full or in part in public media.

[1.1089]
Article 81
Rehearing

(1) A request for rehearing after a final decision of the Court may exceptionally be granted by the Court of Appeal in the following circumstances:
- (a) on discovery of a fact by the party requesting the rehearing, which is of such a nature as to be a decisive factor and which, when the decision was given, was unknown to the party requesting the rehearing; such request may only be granted on the basis of an act which was held, by a final decision of a national court, to constitute a criminal offence; or
- (b) in the event of a fundamental procedural defect, in particular when a defendant who did not appear before the Court was not served with the document initiating the proceedings or an equivalent document in sufficient time and in such a way as to enable him to arrange for the defence.

(2) A request for a rehearing shall be filed within 10 years of the date of the decision but not later than two months from the date of the discovery of the new fact or of the procedural defect. Such request shall not have suspensive effect unless the Court of Appeal decides otherwise.
(3) If the request for a rehearing is well-founded, the Court of Appeal shall set aside, in whole or in part, the decision under review and re-open the proceedings for a new trial and decision, in accordance with the Rules of Procedure.
(4) Persons using patents which are the subject-matter of a decision under review and who act in good faith should be allowed to continue using such patents.

[1.1090]
Article 82
Enforcement of decisions and orders

(1) Decisions and orders of the Court shall be enforceable in any Contracting Member State. An order for the enforcement of a decision shall be appended to the decision by the Court.
(2) Where appropriate, the enforcement of a decision may be subject to the provision of security or an equivalent assurance to ensure compensation for any damage suffered, in particular in the case of injunctions.
(3) Without prejudice to this Agreement and the Statute, enforcement procedures shall be governed by the law of the Contracting Member State where the enforcement takes place. Any decision of the Court shall be enforced under the same conditions as a decision given in the Contracting Member State where the enforcement takes place.
(4) If a party does not comply with the terms of an order of the Court, that party may be sanctioned with a recurring penalty payment payable to the Court. The individual penalty shall be proportionate to the importance of the order to be enforced and shall be without prejudice to the party's right to claim damages or security.

PART IV
TRANSITIONAL PROVISIONS

[1.1091]
Article 83
Transitional regime

(1) During a transitional period of seven years after the date of entry into force of this Agreement, an action for infringement or for revocation of a European patent or an action for infringement or for declaration of invalidity of a supplementary protection certificate issued for a product protected by a European patent may still be brought before national courts or other competent national authorities.

(2) An action pending before a national court at the end of the transitional period shall not be affected by the expiry of this period.

(3) Unless an action has already been brought before the Court, a proprietor of or an applicant for a European patent granted or applied for prior to the end of the transitional period under paragraph 1 and, where applicable, paragraph 5, as well as a holder of a supplementary protection certificate issued for a product protected by a European patent, shall have the possibility to opt out from the exclusive competence of the Court. To this end they shall notify their opt-out to the Registry by the latest one month before expiry of the transitional period. The opt-out shall take effect upon its entry into the register.

(4) Unless an action has already been brought before a national court, proprietors of or applicants for European patents or holders of supplementary protection certificates issued for a product protected by a European patent who made use of the opt-out in accordance with paragraph 3 shall be entitled to withdraw their opt-out at any moment. In this event they shall notify the Registry accordingly. The withdrawal of the opt-out shall take effect upon its entry into the register.

(5) Five years after the entry into force of this Agreement, the Administrative Committee shall carry out a broad consultation with the users of the patent system and a survey on the number of European patents and supplementary protection certificates issued for products protected by European patents with respect to which actions for infringement or for revocation or declaration of invalidity are still brought before the national courts pursuant to paragraph 1, the reasons for this and the implications thereof. On the basis of this consultation and an opinion of the Court, the Administrative Committee may decide to prolong the transitional period by up to seven years.

PART V
FINAL PROVISIONS

[1.1092]
Article 84
Signature, ratification and accession

(1) This Agreement shall be open for signature by any Member State on 19 February 2013.

(2) This Agreement shall be subject to ratification in accordance with the respective constitutional requirements of the Member States. Instruments of ratification shall be deposited with the General Secretariat of the Council of the European Union (hereinafter referred to as "the depositary").

(3) Each Member State having signed this Agreement shall notify the European Commission of its ratification of the Agreement at the time of the deposit of its ratification instrument pursuant to Article 18(3) of Regulation (EU) No 1257/2012.

(4) This Agreement shall be open to accession by any Member State. Instruments of accession shall be deposited with the depositary.

[1.1093]
Article 85
Functions of the depositary

(1) The depositary shall draw up certified true copies of this Agreement and shall transmit them to the governments of all signatory or acceding Member States.

(2) The depositary shall notify the governments of the signatory or acceding Member States of:
- (a) any signature;
- (b) the deposit of any instrument of ratification or accession;
- (c) the date of entry into force of this Agreement.

(3) The depositary shall register this Agreement with the Secretariat of the United Nations.

[1.1094]
Article 86
Duration of the Agreement

This Agreement shall be of unlimited duration.

[1.1095]
Article 87
Revision

(1) Either seven years after the entry into force of this Agreement or once 2000 infringement cases have been decided by the Court, whichever is the later point in time, and if necessary at regular intervals thereafter, a broad consultation with the users of the patent system shall be carried out by the Administrative Committee on the functioning, efficiency and cost-effectiveness of the Court and on the trust and confidence of users of the patent system in the quality of the Court's decisions. On the basis of this consultation and an opinion of the Court, the Administrative Committee may decide to revise this Agreement with a view to improving the functioning of the Court.

(2) The Administrative Committee may amend this Agreement to bring it into line with an international treaty relating to patents or Union law.

(3) A decision of the Administrative Committee taken on the basis of paragraphs 1 and 2 shall not take effect if a Contracting Member State declares within twelve months of the date of the decision, on the basis of its relevant internal decision-making procedures, that it does not wish to be bound by the decision. In this case, a Review Conference of the Contracting Member States shall be convened.

[1.1096]
Article 88
Languages of the Agreement

(1) This Agreement is drawn up in a single original in the English, French and German languages, each text being equally authentic.

(2) The texts of this Agreement drawn up in official languages of Contracting Member States other than those specified in paragraph 1 shall, if they have been approved by the Administrative Committee, be considered as official texts. In the event of divergences between the various texts, the texts referred to in paragraph 1 shall prevail.

[1.1097]
Article 89
Entry into force

(1) This Agreement shall enter into force on 1 January 2014 or on the first day of the fourth month after the deposit of the thirteenth instrument of ratification or accession in accordance with Article 84, including the three Member States in which the highest number of European patents had effect in the year preceding the year in which the signature of the Agreement takes place or on the first day of the fourth month after the date of entry into force of the amendments to Regulation (EU) No 1215/2012 concerning its relationship with this Agreement, whichever is the latest.

(2) Any ratification or accession after the entry into force of this Agreement shall take effect on the first day of the fourth month after the deposit of the instrument of ratification or accession.

In witness whereof the undersigned, being duly authorised thereto, have signed this Agreement,

Done at Brussels on 19 February 2013 in English, French and German, all three texts being equally authentic, in a single copy which shall be deposited in the archives of the General Secretariat of the Council of the European Union.

ANNEX I

STATUTE OF THE UNIFIED PATENT COURT

[1.1098]
Article 1 Scope of the Statute

This Statute contains institutional and financial arrangements for the Unified Patent Court as established under Article 1 of the Agreement.

CHAPTER I
JUDGES

[1.1099]
Article 2 Eligibility of judges

(1) Any person who is a national of a Contracting Member State and fulfils the conditions set out in Article 15 of the Agreement and in this Statute may be appointed as a judge.

(2) Judges shall have a good command of at least one official language of the European Patent Office.

(3) Experience with patent litigation which has to be proven for the appointment pursuant to Article 15(1) of the Agreement may be acquired by training under Article 11(4)(a) of this Statute.

Article 3 Appointment of judges

(1) Judges shall be appointed pursuant to the procedure set out in Article 16 of the Agreement.

(2) Vacancies shall be publicly advertised and shall indicate the relevant eligibility criteria as set out in Article 2. The Advisory Committee shall give an opinion on candidates' suitability to perform the duties of a judge of the Court. The opinion shall comprise a list of most suitable candidates. The list shall contain at least twice as many candidates as there are vacancies. Where necessary, the Advisory Committee may recommend that, prior to the decision on the appointment, a candidate judge receive training in patent litigation pursuant to Article 11(4)(a).

(3) When appointing judges, the Administrative Committee shall ensure the best legal and technical expertise and a balanced composition of the Court on as broad a geographical basis as possible among nationals of the Contracting Member States.

(4) The Administrative Committee shall appoint as many judges as are needed for the proper functioning of the Court. The Administrative Committee shall initially appoint the necessary number of judges for setting up at least one panel in each of the divisions of the Court of First Instance and at least two panels in the Court of Appeal.

(5) The decision of the Administrative Committee appointing full-time or part-time legally qualified judges and full-time technically qualified judges shall state the instance of the Court and/or the division of the Court of First Instance for which each judge is appointed and the field(s) of technology for which a technically qualified judge is appointed.

(6) Part-time technically qualified judges shall be appointed as judges of the Court and shall be included in the Pool of Judges on the basis of their specific qualifications and experience. The appointment of these judges to the Court shall ensure that all fields of technology are covered.

Article 4 Judges' term of office

(1) Judges shall be appointed for a term of six years, beginning on the date laid down in the instrument of appointment. They may be re-appointed.

(2) In the absence of any provision regarding the date, the term shall begin on the date of the instrument of appointment.

Article 5 Appointment of the members of the Advisory Committee

(1) Each Contracting Member State shall propose a member of the Advisory Committee who fulfils the requirements set out in Article 14(2) of the Agreement.

(2) The members of the Advisory Committee shall be appointed by the Administrative Committee acting by common accord.

Article 6 Oath

Before taking up their duties judges shall, in open court, take an oath to perform their duties impartially and conscientiously and to preserve the secrecy of the deliberations of the Court.

Article 7 Impartiality

(1) Immediately after taking their oath, judges shall sign a declaration by which they solemnly undertake that, both during and after their term of office, they shall respect the obligations arising therefrom, in particular the duty to behave with integrity and discretion as regards the acceptance, after they have ceased to hold office, of certain appointments or benefits.

(2) Judges may not take part in the proceedings of a case in which they:

(a) have taken part as adviser;
(b) have been a party or have acted for one of the parties;
(c) have been called upon to pronounce as a member of a court, tribunal, board of appeal, arbitration or mediation panel, a commission of inquiry or in any other capacity;
(d) have a personal or financial interest in the case or in relation to one of the parties; or
(e) are related to one of the parties or the representatives of the parties by family ties.

(3) If, for some special reason, a judge considers that he or she should not take part in the judgement or examination of a particular case, that judge shall so inform the President of the Court of Appeal accordingly or, in the case of judges of the Court of First Instance, the President of the Court of First Instance. If, for some special reason, the President of the Court of Appeal or, in the case of judges of the Court of First Instance, the President of the Court of First Instance considers that a judge should not sit or make submissions in a particular case, the President of the Court of Appeal or the President of the Court of First Instance shall justify this in writing and notify the judge concerned accordingly.

(4) Any party to an action may object to a judge taking part in the proceedings on any of the grounds listed in paragraph 2 or where the judge is suspected, with good reason, of partiality.

(5) Any difficulty arising as to the application of this Article shall be settled by decision of the Presidium, in accordance with the Rules of Procedure. The judge concerned shall be heard but shall not take part in the deliberations.

Article 8 Immunity of judges

(1) The judges shall be immune from legal proceedings. After they have ceased to hold office, they shall continue to enjoy immunity in respect of acts performed by them in relation to their official capacity.

(2) The Presidium may waive the immunity.

(3) Where immunity has been waived and criminal proceedings are instituted against a judge, that judge shall be tried, in any of the Contracting Member States, only by the court competent to judge the members of the highest national judiciary.

(4) The Protocol on the privileges and immunities of the European Union shall apply to the judges of the Court, without prejudice to the provisions relating to immunity from legal proceedings of judges which are set out in this Statute.

Article 9 End of duties

(1) Apart from replacement after expiry of a judge's term pursuant to Article 4, or death, the duties of a judge shall end when that judge resigns.

(2) Where a judge resigns, the letter of resignation shall be addressed to the President of the Court of Appeal or, in the case of judges of the Court of First Instance, the President of the Court of First Instance for transmission to the Chairman of the Administrative Committee.

(3) Save where Article 10 applies, a judge shall continue to hold office until that judge's successor takes up his or her duties.

(4) Any vacancy shall by filled by the appointment of a new judge for the remainder of his or her predecessor's term.

Article 10 Removal from office

(1) A judge may be deprived of his or her office or of other benefits only if the Presidium decides that that judge no longer fulfils the requisite conditions or meets the obligations arising from his or her office. The judge concerned shall be heard but shall not take part in the deliberations.

(2) The Registrar of the Court shall communicate this decision to the Chairman of the Administrative Committee.

(3) In the case of a decision depriving a judge of his or her office, a vacancy shall arise upon that notification.

Article 11 Training

(1) Appropriate and regular training of judges shall be provided for within the training framework set up under Article 19 of the Agreement. The Presidium shall adopt Training Regulations ensuring the implementation and overall coherence of the training framework.

(2) The training framework shall provide a platform for the exchange of expertise and a forum for discussion, in particular by:

- (a) organising courses, conferences, seminars, workshops and symposia;
- (b) cooperating with international organisations and education institutes in the field of intellectual property; and
- (c) promoting and supporting further vocational training.

(3) An annual work programme and training guidelines shall be drawn up, which shall include for each judge an annual training plan identifying that judge's main training needs in accordance with the Training Regulations.

(4) The training framework shall in addition:

- (a) ensure appropriate training for candidate-judges and newly appointed judges of the Court;
- (b) support projects aimed at facilitating cooperation between representatives, patent attorneys and the Court.

Article 12 Remuneration

The Administrative Committee shall set the remuneration of the President of the Court of Appeal, the President of the Court of First Instance, the judges, the Registrar, the Deputy-Registrar and the staff.

CHAPTER II
ORGANISATIONAL PROVISIONS

SECTION 1
COMMON PROVISIONS

[1.1100]
Article 13 President of the Court of Appeal

(1) The President of the Court of Appeal shall be elected by all judges of the Court of Appeal for a term of three years, from among their number. The President of the Court of Appeal may be re-elected twice.

(2) The elections of the President of the Court of Appeal shall be by secret ballot. A judge obtaining an absolute majority shall be elected. If no judge obtains an absolute majority, a second ballot shall be held and the judge obtaining the most votes shall be elected.

(3) The President of the Court of Appeal shall direct the judicial activities and the administration of the Court of Appeal and chair the Court of Appeal sitting as a full Court.

(4) If the office of the President of the Court of Appeal falls vacant before the date of expiry of his or her term, a successor shall be elected for the remainder thereof.

Article 14 President of the Court of First Instance

(1) The President of the Court of First Instance shall be elected by all judges of the Court of First Instance who are full-time judges, for a term of three years, from among their number. The President of the Court of First Instance may be re-elected twice.

(2) The first President of the Court of First Instance shall be a national of the Contracting Member State hosting the seat of the central division.

(3) The President of the Court of First Instance shall direct the judicial activities and the administration of the Court of First Instance.

(4) Article 13(2) and (4), shall by analogy apply to the President of the Court of First Instance.

Article 15 Presidium

(1) The Presidium shall be composed of the President of the Court of Appeal, who shall act as chairperson, the President of the Court of First Instance, two judges of the Court of Appeal elected from among their number, three judges of the Court of First Instance who are full-time judges of the Court elected from among their number, and the Registrar as a non-voting member.

(2) The Presidium shall exercise its duties in accordance with this Statute. It may, without prejudice to its own responsibility, delegate certain tasks to one of its members.

(3) The Presidium shall be responsible for the management of the Court and shall in particular:

(a) draw up proposals for the amendment of the Rules of Procedure in accordance with Article 41 of the Agreement and proposals regarding the Financial Regulations of the Court;

(b) prepare the annual budget, the annual accounts and the annual report of the Court and submit them to the Budget Committee;

(c) establish the guidelines for the training programme for judges and supervise the implementation thereof;

(d) take decisions on the appointment and removal of the Registrar and the Deputy-Registrar;

(e) lay down the rules governing the Registry including the sub-registries;

(f) give an opinion in accordance with Article 83(5) of the Agreement.

(4) Decisions of the Presidium referred to in Articles 7, 8, 10 and 22 shall be taken without the participation of the Registrar.

(5) The Presidium can take valid decisions only when all members are present or duly represented. Decisions shall be taken by a majority of the votes.

Article 16 Staff

(1) The officials and other servants of the Court shall have the task of assisting the President of the Court of Appeal, the President of the Court of First Instance, the judges and the Registrar. They shall be responsible to the Registrar, under the authority of the President of the Court of Appeal and the President of the Court of First Instance.

(2) The Administrative Committee shall establish the Staff Regulations of officials and other servants of the Court.

Article 17 Judicial vacations

(1) After consulting the Presidium, the President of the Court of Appeal shall establish the duration of judicial vacations and the rules on observing official holidays.

(2) During the period of judicial vacations, the functions of the President of the Court of Appeal and of the President of the Court of First Instance may be exercised by any judge invited by the respective President to that effect. In cases of urgency, the President of the Court of Appeal may convene the judges.

(3) The President of the Court of Appeal or the President of the Court of First Instance may, in proper circumstances, grant leave of absence to respectively judges of the Court of Appeal or judges of the Court of First Instance.

SECTION 2
THE COURT OF FIRST INSTANCE

Article 18 Setting up and discontinuance of a local or regional division

(1) A request from one or more Contracting Member States for the setting up of a local or regional division shall be addressed to the Chairman of the Administrative Committee. It shall indicate the seat of the local or regional division.

(2) The decision of the Administrative Committee setting up a local or regional division shall indicate the number of judges for the division concerned and shall be public.

(3) The Administrative Committee shall decide to discontinue a local or regional division at the request of the Contracting Member State hosting the local division or the Contracting Member States participating in the regional division. The decision to discontinue a local or regional division shall state the date after which no new cases may be brought before the division and the date on which the division will cease to exist.

(4) As from the date on which a local or regional division ceases to exist, the judges assigned to that local or regional division shall be assigned to the central division, and cases still pending before that local or regional division together with the sub-registry and all of its documentation shall be transferred to the central division.

Article 19 Panels

(1) The allocation of judges and the assignment of cases within a division to its panels shall be governed by the Rules of Procedure. One judge of the panel shall be designated as the presiding judge, in accordance with the Rules of Procedure.

(2) The panel may delegate, in accordance with the Rules of Procedure, certain functions to one or more of its judges.

(3) A standing judge for each division to hear urgent cases may be designated in accordance with the Rules of Procedure.

(4) In cases where a single judge in accordance with Article 8(7) of the Agreement, or a standing judge, in accordance with paragraph 3 of this Article, hears a case that judge shall carry out all functions of a panel.

(5) One judge of the panel shall act as Rapporteur, in accordance with the Rules of Procedure.

Article 20 Pool of Judges

(1) A list with the names of the judges included in the Pool of Judges shall be drawn up by the Registrar. In relation to each judge, the list shall at least indicate the linguistic skills, the field of technology and experience of, as well as the cases previously handled by, that judge.

(2) A request addressed to the President of the Court of First Instance to assign a judge from the Pool of Judges shall indicate, in particular, the subject matter of the case, the official language of the European Patent Office used by the judges of the panel, the language of the proceedings and the field of technology required.

SECTION 3
THE COURT OF APPEAL

Article 21 Panels

(1) The allocation of judges and the assignment of cases to panels shall be governed by the Rules of Procedure. One judge of the panel shall be appointed as the presiding judge, in accordance with the Rules of Procedure.

(2) When a case is of exceptional importance, and in particular when the decision may affect the unity and consistency of the case law of the Court, the Court of Appeal may decide, on the basis of a proposal from the presiding judge, to refer the case to the full Court.

(3) The panel may delegate, in accordance with the Rules of Procedure, certain functions to one or more of its judges.

(4) One judge of the panel shall act as Rapporteur, in accordance with the Rules of Procedure.

SECTION 4
THE REGISTRY

Article 22 Appointment and removal from office of the Registrar

(1) The Presidium shall appoint the Registrar of the Court for a term of six years. The Registrar may be re-appointed.

(2) Two weeks before the date fixed for appointing the Registrar, the President of the Court of Appeal shall inform the Presidium of the applications which have been submitted for the post.

(3) Before taking up his or her duties, the Registrar shall take oath before the Presidium to perform the duties of the Registrar impartially and conscientiously.

(4) The Registrar may be removed from office only if the Registrar no longer meets the obligations arising from his or her office. The Presidium shall take its decision after having heard the Registrar.

(5) If the office of the Registrar falls vacant before the date of expiry of the term thereof, the Presidium shall appoint a new Registrar for a term of six years.

(6) If the Registrar is absent or prevented from attending or where such post is vacant, the President of the Court of Appeal after having consulted the Presidium shall designate a member of the staff of the Court to carry out the duties of the Registrar.

Article 23 Duties of the Registrar

(1) The Registrar shall assist the Court, the President of the Court of Appeal, the President of the Court of First Instance and the judges in the performance of their functions. The Registrar shall be responsible for the organisation and activities of the Registry under the authority of the President of the Court of Appeal.

(2) The Registrar shall in particular be responsible for:
(a) keeping the register which shall include records of all cases before the Court;
(b) keeping and administering lists drawn up in accordance with Articles 18, 48(3) and 57(2) of the Agreement;
(c) keeping and publishing a list of notifications and withdrawals of opt-outs in accordance with Article 83 of the Agreement;
(d) publishing the decisions of the Court, subject to the protection of confidential information;
(e) publishing annual reports with statistical data; and
(f) ensuring that the information on opt-outs in accordance with Article 83 of the Agreement is notified to the European Patent Office.

Article 24 Keeping of the register

(1) Detailed rules for keeping the register of the Court shall be prescribed in the Rules governing the Registry, adopted by the Presidium.

(2) The rules on access to documents of the Registry shall be provided for in the Rules of Procedure.

Article 25 Sub-registries and Deputy-Registrar

(1) A Deputy-Registrar shall be appointed for a term of six years by the Presidium. The Deputy-Registrar may be re-appointed.

(2) Article 22(2) to (6) shall apply by analogy.

(3) The Deputy-Registrar shall be responsible for the organisation and activities of sub-registries under the authority of the Registrar and the President of the Court of First Instance. The duties of the Deputy-Registrar shall in particular include:
(a) keeping records of all cases before the Court of First Instance;
(b) notifying every case before the Court of First Instance to the Registry.

(4) The Deputy-Registrar shall also provide administrative and secretarial assistance to the divisions of the Court of First Instance.

CHAPTER III
FINANCIAL PROVISIONS

[1.1101]
Article 26 Budget

(1) The budget shall be adopted by the Budget Committee on a proposal from the Presidium. It shall be drawn up in accordance with the generally accepted accounting principles laid down in the Financial Regulations, established in accordance with Article 33.

(2) Within the budget, the Presidium may, in accordance with the Financial Regulations, transfer funds between the various headings or subheadings.

(3) The Registrar shall be responsible for the implementation of the budget in accordance with the Financial Regulations.

(4) The Registrar shall annually make a statement on the accounts of the preceding financial year relating to the implementation of the budget which shall be approved by the Presidium.

Article 27 Authorisation for expenditure

(1) The expenditure entered in the budget shall be authorised for the duration of one accounting period unless the Financial Regulations provide otherwise.

(2) In accordance with the Financial Regulations, any appropriations, other than those relating to staff costs, which are unexpended at the end of the accounting period may be carried forward, but not beyond the end of the following accounting period.

(3) Appropriations shall be set out under different headings according to type and purpose of the expenditure, and subdivided, to the extent necessary, in accordance with the Financial Regulations.

Article 28 Appropriations for unforeseeable expenditure

(1) The budget of the Court may include appropriations for unforeseeable expenditure.

(2) The employment of these appropriations by the Court shall be subject to the prior approval of the Budget Committee.

Article 29 Accounting period

The accounting period shall commence on 1 January and end on 31 December.

Article 30 Preparation of the budget

The Presidium shall submit the draft budget of the Court to the Budget Committee no later than the date prescribed in the Financial Regulations.

Article 31 Provisional budget

(1) If, at the beginning of the accounting period, the budget has not been adopted by the Budget Committee, expenditure may be effected on a monthly basis per heading or other division of the budget, in accordance with the Financial Regulations, up to one-twelfth of the budget appropriations for the preceding accounting period, provided that the appropriations thus made available to the Presidium do not exceed one-twelfth of those provided for in the draft budget.

(2) The Budget Committee may, subject to the observance of the other provisions laid down in paragraph 1, authorise expenditure in excess of one-twelfth of the budget appropriations for the preceding accounting period.

Article 32 Auditing of accounts

(1) The annual financial statements of the Court shall be examined by independent auditors. The auditors shall be appointed and if necessary dismissed by the Budget Committee.

(2) The audit, which shall be based on professional auditing standards and shall take place, if necessary, in situ, shall ascertain that the budget has been implemented in a lawful and proper manner and that the financial administration of the Court has been conducted in accordance with the principles of economy and sound financial management. The auditors shall draw up a report after the end of each accounting period containing a signed audit opinion.

(3) The Presidium shall submit to the Budget Committee the annual financial statements of the Court and the annual budget implementation statement for the preceding accounting period, together with the auditors' report.

(4) The Budget Committee shall approve the annual accounts together with the auditors' report and shall discharge the Presidium in respect of the implementation of the budget.

Article 33 Financial Regulations

(1) The Financial Regulations shall be adopted by the Administrative Committee. They shall be amended by the Administrative Committee on a proposal from the Court.

(2) The Financial Regulations shall lay down in particular:

(a) arrangements relating to the establishment and implementation of the budget and for the rendering and auditing of accounts;

(b) the method and procedure whereby the payments and contributions, including the initial financial contributions provided for in Article 37 of the Agreement are to be made available to the Court;

(c) the rules concerning the responsibilitics of authorising and accounting officers and the arrangements for their supervision; and

(d) the generally accepted accounting principles on which the budget and the annual financial statements are to be based.

CHAPTER IV
PROCEDURAL PROVISIONS

[1.1102]

Article 34 Secrecy of deliberations

The deliberations of the Court shall be and shall remain secret.

Article 35 Decisions

(1) When a panel sits in composition of an even number of judges, decisions of the Court shall be taken by a majority of the panel. In case of equal vote, the vote of the presiding judge shall prevail.

(2) In the event of one of the judges of a panel being prevented from attending, a judge from another panel may be called upon to sit in accordance with the Rules of Procedure.

(3) In cases where this Statute provides that the Court of Appeal shall take a decision sitting as a full court, such decision shall be valid only if it is taken by at least 3/4 of the judges comprising the full court.

(4) Decisions of the Court shall contain the names of the judges deciding the case.

(5) Decisions shall be signed by the judges deciding the case, by the Registrar for decisions of the Court of Appeal, and by the Deputy-Registrar for decisions of the Court of First Instance. They shall be read in open court.

Article 36 Dissenting opinions

A dissenting opinion expressed separately by a judge of a panel in accordance with Article 78 of the Agreement shall be reasoned, given in writing and shall be signed by the judge expressing this opinion.

Article 37 Decision by default

(1) At the request of a party to an action, a decision by default may be given in accordance with the Rules of Procedure, where the other party, after having been served with a document instituting proceedings or with an equivalent document, fails to file written submissions in defence or fails to appear at the oral hearing. An objection may be lodged against that decision within one month of it being notified to the party against which the default decision has been given.

(2) The objection shall not have the effect of staying enforcement of the decision by default unless the Court decides otherwise.

Article 38 Questions referred to the Court of Justice of the European Union

(1) The procedures established by the Court of Justice of the European Union for referrals for preliminary rulings within the European Union shall apply.

(2) Whenever the Court of First Instance or the Court of Appeal has decided to refer to the Court of Justice of the European Union a question of interpretation of the Treaty on European Union or of the Treaty on the Functioning of the European Union or a question on the validity or interpretation of acts of the institutions of the European Union, it shall stay its proceedings.

ANNEX II

[1.1103]

Distribution of cases within the central division[1]

LONDON Section	PARIS Seat	MUNICH Section
	President's Office	
(A) Human necessities	(B) Performing operations, transporting	(F) Mechanical engineering, lighting, heating, weapons, blasting
(C) Chemistry, metallurgy	(D) Textiles, paper	
	(E) Fixed constructions	
	(G) Physics	
	(H) Electricity	

NOTES

[1] The classification into 8 sections (A to H) is based on the International Patent Classification of the World Intellectual Property Organisation (www.wipo.int/classifications/ipc/en).

PRELIMINARY SET OF PROVISIONS FOR THE RULES OF PROCEDURE OF THE UNIFIED PATENT COURT

NOTES

The original source of these Rules is the Unified Patent Court website at www.unified-patent-court.org.

Status

(1) First draft dated 29 May 2009
- Discussed in expert meetings on 5 June and 19 June 2009

(2) Second draft (Part 1, Chapter 1) dated 9 July 2009, Working paper from the Commission Services, Council working document 11813/09
- Discussed in Council Working Party on Intellectual Property (Patents) on 22nd July 2009

(3) Third draft dated 25 September 2009
- Discussed in expert meeting on 2nd October 2009

(4) Fourth draft dated 16 October 2009
- Discussed at the 5th European Patent Judges' Forum on 30 and 31st October 2009

(5) Fifth draft dated 27 January 2012
- Discussed in expert meeting on 3rd February 2012

(6) Sixth draft dated 22nd February 2012
- Discussed by the Drafting Committee on 25 and 26 February 2012

(7) Seventh draft dated 20 March 2012
- Discussed by the Drafting Committee on 24 and 25 March 2012

(8) Eighth draft dated 30 March 2012
- For technical consultation

(9) Ninth draft dated 24 May 2012

(10) Eleventh draft dated 7 November 2012
- Discussed by Drafting Committee on 9 and 10 November 2012

(11) Twelfth draft dated 29 November

(12) 13th draft dated 14 January 2013
- Renumbered version

(13) 14th draft dated 31st January 2013
- For further informal comment prior to the public consultation

(14) 15th draft dated 31st May 2013
- For public consultation

(15) 16th draft dated 31st January 2014
- Discussed by Drafting Committee on 16 and 17 November and 14 December 2013 in light of comments from public consultation
- Provided to Preparatory Committee on 31st January 2014

(16) 17th draft dated 31st October 2014
- Discussed by Legal Group of the Preparatory Committee on 20 February, 10 April, 20 June
- Discussed by Legal Group of the Preparatory Committee and the Drafting Committee on 24 and 25 September 2014

(17) 18th draft dated 1st July 2015
- Discussed by the Legal Group of the Preparatory Committee and the Drafting Committee on 25 and 26 June 2015
- Provided to the Preparatory Committee on 10 July 2015
- Adopted by the Preparatory Committee on 19 October 2015
- Consequential amendments following the agreement on Court fees and the ceiling for recoverable costs submitted to the Preparatory Committee on 30 June 2016
- Amendments by the Preparatory Committee on 10 October 2016
- Amendments by the Preparatory Committee on 15 March 2017

Abbreviations

Agreement: Agreement on a Unified Patent Court of 19 February 2013 (OJ C175, 20.6.2013, p 1) including any subsequent amendments

Directive 98/5/EC: Directive 98/5/EC of the European Parliament and of the Council of 16 February 1998 to facilitate practice of the profession of lawyer on a permanent basis in a Member State other than that in which the qualification was obtained (OJ L77, 14.3.1998, p 36) including any subsequent amendments

EPC: Convention on the Grant of European Patents of 5 October 1973 (European Patent Convention) including any subsequent amendments

The Hague Convention: Convention on the Service Abroad of Judicial and Extrajudicial Documents in Civil or Commercial Matters of 15 November 1965 including any subsequent amendments

Lugano Convention: Convention on Jurisdiction and the Recognition and Enforcement of Judgments in Civil and Commercial Matters of 30 October 2007 (OJ L147, 10.6.2009, p 5) including any subsequent amendments

Regulation (EC) No 1206/2001: Regulation (EC) No 1206/2001 of the Council of 28 May 2001 on cooperation between the courts of the Member States in the taking of evidence in civil or commercial matters (OJ L174, 27.6.2001, p 1) including any subsequent amendments

Regulation (EU) No 1215/2012: Regulation (EU) No 1215/2012 of the European Parliament and of the Council of 12 December 2012 on jurisdiction and the recognition and enforcement of judgments in civil and commercial matters (OJ L351, 20.12.2012, p 1) including any subsequent amendments

Regulation (EU) No 1257/2012: Regulation (EU) No 1257/2012 of the European Parliament and of the Council of 17 December 2012 implementing enhanced cooperation in the area of the creation of unitary patent protection (OJ L361, 31.12.2012, p 1) including any subsequent amendments

Regulation (EU) No 1260/2012: Regulation (EU) No 1260/2012 of the Council of 17 December 2012 implementing enhanced cooperation in the area of the creation of unitary patent protection with regard to the applicable translation arrangements (OJ L361, 31.12.2012, p 89) including any subsequent amendments

Regulation (EC) No 1393/2007: Regulation (EC) No 1393/2007 of the European Parliament and of the Council of 13 November 2007 on the service in the Member States of judicial and extrajudicial documents in civil or commercial matters (service of documents), and repealing Council Regulation (EC) No 1348/2000 (OJ L324, 10.12.2007, p 79) including any subsequent amendments

Statute: Statute of the Unified Patent Court (OJ C175, 20.6.2013, p 29) including any subsequent amendments

PREAMBLE

[1.1106]

1. The Court shall conduct proceedings in accordance with the Agreement, the Statute and these Rules. In the event of a conflict between the provisions of the Agreement and/or the Statute on the one hand and of the Rules on the other hand, the provisions of the Agreement and/or the Statute shall prevail.
2. The Rules shall be applied and interpreted in accordance with Articles 41(3), 42 and 52(1) of the Agreement on the basis of the principles of proportionality, flexibility, fairness and equity.
3. Proportionality shall be ensured by giving due consideration to the nature and complexity of each action and its importance.
4. Flexibility shall be ensured by applying all procedural rules in a flexible and balanced manner with the required level of discretion for the judges to organise the proceedings in the most efficient and cost effective manner.
5. Fairness and equity shall be ensured by having regard to the legitimate interests of all parties.
6. In accordance with these principles, the Court shall apply and interpret the Rules in a way which shall ensure decisions of the highest quality.

7. In accordance with these principles, proceedings shall be conducted in a way which will normally allow the final oral hearing on the issues of infringement and validity at first instance to take place within one year whilst recognising that complex actions may require more time and procedural steps and simple actions less time and fewer procedural steps. Decisions on costs and/or damages may take place at the same time or as soon as practicable thereafter. Case management shall be organised in accordance with these objectives. Parties shall cooperate with the Court and set out their full case as early as possible in the proceedings.
8. The Court shall endeavour to ensure consistent application and interpretation of these Rules by all first instance divisions and the Court of Appeal. Due consideration shall also be given to this objective in any decision concerning leave to appeal against procedural orders.

APPLICATION AND INTERPRETATION OF THE RULES

[1.1107]
Rule 1
Application of the Rules and general principles of interpretation
1. The Court shall conduct proceedings in accordance with the Agreement, the Statute and these Rules, which include the Preamble to these Rules and the principles set out therein. In the event of a conflict between the provisions of the Agreement and/or the Statute on the one hand and of the Rules on the other hand, the provisions of the Agreement and/or the Statute shall prevail.
2. Where these Rules provide for the Court to perform any act other than an act exclusively reserved for a panel of the Court, the President of the Court of First Instance or the President of the Court of Appeal, that act may be performed by:
(a) the presiding judge or the judge-rapporteur of the panel to which the action has been assigned;
(b) a single legally qualified judge where the action has been assigned to a single judge;
(c) the standing judge designated pursuant to Rule 345.5.
3. References to persons in these Rules may apply to legal persons as well as natural persons. Words importing the masculine gender shall include the feminine and vice versa. Unless the contrary intention appears, words in the singular include the plural and vice versa.
Relation with Agreement: Article 8(7)
Relation with Statute: Article 19(3) and (4)

Rule 2
Supplementary protection certificate
1. Subject to paragraph 2, in these Rules with the exception of Rule 5 the expression "patent" and "proprietor" shall whenever appropriate include, respectively, a supplementary protection certificate as defined in Article 2(h) of the Agreement and granted in respect of the patent and the holder of such certificate.
2. References in these Rules to the language in which the patent was granted shall mean that language and not the language in which a supplementary protection certificate in respect of the patent was granted.

Rule 3
Power of staff of the Registry and a sub-registry to perform functions of the Registry
Where these Rules refer to the Registry or Registrar and provide for the Registry to perform any act that reference shall include – where applicable – the Deputy-Registrar and the relevant sub-registry and that act may be performed by the Registrar, the Deputy Registrar or by a member of staff of the Registry or sub-registry of the relevant division.

Rule 4
Lodging of documents
1. Written pleadings and other documents shall be lodged at the Registry or relevant sub-registry in electronic form. Parties shall make use of the official forms available online. The receipt of documents shall be confirmed by the automatic issue of an electronic receipt, which shall indicate the date and local time of receipt.
2. Where it is not possible to lodge a document electronically for any reason a party may lodge the document in hard-copy form. An electronic copy of the document shall be lodged as soon as practicable thereafter.
Relation with Agreement: Article 44

Rule 5

Lodging of an Application to opt out and withdrawal of an opt-out

1. The proprietor of a European patent (including a European patent that has expired) or the applicant for a published application for a European patent (hereinafter in this Rule 5 an "application") who wishes to opt out that patent or application from the exclusive competence of the Court in accordance with Article 83(3) of the Agreement shall lodge an Application (hereinafter in this Rule 5 an "Application to opt out") with the Registry.

(a) Where the patent or application is owned by two or more proprietors or applicants, all proprietors or applicants shall lodge the Application to opt out. Where the person lodging an Application to opt out is not recorded as the proprietor or applicant in the registers referred to in Rule 8.5(a) and (b), respectively, the person shall lodge a declaration pursuant to paragraph 3(e).

(b) The Application to opt out shall be made in respect of all of the Contracting Member States for which the European patent has been granted or which have been designated in the application.

2. An Application to opt out or an Application to withdraw an opt-out pursuant to paragraph 7 (hereinafter in this Rule 5 an "Application to withdraw") shall extend to any supplementary protection certificate based on the European patent.

(a) Where any such supplementary protection certificate has been granted at the date of lodging the Application to opt out or the Application to withdraw, the holder of the supplementary protection certificate shall, if different from the proprietor of the patent, lodge the Application to opt out or the Application to withdraw together with the proprietor.

(b) Where any such supplementary protection certificate is granted subsequent to lodging the Application to opt out, the opt-out shall take effect automatically on grant of said supplementary protection certificate.

(c) Paragraphs 6 and 8 shall apply *mutatis mutandis*. For the purposes of paragraphs 6 and 8, reference to actions

(i) in respect of a European patent shall apply to all supplementary protection certificates based on that European patent, and

(ii) in respect of a supplementary protection certificate shall apply to the European patent on which such supplementary protection certificate is based and

(iii) in respect of a supplementary protection certificate shall apply to all other supplementary protection certificates based on the same European patent.

(d) For the avoidance of doubt, it is not possible to opt out supplementary protection certificates, whether granted by the authorities of a Contracting Member State or otherwise, based on a European patent with unitary effect.

3. The Application to opt out shall contain:

(a) the name of each proprietor or applicant for the European patent or application and of the holder of any supplementary protection certificate based on the European patent in question, and all relevant postal and, where applicable, electronic addresses;

(b) the name and postal address and electronic address of (i) the representative appointed by the applicant or the proprietor in accordance with Article 48 of the Agreement or (ii) any other person lodging the Application to opt out on behalf of the proprietor or the applicant and the mandate for lodging the Application to opt out;

(c) details of the patent and/or application including the number;

(d) details of any supplementary protection certificate granted based on the patent concerned, including the number; and

(e) for the purposes of paragraph 1(a), a declaration by or on behalf of each proprietor or applicant pursuant to Rule 8.5 that he is entitled to be registered in the national patent register.

4. Rule 8 shall not apply to Applications to opt out and to Applications to withdraw made pursuant to this Rule 5. Where a representative is appointed, such a representative may include professional representatives and legal practitioners as defined in Article 134 EPC in addition to those referred to in Article 48 of the Agreement.

5. The Registrar shall as soon as practicable enter the Application to opt out in the register. Subject to paragraph 6, the opt-out which meets the requirements laid down in this Rule shall be regarded as effective from the date of entry in the register. If the requirements recorded in the register are missing or incorrect, a correction may be lodged with the Registry. The date of entry of the correction shall be noted in the register. The opt-out shall be effective from the date of correction.

6. In the event that an action has been commenced before the Court in respect of a patent and/or an application contained in an Application to opt out prior to the date of entry of the Application to opt out in the register or prior to the date of correction pursuant to paragraph 5, the Application to opt out shall be ineffective in respect of the patent and/or application in question, irrespective of whether the action is pending or has been concluded.

7. A proprietor of a patent or an application the subject of an opt-out pursuant to this Rule may lodge an Application to withdraw in respect of the patent or application, but not in respect of different Contracting Member States for which the European patent has been granted or which have

been designated in the application. The Application to withdraw shall contain the particulars in accordance with paragraph 3. The Registrar shall as soon as practicable enter the Application to withdraw in the register and the withdrawal shall be regarded as effective from the date of entry in the register. Paragraphs 1(a) and 5 shall apply *mutatis mutandis*.

8. In the event that an action has been commenced before a court of a Contracting Member State in a matter over which the Court also has jurisdiction pursuant to Article 32 of the Agreement in respect of a patent or application contained in an Application to withdraw, prior to the entry of the Application to withdraw in the register or any time before the date pursuant to paragraph 5, the Application to withdraw shall be ineffective in respect of the patent or application in question, irrespective of whether the action is pending or has been concluded.

9. Where an application for a European patent subject to an opt-out pursuant to this Rule proceeds to grant as a European patent with unitary effect the opt-out shall be deemed to have been withdrawn and the Registrar shall as soon as practicable enter the withdrawal in the register.

10. A patent or application the subject of an Application to withdraw which has been entered on the register may not thereafter be the subject of a further Application to opt out.

11. The Registrar shall as soon as practicable notify the European Patent Office and the national patent office of any Contracting Member States concerned of the entries in the register pursuant to paragraphs 5 and 7.

12. Applications accepted by the Registry before the entry into force of the Agreement shall be treated as entered on the register on the date of entry into force of the Agreement.

Relation with Agreement: Article 83(3) and (4)

Rule 6

Service and supply of orders, decisions, written pleadings and other documents

1. The Registry shall as soon as practicable serve, in accordance with Part 5, Chapter 2:
   (a) orders and decisions of the Court on the parties;
   (b) written pleadings and other documents of a party on the other party.

Where applicable, the Registry shall inform the parties of the opportunity to reply or to take any other appropriate step in the proceedings and of any time period for so doing.

2. The Registry shall also as soon as practicable supply to the parties copies of documents referred to in these Rules and lodged with pleadings and written evidence.

3. Where the postal or electronic address for service provided by a party pursuant to these Rules has changed that party shall give notice to the Registry and to every other party as soon as such change has taken place.

Rule 7

Language of written pleadings and written evidence

1. Written pleadings and other documents, including written evidence, shall be lodged in the language of the proceedings unless the Court or these Rules otherwise provide.

2. Where these Rules or the Court require a pleading or other document to be translated it shall not be necessary to provide a formal certification by the translator as to the accuracy of such translation unless the accuracy is challenged by a party or such certification is ordered by the Court or required by these Rules.

Rule 8

Party and party's representative

1. A party shall be represented in accordance with Article 48 of the Agreement unless otherwise provided by these Rules [Rules 5, 88.4 and 378.5].

2. For the purpose of all proceedings in relation to a patent, where these Rules provide that a party performs any act or that any act be performed upon a party that act shall be performed by or upon the representative for the time being of the party.

3. Except where these Rules provide otherwise, a party shall not communicate with the Court without informing the other party. Where such communication is in writing, the communication should be copied to the other party unless these Rules provide that the Court will supply a copy to the other party.

4. For the purposes of proceedings under these Rules in relation to the proprietor of a European patent with unitary effect, the person shown in the Register for unitary patent protection [Regulation (EU) No 1257/2012, Article 2(e)] as the proprietor shall be treated as such. If during proceedings before the Court a new proprietor is recorded in the Register for unitary patent protection, the former registered proprietor may apply to the Court pursuant to Rule 305.1(c) for the substitution of the new proprietor.

5. Subject to paragraph 6, for the purposes of proceedings under these Rules:
   (a) in relation to the proprietor of a European patent, the person entitled to be registered as proprietor under the law of each Contracting Member State in which such European patent has been validated shall be treated as the proprietor whether or not such person is in fact recorded in the register of patents maintained in such Contracting Member State (hereinafter "national patent register"); and

(b) in relation to the applicant for a European patent, the person entitled to be registered as applicant whether or not such person is in fact recorded as such in the European Patent Register kept by the European Patent Office.

(c) For the purposes of paragraph 5, there shall be a rebuttable presumption that the person shown in each national patent register and the European Patent Register kept by the European Patent Office is the person entitled to be registered as proprietor or applicant as the case may be.

6. For the purposes of proceedings pursuant to Rules 42 and 61 in relation to a European patent, the person shown in the national patent register [Rule 8.5(a)] as the proprietor shall be treated as such for each Contracting Member State or, as far as no such person is registered in a national patent register, the last person shown recorded as proprietor in the European Patent Register kept by the European Patent Office.

Relation with Agreement: Article 48

Rule 9

Powers of the Court

1. The Court may, at any stage of the proceedings, of its own motion or on a reasoned request by a party, make a procedural order such as to order a party to take any step, answer any question or provide any clarification or evidence, within time periods to be specified.

2. The Court may disregard any step, fact, evidence or argument which a party has not taken or submitted in accordance with a time limit set by the Court or these Rules.

3. Subject to paragraph 4, on a reasoned request by a party, the Court may:

(a) extend, even retrospectively, a time period referred to in these Rules or imposed by the Court; and

(b) shorten any such time period.

4. The Court shall not extend the time periods referred to in Rules 198.1, 213.1 and 224.1.

PART 1
PROCEDURES BEFORE THE COURT OF FIRST INSTANCE

[1.1108]

Rule 10

Stages of the proceedings (*inter partes* proceedings)

Proceedings before the Court of First Instance shall consist of the following stages:

(a) a written procedure;

(b) an interim procedure, which may include an interim conference with the parties;

(c) an oral procedure which, subject to Rules 116.1 and 117, shall include an oral hearing of the parties unless the Court dispenses with the oral hearing with the agreement of the parties;

(d) a procedure for the award of damages, which may include a procedure to lay open books;

(e) a procedure for cost decisions.

Relation with Agreement: Articles 52, 68 and 69

Rule 11

Settlement

1. At any stage of the proceedings, if the Court is of the opinion that the dispute is suitable for a settlement, it may propose that the parties make use of the facilities of the Patent Mediation and Arbitration Centre ("the Centre") in order to settle or to explore a settlement of the dispute. In particular the judge-rapporteur shall during the interim procedure, especially at an interim conference in accordance with Rule 104(d), explore with the parties the possibility of a settlement, including through mediation and/or arbitration, using the facilities of the Centre. Parties who choose mediation in an attempt to settle a dispute are subsequently not prevented from initiating judicial proceedings before the Court in relation to that dispute by the expiry of limitation or prescription periods during the mediation process, which will stay the limitation or prescription periods until the end of the mediation process. If mediation proceedings are terminated without a dispute settlement agreement, the period shall continue to run from that moment.

2. Pursuant to Rule 365 the Court shall, if requested by the parties, by decision confirm the terms of any settlement or arbitral award by consent (irrespective of whether it was reached using the facilities of the Centre or otherwise), including a term which obliges the patent owner to limit, surrender or agree to the revocation of a patent or not to assert it against the other party and/or third parties. The parties may agree on costs to be awarded or may request the Court to decide on costs to be awarded in accordance with Rules 150 to 156 *mutatis mutandis*.

3. Save for the purpose of enforcing the terms of any such settlement agreement by any person no opinion expressed, suggestion made, proposal put forward, concession made or document drawn up for the purposes of settlement may be relied on as evidence by the Court or the parties in proceedings before the Court or any other court unless such matter was expressed to be made on an open basis and freely disclosable to the Court or any other court.

Relation with Agreement: Articles 35, 52(2) and 79

CHAPTER 1
WRITTEN PROCEDURE

SECTION 1
INFRINGEMENT ACTION

[1.1109]
Rule 12
Exchange of written pleadings (infringement action)

1. The written procedure shall consist of:
   (a) the lodging of a Statement of claim (by the claimant) [Rule 13];
   (b) the lodging of a Statement of defence (by the defendant) [Rules 23 and 24]; and, optionally
   (c) the lodging of a Reply to the Statement of defence (by the claimant) [Rule 29(b)]; and
   (d) the lodging of a Rejoinder to the Reply (by the defendant) [Rule 29(c)].
2. The Statement of defence may include a Counterclaim for revocation [Rule 25.1].
3. If a Counterclaim for revocation is lodged:
   (a) the claimant and any proprietor who becomes a party pursuant to Rule 25.2 (hereinafter in this Rule 12 and Rules 29 to 32, "the proprietor") shall lodge a Defence to the Counterclaim for revocation [Rule 29(a)], which may include an Application to amend the patent by the proprietor [Rule 30];
   (b) the defendant may lodge a Reply to the Defence to the Counterclaim [Rule 29(d)]; and
   (c) the claimant and the proprietor may lodge a Rejoinder to the Reply to the Defence to the Counterclaim [Rule 29(e)].
4. If an Application to amend the patent is lodged by the proprietor, the defendant shall lodge a Defence to the Application to amend the patent in the Reply to the Defence to the Counterclaim, the proprietor may lodge a Reply to the Defence to the Application to amend and the defendant may lodge a Rejoinder to such Reply [Rule 32].
5. The judge-rapporteur may allow the exchange of further written pleadings, within time periods to be specified [Rule 36].

Statement of Claim

Rule 13
Contents of the Statement of claim

1. The claimant shall lodge a Statement of claim with the division chosen by him [Article 33 of the Agreement] which shall contain:
   (a) the name of the claimant, and, where the claimant is a corporate entity, the location of its registered office, and of the claimant's representative;
   (b) the name of the party against whom the Statement is made (the defendant), and, where the defendant is a corporate entity, the location of its registered office;
   (c) postal and electronic addresses for service on the claimant and the names of the persons authorised to accept service;
   (d) postal and, where available, electronic addresses for service on the defendant and the names of the persons authorised to accept service, if known;
   (e) where the claimant is not the proprietor or not the only proprietor of the patent concerned, postal and where available, electronic addresses for service on the proprietor and the names and addresses of the persons authorised to accept service, if known;
   (f) where the claimant is not the proprietor of the patent concerned, or not the only proprietor, evidence to show the claimant is entitled to commence proceedings [Article 47(2) and (3) of the Agreement];
   (g) details of the patent concerned, including the number;
   (h) where applicable, information about any prior or pending proceedings relating to the patent concerned before the Court including any action for revocation or a declaration of non-infringement pending before the central division and the date of any such action, the European Patent Office or any other court or authority;
   (i) an indication of the division which shall hear the action [Article 33(1) to (6) of the Agreement] with an explanation of why that division has competence; where the parties have agreed in accordance with Article 33(7) of the Agreement, the indication of the division which shall hear the action shall be accompanied by evidence of the defendant's agreement;
   (j) where applicable, an indication that the action shall be heard by a single judge [Article 8(7) of the Agreement], accompanied by evidence of the defendant's agreement;
   (k) the nature of the claim, the order or the remedy sought by the claimant;
   (l) an indication of the facts relied on, in particular:
      (i) one or more instances of alleged infringements or threatened infringements specifying the date and place of each;
      (ii) the identification of the patent claims alleged to be infringed;
   (m) the evidence relied on [Rule 170.1], where available, and an indication of any further evidence which will be offered in support;

(n) the reasons why the facts relied on constitute an infringement of the patent claims, including arguments of law and where appropriate an explanation of the proposed claim interpretation;
(o) an indication of any order the claimant will seek during the interim procedure [Rule 104(e)];
(p) where the claimant assesses that the value of the infringement action exceeds EUR500.000, an indication of the value; and
(q) a list of the documents, including any witness statements, referred to in the Statement of claim, together with any request that all or part of any such document need not be translated and/or any request pursuant to Rule 262.1.

2. The claimant shall at the same time supply a copy of each of the documents referred to in the Statement of claim.
3. The judge-rapporteur shall decide on any request made pursuant to paragraph 1(q) as soon as practicable after his designation pursuant to Rule 18.

Rule 14
Use of languages under Article 49(1) and (2) of the Agreement
1. Without prejudice to Articles 49(3) to (6) of the Agreement and subject to paragraph 2 and Rules 271.7, 321 to 323, proceedings shall be conducted:
(a) in the official language or one of the official languages designated as language(s) of proceedings pursuant to Article 49(1) of the Agreement; or
(b) in a language designated as language of proceedings by a Contracting Member State pursuant to Article 49(2) of the Agreement.

2. Where a Contracting Member State hosts a local division or participates in a regional division for which several languages have been designated pursuant to Article 49(1) and/or Article 49(2) of the Agreement.
(a) subject to paragraphs 2(b) and (c), the claimant may choose as the language of proceedings any of the language(s) designated pursuant to Article 49(1) and/or Article 49(2) of the Agreement;
(b) in proceedings before a local or regional division in a Contracting Member State against a defendant who has his domicile or principal place of business in that Contracting Member State where the action could not be brought pursuant to Article 33(1)(a) of the Agreement before any other local or regional division, proceedings shall be conducted in the official language of the Contracting Member State (paragraph 1(a)). Where a designation by a Contracting Member State having several official regional languages so indicates, proceedings shall be conducted in the official language of the region in which the defendant has his domicile or principal place of business. Where there are two or more such defendants whose domicile or principle place of business has different regional languages, the claimant may choose the language from the regional languages in question. Where a designation by a Contracting Member State having several official languages so indicates, proceedings shall be conducted in the official language of the defendant. Where there are two or more such defendants with different official languages, the claimant may choose the language from the official languages in question.
(c) Where a designation of a language under Article 49(2) of the Agreement for a regional division or for one or more local division(s) hosted in a Member State so indicates, the judge-rapporteur may order in the interest of the panel to provide that judges may use in the oral proceedings the language according to paragraph 1(a) and/or to provide that the Court may make any order and deliver any decision in the language according to paragraph 1(a) together with a certified translation for the purpose of Rule 118.8 into the language according to paragraph 1(b).

3. The Registrar shall maintain a list of languages communicated by Contracting Member States pursuant to Article 49(1) and Article 49(2) of the Agreement as well as designations by Contracting Member States made pursuant to paragraph 2(b) and (c). The list shall be made publically available online.
4. The Registrar shall return any pleading lodged in a language other than the language of proceedings.

Rule 15
Fee for the infringement action
1. The claimant shall pay the fixed fee and, where applicable, the value based fee for the infringement action in accordance with Part 6.
2. The Statement of claim shall not be deemed to have been lodged until the fixed fee and, where applicable, the value based fee for the infringement action has been paid, unless otherwise provided.
Relation with Agreement: Articles 36(3), 70 and 71

Rule 16
Examination as to formal requirements of the Statement of claim
1. The Registry shall as soon as practicable check whether the patent concerned is the subject of an opt-out pursuant to Article 83(3) of the Agreement and Rule 5. In the event of an opt-out the Registry shall as soon as practicable inform the claimant who may withdraw or amend the Statement of claim as appropriate.
2. The Registry shall, as soon as practicable after the lodging of the Statement of claim, examine whether the requirements of Rules 13.1 (a) to (j), .2, 14 and 15.1 have been complied with.
3. If the claimant has not complied with the requirements referred to in paragraph 2, the Registry shall as soon as practicable invite the claimant to:
(a) correct the deficiencies within 14 days of service of such notification; and
(b) where applicable, pay the fee for the infringement action within said 14 days.
4. The Registry shall at the same time inform the claimant that if the claimant fails to correct the deficiencies or pay the fee within the time stated, a decision by default may be given, in accordance with Rule 355.
5. If the claimant fails to correct the deficiencies or pay the fee, the Registry shall inform a judge of the division who may reject the action as inadmissible by a decision by default. The judge may give the claimant an opportunity to be heard beforehand.

Rule 17
Recording in the register and assignment (Court of First Instance, infringement action)
1. If the requirements referred to in Rule 16.2 have been complied with, the Registry shall as soon as practicable:
(a) record the date of receipt of the Statement of claim and attribute an action number to the file;
(b) record the file in the register; and
(c) inform the claimant of the action number of the file and the date of receipt.
2. The action shall be assigned to a panel of a division according to Rule 345.3. Where requested by the parties the action shall be assigned to a single judge in accordance with Rule 345.6.
3. The following shall determine the distribution of actions between the seat of the central division and its sections.
(a) Where an action involves a single patent having a single classification, the Registry shall allocate the action to the seat or the section of the central division appropriate to the classification of the patent according to Annex II of the Agreement. The Registry shall assign the action to a panel in accordance with Rule 345.3.
(b) Where an action involves more than one patent and a majority of the patents have a single classification appropriate to the seat or a single section of the central division according to Annex II of the Agreement, the Registry shall allocate the action to the seat or that section of the central division. The Registry shall assign the action to a panel in accordance with Rule 345.3.
(c) Where neither paragraph (a) nor (b) applies, especially where
(i) the action involves a single patent having more than one classification or
(ii) where the action involves more than one patent and no majority of the patents have a single classification corresponding to the seat or to one of the sections of the central division,
the Registry shall assign the action in accordance with Rule 345.3 to the panel at the seat or the section appropriate to the first classification of either the single patent or, where the action involves more than one patent, the patent first listed in the Statement of claim, according to Annex II of the Agreement. If the presiding judge of the respective panel considers that the reference of the action is appropriate, he shall accept it. If he considers otherwise, he shall instruct the Registry to refer the action in accordance with Rule 345.3 to the presiding judge of a panel of either the seat or the other section of the central division he considers appropriate, who shall likewise consider whether the re-allocation of the action is appropriate. If that presiding judge considers otherwise, he shall inform the President of the Court of First Instance, who shall allocate the action to the seat or the section of the central division he considers appropriate. The Registry shall assign the action to a panel in accordance with Rule 345.3.
4. The action shall be regarded as having commenced before the Court as from the date of receipt attributed to the Statement of claim.
Relation with Agreement: Article 7(2), Article 10

Rule 18
Designation of the judge-rapporteur
The presiding judge of the panel to which the action has been assigned [Rule 17.2] shall designate one legally qualified judge of the panel as judge-rapporteur. The presiding judge may designate himself as judge-rapporteur. The Registry shall as soon as practicable notify the claimant and defendant of the identity of the judge-rapporteur.

Procedure When the Defendant Raises a Preliminary Objection

Rule 19
Preliminary objection

1. Within one month of service of the Statement of claim, the defendant may lodge a Preliminary objection concerning:
   (a) the jurisdiction and competence of the Court, including any objection that an opt-out pursuant to Rule 5 applies to the patent that is the subject of the proceedings;
   (b) the competence of the division indicated by the claimant [Rule 13.1(i)];
   (c) the language of the Statement of claim [Rule 14].
2. A Preliminary objection shall contain:
   (a) particulars in accordance with Rule 24(a) to (c);
   (b) the decision or order sought by the defendant;
   (c) the grounds upon which the Preliminary objection is based; and
   (d) where appropriate the facts and evidence relied on.
3. The Preliminary objection shall be drawn up in the language pursuant to Rule 14.
4. If the action has been commenced before a regional division the defendant may by a Preliminary objection request a transfer of the action to the central division pursuant to Article 33(2) of the Agreement. The Preliminary objection shall in such a case contain all facts and evidence supporting the existence of the same infringement in the territories of three or more regional divisions.
5. The Registry shall as soon as practicable invite the claimant to comment on the Preliminary objection. Where applicable, the claimant may of his own motion correct any deficiency [paragraph 1(b) or (c)], within 14 days of service of notification of the Preliminary objection. Alternatively the claimant may submit written comments within the same period. The judge-rapporteur shall be informed of any correction made or written comments submitted by the claimant. If the deficiency referred to in paragraph 1(b) is corrected and the claimant has indicated another division, which is competent, the judge-rapporteur shall refer the action to the division indicated by the claimant.
6. The period for lodging the Statement of defence [Rule 23] shall not be affected by the lodging of a Preliminary objection, unless the judge-rapporteur decides otherwise.
7. The defendant's failure to lodge a Preliminary objection within the time period referred to in paragraph 1 shall be treated as a submission to the jurisdiction and competence of the Court and the competence of the division chosen by the claimant.

Rule 20
Decision or order on a Preliminary objection

1. As soon as practicable after the expiry of the period referred to in Rule 19.5, the judge-rapporteur shall decide the Preliminary objection. The judge-rapporteur shall give the parties an opportunity to be heard. The decision shall include instructions to the parties and to the Registry concerning the next step in the proceedings.
2. Where the Preliminary objection is to be dealt with in the main proceedings, the judge-rapporteur shall inform the parties.

Rule 21
Appeal against decision or order on a Preliminary objection

1. A decision of the judge-rapporteur allowing the Preliminary objection may be appealed pursuant to Rule 220.1(a). An order of the judge-rapporteur rejecting the Preliminary objection may only be appealed pursuant to Rule 220.2.
2. If an appeal is lodged, proceedings at first instance may be stayed by the judge-rapporteur or the Court of Appeal on a reasoned request by a party.

Value-Based Fee for the Infringement Action

Rule 22
Determination of value-based fee for the infringement action

1. The value of the infringement action shall be determined by the judge-rapporteur under Rule 370.6, taking into account the value as assessed by the parties, by way of an order during the interim procedure.
2. Where the value of the infringement action exceeds EUR 500.000, the claimant shall pay a value-based fee for the infringement action, in accordance with Part 6. Rule 16.3 to .5 shall apply *mutatis mutandis*.

Statement of Defence

Rule 23
Lodging of the Statement of defence
The defendant shall lodge a Statement of defence within three months of service of the Statement of claim.

Rule 24
Contents of the Statement of defence
The Statement of defence shall contain:
(a) the names of the defendant and of the defendant's representative;
(b) postal and electronic addresses for service on the defendant and the names and addresses of the persons authorised to accept service;
(c) the action number of the file;
(d) an indication whether the defendant has lodged a Preliminary objection [Rule 19];
(e) an indication of the facts relied on, including any challenge to the facts relied on by the claimant;
(f) the evidence relied on [Rule 170.1], where available, and an indication of any further evidence which will be offered in support;
(g) the reasons why the action shall fail, arguments of law and any argument arising from the provisions of Article 28 of the Agreement and where appropriate any challenge to the claimant's proposed claim interpretation;
(h) an indication of any order the defendant will seek in respect of the infringement action during the interim procedure [Rule 104(e)];
(i) a statement whether the defendant disputes the claimant's assessment of the value of the infringement action and the grounds for such dispute; and
(j) a list of the documents, including any witness statements, referred to in the Statement of defence together with any request that all or part of any such document need not be translated and/or any request pursuant to Rule 262.1. Rule 13.2 and .3 shall apply *mutatis mutandis*.

Rule 25
Counterclaim for revocation
1. If the Statement of defence includes an assertion that the patent alleged to be infringed is invalid the Statement of defence shall include a Counterclaim against the proprietor of the patent for revocation of said patent in accordance with Rule 42. The Counterclaim for revocation shall contain:
(a) an indication of the extent to which revocation of the patent is requested;
(b) one or more grounds for revocation, which shall as far as possible be supported by arguments of law, and where appropriate an explanation of the defendant's proposed claim construction;
(c) an indication of the facts relied on;
(d) the evidence relied on, where available, and an indication of any further evidence which will be offered in support;
(e) an indication of any order the defendant will seek during the interim procedure [Rule 104(e)];
(f) a statement of his position, if any, on the options provided for in Article 33(3) of the Agreement and Rule 37.4;
(g) a list of the documents, including any witness statements, referred to in the Counterclaim for revocation together with any request that all or part of any such documents need not be translated. Rule 13.2 and .3 shall apply *mutatis mutandis;* and
(h) insofar as the proprietor of the patent is not claimant in the infringement proceedings, the information required by Rule 13.1(b) and (d) in respect of said proprietor.

2. Where the claimant is not the proprietor or not the only proprietor of the patent concerned, the Registry shall as soon as practicable serve a copy of the Counterclaim for revocation on the relevant proprietor in accordance with Rule 13.1(e) and shall supply a copy of each document referred to in paragraph 1(h). Rule 271 shall apply *mutatis mutandis*. The proprietor in question shall become a party to the revocation proceedings and shall be treated as defendant in all subsequent proceedings. The proprietor shall provide details pursuant to Rule 13.1(e) if not already provided by the claimant.

Rule 26
Fee for the Counterclaim for revocation
The defendant shall pay the fee for the Counterclaim for revocation in accordance with Part 6. Rule 15.2 shall apply *mutatis mutandis*.

Rule 27
Examination as to formal requirements of the Statement of defence

1. The Registry shall, as soon as practicable after the lodging of the Statement of defence:
   (a) examine whether the requirements of Rule 24(a) to (d) have been complied with; and
   (b) if the Statement of defence includes a Counterclaim for revocation, examine whether the obligation to pay the fee pursuant to Rule 26 has been complied with.

2. If the Registry considers that the Statement of defence or the Counterclaim for revocation does not comply with any of the requirements referred to in paragraph 1, it shall as soon as practicable invite the defendant to:
   (a) correct the deficiencies noted, within 14 days of service of such notification; and
   (b) where applicable, pay the fee for the Counterclaim for revocation, within said 14 days.

3. The Registry shall at the same time inform the defendant that if the defendant fails to correct the deficiencies or pay the fee within the time stated, a decision by default may be given, in accordance with Rule 355.

4. If the defendant fails to correct the deficiencies or to pay the fee for the Counterclaim for revocation, as appropriate, within said 14 days, the Registry shall inform the judge-rapporteur who may give a decision by default. He may give the defendant an opportunity to be heard beforehand.

Rule 28
Further schedule

As soon as practicable after service of the Statement of defence, the judge-rapporteur shall, after consulting the parties, set a date and time for an interim conference (where necessary [Rule 101.1]) and set a date for the oral hearing. The judge-rapporteur may set one alternative date.

Defence to the Counterclaim for Revocation, reply to the statement of the defence and Application to Amend the Patent and rejoinder to the reply

Rule 29
Lodging of Defence to the Counterclaim for revocation, Reply to the Statement of defence and Rejoinder to the Reply

(a) Within two months of service of a Statement of defence which includes a Counterclaim for revocation, the claimant shall lodge a Defence to the Counterclaim for revocation together with any Reply to the Statement of defence and any Application to amend the patent pursuant to Rule 30, if applicable.
(b) Within two months of service of a Statement of defence which does not include a Counterclaim for revocation, the claimant may lodge a Reply to the Statement of defence.
(c) Within one month of service of a Reply to the Statement of defence which does not include a Counterclaim for revocation the defendant may lodge a Rejoinder to the Reply to the Statement of defence. The Rejoinder to the Reply to the Statement of defence shall be limited to a response to the matters raised in the Reply to the Statement of defence.
(d) Within two months of service of the Defence to Counterclaim the defendant may lodge a Reply to the Defence to the Counterclaim together with any Rejoinder to the Reply to the Statement of defence and any Defence to an Application to amend the patent pursuant to Rule 32, if applicable.
(e) Within one month of the service of the Reply to the Defence to the Counterclaim, the claimant may lodge a Rejoinder to the Reply together with any Reply to the Defence to an Application to amend the patent pursuant to Rule 32, if applicable. The Rejoinder to the Reply to the Statement of defence shall be limited to a response to the matters raised in the Reply to the Statement of defence.
(f) Where the claimant is not the proprietor of the patent, all references to the claimant in this Rule 29 regarding an Application to amend the patent shall be read as including the proprietor.

Rule 29A
Contents of the Defence to the Counterclaim

The Defence to the Counterclaim for revocation shall contain:
(a) an indication of the facts relied on, including any challenge to the facts relied on by the defendant;
(b) the evidence relied on [Rule 170.1], where available, and an indication of any further evidence which will be offered in support;
(c) the reasons why the Counterclaim for revocation shall fail, including arguments of law and any argument as to why any dependent claim of the patent is independently valid;
(d) an indication of any order the claimant and the proprietor will seek in respect of the revocation action at the interim conference [Rule 104(e)];
(e) the claimant's and the proprietor's response to the defendant's choice of option, if any, provided for in Article 33(3) of the Agreement and Rule 37.4;and

(f) a list of the documents, including any witness statements, referred to in the Defence to the Counterclaim together with any request that all or part of any such document shall not be translated and/or any request pursuant to Rule 262.1. Rule 13.2 and .3 shall apply *mutatis mutandis.*

Rule 30
Application to amend the patent

1. The Defence to the Counterclaim for revocation may include an Application by the proprietor of the patent to amend the patent which shall contain:

(a) the proposed amendments of the claims of the patent concerned and/or specification, including where applicable and appropriate one or more alternative sets of claims (auxiliary requests), in the language in which the patent was granted; where the language of the proceedings [Rule 14.3] is not the language in which the patent was granted, the proprietor shall lodge a translation of the proposed amendments in the language of the proceedings, and where the patent is a European patent with unitary effect in the language of the defendant's domicile in a Member State of the EU or of the place of the alleged infringement or threatened infringement in a Contracting Member State if so requested by the defendant;

(b) an explanation as to why the amendments satisfy the requirements of Articles 84 and 123(2), (3) EPC and why the proposed amended claims are valid and, if applicable, why they are infringed; and

(c) an indication whether the proposals are conditional or unconditional; the proposed amendments, if conditional, must be reasonable in number in the circumstances of the case.

2. Any subsequent request to amend the patent may only be admitted into the proceedings with the permission of the Court.

3. Where other proceedings involving the patent subject to an Application to amend the patent are pending, the claimant shall notify the Court or the authority in question that such an Application has been made and provide the information required in paragraph 1(a).

DEFENCE TO THE APPLICATION TO AMEND THE PATENT

Rule 32
Lodging of the Defence to the Application to amend the patent, the Reply to the Defence and the Rejoinder to the Reply

1. Within two months of service of an Application to amend the patent, the defendant shall lodge a Defence to the Application to amend the patent setting out whether he opposes the Application to amend the patent and, if so, why:

(a) the proposed amendments are not allowable; and

(b) the patent cannot be maintained as requested.

2. Where appropriate in view of the proposed amendments, the Defence to the Application to amend the patent may contain submissions in accordance with Rule 44(d) to (h) and alternative non-infringement submissions.

3. The proprietor may lodge a Reply to the Defence to the Application to amend the patent within one month of service of the Defence and the defendant may within one month of the service of the Reply lodge a Rejoinder to the Reply. The Rejoinder shall be limited to the matters raised in the Reply.

APPLICATION FOR ALLOCATING A TECHNICALLY QUALIFIED JUDGE TO THE PANEL

Rule 33
Application by a party for allocating a technically qualified judge

1. Any party to the proceedings may lodge an Application for allocating a technically qualified judge to the panel which shall contain an indication of the relevant field of technology.

2. The Application shall be lodged as early as possible in the written procedure. An Application lodged after the closure of the written procedure [Rule 35] shall only be granted if justified in view of changed circumstances, such as new submissions presented by the other party, and allowed by the Court.

3. If the requirements of paragraphs 1 and 2 have been complied with, the President of the Court of First Instance shall allocate a technically qualified judge to the panel, after consulting the judge-rapporteur.

Rule 34
Request by the judge-rapporteur for allocating a technically qualified judge

1. The judge-rapporteur may at any time during the written procedure, after consulting the presiding judge and the parties, request the President of the Court of First Instance to allocate a technically qualified judge to the panel.

2. Where a technically qualified judge is allocated to the panel, the judge-rapporteur may at any time consult the technically qualified judge.

LAST STEPS IN THE WRITTEN PROCEDURE

Rule 35
Closure of the written procedure
Following the exchange of written pleadings in accordance with Rule 12.1 and, where applicable, in accordance with Rule 12.2 to .4, the judge-rapporteur shall:
(a) inform the parties of the date on which he intends to close the written procedure, without prejudice to Rule 36; and
(b) where an interim conference is necessary [Rules 28 and 101.1], confirm the date and the time set for the interim conference [Rule 28] or inform the parties that an interim conference will not be held.

Rule 36
Further exchanges of written pleadings
Without prejudice to the powers of the judge-rapporteur pursuant to Rule 110.1, on a reasoned request by a party lodged before the date on which the judge-rapporteur intends to close the written procedure [Rule 35(a)], the judge-rapporteur may allow the exchange of further written pleadings, within a period to be specified. Where the exchange of further written pleadings is allowed, the written procedure shall be deemed closed upon expiry of the specified period.

Rule 37
Application of Article 33(3) of the Agreement
1. As soon as practicable after the closure of the written procedure the panel shall decide by way of order how to proceed with respect to the application of Article 33(3) of the Agreement. The parties shall be given an opportunity to be heard [Rule 264]. The panel shall set out in its order brief reasons for its decision.
2. The Panel may by order take an earlier decision if appropriate having considered the parties' pleadings and having given the parties an opportunity to be heard [Rule 264].
3. Where the panel decides to proceed in accordance with Article 33(3)(a) of the Agreement, the judge-rapporteur shall request the President of the Court of First Instance to allocate to the panel a technically qualified judge if not already allocated pursuant to Rules 33 and 34.
4. Where the panel decides to proceed in accordance with Article 33(3)(b) of the Agreement, the panel may stay the infringement proceedings pending a final decision in the revocation proceedings and shall stay the infringement proceedings where there is a high likelihood that the relevant claims of the patent will be held to be invalid on any ground by the final decision in the revocation proceedings.
5. Where the panel decides to proceed in accordance with Article 33(3)(b) of the Agreement and not to stay the proceedings, the judge-rapporteur of the regional or local division shall communicate to the central division the dates set for the interim conference and for the oral hearing according to Rule 28.

COUNTERCLAIM FOR REVOCATION REFERRED TO THE CENTRAL DIVISION UNDER ARTICLE 33(3)(B) OF THE AGREEMENT

Rule 38
Written procedure when the central division deals with a Counterclaim for revocation under Article 33(3)(b) of the Agreement
When a Counterclaim for revocation is referred to the central division, it shall be dealt with as follows:
(a) Rule 17.2 and .3 shall apply *mutatis mutandis;*
(b) Rule 18 shall apply *mutatis mutandis:* the presiding judge of the panel to which the Counterclaim for revocation has been assigned shall designate one legally qualified judge of the panel as judge-rapporteur;
(c) The judge-rapporteur shall give any further directions necessary for the future conduct of the written procedure before the central division;
(d) Rule 28 shall apply *mutatis mutandis:* the judge-rapporteur shall after consulting the parties set a date and a time for the interim conference (where necessary [Rules 28 and 101]) and set a date, and one alternative date, for the oral hearing.

Rule 39
Language of the proceedings before the central division
1. Where the language of the proceedings before the local division or the regional division which referred the Counterclaim for revocation to the central division is not the language in which the patent was granted, the judge-rapporteur may order that the parties lodge, within a period of one month, a translation in the language in which the patent was granted of any written pleadings and such other documents lodged during the written procedure as the judge-rapporteur may direct.

2. Where appropriate, the judge-rapporteur may specify in his order that only excerpts of parties' written pleadings and other documents shall be translated.
3. Where the language of the proceedings before the local division or the regional division is the language in which the patent was granted the pleadings served in accordance with Rules 24, 25, 29, 29a, 30 and 32 shall stand.

Rule 40
Accelerated proceedings before the central division
The judge-rapporteur shall accelerate proceedings before the central division where
(a) an Application for provisional measures has been lodged [Rule 206]; or
(b) the regional or local division has referred the Counterclaim for revocation to the central division and where the infringement action has not been stayed.
In the latter case, the judge-rapporteur of the panel of the central division shall endeavour to set a date for the oral hearing on the revocation action prior to the date of the oral hearing of the infringement action.

ACTION REFERRED TO THE CENTRAL DIVISION UNDER ARTICLE 33(3)(C) OF THE AGREEMENT

Rule 41
Written procedure when the central division deals with the action under Article 33(3)(c) of the Agreement
When an action is referred to the central division under Article 33(3)(c) of the Agreement, it shall be dealt with as follows:
(a) Rule 17.2 and .3 shall apply *mutatis mutandis.* The parties may request that the action be heard by a single judge;
(b) Rule 18 shall apply *mutatis mutandis:* the presiding judge of the panel to which the action has been assigned shall designate one judge of the panel as judge-rapporteur;
(c) dates already set under Rule 28 shall be confirmed wherever possible;
(d) Rule 39 shall apply *mutatis mutandis:* the judge-rapporteur may order that the parties lodge a translation in the language in which the patent was granted of any written pleadings lodged during the written procedure; where appropriate, the judge-rapporteur may specify in his order that only excerpts of parties' written pleadings and other documents shall be translated. Otherwise the pleadings lodged during the written procedure shall stand;
(e) The judge-rapporteur shall give any further directions necessary for the future conduct of the written procedure before the central division.

SECTION 2
REVOCATION ACTION

Rule 42
Action to be directed against the patent proprietor
1. Any action for the revocation of a patent shall be directed against the proprietor of the patent.
2. If the action for revocation is directed against the proprietor in accordance with Rule 8.6 ("the registered proprietor") but the registered proprietor is not a proprietor within the meaning of Rule 8.5(a) or (b) ("the Rule 8.5 proprietor") each such registered proprietor shall as soon as practicable after service of the Statement for revocation apply to the Court pursuant to Rule 305.1(c) for the substitution of the registered proprietor by the Rule 8.5 proprietor.
Relation with Agreement: Articles 47(5) and 65(1)

Rule 43
Exchange of written pleadings (revocation action)
1. The written procedure shall consist of:
(a) the lodging of a Statement for revocation (by the claimant) [Rule 44]; and
(b) the lodging of a Defence to revocation (by the defendant) [Rule 49]; and optionally
(c) the lodging of a Reply to the Defence to revocation (by the claimant) [Rule 51];
(d) the lodging of a Rejoinder to the Reply (by the defendant) [Rule 52].
2. The Defence to revocation may include:
(a) an Application to amend the patent; and
(b) a Counterclaim for infringement by the proprietor of the patent.
3. If an Application to amend the patent is lodged, the claimant shall lodge a Defence to the Application to amend the patent. The defendant may lodge a Reply to the Defence to the Application. The claimant may lodge a Rejoinder to the Reply. The Rejoinder shall be limited to a response to the matters raised in the Reply.
4. If a Counterclaim for infringement is lodged, the claimant shall lodge a Defence to the Counterclaim for infringement [Rule 56], the defendant may lodge a Reply to the Defence to the Counterclaim [Rule 56.3] and the claimant may lodge a Rejoinder to the Reply [Rule 56.4].
5. Rule 12.5 shall apply.

STATEMENT FOR REVOCATION

Rule 44
Contents of the Statement for revocation
The claimant shall, subject to point (b), lodge a Statement for revocation at the Registry in accordance with Article 7(2) of the Agreement and Annex II thereto. The Statement for revocation shall contain:
(a) particulars in accordance with Rule 13.1(a) to (d) and (g), (h);
(b) where the parties have agreed to bring the action before a local division or a regional division in accordance with Article 33(7) of the Agreement, an indication of the division which shall hear the action, accompanied by evidence of the defendant's agreement;
(c) where applicable, an indication that the action shall be heard by a single judge [Article 8(7) of the Agreement], accompanied by evidence of the defendant's agreement;
(d) an indication of the extent to which revocation of the patent is requested;
(e) one or more grounds for revocation, which shall as far as possible be supported by arguments of law, and where appropriate an explanation of the claimant's proposed claim construction;
(f) an indication of the facts relied on;
(g) the evidence relied on, where available, and an indication of any further evidence which will be offered in support;
(h) an indication of any order the claimant will seek during the interim procedure [Rule 104(e)];
and(i) a list of the documents, including any witness statements, referred to in the Statement for revocation together with any request that all or part of any such document need not be translated and/or any request pursuant to Rule 262.1. Rule 13.2 and .3 shall apply *mutatis mutandis.*

Rule 45
Language of the Statement for revocation
1. Subject to paragraph 2, the Statement for revocation shall be drawn up in the language in which the patent was granted.
2. Where the parties have agreed to bring the action before a local or a regional division in accordance with Article 33(7) of the Agreement, the Statement for revocation shall be drawn up in one of the languages referred to in Rule 14.1(a) and (b).
Relation with Agreement: Article 49

Rule 46
Fee for the revocation action
The claimant shall pay the fee for the revocation action in accordance with Part 6. Rule 15.2 shall apply *mutatis mutandis.*
Relation with Agreement: Articles 70 and 71

Rule 47
Examination as to formal requirements, recording in the register, assignment (Court of First Instance, revocation action) and designation of the judge-rapporteur
1. Rules 16 to 18 shall apply *mutatis mutandis.*
2. The Registrar shall notify the European Patent Office that the patent in question is subject to an action for revocation.
Relation with Agreement: Articles 10 and 33

Rule 48
Preliminary objection
Rule 19.1 to .3 and .5 to .7 as well as Rules 20 and 21 shall apply *mutatis mutandis.*

DEFENCE TO REVOCATION

Rule 49
Lodging of the Defence to revocation
1. The defendant shall lodge a Defence to revocation within two months of service of the Statement for revocation.
2. The Defence to revocation may include:
(a) an Application to amend the patent;
(b) a Counterclaim for infringement.

Rule 50
Contents of the Defence to revocation and Counterclaim for infringement

1. The Defence to revocation shall contain the matters referred to in Rule 24(a) to (c). Rule 29A(a) to (d) and (f) to (g) shall apply *mutatis mutandis*.
2. Any Application to amend the patent shall contain the matters referred to in Rule 30.1(a), (c) and an explanation as to why the amendments satisfy the requirements of Articles 84 and 123(2), (3) EPC and why the proposed amended claims are valid. Rule 30.2 shall apply.
3. Any Counterclaim for infringement shall contain the matters referred to in Rule 13.1 (k) to (q). Rule 13.2 and .3 shall apply.

Rule 51
Reply to Defence to revocation

Within two months of service of the Defence to revocation the claimant may lodge a Reply to the Defence to revocation together with any Defence to an Application to amend the patent pursuant to Rule 43.3 and 55 as well as any Defence to the Counterclaim for infringement pursuant to Rule 56.1, if applicable.

Rule 52
Rejoinder to the Reply

Within one month of the service of the Reply the defendant may lodge a Rejoinder to the Reply to the Defence to revocation together with any Reply to the Defence to an Application to amend the patent pursuant to Rule 43.3 and 55 as well as any Reply to the Defence to the Counterclaim for infringement pursuant to Rule 56.3, if applicable. The Rejoinder shall be limited to a response to the matters raised in the Reply.

Rule 53
Fee for the Counterclaim for infringement

The defendant shall pay the fixed fee and, where applicable, the value based fee for the Counterclaim for infringement in accordance with Part 6. Rule 15 and Rule 16.3 to 5 shall apply *mutatis mutandis*.

Rule 54
Examination as to formal requirements and further schedule

Rules 27 and 28 shall apply *mutatis mutandis*.

DEFENCE TO THE APPLICATION TO AMEND THE PATENT AND DEFENCE TO THE COUNTERCLAIM FOR INFRINGEMENT

Rule 55
Lodging of the Defence to the Application to amend the patent, the Reply to the Defence and the Rejoinder to the Reply

Rule 32 shall apply *mutatis mutandis*.

Rule 56
Lodging of the Defence to the Counterclaim for infringement

1. Within two months of service of a Counterclaim for infringement, the claimant shall lodge a Defence to the Counterclaim for infringement.
2. The Defence to the Counterclaim for infringement shall contain the matters referred to in Rule 24.1(e) to (h) and (j) and a statement whether the claimant disputes the defendant's assessment of the value of the Counterclaim pursuant to Rule 50.3 and the reasons for such dispute.
3. The defendant may lodge a Reply to the Defence to the Counterclaim for infringement within one month.
4. Within one month of the service of the Reply to the Defence to the Counterclaim for infringement the claimant may lodge a Rejoinder to the Reply together with any Rejoinder to the Reply to the Defence to the Application to amend the patent pursuant to Rule 43.3 and 55. The Rejoinder shall be limited to matters raised in the Reply.

Rule 57
Request for allocating a technically qualified judge

Rules 33 and 34 shall apply *mutatis mutandis*.

Rule 58
Closure of the written procedure subject to the possible exchange of further pleadings

Rules 35 and 36 shall apply *mutatis mutandis*.

Rule 60
Determination of the value-based fee for the Counterclaim for infringement
1. The value of the Counterclaim for infringement shall be determined by the judge-rapporteur under Rule 370.6, taking into account the value as assessed by the parties, by way of an order during the interim procedure.
2. Where the value of the Counterclaim for infringement exceeds EUR 500.000, the defendant shall pay a value-based fee in accordance with Part 6. Rule 16.3 to .5 shall apply *mutatis mutandis.*

SECTION 3
ACTION FOR DECLARATION OF NON-INFRINGEMENT

Rule 61
Declaration of non-infringement
1. A declaration that the performance of a specific act does not, or a proposed act would not, constitute an infringement of a patent may be made by the Court in proceedings between the person doing or proposing to do the act and the patent proprietor or licensee entitled to commence infringement proceedings pursuant to Article 47 of the Agreement, if the patent proprietor or such licensee has asserted that the act is an infringement, or, if no such assertion has been made by the patent proprietor or licensee, if:
(a) that person has applied in writing to the proprietor or licensee for a written acknowledgment to the effect of the declaration claimed, and has provided him with full particulars in writing of the act in question; and
(b) the proprietor or licensee has refused or failed to give any such acknowledgment within one month.
2. The action for a declaration shall be directed against the proprietor of the patent or the licensee who has asserted an infringement or refused or failed to give an acknowledgement pursuant to paragraph 1(b).
3. If the action for a declaration of non-infringement is directed against the proprietor of the patent in accordance with Rule 8.6 ("the registered proprietor") but the registered proprietor is not a proprietor within the meaning of Rule 8.5(a) or (b) ("the Rule 8.5 proprietor") each such registered proprietor shall as soon as possible after service of the Statement for a declaration of non-infringement apply to the Court pursuant to Rule 305.1(c) for the substitution of the registered proprietor by the Rule 8.5 proprietor.

Rule 62
Exchange of written pleadings (action for declaration of non-infringement)
1. The written procedure shall consist of:
(a) the lodging of a Statement for a declaration of non-infringement (by the claimant) [Rule 63];
(b) the lodging of a Defence to the Statement for a declaration of non-infringement (by the defendant) [Rules 67 and 68]; and, optionally
(c) the lodging of a Reply to the Defence to the Statement for a declaration of non-infringement [Rule 69];
(d) the lodging of a Rejoinder to the Reply [Rule 69].
2. Rule 12.5 shall apply.

Rule 63
Contents of the Statement for a declaration of non-infringement
The claimant shall, subject to point (b), lodge at the Registry in accordance with Article 33(4), Article 7(2) of the Agreement and Annex II thereto, a Statement for a declaration of non-infringement which shall contain:
(a) particulars in accordance with Rule 13.1(a) to (h) and particulars confirming that the requirements of Rule 61 are met;
(b) where the parties have agreed to bring the action before a local division or a regional division in accordance with Article 33(7) of the Agreement, an indication of the division which shall hear the action, accompanied by evidence of the defendant's agreement;
(c) where applicable, an indication that the action shall be heard by a single judge [Article 8(7) of the Agreement], accompanied by evidence of the defendant's agreement;
(d) the declaration sought by the claimant;
(e) the reasons why the performance of a specific act does not, or a proposed act would not, constitute an infringement of the patent concerned, including arguments of law and where appropriate an explanation of the claimant's proposed claim construction;
(f) an indication of the facts relied on;
(g) the evidence relied on, where available, and an indication of any further evidence which will be offered in support;
(h) an indication of any order the claimant will seek at the interim conference [Rule 104(e)];

(i) where the claimant assesses that the value of the declaratory action exceeds EUR 500.000, an indication of the value; and

(j) a list of the documents, including any witness statements, referred to in the Statement for a declaration together with any request that all or part of any such document need not be translated and/or any request pursuant to Rule 262.1. Rule 13.2 and .3 shall apply *mutatis mutandis.*

Rule 64
Language of the Statement for a declaration of non-infringement
Rule 45 shall apply *mutatis mutandis.*

Rule 65
Examination as to formal requirements, recording in the register, assignment and designation of the judge-rapporteur
Rules 16 to 18 shall apply *mutatis mutandis.*

Rule 66
Preliminary objection
Rule 19.1 to .3 and .5 to .7 as well as Rules 20 and 21 shall apply *mutatis mutandis.*

Rule 67
Lodging of the Defence to the Statement for a declaration of non-infringement
The defendant shall lodge a Defence to the Statement for a declaration of non-infringement within two months of service of the Statement for a declaration of non-infringement.

Rule 68
Contents of the Defence to the Statement for a declaration of non-infringement
The Defence to the Statement for a declaration of non-infringement shall contain the matters referred to in Rule 24(a) to (j). Rule 13.2 and .3 shall apply *mutatis mutandis.*

Rule 69
Reply to Defence to the Statement for a declaration of non-infringement and Rejoinder to the Reply
1. The claimant may lodge a Reply to the Defence to the Statement for a declaration of non-infringement within one month.
2. The defendant may lodge a Rejoinder to the Reply within one month of service of the Reply. The Rejoinder shall be limited to the matters raised in the Reply.

Rule 70
Fee for the action for a declaration of non-infringement
The claimant shall pay the fixed fee and, where applicable, the value based fee for the action for a declaration of non-infringement in accordance with Part 6. Rule 15.2 and Rule 16.3 to .5 shall apply *mutatis mutandis.*

Rule 71
Examination as to formal requirements and further schedule
Rules 27 and 28 shall apply *mutatis mutandis.*

Rule 72
Request for allocating a technically qualified judge
Rules 33 and 34 shall apply *mutatis mutandis.*

Rule 73
Closure of the written procedure subject to the possible exchange of further pleadings
Rules 35 and 36 shall apply *mutatis mutandis.*

Rule 74
Value-based fee for the action for a declaration of non-infringement
1. The value of the action for a declaration of non-infringement shall be determined by the judge-rapporteur under Rule 370.6, taking into account the value as assessed by the parties, by way of an order during the interim procedure.
2. Where the value exceeds EUR500.000 the claimant shall pay a value-based fee for the action for a declaration of non-infringement in accordance with Part 6. Rule 16.3 to .5 shall apply *mutatis mutandis.*

SECTION 4
ACTIONS WITHIN ARTICLE 33(5) AND (6) OF THE AGREEMENT

Rule 75
Revocation action and subsequent infringement action in a local or regional division (Article 33(5) of the Agreement).

1. Where a claimant has lodged a Statement for revocation [Rule 44] before the central division and the defendant or a licensee entitled to commence proceedings pursuant to Article 47 of the Agreement subsequently initiates an infringement action in a local or regional division against the claimant in respect of the same patent the following procedures shall apply.
2. The Registry at the local or regional division shall proceed in accordance with Rules 16 and 17. The Registry shall as soon as practicable notify the President of the Court of First Instance of the revocation action in the central division, the infringement action in the local or regional division and any Counterclaim for revocation in the infringement action. The presiding judges of the panels seized shall be informed likewise about actions in the other divisions.
3. Where a Counterclaim for revocation is brought in the infringement action and there is identity of parties as between the two actions, unless otherwise agreed by the parties, the panel appointed in the central division to hear the revocation action shall stay all further proceedings in the revocation action pending a decision of the panel hearing the action for infringement pursuant to Article 33(3) of the Agreement and Rule 37.
4. The panel hearing the action for infringement shall when exercising its discretion under Article 33(3) of the Agreement take into consideration how far the revocation action in the central division was advanced prior to the stay referred to in paragraph 3.
5. Where the panel hearing the action for infringement decides to proceed in accordance with Article 33(3)(a) of the Agreement, Rules 33 and 34 shall apply *mutatis mutandis* to the action for infringement.
6. Where the panel hearing the action for infringement decides to proceed in accordance with Article 33(3)(b) or (c) of the Agreement, Rules 37.4 and 39 to 41 shall apply *mutatis mutandis.*

Rule 76
Actions for declaration of non-infringement within Article 33(6) of the Agreement

1. Where a claimant has lodged an action for declaration of non-infringement (Rule 61) before the central division against the patent proprietor or a licensee entitled to commence infringement proceedings pursuant to Article 47 of the Agreement and the defendant proprietor or licensee subsequently initiates an action for infringement in a local or regional division against the claimant in respect of the same patent and with respect to the same alleged infringement the following procedure shall apply.
2. The Registry shall proceed in accordance with Rule 16 and 17. The Registry shall as soon as practicable notify the President of the Court of First Instance of the co-pending actions and the dates attributed to them. The presiding judges of the panels seized shall be informed likewise about the action in the other division.
3. If the date attributed by the Registry to the action for infringement pursuant to Rule 17.1(a) is within three months of the date attributed to the action for declaration of non-infringement the panel of the central division shall stay all further proceedings in the action for a declaration. If the date attributed to the action for infringement is outside the said three month period there shall be no stay but the presiding judges of the central division and the local or regional division concerned shall consult to agree on the future progress of proceedings including the possibility of a stay of one action pursuant to Rule 295(k).

Rule 77
Action for declaration of non-infringement and action for revocation

An action for declaration of non-infringement may be lodged together with an action for revocation of the patent in question. Fees shall be paid in accordance with both Rules 46 and Rules 70 and 74.

SECTION 5
ACTION FOR COMPENSATION FOR LICENCES ON THE BASIS OF ARTICLE 8 OF REGULATION (EU) NO 1257/2012

Rule 80
Compensation for a licence of right

1. The Application for appropriate compensation [Article 32(1)(h) of the Agreement] shall contain:
   (a) particulars in accordance with Rule 13.1(a) to (d);
   (b) information on the filing of the statement as referred to in Article 8(1) of Regulation (EU) No 1257/2012;
   (c) the licence agreement referred to in Article 8(2) of Regulation (EU) No 1257/2012.

2. Rules 132, 133, 134, 135 and 137 to 140 apply *mutatis mutandis* to the procedure for appropriate compensation.
Relation with Agreement: Article 32(1)(h)

SECTION 6
ACTION AGAINST DECISIONS OF THE EUROPEAN PATENT OFFICE IN CARRYING OUT THE TASKS REFERRED TO IN ARTICLE 9 OF REGULATION (EU) NO 1257/2012

Relation with Agreement: Articles 32(1)(i), 47(7) and 66

Rule 85
Stages of the proceedings (*ex parte* proceedings)
1. Subject to paragraph 2, where an action is brought against a decision of the European Patent Office in carrying out the tasks referred to in Article 9 of Regulation (EU) No 1257/2012 (hereinafter "decision of the Office"), proceedings before the Court of First Instance shall consist of:
(a) a written procedure, which shall include a possibility for interlocutory review by the European Patent Office;
(b) an interim procedure, which may include an interim conference; and
(c) an oral procedure which, at the request of the claimant or at the instance of the Court, may include an oral hearing.
2. This Rule and Rules 88 (save as expressly provided for in Rule 97.2), 89 and 91 to 96 shall not apply to an expedited action against a decision of the Office pursuant to Rule 97.

Rule 86
Suspensive effect
An action against a decision of the Office shall have suspensive effect.

Rule 87
Grounds for annulling or altering a decision of the Office
An action against a decision of the Office may be brought on grounds of:
(a) infringement of Regulation (EU) No 1257/2012 or of Regulation (EU) No 1260/2012 or of any rule of law relating to their application;
(b) infringement of any of the implementing rules of the European Patent Office for carrying out the tasks referred to in Article 9(1) of Regulation (EU) No 1257/2012;
(c) infringement of an essential procedural requirement;
(d) misuse of power.

Rule 88
Application to annul or alter a decision of the Office
1. The claimant shall lodge an Application at the Registry, in accordance with Article 7(2) of the Agreement and Annex II thereto, to annul or alter a decision of the Office in the language in which the patent was granted, within two months of service of the decision of the Office.
2. The Application to annul or alter a decision of the Office shall contain:
(a) the names of the claimant and, where applicable, of the claimant's representative;
(b) where the claimant is not the proprietor of or applicant for the European patent with unitary effect, an explanation and evidence that he is adversely affected by the decision of the Office and entitled to start proceedings [Article 47(7) of the Agreement];
(c) postal and electronic addresses for service on the claimant and the names and addresses of the persons authorised to accept service;
(d) a reference to the contested decision of the Office;
(e) where applicable, information about any prior or pending proceedings relating to the patent concerned before the Court, the European Patent Office or any other court or authority;
(f) an indication whether the action shall be heard by a single judge;
(g) the order or the remedy sought by the claimant;
(h) one or more grounds for annulling or altering the contested decision, in accordance with Rule 87;
(i) the facts, evidence and arguments relied on; and
(j) a list of the documents, including any witness statements, referred to in the Application together with any request that all or part of any such document need not be translated and/ or any request pursuant to Rule 262.1. Rule 13.2 and 3 shall apply *mutatis mutandis.*
3. The claimant shall pay the fee for the action against a decision of the Office, in accordance with Part 6. Rule 15.2 shall apply *mutatis mutandis.*
4. Rule 8 shall not apply.
Relation with Agreement: Articles 32(1)(i), 33(9), 47(7), 48(7) and 49(6)

Rule 89
Examination as to formal requirements (ex *parte* proceedings)

1. The Registry shall, as soon as practicable after an Application to annul or alter a decision of the Office has been lodged, examine whether the requirements of Articles 47(7) and 49(6) of the Agreement and Rule 88.1, .2(a) to (d) and .3 have been complied with.

2. If the Registry considers that any of the requirements referred to in paragraph 1 has not been complied with, it shall invite the claimant to:

(a) correct the deficiencies noted, within 14 days from the date of service of such notification; and

(b) where applicable, pay the fee for the action against a decision of the Office, within said 14 days.

3. The Registry shall at the same time inform the claimant that if the claimant fails to correct the deficiencies or pay the fee within the time stated, a decision by default may be given in accordance with Rule 355.

4. If the claimant fails to correct the deficiencies noted or to pay the fee for the action against a decision of the Office, the Registry shall inform the President of the Court of First Instance who may reject the action as inadmissible by a decision by default. He may give the claimant an opportunity to be heard beforehand.

Rule 90
Recording in the register (*ex parte* proceedings)

If the requirements referred to in Rule 89.1 have been complied with, the Registry shall as soon as practicable:

(a) record the date of receipt of the Application to annul or alter a decision of the Office and attribute an action number to the file;

(b) record the file in the register;

(c) inform the claimant of the action number of the file and the date of receipt; and

(d) forward the Application to the European Patent Office, with an indication that the Application is admissible.

Rule 91
Interlocutory revision by the European Patent Office

1. If the European Patent Office considers that the Application to annul or alter a decision of the Office is well founded, it shall within two months of the date of receipt of the Application:

(a) rectify the contested decision in accordance with the order or remedy sought by the claimant [Rule 88.2(g)]; and

(b) inform the Court that the decision has been rectified.

2. Where the Court is informed by the European Patent Office that the contested decision has been rectified, it shall inform the claimant that the action is closed. It may order full or partial reimbursement of the fee for the action against a decision of the Office, in accordance with Part 6.

Rule 92
Assignment to panel or to single judge, designation of judge-rapporteur

Where the action is not closed in accordance with Rule 91.2, the action shall, as soon as practicable after the expiry of the period referred to in Rule 91.1, be assigned to a panel of the central division or to a single judge if requested by the claimant [Rule 88.2(f)] in accordance with Rule 345.3. Rule 18 shall apply.

Rule 93
Examination of the Application to annul or alter a decision of the Office

1. In the examination of the Application to annul or alter a decision of the Office, the judge-rapporteur may invite the claimant to lodge further written pleadings, within a time period to be specified.

2. Where appropriate, the judge-rapporteur may, after consulting the claimant, set a date and time for an interim conference.

3. Rule 35 shall apply *mutatis mutandis.*

Rule 94
Invitation to the President of the European Patent Office to comment

The judge-rapporteur may, on his own initiative or on request by the President of the European Patent Office, invite the President of the European Patent Office to comment in writing on any question arising in the course of proceedings under this Section including any appeal by the claimant pursuant to Rule 220. The claimant shall be entitled to submit his observations on the President's comments.

Rule 95
***Lex specialis* for the interim procedure (*ex parte* procedure)**
During the interim procedure, the judge-rapporteur shall invite the claimant to indicate whether he wishes that an oral hearing be convened. The judge-rapporteur may convene an oral hearing at his own instance.

Rule 96
***Lex specialis* for the oral procedure (*ex parte* procedure)**
1. Rules 110.3, 111, 115 and 118.6 shall apply to the oral hearing and to the decision of the Court.
2. If an oral hearing is not convened, the panel shall decide in accordance with Rule 117.

Rule 97
Application to annul a decision of the Office to reject a request for unitary effect
1. The proprietor of a patent whose request for unitary effect has been rejected by the Office shall lodge an Application at the Registry in accordance with Article 7(2) of the Agreement and Annex II thereto, to reverse the decision of the Office, in the language in which the patent was granted, within three weeks of service of the decision of the European Patent Office.
2. The Application shall contain particulars in accordance with Rule 88.2(a), (c), (d) and (g) to (j) and the proprietor shall pay the fee for the action against the decision of the Office in accordance with Part 6. Rule 15.2 and Rule 89 shall apply *mutatis mutandis.*
3. If the requirements referred to in paragraph 2 have been complied with, Rule 90 shall apply *mutatis mutandis.*
4. The Registry shall as soon as practicable forward the Application to the standing judge who may invite the President of the European Patent Office to comment on the Application, but shall in any event decide the Application within three weeks of the date of receipt of the Application.
5. A Statement of appeal by the proprietor of the patent or the President of the European Patent Office against the decisions of the standing judge pursuant to paragraph 4 may be lodged within three weeks of service of the said decision. The Statement of appeal shall contain the particulars previously lodged pursuant to paragraph 2 and also the reasons for setting aside the contested decision. The appellant shall pay the fee for the appeal in accordance with Part 6. Rule 15.2 shall apply *mutatis mutandis.* If the requirements of this paragraph 5 have been complied with, the Registry shall record the appeal in accordance with Rule 230.1 and shall as soon as practicable assign the appeal to the standing judge of the Court of Appeal [Rule 345.5 and 345.8] who may invite the other party to comment on the appeal but shall in any event decide the appeal within three weeks of receipt by the Registry of the Statement of appeal.
6. The Registry shall as soon as practicable notify the Office of the decision on the Application or on the appeal as the case may be.

Rule 98
Costs
The parties shall bear their own costs in any action pursuant to Rule 85 or 97.

CHAPTER 2
INTERIM PROCEDURE

[1.1110]
Rule 101
Role of the judge-rapporteur (Case management)
1. During the interim procedure, the judge-rapporteur shall make all necessary preparations for the oral hearing. He may in particular, where appropriate, and subject to the mandate of the panel, hold an interim conference with the parties which may be held on more than one occasion and may exercise the powers provided for in Rule 334.
2. The judge-rapporteur shall have the obligation to ensure a fair, orderly and efficient interim procedure.
3. Without prejudice to the principle of proportionality, the judge-rapporteur shall complete the interim procedure within three months of the closure of the written procedure.
Relation with Agreement: Articles 43 and 52(2)

Rule 102
Referral to the panel
1. The judge-rapporteur may refer any matter to the panel for decision and the panel may of its own motion review any decision or order of the judge-rapporteur or the conduct of the interim procedure.
2. Any party may request that a decision or order of the judge-rapporteur be referred to the panel for a review pursuant to Rule 333. Pending review, the decision or order of the judge-rapporteur shall be effective.

Rule 103
Preparation for the interim conference

1. Whether or not the judge-rapporteur decides to hold an interim conference, he may order the parties, within time periods to be specified, in particular to:
   (a) provide further clarification on specific points;
   (b) answer specific questions;
   (c) produce evidence;
   (d) lodge specific documents including each party's summary of the orders to be sought at the interim conference.

The judge-rapporteur shall at the same time inform the party concerned that if the party fails to comply with the order within the time period specified, a decision by default may be given in accordance with Rule 355.

2. If a party fails to comply with an order of the judge-rapporteur within the time period specified, the judge-rapporteur may give a decision by default pursuant to Rule 355.

Interim Conference

Rule 104
Aim of the interim conference

The interim conference shall enable the judge-rapporteur to:
   (a) identify main issues and determine which relevant facts are in dispute;
   (b) where appropriate, clarify the position of the parties as regards those issues and facts;
   (c) establish a schedule for the further progress of the proceedings;
   (d) explore with the parties the possibilities to settle the dispute or to make use of the facilities of the Centre;
   (e) where appropriate, issue orders regarding production of further pleadings, documents, experts (including court experts), experiments, inspections, further written evidence, the matters to be the subject of oral evidence and the scope of questions to be put to the witnesses;
   (f) where appropriate, but only in the presence of the parties, hold preparatory discussions with witnesses and experts with a view to properly preparing for the oral hearing;
   (g) make any other decision or order as he deems necessary for the preparation of the oral hearing including, after consultation with the presiding judge, an order for a separate hearing of witnesses and experts before the panel;
   (h) set a date for any separate hearing pursuant to point (g) of this Rule and confirm the date for the oral hearing;
   (i) decide the value of the action in accordance with Rule 370.6.;
   (j) decide the value of the proceeding for the purpose of applying the scale of ceilings for recoverable costs (Rule 152.3);
   (k) order the parties to submit, in advance of the decision at the oral hearing, a preliminary estimate of the legal costs that they will seek to recover.

Relation with Agreement: Article 52(2)

Rule 105
Holding the interim conference

1. The interim conference should, where practicable, be held by telephone conference or by video conference.

2. On request by a party, subject to paragraph 1 and the approval of the judge-rapporteur, the interim conference may be held in Court. If the interim conference is held in Court, it shall be open to the public unless the Court decides to make it, to the extent necessary, confidential in the interests of one or both parties or third parties or in the general interests of justice or public order.

3. The judge-rapporteur may hold the interim conference in any language agreed by the parties' representatives.

4. Rule 103 shall apply *mutatis mutandis*.

5. Following the interim conference, the judge-rapporteur shall issue an order setting out the decisions taken.

Rule 106
Recording of the interim conference

The interim conference shall be audio recorded. The recording shall be made available at the premises of the Court to the parties or their representatives after the hearing.

Relation with Agreement: Articles 44 and 45

Preparation for the Oral Hearing

Rule 108
Summons to the oral hearing
The judge-rapporteur shall summon the parties to the oral hearing which shall take place before the panel on the date(s) set under Rules 28 and/or 41(c) and 104(h). If no date(s) have been set the judge-rapporteur shall set a date for the oral hearing. At least two months' notice shall be given, unless the parties agree to a shorter time period.

Rule 109
Simultaneous interpretation during oral hearings
1. At the latest one month before the oral hearing including any separate hearing of witnesses and experts a party may lodge a Request for simultaneous interpretation which shall contain:
(a) an indication of the language to or from which the party requests simultaneous interpretation during the oral hearing;
(b) the reasons for the Request;
(c) the field of technology concerned;
(d) any other information of relevance for the Request.
2. The judge-rapporteur shall decide whether and to what extent simultaneous interpretation is appropriate and shall instruct the Registry to make all necessary arrangements for simultaneous interpretation. In the event that the judge-rapporteur refuses to order simultaneous interpretation the parties may request arrangements to be made, so far as practically possible, for simultaneous interpretation at their cost.
3. The judge-rapporteur may decide of his own motion to order simultaneous interpretation and shall instruct the Registry and inform the parties accordingly.
4. A party wishing to engage an interpreter at its own expense shall inform the Registry at the latest two weeks before the oral hearing.
5. Costs for simultaneous interpretation are costs of the proceedings to be decided upon under Rule 150 except where a party engages an interpreter at its own expense under paragraph 4; these costs are borne solely by that party.
Relation with Agreement: Article 51 (2)

Rule 110
Closure of the interim procedure
1. As soon as the judge-rapporteur considers that the state of preparation of the file is adequate, he shall inform the presiding judge and the parties that the interim procedure is closed in view of the oral hearing.
2. Where final dates have been set pursuant to Rules 103 and 104 the interim procedure shall be deemed closed on the last date set.
3. The oral procedure shall start immediately after the interim procedure is closed. The presiding judge shall, in consultation with the judge-rapporteur, take over the management of the action.

CHAPTER 3
ORAL PROCEDURE

[1.1111]
Rule 111
Role of the presiding judge (Case management)
The presiding judge shall:
(a) have all authority to ensure a fair, orderly and efficient oral procedure; and
(b) ensure that the action is ready for decision on the merits at the end of the oral hearing.

Rule 112
Conduct of the oral hearing
1. The oral hearing shall be held before the panel and shall be under the control of the presiding judge.
2. The oral hearing shall consist of:
(a) the hearing of the parties' oral submissions;
(b) if ordered during the interim procedure, the hearing of witnesses and experts under the control of the presiding judge.
3. The presiding judge and the judges of the panel may provide a preliminary introduction to the action and put questions to the parties, to the parties' representatives and to any witness or expert.
4. Under the control of the presiding judge, the parties may put questions to the witness or expert. The presiding judge may prohibit any question which is not designed to adduce admissible evidence.
5. With the consent of the Court a witness may give evidence in a language other than the language of proceedings.

Relation with Agreement: Articles 52(3) and 53(1)

Rule 113
Duration of the oral hearing
1. Without prejudice to the application of the principle of proportionality, the presiding judge shall endeavour to complete the oral hearing within one day. The presiding judge may set time limits for parties' oral submissions in advance of the oral hearing.
2. Oral testimony at the oral hearing or at any separate hearing shall be limited to issues identified by the judge-rapporteur or the presiding judge as having to be decided on the basis of oral evidence.
3. The presiding judge may, after consulting the panel, limit a party's oral submissions if the panel is sufficiently informed.

Rule 114
Adjournment where the Court considers that further evidence is required
In exceptional cases, the Court may, after hearing the parties' oral submissions, decide to adjourn proceedings and call for further evidence.

Rule 115
The oral hearing
The oral hearing and any separate hearing of witnesses shall be open to the public unless the Court decides to make a hearing, to the extent necessary, confidential in the interests of one or both parties or third parties or in the general interests of justice or public order. The hearing shall be audio recorded. The recording shall be made available to the parties or their representatives at the premises of the Court after the hearing. Rule 103 shall apply *mutatis mutandis*.
Relation with Agreement: Article 45

Rule 116
Absence of a party from the oral hearing
1. A party which does not wish to be represented at the oral hearing shall inform the Registry in good time. Where both parties have informed the Registry that they do not wish to be represented at the oral hearing, the Court may decide the action in accordance with Rule 117.
2. The Court shall not be obliged to delay any step in the procedure, including the decision on the merits, by reason only of the absence of a party from the oral hearing.
3. A party that is not represented at the oral hearing shall be treated as relying only on its written case.
4. If due to an exceptional occurrence a party is prevented from being represented at the oral hearing, the Court shall on a reasoned request of that party, adjourn the oral hearing.
5. The provisions of this Rule are without prejudice to the power of the Court to give a decision by default pursuant to Rule 355.

Rule 117
Absence of both parties from the oral hearing
Where both parties have informed the Registry that they do not wish to be represented at the oral hearing the Court shall take a decision on the merits on the basis of the pleadings and evidence submitted by the parties and the court expert, if applicable, and otherwise in accordance with Rules 118 and 350 to 354.

Rule 118
Decision on the merits
1. In addition to the orders and measures and without prejudice to the discretion of the Court referred to in Articles 63, 64, 67 and 80 of the Agreement the Court may, if requested, order the payment of damages or compensation according to Articles 68 and 32(1)(f) of the Agreement. The amount of the damages or the compensation may be stated in the order or determined in separate proceedings [Rules 125-144].
2. If, while there are infringement proceedings before a local or regional division, a revocation action is pending between the same parties before the central division or an opposition is pending before the European Patent Office, the local or regional division:
   (a) may render its decision on the merits of the infringement claim, including its orders, under the condition subsequent pursuant to Article 56(1) of the Agreement that the patent is not held to be wholly or partially invalid by the final decision in the revocation proceedings or a final decision of the European Patent Office or under any other term or condition; or
   (b) may stay the infringement proceedings pending a decision in the revocation procedure or a decision of the European Patent Office and shall stay the infringement proceedings if it is of the view that there is a high likelihood that the relevant claims of the patent will be held

to be invalid on any ground by the final decision in the revocation proceedings or of the European Patent Office where such decision of the European Patent Office may be expected to be given rapidly.

3. Where, in the decision on the merits of a revocation action, the patent is found to be entirely or partially invalid, the Court shall revoke the patent entirely or partially according to Article 65 of the Agreement.

4. Where the Court has made orders in accordance with paragraph 2(a) any party may apply to the local or regional division within two months following a final decision of the central division or the Court of Appeal or the European Patent Office as the case may be on the validity of the patent for orders consequential on such final decision [Rule 354.2].

5. The Court shall decide in principle on the obligation to bear legal costs in accordance with Article 69 of the Agreement. The Court may order in advance of the decision that the parties submit a preliminary estimate of the legal costs that they will seek to recover.

6. The Court shall give the decision on the merits as soon as possible after the closure of the oral hearing. The Court shall endeavour to issue the decision on the merits in writing within six weeks of the oral hearing. The Court shall give reasons for its decision.

7. The Court may give its decision immediately after the closure of the oral hearing and provide its reasons on a subsequent date.

8. The orders of the Court referred to in paragraphs 1 and 2(a) shall be enforceable on the defendant only after the claimant has notified the Court which part of the orders he intends to enforce, a certified translation of the orders in accordance with Rule 7.2, where applicable, into the official language of a Contracting Member State in which the enforcement shall take place has been provided by the claimant and the said notice and, where applicable, a certified translation of the orders have been served on the defendant by the Registry. The Court may subject any order or measure to a security to be given by the successful party to the unsuccessful party as determined by the Court in accordance with Rule 352.

Relation with Agreement: Article 77

Rule 119

Interim award of damages

The Court may order an interim award of damages to the successful party in the decision on the merits, subject to any conditions that the Court may order. Such award shall at least cover the expected costs of the procedure for the award of damages and compensation on the part of the successful party.

CHAPTER 4
PROCEDURE FOR THE DETERMINATION OF DAMAGES AND COMPENSATION

[1.1112]

Rule 125

Separate proceedings for determining the amount of damages ordered

The determination of the amount of damages ordered for the successful party may be the subject of separate proceedings. The determination shall include the determination of the amount of compensation, if any, to be awarded as a result of the provisional protection conferred by a published European patent application [Article 32(1)(f) of the Agreement, Article 67 EPC] and compensation to be paid pursuant to Rules 118.1, 198.2, 213.2 and 354.2. The expression "damages" used in Chapter 4 shall be deemed to include such compensation and interest at the rate and for the period that the Court shall decide.

Rule 126

Start of proceedings for the determination of damages

Where the successful party wishes to have the amount of damages determined, it shall no later than one year from service of the final decision on the merits (including any final decision on appeal) on both infringement and validity (or in the case of an award under Rules 118.1, 198.2, 213.2 or 354.2 from the date of the order for such award) lodge an Application for the determination of damages, which may include a request for an order to lay open books.

Relation with Agreement: Article 68

SECTION 1
Application for the Determination of Damages

Rule 131

Contents of the Application for the determination of damages

1. The Application for the determination of damages shall contain:
   (a) particulars in accordance with Rule 13.1(a) to (d);
   (b) the date of the decision on the merits and the action number of the file;
   (c) if required a request for an order to lay open books (Rules 141 to 144) in which case the applicant shall provide the matters set out in Rule 141(b) to (e).

2. After any procedure for the laying open of books is complete, or, if that has not been requested in the Application referred to in paragraph 1 the applicant shall indicate:
   (a) the redress (damages, licence fees, profits) and the interest thereon requested by him;
   (b) an indication of the facts relied on, in particular calculations concerning lost profits or profits made by the unsuccessful party;
   (c) the evidence relied on;
   (d) a statement as to whether the decision on the merits is the subject of an appeal;
   (e) his assessment of the amount of damages due to him.

Rule 132
Fee for the Application for the determination of damages
The applicant shall pay the fixed fee and, where applicable, the value based fee for the determination of damages in accordance with Part 6. Rule 15.2 shall apply *mutatis mutandis*.

Rule 133
Determination of the value-based fee for the determination of damages
Where the value of the action exceeds EUR500.000 the applicant shall pay a value based fee for the determination of damages in accordance with Part 6.

Rule 134
Examination as to formal requirements of the Application for the determination of damages
1. The Registry shall, as soon as practicable after the lodging of the Application for the determination of damages, examine whether the requirements of Rules 126, 131.1 and .2(d) and (e) and 132 have been complied with.
2. If the Application for the determination of damages does not comply with the requirements referred to in paragraph 1, the Registry shall invite the applicant to correct the deficiencies noted within a time period to be specified.
3. Rule 16.4 to .5 shall apply *mutatis mutandis*.

Rule 135
Recording in the register (Application for the determination of damages) and service
1. If the requirements referred to in Rule 131.1 and .2(d) and (e) have been complied with, the Registry shall as soon as practicable:
   (a) record the date of receipt of the Application for the determination of damages;
   (b) record the Application in the register;
   (c) inform the applicant of the date of receipt;
   (d) inform the panel which has given the decision on the merits on infringement that an Application for the determination of damages has been lodged;
   (e) serve the Application upon the unsuccessful party.
2. The panel which has given the decision on the merits on infringement shall be the panel for the determination of damages unless for any reason this is not possible or practical in which case the presiding judge of the division concerned shall appoint a fresh panel. Rules 17.2 and 18 shall apply *mutatis mutandis*.

Rule 136
Stay of the Application for a determination of damages
The Court may stay the Application for a determination of damages pending any appeal on the merits pursuant to Rule 295(g) on a reasoned request by the unsuccessful party. The applicant shall be given the opportunity to be heard. If the Court continues the proceedings on the Application it may order the applicant to render a security according to Rule 352.

Rule 137
Reply of the unsuccessful party
1. If the unsuccessful party accepts the claim made in the Application for the determination of damages, it shall within two months inform the Registry. The judge-rapporteur shall make the order for the determination of damages in accordance with the Application for the determination of damages.
2. If the unsuccessful party contests the claim made in the Application for the determination of damages, it shall within two months of service of the Application for the determination of damages or, where there was a procedure for the laying open of books, within two months of service of the indication pursuant to Rule 131.2, lodge a Defence to the Application for the determination of damages.

Rule 138
Contents of the Defence to the Application for the determination of damages
The Defence to the Application for the determination of damages shall contain:

(a) the names of the unsuccessful party and of that party's representative;
(b) postal and electronic addresses for service on the unsuccessful party and the names and addresses of the persons authorised to accept service;
(c) the action number attributed to the file;
(d) the reasons why the Application for the award of damages is contested;
(e) an indication of the facts relied on; and
(f) the evidence relied on.

Rule 139
Reply to the Defence to the Application for the determination of damages and Rejoinder to the Reply
The applicant may within one month lodge a Reply to the Defence to the Application for the determination of damages, limited to the matters raised in the Defence. The unsuccessful party may lodge a Rejoinder to the Reply within one month of service of the Reply, limited to the matters raised in the Reply.

Rule 140
Further procedure (Application for the determination of damages)
1. The judge-rapporteur may order further exchange of written pleadings, within time periods to be specified.
2. The provisions of Part 1, Chapters 2 (Interim procedure) and 3 (Oral procedure) shall apply *mutatis mutandis* but with such reduced timetable as the judge-rapporteur may order. He shall decide on the obligation to bear the legal costs of the proceedings for the determination of damages in accordance with Article 69 of the Agreement.

SECTION 2
Request to Lay open Books

Rule 141
Contents of the Request to lay open books
If the applicant has made a request pursuant to Rule 131.1(c), Rules 134 to 136 shall apply *mutatis mutandis*. The Request shall contain:
(a) particulars in accordance with Rule 131.1(a) and (b);
(b) details of any information ordered by the Court and given by the other party pursuant to Rule 191;
(c) a description of the information held by the unsuccessful party to which the applicant requests access, in particular documents relating to turnover and profits generated by the infringing products or regarding the extent of use of the infringing process as well as accounts and bank documents, and any related document concerning the infringement;
(d) the reasons why the applicant needs access to this information;
(e) the facts relied on; and
(f) the evidence offered in support.

Rule 142
Defence of the unsuccessful party, Reply to the Defence and Rejoinder to the Reply
1. If the unsuccessful party accepts the Request to lay open books, it shall within two months of service of the Request to lay open books inform the Registry. The judge-rapporteur shall make the order to lay open books in accordance with the Request to lay open books.
2. If the unsuccessful party contests the Request to lay open books, it shall within two months of service of the Request to lay open books lodge a Defence to the Request to lay open books.
3. The applicant may within 14 days of service of the Defence to the Request lodge a Reply to the Defence to the Request to lay open books, limited to the matters raised in the Defence. The unsuccessful party may within 14 days of service of the Reply lodge a Rejoinder, limited to the matters raised in the Reply.

Rule 143
Further procedure
Rule 140 shall apply *mutatis mutandis*.

Rule 144
Decision on the Request to lay open books
1. The Court may:
(a) order the unsuccessful party to open its books to the applicant within a time period to be specified and subject to such terms as the Court may deem appropriate having regard *inter alia* to Article 58 of the Agreement and Rule 190.1 and .4;

(b) inform the applicant and specify a time period within which the procedure for the award of damages shall be continued.

2. Where the Request to lay open books is not allowable, the Court shall inform the applicant and specify a time period within which the procedure for the award of damages shall be continued [Rule 131.2].

CHAPTER 5
PROCEDURE FOR COST DECISION

[1.1113]
Rule 150
Separate proceedings for cost decision

1. A cost decision may be the subject of separate proceedings following a decision on the merits and, if applicable, a decision for the determination of damages. The cost decision shall cover costs incurred in the proceedings by the Court such as costs for simultaneous interpretation and costs incurred pursuant to Rules 180.1, 185.7, 188, 201 and 202 and, subject to the Rules 152 to 156, the costs of the successful party including Court fees paid by that party [Rule 151(d)]. Costs for interpretation and translation which is necessary for the judges of the Court in order to conduct the case in the language of proceedings are borne solely by the Court.

2. The Court may order an interim award of costs to the successful party in the decision on the merits [Rule 119] or in a decision for the determination of damages, subject to any conditions that the Court may decide.

Rule 151
Start of proceedings for cost decision

Where the successful party (hereinafter "the applicant") wishes to seek a cost decision, it shall within one month of service of the decision lodge an Application for a cost decision which shall contain:

(a) particulars in accordance with Rule 13.1(a) to (d);
(b) the date of the decision and the action number of the file;
(c) a statement as to whether the decision on the merits is the subject of an appeal, if known at the date of the Application;
(d) an indication of the costs for which compensation is requested, which may include recovery of court fees and costs of representation, of witnesses, of experts, and other expenses; and
(e) the preliminary estimate of the legal costs that the party submitted pursuant to Rule 118.5.

Rule 152
Compensation for representation costs

1. The applicant shall be entitled to recover reasonable and proportionate costs for representation.
2. The Administrative Committee shall adopt a scale of ceilings for recoverable costs by reference to the value of the proceedings. The scale may be adjusted from time to time.
3. Where a claim, counterclaim, application, request or appeal subject to only a fixed fee is made, the party concerned shall, in the first submission, assess its respective value for the purpose of calculating the applicable ceiling. The other party shall be heard. Rule 370.6 shall apply *mutatis mutandis*.

Rule 153
Compensation for costs of experts

The compensation for costs of experts of the parties [Rule 181] exceeding the expenses referred to in Rule 180.1 shall be based on the rates that are customary in the respective sector, with due regard to the required expertise, the complexity of the issue and the time spent by the expert for the services rendered.

Rule 154
Compensation for costs of witnesses

Where the Court has ordered the deposit of a sum sufficient to cover the expenses of a witness in accordance with Rule 180.2 or of a party's expert in accordance with Rule 181, compensation may be requested for payments made by the Registry towards the expenses incurred by a witness or an expert.

Rule 155
Compensation for costs of interpreters and translators

1. The compensation for costs of interpreters shall be the rates that are customary in the country of the division in question, depending on the interpreter's training and professional experience.
2. The compensation for costs of translators shall be the rates that are customary in the country of the division in question, depending on the translator's training and professional experience.

Rule 156
Further procedure
1. The judge-rapporteur may request the applicant to provide written evidence of all costs requested in Rule 151(d). The judge-rapporteur shall allow the unsuccessful party an opportunity to comment in writing on the costs requested including any item of costs that should be apportioned or borne by each party in accordance with Article 69(1) to (3) of the Agreement.
2. The judge-rapporteur shall decide in writing on the costs to be awarded or apportioned in accordance with Article 69(1) to (3) of the Agreement.
3. The costs shall be paid within the period ordered by the judge-rapporteur.

Rule 157
Appeal against the cost decision
The decision of the judge-rapporteur as to costs only may be appealed to the Court of Appeal in accordance with Rule 221.
Relation with Agreement: Article 69

CHAPTER 6
SECURITY FOR COSTS

[1.1114]
Rule 158
Security for costs of a party
1. At any time during proceedings, following a reasoned request by one party, the Court may order the other party to provide, within a specified time period, adequate security for the legal costs and other expenses incurred and/or to be incurred by the requesting party, which the other party may be liable to bear. Where the Court decides to order such security, it shall decide whether it is appropriate to order the security by deposit or bank guarantee.
2. The Court shall give the parties an opportunity to be heard before making an order for security. Rule 354 shall apply to the enforcement of the order.
3. The order for security shall indicate that an appeal may be lodged in accordance with Article 73 of the Agreement and Rule 220.2.
4. The Court shall, when specifying the time period in paragraph 1, inform the party concerned that if the party fails to provide adequate security within the time stated, a decision by default may be given, in accordance with Rule 355.
5. If a party fails to provide adequate security within the time stated, the Court may give a decision by default pursuant to Rule 355.
Relation with the Agreement: Article 69(4)

Rule 159
Security for costs of the Court
Except where deposits are rendered pursuant to Rule 180.2, the Court may order that either or both parties provide adequate security (either by deposit or bank guarantee) to cover costs incurred and/ or to be incurred in the proceedings by the Court, pending a cost decision pursuant to Rule 150.1. Rule 158.2 and .3 shall apply.

PART 2
EVIDENCE

[1.1115]
Rule 170
Means of evidence and means of obtaining evidence
1. In proceedings before the Court, the means of evidence shall include in particular the following:
(a) written evidence, whether printed, hand-written or drawn, in particular documents, written witness statements, plans, drawings, photographs;
(b) expert reports and reports on experiments carried out for the purpose of the proceedings;
(c) physical objects, in particular devices, products, embodiments, exhibits, models;
(d) electronic files and audio/video recordings.
2. Means of obtaining evidence shall include in particular the following:
(a) hearing of the parties;
(b) requests for information;
(c) production of documents;
(d) summoning, hearing and questioning of witnesses;
(e) appointing, receiving opinions from, summoning and hearing and questioning of experts;
(f) ordering inspection of a place or a physical object;
(g) conducting comparative tests and experiments;
(h) sworn statements in writing (written witness statements).
3. Means of obtaining evidence shall further include [Article 59 and 60 of the Agreement]:

(a) ordering a party or a third party to produce evidence;
(b) ordering measures to preserve evidence.

Rule 171
Offering of evidence
1. A party making a statement of fact that is contested or likely to be contested by the other party shall indicate the means of evidence to prove it. In case of failure to indicate the means of evidence regarding a contested fact, the Court shall take such failure into account when deciding the issue in question.
2. A statement of fact that is not specifically contested by any party shall be held to be true as between the parties.

Rule 172
Duty to produce evidence
1. Evidence available to a party regarding a statement of fact that is contested or likely to be contested by the other party must be produced by the party making that statement of fact.
2. The Court may at any time during the proceedings order a party making a statement of fact to produce evidence that lies in the control of that party. If the party fails to produce the evidence, the Court shall take such failure into account when deciding on the issue in question.
Relation with Agreement: Article 53

Rule 173
Cooperation between the courts of the Member States in the taking of evidence
For the taking of evidence in the European Union, the Regulation (EC) No 1206/2001 shall apply.

CHAPTER 1
WITNESSES AND EXPERTS OF THE PARTIES

[1.1116]
Rule 175
Written witness statement
1. A party seeking to offer witness evidence shall lodge a written witness statement or a written summary of the evidence to be given.
2. A written witness statement shall be signed by the witness and shall include a statement of the witness that he is aware of his obligation to tell the truth and of his liability under applicable national law in the event of any breach of this obligation. The statement shall set out the language in which the witness shall give oral evidence, if necessary.
3. The written witness statement or written summary of the evidence to be given shall set out:
(a) any current or past relationship between the witness and the party offering the evidence; and
(b) any actual or potential conflict of interest that may affect the impartiality of the witness.

Rule 176
Application for the hearing of a witness in person
Subject to the orders of the Court referred to in Rules 104(e) and 112.2(b) a party seeking to offer oral witness evidence shall make an Application for the hearing of a witness in person which shall set out:
(a) the reasons why the witness should be heard in person;
(b) the facts which the party expects the witness to confirm; and
(c) the language in which the witness shall give evidence.

Rule 177
Summoning of witnesses to the oral hearing
1. The Court may order that a witness be heard in person:
(a) of its own motion;
(b) where a written witness statement is challenged by the other party; or
(c) on an Application for the hearing of a witness in person [Rule 176].
2. An order of the Court summoning a witness to the oral hearing shall in particular indicate:
(a) the name, address and description of the witness;
(b) the date and place of the oral hearing;
(c) an indication of the facts of the action about which the witness is to be examined;
(d) information about the reimbursement of expenses incurred by the witness;
(e) a statement that the witness will be questioned by the Court and the parties; and
(f) he language of the proceedings and the possibility of arranging simultaneous interpretation between that language and the language of the witness, if necessary [Rule 109].

3. In its order summoning the witness, the Court shall also inform the witness of his duties and rights as a witness under Rules 178 and 179, including the sanctions which may be imposed on a defaulting witness.

Rule 178
Hearing of witnesses
1. After the identity of the witness has been established and before hearing his evidence, the presiding judge shall ask the witness to make the following declaration:
"I solemnly, sincerely and truly declare and affirm that the evidence I shall give shall be the truth, the whole truth and nothing but the truth."
2. The witness shall give his evidence to the Court.
3. The hearing of a witness who has signed a written witness statement shall begin with the confirmation of the evidence given therein. The witness may elaborate on the evidence contained in his written witness statement.
4. The presiding judge and the judges of the panel may put questions to the witness.
5. Under the control of the presiding judge, the parties may put questions to the witness. The presiding judge may prohibit any question which is not designed to adduce admissible evidence.
6. The Court may allow a witness to give evidence through electronic means, such as video conference. Paragraphs 1 to 5 and 7 shall apply.
7. With the consent of the Court a witness may give evidence in a language other than the language of proceedings.

Rule 179
Duties of witnesses
1. Witnesses who have been duly summoned shall obey the summons and attend the oral hearing.
2. Without prejudice to paragraph 3, if a witness who has been duly summoned fails to appear before the Court or refuses to give evidence or to make the declaration referred to in Rule 178.1, the Court may impose upon him a pecuniary sanction not exceeding EUR50.000 and may order that a further summons be served at the witness's own expense. The Court may send a letter rogatory to the competent national court pursuant to Rule 202.
3. Nobody shall be obliged to sign a written witness statement or to give evidence at an oral hearing if he is a spouse, partner equal to a spouse under applicable national law, descendant, sibling or parent of a party. A witness may also refuse to answer questions if answering them would violate a professional privilege or other duty of confidentiality imposed by the national law applicable to the witness or expose him or his spouse, partner equal to a spouse under applicable national law, descendant, sibling or parent to criminal prosecution under applicable national law.
4. The Court may decide to report to the competent authorities of the Contracting Member States whose courts have criminal jurisdiction in case of the giving of false evidence on the part of a witness.

Rule 180
Reimbursement of expenses of witnesses
1. A witness shall be entitled to reimbursement of:
(a) expenses for travelling and stay; and
(b) loss of income caused by his hearing in person.

After the witness has carried out his duties and upon his request, the Registry shall make a payment to the witness towards the expenses incurred.
2. The Court shall make the summoning of a witness conditional upon the deposit by the party relying on the witness of a sum sufficient to cover the expenses referred to in paragraph 1.

Rule 181
Experts of the parties
1. Subject to the orders of the Court referred to in Rules 104(e) and 112.2(b) a party may provide any expert evidence that it considers necessary. Rules 175 to 180 shall apply *mutatis mutandis* to experts of the parties.
2. An order of the Court under Rule 177 summoning the expert shall additionally set out that:
(a) an expert has a duty to assist the Court impartially on matters relevant to his area of expertise which overrides any duty to the party retaining him; and
(b) an expert is to be independent and objective, and shall not act as an advocate for any party to the proceedings.

CHAPTER 2
COURT EXPERTS

[1.1117]
Rule 185
Appointment of a court expert

1. Where the Court must resolve a specific technical or other question in relation to the action, it may of its own motion, and after hearing the parties, appoint a court expert.
2. The parties may make suggestions regarding the identity of the court expert, his technical or other relevant background and the questions to be put to him.
3. The court expert shall be responsible to the Court and shall possess the expertise, independence and impartiality required for being appointed as court expert. The parties shall be entitled to be heard on the expertise, independence and impartiality of the court expert.
4. The Court shall appoint a court expert by way of order which shall in particular specify:
   (a) the name and address of the expert appointed;
   (b) a short description of the facts of the action;
   (c) the evidence submitted by the parties in respect of the technical or other question;
   (d) the questions put to the expert, with the appropriate level of detail, including where appropriate suggestions relating to any experiments to be carried out;
   (e) when and under what conditions the expert may receive other relevant information;
   (f) the time period for the presentation of the expert report;
   (g) information about the reimbursement of expenses incurred by the expert;
   (h) information about the sanctions which may be imposed on a defaulting expert; and
   (i) his duties under Rule 186.
5. The expert shall receive a copy of the order, together with the documents and other evidence that the Court considers to be necessary for carrying out his task.
6. The expert shall be required upon receipt of the order to confirm in writing that he will present the expert report within the time period specified by the Court.
7. The Court shall agree with the expert on a fee covering his written expert report and his participation in the oral hearing. The Court may reduce this fee by an equitable amount if the expert does not deliver his report within the time period specified by the Court or if the report did not have the quality to be expected of the expert.
8. If an appointed court expert does not present his report within the time period specified or, if extended at the expert's request, the extended period, the Court may appoint another expert in his place. The Court may hold the expert liable for all or part of the costs of appointing and reimbursing another expert.
9. The Registry shall maintain an indicative list of technical experts.

Rule 186
Duties of a court expert

1. The court expert shall present an expert report in writing within the time period specified by the Court [Rule 185.4(f)].
2. The court expert shall be under the supervision of the Court and shall inform the Court of his progress in carrying out his task.
3. The court expert shall give expert advice only on questions which have been put to him.
4. The court expert shall not communicate with one party without the other party being present or without the consent of the other party. He shall document all communications with the parties in his report.
5. The court expert shall not communicate the contents of his report to third parties.
6. The court expert shall attend the oral hearing if requested to do so by the Court and shall answer questions from the Court and the parties.
7. The court expert has an overriding duty to assist the Court impartially on matters relevant to his area of expertise. He is to be independent and objective, and shall not act as an advocate for any party to the proceedings.

Rule 187
Expert report

Once the report of the court expert has been presented to the Court, the Court shall invite the parties to comment on it either in writing or during the oral hearing.

Rule 188
Hearing of a court expert

Rules 178 to 180 shall apply *mutatis mutandis* to a court expert.
Relation with Agreement: Article 57

CHAPTER 3
ORDER TO PRODUCE EVIDENCE AND TO COMMUNICATE INFORMATION

Order to Produce Evidence

[1.1118]
Rule 190
Order to produce evidence

1. Where a party has presented reasonably available and plausible evidence in support of its claims and has, in substantiating those claims, specified evidence which lies in the control of the other party or a third party, the Court may on a reasoned request by the party specifying such evidence, order that other party or third party to produce such evidence. For the protection of confidential information the Court may order that the evidence be disclosed to certain named persons only and be subject to appropriate terms of non-disclosure.
2. During the written and interim procedures, a party may request such an order to produce evidence.
3. The judge-rapporteur may make such order in the written procedure or in the interim procedure having given the other/third party an opportunity to be heard.
4. An order to produce evidence shall in particular specify:
   (a) under which conditions, in what form and within what time period the evidence shall be produced;
   (b) any sanction which may be imposed if the evidence is not produced according to the order.
5. Where the Court orders a third party to produce evidence, the interests of that third party shall be duly taken into account.
6. An order to produce evidence shall be subject to the provisions of Rules 179.3, 287 and 288. The order shall indicate that an appeal may be brought in accordance with Article 73 of the Agreement and Rule 220.1.
7. If a party fails to comply with an order to produce evidence, the Court shall take such failure into account when deciding on the issue in question.

Relation with Agreement: Article 59

Order to Communicate Information

Rule 191
Application for order to communicate information

The Court may in response to a reasoned request by a party order the other party or any third party to communicate such information in the control of that other party or third party as is specified in Article 67 of the Agreement or such other information as is reasonably necessary for the purpose of advancing that party's case. Rule 190.1 second sentence, .5 and .6 shall apply *mutatis mutandis*.
Relation with the Agreement: Article 67

CHAPTER 4
ORDER TO PRESERVE EVIDENCE (SAISIE) AND ORDER FOR INSPECTION

Order to Preserve Evidence (Saisie)

[1.1119]
Rule 192
Application for preserving evidence

1. An Application for preserving evidence may be lodged by a party (within the meaning of Article 47 of the Agreement) (hereinafter "the applicant") at the division where the applicant has commenced infringement proceedings on the merits. If the application is lodged before proceedings on the merits have been started it shall be lodged at the division where the applicant intends to start proceedings on the merits.
2. The Application for preserving evidence shall contain:
   (a) particulars in accordance with Rule 13.1(a) to (i);
   (b) a clear indication of the measures requested [Rule 196.1], including the exact location of the evidence to be preserved where it is known or suspected with good reason;
   (c) the reasons why the proposed measures are needed to preserve relevant evidence; and
   (d) the facts and evidence relied on in support of the Application.

Where main proceedings on the merits of the case have not yet been started before the Court, the Application shall in addition contain a concise description of the action which will be started before the Court, including an indication of the facts and evidence which may be relied on in support.
3. Where the applicant requests that measures to preserve evidence be ordered without hearing the other party (hereinafter "the defendant"), the Application for preserving evidence shall in addition set out the reasons for not hearing the defendant having regard in particular to Rule 197. The applicant shall be under a duty to disclose any material fact known to it which might influence the Court in deciding whether to make an order without hearing the defendant. The application shall not be entered on the register until notice has been given to the defendant pursuant to Rule 197.2.

4. Where the Application for preserving evidence is lodged after main proceedings on the merits of the case have been started before the Court, the Application shall be drawn up in the language of the proceedings. Where the Application is lodged before main proceedings on the merits of the case have been started before the Court, Rule 14 shall apply *mutatis mutandis*.
5. The applicant shall pay the fee for the Application for preserving evidence, in accordance with Part 6. Rule 15.2 shall apply *mutatis mutandis*.
Relation with Agreement: Article 60

Rule 193
Examination as to formal requirements, recording in the register, assignment to panel, designation of judge-rapporteur, single judge
1. Where main proceedings on the merits of the case have not yet been started before the Court, the Application for preserving evidence shall be dealt with in accordance with Rule 16 (formalities examination by Registry), Rule 17.1(a) to (c) and .2 (date of receipt, recording in the register, action number, assignment to panel) and Rule 18 (designation only of judge-rapporteur by presiding judge).
2. Where main proceedings on the merits of the case have already been started before the Court, an Application for preserving evidence shall immediately be examined by the Registry in accordance with Rule 16 and forwarded to the panel to which the action has been assigned or to the judge to whom the action has been assigned [Rules 17.2, 194.3 and .4].
3. The judge deciding on an Application for preserving evidence shall have all necessary powers of the Court.

Rule 194
Examination of the Application for preserving evidence
1. The Court shall have the discretion to:
 (a) inform the defendant about the Application and invite him to lodge, within a time period to be specified, an Objection to the Application for preserving evidence which shall contain:
  (i) the reasons why the Application shall fail;
  (ii) the facts and evidence relied on, in particular any challenge to the facts and evidence relied on by the applicant;
  (iii) where main proceedings on the merits of the case have not yet been started before the Court, the reasons why the action which will be started before the Court shall fail and an indication of the facts and evidence relied on in support;
 (b) summon the parties to an oral hearing;
 (c) summon the applicant to an oral hearing without the presence of the defendant;
 (d) decide the Application without having heard the defendant.
2. In exercising its discretion, the Court shall take into account:
 (a) the urgency of the action;
 (b) whether the reasons for not hearing the defendant [Rules 192.3 and 197] appear well-founded;
 (c) the probability that evidence may be destroyed or otherwise cease to be available [Rule 197].
3. The presiding judge may decide that he or the judge-rapporteur or other single judge or the standing judge may decide on the Application.
4. In cases of extreme urgency the applicant may apply without formality for an order to preserve evidence to the standing judge designated in accordance with Rule 345.5. The standing judge shall decide the procedure to be followed on the Application, which may include a subsequent written Application.
5. If the Court decides to inform the defendant about the Application the Court will first give the applicant the possibility to withdraw the Application. In the event of such withdrawal the applicant may request that the Court shall order that the Application and its contents shall remain confidential.
6. If the patent the subject of the Application is also the subject of a Protective letter pursuant to Rule 207 the applicant may withdraw the Application pursuant to paragraph 5.

Rule 195
Oral hearing
1. Where the Court decides to summon the parties to an oral hearing, the date for the oral hearing shall be set as soon as possible after the date of receipt of the Application for preserving evidence.
2. Rules 111 to 116 shall apply *mutatis mutandis*. Where the applicant is absent from the oral hearing without a reasonable excuse, the Court shall reject the Application for preserving evidence.
3. The decision of the Court on the Application for preserving evidence shall be given in writing as soon as possible after the closure of the oral hearing. If the Court deems appropriate, the decision may be given orally to the parties at the end of the oral hearing but shall as soon as practicable thereafter be given in writing.
Relation with Agreement: Article 60

Rule 196
Order on the Application for preserving evidence

1. The Court may order, in particular, the following:
   (a) preserving evidence by detailed description, with or without the taking of samples;
   (b) physical seizure of allegedly infringing goods;
   (c) physical seizure of the materials and implements used in the production and/or distribution of these goods and any related document;
   (d) the preservation and disclosure of digital media and data and the disclosure of any passwords necessary to access them.

For the protection of confidential information the Court may order that any of the above be disclosed only to certain named persons and subject to appropriate terms of non-disclosure.

2. An order to preserve evidence shall specify that, unless otherwise ordered by the Court, the outcome of the measures to preserve evidence may only be used in the proceedings on the merits of the case.
3. The order to preserve evidence shall be enforceable immediately, unless the Court decides otherwise. The Court may set conditions to the enforceability of the order, specifying in particular:
   (a) who may represent the applicant when the measures to preserve evidence are being carried out and under what conditions;
   (b) any security which shall be provided by the applicant.

If necessary, the Court may set penalties applicable to the applicant if these conditions are not observed.

4. The order to preserve evidence shall specify a person who shall carry out the measures referred to in paragraph 1 and present a written Report on the measures to preserve evidence, all in accordance with the national law of the place where the measures are executed, to the Court within a time period to be specified.
5. The person referred to in paragraph 4 shall be a professional person or expert, who guarantees expertise, independence and impartiality. Where appropriate and allowed under applicable national law, the person may be a bailiff or assisted by a bailiff. In no circumstances may an employee or director of the applicant be present at the execution of the measures.
6. The Court may order the applicant to provide adequate security for the legal costs and other expenses and compensation for any injury incurred or likely to be incurred by the defendant which the applicant may be liable to bear. The Court shall do so where the order to preserve evidence was made without the defendant having been heard, unless there are special circumstances not to do so. The Court shall decide whether it is appropriate to order the security by deposit or bank guarantee.
7. The order to preserve evidence shall indicate that an appeal may be lodged in accordance with Article 73 of the Agreement and Rule 220.1.

Relation with Agreement: Article 60(1)-(4)

Rule 197
Order to preserve evidence without hearing the defendant

1. The Court may order measures to preserve evidence [Rule 196.1] without the defendant having been heard, in particular where any delay is likely to cause irreparable harm to the applicant or where there is a demonstrable risk of evidence being destroyed or otherwise ceasing to be available.
2. Where measures to preserve evidence are ordered without the defendant having been heard, Rule 195 shall apply *mutatis mutandis* to the oral hearing without the presence of the defendant. In such cases, the defendant shall be given notice, immediately at the time of the execution of the measures.
3. Within 30 days after the execution of the measures, the defendant may request a review of the order to preserve evidence. The Request for review shall set out:
   (a) the reasons why the order to preserve evidence shall be revoked or modified; and
   (b) the facts and evidence relied on.
4. The Court shall order an oral hearing to review the order without delay. Rule 195 shall apply. The Court may modify, revoke or confirm the order. In case the order is modified or revoked the Court shall oblige the persons to whom confidential information has been disclosed to keep this information confidential [Rule 196.1].

Relation with Agreement: Article 60(6)

Rule 198
Revocation of an order to preserve evidence

1. The Court shall ensure that an order to preserve evidence is revoked or otherwise cease to have effect, upon request of the defendant, without prejudice to the damages which may be claimed, if, within a time period not exceeding 31 calendar days or 20 working days, whichever is the longer, from the date specified in the Court's order with due account to the date where the Report referred to in Rule 196.4 shall be presented, the applicant does not start proceedings on the merits of the case before the Court.

2. Where the measures to preserve evidence are revoked, or where they lapse due to any act or omission by the applicant, or where it is subsequently found that there has been no infringement or threat of infringement of the patent, the Court may order the applicant, upon request of the defendant, to provide the defendant appropriate compensation for any injury caused by those measures [Rule 354.2].
Relation with Agreement: Article 60(8) and (9)

Order for Inspection

Rule 199
Order for inspection
1. The Court may, on a reasoned request by a party, order an inspection of products, devices, methods, premises or local situations *in situ*. For the protection of confidential information the Court may order that any of the above be disclosed only to certain named persons and subject to appropriate terms of non-disclosure in accordance with Article 58 of the Agreement.
2. Rules 192 to 198 shall apply *mutatis mutandis*.
Relation with Agreement: Article 60

CHAPTER 5
OTHER EVIDENCE

[1.1120]
Rule 200
Order to freeze assets
1. Where a party has presented reasonably available and plausible evidence in support of its claim that a patent has been or is about to be infringed the Court may, whether before or after proceedings have been commenced, order a party not to remove from its jurisdiction any assets or particular assets located therein nor to deal in any assets, whether located within its jurisdiction or not.
2. Rules 192 to 198 shall apply *mutatis mutandis*.
Relation with Agreement: Article 61

Rule 201
Experiments ordered by the Court
1. Without prejudice to the possibility for parties or parties' experts to carry out experiments, the Court may, on a reasoned request by a party, order an experiment to prove a statement of fact for the purpose of proceedings before the Court.
2. A party requesting to be allowed to prove a statement of fact by means of experiments shall lodge a request as soon as practicable in the written procedure or the interim procedure to carry out experiments which shall:
- (a) identify the facts intended to be established by the experiments, describe the proposed experiments in detail and the reasons for carrying out the proposed experiments;
- (b) propose an expert to carry out such experiments; and
- (c) disclose any previous attempts to carry out similar experiments.

3. Other parties to the proceedings shall be invited to state whether they dispute the facts intended to be established by the experiments. They shall also be invited to comment on the request, including the identity of the expert proposed and the description of the experiments.
4. Unless otherwise ordered by the Court the party requesting experiments shall initially bear the costs of the experiment.
5. The order of the Court allowing the experiments shall specify the detailed experiments and:
- (a) the name and address of the expert who is to carry out the experiments as Court's expert and draw up the report on the experiments;
- (b) the time period for carrying out the experiments and, where appropriate, the exact time and place where they are to be carried out;
- (c) if necessary, other conditions for carrying out the experiments; and
- (d) the time period for presenting the report on the experiments and, where appropriate, directions relating to the contents of the report.

6. Where appropriate, the Court may order that the experiments be carried out in the presence of the parties and their experts.
7. Once the report on the experiments is presented to the Court, it shall invite the parties to comment on it either in writing or during the oral hearing. The expert may be summoned to the oral hearing.

Rule 202
Letters rogatory
1. The Court may, of its own motion, but only after hearing the parties, or on a reasoned request by a party, issue letters rogatory for the production of documents or the hearing of witnesses or experts by other competent courts or authorities outside the European Union. Rule 180 shall apply.

2. The Court shall draw up letters rogatory in the language of the competent court or authority or shall attach to such letters a translation into that language.
3. Subject to paragraph 4, the competent court or authority shall apply national law as to the procedures to be followed in executing such requests and, in particular, as to the appropriate measures of compulsion.
4. The Court shall be informed of the time when, and the place where, the enquiry or other legal measure is to take place. It may inform the parties, witnesses and experts concerned.

PART 3
PROVISIONAL MEASURES

[1.1121]
Rule 205
Stages of the proceedings (summary proceedings)
Provisional measures are treated by way of summary proceedings which shall consist of the following stages:
(a) a written procedure; and
(b) an oral procedure, which may include an oral hearing of the parties or of one of the parties.

Rule 206
Application for provisional measures
1. An Application for provisional measures may be lodged by a party (hereinafter "the applicant") before or after main proceedings on the merits of the case have been started before the Court.
2. An Application for provisional measures shall contain:
(a) particulars in accordance with Rule 13.1(a) to (i);
(b) a indication of the provisional measures which are being requested [Rule 211.1];
(c) the reasons why provisional measures are necessary to prevent a threatened infringement, to forbid the continuation of an alleged infringement or to make such continuation subject to the lodging of guarantees;
(d) the facts and evidence relied on in support of the Application, including evidence to support the claim that provisional measures are necessary including the matters referred to in Rule 211.2 and .3; and
(e) a concise description of the action which will be started before the Court, including an indication of the facts and evidence which will be relied on in support of the main proceedings on the merits of the case.
3. Where the applicant requests that provisional measures be ordered without hearing the other party (hereinafter "the defendant"), the Application for provisional measures shall in addition contain:
(a) the reasons for not hearing the defendant having regard in particular to Rule 197; and
(b) information about any prior correspondence between the parties concerning the alleged infringement.
4. The applicant shall be under a duty to disclose any material fact known to it which might influence the Court in deciding whether to make an order without hearing the defendant including any pending proceedings and/or any unsuccessful attempt in the past to obtain provisional measures in respect of the patent.
5. Rule 14 shall apply *mutatis mutandis*. The applicant shall pay the fee for the Application for provisional measures, in accordance with Part 6. Rule 15.2 shall apply *mutatis mutandis*.
Relation with Agreement: Articles 32(1)(c) and 62

Rule 207
Protective letter
1. If a person entitled to start proceedings under Article 47 of the Agreement considers it likely that an Application for provisional measures against him as a defendant may be lodged before the Court in the near future, he may file a Protective letter.
2. The Protective letter shall be filed with the Registry in the language of the patent and shall contain:
(a) the name of the defendant or defendants filing the Protective letter and of the defendant's representative;
(b) the name of the presumed applicant for provisional measures;
(c) postal and electronic addresses for service on the defendant filing the Protective letter and the names of the persons authorised to accept service;
(d) postal and, where available, electronic addresses for service on the presumed applicant for provisional measures and the names of the persons authorised to accept service if known;
(e) where available, the number of the patent concerned and, where applicable, information about any prior or pending proceedings referred to in Rule 13.1(h); and
(f) the statement that the letter is a Protective letter.
3. The Protective letter may contain:

(a) an indication of the facts relied on, which may include a challenge to the facts expected to be relied on by the presumed applicant and/or, where applicable, any assertion that the patent is invalid and the grounds for such assertion;
(b) any available written evidence relied on;
(c) the arguments of law, including the reasons why any Application for provisional measures should be rejected.

4. The defendant or defendants filing the Protective letter shall pay the fee for filing a Protective letter, in accordance with Part 6. Rule 15.2 shall apply *mutatis mutandis*.

5. The Registry shall as soon as practicable examine whether the requirements of paragraphs 2(a) to (f) and 3 have been complied with. If these requirements have been complied with, the Registry shall as soon as practicable:
(a) record the date of receipt and assign a number to the Protective letter;
(b) subject to paragraph 7, record the Protective letter in the register;
(c) provide details of the Protective letter to all divisions; and
(d) where an Application for provisional measures has already been lodged, inform the panel or the single judge dealing with the Application about the filing of the Protective letter.

6. If the defendant has not complied with the requirements of paragraph 2 the Registry shall as soon as practicable invite the defendant to:
(a) correct the deficiencies within 14 days of service of such notification; and
(b) where applicable, pay the fee referred to in paragraph 3.

7. The protective letter shall not be publicly available on the register until it has been forwarded to the applicant pursuant to paragraph 8.

8. Where an Application for provisional measures is subsequently lodged the Registrar shall forward a copy of the protective letter to the panel or judge appointed under Rule 208 together with the Application for provisional measures and shall forward a copy to the applicant as soon as practicable.

9. If no Application for provisional measures has been lodged within six months from the date of receipt of the Protective letter, the Protective letter shall be removed from the register unless the person who has lodged the Protective letter has prior to the expiry of such period applied for an extension of six months and paid a fee for the extension in accordance with Part 6. Further extensions may be obtained on further payments of the fee.

10. Rule 15.2 shall apply *mutatis mutandis*.

Rule 208

Examination as to formal requirements, recording in the register, assignment to panel, designation of judge-rapporteur, single judge

1. The Application for provisional measures shall be examined by the Registry in accordance with Rule 16. The Registry shall in addition examine whether any Protective letter relevant for the Application is recorded in the register.

2. Where main proceedings on the merits of the case have not yet been started before the Court, Rule 17 (date of receipt, recording in the register, action number, assignment to panel) and Rule 18 (designation of judge-rapporteur by presiding judge) shall apply *mutatis mutandis*. In urgent cases, the presiding judge may decide that he or an experienced judge of the panel, acting as single judge, may decide on the Application in accordance with Rules 209 to 213 with a reduced time-table.

3. Where main proceedings on the merits of the case have already been started before the Court, the Application for provisional measures shall immediately be forwarded to the panel to which the action has been assigned or to the single judge. In urgent cases (where the action has not been assigned to a single judge), the presiding judge may decide that he or the judge-rapporteur, acting as single judge, may decide on the Application in accordance with Rules 209 to 213 with a reduced time-table.

4. The single judge deciding on the Application for provisional measures shall have all necessary powers of the Court.

Relation with Statute: Article 19

Rule 209

Examination of the Application for provisional measures

1. Without prejudice to the Court's decision on the Application for provisional measures, the Court shall have the discretion to:
(a) inform the defendant about the Application and invite him to lodge, within a time period to be specified, an Objection to the Application for provisional measures which shall contain:
    (i) the reasons why the Application shall fail;
    (ii) the facts and evidence relied on, in particular any challenge to the facts and evidence relied on by the applicant; and
    (iii) where main proceedings on the merits of the case have not yet been started before the Court, the reasons why the action which will be started before the Court shall fail and the facts and evidence relied on in support;
(b) summon the parties to an oral hearing;
(c) summon the applicant to an oral hearing without the presence of the defendant.

2. In exercising its discretion pursuant to paragraph 1, the Court shall in particular take into account:

(a) whether the patent has been upheld in an opposition procedure before the European Patent Office or has been the subject of proceedings in any other court;
(b) the urgency of the action;
(c) whether the applicant has requested provisional measures without hearing the defendant and whether the reasons for not hearing the defendant appear well-founded; and
(d) any Protective letter filed by the defendant; the Court shall in particular consider summoning parties to an oral hearing if a relevant Protective letter has been filed by the defendant.

3. In cases of extreme urgency the standing judge appointed in accordance with Rule 345.5 may decide immediately on the Application for provisional measures and the procedure to be followed on the Application.
4. If the applicant has applied for provisional measures without hearing the defendant and the Court decides not to grant provisional measures without hearing the defendant the applicant may withdraw the Application and may request that the Court order that the Application and the contents of the Application remain confidential.
5. If the patent the subject of the Application is also the subject of a protective letter pursuant to Rule 207 the applicant may withdraw the Application pursuant to paragraph 4.

Rule 210
Oral hearing

1. Where the Court decides to summon the parties to an oral hearing, the date for the oral hearing shall be set as soon as possible after the date of receipt of the Application for provisional measures.
2. The Court may order the parties to provide further information, documents and other evidence before or during the oral hearing, including evidence to enable the Court to make its decision in accordance with Rule 211. Part 2 of these Rules on Evidence shall be applicable only to the extent determined by the Court.
3. Rules 111 to 116 shall apply *mutatis mutandis*. Where the applicant is absent from the oral hearing without a reasonable excuse, the Court shall reject the Application for provisional measures.
4. The decision of the Court on the Application for provisional measures shall be given in writing as soon as possible after the closure of the oral hearing. If the Court deems appropriate, its decision may be given orally to the parties at the end of the oral hearing, prior to providing its decision in writing.

Rule 211
Order on the Application for provisional measures

1. The Court may in particular order the following provisional measures:

(a) injunctions against a defendant;
(b) the seizure or delivery up of the goods suspected of infringing a patent right so as to prevent their entry into or movement within the channels of commerce;
(c) if an applicant demonstrates circumstances likely to endanger the recovery of damages, a precautionary seizure of the movable and immovable property of the defendant, including the blocking of his bank accounts and other assets;
(d) an interim award of costs.

2. In taking its decision the Court may require the applicant to provide reasonable evidence to satisfy the Court with a sufficient degree of certainty that the applicant is entitled to commence proceedings pursuant to Article 47, that the patent in question is valid and that his right is being infringed, or that such infringement is imminent.
3. In taking its decision the Court shall in the exercise of its discretion weigh up the interests of the parties and, in particular, take into account the potential harm for either of the parties resulting from the granting or the refusal of the injunction.
4. The Court shall have regard to any unreasonable delay in seeking provisional measures.
5. The Court may order the applicant to provide adequate security for appropriate compensation for any injury likely to be caused to the defendant which the applicant may be liable to bear in the event that the Court revokes the order for provisional measures. The Court shall do so where interim measures are ordered without the defendant having been heard unless there are special circumstances not to do so. The Court shall decide whether it is appropriate to order the security by deposit or bank guarantee. The order shall be effective only after the security has been given to the defendant in accordance with the Court's decision.
6. The order on provisional measures shall indicate that an appeal may be brought in accordance with Article 73 of the Agreement and Rule 220.1.

Relation with Agreement: Article 62(2) and (4)

Rule 212
Order on provisional measures without hearing the defendant
1. The Court may order provisional measures without the defendant having been heard, in particular where any delay is likely to cause irreparable harm to the applicant or where there is a demonstrable risk of evidence being destroyed. Rule 197 shall apply *mutatis mutandis*.
2. Where provisional measures are ordered without the defendant having been heard, Rule 210 shall apply *mutatis mutandis* to the oral hearing without the presence of the defendant. In such cases, the defendant shall be given notice of the provisional measures without delay and at the latest immediately at the time of execution of the measures.
3. The defendant may request a review. Rule 197.3 and .4 shall apply *mutatis mutandis*.
Relation with Agreement: Article 60(5) and (6)
Rule 213 – Revocation of provisional measures
1. The Court shall ensure that provisional measures are revoked or otherwise cease to have effect, upon request of the defendant, without prejudice to the damages which may be claimed, if, within a time period not exceeding 31 calendar days or 20 working days, whichever is the longer, from the date specified in the Court's order, the applicant does not start proceedings on the merits of the case before the Court. When specifying the date, the Court shall take due account, where applicable, of the date on which the Report referred to in Rule 196.4 shall be presented.
2. Where provisional measures are revoked, or where they lapse due to any act or omission by the applicant, or where it is subsequently found that there has been no infringement or threat of infringement of the patent, the Court may order the applicant, upon request of the defendant, to provide the defendant with appropriate compensation for any injury caused by those measures [Rule 354.2].
Relation with Agreement: Article 60(9).

PART 4
PROCEDURES BEFORE THE COURT OF APPEAL

[1.1122]
Rule 220
Appealable decisions
1. An appeal by a party adversely affected may be brought against:
   (a) final decisions of the Court of First Instance;
   (b) decisions terminating proceedings as regards one of the parties;
   (c) orders referred to in Articles 49(5), 59, 60, 61, 62 or 67 of the Agreement.
2. Orders other than those referred to in paragraph 1 and Rule 97.5, may be either the subject of an appeal together with the appeal against the decision or may be appealed with the leave of the Court of First Instance within 15 days of service of the Court's decision to that effect.
3. In the event of a refusal of the Court of First Instance to grant leave within 15 days of the order of one of its panels a request for a discretionary review to the Court of Appeal may be made within 15 calendar days from the end of that period. Rule 333.3 shall apply *mutatis mutandis*. The request shall set out the matters referred to in Rule 221.2.
4. The Registrar shall assign the request for a discretionary review to the standing judge (Rule 345.5 and .8). The standing judge may deny the request without giving reasons. If the standing judge allows the request after having heard the other party, he shall order what further steps, if any, the parties shall take and within what time limits and the President of the Court of Appeal shall assign the review to a panel of the Court of Appeal for a decision. The Court of Appeal may consult the presiding judge or the judge-rapporteur of the panel of the Court of First Instance which has refused the leave order.
5. The Court of Appeal may hear appeals against separate decisions on the merits in infringement proceedings and in validity proceedings together.
Relation with Agreement: Article 73

Rule 221
Application for leave to appeal against cost decisions
1. A party adversely affected by a decision referred to in Rule 157 may lodge an Application for leave to appeal to the Court of Appeal within 15 days of service of the decision of the Court.
2. The Application for leave to appeal shall set out:
   (a) the reasons why the appeal should be heard;
   (b) where necessary, the facts, evidence and arguments relied on.
3. The Application for leave to appeal shall be assigned to the standing judge (Rule 345.5 and .8) who shall decide on granting leave to appeal.
4. If leave to appeal a cost decision is granted the standing judge shall decide the appeal.

Rule 222
Subject-matter of the proceedings before the Court of Appeal
1. Requests, facts, evidence and arguments submitted by the parties under Rules 221, 225, 226, 236 and 238 shall, subject to paragraph 2, constitute the subject-matter of the proceedings before the Court of Appeal. The Court of Appeal shall consult the file of the proceedings before the Court of First Instance.
2. Requests, facts and evidence which have not been submitted by a party during proceedings before the Court of First Instance may be disregarded by the Court of Appeal. When exercising discretion, the Court shall in particular take into account:
(a) whether a party seeking to lodge new submissions is able to justify that the new submissions could not reasonably have been made during proceedings before the Court of First Instance;
(b) the relevance of the new submissions for the decision on the appeal;
(c) the position of the other party regarding the lodging of the new submissions.
Relation with Agreement: Article 73(4)

Rule 223
Application for suspensive effect
1. A party may lodge an Application for suspensive effect, in accordance with Article 74 of the Agreement.
2. The Application for suspensive effect shall set out:
(a) the reasons why the lodging of the appeal shall have suspensive effect;
(b) the facts, evidence and arguments relied on.
3. The Court of Appeal shall decide the Application without delay.
4. In cases of extreme urgency the applicant may apply at any time without formality for an order for suspensive effect to the standing judge [Rule 345.5 and .8]. The standing judge shall have all the powers of the Court of Appeal and shall decide the procedure to be followed on the application, which may include a subsequent written Application.
5. There shall be no suspensive effect for an appeal of an order pursuant to Rule 220.2.
Relation with Agreement: Article 74

CHAPTER 1
WRITTEN PROCEDURE

SECTION 1
STATEMENT OF APPEAL, STATEMENT OF GROUNDS OF APPEAL

[1.1123]
Rule 224
Time periods for lodging the Statement of appeal and the Statement of grounds of appeal
1. A Statement of appeal shall be lodged by the appellant:
(a) within two months of service of a decision referred to in Rule 220.1 (a) and (b); or
(b) within 15 days of service of an order referred to in Rule 220.1(c) or a decision referred to in Rule 220.2 or 221.3.
2. The Statement of grounds of appeal shall be lodged by the appellant:
(a) within four months of service of a decision referred to in Rule 220.1 (a) and (b); or
(b) within 15 days of service of an order referred to in Rule 220.1(c) or a decision referred to in Rule 220.2 or 221.3.
Relation with Agreement: Article 73(1) and (2)

Rule 225
Contents of the Statement of appeal
The Statement of appeal shall contain:
(a) the names of the appellant and of the appellant's representative;
(b) the names of the respondent and of the respondent's representative;
(c) postal and electronic addresses for service on the appellant and on the respondent, as well as the names of the persons authorised to accept service;
(d) the date of the decision or order appealed against and the action number attributed to the file in proceedings before the Court of First Instance; and
(e) the order or remedy sought by the appellant, including any order for expedition of the appeal pursuant to Rule 9.3(b) and the reasons justifying such order for expedition.

Rule 226 – Contents of the Statement of grounds of appeal
The Statement of grounds of appeal shall contain:
(a) an indication of which parts of the decision or order are contested;
(b) the reasons for setting aside the contested decision or order; and
(c) an indication of the facts and evidence on which the appeal is based in accordance with Rule 222.1 and .2.

Rule 227
Language of the Statement of appeal and of the Statement of grounds of appeal

1. The Statement of appeal and the Statement of grounds of appeal shall be drawn up:
   (a) without prejudice to Article 50(3) of the Agreement, in the language of the proceedings before the Court of First Instance; or
   (b) where the parties have agreed in accordance with Article 50(2) of the Agreement, in the language in which the patent was granted. Where the parties have agreed in accordance with Article 50(2) of the Agreement, evidence of the respondent's agreement shall be lodged by the appellant together with the Statement of appeal.

Relationship with Agreement: Article 50

Rule 228
Fee for the appeal

The appellant shall pay the fixed fee and, where applicable, the value based fee for the appeal, in accordance with Part 6. Rule 15.2 shall apply *mutatis mutandis*.

Rule 229
Examination as to formal requirements of the Statement of appeal

1. The Registry shall, as soon as practicable after the lodging of the Statement of appeal, examine whether the requirements of Rules 224.1, 225, 227 and 228 have been complied with.
2. If the appellant has not complied with the requirements referred to in Rules 225, 227 or 228, the Registry shall invite the appellant to:
   (a) correct the deficiencies within 14 days of service of such notification; and
   (b) where applicable, pay the fee for the appeal within said 14 days.
3. The Registry shall at the same time inform the appellant that if the appellant fails to correct the deficiencies or to pay the fee within the time stated, a decision by default may be given in accordance with Rule 357.
4. If the appellant has not met the requirements of Rules 225, 227 and 228 and fails to correct the deficiencies or pay the fee the Registry shall inform the President of the Court of Appeal who shall reject the appeal as inadmissible by a decision by default. He may give the appellant an opportunity to be heard beforehand.
5. If the appellant has not met the requirements of Rule 224.1, the Registry shall inform the President of the Court of Appeal who shall reject the appeal as inadmissible. He may give the appellant an opportunity to be heard beforehand.

Rule 230
Recording in the register (Court of Appeal)

1. If the Statement of appeal complies with the requirements referred to in Rule 229.1, the Registry shall:
   (a) record the date of receipt to the Statement of appeal and an action number to the appeal file;
   (b) record the appeal file in the register;
   (c) inform the appellant of the action number and the date of receipt; and
   (d) serve the Statement of appeal on all parties to the proceedings at first instance.
2. The action shall be assigned to a panel according to Rule 345.3 and .8.
3. The panel shall as soon as practicable decide whether to grant any order for expedition pursuant to Rule 225(e) having given the parties an opportunity to be heard.

Rule 231
Designation of the judge-rapporteur

The presiding judge of the panel to which the action has been assigned shall designate one legally qualified judge of the panel as judge-rapporteur. The presiding judge may designate himself as the judge-rapporteur. The Registry shall as soon as practicable notify the appellant and respondent of the identity of the judge-rapporteur.

Rule 232
Translation of file

1. If the language of the proceedings before the Court of Appeal is not the language of the proceedings before the Court of First Instance, the judge-rapporteur may order the appellant to lodge, within a time period to be specified, translations into the language of the proceedings before the Court of Appeal of:
   (a) written pleadings and other documents lodged by the parties before the Court of First Instance, as specified by the judge-rapporteur;
   (b) decisions or orders of the Court of First Instance.

The judge-rapporteur shall at the same time inform the appellant that if the appellant fails to lodge the translations within the time period specified, a decision by default may be given in accordance with Rule 357.

2. If the appellant fails to lodge the translations under paragraph 1 within the time period specified, the judge-rapporteur shall reject the appeal by a decision by default in accordance with Rule 357. He may give the appellant an opportunity to be heard beforehand.
3. The appellant may request that documented costs of translations be taken into account when the Court fixes the amount of costs in accordance with Part 1, Chapter 5.
Relation with Agreement: Article 50(2) and (3)

Rule 233
Preliminary examination of the Statement of grounds of appeal
1. The judge-rapporteur shall examine whether the Statement of grounds of appeal satisfies the requirements of Rule 226.
2. If the Statement of grounds of appeal does not comply with the requirements of Rule 226, the judge-rapporteur shall give the appellant leave to amend the Statement of grounds of appeal within such period as he may decide. If the appellant fails to amend the Statement within such period the judge-rapporteur may reject the appeal as inadmissible. He shall give the appellant an opportunity to be heard beforehand.
3. Grounds of appeal which are not raised within the period specified for the Statement of grounds of appeal in Rule 224.2 shall not be admissible.

Rule 234
Challenge to the decision to reject an appeal as inadmissible
1. The appellant may challenge a decision to reject the appeal as inadmissible under Rules 224.1 or 233.2 within one month of service of the decision, without providing new grounds of appeal.
2. The action shall be assigned to a panel according to Rule 345.3 and .8.
3. If a decision to reject an appeal as inadmissible is set aside, the appeal shall take its normal course.

SECTION 2
STATEMENT OF RESPONSE

Rule 235
Statement of response
1. Within three months of service of the Statement of grounds of appeal pursuant to Rule 224.2(a), any other party to proceedings before the Court of First Instance (hereinafter "respondent") may lodge a Statement of response, which shall be served on the appellant.
2. Within 15 days of service of grounds of appeal pursuant to Rule 224.2(b), any other party to proceedings before the Court of First Instance (hereinafter "respondent") may lodge a Statement of response, which shall be served on the appellant.
3. If the respondent fails to lodge a Statement of response, the Court of Appeal may give a reasoned decision.

Rule 236
Contents of the Statement of response
1. The Statement of response shall contain:
(a) the names of the respondent and the respondent's representative;
(b) postal and electronic addresses for service on the respondent and the names and addresses of the persons authorised to accept service;
(c) the action number of the appeal file; and
(d) a response to the grounds of appeal.
2. The respondent may support the decision of the Court of First Instance on grounds other than those given in the decision.

Rule 237
Statement of cross-appeal
1. A party who has not lodged a Statement of appeal within the period referred to in Rule 224.1 may still bring an appeal by way of cross-appeal within the period referred to in Rule 235 if one of the other parties has lodged a Statement of appeal.
2. A Statement of cross-appeal shall be included in the Statement of response. It shall comply with the requirements of Rules 225 and 226. Rules 229, 233 and 234 shall apply *mutatis mutandis* to the Statement of cross-appeal.
3. A Statement of cross-appeal shall not be admissible in any other way or at any other time.
4. A cross-appeal shall be treated as an appeal as far as the fee for the appeal is concerned. Rule 228 shall apply *mutatis mutandis*.
5. If the Statement of appeal is withdrawn, any Statement of cross-appeal shall be deemed to be withdrawn.

SECTION 3
Reply to a Statement of Cross-Appeal

Rule 238
Reply to a Statement of cross-appeal and further schedule
1. The appellant may, within two months of service of any Statement of cross-appeal under Rules 237, 235.1, lodge a Reply to the Statement of cross-appeal which shall contain a response to the grounds of appeal raised in the Statement of cross-appeal.
2. The appellant may, within 15 days of service of the Statement of cross-appeal under Rules 237 and 235.2, lodge a Reply to the Statement of cross-appeal which shall contain a response to the grounds of appeal raised in the Statement of cross-appeal.
3. Rule 28 shall apply *mutatis mutandis*.

SECTION 4
Referral to the Full Court

Rule 238A
Decision to refer
1. The panel to which the action has been assigned may refer it to the full Court of Appeal if the panel considers, on a proposal from the presiding judge, the case to be of exceptional importance and, in particular, where the decision in the action may affect the consistency and unity of the case law of the Court.
2. The presiding judge of the panel shall request that the President of the Court of Appeal and the two judges of the Court of Appeal who are members of the Presidium to appoint the judges of the Court of Appeal to the full Court. The appointees shall be the President of the Court of Appeal and not less than ten (legally and technically qualified) judges of the Court of Appeal to represent the initial two panels of the Court of Appeal. In the event that the Court of Appeal shall have more than two panels the appointees to the full Court shall increase by five judges, (legally and technically qualified), for each additional panel.
3. Decisions of the full Court shall be by no less than a three-quarters majority of the judges of the full Court.

CHAPTER 2
INTERIM PROCEDURE

[1.1124]
Rule 239
Role of the judge-rapporteur
1. Upon the expiry of the periods specified in Rules 224 to 238 the judge-rapporteur shall make all necessary preparations for the oral hearing. Subject always to the provisions of Rule 222, the judge-rapporteur shall, to the extent appropriate, have the powers and exercise the duties set out in Rules 101 to 110 *mutatis mutandis*.
2. As soon as the judge-rapporteur considers that the appeal is ready for oral hearing he shall summon the parties to the oral hearing. Except for appeals against the orders referred to in Rule 220.1(c) and 220.2, and subject to any order for expedition pursuant to Rule 230.3, at least two months' notice shall be given unless the parties agree to a shorter time period. The interim procedure shall be deemed closed and oral procedure shall start immediately on the giving of such summons. The presiding judge shall, in consultation with the judge-rapporteur take over the management of the action.

CHAPTER 3
ORAL PROCEDURE

[1.1125]
Rule 240
Conduct of the oral hearing
Subject to Rule 241 the oral hearing shall be held before the panel and shall be directed by the presiding judge. Subject always to Rule 222, Rules 111, 112, 115, 116 and 117 shall apply *mutatis mutandis*.

Rule 241
Conduct of the oral hearing for an appeal of a cost decision
The oral hearing for an appeal of a cost decision pursuant to Rule 157 shall be heard by the standing judge [Rule 345.5 and .8] who shall have all the powers of the Court of Appeal.

CHAPTER 4
DECISIONS AND EFFECT OF DECISIONS

[1.1126]
Rule 242
Decision of the Court of Appeal
1. The Court of Appeal shall either reject the appeal or set the decision or order aside totally or in part substituting its own decision or order, including an order for costs both in respect of the proceedings at first instance and on appeal.
2. The Court of Appeal may:
   (a) exercise any power within the competence of the Court of First Instance;
   (b) in exceptional circumstances refer the action back to the Court of First Instance for decision or for retrial [Rule 243]. It shall not normally be an exceptional circumstance justifying a referral back that the Court of First Instance failed to decide an issue which it is necessary for the Court of Appeal to decide on appeal.

Relation with Agreement: Article 75

Rule 243
Referral back
1. The decision referring an action back to the Court of First Instance shall specify whether the same panel whose earlier decision or order is revoked shall deal further with the action or whether another panel shall be appointed by the presiding judge of the division concerned.
2. Where an action is referred back to the Court of First Instance, the Court shall be bound by the decision of the Court of Appeal and its *ratio decidendi*.

Relation with Agreement: Article 75

CHAPTER 5
PROCEDURE FOR APPLICATION FOR REHEARING

[1.1127]
Rule 245
Lodging of an Application for rehearing
1. An Application for rehearing may be lodged by any party adversely affected by a final decision (hereinafter "the final decision") of the Court of First Instance for which the time for lodging an appeal has expired or of the Court of Appeal (hereinafter "the petitioner").
2. The Application for rehearing shall be lodged at the Court of Appeal within the following periods:
   (a) where the Application for rehearing is based on the ground of a fundamental procedural defect, within two months of the discovery of the fundamental defect or of service of the final decision, whichever is the later;
   (b) where the Application for rehearing is based on an act which has been held, by a final court decision, to constitute a criminal offence, within two months of the date on which the criminal offence has been so held or service of the final decision, whichever is the later;
   (c) but in any event no later than ten years of service of the final decision.

Relation with Agreement: Article 81

Rule 246
Contents of the Application for rehearing
1. The Application for rehearing shall contain:
   (a) the names of the petitioner and of the petitioner's representative;
   (b) postal and electronic addresses for service on the petitioner and the names and addresses of the persons authorised to accept service; and
   (c) an indication of the decision to be reviewed.
2. The Application for rehearing shall indicate the reasons for setting aside the final decision, as well as the facts and evidence on which the Application is based.

Rule 247
Fundamental procedural defects
A fundamental procedural defect under Article 81(1) of the Agreement may have occurred, for example, where:
   (a) a judge of the Court took part in the decision in breach of Article 17 of the Agreement or Article 7 of the Statute;
   (b) a person not appointed as a judge of the Court sat on the panel which took the final decision;
   (c) a fundamental violation of Article 76 of the Agreement occurred in the proceedings which have led to the final decision;
   (d) the decision was made without deciding on a request relevant to that decision; or

(e) a breach of Article 6 of the Convention for the Protection of Human Rights and Fundamental Freedoms has occurred.

Rule 248
Obligation to raise objections
1. An Application for rehearing based on the ground of a fundamental procedural defect is only admissible where an objection in respect of the procedural defect was raised during the proceedings before the Court of First Instance or the Court of Appeal and dismissed by the Court, except where such objection could not have been raised during the proceedings before the Court of First Instance or the Court of Appeal.
2. An application for rehearing based upon the ground of a fundamental procedural defect is not admissible where the party could have brought an appeal in respect of the defect but failed to do so.

Rule 249
Definition of criminal offence
A criminal offence shall only be considered to have occurred if it is finally held to be such an offence by a competent court or authority. A conviction is not necessary.

Rule 250
Fee for the rehearing
The petitioner shall pay the fee for the rehearing, in accordance with Part 6. Rule 15.2 shall apply *mutatis mutandis*. The Court may waive payment of the fee in the circumstances contemplated by Rule 245.2(a) or (b).

Rule 251
Recording in the register
Rule 230.1 shall apply *mutatis mutandis*.

Rule 252
Suspensive effect
The lodging of an Application for rehearing shall not have suspensive effect unless the Court of Appeal decides otherwise.
Relation with Agreement: Article 81(2)

Rule 253
Examination as to formal requirements of the Application for rehearing
1. The Registry shall, as soon as practicable after the lodging of the Application for rehearing, examine whether the requirements of Rules 245, 246 and 250 have been complied with.
2. If the petitioner has not complied with the requirements referred to in paragraph 1, the Registry shall invite the petitioner to:
(a) correct the deficiencies within 14 days; and
(b) where applicable, pay the fee for the rehearing within 14 days.
If the petitioner fails to correct the deficiencies or pay the fee the case shall be assigned to the standing judge by the Registrar (Rule 345.5 and .8) who may reject the Application for rehearing as inadmissible. He shall give the petitioner an opportunity to be heard beforehand.

Rule 254
Assignment of Application for rehearing to a panel
1. Immediately after the Application for rehearing has been recorded in the register, the Registry shall serve a copy of the Application for rehearing on all other parties and shall inform the President of the Court of Appeal that a Request for rehearing has been lodged.
2. The action shall be assigned to a panel consisting of three legally qualified judges. The President of the Court of Appeal may order that judges of the Court who participated in taking the decision to be reviewed shall not sit on the panel.

Rule 255
Examination of the Application for rehearing
After hearing the parties the panel may make:
(a) a decision to reject the Application for rehearing as not allowable; such a decision shall be by a majority vote of the judges on the panel.
(b) a decision to allow the Application for rehearing; such a decision shall set aside or suspend the decision under review, in whole or in part, and re-open the proceedings for a new hearing and decisions. Where proceedings are re-opened, the panel shall give directions for the future proceedings.
Relation with Agreement: Article 81(3)

PART 5
GENERAL PROVISIONS

CHAPTER 1
GENERAL PROCEDURAL PROVISIONS

[1.1128]
Rule 260
Examination by the Registry of its own motion
1. In any proceedings before the Court, the Registry shall, as soon as practicable in the proceedings, of its own motion, examine whether an opt-out has effect for the patent concerned.
2. Where the Registry notes that two or more actions concerning the same patent are initiated before several divisions (whether or not between the same parties), it shall as soon as practicable inform the divisions concerned.
Relation with Agreement: Article 83(3) and (4)
Relation with Statute: Articles 23 and 24

Rule 261
Date of pleadings
All pleadings and documents lodged with pleadings shall bear a time and a date which shall be the time and date of receipt of pleadings at the Registry. The time shall be the local time of the Registry. The Registrar shall be responsible for time and date marking.

Rule 262
Public access to the register
1. Without prejudice to Articles 58 and 60(1) of the Agreement and subject to Rules 190.1, 194.5, 196.1, 197.4, 199.1, 207.7, 209.4, 315.2 and 365.2, written pleadings, written evidence, decisions and orders lodged at or made by the Court and recorded by the Registry shall be available to the public, unless a party has requested that certain information be kept confidential and provided specific reasons for such confidentiality. The Registrar shall ensure that information subject of such a request shall not be made available pending an Application pursuant to paragraph 2 or an appeal pursuant to Rule 220.2. Where a party requests that parts of written pleadings or written evidence shall be kept confidential, he shall also provide copies of the said documents with the relevant parts redacted when making the request.
2. A member of the public may lodge an Application with the Court for an order that any information excluded from public access pursuant to paragraph 1 may be made available to the applicant.
3. The Application shall contain:
- (a) details of the information alleged to be confidential, so far as possible;
- (b) the grounds upon which the applicant believes the reasons for confidentiality should not be accepted; and
- (c) the purpose for which the information is needed.

4. The Court shall invite written comments from the parties prior to making any order.
5. The Court shall allow the Application unless legitimate reasons given by the party concerned for the confidentiality of the information outweigh the interest of the applicant to access such information.
6. The Registrar shall as soon as practicable take all such steps with regard to access to the register as may be necessary to give effect to an order of the Court under this Rule.
Relation with Agreement: Articles 10, 45, 58 and 60(1)
Relation with Statute: Article 24(2)

Rule 263
Leave to change claim or amend case
1. A party may at any stage of the proceedings apply to the Court for leave to change its claim or to amend its case, including adding a counterclaim. Any such application shall explain why such change or amendment was not included in the original pleading.
2. Subject to paragraph 3, leave shall not be granted if, all circumstances considered, the party seeking the amendment cannot satisfy the Court that:
- (a) the amendment in question could not have been made with reasonable diligence at an earlier stage; and
- (b) the amendment will not unreasonably hinder the other party in the conduct of its action.

3. Leave to limit a claim in an action unconditionally shall always be granted.
4. The Court may re-consider fees already paid in the light of an amendment.

Rule 264
An opportunity to be heard
Where these Rules provide that a party shall or may be given an opportunity to be heard before the Court makes an order or takes some action, the Court shall or may (as the case may be) request the parties to provide written submissions within a specified period and/or shall or may invite the parties to an oral hearing on a fixed date by the Court. The Court may also order that a hearing takes place by telephone or video conference. Rules 105 and 106 shall apply *mutatis mutandis*.

Rule 265
Withdrawal
1. As long as there is no final decision in an action, a claimant may apply to withdraw his action. The Court shall decide the application after hearing the other party. The application to withdraw shall not be permitted if the other party has a legitimate interest in the action being decided by the Court.
2. If withdrawal is permitted, the Court shall:
 (a) give a decision declaring the proceedings closed;
 (b) order the decision to be entered on the register; and
 (c) issue a cost decision in accordance with Part 1, Chapter 5.
The withdrawal of an action by the claimant shall have no effect on any counterclaim in the action. The Court may however refer any counterclaim for revocation to the Central Division.

Rule 266
Preliminary references to the Court of Justice of the European Union
1. At any stage of the proceedings where a question is raised before the Court and the Court considers that a decision on the question by the Court of Justice of the European Union ("CJEU") is necessary before the Court can give judgment, the Court of First Instance may and the Court of Appeal shall request the CJEU to give a ruling thereon.
2. The Court shall in requesting a ruling follow the procedure set out in the Rules of the CJEU.
3. If the Court requests the CJEU to apply its expedited procedure the request shall in addition set out:
 (a) the matters of fact and law which establish its urgency; and
 (b) the reasons why an expedited ruling is appropriate.
4. The Registrar shall as soon as practicable forward the request and any request to apply the expedited procedure to the Registrar of the CJEU.
5. The Court may stay the proceedings. Where it does not stay proceedings, it shall not give judgement until the CJEU has given a ruling on the question.

Rule 267
Actions pursuant to Article 22 of the Agreement
Where an action for damages has been brought against a Contracting Member State pursuant to Article 22 of the Agreement, the President of the Court of Appeal shall, as soon as practicable following a request from the competent authority in the Contracting Member State, provide the competent authority with copies of all pleadings, evidence, decisions and orders available to the Court in its proceedings that are relevant to the action for damages. The President of the Court of Appeal shall have an opportunity to comment.

CHAPTER 2
SERVICE

SECTION 1
SERVICE WITHIN THE CONTRACTING MEMBER STATES

[1.1129]
Rule 270
Scope of this Section
1. For service of the Statement of claim the rules set out in this Section and the Regulation (EC) No 1393/2007 shall apply.
2. For the purpose of Rules 270 to 275 the term Statement of claim shall, where appropriate, mean all originating pleadings in actions referred to in Article 32(1) of the Agreement.

Rule 271
Service of the Statement of claim
1. For service within the Contracting Member States, the Registry may serve the Statement of claim on the defendant at an electronic address which the defendant has provided for the purpose of service in the proceedings provided that the service is effected using appropriately high technical standards guaranteeing
 (a) the identity of the sender;

(b) the safe transmission; and
(c) the possibility for the addressee to take notice of the documents.

A list of secure identification and transmission standards is contained in Annex I of the Rules of Procedure.

2. The Registry may, under the conditions of paragraph 1(a) to (c), serve the Statement of claim where:
(a) the defendant has provided the electronic address of a representative pursuant to Rule 8.1 as an address at which the defendant may be served with the Statement of claim; or
(b) a representative pursuant to Rule 8.1 acting for the defendant has notified the Registry or the claimant that he accepts service of the Statement of claim on behalf of the defendant at an electronic address,

at the electronic address of that representative.

3. For the purpose of serving a Statement for revocation [Rule 44] or of serving a Statement for declaration of non-infringement [Rule 63], reference to representative under paragraph 2(a) or (b) shall additionally include professional representatives and legal practitioners as defined in Article 134 EPC who are recorded as the appointed representative for the patent, the subject of the proceedings, in the Register for unitary patent protection [Regulation (EU) No 1257/2012, Article 2(e)] or in the national patent register [Rule 8.5(a)].

4. Where service by means of electronic communication cannot be effected, the Registry shall serve the Statement of claim on the defendant by:
(a) any other method foreseen in the Regulation (EC) No 1393/2007, in particular by registered letter according to Article 14 of that regulation with advice of delivery;
(b) fax provided that the requirements of paragraph 1(a) to (c) are observed; or
(c) where service in accordance with paragraphs 4(a) and 4(b) could not be effected any method permitted by the law of the Member State of the European Union where service is to be effected or authorised by the Court under Rule 275.

5. Service under paragraph 4(a) shall be effected at the following place:
(a) where the defendant is a company or other legal person, at its statutory seat, central administration or principal place of business within the Contracting Member States or at any place within the Contracting Member States where the company or other legal person has a permanent or temporary place of business;
(b) where the defendant is an individual: at his usual or last known residence within the Contracting Member States; or
(c) for the purpose of serving a Statement for revocation [Rule 44] or of serving a Statement for a declaration of non-infringement [Rule 63], at the place of business of a professional representative or legal practitioner as defined in Article 134 EPC who is recorded as the appointed representative for the patent, the subject of the proceedings, in the Register for unitary patent protection [Regulation (EU) No 1257/2012, Article 2(e)] or of the patent office of a Contracting Member State.

6. Subject to Rule 272.2 and .3, a Statement of claim served in accordance with paragraphs 1 to 5 is deemed to be served on the defendant:
(a) where service takes place by means of electronic communication or by fax, on the day when the relevant electronic message was sent or the transmission of the fax was completed (GMT+1); or
(b) where service takes place by registered letter with advice of delivery such letter shall be deemed to be served on the addressee on the tenth day following posting unless it has failed to reach the addressee, has in fact reached him on a later date or the advice of delivery has not been returned. Such service shall, except where paragraph 7 applies, be deemed effective even if acceptance of the letter has been refused.

7. Where the defendant is entitled to refuse service according to Article 8 of the Regulation (EC) No 1393/2007 and where he has notified the refusal to the Registry within one week of the attempted service together with an indication of the language(s) he understands, the Registry shall inform the claimant. The claimant shall provide to the Registry translations of at least the Statement of claim and the information required in Rule 13.1(a) to (p) in a language provided for by Article 8(1)(a) or (b) of the Regulation (EC) No 1393/2007. For the determination of the date of service Articles 8(3) and 9 of the Regulation (EC) No 1393/2007 shall apply. When serving the Statement of claim the defendant shall be informed of these rights.

Rule 272
Notice of service and non-service of the Statement of claim

1. The Registry shall inform the claimant of the date on which the Statement of claim is deemed served under Rule 271.6.

2. Where the Registry has served the Statement of claim by registered letter with advice of delivery and the Statement of claim is returned to the Registry for any reason, the Registry shall inform the claimant.

3. Paragraph 2 shall apply *mutatis mutandis* where the Registry has served the Statement of claim by means of electronic communication or fax and the relevant electronic message or fax appears not to have been received.

SECTION 2
SERVICE OUTSIDE THE CONTRACTING MEMBER STATES

Rule 273
Scope of this Section
This Section applies to service of a Statement of claim outside the Contracting Member States.

Rule 274
Service outside the Contracting Member States
1. Where a Statement of claim is to be served outside the Contracting Member States, it may be so served by the Registry:
(a) by any method provided by:
(i) the Regulation (EC) No 1393/2007 where it applies respecting the rights of the recipient granted by the Regulation;
(ii) The Hague Convention or any other applicable convention or agreement where it applies; or
(iii) to the extent that there is no such convention or agreement in force, either by service through diplomatic or consular channels from the Contracting Member State in which the sub-registry of the relevant division is established;
(b) where service in accordance with paragraph 1(a) could not be effected by any method permitted by the law of the state where service is to be effected or as authorised by the Court under Rule 275.
2. No Statement of claim may be served under this Rule 274 in a manner which is contrary to the law of the state where service is effected.
3. The Registry shall inform the claimant of the date on which the Statement of claim is deemed served under paragraph 1.
4. The Registry shall inform the claimant if for any reason service pursuant to paragraph 1 cannot be effected.

SECTION 3
SERVICE BY AN ALTERNATIVE METHOD

Rule 275
Service of the Statement of claim by an alternative method or at an alternative place
1. Where it appears to the Court on an application by the claimant that there is a good reason to authorise service by a method or at a place not otherwise permitted by this Chapter, the Court may by way of order permit service by an alternative method or at an alternative place.
2. On a reasoned request by the claimant, the Court may order that steps already taken to bring the Statement of claim to the attention of the defendant by an alternative method or at an alternative place is good service.
3. An order under this rule shall specify:
(a) the method or place of service;
(b) the date on which the Statement of claim is deemed served; and
(c) the period for filing the Statement of defence.
4. No order for alternative service under this Rule shall be made permitting service in a manner that is contrary to the law of the state where service is to be effected.

SECTION 4
SERVICE OF ORDERS, DECISIONS AND WRITTEN PLEADINGS

Rule 276
Service of orders and decisions
1. Any order or decision of the Court shall be served on each of the parties in accordance with the provisions of Sections 1, 2 or 3 of this Chapter 2, as the case may be.
2. Decisions by default pursuant to Rule 355 resulting from failure of the defendant to lodge a Defence to revocation [Rule 50] or failure to lodge a Defence to the Statement for a declaration of non-infringement [Rule 67] within the time limit set by these Rules or by the Court, may be served on the defendant at the place of business of a professional representative or legal practitioner as defined in Article 134 EPC who is recorded as the appointed representative for the subject European patent with unitary effect, the subject of the proceedings, in the Register for unitary patent protection [Regulation (EU) No 1257/2012, Article 2(e)] or in the national patent register [Rule 8.5(a)].

Rule 277
Decisions by default under Part 5, Chapter 11
No decision by default shall be entered under Part 5, Chapter 11 unless the Court is satisfied that either:

(a) the Statement of claim was served by a method prescribed by the internal law of the state addressed for the service of documents in domestic actions upon persons who are within its territory; or
(b) the Statement of claim was actually served on the defendant under this Chapter 2.

Rule 278
Service of written pleadings and other documents
1. As soon as practicable after written pleadings have been received at the Registry, the Registry shall serve the pleadings and any other document lodged with the pleadings on the other party by means of electronic communication except if the pleading contains a request for an *ex parte* proceeding.
2. Where service by means of electronic communication cannot be effected, the Registry shall serve the written pleadings on the party by:
(a) registered letter with advice of delivery;
(b) fax; or
(c) any method authorised by the Court under Rule 275.
3. Service under paragraph 2(a) shall be effected at the following place:
(a) where the party is a company or other legal person: at its statutory seat, central administration, principal place of business or at any place within the Contracting Member States where the company or other legal person has a place of business;
(b) where the party is an individual: at his usual or last known residence within the Contracting Member States.
4. Rule 271.6 and 272 shall apply *mutatis mutandis.*
5. Where a party is represented pursuant to Rule 8, the pleadings and other documents referred to in paragraph 1 shall be served on that representative. Paragraph 2 shall apply *mutatis mutandis.*

Rule 279
Change of electronic address for service
Where the electronic address for service of a party changes, that party must give notice in writing of the change as soon as it has taken place to the Registry and every other party [Rule 6.3].

CHAPTER 3
RIGHTS AND OBLIGATIONS OF REPRESENTATIVES

[1.1130]
Rule 284
Duty of representatives not to misrepresent facts or cases
A representative of a party shall not misrepresent cases or facts before the Court either knowingly or with good reasons to know.
Relation to Agreement: Article 48(6)

Rule 285
Powers of attorney
A representative who claims to be representing a party shall be accepted as such provided however the Court may order a representative to produce a written authority if his representative powers are challenged.

Rule 286
Certificate that a representative is authorised to practice before the Court
1. A representative pursuant to Article 48(1) of the Agreement shall lodge at the Registry a certificate that he is a lawyer authorised to practise before a court of a Member State of the European Union. A lawyer within the meaning of Article 48(1) of the Agreement is a person who is authorised to pursue professional activities under a title referred to in Article 1 of Directive 98/5/EC and by way of exception a person with equivalent legal professional qualifications who, owing to national rules, is permitted to practice in patent infringement and invalidity litigation but not under such title. In subsequent actions the representative may refer to the certificate previously lodged.
2. A representative pursuant to Article 48(2) of the Agreement shall lodge at the Registry the European Patent Litigation Certificate as defined by the Administrative Committee or otherwise justify that he has appropriate qualifications to represent a party before the Court. In subsequent actions such representative may refer to the certificate or other evidence of appropriate qualification previously lodged.

Rule 287
Attorney-client privilege

1. Where a client seeks advice from a lawyer or a patent attorney he has instructed in a professional capacity, whether in connection with proceedings before the Court or otherwise, then any confidential communication (whether written or oral) between them relating to the seeking or the provision of that advice is privileged from disclosure, whilst it remains confidential, in any proceedings before the Court or in arbitration or mediation proceedings before the Centre.
2. This privilege applies also to communications between a client and a lawyer or patent attorney employed by the client and instructed to act in a professional capacity, whether in connection with proceedings before the Court or otherwise.
3. This privilege extends to the work product of the lawyer or patent attorney (including communications between lawyers and/or patent attorneys employed in the same firm or entity or between lawyers and/or patent attorneys employed by the same client) and to any record of a privileged communication.
4. This privilege prevents the lawyer or patent attorney and his client from being questioned or examined about the contents or nature of their communications.
5. This privilege may be expressly waived by the client.
6. For the purpose of Rules 287 and 288:
   (a) the expression "lawyer" shall mean a person as defined in Rule 286.1 and any other person who is qualified to practise as a lawyer and to give legal advice under the law of the state where he practises and who is professionally instructed to give such advice.
   (b) the expression "patent attorney" shall include a person who is recognised as eligible to give advice under the law of the state where he practises in relation to the protection of any invention or to the prosecution or litigation of any patent or patent application and is professionally consulted to give such advice.
7. The expression "patent attorney" shall also include a professional representative before the European Patent Office pursuant to Article 134 (1) EPC.

Relation to Agreement: Article 48(4)

Rule 288
Litigation privilege

Where a client, or a lawyer or patent attorney as specified in Rule 287.1, .2, .6 and .7 instructed by a client in a professional capacity, communicates confidentially with a third party for the purposes of obtaining information or evidence of any nature for the purpose of or for use in any proceedings, including proceedings before the European Patent Office, such communications shall be privileged from disclosure in the same way and to the same extent as provided for in Rule 287.

Relation to Agreement: Article 48(5)

Rule 289
Privileges, immunities and facilities

1. Representatives appearing before the Court or before any judicial authority to which it has addressed letters rogatory [Rule 202] shall enjoy immunity in respect of words spoken or written by them concerning the action or the parties.
2. Representatives shall enjoy the following further privileges and facilities:
   (a) papers and documents relating to the proceedings shall be exempt from both search and seizure;
   (b) any allegedly infringing product or device relating to the proceedings shall be exempt from both search and seizure when brought to the Court for the purposes of the proceedings.

In the event of a dispute, customs officials or police may seal those papers, documents or allegedly infringing products or devices. They shall then be immediately forwarded to the Court for inspection in the presence of the Registrar and of the person concerned.

3. Representatives shall be entitled to travel in the course of duty without hindrance.
4. The privileges, immunities and facilities specified in paragraphs 1 to 3 are granted exclusively in the interests of the proper conduct of proceedings.
5. The Court may waive the immunity where it considers that a representative is guilty of conduct which is contrary to the proper conduct of proceedings.

Relation with Agreement: Article 48

Rule 290
Powers of the Court as regards representatives

1. As regards representatives who appear before it, the Court shall have the powers normally accorded to courts of law, under the conditions laid down in Rule 291.
2. Representatives who appear before the Court shall strictly comply with any code of conduct adopted for such representatives by the Administrative Committee.

Rule 291
Exclusion from the proceedings

1. If the Court considers that the conduct of a party's representative towards the Court, towards any judge of the Court or towards any member of the staff of the Registry is incompatible with the dignity of the Court or with the requirements of the proper administration of justice, or that such representative uses his rights for purposes other than those for which they were granted, or that such representative is otherwise in breach of any code of conduct adopted pursuant to Rule 290.2 it shall so inform the person concerned. On the same grounds, the Court may at any time, after having given the person concerned an opportunity to be heard, exclude that person from the proceedings by way of order. That order shall have immediate effect.
2. Where a party's representative is excluded from the proceedings, the proceedings shall be stayed for a period fixed by the presiding judge in order to enable the party concerned to appoint another representative.

Rule 292
Patent attorneys' right of audience

1. For the purposes of Article 48(4) of the Agreement, the term "patent attorneys" assisting a representative referred to in Article 48(1) and/or (2) of the Agreement shall mean persons meeting the requirements of Rule 287.6(b) or .7 and practising in a Contracting Member State.
2. Such patent attorneys shall be allowed to speak at hearings of the Court at the discretion of the Court and subject to the representative's responsibility to coordinate the presentation of a party's case.
3. Rules 287 to 291 shall apply *mutatis mutandis.*

Relation with Agreement: Article 48(4)

Rule 293
Change of a representative

Any change of representative shall take effect from the receipt by the Registry of notification that a new representative shall in future be representing the party concerned. Until the moment where such statement is received, the former representative remains responsible for the conduct of the proceedings and for communications between the Court and the party concerned.

CHAPTER 4
STAY OF PROCEEDINGS

[1.1131]
Rule 295
Stay of proceedings

The Court may stay proceedings:

(a) where it is seized of an action relating to a patent which is also the subject of opposition proceedings or limitation proceedings (including subsequent appeal proceedings) before the European Patent Office or a national authority where a decision in such proceedings may be expected to be given rapidly;
(b) where it is seized of an action relating to a supplementary protection certificate which is also the subject of proceedings before a national court or authority;
(c) where an appeal is brought before the Court of Appeal against a decision or order of the Court of First Instance:
(i) disposing of the substantive issues in part only;
(ii) disposing of an admissibility issue or a Preliminary objection;
(d) at the joint request of the parties;
(e) pursuant to Rule 37;
(f) pursuant to Rules 75 an 76;
(g) pursuant to Rule 118;
(h) pursuant to Rule 136;
(i) pursuant to Rule 266;
(j) pursuant to Rules 310 and 311;
(k) to give effect to Union law, in particular the provisions of Regulation (EU) No 1215/2012 and the Lugano Convention;
(l) in any other case where the proper administration of justice so requires.

Rule 296
Duration and effects of a stay of proceedings

1. The stay of proceedings shall take effect on the date indicated in the order to stay or, in the absence of such an indication, on the date of that order. The Court shall stipulate what effect the stay shall have on any existing orders.
2. Where the order to stay does not fix the length of the stay, it shall end on the date indicated in the order to resume proceedings or, in the absence of such indication, on the date of the order to resume.

3. While proceedings are stayed, time shall cease to run for the purposes of procedural periods. Time shall begin to run afresh for the purposes of procedural periods from the date on which the stay of proceedings comes to an end.

Rule 297
Resumption of proceedings
Any decision referred to in Rule 296.2 ordering the resumption of proceedings before the end of the stay shall be made by order of the judge-rapporteur after hearing the parties. The judge-rapporteur may refer the matter to the panel.

Rule 298
Accelerated proceedings before the European Patent Office
The Court may of its own motion or at the request of a party request that opposition proceedings or limitation proceedings (including any subsequent appeal proceedings) before the European Patent Office be accelerated in accordance with the proceedings of the European Patent Office. The Court may stay its proceedings in accordance with Rule 295(a) pending the outcome of such request and any subsequent accelerated proceedings.

CHAPTER 5
TIME PERIODS

[1.1132]
Rule 300
Calculation of periods
Any period of time prescribed by the Agreement, the Statute, these Rules or any order of the Court for the taking of any procedural step shall be laid down in terms of full days, weeks, months or years and shall be reckoned as follows:

(a) computation shall start on the day following the day on which the relevant event occurred; in the case of service of a document, the relevant event shall be the receipt of that document in accordance with Part 5, Chapter 2;
(b) when a period is expressed as one year or a certain number of years, it shall expire in the relevant subsequent year in the month having the same name and on the day having the same number as the month and the day on which the said event occurred. If the relevant subsequent month has no day with the same number, the period shall expire on the last day of that month;
(c) when a period is expressed as one month or a certain number of months, it shall expire in the relevant subsequent month on the day which has the same number as the day on which the said event occurred. If the relevant subsequent month has no day with the same number, the period shall expire on the last day of that month;
(d) when a period is expressed as one week or a certain number of weeks, it shall expire in the relevant subsequent week on the day having the same name as the day on which the said event occurred;
(e) day shall mean a calendar day unless expressed as a working day;
(f) calendar days shall include official holidays of the Contracting Member State in which the division or the seat of the central division or its section concerned or the Court of Appeal is located, Saturdays and Sundays;
(g) working days shall not include official holidays of the Contracting Member State in which the division or the seat of the central division or its section concerned or the Court of Appeal is located, Saturdays and Sundays;
(h) periods shall not be suspended during the judicial vacations.

Rule 301
Automatic extension of periods
1. If a period expires on a Saturday, Sunday or official holiday of the Contracting Member State in which the division or the seat of the central division or its section concerned or the Court of Appeal is located, it shall be extended until the end of the first following working day.
2. Paragraph 1 shall apply *mutatis mutandis* if documents filed in electronic form cannot be received by the Court.

CHAPTER 6
PARTIES TO PROCEEDINGS

SECTION 1
PLURALITY OF PARTIES

[1.1133]
Rule 302
Plurality of claimants or patents
1. The Court may order that proceedings commenced by a plurality of claimants or in respect of a plurality of patents be heard in separate proceedings.
2. Where the Court orders a separation of proceedings the Court shall decide on the payment of a new court fee or court fees in accordance with Part 6.
3. The Court may order that parallel infringement or revocation proceedings relating to the same patent or patents and before the same local or regional division or the central division or the Court of Appeal be heard together where it is in the interests of justice to do so.

Rule 303
Plurality of defendants
1. Proceedings may be started against a plurality of defendants if the Court has competence in respect of all of them.
2. The Court may separate the proceedings into two or more separate proceedings against different defendants.
3. Where the Court orders a separation of proceedings under paragraph 2, the claimants in the new proceedings shall pay a new court fee in accordance with Part 6, unless the Court decides otherwise.

SECTION 2
CHANGE IN PARTIES

Rule 305
Change in parties
1. The Court may, on application by a party, order a person to:
(a) be added as a party;
(b) cease to be a party;
(c) be substituted for a party.
2. The Court shall invite other parties to the proceedings to comment on the application, as soon as practicable after service of the application.
3. When ordering that a person shall become a party or shall cease to be a party, the Court may make appropriate orders as to payment of court fees and costs as regards such party.

Rule 306
Consequences for the proceedings
1. Where the Court orders that a party be added, removed or substituted under Rule 305.1, it shall give directions to regulate the consequences as to case management.
2. The Court shall also determine the extent to which a new party is bound by the proceedings as then constituted.

SECTION 3
DEATH, DEMISE OR INSOLVENCY OF A PARTY

Rule 310
Death or demise of a party
1. If a party dies or ceases to exist during proceedings, the proceedings shall be stayed until such party is replaced by his successor. The Court may specify a period in this respect.
2. If there are more than two parties to the proceedings, the Court may decide that:
(a) proceedings between the remaining parties be continued separately; and
(b) the stay shall only concern the proceedings regarding the party that no longer exists.
3. If the successor of the party that died or ceased to exist does not continue the proceedings of his own motion, within a period specified by the Court, any other party may apply to have the successor added to or substituted for a party.
4. The Court shall decide who shall be added or substituted as a party pursuant to Rule 305 and 306 shall apply *mutatis mutandis.*

Rule 311
Insolvency of a party
1. If a party is declared insolvent under the law applicable to the insolvency proceedings the Court shall stay the proceedings up to three months. They may be stayed until the competent national authority or person dealing with the insolvency has decided whether to continue the proceedings or not. Where the competent national authority or person dealing with the insolvency decides not to continue the proceedings, the Court may decide, upon a reasoned request by the other party, that the proceedings should be continued in accordance with the applicable national insolvency law.
2. Proceedings may also be stayed at the request of a temporary administrator who has been appointed before a party is declared insolvent.
3. The claimant may withdraw the action against an insolvent defendant in accordance with Rule 265 and a defendant may withdraw a Counterclaim against an insolvent claimant. Such withdrawal shall not prejudice the action against other parties.
4. If proceedings are continued, the effect of a decision of the Court as regards the insolvent party in the action shall be determined by the law applicable to the insolvency proceedings.

SECTION 4
Transfer of Patent

Rule 312
Transfer of the patent or patent application during proceedings
1. If a patent or patent application is transferred, for one or more Contracting Member States, to another proprietor after proceedings have been started before the Court, the Court may authorise the new proprietor to be added as a party or substituted for a party pursuant to Rule 305 to the extent that the patent and the claims in the proceedings have been assigned to the new proprietor. Rule 306 shall apply *mutatis mutandis*.
2. If the new proprietor takes over the proceedings, no new court fee shall be payable, even if the new proprietor is represented by a new representative.
3. If the new proprietor chooses not to take over the proceedings, any decision in proceedings that have been recorded in the register shall be binding upon him.

SECTION 5
Intervention

Rule 313
Application to intervene
1. An Application to intervene may be lodged at any stage of the proceedings before the Court of First Instance or the Court of Appeal by any person establishing a legal interest in the result of an action submitted to the Court (hereinafter "the intervener").
2. An Application to intervene shall be admissible only if it is made in support, in whole or in part, of a claim, order or remedy sought by one of the parties and is made before the closure of the written procedure unless the Court of First Instance or Court of Appeal orders otherwise.
3. The intervener shall be represented in accordance with Article 48 of the Agreement.
4. The Application to intervene shall contain:
   (a) a reference to the action number of the file;
   (b) the names of the intervener and of the intervener's representative, as well as postal and electronic addresses for service and the names of the persons authorised to accept service;
   (c) the claim, order or remedy in support of which intervention is sought by the intervener; and
   (d) a statement of the facts establishing the right to intervene under paragraphs 1 and 2.

Rule 314
Order on Application to intervene
The judge-rapporteur shall decide on the admissibility of the Application to intervene by way of order. The other parties shall be given an opportunity to be heard beforehand.

Rule 315
Statement in intervention
1. If an Application to intervene is admissible, the judge-rapporteur or the presiding judge shall:
   (a) inform the parties to proceedings; and
   (b) specify a period within which the intervener may lodge a Statement in intervention.
2. The Registry shall as soon as practicable serve on the intervener any written pleading served by the parties. On a reasoned request by a party the Court may for the protection of confidential information order that a pleading or part of a pleading be disclosed only to certain named persons and subject to appropriate terms of non-disclosure.
3. The Statement in intervention shall contain:

(a) a statement as to the issues involving the intervener and one or more of the parties, and their connection to the matters in dispute;
(b) the arguments of law; and
(c) the facts and evidence relied on.
4. The intervener shall be treated as a party, unless otherwise ordered by the Court.

Rule 316
Invitation to intervene
1. The judge-rapporteur or the presiding judge may, of his own motion after hearing the parties, or on a reasoned request from a party, invite any person concerned by the outcome of the dispute to inform the Court, within a period to be specified, whether he wishes to intervene in the proceedings.
2. If the person wishes to intervene, he shall present his Application to intervene within one month of service of the invitation and his Statement in intervention within such further period to be specified by the judge-rapporteur or the presiding judge. Rules 313.3, .4, 314 and 315 shall apply *mutatis mutandis.*
3. An intervener shall be bound by the decision in the action.

Rule 316A
Forced intervention
1. A party who contends that the person should be bound by the decision in the action even if he refuses to intervene shall give reasons for this contention in its reasoned request. In such a case the invitation must include these reasons and must state that the party making the request contends that the person should be bound by the decision in the action even if that person refuses to intervene.
2. If the person invited to intervene pursuant to Rule 316.1 does not intervene but wishes to contend that he should not be bound by the decision in the action, he shall lodge a statement to that effect within the one month period referred to in Rule 316.2. If no such statement is lodged within the time specified he shall be bound by the decision in the action as between himself and any other party to the action and shall not be entitled to argue that the decision in the action was wrong or that the inviting party did not conduct the proceedings leading to the decision in the action properly. If a statement is lodged within the time specified then the Court shall decide whether the person invited to intervene shall be bound having heard the parties and the person invited to intervene. If the Court so decides, the person invited to intervene may present an Application to intervene within one month of service of the Court's decision. Rule 316.2 shall apply. If the person invited to intervene fails to present such an application, he shall be bound by the decision in the action.

Rule 317
No appeal against an order on the Application to intervene
There shall be no appeal against an order refusing an Application to intervene.

SECTION 6
RE-ESTABLISHMENT OF RIGHTS

Rule 320
Re-establishment of rights
1. Where a party has failed to observe a time-limit set by these Rules or the Court for a cause which, despite all due care having been taken by the party, was outside his control and the non-observance of this time limit has had the direct consequence of causing the party to lose a right or means of redress, the relevant panel of the Court may upon the request of that party re-establish the right or means of redress.
2. The Application for Re-establishment of rights shall be lodged with the Registry within one month of the removal of the cause for non-observance of the time-limit but in any event within six months of the non-observed time-limit. Within that time-limit a fee shall be paid for a Request for Re-establishment of rights, in accordance with Part 6.
3. The Application shall:
(a) state the grounds on which it is based and shall set out the facts on which it relies; and
(b) contain the evidence relied on in the form of affidavits from all persons involved in the non-observance of the time-limit and the persons involved in establishing the precautionary measures of due care taken in order to avoid such cases of non-compliance.
4. The omitted act shall be performed or completed together with Application for Re-establishment within the time-limit mentioned in paragraph 2.
5. There shall be no grant of Re-establishment of rights in respect of the non-observance of the time limit mentioned in paragraphs 2 and 4 of this Rule.
6. The panel shall decide on the Application for Re-establishment of rights by way of order. The other parties shall be given an opportunity to be heard beforehand.
7. There shall be no right to appeal from an order rejecting an Application for Re-establishment of rights or from an order granting Re-establishment of rights.

CHAPTER 7
MISCELLANEOUS PROVISIONS ON LANGUAGES

[1.1134]
Rule 321
Application by both parties to use of the language in which the patent was granted as language of the proceedings

1. At any time during the written procedure, any party may lodge an Application by both parties to use the language in which the patent was granted as language of the proceedings, in accordance with Article 49(3) of the Agreement. The Application shall state that both parties agree to use the language in which the patent was granted as the language of the proceedings.
2. As soon as practicable, the Registry shall forward the Application to the panel.
3. The panel shall, as soon as practicable, decide whether it approves the Application by both parties to use the language in which the patent was granted as the language of the proceedings. Where the panel does not approve the Application, the Registry shall as soon as practicable inform the parties who may request, within 10 days, that the action be referred to the central division and the action shall be transferred accordingly.
4. Where the action is transferred to the central division Rule 41 shall apply *mutatis mutandis*.

Relation with Agreement: Article 49(3)

Rule 322
Proposal from the judge-rapporteur to use of the language in which the patent was granted as language of the proceedings

At any time during the written procedure and the interim procedure, the judge-rapporteur may, of his own motion or on a request by a party, after consulting the panel, propose to the parties that the language of the proceedings be changed to the language in which the patent was granted, in accordance with Article 49(4) of the Agreement. If the parties and panel agree the language of the proceedings shall be changed.

Relation with Agreement: Article 49(4)

Rule 323
Application by one party to use the language in which the patent was granted as language of the proceedings

1. If a party wishes to use the language in which the patent was granted as language of the proceedings, in accordance with Article 49(5) of the Agreement, the party shall include such Application in the Statement of Claim, in the case of a claimant, or in the Statement of Defence, in the case of a defendant. The judge-rapporteur shall forward the Application to the President of the Court of First Instance.
2. The President shall invite the other party to indicate, within 10 days, its position on the use of the language in which the patent was granted as language of the proceedings.
3. The President, having consulted the panel of the division, may order that the language in which the patent was granted shall be the language of the proceedings and may make the order conditional on specific translation or interpretation arrangements.

Relation with Agreement: Article 49(5)

Rule 324
Consequences where the language of the proceedings is changed in the course of the proceedings

An Application under Rule 321.1 or 323.1 shall specify whether existing pleadings and other documents should be translated and at whose cost. If the parties cannot agree the judge-rapporteur or the President of the Court of First Instance, as the case may be, shall decide in accordance with Rule 323.3.

CHAPTER 8
CASE MANAGEMENT

Relation with Agreement: Article 43

[1.1135]
Rule 331
Responsibility for case management

1. During the written procedure and the interim procedure, case management shall be the responsibility of the judge-rapporteur subject to Rules 102 and 333.
2. The judge-rapporteur may refer a proposed order to the panel.
3. After the closure of the interim conference, case management shall be the responsibility of the presiding judge in consultation with the judge-rapporteur.
4. The Registry shall serve any case management orders on the parties as soon as practicable after the decision of the judge-rapporteur, presiding judge or panel.

Rule 332
General principles of case management
Active case management includes:
(a) encouraging the parties to co-operate with each other during the proceedings;
(b) identifying the issues at an early stage;
(c) deciding promptly which issues need full investigation and disposing summarily of other issues;
(d) deciding the order in which issues are to be resolved;
(e) encouraging the parties to make use of the Centre and facilitating the use of the Centre;
(f) helping the parties to settle the whole or part of the action;
(g) fixing timetables or otherwise controlling the progress of the action;
(h) considering whether the likely benefits of taking a particular step justify the cost of taking it;
(i) dealing with as many aspects of the action as the Court can on the same occasion;
(j) dealing with the action without the parties needing to attend in person;
(k) making use of available technical means; and
(l) giving directions to ensure that the hearing of the action proceeds quickly and efficiently.

Rule 333
Review of case management orders
1. Case management decisions or orders made by the judge-rapporteur or the presiding judge shall be reviewed by the panel, on a reasoned Application by a party.
2. An Application for the review of a case management order shall be lodged within 15 days of service of the order. The Application shall set out the grounds for review and the evidence, if any, in support of the grounds The other party shall be given an opportunity to be heard.
3. The party seeking a review shall pay the fee for the review of a case management order, in accordance with Part 6. Rule 15.2 shall apply *mutatis mutandis.*
4. The panel shall as soon as practicable decide the Application for review and make any necessary revised case management order.
5. A decision of the panel on an Application for review is a procedural decision for the purposes of Rule 220.2.

Rule 334
Case management powers
Except where the Agreement, the Statute or these Rules provide otherwise, the judge-rapporteur, the presiding judge or the panel may:
(a) extend or shorten the period for compliance with any rule or order [Rule 9.3];
(b) adjourn or bring forward the interim conference or the oral hearing;
(c) communicate with the parties to instruct them about wishes or requirements of the Court;
(d) direct a separate hearing of any issue;
(e) decide the order in which issues are to be decided;
(f) exclude an issue from consideration;
(g) dismiss or decide on a claim after a decision on a preliminary issue makes a decision on further issues irrelevant to the outcome of the action;
(h) dismiss a claim summarily if it has no prospect of succeeding;
(i) consolidate any matter or issue or order them to be heard together;
(j) make any order pursuant to Rules 103 to 109.

Rule 335
Varying or revoking orders
The power of the Court to make a case management order includes a power to vary or revoke such order.

Rule 336
Exercise of case management powers
The Court may exercise its case management powers on the application by a party or of its own motion, unless otherwise provided.

Rule 337
Orders of the Court's own motion
Where the Court proposes to make an order of its own motion, it may do so but only after hearing the parties.

Rule 340
Connection Joinder

1. In the interests of the proper administration of justice and of avoiding inconsistent decisions, where more than one action concerning the same patent (whether or not between the same parties) is pending before:

(a) different panels (whether in the same or different divisions); or
(b) different panels of the Court of Appeal,

the panels may by agreement, at any time, after hearing the parties, order that two or more actions shall, on account of the connection between them, be heard together. Article 33 of the Agreement shall be respected.

2. The actions may subsequently be disjoined.

CHAPTER 9
RULES RELATING TO THE ORGANISATION OF THE COURT

[1.1136]
Rule 341
Precedence

1. With the exception of the President of the Court of Appeal and the President of the Court of First Instance, the judges shall rank in precedence according to their seniority in office.
2. Where there is equal seniority in officc, precedence shall be determined by age.
3. Retiring judges who are reappointed shall retain their former precedence.
4. The Presidium may determine the presiding judge of a panel. In the absence of such a determination by the Presidium and unless otherwise agreed by the panel the most senior judge shall be the presiding judge.

Rule 342
Dates, times and place of the sittings of the Court

1. The duration of judicial vacations shall be fixed by the President of the Court of Appeal, on a proposal from the Presidium. The dates and times of the sittings of the Court shall be decided by the presiding judge of the panel in question.
2. The Court may choose to hold one or more particular sittings in a place other than that in which it has its seat. Subject to any rules agreed by the relevant Contracting Member States pursuant to Article 7(5) of the Agreement where an action is pending before a regional division the judge-rapporteur or the presiding judge shall designate the place within the region for each hearing having regard to the residence or place of business of the defendant and all other relevant circumstances such as the facilities available, the financial means of the parties and the place of actual or threatened infringement.

Relation with Statute: Article 17

Rule 343
Order in which actions are to be dealt with

1. The Court shall deal with the actions before it in the order in which they become ready for hearing in accordance with Rule 108.
2. The presiding judge of a panel may, after hearing the parties [Rule 264]:

(a) direct that a particular action be given priority and that time limits provided for in these Rules be shortened;
(b) defer an action to be dealt with later, in particular with a view to facilitating an amicable settlement of the disputc.

Rule 344
Deliberations

1. The Court shall deliberate in closed session.
2. The presiding judge shall preside over the deliberations. Only those judges who were present at the oral hearing may take part in the deliberations on the decision.
3. The deliberation of the Court shall take place as soon as possible after the closure of the oral hearing.

Rule 345
Composition of panels and assignment of actions

1. The President of the Court of First Instance or a judge to whom he has delegated this task in a division, the seat of the central division or one of its sections shall allocate the judges to the panels of the local and regional divisions, the seat of the central division and its sections.
2. The allocation shall be in conformity with Article 8 of the Agreement.
3. The actions pending in the division, the seat of the central division or one of its sections shall be assigned to the panels by the Registrar following an action-distribution-scheme established by the presiding judge of each local or regional division, the seat of the central division and its

sections (being the judge appointed by the Presidium as the presiding judge) for the duration of one calendar year, preferably distributing the actions according to the date of receipt of the actions at the division or section.

4. Each panel may delegate to one of more judges of the panel:
   (a) the function of acting as a single judge; or
   (b) the function of acting for the panel in the procedures of Part 1 Chapter 4 (Procedure for the Determination of Damages and Compensation, including the procedure for the laying open of books) and Chapter 5 (Procedure for Cost Decisions). These functions may be delegated to the judge-rapporteur who has prepared the action for the oral hearing.

5. The President of the Court of First Instance or a judge to whom he has delegated this task in a division, the seat of the central division or one of its sections shall designate the judges assigned to each division, the seat of the central division and each of its sections as standing judges for urgent actions. The assignment may be limited to certain periods of time.

6. If all parties agree to having the action heard by a single judge, the presiding judge of the panel to which the action is allocated shall assign the action to a legally qualified judge of the panel.

7. Where paragraphs 1 to 6 apply to decisions by the presiding judge of the seat of the central division or one of its sections, the President of the Court of First Instance may of his own motion review that decision.

8. Paragraphs 1 to 6 shall apply *mutatis mutandis* to the Court of Appeal; the President of the Court of Appeal exercising the respective functions.

Relation with Statute: Article 19

Rule 346
Application of Article 7 of the Statute

1. If a party objects to a judge taking part in proceedings pursuant to Article 7(4) of the Statute, the presiding judge of the local or regional division to which the judge is allocated or, if the action is pending before the seat of the central division or one of its sections, the respective presiding judge shall, after hearing the judge concerned, decide whether the objection is admissible having regard to Article 7(2) of the Statute.

2. If the objection is admissible, the respective presiding judge shall refer the action to the Presidium which shall hear the judge concerned and shall decide whether the objection shall stand or not.

3. Paragraphs 1 and 2 shall apply to a judge of the Court of Appeal. The presiding judge of the panel shall perform the functions attributed to the presiding judge of the division, the seat of the central division or one of its sections in these paragraphs.

Relation with Statute: Article 7

CHAPTER 10
DECISIONS AND ORDERS

[1.1137]

Rule 350
Decisions

1. Any decision shall contain:
   (a) the statement that it is a decision of the Court;
   (b) the date of its delivery;
   (c) the names of the presiding judge, the judge-rapporteur and other judges taking part in it;
   (d) the names of the parties and of the parties' representatives;
   (e) an indication of the claim, order or remedy sought by the parties;
   (f) a summary of the facts; and
   (g) the grounds for the decision.

2. The order of the Court consequential upon the decision (other than costs) including any order giving immediate effect to an injunction, shall be appended to the decision. The order shall comply with Rule 351.

3. Any dissenting opinion shall be attached to the Court's decision.

4. The decision of the Court of First Instance shall contain a summary of the requests and facts submitted by the parties and a statement of the facts and arguments on which the Court bases its decision.

5. All decisions shall be recorded in the register.

Relation with Statute: Article 35(4)

Rule 351
Orders

1. Every order shall contain:
   (a) the statement that it is an order of the judge-rapporteur, of the standing judge, of the single judge, of the presiding judge, of a President of the Court or of the Court;
   (b) the date of its adoption;
   (c) the names of any judge taking part in its adoption;

(d) the names of the parties and of the parties' representatives; and
(e) the operative part of the order.
2. Where, in accordance with these Rules the Court grants leave to appeal an order the order shall in addition contain:
(a) a statement of the forms of order sought by the parties;
(b) a summary of the facts; and
(c) the grounds for the order.
3. All orders shall be recorded in the register.

Rule 352
Binding effect of decisions or orders subject to security
1. Decisions and orders may be subject to the rendering of a security (whether by deposit or bank guarantee or otherwise) by a party to the other party for legal costs and other expenses and compensation for any damage incurred or likely to be incurred by the other party if the decisions and orders are enforced and subsequently revoked.
2. The Court may upon the application of a party release a security by order.

Rule 353
Rectification of decisions and orders
The Court may, by way of order, of its own motion or on application by a party made within one month of service of the decision or order to be rectified, after hearing the parties, rectify clerical mistakes, errors in calculation and obvious slips in the decision or order.

Rule 354
Enforcement
1. Subject to Rule 118.8 and 352 decisions and orders of the Court shall be directly enforceable from their date of service in each Contracting Member State. Enforcement shall take place in accordance with the enforcement procedures and conditions governed by the law of the particular Contracting Member State where enforcement takes place.
2. Where during an action an enforceable decision or order of the Court is subsequently varied or revoked, the Court may order the party which has enforced such decision or order, upon the request of the party against whom the decision or order has been enforced, to provide appropriate compensation for any injury caused by the enforcement. Rule 125 shall apply *mutatis mutandis*. Where an enforceable decision or order has been made pursuant to a finding of infringement of a patent and, following the conclusion of the action, the patent is amended or revoked, the Court may order, upon the request of the party against whom the decision or order would be enforceable, that the decision or order ceases to be enforceable.
3. The Court's decisions and orders may provide for periodic penalty payments payable to the Court in the event that a party fails to comply with the terms of the order or an earlier order. The value of such payments shall be set by the Court having regard to the importance of the order in question.
4. If it is alleged that a party has failed to comply with the terms of the order of the Court, the first instance panel of the division in question may decide on penalty payments provided for in the order upon the request of the other party or of its own motion. The procedure foreseen in Rule 264 shall apply. After having heard both parties the Court may make an appropriate order which may be subject to an appeal pursuant to Rule 220.2.
Relation with Agreement: Article 82

CHAPTER 11
DECISION BY DEFAULT

[1.1138]
Rule 355
Decision by default (Court of First Instance)
1. Upon request a decision by default may be given against a party where:
(a) the Rules of Procedure so provide if a party fails to take a step within the time limit foreseen in these Rules or set by the Court; or
(b) without prejudice to Rules 116 and 117, the party which was duly summoned fails to appear at an oral hearing.
2. A decision by default against the defendant of the claim or counterclaim may only be given where the facts put forward by the claimant justify the remedy sought.
3. A decision by default against the defendant of the claim or counterclaim may only be given where the time limits for the defence to the claim or counterclaim have expired.
4. A decision by default shall be enforceable. The Court may, however:
(a) grant a stay of enforcement until it has given its decision on any Application under Rule 356; or
(b) make enforcement subject to the provision of security; this security shall be released if no Application is made or if the Application fails.

Rule 356
Application to set aside a decision by default
1. A party against whom a decision by default has been given may lodge an Application to set aside that decision within one month of service of the decision.
2. The Application to set aside a decision by default shall contain the party's explanation for the default. It shall mention the date and number of the decision by default. The party shall pay a fee for the Application to set aside the decision by default, in accordance with Part 6. In the case of Rule 355.1(a) the Application shall be accompanied by the step the party has failed to take.
3. If the provisions of paragraph 2 are met the Application shall be allowed unless a party has been put on notice in an earlier decision that a further decision by default shall be final. If the Application is allowed, a note of allowance shall be included in any publication of the decision by default.
Relation with Statute: Article 37

Rule 357
Decision by default (Court of Appeal)
1. Rules 355 and 356 shall apply *mutatis mutandis*, in particular where a respondent on whom a Statement of appeal and a Statement of the grounds of appeal have been duly served fails to lodge a Statement of response or where a party fails to file a Reply to a Statement of Cross-Appeal or translations ordered by the judge-rapporteur.
2. When considering whether to give a decision by default, the Court of Appeal may consider the merits of the appeal.
3. Rules 355 and 356 shall apply *mutatis mutandis* where the appellant fails to correct the deficiencies or to pay the fee pursuant to Rule 229.4 or to lodge the translations pursuant to Rule 232.1 within the period specified.

CHAPTER 12
ACTIONS BOUND TO FAIL OR MANIFESTLY INADMISSIBLE

[1.1139]
Rule 360
No need to adjudicate
If the Court finds that an action has become devoid of purpose and that there is no longer any need to adjudicate on it, it may at any time, on the application of a party or of its own motion, after giving the parties an opportunity to be heard, dispose of the action by way of order.

Rule 361
Action manifestly bound to fail
Where it is clear that the Court has no jurisdiction to take cognisance of an action or of certain of the claims therein or where the action or defence is, in whole or in part, manifestly inadmissible or manifestly lacking any foundation in law, the Court may, after giving the parties an opportunity to be heard, give a decision by way of order.

Rule 362
Absolute bar to proceeding with an action
The Court may at any time, on the application of a party or of its own motion, after giving the parties an opportunity to be heard, decide that there exists an absolute bar to proceeding with an action, for example because of the application of the principle of *res judicata.*

Rule 363
Orders dismissing manifestly inadmissible claims
1. Orders under Rules 360, 361 and 362 shall be taken by the panel upon the recommendation of the judge-rapporteur.
2. Where the decision is taken by the Court of First Instance pursuant to Rules 360, 361 and 362 it is a final decision within the meaning of Rule 220.1(a).

CHAPTER 13
SETTLEMENT

[1.1140]
Rule 365
Confirmation by the Court of a settlement
1. Where the parties have concluded their action by way of settlement, they shall inform the judge-rapporteur. The Court shall confirm the settlement by decision of the Court [Rule 11.2], if requested by the parties, and the decision may be enforced as a final decision of the Court.
2. At the request of the parties the Court may order that details of the settlement are confidential.
3. Subject to paragraph 2 the decision of the Court under paragraph 1 shall be entered on the register.

4. The judge-rapporteur shall give a decision as to costs in accordance with the terms of the settlement or, failing that, at his discretion.
Relation with Agreement: Article 79

PART 6
FEES AND LEGAL AID
Court Fees

[1.1141]
Rule 370
Court fees

1. Court fees provided for in these Rules shall be paid in accordance with the provisions contained in this Part and the table of fees adopted by the Administrative Committee pursuant to Article 36 (3) of the Agreement (hereinafter: table of fees).
2. A fixed fee shall be paid in accordance with Section I (fixed fees) of the table of fees for the following actions at the Court of First Instance:
   (a) Infringement action [Rule 15],
   (b) Counterclaim for infringement [Rule 53],
   (c) Action for declaration of non-infringement [Rule 70],
   (d) Action for compensation for licence of right [Rule 80.3],
   (e) Application to determine damages [Rule 132].
3. In addition to the fixed fee a value-based fee shall be paid in accordance with Section II (value-based fees) of the table of fees for those actions at the Court of First Instance set out in paragraph 2, which exceed a value of 500.000 €.
4. For the following procedures and actions at the Court of First Instance a fee shall be paid in accordance with Section III (other procedures and actions) of the table of fees adopted by the Administrative Committee:
   (a) Revocation action [Rule 46],
   (b) Counterclaim for revocation [Rule 26],
   (c) Application for provisional measures [Rule 206.5],
   (d) Action against a decision of the European Patent Office [Rule 88.3, 97.2],
   (e) Application to preserve evidence [Rule 192.5],
   (f) Application for an order for inspection [Rule 199.2],
   (g) Application for an order to freeze assets [Rule 200.2],
   (h) Filing a protective letter [Rule 207.3],
   (i) Application to prolong the period of a protective letter to be kept on the register [Rule.207.9],
   (j) Application for rehearing [Rule 250],
   (k) Application for re-establishment of rights [Rule 320.2],
   (l) Application to review a case management order [Rule 333.3],
   (m) Application to set aside decision by default [Rule 356.2].
5. For the following procedures at the Court of Appeal a fixed fee and, where applicable, a value based fee shall be paid in accordance with Section IV. of the table of fees:
   (a) Appeal pursuant to Rule 220.1 (a) and (b) [Rule 228],
   (b) Interlocutory appeal pursuant to Rule 220.1 (c) [Rule 228],
   (c) Application for leave to appeal against cost decision pursuant to Rule-. 221[Rule 228],
   (d) Request for discretionary review pursuant to Rule 220.3, [Rule 228],
   (e) Application for re-establishment of rights [Rule 320.2],
   (f) Application to review a case management order pursuant to Rule 220.2 [R. 333.3],
   (g) Application to set aside decision by default pursuant to Rule 357 [Rule 356.2],
   (h) Application for rehearing pursuant to Rule 245.2 [Rule 250].
6. The assessment of the value of the relevant action in paragraphs 3 and 5 shall reflect the objective interest pursued by the filing party at the time of filing the action. In deciding on the value, the Court may in particular take into account the guidelines laid down in a decision of the Administrative Committee for this purpose.
7. If an action has more than one claimant and/or more than one defendant or if an action concerns a plurality of patents only one fixed fee and, if applicable, one value-based fee shall apply.
8. Small enterprises and micro-enterprises are required to pay only 60 % of the fees provided for in paragraphs 2 to 5 above (hereinafter: regular fees) subject to the following:
   (a) In the Statement of claim or Counterclaim or in the application for a procedure or an appeal the party shall lodge with the Registry a notification in an electronic form in the language of the proceedings. In this notification the party shall provide an affirmation that he fulfils either the criteria of a "small enterprise" or a "micro-enterprise" as defined in Title I of the Annex to the Recommendation of the European Commission n° 2003/361 of 6 May 2003.
   (b) If the requirements referred to above have not been met Rule 16.3 to .5 shall apply *mutatis mutandis.*

(c) The Court may, of its own motion, order the party to supply further documentation including any document relating to that party's financial resources. The application shall be dealt with by the Court as soon as practicable.

(d) The Court may, at any time, of its own motion, and after having heard the party order payment of

 (i) the remainder of the regular fee, in the event that payment of 60 % of the regular fees is manifestly disproportionate and unreasonable having regard to the financial capacity of the party;

 (ii) the remainder of the regular fee plus an additional 50 % of that regular fee, if the affirmation provided by the party is found to be wholly or partially incorrect. An order for the payment of an additional fee pursuant to (i) and (ii) above shall state the reasons for such order.

(e) If the additional fee is not paid within the time limit set by the Court, a decision by default against the party shall be given by the Court pursuant to Rule 355.

9. Fixed and value-based fees may be reimbursed as follows:

(a) If the action is heard by a single judge [Rule 345.6.] the party liable for the Court fee will be reimbursed by 25 % of the fee.

(b) In case of the withdrawal of an action [Rule 265] the party liable for the Court fees will be reimbursed by:

 (i) 60 % if the action is withdrawn before the closure of the written procedure
 (ii) 40 % if the action is withdrawn before the closure of the interim procedure
 (iii) 20 % if the action is withdrawn before the closure of the oral procedure

(c) If the parties have concluded their action by way of settlement the party liable for the Court fees will be reimbursed by:

 (i) 60 % if the action is settled before the closure of the written procedure
 (ii) 40 % if the action is settled before the closure of the interim procedure
 (iii) 20 % if the action is settled before the closure of the oral procedure

(d) Only one of the reimbursements referred to in paragraph 9 (a), (b) and (c) will apply per action and party. Where more than one reimbursement is applicable, the larger will be applied for each party.

(e) In exceptional cases, having regard, in particular, to the stage of the proceedings and the procedural behaviour of the party, the Court may deny or decrease the reimbursement payable according to paragraph 9 (b) and (c) of the aforementioned provisions.

10. If the amount of Court fees threatens the economic existence of a party who is not a natural person, and has presented reasonably available and plausible evidence to support that the amount of Court fees threatens its economic existence, the Court may upon request by that party, wholly or partially reimburse the fixed and value-based fee. In reaching a decision the Court shall reflect on all circumstances of the case including the procedural behaviour of the party. Before making such a decision the Court may give the other party an opportunity to be heard.

11. The party seeking reimbursement under paragraphs 9 and 10 shall lodge a reasoned Application for reimbursement to the Court. The Court shall deal with the application without delay and if satisfied that the reimbursement is appropriate shall direct the Registrar to make the payment as soon as practicable.

Rule 371
Time periods for paying court fees

1. The fixed fees provided for in Section I and Section IV of the table of fees and fees for other procedures and actions provided for in Section III of the table of fees shall be paid at the time of lodging the relevant pleading or application. The payment shall be made to one of the bank accounts indicated by the Court and it shall indicate the paying party or its representative together with the number of the patent involved and the number of the case.

2. Proof of payment shall be provided together with the relevant pleading or application.

3. In cases of urgency, where a payment in advance is not possible, the representative of the party in question shall pay the fixed fee within the period set by the Court and the Court may order that the relevant pleading or application shall be deemed lodged and effective when received by the Registry if payment of the fixed fee is made within such period.

4. The value-based fee provided for in Section II of the table of fees shall be paid according to the claimant's assessment of the value at the time of lodging the relevant pleading or application. In the event that a higher value is determined by the judge-rapporteur the remaining fees due shall be paid within 10 days of service of the order determining the value of the action in accordance with the Rules 22, 60, 74, and 133. Where the value is lower, the Court will reimburse overpaid fees.

5. Where an Application for legal aid has been lodged in accordance with Rule 377, the rules on the obligation as to the time when to pay the fees under paragraph 1 shall not apply.

Relation with Agreement: Article 70

Legal Aid

Rule 375
Aim and scope

1. In order to ensure effective access to justice, the Court may grant legal aid to a party (hereinafter "the applicant").
2. Legal aid may be granted in respect of any proceedings before the Court.

Rule 376
Costs eligible for legal aid

1. Subject to Article 71(3) of the Agreement, legal aid may cover, in whole or in part, the following costs:
   - (a) court fees;
   - (b) costs of legal assistance and representation regarding:
     - (i) pre-litigation advice with a view to reaching a settlement prior to commencing legal proceedings;
     - (ii) commencing and maintaining proceedings before the Court;
     - (iii) all costs relating to proceedings including the application for legal aid;
     - (iv) enforcement of decisions;
   - (c) other necessary costs related to the proceedings to be borne by a party, including costs of witnesses, experts, interpreters and translators and necessary travel, accommodation and subsistence costs of the applicant and his representative.
2. Subject to Article 71(3) of the Agreement, legal aid may also cover the costs awarded to the successful party, in the event that the applicant loses the action.

Rule 376A
Maximum amount to be paid for representation

1. For the costs of representation pursuant to Rule 376.1(b) the maximum level of legal aid that may be granted by the Court shall be the maximum amount of recoverable costs laid down in the decision of the Administrative Committee pursuant to Article 69(1) of the Agreement and Rule 152.2.
2. The Administrative Committee may define thresholds below the level set in paragraph 1 for the maximum level of legal aid for representation pursuant to Rule 376.1(b), taking into account necessary costs for legal representation in the Contracting Member States and the need to guarantee adequate access to justice.

Rule 377
Conditions for granting legal aid

1. The applicant shall be entitled to apply for legal aid where:
   - (a) owing to his economic situation, he is wholly or partly unable to meet the costs referred to in Rule 376; and
   - (b) the action in respect of which the application for legal aid is made has a reasonable prospect of success, considering the applicant's procedural position; and
   - (c) the claimant applying for legal aid is entitled to bring actions under Article 47 of the Agreement.
2. The Administrative Committee may define thresholds above which legal aid applicants are deemed wholly or partly able to bear the costs of proceedings set out in Rule 376. These thresholds may not prevent applicants whose economic situation is above the thresholds from being granted legal aid if they prove that they are in fact unable to pay the costs of the proceedings referred to in Rule 376 as a result of the high level of the cost of living in the Contracting Member State of domicile or habitual residence.
3. When deciding on the grant of legal aid the Court shall, without prejudice to paragraph 1(a), consider all relevant circumstances including the importance of the action to the applicant and also the nature of the action when the application concerns a claim arising directly out of the applicant's trade or self-employed profession.

Rule 377A
Conditions regarding the financial situation of the applicant

1. When assessing a party's financial situation, his income and assets must be taken into account.
2. Income shall include all earnings in money or equivalent value after deducting all costs required by the applicant and dependent persons in order to cover their reasonable living expenses (disposable income).
3. The Administrative Committee shall define the deductions from income and assets to be taken into account when assessing the applicant's financial situation. It shall also define levels of monthly instalments to be paid by the applicant. All thresholds set by the Administrative Committee shall be adapted regularly to price and income indices.

Rule 378
Application for legal aid

1. An application for legal aid may be lodged before or after proceedings have been started before the Court.
2. The Application for legal aid shall contain in a language of a Contracting Member State:
   (a) the name of the applicant;
   (b) postal and electronic addresses for service on the applicant and the names of the persons authorised to accept service;
   (c) the name of the other party as well as postal and electronic addresses for service on the other party where available and the names of the persons authorised to accept service, if known;
   (d) the action number of the action in respect of which the application is made or, where the application is lodged before the action has been brought, a brief description of the action;
   (e) an indication of the value of the action and the costs to be covered by legal aid;
   (f) where legal aid is requested for costs of legal assistance and representation, the name of the proposed representative;
   (g) an indication of the applicant's financial resources, such as income, assets and capital, and of the applicant's family situation including an assessment of the resources of persons who are financially dependent on the applicant;
   (h) where appropriate, a reasoned request for suspension of a time limit which would otherwise need to be observed until the date of notification of the order deciding on legal aid.
3. The application for legal aid must be supported by:
   (a) evidence of the applicant's need for assistance, such as certificates attesting his income, assets and capital and family situation; and
   (b) where the application is lodged before the action has been brought, an indication of the evidence in support of the action.
4. In the event of an appeal, a new application shall be lodged.
5. Rule 8 shall not apply.

Rule 378A
Type of proof

1. To be admissible, the application must contain a statement of the facts and legal situation, with specific mention of the evidence to be presented. The application must also contain a statement regarding the economic and financial situation of the applicant. The following documents shall be attached to the application:
   (a) latest property and income declarations of the applicant;
   (b) a document showing the personal monthly income for the previous year, or a declaration of unemployment delivered by the competent authorities, or a certificate proving that the applicant is receiving aid or financial support under a social welfare scheme;
   (c) a certificate of composition of household;
   (d) any other official document that can provide proof of the financial situation of the applicant.
2. Where appropriate, a certificate relating to the income of other members of the household of the applicant should also be attached to the application. The official documents shall not be older than 3 months. At the request of the Court, the applicant shall produce further documentation and, if so requested, an affidavit of the truthfulness of his statements, otherwise the application will not be admissible.

Rule 379
Examination and decision

1. The Registry shall examine the formal admissibility of the application for legal aid and the conditions regarding the financial situation of the applicant pursuant to Rules 377.1(a), .2 and 377A.
2. If the requirements referred to in Rules 377.1(a), .2, 377A, 378 and 378A have not been met, the applicant shall, as soon as practicable, be invited to correct the deficiencies within 14 days.
3. If the requirements referred to in Rules 377.1(a), .2, 377A, 378 and 378A have been met, the decision on such application shall be taken, by way of order, by the judge-rapporteur or, where the application is lodged before the action has been brought, by the standing judge.
4. Before making a decision on an application for legal aid, the Court shall invite the other party to submit written observations unless it is already apparent from the information submitted that the conditions referred to in Rule 377.1(b) have not been met. Documents regarding the economic and financial situation of the applicant shall be made accessible to the other party only where the applicant has consented or the applicant's refusal of consent is unreasonable or in the view of the Court the other party has a right to information on the economic or financial situation of the applicant.
5. An order refusing legal aid shall state the reasons on which it is based.
6. An order granting legal aid may provide for:

(a) an exemption, wholly or partly, from Court fees;
(b) an interim amount to be paid to enable the applicant and/or the representative of the applicant to meet any request of the judge-rapporteur or standing judge prior to making a final order;
(c) an amount to be paid to the representative of the applicant or a limit which the representative's disbursements and fees may not exceed;
(d) a contribution to be made by the applicant to the costs referred to in Rule 376.1(c).

7. Legal aid may be granted only for the period from receipt of the application with the Court.
8. Where the legal aid covers, in whole or in part, the costs of legal assistance and representation the order granting legal aid shall designate the representative of the applicant.
9. On a request by the designated representative, the Court may order that an amount shall be paid by way of advance.
10. Where requested by the applicant in accordance with Rule 378.2(h), the Court shall decide on the suspension of any time limit.

Rule 379A
Alteration of economic situation
The applicant shall inform the Court promptly of any alteration in his economic situation.

Rule 380
Withdrawal of legal aid
1. If the economic situation of the applicant which has led to the grant of legal aid according to Rule 377.1(a) alters during the proceedings, the Court may at any time, of his own motion or on a reasoned request by the other party, withdraw wholly or partly legal aid but only after having heard the applicant.
2. The Court may withdraw wholly or partly legal aid if the applicant:
(a) by inaccurately representing the circumstances of the case, has misrepresented its prospects of success, which are determinative for the approval of assistance with Court costs; or
(b) has grossly negligently made false statements as to his personal or economic circumstances; or
(c) has not immediately informed the Court of a considerable improvement to his financial circumstances;
(d) has been in arrears for longer than three months with the payment of a monthly instalment or with the payment of any other amount.
3. An order withdrawing legal aid shall state the reasons on which it is based.

Rule 381
Appeal
An order wholly or partly refusing or withdrawing legal aid may be appealed to the Court of Appeal. The appeal shall be filed with the Court of Appeal within a period of one month after receiving the order. The Court of Appeal may grant legal aid for the conduct of the appeal pursuant to the provisions of Rules 377 to 379.

Rule 382
Recovery
1. Where the Court has ordered another party to pay the costs of the applicant for legal aid, that other party shall be required to refund to the Court any sums advanced by way of legal aid. In the event of a shortfall between the costs so ordered and the sums advanced by way of legal aid the applicant may be required to meet such shortfall from any damages or compensation awarded by the Court or from any sum received by way of settlement.
2. In the event of withdrawal of legal aid under Rule 380, the applicant may be required to refund to the Court any sums advanced by way of legal aid.

ANNEX I[3]
[SEE RULE 271.1]

[1.1142]

. . .

NOTES

3 (The list of methods available for secure electronic service will be updated at the time of adoption of the Rules of Procedure by the Administrative Committee.)

[1.1143]

Table 1 – Infringement proceedings

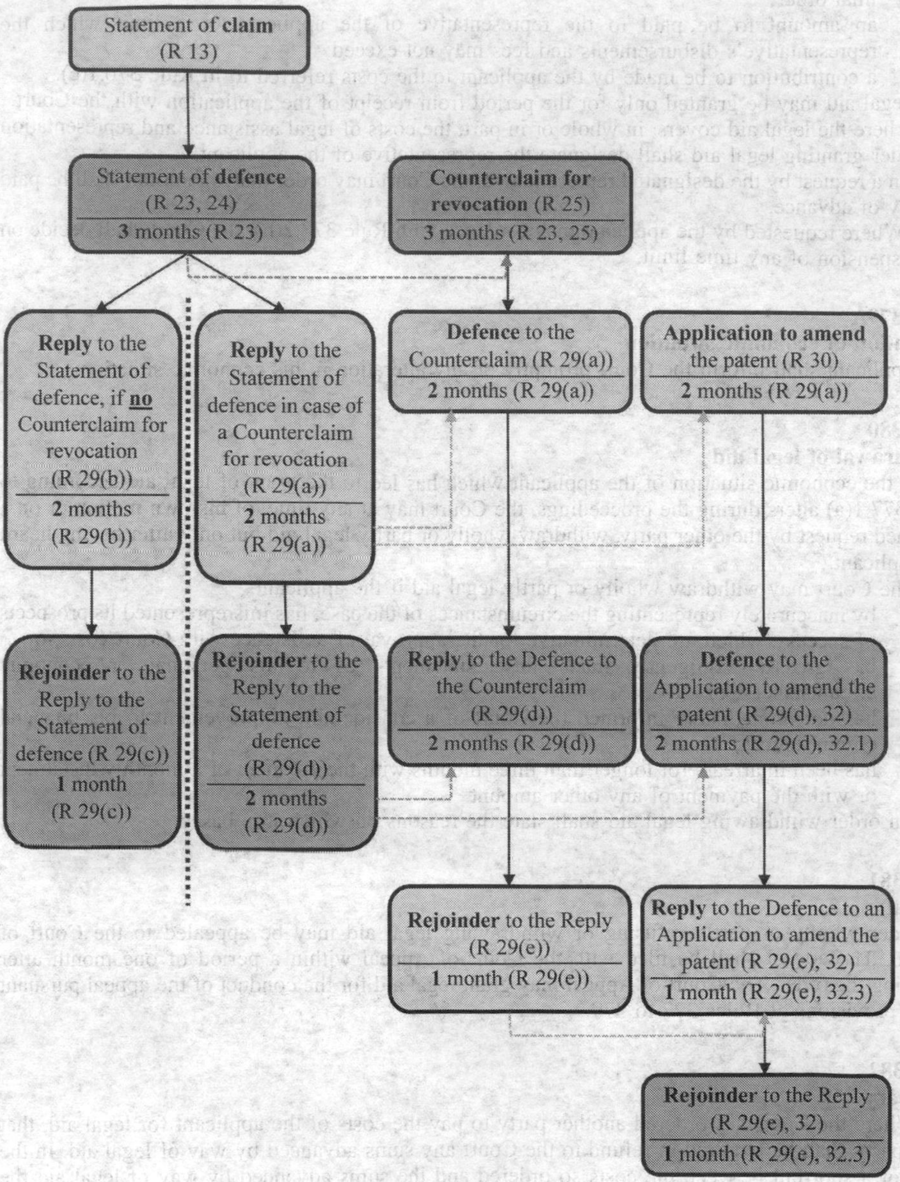

[1.1144]

Table 2 – Revocation proceedings

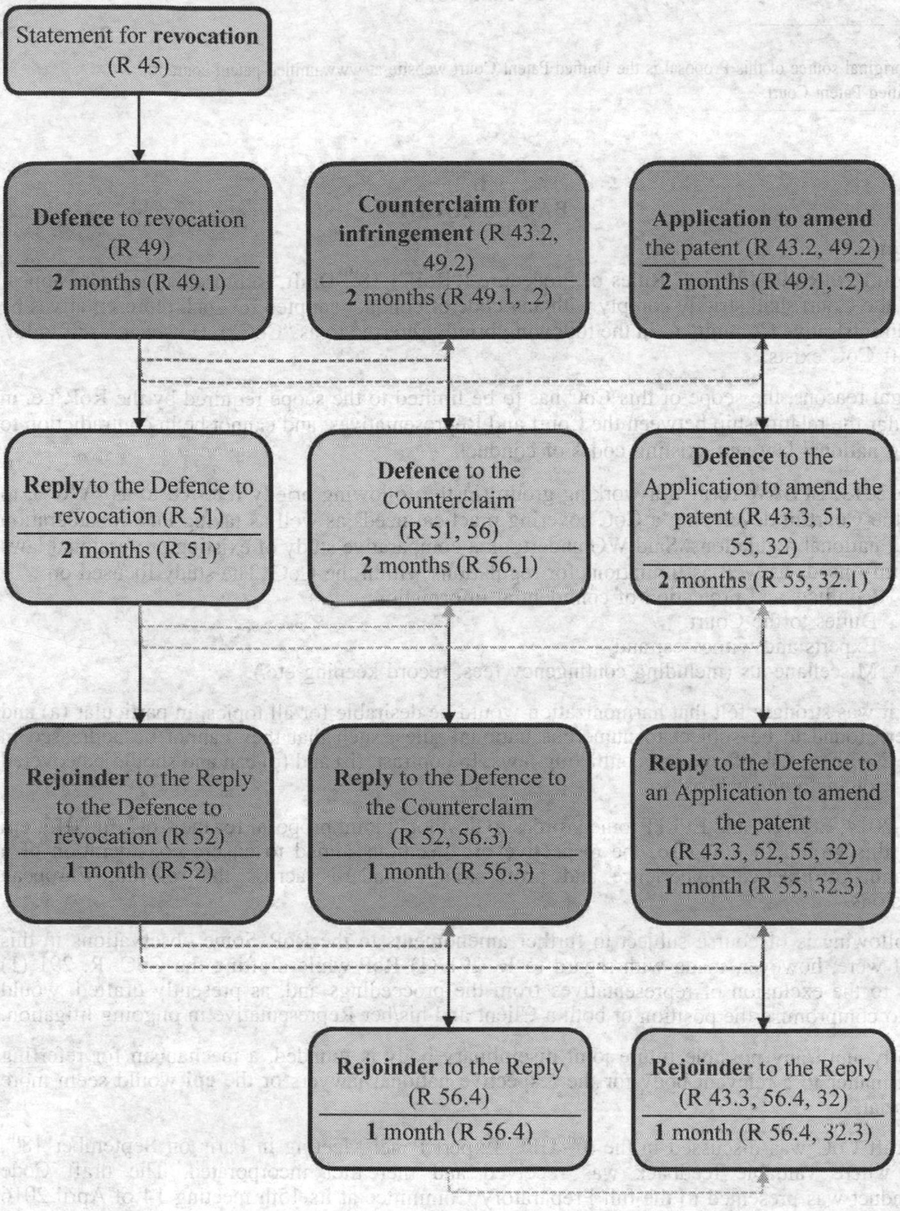

UNIFIED PATENT COURT: PROPOSAL FOR A CODE OF CONDUCT

(22 June 2016)

NOTES

The original source of this Proposal is the Unified Patent Court website at www.unified-patent-court.org.

I.
BACKGROUND

[1.1145]

According to R 290 (2) UPC Rules of Procedure ("RoP") 18th Draft, Representatives who appear before the Court shall strictly comply with any code of conduct adopted for such representatives by the Administrative Committee (in the following briefly referred to as "CoC"). However, as of today, no draft CoC exists.

For legal reasons, the scope of this CoC has to be limited to the scope required by the RoP, i.e. in particular the relationship between the Court and Representatives, and cannot be in contradiction to binding national law and existing codes of conduct.

In late 2013, EPLAW formed a working group (in the following briefly referred to as "WG"), to assist the Court in developing a CoC covering practical needs as well as taking into consideration binding national regulations. Said WG undertook a comparative study of existing professional laws to identify needs as well as limitations for regulations within the CoC. The study focused on:

(a) Conflicts and protection of confidential information;
(b) Duties to the Court;
(c) Experts and witnesses; and
(d) Miscellaneous (including contingency fees, record keeping etc.).

While it was strongly felt that harmonization would be desirable for all topics, in particular (a) and (d) were found to be subject to numerous national rules, such that they cannot be addressed in the CoC without risk of creating conflicting laws. In contrast, (b) and (c) can and should be covered by the CoC without such risks.

In late 2014, EPLAW and EPLIT joined forces to develop a joint proposal for the CoC. In 2015, **epi** joined this group. In doing so, the respective organizations aimed to ensure consideration of a maximum of practical experience and professional standards across the relevant European professions.

The following is of course subject to further amendments to the RoP. Some observations in this respect were, however, made with regard to R. 291 (1) RoP while drafting the CoC. R. 291 (1) relates to the exclusion of representatives from the proceedings and, as presently drafted, would seem to compromise the position of both a Client and his/her Representative in ongoing litigation.

Presently, until any possible future joint disciplinary body is founded, a mechanism for referring such a matter to a relevant body for the respective national lawyers or the **epi** would seem more appropriate.

The draft CoC was discussed in the 3rd UPC Expert Panel Meeting in Paris on September 18th, 2015, where valuable feedback was received and thereafter incorporated. The draft Code of Conduct was presented to the full Preparatory Committee at its 15th meeting 14 of April 2016 where it met with general approval from Member States delegations. Furthermore, EPLAW, EPLIT and **epi** are grateful that experts in particular from IPLA and CCBE proposed amendments to the draft CoC from April to June 2016, which are mostly incorporated in the current version. All this was helpful to further improve the quality and acceptance of the CoC.

Finally, we note that once decided for the judges, some provision on the dress code for Representatives should be added to avoid possible discrimination.

II.
PROPOSAL FOR A COC

[1.1146]

1.

Field of Application

This Code is the Code of Conduct referred to in R. 290 (2) RoP. It shall apply to Representatives under Art. 48 (1) or (2) of the Agreement on a Unified Patent Court ("Agreement") with respect to all activities related to proceedings before the Unified Patent Court ("Court"), considering that said

Representatives may at the same time be subject to other professional and commercial codes and laws, including disciplinary measures. For the avoidance of doubt, in case of any conflict between this CoC and the RoP, the latter shall prevail.

Note: The reference to national professional laws is intended to remind practitioners that they may, in addition to this CoC, be subject to national, regional (e.g. ***epi*** *or CCBE) or other codes of conduct which may include disciplinary measures. Also, for legal reasons, the scope of this CoC has to be limited to the scope required by the RoP, i.e. in particular the relationship between the Court and Representatives, and cannot be in contradiction to binding national law.*

2.
General Conduct

2.1 Relationship with the Court

In all dealings with the Court, any judge of the Court or any member of the staff of the Registry, a Representative shall act respectfully and courteously and - based on sufficient education on the law and Rules governing the Court and proceedings before the Court - competently, and shall do everything possible to uphold the good reputation of his or her respective professional association.

Note: While the term "competently" is not and cannot be intended to impose any formal requirement for Continuing Professional Education (CPE), it seems important for enabling the Court to reach the objective of ensuring decisions of the highest quality (see Preamble of RoP) that Representatives inform themselves sufficiently about the new system and applicable law to prepare their cases correspondingly.

2.2. Fair Conduct of Proceedings

A Representative must always have due regard for the fair conduct of proceedings. He or she shall exercise his or her rights in good faith and shall not abuse the Court process. He or she shall be reasonably accommodating and flexible regarding scheduling and routine matters.

2.3 Contact with Judges of the Court

Save to the extent necessary for *ex parte* procedures, no Representative shall contact a judge about a specific case without the participation or prior consent of the Representative of every other party to those proceedings.

2.4. Demeanour in Court

2.4.1 A Representative shall act towards the Court as an independent counsellor by serving the interests of his or her Clients in an unbiased manner without regard to his or her personal feelings or interests.

2.4.2 A Representative shall act courteously towards other Representatives, persons accompanying the Representatives, parties, witnesses and experts.

2.4.3 A Representative is responsible for taking appropriate steps to ensure the appropriate demeanour in Court of anyone accompanying him or her.

Note: "Accompanying" means attending in person or otherwise, e.g. by telephone or video link. "In Court" includes interim conferences, telephone conferences, video conferences or anything where there is an official communication between the Representative and Court. "Anyone" includes inter alia clients and patent attorneys assisting under Art. 48 (4) of the Agreement.

2.5. False or Misleading Information

If a Representative becomes aware that he or she has inadvertently misled the Court, or that a witness has given evidence which is not true, the Representative shall seek the Client's consent to inform the Court as appropriate.

Note: This addresses the situation where non-witness evidence is provided to Court by the Representative in good faith which turns out to be misleading later-on, or that witness evidence turns out to be incorrect. While this is important to achieve the objective of Art. 48 (6) of the Agreement, the intention is not to introduce a US-style inequitable conduct doctrine.

2.6 *Information unrelated to the subject matter of the proceedings*

Where a Representative who represents an applicant obtains information not related to the case when carrying out measures ordered by the Court to preserve or gather evidence (including inspection of premises), the Representative shall not use that information for any purpose or disclose the same to any person, including his or her client.

3.
Dealings with Witnesses and Party Experts

3.1. Information on legal obligations

A Representative shall ensure that witnesses are at all times fully informed about their obligation to tell the truth and of their liability under applicable national law in the event of any breach of this obligation. Equally, a Representative shall ensure that party experts are fully informed about their obligation to assist the court impartially, being independent and objective and not advocating for any party.

3.2. Contact

Subject to Clause 3.1 and to the extent necessary, a Representative may contact witnesses and party experts out of court in the context of a specific pending case in which they are involved, to verify the eligibility for their respective roles, to explain their roles, and to assist with the preparation of their evidence. A Representative must do everything to ensure that the substance of the evidence of a witness or party expert solely reflects the witness's or expert's respective recollection or opinion.

3.3. Compensation

If required, the Representative may arrange for reasonable compensation for the time spent to prepare and present evidence of witnesses and party experts.
The Representative must upon request of the Court or upon reasonable request of a party inform the Court about the extent of that compensation.

Note: While the Court has discretion to give or withhold grounds for such a request, any party should give reasons for their request to avoid unnecessary disclosure or related obligations; whether such request is reasonable is up to the Court. Party experts are included alongside fact witnesses as their role under the Rules of Procedure is to provide for independent evidence. As part of a "reasonable compensation", appropriate accommodation, travel costs, etc. for preparatory purposes should be allowable.

4.
Change of representation

In the event of a change of representation in accordance with R. 293 RoP, the former Representative shall, unless the circumstances dictate otherwise, be responsible for effecting notification of the change to the Registry without undue delay.
The former Representative shall without undue delay transfer or copy to the new Representative all documents that are necessary for the handling of the case and are not available from the database of the Court.

PROTOCOL ON PRIVILEGES AND IMMUNITIES OF THE UNIFIED PATENT COURT

(29 June 2016)

NOTES

The original source of this Protocol is the Unified Patent Court website at www.unified-patent-court.org.

The undersigning Contracting Member States of the Agreement on a Unified Patent Court,

CONSIDERING that the Unified Patent Court has been established by the Agreement on a Unified Patent Court of 19 February 2013 as an international organisation with legal personality in each Contracting Member State;

RECALLING that the Agreement on a Unified Patent Court provides, in Article 37(1), that Contracting Member States hosting the central division of the Court of First Instance or one of its sections, a local or regional division of the Court of First Instance or the Court of Appeal of the Unified Patent Court shall provide facilities and, during the initial seven years, also administrative support staff;

RECALLING that the Statute of the Unified Patent Court provides, in Article 8, that the Protocol on the privileges and immunities of the European Union shall apply to the judges of the Unified Patent Court;

RECALLING that Article 8(4) of the Statute of the Unified Patent Court covers both the privileges and immunities of the judges of the Unified Patent Court and that the application of the Protocol on the privileges and immunities of the European Union to the judges of the Unified Patent Court has been foreseen because of the intrinsic link of the latter with the European patent with unitary effect and cannot create any precedent for the application of that Protocol to other international organizations with regard to the host nation policies of the Contracting Member States;

RECALLING that the Administrative Committee has the competence to set up an internal tax and a social security scheme under the powers of administration which are conferred to it by the Unified Patent Court Agreement;

RECALLING that the Agreement on a Unified Patent Court provides, in Article 4, that the Unified Patent Court shall enjoy the most extensive legal capacity accorded to legal persons under the national law of that State;

RECOGNIZING that the Unified Patent Court needs to benefit from privileges and immunities which are necessary for the exercise of its functions;

CONSIDERING that a common approach on how to address issues of privileges and immunities is essential in view of the needs of the Unified Patent Court and of the Contracting Member States;

RECOGNIZING that additional bilateral Headquarter Agreements may be concluded between the Unified Patent Court and Contracting Member States hosting the central division of the Court of First Instance or one of its sections, a local or regional division of the Court of First Instance or the Court of Appeal of the Unified Patent Court.

Have agreed as follows:

[1.1147]
Article 1
Use of terms

For the purpose of this Protocol:

a) "Agreement" means the Agreement on a Unified Patent Court of 19 February 2013;
b) "Statute" means the Statute of the Unified Patent Court as set out in Annex I of the Agreement;
c) "State Party" means a State party to this Protocol;
d) "Contracting Member State" means a State party to the Agreement;
e) "Court" means the Unified Patent Court created by the Agreement;
f) "Court of Appeal" means the Court of Appeal of the Court;
g) "The official activities of the Court" means the activities that are necessary for the fulfilment by the Court of the purposes and functions it has been entrusted with in accordance with the provisions of the Agreement;
h) "Premises of the Court" means land and buildings made available to the Court by the Contracting Member State in accordance with Article 37 of the Agreement and used for the official activities of the Court;
i) "Judge" means a Judge of the Court.
j) "Registrar" means the Registrar *and* the Deputy-Registrar of the Court.
k) "Staff" means all personnel employed by the Court as officials and other servants of the Court except the Judges and the Registrar.
l) "Family" means, with respect to any person, the spouse and dependent members of the immediate family of such person forming part of such person's household, as recognised by the hosting Contracting Member State;
m) "Representatives of the parties" means the lawyers, European patent attorneys or patent attorneys authorised to practice or assist before the Court under Article 48 of the Agreement.

[1.1148]
Article 2
General provisions on privileges and immunities of the Court

The Court shall enjoy in the territory of each State Party such privileges and immunities as are necessary for the exercise of its official activities.

[1.1149]
Article 3
Inviolability of the premises of the Court
The premises of the Court shall be inviolable, subject to such conditions as may be agreed with the State Party concerned and subject to the responsibility of the State Party hosting the central division of the Court of First Instance or one of its sections, a local or regional division of the Court of First Instance or the Court of Appeal with respect to the facilities that are to be provided by such a State Party.

[1.1150]
Article 4
Inviolability of archives and documents
The archives of the Court, and all papers and documents in whatever form belonging to it, held by it or addressed to it shall be inviolable at all times and wherever they may be located.

[1.1151]
Article 5
Immunity of the Court, its property, assets and funds
1. The Court shall enjoy immunity from legal process, except:
a. insofar as in any particular case it has expressly waived its immunity;
b. as in the event of civil proceedings against it with respect to contractual liability brought by persons others than the Judges, the Registrar or the Staff of the Court;
c. as in cases of civil proceedings against it with respect to non-contractual liability except where the claim is based on the performance of the Court's jurisprudence or
d. in the case of a civil proceeding brought by a third party for damages resulting from an accident caused by a motor vehicle belonging to, or operated on behalf of, the Court, or in respect of a motor traffic offence involving such a vehicle.
2. The Court shall enjoy immunity from legal process in respect of search, requisition, confiscation, seizure or expropriation of, or any other form of interference with, the property, assets and funds of the Court, wherever located, without the authorisation of the Court.
3. To the extent necessary to exercise its official activities, the property, assets and funds of the Court shall be exempt from restrictions, regulations, controls and moratoria of any nature.

[1.1152]
Article 6
Immunity of Representatives of a State Party
1. Representatives of a State Party shall enjoy, while attending meetings of the Administrative Committee, the Budget Committee and the Advisory Committee immunities from legal process in respect of all acts performed by them in their official capacity, including their words spoken or written. This immunity shall continue to be accorded even after the termination of their mission.
2. Their official papers and documents shall be inviolable.
3. No State Party is obliged to extend the immunities referred to in paragraph 1 and 2 to its own nationals or any person who at the time of taking up his functions with the Court has his permanent residence in that State.

[1.1153]
Article 7
Exemption from taxes
1. The Court, its property and assets, shall be exempt from all direct taxes.
2. The Court shall
a. be exempt from or accorded a refund of value added taxes paid on any substantial purchase of goods and services which are necessary and supplied for the official activities of the Court, subject to the limitations laid down by the host State Party;
b. however not be exempt from taxes and dues which amount to charges for public utility services.
3. Goods purchased under such an exemption or reimbursement shall not be sold or otherwise disposed of in that State Party or in another Member State of the European Union, except in accordance with the conditions laid down by the State Party which granted the exemption or reimbursement.
4. Without prejudice to the obligations arising for the State Parties under European Union law and the application of laws and regulations, the conditions and procedure shall be determined by the competent fiscal authorities of each State Party.

[1.1154]
Article 8
Funds and freedom from currency restrictions
The State Parties shall accord the Court the freedom of currency restrictions which is necessary for the exercise of its official activities.

[1.1155]
Article 9
Privileges and Immunities of the Judges and the Registrar

1. The privileges and immunities of the Judges are governed by Article 8 of the Statute and by reference in Article 8 of the Statute by the Protocol on the privileges and immunities of the European Union.

2. Article 8 of the Statute and the Protocol on the privileges and immunities of the European Union shall apply to the Registrar.

3. When applied in accordance with paragraph 1 and 2, only Article 11(b-e) to 14 of the Protocol on the privileges and immunities of the European Union are to be applied in analogy adapted to the specific circumstances of the Court. This means in particular that the Judges and the Registrar shall:

a. be liable to an internal tax for the benefit of the Court on salaries, wages and emoluments paid to them by the Court;

b. from the date on which the internal tax under letter (a) is applied, be exempted from national taxation on the salaries, wages and emoluments, paid to them by the Court, but not on pensions and annuities, paid to them by the Court;

c. from the date on which the Judges and the Registrar are subject to a social security and health scheme established by the Court, with respect to services rendered for the Court, be exempted from all compulsory contributions to national social security and health schemes.

[1.1156]
Article 10
Immunities and privileges of the Staff

1. The Staff shall be immune from legal process in respect of all acts performed by them in their official capacity, including their words spoken or written. This immunity shall continue to be accorded even after the termination of their employment with the Court.

2. The Staff shall,

a. be liable to an internal tax for the benefit of the Court on salaries, wages and emoluments paid to them by the Court;

b. from the date on which the internal tax under letter (a) is applied, be exempted from national taxation on the salaries, wages and emoluments, but not on pensions and annuities, paid to them by the Court; these salaries, wages and emoluments may be taken into account by the State Parties for the purpose of assessing the amount of taxation to be applied to income from other sources;

c. from the date on which the Staff is subject to a social security and health scheme established by the Court, with respect to services rendered for the Court, be exempted from all compulsory contributions to national social security and health schemes.

3. No State Party is obliged to extend the privileges referred to in paragraph 2 to its own nationals or to a person who immediately prior to the employment by the Court was a resident of that State Party.

[1.1157]
Article 11
Emblem and flag

The Court shall be entitled to display its emblem and flag at its premises subject to such conditions as may be agreed with the State Party concerned, on vehicles used for official purposes as well as on its website and documents.

[1.1158]
Article 12
Cooperation with the authorities of State Parties

1. Without prejudice to their privileges and immunities, it is the duty of all persons enjoying privileges and immunities under Article 6, 9 and 10 to respect the laws and regulations of the State Party in whose territory they may operate in their official capacity.

2. The Court shall cooperate at all times with the appropriate authorities of State Parties to facilitate the enforcement of their laws and to prevent the occurrence of any abuse in connection with the privileges, immunities and facilities referred to in this Protocol.

[1.1159]
Article 13
Purpose and waiver of privileges and immunities provided for in Article 6, 9 and 10

1. The privileges and immunities provided for in this Protocol are not established for the personal benefit of those persons in whose favour they are granted. Their purpose is solely in the interest of the Court, especially to ensure, in all circumstances, the freedom of action of the Court and the complete independence of the persons concerned.

2. The Presidium of the Court shall have not only the right but also the duty to waive the immunity of Judges, the Registrar and the Staff under Articles 9 and 10, when it considers that such immunity would hinder the normal course of justice, and that it is possible to waive such immunity

without prejudicing the interests of the Court. A State Party has the same right regarding its representatives in the Administrative Committee and the Budget Committee (Article 6). The Administrative Committee shall have the same right and obligation regarding the members of the Advisory Committee.

[1.1160]
Article 14
Access, residence and departure

Without prejudice to European Union law, the concerned State Party shall take all the necessary steps to facilitate;

a. the entry into, departure from and residence in its territory of all persons who are performing official duties for the Court, namely the Judges, the Registrar, Staff employed by the Court and staff provided by the State Parties as well as, where persons performing official duties for the Court are based in the State Party and are not nationals or permanent residents of that State Party, dependent members of their families, and

b. the entry into and departure from its territory of all persons who are called to or summoned by the Court in an official capacity, namely parties, Representatives of parties, interpreters, witnesses and experts before the Court.

[1.1161]
Article 15
Notification

The Registrar shall communicate within one month of the entry into force of this Protocol to all State Parties the names of the Judges, the Registrar and the Staff to whom this Protocol applies. In addition to above, appointment/arrival of any Judge, Registrar or Staff to the Court and any change of circumstances shall be reported as soon as possible and at the latest within one month of the date of the relevant change of circumstance.

[1.1162]
Article 16
Settlement of disputes

1. The Court shall make provisions for appropriate modes of settlement of disputes involving any person referred to in this Protocol who by reason of his or her official position enjoys immunity or the Court in cases when it enjoys immunity under Article 5, if such immunity has not been waived.

2. All disputes arising out of the interpretation or application of this Protocol shall be referred to an arbitral tribunal unless the parties have agreed to another mode of settlement. If a dispute arises between the Court and a State Party which is not settled by consultation, negotiation or other agreed mode of settlement within three months following a request by one of the parties to the dispute, it shall at the request of either party be referred for final decision to a panel of three arbitrators: one to be chosen by the Court, one to be chosen by the State Party and the third, who shall be Chairman of the panel, to be chosen by the first two arbitrators. If either party has failed to make its appointment of an arbitrator within two months of the appointment of an arbitrator by the other party, the President of the European Court of Justice shall make such appointment. Should the first two arbitrators fail to agree upon the appointment of the third arbitrator within three months following the appointment of the first two arbitrators the third arbitrator shall be chosen by the President of the European Court of Justice upon the request of the Court or the State Party.

[1.1163]
Article 17
Signature, ratification, acceptance, approval or accession and deposition

1. This Protocol shall be open for signature by all Contracting Member States from 29 June 2016 until 29 June 2017 at the Council of the European Union in Brussels.

2. This Protocol is subject to ratification, acceptance or approval. Instruments of ratification, acceptance or approval shall be deposited with the General Secretariat of the Council of the European Union, hereinafter referred to as the depositary.

3. After 29 June 2017 this Protocol shall remain open for accession by all Contracting Member States. The instruments of accession shall be deposited with the depositary.

[1.1164]
Article 18
Entry into force

1. This Protocol shall enter into force 30 days after the date on which the last of the four State Parties — France, Germany, Luxemburg and the United Kingdom — has deposited its instrument of ratification, acceptance approval or accession.

2. For each State Party, which deposits its instrument after the date referred to in paragraph 1, this Protocol shall enter into force 30 days after the date of deposit of its instrument of ratification, acceptance, approval or accession.

[1.1165]
Article 19
Provisional application

A Contracting Member State may at any time notify the depositary that it will apply this Protocol provisionally.

IN WITNESS WHEREOF, the undersigned, being duly authorized thereto, have signed this Protocol.

Done at Brussels this 29th of June 2016 in the English, French and German languages, all three texts being equally authentic, in a single copy, which shall be deposited with the depositary who shall transmit a certified true copy to all signatory and acceding States.

PATENTS ACT 1977: PATENTABLE SUBJECT MATTER

(2 November 2006)

NOTES

The original source is the UK Intellectual Property Office, an operating name of the Patent Office. See www.gov.uk/government/organisations/intellectual-property-office.

[1.1166]

1. This notice announces an immediate change in the way patent examiners will assess whether inventions are for patentable subject matter. The change results from the recent judgment of the Court of Appeal in the matters of *Aerotel Ltd v Telco Holdings Ltd (and others) and Macrossan's Application* [2006] EWCA Civ 1371 (236Kb) ("*Aerotel/Macrossan*").

BACKGROUND

2. *Aerotel/Macrossan* is a single judgment covering two cases which both concerned the interpretation of section 1(2) of the Patents Act 1977 and its equivalent in the European Patent Convention (EPC), Article 52. The judgment was handed down on 27 October 2006.

3. The Court was clearly mindful of the desirability of consistency of practice across Europe, and took due account of the way that the courts of other EPC Contracting States and the Boards of Appeal of the European Patent Office (EPO) interpret these provisions. However, the Court decided not to follow EPO practice, which they did not consider to have stabilised sufficiently. Instead, the Court approved a 4 step test that had been proposed by the Office.

4. In reaching its judgment, the Court also fully considered all the precedent UK case law in this area. Following the principles discussed in, for example, *Colchester Estates (Cardiff) v Carlton Industries* [1986] 1 Ch 80, [1984] 2 All ER 601 and [1984] 3 WLR 693, the Office takes the view that *Aerotel/Macrossan* must be treated as a definitive statement of how the law on patentable subject matter is now to be applied in the United Kingdom (UK). It should therefore rarely be necessary to refer back to previous UK or EPO case law.

THE NEW TEST

5. The test approved by the Court comprises the following steps:

(1) properly construe the claim
(2) identify the actual contribution
(3) ask whether it falls solely within the excluded subject matter
(4) check whether the actual or alleged contribution is actually technical in nature.

The Court decided that the new approach provided a structured and more helpful way of applying the statutory test for assessing patentability which was consistent with previous decisions of the Court. This test will be applied by examiners with immediate effect.

DETAILS OF THE NEW APPROACH

6. The Court saw the first step, properly construing the claim, as something that always has to be done and involves deciding what the monopoly is before going on to the question of whether it is excluded. If, as can happen when dealing with applications from unrepresented applicants, examiners are faced with no meaningful statement of the monopoly sought, they will do their best to assess what it might be.

7. The Court equated the second step to identifying what the inventor has really added to the stock of human knowledge. The Court re-affirmed that in identifying the contribution, it is the substance of the invention that is important rather than the form of the claim adopted. Thus in the *Macrossan* case it held that the presence of conventional hardware elements in the claim did not change the contribution.

8. What the applicant alleges he/she has contributed is not conclusive and ultimately it is the actual contribution that counts. However, the Court acknowledged that at the application stage, it is quite in order to consider the third and fourth steps on the basis of the alleged contribution. Thus it will not always be necessary to conduct a search to identify the actual contribution before any objection can be raised. Accordingly, examiners will continue the existing practice of issuing a report under section 17(5)(b) that a search would not serve any useful purpose if the application seems to have little prospect of maturing into a valid patent and a search is not necessary for the purposes of the second step. The Office does not consider that informing decisions on filing abroad constitutes a "useful purpose" within the meaning of section 17(5).

9. The third step comprises deciding whether the contribution is solely unpatentable subject matter, ie, matter listed in Article 52(2). The Court saw "solely" as merely an expression of the "as such" qualification of Article 52(3). Thus if the contribution falls wholly within one or more of the listed categories, it is not a patentable invention. If it falls partly within one or more of the listed categories and partly outside, it passes the third step.

10. If the invention passes the third step, one must then check whether the contribution is technical in nature. Of course it is not necessary to apply this fourth step if the invention has failed at the third, and the Court effectively acknowledged this, although it chose to apply it anyway in *Macrossan*.

CONSTRUING THE LIST OF EXCLUDED MATTER

11. In paragraph 12 of its judgment, the Court said that Article 52(2) is not a list of exceptions. Rather, it sets out positive categories of things which are not to be regarded as inventions. Accordingly, the general UK and European principle of statutory interpretation that exceptions should be construed narrowly does not apply to them.

12. Adopting this approach, the Court of Appeal rejected the narrow interpretation afforded to the business method category by Mann J in the court below in the *Macrossan* [2006] EWHC 705 Ch. At paragraph 30 of his judgment, Mann J concluded that this category "is aimed more at the underlying abstraction of business method" rather than a tool or activity which might be used in a business activity. In rejecting that, the Court of Appeal decided that the categories in Article 52(2) are not limited to abstract things and that business methods are not limited to completed transactions. "Methods for doing business" will be interpreted by examiners accordingly in future.

13. The judgment leaves open the question of how to interpret the reference in Article 52(2) to a scheme, rule or method for performing a mental act. In paragraph 62 of its judgment the Court said it was doubtful as to whether this extended to electronic means of doing what could otherwise have been done mentally, but in the earlier case of *Fujitsu Limited's Application* [1997] RPC 608 the Court had expressed a different view. However, both comments were obiter, so the correct interpretation will remain uncertain until the point is decided by the courts. In the meantime, examiners will lean towards the view expressed in the current judgment, on the grounds that this is probably a better reflection of current judicial thinking.

14. Also left open is a question over permissible forms of claim: can claims to a computer program (or a program on a carrier) be allowable when other claims in a different form, claims covering the use of that particular program, would be allowed? In the past, the Office has allowed such claims on the basis that substance should prevail over form. Whilst the judgment maintains the emphasis on substance over form, it also characterises the first step as deciding what the monopoly is, and if the monopoly does not go beyond the program, the contribution is also unlikely to go beyond "a program for a computer". Accordingly, whilst examiners will continue to assess each case on its merits, it seems likely that few claims to programs in themselves (or programs on a carrier) will pass the third test.

NOTES

See further Patent Office Practice Notice "Patents Act 1977: Patentable subject matter", dated 7 February 2008, at **[1.1167]**.

BENEFIT OF THE DOUBT

15. In paragraph 5 of its judgment, the Court makes it clear that whether an invention covers patentable subject matter is a question of law which should be decided during prosecution of the patent application. It is not a question on which applicants are entitled to the benefit of the doubt. Consequently examiners will assess the position fully and not simply drop objections merely because the applicant has managed to put up what at first sight may be a plausible argument that the invention relates to patentable subject matter.

16. As the judgment says, giving benefit of reasonable doubt at the application stage may still be appropriate if debatable questions of pure fact, not law, arise—for example, determining the date of a particular disclosure or the correct amount of common general knowledge to impute to the person skilled in the art. However, this is more likely to occur when considering novelty or obviousness, not patentable subject matter.

EFFECT OF THE NEW APPROACH

17. It is the Office's view that the change in approach does not fundamentally change the boundary between what is and is not patentable in the UK although we recognise that there will inevitably be the odd case right on the boundary that may be decided differently under different tests. To illustrate this, the Office is issuing separately an assessment of how a sample of applications that were refused by hearing officers earlier this year would have fared under the *Aerotel/Macrossan* approach.

18. Furthermore, whilst that approach is different from the one currently adopted in the EPO (as exemplified by the Board of Appeal decision in *Hitachi* T 0258/03 we consider that the end result will be the same in nearly every case irrespective of whether the approach followed is the Court of Appeal's or that of the EPO. The Court suggested that the issue was one which might benefit from a reference to the Enlarged Board of Appeal. However, the President of the EPO has decided not to take this forward at this time. The text of the President of the EPO's letter to Jacob LJ is available.

PENDING APPLICATIONS

19. If an application is currently in the examination process with an outstanding objection from the examiner under section 1(2), the examiner will re-assess the position in the light of *Aerotel/Macrossan* when the applicant replies to the last examination report. Given the Court's view that the new test is consistent with the precedents, it is likely that the examiner will conclude the objection still stands, but the reasoning for that conclusion may be different. Accordingly, in preparing their reply, applicants do not need to make a detailed response to arguments raised by the examiner based on what is now old case law. Instead, it would be helpful if applicants submitted their own assessment of how the invention fares under *Aerotel/Macrossan.*

20. If an application is currently either awaiting a decision of a hearing officer as to whether it is allowable under section 1(2) or awaiting a hearing on the issue, thc Office will contact the applicant to give them an opportunity to submit new arguments based on *Aerotel/Macrossan*. The examiner may also be asked to make a fresh assessment.

PREVIOUS PRACTICE NOTICES

21. This notice supersedes the following Practice Notices:

— **Patents Act 1977: Examining for Patentability** (29 July 2005)
— **Handling Patent Applications for Excluded Subject Matter** (8 February 2002)
— **Patents Act 1977: interpreting section 1(2)** (24 April 2002)
— **Claims to Programs for computers** (19 April 1999)

22. Other Practice Notices on the question of patentable subject matter still stand save as follows:

— **Patentability of games** (25 November 2005): Paragraph 4 is superseded by the present Notice. The rest of this Notice, which explained the comptroller would no longer rely on the Official Ruling 1926(A), still stands.
— **Patent applications relating to methods of doing business** (24 November 2004): This said the Office would bring appropriate cases to a hearing at an earlier stage and issue abbreviated decisions. This still stands, and indeed may become even more relevant now that *Aerotel/Macrossan* has simplified the approach.

23. Whilst they will be guided by the contents of this Notice, examiners and hearing officers will, as always, assess each case individually on its merits and take full account of any arguments advanced by the Applicant. Any enquiries about this notice should be sent to:

Concept House
Cardiff Road
Newport
South Wales NP10 8QQ
Tel: +44 (0)1633 813677
Email: enquiries@ipo.gov.uk

Sean Dennehey

Director of Patents

2 November 2006

PATENTS ACT 1977: PATENTABLE SUBJECT MATTER

(7 February 2008)

NOTES

The original source is the UK Intellectual Property Office, an operating name of the Patent Office. See www.gov.uk/government/organisations/intellectual-property-office.

[1.1167]

1. The Office's Practice Notice dated 2 November 2006 detailed the way patent examiners should assess whether inventions are for patentable subject matter following the judgment of the Court of Appeal in the matters of *Aerotel Ltd v Telco Holdings Ltd (and others)* and *Macrossan's Application*

[2007] RPC 7 ("*Aerotel/Macrossan*"). Among other things, paragraph 14 of that Notice recorded the Office's view that *Aerotel/Macrossan* left open a question over permissible forms of claim: can claims to a computer program (or a program on a carrier) be allowable when other claims in a different form, claims covering the use of that particular program, would be allowed? For reasons the Notice explained, the Office concluded that claims to computer programs or to programs on a carrier were not allowable.

2. In his judgment in *Astron Clinica and other's Applications* [2008] EWHC 85 (Pat) ("*Astron Clinica*"), Kitchin J has now clarified the law in this area. He has decided that where, as a result of applying the test formulated in *Aerotel/Macrossan*, claims to a method performed by running a suitably programmed computer or to a computer programmed to carry out the method are allowable then, in principle, a claim to the program itself should also be allowable. However, Kitchin J made it clear that the claim to the computer program must be drawn to reflect the features of the invention which would ensure the patentability of the method which the program is intended to carry out when it is run. **Where, but only where, these conditions are met, examiners will no longer object to claims to a computer program or a program on a carrier.**

3. The Office will implement this change in approach immediately. **Apart from this one change, the practice of the UK-IPO remains as set out in the Practice Notice of 2 November 2006.**

4. Any enquiries about this notice should be sent to:

Sarah Barker
UK Intellectual Property Office
Concept House
Cardiff Road
Newport
South Wales NP10 8QQ
United Kingdom

Tel: +44 (0)1633 814 807

Sean Dennehey

Director of Patents

UK Intellectual Property Office

7 February 2008

REGULATION OF THE EUROPEAN PARLIAMENT AND OF THE COUNCIL

(816/2006/EC)

of 17 May 2006

on compulsory licensing of patents relating to the manufacture of pharmaceutical products for export to countries with public health problems

NOTES

Date of publication in OJ: OJ L157, 9.6.2006, p 1.

THE EUROPEAN PARLIAMENT AND THE COUNCIL OF THE EUROPEAN UNION,

Having regard to the Treaty establishing the European Community, and in particular Articles 95 and 133 thereof,

Having regard to the proposal from the Commission,

Having regard to the opinion of the European Economic and Social Committee,[1]

Acting in accordance with the procedure laid down in Article 251 of the Treaty,[2]

Whereas:

(1) On 14 November 2001 the Fourth Ministerial Conference of the World Trade Organisation (WTO) adopted the Doha Declaration on the Agreement on Trade-Related Aspects of Intellectual Property Rights (TRIPS Agreement) and Public Health. The Declaration recognises that each WTO Member has the right to grant compulsory licences and the freedom to determine the grounds upon which such licences are granted. It also recognises that WTO Members with insufficient or no manufacturing capacity in the pharmaceutical sector could face difficulties in making effective use of compulsory licensing.

(2) On 30 August 2003 the WTO General Council, in the light of the statement read out by its Chairman, adopted the Decision on the implementation of paragraph 6 of the Doha Declaration on the TRIPS Agreement and Public Health (the Decision). Subject to certain conditions, the Decision

waives certain obligations concerning the issue of compulsory licences set out in the TRIPS Agreement in order to address the needs of WTO Members with insufficient manufacturing capacity.

(3) Given the Community's active role in the adoption of the Decision, its commitment made to the WTO to fully contribute to the implementation of the Decision and its appeal to all WTO Members to ensure that the conditions are put in place which will allow the system set up by the Decision to operate efficiently, it is important for the Community to implement the Decision in its legal order.

(4) Uniform implementation of the Decision is needed to ensure that the conditions for the granting of compulsory licences for the manufacture and sale of pharmaceutical products, when such products are intended for export, are the same in all Member States and to avoid distortion of competition for operators in the single market. Uniform rules should also be applied to prevent re-importation into the territory of the Community of pharmaceutical products manufactured pursuant to the Decision.

(5) This Regulation is intended to be part of wider European and international action to address public health problems faced by least developed countries and other developing countries, and in particular to improve access to affordable medicines which are safe and effective, including fixed-dose combinations, and whose quality is guaranteed. In that connection, the procedures laid down in Community pharmaceutical legislation guaranteeing the scientific quality of such products will be available, in particular that provided for in Article 58 of Regulation (EC) No 726/2004 of the European Parliament and of the Council of 31 March 2004 laying down Community procedures for the authorisation and supervision of medicinal products for human and veterinary use and establishing a European Medicines Agency.[3]

(6) As the compulsory licensing system set up by this Regulation is intended to address public health problems, it should be used in good faith. This system should not be used by countries to pursue industrial or commercial policy objectives. This Regulation is designed to create a secure legal framework and to discourage litigation.

(7) As this Regulation is part of wider action to address the issue of access to affordable medicines for developing countries, complementary actions are set out in the Commission Programme for Action: Accelerated action on HIV/AIDS, malaria and tuberculosis in the context of poverty reduction and in the Commission Communication on a Coherent European Policy Framework for External Action to Confront HIV/AIDS, malaria and tuberculosis. Continued urgent progress is necessary, including actions to support research to combat these diseases and to enhance capacity in developing countries.

(8) It is imperative that products manufactured pursuant to this Regulation reach only those who need them and are not diverted from those for whom they were intended. The issuing of compulsory licences under this Regulation must therefore impose clear conditions upon the licensee as regards the acts covered by the licence, the identification of the pharmaceutical products manufactured under the licence and the countries to which the products will be exported.

(9) Provision should be made for customs action at external borders to deal with products manufactured and sold for export under a compulsory licence which a person attempts to reimport into the territory of the Community.

(10) Where pharmaceutical products produced under a compulsory licence have been seized under this Regulation, the competent authority may, in accordance with national legislation and with a view to ensuring that the intended use is made of the seized pharmaceutical products, decide to send the products to the relevant importing country according to the compulsory licence which has been granted.

(11) To avoid facilitating overproduction and possible diversion of products, the competent authorities should take into account existing compulsory licences for the same products and countries, as well as parallel applications indicated by the applicant.

(12) Since the objectives of this Regulation, in particular the establishment of harmonised procedures for the granting of compulsory licences which contribute to the effective implementation of the system set up by the Decision, cannot be sufficiently achieved by the Member States because of the options available to exporting countries under the Decision and can therefore, by reason of the potential effects on operators in the internal market, be better achieved at Community level, the Community may adopt measures, in accordance with the principle of subsidiarity as set out in Article 5 of the Treaty. In accordance with the principle of proportionality, as set out in that Article, this Regulation does not go beyond what is necessary in order to achieve those objectives.

(13) The Community recognises the utmost desirability of promoting the transfer of technology and capacitybuilding to countries with insufficient or no manufacturing capacity in the pharmaceutical sector, in order to facilitate and increase the production of pharmaceutical products by those countries.

(14) In order to ensure the efficient processing of applications for compulsory licences under this Regulation, Member States should have the ability to prescribe purely formal or administrative requirements, such as rules on the language of the application, the form to be used, the identification of the patent(s) and/or supplementary protection certificate(s) in respect of which a compulsory

licence is sought, and rules on applications made in electronic form.

(15) The simple formula for setting remuneration is intended to accelerate the process of granting a compulsory licence in cases of national emergency or other circumstances of extreme urgency or in cases of public noncommercial use under Article 31(b) of the TRIPS Agreement. The figure of 4% could be used as a reference point for deliberations on adequate remuneration in circumstances other than those listed above,

NOTES

1 OJ C286, 17.11.2005, p 4.

2 Opinion of the European Parliament of 1.12.2005 (not yet published in the Official Journal), and Council Decision of 28 April 2006.

3 OJ L136, 30.4.2004, p 1.

HAVE ADOPTED THIS REGULATION:

[1.1168]
Article 1
Scope

This Regulation establishes a procedure for the grant of compulsory licences in relation to patents and supplementary protection certificates concerning the manufacture and sale of pharmaceutical products, when such products are intended for export to eligible importing countries in need of such products in order to address public health problems. Member States shall grant a compulsory licence to any person making an application in accordance with Article 6 and subject to the conditions set out in Articles 6 to 10.

[1.1169]
Article 2
Definitions

For the purposes of this Regulation, the following definitions shall apply:

(1) 'pharmaceutical product' means any product of the pharmaceutical sector, including medicinal products as defined in Article 1(2) of Directive 2001/83/EC of the European Parliament and of the Council of 6 November 2001 on the Community code relating to medicinal products for human use,[1] active ingredients and diagnostic kits ex vivo;

(2) 'rights-holder' means the holder of any patent or supplementary protection certificate in relation to which a compulsory licence has been applied for under this Regulation;

(3) 'importing country' means the country to which the pharmaceutical product is to be exported;

(4) 'competent authority' for the purposes of Articles 1 to 11, 16 and 17 means any national authority having competence to grant compulsory licences under this Regulation in a given Member State.

NOTES

1 OJ L311, 28.11.2001, p 67. Directive as last amended by Directive 2004/27/EC (OJ L136, 30.4.2004, p 34).

[1.1170]
Article 3
Competent authority

The competent authority as defined in Article 2(4) shall be that which has competence for the granting of compulsory licences under national patent law, unless the Member State determines otherwise.

Member States shall notify the Commission of the designated competent authority as defined in Article 2(4). Notifications shall be published in the Official Journal of the European Union.

[1.1171]
Article 4
Eligible importing countries

The following are eligible importing countries:

(a) any least-developed country appearing as such in the United Nations list;

(b) any member of the WTO, other than the least-developed country members referred to in point (a), that has made a notification to the Council for TRIPs of its intention to use the system as an importer, including whether it will use the system in whole or in a limited way;

(c) any country that is not a member of the WTO, but is listed in the OECD Development Assistance Committee's list of low-income countries with a gross national product per capita of less than USD 745, and has made a notification to the Commission of its intention to use the system as an importer, including whether it will use the system in whole or in a limited way.

However, any WTO member that has made a declaration to the WTO that it will not use the system as an importing WTO member is not an eligible importing country.

[1.1172]
Article 5
Extension to least-developed and developing countries which are not members of the WTO
The following provisions shall apply to importing countries eligible under Article 4 which are not WTO members:
(a) the importing country shall make the notification referred to in Article 8(1) directly to the Commission;
(b) the importing country shall, in the notification referred to in Article 8(1), state that it will use the system to address public health problems and not as an instrument to pursue industrial or commercial policy objectives and that it will adopt the measures referred to in paragraph 4 of the Decision;
(c) the competent authority may, at the request of the rightsholder, or on its own initiative if national law allows the competent authority to act on its own initiative, terminate a compulsory licence granted pursuant to this Article if the importing country has failed to honour its obligations referred to in point (b). Before terminating a compulsory licence, the competent authority shall take into account any views expressed by the bodies referred to in Article 6(3)(f).

[1.1173]
Article 6
Application for a compulsory licence
1. Any person may submit an application for a compulsory licence under this Regulation to a competent authority in the Member State or States where patents or supplementary protection certificates have effect and cover his intended activities of manufacture and sale for export.
2. If the person applying for a compulsory licence is submitting applications to authorities in more than one country for the same product, he shall indicate that fact in each application, together with details of the quantities and importing countries concerned.
3. The application pursuant to paragraph 1 shall set out the following:
(a) the name and contact details of the applicant and of any agent or representative whom the applicant has appointed to act for him before the competent authority;
(b) the non-proprietary name of the pharmaceutical product or products which the applicant intends to manufacture and sell for export under the compulsory licence;
(c) the amount of pharmaceutical product which the applicant seeks to produce under the compulsory licence;
(d) the importing country or countries;
(e) where applicable, evidence of prior negotiation with the rights-holder pursuant to Article 9;
(f) evidence of a specific request from:
(i) authorised representatives of the importing country or countries; or
(ii) a non-governmental organisation acting with the formal authorisation of one or more importing countries; or
(iii) UN bodies or other international health organisations acting with the formal authorisation of one or more importing countries,
indicating the quantity of product required.
4. Purely formal or administrative requirements necessary for the efficient processing of the application may be prescribed under national law. Such requirements shall not add unnecessarily to the costs or burdens placed upon the applicant and, in any event, shall not render the procedure for granting compulsory licences under this Regulation more burdensome than the procedure for the granting of other compulsory licences under national law.

[1.1174]
Article 7
Rights of the rights-holder
The competent authority shall notify the rights-holder without delay of the application for a compulsory licence. Before the grant of the compulsory licence, the competent authority shall give the rights-holder an opportunity to comment on the application and to provide the competent authority with any relevant information regarding the application.

[1.1175]
Article 8
Verification
1. The competent authority shall verify that:
(a) each importing country cited in the application which is a WTO member has made a notification to the WTO pursuant to the Decision, or
(b) each importing country cited in the application which is not a WTO member has made a notification to the Commission pursuant to this Regulation in respect of each of the products covered by the application that:
(i) specifies the names and expected quantities of the product(s) needed;
(ii) unless the importing country is a least-developed country, confirms that the country has established that it had insufficient or no manufacturing capacity in the

pharmaceutical sector in relation to a particular product or products in one of the ways set out in the Annex to the Decision;

(iii) confirms that where a pharmaceutical product is patented in the territory of the importing country, that importing country has granted or intends to grant a compulsory licence for import of the product concerned in accordance with Article 31 of the TRIPS Agreement and the provisions of the Decision.

This paragraph is without prejudice to the flexibility that least-developed countries have under the Decision of the Council for TRIPS of 27 June 2002.

2. The competent authority shall verify that the quantity of product cited in the application does not exceed that notified to the WTO by an importing country which is a WTO member, or to the Commission by an importing country which is not a WTO member, and that, taking into account other compulsory licences granted elsewhere, the total amount of product authorised to be produced for any importing country does not significantly exceed the amount notified by that country to the WTO, in the case of importing countries which are WTO members, or to the Commission, in the case of importing countries which are not WTO members.

[1.1176]
Article 9
Prior negotiation

1. The applicant shall provide evidence to satisfy the competent authority that he has made efforts to obtain authorisation from the rights-holder and that such efforts have not been successful within a period of thirty days before submitting the application.

2. The requirement in paragraph 1 shall not apply in situations of national emergency or other circumstances of extreme urgency or in cases of public non-commercial use under Article 31(b) of the TRIPS Agreement.

[1.1177]
Article 10
Compulsory licence conditions

1. The licence granted shall be non-assignable, except with that part of the enterprise or goodwill which enjoys the licence, and non-exclusive. It shall contain the specific conditions set out in paragraphs 2 to 9 to be fulfilled by the licensee.

2. The amount of product(s) manufactured under the licence shall not exceed what is necessary to meet the needs of the importing country or countries cited in the application, taking into account the amount of product(s) manufactured under other compulsory licences granted elsewhere.

3. The duration of the licence shall be indicated.

4. The licence shall be strictly limited to all acts necessary for the purpose of manufacturing the product in question for export and distribution in the country or countries cited in the application. No product made or imported under the compulsory licence shall be offered for sale or put on the market in any country other than that cited in the application, except where an importing country avails itself of the possibilities under subparagraph 6(i) of the Decision to export to fellow members of a regional trade agreement that share the health problem in question.

5. Products made under the licence shall be clearly identified, through specific labelling or marking, as being produced pursuant to this Regulation. The products shall be distinguished from those made by the rights-holder through special packaging and/or special colouring/shaping, provided that such distinction is feasible and does not have a significant impact on price. The packaging and any associated literature shall bear an indication that the product is subject to a compulsory licence under this Regulation, giving the name of the competent authority and any identifying reference number, and specifying clearly that the product is exclusively for export to and distribution in the importing country or countries concerned.

Details of the product characteristics shall be made available to the customs authorities of the Member States.

6. Before shipment to the importing country or countries cited in the application, the licensee shall post on a website the following information:

(a) the quantities being supplied under the licence and the importing countries to which they are supplied;

(b) the distinguishing features of the product or products concerned.

The website address shall be communicated to the competent authority.

7. If the product(s) covered by the compulsory licence are patented in the importing countries cited in the application, the product(s) shall only be exported if those countries have issued a compulsory licence for the import, sale and/or distribution of the products.

8. The competent authority may at the request of the rightsholder or on its own initiative, if national law allows the competent authority to act on its own initiative, request access to books and records kept by the licensee, for the sole purpose of checking whether the terms of the licence, and in particular those relating to the final destination of the products, have been met. The books and records shall include proof of exportation of the product, through a declaration of exportation certified by the customs authority concerned, and proof of importation from one of the bodies referred to in Article 6(3)(f).

9. The licensee shall be responsible for the payment of adequate remuneration to the rights-holder as determined by the competent authority as follows:
(a) in the cases referred to in Article 9(2), the remuneration shall be a maximum of 4 % of the total price to be paid by the importing country or on its behalf;
(b) in all other cases, the remuneration shall be determined taking into account the economic value of the use authorised under the licence to the importing country or countries concerned, as well as humanitarian or noncommercial circumstances relating to the issue of the licence.

10. The licence conditions are without prejudice to the method of distribution in the importing country.

Distribution may be carried out for example by any of the bodies listed in Article 6(3)(f) and on commercial or noncommercial terms including completely without charge.

[1.1178]
Article 11
Refusal of the application

The competent authority shall refuse an application if any of the conditions set out in Articles 6 to 9 are not met, or if the application does not contain the elements necessary to allow the competent authority to grant the licence in accordance with Article 10. Before refusing an application, the competent authority shall give the applicant an opportunity to rectify the situation and to be heard.

[1.1179]
Article 12
Notification

When a compulsory licence has been granted, the Member State shall notify the Council for TRIPS through the intermediary of the Commission of the grant of the licence, and of the specific conditions attached to it.

The information provided shall include the following details of the licence:
(a) the name and address of the licensee;
(b) the product or products concerned;
(c) the quantity to be supplied;
(d) the country or countries to which the product or products are to be exported;
(e) the duration of the licence;
(f) the address of the website referred to in Article 10(6).

[1.1180]
Article 13
Prohibition of importation

1. The import into the Community of products manufactured under a compulsory licence granted pursuant to the Decision and/or this Regulation for the purposes of release for free circulation, re-export, placing under suspensive procedures or placing in a free zone or free warehouse shall be prohibited.

2. Paragraph 1 shall not apply in the case of re-export to the importing country cited in the application and identified in the packaging and documentation associated with the product, or placing under a transit or customs warehouse procedure or in a free zone or free warehouse for the purpose of re-export to that importing country.

[1.1181]
Article 14
Action by customs authorities

1. If there are sufficient grounds for suspecting that products manufactured under a compulsory licence granted pursuant to the Decision and/or this Regulation are being imported into the Community contrary to Article 13(1), customs authorities shall suspend the release of, or detain, the products concerned for the time necessary to obtain a decision of the competent authority on the character of the merchandise. Member States shall ensure that a body has the authority to review whether such importation is taking place. The period of suspension or detention shall not exceed 10 working days unless special circumstances apply, in which case the period may be extended by a maximum of 10 working days. Upon expiry of that period, the products shall be released, provided that all customs formalities have been complied with.

2. The competent authority, the rights-holder and the manufacturer or exporter of the products concerned shall be informed without delay of the suspended release or detention of the products and shall be given all information available with respect to the products concerned. Due account shall be taken of national provisions on the protection of personal data and commercial and industrial secrecy and professional and administrative confidentiality.

The importer, and where appropriate, the exporter shall be given ample opportunity to supply the competent authority with the information which it deems appropriate regarding the products.

3. If it is confirmed that products suspended for release or detained by customs authorities were intended for import into the Community contrary to the prohibition in Article 13(1), the competent authority shall ensure that the products are seized and disposed of in accordance with national legislation.

4. The procedure of suspension or detention or seizure of the goods shall be carried out at the expense of the importer. If it is not possible to recover those expenses from the importer, they may, in accordance with national legislation, be recovered from any other person responsible for the attempted illicit importation.
5. If the products suspended for release or detained by customs authorities are subsequently found not to violate the prohibition in Article 13(1), the customs authorities shall release the products to the consignee, provided that all customs formalities have been complied with.
6. The competent authority shall inform the Commission of any decisions on seizure or destruction adopted pursuant to this Regulation.

[1.1182]
Article 15
Personal luggage exception
Articles 13 and 14 shall not apply to goods of a non-commercial nature contained in travellers' personal luggage for personal use within the limits laid down in respect of relief from customs duty.

[1.1183]
Article 16
Termination or review of the licence
1. Subject to adequate protection of the legitimate interests of the licensee, a compulsory licence granted pursuant to this Regulation may be terminated by a decision of the competent authority or by one of the bodies referred to in Article 17 if the licence conditions are not respected by the licensee.

The competent authority shall have the authority to review, upon reasoned request by the rights-holder or the licensee, whether the licence conditions have been respected. This review shall be based on the assessment made in the importing country where appropriate.
2. Termination of a licence granted under this Regulation shall be notified to the Council for TRIPS through the intermediary of the Commission.
3. Following termination of the licence, the competent authority, or any other body appointed by the Member State, shall be entitled to establish a reasonable period of time within which the licensee shall arrange for any product in his possession, custody, power or control to be redirected at his expense to countries in need as referred to in Article 4 or otherwise disposed of as prescribed by the competent authority, or by another body appointed by the Member State, in consultation with the rights-holder.
4. When notified by the importing country that the amount of pharmaceutical product has become insufficient to meet its needs, the competent authority may, following an application by the licensee, modify the conditions of the licence permitting the manufacture and export of additional quantities of the product to the extent necessary to meet the needs of the importing country concerned. In such cases the licensee's application shall be processed in accordance with a simplified and accelerated procedure, whereby the information set out in Article 6(3), points (a) and (b), shall not be required provided that the original compulsory licence is identified by the licensee. In situations where Article 9(1) applies but the derogation set out in Article 9(2) does not apply, no further evidence of negotiation with the rights-holder will be required, provided that the additional amount requested does not exceed 25 % of the amount granted under the original licence. In situations where Article 9(2) applies, no evidence of negotiation with the rights-holder will be required.

[1.1184]
Article 17
Appeals
1. Appeals against any decision of the competent authority, and disputes concerning compliance with the conditions of the licence, shall be heard by the appropriate body responsible under national law.
2. Member States shall ensure that the competent authority and/or the body referred to in paragraph 1 have the power to rule that an appeal against a decision granting a compulsory licence shall have suspensory effect.

[1.1185]
Article 18
Safety and efficacy of medicinal products
1. Where the application for a compulsory licence concerns a medicinal product, the applicant may avail himself of:
  (a) the scientific opinion procedure as provided for under Article 58 of Regulation (EC) No 726/2004, or
  (b) any similar procedures under national law, such as scientific opinions or export certificates intended exclusively for markets outside the Community.
2. If a request for any of the above procedures concerns a product which is a generic of a reference medicinal product which is or has been authorised under Article 6 of Directive 2001/83/EC, the protection periods set out in Article 14(11) of Regulation (EC) No 726/2004 and in Articles 10(1) and 10(5) of Directive 2001/83/EC shall not apply.

[1.1186]
Article 19
Review

Three years after the entry into force of this Regulation, and every three years thereafter, the Commission shall present a report to the European Parliament, the Council, and the European Economic and Social Committee on the operation of this Regulation including any appropriate plans for amendments.

The report shall cover, in particular:

(a) the application of Article 10(9) on determining the remuneration of the rights-holder;
(b) the application of the simplified and accelerated procedure referred to in Article 16(4);
(c) the sufficiency of the requirements under Article 10(5) to prevent trade diversion, and
(d) the contribution this Regulation has made to the implementation of the system established by the Decision.

[1.1187]
Article 20
Entry into force

This Regulation shall enter into force on the 20th day following that of its publication in the *Official Journal of the European Union*.

This Regulation shall be binding in its entirety and directly applicable in all Member States.

REGULATION OF THE EUROPEAN PARLIAMENT AND OF THE COUNCIL

(469/2009/EC)

of 6 May 2009

concerning the supplementary protection certificate for medicinal products

(codified version)

(Text with EEA relevance)

NOTES

Date of publication in OJ: OJ L152, 16.6.2009, p 1.

THE EUROPEAN PARLIAMENT AND THE COUNCIL OF THE EUROPEAN UNION,

Having regard to the Treaty establishing the European Community, and in particular Article 95 thereof,

Having regard to the proposal from the Commission,

Having regard to the opinion of the European Economic and Social Committee,[1]

Acting in accordance with the procedure laid down in Article 251 of the Treaty,[2]

Whereas:

(1) Council Regulation (EEC) No 1768/92 of 18 June 1992 concerning the creation of a supplementary protection certificate for medicinal products[3] has been substantially amended several times.[4] In the interests of clarity and rationality the said Regulation should be codified.

(2) Pharmaceutical research plays a decisive role in the continuing improvement in public health.

(3) Medicinal products, especially those that are the result of long, costly research will not continue to be developed in the Community and in Europe unless they are covered by favourable rules that provide for sufficient protection to encourage such research.

(4) At the moment, the period that elapses between the filing of an application for a patent for a new medicinal product and authorisation to place the medicinal product on the market makes the period of effective protection under the patent insufficient to cover the investment put into the research.

(5) This situation leads to a lack of protection which penalises pharmaceutical research.

(6) There exists a risk of research centres situated in the Member States relocating to countries that offer greater protection.

(7) A uniform solution at Community level should be provided for, thereby preventing the heterogeneous development of national laws leading to further disparities which would be likely to create obstacles to the free movement of medicinal products within the Community and thus directly affect the functioning of the internal market.

(8) Therefore, the provision of a supplementary protection certificate granted, under the same conditions, by each of the Member States at the request of the holder of a national or European patent relating to a medicinal product for which marketing authorisation has been granted is necessary. A

regulation is therefore the most appropriate legal instrument.

(9) The duration of the protection granted by the certificate should be such as to provide adequate effective protection. For this purpose, the holder of both a patent and a certificate should be able to enjoy an overall maximum of 15 years of exclusivity from the time the medicinal product in question first obtains authorisation to be placed on the market in the Community.

(10) All the interests at stake, including those of public health, in a sector as complex and sensitive as the pharmaceutical sector should nevertheless be taken into account. For this purpose, the certificate cannot be granted for a period exceeding five years. The protection granted should furthermore be strictly confined to the product which obtained authorisation to be placed on the market as a medicinal product.

(11) Provision should be made for appropriate limitation of the duration of the certificate in the special case where a patent term has already been extended under a specific national law,

NOTES

1 OJ C77, 31.3.2009, p 42.

2 Opinion of the European Parliament of 21 October 2008 (not yet published in the Official Journal) and Council Decision of 6 April 2009.

3 OJ L182, 2.7.1992, p 1.

4 See Annex I.

HAVE ADOPTED THIS REGULATION:

[1.1188]
Article 1
Definitions

For the purposes of this Regulation, the following definitions shall apply:

(a) "medicinal product" means any substance or combination of substances presented for treating or preventing disease in human beings or animals and any substance or combination of substances which may be administered to human beings or animals with a view to making a medical diagnosis or to restoring, correcting or modifying physiological functions in humans or in animals;

(b) "product" means the active ingredient or combination of active ingredients of a medicinal product;

(c) "basic patent" means a patent which protects a product as such, a process to obtain a product or an application of a product, and which is designated by its holder for the purpose of the procedure for grant of a certificate;

(d) "certificate" means the supplementary protection certificate;

(e) "application for an extension of the duration" means an application for an extension of the duration of the certificate pursuant to Article 13(3) of this Regulation and Article 36 of Regulation (EC) No 1901/2006 of the European Parliament and of the Council of 12 December 2006 on medicinal products for paediatric use.[1]

NOTES

1 OJ L378, 27.12.2006, p 1.

[1.1189]
Article 2
Scope

Any product protected by a patent in the territory of a Member State and subject, prior to being placed on the market as a medicinal product, to an administrative authorisation procedure as laid down in Directive 2001/83/EC of the European Parliament and of the Council of 6 November 2001 on the Community code relating to medicinal products for human use[1] or Directive 2001/82/EC of the European Parliament and of the Council of 6 November 2001 on the Community code relating to veterinary medicinal products[2] may, under the terms and conditions provided for in this Regulation, be the subject of a certificate.

NOTES

1 OJ L311, 28.11.2001, p 67.

2 OJ L311, 28.11.2001, p 1.

[1.1190]
Article 3
Conditions for obtaining a certificate

A certificate shall be granted if, in the Member State in which the application referred to in Article 7 is submitted and at the date of that application:

(a) the product is protected by a basic patent in force;

(b) a valid authorisation to place the product on the market as a medicinal product has been granted in accordance with Directive 2001/83/EC or Directive 2001/82/EC, as appropriate;
(c) the product has not already been the subject of a certificate;
(d) the authorisation referred to in point (b) is the first authorisation to place the product on the market as a medicinal product.

[1.1191]
Article 4
Subject matter of protection

Within the limits of the protection conferred by the basic patent, the protection conferred by a certificate shall extend only to the product covered by the authorisation to place the corresponding medicinal product on the market and for any use of the product as a medicinal product that has been authorised before the expiry of the certificate.

[1.1192]
Article 5
Effects of the certificate

Subject to the provisions of Article 4, the certificate shall confer the same rights as conferred by the basic patent and shall be subject to the same limitations and the same obligations.

[1.1193]
Article 6
Entitlement to the certificate

The certificate shall be granted to the holder of the basic patent or his successor in title.

[1.1194]
Article 7
Application for a certificate

1. The application for a certificate shall be lodged within six months of the date on which the authorisation referred to in Article 3(b) to place the product on the market as a medicinal product was granted.
2. Notwithstanding paragraph 1, where the authorisation to place the product on the market is granted before the basic patent is granted, the application for a certificate shall be lodged within six months of the date on which the patent is granted.
3. The application for an extension of the duration may be made when lodging the application for a certificate or when the application for the certificate is pending and the appropriate requirements of Article 8(1)(d) or Article 8(2), respectively, are fulfilled.
4. The application for an extension of the duration of a certificate already granted shall be lodged not later than two years before the expiry of the certificate.
5. Notwithstanding paragraph 4, for five years following the entry into force of Regulation (EC) No 1901/2006, the application for an extension of the duration of a certificate already granted shall be lodged not later than six months before the expiry of the certificate.

[1.1195]
Article 8
Content of the application for a certificate

1. The application for a certificate shall contain:
(a) a request for the grant of a certificate, stating in particular:
(i) the name and address of the applicant;
(ii) if hc has appointed a representative, the name and address of the representative;
(iii) the number of the basic patent and the title of the invention;
(iv) the number and date of the first authorisation to place the product on the market, as referred to in Article 3(b) and, if this authorisation is not the first authorisation for placing the product on the market in the Community, the number and date of that authorisation;
(b) a copy of the authorisation to place the product on the market, as referred to in Article 3(b), in which the product is identified, containing in particular the number and date of the authorisation and the summary of the product characteristics listed in Article 11 of Directive 2001/83/EC or Article 14 of Directive 2001/82/EC;
(c) if the authorisation referred to in point (b) is not the first authorisation for placing the product on the market as a medicinal product in the Community, information regarding the identity of the product thus authorised and the legal provision under which the authorisation procedure took place, together with a copy of the notice publishing the authorisation in the appropriate official publication;
(d) where the application for a certificate includes a request for an extension of the duration:
(i) a copy of the statement indicating compliance with an agreed completed paediatric investigation plan as referred to in Article 36(1) of Regulation (EC) No 1901/2006;

(ii) where necessary, in addition to the copy of the authorisation to place the product on the market as referred to in point (b), proof of possession of authorisations to place the product on the market of all other Member States, as referred to in Article 36(3) of Regulation (EC) No 1901/2006.

2. Where an application for a certificate is pending, an application for an extended duration in accordance with Article 7(3) shall include the particulars referred to in paragraph 1(d) of this Article and a reference to the application for a certificate already filed.
3. The application for an extension of the duration of a certificate already granted shall contain the particulars referred to in paragraph 1(d) and a copy of the certificate already granted.
4. Member States may provide that a fee is to be payable upon application for a certificate and upon application for the extension of the duration of a certificate.

[1.1196]
Article 9
Lodging of an application for a certificate

1. The application for a certificate shall be lodged with the competent industrial property office of the Member State which granted the basic patent or on whose behalf it was granted and in which the authorisation referred to in Article 3(b) to place the product on the market was obtained, unless the Member State designates another authority for the purpose.

The application for an extension of the duration of a certificate shall be lodged with the competent authority of the Member State concerned.

2. Notification of the application for a certificate shall be published by the authority referred to in paragraph 1. The notification shall contain at least the following information:
(a) the name and address of the applicant;
(b) the number of the basic patent;
(c) the title of the invention;
(d) the number and date of the authorisation to place the product on the market, referred to in Article 3(b), and the product identified in that authorisation;
(e) where relevant, the number and date of the first authorisation to place the product on the market in the Community;
(f) where applicable, an indication that the application includes an application for an extension of the duration.

3. Paragraph 2 shall apply to the notification of the application for an extension of the duration of a certificate already granted or where an application for a certificate is pending. The notification shall additionally contain an indication of the application for an extended duration of the certificate.

[1.1197]
Article 10
Grant of the certificate or rejection of the application for a certificate

1. Where the application for a certificate and the product to which it relates meet the conditions laid down in this Regulation, the authority referred to in Article 9(1) shall grant the certificate.
2. The authority referred to in Article 9(1) shall, subject to paragraph 3, reject the application for a certificate if the application or the product to which it relates does not meet the conditions laid down in this Regulation.
3. Where the application for a certificate does not meet the conditions laid down in Article 8, the authority referred to in Article 9(1) shall ask the applicant to rectify the irregularity, or to settle the fee, within a stated time.
4. If the irregularity is not rectified or the fee is not settled under paragraph 3 within the stated time, the authority shall reject the application.
5. Member States may provide that the authority referred to in Article 9(1) is to grant certificates without verifying that the conditions laid down in Article 3(c) and (d) are met.
6. Paragraphs 1 to 4 shall apply *mutatis mutandis* to the application for an extension of the duration.

[1.1198]
Article 11
Publication

1. Notification of the fact that a certificate has been granted shall be published by the authority referred to in Article 9(1). The notification shall contain at least the following information:
(a) the name and address of the holder of the certificate;
(b) the number of the basic patent;
(c) the title of the invention;
(d) the number and date of the authorisation to place the product on the market referred to in Article 3(b) and the product identified in that authorisation;
(e) where relevant, the number and date of the first authorisation to place the product on the market in the Community;
(f) the duration of the certificate.

2. Notification of the fact that the application for a certificate has been rejected shall be published by the authority referred to in Article 9(1). The notification shall contain at least the information listed in Article 9(2).
3. Paragraphs 1 and 2 shall apply to the notification of the fact that an extension of the duration of a certificate has been granted or of the fact that the application for an extension has been rejected.

[1.1199]
Article 12
Annual fees
Member States may require that the certificate be subject to the payment of annual fees.

[1.1200]
Article 13
Duration of the certificate
1. The certificate shall take effect at the end of the lawful term of the basic patent for a period equal to the period which elapsed between the date on which the application for a basic patent was lodged and the date of the first authorisation to place the product on the market in the Community, reduced by a period of five years.
2. Notwithstanding paragraph 1, the duration of the certificate may not exceed five years from the date on which it takes effect.
3. The periods laid down in paragraphs 1 and 2 shall be extended by six months in the case where Article 36 of Regulation (EC) No 1901/2006 applies. In that case, the duration of the period laid down in paragraph 1 of this Article may be extended only once.
4. Where a certificate is granted for a product protected by a patent which, before 2 January 1993, had its term extended or for which such extension was applied for, under national law, the term of protection to be afforded under this certificate shall be reduced by the number of years by which the term of the patent exceeds 20 years.

[1.1201]
Article 14
Expiry of the certificate
The certificate shall lapse:
(a) at the end of the period provided for in Article 13;
(b) if the certificate holder surrenders it;
(c) if the annual fee laid down in accordance with Article 12 is not paid in time;
(d) if and as long as the product covered by the certificate may no longer be placed on the market following the withdrawal of the appropriate authorisation or authorisations to place on the market in accordance with Directive 2001/83/EC or Directive 2001/82/EC. The authority referred to in Article 9(1) of this Regulation may decide on the lapse of the certificate either of its own motion or at the request of a third party.

[1.1202]
Article 15
Invalidity of the certificate
1. The certificate shall be invalid if:
(a) it was granted contrary to the provisions of Article 3;
(b) the basic patent has lapsed before its lawful term expires;
(c) the basic patent is revoked or limited to the extent that the product for which the certificate was granted would no longer be protected by the claims of the basic patent or, after the basic patent has expired, grounds for revocation exist which would have justified such revocation or limitation.
2. Any person may submit an application or bring an action for a declaration of invalidity of the certificate before the body responsible under national law for the revocation of the corresponding basic patent.

[1.1203]
Article 16
Revocation of an extension of the duration
1. The extension of the duration may be revoked if it was granted contrary to the provisions of Article 36 of Regulation (EC) No 1901/2006.
2. Any person may submit an application for revocation of the extension of the duration to the body responsible under national law for the revocation of the corresponding basic patent.

[1.1204]
Article 17
Notification of lapse or invalidity
1. If the certificate lapses in accordance with point (b), (c) or (d) of Article 14, or is invalid in accordance with Article 15, notification thereof shall be published by the authority referred to in Article 9(1).

2. If the extension of the duration is revoked in accordance with Article 16, notification thereof shall be published by the authority referred to in Article 9(1).

[1.1205]
Article 18
Appeals

The decisions of the authority referred to in Article 9(1) or of the bodies referred to in Articles 15(2) and 16(2) taken under this Regulation shall be open to the same appeals as those provided for in national law against similar decisions taken in respect of national patents.

[1.1206]
Article 19
Procedure

1. In the absence of procedural provisions in this Regulation, the procedural provisions applicable under national law to the corresponding basic patent shall apply to the certificate, unless the national law lays down special procedural provisions for certificates.
2. Notwithstanding paragraph 1, the procedure for opposition to the granting of a certificate shall be excluded.

[1.1207]
Article 20
Additional provisions relating to the enlargement of the Community

Without prejudice to the other provisions of this Regulation, the following provisions shall apply:

(a) any medicinal product protected by a valid basic patent and for which the first authorisation to place it on the market as a medicinal product was obtained after 1 January 2000 may be granted a certificate in Bulgaria, provided that the application for a certificate was lodged within six months from 1 January 2007;

(b) any medicinal product protected by a valid basic patent in the Czech Republic and for which the first authorisation to place it on the market as a medicinal product was obtained:
  (i) in the Czech Republic after 10 November 1999 may be granted a certificate, provided that the application for a certificate was lodged within six months of the date on which the first market authorisation was obtained;
  (ii) in the Community not earlier than six months prior to 1 May 2004 may be granted a certificate, provided that the application for a certificate was lodged within six months of the date on which the first market authorisation was obtained;

(c) any medicinal product protected by a valid basic patent and for which the first authorisation to place it on the market as a medicinal product was obtained in Estonia prior to 1 May 2004 may be granted a certificate, provided that the application for a certificate was lodged within six months of the date on which the first market authorisation was obtained or, in the case of those patents granted prior to 1 January 2000, within the six months provided for in the Patents Act of October 1999;

(d) any medicinal product protected by a valid basic patent and for which the first authorisation to place it on the market as a medicinal product was obtained in Cyprus prior to 1 May 2004 may be granted a certificate, provided that the application for a certificate was lodged within six months of the date on which the first market authorisation was obtained; notwithstanding the above, where the market authorisation was obtained before the grant of the basic patent, the application for a certificate must be lodged within six months of the date on which the patent was granted;

(e) any medicinal product protected by a valid basic patent and for which the first authorisation to place it on the market as a medicinal product was obtained in Latvia prior to 1 May 2004 may be granted a certificate. In cases where the period provided for in Article 7(1) has expired, the possibility of applying for a certificate shall be open for a period of six months starting no later than 1 May 2004;

(f) any medicinal product protected by a valid basic patent applied for after 1 February 1994 and for which the first authorisation to place it on the market as a medicinal product was obtained in Lithuania prior to 1 May 2004 may be granted a certificate, provided that the application for a certificate was lodged within six months from 1 May 2004;

(g) any medicinal product protected by a valid basic patent and for which the first authorisation to place it on the market as a medicinal product was obtained after 1 January 2000 may be granted a certificate in Hungary, provided that the application for a certificate was lodged within six months from 1 May 2004;

(h) any medicinal product protected by a valid basic patent and for which the first authorisation to place it on the market as a medicinal product was obtained in Malta prior to 1 May 2004 may be granted a certificate. In cases where the period provided for in Article 7(1) has expired, the possibility of applying for a certificate shall be open for a period of six months starting no later than 1 May 2004;

(i) any medicinal product protected by a valid basic patent and for which the first authorisation to place it on the market as a medicinal product was obtained after 1 January 2000 may be granted a certificate in Poland, provided that the application for a certificate was lodged within six months starting no later than 1 May 2004;

(j) any medicinal product protected by a valid basic patent and for which the first authorisation to place it on the market as a medicinal product was obtained after 1 January 2000 may be granted a certificate in Romania. In cases where the period provided for in Article 7(1) has expired, the possibility of applying for a certificate shall be open for a period of six months starting no later than 1 January 2007;

(k) any medicinal product protected by a valid basic patent and for which the first authorisation to place it on the market as a medicinal product was obtained in Slovenia prior to 1 May 2004 may be granted a certificate, provided that the application for a certificate was lodged within six months from 1 May 2004, including in cases where the period provided for in Article 7(1) has expired;

(l) any medicinal product protected by a valid basic patent and for which the first authorisation to place it on the market as a medicinal product was obtained in Slovakia after 1 January 2000 may be granted a certificate, provided that the application for a certificate was lodged within six months of the date on which the first market authorisation was obtained or within six months of 1 July 2002 if the market authorisation was obtained before that date.

[(m) any medicinal product protected by a valid basic patent and for which the first authorisation to place it on the market as a medicinal product was obtained after 1 January 2003 may be granted a certificate in Croatia, provided that the application for a certificate is lodged within six months from the date of accession.]

NOTES

Para (m): added by the Treaty between the Member States of the European Union and the Republic of Croatia concerning the accession of the Republic of Croatia to the European Union, Art 15, Annex III, para 2.II.2(a).

[1.1208]
Article 21
Transitional provisions

1. This Regulation shall not apply to certificates granted in accordance with the national legislation of a Member State before 2 January 1993 or to applications for a certificate filed in accordance with that legislation before 2 July 1992.

With regard to Austria, Finland and Sweden, this Regulation shall not apply to certificates granted in accordance with their national legislation before 1 January 1995.

[2. This Regulation shall apply to supplementary protection certificates granted in accordance with the national legislation of the Czech Republic, Estonia, Croatia, Cyprus, Latvia, Lithuania, Malta, Poland, Romania, Slovenia and Slovakia prior to their respective date of accession.]

NOTES

Para 2: substituted by the Treaty between the Member States of the European Union and the Republic of Croatia concerning the accession of the Republic of Croatia to the European Union, Art 15, Annex III, para 2.II.2(b).

[1.1209]
Article 22
Repeal

Regulation (EEC) No 1768/92, as amended by the acts listed in Annex I, is repealed.

References to the repealed Regulation shall be construed as references to this Regulation and shall be read in accordance with the correlation table in Annex II.

[1.1210]
Article 23
Entry into force

This Regulation shall enter into force on the 20th day following its publication in the *Official Journal of the European Union*.

This Regulation shall be binding in its entirety and directly applicable in all Member States.

ANNEX I
REPEALED REGULATION WITH ITS SUCCESSIVE AMENDMENTS

[1.1211]

(referred to in Article 22)

Council Regulation (EEC) No 1768/92
(OJ L182, 2.7.1992, p 1)

Annex I, point XI.F.I, of the 1994 Act of Accession
(OJ C241, 29.8.1994, p 233)
Annex II, point 4.C.II, of the 2003 Act of Accession

(OJ L236, 23.9.2003, p 342)	
Annex III, point 1.II, of the 2005 Act of Accession	
(OJ L157, 21.6.2005, p 56)	
Regulation (EC) No 1901/2006 of the European Parliament and of the Council	Only Article 52
(OJ L378, 27.12.2006, p 1)	

ANNEX II
CORRELATION TABLE

[1.1212]

Regulation (EEC) No 1768/92	This Regulation
—	Recital 1
Recital 1	Recital 2
Recital 2	Recital 3
Recital 3	Recital 4
Recital 4	Recital 5
Recital 5	Recital 6
Recital 6	Recital 7
Recital 7	Recital 8
Recital 8	Recital 9
Recital 9	Recital 10
Recital 10	—
Recital 11	—
Recital 12	—
Recital 13	Recital 11
Article 1	Article 1
Article 2	Article 2
Article 3, introductory wording	Article 3, introductory wording
Article 3, point (a)	Article 3, point (a)
Article 3, point (b), first sentence	Article 3, point (b)
Article 3, point (b), second sentence	—
Article 3, points (c) and (d)	Article 3, points (c) and (d)
Articles 4 to 7	Articles 4 to 7
Article 8(1)	Article 8(1)
Article 8(1a)	Article 8(2)
Article 8(1b)	Article 8(3)
Article 8(2)	Article 8(4)
Articles 9 to 12	Articles 9 to 12
Article 13(1), (2) and (3)	Article 13(1), (2) and (3)
Articles 14 and 15	Articles 14 and 15
Article 15a	Article 16
Articles 16, 17 and 18	Articles 17, 18 and 19
Article 19	—
Article 19a, introductory wording	Article 20, introductory wording
Article 19a, point (a), points (i) and (ii)	Article 20, point (b), introductory wording, points (i) and (ii)
Article 19a, point (b)	Article 20, point (c)
Article 19a, point (c)	Article 20, point (d)
Article 19a, point (d)	Article 20, point (e)
Article 19a, point (e)	Article 20, point (f)
Article 19a, point (f)	Article 20, point (g)
Article 19a, point (g)	Article 20, point (h)
Article 19a, point (h)	Article 20, point (i)

Regulation (EEC) No 1768/92	This Regulation
Article 19a, point (i)	Article 20, point (k)
Article 19a, point (j)	Article 20, point (l)
Article 19a, point (k)	Article 20, point (a)
Article 19a, point (l)	Article 20, point (j)
Article 20	Article 21
Article 21	—
Article 22	Article 13(4)
—	Article 22
Article 23	Article 23
—	Annex I
—	Annex II

REGULATION OF THE EUROPEAN PARLIAMENT AND OF THE COUNCIL

(1257/2012/EU)

of 17 December 2012

implementing enhanced cooperation in the area of the creation of unitary patent protection

NOTES

Date of publication in OJ: OJ L361, 31.12.2012, p 1.

THE EUROPEAN PARLIAMENT AND THE COUNCIL OF THE EUROPEAN UNION,

Having regard to the Treaty on the Functioning of the European Union and in particular the first paragraph of Article 118 thereof,

Having regard to Council Decision 2011/167/EU of 10 March 2011 authorising enhanced cooperation in the area of the creation of unitary patent protection,[1]

Having regard to the proposal from the European Commission,

After transmission of the draft legislative act to the national parliaments,

Acting in accordance with the ordinary legislative procedure,[2]

Whereas:

(1) The creation of the legal conditions enabling undertakings to adapt their activities in manufacturing and distributing products across national borders and providing them with greater choice and more opportunities contributes to the attainment of the objectives of the Union set out in Article 3(3) of the Treaty on European Union. Uniform patent protection within the internal market, or at least a significant part thereof, should feature amongst the legal instruments which undertakings have at their disposal.

(2) Pursuant to the first paragraph of Article 118 of the Treaty on the Functioning of the European Union (TFEU), measures to be taken in the context of the establishment and functioning of the internal market include the creation of uniform patent protection throughout the Union and the establishment of centralised Union-wide authorisation, coordination and supervision arrangements.

(3) On 10 March 2011, the Council adopted Decision 2011/167/EU authorising enhanced cooperation between Belgium, Bulgaria, the Czech Republic, Denmark, Germany, Estonia, Ireland, Greece, France, Cyprus, Latvia, Lithuania, Luxembourg, Hungary, Malta, the Netherlands, Austria, Poland, Portugal, Romania, Slovenia, Slovakia, Finland, Sweden and the United Kingdom (hereinafter 'participating Member States') in the area of the creation of unitary patent protection.

(4) Unitary patent protection will foster scientific and technological advances and the functioning of the internal market by making access to the patent system easier, less costly and legally secure. It will also improve the level of patent protection by making it possible to obtain uniform patent protection in the participating Member States and eliminate costs and complexity for undertakings throughout the Union. It should be available to proprietors of a European patent from both the participating Member States and from other States, regardless of their nationality, residence or place of establishment.

(5) The Convention on the Grant of European Patents of 5 October 1973, as revised on 17 December 1991 and on 29 November 2000 (hereinafter 'EPC'), established the European Patent Organisation and entrusted it with the task of granting European patents. This task is carried out by the European Patent Office (hereinafter 'EPO'). A European patent granted by the EPO should, at the request of the patent proprietor, benefit from unitary effect by virtue of this Regulation in the

participating Member States. Such a patent is hereinafter referred to as a 'European patent with unitary effect'.

(6) In accordance with Part IX of the EPC a group of Contracting States to the EPC may provide that European patents granted for those States have a unitary character. This Regulation constitutes a special agreement within the meaning of Article 142 of the EPC, a regional patent treaty within the meaning of Article 45(1) of the Patent Cooperation Treaty of 19 June 1970 as last modified on 3 February 2001 and a special agreement within the meaning of Article 19 of the Convention for the Protection of Industrial Property, signed in Paris on 20 March 1883 and last amended on 28 September 1979.

(7) Unitary patent protection should be achieved by attributing unitary effect to European patents in the post-grant phase by virtue of this Regulation and in respect of all the participating Member States. The main feature of a European patent with unitary effect should be its unitary character, i.e. providing uniform protection and having equal effect in all the participating Member States. Consequently, a European patent with unitary effect should only be limited, transferred or revoked, or lapse, in respect of all the participating Member States. It should be possible for a European patent with unitary effect to be licensed in respect of the whole or part of the territories of the participating Member States. To ensure the uniform substantive scope of protection conferred by unitary patent protection, only European patents that have been granted for all the participating Member States with the same set of claims should benefit from unitary effect. Finally, the unitary effect attributed to a European patent should have an accessory nature and should be deemed not to have arisen to the extent that the basic European patent has been revoked or limited.

(8) In accordance with the general principles of patent law and Article 64(1) of the EPC, unitary patent protection should take effect retroactively in the participating Member States as from the date of publication of the mention of the grant of the European patent in the European Patent Bulletin. Where unitary patent protection takes effect, the participating Member States should ensure that the European patent is deemed not to have taken effect on their territory as a national patent, so as to avoid any duplication of patent protection.

(9) The European patent with unitary effect should confer on its proprietor the right to prevent any third party from committing acts against which the patent provides protection. This should be ensured through the establishment of a Unified Patent Court. In matters not covered by this Regulation or by Council Regulation (EU) No 1260/2012 of 17 December 2012 implementing enhanced cooperation in the area of unitary patent protection with regard to the applicable translation arrangements,[3] the provisions of the EPC, the Agreement on a Unified Patent Court, including its provisions defining the scope of that right and its limitations, and national law, including rules of private international law, should apply.

(10) Compulsory licences for European patents with unitary effect should be governed by the laws of the participating Member States as regards their respective territories.

(11) In its report on the operation of this Regulation, the Commission should evaluate the functioning of the applicable limitations and, where necessary, make appropriate proposals, taking account of the contribution of the patent system to innovation and technological progress, the legitimate interests of third parties and overriding interests of society. The Agreement on a Unified Patent Court does not preclude the European Union from exercising its powers in this field.

(12) In accordance with the case-law of the Court of Justice of the European Union, the principle of the exhaustion of rights should also be applied to European patents with unitary effect. Therefore, rights conferred by a European patent with unitary effect should not extend to acts concerning the product covered by that patent which are carried out within the participating Member States after that product has been placed on the market in the Union by the patent proprietor.

(13) The regime applicable to damages should be governed by the laws of the participating Member States, in particular the provisions implementing Article 13 of Directive 2004/48/EC of the European Parliament and of the Council of 29 April 2004 on the enforcement of intellectual property rights.[4]

(14) As an object of property, a European patent with unitary effect should be dealt with in its entirety, and in all the participating Member States, as a national patent of the participating Member State determined in accordance with specific criteria such as the applicant's residence, principal place of business or place of business.

(15) In order to promote and facilitate the economic exploitation of an invention protected by a European patent with unitary effect, the proprietor of that patent should be able to offer it to be licensed in return for appropriate consideration. To that end, the patent proprietor should be able to file a statement with the EPO that he is prepared to grant a license in return for appropriate consideration. In that case, the patent proprietor should benefit from a reduction of the renewal fees as from the EPO's receipt of such statement.

(16) The group of Member States making use of the provisions of Part IX of the EPC may give tasks to the EPO and set up a select committee of the Administrative Council of the European Patent Organisation (hereinafter 'Select Committee').

(17) The participating Member States should give certain administrative tasks relating to European patents with unitary effect to the EPO, in particular as regards the administration of requests for unitary effect, the registration of unitary effect and of any limitation, licence, transfer, revocation or lapse of European patents with unitary effect, the collection and distribution of renewal fees, the publication of translations for information purposes during a transitional period and the administration of a compensation scheme for the reimbursement of translation costs incurred by applicants filing European patent applications in a language other than one of the official languages of the EPO.

(18) In the framework of the Select Committee, the participating Member States should ensure the governance and supervision of the activities related to the tasks entrusted to the EPO by the participating Member States, ensure that requests for unitary effect are filed with the EPO within one month of the date of publication of the mention of the grant in the European Patent Bulletin and ensure that such requests are submitted in the language of the proceedings before the EPO together with the translation prescribed, during a transitional period, by Regulation (EU) No 1260/2012. The participating Member States should also ensure the setting, in accordance with the voting rules laid down in Article 35(2) of the EPC, of the level of the renewal fees and the share of the distribution of the renewal fees in accordance with the criteria set out in this Regulation.

(19) Patent proprietors should pay a single annual renewal fee for a European patent with unitary effect. Renewal fees should be progressive throughout the term of the patent protection and, together with the fees to be paid to the European Patent Organisation during the pre-grant stage, should cover all costs associated with the grant of the European patent and the administration of the unitary patent protection. The level of the renewal fees should be set with the aim of facilitating innovation and fostering the competitiveness of European businesses, taking into account the situation of specific entities such as small and medium-sized enterprises, for example in the form of lower fees. It should also reflect the size of the market covered by the patent and be similar to the level of the national renewal fees for an average European patent taking effect in the participating Member States at the time when the level of the renewal fees is first set.

(20) The appropriate level and distribution of renewal fees should be determined in order to ensure that, in relation to the unitary patent protection, all costs of the tasks entrusted to the EPO are fully covered by the resources generated by the European patents with unitary effect and that, together with the fees to be paid to the European Patent Organisation during the pre-grant stage, the revenues from the renewal fees ensure a balanced budget of the European Patent Organisation.

(21) Renewal fees should be paid to the European Patent Organisation. The EPO should retain an amount to cover the expenses generated at the EPO in carrying out tasks in relation to the unitary patent protection in accordance with Article 146 of the EPC. The remaining amount should be distributed among the participating Member States and should be used for patent-related purposes. The share of distribution should be set on the basis of fair, equitable and relevant criteria, namely the level of patent activity and the size of the market, and should guarantee a minimum amount to be distributed to each participating Member State in order to maintain a balanced and sustainable functioning of the system. The distribution should provide compensation for having an official language other than one of the official languages of the EPO, having a disproportionately low level of patenting activity established on the basis of the European Innovation Scoreboard, and/or having acquired membership of the European Patent Organisation relatively recently.

(22) An enhanced partnership between the EPO and central industrial property offices of the Member States should enable the EPO to make regular use, where appropriate, of the result of any search carried out by central industrial property offices on a national patent application the priority of which is claimed in a subsequent European patent application. All central industrial property offices, including those which do not perform searches in the course of a national patent-granting procedure, can play an essential role under the enhanced partnership, inter alia, by giving advice and support to potential patent applicants, in particular small and medium-sized enterprises, by receiving applications, by forwarding applications to the EPO and by disseminating patent information.

(23) This Regulation is complemented by Regulation (EU) No 1260/2012, adopted by the Council in accordance with the second paragraph of Article 118 of the TFEU.

(24) Jurisdiction in respect of European patents with unitary effect should be established and governed by an instrument setting up a unified patent litigation system for European patents and European patents with unitary effect.

(25) Establishing a Unified Patent Court to hear cases concerning the European patent with unitary effect is essential in order to ensure the proper functioning of that patent, consistency of case-law and hence legal certainty, and cost-effectiveness for patent proprietors. It is therefore of paramount importance that the participating Member States ratify the Agreement on a Unified Patent Court in accordance with their national constitutional and parliamentary procedures and take the necessary steps for that Court to become operational as soon as possible.

(26) This Regulation should be without prejudice to the right of the participating Member States to grant national patents and should not replace the participating Member States' laws on patents. Patent applicants should remain free to obtain either a national patent, a European patent with unitary effect, a European patent taking effect in one or more of the Contracting States to the EPC or a

European patent with unitary effect validated in addition in one or more other Contracting States to the EPC which are not among the participating Member States.

(27) Since the objective of this Regulation, namely the creation of unitary patent protection, cannot be sufficiently achieved by the Member States and can therefore, by reason of the scale and effects of this Regulation, be better achieved at Union level, the Union may adopt measures, where appropriate by means of enhanced cooperation, in accordance with the principle of subsidiarity as set out in Article 5 of the Treaty on European Union. In accordance with the principle of proportionality, as set out in that Article, this Regulation does not go beyond what is necessary in order to achieve that objective,

NOTES

[1] OJ L76, 22.3.2011, p 53.

[2] Position of the European Parliament of 11 December 2012 (not yet published in the Official Journal) and decision of the Council of 17 December 2012.

[3] See page 89 of this Official Journal.

[4] OJ L157, 30.4.2004, p 45.

HAVE ADOPTED THIS REGULATION:

CHAPTER I
GENERAL PROVISIONS

[1.1213]
Article 1
Subject matter

1. This Regulation implements enhanced cooperation in the area of the creation of unitary patent protection, authorised by Decision 2011/167/EU.

2. This Regulation constitutes a special agreement within the meaning of Article 142 of the Convention on the Grant of European Patents of 5 October 1973, as revised on 17 December 1991 and on 29 November 2000 (hereinafter 'EPC').

[1.1214]
Article 2
Definitions

For the purposes of this Regulation, the following definitions shall apply:

(a) 'Participating Member State' means a Member State which participates in enhanced cooperation in the area of the creation of unitary patent protection by virtue of Decision 2011/167/EU, or by virtue of a decision adopted in accordance with the second or third subparagraph of Article 331(1) of the TFEU, at the time the request for unitary effect as referred to in Article 9 is made;

(b) 'European patent' means a patent granted by the European Patent Office (hereinafter 'EPO') under the rules and procedures laid down in the EPC;

(c) 'European patent with unitary effect' means a European patent which benefits from unitary effect in the participating Member States by virtue of this Regulation;

(d) 'European Patent Register' means the register kept by the EPO under Article 127 of the EPC;

(e) 'Register for unitary patent protection' means the register constituting part of the European Patent Register in which the unitary effect and any limitation, licence, transfer, revocation or lapse of a European patent with unitary effect are registered;

(f) 'European Patent Bulletin' means the periodical publication provided for in Article 129 of the EPC.

[1.1215]
Article 3
European patent with unitary effect

1. A European patent granted with the same set of claims in respect of all the participating Member States shall benefit from unitary effect in the participating Member States provided that its unitary effect has been registered in the Register for unitary patent protection.

A European patent granted with different sets of claims for different participating Member States shall not benefit from unitary effect.

2. A European patent with unitary effect shall have a unitary character. It shall provide uniform protection and shall have equal effect in all the participating Member States.

It may only be limited, transferred or revoked, or lapse, in respect of all the participating Member States.

It may be licensed in respect of the whole or part of the territories of the participating Member States.

3. The unitary effect of a European patent shall be deemed not to have arisen to the extent that the European patent has been revoked or limited.

[1.1216]
Article 4
Date of effect

1. A European patent with unitary effect shall take effect in the participating Member States on the date of publication by the EPO of the mention of the grant of the European patent in the European Patent Bulletin.

2. The participating Member States shall take the necessary measures to ensure that, where the unitary effect of a European patent has been registered and extends to their territory, that European patent is deemed not to have taken effect as a national patent in their territory on the date of publication of the mention of the grant in the European Patent Bulletin.

CHAPTER II
EFFECTS OF A EUROPEAN PATENT WITH UNITARY EFFECT

[1.1217]
Article 5
Uniform protection

1. The European patent with unitary effect shall confer on its proprietor the right to prevent any third party from committing acts against which that patent provides protection throughout the territories of the participating Member States in which it has unitary effect, subject to applicable limitations.

2. The scope of that right and its limitations shall be uniform in all participating Member States in which the patent has unitary effect.

3. The acts against which the patent provides protection referred to in paragraph 1 and the applicable limitations shall be those defined by the law applied to European patents with unitary effect in the participating Member State whose national law is applicable to the European patent with unitary effect as an object of property in accordance with Article 7.

4. In its report referred to in Article 16(1), the Commission shall evaluate the functioning of the applicable limitations and shall, where necessary, make appropriate proposals.

[1.1218]
Article 6
Exhaustion of the rights conferred by a European patent with unitary effect

The rights conferred by a European patent with unitary effect shall not extend to acts concerning a product covered by that patent which are carried out within the participating Member States in which that patent has unitary effect after that product has been placed on the market in the Union by, or with the consent of, the patent proprietor, unless there are legitimate grounds for the patent proprietor to oppose further commercialisation of the product.

CHAPTER III
A EUROPEAN PATENT WITH UNITARY EFFECT AS AN OBJECT OF PROPERTY

[1.1219]
Article 7
Treating a European patent with unitary effect as a national patent

1. A European patent with unitary effect as an object of property shall be treated in its entirety and in all the participating Member States as a national patent of the participating Member State in which that patent has unitary effect and in which, according to the European Patent Register:

(a) the applicant had his residence or principal place of business on the date of filing of the application for the European patent; or

(b) where point (a) does not apply, the applicant had a place of business on the date of filing of the application for the European patent.

2. Where two or more persons are entered in the European Patent Register as joint applicants, point (a) of paragraph 1 shall apply to the joint applicant indicated first. Where this is not possible, point (a) of paragraph 1 shall apply to the next joint applicant indicated in the order of entry. Where point (a) of paragraph 1 does not apply to any of the joint applicants, point (b) of paragraph 1 shall apply accordingly.

3. Where no applicant had his residence, principal place of business or place of business in a participating Member State in which that patent has unitary effect for the purposes of paragraphs 1 or 2, the European patent with unitary effect as an object of property shall be treated in its entirety and in all the participating Member States as a national patent of the State where the European Patent Organisation has its headquarters in accordance with Article 6(1) of the EPC.

4. The acquisition of a right may not be dependent on any entry in a national patent register.

[1.1220]
Article 8
Licences of right

1. The proprietor of a European patent with unitary effect may file a statement with the EPO to the effect that the proprietor is prepared to allow any person to use the invention as a licensee in return for appropriate consideration.

2. A licence obtained under this Regulation shall be treated as a contractual licence.

CHAPTER IV
INSTITUTIONAL PROVISIONS

[1.1221]
Article 9
Administrative tasks in the framework of the European Patent Organisation

1. The participating Member States shall, within the meaning of Article 143 of the EPC, give the EPO the following tasks, to be carried out in accordance with the internal rules of the EPO:
   (a) to administer requests for unitary effect by proprietors of European patents;
   (b) to include the Register for unitary patent protection within the European Patent Register and to administer the Register for unitary patent protection;
   (c) to receive and register statements on licensing referred to in Article 8, their withdrawal and licensing commitments undertaken by the proprietor of the European patent with unitary effect in international standardisation bodies;
   (d) to publish the translations referred to in Article 6 of Regulation (EU) No 1260/2012 during the transitional period referred to in that Article;
   (e) to collect and administer renewal fees for European patents with unitary effect, in respect of the years following the year in which the mention of the grant is published in the European Patent Bulletin; to collect and administer additional fees for late payment of renewal fees where such late payment is made within six months of the due date, as well as to distribute part of the collected renewal fees to the participating Member States;
   (f) to administer the compensation scheme for the reimbursement of translation costs referred to in Article 5 of Regulation (EU) No 1260/2012;
   (g) to ensure that a request for unitary effect by a proprietor of a European patent is submitted in the language of the proceedings as defined in Article 14(3) of the EPC no later than one month after the mention of the grant is published in the European Patent Bulletin; and
   (h) to ensure that the unitary effect is indicated in the Register for unitary patent protection, where a request for unitary effect has been filed and, during the transitional period provided for in Article 6 of Regulation (EU) No 1260/2012, has been submitted together with the translations referred to in that Article, and that the EPO is informed of any limitations, licences, transfers or revocations of European patents with unitary effect.

2. The participating Member States shall ensure compliance with this Regulation in fulfilling their international obligations undertaken in the EPC and shall cooperate to that end. In their capacity as Contracting States to the EPC, the participating Member States shall ensure the governance and supervision of the activities related to the tasks referred to in paragraph 1 of this Article and shall ensure the setting of the level of renewal fees in accordance with Article 12 of this Regulation and the setting of the share of distribution of the renewal fees in accordance with Article 13 of this Regulation.

To that end they shall set up a select committee of the Administrative Council of the European Patent Organisation (hereinafter 'Select Committee') within the meaning of Article 145 of the EPC.

The Select Committee shall consist of the representatives of the participating Member States and a representative of the Commission as an observer, as well as alternates who will represent them in their absence. The members of the Select Committee may be assisted by advisers or experts.

Decisions of the Select Committee shall be taken with due regard for the position of the Commission and in accordance with the rules laid down in Article 35(2) of the EPC.

3. The participating Member States shall ensure effective legal protection before a competent court of one or several participating Member States against the decisions of the EPO in carrying out the tasks referred to in paragraph 1.

CHAPTER V
FINANCIAL PROVISIONS

[1.1222]
Article 10
Principle on expenses

The expenses incurred by the EPO in carrying out the additional tasks given to it, within the meaning of Article 143 of the EPC, by the participating Member States shall be covered by the fees generated by the European patents with unitary effect.

[1.1223]
Article 11
Renewal fees

1. Renewal fees for European patents with unitary effect and additional fees for their late payment shall be paid to the European Patent Organisation by the patent proprietor. Those fees shall be due in respect of the years following the year in which the mention of the grant of the European patent which benefits from unitary effect is published in the European Patent Bulletin.

2. A European patent with unitary effect shall lapse if a renewal fee and, where applicable, any additional fee have not been paid in due time.
3. Renewal fees which fall due after receipt of the statement referred to in Article 8(1) shall be reduced.

[1.1224]
Article 12
Level of renewal fees
1. Renewal fees for European patents with unitary effect shall be:
 (a) progressive throughout the term of the unitary patent protection;
 (b) sufficient to cover all costs associated with the grant of the European patent and the administration of the unitary patent protection; and
 (c) sufficient, together with the fees to be paid to the European Patent Organisation during the pre-grant stage, to ensure a balanced budget of the European Patent Organisation.
2. The level of the renewal fees shall be set, taking into account, among others, the situation of specific entities such as small and medium-sized enterprises, with the aim of:
 (a) facilitating innovation and fostering the competitiveness of European businesses;
 (b) reflecting the size of the market covered by the patent; and
 (c) being similar to the level of the national renewal fees for an average European patent taking effect in the participating Member States at the time the level of the renewal fees is first set.
3. In order to attain the objectives set out in this Chapter, the level of renewal fees shall be set at a level that:
 (a) is equivalent to the level of the renewal fee to be paid for the average geographical coverage of current European patents;
 (b) reflects the renewal rate of current European patents; and
 (c) reflects the number of requests for unitary effect.

[1.1225]
Article 13
Distribution
1. The EPO shall retain 50 per cent of the renewal fees referred to in Article 11 paid for European patents with unitary effect. The remaining amount shall be distributed to the participating Member States in accordance with the share of distribution of the renewal fees set pursuant to Article 9(2).
2. In order to attain the objectives set out in this Chapter, the share of distribution of renewal fees among the participating Member States shall be based on the following fair, equitable and relevant criteria:
 (a) the number of patent applications;
 (b) the size of the market, while ensuring a minimum amount to be distributed to each participating Member State;
 (c) compensation to the participating Member States which have:
  (i) an official language other than one of the official languages of the EPO;
  (ii) a disproportionately low level of patenting activity; and/or
  (iii) acquired membership of the European Patent Organisation relatively recently.

CHAPTER VI
FINAL PROVISIONS

[1.1226]
Article 14
Cooperation between the Commission and the EPO
The Commission shall establish a close cooperation through a working agreement with the EPO in the fields covered by this Regulation. This cooperation shall include regular exchanges of views on the functioning of the working agreement and, in particular, on the issue of renewal fees and their impact on the budget of the European Patent Organisation.

[1.1227]
Article 15
Application of competition law and the law relating to unfair competition
This Regulation shall be without prejudice to the application of competition law and the law relating to unfair competition.

[1.1228]
Article 16
Report on the operation of this Regulation
1. Not later than three years from the date on which the first European patent with unitary effect takes effect, and every five years thereafter, the Commission shall present to the European Parliament and the Council a report on the operation of this Regulation and, where necessary, make appropriate proposals for amending it.

2. The Commission shall regularly submit to the European Parliament and the Council reports on the functioning of the renewal fees referred to in Article 11, with particular emphasis on compliance with Article 12.

[1.1229]
Article 17
Notification by the participating Member States
1. The participating Member States shall notify the Commission of the measures adopted in accordance with Article 9 by the date of application of this Regulation.
2. Each participating Member State shall notify the Commission of the measures adopted in accordance with Article 4(2) by the date of application of this Regulation or, in the case of a participating Member State in which the Unified Patent Court does not have exclusive jurisdiction with regard to European patents with unitary effect on the date of application of this Regulation, by the date from which the Unified Patent Court has such exclusive jurisdiction in that participating Member State.

[1.1230]
Article 18
Entry into force and application
1. This Regulation shall enter into force on the twentieth day following that of its publication in the *Official Journal of the European Union*.
2. It shall apply from 1 January 2014 or the date of entry into force of the Agreement on a Unified Patent Court (the 'Agreement'), whichever is the later.
By way of derogation from Articles 3(1), 3(2) and 4(1), a European patent for which unitary effect is registered in the Register for unitary patent protection shall have unitary effect only in those participating Member States in which the Unified Patent Court has exclusive jurisdiction with regard to European patents with unitary effect at the date of registration.
3. Each participating Member State shall notify the Commission of its ratification of the Agreement at the time of deposit of its ratification instrument. The Commission shall publish in the *Official Journal of the European Union* the date of entry into force of the Agreement and a list of the Member States who have ratified the Agreement at the date of entry into force. The Commission shall thereafter regularly update the list of the participating Member States which have ratified the Agreement and shall publish such updated list in the *Official Journal of the European Union*.
4. The participating Member States shall ensure that the measures referred to in Article 9 are in place by the date of application of this Regulation.
5. Each participating Member State shall ensure that the measures referred to in Article 4(2) are in place by the date of application of this Regulation or, in the case of a participating Member State in which the Unified Patent Court does not have exclusive jurisdiction with regard to European patents with unitary effect on the date of application of this Regulation, by the date from which the Unified Patent Court has such exclusive jurisdiction in that participating Member State.
6. Unitary patent protection may be requested for any European patent granted on or after the date of application of this Regulation.
This Regulation shall be binding in its entirety and directly applicable in the participating Member States in accordance with the Treaties.

COUNCIL REGULATION

(1260/2012/EU)

of 17 December 2012

implementing enhanced cooperation in the area of the creation of unitary patent protection with regard to the applicable translation arrangements

NOTES
Date of publication in OJ: OJ L361, 31.12.2012, p 89.

THE COUNCIL OF THE EUROPEAN UNION,
Having regard to the Treaty on the Functioning of the European Union, and in particular the second paragraph of Article 118 thereof,
Having regard to Council Decision 2011/167/EU of 10 March 2011 authorising enhanced cooperation in the area of the creation of unitary patent protection,[1]
Having regard to the proposal from the European Commission,
After transmission of the draft legislative act to the national parliaments,
Having regard to the opinion of the European Parliament,
Acting in accordance with a special legislative procedure,
Whereas:
(1) Pursuant to Decision 2011/167/EU, Belgium, Bulgaria, the Czech Republic, Denmark,

Germany, Estonia, Ireland, Greece, France, Cyprus, Latvia, Lithuania, Luxembourg, Hungary, Malta, the Netherlands, Austria, Poland, Portugal, Romania, Slovenia, Slovakia, Finland, Sweden and the United Kingdom (hereinafter "participating Member States") were authorised to establish enhanced cooperation between themselves in the area of the creation of unitary patent protection.

(2) Under Regulation (EU) No 1257/2012 of the European Parliament and of the Council of 17 December 2012 implementing enhanced cooperation in the area of the creation of unitary patent protection,[2] certain European patents granted by the European Patent Office (hereinafter 'EPO') under the rules and procedures of the Convention on the Grant of European Patents of 5 October 1973, as revised on 17 December 1991 and on 29 November 2000 (hereinafter 'EPC') should, at the request of the patent proprietor, benefit from unitary effect in the participating Member States.

(3) Translation arrangements for European patents benefiting from unitary effect in the participating Member States (hereinafter 'European patent with unitary effect') should be established by means of a separate Regulation, in accordance with the second paragraph of Article 118 of the Treaty on the Functioning of the European Union (TFEU).

(4) In accordance with Decision 2011/167/EU the translation arrangements for European patents with unitary effect should be simple and cost-effective. They should correspond to those provided for in the proposal for a Council Regulation on the translation arrangements for the European Union patent, presented by the Commission on 30 June 2010, combined with the elements of compromise proposed by the Presidency in November 2010 that had wide support in the Council.

(5) Such translation arrangements should ensure legal certainty and stimulate innovation and should, in particular, benefit small and medium-sized enterprises (SMEs). They should make access to the European patent with unitary effect and to the patent system as a whole easier, less costly and legally secure.

(6) Since the EPO is responsible for the grant of European patents, the translation arrangements for the European patent with unitary effect should be built on the current procedure in the EPO. Those arrangements should aim to achieve the necessary balance between the interests of economic operators and the public interest, in terms of the cost of proceedings and the availability of technical information.

(7) Without prejudice to the transitional arrangements, where the specification of a European patent with unitary effect has been published in accordance with Article 14(6) of the EPC, no further translations should be required. Article 14(6) of the EPC provides that the specification of a European patent is published in the language of the proceedings before the EPO and includes a translation of the claims into the other two official languages of the EPO.

(8) In the event of a dispute concerning a European patent with unitary effect, it is a legitimate requirement that the patent proprietor at the request of the alleged infringer should provide a full translation of the patent into an official language of either the participating Member State in which the alleged infringement took place or the Member State in which the alleged infringer is domiciled. The patent proprietor should also be required to provide, at the request of a court competent in the participating Member States for disputes concerning the European patent with unitary effect, a full translation of the patent into the language used in the proceedings of that court. Such translations should not be carried out by automated means and should be provided at the expense of the patent proprietor.

(9) In the event of a dispute concerning a claim for damages, the court hearing the dispute should take into consideration the fact that, before having been provided with a translation in his own language, the alleged infringer may have acted in good faith and may have not known or had reasonable grounds to know that he was infringing the patent. The competent court should assess the circumstances of the individual case and, inter alia, should take into account whether the alleged infringer is a SME operating only at local level, the language of the proceedings before the EPO and, during the transitional period, the translation submitted together with the request for unitary effect.

(10) In order to facilitate access to European patents with unitary effect, in particular for SMEs, applicants should be able to file their patent applications at the EPO in any official language of the Union. As a complementary measure, certain applicants obtaining European patents with unitary effect, having filed a European patent application in one of the official languages of the Union, which is not an official language of the EPO, and having their residence or principal place of business within a Member State, should receive additional reimbursements of the costs of translating from the language of the patent application into the language of the proceedings of the EPO, beyond what is currently in place at the EPO. Such reimbursements should be administered by the EPO in accordance with Article 9 of Regulation (EU) No 1257/2012.

(11) In order to promote the availability of patent information and the dissemination of technological knowledge, machine translations of patent applications and specifications into all official languages of the Union should be available as soon as possible. Machine translations are being developed by the EPO and are a very important tool in seeking to improve access to patent information and to widely disseminate technological knowledge. The timely availability of high quality machine translations of European patent applications and specifications into all official languages of the Union would benefit all users of the European patent system. Machine translations

are a key feature of European Union policy. Such machine translations should serve for information purposes only and should not have any legal effect.

(12) During the transitional period, before a system of high quality machine translations into all official languages of the Union becomes available, a request for unitary effect as referred to in Article 9 of Regulation (EU) No 1257/2012 should be accompanied by a full translation of the specification of the patent into English where the language of the proceedings before the EPO is French or German, or into any official language of the Member States that is an official language of the Union where the language of the proceedings before the EPO is English. Those arrangements would ensure that during a transitional period all European patents with unitary effect are made available in English which is the language customarily used in the field of international technological research and publications. Furthermore, such arrangements would ensure that with respect to European patents with unitary effect, translations would be published in other official languages of the participating Member States. Such translations should not be carried out by automated means and their high quality should contribute to the training of translation engines by the EPO. They would also enhance the dissemination of patent information.

(13) The transitional period should terminate as soon as high quality machine translations into all official languages of the Union are available, subject to a regular and objective evaluation of the quality by an independent expert committee established by the participating Member States in the framework of the European Patent Organisation and composed of the representatives of the EPO and the users of the European patent system. Given the state of technological development, the maximum period for the development of high quality machine translations cannot be considered to exceed 12 years. Consequently, the transitional period should lapse 12 years from the date of application of this Regulation, unless it has been decided to terminate that period earlier.

(14) Since the substantive provisions applicable to a European patent with unitary effect are governed by Regulation (EU) No 1257/2012 and are completed by the translation arrangements provided for in this Regulation, this Regulation should apply from the same date as Regulation (EU) No 1257/2012.

(15) This Regulation is without prejudice to the rules governing the languages of the Institutions of the Union established in accordance with Article 342 of the TFEU and to Council Regulation No 1 of 15 April 1958 determining the languages to be used by the European Economic Community.[3] This Regulation is based on the linguistic regime of the EPO and should not be considered as creating a specific linguistic regime for the Union, or as creating a precedent for a limited language regime in any future legal instrument of the Union.

(16) Since the objective of this Regulation, namely the creation of a uniform and simple translation regime for European patents with unitary effect, cannot be sufficiently achieved by the Member States and can therefore, by reasons of the scale and effects of this Regulation, be better achieved at Union level, the Union may adopt measures, where appropriate by means of enhanced cooperation, in accordance with the principle of subsidiarity as set out in Article 5 of the Treaty on European Union. In accordance with the principle of proportionality, as set out in that Article, this Regulation does not go beyond what is necessary in order to achieve that objective,

NOTES

1 OJ L76, 22.3.2011, p 53.

2 See page 1 of this Official Journal.

3 OJ 17, 6.10.1958, p 385/58.

HAS ADOPTED THIS REGULATION:

[1.1231]
Article 1
Subject matter

This Regulation implements enhanced cooperation in the area of the creation of unitary patent protection authorised by Decision No 2011/167/EU with regard to the applicable translation arrangements.

[1.1232]
Article 2
Definitions

For the purposes of this Regulation, the following definitions shall apply:

(a) 'European patent with unitary effect' means a European patent which benefits from unitary effect in the participating Member States by virtue of Regulation (EU) No 1257/2012;

(b) 'Language of the proceedings' means the language used in the proceedings before the EPO as defined in Article 14(3) of the Convention on the Grant of European Patents of 5 October 1973, as revised on 17 December 1991 and on 29 November 2000 (hereinafter 'EPC').

[1.1233]
Article 3
Translation arrangements for the European patent with unitary effect

1. Without prejudice to Articles 4 and 6 of this Regulation, where the specification of a European patent, which benefits from unitary effect has been published in accordance with Article 14(6) of the EPC, no further translations shall be required.
2. A request for unitary effect as referred to in Article 9 of Regulation (EU) No 1257/2012 shall be submitted in the language of the proceedings.

[1.1234]
Article 4
Translation in the event of a dispute

1. In the event of a dispute relating to an alleged infringement of a European patent with unitary effect, the patent proprietor shall provide at the request and the choice of an alleged infringer, a full translation of the European patent with unitary effect into an official language of either the participating Member State in which the alleged infringement took place or the Member State in which the alleged infringer is domiciled.
2. In the event of a dispute relating to a European patent with unitary effect, the patent proprietor shall provide in the course of legal proceedings, at the request of a court competent in the participating Member States for disputes concerning European patents with unitary effect, a full translation of the patent into the language used in the proceedings of that court.
3. The cost of the translations referred to in paragraphs 1 and 2 shall be borne by the patent proprietor.
4. In the event of a dispute concerning a claim for damages, the court hearing the dispute shall assess and take into consideration, in particular where the alleged infringer is a SME, a natural person or a non-profit organisation, a university or a public research organisation, whether the alleged infringer acted without knowing or without reasonable grounds for knowing, that he was infringing the European patent with unitary effect before having been provided with the translation referred to in paragraph 1.

[1.1235]
Article 5
Administration of a compensation scheme

1. Given the fact that European patent applications may be filed in any language under Article 14(2) of the EPC, the participating Member States shall in accordance with Article 9 of Regulation (EU) No 1257/2012, give, within the meaning of Article 143 of the EPC, the EPO the task of administering a compensation scheme for the reimbursement of all translation costs up to a ceiling, for applicants filing patent applications at the EPO in one of the official languages of the Union that is not an official language of the EPO.
2. The compensation scheme referred to in paragraph 1 shall be funded through the fees referred to in Article 11 of Regulation (EU) No 1257/2012 and shall be available only for SMEs, natural persons, non-profit organisations, universities and public research organisations having their residence or principal place of business within a Member State.

[1.1236]
Article 6
Transitional measures

1. During a transitional period starting on the date of application of this Regulation a request for unitary effect as referred to in Article 9 of Regulation (EU) No 1257/2012 shall be submitted together with the following:
   (a) where the language of the proceedings is French or German, a full translation of the specification of the European patent into English; or
   (b) where the language of the proceedings is English, a full translation of the specification of the European patent into any other official language of the Union.
2. In accordance with Article 9 of Regulation (EU) No 1257/2012, the participating Member States shall give, within the meaning of Article 143 of the EPC, the EPO the task of publishing the translations referred to in paragraph 1 of this Article as soon as possible after the date of the submission of a request for unitary effect as referred to in Article 9 of Regulation (EU) No 1257/2012. The text of such translations shall have no legal effect and shall be for information purposes only.
3. Six years after the date of application of this Regulation and every two years thereafter, an independent expert committee shall carry out an objective evaluation of the availability of high quality machine translations of patent applications and specifications into all the official languages of the Union as developed by the EPO. This expert committee shall be established by the participating Member States in the framework of the European Patent Organisation and shall be composed of representatives of the EPO and of the non-governmental organisations representing users of the European patent system invited by the Administrative Council of the European Patent Organisation as observers in accordance with Article 30(3) of the EPC.

4. On the basis of the first of the evaluations referred to in paragraph 3 of this Article and every two years thereafter on the basis of the subsequent evaluations, the Commission shall present a report to the Council and, if appropriate, make proposals for terminating the transitional period.
5. If the transitional period is not terminated on the basis of a proposal of the Commission, it shall lapse 12 years from the date of application of this Regulation.

[1.1237]
Article 7
Entry into force
1. This Regulation shall enter into force on the twentieth day following that of its publication in the *Official Journal of the European Union*.
2. It shall apply from 1 January 2014 or the date of entry into force of the Agreement on a Unified Patent Court, whichever is the later.
This Regulation shall be binding in its entirety and directly applicable in the participating Member States in accordance with the Treaties.

PART 2
COPYRIGHT

PUBLIC LENDING RIGHT ACT 1979

(1979 c 10)

ARRANGEMENT OF SECTIONS

SCHEDULES

An Act to provide public lending right for authors, and for connected purposes

[22 March 1979]

[2.1]

1 Establishment of public lending right

(1) In accordance with a scheme to be prepared and brought into force by [the Secretary of State], there shall be conferred on authors a right, known as "public lending right", to receive from time to time out of a Central Fund payments in respect of such of their books as are lent out to the public by local library authorities in the United Kingdom.

(2) The classes, descriptions and categories of books in respect of which public lending right subsists, and the scales of payments to be made from the Central Fund in respect of it, shall be determined by or in accordance with the scheme; and in preparing the scheme [the Secretary of State] shall consult with representatives of authors and library authorities and of others who appear to be likely to be affected by it.

(3) . . . The Schedule to this Act has effect . . .

(4) The [Board] shall be charged with the duty of establishing and maintaining in accordance with the scheme a register showing the books in respect of which public lending right subsists and the persons entitled to the right in respect of any registered book.

(5) The [Board] shall, in the case of any registered book determine in accordance with the scheme the sums (if any) due by way of public lending right; and any sum so determined to be due shall be recoverable form the [Board] as a debt due to the person for the time being entitled to that right in respect of the book.

(6) Subject to any provision made by the scheme, the duration of public lending right in respect of a book shall be from the date of the book's first publication (or, if later, the beginning of the year in which application is made for it to be registered) until 50 years have elapsed since the end of the year in which the author died.

(7) Provision shall be made by the scheme for the right—

(a) to be established by registration;

(b) to be transmissible by assignment or assignation, by testamentary disposition or by operation of law, as personal or moveable property;

(c) to be claimed by or on behalf of the person for the time being entitled;

(d) to be renounced (either in whole or in part, and either temporarily or for all time) on notice being given to the [Board] to that effect.

NOTES

Sub-ss (1), (2): words in square brackets substituted by virtue of the Transfer of Functions (National Heritage) Order 1992, SI 1992/1311, art 3(1), Sch 1, Part I.

Sub-s (3): words omitted repealed by the Public Bodies (Abolition of the Registrar of Public Lending Right) Order 2013, SI 2013/2352, art 7(1), Sch 1, paras 6, 7(1), (2).

Sub-ss (4), (5), (7): words in square brackets substituted by SI 2013/2352, art 7(1), Sch 1, paras 6, 7(1), (3).

[2.2]

2 The Central Fund

(1) The Central Fund shall be constituted by [the Secretary of State] and placed under the control and management of the [Board].

(2) There shall be paid into the Fund from time to time such sums, out of money provided by Parliament, as [the Secretary of State] with Treasury approval determines to be required for the purpose of satisfying the liabilities of the Fund; but in respect of the liabilities of any one financial year of the Fund the total of those sums shall not exceed £2 million . . .

(3) With the consent of the Treasury, [the Secretary of State] may from time to time by order in a statutory instrument increase the limit on the sums to be paid under subsection (2) above in respect of financial years beginning after that in which the order is made; but no such order shall be made unless a draft of it has been laid before the House of Commons and approved by a resolution of that House.

[(4) There are to be paid out of the Central Fund such sums as may in accordance with the scheme be due from time to time in respect of public lending right.]

[(5) There is to be paid into the Central Fund—

(a) money received by the Board in respect of property disposed of in connection with its functions in relation to public lending right, and

(b) money otherwise received by the Board in the course of its functions in relation to public lending right, or under this Act,

after deduction of any costs associated with the disposal of the property or otherwise referable to the money received.

(5A) But an amount required to be paid into the Central Fund under subsection (5) is instead to be paid into the Consolidated Fund if the Secretary of State, with the consent of the Treasury, so directs.]

(6) . . .

NOTES

Sub-s (1): words in first pair of square brackets substituted by virtue of the Transfer of Functions (National Heritage) Order 1992, SI 1992/1311, art 3(1), Sch 1, Part I; word in second pair of square brackets substituted by the Public Bodies (Abolition of the Registrar of Public Lending Right) Order 2013, SI 2013/2352, art 7(1), Sch 1, paras 6, 8(1), (2).

Sub-s (2): words in square brackets substituted by virtue of SI 1992/1311, art 3(1), Sch 1, Part I; words omitted repealed by SI 2013/2352, art 7(1), Sch 1, paras 6, 8(1), (3).

Sub-s (3): words in square brackets substituted by virtue of SI 1992/1311, art 3(1), Sch 1, Part I.

Sub-s (4): substituted by SI 2013/2352, art 7(1), Sch 1, paras 6, 8(1), (4).

Sub-ss (5), (5A): substituted for original sub-s (5), by SI 2013/2352, art 7(1), Sch 1, paras 6, 8(1), (5).

Sub-s (6): repealed by SI 2013/2352, art 7(1), Sch 1, paras 6, 8(1), (6).

Orders: the Public Lending Right (Increase of Limit) Order 2003, SI 2003/839.

[2.3]

3 The scheme and its administration

(1) As soon as may be after this Act comes into force, [the Secretary of State] shall prepare the draft of a scheme for its purposes and lay a copy of the draft before each House of Parliament.

(2) If the draft scheme is approved by a resolution of each House, [the Secretary of State] shall bring the scheme into force (in the form of the draft) by means of an order in a statutory instrument, to be laid before Parliament after it is made; and the order may provide for different provisions of the scheme to come into force on different dates.

(3) The scheme shall be so framed as to make entitlement to public lending right dependent on, and its extent ascertainable by reference to, the number of occasions on which books are lent out from particular libraries, to be specified by the scheme or identified in accordance with provision made by it.

(4) For this purpose, "library"—

(a) means any one of a local library authority's collections of books held by them for the purpose of being borrowed by the public; and

(b) includes any such collection which is taken about from place to place.

(5) The scheme may provide for requiring local library authorities—

(a) to give information as and when, and in the from in which, the [Board] may call for it or [the Secretary of State] may direct, as to loans made by them to the public of books in respect of which public lending right subsists, or of other books; and

(b) to arrange for books to be numbered, or otherwise marked or coded, with a view to facilitating the maintenance of the register and the ascertainment and administration of public lending right.

(6) The [Board] shall . . . reimburse to local library authorities any expenditure incurred by them in giving effect to the scheme, the amount of that expenditure being ascertained in accordance with such calculations as the scheme may prescribe.

(7) Subject to the provisions of this Act (and in particular to the foregoing provisions of this section), the scheme may be varied from time to time by [the Secretary of State], after such consultation as is mentioned in section 1 (2) above, and the variation brought into force by an order in a statutory instrument, subject to annulment in pursuance of a resolution of either House of Parliament; and the variation may comprise such incidental and transitional provisions as [the Secretary of State] thinks appropriate for the purposes of continuing the scheme as varied.

(8) . . .

NOTES

Sub-ss (1), (2), (7): words in square brackets substituted by virtue of the Transfer of Functions (National Heritage) Order 1992, SI 1992/1311, art 3(1), Sch 1, Part I.

Sub-s (5): word in first pair of square brackets substituted by the Public Bodies (Abolition of the Registrar of Public Lending Right) Order 2013, SI 2013/2352, art 7(1), Sch 1, paras 6, 9(1), (2); words in second pair of square brackets substituted by virtue of SI 1992/1311, art 3(1), Sch 1, Part I.

Sub-s (6): word in square brackets substituted and words omitted repealed, by SI 2013/2352, art 7(1), Sch 1, paras 6, 9(1)–(3).

Sub-s (8): repealed by SI 2013/2352, art 7(1), Sch 1, paras 6, 9(1), (4).

Orders: the Public Lending Right Scheme 1982 (Commencement) Order 1982, SI 1982/719 at **[2.444]**.

[2.4]
4 The register

(1) The register shall be kept in such form, and contain such particulars of books and their authors, as may be prescribed.

(2) No application for an entry in the register is to be entertained in the case of any book unless it falls within a class, description or category of books prescribed as one in respect of which public lending right subsists.

(3) The scheme shall provide for the register to be conclusive both as to whether public lending right subsists in respect of a particular book and also as to the persons (if any) who are for the time being entitled to the right.

(4) Provision shall be included in the scheme for entries in the register to be made and amended, on application made in the prescribed manner and supported by prescribed particulars (verified as prescribed) so as to indicate, in the case of any book who (if any one) is for the time being entitled to public lending right in respect of it.

(5) The [Board] may direct the removal from the register of every entry relating to a book in whose case no sum has become due by way of public lending right for a period of at least 10 years, but without prejudice to a subsequent application for the entries to be restored to the register.

[(6) The Board may require the payment of fees, according to prescribed scales and rates, for supplying copies of entries in the register.

(6A) A copy of an entry in the register is, in all legal proceedings, admissible in evidence as of equal validity with the original if it is certified in writing by—

(a) a member of the Board,

(b) a person employed by, or contracted to provide services for, the Board with authority in that behalf (which authority it is unnecessary to prove).]

(7) It shall be an offence for any person, in connection with the entry of any matter whatsoever in the register, to make any statement which he knows to be false in a material particular or recklessly to make any statement which is false in a material particular; and a person who commits an offence under this section shall be liable on summary conviction to a fine of not more than [level 5 on the standard scale].

(8) Where an offence under subsection (7) above which has been committed by a body corporate is proved to have been committed with the consent or connivance of, or to be attributable to any neglect on the part of, a director, manager, secretary or other similar officer of the body corporate, or any person who was purporting to act in any such capacity, he (as well as the body corporate) shall be guilty of that offence and be liable to be proceeded against accordingly.

Where the affairs of a body corporate are managed by its members, this subsection applies in relation to the acts and defaults of a member in connection with his functions of management as if he were a director of the body corporate.

NOTES

Sub-s (5): word in square brackets substituted by the Public Bodies (Abolition of the Registrar of Public Lending Right) Order 2013, SI 2013/2352, art 7(1), Sch 1, paras 6, 10(1), (2).

Sub-ss (6), (6A): substituted for original sub-s (6), by SI 2013/2352, art 7(1), Sch 1, paras 6, 10(1), (3).

Sub-s (7): words in square brackets substituted by virtue of the Criminal Justice Act 1982, ss 37, 46.

[2.5]
5 Citation, etc

(1) This Act may be cited as the Public Lending Right Act 1979.

(2) In this Act any reference to "the scheme" is to the scheme prepared and brought into force by [the Secretary of State] in accordance with sections 1 and 3 of this Act (including the scheme as varied from time to time under section 3(7); and—

["author", in relation to a work recorded as a sound recording, includes a producer or narrator;

["the Board" means the British Library Board established under section 1(2) of the British Library Act 1972;]

"book" includes—

(a) a work recorded as a sound recording and consisting mainly of spoken words (an "audio-book"), and

(b) a work, other than an audio-book, recorded in electronic form and consisting mainly of (or of any combination of) written or spoken words or still pictures (an "e-book");

"lent out"—

(a) means made available to a member of the public for use away from library premises for a limited time, but

(b) does not include being communicated by means of electronic transmission to a place other than library premises,

and "loan" and "borrowed" are to be read accordingly;

"library premises" has the meaning given in section 8(7) of the Public Libraries and Museums Act 1964;]

"local library authority" means—

(a) a library authority under the Public Libraries and Museums Act 1964,

(b) a statutory library authority within the Public Libraries (Scotland) Act 1955, and

(c) an Education and Library Board within the Education and Libraries (Northern Ireland) Order 1972;

"prescribed" means prescribed by the scheme;

["producer" has the meaning given in section 178 of the Copyright, Designs and Patents Act 1988;]

"the register" means the register required by section 1(4) to be established and maintained by the [Board]; . . .

. . .

["sound recording" has the meaning given in section 5A(1) of the Copyright, Designs and Patents Act 1988].

(3) This Act comes into force on a day to be appointed by an order made by [the Secretary of State] in a statutory instrument to be laid before Parliament after it has been made.

(4) This Act extends to Northern Ireland.

NOTES

Sub-s (2) is amended as follows:

words in first pair of square brackets substituted by virtue of the Transfer of Functions (National Heritage) Order 1992, SI 1992/1311, art 3(1), Sch 1, Part I;

definition "the Board" inserted, word in square brackets in definition "the register" substituted and definition "the Registrar" (omitted) repealed by the Public Bodies (Abolition of the Registrar of Public Lending Right) Order 2013, SI 2013/2352, art 7(1), Sch 1, paras 6, 11;

definitions "author", "book", "lent out", "library premises", "producer" and "sound recording" inserted, and word omitted from definition "the register" repealed by the Digital Economy Act 2010, ss 43, 45, Sch 2;

definition "lent out" substituted by the Digital Economy Act 2017, s 31(1), as from a day to be appointed, as follows—

> ""lent out" means made available to a member of the public for use away from library premises for a limited time (including by being communicated by means of electronic transmission to a place other than library premises) and "loan" and "borrowed" are to be read accordingly;".

Sub-s (3): words in square brackets substituted by virtue of SI 1992/1311, art 3(1), Sch 1, Part I.

Orders: the Public Lending Right Act 1979 (Commencement) Order 1980, SI 1980/83.

SCHEDULE
[PUBLIC LENDING RIGHT: SUPPLEMENTARY PROVISION]

Section 1(3)

[2.6]

1–5 . . .

[**6** The Documentary Evidence Act 1868 shall have effect as if the Board were included in the first column of the Schedule to that Act, as if any person authorised to act on behalf of the Board were mentioned in the second column of that Schedule, and as if the regulations referred to in that Act included any documents issued by the Board, or by any such person, in relation to the Board's functions under this Act or the scheme.]

7 . . .

8 Anything authorised or required under this Act . . . , or by or under the scheme, to be done by the [Board] may be done by any [person] who is authorised generally or specially in that behalf in writing by the [Board].

NOTES

Schedule heading: substituted by the Public Bodies (Abolition of the Registrar of Public Lending Right) Order 2013, SI 2013/2352, art 7(1), Sch 1, paras 6, 12(1), (6).

Paras 1–5, 7: repealed by SI 2013/2352, art 7(1), Sch 1, paras 6, 12(1), (2), (4).

Para 6: substituted by SI 2013/2352, art 7(1), Sch 1, paras 6, 12(1), (3).

Para 8: words omitted repealed and words in square brackets substituted by SI 2013/2352, art 7(1), Sch 1, paras 6, 12(1), (5).

COPYRIGHT, DESIGNS AND PATENTS ACT 1988

(1988 c 48)

ARRANGEMENT OF SECTIONS

PART I
COPYRIGHT

CHAPTER I
SUBSISTENCE, OWNERSHIP AND DURATION OF COPYRIGHT

Introductory

Education

Libraries and archives

Orphan works

Public administration

Computer programs: lawful users

Databases: permitted acts

Designs

Typefaces

Works in electronic form

Miscellaneous: literary, dramatic, musical and artistic works

Miscellaneous: lending of works and playing of sound recordings

Duration of rights

Performers' property rights

Non-property rights

Delivery up or seizure of illicit recordings

Offences

Supplementary provisions with respect to delivery up and seizure

Licensing of performers' rights

Jurisdiction of Copyright Tribunal

CHAPTER 3
MORAL RIGHTS

Right to be identified as performer

Right to object to derogatory treatment

Supplementary

CHAPTER 4
QUALIFICATION FOR PROTECTION, EXTENT AND INTERPRETATION

Qualification for protection and extent

Interpretation

Supplementary

PART III
DESIGN RIGHT

CHAPTER I
DESIGN RIGHT IN ORIGINAL DESIGNS

Introductory

Qualification for design right protection

Dealings with design right

CHAPTER II
RIGHTS OF DESIGN RIGHT OWNER AND REMEDIES

Infringement of design right

Remedies for infringement

CHAPTER III
EXCEPTIONS TO RIGHTS OF DESIGN RIGHT OWNERS

Infringement of copyright

An Act to restate the law of copyright, with amendments; to make fresh provision as to the rights of performers and others in performances; to confer a design right in original designs; to amend the Registered Designs Act 1949; to make provision with respect to patent agents and trade mark agents; to confer patents and designs jurisdiction on certain county courts; to amend the law of patents; to make provision with respect to devices designed to circumvent copy-protection of works in electronic form; to make fresh provision penalising the fraudulent reception of transmissions; to make the fraudulent application or use of a trade mark an offence; to make provision for the benefit of the Hospital for Sick Children, Great Ormond Street, London; to enable financial assistance to be given to certain international bodies; and for connected purposes

[15 November 1988]

NOTES

Modification: this Act is modified in its application to the Isle of Man, by the Registered Designs (Isle of Man) Order 2013, SI 2013/2533, art 3(2), Sch 2.

References to trade marks or registered trade marks within the meaning of the Trade Marks Act 1938 shall, unless the context otherwise requires, be construed as references to trade marks or registered trademarks within the meaning of the Trade Marks Act 1994; see the Trade Marks Act 1994, s 106(1), Sch 4, para 1.

Application: as to the application of this Act to works originating from other countries and performances connected with certain countries, see the Copyright and Performances (Application to Other Countries) Order 2016, SI 2016/1219 at **[2.730]**.

PART I
COPYRIGHT

NOTES

Transitional provisions: for transitional provisions and savings relating to works made, and acts or events occurring, before the commencement of this Act; see s 170 and Sch 1, at **[2.226]** and **[2.409]**.

CHAPTER I
SUBSISTENCE, OWNERSHIP AND DURATION OF COPYRIGHT

Introductory

[2.7]
1 Copyright and copyright works

(1) Copyright is a property right which subsists in accordance with this Part in the following descriptions of work—
- (a) original literary, dramatic, musical or artistic works,
- (b) sound recordings, films [or broadcasts], and
- (c) the typographical arrangement of published editions.

(2) In this Part "copyright work" means a work of any of those descriptions in which copyright subsists.

(3) Copyright does not subsist in a work unless the requirements of this Part with respect to qualification for copyright protection are met (see section 153 and the provisions referred to there).

NOTES

Sub-s (1): words in square brackets in para (b) substituted by the Copyright and Related Rights Regulations 2003, SI 2003/2498, regs 3, 5(2), subject to transitional provisions as noted below.

Transitional provisions: the Copyright and Related Rights Regulations 2003, SI 2003/2498 came into force on 31 October 2003 and, except as expressly provided, apply to: (i) works made, (ii) performances given, (iii) databases in which database right vests which are made, and (iv) works in which publication right vests which are first published, before or after that date (see reg 31 of the 2003 Regulations, at **[2.550]**). Savings and transitional provisions are provided for in regs 32–40 of those Regulations, at **[2.551]–[2.559]**.

[2.8]
2 Rights subsisting in copyright works

(1) The owner of the copyright in a work of any description has the exclusive right to do the acts specified in Chapter II as the acts restricted by the copyright in a work of that description.

(2) In relation to certain descriptions of copyright work the following rights conferred by Chapter IV (moral rights) subsist in favour of the author, director or commissioner of the work, whether or not he is the owner of the copyright—

(a) section 77 (right to be identified as author or director),
(b) section 80 (right to object to derogatory treatment of work), and
(c) section 85 (right to privacy of certain photographs and films).

Descriptions of work and related provisions

[2.9]

3 Literary, dramatic and musical works

(1) In this Part—

"literary work" means any work, other than a dramatic or musical work, which is written, spoken or sung, and accordingly includes—

(a) a table or compilation [other than a database], . . .
(b) a computer program[, . . .
(c) preparatory design material for a computer program] [and;
(d) a database;]

"dramatic work" includes a work of dance or mime; and

"musical work" means a work consisting of music, exclusive of any words or action intended to be sung, spoken or performed with the music.

(2) Copyright does not subsist in a literary, dramatic or musical work unless and until it is recorded, in writing or otherwise; and references in this Part to the time at which such a work is made are to the time at which it is so recorded.

(3) It is immaterial for the purposes of subsection (2) whether the work is recorded by or with the permission of the author; and where it is not recorded by the author, nothing in that subsection affects the question whether copyright subsists in the record as distinct from the work recorded.

NOTES

Sub-s (1): words in square brackets in para (a) inserted, word omitted from para (b) repealed and para (d) added, by the Copyright and Rights in Databases Regulations 1997, SI 1997/3032, reg 5, subject to savings and transitional provisions specified in regs 26–30 of those Regulations, at **[2.541]–[2.545]**; word omitted from para (a) repealed, and para (c) and word immediately preceding it inserted, by the Copyright (Computer Programs) Regulations 1992, SI 1992/3233, regs 2, 3, subject to reg 12(2) of those Regulations (agreements entered into before 1 January 1993 to remain unaffected).

[2.10]

[3A Databases

(1) In this Part "database" means a collection of independent works, data or other materials which—

(a) are arranged in a systematic or methodical way, and
(b) are individually accessible by electronic or other means.

(2) For the purposes of this Part a literary work consisting of a database is original if, and only if, by reason of the selection or arrangement of the contents of the database the database constitutes the author's own intellectual creation.]

NOTES

Inserted by the Copyright and Rights in Databases Regulations 1997, SI 1997/3032, reg 6, subject to savings and transitional provisions specified in regs 26–30 of those Regulations, at **[2.541]–[2.545]**.

[2.11]

4 Artistic works

(1) In this Part "artistic work" means—

(a) a graphic work, photograph, sculpture or collage, irrespective of artistic quality,
(b) a work of architecture being a building or a model for a building, or
(c) a work of artistic craftsmanship.

(2) In this Part—

"building" includes any fixed structure, and a part of a building or fixed structure;

"graphic work" includes—

(a) any painting, drawing, diagram, map, chart or plan, and
(b) any engraving, etching, lithograph, woodcut or similar work;

"photograph" means a recording of light or other radiation on any medium on which an image is produced or from which an image may by any means be produced, and which is not part of a film;

"sculpture" includes a cast or model made for purposes of sculpture.

[2.12]

[5A Sound recordings

(1) In this Part "sound recording" means—

(a) a recording of sounds, from which the sounds may be reproduced, or
(b) a recording of the whole or any part of a literary, dramatic or musical work, from which sounds reproducing the work or part may be produced,

regardless of the medium on which the recording is made or the method by which the sounds are reproduced or produced.

(2) Copyright does not subsist in a sound recording which is, or to the extent that it is, a copy taken from a previous sound recording.]

NOTES

Substituted, together with s 5B, for original s 5, by the Duration of Copyright and Rights in Performances Regulations 1995, SI 1995/3297, regs 4, 9(1), subject to transitional provisions and savings specified in regs 12–34 of those Regulations, at **[2.478]–[2.499]**.

[2.13]

[5B Films

(1) In this Part "film" means a recording on any medium from which a moving image may by any means be produced.

(2) The sound track accompanying a film shall be treated as part of the film for the purposes of this Part.

(3) Without prejudice to the generality of subsection (2), where that subsection applies—

(a) references in this Part to showing a film include playing the film sound track to accompany the film, . . .

[(b) references in this Part to playing a sound recording, or to communicating a sound recording to the public, do not include playing or communicating the film sound track to accompany the film,

(c) references in this Part to copying a work, so far as they apply to a sound recording, do not include copying the film sound track to accompany the film, and

(d) references in this Part to the issuing, rental or lending of copies of a work, so far as they apply to a sound recording, do not include the issuing, rental or lending of copies of the sound track to accompany the film.]

(4) Copyright does not subsist in a film which is, or to the extent that it is, a copy taken from a previous film.

(5) Nothing in this section affects any copyright subsisting in a film sound track as a sound recording.]

NOTES

Substituted as noted to s 5A at **[2.12]**.

Sub-s (3): word omitted from para (a) repealed, and paras (b)–(d) substituted for original para (b), by the Performances (Moral Rights, etc) Regulations 2006, SI 2006/18, reg 2, Schedule, paras 1, 2.

[2.14]

6 Broadcasts

[(1) In this Part a "broadcast" means an electronic transmission of visual images, sounds or other information which—

(a) is transmitted for simultaneous reception by members of the public and is capable of being lawfully received by them, or

(b) is transmitted at a time determined solely by the person making the transmission for presentation to members of the public,

and which is not excepted by subsection (1A); and references to broadcasting shall be construed accordingly.

(1A) Excepted from the definition of "broadcast" is any internet transmission unless it is—

(a) a transmission taking place simultaneously on the internet and by other means,

(b) a concurrent transmission of a live event, or

(c) a transmission of recorded moving images or sounds forming part of a programme service offered by the person responsible for making the transmission, being a service in which programmes are transmitted at scheduled times determined by that person.]

(2) An encrypted transmission shall be regarded as capable of being lawfully received by members of the public only if decoding equipment has been made available to members of the public by or with the authority of the person making the transmission or the person providing the contents of the transmission.

(3) References in this Part to the person making a broadcast [or a transmission which is a broadcast] are—

(a) to the person transmitting the programme, if he has responsibility to any extent for its contents, and

(b) to any person providing the programme who makes with the person transmitting it the arrangements necessary for its transmission;

and references in this Part to a programme, in the context of broadcasting, are to any item included in a broadcast.

[(4) For the purposes of this Part, the place from which a [wireless] broadcast is made is the place where, under the control and responsibility of the person making the broadcast, the programme-carrying signals are introduced into an uninterrupted chain of communication (including, in the case of a satellite transmission, the chain leading to the satellite and down towards the earth).]

[(4A) Subsections (3) and (4) have effect subject to section 6A (safeguards in case of certain satellite broadcasts).]

(5) References in this Part to the reception of a broadcast include reception of a broadcast relayed by means of a telecommunications system.
[(5A) The relaying of a broadcast by reception and immediate re-transmission shall be regarded for the purposes of this Part as a separate act of broadcasting from the making of the broadcast which is so re-transmitted.]
(6) Copyright does not subsist in a broadcast which infringes, or to the extent that it infringes, the copyright in another broadcast . . .

NOTES

Sub-ss (1), (1A): substituted, for original sub-s (1), by the Copyright and Related Rights Regulations 2003, SI 2003/2498, regs 3, 4(a), subject to transitional provisions as noted to s 1 of this Act at **[2.7]**.

Sub-s (3): words in square brackets substituted by SI 2003/2498, regs 3, 4(b), subject to transitional provisions as noted to s 1 of this Act at **[2.7]**.

Sub-s (4): substituted by the Copyright and Related Rights Regulations 1996, SI 1996/2967, regs 4, 5, subject to transitional provisions and savings specified in regs 25–36 of those Regulations, at **[2.510]–[2.521]**; word in square brackets inserted by SI 2003/2498, regs 3, 4(c), subject to transitional provisions as noted to s 1 of this Act at **[2.7]**.

Sub-s (4A): inserted by SI 1996/2967, regs 4, 6(1), subject to transitional provisions and savings specified in regs 25–36 of those Regulations, at **[2.510]–[2.521]**.

Sub-s (5A): inserted by SI 2003/2498, regs 3, 4(d), subject to transitional provisions as noted to s 1 of this Act at **[2.7]**.

Sub-s (6): words omitted repealed by SI 2003/2498, reg 2(2), Sch 2, subject to transitional provisions as noted as noted to s 1 of this Act at **[2.7]**.

[2.15]
[6A Safeguards in relation to certain satellite broadcasts
(1) This section applies where the place from which a broadcast by way of satellite transmission is made is located in a country other than an EEA State and the law of that country fails to provide at least the following level of protection—
- (a) exclusive rights in relation to [wireless] broadcasting equivalent to those conferred by section 20 ([infringement by communication to the public]) on the authors of literary, dramatic, musical and artistic works, films and broadcasts;
- (b) a right in relation to live [wireless] broadcasting equivalent to that conferred on a performer by section 182(1)(b) (consent required for live broadcast of performance); and
- (c) a right for authors of sound recordings and performers to share in a single equitable remuneration in respect of the [wireless] broadcasting of sound recordings.

(2) Where the place from which the programme-carrying signals are transmitted to the satellite ("the uplink station") is located in an EEA State—
- (a) that place shall be treated as the place from which the broadcast is made, and
- (b) the person operating the uplink station shall be treated as the person making the broadcast.

(3) Where the uplink station is not located in an EEA State but a person who is established in an EEA State has commissioned the making of the broadcast—
- (a) that person shall be treated as the person making the broadcast, and
- (b) the place in which he has his principal establishment in the European Economic Area shall be treated as the place from which the broadcast is made.]

NOTES

Inserted by the Copyright and Related Rights Regulations 1996, SI 1996/2967, regs 4, 6(2), subject to transitional provisions and savings specified in regs 25–36 of those Regulations, at **[2.510]–[2.521]**.

Sub-s (1): words in second pair of square brackets in para (a) substituted, and other words in square brackets inserted, by the Copyright and Related Rights Regulations 2003, SI 2003/2498, regs 3, 5(3), subject to transitional provisions as noted to s 1 of this Act at **[2.7]**.

7 (*Repealed by the Copyright and Related Rights Regulations 2003, SI 2003/2498, regs 3, 5(1), subject to transitional provisions in regs 31–40 thereof at* **[2.551]–[2.559]**.)

[2.16]
8 Published editions
(1) In this Part "published edition", in the context of copyright in the typographical arrangement of a published edition, means a published edition of the whole or any part of one or more literary, dramatic or musical works.
(2) Copyright does not subsist in the typographical arrangement of a published edition if, or to the extent that, it reproduces the typographical arrangement of a previous edition.

Authorship and ownership of copyright

[2.17]
9 Authorship of work
(1) In this Part "author", in relation to a work, means the person who creates it.
(2) That person shall be taken to be—
- [(aa) in the case of a sound recording, the producer;
- (ab) in the case of a film, the producer and the principal director;]

(b) in the case of a broadcast, the person making the broadcast (see section 6(3)) or, in the case of a broadcast which relays another broadcast by reception and immediate re-transmission, the person making that other broadcast;

(c) . . .

(d) in the case of the typographical arrangement of a published edition, the publisher.

(3) In the case of a literary, dramatic, musical or artistic work which is computer-generated, the author shall be taken to be the person by whom the arrangements necessary for the creation of the work are undertaken.

(4) For the purposes of this Part a work is of "unknown authorship" if the identity of the author is unknown or, in the case of a work of joint authorship, if the identity of none of the authors is known.

(5) For the purposes of this Part the identity of an author shall be regarded as unknown if it is not possible for a person to ascertain his identity by reasonable inquiry; but if his identity is once known it shall not subsequently be regarded as unknown.

NOTES

Sub-s (2): paras (aa), (ab) substituted, for original para (a), by the Copyright and Related Rights Regulations 1996, SI 1996/2967, regs 4, 18(1), subject to transitional provisions and savings specified in regs 25–36 of those Regulations, at **[2.510]–[2.521]**; para (c) repealed by the Copyright and Related Rights Regulations 2003, SI 2003/2498, regs 2(2), 3, 5(4), Sch 2, subject to transitional provisions as noted to s 1 of this Act at **[2.7]**.

[2.18]

10 Works of joint authorship

(1) In this Part a "work of joint authorship" means a work produced by the collaboration of two or more authors in which the contribution of each author is not distinct from that of the other author or authors.

[(1A) A film shall be treated as a work of joint authorship unless the producer and the principal director are the same person.]

(2) A broadcast shall be treated as a work of joint authorship in any case where more than one person is to be taken as making the broadcast (see section 6(3)).

(3) References in this Part to the author of a work shall, except as otherwise provided, be construed in relation to a work of joint authorship as references to all the authors of the work.

NOTES

Sub-s (1A): inserted by the Copyright and Related Rights Regulations 1996, SI 1996/2967, regs 4, 18(2), subject to transitional provisions and savings specified in regs 25–36 of those Regulations, at **[2.510]–[2.521]**.

[2.19]

[10A Works of co-authorship

(1) In this Part a "work of co-authorship" means a work produced by the collaboration of the author of a musical work and the author of a literary work where the two works are created in order to be used together.

(2) References in this Part to a work or the author of a work shall, except as otherwise provided, be construed in relation to a work of co-authorship as references to each of the separate musical and literary works comprised in the work of co-authorship and to each of the authors of such works.]

NOTES

Commencement: 1 November 2013.

Inserted by the Copyright and Duration of Rights in Performances Regulations 2013, SI 2013/1782, regs 3, 4, subject to savings and transitional provisions in regs 11–26 of those Regulations at **[2.665]–[2.680]**.

[2.20]

11 First ownership of copyright

(1) The author of a work is the first owner of any copyright in it, subject to the following provisions.

(2) Where a literary, dramatic, musical or artistic work[, or a film,] is made by an employee in the course of his employment, his employer is the first owner of any copyright in the work subject to any agreement to the contrary.

(3) This section does not apply to Crown copyright or Parliamentary copyright (see sections 163 and 165) or to copyright which subsists by virtue of section 168 (copyright of certain international organisations).

NOTES

Sub-s (2): words in square brackets inserted by the Copyright and Related Rights Regulations 1996, SI 1996/2967, regs 4, 18(3), subject to transitional provisions and savings specified in regs 25–36 of those Regulations, at **[2.510]–[2.521]**.

Duration of copyright

[2.21]

[12 Duration of copyright in literary, dramatic, musical or artistic works

(1) The following provisions have effect with respect to the duration of copyright in a literary, dramatic, musical or artistic work.

(2) Copyright expires at the end of the period of 70 years from the end of the calendar year in which the author dies, subject as follows.

(3) If the work is of unknown authorship, copyright expires—

(a) at the end of the period of 70 years from the end of the calendar year in which the work was made, or

(b) if during that period the work is made available to the public, at the end of the period of 70 years from the end of the calendar year in which it is first so made available,

subject as follows.

(4) Subsection (2) applies if the identity of the author becomes known before the end of the period specified in paragraph (a) or (b) of subsection (3).

(5) For the purposes of subsection (3) making available to the public includes—

(a) in the case of a literary, dramatic or musical work—

(i) performance in public, or

[(ii) communication to the public;]

(b) in the case of an artistic work—

(i) exhibition in public,

(ii) a film including the work being shown in public, or

[(iii) communication to the public;]

but in determining generally for the purposes of that subsection whether a work has been made available to the public no account shall be taken of any unauthorised act.

(6) Where the country of origin of the work is not an EEA state and the author of the work is not a national of an EEA state, the duration of copyright is that to which the work is entitled in the country of origin, provided that does not exceed the period which would apply under subsections (2) to (5).

(7) If the work is computer-generated the above provisions do not apply and copyright expires at the end of the period of 50 years from the end of the calendar year in which the work was made.

(8) The provisions of this section are adapted as follows in relation to a work of joint authorship [or a work of co–authorship]—

(a) the reference in subsection (2) to the death of the author shall be construed—

(i) if the identity of all the authors is known, as a reference to the death of the last of them to die, and

(ii) if the identity of one or more of the authors is known and the identity of one or more others is not, as a reference to the death of the last whose identity is known;

(b) the reference in subsection (4) to the identity of the author becoming known shall be construed as a reference to the identity of any of the authors becoming known;

(c) the reference in subsection (6) to the author not being a national of an EEA state shall be construed as a reference to none of the authors being a national of an EEA state.

(9) This section does not apply to Crown copyright or Parliamentary copyright (see sections 163 to [166D]) or to copyright which subsists by virtue of section 168 (copyright of certain international organisations).]

NOTES

Substituted by the Duration of Copyright and Rights in Performances Regulations 1995, SI 1995/3297, regs 4, 5(1), subject to transitional provisions and savings specified in regs 12–34 of those Regulations, at **[2.478]–[2.499]**.

Sub-s (5): sub-paras (a)(ii) and (b)(iii) substituted by the Copyright and Related Rights Regulations 2003, SI 2003/2498, reg 2(1), Sch 1, Pt 1, paras 1, 4(1), subject to transitional provisions as noted to s 1 of this Act at **[2.7]**.

Sub-s (8): words in square brackets inserted by the Copyright and Duration of Rights in Performances Regulations 2013, SI 2013/1782, regs 3, 5, subject to savings and transitional provisions in regs 11–26 of those Regulations at **[2.665]–[2.680]**.

Sub-s (9): reference in square brackets substituted by the Government of Wales Act 2006, s 160(1), Sch 10, paras 22, 23.

[2.22]

[13A Duration of copyright in sound recordings

(1) The following provisions have effect with respect to the duration of copyright in a sound recording.

[(2) Subject to subsections (4) and (5) [and section 191HA(4)], copyright expires—

(a) at the end of the period of 50 years from the end of the calendar year in which the recording is made, or

(b) if during that period the recording is published, [70] years from the end of the calendar year in which it is first published, or

(c) if during that period the recording is not published but is made available to the public by being played in public or communicated to the public, [70] years from the end of the calendar year in which it is first so made available,

but in determining whether a sound recording has been published, played in public or communicated to the public, no account shall be taken of any unauthorised act.]

(3) . . .
(4) Where the author of a sound recording is not a national of an EEA state, the duration of copyright is that to which the sound recording is entitled in the country of which the author is a national, provided that does not exceed the period which would apply under [subsection (2)].
(5) If or to the extent that the application of subsection (4) would be at variance with an international obligation to which the United Kingdom became subject prior to 29th October 1993, the duration of copyright shall be as specified in [subsection (2)].]

NOTES

Substituted, together with s 13B for original s 13, by the Duration of Copyright and Rights in Performances Regulations 1995, SI 1995/3297, regs 4, 6(1), subject to transitional provisions and savings specified in regs 12–34 of those Regulations, at **[2.478]–[2.499]**.

Sub-s (2): substituted by the Copyright and Related Rights Regulations 2003, SI 2003/2498, regs 3, 29(a), subject to transitional provisions as noted to s 1 of this Act at **[2.7]**; words in first pair of square brackets inserted and figure in square brackets in paras (b) and (c) substituted, by the Copyright and Duration of Rights in Performances Regulations 2013, SI 2013/1782, regs 3, 6, subject to savings and transitional provisions in regs 11–26 of those Regulations at **[2.665]–[2.680]**.

Sub-s (3): repealed by SI 2003/2498, regs 2(2), 3, 29(b), Sch 2, subject to transitional provisions as noted to s 1 of this Act at **[2.7]**.

Sub-ss (4), (5): words in square brackets substituted by SI 2003/2498, regs 3, 29(c), subject to transitional provisions as noted to s 1 of this Act at **[2.7]**.

[2.23]
[13B Duration of copyright in films

(1) The following provisions have effect with respect to the duration of copyright in a film.
(2) Copyright expires at the end of the period of 70 years from the end of the calendar year in which the death occurs of the last to die of the following persons—
(a) the principal director,
(b) the author of the screenplay,
(c) the author of the dialogue, or
(d) the composer of music specially created for and used in the film;
subject as follows.
(3) If the identity of one or more of the persons referred to in subsection (2)(a) to (d) is known and the identity of one or more others is not, the reference in that subsection to the death of the last of them to die shall be construed as a reference to the death of the last whose identity is known.
(4) If the identity of the persons referred to in subsection (2)(a) to (d) is unknown, copyright expires at—
(a) the end of the period of 70 years from the end of the calendar year in which the film was made, or
(b) if during that period the film is made available to the public, at the end of the period of 70 years from the end of the calendar year in which it is first so made available.
(5) Subsections (2) and (3) apply if the identity of any of those persons becomes known before the end of the period specified in paragraph (a) or (b) of subsection (4).
(6) For the purposes of subsection (4) making available to the public includes—
(a) showing in public, or
[(b) communicating to the public;]
but in determining generally for the purposes of that subsection whether a film has been made available to the public no account shall be taken of any unauthorised act.
(7) Where the country of origin is not an EEA state and the author of the film is not a national of an EEA state, the duration of copyright is that to which the work is entitled in the country of origin, provided that does not exceed the period which would apply under subsections (2) to (6).
(8) In relation to a film of which there are joint authors, the reference in subsection (7) to the author not being a national of an EEA state shall be construed as a reference to none of the authors being a national of an EEA state.
(9) If in any case there is no person falling within paragraphs (a) to (d) of subsection (2), the above provisions do not apply and copyright expires at the end of the period of 50 years from the end of the calendar year in which the film was made.
(10) For the purposes of this section the identity of any of the persons referred to in subsection (2)(a) to (d) shall be regarded as unknown if it is not possible for a person to ascertain his identity by reasonable inquiry; but if the identity of any such person is once known it shall not subsequently be regarded as unknown.]

NOTES

Substituted as noted to s 13A at **[2.22]**.

Sub-s (6): para (b) substituted by the Copyright and Related Rights Regulations 2003, SI 2003/2498, reg 2(1), Sch 1, Pt 1, paras 1, 4(3), subject to transitional provisions as noted to s 1 of this Act at **[2.7]**.

[2.24]
[14 Duration of copyright in broadcasts . . .

(1) The following provisions have effect with respect to the duration of copyright in a broadcast . . .

(2) Copyright in a broadcast . . . expires at the end of the period of 50 years from the end of the calendar year in which the broadcast was made . . ., subject as follows.
(3) Where the author of the broadcast . . . is not a national of an EEA state, the duration of copyright in the broadcast . . . is that to which it is entitled in the country of which the author is a national, provided that does not exceed the period which would apply under subsection (2).
(4) If or to the extent that the application of subsection (3) would be at variance with an international obligation to which the United Kingdom became subject prior to 29th October 1993, the duration of copyright shall be as specified in subsection (2).
(5) Copyright in a repeat broadcast . . . expires at the same time as the copyright in the original broadcast . . . ; and accordingly no copyright arises in respect of a repeat broadcast . . . which is broadcast . . . after the expiry of the copyright in the original broadcast . . .
(6) A repeat broadcast . . . means one which is a repeat . . . of a broadcast previously made . . .]

NOTES

Substituted by the Duration of Copyright and Rights in Performances Regulations 1995, SI 1995/3297, regs 4, 7(1), subject to transitional provisions and savings specified in regs 12–34 of those Regulations, at **[2.478]–[2.499]**.

Section heading, sub-ss (1), (3), (5), (6): words omitted repealed by the Copyright and Related Rights Regulations 2003, SI 2003/2498, reg 2(2), Sch 2, subject to transitional provisions as noted to s 1 of this Act at **[2.7]**.

[2.25]
15 Duration of copyright in typographical arrangement of published editions
Copyright in the typographical arrangement of a published edition expires at the end of the period of 25 years from the end of the calendar year in which the edition was first published.

[2.26]
[15A Meaning of country of origin
(1) For the purposes of the provisions of this Part relating to the duration of copyright the country of origin of a work shall be determined as follows.
(2) If the work is first published in a Berne Convention country and is not simultaneously published elsewhere, the country of origin is that country.
(3) If the work is first published simultaneously in two or more countries only one of which is a Berne Convention country, the country of origin is that country.
(4) If the work is first published simultaneously in two or more countries of which two or more are Berne Convention countries, then—
(a) if any of those countries is an EEA state, the country of origin is that country; and
(b) if none of those countries is an EEA state, the country of origin is the Berne Convention country which grants the shorter or shortest period of copyright protection.
(5) If the work is unpublished or is first published in a country which is not a Berne Convention country (and is not simultaneously published in a Berne Convention country), the country of origin is—
(a) if the work is a film and the maker of the film has his headquarters in, or is domiciled or resident in a Berne Convention country, that country;
(b) if the work is—
(i) a work of architecture constructed in a Berne Convention country, or
(ii) an artistic work incorporated in a building or other structure situated in a Berne Convention country,
that country;
(c) in any other case, the country of which the author of the work is a national.
(6) In this section—
(a) a "Berne Convention country" means a country which is a party to any Act of the International Convention for the Protection of Literary and Artistic Works signed at Berne on 9th September 1886; and
(b) references to simultaneous publication are to publication within 30 days of first publication.]

NOTES

Inserted by the Duration of Copyright and Rights in Performances Regulations 1995, SI 1995/3297, regs 4, 8(1), subject to transitional provisions and savings specified in regs 12–34 of those Regulations, at **[2.478]–[2.499]**.

CHAPTER II
RIGHTS OF COPYRIGHT OWNER

The acts restricted by copyright

[2.27]
16 The acts restricted by copyright in a work
(1) The owner of the copyright in a work has, in accordance with the following provisions of this Chapter, the exclusive right to do the following acts in the United Kingdom—
(a) to copy the work (see section 17);
(b) to issue copies of the work to the public (see section 18);

[(ba) to rent or lend the work to the public (see section 18A);]
(c) to perform, show or play the work in public (see section 19);
[(d) to communicate the work to the public (see section 20);]
(e) to make an adaptation of the work or do any of the above in relation to an adaptation (see section 21);

and those acts are referred to in this Part as the "acts restricted by the copyright".

(2) Copyright in a work is infringed by a person who without the licence of the copyright owner does, or authorises another to do, any of the acts restricted by the copyright.

(3) References in this Part to the doing of an act restricted by the copyright in a work are to the doing of it—
(a) in relation to the work as a whole or any substantial part of it, and
(b) either directly or indirectly;

and it is immaterial whether any intervening acts themselves infringe copyright.

(4) This Chapter has effect subject to—
(a) the provisions of Chapter III (acts permitted in relation to copyright works), and
(b) the provisions of Chapter VII (provisions with respect to copyright licensing).

NOTES

Sub-s (1): para (ba) inserted by the Copyright and Related Rights Regulations 1996, SI 1996/2967, regs 4, 10(1), subject to transitional provisions and savings specified in regs 25–36 of those Regulations, at **[2.510]–[2.521]**; para (d) substituted by the Copyright and Related Rights Regulations 2003, SI 2003/2498, regs 3, 6(2), subject to transitional provisions as noted to s 1 of this Act at **[2.7]**.

[2.28]

17 Infringement of copyright by copying

(1) The copying of the work is an act restricted by the copyright in every description of copyright work; and references in this Part to copying and copies shall be construed as follows.

(2) Copying in relation to a literary, dramatic, musical or artistic work means reproducing the work in any material form.

This includes storing the work in any medium by electronic means.

(3) In relation to an artistic work copying includes the making of a copy in three dimensions of a two-dimensional work and the making of a copy in two dimensions of a three-dimensional work.

(4) Copying in relation to a film [or broadcast] includes making a photograph of the whole or any substantial part of any image forming part of the film [or broadcast].

(5) Copying in relation to the typographical arrangement of a published edition means making a facsimile copy of the arrangement.

(6) Copying in relation to any description of work includes the making of copies which are transient or are incidental to some other use of the work.

NOTES

Sub-s (4): words in square brackets substituted by the Copyright and Related Rights Regulations 2003, SI 2003/2498, regs 2(1), 3, 5(5), Sch 1, Pt 1, paras 1, 3(a), subject to transitional provisions as noted to s 1 of this Act at **[2.7]**.

[2.29]

18 Infringement by issue of copies to the public

(1) The issue to the public of copies of the work is an act restricted by the copyright in every description of copyright work.

[(2) References in this Part to the issue to the public of copies of a work are to—
(a) the act of putting into circulation in the EEA copies not previously put into circulation in the EEA by or with the consent of the copyright owner, or
(b) the act of putting into circulation outside the EEA copies not previously put into circulation in the EEA or elsewhere.]

[(3) References in this Part to the issue to the public of copies of a work do not include—
(a) any subsequent distribution, sale, hiring or loan of copies previously put into circulation (but see section 18A: infringement by rental or lending), or
(b) any subsequent importation of such copies into the United Kingdom or another EEA state,

except so far as paragraph (a) of subsection (2) applies to putting into circulation in the EEA copies previously put into circulation outside the EEA.]

[(4) References in this Part to the issue of copies of a work include the issue of the original.]

NOTES

Sub-s (2): substituted by the Copyright and Related Rights Regulations 1996, SI 1996/2967, regs 4, 9(2), subject to transitional provisions and savings specified in regs 25–36 of those Regulations, at **[2.510]–[2.521]**.

Sub-s (3): added by the Copyright (Computer Programs) Regulations 1992, SI 1992/3233, reg 4(2); substituted by SI 1996/2967, regs 4, 9(2), subject to transitional provisions and savings specified in regs 25–36 of those Regulations, at **[2.510]–[2.521]**.

Sub-s (4): added by SI 1996/2967, regs 4, 9(3), subject to transitional provisions and savings specified in regs 25–36 of those Regulations, at **[2.510]–[2.521]**.

[2.30]

[18A Infringement by rental or lending of work to the public

(1) The rental or lending of copies of the work to the public is an act restricted by the copyright in—

(a) a literary, dramatic or musical work,

(b) an artistic work, other than—

(i) a work of architecture in the form of a building or a model for a building, or

(ii) a work of applied art, or

(c) a film or a sound recording.

(2) In this Part, subject to the following provisions of this section—

(a) "rental" means making a copy of the work available for use, on terms that it will or may be returned, for direct or indirect economic or commercial advantage, and

(b) "lending" means making a copy of the work available for use, on terms that it will or may be returned, otherwise than for direct or indirect economic or commercial advantage, through an establishment which is accessible to the public.

(3) The expressions "rental" and "lending" do not include—

(a) making available for the purpose of public performance, playing or showing in public, [or communication to the public];

(b) making available for the purpose of exhibition in public; or

(c) making available for on-the-spot reference use.

(4) The expression "lending" does not include making available between establishments which are accessible to the public.

(5) Where lending by an establishment accessible to the public gives rise to a payment the amount of which does not go beyond what is necessary to cover the operating costs of the establishment, there is no direct or indirect economic or commercial advantage for the purposes of this section.

(6) References in this Part to the rental or lending of copies of a work include the rental or lending of the original.]

NOTES

Inserted by the Copyright and Related Rights Regulations 1996, SI 1996/2967, regs 4, 10(2), subject to transitional provisions and savings specified in regs 25–36 of those Regulations, at **[2.510]–[2.521]**.

Sub-s (3): words in square brackets in para (a) substituted by the Copyright and Related Rights Regulations 2003, SI 2003/2498, reg 2(1), Sch 1, Pt 1, paras 1, 6(2)(a), subject to transitional provisions as noted to s 1 of this Act at **[2.7]**.

[2.31]

19 Infringement by performance, showing or playing of work in public

(1) The performance of the work in public is an act restricted by the copyright in a literary, dramatic or musical work.

(2) In this Part "performance", in relation to a work—

(a) includes delivery in the case of lectures, addresses, speeches and sermons, and

(b) in general, includes any mode of visual or acoustic presentation, including presentation by means of a sound recording, film [or broadcast] of the work.

(3) The playing or showing of the work in public is an act restricted by the copyright in a sound recording, film [or broadcast].

(4) Where copyright in a work is infringed by its being performed, played or shown in public by means of apparatus for receiving visual images or sounds conveyed by electronic means, the person by whom the visual images or sounds are sent, and in the case of a performance the performers, shall not be regarded as responsible for the infringement.

NOTES

Sub-ss (2), (3): words in square brackets in both places they appear substituted by the Copyright and Related Rights Regulations 2003, SI 2003/2498, reg 2(1), Sch 1, Pt 1, paras 1, 3(1)(b), (c), subject to transitional provisions as noted to s 1 of this Act at **[2.7]**.

[2.32]

[20 Infringement by communication to the public

(1) The communication to the public of the work is an act restricted by the copyright in—

(a) a literary, dramatic, musical or artistic work,

(b) a sound recording or film, or

(c) a broadcast.

(2) References in this Part to communication to the public are to communication to the public by electronic transmission, and in relation to a work include—

(a) the broadcasting of the work;

(b) the making available to the public of the work by electronic transmission in such a way that members of the public may access it from a place and at a time individually chosen by them.]

NOTES

Substituted by the Copyright and Related Rights Regulations 2003, SI 2003/2498, regs 3, 6(1), subject to transitional provisions as noted to s 1 of this Act at **[2.7]**.

[2.33]

21 Infringement by making adaptation or act done in relation to adaptation

(1) The making of an adaptation of the work is an act restricted by the copyright in a literary, dramatic or musical work.

For this purpose an adaptation is made when it is recorded, in writing or otherwise.

(2) The doing of any of the acts specified in sections 17 to 20, or subsection (1) above, in relation to an adaptation of the work is also an act restricted by the copyright in a literary, dramatic or musical work.

For this purpose it is immaterial whether the adaptation has been recorded, in writing or otherwise, at the time the act is done.

(3) In this Part "adaptation"—

(a) in relation to a literary [work,] [other than a computer program or a database, or in relation to a] dramatic work, means—

(i) a translation of the work;

(ii) a version of a dramatic work in which it is converted into a non-dramatic work or, as the case may be, of a non-dramatic work in which it is converted into a dramatic work;

(iii) a version of the work in which the story or action is conveyed wholly or mainly by means of pictures in a form suitable for reproduction in a book, or in a newspaper, magazine or similar periodical;

[(ab) in relation to a computer program, means an arrangement or altered version of the program or a translation of it;]

[(ac) in relation to a database, means an arrangement or altered version of the database or a translation of it;]

(b) in relation to a musical work, means an arrangement or transcription of the work.

(4) In relation to a computer program a "translation" includes a version of the program in which it is converted into or out of a computer language or code or into a different computer language or code . . .

(5) No inference shall be drawn from this section as to what does or does not amount to copying a work.

NOTES

Sub-s (3): word in first pair of square brackets and para (ab) inserted by the Copyright (Computer Programs) Regulations 1992, SI 1992/3233, regs 2, 5(1), (2), subject to reg 12(2) of those Regulations (agreements entered into before 1 January 1993 to remain unaffected); words in second pair of square brackets substituted, and para (ac) inserted, by the Copyright and Rights in Databases Regulations 1997, SI 1997/3032, reg 7, subject to savings and transitional provisions specified in regs 26–30 of those Regulations, at **[2.541]–[2.545]**.

Sub-s (4): words omitted repealed by SI 1992/3233, regs 2, 5(3), subject to reg 12(2) of those Regulations (agreements entered into before 1 January 1993 to remain unaffected).

Secondary infringement of copyright

[2.34]

22 Secondary infringement: importing infringing copy

The copyright in a work is infringed by a person who, without the licence of the copyright owner, imports into the United Kingdom, otherwise than for his private and domestic use, an article which is, and which he knows or has reason to believe is, an infringing copy of the work.

[2.35]

23 Secondary infringement: possessing or dealing with infringing copy

The copyright in a work is infringed by a person who, without the licence of the copyright owner—

(a) possesses in the course of a business,

(b) sells or lets for hire, or offers or exposes for sale or hire,

(c) in the course of a business exhibits in public or distributes, or

(d) distributes otherwise than in the course of a business to such an extent as to affect prejudicially the owner of the copyright,

an article which is, and which he knows or has reason to believe is, an infringing copy of the work.

[2.36]

24 Secondary infringement: providing means for making infringing copies

(1) Copyright in a work is infringed by a person who, without the licence of the copyright owner—

(a) makes,

(b) imports into the United Kingdom,

(c) possesses in the course of a business, or

(d) sells or lets for hire, or offers or exposes for sale or hire,

an article specifically designed or adapted for making copies of that work, knowing or having reason to believe that it is to be used to make infringing copies.

(2) Copyright in a work is infringed by a person who without the licence of the copyright owner transmits the work by means of a telecommunications system (otherwise than by [communication to the public]), knowing or having reason to believe that infringing copies of the work will be made by means of the reception of the transmission in the United Kingdom or elsewhere.

NOTES

Sub-s (2): words in square brackets substituted by the Copyright and Related Rights Regulations 2003, SI 2003/2498, reg 2(1), Sch 1, Pt 1, paras 1, 5(a), subject to transitional provisions as noted to s 1 of this Act at **[2.7]**.

[2.37]

25 Secondary infringement: permitting use of premises for infringing performance

(1) Where the copyright in a literary, dramatic or musical work is infringed by a performance at a place of public entertainment, any person who gave permission for that place to be used for the performance is also liable for the infringement unless when he gave permission he believed on reasonable grounds that the performance would not infringe copyright.

(2) In this section "place of public entertainment" includes premises which are occupied mainly for other purposes but are from time to time made available for hire for the purposes of public entertainment.

[2.38]

26 Secondary infringement: provision of apparatus for infringing performance, &c

(1) Where copyright in a work is infringed by a public performance of the work, or by the playing or showing of the work in public, by means of apparatus for—

(a) playing sound recordings,

(b) showing films, or

(c) receiving visual images or sounds conveyed by electronic means,

the following persons are also liable for the infringement.

(2) A person who supplied the apparatus, or any substantial part of it, is liable for the infringement if when he supplied the apparatus or part—

(a) he knew or had reason to believe that the apparatus was likely to be so used as to infringe copyright, or

(b) in the case of apparatus whose normal use involves a public performance, playing or showing, he did not believe on reasonable grounds that it would not be so used as to infringe copyright.

(3) An occupier of premises who gave permission for the apparatus to be brought onto the premises is liable for the infringement if when he gave permission he knew or had reason to believe that the apparatus was likely to be so used as to infringe copyright.

(4) A person who supplied a copy of a sound recording or film used to infringe copyright is liable for the infringement if when he supplied it he knew or had reason to believe that what he supplied, or a copy made directly or indirectly from it, was likely to be so used as to infringe copyright.

Infringing copies

[2.39]

27 Meaning of "infringing copy"

(1) In this Part "infringing copy", in relation to a copyright work, shall be construed in accordance with this section.

(2) An article is an infringing copy if its making constituted an infringement of the copyright in the work in question.

(3) [. . .] an article is also an infringing copy if—

(a) it has been or is proposed to be imported into the United Kingdom, and

(b) its making in the United Kingdom would have constituted an infringement of the copyright in the work in question, or a breach of an exclusive licence agreement relating to that work.

[(3A) . . .]

(4) Where in any proceedings the question arises whether an article is an infringing copy and it is shown—

(a) that the article is a copy of the work, and

(b) that copyright subsists in the work or has subsisted at any time,

it shall be presumed until the contrary is proved that the article was made at a time when copyright subsisted in the work.

(5) Nothing in subsection (3) shall be construed as applying to an article which may lawfully be imported into the United Kingdom by virtue of any enforceable [EU] right within the meaning of section 2(1) of the European Communities Act 1972.

(6) In this Part "infringing copy" includes a copy falling to be treated as an infringing copy by virtue of any of the following provisions—

[section 28B(7) and (9) (personal copies for private use),]

[section 29A(3) (copies for text and data analysis for non-commercial research),]

[[section 31A(5) and (6) (disabled persons: copies of works for personal use),]

[section 31B(11) (making and supply of accessible copies by authorised bodies),]

. . .]

. . .

. . .

[section 35(5) (recording by educational establishments of broadcasts),]

. . .

[section 36(8) (copying and use of extracts of works by educational establishments),]

. . .

[section 42A(5)(b) (copying by librarians: single copies of published works),]

[section 43(5)(b) (copying by librarians or archivists: single copies of unpublished works),]

section 56(2) (further copies, adaptations, &c of work in electronic form retained on transfer of principal copy),

[section 61(6)(b) (recordings of folksongs),]

section 63(2) (copies made for purpose of advertising artistic work for sale),

section 68(4) (copies made for purpose of broadcast . . .),

[section 70(2) (recording for the purposes of time-shifting),

section 71(2) (photographs of broadcasts), or]

any provision of an order under section 141 (statutory licence for certain reprographic copying by educational establishments).

NOTES

Sub-s (3): words omitted from square brackets originally inserted by the Copyright (Computer Programs) Regulations 1992, SI 1992/3233, regs 2, 6, and repealed by the Copyright and Related Rights Regulations 1996, SI 1996/2967, regs 4, 9(4), subject to transitional provisions and savings specified in regs 25–36 of those Regulations, at **[2.510]**–**[2.521]**.

Sub-s (3A): inserted by SI 1992/3233, regs 2, 6, and repealed by SI 1996/2967, regs 4, 9(4), subject to transitional provisions and savings specified in regs 25–36 of those Regulations, at **[2.510]**–**[2.521]**.

Sub-s (5): reference in square brackets substituted by the Treaty of Lisbon (Changes in Terminology) Order 2011, SI 2011/1043, art 6(1)(f).

Sub-s (6): entry relating to "section 28B(7) and (9)" inserted by the Copyright and Rights in Performances (Personal Copies for Private Use) Regulations 2014, SI 2014/2361, regs 2, 4(1), subject to transitional provisions and additional notes, as noted to s 28B at **[2.42]**; entries relating to "section 29A(3)", "section 35(5)", "section 36(8)", "section 42A(5)(b)", "section 43(5)(b)" and "section 61(6)(b)" inserted and entries relating to sections 32(5), 35(3), 36(5) and 37(3)(b) (omitted) repealed by the Copyright and Rights in Performances (Research, Education, Libraries and Archives) Regulations 2014, SI 2014/1372, reg 2(2), Schedule, paras 1, 2; entries relating to "section 31A(5) and (6)" and "section 31B(11)" substituted (for entries originally inserted by the Copyright (Visually Impaired Persons) Act 2002, s 7(1)) and entry relating to "section 31C(2)" (also originally inserted by s 7(1) of the 2002 Act) repealed by the Copyright and Rights in Performances (Disability) Regulations 2014, SI 2014/1384, reg 4, Schedule, para 1; in entry relating to "section 68(4)" words omitted repealed and entries relating to "section 70(2)" and "section 71(2)" substituted by the Copyright and Related Rights Regulations 2003, SI 2003/2498, regs 2(2) 3, 20(3), Sch 2, subject to transitional provisions as noted to s 1 of this Act at **[2.7]**.

CHAPTER III
ACTS PERMITTED IN RELATION TO COPYRIGHT WORKS

NOTES

Chapter III: see further, in relation to the duty to provide advance information about television and radio programme services: the Broadcasting Act 1990, s 176, at **[2.416]**, and Sch 17.

Introductory

[2.40]

28 Introductory provisions

(1) The provisions of this Chapter specify acts which may be done in relation to copyright works notwithstanding the subsistence of copyright; they relate only to the question of infringement of copyright and do not affect any other right or obligation restricting the doing of any of the specified acts.

(2) Where it is provided by this Chapter that an act does not infringe copyright, or may be done without infringing copyright, and no particular description of copyright work is mentioned, the act in question does not infringe the copyright in a work of any description.

(3) No inference shall be drawn from the description of any act which may by virtue of this Chapter be done without infringing copyright as to the scope of the acts restricted by the copyright in any description of work.

(4) The provisions of this Chapter are to be construed independently of each other, so that the fact that an act does not fall within one provision does not mean that it is not covered by another provision.

General

[2.41]

[28A Making of temporary copies

Copyright in a literary work, other than a computer program or a database, or in a dramatic, musical or artistic work, the typographical arrangement of a published edition, a sound recording or a film, is not infringed by the making of a temporary copy which is transient or incidental, which is an integral and essential part of a technological process and the sole purpose of which is to enable—

(a) a transmission of the work in a network between third parties by an intermediary; or

(b) a lawful use of the work;

and which has no independent economic significance.]

NOTES

Inserted by the Copyright and Related Rights Regulations 2003, SI 2003/2498, regs 3, 8(1), subject to transitional provisions as noted to s 1 of this Act at **[2.7]**.

[2.42]

[28B Personal copies for private use

(1) The making of a copy of a work, other than a computer program, by an individual does not infringe copyright in the work provided that the copy—

(a) is a copy of—

(i) the individual's own copy of the work, or

(ii) a personal copy of the work made by the individual,

(b) is made for the individual's private use, and

(c) is made for ends which are neither directly nor indirectly commercial.

(2) In this section "the individual's own copy" is a copy which—

(a) has been lawfully acquired by the individual on a permanent basis,

(b) is not an infringing copy, and

(c) has not been made under any provision of this Chapter which permits the making of a copy without infringing copyright.

(3) In this section a "personal copy" means a copy made under this section.

(4) For the purposes of subsection (2)(a), a copy "lawfully acquired on a permanent basis"—

(a) includes a copy which has been purchased, obtained by way of a gift, or acquired by means of a download resulting from a purchase or a gift (other than a download of a kind mentioned in paragraph (b)); and

(b) does not include a copy which has been borrowed, rented, broadcast or streamed, or a copy which has been obtained by means of a download enabling no more than temporary access to the copy.

(5) In subsection (1)(b) "private use" includes private use facilitated by the making of a copy—

(a) as a back up copy,

(b) for the purposes of format-shifting, or

(c) for the purposes of storage, including in an electronic storage area accessed by means of the internet or similar means which is accessible only by the individual (and the person responsible for the storage area).

(6) Copyright in a work is infringed if an individual transfers a personal copy of the work to another person (otherwise than on a private and temporary basis), except where the transfer is authorised by the copyright owner.

(7) If copyright is infringed as set out in subsection (6), a personal copy which has been transferred is for all purposes subsequently treated as an infringing copy.

(8) Copyright in a work is also infringed if an individual, having made a personal copy of the work, transfers the individual's own copy of the work to another person (otherwise than on a private and temporary basis) and, after that transfer and without the licence of the copyright owner, retains any personal copy.

(9) If copyright is infringed as set out in subsection (8), any retained personal copy is for all purposes subsequently treated as an infringing copy.

(10) To the extent that a term of a contract purports to prevent or restrict the making of a copy which, by virtue of this section, would not infringe copyright, that term is unenforceable.]

NOTES

Commencement: 1 October 2014.

Inserted by the Copyright and Rights in Performances (Personal Copies for Private Use) Regulations 2014, SI 2014/2361, regs 2, 3(1), subject to transitional provisions as noted below.

Transitional provisions: the Copyright and Rights in Performances (Personal Copies for Private Use) Regulations 2014, SI 2014/2361, reg 5 provides as follows—

"5 Transitional provisions

(1) Paragraph (2) applies to a copy of a work—

(a) made before the date on which these Regulations come into force, and

(b) which could have been made under section 28B of the Act had that section been in force at the time when the copy was made.

(2) On and after the date on which these Regulations come into force, the copy is to be treated as a personal copy of the work made under section 28B of the Act (therefore it is not an infringing copy by virtue of section 27(2) of the Act even if its making infringed copyright).

(3) Paragraph (4) applies to a copy of a recording of a performance—

(a) made before the date on which these Regulations come into force, and

(b) which could have been made under paragraph 1B of Schedule 2 to the Act had that paragraph been in force at the time when the copy was made.

(4) On and after the date on which these Regulations come into force, the copy is to be treated as a personal copy of the recording made under paragraph 1B of Schedule 2 to the Act.".

SI 2014/2361: at the date this Handbook went to press, the validity of the Copyright and Rights in Performances (Personal Copies for Private Use) Regulations 2014, SI 2014/2361 was the subject of litigation. See *R (on the application of*

British Academy of Songwriters Composers and Authors and others) v Secretary of State for Business Innovation and Skills (The Incorporated Society of Musicians intervening) [2015] EWHC 1723 (Admin).

[2.43]

29 Research and private study

[(1) Fair dealing with a . . . work for the purposes of research for a non-commercial purpose does not infringe any copyright in the work provided that it is accompanied by a sufficient acknowledgement.]

[(1B) No acknowledgement is required in connection with fair dealing for the purposes mentioned in subsection (1) where this would be impossible for reasons of practicality or otherwise.

(1C) Fair dealing with a . . . work for the purposes of private study does not infringe any copyright in the work.]

(2) . . .

(3) Copying by a person other than the researcher or student himself is not fair dealing if—

[(a) in the case of a librarian, or a person acting on behalf of a librarian, that person does anything which is not permitted under section 42A (copying by librarians: single copies of published works), or]

(b) in any other case, the person doing the copying knows or has reason to believe that it will result in copies of substantially the same material being provided to more than one person at substantially the same time and for substantially the same purpose.

[(4) It is not fair dealing—

(a) to convert a computer program expressed in a low level language into a version expressed in a higher level language, or

(b) incidentally in the course of so converting the program, to copy it,

(these acts being permitted if done in accordance with section 50B (decompilation)).]

[(4A) It is not fair dealing to observe, study or test the functioning of a computer program in order to determine the ideas and principles which underlie any element of the program (these acts being permitted if done in accordance with section 50BA (observing, studying and testing)).]

[(4B) To the extent that a term of a contract purports to prevent or restrict the doing of any act which, by virtue of this section, would not infringe copyright, that term is unenforceable.]

[(5) . . .]

NOTES

Sub-s (1): substituted by the Copyright and Related Rights Regulations 2003, SI 2003/2498, regs 3, 9(a), subject to transitional provisions as noted to s 1 of this Act at **[2.7]**; words omitted repealed by the Copyright and Rights in Performances (Research, Education, Libraries and Archives) Regulations 2014, SI 2014/1372, regs 2(1), 3(1)(a).

Sub-s (1B): substituted, together with sub-s (1C) for sub-s (1A) (as inserted by SI 1997/3032, reg 8(2)), by SI 2003/2498, regs 3, 9(b), subject to transitional provisions as noted to s 1 of this Act at **[2.7]**.

Sub-s (1C): substituted as noted to sub-s (1B) above; words omitted repealed by SI 2014/1372, regs 2(1), 3(1)(b).

Sub-s (2): repealed by SI 2014/1372, regs 2(1), 3(1)(c).

Sub-s (3): para (a) substituted by SI 2014/1372, regs 2(1), 3(1)(d).

Sub-s (4): added by the Copyright (Computer Programs) Regulations 1992, SI 1992/3233, regs 2, 7, subject to reg 12(2) of those Regulations (agreements entered into before 1 January 1993 to remain unaffected).

Sub-s (4A): inserted by SI 2003/2498, regs 3, 9(d), subject to transitional provisions as noted to s 1 of this Act at **[2.7]**.

Sub-s (4B): inserted by SI 2014/1372, regs 2(1), 3(1)(e).

Sub-s (5): added by SI 1997/3032, reg 8(3); repealed by SI 2003/2498, regs 2, 3, 9(e), Sch 2, subject to transitional provisions as noted to s 1 of this Act at **[2.7]**.

[2.44]

[29A Copies for text and data analysis for non-commercial research

(1) The making of a copy of a work by a person who has lawful access to the work does not infringe copyright in the work provided that—

(a) the copy is made in order that a person who has lawful access to the work may carry out a computational analysis of anything recorded in the work for the sole purpose of research for a non commercial purpose, and

(b) the copy is accompanied by a sufficient acknowledgement (unless this would be impossible for reasons of practicality or otherwise).

(2) Where a copy of a work has been made under this section, copyright in the work is infringed if—

(a) the copy is transferred to any other person, except where the transfer is authorised by the copyright owner, or

(b) the copy is used for any purpose other than that mentioned in subsection (1)(a), except where the use is authorised by the copyright owner.

(3) If a copy made under this section is subsequently dealt with—

(a) it is to be treated as an infringing copy for the purposes of that dealing, and

(b) if that dealing infringes copyright, it is to be treated as an infringing copy for all subsequent purposes.

(4) In subsection (3) "dealt with" means sold or let for hire, or offered or exposed for sale or hire.

(5) To the extent that a term of a contract purports to prevent or restrict the making of a copy which, by virtue of this section, would not infringe copyright, that term is unenforceable.]

NOTES

Commencement: 1 June 2014 (at 00.02 hrs).

Inserted by the Copyright and Rights in Performances (Research, Education, Libraries and Archives) Regulations 2014, SI 2014/1372, regs 2(1), 3(2).

[2.45]

30 Criticism, review[, quotation] and news reporting

(1) Fair dealing with a work for the purpose of criticism or review, of that or another work or of a performance of a work, does not infringe any copyright in the work provided that it is accompanied by a sufficient acknowledgement [(unless this would be impossible for reasons of practicality or otherwise)] [and provided that the work has been made available to the public].

[(1ZA) Copyright in a work is not infringed by the use of a quotation from the work (whether for criticism or review or otherwise) provided that—

(a) the work has been made available to the public,

(b) the use of the quotation is fair dealing with the work,

(c) the extent of the quotation is no more than is required by the specific purpose for which it is used, and

(d) the quotation is accompanied by a sufficient acknowledgement (unless this would be impossible for reasons of practicality or otherwise).]

[(1A) For the purposes of [subsections (1) and (1ZA)] a work has been made available to the public if it has been made available by any means, including—

(a) the issue of copies to the public;

(b) making the work available by means of an electronic retrieval system;

(c) the rental or lending of copies of the work to the public;

(d) the performance, exhibition, playing or showing of the work in public;

(e) the communication to the public of the work,

but in determining generally for the purposes of [those subsections] whether a work has been made available to the public no account shall be taken of any unauthorised act.]

(2) Fair dealing with a work (other than a photograph) for the purpose of reporting current events does not infringe any copyright in the work provided that (subject to subsection (3)) it is accompanied by a sufficient acknowledgement.

(3) No acknowledgement is required in connection with the reporting of current events by means of a sound recording, film [or broadcast where this would be impossible for reasons of practicality or otherwise].

[(4) To the extent that a term of a contract purports to prevent or restrict the doing of any act which, by virtue of subsection (1ZA), would not infringe copyright, that term is unenforceable.]

NOTES

Section heading: word in square brackets inserted by the Copyright and Rights in Performances (Quotation and Parody) Regulations 2014, SI 2014/2356, regs 2, 3(1), (2).

Sub-s (1): words in first pair of square brackets inserted by SI 2014/2356, regs 2, 3(1), (3); words in second pair of square brackets added by the Copyright and Related Rights Regulations 2003, SI 2003/2498, regs 3, 10(1)(a), subject to transitional provisions as noted to s 1 of this Act at **[2.7]**.

Sub-s (1ZA): inserted by SI 2014/2356, regs 2, 3(1), (4).

Sub-s (1A): inserted by SI 2003/2498, regs 3, 10(1)(b), subject to transitional provisions as noted to s 1 of this Act at **[2.7]**; words in both pairs of square brackets substituted by SI 2014/2356, regs 2, 3(1), (5).

Sub-s (3): words in square brackets substituted by SI 2003/2498, regs 3, 10(1)(c), subject to transitional provisions as noted to s 1 of this Act at **[2.7]**.

Sub-s (4): added by SI 2014/2356, regs 2, 3(1), (6).

[2.46]

[30A Caricature, parody or pastiche

(1) Fair dealing with a work for the purposes of caricature, parody or pastiche does not infringe copyright in the work.

(2) To the extent that a term of a contract purports to prevent or restrict the doing of any act which, by virtue of this section, would not infringe copyright, that term is unenforceable.]

NOTES

Commencement: 1 October 2014.

Inserted by the Copyright and Rights in Performances (Quotation and Parody) Regulations 2014, SI 2014/2356, regs 2, 5(1).

[2.47]

31 Incidental inclusion of copyright material

(1) Copyright in a work is not infringed by its incidental inclusion in an artistic work, sound recording, film [or broadcast].

(2) Nor is the copyright infringed by the issue to the public of copies, or the playing, showing [or communication to the public], of anything whose making was, by virtue of subsection (1), not an infringement of the copyright

(3) A musical work, words spoken or sung with music, or so much of a sound recording [or broadcast] as includes a musical work or such words, shall not be regarded as incidentally included in another work if it is deliberately included.

NOTES

Words in square brackets substituted by the Copyright and Related Rights Regulations 2003, SI 2003/2498, reg 2(1), Sch 1, Pt 1, paras 1, 3(1)(d), (e), 6(2)(b), subject to transitional provisions as noted to s 1 of this Act at **[2.7]**.

[Disability

[2.48]

31A Disabled persons: copies of works for personal use

(1) This section applies if—

(a) a disabled person has lawful possession or lawful use of a copy of the whole or part of a work, and

(b) the person's disability prevents the person from enjoying the work to the same degree as a person who does not have that disability.

(2) The making of an accessible copy of the copy of the work referred to in subsection (1)(a) does not infringe copyright if—

(a) the copy is made by the disabled person or by a person acting on behalf of the disabled person,

(b) the copy is made for the disabled person's personal use, and

(c) the same kind of accessible copies of the work are not commercially available on reasonable terms by or with the authority of the copyright owner.

(3) If a person makes an accessible copy under this section on behalf of a disabled person and charges the disabled person for it, the sum charged must not exceed the cost of making and supplying the copy.

(4) Copyright is infringed by the transfer of an accessible copy of a work made under this section to any person other than—

(a) a person by or for whom an accessible copy of the work may be made under this section, or

(b) a person who intends to transfer the copy to a person falling within paragraph (a),

except where the transfer is authorised by the copyright owner.

(5) An accessible copy of a work made under this section is to be treated for all purposes as an infringing copy if it is held by a person at a time when the person does not fall within subsection (4)(a) or (b).

(6) If an accessible copy made under this section is subsequently dealt with—

(a) it is to be treated as an infringing copy for the purposes of that dealing, and

(b) if that dealing infringes copyright, it is to be treated as an infringing copy for all subsequent purposes.

(7) In this section "dealt with" means sold or let for hire or offered or exposed for sale or hire.]

NOTES

Commencement: 1 June 2014 (at 00.01 hrs).

Inserted, together with preceding heading, by the Copyright (Visually Impaired Persons) Act 2002, s 1, and substituted, together with preceding heading, by the Copyright and Rights in Performances (Disability) Regulations 2014, SI 2014/1384, reg 2(1)–(3).

[2.49]

[31B Making and supply of accessible copies by authorised bodies

(1) If an authorised body has lawful possession of a copy of the whole or part of a published work, the body may, without infringing copyright, make and supply accessible copies of the work for the personal use of disabled persons.

(2) But subsection (1) does not apply if the same kind of accessible copies of the work are commercially available on reasonable terms by or with the authority of the copyright owner.

(3) If an authorised body has lawful access to or lawful possession of the whole or part of a broadcast or a copy of a broadcast, the body may, without infringing copyright—

(a) in the case of a broadcast, make a recording of the broadcast, and make and supply accessible copies of the recording or of any work included in the broadcast, and

(b) in the case of a copy of a broadcast, make and supply accessible copies of that copy or of any work included in the broadcast,

for the personal use of disabled persons.

(4) But subsection (3) does not apply if the same kind of accessible copies of the broadcast, or of any work included in it, are commercially available on reasonable terms by or with the authority of the copyright owner.

(5) For the purposes of subsections (1) and (3), supply "for the personal use of disabled persons" includes supply to a person acting on behalf of a disabled person.

(6) An authorised body which is an educational establishment conducted for profit must ensure that any accessible copies which it makes under this section are used only for its educational purposes.

Part 2 Copyright

(7) An accessible copy made under this section must be accompanied by—
(a) a statement that it is made under this section, and
(b) a sufficient acknowledgement (unless this would be impossible for reasons of practicality or otherwise).

(8) If an accessible copy is made under this section of a work which is in copy-protected electronic form, the accessible copy must, so far as is reasonably practicable, incorporate the same or equally effective copy protection (unless the copyright owner agrees otherwise).

(9) An authorised body which has made an accessible copy of a work under this section may supply it to another authorised body which is entitled to make accessible copies of the work under this section for the purposes of enabling that other body to make accessible copies of the work.

(10) If an authorised body supplies an accessible copy it has made under this section to a person or authorised body as permitted by this section and charges the person or body for it, the sum charged must not exceed the cost of making and supplying the copy.

(11) If an accessible copy made under this section is subsequently dealt with—
(a) it is to be treated as an infringing copy for the purposes of that dealing, and
(b) if that dealing infringes copyright, it is to be treated as an infringing copy for all subsequent purposes.

(12) In this section "dealt with" means sold or let for hire or offered or exposed for sale or hire.]

NOTES

Commencement: 1 June 2014 (at 00.01 hrs).

Substituted, together with ss 31BA, 31BB (for s 31B as originally inserted by the Copyright (Visually Impaired Persons) Act 2002, s 2), by the Copyright and Rights in Performances (Disability) Regulations 2014, SI 2014/1384, reg 2(1), (4).

[2.50]

[31BA Making and supply of intermediate copies by authorised bodies

(1) An authorised body which is entitled to make an accessible copy of a work under section 31B may, without infringing copyright, make a copy of the work ("an intermediate copy") if this is necessary in order to make the accessible copy.

(2) An authorised body which has made an intermediate copy of a work under this section may supply it to another authorised body which is entitled to make accessible copies of the work under section 31B for the purposes of enabling that other body to make accessible copies of the work.

(3) Copyright is infringed by the transfer of an intermediate copy made under this section to a person other than another authorised body as permitted by subsection (2), except where the transfer is authorised by the copyright owner.

(4) If an authorised body supplies an intermediate copy to an authorised body under subsection (2) and charges the body for it, the sum charged must not exceed the cost of making and supplying the copy.]

NOTES

Commencement: 1 June 2014 (at 00.01 hrs).

Substituted as noted to s 31B at **[2.49]**.

[2.51]

[31BB Accessible and intermediate copies: records and notification

(1) An authorised body must keep a record of—
(a) accessible copies it makes under section 31B,
(b) intermediate copies it makes under section 31BA, and
(c) the persons to whom such copies are supplied.

(2) An authorised body must allow the copyright owner or a person acting for the copyright owner, on giving reasonable notice, to inspect at any reasonable time—
(a) records kept under subsection (1), and
(b) records of copies made under sections 31B and 31C as those sections were in force before the coming into force of these Regulations.

(3) Within a reasonable time of making an accessible copy under section 31B, an authorised body must—
(a) notify any body which—
  (i) represents particular copyright owners or owners of copyright in the type of work concerned, and
  (ii) has given notice to the Secretary of State of the copyright owners, or the classes of copyright owner, represented by it, or
(b) if there is no such body, notify the copyright owner (unless it is not reasonably possible to ascertain the name and address of the copyright owner).]

NOTES

Commencement: 1 June 2014 (at 00.01 hrs).

Substituted as noted to s 31B at **[2.49]**.

31C–31E (*Inserted by the Copyright (Visually Impaired Persons) Act 2002, ss 3–5 and repealed by the Copyright and Rights in Performances (Disability) Regulations 2014, SI 2014/1384, reg 4, Schedule, para 8.*)

[2.52]
[31F Sections 31A to 31BB: interpretation and general
(1) This section supplements sections 31A to 31BB and includes definitions.
(2) "Disabled person" means a person who has a physical or mental impairment which prevents the person from enjoying a copyright work to the same degree as a person who does not have that impairment, and "disability" is to be construed accordingly.
(3) But a person is not to be regarded as disabled by reason only of an impairment of visual function which can be improved, by the use of corrective lenses, to a level that is normally acceptable for reading without a special level or kind of light.
(4) An "accessible copy" of a copyright work means a version of the work which enables the fuller enjoyment of the work by disabled persons.
(5) An accessible copy—
(a) may include facilities for navigating around the version of the work, but
(b) must not include any changes to the work which are not necessary to overcome the problems suffered by the disabled persons for whom the accessible copy is intended.
(6) "Authorised body" means—
(a) an educational establishment, or
(b) a body that is not conducted for profit.
(7) The "supply" of a copy includes making it available for use, otherwise than for direct or indirect economic or commercial advantage, on terms that it will or may be returned.
(8) To the extent that a term of a contract purports to prevent or restrict the doing of any act which, by virtue of section 31A, 31B or 31BA, would not infringe copyright, that term is unenforceable.]

NOTES
Commencement: 1 June 2014 (at 00.01 hrs).
Inserted by the Copyright (Visually Impaired Persons) Act 2002, s 6; substituted by the Copyright and Rights in Performances (Disability) Regulations 2014, SI 2014/1384, reg 2(1), (5), subject to savings in Schedule, para 9 thereto.

Education

[2.53]
[32 Illustration for instruction
(1) Fair dealing with a work for the sole purpose of illustration for instruction does not infringe copyright in the work provided that the dealing is—
(a) for a non-commercial purpose,
(b) by a person giving or receiving instruction (or preparing for giving or receiving instruction), and
(c) accompanied by a sufficient acknowledgement (unless this would be impossible for reasons of practicality or otherwise).
(2) For the purposes of subsection (1), "giving or receiving instruction" includes setting examination questions, communicating the questions to pupils and answering the questions.
(3) To the extent that a term of a contract purports to prevent or restrict the doing of any act which, by virtue of this section, would not infringe copyright, that term is unenforceable.]

NOTES
Commencement: 1 June 2014 (at 00.02 hrs).
Substituted by the Copyright and Rights in Performances (Research, Education, Libraries and Archives) Regulations 2014, SI 2014/1372, regs 2(1), 4(1).

[2.54]
33 Anthologies for educational use
(1) The inclusion of a short passage from a published literary or dramatic work in a collection which—
(a) is intended for use in educational establishments and is so described in its title, and in any advertisements issued by or on behalf of the publisher, and
(b) consists mainly of material in which no copyright subsists,
does not infringe the copyright in the work if the work itself is not intended for use in such establishments and the inclusion is accompanied by a sufficient acknowledgement.
(2) Subsection (1) does not authorise the inclusion of more than two excerpts from copyright works by the same author in collections published by the same publisher over any period of five years.
(3) In relation to any given passage the reference in subsection (2) to excerpts from works by the same author—
(a) shall be taken to include excerpts from works by him in collaboration with another, and
(b) if the passage in question is from such a work, shall be taken to include excerpts from works by any of the authors, whether alone or in collaboration with another.

(4) References in this section to the use of a work in an educational establishment are to any use for the educational purposes of such an establishment.

[2.55]
34 Performing, playing or showing work in course of activities of educational establishment
(1) The performance of a literary, dramatic or musical work before an audience consisting of teachers and pupils at an educational establishment and other persons directly connected with the activities of the establishment—
(a) by a teacher or pupil in the course of the activities of the establishment, or
(b) at the establishment by any person for the purposes of instruction,
is not a public performance for the purposes of infringement of copyright.
(2) The playing or showing of a sound recording, film [or broadcast] before such an audience at an educational establishment for the purposes of instruction is not a playing or showing of the work in public for the purposes of infringement of copyright.
(3) A person is not for this purpose directly connected with the activities of the educational establishment simply because he is the parent of a pupil at the establishment.

NOTES
Sub-s (2): words in square brackets substituted by the Copyright and Related Rights Regulations 2003, SI 2003/2498, reg 2(1), Sch 1, Pt 1, paras 1, 3(1)(f), subject to transitional provisions as noted to s 1 of this Act at **[2.7]**.

[2.56]
[35 Recording by educational establishments of broadcasts
(1) A recording of a broadcast, or a copy of such a recording, may be made by or on behalf of an educational establishment for the educational purposes of that establishment without infringing copyright in the broadcast, or in any work included in it, provided that—
(a) the educational purposes are non-commercial, and
(b) the recording or copy is accompanied by a sufficient acknowledgement (unless this would be impossible for reasons of practicality or otherwise).
(2) Copyright is not infringed where a recording of a broadcast or a copy of such a recording, made under subsection (1), is communicated by or on behalf of the educational establishment to its pupils or staff for the non-commercial educational purposes of that establishment.
(3) Subsection (2) only applies to a communication received outside the premises of the establishment if that communication is made by means of a secure electronic network accessible only by the establishment's pupils and staff.
(4) Acts which would otherwise be permitted by this section are not permitted if, or to the extent that, licences are available authorising the acts in question and the educational establishment responsible for those acts knew or ought to have been aware of that fact.
(5) If a copy made under this section is subsequently dealt with—
(a) it is to be treated as an infringing copy for the purposes of that dealing, and
(b) if that dealing infringes copyright, it is to be treated as an infringing copy for all subsequent purposes.
(6) In this section "dealt with" means—
(a) sold or let for hire,
(b) offered or exposed for sale or hire, or
(c) communicated otherwise than as permitted by subsection (2).]

NOTES
Commencement: 1 June 2014 (at 00.02 hrs).
Substituted by the Copyright and Rights in Performances (Research, Education, Libraries and Archives) Regulations 2014, SI 2014/1372, regs 2(1), 4(2).

[2.57]
[36 Copying and use of extracts of works by educational establishments
(1) The copying of extracts of a relevant work by or on behalf of an educational establishment does not infringe copyright in the work, provided that—
(a) the copy is made for the purposes of instruction for a non-commercial purpose, and
(b) the copy is accompanied by a sufficient acknowledgement (unless this would be impossible for reasons of practicality or otherwise).
(2) Copyright is not infringed where a copy of an extract made under subsection (1) is communicated by or on behalf of the educational establishment to its pupils or staff for the purposes of instruction for a non-commercial purpose.
(3) Subsection (2) only applies to a communication received outside the premises of the establishment if that communication is made by means of a secure electronic network accessible only by the establishment's pupils and staff.
(4) In this section "relevant work" means a copyright work other than—
(a) a broadcast, or
(b) an artistic work which is not incorporated into another work.

(5) Not more than 5% of a work may be copied under this section by or on behalf of an educational establishment in any period of 12 months, and for these purposes a work which incorporates another work is to be treated as a single work.

(6) Acts which would otherwise be permitted by this section are not permitted if, or to the extent that, licences are available authorising the acts in question and the educational establishment responsible for those acts knew or ought to have been aware of that fact.

(7) The terms of a licence granted to an educational establishment authorising acts permitted by this section are of no effect so far as they purport to restrict the proportion of a work which may be copied (whether on payment or free of charge) to less than that which would be permitted by this section.

(8) If a copy made under this section is subsequently dealt with—
- (a) it is to be treated as an infringing copy for the purposes of that dealing, and
- (b) if that dealing infringes copyright, it is to be treated as an infringing copy for all subsequent purposes.

(9) In this section "dealt with" means—
- (a) sold or let for hire,
- (b) offered or exposed for sale or hire, or
- (c) communicated otherwise than as permitted by subsection (2).]

NOTES

Commencement: 1 June 2014 (at 00.02 hrs).

Substituted by the Copyright and Rights in Performances (Research, Education, Libraries and Archives) Regulations 2014, SI 2014/1372, regs 2(1), 4(3).

[2.58]

[36A Lending of copies by educational establishments

Copyright in a work is not infringed by the lending of copies of the work by an educational establishment.]

NOTES

Inserted by the Copyright and Related Rights Regulations 1996, SI 1996/2967, regs 4, 11(1), subject to transitional provisions and savings specified in regs 25–36 of those Regulations, at **[2.510]–[2.521]**.

Libraries and archives

37–40 *(Repealed by the Copyright and Rights in Performances (Research, Education, Libraries and Archives) Regulations 2014, SI 2014/1372, reg 2(2), Schedule, para 14.)*

[2.59]

[40A Lending of copies by libraries or archives

[(1) Copyright in a work of any description is not infringed by the following acts by a public library in relation to a book within the public lending right scheme—
- (a) lending the book;
- (b) in relation to an audio-book or e-book, copying or issuing a copy of the book as an act incidental to lending it.

[(1ZA) Subsection (1) applies to an e-book or an e-audio-book only if—
- (a) the book has been lawfully acquired by the library, and
- (b) the lending is in compliance with any purchase or licensing terms to which the book is subject.]

(1A) In *subsection (1)*—
- (a) "book", "audio-book" and "e-book" have the meanings given in section 5 of the Public Lending Right Act 1979,
- [(aa) "e-audio-book" means an audio-book (as defined in paragraph (a)) in a form enabling lending of the book by electronic transmission,]
- (b) "the public lending right scheme" means the scheme in force under section 1 of that Act,
- (c) a book is within the public lending right scheme if it is a book within the meaning of the provisions of the scheme relating to eligibility, whether or not it is in fact eligible, and
- (d) "lending" is to be read in accordance with the definition of "lent out" in section 5 of that Act (and section 18A of this Act does not apply).]

(2) Copyright in a work is not infringed by the lending of copies of the work by a . . . library or archive (other than a public library) which is not conducted for profit.]

NOTES

Inserted by the Copyright and Related Rights Regulations 1996, SI 1996/2967, regs 4, 11(2), subject to transitional provisions and savings specified in regs 25–36 of those Regulations, at **[2.510]–[2.521]**.

Sub-s (1): substituted together with sub-s (1A), for original sub-s (1), by the Digital Economy Act 2010, s 43(6), (7).

Sub-s (1ZA): inserted by the Digital Economy Act 2017, s 31(2), (3), as from a day to be appointed.

Sub-s (1A): substituted as noted to sub-s (1) above; for the words in italics there are substituted the words "subsections (1) and (1ZA)" and para (aa) is inserted, by the Digital Economy Act 2017, s 31(2), (4), as from a day to be appointed.

Sub-s (2): word omitted repealed by the Copyright and Rights in Performances (Research, Education, Libraries and Archives) Regulations 2014, SI 2014/1372, reg 2(2), Schedule, paras 1, 3.

[2.60]

[40B Libraries and educational establishments etc: making works available through dedicated terminals

(1) Copyright in a work is not infringed by an institution specified in subsection (2) communicating the work to the public or making it available to the public by means of a dedicated terminal on its premises, if the conditions in subsection (3) are met.

(2) The institutions are—

(a) a library,

(b) an archive,

(c) a museum, and

(d) an educational establishment.

(3) The conditions are that the work or a copy of the work—

(a) has been lawfully acquired by the institution,

(b) is communicated or made available to individual members of the public for the purposes of research or private study, and

(c) is communicated or made available in compliance with any purchase or licensing terms to which the work is subject.]

NOTES

Commencement: 1 June 2014 (at 00.02 hrs).

Inserted by the Copyright and Rights in Performances (Research, Education, Libraries and Archives) Regulations 2014, SI 2014/1372, regs 2(1), 5(1).

[2.61]

[41 Copying by librarians: supply of single copies to other libraries

(1) A librarian may, if the conditions in subsection (2) are met, make a single copy of the whole or part of a published work and supply it to another library, without infringing copyright in the work.

(2) Thc conditions are—

(a) the copy is supplied in response to a request from a library which is not conducted for profit, and

(b) at the time of making the copy the librarian does not know, or could not reasonably find out, the name and address of a person entitled to authorise the making of a copy of the work.

(3) The condition in subsection (2)(b) does not apply where the request is for a copy of an article in a periodical.

(4) Where a library makes a charge for supplying a copy under this section, the sum charged must be calculated by reference to the costs attributable to the production of the copy.

(5) To the extent that a term of a contract purports to prevent or restrict the doing of any act which, by virtue of this section, would not infringe copyright, that term is unenforceable.]

NOTES

Commencement: 1 June 2014 (at 00.02 hrs).

Substituted, together with ss 42, 42A, 43, 43A (for original ss 41–43) by the Copyright and Rights in Performances (Research, Education, Libraries and Archives) Regulations 2014, SI 2014/1372, regs 2(1), 5(2).

Regulations: the Copyright (Librarians and Archivists) (Copying of Copyright Material) Regulations 1989, SI 1989/1212 at **[2.461]**.

[2.62]

[42 Copying by librarians etc: replacement copies of works

(1) A librarian, archivist or curator of a library, archive or museum may, without infringing copyright, make a copy of an item in that institution's permanent collection—

(a) in order to preserve or replace that item in that collection, or

(b) where an item in the permanent collection of another library, archive or museum has been lost, destroyed or damaged, in order to replace the item in the collection of that other library, archive or museum,

provided that the conditions in subsections (2) and (3) are met.

(2) The first condition is that the item is—

(a) included in the part of the collection kept wholly or mainly for the purposes of reference on the institution's premises,

(b) included in a part of the collection not accessible to the public, or

(c) available on loan only to other libraries, archives or museums.

(3) The second condition is that it is not reasonably practicable to purchase a copy of the item to achieve either of the purposes mentioned in subsection (1).

(4) The reference in subsection (1)(b) to a library, archive or museum is to a library, archive or museum which is not conducted for profit.

(5) Where an institution makes a charge for supplying a copy to another library, archive or museum under subsection (1)(b), the sum charged must be calculated by reference to the costs attributable to the production of the copy.

(6) In this section "item" means a work or a copy of a work.

(7) To the extent that a term of a contract purports to prevent or restrict the doing of any act which, by virtue of this section, would not infringe copyright, that term is unenforceable.]

NOTES

Commencement: 1 June 2014 (at 00.02 hrs).

Substituted as noted to s 41 at **[2.61]**.

Regulations: the Copyright (Librarians and Archivists) (Copying of Copyright Material) Regulations 1989, SI 1989/1212 at **[2.461]**.

[2.63]

[42A Copying by librarians: single copies of published works

(1) A librarian of a library which is not conducted for profit may, if the conditions in subsection (2) are met, make and supply a single copy of—

(a) one article in any one issue of a periodical, or

(b) a reasonable proportion of any other published work,

without infringing copyright in the work.

(2) The conditions are—

(a) the copy is supplied in response to a request from a person who has provided the librarian with a declaration in writing which includes the information set out in subsection (3), and

(b) the librarian is not aware that the declaration is false in a material particular.

(3) The information which must be included in the declaration is—

(a) the name of the person who requires the copy and the material which that person requires,

(b) a statement that the person has not previously been supplied with a copy of that material by any library,

(c) a statement that the person requires the copy for the purposes of research for a non-commercial purpose or private study, will use it only for those purposes and will not supply the copy to any other person, and

(d) a statement that to the best of the person's knowledge, no other person with whom the person works or studies has made, or intends to make, at or about the same time as the person's request, a request for substantially the same material for substantially the same purpose.

(4) Where a library makes a charge for supplying a copy under this section, the sum charged must be calculated by reference to the costs attributable to the production of the copy.

(5) Where a person ("P") makes a declaration under this section that is false in a material particular and is supplied with a copy which would have been an infringing copy if made by P—

(a) P is liable for infringement of copyright as if P had made the copy, and

(b) the copy supplied to P is to be treated as an infringing copy for all purposes.

(6) To the extent that a term of a contract purports to prevent or restrict the doing of any act which, by virtue of this section, would not infringe copyright, that term is unenforceable.]

NOTES

Commencement: 1 June 2014 (at 00.02 hrs).

Substituted as noted to s 41 at **[2.61]**.

[2.64]

[43 Copying by librarians or archivists: single copies of unpublished works

(1) A librarian or archivist may make and supply a single copy of the whole or part of a work without infringing copyright in the work, provided that—

(a) the copy is supplied in response to a request from a person who has provided the librarian or archivist with a declaration in writing which includes the information set out in subsection (2), and

(b) the librarian or archivist is not aware that the declaration is false in a material particular.

(2) The information which must be included in the declaration is—

(a) the name of the person who requires the copy and the material which that person requires,

(b) a statement that the person has not previously been supplied with a copy of that material by any library or archive, and

(c) a statement that the person requires the copy for the purposes of research for a non-commercial purpose or private study, will use it only for those purposes and will not supply the copy to any other person.

(3) But copyright is infringed if—

(a) the work had been published or communicated to the public before the date it was deposited in the library or archive, or

(b) the copyright owner has prohibited the copying of the work,

and at the time of making the copy the librarian or archivist is, or ought to be, aware of that fact.

(4) Where a library or archive makes a charge for supplying a copy under this section, the sum charged must be calculated by reference to the costs attributable to the production of the copy.

(5) Where a person ("P") makes a declaration under this section that is false in a material particular and is supplied with a copy which would have been an infringing copy if made by P—

(a) P is liable for infringement of copyright as if P had made the copy, and

(b) the copy supplied to P is to be treated as an infringing copy for all purposes.]

NOTES

Commencement: 1 June 2014 (at 00.02 hrs).
Substituted as noted to s 41 at **[2.61]**.
Regulations: the Copyright (Librarians and Archivists) (Copying of Copyright Material) Regulations 1989, SI 1989/1212 at **[2.461]**.

[2.65]
[43A Sections 40A to 43: interpretation

(1) The following definitions have effect for the purposes of sections 40A to 43.

(2) "Library" means—

(a) a library which is publicly accessible, or
(b) a library of an educational establishment.

(3) "Museum" includes a gallery.

(4) "Conducted for profit", in relation to a library, archive or museum, means a body of that kind which is established or conducted for profit or which forms part of, or is administered by, a body established or conducted for profit.

(5) References to a librarian, archivist or curator include a person acting on behalf of a librarian, archivist or curator.]

NOTES

Commencement: 1 June 2014 (at 00.02 hrs).
Substituted as noted to s 41 at **[2.61]**.

[2.66]
44 Copy of work required to be made as condition of export

If an article of cultural or historical importance or interest cannot lawfully be exported from the United Kingdom unless a copy of it is made and deposited in an appropriate library or archive, it is not an infringement of copyright to make that copy.

[2.67]
[44A Legal deposit libraries

(1) Copyright is not infringed by the copying of a work from the internet by a deposit library or person acting on its behalf if—

(a) the work is of a description prescribed by regulations under section 10(5) of the 2003 Act,
(b) its publication on the internet, or a person publishing it there, is connected with the United Kingdom in a manner so prescribed, and
(c) the copying is done in accordance with any conditions so prescribed.

(2) Copyright is not infringed by the doing of anything in relation to relevant material permitted to be done under regulations under section 7 of the 2003 Act.

(3) The Secretary of State may by regulations make provision excluding, in relation to prescribed activities done in relation to relevant material, the application of such of the provisions of this Chapter as are prescribed.

(4) Regulations under subsection (3) may in particular make provision prescribing activities—

(a) done for a prescribed purpose,
(b) done by prescribed descriptions of reader,
(c) done in relation to prescribed descriptions of relevant material,
(d) done other than in accordance with prescribed conditions.

(5) Regulations under this section may make different provision for different purposes.

(6) Regulations under this section shall be made by statutory instrument which shall be subject to annulment in pursuance of a resolution of either House of Parliament.

(7) In this section—

(a) "the 2003 Act" means the Legal Deposit Libraries Act 2003;
(b) "deposit library", "reader" and "relevant material" have the same meaning as in section 7 of the 2003 Act;
(c) "prescribed" means prescribed by regulations made by the Secretary of State.]

NOTES

Inserted by the Legal Deposit Libraries Act 2003, s 8(1).

[Orphan works

[2.68]
44B Permitted uses of orphan works

(1) Copyright in an orphan work is not infringed by a relevant body in the circumstances set out in paragraph 1(1) of Schedule ZA1 (subject to paragraph 6 of that Schedule).

(2) "Orphan work" and "relevant body" have the meanings given by that Schedule.]

NOTES

Commencement: 29 October 2014.

Inserted, together with preceding heading, by the Copyright and Rights in Performances (Certain Permitted Uses of Orphan Works) Regulations 2014, SI 2014/2861, reg 3(1).

Public administration

[2.69]
45 Parliamentary and judicial proceedings

(1) Copyright is not infringed by anything done for the purposes of parliamentary or judicial proceedings.

(2) Copyright is not infringed by anything done for the purposes of reporting such proceedings; but this shall not be construed as authorising the copying of a work which is itself a published report of the proceedings.

[2.70]
46 Royal Commissions and statutory inquiries

(1) Copyright is not infringed by anything done for the purposes of the proceedings of a Royal Commission or statutory inquiry.

(2) Copyright is not infringed by anything done for the purpose of reporting any such proceedings held in public; but this shall not be construed as authorising the copying of a work which is itself a published report of the proceedings.

(3) Copyright in a work is not infringed by the issue to the public of copies of the report of a Royal Commission or statutory inquiry containing the work or material from it.

(4) In this section—

"Royal Commission" includes a Commission appointed for Northern Ireland by the Secretary of State in pursuance of the prerogative powers of Her Majesty delegated to him under section 7(2) of the Northern Ireland Constitution Act 1973; and

"statutory inquiry" means an inquiry held or investigation conducted in pursuance of a duty imposed or power conferred by or under an enactment.

[2.71]
47 Material open to public inspection or on official register

(1) Where material is open to public inspection pursuant to a statutory requirement, or is on a statutory register, any copyright in the material as a literary work is not infringed by the copying of so much of the material as contains factual information of any description, by or with the authority of the appropriate person, for a purpose which does not involve the issuing of copies to the public.

[(2) Where material is open to public inspection pursuant to a statutory requirement, copyright in the material is not infringed by an act to which subsection (3A) applies provided that—

(a) the act is done by or with the authority of the appropriate person,

(b) the purpose of the act is—

(i) to enable the material to be inspected at a more convenient time or place, or

(ii) to otherwise facilitate the exercise of any right for the purpose of which the statutory requirement is imposed, and

(c) in the case of the act specified in subsection (3A)(c), the material is not commercially available to the public by or with the authority of the copyright owner.

(3) Where material which contains information about matters of general scientific, technical, commercial or economic interest is on a statutory register or is open to public inspection pursuant to a statutory requirement, copyright in the material is not infringed by an act to which subsection (3A) applies provided that—

(a) the act is done by or with the authority of the appropriate person,

(b) the purpose of the act is to disseminate that information, and

(c) in the case of the act specified in subsection (3A)(c), the material is not commercially available to the public by or with the authority of the copyright owner.

(3A) This subsection applies to any of the following acts—

(a) copying the material,

(b) issuing copies of the material to the public, and

(c) making the material (or a copy of it) available to the public by electronic transmission in such a way that members of the public may access it from a place and at a time individually chosen by them.]

(4) The Secretary of State may by order provide that subsection (1), (2) or (3) shall, in such cases as may be specified in the order, apply only to copies marked in such manner as may be so specified.

(5) The Secretary of State may by order provide that subsections (1) to (3) apply, to such extent and with such modifications as may be specified in the order—

(a) to material made open to public inspection by—

(i) an international organisation specified in the order, or

(ii) a person so specified who has functions in the United Kingdom under an international agreement to which the United Kingdom is party, or

(b) to a register maintained by an international organisation specified in the order,

as they apply in relation to material open to public inspection pursuant to a statutory requirement or to a statutory register.

Part 2 Copyright

(6) In this section—
"appropriate person" means the person required to make the material open to public inspection or, as the case may be, the person maintaining the register;
"statutory register" means a register maintained in pursuance of a statutory requirement; and
"statutory requirement" means a requirement imposed by provision made by or under an enactment.
(7) An order under this section shall be made by statutory instrument which shall be subject to annulment in pursuance of a resolution of either House of Parliament.

NOTES

Sub-ss (2), (3), (3A): substituted for original sub-ss (2), (3), by the Copyright (Public Administration) Regulations 2014, SI 2014/1385, reg 2(1).

Orders: the Copyright (Material Open to Public Inspection) (International Organisations) Order 1989, SI 1989/1098; the Copyright (Material Open to Public Inspection) (Marking Copies of Maps) Order 1989, SI 1989/1099; the Copyright (Material Open to Public Inspection) (Marking Copies of Plans and Drawings) Order 1990, SI 1990/1427 at **[2.472]**.

[2.72]
48 Material communicated to the Crown in the course of public business

(1) This section applies where a literary, dramatic, musical or artistic work has in the course of public business been communicated to the Crown for any purpose, by or with the licence of the copyright owner and a document or other material thing recording or embodying the work is owned by or in the custody or control of the Crown.
[(2) The Crown may, without infringing copyright in the work, do an act specified in subsection (3) provided that—
(a) the act is done for the purpose for which the work was communicated to the Crown, or any related purpose which could reasonably have been anticipated by the copyright owner, and
(b) the work has not been previously published otherwise than by virtue of this section.
(3) The acts referred to in subsection (2) are—
(a) copying the work,
(b) issuing copies of the work to the public, and
(c) making the work (or a copy of it) available to the public by electronic transmission in such a way that members of the public may access it from a place and at a time individually chosen by them.]
(4) In subsection (1) "public business" includes any activity carried on by the Crown.
(5) This section has effect subject to any agreement to the contrary between the Crown and the copyright owner.
[(6) In this section "the Crown" includes a health service body, as defined in section 60(7) of the National Health Service and Community Care Act 1990, [the National Health Service Commissioning Board, a clinical commissioning group established under section 14D of the National Health Service Act 2006,] [. . .] [the Care Quality Commission][, Health Education England][, the Health Research Authority] and a National Health Service trust established under [*section 25 of the National Health Service Act 2006,* section 18 of the National Health Service (Wales) Act 2006] or the National Health Service (Scotland) Act 1978 [and an NHS foundation trust] [and also includes a health and social services body, as defined in Article 7(6) of the Health and Personal Social Services (Northern Ireland) Order 1991, and a Health and Social Services trust established under that Order]; and the reference in subsection (1) above to public business shall be construed accordingly.

NOTES

Sub-ss (2), (3): substituted by the Copyright (Public Administration) Regulations 2014, SI 2014/1385, reg 2(2).

Sub-s (6): added by the National Health Service and Community Care Act 1990, s 60, Sch 8, Pt I, para 3; words in first pair of square brackets inserted by the Health and Social Care Act 2012, s 55(2), Sch 5, para 44(a); words omitted from second pair of square brackets inserted by the Health Act 1999 (Supplementary, Consequential etc Provisions) Order 2000, SI 2000/90, art 3(1), Sch 1, para 22 and repealed by the Health and Social Care Act 2012, s 55(2), Sch 5, para 44(b); words in third pair of square brackets substituted by the Health and Social Care Act 2008, s 95, Sch 5, Pt 3, para 60; words in fourth and fifth pairs of square brackets inserted by the Care Act 2014, ss 96(2), s 109(2), Sch 5, Pt 4, para 33, Sch 7, Pt 4, para 25; words in sixth pair of square brackets substituted by the National Health Service (Consequential Provisions) Act 2006, s 2, Sch 1, paras 111, 112 and words in italics therein repealed by the Health and Social Care Act 2012, s 179(6), Sch 14, Pt 2, para 52, as from a day to be appointed;
words in seventh pair of square brackets inserted by the Health and Social Care (Community Health and Standards) Act 2003, s 34, Sch 4, paras 71, 72; words in final pair of square brackets inserted by the Health and Personal Social Services (Northern Ireland) Order 1991, SI 1991/194, art 7(2), Sch 2, Pt I.

[2.73]
49 Public records

Material which is comprised in public records within the meaning of the Public Records Act 1958, the Public Records (Scotland) Act 1937 or the Public Records Act (Northern Ireland) 1923[, or in Welsh public records (as defined in [the Government of Wales Act 2006]),] which are open to public inspection in pursuance of that Act, may be copied, and a copy may be supplied to any person, by or with the authority of any officer appointed under that Act, without infringement of copyright.

NOTES

Words in first (outer) pair of square brackets inserted by the Government of Wales Act 1998, s 125, Sch 12, paras 26, 27; words in second (inner) pair of square brackets substituted by the Government of Wales Act 2006, s 160(1), Sch 10, paras 22, 24.

[2.74]
50 Acts done under statutory authority

(1) Where the doing of a particular act is specifically authorised by an Act of Parliament, whenever passed, then, unless the Act provides otherwise, the doing of that act does not infringe copyright.
(2) Subsection (1) applies in relation to an enactment contained in Northern Ireland legislation as it applies in relation to an Act of Parliament.
(3) Nothing in this section shall be construed as excluding any defence of statutory authority otherwise available under or by virtue of any enactment.

[Computer programs: lawful users

[2.75]
50A Back up copies

(1) It is not an infringement of copyright for a lawful user of a copy of a computer program to make any back up copy of it which it is necessary for him to have for the purposes of his lawful use.
(2) For the purposes of this section and sections 50B[, 50BA] and 50C a person is a lawful user of a computer program if (whether under a licence to do any acts restricted by the copyright in the program or otherwise), he has a right to use the program.
(3) Where an act is permitted under this section, it is irrelevant whether or not there exists any term or condition in an agreement which purports to prohibit or restrict the act (such terms being, by virtue of section 296A, void).]

NOTES

Inserted, together with preceding heading and ss 50B, 50C, by the Copyright (Computer Programs) Regulations 1992, SI 1992/3233, regs 2, 8, subject to reg 12(2) of those Regulations (agreements entered into before 1 January 1993 to remain unaffected).

Sub-s (2): figure in square brackets inserted by the Copyright and Related Rights Regulations 2003, SI 2003/2498, regs 3, 15(2), subject to transitional provisions as noted to s 1 of this Act at **[2.7]**.

[2.76]
[50B Decompilation

(1) It is not an infringement of copyright for a lawful user of a copy of a computer program expressed in a low level language—
  (a) to convert it into a version expressed in a higher level language, or
  (b) incidentally in the course of so converting the program, to copy it,

(that is, to "decompile" it), provided that the conditions in subsection (2) are met.
(2) The conditions are that—
  (a) it is necessary to decompile the program to obtain the information necessary to create an independent program which can be operated with the program decompiled or with another program ("the permitted objective"); and
  (b) the information so obtained is not used for any purpose other than the permitted objective.

(3) In particular, the conditions in subsection (2) are not met if the lawful user—
  (a) has readily available to him the information necessary to achieve the permitted objective;
  (b) does not confine the decompiling to such acts as are necessary to achieve the permitted objective;
  (c) supplies the information obtained by the decompiling to any person to whom it is not necessary to supply it in order to achieve the permitted objective; or
  (d) uses the information to create a program which is substantially similar in its expression to the program decompiled or to do any act restricted by copyright.

(4) Where an act is permitted under this section, it is irrelevant whether or not there exists any term or condition in an agreement which purports to prohibit or restrict the act (such terms being, by virtue of section 296A, void).]

NOTES

Inserted as noted to s 50A at **[2.75]**.

[2.77]
[50BA Observing, studying and testing of computer programs

(1) It is not an infringement of copyright for a lawful user of a copy of a computer program to observe, study or test the functioning of the program in order to determine the ideas and principles which underlie any element of the program if he does so while performing any of the acts of loading, displaying, running, transmitting or storing the program which he is entitled to do.

Part 2 Copyright

(2) Where an act is permitted under this section, it is irrelevant whether or not there exists any term or condition in an agreement which purports to prohibit or restrict the act (such terms being, by virtue of section 296A, void).]

NOTES

Inserted by the Copyright and Related Rights Regulations 2003, SI 2003/2498, regs 3, 14(2), subject to transitional provisions as noted to s 1 of this Act at **[2.7]**.

[2.78]

[50C Other acts permitted to lawful users

(1) It is not an infringement of copyright for a lawful user of a copy of a computer program to copy or adapt it, provided that the copying or adapting—

(a) is necessary for his lawful use; and

(b) is not prohibited under any term or condition of an agreement regulating the circumstances in which his use is lawful.

(2) It may, in particular, be necessary for the lawful use of a computer program to copy it or adapt it for the purpose of correcting errors in it.

(3) This section does not apply to any copying or adapting permitted under [section 50A, 50B or 50BA].]

NOTES

Inserted as noted to s 50A at **[2.75]**.

Sub-s (3): words in square brackets substituted by the Copyright and Related Rights Regulations 2003, SI 2003/2498, regs 3, 15(3), subject to transitional provisions as noted to s 1 of this Act at **[2.7]**.

[Databases: permitted acts

[2.79]

50D Acts permitted in relation to databases

(1) It is not an infringement of copyright in a database for a person who has a right to use the database or any part of the database, (whether under a licence to do any of the acts restricted by the copyright in the database or otherwise) to do, in the exercise of that right, anything which is necessary for the purposes of access to and use of the contents of the database or of that part of the database.

(2) Where an act which would otherwise infringe copyright in a database is permitted under this section, it is irrelevant whether or not there exists any term or condition in any agreement which purports to prohibit or restrict the act (such terms being, by virtue of section 296B, void).]

NOTES

Inserted, together with preceding heading, by the Copyright and Rights in Databases Regulations 1997, SI 1997/3032, reg 9, subject to savings and transitional provisions specified in regs 26–30 of those Regulations, at **[2.541]–[2.545]**.

Designs

[2.80]

51 Design documents and models

(1) It is not an infringement of any copyright in a design document or model recording or embodying a design for anything other than an artistic work or a typeface to make an article to the design or to copy an article made to the design.

(2) Nor is it an infringement of the copyright to issue to the public, or include in a film [or communicate to the public], anything the making of which was, by virtue of subsection (1), not an infringement of that copyright.

(3) In this section—

"design" means the design of . . . the shape or configuration (whether internal or external) of the whole or part of an article, other than surface decoration; and

"design document" means any record of a design, whether in the form of a drawing, a written description, a photograph, data stored in a computer or otherwise.

NOTES

Sub-s (2): words in square brackets substituted by the Copyright and Related Rights Regulations 2003, SI 2003/2498, reg 2(1), Sch 1, Pt 1, paras 1, 8(3), subject to transitional provisions as noted to s 1 of this Act at **[2.7]**.

Sub-s (3): words omitted from definition "design" repealed by the Intellectual Property Act 2014, s 1(2).

[2.81]

52 Effect of exploitation of design derived from artistic work

(1) This section applies where an artistic work has been exploited, by or with the licence of the copyright owner, by—

(a) making by an industrial process articles falling to be treated for the purposes of this Part as copies of the work, and

(b) marketing such articles, in the United Kingdom or elsewhere.

(2) After the end of the period of 25 years from the end of the calendar year in which such articles are first marketed, the work may be copied by making articles of any description, or doing anything for the purpose of making articles of any description, and anything may be done in relation to articles so made, without infringing copyright in the work.

(3) Where only part of an artistic work is exploited as mentioned in subsection (1), subsection (2) applies only in relation to that part.

(4) The Secretary of State may by order make provision—

(a) as to the circumstances in which an article, or any description of article, is to be regarded for the purposes of this section as made by an industrial process;

(b) excluding from the operation of this section such articles of a primarily literary or artistic character as he thinks fit.

(5) An order shall be made by statutory instrument which shall be subject to annulment in pursuance of a resolution of either House of Parliament.

(6) In this section—

(a) references to articles do not include films; and

(b) references to the marketing of an article are to its being sold or let for hire or offered or exposed for sale or hire.

NOTES

Repealed by the Enterprise and Regulatory Reform Act 2013, s 74(1), (2), as from 28 July 2016, subject to savings as noted below.

Orders: the Copyright (Industrial Process and Excluded Articles) (No 2) Order 1989, SI 1989/1070, at **[3.84]**.

Savings: the Enterprise and Regulatory Reform Act 2013 (Commencement No 10 and Saving Provisions) Order 2016, SI 2016/593, arts 4, 5 provide as follows (note the expressions "commencement date" and "depletion date" mentioned in arts 4, 5 are defined in art 2 of the 2016 Order as being 28 July 2016 and 28 January 2017 respectively)—

"**4 Saving Provisions—Articles Made in, or Imported into, the United Kingdom**

(1) This article applies to the following acts done on or after the commencement date but before the depletion date—

(a) the copying of an artistic work;

(b) the provision of means for making a copy of an artistic work; and

(c) the importation into the United Kingdom of a copy of an artistic work.

(2) An act of a kind mentioned in paragraph (1) does not constitute an infringement of copyright if—

(a) that act is done pursuant to a contract entered into before the consultation time; and

(b) before the commencement date that act would not, by virtue of section 52 of the 1988 Act, have constituted an infringement of copyright.

5 The following acts done on or after the commencement date but before the depletion date do not constitute an infringement of copyright in an artistic work if before the commencement date those acts would not, by virtue of section 52 of the 1988 Act, have constituted an infringement of copyright—

(a) the issue of a relevant copy to the public;

(b) the renting or lending of a relevant copy to the public; or

(c) the communication to the public of the artistic work in connection with anything done in reliance on paragraphs (a) or (b).".

[2.82]

53 Things done in reliance on registration of design

(1) The copyright in an artistic work is not infringed by anything done—

(a) in pursuance of an assignment or licence made or granted by a person registered[—

(i)] under the Registered Designs Act 1949 as the proprietor of a corresponding design[, or

(ii) under the Community Design Regulation as the right holder of a corresponding registered Community design], and

(b) in good faith in reliance on the registration and without notice of any proceedings for the cancellation [or invalidation] of the registration or[, in a case of registration under the 1949 Act,] for rectifying the relevant entry in the register of designs;

and this is so notwithstanding that the person registered as the proprietor was not the proprietor of the design for the purposes of the 1949 Act [or, in a case of registration under the Community Design Regulation, that the person registered as the right holder was not the right holder of the design for the purposes of the Regulation].

(2) In subsection (1) a "corresponding design", in relation to an artistic work, means a design within the meaning of the 1949 Act which if applied to an article would produce something which would be treated for the purposes of this Part as a copy of the artistic work.

[(3) In subsection (1), a "corresponding registered Community design", in relation to an artistic work, means a design within the meaning of the Community Design Regulation which if applied to an article would produce something which would be treated for the purposes of this Part as a copy of the artistic work.

(4) In this section, "the Community Design Regulation" means Council Regulation (EC) No 6/2002 of 12 December 2001 on Community designs.]

NOTES

Sub-s (1): words in square brackets in para (a), words in second pair of square brackets in para (b) and final words in square brackets inserted, by the Intellectual Property Act 2014, s 5(1)–(4).

Part 2 Copyright

words in first pair of square brackets in para (b) inserted by the Registered Designs Regulations 2001, SI 2001/3949, reg 9(1), Sch 1, para 16, subject to transitional provisions specified in regs 10–14 of those Regulations, at [3.00]–[3.92].

Sub-ss (3), (4): added by the Intellectual Property Act 2014, s 5(1), (5), (6).

Typefaces

[2.83]

54 Use of typeface in ordinary course of printing

(1) It is not an infringement of copyright in an artistic work consisting of the design of a typeface—

(a) to use the typeface in the ordinary course of typing, composing text, typesetting or printing,

(b) to possess an article for the purpose of such use, or

(c) to do anything in relation to material produced by such use;

and this is so notwithstanding that an article is used which is an infringing copy of the work.

(2) However, the following provisions of this Part apply in relation to persons making, importing or dealing with articles specifically designed or adapted for producing material in a particular typeface, or possessing such articles for the purpose of dealing with them, as if the production of material as mentioned in subsection (1) did infringe copyright in the artistic work consisting of the design of the typeface—

section 24 (secondary infringement: making, importing, possessing or dealing with article for making infringing copy),

sections 99 and 100 (order for delivery up and right of seizure),

section 107(2) (offence of making or possessing such an article), and

section 108 (order for delivery up in criminal proceedings).

(3) The references in subsection (2) to "dealing with" an article are to selling, letting for hire, or offering or exposing for sale or hire, exhibiting in public, or distributing.

[2.84]

55 Articles for producing material in particular typeface

(1) This section applies to the copyright in an artistic work consisting of the design of a typeface where articles specifically designed or adapted for producing material in that typeface have been marketed by or with the licence of the copyright owner.

(2) After the period of 25 years from the end of the calendar year in which the first such articles are marketed, the work may be copied by making further such articles, or doing anything for the purpose of making such articles, and anything may be done in relation to articles so made, without infringing copyright in the work.

(3) In subsection (1) "marketed" means sold, let for hire or offered or exposed for sale or hire, in the United Kingdom or elsewhere.

Works in electronic form

[2.85]

56 Transfers of copies of works in electronic form

(1) This section applies where a copy of a work in electronic form has been purchased on terms which, expressly or impliedly or by virtue of any rule of law, allow the purchaser to copy the work, or to adapt it or make copies of an adaptation, in connection with his use of it.

(2) If there are no express terms—

(a) prohibiting the transfer of the copy by the purchaser, imposing obligations which continue after a transfer, prohibiting the assignment of any licence or terminating any licence on a transfer, or

(b) providing for the terms on which a transferee may do the things which the purchaser was permitted to do,

anything which the purchaser was allowed to do may also be done without infringement of copyright by a transferee; but any copy, adaptation or copy of an adaptation made by the purchaser which is not also transferred shall be treated as an infringing copy for all purposes after the transfer.

(3) The same applies where the original purchased copy is no longer usable and what is transferred is a further copy used in its place.

(4) The above provisions also apply on a subsequent transfer, with the substitution for references in subsection (2) to the purchaser of references to the subsequent transferor.

Miscellaneous: literary, dramatic, musical and artistic works

[2.86]

57 Anonymous or pseudonymous works: acts permitted on assumptions as to expiry of copyright or death of author

(1) Copyright in a literary, dramatic, musical or artistic work is not infringed by an act done at a time when, or in pursuance of arrangements made at a time when—

(a) it is not possible by reasonable inquiry to ascertain the identity of the author, and

(b) it is reasonable to assume—

(i) that copyright has expired, or

(ii) that the author died [70 years] or more before the beginning of the calendar year in which the act is done or the arrangements are made.

(2) Subsection (1)(b)(ii) does not apply in relation to—
(a) a work in which Crown copyright subsists, or
(b) a work in which copyright originally vested in an international organisation by virtue of section 168 and in respect of which an Order under that section specifies a copyright period longer than [70 years].
(3) In relation to a work of joint authorship—
(a) the reference in subsection (1) to its being possible to ascertain the identity of the author shall be construed as a reference to its being possible to ascertain the identity of any of the authors, and
(b) the reference in subsection (1)(b)(ii) to the author having died shall be construed as a reference to all the authors having died.

NOTES

Sub-ss (1), (2): words in square brackets substituted by the Duration of Copyright and Rights in Performances Regulations 1995, SI 1995/3297, regs 4, 5(2), subject to transitional provisions and savings specified in regs 12–34 of those Regulations, at **[2.478]–[2.499]**.

[2.87]

58 Use of notes or recordings of spoken words in certain cases

(1) Where a record of spoken words is made, in writing or otherwise, for the purpose—
(a) of reporting current events, or
(b) of [communicating to the public] the whole or part of the work,

it is not an infringement of any copyright in the words as a literary work to use the record or material taken from it (or to copy the record, or any such material, and use the copy) for that purpose, provided the following conditions are met.
(2) The conditions are that—
(a) the record is a direct record of the spoken words and is not taken from a previous record or from a broadcast . . . ;
(b) the making of the record was not prohibited by the speaker and, where copyright already subsisted in the work, did not infringe copyright;
(c) the use made of the record or material taken from it is not of a kind prohibited by or on behalf of the speaker or copyright owner before the record was made; and
(d) the use is by or with the authority of a person who is lawfully in possession of the record.

NOTES

Sub-s (1): words in square brackets substituted by the Copyright and Related Rights Regulations 2003, SI 2003/2498, reg 2(1), Sch 1, Pt 1, paras 1, 12(a), subject to transitional provisions as noted to s 1 of this Act at **[2.7]**.

Sub-s (2): words omitted from para (a) repealed by SI 2003/2498, reg 2(2), Sch 2, subject to transitional provisions as noted to s 1 of this Act at **[2.7]**.

[2.88]

59 Public reading or recitation

(1) The reading or recitation in public by one person of a reasonable extract from a published literary or dramatic work does not infringe any copyright in the work if it is accompanied by a sufficient acknowledgement.
(2) Copyright in a work is not infringed by the making of a sound recording, or the [communication to the public], of a reading or recitation which by virtue of subsection (1) does not infringe copyright in the work, provided that the recording [or communication to the public] consists mainly of material in relation to which it is not necessary to rely on that subsection.

NOTES

Sub-s (2): words in square brackets substituted by the Copyright and Related Rights Regulations 2003, SI 2003/2498, reg 2(1), Sch 1, Pt 1, paras 1, 5(a), 9(1)(a), subject to transitional provisions as noted to s 1 of this Act at **[2.7]**.

[2.89]

60 Abstracts of scientific or technical articles

(1) Where an article on a scientific or technical subject is published in a periodical accompanied by an abstract indicating the contents of the article, it is not an infringement of copyright in the abstract, or in the article, to copy the abstract or issue copies of it to the public.
(2) This section does not apply if or to the extent that there is a licensing scheme certified for the purposes of this section under section 143 providing for the grant of licences.

[2.90]

61 Recordings of folksongs

(1) A sound recording of a performance of a song may be made for the purpose of including it in an archive maintained by a [body not established or conducted for profit] without infringing any copyright in the words as a literary work or in the accompanying musical work, provided the conditions in subsection (2) below are met.
(2) The conditions are that—
(a) the words are unpublished and of unknown authorship at the time the recording is made,

(b) the making of the recording does not infringe any other copyright, and
(c) its making is not prohibited by any performer.

[(3) A single copy of a sound recording made in reliance on subsection (1) and included in an archive referred to in that subsection may be made and supplied by the archivist without infringing copyright in the recording or the works included in it, provided that—
(a) the copy is supplied in response to a request from a person who has provided the archivist with a declaration in writing which includes the information set out in subsection (4), and
(b) the archivist is not aware that the declaration is false in a material particular.

(4) The information which must be included in the declaration is—
(a) the name of the person who requires the copy and the sound recording which is the subject of the request,
(b) a statement that the person has not previously been supplied with a copy of that sound recording by any archivist, and
(c) a statement that the person requires the copy for the purposes of research for a non-commercial purpose or private study, will use it only for those purposes and will not supply the copy to any other person.

(5) Where an archive makes a charge for supplying a copy under this section, the sum charged must be calculated by reference to the costs attributable to the production of the copy.

(6) Where a person ("P") makes a declaration under this section that is false in a material particular and is supplied with a copy which would have been an infringing copy if made by P—
(a) P is liable for infringement of copyright as if P had made the copy, and
(b) the copy supplied to P is to be treated as an infringing copy for all purposes.

(7) In this section references to an archivist include a person acting on behalf of an archivist.]

NOTES

Sub-s (1): words in square brackets substituted by the Copyright and Rights in Performances (Research, Education, Libraries and Archives) Regulations 2014, SI 2014/1372, regs 2(1), 7(1).

Sub-ss (3)–(7): substituted for original sub-ss (3)–(6), by SI 2014/1372, regs 2(1), 7(2).

Orders: the Copyright (Recording of Folksongs for Archives) (Designated Bodies) Order 1989, SI 1989/1012.

[2.91]

62 Representation of certain artistic works on public display

(1) This section applies to—
(a) buildings, and
(b) sculptures, models for buildings and works of artistic craftsmanship, if permanently situated in a public place or in premises open to the public.

(2) The copyright in such a work is not infringed by—
(a) making a graphic work representing it,
(b) making a photograph or film of it, or
(c) [making a broadcast of] a visual image of it.

(3) Nor is the copyright infringed by the issue to the public of copies, or the [communication to the public], of anything whose making was, by virtue of this section, not an infringement of the copyright.

NOTES

Sub-s (2): words in square brackets substituted by the Copyright and Related Rights Regulations 2003, SI 2003/2498, reg 2(1), Sch 1, Pt 1, paras 1, 14, subject to transitional provisions as noted to s 1 of this Act at **[2.7]**.

Sub-s (3): words in square brackets substituted by SI 2003/2498, reg 2(1), Sch 1, Pt 1, paras 1, 5(c), subject to transitional provisions as noted to s 1 of this Act at **[2.7]**.

[2.92]

63 Advertisement of sale of artistic work

(1) It is not an infringement of copyright in an artistic work to copy it, or to issue copies to the public, for the purpose of advertising the sale of the work.

(2) Where a copy which would otherwise be an infringing copy is made in accordance with this section but is subsequently dealt with for any other purpose, it shall be treated as an infringing copy for the purposes of that dealing, and if that dealing infringes copyright for all subsequent purposes.

For this purpose "dealt with" means sold or let for hire, offered or exposed for sale or hire, exhibited in public[, distributed or communicated to the public].

NOTES

Sub-s (2): words in square brackets substituted by the Copyright and Related Rights Regulations 2003, SI 2003/2498, regs 3, 17, subject to transitional provisions as noted to s 1 of this Act at **[2.7]**.

[2.93]

64 Making of subsequent works by same artist

Where the author of an artistic work is not the copyright owner, he does not infringe the copyright by copying the work in making another artistic work, provided he does not repeat or imitate the main design of the earlier work.

[2.94]
65 Reconstruction of buildings
Anything done for the purposes of reconstructing a building does not infringe any copyright—
(a) in the building, or
(b) in any drawings or plans in accordance with which the building was, by or with the licence of the copyright owner, constructed.

[Miscellaneous: lending of works and playing of sound recordings

[2.95]
66 Lending to public of copies of certain works
(1) The Secretary of State may by order provide that in such cases as may be specified in the order the lending to the public of copies of literary, dramatic, musical or artistic works, sound recordings or films shall be treated as licensed by the copyright owner subject only to the payment of such reasonable royalty or other payment as may be agreed or determined in default of agreement by the Copyright Tribunal.
(2) No such order shall apply if, or to the extent that, there is a licensing scheme certified for the purposes of this section under section 143 providing for the grant of licences.
(3) An order may make different provision for different cases and may specify cases by reference to any factor relating to the work, the copies lent, the lender or the circumstances of the lending.
(4) An order shall be made by statutory instrument; and no order shall be made unless a draft of it has been laid before and approved by a resolution of each House of Parliament.
(5) Nothing in this section affects any liability under section 23 (secondary infringement: possessing or dealing with infringing copy) in respect of the lending of infringing copies.]

NOTES
Substituted, together with preceding heading, by the Copyright and Related Rights Regulations 1996, SI 1996/2967, regs 4, 11(3), subject to transitional provisions and savings specified in regs 25–36 of those Regulations, at **[2.510]**–**[2.521]**.

[Miscellaneous: films and sound recordings

[2.96]
66A Films: acts permitted on assumptions as to expiry of copyright, &c
(1) Copyright in a film is not infringed by an act done at a time when, or in pursuance of arrangements made at a time when—
(a) it is not possible by reasonable inquiry to ascertain the identity of any of the persons referred to in section 13B(2)(a) to (d) (persons by reference to whose life the copyright period is ascertained), and
(b) it is reasonable to assume—
(i) that copyright has expired, or
(ii) that the last to die of those persons died 70 years or more before the beginning of the calendar year in which the act is done or the arrangements are made.
(2) Subsection (1)(b)(ii) does not apply in relation to—
(a) a film in which Crown copyright subsists, or
(b) a film in which copyright originally vested in an international organisation by virtue of section 168 and in respect of which an Order under that section specifies a copyright period longer than 70 years.]

NOTES
Inserted, together with preceding heading, by the Duration of Copyright and Rights in Performances Regulations 1995, SI 1995/3297, regs 4, 6(2), subject to transitional provisions and savings specified in regs 12–34 of those Regulations, at **[2.478]**–**[2.499]**.

67 (*Repealed by the Copyright, Designs and Patents Act 1988 (Amendment) Regulations 2010, SI 2010/2694, reg 3(1).*)

Miscellaneous: broadcasts . . .

[2.97]
68 Incidental recording for purposes of broadcast or cable programme
(1) This section applies where by virtue of a licence or assignment of copyright a person is authorised to broadcast . . . —
(a) a literary, dramatic or musical work, or an adaptation of such a work,
(b) an artistic work, or
(c) a sound recording or film.
(2) He shall by virtue of this section be treated as licensed by the owner of the copyright in the work to do or authorise any of the following for the purposes of the broadcast . . . —
(a) in the case of a literary, dramatic or musical work, or an adaptation of such a work, to make a sound recording or film of the work or adaptation;
(b) in the case of an artistic work, to take a photograph or make a film of the work;
(c) in the case of a sound recording or film, to make a copy of it.
(3) That licence is subject to the condition that the recording, film, photograph or copy in question—

Part 2 Copyright

(a) shall not be used for any other purpose, and
(b) shall be destroyed within 28 days of being first used for broadcasting the work . . .

(4) A recording, film, photograph or copy made in accordance with this section shall be treated as an infringing copy—
(a) for the purposes of any use in breach of the condition mentioned in subsection (3)(a), and
(b) for all purposes after that condition or the condition mentioned in subsection (3)(b) is broken.

NOTES

Words omitted (including from the heading preceding this section) repealed by the Copyright and Related Rights Regulations 2003, SI 2003/2498, reg 2(2), Sch 2, subject to transitional provisions as noted to s 1 of this Act at **[2.7]**.

[2.98]

69 Recording for purposes of supervision and control of broadcasts and [other services]

(1) Copyright is not infringed by the making or use by the British Broadcasting Corporation, for the purpose of maintaining supervision and control over programmes broadcast by them [or included in any on-demand programme service provided by them], of recordings of those programmes.

[(2) Copyright is not infringed by anything done in pursuance of—
[(a) section 167(1) of the Broadcasting Act 1990, section 115(4) or (6) or 117 of the Broadcasting Act 1996 or paragraph 20 of Schedule 12 to the Communications Act 2003;]
(b) a condition which, [by virtue of section 334(1) of the Communications Act 2003], is included in a licence granted under Part I or III of that Act or Part I or II of the Broadcasting Act 1996; . . .
(c) a direction given under section 109(2) of the Broadcasting Act 1990 (power of [OFCOM] to require production of recordings etc);
[(d) section 334(3)[, 368O(1) or (3)] of the Communications Act 2003]].

[(3) Copyright is not infringed by the use by OFCOM in connection with the performance of any of their functions under the Broadcasting Act 1990, the Broadcasting Act 1996 or the Communications Act 2003 of—
(a) any recording, script or transcript which is provided to them under or by virtue of any provision of those Acts; or
(b) any existing material which is transferred to them by a scheme made under section 30 of the Communications Act 2003.

(4) In subsection (3), "existing material" means—
(a) any recording, script or transcript which was provided to the Independent Television Commission or the Radio Authority under or by virtue of any provision of the Broadcasting Act 1990 or the Broadcasting Act 1996; and
(b) any recording or transcript which was provided to the Broadcasting Standards Commission under section 115(4) or (6) or 116(5) of the Broadcasting Act 1996.]

[(5) Copyright is not infringed by the use by an appropriate regulatory authority designated under section 368B of the Communications Act 2003, in connection with the performance of any of their functions under that Act, of any recording, script or transcript which is provided to them under or by virtue of any provision of that Act.

(6) In this section "on-demand programme service" has the same meaning as in the Communications Act 2003 (see section 368A of that Act).]

NOTES

Section heading: words in square brackets substituted by the Copyright and Related Rights Regulations 2003, SI 2003/2498, reg 2(1), Sch 1, Pt 1, paras 1, 2(1), subject to transitional provisions as noted to s 1 of this Act at **[2.7]**.

Sub-s (1): words in square brackets inserted by the Audiovisual Media Services Regulations 2009, SI 2009/2979, reg 12(1), (2)(a).

Sub-s (2): substituted by the Broadcasting Act 1996, s 148(1), Sch 10, para 31; para (a) substituted, word omitted from para (b) repealed, words in square brackets in paras (b), (c) substituted, and para (d) inserted by the Communications Act 2003, s 406(1), (7), Sch 17, para 91(1), (2), Sch 19; words in square brackets in para (d) inserted by SI 2009/2979, reg 12(1), (2)(b).

Sub-ss (3), (4): substituted for original sub-s (3) by the Communications Act 2003, s 406, Sch 17, para 91(1), (3).

Sub-ss (5), (6): inserted by SI 2009/2979, reg 12(1), (2)(c).

[2.99]

70 Recording for purposes of time-shifting

[(1)] The making [in domestic premises] for private and domestic use of a recording of a broadcast . . . solely for the purpose of enabling it to be viewed or listened to at a more convenient time does not infringe any copyright in the broadcast . . . or in any work included in it.

[(2) Where a copy which would otherwise be an infringing copy is made in accordance with this section but is subsequently dealt with—
(a) it shall be treated as an infringing copy for the purposes of that dealing; and
(b) if that dealing infringes copyright, it shall be treated as an infringing copy for all subsequent purposes.

(3) In subsection (2), "dealt with" means sold or let for hire, offered or exposed for sale or hire or communicated to the public.]

NOTES

Sub-s (1): numbered as such, words in square brackets inserted, and words omitted repealed, by the Copyright and Related Rights Regulations 2003, SI 2003/2498, regs 2, 3, 19(1), (2), Sch 2, subject to transitional provisions as noted to s 1 of this Act at **[2.7]**.

Sub-ss (2), (3): added by SI 2003/2498, regs 3, 19(1), (2), subject to transitional provisions as noted to s 1 of this Act at **[2.7]**.

[2.100]

[71 Photographs of broadcasts

(1) The making in domestic premises for private and domestic use of a photograph of the whole or any part of an image forming part of a broadcast, or a copy of such a photograph, does not infringe any copyright in the broadcast or in any film included in it.

(2) Where a copy which would otherwise be an infringing copy is made in accordance with this section but is subsequently dealt with—

- (a) it shall be treated as an infringing copy for the purposes of that dealing; and
- (b) if that dealing infringes copyright, it shall be treated as an infringing copy for all subsequent purposes.

(3) In subsection (2), "dealt with" means sold or let for hire, offered or exposed for sale or hire or communicated to the public.]

NOTES

Substituted by the Copyright and Related Rights Regulations 2003, SI 2003/2498, regs 3, 20(1), subject to transitional provisions as noted to s 1 of this Act at **[2.7]**.

[2.101]

72 Free public showing or playing of broadcast . . .

(1) The showing or playing in public of a broadcast . . . to an audience who have not paid for admission to the place where the broadcast . . . is to be seen or heard does not infringe any copyright in—

[(a) the broadcast; [or]

(b) any sound recording (except so far as it is an excepted sound recording) included in it . . .

(c) . . .]

[(1A) For the purposes of this Part an "excepted sound recording" is a sound recording—

(a) whose author is not the author of the broadcast in which it is included; and

(b) which is a recording of music with or without words spoken or sung.

(1B) Where by virtue of subsection (1) the copyright in a broadcast shown or played in public is not infringed, copyright in any [film or] excepted sound recording included in it is not infringed if the playing or showing of that broadcast in public—

(a) . . .

(b) is necessary for the purposes of—

(i) repairing equipment for the reception of broadcasts;

(ii) demonstrating that a repair to such equipment has been carried out; or

(iii) demonstrating such equipment which is being sold or let for hire or offered or exposed for sale or hire.]

(2) The audience shall be treated as having paid for admission to a place—

(a) if they have paid for admission to a place of which that place forms part; or

(b) if goods or services are supplied at that place (or a place of which it forms part)—

(i) at prices which are substantially attributable to the facilities afforded for seeing or hearing the broadcast . . . , or

(ii) at prices exceeding those usually charged there and which are partly attributable to those facilities.

(3) The following shall not be regarded as having paid for admission to a place—

(a) persons admitted as residents or inmates of the place;

(b) persons admitted as members of a club or society where the payment is only for membership of the club or society and the provision of facilities for seeing or hearing broadcasts . . . is only incidental to the main purposes of the club or society.

(4) Where the making of the broadcast . . . was an infringement of the copyright in a sound recording or film, the fact that it was heard or seen in public by the reception of the broadcast . . . shall be taken into account in assessing the damages for that infringement.

NOTES

Section heading: words omitted repealed by the Copyright and Related Rights Regulations 2003, SI 2003/2498, reg 2(2), Sch 2, subject to transitional provisions as noted to s 1 of this Act at **[2.7]**.

Sub-s (1): words omitted in the first and second places repealed, and paras (a)–(c) substituted, for original paras (a), (b), by SI 2003/2498, regs 3, 21(1)(a), subject to transitional provisions as noted to s 1 of this Act at **[2.7]**; word in square brackets in para (a) inserted, and para (c) repealed together with word preceding it, by the Copyright (Free Public Showing or Playing) (Amendment) Regulations 2016, SI 2016/565, regs 2, 3(a)–(c).

Part 2 Copyright

Sub-s (1A): inserted, together with sub-s (1B), by SI 2003/2498, regs 3, 21(1)(b), subject to transitional provisions as noted to s 1 of this Act at **[2.7]**.

Sub-s (1B): inserted as noted to sub-s (1A) above; words in square brackets inserted by SI 2016/565, regs 2, 3(d); para (a) repealed by the Copyright, Designs and Patents Act 1988 (Amendment) Regulations 2010, SI 2010/2694, reg 4(1).

Sub-ss (2), (3), (4): words omitted repealed by SI 2003/2498, reg 2(2), Sch 2, subject to transitional provisions as noted to s 1 of this Act at **[2.7]**.

[2.102]

[73 Reception and re-transmission of [wireless broadcast by cable]

(1) This section applies where a [wireless] broadcast made from a place in the United Kingdom is [received and immediately re-transmitted by cable].

(2) The copyright in the broadcast is not infringed—

(a) if the [re-transmission by cable] is in pursuance of a relevant requirement, or

(b) if and to the extent that the broadcast is made for reception in the area in which [it is re-transmitted by cable] and forms part of a qualifying service.

(3) The copyright in any work included in the broadcast is not infringed if and to the extent that the broadcast is made for reception in the area in which [it is re-transmitted by cable]; but where the making of the broadcast was an infringement of the copyright in the work, the fact that the broadcast was re-transmitted [by cable] shall be taken into account in assessing the damages for that infringement.

(4) Where—

(a) the [re-transmission by cable] is in pursuance of a relevant requirement, but

(b) to any extent, the area in which the [re-transmission by cable takes place] ("the cable area") falls outside the area for reception in which the broadcast is made ("the broadcast area"),

the [re-transmission by cable] (to the extent that it is provided for so much of the cable area as falls outside the broadcast area) of any work included in the broadcast shall, subject to subsection (5), be treated as licensed by the owner of the copyright in the work, subject only to the payment to him by the person making the broadcast of such reasonable royalty or other payment in respect of the [re-transmission by cable of the broadcast] as may be agreed or determined in default of agreement by the Copyright Tribunal.

(5) Subsection (4) does not apply if, or to the extent that, the [re-transmission of the work by cable] is (apart from that subsection) licensed by the owner of the copyright in the work.

(6) In this section "qualifying service" means, subject to subsection (8), any of the following services—

(a) a regional or national Channel 3 service,

(b) Channel 4, Channel 5 and S4C,

[(c) the public teletext service,

(d) S4C Digital, and]

(e) the television broadcasting services and teletext service of the British Broadcasting Corporation;

[and expressions used in this subsection have the same meanings as in Part 3 of the Communications Act 2003.]

[(7) In this section "relevant requirement" means a requirement imposed by a general condition (within the meaning of Chapter 1 of Part 2 of the Communications Act 2003) the setting of which is authorised under section 64 of that Act (must-carry obligations).]

(8) The Secretary of State may by order amend subsection (6) so as to add any service to, or remove any service from, the definition of "qualifying service".

(9) The Secretary of State may also by order—

(a) provide that in specified cases subsection (3) is to apply in relation to broadcasts of a specified description which are not made as mentioned in that subsection, or

(b) exclude the application of that subsection in relation to broadcasts of a specified description made as mentioned in that subsection.

(10) Where the Secretary of State exercises the power conferred by subsection (9)(b) in relation to broadcasts of any description, the order may also provide for subsection (4) to apply, subject to such modifications as may be specified in the order, in relation to broadcasts of that description.

(11) An order under this section may contain such transitional provision as appears to the Secretary of State to be appropriate.

(12) An order under this section shall be made by statutory instrument which shall be subject to annulment in pursuance of a resolution of either House of Parliament.

[(13) In this section references to re-transmission by cable include the transmission of microwave energy between terrestrial fixed points.]]

NOTES

Substituted, together with s 73A, for original s 73, by the Broadcasting Act 1996, s 138, Sch 9, para 1.

Repealed by the Digital Economy Act 2017, s 34(1)(a), as from a day to be appointed.

Section heading: words in square brackets substituted by the Copyright and Related Rights Regulations 2003, SI 2003/2498, regs 3, 22(1)(a), subject to transitional provisions as noted to s 1 of this Act at **[2.7]**.

Sub-ss (1)–(5): words in square brackets inserted and substituted by SI 2003/2498, regs 3, 22(1)(b)–(g), subject to transitional provisions as noted to s 1 of this Act at **[2.7]**.

Sub-s (6): paras (c), (d), and words in square brackets following para (e) substituted by the Communications Act 2003, s 406(1), Sch 17, para 92(1), (2).

Sub-s (7): substituted by the Communications Act 2003, s 406(1), Sch 17, para 92(1), (3).

Sub-s (13): added by SI 2003/2498, regs 3, 22(1)(h), subject to transitional provisions as noted to s 1 of this Act at **[2.7]**.

[2.103]

[73A Royalty or other sum payable in pursuance of section 73(4)

(1) An application to settle the royalty or other sum payable in pursuance of subsection (4) of section 73 (reception and re-transmission of [wireless broadcast by cable]) may be made to the Copyright Tribunal by the copyright owner or the person making the broadcast.

(2) The Tribunal shall consider the matter and make such order as it may determine to be reasonable in the circumstances.

(3) Either party may subsequently apply to the Tribunal to vary the order, and the Tribunal shall consider the matter and make such order confirming or varying the original order as it may determine to be reasonable in the circumstances.

(4) An application under subsection (3) shall not, except with the special leave of the Tribunal, be made within twelve months from the date of the original order or of the order on a previous application under that subsection.

(5) An order under subsection (3) has effect from the date on which it is made or such later date as may be specified by the Tribunal.]

NOTES

Substituted as noted to s 73, at **[2.102]**.

Repealed by the Digital Economy Act 2017, s 34(1)(a), as from a day to be appointed.

Sub-s (1): words in square brackets substituted by the Copyright and Related Rights Regulations 2003, SI 2003/2498, regs 3, 22(2), subject to transitional provisions as noted to s 1 of this Act at **[2.7]**.

74 (*Repealed by the Copyright and Rights in Performances (Disability) Regulations 2014, SI 2014/1384, reg 4, Schedule, para 8.*)

[2.104]

[75 Recording of broadcast for archival purposes

(1) A recording of a broadcast or a copy of such a recording may be made for the purpose of being placed in an archive maintained by a body which is not established or conducted for profit without infringing any copyright in the broadcast or in any work included in it.

(2) To the extent that a term of a contract purports to prevent or restrict the doing of any act which, by virtue of this section, would not infringe copyright, that term is unenforceable.]

NOTES

Commencement: 1 June 2014 (at 00.02 hrs).

Substituted by the Copyright and Rights in Performances (Research, Education, Libraries and Archives) Regulations 2014, SI 2014/1372, regs 2(1), 8(1).

Adaptations

[2.105]

76 Adaptations

An act which by virtue of this Chapter may be done without infringing copyright in a literary, dramatic or musical work does not, where that work is an adaptation, infringe any copyright in the work from which the adaptation was made.

[CHAPTER 3A

CERTAIN PERMITTED USES OF ORPHAN WORKS

[2.106]

76A Certain permitted uses of orphan works

Schedule ZA1 makes provision about the use by relevant bodies of orphan works.]

NOTES

Commencement: 29 October 2014.

Inserted, together with preceding Chapter heading, by the Copyright and Rights in Performances (Certain Permitted Uses of Orphan Works) Regulations 2014, SI 2014/2861, reg 3(2).

CHAPTER IV
MORAL RIGHTS

Right to be identified as author or director

[2.107]

77 Right to be identified as author or director

(1) The author of a copyright literary, dramatic, musical or artistic work, and the director of a copyright film, has the right to be identified as the author or director of the work in the circumstances mentioned in this section; but the right is not infringed unless it has been asserted in accordance with section 78.

(2) The author of a literary work (other than words intended to be sung or spoken with music) or a dramatic work has the right to be identified whenever—

(a) the work is published commercially, performed in public [or communicated to the public]; or

(b) copies of a film or sound recording including the work are issued to the public;

and that right includes the right to be identified whenever any of those events occur in relation to an adaptation of the work as the author of the work from which the adaptation was made.

(3) The author of a musical work, or a literary work consisting of words intended to be sung or spoken with music, has the right to be identified whenever—

(a) the work is published commercially;

(b) copies of a sound recording of the work are issued to the public; or

(c) a film of which the sound-track includes the work is shown in public or copies of such a film are issued to the public;

and that right includes the right to be identified whenever any of those events occur in relation to an adaptation of the work as the author of the work from which the adaptation was made.

(4) The author of an artistic work has the right to be identified whenever—

(a) the work is published commercially or exhibited in public, or a visual image of it is [communicated to the public];

(b) a film including a visual image of the work is shown in public or copies of such a film are issued to the public; or

(c) in the case of a work of architecture in the form of a building or a model for a building, a sculpture or a work of artistic craftsmanship, copies of a graphic work representing it, or of a photograph of it, are issued to the public.

(5) The author of a work of architecture in the form of a building also has the right to be identified on the building as constructed or, where more than one building is constructed to the design, on the first to be constructed.

(6) The director of a film has the right to be identified whenever the film is shown in public [or communicated to the public] or copies of the film are issued to the public.

(7) The right of the author or director under this section is—

(a) in the case of commercial publication or the issue to the public of copies of a film or sound recording, to be identified in or on each copy or, if that is not appropriate, in some other manner likely to bring his identity to the notice of a person acquiring a copy,

(b) in the case of identification on a building, to be identified by appropriate means visible to persons entering or approaching the building, and

(c) in any other case, to be identified in a manner likely to bring his identity to the attention of a person seeing or hearing the performance, exhibition, showing [or communication to the public] in question;

and the identification must in each case be clear and reasonably prominent.

(8) If the author or director in asserting his right to be identified specifies a pseudonym, initials or some other particular form of identification, that form shall be used; otherwise any reasonable form of identification may be used.

(9) This section has effect subject to section 79 (exceptions to right).

NOTES

Sub-ss (2), (4), (6), (7): words in square brackets substituted by the Copyright and Related Rights Regulations 2003, SI 2003/2498, reg 2(1), Sch 1, Pt 1, paras 1, 8(1)(a), (b), (2)(a), 9(1)(b), subject to transitional provisions as noted to s 1 of this Act at **[2.7]**.

[2.108]

78 Requirement that right be asserted

(1) A person does not infringe the right conferred by section 77 (right to be identified as author or director) by doing any of the acts mentioned in that section unless the right has been asserted in accordance with the following provisions so as to bind him in relation to that act.

(2) The right may be asserted generally, or in relation to any specified act or description of acts—

(a) on an assignment of copyright in the work, by including in the instrument effecting the assignment a statement that the author or director asserts in relation to that work his right to be identified, or

(b) by instrument in writing signed by the author or director.

(3) The right may also be asserted in relation to the public exhibition of an artistic work—

(a) by securing that when the author or other first owner of copyright parts with possession of the original, or of a copy made by him or under his direction or control, the author is identified on the original or copy, or on a frame, mount or other thing to which it is attached, or

(b) by including in a licence by which the author or other first owner of copyright authorises the making of copies of the work a statement signed by or on behalf of the person granting the licence that the author asserts his right to be identified in the event of the public exhibition of a copy made in pursuance of the licence.

(4) The persons bound by an assertion of the right under subsection (2) or (3) are—

(a) in the case of an assertion under subsection (2)(a), the assignee and anyone claiming through him, whether or not he has notice of the assertion;

(b) in the case of an assertion under subsection (2)(b), anyone to whose notice the assertion is brought;

(c) in the case of an assertion under subsection (3)(a), anyone into whose hands that original or copy comes, whether or not the identification is still present or visible;

(d) in the case of an assertion under subsection (3)(b), the licensee and anyone into whose hands a copy made in pursuance of the licence comes, whether or not he has notice of the assertion.

(5) In an action for infringement of the right the court shall, in considering remedies, take into account any delay in asserting the right.

[2.109]

79 Exceptions to right

(1) The right conferred by section 77 (right to be identified as author or director) is subject to the following exceptions.

(2) The right does not apply in relation to the following descriptions of work—

(a) a computer program;

(b) the design of a typeface;

(c) any computer-generated work.

(3) The right does not apply to anything done by or with the authority of the copyright owner where copyright in the work originally [vested in the author's or director's employer by virtue of section 11(2) (works produced in the course of employment)].

(4) The right is not infringed by an act which by virtue of any of the following provisions would not infringe copyright in the work—

(a) section 30 (fair dealing for certain purposes), so far as it relates to the reporting of current events by means of a sound recording, film [or broadcast];

(b) section 31 (incidental inclusion of work in an artistic work, sound recording, film [or broadcast]);

(c) . . .

(d) section 45 (parliamentary and judicial proceedings);

(e) section 46(1) or (2) (Royal Commissions and statutory inquiries);

(f) section 51 (use of design documents and models);

(g) section 52 (effect of exploitation of design derived from artistic work);

(h) [section 57 or 66A (acts permitted on assumptions as to expiry of copyright, &c)].

[(4A) The right is also not infringed by any act done for the purposes of an examination which by virtue of any provision of Chapter 3 of Part 1 would not infringe copyright.]

(5) The right does not apply in relation to any work made for the purpose of reporting current events.

(6) The right does not apply in relation to the publication in—

(a) a newspaper, magazine or similar periodical, or

(b) an encyclopaedia, dictionary, yearbook or other collective work of reference,

of a literary, dramatic, musical or artistic work made for the purposes of such publication or made available with the consent of the author for the purposes of such publication.

(7) The right does not apply in relation to—

(a) a work in which Crown copyright or Parliamentary copyright subsists, or

(b) a work in which copyright originally vested in an international organisation by virtue of section 168,

unless the author or director has previously been identified as such in or on published copies of the work.

NOTES

Sub-s (3): words in square brackets substituted by the Copyright and Related Rights Regulations 2003, SI 2003/2498, reg 2(1), Sch 1, Pt 1, paras 1, 18(1), subject to transitional provisions as noted to s 1 of this Act at **[2.7]**.

Sub-s (4): words in square brackets in paras (a), (b) substituted by SI 2003/2498, reg 2(1), Sch 1, Pt 1, paras 1, 3(1)(g), (h), subject to transitional provisions as noted to s 1 of this Act at **[2.7]**; para (c) repealed by the Copyright and Rights in Performances (Research, Education, Libraries and Archives) Regulations 2014, SI 2014/1372, reg 2(2), Schedule, paras 1, 4(a); para (g) repealed by the Enterprise and Regulatory Reform Act 2013, s 74(1), (3)(a), as from 28 July 2016, subject to savings as noted to s 52 at **[2.81]**; words in square brackets in para (h) substituted by the Duration of Copyright and Rights in Performances Regulations 1995, SI 1995/3297, regs 4, 6(3), subject to transitional provisions and savings specified in regs 12–34 of those Regulations, at **[2.478]–[2.499]**.

Part 2 Copyright

Sub-s (4A): inserted by the Copyright and Rights in Performances (Research, Education, Libraries and Archives) Regulations 2014, SI 2014/1372, reg 2(2), Schedule, paras 1, 4(b).

Right to object to derogatory treatment of work

[2.110]

80 Right to object to derogatory treatment of work

(1) The author of a copyright literary, dramatic, musical or artistic work, and the director of a copyright film, has the right in the circumstances mentioned in this section not to have his work subjected to derogatory treatment.

(2) For the purposes of this section—

(a) "treatment" of a work means any addition to, deletion from or alteration to or adaptation of the work, other than—

(i) a translation of a literary or dramatic work, or

(ii) an arrangement or transcription of a musical work involving no more than a change of key or register; and

(b) the treatment of a work is derogatory if it amounts to distortion or mutilation of the work or is otherwise prejudicial to the honour or reputation of the author or director;

and in the following provisions of this section references to a derogatory treatment of a work shall be construed accordingly.

(3) In the case of a literary, dramatic or musical work the right is infringed by a person who—

(a) publishes commercially, performs in public [or communicates to the public] a derogatory treatment of the work; or

(b) issues to the public copies of a film or sound recording of, or including, a derogatory treatment of the work.

(4) In the case of an artistic work the right is infringed by a person who—

(a) publishes commercially or exhibits in public a derogatory treatment of the work, [or communicates to the public] a visual image of a derogatory treatment of the work,

(b) shows in public a film including a visual image of a derogatory treatment of the work or issues to the public copies of such a film, or

(c) in the case of—

(i) a work of architecture in the form of a model for a building,

(ii) a sculpture, or

(iii) a work of artistic craftsmanship,

issues to the public copies of a graphic work representing, or of a photograph of, a derogatory treatment of the work.

(5) Subsection (4) does not apply to a work of architecture in the form of a building; but where the author of such a work is identified on the building and it is the subject of derogatory treatment he has the right to require the identification to be removed.

(6) In the case of a film, the right is infringed by a person who—

(a) shows in public [or communicates to the public] a derogatory treatment of the film; or

(b) issues to the public copies of a derogatory treatment of the film,

(7) The right conferred by this section extends to the treatment of parts of a work resulting from a previous treatment by a person other than the author or director, if those parts are attributed to, or are likely to be regarded as the work of, the author or director.

(8) This section has effect subject to sections 81 and 82 (exceptions to and qualifications of right).

NOTES

Sub-s (3): words in square brackets substituted by the Copyright and Related Rights Regulations 2003, SI 2003/2498, reg 2(1), Sch 1, Pt 1, paras 1, 10(1)(a), subject to transitional provisions as noted to s 1 of this Act at **[2.7]**.

Sub-s (4): words in square brackets substituted by SI 2003/2498, reg 2(1), Sch 1, Pt 1, paras 1, 13(2), subject to transitional provisions as noted to s 1 of this Act at **[2.7]**.

Sub-s (6): words in square brackets substituted by SI 2003/2498, reg 2(1), Sch 1, Pt 1, paras 1, 10(1)(b), subject to transitional provisions as noted to s 1 of this Act at **[2.7]**; words omitted repealed by the Duration of Copyright and Rights in Performances Regulations 1995, SI 1995/3297, regs 4, 9(2), subject to transitional provisions and savings specified in regs 12–34 of those Regulations, at **[2.478]–[2.499]**.

[2.111]

81 Exceptions to right

(1) The right conferred by section 80 (right to object to derogatory treatment of work) is subject to the following exceptions.

(2) The right does not apply to a computer program or to any computer-generated work.

(3) The right does not apply in relation to any work made for the purpose of reporting current events.

(4) The right does not apply in relation to the publication in—

(a) a newspaper, magazine or similar periodical, or

(b) an encyclopaedia, dictionary, yearbook or other collective work of reference,

of a literary, dramatic, musical or artistic work made for the purposes of such publication or made available with the consent of the author for the purposes of such publication.

Nor does the right apply in relation to any subsequent exploitation elsewhere of such a work without any modification of the published version.

(5) The right is not infringed by an act which by virtue of [section 57 or 66A (acts permitted on assumptions as to expiry of copyright, &c)] would not infringe copyright.

(6) The right is not infringed by anything done for the purpose of—

(a) avoiding the commission of an offence,

(b) complying with a duty imposed by or under an enactment, or

(c) in the case of the British Broadcasting Corporation, avoiding the inclusion in a programme broadcast by them of anything which offends against good taste or decency or which is likely to encourage or incite to crime or to lead to disorder or to be offensive to public feeling,

provided, where the author or director is identified at the time of the relevant act or has previously been identified in or on published copies of the work, that there is a sufficient disclaimer.

NOTES

Sub-s (5): words in square brackets substituted by the Duration of Copyright and Rights in Performances Regulations 1995, SI 1995/3297, regs 4, 6(3), subject to transitional provisions and savings specified in regs 12–34 of those Regulations, at **[2.478]–[2.499]**.

[2.112]

82 Qualification of right in certain cases

(1) This section applies to—

(a) works in which copyright originally vested in the author's [or director's] employer by virtue of section 11(2) (works produced in course of employment) . . . ,

(b) works in which Crown copyright or Parliamentary copyright subsists, and

(c) works in which copyright originally vested in an international organisation by virtue of section 168.

(2) The right conferred by section 80 (right to object to derogatory treatment of work) does not apply to anything done in relation to such a work by or with the authority of the copyright owner unless the author or director—

(a) is identified at the time of the relevant act, or

(b) has previously been identified in or on published copies of the work;

and where in such a case the right does apply, it is not infringed if there is a sufficient disclaimer.

NOTES

Sub-s (1): words in square brackets substituted, and words omitted repealed, by the Copyright and Related Rights Regulations 2003, SI 2003/2498, reg 2, Sch 1, Pt 1, paras 1, 18(2), Sch 2, subject to transitional provisions as noted to s 1 of this Act at **[2.7]**.

[2.113]

83 Infringement of right by possessing or dealing with infringing article

(1) The right conferred by section 80 (right to object to derogatory treatment of work) is also infringed by a person who—

(a) possesses in the course of a business, or

(b) sells or lets for hire, or offers or exposes for sale or hire, or

(c) in the course of a business exhibits in public or distributes, or

(d) distributes otherwise than in the course of a business so as to affect prejudicially the honour or reputation of the author or director,

an article which is, and which he knows or has reason to believe is, an infringing article.

(2) An "infringing article" means a work or a copy of a work which—

(a) has been subjected to derogatory treatment within the meaning of section 80, and

(b) has been or is likely to be the subject of any of the acts mentioned in that section in circumstances infringing that right.

False attribution of work

[2.114]

84 False attribution of work

(1) A person has the right in the circumstances mentioned in this section—

(a) not to have a literary, dramatic, musical or artistic work falsely attributed to him as author, and

(b) not to have a film falsely attributed to him as director;

and in this section an "attribution", in relation to such a work, means a statement (express or implied) as to who is the author or director.

(2) The right is infringed by a person who—

(a) issues to the public copies of a work of any of those descriptions in or on which there is a false attribution, or

(b) exhibits in public an artistic work, or a copy of an artistic work, in or on which there is a false attribution.

(3) The right is also infringed by a person who—

(a) in the case of a literary, dramatic or musical work, performs the work in public [or communicates it to the public] as being the work of a person, or

Part 2 Copyright

(b) in the case of a film, shows it in public [or communicates it to the public] as being directed by a person,

knowing or having reason to believe that the attribution is false.

(4) The right is also infringed by the issue to the public or public display of material containing a false attribution in connection with any of the acts mentioned in subsection (2) or (3).

(5) The right is also infringed by a person who in the course of a business—

(a) possesses or deals with a copy of a work of any of the descriptions mentioned in subsection (1) in or on which there is a false attribution, or

(b) in the case of an artistic work, possesses or deals with the work itself when there is a false attribution in or on it,

knowing or having reason to believe that there is such an attribution and that it is false.

(6) In the case of an artistic work the right is also infringed by a person who in the course of a business—

(a) deals with a work which has been altered after the author parted with possession of it as being the unaltered work of the author, or

(b) deals with a copy of such a work as being a copy of the unaltered work of the author,

knowing or having reason to believe that that is not the case.

(7) References in this section to dealing are to selling or letting for hire, offering or exposing for sale or hire, exhibiting in public, or distributing.

(8) This section applies where, contrary to the fact—

(a) a literary, dramatic or musical work is falsely represented as being an adaptation of the work of a person, or

(b) a copy of an artistic work is falsely represented as being a copy made by the author of the artistic work,

as it applies where the work is falsely attributed to a person as author.

NOTES

Sub-s (3): words in square brackets substituted by the Copyright and Related Rights Regulations 2003, SI 2003/2498, reg 2(1), Sch 1, Pt 1, paras 1, 10(2), subject to transitional provisions as noted to s 1 of this Act at **[2.7]**.

Right to privacy of certain photographs and films

[2.115]

85 Right to privacy of certain photographs and films

(1) A person who for private and domestic purposes commissions the taking of a photograph or the making of a film has, where copyright subsists in the resulting work, the right not to have—

(a) copies of the work issued to the public,

(b) the work exhibited or shown in public, or

(c) the work [communicated to the public];

and, except as mentioned in subsection (2), a person who does or authorises the doing of any of those acts infringes that right.

(2) The right is not infringed by an act which by virtue of any of the following provisions would not infringe copyright in the work—

(a) section 31 (incidental inclusion of work in an artistic work, film [or broadcast]);

(b) section 45 (parliamentary and judicial proceedings);

(c) section 46 (Royal Commissions and statutory inquiries);

(d) section 50 (acts done under statutory authority);

(e) [section 57 or 66A (acts permitted on assumptions as to expiry of copyright, &c)].

NOTES

Sub-s (1): words in square brackets in para (c) substituted by the Copyright and Related Rights Regulations 2003, SI 2003/2498, reg 2(1), Sch 1, Pt 1, paras 1, 83(2)(b), subject to transitional provisions as noted to s 1 of this Act at **[2.7]**.

Sub-s (2): words in square brackets in para (a) substituted by SI 2003/2498, reg 2(1), Sch 1, Pt 1, paras 1, 3(1)(i), subject to transitional provisions as noted to s 1 of this Act at **[2.7]**; words in square brackets in para (e) substituted by the Duration of Copyright and Rights in Performances Regulations 1995, SI 1995/3297, regs 4, 6(3), subject to transitional provisions and savings specified in regs 12–34 of those Regulations, at **[2.478]–[2.499]**.

Supplementary

[2.116]

86 Duration of rights

(1) The rights conferred by section 77 (right to be identified as author or director), section 80 (right to object to derogatory treatment of work) and section 85 (right to privacy of certain photographs and films) continue to subsist so long as copyright subsists in the work.

(2) The right conferred by section 84 (false attribution) continues to subsist until 20 years after a person's death.

[2.117]

87 Consent and waiver of rights

(1) It is not an infringement of any of the rights conferred by this Chapter to do any act to which the person entitled to the right has consented.

(2) Any of those rights may be waived by instrument in writing signed by the person giving up the right.

(3) A waiver—

(a) may relate to a specific work, to works of a specified description or to works generally, and may relate to existing or future works, and

(b) may be conditional or unconditional and may be expressed to be subject to revocation;

and if made in favour of the owner or prospective owner of the copyright in the work or works to which it relates, it shall be presumed to extend to his licensees and successors in title unless a contrary intention is expressed.

(4) Nothing in this Chapter shall be construed as excluding the operation of the general law of contract or estoppel in relation to an informal waiver or other transaction in relation to any of the rights mentioned in subsection (1).

[2.118]

88 Application of provisions to joint works

(1) The right conferred by section 77 (right to be identified as author or director) is, in the case of a work of joint authorship, a right of each joint author to be identified as a joint author and must be asserted in accordance with section 78 by each joint author in relation to himself.

(2) The right conferred by section 80 (right to object to derogatory treatment of work) is, in the case of a work of joint authorship, a right of each joint author and his right is satisfied if he consents to the treatment in question.

(3) A waiver under section 87 of those rights by one joint author does not affect the rights of the other joint authors.

(4) The right conferred by section 84 (false attribution) is infringed, in the circumstances mentioned in that section—

(a) by any false statement as to the authorship of a work of joint authorship, and

(b) by the false attribution of joint authorship in relation to a work of sole authorship;

and such a false attribution infringes the right of every person to whom authorship of any description is, whether rightly or wrongly, attributed.

(5) The above provisions also apply (with any necessary adaptations) in relation to a film which was, or is alleged to have been, jointly directed, as they apply to a work which is, or is alleged to be, a work of joint authorship.

A film is "jointly directed" if it is made by the collaboration of two or more directors and the contribution of each director is not distinct from that of the other director or directors.

(6) The right conferred by section 85 (right to privacy of certain photographs and films) is, in the case of a work made in pursuance of a joint commission, a right of each person who commissioned the making of the work, so that—

(a) the right of each is satisfied if he consents to the act in question, and

(b) a waiver under section 87 by one of them does not affect the rights of the others.

[2.119]

89 Application of provisions to parts of works

(1) The rights conferred by section 77 (right to be identified as author or director) and section 85 (right to privacy of certain photographs and films) apply in relation to the whole or any substantial part of a work.

(2) The rights conferred by section 80 (right to object to derogatory treatment of work) and section 84 (false attribution) apply in relation to the whole or any part of a work.

CHAPTER V
DEALINGS WITH RIGHTS IN COPYRIGHT WORKS

Copyright

[2.120]

90 Assignment and licences

(1) Copyright is transmissible by assignment, by testamentary disposition or by operation of law, as personal or moveable property.

(2) An assignment or other transmission of copyright may be partial, that is, limited so as to apply—

(a) to one or more, but not all, of the things the copyright owner has the exclusive right to do;

(b) to part, but not the whole, of the period for which the copyright is to subsist.

(3) An assignment of copyright is not effective unless it is in writing signed by or on behalf of the assignor.

(4) A licence granted by a copyright owner is binding on every successor in title to his interest in the copyright, except a purchaser in good faith for valuable consideration and without notice (actual or constructive) of the licence or a person deriving title from such a purchaser; and references in this Part to doing anything with, or without, the licence of the copyright owner shall be construed accordingly.

[2.121]
91 Prospective ownership of copyright
(1) Where by an agreement made in relation to future copyright, and signed by or on behalf of the prospective owner of the copyright, the prospective owner purports to assign the future copyright (wholly or partially) to another person, then if, on the copyright coming into existence, the assignee or another person claiming under him would be entitled as against all other persons to require the copyright to be vested in him, the copyright shall vest in the assignee or his successor in title by virtue of this subsection.
(2) In this Part—
"future copyright" means copyright which will or may come into existence in respect of a future work or class of works or on the occurrence of a future event; and
"prospective owner" shall be construed accordingly, and includes a person who is prospectively entitled to copyright by virtue of such an agreement as is mentioned in subsection (1).
(3) A licence granted by a prospective owner of copyright is binding on every successor in title to his interest (or prospective interest) in the right, except a purchaser in good faith for valuable consideration and without notice (actual or constructive) of the licence or a person deriving title from such a purchaser; and references in this Part to doing anything with, or without, the licence of the copyright owner shall be construed accordingly.

[2.122]
92 Exclusive licences
(1) In this Part an "exclusive licence" means a licence in writing signed by or on behalf of the copyright owner authorising the licensee to the exclusion of all other persons, including the person granting the licence, to exercise a right which would otherwise be exercisable exclusively by the copyright owner.
(2) The licensee under an exclusive licence has the same rights against a successor in title who is bound by the licence as he has against the person granting the licence.

[2.123]
93 Copyright to pass under will with unpublished work
Where under a bequest (whether specific or general) a person is entitled, beneficially or otherwise, to—
(a) an original document or other material thing recording or embodying a literary, dramatic, musical or artistic work which was not published before the death of the testator, or
(b) an original material thing containing a sound recording or film which was not published before the death of the testator,

the bequest shall, unless a contrary intention is indicated in the testator's will or a codicil to it, be construed as including the copyright in the work in so far as the testator was the owner of the copyright immediately before his death.

[2.124]
[93A Presumption of transfer of rental right in case of film production agreement
(1) Where an agreement concerning film production is concluded between an author and a film producer, the author shall be presumed, unless the agreement provides to the contrary, to have transferred to the film producer any rental right in relation to the film arising by virtue of the inclusion of a copy of the author's work in the film.
(2) In this section "author" means an author, or prospective author, of a literary, dramatic, musical or artistic work.
(3) Subsection (1) does not apply to any rental right in relation to the film arising by virtue of the inclusion in the film of the screenplay, the dialogue or music specifically created for and used in the film.
(4) Where this section applies, the absence of signature by or on behalf of the author does not exclude the operation of section 91(1) (effect of purported assignment of future copyright).
(5) The reference in subsection (1) to an agreement concluded between an author and a film producer includes any agreement having effect between those persons, whether made by them directly or through intermediaries.
(6) Section 93B (right to equitable remuneration on transfer of rental right) applies where there is a presumed transfer by virtue of this section as in the case of an actual transfer.]

NOTES
Inserted by the Copyright and Related Rights Regulations 1996, SI 1996/2967, regs 4, 12, subject to transitional provisions and savings specified in regs 25–36 of those Regulations, at **[2.510]–[2.521]**.

[Right to equitable remuneration where rental right transferred

[2.125]
93B Right to equitable remuneration where rental right transferred
(1) Where an author to whom this section applies has transferred his rental right concerning a sound recording or a film to the producer of the sound recording or film, he retains the right to equitable remuneration for the rental.
The authors to whom this section applies are—

(a) the author of a literary, dramatic, musical or artistic work, and
(b) the principal director of a film.

(2) The right to equitable remuneration under this section may not be assigned by the author except to a collecting society for the purpose of enabling it to enforce the right on his behalf.

The right is, however, transmissible by testamentary disposition or by operation of law as personal or moveable property; and it may be assigned or further transmitted by any person into whose hands it passes.

(3) Equitable remuneration under this section is payable by the person for the time being entitled to the rental right, that is, the person to whom the right was transferred or any successor in title of his.

(4) The amount payable by way of equitable remuneration is as agreed by or on behalf of the persons by and to whom it is payable, subject to section 93C (reference of amount to Copyright Tribunal).

(5) An agreement is of no effect in so far as it purports to exclude or restrict the right to equitable remuneration under this section.

(6) References in this section to the transfer of rental right by one person to another include any arrangement having that effect, whether made by them directly or through intermediaries.

(7) In this section a "collecting society" means a society or other organisation which has as its main object, or one of its main objects, the exercise of the right to equitable remuneration under this section on behalf of more than one author.]

NOTES

Inserted, together with preceding heading and s 93C, by the Copyright and Related Rights Regulations 1996, SI 1996/2967, regs 4, 14(1), subject to transitional provisions and savings specified in regs 25–36 of those Regulations, at **[2.510]–[2.521]**.

[2.126]

[93C Equitable remuneration: reference of amount to Copyright Tribunal

(1) In default of agreement as to the amount payable by way of equitable remuneration under section 93B, the person by or to whom it is payable may apply to the Copyright Tribunal to determine the amount payable.

(2) A person to or by whom equitable remuneration is payable under that section may also apply to the Copyright Tribunal—

(a) to vary any agreement as to the amount payable, or
(b) to vary any previous determination of the Tribunal as to that matter;

but except with the special leave of the Tribunal no such application may be made within twelve months from the date of a previous determination.

An order made on an application under this subsection has effect from the date on which it is made or such later date as may be specified by the Tribunal.

(3) On an application under this section the Tribunal shall consider the matter and make such order as to the method of calculating and paying equitable remuneration as it may determine to be reasonable in the circumstances, taking into account the importance of the contribution of the author to the film or sound recording.

(4) Remuneration shall not be considered inequitable merely because it was paid by way of a single payment or at the time of the transfer of the rental right.

(5) An agreement is of no effect in so far as it purports to prevent a person questioning the amount of equitable remuneration or to restrict the powers of the Copyright Tribunal under this section.]

NOTES

Inserted as noted to s 93B at **[2.125]**.

Moral rights

[2.127]

94 Moral rights not assignable

The rights conferred by Chapter IV (moral rights) are not assignable.

[2.128]

95 Transmission of moral rights on death

(1) On the death of a person entitled to the right conferred by section 77 (right to identification of author or director), section 80 (right to object to derogatory treatment of work) or section 85 (right to privacy of certain photographs and films)—

(a) the right passes to such person as he may by testamentary disposition specifically direct,
(b) if there is no such direction but the copyright in the work in question forms part of his estate, the right passes to the person to whom the copyright passes, and
(c) if or to the extent that the right does not pass under paragraph (a) or (b) it is exercisable by his personal representatives.

(2) Where copyright forming part of a person's estate passes in part to one person and in part to another, as for example where a bequest is limited so as to apply—

(a) to one or more, but not all, of the things the copyright owner has the exclusive right to do or authorise, or

(b) to part, but not the whole, of the period for which the copyright is to subsist,

any right which passes with the copyright by virtue of subsection (1) is correspondingly divided.

(3) Where by virtue of subsection (1)(a) or (b) a right becomes exercisable by more than one person—

(a) it may, in the case of the right conferred by section 77 (right to identification of author or director), be asserted by any of them;

(b) it is, in the case of the right conferred by section 80 (right to object to derogatory treatment of work) or section 85 (right to privacy of certain photographs and films), a right exercisable by each of them and is satisfied in relation to any of them if he consents to the treatment or act in question; and

(c) any waiver of the right in accordance with section 87 by one of them does not affect the rights of the others.

(4) A consent or waiver previously given or made binds any person to whom a right passes by virtue of subsection (1).

(5) Any infringement after a person's death of the right conferred by section 84 (false attribution) is actionable by his personal representatives.

(6) Any damages recovered by personal representatives by virtue of this section in respect of an infringement after a person's death shall devolve as part of his estate as if the right of action had subsisted and been vested in him immediately before his death.

CHAPTER VI
REMEDIES FOR INFRINGEMENT

Rights and remedies of copyright owner

[2.129]

96 Infringement actionable by copyright owner

(1) An infringement of copyright is actionable by the copyright owner.

(2) In an action for infringement of copyright all such relief by way of damages, injunctions, accounts or otherwise is available to the plaintiff as is available in respect of the infringement of any other property right.

(3) This section has effect subject to the following provisions of this Chapter.

[2.130]

97 Provisions as to damages in infringement action

(1) Where in an action for infringement of copyright it is shown that at the time of the infringement the defendant did not know, and had no reason to believe, that copyright subsisted in the work to which the action relates, the plaintiff is not entitled to damages against him, but without prejudice to any other remedy.

(2) The court may in an action for infringement of copyright having regard to all the circumstances, and in particular to—

(a) the flagrancy of the infringement, and

(b) any benefit accruing to the defendant by reason of the infringement,

award such additional damages as the justice of the case may require.

[2.131]

[97A Injunctions against service providers

(1) The High Court (in Scotland, the Court of Session) shall have power to grant an injunction against a service provider, where that service provider has actual knowledge of another person using their service to infringe copyright.

(2) In determining whether a service provider has actual knowledge for the purpose of this section, a court shall take into account all matters which appear to it in the particular circumstances to be relevant and, amongst other things, shall have regard to—

(a) whether a service provider has received a notice through a means of contact made available in accordance with regulation 6(1)(c) of the Electronic Commerce (EC Directive) Regulations 2002 (SI 2002/2013); and

(b) the extent to which any notice includes—

(i) the full name and address of the sender of the notice;

(ii) details of the infringement in question.

(3) In this section "service provider" has the meaning given to it by regulation 2 of the Electronic Commerce (EC Directive) Regulations 2002.]

NOTES

Inserted by the Copyright and Related Rights Regulations 2003, SI 2003/2498, regs 3, 27(1), subject to transitional provisions as noted to s 1 of this Act at **[2.7]**.

[2.132]

98 Undertaking to take licence of right in infringement proceedings

(1) If in proceedings for infringement of copyright in respect of which a licence is available as of right under section 144 (powers exercisable in consequence of report of [Competition and Markets Authority]) the defendant undertakes to take a licence on such terms as may be agreed or, in default of agreement, settled by the Copyright Tribunal under that section—

(a) no injunction shall be granted against him,

(b) no order for delivery up shall be made under section 99, and

(c) the amount recoverable against him by way of damages or on an account of profits shall not exceed double the amount which would have been payable by him as licensee if such a licence on those terms had been granted before the earliest infringement.

(2) An undertaking may be given at any time before final order in the proceedings, without any admission of liability.

(3) Nothing in this section affects the remedies available in respect of an infringement committed before licences of right were available.

NOTES

Sub-s (1): words in square brackets substituted by the Enterprise and Regulatory Reform Act 2013 (Competition) (Consequential, Transitional and Saving Provisions) Order 2014, SI 2014/892, art 2, Sch 1, Pt 2, paras 55, 56.

[2.133]

99 Order for delivery up

(1) Where a person—

(a) has an infringing copy of a work in his possession, custody or control in the course of a business, or

(b) has in his possession, custody or control an article specifically designed or adapted for making copies of a particular copyright work, knowing or having reason to believe that it has been or is to be used to make infringing copies,

the owner of the copyright in the work may apply to the court for an order that the infringing copy or article be delivered up to him or to such other person as the court may direct.

(2) An application shall not be made after the end of the period specified in section 113 (period after which remedy of delivery up not available); and no order shall be made unless the court also makes, or it appears to the court that there are grounds for making, an order under section 114 (order as to disposal of infringing copy or other article).

(3) A person to whom an infringing copy or other article is delivered up in pursuance of an order under this section shall, if an order under section 114 is not made, retain it pending the making of an order, or the decision not to make an order, under that section.

(4) Nothing in this section affects any other power of the court.

[2.134]

100 Right to seize infringing copies and other articles

(1) An infringing copy of a work which is found exposed or otherwise immediately available for sale or hire, and in respect of which the copyright owner would be entitled to apply for an order under section 99, may be seized and detained by him or a person authorised by him.

The right to seize and detain is exercisable subject to the following conditions and is subject to any decision of the court under section 114.

(2) Before anything is seized under this section notice of the time and place of the proposed seizure must be given to a local police station.

(3) A person may for the purpose of exercising the right conferred by this section enter premises to which the public have access but may not seize anything in the possession, custody or control of a person at a permanent or regular place of business of his, and may not use any force.

(4) At the time when anything is seized under this section there shall be left at the place where it was seized a notice in the prescribed form containing the prescribed particulars as to the person by whom or on whose authority the seizure is made and the grounds on which it is made.

(5) In this section—

"premises" includes land, buildings, moveable structures, vehicles, vessels, aircraft and hovercraft; and

"prescribed" means prescribed by order of the Secretary of State.

(6) An order of the Secretary of State under this section shall be made by statutory instrument which shall be subject to annulment in pursuance of a resolution of either House of Parliament.

NOTES

Orders: the Copyright and Rights in Performances (Notice of Seizure) Order 1989, SI 1989/1006, at **[2.447]**.

Rights and remedies of exclusive licensee

[2.135]
101 Rights and remedies of exclusive licensee

(1) An exclusive licensee has, except against the copyright owner, the same rights and remedies in respect of matters occurring after the grant of the licence as if the licence had been an assignment.

(2) His rights and remedies are concurrent with those of the copyright owner; and references in the relevant provisions of this Part to the copyright owner shall be construed accordingly.

(3) In an action brought by an exclusive licensee by virtue of this section a defendant may avail himself of any defence which would have been available to him if the action had been brought by the copyright owner.

[2.136]
[101A Certain infringements actionable by a non-exclusive licensee

(1) A non-exclusive licensee may bring an action for infringement of copyright if—

(a) the infringing act was directly connected to a prior licensed act of the licensee; and

(b) the licence—

(i) is in writing and is signed by or on behalf of the copyright owner; and

(ii) expressly grants the non-exclusive licensee a right of action under this section.

(2) In an action brought under this section, the non-exclusive licensee shall have the same rights and remedies available to him as the copyright owner would have had if he had brought the action.

(3) The rights granted under this section are concurrent with those of the copyright owner and references in the relevant provisions of this Part to the copyright owner shall be construed accordingly.

(4) In an action brought by a non-exclusive licensee by virtue of this section a defendant may avail himself of any defence which would have been available to him if the action had been brought by the copyright owner.

(5) Subsections (1) to (4) of section 102 shall apply to a non-exclusive licensee who has a right of action by virtue of this section as it applies to an exclusive licensee.

(6) In this section a "non-exclusive licensee" means the holder of a licence authorising the licensee to exercise a right which remains exercisable by the copyright owner.]

NOTES

Inserted by the Copyright and Related Rights Regulations 2003, SI 2003/2498, regs 3, 28, subject to transitional provisions as noted to s 1 of this Act at **[2.7]**.

[2.137]
102 Exercise of concurrent rights

(1) Where an action for infringement of copyright brought by the copyright owner or an exclusive licensee relates (wholly or partly) to an infringement in respect of which they have concurrent rights of action, the copyright owner or, as the case may be, the exclusive licensee may not, without the leave of the court, proceed with the action unless the other is either joined as a plaintiff or added as a defendant.

(2) A copyright owner or exclusive licensee who is added as a defendant in pursuance of subsection (1) is not liable for any costs in the action unless he takes part in the proceedings.

(3) The above provisions do not affect the granting of interlocutory relief on an application by a copyright owner or exclusive licensee alone.

(4) Where an action for infringement of copyright is brought which relates (wholly or partly) to an infringement in respect of which the copyright owner and an exclusive licensee have or had concurrent rights of action—

(a) the court shall in assessing damages take into account—

(i) the terms of the licence, and

(ii) any pecuniary remedy already awarded or available to either of them in respect of the infringement;

(b) no account of profits shall be directed if an award of damages has been made, or an account of profits has been directed, in favour of the other of them in respect of the infringement; and

(c) the court shall if an account of profits is directed apportion the profits between them as the court considers just, subject to any agreement between them;

and these provisions apply whether or not the copyright owner and the exclusive licensee are both parties to the action.

(5) The copyright owner shall notify any exclusive licensee having concurrent rights before applying for an order under section 99 (order for delivery up) or exercising the right conferred by section 100 (right of seizure); and the court may on the application of the licensee make such order under section 99 or, as the case may be, prohibiting or permitting the exercise by the copyright owner of the right conferred by section 100, as it thinks fit having regard to the terms of the licence.

Remedies for infringement of moral rights

[2.138]

103 Remedies for infringement of moral rights

(1) An infringement of a right conferred by Chapter IV (moral rights) is actionable as a breach of statutory duty owed to the person entitled to the right.

(2) In proceedings for infringement of the right conferred by section 80 (right to object to derogatory treatment of work) the court may, if it thinks it is an adequate remedy in the circumstances, grant an injunction on terms prohibiting the doing of any act unless a disclaimer is made, in such terms and in such manner as may be approved by the court, dissociating the author or director from the treatment of the work.

Presumptions

[2.139]

104 Presumptions relevant to literary, dramatic, musical and artistic works

(1) The following presumptions apply in proceedings brought by virtue of this Chapter with respect to a literary, dramatic, musical or artistic work.

(2) Where a name purporting to be that of the author appeared on copies of the work as published or on the work when it was made, the person whose name appeared shall be presumed, until the contrary is proved—

(a) to be the author of the work;

(b) to have made it in circumstances not falling within section 11(2), 163, 165 or 168 (works produced in course of employment, Crown copyright, Parliamentary copyright or copyright of certain international organisations).

(3) In the case of a work alleged to be a work of joint authorship, subsection (2) applies in relation to each person alleged to be one of the authors.

(4) Where no name purporting to be that of the author appeared as mentioned in subsection (2) but—

(a) the work qualifies for copyright protection by virtue of section 155 (qualification by reference to country of first publication), and

(b) a name purporting to be that of the publisher appeared on copies of the work as first published,

the person whose name appeared shall be presumed, until the contrary is proved, to have been the owner of the copyright at the time of publication.

(5) If the author of the work is dead or the identity of the author cannot be ascertained by reasonable inquiry, it shall be presumed, in the absence of evidence to the contrary—

(a) that the work is an original work, and

(b) that the plaintiff's allegations as to what was the first publication of the work and as to the country of first publication are correct.

[2.140]

105 Presumptions relevant to sound recordings and films

(1) In proceedings brought by virtue of this Chapter with respect to a sound recording, where copies of the recording as issued to the public bear a label or other mark stating—

(a) that a named person was the owner of copyright in the recording at the date of issue of the copies, or

(b) that the recording was first published in a specified year or in a specified country,

the label or mark shall be admissible as evidence of the facts stated and shall be presumed to be correct until the contrary is proved.

(2) In proceedings brought by virtue of this Chapter with respect to a film, where copies of the film as issued to the public bear a statement—

(a) that a named person was the [director or producer] of the film,

[(aa) that a named person was the principal director, the author of the screenplay, the author of the dialogue or the composer of music specifically created for and used in the film,]

(b) that a named person was the owner of copyright in the film at the date of issue of the copies, or

(c) that the film was first published in a specified year or in a specified country,

the statement shall be admissible as evidence of the facts stated and shall be presumed to be correct until the contrary is proved.

(3) In proceedings brought by virtue of this Chapter with respect to a computer program, where copies of the program are issued to the public in electronic form bearing a statement—

(a) that a named person was the owner of copyright in the program at the date of issue of the copies, or

(b) that the program was first published in a specified country or that copies of it were first issued to the public in electronic form in a specified year,

the statement shall be admissible as evidence of the facts stated and shall be presumed to be correct until the contrary is proved.

(4) The above presumptions apply equally in proceedings relating to an infringement alleged to have occurred before the date on which the copies were issued to the public.

(5) In proceedings brought by virtue of this Chapter with respect to a film, where the film as shown in public [or communicated to the public] bears a statement—

(a) that a named person was the [director or producer] of the film, or

[(aa) that a named person was the principal director of the film, the author of the screenplay, the author of the dialogue or the composer of music specifically created for and used in the film, or,]

(b) that a named person was the owner of copyright in the film immediately after it was made,

the statement shall be admissible as evidence of the facts stated and shall be presumed to be correct until the contrary is proved.

This presumption applies equally in proceedings relating to an infringement alleged to have occurred before the date on which the film was shown in public [or communicated to the public].

[(6) For the purposes of this section, a statement that a person was the director of a film shall be taken, unless a contrary indication appears, as meaning that he was the principal director of the film.]

NOTES

Sub-s (2): words in square brackets in para (a) substituted by the Copyright and Related Rights Regulations 1996, SI 1996/2967, regs 4, 18(4)(a), subject to transitional provisions and savings specified in regs 25–36 of those Regulations, at **[2.510]–[2.521]**; para (aa) inserted by the Duration of Copyright and Rights in Performances Regulations 1995, SI 1995/3297, regs 4, 6(4), subject to transitional provisions and savings specified in regs 12–34 of those Regulations, at **[2.478]–[2.499]**.

Sub-s (5): words in first and last pairs of square brackets substituted by the Copyright and Related Rights Regulations 2003, SI 2003/2498, reg 2(1), Sch 1, Pt 1, paras 1, 8(1)(c), subject to transitional provisions as noted to s 1 of this Act at **[2.7]**; words in square brackets in para (a) substituted, and para (aa) inserted, by SI 1996/2967, regs 4, 18(4)(b), subject to transitional provisions and savings specified in regs 25–36 of those Regulations, at **[2.510]–[2.521]**.

Sub-s (6): added by SI 1996/2967, regs 4, 18(4)(c), subject to transitional provisions and savings specified in regs 25–36 of those Regulations, at **[2.510]–[2.521]**.

[2.141]

106 Presumptions relevant to works subject to Crown copyright

In proceedings brought by virtue of this Chapter with respect to a literary, dramatic or musical work in which Crown copyright subsists, where there appears on printed copies of the work a statement of the year in which the work was first published commercially, that statement shall be admissible as evidence of the fact stated and shall be presumed to be correct in the absence of evidence to the contrary.

Offences

[2.142]

107 Criminal liability for making or dealing with infringing articles, &c

(1) A person commits an offence who, without the licence of the copyright owner—

(a) makes for sale or hire, or

(b) imports into the United Kingdom otherwise than for his private and domestic use, or

(c) possesses in the course of a business with a view to committing any act infringing the copyright, or

(d) in the course of a business—

(i) sells or lets for hire, or

(ii) offers or exposes for sale or hire, or

(iii) exhibits in public, or

(iv) distributes, or

(e) distributes otherwise than in the course of a business to such an extent as to affect prejudicially the owner of the copyright,

an article which is, and which he knows or has reason to believe is, an infringing copy of a copyright work.

(2) A person commits an offence who—

(a) makes an article specifically designed or adapted for making copies of a particular copyright work, or

(b) has such an article in his possession,

knowing or having reason to believe that it is to be used to make infringing copies for sale or hire or for use in the course of a business.

[(2A) A person who infringes copyright in a work by communicating the work to the public—

(a) in the course of a business, or

(b) otherwise than in the course of a business to such an extent as to affect prejudicially the owner of the copyright,

commits an offence if he knows or has reason to believe that, by doing so, he is infringing copyright in that work.]

(3) Where copyright is infringed (otherwise than by reception of a [communication to the public])—

(a) by the public performance of a literary, dramatic or musical work, or

(b) by the playing or showing in public of a sound recording or film,

any person who caused the work to be so performed, played or shown is guilty of an offence if he knew or had reason to believe that copyright would be infringed.

(4) A person guilty of an offence under subsection (1)(a), (b), (d)(iv) or (e) is liable—
(a) on summary conviction to imprisonment for a term not exceeding six months or *a fine not exceeding [£50,000]*, or both;
(b) on conviction on indictment to a fine or imprisonment for a term not exceeding [ten] years, or both.
[(4A) A person guilty of an offence under subsection (2A) is liable—
(a) on summary conviction to imprisonment for a term not exceeding three months or *a fine not exceeding [£50,000]*, or both;
(b) on conviction on indictment to a fine or imprisonment for a term not exceeding *two* years, or both.]
(5) A person guilty of any other offence under this section is liable on summary conviction to imprisonment for a term not exceeding [three] months or a fine not exceeding level 5 on the standard scale, or both.
(6) Sections 104 to 106 (presumptions as to various matters connected with copyright) do not apply to proceedings for an offence under this section; but without prejudice to their application in proceedings for an order under section 108 below.

NOTES

Sub-s (2A): inserted by the Copyright and Related Rights Regulations 2003, SI 2003/2498, regs 3, 26(1)(a), subject to transitional provisions as noted to s 1 of this Act at **[2.7]**; substituted by new sub-ss (2A), (2B), by the Digital Economy Act 2017, s 32(1), (2), (6), as from a day to be appointed and except in relation to offences committed before this amendment comes into force, as follows—

"(2A) A person ("P") who infringes copyright in a work by communicating the work to the public commits an offence if P—
(a) knows or has reason to believe that P is infringing copyright in the work, and
(b) either—
(i) intends to make a gain for P or another person, or
(ii) knows or has reason to believe that communicating the work to the public will cause loss to the owner of the copyright, or will expose the owner of the copyright to a risk of loss.
(2B) For the purposes of subsection (2A)—
(a) "gain" and "loss"—
(i) extend only to gain or loss in money, and
(ii) include any such gain or loss whether temporary or permanent, and
(b) "loss" includes a loss by not getting what one might get.".

Sub-s (3): words in square brackets substituted by SI 2003/2498, reg 2(1), Sch 1, Pt 1, paras 1, 9(2), subject to transitional provisions as noted to s 1 of this Act at **[2.7]**.

Sub-s (4): for the words in italics in para (a) there are substituted the words "a fine" in relation to England and Wales only, by the Legal Aid, Sentencing and Punishment of Offenders Act 2012 (Fines on Summary Conviction) Regulations 2015, SI 2015/664, reg 4(1), Sch 4, Pt 1, para 17(1), (2)(a), subject to transitional provisions and savings in reg 5 thereof; sum in square brackets in para (a) substituted by the Digital Economy Act 2010, s 42(1), (2); word in square brackets in para (b) substituted by the Copyright, etc and Trade Marks (Offences and Enforcement) Act 2002, s 1(1), (2), except in relation to offences committed before 20 November 2002.

Sub-s (4A): inserted by SI 2003/2498, regs 3, 26(1)(b), subject to transitional provisions as noted to s 1 of this Act at **[2.7]**; for the words in italics in para (a) there are substituted the words "a fine" in relation to England and Wales only, by SI 2015/664, reg 4(1), Sch 4, Pt 1, para 17(1), (2)(b), subject to transitional provisions and savings in reg 5 thereof; sum in square brackets in para (a) substituted by the Digital Economy Act 2010, s 42(1), (2); for the word in italics in para (b) there is substituted the word "ten" by the Digital Economy Act 2017, s 32(1), (3), (6), as from a day to be appointed and except in relation to offences committed before this amendment comes into force.

Sub-s (5): word in square brackets substituted by the Copyright, Designs and Patents Act 1988 (Amendment) Regulations 2010, SI 2010/2694, reg 5.

[2.143]

[107A Enforcement by local weights and measures authority

(1) It is the duty of every local weights and measures authority to enforce within their area the provisions of section 107.
(2) . . .
(3) Subsection (1) above does not apply in relation to the enforcement of section 107 in Northern Ireland, but it is the duty of the Department of Economic Development to enforce that section in Northern Ireland.

. . .

[(3A) For the investigatory powers available to a local weights and measures authority or the Department of Enterprise, Trade and Investment in Northern Ireland for the purposes of the duties in this section, see Schedule 5 to the Consumer Rights Act 2015.]
(4) Any enactment which authorises the disclosure of information for the purpose of facilitating the enforcement of the Trade Descriptions Act 1968 shall apply as if section 107 were contained in that Act and as if the functions of any person in relation to the enforcement of that section were functions under that Act.
(5) Nothing in this section shall be construed as authorising a local weights and measures authority to bring proceedings in Scotland for an offence.]

NOTES

Inserted by the Criminal Justice and Public Order Act 1994, s 165(1), (2).

Sub-s (2): repealed by the Consumer Rights Act 2015, s 77(2), Sch 6, paras 48, 49(1), (2).

Sub-s (3): words omitted repealed by the Consumer Rights Act 2015, s 77(2), Sch 6, paras 48, 49(1), (3).

Sub-s (3A): inserted by the Consumer Rights Act 2015, s 77(2), Sch 6, paras 48, 49(1), (4).

[2.144]

108 Order for delivery up in criminal proceedings

(1) The court before which proceedings are brought against a person for an offence under section 107 may, if satisfied that at the time of his arrest or charge—

(a) he had in his possession, custody or control in the course of a business an infringing copy of a copyright work, or

(b) he had in his possession, custody or control an article specifically designed or adapted for making copies of a particular copyright work, knowing or having reason to believe that it had been or was to be used to make infringing copies,

order that the infringing copy or article be delivered up to the copyright owner or to such other person as the court may direct.

(2) For this purpose a person shall be treated as charged with an offence—

(a) in England, Wales and Northern Ireland, when he is orally charged or is served with a summons or indictment;

(b) in Scotland, when he is cautioned, charged or served with a complaint or indictment.

(3) An order may be made by the court of its own motion or on the application of the prosecutor (or, in Scotland, the Lord Advocate or procurator-fiscal), and may be made whether or not the person is convicted of the offence, but shall not be made—

(a) after the end of the period specified in section 113 (period after which remedy of delivery up not available), or

(b) if it appears to the court unlikely that any order will be made under section 114 (order as to disposal of infringing copy or other article).

(4) An appeal lies from an order made under this section by a magistrates' court—

(a) in England and Wales, to the Crown Court, and

(b) in Northern Ireland, to the county court;

and in Scotland, where an order has been made under this section, the person from whose possession, custody or control the infringing copy or article has been removed may, without prejudice to any other form of appeal under any rule of law, appeal against that order in the same manner as against sentence.

(5) A person to whom an infringing copy or other article is delivered up in pursuance of an order under this section shall retain it pending the making of an order, or the decision not to make an order, under section 114.

(6) Nothing in this section affects the powers of the court under [section 143 of the Powers of Criminal Courts (Sentencing) Act 2000], [Part II of the Proceeds of Crime (Scotland) Act 1995] or [Article 11 of the Criminal Justice (Northern Ireland) Order 1994] (general provisions as to forfeiture in criminal proceedings).

NOTES

Sub-s (6): words in first pair of square brackets substituted by the Powers of Criminal Courts (Sentencing) Act 2000, s 165(1), Sch 9, para 115; words in second pair of square brackets substituted by the Criminal Procedure (Consequential Provisions) (Scotland) Act 1995, ss 4, 5, Sch 3, Sch 4, para 70(2), subject to transitional provisions and savings; words in final pair of square brackets substituted by the Criminal Justice (Northern Ireland) Order 1994, SI 1994/2795, art 26(1), Sch 2, para 13.

Lord Advocate: by virtue of the Scotland Act 1998, s 44(1)(c), the Lord Advocate ceased, on 20 May 1999 (see SI 1998/3178), to be a Minister of the Crown and became a member of the Scottish Executive. Accordingly, certain functions of the Lord Advocate are transferred to the Secretary of State (or as the case may be the Secretary of State for Scotland), or the Advocate General for Scotland: see the Transfer of Functions (Lord Advocate and Secretary of State) Order 1999, SI 1999/678 and the Transfer of Functions (Lord Advocate and Advocate General for Scotland) Order 1999, SI 1999/679.

[2.145]

109 Search warrants

(1) Where a justice of the peace (in Scotland, a sheriff or justice of the peace) is satisfied by information on oath given by a constable (in Scotland, by evidence on oath) that there are reasonable grounds for believing—

(a) that an offence under [section 107(1), (2) or (2A)] has been or is about to be committed in any premises, and

(b) that evidence that such an offence has been or is about to be committed is in those premises,

he may issue a warrant authorising a constable to enter and search the premises, using such reasonable force as is necessary.

(2) The power conferred by subsection (1) does not, in England and Wales, extend to authorising a search for material of the kinds mentioned in section 9(2) of the Police and Criminal Evidence Act 1984 (certain classes of personal or confidential material).

(3) A warrant under this section—
  (a) may authorise persons to accompany any constable executing the warrant, and
  (b) remains in force for [three months] from the date of its issue.

(4) In executing a warrant issued under this section a constable may seize an article if he reasonably believes that it is evidence that any offence under [section 107(1), (2) or (2A)] has been or is about to be committed.

(5) In this section "premises" includes land, buildings, [fixed or] moveable structures, vehicles, vessels, aircraft and hovercraft.

NOTES

Sub-s (1): words in square brackets substituted by the Copyright and Related Rights Regulations 2003, SI 2003/2498, regs 3, 26(2)(i), subject to transitional provisions as noted to s 1 of this Act at **[2.7]**.

Sub-s (3): words in square brackets substituted by the Serious Organised Crime and Police Act 2005, s 174(1), Sch 16, para 6(1), (2), in relation to England and Wales.

Sub-s (4): words in square brackets substituted by SI 2003/2498, regs 3, 26(2)(ii), subject to transitional provisions as noted to s 1 of this Act at **[2.7]**.

Sub-s (5): words in square brackets inserted by the Copyright, etc and Trade Marks (Offences and Enforcement) Act 2002, s 2(1), (2)(c).

Seize an article: the powers of seizure conferred by sub-s (4) are powers to which the Criminal Justice and Police Act 2001, s 50 apply (additional powers of seizure from premises); see s 50 of, and Sch 1, Pt 1, para 48 to, that Act.

[2.146]

110 Offence by body corporate: liability of officers

(1) Where an offence under section 107 committed by a body corporate is proved to have been committed with the consent or connivance of a director, manager, secretary or other similar officer of the body, or a person purporting to act in any such capacity, he as well as the body corporate is guilty of the offence and liable to be proceeded against and punished accordingly.

(2) In relation to a body corporate whose affairs are managed by its members "director" means a member of the body corporate.

Provision for preventing importation of infringing copies

[2.147]

111 Infringing copies may be treated as prohibited goods

(1) The owner of the copyright in a published literary, dramatic or musical work may give notice in writing to the Commissioners of Customs and Excise—
  (a) that he is the owner of the copyright in the work, and
  (b) that he requests the Commissioners, for a period specified in the notice, to treat as prohibited goods printed copies of the work which are infringing copies.

(2) The period specified in a notice under subsection (1) shall not exceed five years and shall not extend beyond the period for which copyright is to subsist.

(3) The owner of the copyright in a sound recording or film may give notice in writing to the Commissioners of Customs and Excise—
  (a) that he is the owner of the copyright in the work,
  (b) that infringing copies of the work are expected to arrive in the United Kingdom at a time and a place specified in the notice, and
  (c) that he requests the Commissioners to treat the copies as prohibited goods.

[(3A) The Commissioners may treat as prohibited goods only infringing copies of works which arrive in the United Kingdom—
  (a) from outside the European Economic Area, or
  (b) from within that Area but not having been entered for free circulation.

[(3B) This section does not apply to goods placed in, or expected to be placed in, one of the situations referred to in Article 1(1), in respect of which an application may be made under Article 5(1), of Council Regulation (EC) No 1383/2003 concerning customs action against goods suspected of infringing certain intellectual property rights and the measures to be taken against goods found to have infringed such rights.]]

(4) When a notice is in force under this section the importation of goods to which the notice relates, otherwise than by a person for his private and domestic use, [subject to subsections (3A) and (3B), is prohibited]; but a person is not by reason of the prohibition liable to any penalty other than forfeiture of the goods.

NOTES

Sub-s (3A): inserted by the Copyright (EC Measures Relating to Pirated Goods and Abolition of Restrictions on the Import of Goods) Regulations 1995, SI 1995/1445, reg 2(1), (2).

Sub-s (3B): inserted by SI 1995/1445, reg 2(1), (2); substituted by the Goods Infringing Intellectual Property Rights (Customs) Regulations 2004, SI 2004/1473, reg 12.

Sub-s (4): words in square brackets substituted by SI 1995/1445, reg 2(1), (3).

[2.148]

112 Power of Commissioners of Customs and Excise to make regulations

(1) The Commissioners of Customs and Excise may make regulations prescribing the form in which notice is to be given under section 111 and requiring a person giving notice—

(a) to furnish the Commissioners with such evidence as may be specified in the regulations, either on giving notice or when the goods are imported, or at both those times, and
(b) to comply with such other conditions as may be specified in the regulations.

(2) The regulations may, in particular, require a person giving such a notice—
(a) to pay such fees in respect of the notice as may be specified by the regulations;
(b) to give such security as may be so specified in respect of any liability or expense which the Commissioners may incur in consequence of the notice by reason of the detention of any article or anything done to an article detained;
(c) to indemnify the Commissioners against any such liability or expense, whether security has been given or not.

(3) The regulations may make different provision as respects different classes of case to which they apply and may include such incidental and supplementary provisions as the Commissioners consider expedient.

(4) Regulations under this section shall be made by statutory instrument which shall be subject to annulment in pursuance of a resolution of either House of Parliament.

(5) . . .

NOTES

Sub-s (5): repealed by the Commissioners for Revenue and Customs Act 2005, ss 50(6), 52(2), Sch 4, para 38, Sch 5.
Regulations: the Copyright (Customs) Regulations 1989, SI 1989/1178, at **[2.450]**.

Supplementary

[2.149]

113 Period after which remedy of delivery up not available

(1) An application for an order under section 99 (order for delivery up in civil proceedings) may not be made after the end of the period of six years from the date on which the infringing copy or article in question was made, subject to the following provisions.

(2) If during the whole or any part of that period the copyright owner—
(a) is under a disability, or
(b) is prevented by fraud or concealment from discovering the facts entitling him to apply for an order,

an application may be made at any time before the end of the period of six years from the date on which he ceased to be under a disability or, as the case may be, could with reasonable diligence have discovered those facts.

(3) In subsection (2) "disability"—
(a) in England and Wales, has the same meaning as in the Limitation Act 1980;
(b) in Scotland, means legal disability within the meaning of the Prescription and Limitation (Scotland) Act 1973;
(c) in Northern Ireland, has the same meaning as in the Statute of Limitations (Northern Ireland) 1958.

(4) An order under section 108 (order for delivery up in criminal proceedings) shall not, in any case, be made after the end of the period of six years from the date on which the infringing copy or article in question was made.

[2.150]

114 Order as to disposal of infringing copy or other article

(1) An application may be made to the court for an order that an infringing copy or other article delivered up in pursuance of an order under section 99 or 108, or seized and detained in pursuance of the right conferred by section 100, shall be—
(a) forfeited to the copyright owner, or
(b) destroyed or otherwise dealt with as the court may think fit,

or for a decision that no such order should be made.

(2) In considering what order (if any) should be made, the court shall consider whether other remedies available in an action for infringement of copyright would be adequate to compensate the copyright owner and to protect his interests.

(3) Provision shall be made by rules of court as to the service of notice on persons having an interest in the copy or other articles, and any such person is entitled—
(a) to appear in proceedings for an order under this section, whether or not he was served with notice, and
(b) to appeal against any order made, whether or not he appeared;

and an order shall not take effect until the end of the period within which notice of an appeal may be given or, if before the end of that period notice of appeal is duly given, until the final determination or abandonment of the proceedings on the appeal.

(4) Where there is more than one person interested in a copy or other article, the court shall make such order as it thinks just and may (in particular) direct that the article be sold, or otherwise dealt with, and the proceeds divided.

(5) If the court decides that no order should be made under this section, the person in whose possession, custody or control the copy or other article was before being delivered up or seized is entitled to its return.

(6) References in this section to a person having an interest in a copy or other article include any person in whose favour an order could be made in respect of it—

[(a) under this section or under section 204 or 231 of this Act;
(b) under section 24D of the Registered Designs Act 1949;
(c) under section 19 of Trade Marks Act 1994 (including that section as applied by regulation 4 of the Community Trade Mark Regulations 2006 (SI 2006/1027)); or
(d) under regulation 1C of the Community Design Regulations 2005 (SI 2005/2339)].

NOTES

Sub-s (6): paras (a)–(d) substituted by the Intellectual Property (Enforcement, etc) Regulations 2006, SI 2006/1028, reg 2(2), Sch 2, paras 6, 7.

[2.151]

[114A Forfeiture of infringing copies, etc: England and Wales or Northern Ireland

(1) In England and Wales or Northern Ireland where there have come into the possession of any person in connection with the investigation or prosecution of a relevant offence—

(a) infringing copies of a copyright work, or
(b) articles specifically designed or adapted for making copies of a particular copyright work,

that person may apply under this section for an order for the forfeiture of the infringing copies or articles.

(2) For the purposes of this section "relevant offence" means—

(a) an offence under [section 107(1), (2) or (2A)] (criminal liability for making or dealing with infringing articles, etc),
(b) an offence under the Trade Descriptions Act 1968 (c 29),
[(ba) an offence under the Business Protection from Misleading Marketing Regulations 2008,
(bb) an offence under the Consumer Protection from Unfair Trading Regulations 2008, or]
(c) an offence involving dishonesty or deception.

(3) An application under this section may be made—

(a) where proceedings have been brought in any court for a relevant offence relating to some or all of the infringing copies or articles, to that court, or
(b) where no application for the forfeiture of the infringing copies or articles has been made under paragraph (a), by way of complaint to a magistrates' court.

(4) On an application under this section, the court shall make an order for the forfeiture of any infringing copies or articles only if it is satisfied that a relevant offence has been committed in relation to the infringing copies or articles.

(5) A court may infer for the purposes of this section that such an offence has been committed in relation to any infringing copies or articles if it is satisfied that such an offence has been committed in relation to infringing copies or articles which are representative of the infringing copies or articles in question (whether by reason of being of the same design or part of the same consignment or batch or otherwise).

(6) Any person aggrieved by an order made under this section by a magistrates' court, or by a decision of such a court not to make such an order, may appeal against that order or decision—

(a) in England and Wales, to the Crown Court, or
(b) in Northern Ireland, to the county court.

(7) An order under this section may contain such provision as appears to the court to be appropriate for delaying the coming into force of the order pending the making and determination of any appeal (including any application under section 111 of the Magistrates' Courts Act 1980 (c 43) or Article 146 of the Magistrates' Courts (Northern Ireland) Order 1981 (SI 1981/1675 (NI 26)) (statement of case)).

(8) Subject to subsection (9), where any infringing copies or articles are forfeited under this section they shall be destroyed in accordance with such directions as the court may give.

(9) On making an order under this section the court may direct that the infringing copies or articles to which the order relates shall (instead of being destroyed) be forfeited to the owner of the copyright in question or dealt with in such other way as the court considers appropriate.]

NOTES

Inserted, together with s 114B, by the Copyright, etc and Trade Marks (Offences and Enforcement) Act 2002, s 3.

Sub-s (2): words in square brackets in para (a) substituted by the Copyright and Related Rights Regulations 2003, SI 2003/2498, regs 3, 26(2)(iii), subject to transitional provisions as noted to s 1 of this Act at **[2.7]**; paras (ba), (bb) substituted for original word "or" by the Consumer Protection from Unfair Trading Regulations 2008, SI 2008/1277, reg 30(1), Sch 2, Pt 1, paras 39, 40.

[2.152]

[114B Forfeiture of infringing copies, etc: Scotland

(1) In Scotland the court may make an order under this section for the forfeiture of any—

(a) infringing copies of a copyright work, or
(b) articles specifically designed or adapted for making copies of a particular copyright work.

(2) An order under this section may be made—

(a) on an application by the procurator-fiscal made in the manner specified in section 134 of the Criminal Procedure (Scotland) Act 1995 (c 46), or

Part 2 Copyright

(b) where a person is convicted of a relevant offence, in addition to any other penalty which the court may impose.

(3) On an application under subsection (2)(a), the court shall make an order for the forfeiture of any infringing copies or articles only if it is satisfied that a relevant offence has been committed in relation to the infringing copies or articles.

(4) The court may infer for the purposes of this section that such an offence has been committed in relation to any infringing copies or articles if it is satisfied that such an offence has been committed in relation to infringing copies or articles which are representative of the infringing copies or articles in question (whether by reason of being of the same design or part of the same consignment or batch or otherwise).

(5) The procurator-fiscal making the application under subsection (2)(a) shall serve on any person appearing to him to be the owner of, or otherwise to have an interest in, the infringing copies or articles to which the application relates a copy of the application, together with a notice giving him the opportunity to appear at the hearing of the application to show cause why the infringing copies or articles should not be forfeited.

(6) Service under subsection (5) shall be carried out, and such service may be proved, in the manner specified for citation of an accused in summary proceedings under the Criminal Procedure (Scotland) Act 1995.

(7) Any person upon whom notice is served under subsection (5) and any other person claiming to be the owner of, or otherwise to have an interest in, infringing copies or articles to which an application under this section relates shall be entitled to appear at the hearing of the application to show cause why the infringing copies or articles should not be forfeited.

(8) The court shall not make an order following an application under subsection (2)(a)—

- (a) if any person on whom notice is served under subsection (5) does not appear, unless service of the notice on that person is proved, or
- (b) if no notice under subsection (5) has been served, unless the court is satisfied that in the circumstances it was reasonable not to serve such notice.

(9) Where an order for the forfeiture of any infringing copies or articles is made following an application under subsection (2)(a), any person who appeared, or was entitled to appear, to show cause why infringing copies or articles should not be forfeited may, within 21 days of the making of the order, appeal to the High Court by Bill of Suspension.

(10) Section 182(5)(a) to (e) of the Criminal Procedure (Scotland) Act 1995 (c 46) shall apply to an appeal under subsection (9) as it applies to a stated case under Part 2 of that Act.

(11) An order following an application under subsection (2)(a) shall not take effect—

- (a) until the end of the period of 21 days beginning with the day after the day on which the order is made, or
- (b) if an appeal is made under subsection (9) above within that period, until the appeal is determined or abandoned.

(12) An order under subsection (2)(b) shall not take effect—

- (a) until the end of the period within which an appeal against the order could be brought under the Criminal Procedure (Scotland) Act 1995, or
- (b) if an appeal is made within that period, until the appeal is determined or abandoned.

(13) Subject to subsection (14), infringing copies or articles forfeited under this section shall be destroyed in accordance with such directions as the court may give.

(14) On making an order under this section the court may direct that the infringing copies or articles to which the order relates shall (instead of being destroyed) be forfeited to the owner of the copyright in question or dealt with in such other way as the court considers appropriate.

(15) For the purposes of this section—

["relevant offence" means—

- (a) an offence under section 107(1), (2) or (2A) (criminal liability for making or dealing with infringing articles, etc),
- (b) an offence under the Trade Descriptions Act 1968,
- (c) an offence under the Business Protection from Misleading Marketing Regulations 2008,
- (d) an offence under the Consumer Protection from Unfair Trading Regulations 2008, or
- (e) any offence involving dishonesty or deception;]

"the court" means—

- (a) in relation to an order made on an application under subsection (2)(a), the sheriff, and
- (b) in relation to an order made under subsection (2)(b), the court which imposed the penalty.]

NOTES

Inserted as noted to s 114A at **[2.151]**.

Sub-s (15): definition "relevant offence" substituted by the Consumer Protection from Unfair Trading Regulations 2008, SI 2008/1277, reg 30(1), Sch 2, Pt 1, paras 39, 41.

[2.153]

115 Jurisdiction of county court and sheriff court

(1) In England [and Wales the county court and in] Northern Ireland a county court may entertain proceedings under—

section 99 (order for delivery up of infringing copy or other article),

section 101(5) (order as to exercise of rights by copyright owner where exclusive licensee has concurrent rights), or

section 114 (order as to disposal of infringing copy or other article),

[save that, in Northern Ireland, a county court may entertain such proceedings only] where the value of the infringing copies and other articles in question does not exceed the county court limit for actions in tort.

(2) In Scotland proceedings for an order under any of those provisions may be brought in the sheriff court.

(3) Nothing in this section shall be construed as affecting the jurisdiction of the High Court or, in Scotland, the Court of Session.

NOTES

Sub-s (1): words in first pair of square brackets substituted by the Crime and Courts Act 2013, s 17(5), Sch 9, Pt 3, para 72; words in second pair of square brackets inserted by the High Court and County Courts Jurisdiction Order 1991, SI 1991/724, art 2(8), Schedule, Pt I.

It is thought that the reference in sub-s (1) to "section 101(5)" should read "section 102(5)".

CHAPTER VII
COPYRIGHT LICENSING

Licensing schemes and licensing bodies

[2.154]

116 Licensing schemes and licensing bodies

(1) In this Part a "licensing scheme" means a scheme setting out—

(a) the classes of case in which the operator of the scheme, or the person on whose behalf he acts, is willing to grant copyright licences, and

(b) the terms on which licences would be granted in those classes of case;

and for this purpose a "scheme" includes anything in the nature of a scheme, whether described as a scheme or as a tariff or by any other name.

(2) In this Chapter a "licensing body" means—

[(a)] a society or other organisation which has as its main object, or one of its main objects, the negotiation or granting, either as owner or prospective owner of copyright or as agent for him, of copyright licences, and whose objects include the granting of licences covering works of more than one author[, or,

(b) any other organisation which is a collective management organisation as defined by regulation 2 of the Collective Management of Copyright (EU Directive) Regulations 2016.]

(3) In this section "copyright licences" means licences to do, or authorise the doing of, any of the acts restricted by copyright.

(4) References in this Chapter to licences or licensing schemes covering works of more than one author do not include licences or schemes covering only—

(a) a single collective work or collective works of which the authors are the same, or

(b) works made by, or by employees of or commissioned by, a single individual, firm, company or group of companies.

For this purpose a group of companies means a holding company and its subsidiaries, within the meaning of [section 1159 of the Companies Act 2006].

[(5) Schedule A1 confers powers to provide for the regulation of licensing bodies.]

NOTES

Sub-s (2): para (a) numbered as such and para (b) inserted together with word preceding it, by the Collective Management of Copyright (EU Directive) Regulations 2016, SI 2016/221, reg 44.

Sub-s (4): words in square brackets substituted by the Companies Act 2006 (Consequential Amendments, Transitional Provisions and Savings) Order 2009, SI 2009/1941, art 2(1), Sch 1, para 98(a).

Sub-s (5): added by the Enterprise and Regulatory Reform Act 2013, s 77(1), (2).

[Orphan works licensing and extended collective licensing

[2.155]

116A Power to provide for licensing of orphan works

(1) The Secretary of State may by regulations provide for the grant of licences in respect of works that qualify as orphan works under the regulations.

(2) The regulations may—

(a) specify a person or a description of persons authorised to grant licences, or

(b) provide for a person designated in the regulations to specify a person or a description of persons authorised to grant licences.

(3) The regulations must provide that, for a work to qualify as an orphan work, it is a requirement that the owner of copyright in it has not been found after a diligent search made in accordance with the regulations.

(4) The regulations may provide for the granting of licences to do, or authorise the doing of, any act restricted by copyright that would otherwise require the consent of the missing owner.

(5) The regulations must provide for any licence—

(a) to have effect as if granted by the missing owner;

(b) not to give exclusive rights;

(c) not to be granted to a person authorised to grant licences.

(6) The regulations may apply to a work although it is not known whether copyright subsists in it, and references to a missing owner and a right or interest of a missing owner are to be read as including references to a supposed owner and a supposed right or interest.]

NOTES

Commencement: 25 April 2013.

Inserted, together with preceding cross-heading, and ss 116B–116D, by the Enterprise and Regulatory Reform Act 2013, s 77(1), (3).

Regulations: the Copyright and Rights in Performances (Licensing of Orphan Works) Regulations 2014, SI 2014/2863.

[2.156]

[116B Extended collective licensing

(1) The Secretary of State may by regulations provide for a licensing body that applies to the Secretary of State under the regulations to be authorised to grant copyright licences in respect of works in which copyright is not owned by the body or a person on whose behalf the body acts.

(2) An authorisation must specify—

(a) the types of work to which it applies, and

(b) the acts restricted by copyright that the licensing body is authorised to license.

(3) The regulations must provide for the copyright owner to have a right to limit or exclude the grant of licences by virtue of the regulations.

(4) The regulations must provide for any licence not to give exclusive rights.

(5) In this section "copyright licences" has the same meaning as in section 116.

(6) Nothing in this section applies in relation to Crown copyright or Parliamentary copyright.]

NOTES

Commencement: 25 April 2013.

Inserted as noted to s 116A at **[2.155]**.

Regulations: the Copyright and Rights in Performances (Extended Collective Licensing) Regulations 2014, SI 2014/2588.

[2.157]

[116C General provision about licensing under sections 116A and 116B

(1) This section and section 116D apply to regulations under sections 116A and 116B.

(2) The regulations may provide for a body to be or remain authorised to grant licences only if specified requirements are met, and for a question whether they are met to be determined by a person, and in a manner, specified in the regulations.

(3) The regulations may specify other matters to be taken into account in any decision to be made under the regulations as to whether to authorise a person to grant licences.

(4) The regulations must provide for the treatment of any royalties or other sums paid in respect of a licence, including—

(a) the deduction of administrative costs;

(b) the period for which sums must be held;

(c) the treatment of sums after that period (as bona vacantia or otherwise).

(5) The regulations must provide for circumstances in which an authorisation to grant licences may be withdrawn, and for determining the rights and obligations of any person if an authorisation is withdrawn.

(6) The regulations may include other provision for the purposes of authorisation and licensing, including in particular provision—

(a) for determining the rights and obligations of any person if a work ceases to qualify as an orphan work (or ceases to qualify by reference to any copyright owner), or if a rights owner exercises the right referred to in section 116B(3), while a licence is in force;

(b) about maintenance of registers and access to them;

(c) permitting the use of a work for incidental purposes including an application or search;

(d) for a right conferred by section 77 to be treated as having been asserted in accordance with section 78;

(e) for the payment of fees to cover administrative expenses.]

NOTES

Commencement: 25 April 2013.

Inserted as noted to s 116A at **[2.155]**.

Regulations: the Copyright and Rights in Performances (Extended Collective Licensing) Regulations 2014, SI 2014/2588; the Copyright and Rights in Performances (Licensing of Orphan Works) Regulations 2014, SI 2014/2863.

[2.158]
[116D Regulations under sections 116A and 116B
(1) The power to make regulations includes power—
(a) to make incidental, supplementary or consequential provision, including provision extending or restricting the jurisdiction of the Copyright Tribunal or conferring powers on it;
(b) to make transitional, transitory or saving provision;
(c) to make different provision for different purposes.
(2) Regulations under any provision may amend this Part, or any other enactment or subordinate legislation passed or made before that provision comes into force, for the purpose of making consequential provision or extending or restricting the jurisdiction of the Copyright Tribunal or conferring powers on it.
(3) Regulations may make provision by reference to guidance issued from time to time by any person.
(4) The power to make regulations is exercisable by statutory instrument.
(5) A statutory instrument containing regulations may not be made unless a draft of the instrument has been laid before and approved by a resolution of each House of Parliament.]

NOTES
Commencement: 25 April 2013.
Inserted as noted to s 116A at **[2.155]**.
Regulations: the Copyright and Rights in Performances (Extended Collective Licensing) Regulations 2014, SI 2014/2588; the Copyright and Rights in Performances (Licensing of Orphan Works) Regulations 2014, SI 2014/2863.

References and applications with respect to licensing schemes

[2.159]
[117 Licensing schemes to which following sections apply
Sections 118 to 123 (references and applications with respect to licensing schemes) apply to licensing schemes which are operated by licensing bodies and cover works of more than one author, so far as they relate to licences for—
(a) copying the work,
(b) rental or lending of copies of the work to the public,
(c) performing, showing or playing the work in public, or
[(d) communicating the work to the public;]
and references in those sections to a licensing scheme shall be construed accordingly.]

NOTES
Substituted by the Copyright and Related Rights Regulations 1996, SI 1996/2967, regs 4, 15(1), (2), subject to transitional provisions and savings specified in regs 25–36 of those Regulations, at **[2.510]–[2.521]**.
Para (d) substituted by the Copyright and Related Rights Regulations 2003, SI 2003/2498, reg 2(1), Sch 1, Pt 1, paras 1, 4(4), subject to transitional provisions as noted to s 1 of this Act at **[2.7]**.

[2.160]
118 Reference of proposed licensing scheme to tribunal
(1) The terms of a licensing scheme proposed to be operated by a licensing body may be referred to the Copyright Tribunal by an organisation claiming to be representative of persons claiming that they require licences in cases of a description to which the scheme would apply, either generally or in relation to any description of case.
(2) The Tribunal shall first decide whether to entertain the reference, and may decline to do so on the ground that the reference is premature.
(3) If the Tribunal decides to entertain the reference it shall consider the matter referred and make such order, either confirming or varying the proposed scheme, either generally or so far as it relates to cases of the description to which the reference relates, as the Tribunal may determine to be reasonable in the circumstances.
(4) The order may be made so as to be in force indefinitely or for such period as the Tribunal may determine.

[2.161]
119 Reference of licensing scheme to tribunal
(1) If while a licensing scheme is in operation a dispute arises between the operator of the scheme and—
(a) a person claiming that he requires a licence in a case of a description to which the scheme applies, or
(b) an organisation claiming to be representative of such persons,
that person or organisation may refer the scheme to the Copyright Tribunal in so far as it relates to cases of that description.
(2) A scheme which has been referred to the Tribunal under this section shall remain in operation until proceedings on the reference are concluded.

(3) The Tribunal shall consider the matter in dispute and make such order, either confirming or varying the scheme so far as it relates to cases of the description to which the reference relates, as the Tribunal may determine to be reasonable in the circumstances.
(4) The order may be made so as to be in force indefinitely or for such period as the Tribunal may determine.

[2.162]
120 Further reference of scheme to tribunal
(1) Where the Copyright Tribunal has on a previous reference of a licensing scheme under [section 118, 119 or 128A], or under this section, made an order with respect to the scheme, then, while the order remains in force—
 (a) the operator of the scheme,
 (b) a person claiming that he requires a licence in a case of the description to which the order applies, or
 (c) an organisation claiming to be representative of such persons,
may refer the scheme again to the Tribunal so far as it relates to cases of that description.
(2) A licensing scheme shall not, except with the special leave of the Tribunal, be referred again to the Tribunal in respect of the same description of cases—
 (a) within twelve months from the date of the order on the previous reference, or
 (b) if the order was made so as to be in force for 15 months or less, until the last three months before the expiry of the order.
(3) A scheme which has been referred to the Tribunal under this section shall remain in operation until proceedings on the reference are concluded.
(4) The Tribunal shall consider the matter in dispute and make such order, either confirming, varying or further varying the scheme so far as it relates to cases of the description to which the reference relates, as the Tribunal may determine to be reasonable in the circumstances.
(5) The order may be made so as to be in force indefinitely or for such period as the Tribunal may determine.

NOTES
Sub-s (1): words in square brackets substituted by the Copyright and Related Rights Regulations 2003, SI 2003/2498, regs 3, 21(4), subject to transitional provisions as noted to s 1 of this Act at **[2.7]**.

[2.163]
121 Application for grant of licence in connection with licensing scheme
(1) A person who claims, in a case covered by a licensing scheme, that the operator of the scheme has refused to grant him or procure the grant to him of a licence in accordance with the scheme, or has failed to do so within a reasonable time after being asked, may apply to the Copyright Tribunal.
(2) A person who claims, in a case excluded from a licensing scheme, that the operator of the scheme either—
 (a) has refused to grant him a licence or procure the grant to him of a licence, or has failed to do so within a reasonable time of being asked, and that in the circumstances it is unreasonable that a licence should not be granted, or
 (b) proposes terms for a licence which are unreasonable, may apply to the Copyright Tribunal.
(3) A case shall be regarded as excluded from a licensing scheme for the purposes of subsection (2) if—
 (a) the scheme provides for the grant of licences subject to terms excepting matters from the licence and the case falls within such an exception, or
 (b) the case is so similar to those in which licences are granted under the scheme that it is unreasonable that it should not be dealt with in the same way.
(4) If the Tribunal is satisfied that the claim is well-founded, it shall make an order declaring that, in respect of the matters specified in the order, the applicant is entitled to a licence on such terms as the Tribunal may determine to be applicable in accordance with the scheme or, as the case may be, to be reasonable in the circumstances.
(5) The order may be made so as to be in force indefinitely or for such period as the Tribunal may determine.

[2.164]
122 Application for review of order as to entitlement to licence
(1) Where the Copyright Tribunal has made an order under section 121 that a person is entitled to a licence under a licensing scheme, the operator of the scheme or the original applicant may apply to the Tribunal to review its order.
(2) An application shall not be made, except with the special leave of the Tribunal—
 (a) within twelve months from the date of the order, or of the decision on a previous application under this section, or
 (b) if the order was made so as to be in force for 15 months or less, or as a result of the decision on a previous application under this section is due to expire within 15 months of that decision, until the last three months before the expiry date.

(3) The Tribunal shall on an application for review confirm or vary its order as the Tribunal may determine to be reasonable having regard to the terms applicable in accordance with the licensing scheme or, as the case may be, the circumstances of the case.

[2.165]
123 Effect of order of tribunal as to licensing scheme
(1) A licensing scheme which has been confirmed or varied by the Copyright Tribunal—
(a) under section 118 (reference of terms of proposed scheme), or
(b) under section 119 or 120 (reference of existing scheme to Tribunal),
shall be in force or, as the case may be, remain in operation, so far as it relates to the description of case in respect of which the order was made, so long as the order remains in force.
(2) While the order is in force a person who in a case of a class to which the order applies—
(a) pays to the operator of the scheme any charges payable under the scheme in respect of a licence covering the case in question or, if the amount cannot be ascertained, gives an undertaking to the operator to pay them when ascertained, and
(b) complies with the other terms applicable to such a licence under the scheme,
shall be in the same position as regards infringement of copyright as if he had at all material times been the holder of a licence granted by the owner of the copyright in question in accordance with the scheme.
(3) The Tribunal may direct that the order, so far as it varies the amount of charges payable, has effect from a date before that on which it is made, but not earlier than the date on which the reference was made or, if later, on which the scheme came into operation.
If such a direction is made—
(a) any necessary repayments, or further payments, shall be made in respect of charges already paid, and
(b) the reference in subsection (2)(a) to the charges payable under the scheme shall be construed as a reference to the charges so payable by virtue of the order.
No such direction may be made where subsection (4) below applies.
(4) An order of the Tribunal under section 119 or 120 made with respect to a scheme which is certified for any purpose under section 143 has effect, so far as it varies the scheme by reducing the charges payable for licences, from the date on which the reference was made to the Tribunal.
(5) Where the Tribunal has made an order under section 121 (order as to entitlement to licence under licensing scheme) and the order remains in force, the person in whose favour the order is made shall if he—
(a) pays to the operator of the scheme any charges payable in accordance with the order or, if the amount cannot be ascertained, gives an undertaking to pay the charges when ascertained, and
(b) complies with the other terms specified in the order,
be in the same position as regards infringement of copyright as if he had at all material times been the holder of a licence granted by the owner of the copyright in question on the terms specified in the order.

References and applications with respect to licensing by licensing bodies

[2.166]
[124 Licences to which following sections apply
Sections 125 to 128 (references and applications with respect to licensing by licensing bodies) apply to licences which are granted by a licensing body otherwise than in pursuance of a licensing scheme and cover works of more than one author, so far as they authorise—
(a) copying the work,
(b) rental or lending of copies of the work to the public,
(c) performing, showing or playing the work in public, or
[(d) communicating the work to the public;]
and references in those sections to a licence shall be construed accordingly.]

NOTES
Substituted by the Copyright and Related Rights Regulations 1996, SI 1996/2967, regs 4, 15(1), (3), subject to transitional provisions and savings specified in regs 25–36 of those Regulations, at **[2.510]–[2.521]**.
Para (d) substituted by the Copyright and Related Rights Regulations 2003, SI 2003/2498, reg 2(1), Sch 1, Pt 1, paras 1, 4(4), subject to transitional provisions as noted to s 1 of this Act at **[2.7]**.

[2.167]
125 Reference to tribunal of proposed licence
(1) The terms on which a licensing body proposes to grant a licence may be referred to the Copyright Tribunal by the prospective licensee.
(2) The Tribunal shall first decide whether to entertain the reference, and may decline to do so on the ground that the reference is premature.
(3) If the Tribunal decides to entertain the reference it shall consider the terms of the proposed licence and make such order, either confirming or varying the terms, as it may determine to be reasonable in the circumstances.

(4) The order may be made so as to be in force indefinitely or for such period as the Tribunal may determine.

[2.168]

126 Reference to tribunal of expiring licence

(1) A licensee under a licence which is due to expire, by effluxion of time or as a result of notice given by the licensing body, may apply to the Copyright Tribunal on the ground that it is unreasonable in the circumstances that the licence should cease to be in force.

(2) Such an application may not be made until the last three months before the licence is due to expire.

(3) A licence in respect of which a reference has been made to the Tribunal shall remain in operation until proceedings on the reference are concluded.

(4) If the Tribunal finds the application well-founded, it shall make an order declaring that the licensee shall continue to be entitled to the benefit of the licence on such terms as the Tribunal may determine to be reasonable in the circumstances.

(5) An order of the Tribunal under this section may be made so as to be in force indefinitely or for such period as the Tribunal may determine.

[2.169]

127 Application for review of order as to licence

(1) Where the Copyright Tribunal has made an order under [section 125, 126 or 128B (where that order did not relate to a licensing scheme)], the licensing body or the person entitled to the benefit of the order may apply to the Tribunal to review its order.

(2) An application shall not be made, except with the special leave of the Tribunal—

(a) within twelve months from the date of the order or of the decision on a previous application under this section, or

(b) if the order was made so as to be in force for 15 months or less, or as a result of the decision on a previous application under this section is due to expire within 15 months of that decision, until the last three months before the expiry date.

(3) The Tribunal shall on an application for review confirm or vary its order as the Tribunal may determine to be reasonable in the circumstances.

NOTES

Sub-s (1): words in square brackets substituted by the Copyright and Related Rights Regulations 2003, SI 2003/2498, regs 3, 21(5), subject to transitional provisions as noted to s 1 of this Act at **[2.7]**.

[2.170]

128 Effect of order of tribunal as to licence

(1) Where the Copyright Tribunal has made an order under section 125 or 126 and the order remains in force, the person entitled to the benefit of the order shall if he—

(a) pays to the licensing body any charges payable in accordance with the order or, if the amount cannot be ascertained, gives an undertaking to pay the charges when ascertained, and

(b) complies with the other terms specified in the order,

be in the same position as regards infringement of copyright as if he had at all material times been the holder of a licence granted by the owner of the copyright in question on the terms specified in the order.

(2) The benefit of the order may be assigned—

(a) in the case of an order under section 125, if assignment is not prohibited under the terms of the Tribunal's order; and

(b) in the case of an order under section 126, if assignment was not prohibited under the terms of the original licence.

(3) The Tribunal may direct that an order under section 125 or 126, or an order under section 127 varying such an order, so far as it varies the amount of charges payable, has effect from a date before that on which it is made, but not earlier than the date on which the reference or application was made or, if later, on which the licence was granted or, as the case may be, was due to expire.

If such a direction is made—

(a) any necessary repayments, or further payments, shall be made in respect of charges already paid, and

(b) the reference in subsection (1)(a) to the charges payable in accordance with the order shall be construed, where the order is varied by a later order, as a reference to the charges so payable by virtue of the later order.

128A, 128B *(Inserted by the Copyright and Related Rights Regulations 2003, SI 2003/2498, regs 3, 21(3); repealed by the Copyright, Designs and Patents Act 1988 (Amendment) Regulations 2010, SI 2010/2694, reg 6.)*

Factors to be taken into account in certain classes of case

[2.171]

129 General considerations: unreasonable discrimination

In determining what is reasonable on a reference or application under this Chapter relating to a licensing scheme or licence, the Copyright Tribunal shall have regard to—

(a) the availability of other schemes, or the granting of other licences, to other persons in similar circumstances, and

(b) the terms of those schemes or licences,

and shall exercise its powers so as to secure that there is no unreasonable discrimination between licensees, or prospective licensees, under the scheme or licence to which the reference or application relates and licensees under other schemes operated by, or other licences granted by, the same person.

[2.172]

130 Licences for reprographic copying

Where a reference or application is made to the Copyright Tribunal under this Chapter relating to the licensing of reprographic copying of published literary, dramatic, musical or artistic works, or the typographical arrangement of published editions, the Tribunal shall have regard to—

(a) the extent to which published editions of the works in question are otherwise available,

(b) the proportion of the work to be copied, and

(c) the nature of the use to which the copies are likely to be put.

[2.173]

131 Licences for educational establishments in respect of works included in broadcasts . . .

(1) This section applies to references or applications under this Chapter relating to licences for the recording by or on behalf of educational establishments of broadcasts . . . which include copyright works, or the making of copies of such recordings, for educational purposes.

(2) The Copyright Tribunal shall, in considering what charges (if any) should be paid for a licence, have regard to the extent to which the owners of copyright in the works included in the broadcast . . . have already received, or are entitled to receive, payment in respect of their inclusion.

NOTES

Words omitted repealed by the Copyright and Related Rights Regulations 2003, SI 2003/2498, reg 2(2), Sch 2, subject to transitional provisions as noted to s 1 of this Act at **[2.7]**.

[2.174]

132 Licences to reflect conditions imposed by promoters of events

(1) This section applies to references or applications under this Chapter in respect of licences relating to sound recordings, films [or broadcasts] which include, or are to include, any entertainment or other event.

(2) The Copyright Tribunal shall have regard to any conditions imposed by the promoters of the entertainment or other event; and, in particular, the Tribunal shall not hold a refusal or failure to grant a licence to be unreasonable if it could not have been granted consistently with those conditions.

(3) Nothing in this section shall require the Tribunal to have regard to any such conditions in so far as they—

(a) purport to regulate the charges to be imposed in respect of the grant of licences, or

(b) relate to payments to be made to the promoters of any event in consideration of the grant of facilities for making the recording, film [or broadcast].

NOTES

Sub-s (1): words in square brackets substituted by the Copyright and Related Rights Regulations 2003, SI 2003/2498, reg 2(1), Sch 1, Pt 1, paras 1, 3(2)(a), subject to transitional provisions as noted to s 1 of this Act at **[2.7]**.

Sub-s (3): words in square brackets substituted by SI 2003/2498, reg 2(1), Sch 1, Pt 1, paras 1, 3(1)(j), subject to transitional provisions as noted to s 1 of this Act at **[2.7]**.

[2.175]

133 Licences to reflect payments in respect of underlying rights

[(1) In considering what charges should be paid for a licence—

(a) on a reference or application under this Chapter relating to licences for the rental or lending of copies of a work, or

(b) on an application under section 142 (royalty or other sum payable for lending of certain works),

the Copyright Tribunal shall take into account any reasonable payments which the owner of the copyright in the work is liable to make in consequence of the granting of the licence, or of the acts authorised by the licence, to owners of copyright in works included in that work.]

(2) On any reference or application under this Chapter relating to licensing in respect of the copyright in sound recordings, films [or broadcasts], the Copyright Tribunal shall take into account, in considering what charges should be paid for a licence, any reasonable payments which the copyright owner is liable to make in consequence of the granting of the licence, or of the acts authorised by the licence, in respect of any performance included in the recording, film [or broadcast].

NOTES

Sub-s (1): substituted by the Copyright and Related Rights Regulations 1996, SI 1996/2967, regs 4, 13(1), subject to transitional provisions and savings specified in regs 25–36 of those Regulations, at **[2.510]–[2.521]**.

Sub-s (2): words in square brackets substituted by the Copyright and Related Rights Regulations 2003, SI 2003/2498, reg 2(1), Sch 1, Pt 1, paras 1, 3(1)(k), (2)(b), subject to transitional provisions as noted to s 1 of this Act at **[2.7]**.

[2.176]

134 Licences in respect of works included in re-transmissions

(1) [*Subject to subsection (3A)*] this section applies to references or applications under this Chapter relating to licences to include in a broadcast . . . —

(a) literary, dramatic, musical or artistic works, or,

(b) sound recordings or films,

where one broadcast . . . ("the first transmission") is, by reception and immediate retransmission, to be further broadcast . . . ("the further transmission").

(2) So far as the further transmission is to the same area as the first transmission, the Copyright Tribunal shall, in considering what charges (if any) should be paid for licences for either transmission, have regard to the extent to which the copyright owner has already received, or is entitled to receive, payment for the other transmission which adequately remunerates him in respect of transmissions to that area.

(3) So far as the further transmission is to an area outside that to which the first transmission was made, the Tribunal shall . . . leave the further transmission out of account in considering what charges (if any) should be paid for licences for the first transmission.

[(3A) This section does not apply in relation to any application under section 73A (royalty or other sum payable in pursuance of section 73(4)).]

(4) . . .

NOTES

Sub-s (1): words in italics in square brackets inserted by the Broadcasting Act 1996, s 138, Sch 9, para 2(2) and repealed by the Digital Economy Act 2017, s 34(2)(a)(i), as from a day to be appointed; words omitted repealed by the Copyright and Related Rights Regulations 2003, SI 2003/2498, reg 2(2), Sch 2, subject to transitional provisions as noted to s 1 of this Act at **[2.7]**.

Sub-s (3): words omitted repealed by SI 2003/2498, reg 2(2), Sch 2, subject to transitional provisions as noted to s 1 of this Act at **[2.7]**.

Sub-s (3A): inserted by the Broadcasting Act 1996, s 138, Sch 9, para 2(3) and repealed by the Digital Economy Act 2017, s 34(2)(a)(i), as from a day to be appointed.

Sub-s (4): repealed by the Broadcasting Act 1990, s 203(3), Sch 21.

[2.177]

135 Mention of specific matters not to exclude other relevant considerations

The mention in sections 129 to 134 of specific matters to which the Copyright Tribunal is to have regard in certain classes of case does not affect the Tribunal's general obligation in any case to have regard to all relevant considerations.

[Use as of right of sound recordings in broadcasts . . .

[2.178]

135A Circumstances in which right available

(1) Section 135C applies to the inclusion in a broadcast . . . of any sound recordings if—

(a) a licence to include those recordings in the broadcast . . . could be granted by a licensing body or such a body could procure the grant of a licence to do so,

(b) the condition in subsection (2) or (3) applies, and

(c) the person including those recordings in the broadcast . . . has complied with section 135B.

(2) Where the person including the recordings in the broadcast . . . does not hold a licence to do so, the condition is that the licensing body refuses to grant, or procure the grant of, such a licence, being a licence—

(a) whose terms as to payment for including the recordings in the broadcast . . . would be acceptable to him or comply with an order of the Copyright Tribunal under section 135D relating to such a licence or any scheme under which it would be granted, and

(b) allowing unlimited needletime or such needletime as he has demanded.

(3) Where he holds a licence to include the recordings in the broadcast . . . the condition is that the terms of the licence limit needletime and the licensing body refuses to substitute or procure the substitution of terms allowing unlimited needletime or such needletime as he has demanded, or refuses to do so on terms that fall within subsection (2)(a).

(4) The references in subsection (2) to refusing to grant, or procure the grant of, a licence, and in subsection (3) to refusing to substitute or procure the substitution of terms, include failing to do so within a reasonable time of being asked.

(5) In the group of sections from this section to section 135G—

["broadcast" does not include any broadcast which is a transmission of the kind specified in section 6(1A)(b) or (c);]

"needletime" means the time in any period (whether determined as a number of hours in the period or a proportion of the period, or otherwise) in which any proceedings may be included in a broadcast . . . ;

"sound recording" does not include a film sound track when accompanying a film.

(6) In sections 135B to 135G, "terms of payment" means terms as to payment for including sound recordings in a broadcast . . .]

NOTES

Inserted, together with preceding heading and ss 135B–135G, by the Broadcasting Act 1990, s 175(1).

Sub-ss (1)–(3), (6), and the heading preceding this section: words omitted repealed by the Copyright and Related Rights Regulations 2003, SI 2003/2498, reg 2(2), Sch 2, subject to transitional provisions as noted to s 1 of this Act at **[2.7]**.

Sub-s (5): definition "broadcast" inserted, and words omitted from definition "needletime" repealed, by SI 2003/2498, reg 2, Sch 1, Pt 1, para 15(1), Sch 2, subject to transitional provisions as noted to s 1 of this Act at **[2.7]**.

[2.179]

[135B Notice of intention to exercise right

(1) A person intending to avail himself of the right conferred by section 135C must—

(a) give notice to the licensing body of his intention to exercise the right, asking the body to propose terms of payment, and

(b) after receiving the proposal or the expiry of a reasonable period, give reasonable notice to the licensing body of the date on which he proposes to begin exercising that right, and the terms of payment in accordance with which he intends to do so.

(2) Where he has a licence to include the recordings in a broadcast . . . , the date specified in a notice under subsection (1)(b) must not be sooner than the date of expiry of that licence except in a case falling within section 135A(3).

(3) Before the person intending to avail himself of the right begins to exercise it, he must—

(a) give reasonable notice to the Copyright Tribunal of his intention to exercise the right, and of the date on which he proposes to begin to do so, and

(b) apply to the Tribunal under section 135D to settle the terms of payment.]

NOTES

Inserted as noted to s 135A at **[2.178]**.

Sub-s (2): words omitted repealed by the Copyright and Related Rights Regulations 2003, SI 2003/2498, reg 2(2), Sch 2, subject to transitional provisions as noted to s 1 of this Act at **[2.7]**.

[2.180]

[135C Conditions for exercise of right

(1) A person who, on or after the date specified in a notice under section 135B(1)(b), includes in a broadcast . . . any sound recordings in circumstances in which this section applies, and who—

(a) complies with any reasonable condition, notice of which has been given to him by the licensing body, as to inclusion in the broadcasting . . . of those recordings,

(b) provides that body with such information about their inclusion in the broadcast . . . as it may reasonably require, and

(c) makes the payments to the licensing body that are required by this section,

shall be in the same position as regards infringement of copyright as if he had at all material times been the holder of a licence granted by the owner of the copyright in question.

(2) Payments are to be made at not less than quarterly intervals in arrears.

(3) The amount of any payment is that determined in accordance with any order of the Copyright Tribunal under section 135D or, if no such order has been made—

(a) in accordance with any proposal for terms of payment made by the licensing body pursuant to a request under section 135B, or

(b) where no proposal has been so made or the amount determined in accordance with the proposal so made is unreasonably high, in accordance with the terms of payment notified to the licensing body under section 135B(1)(b).

(4) Where this section applies to the inclusion in a broadcast . . . of any sound recordings, it does so in place of any licence.]

NOTES

Inserted as noted to s 135A at **[2.178]**.

Sub-ss (1), (4): words omitted repealed by the Copyright and Related Rights Regulations 2003, SI 2003/2498, reg 2(2), Sch 2, subject to transitional provisions as noted to s 1 of this Act at **[2.7]**.

[2.181]
[135D Applications to settle payments

(1) On an application to settle the terms of payment, the Copyright Tribunal shall consider the matter and make such order as it may determine to be reasonable in the circumstances.

(2) An order under subsection (1) has effect from the date the applicant begins to exercise the right conferred by section 135C and any necessary repayments, or further payments, shall be made in respect of amounts that have fallen due.]

NOTES

Inserted as noted to s 135A at **[2.178]**.

[2.182]
[135E References etc about conditions, information and other terms

(1) A person exercising the right conferred by section 135C, or who has given notice to the Copyright Tribunal of his intention to do so, may refer to the Tribunal—

(a) any question whether any condition as to the inclusion in a broadcast . . . of sound recordings, notice of which has been given to him by the licensing body in question, is a reasonable condition, or

(b) any question whether any information is information which the licensing body can reasonably require him to provide.

(2) On a reference under this section, the Tribunal shall consider the matter and make such order as it may determine to be reasonable in the circumstances.]

NOTES

Inserted as noted to s 135A at **[2.178]**.

Sub-s (1): words omitted from para (a) repealed by the Copyright and Related Rights Regulations 2003, SI 2003/2498, reg 2(2), Sch 2, subject to transitional provisions as noted to s 1 of this Act at **[2.7]**.

[2.183]
[135F Application for review of order

(1) A person exercising the right conferred by section 135C or the licensing body may apply to the Copyright Tribunal to review any order under section 135D or 135E.

(2) An application shall not be made, except with the special leave of the Tribunal—

(a) within twelve months from the date of the order, or of the decision on a previous application under this section, or

(b) if the order was made so as to be in force for fifteen months or less, or as a result of a decision on a previous application is due to expire within fifteen months of that decision, until the last three months before the expiry date.

(3) On the application the Tribunal shall consider the matter and make such order confirming or varying the original order as it may determine to be reasonable in the circumstances.

(4) An order under this section has effect from the date on which it is made or such later date as may be specified by the Tribunal.]

NOTES

Inserted as noted to s 135A at **[2.178]**.

[2.184]
[135G Factors to be taken into account

(1) In determining what is reasonable on an application or reference under section 135D or 135E, or on reviewing any order under section 135F, the Copyright Tribunal shall—

(a) have regard to the terms of any orders which it has made in the case of persons in similar circumstances exercising the right conferred by section 135C, and

(b) exercise its powers so as to secure that there is no unreasonable discrimination between persons exercising that right against the same licensing body.

(2) In settling the terms of payment under section 135D, the Tribunal shall not be guided by any order it has made under any enactment other than that section.

(3) Section 134 (factors to be taken into account: retransmissions) applies on an application or reference under sections 135D to 135F as it applies on an application or reference relating to a licence.]

NOTES

Inserted as noted to s 135A at **[2.178]**.

[2.185]
[135H Power to amend sections 135A to 135G

(1) The Secretary of State may by order, subject to such transitional provision as appears to him to be appropriate, amend sections 135A to 135G so as—

(a) to include in any reference to sound recordings any works of a description specified in the order; or

(b) to exclude from any reference to a broadcast . . . any broadcast . . . of a description so specified.

(2) An order shall be made by statutory instrument; and no order shall be made unless a draft of it has been laid before and approved by resolution of each House of Parliament.]

NOTES

Inserted by the Broadcasting Act 1996, s 139(1).

Sub-s (1): words omitted from para (b) repealed by the Copyright and Related Rights Regulations 2003, SI 2003/2498, reg 2(2), Sch 2, subject to transitional provisions as noted to s 1 of this Act at **[2.7]**.

Implied indemnity in schemes or licences for reprographic copying

[2.186]

136 Implied indemnity in certain schemes and licences for reprographic copying

(1) This section applies to—

(a) schemes for licensing reprographic copying of published literary, dramatic, musical or artistic works, or the typographical arrangement of published editions, and

(b) licences granted by licensing bodies for such copying,

where the scheme or licence does not specify the works to which it applies with such particularity as to enable licensees to determine whether a work falls within the scheme or licence by inspection of the scheme or licence and the work.

(2) There is implied—

(a) in every scheme to which this section applies an undertaking by the operator of the scheme to indemnify a person granted a licence under the scheme, and

(b) in every licence to which this section applies an undertaking by the licensing body to indemnify the licensee,

against any liability incurred by him by reason of his having infringed copyright by making or authorising the making of reprographic copies of a work in circumstances within the apparent scope of his licence.

(3) The circumstances of a case are within the apparent scope of a licence if—

(a) it is not apparent from inspection of the licence and the work that it does not fall within the description of works to which the licence applies; and

(b) the licence does not expressly provide that it does not extend to copyright of the description infringed.

(4) In this section "liability" includes liability to pay costs; and this section applies in relation to costs reasonably incurred by a licensee in connection with actual or contemplated proceedings against him for infringement of copyright as it applies to sums which he is liable to pay in respect of such infringement.

(5) A scheme or licence to which this section applies may contain reasonable provision—

(a) with respect to the manner in which, and time within which, claims under the undertaking implied by this section are to be made;

(b) enabling the operator of the scheme or, as the case may be, the licensing body to take over the conduct of any proceedings affecting the amount of his liability to indemnify.

Reprographic copying by educational establishments

[2.187]

137 Power to extend coverage of scheme or licence

(1) This section applies to—

(a) a licensing scheme to which sections 118 to 123 apply (see section 117) and which is operated by a licensing body, or

(b) a licence to which sections 125 to 128 apply (see section 124),

so far as it provides for the grant of licences, or is a licence, authorising the making by or on behalf of educational establishments for the purposes of instruction of reprographic copies of published literary, dramatic, musical or artistic works, or of the typographical arrangement of published editions.

(2) If it appears to the Secretary of State with respect to a scheme or licence to which this section applies that—

(a) works of a description similar to those covered by the scheme or licence are unreasonably excluded from it, and

(b) making them subject to the scheme or licence would not conflict with the normal exploitation of the works or unreasonably prejudice the legitimate interests of the copyright owners,

he may by order provide that the scheme or licence shall extend to those works.

(3) Where he proposes to make such an order, the Secretary of State shall give notice of the proposal to—

(a) the copyright owners,

(b) the licensing body in question, and

(c) such persons or organisations representative of educational establishments, and such other persons or organisations, as the Secretary of State thinks fit.

(4) The notice shall inform those persons of their right to make written or oral representations to the Secretary of State about the proposal within six months from the date of the notice; and if any of them wishes to make oral representations, the Secretary of State shall appoint a person to hear the representations and report to him.
(5) In considering whether to make an order the Secretary of State shall take into account any representations made to him in accordance with subsection (4), and such other matters as appear to him to be relevant.

[2.188]
138 Variation or discharge of order extending scheme or licence
(1) The owner of the copyright in a work in respect of which an order is in force under section 137 may apply to the Secretary of State for the variation or discharge of the order, stating his reasons for making the application.
(2) The Secretary of State shall not entertain an application made within two years of the making of the original order, or of the making of an order on a previous application under this section, unless it appears to him that the circumstances are exceptional.
(3) On considering the reasons for the application the Secretary of State may confirm the order forthwith; if he does not do so, he shall give notice of the application to—
(a) the licensing body in question, and
(b) such persons or organisations representative of educational establishments, and such other persons or organisations, as he thinks fit.
(4) The notice shall inform those persons of their right to make written or oral representations to the Secretary of State about the application within the period of two months from the date of the notice; and if any of them wishes to make oral representations, the Secretary of State shall appoint a person to hear the representations and report to him.
(5) In considering the application the Secretary of State shall take into account the reasons for the application, any representations made to him in accordance with subsection (4), and such other matters as appear to him to be relevant.
(6) The Secretary of State may make such order as he thinks fit confirming or discharging the order (or, as the case may be, the order as previously varied), or varying (or further varying) it so as to exclude works from it.

[2.189]
139 Appeals against orders
(1) The owner of the copyright in a work which is the subject of an order under section 137 (order extending coverage of scheme or licence) may appeal to the Copyright Tribunal which may confirm or discharge the order, or vary it so as to exclude works from it, as it thinks fit having regard to the considerations mentioned in subsection (2) of that section.
(2) Where the Secretary of State has made an order under section 138 (order confirming, varying or discharging order extending coverage of scheme or licence)—
(a) the person who applied for the order, or
(b) any person or organisation representative of educational establishments who was given notice of the application for the order and made representations in accordance with subsection (4) of that section,

may appeal to the Tribunal which may confirm or discharge the order or make any other order which the Secretary of State might have made.
(3) An appeal under this section shall be brought within six weeks of the making of the order or such further period as the Tribunal may allow.
(4) An order under section 137 or 138 shall not come into effect until the end of the period of six weeks from the making of the order or, if an appeal is brought before the end of that period, until the appeal proceedings are disposed of or withdrawn.
(5) If an appeal is brought after the end of that period, any decision of the Tribunal on the appeal does not affect the validity of anything done in reliance on the order appealed against before that decision takes effect.

[2.190]
140 Inquiry whether new scheme or general licence required
(1) The Secretary of State may appoint a person to inquire into the question whether new provision is required (whether by way of a licensing scheme or general licence) to authorise the making by or on behalf of educational establishments for the purposes of instruction of reprographic copies of—
(a) published literary, dramatic, musical or artistic works, or
(b) the typographical arrangement of published editions,

of a description which appears to the Secretary of State not to be covered by an existing licensing scheme or general licence and not to fall within the power conferred by section 137 (power to extend existing schemes and licences to similar works).
(2) The procedure to be followed in relation to an inquiry shall be such as may be prescribed by regulations made by the Secretary of State.
(3) The regulations shall, in particular, provide for notice to be given to—

(a) persons or organisations appearing to the Secretary of State to represent the owners of copyright in works of that description, and

(b) persons or organisations appearing to the Secretary of State to represent educational establishments,

and for the making of written or oral representations by such persons; but without prejudice to the giving of notice to, and the making of representations by, other persons and organisations.

(4) The person appointed to hold the inquiry shall not recommend the making of new provision unless he is satisfied—

(a) that it would be of advantage to educational establishments to be authorised to make reprographic copies of the works in question, and

(b) that making those works subject to a licensing scheme or general licence would not conflict with the normal exploitation of the works or unreasonably prejudice the legitimate interests of the copyright owners.

(5) If he does recommend the making of new provision he shall specify any terms, other than terms as to charges payable, on which authorisation under the new provision should be available.

(6) Regulations under this section shall be made by statutory instrument which shall be subject to annulment in pursuance of a resolution of either House of Parliament.

(7) In this section (and section 141) a "general licence" means a licence granted by a licensing body which covers all works of the description to which it applies.

[2.191]

141 Statutory licence where recommendation not implemented

(1) The Secretary of State may, within one year of the making of a recommendation under section 140 by order provide that if, or to the extent that, provision has not been made in accordance with the recommendation, the making by or on behalf of an educational establishment, for the purposes of instruction, of reprographic copies of the works to which the recommendation relates shall be treated as licensed by the owners of the copyright in the works.

(2) For that purpose provision shall be regarded as having been made in accordance with the recommendation if—

(a) a certified licensing scheme has been established under which a licence is available to the establishment in question, or

(b) a general licence has been—

(i) granted to or for the benefit of that establishment, or

(ii) referred by or on behalf of that establishment to the Copyright Tribunal under section 125 (reference of terms of proposed licence), or

(iii) offered to or for the benefit of that establishment and refused without such a reference,

and the terms of the scheme or licence accord with the recommendation.

(3) The order shall also provide that any existing licence authorising the making of such copies (not being a licence granted under a certified licensing scheme or a general licence) shall cease to have effect to the extent that it is more restricted or more onerous than the licence provided for by the order.

(4) The order shall provide for the licence to be free of royalty but, as respects other matters, subject to any terms specified in the recommendation and to such other terms as the Secretary of State may think fit.

(5) The order may provide that where a copy which would otherwise be an infringing copy is made in accordance with the licence provided by the order but is subsequently dealt with, it shall be treated as an infringing copy for the purposes of that dealing, and if that dealing infringes copyright for all subsequent purposes.

In this subsection "dealt with" means sold or let for hire, offered or exposed for sale or hire, or exhibited in public.

(6) The order shall not come into force until at least six months after it is made.

(7) An order may be varied from time to time, but not so as to include works other than those to which the recommendation relates or remove any terms specified in the recommendation, and may be revoked.

(8) An order under this section shall be made by statutory instrument which shall be subject to annulment in pursuance of a resolution of either House of Parliament.

(9) In this section a "certified licensing scheme" means a licensing scheme certified for the purposes of this section under section 143.

[Royalty or other sum payable for lending of certain works

[2.192]

142 Royalty or other sum payable for lending of certain works

(1) An application to settle the royalty or other sum payable in pursuance of section 66 (lending of copies of certain copyright works) may be made to the Copyright Tribunal by the copyright owner or the person claiming to be treated as licensed by him.

(2) The Tribunal shall consider the matter and make such order as it may determine to be reasonable in the circumstances.

(3) Either party may subsequently apply to the Tribunal to vary the order, and the Tribunal shall consider the matter and make such order confirming or varying the original order as it may determine to be reasonable in the circumstances.
(4) An application under subsection (3) shall not, except with the special leave of the Tribunal, be made within twelve months from the date of the original order or of the order on a previous application under that subsection.
(5) An order under subsection (3) has effect from the date on which it is made or such later date as may be specified by the Tribunal.]

NOTES

Substituted, together with preceding heading, by the Copyright and Related Rights Regulations 1996, SI 1996/2967, regs 4, 13(2), subject to transitional provisions and savings specified in regs 25–36 of those Regulations, at **[2.510]**–**[2.521]**.

Certification of licensing schemes

[2.193]

143 Certification of licensing schemes

(1) A person operating or proposing to operate a licensing scheme may apply to the Secretary of State to certify the scheme for the purposes of—
 (a) . . .
 (b) section 60 (abstracts of scientific or technical articles),
 [(c) section 66 (lending to public of copies of certain works),]
 (d) . . . or
 (e) section 141 (reprographic copying of published works by educational establishments).
(2) The Secretary of State shall by order made by statutory instrument certify the scheme if he is satisfied that it—
 (a) enables the works to which it relates to be identified with sufficient certainty by persons likely to require licences, and
 (b) sets out clearly the charges (if any) payable and the other terms on which licences will be granted.
(3) The scheme shall be scheduled to the order and the certification shall come into operation for the purposes of section . . . 60, 66 . . . or 141, as the case may be—
 (a) on such date, not less than eight weeks after the order is made, as may be specified in the order, or
 (b) if the scheme is the subject of a reference under section 118 (reference of proposed scheme), any later date on which the order of the Copyright Tribunal under that section comes into force or the reference is withdrawn.
(4) A variation of the scheme is not effective unless a corresponding amendment of the order is made; and the Secretary of State shall make such an amendment in the case of a variation ordered by the Copyright Tribunal on a reference under section 118, 119 or 120, and may do so in any other case if he thinks fit.
(5) The order shall be revoked if the scheme ceases to be operated and may be revoked if it appears to the Secretary of State that it is no longer being operated according to its terms.

NOTES

Sub-s (1): para (a) repealed by the Copyright and Rights in Performances (Research, Education, Libraries and Archives) Regulations 2014, SI 2014/1372, reg 2(2), Schedule, paras 1, 5(a); para (c) substituted by the Copyright and Related Rights Regulations 1996, SI 1996/2967, regs 4, 11(4), subject to transitional provisions and savings specified in regs 25–36 of those Regulations, at **[2.510]**–**[2.521]**; para (d) repealed by the Copyright and Rights in Performances (Disability) Regulations 2014, SI 2014/1384, reg 4, Schedule, para 2(a).

Sub-s (3): first figure omitted repealed by SI 2014/1372, reg 2(2), Schedule, paras 1, 5(b); second figure omitted repealed by SI 2014/1384, reg 4, Schedule, para 2(b).

Orders: the Copyright (Certification of Licensing Scheme for Educational Recording of Broadcasts) (Open University) Order 2003, SI 2003/187; the Copyright (Certification of Licensing Scheme for Educational Recording of Broadcasts) (Educational Recording Agency Limited) Order 2007, SI 2007/266 at **[2.578]**.

Powers exercisable in consequence of competition report

[2.194]

144 Powers exercisable in consequence of report of [Competition and Markets Authority]

[(1) Subsection (1A) applies where whatever needs to be remedied, mitigated or prevented by the Secretary of State [or (as the case may be) the Competition and Markets Authority] under section 12(5) of the Competition Act 1980 or section 41(2), 55(2), 66(6), 75(2), 83(2), 138(2), 147(2)[, 147A(2)] or 160(2) of, or paragraph 5(2) or 10(2) of Schedule 7 to, the Enterprise Act 2002 (powers to take remedial action following references to the [Competition and Markets Authority] in connection with public bodies and certain other persons, mergers or market investigations) consists of or includes—
 (a) conditions in licences granted by the owner of copyright in a work restricting the use of the work by the licensee or the right of the copyright owner to grant other licences; or
 (b) a refusal of a copyright owner to grant licences on reasonable terms.

(1A) The powers conferred by Schedule 8 to the Enterprise Act 2002 include power to cancel or modify those conditions and, instead or in addition, to provide that licences in respect of the copyright shall be available as of right.
(2) The references to anything permitted by Schedule 8 to the Enterprise Act 2002 in section 12(5A) of the Competition Act 1980 and in sections 75(4)(a), 83(4)(a), 84(2)(a), 89(1), 160(4)(a), 161(3)(a) and 164(1) of, and paragraphs 5, 10 and 11 of Schedule 7 to, the Act of 2002 shall be construed accordingly.]
(3) [The Secretary of State] [or (as the case may be) the Competition and Markets Authority] shall only exercise the powers available by virtue of this section if he [or it] is satisfied that to do so does not contravene any Convention relating to copyright to which the United Kingdom is a party.
(4) The terms of a licence available by virtue of this section shall, in default of agreement, be settled by the Copyright Tribunal on an application by the person requiring the licence; and terms so settled shall authorise the licensee to do everything in respect of which a licence is so available.
(5) Where the terms of a licence are settled by the Tribunal, the licence has effect from the date on which the application to the Tribunal was made.

NOTES

Section heading: words in square brackets substituted by the Enterprise and Regulatory Reform Act 2013 (Competition) (Consequential, Transitional and Saving Provisions) Order 2014, SI 2014/892, art 2, Sch 1, Pt 2, paras 55, 57(1), (4).

Sub-s (1): substituted together with sub-ss (1A), (2) for original sub-ss (1), (2), by the Enterprise Act 2002, s 278, Sch 25, para 18(1), (2), subject to transitional provisions and savings in s 276 of, and Sch 24, paras 2–12, 14–19 to, the 2002 Act, and SI 2004/3233, arts 3–5; words in first and third pairs of square brackets substituted and figure in second pair of square brackets inserted by SI 2014/892, art 2, Sch 1, Pt 2, paras 55, 57(1), (2).

Sub-s (1A): substituted as noted to sub-s (1) above.

Sub-s (2): substituted as noted to sub-s (1) above.

Sub-s (3): words in first and third pairs of square brackets inserted by the Enterprise Act 2002, s 278, Sch 25, para 18(1), (3), subject to transitional provisions and savings in s 276 of, Sch 24, paras 2–12 to, the 2002 Act, and SI 2004/3233, arts 3–5; words in second pair of square brackets substituted by SI 2014/892, art 2, Sch 1, Pt 2, paras 55, 57(1), (3).

Modification: The reference in sub-s (1) to the Enterprise Act 2002, s 66(6), Sch 7, paras 5(2), 10(2) shall have effect as if it included a reference to the Enterprise Act 2002 (Protection of Legitimate Interests) Order 2003, SI 2003/1592, art 12(7), Sch 2, paras 5(2), 10(2) respectively and the reference in sub-s (2) to the 2002 Act, Sch 7, paras 5, 10, 11 shall have effect as if it included a reference to SI 2003/1592, Sch 2, paras 5, 10, 11 respectively; see SI 2003/1592, Sch 4, para 7(1).

[Compulsory collective administration of certain rights

[2.195]

144A Collective exercise of certain rights in relation to cable re-transmission

(1) This section applies to the right of the owner of copyright in a literary, dramatic, musical or artistic work, sound recording or film to grant or refuse authorisation for cable re-transmission of a [wireless] broadcast from another EEA . . . state in which the work is included.

That right is referred to below as "cable re-transmission right".

(2) Cable re-transmission right may be exercised against a cable operator only through a licensing body.
(3) Where a copyright owner has not transferred management of his cable re-transmission right to a licensing body, the licensing body which manages rights of the same category shall be deemed to be mandated to manage his right.

Where more than one licensing body manages rights of that category, he may choose which of them is deemed to be mandated to manage his right.

(4) A copyright owner to whom subsection (3) applies has the same rights and obligations resulting from any relevant agreement between the cable operator and the licensing body as have copyright owners who have transferred management of their cable re-transmission right to that licensing body.
(5) Any rights to which a copyright owner may be entitled by virtue of subsection (4) must be claimed within the period of three years beginning with the date of the cable re-transmission concerned.
(6) This section does not affect any rights exercisable by the maker of the broadcast, whether in relation to the broadcast or a work included in it.
[(7) In this section—

"cable operator" means a person responsible for cable re-transmission of a wireless broadcast; and

"cable re-transmission" means the reception and immediate re-transmission by cable, including the transmission of microwave energy between terrestrial fixed points, of a wireless broadcast.]]

NOTES

Inserted, together with preceding heading, by the Copyright and Related Rights Regulations 1996, SI 1996/2967, regs 4, 7, subject to transitional provisions and savings specified in regs 25–36 of those Regulations, at **[2.510]–[2.521]**.

Sub-s (1): word in square brackets inserted by the Copyright and Related Rights Regulations 2003, SI 2003/2498, regs 3, 5(6), subject to transitional provisions as noted to s 1 of this Act at **[2.7]**; word omitted repealed by the Intellectual Property (Enforcement, etc) Regulations 2006, SI 2006/1028, reg 2(4), Sch 4.

Sub-s (7): substituted by SI 2003/2498, reg 2(1), Sch 1, Pt 1, para 15(2), subject to transitional provisions as noted to s 1 of this Act at **[2.7]**.

CHAPTER VIII
THE COPYRIGHT TRIBUNAL

The Tribunal

[2.196]
145 The Copyright Tribunal

(1) The Tribunal established under section 23 of the Copyright Act 1956 is renamed the Copyright Tribunal.

(2) The Tribunal shall consist of a chairman and two deputy chairmen appointed by the Lord Chancellor, after consultation with the [Secretary of State], and not less than two or more than eight ordinary members appointed by the Secretary of State.

(3) A person is not eligible for appointment as chairman or deputy chairman [unless—

[(a) he satisfies the judicial-appointment eligibility condition on a 5-year basis;]

(b) he is an advocate or solicitor in Scotland of at least [5] years' standing;

(c) he is a member of the Bar of Northern Ireland or [solicitor of the Court of Judicature of Northern Ireland] of at least [5] years' standing; or

(d) he has held judicial office.]

NOTES

Sub-s (2): words in square brackets substituted by virtue of the Transfer of Functions (Lord Advocate and Secretary of State) Order 1999, SI 1999/678, art 2(1), Schedule.

Sub-s (3): words in first (outer) pair of square brackets substituted by the Courts and Legal Services Act 1990, s 71(2), Sch 10, para 73; para (a) substituted and in paras (b), (c) numbers in square brackets substituted by the Tribunals, Courts and Enforcement Act 2007, s 50, Sch 10, Pt 1, para 20, subject to transitional provisions in the Tribunals, Courts and Enforcement Act 2007 (Commencement No 5 and Transitional Provisions) Order 2008, SI 2008/1653, arts 3, 4; words in square brackets in para (c) substituted by the Constitutional Reform Act 2005, s 59(5), Sch 11, Pt 3, para 5.

Modification: by virtue of the Scotland Act 1998 (Functions Exercisable in or as Regards Scotland) Order 1999, SI 1999/1748, art 3, Sch 1, para 10, the Secretary of State's functions under this section and s 150, at **[2.201]** are to be treated, for the purposes of the Scotland Act 1998, s 63, as being exercisable in or as regards Scotland.

Copyright Act 1956: repealed by s 303(2) of, and Sch 8 to, this Act.

[2.197]
146 Membership of the Tribunal

(1) The members of the Copyright Tribunal shall hold and vacate office in accordance with their terms of appointment, subject to the following provisions.

(2) A member of the Tribunal may resign his office by notice in writing to the Secretary of State or, in the case of the chairman or a deputy chairman, to the Lord Chancellor.

(3) The Secretary of State or, in the case of the chairman or a deputy chairman, the Lord Chancellor may by notice in writing to the member concerned remove him from office if—

(a) he has become bankrupt or made an arrangement with his creditors or, in Scotland, his estate has been sequestrated or he has executed a trust deed for his creditors or entered into a composition contract, or

(b) he is incapacitated by physical or mental illness,

or if he is in the opinion of the Secretary of State or, as the case may be, the Lord Chancellor otherwise unable or unfit to perform his duties as member.

[(3A) A person who is the chairman or a deputy chairman of the Tribunal shall vacate his office on the day on which he attains the age of 70 years; but this subsection is subject to section 26(4) to (6) of the Judicial Pensions and Retirement Act 1993 (power to authorise continuance in office up to the age of 75 years).]

(4) If a member of the Tribunal is by reason of illness, absence or other reasonable cause for the time being unable to perform the duties of his office, either generally or in relation to particular proceedings, a person may be appointed to discharge his duties for a period not exceeding six months at one time or, as the case may be, in relation to those proceedings.

(5) The appointment shall be made—

(a) in the case of the chairman or deputy chairman, by the Lord Chancellor, who shall appoint a person who would be eligible for appointment to that office, and

(b) in the case of an ordinary member, by the Secretary of State;

and a person so appointed shall have during the period of his appointment, or in relation to the proceedings in question, the same powers as the person in whose place he is appointed.

(6) The Lord Chancellor shall consult the Lord Advocate before exercising his powers under this section.

[(7) The Lord Chancellor may exercise his powers to remove a person under subsection (3) or to appoint a person under subsection (4) only with the concurrence of the appropriate senior judge.

(8) The appropriate senior judge is the Lord Chief Justice of England and Wales, unless—

(a) the person to be removed exercises functions[, or the person to be appointed is to exercise functions,] wholly or mainly in Scotland, in which case it is the Lord President of the Court of Session, or

(b) the person to be removed exercises functions[, or the person to be appointed is to exercise functions,] wholly or mainly in Northern Ireland, in which case it is the Lord Chief Justice of Northern Ireland.

(9) The Lord Chief Justice of England and Wales may nominate a judicial office holder (as defined in section 109(4) of the Constitutional Reform Act 2005) to exercise his functions under subsection (7) in relation to the appointment of a person under subsection (4).
(10) The Lord President of the Court of Session may nominate a judge of the Court of Session who is a member of the First or Second Division of the Inner House of that Court to exercise his functions under subsection (7) in relation to the appointment of a person under subsection (4).
(11) The Lord Chief Justice of Northern Ireland may nominate any of the following to exercise his functions under subsection (7) in relation to the appointment of a person under subsection (4)—
(a) the holder of one of the offices listed in Schedule 1 to the Justice (Northern Ireland) Act 2002;
(b) a Lord Justice of Appeal (as defined in section 88 of that Act).]

NOTES

Sub-s (3A): inserted by the Judicial Pensions and Retirement Act 1993, s 26(10), Sch 6, para 49.
Sub-ss (7), (9)–(11): added, together with sub-s (8), by the Constitutional Reform Act 2005, s 15(1), Sch 4, Pt 1, paras 198, 199.
Sub-s (8): added as noted above; words in square brackets inserted by the Lord Chancellor (Transfer of Functions and Supplementary Provisions) (No 2) Order 2006, SI 2006/1016, art 4, Sch 3.
Lord Advocate: see the note to s 108, at **[2.144]**.

[2.198]
147 Financial provisions

(1) There shall be paid to the members of the Copyright Tribunal such remuneration (whether by way of salaries or fees), and such allowances, as the Secretary of State with the approval of the Treasury may determine.
(2) The Secretary of State may appoint such staff for the Tribunal as, with the approval of the Treasury as to numbers and remuneration, he may determine.
(3) The remuneration and allowances of members of the Tribunal, the remuneration of any staff and such other expenses of the Tribunal as the Secretary of State with the approval of the Treasury may determine shall be paid out of money provided by Parliament.

[2.199]
148 Constitution for purposes of proceedings

(1) For the purposes of any proceedings the Copyright Tribunal shall consist of—
(a) a chairman, who shall be either the chairman or a deputy chairman of the Tribunal, and
(b) two or more ordinary members.
(2) If the members of the Tribunal dealing with any matter are not unanimous, the decision shall be taken by majority vote; and if, in such a case, the votes are equal the chairman shall have a further, casting vote.
(3) Where part of any proceedings before the Tribunal has been heard and one or more members of the Tribunal are unable to continue, the Tribunal shall remain duly constituted for the purpose of those proceedings so long as the number of members is not reduced to less than three.
(4) If the chairman is unable to continue, the chairman of the Tribunal shall—
(a) appoint one of the remaining members to act as chairman, and
(b) appoint a suitably qualified person to attend the proceedings and advise the members on any questions of law arising.
(5) A person is "suitably qualified" for the purposes of subsection (4)(b) if he is, or is eligible for appointment as, a deputy chairman of the Tribunal.

Jurisdiction and procedure

[2.200]
149 Jurisdiction of the Tribunal

[The Copyright Tribunal has jurisdiction under this Part] to hear and determine proceedings under—
[(za) section 73 (determination of royalty or other remuneration to be paid with respect to re-transmission of broadcast including work);]
[(zb) section 93C (application to determine amount of equitable remuneration under section 93B);]
(a) section 118, 119 or 120 (reference of licensing scheme);
(b) section 121 or 122 (application with respect to entitlement to licence under licensing scheme);
(c) section 125, 126 or 127 (reference or application with respect to licensing by licensing body);
[(ca) section 128B (reference by the Secretary of State under section 128A);]
[(cc) section 135D or 135E (application or reference with respect to use as of right of sound recordings in broadcasts . . .);]
(d) section 139 (appeal against order as to coverage of licensing scheme or licence);
(e) section 142 (application to settle royalty or other sum payable for [lending of certain works]);
(f) section 144(4) (application to settle terms of copyright licence available as of right);

[(fa) paragraph 7 of Schedule ZA1 (application to determine compensation for use of orphan works).]

(g), (h) . . .

NOTES

Words in first pair of square brackets and words in square brackets in para (e) substituted, para (zb) inserted, and paras (g), (h) repealed, by the Copyright and Related Rights Regulations 1996, SI 1996/2967, regs 4, 13(3), 14(2), 24(2), subject to transitional provisions and savings specified in regs 25–36 of those Regulations, at **[2.510]–[2.521]**; para (za) inserted by the Broadcasting Act 1996, s 138, Sch 9, para 3 and repealed by the Digital Economy Act 2017, s 34(2)(a)(ii), as from a day to be appointed; para (cc) inserted by the Broadcasting Act 1990, s 175(2); para (ca) inserted, and words omitted from para (cc) repealed, by the Copyright and Related Rights Regulations 2003, SI 2003/2498, regs 2(2), 3, 21(6), Sch 2, subject to transitional provisions as noted to s 1 of this Act at **[2.7]**; para (fa) inserted by the Copyright and Rights in Performances (Certain Permitted Uses of Orphan Works) Regulations 2014, SI 2014/2861, reg 3(3).

See further, in relation to the duty to provide advance information about television and radio programme services: the Broadcasting Act 1990, s 176, at **[2.416]**, and Sch 17.

[2.201]

150 General power to make rules

(1) The Lord Chancellor may, after consultation with the [Secretary of State], make rules for regulating proceedings before the Copyright Tribunal and, subject to the approval of the Treasury, as to the fees chargeable in respect of such proceedings.

[(2) The rules may apply in relation to the Tribunal, as respects proceedings in England and Wales or Northern Ireland, any of the provisions of Part I of the Arbitration Act 1996.]

(3) Provision shall be made by the rules—

(a) prohibiting the Tribunal from entertaining a reference under section 118, 119, or 120 by a representative organisation unless the Tribunal is satisfied that the organisation is reasonably representative of the class of persons which it claims to represent;

(b) specifying the parties to any proceedings and enabling the Tribunal to make a party to the proceedings any person or organisation satisfying the Tribunal that they have a substantial interest in the matter; and

(c) requiring the Tribunal to give the parties to proceedings an opportunity to state their case, in writing or orally as the rules may provide.

(4) The rules may make provision for regulating or prescribing any matters incidental to or consequential upon any appeal from the Tribunal under section 152 (appeal to the court on point of law).

(5) Rules under this section shall be made by statutory instrument which shall be subject to annulment in pursuance of a resolution of either House of Parliament.

NOTES

Sub-s (1): words in square brackets substituted by virtue of the Transfer of Functions (Lord Advocate and Secretary of State) Order 1999, SI 1999/678, art 2(1), Schedule.

Sub-s (2): substituted by the Arbitration Act 1996, s 107(1), Sch 3, para 50, subject to transitional provisions and savings in relation to arbitral proceedings and arbitration applications (etc) commenced before 31 January 1997.

Modification: see note to s 145 at **[2.196]**.

Rules: the Copyright Tribunal Rules 2010, SI 2010/791 at **[2.584]**.

[2.202]

151 Costs, proof of orders, &c

(1) The Copyright Tribunal may order that the costs of a party to proceedings before it shall be paid by such other party as the Tribunal may direct; and the Tribunal may tax or settle the amount of the costs, or direct in what manner they are to be taxed.

(2) A document purporting to be a copy of an order of the Tribunal and to be certified by the chairman to be a true copy shall, in any proceedings, be sufficient evidence of the order unless the contrary is proved.

(3) As respect proceedings in Scotland, the Tribunal has the like powers for securing the attendance of witnesses and the production of documents, and with regard to the examination of witnesses on oath, as an arbiter under a submission.

[2.203]

[151A Award of interest

(1) Any of the following, namely—

(a) a direction under section 123(3) so far as relating to a licence for [communicating a work to the public];

(b) a direction under section 128(3) so far as so relating;

(c) an order under section 135D(1); and

(d) an order under section 135F confirming or varying an order under section 135D(1),

may award simple interest at such rate and for such period, beginning not earlier than the relevant date and ending not later than the date of the order, as the Copyright Tribunal thinks reasonable in the circumstances.

(2) In this section "the relevant date" means—

(a) in relation to a direction under section 123(3), the date on which the reference was made;

(b) in relation to a direction under section 128(3), the date on which the reference or application was made;
(c) in relation to an order under section 135D(1), the date on which the first payment under section 135C(2) became due; and
(d) in relation to an order under section 135F, the date on which the application was made.]

NOTES

Inserted by the Broadcasting Act 1996, s 139(2), (3), except in any case where the reference or application to the Copyright Tribunal was or is made before 1 November 1996.

Sub-s (1): words in square brackets in para (a) substituted by the Copyright and Related Rights Regulations 2003, SI 2003/2498, reg 2(1), Sch 1, Pt 1, paras 1, 7, subject to transitional provisions as noted to s 1 of this Act at **[2.7]**.

Appeals

[2.204]

152 Appeal to the court on point of law

(1) An appeal lies on any point of law arising from a decision of the Copyright Tribunal to the High Court or, in the case of proceedings of the Tribunal in Scotland, to the Court of Session.

(2) Provision shall be made by rules under section 150 limiting the time within which an appeal may be brought.

(3) Provision may be made by rules under that section—
(a) for suspending, or authorising or requiring the Tribunal to suspend, the operation of orders of the Tribunal in cases where its decision is appealed against;
(b) for modifying in relation to an order of the Tribunal whose operation is suspended the operation of any provision of this Act as to the effect of the order;
(c) for the publication of notices or the taking of other steps for securing that persons affected by the suspension of an order of the Tribunal will be informed of its suspension.

NOTES

Rules: the Copyright Tribunal Rules 2010, SI 2010/791 at **[2.584]**.

CHAPTER IX
QUALIFICATION FOR AND EXTENT OF COPYRIGHT PROTECTION

Qualification for copyright protection

[2.205]

153 Qualification for copyright protection

(1) Copyright does not subsist in a work unless the qualification requirements of this Chapter are satisfied as regards—
(a) the author (see section 154), or
(b) the country in which the work was first published (see section 155), or
(c) in the case of a broadcast . . . , the country from which the broadcast was made . . . (see section 156).

(2) Subsection (1) does not apply in relation to Crown copyright or Parliamentary copyright (see sections 163 to [166D]) or to copyright subsisting by virtue of section 168 (copyright of certain international organisations).

(3) If the qualification requirements of this Chapter, or section 163, 165 or 168, are once satisfied in respect of a work, copyright does not cease to subsist by reason of any subsequent event.

NOTES

Sub-s (1): words omitted from para (c) repealed by the Copyright and Related Rights Regulations 2003, SI 2003/2498, reg 2(2), Sch 2, subject to transitional provisions as noted to s 1 of this Act at **[2.7]**.

Sub-s (2): reference in square brackets substituted by the Government of Wales Act 2006, s 160(1), Sch 10, paras 22, 25.

[2.206]

154 Qualification by reference to author

(1) A work qualifies for copyright protection if the author was at the material time a qualifying person, that is—
(a) a British citizen, [a national of another EEA state,] a [British overseas territories citizen], a British National (Overseas), a British Overseas citizen, a British subject or a British protected person within the meaning of the British Nationality Act 1981, or
[(b) an individual domiciled or resident in the United Kingdom or another EEA state or in the Channel Islands, the Isle of Man or Gibraltar or in a country to which the relevant provisions of this Part extend,
(c) a body incorporated under the law of a part of the United Kingdom or another EEA state or of the Channel Islands, the Isle of Man or Gibraltar or of a country to which the relevant provisions of this Part extend.]

(2) Where, or so far as, provision is made by Order under section 159 (application of this Part to countries to which it does not extend), a work also qualifies for copyright protection if at the material time the author was a citizen or subject of, an individual domiciled or resident in, or a body incorporated under the law of, a country to which the Order relates.

(3) A work of joint authorship qualifies for copyright protection if at the material time any of the authors satisfies the requirements of subsection (1) or (2); but where a work qualifies for copyright protection only under this section, only those authors who satisfy those requirements shall be taken into account for the purposes of—

section 11(1) and (2) (first ownership of copyright; entitlement of author or author's employer),

[section 12 (duration of copyright), and section 9(4) (meaning of "unknown authorship") so far as it applies for the purposes of section 12, and]

section 57 (anonymous or pseudonymous works: acts permitted on assumptions as to expiry of copyright or death of author).

(4) The material time in relation to a literary, dramatic, musical or artistic work is—

(a) in the case of an unpublished work, when the work was made or, if the making of the work extended over a period, a substantial part of that period;

(b) in the case of a published work, when the work was first published or, if the author had died before that time, immediately before his death.

(5) The material time in relation to other descriptions of work is as follows—

(a) in the case of a sound recording or film, when it was made;

(b) in the case of a broadcast, when the broadcast was made;

(c) . . .

(d) in the case of the typographical arrangement of a published edition, when the edition was first published.

NOTES

Sub-s (1): words in second pair of square brackets in para (a) substituted by virtue of the British Overseas Territories Act 2002, s 2(3); words in first pair of square brackets in para (a) inserted and paras (b), (c) substituted, by the Intellectual Property Act 2014, s 22(1), as from 6 April 2017, subject to savings as noted below. Paras (b), (c) previously read as follows—

"(b) an individual domiciled or resident in the United Kingdom or another country to which the relevant provisions of this Part extend, or

(c) a body incorporated under the law of a part of the United Kingdom or of another country to which the relevant provisions of this Part extend.".

Sub-s (3): words in square brackets substituted by the Duration of Copyright and Rights in Performances Regulations 1995, SI 1995/3297, regs 4, 5(3), subject to transitional provisions and savings specified in regs 12–34 of those Regulations, at **[2.478]–[2.499]**.

Sub-s (5): para (c) repealed by the Copyright and Related Rights Regulations 2003, SI 2003/2498, reg 2(2), Sch 2, subject to transitional provisions as noted to s 1 of this Act at **[2.7]**.

Savings: the Intellectual Property Act 2014 (Commencement No 5 and Saving Provisions) Order 2016, SI 2016/1139, art 4 provides as follows—

"4 Saving

(1) For the purposes of this article an act is an "excluded act" where—

(a) a person (A) has incurred any expenditure or liability in connection with the act; and

(b) A—

(i) began in good faith to do the act, or

(ii) made in good faith effective and serious preparations to do the act,

at a time when the act neither infringed nor was restricted by the relevant rights in the work or performance.

(2) Where another person (B) acquires those relevant rights as a consequence of the provisions made by section 22 of the Intellectual Property Act 2014, on or after the coming into force of that section under article 3 of this Order, A has the right—

(a) to continue to do the excluded act, or

(b) to do the excluded act,

notwithstanding that the excluded act infringes or is restricted by those relevant rights.

(3) Where B or, as the case may be, B's exclusive licensee in respect of the relevant rights pays reasonable compensation to A, paragraph (2) no longer applies.

(4) Where—

(a) B or, as the case may be, B's exclusive licensee offers to pay compensation to A under paragraph (3), but

(b) A and B or, as the case may be, B's exclusive licensee cannot agree on what compensation is reasonable,

either person may refer the matter to arbitration.

(5) In this article—

(a) "exclusive licensee" means a licensee under an exclusive licence (as defined in section 92(1) or 191D(1) of the Copyright, Designs and Patents Act 1988); and

(b) "relevant rights" means copyright (as defined in section 1 of the Copyright, Designs and Patents Act 1988), the rights conferred by Chapter 4 of Part 1 (moral rights) of that Act and the rights conferred by Part 2 of that Act.

(6) This article extends to England and Wales, Scotland and Northern Ireland.".

[2.207]

155 Qualification by reference to country of first publication

(1) A literary, dramatic, musical or artistic work, a sound recording or film, or the typographical arrangement of a published edition, qualifies for copyright protection if it is first published—

(a) in the United Kingdom[, another EEA state, the Channel Islands, the Isle of Man or Gibraltar], or

(b) in [a country] to which the relevant provisions of this Part extend.

(2) Where, or so far as, provision is made by Order under section 159 (application of this Part to countries to which it does not extend), such a work also qualifies for copyright protection if it is first published in a country to which the Order relates.

(3) For the purposes of this section, publication in one country shall not be regarded as other than the first publication by reason of simultaneous publication elsewhere; and for this purpose publication elsewhere within the previous 30 days shall be treated as simultaneous.

NOTES

Sub-s (1): words in square brackets in para (a) inserted and words in square brackets in para (b) substituted for original words "another country", by the Intellectual Property Act 2014, s 22(2), as from 6 April 2017, subject to savings as noted to s 154 at **[2.206]**.

[2.208]

156 Qualification by reference to place of transmission

(1) A broadcast qualifies for copyright protection if it is made from . . . a place in—

(a) the United Kingdom[, another EEA state, the Channel Islands, the Isle of Man or Gibraltar], or

(b) [a country] to which the relevant provisions of this Part extend.

(2) Where, or so far as, provision is made by Order under section 159 (application of this Part to countries to which it does not extend), a broadcast . . . also qualifies for copyright protection if it is made from . . . a place in a country to which the Order relates.

NOTES

Sub-s (1): words omitted repealed by the Copyright and Related Rights Regulations 2003, SI 2003/2498, reg 2(2), Sch 2, subject to transitional provisions as noted to s 1 of this Act at **[2.7]**; words in square brackets in para (a) inserted and words in square brackets in para (b) substituted for original words "another country", by the Intellectual Property Act 2014, s 22(3), as from 6 April 2017, subject to savings as noted to s 154 at **[2.206]**.

Sub-s (2): words omitted repealed by the Copyright and Related Rights Regulations 2003, SI 2003/2498, reg 2(2), Sch 2, subject to transitional provisions as noted to s 1 of this Act at **[2.7]**.

Extent and application of this Part

[2.209]

157 Countries to which this Part extends

(1) This Part extends to England and Wales, Scotland and Northern Ireland.

(2) Her Majesty may by Order in Council direct that this Part shall extend, subject to such exceptions and modifications as may be specified in the Order, to—

(a) any of the Channel Islands,

(b) the Isle of Man, or

(c) any colony.

(3) That power includes power to extend, subject to such exceptions and modifications as may be specified in the Order, any Order in Council made under the following provisions of this Chapter.

(4) The legislature of a country to which this Part has been extended may modify or add to the provisions of this Part, in their operation as part of the law of that country, as the legislature may consider necessary to adapt the provisions to the circumstances of that country—

(a) as regards procedure and remedies, or

(b) as regards works qualifying for copyright protection by virtue of a connection with that country.

(5) Nothing in this section shall be construed as restricting the extent of paragraph 36 of Schedule 1 (transitional provisions: [British overseas territories] where the Copyright Act 1956 or the Copyright Act 1911 remains in force) in relation to the law of a [British overseas territory] to which this Part does not extend.

NOTES

Sub-s (5): words in square brackets substituted by virtue of the British Overseas Territories Act 2002, s 1(2).

Copyright Act 1911: repealed by the Copyright Act 1956.

Copyright Act 1956: repealed by s 303(2) of, and Sch 8 to, this Act.

Orders: the Copyright (Gibraltar) Order 2005, SI 2005/853; the Copyright (Gibraltar) Revocation Order 2006, SI 2006/1039; the Copyright (Bermuda) Revocation Order 2009, SI 2009/2749; the Copyright (Cayman Islands) Order 2015, SI 2015/795 (as to Orders made under the corresponding provisions of the repealed enactments, see Sch 1 at **[2.409]**).

[2.210]

158 Countries ceasing to be colonies

(1) The following provisions apply where a country to which this Part has been extended ceases to be a colony of the United Kingdom.

(2) As from the date on which it ceases to be a colony it shall cease to be regarded as a country to which this Part extends for the purposes of—

(a) section 160(2)(a) (denial of copyright protection to citizens of countries not giving adequate protection to British works), and

(b) sections 163 and 165 (Crown and Parliamentary copyright).

(3) But it shall continue to be treated as a country to which this Part extends for the purposes of sections 154 to 156 (qualification for copyright protection) until—

(a) an Order in Council is made in respect of that country under section 159 (application of this Part to countries to which it does not extend), or

(b) an Order in Council is made declaring that it shall cease to be so treated by reason of the fact that the provisions of this Part as part of the law of that country have been repealed or amended.

(4) A statutory instrument containing an Order in Council under subsection (3)(b) shall be subject to annulment in pursuance of a resolution of either House of Parliament.

[2.211]

[159 Application of this Part to countries to which it does not extend

(1) Where a country is a party to the Berne Convention or a member of the World Trade Organisation, this Part, so far as it relates to literary, dramatic, musical and artistic works, films and typographical arrangements of published editions—

(a) applies in relation to a citizen or subject of that country or a person domiciled or resident there as it applies in relation to a person who is a British citizen or is domiciled or resident in the United Kingdom,

(b) applies in relation to a body incorporated under the law of that country as it applies in relation to a body incorporated under the law of a part of the United Kingdom, and

(c) applies in relation to a work first published in that country as it applies in relation to a work first published in the United Kingdom.

(2) Where a country is a party to the Rome Convention, this Part, so far as it relates to sound recordings and broadcasts—

(a) applies in relation to that country as mentioned in paragraphs (a), (b) and (c) of subsection (1), and

(b) applies in relation to a broadcast made from that country as it applies to a broadcast made from the United Kingdom.

(3) Where a country is a party to the WPPT, this Part, so far as relating to sound recordings, applies in relation to that country as mentioned in paragraphs (a), (b) and (c) of subsection (1).

(4) Her Majesty may by Order in Council—

(a) make provision for the application of this Part to a country by subsection (1), (2) or (3) to be subject to specified restrictions;

(b) make provision for applying this Part, or any of its provisions, to a specified country;

(c) make provision for applying this Part, or any of its provisions, to any country of a specified description;

(d) make provision for the application of legislation to a country under paragraph (b) or (c) to be subject to specified restrictions.

(5) Provision made under subsection (4) may apply generally or in relation to such classes of works, or other classes of case, as are specified.

(6) Her Majesty may not make an Order in Council containing provision under subsection (4)(b) or (c) unless satisfied that provision has been or will be made under the law of the country or countries in question, in respect of the classes to which the provision under subsection (4)(b) or (c) relates, giving adequate protection to the owners of copyright under this Part.

(7) Application under subsection (4)(b) or (c) is in addition to application by subsections (1) to (3).

(8) Provision made under subsection (4)(c) may cover countries that become (or again become) of the specified description after the provision comes into force.

(9) In this section—

"the Berne Convention" means any Act of the International Convention for the Protection of Literary and Artistic Works signed at Berne on 9 September 1886;

"the Rome Convention" means the International Convention for the Protection of Performers, Producers of Phonograms and Broadcasting Organisations done at Rome on 26 October 1961;

"the WPPT" means the World Intellectual Property Organisation Performances and Phonograms Treaty adopted in Geneva on 20 December 1996.

(10) A statutory instrument containing an Order in Council under this section is subject to annulment in pursuance of a resolution of either House of Parliament.]

NOTES

Commencement: 1 December 2016 (for the purpose of making Orders in Council); 6 April 2017 (otherwise).

Substituted by the Intellectual Property Act 2014, s 22(4), subject to savings as noted to s 154 at **[2.206]**. Section 159 and the notes relating to it previously read as follows—

"159 Application of this Part to countries to which it does not extend

(1) Her Majesty may by Order in Council make provision for applying in relation to a country to which this Part does not extend any of the provisions of this Part specified in the Order, so as to secure that those provisions—

(a) apply in relation to persons who are citizens or subjects of that country or are domiciled or resident there, as they apply to persons who are British citizens or are domiciled or resident in the United Kingdom, or

(b) apply in relation to bodies incorporated under the law of that country as they apply in relation to bodies incorporated under the law of a part of the United Kingdom, or

(c) apply in relation to works first published in that country as they apply in relation to works first published in the United Kingdom, or

(d) apply in relation to broadcasts made from . . . that country as they apply in relation to broadcasts made from . . . the United Kingdom.

(2) An Order may make provision for all or any of the matters mentioned in subsection (1) and may—

(a) apply any provisions of this Part subject to such exceptions and modifications as are specified in the Order; and

(b) direct that any provisions of this Part apply either generally or in relation to such classes of works, or other classes of case, as are specified in the Order.

(3) Except in the case of a Convention country or another member State of the European Economic Community, Her Majesty shall not make an Order in Council under this section in relation to a country unless satisfied that provision has been or will be made under the law of that country, in respect of the class of works to which the Order relates, giving adequate protection to the owners of copyright under this Part.

(4) In subsection (3) "Convention country" means a country which is a party to a Convention relating to copyright to which the United Kingdom is also a party.

(5) A statutory instrument containing an Order in Council under this section shall be subject to annulment in pursuance of a resolution of either House of Parliament.

NOTES

Sub-s (1): words omitted from para (d) repealed by the Copyright and Related Rights Regulations 2003, SI 2003/2498, reg 2(2), Sch 2, subject to transitional provisions as noted to s 1 of this Act at **[2.7]**.".

Orders: the Copyright and Performances (Application to Other Countries) Order 2016, SI 2016/1219 at **[2.730]**.

[2.212]

160 Denial of copyright protection to citizens of countries not giving adequate protection to British works

(1) If it appears to Her Majesty that the law of a country fails to give adequate protection to British works to which this section applies, or to one or more classes of such works, Her Majesty may make provision by Order in Council in accordance with this section restricting the rights conferred by this Part in relation to works of authors connected with that country.

(2) An Order in Council under this section shall designate the country concerned and provide that, for the purposes specified in the Order, works first published after a date specified in the Order shall not be treated as qualifying for copyright protection by virtue of such publication if at that time the authors are—

(a) citizens or subjects of that country (not domiciled or resident in the United Kingdom or another country to which the relevant provisions of this Part extend), or

(b) bodies incorporated under the law of that country;

and the Order may make such provision for all the purposes of this Part or for such purposes as are specified in the Order, and either generally or in relation to such class of cases as are specified in the Order, having regard to the nature and extent of that failure referred to in subsection (1).

(3) This section applies to literary, dramatic, musical and artistic works, sound recordings and films; and "British works" means works of which the author was a qualifying person at the material time within the meaning of section 154.

(4) A statutory instrument containing an Order in Council under this section shall be subject to annulment in pursuance of a resolution of either House of Parliament.

Supplementary

[2.213]

161 Territorial waters and the continental shelf

(1) For the purposes of this Part the territorial waters of the United Kingdom shall be treated as part of the United Kingdom.

(2) This Part applies to things done in the United Kingdom sector of the continental shelf on a structure or vessel which is present there for purposes directly connected with the exploration of the sea bed or subsoil or the exploitation of their natural resources as it applies to things done in the United Kingdom.

(3) The United Kingdom sector of the continental shelf means the areas designated by order under section 1(7) of the Continental Shelf Act 1964.

[2.214]

162 British ships, aircraft and hovercraft

(1) This Part applies to things done on a British ship, aircraft or hovercraft as it applies to things done in the United Kingdom.

(2) In this section—

"British ship" means a ship which is a British ship for the purposes of the [Merchant Shipping Act 1995] otherwise than by virtue of registration in a country outside the United Kingdom; and

"British aircraft" and "British hovercraft" mean an aircraft or hovercraft registered in the United Kingdom.

NOTES

Sub-s (2): in definition "British ship" words in square brackets substituted by the Merchant Shipping Act 1995, s 314(2), Sch 13, para 84(a).

Part 2 Copyright

CHAPTER X
MISCELLANEOUS AND GENERAL

Crown and Parliamentary copyright

[2.215]
163 Crown copyright

(1) Where a work is made by Her Majesty or by an officer or servant of the Crown in the course of his duties—

(a) the work qualifies for copyright protection notwithstanding section 153(1) (ordinary requirement as to qualification for copyright protection), and

(b) Her Majesty is the first owner of any copyright in the work.

[(1A) . . .]

(2) Copyright in such a work is referred to in this Part as "Crown copyright", notwithstanding that it may be, or have been, assigned to another person.

(3) Crown copyright in a literary, dramatic, musical or artistic work continues to subsist—

(a) until the end of the period of 125 years from the end of the calendar year in which the work was made, or

(b) if the work is published commercially before the end of the period of 75 years from the end of the calendar year in which it was made, until the end of the period of 50 years from the end of the calendar year in which it was first so published.

(4) In the case of a work of joint authorship where one or more but not all of the authors are persons falling within subsection (1), this section applies only in relation to those authors and the copyright subsisting by virtue of their contribution to the work.

(5) Except as mentioned above, and subject to any express exclusion elsewhere in this Part, the provisions of this Part apply in relation to Crown copyright as to other copyright.

(6) This section does not apply to work if, or to the extent that, Parliamentary copyright subsists in the work (see sections 165 [to [166D]]).

NOTES

Sub-s (1A): inserted by the Government of Wales Act 1998, s 125, Sch 12, paras 26, 28; repealed by the Government of Wales Act 2006, ss 160(1), 163, Sch 10, paras 22, 26(1), (2), Sch 12.

Sub-s (6): word in first (outer) pair of square brackets substituted by the Scotland Act 1998, s 125(1), Sch 8, para 25(1), (4); reference in second (inner) pair of square brackets substituted by the Government of Wales Act 2006, s 160(1), Sch 10, paras 22, 26(1), (3).

[2.216]
164 Copyright in Acts and Measures

(1) Her Majesty is entitled to copyright in every Act of Parliament [Act of the Scottish Parliament][, [Measure of the National Assembly for Wales, Act of the National Assembly for Wales,] Act of the Northern Ireland Assembly] or Measure of the General Synod of the Church of England.

(2) The copyright subsists[—

(a) in the case of an Act or a Measure of the General Synod of the Church of England, until the end of the period of 50 years from the end of the calendar year in which Royal Assent was given, and

(b) in the case of a Measure of the National Assembly for Wales, until the end of the period of 50 years from the end of the calendar year in which the Measure was approved by Her Majesty in Council.]

(3) References in this Part to Crown copyright (except in section 163) include copyright under this section; and, except as mentioned above, the provisions of this Part apply in relation to copyright under this section as to other Crown copyright.

(4) No other copyright, or right in the nature of copyright, subsists in an Act or Measure.

NOTES

Sub-s (1): words in first pair of square brackets inserted by the Scotland Act 1998, s 125(1), Sch 8, para 25(1), (5); words in second (outer) pair of square brackets inserted by the Northern Ireland Act 1998, s 99, Sch 13, para 8(1), (5); words in third (inner) pair of square brackets inserted by the Government of Wales Act 2006, s 160(1), Sch 10, paras 22, 27(1), (2).

Sub-s (2): words in square brackets substituted by the Government of Wales Act 2006, s 160(1), Sch 10, paras 22, 27(1), (3).

[2.217]
165 Parliamentary copyright

(1) Where a work is made by or under the direction or control of the House of Commons or the House of Lords—

(a) the work qualifies for copyright protection notwithstanding section 153(1) (ordinary requirement as to qualification for copyright protection), and

(b) the House by whom, or under whose direction or control, the work is made is the first owner of any copyright in the work, and if the work is made by or under the direction or control of both Houses, the two Houses are joint first owners of copyright.

(2) Copyright in such a work is referred to in this Part as "Parliamentary copyright", notwithstanding that it may be, or have been, assigned to another person.

(3) Parliamentary copyright in a literary, dramatic, musical or artistic work continues to subsist until the end of the period of 50 years from the end of the calendar year in which the work was made.
(4) For the purposes of this section, works made by or under the direction or control of the House of Commons or the House of Lords include—
   (a) any work made by an officer or employee of that House in the course of his duties, and
   (b) any sound recording, film [or live broadcast] of the proceedings of that House;
but a work shall not be regarded as made by or under the direction or control of either House by reason only of its being commissioned by or on behalf of that House.
(5) In the case of a work of joint authorship where one or more but not all of the authors are acting on behalf of, or under the direction or control of, the House of Commons or the House of Lords, this section applies only in relation to those authors and the copyright subsisting by virtue of their contribution to the work.
(6) Except as mentioned above, and subject to any express exclusion elsewhere in this Part, the provisions of this Part apply in relation to Parliamentary copyright as to other copyright.
(7) The provisions of this section also apply, subject to any exceptions or modifications specified by Order in Council, to works made by or under the direction or control of any other legislative body of a country to which this Part extends; and references in this Part to "Parliamentary copyright" shall be construed accordingly.
(8) A statutory instrument containing an Order in Council under subsection (7) shall be subject to annulment in pursuance of a resolution of either House of Parliament.

NOTES

Sub-s (4): words in square brackets in para (b) substituted by the Copyright and Related Rights Regulations 2003, SI 2003/2498, reg 2(1), Sch 1, Pt 1, paras 1, 11(b), subject to transitional provisions as noted to s 1 of this Act at **[2.7]**.

Modified, in relation to works made by or under the direction or control of the National Assembly for Wales, by the Parliamentary Copyright (National Assembly for Wales) Order 2007, SI 2007/1116, art 2, at **[2.583]**.

Orders: the Parliamentary Copyright (Scottish Parliament) Order 1999, SI 1999/676; the Parliamentary Copyright (Northern Ireland Assembly) Order 1999, SI 1999/3146; the Parliamentary Copyright (National Assembly for Wales) Order 2007, SI 2007/1116 at **[2.582]**.

[2.218]
166 Copyright in Parliamentary Bills
(1) Copyright in every Bill introduced into Parliament belongs, in accordance with the following provisions, to one or both of the Houses of Parliament.
(2) Copyright in a public Bill belongs in the first instance to the House into which the Bill is introduced, and after the Bill has been carried to the second House to both Houses jointly, and subsists from the time when the text of the Bill is handed in to the House in which it is introduced.
(3) Copyright in a private Bill belongs to both Houses jointly and subsists from the time when a copy of the Bill is first deposited in either House.
(4) Copyright in a personal Bill belongs in the first instance to the House of Lords, and after the Bill has been carried to the House of Commons to both Houses jointly, and subsists from the time when it is given a First Reading in the House of Lords.
(5) Copyright under this section ceases—
   (a) on Royal Assent, or
   (b) if the Bill does not receive Royal Assent, on the withdrawal or rejection of the Bill or the end of the Session:

Provided that, copyright in a Bill continues to subsist notwithstanding its rejection in any Session by the House of Lords if, by virtue of the Parliament Acts 1911 and 1949, it remains possible for it to be presented for Royal Assent in that Session.
(6) References in this Part to Parliamentary copyright (except in section 165) include copyright under this section; and, except as mentioned above, the provisions of this Part apply in relation to copyright under this section as to other Parliamentary copyright.
(7) No other copyright, or right in the nature of copyright, subsists in a Bill after copyright has once subsisted under this section; but without prejudice to the subsequent operation of this section in relation to a Bill which, not having passed in one Session, is reintroduced in a subsequent Session.

[2.219]
[166A Copyright in Bills of the Scottish Parliament
(1) Copyright in every Bill introduced into the Scottish Parliament belongs to the Scottish Parliamentary Corporate Body.
(2) Copyright under this section subsists from the time when the text of the Bill is handed in to the Parliament for introduction—
   (a) until the Bill receives Royal Assent, or
   (b) if the Bill does not receive Royal Assent, until it is withdrawn or rejected or no further parliamentary proceedings may be taken in respect of it.
(3) References in this Part to Parliamentary copyright (except in section 165) include copyright under this section; and, except as mentioned above, the provisions of this Part apply in relation to copyright under this section as to other Parliamentary copyright.

(4) No other copyright, or right in the nature of copyright, subsists in a Bill after copyright has once subsisted under this section; but without prejudice to the subsequent operation of this section in relation to a Bill which, not having received Royal Assent, is later reintroduced into the Parliament.]

NOTES

Inserted by the Scotland Act 1998, s 125(1), Sch 8, para 25(1), (6).

[2.220]

[166B Copyright in Bills of the Northern Ireland Assembly

(1) Copyright in every Bill introduced into the Northern Ireland Assembly belongs to the Northern Ireland Assembly Commission.

(2) Copyright under this section subsists from the time when the text of the Bill is handed in to the Assembly for introduction—

(a) until the Bill receives Royal Assent, or

(b) if the Bill does not receive Royal Assent, until it is withdrawn or rejected or no further proceedings of the Assembly may be taken in respect of it.

(3) References in this Part to Parliamentary copyright (except in section 165) include copyright under this section; and, except as mentioned above, the provisions of this Part apply in relation to copyright under this section as to other Parliamentary copyright.

(4) No other copyright, or right in the nature of copyright, subsists in a Bill after copyright has once subsisted under this section; but without prejudice to the subsequent operation of this section in relation to a Bill which, not having received Royal Assent, is later reintroduced into the Assembly.]

NOTES

Inserted by the Northern Ireland Act 1998, s 99, Sch 13, para 8(1), (6).

[2.221]

[166C Copyright in proposed Measures of the National Assembly for Wales

(1) Copyright in every proposed Assembly Measure introduced into the National Assembly for Wales belongs to the National Assembly for Wales Commission.

(2) Copyright under this section subsists from the time when the text of the proposed Assembly Measure is handed in to the Assembly for introduction—

(a) until the proposed Assembly Measure is approved by Her Majesty in Council, or

(b) if the proposed Assembly Measure is not approved by Her Majesty in Council, until it is withdrawn or rejected or no further proceedings of the Assembly may be taken in respect of it.

(3) References in this Part to Parliamentary copyright (except in section 165) include copyright under this section; and, except as mentioned above, the provisions of this Part apply in relation to copyright under this section as to other Parliamentary copyright.

(4) No other copyright, or right in the nature of copyright, subsists in a proposed Assembly Measure after copyright has once subsisted under this section; but without prejudice to the subsequent operation of this section in relation to a proposed Assembly Measure which, not having been approved by Her Majesty in Council, is later reintroduced into the Assembly.]

NOTES

Inserted, together with s 166D, by the Government of Wales Act 2006, s 160(1), Sch 10, paras 22, 28.

[2.222]

[166D Copyright in Bills of the National Assembly for Wales

(1) Copyright in every Bill introduced into the National Assembly for Wales belongs to the National Assembly for Wales Commission.

(2) Copyright under this section subsists from the time when the text of the Bill is handed in to the Assembly for introduction—

(a) until the Bill receives Royal Assent, or

(b) if the Bill does not receive Royal Assent, until it is withdrawn or rejected or no further proceedings of the Assembly may be taken in respect of it.

(3) References in this Part to Parliamentary copyright (except in section 165) include copyright under this section; and, except as mentioned above, the provisions of this Part apply in relation to copyright under this section as to other Parliamentary copyright.

(4) No other copyright, or right in the nature of copyright, subsists in a Bill after copyright has once subsisted under this section; but without prejudice to the subsequent operation of this section in relation to a Bill which, not having received Royal Assent, is later reintroduced into the Assembly.]

NOTES

Inserted as noted to s 166C, at **[2.221]**.

[2.223]

167 Houses of Parliament: supplementary provisions with respect to copyright

(1) For the purposes of holding, dealing with and enforcing copyright, and in connection with all legal proceedings relating to copyright, each House of Parliament shall be treated as having the legal capacities of a body corporate, which shall not be affected by a prorogation or dissolution.

(2) The functions of the House of Commons as owner of copyright shall be exercised by the Speaker on behalf of the House; and if so authorised by the Speaker, or in case of a vacancy in the office of Speaker, those functions may be discharged by the Chairman of Ways and Means or a Deputy Chairman.

(3) For this purpose a person who on the dissolution of Parliament was Speaker of the House of Commons, Chairman of Ways and Means or a Deputy Chairman may continue to act until the corresponding appointment is made in the next Session of Parliament.

(4) The functions of the House of Lords as owner of copyright shall be exercised by the Clerk of the Parliaments on behalf of the House; and if so authorised by him, or in case of a vacancy in the office of Clerk of the Parliaments, those functions may be discharged by the Clerk Assistant or the Reading Clerk.

(5) Legal proceedings relating to copyright—

(a) shall be brought by or against the House of Commons in the name of "The Speaker of the House of Commons"; and

(b) shall be brought by or against the House of Lords in the name of "The Clerk of the Parliaments".

Other miscellaneous provisions

[2.224]

168 Copyright vesting in certain international organisations

(1) Where an original literary, dramatic, musical or artistic work—

(a) is made by an officer or employee of, or is published by, an international organisation to which this section applies, and

(b) does not qualify for copyright protection under section 154 (qualification by reference to author) or section 155 (qualification by reference to country of first publication),

copyright nevertheless subsists in the work by virtue of this section and the organisation is first owner of that copyright.

(2) The international organisations to which this section applies are those as to which Her Majesty has by Order in Council declared that it is expedient that this section should apply.

(3) Copyright of which an international organisation is first owner by virtue of this section continues to subsist until the end of the period of 50 years from the end of the calendar year in which the work was made or such longer period as may be specified by Her Majesty by Order in Council for the purpose of complying with the international obligations of the United Kingdom.

(4) An international organisation to which this section applies shall be deemed to have, and to have had at all material times, the legal capacities of a body corporate for the purpose of holding, dealing with and enforcing copyright and in connection with all legal proceedings relating to copyright.

(5) A statutory instrument containing an Order in Council under this section shall be subject to annulment in pursuance of a resolution of either House of Parliament.

NOTES

Orders: the Copyright (International Organisations) Order 1989, SI 1989/989. In addition, by virtue of s 170 of, and Sch 1, para 4(1), (3) to, this Act, at **[2.226]**, **[2.409]**, the Copyright (International Organisations) Order 1957, SI 1957/1524 has effect as if made under sub-s (2) above.

[2.225]

169 Folklore, &c: anonymous unpublished works

(1) Where in the case of an unpublished literary, dramatic, musical or artistic work of unknown authorship there is evidence that the author (or, in the case of a joint work, any of the authors) was a qualifying individual by connection with a country outside the United Kingdom, it shall be presumed until the contrary is proved that he was such a qualifying individual and that copyright accordingly subsists in the work, subject to the provisions of this Part.

(2) If under the law of that country a body is appointed to protect and enforce copyright in such works, Her Majesty may by Order in Council designate that body for the purposes of this section.

(3) A body so designated shall be recognised in the United Kingdom as having authority to do in place of the copyright owner anything, other than assign copyright, which it is empowered to do under the law of that country; and it may, in particular, bring proceedings in its own name.

(4) A statutory instrument containing an Order in Council under this section shall be subject to annulment in pursuance of a resolution of either House of Parliament.

(5) In subsection (1) a "qualifying individual" means an individual who at the material time (within the meaning of section 154) was a person whose works qualified under that section for copyright protection.

(6) This section does not apply if there has been an assignment of copyright in the work by the author of which notice has been given to the designated body; and nothing in this section affects the validity of an assignment of copyright made, or licence granted, by the author or a person lawfully claiming under him.

Transitional provisions and savings

[2.226]

170 Transitional provisions and savings

[(1)] Schedule 1 contains transitional provisions and savings relating to works made, and acts or events occurring, before the commencement of this Part, and otherwise with respect to the operation of the provisions of this Part.

[(2) The Secretary of State may by regulations amend Schedule 1 to reduce the duration of copyright in existing works which are unpublished, other than photographs or films.

(3) The regulations may provide for the copyright to expire—

(a) with the end of the term of protection of copyright laid down by Directive 2006/116/EC or at any later time;

(b) subject to that, on the commencement of the regulations or at any later time.

(4) "Existing works" has the same meaning as in Schedule 1.

(5) Regulations under subsection (2) may—

(a) make different provision for different purposes;

(b) make supplementary or transitional provision;

(c) make consequential provision, including provision amending any enactment or subordinate legislation passed or made before that subsection comes into force

(6) The power to make regulations under subsection (2) is exercisable by statutory instrument.

(7) A statutory instrument containing regulations under subsection (2) may not be made unless a draft of the instrument has been laid before and approved by resolution of each House of Parliament.]

NOTES

Sub-s (1): numbered as such by the Enterprise and Regulatory Reform Act 2013, s 76(1), (2).

Sub-ss (2)–(7): added by the Enterprise and Regulatory Reform Act 2013, s 76(1), (3).

[2.227]

171 Rights and privileges under other enactments or the common law

(1) Nothing in this Part affects—

(a) any right or privilege of any person under any enactment (except where the enactment is expressly repealed, amended or modified by this Act);

(b) any right or privilege of the Crown subsisting otherwise than under an enactment;

(c) any right or privilege of either House of Parliament;

(d) the right of the Crown or any person deriving title from the Crown to sell, use or otherwise deal with articles forfeited under the laws relating to customs and excise;

(e) the operation of any rule of equity relating to breaches of trust or confidence.

(2) Subject to those savings, no copyright or right in the nature of copyright shall subsist otherwise than by virtue of this Part or some other enactment in that behalf.

(3) Nothing in this Part affects any rule of law preventing or restricting the enforcement of copyright, on grounds of public interest or otherwise.

(4) Nothing in this Part affects any right of action or other remedy, whether civil or criminal, available otherwise than under this Part in respect of acts infringing any of the rights conferred by Chapter IV (moral rights).

(5) The savings in subsection (1) have effect subject to section 164(4) and section 166(7) (copyright in Acts, Measures and Bills: exclusion of other rights in the nature of copyright).

Interpretation

[2.228]

172 General provisions as to construction

(1) This Part restates and amends the law of copyright, that is, the provisions of the Copyright Act 1956, as amended.

(2) A provision of this Part which corresponds to a provision of the previous law shall not be construed as departing from the previous law merely because of a change of expression.

(3) Decisions under the previous law may be referred to for the purpose of establishing whether a provision of this Part departs from the previous law, or otherwise for establishing the true construction of this Part.

[2.229]

[172A [Meaning of EEA and related expressions

[(1) In this Part—

"the EEA" means the European Economic Area; and

"EEA state" means a member State, Iceland, Liechtenstein or Norway.]]

(2) References in this Part to a person being [a national of an EEA State] shall be construed in relation to a body corporate as references to its being incorporated under the law of an EEA state.

(3) . . .]

NOTES

Inserted by the Duration of Copyright and Rights in Performances Regulations 1995, SI 1995/3297, regs 4, 11(1), subject to transitional provisions and savings specified in regs 12–34 of those Regulations, at **[2.478]–[2.499]**.

Section heading, sub-s (1): substituted by the Copyright and Related Rights Regulations 1996, SI 1996/2967, regs 4, 9(5); sub-s (1) further substituted by the Intellectual Property (Enforcement, etc) Regulations 2006, SI 2006/1028, reg 2(2), Sch 2, paras 6, 8(1), (2).

Sub-s (2): words in square brackets substituted by SI 2006/1028, reg 2(2), Sch 2, paras 6, 8(1), (3).

Sub-s (3): repealed by SI 2006/1028, reg 2(4), Sch 4.

[2.230]

173 Construction of references to copyright owner

(1) Where different persons are (whether in consequence of a partial assignment or otherwise) entitled to different aspects of copyright in a work, the copyright owner for any purpose of this Part is the person who is entitled to the aspect of copyright relevant for that purpose.

(2) Where copyright (or any aspect of copyright) is owned by more than one person jointly, references in this Part to the copyright owner are to all the owners, so that, in particular, any requirement of the licence of the copyright owner requires the licence of all of them.

[2.231]

174 Meaning of "educational establishment" and related expressions

(1) The expression "educational establishment" in a provision of this Part means—

(a) any school, and

(b) any other description of educational establishment specified for the purposes of this Part, or that provision, by order of the Secretary of State.

(2) The Secretary of State may by order provide that the provisions of this Part relating to educational establishments shall apply, with such modifications and adaptations as may be specified in the order, in relation to teachers who are employed by a [local authority (as defined in section 579(1) of the Education Act 1996) or (in Northern Ireland) a local education authority,] to give instruction elsewhere to pupils who are unable to attend an educational establishment.

(3) In subsection (1)(a) "school"—

(a) in relation to England and Wales, has the same meaning as in [the Education Act 1996];

(b) in relation to Scotland, has the same meaning as in the Education (Scotland) Act 1962, except that it includes an approved school within the meaning of the Social Work (Scotland) Act 1968; and

(c) in relation to Northern Ireland, has the same meaning as in the Education and Libraries (Northern Ireland) Order 1986.

(4) An order under subsection (1)(b) may specify a description of educational establishment by reference to the instruments from time to time in force under any enactment specified in the order.

(5) In relation to an educational establishment the expressions "teacher" and "pupil" in this Part include, respectively, any person who gives and any person who receives instruction.

(6) References in this Part to anything being done "on behalf of" an educational establishment are to its being done for the purposes of that establishment by any person.

(7) An order under this section shall be made by statutory instrument which shall be subject to annulment in pursuance of a resolution of either House of Parliament.

NOTES

Sub-s (2): words in square brackets substituted by the Local Education Authorities and Children's Services Authorities (Integration of Functions) Order 2010, SI 2010/1158, art 5(1), Sch 2, Pt 2, para 36.

Sub-s (3): words in square brackets substituted by the Education Act 1996, s 582(1), Sch 37, Pt I, para 83.

Orders: the Copyright (Application of Provisions relating to Educational Establishments to Teachers) (No 2) Order 1989, SI 1989/1067; the Copyright (Educational Establishments) Order 2005, SI 2005/223.

[2.232]

175 Meaning of publication and commercial publication

(1) In this Part "publication", in relation to a work—

(a) means the issue of copies to the public, and

(b) includes, in the case of a literary, dramatic, musical or artistic work, making it available to the public by means of an electronic retrieval system;

and related expressions shall be construed accordingly.

(2) In this Part "commercial publication", in relation to a literary, dramatic, musical or artistic work means—

(a) issuing copies of the work to the public at a time when copies made in advance of the receipt of orders are generally available to the public, or

(b) making the work available to the public by means of an electronic retrieval system;

and related expressions shall be construed accordingly.

(3) In the case of a work of architecture in the form of a building, or an artistic work incorporated in a building, construction of the building shall be treated as equivalent to publication of the work.

(4) The following do not constitute publication for the purposes of this Part and references to commercial publication shall be construed accordingly—

(a) in the case of a literary, dramatic or musical work—
 (i) the performance of the work, or
 (ii) the [communication to the public of the work] (otherwise than for the purposes of an electronic retrieval system);

(b) in the case of an artistic work—
 (i) the exhibition of the work,
 (ii) the issue to the public of copies of a graphic work representing, or of photographs of, a work of architecture in the form of a building or a model for a building, a sculpture or a work of artistic craftsmanship,
 (iii) the issue to the public of copies of a film including the work, or
 (iv) the [communication to the public of the work] (otherwise than for the purposes of an electronic retrieval system);

(c) in the case of a sound recording or film—
 (i) the work being played or shown in public, or
 (ii) the [communication to the public of the work].

(5) References in this Part to publication or commercial publication do not include publication which is merely colourable and not intended to satisfy the reasonable requirements of the public.

(6) No account shall be taken for the purposes of this section of any unauthorised act.

NOTES

Sub-s (4): words in square brackets substituted by the Copyright and Related Rights Regulations 2003, SI 2003/2498, reg 2(1), Sch 1, Pt 1, paras 1, 6(1), subject to transitional provisions as noted to s 1 of this Act at **[2.7]**.

[2.233]

176 Requirement of signature: application in relation to body corporate

(1) The requirement in the following provisions that an instrument be signed by or on behalf of a person is also satisfied in the case of a body corporate by the affixing of its seal—

section 78(3)(b) (assertion by licensor of right to identification of author in case of public exhibition of copy made in pursuance of the licence),
section 90(3) (assignment of copyright),
section 91(1) (assignment of future copyright),
section 92(1) (grant of exclusive licence).

(2) The requirement in the following provisions that an instrument be signed by a person is satisfied in the case of a body corporate by signature on behalf of the body or by the affixing of its seal—

section 78(2)(b) (assertion by instrument in writing of right to have author identified),
section 87(2) (waiver of moral rights).

[2.234]

177 Adaptation of expressions for Scotland

In the application of this Part to Scotland—

"account of profits" means accounting and payment of profits;
"accounts" means count, reckoning and payment;
"assignment" means assignation;
"costs" means expenses;
"defendant" means defender;
"delivery up" means delivery;
"estoppel" means personal bar;
"injunction" means interdict;
"interlocutory relief" means interim remedy; and
"plaintiff" means pursuer.

[2.235]

178 Minor definitions

In this Part—

"article", in the context of an article in a periodical, includes an item of any description;
"business" includes a trade or profession;
"collective work" means—
 (a) a work of joint authorship, or
 (b) a work in which there are distinct contributions by different authors or in which works or parts of works of different authors are incorporated;
"computer-generated", in relation to a work, means that the work is generated by computer in circumstances such that there is no human author of the work;
"country" includes any territory;
"the Crown" includes the Crown in right of [the Scottish administration[, of the Welsh Assembly Government] or of] Her Majesty's Government in Northern Ireland or in any country outside the United Kingdom to which this Part extends;

"electronic" means actuated by electric, magnetic, electro-magnetic, electro-chemical or electro-mechanical energy, and "in electronic form" means in a form usable only by electronic means;

"employed", "employee", "employer" and "employment" refer to employment under a contract of service or of apprenticeship;

"facsimile copy" includes a copy which is reduced or enlarged in scale;

"international organisation" means an organisation the members of which include one or more states;

"judicial proceedings" includes proceedings before any court, tribunal or person having authority to decide any matter affecting a person's legal rights or liabilities;

"parliamentary proceedings" includes proceedings of the Northern Ireland Assembly [of the Scottish Parliament][. . .] or of the European Parliament [and Assembly proceedings within the meaning of section 1(5) of the Government of Wales Act 2006];

["private study" does not include any study which is directly or indirectly for a commercial purpose;]

["producer", in relation to a sound recording or a film, means the person by whom the arrangements necessary for the making of the sound recording or film are undertaken;]

["public library" means a library administered by or on behalf of—

(a) in England and Wales, a library authority within the meaning of the Public Libraries and Museums Act 1964;

(b) in Scotland, a statutory library authority within the meaning of the Public Libraries (Scotland) Act 1955;

(c) in Northern Ireland, an Education or Library Board within the meaning of the Education and Libraries (Northern Ireland) Order 1986;]

. . .

["rental right" means the right of a copyright owner to authorise or prohibit the rental of copies of the work (see section 18A);]

"reprographic copy" and "reprographic copying" refer to copying by means of a reprographic process;

"reprographic process" means a process—

(a) for making facsimile copies, or

(b) involving the use of an appliance for making multiple copies,

and includes, in relation to a work held in electronic form, any copying by electronic means, but does not include the making of a film or sound recording;

"sufficient acknowledgement" means an acknowledgement identifying the work in question by its title or other description, and identifying the author unless—

(a) in the case of a published work, it is published anonymously;

(b) in the case of an unpublished work, it is not possible for a person to ascertain the identity of the author by reasonable inquiry;

"sufficient disclaimer", in relation to an act capable of infringing the right conferred by section 80 (right to object to derogatory treatment of work), means a clear and reasonably prominent indication—

(a) given at the time of the act, and

(b) if the author or director is then identified, appearing along with the identification, that the work has been subjected to treatment to which the author or director has not consented;

"telecommunications system" means a system for conveying visual images, sounds or other information by electronic means;

"typeface" includes an ornamental motif used in printing;

"unauthorised", as regards anything done in relation to a work, means done otherwise than—

(a) by or with the licence of the copyright owner, or

(b) if copyright does not subsist in the work, by or with the licence of the author or, in a case where section 11(2) would have applied, the author's employer or, in either case, persons lawfully claiming under him, or

(c) in pursuance of section 48 (copying, &c of certain material by the Crown);

["wireless broadcast" means a broadcast by means of wireless telegraphy;]

"wireless telegraphy" means the sending of electro-magnetic energy over paths not provided by a material substance constructed or arranged for that purpose[, but does not include the transmission of microwave energy between terrestrial fixed points];

"writing" includes any form of notation or code, whether by hand or otherwise and regardless of the method by which, or medium in or on which, it is recorded, and "written" shall be construed accordingly.

NOTES

In definition "the Crown" words in first (outer) pair of square brackets inserted by the Scotland Act 1998, s 125(1), Sch 8, para 25(1), (7)(a); words in second (inner) pair of square brackets inserted by the Government of Wales Act 2006, s 160(1), Sch 10, paras 22, 29(1), (2).

In definition "parliamentary proceedings" words in first pair of square brackets inserted, by the Scotland Act 1998, s 125(1), Sch 8, para 25(1), (7)(b); words omitted from second pair of square brackets originally inserted by the Northern Ireland

(Elections) Act 1998, s 1(6), Schedule, para 9, and repealed by the Northern Ireland Act 1998, s 99, Sch 13, para 8(1), (7); words in third pair of square brackets inserted by the Government of Wales Act 2006, s 160(1), Sch 10, paras 22, 29(1), (3).

Definitions "private study" and "wireless broadcast" inserted by the Copyright and Related Rights Regulations 2003, SI 2003/2498, reg 2(1), Sch 1, Pt 1, paras 1, 15(3), subject to transitional provisions as noted to s 1 of this Act at **[2.7]**.

Definitions "producer", "public library" and "rental right" inserted, definition omitted repealed, and in definition "wireless telegraphy" words in square brackets added, by the Copyright and Related Rights Regulations 1996, SI 1996/2967, regs 4, 8, 10(3), 11(5), 18(5), subject to transitional provisions and savings specified in regs 25–36 of those Regulations, at **[2.510]–[2.521]**.

[2.236]

179 Index of defined expressions

The following Table shows provisions defining or otherwise explaining expressions used in this Part (other than provisions defining or explaining an expression used only in the same section)—

[accessible copy (in sections 31A to 31F)	section 31F(4)]
account of profits and accounts (in Scotland)	section 177
acts restricted by copyright	section 16(1)
adaptation	section 21(3)
[. . .	. . .]
[archivist (in sections 40A to 43)	section 43A(5),]
article (in a periodical)	section 178
artistic work	section 4(1)
assignment (in Scotland)	section 177
author	sections 9 and 10(3)
[authorised body (in sections 31B to 31BB)	section 31F(6)]
broadcast (and related expressions)	section 6
building	section 4(2)
business	section 178
. . .	. . .
collective work	section 178
commencement (in Schedule 1)	paragraph 1(2) of that Schedule
commercial publication	section 175
[communication to the public	section 20]
computer-generated	section 178
[conducted for profit (in sections 40A to 43)	section 43A(4)]
Copy and copying	section 17
copyright (generally)	section 1
copyright (in Schedule 1)	paragraph 2(2) of that Schedule
copyright owner	sections 101(2) and 173
Copyright Tribunal	section 145
copyright work	section 1(2)
costs (in Scotland)	section 177
country	section 178
[country of origin	section 15A]
the Crown	section 178
Crown copyright	sections 163(2) and 164(3)
[curator (in sections 40A to 43)	section 43A(5)]
[database	section 3A(1)]
defendant (in Scotland)	section 177
delivery up (in Scotland)	section 177
[disabled person (in sections 31A to 31F)	section 31F(2) and (3)]
dramatic work	section 3(1)
educational establishment	section 174(1) to (4)
[[the EEA, EEA state and national of an EEA state]	section 172A]
electronic and electronic form	section 178

employed, employee, employer and employment	section 178
[excepted sound recording	section 72(1A)]
exclusive licence	section 92(1)
existing works (in Schedule 1)	paragraph 1(3) of that Schedule
facsimile copy	section 178
film	[section 5B]
future copyright	section 91(2)
general licence (in sections 140 and 141)	section 140(7)
graphic work	section 4(2)
infringing copy	section 27
injunction (in Scotland)	section 177
interlocutory relief (in Scotland)	section 177
international organisation	section 178
Issue of copies to the public	[section 18]
joint authorship (work of)	sections 10(1) and (2)
judicial proceedings	section 178
[lawful user (in sections 50A to 50C)	section 50A(2)]
[lending	section 18A(2) to (6)]
[librarian (in sections 40A to 43)	section 43A(5)]
[library (in sections 40A to 43)	section 43A(2)]
licence (in sections 125 to 128)	section 124
licence of copyright owner	sections 90(4), 91(3) and 173
licensing body (in Chapter VII)	section 116(2)
licensing scheme (generally)	section 116(1)
licensing scheme (in sections 118 to 121)	section 117
literary work	section 3(1)
made (in relation to a literary, dramatic or musical work)	section 3(2)
[museum (in sections 40A to 43)	section 43A(3)]
musical work	section 3(1)
[needletime	section 135A]
the new copyright provisions (in Schedule 1)	paragraph 1(1) of that Schedule
the 1911 Act (in Schedule 1)	paragraph 1(1) of that Schedule
the 1956 Act (in Schedule 1)	paragraph 1(1) of that Schedule
on behalf of (in relation to an educational establishment)	section 174(5)
[original (in relation to a database	section 3A(2)]
Parliamentary copyright	sections 165(2) and (7) [166(6) [166A(3) [166B(3) 166C(3) and 166D(3)]]]
parliamentary proceedings	section 178
performance	section 19(2)
photograph	section 4(2)
plaintiff (in Scotland)	section 177
. . .	. . .
. . .	. . .
[private study	section 178]
[producer (in relation to a sound recording or film)	section 178]
programme (in the context of broadcasting)	section 6(3)
prospective owner (of copyright)	section 91(2)
[public library	section 178]
publication and related expressions	section 175

Part 2 Copyright

published edition (in the context of copyright in the typographical arrangement)	section 8
Pupil	section 174(5)
rental	[section 18A(2) to (6)]
[rental right	section 178]
reprographic copies and reprographic copying	section 178
reprographic process	section 178
sculpture	section 4(2)
signed	section 176
sound recording	[sections 5A and 135A]
sufficient acknowledgement	section 178
sufficient disclaimer	section 178
[supply (in sections 31B to 31BB)	section 31F(7)]
teacher	section 174(5)
telecommunications system	section 178
[terms of payment	section 135A]
typeface	section 178
unauthorised (as regards things done in relation to a work)	section 178
unknown (in relation to the author of a work)	section 9(5)
unknown authorship (work of)	section 9(4)
[. . .	. . .]
[wireless broadcast	section 178]
wireless telegraphy	section 178
work (in Schedule 1)	paragraph 2(1) of that Schedule
work of more than one author (in Chapter VII)	section 116(4)
writing and written	section 178

NOTES

Entry "accessible copy" inserted by the Copyright (Visually Impaired Persons) Act 2002, s 7(2) and substituted by the Copyright and Rights in Performances (Disability) Regulations 2014, SI 2014/1384, reg 4, Schedule, para 3(a).

Entries "approved body" and "visually impaired person" (omitted) inserted by the Copyright (Visually Impaired Persons) Act 2002, s 7(2) and repealed by SI 2014/1384, reg 4, Schedule, para 3(c).

Entries "archivist" and "librarian" substituted, entries "conducted for profit", "curator", "library" and "museum" inserted and entries "prescribed conditions" and "prescribed library or archive" (omitted) repealed by the Copyright and Rights in Performances (Research, Education, Libraries and Archives) Regulations 2014, SI 2014/1372, reg 2(2), Schedule, paras 1, 6.

Entries "authorised body", "disabled person" and "supply" inserted by SI 2014/1384, reg 4, Schedule, para 3(b).

Entry "country of origin" inserted, and words in square brackets in entries "film" and "sound recording" substituted, by the Duration of Copyright and Rights in Performances Regulations 1995, SI 1995/3297, regs 4, 8(2), 9(5), subject to transitional provisions and savings specified in regs 12–34 of those Regulations, at **[2.478]**–**[2.499]**.

Entry "database" and entry "original (in relation to a database)" inserted by the Copyright and Rights in Databases Regulations 1997, SI 1997/3032, reg 11, subject to savings and transitional provisions specified in regs 26–30 of those Regulations, at **[2.541]**–**[2.545]**.

Entry beginning "EEA," inserted by SI 1995/3297, regs 4, 11(2), subject to transitional provisions and savings specified in regs 12–34 of those Regulations, at **[2.478]**–**[2.499]**, and word in square brackets therein substituted by the Intellectual Property (Enforcement, etc) Regulations 2006, SI 2006/1028, reg 2(2), Sch 2, paras 6, 9.

Entries "communication to the public", "excepted sound recording", "private study" and "wireless broadcast" inserted, and entry "cable programme, cable programme service (and related expressions)" (omitted) repealed, by the Copyright and Related Rights Regulations 2003, SI 2003/2498, regs 2, 3, 21(7), Sch 2, subject to transitional provisions as noted to s 1 of this Act at **[2.7]**.

Words in square brackets in entries "issue of copies to the public" and "rental" substituted, and entries "lending", "producer", "public library" and "rental right" inserted, by SI 1996/2967, regs 4, 9(6)(b), 10(4), 11(6), 18(6), subject to transitional provisions and savings specified in regs 25–36 of those Regulations, at **[2.510]**–**[2.521]**.

Entry "lawful user" inserted by the Copyright (Computer Programs) Regulations 1992, SI 1992/3233, regs 2, 9, 12(2), although not so as to affect agreements entered into before 1 January 1993.

Entries "needletime" and "terms of payment" inserted by the Broadcasting Act 1990, s 175(3).

In entry "Parliamentary copyright" reference in first (outer) pair of square brackets substituted by the Scotland Act 1998, s 125(1), Sch 8, para 25(1), (8), words in second (inner) pair of square brackets substituted by the Northern Ireland Act 1998, s 99, Sch 13, para 8(1), (8); words in third (inner) pair of square brackets substituted by the Government of Wales Act 2006, s 160(1), Sch 10, paras 22, 30.

PART II
RIGHTS IN PERFORMANCES

[CHAPTER 1
INTRODUCTORY]

. . .

[2.237]

180 Rights conferred on performers and persons having recording rights

(1) [Chapter 2 of this Part (economic rights)] confers rights—

(a) on a performer, by requiring his consent to the exploitation of his performances (see sections 181 to 184), and

(b) on a person having recording rights in relation to a performance, in relation to recordings made without his consent or that of the performer (see sections 185 to 188),

and creates offences in relation to dealing with or using illicit recordings and certain other related acts (see sections 198 and 201).

[(1A) Rights are also conferred on a performer by the following provisions of Chapter 3 of this Part (moral rights)—

(a) section 205C (right to be identified);

(b) section 205F (right to object to derogatory treatment of performance).]

(2) In this Part—

"performance" means—

(a) a dramatic performance (which includes dance and mime),

(b) a musical performance,

(c) a reading or recitation of a literary work, or

(d) a performance of a variety act or any similar presentation,

which is, or so far as it is, a live performance given by one or more individuals; and

"recording", in relation to a performance, means a film or sound recording—

(a) made directly from the live performance,

(b) made from a broadcast of . . . the performance, or

(c) made, directly or indirectly, from another recording of the performance.

(3) The rights conferred by this Part apply in relation to performances taking place before the commencement of this Part; but no act done before commencement, or in pursuance of arrangements made before commencement, shall be regarded as infringing those rights.

(4) The rights conferred by this Part are independent of—

(a) any copyright in, or moral rights relating to, any work performed or any film or sound recording of, or broadcast . . . including, the performance, and

(b) any other right or obligation arising otherwise than under this Part.

NOTES

Chapter heading: inserted by the Performances (Moral Rights, etc) Regulations 2006, SI 2006/18, regs 3, 4(2).

Cross-heading: repealed by SI 2006/18, regs 3, 4(1).

Sub-s (1): words in square brackets substituted by SI 2006/18, regs 3, 5(1).

Sub-s (1A): inserted by SI 2006/18, regs 3, 5(2).

Sub-ss (2), (4): words omitted repealed by the Copyright and Related Rights Regulations 2003, SI 2003/2498, reg 2(2), Sch 2, subject to transitional provisions as noted to s 1 of this Act at **[2.7]**.

. . .

[2.238]

181 Qualifying performances

A performance is a qualifying performance for the purposes of the provisions of this Part relating to performers' rights if it is given by a qualifying individual (as defined in section 206) or takes place in a qualifying country (as so defined).

NOTES

Cross-heading: repealed by the Performances (Moral Rights, etc) Regulations 2006, SI 2006/18, SI 2006/18, regs 3, 4(3).

[CHAPTER 2
ECONOMIC RIGHTS

Performers' rights]

[2.239]

[182 Consent required for recording, &c of live performance

(1) A performer's rights are infringed by a person who, without his consent—

(a) makes a recording of the whole or any substantial part of a qualifying performance directly from the live performance,

(b) broadcasts live . . . the whole or any substantial part of a qualifying performance,

(c) makes a recording of the whole or any substantial part of a qualifying performance directly from a broadcast of . . . the live performance.

(2) . . .

(3) In an action for infringement of a performer's rights brought by virtue of this section damages shall not be awarded against a defendant who shows that at the time of the infringement he believed on reasonable grounds that consent had been given.]

NOTES

Chapter heading and cross-heading: inserted by the Performances (Moral Rights, etc) Regulations 2006, SI 2006/18, regs 3, 4(4), (5).

Substituted by the Copyright and Related Rights Regulations 1996, SI 1996/2967, regs 4, 20(1), subject to transitional provisions and savings specified in regs 25–36 of those Regulations, at **[2.510]–[2.521]**.

Sub-s (1): words omitted from paras (b), (c) repealed by the Copyright and Related Rights Regulations 2003, SI 2003/2498, reg 2(2), Sch 2, subject to transitional provisions as noted to s 1 of this Act at **[2.7]**.

Sub-s (2): repealed by SI 2003/2498, reg 2(2), Sch 2, subject to transitional provisions as noted to s 1 of this Act at **[2.7]**.

[2.240]

[182A Consent required for copying of recording

(1) A performer's rights are infringed by a person who, without his consent, makes . . . a copy of a recording of the whole or any substantial part of a qualifying performance.

[(1A) In subsection (1), making a copy of a recording includes making a copy which is transient or is incidental to some other use of the original recording.]

(2) It is immaterial whether the copy is made directly or indirectly

(3) The right of a performer under this section to authorise or prohibit the making of such copies is referred to in [this Chapter] as "reproduction right".]

NOTES

Inserted, together with ss 182B–182D, by the Copyright and Related Rights Regulations 1996, SI 1996/2967, regs 4, 20(2), subject to transitional provisions and savings specified in regs 25–36 of those Regulations, at **[2.510]–[2.521]**.

Sub-s (1): words omitted repealed by the Copyright and Related Rights Regulations 2003, SI 2003/2498, reg 2(2), Sch 2, subject to transitional provisions as noted to s 1 of this Act at **[2.7]**.

Sub-s (1A): inserted by SI 2003/2498, regs 3, 8(3), subject to transitional provisions as noted to s 1 of this Act at **[2.7]**.

Sub-s (3): words in square brackets substituted by the Performances (Moral Rights, etc) Regulations 2006, SI 2006/18, reg 2, Schedule, paras 1, 8.

[2.241]

[182B Consent required for issue of copies to the public

(1) A performer's rights are infringed by a person who, without his consent, issues to the public copies of a recording of the whole or any substantial part of a qualifying performance.

(2) References in this Part to the issue to the public of copies of a recording are to—

(a) the act of putting into circulation in the EEA copies not previously put into circulation in the EEA by or with the consent of the performer, or

(b) the act of putting into circulation outside the EEA copies not previously put into circulation in the EEA or elsewhere.

(3) References in this Part to the issue to the public of copies of a recording do not include—

(a) any subsequent distribution, sale, hiring or loan of copies previously put into circulation (but see section 182C: consent required for rental or lending), or

(b) any subsequent importation of such copies into the United Kingdom or another EEA state,

except so far as paragraph (a) of subsection (2) applies to putting into circulation in the EEA copies previously put into circulation outside the EEA.

(4) References in this Part to the issue of copies of a recording of a performance include the issue of the original recording of the live performance.

(5) The right of a performer under this section to authorise or prohibit the issue of copies to the public is referred to in [this Chapter] as "distribution right".]

NOTES

Inserted as noted to s 182A, at **[2.240]**.

Sub-s (5): words in square brackets substituted by the Performances (Moral Rights, etc) Regulations 2006, SI 2006/18, reg 2, Schedule, paras 1, 8.

[2.242]

[182C Consent required for rental or lending of copies to public

(1) A performer's rights are infringed by a person who, without his consent, rents or lends to the public copies of a recording of the whole or any substantial part of a qualifying performance.

(2) In [this Chapter], subject to the following provisions of this section—

(a) "rental" means making a copy of a recording available for use, on terms that it will or may be returned, for direct or indirect economic or commercial advantage, and

(b) "lending" means making a copy of a recording available for use, on terms that it will or may be returned, otherwise than for direct or indirect economic or commercial advantage, through an establishment which is accessible to the public.

(3) The expressions "rental" and "lending" do not include—

(a) making available for the purpose of public performance, playing or showing in public [or communication to the public];

(b) making available for the purpose of exhibition in public; or

(c) making available for on-the-spot reference use.

(4) The expression "lending" does not include making available between establishments which are accessible to the public.

(5) Where lending by an establishment accessible to the public gives rise to a payment the amount of which does not go beyond what is necessary to cover the operating costs of the establishment, there is no direct or indirect economic or commercial advantage for the purposes of this section.

(6) References in [this Chapter] to the rental or lending of copies of a recording of a performance include the rental or lending of the original recording of the live performance.

(7) In [this Chapter]—

"rental right" means the right of a performer under this section to authorise or prohibit the rental of copies to the public, and

"lending right" means the right of a performer under this section to authorise or prohibit the lending of copies to the public.

NOTES

Inserted as noted to s 182A, at **[2.240]**.

Sub-ss (2), (6), (7): words in square brackets substituted by the Performances (Moral Rights, etc) Regulations 2006, SI 2006/18, reg 2, Schedule, paras 1, 8.

Sub-s (3): words in square brackets in para (a) substituted by the Copyright and Related Rights Regulations 2003, SI 2003/2498, reg 2(1), Sch 1, Pt 1, paras 1, 6(2)(c), subject to transitional provisions as noted to s 1 of this Act at **[2.7]**.

[2.243]

[182CA Consent required for making available to the public

[(1) A performer's rights are infringed by a person who, without his consent, makes available to the public a recording of the whole or any substantial part of a qualifying performance by electronic transmission in such a way that members of the public may access the recording from a place and at a time individually chosen by them.

(2) The right of a performer under this section to authorise or prohibit the making available to the public of a recording is referred to in [this Chapter] as "making available right".]

NOTES

Inserted by the Copyright and Related Rights Regulations 2003, SI 2003/2498, regs 3, 7(1), subject to transitional provisions as noted to s 1 of this Act at **[2.7]**.

Sub-s (2): words in square brackets substituted by the Performances (Moral Rights, etc) Regulations 2006, SI 2006/18, reg 2, Schedule, paras 1, 8.

[2.244]

[182D Right to equitable remuneration for exploitation of sound recording

(1) Where a commercially published sound recording of the whole or any substantial part of a qualifying performance—

(a) is played in public, or

[(b) is communicated to the public otherwise than by its being made available to the public in the way mentioned in section 182CA(1),]

the performer is entitled to equitable remuneration from the owner of the copyright in the sound recording [or, where copyright in the sound recording has expired pursuant to section 191HA(4), from a person who plays the sound recording in public or communicates the sound recording to the public].

[(1A) In subsection (1), the reference to publication of a sound recording includes making it available to the public by electronic transmission in such a way that members of the public may access it from a place and at a time individually chosen by them.]

(2) The right to equitable remuneration under this section may not be assigned by the performer except to a collecting society for the purpose of enabling it to enforce the right on his behalf.

The right is, however, transmissible by testamentary disposition or by operation of law as personal or moveable property; and it may be assigned or further transmitted by any person into whose hands it passes.

(3) The amount payable by way of equitable remuneration is as agreed by or on behalf of the persons by and to whom it is payable, subject to the following provisions.

(4) In default of agreement as to the amount payable by way of equitable remuneration, the person by or to whom it is payable may apply to the Copyright Tribunal to determine the amount payable.

(5) A person to or by whom equitable remuneration is payable may also apply to the Copyright Tribunal—

(a) to vary any agreement as to the amount payable, or

(b) to vary any previous determination of the Tribunal as to that matter;

but except with the special leave of the Tribunal no such application may be made within twelve months from the date of a previous determination.

An order made on an application under this subsection has effect from the date on which it is made or such later date as may be specified by the Tribunal.

Part 2 Copyright

(6) On an application under this section the Tribunal shall consider the matter and make such order as to the method of calculating and paying equitable remuneration as it may determine to be reasonable in the circumstances, taking into account the importance of the contribution of the performer to the sound recording.

(7) An agreement is of no effect in so far as it purports—

(a) to exclude or restrict the right to equitable remuneration under this section, or

(b) to prevent a person questioning the amount of equitable remuneration or to restrict the powers of the Copyright Tribunal under this section.]

[(8) In this section "collecting society" means a society or other organisation which has as its main object, or one of its main objects, the exercise of the right to equitable remuneration on behalf of more than one performer.]

NOTES

Inserted as noted to s 182A at **[2.240]**.

Sub-s (1): para (b) substituted by the Copyright and Related Rights Regulations 2003, SI 2003/2498, regs 3, 7(2), subject to transitional provisions as noted to s 1 of this Act at **[2.7]**; final words in square brackets added by the Copyright and Duration of Rights in Performance Regulations 2013, SI 2013/1782, regs 3, 7, subject to savings and transitional provisions in regs 11–26 of those Regulations at **[2.665]–[2.680]**.

Sub-s (1A): inserted by the Performances (Moral Rights, etc) Regulations 2006, SI 2006/18, reg 2, Schedule, paras 1, 3(1), (2).

Sub-s (8): added by SI 2006/18, reg 2, Schedule, paras 1, 3(1), (3).

[2.245]

183 Infringement of performer's rights by use of recording made without consent

A performer's rights are infringed by a person who, without his consent—

(a) shows or plays in public the whole or any substantial part of a qualifying performance, or

(b) [communicates to the public] the whole or any substantial part of a qualifying performance,

by means of a recording which was, and which that person knows or has reason to believe was, made without the performer's consent.

NOTES

Words in square brackets in para (b) substituted by the Copyright and Related Rights Regulations 2003, SI 2003/2498, reg 2(1), Sch 1, Pt 1, paras 1, 13(1)(a), subject to transitional provisions as noted to s 1 of this Act at **[2.7]**.

[2.246]

184 Infringement of performer's rights by importing, possessing or dealing with illicit recording

(1) A performer's rights are infringed by a person who, without his consent—

(a) imports into the United Kingdom otherwise than for his private and domestic use, or

(b) in the course of a business possesses, sells or lets for hire, offers or exposes for sale or hire, or distributes,

a recording of a qualifying performance which is, and which that person knows or has reason to believe is, an illicit recording.

(2) Where in an action for infringement of a performer's rights brought by virtue of this section a defendant shows that the illicit recording was innocently acquired by him or a predecessor in title of his, the only remedy available against him in respect of the infringement is damages not exceeding a reasonable payment in respect of the act complained of.

(3) In subsection (2) "innocently acquired" means that the person acquiring the recording did not know and had no reason to believe that it was an illicit recording.

Rights of person having recording rights

[2.247]

185 Exclusive recording contracts and persons having recording rights

(1) In [this Chapter] an "exclusive recording contract" means a contract between a performer and another person under which that person is entitled to the exclusion of all other persons (including the performer) to make recordings of one or more of his performances with a view to their commercial exploitation.

(2) References in [this Chapter] to a "person having recording rights", in relation to a performance, are (subject to subsection (3)) to a person—

(a) who is party to and has the benefit of an exclusive recording contract to which the performance is subject, or

(b) to whom the benefit of such a contract has been assigned,

and who is a qualifying person.

(3) If a performance is subject to an exclusive recording contract but the person mentioned in subsection (2) is not a qualifying person, references in [this Chapter] to a "person having recording rights" in relation to the performance are to any person—

(a) who is licensed by such a person to make recordings of the performance with a view to their commercial exploitation, or

(b) to whom the benefit of such a licence has been assigned,

and who is a qualifying person.

(4) In this section "with a view to commercial exploitation" means with a view to the recordings being sold or let for hire, or shown or played in public.

NOTES

Sub-ss (1)–(3): words in square brackets substituted by the Performances (Moral Rights, etc) Regulations 2006, SI 2006/18, reg 2, Schedule, paras 1, 8.

[2.248]

186 Consent required for recording of performance subject to exclusive contract

(1) A person infringes the rights of a person having recording rights in relation to a performance who, without his consent or that of the performer, makes a recording of the whole or any substantial part of the performance . . .

(2) In an action for infringement of those rights brought by virtue of this section damages shall not be awarded against a defendant who shows that at the time of the infringement he believed on reasonable grounds that consent had been given.

NOTES

Sub-s (1): words omitted repealed by the Copyright and Related Rights Regulations 2003, SI 2003/2498, reg 2(2), Sch 2, subject to transitional provisions as noted to s 1 of this Act at **[2.7]**.

[2.249]

187 Infringement of recording rights by use of recording made without consent

(1) A person infringes the rights of a person having recording rights in relation to a performance who, without his consent or, in the case of a qualifying performance, that of the performer—

(a) shows or plays in public the whole or any substantial part of the performance, or

(b) [communicates to the public] the whole or any substantial part of the performance,

by means of a recording which was, and which that person knows or has reason to believe was, made without the appropriate consent.

(2) The reference in subsection (1) to "the appropriate consent" is to the consent of—

(a) the performer, or

(b) the person who at the time the consent was given had recording rights in relation to the performance (or, if there was more than one such person, of all of them).

NOTES

Sub-s (1): words in square brackets in para (b) substituted by the Copyright and Related Rights Regulations 2003, SI 2003/2498, reg 2(1), Sch 1, Pt 1, paras 1, 13(1)(b), subject to transitional provisions as noted to s 1 of this Act at **[2.7]**.

[2.250]

188 Infringement of recording rights by importing, possessing or dealing with illicit recording

(1) A person infringes the rights of a person having recording rights in relation to a performance who, without his consent or, in the case of a qualifying performance, that of the performer—

(a) imports into the United Kingdom otherwise than for his private and domestic use, or

(b) in the course of a business possesses, sells or lets for hire, offers or exposes for sale or hire, or distributes,

a recording of the performance which is, and which that person knows or has reason to believe is, an illicit recording.

(2) Where in an action for infringement of those rights brought by virtue of this section a defendant shows that the illicit recording was innocently acquired by him or a predecessor in title of his, the only remedy available against him in respect of the infringement is damages not exceeding a reasonable payment in respect of the act complained of.

(3) In subsection (2) "innocently acquired" means that the person acquiring the recording did not know and had no reason to believe that it was an illicit recording.

Exceptions to rights conferred

[2.251]

189 Acts permitted notwithstanding rights conferred by [this Chapter]

The provisions of Schedule 2 specify acts which may be done notwithstanding the rights conferred by [this Chapter], being acts which correspond broadly to certain of those specified in Chapter III of Part I (acts permitted notwithstanding copyright).

NOTES

Words in square brackets substituted by the Performances (Moral Rights, etc) Regulations 2006, SI 2006/18, reg 2, Schedule, paras 1, 8.

[2.252]

190 Power of tribunal to give consent on behalf of performer in certain cases

[(1) The Copyright Tribunal may, on the application of a person wishing to make a copy of a recording of a performance, give consent in a case where the identity or whereabouts of the person entitled to the reproduction right cannot be ascertained by reasonable inquiry.]

(2) Consent given by the Tribunal has effect as consent of [the person entitled to the reproduction right] for the purposes of—

(a) the provisions of [this Chapter] relating to performers' rights, and

(b) section 198(3)(a) (criminal liability: sufficient consent in relation to qualifying performances),

and may be given subject to any conditions specified in the Tribunal's order.

(3) The Tribunal shall not give consent under subsection (1)(a) except after the service or publication of such notices as may be required by rules made under section 150 (general procedural rules) or as the Tribunal may in any particular case direct.

(4) . . .

(5) In any case the Tribunal shall take into account the following factors—

(a) whether the original recording was made with the performer's consent and is lawfully in the possession or control of the person proposing to make the further recording;

(b) whether the making of the further recording is consistent with the obligations of the parties to the arrangements under which, or is otherwise consistent with the purposes for which, the original recording was made.

(6) Where the Tribunal gives consent under this section it shall, in default of agreement between the applicant and [the person entitled to the reproduction right], make such order as it thinks fit as to the payment to be made to [that person] in consideration of consent being given.

NOTES

Sub-s (1): substituted by the Copyright and Related Rights Regulations 1996, SI 1996/2967, regs 4, 23(2), subject to transitional provisions and savings specified in regs 25–36 of those Regulations, at **[2.510]–[2.521]**.

Sub-s (2): words in first pair of square brackets substituted by SI 1996/2967, regs 4, 23(3), (5), subject to transitional provisions and savings specified in regs 25–36 of those Regulations, at **[2.510]–[2.521]**; in para (a) words in square brackets substituted by the Performances (Moral Rights, etc) Regulations 2006, SI 2006/18, reg 2, Schedule, paras 1, 8.

Sub-s (4): repealed by SI 1996/2967, regs 4, 23(4), subject to transitional provisions and savings specified in regs 25–36 of those Regulations, at **[2.510]–[2.521]**.

Sub-s (6): words in square brackets substituted by SI 1996/2967, regs 4, 23(3), (5), subject to transitional provisions and savings specified in regs 25–36 of those Regulations, at **[2.510]–[2.521]**.

[Duration of rights]

[2.253]

[191 Duration of rights

(1) The following provisions have effect with respect to the duration of the rights conferred by [this Chapter].

(2) The rights conferred by [this Chapter] in relation to a performance expire—

(a) at the end of the period of 50 years from the end of the calendar year in which the performance takes place, or

(b) if during that period a recording of the performance[, other than a sound recording,] is released, 50 years from the end of the calendar year in which it is released, [or

(c) if during that period a sound recording of the performance is released, 70 years from the end of the calendar year in which it is released,]

subject as follows.

(3) For the purposes of subsection (2) a recording is "released" when it is first published, played or shown in public [or communicated to the public]; but in determining whether a recording has been released no account shall be taken of any unauthorised act.

(4) Where a performer is not a national of an EEA state, the duration of the rights conferred by [this Chapter] in relation to his performance is that to which the performance is entitled in the country of which he is a national, provided that does not exceed the period which would apply under subsections (2) and (3).

(5) If or to the extent that the application of subsection (4) would be at variance with an international obligation to which the United Kingdom became subject prior to 29th October 1993, the duration of the rights conferred by [this Chapter] shall be as specified in subsections (2) and (3).]

NOTES

Cross-heading preceding this section substituted by the Copyright and Related Rights Regulations 1996, SI 1996/2967, regs 4, 21(5)(a), subject to transitional provisions and savings specified in regs 25–36 of those Regulations, at **[2.510]–[2.521]**.

Substituted by the Duration of Copyright and Rights in Performances Regulations 1995, SI 1995/3297, regs 4, 10, subject to transitional provisions and savings specified in regs 12–34 of those Regulations, at **[2.478]–[2.499]**.

Sub-ss (1), (4), (5): words in square brackets substituted by the Performances (Moral Rights, etc) Regulations 2006, SI 2006/18, reg 2, Schedule, paras 1, 8.

Sub-s (2): words in first pair of square brackets substituted by the Performances (Moral Rights, etc) Regulations 2006, SI 2006/18, reg 2, Schedule, paras 1, 8; words in second and third pairs of square brackets inserted by the Copyright and Duration of Rights in Performance Regulations 2013, SI 2013/1782, regs 3, 8, subject to savings and transitional provisions in regs 11–26 of those Regulations at **[2.665]–[2.680]**.

Sub-s (3): words in square brackets substituted by the Copyright and Related Rights Regulations 2003, SI 2003/2498, reg 2(1), Sch 1, Pt 1, paras 1, 8(1)(d), subject to transitional provisions as noted to s 1 of this Act at **[2.7]**.

[Performers' property rights

[2.254]

191A Performers' property rights

(1) The following rights conferred by [this Chapter] on a performer—
reproduction right (section 182A),
distribution right (section 182B),
rental right and lending right (section 182C),
[making available right (section 182CA),]
are property rights (" . . . performer's property rights").

(2) References in [this Chapter] to the consent of the performer shall be construed in relation to a performer's property rights as references to the consent of the rights owner.

(3) Where different persons are (whether in consequence of a partial assignment or otherwise) entitled to different aspects of a performer's property rights in relation to a performance, the rights owner for any purpose of [this Chapter] is the person who is entitled to the aspect of those rights relevant for that purpose.

(4) Where a performer's property rights (or any aspect of them) is owned by more than one person jointly, references in [this Chapter] to the rights owner are to all the owners, so that, in particular, any requirement of the licence of the rights owner requires the licence of all of them.]

NOTES

Inserted, together with preceding cross-heading and ss 191B–191M, by the Copyright and Related Rights Regulations 1996, SI 1996/2967, regs 4, 21(1), subject to transitional provisions and savings specified in regs 25–36 of those Regulations, at **[2.510]**–**[2.521]**.

Sub-s (1): words in first pair of square brackets substituted and word omitted repealed by the Performances (Moral Rights, etc) Regulations 2006, SI 2006/18, reg 2, Schedule, paras 1, 4, 8; words in second pair of square brackets inserted by the Copyright and Related Rights Regulations 2003, SI 2003/2498, regs 3, 7(3), subject to transitional provisions as noted to s 1 of this Act at **[2.7]**.

Sub-ss (2)–(4): words in square brackets substituted by SI 2006/18, reg 2, Schedule, paras 1, 8.

[2.255]

[191B Assignment and licences

(1) A performer's property rights are transmissible by assignment, by testamentary disposition or by operation of law, as personal or moveable property

(2) An assignment or other transmission of a performer's property rights may be partial, that is, limited so as to apply—

(a) to one or more, but not all, of the things requiring the consent of the rights owner;
(b) to part, but not the whole, of the period for which the rights are to subsist.

(3) An assignment of a performer's property rights is not effective unless it is in writing signed by or on behalf of the assignor.

(4) A licence granted by the owner of a performer's property rights is binding on every successor in title to his interest in the rights, except a purchaser in good faith for valuable consideration and without notice (actual or constructive) of the licence or a person deriving title from such a purchaser; and references in [this Chapter] to doing anything with, or without, the licence of the rights owner shall be construed accordingly.]

NOTES

Inserted as noted to s 191A at **[2.254]**.

Sub-s (4): words in square brackets substituted by the Performances (Moral Rights, etc) Regulations 2006, SI 2006/18, reg 2, Schedule, paras 1, 8.

[2.256]

[191C Prospective ownership of a performer's property rights

(1) This section applies where by an agreement made in relation to a future recording of a performance, and signed by or on behalf of the performer, the performer purports to assign his performer's property rights (wholly or partially) to another person.

(2) If on the rights coming into existence the assignee or another person claiming under him would be entitled as against all other persons to require the rights to be vested in him, they shall vest in the assignee or his successor in title by virtue of this subsection.

(3) A licence granted by a prospective owner of a performer's property rights is binding on every successor in title to his interest (or prospective interest) in the rights, except a purchaser in good faith for valuable consideration and without notice (actual or constructive) of the licence or a person deriving title from such a purchaser.

References in [this Chapter] to doing anything with, or without, the licence of the rights owner shall be construed accordingly.

(4) In subsection (3) "prospective owner" in relation to a performer's property rights means a person who is prospectively entitled to those rights by virtue of such an agreement as is mentioned in subsection (1).]

NOTES

Inserted as noted to s 191A at **[2.254]**.

Sub-s (3): words in square brackets substituted by the Performances (Moral Rights, etc) Regulations 2006, SI 2006/18, reg 2, Schedule, paras 1, 8.

[2.257]
[191D Exclusive licences
(1) In [this Chapter] an "exclusive licence" means a licence in writing signed by or on behalf of the owner of a performer's property rights authorising the licensee to the exclusion of all other persons, including the person granting the licence, to do anything requiring the consent of the rights owner.
(2) The licensee under an exclusive licence has the same rights against a successor in title who is bound by the licence as he has against the person granting the licence.]

NOTES
Inserted as noted to s 191A at **[2.254]**.
Sub-s (1): words in square brackets substituted by the Performances (Moral Rights, etc) Regulations 2006, SI 2006/18, reg 2, Schedule, paras 1, 8.

[2.258]
[191E Performer's property right to pass under will with unpublished original recording
Where under a bequest (whether general or specific) a person is entitled beneficially or otherwise to any material thing containing an original recording of a performance which was not published before the death of the testator, the bequest shall, unless a contrary intention is indicated in the testator's will or a codicil to it, be construed as including any performer's rights in relation to the recording to which the testator was entitled immediately before his death.]

NOTES
Inserted as noted to s 191A at **[2.254]**.

[2.259]
[191F Presumption of transfer of rental right in case of film production agreement
(1) Where an agreement concerning film production is concluded between a performer and a film producer, the performer shall be presumed, unless the agreement provides to the contrary, to have transferred to the film producer any rental right in relation to the film arising from the inclusion of a recording of his performance in the film.
(2) Where the section applies, the absence of signature by or on behalf of the performer does not exclude the operation of section 191C (effect of purported assignment of future rights).
(3) The reference in subsection (1) to an agreement concluded between a performer and a film producer includes any agreement having effect between those persons, whether made by them directly or through intermediaries.
(4) Section 191G (right to equitable remuneration on transfer of rental right) applies where there is a presumed transfer by virtue of this section as in the case of an actual transfer.]

NOTES
Inserted as noted to s 191A at **[2.254]**.

[2.260]
[191G Right to equitable remuneration where rental right transferred
(1) Where a performer has transferred his rental right concerning a sound recording or a film to the producer of the sound recording or film, he retains the right to equitable remuneration for the rental.

The reference above to the transfer of rental right by one person to another includes any arrangement having that effect, whether made by them directly or through intermediaries.
(2) The right to equitable remuneration under this section may not be assigned by the performer except to a collecting society for the purpose of enabling it to enforce the right on his behalf.

The right is, however, transmissible by testamentary disposition or by operation of law as personal or moveable property; and it may be assigned or further transmitted by any person into whose hands it passes.
(3) Equitable remuneration under this section is payable by the person for the time being entitled to the rental right, that is, the person to whom the right was transferred or any successor in title of his.
(4) The amount payable by way of equitable remuneration is as agreed by or on behalf of the persons by and to whom it is payable, subject to section 191H (reference of amount to Copyright Tribunal).
(5) An agreement is of no effect in so far as it purports to exclude or restrict the right to equitable remuneration under this section.
(6) In this section a "collecting society" means a society or other organisation which has as its main object, or one of its main objects, the exercise of the right to equitable remuneration on behalf of more than one performer.]

NOTES

Inserted as noted to s 191A at **[2.254]**.

[2.261]

[191H Equitable remuneration: reference of amount to Copyright Tribunal

(1) In default of agreement as to the amount payable by way of equitable remuneration under section 191G, the person by or to whom it is payable may apply to the Copyright Tribunal to determine the amount payable.

(2) A person to or by whom equitable remuneration is payable may also apply to the Copyright Tribunal—

(a) to vary any agreement as to the amount payable, or

(b) to vary any previous determination of the Tribunal as to that matter;

but except with the special leave of the Tribunal no such application may be made within twelve months from the date of a previous determination.

An order made on an application under this subsection has effect from the date on which it is made or such later date as may be specified by the Tribunal.

(3) On an application under this section the Tribunal shall consider the matter and make such order as to the method of calculating and paying equitable remuneration as it may determine to be reasonable in the circumstances, taking into account the importance of the contribution of the performer to the film or sound recording.

(4) Remuneration shall not be considered inequitable merely because it was paid by way of a single payment or at the time of the transfer of the rental right.

(5) An agreement is of no effect in so far as it purports to prevent a person questioning the amount of equitable remuneration or to restrict the powers of the Copyright Tribunal under this section.]

NOTES

Inserted as noted to s 191A at **[2.254]**.

[2.262]

[191HA Assignment of performer's property rights in a sound recording

(1) This section applies where a performer has [by an agreement] assigned the following rights concerning a sound recording to the producer of the sound recording—

(a) reproduction, distribution and making available rights, or

(b) performer's property rights.

(2) If, at the end of the 50-year period, the producer has failed to meet one or both of the following conditions, the performer may give a notice in writing to the producer of the performer's intention to terminate the agreement—

(a) condition 1 is to issue to the public copies of the sound recording in sufficient quantities;

(b) condition 2 is to make the sound recording available to the public by electronic transmission in such a way that a member of the public may access the recording from a place and at a time chosen by him or her.

(3) If, at any time after the end of the 50-year period, the producer, having met one or both of the conditions referred to in subsection (2), fails to do so, the performer may give a notice in writing to the producer of the performer's intention to terminate the agreement.

(4) If at the end of the period of 12 months beginning with the date of the notice, the producer has not met the conditions referred to in subsection (2), the agreement terminates and the copyright in the sound recording expires with immediate effect.

(5) An agreement is of no effect in so far as it purports to exclude or restrict the right to give a notice under subsection (2) or (3).

(6) A reference in this section to the assignment of rights includes any arrangement having that effect, whether made directly between the parties or through intermediaries.

(7) In this section—

"50-year period" means

(a) where the sound recording is published during the initial period, the period of 50 years from the end of the calendar year in which the sound recording is first published, or

(b) where during the initial period the sound recording is not published but is made available to the public by being played in public or communicated to the public, the period of 50 years from the end of the calendar year in which it was first made available to the public,

but in determining whether a sound recording has been published, played in public or communicated to the public, no account shall be taken of any unauthorised act,

"initial period" means the period beginning on the date the recording is made and ending 50 years from the end of the calendar year in which the sound recording is made,

"producer" means the person for the time being entitled to the copyright in the sound recording,

"sufficient quantities" means such quantity as to satisfy the reasonable requirements of the public for copies of the sound recording,

"unauthorised act" has the same meaning as in section 178.]

Part 2 Copyright

NOTES

Commencement: 1 November 2013.

Inserted, together with s 191HB, by the Copyright and Duration of Rights in Performances Regulations 2013, SI 2013/1782, regs 3, 9, subject to savings and transitional provisions in regs 11–26 of those Regulations at **[2.665]–[2.680]**.

Sub-s (1): words in square brackets inserted by the Copyright and Duration of Rights in Performances (Amendment) Regulations 2014, SI 2014/434, reg 2.

[2.263]

[191HB Payment in consideration of assignment

(1) A performer who, under an agreement relating to the assignment of rights referred to in section 191HA(1) (an "assignment agreement"), is entitled to a non-recurring payment in consideration of the assignment, is entitled to an annual payment for each relevant period from—

(a) the producer, or

(b) where the producer has granted an exclusive licence of the copyright in the sound recording, the licensee under the exclusive licence (the "exclusive licensee").

(2) In this section, "relevant period" means—

(a) the period of 12 months beginning at the end of the 50-year period, and

(b) each subsequent period of 12 months beginning with the end of the previous period, until the date on which copyright in the sound recording expires.

(3) The producer or, where relevant, the exclusive licensee gives effect to the entitlement under subsection (1) by remitting to a collecting society for distribution to the performer in accordance with its rules an amount for each relevant period equal to 20% of the gross revenue received during that period in respect of—

(a) the reproduction and issue to the public of copies of the sound recording, and

(b) the making available to the public of the sound recording by electronic transmission in such a way that members of the public may access it from a place and at a time individually chosen by them.

(4) The amount required to be remitted under subsection (3) is payable within 6 months of the end of each relevant period and is recoverable by the collecting society as a debt.

(5) Subsection (6) applies where—

(a) the performer makes a written request to the producer or, where relevant, the exclusive licensee for information in that person's possession or under that person's control to enable the performer—

(i) to ascertain the amount of the annual payment to which the performer is entitled under subsection (1), or

(ii) to secure its distribution by the collecting society, and

(b) the producer or, where relevant, the exclusive licensee does not supply the information within the period of 90 days beginning with the date of the request.

(6) The performer may apply to the county court, or in Scotland to the sheriff, for an order requiring the producer or, where relevant, the exclusive licensee to supply the information.

(7) An agreement is of no effect in so far as it purports to exclude or restrict the entitlement under subsection (1).

(8) In the event of any dispute as to the amount required to be remitted under subsection (3), the performer may apply to the Copyright Tribunal to determine the amount payable.

(9) Where a performer is entitled under an assignment agreement to recurring payments in consideration of the assignment, the payments must, from the end of the 50-year period, be made in full, regardless of any provision in the agreement which entitles the producer to withhold or deduct sums from the amounts payable.

(10) In this section—

"producer" and "50-year period" each has the same meaning as in section 191HA,

"exclusive licence" has the same meaning as in section 92, and

"collecting society" has the same meaning as in section 191G.]

NOTES

Commencement: 1 November 2013.

Inserted as noted to s 191HA at **[2.262]**.

[2.264]

[191I Infringement actionable by rights owner

(1) An infringement of a performer's property rights is actionable by the rights owner.

(2) In an action for infringement of a performer's property rights all such relief by way of damages, injunctions, accounts or otherwise is available to the plaintiff as is available in respect of the infringement of any other property right.

(3) This section has effect subject to the following provisions of [this Chapter].]

NOTES

Inserted as noted to s 191A at **[2.254]**.

Sub-s (3): words in square brackets substituted by the Performances (Moral Rights, etc) Regulations 2006, SI 2006/18, reg 2, Schedule, paras 1, 8.

[2.265]
[191J Provisions as to damages in infringement action

(1) Where in an action for infringement of a performer's property rights it is shown that at the time of the infringement the defendant did not know and had no reason to believe, that the rights subsisted in the recording to which the action relates, the plaintiff is not entitled to damages against him, but without prejudice to any other remedy.
(2) The court may in an action for infringement of a performer's property rights having regard to all the circumstances, and in particular to—
(a) the flagrancy of the infringement, and
(b) any benefit accruing to the defendant by reason of the infringement,
award such additional damages as the justice of the case may require.]

NOTES
Inserted as noted to s 191A at **[2.254]**.

[2.266]
[191JA Injunctions against service providers

(1) The High Court (in Scotland, the Court of Session) shall have power to grant an injunction against a service provider, where that service provider has actual knowledge of another person using their service to infringe a performer's property right.
(2) In determining whether a service provider has actual knowledge for the purpose of this section, a court shall take into account all matters which appear to it in the particular circumstances to be relevant and, amongst other things, shall have regard to—
(a) whether a service provider has received a notice through a means of contact made available in accordance with regulation 6(1)(c) of the Electronic Commerce (EC Directive) Regulations 2002 (SI 2002/2013); and
(b) the extent to which any notice includes—
(i) the full name and address of the sender of the notice;
(ii) details of the infringement in question.
(3) In this section "service provider" has the meaning given to it by regulation 2 of the Electronic Commerce (EC Directive) Regulations 2002.
(4) Section 177 applies in respect of this section as it applies in respect of Part 1.]

NOTES
Inserted by the Copyright and Related Rights Regulations 2003, SI 2003/2498, regs 3, 27(2), subject to transitional provisions as noted to s 1 of this Act at **[2.7]**.

[2.267]
[191K Undertaking to take licence of right in infringement proceedings

(1) If in proceedings for infringement of a performer's property rights in respect of which a licence is available as of right under paragraph 17 of Schedule 2A (powers exercisable in consequence of competition report) the defendant undertakes to take a licence on such terms as may be agreed or, in default of agreement, settled by the Copyright Tribunal under that paragraph—
(a) no injunction shall be granted against him,
(b) no order for delivery up shall be made under section 195, and
(c) the amount recoverable against him by way of damages or on an account of profits shall not exceed double the amount which would have been payable by him as licensee if such a licence on those terms had been granted before the earliest infringement.
(2) An undertaking may be given at any time before final order in the proceedings, without any admission of liability.
(3) Nothing in this section affects the remedies available in respect of an infringement committed before licences of right were available.]

NOTES
Inserted as noted to s 191A at **[2.254]**.

[2.268]
[191L Rights and remedies for exclusive licensee

(1) An exclusive licensee has, except against the owner of a performer's property rights, the same rights and remedies in respect of matters occurring after the grant of the licence as if the licence had been an assignment.
(2) His rights and remedies are concurrent with those of the rights owner; and references in the relevant provisions of [this Chapter] to the rights owner shall be construed accordingly.
(3) In an action brought by an exclusive licensee by virtue of this section a defendant may avail himself of any defence which would have been available to him if the action had been brought by the rights owner.]

NOTES

Inserted as noted to s 191A at **[2.254]**.

Sub-s (2): words in square brackets substituted by the Performances (Moral Rights, etc) Regulations 2006, SI 2006/18, reg 2, Schedule, paras 1, 8.

[2.269]

[191M Exercise of concurrent rights

(1) Where an action for infringement of a performer's property rights brought by the rights owner or an exclusive licensee relates (wholly or partly) to an infringement in respect of which they have concurrent rights of action, the rights owner or, as the case may be, the exclusive licensee may not, without the leave of the court, proceed with the action unless the other is either joined as plaintiff or added as a defendant.

(2) A rights owner or exclusive licensee who is added as a defendant in pursuance of subsection (1) is not liable for any costs in the action unless he takes part in the proceedings.

(3) The above provisions do not affect the granting of interlocutory relief on an application by the rights owner or exclusive licensee alone.

(4) Where an action for infringement of a performer's property rights is brought which relates (wholly or partly) to an infringement in respect of which the rights owner and an exclusive licensee have or had concurrent rights of action—

(a) the court shall in assessing damages take into account—

(i) the terms of the licence, and

(ii) any pecuniary remedy already awarded or available to either of them in respect of the infringement;

(b) no account of profits shall be directed if an award of damages has been made, or an account of profits has been directed, in favour of the other of them in respect of the infringement; and

(c) the court shall if an account of profits is directed apportion the profits between them as the court considers just, subject to any agreement between them;

and these provisions apply whether or not the rights owner and the exclusive licensee are both parties to the action.

(5) The owner of a performer's property rights shall notify any exclusive licensee having concurrent rights before applying for an order under section 195 (order for delivery up) or exercising the right conferred by section 196 (right of seizure); and the court may on the application of the licensee make such order under section 195 or, as the case may be, prohibiting or permitting the exercise by the rights owner of the right conferred by section 196, as it thinks fit having regard to the terms of the licence.]

NOTES

Inserted as noted to s 191A at **[2.254]**.

[Non-property rights

[2.270]

192A Performers' non-property rights

(1) The rights conferred on a performer by—

section 182 (consent required for recording, &c of live performance),

section 183 (infringement of performer's rights by use of recording made without consent),

section 184 (infringement of performer's rights importing, possessing or dealing with illicit recording),

[section 191HA (assignment of performer's property rights in a sound recording), and

section 191HB (payment in consideration of assignment),]

are not assignable or transmissible, except to the following extent.

They are referred to in [this Chapter] as " . . . performer's non-property rights".

(2) On the death of a person entitled to any such right—

(a) the right passes to such person as he may by testamentary disposition specifically direct, and

(b) if or to the extent that there is no such direction, the right is exercisable by his personal representatives.

(3) References in [this Chapter] to the performer, in the context of the person having any such right, shall be construed as references to the person for the time being entitled to exercise those rights.

(4) Where by virtue of subsection (2)(a) a right becomes exercisable by more than one person, it is exercisable by each of them independently of the other or others.

(5) Any damages recovered by personal representatives by virtue of this section in respect of an infringement after a person's death shall devolve as part of his estate as if the right of action had subsisted and been vested in him immediately before his death.]

NOTES

Substituted, together with preceding heading and s 192B, for original s 192, by the Copyright and Related Rights Regulations 1996, SI 1996/2967, regs 4, 21(2), subject to transitional provisions and savings specified in regs 25–36 of those Regulations, at **[2.510]–[2.521]**.

Sub-s (1): first word omitted repealed and words in first pair of square brackets inserted, by the Copyright and Duration of Rights in Performances Regulations 2013, SI 2013/1782, regs 3, 10, subject to savings and transitional provisions in regs 11–26 of those Regulations at **[2.665]–[2.680]**; words in second pair of square brackets substituted and second word omitted repealed by the Performances (Moral Rights, etc) Regulations 2006, SI 2006/18, reg 2, Schedule, paras 1, 5, 8.

Sub-s (3): words in square brackets substituted by SI 2006/18, reg 2, Schedule, paras 1, 8.

[2.271]

[192B Transmissibility of rights of person having recording rights

(1) The rights conferred by [this Chapter] on a person having recording rights are not assignable or transmissible.

(2) This does not affect section 185(2)(b) or (3)(b), so far as those provisions confer rights under [this Chapter] on a person to whom the benefit of a contract or licence is assigned.]

NOTES

Substituted as noted to s 192A at **[2.270]**.

Sub-ss (1), (2): words in square brackets substituted by the Performances (Moral Rights, etc) Regulations 2006, SI 2006/18, reg 2, Schedule, paras 1, 8.

[2.272]

193 Consent

(1) Consent for the purposes of [this Chapter] [by a person having a performer's non-property rights, or by a person having recording rights,] may be given in relation to a specific performance, a specified description of performances or performances generally, and may relate to past or future performances.

(2) A person having recording rights in a performance is bound by any consent given by a person through whom he derives his rights under the exclusive recording contract or licence in question, in the same way as if the consent had been given by him.

(3) Where [a performer's non-property right] passes to another person, any consent binding on the person previously entitled binds the person to whom the right passes in the same way as if the consent had been given by him.

NOTES

Sub-s (1): words in first pair of square brackets substituted by the Performances (Moral Rights, etc) Regulations 2006, SI 2006/18, reg 2, Schedule, paras 1, 8; words in second pair of square brackets inserted by the Copyright and Related Rights Regulations 1996, SI 1996/2967, regs 4, 21(3)(a), subject to transitional provisions and savings specified in regs 25–36 of those Regulations, at **[2.510]–[2.521]**.

Sub-s (3): words in square brackets substituted by SI 1996/2967, regs 4, 21(3)(b), subject to transitional provisions and savings specified in regs 25–36 of those Regulations, at **[2.510]–[2.521]**.

. . .

[2.273]

194 Infringement actionable as breach of statutory duty

An infringement of[—

(a) a performer's non-property rights, or

(b) any right conferred by [this Chapter] on a person having recording rights,]

is actionable by the person entitled to the right as a breach of statutory duty.

NOTES

Cross-heading preceding this section repealed by the Copyright and Related Rights Regulations 1996, SI 1996/2967, regs 4, 21(5)(b), subject to transitional provisions and savings specified in regs 25–36 of those Regulations, at **[2.510]–[2.521]**.

Words in first (outer) pair of square brackets substituted by SI 1996/2967, regs 4, 21(4), subject to transitional provisions and savings specified in regs 25–36 of those Regulations, at **[2.510]–[2.521]**; words in second (inner) pair of square brackets substituted by the Performances (Moral Rights, etc) Regulations 2006, SI 2006/18, reg 2, Schedule, paras 1, 8.

[Delivery up or seizure of illicit recordings]

[2.274]

195 Order for delivery up

(1) Where a person has in his possession, custody or control in the course of a business an illicit recording of a performance, a person having performer's rights or recording rights in relation to the performance under [this Chapter] may apply to the court for an order that the recording be delivered up to him or to such other person as the court may direct.

(2) An application shall not be made after the end of the period specified in section 203; and no order shall be made unless the court also makes, or it appears to the court that there are grounds for making, an order under section 204 (order as to disposal of illicit recording).

(3) A person to whom a recording is delivered up in pursuance of an order under this section shall, if an order under section 204 is not made, retain it pending the making of an order, or the decision not to make an order, under that section.

(4) Nothing in this section affects any other power of the court.

NOTES

Cross-heading preceding this section inserted by the Copyright and Related Rights Regulations 1996, SI 1996/2967, regs 4, 21(5)(c), subject to transitional provisions and savings specified in regs 25–36 of those Regulations, at **[2.510]**–**[2.521]**.

Sub-s (1): words in square brackets substituted by the Performances (Moral Rights, etc) Regulations 2006, SI 2006/18, reg 2, Schedule, paras 1, 8.

[2.275]

196 Right to seize illicit recordings

(1) An illicit recording of a performance which is found exposed or otherwise immediately available for sale or hire, and in respect of which a person would be entitled to apply for an order under section 195, may be seized and detained by him or a person authorised by him.

The right to seize and detain is exercisable subject to the following conditions and is subject to any decision of the court under section 204 (order as to disposal of illicit recording).

(2) Before anything is seized under this section notice of the time and place of the proposed seizure must be given to a local police station.

(3) A person may for the purpose of exercising the right conferred by this section enter premises to which the public have access but may not seize anything in the possession, custody or control of a person at a permanent or regular place of business of his and may not use any force.

(4) At the time when anything is seized under this section there shall be left at the place where it was seized a notice in the prescribed form containing the prescribed particulars as to the person by whom or on whose authority the seizure is made and the grounds on which it is made.

(5) In this section—

"premises" includes land, buildings, fixed or moveable structures, vehicles, vessels, aircraft and hovercraft; and

"prescribed" means prescribed by order of the Secretary of State.

(6) An order of the Secretary of State under this section shall be made by statutory instrument which shall be subject to annulment in pursuance of a resolution of either House of Parliament.

NOTES

Orders: the Copyright and Rights in Performances (Notice of Seizure) Order 1989, SI 1989/1006, at **[2.447]**.

[2.276]

197 Meaning of "illicit recording"

(1) In [this Chapter] "illicit recording", in relation to a performance, shall be construed in accordance with this section.

(2) For the purposes of a performer's rights, a recording of the whole or any substantial part of a performance of his is an illicit recording if it is made, otherwise than for private purposes, without his consent.

(3) For the purposes of the rights of a person having recording rights, a recording of the whole or any substantial part of a performance subject to the exclusive recording contract is an illicit recording if it is made, otherwise than for private purposes, without his consent or that of the performer.

(4) For the purposes of sections 198 and 199 (offences and orders for delivery up in criminal proceedings), a recording is an illicit recording if it is an illicit recording for the purposes mentioned in subsection (2) or subsection (3).

(5) In [this Chapter] "illicit recording" includes a recording falling to be treated as an illicit recording by virtue of any of the following provisions of Schedule 2—

[paragraph 1B(5) and (7) (personal copies of recordings for private use),]

[paragraph 1D(3) (copies for text and data analysis for non-commercial research),]

[paragraph 3A(5) or (6) or 3B(10) (accessible copies of recordings made for disabled persons)], . . .

[paragraph 6(5) (recording by educational establishments of broadcasts),]

[paragraph 6ZA(7) (copying and use of extracts of recordings by educational establishments),]

[paragraph 6F(5)(b) (copying by librarians: single copies of published recordings),]

[paragraph 6G(5)(b) (copying by librarians or archivists: single copies of unpublished recordings),]

paragraph 12(2) (recordings of performance in electronic form retained on transfer of principal recording), . . .

[paragraph 14(6)(b) (recordings of folksongs),]

paragraph 16(3) (recordings made for purposes of broadcast . . .),

[paragraph 17A(2) (recording for the purposes of time-shifting), or

paragraph 17B(2) (photographs of broadcasts),]

but otherwise does not include a recording made in accordance with any of the provisions of that Schedule.

(6) It is immaterial for the purposes of this section where the recording was made.

NOTES

Sub-s (1): words in square brackets substituted by the Performances (Moral Rights, etc) Regulations 2006, SI 2006/18, reg 2, Schedule, paras 1, 8.

Sub-s (5) is amended as follows:

words "this Chapter" in square brackets substituted by SI 2006/18, reg 2, Schedule, paras 1, 8;

entry relating to "paragraph 1B(5) and (7)" inserted by the Copyright and Rights in Performances (Personal Copies for Private Use) Regulations 2014, SI 2014/2361, regs 2, 4(2), subject to transitional provisions and additional notes, as noted to s 28B at **[2.42]**;

entries relating to "paragraph 1D(3)", "paragraph 6ZA(7)", "paragraph 6F(5)(b)", "paragraph 6G(5)(b)", "paragraph 14(6)(b)" inserted, entry relating to "paragraph 4(3)" (omitted) repealed and entry relating to "paragraph 6(5)" substituted by the Copyright and Rights in Performances (Research, Education, Libraries and Archives) Regulations 2014, SI 2014/1372, reg 2(2), Schedule, paras 1, 7;

in entries relating to "paragraph 12(2)" and "paragraph 16(3)" words omitted repealed entries relating to "paragraph 17A(2)" and "paragraph 17B(2)" inserted by the Copyright and Related Rights Regulations 2003, SI 2003/2498, regs 2, 3, 20(4), Sch 2, subject to transitional provisions as noted to s 1 of this Act at **[2.7]**;

entry relating to "paragraph 3A(5) or (6) or 3B(10)" inserted by the Copyright and Rights in Performances (Disability) Regulations 2014, SI 2014/1384, reg 4, Schedule, para 4.

[2.277]

[197A Presumptions relevant to recordings of performances

(1) In proceedings brought by virtue of this Part with respect to the rights in a performance, where copies of a recording of the performance as issued to the public bear a statement that a named person was the performer, the statement shall be admissible as evidence of the fact stated and shall be presumed to be correct until the contrary is proved.

(2) Subsection (1) does not apply to proceedings for an offence under section 198 (criminal liability for making etc illicit recordings); but without prejudice to its application in proceedings for an order under section 199 (order for delivery up in criminal proceedings).]

NOTES

Inserted by the Intellectual Property (Enforcement, etc) Regulations 2006, SI 2006/1028, reg 2(2), Sch 2, paras 6, 10.

Offences

[2.278]

198 Criminal liability for making, dealing with or using illicit recordings

(1) A person commits an offence who without sufficient consent—

(a) makes for sale or hire, or

(b) imports into the United Kingdom otherwise than for his private and domestic use, or

(c) possesses in the course of a business with a view to committing any act infringing the rights conferred by [this Chapter], or

(d) in the course of a business—

(i) sells or lets for hire, or

(ii) offers or exposes for sale or hire, or

(iii) distributes,

a recording which is, and which he knows or has reason to believe is, an illicit recording.

[(1A) A person who infringes a performer's making available right—

(a) in the course of a business, or

(b) otherwise than in the course of a business to such an extent as to affect prejudicially the owner of the making available right,

commits an offence if he knows or has reason to believe that, by doing so, he is infringing the making available right in the recording.]

(2) A person commits an offence who causes a recording of a performance made without sufficient consent to be—

(a) shown or played in public, or

[(b) communicated to the public,]

thereby infringing any of the rights conferred by [this Chapter], if he knows or has reason to believe that those rights are thereby infringed.

(3) In subsections (1) and (2) "sufficient consent" means—

(a) in the case of a qualifying performance, the consent of the performer, and

(b) in the case of a non-qualifying performance subject to an exclusive recording contract—

(i) for the purposes of subsection (1)(a) (making of recording), the consent of the performer or the person having recording rights, and

(ii) for the purposes of subsection (1)(b), (c) and (d) and subsection (2) (dealing with or using recording), the consent of the person having recording rights.

The references in this subsection to the person having recording rights are to the person having those rights at the time the consent is given or, if there is more than one such person, to all of them.

(4) No offence is committed under subsection (1) or (2) by the commission of an act which by virtue of any provision of Schedule 2 may be done without infringing the rights conferred by [this Chapter].

(5) A person guilty of an offence under subsection (1)(a), (b) or (d)(iii) is liable—

(a) on summary conviction to imprisonment for a term not exceeding six months or *a fine not exceeding [£50,000]*, or both;
(b) on conviction on indictment to a fine or imprisonment for a term not exceeding [ten] years, or both.

[(5A) A person guilty of an offence under subsection (1A) is liable—
(a) on summary conviction to imprisonment for a term not exceeding three months or *a fine not exceeding [£50,000]*, or both;
(b) on conviction on indictment to a fine or imprisonment for a term not exceeding *two* years, or both.]

(6) A person guilty of any other offence under this section is liable on summary conviction to a fine not exceeding level 5 on the standard scale or imprisonment for a term not exceeding six months, or both.

NOTES

Sub-ss (1), (4): words in square brackets substituted by the Performances (Moral Rights, etc) Regulations 2006, SI 2006/18, reg 2, Schedule, paras 1, 8.

Sub-s (1A): inserted by the Copyright and Related Rights Regulations 2003, SI 2003/2498, regs 3, 26(3)(a), subject to transitional provisions as noted to s 1 of this Act at **[2.7]**; substituted by new sub-ss (1A), (1B), by the Digital Economy Act 2017, s 32(1), (4), (6), as from a day to be appointed and except in relation to offences committed before this amendment comes into force, as follows—

"(1A) A person ("P") who infringes a performer's making available right in a recording commits an offence if P—
(a) knows or has reason to believe that P is infringing the right, and
(b) either—
(i) intends to make a gain for P or another person, or
(ii) knows or has reason to believe that infringing the right will cause loss to the owner of the right, or expose the owner of the right to a risk of loss.
(1B) For the purposes of subsection (1A)—
(a) "gain" and "loss"—
(i) extend only to gain or loss in money, and
(ii) include any such gain or loss whether temporary or permanent, and
(b) "loss" includes a loss by not getting what one might get.".

Sub-s (2): para (b) substituted by SI 2003/2498, reg 2(1), Sch 1, Pt 1, paras 1, 4(5), subject to transitional provisions as noted to s 1 of this Act at **[2.7]**; words in second pair of square brackets substituted by SI 2006/18, reg 2, Schedule, paras 1, 8.

Sub-s (5): for the words in italics in para (a) there are substituted the words "a fine" in relation to England and Wales only, by the Legal Aid, Sentencing and Punishment of Offenders Act 2012 (Fines on Summary Conviction) Regulations 2015, SI 2015/664, reg 4(1), Sch 4, Pt 1, para 17(1), (3)(a), subject to transitional provisions and savings in reg 5 thereof; sum in square brackets in para (a) substituted by the Digital Economy Act 2010, s 42(1), (3); word in square brackets in para (b) substituted by the Copyright, etc and Trade Marks (Offences and Enforcement) Act 2002, s 1(1), (3), except in relation to offences committed before 20 November 2002.

Sub-s (5A): inserted by SI 2003/2498, regs 3, 26(3)(b), subject to transitional provisions as noted to s 1 of this Act at **[2.7]**; for the words in italics in para (a) there are substituted the words "a fine" in relation to England and Wales only, by SI 2015/664, reg 4(1), Sch 4, Pt 1, para 17(1), (3)(b), subject to transitional provisions and savings in reg 5 thereof; sum in square brackets in para (a) substituted by the Digital Economy Act 2010, s 42(1), (3); for the word in italics in para (b) there is substituted the word "ten" by the Digital Economy Act 2017, s 32(1), (5), (6), as from a day to be appointed and except in relation to offences committed before this amendment comes into force.

[2.279]
[198A Enforcement by local weights and measures authority

(1) It is the duty of every local weights and measures authority to enforce within their area the provisions of section 198.

(2) . . .

(3) Subsection (1) above does not apply in relation to the enforcement of section 198 in Northern Ireland, but it is the duty of the Department of Economic Development to enforce that section in Northern Ireland.

. . .

[(3A) For the investigatory powers available to a local weights and measures authority or the Department of Enterprise, Trade and Investment in Northern Ireland for the purposes of the duties in this section, see Schedule 5 to the Consumer Rights Act 2015.]

(4) Any enactment which authorises the disclosure of information for the purpose of facilitating the enforcement of the Trade Descriptions Act 1968 shall apply as if section 198 were contained in that Act and as if the functions of any person in relation to the enforcement of that section were functions under that Act.

(5) Nothing in this section shall be construed as authorising a local weights and measures authority to bring proceedings in Scotland for an offence.]

NOTES

Inserted by the Criminal Justice and Public Order Act 1994, s 165(1), (3).

Sub-s (2): repealed by the Consumer Rights Act 2015, s 77(2), Sch 6, paras 48, 50(1), (2).

Sub-s (3): words omitted repealed by the Consumer Rights Act 2015, s 77(2), Sch 6, paras 48, 50(1), (3).

Sub-s (3A): inserted by the Consumer Rights Act 2015, s 77(2), Sch 6, paras 48, 50(1), (4).

[2.280]
199 Order for delivery up in criminal proceedings

(1) The court before which proceedings are brought against a person for an offence under section 198 may, if satisfied that at the time of his arrest or charge he had in his possession, custody or control in the course of a business an illicit recording of a performance, order that it be delivered up to a person having performers' rights or recording rights in relation to the performance or to such other person as the court may direct.

(2) For this purpose a person shall be treated as charged with an offence—

(a) in England, Wales and Northern Ireland, when he is orally charged or is served with a summons or indictment;

(b) in Scotland, when he is cautioned, charged or served with a complaint or indictment.

(3) An order may be made by the court of its own motion or on the application of the prosecutor (or, in Scotland, the Lord Advocate or procurator-fiscal), and may be made whether or not the person is convicted of the offence, but shall not be made—

(a) after the end of the period specified in section 203 (period after which remedy of delivery up not available), or

(b) if it appears to the court unlikely that any order will be made under section 204 (order as to disposal of illicit recording).

(4) An appeal lies from an order made under this section by a magistrates' court—

(a) in England and Wales, to the Crown Court, and

(b) in Northern Ireland, to the county court;

and in Scotland, where an order has been made under this section, the person from whose possession, custody or control the illicit recording has been removed may, without prejudice to any other form of appeal under any rule of law, appeal against that order in the same manner as against sentence.

(5) A person to whom an illicit recording is delivered up in pursuance of an order under this section shall retain it pending the making of an order, or the decision not to make an order, under section 204.

(6) Nothing in this section affects the powers of the court under [section 143 of the Powers of Criminal Courts (Sentencing) Act 2000], [Part II of the Proceeds of Crime (Scotland) Act 1995] or [Article 11 of the Criminal Justice (Northern Ireland) Order 1994] (general provisions as to forfeiture in criminal proceedings).

NOTES

Sub-s (6): words in first pair of square brackets substituted by the Powers of Criminal Courts (Sentencing) Act 2000, s 165(1), Sch 9, para 116; words in second pair of square brackets substituted by the Criminal Procedure (Consequential Provisions) (Scotland) Act 1995, s 5, Sch 4, para 70(3), subject to transitional provisions and savings; words in final pair of square brackets substituted by the Criminal Justice (Northern Ireland) Order 1994, SI 1994/2795, art 26(1), Sch 2, para 14.

Lord Advocate: see the note to s 108, at **[2.144]**.

[2.281]
200 Search warrants

(1) Where a justice of the peace (in Scotland, a sheriff or justice of the peace) is satisfied by information on oath given by a constable (in Scotland, by evidence on oath) that there are reasonable grounds for believing—

(a) that an offence under [section 198(1) or (1A)] (offences of making, importing[, possessing, selling etc] or distributing illicit recordings) has been or is about to be committed in any premises, and

(b) that evidence that such an offence has been or is about to be committed is in those premises,

he may issue a warrant authorising a constable to enter and search the premises, using such reasonable force as is necessary.

(2) The power conferred by subsection (1) does not, in England and Wales, extend to authorising a search for material of the kinds mentioned in section 9(2) of the Police and Criminal Evidence Act 1984 (certain classes of personal or confidential material).

(3) A warrant under subsection (1)—

(a) may authorise persons to accompany any constable executing the warrant, and

(b) remains in force for [three months] from the date of its issue.

[(3A) In executing a warrant issued under subsection (1) a constable may seize an article if he reasonably believes that it is evidence that any offence under [section 198(1) or (1A)] has been or is about to be committed.]

(4) In this section "premises" includes land, buildings, fixed or moveable structures, vehicles, vessels, aircraft and hovercraft.

NOTES

Sub-s (1): words in first pair of square brackets substituted by the Copyright and Related Rights Regulations 2003, SI 2003/2498, regs 3, 26(4)(a), subject to transitional provisions as noted to s 1 of this Act at **[2.7]**; words in second pair of square brackets inserted by the Copyright, etc and Trade Marks (Offences and Enforcement) Act 2002, s 2(1), (3)(a).

Sub-s (3): words in square brackets substituted for the words "28 days" by the Serious Organised Crime and Police Act 2005, s 174(1), Sch 16, para 6(1), (3), in relation to England and Wales.

Sub-s (3A): inserted by the Copyright, etc and Trade Marks (Offences and Enforcement) Act 2002, s 2(1), (3)(b); words in square brackets substituted by SI 2003/2498, regs 3, 26(4)(b), subject to transitional provisions as noted to s 1 of this Act at [2.7].

[2.282]

201 False representation of authority to give consent

(1) It is an offence for a person to represent falsely that he is authorised by any person to give consent for the purposes of [this Chapter] in relation to a performance, unless he believes on reasonable grounds that he is so authorised.

(2) A person guilty of an offence under this section is liable on summary conviction to imprisonment for a term not exceeding six months or a fine not exceeding level 5 on the standard scale or both.

NOTES

Sub-s (1): words in square brackets substituted by the Performances (Moral Rights, etc) Regulations 2006, SI 2006/18, reg 2, Schedule, paras 1, 8.

[2.283]

202 Offence by body corporate: liability of officers

(1) Where an offence under [this Chapter] committed by a body corporate is proved to have been committed with the consent or connivance of a director, manager, secretary or other similar officer of the body, or a person purporting to act in any such capacity, he as well as the body corporate is guilty of the offence and liable to be proceeded against and punished accordingly.

(2) In relation to a body corporate whose affairs are managed by its members "director" means a member of the body corporate.

NOTES

Sub-s (1): words in square brackets substituted by the Performances (Moral Rights, etc) Regulations 2006, SI 2006/18, reg 2, Schedule, paras 1, 8.

Supplementary provisions with respect to delivery up and seizure

[2.284]

203 Period after which remedy of delivery up not available

(1) An application for an order under section 195 (order for delivery up in civil proceedings) may not be made after the end of the period of six years from the date on which the illicit recording in question was made, subject to the following provisions.

(2) If during the whole or any part of that period a person entitled to apply for an order—

(a) is under a disability, or

(b) is prevented by fraud or concealment from discovering the facts entitling him to apply,

an application may be made by him at any time before the end of the period of six years from the date on which he ceased to be under a disability or, as the case may be, could with reasonable diligence have discovered those facts.

(3) In subsection (2) "disability"—

(a) in England and Wales, has the same meaning as in the Limitation Act 1980;

(b) in Scotland, means legal disability within the meaning of the Prescription and Limitations (Scotland) Act 1973;

(c) in Northern Ireland, has the same meaning as in the Statute of Limitation (Northern Ireland) 1958.

(4) An order under section 199 (order for delivery up in criminal proceedings) shall not, in any case, be made after the end of the period of six years from the date on which the illicit recording in question was made.

[2.285]

204 Order as to disposal of illicit recording

(1) An application may be made to the court for an order that an illicit recording of a performance delivered up in pursuance of an order under section 195 or 199, or seized and detained in pursuance of the right conferred by section 196, shall be—

(a) forfeited to such person having performer's rights or recording rights in relation to the performance as the court may direct, or

(b) destroyed or otherwise dealt with as the court may think fit,

or for a decision that no such order should be made.

(2) In considering what order (if any) should be made, the court shall consider whether other remedies available in an action for infringement of the rights conferred by [this Chapter] would be adequate to compensate the person or persons entitled to the rights and to protect their interests.

(3) Provision shall be made by rules of court as to the service of notice on persons having an interest in the recording, and any such person is entitled—

(a) to appear in proceedings for an order under this section, whether or not he was served with notice, and

(b) to appeal against any order made, whether or not he appeared;

and an order shall not take effect until the end of the period within which notice of an appeal may be given or, if before the end of that period notice of appeal is duly given, until the final determination or abandonment of the proceedings on the appeal.

(4) Where there is more than one person interested in a recording, the court shall make such order as it thinks just and may (in particular) direct that the recording be sold, or otherwise dealt with, and the proceeds divided.

(5) If the court decides that no order should be made under this section, the person in whose possession, custody or control the recording was before being delivered up or seized is entitled to its return.

(6) References in this section to a person having an interest in a recording include any person in whose favour an order could be made in respect of the recording—

[(a) under this section or under section 114 or 231 of this Act;
(b) under section 24D of the Registered Designs Act 1949;
(c) under section 19 of Trade Marks Act 1994 (including that section as applied by regulation 4 of the Community Trade Mark Regulations 2006 (SI 2006/1027)); or
(d) under regulation 1C of the Community Design Regulations 2005 (SI 2005/2339).]

NOTES

Sub-s (2): words in square brackets substituted by the Performances (Moral Rights, etc) Regulations 2006, SI 2006/18, reg 2, Schedule, paras 1, 8.

Sub-s (6): paras (a)–(d) substituted by the Intellectual Property (Enforcement, etc) Regulations 2006, SI 2006/1028, reg 2(2), Sch 2, paras 6, 11.

[2.286]

[204A Forfeiture of illicit recordings: England and Wales or Northern Ireland

(1) In England and Wales or Northern Ireland where illicit recordings of a performance have come into the possession of any person in connection with the investigation or prosecution of a relevant offence, that person may apply under this section for an order for the forfeiture of the illicit recordings.

(2) For the purposes of this section "relevant offence" means—

(a) an offence under [section 198(1) or (1A)] (criminal liability for making or dealing with illicit recordings),
(b) an offence under the Trade Descriptions Act 1968 (c 29),
[(ba) an offence under the Business Protection from Misleading Marketing Regulations 2008,
(bb) an offence under the Consumer Protection from Unfair Trading Regulations 2008, or]
(c) an offence involving dishonesty or deception.

(3) An application under this section may be made—

(a) where proceedings have been brought in any court for a relevant offence relating to some or all of the illicit recordings, to that court, or
(b) where no application for the forfeiture of the illicit recordings has been made under paragraph (a), by way of complaint to a magistrates' court.

(4) On an application under this section, the court shall make an order for the forfeiture of any illicit recordings only if it is satisfied that a relevant offence has been committed in relation to the illicit recordings.

(5) A court may infer for the purposes of this section that such an offence has been committed in relation to any illicit recordings if it is satisfied that such an offence has been committed in relation to illicit recordings which are representative of the illicit recordings in question (whether by reason of being part of the same consignment or batch or otherwise).

(6) Any person aggrieved by an order made under this section by a magistrates' court, or by a decision of such a court not to make such an order, may appeal against that order or decision—

(a) in England and Wales, to the Crown Court, or
(b) in Northern Ireland, to the county court.

(7) An order under this section may contain such provision as appears to the court to be appropriate for delaying the coming into force of the order pending the making and determination of any appeal (including any application under section 111 of the Magistrates' Courts Act 1980 (c 43) or Article 146 of the Magistrates' Courts (Northern Ireland) Order 1981 (SI 1987/1675 (NI 26)) (statement of case)).

(8) Subject to subsection (9), where any illicit recordings are forfeited under this section they shall be destroyed in accordance with such directions as the court may give.

(9) On making an order under this section the court may direct that the illicit recordings to which the order relates shall (instead of being destroyed) be forfeited to the person having the performers' rights or recording rights in question or dealt with in such other way as the court considers appropriate.]

NOTES

Inserted, together with s 204B, by the Copyright, etc and Trade Marks (Offences and Enforcement) Act 2002, s 4.

Sub-s (2): words in square brackets in para (a) substituted by the Copyright and Related Rights Regulations 2003, SI 2003/2498, regs 3, 26(4)(c), subject to transitional provisions as noted to s 1 of this Act at **[2.7]**; paras (ba), (bb) substituted for the word "or" by the Consumer Protection from Unfair Trading Regulations 2008, SI 2008/1277, reg 30(1), Sch 2, Pt 1, paras 39, 42.

[2.287]

[204B Forfeiture: Scotland

(1) In Scotland the court may make an order under this section for the forfeiture of any illicit recordings.

(2) An order under this section may be made—

- (a) on an application by the procurator-fiscal made in the manner specified in section 134 of the Criminal Procedure (Scotland) Act 1995 (c 46), or
- (b) where a person is convicted of a relevant offence, in addition to any other penalty which the court may impose.

(3) On an application under subsection (2)(a), the court shall make an order for the forfeiture of any illicit recordings only if it is satisfied that a relevant offence has been committed in relation to the illicit recordings.

(4) The court may infer for the purposes of this section that such an offence has been committed in relation to any illicit recordings if it is satisfied that such an offence has been committed in relation to illicit recordings which are representative of the illicit recordings in question (whether by reason of being part of the same consignment or batch or otherwise).

(5) The procurator-fiscal making the application under subsection (2)(a) shall serve on any person appearing to him to be the owner of, or otherwise to have an interest in, the illicit recordings to which the application relates a copy of the application, together with a notice giving him the opportunity to appear at the hearing of the application to show cause why the illicit recordings should not be forfeited.

(6) Service under subsection (5) shall be carried out, and such service may be proved, in the manner specified for citation of an accused in summary proceedings under the Criminal Procedure (Scotland) Act 1995.

(7) Any person upon whom notice is served under subsection (5) and any other person claiming to be the owner of, or otherwise to have an interest in, illicit recordings to which an application under this section relates shall be entitled to appear at the hearing of the application to show cause why the illicit recordings should not be forfeited.

(8) The court shall not make an order following an application under subsection (2)(a)—

- (a) if any person on whom notice is served under subsection (5) does not appear, unless service of the notice on that person is proved, or
- (b) if no notice under subsection (5) has been served, unless the court is satisfied that in the circumstances it was reasonable not to serve such notice.

(9) Where an order for the forfeiture of any illicit recordings is made following an application under subsection (2)(a), any person who appeared, or was entitled to appear, to show cause why the illicit recordings should not be forfeited may, within 21 days of the making of the order, appeal to the High Court by Bill of Suspension.

(10) Section 182(5)(a) to (e) of the Criminal Procedure (Scotland) Act 1995 shall apply to an appeal under subsection (9) as it applies to a stated case under Part 2 of that Act.

(11) An order following an application under subsection (2)(a) shall not take effect—

- (a) until the end of the period of 21 days beginning with the day after the day on which the order is made, or
- (b) if an appeal is made under subsection (9) above within that period, until the appeal is determined or abandoned.

(12) An order under subsection (2)(b) shall not take effect—

- (a) until the end of the period within which an appeal against the order could be brought under the Criminal Procedure (Scotland) Act 1995 (c 46), or
- (b) if an appeal is made within that period, until the appeal is determined or abandoned.

(13) Subject to subsection (14), illicit recordings forfeited under this section shall be destroyed in accordance with such directions as the court may give.

(14) On making an order under this section the court may direct that the illicit recordings to which the order relates shall (instead of being destroyed) be forfeited to the person having the performers' rights or recording rights in question or dealt with in such other way as the court considers appropriate.

(15) For the purposes of this section—

["relevant offence" means—

- (a) an offence under section 198(1) or (1A) (criminal liability for making or dealing with illicit recordings),
- (b) an offence under the Trade Descriptions Act 1968,
- (c) an offence under the Business Protection from Misleading Marketing Regulations 2008,
- (d) an offence under the Consumer Protection from Unfair Trading Regulations 2008, or
- (e) any offence involving dishonesty or deception;]

"the court" means—

- (a) in relation to an order made on an application under subsection (2)(a), the sheriff, and
- (b) in relation to an order made under subsection (2)(b), the court which imposed the penalty.]

NOTES

Inserted as noted to s 204A at **[2.286]**.

Sub-s (15): definition "relevant offence" substituted by the Consumer Protection from Unfair Trading Regulations 2008, SI 2008/1277, reg 30(1), Sch 2, Pt 1, paras 39, 43.

[2.288]

205 Jurisdiction of county court and sheriff court

(1) In England [and Wales the county court and in] Northern Ireland a county court may entertain proceedings under—

section 195 (order for delivery up of illicit recording), or

section 204 (order as to disposal of illicit recording),

[save that, in Northern Ireland, a county court may entertain such proceedings only] where the value of the illicit recordings in question does not exceed the county court limit for actions in tort.

(2) In Scotland proceedings for an order under either of those provisions may be brought in the sheriff court.

(3) Nothing in this section shall be construed as affecting the jurisdiction of the High Court or, in Scotland, the Court of Session.

NOTES

Sub-s (1): words in first pair of square brackets substituted by the Crime and Courts Act 2013, s 17(5), Sch 9, Pt 3, para 72; words in second pair of square brackets inserted by the High Court and County Courts Jurisdiction Order 1991, SI 1991/724, art 2(8), Schedule, Pt I.

[Licensing of performers' . . . rights

[2.289]

205A Licensing of performers' . . . rights

The provisions of Schedule 2A have effect with respect to the licensing of performers' . . . rights.]

NOTES

Inserted, together with preceding heading, by the Copyright and Related Rights Regulations 1996, SI 1996/2967, regs 4, 22(1), subject to transitional provisions and savings specified in regs 25–36 of those Regulations, at **[2.510]–[2.521]**.

Words omitted (from provision and preceding heading) repealed by the Enterprise and Regulatory Reform Act 2013, s 77(4), Sch 22, Pt 2, paras 2, 6.

[Jurisdiction of Copyright Tribunal

[2.290]

205B Jurisdiction of Copyright Tribunal

(1) The Copyright Tribunal has jurisdiction under [this Chapter] to hear and determine proceedings under—

(a) section 182D (amount of equitable remuneration for exploitation of commercial sound recording);

(b) section 190 (application to give consent on behalf of owner of reproduction right);

(c) section 191H (amount of equitable remuneration on transfer of rental right);

[(cc) paragraph 19 of Schedule 2 (determination of royalty or other remuneration to be paid with respect to re-transmission of broadcast including performance or recording);]

(d) paragraph 3, 4 or 5 of Schedule 2A (reference of licensing scheme);

(e) paragraph 6 or 7 of that Schedule (application with respect to licence under licensing scheme);

(f) paragraph 10, 11 or 12 of that Schedule (reference or application with respect to licensing by licensing body);

(g) paragraph 15 of that Schedule (application to settle royalty for certain lending);

(h) paragraph 17 of that Schedule (application to settle terms of licence available as of right).

(2) The provisions of Chapter VIII of Part I (general provisions relating to the Copyright Tribunal) apply in relation to the Tribunal when exercising any jurisdiction under [this Chapter].

(3) Provision shall be made by rules under section 150 prohibiting the Tribunal from entertaining a reference under paragraph 3, 4 or 5 of Schedule 2A (reference of licensing scheme) by a representative organisation unless the Tribunal is satisfied that the organisation is reasonably representative of the class of persons which it claims to represent.]

NOTES

Inserted, together with preceding cross-heading, by the Copyright and Related Rights Regulations 1996, SI 1996/2967, regs 4, 24(1), subject to transitional provisions and savings specified in regs 25–36 of those Regulations, at **[2.510]–[2.521]**.

Sub-s (1): words in first pair of square brackets substituted by the Performances (Moral Rights, etc) Regulations 2006, SI 2006/18, reg 2, Schedule, paras 1, 8; para (cc) inserted by the Broadcasting Act 1996, s 138, Sch 9, para 4 and repealed by the Digital Economy Act 2017, s 34(2)(a)(iii), as from a day to be appointed.

Sub-s (2): words in square brackets substituted by SI 2006/18, reg 2, Schedule, paras 1, 8.

[CHAPTER 3
MORAL RIGHTS]

[Right to be identified as performer

[2.291]

205C Right to be identified as performer

(1) Whenever a person—

(a) produces or puts on a qualifying performance that is given in public,

(b) broadcasts live a qualifying performance,

(c) communicates to the public a sound recording of a qualifying performance, or

(d) issues to the public copies of such a recording,

the performer has the right to be identified as such.

(2) The right of the performer under this section is—

(a) in the case of a performance that is given in public, to be identified in any programme accompanying the performance or in some other manner likely to bring his identity to the notice of a person seeing or hearing the performance,

(b) in the case of a performance that is broadcast, to be identified in a manner likely to bring his identity to the notice of a person seeing or hearing the broadcast,

(c) in the case of a sound recording that is communicated to the public, to be identified in a manner likely to bring his identity to the notice of a person hearing the communication,

(d) in the case of a sound recording that is issued to the public, to be identified in or on each copy or, if that is not appropriate, in some other manner likely to bring his identity to the notice of a person acquiring a copy,

or (in any of the above cases) to be identified in such other manner as may be agreed between the performer and the person mentioned in subsection (1).

(3) The right conferred by this section in relation to a performance given by a group (or so much of a performance as is given by a group) is not infringed—

(a) in a case falling within paragraph (a), (b) or (c) of subsection (2), or

(b) in a case falling within paragraph (d) of that subsection in which it is not reasonably practicable for each member of the group to be identified,

if the group itself is identified as specified in subsection (2).

(4) In this section "group" means two or more performers who have a particular name by which they may be identified collectively.

(5) If the assertion under section 205D specifies a pseudonym, initials or some other particular form of identification, that form shall be used; otherwise any reasonable form of identification may be used.

(6) This section has effect subject to section 205E (exceptions to right).]

NOTES

Chapter heading: inserted by the Performances (Moral Rights, etc) Regulations 2006, SI 2006/18, regs 3, 4(6), except in relation to any performance that took place before 1 February 2006: see reg 8 of the 2006 Regulations.

Inserted, together with preceding cross-heading and ss 205D–205N and associated cross-headings, by SI 2006/18, regs 3, 6, except in relation to any performance that took place before 1 February 2006: see reg 8 of the 2006 Regulations.

[2.292]

[205D Requirement that right be asserted

(1) A person does not infringe the right conferred by section 205C (right to be identified as performer) by doing any of the acts mentioned in that section unless the right has been asserted in accordance with the following provisions so as to bind him in relation to that act.

(2) The right may be asserted generally, or in relation to any specified act or description of acts—

(a) by instrument in writing signed by or on behalf of the performer, or

(b) on an assignment of a performer's property rights, by including in the instrument effecting the assignment a statement that the performer asserts in relation to the performance his right to be identified.

(3) The persons bound by an assertion of the right under subsection (2) are—

(a) in the case of an assertion under subsection (2)(a), anyone to whose notice the assertion is brought;

(b) in the case of an assertion under subsection (2)(b), the assignee and anyone claiming through him, whether or not he has notice of the assertion.

(4) In an action for infringement of the right the court shall, in considering remedies, take into account any delay in asserting the right.]

NOTES

Inserted as noted to s 205C at **[2.291]**.

[2.293]

[205E Exceptions to right

(1) The right conferred by section 205C (right to be identified as performer) is subject to the following exceptions.

(2) The right does not apply where it is not reasonably practicable to identify the performer (or, where identification of a group is permitted by virtue of section 205C(3), the group).
(3) The right does not apply in relation to any performance given for the purposes of reporting current events.
(4) The right does not apply in relation to any performance given for the purposes of advertising any goods or services.
(5) The right is not infringed by an act which by virtue of any of the following provisions of Schedule 2 would not infringe any of the rights conferred by Chapter 2—
(a) paragraph 2(1A) (news reporting);
(b) paragraph 3 (incidental inclusion of a performance or recording);
(c) paragraph 4(2) (things done for the purposes of examination);
(d) paragraph 8 (parliamentary and judicial proceedings);
(e) paragraph 9 (Royal Commissions and statutory inquiries).]

NOTES
Inserted as noted to s 205C at **[2.291]**.

[Right to object to derogatory treatment

[2.294]
205F Right to object to derogatory treatment of performance
(1) The performer of a qualifying performance has a right which is infringed if—
(a) the performance is broadcast live, or
(b) by means of a sound recording the performance is played in public or communicated to the public,
with any distortion, mutilation or other modification that is prejudicial to the reputation of the performer.
(2) This section has effect subject to section 205G (exceptions to right).]

NOTES
Inserted as noted to s 205C at **[2.291]**.

[2.295]
[205G Exceptions to right
(1) The right conferred by section 205F (right to object to derogatory treatment of performance) is subject to the following exceptions.
(2) The right does not apply in relation to any performance given for the purposes of reporting current events.
(3) The right is not infringed by modifications made to a performance which are consistent with normal editorial or production practice.
(4) Subject to subsection (5), the right is not infringed by anything done for the purpose of—
(a) avoiding the commission of an offence,
(b) complying with a duty imposed by or under an enactment, or
(c) in the case of the British Broadcasting Corporation, avoiding the inclusion in a programme broadcast by them of anything which offends against good taste or decency or which is likely to encourage or incite crime or lead to disorder or to be offensive to public feeling.
(5) Where—
(a) the performer is identified in a manner likely to bring his identity to the notice of a person seeing or hearing the performance as modified by the act in question; or
(b) he has previously been identified in or on copies of a sound recording issued to the public,
subsection (4) applies only if there is sufficient disclaimer.
(6) In subsection (5) "sufficient disclaimer", in relation to an act capable of infringing the right, means a clear and reasonably prominent indication—
(a) given in a manner likely to bring it to the notice of a person seeing or hearing the performance as modified by the act in question, and
(b) if the performer is identified at the time of the act, appearing along with the identification,
that the modifications were made without the performer's consent.]

NOTES
Inserted as noted to s 205C at **[2.291]**.

[2.296]
[205H Infringement of right by possessing or dealing with infringing article
(1) The right conferred by section 205F (right to object to derogatory treatment of performance) is also infringed by a person who—
(a) possesses in the course of business, or
(b) sells or lets for hire, or offers or exposes for sale or hire, or
(c) distributes,
an article which is, and which he knows or has reason to believe is, an infringing article.

(2) An "infringing article" means a sound recording of a qualifying performance with any distortion, mutilation or other modification that is prejudicial to the reputation of the performer.]

NOTES

Inserted as noted to s 205C at **[2.291]**.

[Supplementary

[2.297]

205I Duration of rights

(1) A performer's rights under this Chapter in relation to a performance subsist so long as that performer's rights under Chapter 2 subsist in relation to the performance.

(2) In subsection (1) "performer's rights" includes rights of a performer that are vested in a successor of his.]

NOTES

Inserted as noted to s 205C at **[2.291]**.

[2.298]

[205J Consent and waiver of rights

(1) It is not an infringement of the rights conferred by this Chapter to do any act to which consent has been given by or on behalf of the person entitled to the right.

(2) Any of those rights may be waived by instrument in writing signed by or on behalf of the person giving up the right.

(3) A waiver—

(a) may relate to a specific performance, to performances of a specified description or to performances generally, and may relate to existing or future performances, and

(b) may be conditional or unconditional and may be expressed to be subject to revocation,

and if made in favour of the owner or prospective owner of a performer's property rights in the performance or performances to which it relates, it shall be presumed to extend to his licensees and successors in title unless a contrary intention is expressed.

(4) Nothing in this Chapter shall be construed as excluding the operation of the general law of contract or estoppel in relation to an informal waiver or other transaction in relation to either of the rights conferred by this Chapter.]

NOTES

Inserted as noted to s 205C at **[2.291]**.

[2.299]

[205K Application of provisions to parts of performances

(1) The right conferred by section 205C (right to be identified as performer) applies in relation to the whole or any substantial part of a performance.

(2) The right conferred by section 205F (right to object to derogatory treatment of performance) applies in relation to the whole or any part of a performance.]

NOTES

Inserted as noted to s 205C at **[2.291]**.

[2.300]

[205L Moral rights not assignable

The rights conferred by this Chapter are not assignable.]

NOTES

Inserted as noted to s 205C at **[2.291]**.

[2.301]

[205M Transmission of moral rights on death

(1) On the death of a person entitled to a right conferred by this Chapter—

(a) the right passes to such person as he may by testamentary disposition specifically direct,

(b) if there is no such direction but the performer's property rights in respect of the performance in question form part of his estate, the right passes to the person to whom the property rights pass,

(c) if or to the extent that the right does not pass under paragraph (a) or (b) it is exercisable by his personal representatives.

(2) Where a performer's property rights pass in part to one person and in part to another, as for example where a bequest is limited so as to apply—

(a) to one or more, but not all, of the things to which the owner has the right to consent, or

(b) to part, but not the whole, of the period for which the rights subsist,

any right which by virtue of subsection (1) passes with the performer's property rights is correspondingly divided.

(3) Where by virtue of subsection (1)(a) or (1)(b) a right becomes exercisable by more than one person—

(a) it is, in the case of the right conferred by section 205F (right to object to derogatory treatment of performance), a right exercisable by each of them and is satisfied in relation to any of them if he consents to the treatment or act in question, and

(b) any waiver of the right in accordance with section 205J by one of them does not affect the rights of the others.

(4) A consent or waiver previously given or made binds any person to whom a right passes by virtue of subsection (1).

(5) Any damages recovered by personal representatives by virtue of this section in respect of an infringement after a person's death shall devolve as part of his estate as if the right of action had subsisted and been vested in him immediately before his death.]

NOTES

Inserted as noted to s 205C at **[2.291]**.

[2.302]

[205N Remedies for infringement of moral rights

(1) An infringement of a right conferred by this Chapter is actionable as a breach of statutory duty owed to the person entitled to the right.

(2) Where—

(a) there is an infringement of a right conferred by this Chapter,

(b) a person falsely claiming to act on behalf of a performer consented to the relevant conduct or purported to waive the right, and

(c) there would have been no infringement if he had been so acting,

that person shall be liable, jointly and severally with any person liable in respect of the infringement by virtue of subsection (1), as if he himself had infringed the right.

(3) Where proceedings for infringement of the right conferred on a performer by this Chapter, it shall be a defence to prove—

(a) that a person claiming to act on behalf of the performer consented to the defendant's conduct or purported to waive the right, and

(b) that the defendant reasonably believed that the person was acting on behalf of the performer.

(4) In proceedings for infringement of the right conferred by section 205F the court may, if it thinks it an adequate remedy in the circumstances, grant an injunction on terms prohibiting the doing of any act unless a disclaimer is made, in such terms and in such manner as may be approved by the court, dissociating the performer from the broadcast or sound recording of the performance.]

NOTES

Inserted as noted to s 205C at **[2.291]**.

[CHAPTER 4
QUALIFICATION FOR PROTECTION, EXTENT AND INTERPRETATION]

Qualification for protection and extent

[2.303]

206 Qualifying countries, individuals and persons

(1) In this Part—

"qualifying country" means—

(a) the United Kingdom,

[(b) another EEA state,]

[(ba) the Channel Islands, the Isle of Man or Gibraltar,

(bb) a country which is a party to the Rome Convention,] or

(c) to the extent that an Order under section 208 so provides, a country designated under that section as enjoying reciprocal protection;

"qualifying individual" means a citizen or subject of, or an individual resident in, a qualifying country; and

"qualifying person" means a qualifying individual or a body corporate or other body having legal personality which—

(a) is formed under the law of a part of the United Kingdom or another qualifying country, and

(b) has in any qualifying country a place of business at which substantial business activity is carried on.

(2) The reference in the definition of "qualifying individual" to a person's being a citizen or subject of a qualifying country shall be construed—

(a) in relation to the United Kingdom, as a reference to his being a British citizen, and

(b) in relation to a colony of the United Kingdom, as a reference to his being a [British overseas territories citizen] by connection with that colony.

Part 2 Copyright

(3) In determining for the purpose of the definition of "qualifying person" whether substantial business activity is carried on at a place of business in any country, no account shall be taken of dealings in goods which are at all material times outside that country.

[(4) Her Majesty may by Order in Council—

(a) make provision for the application of this Part to a country by virtue of paragraph (bb) or (c) of the definition of "qualifying country" in subsection (1) to be subject to specified restrictions;

(b) amend the definition of "qualifying country" in subsection (1) so as to add a country which is not a party to the Rome Convention;

(c) make provision for the application of this Part to a country added under paragraph (b) to be subject to specified restrictions.

(5) A statutory instrument containing an Order in Council under this section is subject to annulment in pursuance of a resolution of either House of Parliament.]

[(6) In this section, "the Rome Convention" means the International Convention for the Protection of Performers, Producers of Phonograms and Broadcasting Organisations done at Rome on 26 October 1961.]

NOTES

Chapter heading: inserted by the Performances (Moral Rights, etc) Regulations 2006, SI 2006/18, regs 3, 4(7).

Sub-s (1): in definition "qualifying country", para (b) substituted (for original words "another member State of the European Economic Community") and paras (ba), (bb) inserted, by the Intellectual Property Act 2014, s 22(5), as from 6 April 2017, subject to savings as noted to s 154 at **[2.206]**.

Sub-s (2): words in square brackets in para (b) substituted by virtue of the British Overseas Territories Act 2002, s 2(3).

Sub-ss (4)–(6): added by the Intellectual Property Act 2014, s 22(6), (7), as from 1 December 2016 (for the purpose of making Orders in Council) and 6 April 2017 (otherwise), subject to savings as noted to s 154 at **[2.206]**.

Orders: the Copyright and Performances (Application to Other Countries) Order 2016, SI 2016/1219 at **[2.730]**.

[2.304]

207 Countries to which this Part extends

This Part extends to England and Wales, Scotland and Northern Ireland.

[2.305]

208 Countries enjoying reciprocal protection

(1) Her Majesty may by Order in Council designate as enjoying reciprocal protection under this Part—

(a) a Convention country, or

(b) a country as to which Her Majesty is satisfied that provision has been or will be made under its law giving adequate protection for British performances.

(2) A "Convention country" means a country which is a party to a Convention relating to performers' rights to which the United Kingdom is also a party.

(3) A "British performance" means a performance—

(a) given by an individual who is a British citizen or resident in the United Kingdom, or

(b) taking place in the United Kingdom.

(4) If the law of that country provides adequate protection only for certain descriptions of performance, an Order under subsection (1)(b) designating that country shall contain provision limiting to a corresponding extent the protection afforded by this Part in relation to performances connected with that country.

(5) The power conferred by subsection (1)(b) is exercisable in relation to . . . any colony of the United Kingdom, as in relation to a foreign country.

(6) A statutory instrument containing an Order in Council under this section shall be subject to annulment in pursuance of a resolution of either House of Parliament.

NOTES

Sub-s (5): words "any of the Channel Islands, the Isle of Man or" (omitted) repealed by the Intellectual Property Act 2014, s 22(8), as from 6 April 2017, subject to savings as noted to s 154 at **[2.206]**.

Orders: the Copyright and Performances (Application to Other Countries) Order 2016, SI 2016/1219 at **[2.730]**.

[2.306]

209 Territorial waters and the continental shelf

(1) For the purposes of this Part the territorial waters of the United Kingdom shall be treated as part of the United Kingdom.

(2) This Part applies to things done in the United Kingdom sector of the continental shelf on a structure or vessel which is present there for purposes directly connected with the exploration of the sea bed or subsoil or the exploitation of their natural resources as it applies to things done in the United Kingdom.

(3) The United Kingdom sector of the continental shelf means the areas designated by order under section 1(7) of the Continental Shelf Act 1964.

[2.307]

210 British ships, aircraft and hovercraft

(1) This Part applies to things done on a British ship, aircraft or hovercraft as it applies to things done in the United Kingdom.

(2) In this section—

"British ship" means a ship which is a British ship for the purposes of the [Merchant Shipping Act 1995] otherwise than by virtue of registration in a country outside the United Kingdom; and

"British aircraft" and "British hovercraft" mean an aircraft or hovercraft registered in the United Kingdom.

NOTES

Sub-s (2): in definition "British ship" words in square brackets substituted by the Merchant Shipping Act 1995, s 314(2), Sch 13, para 84(b).

[2.308]

[210A Requirement of signature: application in relation to body corporate

(1) The requirement in the following provisions that an instrument be signed by or on behalf of a person is also satisfied in the case of a body corporate by the affixing of its seal—

section 191B(3) (assignment of performer's property rights);
section 191C(1) (assignment of future performer's property rights);
section 191D(1) (grant of exclusive licence).

(2) The requirement in the following provisions that an instrument be signed by a person is also satisfied in the case of a body corporate by signature on behalf of the body or by the affixing of its seal—

section 205D(2)(a) (assertion of performer's moral rights);
section 205J(2) (waiver of performer's moral rights).]

NOTES

Inserted by the Performances (Moral Rights, etc) Regulations 2006, SI 2006/18, regs 3, 7.

Interpretation

[2.309]

211 Expressions having same meaning as in copyright provisions

(1) The following expressions have the same meaning in this Part as in Part I (copyright)—

[assignment (in Scotland),]
broadcast,
business,
. . .
. . .
[communication to the public,]
country,
defendant (in Scotland),
delivery up (in Scotland),
[the EEA,
EEA state,]
film,
[injunction (in Scotland),]
literary work,
published, . . .
[sound recording, and]
[wireless broadcast].

(2) [The provisions of—

(a) section 5B(2) and (3) (supplementary provisions relating to films), and

(b) section 6(3) to (5A) and section 19(4) (supplementary provisions relating to broadcasting),

apply] for the purposes of Part I and in relation to an infringement of copyright.

NOTES

Sub-s (1): entries "assignment (in Scotland)" and "signed" inserted by the Performances (Moral Rights, etc) Regulations 2006, SI 2006/18, reg 2, Schedule, paras 1, 6(1), (2); entries omitted repealed, word omitted from entry "published" repealed, entry "sound recording" substituted, and entries "communication to the public", "injunction (in Scotland)" and "wireless broadcast" inserted by the Copyright and Related Rights Regulations 2003, SI 2003/2498, reg 2, Sch 1, Pt 1, paras 1, 15(5)(a), Sch 2, subject to transitional provisions as noted to s 1 of this Act at **[2.7]**; entries "the EEA" and "EEA state" substituted for entry "EEA national", as inserted by the Duration of Copyright and Rights in Performances Regulations 1995, SI 1995/3297, regs 4, 11(3), by the Intellectual Property (Enforcement, etc) Regulations 2006, SI 2006/1028, reg 2(2), Sch 2, paras 6, 12.

Sub-s (2): words in square brackets substituted by SI 2006/18, reg 2, Schedule, paras 1, 6(1), (3).

[2.310]
212 Index of defined expressions
The following Table shows provisions defining or otherwise explaining expressions used in this Part (other than provisions defining or explaining an expression used only in the same section)—

[accessible copy (in paragraphs 3A to 3E of Schedule 2)	paragraph 3E(4) of Schedule 2]
[assignment (in Scotland)	section 211(1) (and section 177)]
broadcast (and related expressions)	section 211 (and section 6)
business	section 211(1) (and section 178)
. . .	. . .
[communication to the public	section 211(1) (and section 20)]
[consent of performer (in relation to performer's property rights)	section 191A(2)]
country	section 211(1) (and section 178)
defendant (in Scotland)	section 211(1) (and section 177)
delivery up (in Scotland)	section 211(1) (and section 177)
[disabled person (in paragraphs 3A to 3E of Schedule 2)	paragraph 3E(2) and (3) of Schedule 2]
[distribution right	section 182B(5)]
[[the EEA and EEA state]	section 211(1) (and section 172A)]
exclusive recording contract	section 185(1)
film	section 211(1) (and [section 5B])
[group	section 205C(4)]
illicit recording	section 197
[injunction (in Scotland)	section 211(1) (and section 177)]
[issue to the public	section 182B]
[lending right	section 182C(7)]
literary work	section 211(1) (and section 3(1))
[making available right	section 182CA]
performance	section 180(2)
[performer's non-property rights	section 192A(1)]
[performer's property rights	section 191A(1)]
published	section 211(1) (and section 175)
qualifying country	section 206(1)
qualifying individual	section 206(1) and (2)
qualifying performance	section 181
qualifying person	section 206(1) and (3)
recording (of a performance)	section 180(2)
recording rights (person having)	section 185(2) and (3)
[rental right	section 182C(7)]
[reproduction right	section 182A(3)]
[rights owner (in relation to performer's property rights)	section 191A(3) and (4)]
[signed	section 211(1) (and section 176)]
sound recording	section 211(1) (and [section 5A])
[wireless broadcast	section 211(1) (and section 178)]

NOTES

Entries "accessible copy" and "disabled person" inserted by the Copyright and Rights in Performances (Disability) Regulations 2014, SI 2014/1384, reg 4, Schedule, para 5.

Entries "assignment in Scotland", "group", "issue to the public", "signed", and "wireless broadcast" inserted by the Performances (Moral Rights, etc) Regulations 2006, SI 2006/18, reg 2, Schedule, paras 1, 7.

Entry omitted repealed, and entries "communication to the public", "injunction (in Scotland)", and "making available right" inserted by the Copyright and Related Rights Regulations 2003, SI 2003/2498, reg 2, Sch 1, Pt 1, paras 1, 15(6), Sch 2, subject to transitional provisions as noted to s 1 of this Act at **[2.7]**.

Entries beginning "consent of performer" and "rights owner", and entries "distribution right", "lending right", "performer's non-property rights", "performer's property rights", "rental right" and "reproduction right" inserted by the Copyright and Related Rights Regulations 1996, SI 1996/2967, regs 4, 20(4), 21(6), subject to transitional provisions and savings specified in regs 25–36 of those Regulations, at **[2.510]–[2.521]**.

Entry "EEA national" inserted by the Duration of Copyright and Rights in Performances Regulations 1995, SI 1995/3297, regs 4, 11(4); words in square brackets substituted by the Intellectual Property (Enforcement, etc) Regulations 2006, SI 2006/1028, reg 2(2), Sch 2, paras 6, 13.

In entries "film" and "sound recording" words in square brackets substituted, by the Duration of Copyright and Rights in Performances Regulations 1995, SI 1995/3297, regs 4, 9(6), subject to transitional provisions and savings specified in regs 12–34 of those Regulations, at **[2.478]–[2.499]**.

[Supplementary

[2.311]

212A Power to amend in consequence of changes to international law

(1) The Secretary of State may by order amend this Part in consequence of changes to international law in the area of performance rights.

(2) An order under this section must be made by statutory instrument; and no order may be made unless a draft of it has been laid before and approved by a resolution of each House of Parliament.]

NOTES

Commencement: 6 April 2017.

Inserted, together with preceding heading, by the Intellectual Property Act 2014, s 22(9), subject to savings as noted to s 154 at **[2.206]**.

PART III
DESIGN RIGHT

NOTES

Part III is modified, in relation to semiconductor topographies by the Design Right (Semiconductor Topographies) Regulations 1989, SI 1989/1100, at **[4.1]**.

CHAPTER I
DESIGN RIGHT IN ORIGINAL DESIGNS

Introductory

[2.312]

213 Design right

(1) Design right is a property right which subsists in accordance with this Part in an original design.

(2) In this Part "design" means the design of . . . the shape or configuration (whether internal or external) of the whole or part of an article.

(3) Design right does not subsist in—

(a) a method or principle of construction,

(b) features of shape or configuration of an article which—

(i) enable the article to be connected to, or placed in, around or against, another article so that either article may perform its function, or

(ii) are dependent upon the appearance of another article of which the article is intended by the designer to form an integral part, or

(c) surface decoration.

(4) A design is not "original" for the purposes of this Part if it is commonplace [in a qualifying country] in the design field in question at the time of its creation[; and "qualifying country" has the meaning given in section 217(3)].

(5) Design right subsists in a design only if the design qualifies for design right protection by reference to—

(a) the designer or the person by whom [the designer was employed] (see sections 218 and 219), or

(b) the person by whom and country in which articles made to the design were first marketed (see section 220),

or in accordance with any Order under section 221 (power to make further provision with respect to qualification).

[(5A) Design right does not subsist in a design which consists of or contains a controlled representation within the meaning of the Olympic Symbol etc (Protection) Act 1995.]

(6) Design right does not subsist unless and until the design has been recorded in a design document or an article has been made to the design.

(7) Design right does not subsist in a design which was so recorded, or to which an article was made, before the commencement of this Part.

NOTES

Sub-s (2): words omitted repealed by the Intellectual Property Act 2014, s 1(1).

Sub-s (4): words in square brackets inserted by the Intellectual Property Act 2014, s 1(3), (4), in relation to designs created after 1 October 2014.

Sub-s (5): words in square brackets in para (a) substituted for original words "the design was commissioned or the designer employed", by the Intellectual Property Act 2014, s 2(2)(a), subject to savings in s 2(3) of the 2014 Act as noted to s 215 at **[2.314]**.

Sub-s (5A): inserted by the Olympic Symbol etc (Protection) Act 1995, s 14, in relation to designs created on or after 20 September 1995.

[2.313]
214 The designer

(1) In this Part the "designer", in relation to a design, means the person who creates it.

(2) In the case of a computer-generated design the person by whom the arrangements necessary for the creation of the design are undertaken shall be taken to be the designer.

[2.314]
215 Ownership of design right

(1) The designer is the first owner of any design right in a design which is not created *in pursuance of a commission or* in the course of employment.

(2) Where a design is created in pursuance of a commission, the person commissioning the design is the first owner of any design right in it.

(3) Where, *in a case not falling within subsection (2)* a design is created by an employee in the course of his employment, his employer is the first owner of any design right in the design.

(4) If a design qualifies for design right protection by virtue of section 220 (qualification by reference to first marketing of articles made to the design), the above rules do not apply and the person by whom the articles in question are marketed is the first owner of the design right.

NOTES

Words in italics in each place repealed by the Intellectual Property Act 2014, s 2(1), subject to s 2(3) of the 2014 Act, which provides that s 2 does not apply to any design created before 1 October 2014, or any design created after that date in pursuance of a commission (irrespective of whether the design was commissioned before or after that date) provided that (i) the designer and the commissioner of the design have entered into a contract relating to the commission of the design, and (ii) the contract was entered into before 1 October 2014.

[2.315]
216 Duration of design right

(1) Design right expires—

(a) fifteen years from the end of the calendar year in which the design was first recorded in a design document or an article was first made to the design, whichever first occurred, or

(b) if articles made to the design are made available for sale or hire within five years from the end of that calendar year, ten years from the end of the calendar year in which that first occurred.

(2) The reference in subsection (1) to articles being made available for sale or hire is to their being made so available anywhere in the world by or with the licence of the design right owner.

Qualification for design right protection

[2.316]
217 Qualifying individuals and qualifying persons

(1) In this Part—

"qualifying individual" means a citizen or subject of, or an individual habitually resident in, a qualifying country; and

["qualifying person" means—

(a) an individual habitually resident in a qualifying country, or

(b) a body corporate or other body having legal personality which—

(i) is formed under the law of a part of the United Kingdom or another qualifying country, and

(ii) has in any qualifying country a place of business at which substantial business activity is carried on].

(2) References in this Part to a qualifying person include the Crown and the government of any other qualifying country.

(3) In this section "qualifying country" means—

(a) the United Kingdom,

(b) a country to which this Part extends by virtue of an Order under section 255,

(c) another member State of the European Economic Community, or

(d) to the extent that an Order under section 256 so provides, a country designated under that section as enjoying reciprocal protection.

(4) The reference in the definition of "qualifying individual" to a person's being a citizen or subject of a qualifying country shall be construed—

(a) in relation to the United Kingdom, as a reference to his being a British citizen, and

(b) in relation to a colony of the United Kingdom, as a reference to his being a [British overseas territories' citizen] by connection with that colony.

(5) In determining for the purpose of the definition of "qualifying person" whether substantial business activity is carried on at a place of business in any country, no account shall be taken of dealings in goods which are at all material times outside that country.

NOTES

Sub-s (1): definition "qualifying individual" repealed and definition "qualifying person" substituted by the Intellectual Property Act 2014, s 3(1), (6), in relation to designs created after 1 October 2014, and the definition "qualifying person" previously read as follows–

""qualifying person" means a qualifying individual or a body corporate or other body having legal personality which—
(a) is formed under the law of a part of the United Kingdom or another qualifying country, and
(b) has in any qualifying country a place of business at which substantial business activity is carried on.".

Sub-s (4): repealed by the Intellectual Property Act 2014, s 3(2), (6), in relation to designs created after 1 October 2014; words in square brackets in para (b) substituted by virtue of the British Overseas Territories Act 2002, s 2(3).

[2.317]

218 Qualification by reference to designer

(1) This section applies to a design which is not created *in pursuance of a commission or* in the course of employment.

(2) A design to which this section applies qualifies for design right protection if the designer is *a qualifying individual or, in the case of a computer-generated design,* a qualifying person.

(3) A joint design to which this section applies qualifies for design right protection if any of the designers is *a qualifying individual or, as the case may be,* a qualifying person.

(4) Where a joint design qualifies for design right protection under this section, only those designers who are *qualifying individuals or* qualifying persons are entitled to design right under section 215(1) (first ownership of design right: entitlement of designer).

NOTES

Sub-s (1): words in italics repealed by the Intellectual Property Act 2014, s 2(2)(b), subject to savings in s 2(3) of the 2014 Act as noted to s 215 at **[2.314]**.

Sub-ss (2)–(4): words in italics repealed by the Intellectual Property Act 2014, s 3(3), (6), in relation to designs created after 1 October 2014.

[2.318]

219 [Qualification by reference to employer]

(1) A design qualifies for design right protection if it is created [n the course of employment with] a qualifying person.

(2) In the case of *a joint commission or* joint employment a design qualifies for design right protection if any of the *commissioners or* employers is a qualifying person.

(3) Where a design which is *jointly commissioned or* created in the course of joint employment qualifies for design right protection under this section, only those *commissioners or* employers who are qualifying persons are entitled to design right under section [215(3)] (first ownership of design right: entitlement of *commissioner or* employer).

NOTES

Section heading: substituted for original words "Qualification by reference to commissioner or employer" by the Intellectual Property Act 2014, s 2(2)(c), subject to savings in s 2(3) of the 2014 Act as noted to s 215 at **[2.314]**.

Sub-s (1): words in square brackets substituted for original words "in pursuance of a commission from, or in the course of employment with,", by the Intellectual Property Act 2014, s 2(2)(c), subject to savings in s 2(3) of the 2014 Act as noted to s 215 at **[2.314]**.

Sub-s (2): words in italics repealed by the Intellectual Property Act 2014, s 2(2)(d), subject to savings in s 2(3) of the 2014 Act as noted to s 215 at **[2.314]**.

Sub-s (3): words in italics repealed and reference in square brackets substituted for original reference to "215(2) or (3)", by the Intellectual Property Act 2014, s 2(2)(e), (f), subject to savings in s 2(3) of the 2014 Act as noted to s 215 at **[2.314]**.

[2.319]

220 Qualification by reference to first marketing

(1) A design which does not qualify for design right protection under section 218 or 219 (qualification by reference to designer, *commissioner* or employer) qualifies for design right protection if the first marketing of articles made to the design—

(a) is by a qualifying person *who is exclusively authorised to put such articles on the market in the United Kingdom*, and

(b) takes place in the United Kingdom, another country to which this Part extends by virtue of an Order under section 255, or another member State of the European Economic Community.

(2) If the first marketing of articles made to the design is done jointly by two or more persons, the design qualifies for design right protection if any of those persons meets the [requirement] specified in subsection (1)(a).

(3) In such a case only the persons who meet [that requirement] are entitled to design right under section 215(4) (first ownership of design right: entitlement of first marketer of articles made to the design).

(4) In subsection (1)(a) "exclusively authorised" refers—

(a) to authorisation by the person who would have been first owner of design right as designer, commissioner of the design or employer of the designer if he had been a qualifying person, or by a person lawfully claiming under such a person, and

(b) to exclusivity capable of being enforced by legal proceedings in the United Kingdom.

NOTES

Sub-s (1): first word in italics repealed by the Intellectual Property Act 2014, s 2(2)(g), subject to savings in s 2(3) of the 2014 Act as noted to s 215 at **[2.314]**; words in italics in para (a) repealed by the Intellectual Property Act 2014, s 3(4)(a), (6), in relation to designs created after 1 October 2014.

Sub-s (2): word in square brackets substituted for original word "requirements" by the Intellectual Property Act 2014, s 3(4)(b), (6), in relation to designs created after 1 October 2014.

Sub-s (3): words in square brackets substituted for original words "those requirements" by the Intellectual Property Act 2014, s 3(4)(c), (6), in relation to designs created after 1 October 2014.

Sub-s (4): repealed by the Intellectual Property Act 2014, s 3(4)(d), (6), in relation to designs created after 1 October 2014; words ", commissioner of the design" in para (a) repealed by the Intellectual Property Act 2014, s 2(2)(h), subject to savings in s 2(3) of the 2014 Act as noted to s 215 at **[2.314]**.

[2.320]
221 Power to make further provision as to qualification

(1) Her Majesty may, with a view to fulfilling an international obligation of the United Kingdom, by Order in Council provide that a design qualifies for design right protection if such requirements as are specified in the Order are met.

(2) An Order may make different provision for different descriptions of design or article; and may make such consequential modifications of the operation of section 215 (ownership of design right) and sections 218 to 220 (other means of qualification) as appear to Her Majesty to be appropriate.

(3) A statutory instrument containing an Order in Council under this section shall be subject to annulment in pursuance of a resolution of either House of Parliament.

Dealings with design right

[2.321]
222 Assignment and licences

(1) Design right is transmissible by assignment, by testamentary disposition or by operation of law, as personal or moveable property.

(2) An assignment or other transmission of design right may be partial, that is, limited so as to apply—

(a) to one or more, but not all, of the things the design right owner has the exclusive right to do;

(b) to part, but not the whole, of the period for which the right is to subsist.

(3) An assignment of design right is not effective unless it is in writing signed by or on behalf of the assignor.

(4) A licence granted by the owner of design right is binding on every successor in title to his interest in the right, except a purchaser in good faith for valuable consideration and without notice (actual or constructive) of the licence or a person deriving title from such a purchaser; and references in this Part to doing anything with, or without, the licence of the design right owner shall be construed accordingly.

[2.322]
223 Prospective ownership of design right

(1) Where by an agreement made in relation to future design right, and signed by or on behalf of the prospective owner of the design right, the prospective owner purports to assign the future design right (wholly or partially) to another person, then if, on the right coming into existence, the assignee or another person claiming under him would be entitled as against all other persons to require the right to be vested in him, the right shall vest in him by virtue of this section.

(2) In this section—

"future design right" means design right which will or may come into existence in respect of a future design or class of designs or on the occurrence of a future event; and

"prospective owner" shall be construed accordingly, and includes a person who is prospectively entitled to design right by virtue of such an agreement as is mentioned in subsection (1).

(3) A licence granted by a prospective owner of design right is binding on every successor in title to his interest (or prospective interest) in the right, except a purchaser in good faith for valuable consideration and without notice (actual or constructive) of the licence or a person deriving title from such a purchaser; and references in this Part to doing anything with, or without, the licence of the design right owner shall be construed accordingly.

[2.323]

224 Assignment of right in registered design presumed to carry with it design right

Where a design consisting of a design in which design right subsists is registered under the Registered Designs Act 1949 and the proprietor of the registered design is also the design right owner, an assignment of the right in the registered design shall be taken to be also an assignment of the design right, unless a contrary intention appears.

[2.324]

225 Exclusive licences

(1) In this Part an "exclusive licence" means a licence in writing signed by or on behalf of the design right owner authorising the licensee to the exclusion of all other persons, including the person granting the licence, to exercise a right which would otherwise be exercisable exclusively by the design right owner.

(2) The licensee under an exclusive licence has the same rights against any successor in title who is bound by the licence as he has against the person granting the licence.

CHAPTER II
RIGHTS OF DESIGN RIGHT OWNER AND REMEDIES

Infringement of design right

[2.325]

226 Primary infringement of design right

(1) The owner of design right in a design has the exclusive right to reproduce the design for commercial purposes—

(a) by making articles to that design, or

(b) by making a design document recording the design for the purpose of enabling such articles to be made.

(2) Reproduction of a design by making articles to the design means copying the design so as to produce articles exactly or substantially to that design, and references in this Part to making articles to a design shall be construed accordingly.

(3) Design right is infringed by a person who without the licence of the design right owner does, or authorises another to do, anything which by virtue of this section is the exclusive right of the design right owner.

(4) For the purposes of this section reproduction may be direct or indirect, and it is immaterial whether any intervening acts themselves infringe the design right.

(5) This section has effect subject to the provisions of Chapter III (exceptions to rights of design right owner).

[2.326]

227 Secondary infringement: importing or dealing with infringing article

(1) Design right is infringed by a person who, without the licence of the design right owner—

(a) imports into the United Kingdom for commercial purposes, or

(b) has in his possession for commercial purposes, or

(c) sells, lets for hire, or offers or exposes for sale or hire, in the course of a business,

an article which is, and which he knows or has reason to believe is, an infringing article.

(2) This section has effect subject to the provisions of Chapter III (exceptions to rights of design right owner).

[2.327]

228 Meaning of "infringing article"

(1) In this Part "infringing article", in relation to a design, shall be construed in accordance with this section.

(2) An article is an infringing article if its making to that design was an infringement of design right in the design.

(3) An article is also an infringing article if—

(a) it has been or is proposed to be imported into the United Kingdom, and

(b) its making to that design in the United Kingdom would have been an infringement of design right in the design or a breach of an exclusive licence agreement relating to the design.

(4) Where it is shown that an article is made to a design in which design right subsists or has subsisted at any time, it shall be presumed until the contrary is proved that the article was made at a time when design right subsisted.

(5) Nothing in subsection (3) shall be construed as applying to an article which may lawfully be imported into the United Kingdom by virtue of any enforceable [EU] right within the meaning of section 2(1) of the European Communities Act 1972.

(6) The expression "infringing article" does not include a design document, notwithstanding that its making was or would have been an infringement of design right.

NOTES

Sub-s (5): reference in square brackets substituted by the Treaty of Lisbon (Changes in Terminology) Order 2011, SI 2011/1043, art 6(1)(f).

Remedies for infringement

[2.328]

229 Rights and remedies of design right owner

(1) An infringement of design right is actionable by the design right owner.

(2) In an action for infringement of design right all such relief by way of damages, injunctions, accounts or otherwise is available to the plaintiff as is available in respect of the infringement of any other property right.

(3) The court may in an action for infringement of design right, having regard to all the circumstances and in particular to—

(a) the flagrancy of the infringement, and

(b) any benefit accruing to the defendant by reason of the infringement,

award such additional damages as the justice of the case may require.

(4) This section has effect subject to section 233 (innocent infringement).

[2.329]

230 Order for delivery up

(1) Where a person—

(a) has in his possession, custody or control for commercial purposes an infringing article, or

(b) has in his possession, custody or control anything specifically designed or adapted for making articles to a particular design, knowing or having reason to believe that it has been or is to be used to make an infringing article,

the owner of the design right in the design in question may apply to the court for an order that the infringing article or other thing be delivered up to him or to such other person as the court may direct.

(2) An application shall not be made after the end of the period specified in the following provisions of this section; and no order shall be made unless the court also makes, or it appears to the court that there are grounds for making, an order under section 231 (order as to disposal of infringing article, &c).

(3) An application for an order under this section may not be made after the end of the period of six years from the date on which the article or thing in question was made, subject to subsection (4).

(4) If during the whole or any part of that period the design right owner—

(a) is under a disability, or

(b) is prevented by fraud or concealment from discovering the facts entitling him to apply for an order,

an application may be made at any time before the end of the period of six years from the date on which he ceased to be under a disability or, as the case may be, could with reasonable diligence have discovered those facts.

(5) In subsection (4) "disability"—

(a) in England and Wales, has the same meaning as in the Limitation Act 1980;

(b) in Scotland, means legal disability within the meaning of the Prescription and Limitation (Scotland) Act 1973;

(c) in Northern Ireland, has the same meaning as in the Statute of Limitations (Northern Ireland) 1958.

(6) A person to whom an infringing article or other thing is delivered up in pursuance of an order under this section shall, if an order under section 231 is not made, retain it pending the making of an order, or the decision not to make an order, under that section.

(7) Nothing in this section affects any other power of the court.

NOTES

Statute of Limitations (Northern Ireland) 1958: repealed and replaced by the Limitation (Northern Ireland) Order 1989, SI 1989/1339.

[2.330]

231 Order as to disposal of infringing articles, &c

(1) An application may be made to the court for an order that an infringing article or other thing delivered up in pursuance of an order under section 230 shall be—

(a) forfeited to the design right owner, or

(b) destroyed or otherwise dealt with as the court may think fit,

or for a decision that no such order should be made.

(2) In considering what order (if any) should be made, the court shall consider whether other remedies available in an action for infringement of design right would be adequate to compensate the design right owner and to protect his interests.

(3) Provision shall be made by rules of court as to the service of notice on persons having an interest in the article or other thing, and any such person is entitled—

(a) to appear in proceedings for an order under this section, whether or not he was served with notice, and
(b) to appeal against any order made, whether or not he appeared;

and an order shall not take effect until the end of the period within which notice of an appeal may be given or, if before the end of that period notice of appeal is duly given, until the final determination or abandonment of the proceedings on the appeal.

(4) Where there is more than one person interested in an article or other thing, the court shall make such order as it thinks just and may (in particular) direct that the thing be sold, or otherwise dealt with, and the proceeds divided.

(5) If the court decides that no order should be made under this section, the person in whose possession, custody or control the article or other thing was before being delivered up . . . is entitled to its return.

(6) References in this section to a person having an interest in an article or other thing include any person in whose favour an order could be made in respect of it under this section—

[(a) under this section or under section 114 or 204 of this Act;
(b) under section 24D of the Registered Designs Act 1949;
(c) under section 19 of Trade Marks Act 1994 (including that section as applied by regulation 4 of the Community Trade Mark Regulations 2006 (SI 2006/1027)); or
(d) under regulation 1C of the Community Design Regulations 2005 (SI 2005/2339).]

NOTES

Sub-s (5): words omitted repealed by the Intellectual Property (Enforcement, etc) Regulations 2006, SI 2006/1028, reg 2(4), Sch 4.

Sub-s (6): paras (a)–(d) substituted by SI 2006/1028, reg 2(2), Sch 2, paras 6, 14.

[2.331]
232 Jurisdiction of county court and sheriff court

(1) In England [and Wales the county court and in] Northern Ireland a county court may entertain proceedings under—

section 230 (order for delivery up of infringing article, &c),
section 231 (order as to disposal of infringing article, &c), or
section 235(5) (application by exclusive licensee having concurrent rights),

[save that, in Northern Ireland, a county court may entertain such proceedings only] where the value of the infringing articles and other things in question does not exceed the county court limit for actions in tort.

(2) In Scotland proceedings for an order under any of those provisions may be brought in the sheriff court.

(3) Nothing in this section shall be construed as affecting the jurisdiction of the High Court or, in Scotland, the Court of Session.

NOTES

Sub-s (1): words in first pair of square brackets substituted by the Crime and Courts Act 2013, s 17(5), Sch 9, Pt 3, para 72; words in second pair of square brackets inserted by the High Court and County Courts Jurisdiction Order 1991, SI 1991/724, art 2(8), Schedule, Pt I.

[2.332]
233 Innocent infringement

(1) Where in an action for infringement of design right brought by virtue of section 226 (primary infringement) it is shown that at the time of the infringement the defendant did not know, and had no reason to believe, that design right subsisted in the design to which the action relates, the plaintiff is not entitled to damages against him, but without prejudice to any other remedy.

(2) Where in an action for infringement of design right brought by virtue of section 227 (secondary infringement) a defendant shows that the infringing article was innocently acquired by him or a predecessor in title of his, the only remedy available against him in respect of the infringement is damages not exceeding a reasonable royalty in respect of the act complained of.

(3) In subsection (2) "innocently acquired" means that the person acquiring the article did not know and had no reason to believe that it was an infringing article.

[2.333]
234 Rights and remedies of exclusive licensee

(1) An exclusive licensee has, except against the design right owner, the same rights and remedies in respect of matters occurring after the grant of the licence as if the licence had been an assignment.

(2) His rights and remedies are concurrent with those of the design right owner; and references in the relevant provisions of this Part to the design right owner shall be construed accordingly.

(3) In an action brought by an exclusive licensee by virtue of this section a defendant may avail himself of any defence which would have been available to him if the action had been brought by the design right owner.

[2.334]
235 Exercise of concurrent rights

(1) Where an action for infringement of design right brought by the design right owner or an exclusive licensee relates (wholly or partly) to an infringement in respect of which they have concurrent rights of action, the design right owner or, as the case may be, the exclusive licensee may not, without the leave of the court, proceed with the action unless the other is either joined as a plaintiff or added as a defendant.

(2) A design right owner or exclusive licensee who is added as a defendant in pursuance of subsection (1) is not liable for any costs in the action unless he takes part in the proceedings.

(3) The above provisions do not affect the granting of interlocutory relief on the application of the design right owner or an exclusive licensee.

(4) Where an action for infringement of design right is brought which relates (wholly or partly) to an infringement in respect of which the design right owner and an exclusive licensee have concurrent rights of action—

- (a) the court shall, in assessing damages, take into account—
  - (i) the terms of the licence, and
  - (ii) any pecuniary remedy already awarded or available to either of them in respect of the infringement;
- (b) no account of profits shall be directed if an award of damages has been made, or an account of profits has been directed, in favour of the other of them in respect of the infringement; and
- (c) the court shall if an account of profits is directed apportion the profits between them as the court considers just, subject to any agreement between them;

and these provisions apply whether or not the design right owner and the exclusive licensee are both parties to the action.

(5) The design right owner shall notify any exclusive licensee having concurrent rights before applying for an order under section 230 (order for delivery up of infringing article, &c); and the court may on the application of the licensee make such order under that section as it thinks fit having regard to the terms of the licence.

CHAPTER III
EXCEPTIONS TO RIGHTS OF DESIGN RIGHT OWNERS

Infringement of copyright

[2.335]
236 Infringement of copyright

Where copyright subsists in a work which consists of or includes a design in which design right subsists, it is not an infringement of design right in the design to do anything which is an infringement of the copyright in that work.

Availability of licences of right

[2.336]
237 Licences available in last five years of design right

(1) Any person is entitled as of right to a licence to do in the last five years of the design right term anything which would otherwise infringe the design right.

(2) The terms of the licence shall, in default of agreement, be settled by the comptroller.

(3) The Secretary of State may if it appears to him necessary in order to—

- (a) comply with an international obligation of the United Kingdom, or
- (b) secure or maintain reciprocal protection for British designs in other countries,

by order exclude from the operation of subsection (1) designs of a description specified in the order or designs applied to articles of a description so specified.

(4) An order shall be made by statutory instrument; and no order shall be made unless a draft of it has been laid before and approved by a resolution of each House of Parliament.

[2.337]
238 Powers exercisable for protection of the public interest

[(1) Subsection (1A) applies where whatever needs to be remedied, mitigated or prevented by the Secretary of State [or (as the case may be) the Competition and Markets Authority] under section 12(5) of the Competition Act 1980 or section 41(2), 55(2), 66(6), 75(2), 83(2), 138(2), 147(2)[, 147A(2)] or 160(2) of, or paragraph 5(2) or 10(2) of Schedule 7 to, the Enterprise Act 2002 (powers to take remedial action following references to the [Competition and Markets Authority] in connection with public bodies and certain other persons, mergers or market investigations etc) consists of or includes—

- (a) conditions in licences granted by a design right owner restricting the use of the design by the licensee or the right of the design right owner to grant other licences, or
- (b) a refusal of a design right owner to grant licences on reasonable terms.

(1A) The powers conferred by Schedule 8 to the Enterprise Act 2002 include power to cancel or modify those conditions and, instead or in addition, to provide that licences in respect of the design right shall be available as of right.

(2) The references to anything permitted by Schedule 8 to the Enterprise Act 2002 in section 12(5A) of the Competition Act 1980 and in sections 75(4)(a), 83(4)(a), 84(2)(a), 89(1), 160(4)(a), 161(3)(a) and 164(1) of, and paragraphs 5, 10 and 11 of Schedule 7 to, the Act of 2002 shall be construed accordingly.]

(3) The terms of a licence available by virtue of this section shall, in default of agreement, be settled by the comptroller.

NOTES

Sub-s (1): substituted together with sub-ss (1A), (2) for original sub-ss (1), (2), by the Enterprise Act 2002, s 278, Sch 25, para 18(1), (4), subject to transitional provisions and savings in s 276 of, Sch 24, paras 2–12, 14–19 to, the 2002 Act, and SI 2004/3233, arts 3–5; words in first and third pairs of square brackets substituted and figure in second pair of square brackets inserted by the Enterprise and Regulatory Reform Act 2013 (Competition) (Consequential, Transitional and Saving Provisions) Order 2014, SI 2014/892, art 2, Sch 1, Pt 2, paras 55, 58.

Sub-s (1A): substituted as noted to sub-s (1) above.

Sub-s (2): substituted as noted to sub-s (1) above.

Modification: The reference in sub-s (1) to the Enterprise Act 2002, s 66(6), Sch 7, paras 5(2), 10(2) shall have effect as if it included a reference to the Enterprise Act 2002 (Protection of Legitimate Interests) Order 2003, SI 2003/1592, art 12(7), Sch 2, paras 5(2), 10(2) respectively and the reference in sub-s (2) to the 2002 Act, Sch 7, paras 5, 10, 11 shall have effect as if it included a reference to SI 2003/1592, Sch 2, paras 5, 10, 11 respectively; see SI 2003/1592, Sch 4, para 7(2).

[2.338]

239 Undertaking to take licence of right in infringement proceedings

(1) If in proceedings for infringement of design right in a design in respect of which a licence is available as of right under section 237 or 238 the defendant undertakes to take a licence on such terms as may be agreed or, in default of agreement, settled by the comptroller under that section—

- (a) no injunction shall be granted against him,
- (b) no order for delivery up shall be made under section 230, and
- (c) the amount recoverable against him by way of damages or on an account of profits shall not exceed double the amount which would have been payable by him as licensee if such a licence on those terms had been granted before the earliest infringement.

(2) An undertaking may be given at any time before final order in the proceedings, without any admission of liability.

(3) Nothing in this section affects the remedies available in respect of an infringement committed before licences of right were available.

Crown use of designs

[2.339]

240 Crown use of designs

(1) A government department, or a person authorised in writing by a government department, may without the licence of the design right owner—

- (a) do anything for the purpose of supplying articles for the services of the Crown, or
- (b) dispose of articles no longer required for the services of the Crown;

and nothing done by virtue of this section infringes the design right.

(2) References in this Part to "the services of the Crown" are to—

- (a) the defence of the realm,
- (b) foreign defence purposes, and
- (c) health service purposes.

(3) The reference to the supply of articles for "foreign defence purposes" is to their supply—

- (a) for the defence of a country outside the realm in pursuance of an agreement or arrangement to which the government of that country and Her Majesty's Government in the United Kingdom are parties; or
- (b) for use by armed forces operating in pursuance of a resolution of the United Nations or one of its organs.

(4) The reference to the supply of articles for "health service purposes" are to their supply for the purpose of providing—

- [(za) primary medical services or primary dental services under [the National Health Service Act 2006 or the National Health Service (Wales) Act 2006,] [or primary medical services under Part 1 of the National Health Service (Scotland) Act 1978]]
- [(a) pharmaceutical services, general medical services or general dental services under—
  - [(i) Chapter 1 of Part 7 of the National Health Service Act 2006, or Chapter 1 of Part 7 of the National Health Service (Wales) Act 2006 (in the case of pharmaceutical services),]
  - (ii) Part II of the National Health Service (Scotland) Act 1978 [(in the case of *pharmaceutical services or* general dental services)], or
  - (iii) the corresponding provisions of the law in force in Northern Ireland; or
- (b) personal medical services or personal dental services in accordance with arrangements made under—
  - (i) . . . ,
  - (ii) section 17C of the 1978 Act [(in the case of personal dental services)], or
  - (iii) the corresponding provisions of the law in force in Northern Ireland;] [or

(c) local pharmaceutical services provided under [the National Health Service Act 2006 or the National Health Service (Wales) Act 2006][; or
(d) pharmaceutical care services under Part 1 of the National Health Service (Scotland) Act 1978].]

(5) In this Part—

"Crown use", in relation to a design, means the doing of anything by virtue of this section which would otherwise be an infringement of design right in the design; and

"the government department concerned", in relation to such use, means the government department by whom or on whose authority the act was done.

(6) The authority of a government department in respect of Crown use of a design may be given to a person either before or after the use and whether or not he is authorised, directly or indirectly, by the design right owner to do anything in relation to the design.

(7) A person acquiring anything sold in the exercise of powers conferred by this section, and any person claiming under him, may deal with it in the same manner as if the design right were held on behalf of the Crown.

NOTES

Sub-s (4) is amended as follows:

Para (za) inserted by the Health and Social Care (Community Health and Standards) Act 2003, s 184, Sch 11, para 52(a); words in first pair of square brackets substituted by the National Health Service (Consequential Provisions) Act 2006, s 2, Sch 1, paras 111, 113(a); words in second pair of square brackets inserted by the Primary Medical Services (Scotland) Act 2004 (Consequential Modifications) Order 2004, SI 2004/957, art 2, Schedule, para 5(a).

Paras (a), (b) substituted by the National Health Service (Primary Care) Act 1997, s 41(10), Sch 2, Pt I, para 63; para (a)(i) substituted by the National Health Service (Consequential Provisions) Act 2006, s 2, Sch 1, paras 111, 113(b); words in square brackets in paras (a)(ii), (b)(ii) inserted by SI 2004/957, art 2, Schedule, para 5(b), (c); words in italics in para (a)(ii) repealed, in relation to England, Wales and Northern Ireland, by the Smoking, Health and Social Care (Scotland) Act 2005 (Consequential Modifications) (England, Wales and Northern Ireland) Order 2006, SI 2006/1056, art 2, Schedule, Pt 1, para 4(a), as from the day on which the Smoking, Health and Social Care (Scotland) Act 2005, s 20 comes into force; para (b)(i) repealed by the Health and Social Care (Community Health and Standards) Act 2003, ss 184, 196, Sch 11, para 52(b), (c), Sch 14.

Para (c) and the word immediately preceding it inserted by the Health and Social Care Act 2001, s 67(1), Sch 5, Pt 1, para 7; words in square brackets substituted by the National Health Service (Consequential Provisions) Act 2006, s 2, Sch 1, paras 111, 113(c).

Para (d) and the word immediately preceding it inserted, in relation to England, Wales and Northern Ireland, by SI 2006/1056, art 2, Schedule, Pt 1, para 4(b), as from the day on which the Smoking, Health and Social Care (Scotland) Act 2005, s 20 comes into force.

[2.340]

241 Settlement of terms for Crown use

(1) Where Crown use is made of a design, the government department concerned shall—
(a) notify the design right owner as soon as practicable, and
(b) give him such information as to the extent of the use as he may from time to time require,

unless it appears to the department that it would be contrary to the public interest to do so or the identity of the design right owner cannot be ascertained on reasonable inquiry.

(2) Crown use of a design shall be on such terms as, either before or after the use, are agreed between the government department concerned and the design right owner with the approval of the Treasury or, in default of agreement, are determined by the court.

In the application of this subsection to Northern Ireland the reference to the Treasury shall, where the government department referred to in that subsection is a Northern Ireland department, be construed as a reference to the Department of Finance and Personnel.

[In the application of this subsection to Scotland, where the government department referred to in that subsection is any part of the Scottish administration, the words "with the approval of the Treasury" are omitted.]

(3) Where the identity of the design right owner cannot be ascertained on reasonable inquiry, the government department concerned may apply to the court who may order that no royalty or other sum shall be payable in respect of Crown use of the design until the owner agrees terms with the department or refers the matter to the court for determination.

NOTES

Sub-s (2): words in square brackets added by the Scotland Act 1998 (Consequential Modifications) (No 2) Order 1999, SI 1999/1820, art 4, Sch 2, Pt I, para 93(1), (2).

[2.341]

242 Rights of third parties in case of Crown use

(1) The provisions of any licence, assignment or agreement made between the design right owner (or anyone deriving title from him or from whom he derives title) and any person other than a government department are of no effect in relation to Crown use of a design, or any act incidental to Crown use, so far as they—
(a) restrict or regulate anything done in relation to the design, or the use of any model, document or other information relating to it, or
(b) provide for the making of payments in respect of, or calculated by reference to such use;

and the copying or issuing to the public of copies of any such model or document in connection with the thing done, or any such use, shall be deemed not to be an infringement of any copyright in the model or document.

(2) Subsection (1) shall not be construed as authorising the disclosure of any such model, document or information in contravention of the licence, assignment or agreement.

(3) Where an exclusive licence is in force in respect of the design—

(a) if the licence was granted for royalties—

(i) any agreement between the design right owner and a government department under section 241 (settlement of terms for Crown use) requires the consent of the licensee, and

(ii) the licensee is entitled to recover from the design right owner such part of the payment for Crown use as may be agreed between them or, in default of agreement, determined by the court;

(b) if the licence was granted otherwise than for royalties—

(i) section 241 applies in relation to anything done which but for section 240 (Crown use) and subsection (1) above would be an infringement of the rights of the licensee with the substitution for references to the design right owner of references to the licensee, and

(ii) section 241 does not apply in relation to anything done by the licensee by virtue of an authority given under section 240.

(4) Where the design right has been assigned to the design right owner in consideration of royalties—

(a) section 241 applies in relation to Crown use of the design as if the references to the design right owner included the assignor, and any payment for Crown use shall be divided between them in such proportion as may be agreed or, in default of agreement, determined by the court; and

(b) section 241 applies in relation to any act incidental to Crown use as it applies in relation to Crown use of the design.

(5) Where any model, document or other information relating to a design is used in connection with Crown use of the design, or any act incidental to Crown use, section 241 applies to the use of the model, document or other information with the substitution for the references to the design right owner of references to the person entitled to the benefit of any provision of an agreement rendered inoperative by subsection (1) above.

(6) In this section—

"act incidental to Crown use" means anything done for the services of the Crown to the order of a government department by the design right owner in respect of a design;

"payment for Crown use" means such amount as is payable by the government department concerned by virtue of section 241; and

"royalties" includes any benefit determined by reference to the use of the design.

[2.342]

243 Crown use: compensation for loss of profit

(1) Where Crown use is made of a design, the government department concerned shall pay—

(a) to the design right owner, or

(b) if there is an exclusive licence in force in respect of the design, to the exclusive licensee,

compensation for any loss resulting from his not being awarded a contract to supply the articles made to the design.

(2) Compensation is payable only to the extent that such a contract could have been fulfilled from his existing manufacturing capacity; but is payable notwithstanding the existence of circumstances rendering him ineligible for the award of such a contract.

(3) In determining the loss, regard shall be had to the profit which would have been made on such a contract and to the extent to which any manufacturing capacity was under-used.

(4) No compensation is payable in respect of any failure to secure contracts for the supply of articles made to the design otherwise than for the services of the Crown.

(5) The amount payable shall, if not agreed between the design right owner or licensee and the government department concerned with the approval of the Treasury, be determined by the court on a reference under section 252; and it is in addition to any amount payable under section 241 or 242.

(6) In the application of this section to Northern Ireland, the reference in subsection (5) to the Treasury shall, where the government department concerned is a Northern Ireland department, be construed as a reference to the Department of Finance and Personnel.

[(7) In the application of this section to Scotland, where the government department referred to in subsection (5) is any part of the Scottish Administration, the words "with the approval of the Treasury" in that subsection are omitted.]

NOTES

Sub-s (7): added by the Scotland Act 1998 (Consequential Modifications) (No 2) Order 1999, SI 1999/1820, art 4, Sch 2, Pt I, para 93(1), (3).

[2.343]
244 Special provision for Crown use during emergency
(1) During a period of emergency the powers exercisable in relation to a design by virtue of section 240 (Crown use) include power to do any act which would otherwise be an infringement of design right for any purpose which appears to the government department concerned necessary or expedient—
(a) for the efficient prosecution of any war in which Her Majesty may be engaged;
(b) for the maintenance of supplies and services essential to the life of the community;
(c) for securing a sufficiency of supplies and services essential to the well-being of the community;
(d) for promoting the productivity of industry, commerce and agriculture;
(e) for fostering and directing exports and reducing imports, or imports of any classes, from all or any countries and for redressing the balance of trade;
(f) generally for ensuring that the whole resources of the community are available for use, and are used, in a manner best calculated to serve the interests of the community; or
(g) for assisting the relief of suffering and the restoration and distribution of essential supplies and services in any country outside the United Kingdom which is in grave distress as the result of war.
(2) References in this Part to the services of the Crown include, as respects a period of emergency, those purposes; and references to "Crown use" include any act which would apart from this section be an infringement of design right.
(3) In this section "period of emergency" means a period beginning with such date as may be declared by Order in Council to be the beginning, and ending with such date as may be so declared to be the end, of a period of emergency for the purposes of this section.
(4) No Order in Council under this section shall be submitted to Her Majesty unless a draft of it has been laid before and approved by a resolution of each House of Parliament.

[Miscellaneous

[2.344]
244A Exception for private acts, experiments and teaching
Design right is not infringed by—
(a) an act which is done privately and for purposes which are not commercial;
(b) an act which is done for experimental purposes; or
(c) an act of reproduction for teaching purposes or for the purpose of making citations provided that—
(i) the act of reproduction is compatible with fair trade practice and does not unduly prejudice the normal exploitation of the design, and
(ii) mention is made of the source.]

NOTES
Commencement: 1 October 2014.
Inserted, together with preceding heading and s 244B, by the Intellectual Property Act 2014, s 4.

[2.345]
[244B Exception for overseas ships and aircraft
Design right is not infringed by—
(a) the use of equipment on ships or aircraft which are registered in another country but which are temporarily in the United Kingdom;
(b) the importation into the United Kingdom of spare parts or accessories for the purpose of repairing such ships or aircraft; or
(c) the carrying out of repairs on such ships or aircraft.]

NOTES
Commencement: 1 October 2014.
Inserted as noted to s 244A at **[2.344]**.

General

[2.346]
245 Power to provide for further exceptions
(1) The Secretary of State may if it appears to him necessary in order to—
(a) comply with an international obligation of the United Kingdom, or
(b) secure or maintain reciprocal protection for British designs in other countries,
by order provide that acts of a description specified in the order do not infringe design right.
(2) An order may make different provision for different descriptions of design or article.
(3) An order shall be made by statutory instrument and no order shall be made unless a draft of it has been laid before and approved by a resolution of each House of Parliament.

CHAPTER IV
JURISDICTION OF THE COMPTROLLER AND THE COURT

Jurisdiction of the comptroller

[2.347]

246 Jurisdiction to decide matters relating to design right

(1) A party to a dispute as to any of the following matters may refer the dispute to the comptroller for his decision—

(a) the subsistence of design right,

(b) the term of design right, or

(c) the identity of the person in whom design right first vested;

and the comptroller's decision on the reference is binding on the parties to the dispute.

(2) No other court or tribunal shall decide any such matter except—

(a) on a reference or appeal from the comptroller,

(b) in infringement or other proceedings in which the issue arises incidentally, or

(c) in proceedings brought with the agreement of the parties or the leave of the comptroller.

(3) The comptroller has jurisdiction to decide any incidental question of fact or law arising in the course of a reference under this section.

[2.348]

247 Application to settle terms of licence of right

(1) A person requiring a licence which is available as of right by virtue of

(a) section 237 (licences available in last five years of design right), or

(b) an order under section 238 (licences made available in the public interest),

may apply to the comptroller to settle the terms of the licence.

(2) No application for the settlement of the terms of a licence available by virtue of section 237 may be made earlier than one year before the earliest date on which the licence may take effect under that section.

(3) The terms of a licence settled by the comptroller shall authorise the licensee to do—

(a) in the case of licence available by virtue of section 237, everything which would be an infringement of the design right in the absence of a licence;

(b) in the case of a licence available by virtue of section 238, everything in respect of which a licence is so available.

(4) In settling the terms of a licence the comptroller shall have regard to such factors as may be prescribed by the Secretary of State by order made by statutory instrument.

(5) No such order shall be made unless a draft of it has been laid before and approved by a resolution of each House of Parliament.

(6) Where the terms of a licence are settled by the comptroller, the licence has effect—

(a) in the case of an application in respect of a licence available by virtue of section 237 made before the earliest date on which the licence may take effect under that section, from that date;

(b) in any other case, from the date on which the application to the comptroller was made.

[2.349]

248 Settlement of terms where design right owner unknown

(1) This section applies where a person making an application under section 247 (settlement of terms of licence of right) is unable on reasonable inquiry to discover the identity of the design right owner.

(2) The comptroller may in settling the terms of the licence order that the licence shall be free of any obligation as to royalties or other payments.

(3) If such an order is made the design right owner may apply to the comptroller to vary the terms of the licence with effect from the date on which his application is made.

(4) If the terms of a licence are settled by the comptroller and it is subsequently established that a licence was not available as of right, the licensee shall not be liable in damages for, or for an account of profits in respect of, anything done before he was aware of any claim by the design right owner that a licence was not available.

[2.350]

249 Appeals as to terms of licence of right

(1) An appeal lies from any decision of the comptroller under section 247 or 248 (settlement of terms of licence of right) to [a person appointed under section 27A of the Registered Designs Act 1949].

(2) . . .

NOTES

Sub-s (1): words in square brackets substituted by the Intellectual Property Act 2014, s 10(7)(a).

Sub-s (2): repealed by the Intellectual Property Act 2014, s 10(7)(b).

[2.351]
[249A Opinions service

The descriptions of designs which may be specified in regulations under subsection (1)(b) of section 28A of the Registered Designs Act 1949 (requests to the comptroller for opinions on designs) include, in particular—

(a) designs in which design right subsists in accordance with this Part, and
(b) designs in relation to which there is a question whether design right so subsists.]

NOTES

Commencement: 1 October 2014.
Inserted by the Intellectual Property Act 2014, s 11(2).

[2.352]
250 Rules

(1) The Secretary of State may make rules for regulating the procedure to be followed in connection with any proceeding before the comptroller under this Part.
(2) Rules may, in particular, make provision—

(a) prescribing forms;
(b) requiring fees to be paid;
(c) authorising the rectification of irregularities of procedure;
(d) regulating the mode of giving evidence and empowering the comptroller to compel the attendance of witnesses and the discovery of and production of documents;
(e) providing for the appointment of advisers to assist the comptroller in proceedings before him;
(f) prescribing time limits for doing anything required to be done (and providing for the alteration of any such limit); and
(g) empowering the comptroller to award costs and to direct how, to what party and from what parties, costs are to be paid.

(3) Rules prescribing fees require the consent of the Treasury.
(4) The remuneration of an adviser appointed to assist the comptroller shall be determined by the Secretary of State with the consent of the Treasury and shall be defrayed out of money provided by Parliament.
(5) Rules shall be made by statutory instrument which shall be subject to annulment in pursuance of a resolution of either House of Parliament.

NOTES

Rules: the Design Right (Proceedings before Comptroller) Rules 1989, SI 1989/1130 at **[4.12]**; the Patents, Trade Marks and Designs (Address For Service and Time Limits, etc) Rules 2006, SI 2006/760; the Patents, Trade Marks and Designs (Address for Service) Rules 2009, SI 2009/546; the Appointed Person (Designs) Rules 2015, SI 2015/169.

Jurisdiction of the court

[2.353]
251 References and appeals on design right matters

(1) In any proceedings before him under section 246 (reference of matter relating to design right), the comptroller may at any time order the whole proceedings or any question or issue (whether of fact or law) to be referred, on such terms as he may direct, to the High Court or, in Scotland, the Court of Session.
(2) The comptroller shall make such an order if the parties to the proceedings agree that he should do so.
(3) On a reference under this section the court may exercise any power available to the comptroller by virtue of this Part as respects the matter referred to it and, following its determination, may refer any matter back to the comptroller.
(4) An appeal lies from any decision of the comptroller in proceedings before him under section 246 (decisions on matters relating to design right) to[—

(a)] the High Court or, in Scotland, the Court of Session[, or
(b) a person appointed under section 27A of the Registered Designs Act 1949].

NOTES

Sub-s (4): words in square brackets inserted by the Intellectual Property Act 2014, s 10(8).

[2.354]
252 Reference of disputes relating to Crown use

(1) A dispute as to any matter which falls to be determined by the court in default of agreement under—

(a) section 241 (settlement of terms for Crown use),
(b) section 242 (rights of third parties in case of Crown use), or
(c) section 243 (Crown use: compensation for loss of profit),

may be referred to the court by any party to the dispute.
(2) In determining a dispute between a government department and any person as to the terms for Crown use of a design the court shall have regard to—

(a) any sums which that person or a person from whom he derives title has received or is entitled to receive, directly or indirectly, from any government department in respect of the design; and
(b) whether that person or a person from whom he derives title has in the court's opinion without reasonable cause failed to comply with a request of the department for the use of the design on reasonable terms.

(3) One of two or more joint owners of design right may, without the concurrence of the others, refer a dispute to the court under this section, but shall not do so unless the others are made parties; and none of those others is liable for any costs unless he takes part in the proceedings.

(4) Where the consent of an exclusive licensee is required by section 242(3)(a)(i) to the settlement by agreement of the terms for Crown use of a design, a determination by the court of the amount of any payment to be made for such use is of no effect unless the licensee has been notified of the reference and given an opportunity to be heard.

(5) On the reference of a dispute as to the amount recoverable as mentioned in section 242(3)(a)(ii) (right of exclusive licensee to recover part of amount payable to design right owner) the court shall determine what is just having regard to any expenditure incurred by the licensee—
(a) in developing the design, or
(b) in making payments to the design right owner in consideration of the licence (other than royalties or other payments determined by reference to the use of the design).

(6) In this section "the court" means—
(a) in England and Wales, the High [Court],
(b) in Scotland, the Court of Session, and
(c) in Northern Ireland, the High Court.

NOTES

Sub-s (6): word in square brackets in para (a) substituted by the Crime and Courts Act 2013, s 17(5), Sch 9, Pt 2, para 30(1), (2).

CHAPTER V
MISCELLANEOUS AND GENERAL

Miscellaneous

[2.355]
253 Remedy for groundless threats of infringement proceedings

(1) Where a person threatens another person with proceedings for infringement of design right, a person aggrieved by the threats may bring an action against him claiming—
(a) a declaration to the effect that the threats are unjustifiable;
(b) an injunction against the continuance of the threats;
(c) damages in respect of any loss which he has sustained by the threats.

(2) If the plaintiff proves that the threats were made and that he is a person aggrieved by them, he is entitled to the relief claimed unless the defendant shows that the acts in respect of which proceedings were threatened did constitute, or if done would have constituted, an infringement of the design right concerned.

(3) Proceedings may not be brought under this section in respect of a threat to bring proceedings for an infringement alleged to consist of making or importing anything.

(4) Mere notification that a design is protected by design right does not constitute a threat of proceedings for the purposes of this section.

NOTES

Section 253 is substituted (by new ss 253, 253A–253E and preceding heading) by the Intellectual Property (Unjustified Threats) Act 2017, s 5(1), (2), as from a day to be appointed, as follows—

"Unjustified threats

253 Threats of infringement proceedings

(1) A communication contains a "threat of infringement proceedings" if a reasonable person in the position of a recipient would understand from the communication that—
(a) design right subsists in a design, and
(b) a person intends to bring proceedings (whether in a court in the United Kingdom or elsewhere) against another person for infringement of the design right by—
(i) an act done in the United Kingdom, or
(ii) an act which, if done, would be done in the United Kingdom.

(2) References in this section and in section 253C to a "recipient" include, in the case of a communication directed to the public or a section of the public, references to a person to whom the communication is directed.

253A Actionable threats

(1) Subject to subsections (2) to (5), a threat of infringement proceedings made by any person is actionable by any person aggrieved by the threat.

(2) A threat of infringement proceedings is not actionable if the infringement is alleged to consist of—
(a) making an article for disposal, or
(b) importing an article for disposal.

Part 2 Copyright

(3) A threat of infringement proceedings is not actionable if the infringement is alleged to consist of an act which, if done, would constitute an infringement of a kind mentioned in subsection (2)(a) or (b).

(4) A threat of infringement proceedings is not actionable if the threat—

(a) is made to a person who has done, or intends to do, an act mentioned in subsection (2)(a) or (b) in relation to an article, and

(b) is a threat of proceedings for an infringement alleged to consist of doing anything else in relation to that article.

(5) A threat of infringement proceedings which is not an express threat is not actionable if it is contained in a permitted communication.

(6) In sections 253C and 253D an "actionable threat" means a threat of infringement proceedings that is actionable in accordance with this section.

253B Permitted communications

(1) For the purposes of section 253A(5), a communication containing a threat of infringement proceedings is a "permitted communication" if—

(a) the communication, so far as it contains information that relates to the threat, is made for a permitted purpose;

(b) all of the information that relates to the threat is information that—

(i) is necessary for that purpose (see subsection (5)(a) to (c) for some examples of necessary information), and

(ii) the person making the communication reasonably believes is true.

(2) Each of the following is a "permitted purpose"—

(a) giving notice that design right subsists in a design;

(b) discovering whether, or by whom, design right in a design has been infringed by an act mentioned in section 253A(2)(a) or (b);

(c) giving notice that a person has a right in or under the design right in a design, where another person's awareness of the right is relevant to any proceedings that may be brought in respect of the design right in the design.

(3) The court may, having regard to the nature of the purposes listed in subsection (2)(a) to (c), treat any other purpose as a "permitted purpose" if it considers that it is in the interests of justice to do so.

(4) But the following may not be treated as a "permitted purpose"—

(a) requesting a person to cease doing, for commercial purposes, anything in relation to an article made to a design,

(b) requesting a person to deliver up or destroy an article made to a design, or

(c) requesting a person to give an undertaking relating to an article made to a design.

(5) If any of the following information is included in a communication made for a permitted purpose, it is information that is "necessary for that purpose" (see subsection (1)(b)(i))—

(a) a statement that design right subsists in a design;

(b) details of the design, or of a right in or under the design right in the design, which—

(i) are accurate in all material respects, and

(ii) are not misleading in any material respect; and

(c) information enabling the identification of articles that are alleged to be infringing articles in relation to the design.

253C Remedies and defences

(1) Proceedings in respect of an actionable threat may be brought against the person who made the threat for—

(a) a declaration that the threat is unjustified;

(b) an injunction against the continuance of the threat;

(c) damages in respect of any loss sustained by the aggrieved person by reason of the threat.

(2) It is a defence for the person who made the threat to show that the act in respect of which proceedings were threatened constitutes (or if done would constitute) an infringement of design right.

(3) It is a defence for the person who made the threat to show—

(a) that, despite having taken reasonable steps, the person has not identified anyone who has done an act mentioned in section 253A(2)(a) or (b) in relation to the article which is the subject of the threat, and

(b) that the person notified the recipient, before or at the time of making the threat, of the steps taken.

253D Professional advisers

(1) Proceedings in respect of an actionable threat may not be brought against a professional adviser (or any person vicariously liable for the actions of that professional adviser) if the conditions in subsection (3) are met.

(2) In this section "professional adviser" means a person who, in relation to the making of the communication containing the threat—

(a) is acting in a professional capacity in providing legal services or the services of a trade mark attorney or a patent attorney, and

(b) is regulated in the provision of legal services, or the services of a trade mark attorney or a patent attorney, by one or more regulatory bodies (whether through membership of a regulatory body, the issue of a licence to practise or any other means).

(3) The conditions are that—

(a) in making the communication the professional adviser is acting on the instructions of another person, and

(b) when the communication is made the professional adviser identifies the person on whose instructions the adviser is acting.

(4) This section does not affect any liability of the person on whose instructions the professional adviser is acting.

(5) It is for a person asserting that subsection (1) applies to prove (if required) that at the material time—

(a) the person concerned was acting as a professional adviser, and

(b) the conditions in subsection (3) were met.

253E Supplementary: proceedings for delivery up etc

In section 253(1)(b) the reference to proceedings for infringement of design right includes a reference to—

(a) proceedings for an order under section 230 (order for delivery up), and

(b) proceedings for an order under section 231 (order as to disposal of infringing articles).".

[Licensee under licence of right not to claim connection with design right owner]

NOTES

Heading inserted by the Intellectual Property (Unjustified Threats) Act 2017, s 5(1), (3), as from a day to be appointed.

[2.356]

254 Licensee under licence of right not to claim connection with design right owner

(1) A person who has a licence in respect of a design by virtue of section 237 or 238 (licences of right) shall not, without the consent of the design right owner—

(a) apply to goods which he is marketing, or proposes to market, in reliance on that licence a trade description indicating that he is the licensee of the design right owner, or

(b) use any such trade description in an advertisement in relation to such goods.

(2) A contravention of subsection (1) is actionable by the design right owner.

(3) In this section "trade description", the reference to applying a trade description to goods and "advertisement" have the same meaning as in the Trade Descriptions Act 1968.

Extent of operation of this Part

[2.357]

255 Countries to which this Part extends

(1) This Part extends to England and Wales, Scotland and Northern Ireland.

(2) Her Majesty may by Order in Council direct that this Part shall extend, subject to such exceptions and modifications as may be specified in the Order, to—

(a) any of the Channel Islands,

(b) the Isle of Man, or

(c) any colony.

(3) That power includes power to extend, subject to such exceptions and modifications as may be specified in the Order, any Order in Council made under section 221 (further provision as to qualification for design right protection) or section 256 (countries enjoying reciprocal protection).

(4) The legislature of a country to which this Part has been extended may modify or add to the provisions of this Part, in their operation as part of the law of that country, as the legislature may consider necessary to adapt the provisions to the circumstances of that country; but not so as to deny design right protection in a case where it would otherwise exist.

(5) Where a country to which this Part extends ceases to be a colony of the United Kingdom, it shall continue to be treated as such a country for the purposes of this Part until—

(a) an Order in Council is made under section 256 designating it as a country enjoying reciprocal protection, or

(b) an Order in Council is made declaring that it shall cease to be so treated by reason of the fact that the provisions of this Part as part of the law of that country have been amended or repealed.

(6) A statutory instrument containing an Order in Council under subsection (5)(b) shall be subject to annulment in pursuance of a resolution of either House of Parliament.

[2.358]

256 Countries enjoying reciprocal protection

(1) Her Majesty may, if it appears to Her that the law of a country provides adequate protection for British designs, by Order in Council designate that country as one enjoying reciprocal protection under this Part.

(2) If the law of a country provides adequate protection only for certain classes of British design, or only for designs applied to certain classes of article, any Order designating that country shall contain provision limiting, to a corresponding extent, the protection afforded by this Part in relation to designs connected with that country.

(3) An Order under this section shall be subject to annulment in pursuance of a resolution of either House of Parliament.

NOTES

Orders: the Design Right (Reciprocal Protection) (No 2) Order 1989, SI 1989/1294.

[2.359]

257 Territorial waters and the continental shelf

(1) For the purposes of this Part the territorial waters of the United Kingdom shall be treated as part of the United Kingdom.

(2) This Part applies to things done in the United Kingdom sector of the continental shelf on a structure or vessel which is present there for purposes directly connected with the exploration of the sea bed or subsoil or the exploitation of their natural resources as it applies to things done in the United Kingdom.

(3) The United Kingdom sector of the continental shelf means the areas designated by order under section 1(7) of the Continental Shelf Act 1964.

Interpretation

[2.360]
258 Construction of references to design right owner
(1) Where different persons are (whether in consequence of a partial assignment or otherwise) entitled to different aspects of design right in a work, the design right owner for any purpose of this Part is the person who is entitled to the right in the respect relevant for that purpose.
(2) Where design right (or any aspect of design right) is owned by more than one person jointly, references in this Part to the design right owner are to all the owners, so that, in particular, any requirement of the licence of the design right owner requires the licence of all of them.

[2.361]
259 Joint designs
(1) In this Part a "joint design" means a design produced by the collaboration of two or more designers in which the contribution of each is not distinct from that of the other or others.
(2) References in this Part to the designer of a design shall, except as otherwise provided, be construed in relation to a joint design as references to all the designers of the design.

[2.362]
260 Application of provisions to articles in kit form
(1) The provisions of this Part apply in relation to a kit, that is, a complete or substantially complete set of components intended to be assembled into an article, as they apply in relation to the assembled article.
(2) Subsection (1) does not affect the question whether design right subsists in any aspect of the design of the components of a kit as opposed to the design of the assembled article.

[2.363]
261 Requirement of signature: application in relation to body corporate
The requirement in the following provisions that an instrument be signed by or on behalf of a person is also satisfied in the case of a body corporate by the affixing of its seal—
section 222(3) (assignment of design right),
section 223(1) (assignment of future design right),
section 225(1) (grant of exclusive licence).

[2.364]
262 Adaptation of expressions in relation to Scotland
In the application of this Part to Scotland—
"account of profits" means accounting and payment of profits;
"accounts" means count, reckoning and payment;
"assignment" means assignation;
"costs" means expenses;
["declaration" means "declarator";]
"defendant" means defender;
"delivery up" means delivery;
"injunction" means interdict;
"interlocutory relief" means interim remedy; and
"plaintiff" means pursuer.

NOTES
Words in square brackets inserted by the Intellectual Property (Unjustified Threats) Act 2017, s 5(1), (4), as from a day to be appointed.

[2.365]
263 Minor definitions
(1) In this Part—
"British design" means a design which qualifies for design right protection by reason of a connection with the United Kingdom of the designer or the person by whom *the design is commissioned or* the designer is employed;
"business" includes a trade or profession;
"commission" means a commission for money or money's worth;
"the comptroller" means the Comptroller-General of Patents, Designs and Trade Marks;
"computer-generated", in relation to a design, means that the design is generated by computer in circumstances such that there is no human designer,
"country" includes any territory;
"the Crown" includes the Crown in right of Her Majesty's Government in Northern Ireland [and the Crown in right of the Scottish Administration] [and the Crown in right of the Welsh Assembly Government];
"design document" means any record of a design, whether in the form of a drawing, a written description, a photograph, data stored in a computer or otherwise;
"employee", "employment" and "employer" refer to employment under a contract of service or of apprenticeship;

"government department" includes a Northern Ireland department [and any part of the Scottish Administration] [and any part of the Welsh Assembly Government].

(2) References in this Part to "marketing", in relation to an article, are to its being sold or let for hire, or offered or exposed for sale or hire, in the course of a business, and related expressions shall be construed accordingly; but no account shall be taken for the purposes of this Part of marketing which is merely colourable and not intended to satisfy the reasonable requirements of the public.

(3) References in this Part to an act being done in relation to an article for "commercial purposes" are to its being done with a view to the article in question being sold or hired in the course of a business.

NOTES

Sub-s (1): words in italics repealed by the Intellectual Property Act 2014, s 2(2)(i), (j), subject to savings in s 2(3) of the 2014 Act as noted to s 215 at **[2.314]**; in definitions "the Crown" and "government department" words in first pair of square brackets added by the Scotland Act 1998 (Consequential Modifications) (No 2) Order 1999, SI 1999/1820, art 4, Sch 2, Pt I, para 93(1), (4), words in second pair of square brackets added by the Government of Wales Act 2006, s 160(1), Sch 10, paras 22, 31.

[2.366]

264 Index of defined expressions

The following Table shows provisions defining or otherwise explaining expressions used in this Part (other than provisions defining or explaining an expression used only in the same section)—

account of profits and accounts (in Scotland)	section 262
assignment (in Scotland)	section 262
British designs	section 263(1)
business	section 263(1)
commercial purposes	section 263(3)
commission	*section 263(1)*
the comptroller	section 263(1)
computer-generated	section 263(1)
costs (in Scotland)	section 262
country	section 263(1)
the Crown	section 263(1)
Crown use	sections 240(5) and 244(2)
defendant (in Scotland)	section 262
delivery up (in Scotland)	section 262
design	section 213(2)
design document	section 263(1)
designer	sections 214 and 259(2)
design right	section 213(1)
design right owner	sections 234(2) and 258
employee, employment and employer	section 263(1)
exclusive licence	section 225(1)
government department	section 263(1)
government department concerned (in relation to Crown use)	section 240(5)
infringing article	section 228
injunction (in Scotland)	section 262
interlocutory relief (in Scotland)	section 262
joint design	section 259(1)
licence (of the design right owner)	sections 222(4), 223(3) and 258
making articles to a design	section 226(2)
marketing (and related expressions)	section 263(2)
original	section 213(4)
plaintiff (in Scotland)	section 262
qualifying individual	*section 217(1)*
qualifying person	sections 217(1) and (2)
signed	section 261

NOTES

Entry "commission" repealed by the Intellectual Property Act 2014, s 2(2)(k), subject to savings in s 2(3) of the 2014 Act as noted to s 215 at **[2.314]**.

Entry "qualifying individual" repealed by the Intellectual Property Act 2014, s 3(5), (6), in relation to designs created after 1 October 2014.

PART IV
REGISTERED DESIGNS

Amendments of the Registered Designs Act 1949

265 *(Repealed by the Registered Designs Regulations 2001, SI 2001/3949, reg 9(2), Sch 2.)*

[2.367]
266 Provisions with respect to certain designs registered in pursuance of application made before commencement

(1) Where a design is registered under the Registered Designs Act 1949 in pursuance of an application made after 12th January 1988 and before the commencement of this Part which could not have been registered under section 1 of that Act as substituted by section 265 above—

- *(a) the right in the registered design expires ten years after the commencement of this Part, if it does not expire earlier in accordance with the 1949 Act, and*
- *(b) any person is, after the commencement of this Part, entitled as of right to a licence to do anything which would otherwise infringe the right in the registered design.*

(2) The terms of a licence available by virtue of this section shall, in default of agreement, be settled by the registrar on an application by the person requiring the licence; and the terms so settled shall authorise the licensee to do everything which would be an infringement of the right in the registered design in the absence of a licence.

(3) In settling the terms of a licence the registrar shall have regard to such factors as may be prescribed by the Secretary of State by order made by statutory instrument.

No such order shall be made unless a draft of it has been laid before and approved by a resolution of each House of Parliament.

(4) Where the terms of a licence are settled by the registrar, the licence has effect from the date on which the application to the registrar was made.

(5) Section 11B of the 1949 Act (undertaking to take licence of right in infringement proceedings), as inserted by section 270 below, applies where a licence is available as of right under this section, as it applies where a licence is available as of right under section 11A of that Act.

(6) Where a licence is available as of right under this section, a person to whom a licence was granted before the commencement of this Part may apply to the registrar for an order adjusting the terms of that licence.

(7) An appeal lies from any decision of the registrar under this section.

(8) This section shall be construed as one with the Registered Designs Act 1949.

NOTES

In view of sub-s (1) above, this section is considered spent.

Registered Designs Act 1949, s 11B: repealed by the Registered Designs Regulations 2001, SI 2001/3949, reg 9(2), Sch 2.

267–271 (S *267 substitutes the Registered Designs Act 1949, s 2(1) and adds s 2(3), (4) of that Act, at* **[3.5]**, *except in relation to an application made before 1 August 1989; s 268 repealed by the Registered Designs Regulations 2001, SI 2001/3949, reg 9(2), Sch 2; s 269 substitutes ss 8, 8A, 8B for the original s 8 of that Act, at* **[3.15]–[3.17]**, *except in relation to the right in a design registered in pursuance of an application made before 1 August 1989; s 270 inserts ss 11A, 11B of that Act, at* **[3.25]**; *s 271 inserts para 2A and substitutes para 3(1) of the First Schedule to that Act, at* **[3.83]**, *in relation to any Crown use of a registered design after 1 August 1989, even if the terms for such use were settled before that date.*)

[2.368]
272 Minor and consequential amendments

The Registered Designs Act 1949 is further amended in accordance with Schedule 3 which contains minor amendments and amendments consequential upon the provisions of this Act.

Supplementary

[2.369]
273 Text of Registered Designs Act 1949 as amended

Schedule 4 contains the text of the Registered Designs Act 1949 as amended.

PART V
PATENT AGENTS AND TRADE MARK AGENTS
Patent agents

[2.370]

274 Persons permitted to carry on business of a patent agent

(1) Any individual, partnership or body corporate may, subject to the following provisions of this Part [and to the Legal Services Act 2007], carry on the business of acting as agent for others for the purpose of—

(a) applying for or obtaining patents, in the United Kingdom or elsewhere, or

(b) conducting proceedings before the comptroller relating to applications for, or otherwise in connection with, patents.

(2) This does not affect any restriction under the European Patent Convention as to who may act on behalf of another for any purpose relating to European patents.

NOTES

Sub-s (1): words in square brackets inserted by the Legal Services Act 2007, s 185(1), (2).

[2.371]

[275 The register of patent attorneys

(1) There is to continue to be a register of persons who act as agent for others for the purpose of applying for or obtaining patents.

(2) In this Part a registered patent attorney means an individual whose name is entered on the register kept under this section.

(3) The register is to be kept by the Chartered Institute of Patent Attorneys.

(4) The Secretary of State may, by order, amend subsection (3) so as to require the register to be kept by the person specified in the order.

(5) Before making an order under subsection (4), the Secretary of State must consult the Legal Services Board.

(6) An order under this section must be made by statutory instrument.

(7) An order under this section may not be made unless a draft of it has been laid before, and approved by a resolution of, each House of Parliament.]

NOTES

Commencement: 1 January 2010.

Substituted, together with s 275A, for original s 275, by the Legal Services Act 2007, s 185(1), (3).

[2.372]

[275A Regulation of patent attorneys

(1) The person who keeps the register under section 275 may make regulations which regulate—

(a) the keeping of the register and the registration of persons;

(b) the carrying on of patent attorney work by registered persons.

(2) Those regulations may, amongst other things, make—

(a) provision as to the educational and training qualifications, and other requirements, which must be satisfied before an individual may be registered or for an individual to remain registered;

(b) provision as to the requirements which must be met by a body (corporate or unincorporate) before it may be registered, or for it to remain registered, including provision as to the management and control of the body;

(c) provision as to the educational, training and other requirements to be met by regulated persons;

(d) provision regulating the practice, conduct and discipline of registered persons or regulated persons;

(e) provision authorising in such cases as may be specified in the regulations the erasure from the register of the name of any person registered in it, or the suspension of a person's registration;

(f) provision requiring the payment of such fees as may be specified in or determined in accordance with the regulations;

(g) provision about the provision to be made by registered persons in respect of complaints made against them;

(h) provision about the keeping by registered persons or regulated persons of records and accounts;

(i) provision for reviews of or appeals against decisions made under the regulations;

(j) provision as to the indemnification of registered persons or regulated persons against losses arising from claims in respect of civil liability incurred by them.

(3) Regulations under this section may make different provision for different purposes.

(4) Regulations under this section which are not regulatory arrangements within the meaning of the Legal Services Act 2007 are to be treated as such arrangements for the purposes of that Act.

(5) Before the appointed day, regulations under this section may be made only with the approval of the Secretary of State.

(6) The powers conferred to make regulations under this section are not to be taken to prejudice—

(a) any other power which the person who keeps the register may have to make rules or regulations (however they may be described and whether they are made under an enactment or otherwise);

(b) any rules or regulations made by that person under any such power.

(7) In this section—

"appointed day" means the day appointed for the coming into force of paragraph 1 of Schedule 4 to the Legal Services Act 2007;

"manager", in relation to a body, has the same meaning as in the Legal Services Act 2007 (see section 207);

"patent attorney work" means work done in the course of carrying on the business of acting as agent for others for the purpose of—

(a) applying for or obtaining patents, in the United Kingdom or elsewhere, or

(b) conducting proceedings before the comptroller relating to applications for, or otherwise in connection with, patents;

"registered person" means—

(a) a registered patent attorney, or

(b) a body (corporate or unincorporate) registered in the register kept under section 275;

"regulated person" means a person who is not a registered person but is a manager or employee of a body which is a registered person.]

NOTES

Commencement: 1 January 2010.

Substituted as noted to s 275 at **[2.371]**.

[2.373]

276 Persons entitled to describe themselves as patent agents

(1) An individual who is not a [registered patent attorney] shall not—

(a) carry on a business (otherwise than in partnership) under any name or other description which contains the words "patent agent" or "patent attorney"; or

(b) in the course of a business otherwise describe himself, or permit himself to be described, as a "patent agent" or "patent attorney".

(2) A partnership [or other unincorporated body] shall not—

(a) carry on a business under any name or other description which contains the words "patent agent" or "patent attorney"; or

(b) in the course of a business otherwise describe itself, or permit itself to be described as, a firm of "patent agents" or "patent attorneys",

unless [the partnership or other body is registered in the register kept under section 275].

(3) A body corporate shall not—

(a) carry on a business (otherwise than in partnership) under any name or other description which contains the words "patent agent" or "patent attorney"; or

(b) in the course of a business otherwise describe itself, or permit itself to be described as, a "patent agent" or "patent attorney",

unless [the body corporate is registered in the register kept under section 275].

(4) Subsection (3) does not apply to a company which began to carry on business as a patent [attorney] before 17th November 1917 if the name of a director or the manager of the company who is a registered patent agent is mentioned as being so registered in all professional advertisements, circulars or letters issued by or with the company's consent on which its name appears.

(5) Where this section would be contravened by the use of the words "patent agent" or "patent attorney" in reference to an individual, partnership or body corporate, it is equally contravened by the use of other expressions in reference to that person, or his business or place of business, which are likely to be understood as indicating that he is entitled to be described as a "patent agent" or "patent attorney".

(6) A person who contravenes this section commits an offence and is liable on summary conviction to a fine not exceeding level 5 on the standard scale; and proceedings for such an offence may be begun at any time within a year from the date of the offence.

(7) This section has effect subject to—

(a) section 277 (persons entitled to describe themselves as European patent attorneys, &c), and

(b) section 278(1) (use of term "patent attorney" in reference to solicitors).

NOTES

Sub-s (1): words in square brackets substituted by the Legal Services Act 2007, s 208, Sch 21, paras 75, 76(a).

Sub-s (2): words in first pair of square brackets inserted and words in second pair of square brackets substituted by the Legal Services Act 2007, s 185(1), (4)(a).

Sub-s (3): words in square brackets substituted by the Legal Services Act 2007, s 185(1), (4)(b).

Sub-s (4): word in square brackets substituted by the Legal Services Act 2007, s 208, Sch 21, paras 75, 76(b).

Solicitors: references to solicitors are modified so as to include references to: (a) recognised bodies within the meaning of the Administration of Justice Act 1985, s 9, by the Solicitors' Recognised Bodies Order 1991, SI 1991/2684, arts 3–5, Sch 1; and

(b) a body which holds a licence issued by the Law Society which is in force under the Legal Services Act 2007, Pt 5, by the Legal Services Act 2007 (Designation as a Licensing Authority) (No 2) Order 2011, SI 2011/2866, art 8(1), (2), Sch 2.

[2.374]

277 Persons entitled to describe themselves as European patent attorneys, &c

(1) The term "European patent attorney" or "European patent agent" may be used in the following cases without any contravention of section 276.

(2) An individual who is on the European list may—

(a) carry on business under a name or other description which contains the words "European patent attorney" or "European patent agent", or

(b) otherwise describe himself, or permit himself to be described, as a "European patent attorney" or "European patent agent".

(3) A partnership of which not less than the prescribed number or proportion of partners is on the European list may—

(a) carry on a business under a name or other description which contains the words "European patent attorneys" or "European patent agents", or

(b) otherwise describe itself, or permit itself to be described, as a firm which carries on the business of a "European patent attorney" or "European patent agent".

(4) A body corporate of which not less than the prescribed number or proportion of directors is on the European list may—

(a) carry on a business under a name or other description which contains the words "European patent attorney" or "European patent agent", or

(b) otherwise describe itself, or permit itself to be described as, a company which carries on the business of a "European patent attorney" or "European patent agent".

(5) Where the term "European patent attorney" or "European patent agent" may, in accordance with this section, be used in reference to an individual, partnership or body corporate, it is equally permissible to use other expressions in reference to that person, or to his business or place of business, which are likely to be understood as indicating that he is entitled to be described as a "European patent attorney" or "European patent agent."

[2.375]

278 Use of the term "patent attorney": supplementary provisions

(1) The term "patent attorney" may be used in reference to a solicitor [or a licensed body], and a firm of solicitors may be described as a firm of "patent attorneys", without any contravention of section 276.

(2) No offence is committed under the enactments restricting the use of certain expressions in reference to persons not qualified to act as solicitors—

(a) by the use of the term "patent attorney" in reference to a registered patent agent, or

(b) by the use of the term "European patent attorney" in reference to a person on the European list.

(3) The enactments referred to in subsection (2) are section 21 of the Solicitors Act 1974, section 31 of the Solicitors (Scotland) Act 1980 and Article 22 of the Solicitors (Northern Ireland) Order 1976.

NOTES

Sub-s (1): words in square brackets inserted by virtue of the Legal Services Act 2007 (Designation as a Licensing Authority) (No 2) Order 2011, SI 2011/2866, art 8(1), (3), Sch 3.

Solicitors: references to solicitors are modified so as to include references to recognised bodies within the meaning of the Administration of Justice Act 1985, s 9, by the Solicitors' Recognised Bodies Order 1991, SI 1991/2684, arts 3–5, Sch 1.

279 (*Repealed by the Legal Services Act 2007, ss 185(1), (5), 210, Sch 23.*)

[2.376]

280 Privilege for communications with patent agents

(1) This section applies to[—

(a)] communications as to any matter relating to the protection of any invention, design, technical information, [or trade mark], or as to any matter involving passing off[, and

(b) documents, material or information relating to any matter mentioned in paragraph (a).]

[(2) Where a patent attorney acts for a client in relation to a matter mentioned in subsection (1), any communication, document, material or information to which this section applies is privileged from disclosure in like manner as if the patent attorney had at all material times been acting as the client's solicitor.]

(3) In subsection (2) "patent [attorney]" means—

(a) a registered patent [attorney] or a person who is on the European list,

(b) a partnership entitled to describe itself as a firm of patent [attorneys] or as a firm carrying on the business of a European patent attorney, . . .

[(ba) an unincorporated body (other than a partnership) entitled to describe itself as a patent attorney, or]

(c) a body corporate entitled to describe itself as a patent [attorney] or as a company carrying on the business of a European patent attorney.

(4) . . .

NOTES

Sub-s (1): words in first and third pairs of square brackets inserted by the Legal Services Act 2007, s 208, Sch 21, paras 75, 77(a), (b); words in second pair of square brackets substituted by the Trade Marks Act 1994, s 106(1), Sch 4, para 8(1), (3).

Sub-s (2): substituted by the Legal Services Act 2007, s 208, Sch 21, paras 75, 77(c).

Sub-s (3): words in first, second, third and fifth pairs of square brackets substituted, word omitted from para (b) repealed and para (ba) inserted by the Legal Services Act 2007, ss 185(1), (6), 208, 210, Sch 21, paras 75, 77(d), Sch 23.

Sub-s (4): repealed by the Legal Services Act 2007, ss 208, 210, Sch 21, paras 75, 77(e), Sch 23.

Trade marks or registered trade marks: see the note preceding s 1, at **[2.7]**.

[2.377]

281 Power of comptroller to refuse to deal with certain agents

(1) This section applies to business under the Patents Act 1949, the Registered Designs Act 1949 or the Patents Act 1977.

(2) The Secretary of State may make rules authorising the comptroller to refuse to recognise as agent in respect of any business to which this section applies—

(a) a person who has been convicted of an offence under section 88 of the Patents Act 1949, section 114 of the Patents Act 1977 or section 276 of this Act;

(b) [a person] whose name has been erased from and not restored to, or who is suspended from, the register of patent [attorneys] on the ground of misconduct;

(c) a person who is found by the Secretary of State to have been guilty of such conduct as would, in the case of [a person] registered in the register of patent [attorneys], render [the person] liable to have [the person's] name erased from the register on the ground of misconduct;

(d) a partnership or body corporate of which one of the partners or directors is a person whom the comptroller could refuse to recognise under paragraph (a), (b) or (c) above.

(3) The rules may contain such incidental and supplementary provisions as appear to the Secretary of State to be appropriate and may, in particular, prescribe circumstances in which a person is or is not to be taken to have been guilty of misconduct.

(4) Rules made under this section shall be made by statutory instrument which shall be subject to annulment in pursuance of a resolution of either House of Parliament.

(5) The comptroller shall refuse to recognise as agent in respect of any business to which this section applies a person who neither resides nor has a place of business in the United Kingdom, the Isle of Man or another member State of the European Economic Community.

NOTES

Sub-s (2): in paras (b), (c), word "attorneys" in both places it appears substituted by the Legal Services Act 2007, s 208, Sch 21, paras 75, 78, and other words in square brackets substituted by the Legal Services Act 2007 (Consequential Amendments) Order 2009, SI 2009/3348, art 3.

Patents Act 1949, s 88: repealed with savings by the Patents Act 1977, ss 127(6), 132(7), Schs 4, 6.

Rules: the Patent Agents (Non-recognition of Certain Agents by Comptroller) Rules 1990, SI 1990/1454.

282–284 (*Repealed, with savings, by the Trade Marks Act 1994, ss 105, 106(2), Sch 3, para 22(1), Sch 5.*)

Supplementary

[2.378]

285 Offences committed by partnerships and bodies corporate

(1) Proceedings for an offence under this Part alleged to have been committed by a partnership shall be brought in the name of the partnership and not in that of the partners; but without prejudice to any liability of theirs under subsection (4) below.

(2) The following provisions apply for the purposes of such proceedings as in relation to a body corporate—

(a) any rules of court relating to the service of documents;

(b) in England, Wales or Northern Ireland, Schedule 3 to the Magistrates' Courts Act 1980 or Schedule 4 to the Magistrates' Courts (Northern Ireland) Order 1981 (procedure on charge of offence).

(3) A fine imposed on a partnership on its conviction in such proceedings shall be paid out of the partnership assets.

(4) Where a partnership is guilty of an offence under this Part, every partner, other than a partner who is proved to have been ignorant of or to have attempted to prevent the commission of the offence, is also guilty of the offence and liable to be proceeded against and punished accordingly.

(5) Where an offence under this Part committed by a body corporate is proved to have been committed with the consent or connivance of a director, manager, secretary or other similar officer of the body, or a person purporting to act in any such capacity, he as well as the body corporate is guilty of the offence and liable to be proceeded against and punished accordingly.

[2.379]
286 Interpretation
In this Part—

"the comptroller" means the Comptroller-General of Patents, Designs and Trade Marks;

"director", in relation to a body corporate whose affairs are managed by its members, means any member of the body corporate;

"the European list" means the list of professional representatives maintained by the European Patent Office in pursuance of the European Patent Convention;

"registered patent [attorney]" has the meaning given by section 275[(2)];

. . .

NOTES

In definition "registered patent attorney" word and figure in square brackets substituted by the Legal Services Act 2007, s 208, Sch 21, paras 75, 79; definition omitted repealed by the Trade Marks Act 1994, s 106(2), Sch 5.

PART VI
PATENTS

Patents county courts

287–289 (*Repealed by the Crime and Courts Act 2013, s 17(5), Sch 9, Pt 2, para 30(1), (3).*)

[2.380]
290 Limitation of costs where pecuniary claim could have been brought in patents county court

(1) Where an action is commenced in the High Court which could have been commenced in a patents county court and in which a claim for a pecuniary remedy is made, then, subject to the provisions of this section, if the plaintiff recovers less than the prescribed amount, he is not entitled to recover any more costs than those to which he would have been entitled if the action had been brought in the county court.

(2) For this purpose a plaintiff shall be treated as recovering the full amount recoverable in respect of his claim without regard to any deduction made in respect of matters not falling to be taken into account in determining whether the action could have been commenced in a patents county court.

(3) This section does not affect any question as to costs if it appears to the High Court that there was reasonable ground for supposing the amount recoverable in respect of the plaintiff's claim to be in excess of the prescribed amount.

(4) The High Court, if satisfied that there was sufficient reason for bringing the action in the High Court, may make an order allowing the costs or any part of the costs on the High Court scale or on such one of the county court scales as it may direct.

(5) This section does not apply to proceedings brought by the Crown.

(6) In this section "the prescribed amount" means such amount as may be prescribed by Her Majesty for the purposes of this section by Order in Council.

(7) No recommendation shall be made to Her Majesty to make an Order under this section unless a draft of the Order has been laid before and approved by a resolution of each House of Parliament.

NOTES

Repealed by the Courts and Legal Services Act 1990, s 125(7), Sch 20, as from a day to be appointed.

291–294 (*S 291 repealed by the Crime and Courts Act 2013, s 17(5), Sch 9, Pt 2, para 30(1), (3); s 292 repealed by the Legal Services Act 2007, ss 208, 210, Sch 21, paras 75, 80, Sch 23; s 293 amends the Patents Act 1977, Sch 1, para 4(2)(c), and inserts Sch 1, para 4A, at* **[1.151]**; *s 294 inserts Sch 1, para 4B to the 1977 Act, at* **[1.151]**.)

Patents: miscellaneous amendments

[2.381]
295 Patents: miscellaneous amendments
The Patents Act 1949 and the Patents Act 1977 are amended in accordance with Schedule 5.

PART VII
MISCELLANEOUS AND GENERAL

[Circumvention of protection measures

[2.382]
296 Circumvention of technical devices applied to computer programs

(1) This section applies where—

(a) a technical device has been applied to a computer program; and

(b) a person (A) knowing or having reason to believe that it will be used to make infringing copies—

(i) manufactures for sale or hire, imports, distributes, sells or lets for hire, offers or exposes for sale or hire, advertises for sale or hire or has in his possession for commercial purposes any means the sole intended purpose of which is to facilitate the unauthorised removal or circumvention of the technical device; or

(ii) publishes information intended to enable or assist persons to remove or circumvent the technical device.

(2) The following persons have the same rights against A as a copyright owner has in respect of an infringement of copyright—

(a) a person—

(i) issuing to the public copies of, or

(ii) communicating to the public,

the computer program to which the technical device has been applied;

(b) the copyright owner or his exclusive licensee, if he is not the person specified in paragraph (a);

(c) the owner or exclusive licensee of any intellectual property right in the technical device applied to the computer program.

(3) The rights conferred by subsection (2) are concurrent, and sections 101(3) and 102(1) to (4) apply, in proceedings under this section, in relation to persons with concurrent rights as they apply, in proceedings mentioned in those provisions, in relation to a copyright owner and exclusive licensee with concurrent rights.

(4) Further, the persons in subsection (2) have the same rights under section 99 or 100 (delivery up or seizure of certain articles) in relation to any such means as is referred to in subsection (1) which a person has in his possession, custody or control with the intention that it should be used to facilitate the unauthorised removal or circumvention of any technical device which has been applied to a computer program, as a copyright owner has in relation to an infringing copy.

(5) The rights conferred by subsection (4) are concurrent, and section 102(5) shall apply, as respects anything done under section 99 or 100 by virtue of subsection (4), in relation to persons with concurrent rights as it applies, as respects anything done under section 99 or 100, in relation to a copyright owner and exclusive licensee with concurrent rights.

(6) In this section references to a technical device in relation to a computer program are to any device intended to prevent or restrict acts that are not authorised by the copyright owner of that computer program and are restricted by copyright.

(7) The following provisions apply in relation to proceedings under this section as in relation to proceedings under Part 1 (copyright)—

(a) sections 104 to 106 of this Act (presumptions as to certain matters relating to copyright); and

(b) section 72 of the [Senior Courts Act 1981], section 15 of the Law Reform (Miscellaneous Provisions) (Scotland) Act 1985 and section 94A of the Judicature (Northern Ireland) Act 1978 (withdrawal of privilege against self-incrimination in certain proceedings relating to intellectual property);

and section 114 of this Act applies, with the necessary modifications, in relation to the disposal of anything delivered up or seized by virtue of subsection (4).

(8) Expressions used in this section which are defined for the purposes of Part 1 of this Act (copyright) have the same meaning as in that Part.]

NOTES

Substituted, together with preceding cross-heading and ss 296ZA–296ZF, for original s 296 (and preceding cross-heading) by the Copyright and Related Rights Regulations 2003, SI 2003/2498, regs 3, 24(1), subject to transitional provisions as noted to s 1 of this Act at **[2.7]**.

Sub-s (7): words in square brackets in para (b) substituted by the Constitutional Reform Act 2005, s 59(5), Sch 11, Pt 1, para 1.

[2.383]

[296ZA Circumvention of technological measures

(1) This section applies where—

(a) effective technological measures have been applied to a copyright work other than a computer program; and

(b) a person (B) does anything which circumvents those measures knowing, or with reasonable grounds to know, that he is pursuing that objective.

(2) This section does not apply where a person, for the purposes of research into cryptography, does anything which circumvents effective technological measures unless in so doing, or in issuing information derived from that research, he affects prejudicially the rights of the copyright owner.

(3) The following persons have the same rights against B as a copyright owner has in respect of an infringement of copyright—

(a) a person—

(i) issuing to the public copies of, or

(ii) communicating to the public,

the work to which effective technological measures have been applied; and

(b) the copyright owner or his exclusive licensee, if he is not the person specified in paragraph (a).

(4) The rights conferred by subsection (3) are concurrent, and sections 101(3) and 102(1) to (4) apply, in proceedings under this section, in relation to persons with concurrent rights as they apply, in proceedings mentioned in those provisions, in relation to a copyright owner and exclusive licensee with concurrent rights.

(5) The following provisions apply in relation to proceedings under this section as in relation to proceedings under Part 1 (copyright)—

(a) sections 104 to 106 of this Act (presumptions as to certain matters relating to copyright); and

(b) section 72 of the [Senior Courts Act 1981], section 15 of the Law Reform (Miscellaneous Provisions) (Scotland) Act 1985 and section 94A of the Judicature (Northern Ireland) Act 1978 (withdrawal of privilege against self-incrimination in certain proceedings relating to intellectual property).

(6) Subsections (1) to (4) and (5)(b) and any other provision of this Act as it has effect for the purposes of those subsections apply, with any necessary adaptations, to rights in performances, publication right and database right.

(7) The provisions of regulation 22 (presumptions relevant to database right) of the Copyright and Rights in Databases Regulations 1997 (SI 1997/3032) apply in proceedings brought by virtue of this section in relation to database right.]

NOTES

Substituted as noted to s 296 at **[2.382]**.

Sub-s (5): words in square brackets in para (b) substituted by the Constitutional Reform Act 2005, s 59(5), Sch 11, Pt 1, para 1.

[2.384]

[296ZB Devices and services designed to circumvent technological measures

(1) A person commits an offence if he—

(a) manufactures for sale or hire, or

(b) imports otherwise than for his private and domestic use, or

(c) in the course of a business—

(i) sells or lets for hire, or

(ii) offers or exposes for sale or hire, or

(iii) advertises for sale or hire, or

(iv) possesses, or

(v) distributes, or

(d) distributes otherwise than in the course of a business to such an extent as to affect prejudicially the copyright owner,

any device, product or component which is primarily designed, produced, or adapted for the purpose of enabling or facilitating the circumvention of effective technological measures.

(2) A person commits an offence if he provides, promotes, advertises or markets—

(a) in the course of a business, or

(b) otherwise than in the course of a business to such an extent as to affect prejudicially the copyright owner,

a service the purpose of which is to enable or facilitate the circumvention of effective technological measures.

(3) Subsections (1) and (2) do not make unlawful anything done by, or on behalf of, law enforcement agencies or any of the intelligence services—

(a) in the interests of national security; or

(b) for the purpose of the prevention or detection of crime, the investigation of an offence, or the conduct of a prosecution,

and in this subsection "intelligence services" has the meaning given in section 81 of the Regulation of Investigatory Powers Act 2000.

(4) A person guilty of an offence under subsection (1) or (2) is liable—

(a) on summary conviction, to imprisonment for a term not exceeding three months, or to a fine not exceeding the statutory maximum, or both;

(b) on conviction on indictment to a fine or imprisonment for a term not exceeding two years, or both.

(5) It is a defence to any prosecution for an offence under this section for the defendant to prove that he did not know, and had no reasonable ground for believing, that—

(a) the device, product or component; or

(b) the service,

enabled or facilitated the circumvention of effective technological measures.]

NOTES

Substituted as noted to s 296, at **[2.382]**.

Part 2 Copyright

[2.385]

[296ZC Devices and services designed to circumvent technological measures: search warrants and forfeiture

(1) The provisions of sections 297B (search warrants), 297C (forfeiture of unauthorised decoders: England and Wales or Northern Ireland) and 297D (forfeiture of unauthorised decoders: Scotland) apply to offences under section 296ZB with the following modifications.

(2) In section 297B the reference to an offence under section 297A(1) shall be construed as a reference to an offence under section 296ZB(1) or (2).

(3) In sections 297C(2)(a) and 297D(15) the references to an offence under section 297A(1) shall be construed as a reference to an offence under section 296ZB(1).

(4) In sections 297C and 297D references to unauthorised decoders shall be construed as references to devices, products or components for the purpose of circumventing effective technological measures.]

NOTES

Substituted as noted to s 296, at **[2.382]**.

[2.386]

[296ZD Rights and remedies in respect of devices and services designed to circumvent technological measures

(1) This section applies where—

(a) effective technological measures have been applied to a copyright work other than a computer program; and

(b) a person (C) manufactures, imports, distributes, sells or lets for hire, offers or exposes for sale or hire, advertises for sale or hire, or has in his possession for commercial purposes any device, product or component, or provides services which—

(i) are promoted, advertised or marketed for the purpose of the circumvention of, or

(ii) have only a limited commercially significant purpose or use other than to circumvent, or

(iii) are primarily designed, produced, adapted or performed for the purpose of enabling or facilitating the circumvention of,

those measures.

(2) The following persons have the same rights against C as a copyright owner has in respect of an infringement of copyright—

(a) a person—

(i) issuing to the public copies of, or

(ii) communicating to the public,

the work to which effective technological measures have been applied;

(b) the copyright owner or his exclusive licensee, if he is not the person specified in paragraph (a); and

(c) the owner or exclusive licensee of any intellectual property right in the effective technological measures applied to the work.

(3) The rights conferred by subsection (2) are concurrent, and sections 101(3) and 102(1) to (4) apply, in proceedings under this section, in relation to persons with concurrent rights as they apply, in proceedings mentioned in those provisions, in relation to a copyright owner and exclusive licensee with concurrent rights.

(4) Further, the persons in subsection (2) have the same rights under section 99 or 100 (delivery up or seizure of certain articles) in relation to any such device, product or component which a person has in his possession, custody or control with the intention that it should be used to circumvent effective technological measures, as a copyright owner has in relation to any infringing copy.

(5) The rights conferred by subsection (4) are concurrent, and section 102(5) shall apply, as respects anything done under section 99 or 100 by virtue of subsection (4), in relation to persons with concurrent rights as it applies, as respects anything done under section 99 or 100, in relation to a copyright owner and exclusive licensee with concurrent rights.

(6) The following provisions apply in relation to proceedings under this section as in relation to proceedings under Part 1 (copyright)—

(a) sections 104 to 106 of this Act (presumptions as to certain matters relating to copyright); and

(b) section 72 of the [Senior Courts Act 1981], section 15 of the Law Reform (Miscellaneous Provisions) (Scotland) Act 1985 and section 94A of the Judicature (Northern Ireland) Act 1978 (withdrawal of privilege against self-incrimination in certain proceedings relating to intellectual property);

and section 114 of this Act applies, with the necessary modifications, in relation to the disposal of anything delivered up or seized by virtue of subsection (4).

(7) In section 97(1) (innocent infringement of copyright) as it applies to proceedings for infringement of the rights conferred by this section, the reference to the defendant not knowing or having reason to believe that copyright subsisted in the work shall be construed as a reference to his not knowing or having reason to believe that his acts enabled or facilitated an infringement of copyright.
(8) Subsections (1) to (5), (6)(b) and (7) and any other provision of this Act as it has effect for the purposes of those subsections apply, with any necessary adaptations, to rights in performances, publication right and database right.
(9) The provisions of regulation 22 (presumptions relevant to database right) of the Copyright and Rights in Databases Regulations 1997 (SI 1997/3032) apply in proceedings brought by virtue of this section in relation to database right.]

NOTES

Substituted as noted to s 296 at **[2.382]**.

Sub-s (6): words in square brackets in para (b) substituted by the Constitutional Reform Act 2005, s 59(5), Sch 11, Pt 1, para 1.

[2.387]

[296ZE Remedy where effective technological measures prevent permitted acts

(1) In this section—

"permitted act" means an act which may be done in relation to copyright works, notwithstanding the subsistence of copyright, by virtue of a provision of this Act listed in Part 1 of Schedule 5A;

"voluntary measure or agreement" means—

(a) any measure taken voluntarily by a copyright owner, his exclusive licensee or a person issuing copies of, or communicating to the public, a work other than a computer program, or

(b) any agreement between a copyright owner, his exclusive licensee or a person issuing copies of, or communicating to the public, a work other than a computer program and another party,

the effect of which is to enable a person to carry out a permitted act.

(2) Where the application of any effective technological measure to a copyright work other than a computer program prevents a person from carrying out a permitted act in relation to that work then that person or a person being a representative of a class of persons prevented from carrying out a permitted act may issue a notice of complaint to the Secretary of State.
(3) Following receipt of a notice of complaint, the Secretary of State may give to the owner of that copyright work or an exclusive licensee such directions as appear to the Secretary of State to be requisite or expedient for the purpose of—

(a) establishing whether any voluntary measure or agreement relevant to the copyright work the subject of the complaint subsists; or

(b) (where it is established there is no subsisting voluntary measure or agreement) ensuring that the owner or exclusive licensee of that copyright work makes available to the complainant the means of carrying out the permitted act the subject of the complaint to the extent necessary to so benefit from that permitted act.

(4) The Secretary of State may also give directions—

(a) as to the form and manner in which a notice of complaint in subsection (2) may be delivered to him;

(b) as to the form and manner in which evidence of any voluntary measure or agreement may be delivered to him; and

(c) generally as to the procedure to be followed in relation to a complaint made under this section;

and shall publish directions given under this subsection in such manner as in his opinion will secure adequate publicity for them.
(5) It shall be the duty of any person to whom a direction is given under subsection (3)(a) or (b) to give effect to that direction.
(6) The obligation to comply with a direction given under subsection (3)(b) is a duty owed to the complainant or, where the complaint is made by a representative of a class of persons, to that representative and to each person in the class represented; and a breach of the duty is actionable accordingly (subject to the defences and other incidents applying to actions for breach of statutory duty).
(7) Any direction under this section may be varied or revoked by a subsequent direction under this section.
(8) Any direction given under this section shall be in writing.
(9) This section does not apply to copyright works made available to the public on agreed contractual terms in such a way that members of the public may access them from a place and at a time individually chosen by them.
(10) This section applies only where a complainant has lawful access to the protected copyright work, or where the complainant is a representative of a class of persons, where the class of persons have lawful access to the work.

(11) Subsections (1) to (10) apply with any necessary adaptations to—
(a) rights in performances, and in this context the expression "permitted act" refers to an act that may be done by virtue of a provision of this Act listed in Part 2 of Schedule 5A;
(b) database right, and in this context the expression "permitted act" refers to an act that may be done by virtue of a provision of this Act listed in Part 3 of Schedule 5A; and
(c) publication right.]

NOTES

Substituted as noted to s 296, at **[2.382]**.

[2.388]

[296ZEA Remedy where restrictive measures prevent or restrict personal copying

(1) This section applies where an individual is prevented from making a personal copy of a copyright work, or is restricted in the number of personal copies of it which may be made, because of a restrictive measure applied by or on behalf of the copyright owner.

(2) That individual, or a person being a representative of a class of such individuals, may issue a notice of complaint to the Secretary of State.

(3) Following receipt of a notice of complaint, the Secretary of State may give to the owner of that copyright work or an exclusive licensee such directions as appear to the Secretary of State to be requisite or expedient for the purpose of—
(a) establishing whether any voluntary measure or agreement relevant to the copyright work subsists, or
(b) (where it is established there is no subsisting voluntary measure or agreement) ensuring that the owner or exclusive licensee of that copyright work makes available to the complainant or the class of individuals represented by the complainant the means of benefiting from section 28B to the extent necessary to benefit from that section.

(4) In deciding whether to give such directions, the Secretary of State must consider whether the restrictive measure unreasonably prevents or restricts the making of personal copies, in particular having regard to—
(a) the right of the copyright owner to adopt adequate measures limiting the number of personal copies which may be made, and
(b) whether other copies of the work are commercially available on reasonable terms by or with the authority of the copyright owner in a form which does not prevent or unreasonably restrict the making of personal copies.

(5) The Secretary of State may also give directions—
(a) as to the form and manner in which a notice of complaint in subsection (2) may be delivered,
(b) as to the form and manner in which evidence of any voluntary measure or agreement may be delivered, and
(c) generally as to the procedure to be followed in relation to a complaint made under this section,

and shall publish directions given under this subsection in such manner as the Secretary of State thinks will secure adequate publicity for them.

(6) Subsections (5) to (8) of section 296ZE—
(a) apply to directions under subsection (3)(a) or (b) as they apply to directions under section 296ZE(3)(a) or (b), and
(b) apply to directions under subsection (5) as they apply to directions under section 296ZE(4).

(7) This section does not apply to copyright works made available to the public on agreed contractual terms in such a way that members of the public may access them from a place and at a time individually chosen by them.

(8) In this section—

"restrictive measure" means any technology, device or component designed, in the normal course of its operation, to protect the rights of copyright owners, which has the effect of preventing a copyright work from being copied (in whole or in part) or restricting the number of copies which may be made;

"personal copy" means a copy of a copyright work which may be made under section 28B;

"voluntary measure or agreement" has the same meaning as in section 296ZE, except that the reference to carrying out a permitted act is to be read as a reference to making a personal copy.

(9) Subsections (1) to (8) apply with any necessary adaptations to—
(a) rights in performances, and in this context "personal copy" refers to a copy of a recording of a performance which may be made under paragraph 1B of Schedule 2 without infringing the rights conferred by Chapter 2 of Part II (rights in performances), and
(b) publication right.]

NOTES

Commencement: 1 October 2014.

Inserted by the Copyright and Rights in Performances (Personal Copies for Private Use) Regulations 2014, SI 2014/2361, regs 2, 3(2), subject to transitional provisions and additional notes, as noted to s 28B at **[2.42]**.

[2.389]

[296ZF Interpretation of sections 296ZA to [296ZEA]

(1) In sections 296ZA to 296ZE, "technological measures" are any technology, device or component which is designed, in the normal course of its operation, to protect a copyright work other than a computer program.

(2) Such measures are "effective" if the use of the work is controlled by the copyright owner through—

(a) an access control or protection process such as encryption, scrambling or other transformation of the work, or

(b) a copy control mechanism,

which achieves the intended protection.

(3) In this section, the reference to—

(a) protection of a work is to the prevention or restriction of acts that are not authorised by the copyright owner of that work and are restricted by copyright; and

(b) use of a work does not extend to any use of the work that is outside the scope of the acts restricted by copyright.

(4) Expressions used in sections 296ZA to [296ZEA] which are defined for the purposes of Part 1 of this Act (copyright) have the same meaning as in that Part.]

NOTES

Substituted as noted to s 296 at **[2.382]**.

Figure in square brackets in the section heading and sub-s (4) substituted by the Copyright and Rights in Performances (Personal Copies for Private Use) Regulations 2014, SI 2014/2361, regs 2, 4(3), subject to transitional provisions and additional notes, as noted to s 28B at **[2.42]**.

[Rights management information

[2.390]

296ZG Electronic rights management information

(1) This section applies where a person (D), knowingly and without authority, removes or alters electronic rights management information which—

(a) is associated with a copy of a copyright work, or

(b) appears in connection with the communication to the public of a copyright work, and

where D knows, or has reason to believe, that by so doing he is inducing, enabling, facilitating or concealing an infringement of copyright.

(2) This section also applies where a person (E), knowingly and without authority, distributes, imports for distribution or communicates to the public copies of a copyright work from which electronic rights management information—

(a) associated with the copies, or

(b) appearing in connection with the communication to the public of the work,

has been removed or altered without authority and where E knows, or has reason to believe, that by so doing he is inducing, enabling, facilitating or concealing an infringement of copyright.

(3) A person issuing to the public copies of, or communicating, the work to the public, has the same rights against D and E as a copyright owner has in respect of an infringement of copyright.

(4) The copyright owner or his exclusive licensee, if he is not the person issuing to the public copies of, or communicating, the work to the public, also has the same rights against D and E as he has in respect of an infringement of copyright.

(5) The rights conferred by subsections (3) and (4) are concurrent, and sections 101(3) and 102(1) to (4) apply, in proceedings under this section, in relation to persons with concurrent rights as they apply, in proceedings mentioned in those provisions, in relation to a copyright owner and exclusive licensee with concurrent rights.

(6) The following provisions apply in relation to proceedings under this section as in relation to proceedings under Part 1 (copyright)—

(a) sections 104 to 106 of this Act (presumptions as to certain matters relating to copyright); and

(b) section 72 of the [Senior Courts Act 1981], section 15 of the Law Reform (Miscellaneous Provisions) (Scotland) Act 1985 and section 94A of the Judicature (Northern Ireland) Act 1978 (withdrawal of privilege against self-incrimination in certain proceedings relating to intellectual property).

(7) In this section—

(a) expressions which are defined for the purposes of Part 1 of this Act (copyright) have the same meaning as in that Part; and

(b) "rights management information" means any information provided by the copyright owner or the holder of any right under copyright which identifies the work, the author, the copyright owner or the holder of any intellectual property rights, or information about the terms and conditions of use of the work, and any numbers or codes that represent such information.

(8) Subsections (1) to (5) and (6)(b), and any other provision of this Act as it has effect for the purposes of those subsections, apply, with any necessary adaptations, to rights in performances, publication right and database right.

Part 2 Copyright

(9) The provisions of regulation 22 (presumptions relevant to database right) of the Copyright and Rights in Databases Regulations 1997 (SI 1997/3032) apply in proceedings brought by virtue of this section in relation to database right.]

NOTES

Inserted by the Copyright and Related Rights Regulations 2003, SI 2003/2498, regs 3, 25, subject to transitional provisions as noted to s 1 of this Act at **[2.7]**.

Sub-s (6): words in square brackets in para (b) substituted by the Constitutional Reform Act 2005, s 59(5), Sch 11, Pt 1, para 1.

[Computer programs

[2.391]

296A Avoidance of certain terms

(1) Where a person has the use of a computer program under an agreement, any term or condition in the agreement shall be void in so far as it purports to prohibit or restrict—

(a) the making of any back up copy of the program which it is necessary for him to have for the purposes of the agreed use;

(b) where the conditions in section 50B(2) are met, the decompiling of the program; or

[(c) the observing, studying or testing of the functioning of the program in accordance with section 50BA].

(2) In this section, decompile, in relation to a computer program, has the same meaning as in section 50B.]

NOTES

Inserted, together with preceding cross-heading, by the Copyright (Computer Programs) Regulations 1992, SI 1992/3233, regs 2, 11, 12(2), although not so as to affect agreements entered into before 1 January 1993.

Sub-s (1): para (c) substituted by the Copyright and Related Rights Regulations 2003, SI 2003/2498, regs 3, 15(4), subject to transitional provisions as noted to s 1 of this Act at **[2.7]**.

[Databases

[2.392]

296B Avoidance of certain terms relating to databases

Where under an agreement a person has a right to use a database or part of a database, any term or condition in the agreement shall be void in so far as it purports to prohibit or restrict the performance of any act which would but for section 50D infringes the copyright in the database.]

NOTES

Inserted, together with preceding cross-heading, by the Copyright and Rights in Databases Regulations 1997, SI 1997/3032, reg 10, subject to savings and transitional provisions specified in regs 26–30 of those Regulations, at **[2.541]–[2.545]**.

Fraudulent reception of transmissions

[2.393]

297 Offence of fraudulently receiving programmes

(1) A person who dishonestly receives a programme included in a broadcasting . . . service provided from a place in the United Kingdom with intent to avoid payment of any charge applicable to the reception of the programme commits an offence and is liable on summary conviction to a fine not exceeding level 5 on the standard scale.

(2) Where an offence under this section committed by a body corporate is proved to have been committed with the consent or connivance of a director, manager, secretary or other similar officer of the body, or a person purporting to act in any such capacity, he as well as the body corporate is guilty of the offence and liable to be proceeded against and punished accordingly.

In relation to a body corporate whose affairs are managed by its members "director" means a member of the body corporate.

NOTES

Sub-s (1): words omitted repealed by the Copyright and Related Rights Regulations 2003, SI 2003/2498, reg 2(2), Sch 2, subject to transitional provisions as noted to s 1 of this Act at **[2.7]**.

Application of this section: this section applies in relation to programmes included in broadcasting or cable programme services provided from a place in the Bailiwick of Guernsey, and s 298, at **[2.141]** applies in relation to such programmes and to encrypted transmissions of any other description provided or sent from a place in the Bailiwick of Guernsey; see the Fraudulent Reception of Transmissions (Guernsey) Order 1989, SI 1989/2003, art 2.

[2.394]

[297A Unauthorised decoders

(1) A person commits an offence if he—

(a) makes, imports, distributes, sells or lets for hire or offers or exposes for sale or hire any unauthorised decoder;

(b) has in his possession for commercial purposes any unauthorised decoder;

(c) instals, maintains or replaces for commercial purposes any unauthorised decoder; or

(d) advertises any unauthorised decoder for sale or hire or otherwise promotes any unauthorised decoder by means of commercial communications.

(2) A person guilty of an offence under subsection (1) is liable—

[(a) on summary conviction, to imprisonment for a term not exceeding six months, or to a fine not exceeding the statutory maximum, or to both;]

(b) on conviction on indictment, to imprisonment for a term not exceeding [ten] years, or to a fine, or to both.

(3) It is a defence to any prosecution for an offence under this section for the defendant to prove that he did not know, and had no reasonable ground for believing, that the decoder was an unauthorised decoder.

(4) In this section—

"apparatus" includes any device, component or electronic data (including software);

"conditional access technology" means any technical measure or arrangement whereby access to encrypted transmissions in an intelligible form is made conditional on prior individual authorisation;

"decoder" means any apparatus which is designed or adapted to enable (whether on its own or with any other apparatus) an encrypted transmission to be decoded;

"encrypted" includes subjected to scrambling or the operation of cryptographic envelopes, electronic locks, passwords or any other analogous application;

"transmission" means—

(a) any programme included in a broadcasting . . . service which is provided from a place in the United Kingdom or any other member State; or

(b) an information society service (within the meaning of Directive 98/34/EC of the European Parliament and of the Council of 22nd June 1998, as amended by Directive 98/48/EC of the European Parliament and of the Council of 20th July 1998) which is provided from a place in the United Kingdom or any other member State; and

"unauthorised", in relation to a decoder, means that the decoder is designed or adapted to enable an encrypted transmission, or any service of which it forms part, to be accessed in an intelligible form without payment of the fee (however imposed) which the person making the transmission, or on whose behalf it is made, charges for accessing the transmission or service (whether by the circumvention of any conditional access technology related to the transmission or service or by any other means).]

NOTES

Inserted by the Broadcasting Act 1990, s 179(1); substituted by the Conditional Access (Unauthorised Decoders) Regulations 2000, SI 2000/1175, reg 2(1), (2).

Sub-s (2): para (a) substituted, and word in square brackets in para (b) substituted by the Copyright, etc and Trade Marks (Offences and Enforcement) Act 2002, s 1(1), (4), except in relation to offences committed before 20 November 2002.

Sub-s (4): words omitted from definition "transmission" repealed by the Copyright and Related Rights Regulations 2003, SI 2003/2498, reg 2(2), Sch 2, subject to transitional provisions as noted to s 1 of this Act at **[2.7]**.

[2.395]

[297B Search warrants

(1) Where a justice of the peace (in Scotland, a sheriff or justice of the peace) is satisfied by information on oath given by a constable (in Scotland, by evidence on oath) that there are reasonable grounds for believing—

(a) that an offence under section 297A(1) has been or is about to be committed in any premises, and

(b) that evidence that such an offence has been or is about to be committed is in those premises,

he may issue a warrant authorising a constable to enter and search the premises, using such reasonable force as is necessary.

(2) The power conferred by subsection (1) does not, in England and Wales, extend to authorising a search for material of the kinds mentioned in section 9(2) of the Police and Criminal Evidence Act 1984 (c 60) (certain classes of personal or confidential material).

(3) A warrant under subsection (1)—

(a) may authorise persons to accompany any constable executing the warrant, and

(b) remains in force for [three months] from the date of its issue.

(4) In executing a warrant issued under subsection (1) a constable may seize an article if he reasonably believes that it is evidence that any offence under section 297A(1) has been or is about to be committed.

(5) In this section "premises" includes land, buildings, fixed or moveable structures, vehicles, vessels, aircraft and hovercraft.]

NOTES

Inserted by the Copyright, etc and Trade Marks (Offences and Enforcement) Act 2002, s 2(1), (4).

Sub-s (3): words in square brackets substituted for original words "28 days" by the Serious Organised Crime and Police Act 2005, s 174(1), Sch 16, para 6(1), (4), in relation to England and Wales.

[2.396]

[297C Forfeiture of unauthorised decoders: England and Wales or Northern Ireland

(1) In England and Wales or Northern Ireland where unauthorised decoders have come into the possession of any person in connection with the investigation or prosecution of a relevant offence, that person may apply under this section for an order for the forfeiture of the unauthorised decoders.

(2) For the purposes of this section "relevant offence" means—

- (a) an offence under section 297A(1) (criminal liability for making, importing, etc unauthorised decoders),
- (b) an offence under the Trade Descriptions Act 1968,
- [(ba) an offence under the Business Protection from Misleading Marketing Regulations 2008,
- (bb) an offence under the Consumer Protection from Unfair Trading Regulations 2008, or]
- (c) an offence involving dishonesty or deception.

(3) An application under this section may be made—

- (a) where proceedings have been brought in any court for a relevant offence relating to some or all of the unauthorised decoders, to that court, or
- (b) where no application for the forfeiture of the unauthorised decoders has been made under paragraph (a), by way of complaint to a magistrates' court.

(4) On an application under this section, the court shall make an order for the forfeiture of any unauthorised decoders only if it is satisfied that a relevant offence has been committed in relation to the unauthorised decoders.

(5) A court may infer for the purposes of this section that such an offence has been committed in relation to any unauthorised decoders if it is satisfied that such an offence has been committed in relation to unauthorised decoders which are representative of the unauthorised decoders in question (whether by reason of being of the same design or part of the same consignment or batch or otherwise).

(6) Any person aggrieved by an order made under this section by a magistrates' court, or by a decision of such a court not to make such an order, may appeal against that order or decision—

- (a) in England and Wales, to the Crown Court, or
- (b) in Northern Ireland, to the county court.

(7) An order under this section may contain such provision as appears to the court to be appropriate for delaying the coming into force of the order pending the making and determination of any appeal (including any application under section 111 of the Magistrates' Courts Act 1980 (c 43) or Article 146 of the Magistrates' Courts (Northern Ireland) Order 1981 (SI 1981/1675 (NI 26)) (statement of case)).

(8) Subject to subsection (9), where any unauthorised decoders are forfeited under this section they shall be destroyed in accordance with such directions as the court may give.

(9) On making an order under this section the court may direct that the unauthorised decoders to which the order relates shall (instead of being destroyed) be forfeited to a person who has rights or remedies under section 298 in relation to the unauthorised decoders in question, or dealt with in such other way as the court considers appropriate.]

NOTES

Inserted by the Copyright, etc and Trade Marks (Offences and Enforcement) Act 2002, s 5.

Sub-s (2): paras (ba), (bb) substituted for the word "or" by the Consumer Protection from Unfair Trading Regulations 2008, SI 2008/1277, reg 30(1), Sch 2, Pt 1, paras 39, 44.

[2.397]

[297D Forfeiture of unauthorised decoders: Scotland

(1) In Scotland the court may make an order under this section for the forfeiture of unauthorised decoders.

(2) An order under this section may be made—

- (a) on an application by the procurator-fiscal made in the manner specified in section 134 of the Criminal Procedure (Scotland) Act 1995 (c 46), or
- (b) where a person is convicted of a relevant offence, in addition to any other penalty which the court may impose.

(3) On an application under subsection (2)(a), the court shall make an order for the forfeiture of any unauthorised decoders only if it is satisfied that a relevant offence has been committed in relation to the unauthorised decoders.

(4) The court may infer for the purposes of this section that such an offence has been committed in relation to any unauthorised decoders if it is satisfied that such an offence has been committed in relation to unauthorised decoders which are representative of the unauthorised decoders in question (whether by reason of being of the same design or part of the same consignment or batch or otherwise).

(5) The procurator-fiscal making the application under subsection (2)(a) shall serve on any person appearing to him to be the owner of, or otherwise to have an interest in, the unauthorised decoders to which the application relates a copy of the application, together with a notice giving him the opportunity to appear at the hearing of the application to show cause why the unauthorised decoders should not be forfeited.

(6) Service under subsection (5) shall be carried out, and such service may be proved, in the manner specified for citation of an accused in summary proceedings under the Criminal Procedure (Scotland) Act 1995 (c 46).

(7) Any person upon whom notice is served under subsection (5) and any other person claiming to be the owner of, or otherwise to have an interest in, unauthorised decoders to which an application under this section relates shall be entitled to appear at the hearing of the application to show cause why the unauthorised decoders should not be forfeited.

(8) The court shall not make an order following an application under subsection (2)(a)—

(a) if any person on whom notice is served under subsection (5) does not appear, unless service of the notice on that person is proved, or

(b) if no notice under subsection (5) has been served, unless the court is satisfied that in the circumstances it was reasonable not to serve such notice.

(9) Where an order for the forfeiture of any unauthorised decoders is made following an application under subsection (2)(a), any person who appeared, or was entitled to appear, to show cause why the unauthorised decoders should not be forfeited may, within 21 days of the making of the order, appeal to the High Court by Bill of Suspension.

(10) Section 182(5)(a) to (e) of the Criminal Procedure (Scotland) Act 1995 shall apply to an appeal under subsection (9) as it applies to a stated case under Part 2 of that Act.

(11) An order following an application under subsection (2)(a) shall not take effect—

(a) until the end of the period of 21 days beginning with the day after the day on which the order is made, or

(b) if an appeal is made under subsection (9) above within that period, until the appeal is determined or abandoned.

(12) An order under subsection (2)(b) shall not take effect—

(a) until the end of the period within which an appeal against the order could be brought under the Criminal Procedure (Scotland) Act 1995 (c 46), or

(b) if an appeal is made within that period, until the appeal is determined or abandoned.

(13) Subject to subsection (14), where any unauthorised decoders are forfeited under this section they shall be destroyed in accordance with such directions as the court may give.

(14) On making an order under this section the court may direct that the unauthorised decoders to which the order relates shall (instead of being destroyed) be forfeited to a person who has rights or remedies under section 298 in relation to the unauthorised decoders in question, or dealt with in such other way as the court considers appropriate.

(15) For the purposes of this section—

["relevant offence" means—

(a) an offence under section 297A(1) (criminal liability for making, importing, etc unauthorised decoders),

(b) an offence under the Trade Descriptions Act 1968,

(c) an offence under the Business Protection from Misleading Marketing Regulations 2008,

(d) an offence under the Consumer Protection from Unfair Trading Regulations 2008, or

(e) any offence involving dishonesty or deception;]

"the court" means—

(a) in relation to an order made on an application under subsection (2)(a), the sheriff, and

(b) in relation to an order made under subsection (2)(b), the court which imposed the penalty.]

NOTES

Inserted by the Copyright, etc and Trade Marks (Offences and Enforcement) Act 2002, s 5.

Sub-s (15): definition "relevant offence" substituted by the Consumer Protection from Unfair Trading Regulations 2008, SI 2008/1277, reg 30(1), Sch 2, Pt 1, paras 39, 45.

[2.398]

[298 Rights and remedies in respect of apparatus, &c for unauthorised reception of transmissions

(1) A person who—

(a) makes charges for the reception of programmes included in a broadcasting . . . service provided from a place in the United Kingdom or any other member State,

(b) sends encrypted transmissions of any other description from a place in the United Kingdom or any other member State, or

(c) provides conditional access services from a place in the United Kingdom or any other member State,

is entitled to the following rights and remedies.

(2) He has the same rights and remedies against a person—

(a) who—

(i) makes, imports, distributes, sells or lets for hire, offers or exposes for sale or hire, or advertises for sale or hire,

(ii) has in his possession for commercial purposes, or

(iii) instals, maintains or replaces for commercial purposes,

any apparatus designed or adapted to enable or assist persons to access the programmes or other transmissions or circumvent conditional access technology related to the programmes or other transmissions when they are not entitled to do so, or

(b) who publishes or otherwise promotes by means of commercial communications any information which is calculated to enable or assist persons to access the programmes or other transmissions or circumvent conditional access technology related to the programmes or other transmissions when they are not entitled to do so,

as a copyright owner has in respect of an infringement of copyright.

(3) Further, he has the same rights under section 99 or 100 (delivery up or seizure of certain articles) in relation to any such apparatus as a copyright owner has in relation to an infringing copy.

(4) Section 72 of the [Senior Courts Act 1981], section 15 of the Law Reform (Miscellaneous Provisions) (Scotland) Act 1985 and section 94A of the Judicature (Northern Ireland) Act 1978 (withdrawal of privilege against self-incrimination in certain proceedings relating to intellectual property) apply to proceedings under this section as to proceedings under Part I of this Act (copyright).

(5) In section 97(1) (innocent infringement of copyright) as it applies to proceedings for infringement of the rights conferred by this section, the reference to the defendant not knowing or having reason to believe that copyright subsisted in the work shall be construed as a reference to his not knowing or having reason to believe that his acts infringed the rights conferred by this section.

(6) Section 114 applies, with the necessary modifications, in relation to the disposal of anything delivered up or seized by virtue of subsection (3) above.

(7) In this section "apparatus", "conditional access technology" and "encrypted" have the same meanings as in section 297A, "transmission" includes transmissions as defined in that section and "conditional access services" means services comprising the provision of conditional access technology.]

NOTES

Substituted by the Conditional Access (Unauthorised Decoders) Regulations 2000, SI 2000/1175, reg 2(1), (3).

Sub-s (1): words omitted from para (a) repealed by the Copyright and Related Rights Regulations 2003, SI 2003/2498, reg 2(2), Sch 2, subject to transitional provisions as noted to s 1 of this Act at **[2.7]**.

Sub-s (4): words in square brackets substituted by the Constitutional Reform Act 2005, s 59(5), Sch 11, Pt 1, para 1.

Application of this section: see the note to s 297 at **[2.393]**.

[2.399]

299 Supplementary provisions as to fraudulent reception

(1) Her Majesty may by Order in Council—

(a) provide that section 297 applies in relation to programmes included in services provided from a country or territory outside the United Kingdom, and

(b) provide that section 298 applies in relation to such programmes and to encrypted transmissions sent from such a country or territory.

(2) . . .

(3) A statutory instrument containing an Order in Council under subsection (1) shall be subject to annulment in pursuance of a resolution of either House of Parliament.

(4) Where sections 297 and 298 apply in relation to a broadcasting service . . . , they also apply to any service run for the person providing that service, or a person providing programmes for that service, which consists wholly or mainly in the sending by means of a telecommunications system of sounds or visual images, or both

(5) In sections 297[, 297A] and 298, and this section, "programme" [and "broadcasting"], and related expressions, have the same meaning as in Part I (copyright).

NOTES

Sub-s (2): repealed by the Broadcasting Act 1990, ss 179(2), 203(3), Sch 21.

Sub-s (4): words omitted repealed by the Copyright and Related Rights Regulations 2003, SI 2003/2498, reg 2(2), Sch 2, subject to transitional provisions as noted to s 1 of this Act at **[2.7]**.

Sub-s (5): figure in first pair of square brackets inserted by the Broadcasting Act 1990, s 179(2); words in second pair of square brackets substituted by SI 2003/2498, reg 2(1), Sch 1, Pt 1, paras 1, 3(3), subject to transitional provisions as noted to s 1 of this Act at **[2.7]**.

Orders: the Fraudulent Reception of Transmissions (Guernsey) Order 1989, SI 1989/2003.

300 (*Repealed by the Trade Marks Act 1994, s 106(2), Sch 5.*)

Provisions for the benefit of [Great Ormond Street Hospital for Children]

NOTES

Cross-heading: words in square brackets substituted by the NHS (Charitable Trusts Etc) Act 2016, s 3(1), (2)(b).

[2.400]
301 Provisions for the benefit of [Great Ormond Street Hospital for Children]
The provisions of Schedule 6 have effect for conferring on [GOSH Children's Charity for the benefit of Great Ormond Street Hospital for Children] a right to a royalty in respect of the public performance, commercial publication [or communication to the public] of the play "Peter Pan" by Sir James Matthew Barrie, or of any adaptation of that work, notwithstanding that copyright in the work expired on 31st December 1987.

NOTES
Section heading: words in square brackets substituted by the NHS (Charitable Trusts Etc) Act 2016, s 3(1), (2)(a).
Words in first pair of square brackets substituted by the NHS (Charitable Trusts Etc) Act 2016, s 3(1), (3); words in second pair of square brackets substituted by the Copyright and Related Rights Regulations 2003, SI 2003/2498, reg 2(1), Sch 1, Pt 1, paras 1, 6(2)(d), subject to transitional provisions as noted to s 1 of this Act at **[2.7]**.

Financial assistance for certain international bodies

[2.401]
302 Financial assistance for certain international bodies
(1) The Secretary of State may give financial assistance, in the form of grants, loans or guarantees to—
(a) any international organisation having functions relating to trade marks or other intellectual property, or
(b) any [EU] institution or other body established under any of the [EU] Treaties having any such functions,

with a view to the establishment or maintenance by that organisation, institution or body of premises in the United Kingdom.
(2) Any expenditure of the Secretary of State under this section shall be defrayed out of money provided by Parliament; and any sums received by the Secretary of State in consequence of this section shall be paid into the Consolidated Fund.

NOTES
Sub-s (1): reference in square brackets in both places it occurs substituted by the Treaty of Lisbon (Changes in Terminology) Order 2011, SI 2011/1043, art 6(1)(a), (c).
Trade marks or registered trade marks: see the note preceding s 1, at **[2.7]**.

General

[2.402]
303 Consequential amendments and repeals
(1) The enactments specified in Schedule 7 are amended in accordance with that Schedule, the amendments being consequential on the provisions of this Act.
(2) The enactments specified in Schedule 8 are repealed to the extent specified.

[2.403]
304 Extent
(1) Provision as to the extent of Part I (copyright), Part II (rights in performances) and Part III (design right) is to be found in sections 157, 207 and 255 respectively; the extent of the other provisions of this Act is as follows.
(2) Parts IV to VII extend to England and Wales, Scotland and Northern Ireland, except that—
(a) sections 287 to 292 (patents county courts) extend to England and Wales only,
(b) . . . and
(c) the amendments and repeals in Schedules 7 and 8 have the same extent as the enactments amended or repealed.

(3) The following provisions extend to the Isle of Man subject to any modifications contained in an Order made by Her Majesty in Council—
(a) sections 293 and 294 (patents: licences of right), and
(b) paragraphs 24 and 29 of Schedule 5 (patents: effect of filing international application for patent and power to extend time limits).

(4) Her Majesty may by Order in Council direct that the following provisions extend to the Isle of Man, with such exceptions and modifications as may be specified in the Order—
(a) Part IV (registered designs),
(b) Part V (patent agents),
(c) the provisions of Schedule 5 (patents: miscellaneous amendments) not mentioned in subsection (3) above,
(d) sections 297 to 299 (fraudulent reception of transmissions), and
(e) section 300 (fraudulent application or use of trade mark).

(5) Her Majesty may by Order in Council direct that sections 297 to 299 (fraudulent reception of transmissions) extend to any of the Channel Islands, with such exceptions and modifications as may be specified in the Order.

(6) Any power conferred by this Act to make provision by Order in Council for or in connection with the extent of provisions of this Act to a country outside the United Kingdom includes power to extend to that country, subject to any modifications specified in the Order, any provision of this Act which amends or repeals an enactment extending to that country.

NOTES

Sub-s (2): para (b) repealed by the NHS (Charitable Trusts Etc) Act 2016, s 3(1), (4).

Orders: the Copyright, Designs and Patents Act 1988 (Isle of Man) (No 2) Order 1989, SI 1989/1292; the Copyright, Designs and Patents Act 1988 (Guernsey) Order 1989, SI 1989/1997; the Copyright, Designs and Patents Act 1988 (Isle of Man) Order 1990, SI 1990/1505; the Copyright, Designs and Patents Act 1988 (Isle of Man) (No 2) Order 1990, SI 1990/2293; the Registered Designs (Isle of Man) Order 2013, SI 2013/2533.

[2.404]

305 Commencement

(1) The following provisions of this Act come into force on Royal Assent—

paragraphs 24 and 29 of Schedule 5 (patents: effect of filing international application for patent and power to extend time limits);

section 301 and Schedule 6 (provisions for the benefit of the Hospital for Sick Children).

(2) Sections 293 and 294 (licences of right) come into force at the end of the period of two months beginning with the passing of this Act.

(3) The other provisions of this Act come into force on such day as the Secretary of State may appoint by order made by statutory instrument, and different days may be appointed for different provisions and different purposes.

NOTES

Orders: the Copyright, Designs and Patents Act 1988 (Commencement No 1) Order 1989, SI 1989/816; the Copyright, Designs and Patents Act 1988 (Commencement No 2) Order 1989, SI 1989/955; the Copyright, Designs and Patents Act 1988 (Commencement No 3) Order 1989, SI 1989/1032; the Copyright, Designs and Patents Act 1988 (Commencement No 4) Order 1989, SI 1989/1303; the Copyright, Designs and Patents Act 1988 (Commencement No 5) Order 1990, SI 1990/1400; the Copyright, Designs and Patents Act 1988 (Commencement No 6) Order 1990, SI 1990/2168.

[2.405]

306 Short title

This Act may be cited as the Copyright, Designs and Patents Act 1988.

SCHEDULES

[SCHEDULE ZA1
CERTAIN PERMITTED USES OF ORPHAN WORKS

Section 76A

PART 1
GENERAL PROVISIONS

Certain permitted uses of orphan works by relevant bodies

[2.406]

1 (1) A relevant body does not infringe the copyright in a relevant work in its collection which is an orphan work by—

(a) making the orphan work available to the public; or

(b) reproducing the orphan work for the purposes of digitisation, making available, indexing, cataloguing, preservation or restoration.

(2) A relevant body does not infringe the rights conferred by Chapter 2 of Part 2 by doing either of the following in relation to a relevant work in its collection which is an orphan work—

(a) making the orphan work available to the public; or

(b) reproducing the orphan work for the purposes of digitisation, making available, indexing, cataloguing, preservation or restoration.

(3) A relevant body does not commit an offence under section 107 or 198 by using an orphan work in a way which, by virtue of this Schedule, does not infringe copyright or the rights conferred by Chapter 2 of Part 2.

(4) This paragraph is subject to paragraph 6 (further requirements for use of orphan works).

Meaning of "relevant body", "relevant work" and "rightholder"

2 (1) In this Schedule "relevant body" means—

(a) a publicly accessible library, educational establishment or museum,

(b) an archive,

(c) a film or audio heritage institution, or

(d) a public service broadcasting organisation.

(2) Subject to sub-paragraph (4), in this Schedule "relevant work" means a work to which sub-paragraph (3) applies which is—

(a) a work in the form of a book, journal, newspaper, magazine or other writing which is contained in the collection of a publicly accessible library, educational establishment or museum, an archive or a film or audio heritage institution;
(b) a cinematographic or audiovisual work or a sound recording which is contained in the collection of a publicly accessible library, educational establishment or museum, an archive or a film or audio heritage institution; or
(c) a cinematographic or audiovisual work or a sound recording which was commissioned for exclusive exploitation by, or produced by, one or more public service broadcasting organisations on or before 31 December 2002 and is contained in the archives of that organisation or one or more of those organisations.

(3) This sub-paragraph applies to a work if—
(a) it is protected by copyright or rights conferred by Chapter 2 of Part 2, and
(b) the first publication or first broadcast of the work was in a member State.

(4) In this Schedule "relevant work" also includes a work listed in any of paragraphs (a) to (c) of sub-paragraph (2) which—
(a) is protected by copyright or rights conferred by Chapter 2 of Part 2, and
(b) has never been published or broadcast, but
(c) has been made publicly accessible by a relevant body with the consent of the rightholders,

as long as it is reasonable to assume that the rightholders would not oppose the use of the work as mentioned in paragraph 1(1) or (2).

(5) References in this Schedule to a relevant work include—
(a) a work that is embedded or incorporated in, or constitutes an integral part of, a relevant work, and
(b) a performance in relation to which rights are conferred by Chapter 2 of Part 2 and which is embedded or incorporated in, or constitutes an integral part of, a relevant work.

(6) In this Schedule "rightholder" in relation to a relevant work means—
(a) an owner of the copyright in the work,
(b) a licensee under an exclusive licence in relation to the work,
(c) a person with rights under Chapter 2 of Part 2 in relation to a performance recorded by the work, or
(d) a licensee under an exclusive licence in relation to those rights.

(7) In the application of sub-paragraph (6) to a performance by virtue of sub-paragraph (5), the reference in sub-paragraph (6)(c) to a performance recorded by the work is to be read as a reference to the performance.

(8) In this paragraph "public service broadcasting organisation" includes a public service broadcaster within the meaning of section 264 of the Communications Act 2003.

Meaning of "orphan work"

3 (1) For the purposes of this Schedule a relevant work is an orphan work if—
(a) there is a single rightholder in the work and the rightholder has not been identified or located, or
(b) there is more than one rightholder in the work and none of the rightholders has been identified or located,

despite a diligent search for the rightholder or rightholders having been carried out and recorded in accordance with paragraph 5.

(2) Subject as follows, a relevant work with more than one rightholder is also an orphan work for the purposes of this Schedule if—
(a) one or more of the rightholders has been identified or located, and
(b) one or more of the rightholders has not been identified or located despite a diligent search for the rightholder or rightholders having been carried out and recorded in accordance with paragraph 5.

Mutual recognition of orphan work status

4 A relevant work which is designated as an orphan work in another member State is an orphan work for the purposes of this Schedule.

Diligent searches

5 (1) For the purposes of establishing whether a relevant work is an orphan work, a relevant body must ensure that a diligent search is carried out in good faith in respect of the work by consulting the appropriate sources for the category of work in question.

(2) The relevant body must carry out the diligent search prior to the use of the relevant work.

(3) The sources that are appropriate for each category of relevant work must as a minimum include—
(a) the relevant databases maintained by the Office for Harmonization in the Internal Market; and

(b) where there is no record that the relevant work is an orphan work in the databases referred to in paragraph (a), the relevant sources listed in Part 2 of this Schedule for that category.

(4) The Comptroller-General of Patents, Designs and Trade Marks may issue guidance on the appropriate sources to be consulted under this paragraph for any particular category of work.

(5) Subject to sub-paragraphs (6) to (8), a search of the sources mentioned in sub-paragraph (3)(b) must be carried out in the member State in which the relevant work was first published or broadcast.

(6) If the relevant work is a cinematographic or audiovisual work and the producer of the work has his or her headquarters or habitual residence in a member State, the search must be carried out in the member State of the headquarters or habitual residence.

(7) If the relevant work falls within paragraph 2(4), the search must be carried out in the member State where the organisation that made the work publicly accessible with the consent of the rightholders is established.

(8) If there is evidence to suggest that relevant information on rightholders is to be found in other countries, a relevant body carrying out a search in accordance with sub-paragraph (3)(b) must also consult the sources of information available in those other countries.

(9) A relevant body that makes use of orphan works in accordance with this Schedule must maintain records of its diligent searches and must provide the following information to the Office for Harmonization in the Internal Market—

(a) the results of the diligent searches which the relevant body has carried out and which first established that a work is an orphan work;

(b) the use that the relevant body makes of the orphan works;

(c) any change, pursuant to paragraph 7, of the orphan work status of a relevant work that the relevant body has used and in respect of which the relevant body has been supplied with evidence by a rightholder in accordance with paragraph 7(2); and

(d) the contact information for the relevant body.

Further requirements for use of orphan works

6 This Schedule does not prevent the use by a relevant body of an orphan work as mentioned in paragraph 1 from infringing copyright or the rights conferred by Chapter 2 of Part 2 if—

(a) the revenues generated in the course of the use of the orphan work are used otherwise than for the exclusive purpose of covering the costs of the relevant body in digitising orphan works and making them available to the public;

(b) the relevant body uses the orphan work in order to achieve aims which are not related to its public-interest mission (and the aims which are to be treated as related to its public interest mission include, in particular, the preservation of, the restoration of, and the provision of cultural and educational access to, works contained in its collection);

(c) any rightholder who has been identified or located has, in relation to the rightholder's rights, not authorised the relevant body's use of the orphan work as mentioned in paragraph 1; or

(d) the relevant body fails, in the course of the permitted use of the orphan work, to acknowledge the name of any author of or other rightholder in the work who has been identified.

End of orphan work status

7 (1) This paragraph applies to a rightholder who has not been identified or located in relation to a relevant work.

(2) A rightholder may put an end to the orphan work status of a relevant work by providing evidence of his or her ownership of the rights to the Office for Harmonization in the Internal Market or to the relevant body which carried out the diligent search which first established that the relevant work is an orphan work.

(3) A relevant body that is using or has used the orphan work must within a reasonable period provide the rightholder with fair compensation for that body's use of the relevant work together with information on how the fair compensation has been calculated.

(4) If a relevant body and the rightholder cannot agree on the amount of compensation payable, either of them may apply to the Copyright Tribunal to determine the amount.]

NOTES

Commencement: 29 October 2014.

Schedule inserted by the Copyright and Rights in Performances (Certain Permitted Uses of Orphan Works) Regulations 2014, SI 2014/2861, reg 3(5), Schedule.

[PART 2
SOURCES TO BE SEARCHED DURING DILIGENT SEARCH

[2.407]

Category of relevant work	Sources to be searched

1. Published books	(a) legal deposit, library catalogues and authority files maintained by libraries and other institutions; (b) the publishers' and authors' associations in the country in question; (c) existing databases and registries, WATCH (Writers, Artists and their Copyright Holders), the ISBN (International Standard Book Number) and databases listing books in print; (d) the databases of the relevant collecting societies, including reproduction rights organisations; (e) sources that integrate multiple databases and registries, including VIAF (Virtual International Authority Files) and ARROW (Accessible Registries of Rights Information and Orphan Works).
2. Newspapers, magazines, journals and periodicals	(a) the ISSN (International Standard Serial Number) for periodical publications; (b) indexes and catalogues from library holdings and collections; (c) legal deposit; (d) the publishers' associations and the authors' and journalists' associations in the country in question; (e) the databases of relevant collecting societies including reproduction rights organisations.
3. Visual works, including fine art, photography, illustration, design, architecture, sketches of the latter works and other such works that are contained in books, journals, newspapers and magazines or other works	(a) the sources referred to in paragraphs 1 and 2; (b) the databases of the relevant collecting societies, in particular for visual arts, and including reproduction rights organisations; (c) the databases of picture agencies, where applicable.
4. Audiovisual works and sound recordings	(a) legal deposit; (b) the producers' associations in the country in question; (c) databases of film or audio heritage institutions and national libraries; (d) databases with relevant standards and identifiers such as ISAN (International Standard Audiovisual Number) for audiovisual material, ISWC (International Standard Music Work Code) for musical works and ISRC (International Standard Recording Code) for sound recordings; (e) the databases of the relevant collecting societies, in particular for authors, performers, sound recording producers and audiovisual producers; (f) credits and other information appearing on the work's packaging; (g) databases of other relevant associations representing a specific category of rightholders.
5. Relevant works which have not been published or broadcast	Those sources that are listed in paragraphs 1 to 4 above which are appropriate to a relevant work which is unpublished.]

NOTES

Commencement: 29 October 2014.

Inserted as noted to Pt 1 of this Schedule at **[2.406]**.

[SCHEDULE A1
REGULATION OF LICENSING BODIES

Codes of practice

[2.408]

1. (1) The Secretary of State may by regulations make provision for a licensing body to be required to adopt a code of practice that complies with criteria specified in the regulations.

(2) The regulations may provide that, if a licensing body fails to adopt such a code of practice, any code of practice that is approved for the purposes of that licensing body by the Secretary of State, or by a person designated by the Secretary of State under the regulations, has effect as a code of practice adopted by the body.

Part 2 Copyright

(3) The regulations must provide that a code is not to be approved for the purposes of provision under sub-paragraph (2) unless it complies with criteria specified in the regulations.

2. Regulations under paragraph 1 may make provision as to conditions that are to be satisfied, and procedures that are to be followed—

(a) before a licensing body is required to adopt a code of practice as described in paragraph 1(1);

(b) before a code of practice has effect as one adopted by a licensing body as described in paragraph 1(2).

Licensing code ombudsman

3. (1) The Secretary of State may by regulations make provision—

(a) for the appointment of a person (the "licensing code ombudsman") to investigate and determine disputes about a licensing body's compliance with its code of practice;

(b) for the reference of disputes to the licensing code ombudsman;

(c) for the investigation and determination of a dispute so referred.

(2) Provision made under this paragraph may in particular include provision—

(a) about eligibility for appointment as the licensing code ombudsman;

(b) about the disputes to be referred to the licensing code ombudsman;

(c) requiring any person to provide information, documents or assistance to the licensing code ombudsman for the purposes of an investigation or determination;

(d) requiring a licensing body to comply with a determination of the licensing code ombudsman;

(e) about the payment of expenses and allowances to the licensing code ombudsman.

Code reviewer

4. (1) The Secretary of State may by regulations make provision—

(a) for the appointment by the Secretary of State of a person (the "code reviewer") to review and report to the Secretary of State on—

(i) the codes of practice adopted by licensing bodies, and

(ii) compliance with the codes of practice;

(b) for the carrying out of a review and the making of a report by that person.

(2) The regulations must provide for the Secretary of State, before appointing a person as the code reviewer, to consult persons whom the Secretary of State considers represent the interests of licensing bodies, licensees, members of licensing bodies, and the Intellectual Property Office.

(3) The regulations may, in particular, make provision—

(a) requiring any person to provide information, documents or assistance to the code reviewer for the purposes of a review or report;

(b) about the payment of expenses and allowances to the code reviewer.

(4) In this paragraph "member", in relation to a licensing body, means a person on whose behalf the body is authorised to negotiate or grant licences.

Sanctions

5. (1) The Secretary of State may by regulations provide for the consequences of a failure by a licensing body to comply with—

(a) a requirement to adopt a code of practice under provision within paragraph 1(1);

(b) a code of practice that has been adopted by the body in accordance with a requirement under provision within paragraph 1(1), or that has effect as one adopted by the body under provision within paragraph 1(2);

(c) a requirement imposed on the body under any other provision made under this Schedule;

(d) an authorisation under regulations under section 116A or 116B;

(e) a requirement imposed by regulations under section 116A or 116B;

(f) an authorisation under regulations under paragraph 1A or 1B of Schedule 2A;

(g) a requirement imposed by regulations under paragraph 1A or 1B of that Schedule.

(2) The regulations may in particular provide for—

(a) the imposition of financial penalties or other sanctions;

(b) the imposition of sanctions on a director, manager or similar officer of a licensing body or, where the body's affairs are managed by its members, on a member.

(3) The regulations must include provision—

(a) for determining whether there has been a failure to comply with a requirement or code of practice for the purposes of any provision made under sub-paragraph (1);

(b) for determining any sanction that may be imposed in respect of the failure to comply;

(c) for an appeal against a determination within paragraph (a) or (b).

(4) A financial penalty imposed under sub-paragraph (2) must not be greater than £50,000.

(5) The regulations may provide for a determination within sub-paragraph (3)(a) or (3)(b) to be made by the Secretary of State or by a person designated by the Secretary of State under the regulations.

(6) The regulations may make provision for requiring a person to give the person by whom a determination within sub-paragraph (3)(a) falls to be made (the "adjudicator") any information that the adjudicator reasonably requires for the purpose of making that determination.

Fees

6. (1) The Secretary of State may by regulations require a licensing body to which regulations under any other paragraph of this Schedule apply to pay fees to the Secretary of State.

(2) The aggregate amount of fees payable under the regulations must not be more than the cost to the Secretary of State of administering the operation of regulations under this Schedule.

General

7. (1) The power to make regulations under this Schedule includes in particular power—

(a) to make incidental, supplementary or consequential provision, including provision extending or restricting the jurisdiction of the Copyright Tribunal or conferring powers on it;

(b) to make provision for bodies of a particular description, or carrying out activities of a particular description, not to be treated as licensing bodies for the purposes of requirements imposed under regulations under this Schedule;

(c) to make provision that applies only in respect of licensing bodies of a particular description, or only in respect of activities of a particular description;

(d) otherwise to make different provision for different purposes.

(2) Regulations under a paragraph of this Schedule may amend Part 1 or Part 2, or any other enactment or subordinate legislation passed or made before the paragraph in question comes into force, for the purpose of making consequential provision or extending or restricting the jurisdiction of the Copyright Tribunal or conferring powers on it.

(3) The power to make regulations is exercisable by statutory instrument.

(4) A statutory instrument containing regulations may not be made unless a draft of the instrument has been laid before and approved by a resolution of each House of Parliament.

8. References in this Schedule to a licensing body are to a body that is a licensing body for the purposes of Chapter 7 of Part 1 or Chapter 2 of Part 2, and references to licensees are to be construed accordingly.]

NOTES

Commencement: 25 April 2013.

Inserted by the Enterprise and Regulatory Reform Act 2013, s 77(4), Sch 22, Pt 1, para 1.

SCHEDULE 1
COPYRIGHT: TRANSITIONAL PROVISIONS AND SAVINGS

Section 170

Introductory

[2.409]

1. (1) In this Schedule—

"the 1911 Act" means the Copyright Act 1911,

"the 1956 Act" means the Copyright Act 1956, and

"the new copyright provisions" means the provisions of this Act relating to copyright, that is, Part I (including this Schedule) and Schedules 3, 7 and 8 so far as they make amendments or repeals consequential on the provisions of Part I.

(2) References in this Schedule to "commencement", without more, are to the date on which the new copyright provisions come into force.

(3) References in this Schedule to "existing works" are to works made before commencement; and for this purpose a work of which the making extended over a period shall be taken to have been made when its making was completed.

2. (1) In relation to the 1956 Act, references in this Schedule to a work include any work or other subject-matter within the meaning of that Act.

(2) In relation to the 1911 Act—

(a) references in this Schedule to copyright include the right conferred by section 24 of that Act in substitution for a right subsisting immediately before the commencement of that Act;

(b) references in this Schedule to copyright in a sound recording are to the copyright under that Act in records embodying the recording; and

(c) references in this Schedule to copyright in a film are to any copyright under that Act in the film (so far as it constituted a dramatic work for the purposes of that Act) or in photographs forming part of the film.

General principles: continuity of the law

3. The new copyright provisions apply in relation to things existing at commencement as they apply in relation to things coming into existence after commencement, subject to any express provision to the contrary.

4. (1) The provisions of this paragraph have effect for securing the continuity of the law so far as the new copyright provisions re-enact (with or without modification) earlier provisions.

(2) A reference in an enactment, instrument or other document to copyright, or to a work or other subject-matter in which copyright subsists, which apart from this Act would be construed as referring to copyright under the 1956 Act shall be construed, so far as may be required for continuing its effect, as being, or as the case may require, including, a reference to copyright under this Act or to works in which copyright subsists under this Act.

(3) Anything done (including subordinate legislation made), or having effect as done, under or for the purposes of a provision repealed by this Act has effect as if done under or for the purposes of the corresponding provision of the new copyright provisions.

(4) References (expressed or implied) in this Act or any other enactment, instrument or document to any of the new copyright provisions shall, so far as the context permits, be construed as including, in relation to times, circumstances and purposes before commencement, a reference to corresponding earlier provisions.

(5) A reference (express or implied) in an enactment, instrument or other document to a provision repealed by this Act shall be construed, so far as may be required for continuing its effect, as a reference to the corresponding provision of this Act.

(6) The provisions of this paragraph have effect subject to any specific transitional provision or saving and to any express amendment made by this Act.

Subsistence of copyright

5. (1) Copyright subsists in an existing work after commencement only if copyright subsisted in it immediately before commencement.

(2) Sub-paragraph (1) does not prevent an existing work qualifying for copyright protection after commencement—

(a) under section 155 (qualification by virtue of first publication), . . .

(b) by virtue of an Order under section 159 (application of Part I to countries to which it does not extend)[; or

(c) where the work is an artistic work in which copyright subsists as a result of the disapplication of paragraph 6(1) by paragraph 6(1A)].

6. (1) Copyright shall not subsist by virtue of this Act in an artistic work made before 1st June 1957 which at the time when the work was made constituted a design capable of registration under the Registered Designs Act 1949 or under the enactments repealed by that Act, and was used, or intended to be used, as a model or pattern to be multiplied by an industrial process.

[(1A) Sub-paragraph (1) does not apply to an artistic work which was on 1st July 1995 protected under the law of another EEA state relating to copyright or related rights.]

(2) For this purpose a design shall be deemed to be used as a model or pattern to be multiplied by any industrial process—

(a) when the design is reproduced or is intended to be reproduced on more than 50 single articles, unless all the articles in which the design is reproduced or is intended to be reproduced together form only a single set of articles as defined in section 44(1) of the Registered Designs Act 1949, or

(b) when the design is to be applied to—

(i) printed paper hangings,

(ii) carpets, floor cloths or oil cloths, manufactured or sold in lengths or pieces,

(iii) textile piece goods, or textile goods manufactured or sold in lengths or pieces, or

(iv) lace, not made by hand.

7. (1) No copyright subsists in a film, as such, made before 1st June 1957.

(2) Where a film made before that date was an original dramatic work within the meaning of the 1911 Act, the new copyright provisions have effect in relation to the film as if it was an original dramatic work within the meaning of Part I.

(3) The new copyright provisions have effect in relation to photographs forming part of a film made before 1st June 1957 as they have effect in relation to photographs not forming part of a film.

8. (1) A film sound-track to which section 13(9) of the 1956 Act applied before commencement (film to be taken to include sounds in associated sound-track) shall be treated for the purposes of the new copyright provisions not as part of the film, but as a sound recording.

(2) However—

(a) copyright subsists in the sound recording only if copyright subsisted in the film immediately before commencement, and it continues to subsist until copyright in the film expires;
(b) the author and first owner of copyright in the film shall be treated as having been author and first owner of the copyright in the sound recording; and
(c) anything done before commencement under or in relation to the copyright in the film continues to have effect in relation to the sound recording as in relation to the film.

[**9.** No copyright subsists in—
(a) a wireless broadcast made before 1st June 1957, or
(b) a broadcast by cable made before 1st January 1985;
and any such broadcast shall be disregarded for the purposes of section 14(5) (duration of copyright in repeats).]

Authorship of work

10. The question who was the author of an existing work shall be determined in accordance with the new copyright provisions for the purposes of the rights conferred by Chapter IV of Part I (moral rights), and for all other purposes shall be determined in accordance with the law in force at the time the work was made.

First ownership of copyright

11. (1) The question who was first owner of copyright in an existing work shall be determined in accordance with the law in force at the time the work was made.

(2) Where before commencement a person commissioned the making of a work in circumstances falling within—
(a) section 4(3) of the 1956 Act or paragraph (a) of the proviso to section 5(1) of the 1911 Act (photographs, portraits and engravings), or
(b) the proviso to section 12(4) of the 1956 Act (sound recordings),
those provisions apply to determine first ownership of copyright in any work made in pursuance of the commission after commencement.

Duration of copyright in existing works

12. (1) The following provisions have effect with respect to the duration of copyright in existing works.

The question which provision applies to a work shall be determined by reference to the facts immediately before commencement; and expressions used in this paragraph which were defined for the purposes of the 1956 Act have the same meaning as in that Act.

(2) Copyright in the following descriptions of work continues to subsist until the date on which it would have expired under the 1956 Act—
(a) literary, dramatic or musical works in relation to which the period of 50 years mentioned in the proviso to section 2(3) of the 1956 Act (duration of copyright in works made available to the public after the death of the author) has begun to run;
(b) engravings in relation to which the period of 50 years mentioned in the proviso to section 3(4) of the 1956 Act (duration of copyright in works published after the death of the author) has begun to run;
(c) published photographs and photographs taken before 1st June 1957;
(d) published sound recordings and sound recordings made before 1st June 1957;
(e) published films and films falling within section 13(3)(a) of the 1956 Act (films registered under former enactments relating to registration of films).

(3) Copyright in anonymous or pseudonymous literary, dramatic, musical or artistic works (other than photographs) continues to subsist—
(a) if the work is published, until the date on which it would have expired in accordance with the 1956 Act, and
(b) if the work is unpublished, until the end of the period of 50 years from the end of the calendar year in which the new copyright provisions come into force or, if during that period the work is first made available to the public within the meaning of [section 12(3)] (duration of copyright in works of unknown authorship), the date on which copyright expires in accordance with that provision;
unless, in any case, the identity of the author becomes known before that date, in which case [section 12(2)] applies (general rule: life of the author [plus 70] years).

(4) Copyright in the following descriptions of work continues to subsist until the end of the period of 50 years from the end of the calendar year in which the new copyright provisions come into force—
(a) literary, dramatic and musical works of which the author has died and in relation to which none of the acts mentioned in paragraphs (a) to (e) of the proviso to section 2(3) of the 1956 Act has been done;
(b) unpublished engravings of which the author has died;
(c) unpublished photographs taken on or after 1st June 1957.

(5) Copyright in the following descriptions of work continues to subsist until the end of the period of 50 years from the end of the calendar year in which the new copyright provisions come into force—

(a) unpublished sound recordings made on or after 1st June 1957;

(b) films not falling within sub-paragraph (2)(e) above,

unless the recording or film is published before the end of that period in which case copyright in it shall continue until the end of the period of 50 years from the end of the calendar year in which the recording or film is published.

(6) Copyright in any other description of existing work continues to subsist until the date on which copyright in that description of work expires in accordance with sections 12 to 15 of this Act.

(7) The above provisions do not apply to works subject to Crown or Parliamentary copyright (see paragraphs 41 to 43 below).

Perpetual copyright under the Copyright Act 1775

13. (1) The rights conferred on universities and colleges by the Copyright Act 1775 shall continue to subsist until the end of the period of 50 years from the end of the calendar year in which the new copyright provisions come into force and shall then expire.

(2) The provisions of the following Chapters of Part I—

Chapter III (acts permitted in relation to copyright works),
Chapter VI (remedies for infringement),
Chapter VII (provisions with respect to copyright licensing), and
Chapter VIII (the Copyright Tribunal),

apply in relation to those rights as they apply in relation to copyright under this Act.

Acts infringing copyright

14. (1) The provisions of Chapters II and III of Part I as to the acts constituting an infringement of copyright apply only in relation to acts done after commencement; the provisions of the 1956 Act continue to apply in relation to acts done before commencement.

(2) So much of section 18(2) as extends the restricted act of issuing copies to the public to include the rental to the public of copies of sound recordings, films or computer programs does not apply in relation to a copy of a sound recording, film or computer program acquired by any person before commencement for the purpose of renting it to the public.

(3) For the purposes of section 27 (meaning of "infringing copy") the question whether the making of an article constituted an infringement of copyright, or would have done if the article had been made in the United Kingdom, shall be determined—

(a) in relation to an article made on or after 1st June 1957 and before commencement, by reference to the 1956 Act, and

(b) in relation to an article made before 1st June 1957, by reference to the 1911 Act.

(4) For the purposes of the application of sections 31(2), 51(2) and 62(3) (subsequent exploitation of things whose making was, by virtue of an earlier provision of the section, not an infringement of copyright) to things made before commencement, it shall be assumed that the new copyright provisions were in force at all material times.

(5) Section 55 (articles for producing material in a particular typeface) applies where articles have been marketed as mentioned in subsection (1) before commencement with the substitution for the period mentioned in subsection (3) of the period of 25 years from the end of the calendar year in which the new copyright provisions come into force.

(6) Section 56 (transfer of copies, adaptations, &c of work in electronic form) does not apply in relation to a copy purchased before commencement.

(7) In section 65 (reconstruction of buildings) the reference to the owner of the copyright in the drawings or plans is, in relation to buildings constructed before commencement, to the person who at the time of the construction was the owner of the copyright in the drawings or plans under the 1956 Act, the 1911 Act or any enactment repealed by the 1911 Act.

15. (1) Section 57 (anonymous or pseudonymous works: acts permitted on assumptions as to expiry of copyright or death of author) has effect in relation to existing works subject to the following provisions.

(2) Subsection (1)(b)(i) (assumption as to expiry of copyright) does not apply in relation to—

(a) photographs, or

(b) the rights mentioned in paragraph 13 above (rights conferred by the Copyright Act 1775).

(3) . . .

16. The following provisions of section 7 of the 1956 Act continue to apply in relation to existing works—

(a) subsection (6) (copying of unpublished works from manuscript or copy in library, museum or other institution);

(b) subsection (7) (publication of work containing material to which subsection (6) applies), except paragraph (a) (duty to give notice of intended publication);

(c) subsection (8) (subsequent broadcasting, performance, &c of material published in accordance with subsection (7));

and subsection (9)(d) (illustrations) continues to apply for the purposes of those provisions.

17. Where in the case of a dramatic or musical work made before 1st July 1912, the right conferred by the 1911 Act did not include the sole right to perform the work in public, the acts restricted by the copyright shall be treated as not including—

(a) performing the work in public,

[(b) communicating the work to the public, or]

(c) doing any of the above in relation to an adaptation of the work;

and where the right conferred by the 1911 Act consisted only of the sole right to perform the work in public, the acts restricted by the copyright shall be treated as consisting only of those acts.

18. Where a work made before 1st July 1912 consists of an essay, article or portion forming part of and first published in a review, magazine or other periodical or work of a like nature, the copyright is subject to any right of publishing the essay, article, or portion in a separate form to which the author was entitled at the commencement of the 1911 Act, or would if that Act had not been passed, have become entitled under section 18 of the Copyright Act 1842.

Designs

19. (1) Section 51 (exclusion of copyright protection in relation to works recorded or embodied in design document or models) does not apply for ten years after commencement in relation to a design recorded or embodied in a design document or model before commencement.

(2) During those ten years the following provisions of Part III (design right) apply to any relevant copyright as in relation to design right—

(a) sections 237 to 239 (availability of licences of right), and

(b) sections 247 and 248 (application to comptroller to settle terms of licence of right).

(3) In section 237 as it applies by virtue of this paragraph, for the reference in subsection (1) to the last five years of the design right term there shall be substituted a reference to the last five years of the period of ten years referred to in sub-paragraph (1) above, or to so much of those last five years during which copyright subsists.

(4) In section 239 as it applies by virtue of this paragraph, for the reference in subsection (1)(b) to section 230 there shall be substituted a reference to section 99.

(5) Where a licence of right is available by virtue of this paragraph, a person to whom a licence was granted before commencement may apply to the comptroller for an order adjusting the terms of that licence.

(6) The provisions of sections 249 and 250 (appeals and rules) apply in relation to proceedings brought under or by virtue of this paragraph as to proceedings under Part III.

(7) A licence granted by virtue of this paragraph shall relate only to acts which would be permitted by section 51 if the design document or model had been made after commencement.

(8) Section 100 (right to seize infringing copies, &c) does not apply during the period of ten years referred to in sub-paragraph (1) in relation to anything to which it would not apply if the design in question had been first recorded or embodied in a design document or model after commencement.

(9) Nothing in this paragraph affects the operation of any rule of law preventing or restricting the enforcement of copyright in relation to a design.

20. *(1) Where section 10 of the 1956 Act (effect of industrial application of design corresponding to artistic work) applied in relation to an artistic work at any time before commencement, section 52(2) of this Act applies with the substitution for the period of 25 years mentioned there of the relevant period of 15 years as defined in section 10(3) of the 1956 Act.*

(2) Except as provided in sub-paragraph (1), section 52 applies only where articles are marketed as mentioned in subsection (1)(b) after commencement.

Abolition of statutory recording licence

21. Section 8 of the 1956 Act (statutory licence to copy records sold by retail) continues to apply where notice under subsection (1)(b) of that section was given before the repeal of that section by this Act, but only in respect of the making of records—

(a) within one year of the repeal coming into force, and

(b) up to the number stated in the notice as intended to be sold.

Moral rights

22. (1) No act done before commencement is actionable by virtue of any provision of Chapter IV of Part I (moral rights).

(2) Section 43 of the 1956 Act (false attribution of authorship) continues to apply in relation to acts done before commencement.

23. (1) The following provisions have effect with respect to the rights conferred by—

(a) section 77 (right to be identified as author or director), and
(b) section 80 (right to object to derogatory treatment of work).

(2) The rights do not apply—
(a) in relation to a literary, dramatic, musical and artistic work of which the author died before commencement; or
(b) in relation to a film made before commencement.

(3) The rights in relation to an existing literary, dramatic, musical or artistic work do not apply—
(a) where copyright first vested in the author, to anything which by virtue of an assignment of copyright made or licence granted before commencement may be done without infringing copyright;
(b) where copyright first vested in a person other than the author, to anything done by or with the licence of the copyright owner.

(4) The rights do not apply to anything done in relation to a record made in pursuance of section 8 of the 1956 Act (statutory recording licence).

24. The right conferred by section 85 (right to privacy of certain photographs and films) does not apply to photographs taken or films made before commencement.

Assignments and licences

25. (1) Any document made or event occurring before commencement which had any operation—
(a) affecting the ownership of the copyright in an existing work, or
(b) creating, transferring or terminating an interest, right or licence in respect of the copyright in an existing work,

has the corresponding operation in relation to copyright in the work under this Act.

(2) Expressions used in such a document shall be construed in accordance with their effect immediately before commencement.

26. (1) Section 91(1) of this Act (assignment of future copyright: statutory vesting of legal interest on copyright coming into existence) does not apply in relation to an agreement made before 1st June 1957.

(2) The repeal by this Act of section 37(2) of the 1956 Act (assignment of future copyright: devolution of right where assignee dies before copyright comes into existence) does not affect the operation of that provision in relation to an agreement made before commencement.

27. (1) Where the author of a literary, dramatic, musical or artistic work was the first owner of the copyright in it, no assignment of the copyright and no grant of any interest in it, made by him (otherwise than by will) after the passing of the 1911 Act and before 1st June 1957, shall be operative to vest in the assignee or grantee any rights with respect to the copyright in the work beyond the expiration of 25 years from the death of the author.

(2) The reversionary interest in the copyright expectant on the termination of that period may after commencement be assigned by the author during his life but in the absence of any assignment shall, on his death, devolve on his legal personal representatives as part of his estate.

(3) Nothing in this paragraph affects—
(a) an assignment of the reversionary interest by a person to whom it has been assigned,
(b) an assignment of the reversionary interest after the death of the author by his personal representatives or any person becoming entitled to it, or
(c) any assignment of the copyright after the reversionary interest has fallen in.

(4) Nothing in this paragraph applies to the assignment of the copyright in a collective work or a licence to publish a work or part of a work as part of a collective work.

(5) In sub-paragraph (4) "collective work" means—
(a) any encyclopaedia, dictionary, yearbook, or similar work;
(b) a newspaper, review, magazine, or similar periodical; and
(c) any work written in distinct parts by different authors, or in which works or parts of works of different authors are incorporated.

28. (1) This paragraph applies where copyright subsists in a literary, dramatic, musical or artistic work made before 1st July 1912 in relation to which the author, before the commencement of the 1911 Act, made such an assignment or grant as was mentioned in paragraph (a) of the proviso to section 24(1) of that Act (assignment or grant of copyright or performing right for full term of the right under the previous law).

(2) If before commencement any event has occurred or notice has been given which by virtue of paragraph 38 of Schedule 7 to the 1956 Act had any operation in relation to copyright in the work under that Act, the event or notice has the corresponding operation in relation to copyright under this Act.

(3) Any right which immediately before commencement would by virtue of paragraph 38(3) of that Schedule have been exercisable in relation to the work, or copyright in it, is exercisable in relation to the work or copyright in it under this Act.

(4) If in accordance with paragraph 38(4) of that Schedule copyright would, on a date after the commencement of the 1956 Act, have reverted to the author or his personal representatives and that date falls after the commencement of the new copyright provisions—

(a) the copyright in the work shall revert to the author or his personal representatives, as the case may be, and

(b) any interest of any other person in the copyright which subsists on that date by virtue of any document made before the commencement of the 1911 Act shall thereupon determine.

29. Section 92(2) of this Act (rights of exclusive licensee against successors in title of person granting licence) does not apply in relation to an exclusive licence granted before commencement.

Bequests

30. (1) Section 93 of this Act (copyright to pass under will with original document or other material thing embodying unpublished work)—

(a) does not apply where the testator died before 1st June 1957, and

(b) where the testator died on or after that date and before commencement, applies only in relation to an original document embodying a work.

(2) In the case of an author who died before 1st June 1957, the ownership after his death of a manuscript of his, where such ownership has been acquired under a testamentary disposition made by him and the manuscript is of a work which has not been published or performed in public, is prima facie proof of the copyright being with the owner of the manuscript.

Remedies for infringement

31. (1) Sections 96 and 97 of this Act (remedies for infringement) apply only in relation to an infringement of copyright committed after commencement; section 17 of the 1956 Act continues to apply in relation to infringements committed before commencement.

(2) Sections 99 and 100 of this Act (delivery up or seizure of infringing copies, &c) apply to infringing copies and other articles made before or after commencement; section 18 of the 1956 Act, and section 7 of the 1911 Act, (conversion damages, &c), do not apply after commencement except for the purposes of proceedings begun before commencement.

(3) Sections 101 to 102 of this Act (rights and remedies of exclusive licensee) apply where sections 96 to 100 of this Act apply; section 19 of the 1956 Act continues to apply where section 17 or 18 of that Act applies.

(4) Sections 104 to 106 of this Act (presumptions) apply only in proceedings brought by virtue of this Act; section 20 of the 1956 Act continues to apply in proceedings brought by virtue of that Act.

32. Sections 101 and 102 of this Act (rights and remedies of exclusive licensee) do not apply to a licence granted before 1st June 1957.

33. (1) The provisions of section 107 of this Act (criminal liability for making or dealing with infringing articles, &c) apply only in relation to acts done after commencement; section 21 of the 1956 Act (penalties and summary proceedings in respect of dealings which infringe copyright) continues to apply in relation to acts done before commencement.

(2) Section 109 of this Act (search warrants) applies in relation to offences committed before commencement in relation to which section 21A or 21B of the 1956 Act applied; sections 21A and 21B continue to apply in relation to warrants issued before commencement.

Copyright Tribunal: proceedings pending on commencement

34. (1) The Lord Chancellor may, after consultation with the Lord Advocate, by rules make such provision as he considers necessary or expedient with respect to proceedings pending under Part IV of the 1956 Act immediately before commencement.

(2) Rules under this paragraph shall be made by statutory instrument which shall be subject to annulment in pursuance of a resolution of either House of Parliament.

Qualification for copyright protection

35. Every work in which copyright subsisted under the 1956 Act immediately before commencement shall be deemed to satisfy the requirements of Part I of this Act as to qualification for copyright protection.

[British overseas territories]

36. (1) The 1911 Act shall remain in force as part of the law of any [British overseas territory] in which it was in force immediately before commencement until—

(a) the new copyright provisions come into force in that territory by virtue of an Order under section 157 of this Act (power to extend new copyright provisions), or

(b) in the case of any of the Channel Islands, the Act is repealed by Order under sub-paragraph (3) below.

(2) An Order in Council in force immediately before commencement which extends to any [British overseas territory] any provisions of the 1956 Act shall remain in force as part of the law of that territory until—

(a) the new copyright provisions come into force in that territory by virtue of an Order under section 157 of this Act (power to extend new copyright provisions), or

(b) in the case of the Isle of Man, the Order is revoked by Order under sub-paragraph (3) below;

and while it remains in force such an Order may be varied under the provisions of the 1956 Act under which it was made.

(3) If it appears to Her Majesty that provision with respect to copyright has been made in the law of any of the Channel Islands or the Isle of Man otherwise than by extending the provisions of Part I of this Act, Her Majesty may by Order in Council repeal the 1911 Act as it has effect as part of the law of that territory or, as the case may be, revoke the Order extending the 1956 Act there.

(4) A [British overseas territory] in which the 1911 or 1956 Act remains in force shall be treated, in the law of the countries to which Part I extends, as a country to which that Part extends; and those countries shall be treated in the law of such a territory as countries to which the 1911 Act or, as the case may be, the 1956 Act extends.

(5) If a country in which the 1911 or 1956 Act is in force ceases to be a colony of the United Kingdom, section 158 of this Act (consequences of country ceasing to be colony) applies with the substitution for the reference in subsection (3)(b) to the provisions of Part I of this Act of a reference to the provisions of the 1911 or 1956 Act, as the case may be.

(6) In this paragraph "[British overseas territory]" means any of the Channel Islands, the Isle of Man or any colony.

37. (1) This paragraph applies to a country which immediately before commencement was not a [British overseas territory] within the meaning of paragraph 36 above but—

(a) was a country to which the 1956 Act extended, or

(b) was treated as such a country by virtue of paragraph 39(2) of Schedule 7 to that Act (countries to which the 1911 Act extended or was treated as extending);

and Her Majesty may by Order in Council conclusively declare for the purposes of this paragraph whether a country was such a country or was so treated.

(2) A country to which this paragraph applies shall be treated as a country to which Part I extends for the purposes of sections 154 to 156 (qualification for copyright protection) until—

(a) an Order in Council is made in respect of that country under section 159 (application of Part I to countries to which it does not extend), or

(b) an Order in Council is made declaring that it shall cease to be so treated by reason of the fact that the provisions of the 1956 Act or, as the case may be, the 1911 Act, which extended there as part of the law of that country have been repealed or amended.

(3) A statutory instrument containing an Order in Council under this paragraph shall be subject to annulment in pursuance of a resolution of either House of Parliament.

Territorial waters and the continental shelf

38. Section 161 of this Act (application of Part I to things done in territorial waters or the United Kingdom sector of the continental shelf) does not apply in relation to anything done before commencement.

British ships, aircraft and hovercraft

39. Section 162 (British ships, aircraft and hovercraft) does not apply in relation to anything done before commencement.

Crown copyright

40. (1) Section 163 of this Act (general provisions as to Crown copyright) applies to an existing work if—

(a) section 39 of the 1956 Act applied to the work immediately before commencement, and

(b) the work is not one to which section 164, 165 or 166 applies (copyright in Acts, Measures and Bills and Parliamentary copyright: see paragraphs 42 and 43 below).

(2) Section 163(1)(b) (first ownership of copyright) has effect subject to any agreement entered into before commencement under section 39(6) of the 1956 Act.

41. (1) The following provisions have effect with respect to the duration of copyright in existing works to which section 163 (Crown copyright) applies.

The question which provision applies to a work shall be determined by reference to the facts immediately before commencement; and expressions used in this paragraph which were defined for the purposes of the 1956 Act have the same meaning as in that Act.

(2) Copyright in the following descriptions of work continues to subsist until the date on which it would have expired in accordance with the 1956 Act—

(a) published literary, dramatic or musical works;
(b) artistic works other than engravings or photographs;
(c) published engravings;
(d) published photographs and photographs taken before 1st June 1957;
(e) published sound recordings and sound recordings made before 1st June 1957;
(f) published films and films falling within section 13(3)(a) of the 1956 Act (films registered under former enactments relating to registration of films).

(3) Copyright in unpublished literary, dramatic or musical works continues to subsist until—

(a) the date on which copyright expires in accordance with section 163(3), or
(b) the end of the period of 50 years from the end of the calendar year in which the new copyright provisions come into force,

whichever is the later.

(4) Copyright in the following descriptions of work continues to subsist until the end of the period of 50 years from the end of the calendar year in which the new copyright provisions come into force—

(a) unpublished engravings;
(b) unpublished photographs taken on or after 1st June 1957.

(5) Copyright in a film or sound recording not falling within sub-paragraph (2) above continues to subsist until the end of the period of 50 years from the end of the calendar year in which the new copyright provisions come into force, unless the film or recording is published before the end of that period, in which case copyright expires 50 years from the end of the calendar year in which it is published.

42. (1) Section 164 (copyright in Acts and Measures) applies to existing Acts of Parliament and Measures of the General Synod of the Church of England.

(2) References in that section to Measures of the General Synod of the Church of England include Church Assembly Measures.

Parliamentary copyright

43. (1) Section 165 of this Act (general provisions as to Parliamentary copyright) applies to existing unpublished literary, dramatic, musical or artistic works, but does not otherwise apply to existing works.

(2) Section 166 (copyright in Parliamentary Bills) does not apply—

(a) to a public Bill which was introduced into Parliament and published before commencement,
(b) to a private Bill of which a copy was deposited in either House before commencement, or
(c) to a personal Bill which was given a First Reading in the House of Lords before commencement.

Copyright vesting in certain international organisations

44. (1) Any work in which immediately before commencement copyright subsisted by virtue of section 33 of the 1956 Act shall be deemed to satisfy the requirements of section 168(1); but otherwise section 168 does not apply to works made or, as the case may be, published before commencement.

(2) Copyright in any such work which is unpublished continues to subsist until the date on which it would have expired in accordance with the 1956 Act, or the end of the period of 50 years from the end of the calendar year in which the new copyright provisions come into force, whichever is the earlier.

Meaning of "publication"

45. Section 175(3) (construction of building treated as equivalent to publication) applies only where the construction of the building began after commencement.

Meaning of "unauthorised"

46. For the purposes of the application of the definition in section 178 (minor definitions) of the expression "unauthorised" in relation to things done before commencement—

(a) paragraph (a) applies in relation to things done before 1st June 1957 as if the reference to the licence of the copyright owner were a reference to his consent or acquiescence;
(b) paragraph (b) applies with the substitution for the words from "or, in a case" to the end of the words "or any person lawfully claiming under him"; and
(c) paragraph (c) shall be disregarded.

NOTES

Para 5: word omitted from sub-para (2)(a) repealed and sub-para (2)(c) inserted, together with word preceding it, by the Copyright (Amendment) Regulations 2016, SI 2016/1210, reg 2(1), (2).

Para 6: sub-para (1A) inserted by SI 2016/1210, reg 2(1), (3).

Part 2 Copyright

Para 9: substituted by the Copyright and Related Rights Regulations 2003, SI 2003/2498, reg 2(1), Sch 1, Pt 1, paras 1, 16(a), subject to transitional provisions as noted to s 1 of this Act at **[2.7]**.

Para 12: words in square brackets in sub-para (3) substituted by SI 2003/2498, reg 2(1), Sch 1, Pt 1, paras 1, 18(3), subject to transitional provisions as noted to s 1 of this Act at **[2.7]**.

Para 15: sub-para (3) repealed by SI 2003/2498, reg 2, Sch 1, Pt 1, paras 1, 16(b), Sch 2, subject to transitional provisions as noted to s 1 of this Act at **[2.7]**.

Para 17: sub-para (b) substituted by SI 2003/2498, reg 2(1), Sch 1, Pt 1, paras 1, 4(6), subject to transitional provisions as noted to s 1 of this Act at **[2.7]**.

Para 20: repealed by the Enterprise and Regulatory Reform Act 2013, s 74(1), (3)(b), as from 28 July 2016, subject to savings as noted to s 52 at **[2.81]**.

Para 36: the heading preceding this paragraph and the words in square brackets in sub-paras (1), (2), (4), (6) substituted by virtue of the British Overseas Territories Act 2002, s 1(2).

Para 37: words in square brackets substituted by virtue of the British Overseas Territories Act 2002, s 1(2).

Modified in relation to semiconductor topographies by the Design Right (Semiconductor Topographies) Regulations 1989, SI 1989/1100, at **[4.1]**.

See further, in relation to the authorship of pre-1989 photographs: the Copyright and Related Rights Regulations 1996, SI 1996/2967, reg 19, at **[2.509]**.

Lord Advocate: see the note to s 108, at **[2.144]**.

Copyright Act 1956: repealed by s 303(2) of, and Sch 8 to, this Act, subject to s 170, at **[2.226]** and this Schedule.

Orders: the Copyright (Status of Former Dependant Territories) Order 1990, SI 1990/1512.

SCHEDULE 2
RIGHTS IN PERFORMANCES: PERMITTED ACTS

Section 189

Introductory

[2.410]

1. (1) The provisions of this Schedule specify acts which may be done in relation to a performance or recording notwithstanding the rights conferred by [this Chapter]; they relate only to the question of infringement of those rights and do not affect any other right or obligation restricting the doing of any of the specified acts.

(2) No inference shall be drawn from the description of any act which may by virtue of this Schedule be done without infringing the rights conferred by [this Chapter] as to the scope of those rights.

(3) The provisions of this Schedule are to be construed independently of each other, so that the fact that an act does not fall within one provision does not mean that it is not covered by another provision.

[Making of temporary copies

1A. The rights conferred by [this Chapter] are not infringed by the making of a temporary copy of a recording of a performance which is transient or incidental, which is an integral and essential part of a technological process and the sole purpose of which is to enable—

(a) a transmission of the recording in a network between third parties by an intermediary; or

(b) a lawful use of the recording;

and which has no independent economic significance.]

[Personal copies of recordings for private use

1B. (1) The making of a copy of a recording of a performance by an individual does not infringe the rights conferred by this Chapter provided that the copy—

(a) is a copy of—

(i) the individual's own copy of the recording, or

(ii) a personal copy of the recording made by the individual,

(b) is made for the individual's private use, and

(c) is made for ends which are neither directly nor indirectly commercial.

(2) In this paragraph "the individual's own copy" is a copy of a recording which—

(a) has been lawfully acquired by the individual on a permanent basis,

(b) is not an illicit recording, and

(c) has not been made under any provision of this Schedule which permits the making of a copy without infringing the rights conferred by this Chapter.

(3) In this paragraph a "personal copy" means a copy made under this paragraph.

(4) The rights conferred by this Chapter in a recording are infringed if an individual transfers a personal copy of the recording to another person (otherwise than on a private and temporary basis), except where the transfer is authorised by the rights owner.

(5) If the rights conferred by this Chapter are infringed as set out in sub-paragraph (4), a personal copy which has been transferred is for all purposes subsequently treated as an illicit recording.

(6) The rights conferred by this Chapter in a recording are also infringed if an individual, having made a personal copy of the recording, transfers the individual's own copy of the recording to another person (otherwise than on a private and temporary basis) and, after that transfer and without the consent of the rights owner, retains any personal copy.

(7) If the rights conferred by this Chapter are infringed as set out in sub-paragraph (6), any retained personal copy is for all purposes subsequently treated as an illicit recording.

(8) To the extent that a term of a contract purports to prevent or restrict the making of a copy which, by virtue of this paragraph, would not infringe any right conferred by this Chapter, that term is unenforceable.

(9) Expressions used but not defined in this paragraph have the same meaning as in section 28B.]

[Research and private study

1C. (1) Fair dealing with a performance or a recording of a performance for the purposes of research for a non-commercial purpose does not infringe the rights conferred by this Chapter.

(2) Fair dealing with a performance or recording of a performance for the purposes of private study does not infringe the rights conferred by this Chapter.

(3) Copying of a recording by a person other than the researcher or student is not fair dealing if—
- (a) in the case of a librarian, or a person acting on behalf of a librarian, that person does anything which is not permitted under paragraph 6F (copying by librarians: single copies of published recordings), or
- (b) in any other case, the person doing the copying knows or has reason to believe that it will result in copies of substantially the same material being provided to more than one person at substantially the same time and for substantially the same purpose.

(4) To the extent that a term of a contract purports to prevent or restrict the doing of any act which, by virtue of this paragraph, would not infringe any right conferred by this Chapter, that term is unenforceable.

(5) Expressions used in this paragraph have the same meaning as in section 29.

Copies for text and data analysis for non-commercial research

1D. (1) The making of a copy of a recording of a performance by a person who has lawful access to the recording does not infringe any rights conferred by this Chapter provided that the copy is made in order that a person who has lawful access to the recording may carry out a computational analysis of anything recorded in the recording for the sole purpose of research for a non-commercial purpose.

(2) Where a copy of a recording has been made under this paragraph, the rights conferred by this Chapter are infringed if—
- (a) the copy is transferred to any other person, except where the transfer is authorised by the rights owner, or
- (b) the copy is used for any purpose other than that mentioned in sub-paragraph (1), except where the use is authorised by the rights owner.

(3) If a copy of a recording made under this paragraph is subsequently dealt with—
- (a) it is to be treated as an illicit recording for the purposes of that dealing, and
- (b) if that dealing infringes any right conferred by this Chapter, it is to be treated as an illicit recording for all subsequent purposes.

(4) To the extent that a term of a contract purports to prevent or restrict the making of a copy which, by virtue of this paragraph, would not infringe any right conferred by this Chapter, that term is unenforceable.

(5) Expressions used in this paragraph have the same meaning as in section 29A.]

Criticism, reviews[, quotation] and news reporting

2. [(1) Fair dealing with a performance or recording for the purpose of criticism or review, of that or another performance or recording, or of a work, does not infringe any of the rights conferred by [this Chapter] provided that the performance or recording has been made available to the public.

[(1ZA) The rights conferred by this Chapter in a performance or a recording of a performance are not infringed by the use of a quotation from the performance or recording (whether for criticism or review or otherwise) provided that—
- (a) the performance or recording has been made available to the public,
- (b) the use of the quotation is fair dealing with the performance or recording, and
- (c) the extent of the quotation is no more than is required by the specific purpose for which it is used.]

(1A) Fair dealing with a performance or recording for the purpose of reporting current events does not infringe any of the rights conferred by [this Chapter].]

[(1B) To the extent that a term of a contract purports to prevent or restrict the doing of any act which, by virtue of sub-paragraph (1ZA), would not infringe any right conferred by this Chapter, that term is unenforceable.]

(2) Expressions used in this paragraph have the same meaning as in section 30.

[Caricature, parody or pastiche

2A. (1) Fair dealing with a performance or a recording of a performance for the purposes of caricature, parody or pastiche does not infringe the rights conferred by this Chapter in the performance or recording.

(2) To the extent that a term of a contract purports to prevent or restrict the doing of any act which, by virtue of this paragraph, would not infringe any right conferred by this Chapter, that term is unenforceable.

(3) Expressions used in this paragraph have the same meaning as in section 30A.]

Incidental inclusion of performance or recording

3. (1) The rights conferred by [this Chapter] are not infringed by the incidental inclusion of a performance or recording in a sound recording, film [or broadcast].

(2) Nor are those rights infringed by anything done in relation to copies of, or the playing, showing [or communication to the public] of, anything whose making was, by virtue of sub-paragraph (1), not an infringement of those rights.

(3) A performance or recording so far as it consists of music, or words spoken or sung with music, shall not be regarded as incidentally included in a sound recording [or broadcast] if it is deliberately included.

(4) Expressions used in this paragraph have the same meaning as in section 31.

[Disabled persons: copies of recordings for personal use

3A. (1) This paragraph applies if—

(a) a disabled person has lawful possession or lawful use of a copy of the whole or part of a recording of a performance, and

(b) the person's disability prevents the person from enjoying the recording to the same degree as a person who does not have that disability.

(2) The making of an accessible copy of the copy of the recording referred to in sub-paragraph (1)(a) does not infringe the rights conferred by this Chapter if—

(a) the copy is made by the disabled person or by a person acting on behalf of the disabled person,

(b) the copy is made for the disabled person's personal use, and

(c) the same kind of accessible copies of the recording are not commercially available on reasonable terms by or with the authority of the rights owner.

(3) If a person makes an accessible copy under this paragraph on behalf of a disabled person and charges the disabled person for it, the sum charged must not exceed the cost of making and supplying the copy.

(4) The rights conferred by this Chapter are infringed by the transfer of an accessible copy of a recording made under this paragraph to any person other than—

(a) a person by or for whom an accessible copy of the recording may be made under this paragraph, or

(b) a person who intends to transfer the copy to a person falling within paragraph (a),

except where the transfer is authorised by the rights owner.

(5) An accessible copy of a recording made under this paragraph is to be treated for all purposes as an illicit recording if it is held by a person at a time when the person does not fall within sub-paragraph (4)(a) or (b).

(6) If an accessible copy of a recording made under this paragraph is subsequently dealt with—

(a) it is to be treated as an illicit recording for the purposes of that dealing, and

(b) if that dealing infringes any right conferred by this Chapter, it is to be treated as an illicit recording for all subsequent purposes.

Making and supply of accessible copies by authorised bodies

3B. (1) If an authorised body has lawful possession of or lawful access to a copy of the whole or part of a recording of a performance (including a recording of a performance included in a broadcast), the body may, without infringing the rights conferred by this Chapter, make and supply accessible copies of the recording for the personal use of disabled persons.

(2) If an authorised body has lawful access to the whole or part of a broadcast, the body may, without infringing the rights conferred by this Chapter, make a recording of the broadcast, and make and supply accessible copies of the recording, for the personal use of disabled persons.

(3) But sub-paragraphs (1) and (2) do not apply if the same kind of accessible copies of the recording, or of the broadcast, are commercially available on reasonable terms by or with the consent of the rights owner.

(4) For the purposes of sub-paragraphs (1) and (2), supply "for the personal use of disabled persons" includes supply to a person acting on behalf of a disabled person.

(5) An authorised body which is an educational establishment conducted for profit must ensure that any accessible copies which it makes under this paragraph are used only for its educational purposes.

(6) An accessible copy made under this paragraph must be accompanied by a statement that it is made under this paragraph, unless it is accompanied by an equivalent statement in accordance with section 31B(7).

(7) If an accessible copy is made under this paragraph of a recording which is in copy-protected electronic form, the accessible copy must, so far as is reasonably practicable, incorporate the same or equally effective copy protection (unless the rights owner agrees otherwise).

(8) An authorised body which has made an accessible copy of a recording under this paragraph may supply it to another authorised body which is entitled to make accessible copies of the recording under this paragraph for the purposes of enabling that other body to make accessible copies of the recording.

(9) If an authorised body supplies an accessible copy it has made under this paragraph to a person or authorised body as permitted by this paragraph and charges the person or body for it, the sum charged must not exceed the cost of making and supplying the copy.

(10) If an accessible copy of a recording made under this paragraph is subsequently dealt with—
- (a) it is to be treated as an illicit recording for the purposes of that dealing, and
- (b) if that dealing infringes any right conferred by this Chapter, it is to be treated as an illicit recording for all subsequent purposes.

Making and supply of intermediate copies by authorised bodies

3C. (1) An authorised body which is entitled to make an accessible copy of a recording of a performance under paragraph 3B may, without infringing the rights conferred by this Chapter, make a copy of the recording ("an intermediate copy") if this is necessary in order to make the accessible copy.

(2) An authorised body which has made an intermediate copy of a recording under this paragraph may supply it to another authorised body which is entitled to make accessible copies of the recording under paragraph 3B for the purposes of enabling that other body to make accessible copies of the recording.

(3) The rights conferred by this Chapter are infringed by the transfer of an intermediate copy made under this paragraph to a person other than another authorised body as permitted by sub-paragraph (2), except where the transfer is authorised by the rights owner.

(4) If an authorised body supplies an intermediate copy to an authorised body under sub-paragraph (2) and charges the body for it, the sum charged must not exceed the cost of making and supplying the copy.

Accessible and intermediate copies: records

3D. (1) An authorised body must keep a record of—
- (a) accessible copies it makes under paragraph 3B,
- (b) intermediate copies it makes under paragraph 3C, and
- (c) the persons to whom such copies are supplied.

(2) An authorised body must allow the rights owner or a person acting for the rights owner, on giving reasonable notice, to inspect the records at any reasonable time.

Paragraphs 3A to 3D: interpretation and general

3E. (1) This paragraph supplements paragraphs 3A to 3D and includes definitions.

(2) "Disabled person" means a person who has a physical or mental impairment which prevents the person from enjoying a recording of a performance to the same degree as a person who does not have that impairment, and "disability" is to be construed accordingly.

(3) But a person is not to be regarded as disabled by reason only of an impairment of visual function which can be improved, by the use of corrective lenses, to a level that is normally acceptable for reading without a special level or kind of light.

(4) An "accessible copy" of a recording of a performance means a version of the recording which enables the fuller enjoyment of the recording by disabled persons.

(5) An accessible copy—
- (a) may include facilities for navigating around the version of the recording, but
- (b) must not include any changes to the recording which are not necessary to overcome the problems suffered by the disabled persons for whom the accessible copy is intended.

(6) To the extent that a term of a contract purports to prevent or restrict the doing of any act which, by virtue of paragraph 3A, 3B or 3C, would not infringe any right conferred by this Chapter, that term is unenforceable.

(7) "Authorised body" and "supply" have the meaning given in section 31F, and other expressions used in paragraphs 3A to 3D but not defined in this paragraph have the same meaning as in sections 31A to 31BB.]

[Illustration for instruction

4. (1) Fair dealing with a performance or a recording of a performance for the sole purpose of illustration for instruction does not infringe the rights conferred by this Chapter provided that the dealing is—

(a) for a non-commercial purpose, and

(b) by a person giving or receiving instruction (or preparing for giving or receiving instruction).

(2) To the extent that a term of a contract purports to prevent or restrict the doing of any act which, by virtue of this paragraph, would not infringe any right conferred by this Chapter, that term is unenforceable.

(3) Expressions used in this paragraph have the same meaning as in section 32.]

Playing or showing sound recording, film [or broadcast] at educational establishment

5. (1) The playing or showing of a sound recording, film [or broadcast] at an educational establishment for the purposes of instruction before an audience consisting of teachers and pupils at the establishment and other persons directly connected with the activities of the establishment is not a playing or showing of a performance in public for the purposes of infringement of the rights conferred by [this Chapter].

(2) A person is not for this purpose directly connected with the activities of the educational establishment simply because he is the parent of a pupil at the establishment.

(3) Expressions used in this paragraph have the same meaning as in section 34 and any provision made under section 174(2) with respect to the application of that section also applies for the purposes of this paragraph.

[Recording by educational establishments of broadcasts

6. (1) A recording of a broadcast, or a copy of such a recording, may be made by or on behalf of an educational establishment for the educational purposes of that establishment without infringing any of the rights conferred by this Chapter in relation to any performance or recording included in it, provided that the educational purposes are non-commercial.

(2) The rights conferred by this Chapter are not infringed where a recording of a broadcast or a copy of such a recording, made under sub-paragraph (1), is communicated by or on behalf of the educational establishment to its pupils or staff for the non-commercial educational purposes of that establishment.

(3) Sub-paragraph (2) only applies to a communication received outside the premises of the establishment if that communication is made by means of a secure electronic network accessible only by the establishment's pupils and staff.

(4) Acts which would otherwise be permitted by this paragraph are not permitted if, or to the extent that, licences are available authorising the acts in question and the educational establishment responsible for those acts knew or ought to have been aware of that fact.

(5) If a recording made under this paragraph is subsequently dealt with—

(a) it is to be treated as an illicit recording for the purposes of that dealing, and

(b) if that dealing infringes any right conferred by this Chapter, it is to be treated as an illicit recording for all subsequent purposes.

(6) In this paragraph "dealt with" means—

(a) sold or let for hire,

(b) offered or exposed for sale or hire, or

(c) communicated otherwise than as permitted by sub-paragraph (2).

(7) Expressions used in this paragraph (other than "dealt with") have the same meaning as in section 35 and any provision made under section 174(2) with respect to the application of that section also applies for the purposes of this paragraph.

Copying and use of extracts of recordings by educational establishments

6ZA. (1) The copying of extracts of a recording of a performance by or on behalf of an educational establishment does not infringe any of the rights conferred by this Chapter in the recording provided that the copy is made for the purposes of instruction for a non-commercial purpose.

(2) The rights conferred by this Chapter are not infringed where an extract of a recording of a performance, made under sub-paragraph (1), is communicated by or on behalf of the educational establishment to its pupils or staff for the purposes of instruction for a non-commercial purpose.

(3) Sub-paragraph (2) only applies to a communication received outside the premises of the establishment if that communication is made by means of a secure electronic network accessible only by the establishment's pupils and staff.

(4) Not more than 5% of a recording may be copied under this paragraph by or on behalf of an educational establishment in any period of 12 months.

(5) Acts which would otherwise be permitted by this paragraph are not permitted if, or to the extent that, licences are available authorising the acts in question and the educational establishment responsible for those acts knew or ought to have been aware of that fact.

(6) The terms of a licence granted to an educational establishment authorising acts permitted by this paragraph are of no effect so far as they purport to restrict the proportion of a recording which may be copied (whether on payment or free of charge) to less than that which would be permitted by this paragraph.

(7) If a recording made under this paragraph is subsequently dealt with—

(a) it is to be treated as an illicit recording for the purposes of that dealing, and

(b) if that dealing infringes any right conferred by this Chapter, it is to be treated as an illicit recording for all subsequent purposes.

(8) In this paragraph "dealt with" means—

(a) sold or let for hire,

(b) offered or exposed for sale or hire, or

(c) communicated otherwise than as permitted by sub-paragraph (2).

(9) Expressions used in this paragraph (other than "dealt with") have the same meaning as in section 36 and any provision made under section 174(2) with respect to the application of that section also applies for the purposes of this paragraph.]

[Lending of copies by educational establishments

6A. (1) The rights conferred by [this Chapter] are not infringed by the lending of copies of a recording of a performance by an educational establishment.

(2) Expressions used in this paragraph have the same meaning as in section 36A; and any provision with respect to the application of that section made under section 174(2) (instruction given elsewhere than an educational establishment) applies also for the purposes of this paragraph.

Lending of copies by libraries or archives

6B. [(A1) The rights conferred by this Chapter are not infringed by the following acts by a public library in relation to a book within the public lending right scheme—

(a) lending the book;

(b) in relation to an audio-book or e-book, copying or issuing a copy of the book as an act incidental to lending it.

(A2) Expressions used in sub-paragraph (A1) have the same meaning as in section 40A(1).]

(1) The rights conferred by [this Chapter] are not infringed by the lending of copies of a recording of a performance by a . . . library or archive (other than a public library) which is not conducted for profit.

(2) . . .]

[Libraries and educational establishments etc: making recordings of performances available through dedicated terminals

6C. (1) The rights conferred by this Chapter in a recording of a performance are not infringed by an institution specified in sub-paragraph (2) communicating the recording to the public or making it available to the public by means of a dedicated terminal on its premises, if the conditions in sub-paragraph (3) are met.

(2) The institutions are—

(a) a library,

(b) an archive,

(c) a museum, and

(d) an educational establishment.

(3) The conditions are that the recording or a copy of the recording—

(a) has been lawfully acquired by the institution,

(b) is communicated or made available to individual members of the public for the purposes of research or private study, and

(c) is communicated or made available in compliance with any purchase or licensing terms to which the recording is subject.

Copying by librarians: supply of single copies to other libraries

6D. (1) A librarian may, if the conditions in sub-paragraph (2) are met, make a single copy of the whole or part of a published recording of a performance and supply it to another library, without infringing any rights conferred by this Chapter in the recording.

(2) The conditions are—

(a) the copy is supplied in response to a request from a library which is not conducted for profit, and

(b) at the time of making the copy the librarian does not know, or could not reasonably find out, the name and address of a person entitled to authorise the making of a copy of the recording.

(3) Where a library makes a charge for supplying a copy under this paragraph, the sum charged must be calculated by reference to the costs attributable to the production of the copy.

(4) To the extent that a term of a contract purports to prevent or restrict the doing of any act which, by virtue of this paragraph, would not infringe any right conferred by this Chapter, that term is unenforceable.

Copying by librarians etc: replacement copies of recordings

6E. (1) A librarian, archivist or curator of a library, archive or museum may, without infringing any rights conferred by this Chapter, make a copy of a recording of a performance in that institution's permanent collection—

(a) in order to preserve or replace that recording in that collection, or
(b) where a recording in the permanent collection of another library, archive or museum has been lost, destroyed or damaged, in order to replace the recording in the collection of that other library, archive or museum,

provided that the conditions in sub-paragraphs (2) and (3) are met.

(2) The first condition is that the recording is—

(a) included in the part of the collection kept wholly or mainly for the purposes of reference on the institution's premises,
(b) included in a part of the collection not accessible to the public, or
(c) available on loan only to other libraries, archives or museums.

(3) The second condition is that it is not reasonably practicable to purchase a copy of the recording to achieve either of the purposes mentioned in sub-paragraph (1).

(4) The reference in sub-paragraph (1)(b) to a library, archive or museum is to a library, archive or museum which is not conducted for profit.

(5) Where an institution makes a charge for supplying a copy to another library, archive or museum under sub-paragraph (1)(b), the sum charged must be calculated by reference to the costs attributable to the production of the copy.

(6) To the extent that a term of a contract purports to prevent or restrict the doing of any act which, by virtue of this paragraph, would not infringe any right conferred by this Chapter, that term is unenforceable.

Copying by librarians: single copies of published recordings

6F. (1) A librarian of a library which is not conducted for profit may, if the conditions in sub-paragraph (2) are met, make and supply a single copy of a reasonable proportion of a published recording without infringing any of the rights in the recording conferred by this Chapter.

(2) The conditions are—

(a) the copy is supplied in response to a request from a person who has provided the librarian with a declaration in writing which includes the information set out in sub-paragraph (3), and
(b) the librarian is not aware that the declaration is false in a material particular.

(3) The information which must be included in the declaration is—

(a) the name of the person who requires the copy and the material which that person requires,
(b) a statement that the person has not previously been supplied with a copy of that material by any library,
(c) a statement that the person requires the copy for the purposes of research for a non-commercial purpose or private study, will use it only for those purposes and will not supply the copy to any other person, and
(d) a statement that to the best of the person's knowledge, no other person with whom the person works or studies has made, or intends to make, at or about the same time as the person's request, a request for substantially the same material for substantially the same purpose.

(4) Where a library makes a charge for supplying a copy under this paragraph, the sum charged must be calculated by reference to the costs attributable to the production of the copy.

(5) Where a person ("P") makes a declaration under this paragraph that is false in a material particular and is supplied with a copy of a recording which would have been an illicit recording if made by P—

(a) P is liable for infringement of the rights conferred by this Chapter as if P had made the copy, and
(b) the copy supplied to P is to be treated as an illicit recording for all purposes.

(6) To the extent that a term of a contract purports to prevent or restrict the doing of any act which, by virtue of this paragraph, would not infringe any right conferred by this Chapter, that term is unenforceable.

Copying by librarians or archivists: single copies of unpublished recordings

6G. (1) A librarian or archivist may make and supply a single copy of the whole or part of a recording without infringing any of the rights conferred by this Chapter in the recording, provided that—

(a) the copy is supplied in response to a request from a person who has provided the librarian or archivist with a declaration in writing which includes the information set out in sub-paragraph (2), and

(b) the librarian or archivist is not aware that the declaration is false in a material particular.

(2) The information which must be included in the declaration is—

(a) the name of the person who requires the copy and the material which that person requires,

(b) a statement that the person has not previously been supplied with a copy of that material by any library or archive, and

(c) a statement that the person requires the copy for the purposes of research for a non-commercial purpose or private study, will use it only for those purposes and will not supply the copy to any other person.

(3) But the rights conferred by this Chapter are infringed if—

(a) the recording had been published or communicated to the public before the date it was deposited in the library or archive, or

(b) the rights owner has prohibited the copying of the recording,

and at the time of making the copy the librarian or archivist is, or ought to be, aware of that fact.

(4) Where a library or archive makes a charge for supplying a copy under this paragraph, the sum charged must be calculated by reference to the costs attributable to the production of the copy.

(5) Where a person ("P") makes a declaration under this paragraph that is false in a material particular and is supplied with a copy of a recording which would have been an illicit recording if made by P—

(a) P is liable for infringement of the rights conferred by this Chapter as if P had made the copy, and

(b) the copy supplied to P is to be treated as an illicit recording for all purposes.

Paragraphs 6B to 6G: interpretation

6H. Expressions used in paragraphs 6B to 6G have the same meaning as in sections 40A to 43.]

[Certain permitted uses of orphan works

6I. (1) The rights conferred by this Chapter are not infringed by a relevant body in the circumstances set out in paragraph 1(2) of Schedule ZA1 (subject to paragraph 6 of that Schedule).

(2) "Relevant body" has the meaning given by that Schedule.]

Copy of work required to be made as condition of export

7. (1) If an article of cultural or historical importance or interest cannot lawfully be exported from the United Kingdom unless a copy of it is made and deposited in an appropriate library or archive, it is not an infringement of any right conferred by [this Chapter] to make that copy.

(2) Expressions used in this paragraph have the same meaning as in section 44.

Parliamentary and judicial proceedings

8. (1) The rights conferred by [this Chapter] are not infringed by anything done for the purposes of parliamentary or judicial proceedings or for the purpose of reporting such proceedings.

(2) Expressions used in this paragraph have the same meaning as in section 45.

Royal Commissions and statutory inquiries

9. (1) The rights conferred by [this Chapter] are not infringed by anything done for the purposes of the proceedings of a Royal Commission or statutory inquiry or for the purpose of reporting any such proceedings held in public.

(2) Expressions used in this paragraph have the same meaning as in section 46.

Public records

10. (1) Material which is comprised in public records within the meaning of the Public Records Act 1958, the Public Records (Scotland) Act 1937 or the Public Records Act (Northern Ireland) 1923[, or in Welsh public records (as defined in [the Government of Wales Act 2006],] which are open to public inspection in pursuance of that Act, may be copied, and a copy may be supplied to any person, by or with the authority of any officer appointed under that Act, without infringing any right conferred by [this Chapter].

(2) Expressions used in this paragraph have the same meaning as in section 49.

Acts done under statutory authority

11. (1) Where the doing of a particular act is specifically authorised by an Act of Parliament, whenever passed, then, unless the Act provides otherwise, the doing of that act does not infringe the rights conferred by [this Chapter].

(2) Sub-paragraph (1) applies in relation to an enactment contained in Northern Ireland legislation as it applies to an Act of Parliament.

(3) Nothing in this paragraph shall be construed as excluding any defence of statutory authority otherwise available under or by virtue of any enactment.

(4) Expressions used in this paragraph have the same meaning as in section 50.

Transfer of copies of works in electronic form

12. (1) This paragraph applies where a recording of a performance in electronic form has been purchased on terms which, expressly or impliedly or by virtue of any rule of law, allow the purchaser to make further recordings in connection with his use of the recording.

(2) If there are no express terms—

(a) prohibiting the transfer of the recording by the purchaser, imposing obligations which continue after a transfer, prohibiting the assignment of any consent or terminating any consent on a transfer, or

(b) providing for the terms on which a transferee may do the things which the purchaser was permitted to do,

anything which the purchaser was allowed to do may also be done by a transferee without infringement of the rights conferred by [this Chapter], but any recording made by the purchaser which is not also transferred shall be treated as an illicit recording for all purposes after the transfer.

(3) The same applies where the original purchased recording is no longer usable and what is transferred is a further copy used in its place.

(4) The above provisions also apply on a subsequent transfer, with the substitution for references in sub-paragraph (2) to the purchaser of references to the subsequent transferor.

(5) This paragraph does not apply in relation to a recording purchased before the commencement of [this Chapter].

(6) Expressions used in this paragraph have the same meaning as in section 56.

Use of recordings of spoken works in certain cases

13. (1) Where a recording of the reading or recitation of a literary work is made for the purpose—

(a) of reporting current events, or

(b) of [communicating to the public] the whole or part of the reading or recitation,

it is not an infringement of the rights conferred by [this Chapter] to use the recording (or to copy the recording and use the copy) for that purpose, provided the following conditions are met.

(2) The conditions are that—

(a) the recording is a direct recording of the reading or recitation and is not taken from a previous recording or from a broadcast . . . ;

(b) the making of the recording was not prohibited by or on behalf of the person giving the reading or recitation;

(c) the use made of the recording is not of a kind prohibited by or on behalf of that person before the recording was made; and

(d) the use is by or with the authority of a person who is lawfully in possession of the recording.

(3) Expressions used in this paragraph have the same meaning as in section 58.

Recordings of folksongs

14. (1) A recording of a performance of a song may be made for the purpose of including it in an archive maintained by a [body not established or conducted for profit] without infringing any of the rights conferred by [this Chapter], provided the conditions in sub-paragraph (2) below are met.

(2) The conditions are that—

(a) the words are unpublished and of unknown authorship at the time the recording is made,

(b) the making of the recording does not infringe any copyright, and

(c) its making is not prohibited by any performer.

[(3) A single copy of a recording made in reliance on sub-paragraph (1) and included in an archive referred to in that sub-paragraph may be made and supplied by the archivist without infringing any right conferred by this Chapter, provided that—

(a) the copy is supplied in response to a request from a person who has provided the archivist with a declaration in writing which includes the information set out in sub-paragraph (4), and

(b) the archivist is not aware that the declaration is false in a material particular.

(4) The information which must be included in the declaration is—

(a) the name of the person who requires the copy and the recording which is the subject of the request,

(b) a statement that the person has not previously been supplied with a copy of that recording by any archivist, and

(c) a statement that the person requires the copy for the purposes of research for a non-commercial purpose or private study, will use it only for those purposes and will not supply the copy to any other person.

(5) Where an archive makes a charge for supplying a copy under this paragraph, the sum charged must be calculated by reference to the costs attributable to the production of the copy.

(6) Where a person ("P") makes a declaration under this paragraph that is false in a material particular and is supplied with a copy of a recording which would have been an illicit recording if made by P—

(a) P is liable for infringement of the rights conferred by this Chapter as if P had made the copy, and

(b) the copy supplied to P is to be treated as an illicit recording for all purposes.

(7) In this paragraph references to an archivist include a person acting on behalf of an archivist.

(8) Expressions used in this paragraph have the same meaning as in section 61.]

[Lending of certain recordings

14A. (1) The Secretary of State may by order provide that in such cases as may be specified in the order the lending to the public of copies of films or sound recordings shall be treated as licensed by the performer subject only to the payment of such reasonable royalty or other payment as may be agreed or determined in default of agreement by the Copyright Tribunal.

(2) No such order shall apply if, or to the extent that, there is a licensing scheme certified for the purposes of this paragraph under paragraph 16 of Schedule 2A providing for the grant of licences.

(3) An order may make different provision for different cases and may specify cases by reference to any factor relating to the work, the copies lent, the lender or the circumstances of the lending.

(4) An order shall be made by statutory instrument; and no order shall be made unless a draft of it has been laid before and approved by a resolution of each House of Parliament.

(5) Nothing in this section affects any liability under section 184(1)(b) (secondary infringement: possessing or dealing with illicit recording) in respect of the lending of illicit recordings.

(6) Expressions used in this paragraph have the same meaning as in section 66.]

. . .

15. . . .

Incidental recording for purposes of broadcast . . .

16. (1) A person who proposes to broadcast a recording of a performance . . . in circumstances not infringing the rights conferred by [this Chapter] shall be treated as having consent for the purposes of [this Chapter] for the making of a further recording for the purposes of the broadcast . . .

(2) That consent is subject to the condition that the further recording—

(a) shall not be used for any other purpose, and

(b) shall be destroyed within 28 days of being first used for broadcasting the performance . . .

(3) A recording made in accordance with this paragraph shall be treated as an illicit recording—

(a) for the purposes of any use in breach of the condition mentioned in sub-paragraph (2)(a), and

(b) for all purposes after that condition or the condition mentioned in sub-paragraph (2)(b) is broken.

(4) Expressions used in this paragraph have the same meaning as in section 68.

Recordings for purposes of supervision and control of broadcasts and [other services]

17. (1) The rights conferred by [this Chapter] are not infringed by the making or use by the British Broadcasting Corporation, for the purpose of maintaining supervision and control over programmes broadcast by them [or included in any on-demand programme service provided by them], of recordings of those programmes.

[(2) The rights conferred by [this Chapter] are not infringed by anything done in pursuance of—

[(a) section 167(1) of the Broadcasting Act 1990, section 115(4) or (6) or 117 of the Broadcasting Act 1996 or paragraph 20 of Schedule 12 to the Communications Act 2003;]

(b) a condition which, [by virtue of section 334(1) of the Communications Act 2003], is included in a licence granted under Part I or III of that Act or Part I or II of the Broadcasting Act 1996; . . .

(c) a direction given under section 109(2) of the Broadcasting Act 1990 (power of [OFCOM] to require production of recordings etc);

Part 2 Copyright

[(d) section 334(3)[, 368O(1) or (3)] of the Communications Act 2003].

[(3) The rights conferred by [this Chapter] are not infringed by the use by OFCOM in connection with the performance of any of their functions under the Broadcasting Act 1990, the Broadcasting Act 1996 or the Communications Act 2003 of—

(a) any recording, script or transcript which is provided to them under or by virtue of any provision of those Acts; or

(b) any existing material which is transferred to them by a scheme made under section 30 of the Communications Act 2003.

(4) In subsection (3), "existing material" means—

(a) any recording, script or transcript which was provided to the Independent Television Commission or the Radio Authority under or by virtue of any provision of the Broadcasting Act 1990 or the Broadcasting Act 1996; and

(b) any recording or transcript which was provided to the Broadcasting Standards Commission under section 115(4) or (6) or 116(5) of the Broadcasting Act 1996.]]

[(5) The rights conferred by this Chapter are not infringed by the use by the appropriate regulatory authority designated under section 368B of the Communications Act 2003, in connection with the performance of any of their functions under that Act, of any recording, script or transcript which is provided to them under or by virtue of any provision of that Act.

(6) In this paragraph "on-demand programme service" has the same meaning as in the Communications Act 2003 (see section 368A of that Act).]

[Recording for the purposes of time-shifting

17A. (1) The making in domestic premises for private and domestic use of a recording of a broadcast solely for the purpose of enabling it to be viewed or listened to at a more convenient time does not infringe any right conferred by [this Chapter] in relation to a performance or recording included in the broadcast.

(2) Where a recording which would otherwise be an illicit recording is made in accordance with this paragraph but is subsequently dealt with—

(a) it shall be treated as an illicit recording for the purposes of that dealing; and

(b) if that dealing infringes any right conferred by [this Chapter], it shall be treated as an illicit recording for all subsequent purposes.

(3) In sub-paragraph (2), "dealt with" means sold or let for hire, offered or exposed for sale or hire or communicated to the public.

(4) Expressions used in this paragraph have the same meaning as in section 70.]

[Photographs of broadcasts

17B. (1) The making in domestic premises for private and domestic use of a photograph of the whole or any part of an image forming part of a broadcast, or a copy of such a photograph, does not infringe any right conferred by [this Chapter] in relation to a performance or recording included in the broadcast.

(2) Where a recording which would otherwise be an illicit recording is made in accordance with this paragraph but is subsequently dealt with—

(a) it shall be treated as an illicit recording for the purposes of that dealing; and

(b) if that dealing infringes any right conferred by [this Chapter], it shall be treated as an illicit recording for all subsequent purposes.

(3) In sub-paragraph (2), "dealt with" means sold or let for hire, offered or exposed for sale or hire or communicated to the public.

(4) Expressions used in this paragraph have the same meaning as in section 71.]

Free public showing or playing of broadcast . . .

18. (1) The showing or playing in public of a broadcast . . . to an audience who have not paid for admission to the place where the broadcast . . . is to be seen or heard does not infringe any right conferred by [this Chapter] in relation to a performance or recording included in—

(a) the broadcast . . . , or

(b) any sound recording [(except so far as it is an excepted sound recording)] or film which is played or shown in public by reception of the broadcast . . .

[(1A) The showing or playing in public of a broadcast to an audience who have not paid for admission to the place where the broadcast is to be seen or heard does not infringe any right conferred by [this Chapter] in relation to a performance or recording included in any excepted sound recording which is played in public by reception of the broadcast, if the playing or showing of that broadcast in public—

(a) . . .

(b) is necessary for the purposes of—

(i) repairing equipment for the reception of broadcasts;

(ii) demonstrating that a repair to such equipment has been carried out; or

(iii) demonstrating such equipment which is being sold or let for hire or offered or exposed for sale or hire.]

(2) The audience shall be treated as having paid for admission to a place—

(a) if they have paid for admission to a place of which that place forms part; or

(b) if goods or services are supplied at that place (or a place of which it forms part)—

(i) at prices which are substantially attributable to the facilities afforded for seeing or hearing the broadcast . . . , or

(ii) at prices exceeding those usually charged there and which are partly attributable to those facilities.

(3) The following shall not be regarded as having paid for admission to a place—

(a) persons admitted as residents or inmates of the place;

(b) persons admitted as members of a club or society where the payment is only for membership of the club or society and the provision of facilities for seeing or hearing broadcasts . . . is only incidental to the main purposes of the club or society.

(4) Where the making of the broadcast . . . was an infringement of the rights conferred by [this Chapter] in relation to a performance or recording, the fact that it was heard or seen in public by the reception of the broadcast . . . shall be taken into account in assessing the damages for that infringement.

(5) Expressions used in this paragraph have the same meaning as in section 72.

[Reception and re-transmission of [wireless broadcast by cable]

19. *(1) This paragraph applies where a [wireless] broadcast made from a place in the United Kingdom is [received and immediately re-transmitted by cable].*

(2) The rights conferred by [this Chapter] in relation to a performance or recording included in the broadcast are not infringed if and to the extent that the broadcast is made for reception in the area in which [it is re-transmitted by cable]; but where the making of the broadcast was an infringement of those rights, the fact that the broadcast was re-transmitted [by cable] shall be taken into account in assessing the damages for that infringement.

(3) Where—

(a) the [re-transmission by cable] is in pursuance of a relevant requirement, but

(b) to any extent, the area in which the cable programme service is provided ("the cable area") falls outside the area for reception in which the broadcast is made ("the broadcast area"),

the [re-transmission by cable] (to the extent that it is provided for so much of the cable area as falls outside the broadcast area) of any performance or recording included in the broadcast shall, subject to sub-paragraph (4), be treated as licensed by the owner of the rights conferred by [this Chapter] in relation to the performance or recording, subject only to the payment to him by the person making the broadcast of such reasonable royalty or other payment in respect of the [re-transmission by cable of the broadcast] as may be agreed or determined in default of agreement by the Copyright Tribunal.

(4) Sub-paragraph (3) does not apply if, or to the extent that, the [re-transmission of the performance or recording by cable] is (apart from that sub-paragraph) licensed by the owner of the rights conferred by [this Chapter] in relation to the performance or recording.

(5) The Secretary of State may by order—

(a) provide that in specified cases sub-paragraph (2) is to apply in relation to broadcasts of a specified description which are not made as mentioned in that sub-paragraph, or

(b) exclude the application of that sub-paragraph in relation to broadcasts of a specified description made as mentioned in that sub-paragraph.

(6) Where the Secretary of State exercises the power conferred by sub-paragraph (5)(b) in relation to broadcasts of any description, the order may also provide for sub-paragraph (3) to apply, subject to such modifications as may be specified in the order, in relation to broadcasts of that description.

(7) An order under this paragraph may contain such transitional provision as appears to the Secretary of State to be appropriate.

(8) An order under this paragraph shall be made by statutory instrument which shall be subject to annulment in pursuance of a resolution of either House of Parliament.

(9) Expressions used in this paragraph have the same meaning as in section 73.]

[19A. *(1) An application to settle the royalty or other sum payable in pursuance of sub-paragraph (3) of paragraph 19 may be made to the Copyright Tribunal by the owner of the rights conferred by [this Chapter] or the person making the broadcast.*

(2) The Tribunal shall consider the matter and make such order as it may determine to be reasonable in the circumstances.

(3) Either party may subsequently apply to the Tribunal to vary the order, and the Tribunal shall consider the matter and make such order confirming or varying the original order as it may determine to be reasonable in the circumstances.

(4) An application under sub-paragraph (3) shall not, except with the special leave of the Tribunal, be made within twelve months from the date of the original order or of the order on a previous application under that sub-paragraph.

(5) An order under sub-paragraph (3) has effect from the date on which it is made or such later date as may be specified by the Tribunal.]

. . .

20. . . .

[Recording of broadcast for archival purposes

21. (1) A recording of a broadcast or a copy of such a recording may be made for the purpose of being placed in an archive maintained by a body which is not established or conducted for profit without infringing any right conferred by this Chapter in relation to a performance or recording included in the broadcast.

(2) To the extent that a term of a contract purports to prevent or restrict the doing of any act which, by virtue of this paragraph, would not infringe any right conferred by this Chapter, that term is unenforceable.

(3) Expressions used in this paragraph have the same meaning as in section 75.]

NOTES

Except as noted below, all amendments to this Schedule were made by the Copyright and Related Rights Regulations 2003, SI 2003/2498, subject to transitional provisions as noted to s 1 of this Act at **[2.7]**.

Words "this Chapter" in square brackets, wherever they appear, substituted by the Performances (Moral Rights, etc) Regulations 2006, SI 2006/18, reg 2, Schedule, paras 1, 9, 10.

Para 1B: inserted by the Copyright and Rights in Performances (Personal Copies for Private Use) Regulations 2014, SI 2014/2361, regs 2, 3(3), subject to transitional provisions and additional notes, as noted to s 28B at **[2.42]**.

Paras 1C, 1D: inserted by the Copyright and Rights in Performances (Research, Education, Libraries and Archives) Regulations 2014, SI 2014/1372, regs 2(1), 3(3).

Para 2: word in square brackets in heading and sub-paras (1ZA), (1B) inserted by the Copyright and Rights in Performances (Quotation and Parody) Regulations 2014, SI 2014/2356, regs 2, 4.

Para 2A: inserted by SI 2014/2356, regs 2, 5(2).

Paras 3A–3E: inserted by the Copyright and Rights in Performances (Disability) Regulations 2014, SI 2014/1384, reg 3.

Para 4: substituted by SI 2014/1372, regs 2(1), 4(4).

Paras 6, 6ZA: substituted (for original para 6) by SI 2014/1372, regs 2(1), 4(5).

Para 6A: inserted by the Copyright and Related Rights Regulations 1996, SI 1996/2967, regs 4, 20(3), subject to transitional provisions and savings in regs 25–36 thereof at **[2.510]–[2.521]**.

Para 6B: inserted by SI 1996/2967, regs 4, 20(3), subject to transitional provisions and savings in regs 25–36 thereof at **[2.510]–[2.521]**; sub-paras (A1), (A2) inserted by the Digital Economy Act 2010, s 43(6), (8)(a); word omitted from sub-para (1), and sub-para (2) repealed by the Copyright and Rights in Performances (Research, Education, Libraries and Archives) Regulations 2014, SI 2014/1372, reg 2(2), Schedule, paras 1, 8.

Paras 6C–6H: inserted by SI 2014/1372, regs 2(1), 6.

Para 6I: inserted by the Copyright and Rights in Performances (Certain Permitted Uses of Orphan Works) Regulations 2014, SI 2014/2861, reg 3(4).

Para 10: words in first (outer) pair of square brackets inserted by the Government of Wales Act 1998, s 125, Sch 12, paras 26, 29; words in second (inner) pair of square brackets substituted by the Government of Wales Act 2006, s 160(1), Sch 10, paras 22, 32.

Para 14: words in first pair of square brackets in sub-para (1) substituted and sub-paras (3)–(8) substituted for original sub-paras (3), (4), by SI 2014/1372, regs 2(1), 7(3), (4).

Para 14A: inserted by SI 1996/2967, regs 4, 20(3), subject to transitional provisions and savings in regs 25–36 thereof at **[2.510]–[2.521]**.

Para 15: repealed by the Copyright, Designs and Patents Act 1988 (Amendment) Regulations 2010, SI 2010/2694, reg 3(2).

Para 17: words in second pair of square brackets in sub-para (1) inserted, words in square brackets in sub-para (2)(d) inserted, and sub-paras (5), (6) inserted, by the Audiovisual Media Services Regulations 2009, SI 2009/2979, reg 12(1), (3)(a); sub-paras (2), (3) substituted, for original sub-paras (2)–(4), by the Broadcasting Act 1990, s 203(1), Sch 20, para 50(2) and further substituted by the Broadcasting Act 1996, s 148(1), Sch 10, para 32; sub-para (2)(a) substituted, word omitted from sub-para (2)(b) repealed, words in square brackets in sub-para (2)(b), (c) substituted, sub-para (2)(d) added, and sub-paras (3), (4) further substituted for sub-para (3) by the Communications Act 2003, s 406(1), (7), Sch 17, para 93, Sch 19.

Para 18: sub-para (1A)(a) repealed by SI 2010/2694, reg 4(2).

Para 19: substituted by the Broadcasting Act 1996, s 138, Sch 9, para 5; repealed by the Digital Economy Act 2017, s 34(1)(b), as from a day to be appointed.

Para 19A: inserted by the Broadcasting Act 1996, s 138, Sch 9, para 6; repealed by the Digital Economy Act 2017, s 34(1)(b), as from a day to be appointed.

Para 20: repealed by the Copyright and Rights in Performances (Disability) Regulations 2014, SI 2014/1384, reg 4, Schedule, para 8.

Para 21: substituted by SI 2014/1372, regs 2(1), 8(2).

[SCHEDULE 2A
LICENSING OF PERFORMER'S . . . RIGHTS

Section 205A

Licensing schemes and licensing bodies

[2.411]

1. (1) In [this Chapter] a "licensing scheme" means a scheme setting out—

(a) the classes of case in which the operator of the scheme, or the person on whose behalf he acts, is willing to grant performers' property right licences, and

(b) the terms on which licences would be granted in those classes of case;

and for this purpose a "scheme" includes anything in the nature of a scheme, whether described as a scheme or as a tariff or by any other name.

(2) In [this Chapter] a "licensing body" means a society or other organisation which has as its main object, or one of its main objects, the negotiating or granting, whether as owner or prospective owner of a performer's property rights or as agent for him, of performers' property right licences, and whose objects include the granting of licences covering the performances of more than one performer.

(3) In this paragraph "performers' property right licences" means licences to do, or authorise the doing of, any of the things for which consent is required under section [182B, 182C or 182CA].

(4) References in [this Chapter] to licences or licensing schemes covering the performances of more than one performer do not include licences or schemes covering only—

(a) performances recorded in a single recording,

(b) performances recorded in more than one recording where—

(i) the performers giving the performances are the same, or

(ii) the recordings are made by, or by employees of or commissioned by, a single individual, firm, company or group of companies.

For purpose a group of companies means a holding company and its subsidiaries within the meaning of [section 1159 of the Companies Act 2006].

[(5) Schedule A1 confers powers to provide for the regulation of licensing bodies.]

[Power to provide for licensing of orphan rights

1A. (1) The Secretary of State may by regulations provide for the grant of licences to do, or authorise the doing of, acts to which section 182, 182A, 182B, 182C, 182CA, 183 or 184 applies in respect of a performance, where—

(a) the performer's consent would otherwise be required under that section, but

(b) the right to authorise or prohibit the act qualifies as an orphan right under the regulations.

(2) The regulations may—

(a) specify a person or a description of persons authorised to grant licences, or

(b) provide for a person designated in the regulations to specify a person or a description of persons authorised to grant licences.

(3) The regulations must provide that, for a right to qualify as an orphan right, it is a requirement that the owner of the right has not been found after a diligent search made in accordance with the regulations.

(4) The regulations must provide for any licence—

(a) to have effect as if granted by the missing owner;

(b) not to give exclusive rights;

(c) not to be granted to a person authorised to grant licences.

(5) The regulations may apply in a case where it is not known whether a performer's right subsists, and references to a right, to a missing owner and to an interest of a missing owner are to be read as including references to a supposed right, owner or interest.]

Extended collective licensing

1B. (1) The Secretary of State may by regulations provide for a licensing body that applies to the Secretary of State under the regulations to be authorised to grant licences to do, or authorise the doing of, acts to which section 182, 182A, 182B, 182C, 182CA, 183 or 184 applies in respect of a performance, where the right to authorise or prohibit the act is not owned by the body or a person on whose behalf the body acts.

(2) An authorisation must specify the acts to which any of those sections applies that the licensing body is authorised to license.

(3) The regulations must provide for the rights owner to have a right to limit or exclude the grant of licences by virtue of the regulations.

(4) The regulations must provide for any licence not to give exclusive rights.

General provision about licensing

1C. (1) This paragraph and paragraph 1D apply to regulations under paragraphs 1A and 1B.

(2) The regulations may provide for a body to be or remain authorised to grant licences only if specified requirements are met, and for a question whether they are met to be determined by a person, and in a manner, specified in the regulations.

(3) The regulations may specify other matters to be taken into account in any decision to be made under the regulations as to whether to authorise a person to grant licences.

(4) The regulations must provide for the treatment of any royalties or other sums paid in respect of a licence, including—

(a) the deduction of administrative costs;
(b) the period for which sums must be held;
(c) the treatment of sums after that period (as bona vacantia or otherwise).

(5) The regulations must provide for circumstances in which an authorisation to grant licences may be withdrawn, and for determining the rights and obligations of any person if an authorisation is withdrawn.

(6) The regulations may include other provision for the purposes of authorisation and licensing, including in particular provision—
(a) for determining the rights and obligations of any person if a right ceases to qualify as an orphan right (or ceases to qualify by reference to any rights owner), or if a rights owner exercises the right referred to in paragraph 1B(3), while a licence is in force;
(b) about maintenance of registers and access to them;
(c) permitting the use of a work for incidental purposes including an application or search;
(d) for a right conferred by section 205C to be treated as having been asserted under section 205D;
(e) for the payment of fees to cover administrative expenses.

1D. (1) The power to make regulations includes power—
(a) to make incidental, supplementary or consequential provision, including provision extending or restricting the jurisdiction of the Copyright Tribunal or conferring powers on it;
(b) to make transitional, transitory or saving provision;
(c) to make different provision for different purposes.

(2) Regulations under any provision may amend this Part, or any other enactment or subordinate legislation passed or made before that provision comes into force, for the purpose of making consequential provision or extending or restricting the jurisdiction of the Copyright Tribunal or conferring powers on it.

(3) Regulations may make provision by reference to guidance issued from time to time by any person.

(4) The power to make regulations is exercisable by statutory instrument.

(5) A statutory instrument containing regulations may not be made unless a draft of the instrument has been laid before and approved by a resolution of each House of Parliament.]

References and applications with respect to licensing schemes

2. Paragraphs 3 to 8 (references and applications with respect to licensing schemes) apply to licensing schemes operated by licensing bodies in relation to a performer's property rights which cover the performances of more than one performer, so far as they relate to licences for—
(a) copying a recording of the whole or any substantial part of a qualifying performance,
[(aa) making such a recording available to the public in the way mentioned in section 182CA(1), or]
(b) renting or lending copies of a recording to the public;
and in those paragraphs "licensing scheme" means a licensing scheme of any of those descriptions.

Reference of proposed licensing scheme to tribunal

3. (1) The terms of a licensing scheme proposed to be operated by a licensing body may be referred to the Copyright Tribunal by an organisation claiming to be representative of persons claiming that they require licences in cases of a description to which the scheme would apply, either generally or in relation to any description of case.

(2) The Tribunal shall first decide whether to entertain the reference, and may decline to do so on the ground that the reference is premature.

(3) If the Tribunal decides to entertain the reference it shall consider the matter referred and make such order, either confirming or varying the proposed scheme, either generally or so far as it relates to cases of the description to which the reference relates, as the Tribunal may determine to be reasonable in the circumstances.

(4) The order may be made so as to be in force indefinitely or for such period as the Tribunal may determine.

Reference of licensing scheme to tribunal

4. (1) If while a licensing scheme is in operation a dispute arises between the operator of the scheme and—
(a) a person claiming that he requires a licence in a case of a description to which the scheme applies, or
(b) an organisation claiming to be representative of such persons,
that person or organisation may refer the scheme to the Copyright Tribunal in so far as it relates to cases of that description.

(2) A scheme which has been referred to the Tribunal under this paragraph shall remain in operation until proceedings on the reference are concluded.

(3) The Tribunal shall consider the matter in dispute and make such order, either confirming or varying the scheme so far as it relates to cases of the description to which the reference relates, as the Tribunal may determine to be reasonable in the circumstances.

(4) The order may be made so as to be in force indefinitely or for such period as the Tribunal may determine.

Further reference of scheme to tribunal

5. (1) Where the Copyright Tribunal has on a previous reference of a licensing scheme under paragraph 3 or 4, or under this paragraph, made an order with respect to the scheme, then, while the order remains in force—

- (a) the operator of the scheme,
- (b) a person claiming that he requires a licence in a case of the description to which the order applies, or
- (c) an organisation claiming to be representative of such persons,

may refer the scheme again to the Tribunal so far as it relates to cases of that description.

(2) A licensing scheme shall not, except with the special leave of the Tribunal, be referred again to the Tribunal in respect of the same description of cases—

- (a) within twelve months from the date of the order on the previous reference, or
- (b) if the order was made so as to be in force for 15 months or less, until the last three months before the expiry of the order.

(3) A scheme which has been referred to the Tribunal under this paragraph shall remain in operation until proceedings on the reference are concluded.

(4) The Tribunal shall consider the matter in dispute and make such order, either confirming, varying or further varying the scheme so far as it relates to cases of the description to which the reference relates, as the Tribunal may determine to be reasonable in the circumstances.

(5) The order may be made so as to be in force indefinitely or for such period as the Tribunal may determine.

Application for grant of licence in connection with licensing scheme

6. (1) A person who claims, in a case covered by a licensing scheme, that the operator of the scheme has refused to grant him or procure the grant to him of a licence in accordance with the scheme, or has failed to do so within a reasonable time after being asked, may apply to the Copyright Tribunal.

(2) A person who claims, in a case excluded from a licensing scheme, that the operator of the scheme either—

- (a) has refused to grant him a licence or procure the grant to him of a licence, or has failed to do so within a reasonable time of being asked, and that in the circumstances it is unreasonable that a licence should not be granted, or
- (b) proposes terms for a licence which are unreasonable,

may apply to the Copyright Tribunal.

(3) A case shall be regarded as excluded from a licensing scheme for the purposes of sub-paragraph (2) if—

- (a) the scheme provides for the grant of licences subject to terms excepting matters from the licence and the case falls within such an exception, or
- (b) the case is so similar to those in which licences are granted under the scheme that it is unreasonable that it should not be dealt with in the same way.

(4) If the Tribunal is satisfied that the claim is well-founded, it shall make an order declaring that, in respect of the matters specified in the order, the applicant is entitled to a licence on such terms as the Tribunal may determine to be applicable in accordance with the scheme or, as the case may be, to be reasonable in the circumstances.

(5) The order may be made so as to be in force indefinitely or for such period as the Tribunal may determine.

Application for review of order as to entitlement to licence

7. (1) Where the Copyright Tribunal has made an order under paragraph 6 that a person is entitled to a licence under a licensing scheme, the operator of the scheme or the original applicant may apply to the Tribunal to review its order.

(2) An application shall not be made, except with the special leave of the Tribunal—

- (a) within twelve months from the date of the order, or of the decision on a previous application under this paragraph, or
- (b) if the order was made so as to be in force for 15 months or less, or as a result of the decision on a previous application under this paragraph is due to expire within 15 months of that decision, until the last three months before the expiry date.

(3) The Tribunal shall on an application for review confirm or vary its order as the Tribunal may determine to be reasonable having regard to the terms applicable in accordance with the licensing scheme or, as the case may be, the circumstances of the case.

Effect of order of tribunal as to licensing scheme

8. (1) A licensing scheme which has been confirmed or varied by the Copyright Tribunal—

(a) under paragraph 3 (reference of terms of proposed scheme), or

(b) under paragraph 4 or 5 (reference of existing scheme to Tribunal),

shall be in force or, as the case may be, remain in operation, so far as it relates to the description of case in respect of which the order was made, so long as the order remains in force.

(2) While the order is in force a person who in a case of a class to which the order applies—

(a) pays to the operator of the scheme any charges payable under the scheme in respect of a licence covering the case in question or, if the amount cannot be ascertained, gives an undertaking to the operator to pay them when ascertained, and

(b) complies with the other terms applicable to such a licence under the scheme,

shall be in the same position as regards infringement of performers' property rights as if he had at all material times been the holder of a licence granted by the rights owner in question in accordance with the scheme.

(3) The Tribunal may direct that the order, so far as it varies the amount of charges payable, has effect from a date before that on which it is made, but not earlier than the date on which the reference was made or, if later, on which the scheme came into operation.

If such a direction is made—

(a) any necessary repayments, or further payments, shall be made in respect of charges already paid, and

(b) the reference in sub-paragraph (2)(a) to the charges payable under the scheme shall be construed as a reference to the charges so payable by virtue of the order.

No such direction may be made where sub-paragraph (4) below applies.

(4) An order of the Tribunal under paragraph 4 or 5 made with respect to a scheme which is certified for any purpose under paragraph 16 has effect, so far as it varies the scheme by reducing the charges payable for licences, from the date on which the reference was made to the Tribunal.

(5) Where the Tribunal has made an order under paragraph 6 (order as to entitlement to licence under licensing scheme) and the order remains in force, the person in whose favour the order is made shall if he—

(a) pays to the operator of the scheme any charges payable in accordance with the order or, if the amount cannot be ascertained, gives an undertaking to pay the charges when ascertained, and

(b) complies with the other terms specified in the order,

be in the same position as regards infringement of performers' property rights as if he had at all material times been the holder of a licence granted by the rights owner in question on the terms specified in the order.

References and applications with respect to licensing by licensing bodies

9. Paragraphs 10 to 13 (references and applications with respect to licensing by licensing bodies) apply to licences relating to a performer's property rights which cover the performance of more than one performer granted by a licensing body otherwise than in pursuance of a licensing scheme, so far as the licences authorise—

(a) copying a recording of the whole or any substantial part of a qualifying performance,

[(aa) making such a recording available to the public in the way mentioned in section 182CA(1), or]

(b) renting or lending copies of a recording to the public;

and references in those paragraphs to a licence shall be construed accordingly.

Reference to tribunal of proposed licence

10. (1) The terms on which a licensing body proposes to grant a licence may be referred to the Copyright Tribunal by the prospective licensee.

(2) The Tribunal shall first decide whether to entertain the reference, and may decline to do so on the ground that the reference is premature.

(3) If the Tribunal decides to entertain the reference it shall consider the terms of the proposed licence and make such order, either confirming or varying the terms as it may determine to be reasonable in the circumstances.

(4) The order may be made so as to be in force indefinitely or for such period as the Tribunal may determine.

Reference to tribunal of expiring licence

11. (1) A licensee under a licence which is due to expire, by effluxion of time or as a result of notice given by the licensing body, may apply to the Copyright Tribunal on the ground that it is unreasonable in the circumstances that the licence should cease to be in force.

(2) Such an application may not be made until the last three months before the licence is due to expire.

(3) A licence in respect of which a reference has been made to the Tribunal shall remain in operation until proceedings on the reference are concluded.

(4) If the Tribunal finds the application well-founded, it shall make an order declaring that the licensee shall continue to be entitled to the benefit of the licence on such terms as the Tribunal may determine to be reasonable in the circumstances.

(5) An order of the Tribunal under this paragraph may be made so as to be in force indefinitely or for such period as the Tribunal may determine.

Application for review of order as to licence

12. (1) Where the Copyright Tribunal has made an order under paragraph 10 or 11, the licensing body or the person entitled to the benefit of the order may apply to the Tribunal to review its order.

(2) An application shall not be made, except with the special leave of the Tribunal—

(a) within twelve months from the date of the order or of the decision on a previous application under this paragraph, or

(b) if the order was made so as to be in force for 15 months or less, or as a result of the decision on a previous application under this paragraph is due to expire within 15 months of that decision, until the last three months before the expiry date.

(3) The Tribunal shall on an application for review confirm or vary its order as the Tribunal may determine to be reasonable in the circumstances.

Effect of order of tribunal as to licence

13. (1) Where the Copyright Tribunal has made an order under paragraph 10 or 11 and the order remains in force, the person entitled to the benefit of the order shall if he—

(a) pays to the licensing body any charges payable in accordance with the order or, if the amount cannot be ascertained, gives an undertaking to pay the charges when ascertained, and

(b) complies with the other terms specified in the order,

be in the same position as regards infringement of performers' property rights as if he had at all material times been the holder of a licence granted by the rights owner in question on the terms specified in the order.

(2) The benefit of the order may be assigned—

(a) in the case of an order under paragraph 10, if assignment is not prohibited under the terms of the Tribunal's order; and

(b) in the case of an order under paragraph 11, if assignment was not prohibited under the terms of the original licence.

(3) The Tribunal may direct that an order under paragraph 10 or 11, or an order under paragraph 12 varying such an order, so far as it varies the amount of charges payable, has effect from a date before that on which it is made, but not earlier than the date on which the reference or application was made or, if later, on which the licence was granted or, as the case may be, was due to expire.

If such a direction is made—

(a) any necessary repayments, or further payments, shall be made in respect of charges already paid, and

(b) the reference in sub-paragraph (1)(a) to the charges payable in accordance with the order shall be construed, where the order is varied by a later order, as a reference to the charges so payable by virtue of the later order.

General considerations: unreasonable discrimination

14. (1) In determining what is reasonable on a reference or application under this Schedule relating to a licensing scheme or licence, the Copyright Tribunal shall have regard to—

(a) the availability of other schemes, or the granting of other licences, to other persons in similar circumstances, and

(b) the terms of those schemes or licences,

and shall exercise its powers so as to secure that there is no unreasonable discrimination between licensees, or prospective licensees, under the scheme or licence to which the reference or application relates and licensees under other schemes operated by, or other licences granted by, the same person.

(2) This does not affect the Tribunal's general obligation in any case to have regard to all relevant circumstances.

Application to settle royalty or other sum payable for lending

15. (1) An application to settle the royalty or other sum payable in pursuance of paragraph 14A of Schedule 2 (lending of certain recordings) may be made to the Copyright Tribunal by the owner of a performer's property rights or the person claiming to be treated as licensed by him.

(2) The Tribunal shall consider the matter and make such order as it may determine to be reasonable in the circumstances.

(3) Either party may subsequently apply to the Tribunal to vary the order, and the Tribunal shall consider the matter and make such order confirming or varying the original order as it may determine to be reasonable in the circumstances.

(4) An application under sub-paragraph (3) shall not, except with the special leave of the Tribunal, be made within twelve months from the date of the original order or of the order on a previous application under that sub-paragraph.

(5) An order under sub-paragraph (3) has effect from the date on which it is made or such later date as may be specified by the Tribunal

Certification of licensing schemes

16. (1) A person operating or proposing to operate a licensing scheme may apply to the Secretary of State to certify the scheme for the purposes of [paragraph . . . . 14A . . . . of Schedule 2 (. . . . lending of certain recordings . . . .)].

(2) The Secretary of State shall by order made by statutory instrument certify the scheme if he is satisfied that it—

(a) enables the works to which it relates to be identified with sufficient certainty by persons likely to require licences, and

(b) sets out clearly the charges (if any) payable and the other terms on which licences will be granted.

(3) The scheme shall be scheduled to the order and the certification shall come into operation for the purposes of [the relevant paragraph] of Schedule 2—

(a) on such date, not less than eight weeks after the order is made, as may be specified in the order, or

(b) if the scheme is the subject of a reference under paragraph 3 (reference of proposed scheme), any later date on which the order of the Copyright Tribunal under that paragraph comes into force or the reference is withdrawn.

(4) A variation of the scheme is not effective unless a corresponding amendment of the order is made; and the Secretary of State shall make such an amendment in the case of a variation ordered by the Copyright Tribunal on a reference under paragraph 3, 4 or 5, and may do so in any other case if he thinks fit.

(5) The order shall be revoked if the scheme ceases to be operated and may be revoked if it appears to the Secretary of State that it is no longer being operated according to its terms.

Powers exercisable in consequence of competition report

17. [(1) Sub-paragraph (1A) applies where whatever needs to be remedied, mitigated or prevented by the Secretary of State [or (as the case may be) the Competition and Markets Authority] under section 12(5) of the Competition Act 1980 or section 41(2), 55(2), 66(6), 75(2), 83(2), 138(2), 147(2)[, 147A(2)] or 160(2) of, or paragraph 5(2) or 10(2) of Schedule 7 to, the Enterprise Act 2002 (powers to take remedial action following references to the [Competition and Markets Authority] in connection with public bodies and certain other persons, mergers or market investigations etc) consists of or includes—

(a) conditions in licences granted by the owner of a performer's property rights restricting the use to which a recording may be put by the licensee or the right of the owner to grant other licenses, or

(b) a refusal of an owner of a performer's property rights to grant licences on reasonable terms.

(1A) The powers conferred by Schedule 8 to the Enterprise Act 2002 include power to cancel or modify those conditions and, instead or in addition, to provide that licences in respect of the performer's property rights shall be available as of right.

(2) The references to anything permitted by Schedule 8 to the Enterprise Act 2002 in section 12(5A) of the Competition Act 1980 and in sections 75(4)(a), 83(4)(a), 84(2)(a), 89(1), 160(4)(a), 161(3)(a) and 164(1) of, and paragraphs 5, 10 and 11 of Schedule 7 to, the Act of 2002 shall be construed accordingly.]

(3) [The Secretary of State] [or (as the case may be) the Competition and Markets Authority] shall only exercise the powers available by virtue of this paragraph if he [or it] is satisfied that to do so does not contravene any Convention relating to performers' rights to which the United Kingdom is a party.

(4) The terms of a licence available by virtue of this paragraph shall, in default of agreement, be settled by the Copyright Tribunal on an application by the person requiring the licence; and terms so settled shall authorise the licensee to do everything in respect of which a licence is so available.

(5) Where the terms of a licence are settled by the Tribunal, the licence has effect from the date on which the application to the Tribunal was made.]

NOTES

Inserted by the Copyright and Related Rights Regulations 1996, SI 1996/2967, regs 4, 22(2), subject to transitional provisions and savings specified in regs 25–36 of those Regulations, at **[2.510]–[2.521]**.

Schedule heading: word omitted repealed by the Enterprise and Regulatory Reform Act 2013, s 77(4), Sch 22, Pt 2, paras 2, 3.

Para 1: words in square brackets in sub-paras (1), (2), and words in first pair of square brackets in sub-para (4) substituted by the Performances (Moral Rights, etc) Regulations 2006, SI 2006/18, reg 2, Schedule, paras 1, 8, 9; words in square brackets in sub-para (3) substituted by the Copyright and Related Rights Regulations 2003, SI 2003/2498, regs 3, 7(4)(a), subject to transitional provisions as noted to s 1 of this Act at **[2.7]**; words in second pair of square brackets in sub-para (4) substituted by the Companies Act 2006 (Consequential Amendments, Transitional Provisions and Savings) Order 2009, SI 2009/1941, art 2(1), Sch 1, para 98(b); sub-para (5) inserted by the Enterprise and Regulatory Reform Act 2013, s 77(4), Sch 22, Pt 2, paras 2, 4.

Paras 1A–1D: inserted by the Enterprise and Regulatory Reform Act 2013, s 77(4), Sch 22, Pt 2, paras 2, 5.

Paras 2, 9: sub-para (aa) substituted for the original word "or" at the end of sub-para (a) by SI 2003/2498, regs 3, 7(4)(b), subject to transitional provisions as noted to s 1 of this Act at **[2.7]**.

Para 16: words in square brackets substituted by SI 2003/2498, reg 2(1), Sch 1, Pt 1, paras 1, 17, subject to transitional provisions as noted to s 1 of this Act at **[2.7]**; words omitted in first and third places omitted repealed by the Copyright and Rights in Performances (Research, Education, Libraries and Archives) Regulations 2014, SI 2014/1372, reg 2(2), Schedule, paras 1, 9; words omitted in second and fourth places repealed by the Copyright and Rights in Performances (Disability) Regulations 2014, SI 2014/1384, reg 4, Schedule, para 6.

Para 17: sub-paras (1), (1A), (2) substituted, for original sub-paras (1), (2), and words in first and third pairs of square brackets in sub-para (3) substituted, by the Enterprise Act 2002, s 278(1), Sch 25, para 18(1), (5), subject to transitional provisions and savings in s 276 of, Sch 24, paras 2 12, 14–19 to, the 2002 Act, and SI 2004/3233, arts 3–5; in sub-para (1) words in first and third pairs of square brackets substituted and figure in second pair of square brackets inserted, and words in second pair of square brackets in sub-para (3) substituted by the Enterprise and Regulatory Reform Act 2013 (Competition) (Consequential, Transitional and Saving Provisions) Order 2014, SI 2014/892, art 2, Sch 1, Pt 2, paras 55, 59.

Modification: In para 17, the reference in sub-s (1) to the Enterprise Act 2002, s 66(6), Sch 7, paras 5(2), 10(2) shall have effect as if it included a reference to the Enterprise Act 2002 (Protection of Legitimate Interests) Order 2003, SI 2003/1592, art 12(7), Sch 2, paras 5(2), 10(2) respectively and the reference in sub-s (2) to the 2002 Act, Sch 7, paras 5, 10, 11 shall have effect as if it included a reference to SI 2003/1592, Sch 2, paras 5, 10, 11 respectively; see SI 2003/1592, Sch 4, para 7(3).

Orders: the Copyright (Certification of Licensing Scheme for Educational Recording of Broadcasts) (Educational Recording Agency Limited) Order 2007, SI 2007/266 at **[2.578]**.

Regulations: the Copyright and Rights in Performances (Extended Collective Licensing) Regulations 2014, SI 2014/2588; the Copyright and Rights in Performances (Licensing of Orphan Works) Regulations 2014, SI 2014/2863.

SCHEDULES 3–5

(Sch 3 in so far as unrepealed, amends the Registered Designs Act 1949; Sch 4 sets out the text of the 1949 Act, as amended by this Act; Sch 5 amends the Patents Act 1949 and the Patents Act 1977.)

[SCHEDULE 5A
PERMITTED ACTS TO WHICH SECTION 296ZE APPLIES

Section 296ZE

PART 1
COPYRIGHT EXCEPTIONS

[2.412]

section 29 (research and private study)

[section 29A (copies for text and data analysis for non-commercial research)]

section 31A [(disabled persons: copies of works for personal use)]

section 31B [(making and supply of accessible copies by authorised bodies)]

[section 31BA (making and supply of intermediate copies by authorised bodies)]

[section 32 (illustration for instruction)]

section 35 (recording by educational establishments of broadcasts)

[section 36 (copying and use of extracts of works by educational establishments)]

. . .

. . .

[section 41 (copying by librarians: supply of single copies to other libraries)[

[section 42 (copying by librarians etc: replacement copies of works)[

[section 42A (copying by librarians: single copies of published works)[

[section 43 (copying by librarians or archivists: single copies of unpublished works)] section 44 (copy of work required to be made as condition of export)

section 45 (Parliamentary and judicial proceedings)

section 46 (Royal Commissions and statutory inquiries)

section 47 (material open to public inspection or on official register)

section 48 (material communicated to the Crown in the course of public business)

section 49 (public records)

section 50 (acts done under statutory authority)

section 61 (recordings of folksongs)

section 68 (incidental recording for purposes of broadcast)

section 69 (recording for purposes of supervision and control of broadcasts)

section 70 (recording for purposes of time-shifting)

section 71 (photographs of broadcasts)

. . .

[section 75 (recording of broadcast for archival purposes)]]

NOTES

Inserted by the Copyright and Related Rights Regulations 2003, SI 2003/2498, regs 3, 24(2), subject to transitional provisions as noted to s 1 of this Act at **[2.7]**.

Words in square brackets in entries relating to ss 31A, 31B substituted, entry relating to s 31BA substituted for original entry relating to s 31C, and entry relating to s 74 (omitted) repealed, by the Copyright and Rights in Performances (Disability) Regulations 2014, SI 2014/1384, reg 4, Schedule, para 7(1), (2).

Entries relating to ss 29A, 42A inserted, entries relating to ss 32, 36, 41, 42, 43, 75 substituted, and entries relating to ss 38, 39 (omitted) repealed by the Copyright and Rights in Performances (Research, Education, Libraries and Archives) Regulations 2014, SI 2014/1372, reg 2(2), Schedule, paras 1, 10(1), (2).

[PART 2
RIGHTS IN PERFORMANCES EXCEPTIONS

[2.413]

[paragraph 1C of Schedule 2 (research and private study)]

[paragraph 1D of Schedule 2 (copies for text and data analysis for non-commercial research)]

[paragraph 3A of Schedule 2 (disabled persons: copies of recordings for personal use)

paragraph 3B of Schedule 2 (making and supply of accessible copies by authorised bodies)

paragraph 3C of Schedule 2 (making and supply of intermediate copies by authorised bodies)]

[paragraph 4 of Schedule 2 (illustration for instruction)]

[paragraph 6 of Schedule 2 (recording by educational establishments of broadcasts)]

[paragraph 6ZA of Schedule 2 (copying and use of extracts of recordings by educational establishments)]

[paragraph 6D of Schedule 2 (copying by librarians: supply of single copies to other libraries)]

[paragraph 6E of Schedule 2 (copying by librarians etc: replacement copies of recordings)]

[paragraph 6F of Schedule 2 (copying by librarians: single copies of published recordings)]

[paragraph 6G of Schedule 2 (copying by librarians or archivists: single copies of unpublished recordings)]

paragraph 7 of Schedule 2 (copy of work required to be made as condition of export)

paragraph 8 of Schedule 2 (Parliamentary and judicial proceedings)

paragraph 9 of Schedule 2 (Royal Commissions and statutory inquiries)

paragraph 10 of Schedule 2 (public records)

paragraph 11 of Schedule 2 (acts done under statutory authority)

paragraph 14 of Schedule 2 (recordings of folksongs)

paragraph 16 of Schedule 2 (incidental recording for purposes of broadcast) paragraph 17 of Schedule 2 (recordings for purposes of supervision and control of broadcasts)

paragraph 17A of Schedule 2 (recording for the purposes of time-shifting)

paragraph 17B of Schedule 2 (photographs of broadcasts)

. . .

paragraph 21 of Schedule 2 (recording of broadcast for archival purposes)]

NOTES

Inserted by the Copyright and Related Rights Regulations 2003, SI 2003/2498, regs 3, 24(2), subject to transitional provisions as noted to s 1 of this Act at **[2.7]**.

Entries relating to paragraphs 1C, 1D, 6ZA, 6D, 6E, 6F, 6G inserted and entries relating to paragraphs 4 and 6 substituted by the Copyright and Rights in Performances (Research, Education, Libraries and Archives) Regulations 2014, SI 2014/1372, reg 2(2), Schedule, paras 1, 10(1), (3).

Entries relating to paragraphs 3A, 3B and 3C inserted, and entry relating to paragraph 20 (omitted) repealed, by the Copyright and Rights in Performances (Disability) Regulations 2014, SI 2014/1384, reg 4, Schedule, para 7(1), (3).

[PART 3
DATABASE RIGHT EXCEPTIONS

[2.414]
regulation 20 of and Schedule 1 to the Copyright and Rights in Databases Regulations 1997 (SI 1997/3032)]

NOTES

Inserted by the Copyright and Related Rights Regulations 2003, SI 2003/2498, regs 3, 24(2), subject to transitional provisions as noted to s 1 of this Act at **[2.7]**.

Part 2 Copyright

SCHEDULE 6
PROVISIONS FOR THE BENEFIT OF [GREAT ORMOND STREET HOSPITAL FOR CHILDREN]

Section 301

Interpretation

[2.415]
1. (1) In this Schedule—

["GOSH Children's Charity" means Great Ormond Street Hospital Children's Charity (company registration number 9338724);]

"the Hospital" means [Great Ormond Street Hospital for Children];

. . . and

"the work" means the play "Peter Pan" by Sir James Matthew Barrie.

(2) Expressions used in this Schedule which are defined for the purposes of Part I of this Act (copyright) have the same meaning as in that Part.

Entitlement to royalty

2. (1) [GOSH Children's Charity is] entitled, subject to the following provisions of this Schedule, to a royalty in respect of any public performance, commercial publication [or communication to the public] of the whole or any substantial part of the work or an adaptation of it.

(2) Where [GOSH Children's Charity is] or would be entitled to a royalty, another form of remuneration may be agreed.

Exceptions

3. No royalty is payable in respect of—

(a) anything which immediately before copyright in the work expired on 31st December 1987 could lawfully have been done without the licence, or further licence, of the [copyright owner at that time]; or

(b) anything which if copyright still subsisted in the work could, by virtue of any provision of Chapter III of Part I of this Act (acts permitted notwithstanding copyright), be done without infringing copyright.

Saving

4. No royalty is payable in respect of anything done in pursuance of arrangements made before the passing of this Act.

Procedure for determining amount payable

5. (1) In default of agreement application may be made to the Copyright Tribunal which shall consider the matter and make such order regarding the royalty or other remuneration to be paid as it may determine to be reasonable in the circumstances.

(2) Application may subsequently be made to the Tribunal to vary its order, and the Tribunal shall consider the matter and make such order confirming or varying the original order as it may determine to be reasonable in the circumstances.

(3) An application for variation shall not, except with the special leave of the Tribunal, be made within twelve months from the date of the original order or of the order on a previous application for variation.

(4) A variation order has effect from the date on which it is made or such later date as may be specified by the Tribunal.

[(5) The provisions of Chapter VIII of Part I (general provisions relating to the Copyright Tribunal) apply in relation to the Tribunal when exercising any jurisdiction under this paragraph.]

[Sums received to be held for the benefit of the Hospital

6. The sums received by GOSH Children's Charity by virtue of this Schedule, after deduction of any relevant expenses, are to be held by it for the purposes of the Hospital.]

Right only for the benefit of the Hospital

7. (1) The right of [GOSH Children's Charity] under this Schedule may not be assigned and shall cease if [GOSH Children's Charity purports] to assign or charge it.

(2) The right . . . shall cease if the Hospital ceases to have a separate identity or ceases to have purposes which include the care of sick children.

(3) . . .

NOTES

Schedule heading: words in square brackets substituted by the NHS (Charitable Trusts Etc) Act 2016, s 3(1), (5).

Para 1: in sub-para (1) definition "GOSH Children's Charity" inserted, in definition "the Hospital" words in square brackets substituted and definition "the trustees" (omitted) repealed, by the NHS (Charitable Trusts Etc) Act 2016, s 3(1), (6), (7).

Para 2: words in first pair of square brackets in sub-para (1) and words in square brackets in sub-para (2) substituted by the NHS (Charitable Trusts Etc) Act 2016, s 3(1), (6), (8); words in second pair of square brackets in sub-para (1) substituted by the Copyright and Related Rights Regulations 2003, SI 2003/2498, reg 2(1), Sch 1, Pt 1, paras 1, 6(2)(f), subject to transitional provisions as noted to s 1 of this Act at **[2.7]**.

Para 3: in sub-para (a) words in square brackets substituted by the NHS (Charitable Trusts Etc) Act 2016, s 3(1), (6), (9).

Para 5: sub-para (5) added by the Copyright and Related Rights Regulations 1996, SI 1996/2967, regs 4, 24(3), subject to transitional provisions and savings specified in regs 25–36 of those Regulations, at **[2.510]–[2.521]**.

Para 6: substituted (together with preceding heading) by the NHS (Charitable Trusts Etc) Act 2016, s 3(1), (6), (10).

Para 7: words in square brackets in sub-para (1) substituted, words omitted from sub-para (2) repealed and sub-para (3) repealed by the NHS (Charitable Trusts Etc) Act 2016, s 3(1), (6), (11).

SCHEDULES 7 AND 8

(Sch 7 contains consequential amendments which, in so far as relevant to this work, have been incorporated at the appropriate place; Sch 8 contains repeals only.)

BROADCASTING ACT 1990

(1990 c 42)

An Act to make new provision with respect to the provision and regulation of independent television and sound programme services and of other services provided on television or radio frequencies; to make provision with respect to the provision and regulation of local delivery services; to amend in other respects the law relating to broadcasting and the provision of television and sound programme services and to make provision with respect to the supply and use of information about programmes; to make provision with respect to the transfer of the property, rights and liabilities of the Independent Broadcasting Authority and the Cable Authority and the dissolution of those bodies; to make new provision relating to the Broadcasting Complaints Commission; to provide for the establishment and functions of a Broadcasting Standards Council; to amend the Wireless Telegraphy Acts 1949 to 1967 and the Marine, &c, Broadcasting (Offences) Act 1967; to revoke a class licence granted under the Telecommunications Act 1984 to run broadcast relay systems; and for connected purposes

[1 November 1990]

1–174 *((Pts I–VIII) outside the scope of this work.)*

PART IX
COPYRIGHT AND RELATED MATTERS

175 *(Outside the scope of this work.)*

[2.416]
176 Duty to provide advance information about programmes

(1) A person providing a programme service to which this section applies must make available in accordance with this section information relating to the programmes to be included in the service to any person (referred to in this section and Schedule 17 to this Act as "the publisher") wishing to publish in the United Kingdom any such information.

(2) The duty imposed by subsection (1) is to make available information as to the titles of the programmes which are to be, or may be, included in the service on any date, and the time of their inclusion, to any publisher who has asked the person providing the programme service to make such information available to him and reasonably requires it.

(3) Information to be made available to a publisher under this section is to be made available as soon after it has been prepared as is reasonably practicable but, in any event—

(a) not later than when it is made available to any other publisher, and

(b) in the case of information in respect of all the programmes to be included in the service in any period of seven days, not later than the beginning of the preceding period of fourteen days, or such other number of days as may be prescribed by the Secretary of State by order.

(4) An order under subsection (3) shall be subject to annulment in pursuance of a resolution of either House of Parliament.

(5) The duty imposed by subsection (1) is not satisfied by providing the information on terms, other than terms as to copyright, prohibiting or restricting publication in the United Kingdom by the publisher.

(6) Schedule 17 applies to any information or future information which the person providing a programme service to which this section applies is or may be required to make available under this section.

(7) For the purposes of this section and that Schedule, the following table shows the programme services to which the section and Schedule apply and the persons who provide them or are to be treated as providing them.

Programme service	Provider of service
Services other than services under the Act	
Television and national radio services provided by the BBC for reception in the United Kingdom	The BBC
Services under the Act	
Television programme services subject to [regulation by OFCOM]	The person licensed to provide the service
[The public television services of the Welsh Authority (within the meaning of Part 2 of Schedule 12 to the Communications Act 2003)]	The Authority
Any national service (see [section 126(1)]) subject to regulation by [OFCOM][, any simulcast radio service (within the meaning of Part II of the Broadcasting Act 1996), and any national digital sound programme service (within the meaning of that Part of that Act) subject to regulation by [OFCOM]]	The person licensed to provide the service
Services provided during interim period only	
Television broadcasting services provided by the Independent Television Commission in accordance with Schedule 11, other than Channel 4	The programme contractor
Channel 4, as so provided	The body corporate referred to in section 12(2) of the Broadcasting Act 1981

(8) This section does not require any information to be given about any advertisement.

NOTES

Sub-s (7): in the Table, words in first, second, third, fourth and sixth (inner) pairs of square brackets substituted by the Communications Act 2003, s 360(3), Sch 15, Pt 1, para 60, subject to transitional provisions in s 406(6) of, and Sch 18, paras 30, 64 to, that Act; words in fifth (outer) pair of square brackets inserted by the Broadcasting Act 1996, s 148(1), Sch 10, Pt I, para 10.

Broadcasting Act 1981, s 12(2): repealed (subject to transitional provisions) by s 203(3) of, and Sch 21 to, this Act.

PART X
MISCELLANEOUS AND GENERAL

177–194A (*Outside the scope of this work.*)

Part 2 Copyright

General

195–200 (*Outside the scope of this work.*)

[2.417]

201 Programme services

(1) In this Act "programme service" means any of the following services (whether or not it is, or it requires to be, licensed . . .), namely—

[(aa) any service which is a programme service within the meaning of the Communications Act 2003;]

(c) any other service which consists in the sending, by means of [an electronic communications network (within the meaning of the Communications Act 2003)], of sounds or visual images or both either—

(i) for reception at two or more places in the United Kingdom (whether they are so sent for simultaneous reception or at different times in response to requests made by different users of the service); or

(ii) for reception at a place in the United Kingdom for the purpose of being presented there to members of the public or to any group of persons.

[(2A) Subsection (1)(c) does not apply to so much of a service consisting only of sound programmes as—

(a) is a two-way service (within the meaning of section 248(4) of the Communications Act 2003);

(b) satisfies the conditions in section 248(5) of that Act; or

(c) is provided for the purpose only of being received by persons who have qualified as users of the service by reason of being persons who fall within paragraph (a) or (b) of section 248(7) of that Act.

(2B) Subsection (1)(c) does not apply to so much of a service not consisting only of sound programmes as—

(a) is a two-way service (within the meaning of section 232 of the Communications Act 2003);

(b) satisfies the conditions in section 233(5) of that Act; or

(c) is provided for the purpose only of being received by persons who have qualified as users of the service by reason of being persons who fall within paragraph (a) or (b) of section 233(7) of that Act.]

NOTES

Sub-s (1): words omitted repealed, para (aa) substituted for original paras (a), (b), (bb) (as inserted in the case of para (bb) by the Broadcasting Act 1996, s 148(1), Sch 10, Pt I, para 11), and words in square brackets in para (c) substituted by the Communications Act 2003, ss 360(1), 406(7), Sch 19.

Sub-ss (2A), (2B): substituted for original sub-s (2) by the Communications Act 2003, s 360(2).

202 (*Outside the scope of this work.*)

[2.418]

203 Consequential and transitional provisions

(1) The enactments mentioned in Schedule 20 to this Act shall have effect subject to the amendments there specified (being minor amendments or amendments consequential on the provisions of this Act).

(2) Unless the context otherwise requires, in any enactment amended by this Act—

"programme", in relation to a programme service, includes any item included in that service; and "television programme" includes a teletext transmission.

(3) The enactments mentioned in Schedule 21 to this Act (which include certain spent provisions) are hereby repealed to the extent specified in the third column of that Schedule.

(4) The transitional provisions and savings contained in Schedule 22 to this Act shall have effect.

[2.419]

204 Short title, commencement and extent

(1) This Act may be cited as the Broadcasting Act 1990.

(2) This Act shall come into force on such day as the Secretary of State may by order appoint; and different days may be so appointed for different provisions or for different purposes.

(3)–(6) (*Outside the scope of this work.*)

NOTES

Orders: the Broadcasting Act 1990 (Commencement No 1 and Transitional Provisions) Order 1990, SI 1990/2347.

SCHEDULES 1–22

(*Schs 1–22 outside the scope of this work.*)

BROADCASTING ACT 1996

(1996 c 55)

An Act to make new provision about the broadcasting in digital form of television and sound programme services and the broadcasting in that form on television or radio frequencies of other services; to amend the Broadcasting Act 1990; to make provision about rights to televise sporting or other events of national interest; to amend in other respects the law relating to the provision of television and sound programme services; to provide for the establishment and functions of a Broadcasting Standards Commission and for the dissolution of the Broadcasting Complaints Commission and the Broadcasting Standards Council; to make provision for the transfer to other persons of property, rights and liabilities of the British Broadcasting Corporation relating to their transmission network; and for connected purposes

[24 July 1996]

1–136 (*(Pts I–VI) outside the scope of this work.*)

PART VII
COPYRIGHT AND RELATED MATTERS

[2.420]

137 Avoidance of certain terms relating to use for purpose of news reporting of visual images from broadcast or cable programme

(1) Any provision in an agreement is void in so far as it purports to prohibit or restrict relevant dealing with a broadcast . . . in any circumstances where by virtue of section 30(2) of the Copyright, Designs and Patents Act 1988 (fair dealing for the purpose of reporting current events) copyright in the broadcast . . . is not infringed.

(2) In subsection (1)—

[(a) "relevant dealing", in relation to a broadcast, means dealing by communicating to the public any visual images taken from that broadcast, and]

(b) "broadcast" and "[communicating to the public]" have the same meaning as in Part I of the Copyright, Designs and Patents Act 1988.

NOTES

Sub-s (1): words omitted repealed by the Copyright and Related Rights Regulations 2003, SI 2003/2498, reg 2(2), Sch 2, subject to transitional provisions as noted below.

Sub-s (2): para (a), and the words in square brackets in para (b) substituted, by SI 2003/2498, reg 2(1), Sch 1, Pt 2, para 21, subject to transitional provisions as noted below.

Transitional provisions: the Copyright and Related Rights Regulations 2003, SI 2003/2498 came into force on 31 October 2003 and, except as expressly provided, apply to: (i) works made, (ii) performances given, (iii) databases in which database right vests which are made, and (iv) works in which publication right vests which are first published, before or after that date (see reg 31 of the 2003 Regulations, at **[2.550]**). Savings and transitional provisions are provided for in regs 32–40 of those Regulations, at **[2.551]**–**[2.559]**.

138–141 (*S 138 introduces Sch 9 which amends the Copyright, Designs and Patents Act 1988 (and is revoked by the Digital Economy Act 2017, s 34(2)(b), as from a day to be appointed); ss 139–141 outside the scope of this work.*)

PART VIII
MISCELLANEOUS AND GENERAL

142–146 (*Outside the scope of this work.*)

General

147, 148 (*Outside the scope of this work.*)

[2.421]

149 Commencement and transitional provisions

(1) The following provisions of this Act—

(a) paragraphs 7 to 9 of Schedule 2 so far as relating to BBC companies (as defined by section 202(1) of the 1990 Act), and section 73 so far as relating to those paragraphs in their application to such companies,

(b) sections 74 to 78,

(c) section 80,

(d) section 83,

(e) sections 88, 90 and 92,

(f) Part VI (and Schedules 5 to 8),

(g) section 147(1),

(h) paragraphs 15 and 19 of Schedule 10 so far as relating to BBC companies (as defined by section 202(1) of the 1990 Act), and section 148(1) so far as relating to those paragraphs in their application to such companies,

(i) the entries in Schedule 11 relating to sections 32(9), 45(8) and (9) and 47(11) and (12) of the 1990 Act, and section 148(2) so far as relating to those entries, and

(j) this section and section 150,

shall come into force on the passing of this Act.

(2) The other provisions of this Act shall come into force on such day as the Secretary of State may by order made by statutory instrument appoint; and different days may be appointed for different purposes.

(3) The power to make an order under this section includes power to make such transitional provisions and savings as the Secretary of State considers appropriate.

NOTES

Orders: the Broadcasting Act 1996 (Commencement No 1 and Transitional Provisions) Order 1996, SI 1996/2120; the Broadcasting Act 1996 (Commencement No 2) Order 1997, SI 1997/1005; the Broadcasting Act 1996 (Commencement No 3) Order 1998, SI 1998/188.

[2.422]

150 Short title and extent

(1) This Act may be cited as the Broadcasting Act 1996.

(2) This Act, except paragraph 27 of Schedule 10, extends to Northern Ireland.

(3) Section 204(6) of the 1990 Act (power to extend to Isle of Man and Channel Islands) applies to the provisions of this Act amending that Act.

(4) Her Majesty may by Order in Council direct that any of the other provisions of this Act shall extend to the Isle of Man or any of the Channel Islands with such modifications, if any, as appear to Her Majesty to be appropriate.

SCHEDULES 1–11

(Schs 1–8, 10, 11 outside the scope of this work; Sch 9 (revoked by the Digital Economy Act 2017, s 34(2)(b), as from a day to be appointed) substitutes the Copyright, Designs and Patents Act 1988, ss 73, 73A, Sch 2, para 19, at **[2.102]**, **[2.103]**, **[2.410]**, *amends ss 134, 149, 205B, at* **[2.176]**, **[2.200]**, **[2.290]**, *and adds Sch 2, para 19A to that Act, at* **[2.410]**.)

COMMUNICATIONS ACT 2003

(2003 c 21)

ARRANGEMENT OF SECTIONS

An Act to confer functions on the Office of Communications; to make provision about the regulation of the provision of electronic communications networks and services and of the use of the electro-magnetic spectrum; to make provision about the regulation of broadcasting and of the provision of television and radio services; to make provision about mergers involving newspaper and other media enterprises and, in that connection, to amend the Enterprise Act 2002; and for connected purposes.

[17 July 2003]

NOTES

Only provisions of this Act relevant to this work are reproduced. Provisions not reproduced are not annotated.

PART 2
NETWORKS, SERVICES AND THE RADIO SPECTRUM

CHAPTER 1
ELECTRONIC COMMUNICATIONS NETWORKS AND SERVICES

[Online infringement of copyright: obligations of internet service providers

[2.423]

124A Obligation to notify subscribers of copyright infringement reports

(1) This section applies if it appears to a copyright owner that—

(a) a subscriber to an internet access service has infringed the owner's copyright by means of the service; or

(b) a subscriber to an internet access service has allowed another person to use the service, and that other person has infringed the owner's copyright by means of the service.

(2) The owner may make a copyright infringement report to the internet service provider who provided the internet access service if a code in force under section 124C or 124D (an "initial obligations code") allows the owner to do so.

(3) A "copyright infringement report" is a report that—

(a) states that there appears to have been an infringement of the owner's copyright;

(b) includes a description of the apparent infringement;

(c) includes evidence of the apparent infringement that shows the subscriber's IP address and the time at which the evidence was gathered;

(d) is sent to the internet service provider within the period of 1 month beginning with the day on which the evidence was gathered; and

(e) complies with any other requirement of the initial obligations code.

(4) An internet service provider who receives a copyright infringement report must notify the subscriber of the report if the initial obligations code requires the provider to do so.

(5) A notification under subsection (4) must be sent to the subscriber within the period of 1 month beginning with the day on which the provider receives the report.

(6) A notification under subsection (4) must include—

(a) a statement that the notification is sent under this section in response to a copyright infringement report;

(b) the name of the copyright owner who made the report;

(c) a description of the apparent infringement;

(d) evidence of the apparent infringement that shows the subscriber's IP address and the time at which the evidence was gathered;

(e) information about subscriber appeals and the grounds on which they may be made;

(f) information about copyright and its purpose;

(g) advice, or information enabling the subscriber to obtain advice, about how to obtain lawful access to copyright works;

(h) advice, or information enabling the subscriber to obtain advice, about steps that a subscriber can take to protect an internet access service from unauthorised use; and

(i) anything else that the initial obligations code requires the notification to include.

(7) For the purposes of subsection (6)(h) the internet service provider must take into account the suitability of different protection for subscribers in different circumstances.

(8) The things that may be required under subsection (6)(i), whether in general or in a particular case, include in particular—

(a) a statement that information about the apparent infringement may be kept by the internet service provider;

(b) a statement that the copyright owner may require the provider to disclose which copyright infringement reports made by the owner to the provider relate to the subscriber;

(c) a statement that, following such a disclosure, the copyright owner may apply to a court to learn the subscriber's identity and may bring proceedings against the subscriber for copyright infringement; and

(d) where the requirement for the provider to send the notification arises partly because of a report that has already been the subject of a notification under subsection (4), a statement that the number of copyright infringement reports relating to the subscriber may be taken into account for the purposes of any technical measures.

(9) In this section "notify", in relation to a subscriber, means send a notification to the electronic or postal address held by the internet service provider for the subscriber (and sections 394 to 396 do not apply).]

NOTES

Inserted, together with preceding cross heading, by the Digital Economy Act 2010, s 3.

[2.424]

[124B Obligation to provide copyright infringement lists to copyright owners

(1) An internet service provider must provide a copyright owner with a copyright infringement list for a period if—

(a) the owner requests the list for that period; and

(b) an initial obligations code requires the internet service provider to provide it.

(2) A "copyright infringement list" is a list that—

(a) sets out, in relation to each relevant subscriber, which of the copyright infringement reports made by the owner to the provider relate to the subscriber, but

(b) does not enable any subscriber to be identified.

(3) A subscriber is a "relevant subscriber" in relation to a copyright owner and an internet service provider if copyright infringement reports made by the owner to the provider in relation to the subscriber have reached the threshold set in the initial obligations code.]

NOTES

Inserted by the Digital Economy Act 2010, s 4.

[2.425]

[124C Approval of code about the initial obligations

(1) The obligations of internet service providers under sections 124A and 124B are the "initial obligations".

(2) If it appears to OFCOM—

(a) that a code has been made by any person for the purpose of regulating the initial obligations; and

(b) that it would be appropriate for them to approve the code for that purpose,

they may by order approve it, with effect from the date given in the order.

(3) The provision that may be contained in a code and approved under this section includes provision that—

(a) specifies conditions that must be met for rights and obligations under the copyright infringement provisions or the code to apply in a particular case;

(b) requires copyright owners or internet service providers to provide any information or assistance that is reasonably required to determine whether a condition under paragraph (a) is met.

(4) The provision mentioned in subsection (3)(a) may, in particular, specify that a right or obligation does not apply in relation to a copyright owner unless the owner has made arrangements with an internet service provider regarding—

(a) the number of copyright infringement reports that the owner may make to the provider within a particular period; and

(b) payment in advance of a contribution towards meeting costs incurred by the provider.

(5) The provision mentioned in subsection (3)(a) may also, in particular, provide that—

(a) except as provided by the code, rights and obligations do not apply in relation to an internet service provider unless the number of copyright infringement reports the provider receives within a particular period reaches a threshold set in the code; and

(b) if the threshold is reached, rights or obligations apply with effect from the date when it is reached or from a later time.

(6) OFCOM must not approve a code under this section unless satisfied that it meets the criteria set out in section 124E.

(7) Not more than one approved code may have effect at a time.

(8) OFCOM must keep an approved code under review.

(9) OFCOM may by order, at any time, for the purpose mentioned in subsection (2)—

(a) approve modifications that have been made to an approved code; or

(b) withdraw their approval from an approved code,

with effect from the date given in the order, and must do so if the code ceases to meet the criteria set out in section 124E.

(10) The consent of the Secretary of State is required for the approval of a code or the modification of an approved code.

(11) An order made by OFCOM under this section approving a code or modification must set out the code or modification.

(12) Section 403 applies to the power of OFCOM to make an order under this section.

(13) A statutory instrument containing an order made by OFCOM under this section is subject to annulment in pursuance of a resolution of either House of Parliament.]

NOTES

Inserted by the Digital Economy Act 2010, s 5.

[2.426]

[124D Initial obligations code by OFCOM in the absence of an approved code

(1) For any period when sections 124A and 124B are in force but for which there is no approved initial obligations code under section 124C, OFCOM must by order make a code for the purpose of regulating the initial obligations.

(2) OFCOM may but need not make a code under subsection (1) for a time before the end of—

(a) the period of six months beginning with the day on which sections 124A and 124B come into force, or

(b) such longer period as the Secretary of State may specify by notice to OFCOM.

(3) The Secretary of State may give a notice under subsection (2)(b) only if it appears to the Secretary of State that it is not practicable for OFCOM to make a code with effect from the end of the period mentioned in subsection (2)(a) or any longer period for the time being specified under subsection (2)(b).

(4) A code under this section may do any of the things mentioned in section 124C(3) to (5).

(5) A code under this section may also—

(a) confer jurisdiction with respect to any matter (other than jurisdiction to determine appeals by subscribers) on OFCOM themselves;

(b) provide for OFCOM, in exercising such jurisdiction, to make awards of compensation, to direct the reimbursement of costs, or to do both;

(c) provide for OFCOM to enforce, or to participate in the enforcement of, any awards or directions made under the code;

(d) make other provision for the enforcement of such awards and directions;

(e) establish a body corporate, with the capacity to make its own rules and establish its own procedures, for the purpose of determining subscriber appeals;

(f) provide for a person with the function of determining subscriber appeals to enforce, or to participate in the enforcement of, any awards or directions made by the person;

(g) make other provision for the enforcement of such awards and directions; and

(h) make other provision for the purpose of regulating the initial obligations.

(6) OFCOM must not make a code under this section unless they are satisfied that it meets the criteria set out in section 124E.

(7) OFCOM must—

(a) keep a code under this section under review; and

(b) by order make any amendment of it that is necessary to ensure that while it is in force it continues to meet the criteria set out in section 124E.

(8) The consent of the Secretary of State is required for the making or amendment by OFCOM of a code under this section.

(9) Section 403 applies to the power of OFCOM to make an order under this section.

(10) A statutory instrument containing an order made by OFCOM under this section is subject to annulment in pursuance of a resolution of either House of Parliament.]

NOTES

Inserted by the Digital Economy Act 2010, s 6.

[2.427]

[124E Contents of initial obligations code

(1) The criteria referred to in sections 124C(6) and 124D(6) are—

(a) that the code makes the required provision about copyright infringement reports (see subsection (2));

(b) that it makes the required provision about the notification of subscribers (see subsections (3) and (4));

(c) that it sets the threshold applying for the purposes of determining who is a relevant subscriber within the meaning of section 124B(3) (see subsections (5) and (6));

(d) that it makes provision about how internet service providers are to keep information about subscribers;

(e) that it limits the time for which they may keep that information;

(f) that it makes any provision about contributions towards meeting costs that is required to be included by an order under section 124M;

(g) that the requirements concerning administration and enforcement are met in relation to the code (see subsections (7) and (8));

(h) that the requirements concerning subscriber appeals are met in relation to the code (see section 124K);

(i) that the provisions of the code are objectively justifiable in relation to the matters to which it relates;

(j) that those provisions are not such as to discriminate unduly against particular persons or against a particular description of persons;

(k) that those provisions are proportionate to what they are intended to achieve; and

(l) that, in relation to what those provisions are intended to achieve, they are transparent.

(2) The required provision about copyright infringement reports is provision that specifies—

(a) requirements as to the means of obtaining evidence of infringement of copyright for inclusion in a report;
(b) the standard of evidence that must be included, and
(c) the required form of the report.

(3) The required provision about the notification of subscribers is provision that specifies, in relation to a subscriber in relation to whom an internet service provider receives one or more copyright infringement reports—
(a) requirements as to the means by which the provider identifies the subscriber;
(b) which of the reports the provider must notify the subscriber of; and
(c) requirements as to the form, contents and means of the notification in each case.

(4) The provision mentioned in subsection (3) must not permit any copyright infringement report received by an internet service provider more than 12 months before the date of a notification of a subscriber to be taken into account for the purposes of the notification.

(5) The threshold applying in accordance with subsection (1)(c) may, subject to subsection (6), be set by reference to any matter, including in particular one or more of—
(a) the number of copyright infringement reports;
(b) the time within which the reports are made; and
(c) the time of the apparent infringements to which they relate.

(6) The threshold applying in accordance with subsection (1)(c) must operate in such a way that a copyright infringement report received by an internet service provider more than 12 months before a particular date does not affect whether the threshold is met on that date; and a copyright infringement list provided under section 124B must not take into account any such report.

(7) The requirements concerning administration and enforcement are—
(a) that OFCOM have, under the code, the functions of administering and enforcing it, including the function of resolving owner-provider disputes;
(b) that there are adequate arrangements under the code for OFCOM to obtain any information or assistance from internet service providers or copyright owners that OFCOM reasonably require for the purposes of administering and enforcing the code; and
(c) that there are adequate arrangements under the code for the costs incurred by OFCOM in administering and enforcing the code to be met by internet service providers and copyright owners.

(8) The provision mentioned in subsection (7) may include, in particular—
(a) provision for the payment, to a person specified in the code, of a penalty not exceeding the maximum penalty for the time being specified in section 124L(2);
(b) provision requiring a copyright owner to indemnify an internet service provider for any loss or damage resulting from the owner's failure to comply with the code or the copyright infringement provisions.

(9) In this section "owner-provider dispute" means a dispute that—
(a) is between persons who are copyright owners or internet service providers; and
(b) relates to an act or omission in relation to an initial obligation or an initial obligations code.]

NOTES

Inserted by the Digital Economy Act 2010, s 7.

[2.428]

[124F Progress reports

(1) OFCOM must prepare the following reports for the Secretary of State about the infringement of copyright by subscribers to internet access services.

(2) OFCOM must prepare a full report for—
(a) the period of 12 months beginning with the first day on which there is an initial obligations code in force; and
(b) each successive period of 12 months.

(3) OFCOM must prepare an interim report for—
(a) the period of 3 months beginning with the first day on which there is an initial obligations code in force; and
(b) each successive period of 3 months, other than one ending at the same time as a period of 12 months under subsection (2).

But this is subject to any direction by the Secretary of State under subsection (4).

(4) The Secretary of State may direct that subsection (3) no longer applies, with effect from the date given in the direction.

(5) A full report under this section must include—
(a) an assessment of the current level of subscribers' use of internet access services to infringe copyright;
(b) a description of the steps taken by copyright owners to enable subscribers to obtain lawful access to copyright works;
(c) a description of the steps taken by copyright owners to inform, and change the attitude of, members of the public in relation to the infringement of copyright;
(d) an assessment of the extent of the steps mentioned in paragraphs (b) and (c);

(e) an assessment of the extent to which copyright owners have made copyright infringement reports;
(f) an assessment of the extent to which they have brought legal proceedings against subscribers in relation to whom such reports have been made;
(g) an assessment of the extent to which any such proceedings have been against subscribers in relation to whom a substantial number of reports have been made; and
(h) anything else that the Secretary of State directs OFCOM to include in the report.

(6) An interim report under this section must include—
(a) the assessments mentioned in subsection (5)(a), (e) and (f); and
(b) anything else that the Secretary of State directs OFCOM to include in the report.

(7) OFCOM must send a report prepared under this section to the Secretary of State as soon as practicable after the end of the period for which it is prepared.

(8) OFCOM must publish every full report under this section—
(a) as soon as practicable after they send it to the Secretary of State, and
(b) in such manner as they consider appropriate for bringing it to the attention of persons who, in their opinion, are likely to have an interest in it.

(9) OFCOM may exclude information from a report when it is published under subsection (8) if they consider that it is information that they could refuse to disclose in response to a request under the Freedom of Information Act 2000.]

NOTES

Inserted by the Digital Economy Act 2010, s 8.

[2.429]

[124G Obligations to limit internet access: assessment and preparation

(1) The Secretary of State may direct OFCOM to—
(a) assess whether one or more technical obligations should be imposed on internet service providers;
(b) take steps to prepare for the obligations;
(c) provide a report on the assessment or steps to the Secretary of State.

(2) A "technical obligation", in relation to an internet service provider, is an obligation for the provider to take a technical measure against some or all relevant subscribers to its service for the purpose of preventing or reducing infringement of copyright by means of the internet.

(3) A "technical measure" is a measure that—
(a) limits the speed or other capacity of the service provided to a subscriber;
(b) prevents a subscriber from using the service to gain access to particular material, or limits such use;
(c) suspends the service provided to a subscriber; or
(d) limits the service provided to a subscriber in another way.

(4) A subscriber to an internet access service is "relevant" if the subscriber is a relevant subscriber, within the meaning of section 124B(3), in relation to the provider of the service and one or more copyright owners.

(5) The assessment and steps that the Secretary of State may direct OFCOM to carry out or take under subsection (1) include, in particular—
(a) consultation of copyright owners, internet service providers, subscribers or any other person;
(b) an assessment of the likely efficacy of a technical measure in relation to a particular type of internet access service; and
(c) steps to prepare a proposed technical obligations code.

(6) Internet service providers and copyright owners must give OFCOM any assistance that OFCOM reasonably require for the purposes of complying with any direction under this section.

(7) The Secretary of State must lay before Parliament any direction under this section.

(8) OFCOM must publish every report under this section—
(a) as soon as practicable after they send it to the Secretary of State, and
(b) in such manner as they consider appropriate for bringing it to the attention of persons who, in their opinion, are likely to have an interest in it.

(9) OFCOM may exclude information from a report when it is published under subsection (8) if they consider that it is information that they could refuse to disclose in response to a request under the Freedom of Information Act 2000.]

NOTES

Inserted by the Digital Economy Act 2010, s 9.

[2.430]

[124H Obligations to limit internet access

(1) The Secretary of State may by order impose a technical obligation on internet service providers if—
(a) OFCOM have assessed whether one or more technical obligations should be imposed on internet service providers; and

Part 2 Copyright

(b) taking into account that assessment, reports prepared by OFCOM under section 124F, and any other matter that appears to the Secretary of State to be relevant, the Secretary of State considers it appropriate to make the order.

(2) No order may be made under this section within the period of 12 months beginning with the first day on which there is an initial obligations code in force.

(3) An order under this section must specify the date from which the technical obligation is to have effect, or provide for it to be specified.

(4) The order may also specify—

(a) the criteria for taking the technical measure concerned against a subscriber;

(b) the steps to be taken as part of the measure and when they are to be taken.

(5) No order is to be made under this section unless—

(a) the Secretary of State has complied with subsections (6) to (10), and

(b) a draft of the order has been laid before Parliament and approved by a resolution of each House.

(6) If the Secretary of State proposes to make an order under this section, the Secretary of State must lay before Parliament a document that—

(a) explains the proposal, and

(b) sets it out in the form of a draft order.

(7) During the period of 60 days beginning with the day on which the document was laid under subsection (6) ("the 60-day period"), the Secretary of State may not lay before Parliament a draft order to give effect to the proposal (with or without modifications).

(8) In preparing a draft order under this section to give effect to the proposal, the Secretary of State must have regard to any of the following that are made with regard to the draft order during the 60-day period—

(a) any representations, and

(b) any recommendations of a committee of either House of Parliament charged with reporting on the draft order.

(9) When laying before Parliament a draft order to give effect to the proposal (with or without modifications), the Secretary of State must also lay a document that explains any changes made to the proposal contained in the document laid before Parliament under subsection (6).

(10) In calculating the 60-day period, no account is to be taken of any time during which Parliament is dissolved or prorogued or during which either House is adjourned for more than 4 days.]

NOTES

Inserted by the Digital Economy Act 2010, s 10.

[2.431]

[124I Code by OFCOM about obligations to limit internet access

(1) For any period during which there are one or more technical obligations in force under section 124H, OFCOM must by order make a technical obligations code for the purpose of regulating those obligations.

(2) The code may be made separately from, or in combination with, any initial obligations code under section 124D.

(3) A code under this section may—

(a) do any of the things mentioned in section 124C(3) to (5) or section 124D(5)(a) to (g); and

(b) make other provision for the purpose of regulating the technical obligations.

(4) OFCOM must not make a code under this section unless they are satisfied that it meets the criteria set out in section 124J.

(5) OFCOM must—

(a) keep a code under this section under review; and

(b) by order make any amendment of it that is necessary to ensure that while it is in force it continues to meet the criteria set out in section 124J.

(6) The consent of the Secretary of State is required for the making or amendment by OFCOM of a code under this section.

(7) Section 403 applies to the power of OFCOM to make an order under this section.

(8) A statutory instrument containing an order made by OFCOM under this section is subject to annulment in pursuance of a resolution of either House of Parliament.]

NOTES

Inserted by the Digital Economy Act 2010, s 11.

[2.432]

[124J Contents of code about obligations to limit internet access

(1) The criteria referred to in section 124I(4) are—

(a) that the requirements concerning enforcement and related matters are met in relation to the code (see subsections (2) and (3));

(b) that the requirements concerning subscriber appeals are met in relation to the code (see section 124K);

(c) that it makes any provision about contributions towards meeting costs that is required to be included by an order under section 124M;
(d) that it makes any other provision that the Secretary of State requires it to make;
(e) that the provisions of the code are objectively justifiable in relation to the matters to which it relates;
(f) that those provisions are not such as to discriminate unduly against particular persons or against a particular description of persons;
(g) that those provisions are proportionate to what they are intended to achieve; and
(h) that, in relation to what those provisions are intended to achieve, they are transparent.

(2) The requirements concerning enforcement and related matters are—
(a) that OFCOM have, under the code, the functions of administering and enforcing it, including the function of resolving owner-provider disputes;
(b) that there are adequate arrangements under the code for OFCOM to obtain any information or assistance from internet service providers or copyright owners that OFCOM reasonably require for the purposes of administering and enforcing the code; and
(c) that there are adequate arrangements under the code for the costs incurred by OFCOM in administering and enforcing the code to be met by internet service providers and copyright owners.

(3) The provision made concerning enforcement and related matters may also (unless the Secretary of State requires otherwise) include, in particular—
(a) provision for the payment, to a person specified in the code, of a penalty not exceeding the maximum penalty for the time being specified in section 124L(2);
(b) provision requiring a copyright owner to indemnify an internet service provider for any loss or damage resulting from the owner's infringement or error in relation to the code or the copyright infringement provisions.

(4) In this section "owner-provider dispute" means a dispute that—
(a) is between persons who are copyright owners or internet service providers; and
(b) relates to an act or omission in relation to a technical obligation or a technical obligations code.]

NOTES

Inserted by the Digital Economy Act 2010, s 12.

[2.433]

[124K Subscriber appeals

(1) The requirements concerning subscriber appeals are—
(a) for the purposes of section 124E(1)(h), the requirements of subsections (2) to (8); and
(b) for the purposes of section 124J(1)(b), the requirements of subsections (2) to (11).

(2) The requirements of this subsection are—
(a) that the code confers on subscribers the right to bring a subscriber appeal and, in the case of a technical obligations code, a further right of appeal to the First-tier Tribunal;
(b) that there is a person who, under the code, has the function of determining subscriber appeals;
(c) that that person is for practical purposes independent (so far as determining subscriber appeals is concerned) of internet service providers, copyright owners and OFCOM; and
(d) that there are adequate arrangements under the code for the costs incurred by that person in determining subscriber appeals to be met by internet service providers, copyright owners and the subscriber concerned.

(3) The code must provide for the grounds of appeal (so far as an appeal relates to, or to anything done by reference to, a copyright infringement report) to include the following—
(a) that the apparent infringement to which the report relates was not an infringement of copyright;
(b) that the report does not relate to the subscriber's IP address at the time of the apparent infringement.

(4) The code must provide for the grounds of appeal to include contravention by the copyright owner or internet service provider of the code or of an obligation regulated by the code.

(5) The code must provide that an appeal on any grounds must be determined in favour of the subscriber unless the copyright owner or internet service provider shows that, as respects any copyright infringement report to which the appeal relates or by reference to which anything to which the appeal relates was done (or, if there is more than one such report, as respects each of them)—
(a) the apparent infringement was an infringement of copyright, and
(b) the report relates to the subscriber's IP address at the time of that infringement.

(6) The code must provide that, where a ground mentioned in subsection (3) is relied on, the appeal must be determined in favour of the subscriber if the subscriber shows that—
(a) the act constituting the apparent infringement to which the report relates was not done by the subscriber, and
(b) the subscriber took reasonable steps to prevent other persons infringing copyright by means of the internet access service.

Part 2 Copyright

(7) The powers of the person determining subscriber appeals must include power—
(a) to secure so far as practicable that a subscriber is not prejudiced for the purposes of the copyright infringement provisions by an act or omission in respect of which an appeal is determined in favour of the subscriber;
(b) to make an award of compensation to be paid by a copyright owner or internet service provider to a subscriber affected by such an act or omission; and
(c) where the appeal is determined in favour of the subscriber, to direct the copyright owner or internet service provider to reimburse the reasonable costs of the subscriber.

(8) The code must provide that the power to direct the reimbursement of costs under subsection (7)(c) is to be exercised to award reasonable costs to a subscriber whose appeal is successful, unless the person deciding the appeal is satisfied that it would be unjust to give such a direction having regard to all the circumstances including the conduct of the parties before and during the proceedings.

(9) In the case of a technical obligations code, the powers of the person determining subscriber appeals must include power—
(a) on an appeal in relation to a technical measure or proposed technical measure—
(i) to confirm the measure;
(ii) to require the measure not to be taken or to be withdrawn;
(iii) to substitute any other technical measure that the internet service provider has power to take;
(b) to exercise the power mentioned in paragraph (a)(ii) or (iii) where an appeal is not upheld but the person determining it is satisfied that there are exceptional circumstances that justify the exercise of the power;
(c) to take any steps that OFCOM could take in relation to the act or omission giving rise to the technical measure; and
(d) to remit the decision whether to confirm the technical measure, or any matter relating to that decision, to OFCOM.

(10) In the case of a technical obligations code, the code must make provision—
(a) enabling a determination of a subscriber appeal to be appealed to the First-tier Tribunal, including on grounds that it was based on an error of fact, wrong in law or unreasonable;
(b) giving the First-tier Tribunal, in relation to an appeal to it, the powers mentioned in subsections (7) and (9); and
(c) in relation to recovery of costs awarded by the Tribunal.

(11) In the case of a technical obligations code, the code must include provision to secure that a technical measure is not taken against a subscriber until—
(a) the period for bringing a subscriber appeal, or any further appeal to the First-tier Tribunal, in relation to the proposed measure has ended (or the subscriber has waived the right to appeal); and
(b) any such subscriber appeal or further appeal has been determined, abandoned or otherwise disposed of.]

NOTES

Inserted by the Digital Economy Act 2010, s 13.

[2.434]

[124L Enforcement of obligations

(1) Sections 94 to 96 apply in relation to a contravention of an initial obligation or a technical obligation, or a contravention of an obligation under section 124G(6), as they apply in relation to a contravention of a condition set out under section 45.

(2) The amount of the penalty imposed under section 96 as applied by this section is to be such amount not exceeding £250,000 as OFCOM determine to be—
(a) appropriate; and
(b) proportionate to the contravention in respect of which it is imposed.

(3) In making that determination OFCOM must have regard to—
(a) any representations made to them by the internet service provider or copyright owner on whom the penalty is imposed;
(b) any steps taken by the provider or owner towards complying with the obligations contraventions of which have been notified to the provider or owner under section 94 (as applied); and
(c) any steps taken by the provider or owner for remedying the consequences of those contraventions.

(4) The Secretary of State may by order amend this section so as to substitute a different maximum penalty for the maximum penalty for the time being specified in subsection (2).

(5) No order is to be made containing provision authorised by subsection (4) unless a draft of the order has been laid before Parliament and approved by a resolution of each House.]

NOTES

Inserted by the Digital Economy Act 2010, s 14.

[2.435]
[124M Sharing of costs
(1) The Secretary of State may by order specify provision that must be included in an initial obligations code or a technical obligations code about payment of contributions towards costs incurred under the copyright infringement provisions.
(2) Any provision specified under subsection (1) must relate to payment of contributions by one or more of the following only—
(a) copyright owners;
(b) internet service providers;
(c) in relation to a subscriber appeal or a further appeal by a subscriber to the First-tier Tribunal, the subscriber.
(3) Provision specified under subsection (1) may relate to, in particular—
(a) payment by a copyright owner of a contribution towards the costs that an internet service provider incurs;
(b) payment by a copyright owner or internet service provider of a contribution towards the costs that OFCOM incur.
(4) Provision specified under subsection (1) may include, in particular—
(a) provision about costs incurred before the provision is included in an initial obligations code or a technical obligations code;
(b) provision for payment in advance of expected costs (and for reimbursement of overpayments where the costs incurred are less than expected);
(c) provision about how costs, expected costs or contributions must be calculated;
(d) other provision about when and how contributions must be paid.
(5) No order is to be made under this section unless a draft of the order has been laid before Parliament and approved by a resolution of each House.]

NOTES
Inserted by the Digital Economy Act 2010, s 15.

[2.436]
[124N Interpretation
In sections 124A to 124M and this section—
"apparent infringement", in relation to a copyright infringement report, means the infringement of copyright that the report states appears to have taken place;
"copyright infringement list" has the meaning given in section 124B(2);
"copyright infringement provisions" means sections 124A to 124M and this section;
"copyright infringement report" has the meaning given in section 124A(3);
"copyright owner" means—
(a) a copyright owner within the meaning of Part 1 of the Copyright, Designs and Patents Act 1988 (see section 173 of that Act); or
(b) someone authorised by that person to act on the person's behalf;
"copyright work" has the same meaning as in Part 1 of the Copyright, Designs and Patents Act 1988 (see section 1(2) of that Act);
"initial obligations" has the meaning given in section 124C(1);
"initial obligations code" has the meaning given in section 124A(2);
"internet access service" means an electronic communications service that—
(a) is provided to a subscriber;
(b) consists entirely or mainly of the provision of access to the internet; and
(c) includes the allocation of an IP address or IP addresses to the subscriber to enable that access;
"internet service provider" means a person who provides an internet access service;
"IP address" means an internet protocol address;
"subscriber", in relation to an internet access service, means a person who—
(a) receives the service under an agreement between the person and the provider of the service; and
(b) does not receive it as a communications provider;
"subscriber appeal" means—
(a) in relation to an initial obligations code, an appeal by a subscriber on grounds specified in the code in relation to—
(i) the making of a copyright infringement report;
(ii) notification under section 124A(4);
(iii) the inclusion or proposed inclusion of an entry in a copyright infringement list; or
(iv) any other act or omission in relation to an initial obligation or an initial obligations code;
(b) in relation to a technical obligations code, an appeal by a subscriber on grounds specified in the code in relation to—
(i) the proposed taking of a technical measure; or

(ii) any other act or omission in relation to a technical obligation or a technical obligations code;

"technical measure" has the meaning given in section 124G(3);

"technical obligation" has the meaning given in section 124G(2);

"technical obligations code" means a code in force under section 124I.]

NOTES

Inserted by the Digital Economy Act 2010, s 16(1).

[Powers in relation to internet domain registries

[2.437]

124O Notification of failure in relation to internet domain registry

(1) This section applies where the Secretary of State—

(a) is satisfied that a serious relevant failure in relation to a qualifying internet domain registry is taking place or has taken place, and

(b) wishes to exercise the powers under section 124P or 124R.

(2) The Secretary of State must notify the internet domain registry, specifying the failure and a period during which the registry has the opportunity to make representations to the Secretary of State.

(3) There is a relevant failure in relation to a qualifying internet domain registry if—

(a) the registry, or any of its registrars or end-users, engages in prescribed practices that are unfair or involve the misuse of internet domain names, or

(b) the arrangements made by the registry for dealing with complaints in connection with internet domain names do not comply with prescribed requirements.

(4) A relevant failure is serious, for the purposes of this section, if it has adversely affected or is likely adversely to affect—

(a) the reputation or availability of electronic communications networks or electronic communications services provided in the United Kingdom or a part of the United Kingdom, or

(b) the interests of consumers or members of the public in the United Kingdom or a part of the United Kingdom.

(5) In subsection (3) "prescribed" means prescribed by regulations made by the Secretary of State.

(6) Before making regulations under subsection (3) the Secretary of State must consult such persons as the Secretary of State considers appropriate.

(7) In this section and sections 124P to 124R—

"end-user", in relation to a qualifying internet domain registry, means a person who has been or wants to be allocated an internet domain name that is or would be included in the register maintained by the registry;

"qualifying internet domain registry" means a relevant body that—

(a) maintains a relevant register of internet domain names, and

(b) operates a computer program or server that forms part of the system that enables the names included in the register to be used to access internet protocol addresses or other information by means of the internet;

"registrar", in relation to a qualifying internet domain registry, means a person authorised by the registry to act on behalf of end-users in connection with the registration of internet domain names;

"relevant body" means a company formed and registered under the Companies Act 2006 or a limited liability partnership;

"relevant register of internet domain names" means a register of—

(a) the names of second level internet domains that form part of the same UK-related top level internet domain, or

(b) the names of third level internet domains that form part of the same UK-related second level internet domain;

"second level internet domain" means an internet domain indicated by the last two elements of an internet domain name;

"third level internet domain" means an internet domain indicated by the last three elements of an internet domain name;

"top level internet domain" means an internet domain indicated by the last element of an internet domain name.

(8) An internet domain is "UK-related" if, in the opinion of the Secretary of State, the last element of its name is likely to cause users of the internet, or a class of such users, to believe that the domain and its sub-domains are connected with the United Kingdom or a part of the United Kingdom.]

NOTES

Commencement: to be appointed.

Inserted, together with preceding cross-heading, by the Digital Economy Act 2010, s 19, as from a day to be appointed.

[2.438]

[124P Appointment of manager of internet domain registry

(1) This section applies where—

(a) the Secretary of State has given a notification under section 124O to a qualifying internet domain registry specifying a failure,

(b) the period allowed for making representations has expired, and

(c) the Secretary of State is satisfied that the registry has not taken the steps that the Secretary of State considers appropriate for remedying the failure.

(2) The Secretary of State may by order appoint a manager in respect of the property and affairs of the internet domain registry for the purpose of securing that the registry takes the steps described in subsection (1)(c).

(3) The person appointed may be anyone whom the Secretary of State thinks appropriate.

(4) The appointment of the manager does not affect—

(a) a right of a person to appoint a receiver of the registry's property, or

(b) the rights of a receiver appointed by a person other than the Secretary of State.

(5) The Secretary of State must—

(a) keep the order under review, and

(b) if appropriate, discharge all or part of the order.

(6) The Secretary of State must discharge the order on the appointment of a person to act as administrative receiver, administrator, provisional liquidator or liquidator of the registry.

(7) The Secretary of State must discharge the order before the end of the period of 2 years beginning with the day on which it was made (but this does not prevent the Secretary of State from making a further order in the same or similar terms).

(8) When discharging an order under this section, the Secretary of State may make savings and transitional provision.

(9) The Secretary of State must send a copy of an order made under this section to the registry as soon as practicable after it is made.

(10) In subsection (4), "receiver" includes a manager (other than a manager appointed by the registry) and a person who is appointed as both receiver and manager.

(11) In subsection (6)—

"administrative receiver" means an administrative receiver within the meaning of section 251 of the Insolvency Act 1986 or Article 5(1) of the Insolvency (Northern Ireland) Order 1989 (SI 1989/2405 (N.I. 19));

"administrator" means a person appointed to manage the affairs, business and property of the registry under Schedule B1 to that Act or Schedule B1 to that Order.]

NOTES

Commencement: to be appointed.

Inserted, together with s 124Q, by the Digital Economy Act 2010, s 20(1), as from a day to be appointed.

[2.439]

[124Q Functions of manager etc

(1) An order under section 124P may make provision about the functions to be exercised by, and the powers of, the manager.

(2) The order may, in particular—

(a) provide for the manager to have such of the functions of the registry's directors as are specified in the order (including functions exercisable only by a particular director or class of directors), and

(b) provide for one or more of the registry's directors to be prevented from exercising any of those functions.

(3) The order may make provision about the remuneration of the manager, including in particular—

(a) provision for the amount of the remuneration to be determined by the Secretary of State, and

(b) provision for the remuneration to be payable from the property of the registry.

(4) In carrying out the functions conferred by the order, the manager acts as the registry's agent.

(5) The Secretary of State may apply to the court for directions in relation to any matter arising in connection with the functions or powers of the manager (and the costs of the application are to be paid by the registry).

(6) On an application under subsection (5) the court may give such directions or make such orders as it thinks fit.

(7) In this section "the court" means—

(a) in England and Wales, the High Court or [the county court],

(b) in Scotland, the Court of Session or the sheriff, and

(c) in Northern Ireland, the High Court.

(8) Where the registry is a limited liability partnership, this section applies as if references to a director of the registry were references to a member of the limited liability partnership.]

NOTES

Commencement: to be appointed.

Inserted as noted to s 124P at **[2.438]**.

Sub-s (7): words in square brackets substituted by the Crime and Courts Act 2013, s 17(5), Sch 9, Pt 3, para 52(1)(b), (2).

[2.440]

[124R Application to court to alter constitution of internet domain registry

(1) This section applies where—

(a) the Secretary of State has given a notification under section 124O to a qualifying internet domain registry specifying a failure,

(b) the period allowed for making representations has expired, and

(c) the Secretary of State is satisfied that the registry has not taken the steps that the Secretary of State considers appropriate for remedying the failure.

(2) The Secretary of State may apply to the court (as defined in section 124Q) for an order under this section.

(3) The court may make an order—

(a) making alterations of the registry's constitution, and

(b) requiring the registry not to make any alterations, or any specified alterations, of its constitution without the leave of the court.

(4) An order under this section may contain only such provision as the court considers appropriate for securing that the registry remedies the failure specified in the notification under section 124O.

(5) In this section—

"constitution" means, in the case of a company, the articles of association and, in the case of a limited liability partnership, the limited liability partnership agreement;

"limited liability partnership agreement" means the agreement or agreements, whether express or implied, between the members of a limited liability partnership, and between the partnership and the members of the partnership, determining—

(a) the mutual rights and duties of the members, and

(b) their rights and duties in relation to the partnership.]

NOTES

Commencement: to be appointed.

Inserted by the Digital Economy Act 2010, s 21, as from a day to be appointed.

DIGITAL ECONOMY ACT 2010

(2010 c 24)

An Act to make provision about the functions of the Office of Communications; to make provision about the online infringement of copyright and about penalties for infringement of copyright and performers' rights; to make provision about internet domain registries; to make provision about the functions of the Channel Four Television Corporation; to make provision about the regulation of television and radio services; to make provision about the regulation of the use of the electromagnetic spectrum; to amend the Video Recordings Act 1984; to make provision about public lending right in relation to electronic publications; and for connected purposes.

[8 April 2010]

1, 2 (*Outside the scope of this work.*)

Online infringement of copyright

3–43 (*Ss 3–15, 16(1) insert the Communications Act 2003, ss 124A–124N at* **[2.423]**–**[2.436]**; *s 16(2), (3) outside the scope of this work; ss 17, 18 repealed by the Deregulation Act 2015, s 56; ss 19, 20(1), 21 insert the Communications Act 2003, ss 124O–124R at* **[2.437]**–**[2.440]**; *ss 20(2), (3), 22–38, 40, 41 outside the scope of this work; s 39 repealed by the Digital Economy Act 2017, s 9(12); ss 42, 43 amend the Copyright, Designs and Patents Act 1988 at* **[2.7]** *et seq and the Public Lending Right Act 1979, s 5 at* **[2.5]**.)

General

44–46 (*Outside the scope of this work.*)

[2.441]

47 Commencement

(1) This Act comes into force at the end of the period of two months beginning with the day on which it is passed, but this is subject to—

(a) section 28(8), and

(b) subsections (2) and (3).

(2) The following come into force on the day on which this Act is passed—

(a) sections 5, 6, 7, 15 and 16(1),

(b) (*outside the scope of this work.*)
(c) this section and sections 46 and 48.

(3) The following come into force on such day as the Secretary of State may by order made by statutory instrument appoint—

(a) sections 19 to 21,
(b) (*outside the scope of this work.*)
(c) (*outside the scope of this work.*)
(d) section 43 and the entry in Schedule 2 relating to the Public Lending Right Act 1979 (and section 45 so far as it relates to that entry).

(4) The Secretary of State may appoint different days for different purposes.

NOTES

Orders: the Digital Economy Act 2010 (Appointed Day No 1) Order 2011, SI 2011/1170; the Digital Economy Act 2010 (Appointed Day No 2) Order 2012, SI 2012/1164; the Digital Economy Act 2010 (Appointed Day No 3) Order 2012, SI 2012/1766; the Digital Economy Act 2010 (Appointed Day No 4) Order 2014, SI 2014/1659.

[2.442]
48 Short title

This Act may be cited as the Digital Economy Act 2010.

SCHEDULES 1, 2

(Sch 1 outside the scope of this work; Sch 2 contains repeals which, in so far as relevant to this work, have been incorporated at the appropriate place in this work.)

ENTERPRISE AND REGULATORY REFORM ACT 2013

(2013 c 24)

An Act to make provision about the UK Green Investment Bank; to make provision about employment law; to establish and make provision about the Competition and Markets Authority and to abolish the Competition Commission and the Office of Fair Trading; to amend the Competition Act 1998 and the Enterprise Act 2002; to make provision for the reduction of legislative burdens; to make provision about copyright and rights in performances; to make provision about payments to company directors; to make provision about redress schemes relating to lettings agency work and property management work; to make provision about the supply of customer data; to make provision for the protection of essential supplies in cases of insolvency; to make provision about certain bodies established by Royal Charter; to amend section 9(5) of the Equality Act 2010; and for connected purposes.

[25 April 2013]

[2.443]

NOTES

Only provisions of this Act relevant to this work are reproduced. Provisions not reproduced are not annotated.

PART 6
MISCELLANEOUS AND GENERAL

Copyright and rights in performances

74–78 (*S 74 repeals the Copyright, Designs and Patents Act 1988, ss 52, 79(4)(g), Sch 1, para 20; s 75 disapplies the European Communities Act 1972, Sch 2, para 1(1)(d) for the purposes of provision under s 2(2) of that Act amending the Copyright, Designs and Patents Act 1988, Pt 1, Chapter 3 or Sch 2; s 76 renumbers the existing Copyright, Designs and Patents Act 1988, s 170 as s 170(1) and inserts s 170(2)–(7) at* **[2.105]**; *s 77(1) amends the Copyright, Designs and Patents Act 1988, s 116 at* **[2.154]**; *s 77(2) inserts ss 116A–116D of the 1988 Act at* **[2.155]**–**[2.158]**; *s 78 disapplies the European Communities Act 1972, Sch 2, para 1(1)(d) for the purposes of provision under s 2(2) of that Act implementing Directive 2011/77/EU amending Directive 2006/116/EC.*)

SCHEDULE 22
LICENSING OF COPYRIGHT AND PERFORMERS' RIGHTS

(*Sch 22, Pt 1 inserts the Copyright, Designs and Patents Act 1988, Sch A1 at* **[2.408]**; *Pt 2 amends s 205A, Sch 2A of that Act at* **[2.215]** *and* **[2.411]** *respectively.*)

PUBLIC LENDING RIGHT SCHEME 1982 (COMMENCEMENT) ORDER 1982

(SI 1982/719)

NOTES

Made: 17 May 1982.
Authority: Public Lending Right Act 1979, s 3(2).
Commencement: 14 June 1982.

[2.444]
1
This Order may be cited as the Public Lending Right Scheme 1982 (Commencement) Order 1982 and shall come into operation on 14th June 1982.

[2.445]
2
(1) The Scheme set out in the Appendix hereto, which has been approved by a resolution of each House of Parliament, shall come into force in the manner hereinafter provided.

(2) The provisions of the Scheme specified in column 1 of the table set out below shall come into force on the dates specified in relation thereto in column 2 of that table:

(1) Provisions of the Scheme	(2) Date on which provisions come into force
Part I, II and IV, Schedule 2 and Schedule 3 Part I	14th June 1982
Part III and Schedule 1	1st September 1982
Part V, Schedule 3 Part II and Schedule 4	1st July 1983

APPENDIX
PUBLIC LENDING RIGHT SCHEME 1982

Article 2

PART I
TITLE AND INTERPRETATION

[2.446]

Article 1 Citation and extent

This Scheme may be cited as the Public Lending Right Scheme 1982, and shall extend to the whole of the United Kingdom.

Article 2 General definitions

(1) In this Scheme, except where the context otherwise requires, the following expressions have the meanings hereby respectively assigned to them, that is to say—

"the Act" means the Public Lending Right Act 1979;

"author", in relation to an eligible book, means a person who is, or one of a number of persons who are, treated as such by Article 4;

["the Board" has the meaning assigned thereto by section 5(2) of the Act;]

["EEA State" means a member State, Norway, Iceland and Lichtenstein;]

"eligible author", in relation to an eligible book, means an author of that book who is an eligible person;

"eligible book" has the meaning assigned thereto by Article 6;

"eligible person", in relation to an author, has the meaning assigned thereto by Article 5;

"financial year" means a period of twelve months ending on the 31st March;

"identifying number" means the number entered in the Register in pursuance of Article 8(1)(a)(iv);

"local library authority" has the meaning assigned thereto by section 5(2) of the Act;

"posthumously eligible book" has the meaning assigned thereto by article 6A;

"posthumously eligible person" has the meaning assigned thereto by article 5A;

. . . "the Register" [has] the [meaning] assigned thereto by section 5(2) of the Act;

"registered interest" means the interest (being the whole or a share thereof), in the Public Lending Right in respect of a particular book, shown on the Register as belonging to a particular person, and "registered owner" means the person for the time being so registered;

"the registry" means the place at which the Register is for the time being maintained in pursuance of Article 7;

"sampling year" has the meaning assigned thereto by Article 36.

(2) In this Scheme, except where the context otherwise requires, any reference to an Article or to a Part or to a Schedule shall be construed as a reference to an Article contained in, or to a Part of or a Schedule to, this Scheme, as the case may be, and any reference in any Article to a paragraph shall be construed as a reference to a paragraph in that Article.

Article 3 Delivery of documents and service of notice

Unless the context otherwise requires, any requirement in this Scheme for—

(a) a document or an application to be delivered at the registry or produced to the [Board] or for notice to be given to [the Board], shall be satisfied if the same is either—

(i) delivered in person at the registry between the hours of 11 am and 3 pm on a working day; or

(ii) sent through the post by recorded delivery;

(b) a local library authority or a registered owner to be notified of any matter shall be satisfied if such notification is sent through the post.

PART II

BOOKS AND AUTHORS ELIGIBLE UNDER THE SCHEME

Article 4 Authors

(1) Subject to paragraph (2), a person shall be treated as an author of a book for the purpose of this Scheme if he is either—

(a) a writer of the book, including without prejudice to the generality of that expression,

(i) a translator thereof, and

(ii) an editor or compiler thereof, who in either case has contributed more than ten per cent of the contents of the book or more than ten pages of the contents, whichever is the less[, or who is entitled to a royalty payment from the publisher in respect of the book][; and]

[(iii) in relation to an audio-book, a producer or narrator thereof; or;]

(b) an illustrator thereof, which for this purpose includes the author of a photograph . . .

(2) Notwithstanding paragraph (1), a person shall not be treated as an author of a book unless the fact that he is an author within the meaning of paragraph (1)—

(a) is evidenced by his being named on the title page of the book; or

[(b) is evidenced by his entitlement to a royalty payment from the publisher in respect of the book; or

(c) in the case of a book without a title page, is evidenced—

(i) by his being named elsewhere in the book and in the view of the [Board], his contribution to the book was such that he would have merited a mention on the title page had there been one, or

(ii) by his entitlement to a royalty payment from the publisher in respect of the book; or

[(iii) by his being named on the case with which the audio-book is sold; or;

(iv) is evidenced by reference to a written contract with the publisher of the audio-book which refers expressly to his being an author within the meaning of paragraph (1).]

(d) is evidenced by a statement, signed by all the other authors of the book in respect of whom the fact that they are authors of the book is evidenced in accordance with paragraphs (a) to (c), that his contribution to the book was such that it is appropriate that he should be treated as an author of the book and the [Board] is satisfied that it is appropriate so to treat him.]

Article 5 Eligible persons

(1) For the purposes of the Scheme, and in relation to each application by a person relating to an eligible book, the applicant is an eligible person if he is an author (within the meaning of Article 4) of that book who at the date of the application has his only or principal home [in an EEA State or, if he has no home, has been present in an EEA State] for not less than twelve months out of the preceding twenty-four months.

(2) In this Article, "principal home", in the case of a person having more than one home means that one of those homes at which he has been for the longest aggregate period during the twenty-four months immediately preceding the application for registration.

Article 5A Posthumously eligible persons

For the purposes of the Scheme, and in relation to each application relating to a posthumously eligible book, an author who is dead is a posthumously eligible person if, had he been an applicant for first registration of Public Lending Right in relation to that book at the date of his death, he would have been an eligible person in accordance with article 5.

Article 6 Eligible books

(1) For the purposes of this Scheme, an eligible book is a book (as defined in paragraph (2)) the sole author, or at least one of the authors, of which is eligible person; and there shall be treated as a separate book—

(a) each volume of a work published in two or more volumes, and
(b) each new edition of a book.

(2) In paragraph (1) "book" means a printed and bound publication (including a paper-back edition [or an audio-book or an e-book]) but does not include—

(a) a book bearing, in lieu of the name of an author who is a natural person, the name of a body corporate or an unincorporated association;
(b) . . .
(c) a book which is wholly or mainly a musical score;
(d) a book the copyright of which is vested in the Crown;
(e) a book which has not been offered for sale to the public;
(f) a serial publication including, without prejudice to the generality of that expression, a newspaper, magazine, journal or periodical; or
[(g) a book which does not have an International Standard Book Number].

Article 6A Posthumously eligible books

For the purposes of the Scheme, a book is a posthumously eligible book if—

(a) it is a book within the meaning of article 6(2),
(b) the sole author, or at least one of the authors of the book is a posthumously eligible person, and
(c) the book is either—
(i) published within one year before or ten years after the date of that person's death and that person had made a successful application during his lifetime for registration of Public Lending Right or of an eligible author's share of the Right in respect of at least one other book, or
(ii) a book which consists of or incorporates a work of that person which had previously been the constituent of or incorporated in a book in relation to which that person had made such an application as aforesaid.

PART III
REGISTRATION OF PUBLIC LENDING RIGHT

The Register

Article 7 The Register

The [Board] shall establish and maintain a Public Lending Right Register at such place as the Secretary of State may from time to time determine, and upon each such determination notice shall be published in the London Gazette, the Edinburgh Gazette and the Belfast Gazette, of such place and the time of the commencement of registration thereat.

Article 8 The content of the Register

(1) The Register shall contain—

(a) particulars of each book in respect of which Public Lending Right subsists, including—
(i) the title of the book;
(ii) the name or names of the persons appearing on the title page as the authors thereof;
(iii) the true identity of an author if different from (ii) above;
(iv) a number for that book, determined by, or in accordance with arrangements made by, the [Board];
(b) the name and address of each person entitled to the Right in respect of each such book and, if more than one, the share of each such person in such Right.

(2) The [Board] shall also keep at the registry an index whereby all entries in the Register can readily be traced, and for this purpose "index" includes any device or combination of devices serving the purpose of an index.

Article 9 Registration

(1) Public Lending Right in respect of a book may, and may only, be registered if—

(a) the book is an eligible book and application in that behalf is made in accordance with articles 14 and 17, or
(b) the book is a posthumously eligible book and application in that behalf is made in accordance with articles 14A and 17B.

(2) Subject to paragraph (3), an eligible author's share of the Public Lending Right in respect of an eligible book with two or more authors (including any who are not eligible persons) may, and only, be registered on application in that behalf made in accordance with articles 14 and 17.

(3) The share of the Public Lending Right in such a book as is mentioned in paragraph (2) of an author who was not an eligible person at the time when application was first made for the registration of the share of the Right of any co-author may, and may only, be registered if—

(a) he has become and remains an eligible person, and

(b) application in that behalf is made in accordance with Articles 14 and 17.

(4) A posthumously eligible person's share of the Public Lending Right in respect of a posthumously eligible book with two or more authors (including any who are not eligible persons) may, and may only, be registered on application made in accordance with articles 14A and 17B.

Article 9A Shares in Public Lending Right

(1) Subject to the following paragraphs an eligible person's registered share of Public Lending Right in respect of a book [other than an audio-book,] of which he is author shall be the whole of that Right or, where a book has two or more authors (including any who are not eligible persons), such share of the Public Lending Right as may be specified in accordance with Article 17(1)(c) in the application for first registration of the Right.

(2) A translator's share of Public Lending Right in respect of a book [other than an audio-book,] shall be thirty per cent of that Right, or if there is more than one translator (including any who are not eligible persons), an equal share of thirty per cent, but this paragraph shall not apply where a translator is an author of the book in another capacity unless he makes an application in accordance with Article 17(1)(c)(ii).

(3) An editor's or compiler's share of Public Lending Right in respect of a book [other than an audio-book,] shall be

(a) twenty per cent of that Right, or

(b) if he satisfies the [Board] that he has contributed more than twenty per cent of the contents of the book, the percentage equal to that percentage contribution, or

(c) if there is more than one editor or compiler (including any who are not eligible persons), an equal share of twenty per cent or the higher percentage attributable to the editors or compilers in accordance with sub-paragraph (b).

[(4) Each eligible person's share of Public Lending Right in respect of a book [other than an audio-book,] with two or more authors (including any who are not eligible persons but disregarding a translator, editor or compiler) shall not exceed fifty per cent of that Right unless the [Board] is satisfied that any share exceeding fifty per cent which is specified in accordance with article 17(1)(c) in the application for first registration of the Right or in accordance with article 17(2) in the application for first registration of an eligible author's share of the Right is reasonable in relation to that author's contribution.]

(5) Where a book [other than an audio-book,] has two or more authors (including any who are not eligible persons) and the [Board] is satisfied that one or more of them is dead or cannot be traced at the date of application despite all reasonable steps having been taken to do so, the Public Lending Right shall be apportioned amongst all the authors (including any who are not eligible persons)

(a) by attributing to each author the same share of Public Lending Right as has been attributed to that author in respect of any other book by the same authors or, if there is more than one such other book, the most recent book by those authors in respect of which Public Lending Right has been registered, if the [Board] is satisfied that there has been no significant change in the respective contributions of the authors;

(b) where paragraph (a) does not apply, equally, subject to

(i) the prior application of paragraphs (2), (3) and (7), and

(ii) where the book is illustrated,

(aa) the attribution of twenty per cent of the Public Lending Right to the illustrator, or

(bb) if he satisfies the [Board] that he has contributed more than twenty per cent of the contents of the book, the attribution of the percentage equal to that percentage contribution, or

(cc) if there is more than one illustrator (including any who are not eligible persons), the attribution of an equal share of twenty per cent or the higher percentage attributable to illustrators in accordance with sub-paragraph (bb).

(6) Where paragraph 5(b)(ii) applies, an illustrator who is also an author of a book in another capacity shall, in addition to any share of Public Lending Right to which he is entitled under that paragraph, be entitled to any further share of the Right which is attributable to him as author in that other capacity.

(7) Where all the persons (including the personal representatives of a posthumously eligible person) amongst whom the Public Lending Right would otherwise be apportioned equally in accordance with paragraph 5(b) jointly notify the [Board] in writing that they wish the Right to be apportioned in a manner other than equally, the apportionment specified by them shall apply if the [Board] is satisfied that it is reasonable in that case.

(8) Where all the authors who are party to an application under article 17(1)(c) and who are entitled under paragraphs (2), (3), and 5(b)(ii) to a share of a percentage of Public Lending Rights in respect of the relevant book specify in accordance with article 17(1)(c) that the said percentage shall be apportioned in a manner other than that provided for by those paragraphs the specified apportionment shall apply if the [Board] is satisfied that it is reasonable in that case.

[Article 9B Shares in Public Lending Right in respect of audio-books

(1) In respect of an audio-book for which there is a writer, narrator and producer, but no editor or translator—
- (a) the writer's share shall be sixty per cent of the Public Lending Right,
- (b) the narrator's share shall be twenty per cent of that Right, and
- (c) the producer's share shall be twenty per cent of that Right.

(2) In respect of the audio-book for which there is both an editor and a translator—
- (a) the writer's share shall be thirty per cent of the Public Lending Right,
- (b) the narrator's share shall be twenty per cent of that Right,
- (c) the producer's share shall be twenty per cent of the Right,
- (d) the editor's share shall be twelve per cent of that Right,
- (e) the translator's share shall be eighteen percent of that Right.

(3) In respect of an audio-book for which there is an editor, but no translator—
- (a) the writer's share shall be forty-eight per cent of that Right,
- (b) the narrator's share shall be twenty per cent of that Right,
- (c) the producer's share shall be twenty per cent of that Right, and
- (d) the editor's share shall be twelve per cent of that Right.

(4) In respect of an audio-book for which there is a translator, but no editor—
- (a) the writer's share shall be forty-two per cent of the Public Lending Right,
- (b) the narrator's share shall be twenty per cent of that Right,
- (c) the producer's share shall be twenty per cent of that Right, and
- (d) the translator's share shall be eighteen per cent of that Right.

(5) In the case of an audio-book for which the number of writers, narrators, producers, editors or translators is greater than one (including any who are not eligible persons) the respective shares of the Public Lending Right referred to in paragraph (1) to (4) shall be divided equally.]

Article 10 Dealings to be effected only on the Register

No Public Lending Right in respect of a particular book shall subsist and no transmission of a registered interest shall be effective until such Right or such transmission has been entered in the Register by the [Board].

Article 11 Register to be conclusive

The Register shall be conclusive as to whether Public Lending Right subsists in respect of a particular book and also as to the persons (if any) who are for the time being entitled to the Right.

Article 12 Amendment of the Register

The Register may be amended pursuant to an Order of a Court of competent jurisdiction or by the decision of the [Board] in any of the following cases—
- (a) in any case and at any time with the consent of the registered owner or owners of the Right in respect of a particular book;
- (b) where a Court of competent jurisdiction or the [Board] is satisfied that an entry in the Register has been obtained by fraud;
- (c) where a decision of a Court of competent jurisdiction affects any interest in an eligible book and, in consequence thereof, the [Board] is of the opinion that amendment of the Register is required;
- (d) where two or more persons are erroneously registered as being entitled to the same interest in Public Lending Right in respect of a particular book;
- (e) where an entry erroneously relates to a book which is not an eligible book;
- (f) in any other case where by reason of any error or omission in the Register, or by reason of any entry made under a mistake, it appears to the [Board] just to amend the Register.

Article 13 Payments consequent upon amendment

The person who, as a result of an amendment of the Register pursuant to Article 12 or 17A becomes the registered owner of a registered interest shall be entitled to the payment of Public Lending Right in respect of that interest from the date upon which the Register was amended.

Procedure for Registration

Article 14 Forms of application

Any application required under this Scheme other than an application required under article 14A—
- (a) for first registration of Public Lending Right or of an eligible author's share of the Right;

(b) for the transfer of a registered interest, or
(c) for renunciation of a registered interest,

shall be made in writing to the [Board] and provide the information specified in Part I, II or III of Schedule 1 (as the case may be) in such form as [the Board] may from time to time require.

Article 14A Forms of application in respect of posthumously eligible books

An application under article 17B for first registration of Public Lending Right, or of a posthumously eligible person's share of the Right, in relation to a posthumously eligible book shall be made in writing to the [Board] and shall provide in such form as [the Board] may from time to time require—

(a) the information specified in paragraphs 1 to 4 of Part I of Schedule 1 other than the address specified in paragraph 4,
(b) a statement signed by the personal representatives of the posthumously eligible person that the conditions as to eligibility specified in articles 5A and 6A are satisfied, and
(c) in the case of a work by more than one author, a statement signed as aforesaid that the posthumously eligible person in relation to whom the application is being made was translator, editor or compiler or illustrator [or narrator or producer] of the book and that the claim to Public Lending Right in respect thereof is limited to the percentage prescribed in article 9A(2), (3)[, (5)(b)(ii) or article 9B] or that the other author, or one of the other authors, of the work is a translator and that the claim to Public Lending Right in respect thereof is limited to that share or to a share of that share to which the translator is not entitled,

and shall be accompanied, when the personal representatives have not previously made an application under article 17B in relation to that posthumously eligible person, by—

(i) the probate, letters of administration or confirmation of executors of the posthumously eligible person in relation to whom the application is being made, and
(ii) a certificate signed by a Member of Parliament, [a member of the Scottish Parliament,] Justice of the Peace, Minister of Religion, lawyer, bank officer, school teacher, police officer, [registered medical practitioner, who need not hold a licence to practise,] or other person accepted by the [Board] as being of similar standing and stating that he had known the posthumously eligible person in relation to whom the application is being made for at least two years before the date of his death, that he was not related to him and that to the best of his knowledge the contents of the statement referred to in paragraph (b) are true.

Article 15 Recording of receipt of application

The [Board] shall record the date upon which each application for first registration is received by [the Board].

Article 16 Completion of registration

(1) When the [Board] is satisfied as to the eligibility of a book for registration and as to the persons entitled to Public Lending Right in respect of that book and, if more than one, of their respective shares therein, the registration shall be completed and, as regards a first registration of the Right, each registration shall be effective as from the day the application was recorded by the [Board] as have been received by [the Board].

(2) On completion of a registration the [Board] shall issue to any person so entered in the Register as having an interest in the Public Lending Right in respect of the book to which the entry relates, an acknowledgement of registration in the form of a copy of the relevant entry, indicating therein the date from which the entry takes effect.

First Registration

Article 17 Application for first registration

(1) An application for first registration of Public Lending Right in respect of an eligible book—
(a) shall satisfy the requirements of Article 14 and be made by delivery at the registry;
(b) shall be made by an eligible author, and
(c) where the book has two or more authors (including any who are not eligible persons), shall specify the shares of each of them and for that purpose each of those authors who is alive at the date of application shall be a party to the application, unless—
(i) the [Board] is satisfied that he cannot be traced, despite all reasonable steps having been taken to do so, or
(ii) the application is made by the translator or editor or compiler [or narrator or producer] of the book and he specifies that he is making the application only in his capacity as such,
(iii) any author of the book who is not a party to the application is a translator and the application specifies that it relates only to that share of Public Lending Right in the book to which the translator is not entitled or

Part 2 Copyright

(iv) the application is made by an author of the book and he specifies that he is making the application otherwise than wholly or partly in the capacity of translator, editor, or compiler [or narrator or producer] of the book, and—

(aa) there is at the date of the application an effective agreement or arrangement between each person who is an author of the book (including any author who is not an eligible person or who does not wish to register);

(bb) each such person is a party to the agreement or arrangement otherwise than wholly or partly in the capacity of translator, editor or compiler [or narrator or producer] of the book; and

(cc) the agreement or arrangement relates to the apportionment of shares of Public Lending Right in the book or, where there is any eligible person who would be entitled to a share of the Right by virtue of being a translator, editor, or compiler [or narrator or producer], to the apportionment of shares in such proportion of the Right as would remain after taking account of any such entitlement.

(2) An application for first registration of an eligible author's share of Public Lending Right in respect of an eligible book with two or more authors (including any who are not eligible persons)—

(a) shall satisfy the requirements of Article 14 and be made by delivery at the registry,

(b) shall be made by the author concerned, and

(c) shall, when made by an author otherwise than wholly or partly in the capacity of translator, editor or compiler [or narrator or producer] of the book, satisfy the requirements of paragraph (1)(c)(iv).

(3) Anything which falls to be done by an author under this Article shall, if he is not of full age, be done by his parent or guardian and that parent or guardian shall be recorded in the Register as the person to whom are payable sums in respect of any registered interest of the author until such time as a transfer of the registration into the author's own name has been recorded in pursuance of Article 25.

Article 17A Transitional provisions for translators, editors and compilers

(1) Where an application for first registration of Public Lending Right in respect of a book was made before 28th December 1984 and a translator, editor or compiler thereof would have been party to the said application if it had been made on or after that date he may, if he is an eligible person, make an application for the registered shares of the Right to be revised.

(2) Subject to the following paragraphs, the provisions of this Scheme shall apply to an application under paragraph (1) as though it were an application for first registration of Public Lending Right.

(3) Where a successful application is made under paragraph (1)—

(a) the applicant's share of the Public Lending Right shall be that prescribed in Article 9A(2) or (3) as the case may be, and

(b) the relevant shares of his co-authors, one to another, shall remain unaltered, unless all the authors who were party to the original application before 28th December 1984 are party to the application under paragraph (1) and specify an apportionment of their shares in a different manner and the [Board] is satisfied that such apportionment is reasonable.

(4) Where a successful application is made in accordance with paragraph (1) the [Board] shall amend the Register accordingly.

Article 17B Application for first registration in respect of posthumously eligible books

An application for first registration of Public Lending Right in respect of a posthumously eligible book and an application for first registration of a posthumously eligible person's share of Public Lending Right in respect of such a book with two or more authors (including any who are not eligible persons)—

(a) shall satisfy the requirements of article 14A and be made by delivery at the registry, and

(b) shall be made by the personal representatives of the posthumously eligible person concerned.

Article 18 Evidence required in connection with the applications

The [Board] may require the submission of evidence to satisfy [the Board] that—

(a) a book is an eligible book,

(b) a person applying as author for the first registration of Public Lending Right, or the registration of a share of the Right, is in fact the author of that book and is an eligible person,

(c) any co-author who is not a party to an application for first registration of Public Lending Right is dead or cannot be traced despite all reasonable steps having been taken to do so, and

(d) where such an application as is mentioned in article 17(1)(c)(iv) has been made in accordance with paragraph (1) or (2) of that article—

(i) there is such an agreement or arrangement as is mentioned in article 17(1)(c)(iv), and

(ii) the share of Public Lending Right of the person making the application is as specified in that agreement or arrangement.

and may for the purpose of obtaining any such evidence require a statutory declaration to be made by any person.

Subsequent dealings with Public Lending Right

Article 19 Public Lending Right to be transmissible

A registered interest shall be transmissible by assignment or assignation, by testamentary disposition or by operation of law, as personal or movable property, so long, as regards a particular book, as the Right in respect of that book is capable of subsisting.

Article 20 Period during which the Right may be transferred

The duration of Public Lending Right in respect of any book and the period during which there may be dealings therein shall be from the date of the book's first publication (or, if later, the beginning of the sampling year in which application is made for it to be registered) until [seventy] years have elapsed since the end of the sampling year in which the author died or, if the book is registered as the work of more than one author, as regards dealings in the share of the Right attributable to that author, the end of the year in which that author died.

Article 21 Whole interest to be assigned

(1) The disposition of Public Lending Right, after the first registration thereof, shall, as respects each registered interest in any book, be for the whole of that interest.

(2) On such disposition the interest may be registered in the name of joint owners, being not more than four in number and all being of full age, but in such case the senior only shall be deemed, for the purposes of the Scheme, to be the registered owner; seniority shall be determined by the order in which names stand in the Register.

(3) Subject to Articles 29 and 30, no notice of any trusts expressed, implied or constructive, shall be entered on the Register or be receivable by the [Board].

Article 22 Applications for transfer

Every application for registration of a transfer of Public Lending Right shall satisfy the requirements of Article 14 and be made by delivery at the registry.

Article 23 Stamp duty

(1) An application for transfer shall bear the proper Inland Revenue stamp impressed thereon to show that all duty payable (if any) in respect of the transaction has been paid.

(2) Where an application for transfer is submitted for the purpose of giving effect to a transaction under a deed or other instrument on which the Inland Revenue stamp has already been impressed, such stamped instrument shall, before completion of the registration, be produced to the [Board] to show that all duty payable (if any) in respect of the transaction has been paid.

Article 24 Proof of author's existence

It shall be a condition of registration of every transfer that the transferee provides, and gives an undertaking to the [Board] in future to provide at such intervals and in such form as the [Board] may require, evidence that the author is still alive, or, as the case may be, evidence of the author's death.

Article 25 Registration by an author on attainment of full age

An author whose interest is, pursuant to Article 17(3), registered in the name of his parent or guardian may, on attaining full age, make application to the [Board] in accordance with Articles 21 to 23, so far as they are applicable, for the transfer of the registration of the Right into his own name, and until such transfer has been recorded the [Board] shall be entitled to remit any sums due in respect of the Right to such parent or guardian.

Transmission on death

Article 26 Registration of personal representatives

On production of the probate, letters of administration, or confirmation of executors of a registered owner, the personal representatives named in such probate, letters or confirmation shall, on production of the same to the [Board], be registered as owner in place of the deceased owner with the addition of the words "executor *or* executrix (*or* administrator *or* administratrix) of *(name)* deceased".

Part 2 Copyright

Article 27 Transfer by personal representatives

The personal representatives registered under the preceding Article may transfer the interest of the deceased owner, such transfer being in accordance with Articles 21 to 24 or such provisions thereof as are applicable in the circumstances of the case.

Transfer on bankruptcy, liquidation or sequestration

Article 28 Registration of Official Receiver, Official Assignees or Judicial Factor

(1) On the production to the [Board] of an office copy of an Order of a Court having jurisdiction in bankruptcy adjudging a registered owner bankrupt or directing the estate of a deceased registered owner to be administered in accordance with an order under section 421 of the Insolvency Act 1986 or section 21 of the Bankruptcy Amendment Act (Northern Ireland) 1929, together with a certificate signed by the Official Receiver or Official Assignee, as the case may be, that any registered interest in the name of the bankrupt registered owner, or deceased registered owner, is part of his property divisible amongst his creditors, the Official Receiver or the Official Assignee may be registered as the registered owner in place of the bankrupt or deceased registered owner.

(2) Where there is produced to the [Board] a certified copy of an Order of a Court having competent jurisdiction in Scotland awarding sequestration of the estate of a registered owner (including a deceased registered owner) and appointing a judicial factor the [Board] shall on receipt of such a copy enter in the Register the name of the judicial factor as registered owner with the addition of the words "judicial factor in the estate of *(name)*".

Article 29 Registration of Trustee in Bankruptcy in place of Official Receiver, Assignees in Bankruptcy or Judicial Factor

(1) Where the Official Receiver or the Official Assignee has been registered as registered owner and some other person is subsequently appointed trustee, or, in Northern Ireland, a creditor's assignee is appointed, the trustee or the assignee may be registered as registered owner in place of the Official Receiver, or the Official Assignee, on production of an office copy of the certificate by the Department of Trade of his appointment as trustee, or in Northern Ireland an office copy of the certificate under section 90 of the Bankruptcy (Ireland) Amendment Act 1872 or of the certificate of the vesting of the estate and effects of the registered owner in the assignee.

(2) Where a judicial factor has been registered as an owner in terms of Article 28(2) and some other person is subsequently elected as a trustee for behoof of the creditors of the former registered owner, the [Board], on receipt of the notification of such election and of sufficient evidence to demonstrate that that person has been so elected, shall enter in the Register the name of the trustee as registered owner with the addition of the words "trustee in the estate of *(name)*".

(3) If the Official Receiver or the Official Assignee has not been entered on the Register under Article 28(1) the trustee or the assignee may be registered as registered owner on production of office copies of the Order adjudging the registered owner bankrupt and the appropriate certificate referred to in paragraph (1) with a certificate signed by the trustee or the assignee that the registered interest in part of the property of the bankrupt divisible amongst his creditors.

(4) If a judicial factor has not been entered in the Register as owner under Article 28(2) the [Board] shall, on receipt of the certified copy of an Order of a Court under Article 28(2) together with the notification and evidence referred to in paragraph (2), enter in the Register as registered owner the name of the duly elected trustee with the addition of the words "trustee in the estate of *(name)*".

Article 30 Registration of a trust under a Scheme of Arrangement or an Arrangement under the control of the Court

(1) If any registered interest is vested in a trustee under the provisions of a Scheme of Arrangement approved by a Court having jurisdiction in bankruptcy, the Official Receiver or other trustee may be registered as owner in like manner as a trustee in bankruptcy upon production of an office copy of the Scheme of Arrangement, a certificate signed by the Official Receiver, or such other trustee, that the registered interest was part of the property vested in him under the provisions of the Scheme, and in the case of a trustee other than the Official Receiver, an office copy of the certificate by the Department of Trade of his appointment as trustee.

(2) If any registered interest of an arranging debtor who is a registered owner is vested in the Official Assignee alone or jointly with other persons under section 349 of the Irish Bankrupt and Insolvent Act 1857, the Official Assignee and such other persons (if any) may be registered as owner in his place on production of an office copy of the Order of the Court approving and confirming the resolution or agreement referred to in the said section with a certificate by the Official Assignee identifying the arranging debtor named in the Order of the Court with the registered owner endorsed thereon and a certificate signed by the Official Assignee and other such person (if any) that the registered interest was part of the property vested under the resolution or agreement.

(3) If, as regards Scotland, a registered owner—

(a) has entered into a deed of arrangement for behoof of his creditors, the [Board] shall, on receiving a certified copy of the Order of the Court approving such arrangement, enter on the Register as owner the name of the person who is under the said deed of arrangement to receive any payments due to the owner (where that person is not the registered owner at the date of approval of the arrangement);

(b) has entered into a private trust deed or composition contract for behoof of his creditors, the trustee under such deed or contract may made an application, accompanied by such evidence as the [Board] may require, for transmission of the registered interest into his name as such trustee; and on receipt of such an application the [Board] shall make the appropriate entry in the Register.

Article 31 Liquidation of a company

In the liquidation of a company in which an interest in Public Lending Right is vested, any resolution or order appointing a liquidator may be filed and referred to on the Register, and, when so registered, shall be deemed to be in force until it is cancelled or superseded on the Register.

Article 32 Renunciation

(1) On making application in that behalf which satisfies the requirements of Article 14, the registered owner of a registered interest may absolutely and unconditionally renounce that interest as provided in paragraph (2).

(2) Such renunciation may, as to extent, be in respect of either the whole or a half share of the registered interest and may be effective for all time, or in respect of such financial years as shall be specified by the registered owner.

(3) An application for renunciation shall bear the proper Inland Revenue stamp impressed thereon.

(4) The [Board] shall as at the date from which the renunciation is to have effect amend the Register—

(a) in the case of a renunciation for all time of the whole of the registered interest by removing from the Register the entry relating to the registered owner and, if that interest represents the whole of the Public Lending Right in a book, the entry relating to that book; or

(b) in all other cases, by noting against the relevant entry in the Register the extent of the renunciation and the period during which it is effective.

(5) Immediately upon the amendment of the Register as provided in paragraph (4), any sum due by way of Public Lending Right which, apart from the renunciation would become payable to the registered owner by 31st March in any year falling within the period to which the renunciation applies, shall cease to be so payable.

General

Article 33 Neglected applications for registrations

Where in the case of any application for first or any subsequent registration an applicant has failed to provide within three months information requested by the [Board], notice may be given to the applicant that the application will be treated as abandoned unless the information is duly furnished within a time (not being less than one month) determined by the [Board] and specified in the notice; and if, at the expiration of that time, the information so requested is not furnished, the application may be treated as abandoned.

Article 34 Removal of entries from the Register

Where the [Board], pursuant to section 4(5) of the Act, directs the removal from the Register of any entry relating to a book in whose case no sum has become due by way of Public Lending Right for a period of at least ten years, any subsequent application for the entry to be restored to the Register may be made only by the person who, at the date of the removal of the entry, was the registered owner; or by his legal personal representatives.

Article 35 Copies of entries in the Register

(1) The [Board] shall not supply a copy of any entry in the Register otherwise than to—

(a) a registered owner, as regards any entry which relates to his registered interest; or

(b) such other person as the registered owner may direct, but if the entry in question also relates to other registered owners, only with the consent of all such owners.

(2) The [Board] may require a payment of a fee for supplying a copy of an entry in the Register, not exceeding £5 in respect of each such entry.

PART IV

ASCERTAINMENT OF THE NUMBER OF LOANS OF BOOKS

Article 36 Special definitions

In this Part, unless the context otherwise requires—

Part 2 Copyright

"copy" means an individual copy of a particular book, and "copy number" means a number which distinguishes the copy to which it is applied from other copies of the same book in the same library;

"group", in relation to service points, means a group specified in Schedule 2;

"library" has the meaning assigned to it by section 3(4) of the Act;

"loans" means loans whereby books are lent out from a service point to individual borrowers, and includes loans of books not normally held at that service point;

"mobile library service point" means a service point which is taken about from place to place;

"month" means one of the twelve months in the calendar year;

"operative sampling point" means a sampling point at which loans are for the time being required to be recorded in pursuance of Article 40(1);

"ordinary service point" means a service point from which fewer than 500,000 loans were made during the preceding period of twelve months;

"participating period", in relation to a sampling point, means the period commencing on the date on which the local library authority having responsibility for it receives from the [Board] notice of designation pursuant to Article [38(5)] and ending on the date specified in a notice given thereunder as the date upon which it is to cease to act as a sampling point;

"principal service point", in relation to a library authority, means any of the following—

(a) whichever of the service points for which that authority is responsible is the service point from which the greatest number of loans were made during the preceding period of twelve months;

(b) any service point for which that authority is responsible, the number of loans from which during the preceding period of twelve months was not less than three-quarters of the number of loans made from the service point referred to in paragraph (a) during the same period;

(c) any other such service point from which 500,000 or more loans were made during the aforesaid period;

and "principal service points" means every service point which is a principal service point in relation to any library authority;

"sampling point" means any principal service point, ordinary service point or mobile library service point, or any number of such points in relation to any local library authority, which has been designated, for the time being, by the [Board] under article 38;

"sampling year" means the period of twelve months ending on 30th June;

"service point" means a place from which books comprised in a library are lent out to the public at large.

Article 37 Number of loans to be ascertained by means of a sample

The number of occasions on which a book is lent out shall be determined by means of a sample of the lendings of that book from particular service points, designated in accordance with the provisions of this Part; and for the purpose of the sample, service points shall be classified into the groups, according to local library authority areas, specified in Schedule 2.

Article 38 Designation of sampling points

(1) Such local library authorities as the [Board] may require shall, not later than 30th September in each year, furnish to the [Board] lists, as at 31st March of that year, of all their principal, ordinary and mobile service points. The [Board] shall, not later than 31st December of that year, designate in accordance with paragraph (5) those service points which are to be operative sampling points or which are to be included in operative sampling points as from the beginning of the ensuing sampling year.

(1A) The [Board] may, at any time after he has designated a sampling point in accordance with paragraph (1), discontinue the designation of that point and designate a new sampling point, such discontinuance and new point to take effect from 1st January in the ensuing sampling year. Notice of discontinuance and designation pursuant to this paragraph shall be given in accordance with paragraph (5).

(2) The [Board] shall so exercise [the Board's] powers under this article as to secure, subject to paragraph (4), that—

(a) at all times there shall be not less than 30 operative sampling points comprising—

(i) 5 points falling within not less than 3 local library authority areas in Group A and 5 points falling within not less than 4 local library authority areas in Group D in Schedule 2,

(ii) 4 points falling within not less than 3 local library authority areas in each of Groups B, C and E in Schedule 2,

(iii) 3 points falling within not less than 3 local library authority areas in each of Groups F and G in Schedule 2, and

(iv) 2 points falling within not less than 2 local library authority areas in Group H in Schedule 2;

(b) at all times the operative sampling points falling within each Group in Schedule 2 shall include, subject to paragraph (3), a principal service point and an ordinary service point;

[(c) at all times one of the 3 operative sampling points falling within Group F in Schedule 2 shall be within one of the following principal areas: Carmarthenshire, Pembrokeshire, Ceredigion, Isle of Anglesey, Gwynedd, Conwy, Denbighshire or Powys;]

(d) at all times one of the 3 operative sampling points falling within Group G in Schedule 2 shall be outside the [Cities] of Edinburgh and Glasgow;

(e) no operative sampling point shall consist of a mobile library service point other than an operative sampling point falling within [a principal area specified in sub-paragraph (c) above];

(f) during each sampling year at least [7] operative sampling points shall be replaced by new such points; and

(g) no operative sampling point shall remain as such for a continuous period of more than 4 years[, unless it is in Group H in Schedule 2].

(3) The relevant local library authority shall notify the [Board] of any change in the categorisation of a sampling point which consists of a single principal, ordinary or mobile service point but the [Board] shall not be required by paragraph (2)(a) to discontinue the designation of the point as a sampling point before the expiry of the sampling year in which he receives such notice or, if that year has less than six months to run, before the expiry of the next following sampling year.

For the purposes of this paragraph and of paragraph (2)(a), a change in the categorisation of a sampling point shall be disregarded if it is occasioned by an increase or decrease of less than 10 per cent in the number of loans made therefrom.

(4) The local library authority shall notify the [Board] of any decision to close a service point which is or is included in a sampling point and the date on which the closure takes effect but, if it is not reasonably practicable for the [Board] to satisfy the requirements of paragraph (2) before the closure takes effect, those requirements shall be treated as satisfied if satisfied as soon as is reasonably practicable thereafter.

(5) The [Board] shall give to the local library authority responsible for a sampling point—

(a) for the purposes of designating that point under paragraphs (1) or (1A), notice in writing of such designation specifying the period ending on 31st December or 30th June, in any sampling year for which he intends the point to be an operative sampling point;

(b) for the purpose of discontinuing that point as a sampling point, not less than six months notice in writing of such discontinuance.

Article 39 Provision by libraries of recording facilities

Upon receipt of a notice under Article [38(5)(a)] a local library authority shall—

(a) arrange for every book which may be lent out from the sampling point to which the designation refers [to be separately identified], in such form as the [Board] may require, with its identifying number and (where more than one copy may be lent out) copy number, and shall notify the [Board] at such time and in such manner as he may direct of the number of books [so identified]; and

(b) acquire, in accordance with arrangements approved by the [Board], such equipment (including computer programs) as may be necessary to enable the authority to comply with the provision of Article 40 regarding the furnishing of information to the [Board].

Article 40 Duty to record lendings

(1) A local library authority which has received a notice under Article [38(5)(a)] shall, for such period as is specified in the notice, record every occasion on which a copy of a book is lent out to the public from the sampling point to which the notice refers and shall furnish to the [Board], in such form and at such intervals as [the Board] may direct, details of such lendings, including the identifying number and any copy number of the copy in question.

(2) For the purpose of this Article each volume of a work published in two or more volumes shall be treated as a separate book.

Article 41 Provision of book loan data

Each local library authority shall submit to the [Board], in such form, at such intervals and in respect of such periods as [the Board] may direct, a return of the total number of occasions on which the books comprised in all its collections were the subject of loans.

Article 42 Method of determining the number of notional loans

(1) The [Board] shall, from the details of loans furnished to [the Board] by local library authorities pursuant to the provisions of this Part (upon the accuracy of which the [Board] shall be entitled to rely), calculate, in accordance with paragraph (2), the number of notional loans of each book in respect of which Public Lending Right subsists in each sampling year.

(2) The number of notional loans of each book made during a sampling year shall be the aggregate of the number of notional loans of that book made in all groups; and the number of notional loans for a group shall be determined in accordance with the following formula:—

Total notional loans in the group—

$$(A/B) \times C$$

Where—

A represents the number of loans of that book recorded during the sampling year at the operative sampling points in that group;

B represents the total number of loans of books made to the public during the sampling year from the operative sampling points in that group; and

C represents the aggregate of the loans of all books made to the public from all libraries (within the meaning of section 3(4) of the Act) in the area of the group during the financial year ending in the sampling year in question, or, as regards any particular library for which loan data relating to that financial year is not available to the [Board], the most recent financial year for which [the Board] has such data.

(3) For the purposes of paragraph (2)—

(a) Groups A, B and C in Schedule 2 shall be treated as one group;

(b) if on any occasion on which any details of lendings at a particular sampling point which consists of a single service part are furnished to the [Board] in accordance with article 40 and record loans of a copy of a book in excess of an average of one loan for each period of five days covered by the details, the loans in excess of that average shall be disregarded; and

[(c) the [Board] may disregard any loan of a book reported from a sampling point in accordance with Article 40 where the local library authority does not specify an International Standard Book Number in respect of the book].

Article 43 Reimbursement of local library authorities

(1) The [Board] shall, subject to the provisions of this Article and Article 44, reimburse to local library authorities the net expenditure incurred by them in giving effect to this Scheme.

(2) It shall be the duty of local library authorities to keep proper accounts and records in respect of the expenditure (including overhead expenses) incurred by them in giving effect to this Scheme and the [Board] may withhold payment to a local library authority, in whole or in part, until such time as such authority has furnished to [the Board] sufficient evidence as to the amount of the expenditure so incurred.

Article 44 Expense incurred in respect of sampling points

(1) Without prejudice to the generality of Article 43(2) each local library authority to which a notice has been given under Article [38(5)(a)] shall submit to the [Board] at such time and in such form as [the Board] may require estimates of the net expenditure to be incurred in giving effect to this Scheme at the sampling point or points specified in such notice.

(2) Such local library authority may from time to time during the participating period submit to the [Board] claims in respect of the expenditure incurred, or estimated to have been incurred by it, and the [Board] shall be entitled to rely upon the accuracy of such claims and to make payments on account of the expenditure incurred by that authority in giving effect to the Scheme.

(3) The total amount payable by way of reimbursement to such local library authority shall be finally determined by the [Board] after examination of such audited financial statements and such books, records, documents, and accounts relating thereto as [the Board] may require; and any balance found after such final determination to be due by or to the [Board] in account with the local library authority in question shall be paid to or recovered from such local library authority.

(4) In reckoning the net expenditure for the purposes of this Article and of Article 43, the following shall be deducted from the gross expenditure incurred by a local library authority in connection with a sampling point—

(a) any sum received in connection with the disposal (by safe, lease or otherwise) of any property or equipment purchased pursuant to paragraph (b) of Article 39;

(b) any sum which it might reasonably be expected would have been received on such a disposal (whether or not there has been a disposal of the property or equipment in question);

(c) any insurance monies received in respect of the loss or destruction of or damage to any such property or equipment;

(d) an amount representing the appropriate proportion of the net cost (whether by way of purchase, lease, or otherwise) of any property or equipment which is used by a local library authority partly in connection with this Scheme and partly for other purposes not connected therewith:

Provided that where deductions are made under both sub-paragraphs (a) and (b) in respect of the same property or equipment, the aggregate deductions thereunder shall not exceed whichever is the greater of the sums mentioned in those sub-paragraphs.

(5) In determining the amount finally to be paid to or recovered from a local library authority pursuant to paragraph (3), account shall be taken of any expenditure reasonably incurred by that authority in discontinuing the sampling point.

PART V
CALCULATION AND PAYMENT OF PUBLIC LENDING RIGHT

Article 46 Determination of the sum due in respect of Public Lending Right

(1) For any financial year, the sum due by way of Public Lending Right in respect of a registered interest to the registered owner thereof shall be ascertained by reference to—

(a) the product of the number of notional loans attributable to that interest (calculated in accordance with paragraph (4)) and [7.82p], and

(b) the aggregate amount of that product and the like products in the case of all other registered interests which initially were registered interests of the same author or were interests registered by the personal representatives of the same author.

(2) Subject to paragraph (3) the sum so due for the financial year shall be—

(a) except where the following sub-paragraph applies, the product mentioned in paragraph (1)(a);

(b) if the aggregate amount mentioned in paragraph (1)(b) exceeds [£6,600], the product of x/y and [£6,600] where—

x is the number of notional loans attributable to the interest in question, and

y is the aggregate of that number and the number of notional loans attributable to all other registered interests which initially were registered interests of the same author or were interests registered by the personal representatives of the same author.

(3) If the aggregate of the amounts determined in accordance with paragraph (2) in respect of each registered interest of the registered owner thereof is less than [£1], the sum due in respect of the registered interest shall be nil.

(4) For the purposes of paragraphs (1) and (2)(b), the number of notional loans attributable to any registered interest in any financial year shall be calculated by ascertaining, in accordance with Article 42(2), the number of notional loans of the book to which it relates which were made during the sampling year ending in that financial year, and shall be—

(a) if the registered interest represents the whole of the Public Lending Right in respect of that book, the total notional loans of the book in question;

(b) if the registered interest relates only to a share of the Public Lending Right in respect of that book, such proportion of the total notional loans of the book as the registered interest bears to the whole of the Public Lending Right in that book, fractions of a loan being disregarded;

(c) if the Right in respect of that registered interest has been renounced in part, such proportion of the notional loans attributable to the registered interest under sub-paragraph (a) or (b), as the case may be, which the unrenounced share bears to the whole of the registered interest, fractions of a loan being disregarded;

(d) nil, if the Right in respect of the registered interest has been wholly renounced for the financial year in question.

(5) For the purposes of paragraphs (1) and (2)(b), the references to interests which were initially registered interests of the same author include interests which, in pursuance of Article 17(3), were registered in the name of his parent or guardian.

Article 47 Persons to whom the payment is due

The person entitled to the Public Lending Right in respect of any registered book in any financial year shall be the registered owner thereof as at 30th June of that year.

Article 48 Right to be claimed

(1) No payment shall be made in respect of Public Lending Right unless that Right has been claimed by or on behalf of the person for the time being entitled.

(2) A claim in respect of the Right may be made for—

(a) a specified period;

(b) an unspecified period determinable by not less than three months written notice of termination given to the [Board] by or on behalf of the person for the time being entitled to the Right.

(3) A claim shall automatically lapse in the event of any change of ownership recorded on the Register, subsequent to first registration thereof, in respect of the Right to which the claim relates.

Article 49 Notification of entitlement and payment of sums due under the Scheme

(1) Any sum payable by way of Public Lending Right in respect of a registered interest, for any financial year, shall (unless sooner paid) fall due for payment on the last day of that year.

(2) Any such sum may be paid by cheque or warrant sent through the post directed to the registered address of the registered owner or, in the case of joint owners, to the registered address of the senior owner (as defined in Article 21(2)), or to such person and to such address as the owner or joint owners may direct by a written payment mandate to the [Board], delivered at the registry, in the form set out in Schedule 4 or a form to the like effect; every such cheque or warrant shall be made payable to the order of the person to whom it is sent and any one of two or more joint owners may give a good receipt for any money due to them under this Scheme.

(3) The [Board] shall at the end of each financial year, or as soon as is reasonably practicable thereafter, inform each registered owner, by notice posted to his registered address of—

- (a) the notional number of lendings for that year of each book in respect of which he is a registered owner to whom a sum is payable by way of Public Lending Right in respect of that year; and
- (b) the amount of such sum.

(4) If, after the [Board] has notified the registered owner as provided in paragraph (3), the cheque or warrant for the sum referred to therein is not presented for payment and thereby lapses—

- (a) there shall be no further duty on the part of the [Board] to take steps to trace the registered owner and it shall be the responsibility of such owner to make application to the [Board] for payment; and
- (b) if at the end of six years from the date upon which a payment in respect of Public Lending Right becomes due no such application has been made by the person entitled thereto, the entitlement to such payment shall lapse.

(5) At the request of a registered owner to whom no notice is required to be given under paragraph (3) in respect of any financial year, the [Board] shall supply to him particulars (calculated in accordance with article 42) of the number of notional loans during the sampling year ending in that financial year of any book in respect of which he is the registered owner, provided the request is made no later than six months after the end of that financial year.

Article 50 Power to call for information

The [Board] may at any time require a statutory declaration or other sufficient evidence that an author or any registered owner is alive and is the person to whom money is payable under this Scheme, and may withhold payment until such declaration or evidence as he may require is produced.

Article 51 Interest

No sum determined to be due under this Scheme shall carry interest.

SCHEDULE 1

INFORMATION TO BE PROVIDED IN CONNECTION WITH APPLICATIONS

Part I

Application for first registration

Each application shall provide the [Board], in such form as [the Board] may from time to time require, with the following—

1. The title of the book to which the application relates.

[2. The name of every author (within the meaning of article 4) and the evidence on which each author relies for the purpose of being treated as an author in accordance with article 4(2).]

3. The true identity (if different from 2 above) of each such person, and his address.

4. The International Standard Book Number (if any) of the book.

5. A statement signed by each applicant that in each case the conditions as to eligibility specified in Part II of the Scheme are satisfied at the date of application, accompanied, when the applicant has not previously made an application under Article 17 of this Scheme, by a certificate signed by a Member of Parliament, [a member of the Scottish Parliament,] Justice of the Peace, Minister of Religion, lawyer, bank officer, school teacher, police officer, [registered medical practitioner, who need not hold a licence to practise,] or other person accepted by the [Board] as being of similar standing and stating that he has known the applicant for at least two years, that he is not related to the applicant and that to the best of his knowledge the contents of the statement by the applicant are true.

6. In the case of a work by more than one author—
   - (a) a statement signed by all the authors who are alive and can be traced at the date of application specifying—
     - (i) the agreed share in the Public Lending Right of each author, and
     - (ii) whether any author is translator, editor, compiler or, if any author is dead or untraced at the date of application, illustrator of the book and, if so, whether he is also an author of the book in another capacity, or

(b) a statement by the applicant that he is translator, editor or compiler of the book and that his claim to the Public Lending Right in respect thereof is limited to the percentage prescribed in Article 9A(2) or (3) as the case may be, or

(c) where one of the authors of the work is a translator, a statement signed by the other author or, if more than one, all the other authors who are alive and can be traced at the date of application specifying—

(i) that another author of the book who is not a party to the application is a translator,

(ii) that the claim to Public Lending Right in respect thereof is limited to that share to which the translator is not entitled, and

(iii) where there is more than one author other than the translator

(aa) the agreed share of each such author in that share of the Public Lending Right to which the translator is not entitled, and

(bb) whether any such author is editor or compiler or, if any such author is dead or untraced at the date of application, illustrator of the book and, if so, whether he is also an author of the book in another capacity, or

(d) where such an application as is mentioned in paragraph (1)(*c*)(iv) of article 17 is made in accordance with paragraph (1) or (2) of that article, a statement specifying the names of all other persons whether or not party to such agreement or arrangement as is mentioned in paragraph (1)(*c*)(iv) of article 17, who are eligible for a share of Public Lending Right in respect of the book.

7. Where an editor or compiler of a book wishes to claim, or claim an equal share of, more than twenty per cent of the Public Lending Right in accordance with Article 9A(3), particulars indicating evidence of the percentage that he has, or where there are two or more editors or compilers that they have jointly, contributed to the contents of the book.

8. In the case of an author not of full age, a declaration by the applicant that he is the parent or guardian, as the case may be, of the author, and a copy of the author's birth certificate.

Part II

Application for transfer of registered interest

Each application shall provide the [Board], in such form as [the Board] may from time to time require, with the following—

1. The title of the book.
2. The International Standard Book Number (if any) of the book.
3. The name and address of the transferor.
4. The name and address of transferee.
5. An undertaking by the transferee to furnish to the [Board], whenever so required, proof that the author is still alive.

Part III

Application for renunciation of registered interest

Each application shall provide the [Board], in such form as [the Board] may from time to time require, with the following—

1. The name and address of the person renouncing.
2. The title of the book to which the renunciation relates.
3. The International Standard Book Number (if any) of the book.
4. The extent of the Right being renounced.
5. The period in respect of which the Right is renounced.

SCHEDULE 2

GROUPING OF SERVICE POINTS (ARTS 36–38)

Service points shall be grouped according to local library authority areas as follows—

[GROUP A

Those within the areas of the following districts or, as the case may be, counties—

Bedfordshire	Kent	Slough
Bracknell Forest	Luton	Southend
Brighton and Hove	Milton Keynes	Thurrock
Buckinghamshire	Newbury	Suffolk
Cambridgeshire	Norfolk	Surrey
East Sussex	Northamptonshire	West Sussex
Essex	Oxfordshire	Windsor and Maidenhead

Hertfordshire	Peterborough	Wokingham
Medway Council	Reading	

GROUP B

Those within the areas of the following districts or, as the case may be, counties—

Bath and North East Somerset	Gloucestershire	Somerset
Bournemouth	Hampshire	South Gloucestershire
City of Bristol	Herefordshire	Staffordshire
City of Portsmouth	The Isle of Wight	Swindon
City of Southampton	The Isles of Scilly	Torbay
City of Stoke-on-Trent	North Somerset	Warwickshire
Cornwall	Plymouth	Wiltshire
Devon	Poole	Worcestershire
Dorset	Shropshire	The Wrekin

GROUP C

Those within the areas of the following districts or, as the case may be, counties—

Blackburn	East Riding of Yorkshire	North Lincolnshire
Blackpool	Halton	Northumberland
Cheshire	Hartlepool	North Yorkshire
City of Derby	Lancashire	Nottinghamshire
City of Kingston upon Hull	Leicestershire	Redcar and Cleveland
City of Leicester	Lincolnshire	Rutland
Cumbria	Nottingham	Stockton-on-Tees
Darlington	Middlesborough	Warrington
Derbyshire	North East Lincolnshire	York
Durham		

GROUP D

Those within the areas of the metropolitan districts of England.

GROUP E

Those within the area of Greater London.

GROUP F

Those in Wales.

GROUP G

Those in Scotland.

GROUP H

Those in Northern Ireland.]

SCHEDULE 3

. . .

SCHEDULE 4
PAYMENT MANDATE

"Please forward, until further notice, all sums that may from time to time become due to me/us or the survivor(s) of us by way of Public Lending Right to *(here state full name and address of the bank, firm or person to whom payments are to be sent)* or *(where payment is to be made to a Bank)* to such other Branch of that Bank as the Bank may from time to time request. Your compliance with this request shall discharge the [Board's] liability in respect of such sums."

Date . . . . Signature . . . .

Name . . . .
(Block Capitals)

Address . . . .

. . . .

. . . .

SCHEDULE 5

. . .

NOTES

This Appendix was set out, incorporating all amendments as in force on 27 December 1990, by the Public Lending Right Scheme 1982 (Commencement of Variations) Order 1990, SI 1990/2360, art 2, Appendix 2, and has been subsequently amended as follows:

In each place they appear in square brackets, the words "Board", "the Board" and "the Board's" are substituted by the Public Bodies (Abolition of the Registrar of Public Lending Right) Order 2013, SI 2013/2352, art 7(2), Sch 2, para 1.

Art 2: definition "the Board" inserted, and in definition "the Register" words omitted revoked and words in square brackets substituted by SI 2013/2352, art 7(2), Sch 2, para 1; definition "EEA State" in para (1) inserted by the Public Lending Right Scheme 1982 (Commencement of Variations) Order 2004, SI 2004/1258, art 2, Appendix, para (a).

Art 4: words in first pair of square brackets in para (1) inserted by the Public Lending Right Scheme 1982 (Commencement of Variations) Order 1991, SI 1991/2618, art 2, Appendix; words omitted revoked by the Public Lending Right Scheme 1982 (Commencement of Variations) Order 1997, SI 1997/1576, art 2, Appendix, para 1; word in square brackets in para (1)(a)(ii) substituted and paras (1)(a)(iii), (2)(c)(iii), (iv) inserted by the Public Lending Right Scheme 1982 (Commencement of Variations) Order 2014, SI 2014/1457, art 2, Appendix, para 1; para (2)(b)–(d) substituted for original para (2)(b), by SI 1991/2618, art 2, Appendix;

Art 5: words in square brackets in para (1) substituted by SI 2004/1258, art 2, Appendix, para (b).

Art 6: words in first pair of square brackets in para (2) inserted by SI 2014/1457, art 2, Appendix, para 2; para (2)(b) revoked by SI 1991/2618, art 2, Appendix; para (2)(g) substituted by the Public Lending Right Scheme 1982 (Commencement of Variations) Order 1999, SI 1999/420, art 2, Appendix.

Art 9A: para (4) substituted by SI 1997/1576, art 2, Appendix, para 2; other words in square brackets in each place they appear inserted by SI 2014/1457, art 2, Appendix, para 3.

Art 9B: inserted by SI 2014/1457, art 2, Appendix, para 4; substituted by the Public Lending Right Scheme 1982 (Commencement of Variation and Amendment) Order 2014, SI 2014/1945, Appendix, para 1.

Art 14A: in para (c), words in first pair of square brackets inserted and words in second pair of square brackets substituted by SI 2014/1457, art 2, Appendix, para 5; words in first pair of square brackets in para (ii) inserted by the Scotland Act 1998 (Consequential Modifications) (No 1) Order 1999, SI 1999/1042, art 3, Sch 1, para 19; words in second pair of square brackets in para (ii) substituted by the Medical Act 1983 (Amendment) Order 2002, SI 2002/3135, art 16(1), Sch 1, Pt II, para 23.

Art 17: words in square brackets inserted by SI 2014/1457, art 2, Appendix, para 6.

Art 20: word in square brackets substituted by SI 1997/1576, art 2, Appendix, para 3.

Art 36: number in square brackets in definition "participating period" substituted by SI 1997/1576, art 2, Appendix, para 4.

Art 38: para (2)(c), and words in square brackets in para (2)(d), (e) substituted, by the Public Lending Right Scheme 1982 (Commencement of Variations) Order 1996, SI 1996/1338, art 2, Appendix, para 1; number in square brackets in para (2)(f) substituted and words in square brackets in para (2)(g) inserted by the Public Lending Right Scheme 1982 (Commencement of Variations) Order 2005, SI 2005/1519, art 2(a), Appendix, Pt 1, para 1.

Art 39: number in square brackets substituted by SI 1997/1576, art 2, Appendix, para 5; words in second and fifth pairs of square brackets inserted by SI 2014/1457, art 2, Appendix, para 7.

Art 40: number in square brackets substituted by SI 1997/1576, art 2, Appendix, para 5.

Art 42: para (3)(c) substituted by SI 1999/420, art 2, Appendix.

Art 44: number in square brackets in para (1) substituted by SI 1997/1576, art 2, Appendix, para 5.

Art 46: in para (1)(a), sum in square brackets substituted by the Public Lending Right Scheme 1982 (Commencement of Variation) Order 2017, SI 2017/7, art 2; in para (2)(b) sum in square brackets in both places it occurs substituted by SI 2005/1519, art 2(b), Appendix, Pt 2, para 2; in para (3), sum in square brackets substituted by SI 2005/1519, art 2(b), Appendix, Pt 2, para 3.

Sch 1, Pt I: para 2 substituted by SI 1991/2618, art 2, Appendix; in para 5, words in first pair of square brackets inserted by SI 1999/1042, art 3, Sch 1, para 19, and words in second pair of square brackets substituted by SI 2002/3135, art 16(1), Sch 1, Pt II, para 23.

Sch 2: Groups A–H substituted by the Public Lending Right Scheme 1982 (Commencement of Variations) Order 1998, SI 1998/1218, art 2, Appendix, para 1.

Sch 3: revoked by SI 1984/1847, Schedule.

Sch 5: revoked by SI 2004/1258, art 2, Appendix, para (c).

COPYRIGHT AND RIGHTS IN PERFORMANCES (NOTICE OF SEIZURE) ORDER 1989

(SI 1989/1006)

NOTES

Made: 13 June 1989.
Authority: Copyright, Designs and Patents Act 1988, ss 100(4), (5), 196(4), (5).
Commencement: 1 August 1989.

[2.447]
1

This Order may be cited as the Copyright and Rights in Performances (Notice of Seizure) Order 1989 and shall come into force on 1st August 1989.

[2.448]
2

The form set out in the Schedule to this Order is hereby prescribed for the notice required under section 100(4) and section 196(4), respectively, of the Act.

SCHEDULE
THE COPYRIGHT AND RIGHTS IN PERFORMANCES (NOTICE OF SEIZURE) ORDER 1989

Article 2

NOTICE OF SEIZURE

[2.449]
To Whom it May Concern

1. Goods in which you were trading have been seized. This notice tells you who carried out the seizure, the legal grounds on which this has been done and the goods which have been seized and detained. As required by the Copyright, Designs and Patents Act 1988, notice of the proposed seizure was given to the police station at (state address).

Person carrying out seizure

2. (State name and address)

*acting on the authority of (state name and address).

Legal grounds for seizure and detention

3. This action has been taken under *section 100/section 196 of the Act which (subject to certain conditions) permits a copyright owner, or a person having performing rights or recording rights, to seize and detain infringing copies or illicit recordings found exposed or immediately available for sale or hire, or to authorise such seizure. The right to seize and detain is subject to a decision of the court under *section 114/section 204 of the Act (order as to disposal of goods seized and detained).

Nature of the goods seized and detained

*4. Infringing copies of works (within the meaning of section 27 of the Act)—(specify all articles seized)

Illicit recordings (within the meaning of section 197 of the Act)—(specify all articles seized)

Signed . . . . Date . . . .

* Delete as necessary

COPYRIGHT (CUSTOMS) REGULATIONS 1989

(SI 1989/1178)

NOTES

Made: 10 July 1989.
Authority: Copyright, Designs and Patents Act 1988, s 112(1), (2), (3).
Commencement: 1 August 1989.

[2.450]
1

These Regulations may be cited as the Copyright (Customs) Regulations 1989 and shall come into force on 1st August 1989.

[2.451]
2

(1) Notice given under section 111(1) of the Copyright, Designs and Patents Act 1988 shall be in the form set out in Schedule 1 or a form to the like effect approved by the Commissioners; and a separate notice shall be given in respect of each work.

(2) Notice given under section 111(3) of that Act shall be in the form set out in Schedule 2 or a form to the like effect approved by the Commissioners; and a separate notice shall be given in respect of each work and in respect of each expected importation into the United Kingdom.

(3) In regulations 3 to 9 notice means a notice given under either of those subsections.

[2.452]
3

The notice shall contain full particulars of the matters specified therein and shall contain a declaration by the signatory that the information given by him in the notice is true.

[2.453]
4

A fee of £30 (plus value added tax) in respect of the notice shall be paid to the Commissioners at the time it is given.

[2.454]
5

The person giving the notice shall furnish to the Commissioners a copy of the work specified in the notice at the time the notice is given and at that time or at the time the goods to which the notice relates are imported shall furnish to them such evidence as they may reasonably require to establish—

(a) his ownership of the copyright in such work;
(b) that goods detained are infringing copies; or
(c) that a person who has signed the notice as agent is duly authorised.

[2.455]
6

The person giving the notice shall give security or further security within such time and in such manner, whether by bond or by deposit of a sum of money, as the Commissioners may require, in respect of any liability or expense which they may incur in consequence of the notice by reason of the detention of any article or anything done to an article detained.

[2.456]
7

In every case, whether any security or further security is given or not, the person who has given the notice shall keep the Commissioners indemnified against all such liability and expense as is mentioned in regulation 6.

[2.457]
8

The person giving the notice shall notify the Commissioners in writing of any change in the ownership of the copyright in the work specified in the notice or other change affecting the notice within fourteen days of such change.

[2.458]
9

The notice shall be deemed to have been withdrawn—

(a) as from the expiry of fourteen days from any change in ownership of the copyright specified in the notice, whether notified to the Commissioners in accordance with regulation 8 or not; or
(b) if the person giving the notice has failed to comply with any requirement of these Regulations.

10 (*Revokes the Copyright (Customs) Regulations 1957, SI 1957/875 and the Copyright (Customs) (Amendment) Regulations 1982, SI 1982/766.*)

SCHEDULES

SCHEDULE 1

NOTICE UNDER THE COPYRIGHT, DESIGNS & PATENTS ACT 1988 REQUESTING INFRINGING COPIES OF A LITERARY, DRAMATIC OR MUSICAL WORK TO BE TREATED AS PROHIBITED GOODS

Regulation 2(1)

Please read these notes before completing this notice.

[2.459]

1. This notice may only be given by the owner of the copyright in a published literary, dramatic or musical work or a person acting on his behalf. A separate notice must be given for each work.

2. The period specified in part 1 shall not exceed 5 years and shall not extend beyond the period for which copyright is to subsist.

3. A fee of £30 (plus VAT) is payable. Please enclose a cheque for the required amount made payable to "Commissioners of Customs and Excise".

4. A copy of the work specified in part 2 should be enclosed.

5. The person who has given the notice shall keep the Commissioners of Customs and Excise indemnified against any liability or expense which they may incur as a result of detaining any article or anything done to an article detained because of this notice. You may need to provide the Commissioners with security to cover this indemnity. You will be informed when this is required.

6. Part 3 is not obligatory, but please give as many details as possible.

Part 1.

I, ... give notice that

Full name of signatory in BLOCK LETTERS

. . . .

Name and address of Owner of Copyright

. . . .

. . . .

is the owner of the copyright in the work specified below which subsists under the Copyright, Designs and Patents Act 1988 and I request that any infringing copies of the said work be treated as prohibited goods for a period starting on . . . . and ending on . . . .

Part 2.
Particulars of Work

Title: . . . .

. . . .

Full name of author/authors: . . . .

. . . .

Date copyright expires: . . . .

Part 3.
Details of expected importation

a) Date of importation . . . .

b) Place of customs declaration . . . .

c) Place of unloading . . . .

d) Country of origin . . . .

e) Country from which goods consigned . . . .

f) Bill of lading/airway bill/consignment reference number . . . .

g) Name of ship/aircraft flight number/vehicle registration number . . . .

h) Name and address of importer/consignee . . . .

i) Tariff classification and commodity code . . . .

Part 4.
Declaration

I declare that the information given by me in this notice is true.

Signature . . . .
(*Owner of copyright/Authorised agent)

Date . . . .

* Delete as necessary

Part 5.

Please send the completed notice, enclosing fee and a copy of the work, to:

HM Customs and Excise
CDB3(B)
Dorset House
Stamford Street
LONDON SE1 9PS

SCHEDULE 2
NOTICE UNDER THE COPYRIGHT, DESIGNS & PATENTS ACT 1988 REQUESTING INFRINGING COPIES OF A SOUND RECORDING OR FILM TO BE TREATED AS PROHIBITED GOODS

Regulation 2(2)

Please read these notes before completing this notice.

[2.460]
1. This notice may only be given by the owner of the copyright in a sound recording or film or a person acting on his behalf. A separate notice must be given in respect of each work and each expected importation of infringing copies of the work.

2. A fee of £30 (plus VAT) is payable. Please enclose a cheque for the required amount made payable to "Commissioners of Customs and Excise".

3. A copy of the work specified in part 2 should be enclosed.

4. The person who has given the notice shall keep the Commissioners of Customs and Excise indemnified against any liability or expense which they may incur as a result of detaining any article or anything done to an article detained because of this notice. You may need to provide the Commissioners with security to cover this indemnity. You will be informed when this is required.

5. **Part 4 is not obligatory, but please give as many details as possible.**

Part 1.

I, ... give notice that

Full name of signatory in BLOCK LETTERS

. . . .

Name and address of Owner of Copyright

....

....

is the owner of the copyright in the work specified below which subsists under the Copyright, Designs and Patents Act 1988 and that infringing copies of the work are expected to be imported into the United Kingdom and I request that these copies be treated as prohibited goods.

Part 2.
Particulars of Work

Title: ....

Label, Marking or Statement borne by work: ....

....

Date copyright expires: ....

Part 3.
Expected arrival in United Kingdom

Date: ....

Place: ....

Part 4.
Details of expected importation

a) Place of customs declaration ....

b) Place of unloading ....

c) Country of origin ....

d) Country from which goods consigned ....

e) Bill of lading/airway bill/consignment reference number ....

f) Name of ship/aircraft flight number/vehicle registration number ....

g) Name and address of importer/consignee ....

h) Tariff classification and commodity code ....

Part 5.
Declaration

I declare that the information given by me in this notice is true.

Signature . . . . Date . . . .

(*Owner of copyright/Authorised agent)

* Delete as necessary

Part 6.

Please send the completed notice, enclosing fee and a copy of the work, to:

HM Customs and Excise
CDB3(B)
Dorset House

Stamford Street
LONDON SE1 9PS

COPYRIGHT (LIBRARIANS AND ARCHIVISTS) (COPYING OF COPYRIGHT MATERIAL) REGULATIONS 1989

(SI 1989/1212)

NOTES

Made: 14 July 1989.
Authority: Copyright, Designs and Patents Act 1988, ss 37(1), (2), (4), 38, 39, 40, 41, 42, 43.
Commencement: 1 August 1989.

ARRANGEMENT OF REGULATIONS

[2.461]
1 Citation and commencement

These Regulations may be cited as the Copyright (Librarians and Archivists) (Copying of Copyright Material) Regulations 1989 and shall come into force on 1st August 1989.

[2.462]
2 Interpretation

In these Regulations—

"the Act" means the Copyright, Designs and Patents Act 1988;
"the archivist" means the archivist of a prescribed archive;
"the librarian" means the librarian of a prescribed library;
"prescribed archive" means an archive of the descriptions specified in paragraph (4) of regulation 3 below;
"prescribed library" means a library of the descriptions specified in paragraphs (1), (2) and (3) of regulation 3 below.

[2.463]
3 Descriptions of libraries and archives

(1) The descriptions of libraries specified in Part A of Schedule 1 to these Regulations are prescribed for the purposes of section 38 and 39 of the Act:

Provided that any library conducted for profit shall not be a prescribed library for the purposes of those sections.

(2) All libraries in the United Kingdom are prescribed for the purposes of sections 41, 42 and 43 of the Act as libraries the librarians of which may make and supply copies of any material to which those sections relate.

(3) Any library of a description specified in Part A of Schedule 1 to these Regulations which is not conducted for profit and any library of the description specified in Part B of that Schedule which is not conducted for profit are prescribed for the purposes of sections 41 and 42 of the Act as libraries for which copies of any material to which those sections relate may be made and supplied by the librarian of a prescribed library.

(4) All archives in the United Kingdom are prescribed for the purposes of sections 42 and 43 of the Act as archives which may make and supply copies of any material to which those sections relate and any archive within the United Kingdom which is not conducted for profit is prescribed for the purposes of section 42 of the Act as an archive for which copies of any material to which that section relates may be made and supplied by the archivist of a prescribed archive.

(5) In this regulation conducted for profit, in relation to a library or archive, means a library or archive which is established or conducted for profit or which forms part of, or is administered by, a body established or conducted for profit.

[2.464]

4 Copying by librarian of article or part of published work

(1) For the purposes of sections 38 and 39 of the Act the conditions specified in paragraph (2) of this regulation are prescribed as the conditions which must be complied with when the librarian of a prescribed library makes and supplies a copy of any article in a periodical or, as the case may be, of a part of a literary, dramatic or musical work from a published edition to a person requiring the copy.

(2) The prescribed conditions are—

(a) that no copy of any article or any part of a work shall be supplied to the person requiring the same unless—

(i) he satisfies the librarian that he requires the copy for purposes of research [for a non-commercial purpose] or private study and will not use it for any other purpose; and

(ii) he has delivered to the librarian a declaration in writing, in relation to that article or part of a work, substantially in accordance with Form A in Schedule 2 to these Regulations and signed in the manner therein indicated;

(b) that the librarian is satisfied that the requirement of such person and that of any other person—

(i) are not similar, that is to say, the requirements are not for copies of substantially the same article or part of a work at substantially the same time and for substantially the same purpose; and

(ii) are not related, that is to say, he and that person do not receive instruction to which the article or part of the work is relevant at the same time and place;

(c) that such person is not furnished—

(i) in the case of an article, with more than one copy of the article or more than one article contained in the same issue of a periodical; or

(ii) in the case of a part of a published work, with more than one copy of the same material or with a copy of more than a reasonable proportion of any work; and

(d) that such person is required to pay for the copy a sum not less than the cost (including a contribution to the general expenses of the library) attributable to its production.

(3) Unless the librarian is aware that the signed declaration delivered to him pursuant to paragraph (2)(a)(ii) above is false in a material particular, he may rely on it as to the matter he is required to be satisfied on under paragraph (2)(a)(i) above before making or supplying the copy.

NOTES

Para (2): words in square brackets inserted by the Copyright and Related Rights Regulations 2003, SI 2003/2498, reg 2(1), Sch 1, Pt 3, para 26(a), subject to transitional provisions as noted below.

Transitional provisions: the Copyright and Related Rights Regulations 2003, SI 2003/2498 came into force on 31 October 2003 and, except as expressly provided, apply to: (i) works made, (ii) performances given, (iii) databases in which database right vests which are made, and (iv) works in which publication right vests which are first published, before or after that date (see reg 31 of the 2003 Regulations, at **[2.550]**). Savings and transitional provisions are provided for in regs 32–40 of those Regulations, at **[2.423]**–**[2.436]**.

[2.465]

5 Copying by librarian to supply other libraries

(1) For the purposes of section 41 of the Act the conditions specified in paragraph (2) of this regulation are prescribed as the conditions which must be complied with when the librarian of a prescribed library makes and supplies to another prescribed library a copy of any article in a periodical or, as the case may be, of the whole or part of a published edition of a literary, dramatic or musical work required by that other prescribed library.

(2) The prescribed conditions are—

(a) that the other prescribed library is not furnished with more than one copy of the article or of the whole or part of the published edition; or

(b) that, where the requirement is for a copy of more than one article in the same issue of a periodical, or for a copy of the whole or part of a published edition, the other prescribed library furnishes a written statement to the effect that it is a prescribed library and that it does not know, and could not by reasonable inquiry ascertain, the name and address of a person entitled to authorise the making of the copy; and

(c) that the other prescribed library shall be required to pay for the copy a sum [equivalent to but not exceeding] the cost (including a contribution to the general expenses of the library) attributable to its production.

NOTES

Para (2): words in square brackets in para (c) substituted by the Copyright and Related Rights Regulations 2003, SI 2003/2498, reg 2(1), Sch 1, Pt 3, para 26(b), subject to transitional provisions as noted to reg 4 at **[2.464]**.

[2.466]

6 Copying by librarian or archivist for the purposes of replacing items in a permanent collection

(1) For the purposes of section 42 of the Act the conditions specified in paragraph (2) of this regulation are prescribed as the conditions which must be complied with before the librarian or, as the case may be, the archivist makes a copy from any item in the permanent collection of the library or archive in order to preserve or replace that item in the permanent collection of that library or archive or in the permanent collection of another prescribed library or archive.

(2) The prescribed conditions are—

(a) that the item in question is an item in the part of the permanent collection maintained by the library or archive wholly or mainly for the purposes of reference on the premises of the library or archive, or is an item in the permanent collection of the library or archive which is available on loan only to other libraries or archives;

(b) that it is not reasonably practicable for the librarian or archivist to purchase a copy of that item to fulfil the purpose under section 42(1)(a) or (b) of the Act;

(c) that the other prescribed library or archive furnishes a written statement to the effect that the item has been lost, destroyed or damaged and that it is not reasonably practicable for it to purchase a copy of that item, and that if a copy is supplied it will only be used to fulfil the purpose under section 42(1)(b) of the Act; and

(d) that the other prescribed library or archive shall be required to pay for the copy a sum [equivalent to but not exceeding] the cost (including a contribution to the general expenses of the library or archive) attributable to its production.

NOTES

Para (2): words in square brackets in para (d) substituted by the Copyright and Related Rights Regulations 2003, SI 2003/2498, reg 2(1), Sch 1, Pt 3, para 26(b), subject to transitional provisions as noted to reg 4 at **[2.464]**.

[2.467]

7 Copying by librarian or archivist of certain unpublished works

(1) For the purposes of section 43 of the Act the conditions specified in paragraph (2) of this regulation are prescribed as the conditions which must be complied with in the circumstances in which that section applies when the librarian or, as the case may be, the archivist makes and supplies a copy of the whole or part of a literary, dramatic or musical work from a document in the library or archive to a person requiring the copy.

(2) The prescribed conditions are—

(a) that no copy of the whole or part of the work shall be supplied to the person requiring the same unless—

(i) he satisfies the librarian or archivist that he requires the copy for purposes of research [for a non-commercial purpose] or private study and will not use it for any other purpose; and

(ii) he has delivered to the librarian or, as the case may be, the archivist a declaration in writing, in relation to that work, substantially in accordance with Form B in Schedule 2 to these Regulations and signed in the manner therein indicated;

(b) that such person is not furnished with more than one copy of the same material; and

(c) that such person is required to pay for the copy a sum not less than the cost (including a contribution to the general expenses of the library or archive) attributable to its production.

(3) Unless the librarian or archivist is aware that the signed declaration delivered to him pursuant to paragraph (2)(a)(ii) above is false in a material particular, he may rely on it as to the matter he is required to be satisfied on under paragraph (2)(a)(i) above before making or supplying the copy.

NOTES

Para (2): words in square brackets inserted by the Copyright and Related Rights Regulations 2003, SI 2003/2498, reg 2(1), Sch 1, Pt 3, para 26(a), subject to transitional provisions as noted to reg 4 at **[2.464]**.

8 (*Introduces Sch 3 to these Regulations, which contains revocations only.*)

SCHEDULES

SCHEDULE 1

Regulation 3

PART A

[2.468]
Regulation 3(1), (3)

1. Any library administered by—
- (a) a library authority within the meaning of the Public Libraries and Museums Act 1964 in relation to England and Wales;
- (b) a statutory library authority within the meaning of the Public Libraries (Scotland) Act 1955, in relation to Scotland;
- (c) an Education and Library Board within the meaning of the Education and Libraries (Northern Ireland) Order 1986, in relation to Northern Ireland.

2. The British Library, the National Library of Wales, the National Library of Scotland, the Bodleian Library, Oxford and the University Library, Cambridge.

3. Any library of a school within the meaning of section 174 of the Act and any library of a description of educational establishment specified under that section in the Copyright (Educational Establishments) (No 2) Order 1989.

4. Any parliamentary library or library administered as part of a government department, including a Northern Ireland department, [or as part of the Scottish Administration] or any library conducted for or administered by an agency which is administered by a Minister of the Crown.

5. Any library administered by—
- (a) in England and Wales, a local authority within the meaning of the Local Government Act 1972, the Common Council of the City of London or the Council of the Isles of Scilly;
- (b) in Scotland, a local authority within the meaning of the Local Government (Scotland) Act 1973;
- (c) in Northern Ireland, a district council established under the Local Government Act (Northern Ireland) 1972.

6. Any other library conducted for the purpose of facilitating or encouraging the study of bibliography, education, fine arts, history, languages, law, literature, medicine, music, philosophy, religion, science (including natural and social science) or technology, or administered by any establishment or organisation which is conducted wholly or mainly for such a purpose.

PART B

[2.469]
Regulation 3(3)

Any library outside the United Kingdom which is conducted wholly or mainly for the purpose of facilitating or encouraging the study of bibliography, education, fine arts, history, languages, law, literature, medicine, music, philosophy, religion, science (including natural and social science) or technology.

NOTES

Para 4: words in square brackets inserted by the Scotland Act 1998 (Consequential Modifications) (No 1) Order 1999, SI 1999/1042, art 3, Sch 1, Pt II, para 15.

SCHEDULE 2

Regulations 4, 7

FORM A

Declaration: Copy of article or part of published work

[2.470]
To:

The Librarian of . . . . Library

[Address of Library]

Please supply me with a copy of:

*the article in the periodical, the particulars of which are [ ] *the part of the published work, the particulars of which are [ ]

required by me for the purposes of research or private study.

2. I declare that—

(a) I have not previously been supplied with a copy of the same material by you or any other librarian;

(b) I will not use the copy except for research [for a non-commercial purpose] or private study and will not supply a copy of it to any other person; and

(c) to the best of my knowledge no other person with whom I work or study has made or intends to make, at or about the same time as this request, a request for substantially the same material for substantially the same purpose.

3. I understand that if the declaration is false in a material particular the copy supplied to me by you will be an infringing copy and that I shall be liable for infringement of copyright as if I had made the copy myself.

† Signature . . . .

Date . . . .

Name . . . .

Address . . . .

. . . .

. . . .

* Delete whichever is inappropriate.

† This must be the personal signature of the person making the request. A stamped or typewritten signature, or the signature of an agent, is NOT acceptable.

NOTES

Para 2: words in square brackets inserted by the Copyright and Related Rights Regulations 2003, SI 2003/2498, reg 2(1), Sch 1, Pt 3, para 26(c), subject to transitional provisions as noted to reg 4 at **[2.464]**.

FORM B

Declaration: Copy of whole or part of unpublished work

[2.471]
To:

The *Librarian/Archivist of . . . . *Library/Archive

[Address of Library/Archive]

Please supply me with a copy of:

the *whole/following part [particulars of part] of the [particulars of the unpublished work]

required by me for the purposes of research or private study.

2. I declare that—

(a) I have not previously been supplied with a copy of the same material by you or any other librarian or archivist;

(b) I will not use the copy except for research [for a non-commercial purpose] or private study and will not supply a copy of it to any other person; and

(c) to the best of my knowledge the work had not been published before the document was deposited in your *library/archive and the copyright owner has not prohibited copying of the work.

3. I understand that if the declaration is false in a material particular the copy supplied to me by you will be an infringing copy and that I shall liable for infringement of copyright as if I had made the copy myself.

† Signature . . . .

Date . . . .

Name . . . .

Address . . . .

. . . .

. . . .

* Delete whichever is inappropriate.

† This must be the personal signature of the person making the request. A stamped or typewritten signature, or the signature of an agent, is NOT acceptable.

NOTES

Para 2: words in square brackets inserted by the Copyright and Related Rights Regulations 2003, SI 2003/2498, reg 2(1), Sch 1, Pt 3, para 26(c), subject to transitional provisions as noted to reg 4 at **[2.464]**.

SCHEDULE 3

(*Schedule 3 contains revocations only.*)

COPYRIGHT (MATERIAL OPEN TO PUBLIC INSPECTION) (MARKING OF COPIES OF PLANS AND DRAWINGS) ORDER 1990

(SI 1990/1427)

NOTES

Made: 16 July 1990.
Authority: Copyright, Designs and Patents Act 1988, s 47(4).
Commencement: 15 August 1990.

[2.472]
1

This Order may be cited as the Copyright (Material Open to Public Inspection) (Marking of Copies of Plans and Drawings) Order 1990 and shall come into force on 15th August 1990.

[2.473]
2

Subsection (2) of section 47 of the Copyright, Designs and Patents Act 1988 shall, in the case of a plan or drawing which is open to public inspection pursuant to a statutory requirement, apply only to copies of the plan or drawing marked in the following manner—

"This copy has been made by or with the authority of (insert the name of the person required to make the plan or drawing open to public inspection) pursuant to section 47 of the Copyright, Designs and Patents Act 1988. Unless that Act provides a relevant exception to copyright, the copy must not be copied without the prior permission of the copyright owner."

DURATION OF COPYRIGHT AND RIGHTS IN PERFORMANCES REGULATIONS 1995

(SI 1995/3297)

NOTES

Made: 19 December 1995.
Authority: European Communities Act 1972, s 2(2), (4).

Commencement: 1 January 1996.

ARRANGEMENT OF REGULATIONS

PART I
INTRODUCTORY PROVISIONS

PART III
SAVINGS AND TRANSITIONAL PROVISIONS

Introductory

Copyright

Rights in performances

Supplementary

PART I
INTRODUCTORY PROVISIONS

[2.474]
1 Citation, commencement and extent

(1) These Regulations may be cited as the Duration of Copyright and Rights in Performances Regulations 1995.

(2) These Regulations come into force on 1st January 1996.

(3) These Regulations extend to the whole of the United Kingdom.

[2.475]
2 Interpretation

In these Regulations—

"EEA Agreement" means the Agreement on the European Economic Area signed at Oporto on 2nd May 1992, as adjusted by the Protocol signed at Brussels on 17th March 1993; and

["EEA state" means a member State, Iceland, Liechtenstein or Norway.]

NOTES

Definition "EEA state" substituted by the Intellectual Property (Enforcement, etc) Regulations 2006, SI 2006/1028, reg 2(3), Sch 3, para 1.

[2.476]
3 Implementation of Directive, &c

These Regulations make provision for the purpose of implementing—

(a) the main provisions of Council Directive No 93/98/EEC of 29th October 1993 harmonising the term of protection of copyright and certain related rights; and

(b) certain obligations of the United Kingdom created by or arising under the EEA Agreement so far as relevant to the implementation of that Directive.

[2.477]
4 Scheme of the regulations

The Copyright, Designs and Patents Act 1988 is amended in accordance with the provisions of Part II of these Regulations, subject to the savings and transitional provisions in Part III of these Regulations.

5–11 *((Pt II) amend the Copyright, Designs and Patents Act 1988, at* **[2.7]** *et seq.)*

PART III
SAVINGS AND TRANSITIONAL PROVISIONS

Introductory

[2.478]
12 Introductory

(1) References in this Part to "commencement", without more, are to the date on which these Regulations come into force.

(2) In this Part—

"the 1988 Act" means the Copyright, Designs and Patents Act 1988;

"the 1988 provisions" means the provisions of that Act as they stood immediately before commencement (including the provisions of Schedule 1 to that Act continuing the effect of earlier enactments); and

"the new provisions" means the provisions of that Act as amended by these Regulations.

(3) Expressions used in this Part which are defined for the purposes of Part I or II of the 1988 Act, in particular references to the copyright owner, have the same meaning as in that Part.

[2.479]
13 Films not protected as such

In relation to a film in which copyright does not or did not subsist as such but which is or was protected—

(a) as an original dramatic work, or

(b) by virtue of the protection of the photographs forming part of the film,

references in the new provisions, and in this Part, to copyright in a film are to any copyright in the film as an original dramatic work or, as the case may be, in photographs forming part of the film.

Copyright

[2.480]
14 Copyright: interpretation

(1) In the provisions of this Part relating to copyright—

(a) "existing", in relation to a work, means made before commencement; and

(b) "existing copyright work" means a work in which copyright subsisted immediately before commencement.

(2) For the purposes of those provisions a work of which the making extended over a period shall be taken to have been made when its making was completed.

(3) References in those provisions to "moral rights" are to the rights conferred by Chapter IV of Part I of the 1988 Act.

[2.481]
15 Duration of copyright: general saving

(1) Copyright in an existing copyright work shall continue to subsist until the date on which it would have expired under the 1988 provisions if that date is later than the date on which copyright would expire under the new provisions.

(2) Where paragraph (1) has effect, section 57 of the 1988 Act (anonymous or pseudonymous works: acts permitted on assumptions as to expiry of copyright or death of author) applies as it applied immediately before commencement (that is, without the amendments made by Regulation 5(2)).

[2.482]
16 Duration of copyright: application of new provisions

The new provisions relating to duration of copyright apply—

(a) to copyright works made after commencement;

(b) to existing works which first qualify for copyright protection after commencement;
(c) to existing copyright works, subject to Regulation 15 (general saving for any longer period applicable under 1988 provisions); . . .
(d) to existing works in which copyright expired before 31st December 1995 but which were on 1st July 1995 protected in another EEA state under legislation relating to copyright or related rights[; and
(e) to existing works which qualify for copyright protection as a result of the disapplication of paragraph 6(1) of Schedule 1 to the 1988 Act by sub-paragraph (1A) of paragraph 6 of Schedule 1 to the 1988 Act.]

NOTES

Word omitted from para (c) revoked and para (e) inserted, together with word preceding it, by the Copyright (Amendment) Regulations 2016, SI 2016/1210, reg 3(1), (2).

[2.483]
17 Extended and revived copyright

In the following provisions of this Part—
"extended copyright" means any copyright which subsists by virtue of the new provisions after the date on which it would have expired under the 1988 provisions; and
"revived copyright" means any copyright which subsists by virtue of the new provisions after having expired under the 1988 provisions or any earlier enactment relating to copyright.

[2.484]
18 Ownership of extended copyright

(1) The person who is the owner of the copyright in a work immediately before commencement is as from commencement the owner of any extended copyright in the work, subject as follows.

(2) If he is entitled to copyright for a period less than the whole of the copyright period under the 1988 provisions, any extended copyright is part of the reversionary interest expectant on the termination of that period.

[2.485]
19 Ownership of revived copyright

(1) The person who was the owner of the copyright in a work immediately before it expired (the "former copyright owner") is as from commencement the owner of any revived copyright in the work, subject as follows.

(2) If the former copyright owner has died before commencement, or in the case of a legal person has ceased to exist before commencement, the revived copyright shall vest—
(a) in the case of a film, in the principal director of the film or his personal representatives, and
(b) in any other case, in the author of the work or his personal representatives.

(3) Where revived copyright vests in personal representatives by virtue of paragraph (2), it shall be held by them for the benefit of the person who would have been entitled to it had it been vested in the principal director or author immediately before his death and had devolved as part of his estate.

[2.486]
20 Prospective ownership of extended or revived copyright

(1) Where by an agreement made before commencement in relation to extended or revived copyright, and signed by or on behalf of the prospective owner of the copyright, the prospective owner purports to assign the extended or revived copyright (wholly or partially) to another person, then if, on commencement the assignee or another person claiming under him would be entitled as against all other persons to require the copyright to be vested in him, the copyright shall vest in the assignee or his successor in title by virtue of this paragraph.

(2) A licence granted by a prospective owner of extended or revived copyright is binding on every successor in title to his interest (or prospective interest) in the right, except a purchaser in good faith for valuable consideration and without notice (actual or constructive) of the licence or a person deriving title from such a purchaser; and references in Part I of the 1988 Act to doing anything with, or without, the licence of the copyright owner shall be construed accordingly.

(3) In paragraph (2) "prospective owner" includes a person who is prospectively entitled to extended or revived copyright by virtue of such an agreement as is mentioned in paragraph (1).

[2.487]
21 Extended copyright: existing licences, agreement, &c

(1) Any copyright licence, any term or condition of an agreement relating to the exploitation of a copyright work, or any waiver or assertion of moral rights, which—
(a) subsists immediately before commencement in relation to an existing copyright work, and
(b) is not to expire before the end of the copyright period under the 1988 provisions,
shall continue to have effect during the period of any extended copyright, subject to any agreement to the contrary.

(2) Any copyright licence, or term or condition relating to the exploitation of a copyright work, imposed by order of the Copyright Tribunal which—

(a) subsists immediately before commencement in relation to an existing copyright work, and

(b) is not to expire before the end of the copyright period under the 1988 provisions,

shall continue to have effect during the period of any extended copyright, subject to any further order of the Tribunal.

[2.488]

22 Revived copyright: exercise of moral rights

(1) The following provisions have effect with respect to the exercise of moral rights in relation to a work in which there is revived copyright.

(2) Any waiver or assertion of moral rights which subsisted immediately before the expiry of copyright shall continue to have effect during the period of revived copyright.

(3) Moral rights are exercisable after commencement by the author of a work or, as the case may be, the director of a film in which revived copyright subsists, as with any other copyright work.

(4) Where the author or director died before commencement—

(a) the rights conferred by—

section 77 (right to identification as author or director),

section 80 (right to object to derogatory treatment of work), or

section 85 (right to privacy of certain photographs and films),

are exercisable after commencement by his personal representatives, and

(b) any infringement after commencement of the right conferred by section 84 (false attribution) is actionable by his personal representatives.

(5) Any damages recovered by personal representatives by virtue of this Regulation in respect of an infringement after a person's death shall devolve as part of his estate as if the right of action had subsisted and been vested in him immediately before his death.

(6) Nothing in these Regulations shall be construed as causing a moral right to be exercisable if, or to the extent that, the right was excluded by virtue of paragraph 23 or 24 of Schedule 1 on the commencement of the 1988 Act or would have been so excluded if copyright had not previously expired.

[2.489]

23 Revived copyright: saving for acts of exploitation when work in public domain, &c

(1) No act done before commencement shall be regarded as infringing revived copyright in a work.

(2) It is not an infringement of revived copyright in a work—

(a) to do anything after commencement in pursuance of arrangements made before 1st January 1995 at a time when copyright did not subsist in the work, or

(b) to issue to the public after commencement copies of the work made before 1st July 1995 at a time when copyright did not subsist in the work.

(3) It is not an infringement of revived copyright in a work to do anything after commencement in relation to a literary, dramatic, musical or artistic work or a film made before commencement, or made in pursuance of arrangements made before commencement, which contains a copy of that work or is an adaptation of that work if—

(a) the copy or adaptation was made before 1st July 1995 at a time when copyright did not subsist in the work in which revived copyright subsists, or

(b) the copy or adaptation was made in pursuance of arrangements made before 1st July 1995 at a time when copyright did not subsist in the work in which revived copyright subsists.

(4) It is not an infringement of revived copyright in a work to do after commencement anything which is a restricted act in relation to the work if the act is done at a time when, or is done in pursuance of arrangements made at a time when, the name and address of a person entitled to authorise the act cannot by reasonable inquiry be ascertained.

(5) In this Regulation "arrangements" means arrangements for the exploitation of the work in question.

(6) It is not an infringement of any moral right to do anything which by virtue of this Regulation is not an infringement of copyright.

[2.490]

24 Revived copyright: use as of right subject to reasonable royalty

(1) In the case of a work in which revived copyright subsists any acts restricted by the copyright shall be treated as licensed by the copyright owner, subject only to the payment of such reasonable royalty or other remuneration as may be agreed or determined in default of agreement by the Copyright Tribunal.

(2) A person intending to avail himself of the right conferred by this Regulation must give reasonable notice of his intention to the copyright owner, stating when he intends to begin to do the acts.

(3) If he does not give such notice, his acts shall not be treated as licensed.

(4) If he does give such notice, his acts shall be treated as licensed and a reasonable royalty or other remuneration shall be payable in respect of them despite the fact that its amount is not agreed or determined until later.

(5) This Regulation does not apply if or to the extent that a licence to do the acts could be granted by a licensing body (within the meaning of section 116(2) of the 1988 Act), whether or not under a licensing scheme.

(6) No royalty or other remuneration is payable by virtue of this Regulation in respect of anything for which a royalty or other remuneration is payable under Schedule 6 to the 1988 Act.

NOTES

Revoked by the Copyright (Amendment) Regulations 2016, SI 2016/1210, regs 3(1), (3), subject to savings in reg 4 thereof which provides that reg 24 continues to apply on or after 6 April 2017 in relation to acts restricted by copyright done in relation to a work in which revived copyright subsists but only where, in relation to those acts, a royalty or remuneration is agreed or determined for the purposes of that regulation before 6 April 2017.

25 (*Revoked by the Copyright (Amendment) Regulations 2016, SI 2016/1210, reg 3(1), (4).*)

[2.491]
26 Film sound tracks: application of new provisions

(1) The new provisions relating to the treatment of film sound tracks apply to existing sound tracks as from commencement.

(2) The owner of any copyright in a film has as from commencement corresponding rights as copyright owner in any existing sound track treated as part of the film; but without prejudice to any rights of the owner of the copyright in the sound track as a sound recording.

(3) Anything done before commencement under or in relation to the copyright in the sound recording continues to have effect and shall have effect, so far as concerns the sound track, in relation to the film as in relation to the sound recording.

(4) It is not an infringement of the copyright in the film (or of any moral right in the film) to do anything after commencement in pursuance of arrangements for the exploitation of the sound recording made before commencement.

Rights in performances

[2.492]
27 Rights in performances: interpretation

(1) In the provisions of this Part relating to rights in performances—

(a) "existing", in relation to a performance, means given before commencement; and

(b) "existing protected performance" means a performance in relation to which rights under Part II of the 1988 act (rights in performances) subsisted immediately before commencement.

(2) References in this Part to performers' rights are to the rights given by section 180(1)(a) of the 1988 Act and references to recording rights are to the rights given by section 180(1)(b) of that Act.

[2.493]
28 Duration of rights in performances: general saving

Any rights under Part II of the 1988 Act in an existing protected performance shall continue to subsist until the date on which they would have expired under the 1988 provisions if that date is later than the date on which the rights would expire under the new provisions.

[2.494]
29 Duration of rights in performances: application of new provisions

The new provisions relating to the duration of rights under Part II of the 1988 Act apply—

(a) to performances taking place after commencement;

(b) to existing performances which first qualify for protection under Part II of the 1988 Act after commencement;

(c) to existing protected performances, subject to Regulation 28 (general saving for any longer period applicable under 1988 provisions); and

(d) to existing performances—

(i) in which rights under Part II of the 1988 Act expired after the commencement of that Part and before 31st December 1995, or

(ii) which were protected by earlier enactments relating to the protection of performers and in which rights under that Part did not arise by reason only that the performance was given at a date such that the rights would have ceased to subsist before the commencement of that Part,

but which were on 1st July 1995 protected in another EEA state under legislation relating to copyright or related rights.

Part 2 Copyright

[2.495]
30 Extended and revived performance rights

In the following provisions of this Part—

"extended performance rights" means rights under Part II of the 1988 Act which subsist by virtue of the new provisions after the date on which they would have expired under the 1988 provisions; and

"revived performance rights" means rights under Part II of the 1988 Act which subsist by virtue of the new provisions—

(a) after having expired under the 1988 provisions, or

(b) in relation to a performance which was protected by earlier enactments relating to the protection of performers and in which rights under that Part did not arise by reason only that the performance was given at a date such that the rights would have ceased to subsist before the commencement of that Part.

References in the following provisions of this Part to "revived pre-1988 rights" are to revived performance rights within paragraph (b) of the above definition.

[2.496]
31 Entitlement to extended or revived performance rights

(1) Any extended performance rights are exercisable as from commencement by the person who was entitled to exercise those rights immediately before commencement, that is—

(a) in the case of performers' rights, the performer or (if he has died) the person entitled by virtue of section 192(2) of the 1988 Act to exercise those rights;

(b) in the case of recording rights, the person who was within the meaning of section 185 of the 1988 Act the person having those rights.

(2) Any revived performance rights are exercisable as from commencement—

(a) in the case of rights which expired after the commencement of the 1988 Act, by the person who was entitled to exercise those rights immediately before they expired;

(b) in the case of revived pre-1988 performers' rights, by the performer or his personal representatives;

(c) in the case of revived pre-1988 recording rights, by the person who would have been the person having those rights immediately before the commencement of the 1988 Act or, if earlier, immediately before the death of the performer, applying the provisions of section 185 of that Act to the circumstances then obtaining.

(3) Any remuneration or damages received by a person's personal representatives by virtue of a right conferred on them by paragraph (1) or (2) shall devolve as part of that person's estate as if the right had subsisted and been vested in him immediately before his death.

[2.497]
32 Extended performance rights: existing consents, agreement, &c

Any consent, or any term or condition of an agreement, relating to the exploitation of an existing protected performance which—

(a) subsists immediately before commencement, and

(b) is not to expire before the end of the period for which rights under Part II of the 1988 Act subsist in relation to that performance,

shall continue to subsist during the period of any extended performance rights, subject to any agreement to the contrary.

[2.498]
33 Revived performance rights: saving for acts of exploitation when performance in public domain, &c

(1) No act done before commencement shall be regarded as infringing revived performance rights in a performance.

(2) It is not an infringement of revived performance rights in a performance—

(a) to do anything after commencement in pursuance of arrangements made before 1st January 1995 at a time when the performance was not protected, or

(b) to issue to the public after commencement a recording of a performance made before 1st July 1995 at a time when the performance was not protected.

(3) It is not an infringement of revived performance rights in a performance to do anything after commencement in relation to a sound recording or film made before commencement, or made in pursuance of arrangements made before commencement, which contains a recording of the performance if—

(a) the recording of the performance was made before 1st July 1995 at a time when the performance was not protected, or

(b) the recording of the performance was made in pursuance of arrangements made before 1st July 1995 at a time when the performance was not protected.

(4) It is not an infringement of revived performance rights in a performance to do after commencement anything at a time when, or in pursuance of arrangements made at a time when, the name and address of a person entitled to authorise the act cannot by reasonable inquiry be ascertained.

(5) In this Regulation "arrangements" means arrangements for the exploitation of the performance in question.

(6) References in this Regulation to a performance being protected are—

(a) in relation to the period after the commencement of the 1988 Act, to rights under Part II of that Act subsisting in relation to the performance, and

(b) in relation to earlier periods, to the consent of the performer being required under earlier enactments relating to the protection of performers.

[2.499]

34 Revived performance rights: use as of right subject to reasonable remuneration

(1) In the case of a performance in which revived performance rights subsist any acts which require the consent of any person under Part II of the 1988 Act (the "rights owner") shall be treated as having that consent, subject only to the payment of such reasonable remuneration as may be agreed or determined in default of agreement by the Copyright Tribunal.

(2) A person intending to avail himself of the right conferred by this Regulation must give reasonable notice of his intention to the rights owner, stating when he intends to begin to do the acts.

(3) If he does not give such notice, his acts shall not be treated as having consent.

(4) If he does give such notice, his acts shall be treated as having consent and reasonable remuneration shall be payable in respect of them despite the fact that its amount is not agreed or determined until later.

NOTES

Revoked by the Copyright (Amendment) Regulations 2016, SI 2016/1210, reg 3(1), (5), subject to savings in reg 5 thereof which provides that reg 34 continues to apply on or after 6 April 2017 in relation to acts which require the consent of the rights owner done in relation to a performance in which revived performance rights subsist but only where, in relation to those acts, remuneration is agreed or determined for the purposes of that regulation before 6 April 2017.

35 *(Revoked by the Copyright (Amendment) Regulations 2016, SI 2016/1210, reg 3(1), (6).)*

Supplementary

[2.500]

36 Construction of references to EEA states

(1) For the purpose of the new provisions relating to the term of copyright protection applicable to a work of which the country of origin is not an EEA state and of which the author is not a national of an EEA state—

(a) a work first published before 1st July 1995 shall be treated as published in an EEA state if it was on that date regarded under the law of the United Kingdom or another EEA state as having been published in that state;

(b) an unpublished film made before 1st July 1995 shall be treated as originating in an EEA state if it was on that date regarded under the law of the United Kingdom or another EEA state as a film whose maker had his headquarters in, or was domiciled or resident in, that state; and

(c) the author of a work made before 1st July 1995 shall be treated as an EEA national if he was on that date regarded under the law of the United Kingdom or another EEA state as a national of that state.

The references above to the law of another EEA state are to the law of that state having effect for the purposes of rights corresponding to those provided for in Part I of the 1988 Act.

(2) For the purposes of the new provisions relating to the term of protection applicable to a performance where the performer is not a national of an EEA state, the performer of a performance given before 1st July 1995 shall be treated as an EEA national if he was on that date regarded under the law of the United Kingdom or another EEA state as a national of that state.

The reference above to the law of another EEA state is to the law of that state having effect for the purposes of rights corresponding to those provided for in Part II of the 1988 Act.

(3) In this Regulation "another EEA state" means an EEA state other than the United Kingdom.

COPYRIGHT AND RELATED RIGHTS REGULATIONS 1996

(SI 1996/2967)

NOTES

Made: 26 November 1996.
Authority: European Communities Act 1972, s 2(2), (4).

Commencement: 1 December 1996.

ARRANGEMENT OF REGULATIONS

PART I
INTRODUCTORY PROVISIONS

PART II
AMENDMENTS OF THE COPYRIGHT, DESIGNS AND PATENTS ACT 1988

Publication right

Authorship of films and certain photographs

PART III
TRANSITIONAL PROVISIONS AND SAVINGS

General provisions

Special provisions

PART I
INTRODUCTORY PROVISIONS

[2.501]

1 Citation, commencement and extent

(1) These Regulations may be cited as the Copyright and Related Rights Regulations 1996.

(2) These Regulations come into force on 1st December 1996.

(3) These Regulations extend to the whole of the United Kingdom.

[2.502]

2 Interpretation

In these Regulations—

"EEA Agreement" means the Agreement on the European Economic Area signed at Oporto on 2nd May 1992, as adjusted by the Protocol signed at Brussels on 17th March 1993; and

["EEA state" means a member State, Iceland, Liechtenstein or Norway].

NOTES

Definition "EEA state" substituted by the Intellectual Property (Enforcement, etc) Regulations 2006, SI 2006/1028, reg 2(3), Sch 3, paras 2, 3.

[2.503]

3 Implementation of Directives, &c

These Regulations make provision for the purpose of implementing—

(a) Council Directive No 92/100/EEC of 19 November 1992 on rental right and lending right and on certain rights related to copyright in the field of intellectual property;

(b) Council Directive No 93/83/EEC of 27 September 1993 on the coordination of certain rules concerning copyright and rights related to copyright applicable to satellite broadcasting and cable retransmission;

(c) the provisions of Council Directive No 93/98/EEC of 29 October 1993 harmonising the term of protection of copyright and certain related rights, so far as not implemented by the Duration of Copyright and Rights in Performances Regulations 1995; and

(d) certain obligations of the United Kingdom created by or arising under the EEA Agreement so far as relevant to the implementation of those Directives.

[2.504]

4 Scheme of the regulations

The Copyright, Designs, and Patents Act 1988 is amended in accordance with the provisions of Part II of these Regulations, subject to the savings and transitional provisions in Part III of these Regulations.

PART II
AMENDMENTS OF THE COPYRIGHT, DESIGNS AND PATENTS ACT 1988

5–15 (*Amend the Copyright, Designs and Patents Act 1988, at* **[2.7]** *et seq, the Public Libraries (Scotland) Act 1955, the Public Libraries and Museums Act 1964, and the Education and Libraries (Northern Ireland) Order 1986, SI 1986/594.*)

Publication right

[2.505]

16 Publication right

(1) A person who after the expiry of copyright protection, publishes for the first time a previously unpublished work has, in accordance with the following provisions, a property right ("publication right") equivalent to copyright.

(2) For this purpose publication includes any [making available] to the public, in particular—

(a) the issue of copies to the public;

(b) making the work available by means of an electronic retrieval system;

(c) the rental or lending of copies of the work to the public;

(d) the performance, exhibition or showing of the work in public; or

[(e) communicating the work to the public.]

(3) No account shall be taken for this purpose of any unauthorised act.

In relation to a time when there is no copyright in the work, an unauthorised act means an act done without the consent of the owner of the physical medium in which the work is embodied or on which it is recorded.

(4) A work qualifies for publication right protection only if—

(a) first publication is in the European Economic Area, and

(b) the publisher of the work is at the time of first publication a national of an EEA state.

Where two or more persons jointly publish the work, it is sufficient for the purposes of paragraph (b) if any of them is a national of an EEA state.

(5) No publication right arises from the publication of a work in which Crown copyright or Parliamentary copyright subsisted.

(6) Publication right expires at the end of the period of 25 years from the end of the calendar year in which the work was first published.

(7) In this regulation [and regulation 17A] a "work" means a literary, dramatic, musical or artistic work or a film.

(8) Expressions used in this regulation (other than "publication") have the same meaning as in Part I.

NOTES

Para (2): words in first pair of square brackets substituted, and sub-para (e) substituted, by the Copyright and Related Rights Regulations 2003, SI 2003/2498, reg 2(1), Sch 1, Pt 3, para 27, subject to transitional provisions as noted below.

Para (7): words in square brackets inserted by the Intellectual Property (Enforcement, etc) Regulations 2006, SI 2006/1028, reg 2(3), Sch 3, paras 2, 4.

Transitional provisions: the Copyright and Related Rights Regulations 2003, SI 2003/2498 came into force on 31 October 2003 and, except as expressly provided, apply to: (i) works made, (ii) performances given, (iii) databases in which database right vests which are made, and (iv) works in which publication right vests which are first published, before or after that date (see reg 31 of the 2003 Regulations, at **[2.550]**). Savings and transitional provisions are provided for in regs 32–40 of those Regulations, at **[2.551]**–**[2.559]**.

[2.506]

17 Application of copyright provisions to publication right

(1) The substantive provisions of Part I relating to copyright (but not moral rights in copyright works), that is, the relevant provisions of—

Chapter II (rights of copyright owner),

Part 2 Copyright

Chapter III (acts permitted in relation to copyright works),
Chapter V (dealings with rights in copyright works),
Chapter VI (remedies for infringement), and
Chapter VII (copyright licensing),

apply in relation to publication right as in relation to copyright, subject to the following exceptions and modifications.

(2) The following provisions do not apply—

(a) in Chapter III (acts permitted in relation to copyright works), sections 57, 64, 66A and 67;
(b) in Chapter VI (remedies for infringement), sections 104 to 106;
(c) in Chapter VII (copyright licensing), section 116(4).

(3) The following provisions have effect with the modifications indicated—

(a) in section 107(4) and (5) (offences of making or dealing in infringing articles, &c), the maximum punishment on summary conviction is imprisonment for a term not exceeding three months or a fine not exceeding level 5 on the standard scale, or both;
(b) in sections 116(2), 117 and 124 for "works of more than one author" substitute "works of more than one publisher".

(4) The other relevant provisions of Part I, that is—

in Chapter I, provisions defining expressions used generally in Part I,
Chapter VIII (the Copyright Tribunal),
in Chapter IX—
section 161 (territorial waters and the continental shelf), and
section 162 (British ships, aircraft and hovercraft), and
in Chapter X—
section 171(1) and (3) (savings for other rules of law, &c), and
sections 172 to 179 (general interpretation provisions),

apply, with any necessary adaptations, for the purposes of supplementing the substantive provisions of that Part as applied by this regulation.

(5) Except where the context otherwise requires, any other enactment relating to copyright (whether passed or made before or after these regulations) applies in relation to publication right as in relation to copyright.

In this paragraph "enactment" includes an enactment contained in subordinate legislation within the meaning of the Interpretation Act 1978.

[2.507]
[17A Presumptions relevant to works subject to publication right

In proceedings brought by virtue of Chapter 6 of Part 1 of the Copyright, Designs and Patents Act 1988, as applied to publication right by regulation 17, with respect to a work, where copies of the work as issued to the public bear a statement that a named person was the owner of publication right in the work at the date of issue of the copies, the statement shall be admissible as evidence of the fact stated and shall be presumed to be correct until the contrary is proved.]

NOTES

Inserted, together with reg 17B, by the Intellectual Property (Enforcement, etc) Regulations 2006, SI 2006/1028, reg 2(3), Sch 3, paras 2, 5.

[2.508]
[17B Application of presumptions in relation to an order for delivery up in criminal proceedings

Regulation 17A does not apply to proceedings for an offence under section 107 of the Copyright, Designs and Patents Act 1988 as applied and modified by regulation 17 in relation to publication right; but without prejudice to its application in proceedings for an order under section 108 of the Copyright, Designs and Patents Act 1988 as that section applies to publication right by virtue of regulation 17.]

NOTES

Inserted as noted to reg 17A at **[2.507]**.

Authorship of films and certain photographs

18 (*Amends the Copyright, Designs and Patents Act 1988 at* **[2.7]** *et seq.*)

[2.509]
19 Clarification of transitional provisions relating to pre-1989 photographs

Any question arising, in relation to photographs which were existing works within the meaning of Schedule 1, as to who is to be regarded as the author for the purposes of—

(a) regulations 15 and 16 of the Duration of Copyright and Rights in Performances Regulations 1995 (duration of copyright: application of new provisions subject to general saving), or
(b) regulation 19(2)(b) of those regulations (ownership of revived copyright),

is to be determined in accordance with section 9 as in force on the commencement of those regulations (and not, by virtue of paragraph 10 of Schedule 1, in accordance with the law in force at the time when the work was made).

20–24 (*Amend the Copyright, Designs and Patents Act 1988 at* **[2.7]** *et seq.*)

PART III
TRANSITIONAL PROVISIONS AND SAVINGS

General provisions

[2.510]
25 Introductory

(1) In this Part—

"commencement" means the commencement of these Regulations; and

"existing", in relation to a work or performance, means made or given before commencement.

(2) For the purposes of this Part a work of which the making extended over a period shall be taken to have been made when its making was completed.

(3) In this Part a "new right" means a right arising by virtue of these Regulations, in relation to a copyright work or a qualifying performance, to authorise or prohibit an act.

The expression does not include—

(a) a right corresponding to a right which existed immediately before commencement, or

(b) a right to remuneration arising by virtue of these Regulations.

(4) Expressions used in this Part have the same meaning in relation to copyright as they have in Part I of the Copyright, Designs and Patents Act 1988, and in relation to performances as in Part II of that Act.

[2.511]
26 General rules

(1) Subject to anything in regulations 28 to 36 (special transitional provisions and savings), these regulations apply to copyright works made, and to performances given, before or after commencement.

(2) No act done before commencement shall be regarded as an infringement of any new right, or as giving rise to any right to remuneration arising by virtue of these Regulations.

[2.512]
27 Saving for certain existing agreements

(1) Except as otherwise expressly provided, nothing in these Regulations affects an agreement made before 19th November 1992.

(2) No act done in pursuance of any such agreement after commencement shall be regarded as an infringement of any new right.

Special provisions

[2.513]
28 Broadcasts

The provisions of—

regulation 5 (place where broadcast treated as made) and

regulation 6 (safeguards in relation to certain satellite broadcasts),

have effect in relation to broadcasts made after commencement.

[2.514]
29 Satellite broadcasting: international co-production agreements

(1) This regulation applies to an agreement concluded before 1st January 1995—

(a) between two or more co-producers of a film, one of whom is a national of an EEA state, and

(b) the provisions of which grant to the parties exclusive rights to exploit all communication to the public of the film in separate geographical areas.

(2) Where such an agreement giving such exclusive exploitation rights in relation to the United Kingdom does not expressly or by implication address satellite broadcasting from the United Kingdom, the person to whom those exclusive rights have been granted shall not make any such broadcast without the consent of any other party to the agreement whose language-related exploitation rights would be adversely affected by that broadcast.

[2.515]
30 New rights: exercise of rights in relation to performances

(1) Any new right conferred by these Regulations in relation to a qualifying performance is exercisable as from commencement by the performer or (if he has died) by the person who immediately before commencement was entitled by virtue of section 192(2) to exercise the rights conferred on the performer by Part II in relation to that performance.

(2) Any remuneration or damages received by a person's personal representatives by virtue of a right conferred on them by paragraph (1) shall devolve as part of that person's estate as if the right had subsisted and been vested in him immediately before his death.

[2.516]
31 New rights: effect of pre-commencement authorisation of copying

Where before commencement—

(a) the owner or prospective owner of copyright in a literary, dramatic, musical or artistic work has authorised a person to make a copy of the work, or

(b) the owner or prospective owner of performers' rights in a performance has authorised a person to make a copy of a recording of the performance,

any new right in relation to that copy shall vest on commencement in the person so authorised, subject to any agreement to the contrary.

[2.517]
32 New rights: effect of pre-commencement film production agreement

(1) Sections 93A and 191F (presumption of transfer of rental right in case of production agreement) apply in relation to an agreement concluded before commencement.

As section 93A so applies, the restriction in subsection (3) of that section shall be omitted (exclusion of presumption in relation to screenplay, dialogue or music specifically created for the film).

(2) Sections 93B and 191G (right to equitable remuneration where rental right transferred) have effect accordingly, but subject to regulation 33 (right to equitable remuneration applicable to rental after 1st April 1997).

[2.518]
33 Right to equitable remuneration applicable to rental after 1st April 1997

No right to equitable remuneration under section 93B or 191G (right to equitable remuneration where rental right transferred) arises—

(a) in respect of any rental of a sound recording or film before 1st April 1997, or

(b) in respect of any rental after that date of a sound recording or film made in pursuance of an agreement entered into before 1st July 1994, unless the author or performer (or a successor in title of his) has before 1st January 1997 notified the person by whom the remuneration would be payable that he intends to exercise that right.

[2.519]
34 Savings for existing stocks

(1) Any new right in relation to a copyright work does not apply to a copy of the work acquired by a person before commencement for the purpose of renting or lending it to the public.

(2) Any new right in relation to a qualifying performance does not apply to a copy of a recording of the performance acquired by a person before commencement for the purpose of renting or lending it to the public.

[2.520]
35 Lending of copies by libraries or archives

Until the making of regulations under section 37 of the Copyright, Designs and Patents Act 1988 for the purposes of section 40A(2) of that Act (lending of copies by libraries or archives), the reference in section 40A(2) (and in paragraph 6B of Schedule 2) to a prescribed library or archive shall be construed as a reference to any library or archive in the United Kingdom prescribed by paragraphs 2 to 6 of Part A of Schedule 1 to the Copyright (Librarians and Archivists) (Copying of Copyright Material) Regulations 1989.

[2.521]
36 Authorship of films

(1) Regulation 18 (authorship of films) applies as from commencement in relation to films made on or after 1st July 1994.

(2) It is not an infringement of any right which the principal director has by virtue of these Regulations to do anything after commencement in pursuance of arrangements for the exploitation of the film made before 19th November 1992.

This does not affect any right of his to equitable remuneration under section 93B.

COPYRIGHT AND RIGHTS IN DATABASES REGULATIONS 1997

(SI 1997/3032)

NOTES

Made: 18 December 1997.

Authority: European Communities Act 1972, s 2(2), (4).

Commencement: 1 January 1998.

ARRANGEMENT OF REGULATIONS

PART I
INTRODUCTORY PROVISIONS

PART I
INTRODUCTORY PROVISIONS

[2.522]
1 Citation, commencement and extent

(1) These Regulations may be cited as the Copyright and Rights in Databases Regulations 1997.

(2) These Regulations come into force on 1st January 1998.

(3) These Regulations extend to the whole of the United Kingdom.

[2.523]
2 Implementation of Directive

(1) These Regulations make provision for the purpose of implementing—

(a) Council Directive No 96/9/EC of 11 March 1996 on the legal protection of databases, . . .

(b) certain obligations of the United Kingdom created by or arising under the EEA Agreement so far as relating to the implementation of that Directive[, and]

[(c) an Agreement in the form of an exchange of letters between the United Kingdom of Great Britain and Northern Ireland on behalf of the Isle of Man and the European Community extending to the Isle of Man the legal protection of databases as provided for in Chapter III of that Directive.]

(2) In this Regulation "the EEA Agreement" means the Agreement on the European Economic Area signed at Oporto on 2nd May 1992, as adjusted by the Protocol signed at Brussels on 17th March 1993.

NOTES

Para (1): word omitted in sub-para (a) revoked, word in square brackets in sub-para (b) substituted, sub-para (c) inserted, by the Copyright and Rights in Databases (Amendment) Regulations 2003, SI 2003/2501, regs 2, 3.

[2.524]
3 Interpretation

In these Regulations "the 1988 Act" means the Copyright, Designs and Patents Act 1988.

[2.525]
4 Scheme of the Regulations

(1) The 1988 Act is amended in accordance with the provisions of Part II of these Regulations, subject to the savings and transitional provisions in Part IV of these Regulations.

(2) Part III of these Regulations has effect subject to those savings and transitional provisions.

5–11 *((Pt II) amend the Copyright Designs and Patents Act 1988, ss 3, 21, 29, 179 at* **[2.9]**, **[2.33]**, **[2.43]**, **[2.236]**, *and insert ss 3A, 50D and 296B of that Act at* **[2.10]**, **[2.79]**, **[2.392]**.)

PART III
DATABASE RIGHT

[2.526]
12 Interpretation

(1) In this Part—

"database" has the meaning given by section 3A(1) of the 1988 Act (as inserted by Regulation 6);

"extraction", in relation to any contents of a database, means the permanent or temporary transfer of those contents to another medium by any means or in any form;

"insubstantial", in relation to part of the contents of a database, shall be construed subject to Regulation 16(2);

"investment" includes any investment, whether of financial, human or technical resources;

"jointly", in relation to the making of a database, shall be construed in accordance with Regulation 14(6);

"lawful user", in relation to a database, means any person who (whether under a licence to do any of the acts restricted by any database right in the database or otherwise) has a right to use the database;

"maker", in relation to a database, shall be construed in accordance with Regulation 14;

"re-utilisation", in relation to any contents of a database, means making those contents available to the public by any means;

"substantial", in relation to any investment, extraction or re-utilisation, means substantial in terms of quantity or quality or a combination of both.

(2) The making of a copy of a database available for use, on terms that it will or may be returned, otherwise than for direct or indirect economic or commercial advantage, through an establishment which is accessible to the public shall not be taken for the purposes of this Part to constitute extraction or re-utilisation of the contents of the database.

(3) Where the making of a copy of a database available through an establishment which is accessible to the public gives rise to a payment the amount of which does not go beyond what is necessary to cover the costs of the establishment, there is no direct or indirect economic or commercial advantage for the purposes of paragraph (2).

(4) Paragraph (2) does not apply to the making of a copy of a database available for on-the-spot reference use.

(5) Where a copy of a database has been sold within the EEA [or the Isle of Man] by, or with the consent of, the owner of the database right in the database, the further sale within the EEA [or the Isle of Man] of that copy shall not be taken for the purposes of this Part to constitute extraction or re-utilisation of the contents of the database.

NOTES

Para (5): words in square brackets inserted by the Copyright and Rights in Databases (Amendment) Regulations 2003, SI 2003/2501, regs 2, 4.

[2.527]
13 Database right

(1) A property right ("database right") subsists, in accordance with this Part, in a database if there has been a substantial investment in obtaining, verifying or presenting the contents of the database.

(2) For the purposes of paragraph (1) it is immaterial whether or not the database or any of its contents is a copyright work, within the meaning of Part I of the 1988 Act.

(3) This Regulation has effect subject to Regulation 18.

[2.528]

14 The maker of a database

(1) Subject to paragraphs (2) to (4), the person who takes the initiative in obtaining, verifying or presenting the contents of a database and assumes the risk of investing in that obtaining, verification or presentation shall be regarded as the maker of, and as having made, the database.

(2) Where a database is made by an employee in the course of his employment, his employer shall be regarded as the maker of the database, subject to any agreement to the contrary.

(3) Subject to paragraph (4), where a database is made by Her Majesty or by an officer or servant of the Crown in the course of his duties, Her Majesty shall be regarded as the maker of the database.

(4) Where a database is made by or under the direction or control of the House of Commons or the House of Lords—

(a) the House by whom, or under whose direction or control, the database is made shall be regarded as the maker of the database, and

(b) if the database is made by or under the direction or control of both Houses, the two Houses shall be regarded as the joint makers of the database.

[(4A) Where a database is made by or under the direction of control of the Scottish Parliament, the Scottish Parliamentary Corporate Body shall be regarded as the maker of the database.]

(5) For the purposes of this Part a database is made jointly if two or more persons acting together in collaboration take the initiative in obtaining, verifying or presenting the contents of the database and assume the risk of investing in that obtaining, verification or presentation.

(6) References in this Part to the maker of a database shall, except as otherwise provided, be construed, in relation to a database which is made jointly, as references to all the makers of the database.

NOTES

Para (4A): inserted by the Scotland Act 1998 (Consequential Modifications) (No 1) Order 1999, SI 1999/1042, art 3, Sch 1, Pt II, para 26.

[2.529]

15 First ownership of database right

The maker of a database is the first owner of database right in it.

[2.530]

16 Acts infringing database right

(1) Subject to the provisions of this Part, a person infringes database right in a database if, without the consent of the owner of the right, he extracts or re-utilises all or a substantial part of the contents of the database.

(2) For the purposes of this Part, the repeated and systematic extraction or re-utilisation of insubstantial parts of the contents of a database may amount to the extraction or re-utilisation of a substantial part of those contents.

[2.531]

17 Term of protection

(1) Database right in a database expires at the end of the period of fifteen years from the end of the calendar year in which the making of the database was completed.

(2) Where a database is made available to the public before the end of the period referred to in paragraph (1), database right in the database shall expire fifteen years from the end of the calendar year in which the database was first made available to the public.

(3) Any substantial change to the contents of a database, including a substantial change resulting from the accumulation of successive additions, deletions or alterations, which would result in the database being considered to be a substantial new investment shall qualify the database resulting from that investment for its own term of protection.

(4) This Regulation has effect subject to Regulation 30.

[2.532]

18 Qualification for database right

(1) Database right does not subsist in a database unless, at the material time, its maker, or if it was made jointly, one or more of its makers, was—

(a) an individual who was a national of an EEA state or habitually resident within the EEA,

(b) a body which was incorporated under the law of an EEA state and which, at that time, satisfied one of the conditions in paragraph (2), . . .

(c) a partnership or other unincorporated body which was formed under the law of an EEA state and which, at that time, satisfied the condition in paragraph (2)(a)[,]

[(d) an individual who was habitually resident within the Isle of Man,

(e) a body which was incorporated under the law of the Isle of Man and which, at that time, satisfied one of the conditions in paragraph (2A), or

(f) a partnership or other unincorporated body which was formed under the law of the Isle of Man and which, at that time, satisfied the condition in paragraph (2A)(a).]

(2) The conditions mentioned in paragraphs (1)(b) and (c) are—

(a) that the body has its central administration or principal place of business within the EEA, or

(b) that the body has its registered office within the EEA and the body's operations are linked on an ongoing basis with the economy of an EEA state.

[(2A) The conditions mentioned in paragraphs (1)(e) and (f) are—

(a) that the body has its central administration or principal place of business within the Isle of Man, or

(b) that the body has its registered office within the Isle of Man and the body's operations are linked on an ongoing basis with the economy of the Isle of Man.]

(3) Paragraph (1) does not apply in any case falling within Regulation 14(4).

(4) In this Regulation—

(a) "EEA" and "EEA state" have the meaning given by section 172A of the 1988 Act;

(b) "the material time" means the time when the database was made, or if the making extended over a period, a substantial part of that period.

NOTES

Para (1): word omitted in sub-para (b) revoked, comma in square brackets in sub-para (c) substituted, and sub-paras (d)–(f) inserted, by the Copyright and Rights in Databases (Amendment) Regulations 2003, SI 2003/2501, regs 2, 5(a)–(c).

Para (2A): inserted by SI 2003/2501, regs 2, 5(d).

[2.533]

19 Avoidance of certain terms affecting lawful users

(1) A lawful user of a database which has been made available to the public in any manner shall be entitled to extract or re-utilise insubstantial parts of the contents of the database for any purpose.

(2) Where under an agreement a person has a right to use a database, or part of a database, which has been made available to the public in any manner, any term or condition in the agreement shall be void in so far as it purports to prevent that person from extracting or re-utilising insubstantial parts of the contents of the database, or of that part of the database, for any purpose.

[2.534]

20 Exceptions to database right

(1) Database right in a database which has been made available to the public in any manner is not infringed by fair dealing with a substantial part of its contents if—

(a) that part is extracted from the database by a person who is apart from this paragraph a lawful user of the database,

(b) it is extracted for the purpose of illustration for teaching or research and not for any commercial purpose, and

(c) the source is indicated.

(2) The provisions of Schedule 1 specify other acts which may be done in relation to a database notwithstanding the existence of database right.

[2.535]

[20A Exceptions to database right: deposit libraries

(1) Database right in a database is not infringed by the copying of a work from the internet by a deposit library or person acting on its behalf if—

(a) the work is of a description prescribed by regulations under section 10(5) of the 2003 Act,

(b) its publication on the internet, or a person publishing it there, is connected with the United Kingdom in a manner so prescribed, and

(c) the copying is done in accordance with any conditions so prescribed.

(2) Database right in a database is not infringed by the doing of anything in relation to relevant material permitted to be done under regulations under section 7 of the 2003 Act.

(3) Regulations under section 44A(3) of the 1988 Act exclude the application of paragraph (2) in relation to prescribed activities in relation to relevant material as (and to the extent that) they exclude the application of section 44A(2) of that Act in relation to those activities.

(4) In this Regulation—

(a) "the 2003 Act" means the Legal Deposit Libraries Act 2003;

(b) "deposit library" and "relevant material" have the same meaning as in section 7 of the 2003 Act.]

NOTES

Inserted by the Legal Deposit Libraries Act 2003, s 8(2).

[2.536]
21 Acts permitted on assumption as to expiry of database right

(1) Database right in a database is not infringed by the extraction or re-utilisation of a substantial part of the contents of the database at a time when, or in pursuance of arrangements made at a time when—

(a) it is not possible by reasonable inquiry to ascertain the identity of the maker, and
(b) it is reasonable to assume that database right has expired.

(2) In the case of a database alleged to have been made jointly, paragraph (1) applies in relation to each person alleged to be one of the makers.

[2.537]
22 Presumptions relevant to database right

(1) The following presumptions apply in proceedings brought by virtue of this Part of these Regulations with respect to a database.

(2) Where a name purporting to be that of the maker appeared on copies of the database as published, or on the database when it was made, the person whose name appeared shall be presumed, until the contrary is proved—

(a) to be the maker of the database, and
(b) to have made it in circumstances not falling within Regulation 14(2) to (4).

(3) Where copies of the database as published bear a label or a mark stating—

(a) that a named person was the maker of the database, or
(b) that the database was first published in a specified year,

the label or mark shall be admissible as evidence of the facts stated and shall be presumed to be correct until the contrary is proved.

(4) In the case of a database alleged to have been made jointly, paragraphs (2) and (3), so far as is applicable, apply in relation to each person alleged to be one of the makers.

[2.538]
[23 Application of copyright provisions to database right

The following provisions of the 1988 Act apply in relation to database right and databases in which that right subsists as they apply in relation to copyright and copyright works—

sections 90 to 93 (dealing with rights in copyright works)
sections 96 to 102 (rights and remedies of copyright owner and exclusive licensee)
sections 113 and 114 (supplementary provisions relating to delivery up)
section 115 (jurisdiction of county court and sheriff court).]

NOTES

Substituted by the Intellectual Property (Enforcement, etc) Regulations 2006, SI 2006/1028, reg 2(3), Sch 3, para 6.

[2.539]
24 Licensing of database right

The provisions of Schedule 2 have effect with respect to the licensing of database right.

[2.540]
25 Database right: jurisdiction of Copyright Tribunal

(1) The Copyright Tribunal has jurisdiction under this Part to hear and determine proceedings under the following provisions of Schedule 2—

(a) paragraph 3, 4 or 5 (reference of licensing scheme);
(b) paragraph 6 or 7 (application with respect to licence under licensing scheme);
(c) paragraph 10, 11 or 12 (reference or application with respect to licence by licensing body).

(2) The provisions of Chapter VIII of Part I of the 1988 Act (general provisions relating to the Copyright Tribunal) apply in relation to the Tribunal when exercising any jurisdiction under this Part.

(3) Provision shall be made by rules under section 150 of the 1988 Act prohibiting the Tribunal from entertaining a reference under paragraph 3, 4 or 5 of Schedule 2 (reference of licensing scheme) by a representative organisation unless the Tribunal is satisfied that the organisation is reasonably representative of the class of persons which it claims to represent.

PART IV
SAVINGS AND TRANSITIONAL PROVISIONS

[2.541]
[26 Introductory

Expressions used in this Part which are defined for the purposes of Part I of the 1988 Act have the same meaning as in that Part.]

Part 2 Copyright

NOTES

Substituted by the Copyright and Rights in Databases (Amendment) Regulations 2003, SI 2003/2501, regs 2, 6.

[2.542]

27 General rule

Subject to Regulations 28 and 29, these Regulations apply to databases made before or after [1st January 1998].

NOTES

Words in square brackets substituted by the Copyright and Rights in Databases (Amendment) Regulations 2003, SI 2003/2501, regs 2, 7.

[2.543]

[28 General savings

(1) Nothing in these Regulations affects any agreement made before 1st January 1998.

(2) Nothing in these Regulations affects any agreement made after 31st December 1997 and before 1st November 2003 in so far as the effect would only arise as a result of the amendment of these Regulations by the Copyright and Rights in Databases (Amendment) Regulations 2003.

(3) No act done in respect of any database, in which database right subsists by virtue of the maker of the database (or one or more of its makers) falling within one of the provisions contained in Regulations 14(4) and 18(1)(a), (b) and (c),—

(a) before 1st January 1998, or

(b) after 31st December 1997, in pursuance of an agreement made before 1st January 1998,

shall be regarded as an infringement of database right in the database.

(4) No act done in respect of any database, in which database right subsists by virtue of its maker (or one or more of its makers) falling within one of the provisions contained in Regulation 18(1)(d), (e) and (f),—

(a) before 1st November 2003, or

(b) after 31st October 2003, in pursuance of an agreement made before 1st November 2003,

shall be regarded as an infringement of database right in the database.]

NOTES

Substituted by the Copyright and Rights in Databases (Amendment) Regulations 2003, SI 2003/2501, regs 2, 8.

[2.544]

29 Saving for copyright in certain existing databases

(1) Where a database—

(a) was created on or before 27th March 1996, and

(b) is a copyright work immediately before [1st January 1998],

copyright shall continue to subsist in the database for the remainder of its copyright term.

(2) In this Regulation "copyright term" means the period of the duration of copyright under section 12 of the 1988 Act (duration of copyright in literary, dramatic, musical or artistic works).

NOTES

Para (1): words in square brackets in sub-para (b) substituted by the Copyright and Rights in Databases (Amendment) Regulations 2003, SI 2003/2501, regs 2, 9.

[2.545]

[30 Database right: term applicable to certain existing databases

Where—

(a) the making of any database is completed on or after 1st January 1983, and before 1st January 1998, and

(b) either—

(i) the database is a database in which database right subsists by virtue of the maker of the database (or one or more of its makers) falling within one of the provisions contained in Regulations 14(4) and 18(1)(a), (b) and (c) and database right begins to subsist in the database on 1st January 1998, or

(ii) the database is a database in which database right subsists by virtue of its maker (or one or more of its makers) falling within one of the provisions contained in Regulation 18(1)(d), (e) and (f) and database right begins to subsist in the database on 1st November 2003,

then database right shall subsist in the database for a period of fifteen years beginning with 1st January 1998.]

NOTES

Substituted by the Copyright and Rights in Databases (Amendment) Regulations 2003, SI 2003/2501, regs 2, 10.

SCHEDULES

SCHEDULE 1
EXCEPTIONS TO DATABASE RIGHT FOR PUBLIC ADMINISTRATION

Regulation 20(2)

Parliamentary and judicial proceedings

[2.546]

1. Database right in a database is not infringed by anything done for the purposes of parliamentary or judicial proceedings or for the purposes of reporting such proceedings.

Royal Commissions and statutory inquiries

2. (1) Database right in a database is not infringed by anything done for—

(a) the purposes of the proceedings of a Royal Commission or statutory inquiry, or

(b) the purpose of reporting any such proceedings held in public.

(2) Database right in a database is not infringed by the issue to the public of copies of the report of a Royal Commission or statutory inquiry containing the contents of the database.

(3) In this paragraph "Royal Commission" and "statutory inquiry" have the same meaning as in section 46 of the 1988 Act.

Material open to public inspection or on official register

3. (1) Where the contents of a database are open to public inspection pursuant to a statutory requirement, or are on a statutory register, database right in the database is not infringed by the extraction of all or a substantial part of the contents containing factual information of any description, by or with the authority of the appropriate person, for a purpose which does not involve re-utilisation of all or a substantial part of the contents.

(2) Where the contents of a database are open to public inspection pursuant to a statutory requirement, database right in the database is not infringed by the extraction or re-utilisation of all or a substantial part of the contents, by or with the authority of the appropriate person, for the purpose of enabling the contents to be inspected at a more convenient time or place or otherwise facilitating the exercise of any right for the purpose of which the requirement is imposed.

(3) Where the contents of a database which is open to public inspection pursuant to a statutory requirement, or which is on a statutory register, contain information about matters of general scientific, technical, commercial or economic interest, database right in the database is not infringed by the extraction or re-utilisation of all or a substantial part of the contents, by or with the authority of the appropriate person, for the purpose of disseminating that information.

(4) In this paragraph—

"appropriate person" means the person required to make the contents of the database open to public inspection or, as the case may be, the person maintaining the register;

"statutory register" means a register maintained in pursuance of a statutory requirement; and

"statutory requirement" means a requirement imposed by provision made by or under an enactment.

Material communicated to the Crown in the course of public business

4. (1) This paragraph applies where the contents of a database have in the course of public business been communicated to the Crown for any purpose, by or with the licence of the owner of the database right and a document or other material thing recording or embodying the contents of the database is owned by or in the custody or control of the Crown.

(2) The Crown may, for the purpose for which the contents of the database were communicated to it, or any related purpose which could reasonably have been anticipated by the owner of the database right in the database, extract or re-utilise all or a substantial part of the contents without infringing database right in the database.

(3) The Crown may not re-utilise the contents of a database by virtue of this paragraph if the contents have previously been published otherwise than by virtue of this paragraph.

(4) In sub-paragraph (1) "public business" includes any activity carried on by the Crown.

(5) This paragraph has effect subject to any agreement to the contrary between the Crown and the owner of the database right in the database.

Public records

5. The contents of a database which are comprised in public records within the meaning of the Public Records Act 1958, the Public Records (Scotland) Act 1937 or the Public Records Act (Northern Ireland) 1923 which are open to public inspection in pursuance of that Act, may be re-utilised by or with the authority of any officer appointed under that Act, without infringement of database right in the database.

Acts done under statutory authority

6. (1) Where the doing of a particular act is specifically authorised by an Act of Parliament, whenever passed, then, unless the Act provides otherwise, the doing of that act does not infringe database right in a database.

(2) Sub-paragraph (1) applies in relation to an enactment contained in Northern Ireland legislation as it applies in relation to an Act of Parliament.

(3) Nothing in this paragraph shall be construed as excluding any defence of statutory authority otherwise available under or by virtue of any enactment.

SCHEDULE 2
LICENSING OF DATABASE RIGHT

Regulation 24

Licensing scheme and licensing bodies

[2.547]

1. (1) In this Schedule a "licensing scheme" means a scheme setting out—

(a) the classes of case in which the operator of the scheme, or the person on whose behalf he acts, is willing to grant database right licences, and

(b) the terms on which licences would be granted in those classes of case;

and for this purpose a "scheme" includes anything in the nature of a scheme, whether described as a scheme or as a tariff or by any other name.

(2) In this Schedule a "licensing body" means a society or other organisation which has as its main object, or one of its main objects, the negotiating or granting, whether as owner or prospective owner of a database right or as agent for him, of database right licences, and whose objects include the granting of licences covering the databases of more than one maker.

(3) In this paragraph "database right licences" means licences to do, or authorise the doing of, any of the things for which consent is required under Regulation 16.

2. Paragraphs 3 to 8 apply to licensing schemes which are operated by licensing bodies and cover databases of more than one maker so far as they relate to licences for extracting or re-utilising all or a substantial part of the contents of a database; and references in those paragraphs to a licensing scheme shall be construed accordingly.

Reference of proposed licensing scheme to tribunal

3. (1) The terms of a licensing scheme proposed to be operated by a licensing body may be referred to the Copyright Tribunal by an organisation claiming to be representative of persons claiming that they require licences in cases of a description to which the scheme would apply, either generally or in relation to any description of case.

(2) The Tribunal shall first decide whether to entertain the reference, and may decline to do so on the ground that the reference is premature.

(3) If the Tribunal decides to entertain the reference it shall consider the matter referred and make such order, either confirming or varying the proposed scheme, either generally or so far as it relates to cases of the description to which the reference relates, as the Tribunal may determine to be reasonable in the circumstances.

(4) The order may be made so as to be in force indefinitely or for such period as the Tribunal may determine.

Reference of licensing scheme to tribunal

4. (1) If while a licensing scheme is in operation a dispute arises between the operator of the scheme and—

(a) a person claiming that he requires a licence in a case of a description to which the scheme applies, or

(b) an organisation claiming to be representative of such persons,

that person or organisation may refer the scheme to the Copyright Tribunal in so far as it relates to cases of that description.

(2) A scheme which has been referred to the Tribunal under this paragraph shall remain in operation until proceedings on the reference are concluded.

(3) The Tribunal shall consider the matter in dispute and make such order, either confirming or varying the scheme so far as it relates to cases of the description to which the reference relates, as the Tribunal may determine to be reasonable in the circumstances.

(4) The order may be made so as to be in force indefinitely or for such period as the Tribunal may determine.

Further reference of scheme to tribunal

5. (1) Where the Copyright Tribunal has on a previous reference of a licensing scheme under paragraph 3 or 4, or under this paragraph, made an order with respect to the scheme, then, while the order remains in force—

(a) the operator of the scheme,

(b) a person claiming that he requires a licence in a case of the description to which the order applies, or

(c) an organisation claiming to be representative of such persons,

may refer the scheme again to the Tribunal so far as it relates to cases of that description.

(2) A licensing scheme shall not, except with the special leave of the Tribunal, be referred again to the Tribunal in respect of the same description of cases—

(a) within twelve months from the date of the order on the previous reference, or

(b) if the order was made so as to be in force for 15 months or less, until the last three months before the expiry of the order.

(3) A scheme which has been referred to the Tribunal under this section shall remain in operation until proceedings on the reference are concluded.

(4) The Tribunal shall consider the matter in dispute and make such order, either confirming, varying or further varying the scheme so far as it relates to cases of the description to which the reference relates, as the Tribunal may determine to be reasonable in the circumstances.

(5) The order may be made so as to be in force indefinitely or for such period as the Tribunal may determine.

Application for grant of licence in connection with licensing scheme

6. (1) A person who claims, in a case covered by a licensing scheme, that the operator of the scheme has refused to grant him or procure the grant to him of a licence in accordance with the scheme, or has failed to do so within a reasonable time after being asked, may apply to the Copyright Tribunal.

(2) A person who claims, in a case excluded from a licensing scheme, that the operator of the scheme either—

(a) has refused to grant him a licence or procure the grant to him of a licence, or has failed to do so within a reasonable time of being asked, and that in the circumstances it is unreasonable that a licence should not be granted, or

(b) proposes terms for a licence which are unreasonable,

may apply to the Copyright Tribunal.

(3) A case shall be regarded as excluded from a licensing scheme for the purposes of sub-paragraph (2) if—

(a) the scheme provides for the grant of licences subject to terms excepting matters from the licence and the case falls within such an exception, or

(b) the case is so similar to those in which licences are granted under the scheme that it is unreasonable that it should not be dealt with in the same way.

(4) If the Tribunal is satisfied that the claim is well-founded, it shall make an order declaring that, in respect of the matters specified in the order, the applicant is entitled to a licence on such terms as the Tribunal may determine to be applicable in accordance with the scheme or, as the case may be, to be reasonable in the circumstances.

(5) The order may be made so as to be in force indefinitely or for such period as the Tribunal may determine.

Application for review of order as to entitlement to licence

7. (1) Where the Copyright Tribunal has made an order under paragraph 6 that a person is entitled to a licence under a licensing scheme, the operator of the scheme or the original applicant may apply to the Tribunal to review its order.

(2) An application shall not be made, except with the special leave of the Tribunal—

(a) within twelve months from the date of the order, or of the decision on a previous application under this section, or

(b) if the order was made so as to be in force for 15 months or less, or as a result of the decision on a previous application under this section is due to expire within 15 months of that decision, until the last three months before the expiry date.

(3) The Tribunal shall on an application for review confirm or vary its order as the Tribunal may determine to be reasonable having regard to the terms applicable in accordance with the licensing scheme or, as the case may be, the circumstances of the case.

Effect of order of tribunal as to licensing scheme

8. (1) A licensing scheme which has been confirmed or varied by the Copyright Tribunal—

(a) under paragraph 3 (reference of terms of proposed scheme), or

(b) under paragraph 4 or 5 (reference of existing scheme to Tribunal), shall be in force or, as the case may be, remain in operation, so far as it relates to the description of case in respect of which the order was made, so long as the order remains in force.

(2) While the order is in force a person who in a case of a class to which the order applies—

(a) pays to the operator of the scheme any charges payable under the scheme in respect of a licence covering the case in question or, if the amount cannot be ascertained, gives an undertaking to the operator to pay them when ascertained, and

(b) complies with the other terms applicable to such a licence under the scheme,

shall be in the same position as regards infringement of database right as if he had at all material times been the holder of a licence granted by the owner of the database right in question in accordance with the scheme.

(3) The Tribunal may direct that the order, so far as it varies the amount of charges payable, has effect from a date before that on which it is made, but not earlier than the date on which the reference was made or, if later, on which the scheme came into operation.

If such a direction is made—

(a) any necessary repayments, or further payments, shall be made in respect of charges already paid, and

(b) the reference in sub-paragraph (2)(a) to the charges payable under the scheme shall be construed as a reference to the charges so payable by virtue of the order.

No such direction may be made where sub-paragraph (4) below applies.

(4) Where the Tribunal has made an order under paragraph 6 (order as to entitlement to licence under licensing scheme) and the order remains in force, the person in whose favour the order is made shall if he—

(a) pays to the operator of the scheme any charges payable in accordance with the order or, if the amount cannot be ascertained, gives an undertaking to pay the charges when ascertained, and

(b) complies with the other terms specified in the order,

be in the same position as regards infringement of database right as if he had at all material times been the holder of a licence granted by the owner of the database right in question on the terms specified in the order.

References and applications with respect to licences by licensing bodies

9. Paragraphs 10 to 13 (references and applications with respect to licensing by licensing bodies) apply to licences relating to database right which cover databases of more than one maker granted by a licensing body otherwise than in pursuance of a licensing scheme, so far as the licences authorise extracting or re-utilising all or a substantial part of the contents of a database; and references in those paragraphs to a licence shall be construed accordingly.

Reference to tribunal of proposed licence

10. (1) The terms on which a licensing body proposes to grant a licence may be referred to the Copyright Tribunal by the prospective licensee.

(2) The Tribunal shall first decide whether to entertain the reference, and may decline to do so on the ground that the reference is premature.

(3) If the Tribunal decides to entertain the reference it shall consider the terms of the proposed licence and make such order, either confirming or varying the terms, as it may determine to be reasonable in the circumstances.

(4) The order may be made so as to be in force indefinitely or for such period as the Tribunal may determine.

Reference to tribunal of expiring licence

11. (1) A licensee under a licence which is due to expire, by effluxion of time or as a result of notice given by the licensing body, may apply to the Copyright Tribunal on the ground that it is unreasonable in the circumstances that the licence should cease to be in force.

(2) Such an application may not be made until the last three months before the licence is due to expire.

(3) A licence in respect of which a reference has been made to the Tribunal shall remain in operation until proceedings on the reference are concluded.

(4) If the Tribunal finds the application well-founded, it shall make an order declaring that the licensee shall continue to be entitled to the benefit of the licence on such terms as the Tribunal may determine to be reasonable in the circumstances.

(5) An order of the Tribunal under this section may be made so as to be in force indefinitely or for such period as the Tribunal may determine.

Application for review of order as to licence

12. (1) Where the Copyright Tribunal has made an order under paragraph 10 or 11, the licensing body or the person entitled to the benefit of the order may apply to the Tribunal to review its order.

(2) An application shall not be made, except with the special leave of the Tribunal—

(a) within twelve months from the date of the order or of the decision on a previous application under this paragraph, or
(b) if the order was made so as to be in force for 15 months or less, or as a result of the decision on a previous application under this section is due to expire within 15 months of that decision, until the last three months before the expiry date.

(3) The Tribunal shall on an application for review confirm or vary its order as the Tribunal may determine to be reasonable in the circumstances.

Effect of order of tribunal as to licence

13. (1) Where the Copyright Tribunal has made an order under paragraph 10 or 11 and the order remains in force, the person entitled to the benefit of the order shall if he—
(a) pays to the licensing body any charges payable in accordance with the order or, if the amount cannot be ascertained, gives an undertaking to pay the charges when ascertained, and
(b) complies with the other terms specified in the order,
be in the same position as regards infringement of database right as if he had at all material times been the holder of a licence granted by the owner of the database right in question on the terms specified in the order.

(2) The benefit of the order may be assigned—
(a) in the case of an order under paragraph 10, if assignment is not prohibited under the terms of the Tribunal's order; and
(b) in the case of an order under paragraph 11, if assignment was not prohibited under the terms of the original licence.

(3) The Tribunal may direct that an order under paragraph 10 or 11, or an order under paragraph 12 varying such an order, so far as it varies the amount of charges payable, has effect from a date before that on which it is made, but not earlier than the date on which the reference or application was made or, if later, on which the licence was granted or, as the case may be, was due to expire.

If such a direction is made—
(a) any necessary repayments, or further payments, shall be made in respect of charges already paid, and
(b) the reference in sub-paragraph (1)(a) to the charges payable in accordance with the order shall be construed, where the order is varied by a later order, as a reference to the charges so payable by virtue of the later order.

General considerations: unreasonable discrimination

14. In determining what is reasonable on a reference or application under this Schedule relating to a licensing scheme or licence, the Copyright Tribunal shall have regard to—
(a) the availability of other schemes, or the granting of other licences, to other persons in similar circumstances, and
(b) the terms of those schemes or licences,
and shall exercise its powers so as to secure that there is no unreasonable discrimination between licensees, or prospective licensees, under the scheme or licence to which the reference or application relates and licensees under other schemes operated by, or other licences granted by, the same person.

Powers exercisable in consequence of competition report

15. [(1) Sub-paragraph (1A) applies where whatever needs to be remedied, mitigated or prevented by the Secretary of State [or (as the case may be) the Competition and Markets Authority] under section 12(5) of the Competition Act 1980 or section 41(2), 55(2), 66(6), 75(2), 83(2), 138(2), 147(2)[, 147A(2)] or 160(2) of, or paragraph 5(2) or 10(2) of Schedule 7 to, the Enterprise Act 2002 (powers to take remedial action following references [to the chair of the Competition and Markets Authority for the constitution of a group] in connection with public bodies and certain other persons, mergers or market investigations) or article 12(7) of, or paragraph 5(2) or 10(2) of Schedule 2 to, the Enterprise Act 2002 (Protection of Legitimate Interests) Order 2003 (power to take remedial action following references [to the chair of the Competition and Markets Authority for the constitution of a group] in connection with European mergers) consists of or includes—
(a) conditions in licences granted by the owner of database right in a database restricting the use of the database by the licensee or the right of the owner of the database right to grant other licences; or
(b) a refusal of an owner of database right to grant licences on reasonable terms.

(1A) The powers conferred by Schedule 8 to the Enterprise Act 2002 include power to cancel or modify those conditions and, instead or in addition, to provide that licences in respect of the database right shall be available as of right.

Part 2 Copyright

(2) The references to anything permitted by Schedule 8 to the Enterprise Act 2002 in section 12(5A) of the Competition Act 1980 and in sections 75(4)(a), 83(4)(a), 84(2)(a), 89(1), 160(4)(a), 161(3)(a) and 164(1) of, and paragraphs 5, 10 and 11 of Schedule 7 to, the Act of 2002 and paragraphs 5, 10 and 11 of Schedule 2 to the Enterprise Act 2002 (Protection of Legitimate Interests) Order 2003 shall be construed accordingly.]

(3) The terms of a licence available by virtue of this paragraph shall, in default of agreement, be settled by the Copyright Tribunal on an application by the person requiring the licence; and terms so settled shall authorise the licensee to do everything in respect of which a licence is so available.

(4) Where the terms of a licence are settled by the Tribunal, the licence has effect from the date on which the application to the Tribunal was made.

NOTES

Para 15: sub-paras (1), (1A), (2) substituted, for original sub-paras (1), (2), by the Enterprise Act 2002 (Consequential and Supplemental Provisions) Order 2003, SI 2003/1398, art 2, Schedule, para 31; in sub-para (1), words in first, third and fourth pairs of square brackets substituted and figure in second pair of square brackets inserted, by the Enterprise and Regulatory Reform Act 2013 (Competition) (Consequential, Transitional and Saving Provisions) (No 2) Order 2014, SI 2014/549, art 2, Sch 1, Pt 2, para 27.

COPYRIGHT AND RELATED RIGHTS REGULATIONS 2003

(SI 2003/2498)

NOTES

Made: 27 September 2003.
Authority: European Communities Act 1972, s 2(2).
Commencement: 31 October 2003.

ARRANGEMENT OF REGULATIONS

PART 1
INTRODUCTORY PROVISIONS

[2.548]

1 Citation and commencement

These Regulations may be cited as the Copyright and Related Rights Regulations 2003 and shall come into force on 31st October 2003.

2–29 (*Reg 2 introduces Schs 1, 2 to these Regulations; regs 3–29 (Pt 3) amend the Copyright, Designs and Patents Act 1988 at* **[2.7]** *et seq. Reg 22 is revoked by the Digital Economy Act 2017, s 34(2)(c), as from a day to be appointed.*)

PART 3
SAVINGS AND TRANSITIONAL PROVISIONS

General provisions

[2.549]
30 Introductory

(1) In this Part—

"commencement" means the date upon which these regulations come into force;

"extended copyright" means any copyright in sound recordings which subsists by virtue of section 13A of the 1988 Act (as amended by regulation 29) after the date on which it would have expired under the 1988 provisions;

"prospective owner" includes a person who is prospectively entitled to extended copyright in a sound recording by virtue of such an agreement as is mentioned in regulation 37(1);

"the 1988 Act" means the Copyright, Designs and Patents Act 1988; and

"the 1988 provisions" means the provisions of the 1988 Act as they stood immediately before commencement (including the provisions of Schedule 1 to that Act continuing the effect of earlier enactments).

(2) Expressions used in this Part which are defined for the purposes of Part 1 or 2 of the 1988 Act have the same meaning as in that Part.

[2.550]
31 General rules

(1) Subject to regulation 32, these Regulations apply to—

(a) copyright works made,
(b) performances given,
(c) databases, in which database right vests, made, and
(d) works, in which publication right vests, first published,

before or after commencement.

(2) No act done before commencement shall be regarded as an infringement of any new or extended right arising by virtue of these Regulations.

[2.551]
32 Savings for certain existing agreements

(1) Nothing in these Regulations affects any agreement made before 22nd December 2002.

(2) No act done after commencement, in pursuance of an agreement made before 22nd December 2002, shall be regarded as an infringement of any new or extended right arising by virtue of these Regulations.

Special provisions

[2.552]
33 Permitted acts

The provisions of Chapter 3 of Part 1 (acts permitted in relation to copyright works) and Schedule 2 (rights in performances: permitted acts) in the 1988 provisions shall continue to apply to anything done after commencement in completion of an act begun before commencement which was permitted by those provisions.

[2.553]
34 Performers' rights: making available to the public

(1) Those parts of section 182D in the 1988 provisions which confer a right to equitable remuneration in relation to the making available to the public in the way mentioned in section 182CA(1) (regulation 7) of a commercially published sound recording shall cease to apply on commencement.

(2) Any assignment made before commencement under the provisions of section 182D(2) shall, on commencement, cease to apply insofar as it relates to the new making available to the public right conferred by section 182CA (regulation 7).

[2.554]
35 Exercise of rights in relation to performances

(1) The new right conferred by section 182CA (consent required for making available to the public) (in regulation 7) is exercisable as from commencement by the performer or (if he has died) by the person who immediately before commencement was entitled by virtue of section 192A(2) to exercise the rights conferred on the performer by Part 2 in relation to that performance.

(2) Any damages received by a person's personal representatives by virtue of the right conferred by paragraph (1) shall devolve as part of that person's estate as if the right had subsisted and been vested in him immediately before his death.

[2.555]
36 Ownership of extended copyright in sound recordings

The person who is the owner of the copyright in a sound recording immediately before commencement is as from commencement the owner of any extended copyright in that sound recording.

[2.556]
37 Prospective ownership of extended copyright in sound recordings

(1) Where by an agreement made before commencement in relation to extended copyright in a sound recording, and signed by or on behalf of the prospective owner of the copyright, the prospective owner purports to assign the extended copyright (wholly or partially) to another person, then, if on commencement the assignee or another person claiming under him would be entitled as against all other persons to require the copyright to be vested in him, the copyright shall vest in the assignee or his successor in title by virtue of this paragraph.

(2) A licence granted by a prospective owner of extended copyright in a sound recording is binding on every successor in title to his interest (or prospective interest) in the right, except a purchaser in good faith for valuable consideration and without notice (actual or constructive) of the licence or a person deriving title from such a purchaser; and references in Part 1 of the 1988 Act to doing anything with, or without, the licence of the copyright owner shall be construed accordingly.

[2.557]
38 Extended copyright in sound recordings: existing licences, agreements, etc

(1) Any copyright licence or any term or condition of an agreement relating to the exploitation of a sound recording which—

(a) subsists immediately before commencement in relation to an existing sound recording, and
(b) is not to expire before the end of the copyright period under the 1988 provisions,

shall continue to have effect during the period of any extended copyright in that sound recording, subject to any agreement to the contrary.

(2) Any copyright licence, or term or condition relating to the exploitation of a sound recording, imposed by order of the Copyright Tribunal which—

(a) subsists immediately before commencement in relation to an existing sound recording, and
(b) is not to expire before the end of the copyright period under the 1988 provisions,

shall continue to have effect during the period of any extended copyright, subject to any further order of the Tribunal.

[2.558]
39 Duration of copyright in sound recordings: general saving

Copyright in an existing sound recording shall continue to subsist until the date it would have expired under Regulation 15 of the Duration of Copyright and Rights in Performances Regulations 1995 (SI 1995/3297) if that date is later than the date on which copyright would expire under the provisions of section 13A of the 1988 Act as amended by regulation 29.

[2.559]
40 Sanctions and remedies

(1) Section 296 in the 1988 provisions (devices designed to circumvent copy-protection) shall continue to apply to acts done in relation to computer programs or other works prior to commencement.

(2) Section 296 as substituted by regulation 24(1) (circumvention of technical devices applied to computer programs), and sections 296ZA (circumvention of technological measures) and 296ZD (rights and remedies in respect of devices designed to circumvent technological measures), introduced by regulation 24(1), shall apply to acts done in relation to computer programs or other works on or after commencement.

(3) Sections 107(2A), 198(1A) and 296ZB(1) and (2) (offences) do not have effect in relation to any act committed before commencement.

SCHEDULES 1–3

(*Schs 1, 2 contain consequential amendments and repeals which, in so far as relevant to this work, have been incorporated at the appropriate place; Sch 3 inserts Sch 5A to the Copyright, Designs and Patents Act 1988 at* **[2.412]–[2.414]**.)

ARTIST'S RESALE RIGHT REGULATIONS 2006

(SI 2006/346)

NOTES

Made: 13 February 2006.
Commencement: see reg 1(1).
Authority: European Communities Act 1972, s 2(2).

ARRANGEMENT OF REGULATIONS

SCHEDULES

[2.560]
1 Citation, commencement and extent

(1) These Regulations may be cited as the Artist's Resale Right Regulations 2006 and shall come into force on the day after the day on which they are made.

(2) These Regulations extend to the whole of the United Kingdom.

[2.561]
2 Interpretation

In these Regulations—

"author", in relation to a work, means the person who creates it;

"collecting society" has the meaning given in regulation 14(5);

"contract date", in relation to a sale, means the time at which the contract of sale was made (and "contract of sale" has the meaning given in section 2 of the Sale of Goods Act 1979);

"copyright" has the meaning given in section 1 of the Copyright, Designs and Patents Act 1988;

"EEA state" means a member State, Iceland, Liechtenstein or Norway;

"qualifying body" has the meaning given in regulation 7(4);

. . .

"resale" is to be construed in accordance with regulation 12;

"resale right" has the meaning given in regulation 3 (and, unless the context otherwise requires, includes a share in resale right);

"resale royalty" has the meaning given in regulation 3;

"sale" has the meaning given in section 2 of the Sale of Goods Act 1979;

"sale price" has the meaning given in regulation 3(4);

"trustee in bankruptcy" means, in relation to Scotland, an interim or permanent trustee appointed under the Bankruptcy (Scotland) Act 1985;

"work" has the meaning given in regulation 4;

"work of joint authorship" has the meaning given in regulation 5(4).

NOTES

Definition omitted revoked by the Artist's Resale Right (Amendment) Regulations 2011, SI 2011/2873, regs 2, 3.

[2.562]
3 Artist's resale right

(1) The author of a work in which copyright subsists shall, in accordance with these Regulations, have a right ("resale right") to a royalty on any sale of the work which is a resale subsequent to the first transfer of ownership by the author ("resale royalty").

(2) Resale right in a work shall continue to subsist so long as copyright subsists in the work.

(3) The royalty shall be an amount based on the sale price which is calculated in accordance with Schedule 1.

(4) The sale price is the price obtained for the sale, net of the tax payable on the sale, and converted into euro at the European Central Bank reference rate prevailing at the contract date.

(5) For the purposes of paragraph (1), "transfer of ownership by the author" includes in particular—

(a) transmission of the work from the author by testamentary disposition, or in accordance with the rules of intestate succession;

(b) disposal of the work by the author's personal representatives for the purposes of the administration of his estate; and

(c) disposal of the work by an official receiver (or, in Northern Ireland, the Official Receiver for Northern Ireland) or a trustee in bankruptcy, for the purposes of the realisation of the author's estate.

[2.563]
4 Works covered

(1) For the purposes of these Regulations, "work" means any work of graphic or plastic art such as a picture, a collage, a painting, a drawing, an engraving, a print, a lithograph, a sculpture, a tapestry, a ceramic, an item of glassware or a photograph.

(2) However, a copy of a work is not to be regarded as a work unless the copy is one of a limited number which have been made by the author or under his authority.

[2.564]
5 Joint authorship

(1) In the case of a work of joint authorship, the resale right shall belong to the authors as owners in common.

(2) The right shall be held in equal shares or in such other shares as may be agreed.

(3) Such an agreement must be in writing signed by or on behalf of each party to the agreement.

(4) "Work of joint authorship" means a work created by two or more authors.

[2.565]
6 Proof of authorship

(1) Where a name purporting to be that of the author appeared on the work when it was made, the person whose name appeared shall, unless the contrary is proved, be presumed to be the author of the work.

(2) In the case of a work alleged to be a work of joint authorship, paragraph (1) applies in relation to each person alleged to be one of the authors.

[2.566]
7 Assignment etc

(1) Resale right is not assignable.

(2) Any charge on a resale right is void.

(3) Paragraph (1) does not prevent the transfer of a resale right which was transmitted to a qualifying body under regulation 9 (or is deemed to have been so transmitted under regulation 16), provided that the transfer is to another qualifying body.

(4) A qualifying body is a body which—

(a) is a charity within the meaning of section 96(1) of the Charities Act 1993 or section 35 of the Charities Act (Northern Ireland) 1964;

(b) is a Scottish charity; or

[(c) is a foreign charity.]

(5) In paragraph (4)—

(a) "Scottish charity" means—

(i) a body entered in the Scottish Charity Register under section 3 of the Charities and Trustee Investment (Scotland) Act 2005; or

(ii) a "recognised body" within the meaning of section 1(7) of the Law Reform (Miscellaneous Provisions) (Scotland) Act 1990; and

(b) "foreign charity" means a body which is established outside the United Kingdom for purposes similar to those for which a body within paragraph (4)(a) or (b) may be established, and which is subject to similar rules regarding the distribution and application of its assets.

NOTES

Para (4): sub-para (c) substituted by the Artist's Resale Right (Amendment) Regulations 2011, SI 2011/2873, regs 2, 4.

[2.567]
8 Waiver etc

(1) A waiver of a resale right shall have no effect.

(2) An agreement to share or repay resale royalties shall be void.

(3) Paragraph (2) does not affect any agreement made for the purposes of the management of resale right in accordance with regulation 14.

[2.568]
[9 Transmission and vesting of resale right

(1) Whereby virtue of this regulation resale right is transmitted to, or vests in, any person, it may be exercised by that person.

(2) Resale right—

- (a) is transmissible as personal or moveable property by testamentary disposition or in accordance with the rules of intestate succession but only to a natural person or a qualifying body; and
- (b) may vest by operation of law in the personal representative of a deceased person.

(3) Resale right may be further transmitted to a natural person or a qualifying body by any person to whom it passes under paragraph (2)(a).

(4) Resale right may be transmitted as bona vacantia.

(5) Resale right may vest by operation of law in an official receiver (or in Northern Ireland, the Official Receiver for Northern Ireland) or a trustee in bankruptcy.

(6) Where resale right is transmitted to more than one person it belongs to them as owners in common.]

NOTES

Commencement: 1 January 2012.

Substituted by the Artist's Resale Right (Amendment) Regulations 2011, SI 2011/2873, regs 2, 5.

[2.569]
[10 Requirements as to nationality

Resale right may only be exercised in respect of the sale of a work where its author is—

- (a) living at the date of the sale and is at that date a national of—
  - (i) an EEA state; or
  - (ii) a state the legislation of which permits resale right protection for authors from EEA states and their successors in title; or
- (b) deceased at the date of the sale and, at the date of the author's death, the author was a national of a state falling within paragraph (a)(i) or (ii).]

NOTES

Commencement: 1 January 2012.

Substituted by the Artist's Resale Right (Amendment) Regulations 2011, SI 2011/2873, regs 2, 6.

[2.570]
11 Trusts

Nothing in regulations 7, 9 or 10 prevents a resale right from being—

- (a) held, and exercised in respect of a sale, by any person acting as trustee for the person who would otherwise be entitled to exercise the right ("the beneficiary"); or
- (b) transferred to such a trustee, or from the trustee to the beneficiary.

[2.571]
12 "Resale"

(1) The sale of a work may be regarded as a resale notwithstanding that the first transfer of ownership was not made for a money (or any) consideration.

(2) The sale of a work may regarded as a resale only if the conditions mentioned in paragraph (3) are satisfied in respect of that sale.

(3) The conditions are that—

- (a) the buyer or the seller, or (where the sale takes place through an agent) the agent of the buyer or the seller, is acting in the course of a business of dealing in works of art; and
- (b) the sale price is not less than 1,000 euro.

(4) The sale of a work is not to be regarded as a resale if—

- (a) the seller previously acquired the work directly from the author less than three years before the sale; and
- (b) the sale price does not exceed 10,000 euro.

[2.572]
13 Liability to pay resale royalty

(1) The following shall be jointly and severally liable to pay the resale royalty due in respect of a sale—
- (a) the seller; and
- (b) the relevant person (within the meaning of paragraph (2)).

(2) The relevant person is a person who satisfies the condition mentioned in regulation 12(3)(a) and who is—
- (a) the agent of the seller; or
- (b) where there is no such agent, the agent of the buyer; or
- (c) where there are no such agents, the buyer.

(3) Liability shall arise on the completion of the sale; however, a person who is liable may withhold payment until evidence of entitlement to be paid the royalty is produced.

(4) Any liability to pay resale royalty in respect of a resale right which belongs to two or more persons as owners in common is discharged by a payment of the total amount of royalty to one of those persons.

[2.573]
14 Collective management

(1) Resale right may be exercised only through a collecting society.

(2) Where the holder of the resale right has not transferred the management of his right to a collecting society, the collecting society which manages copyright on behalf of artists shall be deemed to be mandated to manage his right.

(3) Where there is more than one such collecting society, the holder may choose which of them is so mandated.

(4) A holder to whom paragraph (2) applies has the same rights and obligations, in respect of the management of his right, as have holders who have transferred the management of their right to the collecting society concerned.

(5) For those purposes—
- (a) "collecting society" means a society or other organisation which has as its main object, or one of its main objects, the administration of rights on behalf of more than one artist; and
- (b) the management of resale right is the collection of resale royalty on behalf of the holder of the right in return for a fixed fee or a percentage of the royalty.

[2.574]
15 Right to information

(1) A holder of resale right in respect of a sale, or a person acting on his behalf, shall have the right to obtain information by making a request under this regulation.

(2) Such a request—
- (a) may be made to any person who (in relation to that sale) satisfies the condition mentioned in regulation 12(3)(a); but
- (b) must be made within three years of the sale to which it relates.

(3) The information that may be so requested is any that may be necessary in order to secure payment of the resale royalty, and in particular to ascertain—
- (a) the amount of royalty that is due; and
- (b) where the royalty is not paid by the person to whom the request is made, the name and address of any person who is liable.

(4) The person to whom the request is made shall do everything within his power to supply the information requested within 90 days of the receipt of the request.

(5) If that information is not supplied within the period mentioned in paragraph (4), the person making the request may, in accordance with rules of court, apply to the county court for an order requiring the person to whom the request is made to supply the information.

(6) In Scotland, such an application shall be by way of summary application to the sheriff, and the procedure for breach of an order shall proceed in like manner as for a contempt of court.

(7) Information obtained under this regulation shall be treated as confidential.

[2.575]
16 Transitional provisions

(1) These Regulations—
- (a) do not apply to sales where the contract date preceded the commencement of the Regulations; but
- (b) apply notwithstanding that the work sold was made before that commencement.

(2) Where the author of a work (or a person to whom the resale right in that work is deemed to have been transmitted under this regulation) died before the commencement of these Regulations, and was at the time of his death a qualifying individual [within the meaning of regulation 10(3) as originally enacted]—

- (a) if he was the owner of the copyright in the work immediately before his death, and on his death a qualifying person became beneficially entitled to that copyright (or to part of it), the resale right in the work shall be deemed to have been transmitted to that person;
- (b) if he was the owner of the work (but not the copyright in it) immediately before his death, and on his death a qualifying person became beneficially entitled to the work, the resale right shall be deemed to have been transmitted to that person;
- (c) otherwise, the resale right shall be deemed to have been transmitted to the qualifying persons who were beneficially entitled to the residue of his personal estate.

(3) Where the author of the work was one of a number of joint authors, the right deemed to have been transmitted by the author under this regulation is one of that number of equal shares in the resale right.

(4) Where a resale right is deemed to have been transmitted to more than one person under paragraph (2)(a), (b) or (c), the resale right shall be deemed to have been transmitted to them in equal shares as owners in common.

(5) In this regulation, "qualifying person" means a person to whom a resale right may be transmitted under regulation 9(2) and (3) [as originally enacted].

NOTES

Paras (2), (5): words in square brackets inserted by the Artist's Resale Right (Amendment) Regulations 2011, SI 2011/2873, regs 2, 7.

[2.576]

[17 Review of Regulations

(1) The Secretary of State must from time to time—

- (a) carry out a review of these Regulations,
- (b) set out the conclusions of the review in the report, and
- (c) publish the report.

(2) In carrying out the review the Secretary of State must, so far as is reasonable, have regard to how Directive 2001/84/EC of the European Parliament and of the Council of 27th September 2001 on the resale right for the benefit of the author of an original work of art (which is implemented by means of these Regulations) is implemented in other member States.

(3) The report must in particular—

- (a) set out the objectives intended to be achieved by the regulatory system established by these Regulations,
- (b) assess the extent to which those objectives are achieved, and
- (c) assess whether those objectives remain appropriate and, if so, the extent to which they could be achieved with a system that imposes less regulation.

(4) The first report under this regulation must be published before the end of the period of five years beginning with the 1st January 2012.

(5) Reports under this regulation are afterwards to be published at intervals not exceeding five years.]

NOTES

Commencement: 1 January 2012.

Substituted by the Artist's Resale Right (Amendment) Regulations 2011, SI 2011/2873, regs 2, 8.

SCHEDULE 1
CALCULATION OF RESALE ROYALTY

Regulation 3(3)

[2.577]

1. The resale royalty payable on the sale of a work shall be the sum of the following amounts, being percentage amounts of consecutive portions of the sale price—

Portion of the sale price	*Percentage amount*
From 0 to 50,000 euro	4%
From 50,000.01 to 200,000 euro	3%
From 200,000.01 to 350,000 euro	1%
From 350,000.01 to 500,000 euro	0.5%
Exceeding 500,000 euro	0.25%

Part 2 Copyright

2. However, the total amount of royalty payable on the sale shall not in any event exceed 12,500 euro.

SCHEDULE 2

(*Sch 2 revoked by the Artist's Resale Right (Amendment) Regulations 2011, SI 2011/2873, regs 2, 9.*)

COPYRIGHT (CERTIFICATION OF LICENSING SCHEME FOR EDUCATIONAL RECORDING OF BROADCASTS) (EDUCATIONAL RECORDING AGENCY LIMITED) ORDER 2007

(SI 2007/266)

NOTES

Made: 1 February 2007.
Authority: Copyright, Designs and Patents Act 1988, s 143, Sch 2A, para 16.
Commencement: 1 April 2007.

[2.578]
1

This Order may be cited as the Copyright (Certification of Licensing Scheme for Educational Recording of Broadcasts) (Educational Recording Agency Limited) Order 2007.

[2.579]
2

The licensing scheme set out in the Schedule to this Order is certified for the purposes of section 35 of, and paragraph 6 of Schedule 2 to, the Copyright, Designs and Patents Act 1988.

[2.580]
3

The certification under article 2 shall come into operation on 1st April 2007.

SCHEDULE
THE EDUCATIONAL RECORDING AGENCY LIMITED LICENSING SCHEME

Article 2

Nature of the Licence

[2.581]

1. The Educational Recording Agency Limited (known as "ERA") is authorised to operate a Licensing Scheme for the purposes of both section 35 of, and paragraph 6 of Schedule 2 to the Copyright, Designs and Patents Act 1988.

2. "The Act" refers to the Copyright, Designs and Patents Act 1988 or any relevant law amending, modifying or re-enacting it from time to time.

3. Set out below are the terms of the Licensing Scheme which ERA has been authorised to operate to the extent that the same has been certified for the purposes of both section 35 of the Act and paragraph 6 of Schedule 2 to the Act ("the Licensing Scheme").

4. These terms shall form part of licences issued under the Licensing Scheme ("the Licence").

5. The Licensing Scheme and Licences issued under it shall apply only to Relevant Rights when used for non-commercial educational purposes within or on behalf of an Educational Establishment. All licensees under the Licensing Scheme shall either be or represent an Educational Establishment ("Licensee").

[**6.** "Educational Establishment" shall mean any school or other description of educational establishment defined by section 174 of the Act or as may be specified by order of the Secretary of State for the purposes of that section.]

ERA Repertoire and Licensor Members

7. (1) The copyright works and rights in performances relevant to a Licence granted under the Licensing Scheme ("ERA Repertoire") are the works and performances in respect of which and to the extent to which the Licensor Members of ERA (or persons represented by the Licensor Members) own or control Relevant Rights.

(2) "Relevant Rights" shall comprise the right:

(a) to cause or authorise the making of recordings of a broadcast and copies of such a recording and (only as a direct result of their inclusion in a broadcast) of copyright works and/or performances contained in the recorded broadcast by or on behalf of an Educational Establishment for the educational purposes of that Educational Establishment ("ERA Recordings"); and

(b) to authorise ERA Recordings to be communicated to the public by a person situated within the premises of an Educational Establishment but only to the extent that the communication cannot be received by any person situated outside the premises of that Educational Establishment.

[In addition this Licence may be relevant to terms and conditions for online services that authorise defined rights of non-commercial educational access or use to educational establishments on the condition that they hold a current licence from ERA.]

[8. The Licensor Members of ERA and the works and performances forming part of ERA Repertoire in respect of which the Relevant Rights are owned or controlled by such Licensors will for the purposes of Licences issued under the Licensing Scheme comprise:

AUTHORS' LICENSING AND COLLECTING SOCIETY LIMITED ("ALCS")

Those literary and dramatic works which are owned by or controlled by persons represented by ALCS and which are included in any broadcast.

[ASSOCIATION DE GESTION INTERNATIONALE COLLECTIVE DES OEUVRES AUDIOVISUELLES ("AGICOA")]

The films which are owned or controlled by persons represented by AGICOA and which are included in any broadcast from which an ERA Recording is made.

BBC WORLDWIDE LIMITED

The broadcasts of the British Broadcasting Corporation and all those copyright works owned or controlled by the British Broadcasting Corporation which are included in any broadcast.

BPI (BRITISH RECORDED MUSIC INDUSTRY) LIMITED ("BPI")

Those sound recordings which are owned or controlled by persons represented by BPI and which are included in any broadcast from which an ERA Recording is made.

CHANNEL FOUR TELEVISION CORPORATION ("Channel 4")

The broadcasts made on Channel 4, E4 and/or Film Four and/or any other broadcast service operated by Channel 4 or any of its subsidiary companies and all those copyright works owned or controlled by Channel 4 or any of its subsidiary companies included in any broadcast.

CHANNEL 5 BROADCASTING LIMITED ("Channel 5")

The broadcasts made on Five and/or any other broadcast service operated by Channel 5 or any of its subsidiary companies and all those copyright works owned or controlled by Channel 5 or any of its subsidiary companies included in any broadcast.

[COMPACT COLLECTION LIMITED ("COMPACT") acting as agent for

(i) DISCOVERY COMMUNICATIONS EUROPE LIMITED concerning the broadcasts made on the broadcast services operated by Discovery Communications Europe Limited including Discovery Science and all those copyright works owned or controlled by Discovery Communications Europe Limited or any of its subsidiary or associated companies included in any broadcast;

(ii) NGC EUROPE LIMITED concerning the broadcasts made on the broadcast services operated by NGC Europe Limited including National Geographic Channel, National Geographic Channel HD, Wild UK, Nat Geo Wild (Europe) and Wild HD and all those copyright works owned or controlled by NGC Europe Limited or any of its subsidiary or associated companies included in any broadcast; and

(iii) AETN UK concerning the broadcasts of AETN UK or any of its subsidiary companies and all those copyright works owned or controlled by AETN UK or any of its subsidiary companies which are included in any broadcast.]

DESIGN AND ARTISTS COPYRIGHT SOCIETY ("DACS")

Those artistic works (as defined in the Act) in which the copyright is owned or controlled by the members of DACS or the members of copyright societies represented by DACS and which are included in any broadcast.

DIRECTORS UK LIMITED ("Directors UK")

The copyright works which are owned or controlled by, or in which authorship is owned or controlled by, persons represented by Directors UK and which are included in any broadcast from which an ERA Recording is made.

EQUITY

The performances by persons represented by Equity which are included in any broadcast.

[FOCAL INTERNATIONAL LIMITED (The Federation of Commercial Audio Visual Libraries) ("FOCAL")

The film and videotape clips and stills which are owned or controlled by persons represented by FOCAL or its subsidiary or associated companies and which are included in any broadcast from which an ERA Recording is made.]

THE INCORPORATED SOCIETY OF MUSICIANS ("ISM")

The literary and musical works which are owned by or controlled by persons represented by ISM and the performances by persons who are represented by ISM which are included in any broadcast.

ITV NETWORK LIMITED ("ITV Network")

The broadcasts made on the channel branded as ITV1 in England and Wales, as the STV regions (formerly known as Grampian TV and Scottish TV) in Scotland, as Ulster in Northern Ireland, and as Channel TV in the Channel Islands, on ITV 2, on ITV 3, on the ITV News Channel and/or any other broadcast service operated by ITV Network Limited or any of its associated or subsidiary companies and all those copyright works owned or controlled by ITV Network Limited or any of its subsidiary or associated companies included in any broadcast.

MECHANICAL COPYRIGHT PROTECTION SOCIETY LIMITED ("MCPS")

Those musical works and sound recordings which are owned or controlled by members of MCPS and entrusted by its members to MCPS and which are included in any broadcast from which an ERA Recording is made.

MUSICIANS' UNION ("the MU")

The performances by persons represented by the MU which are included in any broadcast.

[OPEN UNIVERSITY WORLDWIDE LIMITED

The films and other copyright works which are owned or represented by Open University Worldwide Limited or any of its subsidiary or associated companies and which are included in any broadcast made by the British Broadcasting Corporation or any other broadcast on behalf of the Open University Worldwide Limited from which an ERA Recording is made.]

THE PERFORMING RIGHT SOCIETY LIMITED ("PRS")

The musical works which are owned or controlled by the PRS or by persons represented by the PRS and which are included in any broadcast from which an ERA Recording has been made.

PHONOGRAPHIC PERFORMANCE LIMITED ("PPL")

Those sound recordings which are owned or represented by PPL and which are included in any broadcast from which an ERA Recording is made.

[RADIO INDEPENDENTS GROUP ("RIG")

The sound recordings and any other copyright audio works owned or controlled by members of RIG and entrusted by its members to RIG and which are included in any broadcast from which an ERA recording is made.]

SIANEL PEDWAR CYMRU ("S4C")

The broadcasts made on S4C, S4C Digital and/or S4C2 and/or any other broadcast service operated by S4C or any of its subsidiary companies and all those copyright works owned or controlled by S4C or any of its subsidiary companies included in any broadcast.

For the above purposes "broadcast" shall have the meaning provided by section 6 of the Act.

. . . If the Licensee is in any doubt as to whether a Licence covers a particular right or a particular copyright work the Licensee shall be entitled to contact ERA who shall be obliged within a reasonable time (by one of the Licensor Members) to confirm whether or not a particular right is owned or controlled by one of the Licensors.]

9. No recording or copying of a broadcast under any Licence shall be made except by or on behalf of an Educational Establishment and any such recording or copying shall be made either:

(a) on the premises of the Educational Establishment by or under the direct supervision of a teacher or employee of the Licensee; or

(b) at the residence of a teacher employed by the Licensee by that teacher; or

(c) at the premises of a third party authorised by the Licensee to make recordings or copies on behalf of the Licensee under written contractual terms and conditions which prevent the retention or use of any recordings or copies by that third party or any other third party unless ERA shall have expressly agreed that a specific third party may retain any recordings or copies for subsequent use only by authorised Licensees of ERA in accordance with the provisions of the Licensing Scheme.

Maintaining records

10. [Licensees shall be required to ensure that all ERA Recordings or copies comprising ERA Recordings made under a Licence provide for sufficient acknowledgement of the service from which the ERA Recording was acquired to be given; with each ERA Recording being marked with the name of the source, the date upon which the recording was secured by or for the Educational establishment and the title of the recording.]

To provide sufficient acknowledgement all copies shall be marked with a statement in clear and bold lettering reading:

"This recording is to be used only for non-commercial educational purposes under the terms of the ERA Licence"

or such other wording or statement as ERA shall reasonably require from time to time.

Physical copies shall include the statement on the exterior of the copy, and/or its packaging.

When under the Licence copies are made and stored in digital form for access through a computer server, the statement shall also be included as a written opening credit or webpage which must be viewed or listened to before access to the ERA Recording is permitted.

11. Licensees may be required to record and maintain at the request of ERA details of [how ERA Recordings are acquired or accessed] and the number of copies of such recordings made under a Licence and to make available to ERA such records for inspection.

12. Licensees shall undertake that if and when any ERA Recordings are communicated to the public by a person situated within the premises of an Educational Establishment under the Licence suitable password, and other digital rights management or technological protection systems are operated and applied by the Licensee to ensure that such communication is not received or receivable by persons situated outside the premises of the licensed Educational Establishment.

13. Licensees may be required to maintain further records and answer questionnaires or surveys as ERA may reasonably require for the proper operation of the Licensing Scheme [and any agreements with third parties relevant to clause 9(c).].

14. ERA shall be entitled to inspect and Licensees shall provide for ERA to have access to all records that Licensees and licensed Educational Establishments are required to maintain under the above provisions, and further to have access to all ERA Recordings however stored under the terms of a Licence, in order to inspect the same to check compliance with the Licence.

Period of Licence and Fees

15. Licences shall be granted in consideration of payment of the agreed Licence fees and may be granted for such period or periods as may from time to time be specified by or agreed with ERA.

16. The Licence fee shall be calculated by reference to the period for which the Licence is granted and to the tariff applicable in respect of that period.

[17A. The annual tariff for students in Educational Establishments relevant to this clause 17A shall apply for each student.

For Licences taking effect on or after 1st April 2013 the annual tariff shall be:	
Students in Primary schools (including Educational Establishments known as Preparatory Schools)	33p per head
Students in Secondary schools undertaking Secondary education	59p per head
Students in Educational Establishments of Further Education (including former Sixth Form Colleges) who have not attained the age of 18 at the start of the education year	59p per head

Discounted rates may be negotiated at ERA's discretion to cover groups of Educational Establishments relevant to this clause.

17B. The annual tariff for students relevant to this clause 17B shall be calculated on a full-time or full-time equivalent basis by category of student in an Educational Establishment.

For Licences taking effect on or after 1st April 2013 the annual tariff shall be:	
Students who have attained the age of 18 at the start of the educational year in Educational Establishments of Further Education undertaking courses of further education	£1.11p
Students in Educational Establishments of Higher Education and Students of other Educational Establishments who have attained the age of 18 at the start of the educational year when undertaking courses of Higher Education	£1.75p
Students in Educational Establishments not relevant to clause 17A or otherwise under this clause 17B but specified from time to time by the Secretary of State under s 174 of the Act	£1.75p

Discounted rates may be negotiated at ERA's discretion to cover groups of Educational Establishments relevant to this clause.]

18. Licence fees for Licences running for a period of less than one year shall be calculated on a pro-rata basis against the applicable annual tariff.

Part 2 Copyright

19. Licensees shall pay agreed Licence fees together with any VAT and any other Government tax which may be applicable from time to time in addition to such Licence Fee on such a date or dates as may from time to time be required by ERA in the Licence and within 28 days of invoice.

Termination

20. ERA shall be entitled to terminate Licences granted:

(a) if Licence Fees are not paid when due; or

(b) for any other substantial breach of the conditions of the Licence,

provided that ERA shall have given to the Licensee written notice identifying the nature of late payment or the nature of the breach.

The termination will become effective twenty eight days after receipt of the written notice unless during the relevant period of twenty eight days the Licensee makes payment of outstanding fees or remedies the breach.

21. Licences will automatically terminate:

(a) if and when an administrator, receiver, administrative receiver or other encumbrancer takes possession of, or is appointed over, the whole or any substantial part of the assets of a Licensee;

(b) if the Licensee enters into an arrangement or composition with or for the benefit of its creditors (including any voluntary arrangement under the Insolvency Act 1986);

(c) if a petition is presented for the purpose of considering a resolution for the making of an administration order, the winding-up or dissolution of the Licensee.

22. If punctual payment of agreed Licence Fees is not made, ERA shall be entitled to charge interest on amounts unpaid at the rate of statutory interest prescribed under section 6 of the Late Payment of Commercial Debts (Interest) Act 1998.

23. Upon expiry of a Licence without renewal or when a Licence is terminated by ERA it shall be entitled to require a Licensee to delete all ERA Recordings or copies made by the Educational Establishment to which the Licence related.

24. If a Licensee is in breach of the terms of a Licence and ERA incurs costs and expenses either in monitoring and discovering any breach of the terms of a Licence or in enforcing the conditions of any Licence, the Licensee shall be required to indemnify ERA in respect of any such costs and expenses so incurred.

25. Licensees shall be required to take all reasonable steps to ensure that rights granted by a Licence are not exceeded or abused by teachers, employees, pupils or other persons.

26. Licences issued shall be governed and interpreted in accordance with the laws of England and Wales.

NOTES

Para 6: substituted by the Copyright (Certification of Licensing Scheme for Educational Recording of Broadcasts) (Educational Recording Agency Limited) (Amendment) Order 2013, SI 2013/158, art 2(1), (2).

Paras 7, 13: words in square brackets added by SI 2013/158, art 2(1), (3), (7).

Para 8: substituted by the Copyright (Certification of Licensing Scheme for Educational Recording of Broadcasts) (Educational Recording Agency Limited) (Revocation and Amendment) Order 2008, SI 2008/211, art 3, Sch 1; words in square brackets in entry "AGICOA" substituted by the Copyright (Certification of Licensing Scheme for Educational Recording of Broadcasts) (Educational Recording Agency Limited) (Amendment) Order 2009, SI 2009/20, art 2(1), (2); entries "COMPACT" and "FOCAL" inserted by the Copyright (Certification of Licensing Scheme for Educational Recording of Broadcasts) (Educational Recording Agency Limited) (Amendment) Order 2011, SI 2011/159, art 2(1), (2); entry "RADIO INDEPENDENTS GROUP ("RIG")" inserted by SI 2013/158, art 2(1), (4); entry "OPEN UNIVERSITY" inserted by the Copyright (Certification of Licensing Scheme for Educational Recording of Broadcasts) (Educational Recording Agency Limited) (Amendment No 2) Order 2013, SI 2013/1924, art 2.

Paras 10, 11: words in square brackets substituted by SI 2013/158, art 2(1), (5), (6).

Paras 17A, 17B: substituted for original para 17 by SI 2013/158, art 2(1), (8).

PARLIAMENTARY COPYRIGHT (NATIONAL ASSEMBLY FOR WALES) ORDER 2007

(SI 2007/1116)

NOTES

Made: 4 April 2007.

Authority: Copyright, Designs and Patents Act 1988, s 165(7).

Commencement: 4 May 2007.

[2.582]
1 Citation and commencement

(1) This Order may be cited as the Parliamentary Copyright (National Assembly for Wales) Order 2007.

(2) This Order shall come into force immediately after the ordinary election under section 3 of the Government of Wales Act 1998 held in 2007.

[2.583]
2 Modification of section 165 of the Copyright, Designs and Patents Act 1988

(1) This article modifies the effect of section 165 of the Copyright, Designs and Patents Act 1988 (parliamentary copyright) in its application to works made by or under the direction or control of the National Assembly for Wales.

(2) The section has effect as if for subsection (1) there were substituted—

"(1) Where a work is made by or under the direction or control of the National Assembly for Wales—

(a) the work qualifies for copyright protection notwithstanding section 153(1) (ordinary requirement as to qualification for copyright protection), and

(b) the National Assembly for Wales Commission is the first owner of any copyright in the work.".

(3) The section has effect as if for subsection (4) there were substituted—

"(4) For the purposes of this section, works made by or under the direction or control of the National Assembly for Wales include—

(a) any work made by a relevant person in the course of his duties, and

(b) any sound recording, film or live broadcast of the proceedings of the Assembly (including proceedings of a committee or sub-committee of the Assembly),

but a work shall not be regarded as made by or under the direction or control of the Assembly by reason only of its being commissioned by or on behalf of the Assembly.

(4A) The following are relevant persons for the purposes of subsection (4)—

(a) the presiding officer of the National Assembly for Wales elected under section 25 of the Government of Wales Act 2006,

(b) the deputy presiding officer of the Assembly elected under that section,

(c) the members of the Assembly Commission appointed under the standing orders of the Assembly by virtue of section 27(3) of that Act, and

(d) the members of the staff of the Assembly, within the meaning of that Act (see paragraph 3(2) of Schedule 2 to that Act).".

(4) The section has effect as if in subsection (5) for "the House of Commons or the House of Lords" there were substituted "the National Assembly for Wales".

COPYRIGHT TRIBUNAL RULES 2010

(SI 2010/791)

NOTES

Made: 15 March 2010.
Authority: Copyright, Designs and Patents Act 1988, ss 150, 152(2).
Commencement: 6 April 2010.

ARRANGEMENT OF RULES

PART I
PRELIMINARY

PART II
COMMENCING PROCEEDINGS

Part 2 Copyright

PART III
RESPONSE TO THE PROCEEDINGS

PART IV
INTERVENTION AND CONSOLIDATION

PART V
ALLOCATION

PART VI
CASE MANAGEMENT AND PREPARATION FOR HEARING

PART VII
THE HEARING

PART VIII
DELIVERY OF THE DECISION

PART IX
APPEALS FROM THE TRIBUNAL

PART X
INTERIM ORDERS AND AWARDS

PART XI
SUPPLEMENTARY

PART XII
TRANSITIONAL AND REVOCATION

SCHEDULES

PART I
PRELIMINARY

[2.584]
1 Citation and Commencement

These Rules may be cited as the Copyright Tribunal Rules 2010 and shall come into force on 6th April 2010.

[2.585]
2 Interpretation

(1) In these Rules—

"the Act" means the Copyright, Designs and Patents Act 1988;

"applicant" means a person or organisation who has made a reference or application to the Tribunal in accordance with rule 7;

"application" means the application form and statement of grounds filed with the Tribunal in accordance with rule 7(1);

"application form" means the form set out in Schedule 1;

"bank holiday" has the meaning conferred by section 1 of the Banking and Financial Dealings Act 1971;

"the Chairman" means the Chairman of the Tribunal or a deputy chairman or any other member of the Tribunal appointed to act as chairman;

"costs", in relation to proceedings in Scotland, means "expenses";

"court" means—

(a) as respects England and Wales, the High Court;
(b) as respects Scotland, the Court of Session;
(c) as respects Northern Ireland, the High Court of Northern Ireland;

"intervener" means a person or organisation who has applied under rule 15 to be made a party to proceedings;

"the office" means the office for the time being of the Tribunal;

"proceedings" means proceedings in respect of an application before the Tribunal;

"relevant fee" means the fee payable to the Tribunal as set out in Schedule 2;

"the Secretary" means the Secretary for the time being of the Tribunal;

"small application" has the meaning given in rule 17(6);

"standard application" has the meaning given in rule 17(6);

"statement of truth" means—

(a) in Northern Ireland, an affidavit;
(b) in England and Wales and Scotland a statement which meets the requirements of paragraphs (2) and (3) below;

"the Tribunal" means the Copyright Tribunal;

"the Tribunal address for service" has the meaning set out in rule 4; and

"the Tribunal Website" has the meaning set out in rule 5.

(2) A statement of truth is a statement that—

(a) The party putting forward the document, or
(b) in the case of a witness statement, the maker of the witness statement

believes the facts stated in the document are true.

(3) A statement of truth must be signed by—

(a) In the case of a statement of grounds, a response or a request for permission to intervene, the party or the legal representative of the party and
(b) In the case of a witness statement, the maker of the statement.

(4) The powers conferred on the Tribunal by rules 39(3) and 42 may be exercised by either the Chairman or the Tribunal.

[2.586]
3 Overriding objective

(1) The Rules set out a procedural code with the overriding objective of enabling the Tribunal to deal with cases justly.

(2) Dealing with a case justly includes, so far as practicable—

(a) ensuring that the parties are on an equal footing;
(b) saving expense;
(c) dealing with the case in ways which are proportionate—
    (i) to the amount of money involved,
    (ii) to the importance of the case,
    (iii) to the complexity of the issues, and
    (iv) to the financial position of each party;
(d) ensuring that it is dealt with expeditiously and fairly; and
(e) allotting to it an appropriate share of the resources available to the Tribunal, while taking into account the need to allot resources to other cases.

(3) The parties are required to help the Tribunal to further the overriding objective.

[2.587]

4 Tribunal address for service

The address for service of documents on the Tribunal is: The Secretary of the Copyright Tribunal, 21 Bloomsbury Street, London WC1B 3HF or such other address as may be notified in the London, Edinburgh and Belfast Gazettes and on the Tribunal Website.

[2.588]

5 Tribunal Website

The location of the Tribunal Website is: www.ipo.gov.uk/ctribunal.htm or such other location as may be notified from time to time in such manner as the Chairman may direct.

[2.589]

6 Representation and rights of audience

In proceedings a party may be represented by—

(a) a person who, for the purposes of the Legal Services Act 2007 is an authorised person in relation to an activity which constitutes the exercise of a right of audience or the conduct of litigation within the meaning of that Act;

(b) an advocate or solicitor in Scotland or a barrister or solicitor in Northern Ireland; or

(c) any other person allowed by the Tribunal to appear on his behalf.

PART II
COMMENCING PROCEEDINGS

[2.590]

7 Commencing proceedings

(1) Proceedings are started when a person files—

(a) an application form;

(b) a statement of grounds; and

(c) the relevant fee.

(2) The statement of grounds must—

(a) contain a concise statement of the facts on which the applicant relies;

(b) state the statutory provision under which the application is made;

(c) where appropriate include the terms of payment or terms of licence which the applicant believes to be unreasonable;

(d) specify the relief sought;

(e) be verified by a statement of truth.

[2.591]

8 Defective applications

(1) If the Tribunal considers that an application does not comply with rule 7, or is materially incomplete, or is lacking in clarity, it may give such directions as may be necessary to ensure that those defects are remedied.

(2) The Tribunal may, if satisfied that the efficient conduct of the proceedings so requires, instruct the Secretary to defer service of the application on the respondent until after the directions referred to in paragraph (1) have been complied with.

[2.592]

9 Power to reject

(1) The Tribunal may, after giving the parties an opportunity to be heard, reject an application in whole or in part at any stage in the proceedings if—

(a) it considers that the Tribunal has no jurisdiction to hear the application;

(b) it considers that the applicant

  (i) does not have a sufficient interest in the application; or

  (ii) is not an organisation that is representative of a class of persons that have a sufficient interest in the application;

(c) it considers, in accordance with relevant provision of the Act, that the application is premature;

(d) it considers that the application is an abuse of the Tribunal's process;

(e) it considers that the application discloses no reasonable grounds for bringing the application.

(2) When the Tribunal rejects an application it may make any consequential order it considers appropriate.

(3) For the purposes of paragraph (1)(c), the relevant provision means—

(a) section 118(2), where the reference is made under section 118;

(b) section 125(2), where the reference is made under section 125;

(c) paragraph 3(2) of Schedule 2A, where the reference is made under paragraph 3 of Schedule 2A and

(d) paragraph 10(2) of Schedule 2A, where the reference is made under paragraph 10 of Schedule 2A.

[2.593]
10 Amendment of application

(1) The applicant may amend the application only with the permission of the Tribunal.

(2) Where the Tribunal grants permission under paragraph (1) it may do so on such terms as it thinks fit, and shall give such further or consequential directions as may be necessary.

[2.594]
11 Withdrawal of the application

(1) The applicant may withdraw an application only with the permission of the Tribunal.

(2) Where the Tribunal gives permission under paragraph (1) it may—
(a) do so on such terms as it thinks fit; and
(b) instruct the Secretary to publish notice of the withdrawal on the Tribunal Website or in such other manner as the Tribunal may direct.

(3) Where an application is withdrawn any interim order of the Tribunal, other than an order made in respect of costs, shall immediately cease to have effect, unless the Tribunal directs otherwise.

PART III
RESPONSE TO THE PROCEEDINGS

[2.595]
12 Acknowledgement and notification

(1) On receiving an application the Secretary must—
(a) send an acknowledgement of its receipt to the applicant; and
(b) subject to rules 8(2) and 9 send a copy of the application to the respondent marked to show the date on which that copy is sent.

[2.596]
13 The response

(1) The respondent must send to the Secretary a response in the form required by this rule so that the response is received within 28 days (or such further time as the Tribunal may allow) of the date on which the Secretary sent a copy of the application to the respondent in accordance with rule 12(b).

(2) The response filed by the respondent must state—
(a) the name and address of the respondent;
(b) the name and address of the respondent's legal representatives, if any;
(c) an address for service in the European Economic Area;
and must be signed and dated by the respondent, or on the respondent's behalf by a duly authorised officer or legal representative.

(3) The response must contain—
(a) a concise statement of the facts on which the respondent relies;
(b) any relief sought by the respondent; and
(c) any directions sought pursuant to rule 20.

(4) The response must be verified by a statement of truth.

(5) Rules 8 and 10 shall apply to the response.

(6) On receiving the response, the Secretary shall send a copy to the applicant.

PART IV
INTERVENTION AND CONSOLIDATION

[2.597]
14 Publication of application

(1) Subject to rules 8 and 9 the Secretary must as soon as practicable upon receipt of an application publish a notice on the Tribunal Website and in any other manner the Chairman may direct.

(2) The notice referred to in paragraph (1) must state—
(a) that an application has been received;
(b) the section of the Act under which the application is made;
(c) the name of the applicant;
(d) the particulars of the relief sought by the applicant;
(e) a summary of the principal grounds relied on; and
(f) that any person—
(i) with substantial interest in the proceedings;
(ii) who objects to the application on the basis that the applicant does not have a sufficient interest in the application; or

(iii) who objects to the application on the basis that the applicant is not representative of a class of persons that have a sufficient interest in the application,

may apply to intervene in the proceedings, in accordance with rule 15, within 28 days of publication of the notice or such other period as the Chairman may direct.

[2.598]
15 Intervention

(1) Any person with substantial interest in the outcome of proceedings may make a request to the Tribunal for permission to intervene in those proceedings.

(2) The request must be sent to the Secretary within 28 days of the publication of the notice in accordance with rule 14.

(3) The Secretary shall give notice of the request for permission to intervene to the respondent and all other parties to the proceedings and invite their observations on that request within a specified period.

(4) A request for permission to intervene must state—

(a) the title of the proceedings to which that request relates;
(b) the name and address of the person wishing to intervene;
(c) the name and address of their legal representative, if any;
(d) an address for service in the European Economic Area;
(e) the facts on which the person wishing to intervene relies and the relief sought.

(5) The request must be verified by a statement of truth and accompanied by the relevant fee.

(6) The Tribunal may permit the intervention on such terms and conditions as it thinks fit, if satisfied, having taken into account the observations of the parties, that the intervening party has a substantial interest.

(7) On granting permission in accordance with paragraph (6), the Tribunal shall give all such consequential directions as it considers necessary with regard, in particular, to the service on the intervener of the documents lodged with the Secretary, the submission by the intervener of a statement of intervention and, if appropriate, the submission by the principal parties of a response to the statement of intervention.

(8) The statement of intervention and any response to it shall contain—

(a) a concise statement of the facts supporting the intervention or response; and
(b) any relief sought by the intervener or the party responding to the intervention.

(9) The statement of intervention and any response shall be verified by a statement of truth.

(10) Rules 8 and 10 shall apply to the statement of intervention.

[2.599]
16 Consolidation

(1) Where two or more applications are made relating to the same licensing scheme or proposed licensing scheme, or which involve the same or similar issues, the Tribunal may on its own initiative, or on the request of a party, order that the proceedings or any particular issue or matter raised in the proceedings be consolidated or heard together.

(2) Before making an order under this rule, the Tribunal must invite the parties to the relevant proceedings to submit their observations.

PART V
ALLOCATION

[2.600]
17 Allocation

(1) The Tribunal shall allocate an application to the small applications track or to the standard applications track, taking into account the factors set out in this rule;

(2) When the Tribunal makes an allocation it shall have regard to—

(a) the financial value of the application to each of the parties;
(b) whether the facts, legal issues, relief requested or procedures involved are simple or complex; and
(c) the importance of the outcome of the application to other licensees or putative licensees of a licensing body.

(3) The small applications track is the normal track for an application where its financial value is less than £50,000 to each party and the facts and legal issues involved are simple.

(4) The standard track is the normal track for all other applications.

(5) When the Tribunal has allocated an application to a track the Secretary shall serve a notice of allocation on every party.

(6) Applications allocated to the small applications track are referred to as "small applications" and all other applications are referred to as "standard applications".

(7) The Rules apply to small applications with the exception of rules 22(1), (2) and (3), 23, 35 and 36.

(8) The Rules apply to standard applications with the exception of rule 21.

[2.601]
18 Change of track

The Tribunal may at any time on the request of a party or of its own initiative order, having considered the factors set out in rule 17(2), that—

(a) proceedings allocated to the small applications track be transferred to the standard applications track; or

(b) proceedings allocated to the standard applications track be transferred to the small applications track.

PART VI
CASE MANAGEMENT AND PREPARATION FOR HEARING

[2.602]
19 Case management—general

(1) In determining applications the Tribunal shall actively exercise its powers set out in rules 16 (consolidation), 17 (allocation), 18 (change of track), 20 (directions), 21 (procedure for small applications) 22 (case management of standard applications) 23 (oral hearing of a standard application) 24 (evidence), 25 (expert evidence) 26 (summoning of witnesses and order to answer questions or produce documents) and 27 (failure to comply with directions) with a view to ensuring that the application is dealt with justly.

(2) The Tribunal may in particular—

(a) encourage and facilitate the use of an alternative dispute resolution procedure if it considers it appropriate; and

(b) dispense with the need for the parties to attend any hearing.

[2.603]
20 Directions

(1) The Tribunal may at any time, on the request of a party or of its own initiative, at a case management conference, pre-hearing review, on an application for appeal or otherwise, give such directions as are provided for in paragraph (2) below or such other directions as it thinks fit to secure the just, expeditious and economical conduct of the proceedings.

(2) Where a party requests directions in accordance with paragraph (1) the request must be accompanied by the relevant fee.

(3) The Tribunal may give directions—

(a) as to the manner in which the proceedings are to be conducted, including any time limits to be observed in the conduct of an oral hearing;

(b) that the parties file a reply, rejoinder or other additional statements or particulars;

(c) that part of any of the proceedings be dealt with as a preliminary issue;

(d) that any part of the application, response or intervention be struck out;

(e) for the dismissal of the proceedings;

(f) to stay or, where the proceedings are in Scotland, to sist the whole or part of any proceedings or order or decision of the Tribunal either generally or until after a specified date;

(g) for the preparation and exchange of skeleton arguments;

(h) in relation to proceedings in England and Wales or Northern Ireland, requiring persons to attend and give evidence or to produce documents;

(i) as to the evidence which may be required or admitted in proceedings before the Tribunal and the extent to which it shall be oral or written;

(j) as to the submission in advance of a hearing of any witness statements or expert reports;

(k) as to the cross-examination of witnesses;

(l) as to the fixing of time limits with respect to any aspect of the proceedings;

(m) as to the abridgement or extension of any time limits, whether or not expired;

(n) for the disclosure between, or the production by, the parties of documents or classes of documents;

(o) for the appointment and instruction of experts, whether by the Tribunal or by the parties and the manner in which expert evidence is to be given;

(p) as to the use or further disclosure of a document which has been disclosed in the proceedings, whether or not it has been read to or by the Chairman or Tribunal or referred to at a hearing which has been held in public;

(q) for the award of costs; and

(r) for hearing a person who is not a party where, in any proceedings, it is proposed to make an order or give a direction in relation to that person.

(4) The Tribunal may, in particular, of its own initiative—

(a) put questions to the parties;

(b) invite the parties to make written or oral submissions on certain aspects of the proceedings;
(c) ask the parties or other persons for information or particulars;
(d) ask for documents or any papers relating to the case to be produced;
(e) summon the parties' representatives or the parties in person to meetings.

(5) A request by a party for directions shall be made in writing as soon as practicable and shall be served by the Secretary on any other party who might be affected by such directions and determined by the Tribunal taking into account the observations of the parties.

[2.604]
21 Procedure for small applications

(1) This rule contains the procedure for small applications.

(2) As soon as possible after an allocation is made in accordance with rule 17 or 18 the Tribunal shall give directions and notify the parties of the date on which the decision shall be delivered in accordance with rule 30.

(3) If any party requests a hearing or the Tribunal considers that a hearing is required, either before or after the Tribunal has given directions in accordance with paragraph (2) the Tribunal must give directions (which may include directions for a case management conference or a pre-hearing review), fix a date for the hearing and notify the parties in writing of the date, time and place of that oral hearing.

[2.605]
22 Case management of standard applications

(1) This rule applies to the case management of standard applications. Paragraphs (4) and (5) of this rule apply to small applications if the Tribunal gives directions in accordance with rule 21(3).

(2) Where it appears to the Tribunal that any proceedings would be facilitated by holding a case management conference or pre-hearing review the Tribunal may, on the request of a party or of its own initiative, give directions for such a conference or review to be held.

(3) Unless the Tribunal otherwise directs, a case management conference must be held as soon as practicable after allocation in accordance with rule 17 or rule 18(a).

(4) A case management conference or pre-hearing review shall be held in private unless the Tribunal otherwise directs.

(5) The purpose of a case management conference or pre-hearing review is—
(a) to ensure the efficient conduct of the proceedings;
(b) to determine the points on which the parties must present further argument or which call for further evidence to be produced;
(c) to clarify the forms of order sought by the parties, their arguments of fact and law and the points at issue between them;
(d) to ensure that all agreements that can be reached between the parties about the matters in issue and the conduct of the proceedings are made and recorded;
(e) to facilitate the settlement of the proceedings;
(f) to set a timetable outlining the steps to be taken by the parties pursuant to directions in preparation for the oral hearing of the proceedings;
(g) to set the dates within which the hearing shall take place.

[2.606]
23 Oral hearing of a standard application

As soon as practicable after the case management conference or pre-hearing review, the Secretary shall, after discussions with the parties, notify the parties in writing of the date, time and place for the oral hearing and of any timetable for that hearing.

[2.607]
24 Evidence

(1) The Tribunal may control the evidence by giving directions as to—
(a) the issues on which evidence is required;
(b) the nature of the evidence required to decide those issues; and
(c) the way in which the evidence is to be placed before the Tribunal.

(2) The Tribunal may use its power to exclude evidence that would otherwise be admissible where—
(a) the evidence was not provided within the time allowed by a direction;
(b) the evidence was provided in a manner that did not comply with a direction;
(c) it would be unfair to admit the evidence;
(d) the evidence is not proportionate to the issues of the case; or
(e) the evidence is not necessary for the fair disposal of the case.

(3) The Tribunal may require any witness to give evidence on oath or affirmation or, if in writing, by way of a witness statement verified by a statement of truth.

(4) The Tribunal may allow a witness to give evidence through a video link or by other means.

[2.608]
25 Expert evidence

(1) Expert evidence shall be restricted to that which is proportionate to the issues of the case and necessary for the fair disposal of the case.

(2) No party may call an expert or put in expert evidence without the permission of the Tribunal.

(3) When a party applies for permission to call an expert or put in expert evidence it must identify—

(a) the field in which expert evidence shall be relied upon;

(b) the expert in that field whose evidence shall be relied upon and, if applicable, the organisation by whom the expert is employed and

(c) the principal issues which the expert will be expected to address.

(4) If the Tribunal grants permission under this rule it must be only in relation to the expert named and the field and on the issues identified in the application.

(5) The Tribunal may limit the fees and expenses of an expert that can be recovered from the parties to the litigation that did not instruct that expert.

[2.609]
26 Summoning of witnesses and orders to answer questions or produce documents

(1) On the application of a party or on its own initiative, the Tribunal may—

(a) by summons require any person to attend as a witness at a hearing at the time and place specified in the summons; or

(b) order any person to answer any questions or produce any documents in that person's possession or control which relate to any issue in the proceedings.

(2) A summons under paragraph (1)(a) must—

(a) give the person required to attend not less than 14 days' notice of the hearing or such shorter period as the Tribunal may direct; and

(b) where the person is not a party, make provision for the person's necessary expenses of attendance to be paid, and state who is to pay them.

(3) No person may be compelled to give any evidence or produce any document that the person could not be compelled to give or produce on a trial of an action in a court of law in the part of the United Kingdom where the proceedings are due to be determined.

(4) This rule shall only apply to proceedings in England and Wales and Northern Ireland.

[2.610]
27 Failure to comply with directions

If any party fails to comply with any direction given in accordance with these Rules, the Tribunal may, if it considers that the justice of the case so requires, order that such party be debarred from taking any further part in the proceedings without the permission of the Tribunal.

PART VII
THE HEARING

[2.611]
28 Hearing to be in public

Except where the Tribunal orders otherwise, the hearing of any application must be in public.

[2.612]
29 Procedure at the hearing

(1) The proceedings must be opened and directed by the Chairman who is responsible for the proper conduct of the hearing.

(2) The Tribunal shall, so far as it appears to it appropriate, seek to avoid formality in its proceedings and shall conduct the hearing in such manner as it considers most appropriate for the clarification of the issues before it and generally to the just, expeditious and economical handling of the proceedings.

(3) Unless the Tribunal otherwise directs, no witness of fact or expert may be heard unless the relevant witness statement or expert report has been submitted in advance of the hearing and in accordance with any directions of the Tribunal.

(4) The Tribunal may limit cross-examination of witnesses to any extent or in any manner it deems appropriate.

PART VIII
DELIVERY OF THE DECISION

[2.613]
30 Delivery of the decision

(1) The decision of the Tribunal on an application must be given in writing and must include a statement of the Tribunal's reasons.

(2) The Secretary must as soon as practicable serve on every party to the proceedings a copy of the Tribunal's decision.

(3) The Chairman must arrange for the decision of the Tribunal to be published in such manner as considered appropriate.

[2.614]
31 Orders for costs

(1) The Tribunal may, at its discretion, at any stage of the proceedings make any order it thinks fit in relation to the payment of costs by one party to another in respect of the whole or part of the proceedings.

(2) Any party against whom an order for costs is made shall, if the Tribunal so directs, pay to any other party a lump sum by way of costs, or such proportion of the costs as may be just, and in the last mentioned case the Tribunal may assess the sum to be paid or may direct that it be assessed or, where appropriate, taxed by—

(a) the Chairman;
(b) a costs officer of the High Court;
(c) the Master (Taxing Office) of the High Court of Northern Ireland; or
(d) the Auditor of the Court of Session.

[2.615]
32 Effective date of order

Except where the operation of the order is suspended under rule 33 or 34, an order of the Tribunal shall take effect from such date, and shall remain in force for such period, as is specified in the order.

PART IX
APPEALS FROM THE TRIBUNAL

[2.616]
33 Commencement of appeal proceedings

(1) An appeal to the court under section 152 of the Act arising from a decision of the Tribunal must be brought within 28 days of the date of decision of the Tribunal or within such further period as the court may, on application to it, allow.

(2) A party appealing to the court must as soon as may be practicable serve on the Secretary a notice of such appeal accompanied by the relevant fee and shall serve a copy of the notice on every person who was a party to the proceedings giving rise to that decision.

(3) Following receipt of the notice of appeal by the Secretary the Tribunal may on its own initiative suspend the operation of any order contained in its decision.

[2.617]
34 Suspension of order

(1) Unless the Tribunal orders otherwise an appeal to the Court shall not operate as a stay of any decision or order of the Tribunal.

(2) The Tribunal may endorse a consent order where all parties to an action have consented to the suspension of the operation of an order.

(3) An application to the Tribunal for an endorsement under paragraph (2) must be accompanied by the relevant fee.

(4) Where any order of the Tribunal has been suspended by the Tribunal in accordance with rule 33(3) or upon the application of a party to the proceedings in accordance with rule 34(2) the Secretary must serve notice of the suspension on all parties to the proceedings, and if particulars of the order have been advertised must cause notice of the suspension to be advertised in the same manner.

(5) Rule 30(3) applies to the publication of a decision to suspend an order.

PART X
INTERIM ORDERS AND AWARDS

[2.618]
35 Power to make provisional awards

Subject to rule 36, the Tribunal shall have power to order on a provisional basis any relief which it would have power to grant in a final decision.

[2.619]
36 Awards on different issues

(1) The Tribunal may make more than one award at different times on different aspects of the matters to be determined.

(2) The Tribunal may, in particular, make an award relating to—

(a) an issue affecting the whole claim, or

(b) a part only of the claims or cross-claims submitted to it for decision.

(3) If the Tribunal makes an award under paragraph (2) it shall specify in its award the issue, or the claim or part of a claim, which is the subject matter of that award.

PART XI SUPPLEMENTARY

[2.620]

37 Enforcement—England and Wales and Northern Ireland

A decision made by the Tribunal may, by leave of the court, be enforced in England and Wales or Northern Ireland in the same manner as a judgment or order of the court to the same effect.

[2.621]

38 Enforcement of Tribunal's orders in Scotland

Any decision of the Tribunal may be enforced in Scotland in the same way as a recorded decree arbitral.

[2.622]

39 Service of documents

(1) Any notice or other document required by these Rules to be served on any person may be sent by pre-paid post to its address for service, or, where no address for service has been given, to its registered office, principal place of business or last known address, and every notice or other document required to be served on the Secretary may be sent by pre-paid post to the Secretary the Tribunal address for service during office hours.

(2) Any notice or other document required to be served on a licensing body or organisation which is not a body corporate may be sent to the secretary, manager or other similar officer.

(3) The Tribunal may direct that service of any notice or other document be dispensed with or effected otherwise than in the manner provided by these Rules.

(4) Service of any notice or document on a party's solicitor or agent shall be deemed to be service on such party, and service on a solicitor or agent acting for more than one party shall be deemed to be service on every party for whom such a solicitor or agent acts.

[2.623]

40 Time

(1) Where a period expressed in days, weeks or months is to be calculated from the moment at which an event occurs or an action takes place, the day during which that event occurs or that action takes place shall not be counted as falling within the period in question.

(2) A period expressed in weeks or months shall end with the expiry of whichever day in the last week or month is the same day of the week or falls on the same date in the month, as the day during which the event or action from which the period is to be calculated occurred or took place. If, in a period expressed in months, the day on which it should expire does not occur in the last month, the period shall end with the expiry of the last day of that month.

(3) Where the time for doing any act expires on a Saturday, Sunday, Christmas Day, Good Friday or bank holiday, the act is in time if done on the next following day which is not a Saturday, a Sunday, Christmas Day, Good Friday or bank holiday in any part of the United Kingdom.

[2.624]

41 Office hours

The office shall be open between 10.00 am and 4.00 pm Monday to Friday, excluding Good Friday, Christmas Day and bank holidays in England and Wales.

[2.625]

42 Clerical mistakes and accidental slips or omissions

The Tribunal may at any time correct any clerical mistake or other accidental slip or omission in a decision, direction or any document produced by it, by—

(a) sending notification of the amended decision or direction, or a copy of the amended document, to each party; and

(b) making any necessary amendment to any information published in relation to the decision, direction or document.

[2.626]

43 Power of Tribunal to regulate procedure

Subject to the provisions of the Act and these Rules, the Tribunal shall have power to regulate its own procedure.

PART XII
TRANSITIONAL AND REVOCATION

[2.627]
44 Transitional provisions

Any proceedings commenced under the Act before these Rules come into force shall continue in accordance with these Rules.

45 (*Revokes the Copyright Tribunal Rules 1989, SI 1989/1129.*)

SCHEDULES

SCHEDULE 1
APPLICATION FORM

Rule 2

[2.628]

APPLICATION FORM	
Tribunal reference: Issue date	
Applicant's name and address, email address and telephone number:	
Respondent's name and address, email address and telephone number:	
Either (a) the section number of the Copyright Designs and Patents Act 1988 or Broadcasting Act 1990 or (b) name of the Regulations under which the claim is brought:	
Brief details of the facts upon which the applicant relies:	
Applicant's address for service, if different from the address above:	
Date:	

SCHEDULE 2
FEES

Rule 2

[2.629]

1. The relevant fee is £15 for an application for directions in accordance with rule 20, other than an application for a direction under rule 20(3)(d).

2. The relevant fee is £25 for

(a) an application for directions under rule 20(3)(d);

(b) a request for permission to intervene made under rule 15;

(c) a notice of appeal served in accordance with rule 33;

(d) an application for endorsement of a consent order made in accordance with rule 34(3);

(e) an application to the Tribunal made under rule 7 where the application is

(i) for special leave made under section 120, 122, 127, 135F, 142 or paragraph 5 of Schedule 6 to the Act or paragraph 6(2) of Schedule 17 to the Broadcasting Act 1990;

(ii) a reference made under section 125 or 126 of the Act;

(iii) an appeal made under section 139 of the Act;

(iv) made under section 135F(2) of the Act for review of an order;

(v) made under section 142 of the Act to settle royalty or other sums payable;

(vi) made under section 144 of the Act to settle terms of a licence of right;

(vii) made under paragraph 6(1) of Schedule 17 to the Broadcasting Act 1990.

3. The relevant fee is £50 for an application made under rule 7, other than an application listed in paragraph 2(e) above.

LEGAL DEPOSIT LIBRARIES (NON-PRINT WORKS) REGULATIONS 2013

(SI 2013/777)

NOTES

Made: 5 April 2013.
Authority: Legal Deposit Libraries Act 2003, ss 1(4), 2(2), 6(1), 7(3), 10(5), 11(1).
Commencement: 6 April 2013.

ARRANGEMENT OF REGULATIONS

PART 1
INTRODUCTORY

[2.630]

1 Citation and commencement

(1) These Regulations may be cited as the Legal Deposit Libraries (Non-Print Works) Regulations 2013.

(2) They come into force on the day after the day on which they are made.

NOTES

Commencement: 6 April 2013.

[2.631]

2 Interpretation

(1) In these Regulations—

"the Act" means the Legal Deposit Libraries Act 2003;

"computer terminal" means a terminal on library premises controlled by the deposit library from which a reader is permitted to view relevant material;

"database right" has the same meaning as in regulation 13 of the Copyright and Rights in Databases Regulations 1997;

"IP address" means internet protocol address;

"permanent collection" means the permanent collection held by a deposit library of non-print work delivered or copied under these Regulations;

"personal data" has the same meaning as in section 1 of the Data Protection Act 1998;

"publisher" means, in relation to a work to which the Act applies, the person to whom the obligation in section 1(1) of the Act applies in respect of that work;

"web harvester" means a computer program which is used to search the internet in order to request delivery of on line work on behalf of a deposit library;

(2) a reference to "in writing" includes text which is—

(a) transmitted by electronic means;

(b) received in legible form; and

(c) capable of being used for subsequent reference;

(3) a reference to a deposit library (whether or not to a specific deposit library) includes a person acting on behalf of the deposit library.

NOTES

Commencement: 6 April 2013.

[2.632]

3

In regulations 20 and 23 to 31 references to a deposit library include reference to the Faculty of Advocates.

NOTES

Commencement: 6 April 2013.

PART 2
EXEMPTION FOR EXISTING MICRO-BUSINESSES AND NEW BUSINESSES

[2.633]

4 The exemption

(1) During the exemption period, regulations 13(1)(a), 14(2), 15, 16(3) to 16(7) and 17 do not apply in relation to a work published in a medium other than print where a person publishes the work in the course of a business, if the business is—

(a) an existing micro-business, or

(b) a new business.

(2) In relation to a work published off line that is subject to the exemption in paragraph (1)—

(a) paragraphs (1) and (2) of regulation 15 shall not require delivery of any such work;

(b) paragraph (3) of regulation 15 shall have effect as if it provided for the British Library Board (in addition to other deposit libraries) to be entitled to delivery of the work if it requests it, and paragraphs (4) to (10) of that regulation have effect accordingly.

NOTES

Commencement: 6 April 2013.

[2.634]

5 Micro-businesses

A micro-business is a business that has fewer than 10 employees (see regulations 9 to 11).

NOTES

Commencement: 6 April 2013.

[2.635]

6 Existing micro-businesses

An existing micro-business is a business that was a micro-business immediately before the commencement date.

NOTES

Commencement: 6 April 2013.

[2.636]

7 New businesses

(1) A new business is a business which a person, or a number of persons, ("P") begins to carry on during the period beginning with the commencement date and ending with 31 March 2014.

(2) But a business is not a new business if—

(a) P has, at any time during the period of 6 months ending immediately before the date on which P begins to carry on the business, carried on another business consisting of the activities of which the business consists (or most of them), or

(b) P carries on the business as a result of a transfer (within the meaning of paragraph (4)).

(3) Paragraph (2)(a) does not apply if the other business referred to in that paragraph was a new business (within the meaning of this regulation).

(4) P carries on a business as a result of a transfer if P begins to carry on the business on another person ceasing to carry on the activities of which it consists (or most of them) in consequence of arrangements involving P and the other person.

(5) For this purpose, P is to be taken to begin to carry on a business on another person ceasing to carry on such activities if—

(a) P begins to carry on the business otherwise than in partnership on such activities ceasing to be carried on by persons in partnership, or

(b) P is a number of persons in partnership who begin to carry on the business on such activities ceasing to be carried on—

(i) by a person, or a number of persons, otherwise than in partnership,

(ii) by persons in partnership who do not consist only of all the persons who constitute P, or

(iii) partly as mentioned in paragraph (i) and partly as mentioned in paragraph (ii).

(6) Paragraph (2)(b) does not apply if the activities referred to in paragraph (4) were, when carried on by the person who is not P referred to in that paragraph, activities of a new business (within the meaning of this regulation).

(7) P is not to be regarded as beginning to carry on a business for the purposes of paragraph (1) if—

(a) before P begins to carry on the business, P is a party to arrangements under which P may (at any time during the period beginning with the commencement date and ending with 31 March 2014) carry on, as part of the business, activities carried on by any other person, and

(b) the business would have been prevented by paragraph (2)(b) from being a new business if—

(i) P had begun to carry on the activities when beginning to carry on the business, and

(ii) the other person had at that time ceased to carry them on.

(8) "Arrangements" includes an agreement, understanding, scheme, transaction or series of transactions (whether or not legally enforceable).

NOTES

Commencement: 6 April 2013.

[2.637]

8 The exemption period

(1) The exemption period in relation to an existing micro-business starts with the commencement date and ends with 31 March 2014.

(2) The exemption period in relation to a new business starts with the date on which P begins to carry on the business and ends with 31 March 2014.

NOTES

Commencement: 6 April 2013.

[2.638]

9 Number of employees of a business

For the purposes of this Part, the number of employees of a business is calculated as follows—

TH / 37.5

where TH is the total number of hours per week for which all the employees of the business are contracted to work.

NOTES

Commencement: 6 April 2013.

[2.639]

10 Employees of a business

For the purposes of this Part, the employees of a business are the persons who are employed for the purposes of the business.

NOTES

Commencement: 6 April 2013.

[2.640]
11 Employees

(1) In this Part, "employee" means an individual who has entered into or works under a contract of employment.

(2) In paragraph (1) "contract of employment" means a contract of service, whether express or implied, and (if it is express) whether oral or in writing.

NOTES
Commencement: 6 April 2013.

[2.641]
12 The commencement date

For the purposes of this Part, "the commencement date" means the date on which these Regulations come into force.

NOTES
Commencement: 6 April 2013.

PART 3
DEPOSIT

[2.642]
13 Non-print work to which the Act applies

(1) The Act applies to the following descriptions of work published in a medium other than print—
- (a) work that is published off line, and
- (b) work that is published on line.

(2) But, the descriptions of work prescribed in paragraph (1) do not include—
- (a) work consisting only of—
  - (i) a sound recording or film or both, or
  - (ii) such material and other material which is merely incidental to it;
- (b) work which contains personal data and which is only made available to a restricted group of persons; or
- (c) work published before these Regulations were made.

(3) The description of work that is prescribed for the purposes of section 10(5)(a) of the Act is work that is published on the internet and that does not fall within the description given in paragraph (2)(a) or (b).

NOTES
Commencement: 6 April 2013.

[2.643]
14 New and alternative editions

(1) Where substantially the same work is published in the United Kingdom in print and in one or more non-print media, the duty under section 1(1) of the Act applies only in relation to its publication in print unless the publisher and the deposit library agree that instead the duty under section 1(1) of the Act applies in relation to its publication in one of the non-print media in which the work is published.

(2) Where substantially the same work is published in the United Kingdom in two or more non-print media (and is not published in print), the publisher and the deposit library may agree one of those non-print media as the medium in relation to which the duty under section 1(1) of the Act applies and, in the absence of agreement, the publisher may decide the non-print medium (which must be one in which the work is published) in relation to which the duty under section 1(1) of the Act applies.

NOTES
Commencement: 6 April 2013.

[2.644]
15 Entitlement to delivery: off line work

(1) The British Library Board is entitled to delivery under section 1 of the Act of a copy of every work published off line.

(2) A copy must be delivered to the British Library Board within one month beginning with the day of publication.

(3) Each deposit library other than the British Library Board is entitled to delivery under section 1 of the Act of a copy of any work published off line which it requests.

(4) The following provisions apply to a request made under paragraph (3)—

(a) it must be in writing;
(b) it must be made—
(i) within 12 months beginning with the day of publication, or
(ii) (in relation to a work published off line that is subject to the exemption in regulation 4) if later, by 30 April 2014;
(c) it may be made before publication;
(d) it may relate to all future numbers or parts of an encyclopaedia, newspaper, magazine or other non-print work.

(5) The copy must be delivered within one month beginning with—
(a) the day of publication, or
(b) if later, the day on which the request is received.

(6) The copy delivered pursuant to paragraphs (1) and (3) must be of a quality most suitable for the preservation of the work.

(7) The quality most suitable for the preservation of the work may be as agreed between the publisher and the deposit library or, in the absence of agreement, a quality which the publisher decides.

(8) Each deposit library must give a receipt in writing for the copies of work published off line that it receives.

NOTES

Commencement: 6 April 2013.

[2.645]
16 Entitlement to delivery: on line work

(1) Each deposit library is entitled to delivery under section 1 of the Act of a copy of any work published on line which it requests provided that such a request is made in accordance with paragraph (2) or (3).

(2) Where there is an agreement between a publisher and a deposit library regarding the method by which a work, or works of a particular description, will be delivered—
(a) the request for delivery of the work must be made in writing; and
(b) the work must be delivered to the deposit library by the agreed method within one month of the request being made, and must be of a quality which is most suitable for its preservation.

(3) Where no such agreement is in place, any request for delivery of a work must be made by the deposit library by means of a web harvester from one or more IP addresses dedicated for the purpose of making requests under this paragraph to the IP address from which the work is made available to the public.

(4) A request by a deposit library under paragraph (3) made in respect of a webpage which contains a login facility will be deemed to be a request for the work or works available behind that login facility provided that the deposit library has given the publisher at least one month's notice in writing before making the request.

(5) Delivery of a work requested under paragraph (3) must be by electronic means and by automated response to the request made by the web harvester.

(6) When making a request under paragraph (3) for work or works available behind a login facility, a deposit library must use any relevant login details provided to it by the publisher.

(7) A deposit library must not use such login details for any purpose except for compliance with these Regulations.

(8) For the purposes of paragraph (2)(b), the quality most suitable for the preservation of a work shall be such as may be agreed between the publisher and the deposit library or, in the absence of agreement, shall be decided by the publisher.

NOTES

Commencement: 6 April 2013.

[2.646]
17 Delivery of additional information

The publisher of a work delivered under regulation 15 or regulation 16(2) must deliver at the same time—
(a) a copy of any computer program or any other data or information necessary to access the work; and
(b) a copy of any manual and other material that accompanies the work and is made available to the public.

NOTES

Commencement: 6 April 2013.

[2.647]
18 On line work: published in the United Kingdom

(1) Subject to paragraph (2), a work published on line shall be treated as published in the United Kingdom if—

(a) it is made available to the public from a website with a domain name which relates to the United Kingdom or to a place within the United Kingdom; or

(b) it is made available to the public by a person and any of that person's activities relating to the creation or the publication of the work take place within the United Kingdom.

(2) A work published on line shall not be treated as published in the United Kingdom if access to the work is only made available to persons outside the United Kingdom.

(3) Where work is published on the internet and the publication of that work or a person publishing it there is connected with the United Kingdom in the manner prescribed in paragraphs (1) and (2), that manner of connection with the United Kingdom is also prescribed for the purposes of section 10(5)(b) of the Act.

NOTES

Commencement: 6 April 2013.

PART 4
PERMITTED ACTIVITIES

[2.648]
19 Use etc of relevant material by deposit libraries

A deposit library may transfer or lend relevant material to any other deposit library.

NOTES

Commencement: 6 April 2013.

[2.649]
20

A deposit library may use relevant material for the purposes of—

(a) reviewing and maintaining the relevant material, and

(b) the deposit library's own non-commercial research (whether the subject matter of the research is the permanent collection or not).

NOTES

Commencement: 6 April 2013.

[2.650]
21

The National Library of Scotland may permanently transfer any relevant material that is an off line legal publication to the Faculty of Advocates.

NOTES

Commencement: 6 April 2013.

[2.651]
22

The National Library of Scotland may transfer or lend any relevant material that is an on line legal publication to the Faculty of Advocates.

NOTES

Commencement: 6 April 2013.

[2.652]
23 Reader access to relevant material

A deposit library must ensure that only one computer terminal is available to readers to access the same relevant material at any one time.

NOTES

Commencement: 6 April 2013.

[2.653]
24

In the case of relevant material which is work published on line, at least seven days must elapse from the date of delivery of that relevant material to the deposit library before a reader may be permitted to view it.

NOTES

Commencement: 6 April 2013.

[2.654]

25

(1) A copyright owner or database right owner in relation to relevant material may make a request in writing to a deposit library to withhold access to that relevant material from readers for a specified period of time.

(2) The deposit library receiving the request must comply with that request if the following conditions are met—

(a) the period specified in the request does not exceed three years from the date on which the request is made;

(b) the deposit library is satisfied on reasonable grounds that, for the period specified in the request, viewing of the relevant material by a reader would, or would be likely to, unreasonably prejudice the interests of the person making the request.

(3) The entitlement to make a request under paragraph (1) includes an entitlement to make subsequent requests, and (subject to paragraph (4)) a deposit library must comply with a subsequent request if the conditions in paragraph (2) are met in relation to that request.

(4) If a subsequent request seeks to extend the specified period of time relating to an earlier request made under paragraph (1), that subsequent request must be made at least one month before the specified period expires.

NOTES

Commencement: 6 April 2013.

[2.655]

26 Reader access to relevant material: visually impaired persons

(1) A deposit library may make and supply for use on its premises accessible copies of relevant material for a visually impaired person if copies of the relevant material are not commercially available in a form that is accessible to the visually impaired person.

(2) Paragraph (1) does not apply in relation to relevant material that is a database in which copyright or database right subsists.

(3) A deposit library must ensure that only one reader uses an accessible copy of the same relevant material made under this regulation at any one time.

(4) An accessible copy made under paragraph (1) must be accompanied by—

(a) a statement that it is made under this regulation; and

(b) a sufficient acknowledgement.

(5) A deposit library entitled to make accessible copies under paragraph (1) may hold an intermediate copy of the relevant material which is necessarily made during the production of the accessible copies, but only—

(a) if and so long as the deposit library continues to be entitled to make accessible copies of that relevant material; and

(b) for the purposes of the production of further accessible copies.

(6) A deposit library may lend or transfer the intermediate copy to another deposit library which is entitled to make accessible copies of the relevant material under paragraph (1) provided that the intermediate copy is used only for the purposes of the production of further accessible copies.

(7) A deposit library must—

(a) keep records of accessible copies made under this regulation and of the persons to whom they are supplied;

(b) keep records of any intermediate copy lent or transferred under this regulation and of the deposit libraries to whom it is lent or transferred;

(c) allow a copyright owner or a person acting for a copyright owner, on giving reasonable notice, to inspect the records at any reasonable time.

(8) Within a reasonable time of making an accessible copy under paragraph (1) or lending or transferring an intermediate copy under paragraph (6), the deposit library must notify—

(a) each representative body; or

(b) if there is no such body, the copyright owner.

(9) A representative body is a body which—

(a) represents particular copyright owners, or owners of copyright in the type of copyright work concerned; and

(b) has given notice to the Secretary of State of the copyright owners, or the classes of copyright owner, represented by it.

(10) The requirement to notify the copyright owner under paragraph (8) does not apply—

(a) if it is not reasonably possible for the deposit library to ascertain the name and address of the copyright owner; or

(b) (where there is more than one copyright owner of the work to which the notification relates) in respect of those persons for whom it is not reasonably possible for the deposit library to ascertain their names and addresses.

(11) In this regulation—

(a) "accessible copy" and "visually impaired" have the same meaning as in section 31F of the Copyright, Designs and Patents Act 1988 ("the 1988 Act");

(b) "database" has the same meaning as in section 3A of the 1988 Act;

(c) "sufficient acknowledgement" has the same meaning as in section 178 of the 1988 Act.

NOTES

Commencement: 6 April 2013.

[2.656]

27 Supplying copies for research etc

(1) A deposit library may, if the conditions set out in paragraph (2) are met, produce and supply to a person a copy of relevant material.

(2) Those conditions are that—

(a) in relation to relevant material in which database right does not subsist, the deposit library is satisfied that the copy is required by that person for the purposes of non-commercial research or private study, criticism or review or reporting current events, parliamentary or judicial proceedings or a Royal Commission or statutory inquiry and will not be used for any other purpose;

(b) in relation to relevant material in which database right subsists, the deposit library is satisfied that the copy is required by that person for the purposes of parliamentary or judicial proceedings or a Royal Commission or statutory inquiry and will not be used for any other purpose;

(c) that person has delivered to the deposit library a signed declaration in writing in relation to the relevant material substantially in accordance with the Form in the Schedule to these Regulations;

(d) in relation to a copy of relevant material required for the purposes of non-commercial research or private study, the deposit library is satisfied that the requirement of the person requiring the copy is not related and similar to that of another person.

(3) For the purposes of paragraph (2)(d)—

(a) requirements shall be regarded as similar if the requirements are for copies of substantially the same relevant material at substantially the same time and for substantially the same purpose; and

(b) requirements of persons shall be regarded as related if those persons receive instruction to which the relevant material is relevant at the same time and place.

(4) Unless the deposit library is aware that the signed declaration delivered under paragraph (2)(c) is false in a material particular, the deposit library may rely on it in order to determine whether a copy is required for any of the purposes specified in paragraph (2)(a) or 2(b) and may rely on it in relation to paragraph (2)(d).

NOTES

Commencement: 6 April 2013.

[2.657]

28

(1) The supply by a deposit library of a copy of relevant material under regulation 27 is subject to the following provisions of this regulation.

(2) Where the relevant material is capable of being supplied in print, a deposit library must supply a copy of the relevant material in print unless the copyright owner or database right owner (as the case may be) has given permission for a copy to be supplied in a medium other than print in which case it may be supplied in that medium.

(3) Where the relevant material is not capable of being supplied in print, a deposit library may only supply a copy of the relevant material in a medium other than print if the copyright owner or database right owner (as the case may be) has given permission for the deposit library to supply a copy in that medium.

(4) In relation to a copy of relevant material required for the purposes of non-commercial research or private study—

(a) a deposit library must not supply a person with more than one copy of the same relevant material;

(b) the copy of the relevant material supplied by a deposit library must not represent more than a reasonable proportion of the relevant material of which the element copied forms a part;

(c) if the relevant material being copied is an article in a periodical, a deposit library must not supply a person with more than one copy of that article or more than one article contained in the same edition of that periodical.

(5) The person requiring the copy of the relevant material is required to pay for that copy a sum not less than the cost (including a contribution to general expenses) attributable to its production.

NOTES

Commencement: 6 April 2013.

[2.658]

29 Copying relevant material for the purposes of preservation

(1) A deposit library may copy relevant material if the copy is made in any of the circumstances falling within paragraph (2).

(2) The circumstances are that the copy is made (whether from the relevant material itself or from a copy made by the deposit library by virtue of this regulation) in order—

(a) to preserve or replace the relevant material by placing the copy in the permanent collection in addition to or in place of the relevant material;

(b) to replace the relevant material in the permanent collection of another deposit library if that relevant material has been lost, destroyed or damaged.

(3) A copy may be made by virtue of this regulation in a different medium or format from the relevant material if the deposit library considers the change is necessary or expedient for the purpose for which the copy is made.

(4) Paragraph (1) does not apply if database right subsists in the relevant material.

NOTES

Commencement: 6 April 2013.

[2.659]

30 Adapting relevant material for the purposes of preservation

(1) A deposit library may adapt relevant material if the adaptation is made in any of the circumstances falling within paragraph (2).

(2) The circumstances are that the adaptation is made (whether from the relevant material itself or from a copy made by the deposit library by virtue of regulation 29) for the following purposes—

(a) to preserve or replace the relevant material by placing the adaptation in the permanent collection in addition to or in place of the relevant material;

(b) to replace the relevant material in the permanent collection of another deposit library if that relevant material has been lost, destroyed or damaged.

(3) An adaptation may be made by virtue of this regulation in a different medium or format from the relevant material if the deposit library considers the change is necessary or expedient for the purpose for which the adaptation is made.

(4) Paragraph (1) does not apply if database right subsists in the relevant material.

NOTES

Commencement: 6 April 2013.

[2.660]

31 Disposing of relevant material

(1) A deposit library may dispose of relevant material, or copies or adaptations of relevant material, by destroying it but must retain at least one version of any relevant material.

(2) The version or versions retained by a deposit library must be the version or versions which the deposit library considers most suitable for the preservation of the relevant material.

NOTES

Commencement: 6 April 2013.

SCHEDULE
FORM OF DECLARATION: COPY OF RELEVANT MATERIAL

Regulation 27

[2.661]

1 To . . . . (Name and address of deposit library)

Please supply me with a copy of the following:

[Description of work]

2 I declare that:

(a) I will not use the copy except for the purposes of [research for a non-commercial purpose] [private study] [criticism or review or reporting current events] [parliamentary or judicial proceedings] [a Royal Commission or statutory inquiry] (delete whichever is inappropriate).

(b) In relation to a copy of relevant material required for the purposes of non-commercial research or private study:

(i) I have not previously been supplied with a copy of the same material by you or by another deposit library; and

(ii) to the best of my knowledge, no person with whom I work or study has made or intends to make, at or about the same time as this request, a request for substantially the same material for substantially the same purpose.

3 I understand that, if the declaration in paragraph 2 is false in a material particular, the copy supplied to me by you will be an infringing copy and that I shall be liable for infringement of copyright in the same way as if I had made the copy myself.

NOTES

Commencement: 6 April 2013.

COPYRIGHT AND DURATION OF RIGHTS IN PERFORMANCES REGULATIONS 2013

(SI 2013/1782)

NOTES

Made: 17 July 2013.
Authority: European Communities Act 1972, s 2(2); Enterprise and Regulatory Reform Act 2013, s 78.
Commencement: 1 November 2013.

PART 1
INTRODUCTORY PROVISIONS

[2.662]
1 Citation and commencement

These Regulations may be cited as the Copyright and Duration of Rights in Performances Regulations 2013 and come into force on 1st November 2013.

[2.663]
2 Interpretation

In these Regulations "the Act" means the Copyright, Designs and Patents Act 1988.

NOTES

Commencement: 1 November 2013.

[2.664]
3 Scheme of the Regulations

The Act is amended in accordance with the provisions of Part 2 of these Regulations, subject to the savings and transitional provisions in Part 3 of these Regulations.

NOTES

Commencement: 1 November 2013.

PART 2
AMENDMENTS TO THE COPYRIGHT, DESIGNS AND PATENTS ACT 1988

4–10 (*Reg 4 inserts the Copyright, Designs and Patents Act 1988, s 10A at* **[2.19]**; *reg 5 amends s 12(8) of the 1988 Act at* **[2.21]**; *reg 6 amends s 13A(2) of the 1988 Act at* **[2.22]**; *reg 7 amends s 182D(1) of the 1988 Act at* **[2.244]**; *reg 8 amends s 191(2) of the 1988 Act at* **[2.253]**; *reg 9 inserts ss 191HA, 191HB of the 1988 Act at* **[2.262]**, **[2.263]**; *reg 10 amends s 192A(1) of the 1988 Act at* **[2.270]**.)

PART 3
SAVINGS, TRANSITIONAL AND REVIEW PROVISIONS

Introductory

[2.665]
11 Introductory

(1) References in this Part to "commencement", without more, are to the date on which these Regulations come into force.

(2) In this Part—

"the 1988 provisions" means the provisions of the Act as they stood immediately before commencement (including the provisions of Schedule 1 to the Act continuing the effect of earlier enactments); and

"the new provisions" means the provisions of the Act as amended by these Regulations.

(3) Expressions used in this Part which are defined for the purposes of Part 1 or Part 2 of the Act have the same meaning as in that Part.

NOTES

Commencement: 1 November 2013.

Copyright

[2.666]

12 Copyright: interpretation

(1) In the provisions of this Part relating to copyright—

(a) "existing" in relation to a work, means made before commencement; and

(b) "existing copyright work" means a work in which copyright subsisted immediately before commencement.

(2) For the purposes of those provisions a work of which the making extended over a period shall be taken to have been made when its making was completed.

(3) References in those provisions to "moral rights" are to the rights conferred by Chapter IV of Part I of the Act.

NOTES

Commencement: 1 November 2013.

[2.667]

13 Duration of copyright: general saving

Copyright in an existing copyright work shall continue to subsist until the date on which it would have expired under the 1988 provisions if that date is later than the date on which copyright would expire under the new provisions.

NOTES

Commencement: 1 November 2013.

[2.668]

14 Duration of copyright: application of new provisions

The new provisions relating to duration of copyright in sound recordings and works comprised in works of co-authorship apply—

(a) to sound recordings and works of co-authorship made after commencement;

(b) to existing sound recordings and works of co-authorship which first qualify for copyright protection after commencement;

(c) to existing sound recordings in which copyright subsisted immediately before commencement;

(d) to works of co-authorship of which either or both the musical work and the literary work were existing copyright works; and

(e) to works of co-authorship of which the musical work or the literary work were on commencement protected as copyright works in another EEA state under legislation relating to copyright or related rights.

NOTES

Commencement: 1 November 2013.

[2.669]

15 Extended and revived copyright

In the following provisions of this Part—

(a) "extended copyright" means any copyright which subsists by virtue of the new provisions after the date on which it would have expired under the 1988 provisions; and

(b) "revived copyright" means any copyright in a musical or literary work comprised in a work of co-authorship which subsists by virtue of the new provisions after having expired under the 1988 provisions or any earlier enactment relating to copyright.

NOTES

Commencement: 1 November 2013.

Part 2 Copyright

[2.670]
16 Ownership of extended copyright

(1) The person who is the owner of the copyright in a sound recording or in a work comprised in a work of co-authorship immediately before commencement is as from commencement the owner of any extended copyright in the sound recording or work, subject as follows.

(2) If he or she is entitled to copyright for a period less than the whole of the copyright period under the 1988 provisions, any extended copyright is part of the reversionary interest expectant on the termination of that period.

NOTES

Commencement: 1 November 2013.

[2.671]
17 Ownership of revived copyright in works of co-authorship

(1) The person who was the owner of the copyright in a musical or literary work comprised in the work of co-authorship immediately before it expired (the "former copyright owner") is as from commencement the owner of any revived copyright in the work, subject as follows.

(2) If the former copyright owner has died before commencement, or in the case of a legal person has ceased to exist before commencement, the revived copyright shall vest in the author of the work or his or her personal representatives.

(3) Where revived copyright vests in personal representatives by virtue of paragraph (2), it shall be held by them for the benefit of the person who would have been entitled to it had it been vested in the author immediately before his or her death and had devolved as part of his or her estate.

NOTES

Commencement: 1 November 2013.

[2.672]
18 Prospective ownership of extended or revived copyright

(1) Where by an agreement made before commencement in relation to extended or revived copyright, and signed by or on behalf of the prospective owner of the copyright, the prospective owner purports to assign the extended or revived copyright (wholly or partially) to another person, then if, on commencement the assignee or another person claiming under the assignee would be entitled as against all other persons to require the copyright to be vested in him or her, the copyright shall vest in the assignee or his or her successor in title by virtue of this paragraph.

(2) A licence granted by a prospective owner of extended or revived copyright is binding on every successor in title to the prospective owner's interest (or prospective interest) in the right, except a purchaser in good faith for valuable consideration and without notice (actual or constructive) of the licence or a person deriving title from such a purchaser and references in Part 1 of the Act to do anything with, or without, the licence of the copyright owner shall be construed accordingly.

(3) In paragraph (2) "prospective owner" includes a person who is prospectively entitled to extended or revived copyright by virtue of such an agreement as is mentioned in paragraph (1).

NOTES

Commencement: 1 November 2013.

[2.673]
19 Extended copyright: existing licences, agreements, &c

(1) Subject to sections 191HA(5) and 191HB(7) and (9), any copyright licence, any term or condition of an agreement relating to the exploitation of a copyright work, or any waiver or assertion of moral rights, which—

(a) subsists immediately before commencement in relation to an existing copyright work, and
(b) is not to expire before the end of the copyright period under the 1988 provisions,

shall continue to have effect during the period of any extended copyright, subject to any agreement to the contrary.

(2) Any copyright licence, or term or condition relating to the exploitation of a copyright work, imposed by order of the Copyright Tribunal which—

(a) subsists immediately before commencement in relation to an existing copyright work, and
(b) is not to expire before the end of the copyright period under the 1988 provisions,

shall continue to have effect during the period of any extended copyright, subject to any further order of the Tribunal.

NOTES

Commencement: 1 November 2013.

[2.674]

20 Revived copyright: exercise of moral rights

(1) The following provisions have effect with respect to the exercise of moral rights in relation to a work comprised in a work of co-authorship in which there is revived copyright.

(2) Any waiver or assertion of moral rights which subsisted immediately before the expiry of copyright shall continue to have effect during the period of revived copyright.

(3) Moral rights are exercisable after commencement by the author of a work as with any other copyright work.

(4) Where the author died before commencement—

(a) the rights conferred by—

(i) section 77 (right to identification as author or director); or

(ii) section 80 (right to object to derogatory treatment of work),

are exercisable after commencement by his personal representatives, and

(b) any infringement after commencement of the right conferred by section 84 (false attribution) is actionable by his personal representatives.

(5) Any damages recovered by personal representatives by virtue of this regulation in respect of an infringement after a person's death shall devolve as part of his or her estate as if the right of action had subsisted and been vested in him or her immediately before his or her death.

(6) Nothing in these Regulations shall be construed as causing a moral right to be exercisable if, or to the extent that, the right was excluded by virtue of paragraph 23 of Schedule 1 on the commencement of the Act or would have been so excluded if copyright had not previously expired.

NOTES

Commencement: 1 November 2013.

[2.675]

21 Revived copyright: saving for acts of exploitation when work in public domain, &c

(1) No act done before commencement shall be regarded as infringing revived copyright in a work.

(2) It is not an infringement of revived copyright in a work—

(a) to do anything after commencement in pursuance of arrangements made before commencement at a time when copyright did not subsist in the work, or

(b) to issue to the public after commencement copies of the work made before commencement at a time when copyright did not subsist in the work.

(3) It is not an infringement of revived copyright in a work to do anything after commencement in relation to a literary, dramatic or musical work or a film made before commencement or made in pursuance of arrangements made before commencement, which contains a copy of that work or is an adaptation of that work if—

(a) the copy or adaptation was made before commencement at a time when copyright did not subsist in the work in which revived copyright subsists, or

(b) the copy or adaptation was made in pursuance of arrangements made before commencement at a time when copyright did not subsist in the work in which revived copyright subsists.

(4) It is not an infringement of revived copyright in a work to do after commencement anything which is a restricted act in relation to the work if the act is done at a time when, or is done in pursuance of arrangements made at a time when, the name and address of a person entitled to authorise the act cannot by reasonable inquiry be ascertained.

(5) In this regulation "arrangements" means arrangements for the exploitation of the work in question.

(6) It is not an infringement of any moral right to do anything which by virtue of this regulation is not an infringement of copyright.

NOTES

Commencement: 1 November 2013.

Rights in Performances

[2.676]

22 Rights in performances: interpretation

(1) In the provisions of this Part relating to rights in performances—

"existing protected performance" means a performance in a sound recording in relation to which rights under Part II of the Act (rights in performances) subsisted immediately before commencement,

"a new right" means a right arising by virtue of regulation 9 in relation to an assignment of a performer's property rights in a sound recording.

References in this Part to performers' rights are to the rights given by section 180(1)(a) of the Act.

NOTES

Commencement: 1 November 2013.

[2.677]

23 Rights in performances: application of new provisions

The new provisions relating to the duration of performers' rights in sound recordings and rights in relation to an assignment of performers' rights in a sound recording apply—

(a) to performances taking place after commencement;

(b) to existing performances which first qualify for protection under Part II of the 1988 Act after commencement; and

(c) to existing protected performances.

NOTES

Commencement: 1 November 2013.

[2.678]

24 Extended performance rights

In the following provisions of this Part "extended performance rights" means rights under Part II of the Act which subsist by virtue of the new provisions after the date on which they would have expired under the 1988 provisions.

NOTES

Commencement: 1 November 2013.

[2.679]

25 Entitlement to extended performance rights and new rights

(1) Any extended performance rights and any new rights are exercisable as from commencement by the performer or (if he or she has died) the person entitled to exercise those rights by virtue of section 191B(1) or 192A of the Act.

(2) Any remuneration or damages received by a person's personal representatives by virtue of a right conferred on them by paragraph (1) shall devolve as part of that person's estate as if the right had subsisted and been vested in him or her immediately before his or her death.

NOTES

Commencement: 1 November 2013.

[2.680]

26 Extended performance rights: existing consents, agreements, &c

Subject to the provisions of sections 191HA(5) and 191HB(7) and (9), any consent, or any term or condition of an agreement, relating to the exploitation of an existing protected performance which—

(a) subsists immediately before commencement, and

(b) is not to expire before the end of the period for which rights under Part II of the Act subsist in relation to that performance,

shall continue to subsist during the period of any extended performance rights, subject to any agreement to the contrary.

NOTES

Commencement: 1 November 2013.

[2.681]

27 Review

(1) Before the end of each review period, the Secretary of State must—

(a) carry out a review of regulations 4 to 26,

(b) set out the conclusions of the review in a report, and

(c) lay the report before Parliament.

(2) In carrying out the review the Secretary of State must, so far as is reasonable, have regard to how the Directive (which is implemented by means of regulations 4 to 26) is implemented in other Member States and must in particular—

(a) consider whether and if so, to what extent certain producers should be subject to the obligation to pay the annual payment referred to in section 191HB of the Act (as inserted by regulation 9) having regard to the provisions of Recital (12) of the Directive, and

(b) consider whether to implement the provision set out in Article 10a, paragraph 2 of Directive 2006/116/EC as inserted by Article 1(4) of the Directive.

(3) The report must in particular—

(a) set out the objectives intended to be achieved by the regulatory system established by those regulations,

(b) assess the extent to which those objectives are achieved, and

(c) assess whether those objectives remain appropriate and, if so, the extent to which they could be achieved with a system that imposes less regulation.

(4) In this Regulation—

"Directive" means Directive 2011/77/EU of the European Parliament and of the Council of 27th September 2011 amending Directive 2006/116/EC on the term of protection of copyright and related rights;

"Review period" means—

(a) the period of five years beginning with the day on which regulations 4 to 26 come into force, and

(b) subject to paragraph (5), each successive period of five years.

(5) If a report under this regulation is laid before Parliament before the last day of the review period to which it relates, the following review period is to begin with the day on which that report is laid.

NOTES

Commencement: 1 November 2013.

COLLECTIVE MANAGEMENT OF COPYRIGHT (EU DIRECTIVE) REGULATIONS 2016

(SI 2016/221)

NOTES

Made: 24 February 2016.
Authority: European Communities Act 1972, s 2(2).
Commencement: 10 April 2016.
These Regulations implement European Parliament and Council Directive 2014/26/EU at **[2.809]**.

PART 1
INTRODUCTION

[2.682]

1 Citation and commencement

These Regulations may be cited as the Collective Management of Copyright (EU Directive) Regulations 2016 and come into force on 10th April 2016.

NOTES

Commencement: 10 April 2016.

[2.683]

2 Interpretation and application

(1) In these Regulations—

"collective management organisation" means an organisation which—

(a) is authorised by law or by way of assignment, licence or any other contractual arrangement to manage copyright or rights related to copyright on behalf of more than one right holder, for the collective benefit of those right holders, as its sole or main purpose; and

(b) is either owned or controlled by its members or is organised on a not for profit basis, or both;

"general assembly of members" means the body in the collective management organisation through which members participate and exercise their voting rights;

"independent management entity" means an organisation which—

(a) is authorised by law or by way of assignment, licence or any other contractual arrangement to manage copyright or rights related to copyright on behalf of more than one right holder, for the collective benefit of those right holders, as its sole or main purpose;

(b) is neither owned nor controlled, directly or indirectly, wholly or in part, by right holders; and

(c) is organised on a for profit basis;

"management fees" means the amounts charged, deducted or offset by a collective management organisation from rights revenue or from any income arising from the investment of rights revenue in order to cover the costs of its management of copyright or related rights;

"member" means a right holder or an entity representing right holders, including other collective management organisations and associations of right holders, fulfilling the membership requirements of the collective management organisation and admitted by it;

"multi-territorial licence" means a licence which covers the territory of more than one member State;

"non-distributable", in relation to amounts due to right holders, is construed in accordance with regulation 12(9);

"online rights in musical works" means any of the rights of an author in a musical work provided for under articles 2 and 3 of Directive 2001/29/EC of the European Parliament and of the Council of 22 May 2001 which are required for the provision of an online service;

"online service provider" means a user who is an online service provider referred to in Part 3 of these Regulations;

"repertoire" means the works in respect of which a collective management organisation manages rights;

"representation agreement" means an agreement between collective management organisations whereby one collective management organisation mandates another collective management organisation to manage the rights it represents, including an agreement concluded under regulations 28 (agreements between collective management organisations) and 29 (representation of other collective management organisations);

"right holder" means any person, other than a collective management organisation, that—
- (a) holds a copyright or related right; or
- (b) under an agreement for the exploitation of rights or by law is entitled to a share of the rights revenue;

"rights revenue" means income collected by a collective management organisation on behalf of right holders, whether deriving from an exclusive right, a right to remuneration or a right to compensation;

"statute" means the memorandum and articles of association, the statute, the rules or documents of constitution of a collective management organisation;

"user" means a person who—
- (a) is carrying out acts subject to the authorisation of right holders, remuneration of right holders or payment of compensation to right holders; and
- (b) is not acting in the capacity of a consumer.

(2) The obligations of a collective management organisation in Parts 2 and 4 of these Regulations apply to a collective management organisation established in the United Kingdom.

(3) The obligations of a collective management organisation in Part 3 of these Regulations apply to a collective management organisation in accordance with regulation 22.

(4) Where an entity which is directly or indirectly owned or controlled, wholly or in part, by a collective management organisation carries on an activity which, if carried on by the collective management organisation, would be subject to the provisions of these Regulations then those provisions apply to that entity.

(5) The following provisions of these Regulations apply to an independent management entity established in the United Kingdom—
- (a) paragraph (1) of regulation 15 (licensing);
- (b) regulation 17 (information to be provided to right holders);
- (c) paragraph (1)(b) of regulation 19 (information to be provided on request);
- (d) paragraph (2) of regulation 20 (disclosure of information to the public); and
- (e) paragraph 1(f) of regulation 36 (power to request information).

NOTES

Commencement: 10 April 2016.

PART 2
COLLECTIVE MANAGEMENT ORGANISATIONS

[2.684]

3 General obligations of collective management organisations in relation to right holders

A collective management organisation—
- (a) must act in the best interests of right holders whose rights it represents; and
- (b) must not impose on such right holders any obligations which are not objectively necessary for the protection of their rights and interests or for the effective management of their rights.

NOTES

Commencement: 10 April 2016.

[2.685]

4 Particular obligations of collective management organisations in relation to right holders

A collective management organisation must ensure that—
- (a) right holders have the right to authorise a collective management organisation of their choice to manage—
  - (i) the rights,

(ii) categories of rights,
(iii) types of works, and
(iv) other subject matter,

of their choice, for the territory of their choice irrespective of the member State of nationality, residence or establishment of either the collective management organisation or the right holder;

(b) it manages the matters referred to in paragraph (a)(i) to (iv) provided that the management of these matters falls within the scope of its activity or unless it has objectively justified reasons to refuse management;

(c) right holders have the right to grant licences for non-commercial uses of any of the matters referred to in paragraph (a)(i) to (iv) that they may choose;

(d) right holders have the right—

(i) to terminate the authorisation to manage the matters referred to in paragraph (a)(i) to (iv) granted by them to a collective management organisation, or

(ii) to withdraw from a collective management organisation the matters of their choice referred to in paragraph (a)(i) to (iv) for the territory of their choice,

upon serving reasonable notice not exceeding six months unless the collective management organisation decides that such termination or withdrawal is to take place at the end of its financial year;

(e) if there are amounts due to a right holder for acts of exploitation which occurred, or under a licence granted, before the time when termination or withdrawal under paragraph (d) took effect, the right holder retains the rights under regulations 11 (deductions), 12 (distributions), 17 (information), 19 (information on request), 27 (payment) and 31 (complaints);

(f) it does not restrict the exercise of rights referred to in paragraphs (d) and (e) by requiring, as a condition for the exercise of those rights, that the management of the matters referred to in paragraph (a)(i) to (iv) which are subject to the termination or the withdrawal are entrusted to another collective management organisation;

(g) where a right holder authorises a collective management organisation to manage that right holder's rights—

(i) the right holder gives consent specifically for each of the matters referred to in paragraph (a)(i) to (iv) which the right holder authorises the collective management organisation to manage; and

(ii) that consent is evidenced in documentary form;

(h) it informs a right holder of their rights under paragraphs (a) to (g) and any conditions attached to the right in paragraph (c) before obtaining the right holder's consent to its managing the matters set out in paragraph (a)(i) to (iv);

(i) by 10th October 2016 it informs right holders who have authorised it by 9th April 2016 of their rights under paragraphs (a) to (g) as well as of any conditions attached to the right set out in paragraph (c); and

(j) the rights under paragraphs (a) to (i) are set out in the statute or membership terms of the collective management organisation.

NOTES

Commencement: 10 April 2016.

[2.686]

5 Membership rules of collective management organisations

(1) A collective management organisation must—

(a) accept as members—

(i) right holders, and

(ii) entities representing right holders, including other collective managements organisations and associations of right holders,

if they fulfil the membership requirements (see paragraph (2)); and

(b) in cases where it refuses to accept a request for membership, provide the right holder with a clear explanation of the reasons for its decision.

(2) A collective management organisation must ensure that its membership requirements—

(a) are based on objective, transparent and non-discriminatory criteria;

(b) are included in its statute or membership terms; and

(c) are made publicly available.

NOTES

Commencement: 10 April 2016.

[2.687]

6 Collective management organisations and their members

A collective management organisation must—

(a) ensure that its statute provides for appropriate and effective mechanisms for the participation of its members in the decision-making process of that organisation;

(b) ensure that the representation of the different categories of members in the decision-making process is fair and balanced;

(c) allow—

(i) its members, and

(ii) right holders who are not members but who have a direct legal relationship with it by law or by way of assignment, licence or other contractual arrangement,

to communicate with it by electronic means including, in the case of its members, for the purposes of exercising members' rights; and

(d) keep records of its members and regularly update those records.

NOTES

Commencement: 10 April 2016.

[2.688]

7 General assembly of members of collective management organisations

(1) A collective management organisation must ensure that—

(a) the general assembly of members is convened at least once a year;

(b) the general assembly of members decides on amendments to the statute and the membership terms of the collective management organisation, where those terms are not regulated by the statute;

(c) the general assembly of members decides on the appointment and dismissal of the directors, reviews their general performance and approves their remuneration and other benefits such as—

(i) monetary and non-monetary benefits;

(ii) pension awards and entitlements;

(iii) rights to other awards; and

(iv) rights to severance pay;

(but see paragraph (12));

(d) in accordance with regulations 10 (rights revenue), 11 (deductions) and 12 (distribution) and subject to paragraph (2) the general assembly of members decides on at least—

(i) the general policy on the distribution of amounts due to right holders;

(ii) the general policy on the use of non-distributable amounts;

(iii) the general investment policy with regards to rights revenue and to any income arising from the investment of rights revenue;

(iv) the general policy on deductions from rights revenue and from any income arising from the investment of rights revenue;

(v) the use of non-distributable amounts;

(vi) the risk management policy;

(vii) the approval of any acquisition, sale or hypothecation of immovable property;

(viii) the approval of—

(aa) mergers and alliances;

(bb) the setting-up of subsidiaries;

(cc) the acquisition of other entities or shares or rights in other entities;

and

(ix) the approval of taking out loans, granting loans or providing security for loans;

(e) the general assembly of members controls the activities of the collective management organisation by at least—

(i) deciding on the appointment and removal of the auditor (but see paragraph (3)); and

(ii) approving the annual transparency report referred to in regulation 21 (annual transparency report);

(f) all members of the collective management organisation have the right to participate in, and the right to vote at, the general assembly of members (but see paragraph (4));

(g) every member of a collective management organisation has a right to appoint another person as a proxy to participate in, and vote at, the general assembly of members on the member's behalf provided that the appointment does not result in a conflict of interest; and

(h) in relation to the right in sub-paragraph (g)—

(i) each proxy is valid for a single general assembly of members;

(ii) the proxy holder enjoys the same rights in the general assembly of members as those to which the appointing member would be entitled;

(iii) the proxy holder casts votes in accordance with the instructions issued by the appointing member.

(2) The requirement in paragraph (1)(d)(vi) to (ix) may be satisfied where the general assembly of members delegates to the body exercising the supervisory function referred in regulation 8 (supervisory function) the functions referred to in those sub-paragraphs by a resolution or by a provision in the statute.

(3) The requirement in paragraph (1)(e)(i) may be satisfied where an auditor is appointed under Chapter 2 of Part 16 of the Companies Act 2006.

(4) The requirement in paragraph (1)(f) may be satisfied—
  (a) where a collective management organisation restricts the rights of members referred to in that sub-paragraph on the basis or either or both the following criteria—
    (i) duration of membership, or
    (ii) amounts received or due to a member;
    and
  (b) where these criteria—
    (i) are determined and applied in a manner which is fair and proportionate; and
    (ii) are included in the statute or the membership terms of the collective management organisation and are made publicly available in accordance with regulation 20 (disclosure of information to the public).

(5) This paragraph applies where a collective management organisation by reason of its legal form does not have a general assembly of members.

(6) Where paragraph (5) applies—
  (a) the collective management organisation must ensure that the functions of the general assembly of members referred to in paragraph (1)(b) to (e) are exercised by the body exercising the supervisory function referred to in regulation 8 (collective management organisation: supervisory function); and
  (b) this regulation applies with the following modifications—
    (i) in paragraph (1), sub-paragraphs (a), (b), (c), (d) and (e) apply as if the references to "general assembly of members" were references to "body exercising the supervisory function referred to in regulation 8";
    (ii) in paragraph (1), sub-paragraphs (f), (g) and (h) do not apply; and
    (iii) paragraphs (2) and (4) do not apply.

(7) This paragraph applies where—
  (a) a collective management organisation decides that the functions of the general assembly of members referred to in paragraph (1)(b) to (e) are to be exercised by an assembly of delegates elected at least every four years by the members of the collective management organisation;
  (b) appropriate and effective participation of members in the collective management organisation's decision-making process is ensured; and
  (c) the representation of the different categories of members in the assembly of delegates is fair and balanced.

(8) Where paragraph (7) applies this regulation applies with the following modifications—
  (a) in paragraph (1), sub-paragraphs (a), (b), (c), (d) and (e) apply as if the references to "general assembly of members" were references to " assembly of delegates";
  (b) in paragraph (1), sub-paragraph (f) applies as if it read "all delegates elected to the assembly of delegates have the right to participate in, and vote at, the assembly of delegates;";
  (c) in paragraph (1), sub-paragraph (g) applies as if the reference to—
    (i) "member of a collective management organisation" read "delegate elected to the assembly of delegates";
    (ii) "general assembly of members" read "assembly of delegates"; and
    (iii) "member's behalf" read "delegate's behalf";
  (d) in paragraph (1), sub-paragraph (h) applies as if—
      (aa) both references to "general assembly of members" were references to "assembly of delegates"; and
      (bb) both references to "appointing member" were to "appointing delegate";
  (e) paragraph (2) applies as if the reference to "general assembly of members" were a reference to "assembly of delegates"; and
  (f) paragraph (4) does not apply.

(9) This paragraph applies where—
  (a) a collective management organisation only has members who represent right holders; and
  (b) the collective management organisation decides that one or more of the functions of the general assembly of members referred to in paragraph (1)(b) to (e) are to be exercised by an assembly of those right holders.

(10) Where paragraph (9) applies and the collective management organisation has decided that all the functions of the general assembly of members are to be exercised by an assembly of right holders then this regulation applies with the following modifications—
  (a) in paragraph (1), sub-paragraphs (a), (b), (c), (d) and (e) apply as if references to "general assembly of members" were references to "assembly of right holders";
  (b) in paragraph (1), sub-paragraph (f) applies as if it read "all right holders who are represented by members have the right to participate in, and the right to vote at, the assembly of right holders;";
  (c) in paragraph (1), sub-paragraph (g) applies as if the reference to—

(i) "member of a collective management organisation" read "right holder who is represented by a member"; and

(ii) "general assembly of members on the member's behalf" read "assembly of right holders on the right holder's behalf";

(d) in paragraph (1), sub-paragraph (h) applies as if—

(i) both references to "general assembly of members" were references to "assembly of right holders"; and

(ii) both references to "appointing member" were to "appointing right holder";

(e) paragraph (2) applies as if the reference to "general assembly of members" were a reference to "assembly of right holders"; and

(f) paragraph (4) does not apply.

(11) Where paragraph (9) applies and the collective management organisation has decided that some of the functions of the general assembly of members are to be exercised by an assembly of right holders then this regulation applies with the following modifications—

(a) in paragraph (1), sub-paragraph (a) applies as if after the words "general assembly of members" there were added "and the assembly of right holders";

(b) a reference in paragraph (1) (b), (c), (d) and (e) to the general assembly of members is to be read as a reference to an assembly of right holders so far as that reference relates to a function that the collective management organisation has decided is to be exercised by an assembly of right holders;

(c) in paragraph (1), sub-paragraph (f) applies as if after "(but see paragraph (4))" there were added "and all right holders who are represented by members have the right to participate in, and vote at, the assembly of right holders";

(d) in paragraph (1), sub-paragraph (g) applies as if after "general assembly of members on the member's behalf" there were added " and every right holder who is represented by a member has a right to appoint another person as a proxy to participate in, and vote at, the assembly of right holders on the right holder's behalf";

(e) in paragraph (1), sub-paragraph (h) applies as if—

(i) at the end of sub-paragraph (i) there were added "or for a single assembly of right holders";

(ii) in sub-paragraph (ii)—

(aa) after the reference to "the general assembly of members" there were added "or the assembly of right holders"; and

(bb) after the reference to "appointing member" there were added "or appointing right holder";

and

(iii) in sub-paragraph (iii) after the reference to "appointing member" there were added "or the appointing right holder";

(f) paragraph (2) applies as if after the reference to the "general assembly of members" there were added "or the assembly of right holders"; and

(g) paragraph (4) applies only in relation to the requirement in paragraph (1)(f) concerning the rights of members in relation to the general assembly of members.

(12) Where the statute of a collective management organisation provides for a dual board the collective management organisation must ensure that the general assembly of members does not—

(a) decide on the appointment and dismissal of members of the management board, or

(b) approve their remuneration and other benefits,

to the extent those powers are delegated to the supervisory board.

(13) In paragraph (1)(c) "director" means—

(a) any member of the administrative board of the collective management organisation; or

(b) where the statute of the collective management organisation provides for a dual board, any member of the management board or supervisory board.

NOTES

Commencement: 10 April 2016.

[2.689]

8 Collective management organisations: supervisory function

(1) A collective management organisation must ensure that it has in place a supervisory function for continuously monitoring the activities and the performance of the duties of the persons who manage the business of the organisation which satisfies the requirements of this regulation.

(2) The requirements of this regulation are—

(a) there is a fair and balanced representation of the different categories of members of the collective management organisation in the body exercising the supervisory function;

(b) each person exercising the supervisory function makes an annual individual statement to the general assembly of members on conflicts of interest, containing the information referred in paragraph (3) of regulation 9 (management);

(c) the body exercising the supervisory function meets regularly and has at least the following powers—
  (i) to exercise the powers delegated to it by the general assembly of members, including the delegation of functions referred to in paragraph (2) of regulation 7 (general assembly of members); and
  (ii) to monitor the activities and the performance of the duties of persons referred to in regulation 9, including the implementation of the decisions of the general assembly of members and, in particular, of the general policies referred to in paragraph (1)(d)(i) to (iv) of regulation 7 (general assembly of members);

and

(d) the body exercising the supervisory function reports on the exercise of its powers to the general assembly of members at least once a year.

NOTES

Commencement: 10 April 2016.

[2.690]

9 Collective management organisations: management

(1) A collective management organisation must ensure that persons who manage its business do so in a sound, prudent and appropriate manner, using sound administrative and accounting procedures and internal control mechanisms.

(2) A collective management organisation must put in place and apply procedures (see paragraph (3))—
  (a) to avoid conflicts of interest; and
  (b) where such conflicts cannot be avoided, to identify, manage, monitor and disclose actual or potential conflicts of interest in such a way as to prevent them from adversely affecting the collective interests of the right holders whom the organisation represents.

(3) The procedures referred to in paragraph (2) include an annual individual statement by each of the persons referred to in paragraph (1) to the general assembly of members, containing the following information—
  (a) any interests in the collective management organisation;
  (b) any remuneration received in the preceding financial year from the collective management organisation, including in the form of pension schemes, benefits in kind and other types of benefits;
  (c) any amount received in the preceding financial year as a right holder from the collective management organisation; and
  (d) a declaration concerning any actual or potential conflict between—
    (i) any personal interests and those of the collective management organisation; and
    (ii) any obligations owed to the collective management organisation and any duty owed to any other person.

(4) A collective management organisation must ensure that its staff training procedures for employees, agents and representatives include appropriate training about conduct that complies with its obligations under these Regulations (but see paragraph (5)).

(5) Paragraph (4) does not apply where the collective management organisation is a business with fewer than ten employees and which has a turnover or balance sheet of less than 2 million euros per annum.

NOTES

Commencement: 10 April 2016.

[2.691]

10 Collection and use of rights revenue

A collective management organisation must ensure—
  (a) that it is diligent in the collection and management of rights revenue;
  (b) that it keeps separate in its accounts—
    (i) rights revenue and any income arising from the investment of rights revenue; and
    (ii) any own assets it may have and income arising from such assets, from management fees or from other activities;
  (c) that it does not use rights revenue or any income arising from the investment of rights revenue for purposes other than distribution to right holders, except where it is allowed—
    (i) to deduct or offset its management fees in compliance with a decision taken in accordance with paragraph (1)(d)(iv) of regulation 7 (general assembly of members); or
    (ii) to use the rights revenue or any income arising from the investment of rights revenue in compliance with a decision taken in accordance with regulation 7(1)(d);

  and

  (d) that where it invests rights revenue, or any income arising from the investment of rights revenue, it does so—

Part 2 Copyright

(i) in the best interests of the right holders whose rights it represents;

(ii) in accordance with the general investment and risk management policy referred to in paragraph (1)(d)(iii) and (vi) of regulation 7 (general assembly of members); and

(iii) having regard to the following—

(aa) where there is any potential conflict of interest, the collective management organisation must ensure that the investment is made in the sole interest of those right holders;

(bb) the assets are invested in order to ensure the security, quality, liquidity and profitability of the portfolio as a whole; and

(cc) the assets are properly diversified in order to avoid excessive reliance on any particular asset and accumulation of risks in the portfolio as a whole.

NOTES

Commencement: 10 April 2016.

[2.692]

11 Deductions

(1) A collective management organisation must ensure that where a right holder authorises it to manage that right holder's rights, the collective management organisation provides the right holder with information on—

(a) management fees (see paragraph (3)), and

(b) other deductions from the rights revenue and from any income arising from the investment of the rights revenue (see paragraph (2)),

before obtaining the right holder's consent to manage the right holder's rights.

(2) A collective management organisation must ensure that deductions—

(a) are reasonable in relation to the services provided by the collective management organisation to right holders (including, where appropriate, the services referred to in paragraph (5)); and

(b) are established on the basis of objective criteria.

(3) A collective management organisation must ensure that management fees do not exceed the justified and documented costs incurred by the collective management organisation in managing copyright and related rights.

(4) A collective management organisation must ensure that the requirements in these Regulations relating to the use, and the transparency of the use, of amounts deducted or offset in respect of management fees apply to any other deductions made in order to cover the costs of managing copyright and related rights.

(5) A collective management organisation must ensure that where it provides social, cultural or educational services funded through deductions from rights revenue or from any income arising from the investment of rights revenue, such services are provided on the basis of fair criteria, in particular in relation to access to, and the extent of, those services.

NOTES

Commencement: 10 April 2016.

[2.693]

12 Distributions of amounts to right holders

(1) A collective management organisation must regularly, diligently and accurately distribute and pay amounts due to right holders in accordance with the general policy on distribution referred to in paragraph (1)(d)(i) of regulation 7 (general assembly of members) subject to paragraph (3) of regulation 14 (deductions and payments) and regulation 27 (payment).

(2) A collective management organisation or, a member of it which is an entity representing right holders, must distribute and pay the amounts referred to in paragraph (1) to right holders as soon as possible but in any event no later than the beginning of the period which starts 9 months from the end of the financial year in which the rights revenue was collected unless paragraph (3) applies.

(3) This paragraph applies where there are objective reasons which prevent the collective management organisation or its member referred to in paragraph (2) from distributing or paying the amounts within the time specified in that paragraph.

(4) The objective reasons referred to in paragraph (3) may relate in particular to—

(a) reporting by users;

(b) identification of rights or right holders; or

(c) matching of information on works and other subject matter with right holders.

(5) A collective management organisation must ensure that amounts due to right holders are kept separate in the accounts of the collective management organisation where—

(a) those amounts cannot be distributed within the time specified in paragraph (2) because the relevant right holders cannot be identified or located; and

(b) paragraph (3) does not apply.

(6) A collective management organisation must take all necessary measures to identify and locate right holders consistent with the requirements of paragraph (1) (see paragraph 7).

(7) The measures referred to in paragraph (6) include in particular—
- (a) the collective management organisation making available, at the latest 3 months after the beginning of the period specified in paragraph (2), information on works and other subject matter (see paragraph (8)) for which a right holder has not been identified or located to—
  - (i) the right holders that the collective management organisation represents or entities which are its members and which represent right holders; and
  - (ii) the collective management organisations with which it has concluded representation agreements.
- (b) the collective management organisation—
  - (i) verifying the records referred in in paragraph (d) of regulation 6 (collective management organisation and its members) and other readily available records; and
  - (ii) where right holders remain unidentified or not located, making the information referred to in sub-paragraph (a) available to the public no later than one year after the end of the 3 month period referred to in that sub-paragraph.

(8) The information referred to in paragraph (7) includes, where available—
- (a) the title of the work or other subject matter;
- (b) the name of the right holder;
- (c) the name of the relevant publisher or producer; and
- (d) any other relevant information available which could assist in identifying the right holder.

(9) Amounts due to right holders are non-distributable for the purposes of these Regulations where—
- (a) they cannot be distributed before the end of the period of 3 years from the end of the financial year in which collection of the rights revenue occurred; and
- (b) the collective management organisation has taken all necessary measures to identify and locate the right holders referred to in paragraph (6).

(10) The decision on the use of non-distributable amounts referred to in regulation 7(1)(d) is without prejudice to the right of a right holder to claim such amounts from the copyright management organisation in accordance with the law providing for a limitation period applicable to the bringing of proceedings.

NOTES

Commencement: 10 April 2016.

[2.694]

13 Rights managed under representation agreements

A collective management organisation must not discriminate against any right holder whose rights it manages under a representation agreement in particular with respect to—
- (a) applicable tariffs;
- (b) management fees; and
- (c) the conditions for—
  - (i) the collection of rights revenue; and
  - (ii) distribution of amounts due to right holders.

NOTES

Commencement: 10 April 2016.

[2.695]

14 Deductions and payments in representation agreements

(1) A collective management organisation must not make deductions (other than in respect of management fees)—
- (a) from the rights revenue derived from the rights it manages on the basis of a representation agreement, or
- (b) from any income arising from the investment of that rights revenue,

unless the other collective management organisation that is party to the representation agreement expressly consents to such deductions.

(2) A collective management organisation must regularly, diligently and accurately distribute and pay amounts due to other collective management organisations.

(3) A collective management organisation must carry out the distribution and payments referred to in paragraph (2) as soon as possible but in any event no later than the beginning of the period which starts 9 months from the end of the financial year in which the rights revenue was collected unless paragraph (4) applies.

(4) This paragraph applies where there are objective reasons which prevent the collective management organisation from distributing or paying the amounts within the time specified in paragraph (3).

(5) The objective reasons referred to in paragraph (4) may, in particular, relate to—

(a) reporting by users;
(b) identification of rights or right holders; or
(c) matching of information on works and other subject matter with right holders.

(6) The other collective management organisation referred to in paragraph (1) or, where it has a member which is an entity representing right holders, that member must ensure that it distributes and pays the amounts due to right holders as soon as possible but in any event no later than the beginning of the period which starts 6 months from the receipt of those amounts unless paragraph (7) applies.

(7) This paragraph applies where there are objective reasons which prevent the collective management organisation or its member referred to in paragraph (6) from distributing and paying the amounts within the time specified in paragraph (6).

(8) The objective reasons referred to in paragraph (6) may, in particular, relate to—
(a) reporting by users;
(b) identification of rights or right holders; or
(c) matching of information on works and other subject matter with right holders.

NOTES

Commencement: 10 April 2016.

[2.696]
15 Licensing

(1) A collective management organisation and a user and an independent management entity and a user must—
(a) conduct negotiations for the licensing of rights in good faith; and
(b) provide each other with all necessary information.

(2) A collective management organisation must ensure that licensing terms are based on objective and non-discriminatory criteria (but see paragraph (3)).

(3) Paragraph (2) does not require a collective management organisation to use as a precedent for other online services licensing terms agreed with a user where the user is providing a new type of online service which has been available to the public in a member State for less than 3 years.

(4) A collective management organisation must ensure that—
(a) right holders receive appropriate remuneration for the use of their rights;
(b) tariffs it determines for exclusive rights and rights to remuneration are reasonable in relation to matters such as—
(i) the economic value of the use of the rights in trade taking into account the nature and scope of the use of the work and other subject matter; and
(ii) the economic value of the service provided by the collective management organisation;
and
(c) it informs the user concerned of the criteria used for the setting of those tariffs.

(5) A collective management organisation must—
(a) reply without undue delay to requests from users indicating, amongst other things, the information needed in order for the collective management organisation to offer a licence;
(b) upon receipt of all relevant information without undue delay either—
(i) offer a licence; or
(ii) provide the user with a reasoned statement explaining why it does not intend to license a particular service;
(c) allow users to communicate with it by electronic means, including, where appropriate, for the purpose of reporting on the use of the licence; and
(d) after giving a user a licence, treat that user in good faith (but see paragraph (6)).

(6) Paragraph 5(d) does not apply where the collective management organisation is a business with fewer than ten employees and has a turnover or balance sheet total of less than 2 million euros per annum.

NOTES

Commencement: 10 April 2016.

[2.697]
16 Users' obligations

(1) A user must provide a collective management organisation within an agreed or pre-established time and in an agreed or pre-established format with such relevant information at its disposal on the use of the rights represented by the collective management organisation as is necessary for—
(a) the collection of rights revenue; and
(b) the distribution and payment of amounts due to right holders.

(2) A collective management organisation and a user must ensure that they take into account, as far as possible, voluntary industry standards in deciding on the format for the information referred to in paragraph (1).

NOTES

Commencement: 10 April 2016.

[2.698]

17 Information provided to right holders

(1) A collective management organisation and an independent management entity must make available not less than once a year to each right holder to whom—

(a) it has attributed rights revenue, or

(b) made payments,

in the period to which the information relates, at least the information specified in paragraph (2).

(2) The information specified in this paragraph is—

(a) contact details which the right holder has authorised the collective management organisation or the independent management entity to use in order to identify and locate the right holder;

(b) the rights revenue attributed to the right holder;

(c) the amount paid by the collective management organisation or the independent management entity to the right holder for each category of right managed and for each type of use;

(d) the period during which the use took place for which amounts were attributed and paid to the right holder unless objective reasons relating to reporting by users prevent the collective management organisation or the independent management entity from providing this information;

(e) deductions made in respect of management fees;

(f) deductions made for any other purpose other than in respect of management fees, including those that may be legally required for the provision of social, cultural or educational services; and

(g) rights revenue attributed to the right holder which is outstanding for a period.

(3) A collective management organisation and an independent management entity must provide the information specified in paragraph (2) to the person referred to in sub-paragraph (b) where—

(a) it attributes rights revenue to right holders;

(b) it has a member an entity which is responsible for the distribution of rights revenue to right holders; and

(c) that member does not have that information in their possession.

(4) The member to whom information is supplied under paragraph (3) must make available not less than once a year the information specified in paragraph (2) to each right holder to whom the member has attributed rights revenue or made payments in the period to which the information relates.

NOTES

Commencement: 10 April 2016.

[2.699]

18 Information provided to other collective management organisations

(1) A collective management organisation must make available at least the information specified in paragraph (2) by electronic means no less than once a year to collective management organisations on whose behalf it manages rights under a representation agreement for the period to which the information relates.

(2) The information specified in this paragraph is—

(a) the rights revenue attributed for the rights it manages under the representation agreement;

(b) the amounts paid by the collective management organisation—

(i) for each category of rights managed, and

(ii) for each type of use,

for the rights it manages under the representation agreement;

(c) rights revenue attributed which is outstanding for any period;

(d) deductions made in respect of management fees;

(e) deductions made for a purpose other than in respect of management fees referred to in regulation 14 (deductions and payments);

(f) information on any licences grated or refused with regard to works and other subject matter covered by the representation agreement; and

(g) resolutions adopted by the general assembly of members in so far as those resolutions are relevant to the management of the rights under the representation agreement.

NOTES

Commencement: 10 April 2016.

Part 2 Copyright

[2.700]

19 Information provided to right holders, other collective management organisations and users on request

(1) Subject to regulation 24 (transparency of multi-territorial repertoire information)—

(a) a collective management organisation must make the information specified in paragraph (2) or, where it applies, paragraph (4) available by electronic means and without undue delay, in response to a duly justified request, to—

(i) a collective management organisation on whose behalf it manages rights under a representation agreement;

(ii) a right holder; or

(iii) a user;

and

(b) an independent management entity must make the information specified in paragraph (2) or, where it applies, paragraph (4) available by electronic means and without undue delay, in response to a duly justified request, to—

(i) a right holder; or

(ii) a user.

(2) The information specified in this paragraph is—

(a) the works or other subject matter the collective management organisation or the independent management entity represents;

(b) the rights the collective management organisation or the independent management entity manages directly or the collective management organisation manages under representation agreements; and

(c) the territories covered.

(3) Paragraph (4) applies where, due to the scope of the activity of the collective management organisation or the independent management entity, the work or other subject matter which it represents cannot be determined.

(4) The information specified in this paragraph is—

(a) the types of works of other subject matter the collective management organisation or the independent management entity represents;

(b) the rights the collective management organisation or the independent management entity manages; and

(c) the territories covered.

NOTES

Commencement: 10 April 2016.

[2.701]

20 Disclosure of information to the public

(1) A collective management organisation must—

(a) make public the information specified in paragraph (3); and

(b) publish and keep up to date on its public website the information specified in that paragraph.

(2) An independent management entity must make public the information specified in paragraph (3)(a), (b), (c), (e), (f) and (g).

(3) The information specified in this paragraph is—

(a) its statute;

(b) its membership terms and the terms of termination of authorisation to manage rights, if these are not included in the statute;

(c) standard licensing contracts and standard applicable tariffs including discounts;

(d) the list of persons referred to in regulation 9(1) (management);

(e) its general policy on distribution of amounts due to right holders;

(f) its general policy on management fees;

(g) its general policy on deductions, other than in respect of management fees, from—

(i) rights revenue; and

(ii) income arising from the investment of rights revenue including deductions for the purposes of social, cultural and educational services;

(h) a list of—

(i) the representation agreements it has entered into; and

(ii) the names of the collective management organisations with which those representation agreements have been concluded;

(i) the general policy on the use of non-distributable amounts; and

(j) the complaint handling and dispute resolution procedures available in accordance with regulations 31 (complaints procedure) and 32 (alternative dispute resolution procedure) and under Part 1, Chapter 7 of the Copyright, Designs and Patents Act 1988.

NOTES

Commencement: 10 April 2016.

[2.702]

21 Annual transparency report

(1) A collective management organisation must—

(a) draw up and make public an annual transparency report, including the special report referred to in paragraph (3), for each financial year no later than 8 months following the end of that financial year;

(b) publish on its website the annual transparency report; and

(c) ensure that the annual transparency report remains available on its website for at least 5 years.

(2) The annual transparency report referred to in paragraph (1) must—

(a) contain at least the information specified in paragraph (4);

(b) be audited by a person who is eligible for appointment as a statutory auditor under Part 42 of the Companies Act 2006 in respect of the accounting information referred to in paragraph (4)(a), (g), (h), (i), (j) and (k) included in the report; and

(c) reproduce in full the audit report including any qualifications to that report.

(3) The special report referred to in paragraph (1)(a) must address the use of the amounts deducted for the purposes of social, cultural and educational services and must contain at least the information specified in paragraph (5).

(4) The information specified in this paragraph is—

(a) financial statements comprising a balance sheet or a statement of assets and liabilities, an income and expenditure account for the financial year and a cash flow statement;

(b) a report on the activities in the financial year;

(c) information on refusals to grant a licence in accordance with paragraph (5)(b)(ii) of regulation 15 (licensing);

(d) a description of the legal and governance structure of the collective management organisation;

(e) information on entities directly or indirectly owned or controlled, wholly or in part, by the collective management organisation;

(f) information on the total amount of remuneration paid to the persons referred to in paragraph (2)(b) of regulation 8 (supervisory function) and regulation 9 (management) in the previous year and on other benefits granted to them;

(g) a special report on the use of any amounts deducted for the purpose of social, cultural and educational services referred to in paragraph (5);

(h) financial information on rights revenue for each category of rights managed and for each type of use (for example broadcasting, online and public performance), including information on—

  (i) the income arising from the investment of rights revenue; and

  (ii) use of such income (whether it is distributed to right holders or other collective management organisations or otherwise used);

(i) financial information on the cost of rights management and other services provided by the collective management organisation to right holders with a comprehensive description of at least the following—

  (i) all operating and financial costs, with a breakdown for each category of rights managed and, where costs are indirect and cannot be attributed to one or more categories of rights, an explanation of the method used to allocate such indirect costs;

  (ii) operating and financial costs with a breakdown for each category of rights managed and, where costs are indirect and cannot be attributed to one or more categories of rights, an explanation of the method used to allocate such indirect costs, only with regard to the management of rights, including management fees deducted from or offset against—

    (aa) rights revenue, or

    (bb) income arising from the investment of rights revenue in accordance with paragraph (c) of regulation 10 (collection and use of rights revenue) and paragraphs (1) to (3) of regulation 11 (deductions);

  (iii) operating and financial costs with regard to services other than the management of rights but including social, cultural and educational services;

  (iv) resources used to cover costs;

  (v) deductions made from rights revenue with a breakdown for each category of rights managed and for each type of use and the purpose of the deduction (such as costs relating to the management of rights or to social, cultural or educational services);

  (vi) the percentages that the cost of the rights management and other services provided by the collective management organisation to right holders represents compared to the rights revenue in the relevant financial year for each category of rights managed; and

(vii) where the costs in sub-paragraph (vi) are indirect and cannot be attributed to one or more categories of rights, an explanation of the method used to allocate such indirect costs;

(j) financial information on amounts due to right holders with a comprehensive description of at least the following—

(i) the total amount attributed to right holders with a breakdown for each category of rights managed and type of use;

(ii) the total amount paid to right holders, with a breakdown for each category of rights managed and type of use;

(iii) the frequency of payments with a breakdown for each category of rights managed and type of use;

(iv) the total amount collected but not yet attributed to right holders with a breakdown for each category of rights managed and type of use and indicating the financial year in which those amounts were collected;

(v) the total amount attributed to, but not yet distributed to, right holders with a breakdown for each category of rights managed and type of use and indicating the financial year in which those amounts were collected;

(vi) where a collective management organisation has not carried out the distribution and payments within the period provided for in paragraph (2) in regulation 12 (distribution), the reason for the delay; and

(vii) the total non-distributable amounts along with an explanation of the use to which those amounts have been put;

and

(k) information on relationships with other collective management organisations, with a description of at least the following—

(i) amounts received from and paid to other collective management organisations with a breakdown for each category of rights, for each type of use and for each organisation;

(ii) management fees and other deductions from the rights revenue due to other collective management organisations with a breakdown for each category of rights, for each type of use and for each organisation;

(iii) management fees and other deductions from the amounts paid by other collective management organisations with a breakdown for each category of rights and for each organisation; and

(iv) amounts distributed directly to right holders originating from other collective management organisations with a breakdown for each category of rights and for each organisation.

(5) The information specified in this paragraph is—

(a) the amounts deducted for the purposes of social, cultural and educational services in the financial year, with a breakdown for each type of purpose and, for each type of purpose, with a breakdown for each category of rights managed and for each type of use; and

(b) an explanation of the use of those amounts with a breakdown for each type of purpose including costs of managing amounts deducted to fund social, cultural and educational services and of the separate amounts used for social, cultural and educational services.

NOTES

Commencement: 10 April 2016.

PART 3
MULTI-TERRITORIAL LICENSING AND COLLECTIVE MANAGEMENT ORGANISATIONS

[2.703]
22 Application

(1) The obligations of a collective management organisation in this Part apply to a collective management organisation established in the United Kingdom managing authors' rights in musical works for online use on a multi-territorial basis (but see paragraphs (2) and (3)).

(2) The obligations of a collective management organisation in this Part do not apply to a collective management organisation when it grants, on the basis of the voluntary aggregation of the required rights, in compliance with the competition rules under Articles 101 and 102 of the Treaty on the Functioning of the European Union a multi-territorial licence for—

(a) the online rights in musical works required by a broadcaster to communicate or make available to the public its radio or television programmes simultaneously with or after their initial broadcast; and

(b) any online material, including previews, produced by or for the broadcaster which is ancillary to the initial broadcast of its radio or television programmes.

(3) Regulation 30 (access to multi-territorial licensing) applies in accordance with paragraph (1) of that regulation.

NOTES

Commencement: 10 April 2016.

[2.704]

23 Capacity to process multi-territorial licences

(1) A collective management organisation which grants multi-territorial licences for online rights in musical works must ensure that it has sufficient capacity to process electronically, in an efficient and transparent manner, data needed for the administration of a multi-territorial licence for online rights in musical works.

(2) For the purposes of paragraph (1) "sufficient capacity" includes sufficient capacity for the purposes of—

(a) identifying the repertoire and monitoring its use;
(b) invoicing users;
(c) collecting rights revenue; and
(d) distributing amounts due to right holders.

(3) For the purposes of paragraph (1) a collective management organisation must—

(a) have the ability to identify accurately the musical works, wholly or in part, which the collective management organisation is authorised to represent;
(b) have the ability to identify accurately, wholly or in part, with respect to each relevant territory, the rights and their corresponding right holders for each musical work, or share in such work, which the collective management organisation is authorised to represent;
(c) make use of unique identifiers in order to identify right holders and musical works, taking into account, as far as possible, voluntary industry standards and practices developed at international level or at the level of the European Union; and
(d) make use of adequate means in order to identify and resolve in a timely and effective manner inconsistencies in data held by other collective management organisations granting multi-territorial licences for online rights in musical works.

NOTES

Commencement: 10 April 2016.

[2.705]

24 Transparency of multi-territorial repertoire information

(1) In response to a duly justified request a collective management organisation which grants multi-territorial licences for online rights in musical works must provide, by electronic means, to—

(a) online service providers,
(b) right holders whose rights it represents, and
(c) other collective management organisations,

up-to-date information allowing the identification of the online music repertoire it represents (but see paragraph (3)).

(2) The information referred to in paragraph (1) includes—

(a) the musical works represented;
(b) the rights represented wholly or in part; and
(c) the territories covered.

(3) In complying with paragraph (1) a collective management organisation may take reasonable measures, where necessary, to—

(a) protect the accuracy and integrity of the data;
(b) control their reuse; and
(c) protect commercially sensitive information.

NOTES

Commencement: 10 April 2016.

[2.706]

25 Accuracy of multi-territorial repertoire information

(1) A collective management organisation which grants multi-territorial licences for online rights in musical works must have in place arrangements to enable—

(a) a right holder,
(b) another collective management organisation, and
(c) an online service provider,

to request a correction of the data referred to in paragraph (3) of regulation 23 (capacity to process) or the information referred to in paragraph (1) of regulation 24 (transparency) where a person referred to in sub-paragraphs (a) to (c) believes on the basis of reasonable evidence that the information or data is inaccurate in respect of their online rights in musical works.

(2) Where a claim under paragraph (1) is sufficiently substantiated the collective management organisation must correct the information without undue delay.

(3) A collective management organisation must provide—

(a) right holders whose musical works are included in its own music repertoire, and

(b) right holders who have entrusted the management of their online rights in musical works to it in accordance with regulation 30 (access to multi-territorial licensing),

with the means of submitting to it in electronic form information concerning their musical works, their rights in those works and the territories in respect of which the right holders authorise the organisation.

(4) When information is submitted in accordance with paragraph (3), the collective management organisation and the right holder must take into account, as far as possible, voluntary industry standards or practices regarding the exchange of data developed at international level or at the level of the European Union allowing right holders to specify—

(a) the musical work, wholly or in part;

(b) the online rights, wholly or in part; and

(c) the territories in respect of which they authorise the organisation.

(5) A collective management organisation which has been mandated by another collective management organisation ("the mandating collective management organisation") to grant multi-territorial licences for online rights in musical works under—

(a) regulation 28 (agreements between collective management organisations), or

(b) regulation 29 (representation of collective management organisations),

must comply with paragraph (3) with respect to the right holders whose musical works are included in the repertoire of the mandating collective management organisation unless the collective management organisations agree otherwise.

NOTES

Commencement: 10 April 2016.

[2.707]

26 Reporting and invoicing

(1) A collective management organisation must monitor the use of online rights in musical works which it represents, wholly or in part, by online service providers to which it has granted a multi-territorial licence for those rights.

(2) A collective management organisation must offer online service providers the possibility of reporting by electronic means the actual use of online rights in musical works.

(3) A collective management organisation must offer the use of at least one method of reporting the matters referred to in paragraph (2) which takes account of voluntary industry standards or practices developed at international level or at the level of the European Union for the electronic exchange of such data.

(4) A collective management organisation may refuse to accept reporting by the online service provider in a proprietary format if the organisation allows for reporting using an industry standard for the electronic exchange of data.

(5) An online service provider must accurately report the use of the works referred to in paragraph (2).

(6) A collective management organisation must invoice the online service provider by electronic means in accordance with paragraphs (7) and (8).

(7) The collective management organisation must offer the use of at least one format which takes into account voluntary industry standards or practices developed at international level or at the level of the European Union.

(8) The invoice must identify—

(a) the works and rights which are licensed, wholly or in part, on the basis of the data referred to in paragraph (3) of regulation 23 (capacity to process); and

(b) the corresponding actual uses, to the extent this is possible on the basis of the information provided by the online service provider and the format used to provide that information.

(9) The online service provider may not refuse to accept the invoice because of its format if the collective management organisation is using an industry standard.

(10) The collective management organisation must invoice the online service provider accurately and without delay after the actual use of the online rights in that musical work is reported except where this is not possible for reasons attributable to the online service provider.

(11) The collective management organisation must have in place adequate arrangements enabling the online service provider to challenge the accuracy of the invoice including when the online service provider receives invoices from one or more collective management organisations for the same online rights in the same musical work.

NOTES

Commencement: 10 April 2016.

[2.708]

27 Payment to right holders

(1) A collective management organisation which grants multi-territorial licences for online rights in musical works must distribute amounts due to a right holder accruing from multi-territorial licences for online rights in musical works accurately and without delay after the actual use of the work is reported unless this is not possible for reasons attributable to the online service provider (but see paragraph (3)).

(2) A collective management organisation must provide at least the following information to a right holder together with each payment it makes under paragraph (1) (but see paragraph (3))—

(a) the period during which the uses took place for which amounts are due to the right holder and the territories in which the uses took place;

(b) the amounts collected, deductions made and amounts distributed by the collective management organisation for each online right in any musical work which the right holder has authorised the collective management organisation to represent wholly or in part; and

(c) the amounts collected for the right holder, deductions made and amounts distributed by the collective management organisation in respect of each online service provider.

(3) Where a collective management organisation ("the mandating collective management organisation") mandates another collective management organisation ("the mandated collective management organisation") to grant multi-territorial licences for online rights in musical works under regulations 28 (agreements between collective management organisations) and 29 (representation of other collective management organisations) then—

(a) the mandated collective management organisation must—

(i) distribute the amounts referred to in paragraph (1) accurately and without delay to the mandating collective management organisation; and

(ii) provide the information referred to in paragraph (2) to the mandating collective management organisation;

and

(b) the mandating collective management organisation has responsibility for—

(i) the subsequent distribution of the amounts referred to in sub-paragraph (a)(i) to right holders, and

(ii) the subsequent provision of the information referred to in sub-paragraph (a)(ii) to right holders,

unless the mandating and mandated collective management organisations agree otherwise.

NOTES

Commencement: 10 April 2016.

[2.709]

28 Agreements between collective management organisations for multi-territorial licensing

(1) A collective management organisation ("the mandating collective management organisation") must—

(a) ensure that a representation agreement under which the organisation mandates another collective management organisation ("the mandated collective management organisation") to grant multi-territorial licences for the online rights in musical works in its musical repertoire is of a non-exclusive nature; and

(b) inform—

(i) its members, and

(ii) right holders who are not its members but who have a direct legal relationship with it by law or by way of assignment, licence or other contractual arrangement,

of the main terms of that agreement including its duration and the costs of the services provided by the mandated collective management organisation.

(2) The mandated collective management organisation must—

(a) manage the online rights referred to in paragraph (1) on a non-discriminatory basis; and

(b) inform the mandating collective management organisation of the main terms according to which the mandating collective management organisation's online rights are to be licensed including—

(i) the nature of the exploitation;

(ii) all provisions which relate to or affect the licence fee;

(iii) the duration of the licence;

(iv) the accounting periods; and

(v) the territories covered.

NOTES

Commencement: 10 April 2016.

[2.710]
29 Representation of other collective management organisations in relation to multi-territorial licensing

(1) This regulation applies where a collective management organisation ("the requesting collective management organisation")—

(a) does not grant or offer to grant multi-territorial licences for the online rights in musical works in its own repertoire; and

(b) requests another collective management organisation ("the requested collective management organisation") to enter into a representation agreement to represent the rights referred to in sub-paragraph (a).

(2) Where this regulation applies—

(a) the requested collective management organisation must agree to the request referred to in paragraph (1)(b) if that organisation is already granting or offering to grant multi-territorial licences for the same category of online rights in musical works in the repertoire of one or more other collective management organisations;

(b) the requested collective management organisation must respond to the requesting collective management organisation in writing without undue delay;

(c) the requested collective management organisation must manage the represented repertoire of the requesting collective management organisation on the same conditions as those which it applies to the management of its own repertoire (but see sub-paragraphs (e) and (f);

(d) the requested collective management organisation must include the represented repertoire of the requesting collective management organisation in all offers it addresses to online service providers;

(e) the requested collective management organisation must ensure that the management fee for the service provided by the requested management organisation to the requesting management organisation does not exceed the costs reasonably incurred by the requested collective management organisation; and

(f) the requesting collective management organisation must make available to the requested collective management organisation information relating to its own music repertoire required for the provision of multi-territorial licences for online rights in musical works.

(3) Where the information provided under paragraph (2)(f) is insufficient or provided in a form that does not allow the requested collective management organisation to meet the requirements of this Part, paragraph (2) does not prevent the requested collective management organisation from—

(a) charging for the costs reasonably incurred in meeting the requirements of this Part; or

(b) excluding the online rights in musical works for which information made available under paragraph (2)(f) is insufficient or cannot be used.

NOTES

Commencement: 10 April 2016.

[2.711]
30 Access to multi-territorial licensing

(1) This regulation applies to a collective management organisation established in the United Kingdom which by 10th April 2017—

(a) does not grant or offer to grant multi-territorial licences for online rights in musical works; or

(b) does not allow another collective management organisation to represent those rights for such purpose.

(2) A collective management organisation to which this regulation applies must ensure that a right holder who has authorised that collective management organisation to represent their online rights in musical works can withdraw from that collective management organisation the online rights in musical works under the conditions provided in paragraph (3).

(3) The conditions provided in this paragraph are—

(a) the withdrawal referred to in paragraph (2) is for the purpose of multi-territorial licensing in respect of all territories in order to—

(i) grant multi-territorial licenses for the right holder's online rights in musical works by that right holder; or

(ii) grant multi-territorial licences for those works through any other person the right holder authorises or through any collective management organisation complying with the provisions of this Part;

and

(b) the withdrawal does not require withdrawal of online rights in musical works for the purposes of mono-territorial licensing.

NOTES

Commencement: 10 April 2016.

PART 4
DISPUTE RESOLUTION AND ENFORCEMENT

[2.712]
31 Complaints procedure

(1) A collective management organisation must make available to—
- (a) its members,
- (b) right holders who are not its members but who have a direct legal relationship with it by law or by way of assignment, licence or other contractual arrangement,
- (c) collective management organisations on whose behalf it manages rights under representation agreement, and
- (d) users,

effective and timely procedures for dealing with complaints.

(2) The matters covered by the procedures for dealing with complaints referred to in paragraph (1) relate in particular to—
- (a) authorisation to manage rights;
- (b) termination or withdrawal of rights;
- (c) membership terms;
- (d) the collection of amounts due to right holders;
- (e) deductions and distributions; and
- (f) the service provided.

(3) A collective management organisation must—
- (a) respond in writing to complaints; and
- (b) give reasons where it rejects a complaint.

(4) Paragraph (1)(d) does not apply where the collective management organisation is a business with fewer than ten employees and which has a turnover or balance sheet of less than 2 million euros per annum.

NOTES

Commencement: 10 April 2016.

[2.713]
32 Alternative dispute resolution procedures

(1) A collective management organisation must ensure that disputes to which—
- (a) paragraph (2) applies, or
- (b) paragraph (3) applies,

can be submitted to an independent and impartial alternative dispute resolution procedure.

(2) This paragraph applies to disputes between a collective management organisation and one of its members, a right holder, a user or another collective management organisation concerning compliance with these Regulations other than—
- (a) a dispute to which paragraph (3) applies; or
- (b) a dispute concerning paragraph (4)(b) of regulation 15 (tariffs).

(3) This paragraph applies to disputes between a collective management organisation to which Part 3 of these Regulations applies which grants or offers to grant multi-territorial licences for online rights in musical works with—
- (a) an actual or potential online service provider regarding compliance with regulations 15 (licensing), 24 (transparency), 25 (accuracy of multi-territorial repertoire information) and 26 (reporting and invoicing);
- (b) a right holder regarding compliance with regulations 24, 25, 26, 27 (payment to right holders), 28 (agreements between collective management organisations), 29 (representation of other collective management organisations) and 30 (access to multi-territorial licensing); and
- (c) another collective management organisation regarding compliance with regulations 24, 25, 26, 27, 28 and 29.

(4) Paragraph (1)(a) does not apply where the collective management organisation is a business with fewer than ten employees and which has a turnover or balance sheet of less than 2 million euros per annum.

NOTES

Commencement: 10 April 2016.

[2.714]
33 Right of right holders in relation to a breach of regulation 4

(1) The obligation of a collective management organisation to comply with regulation 4 (particular obligations of collective management organisations to right holders) is a duty owed to any right holder who may be affected by the contravention of that regulation.

Part 2 Copyright

(2) Where a duty is owed by virtue of paragraph (1) to a right holder, a breach of that duty which causes that right holder to sustain loss or damage shall be actionable by the right holder.

NOTES

Commencement: 10 April 2016.

[2.715]

34 Monitoring of compliance

The Secretary of State must monitor compliance with these Regulations.

NOTES

Commencement: 10 April 2016.

[2.716]

35 Evidence of non-compliance

The Secretary of State must have regard to evidence which is notified to the Secretary of State of activities or circumstances which may constitute a breach of these Regulations.

NOTES

Commencement: 10 April 2016.

[2.717]

36 Power to request information

(1) The Secretary of State may give notice to—

(a) a collective management organisation,
(b) a member,
(c) a right holder or a body representing the interests of right holders,
(d) a user or a body representing the interests of users,
(e) an entity to which a provision of these Regulations applies under paragraph (4) of regulation 2 (interpretation and application), or
(f) an independent management entity,

requiring it to supply to the Secretary of State such information or document as may be specified or described in the notice for the purpose of ascertaining whether these Regulations have been complied with.

(2) The notice may require the person to whom it is given to supply the information or document referred to in paragraph (1) at a time and a place and in a form and manner which is specified.

(3) The person to whom the notice is given shall supply to the Secretary of State the information or document which is specified or described in the notice under paragraph (1) in accordance with what is specified under paragraph (2).

(4) The Secretary of State may, for the purpose described in paragraph (1), copy any document or information provided.

(5) Nothing in this regulation gives the Secretary of State any power to require a person to supply any information or document which the person would be entitled to refuse to supply in proceedings in the High Court on the grounds of legal professional privilege or (in Scotland) in proceedings in the Court of Session on the grounds of confidentiality of communications.

(6) In paragraph (5) "communications" means—

(a) communications between a professional legal adviser and the adviser's client; or
(b) communications made in connection with, or in contemplation of, legal proceedings and for the purposes of those proceedings.

(7) Nothing in this regulation shall be construed as requiring a person to provide information if to do so might incriminate that person.

(8) A reference in this regulation to the supply of a document is a reference to the supply of a legible and intelligible copy of information recorded otherwise than in legible form.

NOTES

Commencement: 10 April 2016.

[2.718]

37 Compliance notice

(1) Where the Secretary of State thinks that—

(a) a collective management organisation,
(b) a member,
(c) a right holder or a body representing the interests of right holders,
(d) a user or a body representing the interests of users,
(e) an entity to which a provision of these Regulations applies under paragraph (4) of regulation 2, or
(f) an independent management entity,

has failed to comply with its obligations under Part 2 or 3 of these Regulations or under regulation 31 (complaints procedure), 32 (alternative dispute resolution procedures) or 36 (information) the Secretary of State may give a notice ("a compliance notice") to that person.

(2) A compliance notice must be in writing and must—

(a) state that the Secretary of State thinks that the person has not complied with a provision of these Regulations;

(b) specify the provision in question and state the acts or omissions which the Secretary of State thinks contravene that provision;

(c) request the person, where non-compliance with the provision is continuing,—

(i) to end the non-compliance within such time as the notice may specify;

(ii) to provide such evidence within that period to the satisfaction of the Secretary of State that the non-compliance has ended;

(d) if the Secretary of State thinks fit, request the person to provide a written undertaking in a form which is satisfactory to the Secretary of State, that non-compliance with the provision will not be repeated; and

(e) warn the person that if—

(i) the person does not comply with the compliance notice, or

(ii) the person fails to comply with a written undertaking provided in respect of the compliance notice,

further action may be taken under these Regulations.

(3) The Secretary of State may rescind a compliance notice given to a person under paragraph (1) and where doing so must give the person notice of the rescission.

(4) Where a compliance notice has been given in relation to a failure to comply with these Regulations no action to impose a penalty under regulation 38 (financial penalties) may be taken in relation to that failure unless the person to whom it has been given has failed—

(a) to comply with the compliance notice; or

(b) to comply with a written undertaking provided in respect of a compliance notice.

NOTES

Commencement: 10 April 2016.

[2.719]

38 Financial penalties for non-compliance

(1) The Secretary of State may impose a financial penalty on—

(a) a collective management organisation,

(b) a member,

(c) a right holder or a body representing the interests of right holders,

(d) a user or a body representing the interests of users,

(e) an entity to which a provision of these Regulations applies under paragraph (4) of regulation 2, or

(f) an independent management entity,

if the Secretary of State is satisfied that the person referred to in paragraph (1)(a) to (f) has failed to comply with its obligations under Part 2 or 3 of these Regulations or regulation 31, 32 or 36.

(2) If the Secretary of State may impose a financial penalty on a collective management organisation under paragraph (1) the Secretary of State may instead impose a financial penalty on a director, manager or similar officer of that collective management organisation or, where the organisation's affairs are managed by its members, a member.

(3) The amount of the financial penalty must be such amount as the Secretary of State considers appropriate.

(4) In deciding what amount is appropriate the Secretary of State must have regard to the nature of the failure of compliance.

(5) A financial penalty may comprise of either—

(a) a sum not exceeding £50,000; or

(b) a sum not exceeding £5,000 together with a sum not exceeding £500 for each day that the person referred to in paragraph (1) continues to fail to comply with its obligations under these Regulations not exceeding in total £50,000.

(6) A financial penalty is payable to the Secretary of State.

NOTES

Commencement: 10 April 2016.

[2.720]

39 Financial penalties: procedure

(1) As soon as practicable after imposing a financial penalty, the Secretary of State must give notice of the financial penalty to the person on whom it is imposed.

(2) The notice must state—

(a) that the Secretary of State has imposed a financial penalty;

(b) the amount of the financial penalty;
(c) the acts or omissions which the Secretary of State considers contravene the Regulations;
(d) the provisions of these Regulation which the Secretary of State considers are contravened;
(e) any other facts which the Secretary of State considers justify the imposition of a financial penalty;
(f) the period (not less than 28 days from the date the notice is received by the person) within which the financial penalty is to be paid.

(3) The Secretary of State may rescind a penalty which has been imposed on a person under regulation 38 (financial penalties) and where doing so must give the person notice of the rescission.

NOTES
Commencement: 10 April 2016.

[2.721]
40 Appeals

(1) If a person on whom a financial penalty is imposed is aggrieved by the imposition or the amount of a financial penalty, the person may appeal to the First-tier Tribunal.

(2) On an appeal under this regulation, the First-tier Tribunal may make such order as it considers appropriate.

(3) In this regulation "First-tier Tribunal" means the First-tier Tribunal established by section 3(1) of the Tribunals, Courts and Enforcement Act 2007.

NOTES
Commencement: 10 April 2016.

[2.722]
41 Recovery of a financial penalty

(1) Where a financial penalty, or any portion of it, has not been paid by the time which it is required to be paid and paragraph (2) applies the Secretary of State may recover from the person on whom the penalty is imposed any of the penalty which has not been paid as a debt due to the Secretary of State.

(2) This paragraph applies where—
(a) no appeal relating to the penalty has been made under regulation 40; or
(b) an appeal has been made under that regulation and that appeal has been determined, withdrawn or otherwise dealt with.

NOTES
Commencement: 10 April 2016.

[2.723]
42 Notices

(1) Where a notice is to be given under these Regulations, it may be given—
(a) by being delivered personally to a person;
(b) by being sent to the proper address of the person—
(i) by a registered post service (as defined in section 125(1) of the Postal Services Act 2000); or
(ii) by a postal service which provides for the delivery of the document to be recorded;
(c) by being sent to the person using electronic communications to that person's last known electronic address.

(2) For the purpose of paragraph (1)(b) the proper address of a person is—
(a) in the case of a body corporate, the address of the registered office or principal office of the body,
(b) in the case of a partnership, the address of the principal office of the partnership,
(c) in any other case, the last known address of that person.

(3) Where a notice has been given as mentioned in paragraph (1)(b) or (c) it is to be taken to have been received 48 hours after it is sent unless the contrary is shown.

NOTES
Commencement: 10 April 2016.

[2.724]
43 Computation of time

(1) If the time specified in these Regulations for doing any act ends on a day other than a working day, the act is done in time if it is done on the next working day.

(2) In this regulation "working day" means any day except a Saturday or Sunday, Christmas Day, Good Friday or a day which is a bank holiday in any part of the United Kingdom under section 1 of the Banking and Financial Dealings Act 1971.

NOTES

Commencement: 10 April 2016.

PART 5
AMENDMENTS AND TRANSITIONAL PROVISION

44–46 *(Reg 44 amends the Copyright, Designs and Patents Act 1988, s 116 at* **[2.154]**; *reg 45 revokes the Copyright (Regulation of Relevant Licensing Bodies) Regulations 2014, SI 2014/898; reg 46 amends the Copyright and Rights in Performances (Extended Collective Licensing) Regulations 2014, SI 2014/2588.)*

[2.725]

47 Transitional provisions

Despite the revocation by these Regulations of the Copyright (Regulation of Relevant Licensing Bodies) Regulations 2014—

(a) regulation 2 (interpretation) shall continue to apply for the purposes of the regulations referred to in paragraphs (b) to (g);

(b) regulation 6 (code reviewer) shall continue to apply in relation to a review and report on a code of practice in respect of a period before the date on which these Regulations come into force;

(c) regulation 7 (licensing code ombudsman) shall continue to apply in relation to a dispute concerning compliance with a code of practice before the date on which these Regulations come into force;

(d) regulation 8 (recovery of fees) shall continue to apply in relation to the cost of administering the operation of those Regulations;

(e) regulation 9 (power to request information) shall continue to apply in relation to information relating to licensing activities before the date on which these Regulations come into force;

(f) regulation 10 (financial penalties) shall continue to apply in relation to a failure to comply with the obligations specified under that regulation; and

(g) regulation 11 (imposition of penalty) and 12 (appeals) shall continue to apply in relation to a financial penalty imposed under regulation 10.

NOTES

Commencement: 10 April 2016.

[2.726]

48

Despite the omission by these Regulations of the definitions "code of practice", "Codes Regulations" and "specified criteria" in regulation 2 of the Copyright and Rights in Performances (Extended Collective Licensing) Regulations 2014 those definitions shall continue to apply for the purposes of regulation 10(2)(g), 11(1)(c) and 14(2)(c) of those Regulations.

NOTES

Commencement: 10 April 2016.

[2.727]

49

Despite the revocation by these Regulations of regulations 10(2)(g) and 11(1)(c) of the Copyright and Rights in Performances (Extended Collective Licensing) Regulations 2014, those sub-paragraphs shall continue to have effect in relation to a report to which they apply which has been produced.

NOTES

Commencement: 10 April 2016.

[2.728]

50

Despite the revocation by these Regulations of regulation 14(2)(c) of the Copyright and Rights in Performances (Extended Collective Licensing) Regulations 2014 that sub-paragraph shall continue to apply in relation to a failure to comply which occurred before the date on which these Regulations come into force.

NOTES

Commencement: 10 April 2016.

[2.729]

51 Review

(1) The Secretary of State must from time to time—

(a) carry out of review of these Regulations;

(b) set out the conclusions of the review in a report; and

(c) publish the report.

(2) In carrying out the review the Secretary of State must, so far as is reasonable, have regard to how Directive 2014/26/EU of 26 February 2014 (which is implemented by means of these Regulations) is implemented in other member States.

(3) The report must in particular—

(a) set out the objectives to be achieved by the regulatory system established by these Regulations;

(b) assess the extent to which those objectives are achieved; and

(c) assess whether those objectives remain appropriate and, if so, the extent to which they could be achieved with a system that imposes less regulation.

(4) The first report under this regulation must be published before the end of the period of five years beginning with the day on which this regulation comes into force.

(5) Reports under this regulation are afterwards to be published at intervals not exceeding five years.

NOTES

Commencement: 10 April 2016.

COPYRIGHT AND PERFORMANCES (APPLICATION TO OTHER COUNTRIES) ORDER 2016

(SI 2016/1219)

NOTES

Made: 14 December 2016.

Authority: European Communities Act 1972, s 2(2), Copyright, Designs and Patents Act 1988, ss 159, 206(4), 208.

Commencement: 6 April 2017.

ARRANGEMENT OF ARTICLES

SCHEDULES

PART 1
INTRODUCTORY

[2.730]

1 Citation, commencement, interpretation and revocation

(1) This Order may be cited as the Copyright and Performances (Application to Other Countries) Order 2016 and comes into force on 6th April 2017.

(2) In this Order—

"the Act" means the Copyright, Designs and Patents Act 1988 and references to a numbered section are references to the section bearing that number in that Act;

"relevant country" means a country other than the United Kingdom, another EEA state, the Channel Islands, the Isle of Man or Gibraltar;

"WPPT" means the World Intellectual Property Organisation Performances and Phonograms Treaty adopted in Geneva on 20th December 1996; and

"WTO" means the World Trade Organisation.

(3) The Copyright and Performances (Application to Other Countries) Order 2013 and the Copyright and Performances (Application to Other Countries) (Amendment) Order 2015 are revoked.

NOTES

Commencement: 6 April 2017.

PART 2
LITERARY, DRAMATIC, MUSICAL AND ARTISTIC WORKS, FILMS AND TYPOGRAPHICAL ARRANGEMENTS OF PUBLISHED EDITIONS

[2.731]

2 Restrictions on the application of Part 1 of the Act by virtue of section 159(1) to certain works first published before 1st June 1957

(1) The application of Part 1 of the Act by virtue of section 159(1) (countries that are parties to the Berne Convention or WTO members) is subject to the restriction specified in paragraph (2).

(2) A literary, dramatic, musical or artistic work first published before 1st June 1957 does not qualify for copyright protection under section 154 (qualification by reference to author).

NOTES

Commencement: 6 April 2017.

PART 3
SOUND RECORDINGS

[2.732]

3 Restricted application of section 159(3) in relation to certain sound recordings

(1) The application of Part 1 of the Act by virtue of section 159(3) (countries that are parties to the WPPT) is subject to the restrictions set out in paragraph (2).

(2) Where a country is a party to the WPPT but not the Rome Convention, Part 1 of the Act applies except that—

(a) section 18A (infringement by rental or lending of work to the public) does not apply in so far as it relates to lending;

(b) section 20 (infringement by communication to the public) does not apply to the broadcasting of a sound recording; and

(c) section 107(2A) (criminal liability for communicating to the public) does not apply in relation to the broadcasting of a sound recording.

NOTES

Commencement: 6 April 2017.

[2.733]

4 Sound recordings—application of Part 1 of the Act—parties to the Berne Convention and WTO Members

(1) This article applies to a relevant country that—

(a) is not a party to the Rome Convention or the WPPT; and
(b) satisfies either or both of the following criteria—
  (i) the country is a party to the Berne Convention; and
  (ii) the country is a member of the WTO.

(2) Where this article applies to a country, Part 1 of the Act so far as it relates to sound recordings—
(a) applies in relation to a person who is a citizen or subject of that country or a person domiciled or resident there as it applies in relation to a person who is a British citizen or is domiciled or resident in the United Kingdom,
(b) applies in relation to a body incorporated under the law of that country as it applies in relation to a body incorporated under the law of a part of the United Kingdom, and
(c) applies in relation to a sound recording first published in that country as it applies in relation to a sound recording first published the United Kingdom,

(but see paragraph (3)).

(3) The application of Part 1 of the Act by virtue of paragraph (2) is subject to the following modifications—
(a) section 18A (infringement by rental or lending of work to the public) does not apply in so far as it relates to lending;
(b) the following provisions do not apply—
  (i) section 19 (infringement by showing or playing of work in public);
  (ii) section 20 (infringement by communication to the public);
  (iii) section 26 (secondary infringement: provision of apparatus for infringing performance, &c); and
  (iv) section 107(2A) and (3) (criminal liability for communicating to the public or playing sound recording).

NOTES

Commencement: 6 April 2017.

[2.734]

5 Sound recordings—application of Part 1 of the Act—miscellaneous countries

(1) This article applies to the countries listed in Part 1 of the Schedule to this Order.

(2) Where this article applies to a country, Part 1 of the Act so far as it relates to sound recordings—
(a) applies in relation to a person who is a citizen or subject of that country or a person domiciled or resident there as it applies in relation to a person who is a British citizen or is domiciled or resident in the United Kingdom;
(b) applies in relation to a body incorporated under the law of that country as it applies in relation to a body incorporated under the law of a part of the United Kingdom; and
(c) applies in relation to a sound recording first published in that country as it applies in relation to a sound recording first published in the United Kingdom.

NOTES

Commencement: 6 April 2017.

PART 4
BROADCASTS

[2.735]

6 Restrictions on the application of Part 1 of the Act to broadcasts

(1) The application of Part 1 of the Act to broadcasts by virtue of section 159(2) is subject to the restrictions specified in paragraphs (2) and (3).

(2) Part 1 of the Act only applies by virtue of section 159(2) to a wireless broadcast made from a country on or after the date that country became a party to the Rome Convention.

(3) Part 1 of the Act only applies by virtue of section 159(2) to a broadcast, which is not a wireless broadcast, where that broadcast is made from Switzerland.

NOTES

Commencement: 6 April 2017.

[2.736]

7 Application of Part 1 of the Act under section 159(4)—WTO members

(1) This article applies to a relevant country that is a member of the WTO but not a party to the Rome Convention.

(2) Where this article applies to a relevant country, Part 1 of the Act applies to a wireless broadcast in relation to that country in the manner set out in paragraph (4) subject to paragraph (3).

(3) The application of Part 1 of the Act by virtue of paragraph (2) is subject to the following modifications—

(a) section 18A (infringement by rental of work to the public) does not apply;

(b) section 19 (infringement by showing or playing the work in public) only applies in relation to television broadcasts;

(c) section 20 (infringement by communication to the public) only applies in relation to broadcasting by wireless telegraphy;

(d) section 26 (secondary infringement: provision of apparatus for infringing performance, &c) does not apply in so far as it relates to television broadcasts;

(e) section 107(2A) (criminal liability for communicating to the public) only applies in relation to broadcasting by wireless telegraphy; and

(f) Part 1 of the Act only applies to a broadcast made on or after 1st January 1996 or, if later, the date on which the relevant country became a member of the WTO.

(4) Part 1 of the Act applies in relation to—

(a) a person who is a citizen or subject of a relevant country or a person domiciled or resident there as it applies in relation to a person who is a British citizen or is domiciled or resident in the United Kingdom;

(b) a body incorporated under the law of a relevant country as it applies in relation to a body incorporated under the law of a part of the United Kingdom; and

(c) a wireless broadcast made from that country as it applies in relation to a wireless broadcast made from the United Kingdom.

NOTES

Commencement: 6 April 2017.

[2.737]

8 Application of Part 1 of the Act under section 159(4)—miscellaneous countries

(1) This paragraph applies to the following countries—

(a) Indonesia; and

(b) Singapore.

(2) This paragraph applies to the following countries—

(a) Hong Kong;

(b) Indonesia;

(c) Malawi;

(d) Malaysia; and

(e) Singapore.

(3) Where paragraph (1) applies to a country, Part 1 of the Act applies to a broadcast which is not a wireless broadcast in relation to that country in the manner set out in paragraph (5)(a), (b) and (d).

(4) Where paragraph (2) applies to a country, Part 1 of the Act applies to a wireless broadcast in relation to that country in the manner set out in paragraph (5)(a), (b) and (c) subject to paragraph (6).

(5) Part 1 of the Act applies in relation to—

(a) a person who is a citizen or subject of that country or a person domiciled or resident there as it applies in relation to a person who is a British citizen or is domiciled or resident in the United Kingdom;

(b) a body incorporated under the law of that country as it applies in relation to a body incorporated under the law of a part of the United Kingdom;

(c) a wireless broadcast made from that country as it applies in relation to a wireless broadcast made from the United Kingdom; and

(d) a broadcast which is not a wireless broadcast made from that country as it applies in relation to a broadcast which is not a wireless broadcast made from the United Kingdom.

(6) Part 1 of the Act only applies to a wireless broadcast made on or after 1st June 1957 or, in the case of Malawi, on or after 22nd June 1989.

NOTES

Commencement: 6 April 2017.

PART 5
PERFORMANCES

[2.738]

9 Restrictions on the application of Part 2 of the Act in respect of countries that have made declarations under Article 16(1)(a)(i) of the Rome Convention

(1) This article applies to a country which is a party to the Rome Convention and has made a declaration under Article 16(1)(a) of the Rome Convention that it will not apply the provisions of Article 12 (which provides for the payment of a single equitable remuneration).

(2) Where this article applies, to the extent that the declaration referred to in paragraph (1) is in force in the law of the country in relation to British performances, the provisions of Part 2 of the Act shall not apply to grant the protection provided for under Article 12 of the Rome Convention unless the recording has been first published in a country which—

(a) is a party to the Rome Convention; and
(b) has not made a declaration of the kind referred to in paragraph (1).

NOTES

Commencement: 6 April 2017.

[2.739]

10 Application of Part 2 of the Act to WPPT countries which have made a declaration under Article 15(3) of the WPPT and which are party to the Rome Convention

(1) This article applies to—

(a) Australia (including Norfolk Island);
(b) Chile;
(c) Costa Rica;
(d) Korea, Republic of; and
(e) Macedonia, The Former Yugoslav Republic of.

(2) This article does not affect the application of Part 2 of the Act to a country to which this article applies by virtue of paragraph (bb) (countries party to the Rome Convention) of the definition of "qualifying country" in subsection (1) of section 206 (qualifying countries).

(3) A country to which this article applies is, subject to paragraph (4), designated as enjoying reciprocal protection under Part 2 of the Act.

(4) Part 2 of the Act applies subject to the following modifications—

(a) the definition of recording in section 180(2) (rights conferred on performers and persons having recording rights), shall be construed as applying only to sound recordings (and not to films);
(b) the following provisions do not apply—
  (i) section 182C (consent required for rental or lending of copies to the public), in so far as it relates to lending;
  (ii) section 183 (infringement of performer's rights by use of recording made without consent);
  (iii) sections 185 to 188 (rights of persons having recording rights); and
  (iv) section 198(2) (criminal liability for making available to the public);
  and
(c) the provisions of Part 2 of the Act shall not apply to protect the right provided for in Article 15(1) of the WPPT to the extent that a declaration is in force in the law of a country to which this article applies in relation to British performances.

(5) In paragraph (4)(c) "declaration" means a declaration made under Article 15(3) of the WPPT by a country to which this article applies that—

(a) it will apply the provisions of Article 15(1) of the WPPT (which confers on performers and producers of phonograms a right to remuneration for broadcasting and communication to the public) only in respect of certain uses;
(b) it will limit the application of the provisions of Article 15(1) of the WPPT in some other way; or
(c) it will not apply the provisions of Article 15(1) of the WPPT at all.

NOTES

Commencement: 6 April 2017.

[2.740]

11 Application of Part 2 of the Act to WPPT countries not party to the Rome Convention

(1) This article applies to the countries listed in Part 2 of the Schedule where this article is specified in the entry relating to that country (countries party to the WPPT but not the Rome Convention).

(2) A country to which this article applies is, subject to paragraphs (3) and (4), designated as enjoying reciprocal protection under Part 2 of the Act.

(3) Part 2 of the Act applies subject to the following modifications—

(a) the definition of recording in section 180(2) (rights conferred on performers and persons having recording rights), shall be construed as applying only to sound recordings (and not to films);
(b) the following provisions do not apply—
  (i) section 182C (consent required for rental or lending of copies to public), in so far as it relates to lending;
  (ii) section 183 (infringement of performer's rights by use of recording made without consent);

(iii) sections 185 to 188 (rights of persons having recording rights); and
(iv) section 198(2) (criminal liability for making available to the public).

(4) Where a country to which this article applies has made a declaration under Article 15(3) of the WPPT that—

(a) it will apply the provisions of Article 15(1) of the WPPT (which confers on performers and producers of phonograms a right to remuneration for broadcasting and communication to the public) only in respect of certain uses,
(b) it will limit the application of the provisions of Article 15(1) of the WPPT in some other way, or
(c) it will not apply the provisions of Article 15(1) of the WPPT at all,

the provisions of Part 2 of the Act shall not apply to protect the right provided for in Article 15(1) of the WPPT to the extent that the declaration is in force in the law of that country in relation to British performances.

NOTES

Commencement: 6 April 2017.

[2.741]

12 Application of Part 2 of the Act to WTO countries

(1) This article applies to a country listed in Part 2 of the Schedule to this Order where this article is specified in the entry relating to that country (WTO members not party to the Rome Convention or the WPPT).

(2) A country to which this article applies is, subject to paragraph (3), designated as enjoying reciprocal protection under Part 2 of the Act.

(3) Part 2 of the Act applies subject to the following modifications—

(a) the definition of recording in section 180(2) (rights conferred on performers and persons having recording rights), shall be construed as applying only to sound recordings (and not to films); and
(b) the following provisions do not apply—
(i) section 182C (consent required for rental or lending of copies to public), in so far as it relates to lending;
(ii) section 182CA (consent required for making available to the public);
(iii) section 182D (right to equitable remuneration for exploitation of sound recording);
(iv) section 183 (infringement of performer's rights by use of recording made without consent);
(v) sections 185 to 188 (rights of persons having recording rights); and
(vi) section 198(1A) and (2) (criminal liability for making available to the public).

NOTES

Commencement: 6 April 2017.

[2.742]

13 Saving

(1) For the purposes of this article an act is an "excluded act" where—

(a) a person (A) has incurred any expenditure or liability in connection with the act; and
(b) A—
(i) began in good faith to do the act, or
(ii) made in good faith effective and serious preparations to do the act,

at a time when the act neither infringed nor was restricted by the relevant rights in the work or performance.

(2) Where another person (B) acquires those relevant rights as a consequence of the provisions of this Order on or after its coming into force, A has the right—

(a) to continue to do the excluded act, or
(b) to do the excluded act,

notwithstanding that the excluded act infringes or is restricted by those relevant rights.

(3) Where B or, as the case may be, B's exclusive licensee in respect of the relevant rights pays reasonable compensation to A, paragraph (2) no longer applies.

(4) Where—

(a) B or, as the case may be, B's exclusive licensee offers to pay compensation to A under paragraph (3), but
(b) A and B or, as the case may be, B's exclusive licensee cannot agree on what compensation is reasonable,

either person may refer the matter to arbitration.

(5) In this article—

(a) "exclusive licensee" means a licensee under an exclusive licence (as defined in section 92(1) or 191D(1)); and

(b) "relevant rights" means copyright, the rights conferred by Chapter 4 of Part 1 of the Act (moral rights) and the rights conferred by Part 2 of the Act.

NOTES

Commencement: 6 April 2017.

SCHEDULE

Articles 5, 11 and 12

PART 1
SOUND RECORDINGS—APPLICATION OF PART 1 OF THE ACT—MISCELLANEOUS COUNTRIES

[2.743]

Bangladesh

Ghana

Hong Kong

India

Indonesia

Malawi

Malaysia

New Zealand

Pakistan

Taiwan

Thailand

NOTES

Commencement: 6 April 2017.

PART 2
COUNTRIES WHICH ARE NOT PARTIES TO THE ROME CONVENTION—APPLICATION OF PART 2 OF THE ACT UNDER ARTICLES 11 AND 12

[2.744]

Country	*Applicable article*
Afghanistan	Article 12
Angola	Article 12
Antigua and Barbuda	Article 12
Bangladesh	Article 12
Belize	Article 12
Benin	Article 11
Botswana	Article 11
Brunei Darussalam	Article 12
Burundi	Article 12
Cambodia	Article 12
Cameroon	Article 12
Canada	Article 11
Central African Republic	Article 12
Chad	Article 12
China	Article 11
Côte d'Ivoire	Article 12
Cuba	Article 12
Democratic Republic of Congo	Article 12
Djibouti	Article 12
Egypt	Article 12

Gabon	Article 11
Gambia	Article 12
Ghana	Article 11
Grenada	Article 12
Guinea	Article 11
Guinea-Bissau	Article 12
Guyana	Article 12
Haiti	Article 12
Hong Kong	Article 11
India	Article 12
Indonesia	Article 11
Jordan	Article 11
Kenya	Article 12
Kuwait	Article 12
Lao People's Democratic Republic	Article 12
Macao	Article 11
Madagascar	Article 11
Malawi	Article 12
Malaysia	Article 11
Maldives	Article 12
Mali	Article 11
Mauretania	Article 12
Mauritius	Article 12
Mongolia	Article 11
Morocco	Article 11
Mozambique	Article 12
Myanmar	Article 12
Namibia	Article 12
Nepal	Article 12
Netherlands Antilles, Curaçao, Sint Maarten and Aruba	Article 11
New Zealand	Article 12
Oman	Article 11
Pakistan	Article 12
Papua New Guinea	Article 12
Qatar	Article 11
Rwanda	Article 12
Saint Kitts and Nevis	Article 12
Saint Vincent and the Grenadines	Article 11
Samoa	Article 12
Saudi Arabia	Article 12
Senegal	Article 11
Seychelles	Article 12
Sierra Leone	Article 12
Singapore	Article 11
Solomon Islands	Article 12
South Africa	Article 12
Sri Lanka	Article 12
Suriname	Article 12
Swaziland	Article 12
Taiwan	Article 12
Tanzania, United Republic of	Article 12
Thailand	Article 12

Part 2 Copyright

Tonga	Article 12
Trinidad and Tobago	Article 11
Tunisia	Article 12
Uganda	Article 12
United States of America (including Puerto Rico and all territories and possessions)	Article 11
Vanuatu	Article 12
Yemen	Article 12
Zambia	Article 12
Zimbabwe	Article 12

NOTES

Commencement: 6 April 2017.

COUNCIL DIRECTIVE

(93/83/EEC)

of 27 September 1993

on the coordination of certain rules concerning copyright and rights related to copyright applicable to satellite broadcasting and cable retransmission

NOTES

Date of publication in OJ: OJ L248, 6.10.93, p 15.

THE COUNCIL OF THE EUROPEAN COMMUNITIES,

Having regard to the Treaty establishing the European Economic Community, and in particular Articles 57(2) and 66 thereof,

Having regard to the proposal from the Commission,[1]

In cooperation with the European Parliament,[2]

Having regard to the opinion of the Economic and Social Committee,[3]

Whereas the objectives of the Community as laid down in the Treaty include establishing an ever closer union among the peoples of Europe, fostering closer relations between the States belonging to the Community and ensuring the economic and social progress of the Community countries by common action to eliminate the barriers which divide Europe;

Whereas, to that end, the Treaty provides for the establishment of a common market and an area without internal frontiers; whereas measures to achieve this include the abolition of obstacles to the free movement of services and the institution of a system ensuring that competition in the common market is not distorted; whereas, to that end, the Council may adopt directives for the coordination of the provisions laid down by law, regulation or administrative action in Member States concerning the taking up and pursuit of activities as self-employed persons;

Whereas broadcasts transmitted across frontiers within the Community, in particular by satellite and cable, are one of the most important ways of pursuing these Community objectives, which are at the same time political, economic, social, cultural and legal;

Whereas the Council has already adopted Directive 89/552/EEC of 3 October 1989 on the coordination of certain provisions laid down by law, regulation or administrative action in Member States concerning the pursuit of television broadcasting activities,[4] which makes provision for the promotion of the distribution and production of European television programmes and for advertising and sponsorship, the protection of minors and the right of reply;

Whereas, however, the achievement of these objectives in respect of cross-border satellite broadcasting and the cable retransmission of programmes from other Member States is currently still obstructed by a series of differences between national rules of copyright and some degree of legal uncertainty; whereas this means that holders of rights are exposed to the threat of seeing their works exploited without payment of remuneration or that the individual holders of exclusive rights in various Member States block the exploitation of their rights; whereas the legal uncertainty in particular constitutes a direct obstacle in the free circulation of programmes within the Community;

Whereas a distinction is currently drawn for copyright purposes between communication to the public by direct satellite and communication to the public by communications satellite; whereas, since individual reception is possible and affordable nowadays with both types of satellite, there is no longer any justification for this differing legal treatment;

Whereas the free broadcasting of programmes is further impeded by the current legal uncertainty over whether broadcasting by a satellite whose signals can be received directly affects the rights in the country of transmission only or in all countries of reception together; whereas, since communications satellites and direct satellites are treated alike for copyright purposes, this legal uncertainty now affects almost all programmes broadcast in the Community by satellite;

Whereas, furthermore, legal certainty, which is a prerequisite for the free movement of broadcasts within the Community, is missing where programmes transmitted across frontiers are fed into and retransmitted through cable networks;

Whereas the development of the acquisition of rights on a contractual basis by authorisation is already making a vigorous contribution to the creation of the desired European audiovisual area; whereas the continuation of such contractual agreements should be ensured and their smooth application in practice should be promoted wherever possible;

Whereas at present cable operators in particular cannot be sure that they have actually acquired all the programme rights covered by such an agreement;

Whereas, lastly, parties in different Member States are not all similarly bound by obligations which prevent them from refusing without valid reason to negotiate on the acquisition of the rights necessary for cable distribution or allowing such negotiations to fail;

Whereas the legal framework for the creation of a single audiovisual area laid down in Directive 89/552/EEC must, therefore, be supplemented with reference to copyright;

Whereas, therefore, an end should be put to the differences of treatment of the transmission of programmes by communications satellite which exist in the Member States, so that the vital distinction throughout the Community becomes whether works and other protected subject matter are communicated to the public; whereas this will also ensure equal treatment of the suppliers of cross-border broadcasts, regardless of whether they use a direct broadcasting satellite or a communications satellite;

Whereas the legal uncertainty regarding the rights to be acquired which impedes cross-border satellite broadcasting should be overcome by defining the notion of communication to the public by satellite at a Community level; whereas this definition should at the same time specify where the act of communication takes place; whereas such a definition is necessary to avoid the cumulative application of several national laws to one single act of broadcasting; whereas communication to the public by satellite occurs only when, and in the Member State where, the programme-carrying signals are introduced under the control and responsibility of the broadcasting organisation into an uninterrupted chain of communication leading to the satellite and down towards the earth; whereas normal technical procedures relating to the programme-carrying signals should not be considered as interruptions to the chain of broadcasting;

Whereas the acquisition on a contractual basis of exclusive broadcasting rights should comply with any legislation on copyright and rights related to copyright in the Member State in which communication to the public by satellite occurs;

Whereas the principle of contractual freedom on which this Directive is based will make it possible to continue limiting the exploitation of these rights, especially as far as certain technical means of transmission or certain language versions are concerned;

Whereas, in arriving at the amount of the payment to be made for the rights acquired, the parties should take account of all aspects of the broadcast, such as the actual audience, the potential audience and the language version;

Whereas the application of the country-of-origin principle contained in this Directive could pose a problem with regard to existing contracts; whereas this Directive should provide for a period of five years for existing contracts to be adapted, where necessary, in the light of the Directive; whereas the said country-of-origin principle should not, therefore, apply to existing contracts which expire before 1 January 2000; whereas if by that date parties still have an interest in the contract, the same parties should be entitled to renegotiate the conditions of the contract;

Whereas existing international co-production agreements must be interpreted in the light of the economic purpose and scope envisaged by the parties upon signature; whereas in the past international co-production agreements have often not expressly and specifically addressed communication to the public by satellite within the meaning of this Directive a particular form of exploitation; whereas the underlying philosophy of many existing international co-production agreements is that the rights in the co-production are exercised separately and independently by each co-producer, by dividing the exploitation rights between them along territorial lines; whereas, as a general rule, in the situation where a communication to the public by satellite authorised by one co-producer would prejudice the value of the exploitation rights of another co-producer, the interpretation of such an existing agreement would normally suggest that the latter co-producer would have to give his consent to the authorisation, by the former co-producer, of the communication to the public by satellite; whereas the language exclusivity of the latter co-producer will be prejudiced where the language version or versions of the communication to the public, including where the version is dubbed or subtitled, coincide(s) with the language or the languages widely understood in the territory allotted by the agreement to the latter co-producer; whereas the notion of exclusivity should be understood in a wider sense where the communication to the public by satellite concerns a work which consists merely of images and contains no dialogue or subtitles; whereas a clear rule is necessary in cases where the international co-production agreement does not expressly regulate the division of rights in the specific case of communication to the public by satellite within the meaning of this Directive;

Whereas communications to the public by satellite from non-member countries will under certain conditions be deemed to occur within a Member State of the Community;

Whereas it is necessary to ensure that protection for authors, performers, producers of phonograms and broadcasting organisations is accorded in all Member States and that this protection is not subject to a statutory licence system; whereas only in this way is it possible to ensure that any difference in the level of protection within the common market will not create distortions of competition;

Whereas the advent of new technologies is likely to have an impact on both the quality and the quantity of the exploitation of works and other subject matter;

Whereas in the light of these developments the level of protection granted pursuant to this Directive to all rightholders in the areas covered by this Directive should remain under consideration;

Whereas the harmonisation of legislation envisaged in this Directive entails the harmonisation of the provisions ensuring a high level of protection of authors, performers, phonogram producers and broadcasting organisations; whereas this harmonisation should not allow a broadcasting organisation to take advantage of differences in levels of protection by relocating activities, to the detriment of audiovisual productions;

Whereas the protection provided for rights related to copyright should be aligned on that contained in Council Directive 92/100/EEC of 19 November 1992 on rental right and lending right and on certain rights related to copyright in the field of intellectual property[5] for the purposes of communication to the public by satellite; whereas, in particular, this will ensure that performers and phonogram producers are guaranteed an appropriate remuneration for the communication to the public by satellite of their performances or phonograms;

Whereas the provisions of Article 4 do not prevent Member States from extending the presumption set out in Article 2(5) of Directive 92/100/EEC to the exclusive rights referred to in Article 4; whereas, furthermore, the provisions of Article 4 do not prevent Member States from providing for a rebuttable presumption of the authorisation of exploitation in respect of the exclusive rights of performers referred to in that Article, in so far as such presumption is compatible with the International Convention for the Protection of Performers, Producers of Phonograms and Broadcasting Organisations;

Whereas the cable retransmission of programmes from other Member States is an act subject to copyright and, as the case may be, rights related to copyright; whereas the cable operator must, therefore, obtain the authorisation from every holder of rights in each part of the programme retransmitted; whereas, pursuant to this Directive, the authorisations should be granted contractually unless a temporary exception is provided for in the case of existing legal licence schemes;

Whereas, in order to ensure that the smooth operation of contractual arrangements is not called into question by the intervention of outsiders holding rights in individual parts of the programme, provision should be made, through the obligation to have recourse to a collecting society, for the exclusive collective exercise of the authorisation right to the extent that this is required by the special features of cable retransmission; whereas the authorisation right as such remains intact and only the exercise of this right is regulated to some extent, so that the right to authorise a cable retransmission can still be assigned; whereas this Directive does not affect the exercise of moral rights;

Whereas the exemption provided for in Article 10 should not limit the choice of holders of rights to transfer their rights to a collecting society and thereby have a direct share in the remuneration paid by the cable distributor for cable retransmission;

Whereas contractual arrangements regarding the authorisation of cable retransmission should be promoted by additional measures; whereas a party seeking the conclusion of a general contract should, for its part, be obliged to submit collective proposals for an agreement; whereas, furthermore, any party shall be entitled, at any moment, to call upon the assistance of impartial mediators whose task is to assist negotiations and who may submit proposals; whereas any such proposals and any opposition thereto should be served on the parties concerned in accordance with the applicable rules concerning the service of legal documents, in particular as set out in existing international conventions; whereas, finally, it is necessary to ensure that the negotiations are not blocked without valid justification or that individual holders are not prevented without valid justification from taking part in the negotiations; whereas none of these measures for the promotion of the acquisition of rights calls into question the contractual nature of the acquisition of cable retransmission rights;

Whereas for a transitional period Member States should be allowed to retain existing bodies with jurisdiction in their territory over cases where the right to retransmit a programme by cable to the public has been unreasonably refused or offered on unreasonable terms by a broadcasting organisation; whereas it is understood that the right of parties concerned to be heard by the body should be guaranteed and that the existence of the body should not prevent the parties concerned from having normal access to the courts;

Whereas, however, Community rules are not needed to deal with all of those matters, the effects of which perhaps with some commercially insignificant exceptions, are felt only inside the borders of a single Member State;

Whereas minimum rules should be laid down in order to establish and guarantee free and uninterrupted cross-border broadcasting by satellite and simultaneous, unaltered cable retransmission of programmes broadcast from other Member States, on an essentially contractual basis;

Whereas this Directive should not prejudice further harmonisation in the field of copyright and rights related to copyright and the collective administration of such rights; whereas the possibility for Member States to regulate the activities of collecting societies should not prejudice the freedom of contractual negotiation of the rights provided for in this Directive, on the understanding that such negotiation takes place within the framework of general or specific national rules with regard to competition law or the prevention of abuse of monopolies;

Whereas it should, therefore, be for the Member States to supplement the general provisions needed to achieve the objectives of this Directive by taking legislative and administrative measures in their domestic law, provided that these do not run counter to the objectives of this Directive and are compatible with Community law;

Whereas this Directive does not affect the applicability of the competition rules in Articles 85 and 86 of the Treaty,

NOTES

1 OJ C255, 1.10.1991, p 3 and OJ C25, 28.1.1993, p 43.

2 OJ C305, 23.11.1992, p 129 and OJ C255, 20.9.1993.

3 OJ C98, 21.4.1992, p 44.

4 OJ L298, 17.10.1989, p 23.

5 OJ L346, 27.11.1992, p 61.

HAS ADOPTED THIS DIRECTIVE—

CHAPTER I
DEFINITIONS

[2.745]
Article 1
Definitions

1. For the purpose of this Directive, 'satellite' means any satellite operating on frequency bands which, under telecommunications law, are reserved for the broadcast of signals for reception by the public or which are reserved for closed, point-to-point communication. In the latter case, however, the circumstances in which individual reception of the signals takes place must be comparable to those which apply in the first case.

2.

(a) For the purpose of this Directive, "communication to the public by satellite" means the act of introducing, under the control and responsibility of the broadcasting organisation, the programme-carrying signals intended for reception by the public into an uninterrupted chain of communication leading to the satellite and down towards the earth.

(b) The act of communication to the public by satellite occurs solely in the Member State where, under the control and responsibility of the broadcasting organisation, the programme-carrying signals are introduced into an uninterrupted chain of communication leading to the satellite and down towards the earth.

(c) If the programme-carrying signals are encrypted, then there is communication to the public by satellite on condition that the means for decrypting the broadcast are provided to the public by the broadcasting organisation or with its consent.

(d) Where an act of communication to the public by satellite occurs in a non-Community State which does not provide the level of protection provided for under Chapter II,

- (i) if the programme-carrying signals are transmitted to the satellite from an uplink situation situated in a Member State, that act of communication to the public by satellite shall be deemed to have occurred in that Member State and the rights provided for under Chapter II shall be exercisable against the person operating the uplink station; or
- (ii) if there is no use of an uplink station situated in a Member State but a broadcasting organisation established in a Member State has commissioned the act of communication to the public by satellite, that act shall be deemed to have occurred in the Member State in which the broadcasting organisation has its principal establishment in the Community and the rights provided for under Chapter II shall be exercisable against the broadcasting organisation.

3. For the purposes of this Directive, "cable retransmission" means the simultaneous, unaltered and unabridged retransmission by a cable or microwave system for reception by the public of an initial transmission from another Member State, by wire or over the air, including that by satellite, of television or radio programmes intended for reception by the public.

4. For the purposes of this Directive "collecting society" means any organisation which manages or administers copyright or rights related to copyright as its sole purpose or as one of its main purposes.

5. For the purposes of this Directive, the principal director of a cinematographic or audiovisual work shall be considered as its author or one of its authors. Member States may provide for others to be considered as its co-authors.

CHAPTER II
BROADCASTING OF PROGRAMMES BY SATELLITE

[2.746]
Article 2
Broadcasting right
Member States shall provide an exclusive right for the author to authorise the communication to the public by satellite of copyright works, subject to the provisions set out in this chapter.

[2.747]
Article 3
Acquisition of broadcasting rights
1. Member States shall ensure that the authorisation referred to in Article 2 may be acquired only by agreement.
2. A Member State may provide that a collective agreement between a collecting society and a broadcasting organisation concerning a given category of works may be extended to rightholders of the same category who are not represented by the collecting society, provided that—
— the communication to the public by satellite simulcasts a terrestrial broadcast by the same broadcaster, and
— the unrepresented rightholder shall, at any time, have the possibility of excluding the extension of the collective agreement to his works and of exercising his rights either individually or collectively.
3. Paragraph 2 shall not apply to cinematographic works, including works created by a process analogous to cinematography.
4. Where the law of a Member State provides for the extension of a collective agreement in accordance with the provisions of paragraph 2, that Member State shall inform the Commission which broadcasting organisations are entitled to avail themselves of that law. The Commission shall publish this information in the *Official Journal of the European Communities* (C series).

[2.748]
Article 4
Rights of performers, phonogram producers and broadcasting organisations
1. For the purposes of communication to the public by satellite, the rights of performers, phonogram producers and broadcasting organisations shall be protected in accordance with the provisions of Articles 6, 7, 8 and 10 of Directive 92/100/EEC.
2. For the purposes of paragraph 1, "broadcasting by wireless means" in Directive 92/100/EEC shall be understood as including communication to the public by satellite.
3. With regard to the exercise of the rights referred to in paragraph 1, Articles 2(7) and 12 of Directive 92/100/EEC shall apply.

[2.749]
Article 5
Relation between copyright and related rights
Protection of copyright-related rights under this Directive shall leave intact and shall in no way affect the protection of copyright.

[2.750]
Article 6
Minimum protection
1. Member States may provide for more far-reaching protection for holders of rights related to copyright than that required by Article 8 of Directive 92/100/EEC.
2. In applying paragraph 1 Member States shall observe the definitions contained in Article 1(1) and (2).

[2.751]
Article 7
Transitional provisions
1. With regard to the application in time of the rights referred to in Article 4(1) of this Directive, Article 13(1), (2), (6) and (7) of Directive 92/100/EEC shall apply. Article 13(4) and (5) of Directive 92/100/EEC shall apply *mutatis mutandis*.
2. Agreements concerning the exploitation of works and other protected subject matter which are in force on the date mentioned in Article 14(1) shall be subject to the provisions of Articles 1(2), 2 and 3 as from 1 January 2000 if they expire after that date.
3. When an international co-production agreement concluded before the date mentioned in Article 14(1) between a co-producer from a Member State and one or more co-producers from other Member States or third countries expressly provides for a system of division of exploitation rights

between the co-producers by geographical areas for all means of communication to the public, without distinguishing the arrangement applicable to communication to the public by satellite from the provisions applicable to the other means of communication, and where communication to the public by satellite of the co-production would prejudice the exclusivity, in particular the language exclusivity, of one of the co-producers or his assignees in a given territory, the authorisation by one of the co-producers or his assignees for a communication to the public by satellite shall require the prior consent of the holder of that exclusivity, whether co-producer or assignee.

CHAPTER III
CABLE RETRANSMISSION

[2.752]
Article 8
Cable retransmission right

1. Member States shall ensure that when programmes from other Member States are retransmitted by cable in their territory the applicable copyright and related rights are observed and that such retransmission takes place on the basis of individual or collective contractual agreements between copyright owners, holders of related rights and cable operators.
2. Notwithstanding paragraph 1, Member States may retain until 31 December 1997 such statutory licence systems which are in operation or expressly provided for by national law on 31 July 1991.

[2.753]
Article 9
Exercise of the cable retransmission right

1. Member States shall ensure that the right of copyright owners and holders or related rights to grant or refuse authorisation to a cable operator for a cable retransmission may be exercised only through a collecting society.
2. Where a rightholder has not transferred the management of his rights to a collecting society, the collecting society which manages rights of the same category shall be deemed to be mandated to manage his rights. Where more than one collecting society manages rights of that category, the rightholder shall be free to choose which of those collecting societies is deemed to be mandated to manage his rights. A rightholder referred to in this paragraph shall have the same rights and obligations resulting from the agreement between the cable operator and the collecting society which is deemed to be mandated to manage his rights as the rightholders who have mandated that collecting society and he shall be able to claim those rights within a period, to be fixed by the Member State concerned, which shall not be shorter than three years from the date of the cable retransmission which includes his work or other protected subject matter.
3. A Member State may provide that, when a right-holder authorises the initial transmission within its territory of a work or other protected subject matter, he shall be deemed to have agreed not to exercise his cable retransmission rights on an individual basis but to exercise them in accordance with the provisions of this Directive.

[2.754]
Article 10
Exercise of the cable retransmission right by broadcasting organisations

Member States shall ensure that Article 9 does not apply to the rights exercised by a broadcasting organisation in respect of its own transmission, irrespective of whether the rights concerned are its own or have been transferred to it by other copyright owners and/or holders of related rights.

[2.755]
Article 11
Mediators

1. Where no agreement is concluded regarding authorisation of the cable retransmission of a broadcast. Member States shall ensure that either party may call upon the assistance of one or more mediators.
2. The task of the mediators shall be to provide assistance with negotiation. They may also submit proposals to the parties.
3. It shall be assumed that all the parties accept a proposal as referred to in paragraph 2 if none of them expresses its opposition within a period of three months. Notice of the proposal and of any opposition thereto shall be served on the parties concerned in accordance with the applicable rules concerning the service of legal documents.
4. The mediators shall be so selected that their independence and impartiality are beyond reasonable doubt.

Part 2 Copyright

[2.756]
Article 12
Prevention of the abuse of negotiating positions
1. Member States shall ensure by means of civil or administrative law, as appropriate, that the parties enter and conduct negotiations regarding authorisation for cable retransmission in good faith and do not prevent or hinder negotiation without valid justification.
2. A Member State which, on the date mentioned in Article 14(1), has a body with jurisdiction in its territory over cases where the right to retransmit a programme by cable to the public in that Member State has been unreasonably refused or offered on unreasonable terms by a broadcasting organisation may retain that body.
3. Paragraph 2 shall apply for a transitional period of eight years from the date mentioned in Article 14(1).

CHAPTER IV
GENERAL PROVISIONS

[2.757]
Article 13
Collective administration of rights
This Directive shall be without prejudice to the regulation of the activities of collecting societies by the Member States.

[2.758]
Article 14
Final provisions
1. Member States shall bring into force the laws, regulations and administrative provisions necessary to comply with this Directive before 1 January 1995. They shall immediately inform the Commission thereof.

When Member States adopt these measures, the latter shall contain a reference to this Directive or shall be accompanied by such reference at the time of their official publication. The methods of making such a reference shall be laid down by the Member States.
2. Member States shall communicate to the Commission the provisions of national law which they adopt in the field covered by this Directive.
3. Not later than 1 January 2000, the Commission shall submit to the European Parliament, the Council and the Economic and Social Committee a report on the application of this Directive and, if necessary, make further proposals to adapt it to developments in the audio and audiovisual sector.

[2.759]
Article 15
This Directive is addressed to the Member States.

DIRECTIVE OF THE EUROPEAN PARLIAMENT AND OF THE COUNCIL

(2006/115/EC)

of 12 December 2006

on rental right and lending right and on certain rights related to copyright in the field of intellectual property

(codified version)

NOTES

Date of publication in OJ: OJ L376, 27.12.2006, p 28.

THE EUROPEAN PARLIAMENT AND THE COUNCIL OF THE EUROPEAN UNION,

Having regard to the Treaty establishing the European Community, and in particular Articles 47(2), 55 and 95 thereof,

Having regard to the proposal from the Commission,

Having regard to the opinion of the European Economic and Social Committee,

Acting in accordance with the procedure laid down in Article 251 of the Treaty,[1]

Whereas:

(1) Council Directive 92/100/EEC of 19 November 1992 on rental right and lending right and on certain rights related to copyright in the field of intellectual property[2] has been substantially amended several times.[3] In the interests of clarity and rationality the said Directive should be codified.

(2) Rental and lending of copyright works and the subject matter of related rights protection is playing an increasingly important role in particular for authors, performers and producers of phonograms and films. Piracy is becoming an increasing threat.

(3) The adequate protection of copyright works and subject matter of related rights protection by rental and lending rights as well as the protection of the subject matter of related rights protection by the fixation right, distribution right, right to broadcast and communication to the public can accordingly be considered as being of fundamental importance for the economic and cultural development of the Community.

(4) Copyright and related rights protection must adapt to new economic developments such as new forms of exploitation.

(5) The creative and artistic work of authors and performers necessitates an adequate income as a basis for further creative and artistic work, and the investments required particularly for the production of phonograms and films are especially high and risky. The possibility of securing that income and recouping that investment can be effectively guaranteed only through adequate legal protection of the rightholders concerned.

(6) These creative, artistic and entrepreneurial activities are, to a large extent, activities of self-employed persons. The pursuit of such activities should be made easier by providing a harmonised legal protection within the Community. To the extent that these activities principally constitute services, their provision should equally be facilitated by a harmonised legal framework in the Community.

(7) The legislation of the Member States should be approximated in such a way as not to conflict with the international conventions on which the copyright and related rights laws of many Member States are based.

(8) The legal framework of the Community on the rental right and lending right and on certain rights related to copyright can be limited to establishing that Member States provide rights with respect to rental and lending for certain groups of rightholders and further to establishing the rights of fixation, distribution, broadcasting and communication to the public for certain groups of rightholders in the field of related rights protection.

(9) It is necessary to define the concepts of rental and lending for the purposes of this Directive.

(10) It is desirable, with a view to clarity, to exclude from rental and lending within the meaning of this Directive certain forms of making available, as for instance making available phonograms or films for the purpose of public performance or broadcasting, making available for the purpose of exhibition, or making available for on-the-spot reference use. Lending within the meaning of this Directive should not include making available between establishments which are accessible to the public.

(11) Where lending by an establishment accessible to the public gives rise to a payment the amount of which does not go beyond what is necessary to cover the operating costs of the establishment, there is no direct or indirect economic or commercial advantage within the meaning of this Directive.

(12) It is necessary to introduce arrangements ensuring that an unwaivable equitable remuneration is obtained by authors and performers who must remain able to entrust the administration of this right to collecting societies representing them.

(13) The equitable remuneration may be paid on the basis of one or several payments at any time on or after the conclusion of the contract. It should take account of the importance of the contribution of the authors and performers concerned to the phonogram or film.

(14) It is also necessary to protect the rights at least of authors as regards public lending by providing for specific arrangements. However, any measures taken by way of derogation from the exclusive public lending right should comply in particular with Article 12 of the Treaty.

(15) The provisions laid down in this Directive as to rights related to copyright should not prevent Member States from extending to those exclusive rights the presumption provided for in this Directive with regard to contracts concerning film production concluded individually or collectively by performers with a film producer. Furthermore, those provisions should not prevent Member States from providing for a rebuttable presumption of the authorisation of exploitation in respect of the exclusive rights of performers provided for in the relevant provisions of this Directive, in so far as such presumption is compatible with the International Convention for the Protection of Performers, Producers of Phonograms and Broadcasting Organisations (hereinafter referred to as the Rome Convention).

(16) Member States should be able to provide for more far-reaching protection for owners of rights related to copyright than that required by the provisions laid down in this Directive in respect of broadcasting and communication to the public.

(17) The harmonised rental and lending rights and the harmonised protection in the field of rights related to copyright should not be exercised in a way which constitutes a disguised restriction on trade between Member States or in a way which is contrary to the rule of media exploitation chronology, as recognised in the judgment handed down in Société Cinéthèque v FNCF[4].

(18) This Directive should be without prejudice to the obligations of the Member States relating to the time-limits for transposition into national law of the Directives as set out in Part B of Annex I,

NOTES

[1] Opinion of the European Parliament delivered on 12 October 2006 (not yet published in the Official Journal).

[2] OJ L346, 27.11.1992, p 61. Directive as last amended by Directive 2001/29/EC of the European Parliament and of the Council (OJ L167, 22.6.2001, p 10).

[3] See Annex I, Part A.

[4] Joined Cases 60/84 and 61/84 [1985] ECR 2 605.

HAVE ADOPTED THIS DIRECTIVE:

CHAPTER I
RENTAL AND LENDING RIGHT

[2.760]
Article 1
Object of harmonisation

1. In accordance with the provisions of this Chapter, Member States shall provide, subject to Article 6, a right to authorise or prohibit the rental and lending of originals and copies of copyright works, and other subject matter as set out in Article 3(1).
2. The rights referred to in paragraph 1 shall not be exhausted by any sale or other act of distribution of originals and copies of copyright works and other subject matter as set out in Article 3(1).

[2.761]
Article 2
Definitions

1. For the purposes of this Directive the following definitions shall apply:
   (a) "rental" means making available for use, for a limited period of time and for direct or indirect economic or commercial advantage;
   (b) "lending" means making available for use, for a limited period of time and not for direct or indirect economic or commercial advantage, when it is made through establishments which are accessible to the public;
   (c) "film" means a cinematographic or audiovisual work or moving images, whether or not accompanied by sound.
2. The principal director of a cinematographic or audiovisual work shall be considered as its author or one of its authors. Member States may provide for others to be considered as its co-authors.

[2.762]
Article 3
Rightholders and subject matter of rental and lending right

1. The exclusive right to authorise or prohibit rental and lending shall belong to the following:
   (a) the author in respect of the original and copies of his work;
   (b) the performer in respect of fixations of his performance;
   (c) the phonogram producer in respect of his phonograms;
   (d) the producer of the first fixation of a film in respect of the original and copies of his film.
2. This Directive shall not cover rental and lending rights in relation to buildings and to works of applied art.
3. The rights referred to in paragraph 1 may be transferred, assigned or subject to the granting of contractual licences.
4. Without prejudice to paragraph 6, when a contract concerning film production is concluded, individually or collectively, by performers with a film producer, the performer covered by this contract shall be presumed, subject to contractual clauses to the contrary, to have transferred his rental right, subject to Article 5.
5. Member States may provide for a similar presumption as set out in paragraph 4 with respect to authors.
6. Member States may provide that the signing of a contract concluded between a performer and a film producer concerning the production of a film has the effect of authorising rental, provided that such contract provides for an equitable remuneration within the meaning of Article 5. Member States may also provide that this paragraph shall apply mutatis mutandis to the rights included in Chapter II.

[2.763]
Article 4
Rental of computer programs

This Directive shall be without prejudice to Article 4(c) of Council Directive 91/250/EEC of 14 May 1991 on the legal protection of computer programs.[1]

NOTES

[1] OJ L122, 17.5.1991, p 42. Directive as amended by Directive 93/98/EEC (OJ L290, 24.11.1993, p 9).

[2.764]
Article 5
Unwaivable right to equitable remuneration

1. Where an author or performer has transferred or assigned his rental right concerning a phonogram or an original or copy of a film to a phonogram or film producer, that author or performer shall retain the right to obtain an equitable remuneration for the rental.
2. The right to obtain an equitable remuneration for rental cannot be waived by authors or performers.
3. The administration of this right to obtain an equitable remuneration may be entrusted to collecting societies representing authors or performers.
4. Member States may regulate whether and to what extent administration by collecting societies of the right to obtain an equitable remuneration may be imposed, as well as the question from whom this remuneration may be claimed or collected.

[2.765]
Article 6
Derogation from the exclusive public lending right

1. Member States may derogate from the exclusive right provided for in Article 1 in respect of public lending, provided that at least authors obtain a remuneration for such lending. Member States shall be free to determine this remuneration taking account of their cultural promotion objectives.
2. Where Member States do not apply the exclusive lending right provided for in Article 1 as regards phonograms, films and computer programs, they shall introduce, at least for authors, a remuneration.
3. Member States may exempt certain categories of establishments from the payment of the remuneration referred to in paragraphs 1 and 2.

CHAPTER II
RIGHTS RELATED TO COPYRIGHT

[2.766]
Article 7
Fixation right

1. Member States shall provide for performers the exclusive right to authorise or prohibit the fixation of their performances.
2. Member States shall provide for broadcasting organisations the exclusive right to authorise or prohibit the fixation of their broadcasts, whether these broadcasts are transmitted by wire or over the air, including by cable or satellite.
3. A cable distributor shall not have the right provided for in paragraph 2 where it merely retransmits by cable the broadcasts of broadcasting organisations.

[2.767]
Article 8
Broadcasting and communication to the public

1. Member States shall provide for performers the exclusive right to authorise or prohibit the broadcasting by wireless means and the communication to the public of their performances, except where the performance is itself already a broadcast performance or is made from a fixation.
2. Member States shall provide a right in order to ensure that a single equitable remuneration is paid by the user, if a phonogram published for commercial purposes, or a reproduction of such phonogram, is used for broadcasting by wireless means or for any communication to the public, and to ensure that this remuneration is shared between the relevant performers and phonogram producers. Member States may, in the absence of agreement between the performers and phonogram producers, lay down the conditions as to the sharing of this remuneration between them.
3. Member States shall provide for broadcasting organisations the exclusive right to authorise or prohibit the rebroadcasting of their broadcasts by wireless means, as well as the communication to the public of their broadcasts if such communication is made in places accessible to the public against payment of an entrance fee.

[2.768]
Article 9
Distribution right

1. Member States shall provide the exclusive right to make available to the public, by sale or otherwise, the objects indicated in points (a) to (d), including copies thereof, hereinafter "the distribution right":
   (a) for performers, in respect of fixations of their performances;

(b) for phonogram producers, in respect of their phonograms;
(c) for producers of the first fixations of films, in respect of the original and copies of their films;
(d) for broadcasting organisations, in respect of fixations of their broadcasts as set out in Article 7(2).

2. The distribution right shall not be exhausted within the Community in respect of an object as referred to in paragraph 1, except where the first sale in the Community of that object is made by the rightholder or with his consent.

3. The distribution right shall be without prejudice to the specific provisions of Chapter I, in particular Article 1(2).

4. The distribution right may be transferred, assigned or subject to the granting of contractual licences.

[2.769]
Article 10
Limitations to rights

1. Member States may provide for limitations to the rights referred to in this Chapter in respect of:
(a) private use;
(b) use of short excerpts in connection with the reporting of current events;
(c) ephemeral fixation by a broadcasting organisation by means of its own facilities and for its own broadcasts;
(d) use solely for the purposes of teaching or scientific research.

2. Irrespective of paragraph 1, any Member State may provide for the same kinds of limitations with regard to the protection of performers, producers of phonograms, broadcasting organisations and of producers of the first fixations of films, as it provides for in connection with the protection of copyright in literary and artistic works.

However, compulsory licences may be provided for only to the extent to which they are compatible with the Rome Convention.

3. The limitations referred to in paragraphs 1 and 2 shall be applied only in certain special cases which do not conflict with a normal exploitation of the subject matter and do not unreasonably prejudice the legitimate interests of the rightholder.

CHAPTER III
COMMON PROVISIONS

[2.770]
Article 11
Application in time

1. This Directive shall apply in respect of all copyright works, performances, phonograms, broadcasts and first fixations of films referred to in this Directive which were, on 1 July 1994, still protected by the legislation of the Member States in the field of copyright and related rights or which met the criteria for protection under this Directive on that date.

2. This Directive shall apply without prejudice to any acts of exploitation performed before 1 July 1994.

3. Member States may provide that the rightholders are deemed to have given their authorisation to the rental or lending of an object referred to in points (a) to (d) of Article 3(1) which is proven to have been made available to third parties for this purpose or to have been acquired before 1 July 1994.

However, in particular where such an object is a digital recording, Member States may provide that rightholders shall have a right to obtain an adequate remuneration for the rental or lending of that object.

4. Member States need not apply the provisions of Article 2(2) to cinematographic or audiovisual works created before 1 July 1994.

5. This Directive shall, without prejudice to paragraph 3 and subject to paragraph 7, not affect any contracts concluded before 19 November 1992.

6. Member States may provide, subject to the provisions of paragraph 7, that when rightholders who acquire new rights under the national provisions adopted in implementation of this Directive have, before 1 July 1994, given their consent for exploitation, they shall be presumed to have transferred the new exclusive rights.

7. For contracts concluded before 1 July 1994, the unwaivable right to an equitable remuneration provided for in Article 5 shall apply only where authors or performers or those representing them have submitted a request to that effect before 1 January 1997. In the absence of agreement between rightholders concerning the level of remuneration, Member States may fix the level of equitable remuneration.

[2.771]
Article 12
Relation between copyright and related rights
Protection of copyright-related rights under this Directive shall leave intact and shall in no way affect the protection of copyright.

[2.772]
Article 13
Communication
Member States shall communicate to the Commission the main provisions of national law adopted in the field covered by this Directive.

[2.773]
Article 14
Repeal
Directive 92/100/EEC is hereby repealed, without prejudice to the obligations of the Member States relating to the time-limits for transposition into national law of the Directives as set out in Part B of Annex I.

References made to the repealed Directive shall be construed as being made to this Directive and should be read in accordance with the correlation table in Annex II.

[2.774]
Article 15
Entry into force
This Directive shall enter into force on the twentieth day following that of its publication in the *Official Journal of the European Union*.

[2.775]
Article 16
Addressees
This Directive is addressed to the Member States.

ANNEX I

PART A
REPEALED DIRECTIVE WITH ITS SUCCESSIVE AMENDMENTS

[2.776]

Council Directive 92/100/EEC (OJ L346, 27.11.1992, p 61)	
Council Directive 93/98/EEC (OJ L290, 24.11.1993, p 9)	Article 11(2) only
Directive 2001/29/EC of the European Parliament and of the Council (OJ L167, 22.6.2001, p 10)	Article 11(1) only

PART B
LIST OF TIME-LIMITS FOR TRANSPOSITION INTO NATIONAL LAW

(referred to in Article 14)

Directive	Time-limit for transposition
92/100/EEC	1 July 1994
93/98/EEC	30 June 1995
2001/29/EC	21 December 2002

ANNEX II
CORRELATION TABLE

[2.777]

Directive 92/100/EEC	This Directive
Article 1(1)	Article 1(1)
Article 1(2)	Article 2(1), introductory words and point (a)
Article 1(3)	Article 2(1), point (b)
Article 1(4)	Article 1(2)
Article 2(1), introductory words	Article 3(1), introductory wordsl

Directive 92/100/EEC	This Directive
Article 2(1), first indent	Article 3(1)(a)
Article 2(1), second indent	Article 3(1)(b)
Article 2(1), third indent	Article 3(1)(c)
Article 2(1), fourth indent, first sentence	Article 3(1)(d)
Article 2(1), fourth indent, second sentence	Article 2(1), point (c)
Article 2(2)	Article 2(2)
Article 2(3)	Article 3(2)
Article 2(4)	Article 3(3)
Article 2(5)	Article 3(4)
Article 2(6)	Article 3(5)
Article 2(7)	Article 3(6)
Article 3	Article 4
Article 4	Article 5
Article 5(1) to (3)	Article 6(1) to (3)
Article 5(4)	—
Article 6	Article 7
Article 8	Article 8
Article 9(1), introductory words and final words	Article 9(1), introductory words
Article 9(1), first indent	Article 9(1)(a)
Article 9(1), second indent	Article 9(1)(b)
Article 9(1), third indent	Article 9(1)(c)
Article 9(1), fourth indent	Article 9(1)(d)
Article 9(2), (3) and (4)	Article 9(2), (3) and (4)
Article 10(1)	Article 10(1)
Article 10(2), first sentence	Article 10(2), first subparagraph
Article 10(2), second sentence	Article 10(2), second subparagraph
Article 10(3)	Article 10(3)
Article 13(1) and (2)	Article 11(1) and (2)
Article 13(3), first sentence	Article 11(3), first subparagraph
Article 13(3), second sentence	Article 11(3), second subparagraph
Article 13(4)	Article 11(4)
Article 13(5)	—
Article 13(6)	Article 11(5)
Article 13(7)	Article 11(6)
Article 13(8)	—
Article 13(9)	Article 11(7)
Article 14	Article 12
Article 15(1)	—
Article 15(2)	Article 13
—	Article 14
—	Article 15
Article 16	Article 16
—	Annex I
—	Annex II

DIRECTIVE OF THE EUROPEAN PARLIAMENT AND OF THE COUNCIL

(2006/116/EC)

of 12 December 2006

on the term of protection of copyright and certain related rights

(codified version)

NOTES

Date of publication in OJ: OJ L372, 27.12.2006, p 12.

THE EUROPEAN PARLIAMENT AND THE COUNCIL OF THE EUROPEAN UNION,

Having regard to the Treaty establishing the European Community, and in particular Articles 47(2), 55 and 95 thereof,

Having regard to the proposal from the Commission,

Having regard to the opinion of the European Economic and Social Committee,[1]

Acting in accordance with the procedure laid down in Article 251 of the Treaty,[2]

Whereas:

(1) Council Directive 93/98/EEC of 29 October 1993 harmonising the term of protection of copyright and certain related rights[3] has been substantially amended.[4] In the interests of clarity and rationality the said Directive should be codified.

(2) The Berne Convention for the protection of literary and artistic works and the International Convention for the protection of performers, producers of phonograms and broadcasting organisations (Rome Convention) lay down only minimum terms of protection of the rights they refer to, leaving the Contracting States free to grant longer terms. Certain Member States have exercised this entitlement. In addition, some Member States have not yet become party to the Rome Convention.

(3) There are consequently differences between the national laws governing the terms of protection of copyright and related rights, which are liable to impede the free movement of goods and freedom to provide services and to distort competition in the common market. Therefore, with a view to the smooth operation of the internal market, the laws of the Member States should be harmonised so as to make terms of protection identical throughout the Community.

(4) It is important to lay down not only the terms of protection as such, but also certain implementing arrangements, such as the date from which each term of protection is calculated.

(5) The provisions of this Directive should not affect the application by the Member States of the provisions of Article 14 bis (2)(b), (c) and (d) and (3) of the Berne Convention.

(6) The minimum term of protection laid down by the Berne Convention, namely the life of the author and 50 years after his death, was intended to provide protection for the author and the first two generations of his descendants. The average lifespan in the Community has grown longer, to the point where this term is no longer sufficient to cover two generations.

(7) Certain Member States have granted a term longer than 50 years after the death of the author in order to offset the effects of the world wars on the exploitation of authors' works.

(8) For the protection of related rights certain Member States have introduced a term of 50 years after lawful publication or lawful communication to the public.

(9) The Diplomatic Conference held in December 1996, under the auspices of the World Intellectual Property Organization (WIPO), led to the adoption of the WIPO Performances and Phonograms Treaty, which deals with the protection of performers and producers of phonograms. This Treaty took the form of a substantial up-date of the international protection of related rights.

(10) Due regard for established rights is one of the general principles of law protected by the Community legal order. Therefore, the terms of protection of copyright and related rights established by Community law cannot have the effect of reducing the protection enjoyed by rightholders in the Community before the entry into force of Directive 93/98/EEC. In order to keep the effects of transitional measures to a minimum and to allow the internal market to function smoothly, those terms of protection should be applied for long periods.

(11) The level of protection of copyright and related rights should be high, since those rights are fundamental to intellectual creation. Their protection ensures the maintenance and development of creativity in the interest of authors, cultural industries, consumers and society as a whole.

(12) In order to establish a high level of protection which at the same time meets the requirements of the internal market and the need to establish a legal environment conducive to the harmonious development of literary and artistic creation in the Community, the term of protection for copyright should be harmonised at 70 years after the death of the author or 70 years after the

work is lawfully made available to the public, and for related rights at 50 years after the event which sets the term running.

(13) Collections are protected according to Article 2(5) of the Berne Convention when, by reason of the selection and arrangement of their content, they constitute intellectual creations. Those works are protected as such, without prejudice to the copyright in each of the works forming part of such collections. Consequently, specific terms of protection may apply to works included in collections.

(14) In all cases where one or more physical persons are identified as authors, the term of protection should be calculated after their death. The question of authorship of the whole or a part of a work is a question of fact which the national courts may have to decide.

(15) Terms of protection should be calculated from the first day of January of the year following the relevant event, as they are in the Berne and Rome Conventions.

(16) The protection of photographs in the Member States is the subject of varying regimes. A photographic work within the meaning of the Berne Convention is to be considered original if it is the author's own intellectual creation reflecting his personality, no other criteria such as merit or purpose being taken into account. The protection of other photographs should be left to national law.

(17) In order to avoid differences in the term of protection as regards related rights it is necessary to provide the same starting point for the calculation of the term throughout the Community. The performance, fixation, transmission, lawful publication, and lawful communication to the public, that is to say the means of making a subject of a related right perceptible in all appropriate ways to persons in general, should be taken into account for the calculation of the term of protection regardless of the country where this performance, fixation, transmission, lawful publication, or lawful communication to the public takes place.

(18) The rights of broadcasting organisations in their broadcasts, whether these broadcasts are transmitted by wire or over the air, including by cable or satellite, should not be perpetual. It is therefore necessary to have the term of protection running from the first transmission of a particular broadcast only. This provision is understood to avoid a new term running in cases where a broadcast is identical to a previous one.

(19) The Member States should remain free to maintain or introduce other rights related to copyright in particular in relation to the protection of critical and scientific publications. In order to ensure transparency at Community level, it is however necessary for Member States which introduce new related rights to notify the Commission.

(20) It should be made clear that this Directive does not apply to moral rights.

(21) For works whose country of origin within the meaning of the Berne Convention is a third country and whose author is not a Community national, comparison of terms of protection should be applied, provided that the term accorded in the Community does not exceed the term laid down in this Directive.

(22) Where a rightholder who is not a Community national qualifies for protection under an international agreement, the term of protection of related rights should be the same as that laid down in this Directive. However, this term should not exceed that fixed in the third country of which the rightholder is a national.

(23) Comparison of terms should not result in Member States being brought into conflict with their international obligations.

(24) Member States should remain free to adopt provisions on the interpretation, adaptation and further execution of contracts on the exploitation of protected works and other subject matter which were concluded before the extension of the term of protection resulting from this Directive.

(25) Respect of acquired rights and legitimate expectations is part of the Community legal order. Member States may provide in particular that in certain circumstances the copyright and related rights which are revived pursuant to this Directive may not give rise to payments by persons who undertook in good faith the exploitation of the works at the time when such works lay within the public domain.

(26) This Directive should be without prejudice to the obligations of the Member States relating to the time-limits for transposition into national law and application of the Directives, as set out in Part B of Annex I,

NOTES

1 Opinion of 26 October 2006 (not yet published in the Official Journal).

2 Opinion of the European Parliament of 12 October 2006 (not yet published in the Official Journal) and Council Decision of 30 November 2006.

3 OJ L290, 24.11.1993, p 9. Directive as amended by Directive 2001/29/EC of the European Parliament and of the Council (OJ L167, 22.6.2001, p 10).

4 See Annex I, Part A.

HAVE ADOPTED THIS DIRECTIVE:

[2.778]
Article 1
Duration of authors' rights

1. The rights of an author of a literary or artistic work within the meaning of Article 2 of the Berne Convention shall run for the life of the author and for 70 years after his death, irrespective of the date when the work is lawfully made available to the public.
2. In the case of a work of joint authorship, the term referred to in paragraph 1 shall be calculated from the death of the last surviving author.
3. In the case of anonymous or pseudonymous works, the term of protection shall run for 70 years after the work is lawfully made available to the public. However, when the pseudonym adopted by the author leaves no doubt as to his identity, or if the author discloses his identity during the period referred to in the first sentence, the term of protection applicable shall be that laid down in paragraph 1.
4. Where a Member State provides for particular provisions on copyright in respect of collective works or for a legal person to be designated as the rightholder, the term of protection shall be calculated according to the provisions of paragraph 3, except if the natural persons who have created the work are identified as such in the versions of the work which are made available to the public. This paragraph is without prejudice to the rights of identified authors whose identifiable contributions are included in such works, to which contributions paragraph 1 or 2 shall apply.
5. Where a work is published in volumes, parts, instalments, issues or episodes and the term of protection runs from the time when the work was lawfully made available to the public, the term of protection shall run for each such item separately.
6. In the case of works for which the term of protection is not calculated from the death of the author or authors and which have not been lawfully made available to the public within 70 years from their creation, the protection shall terminate.
[7. The term of protection of a musical composition with words shall expire 70 years after the death of the last of the following persons to survive, whether or not those persons are designated as co-authors: the author of the lyrics and the composer of the musical composition, provided that both contributions were specifically created for the respective musical composition with words.]

NOTES

Para 7: added by European Parliament and Council Directive 2011/77/EU, Art 1(1).

[2.779]
Article 2
Cinematographic or audiovisual works

1. The principal director of a cinematographic or audiovisual work shall be considered as its author or one of its authors. Member States shall be free to designate other co-authors.
2. The term of protection of cinematographic or audiovisual works shall expire 70 years after the death of the last of the following persons to survive, whether or not these persons are designated as co-authors: the principal director, the author of the screenplay, the author of the dialogue and the composer of music specifically created for use in the cinematographic or audiovisual work.

[2.780]
Article 3
Duration of related rights

1. The rights of performers shall expire 50 years after the date of the performance. [However,
   — if a fixation of the performance otherwise than in a phonogram is lawfully published or lawfully communicated to the public within this period, the rights shall expire 50 years from the date of the first such publication or the first such communication to the public, whichever is the earlier,
   — if a fixation of the performance in a phonogram is lawfully published or lawfully communicated to the public within this period, the rights shall expire 70 years from the date of the first such publication or the first such communication to the public, whichever is the earlier.]
2. The rights of producers of phonograms shall expire 50 years after the fixation is made. However, if the phonogram has been lawfully published within this period, the said rights shall expire [70] years from the date of the first lawful publication. If no lawful publication has taken place within the period mentioned in the first sentence, and if the phonogram has been lawfully communicated to the public within this period, the said rights shall expire [70] years from the date of the first lawful communication to the public.

However, this paragraph shall not have the effect of protecting anew the rights of producers of phonograms where, through the expiry of the term of protection granted them pursuant to Article 3(2) of Directive 93/98/EEC in its version before amendment by Directive 2001/29/EEC, they were no longer protected on 22 December 2002.

[2a. If, 50 years after the phonogram was lawfully published or, failing such publication, 50 years after it was lawfully communicated to the public, the phonogram producer does not offer copies of the phonogram for sale in sufficient quantity or does not make it available to the public, by wire or wireless means, in such a way that members of the public may access it from a place and at a time

Part 2 Copyright

individually chosen by them, the performer may terminate the contract by which the performer has transferred or assigned his rights in the fixation of his performance to a phonogram producer (hereinafter a "contract on transfer or assignment"). The right to terminate the contract on transfer or assignment may be exercised if the producer, within a year from the notification by the performer of his intention to terminate the contract on transfer or assignment pursuant to the previous sentence, fails to carry out both of the acts of exploitation referred to in that sentence. This right to terminate may not be waived by the performer. Where a phonogram contains the fixation of the performances of a plurality of performers, they may terminate their contracts on transfer or assignment in accordance with applicable national law. If the contract on transfer or assignment is terminated pursuant to this paragraph, the rights of the phonogram producer in the phonogram shall expire.

2b. Where a contract on transfer or assignment gives the performer a right to claim a non-recurring remuneration, the performer shall have the right to obtain an annual supplementary remuneration from the phonogram producer for each full year immediately following the 50th year after the phonogram was lawfully published or, failing such publication, the 50th year after it was lawfully communicated to the public. The right to obtain such annual supplementary remuneration may not be waived by the performer.

2c. The overall amount to be set aside by a phonogram producer for payment of the annual supplementary remuneration referred to in paragraph 2b shall correspond to 20 % of the revenue which the phonogram producer has derived, during the year preceding that for which the said remuneration is paid, from the reproduction, distribution and making available of the phonogram in question, following the 50th year after it was lawfully published or, failing such publication, the 50th year after it was lawfully communicated to the public.

Member States shall ensure that phonogram producers are required on request to provide to performers who are entitled to the annual supplementary remuneration referred to in paragraph 2b any information which may be necessary in order to secure payment of that remuneration.

2d. Member States shall ensure that the right to obtain an annual supplementary remuneration as referred to in paragraph 2b is administered by collecting societies.

2e. Where a performer is entitled to recurring payments, neither advance payments nor any contractually defined deductions shall be deducted from the payments made to the performer following the 50th year after the phonogram was lawfully published or, failing such publication, the 50th year after it was lawfully communicated to the public.]

3. The rights of producers of the first fixation of a film shall expire 50 years after the fixation is made. However, if the film is lawfully published or lawfully communicated to the public during this period, the rights shall expire 50 years from the date of the first such publication or the first such communication to the public, whichever is the earlier. The term "film" shall designate a cinematographic or audiovisual work or moving images, whether or not accompanied by sound.

4. The rights of broadcasting organisations shall expire 50 years after the first transmission of a broadcast, whether this broadcast is transmitted by wire or over the air, including by cable or satellite.

NOTES

Para 1: words in square brackets substituted by European Parliament and Council Directive 2011/77/EU, Art 1(2)(a).

Para 2: figures in square brackets substituted by European Parliament and Council Directive 2011/77/EU, Art 1(2)(b).

Paras 2a–2e: inserted by European Parliament and Council Directive 2011/77/EU, Art 1(2)(c).

[2.781]
Article 4
Protection of previously unpublished works

Any person who, after the expiry of copyright protection, for the first time lawfully publishes or lawfully communicates to the public a previously unpublished work, shall benefit from a protection equivalent to the economic rights of the author. The term of protection of such rights shall be 25 years from the time when the work was first lawfully published or lawfully communicated to the public.

[2.782]
Article 5
Critical and scientific publications

Member States may protect critical and scientific publications of works which have come into the public domain. The maximum term of protection of such rights shall be 30 years from the time when the publication was first lawfully published.

[2.783]
Article 6
Protection of photographs

Photographs which are original in the sense that they are the author's own intellectual creation shall be protected in accordance with Article 1. No other criteria shall be applied to determine their eligibility for protection. Member States may provide for the protection of other photographs.

[2.784]
Article 7
Protection vis-à-vis third countries

1. Where the country of origin of a work, within the meaning of the Berne Convention, is a third country, and the author of the work is not a Community national, the term of protection granted by the Member States shall expire on the date of expiry of the protection granted in the country of origin of the work, but may not exceed the term laid down in Article 1.
2. The terms of protection laid down in Article 3 shall also apply in the case of rightholders who are not Community nationals, provided Member States grant them protection. However, without prejudice to the international obligations of the Member States, the term of protection granted by Member States shall expire no later than the date of expiry of the protection granted in the country of which the rightholder is a national and may not exceed the term laid down in Article 3.
3. Member States which, on 29 October 1993, in particular pursuant to their international obligations, granted a longer term of protection than that which would result from the provisions of paragraphs 1 and 2 may maintain this protection until the conclusion of international agreements on the term of protection of copyright or related rights.

[2.785]
Article 8
Calculation of terms

The terms laid down in this Directive shall be calculated from the first day of January of the year following the event which gives rise to them.

[2.786]
Article 9
Moral rights

This Directive shall be without prejudice to the provisions of the Member States regulating moral rights.

[2.787]
Article 10
Application in time

1. Where a term of protection which is longer than the corresponding term provided for by this Directive was already running in a Member State on 1 July 1995, this Directive shall not have the effect of shortening that term of protection in that Member State.
2. The terms of protection provided for in this Directive shall apply to all works and subject matter which were protected in at least one Member State on the date referred to in paragraph 1, pursuant to national provisions on copyright or related rights, or which meet the criteria for protection under [Council Directive 92/100/EEC of 19 November 1992 on rental right and lending right and on certain rights related to copyright in the field of intellectual property][1].
3. This Directive shall be without prejudice to any acts of exploitation performed before the date referred to in paragraph 1. Member States shall adopt the necessary provisions to protect in particular acquired rights of third parties.
4. Member States need not apply the provisions of Article 2(1) to cinematographic or audiovisual works created before 1 July 1994.
[5. Article 3(1) to (2e) in the version thereof in force on 31 October 2011 shall apply to fixations of performances and phonograms in regard to which the performer and the phonogram producer are still protected, by virtue of those provisions in the version thereof in force on 30 October 2011, as at 1 November 2013 and to fixations of performances and phonograms which come into being after that date.
6. Article 1(7) shall apply to musical compositions with words of which at least the musical composition or the lyrics are protected in at least one Member State on 1 November 2013, and to musical compositions with words which come into being after that date.

The first subparagraph of this paragraph shall be without prejudice to any acts of exploitation performed before 1 November 2013. Member States shall adopt the necessary provisions to protect, in particular, acquired rights of third parties.]

NOTES

Paras 5, 6: added by European Parliament and Council Directive 2011/77/EU, Art 1(3).

[1] OJ L346, 27.11.1992, p 61. Directive as last amended by Directive 2001/29/EC.

[2.788]
[Article 10a
Transitional measures

1. In the absence of clear contractual indications to the contrary, a contract on transfer or assignment concluded before 1 November 2013 shall be deemed to continue to produce its effects beyond the moment at which, by virtue of Article 3(1) in the version thereof in force on 30 October 2011, the performer would no longer be protected.

Part 2 Copyright

2. Member States may provide that contracts on transfer or assignment which entitle a performer to recurring payments and which are concluded before 1 November 2013 can be modified following the 50th year after the phonogram was lawfully published or, failing such publication, the 50th year after it was lawfully communicated to the public.]

NOTES

Inserted by European Parliament and Council Directive 2011/77/EU, Art 1(4).

[2.789]
Article 11
Notification and communication

1. Member States shall immediately notify the Commission of any governmental plan to grant new related rights, including the basic reasons for their introduction and the term of protection envisaged.

2. Member States shall communicate to the Commission the texts of the provisions of internal law which they adopt in the field governed by this Directive.

[2.790]
Article 12
Repeal

Directive 93/98/EEC is hereby repealed, without prejudice to the obligations of the Member States relating to the time-limits for transposition into national law, as set out in Part B of Annex I, of the Directives, and their application.

References made to the repealed Directive shall be construed as being made to this Directive and should be read in accordance with the correlation table in Annex II.

[2.791]
Article 13
Entry into force

This Directive shall enter into force on the twentieth day following that of its publication in the *Official Journal of the European Union*.

[2.792]
Article 14
Addressees

This Directive is addressed to the Member States.

ANNEX I

PART A
REPEALED DIRECTIVE WITH ITS AMENDMENT

[2.793]

Council Directive 92/100/EEC
(OJ L346, 27.11.1992, p 61)

Council Directive 93/98/EEC (OJ L290, 24.11.1993, p 9)	Article 11(2) only
Directive 2001/29/EC of the European Parliament and of the Council (OJ L167, 22.6.2001, p 10)	Article 11(1) only

PART B
LIST OF TIME-LIMITS FOR TRANSPOSITION INTO NATIONAL LAW AND APPLICATION

(referred to in Article 12)

Directive	Time-limit for transposition	Date of application
93/98/EEC	1 July 1995 (Articles 1 to 11)	19 November 1993 (Article 12) 1 July 1997 at the latest as regards Article 2(1) (Article 10(5))
2001/29/EC	22 December 2002	

ANNEX II
CORRELATION TABLE

[2.794]

Directive 93/98/EEC	This Directive
Articles 1 to 9	Articles 1 to 9
Article 10(1) to (4)	Article 10(1) to (4)
Article 10(5)	—
Article 11	—
Article 12	Article 11(1)
Article 13(1), first subparagraph	—
Article 13(1), second subparagraph	—
Article 13(1), third subparagraph	Article 11(2)
Article 13(2)	
—	Article 12
—	Article 13
Article 14	Article 14
—	Annex I
—	Annex II

DIRECTIVE OF THE EUROPEAN PARLIAMENT AND OF THE COUNCIL

(2009/24/EC)

of 23 April 2009

on the legal protection of computer programs ('Software Directive')

(codified version)

(Text with EEA relevance)

NOTES

Date of publication in OJ: OJ L111, 5.5.2009, p 16.

THE EUROPEAN PARLIAMENT AND THE COUNCIL OF THE EUROPEAN UNION,

Having regard to the Treaty establishing the European Community, and in particular Article 95 thereof,

Having regard to the proposal from the Commission,

Having regard to the opinion of the European Economic and Social Committee,[1]

Acting in accordance with the procedure laid down in Article 251 of the Treaty,[2]

Whereas:

(1) The content of Council Directive 91/250/EEC of 14 May 1991 on the legal protection of computer programs[3] has been amended[4] In the interests of clarity and rationality the said Directive should be codified.

(2) The development of computer programs requires the investment of considerable human, technical and financial resources while computer programs can be copied at a fraction of the cost needed to develop them independently.

(3) Computer programs are playing an increasingly important role in a broad range of industries and computer program technology can accordingly be considered as being of fundamental importance for the Community's industrial development.

(4) Certain differences in the legal protection of computer programs offered by the laws of the Member States have direct and negative effects on the functioning of the internal market as regards computer programs.

(5) Existing differences having such effects need to be removed and new ones prevented from arising, while differences not adversely affecting the functioning of the internal market to a substantial degree need not be removed or prevented from arising.

(6) The Community's legal framework on the protection of computer programs can accordingly in the first instance be limited to establishing that Member States should accord protection to

computer programs under copyright law as literary works and, further, to establishing who and what should be protected, the exclusive rights on which protected persons should be able to rely in order to authorise or prohibit certain acts and for how long the protection should apply.

(7) For the purpose of this Directive, the term 'computer program' shall include programs in any form, including those which are incorporated into hardware. This term also includes preparatory design work leading to the development of a computer program provided that the nature of the preparatory work is such that a computer program can result from it at a later stage.

(8) In respect of the criteria to be applied in determining whether or not a computer program is an original work, no tests as to the qualitative or aesthetic merits of the program should be applied.

(9) The Community is fully committed to the promotion of international standardisation.

(10) The function of a computer program is to communicate and work together with other components of a computer system and with users and, for this purpose, a logical and, where appropriate, physical interconnection and interaction is required to permit all elements of software and hardware to work with other software and hardware and with users in all the ways in which they are intended to function. The parts of the program which provide for such interconnection and interaction between elements of software and hardware are generally known as 'interfaces'. This functional interconnection and interaction is generally known as 'interoperability'; such interoperability can be defined as the ability to exchange information and mutually to use the information which has been exchanged.

(11) For the avoidance of doubt, it has to be made clear that only the expression of a computer program is protected and that ideas and principles which underlie any element of a program, including those which underlie its interfaces, are not protected by copyright under this Directive. In accordance with this principle of copyright, to the extent that logic, algorithms and programming languages comprise ideas and principles, those ideas and principles are not protected under this Directive. In accordance with the legislation and case-law of the Member States and the international copyright conventions, the expression of those ideas and principles is to be protected by copyright.

(12) For the purposes of this Directive, the term 'rental' means the making available for use, for a limited period of time and for profit-making purposes, of a computer program or a copy thereof. This term does not include public lending, which, accordingly, remains outside the scope of this Directive.

(13) The exclusive rights of the author to prevent the unauthorised reproduction of his work should be subject to a limited exception in the case of a computer program to allow the reproduction technically necessary for the use of that program by the lawful acquirer. This means that the acts of loading and running necessary for the use of a copy of a program which has been lawfully acquired, and the act of correction of its errors, may not be prohibited by contract. In the absence of specific contractual provisions, including when a copy of the program has been sold, any other act necessary for the use of the copy of a program may be performed in accordance with its intended purpose by a lawful acquirer of that copy.

(14) A person having a right to use a computer program should not be prevented from performing acts necessary to observe, study or test the functioning of the program, provided that those acts do not infringe the copyright in the program.

(15) The unauthorised reproduction, translation, adaptation or transformation of the form of the code in which a copy of a computer program has been made available constitutes an infringement of the exclusive rights of the author. Nevertheless, circumstances may exist when such a reproduction of the code and translation of its form are indispensable to obtain the necessary information to achieve the interoperability of an independently created program with other programs. It has therefore to be considered that, in these limited circumstances only, performance of the acts of reproduction and translation by or on behalf of a person having a right to use a copy of the program is legitimate and compatible with fair practice and must therefore be deemed not to require the authorisation of the rightholder. An objective of this exception is to make it possible to connect all components of a computer system, including those of different manufacturers, so that they can work together. Such an exception to the author's exclusive rights may not be used in a way which prejudices the legitimate interests of the rightholder or which conflicts with a normal exploitation of the program.

(16) Protection of computer programs under copyright laws should be without prejudice to the application, in appropriate cases, of other forms of protection. However, any contractual provisions contrary to the provisions of this Directive laid down in respect of decompilation or to the exceptions provided for by this Directive with regard to the making of a back-up copy or to observation, study or testing of the functioning of a program should be null and void.

(17) The provisions of this Directive are without prejudice to the application of the competition rules under Articles 81 and 82 of the Treaty if a dominant supplier refuses to make information available which is necessary for interoperability as defined in this Directive.

(18) The provisions of this Directive should be without prejudice to specific requirements of Community law already enacted in respect of the publication of interfaces in the telecommuni-

cations sector or Council Decisions relating to standardisation in the field of information technology and telecommunication.

(19) This Directive does not affect derogations provided for under national legislation in accordance with the Berne Convention on points not covered by this Directive.

(20) This Directive should be without prejudice to the obligations of the Member States relating to the time-limits for transposition into national law of the Directives set out in Annex I, Part B,

NOTES

[1] OJ C204, 9.8.2008, p 24.

[2] Opinion of the European Parliament of 17 June 2008 (not yet published in the Official Journal) and Council Decision of 23 March 2009.

[3] OJ L122, 17.5.1991, p 42.

[4] See Annex I, Part A.

HAVE ADOPTED THIS DIRECTIVE:

[2.795]
Article 1
Object of protection

1. In accordance with the provisions of this Directive, Member States shall protect computer programs, by copyright, as literary works within the meaning of the Berne Convention for the Protection of Literary and Artistic Works. For the purposes of this Directive, the term 'computer programs' shall include their preparatory design material.
2. Protection in accordance with this Directive shall apply to the expression in any form of a computer program. Ideas and principles which underlie any element of a computer program, including those which underlie its interfaces, are not protected by copyright under this Directive.
3. A computer program shall be protected if it is original in the sense that it is the author's own intellectual creation. No other criteria shall be applied to determine its eligibility for protection.
4. The provisions of this Directive shall apply also to programs created before 1 January 1993, without prejudice to any acts concluded and rights acquired before that date.

[2.796]
Article 2
Authorship of computer programs

1. The author of a computer program shall be the natural person or group of natural persons who has created the program or, where the legislation of the Member State permits, the legal person designated as the rightholder by that legislation. Where collective works are recognised by the legislation of a Member State, the person considered by the legislation of the Member State to have created the work shall be deemed to be its author.
2. In respect of a computer program created by a group of natural persons jointly, the exclusive rights shall be owned jointly.
3. Where a computer program is created by an employee in the execution of his duties or following the instructions given by his employer, the employer exclusively shall be entitled to exercise all economic rights in the program so created, unless otherwise provided by contract.

[2.797]
Article 3
Beneficiaries of protection

Protection shall be granted to all natural or legal persons eligible under national copyright legislation as applied to literary works.

[2.798]
Article 4
Restricted acts

1. Subject to the provisions of Articles 5 and 6, the exclusive rights of the rightholder within the meaning of Article 2 shall include the right to do or to authorise:
   (a) the permanent or temporary reproduction of a computer program by any means and in any form, in part or in whole; in so far as loading, displaying, running, transmission or storage of the computer program necessitate such reproduction, such acts shall be subject to authorisation by the rightholder;
   (b) the translation, adaptation, arrangement and any other alteration of a computer program and the reproduction of the results thereof, without prejudice to the rights of the person who alters the program;
   (c) any form of distribution to the public, including the rental, of the original computer program or of copies thereof.
2. The first sale in the Community of a copy of a program by the rightholder or with his consent shall exhaust the distribution right within the Community of that copy, with the exception of the right to control further rental of the program or a copy thereof.

[2.799]
Article 5
Exceptions to the restricted acts

1. In the absence of specific contractual provisions, the acts referred to in points (a) and (b) of Article 4(1) shall not require authorisation by the rightholder where they are necessary for the use of the computer program by the lawful acquirer in accordance with its intended purpose, including for error correction.

2. The making of a back-up copy by a person having a right to use the computer program may not be prevented by contract in so far as it is necessary for that use.

3. The person having a right to use a copy of a computer program shall be entitled, without the authorisation of the rightholder, to observe, study or test the functioning of the program in order to determine the ideas and principles which underlie any element of the program if he does so while performing any of the acts of loading, displaying, running, transmitting or storing the program which he is entitled to do.

[2.800]
Article 6
Decompilation

1. The authorisation of the rightholder shall not be required where reproduction of the code and translation of its form within the meaning of points (a) and (b) of Article 4(1) are indispensable to obtain the information necessary to achieve the interoperability of an independently created computer program with other programs, provided that the following conditions are met:
  (a) those acts are performed by the licensee or by another person having a right to use a copy of a program, or on their behalf by a person authorised to do so;
  (b) the information necessary to achieve interoperability has not previously been readily available to the persons referred to in point (a); and (c) those acts are confined to the parts of the original program which are necessary in order to achieve interoperability.

2. The provisions of paragraph 1 shall not permit the information obtained through its application:
  (a) to be used for goals other than to achieve the interoperability of the independently created computer program;
  (b) to be given to others, except when necessary for the interoperability of the independently created computer program; or
  (c) to be used for the development, production or marketing of a computer program substantially similar in its expression, or for any other act which infringes copyright.

3. In accordance with the provisions of the Berne Convention for the protection of Literary and Artistic Works, the provisions of this Article may not be interpreted in such a way as to allow its application to be used in a manner which unreasonably prejudices the rightholder's legitimate interests or conflicts with a normal exploitation of the computer program.

[2.801]
Article 7
Special measures of protection

1. Without prejudice to the provisions of Articles 4, 5 and 6, Member States shall provide, in accordance with their national legislation, appropriate remedies against a person committing any of the following acts:
  (a) any act of putting into circulation a copy of a computer program knowing, or having reason to believe, that it is an infringing copy;
  (b) the possession, for commercial purposes, of a copy of a computer program knowing, or having reason to believe, that it is an infringing copy;
  (c) any act of putting into circulation, or the possession for commercial purposes of, any means the sole intended purpose of which is to facilitate the unauthorised removal or circumvention of any technical device which may have been applied to protect a computer program.

2. Any infringing copy of a computer program shall be liable to seizure in accordance with the legislation of the Member State concerned. 3. Member States may provide for the seizure of any means referred to in point (c) of paragraph 1.

[2.802]
Article 8
Continued application of other legal provisions

The provisions of this Directive shall be without prejudice to any other legal provisions such as those concerning patent rights, trade-marks, unfair competition, trade secrets, protection of semi-conductor products or the law of contract. Any contractual provisions contrary to Article 6 or to the exceptions provided for in Article 5(2) and (3) shall be null and void.

[2.803]
Article 9
Communication

Member States shall communicate to the Commission the provisions of national law adopted in the field governed by this Directive.

[2.804]
Article 10
Repeal
Directive 91/250/EEC, as amended by the Directive indicated in Annex I, Part A, is repealed, without prejudice to the obligations of the Member States relating to the time-limits for transposition into national law of the Directives set out in Annex I, Part B.

References to the repealed Directive shall be construed as references to this Directive and shall be read in accordance with the correlation table in Annex II.

[2.805]
Article 11
Entry into force
This Directive shall enter into force on the 20th day following its publication in the *Official Journal of the European Union*.

[2.806]
Article 12
Addressees
This Directive is addressed to the Member States.

ANNEX I

PART A
REPEALED DIRECTIVE WITH ITS AMENDMENT

(referred to in Article 10)
[2.807]

Council Directive 91/250/EEC
(OJ L122, 17.5.1991, p 42)

Council Directive 93/98/EEC (OJ L290, 24.11.1993, p 9)	Article 11(1) only

PART B
LIST OF TIME-LIMITS FOR TRANSPOSITION INTO NATIONAL LAW

(referred to in Article 10)

Directive	Time-limit for transposition
91/250/EEC	31 December 1992
93/98/EEC	30 June 1995

ANNEX II
CORRELATION TABLE

[2.808]

Directive 91/250/EEC	This Directive
Article 1(1), (2) and (3)	Article 1(1), (2) and (3)
Article 2(1), first sentence	Article 2(1), first subparagraph
Article 2(1), second sentence	Article 2(1), second subparagraph
Article 2(2) and (3)	Article 2(2) and (3)
Article 3	Article 3
Article 4, introductory words	Article 4(1), introductory words
Article 4(a)	Article 4(1), point (a)
Article 4(b)	Article 4(1), point (b)
Article 4(c), first sentence	Article 4(1), point (c)
Article 4(c), second sentence	Article 4(2)
Articles 5, 6 and 7	Articles 5, 6 and 7
Article 9(1), first sentence	Article 8, first paragraph
Article 9(1), second sentence	Article 8, second paragraph
Article 9(2)	Article 1(4)
Article 10(1)	—
Article 10(2)	Article 9

Part 2 Copyright

Directive 91/250/EEC	This Directive
—	Article 10
—	Article 11
Article 11	Article 12
—	Annex I
—	Annex II

DIRECTIVE OF THE EUROPEAN PARLIAMENT AND OF THE COUNCIL

(2014/26/EU)

of 26 February 2014

on collective management of copyright and related rights and multi-territorial licensing of rights in musical works for online use in the internal market

(Text with EEA relevance)

NOTES

Date of publication in OJ: OJ L84, 20.3.2014, p 72.

THE EUROPEAN PARLIAMENT AND THE COUNCIL OF THE EUROPEAN UNION,

Having regard to the Treaty on the Functioning of the European Union, and in particular Articles 50(1) and 53(1) and Article 62 thereof,

Having regard to the proposal from the European Commission,

After transmission of the draft legislative act to the national parliaments,

Having regard to the opinion of the European Economic and Social Committee,[1]

Acting in accordance with the ordinary legislative procedure,[2]

Whereas:

(1) The Union Directives which have been adopted in the area of copyright and related rights already provide a high level of protection for rightholders and thereby a framework wherein the exploitation of content protected by those rights can take place. Those Directives contribute to the development and maintenance of creativity. In an internal market where competition is not distorted, protecting innovation and intellectual creation also encourages investment in innovative services and products.

(2) The dissemination of content which is protected by copyright and related rights, including books, audiovisual productions and recorded music, and services linked thereto, requires the licensing of rights by different holders of copyright and related rights, such as authors, performers, producers and publishers. It is normally for the rightholder to choose between the individual or collective management of his rights, unless Member States provide otherwise, in compliance with Union law and the international obligations of the Union and its Member States. Management of copyright and related rights includes granting of licences to users, auditing of users, monitoring of the use of rights, enforcement of copyright and related rights, collection of rights revenue derived from the exploitation of rights and the distribution of the amounts due to rightholders. Collective management organisations enable rightholders to be remunerated for uses which they would not be in a position to control or enforce themselves, including in non-domestic markets.

(3) Article 167 of the Treaty on the Functioning of the European Union (TFEU) requires the Union to take cultural diversity into account in its action and to contribute to the flowering of the cultures of the Member States, while respecting their national and regional diversity and at the same time bringing the common cultural heritage to the fore. Collective management organisations play, and should continue to play, an important role as promoters of the diversity of cultural expression, both by enabling the smallest and less popular repertoires to access the market and by providing social, cultural and educational services for the benefit of their rightholders and the public.

(4) When established in the Union, collective management organisations should be able to enjoy the freedoms provided by the Treaties when representing rightholders who are resident or established in other Member States or granting licences to users who are resident or established in other Member States.

(5) There are significant differences in the national rules governing the functioning of collective management organisations, in particular as regards their transparency and accountability to their members and rightholders. This has led in a number of instances to difficulties, in particular for non-domestic rightholders when they seek to exercise their rights, and to poor financial management of the revenues collected. Problems with the functioning of collective management organisations

lead to inefficiencies in the exploitation of copyright and related rights across the internal market, to the detriment of the members of collective management organisations, rightholders and users.

(6) The need to improve the functioning of collective management organisations has already been identified in Commission Recommendation 2005/737/EC.[3] That Recommendation set out a number of principles, such as the freedom of rightholders to choose their collective management organisations, equal treatment of categories of rightholders and equitable distribution of royalties. It called on collective management organisations to provide users with sufficient information on tariffs and repertoire in advance of negotiations between them. It also contained recommendations on accountability, rightholder representation in the decision-making bodies of collective management organisations and dispute resolution. However, the Recommendation has been unevenly followed.

(7) The protection of the interests of the members of collective management organisations, rightholders and third parties requires that the laws of the Member States relating to copyright management and multi-territorial licensing of online rights in musical works should be coordinated with a view to having equivalent safeguards throughout the Union. Therefore, this Directive should have as a legal base Article 50(1) TFEU.

(8) The aim of this Directive is to provide for coordination of national rules concerning access to the activity of managing copyright and related rights by collective management organisations, the modalities for their governance, and their supervisory framework, and it should therefore also have as a legal base Article 53(1) TFEU. In addition, since it is concerned with a sector offering services across the Union, this Directive should have as a legal base Article 62 TFEU.

(9) The aim of this Directive is to lay down requirements applicable to collective management organisations, in order to ensure a high standard of governance, financial management, transparency and reporting. This should not, however, prevent Member States from maintaining or imposing, in relation to collective management organisations established in their territories, more stringent standards than those laid down in Title II of this Directive, provided that such more stringent standards are compatible with Union law.

(10) Nothing in this Directive should preclude a Member State from applying the same or similar provisions to collective management organisations which are established outside the Union but which operate in that Member State.

(11) Nothing in this Directive should preclude collective management organisations from concluding representation agreements with other collective management organisations — in compliance with the competition rules laid down by Articles 101 and 102 TFEU — in the area of rights management in order to facilitate, improve and simplify the procedures for granting licences to users, including for the purposes of single invoicing, under equal, non-discriminatory and transparent conditions, and to offer multi-territorial licences also in areas other than those referred to in Title III of this Directive.

(12) This Directive, while applying to all collective management organisations, with the exception of Title III, which applies only to collective management organisations managing authors' rights in musical works for online use on a multi-territorial basis, does not interfere with arrangements concerning the management of rights in the Member States such as individual management, the extended effect of an agreement between a representative collective management organisation and a user, i.e. extended collective licensing, mandatory collective management, legal presumptions of representation and transfer of rights to collective management organisations.

(13) This Directive does not affect the possibility for Member States to determine by law, by regulation or by any other specific mechanism to that effect, rightholders' fair compensation for exceptions or limitations to the reproduction right provided for in Directive 2001/29/EC of the European Parliament and of the Council[4] and rightholders' remuneration for derogations from the exclusive right in respect of public lending provided for in Directive 2006/115/EC of the European Parliament and of the Council[5] applicable in their territory as well as the conditions applicable for their collection.

(14) This Directive does not require collective management organisations to adopt a specific legal form. In practice, those organisations operate in various legal forms such as associations, cooperatives or limited liability companies, which are controlled or owned by holders of copyright and related rights or by entities representing such rightholders. In some exceptional cases, however, due to the legal form of a collective management organisation, the element of ownership or control is not present. This is, for example, the case for foundations, which do not have members. None the less, the provisions of this Directive should also apply to those organisations. Similarly, Member States should take appropriate measures to prevent the circumvention of the obligations under this Directive through the choice of legal form. It should be noted that entities which represent rightholders, and which are members of collective management organisations, may be other collective management organisations, associations of rightholders, unions or other organisations.

(15) Rightholders should be free to entrust the management of their rights to independent management entities. Such independent management entities are commercial entities which differ from collective management organisations, inter alia, because they are not owned or controlled by rightholders. However, to the extent that such independent management entities carry out the same

activities as collective management organisations, they should be obliged to provide certain information to the rightholders they represent, collective management organisations, users and the public.

(16) Audiovisual producers, record producers and broadcasters license their own rights, in certain cases alongside rights that have been transferred to them by, for instance, performers, on the basis of individually negotiated agreements, and act in their own interest. Book, music or newspaper publishers license rights that have been transferred to them on the basis of individually negotiated agreements and act in their own interest. Therefore audiovisual producers, record producers, broadcasters and publishers should not be regarded as 'independent management entities'. Furthermore, authors' and performers' managers and agents acting as intermediaries and representing rightholders in their relations with collective management organisations should not be regarded as 'independent management entities' since they do not manage rights in the sense of setting tariffs, granting licences or collecting money from users.

(17) Collective management organisations should be free to choose to have certain of their activities, such as the invoicing of users or the distribution of amounts due to rightholders, carried out by subsidiaries or by other entities that they control. In such cases, those provisions of this Directive that would be applicable if the relevant activity were carried out directly by a collective management organisation should be applicable to the activities of the subsidiaries or other entities.

(18) In order to ensure that holders of copyright and related rights can benefit fully from the internal market when their rights are being managed collectively and that their freedom to exercise their rights is not unduly affected, it is necessary to provide for the inclusion of appropriate safeguards in the statute of collective management organisations. Moreover, a collective management organisation should not, when providing its management services, discriminate directly or indirectly between rightholders on the basis of their nationality, place of residence or place of establishment.

(19) Having regard to the freedoms established in the TFEU, collective management of copyright and related rights should entail a rightholder being able freely to choose a collective management organisation for the management of his rights, whether those rights be rights of communication to the public or reproduction rights, or categories of rights related to forms of exploitation such as broadcasting, theatrical exhibition or reproduction for online distribution, provided that the collective management organisation that the rightholder wishes to choose already manages such rights or categories of rights.

The rights, categories of rights or types of works and other subject-matter managed by the collective management organisation should be determined by the general assembly of members of that organisation if they are not already determined in its statute or prescribed by law. It is important that the rights and categories of rights be determined in a manner that maintains a balance between the freedom of rightholders to dispose of their works and other subject-matter and the ability of the organisation to manage the rights effectively, taking into account in particular the category of rights managed by the organisation and the creative sector in which it operates. Taking due account of that balance, rightholders should be able easily to withdraw such rights or categories of rights from a collective management organisation and to manage those rights individually or to entrust or transfer the management of all or part of them to another collective management organisation or another entity, irrespective of the Member State of nationality, residence or establishment of the collective management organisation, the other entity or the rightholder. Where a Member State, in compliance with Union law and the international obligations of the Union and its Member States, provides for mandatory collective management of rights, rightholders' choice would be limited to other collective management organisations.

Collective management organisations managing different types of works and other subject-matter, such as literary, musical or photographic works, should also allow this flexibility to rightholders as regards the management of different types of works and other subject-matter. As far as non-commercial uses are concerned, Member States should provide that collective management organisations take the necessary steps to ensure that their rightholders can exercise the right to grant licences for such uses. Such steps should include, inter alia, a decision by the collective management organisation on the conditions attached to the exercise of that right as well as the provision to their members of information on those conditions. Collective management organisations should inform rightholders of their choices and allow them to exercise the rights related to those choices as easily as possible. Rightholders who have already authorised the collective management organisation may be informed via the website of the organisation. A requirement for the consent of rightholders in the authorisation to the management of each right, category of rights or type of works and other subject-matter should not prevent the rightholders from accepting proposed subsequent amendments to that authorisation by tacit agreement in accordance with the conditions set out in national law. Neither contractual arrangements according to which a termination or withdrawal by rightholders has an immediate effect on licences granted prior to such termination or withdrawal, nor contractual arrangements according to which such licences remain unaffected for a certain period of time after such termination or withdrawal, are, as such, precluded by this Directive. Such arrangements should not, however, create an obstacle to the full application of this Directive. This Directive should not prejudice the possibility for rightholders to manage their rights individually, including for non-commercial uses.

(20) Membership of collective management organisations should be based on objective, transparent and non-discriminatory criteria, including as regards publishers who by virtue of an agreement on the exploitation of rights are entitled to a share of the income from the rights managed by collective management organisations and to collect such income from the collective management organisations. Those criteria should not oblige collective management organisations to accept members the management of whose rights, categories of rights or types of works or other subject-matter falls outside their scope of activity. The records kept by a collective management organisation should allow for the identification and location of its members and rightholders whose rights the organisation represents on the basis of authorisations given by those rightholders.

(21) In order to protect those rightholders whose rights are directly represented by the collective management organisation but who do not fulfil its membership requirements, it is appropriate to require that certain provisions of this Directive relating to members be also applied to such rightholders. Member States should be able also to provide such rightholders with rights to participate in the decision-making process of the collective management organisation.

(22) Collective management organisations should act in the best collective interests of the rightholders they represent. It is therefore important to provide for systems which enable the members of a collective management organisation to exercise their membership rights by participating in the organisation's decision-making process. Some collective management organisations have different categories of members, which may represent different types of rightholders, such as producers and performers. The representation in the decision-making process of those different categories of members should be fair and balanced. The effectiveness of the rules on the general assembly of members of collective management organisations would be undermined if there were no provisions on how the general assembly should be run. Thus, it is necessary to ensure that the general assembly is convened regularly, and at least annually, and that the most important decisions in the collective management organisation are taken by the general assembly.

(23) All members of collective management organisations should be allowed to participate and vote in the general assembly of members. The exercise of those rights should be subject only to fair and proportionate restrictions. In some exceptional cases, collective management organisations are established in the legal form of a foundation, and thus have no members. In such cases, the powers of the general assembly of members should be exercised by the body entrusted with the supervisory function. Where collective management organisations have entities representing rightholders as their members, as may be the case where a collective management organisation is a limited liability company and its members are associations of rightholders, Member States should be able to provide that some or all powers of the general assembly of members are to be exercised by an assembly of those rightholders. The general assembly of members should, at least, have the power to set the framework of the activities of the management, in particular with respect to the use of rights revenue by the collective management organisation. This should, however, be without prejudice to the possibility for Member States to provide for more stringent rules on, for example, investments, mergers or taking out loans, including a prohibition on any such transactions. Collective management organisations should encourage the active participation of their members in the general assembly. The exercise of voting rights should be facilitated for members who attend the general assembly and also for those who do not. In addition to being able to exercise their rights by electronic means, members should be allowed to participate and vote in the general assembly of members through a proxy. Proxy voting should be restricted in cases of conflicts of interest. At the same time, Member States should provide for restrictions as regards proxies only if this does not prejudice the appropriate and effective participation of members in the decision-making process. In particular, the appointment of proxy-holders contributes to the appropriate and effective participation of members in the decision-making process and allows rightholders to have a true opportunity to opt for a collective management organisation of their choice, irrespective of the Member State of establishment of the organisation.

(24) Members should be allowed to participate in the continuous monitoring of the management of collective management organisations. To that end, those organisations should have a supervisory function appropriate to their organisational structure and should allow members to be represented in the body that exercises that function. Depending on the organisational structure of the collective management organisation, the supervisory function may be exercised by a separate body, such as a supervisory board, or by some or all of the directors in the administrative board who do not manage the business of the collective management organisation. The requirement of fair and balanced representation of members should not prevent the collective management organisation from appointing third parties to exercise the supervisory function, including persons with relevant professional expertise and rightholders who do not fulfil the membership requirements or who are represented by the organisation not directly but via an entity which is a member of the collective management organisation.

(25) For reasons of sound management, the management of a collective management organisation must be independent. Managers, whether elected as directors or hired or employed by the organisation on the basis of a contract, should be required to declare, prior to taking up their position

and thereafter on a yearly basis, whether there are conflicts between their interests and those of the rightholders that are represented by the collective management organisation. Such annual statements should be also made by persons exercising the supervisory function. Member States should be free to require collective management organisations to make such statements public or to submit them to public authorities.

(26) Collective management organisations collect, manage and distribute revenue from the exploitation of the rights entrusted to them by rightholders. That revenue is ultimately due to rightholders, who may have a direct legal relationship with the organisation, or may be represented via an entity which is a member of the collective management organisation or via a representation agreement. It is therefore important that a collective management organisation exercise the utmost diligence in collecting, managing and distributing that revenue. Accurate distribution is only possible where the collective management organisation maintains proper records of membership, licences and use of works and other subject-matter. Relevant data that are required for the efficient collective management of rights should also be provided by rightholders and users and verified by the collective management organisation.

(27) Amounts collected and due to rightholders should be kept separately in the accounts from any own assets the organisation may have. Without prejudice to the possibility for Member States to provide for more stringent rules on investment, including a prohibition of investment of the rights revenue, where such amounts are invested, this should be carried out in accordance with the general investment and risk management policy of the collective management organisation. In order to maintain a high level of protection of the rights of rightholders and to ensure that any income that may arise from the exploitation of such rights accrues to their benefit, the investments made and held by the collective management organisation should be managed in accordance with criteria which would oblige the organisation to act prudently, while allowing it to decide on the most secure and efficient investment policy. This should allow the collective management organisation to opt for an asset allocation that suits the precise nature and duration of any exposure to risk of any rights revenue invested and does not unduly prejudice any rights revenue owed to rightholders.

(28) Since rightholders are entitled to be remunerated for the exploitation of their rights, it is important that management fees do not exceed justified costs of the management of the rights and that any deduction other than in respect of management fees, for example a deduction for social, cultural or educational purposes, should be decided by the members of the collective management organisation. The collective management organisations should be transparent towards rightholders regarding the rules governing such deductions. The same requirements should apply to any decision to use the rights revenue for collective distribution, such as scholarships. Rightholders should have access, on a non-discriminatory basis, to any social, cultural or educational service funded through such deductions. This Directive should not affect deductions under national law, such as deductions for the provision of social services by collective management organisations to rightholders, as regards any aspects that are not regulated by this Directive, provided that such deductions are in compliance with Union law.

(29) The distribution and payment of amounts due to individual rightholders or, as the case may be, to categories of rightholders, should be carried out in a timely manner and in accordance with the general policy on distribution of the collective management organisation concerned, including when they are performed via another entity representing the rightholders. Only objective reasons beyond the control of a collective management organisation can justify delay in the distribution and payment of amounts due to rightholders. Therefore, circumstances such as the rights revenue having been invested subject to a maturity date should not qualify as valid reasons for such a delay. It is appropriate to leave it to Member States to decide on rules ensuring timely distribution and the effective search for, and identification of, rightholders in cases where such objective reasons occur. In order to ensure that the amounts due to rightholders are appropriately and effectively distributed, without prejudice to the possibility for Member States to provide for more stringent rules, it is necessary to require collective management organisations to take reasonable and diligent measures, on the basis of good faith, to identify and locate the relevant rightholders. It is also appropriate that members of a collective management organisation, to the extent allowed for under national law, should decide on the use of any amounts that cannot be distributed in situations where rightholders entitled to those amounts cannot be identified or located.

(30) Collective management organisations should be able to manage rights and collect revenue from their exploitation under representation agreements with other organisations. To protect the rights of the members of the other collective management organisation, a collective management organisation should not distinguish between the rights it manages under representation agreements and those it manages directly for its rightholders. Nor should the collective management organisation be allowed to apply deductions to the rights revenue collected on behalf of another collective management organisation, other than deductions in respect of management fees, without the express consent of the other organisation. It is also appropriate to require collective management organisations to distribute and make payments to other organisations on the basis of such representation agreements no later than when they distribute and make payments to their own members and to non-member rightholders whom they represent. Furthermore, the recipient

organisation should in turn be required to distribute the amounts due to the rightholders it represents without delay.

(31) Fair and non-discriminatory commercial terms in licensing are particularly important to ensure that users can obtain licences for works and other subject-matter in respect of which a collective management organisation represents rights, and to ensure the appropriate remuneration of rightholders. Collective management organisations and users should therefore conduct licensing negotiations in good faith and apply tariffs which should be determined on the basis of objective and non-discriminatory criteria. It is appropriate to require that the licence fee or remuneration determined by collective management organisations be reasonable in relation to, inter alia, the economic value of the use of the rights in a particular context. Finally, collective management organisations should respond without undue delay to users' requests for licences.

(32) In the digital environment, collective management organisations are regularly required to license their repertoire for totally new forms of exploitation and business models. In such cases, and in order to foster an environment conducive to the development of such licences, without prejudice to the application of competition law rules, collective management organisations should have the flexibility required to provide, as swiftly as possible, individualised licences for innovative online services, without the risk that the terms of those licences could be used as a precedent for determining the terms for other licences.

(33) In order to ensure that collective management organisations can comply with the obligations set out in this Directive, users should provide those organisations with relevant information on the use of the rights represented by the collective management organisations. This obligation should not apply to natural persons acting for purposes outside their trade, business, craft or profession, who therefore fall outside the definition of user as laid down in this Directive. Moreover, the information required by collective management organisations should be limited to what is reasonable, necessary and at the users' disposal in order to enable such organisations to perform their functions, taking into account the specific situation of small and medium-sized enterprises. That obligation could be included in an agreement between a collective management organisation and a user; this does not preclude national statutory rights to information. The deadlines applicable to the provision of information by users should be such as to allow collective management organisations to meet the deadlines set for the distribution of amounts due to rightholders. This Directive should be without prejudice to the possibility for Member States to require collective management organisations established in their territory to issue joint invoices.

(34) In order to enhance the trust of rightholders, users and other collective management organisations in the management of rights by collective management organisations, each collective management organisation should comply with specific transparency requirements. Each collective management organisation or its member being an entity responsible for attribution or payment of amounts due to rightholders should therefore be required to provide certain information to individual rightholders at least once a year, such as the amounts attributed or paid to them and the deductions made. Collective management organisations should also be required to provide sufficient information, including financial information, to the other collective management organisations whose rights they manage under representation agreements.

(35) In order to ensure that rightholders, other collective management organisations and users have access to information on the scope of activity of the organisation and the works or other subject-matter that it represents, a collective management organisation should provide information on those issues in response to a duly justified request. The question whether, and to what extent, reasonable fees can be charged for providing this service should be left to national law. Each collective management organisation should also make public information on its structure and on the way in which it carries out its activities, including in particular its statutes and general policies on management fees, deductions and tariffs.

(36) In order to ensure that rightholders are in a position to monitor and compare the respective performances of collective management organisations, such organisations should make public an annual transparency report comprising comparable audited financial information specific to their activities. Collective management organisations should also make public an annual special report, forming part of the annual transparency report, on the use of amounts dedicated to social, cultural and educational services. This Directive should not prevent a collective management organisation from publishing the information required by the annual transparency report in a single document, for example as part of its annual financial statements, or in separate reports.

(37) Providers of online services which make use of musical works, such as music services that allow consumers to download music or to listen to it in streaming mode, as well as other services providing access to films or games where music is an important element, must first obtain the right to use such works. Directive 2001/29/EC requires that a licence be obtained for each of the rights in the online exploitation of musical works. In respect of authors, those rights are the exclusive right of reproduction and the exclusive right of communication to the public of musical works, which includes the right of making available. Those rights may be managed by the individual rightholders themselves, such as authors or music publishers, or by collective management organisations that provide collective management services to rightholders. Different collective management organisa-

tions may manage authors' rights of reproduction and communication to the public. Furthermore, there are cases where several rightholders have rights in the same work and may have authorised different organisations to license their respective shares of rights in the work. Any user wishing to provide an online service offering a wide choice of musical works to consumers needs to aggregate rights in works from different rightholders and collective management organisations.

(38) While the internet knows no borders, the online market for music services in the Union is still fragmented, and a digital single market has not yet been fully achieved. The complexity and difficulty associated with the collective management of rights in Europe has, in a number of cases, exacerbated the fragmentation of the European digital market for online music services. This situation is in stark contrast to the rapidly growing demand on the part of consumers for access to digital content and associated innovative services, including across national borders.

(39) Commission Recommendation 2005/737/EC promoted a new regulatory environment better suited to the management, at Union level, of copyright and related rights for the provision of legitimate online music services. It recognised that, in an era of online exploitation of musical works, commercial users need a licensing policy that corresponds to the ubiquity of the online environment and is multi-territorial. However, the Recommendation has not been sufficient to encourage the widespread multi-territorial licensing of online rights in musical works or to address the specific demands of multi-territorial licensing.

(40) In the online music sector, where collective management of authors' rights on a territorial basis remains the norm, it is essential to create conditions conducive to the most effective licensing practices by collective management organisations in an increasingly cross-border context. It is therefore appropriate to provide a set of rules prescribing basic conditions for the provision by collective management organisations of multi-territorial collective licensing of authors' rights in musical works for online use, including lyrics. The same rules should apply to such licensing for all musical works, including musical works incorporated in audiovisual works. However, online services solely providing access to musical works in sheet music form should not be covered. The provisions of this Directive should ensure the necessary minimum quality of cross-border services provided by collective management organisations, notably in terms of transparency of repertoire represented and accuracy of financial flows related to the use of the rights. They should also set out a framework for facilitating the voluntary aggregation of music repertoire and rights, thus reducing the number of licences a user needs to operate a multi-territory, multi-repertoire service. Those provisions should enable a collective management organisation to request another organisation to represent its repertoire on a multi-territorial basis where it cannot or does not wish to fulfil the requirements itself. There should be an obligation on the requested organisation, provided that it already aggregates repertoire and offers or grants multi-territorial licences, to accept the mandate of the requesting organisation. The development of legal online music services across the Union should also contribute to the fight against online infringements of copyright.

(41) The availability of accurate and comprehensive information on musical works, rightholders and the rights that each collective management organisation is authorised to represent in a given territory is of particular importance for an effective and transparent licensing process, for the subsequent processing of the users' reports and the related invoicing of service providers, and for the distribution of amounts due. For that reason, collective management organisations granting multi-territorial licences for musical works should be able to process such detailed data quickly and accurately. This requires the use of databases on ownership of rights that are licensed on a multi-territorial basis, containing data that allow for the identification of works, rights and rightholders that a collective management organisation is authorised to represent and of the territories covered by the authorisation. Any changes to that information should be taken into account without undue delay and the databases should be continually updated. Those databases should also help to match information on works with information on phonograms or any other fixation in which the work has been incorporated. It is also important to ensure that prospective users and rightholders, as well as collective management organisations, have access to the information they need in order to identify the repertoire that those organisations are representing. Collective management organisations should be able to take measures to protect the accuracy and integrity of the data, to control their reuse or to protect commercially sensitive information.

(42) In order to ensure that the data on the music repertoire they process are as accurate as possible, collective management organisations granting multi-territorial licences in musical works should be required to update their databases continuously and without delay as necessary. They should establish easily accessible procedures to enable online service providers, as well as rightholders and other collective management organisations, to inform them of any inaccuracy that the organisations' databases may contain in respect of works they own or control, including rights — in whole or in part — and territories for which they have mandated the relevant collective management organisation to act, without however jeopardising the veracity and integrity of the data held by the collective management organisation. Since Directive 95/46/EC of the European Parliament and of the Council[6] grants to every data subject the right to obtain rectification, erasure or blocking of inaccurate or incomplete data, this Directive should also ensure that inaccurate information regarding rightholders or other collective management organisations in the case of multi-territorial licences is to be corrected without undue delay. Collective management organisa-

tions should also have the capacity to process electronically the registration of works and authorisations to manage rights. Given the importance of information automation for the fast and effective processing of data, collective management organisations should provide for the use of electronic means for the structured communication of that information by rightholders. Collective management organisations should, as far as possible, ensure that such electronic means take into account the relevant voluntary industry standards or practices developed at international or Union level.

(43) Industry standards for music use, sales reporting and invoicing are instrumental in improving efficiency in the exchange of data between collective management organisations and users. Monitoring the use of licences should respect fundamental rights, including the right to respect for private and family life and the right to protection of personal data. In order to ensure that these efficiency gains result in faster financial processing and ultimately in earlier payments to rightholders, collective management organisations should be required to invoice service providers and to distribute amounts due to rightholders without delay. For this requirement to be effective, it is necessary that users provide collective management organisations with accurate and timely reports on the use of works. Collective management organisations should not be required to accept users' reports in proprietary formats when widely used industry standards are available. Collective management organisations should not be prevented from outsourcing services relating to the granting of multi-territorial licences for online rights in musical works. Sharing or consolidation of back-office capabilities should help the organisations to improve management services and rationalise investments in data management tools.

(44) Aggregating different music repertoires for multi-territorial licensing facilitates the licensing process and, by making all repertoires accessible to the market for multi-territorial licensing, enhances cultural diversity and contributes to reducing the number of transactions an online service provider needs in order to offer services. This aggregation of repertoires should facilitate the development of new online services, and should also result in a reduction of transaction costs being passed on to consumers. Therefore, collective management organisations that are not willing or not able to grant multi-territorial licences directly in their own music repertoire should be encouraged on a voluntary basis to mandate other collective management organisations to manage their repertoire on a non-discriminatory basis. Exclusivity in agreements on multi-territorial licences would restrict the choices available to users seeking multi-territorial licences and also restrict the choices available to collective management organisations seeking administration services for their repertoire on a multi-territorial basis. Therefore, all representation agreements between collective management organisations providing for multi-territorial licensing should be concluded on a non-exclusive basis.

(45) The transparency of the conditions under which collective management organisations manage online rights is of particular importance to members of collective management organisations. Collective management organisations should therefore provide sufficient information to their members on the main terms of any agreement mandating any other collective management organisation to represent those members' online music rights for the purposes of multi-territorial licensing.

(46) It is also important to require any collective management organisations that offer or grant multi-territorial licences to agree to represent the repertoire of any collective management organisations that decide not to do so directly. To ensure that this requirement is not disproportionate and does not go beyond what is necessary, the requested collective management organisation should only be required to accept the representation if the request is limited to the online right or categories of online rights that it represents itself. Moreover, this requirement should only apply to collective management organisations which aggregate repertoire and should not extend to collective management organisations which provide multi-territorial licences for their own repertoire only. Nor should it apply to collective management organisations which merely aggregate rights in the same works for the purpose of being able to license jointly both the right of reproduction and the right of communication to the public in respect of such works. To protect the interests of the rightholders of the mandating collective management organisation and to ensure that small and less well-known repertoires in Member States can access the internal market on equal terms, it is important that the repertoire of the mandating collective management organisation be managed on the same conditions as the repertoire of the mandated collective management organisation and that it is included in offers addressed by the mandated collective management organisation to online service providers. The management fee charged by the mandated collective management organisation should allow that organisation to recoup the necessary and reasonable investments incurred. Any agreement whereby a collective management organisation mandates another organisation or organisations to grant multi-territorial licences in its own music repertoire for online use should not prevent the first-mentioned collective management organisation from continuing to grant licences limited to the territory of the Member State where that organisation is established, in its own repertoire and in any other repertoire it may be authorised to represent in that territory.

(47) The objectives and effectiveness of the rules on multi-territorial licensing by collective management organisations would be significantly jeopardised if rightholders were not able to exercise such rights in respect of multi-territorial licences when the collective management

organisation to which they have granted their rights did not grant or offer multi-territorial licences and furthermore did not want to mandate another collective management organisation to do so. For this reason, it would be important in such circumstances to enable rightholders to exercise the right to grant the multi-territorial licences required by online service providers themselves or through another party or parties, by withdrawing from their original collective management organisation their rights to the extent necessary for multi-territorial licensing for online uses, and to leave the same rights with their original organisation for the purposes of mono-territorial licensing.

(48) Broadcasting organisations generally rely on a licence from a local collective management organisation for their own broadcasts of television and radio programmes which include musical works. That licence is often limited to broadcasting activities. A licence for online rights in musical works would be required in order to allow such television or radio broadcasts to be also available online. To facilitate the licensing of online rights in musical works for the purposes of simultaneous and delayed transmission online of television and radio broadcasts, it is necessary to provide for a derogation from the rules that would otherwise apply to the multi-territorial licensing of online rights in musical works. Such a derogation should be limited to what is necessary in order to allow access to television or radio programmes online and to material having a clear and subordinate relationship to the original broadcast produced for purposes such as supplementing, previewing or reviewing the television or radio programme concerned. That derogation should not operate so as to distort competition with other services which give consumers access to individual musical or audiovisual works online, nor lead to restrictive practices, such as market or customer sharing, which would be in breach of Article 101 or 102 TFEU.

(49) It is necessary to ensure the effective enforcement of the provisions of national law adopted pursuant to this Directive. Collective management organisations should offer their members specific procedures for handling complaints. Those procedures should also be made available to other rightholders directly represented by the organisation and to other collective management organisations on whose behalf it manages rights under a representation agreement. Furthermore, Member States should be able to provide that disputes between collective management organisations, their members, rightholders or users as to the application of this Directive can be submitted to a rapid, independent and impartial alternative dispute resolution procedure. In particular, the effectiveness of the rules on multi-territorial licensing of online rights in musical works could be undermined if disputes between collective management organisations and other parties were not resolved quickly and efficiently. As a result, it is appropriate to provide, without prejudice to the right of access to a tribunal, for the possibility of easily accessible, efficient and impartial out-of-court procedures, such as mediation or arbitration, for resolving conflicts between, on the one hand, collective management organisations granting multi-territorial licences and, on the other, online service providers, rightholders or other collective management organisations. This Directive neither prescribes a specific manner in which such alternative dispute resolution should be organised, nor determines which body should carry it out, provided that its independence, impartiality and efficiency are guaranteed. Finally, it is also appropriate to require that Member States have independent, impartial and effective dispute resolution procedures, via bodies possessing expertise in intellectual property law or via courts, suitable for settling commercial disputes between collective management organisations and users on existing or proposed licensing conditions or on a breach of contract.

(50) Member States should establish appropriate procedures by means of which it will be possible to monitor compliance by collective management organisations with this Directive. While it is not appropriate for this Directive to restrict the choice of Member States as to competent authorities, nor as regards the *ex-ante* or *ex-post* nature of the control over collective management organisations, it should be ensured that such authorities are capable of addressing in an effective and timely manner any concern that may arise in the application of this Directive. Member States should not be obliged to set up new competent authorities. Moreover, it should also be possible for members of a collective management organisation, rightholders, users, collective management organisations and other interested parties to notify a competent authority in respect of activities or circumstances which, in their opinion, constitute a breach of law by collective management organisations and, where relevant, users. Member States should ensure that competent authorities have the power to impose sanctions or measures where provisions of national law implementing this Directive are not complied with. This Directive does not provide for specific types of sanctions or measures, provided that they are effective, proportionate and dissuasive. Such sanctions or measures may include orders to dismiss directors who have acted negligently, inspections at the premises of a collective management organisation or, in cases where an authorisation is issued for an organisation to operate, the withdrawal of such authorisation. This Directive should remain neutral as regards the prior authorisation and supervision regimes in the Member States, including a requirement for the representativeness of the collective management organisation, in so far as those regimes are compatible with Union law and do not create an obstacle to the full application of this Directive.

(51) In order to ensure that the requirements for multi-territorial licensing are complied with, specific provisions on the monitoring of their implementation should be laid down. The competent authorities of the Member States and the Commission should cooperate with each other to that end. Member States should provide each other with mutual assistance by way of exchange of information

between their competent authorities in order to facilitate the monitoring of collective management organisations.

(52) It is important for collective management organisations to respect the rights to private life and personal data protection of any rightholder, member, user and other individual whose personal data they process. Directive 95/46/EC governs the processing of personal data carried out in the Member States in the context of that Directive and under the supervision of the Member States' competent authorities, in particular the public independent authorities designated by the Member States. Rightholders should be given appropriate information about the processing of their data, the recipients of those data, time limits for the retention of such data in any database, and the way in which rightholders can exercise their rights to access, correct or delete their personal data concerning them in accordance with Directive 95/46/EC. In particular, unique identifiers which allow for the indirect identification of a person should be treated as personal data within the meaning of that Directive.

(53) Provisions on enforcement measures should be without prejudice to the competencies of national independent public authorities established by the Member States pursuant to Directive 95/46/EC to monitor compliance with national provisions adopted in implementation of that Directive.

(54) This Directive respects the fundamental rights and observes the principles enshrined in the Charter of Fundamental Rights of the European Union ('the Charter'). Provisions in this Directive relating to dispute resolution should not prevent parties from exercising their right of access to a tribunal as guaranteed in the Charter.

(55) Since the objectives of this Directive, namely to improve the ability of their members to exercise control over the activities of collective management organisations, to guarantee sufficient transparency by collective management organisations and to improve the multi-territorial licensing of authors' rights in musical works for online use, cannot be sufficiently achieved by Member States but can rather, by reason of their scale and effects, be better achieved at Union level, the Union may adopt measures in accordance with the principle of subsidiarity as set out in Article 5 of the Treaty on European Union. In accordance with the principle of proportionality, as set out in that Article, this Directive does not go beyond what is necessary in order to achieve those objectives.

(56) The provisions of this Directive are without prejudice to the application of rules on competition, and any other relevant law in other areas including confidentiality, trade secrets, privacy, access to documents, the law of contract and private international law relating to the conflict of laws and the jurisdiction of courts, and workers' and employers' freedom of association and their right to organise.

(57) In accordance with the Joint Political Declaration of 28 September 2011 of Member States and the Commission on explanatory documents,[7] Member States have undertaken to accompany, in justified cases, the notification of their transposition measures with one or more documents explaining the relationship between the components of a directive and the corresponding parts of national transposition instruments. With regard to this Directive, the legislator considers the transmission of such documents to be justified.

(58) The European Data Protection Supervisor was consulted in accordance with Article 28(2) of Regulation (EC) No 45/2001 of the European Parliament and of the Council[8] and delivered an opinion on 9 October 2012,

NOTES

[1] OJ C44, 15.2.2013, p 104.

[2] Position of the European Parliament of 4 February 2014 (not yet published in the Official Journal) and decision of the Council of 20 February 2014.

[3] Commission Recommendation 2005/737/EC of 18 May 2005 on collective cross-border management of copyright and related rights for legitimate online music services (OJ L276, 21.10.2005, p 54).

[4] Directive 2001/29/EC of the European Parliament and of the Council of 22 May 2001 on the harmonisation of certain aspects of copyright and related rights in the information society (OJ L167, 22.6.2001, p 10).

[5] Directive 2006/115/EC of the European Parliament and of the Council of 12 December 2006 on rental right and lending right and on certain rights related to copyright in the field of intellectual property (OJ L376, 27.12.2006, p 28).

[6] Directive 95/46/EC of the European Parliament and of the Council of 24 October 1995 on the protection of individuals with regard to the processing of personal data and on the free movement of such data (OJ L281, 23.11.1995, p 31).

[7] OJ C369, 17.12.2011, p 14.

[8] Regulation (EC) No 45/2001 of the European Parliament and of the Council of 18 December 2000 on the protection of individuals with regard to the processing of personal data by the Community institutions and bodies and on the free movement of such data (OJ L8, 12.1.2001, p 1).

HAVE ADOPTED THIS DIRECTIVE:

TITLE I
GENERAL PROVISIONS

[2.809]
Article 1
Subject-matter

This Directive lays down requirements necessary to ensure the proper functioning of the management of copyright and related rights by collective management organisations. It also lays down requirements for multi-territorial licensing by collective management organisations of authors' rights in musical works for online use.

[2.810]
Article 2
Scope

1. Titles I, II, IV and V with the exception of Article 34(2) and Article 38 apply to all collective management organisations established in the Union.
2. Title III and Article 34(2) and Article 38 apply to collective management organisations established in the Union managing authors' rights in musical works for online use on a multi-territorial basis.
3. The relevant provisions of this Directive apply to entities directly or indirectly owned or controlled, wholly or in part, by a collective management organisation, provided that such entities carry out an activity which, if carried out by the collective management organisation, would be subject to the provisions of this Directive.
4. Article 16(1), Articles 18 and 20, points (a), (b), (c), (e), (f) and (g) of Article 21(1) and Articles 36 and 42 apply to all independent management entities established in the Union.

[2.811]
Article 3
Definitions

For the purposes of this Directive, the following definitions shall apply:

(a) 'collective management organisation' means any organisation which is authorised by law or by way of assignment, licence or any other contractual arrangement to manage copyright or rights related to copyright on behalf of more than one rightholder, for the collective benefit of those rightholders, as its sole or main purpose, and which fulfils one or both of the following criteria:
   (i) it is owned or controlled by its members;
   (ii) it is organised on a not-for-profit basis;

(b) 'independent management entity' means any organisation which is authorised by law or by way of assignment, licence or any other contractual arrangement to manage copyright or rights related to copyright on behalf of more than one rightholder, for the collective benefit of those rightholders, as its sole or main purpose, and which is:
   (i) neither owned nor controlled, directly or indirectly, wholly or in part, by rightholders; and
   (ii) organised on a for-profit basis;

(c) 'rightholder' means any person or entity, other than a collective management organisation, that holds a copyright or related right or, under an agreement for the exploitation of rights or by law, is entitled to a share of the rights revenue;

(d) 'member' means a rightholder or an entity representing rightholders, including other collective management organisations and associations of rightholders, fulfilling the membership requirements of the collective management organisation and admitted by it;

(e) 'statute' means the memorandum and articles of association, the statute, the rules or documents of constitution of a collective management organisation;

(f) 'general assembly of members' means the body in the collective management organisation wherein members participate and exercise their voting rights, regardless of the legal form of the organisation;

(g) 'director' means:
   (i) where national law or the statute of the collective management organisation provides for a unitary board, any member of the administrative board;
   (ii) where national law or the statute of the collective management organisation provides for a dual board, any member of the management board or the supervisory board;

(h) 'rights revenue' means income collected by a collective management organisation on behalf of rightholders, whether deriving from an exclusive right, a right to remuneration or a right to compensation;

(i) 'management fees' means the amounts charged, deducted or offset by a collective management organisation from rights revenue or from any income arising from the investment of rights revenue in order to cover the costs of its management of copyright or related rights;

(j) 'representation agreement' means any agreement between collective management organisations whereby one collective management organisation mandates another collective management organisation to manage the rights it represents, including an agreement concluded under Articles 29 and 30;

(k) 'user' means any person or entity that is carrying out acts subject to the authorisation of rightholders, remuneration of rightholders or payment of compensation to rightholders and is not acting in the capacity of a consumer;

(l) 'repertoire' means the works in respect of which a collective management organisation manages rights;

(m) 'multi-territorial licence' means a licence which covers the territory of more than one Member State;

(n) 'online rights in musical works' means any of the rights of an author in a musical work provided for under Articles 2 and 3 of Directive 2001/29/EC which are required for the provision of an online service.

TITLE II
COLLECTIVE MANAGEMENT ORGANISATIONS

CHAPTER 1
REPRESENTATION OF RIGHTHOLDERS AND MEMBERSHIP AND ORGANISATION OF COLLECTIVE MANAGEMENT ORGANISATIONS

[2.812]
Article 4
General principles

Member States shall ensure that collective management organisations act in the best interests of the rightholders whose rights they represent and that they do not impose on them any obligations which are not objectively necessary for the protection of their rights and interests or for the effective management of their rights.

[2.813]
Article 5
Rights of rightholders

1. Member States shall ensure that rightholders have the rights laid down in paragraphs 2 to 8 and that those rights are set out in the statute or membership terms of the collective management organisation.

2. Rightholders shall have the right to authorise a collective management organisation of their choice to manage the rights, categories of rights or types of works and other subject-matter of their choice, for the territories of their choice, irrespective of the Member State of nationality, residence or establishment of either the collective management organisation or the rightholder. Unless the collective management organisation has objectively justified reasons to refuse management, it shall be obliged to manage such rights, categories of rights or types of works and other subject-matter, provided that their management falls within the scope of its activity.

3. Rightholders shall have the right to grant licences for non-commercial uses of any rights, categories of rights or types of works and other subject-matter that they may choose.

4. Rightholders shall have the right to terminate the authorisation to manage rights, categories of rights or types of works and other subject-matter granted by them to a collective management organisation or to withdraw from a collective management organisation any of the rights, categories of rights or types of works and other subject-matter of their choice, as determined pursuant to paragraph 2, for the territories of their choice, upon serving reasonable notice not exceeding six months. The collective management organisation may decide that such termination or withdrawal is to take effect only at the end of the financial year.

5. If there are amounts due to a rightholder for acts of exploitation which occurred before the termination of the authorisation or the withdrawal of rights took effect, or under a licence granted before such termination or withdrawal took effect, the rightholder shall retain his rights under Articles 12, 13, 18, 20, 28 and 33.

6. A collective management organisation shall not restrict the exercise of rights provided for under paragraphs 4 and 5 by requiring, as a condition for the exercise of those rights, that the management of rights or categories of rights or types of works and other subject-matter which are subject to the termination or the withdrawal be entrusted to another collective management organisation.

7. In cases where a rightholder authorises a collective management organisation to manage his rights, he shall give consent specifically for each right or category of rights or type of works and other subject-matter which he authorises the collective management organisation to manage. Any such consent shall be evidenced in documentary form.

8. A collective management organisation shall inform rightholders of their rights under paragraphs 1 to 7, as well as of any conditions attached to the right set out in paragraph 3, before obtaining their consent to its managing any right or category of rights or type of works and other subject-matter.

A collective management organisation shall inform those rightholders who have already authorised it of their rights under paragraphs 1 to 7, as well as of any conditions attached to the right set out in paragraph 3, by 10 October 2016.

[2.814]
Article 6
Membership rules of collective management organisations

1. Member States shall ensure that collective management organisations comply with the rules laid down in paragraphs 2 to 5.
2. A collective management organisation shall accept rightholders and entities representing rightholders, including other collective management organisations and associations of rightholders, as members if they fulfil the membership requirements, which shall be based on objective, transparent and non-discriminatory criteria. Those membership requirements shall be included in the statute or membership terms of the collective management organisation and shall be made publicly available. In cases where a collective management organisation refuses to accept a request for membership, it shall provide the rightholder with a clear explanation of the reasons for its decision.
3. The statute of a collective management organisation shall provide for appropriate and effective mechanisms for the participation of its members in the organisation's decision-making process. The representation of the different categories of members in the decision-making process shall be fair and balanced.
4. A collective management organisation shall allow its members to communicate with it by electronic means, including for the purposes of exercising members' rights.
5. A collective management organisation shall keep records of its members and shall regularly update those records.

[2.815]
Article 7
Rights of rightholders who are not members of the collective management organisation

1. Member States shall ensure that collective management organisations comply with the rules laid down in Article 6(4), Article 20, Article 29(2) and Article 33 in respect of rightholders who have a direct legal relationship by law or by way of assignment, licence or any other contractual arrangement with them but are not their members.
2. Member States may apply other provisions of this Directive to the rightholders referred to in paragraph 1.

[2.816]
Article 8
General assembly of members of the collective management organisation

1. Member States shall ensure that the general assembly of members is organised in accordance with the rules laid down in paragraphs 2 to 10.
2. A general assembly of members shall be convened at least once a year.
3. The general assembly of members shall decide on any amendments to the statute and to the membership terms of the collective management organisation, where those terms are not regulated by the statute.
4. The general assembly of members shall decide on the appointment or dismissal of the directors, review their general performance and approve their remuneration and other benefits such as monetary and non-monetary benefits, pension awards and entitlements, rights to other awards and rights to severance pay.

In a collective management organisation with a dual board system, the general assembly of members shall not decide on the appointment or dismissal of members of the management board or approve their remuneration and other benefits where the power to take such decisions is delegated to the supervisory board.

5. In accordance with the provisions laid down in Chapter 2 of Title II, the general assembly of members shall decide at least on the following issues:
   (a) the general policy on the distribution of amounts due to rightholders;
   (b) the general policy on the use of non-distributable amounts;
   (c) the general investment policy with regard to rights revenue and to any income arising from the investment of rights revenue;
   (d) the general policy on deductions from rights revenue and from any income arising from the investment of rights revenue;
   (e) the use of non-distributable amounts;
   (f) the risk management policy;
   (g) the approval of any acquisition, sale or hypothecation of immovable property;
   (h) the approval of mergers and alliances, the setting-up of subsidiaries, and the acquisition of other entities or shares or rights in other entities;
   (i) the approval of taking out loans, granting loans or providing security for loans.

6. The general assembly of members may delegate the powers listed in points (f), (g), (h) and (i) of paragraph 5, by a resolution or by a provision in the statute, to the body exercising the supervisory function.
7. For the purposes of points (a) to (d) of paragraph 5, Member States may require the general assembly of members to determine more detailed conditions for the use of the rights revenue and the income arising from the investment of rights revenue.
8. The general assembly of members shall control the activities of the collective management organisation by, at least, deciding on the appointment and removal of the auditor and approving the annual transparency report referred to in Article 22.
Member States may allow alternative systems or modalities for the appointment and removal of the auditor, provided that those systems or modalities are designed to ensure the independence of the auditor from the persons who manage the business of the collective management organisation.
9. All members of the collective management organisation shall have the right to participate in, and the right to vote at, the general assembly of members. However, Member States may allow for restrictions on the right of the members of the collective management organisation to participate in, and to exercise voting rights at, the general assembly of members, on the basis of one or both of the following criteria:
(a) duration of membership;
(b) amounts received or due to a member,
provided that such criteria are determined and applied in a manner that is fair and proportionate.
The criteria laid down in points (a) and (b) of the first subparagraph shall be included in the statute or the membership terms of the collective management organisation and shall be made publicly available in accordance with Articles 19 and 21.
10. Every member of a collective management organisation shall have the right to appoint any other person or entity as a proxy holder to participate in, and vote at, the general assembly of members on his behalf, provided that such appointment does not result in a conflict of interest which might occur, for example, where the appointing member and the proxy holder belong to different categories of rightholders within the collective management organisation.
However, Member States may provide for restrictions concerning the appointment of proxy holders and the exercise of the voting rights of the members they represent if such restrictions do not prejudice the appropriate and effective participation of members in the decision-making process of a collective management organisation.
Each proxy shall be valid for a single general assembly of members. The proxy holder shall enjoy the same rights in the general assembly of members as those to which the appointing member would be entitled. The proxy holder shall cast votes in accordance with the instructions issued by the appointing member.
11. Member States may decide that the powers of the general assembly of members may be exercised by an assembly of delegates elected at least every four years by the members of the collective management organisation, provided that:
(a) appropriate and effective participation of members in the collective management organisation's decision-making process is ensured; and
(b) the representation of the different categories of members in the assembly of delegates is fair and balanced.
The rules laid down in paragraphs 2 to 10 shall apply to the assembly of delegates mutatis mutandis.
12. Member States may decide that where a collective management organisation, by reason of its legal form, does not have a general assembly of members, the powers of that assembly are to be exercised by the body exercising the supervisory function. The rules laid down in paragraphs 2 to 5, 7 and 8 shall apply mutatis mutandis to such body exercising the supervisory function.
13. Member States may decide that where a collective management organisation has members who are entities representing rightholders, all or some of the powers of the general assembly of members are to be exercised by an assembly of those rightholders. The rules laid down in paragraphs 2 to 10 shall apply mutatis mutandis to the assembly of rightholders.

[2.817]
Article 9
Supervisory function
1. Member States shall ensure that each collective management organisation has in place a supervisory function for continuously monitoring the activities and the performance of the duties of the persons who manage the business of the organisation.
2. There shall be fair and balanced representation of the different categories of members of the collective management organisation in the body exercising the supervisory function.
3. Each person exercising the supervisory function shall make an annual individual statement on conflicts of interest, containing the information referred to in the second subparagraph of Article 10(2), to the general assembly of members.
4. The body exercising the supervisory function shall meet regularly and shall have at least the following powers:
(a) to exercise the powers delegated to it by the general assembly of members, including under Article 8(4) and (6);

(b) to monitor the activities and the performance of the duties of the persons referred to in Article 10, including the implementation of the decisions of the general assembly of members and, in particular, of the general policies listed in points (a) to (d) of Article 8(5).

5. The body exercising the supervisory function shall report on the exercise of its powers to the general assembly of members at least once a year.

[2.818]
Article 10
Obligations of the persons who manage the business of the collective management organisation

1. Member States shall ensure that each collective management organisation takes all necessary measures so that the persons who manage its business do so in a sound, prudent and appropriate manner, using sound administrative and accounting procedures and internal control mechanisms.

2. Member States shall ensure that collective management organisations put in place and apply procedures to avoid conflicts of interest, and where such conflicts cannot be avoided, to identify, manage, monitor and disclose actual or potential conflicts of interest in such a way as to prevent them from adversely affecting the collective interests of the rightholders whom the organisation represents.

The procedures referred to in the first subparagraph shall include an annual individual statement by each of the persons referred to in paragraph 1 to the general assembly of members, containing the following information:

(a) any interests in the collective management organisation;

(b) any remuneration received in the preceding financial year from the collective management organisation, including in the form of pension schemes, benefits in kind and other types of benefits;

(c) any amounts received in the preceding financial year as a rightholder from the collective management organisation;

(d) a declaration concerning any actual or potential conflict between any personal interests and those of the collective management organisation or between any obligations owed to the collective management organisation and any duty owed to any other natural or legal person.

CHAPTER 2
MANAGEMENT OF RIGHTS REVENUE

[2.819]
Article 11
Collection and use of rights revenue

1. Member States shall ensure that collective management organisations comply with the rules laid down in paragraphs 2 to 5.

2. A collective management organisation shall be diligent in the collection and management of rights revenue.

3. A collective management organisation shall keep separate in its accounts:

(a) rights revenue and any income arising from the investment of rights revenue; and

(b) any own assets it may have and income arising from such assets, from management fees or from other activities.

4. A collective management organisation shall not be permitted to use rights revenue or any income arising from the investment of rights revenue for purposes other than distribution to rightholders, except where it is allowed to deduct or offset its management fees in compliance with a decision taken in accordance with point (d) of Article 8(5) or to use the rights revenue or any income arising from the investment of rights revenue in compliance with a decision taken in accordance with Article 8(5).

5. Where a collective management organisation invests rights revenue or any income arising from the investment of rights revenue, it shall do so in the best interests of the rightholders whose rights it represents, in accordance with the general investment and risk management policy referred to in points (c) and (f) of Article 8(5) and having regard to the following rules:

(a) where there is any potential conflict of interest, the collective management organisation shall ensure that the investment is made in the sole interest of those rightholders;

(b) the assets shall be invested in order to ensure the security, quality, liquidity and profitability of the portfolio as a whole;

(c) the assets shall be properly diversified in order to avoid excessive reliance on any particular asset and accumulations of risks in the portfolio as a whole.

[2.820]

Article 12

Deductions

1. Member States shall ensure that where a rightholder authorises a collective management organisation to manage his rights, the collective management organisation is required to provide the rightholder with information on management fees and other deductions from the rights revenue and from any income arising from the investment of rights revenue, before obtaining his consent to its managing his rights.

2. Deductions shall be reasonable in relation to the services provided by the collective management organisation to rightholders, including, where appropriate, the services referred to in paragraph 4, and shall be established on the basis of objective criteria.

3. Management fees shall not exceed the justified and documented costs incurred by the collective management organisation in managing copyright and related rights.

Member States shall ensure that the requirements applicable to the use and the transparency of the use of amounts deducted or offset in respect of management fees apply to any other deductions made in order to cover the costs of managing copyright and related rights.

4. Where a collective management organisation provides social, cultural or educational services funded through deductions from rights revenue or from any income arising from the investment of rights revenue, such services shall be provided on the basis of fair criteria, in particular as regards access to, and the extent of, those services.

[2.821]

Article 13

Distribution of amounts due to rightholders

1. Without prejudice to Article 15(3) and Article 28, Member States shall ensure that each collective management organisation regularly, diligently and accurately distributes and pays amounts due to rightholders in accordance with the general policy on distribution referred to in point (a) of Article 8(5).

Member States shall also ensure that collective management organisations or their members who are entities representing rightholders distribute and pay those amounts to rightholders as soon as possible but no later than nine months from the end of the financial year in which the rights revenue was collected, unless objective reasons relating in particular to reporting by users, identification of rights, rightholders or matching of information on works and other subject-matter with rightholders prevent the collective management organisation or, where applicable, its members from meeting that deadline.

2. Where the amounts due to rightholders cannot be distributed within the deadline set in paragraph 1 because the relevant rightholders cannot be identified or located and the exception to that deadline does not apply, those amounts shall be kept separate in the accounts of the collective management organisation.

3. The collective management organisation shall take all necessary measures, consistent with paragraph 1, to identify and locate the rightholders. In particular, at the latest three months after the expiry of the deadline set in paragraph 1, the collective management organisation shall make available information on works and other subject-matter for which one or more rightholders have not been identified or located to:

(a) the rightholders that it represents or the entities representing rightholders, where such entities are members of the collective management organisation; and

(b) all collective management organisations with which it has concluded representation agreements.

The information referred to in the first subparagraph shall include, where available, the following:

(a) the title of the work or other subject-matter;

(b) the name of the rightholder;

(c) the name of the relevant publisher or producer; and

(d) any other relevant information available which could assist in identifying the rightholder.

The collective management organisation shall also verify the records referred to in Article 6(5) and other readily available records. If the abovementioned measures fail to produce results, the collective management organisation shall make that information available to the public at the latest one year after the expiry of the three-month period.

4. Where the amounts due to rightholders cannot be distributed after three years from the end of the financial year in which the collection of the rights revenue occurred, and provided that the collective management organisation has taken all necessary measures to identify and locate the rightholders referred to in paragraph 3, those amounts shall be deemed non-distributable.

5. The general assembly of members of a collective management organisation shall decide on the use of the non-distributable amounts in accordance with point (b) of Article 8(5), without prejudice to the right of rightholders to claim such amounts from the collective management organisation in accordance with the laws of the Member States on the statute of limitations of claims.

6. Member States may limit or determine the permitted uses of non-distributable amounts, inter alia, by ensuring that such amounts are used in a separate and independent way in order to fund social, cultural and educational activities for the benefit of rightholders.

CHAPTER 3
MANAGEMENT OF RIGHTS ON BEHALF OF OTHER COLLECTIVE MANAGEMENT ORGANISATIONS

[2.822]
Article 14
Rights managed under representation agreements
Member States shall ensure that a collective management organisation does not discriminate against any rightholder whose rights it manages under a representation agreement, in particular with respect to applicable tariffs, management fees, and the conditions for the collection of the rights revenue and distribution of amounts due to rightholders.

[2.823]
Article 15
Deductions and payments in representation agreements
1. Member States shall ensure that a collective management organisation does not make deductions, other than in respect of management fees, from the rights revenue derived from the rights it manages on the basis of a representation agreement, or from any income arising from the investment of that rights revenue, unless the other collective management organisation that is party to the representation agreement expressly consents to such deductions.
2. The collective management organisation shall regularly, diligently and accurately distribute and pay amounts due to other collective management organisations.
3. The collective management organisation shall carry out such distribution and payments to the other collective management organisation as soon as possible but no later than nine months from the end of the financial year in which the rights revenue was collected, unless objective reasons relating in particular to reporting by users, identification of rights, rightholders or matching of information on works and other subject-matter with rightholders prevent the collective management organisation from meeting that deadline.
The other collective management organisation, or, where it has as members entities representing rightholders, those members, shall distribute and pay the amounts due to rightholders as soon as possible but no later than six months from receipt of those amounts, unless objective reasons relating in particular to reporting by users, identification of rights, rightholders or matching of information on works and other subject-matter with rightholders prevent the collective management organisation or, where applicable, its members from meeting that deadline.

CHAPTER 4
RELATIONS WITH USERS

[2.824]
Article 16
Licensing
1. Member States shall ensure that collective management organisations and users conduct negotiations for the licensing of rights in good faith. Collective management organisations and users shall provide each other with all necessary information.
2. Licensing terms shall be based on objective and non-discriminatory criteria. When licensing rights, collective management organisations shall not be required to use, as a precedent for other online services, licensing terms agreed with a user where the user is providing a new type of online service which has been available to the public in the Union for less than three years.
Rightholders shall receive appropriate remuneration for the use of their rights. Tariffs for exclusive rights and rights to remuneration shall be reasonable in relation to, inter alia, the economic value of the use of the rights in trade, taking into account the nature and scope of the use of the work and other subject-matter, as well as in relation to the economic value of the service provided by the collective management organisation. Collective management organisations shall inform the user concerned of the criteria used for the setting of those tariffs.
3. Collective management organisations shall reply without undue delay to requests from users, indicating, inter alia, the information needed in order for the collective management organisation to offer a licence.
Upon receipt of all relevant information, the collective management organisation shall, without undue delay, either offer a licence or provide the user with a reasoned statement explaining why it does not intend to license a particular service.
4. A collective management organisation shall allow users to communicate with it by electronic means, including, where appropriate, for the purpose of reporting on the use of the licence.

[2.825]
Article 17
Users' obligations
Member States shall adopt provisions to ensure that users provide a collective management organisation, within an agreed or pre-established time and in an agreed or pre-established format, with such relevant information at their disposal on the use of the rights represented by the collective management organisation as is necessary for the collection of rights revenue and for the distribution

and payment of amounts due to rightholders. When deciding on the format for the provision of such information, collective management organisations and users shall take into account, as far as possible, voluntary industry standards.

CHAPTER 5
TRANSPARENCY AND REPORTING

[2.826]
Article 18
Information provided to rightholders on the management of their rights

1. Without prejudice to paragraph 2 of this Article and Article 19 and Article 28(2), Member States shall ensure that a collective management organisation makes available, not less than once a year, to each rightholder to whom it has attributed rights revenue or made payments in the period to which the information relates, at least the following information:

(a) any contact details which the rightholder has authorised the collective management organisation to use in order to identify and locate the rightholder;
(b) the rights revenue attributed to the rightholder;
(c) the amounts paid by the collective management organisation to the rightholder per category of rights managed and per type of use;
(d) the period during which the use took place for which amounts were attributed and paid to the rightholder, unless objective reasons relating to reporting by users prevent the collective management organisation from providing this information;
(e) deductions made in respect of management fees;
(f) deductions made for any purpose other than in respect of management fees, including those that may be required by national law for the provision of any social, cultural or educational services;
(g) any rights revenue attributed to the rightholder which is outstanding for any period.

2. Where a collective management organisation attributes rights revenue and has as members entities which are responsible for the distribution of rights revenue to rightholders, the collective management organisation shall provide the information listed in paragraph 1 to those entities, provided that they do not have that information in their possession. Member States shall ensure that the entities make at least the information listed in paragraph 1 available, not less than once a year, to each rightholder to whom they have attributed rights revenue or made payments in the period to which the information relates.

[2.827]
Article 19
Information provided to other collective management organisations on the management of rights under representation agreements

Member States shall ensure that a collective management organisation makes at least the following information available, not less than once a year and by electronic means, to collective management organisations on whose behalf it manages rights under a representation agreement, for the period to which the information relates:

(a) the rights revenue attributed, the amounts paid by the collective management organisation per category of rights managed, and per type of use, for the rights it manages under the representation agreement, and any rights revenue attributed which is outstanding for any period;
(b) deductions made in respect of management fees;
(c) deductions made for any purpose other than in respect of management fees as referred to in Article 15;
(d) information on any licences granted or refused with regard to works and other subject-matter covered by the representation agreement;
(e) resolutions adopted by the general assembly of members in so far as those resolutions are relevant to the management of the rights under the representation agreement.

[2.828]
Article 20
Information provided to rightholders, other collective management organisations and users on request

Without prejudice to Article 25, Member States shall ensure that, in response to a duly justified request, a collective management organisation makes at least the following information available by electronic means and without undue delay to any collective management organisation on whose behalf it manages rights under a representation agreement or to any rightholder or to any user:

(a) the works or other subject-matter it represents, the rights it manages, directly or under representation agreements, and the territories covered; or
(b) where, due to the scope of activity of the collective management organisation, such works or other subject-matter cannot be determined, the types of works or of other subject-matter it represents, the rights it manages and the territories covered.

[2.829]
Article 21
Disclosure of information to the public

1. Member States shall ensure that a collective management organisation makes public at least the following information:

(a) its statute;
(b) its membership terms and the terms of termination of authorisation to manage rights, if these are not included in the statute;
(c) standard licensing contracts and standard applicable tariffs, including discounts;
(d) the list of the persons referred to in Article 10;
(e) its general policy on distribution of amounts due to rightholders;
(f) its general policy on management fees;
(g) its general policy on deductions, other than in respect of management fees, from rights revenue and from any income arising from the investment of rights revenue, including deductions for the purposes of social, cultural and educational services;
(h) a list of the representation agreements it has entered into, and the names of the collective management organisations with which those representation agreements have been concluded;
(i) the general policy on the use of non-distributable amounts;
(j) the complaint handling and dispute resolution procedures available in accordance with Articles 33, 34 and 35.

2. The collective management organisation shall publish, and keep up to date, on its public website the information referred to in paragraph 1.

[2.830]
Article 22
Annual transparency report

1. Member States shall ensure that a collective management organisation, irrespective of its legal form under national law, draws up and makes public an annual transparency report, including the special report referred to in paragraph 3, for each financial year no later than eight months following the end of that financial year.
The collective management organisation shall publish on its website the annual transparency report, which shall remain available to the public on that website for at least five years.
2. The annual transparency report shall contain at least the information set out in the Annex.
3. A special report shall address the use of the amounts deducted for the purposes of social, cultural and educational services and shall contain at least the information set out in point 3 of the Annex.
4. The accounting information included in the annual transparency report shall be audited by one or more persons empowered by law to audit accounts in accordance with Directive 2006/43/EC of the European Parliament and of the Council.[1]
The audit report, including any qualifications thereto, shall be reproduced in full in the annual transparency report.
For the purposes of this paragraph, accounting information shall comprise the financial statements referred to in point 1(a) of the Annex and any financial information referred to in points (g) and (h) of point 1 and in point 2 of the Annex.

NOTES

[1] Directive 2006/43/EC of the European Parliament and of the Council of 17 May 2006 on statutory audits of annual accounts and consolidated account, amending Council Directives 78/660/EEC and 83/349/EEC and repealing Council Directive 84/253/EEC (OJ L157, 9.6.2006, p 87).

TITLE III
MULTI-TERRITORIAL LICENSING OF ONLINE RIGHTS IN MUSICAL WORKS BY COLLECTIVE MANAGEMENT ORGANISATIONS

[2.831]
Article 23
Multi-territorial licensing in the internal market

Member States shall ensure that collective management organisations established in their territory comply with the requirements of this Title when granting multi-territorial licences for online rights in musical works.

[2.832]
Article 24
Capacity to process multi-territorial licences

1. Member States shall ensure that a collective management organisation which grants multi-territorial licences for online rights in musical works has sufficient capacity to process electronically, in an efficient and transparent manner, data needed for the administration of such licences, including for the purposes of identifying the repertoire and monitoring its use, invoicing users, collecting rights revenue and distributing amounts due to rightholders.

2. For the purposes of paragraph 1, a collective management organisation shall comply, at least, with the following conditions:

(a) to have the ability to identify accurately the musical works, wholly or in part, which the collective management organisation is authorised to represent;

(b) to have the ability to identify accurately, wholly or in part, with respect to each relevant territory, the rights and their corresponding rightholders for each musical work or share therein which the collective management organisation is authorised to represent;

(c) to make use of unique identifiers in order to identify rightholders and musical works, taking into account, as far as possible, voluntary industry standards and practices developed at international or Union level;

(d) to make use of adequate means in order to identify and resolve in a timely and effective manner inconsistencies in data held by other collective management organisations granting multi-territorial licences for online rights in musical works.

[2.833]
Article 25
Transparency of multi-territorial repertoire information

1. Member States shall ensure that a collective management organisation which grants multi-territorial licences for online rights in musical works provides to online service providers, to rightholders whose rights it represents and to other collective management organisations, by electronic means, in response to a duly justified request, up-to-date information allowing the identification of the online music repertoire it represents. This shall include:

(a) the musical works represented;

(b) the rights represented wholly or in part; and

(c) the territories covered.

2. The collective management organisation may take reasonable measures, where necessary, to protect the accuracy and integrity of the data, to control their reuse and to protect commercially sensitive information.

[2.834]
Article 26
Accuracy of multi-territorial repertoire information

1. Member States shall ensure that a collective management organisation which grants multi-territorial licences for online rights in musical works has in place arrangements to enable rightholders, other collective management organisations and online service providers to request a correction of the data referred to in the list of conditions under Article 24(2) or the information provided under Article 25, where such rightholders, collective management organisations and online service providers, on the basis of reasonable evidence, believe that the data or the information are inaccurate in respect of their online rights in musical works. Where the claims are sufficiently substantiated, the collective management organisation shall ensure that the data or the information are corrected without undue delay.

2. The collective management organisation shall provide rightholders whose musical works are included in its own music repertoire and rightholders who have entrusted the management of their online rights in musical works to it in accordance with Article 31 with the means of submitting to it in electronic form information concerning their musical works, their rights in those works and the territories in respect of which the rightholders authorise the organisation. When doing so, the collective management organisation and the rightholders shall take into account, as far as possible, voluntary industry standards or practices regarding the exchange of data developed at international or Union level, allowing rightholders to specify the musical work, wholly or in part, the online rights, wholly or in part, and the territories in respect of which they authorise the organisation.

3. Where a collective management organisation mandates another collective management organisation to grant multi-territorial licences for the online rights in musical works under Articles 29 and 30, the mandated collective management organisation shall also apply paragraph 2 of this Article with respect to the rightholders whose musical works are included in the repertoire of the mandating collective management organisation, unless the collective management organisations agree otherwise.

[2.835]
Article 27
Accurate and timely reporting and invoicing

1. Member States shall ensure that a collective management organisation monitors the use of online rights in musical works which it represents, wholly or in part, by online service providers to which it has granted a multi-territorial licence for those rights.

2. The collective management organisation shall offer online service providers the possibility of reporting by electronic means the actual use of online rights in musical works and online service providers shall accurately report the actual use of those works. The collective management organisation shall offer the use of a least one method of reporting which takes into account voluntary industry standards or practices developed at international or Union level for the electronic exchange of such data. The collective management organisation may refuse to accept reporting by the online service provider in a proprietary format if the organisation allows for reporting using an industry standard for the electronic exchange of data.

3. The collective management organisation shall invoice the online service provider by electronic means. The collective management organisation shall offer the use of a least one format which takes into account voluntary industry standards or practices developed at international or Union level. The invoice shall identify the works and rights which are licensed, wholly or in part, on the basis of the data referred to in the list of conditions under Article 24(2), and the corresponding actual uses, to the extent that this is possible on the basis of the information provided by the online service provider and the format used to provide that information. The online service provider may not refuse to accept the invoice because of its format if the collective management organisation is using an industry standard.

4. The collective management organisation shall invoice the online service provider accurately and without delay after the actual use of the online rights in that musical work is reported, except where this is not possible for reasons attributable to the online service provider.

5. The collective management organisation shall have in place adequate arrangements enabling the online service provider to challenge the accuracy of the invoice, including when the online service provider receives invoices from one or more collective management organisations for the same online rights in the same musical work.

[2.836]
Article 28
Accurate and timely payment to rightholders

1. Without prejudice to paragraph 3, Member States shall ensure that a collective management organisation which grants multi-territorial licences for online rights in musical works distributes amounts due to rightholders accruing from such licences accurately and without delay after the actual use of the work is reported, except where this is not possible for reasons attributable to the online service provider.

2. Without prejudice to paragraph 3, the collective management organisation shall provide at least the following information to rightholders together with each payment it makes under paragraph 1:
   (a) the period during which the uses took place for which amounts are due to rightholders and the territories in which the uses took place;
   (b) the amounts collected, deductions made and amounts distributed by the collective management organisation for each online right in any musical work which rightholders have authorised the collective management organisation, wholly or in part, to represent;
   (c) the amounts collected for rightholders, deductions made, and amounts distributed by the collective management organisation in respect of each online service provider.

3. Where a collective management organisation mandates another collective management organisation to grant multi-territorial licences for the online rights in musical works under Articles 29 and 30, the mandated collective management organisation shall distribute the amounts referred to in paragraph 1 accurately and without delay, and shall provide the information referred to in paragraph 2 to the mandating collective management organisation. The mandating collective management organisation shall be responsible for the subsequent distribution of such amounts and the provision of such information to rightholders, unless the collective management organisations agree otherwise.

[2.837]
Article 29
Agreements between collective management organisations for multi-territorial licensing

1. Member States shall ensure that any representation agreement between collective management organisations whereby a collective management organisation mandates another collective management organisation to grant multi-territorial licences for the online rights in musical works in its own music repertoire is of a non-exclusive nature. The mandated collective management organisation shall manage those online rights on a non-discriminatory basis.

2. The mandating collective management organisation shall inform its members of the main terms of the agreement, including its duration and the costs of the services provided by the mandated collective management organisation.

3. The mandated collective management organisation shall inform the mandating collective management organisation of the main terms according to which the latter's online rights are to be licensed, including the nature of the exploitation, all provisions which relate to or affect the licence fee, the duration of the licence, the accounting periods and the territories covered.

[2.838]
Article 30
Obligation to represent another collective management organisation for multi-territorial licensing

1. Member States shall ensure that where a collective management organisation which does not grant or offer to grant multi-territorial licences for the online rights in musical works in its own repertoire requests another collective management organisation to enter into a representation agreement to represent those rights, the requested collective management organisation is required to agree to such a request if it is already granting or offering to grant multi-territorial licences for the same category of online rights in musical works in the repertoire of one or more other collective management organisations.
2. The requested collective management organisation shall respond to the requesting collective management organisation in writing and without undue delay.
3. Without prejudice to paragraphs 5 and 6, the requested collective management organisation shall manage the represented repertoire of the requesting collective management organisation on the same conditions as those which it applies to the management of its own repertoire.
4. The requested collective management organisation shall include the represented repertoire of the requesting collective management organisation in all offers it addresses to online service providers.
5. The management fee for the service provided by the requested collective management organisation to the requesting organisation shall not exceed the costs reasonably incurred by the requested collective management organisation.
6. The requesting collective management organisation shall make available to the requested collective management organisation information relating to its own music repertoire required for the provision of multi-territorial licences for online rights in musical works. Where information is insufficient or provided in a form that does not allow the requested collective management organisation to meet the requirements of this Title, the requested collective management organisation shall be entitled to charge for the costs reasonably incurred in meeting such requirements or to exclude those works for which information is insufficient or cannot be used.

[2.839]
Article 31
Access to multi-territorial licensing

Member States shall ensure that where a collective management organisation does not grant or offer to grant multi-territorial licences for online rights in musical works or does not allow another collective management organisation to represent those rights for such purpose by 10 April 2017, rightholders who have authorised that collective management organisation to represent their online rights in musical works can withdraw from that collective management organisation the online rights in musical works for the purposes of multi-territorial licensing in respect of all territories without having to withdraw the online rights in musical works for the purposes of mono-territorial licensing, so as to grant multi-territorial licences for their online rights in musical works themselves or through any other party they authorise or through any collective management organisation complying with the provisions of this Title.

[2.840]
Article 32
Derogation for online music rights required for radio and television programmes

The requirements under this Title shall not apply to collective management organisations when they grant, on the basis of the voluntary aggregation of the required rights, in compliance with the competition rules under Articles 101 and 102 TFEU, a multi-territorial licence for the online rights in musical works required by a broadcaster to communicate or make available to the public its radio or television programmes simultaneously with or after their initial broadcast as well as any online material, including previews, produced by or for the broadcaster which is ancillary to the initial broadcast of its radio or television programme.

TITLE IV
ENFORCEMENT MEASURES

[2.841]
Article 33
Complaints procedures

1. Member States shall ensure that collective management organisations make available to their members, and to collective management organisations on whose behalf they manage rights under a representation agreement, effective and timely procedures for dealing with complaints, particularly in relation to authorisation to manage rights and termination or withdrawal of rights, membership terms, the collection of amounts due to rightholders, deductions and distributions.
2. Collective management organisations shall respond in writing to complaints by members or by collective management organisations on whose behalf they manage rights under a representation agreement. Where the collective management organisation rejects a complaint, it shall give reasons.

[2.842]
Article 34
Alternative dispute resolution procedures

1. Member States may provide that disputes between collective management organisations, members of collective management organisations, rightholders or users regarding the provisions of national law adopted pursuant to the requirements of this Directive can be submitted to a rapid, independent and impartial alternative dispute resolution procedure.
2. Member States shall ensure, for the purposes of Title III, that the following disputes relating to a collective management organisation established in their territory which grants or offers to grant multi-territorial licences for online rights in musical works can be submitted to an independent and impartial alternative dispute resolution procedure:
   (a) disputes with an actual or potential online service provider regarding the application of Articles 16, 25, 26 and 27;
   (b) disputes with one or more rightholders regarding the application of Articles 25, 26, 27, 28, 29, 30 and 31;
   (c) disputes with another collective management organisation regarding the application of Articles 25, 26, 27, 28, 29 and 30.

[2.843]
Article 35
Dispute resolution

1. Member States shall ensure that disputes between collective management organisations and users concerning, in particular, existing and proposed licensing conditions or a breach of contract can be submitted to a court, or if appropriate, to another independent and impartial dispute resolution body where that body has expertise in intellectual property law.
2. Articles 33 and 34 and paragraph 1 of this Article shall be without prejudice to the right of parties to assert and defend their rights by bringing an action before a court.

[2.844]
Article 36
Compliance

1. Member States shall ensure that compliance by collective management organisations established in their territory with the provisions of national law adopted pursuant to the requirements laid down in this Directive is monitored by competent authorities designated for that purpose.
2. Member States shall ensure that procedures exist enabling members of a collective management organisation, rightholders, users, collective management organisations and other interested parties to notify the competent authorities designated for that purpose of activities or circumstances which, in their opinion, constitute a breach of the provisions of national law adopted pursuant to the requirements laid down in this Directive.
3. Member States shall ensure that the competent authorities designated for that purpose have the power to impose appropriate sanctions or to take appropriate measures where the provisions of national law adopted in implementation of this Directive have not been complied with. Those sanctions and measures shall be effective, proportionate and dissuasive.

Member States shall notify the Commission of the competent authorities referred to in this Article and in Articles 37 and 38 by 10 April 2016. The Commission shall publish the information received in that regard.

[2.845]
Article 37
Exchange of information between competent authorities

1. In order to facilitate the monitoring of the application of this Directive, each Member State shall ensure that a request for information received from a competent authority of another Member State, designated for that purpose, concerning matters relevant to the application of this

Directive, in particular with regard to the activities of collective management organisations established in the territory of the requested Member State, is responded to without undue delay by the competent authority designated for that purpose, provided that the request is duly justified.

2. Where a competent authority considers that a collective management organisation established in another Member State but acting within its territory may not be complying with the provisions of the national law of the Member State in which that collective management organisation is established which have been adopted pursuant to the requirements laid down in this Directive, it may transmit all relevant information to the competent authority of the Member State in which the collective management organisation is established, accompanied where appropriate by a request to that authority that it take appropriate action within its competence. The requested competent authority shall provide a reasoned reply within three months.

3. Matters as referred to in paragraph 2 may also be referred by the competent authority making such a request to the expert group established in accordance with Article 41.

[2.846]
Article 38
Cooperation for the development of multi-territorial licensing

1. The Commission shall foster a regular exchange of information between the competent authorities designated for that purpose in Member States, and between those authorities and the Commission, on the situation and development of multi-territorial licensing.

2. The Commission shall conduct regular consultations with representatives of rightholders, collective management organisations, users, consumers and other interested parties on their experience with the application of the provisions of Title III of this Directive. The Commission shall provide competent authorities with all relevant information that emerges from those consultations, within the framework of the exchange of information provided for in paragraph 1.

3. Member States shall ensure that by 10 October 2017, their competent authorities provide the Commission with a report on the situation and development of multi-territorial licensing in their territory. The report shall include information on, in particular, the availability of multi-territorial licences in the Member State concerned and compliance by collective management organisations with the provisions of national law adopted in implementation of Title III of this Directive, together with an assessment of the development of multi-territorial licensing of online rights in musical works by users, consumers, rightholders and other interested parties.

4. On the basis of the reports received pursuant to paragraph 3 and the information gathered pursuant to paragraphs 1 and 2, the Commission shall assess the application of Title III of this Directive. If necessary, and where appropriate on the basis of a specific report, it shall consider further steps to address any identified problems. That assessment shall cover, in particular, the following:

(a) the number of collective management organisations meeting the requirements of Title III;
(b) the application of Articles 29 and 30, including the number of representation agreements concluded by collective management organisations pursuant to those Articles;
(c) the proportion of repertoire in the Member States which is available for licensing on a multi-territorial basis.

TITLE V
REPORTING AND FINAL PROVISIONS

[2.847]
Article 39
Notification of collective management organisations

By 10 April 2016, Member States shall provide the Commission, on the basis of the information at their disposal, with a list of the collective management organisations established in their territories. Member States shall notify any changes to that list to the Commission without undue delay.
The Commission shall publish that information and keep it up to date.

[2.848]
Article 40
Report

By 10 April 2021, the Commission shall assess the application of this Directive and submit to the European Parliament and to the Council a report on the application of this Directive. That report shall include an assessment of the impact of this Directive on the development of cross-border services, on cultural diversity, on the relations between collective management organisations and users and on the operation in the Union of collective management organisations established outside the Union, and, if necessary, on the need for a review. The Commission's report shall be accompanied, if appropriate, by a legislative proposal.

[2.849]
Article 41
Expert group

An expert group is hereby established. It shall be composed of representatives of the competent authorities of the Member States. The expert group shall be chaired by a representative of the Commission and shall meet either on the initiative of the chairman or at the request of the delegation of a Member State. The tasks of the group shall be as follows:

(a) to examine the impact of the transposition of this Directive on the functioning of collective management organisations and independent management entities in the internal market, and to highlight any difficulties;
(b) to organise consultations on all questions arising from the application of this Directive;
(c) to facilitate the exchange of information on relevant developments in legislation and case-law, as well as relevant economic, social, cultural and technological developments, especially in relation to the digital market in works and other subject-matter.

[2.850]
Article 42
Protection of personal data

The processing of personal data carried out within the framework of this Directive shall be subject to Directive 95/46/EC.

[2.851]
Article 43
Transposition

1. Member States shall bring into force the laws, regulations and administrative provisions necessary to comply with this Directive by 10 April 2016. They shall immediately inform the Commission thereof.

When Member States adopt those measures, they shall contain a reference to this Directive or shall be accompanied by such reference on the occasion of their official publication. The methods of making such reference shall be laid down by Member States.

2. Member States shall communicate to the Commission the text of the main measures of national law which they adopt in the field covered by this Directive.

[2.852]
Article 44
Entry into force

This Directive shall enter into force on the twentieth day following that of its publication in the *Official Journal of the European Union*.

[2.853]
Article 45
Addressees

This Directive is addressed to the Member States.

ANNEX

[2.854]

1. Information to be provided in the annual transparency report referred to in Article 22(2):
   (a) financial statements comprising a balance-sheet or a statement of assets and liabilities, an income and expenditure account for the financial year and a cash-flow statement;
   (b) a report on the activities in the financial year;
   (c) information on refusals to grant a licence pursuant to Article 16(3);
   (d) a description of the legal and governance structure of the collective management organisation;
   (e) information on any entities directly or indirectly owned or controlled, wholly or in part, by the collective management organisation;
   (f) information on the total amount of remuneration paid to the persons referred in Article 9(3) and Article 10 in the previous year, and on other benefits granted to them;
   (g) the financial information referred to in point 2 of this Annex;
   (h) a special report on the use of any amounts deducted for the purposes of social, cultural and educational services, containing the information referred to in point 3 of this Annex.

2. Financial information to be provided in the annual transparency report:
   (a) financial information on rights revenue, per category of rights managed and per type of use (e.g. broadcasting, online, public performance), including information on the income arising from the investment of rights revenue and the use of such income (whether it is distributed to rightholders or other collective management organisations, or otherwise used);
   (b) financial information on the cost of rights management and other services provided by the collective management organisation to rightholders, with a comprehensive description of at least the following items:
      (i) all operating and financial costs, with a breakdown per category of rights managed and, where costs are indirect and cannot be attributed to one or more categories of rights, an explanation of the method used to allocate such indirect costs;

(ii) operating and financial costs, with a breakdown per category of rights managed and, where costs are indirect and cannot be attributed to one or more categories of rights, an explanation of the method used to allocate such indirect costs, only with regard to the management of rights, including management fees deducted from or offset against rights revenue or any income arising from the investment of rights revenue in accordance with Article 11(4) and Article 12(1), (2) and (3);

(iii) operating and financial costs with regard to services other than the management of rights, but including social, cultural and educational services;

(iv) resources used to cover costs;

(v) deductions made from rights revenues, with a breakdown per category of rights managed and per type of use and the purpose of the deduction, such as costs relating to the management of rights or to social, cultural or educational services;

(vi) the percentages that the cost of the rights management and other services provided by the collective management organisation to rightholders represents compared to the rights revenue in the relevant financial year, per category of rights managed, and, where costs are indirect and cannot be attributed to one or more categories of rights, an explanation of the method used to allocate such indirect costs;

(c) financial information on amounts due to rightholders, with a comprehensive description of at least the following items:

(i) the total amount attributed to rightholders, with a breakdown per category of rights managed and type of use;

(ii) the total amount paid to rightholders, with a breakdown per category of rights managed and type of use;

(iii) the frequency of payments, with a breakdown per category of rights managed and per type of use;

(iv) the total amount collected but not yet attributed to rightholders, with a breakdown per category of rights managed and type of use, and indicating the financial year in which those amounts were collected;

(v) the total amount attributed to but not yet distributed to rightholders, with a breakdown per category of rights managed and type of use, and indicating the financial year in which those amounts were collected;

(vi) where a collective management organisation has not carried out the distribution and payments within the deadline set in Article 13(1), the reasons for the delay;

(vii) the total non-distributable amounts, along with an explanation of the use to which those amounts have been put;

(d) information on relationships with other collective management organisations, with a description of at least the following items:

(i) amounts received from other collective management organisations and amounts paid to other collective management organisations, with a breakdown per category of rights, per type of use and per organisation;

(ii) management fees and other deductions from the rights revenue due to other collective management organisations, with a breakdown per category of rights, per type of use and per organisation;

(iii) management fees and other deductions from the amounts paid by other collective management organisations, with a breakdown per category of rights and per organisation;

(iv) amounts distributed directly to rightholders originating from other collective management organisations, with a breakdown per category of rights and per organisation.

3. Information to be provided in the special report referred to in Article 22(3):

(a) the amounts deducted for the purposes of social, cultural and educational services in the financial year, with a breakdown per type of purpose and, for each type of purpose, with a breakdown per category of rights managed and per type of use;

(b) an explanation of the use of those amounts, with a breakdown per type of purpose including the costs of managing amounts deducted to fund social, cultural and educational services and of the separate amounts used for social, cultural and educational services.

PART 3
DESIGNS

REGISTERED DESIGNS ACT 1949

(1949 c 88)

NOTES

Modification: this Act is modified in its application to the Isle of Man, by the Registered Designs (Isle of Man) Order 2013, SI 2013/2533, art 3(1), Sch 1.

ARRANGEMENT OF SECTIONS

Registrable designs and proceedings for registration

Part 3 Designs

An Act to consolidate certain enactments relating to registered designs

[16 December 1949]

NOTES

Trade marks and registered trade marks: note that references to trade marks and registered trade marks within the meaning of the Trade Marks Act 1938 shall, unless the context otherwise requires, be construed after the commencement of the Trade Marks Act 1994 as references to trade marks and registered trade marks within the meaning of that Act, by virtue of the Trade Marks Act 1994, s 102(1), Sch 4, para 1.

Registrable designs and proceedings for registration

[3.1]

[1 Registration of designs

(1) A design may, subject to the following provisions of this Act, be registered under this Act on the making of an application for registration.

(2) In this Act "design" means the appearance of the whole or a part of a product resulting from the features of, in particular, the lines, contours, colours, shape, texture or materials of the product or its ornamentation.

(3) In this Act—

"complex product" means a product which is composed of at least two replaceable component parts permitting disassembly and reassembly of the product; and

"product" means any industrial or handicraft item other than a computer program; and, in particular, includes packaging, get-up, graphic symbols, typographic type-faces and parts intended to be assembled into a complex product.]

NOTES

Substituted, together with ss 1A–1D for original s 1, by the Registered Designs Regulations 2001, SI 2001/3949, reg 2; for transitional provisions in relation to certain applications and registrations, see regs 10–14 of those Regulations at **[3.88]**–**[3.92]**.

1A (*Substituted as noted to s 1 at* **[3.1]***; repealed by the Regulatory Reform (Registered Designs) Order 2006, SI 2006/1974, arts 2, 3.*)

[3.2]

[1B Requirement of novelty and individual character

(1) A design shall be protected by a right in a registered design to the extent that the design is new and has individual character.

(2) For the purposes of subsection (1) above, a design is new if no identical design or no design whose features differ only in immaterial details has been made available to the public before the relevant date.

(3) For the purposes of subsection (1) above, a design has individual character if the overall impression it produces on the informed user differs from the overall impression produced on such a user by any design which has been made available to the public before the relevant date.

(4) In determining the extent to which a design has individual character, the degree of freedom of the author in creating the design shall be taken into consideration.

(5) For the purposes of this section, a design has been made available to the public before the relevant date if—

(a) it has been published (whether following registration or otherwise), exhibited, used in trade or otherwise disclosed before that date; and

(b) the disclosure does not fall within subsection (6) below.

(6) A disclosure falls within this subsection if—

(a) it could not reasonably have become known before the relevant date in the normal course of business to persons carrying on business in the European Economic Area and specialising in the sector concerned;

(b) it was made to a person other than the designer, or any successor in title of his, under conditions of confidentiality (whether express or implied);

(c) it was made by the designer, or any successor in title of his, during the period of 12 months immediately preceding the relevant date;

(d) it was made by a person other than the designer, or any successor in title of his, during the period of 12 months immediately preceding the relevant date in consequence of information provided or other action taken by the designer or any successor in title of his; or

(e) it was made during the period of 12 months immediately preceding the relevant date as a consequence of an abuse in relation to the designer or any successor in title of his.

(7) In subsections (2), (3), (5) and (6) above "the relevant date" means the date on which the application for the registration of the design was made or is treated by virtue of section 3B(2), (3) or (5) or 14(2) of this Act as having been made.

(8) For the purposes of this section, a design applied to or incorporated in a product which constitutes a component part of a complex product shall only be considered to be new and to have individual character—

(a) if the component part, once it has been incorporated into the complex product, remains visible during normal use of the complex product; and

(b) to the extent that those visible features of the component part are in themselves new and have individual character.

(9) In subsection (8) above "normal use" means use by the end user; but does not include any maintenance, servicing or repair work in relation to the product.]

NOTES

Substituted as noted to s 1 at **[3.1]**.

[3.3]

[1C Designs dictated by their technical function

(1) A right in a registered design shall not subsist in features of appearance of a product which are solely dictated by the product's technical function.

(2) A right in a registered design shall not subsist in features of appearance of a product which must necessarily be reproduced in their exact form and dimensions so as to permit the product in which the design is incorporated or to which it is applied to be mechanically connected to, or placed in, around or against, another product so that either product may perform its function.
(3) Subsection (2) above does not prevent a right in a registered design subsisting in a design serving the purpose of allowing multiple assembly or connection of mutually interchangeable products within a modular system.]

NOTES

Substituted as noted to s 1 at **[3.1]**.

[3.4]
[1D Designs contrary to public policy or morality

A right in a registered design shall not subsist in a design which is contrary to public policy or to accepted principles of morality.]

NOTES

Substituted as noted to s 1 at **[3.1]**.

[3.5]
2 Proprietorship of designs

[(1) The author of a design shall be treated for the purposes of this Act as the original proprietor of the design, subject to the following provisions.
(1A) Where a design is created in pursuance of a commission for money or money's worth, the person commissioning the design shall be treated as the original proprietor of the design.
(1B) Where, *in a case not falling within subsection (1A),* a design is created by an employee in the course of his employment, his employer shall be treated as the original proprietor of the design.]
(2) Where a design . . . becomes vested, whether by assignment, transmission or operation of law, in any person other than the original proprietor, either alone or jointly with the original proprietor, that other person, or as the case may be the original proprietor and that other person, shall be treated for the purposes of this Act as the proprietor of the design . . .
[(3) In this Act the "author" of a design means the person who creates it.
(4) In the case of a design generated by computer in circumstances such that there is no human author, the person by whom the arrangements necessary for the creation of the design are made shall be taken to be the author.]

NOTES

Sub-ss (1)–(1B): substituted, for original sub-s (1), by the Copyright, Designs and Patents Act 1988, s 267(2), except in relation to applications for registrations before 1 August 1989; sub-s (1A) and words in italics in sub-s (1B) repealed by the Intellectual Property Act 2014, s 6(1), except in relation to any design created before 1 October 2014, or any design created on or after that date in pursuance of a commission (irrespective of whether the design was commissioned before, on or after that date) provided that (i) the designer and the commissioner of the design have entered into a contract relating to the commission of the design, and (ii) the contract was entered into before 1 October 2014.

Sub-s (2): words omitted repealed by the Registered Designs Regulations 2001, SI 2001/3949, reg 9(2), Sch 2; for transitional provisions in relation to certain applications and registrations, see regs 10–14 of those Regulations at **[3.88]**–**[3.92]**.

Sub-ss (3), (4): added by the Copyright, Designs and Patents Act 1988, s 267(3), except in relation to applications for registration before 1 August 1989.

[3.6]
[3 Applications for registration

(1) An application for the registration of a design [or designs] *shall be made in the prescribed form and* shall be filed at the Patent Office in the prescribed manner.
(2) . . .
(3) An application for the registration of a design [or designs] in which national unregistered design right subsists shall be made by the person claiming to be the design right owner.
(4) . . .
(5) An application for the registration of a design which, owing to any default or neglect on the part of the applicant, has not been completed so as to enable registration to be effected within such time as may be prescribed shall be deemed to be abandoned.]

NOTES

Substituted, together with ss 3A–3D for original s 3, by the Registered Designs Regulations 2001, SI 2001/3949, reg 4; for transitional provisions in relation to certain applications and registrations, see regs 10–14 of those Regulations at **[3.88]**–**[3.92]**.

Sub-s (1): words in square brackets inserted by the Regulatory Reform (Registered Designs) Order 2006, SI 2006/1974, arts 2, 11; words in italics repealed by the Intellectual Property Act 2014, s 12(2), as from 1 October 2014, subject to s 12(5) thereof which provides that any rules made in reliance on sub-s (1) above which are in force immediately before 1 October 2014, continue in force until such time as directions about forms of the kind which had been prescribed by the rules take effect.

Sub-s (2): repealed by the Intellectual Property Act 2014, s 6(2).

Sub-s (3): words in square brackets inserted by the Regulatory Reform (Registered Designs) Order 2006, SI 2006/1974, arts 2, 11.

Sub-s (4): repealed by SI 2006/1974, arts 2, 4.

[3.7]

[3A Determination of applications for registration

(1) Subject as follows, the registrar shall not refuse [to register a design included in an application under this Act].

(2) If it appears to the registrar that an application for the registration of a design [or designs] has not been made in accordance with any rules made under this Act, he may refuse [to register any design included in it].

(3) If it appears to the registrar that [the applicant is not under section 3(2) or (3) or 14 entitled to apply for the registration of a design included in the application, he shall refuse to register that design.]

[(4) If it appears to the registrar that the application for registration includes—

(a) something which does not fulfil the requirements of section 1(2) of this Act;

(b) a design that does not fulfil the requirements of section 1C or 1D of this Act; or

(c) a design to which a ground of refusal mentioned in Schedule A1 to this Act applies,

he shall refuse to register that thing or that design.]]

NOTES

Substituted as noted to s 3 at **[3.6]**.

Sub-ss (1), (3): words in square brackets substituted by the Regulatory Reform (Registered Designs) Order 2006, SI 2006/1974, arts 2, 12(1), (2), (4).

Sub-s (2): words in first pair of square brackets inserted and words in second pair of square brackets substituted by SI 2006/1974, arts 2, 12(1), (3).

Sub-s (4): substituted by SI 2006/1974, arts 2, 5.

[3.8]

[3B Modification of applications for registration

(1) The registrar may, at any time before an application for the registration of a design [or designs] is determined, permit the applicant to make such modifications of the application as the registrar thinks fit.

(2) Where an application for the registration of a design [or designs] has been modified before it has been determined in such a way that [any design included in the application] has been altered significantly, the registrar may, for the purpose of deciding whether and to what extent the design is new or has individual character, direct that the application [so far as relating to that design] shall be treated as having been made on the date on which it was so modified.

(3) Where—

(a) an application for the registration of [more than one design] has been modified before it has been determined to exclude one or more designs from the application; and

(b) a subsequent application for the registration of a design so excluded has, within such period (if any) as has been prescribed for such applications, been made by the person who made the earlier application or his successor in title,

the registrar may, for the purpose of deciding whether and to what extent the design is new or has individual character, direct that the subsequent application shall be treated as having been made on the date on which the earlier application was, or is treated as having been, made.

(4) Where . . . the registration of a design has been refused on any ground mentioned in [section 3A(4)(b) or (c)] of this Act, the application [for the design] may be modified by the applicant if it appears to the registrar that—

(a) the identity of the design is retained; and

(b) the modifications have been made in accordance with any rules made under this Act.

(5) An application modified under subsection (4) above shall be treated as the original application and, in particular, as made on the date on which the original application was made or is treated as having been made.

(6) Any modification under this section may, in particular, be effected by making a partial disclaimer in relation to the application.]

NOTES

Substituted as noted to s 3 at **[3.6]**.

Sub-s (1): words in square brackets inserted by the Regulatory Reform (Registered Designs) Order 2006, SI 2006/1974, arts 2, 13(1), (2).

Sub-s (2): words in first and third pairs of square brackets inserted and words in second pair of square brackets substituted by SI 2006/1974, arts 2, 13(1), (3).

Sub-s (3): words in square brackets substituted by SI 2006/1974, arts 2, 13(1), (4).

Sub-s (4): words omitted repealed, words in first pair of square brackets substituted and words in second pair of square brackets inserted, by SI 2006/1974, arts 2, 6, 13(1), (5).

[3.9]

[3C Date of registration of designs

(1) Subject as follows, a design, when registered, shall be registered as of the date on which the application was made or is treated as having been made.

(2) Subsection (1) above shall not apply to an application which is treated as having been made on a particular date by section 14(2) of this Act or by virtue of the operation of section 3B(3) or (5) of this Act by reference to section 14(2) of this Act.

(3) A design, when registered, shall be registered as of—

(a) in the case of an application which is treated as having been made on a particular date by section 14(2) of this Act, the date on which the application was made;

(b) in the case of an application which is treated as having been made on a particular date by virtue of the operation of section 3B(3) of this Act by reference to section 14(2) of this Act, the date on which the earlier application was made;

(c) in the case of an application which is treated as having been made on a particular date by virtue of the operation of section 3B(5) of this Act by reference to section 14(2) of this Act, the date on which the original application was made.]

NOTES

Substituted as noted to s 3 at **[3.6]**.

[3.10]

[3D Appeals in relation to applications for registration

An appeal lies from any decision of the registrar under section 3A or 3B of this Act.]

NOTES

Substituted as noted to s 3 at **[3.6]**.

4 (*Repealed by the Registered Designs Regulations 2001, SI 2001/3949, reg 9(2), Sch 2; for transitional provisions in relation to certain applications and registrations, see regs 10–14 of those Regulations at* **[3.88]**–**[3.92]**).

[3.11]

5 Provisions for secrecy of certain designs

(1) Where, either before or after the commencement of this Act, an application for the registration of a design has been made, and it appears to the registrar that the design is one of a class notified to him by [the Secretary of State] as relevant for defence purposes, he may give directions for prohibiting or restricting the publication of information with respect to the design, or the communication of such information to any person or class of persons specified in the directions.

[(2) The Secretary of State shall by rules make provision for securing that where such directions are given—

(a) the representation or specimen of the design, . . .

(b) . . .

shall not be open to public inspection at the Patent Office during the continuance in force of the directions.]

(3) Where the registrar gives any such directions as aforesaid, he shall give notice of the application and of the directions to [the Secretary of State], and thereupon the following provisions shall have effect, that is to say—

(a) [the Secretary of State] shall, upon receipt of such notice, consider whether the publication of the design would be prejudicial to the defence of the realm and unless a notice under paragraph (c) of this subsection has previously been given by that authority to the registrar, shall reconsider that question before the expiration of nine months from the date of filing of the application for registration of the design and at least once in every subsequent year;

(b) for the purpose aforesaid, [the Secretary of State] may, at any time after the design has been registered or, with the consent of the applicant, at any time before the design has been registered, inspect the representation or specimen of the design [. . .] filed in pursuance of the application;

(c) if upon consideration of the design at any time it appears to [the Secretary of State] that the publication of the design would not, or would no longer, be prejudicial to the defence of the realm, [he] shall give notice to the registrar to that effect;

(d) on the receipt of any such notice the registrar shall revoke the directions and may, subject to such conditions, if any, as he thinks fit, extend the time for doing anything required or authorised to be done by or under this Act in connection with the application or registration, whether or not that time has previously expired.

(4) No person resident in the United Kingdom shall, except under the authority of a written permit granted by or on behalf of the registrar, make or cause to be made any application outside the United Kingdom for the registration of a design of any class prescribed for the purposes of this subsection unless—

(a) an application for registration of the same design has been made in the United Kingdom not less than six weeks before the application outside the United Kingdom; and

(b) either no directions have been given under subsection (1) of this section in relation to the application in the United Kingdom or all such directions have been revoked:

Provided that this subsection shall not apply in relation to a design for which an application for protection has first been filed in a country outside the United Kingdom by a person resident outside the United Kingdom.

(5) . . .

NOTES

Sub-s (1): words in square brackets substituted by the Copyright, Designs and Patents Act 1988, s 272, Sch 3, para 3.

Sub-s (2): substituted by the Copyright, Designs and Patents Act 1988, s 272, Sch 3, para 3; para (b) and word immediately preceding it repealed by the Registered Designs Regulations 2001, SI 2001/3949, reg 9(2), Sch 2, for transitional provisions in relation to certain applications and registrations, see regs 10–14 of those Regulations at **[3.88]–[3.92]**.

Sub-s (3): words in square brackets substituted by the Copyright, Designs and Patents Act 1988, s 272, Sch 3, para 3; words omitted from para (b) repealed by SI 2001/3949, reg 9(2), Sch 2, for transitional provisions in relation to certain applications and registrations, see regs 10–14 of those Regulations at **[3.88]–[3.92]**.

Sub-s (5): repealed by the Copyright, Designs and Patents Act 1988, ss 272, 303(2), Sch 3, para 3, Sch 8.

6 (*Repealed by the Registered Designs Regulations 2001, SI 2001/3949, reg 9(2), Sch 2; for transitional provisions in relation to certain applications and registrations, see regs 10–14 of those Regulations at* **[3.88]–[3.92]**.)

Effect of registration, &c

[3.12]

[7 Right given by registration

(1) The registration of a design under this Act gives the registered proprietor the exclusive right to use the design and any design which does not produce on the informed user a different overall impression.

(2) For the purposes of subsection (1) above and section 7A of this Act any reference to the use of a design includes a reference to—

(a) the making, offering, putting on the market, importing, exporting or using of a product in which the design is incorporated or to which it is applied; or

(b) stocking such a product for those purposes.

(3) In determining for the purposes of subsection (1) above whether a design produces a different overall impression on the informed user, the degree of freedom of the author in creating his design shall be taken into consideration.

(4) The right conferred by subsection (1) above is subject to any limitation attaching to the registration in question (including, in particular, any partial disclaimer or any declaration by the registrar or a court of partial invalidity).]

NOTES

Substituted, together with s 7A, for original s 7, by the Registered Designs Regulations 2001, SI 2001/3949, reg 5; for transitional provisions in relation to certain applications and registrations, see regs 10–14 of those Regulations at **[3.88]–[3.92]**.

[3.13]

[7A Infringements of rights in registered designs

(1) Subject as follows, the right in a registered design is infringed by a person who, without the consent of the registered proprietor, does anything which by virtue of section 7 of this Act is the exclusive right of the registered proprietor.

(2) The right in a registered design is not infringed by—

(a) an act which is done privately and for purposes which are not commercial;

(b) an act which is done for experimental purposes;

(c) an act of reproduction for teaching purposes or for the purpose of making citations provided that the conditions mentioned in subsection (3) below are satisfied;

(d) the use of equipment on ships or aircraft which are registered in another country but which are temporarily in the United Kingdom;

(e) the importation into the United Kingdom of spare parts or accessories for the purpose of repairing such ships or aircraft; or

(f) the carrying out of repairs on such ships or aircraft.

(3) The conditions mentioned in this subsection are—

(a) the act of reproduction is compatible with fair trade practice and does not unduly prejudice the normal exploitation of the design; and

(b) mention is made of the source.

(4) The right in a registered design is not infringed by an act which relates to a product in which any design protected by the registration is incorporated or to which it is applied if the product has been put on the market in the European Economic Area by the registered proprietor or with his consent.

(5) The right in a registered design of a component part which may be used for the purpose of the repair of a complex product so as to restore its original appearance is not infringed by the use for that purpose of any design protected by the registration.

(6) No proceedings shall be taken in respect of an infringement of the right in a registered design committed before the date on which the certificate of registration of the design under this Act is granted.]

NOTES

Substituted as noted to s 7 at **[3.12]**.

[3.14]

[7B Right of prior use

(1) A person who, before the application date, used a registered design in good faith or made serious and effective preparations to do so may continue to use the design for the purposes for which, before that date, the person had used it or made the preparations to use it.

(2) In subsection (1), the "application date", in relation to a registered design, means—

(a) the date on which an application for the registration was made under section 3, or

(b) where an application for the registration was treated as having been made by virtue of section 14(2), the date on which it was treated as having been so made.

(3) Subsection (1) does not apply if the design which the person used, or made preparations to use, was copied from the design which was subsequently registered.

(4) The right conferred on a person by subsection (1) does not include a right to licence another person to use the design.

(5) Nor may the person on whom the right under subsection (1) is conferred assign the right, or transmit it on death (or in the case of a body corporate on its dissolution), unless—

(a) the design was used, or the preparations for its use were made, in the course of a business, and

(b) the right is assigned or transmitted with the part of the business in which the design was used or the preparations for its use were made.]

NOTES

Commencement: 1 October 2014.

Inserted by the Intellectual Property Act 2014, s 7, in relation to designs registered under this Act after 1 October 2014.

[3.15]

[8 Duration of right in registered design

(1) The right in a registered design subsists in the first instance for a period of five years from the date of the registration of the design.

(2) The period for which the right subsists may be extended for a second, third, fourth and fifth period of five years, by applying to the registrar for an extension and paying the prescribed renewal fee.

(3) If the first, second, third or fourth period expires without such application and payment being made, the right shall cease to have effect; and the registrar shall, in accordance with rules made by the Secretary of State, notify the proprietor of that fact.

(4) If during the period of six months immediately following the end of that period an application for extension is made and the prescribed renewal fee and any prescribed additional fee is paid, the right shall be treated as if it had never expired, with the result that—

(a) anything done under or in relation to the right during that further period shall be treated as valid,

(b) an act which would have constituted an infringement of the right if it had not expired shall be treated as an infringement, and

(c) an act which would have constituted use of the design for the services of the Crown if the right had not expired shall be treated as such use.

(5), (6) . . .]

NOTES

Substituted, together with ss 8A, 8B for original s 8, by the Copyright, Designs and Patents Act 1988, s 269, except in relation to rights in designs registered in pursuance of applications made before 1 August 1989.

Sub-ss (5), (6): repealed by the Registered Designs Regulations 2001, SI 2001/3949, reg 9(2), Sch 2; for transitional provisions in relation to certain applications and registrations, see regs 10–14 of those Regulations at **[3.88]–[3.92]**.

[3.16]

[8A Restoration of lapsed right in design

(1) Where the right in a registered design has expired by reason of a failure to extend, in accordance with section 8(2) or (4), the period for which the right subsists, an application for the restoration of the right in the design may be made to the registrar within the prescribed period.

(2) The application may be made by the person who was the registered proprietor of the design or by any other person who would have been entitled to the right in the design if it had not expired; and where the design was held by two or more persons jointly, the application may, with the leave of the registrar, be made by one or more of them without joining the others.

(3) Notice of the application shall be published by the registrar in the prescribed manner.

(4) If the registrar is satisfied that the [failure of the proprietor] to see that the period for which the right subsisted was extended in accordance with section 8(2) or (4) [was unintentional], he shall, on payment of any unpaid renewal fee and any prescribed additional fee, order the restoration of the right in the design.
(5) The order may be made subject to such conditions as the registrar thinks fit, and if the proprietor of the design does not comply with any condition the registrar may revoke the order and give such consequential directions as he thinks fit.
(6) Rules altering the period prescribed for the purposes of subsection (1) may contain such transitional provisions and savings as appear to the Secretary of State to be necessary or expedient.]

NOTES

Substituted as noted to s 8 at **[3.15]**.

Sub-s (4): words in first pair of square brackets substituted and words in second pair of square brackets inserted by the Regulatory Reform (Registered Designs) Order 2006, SI 2006/1974, arts 2, 17.

[3.17]
[8B Effect of order for restoration of right

(1) The effect of an order under section 8A for the restoration of the right in a registered design is as follows.
(2) Anything done under or in relation to the right during the period between expiry and restoration shall be treated as valid.
(3) Anything done during that period which would have constituted an infringement if the right had not expired shall be treated as an infringement—
(a) if done at a time when it was possible for an application for extension to be made under section 8(4); or
(b) if it was a continuation or repetition of an earlier infringing act.
(4) If, after it was no longer possible for such an application for extension to be made and before publication of notice of the application for restoration, a person—
(a) began in good faith to do an act which would have constituted an infringement of the right in the design if it had not expired, or
(b) made in good faith effective and serious preparations to do such an act,
he has the right to continue to do the act or, as the case may be, to do the act, notwithstanding the restoration of the right in the design; but this does not extend to granting a licence to another person to do the act.
(5) If the act was done, or the preparations were made, in the course of a business, the person entitled to the right conferred by subsection (4) may—
(a) authorise the doing of that act by any partners of his for the time being in that business, and
(b) assign that right, or transmit it on death (or in the case of a body corporate on its dissolution), to any person who acquires that part of the business in the course of which the act was done or the preparations were made.
(6) Where [a product] is disposed of to another in exercise of the rights conferred by subsection (4) or subsection (5), that other and any person claiming through him may deal with [the product] in the same way as if it had been disposed of by the registered proprietor of the design.
(7) The above provisions apply in relation to the use of a registered design for the services of the Crown as they apply in relation to infringement of the right in the design.]

NOTES

Substituted as noted to s 8 at **[3.15]**.

Sub-s (6): words in square brackets substituted by the Registered Designs Regulations 2001, SI 2001/3949, reg 9(1), Sch 1, para 2; for transitional provisions in relation to certain applications and registrations, see regs 10–14 of those Regulations at **[3.88]**–**[3.92]**.

9, 10 *(S 9 repealed by the Intellectual Property (Enforcement, etc) Regulations 2006, SI 2006/1028, reg 2(4), Sch 4; s 10 repealed by the Registered Designs Regulations 2001, SI 2001/3949, regs 6(1), 9(2), Sch 2; for transitional provisions in relation to certain applications and registrations, see regs 10–14 of those Regulations at* **[3.88]**–**[3.92]**.)

[3.18]
[11 Cancellation of registration

The registrar may, upon a request made in the prescribed manner by the registered proprietor, cancel the registration of a design.]

NOTES

Substituted, together with ss 11ZA–11ZF for original s 11, by the Registered Designs Regulations 2001, SI 2001/3949, reg 7; for transitional provisions in relation to certain applications and registrations, see regs 10–14 of those Regulations at **[3.88]**–**[3.92]**.

[3.19]
[11ZA Grounds for invalidity of registration

(1) The registration of a design may be declared invalid[—
(a) on the ground that it does not fulfil the requirements of section 1(2) of this Act;

(b) on the ground that it does not fulfil the requirements of sections 1B to 1D of this Act; or
(c) where any ground of refusal mentioned in Schedule A1 to this Act applies.]

[(1A) The registration of a design ("the later design") may be declared invalid if it is not new or does not have individual character when compared to a design which—
(a) has been made available to the public on or after the relevant date; but
[(b) is protected as from a date prior to the relevant date—
(i) by virtue of registration under this Act or the Community Design Regulation or an application for such registration, or
(ii) by virtue of an international registration (within the meaning of Articles 106a to 106f of that Regulation) designating the Community.]

(1B) In subsection (1A) "the relevant date" means the date on which the application for the registration of the later design was made or is treated by virtue of section 3B(2), (3) or (5) or 14(2) of this Act as having been made.]

(2) The registration of a design may be declared invalid on the ground of the registered proprietor not being the proprietor of the design and the proprietor of the design objecting.

(3) The registration of a design involving the use of an earlier distinctive sign may be declared invalid on the ground of an objection by the holder of rights to the sign which include the right to prohibit in the United Kingdom such use of the sign.

(4) The registration of a design constituting an unauthorised use of a work protected by the law of copyright in the United Kingdom may be declared invalid on the ground of an objection by the owner of the copyright.

(5) In this section and sections 11ZB, 11ZC and 11ZE of this Act (other than section 11ZE(1)) references to the registration of a design include references to the former registration of a design; and these sections shall apply, with necessary modifications, in relation to such former registrations.]

NOTES

Substituted as noted to s 11 at **[3.18]**.

Sub-s (1): words in square brackets substituted by the Regulatory Reform (Registered Designs) Order 2006, SI 2006/1974, arts 2, 7(1), (2); for transitional savings in relation to certain registrations, see art 18 of that Order at **[3.111]**.

Sub-s (1A): inserted, together with sub-s (1B), by SI 2006/1974, arts 2, 7(1), (3); for transitional savings in relation to certain registrations, see art 18 of that Order at **[3.111]**; para (b) substituted by the Designs (International Registrations Designating the European Community) Regulations 2007, SI 2007/3378, reg 2.

Sub-s (1B): inserted as noted to sub-s (1A).

[3.20]

[11ZB Applications for declaration of invalidity

(1) Any person interested may make an application to the registrar for a declaration of invalidity [under section 11ZA(1)(a) or (b)] of this Act.

(2) Any person concerned by the use in question may make an application to the registrar for a declaration of invalidity [under section 11ZA(1)(c)] of this Act.

(3) The relevant person may make an application to the registrar for a declaration of invalidity [under section 11ZA(1A)] of this Act.

(4) In subsection (3) above "the relevant person" means, in relation to an earlier design protected by virtue of registration under this Act [or the Community Design Regulation] or an application for such registration, the registered proprietor of the design[, the holder of the registered Community design] or (as the case may be) the applicant.

(5) The person able to make an objection under subsection (2), (3) or (4) of section 11ZA of this Act may make an application to the registrar for a declaration of invalidity [under] that subsection.

(6) An application may be made under this section in relation to a design at any time after the design has been registered.]

NOTES

Substituted as noted to s 11 at **[3.18]**.

Sub-ss (1)–(3), (5): words in square brackets substituted by the Regulatory Reform (Registered Designs) Order 2006, SI 2006/1974, arts 2, 8; for transitional savings in relation to certain registrations, see art 18 of that Order at **[3.111]**.

Sub-s (4): words in square brackets inserted by the Registered Designs Regulations 2003, SI 2003/550, reg 2(1), (3); for transitional provisions in relation to certain applications and registrations, see regs 3–5 of those Regulations at **[3.94]–[3.96]**.

[3.21]

[11ZC Determination of applications for declaration of invalidity

(1) This section applies where an application has been made to the registrar for a declaration of invalidity in relation to a registration.

(2) If it appears to the registrar that the application has not been made in accordance with any rules made under this Act, he may refuse the application.

(3) If it appears to the registrar that the application has not been made in accordance with section 11ZB of this Act, he shall refuse the application.

(4) Subject to subsections (2) and (3) above, the registrar shall make a declaration of invalidity if it appears to him that the ground of invalidity specified in the application has been established in relation to the registration.

(5) Otherwise the registrar shall refuse the application.
(6) A declaration of invalidity may be a declaration of partial invalidity.]

NOTES
Substituted as noted to s 11 at **[3.18]**.

[3.22]
[11ZD Modification of registration
(1) Subsections (2) and (3) below apply where the registrar intends to declare the registration of a design invalid [under section 11ZA(1)(b) or (c), (1A), (3) or (4)] of this Act.
(2) The registrar shall inform the registered proprietor of that fact.
(3) The registered proprietor may make an application to the registrar for the registrar to make such modifications to the registration of the design as the registered proprietor specifies in his application.
(4) Such modifications may, in particular, include the inclusion on the register of a partial disclaimer by the registered proprietor.
(5) If it appears to the registrar that the application has not been made in accordance with any rules made under this Act, the registrar may refuse the application.
(6) If it appears to the registrar that the identity of the design is not retained or the modified registration would be invalid by virtue of section 11ZA of this Act, the registrar shall refuse the application.
(7) Otherwise the registrar shall make the specified modifications.
(8) A modification of a registration made under this section shall have effect, and be treated always to have had effect, from the grant of registration.]

NOTES
Substituted as noted to s 11 at **[3.18]**.
Sub-s (1): words in square brackets substituted by the Regulatory Reform (Registered Designs) Order 2006, SI 2006/1974, arts 2, 9; for transitional savings in relation to certain registrations, see art 18 of that Order at **[3.111]**.

[3.23]
[11ZE Effect of cancellation or invalidation of registration
(1) A cancellation of registration under section 11 of this Act takes effect from the date of the registrar's decision or from such other date as the registrar may direct.
(2) Where the registrar declares the registration of a design invalid to any extent, the registration shall to that extent be treated as having been invalid from the date of registration or from such other date as the registrar may direct.]

NOTES
Substituted as noted to s 11 at **[3.18]**.

[3.24]
[11ZF Appeals in relation to cancellation or invalidation
An appeal lies from any decision of the registrar under section 11 to 11ZE of this Act.]

NOTES
Substituted as noted to s 11 at **[3.18]**.

[3.25]
[11A Powers exercisable for protection of the public interest
(1) Where a report of the [Competition and Markets Authority] has been laid before Parliament containing conclusions to the effect—
(a), (b) . . .
(c) on a competition reference, that a person was engaged in an anti-competitive practice which operated or may be expected to operate against the public interest, or
(d) on a reference under section 11 of the Competition Act 1980 (reference of public bodies and certain other persons), that a person is pursuing a course of conduct which operates against the public interest,

the appropriate Minister or Ministers may apply to the registrar to take action under this section.
(2) Before making an application the appropriate Minister or Ministers shall publish, in such a manner as he or they think appropriate, a notice describing the nature of the proposed application and shall consider any representations which may be made within 30 days of such publication by persons whose interests appear to him or them to be affected.
(3) If on an application under this section it appears to the registrar that the matters specified in the [Competition and Markets Authority's report as being those which in the opinion of the Competition and Markets Authority] operate or operated or may be expected to operate against the public interest include—
(a) conditions in licences granted in respect of a registered design by its proprietor restricting the use of the design by the licensee or the right of the proprietor to grant other licences,
. . .

Part 3 Designs

(b) . . .

he may by order cancel or modify any such condition . . .

(4), (5) . . .

(6) An appeal lies from any order of the registrar under this section.

(7) In this section "the appropriate Minister or Ministers" means the Minister or Ministers to whom the report of the [Competition and Markets Authority] was made.]

NOTES

Inserted by the Copyright, Designs and Patents Act 1988, s 270.

Sub-s (1): words in square brackets substituted by the Enterprise and Regulatory Reform Act 2013 (Competition) (Consequential, Transitional and Saving Provisions) Order 2014, SI 2014/892, art 2, Sch 1, Pt 2, paras 19, 20(1), (2); paras (a), (b) repealed by the Enterprise Act 2002, s 278, Sch 25, para 1(1), (2), Sch 26, except in relation to the making by the Secretary of State of references under the Water Industry Act 1991.

Sub-s (3): words in square brackets substituted by SI 2014/892, art 2, Sch 1, Pt 2, paras 19, 20(1), (3); para (b) and word immediately preceding it, and final words omitted repealed by the Registered Designs Regulations 2001, SI 2001/3949, regs 6(2), 9(2), Sch 2; for transitional provisions in relation to certain applications and registrations, see regs 10–14 of those Regulations at **[3.88]–[3.92]**.

Sub-ss (4), (5): repealed by SI 2001/3949, reg 9(2), Sch 2; for transitional provisions in relation to certain applications and registrations, see regs 10–14 of those Regulations at **[3.88]–[3.92]**.

Sub-s (7): words in square brackets substituted by SI 2014/892, art 2, Sch 1, Pt 2, paras 19, 20(1), (2).

[3.26]

[11AB Powers exercisable following merger and market investigations

(1) Subsection (2) below applies where—

(a) section 41(2), 55(2), 66(6), 75(2), 83(2), 138(2), 147(2)[, 147A(2)] or 160(2) of, or paragraph 5(2) or 10(2) of Schedule 7 to, the Enterprise Act 2002 (powers to take remedial action following merger or market investigations) applies;

(b) the [Competition and Markets Authority] or (as the case may be) the Secretary of State considers that it would be appropriate to make an application under this section for the purpose of remedying, mitigating or preventing a matter which cannot be dealt with under the enactment concerned; and

(c) the matter concerned involves conditions in licences granted in respect of a registered design by its proprietor restricting the use of the design by the licensee or the right of the proprietor to grant other licences.

(2) The [Competition and Markets Authority] or (as the case may be) the Secretary of State may apply to the registrar to take action under this section.

(3) Before making an application the [Competition and Markets Authority] or (as the case may be) the Secretary of State shall publish, in such manner as it or he thinks appropriate, a notice describing the nature of the proposed application and shall consider any representations which may be made within 30 days of such publication by persons whose interests appear to it or him to be affected.

(4) The registrar may, if it appears to him on an application under this section that the application is made in accordance with this section, by order cancel or modify any condition concerned of the kind mentioned in subsection (1)(c) above.

(5) An appeal lies from any order of the registrar under this section.

[(6) References in this section to the Competition and Markets Authority are references to a CMA group except where—

(a) section 75(2) of the Enterprise Act 2002 applies; or

(b) any other enactment mentioned in subsection (1)(a) above applies and the functions of the Competition and Markets Authority under that enactment are being performed by the CMA Board by virtue of section 34C(3) or 133A(2) of the Enterprise Act 2002.]

(7) References in section 35, 36, 47, 63, 134[, 141 or 141A] of the Enterprise Act 2002 (questions to be decided by the [Competition and Markets Authority] in its reports) to taking action under section 41(2), 55, 66, 138[, 147 or 147A] shall include references to taking action under subsection (2) above.

(8) An order made by virtue of this section in consequence of action under subsection (2) above where an enactment mentioned in subsection (1)(a) above applies shall be treated, for the purposes of sections 91(3), 92(1)(a), 162(1) and 166(3) of the Enterprise Act 2002 (duties to register and keep under review enforcement orders etc), as if it were made under the relevant power in Part 3 or (as the case may be) 4 of that Act to make an enforcement order (within the meaning of the Part concerned).

[(9) In subsection (6) "CMA Board" and "CMA group" have the same meaning as in Schedule 4 to the Enterprise and Regulatory Reform Act 2013.]]

NOTES

Inserted by the Enterprise Act 2002, s 278(1), Sch 25, para 1(1), (3).

Sub-s (1): reference in square brackets in para (a) brackets inserted, and words in square brackets in para (b) substituted by the Enterprise and Regulatory Reform Act 2013 (Competition) (Consequential, Transitional and Saving Provisions) Order 2014, SI 2014/892, art 2, Sch 1, Pt 2, paras 19, 21(1), (2).

Sub-ss (2), (3): words in square brackets substituted by SI 2014/892, art 2, Sch 1, Pt 2, paras 19, 21(1), (3).

Sub-s (6): substituted by SI 2014/892, art 2, Sch 1, Pt 2, paras 19, 21(1), (4).

Sub-s (7): words in square brackets substituted by SI 2014/892, art 2, Sch 1, Pt 2, paras 19, 21(1), (5).

Sub-s (9): added by SI 2014/892, art 2, Sch 1, Pt 2, paras 19, 21(1), (6).

Modifications: the reference in sub-s (1)(a) to the Enterprise Act 2002, 66(6) shall have effect as if it included a reference to the Enterprise Act 2002 (Protection of Legitimate Interests) Order 2003, SI 2003/1592, art 12(7); the reference in sub-s (1)(a) to Sch 7, paras 5(2) or 10(2) to that Act shall have effect as if it included a reference to Sch 2, para 5(2) or 10(2) to that Order; the references in sub-s (7) to ss 63 and 66 of that Act shall have effect as if they included references to arts 6 and 12 of that Order respectively; and the reference in sub-s (8) to Part 3 shall have effect as if it included a reference to the Order; see the Enterprise Act 2002 (Protection of Legitimate Interests) Order 2003, SI 2003/1592, art 16, Sch 4, para 2.

11B (*Inserted by the Copyright, Designs and Patents Act 1988, s 270; repealed by the Registered Designs Regulations 2001, SI 2001/3949, reg 9(2), Sch 2, for transitional provisions in relation to certain applications and registrations, see regs 10–14 of those Regulations at* **[3.88]–[3.92]**.)

[3.27]

12 Use for services of Crown

The provisions of the First Schedule to this Act shall have effect with respect to the use of registered designs for the services of the Crown and the rights of third parties in respect of such use.

International Arrangements

[3.28]

13 Orders in Council as to convention countries

(1) His Majesty may, with a view to the fulfilment of a treaty, convention, arrangement or engagement, by Order in Council declare that any country specified in the Order is a convention country for the purposes of this Act:

Provided that a declaration may be made as aforesaid for the purposes either of all or of some only of the provisions of this Act, and a country in the case of which a declaration made for the purposes of some only of the provisions of this Act is in force shall be deemed to be a convention country for the purposes of those provisions only.

(2) His Majesty may by Order in Council direct that any of the Channel Islands, any colony . . . shall be deemed to be a convention country for the purposes of all or any of the provisions of this Act; and an Order made under this subsection may direct that any such provisions shall have effect, in relation to the territory in question, subject to such conditions or limitations, if any, as may be specified in the Order.

(3) For the purposes of subsection (1) of this section, every colony, protectorate, territory subject to the authority or under the suzerainty of another country, and territory administered by another country . . . under the trusteeship system of the United Nations, shall be deemed to be a country in the case of which a declaration may be made under that subsection.

NOTES

Sub-ss (3), (4): words omitted repealed by the Statute Law (Repeals) Act 1986.

Orders: the Designs (Convention Countries) Order 2007, SI 2007/277 at **[3.164]**.

[3.29]

14 Registration of design where application for protection in convention country has been made

(1) An application for registration of a design [or designs] in respect of which protection has been applied for in a convention country may be made in accordance with the provisions of this Act by the person by whom the application for protection was made or his personal representative or assignee:

Provided that no application shall be made by virtue of this section after the expiration of six months from the date of the application for protection in a convention country or, where more than one such application for protection has been made, from the date of the first application.

[(2) Where an application for registration of a design [or designs] is made by virtue of this section, the application shall be treated, for the purpose of determining whether [(and to what extent)] that or any other design is new [or has individual character], as made on the date of the application for protection in the convention country or, if more than one such application was made, on the date of the first such application.

(3) Subsection (2) shall not be construed as excluding the power to give directions under [section 3B(2) or (3)] of this Act in relation to an application made by virtue of this section.]

(4) Where a person has applied for protection for a design by an application which—

(a) in accordance with the terms of a treaty subsisting between two or more convention countries, is equivalent to an application duly made in any one of those convention countries; or

(b) in accordance with the law of any convention country, is equivalent to an application duly made in that convention country,

he shall be deemed for the purposes of this section to have applied in that convention country.

NOTES

Sub-s (1): words in square brackets inserted by the Regulatory Reform (Registered Designs) Order 2006, SI 2006/1974, arts 2, 14(1), (2).

Sub-s (2): substituted by the Copyright, Designs and Patents Act 1988, s 272, Sch 3, para 7; words in first pair of square brackets inserted by SI 2006/1974, arts 2, 14(1), (3); words in second and third pairs of square brackets inserted by the Registered Designs Regulations 2001, SI 2001/3949, reg 9(1), Sch 1, para 4(1), (2); for transitional provisions in relation to certain applications and registrations, see regs 10–14 of those Regulations at **[3.88]–[3.92]**.

Sub-s (3): substituted by the Copyright, Designs and Patents Act 1988, s 272, Sch 3, para 7; words in square brackets substituted by SI 2001/3949, reg 9(1), Sch 1, para 4(1), (3); for transitional provisions in relation to certain applications and registrations, see regs 10–14 of those Regulations at **[3.88]–[3.92]**.

[3.30]

15 Extension of time for applications under s 14 in certain cases

(1) If [the Secretary of State is satisfied] that provision substantially equivalent to the provision to be made by or under this section has been or will be made under the law of any convention country, [he] may make rules empowering the registrar to extend the time for making application under subsection (1) of section fourteen of this Act for registration of a design in respect of which protection has been applied for in that country in any case where the period specified in the proviso to that subsection expires during a period prescribed by the rules.

(2) Rules made under this section—

(a) may, where any agreement or arrangement has been made between His Majesty's Government in the United Kingdom and the government of the convention country for the supply or mutual exchange of information or [products], provide, either generally or in any class of case specified in the rules, that an extension of time shall not be granted under this section unless the design has been communicated in accordance with the agreement or arrangement;

(b) may, either generally or in any class of case specified in the rules, fix the maximum extension which may be granted under this section;

(c) may prescribe or allow any special procedure in connection with applications made by virtue of this section;

(d) may empower the registrar to extend, in relation to an application made by virtue of this section, the time limited by or under the foregoing provisions of this Act for doing any act, subject to such conditions, if any, as may be imposed by or under the rules;

(e) may provide for securing that the rights conferred by registration on an application made by virtue of this section shall be subject to such restrictions or conditions as may be specified by or under the rules and in particular to restrictions and conditions for the protection of persons (including persons acting on behalf of His Majesty) who, otherwise than as the result of a communication made in accordance with such an agreement or arrangement as is mentioned in paragraph (a) of this subsection, and before the date of the application in question or such later date as may be allowed by the rules, may have imported or made [products] to which the design is applied [or in which it is incorporated] or may have made an application for registration of the design.

NOTES

Sub-s (1): words in square brackets substituted by the Copyright, Designs and Patents Act 1988, s 272, Sch 3, para 8.

Sub-s (2): words in first and second pairs of square brackets substituted, and words in final pair of square brackets inserted, by the Registered Designs Regulations 2001, SI 2001/3949, reg 9(1), Sch 1, para 5; for transitional provisions in relation to certain applications and registrations see, regs 10–14 of those Regulations at **[3.88]–[3.92]**.

[3.31]

[15ZA Accession to the Hague Agreement

(1) The Secretary of State may by order make provision for giving effect in the United Kingdom to the provisions of the Geneva Act of the Hague Agreement Concerning the International Registration of Industrial Designs adopted by the Diplomatic Conference on 2 July 1999.

(2) An order under this section may, in particular, make provision about—

(a) the making of applications for international registrations at the Patent Office;

(b) the procedures to be followed where an international registration designates the United Kingdom;

(c) the effect of an international registration which designates the United Kingdom;

(d) the communication of information to the International Bureau;

(e) the payment of fees.

(3) An order under this section may—

(a) amend this Act;

(b) apply specified provisions of this Act with such modifications as may be specified.

(4) An expression used in subsection (2) and in the Agreement referred to in subsection (1) has the same meaning in that subsection as it has in the Agreement.]

NOTES

Commencement: 1 October 2014.

Inserted by the Intellectual Property Act 2014, s 8(1).

[Property in and Dealing with Registered Designs and Applications

[3.32]

15A The nature of registered designs

A registered design or an application for a registered design is personal property (in Scotland, incorporeal moveable property).]

NOTES

Inserted, together with preceding heading and ss 15B, 15C, by the Intellectual Property (Enforcement, etc) Regulations 2006, SI 2006/1028, reg 2(1), Sch 1, paras 1, 2.

[3.33]

[15B Assignment, &c of registered designs and applications for registered designs

(1) A registered design or an application for a registered design is transmissible by assignment, testamentary disposition or operation of law in the same way as other personal or moveable property, subject to the following provisions of this section.

(2) Any transmission of a registered design or an application for a registered design is subject to any rights vested in any other person of which notice is entered in the register of designs, or in the case of applications, notice is given to the registrar.

(3) An assignment of, or an assent relating to, a registered design or application for a registered design is not effective unless it is in writing signed by or on behalf of the assignor or, as the case may be, a personal representative.

(4) Except in Scotland, the requirement in subsection (3) may be satisfied in a case where the assignor or personal representative is a body corporate by the affixing of its seal.

(5) Subsections (3) and (4) apply to assignment by way of security as in relation to any other assignment.

(6) A registered design or application for a registered design may be the subject of a charge (in Scotland, security) in the same way as other personal or moveable property.

(7) The proprietor of a registered design may grant a licence to use that registered design.

(8) Any equities (in Scotland, rights) in respect of a registered design or an application for a registered design may be enforced in like manner as in respect of any other personal or moveable property.]

NOTES

Inserted as noted to s 15A at **[3.32]**.

[3.34]

[15C Exclusive licences

(1) In this Act an "exclusive licence" means a licence in writing signed by or on behalf of the proprietor of the registered design authorising the licensee to the exclusion of all other persons, including the person granting the licence, to exercise a right which would otherwise be exercisable exclusively by the proprietor of the registered design.

(2) The licensee under an exclusive licence has the same rights against any successor in title who is bound by the licence as he has against the person granting the licence.]

NOTES

Inserted as noted to s 15A at **[3.32]**.

16 (*Repealed by the Registered Designs Regulations 2001, SI 2001/3949, reg 9(2), Sch 2; for transitional provisions in relation to certain applications and registrations, see regs 10–14 of those Regulations at* **[3.88]–[3.92]**.)

Register of designs, &c

[3.35]

[17 Register of designs, etc

(1) The registrar shall maintain the register of designs, in which shall be entered—

(a) the names and addresses of proprietors of registered designs;

(b) notices of assignments and of transmissions of registered designs; and

(c) such other matters as may be prescribed or as the registrar may think fit.

(2) No notice of any trust, whether express, implied or constructive, shall be entered in the register of designs, and the registrar shall not be affected by any such notice.

(3) The register need not be kept in documentary form.

(4) Subject to the provisions of this Act and to rules made by the Secretary of State under it, the public shall have a right to inspect the register at the Patent Office at all convenient times.

(5) Any person who applies for a certified copy of an entry in the register or a certified extract from the register shall be entitled to obtain such a copy or extract on payment of a fee prescribed in relation to certified copies and extracts; and rules made by the Secretary of State under this Act may provide that any person who applies for an uncertified copy or extract shall be entitled to such a copy or extract on payment of a fee prescribed in relation to uncertified copies and extracts.

(6) Applications under subsection (5) above or rules made by virtue of that subsection shall be made in such manner as may be prescribed.

(7) In relation to any portion of the register kept otherwise than in documentary form—

(a) the right of inspection conferred by subsection (4) above is a right to inspect the material on the register; and

(b) the right to a copy or extract conferred by subsection (5) above or rules is a right to a copy or extract in a form in which it can be taken away and in which it is visible and legible.

(8) . . . the register shall be prima facie evidence of anything required or authorised to be entered in it and in Scotland shall be sufficient evidence of any such thing.

(9) A certificate purporting to be signed by the registrar and certifying that any entry which he is authorised by or under this Act to make has or has not been made, or that any other thing which he is so authorised to do has or has not been done, shall be prima facie evidence, and in Scotland shall be sufficient evidence, of the matters so certified.

(10) Each of the following—

(a) a copy of an entry in the register or an extract from the register which is supplied under subsection (5) above;

(b) a copy of any representation, specimen or document kept in the Patent Office or an extract from any such document,

which purports to be a certified copy or certified extract shall . . . be admitted in evidence without further proof and without production of any original; and in Scotland such evidence shall be sufficient evidence.

(11) . . .

(12) In this section "certified copy" and "certified extract" mean a copy and extract certified by the registrar and sealed with the seal of the Patent Office.]

NOTES

Substituted by the Patents, Designs and Marks Act 1986, s 1, Sch 1, para 3.

Sub-ss (8), (10): words omitted repealed by the Criminal Justice Act 2003, s 332, Sch 37, Pt 6.

Sub-s (11): repealed by the Youth Justice and Criminal Evidence Act 1999, s 67(3), Sch 6.

[3.36]

18 Certificate of registration

(1) The registrar shall grant a certificate of registration in the prescribed form to the registered proprietor of a design when the design is registered.

(2) The registrar may, in a case where he is satisfied that the certificate of registration has been lost or destroyed, or in any other case in which he thinks it expedient, furnish one or more copies of the certificate.

[3.37]

19 Registration of assignments, etc

(1) Where any person becomes entitled by assignment, transmission or operation of law to a registered design or to a share in a registered design, or becomes entitled as mortgagee, licensee or otherwise to any other interest in a registered design, he shall apply to the registrar in the prescribed manner for the registration of his title as proprietor or co-proprietor or, as the case may be, of notice of his interest, in the register of designs.

(2) Without prejudice to the provisions of the foregoing subsection, an application for the registration of the title of any person becoming entitled by assignment to a registered design or a share in a registered design, or becoming entitled by virtue of a mortgage, licence or other instrument to any other interest in a registered design, may be made in the prescribed manner by the assignor, mortgagor, licensor or other party to that instrument, as the case may be.

(3) Where application is made under this section for the registration of the title of any person, the registrar shall, upon proof of title to his satisfaction—

(a) where that person is entitled to a registered design or a share in a registered design, register him in the register of designs as proprietor or co-proprietor of the design, and enter in that register particulars of the instrument or event by which he derives title; or

(b) where that person is entitled to any other interest in the registered design, enter in that register notice of his interest, with particulars of the instrument (if any) creating it.

[(3A) . . .

(3B) Where [national unregistered design right] subsists in a registered design and the proprietor of the registered design is also the design right owner, an assignment of the [national unregistered design right] shall be taken to be also an assignment of the right in the registered design, unless a contrary intention appears.]

(4) . . .

(5) Except for the purposes of an application to rectify the register under the following provisions of this Act, a document in respect of which no entry has been made in the register of designs under subsection (3) of this section shall not be admitted in any court as evidence of the title of any person to a registered design or share of or interest in a registered design unless the court otherwise directs.

NOTES

Sub-s (3A): inserted, together with sub-s (3B), by the Copyright, Designs and Patents Act 1988, s 272, Sch 3, para 10; repealed by the Intellectual Property Act 2014, s 9(1).

Sub-s (3B): inserted as noted to sub-s (3A) above; words in square brackets substituted by the Registered Designs Regulations 2001, SI 2001/3949, reg 9(1), Sch 1, para 6, for transitional provisions in relation to certain applications and registrations, see regs 10–14 of those Regulations at **[3.88]–[3.92]**.

Sub-s (4): repealed by the Intellectual Property (Enforcement, etc) Regulations 2006, SI 2006/1028, reg 2(4), Sch 4.

[3.38]

20 Rectification of register

(1) The court may, on the application of [the relevant person], order the register of designs to be rectified by the making of any entry therein or the variation or deletion of any entry therein.

[(1A) In subsection (1) above "the relevant person" means—

(a) in the case of an application invoking any ground referred to in [section 11ZA(1)(c)] of this Act, any person concerned by the use in question;

(b) in the case of an application invoking the ground mentioned in [section 11ZA(1A)] of this Act, the appropriate person;

(c) in the case of an application invoking any ground mentioned in section 11ZA(2), (3) or (4) of this Act, the person able to make the objection;

(d) in any other case, any person aggrieved.

(1B) In subsection (1A) above "the appropriate person" means, in relation to an earlier design protected by virtue of registration under this Act [or the Community Design Regulation] or an application for such registration, the registered proprietor of the design[, the holder of the registered Community design] or (as the case may be) the applicant.]

(2) In proceedings under this section the court may determine any question which it may be necessary or expedient to decide in connection with the rectification of the register.

(3) Notice of any application to the court under this section shall be given in the prescribed manner to the registrar, who shall be entitled to appear and be heard on the application, and shall appear if so directed by the court.

(4) Any order made by the court under this section shall direct that notice of the order shall be served on the registrar in the prescribed manner; and the registrar shall, on receipt of the notice, rectify the register accordingly.

[(5) A rectification of the register under this section has effect as follows—

(a) an entry made has effect from the date on which it should have been made,

(b) an entry varied has effect as if it had originally been made in its varied form, and

(c) an entry deleted shall be deemed never to have had effect,

unless, in any case, the court directs otherwise.]

[(6) Orders which may be made by the court under this section include, in particular, declarations of partial invalidity.]

NOTES

Sub-s (1): words in square brackets substituted by the Registered Designs Regulations 2001, SI 2001/3949, reg 8(1), (2); for transitional provisions in relation to certain applications and registrations, see regs 10–14 of those Regulations at **[3.88]–[3.92]**.

Sub-s (1A): inserted, together with sub-s (1B), by SI 2001/3949, reg 8(1), (3); for transitional provisions in relation to certain applications and registrations, see regs 10–14 of those Regulations at **[3.88]–[3.92]**; words in square brackets substituted by the Regulatory Reform (Registered Designs) Order 2006, SI 2006/1974, arts 2, 10; for transitional savings in relation to certain registrations, see art 18 of that Order at **[3.111]**.

Sub-s (1B): inserted, together with sub-s (1A), by SI 2001/3949, reg 8(1), (3), for transitional provisions in relation to certain applications and registrations, see regs 10–14 of those Regulations at **[3.88]–[3.92]**; words in square brackets inserted by the Registered Designs Regulations 2003, SI 2003/550, reg 2(1), (4), for transitional provisions in relation to certain applications and registrations, see regs 3–5 of those Regulations at **[3.94]–[3.96]**.

Sub-s (5): added by the Copyright, Designs and Patents Act 1988, s 272, Sch 3, para 11.

Sub-s (6): added by SI 2001/3949, reg 8(1), (4); for transitional provisions in relation to certain applications and registrations, see regs 10–14 of those Regulations at **[3.88]–[3.92]**.

[3.39]

21 Power to correct clerical errors

(1) The registrar may, in accordance with the provisions of this section, correct any error in an application for the registration or in the representation of a design, or any error in the register of designs.

(2) A correction may be made in pursuance of this section either upon a request in writing made by any person interested and accompanied by the prescribed fee, or without such a request.

(3) Where the registrar proposes to make any such correction as aforesaid otherwise than in pursuance of a request made under this section, he shall give notice of the proposal to the registered proprietor or the applicant for registration of the design, as the case may be, and to any other person who appears to him to be concerned, and shall give them an opportunity to be heard before making the correction.

[3.40]

22 *Inspection of registered designs*

[(1) Where a design has been registered under this Act, there shall be open to inspection at the Patent Office on and after the day on which the certificate of registration is [granted]—

(a) the representation or specimen of the design, [and

(aa) every document kept at the Patent Office in connection with that design.]

(b) . . .

This subsection has effect subject to *[subsection (4)]* and to any rules made under section 5(2) of this Act.]

(2), (3) . . .

[(4) Where registration of a design has been refused pursuant to an application under this Act, or an application under this Act has been abandoned in relation to any design—

(a) the application, so far as relating to that design, and

(b) any representation, specimen or other document which has been filed and relates to that design,

shall not at any time be open to inspection at the Patent Office or be published by the registrar.]

[(5) For the purposes of subsection (1), a document is not to be regarded as open for inspection unless (in addition to being open for inspection in hard copy) it is made available by electronic transmission in such a way that members of the public may access it at a place and time individually chosen by them.

(6) The Secretary of State may by rules specify cases or circumstances in which a document kept at the Patent Office in connection with a registered design may not be inspected.

(7) Rules made under subsection (6) may confer a discretion on the registrar.]

NOTES

Section heading: for the words in italics there are substituted the words "Inspection of registered designs and associated documents" by the Intellectual Property Act 2014, s 9(2), as from a day to be appointed.

Sub-s (1): substituted by the Copyright, Designs and Patents Act 1988, s 272, Sch 3, para 12; para (aa) inserted together with word preceding it, and for the words in italics there are substituted the words "subsections (4) to (7)" by the Intellectual Property Act 2014, s 9(2), (3), as from a day to be appointed; para (b) repealed by the Registered Designs Regulations 2001, SI 2001/3949, reg 9(2), Sch 2, for transitional provisions in relation to certain applications and registrations, see regs 10–14 of those Regulations at **[3.88]–[3.92]**; words in square brackets substituted by the Regulatory Reform (Registered Designs) Order 2006, SI 2006/1974, arts 2, 7(1), (2), except in relation to any registration under this Act which has resulted from an application made before 1 October 2006: see art 19 of the 2006 Order at **[3.112]**.

Sub-ss (2), (3): repealed by SI 2006/1974, arts 2, 16(1), (3), except in relation to any registration under this Act which has resulted from an application made before 1 October 2006: see art 19 of the 2006 Order at **[3.112]**.

Sub-s (4): substituted by SI 2006/1974, arts 2, 15.

Sub-ss (5)–(7): added by the Intellectual Property Act 2014, s 9(4), (5), as from a day to be appointed.

[3.41]

[23 Information as to existence of right in registered design

On the request of a person furnishing such information as may enable the registrar to identify the design, and on payment of the prescribed fee, the registrar shall inform him—

(a) whether the design is registered . . . , and

(b) whether any extension of the period of the right in the registered design has been granted,

and shall state the date of registration and the name and address of the registered proprietor.]

NOTES

Substituted by the Copyright, Designs and Patents Act 1988, s 272, Sch 3, para 13.

Words omitted from para (a) repealed by the Registered Designs Regulations 2001, SI 2001/3949, reg 9(2), Sch 2; for transitional provisions in relation to certain applications and registrations, see regs 10–14 of those Regulations at **[3.88]–[3.92]**.

24 (*Repealed by the Patents, Designs and Marks Act 1986, s 3, Sch 3, Pt I.*)

Legal proceedings and Appeals

NOTES

Heading: for the words in italics there are substituted the words "Legal proceedings: general" by the Intellectual Property (Unjustified Threats) Act 2017, s 4(1), (2), as from a day to be appointed.

[3.42]

[24A Action for infringement

(1) An infringement of the right in a registered design is actionable by the registered proprietor.

(2) In an action for infringement all such relief by way of damages, injunctions, accounts or otherwise is available to him as is available in respect of the infringement of any other property right.

(3) This section has effect subject to section 24B of this Act (exemption of innocent infringer from liability).]

NOTES

Inserted, together with ss 24B–24G, by the Intellectual Property (Enforcement, etc) Regulations 2006, SI 2006/1028, reg 2(1), Sch 1, paras 1, 3.

[3.43]

[24B Exemption of innocent infringer from liability

(1) In proceedings for the infringement of the right in a registered design damages shall not be awarded . . . against a defendant who proves that at the date of the infringement he was not aware, and had no reasonable ground for supposing, that the design was registered.

(2) For the purposes of subsection (1), a person shall not be deemed to have been aware or to have had reasonable grounds for supposing that the design was registered by reason only of the marking of a product with—

(a) the word "registered" or any abbreviation thereof, or

(b) any word or words expressing or implying that the design applied to, or incorporated in, the product has been registered,

unless the number of the design [or a relevant internet link] accompanied the word or words or the abbreviation in question.

[(2A) The reference in subsection (2) to a relevant internet link is a reference to an address of a posting on the internet—

(a) which is accessible to the public free of charge, and

(b) which clearly associates the product with the number of the design.]

(3) Nothing in this section shall affect the power of the court to grant an injunction in any proceedings for infringement of the right in a registered design.]

NOTES

Inserted as noted to s 24A at **[3.42]**.

Sub-s (1): words omitted repealed by the Intellectual Property Act 2014, s 10(1).

Sub-s (2): words in square brackets inserted by the Digital Economy Act 2017, s 33(1), (2), as from a day to be appointed.

Sub-s (2A): inserted by the Digital Economy Act 2017, s 33(1), (3), as from a day to be appointed.

[3.44]

[24C Order for delivery up

(1) Where a person—

(a) has in his possession, custody or control for commercial purposes an infringing article, or

(b) has in his possession, custody or control anything specifically designed or adapted for making articles to a particular design which is a registered design, knowing or having reason to believe that it has been or is to be used to make an infringing article,

the registered proprietor in question may apply to the court for an order that the infringing article or other thing be delivered up to him or to such other person as the court may direct.

(2) An application shall not be made after the end of the period specified in the following provisions of this section; and no order shall be made unless the court also makes, or it appears to the court that there are grounds for making, an order under section 24D of this Act (order as to disposal of infringing article, &c).

(3) An application for an order under this section may not be made after the end of the period of six years from the date on which the article or thing in question was made, subject to subsection (4).

(4) If during the whole or any part of that period the registered proprietor—

(a) is under a disability, or

(b) is prevented by fraud or concealment from discovering the facts entitling him to apply for an order,

an application may be made at any time before the end of the period of six years from the date on which he ceased to be under a disability or, as the case may be, could with reasonable diligence have discovered those facts.

(5) In subsection (4) "disability"—

(a) in England and Wales, has the same meaning as in the Limitation Act 1980;

(b) in Scotland, means legal disability within the meaning of the Prescription and Limitation (Scotland) Act 1973;

(c) in Northern Ireland, has the same meaning as in the Statute of Limitations (Northern Ireland) 1958.

(6) A person to whom an infringing article or other thing is delivered up in pursuance of an order under this section shall, if an order under section 24D of this Act is not made, retain it pending the making of an order, or the decision not to make an order, under that section.

(7) The reference in subsection (1) to an act being done in relation to an article for "commercial purposes" are to its being done with a view to the article in question being sold or hired in the course of a business.

(8) Nothing in this section affects any other power of the court.]

NOTES

Inserted as noted to s 24A at **[3.42]**.

[3.45]
[24D Order as to disposal of infringing articles, &c

(1) An application may be made to the court for an order that an infringing article or other thing delivered up in pursuance of an order under section 24C of this Act shall be—

(a) forfeited to the registered proprietor, or

(b) destroyed or otherwise dealt with as the court may think fit,

or for a decision that no such order should be made.

(2) In considering what order (if any) should be made, the court shall consider whether other remedies available in an action for infringement of the right in a registered design would be adequate to compensate the registered proprietor and to protect his interests.

(3) Where there is more than one person interested in an article or other thing, the court shall make such order as it thinks just and may (in particular) direct that the thing be sold, or otherwise dealt with, and the proceeds divided.

(4) If the court decides that no order should be made under this section, the person in whose possession, custody or control the article or other thing was before being delivered up is entitled to its return.

(5) References in this section to a person having an interest in an article or other thing include any person in whose favour an order could be made in respect of it—

(a) under this section;

(b) under section 19 of Trade Marks Act 1994 (including that section as applied by regulation 4 of the Community Trade Mark Regulations 2006 (SI 2006/1027));

(c) under section 114, 204 or 231 of the Copyright, Designs and Patents Act 1988; or

(d) under regulation 1C of the Community Design Regulations 2005 (SI 2005/2339).]

NOTES

Inserted as noted to s 24A at **[3.42]**.

[3.46]
[24E Jurisdiction of county court and sheriff court

(1) In Northern Ireland a county court may entertain proceedings under the following provisions of this Act—

section 24C (order for delivery up of infringing article, &c),
section 24D (order as to disposal of infringing article, &c), or
section 24F(8) (application by exclusive licensee having concurrent rights),

where the value of the infringing articles and other things in question does not exceed the county court limit for actions in tort.

(2) In Scotland proceedings for an order under any of those provisions may be brought in the sheriff court.

(3) Nothing in this section shall be construed as affecting the jurisdiction of the Court of Session or the High Court in Northern Ireland.]

NOTES

Inserted as noted to s 24A at **[3.42]**.

[3.47]
[24F Rights and remedies of exclusive licensee

(1) In relation to a registered design, an exclusive licensee has, except against the registered proprietor, the same rights and remedies in respect of matters occurring after the grant of the licence as if the licence had been an assignment.

(2) His rights and remedies are concurrent with those of the registered proprietor; and references to the registered proprietor in the provisions of this Act relating to infringement shall be construed accordingly.

(3) In an action brought by an exclusive licensee by virtue of this section a defendant may avail himself of any defence which would have been available to him if the action had been brought by the registered proprietor.

(4) Where an action for infringement of the right in a registered design brought by the registered proprietor or an exclusive licensee relates (wholly or partly) to an infringement in respect of which they have concurrent rights of action, the proprietor or, as the case may be, the exclusive licensee may not, without the leave of the court, proceed with the action unless the other is either joined as a claimant or added as a defendant.

(5) A registered proprietor or exclusive licensee who is added as a defendant in pursuance of subsection (4) is not liable for any costs in the action unless he takes part in the proceedings.

(6) Subsections (4) and (5) do not affect the granting of interlocutory relief on the application of the registered proprietor or an exclusive licensee.

(7) Where an action for infringement of the right in a registered design is brought which relates (wholly or partly) to an infringement in respect of which the registered proprietor and an exclusive licensee have concurrent rights of action—

(a) the court shall, in assessing damages, take into account—

(i) the terms of the licence, and

(ii) any pecuniary remedy already awarded or available to either of them in respect of the infringement;

(b) no account of profits shall be directed if an award of damages has been made, or an account of profits has been directed, in favour of the other of them in respect of the infringement; and

(c) the court shall if an account of profits is directed apportion the profits between them as the court considers just, subject to any agreement between them;

and these provisions apply whether or not the proprietor and the exclusive licensee are both parties to the action.

(8) The registered proprietor shall notify any exclusive licensee having concurrent rights before applying for an order under section 24C of this Act (order for delivery up of infringing article, &c); and the court may on the application of the licensee make such order under that section as it thinks fit having regard to the terms of the licence.]

NOTES

Inserted as noted to s 24A at **[3.42]**.

[3.48]

[24G Meaning of "infringing article"

(1) In this Act "infringing article", in relation to a design, shall be construed in accordance with this section.

(2) An article is an infringing article if its making to that design was an infringement of the right in a registered design.

(3) An article is also an infringing article if—

(a) it has been or is proposed to be imported into the United Kingdom, and

(b) its making to that design in the United Kingdom would have been an infringement of the right in a registered design or a breach of an exclusive licensing agreement relating to that registered design.

(4) Where it is shown that an article is made to a design which is or has been a registered design, it shall be presumed until the contrary is proved that the article was made at a time when the right in the registered design subsisted.

(5) Nothing in subsection (3) shall be construed as applying to an article which may be lawfully imported into the United Kingdom by virtue of an enforceable [EU] right within the meaning of section 2(1) of the European Communities Act 1972.]

NOTES

Inserted as noted to s 24A at **[3.42]**.

Sub-s (5): reference in square brackets substituted by the Treaty of Lisbon (Changes in Terminology) Order 2011, SI 2011/1043, art 6(1)(f).

[3.49]

25 Certificate of contested validity of registration

(1) If in any proceedings before the court the validity of the registration of a design is contested, and it is found by the court that the design is[, to any extent,] validly registered, the court may certify that the validity of the registration of the design was contested in those proceedings.

(2) Where any such certificate has been granted, then if in any subsequent proceedings before the court for infringement of [the right in the registered design] or for [invalidation] of the registration of the design, a final order or judgment is made or given in favour of the registered proprietor, he shall, unless the court otherwise directs, be entitled to his costs as between solicitor and client:

Provided that this subsection shall not apply to the costs of any appeal in any such proceedings as aforesaid.

NOTES

Sub-s (1): words in square brackets inserted by the Registered Designs Regulations 2001, SI 2001/3949, reg 9(1), Sch 1, para 8(1), (2); for transitional provisions in relation to certain applications and registrations, see regs 10–14 of those Regulations at **[3.88]–[3.92]**.

Sub-s (2): words in first pair of square brackets substituted by the Copyright, Designs and Patents Act 1988, s 272, Sch 3, para 14; word in second pair of square brackets substituted by SI 2001/3949, reg 9(1), Sch 1, para 8(1), (3), for transitional provisions in relation to certain applications and registrations, see regs 10–14 of those Regulations at **[3.88]–[3.92]**.

[3.50]

26 Remedy for groundless threats of infringement proceedings

(1) Where any person (whether entitled to or interested in a registered design or an application for registration of a design or not) by circulars, advertisements or otherwise threatens any other person with proceedings for infringement of [the right in a registered design], any person aggrieved thereby may bring an action against him for any such relief as is mentioned in the next following subsection.

(2) Unless in any action brought by virtue of this section the defendant proves that the acts in respect of which proceedings were threatened constitute or, if done, would constitute, an infringement of [the right in a registered design] the registration of which is not shown by the [claimant] to be invalid, the [claimant] shall be entitled to the following relief, that is to say:—

(a) a declaration to the effect that the threats are unjustifiable;

(b) an injunction against the continuance of the threats; and

(c) such damages, if any, as he has sustained thereby.

[(2A) Proceedings may not be brought under this section in respect of a threat to bring proceedings for an infringement alleged to consist of the making or importing of anything.]

(3) For the avoidance of doubt it is hereby declared that a mere notification that a design is registered does not constitute a threat of proceedings within the meaning of this section.

NOTES

Section 26 is substituted (by new ss 26, 26A–26F and the preceding heading) by the Intellectual Property (Unjustified Threats) Act 2017, s 4(1), (3), as from a day to be appointed, as follows—

"Unjustified threats

26 Threats of infringement proceedings

(1) A communication contains a "threat of infringement proceedings" if a reasonable person in the position of a recipient would understand from the communication that—

(a) a registered design exists, and

(b) a person intends to bring proceedings (whether in a court in the United Kingdom or elsewhere) against another person for infringement of the right in the registered design by—

(i) an act done in the United Kingdom, or

(ii) an act which, if done, would be done in the United Kingdom.

(2) References in this section and in section 26C to a "recipient" include, in the case of a communication directed to the public or a section of the public, references to a person to whom the communication is directed.

26A Actionable threats

(1) Subject to subsections (2) to (5), a threat of infringement proceedings made by any person is actionable by any person aggrieved by the threat.

(2) A threat of infringement proceedings is not actionable if the infringement is alleged to consist of—

(a) making a product for disposal, or

(b) importing a product for disposal.

(3) A threat of infringement proceedings is not actionable if the infringement is alleged to consist of an act which, if done, would constitute an infringement of a kind mentioned in subsection (2)(a) or (b).

(4) A threat of infringement proceedings is not actionable if the threat—

(a) is made to a person who has done, or intends to do, an act mentioned in subsection (2)(a) or (b) in relation to a product, and

(b) is a threat of proceedings for an infringement alleged to consist of doing anything else in relation to that product.

(5) A threat of infringement proceedings which is not an express threat is not actionable if it is contained in a permitted communication.

(6) In sections 26C and 26D an "actionable threat" means a threat of infringement proceedings that is actionable in accordance with this section.

26B Permitted communications

(1) For the purposes of section 26A(5), a communication containing a threat of infringement proceedings is a "permitted communication" if—

(a) the communication, so far as it contains information that relates to the threat, is made for a permitted purpose;

(b) all of the information that relates to the threat is information that—

(i) is necessary for that purpose (see subsection (5)(a) to (c) for some examples of necessary information), and

(ii) the person making the communication reasonably believes is true.

(2) Each of the following is a "permitted purpose"—

(a) giving notice that a registered design exists;

(b) discovering whether, or by whom, the right in a registered design has been infringed by an act mentioned in section 26A(2)(a) or (b);

(c) giving notice that a person has a right in or under a registered design, where another person's awareness of the right is relevant to any proceedings that may be brought in respect of the registered design.

(3) The court may, having regard to the nature of the purposes listed in subsection (2)(a) to (c), treat any other purpose as a "permitted purpose" if it considers that it is in the interests of justice to do so.

(4) But the following may not be treated as a "permitted purpose"—

(a) requesting a person to cease doing, for commercial purposes, anything in relation to a product in which a design is incorporated or to which it is applied,

(b) requesting a person to deliver up or destroy a product in which a design is incorporated or to which it is applied, or

(c) requesting a person to give an undertaking relating to a product in which a design is incorporated or to which it is applied.

(5) If any of the following information is included in a communication made for a permitted purpose, it is information that is "necessary for that purpose" (see subsection (1)(b)(i))—

(a) a statement that a right in a registered design exists and is in force or that an application for registration of a design has been made;

(b) details of the registered design, or of a right in or under the right in the registered design, which—

(i) are accurate in all material respects, and

(ii) are not misleading in any material respect; and

(c) information enabling the identification of the products in which the registered design is allegedly incorporated or to which the registered design is allegedly applied.

26C Remedies and defences

(1) Proceedings in respect of an actionable threat may be brought against the person who made the threat for—

(a) a declaration that the threat is unjustified;

(b) an injunction against the continuance of the threat;

(c) damages in respect of any loss sustained by the aggrieved person by reason of the threat.

(2) It is a defence for the person who made the threat to show that the act in respect of which proceedings were threatened constitutes (or if done would constitute) an infringement of the right in the registered design.

(3) It is a defence for the person who made the threat to show—

(a) that, despite having taken reasonable steps, the person has not identified anyone who has done an act mentioned in section 26A(2)(a) or (b) in relation to the product which is the subject of the threat, and

(b) that the person notified the recipient, before or at the time of making the threat, of the steps taken.

26D Professional advisers

(1) Proceedings in respect of an actionable threat may not be brought against a professional adviser (or any person vicariously liable for the actions of that professional adviser) if the conditions in subsection (3) are met.

(2) In this section "professional adviser" means a person who, in relation to the making of the communication containing the threat—

(a) is acting in a professional capacity in providing legal services or the services of a trade mark attorney or a patent attorney, and

(b) is regulated in the provision of legal services, or the services of a trade mark attorney or a patent attorney, by one or more regulatory bodies (whether through membership of a regulatory body, the issue of a licence to practise or any other means).

(3) The conditions are that—

(a) in making the communication the professional adviser is acting on the instructions of another person, and

(b) when the communication is made the professional adviser identifies the person on whose instructions the adviser is acting.

(4) This section does not affect any liability of the person on whose instructions the professional adviser is acting.

(5) It is for a person asserting that subsection (1) applies to prove (if required) that at the material time—

(a) the person concerned was acting as a professional adviser, and

(b) the conditions in subsection (3) were met.

26E Supplementary: pending registration

(1) In sections 26 and 26B references to a registered design include references to a design in respect of which an application for registration has been made under section 3.

(2) Where the threat of infringement proceedings is made after an application for registration has been made (but before registration) the reference in section 26C(2) to "the registered design" is to be treated as a reference to the design registered in pursuance of that application.

26F Supplementary: proceedings for delivery up etc

In section 26(1)(b) the reference to proceedings for infringement of the right in a registered design includes a reference to—

(a) proceedings for an order under section 24C (order for delivery up), and

(b) proceedings for an order under section 24D (order as to disposal of infringing articles).".

Sub-s (1): words in square brackets substituted by the Copyright, Designs and Patents Act 1988, s 272, Sch 3, para 15.

Sub-s (2): words in first pair of square brackets substituted by the Copyright, Designs and Patents Act 1988, s 272, Sch 3, para 15; words in second and third pairs of square brackets substituted by the Intellectual Property (Enforcement, etc) Regulations 2006, SI 2006/1028, reg 2(1), Sch 1, paras 1, 4.

Sub-s (2A): inserted by the Copyright, Designs and Patents Act 1988, s 272, Sch 3, para 15.

[Meaning of "the court" and appeals]

NOTES

Heading inserted by the Intellectual Property (Unjustified Threats) Act 2017, s 4(1), (4), as from a day to be appointed.

[3.51]

[27 The court

(1) In this Act "the court" means—

(a) in England and Wales the High [Court [(subject to section 27A(6))],]

(b) in Scotland, the Court of Session, and

(c) in Northern Ireland, the High Court.

(2) Provision may be made by rules of court with respect to proceedings in the High Court in England and Wales for references and applications under this Act to be dealt with by such judge of that court as the [Lord Chief Justice of England and Wales may, after consulting the Lord Chancellor, select] for the purpose.

[(3) The Lord Chief Justice may nominate a judicial office holder (as defined in section 109(4) of the Constitutional Reform Act 2005) to exercise his functions under subsection (2).]]

NOTES

Substituted by the Copyright, Designs and Patents Act 1988, s 272, Sch 3, para 16.

Sub-s (1): in para (a), word in first (outer) pair of square brackets substituted by the Crime and Courts Act 2013, s 17(5), Sch 9, Pt 2, para 21(1), (2) and words in second (inner) pair of square brackets inserted by the Intellectual Property Act 2014, s 10(3).

Sub-s (2): words in square brackets substituted by the Constitutional Reform Act 2005, s 15(1), Sch 4, Pt 1, paras 35, 36(1), (2).

Sub-s (3): added by the Constitutional Reform Act 2005, s 15(1), Sch 4, Pt 1, paras 35, 36(1), (3).

[3.52]
[27A Appeals from decisions of registrar
(1) An appeal against a decision of the registrar under this Act may be made to—
(a) a person appointed by the Lord Chancellor (an "appointed person"), or
(b) the court.
(2) On an appeal under this section to an appointed person, the appointed person may refer the appeal to the court if—
(a) it appears to the appointed person that a point of general legal importance is involved,
(b) the registrar requests that the appeal be so referred, or
(c) such a request is made by any party to the proceedings before the registrar in which the decision appealed against was made.
(3) Before referring an appeal to the court under subsection (2), the appointed person must give the appellant and any other party to the appeal an opportunity to make representations as to whether it should be so referred.
(4) Where, on an appeal under this section to an appointed person, the appointed person does not refer the appeal to the court—
(a) the appointed person must hear and determine the appeal, and
(b) the appointed person's decision is final.
(5) Sections 30 and 31 (costs, evidence) apply to proceedings before an appointed person as they apply to proceedings before the registrar.
(6) In the application of this section to England and Wales, "the court" means the High Court.]

NOTES
Commencement: 15 July 2014 (for the purposes of appointing the appointed person under sub-s (1)(a)); 6 April 2015 (for remaining purposes).
Inserted, together with s 27B, by the Intellectual Property Act 2014, s 10(2).

[3.53]
[27B Persons appointed to hear and determine appeals
(1) A person is not eligible for appointment under section 27A(1)(a) unless the person—
(a) satisfies the judicial-appointment eligibility condition on a 5-year basis,
(b) is an advocate or solicitor in Scotland of at least 5 years' standing,
(c) is a member of the Bar of Northern Ireland or solicitor of the Court of Judicature of Northern Ireland of at least 5 years' standing, or
(d) has held judicial office.
(2) An appointed person must hold and vacate office in accordance with his terms of appointment, subject to subsections (3) to (5).
(3) An appointed person is to be paid such remuneration (whether by way of salary or fees) and such allowances as the Secretary of State may with the approval of the Treasury decide.
(4) An appointed person may resign office by notice in writing to the Lord Chancellor.
(5) The Lord Chancellor may by notice in writing remove an appointed person ("A") from office if—
(a) A has become bankrupt or made an arrangement with A's creditors or, in Scotland, A's estate has been sequestrated or A has executed a trust deed for A's creditors or entered into a composition contract,
(b) A is incapacitated by physical or mental illness, or
(c) A is, in the opinion of the Lord Chancellor, otherwise unable or unfit to perform A's duties as an appointed person.
(6) Before exercising a power under section 27A or this section, the Lord Chancellor must consult the Secretary of State.
(7) The Lord Chancellor may remove a person from office under subsection (5) only with the concurrence of the appropriate senior judge.
(8) The appropriate senior judge is the Lord Chief Justice of England and Wales, unless—
(a) the person to be removed exercises functions wholly or mainly in Scotland, in which case it is the Lord President of the Court of Session, or
(b) the person to be removed exercises functions wholly or mainly in Northern Ireland, in which case it is the Lord Chief Justice of Northern Ireland.]

NOTES
Commencement: 15 July 2014 (for the purposes of appointing the appointed person under this section); 6 April 2015 (for remaining purposes).
Inserted as noted to s 27A at **[3.52]**.

28 (*Repealed by the Intellectual Property Act 2014, s 10(4).*)

[Opinions service

[3.54]

28A Opinions on designs

(1) The Secretary of State may by regulations make provision about the making of requests to the registrar for an opinion on specified matters relating to—

(a) designs registered under this Act;

(b) designs of such other description as may be specified.

(2) The regulations must require the registrar to give an opinion in response to a request made under the regulations, except—

(a) in specified cases or circumstances, or

(b) where for any reason the registrar considers it inappropriate in all the circumstances to do so.

(3) The regulations may provide that a request made under the regulations must be accompanied by—

(a) a fee of a specified amount;

(b) specified information.

(4) The regulations must provide that an opinion given by the registrar under the regulations is not binding for any purposes.

(5) The regulations must provide that neither the registrar nor any examiner or other officer of the Patent Office is to incur any liability by reason of or in connection with—

(a) any opinion given under the regulations, or

(b) any examination or investigation undertaken for the purpose of giving such an opinion.

(6) An opinion given by the registrar under the regulations is not to be treated as a decision of the registrar for the purposes of section 27A.

(7) But the regulations must provide for an appeal relating to an opinion given under the regulations to be made to a person appointed under section 27A; and the regulations may make further provision in relation to such appeals.

(8) The regulations may confer discretion on the registrar.

(9) Regulations under this section—

(a) may make different provision for different purposes;

(b) may include consequential, incidental, supplementary, transitional, transitory or saving provision.

(10) In this section, "specified" means specified in regulations under this section.]

NOTES

Commencement: 1 October 2014.

Inserted, together with preceding heading, by the Intellectual Property Act 2014, s 11(1).

Powers and Duties of Registrar

[3.55]

29 Exercise of discretionary powers of registrar

Without prejudice to any provisions of this Act requiring the registrar to hear any party to proceedings thereunder, or to give to any such party an opportunity to be heard, [rules made by the Secretary of State under this Act shall require the registrar to give] to any applicant for registration of a design an opportunity to be heard before exercising adversely to the applicant any discretion vested in the registrar by or under this Act.

NOTES

Words in square brackets substituted by the Copyright, Designs and Patents Act 1988, s 272, Sch 3, para 18.

Rules: the Registered Designs Rules 2006, SI 2006/1975 at **[3.113]**.

[3.56]

[30 Costs and security for costs

(1) Rules made by the Secretary of State under this Act may make provision empowering the registrar, in any proceedings before him under this Act—

(a) to award any party such costs as he may consider reasonable, and

(b) to direct how and by what parties they are to be paid.

(2) Any such order of the registrar may be enforced—

(a) in England and Wales or Northern Ireland, in the same way as an order of the High Court;

(b) in Scotland, in the same way as a decree for expenses granted by the Court of Session.

(3) Rules made by the Secretary of State under this Act may make provision empowering the registrar to require a person, in such cases as may be prescribed, to give security for the costs of—

(a) an application for [invalidation] of the registration of a design,

(b) . . .

(c) an appeal from any decision of the registrar under this Act,

and enabling the application or appeal to be treated as abandoned in default of such security being given.]

NOTES

Substituted by the Copyright, Designs and Patents Act 1988, s 272, Sch 3, para 19.

Sub-s (3): word in square brackets in para (a) substituted, and para (b) repealed, by the Registered Designs Regulations 2001, SI 2001/3949, reg 9, Sch 1, para 9, Sch 2; for transitional provisions in relation to certain applications and registrations, see regs 10–14 of those Regulations at **[3.88]–[3.92]**.

Rules: the Registered Designs Rules 2006, SI 2006/1975 at **[3.113]**.

[3.57]

[31 Evidence before registrar

Rules made by the Secretary of State under this Act may make provision—

(a) as to the giving of evidence in proceedings before the registrar under this Act by affidavit or statutory declaration;

(b) conferring on the registrar the powers of an official referee of the [Senior Courts] [or of the Court of Judicature] as regards the examination of witnesses on oath and the discovery and production of documents; and

(c) applying in relation to the attendance of witnesses in proceedings before the registrar the rules applicable to the attendance of witnesses in proceedings before such a referee.]

NOTES

Substituted by the Copyright, Designs and Patents Act 1988, s 272, Sch 3, para 20.

Words in first pair of square brackets substituted and words in second pair of square brackets inserted by the Constitutional Reform Act 2005, s 59(5), Sch 11, Pt 2, para 4(1), (3), Pt 4, para 18.

Rules: the Registered Design Rules 2006, SI 2006/1975 at **[3.113]**.

[3.58]

[31A Power to require use of forms

(1) The registrar may require the use of such forms as the registrar may direct for—

(a) an application for the registration of a design;

(b) representations or specimens of designs or other documents which may be filed at the Patent Office.

(2) The forms, and any directions by the registrar about their use, are to be published in the prescribed manner.]

NOTES

Commencement: 1 October 2014.

Inserted by the Intellectual Property Act 2014, s 12(1).

32 (*Repealed by the Copyright, Designs and Patents Act 1988, ss 272, 303(2), Sch 3, para 21, Sch 8.*)

Offences

[3.59]

33 Offences under s 5

(1) If any person fails to comply with any direction given under section five of this Act or makes or causes to be made an application for the registration of a design in contravention of that section, he shall be guilty of an offence and liable—

[(a) on conviction on indictment to imprisonment for a term not exceeding two years or a fine, or both;

(b) on summary conviction to imprisonment for a term not exceeding six months or a fine not exceeding the statutory maximum, or both.]

(2) . . .

NOTES

Sub-s (1): words in square brackets substituted by the Copyright, Designs and Patents Act 1988, s 272, Sch 3, para 22, except in relation to offences committed before 1 August 1989.

Sub-s (2): repealed by the Copyright, Designs and Patents Act 1988, ss 272, 303(2), Sch 3, para 22, Sch 8, except in relation to offences committed before 1 August 1989.

[3.60]

34 Falsification of register, etc

If any person makes or causes to be made a false entry in the register of designs, or a writing falsely purporting to be a copy of an entry in that register, or produces or tenders or causes to be produced or tendered in evidence any such writing, knowing the entry or writing to be false, he [shall be guilty of an offence and liable—

(a) on conviction on indictment to imprisonment for a term not exceeding two years or a fine, or both;

(b) on summary conviction to imprisonment for a term not exceeding six months or a fine not exceeding the statutory maximum, or both.]

NOTES

Words in square brackets substituted by the Copyright, Designs and Patents Act 1988, s 272, Sch 3, para 23, except in relation to offences committed before 1 August 1989.

[3.61]

35 Fine for falsely representing a design as registered

(1) If any person falsely represents that a design applied to[, or incorporated in, any product] sold by him is registered . . . , he shall be liable on summary conviction to a fine not exceeding [level 3 on the standard scale]; and for the purposes of this provision a person who sells [a product] having stamped, engraved or impressed thereon or otherwise applied thereto the word "registered", or any other word expressing or implying that the design applied to[, or incorporated in, the product] is registered, shall be deemed to represent that the design applied to[, or incorporated in, the product] is registered . . .

(2) If any person, after [the right in a registered design] has expired, marks [any product] to which the design has been applied [or in which it has been incorporated] with the word "registered", or any word or words implying that there is a [subsisting right in the design under this Act], or causes any [such product] to be so marked, he shall be liable on summary conviction [to a fine not exceeding level 1 on the standard scale.]

[(3) For the purposes of this section, the use in the United Kingdom in relation to a design—

(a) of the word "registered", or

(b) of any other word or symbol importing a reference (express or implied) to registration,

shall be deemed to be a representation as to registration under this Act unless it is shown that the reference is to registration elsewhere than in the United Kingdom and that the design is in fact so registered.]

NOTES

Sub-s (1): words in first, third, fourth and fifth pairs of square brackets substituted, and words omitted repealed, by the Registered Designs Regulations 2001, SI 2001/3949, reg 9(1), Sch 1, para 10(1), (2), Sch 2, for transitional provisions in relation to certain applications and registrations, see regs 10–14 of those Regulations at **[3.88]–[3.92]**; words in second pair of square brackets substituted by the Copyright, Designs and Patents Act 1988, s 272, Sch 3, para 24, except in relation to offences committed before 1 August 1989.

Sub-s (2): words in first, fourth and sixth pairs of square brackets substituted by the Copyright, Designs and Patents Act 1988, s 272, Sch 3, para 24; words in second and fifth pairs of square brackets substituted and words in third pair of square brackets inserted by SI 2001/3949, reg 9(1), Sch 1, para 10(1), (3), for transitional provisions in relation to certain applications and registrations, see regs 10–14 of those Regulations at **[3.88]–[3.92]**.

Sub-s (3): added by the Community Design Regulations 2005, SI 2005/2339, reg 6.

[3.62]

[35ZA Offence of unauthorised copying etc of design in course of business

(1) A person commits an offence if—

(a) in the course of a business, the person intentionally copies a registered design so as to make a product—

(i) exactly to that design, or

(ii) with features that differ only in immaterial details from that design, and

(b) the person does so—

(i) knowing, or having reason to believe, that the design is a registered design, and

(ii) without the consent of the registered proprietor of the design.

(2) Subsection (3) applies in relation to a product where a registered design has been intentionally copied so as to make the product—

(a) exactly to the design, or

(b) with features that differ only in immaterial details from the design.

(3) A person commits an offence if—

(a) in the course of a business, the person offers, puts on the market, imports, exports or uses the product, or stocks it for one or more of those purposes,

(b) the person does so without the consent of the registered proprietor of the design, and

(c) the person does so knowing, or having reason to believe, that—

(i) a design has been intentionally copied without the consent of the registered proprietor so as to make the product exactly to the design or with features that differ only in immaterial details from the design, and

(ii) the design is a registered design.

(4) It is a defence for a person charged with an offence under this section to show that the person reasonably believed that the registration of the design was invalid.

(5) It is also a defence for a person charged with an offence under this section to show that the person—

(a) did not infringe the right in the design, or

(b) reasonably believed that the person did not do so.

(6) The reference in subsection (3) to using a product in the course of a business does not include a reference to using it for a purpose which is merely incidental to the carrying on of the business.

(7) In this section "registered design" includes a registered Community design; and a reference to the registered proprietor is, in the case of a registered Community design, to be read as a reference to the holder.

(8) A person guilty of an offence under this section is liable—

(a) on conviction on indictment, to imprisonment for a term not exceeding ten years or to a fine or to both;

(b) on summary conviction in England and Wales or Northern Ireland, to imprisonment for a term not exceeding six months or to a fine not exceeding the statutory maximum or to both;

(c) on summary conviction in Scotland, to imprisonment for a term not exceeding 12 months or to a fine not exceeding the statutory maximum or to both.]

NOTES

Commencement: 1 October 2014.

Inserted, together with ss 35ZB–35ZD, by the Intellectual Property Act 2014, s 13.

[3.63]

[35ZB Section 35ZA: enforcement

(1) . . .

[(1A) For the investigatory powers available to a local weights and measures authority or the Department of Enterprise, Trade and Investment in Northern Ireland for the purposes of the enforcement of section 35ZA, see Schedule 5 to the Consumer Rights Act 2015.]

(2) Any enactment which authorises the disclosure of information for the purpose of facilitating the enforcement of the Trade Descriptions Act 1968 applies—

(a) as if section 35ZA were a provision of that Act, and

(b) as if the functions of any person in relation to the enforcement of that section were functions under that Act.

(3) Nothing in this section is to be construed as authorising a local weights and measures authority to bring proceedings in Scotland.]

NOTES

Commencement: 1 October 2014.

Inserted as noted to s 35ZA at **[3.62]**.

Sub-s (1): repealed by the Consumer Rights Act 2015, s 77(2), Sch 6, para 1(1), (2).

Sub-s (1A): inserted by the Consumer Rights Act 2015, s 77(2), Sch 6, para 1(1), (3).

[3.64]

[35ZC Section 35ZA: forfeiture in England and Wales or Northern Ireland

(1) In England and Wales or Northern Ireland, a person who, in connection with the investigation or prosecution of an offence under section 35ZA, has come into the possession of relevant products or articles may apply under this section for an order for the forfeiture of the products or articles.

(2) "Relevant product" means a product which is made exactly to a registered design, or with features that differ only in immaterial details from a registered design, by copying that design intentionally.

(3) "Relevant article" means an article which is specifically designed or adapted for making copies of a registered design intentionally.

(4) An application under this section may be made—

(a) where proceedings have been brought in any court for an offence under section 35ZA relating to some or all of the products or articles, to that court;

(b) where no application for the forfeiture of the products or articles has been made under paragraph (a), by way of complaint to a magistrates' court.

(5) On an application under this section, the court may make an order for the forfeiture of products or articles only if it is satisfied that an offence under section 35ZA has been committed in relation to the products or articles.

(6) A court may infer for the purposes of this section that such an offence has been committed in relation to any products or articles if it is satisfied that such an offence has been committed in relation to products or articles which are representations of them (whether by reason of being of the same design or part of the same consignment or batch or otherwise).

(7) Any person aggrieved by an order made under this section by a magistrates' court, or by a decision of such a court not to make such an order, may appeal against that order or decision—

(a) in England and Wales, to the Crown Court;

(b) in Northern Ireland, to the county court.

(8) An order so made may contain such provision as appears to the court to be appropriate for delaying the coming into force of the order pending the making and determination of any appeal (including any application under section 111 of the Magistrates' Courts Act 1980 or Article 146 of the Magistrates' Courts (Northern Ireland) Order 1981).

(9) Subject to subsection (10), any products or articles forfeited under this section are to be destroyed in accordance with such directions as the court may give.

(10) On making an order under this section, the court may, if it considers it appropriate to do so, direct that the products or articles to which the order relates shall (instead of being destroyed) be released to such person and on such conditions as the court may specify.]

NOTES

Commencement: 1 October 2014.

Inserted as noted to s 35ZA at **[3.62]**.

[3.65]

[35ZD Section 35ZA: forfeiture in Scotland

(1) In Scotland, the court may make an order for the forfeiture of any relevant products or articles (as defined by section 35ZC).

(2) An order under this section may be made—

(a) on an application by the procurator fiscal made in the manner specified in section 134 of the Criminal Procedure (Scotland) Act 1995, or

(b) where a person is convicted of an offence under section 35ZA, in addition to any other penalty which the court may impose.

(3) On an application under subsection (2)(a), the court may make an order for the forfeiture of relevant products or articles only if it is satisfied that an offence under section 35ZA has been committed in relation to the relevant products or articles.

(4) The court may infer for the purposes of this section that such an offence has been committed in relation to any relevant products or articles [if it is satisfied that such an offence has been committed in relation to products or articles] which are representative of them (whether by reason of being of the same design or part of the same consignment or batch or otherwise).

(5) The procurator fiscal making the application under subsection (2)(a) must serve on any person appearing to the procurator fiscal to be the owner of, or otherwise have an interest in, the products or articles to which [the application relates a copy of the application, together with a notice giving the person the opportunity] to appear at the hearing of the application to show cause why the products or articles should not be forfeited.

(6) Service under subsection (5) must be carried out, and such service may be proved, in the manner specified for citation of an accused in summary proceedings under the Criminal Procedure (Scotland) Act 1995.

(7) Any person upon whom notice is served under subsection (5) and any other person claiming to be the owner of, or otherwise have an interest in, products or articles to which an application under this section relates is entitled to appear at the hearing of the application to show cause why the products or articles should not be forfeited.

(8) The court must not make an order following an application under subsection (2)(a)—

(a) if any person on whom notice is served under subsection (5) does not appear, unless service of the notice on that person is proved, or

(b) if no notice under subsection (5) has been served, unless the court is satisfied that in the circumstances it was reasonable not to serve such notice.

(9) Where an order for the forfeiture of any products or articles is made following an application under subsection (2)(a), any person who appeared, or was entitled to appear, to show cause why goods, material or articles should not be forfeited may, within 21 days of making the order, appeal to the High Court of Justiciary by bill of suspension.

(10) Section 182(5)(a) to (e) of the Criminal Procedure (Scotland) Act 1995 applies to an appeal under subsection (9) as it applies to a stated case under Part 2 of that Act.

(11) An order following an application under subsection (2)(a) does not take effect—

(a) until the end of the period of 21 days beginning with the day after the day on which the order is made, or

(b) if an appeal is made under subsection (9) within that period, until the appeal is dismissed or abandoned.

(12) An order under subsection (2)(b) does not take effect—

(a) until the end of the period within which an appeal against the order could be brought under the Criminal Procedure (Scotland) Act 1995, or

(b) if an appeal is made within that period, until the appeal is determined or abandoned.

(13) Subject to subsection (14), products or articles forfeited under this section must be destroyed in accordance with such directions as the court may give.

(14) On making an order under this section, the court may, if it considers it appropriate to do so, direct that the products or articles to which the order relates shall (instead of being destroyed) be released, to such person and on such conditions as the court may specify.

(15) In this section, "the court" means—

(a) in relation to an order made on an application under subsection (2)(a), the sheriff;

(b) in relation to an order made under subsection (2)(b), the court which imposed the penalty.]

NOTES

Commencement: 1 October 2014.

Inserted as noted to s 35ZA at **[3.62]**.

[3.66]

[35A [Offence by body corporate or partnership: liability of officers or partners]

(1) Where an offence under this Act committed by a body corporate is proved to have been committed with the consent or connivance of a director, manager, secretary or other similar officer of the body, or a person purporting to act in any such capacity, he as well as the body corporate is guilty of the offence and liable to be proceeded against and punished accordingly.

(2) In relation to a body corporate whose affairs are managed by its members "director" means a member of the body corporate.

[(3) Proceedings for an offence under this Act alleged to have been committed by a partnership are to be brought against the partnership in the name of the firm and not in that of the partners; but without prejudice to any liability of the partners under subsection (6) or (7).

(4) The following provisions apply for the purposes of such proceedings as in relation to a body corporate—

(a) any rules of court relating to the service of documents;
(b) in England and Wales, Schedule 3 to the Magistrates' Courts Act 1980;
(c) in Northern Ireland, Schedule 4 to the Magistrates' Courts (Northern Ireland) Order 1981.

(5) A fine imposed on a partnership (other than a Scottish partnership) on its conviction in such proceedings must be paid out of the partnership assets.

(6) Where a partnership (other than a Scottish partnership) is guilty of an offence under this Act, every partner, other than a partner who is proved to have been ignorant of or to have attempted to prevent the commission of the offence, is also guilty of the offence and liable to be proceeded against and punished accordingly.

(7) Where an offence under this Act committed by a Scottish partnership is proved to have been committed with the consent or connivance of a partner in the partnership, or a person purporting to act in that capacity, he as well as the partnership is guilty of the offence and liable to be proceeded against and punished accordingly.]]

NOTES

Inserted by the Copyright, Designs and Patents Act 1988, s 272, Sch 3, para 25, except in relation to offences committed before 1 August 1989.

Section heading: words in square brackets substituted by the Intellectual Property Act 2014, s 14.

Sub-ss (3)–(7): added by the Intellectual Property Act 2014, s 14.

Rules, &c

[3.67]

36 General power of [Secretary of State] to make rules, etc

(1) Subject to the provisions of this Act, [the Secretary of State] may make such rules [as he thinks expedient] for regulating the business of the Patent Office in relation to designs and for regulating all matters by this Act placed under the direction or control of the registrar or [the Secretary of State].

[(1A) Rules may, in particular, make provision—

[(a) requiring the furnishing of copies of such representations or specimens of designs or other documents as may be filed at the Patent Office;]

[(ab) requiring applications for registration of designs to specify—

(i) the products to which the designs are intended to be applied or in which they are intended to be incorporated;

(ii) the classification of the designs by reference to such test as may be prescribed;]

(b) regulating the procedure to be followed in connection with any application or request to the registrar or in connection with any proceeding before him, and authorising the rectification of irregularities of procedure;

(c) providing for the appointment of advisers to assist the registrar in proceedings before him;

(d) regulating the keeping of the register of designs;

(e) authorising the publication and sale of copies of representations of designs and other documents in the Patent Office;

(f) prescribing anything authorised or required by this Act to be prescribed by rules.

(1B) The remuneration of an adviser appointed to assist the registrar shall be determined by the Secretary of State with the consent of the Treasury and shall be defrayed out of money provided by Parliament.]

(2) Rules made under this section may provide for the establishment of branch offices for designs and may authorise any document or thing required by or under this Act to be filed or done at the Patent Office to be filed or done at the branch office at Manchester or any other branch office established in pursuance of the rules.

NOTES

Section heading, sub-s (1): words in square brackets substituted by the Copyright, Designs and Patents Act 1988, s 272, Sch 3, para 26(1), (2).

Sub-s (1A): substituted, together with sub-s (1B) for part of original sub-s (1), by the Copyright, Designs and Patents Act 1988, s 272, Sch 3, para 26(1), (3); para (ab) inserted by the Registered Designs Regulations 2001, SI 2001/3949, reg 9(1), Sch 1, para 11, for transitional provisions in relation to certain applications and registrations, see regs 10–14 of those Regulations at **[3.88]–[3.92]**; para (a) substituted by the Intellectual Property Act 2014, s 12(3), subject to s 12(6) thereof which provides that any rules made in reliance on s 36(1A)(a) which are in force immediately before 1 October 2014, continue in force until such time as directions about forms of the kind which had been prescribed by the rules take effect. Para (a) originally read as follows—

"(a) prescribing the form of applications for registration of designs and of any representations or specimens of designs or other documents which may be filed at the Patent Office, and requiring copies to be furnished of any such representations, specimens or documents;".

Sub-s (1B): substituted as noted to sub-s (1A) above.

Rules: the Designs (Companies Re-registration) Rules 1982, SI 1982/299; the Patents, Trade Marks and Designs (Address For Service and Time Limits, etc) Rules 2006, SI 2006/760; the Registered Designs Rules 2006, SI 2006/1975 at **[3.113]**; the Patents, Trade Marks and Designs (Address for Service) Rules 2009, SI 2009/546; the Appointed Person (Designs) Rules 2015, SI 2015/169; the Registered Designs (Fees) Rules 2016, SI 2016/889.

[3.68]

37 [Provisions as to rules, regulations and orders]

(1) . . .

(2) Any rules made by [the Secretary of State] in pursuance of [section 15 [or 22(6)] of this Act], and any order made, direction given, or other action taken under the rules by the registrar, may be made, given or taken so as to have effect as respects things done or omitted to be done on or after such date, whether before or after the coming into operation of the rules or of this Act, as may be specified in the rules.

(3) Any power to make rules conferred by this Act on [the Secretary of State] . . . [and the power to make an order under section 15ZA] [and the power to make regulations under section 28A] shall be exercisable by statutory instrument; . . .

(4) Any statutory instrument containing rules made by [the Secretary of State] under this Act [or regulations under section 28A] shall be subject to annulment in pursuance of a resolution of either House of Parliament.

[(4A) Subsection (4) does not apply to the first regulations to be made under section 28A, but the Secretary of State may not make those regulations unless a draft of the statutory instrument containing them has been laid before, and approved by a resolution of, each House of Parliament.]

[(4B) The Secretary of State may not make an order under section 15ZA unless a draft of the statutory instrument containing the order has been laid before, and approved by a resolution of, each House of Parliament.]

(5) Any Order in Council made under this Act may be revoked or varied by a subsequent Order in Council.

NOTES

Section heading: words in square brackets substituted by the Intellectual Property Act 2014, s 11(3).

Sub-s (1): repealed by the Copyright, Designs and Patents Act 1988, ss 272, 303(2), Sch 3, para 27(1), (2), Sch 8.

Sub-s (2): words in first pair of square brackets substituted by the Copyright, Designs and Patents Act 1988, s 272, Sch 3, para 27(1), (3); words in second (outer) pair of square brackets substituted by the Registered Designs Regulations 2001, SI 2001/3949, reg 9(1), Sch 1, para 12, for transitional provisions in relation to certain applications and registrations, see regs 10–14 of those Regulations at **[3.88]**–**[3.92]**; words in third (inner) pair of square brackets inserted by the Intellectual Property Act 2014, s 9(6), as from a day to be appointed.

Sub-s (3): words in first pair of square brackets substituted by the Copyright, Designs and Patents Act 1988, s 272, Sch 3, para 27(1), (3); words omitted repealed and words in second and third pairs of square brackets inserted by the Intellectual Property Act 2014, ss 8(2)(a), 10(5), 11(3)(a).

Sub-s (4): words in first pair of square brackets substituted by the Copyright, Designs and Patents Act 1988, s 272, Sch 3, para 27(1), (3); words in second pair of square brackets inserted by the Intellectual Property Act 2014, s 11(3)(b).

Sub-s (4A): inserted by the Intellectual Property Act 2014, s 11(3)(c).

Sub-s (4B): inserted by the Intellectual Property Act 2014, s 8(2)(b).

Orders: the Designs (Convention Countries) Order 2007, SI 2007/277 at **[3.164]**; the Registered Designs (Isle of Man) Order 2013, SI 2013/2533.

[3.69]

[37A Use of electronic communications

(1) The registrar may give directions as to the form and manner in which documents to be delivered to the registrar—

(a) in electronic form; or

(b) using electronic communications,

are to be delivered to him.

(2) A direction under subsection (1) may provide that in order for a document to be delivered in compliance with the direction it shall be accompanied by one or more additional documents specified in the direction.

(3) Subject to subsections (11) and (12), if a document to which a direction under subsection (1) or (2) applies is delivered to the registrar in a form or manner which does not comply with the direction the registrar may treat the document as not having been delivered.

(4) Subsection (5) applies in relation to a case where—

(a) a document is delivered using electronic communications, and

(b) there is a requirement for a fee to accompany the document.

(5) The registrar may give directions specifying—

(a) how the fee shall be paid; and
(b) when the fee shall be deemed to have been paid.

(6) The registrar may give directions specifying that a person who delivers a document to the registrar in electronic form or using electronic communications cannot treat the document as having been delivered unless its delivery has been acknowledged.

(7) The registrar may give directions specifying how a time of delivery is to be accorded to a document delivered to him in electronic form or using electronic communications.

(8) A direction under this section may be given—
(a) generally;
(b) in relation to a description of cases specified in the direction;
(c) in relation to a particular person or persons.

(9) A direction under this section may be varied or revoked by a subsequent direction under this section.

(10) The delivery using electronic communications to any person by the registrar of any document is deemed to be effected, unless the registrar has otherwise specified, by transmitting an electronic communication containing the document to an address provided or made available to the registrar by that person as an address of his for the receipt of electronic communications; and unless the contrary is proved such delivery is deemed to be effected immediately upon the transmission of the communication.

(11) A requirement of this Act that something must be done in the prescribed manner is satisfied in the case of something that is done—
(a) using a document in electronic form, or
(b) using electronic communications,
only if the directions under this section that apply to the manner in which it is done are complied with.

(12) In the case of an application made as mentioned in subsection (11)(a) or (b) above, a reference in this Act to the application not having been made in accordance with rules under this Act includes a reference to its not having been made in accordance with any applicable directions under this section.

(13) This section applies—
(a) to delivery at the Patent Office as it applies to delivery to the registrar; and
(b) to delivery by the Patent Office as it applies to delivery by the registrar.]

NOTES

Inserted by the Registered Designs Act 1949 and Patents Act 1977 (Electronic Communications) Order 2006, SI 2006/1229, art 2.

38 (*Repealed by the Copyright, Designs and Patents Act 1988, ss 272, 303(2), Sch 3, para 28, Sch 8.*)

Supplemental

[3.70]

39 Hours of business and excluded days

(1) [The registrar may give directions specifying] the hour at which the Patent Office shall be deemed to be closed on any day for the purposes of the transaction by the public of business under this Act or of any class of such business, [and specifying] days as excluded days for any such purposes.

(2) Any business done under this Act on any day after the hour specified as aforesaid in relation to business of that class, or on a day which is an excluded day in relation to business of that class, shall be deemed to have been done on the next following day not being an excluded day; and where the time for doing anything under this Act expires on an excluded day, that time shall be extended to the next following day not being an excluded day.

NOTES

Sub-s (1): words in first and second pairs of square brackets substituted for original words "Rules made by the Secretary of State under this Act may specify" and "and may specify" respectively, by the Intellectual Property Act 2014, s 12(4), as from 1 October 2014, subject to s 12(8) thereof which provides that any rules made in reliance on sub-s (1) above which are in force immediately before 1 October 2014, continue in force until such time as directions about the matter specified by the rules take effect.

[3.71]

40 Fees

There shall be paid in respect of the registration of designs and applications therefor, and in respect of other matters relating to designs arising under this Act, such fees as may be prescribed by rules made by [the Secretary of State] with the consent of the Treasury.

NOTES

Words in square brackets substituted by the Copyright, Designs and Patents Act 1988, s 272, Sch 3, para 29.
Rules: the Registered Designs (Fees) Rules 2016, SI 2016/889.

[3.72]

41 Service of notices, etc, by post

Any notice required or authorised to be given by or under this Act, and any application or other document so authorised or required to be made or filed, may be given, made or filed by post.

[3.73]

42 Annual report of registrar

The Comptroller-General of Patents, Designs and Trade Marks shall, in his annual report with respect to the execution of [the Patents Act 1977], include a report with respect to the execution of this Act as if it formed a part of or was included in that Act.

NOTES

Words in square brackets substituted by the Patents Act 1977, s 132(6), Sch 5, para 3.

[3.74]

43 Savings

(1) . . .

(2) Nothing in this Act shall affect the right of the Crown or of any person deriving title directly or indirectly from the Crown to sell or use [products] forfeited under the laws relating to customs or excise.

NOTES

Sub-s (1): repealed by the Registered Designs Regulations 2001, SI 2001/3949, reg 9(2), Sch 2; for transitional provisions in relation to certain applications and registrations, see regs 10–14 of those Regulations at **[3.88]–[3.92]**.

Sub-s (2): word in square brackets substituted by SI 2001/3949, reg 9(1), Sch 1, para 13; for transitional provisions in relation to certain applications and registrations, see regs 10–14 of those Regulations at **[3.88]–[3.92]**.

[3.75]

44 Interpretation

(1) In this Act, except where the context otherwise requires, the following expressions have the meanings hereby respectively assigned by them, that is to say—

. . .

"assignee" includes the personal representative of a deceased assignee, and references to the assignee of any person include references to the assignee of the personal representative or assignee of that person;

["author" in relation to a design, has the meaning given by section 2(3) and (4);]

. . .

["Community Design Regulation" means Council Regulation (EC) 6/2002 of 12th December 2001 on Community Designs;]

["complex product" has the meaning assigned to it by section 1(3) of this Act;]

. . .

"the court" shall be construed in accordance with section 27 of this Act;

"design" has the meaning assigned to it by [[section 1(2)] of this Act];

["electronic communication" has the same meaning as in the Electronic Communications Act 2000;]

"employee", "employment" and "employer" refer to employment under a contract of service or of apprenticeship,

. . .

["national unregistered design right" means design right within the meaning of Part III of the Copyright, Designs and Patents Act 1988;]

"prescribed" means prescribed by rules made by [the Secretary of State] under this Act;

["product" has the meaning assigned to it by section 1(3) of this Act;]

"proprietor" has the meaning assigned to it by section two of this Act;

["registered Community design" means a design that complies with the conditions contained in, and is registered in the manner provided for in, the Community Design Regulation;]

"registered proprietor" means the person or persons for the time being entered in the register of designs as proprietor of the design;

"registrar" means the Comptroller-General of Patents Designs and Trade Marks;

. . .

(2), (3) . . .

(4) For the purposes of subsection (1) of [section 14 of this Act], the expression "personal representative", in relation to a deceased person, includes the legal representative of the deceased appointed in any country outside the United Kingdom.

NOTES

Sub-s (1): definition "Appeal Tribunal" (omitted) repealed by the Intellectual Property Act 2014, s 10(6); definitions "article", "artistic work" (as originally inserted by the Copyright Act 1956, s 44(5)), "copyright", "corresponding design" (as originally inserted by the Copyright Act 1956, s 44(5)), and "set of articles" repealed, and definitions "complex product", "national unregistered design right", and "product", inserted, by the Registered Designs Regulations 2001, SI 2001/3949, reg 9, Sch 1, para 14(1), (3), subject to transitional provisions in regs 10–14 of those Regulations at **[3.88]–[3.92]**; definitions "author", "employee", "employment", and "employer" inserted, definition "the court" substituted, definition "Journal" repealed, and words in square brackets in definition "prescribed" substituted, by the Copyright, Designs and Patents Act 1988, ss 272, 303(2), Sch 3, para 31(1), (3), (6), (8)–(10), Sch 8; definitions "Community Design Regulation" and "registered Community design" inserted by the Registered Designs Regulations 2003, SI 2003/550, reg 2(1), (5); in definition "design" words in first (outer) pair of square brackets substituted by Copyright, Designs and Patents Act 1988, s 272, Sch 3, para 31(1), (7), words in second (inner) pair of square brackets substituted by SI 2001/3949, reg 9(1), Sch 1, para 14(1), (2), subject to transitional provisions in regs 10–14 of those Regulations at **[3.88]–[3.92]**; definition "electronic communication" inserted by the Registered Designs Act 1949 and Patents Act 1977 (Electronic Communications) Order 2006, SI 2006/1229, art 3.

Sub-ss (2), (3): repealed by SI 2001/3949, reg 9(2), Sch 2; for transitional provisions in relation to certain applications and registrations, see regs 10–14 of those Regulations at **[3.88]–[3.92]**.

Sub-s (4): words in square brackets substituted by SI 2001/3949, reg 9(1), Sch 1, para 14(1), (4); for transitional provisions in relation to certain applications and registrations, see regs 10–14 of those Regulations at **[3.88]–[3.92]**.

[3.76]

[45 Application to Scotland

(1) In the application of this Act to Scotland—

"account of profits" means accounting and payment of profits;
"accounts" means count, reckoning and payment;
"arbitrator" means arbiter;
"assignment" means assignation;
"claimant" means pursuer;
"costs" means expenses;
"defendant" means defender;
"delivery up" means delivery;
"injunction" means interdict;
"interlocutory relief" means interim remedy.

[(1A) In the application of section 26C(1)(a) (remedy for unjustified threat of infringement proceedings) to Scotland, "declaration" means "declarator".]

(2) References to the Crown shall be construed as including references to the Crown in right of the Scottish Administration.]

NOTES

Substituted by the Intellectual Property (Enforcement, etc) Regulations 2006, SI 2006/1028, reg 2(1), Sch 1, paras 1, 5.

Sub-s (1A): inserted by the Intellectual Property (Unjustified Threats) Act 2017, s 4(1), (5), as from a day to be appointed.

[3.77]

46 Application to Northern Ireland

In the application of this Act to Northern Ireland—

(1), (2) . . .

[(3) References to enactments include enactments comprised in Northern Ireland legislation:]

[(3A) References to the Crown include the Crown in right of Her Majesty's Government in Northern Ireland:]

(4) References to a Government department shall be construed as including references to [a Northern Ireland department] [and in relation to a Northern Ireland department references to the Treasury shall be construed as references to the Department of Finance and Personnel]:

[(4A) Any reference to a claimant includes a reference to a plaintiff.]

(5) . . .

NOTES

Sub-ss (1), (2): repealed by the Copyright, Designs and Patents Act 1988, ss 272, 303(2), Sch 3, para 33(1), (2), Sch 8.

Sub-s (3): substituted by the Copyright, Designs and Patents Act 1988, s 272, Sch 3, para 33(1), (3).

Sub-s (3A): inserted by the Copyright, Designs and Patents Act 1988, s 272, Sch 3, para 33(1), (4).

Sub-s (4): words in first pair of square brackets substituted, and words in second pair of square brackets inserted, by the Copyright, Designs and Patents Act 1988, s 272, Sch 3, para 33(1), (5).

Sub-s (4A): inserted by the Intellectual Property (Enforcement, etc) Regulations 2006, SI 2006/1028, reg 2(1), Sch 1, paras 1, 6.

Sub-s (5): repealed by the Northern Ireland Act 1962, s 30(2)(d), Sch 4, Pt IV.

[3.78]

[47 Application to Isle of Man

This Act extends to the Isle of Man, subject to any modifications contained in an Order made by Her Majesty in Council, and accordingly, subject to any such Order, references in this Act to the United Kingdom shall be construed as including the Isle of Man.]

NOTES

Substituted by the Copyright, Designs and Patents Act 1988, s 272, Sch 3, para 34.

Orders: the Registered Designs (Isle of Man) Order 2013, SI 2013/2533.

[3.79]

[47A Territorial waters and the continental shelf

(1) For the purposes of this Act the territorial waters of the United Kingdom shall be treated as part of the United Kingdom.

(2) This Act applies to things done in the United Kingdom sector of the continental shelf on a structure or vessel which is present there for purposes directly connected with the exploration of the sea bed or subsoil or the exploitation of their natural resources as it applies to things done in the United Kingdom.

(3) The United Kingdom sector of the continental shelf means the areas designated by order under section 1(7) of the Continental Shelf Act 1964.]

NOTES

Inserted by the Copyright, Designs and Patents Act 1988, s 272, Sch 3, para 35.

[3.80]

48 Repeals, savings, and transitional provisions

(1) . . .

(2) Subject to the provisions of this section, any Order in Council, rule, order, requirement, certificate, notice, decision, direction, authorisation, consent, application, request or thing made, issued, given or done under any enactment repealed by this Act shall, if in force at the commencement of this Act, and so far as it could have been made, issued, given or done under this Act, continue in force and have effect as if made, issued, given or done under the corresponding enactment of this Act.

(3) Any register kept under the Patents and Designs Act 1907, shall be deemed to form part of the corresponding register under this Act.

(4) Any design registered before the commencement of this Act shall be deemed to be registered under this Act in respect of articles of the class in which it is registered.

(5) . . .

(6) Any document referring to any enactment repealed by this Act shall be construed as referring to the corresponding enactment of this Act.

(7) Nothing in the foregoing provisions of this section shall be taken as prejudicing the operation of section thirty-eight of the Interpretation Act 1889, (which relates to the effect of repeals).

NOTES

Sub-s (1): repealed by the Copyright, Designs and Patents Act 1988, ss 272, 303(2), Sch 3, para 36, Sch 8.

Sub-s (5): repealed by the Registered Designs Regulations 2001, SI 2001/3949, reg 9(2), Sch 2; for transitional provisions in relation to certain applications and registrations, see regs 10–14 of those Regulations at **[3.88]–[3.92]**.

Interpretation Act 1889, s 38: repealed by the Interpretation Act 1978, s 25, Sch 3, and replaced by ss 16(1), 17(2)(a) of, and Sch 2, para 3 to, that Act.

[3.81]

49 Short title and commencement

(1) This Act may be cited as the Registered Designs Act 1949.

(2) This Act shall come into operation on the first day of January, nineteen hundred and fifty, immediately after the coming into operation of the Patents and Designs Act 1949.

NOTES

Patents and Designs Act 1949: repealed by the Statute Law (Repeals) Act 1986 (having come into operation on 1 January 1950).

SCHEDULES

[SCHEDULE A1

GROUNDS FOR REFUSAL OF REGISTRATION IN RELATION TO EMBLEMS ETC

Grounds for refusal in relation to certain emblems etc

[3.82]

1. (1) A design shall be refused registration under this Act if it involves the use of—

(a) the Royal arms, or any of the principal armorial bearings of the Royal arms, or any insignia or device so nearly resembling the Royal arms or any such armorial bearing as to be likely to be mistaken for them or it;

(b) a representation of the Royal crown or any of the Royal flags;

(c) a representation of Her Majesty or any member of the Royal family, or any colourable imitation thereof; or

(d) words, letters or devices likely to lead persons to think that the applicant either has or recently has had Royal patronage or authorisation;

unless it appears to the registrar that consent for such use has been given by or on behalf of Her Majesty or (as the case may be) the relevant member of the Royal family.

(2) A design shall be refused registration under this Act if it involves the use of—

(a) the national flag of the United Kingdom (commonly known as the Union Jack); or

Part 3 Designs

(b) the flag of England, Wales, Scotland, Northern Ireland or the Isle of Man,

and it appears to the registrar that the use would be misleading or grossly offensive.

(3) A design shall be refused registration under this Act if it involves the use of—

(a) arms to which a person is entitled by virtue of a grant of arms by the Crown; or

(b) insignia so nearly resembling such arms as to be likely to be mistaken for them;

unless it appears to the registrar that consent for such use has been given by or on behalf of the person concerned and the use is not in any way contrary to the law of arms.

(4) A design shall be refused registration under this Act if it involves the use of a controlled representation within the meaning of the Olympic Symbol etc (Protection) Act 1995 unless it appears to the registrar that—

(a) the application is made by the person for the time being appointed under section 1(2) of the Olympic Symbol etc (Protection) Act 1995 (power of Secretary of State to appoint a person as the proprietor of the Olympics association right); or

(b) consent for such use has been given by or on behalf of the person mentioned in paragraph (a) above.

Grounds for refusal in relation to emblems etc of Paris Convention countries

2. (1) A design shall be refused registration under this Act if it involves the use of the flag of a Paris Convention country unless—

(a) the authorisation of the competent authorities of that country has been given for the registration; or

(b) it appears to the registrar that the use of the flag in the manner proposed is permitted without such authorisation.

(2) A design shall be refused registration under this Act if it involves the use of the armorial bearings or any other state emblem of a Paris Convention country which is protected under the Paris Convention unless the authorisation of the competent authorities of that country has been given for the registration.

(3) A design shall be refused registration under this Act if—

(a) the design involves the use of an official sign or hallmark adopted by a Paris Convention country and indicating control and warranty;

(b) the sign or hallmark is protected under the Paris Convention; and

(c) the design could be applied to or incorporated in goods of the same, or a similar, kind as those in relation to which the sign or hallmark indicates control and warranty;

unless the authorisation of the competent authorities of that country has been given for the registration.

(4) The provisions of this paragraph as to national flags and other state emblems, and official signs or hallmarks, apply equally to anything which from a heraldic point of view imitates any such flag or other emblem, or sign or hallmark.

(5) Nothing in this paragraph prevents the registration of a design on the application of a national of a country who is authorised to make use of a state emblem, or official sign or hallmark, of that country, notwithstanding that it is similar to that of another country.

Grounds for refusal in relation to emblems etc of certain international organisations

3. (1) This paragraph applies to—

(a) the armorial bearings, flags or other emblems; and

(b) the abbreviations and names,

of international intergovernmental organisations of which one or more Paris Convention countries are members.

(2) A design shall be refused registration under this Act if it involves the use of any such emblem, abbreviation or name which is protected under the Paris Convention unless—

(a) the authorisation of the international organisation concerned has been given for the registration; or

(b) it appears to the registrar that the use of the emblem, abbreviation or name in the manner proposed—

(i) is not such as to suggest to the public that a connection exists between the organisation and the design; or

(ii) is not likely to mislead the public as to the existence of a connection between the user and the organisation.

(3) The provisions of this paragraph as to emblems of an international organisation apply equally to anything which from a heraldic point of view imitates any such emblem.

(4) Nothing in this paragraph affects the rights of a person whose *bona fide* use of the design in question began before 4th January 1962 (when the relevant provisions of the Paris Convention entered into force in relation to the United Kingdom).

Paragraphs 2 and 3: supplementary

4. (1) For the purposes of paragraph 2 above state emblems of a Paris Convention country (other than the national flag), and official signs or hallmarks, shall be regarded as protected under the Paris Convention only if, or to the extent that—

(a) the country in question has notified the United Kingdom in accordance with Article 6*ter* (3) of the Convention that it desires to protect that emblem, sign or hallmark;

(b) the notification remains in force; and

(c) the United Kingdom has not objected to it in accordance with Article 6*ter* (4) or any such objection has been withdrawn.

(2) For the purposes of paragraph 3 above the emblems, abbreviations and names of an international organisation shall be regarded as protected under the Paris Convention only if, or to the extent that—

(a) the organisation in question has notified the United Kingdom in accordance with Article 6*ter* (3) of the Convention that it desires to protect that emblem, abbreviation or name;

(b) the notification remains in force; and

(c) the United Kingdom has not objected to it in accordance with Article 6*ter* (4) or any such objection has been withdrawn.

(3) Notification under Article 6*ter* (3) of the Paris Convention shall have effect only in relation to applications for the registration of designs made more than two months after the receipt of the notification.

Interpretation

5. In this Schedule—

"a Paris Convention country" means a country, other than the United Kingdom, which is a party to the Paris Convention; and

"the Paris Convention" means the Paris Convention for the Protection of Industrial Property of 20th March 1883.]

NOTES

Inserted by the Registered Designs Regulations 2001, SI 2001/3949, reg 3; for transitional provisions in relation to certain applications and registrations, see regs 10–14 of those Regulations at **[3.88]–[3.92]**.

FIRST SCHEDULE
PROVISIONS AS TO THE USE OF REGISTERED DESIGNS FOR THE SERVICES OF THE CROWN AND AS TO THE RIGHTS OF THIRD PARTIES IN RESPECT OF SUCH USE

Section 12

[3.83]

1 Use of registered designs for services of the Crown

(1) Notwithstanding anything in this Act, any Government department, and any person authorised in writing by a Government department, may use any registered design for the services of the Crown in accordance with the following provisions of this paragraph.

(2) If and so far as the design has before the date of registration thereof been duly recorded by or applied by or on behalf of a Government department otherwise than in consequence of the communication of the design directly or indirectly by the registered proprietor or any person from whom he derives title, any use of the design by virtue of this paragraph may be made free of any royalty or other payment to the registered proprietor.

(3) If and so far as the design has not been so recorded or applied as aforesaid, any use of the design made by virtue of this paragraph at any time after the date of registration thereof, or in consequence of any such communication as aforesaid, shall be made upon such terms as may be agreed upon, either before or after the use, between the Government department and the registered proprietor with the approval of the Treasury, or as may in default of agreement be determined by the court on a reference under paragraph 3 of this Schedule.

(4) The authority of a Government department in respect of a design may be given under this paragraph either before or after the design is registered and either before or after the acts in respect of which the authority is given are done, and may be given to any person whether or not he is authorised directly or indirectly by the registered proprietor to use the design.

(5) Where any use of a design is made by or with the authority of a Government department under this paragraph, then, unless it appears to the department that it would be contrary to the public interest so to do, the department shall notify the registered proprietor as soon as practicable after the use is begun, and furnish him with such information as to the extent of the use as he may from time to time require.

[(6) For the purposes of this and the next following paragraph "the services of the Crown" shall be deemed to include—

(a) the supply to the government of any country outside the United Kingdom, in pursuance of an agreement or arrangement between Her Majesty's Government in the United Kingdom and the government of that country, of [products] required—
   (i) for the defence of that country; or
   (ii) for the defence of any other country whose government is party to any agreement or arrangement with Her Majesty's said Government in respect of defence matters;

(b) the supply to the United Nations, or to the government of any country belonging to that organisation, in pursuance of an agreement or arrangement between Her Majesty's Government and that organisation or government, of [products] required for any armed forces operating in pursuance of a resolution of that organisation or any organ of that organisation;

and the power of a Government department or a person authorised by a Government department under this paragraph to use a design shall include power to sell to any such government or to the said organisation any [products] the supply of which is authorised by this sub-paragraph, and to sell to any person any [products] made in the exercise of the powers conferred by this paragraph which are no longer required for the purpose for which they were made.]

(7) The purchaser of any [products] sold in the exercise of powers conferred by this paragraph, and any person claiming through him, shall have power to deal with them in the same manner as if the rights in the registered design were held on behalf of His Majesty.

2 Rights of third parties in respect of Crown use

(1) In relation to any use of a registered design, or a design in respect of which an application for registration is pending, made for the services of the Crown—

(a) by a Government department or a person authorised by a Government department under the last foregoing paragraph; or

(b) by the registered proprietor or applicant for registration to the order of a Government department,

the provisions of any licence, assignment or agreement made, whether before or after the commencement of this Act, between the registered proprietor or applicant for registration or any person who derives title from him or from whom he derives title and any person other than a Government department shall be of no effect so far as those provisions restrict or regulate the use of the design, or any model, document or information relating thereto, or provide for the making of payments in respect of any such use, or calculated by reference thereto; and the reproduction or publication of any model or document in connection with the said use shall not be deemed to be an infringement of any copyright [or [national unregistered design right]] subsisting in the model or document.

(2) Where an exclusive licence granted otherwise than for royalties or other benefits determined by reference to the use of the design is in force under the registered design then—

(a) in relation to any use of the design which, but for the provisions of this and the last foregoing paragraph, would constitute an infringement of the rights of the licensee, sub-paragraph (3) of the last foregoing paragraph shall have effect as if for the reference to the registered proprietor there were substituted a reference to the licensee; and

(b) in relation to any use of the design by the licensee by virtue of an authority given under the last foregoing paragraph, that paragraph shall have effect as if the said sub-paragraph (3) were omitted.

(3) Subject to the provisions of the last foregoing sub-paragraph, where the registered design or the right to apply for or obtain registration of the design has been assigned to the registered proprietor in consideration of royalties or other benefits determined by reference to the use of the design, then—

(a) in relation to any use of the design by virtue of paragraph 1 of this Schedule, sub-paragraph (3) of that paragraph shall have effect as if the reference to the registered proprietor included a reference to the assignor, and any sum payable by virtue of that sub-paragraph shall be divided between the registered proprietor and the assignor in such proportion as may be agreed upon between them or as may in default of agreement be determined by the court on a reference under the next following paragraph; and

(b) in relation to any use of the design made for the services of the Crown by the registered proprietor to the order of a Government department, sub-paragraph (3) of paragraph 1 of this Schedule shall have effect as if that use were made by virtue of an authority given under that paragraph.

(4) Where, under sub-paragraph (3) of paragraph 1 of this Schedule, payments are required to be made by a Government department to a registered proprietor in respect of any use of a design, any person being the holder of an exclusive licence under the registered design (not being such a licence as is mentioned in sub-paragraph (2) of this paragraph) authorising him to make use of the design shall be entitled to recover from the registered proprietor such part (if any) of those payments as may be agreed upon between that person and the registered proprietor, or as may in default of agreement be determined by the court under the next following paragraph to be just having regard to any expenditure incurred by that person—

(a) in developing the said design; or

(b) in making payments to the registered proprietor, other than royalties or other payments determined by reference to the use of the design, in consideration of the licence;

and if, at any time before the amount of any such payment has been agreed upon between the Government department and the registered proprietor, that person gives notice in writing of his interest to the department, any agreement as to the amount of that payment shall be of no effect unless it is made with his consent.

(5) In this paragraph "exclusive licence" means a licence from a registered proprietor which confers on the licensee, or on the licensee and persons authorised by him, to the exclusion of all other persons (including the registered proprietor), any right in respect of the registered design.

[2A Compensation for loss of profit

(1) Where Crown use is made of a registered design, the government department concerned shall pay—

(a) to the registered proprietor, or

(b) if there is an exclusive licence in force in respect of the design, to the exclusive licensee,

compensation for any loss resulting from his not being awarded a contract to supply the [products] to which the design is applied [or in which it is incorporated].

(2) Compensation is payable only to the extent that such a contract could have been fulfilled from his existing manufacturing capacity; but is payable notwithstanding the existence of circumstances rendering him ineligible for the award of such a contract.

(3) In determining the loss, regard shall be had to the profit which would have been made on such a contract and to the extent to which any manufacturing capacity was underused.

(4) No compensation is payable in respect of any failure to secure contracts for the supply of [products] to which the design is applied [or in which it is incorporated] otherwise than for the services of the Crown.

(5) The amount payable under this paragraph shall, if not agreed between the registered proprietor or licensee and the government department concerned with the approval of the Treasury, be determined by the court on a reference under paragraph 3; and it is in addition to any amount payable under paragraph 1 or 2 of this Schedule.

(6) In this paragraph—

"Crown use", in relation to a design, means the doing of anything by virtue of paragraph 1 which would otherwise be an infringement of the right in the design; and

"the government department concerned", in relation to such use, means the government department by whom or on whose authority the act was done.]

3 Reference of disputes as to Crown use

[(1) Any dispute as to—

(a) the exercise by a Government department, or a person authorised by a Government department, of the powers conferred by paragraph 1 of this Schedule,

(b) terms for the use of a design for the services of the Crown under that paragraph,

(c) the right of any person to receive any part of a payment made under paragraph 1(3), or

(d) the right of any person to receive a payment under paragraph 2A,

may be referred to the court by either party to the dispute.]

(2) In any proceedings under this paragraph to which a Government department are a party, the department may—

(a) if the registered proprietor is a party to the proceedings [and the department are a relevant person within the meaning of section 20 of this Act], apply for [invalidation] of the registration of the design upon any ground upon which the registration of a design may be [declared invalid] on an application to the court under section twenty of this Act;

(b) in any case [and provided that the department would be the relevant person within the meaning of section 20 of this Act if they had made an application on the grounds for invalidity being raised], put in issue the validity of the registration of the design without applying for its [invalidation].

(3) If in such proceedings as aforesaid any question arises whether a design has been recorded or applied as mentioned in paragraph 1 of this Schedule, and the disclosure of any document recording the design, or of any evidence of the application thereof, would in the opinion of the department be prejudicial to the public interest, the disclosure may be made confidentially to counsel for the other party or to an independent expert mutually agreed upon.

(4) In determining under this paragraph any dispute between a Government department and any person as to terms for the use of a design for the services of the Crown, the court shall have regard to any benefit or compensation which that person or any person from whom he derives title may have received, or may be entitled to receive, directly or indirectly from any Government department in respect of the design in question.

(5) In any proceedings under this paragraph the court may at any time order the whole proceedings or any question or issue of fact arising therein to be referred to a special or official referee or an arbitrator on such terms as the court may direct; and references to the court in the foregoing provisions of this paragraph shall be construed accordingly.

4 Special provisions as to Crown use during emergency

(1) During any period of emergency within the meaning of this paragraph, the powers exercisable in relation to a design by a Government department, or a person authorised by a Government department under paragraph 1 of this Schedule shall include power to use the design for any purpose which appears to the department necessary or expedient—

(a) for the efficient prosecution of any war in which His Majesty may be engaged;
(b) for the maintenance of supplies and services essential to the life of the community;
(c) for securing a sufficiency of supplies and services essential to the well-being of the community;
(d) for promoting the productivity of industry, commerce and agriculture;
(e) for fostering and directing exports and reducing imports, or imports of any classes, from all or any countries and for redressing the balance of trade;
(f) generally for ensuring that the whole resources of the community are available for use, and are used, in a manner best calculated to serve the interests of the community; or
(g) for assisting the relief of suffering and the restoration and distribution of essential supplies and services in any part of His Majesty's dominions or any foreign countries that are in grave distress as the result of war;

and any reference in this Schedule to the services of the Crown shall be construed as including a reference to the purposes aforesaid.

(2) In this paragraph the expression "period of emergency" means [a period] beginning on such date as may be declared by Order in Council to be the commencement, and ending on such date as may be so declared to be the termination, of a period of emergency for the purposes of this paragraph.

[(3) No Order in Council under this paragraph shall be submitted to Her Majesty unless a draft of it has been laid before and approved by a resolution of each House of Parliament.]

NOTES

Para 1: sub-para (6) substituted by the Defence Contracts Act 1958, s 1(1), (4); words in square brackets in sub-paras (6), (7) substituted by Registered Designs Regulations 2001, SI 2001/3949, reg 9(1), Sch 1, para 15(1), (2), for transitional provisions in relation to certain applications and registrations, see regs 10–14 of those Regulations at **[3.88]–[3.92]**.

Para 2: words in first (outer) pair of square brackets in sub-para (1) inserted by the Copyright, Designs and Patents Act 1988, s 272, Sch 3, para 37; words in second (inner) pair of square brackets in that sub-paragraph substituted by SI 2001/3949, reg 9(1), Sch 1, para 15(1), (3), for transitional provisions in relation to certain applications and registrations, see regs 10–14 of those Regulations at **[3.88]–[3.92]**.

Paras 2A: inserted by the Copyright, Designs and Patents Act 1988, s 272, Sch 3, para 37, in relation to any Crown use of a registered design after 1 August 1989, even if the terms of such use were settled before that date; words in first pairs of square brackets in sub-paras (1), (4) substituted, and words in second pairs of square brackets inserted, by SI 2001/3949, reg 9(1), Sch 1, para 15(1), (4), for transitional provisions in relation to certain applications and registrations, see regs 10–14 of those Regulations at **[3.88]–[3.92]**.

Para 3: sub-para (1) substituted by the Copyright, Designs and Patents Act 1988, s 271, in relation to any Crown use of a registered design after 1 August 1989, even if the terms for such use were settled before that date; words in first pair of square brackets in sub-para (2)(a) inserted, and words in second and third pairs of square brackets in that sub-paragraph substituted, and words in first pair of square brackets in sub-para (2)(b) inserted, and words in second pair of square brackets in that sub-paragraph substituted, by the Registered Designs Regulations 2001, SI 2001/3949, reg 9(1), Sch 1, para 15(1), (5), (6), for transitional provisions in relation to certain applications and registrations, see regs 10–14 of those Regulations at **[3.88]–[3.92]**.

Para 4: words in square brackets in sub-para (2), and the whole of sub-para (3) substituted by the Copyright, Designs and Patents Act 1988, s 272, Sch 3, para 37.

SCHEDULE 2

(Sch 2 repealed by the Copyright, Designs and Patents Act 1988, ss 272, 303(2), Sch 3, para 28, Sch 8.)

COPYRIGHT (INDUSTRIAL PROCESS AND EXCLUDED ARTICLES) (NO 2) ORDER 1989

(SI 1989/1070)

NOTES

Made: 26 June 1989.
Authority: Copyright, Designs and Patents Act 1988, s 52(4).
Commencement: 1 August 1989.

[3.84]
1

This Order may be cited as the Copyright (Industrial Process and Excluded Articles) (No 2) Order 1989 and shall come into force on 1st August 1989.

[3.85]
2

An article is to be regarded for the purposes of section 52 of the Act (limitation of copyright protection for design derived from artistic work) as made by an industrial process if—

(a) it is one of more than fifty articles which—

(i) all fall to be treated for the purposes of Part I of the Act as copies of a particular artistic work, but

(ii) do not all together constitute a single set of articles as defined in section 44(1) of the Registered Designs Act 1949; or

(b) it consists of goods manufactured in lengths or pieces, not being hand-made goods.

[3.86]
3

(1) There are excluded from the operation of section 52 of the Act—

(a) works of sculpture, other than casts or models used or intended to be used as models or patterns to be multiplied by any industrial process;

(b) wall plaques, medals and medallions; and

(c) printed matter primarily of a literary or artistic character, including book jackets, calendars, certificates, coupons, dress-making patterns, greetings cards, labels, leaflets, maps, plans, playing cards, postcards, stamps, trade advertisements, trade forms and cards, transfers and similar articles.

(2) Nothing in article 2 of this Order shall be taken to limit the meaning of "industrial process" in paragraph (1)(a) of this article.

4 (*Revokes the Copyright (Industrial Designs) Rules 1957, SI 1957/867 and the Copyright (Industrial Process and Excluded Articles) Order 1989, SI 1989/1010.*)

REGISTERED DESIGNS REGULATIONS 2001

(SI 2001/3949)

NOTES

Made: 8 December 2001.
Authority: European Communities Act 1972, s 2(2).
Commencement: 9 December 2001.

ARRANGEMENT OF REGULATIONS

[3.87]
1 Citation, commencement and extent

(1) These Regulations may be cited as the Registered Designs Regulations 2001 and shall come into force on the day after the day on which they are made.

(2) Subject to paragraph (3), these Regulations extend to England and Wales, Scotland and Northern Ireland.

(3) The amendments made by these Regulations to the Chartered Associations (Protection of Names and Uniforms) Act 1926 do not extend to Northern Ireland.

2–9 (*Reg 2 substitutes the Registered Designs Act 1949, ss 1, 1A–1D for original s 1 at* **[3.1]–[3.4]***; reg 3 inserts Sch A1 to that Act at* **[3.82]***; reg 4 substitutes ss 3, 3A–3D for original s 3 of that Act at* **[3.6]–[3.10]***, reg 5 substitutes ss 7, 7A for original s 7 of that Act at* **[3.12]**, **[3.13]***; reg 6 revokes s 10 and amends s 11A of that Act at* **[3.25]***; reg 7 substitutes ss 11, 11ZA–11ZF for original s 11 of that Act at* **[3.19]–[3.24]***; reg 8 amends s 20 of that Act at* **[3.38]***; reg 9 introduces Sch 1 (consequential amendments) and Sch 2 (repeals).*)

[3.88]
10 Transitional provisions: pending applications

(1) This Regulation applies to applications for registration under the Registered Designs Act 1949 which have been made but not finally determined before the coming into force of these Regulations ("pending applications").

(2) The Act of 1949 as it has effect immediately before the coming into force of these Regulations shall continue to apply in relation to pending applications so far as it relates to the determination of such applications.

(3) Accordingly the amendments and repeals made by these Regulations shall not apply in relation to the determination of such applications.

[3.89]

11 Transitional provisions: transitional registrations

(1) This Regulation applies to any registration under the Registered Designs Act 1949 which results from the determination of a pending application (within the meaning of Regulation 10).

(2) The Act of 1949 as it has effect immediately before the coming into force of these Regulations shall continue to apply in relation to registrations to which this Regulation applies ("transitional registrations") so far as the Act relates to the cancellation or invalidation of such registrations (other than cancellation by virtue of section 11(3) of that Act).

(3) Accordingly the amendments and repeals made by these Regulations shall, so far as they relate to the cancellation or invalidation of registrations, not apply in relation to transitional registrations.

(4) The amendments and repeals made by these Regulations shall otherwise (and subject to paragraphs (5) to (9) and Regulation 14) apply in relation to transitional registrations.

(5) In the application by virtue of paragraph (4) of the amendments made by Regulation 5, the fact that transitional registrations are in respect of any articles, or sets of articles, shall be disregarded.

(6) The amendments made by Regulation 4 shall not operate so as to determine the dates of registration of designs to which transitional registrations apply; and these dates shall be determined by reference to the Act of 1949 as it has effect immediately before the coming into force of these Regulations.

(7) Where—

(a) any such date of registration for the purposes of calculating the period for which the right in a registered design subsists, or any extension of that period, under section 8 of the Act of 1949 is determined by virtue of section 14(2) of that Act; and

(b) that date is earlier than the date which would otherwise have been the date of registration for those purposes;

the difference between the two dates shall be added to the first period of five years for which the right in the registered design is to subsist.

(8) Any reference in section 8 of the Act of 1949 to a period of five years shall, in the case of any such period which is extended by virtue of paragraph (7), be treated as a reference to the extended period.

(9) The repeal by these Regulations of the proviso in section 4(1) of the Act of 1949 and of the reference to it in section 8 of that Act shall not apply to the right in a design to which a transitional registration applies.

[3.90]

12 Transitional provisions: post-1989 registrations

(1) This Regulation applies to—

(a) any registration under the Registered Designs Act 1949 which—

(i) has resulted from an application made on or after 1st August 1989 and before the coming into force of these Regulations; and

(ii) has given rise to a right in a registered design which is in force at the coming into force of these Regulations;

(b) any registration under the Act of 1949 which—

(i) has resulted from an application made on or after 1st August 1989 and before the coming into force of these Regulations; and

(ii) has given rise to a right in a registered design which is not in force at the coming into force of these Regulations but which is capable of being treated as never having ceased to be in force by virtue of section 8(4) of the Act of 1949 or of being restored by virtue of sections 8A and 8B of that Act; and

(c) any registration which subsequently ceases to fall within sub-paragraph (b) because the right in the registered design has been treated or restored as mentioned in paragraph (ii) of that sub-paragraph.

(2) The Act of 1949 as it has effect immediately before the coming into force of these Regulations shall continue to apply in relation to registrations to which this Regulation applies ("post-1989 registrations") so far as the Act relates to the cancellation or invalidation of such registrations (other than cancellation by virtue of section 11(3) of that Act and by reference to an expiry of copyright occurring on or after the coming into force of these Regulations).

(3) Accordingly the amendments and repeals made by these Regulations shall, so far as they relate to the cancellation or invalidation of registrations, not apply in relation to post-1989 registrations.

(4) The amendments and repeals made by these Regulations shall otherwise apply (subject to paragraphs (5) to (9) and Regulation 14) in relation to post-1989 registrations.

(5) In the application by virtue of paragraph (4) of the amendments made by Regulation 5, the fact that post-1989 registrations are in respect of any articles, or sets of articles, shall be disregarded.

(6) The amendments made by Regulation 4 shall not operate so as to alter the dates of registration of designs to which post-1989 registrations apply.

(7) Where—

(a) any such date of registration for the purposes of calculating the period for which the right in a registered design subsists, or any extension of that period, under section 8 of the Act of 1949 was determined by virtue of section 14(2) of that Act; and

(b) that date is earlier than the date which would otherwise have been the date of registration for those purposes;

the difference between the two dates shall be added to any period of five years which is current on the coming into force of these Regulations or, if no such period is current but a subsequent extension or restoration is effected under section 8, or sections 8A and 8B, of the Act of 1949, to the period resulting from that extension or restoration.

(8) Any reference in section 8 of the Act of 1949 to a period of five years shall, in the case of any such period which is extended by virtue of paragraph (7), be treated as a reference to the extended period.

(9) The repeal by these Regulations of the proviso in section 4(1) of the Act of 1949 and the reference to it in section 8 of that Act shall not apply to the right in a design to which a post-1989 registration applies.

[3.91]

13 Transitional provisions: pre-1989 registrations

(1) This Regulation applies to—

(a) any registration under the Registered Designs Act 1949 which—

(i) has resulted from an application made before 1st August 1989; and

(ii) has given rise to a copyright in a registered design which is in force at the coming into force of these Regulations;

(b) any registration under the Act of 1949 which—

(i) has resulted from an application made before 1st August 1989; and

(ii) has given rise to a copyright in a registered design which is not in force at the coming into force of these Regulations but which would be capable of coming back into force by virtue of an extension of the period of copyright under section 8(2) of the Act of 1949 if that provision were amended as set out in paragraph (8); and

(c) any registration which subsequently ceases to fall within sub-paragraph (b) because the copyright in the registered design has come back into force by virtue of an extension of the period of copyright under section 8(2) of the Act of 1949 as amended by paragraph (8).

(2) Subject as follows, the amendments and repeals made by these Regulations shall not apply to any provision of the Act of 1949 which only has effect in relation to applications for registration made before 1st August 1989 or any registrations resulting from such applications.

(3) Any such provision and any other provision of the Act of 1949 as it has effect immediately before the coming into force of these Regulations in relation to registrations which fall within paragraph (1) ("pre-1989 registrations") shall continue to apply so far as it relates to the cancellation or invalidation of pre-1989 registrations (other than cancellation by virtue of section 11(3) of that Act and by reference to an expiry of copyright occurring on or after the coming into force of these Regulations).

(4) Accordingly the amendments and repeals made by these Regulations shall, so far as they relate to the cancellation or invalidation of registrations, not apply in relation to pre-1989 registrations.

(5) The amendments and repeals made by these Regulations shall otherwise apply (subject to paragraphs (2) and (9) to (12) and Regulation 14) in relation to pre-1989 registrations.

(6) Amendments and repeals corresponding to the amendments and repeals made by these Regulations (other than those relating to the cancellation or invalidation of registrations) shall be treated as having effect, with necessary modifications and subject to Regulation 14, in relation to any provision of the Act of 1949 which only has effect in relation to applications for registration made before 1st August 1989 or any registrations resulting from such applications.

(7) In the application by virtue of paragraph (6) of amendments corresponding to those made by Regulation 5, the fact that pre-1989 registrations are in respect of any articles, or sets of articles, shall be disregarded.

(8) In section 8(2) of the Act of 1949 as it has effect in relation to pre-1989 registrations (period of copyright)—

(a) after the words "second period", where they appear for the second time, there shall be inserted "and for a fourth period of five years from the expiration of the third period and for a fifth period of five years from the expiration of the fourth period";

(b) after the words "second or third" there shall be inserted "or fourth or fifth"; and

(c) after the words "second period", where they appear for the third time, there shall be inserted "or the third period or the fourth period".

(9) The amendments made by Regulation 4 shall not operate so as to alter the dates of registration of designs to which pre-1989 registrations apply.

(10) Where—

(a) the date of registration for the purposes of calculating the period of copyright, or any extension of that period, under section 8(2) of the Act of 1949 as it has effect in relation to pre-1989 registrations was determined by virtue of section 14(2) of that Act; and

(b) that date is earlier than the date which would otherwise have been the date of registration for those purposes;

the difference between the two dates shall be added to any period of five years which is current on the coming into force of these Regulations or, if no such period is current but a subsequent extension is effected under section 8 of the Act of 1949 as amended by paragraph (8), to the period resulting from that extension.

(11) Any reference in section 8(2) of the Act of 1949 as amended by paragraph (8) to a period of five years shall, in the case of any such period which is extended by virtue of paragraph (10), be treated as a reference to the extended period.

(12) The repeal by these Regulations of the proviso in section 4(1) of the Act of 1949 shall not apply to the right in a design to which a pre-1989 registration applies.

[3.92]

14 Other transitional provisions

(1) Any licence which—

(a) permits anything which would otherwise be an infringement under the Registered Designs Act 1949 of the right in a registered design or the copyright in a registered design; and

(b) was granted by the registered proprietor of the design, or under section 10 or 11A of the Act of 1949, before the coming into force of these Regulations,

shall continue in force, with necessary modifications, on or after the making of these Regulations.

(2) In determining the effect of any such licence on or after the coming into force of these Regulations, regard shall be had to the purpose for which the licence was granted; and, in particular, a licence granted for the full term or extent of the right in a registered design or the copyright in a registered design shall be treated as applying, subject to its other terms and conditions, to the full term or extent of that right as extended by virtue of these Regulations.

(3) The right in a registered design conferred by virtue of these Regulations in relation to registrations to which Regulation 11, 12 or 13 applies shall not enable the registered proprietor to prevent any person from continuing to carry out acts begun by him before the coming into force of these Regulations and which, at that time, the registered proprietor or, in the case of registrations to which Regulation 11 applies, a registered proprietor would have been unable to prevent.

(4) The right in a registered design conferred by virtue of these Regulations in relation to registrations to which Regulation 12 or 13 applies shall, in particular, not apply in relation to infringements committed in relation to those registrations before the coming into force of these Regulations.

(5) The repeals by these Regulations in section 5 of the Registered Designs Act 1949 shall not apply in relation to any evidence filed in support of an application made before the coming into force of these Regulations.

(6) The amendments and repeals made by these Regulations in section 22 of the Act of 1949 (other than the amendment to the proviso in subsection (2) of that section) shall not apply in relation to any registration which has resulted from an application made before the coming into force of these Regulations.

(7) The amendment to the proviso in section 22(2) of the Act of 1949 shall not apply where—

(a) the registration of the first-mentioned design resulted from an application made before the coming into force of these Regulations; and

(b) the application for the registration of the other design was also made before the coming into force of these Regulations.

(8) The amendments and repeals made by these Regulations in section 35 of the Act of 1949 shall not apply in relation to any offences committed before the coming into force of these Regulations.

(9) The repeal by these Regulations of provisions in section 44 of the Act of 1949 which relate to the meaning of a set of articles shall not apply so far as those provisions are required for the purposes of paragraph 6(2)(a) of Schedule 1 to the Copyright, Designs and Patents Act 1988.

(10) Any amendment or repeal by these Regulations of a provision in section 44 of the Act of 1949 or in any enactment other than the Act of 1949 shall not apply so far as that provision is required for the purposes of any other transitional provision made by these Regulations.

(11) The Act of 1949 as it has effect immediately before the coming into force of these Regulations shall continue to apply in relation to former registrations, whose registration resulted from an application made before the coming into force of these Regulations, so far as the Act relates to the cancellation or invalidation of such registrations.

(12) Paragraph (13) applies in relation to any registration to which Regulation 11, 12 or 13 applies which is in respect of any features of shape, configuration, pattern or ornament which do not fall within the new definition of "design" inserted into section 1 of the Act of 1949 by Regulation 2 of these Regulations.

(13) The Act of 1949 shall, so far as it applies in relation to any such registration, apply as if the features concerned were included within the new definition of "design" in that Act.

SCHEDULES 1 AND 2

(Schs 1, 2 contain consequential amendments and repeals, which in so far as they are relevant to this work have been incorporated at the appropriate place.)

REGISTERED DESIGNS REGULATIONS 2003

(SI 2003/550)

NOTES

Made: 6 March 2003.
Authority: European Communities Act 1972, s 2(2).
Commencement: 1 April 2003.

[3.93]
1 Citation, commencement and extent

(1) These Regulations may be cited as the Registered Designs Regulations 2003 and shall come into force on 1st April 2003.

(2) These Regulations extend to England and Wales, Scotland and Northern Ireland.

2 *(Amends the Registered Designs Act 1949, ss 1A (repealed), 11ZB, 20, 44 at* **[3.20]**, **[3.38]**, **[3.75]**.*)*

[3.94]
3 Transitional provisions: pending applications

(1) This Regulation applies to applications for registration under the Act that have been made after the coming into force of the Registered Designs Regulations 2001 ("2001 Regulations") and before the coming into force of these Regulations but that have not been finally determined before the coming into force of these Regulations ("pending applications").

(2) The Act as it has effect immediately before the coming into force of these Regulations shall continue to apply in relation to pending applications.

(3) Accordingly the amendments made by these Regulations shall not apply in relation to such applications.

[3.95]
4 Transitional provisions: transitional registrations

(1) This Regulation applies to any registration under the Act that results from the determination of a pending application (within the meaning of Regulation 3).

(2) The Act as it has effect immediately before the coming into force of these Regulations shall continue to apply in relation to registrations to which this Regulation applies ("transitional registrations").

(3) Accordingly the amendments made by these Regulations shall not apply in relation to transitional registrations.

[3.96]
5 Transitional provisions: resulting registrations

(1) This Regulation applies to any registration made under the Act before the coming into force of these Regulations that results from the determination of an application made under the Act after the coming into force of the 2001 Regulations.

(2) The Act as it has effect immediately before the coming into force of these Regulations shall continue to apply in relation to registrations to which this Regulation applies ("resulting registrations").

(3) Accordingly the amendments made by these Regulations shall not apply in relation to resulting registrations.

COMMUNITY DESIGNS (DESIGNATION OF COMMUNITY DESIGN COURTS) REGULATIONS 2005

(SI 2005/696)

NOTES

Made: 10 March 2005.
Authority: European Communities Act 1972, s 2(2).
Commencement: 6 April 2005.

[3.97]
1

These Regulations may be cited as the Community Designs (Designation of Community Design Courts) Regulations 2005 and shall come into force on 6th April 2005.

[3.98]
2

(1) For the purposes of Article 80 of the Council Regulation (EC) No 6/2002 of 12th December 2001 on Community designs, the following courts are designated as Community design courts—

(a) in England and Wales—
 (i) the High Court; and
 (ii) any county court designated as a patents county court under section 287(1) of the Copyright, Designs and Patents Act 1988;
(b) in Scotland, the Court of Session; and
(c) in Northern Ireland, the High Court.

(2) For the purpose of hearing appeals from judgments of the courts designated by paragraph (1), the following courts are designated as Community design courts—

(a) in England and Wales, the Court of Appeal;
(b) in Scotland, the Court of Session;
(c) in Northern Ireland, the Court of Appeal.

NOTES

Modification: any reference (however expressed) that is or is deemed to be a reference to a county court held under the County Courts Act 1984, s 1, is to be read as a reference to the county court established by s A1 of that Act; see the Crime and Courts Act 2013, s 17(5), Sch 9, Pt 2, para 11.

Patents county court: s 287 of the Copyright, Designs and Patents Act 1988 is repealed by the Crime and Courts Act 2013, s 17(5), Sch 9, Pt 2, para 30(1), (3). The 2013 Act provides for a unified county court.

COMMUNITY DESIGN REGULATIONS 2005

(SI 2005/2339)

NOTES

Made: 15 August 2005.
Authority: European Communities Act 1972, s 2(2).
Commencement: 1 October 2005.

ARRANGEMENT OF REGULATIONS

SCHEDULES

[3.99]

1 Introductory and interpretation

(1) These Regulations may be cited as the Community Design Regulations 2005 and shall come into force on 1st October 2005.

(2) In these Regulations—

["Community design court" means a court designated as such by the Community Designs (Designation of Community Design Courts) Regulations 2005;]

"the Community Design Regulation" means Council Regulation (EC) 6/2002 of 12th December 2001 on Community Designs; . . .

"Community design", "registered Community design" and "unregistered Community design" have the same meanings as in the Community Design Regulation[; and "international registration" has the same meaning as in Articles 106a to 106f of the Community Design Regulation].

[(3) In addition, references to a Community design and a registered Community design include a reference to a design protected by virtue of an international registration designating the [European Union].]

NOTES

Para (2): definition "Community design court" inserted by the Intellectual Property (Enforcement, etc) Regulations 2006, SI 2006/1028, reg 2(3), Sch 3, paras 7, 8; word omitted from definition "the Community Design Regulation" revoked and in definition "Community design", words in square brackets added by the Designs (International Registrations Designating the European Community) Regulations 2007, SI 2007/3378, reg 3(1), (2)(a).

Para (3): added by SI 2007/3378, reg 3(1), (2)(b); words in square brackets substituted by the Treaty of Lisbon (Changes in Terminology) Order 2011, SI 2011/1043, art 4(1).

[3.100]

[1A Infringement proceedings

(1) This regulation and regulations 1B to 1D are without prejudice to the duties of the Community design court under the provisions of Article 89(1)(a) to (c) of the Community Design Regulation.

(2) [Subject to paragraphs (3) to (5), in an action] for infringement of a Community design all such relief by way of damages, injunctions, accounts or otherwise is available to the holder of the Community design as is available in respect of the infringement of any other property right.

[(3) In an action for the infringement of the right in a registered Community design damages shall not be awarded against a person who proves that at the date of the infringement they were not aware, and had no reasonable ground for supposing, that the design was registered.

(4) For the purpose of paragraph (3), a person shall not be deemed to have been aware or to have had reasonable grounds for supposing that the design was registered by reason only of the marking of a product with—

(a) the word "registered" or any abbreviation of that word, or

(b) any word or words expressing or implying that the design applied to, or incorporated in, the product has been registered,

unless the number of the design accompanied the word or words or the abbreviation in question.

(5) In an action for the infringement of an unregistered Community design, damages shall not be awarded against a person who proves that at the date of the infringement that they were not aware, and had no reason to believe, that the design to which the action relates was protected as an unregistered Community design.]]

NOTES

Inserted, together with regs 1B–1D, by the Intellectual Property (Enforcement, etc) Regulations 2006, SI 2006/1028, reg 2(3), Sch 3, paras 7, 9.

Para (2): words in square brackets substituted by the Community Design (Amendment) Regulations 2014, SI 2014/2400, regs 2, 3(a).

Paras (3)–(5): added by SI 2014/2400, regs 2, 3(b).

[3.101]

[1B Order for delivery up

(1) Where a person—

(a) has in his possession, custody or control for commercial purposes an infringing article, or

(b) has in his possession, custody or control anything specifically designed or adapted for making articles to a particular design which is a Community design, knowing or having reason to believe that it has been or is to be used to make an infringing article,

the holder of the Community design in question may apply to the Community design court for an order that the infringing article or other thing be delivered up to him or to such other person as the court may direct.

(2) An application shall not be made after the end of the period specified in the following provisions of this regulation; and no order shall be made unless the court also makes, or it appears to the court that there are grounds for making, an order under regulation 1C (order as to disposal of infringing articles, &c).

(3) An application for an order under this regulation may not be made after the end of the period of six years from the date on which the article or thing in question was made, subject to paragraph (4).

(4) If during the whole or any part of that period the holder of the Community design—
- (a) is under a disability, or
- (b) is prevented by fraud or concealment from discovering the facts entitling him to apply for an order,

an application may be made at any time before the end of the period of six years from the date on which he ceased to be under a disability or, as the case may be, could with reasonable diligence have discovered those facts.

(5) In paragraph (4) "disability"—
- (a) in England and Wales, has the same meaning as in the Limitation Act 1980;
- (b) in Scotland, means legal disability within the meaning of the Prescription and Limitation (Scotland) Act 1973;
- (c) in Northern Ireland, has the same meaning as in the Statute of Limitations (Northern Ireland) 1958.

(6) A person to whom an infringing article or other thing is delivered up in pursuance of an order under this regulation shall, if an order under regulation 1C is not made, retain it pending the making of an order, or the decision not to make an order, under that regulation.

(7) The reference in paragraph (1) to an act being done in relation to an article for "commercial purposes" are to its being done with a view to the article in question being sold or hired in the course of a business.

(8) Nothing in this regulation affects any other power of the court.]

NOTES

Inserted as noted to reg 1A at **[3.100]**.

[3.102]

[1C Order as to disposal of infringing articles, &c

(1) An application may be made to the Community design court for an order that an infringing article or other thing delivered up in pursuance of an order under regulation 1B shall be—
- (a) forfeited to the holder of the Community design, or
- (b) destroyed or otherwise dealt with as the court may think fit,

or for a decision that no such order should be made.

(2) In considering what order (if any) should be made, the court shall consider whether other remedies available in an action for infringement of the right in a Community design would be adequate to compensate the holder and to protect his interests.

(3) Where there is more than one person interested in an article or other thing, the court shall make such order as it thinks just and may (in particular) direct that the thing be sold, or otherwise dealt with, and the proceeds divided.

(4) If the court decides that no order should be made under this regulation, the person in whose possession, custody or control the article or other thing was before being delivered up is entitled to its return.

(5) References in this regulation to a person having an interest in an article or other thing include any person in whose favour an order could be made in respect of it—
- (a) under this regulation;
- (b) under section 24D of the Registered Designs Act 1949;
- (c) under section 114, 204 or 231 of the Copyright, Designs and Patents Act 1988; or
- (d) under section 19 of the Trade Marks Act 1994 (including that section as applied by regulation 4 of the Community Trade Mark Regulations 2006 (SI 2006/1027)).]

NOTES

Inserted as noted to reg 1A at **[3.100]**.

[3.103]

[1D Meaning of "infringing article"

(1) In these Regulations "infringing article", in relation to a design, shall be construed in accordance with this regulation.

(2) An article is an infringing article if its making to that design was an infringement of a Community design.

(3) An article is also an infringing article if—
- (a) it has been or is proposed to be imported into the United Kingdom, and

(b) its making to that design in the United Kingdom would have been an infringement of a Community design or a breach of an exclusive licensing agreement relating to that Community design.

(4) Where it is shown that an article is made to a design which is or has been a Community design, it shall be presumed until the contrary is proved that the article was made at a time when the right in the Community design subsisted.

(5) Nothing in paragraph (3) shall be construed as applying to an article which may be lawfully imported into the United Kingdom by virtue of an enforceable [EU] right within the meaning of section 2(1) of the European Communities Act 1972.]

NOTES

Inserted as noted to reg 1A at **[3.100]**.

Para (5): words in square brackets substituted by the Treaty of Lisbon (Changes in Terminology) Order 2011, SI 2011/1043, art 6(1)(f).

[3.104]

2 Remedy for groundless threats of infringement proceedings

(1) Where any person (whether entitled to or interested in a Community design or not) by circulars, advertisements or otherwise threatens any other person with proceedings for infringement of a Community design, any person aggrieved thereby may bring an action against him for any such relief as is mentioned in paragraph (2).

(2) Subject to paragraphs (3) and (4), the claimant shall be entitled to the following relief—

(a) a declaration to the effect that the threats are unjustifiable;

(b) an injunction against the continuance of the threats; and

(c) such damages, if any, as he has sustained by reason of the threats.

(3) If the defendant proves that the acts in respect of which proceedings were threatened constitute or, if done, would constitute an infringement of a registered Community design the claimant shall be entitled to the relief claimed only if he shows that the registration is invalid.

(4) If the defendant proves that the acts in respect of which proceedings were threatened constitute or, if done, would constitute an infringement of an unregistered Community design the claimant shall not be entitled to the relief claimed.

(5) Proceedings may not be brought under this regulation in respect of a threat to bring proceedings for an infringement alleged to consist of the making or importing of anything.

(6) Mere notification that a design is—

(a) a registered Community design; or

(b) protected as an unregistered Community design,

does not constitute a threat of proceedings for the purpose of this regulation.

[(6A) In relation to a design protected by virtue of an international registration designating the [European Union], the reference in paragraph (3) to a registration being invalid includes a reference to the effects of the international registration being declared invalid in accordance with Article 106f of the Community Design Regulation.]

(7) . . .

NOTES

Reg 2 is substituted (by new regs 2, 2A–2F) by the Intellectual Property (Unjustified Threats) Act 2017, s 6(1), (2), as from a day to be appointed, as follows—

"**2 Unjustified threats: threats of infringement proceedings**

(1) A communication contains a "threat of infringement proceedings" if a reasonable person in the position of a recipient would understand from the communication that—

(a) a Community design exists, and

(b) a person intends to bring proceedings (whether in a court in the United Kingdom or elsewhere) against another person for infringement of the Community design by—

(i) an act done in the United Kingdom, or

(ii) an act which, if done, would be done in the United Kingdom.

(2) References in this regulation and in regulation 2C to a "recipient" include, in the case of a communication directed to the public or a section of the public, references to a person to whom the communication is directed.

2A Unjustified threats: actionable threats

(1) Subject to paragraphs (2) to (5), a threat of infringement proceedings made by any person is actionable by any person aggrieved by the threat.

(2) A threat of infringement proceedings is not actionable if the infringement is alleged to consist of—

(a) making an article for disposal, or

(b) importing an article for disposal.

(3) A threat of infringement proceedings is not actionable if the infringement is alleged to consist of an act which, if done, would constitute an infringement of a kind mentioned in paragraph (2)(a) or (b).

(4) A threat of infringement proceedings is not actionable if the threat—

(a) is made to a person who has done, or intends to do, an act mentioned in paragraph (2)(a) or (b) in relation to an article, and

(b) is a threat of proceedings for an infringement alleged to consist of doing anything else in relation to that article.

(5) A threat of infringement proceedings which is not an express threat is not actionable if it is contained in a permitted

communication.

(6) In regulations 2C and 2D an "actionable threat" means a threat of infringement proceedings that is actionable in accordance with this regulation.

2B Unjustified threats: permitted communications

(1) For the purposes of regulation 2A(5), a communication containing a threat of infringement proceedings is a "permitted communication" if—

(a) the communication, so far as it contains information that relates to the threat, is made for a permitted purpose;

(b) all of the information that relates to the threat is information that—

(i) is necessary for that purpose (see paragraph (5)(a) to (c) for some examples of necessary information), and

(ii) the person making the communication reasonably believes is true.

(2) Each of the following is a "permitted purpose"—

(a) giving notice that a Community design exists;

(b) discovering whether, or by whom, a Community design has been infringed by an act mentioned in regulation 2A(2)(a) or (b);

(c) giving notice that a person has a right in or under a Community design, where another person's awareness of the right is relevant to any proceedings that may be brought in respect of the Community design.

(3) The court may, having regard to the nature of the purposes listed in paragraph (2)(a) to (c), treat any other purpose as a "permitted purpose" if it considers that it is in the interests of justice to do so.

(4) But the following may not be treated as a "permitted purpose"—

(a) requesting a person to cease doing, for commercial purposes, anything in relation to an article made to a design, in which a design is incorporated or to which it is applied,

(b) requesting a person to deliver up or destroy an article made to a design, in which a design is incorporated or to which it is applied, or

(c) requesting a person to give an undertaking relating to an article made to a design, in which a design is incorporated or to which it is applied.

(5) If any of the following information is included in a communication made for a permitted purpose, it is information that is "necessary for that purpose" (see paragraph (1)(b)(i))—

(a) a statement—

(i) that a design is a registered Community design and the registration is in force,

(ii) that an application for a registered Community design has been made, or

(iii) that a design is protected as an unregistered Community design;

(b) details of the Community design, or of a right in or under the Community design, which—

(i) are accurate in all material respects, and

(ii) are not misleading in any material respect; and

(c) information enabling the identification of the article that is alleged to be infringing an article in relation to the design.

2C Unjustified threats: remedies and defences

(1) Proceedings in respect of an actionable threat may be brought against the person who made the threat for—

(a) a declaration that the threat is unjustified;

(b) an injunction against the continuance of the threat;

(c) damages in respect of any loss sustained by the aggrieved person by reason of the threat.

(2) It is a defence for the person who made the threat to show that the act in respect of which proceedings were threatened constitutes (or if done would constitute) an infringement of the Community design.

(3) It is a defence for the person who made the threat to show—

(a) that, despite having taken reasonable steps, the person has not identified anyone who has done an act mentioned in regulation 2A(2)(a) or (b) in relation to the article which is the subject of the threat, and

(b) that the person notified the recipient, before or at the time of making the threat, of the steps taken.

2D Unjustified threats: professional advisers

(1) Proceedings in respect of an actionable threat may not be brought against a professional adviser (or any person vicariously liable for the actions of that professional adviser) if the conditions in paragraph (3) are met.

(2) In this section "professional adviser" means a person who, in relation to the making of the communication containing the threat—

(a) is acting in a professional capacity in providing legal services or the services of a trade mark attorney or a patent attorney, and

(b) is regulated in the provision of legal services, or the services of a trade mark attorney or a patent attorney, by one or more regulatory bodies (whether through membership of a regulatory body, the issue of a licence to practise or any other means).

(3) The conditions are that—

(a) in making the communication the professional adviser is acting on the instructions of another person, and

(b) when the communication is made the professional adviser identifies the person on whose instructions the adviser is acting.

(4) This section does not affect any liability of the person on whose instructions the professional adviser is acting.

(5) It is for a person asserting that paragraph (1) applies to prove (if required) that at the material time—

(a) the person concerned was acting as a professional adviser, and

(b) the conditions in paragraph (3) were met.

2E Unjustified threats: supplementary: pending registration

(1) In the application of regulations 2 and 2B in relation to a registered Community design, references to a Community design include references to a Community design in respect of which an application for registration has been filed in accordance with Article 35 of the Community Design Regulation.

(2) Where the threat of infringement proceedings is made after an application for registration has been filed (but before registration) the reference in regulation 2C(2) to "the Community design" is to be treated as a reference to the design registered in pursuance of that application.

2F Unjustified threats: supplementary: proceedings for delivery up etc

In regulation 2(1)(b) the reference to proceedings for infringement of the Community design includes a reference to—

(a) proceedings for an order under regulation 1B (order for delivery up), and

(b) proceedings for an order under regulation 1C (order as to disposal of infringing articles).".

Para (6A): added by the Designs (International Registrations Designating the European Community) Regulations 2007, SI 2007/3378, reg 3(1), (3); words in square brackets substituted by the Treaty of Lisbon (Changes in Terminology) Order 2011, SI 2011/1043, art 4(1).

Para (7): revoked by the Intellectual Property (Enforcement, etc) Regulations 2006, SI 2006/1028, reg 2(4), Sch 4.

[3.105]

3 Falsely representing a design as a registered Community design

(1) It is an offence for a person falsely to represent that a design applied to, or incorporated in, any product sold by him is a registered Community design.

(2) It is an offence for a person, after a registered Community design has expired, to represent (expressly or by implication) that a design applied to, or incorporated in, any product sold is still registered in the manner provided for in the Community Design Regulation.

(3) A person guilty of an offence under paragraph (1) is liable on summary conviction to a fine not exceeding level 3 on the standard scale.

(4) A person guilty of an offence under paragraph (2) is liable on summary conviction to a fine not exceeding level 1 on the standard scale.

[3.106]

4 Privilege for communications with those on the special list of professional design representatives

(1) This regulation applies to communications as to any matter relating to the protection of any design.

(2) Any such communication—

(a) between a person and his professional designs representative, or

(b) for the purposes of obtaining, or in response to a request for, information which a person is seeking for the purpose of instructing his professional designs representative,

is privileged from, or in Scotland protected against, disclosure in legal proceedings in the same way as a communication between a person and his solicitor or, as the case may be, a communication for the purpose of obtaining, or in response to a request for, information which a person is seeking for the purpose of instructing his solicitor.

(3) In paragraph (2) "professional designs representative" means a person who is on the special list of professional representatives for design matters referred to in Article 78 of the Community Design Regulation.

[3.107]

5 Use of Community design for services of the Crown

The provisions of the Schedule to these Regulations shall have effect with respect to the use of registered Community designs and unregistered Community designs for the services of the Crown and the rights of third parties in respect of such use.

[3.108]

[5A Application to Scotland and Northern Ireland

(1) In the application of these Regulations to Scotland—

"accounts" means count, reckoning and payment;

"claimant" means pursuer;

["declaration" means "declarator";]

"defendant" means defender;

"delivery up" means delivery;

"injunction" means interdict.

(2) In the application of these Regulations to Northern Ireland, "claimant" includes plaintiff.]

NOTES

Inserted by the Intellectual Property (Enforcement, etc) Regulations 2006, SI 2006/1028, reg 2(3), Sch 3, paras 7, 10.

Words in square brackets inserted by the Intellectual Property (Unjustified Threats) Act 2017, s 6(1), (3), as from a day to be appointed.

6 (*Amends the Registered Designs Act 1949, s 35 at* **[3.61]**).

Part 3 Designs

SCHEDULE
USE OF COMMUNITY DESIGNS FOR SERVICES OF THE CROWN

Regulation 5

Use of Community design for services of the Crown

[3.109]

1. (1) A government department, or a person authorised in writing by a government department, may without the consent of the holder of a Community design—

(a) do anything for the purpose of supplying products for the services of the Crown, or

(b) dispose of products no longer required for the services of the Crown;

and nothing done by virtue of this paragraph infringes the Community design.

(2) References in this Schedule to "the services of the Crown" are limited to those which are necessary for essential defence or security needs.

(3) In this Schedule—

"Crown use", in relation to a Community design, means the doing of anything by virtue of this paragraph which would otherwise be an infringement of the Community design; and

"the government department concerned", in relation to such use, means the government department by whom or on whose authority the act was done.

(4) The authority of a government department in respect of Crown use of a Community design may be given to a person either before or after the use and whether or not he is authorised, directly or indirectly, by the holder of the Community design to do anything in relation to the design.

(5) A person acquiring anything sold in the exercise of powers conferred by this paragraph, and any person claiming under him, may deal with it in the same manner as if the Crown was the holder of the Community design.

Settlement of terms for Crown use

2. (1) Where Crown use is made of a Community design, the government department concerned shall—

(a) notify the holder of the Community design as soon as practicable, and

(b) give him such information as to the extent of the use as he may from time to time require,

unless it appears to the department that it would be contrary to the public interest to do so or the identity of the holder of the Community design cannot be ascertained on reasonable inquiry.

(2) Crown use of a Community design shall be on such terms as, either before or after the use, are agreed between the government department concerned and the holder of the Community design with the approval of the Treasury or, in default of agreement, are determined by the court.

(3) In the application of sub-paragraph (2) to Northern Ireland the reference to the Treasury shall, where the government department referred to in that sub-paragraph is a Northern Ireland department, be construed as a reference to the Department of Finance and Personnel.

(4) In the application of sub-paragraph (2) to Scotland, where the government department referred to in that sub-paragraph is any part of the Scottish Administration, the words "with the approval of the Treasury" are omitted.

(5) Where the identity of the holder of the Community design cannot be ascertained on reasonable inquiry, the government department concerned may apply to the court who may order that no royalty or other sum shall be payable in respect of Crown use of the Community design until the holder agrees terms with the department or refers the matter to the court for determination.

Rights of third parties in case of Crown use

3. (1) The provisions of any licence, assignment or agreement made between the holder of the Community design (or anyone deriving title from him or from whom he derives title) and any person other than a government department are of no effect in relation to Crown use of a Community design, or any act incidental to Crown use, so far as they—

(a) restrict or regulate anything done in relation to the Community design, or the use of any model, document or other information relating to it, or

(b) provide for the making of payments in respect of, or calculated by reference to such use;

and the copying or issuing to the public of copies of any such model or document in connection with the thing done, or any such use, shall be deemed not to be an infringement of any copyright in the model or document.

(2) Sub-paragraph (1) shall not be construed as authorising the disclosure of any such model, document or information in contravention of the licence, assignment or agreement.

(3) Where an exclusive licence is in force in respect of the Community design—

(a) if the licence was granted for royalties—

(i) any agreement between the holder of the Community design and a government department under paragraph 2 (settlement of terms for Crown use) requires the consent of the licensee, and

(ii) the licensee is entitled to recover from the holder of the Community design such part of the payment for Crown use as may be agreed between them or, in default of agreement, determined by the court;

(b) if the licence was granted otherwise than for royalties—

(i) paragraph 2 applies in relation to anything done which but for paragraph 1 (Crown use) and sub-paragraph (1) would be an infringement of the rights of the licensee with the substitution for references to the holder of the Community design of references to the licensee, and

(ii) paragraph 2 does not apply in relation to anything done by the licensee by virtue of an authority given under paragraph 1.

(4) Where the Community design has been assigned to the holder of the Community design in consideration of royalties—

(a) paragraph 2 applies in relation to Crown use of the Community design as if the references to the holder of the Community design included the assignor, and any payment for Crown use shall be divided between them in such proportion as may be agreed or, in default of agreement, determined by the court; and

(b) paragraph 2 applies in relation to any act incidental to Crown use as it applies in relation to Crown use of the Community design.

(5) Where any model, document or other information relating to a Community design is used in connection with Crown use of the design, or any act incidental to Crown use, paragraph 2 applies to the use of the model, document or other information with the substitution for the references to the holder of the Community design of references to the person entitled to the benefit of any provision of an agreement rendered inoperative by sub-paragraph (1).

(6) In this paragraph—

"act incidental to Crown use" means anything done for the services of the Crown to the order of a government department by the holder of the Community design in respect of a design;

"payment for Crown use" means such amount as is payable by the government department concerned by virtue of paragraph 2; and

"royalties" includes any benefit determined by reference to the use of the Community design.

Crown use: compensation for loss of profit

4. (1) Where Crown use is made of a Community design, the government department concerned shall pay—

(a) to the holder of the Community design, or

(b) if there is an exclusive licence in force in respect of the Community design, to the exclusive licensee,

compensation for any loss resulting from his not being awarded a contract to supply the products to which the Community design is applied or in which it is incorporated.

(2) Compensation is payable only to the extent that such a contract could have been fulfilled from his existing manufacturing capacity; but is payable notwithstanding the existence of circumstances rendering him ineligible for the award of such a contract.

(3) In determining the loss, regard shall be had to the profit which would have been made on such a contract and to the extent to which any manufacturing capacity was under-used.

(4) No compensation is payable in respect of any failure to secure contracts for the supply of products to which the Community design is applied or in which it is incorporated otherwise than for the services of the Crown.

(5) The amount payable shall, if not agreed between the holder of the Community design or licensee and the government department concerned with the approval of the Treasury, be determined by the court on a reference under paragraph 5; and it is in addition to any amount payable under paragraph 2 or 3.

(6) In the application of this paragraph to Northern Ireland, the reference in sub-paragraph (5) to the Treasury shall, where the government department concerned is a Northern Ireland department, be construed as a reference to the Department of Finance and Personnel.

(7) In the application of this paragraph to Scotland, where the government department referred to in sub-paragraph (5) is any part of the Scottish Administration, the words "with the approval of the Treasury" in that sub-paragraph are omitted.

Reference of disputes relating to Crown use

5. (1) A dispute as to any matter which falls to be determined by the court in default of agreement under—

(a) paragraph 2 (settlement of terms for Crown use),

(b) paragraph 3 (rights of third parties in case of Crown use), or

(c) paragraph 4 (Crown use: compensation for loss of profit),

may be referred to the court by any party to the dispute.

(2) In determining a dispute between a government department and any person as to the terms for Crown use of a Community design the court shall have regard to—

(a) any sums which that person or a person from whom he derives title has received or is entitled to receive, directly or indirectly, from any government department in respect of the Community design; and
(b) whether that person or a person from whom he derives title has in the court's opinion without reasonable cause failed to comply with a request of the department for the use of the Community design on reasonable terms.

(3) One of two or more joint holders of the Community design may, without the concurrence of the others, refer a dispute to the court under this paragraph, but shall not do so unless the others are made parties; and none of those others is liable for any costs unless he takes part in the proceedings.

(4) Where the consent of an exclusive licensee is required by paragraph 3(3)(a)(i) to the settlement by agreement of the terms for Crown use of a Community design, a determination by the court of the amount of any payment to be made for such use is of no effect unless the licensee has been notified of the reference and given an opportunity to be heard.

(5) On the reference of a dispute as to the amount recoverable as mentioned in paragraph 3(3)(a)(ii) (right of exclusive licensee to recover part of amount payable to holder of Community design) the court shall determine what is just having regard to any expenditure incurred by the licensee—
(a) in developing the design, or
(b) in making payments to the holder of the Community design in consideration of the licence (other than royalties or other payments determined by reference to the use of the design).

(6) In this Schedule "the court" means—
(a) in England and Wales, the High Court or any patents county court having jurisdiction by virtue of an order under section 287 of the Copyright, Designs and Patents Act 1988,
(b) in Scotland, the Court of Session, and
(c) in Northern Ireland, the High Court.

NOTES

Modification: any reference (however expressed) that is or is deemed to be a reference to a county court held under the County Courts Act 1984, s 1, is to be read as a reference to the county court established by s A1 of that Act; see the Crime and Courts Act 2013, s 17(5), Sch 9, Pt 2, para 11.

Patents county court: s 287 of the Copyright, Designs and Patents Act 1988 is repealed by the Crime and Courts Act 2013, s 17(5), Sch 9, Pt 2, para 30(1), (3). The 2013 Act provides for a unified county court.

REGULATORY REFORM (REGISTERED DESIGNS) ORDER 2006

(SI 2006/1974)

NOTES

Made: 26 July 2006.
Authority: Regulatory Reform Act 2001, s 1.
Commencement: 1 October 2006.

[3.110]
1 Introductory

(1) This Order may be cited as the Regulatory Reform (Registered Designs) Order 2006 and it shall come into force on 1st October 2006.

(2) This Order extends to England and Wales, Scotland and Northern Ireland.

2–17 (*Art 2 introduces the amendments to the Registered Designs Act 1949; art 3 revokes s 1A of that Act; arts 4, 11 amend s 3 of that Act at* **[3.6]**; *arts 5, 12 amend s 3A of that Act at* **[3.7]**, *arts 6, 13 amend s 3B of that Act at* **[3.8]**; *art 7 amends s 11ZA of that Act at* **[3.19]**; *art 8 amends s 11ZB of that Act at* **[3.20]**; *art 9 amends s 11ZD of that Act at* **[3.22]**; *art 10 amends s 20 of that Act at* **[3.38]**; *art 14 amends s 14 of that Act at* **[3.29]**; *arts 15, 16 amend s 22 of that Act at* **[3.40]**; *art 17 amends s 8A of that Act at* **[3.16]**.)

[3.111]
18 Transitional provisions

(1) The amendments made to the Registered Designs Act 1949 by articles 7 to 10 shall not apply to post-1989 registrations or pre-1989 registrations.

(2) In paragraph (1)—
"post-1989 registrations" means registrations to which regulation 12 of the Registered Designs Regulations 2001 applies;
"pre-1989 registrations" means registrations which fall within regulation 13(1) of those Regulations.

[3.112]
19

The amendments made to section 22 of the Registered Designs Act 1949 by article 16(2)(b) and (3) shall not apply to any registration under the Act which has resulted from an application made before the coming into force of this Order.

REGISTERED DESIGNS RULES 2006

(SI 2006/1975)

NOTES

Made: 27 July 2006.
Authority: Registered Designs Act 1949, ss 29–31, 36.
Commencement: 1 October 2006.

ARRANGEMENT OF RULES

PART 1
INTRODUCTORY

PART 2
APPLICATIONS FOR REGISTRATION

Applications for registration and formal requirements

Disclaimers

Convention applications

Examination of application, representations for publication and time limits

PART 3
DESIGNS AFTER REGISTRATION

Publication

Duration of rights and surrender

PART 4
PROCEEDINGS HEARD BEFORE THE REGISTRAR

Conduct of proceedings

Miscellaneous

PART 5
THE REGISTER AND OTHER INFORMATION

PART 1
INTRODUCTORY

[3.113]
1 Citation and commencement

These Rules may be cited as the Registered Designs Rules 2006 and shall come into force on 1st October 2006.

[3.114]
2 Interpretation

(1) In these Rules—
"the Act" means the Registered Designs Act 1949;
"the journal" means the journal published under rule 44(1); and
"section" means a section of the Act.

(2) Where a time or period has been altered under rules 19(1) or 39 to 41, any reference in these Rules to the time or period shall be construed as a reference to the time or period as altered.

[3.115]
[2A Directions of the registrar

Any directions given by the registrar under sections 31A or 39 must be published on such website as the registrar considers to be likely to bring them to the attention of those persons likely to be affected by them.]

NOTES

Commencement: 1 October 2014.

Inserted by the Registered Designs (Amendment) Rules 2014, SI 2014/2405, rr 2, 3.

[3.116]

3 Forms

(1) The forms of which the use is required by these Rules are those set out in Schedule 1.

(2) Such a requirement to use a form is satisfied by the use of a form which is acceptable to the registrar and contains the information required by the form as so set out.

PART 2
APPLICATIONS FOR REGISTRATION

Applications for registration and formal requirements

[3.117]

4 Applications

(1) An application for the registration of a design or designs shall be made on Form DF2A and—

(a) shall include the identity of the person making the application; and

(b) in relation to each design, shall either—

(i) include a representation of the design; or

(ii) be accompanied by a specimen of the design,

and it shall be accompanied by the prescribed fee.

(2) But an application for the registration of a design or designs, which is a subsequent application for the purposes of section 3B(3), shall be made on Form DF2B and be accompanied by the prescribed fee.

(3) Where an application includes a representation of the design, the applicant may give his consent for its publication on Form DF2A or Form DF2B.

(4) Where a person purports to file something under section 3(1) and—

(a) it is not in the form prescribed by either paragraph (1) or (2); or

(b) it is not accompanied by the prescribed fee,

the registrar shall notify that person accordingly.

(5) A representation or specimen filed under paragraph (1)(b) may be accompanied by a brief description of the design.

(6) A specimen may not be filed under paragraph (1)(b) if it is hazardous or perishable; and where such a specimen is so filed it shall be disregarded.

(7) An application for the registration of a design which is a repeating surface pattern shall only be treated as such if—

(a) the representation or specimen filed under paragraph (1)(b) includes the complete pattern and a sufficient portion of the repeat in length and width to show how the pattern repeats; and

(b) the application contains a statement that it relates to a repeating surface pattern.

[3.118]

5 Formal requirements

(1) An application for the registration of a design shall comply with the first and second requirement.

(2) The first requirement is that the applicant has specified the product to which the design is intended to be applied or in which it is intended to be incorporated.

(3) The second requirement is that the dimensions of any specimen of the design filed under rule 4(1)(b)(ii) shall not exceed 29.7cm x 21cm x 1cm.

(4) Where the applicant files a representation of the design after being notified under rule 8(1) that the application does not comply with the second requirement—

(a) that representation shall be deemed to have been filed under rule 4(1)(b)(i); and

(b) any specimen filed under rule 4(1)(b)(ii) shall be treated as not having been filed.

(5) Nothing done to comply with the first requirement shall be taken to affect the scope of the protection conferred by the registration of a design.

Disclaimers

[3.119]

6 Partial disclaimers

An application for the registration of a design may be accompanied by a disclaimer which—

(a) limits the scope or extent of protection being applied for in relation to the design; or

(b) Indicates that the application for registration relates to a design that forms only a part of the appearance of a product.

Convention applications

[3.120]

7 Convention applications

(1) Where an application for the registration of a design or designs is made by virtue of section 14 the applicant shall comply with the following provisions.

(2) The application shall contain a declaration specifying—

(a) the date of making of each convention application; and

(b) the country it was made in or in respect of.

(3) The applicant shall, before the end of the period of 3 months [beginning immediately after] the date on which the application was filed, file at the Patent Office a copy of the representation of the design that was the subject of each convention application.

(4) A copy of the representation filed under paragraph (3) shall be—

(a) duly certified by the authority with which it was filed; or

(b) verified to the satisfaction of the registrar.

(5) Paragraph (3) shall not apply where a copy of the convention application is kept at the Patent Office.

(6) Where any document relating to the convention application is in a language other than English or Welsh, the registrar may direct the applicant to provide a translation of the whole or any part of that document.

(7) The translation shall be filed before the end of the period of 3 months [beginning immediately after] the date of the direction.

(8) Where the applicant—

(a) fails to file a copy of the representation of the design which has been certified or verified in accordance with paragraph (4); or

(b) fails to comply with a direction given under paragraph (6),

the convention application shall be disregarded for the purposes of section 14(2).

(9) In this rule "convention application" means an application for the protection of a design which has been made in a convention country.

NOTES

Paras (3), (7): words in square brackets substituted by the Trade Marks and Registered Designs (Amendment) Rules 2013, SI 2013/444, rr 5, 7, Sch 2.

Examination of application, representations for publication and time limits

[3.121]

8 Substantive and formal examination of application

(1) Where it appears to the registrar that he should refuse to register a design included in an application—

(a) by reason of the application for the registration of that design not being made in accordance with any of these Rules, other than rule 9(2) (see section 3A(2)); or

(b) by reason of section 3A(3) or (4),

he shall notify the applicant accordingly.

(2) The notification shall include a statement of why it appears to the registrar that he should refuse to register the design (for the purposes of this rule the "statement of objections").

(3) The applicant may, before the end of the period of 2 months [beginning immediately after] the date of the notification, send his written observations on the statement of objections to the registrar.

(4) The registrar shall give the applicant an opportunity to be heard.

(5) Where the registrar refuses to register a design included in an application, he shall send to the applicant the written reasons for his decision.

(6) The date on which the written reasons were sent to the applicant shall be deemed to be the date of the decision for the purposes of any appeal.

NOTES

Para (3): words in square brackets substituted by the Trade Marks and Registered Designs (Amendment) Rules 2013, SI 2013/444, rr 5, 7, Sch 2.

[3.122]

9 Representation of design for publication

(1) Where the registrar decides that he should not refuse to register the design for the reasons mentioned in rule 8(1)(a) or (b) and—

(a) no representation of the design has been filed; or

(b) a representation has been filed but it is not suitable for publication,

the registrar shall direct the applicant to provide a suitable representation.

(2) Where a direction is given, the applicant shall, before the end of the period of 3 months [beginning immediately after] the date of the direction, file a suitable representation (otherwise the registrar may refuse to register the design: see section 3A(2)).

(3) Where a suitable representation has been filed, the applicant shall file his consent for its publication on Form DF2C

(4) But paragraph (3) shall not apply where the applicant consented to publication in accordance with rule 4(3).

(5) In this rule "suitable representation" means a representation of the design which is suitable for publication.

NOTES

Para (2): words in square brackets substituted by the Trade Marks and Registered Designs (Amendment) Rules 2013, SI 2013/444, rr 5, 7, Sch 2.

[3.123]

10 Time limits under section 3(5) and section 3B

(1) The time prescribed for the purposes of section 3(5) shall be 12 months [beginning immediately after] the date on which the application for registration of the design was made or treated as made (disregarding section 14).

(2) The period prescribed for the purposes of section 3B(3) shall be the period of 2 months [beginning immediately after] the date on which the earlier application was modified under section 3B(3).

NOTES

Words in square brackets substituted by the Trade Marks and Registered Designs (Amendment) Rules 2013, SI 2013/444, rr 5, 7, Sch 2.

PART 3
DESIGNS AFTER REGISTRATION

Publication

[3.124]

11 Publication

(1) When a design has been registered, the registrar shall publish a representation of that design in the journal as soon as possible after the certificate of registration is granted.

(2) When the registrar publishes the representation, he may also publish any other information he thinks is relevant to that design.

(3) The representation published under paragraph (1) shall be the representation filed under rule 4(1)(b)(i) or 9(2) or as mentioned in rule 5(4).

Duration of rights and surrender

[3.125]

12 Extension of duration of right in registered design

(1) An application for an extension under section 8(2) or 8(4) shall be made on Form DF9A.

(2) An application under section 8(2) may only be made during the period of 6 months ending with the date on which the relevant period of 5 years expires.

(3) On receipt of the prescribed renewal fee the registrar shall notify the registered proprietor of the extension of the right in the registered design.

(4) Where the right in a registered design has ceased to have effect by reason of section 8(3), the registrar shall, before the end of the period of 6 weeks [beginning immediately after] the date on which the right ceased, send written notice to the registered proprietor of that fact.

(5) But paragraph (4) shall not apply where the renewal fee and the prescribed additional fee is paid before a notice is sent.

NOTES

Para (4): words in square brackets substituted by the Trade Marks and Registered Designs (Amendment) Rules 2013, SI 2013/444, rr 5, 7, Sch 2.

[3.126]

13 Restoration of a lapsed right in a design under section 8A

(1) An application for the restoration of the right in a design under section 8A shall—

(a) be made on Form DF29; and

(b) be supported by evidence of the statements made in the application.

(2) The period prescribed for the purposes of section 8A(1) shall be the period of 12 months [beginning immediately after] the date on which the registered design ceased to have effect.

(3) The notice of the application shall be published in the journal.

(4) Where, upon consideration of that evidence, the registrar is not satisfied that a case for an order under section 8A has been made out, he shall notify the applicant accordingly.

(5) The applicant may, before the end of the period of 1 month [beginning immediately after] the date of that notification, request to be heard by the registrar.

(6) Where the applicant requests a hearing, the registrar shall give him an opportunity to be heard; after which the registrar shall determine whether the application under section 8A shall be granted or refused.

(7) Where the registrar decides not to make the order he shall give the applicant written reasons for his refusal.

NOTES

Paras (2), (5): words in square brackets substituted by the Trade Marks and Registered Designs (Amendment) Rules 2013, SI 2013/444, rr 5, 7, Sch 2.

[3.127]

14 Cancellation of registration

A request under section 11 to cancel the registration of a design shall be made on Form DF19C.

PART 4
PROCEEDINGS HEARD BEFORE THE REGISTRAR

Conduct of proceedings

[3.128]

15 Procedure for applying for a declaration of invalidity

(1) An application for a declaration of invalidity under section 11ZB shall—

(a) be made on Form DF19A; and
(b) include a statement of the grounds on which the application is made.

(2) The statement of grounds shall include a concise statement of the facts and grounds on which the applicant relies and shall be verified by a statement of truth.

(3) The registrar shall send a copy of Form DF19A and the statement of case to the registered proprietor.

(4) The registrar shall specify a period within which the registered proprietor shall file a counter-statement.

(5) The registered proprietor, within that period, shall—

(a) file his counter-statement on Form DF19B; and
(b) send a copy of it to the applicant,

otherwise the registrar may treat him as not opposing the application.

(6) In his counter-statement the registered proprietor shall—

(a) include a concise statement of the facts on which he relies;
(b) state which of the allegations in the statement of grounds he denies;
(c) state which of the allegations he is unable to admit or deny, but which he requires the applicant to prove;
(d) state which allegations he admits,

and it shall be verified by a statement of truth.

(7) In this Part—

(a) "statement of case" means the statement of grounds filed by the applicant or the counter-statement filed by the registered proprietor; and
(b) references to the statement of case include part of the statement of case.

[3.129]

16 Evidence rounds

(1) When the period specified under rule 15(4) has expired, the registrar shall specify the periods within which evidence may be filed by the parties.

(2) Where the applicant for a declaration of invalidity files no evidence (other than his statement of grounds) in support of his application, the registrar may treat him as having withdrawn his application.

(3) The registrar may, at any time if he thinks fit, give leave to either party to file evidence upon such terms as he thinks fit.

(4) Under this rule, evidence shall only be considered to be filed when—

(a) it has been received by the registrar; and
(b) it has been sent to all other parties to the proceedings.

(5) The registrar shall give the parties an opportunity to be heard.

(6) Where any party requests to be heard, the registrar shall send to the parties notice of a date for the hearing.

[3.130]
17 Decision of registrar on invalidity

(1) When the registrar has made a decision on the application for a declaration of invalidity, he shall send to the parties written notice of it, stating the reasons for his decision.

(2) The date on which the decision was sent to the applicant shall be deemed to be the date of the decision for the purposes of any appeal.

[3.131]
18 Exercise of discretionary powers of registrar

The registrar shall give to any applicant for registration of a design an opportunity to be heard before exercising adversely to the applicant any discretion vested in the registrar by or under the Act.

[3.132]
19 General powers of registrar in relation to proceedings before him

(1) The registrar may extend or shorten (or further extend or shorten) any period which has been specified under any provision of this Part.

(2) At any stage of proceedings before him, the registrar may direct that the parties to the proceedings attend a case management conference or pre-hearing review.

(3) Except where the Act or these Rules otherwise provide, the registrar may give such directions as to the management of the proceedings as he thinks fit, and in particular he may—
- (a) require a document, information or evidence to be filed;
- (b) require a translation of any document;
- (c) require a party or a party's legal representative to attend a hearing;
- (d) hold a hearing and receive evidence by telephone or by using any other method of direct oral communication;
- (e) allow a statement of case to be amended;
- (f) stay the whole, or any part, of the proceedings either generally or until a specified date or event;
- (g) consolidate proceedings;
- (h) direct that part of any proceedings be dealt with as separate proceedings.

(4) The registrar may control the evidence by giving directions as to—
- (a) the issues on which he requires evidence;
- (b) the nature of the evidence which he requires to decide those issues; and
- (c) the way in which the evidence is to be placed before him,

and the registrar may use his power under this paragraph to exclude evidence which would otherwise be admissible.

(5) When the registrar gives directions under any provision of this Part, he may—
- (a) make them subject to conditions; and
- (b) specify the consequences of failure to comply with the directions or a condition.

[3.133]
20 Hearings in public

(1) Subject to paragraphs (3) and (4), any hearing before the registrar of proceedings between two or more parties relating to an application for a registered design or a registered design, shall be held in public.

(2) Any party to the proceedings may apply to the registrar for the hearing to be held in private.

(3) The registrar shall only grant an application under paragraph (2) where—
- (a) it is in the interests of justice for the hearing to be in held in private; and
- (b) all the parties to the proceedings have had an opportunity to be heard on the matter,

and where the application is granted the hearing shall be in private.

(4) Any hearing of an application under paragraph (2) shall be held in private.

(5) In this rule a reference to a hearing includes any part of a hearing.

(6) . . .

NOTES

Para (6): revoked by the Tribunals, Courts and Enforcement Act 2007 (Transitional and Consequential Provisions) Order 2008, SI 2008/2683, art 6(1), Sch 1, para 318.

[3.134]
21 Evidence in proceedings before the registrar

(1) Subject as follows, evidence filed under this Part may be given—
- (a) by witness statement, statement of case, affidavit, statutory declaration; or
- (b) in any other form which would be admissible as evidence in proceedings before the court.

(2) A witness statement or a statement of case may only be given in evidence if it includes a statement of truth.

(3) The general rule is that evidence at hearings is to be by witness statement unless the registrar or any enactment requires otherwise.

(4) For the purposes of this Part, a statement of truth—

(a) means a statement that the person making the statement believes that the facts stated in a particular document are true; and

(b) shall be dated and signed by—

(i) in the case of a witness statement, the maker of the statement,

(ii) in any other case, the party or his legal representative.

(5) In this Part, a witness statement is a written statement signed by a person that contains the evidence which that person would be allowed to give orally.

Miscellaneous

[3.135]

22 Costs of proceedings

The registrar may, in any proceedings before him under the Act, award to any party by order such costs as he considers reasonable, and direct how and by what parties they are to be paid.

[3.136]

23 Security for costs

(1) The registrar may require a person to give security for the costs of any application or appeal mentioned in section 30(3) if—

(a) he is satisfied, having regard to all the circumstances of the case, that it is just to require such security; and

(b) one or more of the conditions in paragraph (2) applies.

(2) The conditions are—

(a) the person is resident outside the United Kingdom but [not resident in]—

(i) . . . a Brussels Contracting State,

(ii) a Lugano Contracting State, or

(iii) a Regulation State,

as defined in section 1(3) of the Civil Jurisdiction and Judgments Act 1982;

(b) the person is a company or other body (whether incorporated inside or outside the United Kingdom) and there is reason to believe that it will be unable to pay the other person's costs if ordered to do so;

(c) the person has changed his address since filing an address for service with a view to evading the consequences of the proceedings;

(d) the person has furnished an incorrect address for service;

(e) the person has taken steps in relation to his assets that would make it difficult to enforce an order for costs against him;

(f) the person has failed to pay a costs order in relation to previous proceedings before the registrar or a court (whether or not the proceedings were between the same parties).

(3) In default of such security being given the registrar may treat the application or appeal as abandoned.

NOTES

Para (2): words in square brackets inserted and words omitted revoked by the Trade Marks and Registered Designs (Amendment) Rules 2013, SI 2013/444, rr 5, 6.

[3.137]

24 Registrar shall have the powers of official referee

The registrar shall have the powers of an official referee of the Supreme Court as regards—

(a) the attendance of witnesses and their examination on oath; and

(b) the discovery and production of documents,

but he shall have no power to punish summarily for contempt.

[3.138]

25 Minimum notice of hearing

The registrar shall not give a person less than 14 days notice of any hearing under the Act.

PART 5
THE REGISTER AND OTHER INFORMATION

Certificate of registration and registrable interests

[3.139]

26 Certificate of registration

(1) The certificate of registration of a design shall include—

(a) the name of the registered proprietor;

(b) the date of registration; and

(c) the registration number of the design.

(2) Any request by the registered proprietor for a copy of the certificate of registration shall—

(a) be in writing; and

(b) be accompanied by the prescribed fee.

(3) Before considering the request, the registrar may require the person making the request to provide such information or evidence as the registrar thinks fit.

[3.140]

27 Registration of interests

(1) The following matters are prescribed for the purposes of section 17(1)(c)—

(a) the registered proprietor's address for service;

(b) the grant or cancellation of a licence under a registered design;

(c) the granting or cancelling of a security interest (whether fixed or floating) over a registered design or any right in or under it;

(d) an order of a court or other competent authority transferring a registered design or any right in or under it.

(2) An application to the registrar to enter in the register a matter not mentioned in section 17(1)(a) or (b) or paragraph (1) shall be made in writing.

(3) An application under section 19(1) or (2) shall be made on Form DF12A.

(4) Where the registrar has doubts about whether he should enter a matter in the register—

(a) he shall inform the person making the application of the reasons for his doubts; and

(b) he may require that person to furnish evidence in support of the application.

Inspection and information about registered designs

[3.141]

28 Inspection of register, representations and specimens

(1) The register and any representation or specimen of a registered design shall be open for inspection at the Patent Office during the hours the Patent Office is open for all classes of public business (see rule 45(2)).

(2) Whilst a direction under section 5(1) in respect of a design remains in force, no representation or specimen of the design shall be open to inspection.

[3.142]

29 Inspection of documents

(1) Where a design has been registered under the Act, there shall be open to inspection at the Patent Office on and after the date on which the certificate of registration is granted every document kept at the Patent Office in connection with that design.

(2) But no document may be inspected—

(a) before the end of the period of 14 days [beginning immediately after] the day—

(i) it was filed at the Patent Office; or

(ii) received by the registrar or the Patent Office;

(b) where that document was prepared by the registrar or the Patent Office for internal use only;

(c) where the document includes matter—

(i) which in the registrar's opinion disparages any person in a way likely to damage him; or

(ii) the inspection of which would in his opinion be generally expected to encourage offensive, immoral or anti-social behaviour.

(3) Unless, in a particular case, the registrar otherwise directs, no document may be inspected—

(a) where—

(i) the document was prepared by the registrar or the Patent Office other than for internal use; and

(ii) it contains information which the registrar considers should remain confidential;

(b) where it is treated as a confidential document (under rule 30).

(4) In this rule and rule 30 references to a document include part of a document.

NOTES

Para (2): words in square brackets substituted by the Trade Marks and Registered Designs (Amendment) Rules 2013, SI 2013/444, rr 5, 7, Sch 2.

[3.143]

30 Confidential information

(1) Where a person files a document at the Patent Office or sends it to the registrar or the Patent Office, any person may request that the document be treated as a confidential document.

(2) A request to treat a document as confidential shall—

(a) be made before the end of the period of 14 days [beginning immediately after] the date on which the document was filed at the Patent Office or received by the registrar or at the Patent Office;

(b) include reasons for the request.

(3) Where a request has been made under paragraph (1), the document shall be treated as confidential until the registrar refuses that request or makes a direction under paragraph (4).

(4) Where it appears that there is good reason for the document to remain confidential, the registrar may direct that the document shall be treated as a confidential document; otherwise he shall refuse the request made under paragraph (1).

(5) But, where the registrar believes there is no longer a good reason for the direction under paragraph (4) to remain in force, he shall revoke it.

NOTES

Para (2): words in square brackets substituted by the Trade Marks and Registered Designs (Amendment) Rules 2013, SI 2013/444, rr 5, 7, Sch 2.

[3.144]

31 Information about rights in registered designs

(1) A request for information under section 23 shall be made on Form DF21 and be accompanied by the prescribed fee.

(2) The request shall—

- (a) where the registration number is known by the person making the request, include that number; or
- (b) in any other case, be accompanied by a representation or specimen of the product—
  - (i) in which the design has been incorporated; or
  - (ii) to which the design has been applied.

Copies of documents

[3.145]

32 Copies of entries in, or extracts from, the register

An application under section 17(5) for a certified copy of an entry in the register or a certified extract from the register shall be made on Form DF23 and be accompanied by the prescribed fee.

[3.146]

33 Copies of representations and specimens

(1) A person may apply to the registrar for a certified copy of any representation or specimen of a design; and that person shall be entitled to such a copy.

(2) an application under paragraph (1) shall be made in writing and be accompanied by the prescribed fee.

Alterations and rectification

[3.147]

34 Alteration of name or address

(1) Any person may request that an alteration to his name or address—

- (a) be entered in the register; or
- (b) be made to any application or other document filed at the Patent Office.

(2) A request under paragraph (1) shall in relation to an alteration to—

- (a) his name, be made on Form DF16A; and
- (b) his address, be made on Form DF16A or in writing.

(3) Where the registrar has doubts about whether he should make the alteration to a name or address—

- (a) he shall inform the person making the request of the reason for his doubts; and
- (b) he may require that person to furnish evidence in support of the request.

(4) Where the registrar has no doubts (or no longer has doubts) about whether he should make the alteration, it shall be entered in the register or made to the application or document.

[3.148]

35 Notice of rectification of the register

(1) The prescribed manner of giving notice to the registrar for the purposes of section 20(3) is by giving written notice.

(2) The prescribed manner of service on the registrar for the purposes of section 20(4) is by filing a copy of the order at the Patent Office.

PART 6
MISCELLANEOUS

Agents and advisers

[3.149]
36 Agents

(1) Any act required or authorised by the Act to be done by or to any person in connection with the registration of a design, or any procedure relating to a registered design, may be done by or to an agent authorised by that person orally or in writing.

(2) But an agent shall only be treated as authorised under paragraph (1) where—
  (a) he was nominated by the applicant at the time of—
    (i) making his application for registration;
    (ii) making his application for a declaration of invalidity under section 11ZB; or
    (iii) making his application under section 19(1) or (2); or
  (b) he has filed Form DF1A.

(3) Where an agent has been authorised under paragraph (1), the registrar may, if he thinks fit in any particular case, require the signature or presence of his principal.

[3.150]
37 Appointing advisers

(1) The registrar may appoint an adviser to assist him in any proceedings before him.

(2) the registrar shall settle any question or instructions to be submitted or given to the adviser.

Correction of irregularities and extensions of time

[3.151]
38 Correction of irregularities

Where the registrar thinks fit, he may rectify any irregularity of procedure—
  (a) after giving the parties such notice, and
  (b) subject to such conditions,
as he may direct.

[3.152]
39 Extension of times or periods prescribed by Rules

(1) The registrar may, if he thinks fit, extend (or further extend) any time or period prescribed by these Rules, except the periods prescribed by—
  (a) rule 10(1) (period prescribed for the purposes of section 3(5)); and
  (b) rule 13(2) (period for making an application for restoration),
(but those periods may be extended under rules 38, 40 and 41).

(2) Any extension under paragraph (1) shall be made—
  (a) after giving the parties such notice, and
  (b) subject to such conditions,
as the registrar may direct.

(3) An extension may be granted under paragraph (1) notwithstanding that the time or period prescribed by the relevant rule has expired.

[3.153]
40 Interrupted days

(1) The registrar may certify any day as an interrupted day where—
  (a) there is an event or circumstance causing an interruption in the normal operation of the Patent Office; or
  (b) there is a general interruption or subsequent dislocation in the postal services of the United Kingdom.

(2) Any certificate of the registrar made under paragraph (1) shall be posted in the Patent Office and advertised in the journal.

(3) The registrar shall, where the time for doing anything under these Rules expires on an interrupted day, extend that time to the next following day not being an interrupted day (or an excluded day).

(4) In this rule—
"interrupted day" means a day which has been certified as such under paragraph (1); and
"excluded day" means a day specified as such by rule 46.

[3.154]
41 Delays in communication services

(1) The registrar shall extend any time or period in these Rules where he is satisfied that the failure to do something under these Rules was wholly or mainly attributed to a delay in, or failure of, a communication service.

(2) Any extension under paragraph (1) shall be—

(a) made after giving the parties such notice; and
(b) subject to such conditions,
as the registrar may direct.

(3) In this rule "communication service" means a service by which documents may be sent and delivered and includes post, electronic communications and courier.

Address for service

[3.155]
42 Address for service

(1) For the purposes of any proceedings under the Act, an address for service shall be furnished by—
(a) an applicant for the registration of a design;
(b) a person who makes an application under section 11ZB for a declaration of invalidity of a registered design;
(c) the registered proprietor of the design who opposes such an application.

(2) The proprietor of a registered design, or any person who has registered any interest in a registered design, may furnish an address for service on Form DF1A.

(3) Where a person has furnished an address for service under paragraph (1) or (2), he may substitute a new address for service by notifying the registrar on Form DF1A.

[(4) An address for service furnished under this Rule shall be an address in the United Kingdom, another EEA state or the Channel Islands.]

(6) In this rule "EEA State" means a member State, Iceland, Liechtenstein or Norway.

NOTES

Para (4): substituted for original paras (4), (5) by the Patents, Trade Marks and Designs (Address for Service) Rules 2009, SI 2009/546, rr 5, 6.

[3.156]
43 Failure to furnish an address for service

(1) Where—
(a) a person has failed to furnish an address for service under rule 42(1); and
(b) the registrar has sufficient information enabling him to contact that person,
the registrar shall direct that person to furnish an address for service.

(2) Where a direction has been given under paragraph (1), the person directed shall, before the end of the period of 2 months [beginning immediately after] the date of the direction, furnish an address for service.

(3) Paragraph (4) applies where—
(a) a direction was given under paragraph (1) and the period prescribed by paragraph (2) has expired; or
(b) the registrar had insufficient information to give a direction under paragraph (1),
and the person has failed to furnish an address for service.

(4) Where this paragraph applies—
(a) in the case of an applicant for the registration of a design, the application shall be treated as withdrawn;
(b) in the case of a person applying under section 11ZB for a declaration of invalidity, his application shall be treated as withdrawn; and
(c) in the case of the proprietor who is opposing an application under section 11ZB, he shall be deemed to have withdrawn from the proceedings.

(5) In this rule an "address for service" means an address which complies with the requirements of rule 42(4) . . .

NOTES

Para (2): words in square brackets substituted by the Trade Marks and Registered Designs (Amendment) Rules 2013, SI 2013/444, rr 5, 7, Sch 2.

Para (5): words omitted revoked by the Patents, Trade Marks and Designs (Address for Service) Rules 2009, SI 2009/546, rr 5, 7.

Miscellaneous

[3.157]
44 The journal

(1) The registrar shall publish a journal which shall contain—
(a) everything which is required by the Act or these Rules to be published; and
(b) any other information that the registrar may consider to be generally useful or important.

(2) In these Rules "the journal" means the journal published under paragraph (1).

[3.158]
45 Hours of business

(1) For the transaction of relevant business by the public the Patent Office shall be open—
- (a) on Monday to Friday between 9.00am and midnight; and
- (b) on Saturday between 9.00am and 1.00pm.

(2) For the transaction of all other business by the public under the Act the Patent Office shall be open between 9.00am and 5.00pm.

(3) In this Part "relevant business" means the filing of any application or other document except—
- (a) an application for an extension under section 8; or
- (b) an application for the registration of a design or designs made by virtue of section 14.

[3.159]
46 Excluded days

(1) The following shall be excluded days for the transaction by the public of business under the Act—
- (a) a Sunday;
- (b) Good Friday;
- (c) Christmas day; or
- (d) a day which is specified or proclaimed to be a bank holiday by or under section 1 of the Banking and Financial Dealings Act 1971.

(2) A Saturday shall be an excluded day for the transaction by the public of business under the Act, except relevant business (see rule 45(1)).

[3.160]
47 Transitional provisions and revocation

(1) Schedule 2 (transitional provisions) shall have effect.

(2) The instruments set out in Schedule 3 (revocations) are revoked to the extent specified.

SCHEDULE 1
FORMS

Rule 3

[3.161]

NOTES

The forms themselves are not reproduced in this work, but their numbers and descriptions are listed below.

Form	*Title*	*Rule*
DF1A	Appointment or change of agent or contact address	36 and 42
DF2A	Application to register one or more designs	4
DF2B	Application to register one or more designs divided from an earlier application	4
DF2C	Application to publish one or more designs	9
DF9A	Renewal of design registration	12
DF12A	Application to record a change of ownership or to record or cancel a licence or security	27
DF16A	Change of proprietor's name or address	34
DF19A	Request to invalidate a design registration	15
DF19B	Notice of counter-statement	15
DF19C	Notice by proprietor to cancel a registration	14
DF21	Request for a search of the UK designs register	31
DF23	Request for a Certified Copy	32
DF29	Request to restore a registration	13

SCHEDULE 2
TRANSITIONAL PROVISIONS

Rule 47(1)

PART 1
PROVISIONS RELATING TO PENDING APPLICATIONS

[3.162]
1 Interpretation

In this Part—

Part 3 Designs

"the old Rules" means the Registered Designs Rules 1995 as they had effect immediately before the coming into force of these Rules; and

"the RRO" means the Regulatory Reform (Registered Designs) Order 2006.

2 Statement of objections

Where—

(a) the registrar sent the applicant a statement of objections under rule 29 of the old Rules; and

(b) the applicant has not sent to the registrar his observations in writing on the objections,

the objections shall be treated as the "statement of objections" under rule 8 of these Rules and the date on which the objections were sent shall be treated as the date on which the applicant was notified under rule 8(1).

3 Period prescribed for the purposes of section 3B(3)

Where—

(a) the period prescribed by rule 10 of these Rules has expired before the date on which these Rules come into force; and

(b) the period prescribed for the purposes of section 3B by rule 36A of the old Rules has not expired before the date on which these Rules come into force,

the period prescribed for the purposes of section 3B(3) shall be that mentioned in rule 36A of the old Rules.

4 Publication

Rules 9 and 11 shall not apply where the application for registration of a design under the Act was made before these Rules come into force.

5 Restoration

An application made in accordance with rule 41(2) of the old Rules shall be treated as made in accordance with rule 13(1) of these Rules.

6 Inspection of register

Where the amendments made to section 22, by article 16(2)(b) and (3) of the RRO, do not apply to a registration under the Act (by reason of article 19 of the RRO), rule 69 of the old Rules shall continue to have effect in relation to that registration.

7 Inspection of documents

Rules 29 and 30 shall not apply to any document filed at the Patent Office before these Rules come into force.

8 Requests for certified copies

A request under rule 72 of the old Rules for a certified copy of any representation, specimen or document kept at the Patent Office shall be treated as an application under rule 33(1) of these Rules.

9 Invalidity proceedings

(1) The time the registrar allowed under rule 53 of the old Rules for the filing of the counter-statement shall be treated as the period specified under rule 15(4) of these Rules.

(2) Where—

(a) an application for a declaration of invalidity which was made before these Rules came into force; and

(b) a counter-statement has been filed by the registered proprietor,

the registrar shall, within 28 days of these Rules coming into force, specify the periods within which any evidence may be filed, in accordance with rule 16(1).

PART 2
PROVISIONS RELATING TO APPLICATIONS UNDER THE OLD ACT

[3.163]

10 Interpretation

In this Part, "the old Act" means the Registered Designs Act 1949 as it had effect on 27th October 2001.

11 Application of this Part

This Part applies to—

(a) transitional registrations, within the meaning of regulation 11 of the Registered Designs Regulations 2001;

(b) post-1989 registrations, within the meaning of regulation 12 of those Regulations; and

(c) pre-1989 registrations, within the meaning of regulation 13 of those Regulations.

12 Meaning of applied industrially

For the purposes of section 6 of the old Act, the circumstances in which a design shall be regarded as "applied industrially" are—

(a) where the design is applied to more than fifty articles, which do not all together constitute a single set of articles (within the meaning of section 44(1) of the old Act); or
(b) where the design is applied to goods manufactured in lengths or pieces, not being hand-made goods.

13 Applications under section 11(2) of old Act

(1) Part 4 of these Rules applies to an application under section 11(2) of the old Act for the cancellation of registration as it applies to an application for a declaration of invalidity under section 11ZB of the Act.

(2) Where an application is made under section 11(2) of the old Act, any reference in rule 15(1) to an application for a declaration of invalidity under section 11ZB of the Act shall be construed as a reference to an application under the relevant provision of the old Act.

(3) For the purposes of rule 23(1), an application under section 11(2) of the old Act shall be treated as if it were mentioned in section 30(3) of the Act.

SCHEDULE 3

(*Sch 3 contains revocations only.*)

DESIGNS (CONVENTION COUNTRIES) ORDER 2007

(SI 2007/277)

NOTES

Made. 7 February 2007.
Authority: Registered Designs Act 1949, ss 13(1), 37(5).
Commencement: 6 April 2007.

[3.164]
1

(1) This Order may be cited as the Designs (Convention Countries) Order 2007 and shall come into force on 6th April 2007.

(2) The Designs (Convention Countries) Order 2006 is revoked.

[3.165]
2

The countries specified in the Schedule are declared to be convention countries for the purposes of all the provisions of the Registered Designs Act 1949.

SCHEDULE
CONVENTION COUNTRIES

Article 2

[3.166]
Albania

Algeria

Andorra

Angola

Antigua and Barbuda

Argentina

Armenia

Australia

Austria

Azerbaijan

Bahamas

Bahrain

Bangladesh

Barbados

Belarus

Belgium

Belize

Benin

Bhutan

Bolivia

Bosnia and Herzegovina

Botswana

Brazil

Brunei Darussalam

Bulgaria

Burkina Faso

Burundi

Cambodia

Cameroon

Canada

[Cape Verde]

Central African Republic

Chad

Chile

China

Columbia

Comoros

Congo

Congo, Democratic Republic of the

Costa Rica

Cote d'lvoire

Croatia

Cuba

Cyprus

Czech Republic

Denmark

Djibouti

Dominica

Dominican Republic

Ecuador

Egypt

El Salvador

Equatorial Guinea

Estonia

Faeroe Islands

Fiji

Finland

France (including overseas Departments and Territories)

Gabon

Gambia

Georgia

Germany

Ghana

Greece

Grenada

Guatemala

Guinea

Guinea-Bissau

Guyana

Haiti

Holy See

Honduras

Hong Kong

Hungary

Iceland

India

Indonesia

Iran, Islamic Republic of

Iraq

Ireland

Israel

Italy

Jamaica

Japan

Jordan

Kazakhstan

Kenya

Korea, Democratic People's Republic of

Korea, Republic of

Kuwait

Kyrgyzstan

Lao People's Democratic Republic

Latvia

Lebanon

Lesotho

Liberia

Libyan Arab Jamahiriya

Liechtenstein

Lithuania

Luxembourg

Macao

Macedonia, Former Yugoslav Republic of

Madagascar

Malawi

Malaysia

Maldives

Mali

Malta

Mauritania

Mauritius

Mexico

Moldova, Republic of

Monaco

Mongolia

Montenegro

Morocco

Mozambique

Myanmar

Namibia

Nepal

Netherlands

Netherlands Antilles and Aruba

New Zealand (including the Cook Islands, Niue and Tokelau)

Nicaragua

Niger

Nigeria

Norway

Oman

Pakistan

Panama

Papua New Guinea

Paraguay

Peru

Philippines

Poland

Portugal

Qatar

Romania

Russian Federation

Rwanda

Saint Kitts and Nevis

Saint Lucia

Saint Vincent and the Grenadines

[Samoa]

San Marino

Sao Tome and Principe

Saudi Arabia

Senegal

Serbia

Seychelles

Sierra Leone

Singapore

Slovakia

Slovenia

Solomon Islands

South Africa

Spain

Sri Lanka

Sudan

Suriname

Swaziland

Sweden

Switzerland

Syrian Arab Republic

Taiwan

Tajikistan

Tanzania, United Republic of

Thailand

Togo

Tonga

Trinidad and Tobago

Tunisia

Turkey

Turkmenistan

Uganda

Ukraine

United Arab Emirates

United States of America (including Puerto Rico and all territories and possessions)

Uruguay

Uzbekistan

[Vanuatu]

Venezuela

Viet Nam

Yemen

Zambia

Zimbabwe

NOTES

Entry "Cape Verde" inserted by the Designs (Convention Countries) (Amendment) Order 2009, SI 2009/2747, art 2.

Entries "Samoa" and "Vanuatu" inserted by the Designs (Convention Countries) (Amendment) Order 2013, SI 2013/539, art 2.

COUNCIL REGULATION

(6/2002/EC)

of 12 December 2001

on Community designs

NOTES

Date of publication in OJ: OJ L3, 5.1.2002, p 1.

THE COUNCIL OF THE EUROPEAN UNION,

Having regard to the Treaty establishing the European Community, and in particular Article 308 thereof,

Having regard to the proposal from the Commission,[1]

Having regard to the opinion of the European Parliament,[2]

Having regard to the opinion of the Economic and Social Committee,[3]

Whereas—

(1) A unified system for obtaining a Community design to which uniform protection is given with uniform effect throughout the entire territory of the Community would further the objectives of the Community as laid down in the Treaty.

(2) Only the Benelux countries have introduced a uniform design protection law. In all the other Member States the protection of designs is a matter for the relevant national law and is confined to the territory of the Member State concerned. Identical designs may be therefore protected differently in different Member States and for the benefit of different owners. This inevitably leads to conflicts in the course of trade between Member States.

(3) The substantial differences between Member States' design laws prevent and distort Community-wide competition. In comparison with domestic trade in, and competition between, products incorporating a design, trade and competition within the Community are prevented and distorted by the large number of applications, offices, procedures, laws, nationally circumscribed exclusive rights and the combined administrative expense with correspondingly high costs and fees for the applicant. Directive 98/71/EC of the European Parliament and of the Council of 13 October 1998 on the legal protection of designs[4] contributes to remedying this situation.

(4) The effect of design protection being limited to the territory of the individual Member States whether or not their laws are approximated, leads to a possible division of the internal market with respect to products incorporating a design which is the subject of national rights held by different individuals, and hence constitutes an obstacle to the free movement of goods.

(5) This calls for the creation of a Community design which is directly applicable in each Member State, because only in this way will it be possible to obtain, through one application made to the Office for Harmonisation in the Internal Market (Trade Marks and Design) in accordance with a single procedure under one law, one design right for one area encompassing all Member States.

(6) Since the objectives of the proposed action, namely, the protection of one design right for one area encompassing all the Member States, cannot be sufficiently achieved by the Member States by reason of the scale and the effects of the creation of a Community design and a Community design authority and can therefore, and can therefore be better achieved at Community level, the Community may adopt measures, in accordance with the principle of subsidiarity as set out in Article 5 of the Treaty. In accordance with the principle of proportionality, as set out in that Article, this Regulation does not go beyond what is necessary in order to achieve those objectives.

(7) Enhanced protection for industrial design not only promotes the contribution of individual designers to the sum of Community excellence in the field, but also encourages innovation and development of new products and investment in their production.

(8) Consequently a more accessible design-protection system adapted to the needs of the internal market is essential for Community industries.

(9) The substantive provisions of this Regulation on design law should be aligned with the respective provisions in Directive 98/71/EC.

(10) Technological innovation should not be hampered by granting design protection to features dictated solely by a technical function. It is understood that this does not entail that a design must have an aesthetic quality. Likewise, the interoperability of products of different makes should not be hindered by extending protection to the design of mechanical fittings. Consequently, those features of a design which are excluded from protection for those reasons should not be taken into consideration for the purpose of assessing whether other features of the design fulfil the requirements for protection.

(11) The mechanical fittings of modular products may nevertheless constitute an important element of the innovative characteristics of modular products and present a major marketing asset, and therefore should be eligible for protection.

(12) Protection should not be extended to those component parts which are not visible during normal use of a product, nor to those features of such part which are not visible when the part is mounted, or which would not, in themselves, fulfil the requirements as to novelty and individual character. Therefore, those features of design which are excluded from protection for these reasons should not be taken into consideration for the purpose of assessing whether other features of the design fulfil the requirements for protection.

(13) Full-scale approximation of the laws of the Member States on the use of protected designs for the purpose of permitting the repair of a complex product so as to restore its original appearance, where the design is applied to or incorporated in a product which constitutes a component part of a complex product upon whose appearance the protected design is dependent, could not be achieved through Directive 98/71/EC. Within the framework of the conciliation procedure on the said Directive, the Commission undertook to review the consequences of the provisions of that Directive three years after the deadline for transposition of the Directive in particular for the industrial sectors which are most affected. Under these circumstances, it is appropriate not to confer any protection as a Community design for a design which is applied to or incorporated in a product which constitutes a component part of a complex product upon whose appearance the design is dependent and which is used for the purpose of the repair of a complex product so as to restore its original appearance, until the Council has decided its policy on this issue on the basis of a Commission proposal.

(14) The assessment as to whether a design has individual character should be based on whether the overall impression produced on an informed user viewing the design clearly differs from that produced on him by the existing design corpus, taking into consideration the nature of the product to which the design is applied or in which it is incorporated, and in particular the industrial sector to which it belongs and the degree of freedom of the designer in developing the design.

(15) A Community design should, as far as possible, serve the needs of all sectors of industry in the Community.

(16) Some of those sectors produce large numbers of designs for products frequently having a short market life where protection without the burden of registration formalities is an advantage and the duration of protection is of lesser significance. On the other hand, there are sectors of industry which value the advantages of registration for the greater legal certainty it provides and which require the possibility of a longer term of protection corresponding to the foreseeable market life of their products.

(17) This calls for two forms of protection, one being a short-term unregistered design and the other being a longer term registered design.

(18) A registered Community design requires the creation and maintenance of a register in which will be registered all those applications which comply with formal conditions and which have been accorded a date of filing. This registration system should in principle not be based upon substantive examination as to compliance with requirements for protection prior to registration, thereby keeping to a minimum the registration and other procedural burdens on applicants.

(19) A Community design should not be upheld unless the design is new and unless it also possesses an individual character in comparison with other designs.

(20) It is also necessary to allow the designer or his successor in title to test the products embodying the design in the market place before deciding whether the protection resulting from a registered Community design is desirable. To this end it is necessary to provide that disclosures of the design by the designer or his successor in title, or abusive disclosures during a period of 12 months prior to the date of the filing of the application for a registered Community design should not be prejudicial in assessing the novelty or the individual character of the design in question.

(21) The exclusive nature of the right conferred by the registered Community design is consistent with its greater legal certainty. It is appropriate that the unregistered Community design should, however, constitute a right only to prevent copying. Protection could not therefore extend to design products which are the result of a design arrived at independently by a second designer. This right should also extend to trade in products embodying infringing designs.

(22) The enforcement of these rights is to be left to national laws. It is necessary therefore to

provide for some basic uniform sanctions in all Member States. These should make it possible, irrespective of the jurisdiction under which enforcement is sought, to stop the infringing acts.

(23) Any third person who can establish that he has in good faith commenced use even for commercial purposes within the Community, or has made serious and effective preparations to that end, of a design included within the scope of protection of a registered Community design, which has not been copied from the latter, may be entitled to a limited exploitation of that design.

(24) It is a fundamental objective of this Regulation that the procedure for obtaining a registered Community design should present the minimum cost and difficulty to applicants, so as to make it readily available to small and medium-sized enterprises as well as to individual designers.

(25) Those sectors of industry producing large numbers of possibly short-lived designs over short periods of time of which only some may be eventually commercialised will find advantage in the unregistered Community design. Furthermore, there is also a need for these sectors to have easier recourse to the registered Community design. Therefore, the option of combining a number of designs in one multiple application would satisfy that need. However, the designs contained in a multiple application may be dealt with independently of each other for the purposes of enforcement of rights, licensing, rights in rem, levy of execution, insolvency proceedings, surrender, renewal, assignment, deferred publication or declaration of invalidity.

(26) The normal publication following registration of a Community design could in some cases destroy or jeopardise the success of a commercial operation involving the design. The facility of a deferment of publication for a reasonable period affords a solution in such cases.

(27) A procedure for hearing actions concerning validity of a registered Community design in a single place would bring savings in costs and time compared with procedures involving different national courts.

(28) It is therefore necessary to provide safeguards including a right of appeal to a Board of Appeal, and ultimately to the Court of Justice. Such a procedure would assist the development of uniform interpretation of the requirements governing the validity of Community designs.

(29) It is essential that the rights conferred by a Community design can be enforced in an efficient manner throughout the territory of the Community.

(30) The litigation system should avoid as far as possible "forum shopping". It is therefore necessary to establish clear rules of international jurisdiction.

(31) This Regulation does not preclude the application to designs protected by Community designs of the industrial property laws or other relevant laws of the Member States, such as those relating to design protection acquired by registration or those relating to unregistered designs, trade marks, patents and utility models, unfair competition or civil liability.

(32) In the absence of the complete harmonisation of copyright law, it is important to establish the principle of cumulation of protection under the Community design and under copyright law, whilst leaving Member States free to establish the extent of copyright protection and the conditions under which such protection is conferred.

(33) The measures necessary for the implementation of this Regulation should be adopted in accordance with Council Decision 1999/468/EC of 28 June 1999 laying down the procedures for the exercise of implementing powers conferred on the Commission,[5]

NOTES

[1] OJ C29, 31.1.1994, p 20 and OJ C248, 29.8.2000, p 3.

[2] OJ C67, 1.3.2001, p 318.

[3] OJ C110, 2.5.1995 and OJ C75, 15.3.2000, p 35.

[4] OJ L289, 28.10.1998, p 28.

[5] OJ L184, 17.7.1999, p 23.

HAS ADOPTED THIS REGULATION—

TITLE I
GENERAL PROVISIONS

[3.167]
Article 1
Community design

1. A design which complies with the conditions contained in this Regulation is hereinafter referred to as a "Community design".

2. A design shall be protected—

(a) by an "unregistered Community design", if made available to the public in the manner provided for in this Regulation;

(b) by a "registered Community design", if registered in the manner provided for in this Regulation.

3. A Community design shall have a unitary character. It shall have equal effect throughout the Community. It shall not be registered, transferred or surrendered or be the subject of a decision declaring it invalid, nor shall its use be prohibited, save in respect of the whole Community. This principle and its implications shall apply unless otherwise provided in this Regulation.

[3.168]
Article 2
Office

The Office for Harmonisation in the Internal Market (Trade Marks and Designs), hereinafter referred to as "the Office", instituted by Council Regulation (EC) No 40/94 of 20 December 1993 on the Community trade mark,[1] hereinafter referred to as the "Regulation on the Community trade mark", shall carry out the tasks entrusted to it by this Regulation.

NOTES

[1] OJ L11, 14.1.1994, p 1. Regulation as last amended by Regulation (EC) No 3288/94 (OJ L349, 31.12.1994, p 83).

TITLE II
THE LAW RELATING TO DESIGNS

SECTION 1
REQUIREMENTS FOR PROTECTION

[3.169]
Article 3
Definitions

For the purposes of this Regulation—

(a) "design" means the appearance of the whole or a part of a product resulting from the features of, in particular, the lines, contours, colours, shape, texture and/or materials of the product itself and/or its ornamentation;

(b) "product" means any industrial or handicraft item, including inter alia parts intended to be assembled into a complex product, packaging, get-up, graphic symbols and typographic typefaces, but excluding computer programs;

(c) "complex product" means a product which is composed of multiple components which can be replaced permitting disassembly and re-assembly of the product.

[3.170]
Article 4
Requirements for protection

1. A design shall be protected by a Community design to the extent that it is new and has individual character.

2. A design applied to or incorporated in a product which constitutes a component part of a complex product shall only be considered to be new and to have individual character—

(a) if the component part, once it has been incorporated into the complex product, remains visible during normal use of the latter; and

(b) to the extent that those visible features of the component part fulfil in themselves the requirements as to novelty and individual character.

3. "Normal use" within the meaning of paragraph (2)(a) shall mean use by the end user, excluding maintenance, servicing or repair work.

[3.171]
Article 5
Novelty

1. A design shall be considered to be new if no identical design has been made available to the public—

(a) in the case of an unregistered Community design, before the date on which the design for which protection is claimed has first been made available to the public;

(b) in the case of a registered Community design, before the date of filing of the application for registration of the design for which protection is claimed, or, if priority is claimed, the date of priority.

2. Designs shall be deemed to be identical if their features differ only in immaterial details.

[3.172]
Article 6
Individual character

1. A design shall be considered to have individual character if the overall impression it produces on the informed user differs from the overall impression produced on such a user by any design which has been made available to the public—

(a) in the case of an unregistered Community design, before the date on which the design for which protection is claimed has first been made available to the public;

(b) in the case of a registered Community design, before the date of filing the application for registration or, if a priority is claimed, the date of priority.

2. In assessing individual character, the degree of freedom of the designer in developing the design shall be taken into consideration.

[3.173]
Article 7
Disclosure

1. For the purpose of applying Articles 5 and 6, a design shall be deemed to have been made available to the public if it has been published following registration or otherwise, or exhibited, used in trade or otherwise disclosed, before the date referred to in Articles 5(1)(a) and 6(1)(a) or in Articles 5(1)(b) and 6(1)(b), as the case may be, except where these events could not reasonably have become known in the normal course of business to the circles specialised in the sector concerned, operating within the Community. The design shall not, however, be deemed to have been made available to the public for the sole reason that it has been disclosed to a third person under explicit or implicit conditions of confidentiality.

2. A disclosure shall not be taken into consideration for the purpose of applying Articles 5 and 6 and if a design for which protection is claimed under a registered Community design has been made available to the public—

(a) by the designer, his successor in title, or a third person as a result of information provided or action taken by the designer or his successor in title; and

(b) during the 12-month period preceding the date of filing of the application or, if a priority is claimed, the date of priority.

3. Paragraph 2 shall also apply if the design has been made available to the public as a consequence of an abuse in relation to the designer or his successor in title.

[3.174]
Article 8
Designs dictated by their technical function and designs of interconnections

1. A Community design shall not subsist in features of appearance of a product which are solely dictated by its technical function.

2. A Community design shall not subsist in features of appearance of a product which must necessarily be reproduced in their exact form and dimensions in order to permit the product in which the design is incorporated or to which it is applied to be mechanically connected to or placed in, around or against another product so that either product may perform its function.

3. Notwithstanding paragraph 2, a Community design shall under the conditions set out in Articles 5 and 6 subsist in a design serving the purpose of allowing the multiple assembly or connection of mutually interchangeable products within a modular system.

[3.175]
Article 9
Designs contrary to public policy or morality

A Community design shall not subsist in a design which is contrary to public policy or to accepted principles of morality.

SECTION 2
SCOPE AND TERM OF PROTECTION

[3.176]
Article 10
Scope of protection

1. The scope of the protection conferred by a Community design shall include any design which does not produce on the informed user a different overall impression.

2. In assessing the scope of protection, the degree of freedom of the designer in developing his design shall be taken into consideration.

[3.177]
Article 11
Commencement and term of protection of the unregistered Community design

1. A design which meets the requirements under Section 1 shall be protected by an unregistered Community design for a period of three years as from the date on which the design was first made available to the public within the Community.

2. For the purpose of paragraph 1, a design shall be deemed to have been made available to the public within the Community if it has been published, exhibited, used in trade or otherwise disclosed in such a way that, in the normal course of business, these events could reasonably have become known to the circles specialised in the sector concerned, operating within the Community. The design shall not, however, be deemed to have been made available to the public for the sole reason that it has been disclosed to a third person under explicit or implicit conditions of confidentiality.

[3.178]
Article 12
Commencement and term of protection of the registered Community design
Upon registration by the Office, a design which meets the requirements under Section 1 shall be protected by a registered Community design for a period of five years as from the date of the filing of the application. The right holder may have the term of protection renewed for one or more periods of five years each, up to a total term of 25 years from the date of filing.

[3.179]
Article 13
Renewal
1. Registration of the registered Community design shall be renewed at the request of the right holder or of any person expressly authorised by him, provided that the renewal fee has been paid.
2. The Office shall inform the right holder of the registered Community design and any person having a right entered in the register of Community designs, referred to in Article 72, hereafter referred to as the "register" in respect of the registered Community design, of the expiry of the registration in good time before the said expiry. Failure to give such information shall not involve the responsibility of the Office.
3. The request for renewal shall be submitted and the renewal fee paid within a period of six months ending on the last day of the month in which protection ends. Failing this, the request may be submitted and the fee paid within a further period of six months from the day referred to in the first sentence, provided that an additional fee is paid within this further period.
4. Renewal shall take effect from the day following the date on which the existing registration expires. The renewal shall be entered in the register.

SECTION 3
RIGHT TO THE COMMUNITY DESIGN

[3.180]
Article 14
Right to the Community design
1. The right to the Community design shall vest in the designer or his successor in title.
2. If two or more persons have jointly developed a design, the right to the Community design shall vest in them jointly.
3. However, where a design is developed by an employee in the execution of his duties or following the instructions given by his employer, the right to the Community design shall vest in the employer, unless otherwise agreed or specified under national law.

[3.181]
Article 15
Claims relating to the entitlement to a Community design
1. If an unregistered Community design is disclosed or claimed by, or a registered Community design has been applied for or registered in the name of, a person who is not entitled to it under Article 14, the person entitled to it under that provision may, without prejudice to any other remedy which may be open to him, claim to become recognised as the legitimate holder of the Community design.
2. Where a person is jointly entitled to a Community design, that person may, in accordance with paragraph 1, claim to become recognised as joint holder.
3. Legal proceedings under paragraphs 1 or 2 shall be barred three years after the date of publication of a registered Community design or the date of disclosure of an unregistered Community design. This provision shall not apply if the person who is not entitled to the Community design was acting in bad faith at the time when such design was applied for or disclosed or was assigned to him.
4. In the case of a registered Community design, the following shall be entered in the register—
(a) the mention that legal proceedings under paragraph 1 have been instituted;
(b) the final decision or any other termination of the proceedings;
(c) any change in the ownership of the registered Community design resulting from the final decision.

[3.182]
Article 16
Effects of a judgement on entitlement to a registered Community design
1. Where there is a complete change of ownership of a registered Community design as a result of legal proceedings under Article 15(1), licences and other rights shall lapse upon the entering in the register of the person entitled.
2. If, before the institution of the legal proceedings under Article 15(1) has been registered, the holder of the registered Community design or a licensee has exploited the design within the Community or made serious and effective preparations to do so, he may continue such

exploitation provided that he requests within the period prescribed by the implementing regulation a non-exclusive licence from the new holder whose name is entered in the register. The licence shall be granted for a reasonable period and upon reasonable terms.
3. Paragraph 2 shall not apply if the holder of the registered Community design or the licensee was acting in bad faith at the time when he began to exploit the design or to make preparations to do so.

[3.183]
Article 17
Presumption in favour of the registered holder of the design
The person in whose name the registered Community design is registered or, prior to registration, the person in whose name the application is filed, shall be deemed to be the person entitled in any proceedings before the Office as well as in any other proceedings.

[3.184]
Article 18
Right of the designer to be cited
The designer shall have the right, in the same way as the applicant for or the holder of a registered Community design, to be cited as such before the Office and in the register. If the design is the result of teamwork, the citation of the team may replace the citation of the individual designers.

SECTION 4
EFFECTS OF THE COMMUNITY DESIGN

[3.185]
Article 19
Rights conferred by the Community design
1. A registered Community design shall confer on its holder the exclusive right to use it and to prevent any third party not having his consent from using it. The aforementioned use shall cover, in particular, the making, offering, putting on the market, importing, exporting or using of a product in which the design is incorporated or to which it is applied, or stocking such a product for those purposes.
2. An unregistered Community design shall, however, confer on its holder the right to prevent the acts referred to in paragraph 1 only if the contested use results from copying the protected design.

The contested use shall not be deemed to result from copying the protected design if it results from an independent work of creation by a designer who may be reasonably thought not to be familiar with the design made available to the public by the holder.
3. Paragraph 2 shall also apply to a registered Community design subject to deferment of publication as long as the relevant entries in the register and the file have not been made available to the public in accordance with Article 50(4).

[3.186]
Article 20
Limitation of the rights conferred by a Community design
1. The rights conferred by a Community design shall not be exercised in respect of—
(a) acts done privately and for non-commercial purposes;
(b) acts done for experimental purposes;
(c) acts of reproduction for the purpose of making citations or of teaching, provided that such acts are compatible with fair trade practice and do not unduly prejudice the normal exploitation of the design, and that mention is made of the source.
2. In addition, the rights conferred by a Community design shall not be exercised in respect of—
(a) the equipment on ships and aircraft registered in a third country when these temporarily enter the territory of the Community;
(b) the importation in the Community of spare parts and accessories for the purpose of repairing such craft;
(c) the execution of repairs on such craft.

[3.187]
Article 21
Exhaustion of rights
The rights conferred by a Community design shall not extend to acts relating to a product in which a design included within the scope of protection of the Community design is incorporated or to which it is applied, when the product has been put on the market in the Community by the holder of the Community design or with his consent.

[3.188]
Article 22
Rights of prior use in respect of a registered Community design

1. A right of prior use shall exist for any third person who can establish that before the date of filing of the application, or, if a priority is claimed, before the date of priority, he has in good faith commenced use within the Community, or has made serious and effective preparations to that end, of a design included within the scope of protection of a registered Community design, which has not been copied from the latter.
2. The right of prior use shall entitle the third person to exploit the design for the purposes for which its use had been effected, or for which serious and effective preparations had been made, before the filing or priority date of the registered Community design.
3. The right of prior use shall not extend to granting a licence to another person to exploit the design.
4. The right of prior use cannot be transferred except, where the third person is a business, along with that part of the business in the course of which the act was done or the preparations were made.

[3.189]
Article 23
Government use

Any provision in the law of a Member State allowing use of national designs by or for the government may be applied to Community designs, but only to the extent that the use is necessary for essential defence or security needs.

SECTION 5
INVALIDITY

[3.190]
Article 24
Declaration of invalidity

1. A registered Community design shall be declared invalid on application to the Office in accordance with the procedure in Titles VI and VII or by a Community design court on the basis of a counterclaim in infringement proceedings.
2. A Community design may be declared invalid even after the Community design has lapsed or has been surrendered.
3. An unregistered Community design shall be declared invalid by a Community design court on application to such a court or on the basis of a counterclaim in infringement proceedings.

[3.191]
Article 25
Grounds for invalidity

1. A Community design may be declared invalid only in the following cases—
   (a) if the design does not correspond to the definition under Article 3(a);
   (b) if it does not fulfil the requirements of Articles 4 to 9;
   (c) if, by virtue of a court decision, the right holder is not entitled to the Community design under Article 14;
   [(d) if the Community design is in conflict with a prior design which has been made available to the public after the date of filing of the application or, if priority is claimed, the date of priority of the Community design, and which is protected from a date prior to the said date—
      (i) by a registered Community design or an application for such a design, or
      (ii) by a registered design right of a Member State, or by an application for such a right, or
      (iii) by a design right registered under the Geneva Act of the Hague Agreement concerning the international registration of industrial designs, adopted in Geneva on 2 July 1999, hereinafter referred to as "the Geneva Act", which was approved by Council Decision 954/2006 and which has effect in the Community, or by an application for such a right;]
   (e) if a distinctive sign is used in a subsequent design, and Community law or the law of the Member State governing that sign confers on the right holder of the sign the right to prohibit such use;
   (f) if the design constitutes an unauthorised use of a work protected under the copyright law of a Member State;
   (g) if the design constitutes an improper use of any of the items listed in Article 6ter of the "Paris Convention" for the Protection of Industrial Property hereafter referred to as the "Paris Convention", or of badges, emblems and escutcheons other than those covered by the said Article 6ter and which are of particular public interest in a Member State.
2. The ground provided for in paragraph (1)(c) may be invoked solely by the person who is entitled to the Community design under Article 14.

Part 3 Designs

3. The grounds provided for in paragraph (1)(d), (e) and (f) may be invoked solely by the applicant for or holder of the earlier right.
4. The ground provided for in paragraph (1)(g) may be invoked solely by the person or entity concerned by the use.
5. Paragraphs 3 and 4 shall be without prejudice to the freedom of Member States to provide that the grounds provided for in paragraphs 1(d) and (g) may also be invoked by the appropriate authority of the Member State in question on its own initiative.
6. A registered Community design which has been declared invalid pursuant to paragraph (1)(b), (e), (f) or (g) may be maintained in an amended form, if in that form it complies with the requirements for protection and the identity of the design is retained. "Maintenance" in an amended form may include registration accompanied by a partial disclaimer by the holder of the registered Community design or entry in the register of a court decision or a decision by the Office declaring the partial invalidity of the registered Community design.

NOTES

Para 1: sub-para (d) substituted by Council Regulation 1891/2006/EC, Art 2(1).

[3.192]
Article 26
Consequences of invalidity

1. A Community design shall be deemed not to have had, as from the outset, the effects specified in this Regulation, to the extent that it has been declared invalid.
2. Subject to the national provisions relating either to claims for compensation for damage caused by negligence or lack of good faith on the part of the holder of the Community design, or to unjust enrichment, the retroactive effect of invalidity of the Community design shall not affect—
   (a) any decision on infringement which has acquired the authority of a final decision and been enforced prior to the invalidity decision;
   (b) any contract concluded prior to the invalidity decision, in so far as it has been performed before the decision; however, repayment, to an extent justified by the circumstances, of sums paid under the relevant contract may be claimed on grounds of equity.

TITLE III
COMMUNITY DESIGNS AS OBJECTS OF PROPERTY

[3.193]
Article 27
Dealing with Community designs as national design rights

1. Unless Articles 28, 29, 30, 31 and 32 provide otherwise, a Community design as an object of property shall be dealt with in its entirety, and for the whole area of the Community, as a national design right of the Member State in which—
   (a) the holder has his seat or his domicile on the relevant date; or
   (b) where point (a) does not apply, the holder has an establishment on the relevant date.
2. In the case of a registered Community design, paragraph 1 shall apply according to the entries in the register.
3. In the case of joint holders, if two or more of them fulfil the condition under paragraph 1, the Member State referred to in that paragraph shall be determined—
   (a) in the case of an unregistered Community design, by reference to the relevant joint holder designated by them by common agreement;
   (b) in the case of a registered Community design, by reference to the first of the relevant joint holders in the order in which they are mentioned in the register.
4. Where paragraphs 1, 2 and 3 do not apply, the Member State referred to in paragraph 1 shall be the Member State in which the seat of the Office is situated.

[3.194]
Article 28
Transfer of the registered Community design

The transfer of a registered Community design shall be subject to the following provisions—
   (a) at the request of one of the parties, a transfer shall be entered in the register and published;
   (b) until such time as the transfer has been entered in the register, the successor in title may not invoke the rights arising from the registration of the Community design;
   (c) where there are time limits to be observed in dealings with the Office, the successor in title may make the corresponding statements to the Office once the request for registration of the transfer has been received by the Office;
   (d) all documents which by virtue of Article 66 require notification to the holder of the registered Community design shall be addressed by the Office to the person registered as holder or his representative, if one has been appointed.

[3.195]
Article 29
Rights in rem on a registered Community design

1. A registered Community design may be given as security or be the subject of rights in rem.
2. On request of one of the parties, the rights mentioned in paragraph 1 shall be entered in the register and published.

[3.196]
Article 30
Levy of execution

1. A registered Community design may be levied in execution.
2. As regards the procedure for levy of execution in respect of a registered Community design, the courts and authorities of the Member State determined in accordance with Article 27 shall have exclusive jurisdiction.
3. On request of one of the parties, levy of execution shall be entered in the register and published.

[3.197]
Article 31
Insolvency proceedings

1. The only insolvency proceedings in which a Community design may be involved shall be those opened in the Member State within the territory of which the centre of a debtor's main interests is situated.
2. In the case of joint proprietorship of a Community design, paragraph 1 shall apply to the share of the joint proprietor.
3. Where a Community design is involved in insolvency proceedings, on request of the competent national authority an entry to this effect shall be made in the register and published in the Community Designs Bulletin referred to in Article 73(1).

[3.198]
Article 32
Licensing

1. A Community design may be licensed for the whole or part of the Community. A licence may be exclusive or non-exclusive.
2. Without prejudice to any legal proceedings based on the law of contract, the holder may invoke the rights conferred by the Community design against a licensee who contravenes any provision in his licensing contract with regard to its duration, the form in which the design may be used, the range of products for which the licence is granted and the quality of products manufactured by the licensee.
3. Without prejudice to the provisions of the licensing contract, the licensee may bring proceedings for infringement of a Community design only if the right holder consents thereto. However, the holder of an exclusive licence may bring such proceedings if the right holder in the Community design, having been given notice to do so, does not himself bring infringement proceedings within an appropriate period.
4. A licensee shall, for the purpose of obtaining compensation for damage suffered by him, be entitled to intervene in an infringement action brought by the right holder in a Community design.
5. In the case of a registered Community design, the grant or transfer of a licence in respect of such right shall, at the request of one of the parties, be entered in the register and published.

[3.199]
Article 33
Effects vis-à-vis third parties

1. The effects vis-à-vis third parties of the legal acts referred to in Articles 28, 29, 30 and 32 shall be governed by the law of the Member State determined in accordance with Article 27.
2. However, as regards registered Community designs, legal acts referred to in Articles 28, 29 and 32 shall only have effect vis-à-vis third parties in all the Member States after entry in the register. Nevertheless, such an act, before it is so entered, shall have effect vis-à-vis third parties who have acquired rights in the registered Community design after the date of that act but who knew of the act at the date on which the rights were acquired.
3. Paragraph 2 shall not apply to a person who acquires the registered Community design or a right concerning the registered Community design by way of transfer of the whole of the undertaking or by any other universal succession.
4. Until such time as common rules for the Member States in the field of insolvency enter into force, the effects vis-à-vis third parties of insolvency proceedings shall be governed by the law of the Member State in which such proceedings are first brought under the national law or the regulations applicable in this field.

[3.200]
Article 34
The application for a registered Community design as an object of property

1. An application for a registered Community design as an object of property shall be dealt with in its entirety, and for the whole area of the Community, as a national design right of the Member State determined in accordance with Article 27.
2. Articles 28, 29, 30, 31, 32 and 33 shall apply *mutatis mutandis* to applications for registered Community designs. Where the effect of one of these provisions is conditional upon an entry in the register, that formality shall be performed upon registration of the resulting registered Community design.

TITLE IV
APPLICATION FOR A REGISTERED COMMUNITY DESIGN

SECTION 1
FILING OF APPLICATIONS AND THE CONDITIONS WHICH GOVERN THEM

[3.201]
Article 35
Filing and forwarding of applications

1. An application for a registered Community design shall be filed, at the option of the applicant—
   (a) at the Office; or
   (b) at the central industrial property office of a Member State; or
   (c) in the Benelux countries, at the Benelux Design Office.
2. Where the application is filed at the central industrial property office of a Member State or at the Benelux Design Office, that office shall take all steps to forward the application to the Office within two weeks after filing. It may charge the applicant a fee which shall not exceed the administrative costs of receiving and forwarding the application.
3. As soon as the Office has received an application which has been forwarded by a central industrial property office of a Member State or by the Benelux Design Office, it shall inform the applicant accordingly, indicating the date of its receipt at the Office.
4. No less than 10 years after the entry into force of this Regulation, the Commission shall draw up a report on the operation of the system of filing applications for registered Community designs, accompanied by any proposals for revision that it may deem appropriate.

[3.202]
Article 36
Conditions with which applications must comply

1. An application for a registered Community design shall contain—
   (a) a request for registration;
   (b) information identifying the applicant;
   (c) a representation of the design suitable for reproduction. However, if the object of the application is a two-dimensional design and the application contains a request for deferment of publication in accordance with Article 50, the representation of the design may be replaced by a specimen.
2. The application shall further contain an indication of the products in which the design is intended to be incorporated or to which it is intended to be applied.
3. In addition, the application may contain—
   (a) a description explaining the representation or the specimen;
   (b) a request for deferment of publication of the registration in accordance with Article 50;
   (c) information identifying the representative if the applicant has appointed one;
   (d) the classification of the products in which the design is intended to be incorporated or to which it is intended to be applied according to class;
   (e) the citation of the designer or of the team of designers or a statement under the applicant's responsibility that the designer or the team of designers has waived the right to be cited.
4. The application shall be subject to the payment of the registration fee and the publication fee. Where a request for deferment under paragraph 3(b) is filed, the publication fee shall be replaced by the fee for deferment of publication.
5. The application shall comply with the conditions laid down in the implementing regulation.
6. The information contained in the elements mentioned in paragraph 2 and in paragraph 3(a) and (d) shall not affect the scope of protection of the design as such.

[3.203]
Article 37
Multiple applications

1. Several designs may be combined in one multiple application for registered Community designs. Except in cases of ornamentation, this possibility is subject to the condition that the products in which the designs are intended to be incorporated or to which they are intended to be applied all belong to the same class of the International Classification for Industrial Designs.
2. Besides the fees referred to in Article 36(4), the multiple application shall be subject to payment of an additional registration fee and an additional publication fee. Where the multiple application contains a request for deferment of publication, the additional publication fee shall be replaced by the additional fee for deferment of publication. The additional fees shall correspond to a percentage of the basic fees for each additional design.
3. The multiple application shall comply with the conditions of presentation laid down in the implementing regulation.
4. Each of the designs contained in a multiple application or registration may be dealt with separately from the others for the purpose of applying this Regulation. It may in particular, separately from the others, be enforced, licensed, be the subject of a right in rem, a levy of execution or insolvency proceedings, be surrendered, renewed or assigned, be the subject of deferred publication or be declared invalid. A multiple application or registration may be divided into separate applications or registrations only under the conditions set out in the implementing regulation.

[3.204]
Article 38
Date of filing

1. The date of filing of an application for a registered Community design shall be the date on which documents containing the information specified in Article 36(1) are filed with the Office by the applicant, or, if the application has been filed with the central industrial property office of a Member State or with the Benelux Design Office, with that office.
2. By derogation from paragraph 1, the date of filing of an application filed with the central industrial property office of a Member State or with the Benelux Design Office and reaching the Office more than two months after the date on which documents containing the information specified in Article 36(1) have been filed shall be the date of receipt of such documents by the Office.

[3.205]
Article 39
Equivalence of Community filing with national filing

An application for a registered Community design which has been accorded a date of filing shall, in the Member States, be equivalent to a regular national filing, including where appropriate the priority claimed for the said application.

[3.206]
Article 40
Classification

For the purpose of this Regulation, use shall be made of the Annex to the Agreement establishing an International Classification for Industrial Designs, signed at Locarno on 8 October 1968.

SECTION 2
PRIORITY

[3.207]
Article 41
Right of priority

1. A person who has duly filed an application for a design right or for a utility model in or for any State party to the Paris Convention for the Protection of Industrial Property, or to the Agreement establishing the World Trade Organisation, or his successors in title, shall enjoy, for the purpose of filing an application for a registered Community design in respect of the same design or utility model, a right of priority of six months from the date of filing of the first application.
2. Every filing that is equivalent to a regular national filing under the national law of the State where it was made or under bilateral or multilateral agreements shall be recognised as giving rise to a right of priority.
3. "Regular national filing" means any filing that is sufficient to establish the date on which the application was filed, whatever may be the outcome of the application.
4. A subsequent application for a design which was the subject of a previous first application, and which is filed in or in respect of the same State, shall be considered as the first application for the purpose of determining priority, provided that, at the date of the filing of the subsequent application, the previous application has been withdrawn, abandoned or refused without being open to public inspection and without leaving any rights outstanding, and has not served as a basis for claiming priority. The previous application may not thereafter serve as a basis for claiming a right of priority.

5. If the first filing has been made in a State which is not a party to the Paris Convention, or to the Agreement establishing the World Trade Organisation, paragraphs 1 to 4 shall apply only in so far as that State, according to published findings, grants, on the basis of a filing made at the Office and subject to conditions equivalent to those laid down in this Regulation, a right of priority having equivalent effect.

[3.208]
Article 42
Claiming priority
An applicant for a registered Community design desiring to take advantage of the priority of a previous application shall file a declaration of priority and a copy of the previous application. If the language of the latter is not one of the languages of the Office, the Office may require a translation of the previous application in one of those languages.

[3.209]
Article 43
Effect of priority right
The effect of the right of priority shall be that the date of priority shall count as the date of the filing of the application for a registered Community design for the purpose of Articles 5, 6, 7, 22, 25(1)(d) and 50(1).

[3.210]
Article 44
Exhibition priority
1. If an applicant for a registered Community design has disclosed products in which the design is incorporated, or to which it is applied, at an official or officially recognised international exhibition falling within the terms of the Convention on International Exhibitions signed in Paris on 22 November 1928 and last revised on 30 November 1972, he may, if he files the application within a period of six months from the date of the first disclosure of such products, claim a right of priority from that date within the meaning of Article 43.
2. An applicant who wishes to claim priority pursuant to paragraph 1, under the conditions laid down in the implementing regulation, must file evidence that he has disclosed at an exhibition the products in or to which the design is incorporated or applied.
3. An exhibition priority granted in a Member State or in a third country does not extend the period of priority laid down in Article 41.

TITLE V
REGISTRATION PROCEDURE

[3.211]
Article 45
Examination as to formal requirements for filing
1. The Office shall examine whether the application complies with the requirements laid down in Article 36(1) for the accordance of a date of filing.
2. The Office shall examine whether—
(a) the application complies with the other requirements laid down in Article 36(2), (3), (4) and (5) and, in the case of a multiple application, Article 37(1) and (2);
(b) the application meets the formal requirements laid down in the implementing regulation for the implementation of Articles 36 and 37;
(c) the requirements of Article 77(2) are satisfied;
(d) the requirements concerning the claim to priority are satisfied, if a priority is claimed.
3. The conditions for the examination as to the formal requirements for filing shall be laid down in the implementing regulation.

[3.212]
Article 46
Remediable deficiencies
1. Where, in carrying out the examination under Article 45, the Office notes that there are deficiencies which may be corrected, the Office shall request the applicant to remedy them within the prescribed period.
2. If the deficiencies concern the requirements referred to in Article 36(1) and the applicant complies with the Office's request within the prescribed period, the Office shall accord as the date of filing the date on which the deficiencies are remedied. If the deficiencies are not remedied within the prescribed period, the application shall not be dealt with as an application for a registered Community design.
3. If the deficiencies concern the requirements, including the payment of fees, as referred to in Article 45(2)(a), (b) and (c) and the applicant complies with the Office's request within the prescribed period, the Office shall accord as the date of filing the date on which the application was originally filed. If the deficiencies or the default in payment are not remedied within the prescribed period, the Office shall refuse the application.

4. If the deficiencies concern the requirements referred to in Article 45(2)(d), failure to remedy them within the prescribed period shall result in the loss of the right of priority for the application.

[3.213]
Article 47
Grounds for non-registrability

1. If the Office, in carrying out the examination pursuant to Article 45, notices that the design for which protection is sought—
   (a) does not correspond to the definition under Article 3(a); or
   (b) is contrary to public policy or to accepted principles of morality, it shall refuse the application.

2. The application shall not be refused before the applicant has been allowed the opportunity of withdrawing or amending the application or of submitting his observations.

[3.214]
Article 48
Registration

If the requirements that an application for a registered Community design must satisfy have been fulfilled and to the extent that the application has not been refused by virtue of Article 47, the Office shall register the application in the Community design Register as a registered Community design. The registration shall bear the date of filing of the application referred to in Article 38.

[3.215]
Article 49
Publication

Upon registration, the Office shall publish the registered Community design in the Community Designs Bulletin as mentioned in Article 73(1). The contents of the publication shall be set out in the implementing regulation.

[3.216]
Article 50
Deferment of publication

1. The applicant for a registered Community design may request, when filing the application, that the publication of the registered Community design be deferred for a period of 30 months from the date of filing the application or, if a priority is claimed, from the date of priority.
2. Upon such request, where the conditions set out in Article 48 are satisfied, the registered Community design shall be registered, but neither the representation of the design nor any file relating to the application shall, subject to Article 74(2), be open to public inspection.
3. The Office shall publish in the Community Designs Bulletin a mention of the deferment of the publication of the registered Community design. The mention shall be accompanied by information identifying the right holder in the registered Community design, the date of filing the application and any other particulars prescribed by the implementing regulation.
4. At the expiry of the period of deferment, or at any earlier date on request by the right holder, the Office shall open to public inspection all the entries in the register and the file relating to the application and shall publish the registered Community design in the Community Designs Bulletin, provided that, within the time limit laid down in the implementing regulation—
   (a) the publication fee and, in the event of a multiple application, the additional publication fee are paid;
   (b) where use has been made of the option pursuant to Article 36(1)(c), the right holder has filed with the Office a representation of the design.

If the right holder fails to comply with these requirements, the registered Community design shall be deemed from the outset not to have had the effects specified in this Regulation.
5. In the case of multiple applications, paragraph 4 need only be applied to some of the designs included therein.
6. The institution of legal proceedings on the basis of a registered Community design during the period of deferment of publication shall be subject to the condition that the information contained in the register and in the file relating to the application has been communicated to the person against whom the action is brought.

TITLE VI
SURRENDER AND INVALIDITY OF THE REGISTERED COMMUNITY DESIGN

[3.217]
Article 51
Surrender

1. The surrender of a registered Community design shall be declared to the Office in writing by the right holder. It shall not have effect until it has been entered in the register.
2. If a Community design which is subject to deferment of publication is surrendered it shall be deemed from the outset not to have had the effects specified in this Regulation.

3. A registered Community design may be partially surrendered provided that its amended form complies with the requirements for protection and the identity of the design is retained.
4. Surrender shall be registered only with the agreement of the proprietor of a right entered in the register. If a licence has been registered, surrender shall be entered in the register only if the right holder in the registered Community design proves that he has informed the licensee of his intention to surrender. This entry shall be made on expiry of the period prescribed by the implementing regulation.
5. If an action pursuant to Article 14 relating to the entitlement to a registered Community design has been brought before a Community design court, the Office shall not enter the surrender in the register without the agreement of the claimant.

[3.218]
Article 52
Application for a declaration of invalidity
1. Subject to Article 25(2), (3), (4) and (5), any natural or legal person, as well as a public authority empowered to do so, may submit to the Office an application for a declaration of invalidity of a registered Community design.
2. The application shall be filed in a written reasoned statement. It shall not be deemed to have been filed until the fee for an application for a declaration of invalidity has been paid.
3. An application for a declaration of invalidity shall not be admissible if an application relating to the same subject matter and cause of action, and involving the same parties, has been adjudicated on by a Community design court and has acquired the authority of a final decision.

[3.219]
Article 53
Examination of the application
1. If the Office finds that the application for a declaration of invalidity is admissible, the Office shall examine whether the grounds for invalidity referred to in Article 25 prejudice the maintenance of the registered Community design.
2. In the examination of the application, which shall be conducted in accordance with the implementing regulation, the Office shall invite the parties, as often as necessary, to file observations, within a period to be fixed by the Office, on communications from the other parties or issued by itself.
3. The decision declaring the registered Community design invalid shall be entered in the register upon becoming final.

[3.220]
Article 54
Participation in the proceedings of the alleged infringer
1. In the event of an application for a declaration of invalidity of a registered Community design being filed, and as long as no final decision has been taken by the Office, any third party who proves that proceedings for infringement of the same design have been instituted against him may be joined as a party in the invalidity proceedings on request submitted within three months of the date on which the infringement proceedings were instituted.

The same shall apply in respect of any third party who proves both that the right holder of the Community design has requested that he cease an alleged infringement of the design and that he has instituted proceedings for a court ruling that he is not infringing the Community design.
2. The request to be joined as a party shall be filed in a written reasoned statement. It shall not be deemed to have been filed until the invalidity fee, referred to in Article 52(2), has been paid. Thereafter the request shall, subject to any exceptions laid down in the implementing regulation, be treated as an application for a declaration of invalidity.

TITLE VII
APPEALS

[3.221]
Article 55
Decisions subject to appeal
1. An appeal shall lie from decisions of the examiners, the Administration of Trade Marks and Designs and Legal Division and Invalidity Divisions. It shall have suspensive effect.
2. A decision which does not terminate proceedings as regards one of the parties can only be appealed together with the final decision, unless the decision allows separate appeal.

[3.222]
Article 56
Persons entitled to appeal and to be parties to appeal proceedings
Any party to proceedings adversely affected by a decision may appeal. Any other parties to the proceedings shall be parties to the appeal proceedings as of right.

[3.223]
Article 57
Time limit and form of appeal
Notice of appeal must be filed in writing at the Office within two months after the date of notification of the decision appealed from. The notice shall be deemed to have been filed only when the fee for appeal has been paid. Within four months after the date of notification of the decision, a written statement setting out the grounds of appeal must be filed.

[3.224]
Article 58
Interlocutory revision
1. If the department whose decision is contested considers the appeal to be admissible and well founded, it shall rectify its decision. This shall not apply where the appellant is opposed by another party to the proceedings.
2. If the decision is not rectified within one month after receipt of the statement of grounds, the appeal shall be remitted to the Board of Appeal without delay and without comment as to its merits.

[3.225]
Article 59
Examination of appeals
1. If the appeal is admissible, the Board of Appeal shall examine whether the appeal is to be allowed.
2. In the examination of the appeal, the Board of Appeal shall invite the parties, as often as necessary, to file observations, within a period to be fixed by the Board of Appeal, on communications from the other parties or issued by itself.

[3.226]
Article 60
Decisions in respect of appeals
1. Following the examination as to the merits of the appeal, the Board of Appeal shall decide on the appeal. The Board of Appeal may either exercise any power within the competence of the department which was responsible for the decision appealed against or remit the case to that department for further prosecution.
2. If the Board of Appeal remits the case for further prosecution to the department whose decision was appealed, that department shall be bound by the *ratio decidendi* of the Board of Appeal, in so far as the facts are the same.
3. The decisions of the Boards of Appeal shall take effect only from the date of expiry of the period referred to in Article 61(5) or, if an action has been brought before the Court of Justice within that period, from the date of rejection of such action.

[3.227]
Article 61
Actions before the Court of Justice
1. Actions may be brought before the Court of Justice against decisions of the Boards of Appeal on appeals.
2. The action may be brought on grounds of lack of competence, infringement of an essential procedural requirement, infringement of the Treaty, of this Regulation or of any rule of law relating to their application or misuse of power.
3. The Court of Justice has jurisdiction to annul or to alter the contested decision.
4. The action shall be open to any party to proceedings before the Board of Appeal adversely affected by its decision.
5. The action shall be brought before the Court of Justice within two months of the date of notification of the decision of the Board of Appeal.
6. The Office shall be required to take the necessary measures to comply with the judgment of the Court of Justice.

TITLE VIII
PROCEDURE BEFORE THE OFFICE

SECTION 1
GENERAL PROVISIONS

[3.228]
Article 62
Statement of reasons on which decisions are based
Decisions of the Office shall state the reasons on which they are based. They shall be based only on reasons or evidence on which the parties concerned have had an opportunity to present their comments.

[3.229]
Article 63
Examination of the facts by the Office of its own motion

1. In proceedings before it the Office shall examine the facts of its own motion. However, in proceedings relating to a declaration of invalidity, the Office shall be restricted in this examination to the facts, evidence and arguments provided by the parties and the relief sought.
2. The Office may disregard facts or evidence which are not submitted in due time by the parties concerned.

[3.230]
Article 64
Oral proceedings

1. If the Office considers that oral proceedings would be expedient, they shall be held either at the instance of the Office or at the request of any party to the proceedings.
2. Oral proceedings, including delivery of the decision, shall be public, unless the department before which the proceedings are taking place decides otherwise in cases where admission of the public could have serious and unjustified disadvantages, in particular for a party to the proceedings.

[3.231]
Article 65
Taking of evidence

1. In any proceedings before the Office the means of giving or obtaining evidence shall include the following—
   (a) hearing the parties;
   (b) requests for information;
   (c) the production of documents and items of evidence;
   (d) hearing witnesses;
   (e) opinions by experts;
   (f) statements in writing, sworn or affirmed or having a similar effect under the law of the State in which the statement is drawn up.
2. The relevant department of the Office may commission one of its members to examine the evidence adduced.
3. If the Office considers it necessary for a party, witness or expert to give evidence orally, it shall issue a summons to the person concerned to appear before it.
4. The parties shall be informed of the hearing of a witness or expert before the Office. They shall have the right to be present and to put questions to the witness or expert.

[3.232]
Article 66
Notification

The Office shall, as a matter of course, notify those concerned of decisions and summonses and of any notice or other communication from which a time limit is reckoned, or of which those concerned must be notified under other provisions of this Regulation or of the implementing regulation, or of which notification has been ordered by the President of the Office.

[3.233]
Article 67
Restitutio in integrum

1. The applicant for or holder of a registered Community design or any other party to proceedings before the Office who, in spite of all due care required by the circumstances having been taken, was unable to observe a time limit vis-à-vis the Office shall, upon application, have his rights re-established if the non-observance in question has the direct consequence, by virtue of the provisions of this Regulation, of causing the loss of any rights or means of redress.
2. The application must be filed in writing within two months of the removal of the cause of non-compliance with the time limit. The omitted act must be completed within this period. The application shall only be admissible within the year immediately following the expiry of the unobserved time limit. In the case of non-submission of the request for renewal of registration or of non-payment of a renewal fee, the further period of six months provided for in the second sentence of Article 13(3) shall be deducted from the period of one year.
3. The application must state the grounds on which it is based and must set out the facts on which it relies. It shall not be deemed to be filed until the fee for the re-establishment of rights has been paid.
4. The department competent to decide on the omitted act shall decide upon the application.
5. The provisions of this Article shall not be applicable to the time limits referred to in paragraph 2 and Article 41(1).
6. Where the applicant for or holder of a registered Community design has his rights re-established, he may not invoke his rights vis-à-vis a third party who, in good faith, in the course of the period between the loss of rights in the application for or registration of the

registered Community design and publication of the mention of re-establishment of those rights, has put on the market products in which a design included within the scope of protection of the registered Community design is incorporated or to which it is applied.

7. A third party who may avail himself of the provisions of paragraph 6 may bring third party proceedings against the decision re-establishing the rights of the applicant for or holder of the registered Community design within a period of two months as from the date of publication of the mention of re-establishment of those rights.

8. Nothing in this Article shall limit the right of a Member State to grant *restitutio in integrum* in respect of time limits provided for in this Regulation and to be complied with vis-à-vis the authorities of such State.

[3.234]
Article 68
Reference to general principles

In the absence of procedural provisions in this Regulation, the implementing regulation, the fees regulation or the rules of procedure of the Boards of Appeal, the Office shall take into account the principles of procedural law generally recognised in the Member States.

[3.235]
Article 69
Termination of financial obligations

1. Rights of the Office to the payment of fees shall be barred four years from the end of the calendar year in which the fee fell due.

2. Rights against the Office for the refunding of fees or sums of money paid in excess of a fee shall be barred after four years from the end of the calendar year in which the right arose.

3. The periods laid down in paragraphs 1 and 2 shall be interrupted, in the case covered by paragraph 1, by a request for payment of the fee and, in the case covered by paragraph 2, by a reasoned claim in writing. On interruption it shall begin again immediately and shall end at the latest six years after the end of the year in which it originally began, unless in the meantime judicial proceedings to enforce the right have begun. In this case the period shall end at the earliest one year after the judgment has acquired the authority of a final decision.

SECTION 2
COSTS

[3.236]
Article 70
Apportionment of costs

1. The losing party in proceedings for a declaration of invalidity of a registered Community design or appeal proceedings shall bear the fees incurred by the other party as well as all costs incurred by him essential to the proceedings, including travel and subsistence and the remuneration of an agent, adviser or advocate, within the limits of scales set for each category of costs under the conditions laid down in the implementing regulation.

2. However, where each party succeeds on some and fails on other heads, or if reasons of equity so dictate, the Invalidity Division or Board of Appeal shall decide a different apportionment of costs.

3. A party who terminates the proceedings by surrendering the registered Community design or by not renewing its registration or by withdrawing the application for a declaration of invalidity or the appeal, shall bear the fees and the costs incurred by the other party as stipulated in paragraphs 1 and 2.

4. Where a case does not proceed to judgment, the costs shall be at the discretion of the Invalidity Division or Board of Appeal.

5. Where the parties conclude before the Invalidity Division or Board of Appeal a settlement of costs differing from that provided for in paragraphs 1, 2, 3 and 4, the body concerned shall take note of that agreement.

6. On request, the registry of the Invalidity Division or Board of Appeal shall fix the amount of the costs to be paid pursuant to the preceding paragraphs. The amount so determined may be reviewed by a decision of the Invalidity Division or Board of Appeal on a request filed within the period prescribed by the implementing regulation.

[3.237]
Article 71
Enforcement of decisions fixing the amount of costs

1. Any final decision of the Office fixing the amount of costs shall be enforceable.

2. Enforcement shall be governed by the rules of civil procedure in force in the State in the territory of which it is carried out. The order for its enforcement shall be appended to the decision, without any other formality than verification of the authenticity of the decision, by the national authority which the government of each Member State shall designate for this purpose and shall make known to the Office and to the Court of Justice.

3. When these formalities have been completed on application by the party concerned, the latter may proceed to enforcement in accordance with the national law, by bringing the matter directly before the competent authority.
4. Enforcement may be suspended only by a decision of the Court of Justice. However, the courts of the Member State concerned shall have jurisdiction over complaints that enforcement is being carried out in an irregular manner.

SECTION 3
INFORMING THE PUBLIC AND THE OFFICIAL AUTHORITIES OF THE MEMBER STATES

[3.238]
Article 72
Register of Community designs
The Office shall keep a register to be known as the register of Community designs, which shall contain those particulars of which the registration is provided for by this Regulation or by the implementing regulation. The register shall be open to public inspection, except to the extent that Article 50(2) provides otherwise.

[3.239]
Article 73
Periodical publications
1. This Office shall periodically publish a Community Designs Bulletin containing entries open to public inspection in the register as well as other particulars the publication of which is prescribed by this Regulation or by the implementing regulation.
2. Notices and information of a general character issued by the President of the Office, as well as any other information relevant to this Regulation or its implementation, shall be published in the Official Journal of the Office.

[3.240]
Article 74
Inspection of files
1. The files relating to applications for registered Community designs which have not yet been published or the files relating to registered Community designs which are subject to deferment of publication in accordance with Article 50 or which, being subject to such deferment, have been surrendered before or on the expiry of that period, shall not be made available for inspection without the consent of the applicant for or the right holder in the registered Community design.
2. Any person who can establish a legitimate interest may inspect a file without the consent of the applicant for or holder of the registered Community design prior to the publication or after the surrender of the latter in the case provided for in paragraph 1.

This shall in particular apply if the interested person proves that the applicant for or the holder of the registered Community design has taken steps with a view to invoking against him the right under the registered Community design.
3. Subsequent to the publication of the registered Community design, the file may be inspected on request.
4. However, where a file is inspected pursuant to paragraph 2 or 3, certain documents in the file may be withheld from inspection in accordance with the provisions of the implementing regulation.

[3.241]
Article 75
Administrative cooperation
Unless otherwise provided in this Regulation or in national laws, the Office and the courts or authorities of the Member States shall on request give assistance to each other by communicating information or opening files for inspection.

Where the Office opens files to inspection by courts, public prosecutors' offices or central industrial property offices, the inspection shall not be subject to the restrictions laid down in Article 74.

[3.242]
Article 76
Exchange of publications
1. The Office and the central industrial property offices of the Member States shall despatch to each other on request and for their own use one or more copies of their respective publications free of charge.
2. The Office may conclude agreements relating to the exchange or supply of publications.

SECTION 4
REPRESENTATION

[3.243]
Article 77
General principles of representation

1. Subject to paragraph 2, no person shall be compelled to be represented before the Office.
2. Without prejudice to the second subparagraph of paragraph 3, natural or legal persons not having either their domicile or their principal place of business or a real and effective industrial or commercial establishment in the Community must be represented before the Office in accordance with Article 78(1) in all proceedings before the Office established by this Regulation, other than in filing an application for a registered Community design; the implementing regulation may permit other exceptions.
3. Natural or legal persons having their domicile or principal place of business or a real and effective industrial or commercial establishment in the Community may be represented before the Office by one of their employees, who must file with it a signed authorisation for inclusion in the files, the details of which are set out in the implementing regulation.

An employee of a legal person to which this paragraph applies may also represent other legal persons which have economic connections with the first legal person, even if those other legal persons have neither their domicile nor their principal place of business nor a real and effective industrial or commercial establishment within the Community.

[3.244]
Article 78
Professional representation

1. Representation of natural or legal persons in proceedings before the Office under this Regulation may only be undertaken by—
   (a) any legal practitioner qualified in one of the Member States and having his place of business within the Community, to the extent that he is entitled, within the said State, to act as a representative in industrial property matters; or
   (b) any professional representatives whose name has been entered on the list of professional representatives referred to in Article 89(1)(b) of the Regulation on the Community trade mark; or
   (c) persons whose names are entered on the special list of professional representatives for design matters referred to in paragraph 4.
2. The persons referred to in paragraph 1(c) shall only be entitled to represent third persons in proceedings on design matters before the Office.
3. The implementing regulation shall provide whether and under what conditions representatives must file with the Office a signed authorisation for insertion on the files.
4. Any natural person may be entered on the special list of professional representatives in design matters, if he fulfils the following conditions—
   (a) he must be a national of one of the Member States;
   (b) he must have his place of business or employment in the Community;
   (c) he must be entitled to represent natural or legal persons in design matters before the central industrial property office of a Member State or before the Benelux Design Office. Where, in that State, the entitlement to represent in design matters is not conditional upon the requirement of special professional qualifications, persons applying to be entered on the list must have habitually acted in design matters before the central industrial property office of the said State for at least five years. However, persons whose professional qualification to represent natural or legal persons in design matters before the central industrial property office of one of the Member States is officially recognised in accordance with the regulations laid by such State shall not be subject to the condition of having exercised the profession.
5. Entry on the list referred to in paragraph 4 shall be effected upon request, accompanied by a certificate furnished by the central industrial property office of the Member State concerned, which must indicate that the conditions laid down in the said paragraph are fulfilled.
6. The President of the Office may grant exemption from—
   (a) the requirement of paragraph 4(a) in special circumstances;
   (b) the requirement of paragraph 4(c), second sentence, if the applicant furnishes proof that he has acquired the requisite qualification in another way.
7. The conditions under which a person may be removed from the list shall be laid down in the implementing regulation.

TITLE IX
JURISDICTION AND PROCEDURE IN LEGAL ACTIONS RELATING TO COMMUNITY DESIGNS

SECTION 1
JURISDICTION AND ENFORCEMENT

[3.245]
Article 79
Application of the Convention on Jurisdiction and Enforcement

1. Unless otherwise specified in this Regulation, the Convention on Jurisdiction and the Enforcement of Judgements in Civil and Commercial Matters, signed in Brussels on 27 September 1968,[1] hereinafter referred to as the "Convention on Jurisdiction and Enforcement", shall apply to proceedings relating to Community designs and applications for registered Community designs, as well as to proceedings relating to actions on the basis of Community designs and national designs enjoying simultaneous protection.
2. The provisions of the Convention on Jurisdiction and Enforcement which are rendered applicable by the paragraph 1 shall have effect in respect of any Member State solely in the text which is in force in respect of that State at any given time.
3. In the event of proceedings in respect of the actions and claims referred to in Article 85—
   (a) Articles 2, 4, 5(1), (3), (4) and (5), 16(4) and 24 of the Convention on Jurisdiction and Enforcement shall not apply;
   (b) Articles 17 and 18 of that Convention shall apply subject to the limitations in Article 82(4) of this Regulation;
   (c) the provisions of Title II of that Convention which are applicable to persons domiciled in a Member State shall also be applicable to persons who do not have a domicile in any Member State but have an establishment therein.
4. The provisions of the Convention on Jurisdiction and Enforcement shall not have effect in respect of any Member State for which that Convention has not yet entered into force. Until such entry into force, proceedings referred to in paragraph 1 shall be governed in such a Member State by any bilateral or multilateral convention governing its relationship with another Member State concerned, or, if no such convention exists, by its domestic law on jurisdiction, recognition and enforcement of decisions.

NOTES

1 OJ L299, 31.12.1972, p 32. Convention as amended by the Conventions on the Accession to that Convention of the States acceding to the European Communities.

SECTION 2
DISPUTES CONCERNING THE INFRINGEMENT AND VALIDITY OF COMMUNITY DESIGNS

[3.246]
Article 80
Community design courts

1. The Member States shall designate in their territories as limited a number as possible of national courts and tribunals of first and second instance (Community design courts) which shall perform the functions assigned to them by this Regulation.
2. Each Member State shall communicate to the Commission not later than 6 March 2005 a list of Community design courts, indicating their names and their territorial jurisdiction.
3. Any change made after communication of the list referred to in paragraph 2 in the number, names or territorial jurisdiction of the Community design courts shall be notified without delay by the Member State concerned to the Commission.
4. The information referred to in paragraphs 2 and 3 shall be notified by the Commission to the Member States and published in the *Official Journal of the European Communities*.
5. As long as a Member State has not communicated the list as stipulated in paragraph 2, jurisdiction for any proceedings resulting from an action covered by Article 81 for which the courts of that State have jurisdiction pursuant to Article 82 shall lie with that court of the State in question which would have jurisdiction *ratione loci* and *ratione materiae* in the case of proceedings relating to a national design right of that State.

[3.247]
Article 81
Jurisdiction over infringement and validity

The Community design courts shall have exclusive jurisdiction—
   (a) for infringement actions and—if they are permitted under national law— actions in respect of threatened infringement of Community designs;
   (b) for actions for declaration of non-infringement of Community designs, if they are permitted under national law;

(c) for actions for a declaration of invalidity of an unregistered Community design;
(d) for counterclaims for a declaration of invalidity of a Community design raised in connection with actions under (a).

[3.248]
Article 82
International jurisdiction

1. Subject to the provisions of this Regulation and to any provisions of the Convention on Jurisdiction and Enforcement applicable by virtue of Article 79, proceedings in respect of the actions and claims referred to in Article 81 shall be brought in the courts of the Member State in which the defendant is domiciled or, if he is not domiciled in any of the Member States, in any Member State in which he has an establishment.
2. If the defendant is neither domiciled nor has an establishment in any of the Member States, such proceedings shall be brought in the courts of the Member State in which the plaintiff is domiciled or, if he is not domiciled in any of the Member States, in any Member State in which he has an establishment.
3. If neither the defendant nor the plaintiff is so domiciled or has such an establishment, such proceedings shall be brought in the courts of the Member State where the Office has its seat.
4. Notwithstanding paragraphs 1, 2 and 3—
(a) Article 17 of the Convention on Jurisdiction and Enforcement shall apply if the parties agree that a different Community design court shall have jurisdiction;
(b) Article 18 of that Convention shall apply if the defendant enters an appearance before a different Community design court.
5. Proceedings in respect of the actions and claims referred to in Article 81(a) and (d) may also be brought in the courts of the Member State in which the act of infringement has been committed or threatened.

[3.249]
Article 83
Extent of jurisdiction on infringement

1. A Community design court whose jurisdiction is based on Article 82(1), (2) (3) or (4) shall have jurisdiction in respect of acts of infringement committed or threatened within the territory of any of the Member States.
2. A Community design court whose jurisdiction is based on Article 82(5) shall have jurisdiction only in respect of acts of infringement committed or threatened within the territory of the Member State in which that court is situated.

[3.250]
Article 84
Action or counterclaim for a declaration of invalidity of a Community design

1. An action or a counterclaim for a declaration of invalidity of a Community design may only be based on the grounds for invalidity mentioned in Article 25.
2. In the cases referred to in Article 25(2), (3), (4) and (5) the action or the counterclaim may be brought solely by the person entitled under those provisions.
3. If the counterclaim is brought in a legal action to which the right holder of the Community design is not already a party, he shall be informed thereof and may be joined as a party to the action in accordance with the conditions set out in the law of the Member State where the court is situated.
4. The validity of a Community design may not be put in issue in an action for a declaration of non-infringement.

[3.251]
Article 85
Presumption of validity – defence as to the merits

1. In proceedings in respect of an infringement action or an action for threatened infringement of a registered Community design, the Community design court shall treat the Community design as valid. Validity may be challenged only with a counterclaim for a declaration of invalidity. However, a plea relating to the invalidity of a Community design, submitted otherwise than by way of counterclaim, shall be admissible in so far as the defendant claims that the Community design could be declared invalid on account of an earlier national design right, within the meaning of Article 25(1)(d), belonging to him.
2. In proceedings in respect of an infringement action or an action for threatened infringement of an unregistered Community design, the Community design court shall treat the Community design as valid if the right holder produces proof that the conditions laid down in Article 11 have been met and indicates what constitutes the individual character of his Community design. However, the defendant may contest its validity by way of a plea or with a counterclaim for a declaration of invalidity.

[3.252]
Article 86
Judgments of invalidity

1. Where in a proceeding before a Community design court the Community design has been put in issue by way of a counterclaim for a declaration of invalidity—
   (a) if any of the grounds mentioned in Article 25 are found to prejudice the maintenance of the Community design, the court shall declare the Community design invalid;
   (b) if none of the grounds mentioned in Article 25 is found to prejudice the maintenance of the Community design, the court shall reject the counterclaim.
2. The Community design court with which a counterclaim for a declaration of invalidity of a registered Community design has been filed shall inform the Office of the date on which the counterclaim was filed. The latter shall record this fact in the register.
3. The Community design court hearing a counterclaim for a declaration of invalidity of a registered Community design may, on application by the right holder of the registered Community design and after hearing the other parties, stay the proceedings and request the defendant to submit an application for a declaration of invalidity to the Office within a time limit which the court shall determine. If the application is not made within the time limit, the proceedings shall continue; the counterclaim shall be deemed withdrawn. Article 91(3) shall apply.
4. Where a Community design court has given a judgment which has become final on a counterclaim for a declaration of invalidity of a registered Community design, a copy of the judgment shall be sent to the Office. Any party may request information about such transmission. The Office shall mention the judgment in the register in accordance with the provisions of the implementing regulation.
5. No counterclaim for a declaration of invalidity of a registered Community design may be made if an application relating to the same subject matter and cause of action, and involving the same parties, has already been determined by the Office in a decision which has become final.

[3.253]
Article 87
Effects of the judgement on invalidity

When it has become final, a judgment of a Community design court declaring a Community design invalid shall have in all the Member States the effects specified in Article 26.

[3.254]
Article 88
Applicable law

1. The Community design courts shall apply the provisions of this Regulation.
2. On all matters not covered by this Regulation, a Community design court shall apply its national law, including its private international law.
3. Unless otherwise provided in this Regulation, a Community design court shall apply the rules of procedure governing the same type of action relating to a national design right in the Member State where it is situated.

[3.255]
Article 89
Sanctions in actions for infringement

1. Where in an action for infringement or for threatened infringement a Community design court finds that the defendant has infringed or threatened to infringe a Community design, it shall, unless there are special reasons for not doing so, order the following measures—
   (a) an order prohibiting the defendant from proceeding with the acts which have infringed or would infringe the Community design;
   (b) an order to seize the infringing products;
   (c) an order to seize materials and implements predominantly used in order to manufacture the infringing goods, if their owner knew the effect for which such use was intended or if such effect would have been obvious in the circumstances;
   (d) any order imposing other sanctions appropriate under the circumstances which are provided by the law of the Member State in which the acts of infringement or threatened infringement are committed, including its private international law.
2. The Community design court shall take such measures in accordance with its national law as are aimed at ensuring that the orders referred to in paragraph 1 are complied with.

[3.256]
Article 90
Provisional measures, including protective measures

1. Application may be made to the courts of a Member State, including Community design courts, for such provisional measures, including protective measures, in respect of a Community design as may be available under the law of that State in respect of national design rights even if, under this Regulation, a Community design court of another Member State has jurisdiction as to the substance of the matter.

2. In proceedings relating to provisional measures, including protective measures, a plea otherwise than by way of counterclaim relating to the invalidity of a Community design submitted by the defendant shall be admissible. Article 85(2) shall, however, apply *mutatis mutandis*.

3. A Community design court whose jurisdiction is based on Article 82(1), (2), (3) or (4) shall have jurisdiction to grant provisional measures, including protective measures, which, subject to any necessary procedure for recognition and enforcement pursuant to Title III of the Convention on Jurisdiction and Enforcement, are applicable in the territory of any Member State. No other court shall have such jurisdiction.

[3.257]
Article 91
Specific rules on related actions

1. A Community design court hearing an action referred to in Article 81, other than an action for a declaration of non-infringement, shall, unless there are special grounds for continuing the hearing, of its own motion after hearing the parties, or at the request of one of the parties and after hearing the other parties, stay the proceedings where the validity of the Community design is already in issue before another Community design court on account of a counterclaim or, in the case of a registered Community design, where an application for a declaration of invalidity has already been filed at the Office.

2. The Office, when hearing an application for a declaration of invalidity of a registered Community design, shall, unless there are special grounds for continuing the hearing, of its own motion after hearing the parties, or at the request of one of the parties and after hearing the other parties, stay the proceedings where the validity of the registered Community design is already in issue on account of a counterclaim before a Community design court. However, if one of the parties to the proceedings before the Community design court so requests, the court may, after hearing the other parties to these proceedings, stay the proceedings. The Office shall in this instance continue the proceedings pending before it.

3. Where the Community design court stays the proceedings it may order provisional measures, including protective measures, for the duration of the stay.

[3.258]
Article 92
Jurisdiction of Community design courts of second instance – further appeal

1. An appeal to the Community design courts of second instance shall lie from judgments of the Community design courts of first instance in respect of proceedings arising from the actions and claims referred to in Article 81.

2. The conditions under which an appeal may be lodged with a Community design court of second instance shall be determined by the national law of the Member State in which that court is located.

3. The national rules concerning further appeal shall be applicable in respect of judgments of Community design courts of second instance.

SECTION 3
OTHER DISPUTES CONCERNING COMMUNITY DESIGNS

[3.259]
Article 93
Supplementary provisions on the jurisdiction of national courts other than Community design courts

1. Within the Member State whose courts have jurisdiction under Article 79(1) or (4), those courts shall have jurisdiction for actions relating to Community designs other than those referred to in Article 81 which would have jurisdiction *ratione loci* and *ratione materiae* in the case of actions relating to a national design right in that State.

2. Actions relating to a Community design, other than those referred to in Article 81, for which no court has jurisdiction pursuant to Article 79(1) and (4) and paragraph 1 of this Article may be heard before the courts of the Member State in which the Office has its seat.

[3.260]
Article 94
Obligation of the national court

A national court which is dealing with an action relating to a Community design other than the actions referred to in Article 81 shall treat the design as valid. Articles 85(2) and 90(2) shall, however, apply *mutatis mutandis*.

TITLE X
EFFECTS ON THE LAWS OF THE MEMBER STATES

[3.261]
Article 95
Parallel actions on the basis of Community designs and national design rights

1. Where actions for infringement or for threatened infringement involving the same cause of action and between the same parties are brought before the courts of different Member States, one seized on the basis of a Community design and the other seized on the basis of a national design right providing simultaneous protection, the court other than the court first seized shall of its own motion decline jurisdiction in favour of that court. The court which would be required to decline jurisdiction may stay its proceedings if the jurisdiction of the other court is contested.
2. The Community design court hearing an action for infringement or threatened infringement on the basis of a Community design shall reject the action if a final judgment on the merits has been given on the same cause of action and between the same parties on the basis of a design right providing simultaneous protection.
3. The court hearing an action for infringement or for threatened infringement on the basis of a national design right shall reject the action if a final judgment on the merits has been given on the same cause of action and between the same parties on the basis of a Community design providing simultaneous protection.
4. Paragraphs 1, 2 and 3 shall not apply in respect of provisional measures, including protective measures.

[3.262]
Article 96
Relationship to other forms of protection under national law

1. The provisions of this Regulation shall be without prejudice to any provisions of Community law or of the law of the Member States concerned relating to unregistered designs, trade marks or other distinctive signs, patents and utility models, typefaces, civil liability and unfair competition.
2. A design protected by a Community design shall also be eligible for protection under the law of copyright of Member States as from the date on which the design was created or fixed in any form. The extent to which, and the conditions under which, such a protection is conferred, including the level of originality required, shall be determined by each Member State.

TITLE XI
SUPPLEMENTARY PROVISIONS CONCERNING THE OFFICE

SECTION 1
GENERAL PROVISIONS

[3.263]
Article 97
General provision

Unless otherwise provided in this Title, Title XII of the Regulation on the Community trade mark shall apply to the Office with regard to its tasks under this Regulation.

[3.264]
Article 98
Language of proceedings

1. The application for a registered Community design shall be filed in one of the official languages of the Community.
2. The applicant must indicate a second language which shall be a language of the Office the use of which he accepts as a possible language of proceedings before the Office.

If the application was filed in a language which is not one of the languages of the Office, the Office shall arrange to have the application translated into the language indicated by the applicant.
3. Where the applicant for a registered Community design is the sole party to proceedings before the Office, the language of proceedings shall be the language used for filing the application. If the application was made in a language other then the languages of the Office, the Office may send written communications to the applicant in the second language indicated by the applicant in his application.
4. In the case of invalidity proceedings, the language of proceedings shall be the language used for filing the application for a registered Community design if this is one of the languages of the Office. If the application was made in a language other than the languages of the Office, the language of proceedings shall be the second language indicated in the application.

The application for a declaration of invalidity shall be filed in the language of proceedings.

Where the language of proceedings is not the language used for filing the application for a registered Community design, the right holder of the Community design may file observations in the language of filing. The Office shall arrange to have those observations translated into the language of proceedings.

The implementing regulation may provide that the translation expenses to be borne by the Office may not, subject to a derogation granted by the Office where justified by the complexity of the case, exceed an amount to be fixed for each category of proceedings on the basis of the average size of statements of case received by the Office. Expenditure in excess of this amount may be allocated to the losing party in accordance with Article 70.

5. Parties to invalidity proceedings may agree that a different official language of the Community is to be the language of the proceedings.

[3.265]
Article 99
Publication and register

1. All information the publication of which is prescribed by this Regulation or the implementing regulation shall be published in all the official languages of the Community.
2. All entries in the Register of Community designs shall be made in all the official languages of the Community.
3. In cases of doubt, the text in the language of the Office in which the application for a registered Community design was filed shall be authentic. If the application was filed in an official language of the Community other than one of the languages of the Office, the text in the second language indicated by the applicant shall be authentic.

[3.266]
Article 100
Supplementary powers of the President

In addition to the functions and powers conferred on the President of the Office by Article 119 of the Regulation on the Community trade mark, the President may place before the Commission any proposal to amend this Regulation, the implementing regulation, the fees regulation and any other rule to the extent that they apply to registered Community designs, after consulting the Administrative Board and, in the case of the fees regulation, the Budget Committee.

[3.267]
Article 101
Supplementary powers of the Administrative Board

In addition to the powers conferred on it by Article 121 *et seq* of the Regulation on the Community trade mark or by other provisions of this Regulation, the Administrative Board;

(a) shall set the date for the first filing of applications for registered Community designs pursuant to Article 111(2);
(b) shall be consulted before adoption of the guidelines for examination as to formal requirements, examination as to grounds for refusal of registration and invalidity proceedings in the Office and in the other cases provided for in this Regulation.

SECTION 2
PROCEDURES

[3.268]
Article 102
Competence

For taking decisions in connection with the procedures laid down in this Regulation the following shall be competent—

(a) examiners;
(b) the Administration of Trade Marks and Designs and Legal Division;
(c) Invalidity Divisions;
(d) Boards of Appeal.

[3.269]
Article 103
Examiners

An examiner shall be responsible for taking decisions on behalf of the Office in relation to an application for a registered Community design.

[3.270]
Article 104
The Administration of Trade Marks and Designs and Legal Division

1. The Administration of Trade Marks and Legal Division provided for by Article 128 of the Regulation on the Community trade mark shall become the Administration of Trade Marks and Designs and Legal Division.
2. In addition to the powers conferred upon it by the Regulation on the Community trade mark, it shall be responsible for taking those decisions required by this Regulation which do not fall within the competence of an examiner or an Invalidity Division. It shall in particular be responsible for decisions in respect of entries in the register.

[3.271]
Article 105
Invalidity Divisions
1. An Invalidity Division shall be responsible for taking decisions in relation to applications for declarations of invalidity of registered Community designs.
2. An Invalidity Division shall consist of three members. At least one of the members must be legally qualified.

[3.272]
Article 106
Boards of Appeal
In addition to the powers conferred upon it by Article 131 of the Regulation on the Community trade mark, the Boards of Appeal instituted by that Regulation shall be responsible for deciding on appeals from decisions of the examiners, the Invalidity Divisions and from the decisions of the Administration of Trade Marks and Designs and Legal Division as regards their decisions concerning Community designs.

[TITLE XIA
INTERNATIONAL REGISTRATION OF DESIGNS

SECTION 1
GENERAL PROVISIONS

[3.273]
Article 106a
Application of provisions
1. Unless otherwise specified in this title, this Regulation and any Regulations implementing this Regulation adopted pursuant to Article 109 shall apply, mutatis mutandis, to registrations of industrial designs in the international register maintained by the International Bureau of the World Intellectual Property Organisation (hereinafter referred to as "international registration" and "the International Bureau") designating the Community, under the Geneva Act.
2. Any recording of an international registration designating the Community in the International Register shall have the same effect as if it had been made in the register of Community designs of the Office, and any publication of an international registration designating the Community in the Bulletin of the International Bureau shall have the same effect as if it had been published in the Community Designs Bulletin.]

NOTES
Title XIa (Arts 106a–106f) inserted by Council Regulation 1891/2006/EC, Art 2(2).

[SECTION 2
INTERNATIONAL REGISTRATIONS DESIGNATING THE COMMUNITY

[3.274]
Article 106b
Procedure for filing the international application
International applications pursuant to Article 4(1) of the Geneva Act shall be filed directly at the International Bureau.]

NOTES
Inserted as noted to Article 106a at **[3.273]**.

[3.275]
[Article 106c
Designation fees
The prescribed designation fees referred to in Article 7(1) of the Geneva Act are replaced by an individual designation fee.]

NOTES
Inserted as noted to Article 106a at **[3.273]**.

[3.276]
[Article 106d
Effects of international registration designating the European Community
1. An international registration designating the Community shall, from the date of its registration referred to in Article 10(2) of the Geneva Act, have the same effect as an application for a registered Community design.
2. If no refusal has been notified or if any such refusal has been withdrawn, the international registration of a design designating the Community shall, from the date referred to in paragraph 1, have the same effect as the registration of a design as a registered Community design.

3. The Office shall provide information on international registrations referred to in paragraph 2, in accordance with the conditions laid down in the Implementing Regulation.]

NOTES

Inserted as noted to Article 106a at **[3.273]**.

[3.277]
[Article 106e
Refusal

1. The Office shall communicate to the International Bureau a notification of refusal not later than six months from the date of publication of the international registration, if in carrying out an examination of an international registration, the Office notices that the design for which protection is sought does not correspond to the definition under Article 3(a), or is contrary to public policy or to accepted principles of morality.
The notification shall state the grounds on which the refusal is based.
2. The effects of an international registration in the Community shall not be refused before the holder has been allowed the opportunity of renouncing the international registration in respect of the Community or of submitting observations.
3. The conditions for the examination as to the grounds for refusal shall be laid down in the Implementing Regulation.]

NOTES

Inserted as noted to Article 106a at **[3.273]**.

[3.278]
[Article 106f
Invalidation of the effects of an international registration

1. The effects of an international registration in the Community may be declared invalid partly or in whole in accordance with the procedure in Titles VI and VII or by a Community design court on the basis of a counterclaim in infringement proceedings.
2. Where the Office is aware of the invalidation, it shall notify it to the International Bureau.]

NOTES

Inserted as noted to Article 106a at **[3.273]**.

TITLE XII
FINAL PROVISIONS

[3.279]
Article 107
Implementing regulation

1. The rules implementing this Regulation shall be adopted in an implementing regulation.
2. In addition to the fees already provided for in this Regulation, fees shall be charged, in accordance with the detailed rules of application laid down in the implementing regulation and in a fees regulation, in the cases listed below—
  (a) late payment of the registration fee;
  (b) late payment of the publication fee;
  (c) late payment of the fee for deferment of publication;
  (d) late payment of additional fees for multiple applications;
  (e) issue of a copy of the certificate of registration;
  (f) registration of the transfer of a registered Community design;
  (g) registration of a licence or another right in respect of a registered Community design;
  (h) cancellation of the registration of a licence or another right;
  (i) issue of an extract from the register;
  (j) inspection of the files;
  (k) issue of copies of file documents;
  (l) communication of information in a file;
  (m) review of the determination of the procedural costs to be refunded;
  (n) issue of certified copies of the application.
3. The implementing regulation and the fees regulation shall be adopted and amended in accordance with the procedure laid down in Article 109(2).

[3.280]
Article 108
Rules of procedure of the Boards of Appeal

The rules of procedure of the Boards of Appeal shall apply to appeals heard by those Boards under this Regulation, without prejudice to any necessary adjustment or additional provision, adopted in accordance with the procedure laid down in Article 109(2).

[3.281]
Article 109
Committee

1. The Commission shall be assisted by a Committee.
2. Where reference is made to this paragraph, Articles 5 and 7 of Decision 1999/468/EC shall apply.
The period laid down in Article 5(6) of Decision 1999/468/EC shall be set at three months.
3. The Committee shall adopt its rules of procedure.

[3.282]
Article 110
Transitional provision

1. Until such time as amendments to this Regulation enter into force on a proposal from the Commission on this subject, protection as a Community design shall not exist for a design which constitutes a component part of a complex product used within the meaning of Article 19(1) for the purpose of the repair of that complex product so as to restore its original appearance.
2. The proposal from the Commission referred to in paragraph 1 shall be submitted together with, and take into consideration, any changes which the Commission shall propose on the same subject pursuant to Article 18 of Directive 98/71/EC.

[3.283]
[Article 110a
Provisions relating to the enlargement of the Community

[1. As of the date of accession of Bulgaria, the Czech Republic, Estonia, Croatia, Cyprus, Latvia, Lithuania, Hungary, Malta, Poland, Romania, Slovenia and Slovakia (hereinafter referred to as 'new Member State(s)'), a Community design protected or applied for pursuant to this Regulation before their respective date of accession shall be extended to the territory of those Member States in order to have equal effect throughout the Community.]
2. The application for a registered Community design may not be refused on the basis of any of the grounds for non-registrability listed in Article 47(1), if these grounds became applicable merely because of the accession of a new Member State.
3. A Community design as referred to in paragraph 1 may not be declared invalid pursuant to Article 25(1) if the grounds for invalidity became applicable merely because of the accession of a new Member State.
4. The applicant or the holder of an earlier right in a new Member State may oppose the use of a Community design falling under Article 25(1)(d), (e) or (f) within the territory where the earlier right is protected. For the purpose of this provision, "earlier right" means a right acquired or applied for in good faith before accession.
5. Paragraphs 1, 3 and 4 above shall also apply to unregistered Community designs. Pursuant to Article 11, a design which has not been made public within the territory of the Community shall not enjoy protection as an unregistered Community design].

NOTES

Inserted by AA5, Annex II(4)(C)(III) (see OJ L236, 23.9.2003, p 33).
Para 1: substituted by Treaty of Accession of Croatia (2012) (see OJ L112, 24.4.2012, p 10).

[3.284]
Article 111
Entry into force

1. This Regulation shall enter into force on the 60th day following its publication in the *Official Journal of the European Communities*.
2. Applications for registered Community designs may be filed at the Office from the date fixed by the Administrative Board on the recommendation of the President of the Office.
3. Applications for registered Community designs filed within three months before the date referred to in paragraph 2 shall be deemed to have been filed on that date.

This Regulation shall be binding in its entirety and directly applicable in all Member States.

COMMISSION REGULATION

(2245/2002/EC)

of 21 October 2002

implementing Council Regulation (EC) No 6/2002 on Community designs

NOTES

Date of publication in OJ: OJ L341, 17.12.2002, p 28.

THE COMMISSION OF THE EUROPEAN COMMUNITIES,

Having regard to the Treaty establishing the European Community,

Having regard to Council Regulation (EC) No 6/2002 of 12 December 2001 on Community designs,[1] and in particular Article 107(3) thereof,

Whereas—

(1) Regulation (EC) No 6/2002 creates a system enabling a design having effect throughout the Community to be obtained on the basis of an application to the Office for Harmonisation in the Internal Market (trade marks and designs) (hereinafter "the Office").

(2) For this purpose, Regulation (EC) No 6/2002 contains the necessary provisions for a procedure leading to the registration of a Community design, as well as for the administration of registered Community designs, for appeals against decisions of the Office and for proceedings for the invalidation of a Community design.

(3) The present Regulation lays down the necessary measures for implementing the provisions of Regulation (EC) No 6/2002.

(4) This Regulation should ensure the smooth and efficient operation of design proceedings before the Office.

(5) The measures provided for in this Regulation are in accordance with the opinion of the Committee established under Article 109 of Regulation (EC) No 6/2002,

NOTES

[1] OJ L3, 5.1.2002, p 1.

HAS ADOPTED THIS REGULATION—

CHAPTER I
APPLICATION PROCEDURE

[3.285]

Article 1

Content of the application

1. The application for a registered Community design shall contain—
   (a) a request for registration of the design as a registered Community design;
   (b) the name, address and nationality of the applicant and the State in which the applicant is domiciled or in which it has its seat or establishment. Names of natural persons shall take the form of the family name and the given name(s). Names of legal entities shall be indicated by their official designation, which may be abbreviated in a customary manner; furthermore, the State whose law governs such entities shall be indicated.
   The telephone numbers as well as fax numbers and details of other data-communications links, such as electronic mail, may be given. Only one address shall, in principle, be indicated for each applicant; where several addresses are indicated, only the address mentioned first shall be taken into account, except where the applicant designates one of the addresses as an address for service. If the Office has given the applicant an identification number, it shall be sufficient to mention that number together with the name of the applicant;
   (c) a representation of the design in accordance with Article 4 of this Regulation or, if the application concerns a two-dimensional design and contains a request for deferment of publication in accordance with Article 50 of Regulation (EC) No 6/2002, a specimen in accordance with Article 5 of this Regulation;
   (d) an indication, in accordance with Article 3(3), of the products in which the design is intended to be incorporated or to which it is intended to be applied;
   (e) if the applicant has appointed a representative, the name of that representative and the address of his/her place of business in accordance with point (b); if the representative has more than one business address or if there are two or more representatives with different business addresses, the application shall indicate which address shall be used as an address for service; where no such indication is made, only the first-mentioned address shall be taken into account as an address for service. If there is more than one applicant, the application may indicate the appointment of one applicant or representative as common representative. If an appointed representative has been given an identification number by the Office, it shall be sufficient to mention that number together with the name of the representative;
   (f) if applicable, a declaration that priority of a previous application is claimed pursuant to Article 42 of Regulation (EC) No 6/2002, stating the date on which the previous application was filed and the country in which or for which it was filed;
   (g) if applicable, a declaration that exhibition priority is claimed pursuant to Article 44 of Regulation (EC) No 6/2002, stating the name of the exhibition and the date of the first disclosure of the products in which the design is incorporated or to which it is applied;
   (h) a specification of the language in which the application is filed, and of the second language pursuant to Article 98(2) of Regulation (EC) No 6/2002;

(i) the signature of the applicant or his/her representative in accordance with Article 65.

2. The application may contain—

(a) a single description per design not exceeding 100 words explaining the representation of the design or the specimen; the description must relate only to those features which appear in the reproductions of the design or the specimen; it shall not contain statements as to the purported novelty or individual character of the design or its technical value;

(b) a request for deferment of publication of registration in accordance with Article 50(1) of Regulation (EC) No 6/2002;

(c) an indication of the "Locarno classification" of the products contained in the application, that is to say, of the class or classes and the subclass or subclasses to which they belong in accordance with the Annex to the Agreement establishing an international classification for industrial designs, signed at Locarno on 8 October 1968 (hereinafter "the Locarno Agreement"), referred to in Article 3 and subject to Article 2(2);

(d) the citation of the designer or of the team of designers or a statement signed by the applicant to the effect that the designer or team of designers has waived the right to be cited under Article 36(3)(e) of Regulation (EC) No 6/2002.

[3.286]
Article 2
Multiple application

1. An application may be a multiple application requesting the registration of several designs.

2. When several designs other than ornamentation are combined in a multiple application, the application shall be divided if the products in which the designs are intended to be incorporated or to which they are intended to be applied belong to more than one class of the Locarno Classification.

3. For each design contained in the multiple application the applicant shall provide a representation of the design in accordance with Article 4 and the indication of the product in which the design is intended to be incorporated or to be applied.

4. The applicant shall number the designs contained in the multiple application consecutively, using arabic numerals.

[3.287]
Article 3
Classification and indication of products

1. Products shall be classified in accordance with Article 1 of the Locarno Agreement, as amended and in force at the date of filing of the design.

2. The classification of products shall serve exclusively administrative purposes.

3. The indication of products shall be worded in such a way as to indicate clearly the nature of the products and to enable each product to be classified in only one class of the Locarno classification, preferably using the terms appearing in the list of products set out therein.

4. The products shall be grouped according to the classes of the Locarno classification, each group being preceded by the number of the class to which that group of products belongs and presented in the order of the classes and subclasses under that classification.

[3.288]
Article 4
Representation of the design

1. The representation of the design shall consist in a graphic or photographic reproduction of the design, either in black and white or in colour. It shall meet the following requirements—

(a) save where the application is filed by electronic means pursuant to Article 67, the representation must be filed on separate sheets of paper or reproduced on the page provided for that purpose in the form made available by the Office pursuant to Article 68;

(b) in the case of separate sheets of paper, the design shall be reproduced on opaque white paper and either pasted or printed directly on it. Only one copy shall be filed and the sheets of paper shall not be folded or stapled;

(c) the size of the separate sheet shall be DIN A4 size (29.7 cm x 21 cm) and the space used for the reproduction shall be no larger than 26.2 cm x 17 cm. A margin of at least 2.5 cm shall be left on the left-hand side; at the top of each sheet of paper the number of views shall be indicated pursuant to paragraph 2 and, in the case of a multiple application, the consecutive number of the design; no explanatory text, wording or symbols, other than the indication "top" or the name or address of the applicant, may be displayed thereon;

(d) where the application is filed by electronic means, the graphic or photographic reproduction of the designs shall be in a data format determined by the President of the Office; the manner of identifying the different designs contained in a multiple application, or the different views, shall be determined by the President of the Office;

(e) the design shall be reproduced on a neutral background and shall not be retouched with ink or correcting fluid. It shall be of a quality permitting all the details of the matter for which protection is sought to be clearly distinguished and permitting it to be reduced or enlarged to a size no greater than 8 cm by 16 cm per view for entry in the Register of Community Designs provided for in Article 72 of Regulation (EC) No 6/2002, hereinafter "the Register", and for direct publishing in the *Community Designs Bulletin* referred to in Article 73 of that Regulation.

2. The representation may contain no more than seven different views of the design. Any one graphic or photographic reproduction may contain only one view. The applicant shall number each view using arabic numerals. The number shall consist of separate numerals separated by a point, the numeral to the left of the point indicating the number of the design, that to the right indicating the number of the view.

In cases where more than seven views are provided, the Office may disregard for registration and publication any of the extra views. The Office shall take the views in the consecutive order in which the views are numbered by the applicant.

3. Where an application concerns a design that consists in a repeating surface pattern, the representation of the design shall show the complete pattern and a sufficient portion of the repeating surface.

The size limits set out in paragraph 1(c) shall apply.

4. Where an application concerns a design consisting in a typographic typeface, the representation of the design shall consist in a string of all the letters of the alphabet, in both upper and lower case, and of all the arabic numerals, together with a text of five lines produced using that typeface, both letters and numerals being in the size pitch 16.

[3.289]
Article 5
Specimens

1. Where the application concerns a two-dimensional design and contains a request for a deferment of publication, in accordance with Article 50(1) of Regulation (EC) No 6/2002, the representation of the design may be replaced by a specimen pasted on a sheet of paper.

Applications for which a specimen is submitted must be sent by a single mail or directly delivered to the office of filing.

Both the application and the specimen shall be submitted at the same time.

2. The specimens shall not exceed 26.2 cm x 17 cm in size, 50 grams in weight or 3 mm in thickness. The specimen shall be capable of being stored, unfolded, alongside documents of the size prescribed in Article 4(1)(c).

3. Specimens that are perishable or dangerous to store shall not be filed.

The specimen shall be filed in five copies; in the case of a multiple application, five copies of the specimen shall be filed for each design.

4. Where the design concerns a repeating surface pattern, the specimen shall show the complete pattern and a sufficient portion of the repeating surface in length and width. The limits set out in paragraph 2 shall apply.

[3.290]
Article 6
Fees for the application

1. The following fees shall be paid at the time when the application is submitted to the Office—
   (a) the registration fee;
   (b) the publication fee or a deferment fee if deferment of publication has been requested;
   (c) an additional registration fee in respect of each additional design included in a multiple application;
   (d) an additional publication fee in respect of each additional design included in a multiple application, or an additional deferment fee in respect of each additional design included in a multiple application if deferment of publication has been requested.

2. Where the application includes a request for deferment of publication of registration, the publication fee and any additional publication fee in respect of each additional design included in a multiple application shall be paid within the time limits specified in Article 15(4).

[3.291]
Article 7
Filing of the application

1. The Office shall mark the documents making up the application with the date of its receipt and the file number of the application.

Each design contained in a multiple application shall be numbered by the Office in accordance with a system determined by the President.

The Office shall issue to the applicant without delay a receipt which shall specify the file number, the representation, description or other identification of the design, the nature and the number of the documents and the date of their receipt.

In the case of a multiple application, the receipt issued by the Office shall specify the first design and the number of designs filed.

2. If the application is filed with the central industrial property office of a Member State or at the Benelux Design Office in accordance with Article 35 of Regulation (EC) No 6/2002, the office of filing shall number each page of the application, using arabic numerals. The office of filing shall mark the documents making up the application with the date of receipt and the number of pages before forwarding the application to the Office.

The office of filing shall issue to the applicant without delay a receipt specifying the nature and the number of the documents and the date of their receipt.

3. If the Office receives an application forwarded by the central industrial property office of a Member State or the Benelux Design Office, it shall mark the application with the date of receipt and the file number and shall issue to the applicant without delay a receipt in accordance with the third and fourth subparagraphs of paragraph 1, indicating the date of receipt at the Office.

[3.292]
Article 8
Claiming priority

1. Where the priority of one or more previous applications is claimed in the application pursuant to Article 42 of Regulation (EC) No 6/2002, the applicant shall indicate the file number of the previous application and file a copy of it within three months of the filing date referred to in Article 38 of that Regulation. The President of the Office shall determine the evidence to be provided by the applicant.

2. Where, subsequent to the filing of the application, the applicant wishes to claim the priority of one or more previous applications pursuant to Article 42 of Regulation (EC) No 6/2002, he/she shall submit, within one month of the filing date, the declaration of priority, stating the date on which and the country in or for which the previous application was made.

The applicant shall submit to the Office the indications and evidence referred to in paragraph 1 within three months of receipt of the declaration of priority.

[3.293]
Article 9
Exhibition priority

1. Where exhibition priority has been claimed in the application pursuant to Article 44 of Regulation (EC) No 6/2002, the applicant shall, together with the application or at the latest within three months of the filing date, file a certificate issued at the exhibition by the authority responsible for the protection of industrial property at the exhibition.

That certificate shall declare that the design was incorporated in or applied to the product and disclosed at the exhibition, and shall state the opening date of the exhibition and, where the first disclosure of the product did not coincide with the opening date of the exhibition, the date of such first disclosure. The certificate shall be accompanied by an identification of the actual disclosure of the product, duly certified by that authority.

2. Where the applicant wishes to claim an exhibition priority subsequent to the filing of the application, the declaration of priority, indicating the name of the exhibition and the date of the first disclosure of the product in which the design was incorporated or to which it was applied, shall be submitted within one month of the filing date. The indications and evidence referred to in paragraph 1 shall be submitted to the Office within three months of receipt of the declaration of priority.

[3.294]
Article 10
Examination of requirements for a filing date and of formal requirements

1. The Office shall notify the applicant that a date of filing cannot be granted if the application does not contain—

(a) a request for registration of the design as a registered Community design;
(b) information identifying the applicant;
(c) a representation of the design pursuant to Article 4(1)(d) and (e) or, where applicable, a specimen.

2. If the deficiencies indicated in paragraph 1 are remedied within two months of receipt of the notification, the date on which all the deficiencies are remedied shall determine the date of filing.

If the deficiencies are not remedied before the time limit expires, the application shall not be dealt with as a Community design application. Any fees paid shall be refunded.

3. The Office shall call upon the applicant to remedy the deficiencies noted within a time limit specified by it where, although a date of filing has been granted, the examination reveals that—

(a) the requirements set out in Articles 1, 2, 4 and 5 or the other formal requirements for applications laid down in the Regulation (EC) No 6/2002 or in this Regulation have not been complied with;
(b) the full amount of the fees payable pursuant to Article 6(1), read in conjunction with Commission Regulation (EC) No 2246/2002, has not been received by the Office;
(c) where priority has been claimed pursuant to Articles 8 and 9, either in the application itself or within one month after the date of filing, the other requirements set out in those Articles have not been complied with;

(d) in the case of a multiple application, the products in which the designs are intended to be incorporated or to which they are intended to be applied belong to more than one class of the Locarno classification.

In particular, the Office shall call upon the applicant to pay the required fees within two months of the date of notification, together with the late payment fees provided for in Article 107(2)(a) to (d) of Regulation (EC) No 6/2002 and as set out in Regulation (EC) No 2246/2002.

In the case of the deficiency referred to in point (d) of the first subparagraph, the Office shall call upon the applicant to divide the multiple application in order to ensure compliance with the requirements under Article 2(2). It shall also call upon the applicant to pay the total amount of the fees for all the applications resulting from the separation of the multiple application, within such a time limit as it may specify.

After the applicant has complied with the request to divide the application within the time limit set, the date of filing of the resulting application or applications shall be the date of filing granted to the multiple application initially filed.

4. If the deficiencies referred to in paragraph 3(a) and (d) are not remedied before the time limit expires, the Office shall reject the application.

5. If the fees payable pursuant to Article 6(1)(a) and (b) are not paid before the time limit expires, the Office shall reject the application.

6. If any additional fees payable pursuant to Article 6(1)(c) or (d) in respect of multiple applications are not paid or not paid in full before the time limit expires, the Office shall reject the application in respect of all the additional designs which are not covered by the amount paid.

In the absence of any criteria for determining which designs are intended to be covered, the Office shall take the designs in the numerical order in which they are represented in accordance with Article 2(4). The Office shall reject the application in so far as it concerns designs for which additional fees have not been paid or have not been paid in full.

7. If the deficiencies referred to in paragraph 3(c) are not remedied before the time limit expires, the right of priority for the application shall be lost.

8. If any of the deficiencies referred to in paragraph 3 is not remedied before the time limit expires and such deficiency concerns only some of the designs contained in a multiple application, the Office shall reject the application, or the right of priority shall be lost, only in so far as those designs are concerned.

[3.295]
Article 11
Examination of grounds for non-registrability

1. Where, pursuant to Article 47 of Regulation (EC) No 6/2002, the Office finds, in the course of carrying out the examination under Article 10 of this Regulation, that the design for which protection is sought does not correspond to the definition of design provided in Article 3(a) of Regulation (EC) No 6/2002 or that the design is contrary to public policy or to accepted principles of morality, it shall inform the applicant that the design is non-registrable, specifying the ground for non-registrability.

2. The Office shall specify a time limit within which the applicant may submit his/her observations, withdraw the application or amend it by submitting an amended representation of the design, provided that the identity of the design is retained.

3. Where the applicant fails to overcome the grounds for non-registrability within the time limit, the Office shall refuse the application. If those grounds concern only some of the designs contained in a multiple application, the Office shall refuse the application only in so far as those designs are concerned.

[3.296]
[Article 11a
Examination of grounds for refusal

1. Where, pursuant to Article 106e(1) of Regulation (EC) No 6/2002, the Office finds, in the course of carrying out an examination of an international registration, that the design for which protection is sought does not correspond to the definition of design provided for in Article 3(a) of that Regulation or that the design is contrary to public policy or to accepted principles of morality, it shall send to the International Bureau of the World Intellectual Property Organisation (hereinafter "the International Bureau") a notification of refusal not later than six months from the date of publication of the international registration, specifying the grounds for refusal pursuant to Article 12(2) of the Geneva Act of the Hague Agreement concerning the International Registration of Industrial Designs adopted on 2 July 1999 (hereinafter "the Geneva Act") approved by Council Decision 2006/954/EC.[1]

2. The Office shall specify a time limit within which the holder of the international registration has the possibility, pursuant to Article 106e(2) of Regulation (EC) No 6/2002, to renounce the international registration in respect of the Community, to limit the international registration to one or some of the industrial designs in respect of the Community or to submit observations.

3. Where the holder of the international registration is obliged to be represented in proceedings before the Office pursuant to Article 77(2) of Regulation (EC) No 6/2002, the notification shall contain a reference to the obligation of the holder to appoint a representative as referred to in Article 78(1) of that Regulation.

The time limit specified in paragraph 2 of this Article shall apply *mutatis mutandis*.

4. If the holder fails to appoint a representative within the specified time limit, the Office shall refuse the protection of the international registration.

5. Where the holder submits observations that would satisfy the Office within the specified time limit, the Office shall withdraw the refusal and notify the International Bureau in accordance with Article 12(4) of the Geneva act.

Where, pursuant to Article 12(2) of the Geneva act, the holder does not submits observations that would satisfy the Office within the specified time limit, the Office shall confirm the decision refusing protection for the international registration. That decision is subject to appeal in accordance with Title VII of Regulation (EC) No 6/2002.

6. Where the holder renounces the international registration or limits the international registration to one or some of the industrial designs in respect of the Community, he shall inform the International Bureau by way of recording procedure in accordance with Article 16(1)(iv) and (v) of the Geneva Act. The holder can inform the Office submitting a corresponding statement.]

NOTES

Inserted by Commission Regulation 876/2007/EC, Art 1(1).

[1] OJ L386, 29.12.2006, p 28.

[3.297]
Article 12
Withdrawal or correction of the application

1. The applicant may at any time withdraw a Community design application or, in the case of a multiple application, withdraw some of the designs contained in the application.

2. Only the name and address of the applicant, errors of wording or of copying, or obvious mistakes may be corrected, at the request of the applicant and provided that such correction does not change the representation of the design.

3. An application for the correction of the application pursuant to paragraph 2 shall contain—

(a) the file number of the application;

(b) the name and the address of the applicant in accordance with Article 1(1)(b);

(c) where the applicant has appointed a representative, the name and the business address of the representative in accordance with Article 1(1)(e);

(d) the indication of the element of the application to be corrected and that element in its corrected version.

4. If the requirements for the correction of the application are not fulfilled, the Office shall communicate the deficiency to the applicant. If the deficiency is not remedied within the time limits specified by the Office, the Office shall reject the application for correction.

5. A single application may be made for the correction of the same element in two or more applications submitted by the same applicant.

6. Paragraphs 2 to 5 shall apply *mutatis mutandis* to applications to correct the name or the business address of a representative appointed by the applicant.

CHAPTER II
REGISTRATION PROCEDURE

[3.298]
Article 13
Registration of the design

1. If the application satisfies the requirements referred to in Article 48 of Regulation (EC) No 6/2002, the design contained in that application and the particulars set out in Article 69(2) of this Regulation shall be recorded in the Register.

2. If the application contains a request for deferment of publication pursuant to Article 50 of Regulation (EC) No 6/2002, that fact and the date of expiry of the period of deferment shall be recorded.

3. The fees payable pursuant to Article 6(1) shall not be refunded even if the design applied for is not registered.

[3.299]
Article 14
Publication of the registration

1. The registration of the design shall be published in the *Community Designs Bulletin*.

2. Subject to paragraph 3, the publication of the registration shall contain—

(a) the name and address of the holder of the Community design (hereinafter "the holder");

(b) where applicable, the name and business address of the representative appointed by the holder other than a representative falling within the first subparagraph of Article 77(3) of

Regulation (EC) No 6/2002; if more than one representative has the same business address, only the name and business address of the first-named representative shall be published, the name being followed by the words "et al"; if there are two or more representatives with different business addresses, only the address for service determined pursuant to Article 1(1)(e) of this Regulation shall be published; where an association of representatives is appointed pursuant to Article 62(9) only the name and business address of the association shall be published;

(c) the representation of the design pursuant to Article 4; where the representation of the design is in colour, the publication shall be in colour;

(d) where applicable, an indication that a description has been filed pursuant to Article 1(2)(a);

(e) an indication of the products in which the design is intended to be incorporated or to which it is intended to be applied, preceded by the number of the relevant classes and subclasses of the Locarno classification, and grouped accordingly;

(f) where applicable, the name of the designer or the team of designers;

(g) the date of filing and the file number and, in the case of a multiple application, the file number of each design;

(h) where applicable, particulars of the claim of priority pursuant to Article 42 of Regulation (EC) No 6/2002;

(i) where applicable, particulars of the claim of exhibition priority pursuant to Article 44 of Regulation (EC) No 6/2002;

(j) the date and the registration number and the date of the publication of the registration;

(k) the language in which the application was filed and the second language indicated by the applicant pursuant to Article 98(2) of Regulation (EC) No 6/2002.

3. If the application contains a request for deferment of publication pursuant to Article 50 of Regulation (EC) No 6/2002, a mention of the deferment shall be published in the *Community Designs Bulletin*, together with the name of the holder, the name of the representative, if any, the date of filing and registration, and the file number of the application. Neither the representation of the design nor any particulars identifying its appearance shall be published.

[3.300]

Article 15

Deferment of publication

1. Where the application contains a request for deferment of publication pursuant to Article 50 of Regulation (EC) No 6/2002, the holder shall, together with the request or at the latest three months before the 30-month deferment period expires—

(a) pay the publication fee referred to in Article 6(1)(b);

(b) in the case of a multiple registration, pay the additional publication fees, referred to in Article 6(1)(d);

(c) in cases where a representation of the design has been replaced by a specimen in accordance with Article 5, file a representation of the design in accordance with Article 4. This applies to all the designs contained in a multiple application for which publication is requested;

(d) in the case of a multiple registration, clearly indicate which of the designs contained therein is to be published or which of the designs are to be surrendered, or, if the period of deferment has not yet expired, for which designs deferment is to be continued.

Where the holder requests publication before the expiry of the 30-month deferment period, he/she shall, at the latest three months before the requested date of publication, comply with the requirements set out in points (a) to (d) of the first paragraph.

2. If the holder fails to comply with the requirements set out in paragraph 1(c) or (d), the Office shall call upon him/her to remedy the deficiencies within a specified time limit which shall in no case expire after the 30-month deferment period.

3. If the holder fails to remedy the deficiencies referred to in paragraph 2 within the applicable time limit—

(a) the registered Community design shall be deemed from the outset not to have had the effects specified in Regulation (EC) No 6/2002;

(b) where the holder has requested earlier publication as provided for under the second subparagraph of paragraph 1, the request shall be deemed not to have been filed.

4. If the holder fails to pay the fees referred to in paragraph 1(a) or (b), the Office shall call upon him/her to pay those fees together with the fees for late payment provided for in Article 107(2)(b) or (d) of Regulation (EC) No 6/2002 and as set out in Regulation (EC) No 2246/2002, within a specified time limit which shall in no case expire after the 30-month deferment period.

If no payment has been made within that time limit, the Office shall notify the holder that the registered Community design has from the outset not had the effects specified in Regulation (EC) No 6/2002.

If, in respect of a multiple registration, a payment is made within that time limit but is insufficient to cover all the fees payable pursuant to paragraph 1(a) and (b), as well as the applicable fee for late payment, all the designs in respect of which the fees have not been paid shall be deemed from the outset not to have had the effects specified in Regulation (EC) No 6/2002.

Unless it is clear which designs the amount paid is intended to cover, and in the absence of other criteria for determining which designs are intended to be covered, the Office shall take the designs in the numerical order in which they are represented in accordance with Article 2(4).

All designs for which the additional publication fee has not been paid or has not been paid in full, together with the applicable fee for late payment, shall be deemed from the outset not to have had the effects specified in Regulation (EC) No 6/2002.

[3.301]
Article 16
Publication after the period for deferment

1. Where the holder has complied with the requirements laid down in Article 15, the Office shall, at the expiry of the period for deferment or in the case of a request for earlier publication, as soon as is technically possible—

(a) publish the registered Community design in the *Community Designs Bulletin*, with the indications set out in Article 14(2), together with an indication of the fact that the application contained a request for deferment of publication pursuant to Article 50 of Regulation (EC) No 6/2002 and, where applicable, that a specimen was filed in accordance with Article 5 of this Regulation;
(b) make available for public inspection any file relating to the design;
(c) open to public inspection all the entries in the Register, including any entries withheld from inspection pursuant to Article 73.

2. Where Article 15(4) applies, the actions referred to in paragraph 1 of this Article shall not take place in respect of those designs contained in the multiple registration which are deemed from the outset not to have had the effects specified in Regulation (EC) No 6/2002.

[3.302]
Article 17
Certificate of registration

1. After publication, the Office shall issue to the holder a certificate of registration which shall contain the entries in the Register provided for in Article 69(2) and a statement to the effect that those entries have been recorded in the Register.

2. The holder may request that certified or uncertified copies of the certificate of registration be supplied to him/her upon payment of a fee.

[3.303]
Article 18
Maintenance of the design in an amended form

1. Where, pursuant to Article 25(6) of Regulation (EC) No 6/2002, the registered Community design is maintained in an amended form, the Community design in its amended form shall be entered in the Register and published in the *Community Designs Bulletin*.

2. Maintenance of a design in an amended form may include a partial disclaimer, not exceeding 100 words, by the holder or an entry in the Register of Community Designs of a court decision or a decision by the Office declaring the partial invalidity of the design right.

[3.304]
Article 19
Change of the name or address of the holder or of his/her registered representative

1. A change of the name or address of the holder which is not the consequence of a transfer of the registered design shall, at the request of the holder, be recorded in the Register.

2. An application for a change of the name or address of the holder shall contain—

(a) the registration number of the design;
(b) the name and the address of the holder as recorded in the Register. If the holder has been given an identification number by the Office, it shall be sufficient to indicate that number together with the name of the holder;
(c) the indication of the name and address of the holder, as changed, in accordance with Article 1(1)(b);
(d) where the holder has appointed a representative, the name and business address of the representative, in accordance with Article 1(1)(e).

3. The application referred to in paragraph 2 shall not be subject to payment of a fee.

4. A single application may be made for a change of the name or address in respect of two or more registrations of the same holder.

5. If the requirements set out in paragraphs 1 and 2 are not fulfilled, the Office shall communicate the deficiency to the applicant.

If the deficiency is not remedied within the time limits specified by the Office, the Office shall reject the application.

6. Paragraphs 1 to 5 shall apply *mutatis mutandis* to a change of the name or address of the registered representative.

7. Paragraphs 1 to 6 shall apply *mutatis mutandis* to applications for Community designs. The change shall be recorded in the files kept by the Office concerning the Community design application.

[3.305]
Article 20
Correction of mistakes and errors in the Register and in the publication of the registration

Where the registration of a design or the publication of the registration contains a mistake or error attributable to the Office, the Office shall correct the error or mistake of its own motion or at the request of the holder.

Where such a request is made by the holder, Article 19 shall apply *mutatis mutandis*. The request shall not be subject to payment of a fee.

The Office shall publish the corrections made pursuant to this Article.

CHAPTER III
RENEWAL OF REGISTRATION

[3.306]
Article 21
Notification of expiry of registration

At least six months before expiry of the registration, the Office shall inform the holder, and any person having a right entered in the Register, including a licence, in respect of the Community design, that the registration is approaching expiry. Failure to give notification shall not affect the expiry of the registration.

[3.307]
[Article 22
Renewal of Community design registration

1. An application for renewal of registration shall contain:
   (a) the name of the person requesting renewal;
   (b) the registration number;
   (c) where applicable, an indication that renewal is requested for all the designs covered by a multiple registration or, if the renewal is not requested for all such designs, an indication of those designs for which renewal is requested.
2. The fees payable pursuant to Article 13 of Regulation (EC) No 6/2002 for the renewal of a registration shall consist of:
   (a) renewal fee, which, in cases where several designs are covered by a multiple registration, shall be proportionate to the number of designs covered by the renewal;
   (b) here applicable, the additional fee for late payment of the renewal fee or late submission of the request for renewal, pursuant to Article 13 of Regulation (EC) No 6/2002, as specified in Regulation (EC) No 2246/2002.
3. If the payment referred to in paragraph 2 of this Article is made according to the provisions of Article 5(1) of the Regulation (EC) No 2246/2002, this shall be deemed to constitute a request for renewal provided that it contains all the indications required under points (a) and (b) of paragraph 1, of this Article and Article 6(1) of that Regulation.
4. Where the application for renewal is filed within the time limits provided for in Article 13(3) of Regulation (EC) No 6/2002, but the other conditions for renewal provided for in Article 13 thereof and in this Regulation are not satisfied, the Office shall inform the applicant of the deficiencies.
5. Where an application for renewal is not submitted or is submitted after expiry of the time limit provided for in the second sentence of Article 13(3) of Regulation (EC) No 6/2002, or if the fees are not paid or are paid only after expiry of the relevant time limit, or if the deficiencies are not remedied within the time limit specified by the Office, the Office shall determine that the registration has expired and shall notify the holder accordingly.

In the case of a multiple registration, where the fees paid are insufficient to cover all the designs for which renewal is requested, such a determination shall be made only after the Office has established which designs the amount paid is intended to cover.

In the absence of other criteria for determining which designs are intended to be covered, the Office shall take the designs in the numerical order in which they are represented in accordance with Article 2(4).

The Office shall determine that the registration has expired with regard to all designs for which the renewal fees have not been paid or have not been paid in full.

6. Where the determination made pursuant to paragraph 5 has become final, the Office shall cancel the design from the Register with effect from the day following the day on which the existing registration expired.
7. Where the renewal fees provided for in paragraph 2 have been paid but the registration is not renewed, those fees shall be refunded.
8. A single application for renewal may be submitted for two or more designs, whether or not part of the same multiple registration, upon payment of the required fees for each of the designs, provided that the holders or the representatives are the same in each case.]

NOTES

Substituted by Commission Regulation 876/2007/EC, Art 1(2).

Part 3 Designs

[3.308]
[Article 22a
Renewals of international registration designating the Community
The international registration shall be renewed directly at the International Bureau in compliance with Article 17 of the Geneva Act.]

NOTES
Inserted by Commission Regulation 876/2007/EC, Art 1(3).

CHAPTER IV
TRANSFER, LICENCES AND OTHER RIGHTS, CHANGES

[3.309]
Article 23
Transfer
1. An application for registration of a transfer pursuant to Article 28 of Regulation (EC) No 6/2002 shall contain—
(a) the registration number of the Community design;
(b) particulars of the new holder in accordance with Article 1(1)(b);
(c) where not all of the designs covered by a multiple registration are included in the transfer, particulars of the registered designs to which the transfer relates;
(d) documents duly establishing the transfer.
2. The application may contain, where applicable, the name and business address of the representative of the new holder, to be set out in accordance with Article 1(1)(e).
3. The application shall not be deemed to have been filed until the required fee has been paid. If the fee is not paid or is not paid in full, the Office shall notify the applicant accordingly.
4. The following shall constitute sufficient proof of transfer under paragraph 1(d)—
(a) the application for registration of the transfer is signed by the registered holder or his/her representative and by the successor in title or his/her representative; or
(b) the application, if submitted by the successor in title, is accompanied by a declaration, signed by the registered holder or his/her representative, that he/she agrees to the registration of the successor in title; or
(c) the application is accompanied by a completed transfer form or document, signed by the registered holder or his/her representative and by the successor in title or his/her representative.
5. Where the conditions applicable to the registration of a transfer are not fulfilled, the Office shall notify the applicant of the deficiencies.
If the deficiencies are not remedied within the time limit specified by the Office, it shall reject the application for registration of the transfer.
6. A single application for registration of a transfer may be submitted for two or more registered Community designs, provided that the registered holder and the successor in title are the same in each case.
7. Paragraphs 1 to 6 shall apply *mutatis mutandis* to the transfer of applications for registered Community designs. The transfer shall be recorded in the files kept by the Office concerning the Community design application.

[3.310]
Article 24
Registration of licences and other rights
1. Article 23(1)(a), (b) and (c) and Article 23(2), (3), (5) and (6) shall apply *mutatis mutandis* to the registration of the grant or transfer of a licence, to registration of the creation or transfer of a right in rem in respect of a registered Community design, and to registration of enforcement measures. However, where a registered Community design is involved in insolvency proceedings, the request of the competent national authority for an entry in the Register to this effect shall not be subject to payment of a fee.
In the case of a multiple registration, each registered Community design may, separately from the others, be licensed, the subject of a right in rem, levy of execution or insolvency proceedings.
2. Where the registered Community design is licensed for only a part of the Community, or for a limited period of time, the application for registration of the licence shall indicate the part of the Community or the period of time for which the licence is granted.
3. Where the conditions applicable to registration of licences and other rights, set out in Articles 29, 30 or 32 of Regulation (EC) No 6/2002, in paragraph 1 of this Article, and in the other applicable Articles of this Regulation are not fulfilled, the Office shall notify the applicant of the deficiencies.
If the deficiencies are not remedied within a time limit specified by the Office, it shall reject the application for registration.
4. Paragraphs 1, 2 and 3 shall apply *mutatis mutandis* to licences and other rights concerning applications for registered Community designs. Licences, rights in rem and enforcement measures shall be recorded in the files kept by the Office concerning the Community design application.

5. The request for a non-exclusive licence pursuant to Article 16(2) of Regulation (EC) No 6/2002 shall be made within three months of the date of the entry in the Register of the newly entitled holder.

[3.311]
Article 25
Special provisions for the registration of a licence

1. A licence in respect of a registered Community design shall be recorded in the Register as an exclusive licence if the holder of the design or the licensee so requests.
2. A licence in respect of a registered Community design shall be recorded in the Register as a sub-licence where it is granted by a licensee whose licence is recorded in the Register.
3. A licence in respect of a registered Community design shall be recorded in the Register as a territorially limited licence if it is granted for a part of the Community.
4. A licence in respect of a registered Community design shall be recorded in the Register as a temporary licence if it is granted for a limited period of time.

[3.312]
Article 26
Cancellation or modification of the registration of licences and other rights

1. A registration effected under Article 24 shall be cancelled upon application by one of the persons concerned.
2. The application shall contain—
   (a) the registration number of the registered Community design, or in the case of a multiple registration, the number of each design; and
   (b) particulars of the right whose registration is to be cancelled.
3. Application for cancellation of the registration of a licence or other right shall not be deemed to have been filed until the required fee has been paid.

If the fee is not paid or is not paid in full, the Office shall notify the applicant accordingly. A request from a competent national authority for cancellation of an entry where a registered Community design is involved in insolvency proceedings shall not be subject to payment of a fee.

4. The application shall be accompanied by documents showing that the registered right no longer exists or by a statement by the licensee or the holder of another right to the effect that he/she consents to cancellation of the registration.
5. Where the requirements for cancellation of the registration are not satisfied, the Office shall notify the applicant of the deficiencies. If the deficiencies are not remedied within the time limit specified by the Office, it shall reject the application for cancellation of the registration.
6. Paragraphs 1, 2, 4 and 5 shall apply *mutatis mutandis* to a request for modification of a registration effected pursuant to Article 24.
7. Paragraphs 1 to 6 shall apply *mutatis mutandis* to entries made in the files pursuant to Article 24(4).

CHAPTER V
SURRENDER AND INVALIDITY

[3.313]
Article 27
Surrender

1. A declaration of surrender pursuant to Article 51 of Regulation (EC) No 6/2002 shall contain—
   (a) the registration number of the registered Community design;
   (b) the name and address of the holder in accordance with Article 1(1)(b);
   (c) where a representative has been appointed, the name and business address of the representative in accordance with Article 1(1)(e);
   (d) where surrender is declared only for some of the designs contained in a multiple registration, an indication of the designs for which the surrender is declared or the designs which are to remain registered;
   (e) where, pursuant to Article 51(3) of Regulation (EC) No 6/2002, the registered Community design is partially surrendered, a representation of the amended design in accordance with Article 4 of this Regulation.
2. Where a right of a third party relating to the registered Community design is entered in the Register, it shall be sufficient proof of his/her agreement to the surrender that a declaration of consent to the surrender is signed by the holder of that right or his/her representative.

Where a licence has been registered, surrender of the design shall be registered three months after the date on which the holder satisfies the Office that he/she has informed the licensee of his/her intention to surrender it. If the holder proves to the Office before the expiry of that period that the licensee has given his/her consent, the surrender shall be registered forthwith.

3. Where a claim relating to the entitlement to a registered Community design has been brought before a court pursuant to Article 15 of Regulation (EC) No 6/2002, a declaration of consent to the surrender, signed by the claimant or his/her representative, shall be sufficient proof of his/her agreement to the surrender.
4. If the requirements governing surrender are not fulfilled, the Office shall communicate the deficiencies to the declarant. If the deficiencies are not remedied within the time limit specified by the Office, the Office shall reject the entry of the surrender in the Register.

[3.314]
Article 28
Application for a declaration of invalidity
1. An application to the Office for a declaration of invalidity pursuant to Article 52 of Regulation (EC) No 6/2002 shall contain—
- (a) as concerns the registered Community design for which the declaration of invalidity is sought—
  - (i) its registration number;
  - (ii) the name and address of its holder;
- (b) as regards the grounds on which the application is based—
  - (i) a statement of the grounds on which the application for a declaration of invalidity is based;
  - (ii) additionally, in the case of an application pursuant to Article 25(1)(d) of Regulation (EC) No 6/2002, the representation and particulars identifying the prior design on which the application for a declaration of invalidity is based and showing that the applicant is entitled to invoke the earlier design as a ground for invalidity pursuant to Article 25(3) of that Regulation;
  - (iii) additionally, in the case of an application pursuant to Article 25(1)(e) or (f) of Regulation (EC) No 6/2002, the representation and particulars identifying the distinctive sign or the work protected by copyright on which the application for a declaration of invalidity is based and particulars showing that the applicant is the holder of the earlier right pursuant to Article 25(3) of that Regulation;
  - (iv) additionally, in the case of an application pursuant to Article 25(1)(g) of the Regulation (EC) No 6/2002, the representation and particulars of the relevant item as referred to in that Article and particulars showing that the application is filed by the person or entity concerned by the improper use pursuant to Article 25(4) of that Regulation;
  - (v) where the ground for invalidity is that the registered Community design does not fulfil the requirements set out in Article 5 or 6 of Regulation (EC) No 6/2002, the indication and the reproduction of the prior designs that could form an obstacle to the novelty or individual character of the registered Community design, as well as documents proving the existence of those earlier designs;
  - (vi) an indication of the facts, evidence and arguments submitted in support of those grounds;
- (c) as concerns the applicant—
  - (i) his/her name and address in accordance with Article 1(1)(b);
  - (ii) if the applicant has appointed a representative, the name and the business address of the representative, in accordance with Article 1(1)(e);
  - (iii) additionally, in the case of an application pursuant to Article 25(1)(c) of Regulation (EC) No 6/2002, particulars showing that the application is made by a person or by persons duly entitled pursuant to Article 25(2) of that Regulation.

2. The application shall be subject to the fee referred to in Article 52(2) of Regulation (EC) No 6/2002.
3. The Office shall inform the holder that an application for declaration of invalidity has been filed.

[3.315]
Article 29
Languages used in invalidity proceedings
1. The application for a declaration of invalidity shall be filed in the language of proceedings pursuant to Article 98(4) of Regulation (EC) No 6/2002.
2. Where the language of proceedings is not the language used for filing the application and the holder has filed his/her observations in the language of filing, the Office shall arrange to have those observations translated into the language of proceedings.
3. Three years after the date fixed in accordance with Article 111(2) of Regulation (EC) No 6/2002, the Commission will submit to the Committee mentioned in Article 109 of Regulation (EC) No 6/2002 a report on the application of paragraph 2 of this Article and, if appropriate, proposals for fixing a limit for the expenses borne by the Office in this respect as provided for in the fourth subparagraph of Article 98(4) of Regulation (EC) No 6/2002.

4. The Commission may decide to submit the report and possible proposals referred to in paragraph 3 at an earlier date, and the Committee shall discuss them as a matter of priority if the facilities in paragraph 2 lead to disproportionate expenditure.
5. Where the evidence in support of the application is not filed in the language of the invalidity proceedings, the applicant shall file a translation of that evidence into that language within two months of the filing of such evidence.
6. Where the applicant for a declaration of invalidity or the holder informs the Office, within two months of receipt by the holder of the communication referred to in Article 31(1) of this Regulation, that they have agreed on a different language of proceedings pursuant to Article 98(5) of Regulation (EC) No 6/2002, the applicant shall, where the application was not filed in that language, file a translation of the application in that language within one month of the said date.

[3.316]
Article 30
Rejection of the application for declaration of invalidity as inadmissible
1. If the Office finds that the application for declaration of invalidity does not comply with Article 52 of Regulation (EC) No 6/2002, Article 28(1) of this Regulation or any other provision of Regulation (EC) No 6/2002 or this Regulation, it shall inform the applicant accordingly and shall call upon him/her to remedy the deficiencies within such time limit as it may specify.

If the deficiencies are not remedied within the specified time limit, the Office shall reject the application as inadmissible.
2. Where the Office finds that the required fees have not been paid, it shall inform the applicant accordingly and shall inform him/her that the application will be deemed not to have been filed if the required fees are not paid within a specified time limit.

If the required fees are paid after the expiry of the time limit specified, they shall be refunded to the applicant.
3. Any decision to reject an application for a declaration of invalidity pursuant to paragraph 1 shall be communicated to the applicant.

Where, pursuant to paragraph 2, an application is deemed not to have been filed, the applicant shall be informed accordingly.

[3.317]
Article 31
Examination of the application for a declaration of invalidity
1. If the Office does not reject the application for declaration of invalidity in accordance with Article 30, it shall communicate such application to the holder and shall request him/her to file his/her observations within such time limits as it may specify.
2. If the holder files no observations, the Office may base its decision concerning invalidity on the evidence before it.
3. Any observations filed by the holder shall be communicated to the applicant, who may be called upon by the Office to reply within specified time limits.
4. All communications pursuant to Article 53(2) of Regulation (EC) No 6/2002 and all observations filed in that respect shall be sent to the parties concerned.
5. The Office may call upon the parties to make a friendly settlement.
[6. Where the Office declares invalid the effects of an international registration in the territory of the Community; it shall notify its decision to the International Bureau upon becoming final.]

NOTES
Para 6: added by Commission Regulation 876/2007/EC, Art 1(4).

[3.318]
Article 32
Multiple applications for a declaration of invalidity
1. Where a number of applications for a declaration of invalidity have been filed relating to the same registered Community design, the Office may deal with them in one set of proceedings.

The Office may subsequently decide no longer to deal with them in that way.
2. If a preliminary examination of one or more applications reveals that the registered Community design may be invalid, the Office may suspend the other invalidity proceedings.

The Office shall inform the remaining applicants of any relevant decisions taken during such proceedings as are continued.
3. Once a decision declaring the invalidity of the design has become final, the applications in respect of which the proceedings have been suspended in accordance with paragraph 2 shall be deemed to have been disposed of and the applicants concerned shall be informed accordingly. Such disposition shall be considered to constitute a case which has not proceeded to judgment for the purposes of Article 70(4) of Regulation (EC) No 6/2002.
4. The Office shall refund 50% of the invalidity fee referred to in Article 52(2) of Regulation (EC) No 6/2002 paid by each applicant whose application is deemed to have been disposed of in accordance with paragraphs 1, 2 and 3 of this Article.

[3.319]
Article 33
Participation of an alleged infringer

Where, pursuant to Article 54 of Regulation (EC) No 6/2002, an alleged infringer seeks to join the proceedings, he/she shall be subject to the relevant provisions of Articles 28, 29 and 30 of this Regulation, and shall in particular file a reasoned statement and pay the fee referred to in Article 52(2) of Regulation (EC) No 6/2002.

CHAPTER VI
APPEALS

[3.320]
Article 34
Content of the notice of appeal

1. The notice of appeal shall contain—
   (a) the name and address of the appellant in accordance with Article 1(1)(b);
   (b) where the appellant has appointed a representative, the name and the business address of the representative in accordance with Article 1(1)(e);
   (c) a statement identifying the decision which is contested and the extent to which amendment or cancellation of the decision is requested.

2. The notice of appeal shall be filed in the language of the proceedings in which the decision subject to the appeal was taken.

[3.321]
Article 35
Rejection of the appeal as inadmissible

1. If the appeal does not comply with Articles 55, 56 and 57 of Regulation (EC) No 6/2002 and Article 34(1)(c) and (2) of this Regulation, the Board of Appeal shall reject it as inadmissible, unless each deficiency has been remedied before the relevant time limit laid down in Article 57 of Regulation (EC) No 6/2002 has expired.

2. If the Board of Appeal finds that the appeal does not comply with other provisions of Regulation (EC) No 6/2002 or other provisions of this Regulation, in particular with Article 34(1)(a) and (b), it shall inform the appellant accordingly and shall request him/her to remedy the deficiencies noted within such time limit as it may specify. If the deficiencies are not remedied in good time, the Board of Appeal shall reject the appeal as inadmissible.

3. If the fee for appeal has been paid after expiry of the time limits for the filing of an appeal pursuant to Article 57 of Regulation (EC) No 6/2002, the appeal shall be deemed not to have been filed and the appeal fee shall be refunded to the appellant.

[3.322]
Article 36
Examination of appeals

1. Save as otherwise provided, the provisions relating to proceedings before the department which has made the decision against which the appeal is brought shall be applicable to appeal proceedings *mutatis mutandis*.

2. The Board of Appeal's decision shall contain—
   (a) a statement that it is delivered by the Board;
   (b) the date when the decision was taken;
   (c) the names of the Chairman and the other members of the Board of Appeal taking part;
   (d) the name of the competent employee of the registry;
   (e) the names of the parties and of their representatives;
   (f) a statement of the issues to be decided;
   (g) a summary of the facts;
   (h) the reasons;
   (i) the order of the Board of Appeal, including, where necessary, a decision on costs.

3. The decision shall be signed by the Chairman and the other members of the Board of Appeal and by the employee of the registry of the Board of Appeal.

[3.323]
Article 37
Reimbursement of appeal fees

The reimbursement of appeal fees shall be ordered in the event of interlocutory revision or where the Board of Appeal deems an appeal to be allowable, if such reimbursement is equitable by reason of a substantial procedural violation. In the event of interlocutory revision, reimbursement shall be ordered by the department whose decision has been impugned, and in other cases by the Board of Appeal.

CHAPTER VII
DECISIONS AND COMMUNICATIONS OF THE OFFICE

[3.324]
Article 38
Form of decisions
1. Decisions of the Office shall be in writing and shall state the reasons on which they are based.
Where oral proceedings are held before the Office, the decision may be given orally. Subsequently, the decision in writing shall be notified to the parties.
2. Decisions of the Office which are open to appeal shall be accompanied by a written communication indicating that notice of appeal must be filed in writing at the Office within two months of the date of notification of the decision from which appeal is to be made. The communications shall also draw the attention of the parties to the provisions laid down in Articles 55, 56 and 57 of Regulation (EC) No 6/2002.
The parties may not plead any failure to communicate the availability of such appeal proceedings.

[3.325]
Article 39
Correction of errors in decisions
In decisions of the Office, only linguistic errors, errors of transcription and obvious mistakes may be corrected. They shall be corrected by the department which took the decision, acting of its own motion or at the request of an interested party.

[3.326]
Article 40
Noting of loss of rights
1. If the Office finds that the loss of any rights results from Regulation (EC) No 6/2002 or this Regulation without any decision having been taken, it shall communicate this to the person concerned in accordance with Article 66 of Regulation (EC) No 6/2002, and shall draw his/her attention to the legal remedies set out in paragraph 2 of this Article.
2. If the person concerned considers that the finding of the Office is inaccurate, he/she may, within two months of notification of the communication referred to in paragraph 1, apply for a decision on the matter by the Office.
Such decision shall be given only if the Office disagrees with the person requesting it; otherwise the Office shall amend its finding and inform the person requesting the decision.

[3.327]
Article 41
Signature, name, seal
1. Any decision, communication or notice from the Office shall indicate the department or division of the Office as well as the name or the names of the official or officials responsible. They shall be signed by the official or officials, or, instead of a signature, carry a printed or stamped seal of the Office.
2. The President of the Office may determine that other means of identifying the department or division of the Office and the name of the official or officials responsible or an identification other than a seal may be used where decisions, communications or notices are transmitted by fax or any other technical means of communication.

CHAPTER VIII
ORAL PROCEEDINGS AND TAKING OF EVIDENCE

[3.328]
Article 42
Summons to oral proceedings
1. The parties shall be summoned to oral proceedings provided for in Article 64 of Regulation (EC) No 6/2002 and their attention shall be drawn to paragraph 3 of this Article. At least one month's notice of the summons shall be given unless the parties agree to a shorter time limit.
2. When issuing the summons, the Office shall draw attention to the points which in its opinion need to be discussed in order for the decision to be taken.
3. If a party who has been duly summoned to oral proceedings before the Office does not appear as summoned, the proceedings may continue without him/her.

[3.329]
Article 43
Taking of evidence by the Office
1. Where the Office considers it necessary to hear the oral evidence of parties, of witnesses or of experts or to carry out an inspection, it shall take a decision to that end, stating the means by which it intends to obtain evidence, the relevant facts to be proved and the date, time and place of the hearing or inspection.

If oral evidence from witnesses and experts is requested by a party, the decision of the Office shall determine the period of time within which the party filing the request must make known to the Office the names and addresses of the witnesses and experts whom the party wishes to be heard.
2. The period of notice given in the summons of a party, witness or expert to give evidence shall be at least one month, unless they agree to a shorter time limit.
The summons shall contain—
(a) an extract from the decision mentioned in the first subparagraph of paragraph 1, indicating in particular the date, time and place of the hearing ordered and stating the facts regarding which the parties, witnesses and experts are to be heard;
(b) the names of the parties to proceedings and particulars of the rights which the witnesses or experts may invoke pursuant to Article 45(2) to (5).

[3.330]
Article 44
Commissioning of experts
1. The Office shall decide in what form the report made by an expert whom it appoints shall be submitted.
2. The terms of reference of the expert shall include—
(a) a precise description of his/her task;
(b) the time limit laid down for the submission of the expert's report;
(c) the names of the parties to the proceedings;
(d) particulars of the claims which the expert may invoke pursuant to Article 45(2), (3) and (4).
3. A copy of any written report shall be submitted to the parties.
4. The parties may object to an expert on grounds of incompetence or on the same grounds as those on which objection may be made to an examiner or to a member of a Division or Board of Appeal pursuant to Article 132(1) and (3) of Council Regulation (EC) No 40/94.[1] The department of the Office concerned shall rule on the objection.

NOTES
[1] OJ L11, 14.1.1994, p 1.

[3.331]
Article 45
Costs of taking of evidence
1. The taking of evidence by the Office may be made conditional upon deposit with it, by the party who has requested the evidence to be taken, of a sum which shall be fixed by reference to an estimate of the costs.
2. Witnesses and experts who are summoned by and appear before the Office shall be entitled to reimbursement of reasonable expenses for travel and subsistence. An advance for those expenses may be granted to them by the Office. The first sentence shall apply also to witnesses and experts who appear before the Office without being summoned by it and who are heard as witnesses or experts.
3. Witnesses entitled to reimbursement under paragraph 2 shall also be entitled to appropriate compensation for loss of earnings, and experts shall be entitled to fees for their services. Those payments shall be made to the witnesses and experts after they have fulfilled their duties or tasks, where such witnesses and experts have been summoned by the Office on its own initiative.
4. The amounts and the advances for expenses to be paid pursuant to paragraphs 1, 2 and 3 shall be determined by the President of the Office and shall be published in the Official Journal of the Office.
The amounts shall be calculated on the same basis as the compensation and salaries received by officials in grades A 4 to A 8 as laid down in the Staff Regulations of officials of the European Communities and in Annex VII thereto.
5. Final liability for the amounts due or paid pursuant to paragraphs 1 to 4 shall lie with—
(a) the Office where the Office, on its own initiative, considered it necessary to hear the oral evidence of witnesses or experts; or
(b) the party concerned where that party requested the giving of oral evidence by witnesses or experts, subject to the decision on apportionment and fixing of costs pursuant to Articles 70 and 71 of Regulation (EC) No 6/2002 and Article 79 of this Regulation.
The party referred to in point (b) of the first subparagraph shall reimburse the Office for any advances duly paid.

[3.332]
Article 46
Minutes of oral proceedings and of evidence
1. Minutes of oral proceedings or the taking of evidence shall be drawn up, containing the essentials of the oral proceedings or of the taking of evidence, the relevant statements made by the parties, the testimony of the parties, witnesses or experts and the result of any inspection.

2. The minutes of the testimony of a witness, expert or party shall be read out or submitted to him/her so that he/she may examine them. It shall be noted in the minutes that this formality has been carried out and that the person who gave the testimony approved the minutes. Where his/her approval is not given, his/her objections shall be noted.
3. The minutes shall be signed by the employee who drew them up and by the employee who conducted the oral proceedings or taking of evidence.
4. The parties shall be provided with a copy of the minutes.
5. Upon request, the Office shall make available to the parties transcripts of recordings of the oral proceedings, in typescript or in any other machine-readable form.

The release of transcripts of those recordings shall be subject to the payment of the costs incurred by the Office in making such transcript. The amount to be charged shall be determined by the President of the Office.

CHAPTER IX
NOTIFICATIONS

[3.333]
Article 47
General provisions on notifications
1. In proceedings before the Office, any notifications to be made by the Office shall take the form of the original document, of a copy thereof certified by, or bearing the seal of, the Office or of a computer print-out bearing such seal. Copies of documents emanating from the parties themselves shall not require such certification.
2. Notifications shall be made—
   (a) by post in accordance with Article 48;
   (b) by hand delivery in accordance with Article 49;
   (c) by deposit in a post box at the Office in accordance with Article 50;
   (d) by fax and other technical means in accordance with Article 51;
   (e) by public notification in accordance with Article 52.

[3. Communications between the Office and the International Bureau shall be in a mutually agreed manner and format, where possible by electronic means. Any reference to forms shall be construed as including forms available in electronic format.]

NOTES
Para 3: added by Commission Regulation 876/2007/EC, Art 1(5).

[3.334]
Article 48
Notification by post
1. Decisions subject to a time limit for appeal, summonses and other documents as determined by the President of the Office shall be notified by registered letter with acknowledgement of delivery.

Decisions and communications subject to another time limit shall be notified by registered letter, unless the President of the Office determines otherwise.

All other communications shall be ordinary mail.
2. Notifications to addressees having neither their domicile nor their principal place of business nor an establishment in the Community and who have not appointed a representative in accordance with Article 77(2) of Regulation (EC) No 6/2002 shall be effected by posting the document requiring notification by ordinary mail to the last address of the addressee known to the Office.

Notification shall be deemed to have been effected when the posting has taken place.
3. Where notification is effected by registered letter, whether or not with acknowledgement of delivery, it shall be deemed to be delivered to the addressee on the 10th day following that of its posting, unless the letter has failed to reach the addressee or has reached him/her at a later date.

In the event of any dispute, it shall be for the Office to establish that the letter has reached its destination or to establish the date on which it was delivered to the addressee, as the case may be.
4. Notification by registered letter, with or without acknowledgement of delivery, shall be deemed to have been effected even if the addressee refuses to accept the letter.
5. To the extent that notification by post is not covered by paragraphs 1 to 4, the law of the State on the territory of which notification is made shall apply.

[3.335]
Article 49
Notification by hand delivery
Notification may be effected on the premises of the Office by hand delivery of the document to the addressee, who shall on delivery acknowledge its receipt.

[3.336]
Article 50
Notification by deposit in a post box at the Office
Notification may also be effected to addressees who have been provided with a post box at the Office, by depositing the document therein. A written notification of deposit shall be inserted in the files. The date of deposit shall be recorded on the document. Notification shall be deemed to have taken place on the fifth day following deposit of the document in the post box at the Office.

[3.337]
Article 51
Notification by fax and other technical means
1. Notification by fax shall be effected by transmitting either the original or a copy, as provided for in Article 47(1), of the document to be notified. The details of such transmission shall be determined by the President of the Office.
2. Details of notification by other technical means of communication shall be determined by the President of the Office.

[3.338]
Article 52
Public notification
1. If the address of the addressee cannot be established, or if notification in accordance with Article 48(1) has proved to be impossible even after a second attempt by the Office, notification shall be effected by public notice.

Such notice shall be published at least in the *Community Designs Bulletin*.
2. The President of the Office shall determine how the public notice is to be given and shall fix the beginning of the time limit of one month on the expiry of which the document shall be deemed to have been notified.

[3.339]
Article 53
Notification to representatives
1. If a representative has been appointed or where the applicant first named in a common application is considered to be the common representative pursuant to Article 61(1), notifications shall be addressed to that appointed or common representative.
2. If several representatives have been appointed for a single interested party, notification to any one of them shall be sufficient, unless a specific address for service has been indicated in accordance with Article 1(1)(e).
3. If several interested parties have appointed a common representative, notification of a single document to the common representative shall be sufficient.

[3.340]
Article 54
Irregularities in notification
Where a document has reached the addressee, if the Office is unable to prove that it has been duly notified or if provisions relating to its notification have not been observed, the document shall be deemed to have been notified on the date established by the Office as the date of receipt.

[3.341]
Article 55
Notification of documents in the case of several parties
Documents emanating from parties which contain substantive proposals, or a declaration of withdrawal of a substantive proposal, shall be notified to the other parties as a matter of course. Notification may be dispensed with where the document contains no new pleadings and the matter is ready for decision.

CHAPTER X
TIME LIMITS

[3.342]
Article 56
Calculation of time limits
1. Time limits shall be laid down in terms of full years, months, weeks or days.
2. The beginning of any time limit shall be calculated starting on the day following the day on which the relevant event occurred, the event being either a procedural step or the expiry of another time limit. Where that procedural step is a notification, the event considered shall be the receipt of the document notified, unless otherwise provided.
3. Where a time limit is expressed as one year or a certain number of years, it shall expire in the relevant subsequent year in the month having the same name and on the day having the same number as the month and the day on which the relevant event occurred. Where the relevant month has no day with the same number the time limit shall expire on the last day of that month.

4. Where a time limit is expressed as one month or a certain number of months, it shall expire in the relevant subsequent month on the day which has the same number as the day on which the relevant event occurred. Where the day on which the relevant event occurred was the last day of a month or where the relevant subsequent month has no day with the same number the time limit shall expire on the last day of that month.
5. Where a time limit is expressed as one week or a certain number of weeks, it shall expire in the relevant subsequent week on the day having the same name as the day on which the relevant event occurred.

[3.343]
Article 57
Duration of time limits
1. Where Regulation (EC) No 6/2002 or this Regulation provide for a time limit to be specified by the Office, such time limit shall, when the party concerned has its domicile or its principal place of business or an establishment within the Community, be not less than one month, or, when those conditions are not fulfilled, not less than two months, and no more than six months.

The Office may, when this is appropriate under the circumstances, grant an extension of a time limit specified if such extension is requested by the party concerned and the request is submitted before the original time limit expires.
2. Where there are two or more parties, the Office may make the extension of a time limit subject to the agreement of the other parties.

[3.344]
Article 58
Expiry of time limits in special cases
1. If a time limit expires on a day on which the Office is not open for receipt of documents or on which, for reasons other than those referred to in paragraph 2, ordinary mail is not delivered in the locality in which the Office is located, the time limit shall extend until the first day thereafter on which the Office is open for receipt of documents and on which ordinary mail is delivered.

The days on which the Office is not open for receipt of documents shall be determined by the President of the Office before the commencement of each calendar year.
2. If a time limit expires on a day on which there is a general interruption or subsequent dislocation in the delivery of mail in a Member State or between a Member State and the Office, the time limit shall extend until the first day following the end of the period of interruption or dislocation, for parties having their residence or registered office in the State concerned or who have appointed representatives with a place of business in that State.

In the event of the Member State concerned being the State in which the Office is located, the first subparagraph shall apply to all parties.

The period referred to in the first subparagraph shall be as determined by the President of the Office.
3. Paragraphs 1 and 2 shall apply *mutatis mutandis* to the time limits provided for in Regulation (EC) No 6/2002 or this Regulation in the case of transactions to be carried out with the competent authority within the meaning of Article 35(1)(b) and (c) of Regulation (EC) No 6/2002.
4. If an exceptional occurrence such as natural disaster or strike interrupts or dislocates the proper functioning of the Office so that any communication from the Office to parties concerning the expiry of a time limit is delayed, acts to be completed within such a time limit may still be validly completed within one month of the notification of the delayed communication.

The date of commencement and the end of any such interruption or dislocation shall be as determined by the President of the Office.

CHAPTER XI
INTERRUPTION OF PROCEEDINGS AND WAIVING OF ENFORCED RECOVERY PROCEDURES

[3.345]
Article 59
Interruption of proceedings
1. Proceedings before the Office shall be interrupted—
   (a) in the event of the death or legal incapacity of the applicant for or holder of a registered Community design or of the person authorised by national law to act on his/her behalf;
   (b) in the event that the applicant for or holder of a registered Community design is, as a result of some action taken against his/her property, prevented for legal reasons from continuing the proceedings before the Office;
   (c) in the event of the death or legal incapacity of the representative of an applicant for or holder of a registered Community design or of his/her being prevented for legal reasons resulting from action taken against his/her property from continuing the proceedings before the Office.

To the extent that the events referred to in point (a) of the first subparagraph do not affect the authorisation of a representative appointed under Article 78 of Regulation (EC) No 6/2002, proceedings shall be interrupted only on application by such representative.

2. When, in the cases referred to in points (a) and (b) of the first subparagraph of paragraph 1, the Office has been informed of the identity of the person authorised to continue the proceedings before the Office, the Office shall communicate to such person and to any interested third parties that the proceedings shall be resumed as from a date to be fixed by the Office.

3. In the case referred to in paragraph 1(c), the proceedings shall be resumed when the Office has been informed of the appointment of a new representative of the applicant or when the Office has notified to the other parties the communication of the appointment of a new representative of the holder of the design.

If, three months after the beginning of the interruption of the proceedings, the Office has not been informed of the appointment of a new representative, it shall communicate that fact to the applicant for or holder of the registered Community design—

(a) where Article 77(2) of Regulation (EC) No 6/2002 is applicable, that the Community design application will be deemed to be withdrawn if the information is not submitted within two months after that communication is notified; or

(b) where Article 77(2) of Regulation (EC) No 6/2002 is not applicable, that the proceedings will be resumed with the applicant for or holder as from the date on which that communication is notified.

4. The time limits, other than the time limit for paying the renewal fees, in force as regards the applicant for or holder of the Community design at the date of interruption of the proceedings, shall begin again as from the day on which the proceedings are resumed.

[3.346]
Article 60
Waiving of enforced recovery procedures

The President of the Office may waive action for the enforced recovery of any sum due where the sum to be recovered is minimal or where such recovery is too uncertain.

CHAPTER XII
REPRESENTATION

[3.347]
Article 61
Appointment of a common representative

1. If there is more than one applicant and the application for a registered Community design does not name a common representative, the applicant first named in the application shall be considered to be the common representative.

However, if one of the applicants is obliged to appoint a professional representative, such representative shall be considered to be the common representative unless the applicant named first in the application has also appointed a professional representative.

The first and second subparagraphs shall apply *mutatis mutandis* to third parties acting in common in applying for a declaration of invalidity, and to joint holders of a registered Community design.

2. If, during the course of proceedings, transfer is made to more than one person, and such persons have not appointed a common representative, paragraph 1 shall apply.

If such application is not possible, the Office shall require such persons to appoint a common representative within two months. If this request is not complied with, the Office shall appoint the common representative.

[3.348]
Article 62
Authorisations

1. Legal practitioners and professional representatives entered on the lists maintained by the Office pursuant to Article 78(1)(b) or (c) of Regulation (EC) No 6/2002 may file with the Office a signed authorisation for inclusion in the files.

Such authorisation shall be filed if the Office expressly requires it or, where there are several parties to the proceedings in which the representative acts before the Office, one of the parties expressly request it.

2. Employees acting on behalf of natural or legal persons pursuant to Article 77(3) of Regulation (EC) No 6/2002 shall file with the Office a signed authorisation for insertion in the files.

3. The authorisation may be filed in any of the official languages of the Community. It may cover one or more applications or registered Community designs or may be in the form of a general authorisation allowing the representative to act in respect of all proceedings before the Office to which the person who has issued it is a party.

4. Where, pursuant to paragraphs 1 or 2, an authorisation has to be filed, the Office shall specify a time limit within which such authorisation shall be filed. If the authorisation is not filed in due time, proceedings shall be continued with the represented person. Any procedural steps other than

the filing of the application taken by the representative shall be deemed not to have been taken if the represented person does not approve them. The application of Article 77(2) of Regulation (EC) No 6/2002 shall remain unaffected.

5. Paragraphs 1, 2 and 3 shall apply *mutatis mutandis* to a document withdrawing an authorisation.

6. Any representative who has ceased to be authorised shall continue to be regarded as the representative until the termination of his/her authorisation has been communicated to the Office.

7. Subject to any provisions to the contrary contained therein, an authorisation shall not terminate vis-à-vis the Office upon the death of the person who gave it.

8. Where several representatives are appointed by the same party, they may, notwithstanding any provisions to the contrary in their authorisations, act either collectively or individually.

9. The authorisation of an association of representatives shall be deemed to be an authorisation of any representative who can establish that he/she practises within that association.

[3.349]

Article 63

Representation

Any notification or other communication addressed by the Office to the duly authorised representative shall have the same effect as if it had been addressed to the represented person.

Any communication addressed to the Office by the duly authorised representative shall have the same effect as if it originated from the represented person.

[3.350]

Article 64

Amendment of the special list of professional representatives for design matters

1. The entry of a professional representative in the special list of professional representatives for design matters, as referred to in Article 78(4) of Regulation (EC) No 6/2002, shall be deleted at his/her request.

2. The entry of a professional representative shall be deleted automatically—

(a) in the event of the death or legal incapacity of the professional representative;

(b) where the professional representative is no longer a national of a Member State, unless the President of the Office has granted an exemption pursuant to Article 78(6)(a) of Regulation (EC) No 6/2002;

(c) where the professional representative no longer has his/her place of business or employment in the Community;

(d) where the professional representative no longer possesses the entitlement referred to in the first sentence of Article 78(4)(c) of Regulation (EC) No 6/2002.

3. The entry of a professional representative shall be suspended of the Office's own motion where his/her entitlement to represent natural or legal persons before the Benelux Design Office or the central industrial property office of the Member State as referred to in the first sentence of Article 78(4)(c) of Regulation (EC) No 6/2002 has been suspended.

4. A person whose entry has been deleted shall, upon request pursuant to Article 78(5) of Regulation (EC) No 6/2002, be reinstated in the list of professional representatives if the conditions for deletion no longer exist.

5. The Benelux Design Office and the central industrial property offices of the Member States concerned shall, where they are aware thereof, promptly inform the Office of any relevant events referred to in paragraphs 2 and 3.

6. The amendments of the special list of professional representatives for design matters shall be published in the Official Journal of the Office.

CHAPTER XIII
WRITTEN COMMUNICATIONS AND FORMS

[3.351]

Article 65

Communication in writing or by other means

1. Subject to paragraph 2, applications for the registration of a Community design as well as any other application or declaration provided for in Regulation (EC) No 6/2002 and all other communications addressed to the Office shall be submitted as follows—

(a) by submitting a signed original of the document in question to the Office, by post, personal delivery, or by any other means; annexes to documents submitted need not be signed;

(b) by transmitting a signed original by fax in accordance with Article 66; or

(c) by transmitting the contents of the communication by electronic means in accordance with Article 67.

2. Where the applicant avails himself of the possibility provided for in Article 36(1)(c) of Regulation (EC) No 6/2002 of filing a specimen of the design, the application and the specimen shall be submitted to the Office by a single mail in the form prescribed in paragraph 1(a) of this

Part 3 Designs

Article. If the application and the specimen, or specimens in the case of a multiple application, are not submitted by a single mail the Office shall not give a filing date until the last item has been received pursuant to Article 10(1) of this Regulation.

[3.352]
Article 66
Communication by fax

1. Where an application for registration of a Community design is submitted by fax and the application contains a reproduction of the design pursuant to Article 4(1) which does not satisfy the requirements of that Article, the required reproduction suitable for registration and publication shall be submitted to the Office in accordance with Article 65(1)(a).

Where the reproduction is received by the Office within a time limit of one month from the date of the receipt of the fax, the application shall be deemed to have been received by the Office on the date on which the fax was received.

Where the reproduction is received by the Office after the expiry of that time limit, the application shall be deemed to have been received by the Office on the date on which the reproduction was received.

2. Where a communication received by fax is incomplete or illegible, or where the Office has reasonable doubts as to the accuracy of the transmission, the Office shall inform the sender accordingly and shall call upon him/her, within a time limit to be specified by the Office, to retransmit the original by fax or to submit the original in accordance with Article 65(1)(a).

Where that request is complied with within the time limit specified, the date of the receipt of the retransmission or of the original shall be deemed to be the date of the receipt of the original communication, provided that where the deficiency concerns the granting of a filing date for an application to register a Community design, the provisions on the filing date shall apply.

Where the request is not complied with within the time limit specified, the communication shall be deemed not to have been received.

3. Any communication submitted to the Office by fax shall be considered to be duly signed if the reproduction of the signature appears on the printout produced by the fax.

4. The President of the Office may determine additional requirements for communication by fax, such as the equipment to be used, technical details of communication, and methods of identifying the sender.

[3.353]
Article 67
Communication by electronic means

1. Applications for registration of a Community design may be submitted by electronic means, including the representation of the design, and notwithstanding Article 65(2) in the case of filing a specimen.

The conditions shall be laid down by the President of the Office.

2. The President of the Office shall determine the requirements for communication by electronic means, such as the equipment to be used, technical details of communication, and methods of identifying the sender.

3. Where a communication is sent by electronic means, Article 66(2) shall apply *mutatis mutandis*.

4. Where a communication is sent to the Office by electronic means, the indication of the name of the sender shall be deemed to be equivalent to the signature.

[3.354]
Article 68
Forms

1. The Office shall make available free of charge forms for the purpose of—
   - (a) filing an application for a registered Community design;
   - (b) applying for the correction of an application or a registration;
   - (c) applying for the registration of a transfer and the transfer form and transfer document referred to in Article 23(4);
   - (d) applying for the registration of a licence;
   - (e) applying for renewal of registration of a registered Community design;
   - (f) applying for a declaration of invalidity of a registered Community design;
   - (g) applying for *restitutio in integrum*;
   - (h) taking an appeal;
   - (i) authorising a representative, in the form of an individual authorisation and in the form of a general authorisation.
2. The Office may make other forms available free of charge.
3. The Office shall make available the forms referred to in paragraphs 1 and 2 in all the official languages of the Community.
4. The Office shall place the forms at the disposal of the Benelux Design Office and of the Member States' central industrial property offices free of charge.
5. The Office may also make available the forms in machine-readable form.

6. Parties to proceedings before the Office should use the forms provided by the Office, or copies of those forms, or forms with the same content and format as those forms, such as forms generated by means of electronic data processing.
7. Forms shall be completed in such a manner as to permit an automated input of the content into a computer, such as by character recognition or scanning.

CHAPTER XIV
INFORMATION TO THE PUBLIC

[3.355]
Article 69
Register of Community Designs

1. The Register may be maintained in the form of an electronic database.
2. The Register shall contain the following entries—
   (a) the date of filing the application;
   (b) the file number of the application and the file number of each individual design included in a multiple application;
   (c) the date of the publication of the registration;
   (d) the name, the address and the nationality of the applicant and the State in which he/she is domiciled or has his/her seat or establishment;
   (e) the name and business address of the representative, other than an employee acting as representative in accordance with the first subparagraph of Article 77(3) of Regulation (EC) No 6/2002; where there is more than one representative, only the name and business address of the first named representative, the name being followed by the words "et al", shall be recorded; where an association of representatives is appointed, only the name and address of the association shall be recorded;
   (f) the representation of the design;
   (g) an indication of the products by their names, preceded by the numbers of the classes and subclasses of the Locarno classification, and grouped accordingly;
   (h) particulars of claims of priority pursuant to Article 42 of Regulation (EC) No 6/2002;
   (i) particulars of claims of exhibition priority pursuant to Article 44 of Regulation (EC) No 6/2002;
   (j) where applicable, the citation of the designer or of the team of designers pursuant to Article 18 of Regulation (EC) No 6/2002, or a statement that the designer or the team of designers has waived the right to be cited;
   (k) the language in which the application was filed and the second language which the applicant has indicated in his/her application, pursuant to Article 98(2) of Regulation (EC) No 6/2002;
   (l) the date of registration of the design in the Register and the registration number;
   (m) a mention of any request for deferment of publication pursuant to Article 50(3) of Regulation (EC) No 6/2002, specifying the date of expiry of the period of deferment;
   (n) a mention that a specimen was filed pursuant to Article 5;
   (o) a mention that a description was filed pursuant to Article 1(2)(a).
3. In addition to the entries set out in paragraph 2 the Register shall contain the following entries, each accompanied by the date of recording such entry—
   (a) changes in the name, the address or the nationality of the holder or in the State in which he/she is domiciled or has his/her seat or establishment;
   (b) changes in the name or business address of the representative, other than a representative falling within the first subparagraph of Article 77(3) of Regulation (EC) No 6/2002;
   (c) when a new representative is appointed, the name and business address of that representative;
   (d) a mention that a multiple application or registration has been divided into separate applications or registrations pursuant to Article 37(4) of Regulation (EC) No 6/2002;
   (e) the notice of an amendment to the design pursuant to Article 25(6) of Regulation (EC) No 6/2002, including, if applicable, a reference to the disclaimer made or the court decision or the decision by the Office declaring the partial invalidity of the design right, as well as corrections of mistakes and errors pursuant to Article 20 of this Regulation;
   (f) a mention that entitlement proceedings have been instituted under Article 15(1) of Regulation (EC) No 6/2002 in respect of a registered Community design;
   (g) the final decision or other termination of proceedings pursuant to Article 15(4)(b) of Regulation (EC) No 6/2002 concerning entitlement proceedings;
   (h) a change of ownership pursuant to Article 15(4)(c) of Regulation (EC) No 6/2002;
   (i) transfers pursuant to Article 28 of Regulation (EC) No 6/2002;
   (j) the creation or transfer of a right in rem pursuant to Article 29 of Regulation (EC) No 6/2002 and the nature of the right in rem;
   (k) levy of execution pursuant to Article 30 of Regulation (EC) No 6/2002 and insolvency proceedings pursuant to Article 31 of that Regulation;

(l) the grant or transfer of a licence pursuant to Article 16(2) or Article 32 of Regulation (EC) No 6/2002 and, where applicable, the type of licence pursuant to Article 25 of this Regulation;
(m) renewal of the registration pursuant to Article 13 of Regulation (EC) No 6/2002 and the date from which it takes effect;
(n) a record of the determination of the expiry of the registration;
(o) a declaration of total or partial surrender by the holder pursuant to Article 51(1) and (3) of Regulation (EC) No 6/2002;
(p) the date of submission of an application or of the filing of a counterclaim for a declaration of invalidity pursuant, respectively, to Article 52 or Article 86(2) of Regulation (EC) No 6/2002;
(q) the date and content of the decision on the application or counterclaim for declaration of invalidity or any other termination of proceedings pursuant, respectively, to Article 53 or Article 86(4) of Regulation (EC) No 6/2002;
(r) a mention pursuant to Article 50(4) of Regulation (EC) No 6/2002 that the registered Community design is deemed from the outset not to have had the effects specified in that Regulation;
(s) the cancellation of the representative recorded pursuant to paragraph 2(e);
(t) the modification or cancellation from the Register of the items referred to in points (j), (k) and (l).

4. The President of the Office may determine that items other than those referred to in paragraphs 2 and 3 shall be entered in the Register.
5. The holder shall be notified of any change in the Register.
6. Subject to Article 73, the Office shall provide certified or uncertified extracts from the Register on request, on payment of a fee.

CHAPTER XV
COMMUNITY DESIGNS BULLETIN AND DATA BASE

[3.356]
Article 70
Community Designs Bulletin

1. The Office shall determine the frequency of the publication of the *Community Designs Bulletin* and the manner in which such publication shall take place.
2. Without prejudice to the provisions of Article 50(2) of Regulation (EC) No 6/2002 and subject to Articles 14 and 16 of this Regulation relating to deferment of publication, the *Community Designs Bulletin* shall contain publications of registration and of entries made in the Register as well as other particulars relating to registrations of designs whose publication is prescribed by Regulation (EC) No 6/2002 or by this Regulation.
3. Where particulars whose publication is prescribed in Regulation (EC) No 6/2002 or in this Regulation are published in the *Community Designs Bulletin*, the date of issue shown on the Bulletin shall be taken as the date of publication of the particulars.
4. The information the publication of which is prescribed in Articles 14 and 16 shall, where appropriate, be published in all the official languages of the Community.

[3.357]
Article 71
Database

1. The Office shall maintain an electronic database with the particulars of applications for registration of Community designs and entries in the Register. The Office may, subject to the restrictions prescribed by Article 50(2) and (3) of Regulation (EC) No 6/2002, make available the contents of that database for direct access or on CD-ROM or in any other machine-readable form.
2. The President of the Office shall determine the conditions of access to the database and the manner in which the contents of this database may be made available in machine-readable form, including the charges for those acts.
[3. The Office shall provide information on international registrations of designs designating the Community in the form of an electronic link to the searchable database maintained by the International Bureau.]

NOTES

Para 3: added by Commission Regulation 876/2007/EC, Art 1(6).

CHAPTER XVI
INSPECTION OF FILES AND KEEPING OF FILES

[3.358]
Article 72
Parts of the file excluded from inspection

The parts of the file which shall be excluded from inspection pursuant to Article 74(4) of Regulation (EC) No 6/2002 shall be—

(a) documents relating to exclusion or objection pursuant to Article 132 of Regulation (EC) No 40/94, the provisions of that Article being considered for this purpose as applying *mutatis mutandis* to registered Community designs and to applications for these;

(b) draft decisions and opinions, and all other internal documents used for the preparation of decisions and opinions;

(c) parts of the file which the party concerned showed a special interest in keeping confidential before the application for inspection of the files was made, unless inspection of such part of the file is justified by overriding legitimate interests of the party seeking inspection.

[3.359]
Article 73
Inspection of the Register of Community Designs

Where the registration is subject to a deferment of publication pursuant to Article 50(1) of Regulation (EC) No 6/2002—

(a) access to the Register to persons other than the holder shall be limited to the name of the holder, the name of any representative, the date of filing and registration, the file number of the application and the mention that publication is deferred;

(b) the certified or uncertified extracts from the Register shall contain only the name of the holder, the name of any representative, the date of filing and registration, the file number of the application and the mention that publication is deferred, except where the request has been made by the holder or his/her representative.

[3.360]
Article 74
Procedures for the inspection of files

1. Inspection of the files of registered Community designs shall either be of the original document, or of copies thereof, or of technical means of storage if the files are so stored.

The request for inspection of the files shall not be deemed to have been made until the required fee has been paid.

The means of inspection shall be determined by the President of the Office.

2. Where inspection of the files relates to an application for a registered Community design or to a registered Community design which is subject to deferment of publication, which, being subject to such deferment, has been surrendered before or on the expiry of that period or which, pursuant to Article 50(4) of Regulation (EC) No 6/2002, is deemed from the outset not to have had the effects specified in that Regulation, the request shall contain an indication and evidence to the effect that—

(a) the applicant for or holder of the Community design has consented to the inspection; or

(b) the person requesting the inspection has established a legitimate interest in the inspection of the file, in particular where the applicant for or holder of the Community design has stated that after the design has been registered he/she will invoke the rights under it against the person requesting the inspection.

3. Inspection of the files shall take place on the premises of the Office.

4. On request, inspection of the files shall be effected by means of issuing copies of file documents. Such copies shall incur fees.

5. The Office shall issue on request certified or uncertified copies of the application for a registered Community design or of those file documents of which copies may be issued pursuant to paragraph 4 upon payment of a fee.

[3.361]
Article 75
Communication of information contained in the files

Subject to the restrictions provided for in Article 74 of Regulation (EC) No 6/2002 and Articles 72 and 73 of this Regulation, the Office may, upon request, communicate information from any file of a Community design applied for or of a registered Community design, subject to payment of a fee.

However, the Office may require the applicant to inspect the file *in situ*, should it deem that to be appropriate in view of the quantity of information to be supplied.

[3.362]
Article 76
Keeping of files

1. The Office shall keep the files relating to Community design applications and to registered Community designs for at least five years from the end of the year in which—

Part 3 Designs

(a) the application is rejected or withdrawn;
(b) the registration of the registered Community design expires definitively;
(c) the complete surrender of the registered Community design is registered pursuant to Article 51 of Regulation (EC) No 6/2002;
(d) the registered Community design is definitively removed from the Register;
(e) the registered Community design is deemed not to have had the effects specified in Regulation (EC) No 6/2002 pursuant to Article 50(4) thereof.

2. The President of the Office shall determine the form in which the files shall be kept.

CHAPTER XVII
ADMINISTRATIVE COOPERATION

[3.363]
Article 77
Exchange of information and communications between the Office and the authorities of the Member States

1. The Office and the central industrial property offices of the Member States and the Benelux Design Office shall, upon request, communicate to each other relevant information about the filing of applications for registered Community designs, Benelux designs or national registered designs and about proceedings relating to such applications and the designs registered as a result thereof. Such communications shall not be subject to the restrictions provided for in Article 74 of Regulation (EC) No 6/2002.

2. Communications between the Office and the courts or authorities of the Member States which arise out of the application of Regulation (EC) No 6/2002 or this Regulation shall be effected directly between those authorities.

Such communication may also be effected through the central industrial property offices of the Member States or the Benelux Design Office.

3. Expenditure in respect of communications pursuant to paragraphs 1 and 2 shall be chargeable to the authority making the communications, which shall be exempt from fees.

[3.364]
Article 78
Inspection of files by or via courts or authorities of the Member States

1. Inspection of files relating to Community designs applied for or registered Community designs by courts or authorities of the Member States shall if so requested be of the original documents or of copies thereof. Article 74 shall not apply.

2. Courts or public prosecutors' offices of the Member States may, in the course of proceedings before them, open files or copies thereof transmitted by the Office to inspection by third parties. Such inspection shall be subject to Article 74 of Regulation (EC) No 6/2002.

3. The Office shall not charge any fee for inspections pursuant to paragraphs 1 and 2.

4. The Office shall, at the time of transmission of the files or copies thereof to the courts or public prosecutors' offices of the Member States, indicate the restrictions to which the inspection of files relating to Community designs applied for or registered Community designs is subject pursuant to Article 74 of Regulation (EC) No 6/2002 and Article 72 of this Regulation.

CHAPTER XVIII
COSTS

[3.365]
Article 79
Apportionment and fixing of costs

1. Apportionment of costs pursuant to Article 70(1) and (2) of Regulation (EC) No 6/2002 shall be dealt with in the decision on the application for a declaration of invalidity of a registered Community design, or in the decision on the appeal.

2. Apportionment of costs pursuant to Article 70(3) and (4) of Regulation (EC) No 6/2002 shall be dealt with in a decision on costs by the Invalidity Division or the Board of Appeal.

3. A bill of costs, with supporting evidence, shall be attached to the request for the fixing of costs provided for in the first sentence of Article 70(6) of Regulation (EC) No 6/2002.

The request shall be admissible only if the decision in respect of which the fixing of costs is required has become final. Costs may be fixed once their credibility is established.

4. The request provided for in the second sentence of Article 70(6) of Regulation (EC) No 6/2002 for a review of the decision of the registry on the fixing of costs, stating the reasons on which it is based, must be filed at the Office within one month of the date of notification of the awarding of costs.

It shall not be deemed to be filed until the fee for reviewing the amount of the costs has been paid.

5. The Invalidity Division or the Board of Appeal, as the case may be, shall take a decision on the request referred to in paragraph 4 without oral proceedings.

6. The fees to be borne by the losing party pursuant to Article 70(1) of Regulation (EC) No 6/2002 shall be limited to the fees incurred by the other party for the application for a declaration of invalidity and/or for the appeal.

7. Costs essential to the proceedings and actually incurred by the successful party shall be borne by the losing party in accordance with Article 70(1) of Regulation (EC) No 6/2002 on the basis of the following maximum rates—

(a) travel expenses of one party for the outward and return journey between the place of residence or the place of business and the place where oral proceedings are held or where evidence is taken, as follows—
  (i) the cost of the first-class rail fare including usual transport supplements where the total distance by rail does not exceed 800 km;
  (ii) the cost of the tourist-class air fare where the total distance by rail exceeds 800 km or the route includes a sea crossing;
(b) subsistence expenses of one party equal to the daily subsistence allowance for officials in grades A 4 to A 8 as laid down in Article 13 of Annex VII to the Staff Regulations of officials of the European Communities;
(c) travel expenses of representatives within the meaning of Article 78(1) of Regulation (EC) No 6/2002 and of witnesses and of experts, at the rates provided for in point (a);
(d) subsistence expenses of representatives within the meaning of Article 78(1) of Regulation (EC) No 6/2002 and of witnesses and experts, at the rates referred to in point (b);
(e) costs entailed in the taking of evidence in the form of examination of witnesses, opinions by experts or inspection, up to EUR 300 per proceedings;
(f) costs of representation, within the meaning of Article 78(1) of Regulation (EC) No 6/2002—
  (i) of the applicant in proceedings relating to invalidity of a registered Community design up to EUR 400;
  (ii) of the holder in proceedings relating to invalidity of a registered Community design up to EUR 400;
  (iii) of the appellant in appeal proceedings up to EUR 500;
  (iv) of the defendant in appeal proceedings up to EUR 500;
(g) where the successful party is represented by more than one representative within the meaning of Article 78(1) of the Regulation (EC) No 6/2002, the losing party shall bear the costs referred to in points (c), (d) and (f) for one such person only;
(h) the losing party shall not be obliged to reimburse the successful party for any costs, expenses and fees other than those referred to in points (a) to (g).

Where the taking of evidence in any of the proceedings referred to in point (f) of the first subparagraph involves the examination of witnesses, opinions by experts or inspection, an additional amount shall be granted for representation costs of up to EUR 600 per proceedings.

CHAPTER XIX
LANGUAGES

[3.366]
Article 80
Applications and declarations

Without prejudice to Article 98(4) of Regulation (EC) No 6/2002—

(a) any application or declaration relating to an application for a registered Community design may be filed in the language used for filing the application or in the second language indicated by the applicant in his/her application;
(b) any application or declaration other than an application for declaration of invalidity pursuant to Article 52 of Regulation (EC) No 6/2002, or declaration of surrender pursuant to Article 51 of that Regulation relating to a registered Community design may be filed in one of the languages of the Office;
(c) when any of the forms provided by the Office pursuant to Article 68 is used, such forms may be used in any of the official languages of the Community, provided that the form is completed in one of the languages of the Office, as far as textual elements are concerned.

[3.367]
Article 81
Written proceedings

1. Without prejudice to Article 98(3) and (5) of Regulation (EC) No 6/2002 and save as otherwise provided in this Regulation, in written proceedings before the Office a party may use any language of the Office.

If the language chosen is not the language of the proceedings, the party shall supply a translation into that language within one month of the date of the submission of the original document.

Where the applicant for a registered Community design is the sole party to proceedings before the Office and the language used for the filing of the application for the registered Community design is not one of the languages of the Office, the translation may also be filed in the second language indicated by the applicant in his/her application.

2. Save as otherwise provided in this Regulation, documents to be used in proceedings before the Office may be filed in any official language of the Community.

Where the language of such documents is not the language of the proceedings the Office may require that a translation be supplied, within a time limit specified by it, in that language or, at the choice of the party to the proceeding, in any language of the Office.

[3.368]
Article 82
Oral proceedings

1. Any party to oral proceedings before the Office may, in place of the language of proceedings, use one of the other official languages of the Community, on condition that he/she makes provision for interpretation into the language of proceedings.

Where the oral proceedings are held in a proceeding concerning the application for registration of a design the applicant may use either the language of the application or the second language indicated by him/her.

2. In oral proceedings concerning the application for registration of a design, the staff of the Office may use either the language of the application or the second language indicated by the applicant.

In all other oral proceedings, the staff of the Office may use, in place of the language of the proceedings, one of the other languages of the Office, on condition that the party or parties to the proceedings agree(s) to such use.

3. With regard to the taking of evidence, any party to be heard, witness or expert who is unable to express himself/herself adequately in the language of proceedings, may use any of the official languages of the Community.

Where the taking of evidence is decided upon following a request by a party to the proceedings, parties to be heard, witnesses or experts who express themselves in languages other than the language of proceedings may be heard only if the party who made the request makes provision for interpretation into that language.

In proceedings concerning the application for registration of a design, in place of the language of the application, the second language indicated by the applicant may be used.

In any proceedings with only one party, the Office may at the request of the party concerned permit derogation from the provisions in this paragraph.

4. If the parties and the Office so agree, any official language of the Community may be used in oral proceedings.

5. The Office shall, if necessary, make provision at its own expense for interpretation into the language of proceedings, or, where appropriate, into its other languages, unless this interpretation is the responsibility of one of the parties to the proceedings.

6. Statements by staff of the Office, by parties to the proceedings and by witnesses and experts, made in one of the languages of the Office during oral proceedings shall be entered in the minutes in the language employed. Statements made in any other language shall be entered in the language of proceedings.

Corrections to the application for or the registration of a Community design shall be entered in the minutes in the language of proceedings.

[3.369]
Article 83
Certification of translations

1. When a translation of any document is to be filed, the Office may require the filing, within a time limit to be specified by it, of a certificate that the translation corresponds to the original text.

Where the certificate relates to the translation of a previous application pursuant to Article 42 of Regulation (EC) No 6/2002, such time limit shall not be less than three months after the date of filing of the application.

Where the certificate is not filed within that time limit, the document shall be deemed not to have been received.

2. The President of the Office may determine the manner in which translations are certified.

[3.370]
Article 84
Legal authenticity of translations

In the absence of evidence to the contrary, the Office may assume that a translation corresponds to the relevant original text.

CHAPTER XX
RECIPROCITY, TRANSITION PERIOD AND ENTRY INTO FORCE

[3.371]
Article 85
Publication of reciprocity

1. If necessary, the President of the Office shall request the Commission to enquire whether a State which is not party to the Paris Convention for the Protection of Industrial Property or to the Agreement establishing the World Trade Organisation grants reciprocal treatment within the meaning of Article 41(5) Regulation (EC) No 6/2002.
2. If the Commission determines that reciprocal treatment in accordance with paragraph 1 is granted, it shall publish a communication to that effect in the *Official Journal of the European Communities*.
3. Article 41(5) of Regulation (EC) No 6/2002 shall apply from the date of publication in the *Official Journal of the European Communities* of the communication referred to in paragraph 2, unless the communication states an earlier date from which it is applicable.

Article 41(5) of Regulation (EC) No 6/2002 shall cease to be applicable from the date of publication in the *Official Journal of the European Communities* of a communication of the Commission stating that reciprocal treatment is no longer granted, unless the communication states an earlier date from which it is applicable.

4. Communications referred to in paragraphs 2 and 3 shall also be published in the Official Journal of the Office.

[3.372]
Article 86
Transition period

1. Any application for registration of a Community design filed no more than three months before the date fixed pursuant to Article 111(2) of Regulation (EC) No 6/2002 shall be marked by the Office with the filing date determined pursuant to that provision and with the actual date of receipt of the application.
2. With regard to the application, the priority period of six months provided for in Articles 41 and 44 of Regulation (EC) No 6/2002 shall be calculated from the date fixed pursuant to Article 111(2) of that Regulation.
3. The Office may issue a receipt to the applicant prior to the date fixed pursuant to Article 111(2) of Regulation (EC) No 6/2002.
4. The Office may examine the applications prior to the date fixed pursuant to Article 111(2) of Regulation (EC) No 6/2002 and communicate with the applicant with a view to remedying any deficiencies prior to that date.

Any decisions with regard to such applications may be taken only after that date.

5. Where the date of receipt of an application for the registration of a Community design by the Office, by the central industrial property office of a Member State or by the Benelux Design Office is before the commencement of the three-month period specified in Article 111(3) of Regulation (EC) No 6/2002 the application shall be deemed not to have been filed.

The applicant shall be informed accordingly and the application shall be sent back to him/her.

[3.373]
Article 87
Entry into force

This Regulation shall enter into force on the seventh day following its publication in the *Official Journal of the European Communities*.

This Regulation shall be binding in its entirety and directly applicable in all Member States.

DPN 1/16: GUIDANCE ON USE OF REPRESENTATIONS WHEN FILING REGISTERED DESIGN APPLICATIONS

1 June 2016

NOTES

INTRODUCTION

[3.374]

1). The Supreme Court's (SC) recent judgment in PMS International Limited v Magmatic Limited[1] has highlighted the extent to which protection conferred by a Registered Design can be determined by the representations used in the course of submitting an application.

2). By necessity, all Registered Design applications must include a 'representation' of the design intended for protection. Apart from a requirement that such representations be 'suitable for publication' (Rule 9(1) of The Registered Designs Rules 2006 refers), the applicant may choose to present a design using whichever illustration 'format' he or she considers to be the most effective and

Part 3 Designs

accurate means of representing the design. Guidance on the use of different representation formats is set out in the IPOs Illustrations Dos and Don'ts factsheet. Most representations are submitted in the form of pencil drawings, black line drawings, photographs, or computer-generated graphic images (such as those generated by Computer Assisted Design (CAD) software).

3). The degree of detail disclosed in a representation can vary depending on the type of representation format used. For example, a high-definition photograph of a three-dimensional object is likely to disclose design features which may not be discernible in a simple line drawing of the same object (a photograph is likely to disclose the visual effect of surface material, whereas a simple black-line drawing may not). That being so, applicants should be careful when selecting representations to ensure that they accurately reflect exactly what the design is intended to protect.

4). The following guidance takes into account the Supreme Court's conclusions in PMS v Magmatic[1], and seeks to help designers understand the possible consequences of selecting one representation format over another.

SHAPE-ONLY VERSUS 'MINIMALIST' DESIGN

5). The SCs judgment places much emphasis upon the distinction between those designs which are intended to protect shape alone, and those which are intended to protect both shape and other features. Designers have frequently sought to protect the former on the basis that it is perceived to provide a wider scope of protection. Where an earlier design registered in respect of shape-only is used as the basis for an infringement action, the like-for-like comparison with a later design is more likely to focus on shape without consideration of any surface decoration, ornamentation, or other visual features present in the allegedly infringing design.

6). When seeking to protect shape alone, the applicant is at liberty to choose whichever form of representation he or she deems the most suitable means of capturing the shape in question. That notwithstanding, evidence indicates that line drawings are the preferred means for representing (and therefore capturing) shape alone. This reflects the Court's judgment in Procter & Gamble Co v Reckitt Benckiser (UK) Ltd[2] where, in relation to the registration of black-line-on-white-background illustrations showing a plain undecorated 'spray can', it determined that:

(i) the registration was 'evidently' for shape
(ii) any like-for-like comparison with a later design should be limited to comparing the respective shapes only
(iii) graphics and other markings on the later design were 'irrelevant'.

7). Although line drawings have been effectively used to signify shape-only, the law does not require that applicants state the 'type' of protection intended when submitting a UK Registered Design application. Where an application does not contain any additional written disclaimers or limitations (see paragraphs 13 and 14 below), protection is granted on the basis of what is shown and disclosed in the supplied representations.

8). Alongside the Court's endorsement of shape-only design protection in cases such as Procter & Gamble, the SC in PMS v Magmatic[1] has also confirmed that absence of decoration can be a (positive) feature of a registered design. At paragraph 44 of its judgment, the Supreme Court stated that:

> . . . simplicity or minimalism can notoriously be an aspect of a design, and it would be very curious if a design right registration system did not cater for it . . . .

At paragraph 60, it goes on to confirm that:

> . . . minimalism can self-evidently be an important aspect of a design just as intensive decoration can be . . . .

9). These conclusions highlight an ongoing tension in the use of 'simple' representations (i.e. those showing outline shape without ornamentation) for the purposes of capturing a design. On the one hand, and in accordance with Procter & Gamble, an application containing basic line drawings may well be interpreted as an attempt to protect shape-only. At the same time, and in light of the SCs judgement in PMS v Magmatic[1], it is also possible that a line drawing may be interpreted as an attempt to register both shape and 'minimalist' ornamentation (i.e. where plain undecorated surfaces are positively intended to be a feature of the design).

WHAT DOES THIS MEAN IN PRACTICE?

10). Following the SCs judgment, applicants should take care when selecting representations for use in UK Registered Design Applications, and it may be useful to consider how the Courts have responded to the following two different types of representation:

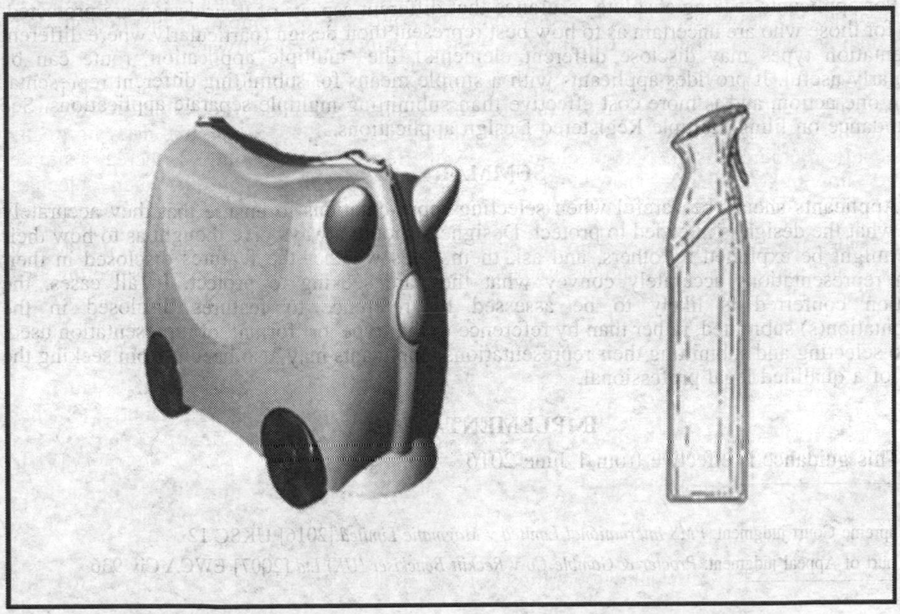

In PMS v Magmatic[1], the Court assessed the greyscale representation shown on the left and concluded that its minimal levels of tonal differentiation were enough to result in the design being assessed as shape 'and more' (reference was made to the design being "not merely a specific shape, but a shape in two contrasting colours – one represented as grey and the other as black on the images"). In contrast, the Court in Procter & Gamble pointed to the line-drawing format shown on the right as being a suitable means for capturing shape-only.

11). Applicants should not interpret the SCs judgment in PMS[1] as discouragement against the general use of CAD representations when filing Registered Designs per se. The Registrar receives applications in a variety of representation formats including line drawings, photographs and CAD representations, and is keen to ensure that the application process remains accessible and flexible for all. However, when selecting representations, one should always bear in mind how the examples presented above were subject to different interpretations by the Court. Applicants may also benefit from seeking the advice of a qualified legal professional prior to submitting an application.

12). When using more detailed CAD-type representations, the visible presence of apparently-incidental features such as, for example, shading and light reflection, may still be taken into account by a Court or Tribunal, and may have the effect of limiting protection to shape 'and more'. Therefore, when seeking to protect shape-only, applicants are advised to use simple line drawings, without any colour or tonal differences, and without any visible surface features or decoration.

13). Reflecting the Court's confirmation in PMS[1] that overall impression can be determined by the representations used, applicants should also note that a combination of representation formats cannot be used in the context of a single application. Where a single application is received consisting of, for example, a simple outline drawing and a tonally-shaded CAD drawing (and where both representations are intended to represent the same design) an objection will be raised and the applicant given an opportunity to modify the application accordingly.

USE AND EFFECT OF DISCLAIMERS AND LIMITATIONS

14). The UK's digital application filing system and the equivalent (paper) application form both provide the applicant with an opportunity to disclaim or limit particular elements or aspects shown in the representation(s), thereby enabling further definition of the design intended for protection. A disclaimer or limitation can be presented in graphic form (for example, by circling those elements which are intended for protection, or by blurring-out those elements which are not), or in written form (by drafting and submitting a statement which explicitly states what is or is not intended for protection).

15). Where an applicant seeks to protect shape only, the Registrar recommends the use of written limitations/disclaimers in order to define the intended protection as explicitly and as accurately as possible. Therefore, in addition to following the advice provided at paragraph 12 above regarding the use of simple line drawings, an applicant may also wish to submit a written disclaimer or limitation such as, for example, 'protection is sought for the shape and contours alone'. See further IPO guidance on disclaimers and limitations.

MULTIPLE DESIGN APPLICATIONS

16). For applicants seeking absolute assurance that different aspects of their design are protected, and/or for those who are uncertain as to how best represent their design (particularly where different representation types may disclose different elements), the 'multiple application' route can be particularly useful. It provides applicants with a simple means for submitting different representations in one action, and is more cost effective than submitting multiple separate applications. See IPO guidance on filing multiple Registered Design applications.

SUMMARY

17). Applicants should be careful when selecting representations to ensure that they accurately reflect what the design is intended to protect. Designers should always give thought as to how their design might be exploited by others, and ask themselves whether the features disclosed in their chosen representations accurately convey what they are seeking to protect. In all cases, the protection conferred is likely to be assessed by reference to features disclosed in the representation(s) submitted, rather than by reference to the 'type' or 'format' of representation used. Prior to selecting and submitting their representations, applicants may also benefit from seeking the advice of a qualified legal professional.

IMPLEMENTATION

18). This guidance is effective from 1 June 2016.

NOTES

1 Supreme Court judgment: *PMS International Limited v Magmatic Limited* [2016] UKSC 12

2 Court of Appeal judgment: *Procter & Gamble Co v Reckitt Benckiser (UK) Ltd* [2007] EWCA Civ 936

DIRECTIONS UNDER 37A OF THE REGISTERED DESIGN ACT GIVEN IN RELATION TO USE OF ELECTRONIC COMMUNICATIONS

Published 31 May 2016

NOTES

DIRECTIONS UNDER SECTION 37A

[3.375]

1. The registrar has given the following Directions under section 37A of the Registered Design Act 1949.

2. These Directions direct the use of electronic communications for form DF2A for making an application to the Patent Office for the registration of a design.

3. These Directions come into force on 31 May 2016.

Lynda Adams
On behalf of Comptroller General of Patents, Designs and Trade Marks
25 May 2016

PART 4
UNREGISTERED DESIGN RIGHT

DESIGN RIGHT (SEMICONDUCTOR TOPOGRAPHIES) REGULATIONS 1989

(SI 1989/1100)

NOTES

Made: 29 June 1989.
Authority: European Communities Act 1972, s 2(2).
Commencement: 1 August 1989.

ARRANGEMENT OF REGULATIONS

SCHEDULES

[4.1]
1 Citation and commencement

These Regulations may be cited as the Design Right (Semiconductor Topographies) Regulations 1989 and shall come into force on 1st August 1989.

[4.2]
2 Interpretation

(1) In these Regulations—

"the Act" means the Copyright, Designs and Patents Act 1988;

"semiconductor product" means an article the purpose, or one of the purposes, of which is the performance of an electronic function and which consists of two or more layers, at least one of which is composed of semiconducting material and in or upon one or more of which is fixed a pattern appertaining to that or another function; and

"semiconductor topography" means a design within the meaning of section 213(2) of the Act which is a design of either of the following—

(a) the pattern fixed, or intended to be fixed, in or upon—

(i) a layer of a semiconductor product, or

(ii) a layer of material in the course of and for the purpose of the manufacture of a semiconductor product, or

(b) the arrangement of the patterns fixed, or intended to be fixed, in or upon the layers of a semiconductor product in relation to one another.

(2) Except where the context otherwise requires, these Regulations shall be construed as one with Part III of the Act (design right).

[4.3]
3 Application of Copyright, Designs and Patents Act 1988, Part III

In its application to a design which is a semiconductor topography, Part III of the Act shall have effect subject to regulation 4 to 9 below.

[4.4]
4 Qualification

(1) Section 213(5) of the Act has effect subject to paragraphs (2) to (4) below.

[(2) Part III of the Act has effect as if for section 217(3) there was substituted the following—

"(3) In this section "qualifying country" means—

(a) the United Kingdom,

(b) another member State,

(c) the Isle of Man, Gibraltar, the Channel Islands or any colony,

(d) a country listed in the Schedule to the Design Right (Semiconductor Topographies) Regulations 1989.".]

(3) Where a semiconductor topography is created in pursuance of a commission or in the course of employment and the designer of the topography is, by virtue of section 215 of the Act (as substituted by regulation 5 below), the first owner of design right in that topography, section 219 of the Act does not apply and section 218(2) to (4) of the Act shall apply to the topography as if it had not been created in pursuance of a commission or in the course of employment.

(4) Section 220 of the Act has effect subject to regulation 7 below and as if for subsection (1) there was substituted the following—

"220

(1) A design which does not qualify for design right protection under section 218 or 219 (as modified by regulation 4(3) of the Design Right (Semiconductor Topographies) Regulations 1989) or under the said regulation 4(3) qualifies for design right protection if the first marketing of articles made to the design—

(a) is by a qualifying person who is exclusively authorised to put such articles on the market in every member State of the European Economic Community, and

(b) takes place within the territory of any member State.";

and subsection (4) of section 220 accordingly has effect as if the words "in the United Kingdom" were omitted.

NOTES

Para (2): substituted by the Design Right (Semiconductor Topographies) (Amendment) Regulations 2006, SI 2006/1833, regs 2, 3.

[4.5]

5 Ownership of design right

Part III of the Act has effect as if for section 215 of the Act there was substituted the following—

"215

(1) The designer is the first owner of any design right in a design which is not created in pursuance of a commission or in the course of employment.

(2) Where a design is created in pursuance of a commission, the person commissioning the design is the first owner of any design right in it subject to any agreement in writing to the contrary.

(3) Where, in a case not falling within subsection (2) a design is created by an employee in the course of his employment, his employer is the first owner of any design right in the design subject to any agreement in writing to the contrary.

(4) If a design qualifies for design right protection by virtue of section 220 (as modified by regulation 4(4) of the Design Right (Semiconductor Topographies) Regulations 1989), the above rules do not apply and, subject to regulation 7 of the said Regulations, the person by whom the articles in question are marketed is the first owner of the design right.".

[4.6]

6 Duration of design right

(1) Part III of the Act has effect as if for section 216 of the Act there was substituted the following—

"216

The design right in a semiconductor topography expires—

(a) ten years from the end of the calendar year in which the topography or articles made to the topography were first made available for sale or hire anywhere in the world by or with the licence of the design right owner, or

(b) if neither the topography nor articles made to the topography are so made available within a period of fifteen years commencing with the earlier of the time when the topography was first recorded in a design document or the time when an article was first made to the topography, at the end of that period.".

(2) Subsection (2) of section 263 of the Act has effect as if the words "or a semiconductor topography" were inserted after the words "in relation to an article".

(3) The substitute provision set out in paragraph (1) above has effect subject to regulation 7 below.

[4.7]

7 Confidential information

In determining, for the purposes of section 215(4), 216 or 220 of the Act (as modified by these Regulations), whether there has been any marketing, or anything has been made available for sale or hire, no account shall be taken of any sale or hire, or any offer or exposure for sale or hire, which is subject to an obligation of confidence in respect of information about the semiconductor topography in question unless either—

(a) the article or semiconductor topography sold or hired or offered or exposed for sale or hire has been sold or hired on a previous occasion (whether or not subject to an obligation of confidence), or

(b) the obligation is imposed at the behest of the Crown, or of the government of any country outside the United Kingdom, for the protection of security in connection with the production of arms, munitions or war material.

[4.8]

8 Infringement

(1) Section 226 of the Act has effect as if for subsection (1) there was substituted the following—

"226

(1) Subject to subsection (1A), the owner of design right in a design has the exclusive right to reproduce the design—

(a) by making articles to that dcsign, or

(b) by making a design document recording the design for the purpose of enabling such articles to be made.

(1A) Subsection (1) does not apply to—

(a) the reproduction of a design privately for non-commercial aims; or

(b) the reproduction of a design for the purpose of analysing or evaluating the design or analysing, evaluating or teaching the concepts, processes, systems or techniques embodied in it.".

(2) Section 227 of the Act does not apply if the article in question has previously been sold or hired within—

(a) the United Kingdom by or with the licence of the owner of design right in the semiconductor topography in question, or

(b) the territory of any other member State of the European Economic Community or the territory of Gibraltar by or with the consent of the person for the time being entitled to import it into or sell or hire it within that territory.

(3) Section 228(6) of the Act does not apply.

(4) It is not an infringement of design right in a semiconductor topography to—

(a) create another original semiconductor topography as a result of an analysis or evaluation of the first topography or of the concepts, processes, systems or techniques embodied in it, or

(b) reproduce that other topography.

(5) Anything which would be an infringement of the design right in a semiconductor topography if done in relation to the topography as a whole is an infringement of the design right in the topography if done in relation to a substantial part of the topography.

[4.9]

9 Licences of right

Section 237 of the Act does not apply.

[4.10]

10 Revocation and transitional provisions

(1) . . .

(2) Sub-paragraph (1) of paragraph 19 of Schedule 1 to the Act shall not apply in respect of a semiconductor topography created between 7th November 1987 and 31st July 1989.

(3) In its application to copyright in a semiconductor topography created before 7th November 1987, sub-paragraph (2) of the said paragraph 19 shall have effect as if the reference to sections 237 to 239 were a reference to sections 238 and 239; and sub-paragraph (3) of that paragraph accordingly shall not apply to such copyright.

NOTES

Para (1): revokes the Semiconductor Products (Protection of Topography) Regulations 1987, SI 1987/1497.

[SCHEDULE
QUALIFYING COUNTRIES

Regulation 4(2)

[4.11]

Albania

Angola

Antigua and Barbuda

Argentina

Armenia

Australia

Bahrain, Kingdom of

Bangladesh

Barbados

Belize

Benin

Bolivia

Botswana

Brazil

Brunei Darussalam

Bulgaria

Burkina Faso

Burundi

Cambodia

Cameroon

Canada

Central African Republic

Chad

Chile

China

Colombia

Congo

Costa Rica

Côte d'Ivoire

Croatia

Cuba

Democratic Republic of the Congo

Djibouti

Dominica

Dominican Republic

Ecuador

Egypt

El Salvador

Fiji

Former Yugoslav Republic of Macedonia

French overseas territories

Gabon

The Gambia

Georgia

Ghana

Grenada

Guatemala

Guinea

Guinea Bissau

Guyana

Haiti

Honduras

Hong Kong

Iceland

India

Indonesia

Israel

Jamaica

Japan

Jordan

Kenya

Korea, Republic of

Kuwait

Kyrgyz Republic

Lesotho

Liechtenstein

Macao, China

Madagascar

Malawi

Malaysia

Maldives

Mali

Mauritania

Mauritius

Mexico

Moldova

Mongolia

Morocco

Mozambique

Myanmar

Namibia

Nepal

Netherlands Antilles

New Zealand

Nicaragua

Niger

Nigeria

Norway

Oman

Pakistan

Panama

Papua New Guinea

Paraguay

Peru

Philippines

Qatar

Romania

Rwanda

Saint Kitts and Nevis

Saint Lucia

Saint Vincent & the Grenadines

Saudi Arabia

Senegal

Sierra Leone

Singapore

Solomon Islands

South Africa

Sri Lanka

Suriname

Swaziland

Switzerland

Chinese Taipei

Tanzania

Thailand

Togo

[Tonga]

Trinidad and Tobago

Tunisia

Turkey

Uganda

[Ukraine]

United Arab Emirates

United States of America

Uruguay

[Vietnam]

Venezuela

Zambia

Zimbabwe]

NOTES

Substituted by the Design Right (Semiconductor Topographies) (Amendment) Regulations 2006, SI 2006/1833, regs 2, 4, Sch 1.

Entries "Tonga", "Ukraine" and "Vietnam" inserted by the Design Right (Semiconductor Topographies) (Amendment) (No 2) Regulations 2008, SI 2008/1434, regs 2, 3.

DESIGN RIGHT (PROCEEDINGS BEFORE COMPTROLLER) RULES 1989

(SI 1989/1130)

NOTES

Made: 4 July 1989.
Authority: Copyright, Designs and Patents Act 1988, s 250.
Commencement: 1 August 1989.

ARRANGEMENT OF RULES

[4.12]
1 Citation and commencement

These Rules may be cited as the Design Right (Proceedings before Comptroller) Rules 1989 and shall come into force on 1st August 1989.

[4.13]
2 Interpretation

(1) In these Rules, unless the context otherwise requires—

"the Act" means the Copyright, Designs and Patents Act 1988;

"applicant" means a person who has referred a dispute or made an application to the Comptroller;

"application" means an application to the Comptroller to settle or vary the terms of a licence of right or to adjust the terms of a licence;

"dispute" means a dispute as to any of the matters referred to in rule 3(1); and

"proceedings" means proceedings before the Comptroller in respect of a dispute or application.

(2) A rule or schedule referred to by number means the rule or schedule so numbered in these Rules; and a requirement under these Rules to use a form set out in Schedule 1 is satisfied by the use either of a replica of that form or of a form which contains the information required by the form set out in the said Schedule and which is acceptable to the Comptroller.

Proceedings in respect of a dispute

[4.14]
3 Commencement of proceedings

(1) Proceedings under section 246 of the Act in respect of a dispute as to—

(a) the subsistence of design right,

(b) the term of design right, or

(c) the identity of the person in whom design right first vested,

shall be commenced by the service by the applicant on the Comptroller of a notice in Form 1 in Schedule 1. There shall be served with that notice a statement in duplicate setting out the name and address of the other party to the dispute (hereinafter in this rule referred to as the respondent), the issues in dispute, the applicant's case and the documents relevant to his case.

(2) Within 14 days of the receipt of the notice the Comptroller shall send a copy of the notice, together with a copy of the applicant's statement, to the respondent.

(3) Within 28 days of the receipt by him of the documents referred to in paragraph (2) above, the respondent shall serve on the Comptroller a counter-statement and shall at the same time serve a copy of it on the applicant. Such counter-statement shall set out full particulars of the grounds on which he contests the applicant's case, any issues on which he and the applicant are in agreement and the documents relevant to his case.

(4) Within 21 days of the service on him of the counter-statement, the applicant may serve a further statement on the Comptroller setting out the grounds on which he contests the respondent's case, and shall at the same time serve a copy of it on the respondent.

(5) No amended statement or further statement shall be served by either party except by leave or direction of the Comptroller.

[4.15]
4 Comptroller's directions

(1) The Comptroller shall give such directions as to the further conduct of proceedings as he considers appropriate [including directing the party or parties to attend a case management conference or a pre-hearing review or both].

(2) If a party fails to comply with any direction given under this rule, the Comptroller may in awarding costs take account of such default.

NOTES

Para (1): words in square brackets added by the Design Right (Proceedings before Comptroller) (Amendment) Rules 1999, SI 1999/3195, rr 2, 3.

[4.16]
5 Procedure and evidence at hearing

(1) Unless the Comptroller otherwise directs, all evidence in the proceedings shall be by statutory declaration[, witness statement] or affidavit.

(2) Where the Comptroller thinks fit in any particular case to take oral evidence in lieu of or in addition to evidence by statutory declaration[, witness statement] or affidavit he may so direct and, unless he directs otherwise, shall allow any witness to be cross-examined on his evidence.

(3) A party to the proceedings who desires to make oral representations shall so notify the Comptroller and the Comptroller shall, unless he and the parties agree to a shorter period, give at least 14 days' notice of the time and place of the hearing to the parties.

(4) If a party intends to refer at a hearing to any document not already referred to in the proceedings, he shall, unless the Comptroller and the other party agree to a shorter period, give 14 days' notice of his intention, together with particulars of every document to which he intends to refer, to the Comptroller and the other party.

(5) At any stage of the proceedings the Comptroller may direct that such documents, information or evidence as he may require shall be filed within such time as he may specify.

(6) The hearing of any proceedings, or part of proceedings, under this rule shall be in public, unless the Comptroller, after consultation with the parties, otherwise directs.

[(7) The Comptroller may give a direction as he thinks fit in any particular case that evidence shall be given by affidavit or statutory declaration instead of or in addition to a witness statement.

(8) Where in proceedings before the Comptroller, a party adduces evidence of a statement made by a person otherwise than while giving oral evidence in the proceedings and does not call that person as a witness, the Comptroller may, if he thinks fit, permit any other party to the proceedings to call that person as a witness and cross-examine him on the statement as if he had been called by the first-mentioned party and as if the statement were his evidence in chief.]

NOTES

Paras (1), (2): words in square brackets inserted by the Design Right (Proceedings before Comptroller) (Amendment) Rules 1999, SI 1999/3195, rr 2, 4(a).

Paras (7), (8): added by SI 1999/3195, rr 2, 4(b).

[4.17]

6 Representation and rights of audience

(1) Any party to the proceedings may appear in person or be represented by counsel or a solicitor (of any part of the United Kingdom) or, subject to paragraph (4) below, a patent [attorney] or any other person whom he desires to represent him.

(2) Anything required or authorised by these Rules to be done by or in relation to any person may be done by or in relation to his agent.

(3) Where after a person has become a party to the proceedings he appoints an agent for the first time or appoints an agent in substitution for another, the newly appointed agent shall give written notice of his appointment to the Comptroller and to every other party to the proceedings.

(4) The Comptroller may refuse to recognise as such an agent in respect of any proceedings before him—

(a) a person who has been convicted of an offence under section 88 of the Patents Act 1949 or section 114 of the Patents Act 1977 [or section 276 of the Act];

(b) [a person] whose name has been erased from and not restored to, or who is suspended from, the register of patent [attorneys] (kept [in accordance with] [section 275 of the Act]) on the ground of misconduct;

(c) a person who is found by the Secretary of State to have been guilty of such conduct as would, in the case of [a person] registered in the register of patent [attorneys], render [the person] liable to have [the person's] name erased from the register on the ground of misconduct;

(d) a partnership or body corporate of which one of the partners or directors is a person whom the Comptroller could refuse to recognise under sub-paragraphs (a), (b) or (c) above.

NOTES

Para (1): word in square brackets substituted by the Legal Services Act 2007 (Consequential Amendments) Order 2009, SI 2009/3348, art 8(a).

Para (4): words in square brackets in sub-para (a) inserted by the Design Right (Proceedings before Comptroller) (Amendment) Rules 1990, SI 1990/1453, r 2; in sub-para (b), words in first, second and third pairs of square brackets substituted by SI 2009/3348, art 8(b) and words in fourth pair of square brackets substituted by SI 1990/1453, r 2; words in square brackets in sub-para (c) substituted by SI 2009/3348, art 8(c).

Patents Act 1949, s 88: repealed by the Patents Act 1977, s 132, Sch 6, subject to savings contained in Sch 4 to that Act at **[1.153]**.

Patents Act 1977, s 114: repealed by the Copyright, Designs and Patents Act 1988, s 303(2), Sch 8.

[4.18]

7 Application to be made a party to proceedings

(1) A person who claims to have a substantial interest in a dispute in respect of which proceedings have been commenced may apply to the Comptroller to be made a party to the dispute in Form 2 in Schedule 1, supported by a statement of his interest. He shall serve a copy of his application, together with his statement, on every party to the proceedings.

(2) The Comptroller shall, upon being satisfied of the substantial interest of that person in the dispute, grant the application and shall give directions or further directions under rule 3(1) as may be necessary to enable that person to participate in the proceedings as a party to the dispute.

[4.19]
8 Withdrawal of reference

A party (including a person made a party to the proceedings under rule 7) may at any time before the Comptroller's decision withdraw from the proceedings by serving a notice to that effect on the Comptroller and every other party to the proceedings, but such withdrawal shall be without prejudice to the Comptroller's power to make an order as to the payment of costs incurred up to the time of service of the notice.

[4.20]
9 Decision of the Comptroller

After hearing the party or parties desiring to be heard, or if none of the parties so desires, then without a hearing, the Comptroller shall decide the dispute and notify his decision to the parties, giving written reasons for his decision if so required by any party.

Proceedings in respect of application to settle terms of licence of right or adjust terms of licence

[4.21]
10 Commencement of proceedings

(1) Proceedings in respect of an application to the Comptroller—

(a) under section 247 of the Act, to settle the terms of a licence available as of right by virtue of section 237 or under an order under section 238 of the Act, or

(b) under paragraph 19(2) of Schedule 1 to the Act, to settle the terms of a licence available as of right in respect of a design recorded or embodied in a design document or model before 1st August 1989, or

(c) brought by virtue of paragraph 19(5) of Schedule 1 to the Act, to adjust the terms of a licence granted before 1st August 1989 in respect of a design referred to in sub-paragraph (b) above,

shall be commenced by the service by the applicant on the Comptroller of a notice in Form 3 in Schedule 1.

(2) There shall be served with the notice a statement in duplicate setting out—

(a) in the case of an application referred to in paragraph (1)(a) or (b) above, the terms of the licence which the applicant requires the Comptroller to settle and, unless the application is one to which rule 13 relates, the name and address of the owner of the design right or, as the case may be, the copyright owner of the design;

(b) in the case of an application referred to in paragraph (1)(c) above, the date and terms of the licence and the grounds on which the applicant requires the Comptroller to adjust those terms and the name and address of the grantor of the licence.

(3) Within 14 days of the receipt of the notice the Comptroller shall send a copy of it, together with a copy of the applicant's statement, to the person (hereinafter in this rule referred to as the respondent) shown in the application as the design right owner, copyright owner or grantor of the licence, as appropriate.

(4) Within 6 weeks of the receipt by him of the notice sent under paragraph (3) above the respondent shall, if he does not agree to the terms of the licence required by the applicant to be settled or, as the case may be, adjusted, serve a notice of objection on the Comptroller with a statement setting out the grounds of his objection and at the same time shall serve a copy of the same on the applicant.

(5) Within 4 weeks of the receipt of the notice of objection the applicant may serve on the Comptroller a counter-statement and at the same time serve a copy of it on the respondent.

(6) No amended statement or further statement shall be served by either party except by leave or direction of the Comptroller.

[4.22]
11 Directions, procedure and evidence

Rules 4, 5, 6 and 8 shall apply in respect of proceedings under rule 10 as they apply in respect of proceedings under rule 3.

[4.23]
12 Decision of the Comptroller

After hearing the party or parties desiring to be heard, or if none of the parties so desires, then without a hearing, the Comptroller shall decide the application and notify his decision to the parties, giving written reasons for his decision if so required by any party.

Settlement of terms where design right owner unknown

[4.24]

13 Commencement of proceedings

(1) Where a person making an application under rule 10(1)(a) or (b) is unable (after making such inquiries as he considers reasonable) to discover the identity of the design right owner or, as the case may be, the copyright owner, he shall serve with his notice under that rule a statement to that effect, setting out particulars of the inquiries made by him as to the identity of the owner of the right and the result of those inquiries.

(2) The Comptroller may require the applicant to make such further inquiries into the identity of the owner of the right as he thinks fit and, may for that purpose, require him to publish in such a manner as the Comptroller considers appropriate particulars of the application.

(3) The Comptroller shall, upon being satisfied from the applicant's statement or the further inquiries made under paragraph (2) above that the identity of the owner of the right cannot be discovered, consider the application and settle the terms of the licence.

Proceedings in respect of application by design right owner to vary terms of licence

[4.25]

14 Commencement of proceedings

(1) Where the Comptroller has, in settling the terms of the licence under rule 13, ordered that the licence shall be free of any obligation as to royalties or other payments, the design right owner or copyright owner (as the case may be) may serve on the Comptroller a notice in Form 4 in Schedule 1 applying for the terms of the licence to be varied from the date of his application. There shall be served with the notice a statement in duplicate setting out the particulars of the grounds for variation and the terms required to be varied.

(2) Within 14 days of the receipt of the notice the Comptroller shall send a copy of the notice, together with the design right or copyright owner's statement, to the applicant under rule 10 (hereinafter in this rule referred to as the licensee).

(3) The licensee shall, if he does not agree to the terms as required to be varied by the design right or copyright owner, within 6 weeks of the receipt of the notice serve notice of objection on the Comptroller with a statement setting out the grounds of his objection and at the same time shall serve a copy on the design right or copyright owner, as the case may be.

(4) Within 4 weeks of the receipt of the notice of objection the design right or copyright owner may serve on the Comptroller a counter-statement, and at the same time shall serve a copy of it on the licensee.

(5) No amended statement or further statement shall be served by either party except by leave or direction of the Comptroller.

[4.26]

15 Directions, procedure and evidence

Rules 4, 5, 6 and 8 shall apply in respect of proceedings under rule 14 as they apply in respect of proceedings under rule 3.

[4.27]

16 Decision of the Comptroller

After hearing the party or parties desiring to be heard, or if none of the parties so desires, then without a hearing, the Comptroller shall decide the application and notify his decision to the parties, giving written reasons for his decision if so required by any party.

General

[4.28]

17 Rectification of irregularities

Any document filed in any proceedings may, if the Comptroller thinks fit, be amended, and any irregularity in procedure may be rectified by the Comptroller on such terms as he may direct.

[4.29]

18 Evidence

(1) Any statutory declaration or affidavit filed in any proceedings shall be made and subscribed as follows—

(a) in the United Kingdom, before any justice of the peace or any commissioner or other officer authorised by law in any part of the United Kingdom to administer an oath for the purpose of any legal proceedings;

(b) in any other part of Her Majesty's dominions or in the Republic of Ireland, before any court, judge, justice of the peace or any officer authorised by law to administer an oath there for the purpose of any legal proceedings; and

(c) elsewhere, before a British Minister, or person exercising the functions of a British Minister, or a Consul, Vice-Consul or other person exercising the functions of a British Consul or before a notary public, judge or magistrate.

(2) Any document purporting to have fixed, impressed or subscribed thereto or thereon the seal or signature of any person authorised by paragraph (1) above to take a declaration may be admitted by the Comptroller without proof of the genuineness of the seal or signature or of the official character of the person or his authority to take the declaration.

(3) In England and Wales, the Comptroller shall, in relation to the giving of evidence (including evidence on oath), the attendance of witnesses and the discovery and production of documents, have all the powers of a judge of the High Court, other than the power to punish summarily for contempt of court.

(4) In Scotland, the Comptroller shall, in relation to the giving of evidence (including evidence on oath), have all the powers which a Lord Ordinary of the Court of Session has in an action before him, other than the power to punish summarily for contempt of court, and, in relation to the attendance of witnesses and the recovery and production of documents, have all the powers of the Court of Session.

[4.30]
[18(A)

Any witness statement filed under these Rules shall—

(a) be a written statement signed and dated by a person which contains the evidence which the person signing it would be allowed to give orally; and

(b) include a statement by the intended witness that he believes the facts in it are true.]

NOTES

Inserted by the Design Right (Proceedings before Comptroller) (Amendment) Rules 1999, SI 1999/3195, rr 2, 5.

[4.31]
19 Appointment of advisers

The Comptroller may appoint an adviser to assist him in any proceedings and shall settle the question or instructions to be submitted or given to such an adviser.

[4.32]
20 Time

[(1) The times or periods prescribed by these Rules for doing any act or taking any proceedings thereunder may be extended or shortened by the Comptroller if he thinks fit, upon such notice and upon such terms as he may direct, and an extension may be granted although the time for doing such act or taking such proceedings has already expired.]

(2) Where the last day for the doing of any act falls on a day on which the Patent Office is closed and by reason thereof the act cannot be done on that day, it may be done on the next day on which the Office is open.

NOTES

Para (1): substituted by the Design Right (Proceedings before Comptroller) (Amendment) Rules 1999, SI 1999/3195, rr 2, 6.

[4.33]
21 Hours of business

For the purposes of these Rules the Patent Office shall be open Monday to Friday—

(a) between [9.00 am] and midnight, for the filing of applications, forms and other documents, and

(b) between [9.00 am] and [5.00 pm] for all other purposes,

excluding Good Friday, Christmas Day[, Tuesday 4th January 2000] and any day specified or proclaimed to be a bank holiday under section 1 of the Banking and Financial Dealings Act 1971.

NOTES

Words in first, second and third pairs of square brackets substituted, and words in final pair of square brackets inserted, by the Design Right (Proceedings before Comptroller) (Amendment) Rules 1999, SI 1999/3195, rr 2, 7.

[4.34]
22 Costs

(1) The Comptroller may, in respect of any proceedings, by order award such costs or, in Scotland, such expenses as he considers reasonable and direct how, to what party and from what parties they are to be paid.

(2) Where any applicant or a person making an application under rule 7 neither resides nor carries on business in the United Kingdom or another member State of the [European Union] the Comptroller may require him to give security for the costs or expenses of the proceedings and in default of such security being given may treat the reference or application as abandoned.

NOTES

Para (2): words in square brackets substituted by the Treaty of Lisbon (Changes in Terminology) Order 2011, SI 2011/1043, art 4(1).

[4.35]

23 Service and translation of documents

(1) Every person concerned in any proceedings to which these Rules relate shall furnish to the Comptroller an address for service . . . , and that address may be treated for all purposes connected with such proceedings as the address of the person concerned.

[(1A) The address for service shall be an address in the United Kingdom, another EEA state or the Channel Islands.]

(2) Where any document or part of a document which is in a language other than English is served on the Comptroller or any party to proceedings or filed with the Comptroller in pursuance of these Rules, it shall be accompanied by a translation into English of the document or part, verified to the satisfaction of the Comptroller as corresponding to the original text.

NOTES

Para (1): words omitted revoked by the Patents, Trade Marks and Designs (Address For Service and Time Limits, etc) Rules 2006, SI 2006/760, rr 2, 3(1), (2).

Para (1A): inserted by SI 2006/760, rr 2, 3(1), (3); substituted by the Patents, Trade Marks and Designs (Address for Service) Rules 2009, SI 2009/546, rr 2, 3.

[4.36]

24 Fees

The fees specified in Schedule 2 shall be payable in respect of the matters there mentioned.

SCHEDULES

SCHEDULE 1
FORMS

Rules 3(1), 7(1), 10(1) and 14(1)

[4.37]

Intellectual Property Office

For Creativity and Innovation

Design Right Form 1
Notice of counter-statement

For Official Use

Reference of dispute to Comptroller

Copyright, Designs & Patents Act 1988

Notes
Please type or write in dark ink using BLOCK LETTERS. For details of prescribed fees please contact the Intellectual Property Office.

Rule 3 of the Design Right (proceedings before Comptroller) Rules 1989 is the main rule governing the completion and filing of this form.

This form must be filed together with a statement in duplicate setting out the matters referred to in Rule 3(1).

4. Identification may be made by providing drawings, photographs or other identifying material.

☑ Please tick correct box where appropriate

1. Your reference

2. Please give full name and address of person making the reference.

Name

Address

Postcode

ADP number (if known)

3. Please give an address for service in the United Kingdom, another EEA state or the Channel Islands to which all correspondence will be sent.

Name

Address

Postcode

ADP number (if known)

4. Please identify the design which is the subject of the proceedings.

5. The dispute to be settled is in respect of:

the subsistence of the design right ☐

the term of the design right ☐

the identity of the person in whom design right first vested ☐

6. Please give the name and address of the other party to the dispute.

Name

Address

Postcode

ADP number (if known)

Signature **Date**

Reminder
Have you attached: the statement case in duplicate? ☐
the prescribed fee? ☐

Issued 2007

Intellectual Property Office is an operating name of the Patent Office

NOTES

Words "Please give an address for service in the United Kingdom, another EEA state or the Channel Islands" substituted by the Patents, Trade Marks and Designs (Address for Service) Rules 2009, SI 2009/546, rr 2, 4.

[4.38]

UK Intellectual Property Office
For Creativity and Innovation

Design Right Form 2

Application to be made a party to proceedings

For Official Use

Copyright, Designs & Patents Act 1988

Notes
Please type or write in dark ink using BLOCK LETTERS. For details of prescribed fees please contact the UK Intellectual Property Office.

Rule 7 of the Design Right (Proceedings before Comptroller) Rules 1989 is the main rule governing the completion and filing of this form.

A statement to show your substantial interest in the dispute in respect of which proceedings have been commenced must accompany this form. You must also serve a copy of the form and statement on every party to the proceedings.

1. Your reference

2. Please give full name and address of person applying to be made a party to dispute.

Name

Address

Postcode

ADP number (if known)

3. Please give an address for service in the United Kingdom, another EEA state or the Channel Islands to which all correspondence will be sent.

Name

Address

Postcode

ADP number (if known)

4. Please identify the proceedings relating to the dispute in which you claim to have a substantial interest.

Signature **Date**

☑ Please tick correct box where appropriate

Reminder
Have you attached:
a statement of your interest? ☐
the prescribed fee? ☐

Issued 2007

UK Intellectual Property Office is an operating name of the Patent Office

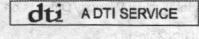

dti A DTI SERVICE

DDU/P640/04/07

NOTES

Words "Please give an address for service in the United Kingdom, another EEA state or the Channel Islands" substituted by the Patents, Trade Marks and Designs (Address for Service) Rules 2009, SI 2009/546, rr 2, 4.

[4.39]

UK Intellectual Property Office
For Creativity and Innovation

Design Right Form 3

Application to settle terms of Licence of Right or to adjust terms of Licence granted before 1st August 1989

For Official Use

Copyright, Designs & Patents Act 1988

Notes
Please type or write in dark ink using BLOCK LETTERS. For details of prescribed fees please contact the UK Intellectual Property Office.

Rule 10 and 13 of the Design Right (Proceedings before Comptroller) Rules 1989 are the main rules governing the completion and filing of this form.

This form must be filed, by the person requiring the settlement or adjustment of the licence, together with a statement in duplicate setting out the terms required. Where the applicant has been unable to discover the identity of the design right or copyright owner a statement must also be filed setting out the particulars of and result of the inquiries made to try to identify the owner.

4. Identification may be made by providing drawings, photographs or other identifying material.

5. Give the name and address of the design right or copyright owner (if known).

☑ Please tick correct box where appropriate

1. Your reference

2. Please give full name and address of applicant.
Name
Address
Postcode
ADP number (if known)

3. Please give an address for service in the United Kingdom, another EEA state or the Channel Islands to which all correspondence will be sent.
Name
Address
Postcode
ADP number (if known)

4. Please identify the design which is the subject of the proceedings.

5. Please give the name and address of the respondent
Name
Address
Postcode
ADP number (if known)

6. Application is made to the Comptroller to settle the terms of a licence for the design which is available as of right by virtue of:
Section 237 ☐
an order under Section 238 ☐

Signature **Date**

Reminder
Have you attached: the statement in duplicate of the terms required? ☐
the prescribed fee? ☐
a statement of inquiries made to identify the design right or copyright owner (if inquiries unsuccessful)? ☐

Issued 2007

UK Intellectual Property Office is an operating name of the Patent Office

dti A DTI SERVICE

DDU/P640/04/07

NOTES
Words "Please give an address for service in the United Kingdom, another EEA state or the Channel Islands" substituted by the Patents, Trade Marks and Designs (Address for Service) Rules 2009, SI 2009/546, rr 2, 4.

[4.40]

UK Intellectual Property Office

For Creativity and Innovation

Design Right Form 4

Application by Design Right or Copyright owner to vary terms of licence of right

For Official Use

Copyright, Designs & Patents Act 1988

Notes

Please type or write in dark ink using BLOCK LETTERS. For details of prescribed fees please contact the UK Intellectual Property Office.

Rule 14 of the Design Right (Proceedings before Comptroller) Rules 1989 is the main rule governing the completion and filing of this form.

This form must be filed together with a statement in duplicate setting out the particular of the grounds for variation and the terms required to be varied.

1. Your reference

2. Please give full name and address of applicant.

Name

Address

Postcode

ADP number (if known)

3. Please give an address for service in the United Kingdom, another EEA state or the Channel Islands to which all correspondence will be sent.

Name

Address

Postcode

ADP number (if known)

4. Please identify the licence which is the subject of the application.

5. Please give the name and address of the licence holder.

Name

Address

Postcode

ADP number (if known)

Signature **Date**

Reminder

Have you attached: a statement in duplicate of the grounds for variation and the terms required? ☐

the prescribed fee? ☐

☑ Please tick correct box where appropriate

Issued 2007

UK Intellectual Property Office is an operating name of the Patent Office

dti A DTI SERVICE

DDU/P640/04/07

NOTES

Words "Please give an address for service in the United Kingdom, another EEA state or the Channel Islands" substituted by the Patents, Trade Marks and Designs (Address for Service) Rules 2009, SI 2009/546, rr 2, 4.

[SCHEDULE 2
FEES

Rule 24

[4.41]

1. On reference of dispute (Form 1) under rule 3(1) £65

2. On application (Form 2) under rule 7(1) £40

3. On application (Form 3) under rule 10(1) £65

4. On application (Form 4) under rule 14(1) £65]

NOTES

Substituted by the Design Right (Proceedings before Comptroller) (Amendment) Rules 1992, SI 1992/615, r 2, Schedule.

PART 5
TRADE MARKS

TRADE MARKS ACT 1994

(1994 c 26)

NOTES

Modification: this Act is modified in its application to the Isle of Man by the Trade Marks (Isle of Man) Order 2013, SI 2013/2601, art 2, Schedule.

See also, in relation to the application of this Act, with modifications, to a European Union trade mark: the Community Trade Mark Regulations 2006, SI 2006/1027 at **[5.129]**.

ARRANGEMENT OF SECTIONS

PART I
REGISTERED TRADE MARKS

Introductory

An Act to make new provision for registered trade marks, implementing Council Directive No 89/104/EEC of 21st December 1988 to approximate the laws of the Member States relating to trade marks; to make provision in connection with Council Regulation (EC) No 40/94 of 20th December 1993 on the Community trade mark; to give effect to the Madrid Protocol Relating to the International Registration of Marks of 27th June 1989, and to certain provisions of the

Paris Convention for the Protection of Industrial Property of 20th March 1883, as revised and amended; and for connected purposes

[21 July 1994]

NOTES

See further, in relation to the application of this Act, with modifications, to International trade marks (UK) and requests for extension: the Trade Marks (International Registration) Order 2008, SI 2008/2206, art 3 at **[5.233]**.

PART I
REGISTERED TRADE MARKS

Introductory

[5.1]

1 Trade Marks

(1) In this Act a "trade mark" means any sign capable of being represented graphically which is capable of distinguishing goods or services of one undertaking from those of other undertakings.

A trade mark may, in particular, consist of words (including personal names), designs, letters, numerals or the shape of goods or their packaging.

(2) References in this Act to a trade mark include, unless the context otherwise requires, references to a collective mark (see section 49) or certification mark (see section 50).

NOTES

See the Harmonisation Directive 2008/95/EC, Arts 1, 2, at **[5.555]**, **[5.556]**.

[5.2]

2 Registered trade marks

(1) A registered trade mark is a property right obtained by the registration of the trade mark under this Act and the proprietor of a registered trade mark has the rights and remedies provided by this Act.

(2) No proceedings lie to prevent or recover damages for the infringement of an unregistered trade mark as such; but nothing in this Act affects the law relating to passing off.

NOTES

See the Harmonisation Directive 2008/95/EC, Preamble, recital 10.

Grounds for refusal of registration

[5.3]

3 Absolute grounds for refusal of registration

(1) The following shall not be registered—

(a) signs which do not satisfy the requirements of section 1(1),

(b) trade marks which are devoid of any distinctive character,

(c) trade marks which consist exclusively of signs or indications which may serve, in trade, to designate the kind, quality, quantity, intended purpose, value, geographical origin, the time of production of goods or of rendering of services, or other characteristics of goods or services,

(d) trade marks which consist exclusively of signs or indications which have become customary in the current language or in the *bona fide* and established practices of the trade:

Provided that, a trade mark shall not be refused registration by virtue of paragraph (b), (c) or (d) above if, before the date of application for registration, it has in fact acquired a distinctive character as a result of the use made of it.

(2) A sign shall not be registered as a trade mark if it consists exclusively of—

(a) the shape which results from the nature of the goods themselves,

(b) the shape of goods which is necessary to obtain a technical result, or

(c) the shape which gives substantial value to the goods.

(3) A trade mark shall not be registered if it is—

(a) contrary to public policy or to accepted principles of morality, or

(b) of such a nature as to deceive the public (for instance as to the nature, quality or geographical origin of the goods or service).

(4) A trade mark shall not be registered if or to the extent that its use is prohibited in the United Kingdom by any enactment or rule of law or by any provision of [EU] law.

(5) A trade mark shall not be registered in the cases specified, or referred to, in section 4 (specially protected emblems).

(6) A trade mark shall not be registered if or to the extent that the application is made in bad faith.

NOTES

Sub-s (4): reference in square brackets substituted by the Treaty of Lisbon (Changes in Terminology) Order 2011, SI 2011/1043, art 6(2)(a), subject to transitional provisions contained in art 3(3) thereof.

See the Harmonisation Directive 2008/95/EC, Art 3(1), (2), at **[5.557]**.

[5.4]
4 Specially protected emblems

(1) A trade mark which consists of or contains—

(a) the Royal arms, or any of the principal armorial bearings of the Royal arms, or any insignia or device so nearly resembling the Royal arms or any such armorial bearing as to be likely to be mistaken for them or it,

(b) a representation of the Royal crown or any of the Royal flags,

(c) a representation of Her Majesty or any member of the Royal family, or any colourable imitation thereof, or

(d) words, letters or devices likely to lead persons to think that the applicant either has or recently has had Royal patronage or authorisation,

shall not be registered unless it appears to the registrar that consent has been given by or on behalf of Her Majesty or, as the case may be, the relevant member of the Royal family.

(2) A trade mark which consists of or contains a representation of—

(a) the national flag of the United Kingdom (commonly known as the Union Jack), or

(b) the flag of England, Wales, Scotland, Northern Ireland or the Isle of Man,

shall not be registered if it appears to the registrar that the use of the trade mark would be misleading or grossly offensive.

Provision may be made by rules identifying the flags to which paragraph (b) applies.

(3) A trade mark shall not be registered in the cases specified in— section 57 (national emblems, &c of Convention countries), or section 58 (emblems, &c of certain international organisations).

(4) Provision may be made by rules prohibiting in such cases as may be prescribed the registration of a trade mark which consists of or contains—

(a) arms to which a person is entitled by virtue of a grant of arms by the Crown, or

(b) insignia so nearly resembling such arms as to be likely to be mistaken for them,

unless it appears to the registrar that consent has been given by or on behalf of that person.

Where such a mark is registered, nothing in this Act shall be construed as authorising its use in any way contrary to the laws of arms.

[(5) A trade mark which consists of or contains a controlled representation within the meaning of the Olympic Symbol etc (Protection) Act 1995 shall not be registered unless it appears to the registrar—

(a) that the application is made by the person for the time being appointed under section 1(2) of the Olympic Symbol etc (Protection) Act 1995 (power of Secretary of State to appoint a person as the proprietor of the Olympics association right), or

(b) that consent has been given by or on behalf of the person mentioned in paragraph (a) above.]

NOTES

Sub-s (5): added by the Olympic Symbol etc (Protection) Act 1995, s 13(2), (3), with effect in relation to applications for registration made on or after 20 September 1995.

See the Harmonisation Directive 2008/95/EC, Art 3(1), (2), at **[5.557]**.

Rules: the Trade Marks Rules 2008, SI 2008/1797, at **[5.146]**.

[5.5]
5 Relative grounds for refusal of registration

(1) A trade mark shall not be registered if it is identical with an earlier trade mark and the goods or services for which the trade mark is applied for are identical with the goods or services for which the earlier trade mark is protected.

(2) A trade mark shall not be registered if because—

(a) it is identical with an earlier trade mark and is to be registered for goods or services similar to those for which the earlier trade mark is protected, or

(b) it is similar to an earlier trade mark and is to be registered for goods or services identical with or similar to those for which the earlier trade mark is protected,

there exists a likelihood of confusion on the part of the public, which includes the likelihood of association with the earlier trade mark.

(3) A trade mark which—

(a) is identical with or similar to an earlier trade mark, . . .

(b) . . .

shall not be registered if, or to the extent that, the earlier trade mark has a reputation in the United Kingdom (or, in the case of a [European Union] trade mark [or international trade mark (EC)], in the [European Union]) and the use of the later mark without due cause would take unfair advantage of, or be detrimental to, the distinctive character or the repute of the earlier trade mark.

(4) A trade mark shall not be registered if, or to the extent that, its use in the United Kingdom is liable to be prevented—

(a) by virtue of any rule of law (in particular, the law of passing off) protecting an unregistered trade mark or other sign used in the course of trade, or

(b) by virtue of an earlier right other than those referred to in subsections (1) to (3) or paragraph (a) above, in particular by virtue of the law of copyright, design right or registered designs.

A person thus entitled to prevent the use of a trade mark is referred to in this Act as the proprietor of an "earlier right" in relation to the trade mark.

(5) Nothing in this section prevents the registration of a trade mark where the proprietor of the earlier trade mark or other earlier right consents to the registration.

NOTES

Sub-s (3): words omitted repealed by the Trade Marks (Proof of Use, etc) Regulations 2004, SI 2004/946, regs 3, 7(1); words in first pair of square brackets substituted by the European Union Trade Mark Regulations 2016, SI 2016/299, reg 15, Schedule, para 1, subject to transitional provisions and savings as noted below; words in second pair of square brackets inserted by the Trade Marks (International Registrations Designating the European Community, etc) Regulations 2004, SI 2004/2332, regs 2, 3; words in final pair of square brackets substituted by the Treaty of Lisbon (Changes in Terminology) Order 2011, SI 2011/1043, art 4(1), subject to transitional provisions contained in art 3(3) thereof.

See the Harmonisation Directive 2008/95/EC, Art 4(1), (2), (4), (5), at **[5.558]**.

Transitional provisions and savings: the European Union Trade Mark Regulations 2016, SI 2016/299, regs 13,14 (in force on 6 April 2016) provide as follows:

13 Transitional Provisions

(1) Anything done or having effect as if done under, for the purposes of, or in reliance on the old Regulation or a provision of the old Regulation has effect, so far as necessary for continuing its effect after the coming into force of these Regulations, as if done under, for the purposes of, or in reliance on the current Regulation or the corresponding provision of that Regulation.

(2) In this regulation—

"the old Regulation" means Council Regulation (EC) No 40/94 of 20th December 1993 on the Community Trade Mark;

"the current Regulation" means Council Regulation (EC) No 207/2009 of 26th February 2009 on the European Union Trade Mark.

14 Saving provision

Subject to the amendments made by regulations 6 to 12, any regulations made under section 52 of the 1994 Act which have effect immediately before the coming into force of these Regulations have effect after then as if made under that section as amended by these Regulations.".

[5.6]

6 Meaning of "earlier trade mark"

(1) In this Act an "earlier trade mark" means—

(a) a registered trade mark, international trade mark (UK)[, [European Union] trade mark or international trade mark (EC)] which has a date of application for registration earlier than that of the trade mark in question, taking account (where appropriate) of the priorities claimed in respect of the trade marks,

[(b) a [European Union] trade mark or international trade mark (EC) which has a valid claim to seniority from an earlier registered trade mark or international trade mark (UK),

(ba) a registered trade mark or international trade mark (UK) which—

(i) has been converted from a [European Union] trade mark or international trade mark (EC) which itself had a valid claim to seniority within paragraph (b) from an earlier trade mark, and

(ii) accordingly has the same claim to seniority, or]

(c) a trade mark which, at the date of application for registration of the trade mark in question or (where appropriate) of the priority claimed in respect of the application, was entitled to protection under the Paris Convention [or the WTO agreement] as a well known trade mark.

(2) References in this Act to an earlier trade mark include a trade mark in respect of which an application for registration has been made and which, if registered, would be an earlier trade mark by virtue of subsection 1(a) or (b), subject to its being so registered.

(3) A trade mark within subsection (1)(a) or (b) whose registration expires shall continue to be taken into account in determining the registrability of a later mark for a period of one year after the expiry unless the registrar is satisfied that there was no *bona fide* use of the mark during the two years immediately preceding the expiry.

NOTES

Sub-s (1): words in first (outer) pair of square brackets in para (a) substituted and paras (b), (ba) substituted for original para (b) by the Trade Marks (International Registrations Designating the European Community, etc) Regulations 2004, SI 2004/2332, regs 2, 4; words in second (inner) pair of square brackets in para (a) and words in square brackets in paras (b), (ba) substituted by the European Union Trade Mark Regulations 2016, SI 2016/299, reg 15, Schedule, para 1, subject to transitional provisions and savings as noted to s 5 at **[5.5]**; words in square brackets in para (c) inserted by the Patents and Trade Marks (World Trade Organisation) Regulations 1999, SI 1999/1899, reg 13(1).

See the Harmonisation Directive 2008/95/EC, Art 4(2), (4), at **[5.558]**.

[5.7]

[6A Raising of relative grounds in opposition proceedings in case of non-use

(1) This section applies where—

(a) an application for registration of a trade mark has been published,

(b) there is an earlier trade mark [of a kind falling within section 6(1)(a), (b) or (ba)] in relation to which the conditions set out in section 5(1), (2) or (3) obtain, and

(c) the registration procedure for the earlier trade mark was completed before the start of the period of five years ending with the date of publication.

(2) In opposition proceedings, the registrar shall not refuse to register the trade mark by reason of the earlier trade mark unless the use conditions are met.

(3) The use conditions are met if—

(a) within the period of five years ending with the date of publication of the application the earlier trade mark has been put to genuine use in the United Kingdom by the proprietor or with his consent in relation to the goods or services for which it is registered, or

(b) the earlier trade mark has not been so used, but there are proper reasons for non-use.

(4) For these purposes—

(a) use of a trade mark includes use in a form differing in elements which do not alter the distinctive character of the mark in the form in which it was registered, and

(b) use in the United Kingdom includes affixing the trade mark to goods or to the packaging of goods in the United Kingdom solely for export purposes.

(5) In relation to a [European Union] trade mark [or international trade mark (EC)], any reference in subsection (3) or (4) to the United Kingdom shall be construed as a reference to the [European Union].

(6) Where an earlier trade mark satisfies the use conditions in respect of some only of the goods or services for which it is registered, it shall be treated for the purposes of this section as if it were registered only in respect of those goods or services.

(7) Nothing in this section affects—

(a) the refusal of registration on the grounds mentioned in section 3 (absolute grounds for refusal) or section 5(4)(relative grounds of refusal on the basis of an earlier right), or

(b) the making of an application for a declaration of invalidity under section 47(2) (application on relative grounds where no consent to registration).]

NOTES

Inserted by the Trade Marks (Proof of Use, etc) Regulations 2004, SI 2004/946, regs 3, 4, except in respect of any application for the registration of a trade mark published before 5 May 2004.

Sub-s (1): words in square brackets in para (b) inserted by the Trade Marks (Earlier Trade Marks) Regulations 2008, SI 2008/1067, regs 3, 4(1), (2), subject to transitional provisions in reg 6 thereof.

Sub-s (5): words in first pair of square brackets substituted by the European Union Trade Mark Regulations 2016, SI 2016/299, reg 15, Schedule, para 1, subject to transitional provisions and savings as noted to s 5 at **[5.5]**; words in second pair of square brackets inserted by SI 2008/1067, regs 3, 4(1), (3); words in third pair of square brackets substituted by the Treaty of Lisbon (Changes in Terminology) Order 2011, SI 2011/1043, art 4(1), subject to transitional provisions contained in art 3(3) thereof.

[5.8]

7 Raising of relative grounds in case of honest concurrent use

(1) This section applies where on an application for the registration of a trade mark it appears to the registrar—

(a) that there is an earlier trade mark in relation to which the conditions set out in section 5(1), (2) or (3) obtain, or

(b) that there is an earlier right in relation to which the condition set out in section 5(4) is satisfied,

but the applicant shows to the satisfaction of the registrar that there has been honest concurrent use of the trade mark for which registration is sought.

(2) In that case the registrar shall not refuse the application by reason of the earlier trade mark or other earlier right unless objection on that ground is raised in opposition proceedings by the proprietor of that earlier trade mark or other earlier right.

(3) For the purposes of this section "honest concurrent use" means such use in the United Kingdom, by the applicant or with his consent, as would formerly have amounted to honest concurrent use for the purposes of section 12(2) of the Trade Marks Act 1938.

(4) Nothing in this section affects—

(a) the refusal of registration on the grounds mentioned in section 3 (absolute grounds for refusal), or

(b) the making of an application for a declaration of invalidity under section 47(2) (application on relative grounds where no consent to registration).

(5) This section does not apply when there is an order in force under section 8 below.

NOTES

Trade Marks Act 1938: repealed by s 106(2) of, and Sch 5 to, this Act.

[5.9]

8 Power to require that relative grounds be raised in opposition proceedings

(1) The Secretary of State may by order provide that in any case a trade mark shall not be refused registration on a ground mentioned in section 5 (relative grounds for refusal) unless objection on that ground is raised in opposition proceedings by the proprietor of the earlier trade mark or other earlier right.

(2) The order may make such consequential provision as appears to the Secretary of State appropriate—

(a) with respect to the carrying out by the registrar of searches of earlier trade marks, and

(b) as to the persons by whom an application for a declaration of invalidity may be made on the grounds specified in section 47(2) (relative grounds).

(3) An order making such provision as is mentioned in subsection (2)(a) may direct that so much of section 37 (examination of application) as requires a search to be carried out shall cease to have effect.

(4) An order making such provision as is mentioned in subsection (2)(b) may provide that so much of section 47(3) as provides that any person may make an application for a declaration of invalidity shall have effect subject to the provisions of the order.

(5) An order under this section shall be made by statutory instrument, and no order shall be made unless a draft of it has been laid before and approved by a resolution of each House of Parliament.

No such draft of an order making such provision as is mentioned in subsection (1) shall be laid before Parliament until after the end of the period of ten years beginning with the day on which applications for Community trade marks may first be filed in pursuance of [Council Regulation (EC) No 40/94 of 20th December 1993 on the Community trade mark].

(6) An order under this section may contain such transitional provisions as appear to the Secretary of State to be appropriate.

NOTES

Sub-s (5): words in square brackets substituted by the European Union Trade Mark Regulations 2016, SI 2016/299, reg 15, Schedule, para 2, subject to transitional provisions and savings as noted to s 5 at **[5.5]**.

Orders: the Trade Marks (Relative Grounds) Order 2007, SI 2007/1976, at **[5.141]**.

Effects of registered trade mark

[5.10]

9 Rights conferred by registered trade mark

(1) The proprietor of a registered trade mark has exclusive rights in the trade mark which are infringed by use of the trade mark in the United Kingdom without his consent.

The acts amounting to infringement, if done without the consent of the proprietor, are specified in section 10.

(2) References in this Act to the infringement of a registered trade mark are to any such infringement of the rights of the proprietor.

(3) The rights of the proprietor have effect from the date of registration (which in accordance with section 40(3) is the date of filing of the application for registration):

Provided that—

(a) no infringement proceedings may be begun before the date on which the trade mark is in fact registered; and

(b) no offence under section 92 (unauthorised use of trade mark, &c in relation to goods) is committed by anything done before the date of publication of the registration.

NOTES

See the Harmonisation Directive 2008/95/EC, Art 5(1), at **[5.559]**.

[5.11]

10 Infringement of registered trade mark

(1) A person infringes a registered trade mark if he uses in the course of trade a sign which is identical with the trade mark in relation to goods or services which are identical with those for which it is registered.

(2) A person infringes a registered trade mark if he uses in the course of trade a sign where because—

(a) the sign is identical with the trade mark and is used in relation to goods or services similar to those for which the trade mark is registered, or

(b) the sign is similar to the trade mark and is used in relation to goods or services identical with or similar to those for which the trade mark is registered,

there exists a likelihood of confusion on the part of the public, which includes the likelihood of association with the trade mark.

(3) A person infringes a registered trade mark if he uses in the course of trade[, in relation to goods or services,] a sign which—

(a) is identical with or similar to the trade mark, . . .

(b) . . .

where the trade mark has a reputation in the United Kingdom and the use of the sign, being without due cause, takes unfair advantage of, or is detrimental to, the distinctive character or the repute of the trade mark.

(4) For the purposes of this section a person uses a sign if, in particular, he—

(a) affixes it to goods or the packaging thereof;

(b) offers or exposes goods for sale, puts them on the market or stocks them for those purposes under the sign, or offers or supplies services under the sign;

(c) imports or exports goods under the sign; or
(d) uses the sign on business papers or in advertising.

(5) A person who applies a registered trade mark to material intended to be used for labelling or packaging goods, as a business paper, or for advertising goods or services, shall be treated as a party to any use of the material which infringes the registered trade mark if when he applied the mark he knew or had reason to believe that the application of the mark was not duly authorised by the proprietor or a licensee.

(6) Nothing in the preceding provisions of this section shall be construed as preventing the use of a registered trade mark by any person for the purpose of identifying goods or services as those of the proprietor or a licensee.

But any such use otherwise than in accordance with honest practices in industrial or commercial matters shall be treated as infringing the registered trade mark if the use without due cause takes unfair advantage of, or is detrimental to, the distinctive character or repute of the trade mark.

NOTES

Sub-s (3): words in square brackets inserted and words omitted repealed by the Trade Marks (Proof of Use, etc) Regulations 2004, SI 2004/946, regs 3, 7(2).

See the Harmonisation Directive 2008/95/EC, Art 5(1)–(3), (5), at **[5.559]**.

[5.12]

11 Limits on effect of registered trade mark

(1) A registered trade mark is not infringed by the use of another registered trade mark in relation to goods or services for which the latter is registered (but see section 47(6) (effect of declaration of invalidity of registration)).

(2) A registered trade mark is not infringed by—
(a) the use by a person of his own name or address,
(b) the use of indications concerning the kind, quality, quantity, intended purpose, value, geographical origin, the time of production of goods or of rendering of services, or other characteristics of goods or services, or
(c) the use of the trade mark where it is necessary to indicate the intended purpose of a product or service (in particular, as accessories or spare parts),

provided the use is in accordance with honest practices in industrial or commercial matters.

(3) A registered trade mark is not infringed by the use in the course of trade in a particular locality of an earlier right which applies only in that locality.

For this purpose an "earlier right" means an unregistered trade mark or other sign continuously used in relation to goods or services by a person or a predecessor in title of his from a date prior to whichever is the earlier of—
(a) the use of the first-mentioned trade mark in relation to those goods or services by the proprietor or a predecessor in title of his, or
(b) the registration of the first-mentioned trade mark in respect of those goods or services in the name of the proprietor or a predecessor in title of his;

and an earlier right shall be regarded as applying in a locality if, or to the extent that, its use in that locality is protected by virtue of any rule of law (in particular, the law of passing off).

NOTES

See the Harmonisation Directive 2008/95/EC, Art 6, at **[5.560]**.

[5.13]

12 Exhaustion of rights conferred by registered trade mark

(1) A registered trade mark is not infringed by the use of the trade mark in relation to goods which have been put on the market in the European Economic Area under that trade mark by the proprietor or with his consent.

(2) Subsection (1) does not apply where there exist legitimate reasons for the proprietor to oppose further dealings in the goods (in particular, where the condition of the goods has been changed or impaired after they have been put on the market).

NOTES

See the Harmonisation Directive 2008/95/EC, Art 7, at **[5.561]**.

[5.14]

13 Registration subject to disclaimer or limitation

(1) An applicant for registration of a trade mark, or the proprietor of a registered trade mark, may—
(a) disclaim any right to the exclusive use of any specified element of the trade mark, or
(b) agree that the rights conferred by the registration shall be subject to a specified territorial or other limitation;

and where the registration of a trade mark is subject to a disclaimer or limitation, the rights conferred by section 9 (rights conferred by registered trade mark) are restricted accordingly.

(2) Provision shall be made by rules as to the publication and entry in the register of a disclaimer or limitation.

NOTES

Rules: the Trade Marks Rules 2008, SI 2008/1797, at **[5.146]**.

Infringement proceedings

[5.15]

14 Action for infringement

(1) An infringement of a registered trade mark is actionable by the proprietor of the trade mark.

(2) In an action for infringement all such relief by way of damages, injunctions, accounts or otherwise is available to him as is available in respect of the infringement of any other property right.

NOTES

See the Harmonisation Directive 2008/95/EC, Art 5(1), at **[5.559]**.

[5.16]

15 Order for erasure, &c of offending sign

(1) Where a person is found to have infringed a registered trade mark, the court may make an order requiring him—

(a) to cause the offending sign to be erased, removed or obliterated from any infringing goods, material or articles in his possession, custody or control, or

(b) if it is not reasonably practicable for the offending sign to be erased, removed or obliterated, to secure the destruction of the infringing goods, material or articles in question.

(2) If an order under subsection (1) is not complied with, or it appears to the court likely that such an order would not be complied with, the court may order that the infringing goods, material or articles be delivered to such person as the court may direct for erasure, removal or obliteration of the sign, or for destruction, as the case may be.

[5.17]

16 Order for delivery up of infringing goods, material or articles

(1) The proprietor of a registered trade mark may apply to the court for an order for the delivery up to him, or such other person as the court may direct, of any infringing goods, material or articles which a person has in his possession, custody or control in the course of a business.

(2) An application shall not be made after the end of the period specified in section 18 (period after which remedy of delivery up not available); and no order shall be made unless the court also makes, or it appears to the court that there are grounds for making, an order under section 19 (order as to disposal of infringing goods, &c).

(3) A person to whom any infringing goods, material or articles are delivered up in pursuance of an order under this section shall, if an order under section 19 is not made, retain them pending the making of an order, or the decision not to make an order, under that section.

(4) Nothing in this section affects any other power of the court.

[5.18]

17 Meaning of "infringing goods, material or articles"

(1) In this Act the expressions "infringing goods", "infringing material" and "infringing articles" shall be construed as follows.

(2) Goods are "infringing goods", in relation to a registered trade mark, if they or their packaging bear a sign identical or similar to that mark and—

(a) the application of the sign to the goods or their packaging was an infringement of the registered trade mark, or

(b) the goods are proposed to be imported into the United Kingdom and the application of the sign in the United Kingdom to them or their packaging would be an infringement of the registered trade mark, or

(c) the sign has otherwise been used in relation to the goods in such a way as to infringe the registered trade mark.

(3) Nothing in subsection (2) shall be construed as affecting the importation of goods which may lawfully be imported into the United Kingdom by virtue of an enforceable [EU] right.

(4) Material is "infringing material", in relation to a registered trade mark if it bears a sign identical or similar to that mark and either—

(a) it is used for labelling or packaging goods, as a business paper, or for advertising goods or services, in such a way as to infringe the registered trade mark, or

(b) it is intended to be so used and such use would infringe the registered trade mark.

(5) "Infringing articles", in relation to a registered trade mark, means articles—

(a) which are specifically designed or adapted for making copies of a sign identical or similar to that mark, and

(b) which a person has in his possession, custody or control, knowing or having reason to believe that they have been or are to be used to produce infringing goods or material.

NOTES

Sub-s (3): reference in square brackets substituted by the Treaty of Lisbon (Changes in Terminology) Order 2011, SI 2011/1043, art 6(1)(f), subject to a transitional provision contained in art 3(3) thereof.

[5.19]

18 Period after which remedy of delivery up not available

(1) An application for an order under section 16 (order for delivery up of infringing goods, material or articles) may not be made after the end of the period of six years from—

(a) in the case of infringing goods, the date on which the trade mark was applied to the goods or their packaging,

(b) in the case of infringing material, the date on which the trade mark was applied to the material, or

(c) in the case of infringing articles, the date on which they were made,

except as mentioned in the following provisions.

(2) If during the whole or part of that period the proprietor of the registered trade mark—

(a) is under a disability, or

(b) is prevented by fraud or concealment from discovering the facts entitling him to apply for an order,

an application may be made at any time before the end of the period of six years from the date on which he ceased to be under a disability or, as the case may be, could with reasonable diligence have discovered those facts.

(3) In subsection (2) "disability"—

(a) in England and Wales, has the same meaning as in the Limitation Act 1980;

(b) in Scotland, means legal disability within the meaning of the Prescription and Limitation (Scotland) Act 1973;

(c) in Northern Ireland, has the same meaning as in the Limitation (Northern Ireland) Order 1989.

[5.20]

19 Order as to disposal of infringing goods, material or articles

(1) Where infringing goods, material or articles have been delivered up in pursuance of an order under section 16, an application may be made to the court—

(a) for an order that they be destroyed or forfeited to such person as the court may think fit, or

(b) for a decision that no such order should be made.

(2) In considering what order (if any) should be made, the court shall consider whether other remedies available in an action for infringement of the registered trade mark would be adequate to compensate the proprietor and any licensee and protect their interests.

(3) Provision shall be made by rules of court as to the service of notice on persons having an interest in the goods, material or articles, and any such person is entitled—

(a) to appear in proceedings for an order under this section, whether or not he was served with notice, and

(b) to appeal against any order made, whether or not he appeared;

and an order shall not take effect until the end of the period within which notice of an appeal may be given or, if before the end of that period notice of appeal is duly given, until the final determination or abandonment of the proceedings on the appeal.

(4) Where there is more than one person interested in the goods, material or articles, the court shall make such order as it thinks just.

(5) If the court decides that no order should be made under this section, the person in whose possession, custody or control the goods, material or articles were before being delivered up is entitled to their return.

(6) References in this section to a person having an interest in goods, material or articles include any person in whose favour an order could be made—

[(a) under this section (including that section as applied by regulation 4 of the Community Trade Mark Regulations 2006 (SI 2006/1027));

(b) under section 24D of the Registered Designs Act 1949;

(c) under section 114, 204 or 231 of the Copyright, Designs and Patents Act 1988; or

(d) under regulation 1C of the Community Design Regulations 2005 (SI 2005/2339).]

NOTES

Sub-s (6): paras (a)–(d) substituted by the Intellectual Property (Enforcement, etc) Regulations 2006, SI 2006/1028, reg 2(2), Sch 2, paras 15, 16.

[5.21]

20 Jurisdiction of sheriff court or county court in Northern Ireland

Proceedings for an order under section 16 (order for delivery up of infringing goods, material or articles) or section 19 (order as to disposal of infringing goods, &c) may be brought—

(a) in the sheriff court in Scotland, or

(b) in a county court in Northern Ireland.

This docs not affect the jurisdiction of the Court of Session or the High Court in Northern Ireland.

[5.22]

21 Remedy for groundless threats of infringement proceedings

(1) Where a person threatens another with proceedings for infringement of a registered trade mark other than—

(a) the application of the mark to goods or their packaging,

(b) the importation of goods to which, or to the packaging of which, the mark has been applied, or

(c) the supply of services under the mark,

any person aggrieved may bring proceedings for relief under this section.

(2) The relief which may be applied for is any of the following—

(a) a declaration that the threats are unjustifiable,

(b) an injunction against the continuance of the threats,

(c) damages in respect of any loss he has sustained by the threats;

and the plaintiff is entitled to such relief unless the defendant shows that the acts in respect of which proceedings were threatened constitute (or if done would constitute) an infringement of the registered trade mark concerned.

(3) If that is shown by the defendant, the plaintiff is nevertheless entitled to relief if he shows that the registration of the trade mark is invalid or liable to be revoked in a relevant respect.

(4) The mere notification that a trade mark is registered, or that an application for registration has been made, does not constitute a threat of proceedings for the purposes of this section.

NOTES

Section 21 is substituted (by new ss 21, 21A–21F and preceding heading) by the Intellectual Property (Unjustified Threats) Act 2017, s 2(1), (2), as from a day to be appointed, as follows—

"Unjustified threats

21 Threats of infringement proceedings

(1) A communication contains a "threat of infringement proceedings" if a reasonable person in the position of a recipient would understand from the communication that—

(a) a registered trade mark exists, and

(b) a person intends to bring proceedings (whether in a court in the United Kingdom or elsewhere) against another person for infringement of the registered trade mark by—

(i) an act done in the United Kingdom, or

(ii) an act which, if done, would be done in the United Kingdom.

(2) References in this section and in section 21C to a "recipient" include, in the case of a communication directed to the public or a section of the public, references to a person to whom the communication is directed.

21A Actionable threats

(1) Subject to subsections (2) to (6), a threat of infringement proceedings made by any person is actionable by any person aggrieved by the threat.

(2) A threat of infringement proceedings is not actionable if the infringement is alleged to consist of—

(a) applying, or causing another person to apply, a sign to goods or their packaging,

(b) importing, for disposal, goods to which, or to the packaging of which, a sign has been applied, or

(c) supplying services under a sign.

(3) A threat of infringement proceedings is not actionable if the infringement is alleged to consist of an act which, if done, would constitute an infringement of a kind mentioned in subsection (2)(a), (b) or (c).

(4) A threat of infringement proceedings is not actionable if the threat—

(a) is made to a person who has done, or intends to do, an act mentioned in subsection (2)(a) or (b) in relation to goods or their packaging, and

(b) is a threat of proceedings for an infringement alleged to consist of doing anything else in relation to those goods or their packaging.

(5) A threat of infringement proceedings is not actionable if the threat—

(a) is made to a person who has done, or intends to do, an act mentioned in subsection (2)(c) in relation to services, and

(b) is a threat of proceedings for an infringement alleged to consist of doing anything else in relation to those services.

(6) A threat of infringement proceedings which is not an express threat is not actionable if it is contained in a permitted communication.

(7) In sections 21C and 21D "an actionable threat" means a threat of infringement proceedings that is actionable in accordance with this section.

21B Permitted communications

(1) For the purposes of section 21A(6), a communication containing a threat of infringement proceedings is a "permitted communication" if—

(a) the communication, so far as it contains information that relates to the threat, is made for a permitted purpose;

(b) all of the information that relates to the threat is information that—

(i) is necessary for that purpose (see subsection (5)(a) to (c) for some examples of necessary information), and

(ii) the person making the communication reasonably believes is true.

(2) Each of the following is a "permitted purpose"—

(a) giving notice that a registered trade mark exists;

(b) discovering whether, or by whom, a registered trade mark has been infringed by an act mentioned in section 21A(2)(a), (b) or (c);
(c) giving notice that a person has a right in or under a registered trade mark, where another person's awareness of the right is relevant to any proceedings that may be brought in respect of the registered trade mark.

(3) The court may, having regard to the nature of the purposes listed in subsection (2)(a) to (c), treat any other purpose as a "permitted purpose" if it considers that it is in the interests of justice to do so.

(4) But the following may not be treated as a "permitted purpose"—
(a) requesting a person to cease using, in the course of trade, a sign in relation to goods or services,
(b) requesting a person to deliver up or destroy goods, or
(c) requesting a person to give an undertaking relating to the use of a sign in relation to goods or services.

(5) If any of the following information is included in a communication made for a permitted purpose, it is information that is "necessary for that purpose" (see subsection (1)(b)(i))—
(a) a statement that a registered trade mark exists and is in force or that an application for the registration of a trade mark has been made;
(b) details of the registered trade mark, or of a right in or under the registered trade mark, which—
(i) are accurate in all material respects, and
(ii) are not misleading in any material respect; and
(c) information enabling the identification of the goods or their packaging, or the services, in relation to which it is alleged that the use of a sign constitutes an infringement of the registered trade mark.

21C Remedies and defences

(1) Proceedings in respect of an actionable threat may be brought against the person who made the threat for—
(a) a declaration that the threat is unjustified;
(b) an injunction against the continuance of the threat;
(c) damages in respect of any loss sustained by the aggrieved person by reason of the threat.

(2) It is a defence for the person who made the threat to show that the act in respect of which proceedings were threatened constitutes (or if done would constitute) an infringement of the registered trade mark.

(3) It is a defence for the person who made the threat to show—
(a) that, despite having taken reasonable steps, the person has not identified anyone who has done an act mentioned in section 21A(2)(a), (b) or (c) in relation to the goods or their packaging or the services which are the subject of the threat, and
(b) that the person notified the recipient, before or at the time of making the threat, of the steps taken.

21D Professional advisers

(1) Proceedings in respect of an actionable threat may not be brought against a professional adviser (or any person vicariously liable for the actions of that professional adviser) if the conditions in subsection (3) are met.

(2) In this section "professional adviser" means a person who, in relation to the making of the communication containing the threat—
(a) is acting in a professional capacity in providing legal services or the services of a trade mark attorney or a patent attorney, and
(b) is regulated in the provision of legal services, or the services of a trade mark attorney or a patent attorney, by one or more regulatory bodies (whether through membership of a regulatory body, the issue of a licence to practise or any other means).

(3) The conditions are that—
(a) in making the communication the professional adviser is acting on the instructions of another person, and
(b) when the communication is made the professional adviser identifies the person on whose instructions the adviser is acting.

(4) This section does not affect any liability of the person on whose instructions the professional adviser is acting.

(5) It is for a person asserting that subsection (1) applies to prove (if required) that at the material time—
(a) the person concerned was acting as a professional adviser, and
(b) the conditions in subsection (3) were met.

21E Supplementary: pending registration

(1) In sections 21 and 21B references to a registered trade mark include references to a trade mark in respect of which an application for registration has been published under section 38.

(2) Where the threat of infringement proceedings is made after an application for registration has been published (but before registration) the reference in section 21C(2) to "the registered trade mark" is to be treated as a reference to the trade mark registered in pursuance of that application.

21F Supplementary: proceedings for delivery up etc

In section 21(1)(b) the reference to proceedings for infringement of a registered trade mark includes a reference to—
(a) proceedings for an order under section 16 (order for delivery up of infringing goods, material or articles), and
(b) proceedings for an order under section 19 (order as to disposal of infringing goods, material or articles).".

Registered trade mark as object of property

[5.23]

22 Nature of registered trade mark

A registered trade mark is personal property (in Scotland, incorporeal moveable property).

[5.24]

23 Co-ownership of registered trade mark

(1) Where a registered trade mark is granted to two or more persons jointly, each of them is entitled, subject to any agreement to the contrary, to an equal undivided share in the registered trade mark.

(2) The following provisions apply where two or more persons are co-proprietors of a registered trade mark, by virtue of subsection (1) or otherwise.

(3) Subject to any agreement to the contrary, each co-proprietor is entitled, by himself or his agents, to do for his own benefit and without the consent of or the need to account to the other or others, any act which would otherwise amount to an infringement of the registered trade mark.

(4) One co-proprietor may not without the consent of the other or others—

(a) grant a licence to use the registered trade mark, or

(b) assign or charge his share in the registered trade mark (or, in Scotland, cause or permit security to be granted over it).

(5) Infringement proceedings may be brought by any co-proprietor, but he may not, without the leave of the court, proceed with the action unless the other, or each of the others, is either joined as a plaintiff or added as a defendant.

A co-proprietor who is thus added as a defendant shall not be made liable for any costs in the action unless he takes part in the proceedings.

Nothing in this subsection affects the granting of interlocutory relief on the application of a single co-proprietor.

(6) Nothing in this section affects the mutual rights and obligations of trustees or personal representatives, or their rights and obligations as such.

[5.25]

24 Assignment, &c of registered trade mark

(1) A registered trade mark is transmissible by assignment, testamentary disposition or operation of law in the same way as other personal or moveable property.

It is so transmissible either in connection with the goodwill of a business or independently.

(2) An assignment or other transmission of a registered trade mark may be partial, that is, limited so as to apply—

(a) in relation to some but not all of the goods or services for which the trade mark is registered, or

(b) in relation to use of the trade mark in a particular manner or a particular locality.

(3) An assignment of a registered trade mark, or an assent relating to a registered trade mark, is not effective unless it is in writing signed by or on behalf of the assignor or, as the case may be, a personal representative.

Except in Scotland, this requirement may be satisfied in a case where the assignor or personal representative is a body corporate by the affixing of its seal.

(4) The above provisions apply to assignment by way of security as in relation to any other assignment.

(5) A registered trade mark may be the subject of a charge (in Scotland, security) in the same way as other personal or moveable property.

(6) Nothing in this Act shall be construed as affecting the assignment or other transmission of an unregistered trade mark as part of the goodwill of a business.

[5.26]

25 Registration of transactions affecting registered trade mark

(1) On application being made to the registrar by—

(a) a person claiming to be entitled to an interest in or under a registered trade mark by virtue of a registrable transaction, or

(b) any other person claiming to be affected by such a transaction,

the prescribed particulars of the transaction shall be entered in the register.

(2) The following are registrable transactions—

(a) an assignment of a registered trade mark or any right in it;

(b) the grant of a licence under a registered trade mark;

(c) the granting of any security interest (whether fixed or floating) over a registered trade mark or any right in or under it;

(d) the making by personal representatives of an assent in relation to a registered trade mark or any right in or under it;

(e) an order of a court or other competent authority transferring a registered trade mark or any right in or under it.

(3) Until an application has been made for registration of the prescribed particulars of a registrable transaction—

(a) the transaction is ineffective as against a person acquiring a conflicting interest in or under the registered trade mark in ignorance of it, and

(b) a person claiming to be a licensee by virtue of the transaction does not have the protection of section 30 or 31 (rights and remedies of licensee in relation to infringement).

(4) Where a person becomes the proprietor or a licensee of a registered trade mark by virtue of a registrable transaction [and the mark is infringed before the prescribed particulars of the transaction are registered, in proceedings for such an infringement, the court shall not award him costs unless—

(a) an application for registration of the prescribed particulars of the transaction is made before the end of the period of six months beginning with its date, or

(b) the court is satisfied that it was not practicable for such an application to be made before the end of that period and that an application was made as soon as practicable thereafter.]

(5) Provision may be made by rules as to—

(a) the amendment of registered particulars relating to a licence so as to reflect any alteration of the terms of the licence, and
(b) the removal of such particulars from the register—
(i) where it appears from the registered particulars that the licence was granted for a fixed period and that period has expired, or
(ii) where no such period is indicated and, after such period as may be prescribed, the registrar has notified the parties of his intention to remove the particulars from the register.

(6) Provision may also be made by rules as to the amendment or removal from the register of particulars relating to a security interest on the application of, or with the consent of, the person entitled to the benefit of that interest.

NOTES

Sub-s (4): words in square brackets substituted by the Intellectual Property (Enforcement, etc) Regulations 2006, SI 2006/1028, reg 2(2), Sch 2, paras 15, 17.

Rules: the Trade Marks Rules 2008, SI 2008/1797, at **[5.146]**.

[5.27]
26 Trusts and equities

(1) No notice of any trust (express, implied or constructive) shall be entered in the register; and the registrar shall not be affected by any such notice.

(2) Subject to the provisions of this Act, equities (in Scotland, rights) in respect of a registered trade mark may be enforced in like manner as in respect of other personal or moveable property.

[5.28]
27 Application for registration of trade mark as an object of property

(1) The provisions of sections 22 to 26 (which relate to a registered trade mark as an object of property) apply, with the necessary modifications, in relation to an application for the registration of a trade mark as in relation to a registered trade mark.

(2) In section 23 (co-ownership of registered trade mark) as it applies in relation to an application for registration the reference in subsection (1) to the granting of the registration shall be construed as a reference to the making of the application.

(3) In section 25 (registration of transactions affecting registered trade marks) as it applies in relation to a transaction affecting an application for the registration of a trade mark, the references to the entry of particulars in the register, and to the making of an application to register particulars, shall be construed as references to the giving of notice to the registrar of those particulars.

Licensing

[5.29]
28 Licensing of registered trade mark

(1) A licence to use a registered trade mark may be general or limited.

A limited licence may, in particular, apply—
(a) in relation to some but not all of the goods or services for which the trade mark is registered, or
(b) in relation to use of the trade mark in a particular manner or a particular locality.

(2) A licence is not effective unless it is in writing signed by or on behalf of the grantor.

Except in Scotland, this requirement may be satisfied in a case where the grantor is a body corporate by the affixing of its seal.

(3) Unless the licence provides otherwise, it is binding on a successor in title to the grantor's interest.

References in this Act to doing anything with, or without, the consent of the proprietor of a registered trade mark shall be construed accordingly.

(4) Where the licence so provides, a sub-licence may be granted by the licensee; and references in this Act to a licence or licensee include a sub-licence or sub-licensee.

NOTES

See the Harmonisation Directive 2008/95/EC, Art 8(1), at **[5.562]**.

[5.30]
29 Exclusive licences

(1) In this Act an "exclusive licence" means a licence (whether general or limited) authorising the licensee to the exclusion of all other persons, including the person granting the licence, to use a registered trade mark in the manner authorised by the licence.

The expression "exclusive licensee" shall be construed accordingly.

(2) An exclusive licensee has the same rights against a successor in title who is bound by the licence as he has against the person granting the licence.

[5.31]

30 General provisions as to rights of licensees in case of infringement

(1) This section has effect with respect to the rights of a licensee in relation to infringement of a registered trade mark.

The provisions of this section do not apply where or to the extent that, by virtue of section 31(1) below (exclusive licensee having rights and remedies of assignee), the licensee has a right to bring proceedings in his own name.

(2) A licensee is entitled, unless his licence, or any licence through which his interest is derived, provides otherwise, to call on the proprietor of the registered trade mark to take infringement proceedings in respect of any matter which affects his interests.

(3) If the proprietor—

(a) refuses to do so, or

(b) fails to do so within two months after being called upon,

the licensee may bring the proceedings in his own name as if he were the proprietor.

(4) Where infringement proceedings are brought by a licensee by virtue of this section, the licensee may not, without the leave of the court, proceed with the action unless the proprietor is either joined as a plaintiff or added as a defendant.

This does not affect the granting of interlocutory relief on an application by a licensee alone.

(5) A proprietor who is added as a defendant as mentioned in subsection (4) shall not be made liable for any costs in the action unless he takes part in the proceedings.

(6) In infringement proceedings brought by the proprietor of a registered trade mark any loss suffered or likely to be suffered by licensees shall be taken into account; and the court may give such directions as it thinks fit as to the extent to which the plaintiff is to hold the proceeds of any pecuniary remedy on behalf of licensees.

(7) The provisions of this section apply in relation to an exclusive licensee if or to the extent that he has, by virtue of section 31(1), the rights and remedies of an assignee as if he were the proprietor of the registered trade mark.

[5.32]

31 Exclusive licensee having rights and remedies of assignee

(1) An exclusive licence may provide that the licensee shall have, to such extent as may be provided by the licence, the same rights and remedies in respect of matters occurring after the grant of the licence as if the licence had been an assignment.

Where or to the extent that such provision is made, the licensee is entitled, subject to the provisions of the licence and to the following provisions of this section, to bring infringement proceedings, against any person other than the proprietor, in his own name.

(2) Any such rights and remedies of an exclusive licensee are concurrent with those of the proprietor of the registered trade mark; and references to the proprietor of a registered trade mark in the provisions of this Act relating to infringement shall be construed accordingly.

(3) In an action brought by an exclusive licensee by virtue of this section a defendant may avail himself of any defence which would have been available to him if the action had been brought by the proprietor of the registered trade mark.

(4) Where proceedings for infringement of a registered trade mark brought by the proprietor or an exclusive licensee relate wholly or partly to an infringement in respect of which they have concurrent rights of action, the proprietor or, as the case may be, the exclusive licensee may not, without the leave of the court, proceed with the action unless the other is either joined as a plaintiff or added as a defendant.

This does not affect the granting of interlocutory relief on an application by a proprietor or exclusive licensee alone.

(5) A person who is added as a defendant as mentioned in subsection (4) shall not be made liable for any costs in the action unless he takes part in the proceedings.

(6) Where an action for infringement of a registered trade mark is brought which relates wholly or partly to an infringement in respect of which the proprietor and an exclusive licensee have or had concurrent rights of action—

(a) the court shall in assessing damages take into account—

(i) the terms of the licence, and

(ii) any pecuniary remedy already awarded or available to either of them in respect of the infringement;

(b) no account of profits shall be directed if an award of damages has been made, or an account of profits has been directed, in favour of the other of them in respect of the infringement; and

(c) the court shall if an account of profits is directed apportion the profits between them as the court considers just, subject to any agreement between them.

The provisions of this subsection apply whether or not the proprietor and the exclusive licensee are both parties to the action; and if they are not both parties the court may give such directions as it thinks fit as to the extent to which the party to the proceedings is to hold the proceeds of any pecuniary remedy on behalf of the other.

(7) The proprietor of a registered trade mark shall notify any exclusive licensee who has a concurrent right of action before applying for an order under section 16 (order for delivery up); and the court may on the application of the licensee make such order under that section as it thinks fit having regard to the terms of the licence.

(8) The provisions of subsections (4) to (7) above have effect subject to any agreement to the contrary between the exclusive licensee and the proprietor.

Application for registered trade mark

[5.33]

32 Application for registration

(1) An application for registration of a trade mark shall be made to the registrar.

(2) The application shall contain—

(a) a request for registration of a trade mark,

(b) the name and address of the applicant,

(c) a statement of the goods or services in relation to which it is sought to register the trade mark, and

(d) a representation of the trade mark.

(3) The application shall state that the trade mark is being used, by the applicant or with his consent, in relation to those goods or services, or that he has a *bona fide* intention that it should be so used.

(4) The application shall be subject to the payment of the application fee and such class fees as may be appropriate.

[5.34]

33 Date of filing

(1) The date of filing of an application for registration of a trade mark is the date on which documents containing everything required by section 32(2) are furnished to the registrar by the applicant.

If the documents are furnished on different days, the date of filing is the last of those days.

(2) References in this Act to the date of application for registration are to the date of filing of the application.

[5.35]

34 Classification of trade marks

(1) Goods and services shall be classified for the purposes of the registration of trade marks according to a prescribed system of classification.

(2) Any question arising as to the class within which any goods or services fall shall be determined by the registrar, whose decision shall be final.

NOTES

Rules: the Trade Marks Rules 2008, SI 2008/1797, at **[5.146]**.

Priority

[5.36]

35 Claim to priority of Convention application

(1) A person who has duly filed an application for protection of a trade mark in a Convention country (a "Convention application"), or his successor in title, has a right to priority, for the purposes of registering the same trade mark under this Act for some or all of the same goods or services, for a period of six months from the date of filing of the first such application.

(2) If the application for registration under this Act is made within that six-month period—

(a) the relevant date for the purposes of establishing which rights take precedence shall be the date of filing of the first Convention application, and

(b) the registrability of the trade mark shall not be affected by any use of the mark in the United Kingdom in the period between that date and the date of the application under this Act.

(3) Any filing which in a Convention country is equivalent to a regular national filing, under its domestic legislation or an international agreement, shall be treated as giving rise to the right of priority.

A "regular national filing" means a filing which is adequate to establish the date on which the application was filed in that country, whatever may be the subsequent fate of the application.

(4) A subsequent application concerning the same subject as the first Convention application, filed in the same Convention country, shall be considered the first Convention application (of which the filing date is the starting date of the period of priority), if at the time of the subsequent application—

(a) the previous application has been withdrawn, abandoned or refused, without having been laid open to public inspection and without leaving any rights outstanding, and

(b) it has not yet served as a basis for claiming a right of priority.

The previous application may not thereafter serve as a basis for claiming a right of priority.

(5) Provision may be made by rules as to the manner of claiming a right to priority on the basis of a Convention application.

(6) A right to priority arising as a result of a Convention application may be assigned or otherwise transmitted, either with the application or independently.

The reference in subsection (1) to the applicant's "successor in title" shall be construed accordingly.

NOTES

Rules: the Trade Marks Rules 2008, SI 2008/1797, at **[5.146]**.

[5.37]

36 Claim to priority from other relevant overseas application

(1) Her Majesty may by Order in Council make provision for conferring on a person who has duly filed an application for protection of a trade mark in—

(a) any of the Channel Islands or a colony, or

(b) a country or territory in relation to which Her Majesty's Government in the United Kingdom have entered into a treaty, convention, arrangement or engagement for the reciprocal protection of trade marks,

a right to priority, for the purpose of registering the same trade mark under this Act for some or all of the same goods or services, for a specified period from the date of filing of that application.

(2) An Order in Council under this section may make provision corresponding to that made by section 35 in relation to Convention countries or such other provision as appears to Her Majesty to be appropriate.

(3) A statutory instrument containing an Order in Council under this section shall be subject to annulment in pursuance of a resolution of either House of Parliament.

NOTES

Orders: the Trade Marks (Claims to Priority from Relevant Countries) Order 1994, SI 1994/2803.

Registration procedure

[5.38]

37 Examination of application

(1) The registrar shall examine whether an application for registration of a trade mark satisfies the requirements of this Act (including any requirements imposed by rules).

(2) For that purpose he shall carry out a search, to such extent as he considers necessary, of earlier trade marks.

(3) If it appears to the registrar that the requirements for registration are not met, he shall inform the applicant and give him an opportunity, within such period as the registrar may specify, to make representations or to amend the application.

(4) If the applicant fails to satisfy the registrar that those requirements are met, or to amend the application so as to meet them, or fails to respond before the end of the specified period, the registrar shall refuse to accept the application.

(5) If it appears to the registrar that the requirements for registration are met, he shall accept the application.

NOTES

Sub-s (2): repealed by the Trade Marks (Relative Grounds) Order 2007, SI 2007/1976, art 3, except in relation to an application for registration of a trade mark which was published before 1 October 2007: see art 6(1) of the 2007 Order at **[5.145]**.

[5.39]

38 Publication, opposition proceedings and observations

(1) When an application for registration has been accepted, the registrar shall cause the application to be published in the prescribed manner.

(2) Any person may, within the prescribed time from the date of the publication of the application, give notice to the registrar of opposition to the registration.

The notice shall be given in writing in the prescribed manner, and shall include a statement of the grounds of opposition.

(3) Where an application has been published, any person may, at any time before the registration of the trade mark, make observations in writing to the registrar as to whether the trade mark should be registered; and the registrar shall inform the applicant of any such observations.

A person who makes observations does not thereby become a party to the proceedings on the application.

NOTES

Rules: the Trade Marks Rules 2008, SI 2008/1797, at **[5.146]**.

[5.40]

39 Withdrawal, restriction or amendment of application

(1) The applicant may at any time withdraw his application or restrict the goods or services covered by the application.

If the application has been published, the withdrawal or restriction shall also be published.

(2) In other respects, an application may be amended, at the request of the applicant, only by correcting—

(a) the name or address of the applicant,

(b) errors of wording or of copying, or

(c) obvious mistakes,

and then only where the correction does not substantially affect the identity of the trade mark or extend the goods or services covered by the application.

(3) Provision shall be made by rules for the publication of any amendment which affects the representation of the trade mark, or the goods or services covered by the application, and for the making of objections by any person claiming to be affected by it.

NOTES

Rules: the Trade Marks Rules 2008, SI 2008/1797, at **[5.146]**.

[5.41]

40 Registration

(1) Where an application has been accepted and—

(a) no notice of opposition is given within the period referred to in section 38(2), or

(b) all opposition proceedings are withdrawn or decided in favour of the applicant,

the registrar shall register the trade mark, unless it appears to him having regard to matters coming to his notice [since the application was accepted that the registration requirements (other than those mentioned in section 5(1), (2) or (3)) were not met at that time.]

(2) A trade mark shall not be registered unless any fee prescribed for the registration is paid within the prescribed period.

If the fee is not paid within that period, the application shall be deemed to be withdrawn.

(3) A trade mark when registered shall be registered as of the date of filing of the application for registration; and that date shall be deemed for the purposes of this Act to be the date of registration.

(4) On the registration of a trade mark the registrar shall publish the registration in the prescribed manner and issue to the applicant a certificate of registration.

NOTES

Sub-s (1): words in square brackets substituted by the Trade Marks (Proof of Use, etc) Regulations 2004, SI 2004/946, regs 3, 5, except in respect of any application for the registration of a trade mark published before 5 May 2004.

Rules: the Trade Marks Rules 2008, SI 2008/1797, at **[5.146]**.

[5.42]

41 Registration: supplementary provisions

(1) Provision may be made by rules as to—

(a) the division of an application for the registration of a trade mark into several applications;

(b) the merging of separate applications or registrations;

(c) the registration of a series of trade marks.

(2) A series of trade marks means a number of trade marks which resemble each other as to their material particulars and differ only as to matters of a non-distinctive character not substantially affecting the identity of the trade mark.

(3) Rules under this section may include provision as to—

(a) the circumstances in which, and conditions subject to which, division, merger or registration of a series is permitted, and

(b) the purposes for which an application to which the rules apply is to be treated as a single application and those for which it is to be treated as a number of separate applications.

NOTES

Rules: the Trade Marks Rules 2008, SI 2008/1797, at **[5.146]**.

Duration, renewal and alteration of registered trade mark

[5.43]

42 Duration of registration

(1) A trade mark shall be registered for a period of ten years from the date of registration.

(2) Registration may be renewed in accordance with section 43 for further periods of ten years.

[5.44]

43 Renewal of registration

(1) The registration of a trade mark may be renewed at the request of the proprietor, subject to payment of a renewal fee.

(2) Provision shall be made by rules for the registrar to inform the proprietor of a registered trade mark, before the expiry of the registration, of the date of expiry and the manner in which the registration may be renewed.

(3) A request for renewal must be made, and the renewal fee paid, before the expiry of the registration.

Failing this, the request may be made and the fee paid within such further period (of not less than six months) as may be prescribed, in which case an additional renewal fee must also be paid within that period.

(4) Renewal shall take effect from the expiry of the previous registration.

(5) If the registration is not renewed in accordance with the above provisions, the registrar shall remove the trade mark from the register.

Provision may be made by rules for the restoration of the registration of a trade mark which has been removed from the register, subject to such conditions (if any) as may be prescribed.

(6) The renewal or restoration of the registration of a trade mark shall be published in the prescribed manner.

NOTES

Rules: the Trade Marks Rules 2008, SI 2008/1797, at **[5.146]**.

[5.45]

44 Alteration of registered trade mark

(1) A registered trade mark shall not be altered in the register, during the period of registration or on renewal.

(2) Nevertheless, the registrar may, at the request of the proprietor, allow the alteration of a registered trade mark where the mark includes the proprietor's name or address and the alteration is limited to alteration of that name or address and does not substantially affect the identity of the mark.

(3) Provision shall be made by rules for the publication of any such alteration and the making of objections by any person claiming to be affected by it.

NOTES

Rules: the Trade Marks Rules 2008, SI 2008/1797, at **[5.146]**.

Surrender, revocation and invalidity

[5.46]

45 Surrender of registered trade mark

(1) A registered trade mark may be surrendered by the proprietor in respect of some or all of the goods or services for which it is registered.

(2) Provision may be made by rules—

(a) as to the manner and effect of a surrender, and

(b) for protecting the interests of other persons having a right in the registered trade mark.

NOTES

Rules: the Trade Marks Rules 2008, SI 2008/1797, at **[5.146]**.

[5.47]

46 Revocation of registration

(1) The registration of a trade mark may be revoked on any of the following grounds—

(a) that within the period of five years following the date of completion of the registration procedure it has not been put to genuine use in the United Kingdom, by the proprietor or with his consent, in relation to the goods or services for which it is registered, and there are no proper reasons for non-use;

(b) that such use has been suspended for an uninterrupted period of five years, and there are no proper reasons for non-use;

(c) that, in consequence of acts or inactivity of the proprietor, it has become the common name in the trade for a product or service for which it is registered;

(d) that in consequence of the use made of it by the proprietor or with his consent in relation to the goods or services for which it is registered, it is liable to mislead the public, particularly as to the nature, quality or geographical origin of those goods or services.

(2) For the purposes of subsection (1) use of a trade mark includes use in a form differing in elements which do not alter the distinctive character of the mark in the form in which it was registered, and use in the United Kingdom includes affixing the trade mark to goods or to the packaging of goods in the United Kingdom solely for export purposes.

(3) The registration of a trade mark shall not be revoked on the ground mentioned in subsection (1)(a) or (b) if such use as is referred to in that paragraph is commenced or resumed after the expiry of the five year period and before the application for revocation is made:

Provided that, any such commencement or resumption of use after the expiry of the five year period but within the period of three months before the making of the application shall be disregarded unless preparations for the commencement or resumption began before the proprietor became aware that the application might be made.

(4) An application for revocation may be made by any person, and may be made either to the registrar or to the court, except that—

(a) if proceedings concerning the trade mark in question are pending in the court, the application must be made to the court; and

(b) if in any other case the application is made to the registrar, he may at any stage of the proceedings refer the application to the court.

(5) Where grounds for revocation exist in respect of only some of the goods or services for which the trade mark is registered, revocation shall relate to those goods or services only.

(6) Where the registration of a trade mark is revoked to any extent, the rights of the proprietor shall be deemed to have ceased to that extent as from—

(a) the date of the application for revocation, or

(b) if the registrar or court is satisfied that the grounds for revocation existed at an earlier date, that date.

NOTES

See the Harmonisation Directive 2008/95/EC, Arts 10(1), 12–14, at **[5.564]**, **[5.566]–[5.568]**.

[5.48]

47 Grounds for invalidity of registration

(1) The registration of a trade mark may be declared invalid on the ground that the trade mark was registered in breach of section 3 or any of the provisions referred to in that section (absolute grounds for refusal of registration).

Where the trade mark was registered in breach of subsection (1)(b), (c) or (d) of that section, it shall not be declared invalid if, in consequence of the use which has been made of it, it has after registration acquired a distinctive character in relation to the goods or services for which it is registered.

(2) The registration of a trade mark may be declared invalid on the ground—

(a) that there is an earlier trade mark in relation to which the conditions set out in section 5(1), (2) or (3) obtain, or

(b) that there is an earlier right in relation to which the condition set out in section 5(4) is satisfied,

unless the proprietor of that earlier trade mark or other earlier right has consented to the registration.

[(2A) But the registration of a trade mark may not be declared invalid on the ground that there is an earlier trade mark unless—

(a) the registration procedure for the earlier trade mark was completed within the period of five years ending with the date of the application for the declaration,

(b) the registration procedure for the earlier trade mark was not completed before that date, or

(c) the use conditions are met.

(2B) The use conditions are met if—

(a) within the period of five years ending with the date of the application for the declaration the earlier trade mark has been put to genuine use in the United Kingdom by the proprietor or with his consent in relation to the goods or services for which it is registered, or

(b) it has not been so used, but there are proper reasons for non-use.

(2C) For these purposes—

(a) use of a trade mark includes use in a form differing in elements which do not alter the distinctive character of the mark in the form in which it was registered, and

(b) use in the United Kingdom includes affixing the trade mark to goods or to the packaging of goods in the United Kingdom solely for export purposes.

(2D) In relation to a [European Union] trade mark [or international trade mark (EC)], any reference in subsection (2B) or (2C) to the United Kingdom shall be construed as a reference to the [European Union].

(2E) Where an earlier trade mark satisfies the use conditions in respect of some only of the goods or services for which it is registered, it shall be treated for the purposes of this section as if it were registered only in respect of those goods or services.]

[(2F) Subsection (2A) does not apply where the earlier trade mark is a trade mark within section 6(1)(c).]

(3) An application for a declaration of invalidity may be made by any person, and may be made either to the registrar or to the court, except that—

(a) if proceedings concerning the trade mark in question are pending in the court, the application must be made to the court; and

(b) if in any other case the application is made to the registrar, he may at any stage of the proceedings refer the application to the court.

(4) In the case of bad faith in the registration of a trade mark, the registrar himself may apply to the court for a declaration of the invalidity of the registration.

(5) Where the grounds of invalidity exist in respect of only some of the goods or services for which the trade mark is registered, the trade mark shall be declared invalid as regards those goods or services only.

(6) Where the registration of a trade mark is declared invalid to any extent, the registration shall to that extent be deemed never to have been made:

Provided that this shall not affect transactions past and closed.

NOTES

Sub-ss (2A)–(2C), (2E): inserted, together with sub-s (2D), by the Trade Marks (Proof of Use, etc) Regulations 2004, SI 2004/946, regs 3, 6, except in respect of an application under sub-s (3) above made before 5 May 2004.

Sub-s (2D): inserted, together with sub-ss (2A)–(2C), (2E), by SI 2004/946, regs 3, 6, except in respect of an application under sub-s (3) above made before 5 May 2004; words in first pair of square brackets substituted by the European Union Trade Mark Regulations 2016, SI 2016/299, reg 15, Schedule, para 1, subject to transitional provisions and savings as noted to s 5 at **[5.5]**; words in second pair of square brackets inserted by the Trade Marks (Earlier Trade Marks) Regulations 2008, SI 2008/1067, regs 3, 5(1), (2); words in third pair of square brackets substituted by the Treaty of Lisbon (Changes in Terminology) Order 2011, SI 2011/1043, art 4(1), subject to transitional provisions contained in art 3(3) thereof.

Sub-s (2F): inserted by SI 2008/1067, regs 3, 5(1), (3), subject to transitional provisions in regs 7, 8 thereof.

See the Harmonisation Directive 2008/95/EC, Arts 3(1)–(3), 4(1), at **[5.557]**, **[5.558]**.

[5.49]
48 Effect of acquiescence

(1) Where the proprietor of an earlier trade mark or other earlier right has acquiesced for a continuous period of five years in the use of a registered trade mark in the United Kingdom, being aware of that use, there shall cease to be any entitlement on the basis of that earlier trade mark or other right—

(a) to apply for a declaration that the registration of the later trade mark is invalid, or

(b) to oppose the use of the later trade mark in relation to the goods or services in relation to which it has been so used,

unless the registration of the later trade mark was applied for in bad faith.

(2) Where subsection (1) applies, the proprietor of the later trade mark is not entitled to oppose the use of the earlier trade mark or, as the case may be, the exploitation of the earlier right, notwithstanding that the earlier trade mark or right may no longer be invoked against his later trade mark.

NOTES

See the Harmonisation Directive 2008/95/EC, Art 9, at **[5.563]**.

Collective marks

[5.50]
49 Collective marks

(1) A collective mark is a mark distinguishing the goods or services of members of the association which is the proprietor of the mark from those of other undertakings.

(2) The provisions of this Act apply to collective marks subject to the provisions of Schedule 1.

Certification marks

[5.51]
50 Certification marks

(1) A certification mark is a mark indicating that the goods or services in connection with which it is used are certified by the proprietor of the mark in respect of origin, material, mode of manufacture of goods or performance of services, quality, accuracy or other characteristics.

(2) The provisions of this Act apply to certification marks subject to the provisions of Schedule 2.

PART II
[EUROPEAN UNION] TRADE MARKS AND INTERNATIONAL MATTERS

NOTES

Part heading: words in square brackets substituted by the European Union Trade Mark Regulations 2016, SI 2016/299, regs 2, 3, subject to transitional provisions and savings as noted to s 5 at **[5.5]**.

[European Union] trade marks

NOTES

Heading: words in square brackets substituted by the European Union Trade Mark Regulations 2016, SI 2016/299, regs 2, 3, subject to transitional provisions and savings as noted to s 5 at **[5.5]**.

[5.52]
[51 Meaning of "European Union trade mark"

In this Act—

"European Union trade mark" has the meaning given by Article 1(1) of the European Union Trade Mark Regulation; and

"the European Union Trade Mark Regulation" means Council Regulation (EC) No 207/2009 of 26 February 2009 on the European Union Trade Mark.]

NOTES

Commencement: 6 April 2016.

Substituted by the European Union Trade Mark Regulations 2016, SI 2016/299, regs 2, 4, subject to transitional provisions and savings as noted to s 5 at **[5.5]**.

[5.53]

52 Power to make provision in connection with [European Union] Trade Mark Regulation

(1) The Secretary of State may by regulations make such provision as he considers appropriate in connection with the operation of the [European Union] Trade Mark Regulation.

(2) Provision may, in particular, be made with respect to—

(a) . . .

(b) the procedures for determining a posteriori the invalidity, or liability to revocation, of the registration of a trade mark from which a [European Union] trade mark claims seniority;

(c) the conversion of a [European Union] trade mark, or an application for a [European Union] trade mark, into an application for registration under this Act;

(d) the designation of courts in the United Kingdom having jurisdiction over proceedings arising out of the [European Union] Trade Mark Regulation.

(3) Without prejudice to the generality of subsection (1), provision may be made by regulations under this section—

(a) applying in relation to a [European Union] trade mark the provisions of—

(i) section 21 (remedy for groundless threats of infringement proceedings);

(ii) sections 89 to 91 (importation of infringing goods, material or articles); and

(iii) sections 92, 93, 95 and 96 (offences); and

(b) making in relation to the list of professional representatives maintained in pursuance of [Article 93] of the [European Union] Trade Mark Regulation, and persons on that list, provision corresponding to that made by, or capable of being made under, sections 84 to 88 in relation to the register of [trade mark attorneys and registered trade mark attorneys].

[(3A) The reference in subsections (1) and (2)(d) to the European Union Trade Mark Regulation includes a reference to Council Regulation (EC) No 40/94 of 20th December 1993 on the Community trade mark.]

(4) Regulations under this section shall be made by statutory instrument which shall be subject to annulment in pursuance of a resolution of either House of Parliament.

NOTES

Section heading, sub-s (1): words in square brackets substituted by the European Union Trade Mark Regulations 2016, SI 2016/299, regs 2, 5(1)–(3), subject to transitional provisions and savings as noted to s 5 at **[5.5]**.

Sub-s (2): para (a) repealed and words in square brackets substituted, by SI 2016/299, regs 2, 5(1), (3), (4), subject to transitional provisions and savings as noted to s 5 at **[5.5]**.

Sub-s (3): words in square brackets in para (a) and words in first and second pairs of square brackets in para (b) substituted by SI 2016/299, regs 2, 5(1), (3), (5), subject to transitional provisions and savings as noted to s 5 at **[5.5]**; para (a)(i) substituted by the Intellectual Property (Unjustified Threats) Act 2017, s 2(1), (3), as from a day to be appointed, as follows—

"(i) sections 21 to 21F (unjustified threats);";

words in third pair of square brackets in para (b) substituted by the Legal Services Act 2007, s 208, Sch 21, paras 109, 110.

Sub-s (3A): inserted by SI 2016/299, regs 2, 5(1), (6), subject to transitional provisions and savings as noted to s 5 at **[5.5]**.

See the Harmonisation Directive 2008/95/EC, Art 14, at **[5.568]**.

Regulations: the Trade Marks (International Registrations Designating the European Community, etc) Regulations 2004, SI 2004/2332; the Community Trade Mark Regulations 2006, SI 2006/1027 at **[5.129]**; the European Union Trade Mark Regulations 2016, SI 2016/299.

The Madrid Protocol: international registration

[5.54]

53 The Madrid Protocol

In this Act—

"the Madrid Protocol" means the Protocol relating to the Madrid Agreement concerning the International Registration of Marks, adopted at Madrid on 27th June 1989;

"the International Bureau" has the meaning given by Article 2(1) of that Protocol;

["international trade mark (EC)" means a trade mark which is entitled to protection in the [European Union] under that Protocol;] and

"international trade mark (UK)" means a trade mark which is entitled to protection in the United Kingdom under that Protocol.

NOTES

Definition "international trade mark (EC)" inserted by the Trade Marks (International Registrations Designating the European Community, etc) Regulations 2004, SI 2004/2332, regs 2, 5; words in square brackets substituted by the Treaty of Lisbon (Changes in Terminology) Order 2011, SI 2011/1043, art 4(1), subject to a transitional provision contained in art 3(3) thereof.

[5.55]

54 Power to make provision giving effect to Madrid Protocol

(1) The Secretary of State may by order make such provision as he thinks fit for giving effect in the United Kingdom to the provisions of the Madrid Protocol.

(2) Provision may, in particular, be made with respect to—

(a) the making of applications for international registrations by way of the Patent Office as office of origin;

(b) the procedures to be followed where the basic United Kingdom application or registration fails or ceases to be in force;

(c) the procedures to be followed where the Patent Office receives from the International Bureau a request for extension of protection to the United Kingdom;

(d) the effects of a successful request for extension of protection to the United Kingdom;

(e) the transformation of an application for an international registration, or an international registration, into a national application for registration;

(f) the communication of information to the International Bureau;

(g) the payment of fees and amounts prescribed in respect of applications for international registrations, extensions of protection and renewals.

(3) Without prejudice to the generality of subsection (1), provision may be made by regulations under this section applying in relation to an international trade mark (UK) the provisions of—

(a) section 21 (remedy for groundless threats of infringement proceedings);

(b) sections 89 to 91 (importation of infringing goods, material or articles); and

(c) sections 92, 93, 95 and 96 (offences).

(4) An order under this section shall be made by statutory instrument which shall be subject to annulment in pursuance of a resolution of either House of Parliament.

NOTES

Sub-s (3): para (a) substituted by the Intellectual Property (Unjustified Threats) Act 2017, s 2(1), (4), as from a day to be appointed, as follows—

"(a) sections 21 to 21F (unjustified threats);".

Orders: the Trade Marks (International Registration) Order 2008, SI 2008/2206 at **[5.231]**.

The Paris Convention: supplementary provisions

[5.56]

55 The Paris Convention

(1) In this Act—

(a) "the Paris Convention" means the Paris Convention for the Protection of Industrial Property of March 20th 1883, as revised or amended from time to time, . . .

[(aa) "the WTO agreement" means the Agreement establishing the World Trade Organisation signed at Marrakesh on 15th April 1974, and]

(b) a "Convention country" means a country, other than the United Kingdom, which is a party to that Convention [or to that Agreement].

(2) The Secretary of State may by order make such amendments of this Act, and rules made under this Act, as appear to him appropriate in consequence of any revision or amendment of the Paris Convention [or the WTO agreement] after the passing of this Act.

(3) Any such order shall be made by statutory instrument which shall be subject to annulment in pursuance of a resolution of either House of Parliament.

NOTES

Sub-s (1): para (aa) inserted, and word immediately preceding it repealed, by the Patents and Trade Marks (World Trade Organisation) Regulations 1999, SI 1999/1899, reg 13(2); in para (b) words in square brackets inserted by the Intellectual Property (Enforcement, etc) Regulations 2006, SI 2006/1028, reg 2(2), Sch 2, paras 15, 18.

Sub-s (2): words in square brackets inserted by SI 1999/1899, reg 13(3).

[5.57]

56 Protection of well-known trade marks: Article 6bis

(1) References in this Act to a trade mark which is entitled to protection under the Paris Convention [or the WTO agreement] as a well known trade mark are to a mark which is well-known in the United Kingdom as being the mark of a person who—

(a) is a national of a Convention country, or

(b) is domiciled in, or has a real and effective industrial or commercial establishment in, a Convention country,

whether or not that person carries on business, or has any goodwill, in the United Kingdom.

References to the proprietor of such a mark shall be construed accordingly.

(2) The proprietor of a trade mark which is entitled to protection under the Paris Convention [or the WTO agreement] as a well known trade mark is entitled to restrain by injunction the use in the United Kingdom of a trade mark which, or the essential part of which, is identical or similar to his mark, in relation to identical or similar goods or services, where the use is likely to cause confusion.

This right is subject to section 48 (effect of acquiescence by proprietor of earlier trade mark).

(3) Nothing in subsection (2) affects the continuation of any *bona fide* use of a trade mark begun before the commencement of this section.

NOTES

Sub-s (1): words in square brackets inserted by the Patents and Trade Marks (World Trade Organisation) Regulations 1999, SI 1999/1899, reg 13(4).

Sub-s (2): words in square brackets inserted by SI 1999/1899, regs 13(4), 14(1), but not so as to affect the continuation of any bona fide use of a trade mark started before 1 January 1996.

See the Harmonisation Directive 2008/95/EC, Art 4(2)(d), at **[5.558]**.

[5.58]

57 National emblems, &c of Convention countries: Article 6ter

(1) A trade mark which consists of or contains the flag of a Convention country shall not be registered without the authorisation of the competent authorities of that country, unless it appears to the registrar that use of the flag in the manner proposed is permitted without such authorisation.

(2) A trade mark which consists of or contains the armorial bearings or any other state emblem of a Convention country which is protected under the Paris Convention [or the WTO agreement] shall not be registered without the authorisation of the competent authorities of that country.

(3) A trade mark which consists of or contains an official sign or hallmark adopted by a Convention country and indicating control and warranty shall not, where the sign or hallmark is protected under the Paris Convention [or the WTO agreement], be registered in relation to goods or services of the same, or a similar kind, as those in relation to which it indicates control and warranty, without the authorisation of the competent authorities of the country concerned.

(4) The provisions of this section as to national flags and other state emblems, and official signs or hallmarks, apply equally to anything which from a heraldic point of view imitates any such flag or other emblem, or sign or hallmark.

(5) Nothing in this section prevents the registration of a trade mark on the application of a national of a country who is authorised to make use of a state emblem, or official sign or hallmark, of that country, notwithstanding that it is similar to that of another country.

(6) Where by virtue of this section the authorisation of the competent authorities of a Convention country is or would be required for the registration of a trade mark, those authorities are entitled to restrain by injunction any use of the mark in the United Kingdom without their authorisation.

NOTES

Sub-ss (2), (3): words in square brackets inserted by the Patents and Trade Marks (World Trade Organisation) Regulations 1999, SI 1999/1899, reg 13(5).

[5.59]

58 Emblems, &c of certain international organisations: Article 6ter

(1) This section applies to—

(a) the armorial bearings, flags or other emblems, and

(b) the abbreviations and names,

of international intergovernmental organisations of which one or more Convention countries are members.

(2) A trade mark which consists of or contains any such emblem, abbreviation or name which is protected under the Paris Convention [or the WTO agreement] shall not be registered without the authorisation of the international organisation concerned, unless it appears to the registrar that the use of the emblem, abbreviation or name in the manner proposed—

(a) is not such as to suggest to the public that a connection exists between the organisation and the trade mark, or

(b) is not likely to mislead the public as to the existence of a connection between the user and the organisation.

(3) The provisions of this section as to emblems of an international organisation apply equally to anything which from a heraldic point of view imitates any such emblem.

(4) Where by virtue of this section the authorisation of an international organisation is or would be required for the registration of a trade mark, that organisation is entitled to restrain by injunction any use of the mark in the United Kingdom without its authorisation.

(5) Nothing in this section affects the rights of a person whose *bona fide* use of the trade mark in question began before 4th January 1962 (when the relevant provisions of the Paris Convention entered into force in relation to the United Kingdom).

NOTES

Sub-s (2): words in square brackets inserted by the Patents and Trade Marks (World Trade Organisation) Regulations 1999, SI 1999/1899, regs 13(4), 14(2), but without prejudice to the rights of a person whose bona fide use of a trade mark started before 1 January 1996.

[5.60]
59 Notification under Article 6ter of the Convention
(1) For the purposes of section 57 state emblems of a Convention country (other than the national flag), and official signs or hallmarks, shall be regarded as protected under the Paris Convention only if, or to the extent that—
(a) the country in question has notified the United Kingdom in accordance with Article 6*ter* (3) of the Convention that it desires to protect that emblem, sign or hallmark,
(b) the notification remains in force, and
(c) the United Kingdom has not objected to it in accordance with Article 6*ter* (4) or any such objection has been withdrawn.
(2) For the purposes of section 58 the emblems, abbreviations and names of an international organisation shall be regarded as protected under the Paris Convention only if, or to the extent that—
(a) the organisation in question has notified the United Kingdom in accordance with Article 6*ter* (3) of the Convention that it desires to protect that emblem, abbreviation or name,
(b) the notification remains in force, and
(c) the United Kingdom has not objected to it in accordance with Article 6*ter* (4) or any such objection has been withdrawn.
(3) Notification under Article 6*ter* (3) of the Paris Convention shall have effect only in relation to applications for registration made more than two months after the receipt of the notification.
(4) The registrar shall keep and make available for public inspection by any person, at all reasonable hours and free of charge, a list of—
(a) the state emblems and official signs or hallmarks, and
(b) the emblems, abbreviations and names of international organisations,
which are for the time being protected under the Paris Convention by virtue of notification under Article 6*ter* (3).
[(5) Any reference in this section to Article 6*ter* of the Paris Convention shall be construed as including a reference to that Article as applied by the WTO agreement.]

NOTES
Sub-s (5): added by the Patents and Trade Marks (World Trade Organisation) Regulations 1999, SI 1999/1899, regs 13(7).

[5.61]
60 Acts of agent or representative: Article 6septies
(1) The following provisions apply where an application for registration of a trade mark is made by a person who is an agent or representative of a person who is the proprietor of the mark in a Convention country.
(2) If the proprietor opposes the application, registration shall be refused.
(3) If the application (not being so opposed) is granted, the proprietor may—
(a) apply for a declaration of the invalidity of the registration, or
(b) apply for the rectification of the register so as to substitute his name as the proprietor of the registered trade mark.
(4) The proprietor may (notwithstanding the rights conferred by this Act in relation to a registered trade mark) by injunction restrain any use of the trade mark in the United Kingdom which is not authorised by him.
(5) Subsections (2), (3) and (4) do not apply if, or to the extent that, the agent or representative justifies his action.
(6) An application under subsection (3)(a) or (b) must be made within three years of the proprietor becoming aware of the registration; and no injunction shall be granted under subsection (4) in respect of a use in which the proprietor has acquiesced for a continuous period of three years or more.

NOTES
See the Harmonisation Directive 2008/95/EC, Art 4(4)(g), at **[5.558]**.

61 (*Repealed by the Finance Act 2000, s 156, Sch 40, Pt III, in relation to instruments executed on or after 28 March 2000.*)

PART III
ADMINISTRATIVE AND OTHER SUPPLEMENTARY PROVISIONS

The registrar

[5.62]
62 The registrar
In this Act "the registrar" means the Comptroller-General of Patents, Designs and Trade Marks.

The register

[5.63]
63 The register

(1) The registrar shall maintain a register of trade marks.

References in this Act to "the register" are to that register; and references to registration (in particular, in the expression "registered trade mark") are, unless the context otherwise requires, to registration in that register.

(2) There shall be entered in the register in accordance with this Act—

(a) registered trade marks,

(b) such particulars as may be prescribed of registrable transactions affecting a registered trade mark, and

(c) such other matters relating to registered trade marks as may be prescribed.

(3) The register shall be kept in such manner as may be prescribed, and provision shall in particular be made for—

(a) public inspection of the register, and

(b) the supply of certified or uncertified copies, or extracts, of entries in the register.

NOTES

Rules: the Trade Marks Rules 2008, SI 2008/1797, at **[5.146]**.

[5.64]
64 Rectification or correction of the register

(1) Any person having a sufficient interest may apply for the rectification of an error or omission in the register:

Provided that an application for rectification may not be made in respect of a matter affecting the validity of the registration of a trade mark.

(2) An application for rectification may be made either to the registrar or to the court, except that—

(a) if proceedings concerning the trade mark in question are pending in the court, the application must be made to the court; and

(b) if in any other case the application is made to the registrar, he may at any stage of the proceedings refer the application to the court.

(3) Except where the registrar or the court directs otherwise the effect of rectification of the register is that the error or omission in question shall be deemed never to have been made.

(4) The registrar may, on request made in the prescribed manner by the proprietor of a registered trade mark, or a licensee, enter any change in his name or address as recorded in the register.

(5) The registrar may remove from the register matter appearing to him to have ceased to have effect.

NOTES

Rules: the Trade Marks Rules 2008, SI 2008/1797, at **[5.146]**.

[5.65]
65 Adaptation of entries to new classification

(1) Provision may be made by rules empowering the registrar to do such things as he considers necessary to implement any amended or substituted classification of goods or services for the purposes of the registration of trade marks.

(2) Provision may in particular be made for the amendment of existing entries on the register so as to accord with the new classification.

(3) Any such power of amendment shall not be exercised so as to extend the rights conferred by the registration, except where it appears to the registrar that compliance with this requirement would involve undue complexity and that any extension would not be substantial and would not adversely affect the rights of any person.

(4) The rules may empower the registrar—

(a) to require the proprietor of a registered trade mark, within such time as may be prescribed, to file a proposal for amendment of the register, and

(b) to cancel or refuse to renew the registration of the trade mark in the event of his failing to do so.

(5) Any such proposal shall be advertised, and may be opposed, in such manner as may be prescribed.

NOTES

Rules: the Trade Marks Rules 2008, SI 2008/1797, at **[5.146]**.

Powers and duties of the registrar

[5.66]
66 Power to require use of forms

(1) The registrar may require the use of such forms as he may direct for any purpose relating to the registration of a trade mark or any other proceeding before him under this Act.

(2) The forms, and any directions of the registrar with respect to their use, shall be published in the prescribed manner.

NOTES

Rules: the Trade Marks Rules 2008, SI 2008/1797, at **[5.146]**.

[5.67]

67 Information about applications and registered trade marks

(1) After publication of an application for registration of a trade mark, the registrar shall on request provide a person with such information and permit him to inspect such documents relating to the application, or to any registered trade mark resulting from it, as may be specified in the request, subject, however, to any prescribed restrictions.

Any request must be made in the prescribed manner and be accompanied by the appropriate fee (if any).

(2) Before publication of an application for registration of a trade mark, documents or information constituting or relating to the application shall not be published by the registrar or communicated by him to any person except—

- (a) in such cases and to such extent as may be prescribed, or
- (b) with the consent of the applicant;

but subject as follows.

(3) Where a person has been notified that an application for registration of a trade mark has been made, and that the applicant will if the application is granted bring proceedings against him in respect of acts done after publication of the application, he may make a request under subsection (1) notwithstanding that the application has not been published and that subsection shall apply accordingly.

NOTES

Rules: the Trade Marks Rules 2008, SI 2008/1797, at **[5.146]**.

[5.68]

68 Costs and security for costs

(1) Provision may be made by rules empowering the registrar, in any proceedings before him under this Act—

- (a) to award any party such costs as he may consider reasonable, and
- (b) to direct how and by what parties they are to be paid.

(2) Any such order of the registrar may be enforced—

- (a) in England and Wales or Northern Ireland, in the same way as an order of the High Court;
- (b) in Scotland, in the same way as a decree for expenses granted by the Court of Session.

(3) Provision may be made by rules empowering the registrar, in such cases as may be prescribed, to require a party to proceedings before him to give security for costs, in relation to those proceedings or to proceedings on appeal, and as to the consequences if security is not given.

NOTES

Rules: the Trade Marks Rules 2008, SI 2008/1797, at **[5.146]**.

[5.69]

69 Evidence before registrar

Provision may be made by rules—

- (a) as to the giving of evidence in proceedings before the registrar under this Act by affidavit or statutory declaration;
- (b) conferring on the registrar the powers of an official referee of the [Senior Courts or of the Court of Judicature] as regards the examination of witnesses on oath and the discovery and production of documents; and
- (c) applying in relation to the attendance of witnesses in proceedings before the registrar the rules applicable to the attendance of witnesses before such a referee.

NOTES

Words in square brackets substituted by the Constitutional Reform Act 2005, s 59(5), Sch 11, Pt 4, para 31.

Rules: the Trade Marks Rules 2008, SI 2008/1797, at **[5.146]**.

[5.70]

70 Exclusion of liability in respect of official acts

(1) The registrar shall not be taken to warrant the validity of the registration of a trade mark under this Act or under any treaty, convention, arrangement or engagement to which the United Kingdom is a party.

(2) The registrar is not subject to any liability by reason of, or in connection with, any examination required or authorised by this Act, or any such treaty, convention, arrangement or engagement, or any report or other proceedings consequent on such examination.

(3) No proceedings lie against an officer of the registrar in respect of any matter for which, by virtue of this section, the registrar is not liable.

[5.71]
71 Registrar's annual report
(1) The Comptroller-General of Patents, Designs and Trade Marks shall in his annual report under section 121 of the Patents Act 1977, include a report on the execution of this Act, including the discharge of his functions under the Madrid Protocol.
(2) The report shall include an account of all money received and paid by him under or by virtue of this Act.

Legal proceedings and appeals

[5.72]
72 Registration to be prima facie evidence of validity
In all legal proceedings relating to a registered trade mark (including proceedings for rectification of the register) the registration of a person as proprietor of a trade mark shall be prima facie evidence of the validity of the original registration and of any subsequent assignment or other transmission of it.

[5.73]
73 Certificate of validity of contested registration
(1) If in proceedings before the court the validity of the registration of a trade mark is contested and it is found by the court that the trade mark is validly registered, the court may give a certificate to that effect.
(2) If the court gives such a certificate and in subsequent proceedings—
(a) the validity of the registration is again questioned, and
(b) the proprietor obtains a final order or judgment in his favour,
he is entitled to his costs as between solicitor and client unless the court directs otherwise.
This subsection does not extend to the costs of an appeal in any such proceedings.

[5.74]
74 Registrar's appearance in proceedings involving the register
(1) In proceedings before the court involving an application for—
(a) the revocation of the registration of a trade mark,
(b) a declaration of the invalidity of the registration of a trade mark, or
(c) the rectification of the register,
the registrar is entitled to appear and be heard, and shall appear if so directed by the court.
(2) Unless otherwise directed by the court, the registrar may instead of appearing submit to the court a statement in writing signed by him, giving particulars of—
(a) any proceedings before him in relation to the matter in issue,
(b) the grounds of any decision given by him affecting it,
(c) the practice of the Patent Office in like cases, or
(d) such matters relevant to the issues and within his knowledge as registrar as he thinks fit;
and the statement shall be deemed to form part of the evidence in the proceedings.
(3) Anything which the registrar is or may be authorised or required to do under this section may be done on his behalf by a duly authorised officer.

[5.75]
75 The court
In this Act, unless the context otherwise requires, "the court" means—
(a) in England and Wales[, the High Court[, or the county court where it has] jurisdiction by virtue of an order made under section 1 of the Courts and Legal Services Act 1990,
(aa) in] Northern Ireland, the High Court, and
(b) in Scotland, the Court of Session.

NOTES
Words in first (outer) pair of square brackets substituted by the High Court and County Courts Jurisdiction (Amendment) Order 2005, SI 2005/587, art 4(1), (2); words in second (inner) pair of square brackets substituted by the Crime and Courts Act 2013, s 17(5), Sch 9, Pt 3, para 134.

[5.76]
76 Appeals from the registrar
(1) An appeal lies from any decision of the registrar under this Act, except as otherwise expressly provided by rules.
For this purpose "decision" includes any act of the registrar in exercise of a discretion vested in him by or under this Act.
(2) Any such appeal may be brought either to an appointed person or to the court.
(3) Where an appeal is made to an appointed person, he may refer the appeal to the court if—
(a) it appears to him that a point of general legal importance is involved,
(b) the registrar requests that it be so referred, or
(c) such a request is made by any party to the proceedings before the registrar in which the decision appealed against was made.

Before doing so the appointed person shall give the appellant and any other party to the appeal an opportunity to make representations as to whether the appeal should be referred to the court.

(4) Where an appeal is made to an appointed person and he does not refer it to the court, he shall hear and determine the appeal and his decision shall be final.

(5) The provisions of sections 68 and 69 (costs and security for costs; evidence) apply in relation to proceedings before an appointed person as in relation to proceedings before the registrar.

[(6) In the application of this section to England and Wales, "the court" means the High Court.]

NOTES

Sub-s (6): added by the High Court and County Courts Jurisdiction (Amendment) Order 2005, SI 2005/587, art 4(1), (3).

Rules: the Trade Marks Rules 2008, SI 2008/1797, at **[5.146]**.

[5.77]

77 Persons appointed to hear and determine appeals

(1) For the purposes of section 76 an "appointed person" means a person appointed by the Lord Chancellor to hear and decide appeals under this Act.

(2) A person is not eligible for such appointment unless—

[(a) he satisfies the judicial-appointment eligibility condition on a 5-year basis;]

(b) he is an advocate or solicitor in Scotland of at least [5] years' standing;

(c) he is a member of the Bar of Northern Ireland or [solicitor of the Court of Judicature of Northern Ireland] of at least [5] years' standing; or

(d) he has held judicial office.

(3) An appointed person shall hold and vacate office in accordance with his terms of appointment, subject to the following provisions—

(a) there shall be paid to him such remuneration (whether by way of salary or fees), and such allowances, as the Secretary of State with the approval of the Treasury may determine;

(b) he may resign his office by notice in writing to the Lord Chancellor;

(c) the Lord Chancellor may by notice in writing remove him from office if—

(i) he has become bankrupt or [a debt relief order (under Part 7A of the Insolvency Act 1986) has been made in respect of him or he has] made an arrangement with his creditors or, in Scotland, his estate has been sequestrated or he has executed a trust deed for his creditors or entered into a composition contract, or

(ii) he is incapacitated by physical or mental illness,

or if he is in the opinion of the Lord Chancellor otherwise unable or unfit to perform his duties as an appointed person.

(4) The Lord Chancellor shall consult the [Secretary of State] before exercising his powers under this section.

[(5) The Lord Chancellor may remove a person from office under subsection (3)(c) only with the concurrence of the appropriate senior judge.

(6) The appropriate senior judge is the Lord Chief Justice of England and Wales, unless—

(a) the person to be removed exercises functions wholly or mainly in Scotland, in which case it is the Lord President of the Court of Session, or

(b) the person to be removed exercises functions wholly or mainly in Northern Ireland, in which case it is the Lord Chief Justice of Northern Ireland.]

NOTES

Sub-s (2): para (a) substituted, and numbers in square brackets in paras (b), (c) substituted by the Tribunals, Courts and Enforcement Act 2007, s 50, Sch 10, Pt 1, para 25; words in square brackets in para (c) substituted by the Constitutional Reform Act 2005, s 59(5), Sch 11, Pt 3, para 5.

Sub-s (3): words in square brackets inserted, in relation to a debt relief order the application for which is made after 1 October 2012, by the Tribunals, Courts and Enforcement Act 2007 (Consequential Amendments) Order 2012, SI 2012/2404, arts 3(2), 5, Sch 2, para 31.

Sub-s (4): words in square brackets substituted by virtue of the Transfer of Functions (Lord Advocate and Secretary of State) Order 1999, SI 1999/678, art 2(1), Schedule.

Sub-ss (5), (6): added by the Constitutional Reform Act 2005, s 15(1), Sch 4, Pt 1, para 238.

Transfer of functions: functions of the Secretary of State under sub-s (4) are transferred, in so far as they are exercisable in or as regards Scotland, to the Scottish Ministers, by the Scotland Act 1998 (Transfer of Functions to the Scottish Ministers etc) Order 1999, SI 1999/1750, art 2, Sch 1.

Rules, fees, hours of business, &c

[5.78]

78 Power of Secretary of State to make rules

(1) The Secretary of State may make rules—

(a) for the purposes of any provision of this Act authorising the making of rules with respect to any matter, and

(b) for prescribing anything authorised or required by any provision of this Act to be prescribed,

and generally for regulating practice and procedure under this Act.

(2) Provision may, in particular, be made—

(a) as to the manner of filing of applications and other documents;

(b) requiring and regulating the translation of documents and the filing and authentication of any translation;
(c) as to the service of documents;
(d) authorising the rectification of irregularities of procedure;
(e) prescribing time limits for anything required to be done in connection with any proceeding under this Act;
(f) providing for the extension of any time limit so prescribed, or specified by the registrar, whether or not it has already expired.

(3) Rules under this Act shall be made by statutory instrument which shall be subject to annulment in pursuance of a resolution of either House of Parliament.

NOTES

Rules: the Patents, Trade Marks and Designs (Address For Service and Time Limits, etc) Rules 2006, SI 2006/760; the Trade Marks Rules 2008, SI 2008/1797 at **[5.146]**; the Patents, Trade Marks and Designs (Address for Service) Rules 2009, SI 2009/546; the European Union Trade Mark Regulations 2016, SI 2016/299.

[5.79]
79 Fees

(1) There shall be paid in respect of applications and registration and other matters under this Act such fees as may be prescribed.
(2) Provision may be made by rules as to—
(a) the payment of a single fee in respect of two or more matters, and
(b) the circumstances (if any) in which a fee may be repaid or remitted.

NOTES

Rules: the Trade Marks (Fees) Rules 2008, SI 2008/1958.

[5.80]
80 Hours of business and business days

(1) The registrar may give directions specifying the hours of business of the Patent Office for the purpose of the transaction by the public of business under this Act, and the days which are business days for that purpose.
(2) Business done on any day after the specified hours of business, or on a day which is not a business day, shall be deemed to have been done on the next business day; and where the time for doing anything under this Act expires on a day which is not a business day, that time shall be extended to the next business day.
(3) Directions under this section may make different provision for different classes of business and shall be published in the prescribed manner.

NOTES

Rules: the Trade Marks Rules 2008, SI 2008/1797 at **[5.146]**.

[5.81]
81 The trade marks journal

Provision shall be made by rules for the publication by the registrar of a journal containing particulars of any application for the registration of a trade mark (including a representation of the mark) and such other information relating to trade marks as the registrar thinks fit.

NOTES

Rules: the Trade Marks Rules 2008, SI 2008/1797 at **[5.146]**.

Trade mark agents, &c

[5.82]
82 Recognition of agents

Except as otherwise provided by rules [and subject to the Legal Services Act 2007], any act required or authorised by this Act to be done by or to a person in connection with the registration of a trade mark, or any procedure relating to a registered trade mark, may be done by or to an agent authorised by that person orally or in writing.

NOTES

Words in square brackets inserted by the Legal Services Act 2007, s 184(1), (2).
Rules: the Trade Marks Rules 2008, SI 2008/1797 at **[5.146]**.

[5.83]
[83 The register of trade mark attorneys

(1) There is to continue to be a register of persons who act as agent for others for the purpose of applying for or obtaining the registration of trade marks.
(2) In this Act a registered trade mark attorney means an individual whose name is entered on the register kept under this section.
(3) The register is to be kept by the Institute of Trade Mark Attorneys.

(4) The Secretary of State may, by order, amend subsection (3) so as to require the register to be kept by the person specified in the order.
(5) Before making an order under subsection (4), the Secretary of State must consult the Legal Services Board.
(6) An order under this section must be made by statutory instrument.
(7) An order under this section may not be made unless a draft of it has been laid before, and approved by a resolution of, each House of Parliament.]

NOTES

Substituted, together with s 83A for original s 83, by the Legal Services Act 2007, s 184(1), (3).

[5.84]

[83A Regulation of trade mark attorneys

(1) The person who keeps the register under section 83 may make regulations which regulate—
 (a) the keeping of the register and the registration of persons;
 (b) the carrying on of trade mark agency work by registered persons.
(2) Those regulations may, amongst other things, make—
 (a) provision as to the educational and training qualifications, and other requirements, which must be satisfied before an individual may be registered or for an individual to remain registered;
 (b) provision as to the requirements which must be met by a body (corporate or unincorporate) before it may be registered or for it to remain registered, including provision as to the management and control of the body;
 (c) provision as to the educational, training or other requirements to be met by regulated persons;
 (d) provision regulating the practice, conduct and discipline of registered persons or regulated persons;
 (e) provision authorising in such cases as may be specified in the regulations the erasure from the register of the name of any person registered in it, or the suspension of a person's registration;
 (f) provision requiring the payment of such fees as may be specified in or determined in accordance with the regulations;
 (g) provision about the provision to be made by registered persons in respect of complaints made against them;
 (h) provision about the keeping of records and accounts by registered persons or regulated persons;
 (i) provision for reviews of or appeals against decisions made under the regulations;
 (j) provision as to the indemnification of registered persons or regulated persons against losses arising from claims in respect of civil liability incurred by them.
(3) Regulations under this section may make different provision for different purposes.
(4) Regulations under this section which are not regulatory arrangements within the meaning of the Legal Services Act 2007 are to be treated as such arrangements for the purposes of that Act.
(5) Before the appointed day, regulations under this section may be made only with the approval of the Secretary of State.
(6) The powers conferred to make regulations under this section are not to be taken to prejudice—
 (a) any other power which the person who keeps the register may have to make rules or regulations (however they may be described and whether they are made under an enactment or otherwise);
 (b) any rules or regulations made by that person under any such power.
(7) In this section—
 "appointed day" means the day appointed for the coming into force of paragraph 1 of Schedule 4 to the Legal Services Act 2007;
 "manager", in relation to a body, has the same meaning as in the Legal Services Act 2007 (see section 207);
 "registered person" means—
  (a) a registered trade mark attorney, or
  (b) a body (corporate or unincorporate) registered in the register kept under section 83;
 "regulated person" means a person who is not a registered person but is a manager or employee of a body which is a registered person;
 "trade mark agency work" means work done in the course of carrying on the business of acting as agent for others for the purpose of—
  (a) applying for or obtaining the registration of trade marks in the United Kingdom [or elsewhere], or
  (b) conducting proceedings before the Comptroller relating to applications for or otherwise in connection with the registration of trade marks.]

NOTES

Substituted as noted to s 83 at **[5.83]**.

Sub-s (7): in definition "trade mark agency work" words in square brackets inserted by the Legal Services Act 2007 (Functions of an Approved Regulator) Order 2009, SI 2009/3339, art 2.

[5.85]

84 Unregistered persons not to be described as registered trade mark [attorneys]

(1) An individual who is not a registered trade mark [attorney] shall not—

(a) carry on a business (otherwise than in partnership) under any name or other description which contains the words "registered trade mark agent" [or registered trade mark attorney]; or

(b) in the course of a business otherwise describe or hold himself out, or permit himself to be described or held out, as a registered trade mark agent [or a registered trade mark attorney].

(2) A partnership [or other unincorporated body] shall not—

(a) carry on a business under any name or other description which contains the words "registered trade mark agent" [or registered trade mark attorney]; or

(b) in the course of a business otherwise describe or hold itself out, or permit itself to be described or held out, as a firm of registered trade mark agents [or registered trade mark attorneys],

unless [the partnership or other body is registered in the register kept under section 83.]

(3) A body corporate shall not—

(a) carry on a business (otherwise than in partnership) under any name or other description which contains the words "registered trade mark agent" [or registered trade mark attorney]; or

(b) in the course of a business otherwise describe or hold itself out, or permit itself to be described or held out, as a registered trade mark agent [or a registered trade mark attorney],

unless [the partnership or other body is registered in the register kept under section 83.]

(4) A person who contravenes this section commits an offence and is liable on summary conviction to a fine not exceeding level 5 on the standard scale; and proceedings for such an offence may be begun at any time within a year from the date of the offence.

NOTES

Section heading: word in square brackets substituted by virtue of the Legal Services Act 2007, s 208, Sch 21, paras 109, 111(a).

Sub-s (1): word in first pair of square brackets substituted and words in square brackets in paras (a), (b) inserted by the Legal Services Act 2007, s 208, Sch 21, paras 109, 111(a).

Sub-s (2): words in first, second and third pairs of square brackets inserted and words in fourth pair of square brackets substituted by the Legal Services Act 2007, ss 184(1), (4)(a), 208, Sch 21, paras 9, 11(b).

Sub-s (3): words in first and second pairs of square brackets inserted and words in third pair of square brackets substituted by the Legal Services Act 2007, ss 184(1), (4)(b), 208, Sch 21, paras 109, 111(c).

85 (*Repealed by the Legal Services Act 2007, ss 184(1), (5), 210, Sch 23.*)

[5.86]

86 Use of the term "trade mark attorney"

(1) No offence is committed under the enactments restricting the use of certain expressions in reference to persons not qualified to act as solicitors by the use of the term "trade mark attorney" in reference to a registered trade mark [attorney].

(2) The enactments referred to in subsection (1) are section 21 of the Solicitors Act 1974, section 31 of the Solicitors (Scotland) Act 1980 and Article 22 of the Solicitors (Northern Ireland) Order 1976.

NOTES

Sub-s (1): word in square brackets substituted by the Legal Services Act 2007, s 208, Sch 21, paras 109, 112.

[5.87]

87 Privilege for communications with registered trade mark agents

(1) This section applies to[—

(a)] communications as to any matter relating to the protection of any design or trade mark, or as to any matter involving passing off[, and

(b) documents, material or information relating to any matter mentioned in paragraph (a).]

[(2) Where a trade mark attorney acts for a client in relation to a matter mentioned in subsection (1), any communication, document, material or information to which this section applies is privileged from disclosure in like manner as if the trade mark attorney had at all material times been acting as the client's solicitor.]

(3) In subsection (2) "trade mark [attorney]" means—

(a) a registered trade mark [attorney], or

(b) a partnership entitled to describe itself as a firm of registered trade mark [attorneys], or

(c) [any other unincorporated body or] a body corporate entitled to describe itself as a registered trade mark [attorney].

NOTES

Sub-s (1): words in square brackets inserted by the Legal Services Act 2007, s 208, Sch 21, paras 109, 113(a), (b).

Sub-s (2): substituted by the Legal Services Act 2007, s 208, Sch 21, paras 109, 113(c).

Sub-s (3): words in first, second, third and fifth pairs of square brackets substituted and words in square brackets in para (c) inserted by the Legal Services Act 2007, ss 184(1), (6), 208, Sch 21, paras 109, 113(d).

[5.88]

88 Power of registrar to refuse to deal with certain agents

(1) The Secretary of State may make rules authorising the registrar to refuse to recognise as agent in respect of any business under this Act—

(a) a person who has been convicted of an offence under section 84 (unregistered persons describing themselves as registered trade mark agents);

(b) [a person] whose name has been erased from and not restored to, or who is suspended from, the register of trade mark [attorneys] on the ground of misconduct;

(c) a person who is found by the Secretary of State to have been guilty of such conduct as would, in the case of [a person] registered in the register of trade mark [attorneys], render [the person] liable to have [the person's] name erased from the register on the ground of misconduct;

(d) a partnership or body corporate of which one of the partners or directors is a person whom the registrar could refuse to recognise under paragraph (a), (b) or (c) above.

(2) The rules may contain such incidental and supplementary provisions as appear to the Secretary of State to be appropriate and may, in particular, prescribe circumstances in which a person is or is not to be taken to have been guilty of misconduct.

NOTES

Sub-s (1): word "attorneys" in square brackets in paras (b), (c) substituted by the Legal Services Act 2007, s 208, Sch 21, paras 109, 114; other words in square brackets in paras (b), (c) substituted by the Legal Services Act 2007 (Consequential Amendments) Order 2009, SI 2009/3348, art 5.

Rules: the Trade Marks Rules 2008, SI 2008/1797 at **[5.146]**.

Importation of infringing goods, material or articles

[5.89]

89 Infringing goods, material or articles may be treated as prohibited goods

(1) The proprietor of a registered trade mark, or a licensee, may give notice in writing to the [Commissioners for Her Majesty's Revenue and Customs]—

(a) that he is the proprietor or, as the case may be, a licensee of the registered trade mark,

(b) that, at a time and place specified in the notice, goods which are, in relation to that registered trade mark, infringing goods, material or articles are expected to arrive in the United Kingdom—

(i) from outside the European Economic Area, or

(ii) from within that Area but not having been entered for free circulation, and

(c) that he requests the Commissioners to treat them as prohibited goods.

(2) When a notice is in force under this section the importation of the goods to which the notice relates, otherwise than by a person for his private and domestic use, is prohibited; but a person is not by reason of the prohibition liable to any penalty other than forfeiture of the goods.

[(3) This section does not apply to goods placed in, or expected to be placed in, one of the situations referred to in Article 1(1), in respect of which an application may be made under Article 5(1), of Council Regulation (EC) No 1383/2003 concerning customs action against goods suspected of infringing certain intellectual property rights and the measures to be taken against goods found to have infringed such rights.]

NOTES

Sub-s (1): words in square brackets substituted by virtue of the Commissioners for Revenue and Customs Act 2005, s 50(1).

Sub-s (3): substituted by the Goods Infringing Intellectual Property Rights (Customs) Regulations 2004, SI 2004/1473, reg 13.

[5.90]

90 Power of [Commissioners for Her Majesty's Revenue and Customs] to make regulations

(1) The [Commissioners for Her Majesty's Revenue and Customs] may make regulations prescribing the form in which notice is to be given under section 89 and requiring a person giving notice—

(a) to furnish the Commissioners with such evidence as may be specified in the regulations, either on giving notice or when the goods are imported, or at both those times, and

(b) to comply with such other conditions as may be specified in the regulations.

(2) The regulations may, in particular, require a person giving such a notice—

(a) to pay such fees in respect of the notice as may be specified by the regulations;

(b) to give such security as may be so specified in respect of any liability or expense which the Commissioners may incur in consequence of the notice by reason of the detention of any goods or anything done to goods detained;

(c) to indemnify the Commissioners against any such liability or expense, whether security has been given or not.

(3) The regulations may make different provision as respects different classes of case to which they apply and may include such incidental and supplementary provisions as the Commissioners consider expedient.

(4) Regulations under this section shall be made by statutory instrument which shall be subject to annulment in pursuance of a resolution of either House of Parliament.

(5) . . .

NOTES

Section heading: words in square brackets substituted by virtue of the Commissioners for Revenue and Customs Act 2005, s 50(1).

Sub-s (1): words in square brackets substituted by virtue of the Commissioners for Revenue and Customs Act 2005, s 50(1).

Sub-s (5): repealed by the Commissioners for Revenue and Customs Act 2005, ss 50(6), 52(2), Sch 4, para 57, Sch 5.

Regulations: the Trade Marks (Customs) Regulations 1994, SI 1994/2625, at **[5.115]**; the Goods Infringing the Olympics and Paralympics Association Rights (Customs) Regulations 2007, SI 2007/1508.

[5.91]

[91 Power of Commissioners for Revenue and Customs to disclose information]

Where information relating to infringing goods, material or articles has been obtained [or is held] by [the Commissioners for her Majesty's Revenue and Customs] for the purposes of, or in connection with, the exercise of [functions of Her Majesty's Revenue and Customs] in relation to imported goods, the Commissioners may authorise the disclosure of that information for the purpose of facilitating the exercise by any person of any function in connection with the investigation or prosecution of [an offence under—

(a) section 92 below (unauthorised use of trade mark, &c in relation to goods),

(b) the Trade Descriptions Act 1968,

(c) the Business Protection from Misleading Marketing Regulations 2008, or

(d) the Consumer Protection from Unfair Trading Regulations 2008.]

NOTES

Section heading: substituted by the Commissioners for Revenue and Customs Act 2005, s 50(6), Sch 4, para 58(2).

Words in first pair of square brackets inserted and words in second and third pairs of square brackets substituted by the Commissioners for Revenue and Customs Act 2005, s 50(6), Sch 4, para 58(1); words in fourth pair of square brackets substituted by the Consumer Protection from Unfair Trading Regulations 2008, SI 2008/1277, reg 30(1), Sch 2, Pt 1, paras 53, 54.

Offences

[5.92]

92 Unauthorised use of trade mark, &c in relation to goods

(1) A person commits an offence who with a view to gain for himself or another, or with intent to cause loss to another, and without the consent of the proprietor—

(a) applies to goods or their packaging a sign identical to, or likely to be mistaken for, a registered trade mark, or

(b) sells or lets for hire, offers or exposes for sale or hire or distributes goods which bear, or the packaging of which bears, such a sign, or

(c) has in his possession, custody or control in the course of a business any such goods with a view to the doing of anything, by himself or another, which would be an offence under paragraph (b).

(2) A person commits an offence who with a view to gain for himself or another, or with intent to cause loss to another, and without the consent of the proprietor—

(a) applies a sign identical to, or likely to be mistaken for, a registered trade mark to material intended to be used—

(i) for labelling or packaging goods,

(ii) as a business paper in relation to goods, or

(iii) for advertising goods, or

(b) uses in the course of a business material bearing such a sign for labelling or packaging goods, as a business paper in relation to goods, or for advertising goods, or

(c) has in his possession, custody or control in the course of a business any such material with a view to the doing of anything, by himself or another, which would be an offence under paragraph (b).

(3) A person commits an offence who with a view to gain for himself or another, or with intent to cause loss to another, and without the consent of the proprietor—

(a) makes an article specifically designed or adapted for making copies of a sign identical to, or likely to be mistaken for, a registered trade mark, or

(b) has such an article in his possession, custody or control in the course of a business,

knowing or having reason to believe that it has been, or is to be, used to produce goods, or material for labelling or packaging goods, as a business paper in relation to goods, or for advertising goods.

(4) A person does not commit an offence under this section unless—

(a) the goods are goods in respect of which the trade mark is registered, or

(b) the trade mark has a reputation in the United Kingdom and the use of the sign takes or would take unfair advantage of, or is or would be detrimental to, the distinctive character or the repute of the trade mark.

(5) It is a defence for a person charged with an offence under this section to show that he believed on reasonable grounds that the use of the sign in the manner in which it was used, or was to be used, was not an infringement of the registered trade mark.

(6) A person guilty of an offence under this section is liable—

(a) on summary conviction to imprisonment for a term not exceeding six months or a fine not exceeding the statutory maximum, or both;

(b) on conviction on indictment to a fine or imprisonment for a term not exceeding ten years, or both.

NOTES

[5.93]

[92A Search warrants

(1) Where a justice of the peace (in Scotland, a sheriff or justice of the peace) is satisfied by information on oath given by a constable (in Scotland, by evidence on oath) that there are reasonable grounds for believing—

(a) that an offence under section 92 (unauthorised use of trade mark, etc in relation to goods) has been or is about to be committed in any premises, and

(b) that evidence that such an offence has been or is about to be committed is in those premises,

he may issue a warrant authorising a constable to enter and search the premises, using such reasonable force as is necessary.

(2) The power conferred by subsection (1) does not, in England and Wales, extend to authorising a search for material of the kinds mentioned in section 9(2) of the Police and Criminal Evidence Act 1984 (c 60) (certain classes of personal or confidential material).

(3) A warrant under subsection (1)—

(a) may authorise persons to accompany any constable executing the warrant, and

(b) remains in force for [three months] from the date of its issue.

(4) In executing a warrant issued under subsection (1) a constable may seize an article if he reasonably believes that it is evidence that any offence under section 92 has been or is about to be committed.

(5) In this section "premises" includes land, buildings, fixed or moveable structures, vehicles, vessels, aircraft and hovercraft.]

NOTES

Inserted by the Copyright, etc and Trade Marks (Offences and Enforcement) Act 2002, s 6.

Sub-s (3): words in square brackets substituted for original words "28 days" in relation to England and Wales by the Serious Organised Crime and Police Act 2005, s 174(1), Sch 16, para 8.

[5.94]

93 Enforcement function of local weights and measures authority

(1) It is the duty of every local weights and measures authority to enforce within their area the provisions of section 92 (unauthorised use of trade mark, &c in relation to goods).

(2) . . .

(3) Subsection (1) above does not apply in relation to the enforcement of section 92 in Northern Ireland, but it is the duty of the Department of Economic Development to enforce that section in Northern Ireland.

. . .

[(3A) For the investigatory powers available to a local weights and measures authority or the Department of Enterprise, Trade and Investment in Northern Ireland for the purposes of the duties in this section, see Schedule 5 to the Consumer Rights Act 2015.]

(4) Any enactment which authorises the disclosure of information for the purpose of facilitating the enforcement of the Trade Descriptions Act 1968 shall apply as if section 92 above were contained in that Act and as if the functions of any person in relation to the enforcement of that section were functions under that Act.

(5) Nothing in this section shall be construed as authorising a local weights and measures authority to bring proceedings in Scotland for an offence.

NOTES

Sub-s (2): repealed by the Consumer Rights Act 2015, s 77(2), Sch 6, para 59(1), (2).

Sub-s (3): words omitted repealed by the Consumer Rights Act 2015, s 77(2), Sch 6, para 59(1), (3).

Sub-s (3A): inserted by the Consumer Rights Act 2015, s 77(2), Sch 6, para 59(1), (4).

[5.95]

94 Falsification of register, &c

(1) It is an offence for a person to make, or cause to be made, a false entry in the register of trade marks, knowing or having reason to believe that it is false.

(2) It is an offence for a person—

(a) to make or cause to be made anything falsely purporting to be a copy of an entry in the register, or

(b) to produce or tender or cause to be produced or tendered in evidence any such thing,

knowing or having reason to believe that it is false.

(3) A person guilty of an offence under this section is liable—

(a) on conviction on indictment, to imprisonment for a term not exceeding two years or a fine, or both;

(b) on summary conviction, to imprisonment for a term not exceeding six months or a fine not exceeding the statutory maximum, or both.

[5.96]

95 Falsely representing trade mark as registered

(1) It is an offence for a person—

(a) falsely to represent that a mark is a registered trade mark, or

(b) to make a false representation as to the goods or services for which a trade mark is registered

knowing or having reason to believe that the representation is false.

(2) For the purposes of this section, the use in the United Kingdom in relation to a trade mark—

(a) of the word "registered", or

(b) of any other word or symbol importing a reference (express or implied) to registration,

shall be deemed to be a representation as to registration under this Act unless it is shown that the reference is to registration elsewhere than in the United Kingdom and that the trade mark is in fact so registered for the goods or services in question.

(3) A person guilty of an offence under this section is liable on summary conviction to a fine not exceeding level 3 on the standard scale.

[5.97]

96 Supplementary provisions as to summary proceedings in Scotland

(1) Notwithstanding anything in [section 136 of the Criminal Procedure (Scotland) Act 1995], summary proceedings in Scotland for an offence under this Act may be begun at any time within six months after the date on which evidence sufficient in the Lord Advocate's opinion to justify the proceedings came to his knowledge.

For this purpose a certificate of the Lord Advocate as to the date on which such evidence came to his knowledge is conclusive evidence.

(2) For the purposes of subsection (1) and of any other provision of this Act as to the time within which summary proceedings for an offence may be brought, proceedings in Scotland shall be deemed to be begun on the date on which a warrant to apprehend or to cite the accused is granted, if such warrant is executed without undue delay.

NOTES

Sub-s (1): words in square brackets substituted by the Criminal Procedure (Consequential Provisions) (Scotland) Act 1995, s 5, Sch 4, para 92(2).

Transfer of functions: by virtue of the Scotland Act 1998, s 44(1)(c), the Lord Advocate ceased, on 20 May 1999 (see SI 1998/3178), to be a Minister of the Crown and became a member of the Scottish Executive. Accordingly, certain functions of the Lord Advocate are transferred to the Secretary of State (or as the case may be the Secretary of State for Scotland), or the Advocate General for Scotland: see the Transfer of Functions (Lord Advocate and Secretary of State) Order 1999, SI 1999/678 and the Transfer of Functions (Lord Advocate and Advocate General for Scotland) Order 1999, SI 1999/679.

Forfeiture of counterfeit goods, &c

[5.98]

97 Forfeiture: England and Wales or Northern Ireland

(1) In England and Wales or Northern Ireland where there has come into the possession of any person in connection with the investigation or prosecution of a relevant offence—

(a) goods which, or the packaging of which, bears a sign identical to or likely to be mistaken for a registered trade mark,

(b) material bearing such a sign and intended to be used for labelling or packaging goods, as a business paper in relation to goods, or for advertising goods, or

(c) articles specifically designed or adapted for making copies of such a sign,

that person may apply under this section for an order for the forfeiture of the goods, material or articles.

(2) An application under this section may be made—

(a) where proceedings have been brought in any court for a relevant offence relating to some or all of the goods, material or articles, to that court;

(b) where no application for the forfeiture of the goods, material or articles has been made under paragraph (a), by way of complaint to a magistrates' court.

(3) On an application under this section the court shall make an order for the forfeiture of any goods, material or articles only if it is satisfied that a relevant offence has been committed in relation to the goods, material or articles.

(4) A court may infer for the purposes of this section that such an offence has been committed in relation to any goods, material or articles if it is satisfied that such an offence has been committed in relation to goods, material or articles which are representative of them (whether by reason of being of the same design or part of the same consignment or batch or otherwise).

(5) Any person aggrieved by an order made under this section by a magistrates' court, or by a decision of such a court not to make such an order, may appeal against that order or decision—

(a) in England and Wales, to the Crown Court;

(b) in Northern Ireland, to the county court;

and an order so made may contain such provision as appears to the court to be appropriate for delaying the coming into force of the order pending the making and determination of any appeal (including any application under section 111 of the Magistrates' Courts Act 1980 or Article 146 of the Magistrates' Courts (Northern Ireland) Order 1981 (statement of case)).

(6) Subject to subsection (7), where any goods, material or articles are forfeited under this section they shall be destroyed in accordance with such directions as the court may give.

(7) On making an order under this section the court may, if it considers it appropriate to do so, direct that the goods, material or articles to which the order relates shall (instead of being destroyed) be released, to such person as the court may specify, on condition that that person—

(a) causes the offending sign to be erased, removed or obliterated and

(b) complies with any order to pay costs which has been made against him in the proceedings for the order for forfeiture.

(8) For the purposes of this section a "relevant offence" means—

[(a) an offence under section 92 above (unauthorised use of trade mark, &c in relation to goods),

(b) an offence under the Trade Descriptions Act 1968,

(c) an offence under the Business Protection from Misleading Marketing Regulations 2008,

(d) an offence under the Consumer Protection from Unfair Trading Regulations 2008, or

(e) any offence involving dishonesty or deception.]

NOTES

Sub-s (8): words in square brackets substituted by the Consumer Protection from Unfair Trading Regulations 2008, SI 2008/1277, reg 30(1), Sch 2, Pt 1, paras 53, 55.

Modification: this section is modified in its application to representations of the Olympic symbol, motto, or protected word, by the Olympic Symbol etc (Protection) Act 1995, s 11.

[5.99]

98 Forfeiture: Scotland

(1) In Scotland the court may make an order for the forfeiture of any—

(a) goods which bear, or the packaging of which bears, a sign identical to or likely to be mistaken for a registered trade mark,

(b) material bearing such a sign and intended to be used for labelling or packaging goods, as a business paper in relation to goods, or for advertising goods, or

(c) articles specifically designed or adapted for making copies of such a sign.

(2) An order under this section may be made—

(a) on an application by the procurator-fiscal made in the manner specified in [section 134 of the Criminal Procedure (Scotland) Act 1995], or

(b) where a person is convicted of a relevant offence, in addition to any other penalty which the court may impose.

(3) On an application under subsection (2)(a), the court shall make an order for the forfeiture of any goods, material or articles only if it is satisfied that a relevant offence has been committed in relation to the goods, material or articles.

(4) The court may infer for the purposes of this section that such an offence has been committed in relation to any goods, material or articles if it is satisfied that such an offence has been committed in relation to goods, material or articles which are representative of them (whether by reason of being of the same design or part of the same consignment or batch or otherwise).

(5) The procurator-fiscal making the application under subsection (2)(a) shall serve on any person appearing to him to be the owner of, or otherwise to have an interest in, the goods, material or articles to which the application relates a copy of the application, together with a notice giving him the opportunity to appear at the hearing of the application to show cause why the goods, material or articles should not be forfeited.

(6) Service under subsection (5) shall be carried out, and such service may be proved, in the manner specified for citation of an accused in summary proceedings under the [Criminal Procedure (Scotland) Act 1995].

(7) Any person upon whom notice is served under subsection (5) and any other person claiming to be the owner of, or otherwise to have an interest in, goods, material or articles to which an application under this section relates shall be entitled to appear at the hearing of the application to show cause why the goods, material or articles should not be forfeited.

(8) The court shall not make an order following an application under subsection (2)(a)—

(a) if any person on whom notice is served under subsection (5) does not appear, unless service of the notice on that person is proved; or

(b) if no notice under subsection (5) has been served, unless the court is satisfied that in the circumstances it was reasonable not to serve such notice.

(9) Where an order for the forfeiture of any goods, material or articles is made following an application under subsection (2)(a), any person who appeared, or was entitled to appear, to show cause why goods, material or articles should not be forfeited may, within 21 days of the making of the order, appeal to the High Court by Bill of Suspension; and [section 182(5)(a) to (e) of the Criminal Procedure (Scotland) Act 1995] shall apply to an appeal under this subsection as it applies to a stated case under Part II of that Act.

(10) An order following an application under subsection (2)(a) shall not take effect—

(a) until the end of the period of 21 days beginning with the day after the day on which the order is made; or

(b) if an appeal is made under subsection (9) above within that period, until the appeal is determined or abandoned.

(11) An order under subsection (2)(b) shall not take effect—

(a) until the end of the period within which an appeal against the order could be brought under the [Criminal Procedure (Scotland) Act 1995]; or

(b) if an appeal is made within that period, until the appeal is determined or abandoned.

(12) Subject to subsection (13), goods, material or articles forfeited under this section shall be destroyed in accordance with such directions as the court may give.

(13) On making an order under this section the court may if it considers it appropriate to do so, direct that the goods, material or articles to which the order relates shall (instead of being destroyed) be released, to such person as the court may specify, on condition that that person causes the offending sign to be erased, removed or obliterated.

(14) For the purposes of this section—

"relevant offence" means—

[(a) an offence under section 92 above (unauthorised use of trade mark, &c in relation to goods),

(b) an offence under the Trade Descriptions Act 1968,

(c) an offence under the Business Protection from Misleading Marketing Regulations 2008,

(d) an offence under the Consumer Protection from Unfair Trading Regulations 2008, or

(e) any offence involving dishonesty or deception;]

"the court" means—

(a) in relation to an order made on an application under subsection (2)(a), the sheriff, and

(b) in relation to an order made under subsection (2)(b), the court which imposed the penalty.

NOTES

Sub-ss (2), (6), (9), (11): words in square brackets substituted by the Criminal Procedure (Consequential Provisions) (Scotland) Act 1995, s 5, Sch 4, para 92(3).

Sub-s (14): in definition "relevant offence" words in square brackets substituted by the Consumer Protection from Unfair Trading Regulations 2008, SI 2008/1277, reg 30(1), Sch 2, Pt 1, paras 53, 56.

Modification: this section is modified in its application to representations of the Olympic symbol, motto, or protected word, by the Olympic Symbol etc (Protection) Act 1995, s 12.

PART IV
MISCELLANEOUS AND GENERAL PROVISIONS

Miscellaneous

[5.100]

99 Unauthorised use of Royal arms, &c

(1) A person shall not without the authority of Her Majesty use in connection with any business the Royal arms (or arms so closely resembling the Royal arms as to be calculated to deceive) in such manner as to be calculated to lead to the belief that he is duly authorised to use the Royal arms.

(2) A person shall not without the authority of Her Majesty or of a member of the Royal family use in connection with any business any device, emblem or title in such a manner as to be calculated to lead to the belief that he is employed by, or supplies goods or services to, Her Majesty or that member of the Royal family.

(3) A person who contravenes subsection (1) commits an offence and is liable on summary conviction to a fine not exceeding level 2 on the standard scale.

(4) Contravention of subsection (1) or (2) may be restrained by injunction in proceedings brought by—

(a) any person who is authorised to use the arms, device, emblem or title in question, or

(b) any person authorised by the Lord Chamberlain to take such proceedings.

(5) Nothing in this section affects any right of the proprietor of a trade mark containing any such arms, device, emblem or title to use that trade mark.

[5.101]
100 Burden of proving use of trade mark
If in any civil proceedings under this Act a question arises as to the use to which a registered trade mark has been put, it is for the proprietor to show what use has been made of it.

[5.102]
101 Offences committed by partnerships and bodies corporate
(1) Proceedings for an offence under this Act alleged to have been committed by a partnership shall be brought against the partnership in the name of the firm and not in that of the partners; but without prejudice to any liability of the partners under subsection (4) below.
(2) The following provisions apply for the purposes of such proceedings as in relation to a body corporate—
(a) any rules of court relating to the service of documents;
(b) in England and Wales or Northern Ireland, Schedule 3 to the Magistrates' Courts Act 1980 or Schedule 4 to the Magistrates' Courts (Northern Ireland) Order 1981 (procedure on charge of offence).
(3) A fine imposed on a partnership on its conviction in such proceedings shall be paid out of the partnership assets.
(4) Where a partnership is guilty of an offence under this Act, every partner, other than a partner who is proved to have been ignorant of or to have attempted to prevent the commission of the offence, is also guilty of the offence and liable to be proceeded against and punished accordingly.
(5) Where an offence under this Act committed by a body corporate is proved to have been committed with the consent or connivance of a director, manager, secretary or other similar officer of the body, or a person purporting to act in any such capacity, he as well as the body corporate is guilty of the offence and liable to be proceeded against and punished accordingly.

Interpretation

[5.103]
102 Adaptation of expressions for Scotland
In the application of this Act to Scotland—
"account of profits" means accounting and payment of profits;
"accounts" means count, reckoning and payment;
"assignment" means assignation;
"costs" means expenses;
"declaration" means declarator;
"defendant" means defender;
"delivery up" means delivery;
"injunction" means interdict;
"interlocutory relief" means interim remedy; and
"plaintiff" means pursuer.

[5.104]
103 Minor definitions
(1) In this Act—
"business" includes a trade or profession;
"director", in relation to a body corporate whose affairs are managed by its members, means any member of the body;
"infringement proceedings", in relation to a registered trade mark, includes proceedings under section 16 (order for delivery up of infringing goods, &c);
"publish" means make available to the public, and references to publication—
(a) in relation to an application for registration, are to publication under section 38(1), and
(b) in relation to registration, are to publication under section 40(4);
"statutory provisions" includes provisions of subordinate legislation within the meaning of the Interpretation Act 1978;
"trade" includes any business or profession.
(2) References in this Act to use (or any particular description of use) of a trade mark, or of a sign identical with, similar to, or likely to be mistaken for a trade mark, include use (or that description of use) otherwise than by means of a graphic representation.
(3) References in this Act to [an] [EU] instrument include references to any instrument amending or replacing that instrument.

NOTES
Sub-s (3): word in first pair of square brackets substituted by the Treaty of Lisbon (Changes in Terminology) Order 2011, SI 2011/1043, art 6(3), subject to a transitional provision contained in art 3(3) thereof; reference in second pair of square brackets substituted by the Treaty of Lisbon (Changes in Terminology) Order 2011, SI 2011/1043, art 6(1)(d), subject to a transitional provision contained in art 3(3) thereof.

[5.105]

104 Index of defined expressions

In this Act the expressions listed below are defined by or otherwise fall to be construed in accordance with the provisions indicated—

account of profits and accounts (in Scotland)	section 102
appointed person (for purposes of section 76)	section 77
assignment (in Scotland)	section 102
business	section 103(1)
certification mark	section 50(1)
collective mark	section 49(1)
commencement (of this Act)	section 109(2)
. . .	. . .
. . .	. . .
Convention country	section 55(1)(b)
costs (in Scotland)	section 102
the court	section 75
date of application	section 33(2)
date of filing	section 33(1)
date of registration	section 40(3)
defendant (in Scotland)	section 102
delivery up (in Scotland)	section 102
director	section 103(1)
earlier right	section 5(4)
earlier trade mark	section 6
[European Union trade mark	section 51]
[European Union Trade Mark Regulation	section 51]
exclusive licence and licensee	section 29(1)
infringement (of registered trade mark)	sections 9(1) and (2) and 10
infringement proceedings	section 103(1)
infringing articles	section 17
infringing goods	section 17
infringing material	section 17
injunction (in Scotland)	section 102
interlocutory relief (in Scotland)	section 102
the International Bureau	section 53
[international trade mark (EC)	section 53]
international trade mark (UK)	section 53
Madrid Protocol	section 53
Paris Convention	section 55(1)(a)
plaintiff (in Scotland)	section 102
prescribed	section 78(1)(b)
protected under the Paris Convention	
—well-known trade marks	section 56(1)
—state emblems and official signs or hallmarks	section 57(1)
—emblems, &c of international organisations	section 58(2)
publish and references to publication	section 103(1)
register, registered (and related expressions)	section 63(1)
registered trade mark [attorney]	section 83[(2)]
registrable transaction	section 25(2)
the registrar	section 62
rules	section 78
statutory provisions	section 103(1)
trade	section 103(1)

trade mark	
—generally	section 1(1)
—includes collective mark or certification mark	section 1(2)
United Kingdom (references include Isle of Man)	section 108(2)
use (of trade mark or sign)	section 103(2)
well-known trade mark (under Paris Convention)	section 56(1)

NOTES

Entries "Community trade mark" and "Community Trade Mark Regulation" (omitted) repealed and entries "European Union trade mark" and "European Union Trade Mark Regulation" inserted, by the European Union Trade Mark Regulations 2016, SI 2016/299, reg 15, Schedule, para 3, subject to transitional provisions and savings as noted to s 5 at **[5.5]**.

Entry "international trade mark (EC)" inserted by the Trade Marks (International Registrations Designating the European Community, etc) Regulations 2004, SI 2004/2332, regs 2, 6.

In entry "registered trade mark agents" word and number in square brackets substituted by the Legal Services Act 2007, s 208, Sch 21, paras 109, 115.

Other general provisions

[5.106]
105 Transitional provisions

The provisions of Schedule 3 have effect with respect to transitional matters, including the treatment of marks registered under the Trade Marks Act 1938, and applications for registration and other proceedings pending under that Act, on the commencement of this Act.

NOTES

Trade Marks Act 1938: repealed by s 106(2) of, and Sch 5 to, this Act.

[5.107]
106 Consequential amendments and repeals

(1) The enactments specified in Schedule 4 are amended in accordance with that Schedule, the amendments being consequential on the provisions of this Act.
(2) The enactments specified in Schedule 5 are repealed to the extent specified.

[5.108]
107 Territorial waters and the continental shelf

(1) For the purposes of this Act the territorial waters of the United Kingdom shall be treated as part of the United Kingdom.
(2) This Act applies to things done in the United Kingdom sector of the continental shelf on a structure or vessel which is present there for purposes directly connected with the exploration of the sea bed or subsoil or the exploitation of their natural resources as it applies to things done in the United Kingdom.
(3) The United Kingdom sector of the continental shelf means the areas designated by order under section 1(7) of the Continental Shelf Act 1964.

[5.109]
108 Extent

(1) This Act extends to England and Wales, Scotland and Northern Ireland.
(2) This Act also extends to the Isle of Man, subject to such exceptions and modifications as Her Majesty may specify by Order in Council; and subject to any such Order references in this Act to the United Kingdom shall be construed as including the Isle of Man.

NOTES

Orders: the Trade Marks (Isle of Man) Order 2013, SI 2013/2601.

[5.110]
109 Commencement

(1) The provisions of this Act come into force on such day as the Secretary of State may appoint by order made by statutory instrument.

Different days may be appointed for different provisions and different purposes.

(2) The references to the commencement of this Act in Schedules 3 and 4 (transitional provisions and consequential amendments) are to the commencement of the main substantive provisions of Parts I and III of this Act and the consequential repeal of the Trade Marks Act 1938.

Provision may be made by order under this section identifying the date of that commencement.

NOTES

Orders: the Trade Marks Act 1994 (Commencement) Order 1994, SI 1994/2550.
Trade Marks Act 1938: repealed by s 106(2) of, and Sch 5 to, this Act.

[5.111]

110 Short title

This Act may be cited as the Trade Marks Act 1994.

SCHEDULES

SCHEDULE 1
COLLECTIVE MARKS

Section 49

General

[5.112]

1. The provisions of this Act apply to collective marks subject to the following provisions.

Signs of which a collective mark may consist

2. In relation to a collective mark the reference in section 1(1) (signs of which a trade mark may consist) to distinguishing goods or services of one undertaking from those of other undertakings shall be construed as a reference to distinguishing goods or services of members of the association which is the proprietor of the mark from those of other undertakings.

Indication of geographical origin

3. (1) Notwithstanding section 3(1)(c), a collective mark may be registered which consists of signs or indications which may serve, in trade, to designate the geographical origin of the goods or services.

(2) However, the proprietor of such a mark is not entitled to prohibit the use of the signs or indications in accordance with honest practices in industrial or commercial matters (in particular, by a person who is entitled to use a geographical name).

Mark not to be misleading as to character or significance

4. (1) A collective mark shall not be registered if the public is liable to be misled as regards the character or significance of the mark, in particular if it is likely to be taken to be something other than a collective mark.

(2) The registrar may accordingly require that a mark in respect of which application is made for registration include some indication that it is a collective mark.

Notwithstanding section 39(2), an application may be amended so as to comply with any such requirement.

Regulations governing use of collective mark

5. (1) An applicant for registration of a collective mark must file with the registrar regulations governing the use of the mark.

(2) The regulations must specify the persons authorised to use the mark, the conditions of membership of the association and, where they exist, the conditions of use of the mark, including any sanctions against misuse.

Further requirements with which the regulations have to comply may be imposed by rules.

Approval of regulations by registrar

6. (1) A collective mark shall not be registered unless the regulations governing the use of the mark—

(a) comply with paragraph 5(2) and any further requirements imposed by rules, and

(b) are not contrary to public policy or to accepted principles of morality.

(2) Before the end of the prescribed period after the date of the application for registration of a collective mark, the applicant must file the regulations with the registrar and pay the prescribed fee.

If he does not do so, the application shall be deemed to be withdrawn.

7. (1) The registrar shall consider whether the requirements mentioned in paragraph 6(1) are met.

(2) If it appears to the registrar that those requirements are not met, he shall inform the applicant and give him an opportunity, within such period as the registrar may specify, to make representations or to file amended regulations.

(3) If the applicant fails to satisfy the registrar that those requirements are met, or to file regulations amended so as to meet them, or fails to respond before the end of the specified period, the registrar shall refuse the application.

(4) If it appears to the registrar that those requirements, and the other requirements for registration, are met, he shall accept the application and shall proceed in accordance with section 38 (publication, opposition proceedings and observations).

8. The regulations shall be published and notice of opposition may be given, and observations may be made, relating to the matters mentioned in paragraph 6(1).

This is in addition to any other grounds on which the application may be opposed or observations made.

Regulations to be open to inspection

9. The regulations governing the use of a registered collective mark shall be open to public inspection in the same way as the register.

Amendment of regulations

10. (1) An amendment of the regulations governing the use of a registered collective mark is not effective unless and until the amended regulations are filed with the registrar and accepted by him.

(2) Before accepting any amended regulations the registrar may in any case where it appears to him expedient to do so cause them to be published.

(3) If he does so, notice of opposition may be given, and observations may be made, relating to the matters mentioned in paragraph 6(1).

Infringement: rights of authorised users

11. The following provisions apply in relation to an authorised user of a registered collective mark as in relation to a licensee of a trade mark—

(a) section 10(5) (definition of infringement: unauthorised application of mark to certain material);

(b) section 19(2) (order as to disposal of infringing goods, material or articles: adequacy of other remedies);

(c) section 89 (prohibition of importation of infringing goods, material or articles: request to [Commissioners for Her Majesty's Revenue and Customs]).

12. (1) Thc following provisions (which correspond to the provisions of section 30 (general provisions as to rights of licensees in case of infringement)) have effect as regards the rights of an authorised user in relation to infringement of a registered collective mark.

(2) An authorised user is entitled, subject to any agreement to the contrary between him and the proprietor, to call on the proprietor to take infringement proceedings in respect of any matter which affects his interests.

(3) If the proprietor—

(a) refuses to do so, or

(b) fails to do so within two months after being called upon,

the authorised user may bring the proceedings in his own name as if he were the proprietor.

(4) Where infringement proceedings are brought by virtue of this paragraph, the authorised user may not, without the leave of the court, proceed with the action unless the proprietor is either joined as a plaintiff or added as a defendant.

This does not affect the granting of interlocutory relief on an application by an authorised user alone.

(5) A proprietor who is added as a defendant as mentioned in sub-paragraph (4) shall not be made liable for any costs in the action unless he takes part in the proceedings.

(6) In infringement proceedings brought by the proprietor of a registered collective mark any loss suffered or likely to be suffered by authorised users shall be taken into account; and the court may give such directions as it thinks fit as to the extent to which the plaintiff is to hold the proceeds of any pecuniary remedy on behalf of such users.

Grounds for revocation of registration

13. Apart from the grounds of revocation provided for in section 46, the registration of a collective mark may be revoked on the ground—

(a) that the manner in which the mark has been used by the proprietor has caused it to become liable to mislead the public in the manner referred to in paragraph 4(1), or

(b) that the proprietor has failed to observe, or to secure the observance of, the regulations governing the use of the mark, or

(c) that an amendment of the regulations has been made so that the regulations—

(i) no longer comply with paragraph 5(2) and any further conditions imposed by rules, or

(ii) are contrary to public policy or to accepted principles of morality.

Grounds for invalidity of registration

14. Apart from the grounds of invalidity provided for in section 47, the registration of a collective mark may be declared invalid on the ground that the mark was registered in breach of the provisions of paragraph 4(1) or 6(1).

NOTES

Para 11: words in square brackets substituted by virtue of the Commissioners for Revenue and Customs Act 2005, s 50(1).
Rules: the Trade Marks Rules 2008, SI 2008/1797, at **[5.146]**.

SCHEDULE 2
CERTIFICATION MARKS

Section 50

General

[5.113]

1. The provisions of this Act apply to certification marks subject to the following provisions.

Signs of which a certification mark may consist

2. In relation to a certification mark the reference in section 1(1) (signs of which a trade mark may consist) to distinguishing goods or services of one undertaking from those of other undertakings shall be construed as a reference to distinguishing goods or services which are certified from those which are not.

Indication of geographical origin

3. (1) Notwithstanding section 3(1)(c), a certification mark may be registered which consists of signs or indications which may serve, in trade, to designate the geographical origin of the goods or services.

(2) However, the proprietor of such a mark is not entitled to prohibit the use of the signs or indications in accordance with honest practices in industrial or commercial matters (in particular, by a person who is entitled to use a geographical name).

Nature of proprietor's business

4. A certification mark shall not be registered if the proprietor carries on a business involving the supply of goods or services of the kind certified.

Mark not to be misleading as to character or significance

5. (1) A certification mark shall not be registered if the public is liable to be misled as regards the character or significance of the mark, in particular if it is likely to be taken to be something other than a certification mark.

(2) The registrar may accordingly require that a mark in respect of which application is made for registration include some indication that it is a certification mark.

Notwithstanding section 39(2), an application may be amended so as to comply with any such requirement.

Regulations governing use of certification mark

6. (1) An applicant for registration of a certification mark must file with the registrar regulations governing the use of the mark.

(2) The regulations must indicate who is authorised to use the mark, the characteristics to be certified by the mark, how the certifying body is to test those characteristics and to supervise the use of the mark, the fees (if any) to be paid in connection with the operation of the mark and the procedures for resolving disputes.

Further requirements with which the regulations have to comply may be imposed by rules.

Approval of regulations, &c

7. (1) A certification mark shall not be registered unless—

(a) the regulations governing the use of the mark—
   (i) comply with paragraph 6(2) and any further requirements imposed by rules, and
   (ii) are not contrary to public policy or to accepted principles of morality, and

(b) the applicant is competent to certify the goods or services for which the mark is to be registered.

(2) Before the end of the prescribed period after the date of the application for registration of a certification mark, the applicant must file the regulations with the registrar and pay the prescribed fee.

If he does not do so, the application shall be deemed to be withdrawn.

8. (1) The registrar shall consider whether the requirements mentioned in paragraph 7(1) are met.

(2) If it appears to the registrar that those requirements are not met, he shall inform the applicant and give him an opportunity, within such period as the registrar may specify, to make representations or to file amended regulations.

(3) If the applicant fails to satisfy the registrar that those requirements are met, or to file regulations amended so as to meet them, or fails to respond before the end of the specified period, the registrar shall refuse the application.

(4) If it appears to the registrar that those requirements, and the other requirements for registration, are met, he shall accept the application and shall proceed in accordance with section 38 (publication, opposition proceedings and observations).

9. The regulations shall be published and notice of opposition may be given, and observations may be made, relating to the matters mentioned in paragraph 7(1).

This is in addition to any other grounds on which the application may be opposed or observations made.

Regulations to he open to inspection

10. The regulations governing the use of a registered certification mark shall be open to public inspection in the same way as the register.

Amendment of regulations

11. (1) An amendment of the regulations governing the use of a registered certification mark is not effective unless and until the amended regulations are filed with the registrar and accepted by him.

(2) Before accepting any amended regulations the registrar may in any case where it appears to him expedient to do so cause them to be published.

(3) If he does so, notice of opposition may be given, and observations may be made, relating to the matters mentioned in paragraph 7(1).

Consent to assignment of registered certification mark

12. The assignment or other transmission of a registered certification mark is not effective without the consent of the registrar.

Infringement: rights of authorised users

13. The following provisions apply in relation to an authorised user of a registered certification mark as in relation to a licensee of a trade mark—

(a) section 10(5) (definition of infringement: unauthorised application of mark to certain material);

(b) section 19(2) (order as to disposal of infringing goods, material or articles: adequacy of other remedies);

(c) section 89 (prohibition of importation of infringing goods, material or articles: request to [Commissioners for Her Majesty's Revenue and Customs]).

14. In infringement proceedings brought by the proprietor of a registered certification mark any loss suffered or likely to be suffered by authorised users shall be taken into account; and the court may give such directions as it thinks fit as to the extent to which the plaintiff is to hold the proceeds of any pecuniary remedy on behalf of such users.

Grounds for revocation of registration

15. Apart from the grounds of revocation provided for in section 46, the registration of a certification mark may be revoked on the ground—

(a) that the proprietor has begun to carry on such a business as is mentioned in paragraph 4,

(b) that the manner in which the mark has been used by the proprietor has caused it to become liable to mislead the public in the manner referred to in paragraph 5(1),

(c) that the proprietor has failed to observe, or to secure the observance of, the regulations governing the use of the mark,

(d) that an amendment of the regulations has been made so that the regulations—

  (i) no longer comply with paragraph 6(2) and any further conditions imposed by rules, or

  (ii) are contrary to public policy or to accepted principles of morality, or

(e) that the proprietor is no longer competent to certify the goods or services for which the mark is registered.

Grounds for invalidity of registration

16. Apart from the grounds of invalidity provided for in section 47, the registration of a certification mark may be declared invalid on the ground that the mark was registered in breach of the provisions of paragraph 4, 5(1) or 7(1).

NOTES

Para 13: words in square brackets substituted by virtue of the Commissioners for Revenue and Customs Act 2005, s 50(1).

Rules: the Trade Marks Rules 2008, SI 2008/1797, at **[5.146]**.

SCHEDULE 3
TRANSITIONAL PROVISIONS

Section 105

Introductory

[5.114]

1. (1) In this Schedule—

"existing registered mark" means a trade mark, certification trade mark or service mark registered under the 1938 Act immediately before the commencement of this Act;

"the 1938 Act" means the Trade Marks Act 1938; and

"the old law" means that Act and any other enactment or rule of law applying to existing registered marks immediately before the commencement of this Act.

(2) For the purposes of this Schedule—

(a) an application shall be treated as pending on the commencement of this Act if it was made but not finally determined before commencement, and

(b) the date on which it was made shall be taken to be the date of filing under the 1938 Act.

Existing registered marks

2. (1) Existing registered marks (whether registered in Part A or B of the register kept under the 1938 Act) shall be transferred on the commencement of this Act to the register kept under this Act and have effect, subject to the provisions of this Schedule, as if registered under this Act.

(2) Existing registered marks registered as a series under section 21(2) of the 1938 Act shall be similarly registered in the new register.

Provision may be made by rules for putting such entries in the same form as is required for entries under this Act.

(3) In any other case notes indicating that existing registered marks are associated with other marks shall cease to have effect on the commencement of this Act.

3. (1) A condition entered on the former register in relation to an existing registered mark immediately before the commencement of this Act shall cease to have effect on commencement.

Proceedings under section 33 of the 1938 Act (application to expunge or vary registration for breach of condition) which are pending on the commencement of this Act shall be dealt with under the old law and any necessary alteration made to the new register.

(2) A disclaimer or limitation entered on the former register in relation to an existing registered mark immediately before the commencement of this Act shall be transferred to the new register and have effect as if entered on the register in pursuance of section 13 of this Act.

Effects of registration: infringement

4. (1) Sections 9 to 12 of this Act (effects of registration) apply in relation to an existing registered mark as from the commencement of this Act and section 14 of this Act (action for infringement) applies in relation to infringement of an existing registered mark committed after the commencement of this Act, subject to sub-paragraph (2) below.

The old law continues to apply in relation to infringements committed before commencement.

(2) It is not an infringement of—

(a) an existing registered mark, or

(b) a registered trade mark of which the distinctive elements are the same or substantially the same as those of an existing registered mark and which is registered for the same goods or services,

to continue after commencement any use which did not amount to infringement of the existing registered mark under the old law.

Infringing goods, material or articles

5. Section 16 of this Act (order for delivery up of infringing goods, material or articles) applies to infringing goods, material or articles whether made before or after the commencement of this Act.

Rights and remedies of licensee or authorised user

6. (1) Section 30 (general provisions as to rights of licensees in case of infringement) of this Act applies to licences granted before the commencement of this Act, but only in relation to infringements committed after commencement.

(2) Paragraph 14 of Schedule 2 of this Act (court to take into account loss suffered by authorised users, &c) applies only in relation to infringements committed after commencement.

Co-ownership of registered mark

7. The provisions of section 23 of this Act (co-ownership of registered mark) apply as from the commencement of this Act to an existing registered mark of which two or more persons were immediately before commencement registered as joint proprietors.

But so long as the relations between the joint proprietors remain such as are described in section 63 of the 1938 Act (joint ownership) there shall be taken to be an agreement to exclude the operation of subsections (1) and (3) of section 23 of this Act (ownership in undivided shares and right of co-proprietor to make separate use of the mark).

Assignment, &c of registered mark

8. (1) Section 24 of this Act (assignment or other transmission of registered mark) applies to transactions and events occurring after the commencement of this Act in relation to an existing registered mark; and the old law continues to apply in relation to transactions and events occurring before commencement.

(2) Existing entries under section 25 of the 1938 Act (registration of assignments and transmissions) shall be transferred on the commencement of this Act to the register kept under this Act and have effect as if made under section 25 of this Act.

Provision may be made by rules for putting such entries in the same form as is required for entries made under this Act.

(3) An application for registration under section 25 of the 1938 Act which is pending before the registrar on the commencement of this Act shall be treated as an application for registration under section 25 of this Act and shall proceed accordingly.

The registrar may require the applicant to amend his application so as to conform with the requirements of this Act.

(4) An application for registration under section 25 of the 1938 Act which has been determined by the registrar but not finally determined before the commencement of this Act shall be dealt with under the old law; and sub-paragraph (2) above shall apply in relation to any resulting entry in the register.

(5) Where before the commencement of this Act a person has become entitled by assignment or transmission to an existing registered mark but has not registered his title, any application for registration after commencement shall be made under section 25 of this Act.

(6) In cases to which sub-paragraph (3) or (5) applies section 25(3) of the 1938 Act continues to apply (and section 25(3) and (4) of this Act do not apply) as regards the consequences of failing to register.

Licensing of registered mark

9. (1) Sections 28 and 29(2) of this Act (licensing of registered trade mark; rights of exclusive licensee against grantor's successor in title) apply only in relation to licences granted after the commencement of this Act; and the old law continues to apply in relation to licences granted before commencement.

(2) Existing entries under section 28 of the 1938 Act (registered users) shall be transferred on the commencement of this Act to the register kept under this Act and have effect as if made under section 25 of this Act.

Provision may be made by rules for putting such entries in the same form as is required for entries made under this Act.

(3) An application for registration as a registered user which is pending before the registrar on the commencement of this Act shall be treated as an application for registration of a licence under section 25(1) of this Act and shall proceed accordingly.

The registrar may require the applicant to amend his application so as to conform with the requirements of this Act.

(4) An application for registration as a registered user which has been determined by the registrar but not finally determined before the commencement of this Act shall be dealt with under the old law; and sub-paragraph (2) above shall apply in relation to any resulting entry in the register.

(5) Any proceedings pending on the commencement of this Act under section 28(8) or (10) of the 1938 Act (variation or cancellation of registration of registered user) shall be dealt with under the old law and any necessary alteration made to the new register.

Pending applications for registration

10. (1) An application for registration of a mark under the 1938 Act which is pending on the commencement of this Act shall be dealt with under the old law, subject as mentioned below, and if registered the mark shall be treated for the purposes of this Schedule as an existing registered mark.

(2) The power of the Secretary of State under section 78 of this Act to make rules regulating practice and procedure, and as to the matters mentioned in subsection (2) of that section, is exercisable in relation to such an application; and different provision may be made for such applications from that made for other applications.

(3) Section 23 of the 1938 Act (provisions as to associated trade marks) shall be disregarded in dealing after the commencement of this Act with an application for registration.

Conversion of pending application

11. (1) In the case of a pending application for registration which has not been advertised under section 18 of the 1938 Act before the commencement of this Act, the applicant may give notice to the registrar claiming to have the registrability of the mark determined in accordance with the provisions of this Act.

(2) The notice must be in the prescribed form, be accompanied by the appropriate fee and be given no later than six months after the commencement of this Act.

(3) Notice duly given is irrevocable and has the effect that the application shall be treated as if made immediately after the commencement of this Act.

Trade marks registered according to old classification

12. The registrar may exercise the powers conferred by rules under section 65 of this Act (adaptation of entries to new classification) to secure that any existing registered marks which do not conform to the system of classification prescribed under section 34 of this Act are brought into conformity with that system.

This applies, in particular, to existing registered marks classified according to the pre-1938 classification set out in Schedule 3 to the Trade Marks Rules 1986.

Claim to priority from overseas application

13. Section 35 of this Act (claim to priority of Convention application) applies to an application for registration under this Act made after the commencement of this Act notwithstanding that the Convention application was made before commencement.

14. (1) Where before the commencement of this Act a person has duly filed an application for protection of a trade mark in a relevant country within the meaning of section 39A of the 1938 Act which is not a Convention country (a "relevant overseas application"), he, or his successor in title, has a right to priority, for the purposes of registering the same trade mark under this Act for some or all of the same goods or services, for a period of six months from the date of filing of the relevant overseas application.

(2) If the application for registration under this Act is made within that six-month period—

(a) the relevant date for the purposes of establishing which rights take precedence shall be the date of filing of the relevant overseas application, and

(b) the registrability of the trade mark shall not be affected by any use of the mark in the United Kingdom in the period between that date and the date of the application under this Act.

(3) Any filing which in a relevant country is equivalent to a regular national filing, under its domestic legislation or an international agreement, shall be treated as giving rise to the right of priority.

A "regular national filing" means a filing which is adequate to establish the date on which the application was filed in that country, whatever may be the subsequent fate of the application.

(4) A subsequent application concerning the same subject as the relevant overseas application, filed in the same country, shall be considered the relevant overseas application (of which the filing date is the starting date of the period of priority), if at the time of the subsequent application—

(a) the previous application has been withdrawn, abandoned or refused, without having been laid open to public inspection and without leaving any rights outstanding, and

(b) it has not yet served as a basis for claiming a right of priority.

The previous application may not thereafter serve as a basis for claiming a right of priority.

(5) Provision may be made by rules as to the manner of claiming a right to priority on the basis of a relevant overseas application.

(6) A right to priority arising as a result of a relevant overseas application may be assigned or otherwise transmitted, either with the application or independently.

The reference in sub-paragraph (1) to the applicant's "successor in title" shall be construed accordingly.

(7) Nothing in this paragraph affects proceedings on an application for registration under the 1938 Act made before the commencement of this Act (see paragraph 10 above).

Duration and renewal of registration

15. (1) Section 42(1) of this Act (duration of original period of registration) applies in relation to the registration of a mark in pursuance of an application made after the commencement of this Act; and the old law applies in any other case.

(2) Sections 42(2) and 43 of this Act (renewal) apply where the renewal falls due on or after the commencement of this Act; and the old law continues to apply in any other case.

(3) In either case it is immaterial when the fee is paid.

Pending application for alteration of registered mark

16. An application under section 35 of the 1938 Act (alteration of registered trade mark) which is pending on the commencement of this Act shall be dealt with under the old law and any necessary alteration made to the new register.

Revocation for non-use

17. (1) An application under section 26 of the 1938 Act (removal from register or imposition of limitation on ground of non-use) which is pending on the commencement of this Act shall be dealt with under the old law and any necessary alteration made to the new register.

(2) An application under section 46(1)(a) or (b) of this Act (revocation for non-use) may be made in relation to an existing registered mark at any time after the commencement of this Act.

Provided that no such application for the revocation of the registration of an existing registered mark registered by virtue of section 27 of the 1938 Act (defensive registration of well-known trade marks) may be made until more than five years after the commencement of this Act.

Application for rectification, &c

18. (1) An application under section 32 or 34 of the 1938 Act (rectification or correction of the register) which is pending on the commencement of this Act shall be dealt with under the old law and any necessary alteration made to the new register.

(2) For the purposes of proceedings under section 47 of this Act (grounds for invalidity of registration) as it applies in relation to an existing registered mark, the provisions of this Act shall be deemed to have been in force at all material times.

Provided that no objection to the validity of the registration of an existing registered mark may be taken on the ground specified in subsection (3) of section 5 of this Act (relative grounds for refusal of registration: conflict with earlier mark registered for different goods or services).

Regulations as to use of certification mark

19. (1) Regulations governing the use of an existing registered certification mark deposited at the Patent Office in pursuance of section 37 of the 1938 Act shall be treated after the commencement of this Act as if filed under paragraph 6 of Schedule 2 to this Act.

(2) Any request for amendment of the regulations which was pending on the commencement of this Act shall be dealt with under the old law.

Sheffield marks

20. (1) For the purposes of this Schedule the Sheffield register kept under Schedule 2 to the 1938 Act shall be treated as part of the register of trade marks kept under that Act.

(2) Applications made to the Cutlers' Company in accordance with that Schedule which are pending on the commencement of this Act shall proceed after commencement as if they had been made to the registrar.

Certificate of validity of contested registration

21. A certificate given before the commencement of this Act under section 47 of the 1938 Act (certificate of validity of contested registration) shall have effect as if given under section 73(1) of this Act.

Trade mark agents

22. (1) Rules in force immediately before the commencement of this Act under section 282 or 283 of the Copyright, Designs and Patents Act 1988 (register of trade mark agents; persons entitled to described themselves as registered) shall continue in force and have effect as if made under section 83 or 85 of this Act.

(2) Rules in force immediately before the commencement of this Act under section 40 of the 1938 Act as to the persons whom the registrar may refuse to recognise as agents for the purposes of business under that Act shall continue in force and have effect as if made under section 88 of this Act.

(3) Rules continued in force under this paragraph may be varied or revoked by further rules made under the relevant provisions of this Act.

NOTES

Trade Marks Act 1938: repealed by s 106(2) of, and Sch 5 to, this Act.

SCHEDULES 4 AND 5

(*Schs 4, 5 contain consequential amendments, repeals and revocations and in so far as relevant to this work, have been incorporated at the appropriate place.*)

TRADE MARKS (CUSTOMS) REGULATIONS 1994

(SI 1994/2625)

NOTES

Made: 11 October 1994.
Authority: Trade Marks Act 1994, s 90(1)–(3).
Commencement: 31 October 1994.

[5.115]
1

These Regulations may be cited as the Trade Marks (Customs) Regulations 1994 and shall come into force on 31st October 1994.

[5.116]
2

If notice is given under section 89(1) of The Trade Marks Act 1994 by the proprietor or licensee of a registered trade mark in respect of certain goods it shall be in the form set out in the Schedule to these Regulations or a form to the like effect approved by the Commissioners; and separate notices shall be given in respect of each arrival of such goods.

[5.117]
3

A fee of £30 (plus value added tax) in respect of each notice shall be paid to the Commissioners at the time it is given.

[5.118]
4

The person giving the notice shall give to the Commissioners such security or further security within such time and in such manner, whether by deposit of a sum of money or guarantee, as the Commissioners may require, in respect of any liability or expense which they may incur in consequence of the notice by reason of the detention of any goods or anything done to goods so detained: and if such security or further security is not given within the time specified by the Commissioners, then (but without prejudice to the operation of regulation 5 below) the notice shall have no effect.

[5.119]
5

In every case, whether any security or further security is given or not, the person who has given the notice shall keep the Commissioners indemnified against all such liability and expense as is mentioned in regulation 4 above.

[5.120]
6

(1) The person giving the notice shall, either on giving notice or when the goods are imported, furnish the Commissioners with the certificate of registration (or a copy of it) issued by the Registrar of Trade Marks on the registration of the trade mark specified in the notice, together with evidence that such registration was duly renewed at all such times as it may have expired.

(2) If such a certificate or copy and, where applicable, evidence of renewal is not furnished in accordance with paragraph (1) above then the goods shall not be detained, or, if detained, shall be released, and (but without prejudice to the operation of regulation 5 above) any notice given in respect of them shall have no effect.

7 (*Revokes the Trade Marks (Customs) Regulations 1970, SI 1970/212.*)

SCHEDULE
NOTICE UNDER SECTION 89 TRADE MARKS ACT 1994 REQUESTING INFRINGING GOODS, MATERIAL OR ARTICLES TO BE TREATED AS PROHIBITED GOODS

Please read these notes before completing this notice

[5.121]

1. This notice may only be given by the proprietor of a registered trade mark, or a licensee. A separate notice must be given in respect of each consignment.

2. Please note that in Part 3 it is not mandatory to provide details other than the time and place of expected arrival of infringing goods but it will greatly increase the prospect of intercepting the consignment concerned if all the details requested are given.

3. A fee of £30 (plus VAT) is payable for each notice given. Please enclose a cheque for the required amount, made payable to "Commissioners of Customs and Excise".

4. A copy of the certificate of registration for the trade mark, as well as the certificate of renewal (where applicable), is to be enclosed with the notice, **or** submitted when the goods are imported.

5. The person who has given notice shall keep the Commissioners of Customs and Excise indemnified against any liability or expense which they may incur in consequence of the notice by reason of the detention of any goods or anything done to goods detained. The person giving the notice may be required to provide a security to cover this indemnity.

1 Person giving notice

*I/We . . . .

Full name of signatory in BLOCK LETTERS

give notice to the Commissioners of Customs and Excise that

. . . .

. . . .

. . . .

Name and address of proprietor or licensee in BLOCK LETTERS

is the *proprietor/licensee of a trade mark registered in the United Kingdom and that infringing goods, material or articles are expected to arrive in the United Kingdom, and *I/we request that they be treated as prohibited goods.

2 Details of infringing goods, material or articles

Trade mark

Infringing goods, material or articles . . . .

Quantity . . . .

Commodity . . . .

Code(s) . . . .

3 Details of expected importation

Place of importation . . . .

Method of importation . . . .

Please include details of ship, aircraft or vehicle, where known

Expected date of arrival . . . .

Country of origin . . . .

Country of consignment . . . .

Importer's details . . . .

Please include VAT number, if known

Consignor's details . . . .

4 Declaration

I declare that the information given by me in this notice is true.

Signature . . . .

(*Sole Proprietor/Partner/Director/Company Secretary/Duly Authorised Person)

Date. . . . .

5 Submission of notice

Please send the completed notice, fee and copies of relevant certificates to:

HM Customs and Excise
CD3A
New King's Beam House
22 Upper Ground London SE1 9PJ

*Delete as necessary

TOBACCO ADVERTISING AND PROMOTION (BRANDSHARING) REGULATIONS 2004

(SI 2004/1824)

NOTES

Made: 13 July 2004.
Authority: Tobacco Advertising and Promotion Act 2002, ss 11, 19(2).
Commencement: 31 July 2005.

ARRANGEMENT OF REGULATIONS

SCHEDULES

[5.122]

1 Citation and commencement

These Regulations may be cited as the Tobacco Advertising and Promotion (Brandsharing) Regulations 2004 and shall come into force on 31st July 2005.

[5.123]

2 Interpretation

In these Regulations:

"A5 size" means the size of an area of any shape which is equal to the area of size A5 in the A series of paper sizes defined in BS EN ISO 216: 2001;

"the Act" means the Tobacco Advertising and Promotion Act 2002;

"advertisement" means a tobacco advertisement;

"the EEA Agreement" means the Agreement on the European Economic Area signed at Oporto on 2nd May 1992 as adjusted by the Protocol signed at Brussels on 17th March 1993;

"European Economic Area" means the territory of—

(a) the [European Union]; and

(b) States which are party to, or otherwise bound by, the EEA Agreement;

"feature" means a name, emblem or other feature, whether alone or in combination;

"gantry or display unit" means any gantry, display cabinet, tray or other product in which tobacco products are held pending sale that is—

(a) fixed to one place within fixed or movable premises; and

(b) primarily used for the display of tobacco products to customers;

"group of companies" means a holding company and its subsidiaries within the meaning of section 736 (interpretation) of the Companies Act 1985 or, as regards Northern Ireland, Article 4 (introductory and interpretation) of Part I of the Companies (Northern Ireland) Order 1986;

"non-tobacco product" means any product other than a tobacco product;

"other feature", in so far as any of the following features are neither a name nor an emblem, means a logo, trademark, symbol, motto, print, type-face, colour or pattern of colour, picture, artwork, imagery, appearance, message or other indication that constitutes all or part of the recognisable identity of a product or service;

"tobacco producer or promoter" means any producer or promoter engaged in the production or promotion of tobacco products.

NOTES

In definition "European Economic Area" words in square brackets substituted by the Treaty of Lisbon (Changes in Terminology) Order 2011, SI 2011/1043, art 4(1).

[5.124]

3 Brandsharing

(1) Subject to paragraph (3) and regulations 4(1) to (4) and 5, the use by a person in connection with any non-tobacco product or service of any feature which is the same as, or is so similar as to be likely to be mistaken for, any feature which is connected with a tobacco product is prohibited if the purpose or effect of that use is to promote a tobacco product in the United Kingdom.

(2) Subject to paragraph (3) and regulations 4(5) to (8) and 5, the use by a person in connection with any tobacco product of any feature which is the same as, or is so similar as to be likely to be mistaken for, any feature which is connected with any non-tobacco product or service is prohibited if the purpose or effect of that use is to promote a tobacco product in the United Kingdom through the association which it has with any non-tobacco product or service.

(3) Paragraphs (1) and (2) apply only to the use in the United Kingdom of a feature in the course of a business.

[5.125]

4 Exceptions

(1) Subject to regulation 5(4), the prohibition in regulation 3(1) does not apply if—

(a) it was not the purpose of the person's use to promote a tobacco product, or (as the case may be) the tobacco product in question; and

(b) the person could not reasonably have foreseen that that would be its effect.

(2) Subject to regulation 5(4), the prohibition in regulation 3(1) does not apply if—

(a) when the person uses any feature in connection with a non-tobacco product or service, he does not do so for the purpose of promoting a tobacco product;

(b) that person is not, and is not employed or commissioned by—

(i) a tobacco producer or promoter,

(ii) a company in the same group of companies as a tobacco producer or promoter, or

(iii) a company which has a common parent company with a tobacco producer or promoter; and

(c) the feature is not used by that person under any agreement or licence, or any series of agreements, licences or both, to which at least one party is a tobacco producer or promoter.

(3) Subject to regulation 5(4), the prohibition in regulation 3(1) does not apply if—

(a) when the person uses any feature in connection with a non-tobacco product or service, he does not do so for the purpose of promoting a tobacco product;

(b) the feature was first used in connection with a non-tobacco product or service on or before 1st September 2002 in an area which was then or has subsequently become part of the European Economic Area; and

(c) the presentation of the feature of the non-tobacco product or service does not make it appear that it belongs to the same brand as any tobacco product.

(4) Subject to regulation 5(4), the prohibition in regulation 3(1) does not apply if—

(a) the person who is using a feature in connection with a non-tobacco product or service does not know that the purpose or effect of using the feature is, or is likely to be, to promote a tobacco product; and

(b) the use of the feature does not make it appear that the same person, firm or company is responsible for the branding of both the tobacco product and the non-tobacco product or service (whether that is in fact so or not).

(5) Subject to regulation 5(4), the prohibition in regulation 3(2) does not apply if—

(a) it was not the purpose of the person's use to promote a tobacco product, or (as the case may be) the tobacco product in question, through the association which any relevant feature has with any non-tobacco product or service; and

(b) the person could not reasonably have foreseen that that would be its effect.

(6) Subject to regulation 5(4), the prohibition in regulation 3(2) does not apply if—

(a) when the person uses any feature in connection with a tobacco product, he does not do so for the purpose of promoting a tobacco product through the association which that feature has with any non-tobacco product or service;

(b) the person is not, and is not employed or commissioned by—

(i) a tobacco producer or promoter,
(ii) a company in the same group of companies as a tobacco producer or promoter, or
(iii) a company which has a common parent company with a tobacco producer or promoter; and

(c) the feature is not used by that person under any agreement or licence, or any series of agreements, licences or both, to which at least one party is a tobacco producer or promoter.

(7) Subject to regulation 5(4), the prohibition in regulation 3(2) does not apply if—

(a) when the person uses any feature in connection with a tobacco product, he does not do so for the purpose of promoting a tobacco product through the association which that feature has with any non-tobacco product or service;

(b) the feature was first used in connection with a tobacco product on or before 1st September 2002 in an area which was then or has subsequently become part of the European Economic Area; and

(c) the presentation of the feature of the tobacco product does not make it appear that it belongs to the same brand as any non-tobacco product or service.

(8) Subject to regulation 5(4), the prohibition in regulation 3(2) does not apply if—

(a) the person who is using a feature in connection with a tobacco product does not know that the purpose or effect of using the feature is, or is likely to be, to promote a tobacco product through the association which the feature has with any non-tobacco product or service; and

(b) the use of the feature does not make it appear that the same person, firm or company is responsible for the branding of both the tobacco product and the non-tobacco product or service (whether that is in fact so or not).

[5.126]

5 Point of sale brandsharing

(1) The prohibitions in regulation 3 do not apply where paragraph (2) or (3) applies.

(2) This paragraph applies where—

(a) any feature is used—
(i) in the course of a business; and
(ii) at a place where tobacco products are sold;
on a gantry or display unit;

(b) the only feature that promotes a tobacco product consists of an advertisement presented in a two dimensional format—
(i) with a surface area which does not exceed A5 size (or two or more advertisements with a surface area which in total does not exceed A5 size); and
(ii) which consists of any feature of the tobacco product and no other information;

(c) the surface area of all advertisements on the gantry or display unit does not in total exceed A5 size;

(d) the advertisement (or if more than one, each of them) contains the health warning and health information in accordance with the Schedule to these Regulations; and

(e) the health warning and health information are parallel to the floor.

(3) This paragraph applies where any feature is used to promote a tobacco product on a vending machine and the only features used on that machine to promote a tobacco product are contained in an advertisement which—

(a) consists only of a single picture of the packet of a tobacco product which is for sale from that vending machine or, if more than one tobacco product is for sale from that machine, a single picture of the packet of some or each of those products;

(b) includes a health warning which is identical to a health warning which is required to be shown on the most visible surface of the tobacco product to which the picture relates and which occupies not less than 30% of the surface area of the advertisement and is surrounded by a black border which—
(i) is not less than 3 millimetres nor more than 4 millimetres in width;
(ii) is outside the area occupied by the health warning; and
(iii) does not interfere with the text of the warning; and

(c) is no larger than the surface area of the largest face of the packet of the tobacco product depicted.

(4) Where paragraph (2) or (3) applies, the exceptions in regulation 4 do not apply.

(5) In paragraph (3) "vending machine" means a tobacco vending machine which contains tobacco products which are not visible prior to purchase.

[5.127]

6 General provisions

(1) A person who uses any feature of any product or service in circumstances set out in one or more of the exceptions in regulation 4(1) to (4) or regulation 5 does not commit an offence under section 2, 3, 9 or 10 of the Act in respect of the use of that feature.

(2) Where a person charged with an offence under section 11(4) of the Act relies on an exception under regulation 4(1) to (3) or (5) to (7) or regulation 5, he shall adduce evidence which is sufficient to raise an issue with respect to that exception.

(3) Where a person charged with an offence under section 2, 3, 9 or 10 of the Act relies on a defence provided by paragraph (1), he shall adduce evidence which is sufficient to raise an issue with respect to that defence.

(4) Where evidence is adduced under paragraph (2) or (3), the court or jury shall assume that the defence is satisfied unless the prosecution proves beyond reasonable doubt that it is not.

SCHEDULES

THE SCHEDULE
HEALTH WARNINGS AND HEALTH INFORMATION

Regulation 5(2)(d)

[5.128]
1. An advertisement to which this Schedule applies shall include an area which is not less than 30% of the total surface area of the advertisement in which is displayed, in accordance with the requirements specified in paragraph 2, the health warning "Smoking kills" or the health warning "Smoking seriously harms you and others around you" and the following information—

"NHS Smoking Helpline 0800 169 0 169".

2. The health warning and information which is required by paragraph 1 shall be—
- (a) indelible;
- (b) legible;
- (c) printed in black Helvetica bold type on a white background;
- (d) in a font size consistent throughout the text which ensures that the text occupies the greatest possible proportion of the area specified for the warning and information;
- (e) in upper case and lower case type as set out in paragraph 1;
- (f) centred in the area in which the text is required to be printed;
- (g) surrounded by a black border outside the area specified for the health warning and information, which shall be not less than 3 millimetres and not more than 4 millimetres in width, which does not interfere with the text of the warning or information; and
- (h) irremovably printed on the advertisement.

COMMUNITY TRADE MARK REGULATIONS 2006

(SI 2006/1027)

NOTES

Made: 5 April 2006.
Authority: Trade Marks Act 1994, s 52.
Commencement: 29 April 2006.

ARRANGEMENT OF REGULATIONS

[5.129]
1 Citation, commencement, extent and revocations

(1) These Regulations may be cited as the Community Trade Mark Regulations 2006 and shall come into force on 29th April 2006.

(2) These Regulations extend to England and Wales, Scotland and Northern Ireland.

(3) The instruments set out in the Schedule (revocations) shall be revoked to the extent specified.

[5.130]

2 Interpretation

(1) In these Regulations—

"[EU trade mark court]" means a court designated by regulation 12;

"international application" means an application to the International Bureau for registration of a trade mark in the International Register;

"international application designating the [European Union]" means an international application in which a request has been made for extension of protection to the [European Union] under Article 3*ter* (1) of the Madrid Protocol;

"International Register" means the register of trade marks maintained by the International Bureau for the purposes of the Madrid Protocol;

"international registration" means the registration of a trade mark in the International Register;

"international registration designating the [European Union]" means an international registration in relation to which a request has been made (either in the relevant international application or subsequently) for extension of protection to the [European Union] under Article 3*ter* (1) or (2) of the Madrid Protocol.

(2) In regulations 3 to 9, a reference to a [European Union trade mark] includes a reference to an international trade mark (EC), and in that case—

(a) a reference to a revocation or declaration of invalidity of the mark is a reference to a revocation or declaration of invalidity of the protection of the mark;

(b) a reference to the goods or services for which the mark is registered is a reference to the goods or services in respect of which the mark is protected.

(3) In these Regulations "the Act" means the Trade Marks Act 1994, and any reference to a section is, unless the context otherwise requires, a reference to a section of that Act.

NOTES

Para (1): words in square brackets in definition "EU trade mark court" substituted by the European Union Trade Mark Regulations 2016, SI 2016/299, regs 6, 7, subject to transitional provisions and savings as noted to the Trade Marks Act 1994, s 5 at **[5.5]**; words in square brackets in definitions "international application designating the European Union" and "international registration designating the European Union" substituted by the Treaty of Lisbon (Changes in Terminology) Order 2011, SI 2011/1043, art 4(1).

Para (2): words in square brackets substituted by SI 2016/299, regs 6, 8, subject to transitional provisions and savings as noted to the Trade Marks Act 1994, s 5 at **[5.5]**.

[5.131]

3 Determination of invalidity and liability to revocation in relation to claims of seniority

(1) Where the proprietor of a [European Union trade mark] claims the seniority of a registered trade mark which—

(a) has been removed from the register under section 43, or

(b) has been surrendered under section 45,

any person may apply to the registrar or to the court for the declaration set out in paragraph (3).

(2) Where such a proprietor claims the seniority of an international trade mark (UK) which has been removed from the International Register or surrendered, any person may apply to the registrar or to the court for the declaration set out in paragraph (3).

(3) The declaration is that if the trade mark had not been so removed or surrendered, it would have been liable to be revoked under section 46 or declared invalid under section 47.

(4) An address for service in the United Kingdom shall be filed by—

(a) the person making an application under paragraph (1) or (2); and

(b) the proprietor of the [European Union trade mark],

unless in a particular case the registrar otherwise directs.

(5) Where the trade mark has been surrendered in respect of some only of the goods or services for which it is registered (or protected), paragraph (1) or (2) shall apply in relation to those goods or services only.

NOTES

Paras (1), (4): words in square brackets substituted by the European Union Trade Mark Regulations 2016, SI 2016/299, regs 6, 8, subject to transitional provisions and savings as noted to the Trade Marks Act 1994, s 5 at **[5.5]**.

[5.132]

4 Procedure for declaration that trade mark would have been liable to be revoked or declared invalid

(1) In proceedings on an application under regulation 3(1) or (2) the registration of a person as proprietor of a trade mark shall be prima facie evidence of the validity of the original registration.

(2) In the case of such proceedings before the registrar, the provisions of [rules 38 to 43, 45, 62 to 79 and 82 of the Trade Marks Rules 2008], with necessary modifications, shall apply.

(3) In the case of such proceedings before the court, the registrar is entitled to appear and be heard, and shall appear if so directed by the court.

(4) Unless otherwise directed by the court, the registrar may instead of appearing submit to the court a statement in writing signed by him, giving particulars of—

(a) any proceedings before him in relation to the matter in issue,

(b) the grounds of any decision given by him affecting it,

(c) the practice of the Patent Office in like cases, or

(d) such matters relevant to the issues and within his knowledge as registrar as he thinks fit;

and the statement shall be deemed to form part of the evidence in the proceedings.

(5) Anything which the registrar is or may be authorised or required to do under this regulation may be done on his behalf by a duly authorised officer.

NOTES

Para (2): words in square brackets substituted by the Community Trade Mark (Amendment) Regulations 2008, SI 2008/1959, reg 2.

[5.133]

5 Remedies in infringement proceedings

(1) This regulation is without prejudice to the duties of the [European Union trade mark] court under [Article 102(1)] of the [European Union Trade Mark Regulation].

(2) In an action for infringement of a [European Union trade mark] all such relief by way of damages, injunctions, accounts or otherwise is available to the proprietor of the [European Union trade mark] as is available in respect of the infringement of any other property right.

(3) The provisions of sections 15 to 19 apply in relation to a [European Union trade mark] as they apply to a registered trade mark; and any reference to the court shall be construed as meaning the [European Union trade mark] court.

NOTES

Words in square brackets substituted by the European Union Trade Mark Regulations 2016, SI 2016/299, regs 6–9, subject to transitional provisions and savings as noted to the Trade Marks Act 1994, s 5 at **[5.5]**.

[5.134]

6 *Groundless threats of infringement proceedings*

(1) The provisions of *section 21* apply in relation to a [European Union trade mark] as they apply to a registered trade mark.

[(1A) In the application of sections 21 and 21B in relation to a European Union trade mark, references to a registered trade mark are to be treated as references to a European Union trade mark in respect of which an application has been published in accordance with Article 39 of the European Union Trade Mark Regulation.

(1B) In the application of section 21C in relation to a European Union trade mark in a case where the threat of infringement proceedings is made after an application has been published (but before registration) the reference in section 21C(2) to "the registered trade mark" is to be treated as a reference to the European Union trade mark registered in pursuance of that application.]

(2) However, in the application of those provisions in relation to an international trade mark (EC)—

(a) the reference in section 21(3) to the registration of the trade mark shall be treated as a reference to the protection of the international trade mark (EC);

(b) the reference in section 21(4) to notification that a trade mark is registered, shall be treated as a reference to notification that a trade mark is an international trade mark (EC); and

(c) the reference in section 21(4) to notification that an application for registration has been made, shall be treated as a reference to notification that a trade mark is the subject of an international application or international registration designating the [European Union].

NOTES

Provision heading: for the words in italics there are substituted the words "Unjustified threats" by the Intellectual Property (Unjustified Threats) Act 2017, s 3(1), (5), as from a day to be appointed.

Para (1): for the words in italics there are substituted the words "sections 21 to 21D and section 21F" by the Intellectual Property (Unjustified Threats) Act 2017, s 3(1), (2), as from a day to be appointed; words in square brackets substituted by the European Union Trade Mark Regulations 2016, SI 2016/299, regs 6, 8, subject to transitional provisions and savings as noted to the Trade Marks Act 1994, s 5 at **[5.5]**.

Paras (1A), (1B): inserted by the Intellectual Property (Unjustified Threats) Act 2017, s 3(1), (3), as from a day to be appointed.

Para (2): words in square brackets substituted by the Treaty of Lisbon (Changes in Terminology) Order 2011, SI 2011/1043, art 4(1); substituted by new paras (2), (3), by the Intellectual Property (Unjustified Threats) Act 2017, s 3(1), (4), as from a day to be appointed, as follows—

"(2) In the application of sections 21 and 21B in relation to an international trade mark (EC), references to a registered trade mark are to be treated as references to an international trade mark (EC) in respect of which particulars of an international registration designating the European Union have been published in accordance with Article 152 of the European Union Trade Mark Regulation.

(3) In the application of section 21C in relation to an international trade mark (EC) in a case where the threat of infringement proceedings is made after particulars have been published (but before registration) the reference in section 21C(2) to "the registered trade mark" is to be treated as a reference to the international trade mark (EC) registered in pursuance of those particulars.".

[5.135]
7 Importation of infringing goods, material or articles

(1) The provisions of—
- (a) section 89 (infringing goods, material or articles may be treated as prohibited goods);
- (b) section 90 and section 91 (power of Commissioners of Customs and Excise to disclose information),

apply in relation to a [European Union trade mark] as they apply in relation to a registered trade mark.

(2) The Trade Marks (Customs) Regulations 1994 shall apply in relation to notices given under section 89 as applied by paragraph (1).

NOTES

Para (1): words in square brackets substituted by the European Union Trade Mark Regulations 2016, SI 2016/299, regs 6, 8, subject to transitional provisions and savings as noted to the Trade Marks Act 1994, s 5 at **[5.5]**.

[5.136]
8 Offences and forfeiture

(1) The provisions of—
- (a) section 92 (unauthorised use of trade mark, etc, in relation to goods);
- (b) section 92A (search warrants);
- (c) section 93 (enforcement function of local weights and measures authority);
- (d) section 97 (forfeiture: England and Wales or Northern Ireland); and
- (e) section 98 (forfeiture: Scotland),

apply in relation to a [European Union trade mark] as they apply in relation to a registered trade mark.

(2) For the purposes of those provisions, references to goods in respect of which a trade mark is registered shall include goods in respect of which an international trade mark (EC) confers protection in the [European Union].

NOTES

Para (1): words in square brackets substituted by the European Union Trade Mark Regulations 2016, SI 2016/299, regs 6, 8, subject to transitional provisions and savings as noted to the Trade Marks Act 1994, s 5 at **[5.5]**.

Para (2): words in square brackets substituted by the Treaty of Lisbon (Changes in Terminology) Order 2011, SI 2011/1043, art 4(1).

[5.137]
9 Falsely representing trade mark as a [European Union trade mark]

(1) It is an offence for a person—
- (a) falsely to represent that a mark is a [European Union trade mark], or
- (b) to make a false representation as to the goods or services for which a [European Union trade mark] is registered,

knowing or having reason to believe that the representation is false.

(2) A person guilty of an offence under this regulation is liable on summary conviction to a fine not exceeding level 3 on the standard scale.

NOTES

Provision heading, para (1): words in square brackets substituted by the European Union Trade Mark Regulations 2016, SI 2016/299, regs 6, 8, subject to transitional provisions and savings as noted to the Trade Marks Act 1994, s 5 at **[5.5]**.

[5.138]
10 Conversion

(1) This regulation applies where, pursuant to [Article 112] of the [European Union Trade Mark Regulation]—
- (a) the applicant for or the proprietor of a [European Union trade mark] requests the conversion of his [European Union trade mark] application or [European Union trade mark] into an application for registration of a trade mark under the Act; or
- (b) the holder of an international registration designating the [European Union] requests (in accordance with [Article 159(1)(a)] of that Regulation) the conversion of that designation into an application for registration of a trade mark under the Act.

(2) Where the request has been transmitted to the registrar under [Article 113(3)] of the [European Union Trade Mark Regulation], it shall be treated as an application for registration of a trade mark under the Act.

(3) A decision of the registrar in relation to the request shall be treated as a decision of the registrar under the Act.

NOTES

Words "European Union" in square brackets in para (1)(b) substituted by the Treaty of Lisbon (Changes in Terminology) Order 2011, SI 2011/1043, art 4(1); all other words in square brackets substituted by the European Union Trade Mark Regulations 2016, SI 2016/299, regs 6, 8, 10, subject to transitional provisions and savings as noted to the Trade Marks Act 1994, s 5 at **[5.5]**.

[5.139]

11 Privilege for communications with those on the list of professional trade marks representatives

(1) This regulation applies to communications as to any matter relating to the protection of any trade mark or as to any matter involving passing off.

(2) Any such communication—

(a) between a person and his professional trade marks representative, or

(b) for the purposes of obtaining, or in response to a request for, information which a person is seeking for the purpose of instructing his professional trade marks representative,

is privileged from, or in Scotland protected against, disclosure in legal proceedings in the same way as a communication between a person and his solicitor or, as the case may be, a communication for the purpose of obtaining, or in response to a request for, information which a person is seeking for the purpose of instructing his solicitor.

(3) In paragraph (2) a person's "professional trade marks representative" means a person who is retained by him and is on the special list of professional representatives for trade marks matters referred to in [Article 93] of the [European Union Trade Mark Regulation].

NOTES

Para (3): words in square brackets substituted by the European Union Trade Mark Regulations 2016, SI 2016/299, regs 6, 8, 11, subject to transitional provisions and savings as noted to the Trade Marks Act 1994, s 5 at **[5.5]**.

[5.140]

12 Designation of [EU trade mark courts]

(1) [For the purposes of Article 95 of the European Union Trade Mark Regulation, the following courts are designated as EU trade mark courts]—

(a) in England and Wales—

(i) the High Court;

(ii) any county court designated as a patents county court under section 287(1) of the Copyright, Designs and Patents Act 1988; and

(iii) the county courts listed in paragraph (2);

(b) in Scotland, the Court of Session; and

(c) in Northern Ireland, the High Court.

(2) The county courts referred to in paragraph (1)(a)(iii) are the county courts at—

(a) Birmingham;

(b) Bristol;

(c) Cardiff;

(d) Leeds;

(e) Liverpool;

(f) Manchester; and

(g) Newcastle upon Tyne.

(3) For the purpose of hearing appeals from judgments of the courts designated by paragraph (1), the following courts are also designated as Community trade mark courts—

(a) in England and Wales, the Court of Appeal;

(b) in Scotland, the Court of Session; and

(c) in Northern Ireland, the Court of Appeal.

NOTES

Provision heading, para (1): words in square brackets substituted by the European Union Trade Mark Regulations 2016, SI 2016/299, regs 6, 12, subject to transitional provisions and savings as noted to the Trade Marks Act 1994, s 5 at **[5.5]**.

Modification: any reference (however expressed) that is or is deemed to be a reference to a county court held under the County Courts Act 1984, s 1, is to be read as a reference to the county court established by s A1 of that Act; see the Crime and Courts Act 2013, s 17(5), Sch 9, Pt 2, para 11.

SCHEDULE

(*The Schedule contains revocations only.*)

TRADE MARKS (RELATIVE GROUNDS) ORDER 2007

(SI 2007/1976)

NOTES

Made: 10 July 2007.

Authority: Trade Marks Act 1994, s 8.

Commencement: 1 October 2007.

See further, in relation to the application of this Order, with modifications, to International trade marks (UK) and requests for extension: the Trade Marks (International Registration) Order 2008, SI 2008/2206, art 3 at **[5.233]**.

[5.141]

1 Citation and commencement

This Order may be cited as the Trade Marks (Relative Grounds) Order 2007 and shall come into force on 1st October 2007.

[5.142]

2 Refusing to register a mark on a ground mentioned in section 5 of the Trade Marks Act 1994

The registrar shall not refuse to register a trade mark on a ground mentioned in section 5 of the Trade Marks Act 1994 (relative grounds for refusal) unless objection on that ground is raised in opposition proceedings by the proprietor of the earlier trade mark or other earlier right.

3 (*Repeals the Trade Marks Act 1994, s 37(2).*)

[5.143]

4

The registrar may, in connection with an examination under section 37(1) of the Trade Marks Act 1994, carry out a search of earlier trade marks for the purpose of notifying the applicant and other persons about the existence of earlier trade marks that might be relevant to the proposed registration.

[5.144]

5

(1) Only the persons specified in paragraph (2) may make an application for a declaration of invalidity on the grounds in section 47(2) of the Trade Marks Act 1994 (relative grounds).

(2) Those persons are—

- (a) in the case of an application on the ground in section 47(2)(a) of that Act, the proprietor or a licensee of the earlier trade mark or, in the case of an earlier collective mark or certification mark, the proprietor or an authorised user of such collective mark or certification mark; and
- (b) in the case of an application on the ground in section 47(2)(b) of that Act, the proprietor of the earlier right.

(3) So much of section 47(3) of that Act as provides that any person may make an application for a declaration of invalidity shall have effect subject to this article.

[5.145]

6 Transitional provisions

(1) Articles 2 to 4 shall not apply to an application for registration of a trade mark which was published before the coming into force of this Order.

(2) Article 5 shall not apply to an application for a declaration of invalidity which relates to a trade mark the application for the registration of which was published before the coming into force of this Order.

TRADE MARKS RULES 2008

(SI 2008/1797)

NOTES

Made: 7 July 2008.

Authority: Trade Marks Act 1994, ss 4(4), 13(2), 25(1), (5), (6), 34(1), 35(5), 38(1), (2), 39(3), 40(4), 41(1), (3), 43(2), (3), (5), (6), 44(3), 45(2), 63(2), (3), 64(4), 65(1), (2), 66(2), 67(1), (2), 68(1), (3), 69, 76(1), 78, 80(3), 81, 82, 88, Sch 1, para 6(2), Sch 2, para 7(2).

Commencement: 1 October 2008.

See further, in relation to the application of these Rules, with modifications, to International trade marks (UK) and requests for extension: the Trade Marks (International Registration) Order 2008, SI 2008/2206, art 3 at **[5.233]**.

ARRANGEMENT OF RULES

Preliminary

Preliminary

[5.146]
1 Citation and commencement

These Rules may be cited as the Trade Marks Rules 2008 and shall come into force on 1st October 2008.

[5.147]
2 Interpretation

(1) In these Rules—

"the Act" means the Trade Marks Act 1994;

["fast track opposition" means an opposition—

(a) brought solely on grounds under section 5(1) or 5(2) of the Act,

(b) based on no more than 3 earlier trade marks, each of which is registered in the UK or in the EU, or is protected in one or another of those territories as an international trade mark (UK) or (EU),

(c) where proof of use of the earlier marks can be provided with the notice of opposition, and

(d) which the opponent considers may be determined without the need for further evidence and without an oral hearing.]

"the Journal" means the Trade Marks Journal published in accordance with rule 81;

"the "Nice Agreement" means the Nice Agreement Concerning the International Classification of Goods and Services for the Purposes of the Registration of Marks of 15th June 1957, which was last amended on 28th September 1979;

"the "Nice Classification" means the system of classification under the Nice Agreement;

["the Office" means the Patent Office which operates under the name "Intellectual Property Office";]

"send" includes give;

"specification" means the statement of goods or services in respect of which a trade mark is registered or proposed to be registered;

"transformation application" means an application to register a trade mark under the Act where that mark was the subject of an international registration prior to that registration being cancelled.

(2) In these Rules a reference to a section is a reference to that section in the Act and a reference to a form is a reference to that form as published under rule 3.

(3) In these Rules references to the filing of any application, notice or other document, unless the contrary intention appears, are to be construed as references to its being delivered to the registrar at the Office.

NOTES

Para (1): definition "fast track opposition" inserted by the Trade Marks (Fast Track Opposition) (Amendment) Rules 2013, SI 2013/2235, r 2(1), (2); definition "the Office" substituted by the Trade Marks and Trade Marks and Patents (Fees) (Amendment) Rules 2009, SI 2009/2089, rr 3, 4.

[5.148]
3 Forms and directions of the registrar; section 66

(1) Any forms required by the registrar to be used for the purpose of registration of a trade mark or any other proceedings before the registrar under the Act pursuant to section 66 and any directions with respect to their use shall be published on the Office website and any amendment or modification of a form or of the directions with respect to its use shall also be published on the Office website.

(2) Except in relation to Forms TM6 and TM7A a requirement under this rule to use a form as published is satisfied by the use either of a replica of that form or of a form which is acceptable to the registrar and contains the information required by the form as published and complies with any directions as to the use of such a form.

[5.149]
4 Requirement as to fees

(1) The fees to be paid in respect of any application, registration or any other matter under the Act and these Rules shall be those (if any) prescribed in relation to such matter by rules under section 79 (fees).

(2) Any form required to be filed with the registrar in respect of any specified matter shall be subject to the payment of the fee (if any) prescribed in respect of that matter by those rules.

Application for Registration

[5.150]

5 Application for registration; section 32 (Form TM3)

[(1) An application for the registration of a trade mark (other than a transformation application, which shall be filed on Form TM4) shall be filed on Form TM3 or, where the application is filed in electronic form using the filing system provided on the Office website, on Form e-TM3.

(1A) Where an application is filed on Form TM3 (a "standard application") the application shall be subject to the payment of the standard application fee and such class and series fees as may be appropriate.

(1B) Where an application is filed on Form e-TM3 (an "electronic application") the application shall be subject to the payment of the e-filed application fee and such class and series fees as may be appropriate, which shall be payable at the time the electronic application is made and if they are not so paid the application shall be subject to the payment of the standard application fee referred to in paragraph (1A) and such class and series fees as may be appropriate.]

(2) [Subject to paragraph (6)] where an application is for the registration of a single trade mark, an applicant may request the registrar to undertake an expedited examination of the application.

(3) A request for expedited examination shall be made on [Form e-TM3] and shall be subject to payment of the prescribed fee.

(4) Where an applicant makes a request for expedited examination, the application fee and any class fees payable in respect of the application shall be payable at the time the application is made and accordingly rule 13 shall not apply insofar as it relates to the failure of an application to satisfy the requirements of section 32(4).

(5) In this rule and rule 15 a "request for expedited examination" means a request that, following an examination under section 37, the registrar notify the applicant within a period of ten business days (as specified in a direction given by the registrar under section 80) beginning on the business day after the date of filing of the application for registration whether or not it appears to the registrar that the requirements for registration are met.

[(6) Where it appears to the registrar that the period (the "routine period") within which applicants are routinely notified of the outcome of an examination under section 37 is equal to or less than the period specified in paragraph (5), the registrar may suspend the right of applicants to file a request for expedited examination until such time as the routine period exceeds the period specified in paragraph (5) and the registrar shall, in each case, publish a notice on the Office website to this effect.]

NOTES

Paras (1), (1A), (1B): substituted for original para (1), by the Trade Marks and Trade Marks and Patents (Fees) (Amendment) Rules 2009, SI 2009/2089, rr 3, 5.

Para (2): words in square brackets inserted by SI 2009/2089, rr 3, 6.

Para (3): words in square brackets substituted by SI 2009/2089, rr 3, 7.

Para (6): added by SI 2009/2089, rr 3, 8.

[5.151]

6 Claim to priority; sections 35 & 36

(1) Where a right to priority is claimed by reason of an application for protection of a trade mark duly filed in a Convention country under section 35 or in another country or territory in respect of which provision corresponding to that made by section 35 is made under section 36 (an "overseas application"), the application for registration under rule 5 shall specify—

- (a) the number accorded to the overseas application by the registering or other competent authority of the relevant country;
- (b) the country in which the overseas application was filed; and
- (c) the date of filing.

(2) The registrar may, in any particular case, by notice require the applicant to file, within such period of not less than one month as the notice may specify, such documentary evidence as the registrar may require certifying, or verifying to the satisfaction of the registrar, the date of the filing of the overseas application, the country or registering or competent authority, the representation of the mark and the goods or services covered by the overseas application.

[5.152]

7 Classification of goods and services; section 34

(1) The prescribed system of classification for the purposes of the registration of trade marks is the Nice Classification.

(2) When a trade mark is registered it shall be classified according to the version of the Nice Classification that had effect on the date of application for registration.

[5.153]
8 Application may relate to more than one class and shall specify the class (Form TM3A)

(1) An application may be made in more than one class of the Nice Classification.

(2) Every application shall specify—

(a) the class in the Nice Classification to which it relates; and

(b) the goods or services which are appropriate to the class and they shall be described in such a way as to indicate clearly the nature of those goods or services and to allow them to be classified in the classes in the Nice Classification.

(3) If the application relates to more than one class in the Nice Classification the specification contained in it shall set out the classes in consecutive numerical order and the specification of the goods or services shall be grouped accordingly.

(4) If the specification contained in the application lists items by reference to a class in the Nice Classification in which they do not fall, the applicant may request, by filing Form TM3A, that the application be amended to include the appropriate class for those items, and upon the payment of such class fee as may be appropriate the registrar shall amend the application accordingly.

[5.154]
9 Determination of classification

(1) Where an application does not satisfy the requirements of rule 8(2) or (3), the registrar shall send notice to the applicant.

(2) A notice sent under paragraph (1) shall specify a period, of not less than one month, within which the applicant must satisfy those requirements.

(3) Where the applicant fails to satisfy the requirements of rule 8(2) before the expiry of the period specified under paragraph (2), the application for registration, insofar as it relates to any goods or services which failed that requirement, shall be treated as abandoned.

(4) Where the applicant fails to satisfy the requirements of rule 8(3) before the expiry of the period specified under paragraph (2), the application for registration shall be treated as abandoned.

[5.155]
10 Prohibition on registration of mark consisting of arms; section 4

Where having regard to matters coming to the notice of the registrar it appears to the registrar that a representation of any arms or insignia as is referred to in section 4(4) appears in a mark, the registrar shall refuse to accept an application for the registration of the mark unless satisfied that the consent of the person entitled to the arms has been obtained.

[5.156]
11 Address for service

(1) For the purposes of any proceedings under the Act or these Rules, an address for service shall be filed by—

(a) an applicant for the registration of a trade mark;

(b) any person who opposes the registration of a trade mark in opposition proceedings;

(c) any person who applies for revocation, a declaration of invalidity or rectification under the Act;

(d) the proprietor of the registered trade mark who opposes such an application.

(2) The proprietor of a registered trade mark, or any person who has registered an interest in a registered trade mark, may file an address for service on Form TM33 or, in the case of an assignment of a registered trade mark, on Form TM16.

(3) Where a person has provided an address for service under paragraph (1) or (2), that person may substitute a new address for service by notifying the registrar on Form TM33.

[(4) An address for service filed under this Rule shall be an address in the United Kingdom, another EEA state or the Channel Islands.]

NOTES

Para (4): substituted for paras (4), (5), as originally enacted, by the Patents, Trade Marks and Designs (Address for Service) Rules 2009, SI 2009/546, rr 11, 12.

[5.157]
12 Failure to provide an address for service

(1) Where—

(a) a person has failed to file an address for service under rule 11(1); and

(b) the registrar has sufficient information enabling the registrar to contact that person,

the registrar shall direct that person to file an address for service.

(2) Where a direction has been given under paragraph (1), the person directed shall, before the end of the period of one month [beginning immediately after] the date of the direction, file an address for service.

(3) Paragraph (4) applies where—

(a) a direction was given under paragraph (1) and the period prescribed by paragraph (2) has expired; or

(b) the registrar had insufficient information to give a direction under paragraph (1),

and the person has failed to provide an address for service.

(4) Where this paragraph applies—

(a) in the case of an applicant for registration of a trade mark, the application shall be treated as withdrawn;

(b) in the case of a person opposing the registration of a trade mark, that person's opposition shall be treated as withdrawn;

(c) in the case of a person applying for revocation, a declaration of invalidity or rectification, that person's application shall be treated as withdrawn; and

(d) in the case of the proprietor opposing such an application, the proprietor shall be deemed to have withdrawn from the proceedings.

(5) In this rule an "address for service" means an address which complies with the requirements of rule 11(4) . . .

NOTES

Para (2): words in square brackets substituted by the Trade Marks and Registered Designs (Amendment) Rules 2013, SI 2013/444, rr 2, 4, Sch 1.

Para (5): words omitted revoked by the Patents, Trade Marks and Designs (Address for Service) Rules 2009, SI 2009/546, rr 11, 13.

[5.158]

13 Deficiencies in application; section 32

(1) Where an application for registration of a trade mark does not satisfy the requirements of section 32(2), (3) or (4) or rule 5(1), the registrar shall send notice to the applicant to remedy the deficiencies or, in the case of section 32(4), the default of payment.

(2) A notice sent under paragraph (1) shall specify a period, of not less than [14 days], within which the applicant must remedy the deficiencies or the default of payment.

(3) Where, before the expiry of the period specified under paragraph (2), the applicant—

(a) fails to remedy any deficiency notified to the applicant in respect of section 32(2), the application shall be deemed never to have been made; or

(b) fails to remedy any deficiency notified to the applicant in respect of section 32(3) or rule 5(1) or fails to make payment as required by section 32(4), the application shall be treated as abandoned.

NOTES

Para (2): words in square brackets substituted by the Trade Marks and Trade Marks and Patents (Fees) (Amendment) Rules 2009, SI 2009/2089, rr 3, 9.

[5.159]

14 Notifying results of search

(1) Where, following any search under article 4 of the Trade Marks (Relative Grounds) Order 2007, it appears to the registrar that the requirements for registration mentioned in section 5 are not met, the registrar shall notify this fact to—

(a) the applicant; and

(b) any relevant proprietor.

[(2) In paragraph (1), "relevant proprietor" means the proprietor of a registered trade mark or international trade mark (UK) which is an earlier trade mark in relation to which it appears to the registrar that the conditions set out in section 5(1) or (2) obtain but does not include a proprietor who does not wish to be notified and who has notified the registrar to this effect.]

(3) References in paragraph (2) to the proprietor of a trade mark include a person who has applied for registration of a trade mark which, if registered, would be an earlier trade mark by virtue of section 6(1)(a) or (b).

(4)–(6) . . .

(7) Rule 63 shall not apply to any decision made in pursuance of this rule.

(8) No decision made in pursuance of this rule shall be subject to appeal.

NOTES

Para (2): substituted by the Trade Marks and Trade Marks (Fees) (Amendment) Rules 2012, SI 2012/1003, r 2(1), (2)(a).

Paras (4)–(6): revoked by SI 2012/1003, r 2(1), (2)(b).

[5.160]

15 Compliance with request for expedited examination

Where the registrar receives a request for expedited examination under rule 5, the date on which the registrar shall be deemed to have notified the applicant whether or not it appears to the registrar that the requirements for registration are met shall be the date on which notice is sent to the applicant.

Publication, Observations, Oppositions and Registration

[5.161]

16 Publication of application for registration; section 38(1)

An application which has been accepted for registration shall be published in the Journal.

[5.162]

17 Opposition proceedings: filing of notice of opposition; section 38(2) (Form TM7)

(1) [Subject to Rule 17A, any] notice to the registrar of opposition to the registration, including the statement of the grounds of opposition, shall be filed on Form TM7.

(2) Unless paragraph (3) applies, the time prescribed for the purposes of section 38(2) shall be the period of two months [beginning immediately after] the date on which the application was published.

(3) This paragraph applies where a request for an extension of time for the filing of Form TM7 has been made on Form TM7A, before the expiry of the period referred to in paragraph (2) and where this paragraph applies, the time prescribed for the purposes of section 38(2) in relation to any person having filed a Form TM7A (or, in the case of a company, any subsidiary or holding company of that company or any other subsidiary of that holding company) shall be the period of three months [beginning immediately after] the date on which the application was published.

(4) Where a person makes a request for an extension of time under paragraph (3), Form TM7A shall be filed electronically using the filing system provided on the Office website or by such other means as the registrar may permit.

(5) Where the opposition is based on a trade mark which has been registered, there shall be included in the statement of the grounds of opposition a representation of that mark and—

- (a) the details of the authority with which the mark is registered;
- (b) the registration number of that mark;
- (c) the goods and services in respect of which—
  - (i) that mark is registered, and
  - (ii) the opposition is based; and
- (d) where the registration procedure for the mark was completed before the start of the period of five years ending with the date of publication, a statement detailing whether during the period referred to in section 6A(3)(a) the mark has been put to genuine use in relation to each of the goods and services in respect of which the opposition is based or whether there are proper reasons for non-use (for the purposes of rule 20 this is the "statement of use").

(6) Where the opposition is based on a trade mark in respect of which an application for registration has been made, there shall be included in the statement of the grounds of opposition a representation of that mark and those matters set out in paragraph (5)(a) to (c), with references to registration being construed as references to the application for registration.

(7) Where the opposition is based on an unregistered trade mark or other sign which the person opposing the application claims to be protected by virtue of any rule of law (in particular, the law of passing off), there shall be included in the statement of the grounds of opposition a representation of that mark or sign and the goods and services in respect of which such protection is claimed.

(8) The registrar shall send a copy of Form TM7 to the applicant and the date upon which this is sent shall, for the purposes of rule 18, be the "notification date".

(9) In this rule "subsidiary" and "holding company" have the same meaning as in the Companies Act 2006.

NOTES

Para (1): words in square brackets substituted by the Trade Marks (Fast Track Opposition) (Amendment) Rules 2013, SI 2013/2235, r 2(1), (3).

Paras (2), (3): words in square brackets substituted by the Trade Marks and Registered Designs (Amendment) Rules 2013, SI 2013/444, rr 2, 4, Sch 1.

[5.163]

[17A Opposition proceedings: filing of notice of fast track opposition; section 38(2) (Form TM7F))

(1) A notice to the registrar of fast track opposition to the registration, including the statement of the grounds of opposition, may be filed on Form TM7F.

(2) A notice of fast track opposition to the registration filed on Form TM7F and a notice of opposition to the registration filed on Form TM7 shall constitute alternatives and an opponent shall not maintain more than one opposition against the same trade mark application.

(3) Unless paragraph (4) applies, the time prescribed for the purposes of section 38(2) shall be the period of two months beginning immediately after the date on which the application was published.

(4) This paragraph applies where a request for an extension of time for the filing of Form TM7 or TM7F has been made on Form TM7A, before the expiry of the period referred to in paragraph (3) and where this paragraph applies, the time prescribed for the purposes of section 38(2) in relation

to any person having filed a Form TM7A (or, in the case of a company, any subsidiary or holding company of that company or any other subsidiary of that holding company) shall be the period of three months beginning immediately after the date on which the application was published.

(5) Forms TM7F and TM7A shall be filed electronically using the filing system provided on the Office website or by such other means as the registrar may permit.

(6) There shall be included in the statement of the grounds of opposition a representation of that mark and—

- (a) the details of the authority with which the mark is registered or protected;
- (b) the registration number of that mark;
- (c) the goods and services in respect of which—
  - (i) that mark is registered, and
  - (ii) the opposition is based;
- (d) the date of completion of the registration procedure or of granting protection to an international trade mark (UK) or (EU); and
- (e) where the registration or protection procedure for the mark was completed before the start of the period of five years ending with the date of publication, a statement detailing whether during the period referred to in section 6A(3)(a) the mark has been put to genuine use in relation to each of the goods and services in respect of which the opposition is based.

(7) Where the earlier mark is subject to proof of use under section 6A of the Act, the proof of use that the opponent wishes to rely upon shall be provided with the notice of fast track opposition.

(8) The registrar shall send a copy of Form TM7F to the applicant and the date upon which this is sent shall, for the purposes of rule 18, be the "notification date".

(9) In this rule "subsidiary" and "holding company" have the same meaning as in the Companies Act 2006.]

NOTES

Commencement: 1 October 2013.

Inserted by the Trade Marks (Fast Track Opposition) (Amendment) Rules 2013, SI 2013/2235, r 2(1), (4).

[5.164]

18 Opposition proceedings: filing of counter-statement and cooling off period (Forms TM8, TM9c & TM9t)

(1) The applicant shall, within the relevant period, file a Form TM8, which shall include a counter-statement.

(2) Where the applicant fails to file a Form TM8 or counter-statement within the relevant period, the application for registration, insofar as it relates to the goods and services in respect of which the opposition is directed, shall, unless the registrar otherwise directs, be treated as abandoned.

(3) Unless either paragraph (4), (5) or (6) applies, the relevant period [is the period of two months beginning immediately after the notification date].

(4) This paragraph applies where—

- (a) the applicant and the person opposing the registration agree to an extension of time for the filing of Form TM8;
- (b) within the period of two months [beginning immediately after] the notification date, either party files Form TM9c requesting an extension of time for the filing of Form TM8; and
- (c) during the period beginning on the date Form TM9c was filed and ending nine months after the notification date, no notice to continue on Form TM9t is filed by the person opposing the registration and no request for a further extension of time for the filing of Form TM8 is filed on Form TM9e,

and where this paragraph applies the relevant period [is the period of nine months beginning immediately after the notification date].

(5) This paragraph applies where—

- (a) a request for an extension of time for the filing of Form TM8 has been filed on Form TM9c in accordance with paragraph (4)(b);
- (b) during the period referred to in paragraph (4)(c), either party files Form TM9e requesting a further extension of time for the filing of Form TM8 which request includes a statement confirming that the parties are seeking to negotiate a settlement of the opposition proceedings; and
- (c) the other party agrees to the further extension of time for the filing of Form TM8,

and where this paragraph applies the relevant period [is the period of eighteen months beginning immediately after the notification date].

(6) This paragraph applies where—

- (a) a request for an extension of time for the filing of Form TM8 has been filed on Form TM9c in accordance with paragraph (4)(b); and
- (b) the person opposing the registration has filed a notice to continue on Form TM9t,

and where this paragraph applies the relevant period shall begin on the notification date and end one month after the date on which Form TM9t was filed or two months [beginning immediately] after the notification date, whichever is the later.

(7) The registrar shall send a copy of Form TM8 to the person opposing the registration.

NOTES

Paras (3)–(5): words in square brackets substituted by the Trade Marks and Registered Designs (Amendment) Rules 2013, SI 2013/444, rr 2, 3(1)–(5).

Para (6): words in square brackets inserted by SI 2013/444, rr 2, 3(1), (6).

[5.165]

19 Opposition proceedings: preliminary indication (Form TM53)

(1) This rule applies if—

(a) the opposition or part of it is based on the relative grounds of refusal set out in section 5(1) or (2); and

(b) the registrar has not indicated to the parties that the registrar thinks that it is inappropriate for this rule to apply.

[(1A) This rule shall not apply to fast track oppositions.]

(2) After considering the statement of the grounds of opposition and the counter-statement the registrar shall send notice to the parties ("the preliminary indication") stating whether it appears to the registrar that—

(a) registration of the mark should not be refused in respect of all or any of the goods and services listed in the application on the grounds set out in section 5(1) or (2); or

(b) registration of the mark should be refused in respect of all or any of the goods and services listed in the application on the grounds set out in section 5(1) or (2).

(3) The date upon which the preliminary indication is sent shall be the "indication date".

(4) Where it appeared to the registrar under paragraph (2) that registration of the mark should not be refused in respect of all or any of the goods or services listed in the application on the grounds set out in section 5(1) or (2), the person opposing the registration shall, within one month of the indication date, file a notice of intention to proceed with the opposition based on those grounds by filing a Form TM53, otherwise that person's opposition to the registration of the mark in relation to those goods or services on the grounds set in section 5(1) or (2) shall be deemed to have been withdrawn

(5) Where it appeared to the registrar under paragraph (2) that registration of the mark should be refused in respect of all or any of the goods or services listed in the application on the grounds set out in section 5(1) or (2), the applicant shall, within one month of the indication date, file a notice of intention to proceed on Form TM53, otherwise the applicant shall be deemed to have withdrawn the request to register the mark in respect of the goods or services for which the registrar indicated registration should be refused.

(6) A person who files a Form TM53 shall, at the same time, send a copy to all other parties to the proceedings.

(7) The registrar need not give reasons for the preliminary indication nor shall the preliminary indication be subject to appeal.

NOTES

Para (1A): inserted by the Trade Marks (Fast Track Opposition) (Amendment) Rules 2013, SI 2013/2235, r 2(1), (5).

[5.166]

20 Opposition proceedings: evidence rounds

(1) Where—

(a) Form TM53 has been filed by either party;

(b) the opposition or part of it is based on grounds other than those set out in section 5(1) or (2) and the applicant has filed a Form TM8; or

(c) the registrar has indicated to the parties that it is inappropriate for rule 19 to apply,

the registrar shall specify the periods within which evidence and submissions may be filed by the parties.

(2) Where—

(a) the opposition is based on an earlier trade mark of a kind falling within section 6(1)(c); or

(b) the opposition or part of it is based on grounds other than those set out in section 5(1) or (2); or

(c) the truth of a matter set out in the statement of use is either denied or not admitted by the applicant,

the person opposing the registration ("the opposer") shall file evidence supporting the opposition.

(3) Where the opposer files no evidence under paragraph (2), the opposer shall be deemed to have withdrawn the opposition to the registration to the extent that it is based on—

(a) the matters in paragraph (2)(a) or (b); or

(b) an earlier trade mark which has been registered and which is the subject of the statement of use referred to in paragraph (2)(c).

(4) The registrar may, at any time, give leave to either party to file evidence upon such terms as the registrar thinks fit.

[(5) Paragraphs (1)–(3) of this Rule shall not apply to fast track oppositions but paragraph (4) shall apply.]

NOTES

Para (5): added by the Trade Marks (Fast Track Opposition) (Amendment) Rules 2013, SI 2013/2235, r 2(1), (6).

[5.167]

21 Procedure for intervention

(1) If the opposition or part of it is based on the relative grounds for refusal set out in section 5(1), (2) or (3), any person in paragraph (3) may file an application to the registrar on Form TM27 for leave to intervene and the registrar may, after hearing the parties concerned if so required, refuse such leave or grant leave upon such terms and conditions (including any undertaking as to costs) as the registrar thinks fit.

(2) Any person granted leave to intervene shall, subject to any terms and conditions imposed in respect of the intervention, be treated as a party to the proceedings for the purposes of the application of the provisions of rules 19, 20 and 62 to 73.

(3) The persons referred to in paragraph (1) are—

- (a) where the opposition is based on an earlier trade mark, a licensee of that mark; and
- (b) where the opposition is based on an earlier collective mark or certification mark, an authorised user of that mark.

[5.168]

22 Observations on application to be sent to applicant; section 38(3)

The registrar shall send to the applicant a copy of any document containing observations made under section 38(3).

[5.169]

23 Publication of registration; section 40

On the registration of the trade mark the registrar shall publish the registration on the Office website, specifying the date upon which the trade mark was entered in the register.

Amendment of Application

[5.170]

24 Amendment of application; section 39 (Form TM21)

A request for an amendment of an application to correct an error or to change the name or address of the applicant or in respect of any amendment requested after publication of the application shall be made on Form TM21.

[5.171]

25 Amendment of application after publication; section 39 (Form TM7)

(1) Where, pursuant to section 39, a request is made for amendment of an application which has been published in the Journal and the amendment affects the representation of the trade mark or the goods or services covered by the application, the amendment or a statement of the effect of the amendment shall also be published in the Journal.

(2) Any person claiming to be affected by the amendment may, within one month of the date on which the amendment or a statement of the effect of the amendment was published under paragraph (1), give notice to the registrar of objection to the amendment on Form TM7 which shall include a statement of the grounds of objection which shall, in particular, indicate why the amendment would not fall within section 39(2).

(3) The registrar shall send a copy of Form TM7 to the applicant and the procedure in rules 17, 18 and 20 shall apply to the proceedings relating to the objection to the amendment as they apply to proceedings relating to opposition to an application for registration, but with the following modifications—

- (a) any reference to—
  - (i) an application for registration shall be construed as a reference to a request for amendment of an application,
  - (ii) the person opposing the registration shall be construed as a reference to the person objecting to the amendment of an application,
  - (iii) the opposition shall be construed as a reference to the objection;
- (b) the relevant period, referred to in rule 18(1), shall for these purposes be the period of two months [beginning immediately after] the date upon which the registrar sent a copy of Form TM7 to the applicant; and
- (c) rules 18(3) to (6), 20(2) and (3) shall not apply.

NOTES

Para (3): words in square brackets substituted by the Trade Marks and Registered Designs (Amendment) Rules 2013, SI 2013/444, rr 2, 4, Sch 1.

Division, Merger and Series of Marks

[5.172]

26 Division of application; section 41 (Form TM12)

(1) At any time before registration an applicant may send to the registrar a request on Form TM12 [to divide the specification] of the application for registration (the original application) into two or more separate applications (divisional applications), indicating for each division the specification of goods or services.

(2) Each divisional application shall be treated as a separate application for registration with the same filing date as the original application.

(3) Where the request to divide an application is sent after publication of the application, any objections in respect of, or opposition to, the original application shall be taken to apply to each divisional application and shall be proceeded with accordingly.

(4) Upon division of an original application in respect of which notice has been given to the registrar of particulars relating to the grant of a licence, or a security interest or any right in or under it, the notice and the particulars shall be deemed to apply in relation to each of the applications into which the original application has been divided.

NOTES

Para (1): words in square brackets substituted by the Trade Marks and Trade Marks and Patents (Fees) (Amendment) Rules 2009, SI 2009/2089, rr 3, 10.

[5.173]

27 Merger of separate applications or registrations; section 41 (Form TM17)

(1), (2) . . .

(3) The proprietor of two or more registrations of a trade mark[, the applications relating to which were filed on the same date,] may request the registrar on Form TM17 to merge them into a single registration and the registrar shall, if satisfied that the registrations are in respect of the same trade mark, merge them into a single registration.

[(3A) No application under paragraph (3) may be granted in respect of the registration of a trade mark which—

(a) is the subject of proceedings for its revocation or invalidation; or

(b) is the subject of an international registration within the meaning of article 2 of the Trade Marks (International Registration) Order 2008 which has not become independent of the trade mark as provided for in accordance with Article 6 of the Madrid Protocol.]

(4) Where any registration of a trade mark to be merged under paragraph (3) is subject to a disclaimer or limitation, the merged registration shall also be restricted accordingly.

(5) Where any registration of a trade mark to be merged under paragraph (3) has had registered in relation to it particulars relating to the grant of a licence or a security interest or any right in or under it, or of any memorandum or statement of the effect of a memorandum, the registrar shall enter in the register the same particulars in relation to the merged registration.

(6) The date of registration of the merged registration shall, where the separate registrations bear different dates of registration, be the latest of those dates.

NOTES

Paras (1), (2): revoked by the Trade Marks and Trade Marks (Fees) (Amendment) Rules 2012, SI 2012/1003, r 2(1), (3)(a).
Para (3): words in square brackets inserted by SI 2012/1003, r 2(1), (3)(b).
Para (3A): inserted by SI 2012/1003, r 2(1), (3)(c).

[5.174]

28 Registration of a series of trade marks; section 41 (Form TM12)

[(1) An application may be made in accordance with rule 5 for the registration of a series of trade marks in a single registration provided that the series comprises of no more than six trade marks.

(1A) Where an application for registration of a series of trade marks comprises three or more trade marks, the application shall be subject to the payment of the prescribed fee for each trade mark in excess of two trade marks.]

(2) Following an application under paragraph (1) the registrar shall, if satisfied that the marks constitute a series, accept the application.

(3) At any time before registration, the applicant under paragraph (1) may request on Form TM12 the division of the application into separate applications in respect of one or more marks in that series and the registrar shall divide the application accordingly, provided that at least one application remaining after such a division would comprise of either—

(a) a single mark; or

(b) two or more marks that would be a series of trade marks within the meaning of section 41(2).

(4) Where the request to divide an application is sent after publication of the application, any objections in respect of, or opposition to, the original application shall be taken to apply to each divisional application and shall be proceeded with accordingly.

(5) At any time the applicant for registration of a series of trade marks or the proprietor of a registered series of trade marks may request the deletion of a mark in that series and, following such request, the registrar shall delete the mark accordingly.

(6) Where under paragraph (5) the registrar deletes a trade mark from an application for registration, the application, in so far as it relates to the deleted mark, shall be treated as withdrawn.

(7) The division of an application into one or more applications under paragraph (3) shall be subject to the payment of a divisional fee and such application and class fees as are appropriate.

NOTES

Paras (1), (1A): substituted for original para (1), by the Trade Marks and Trade Marks and Patents (Fees) (Amendment) Rules 2009, SI 2009/2089, rr 3, 11.

Paras (3), (4), (7): revoked by SI 2009/2089, rr 3, 12, 23, except in relation to an application for registration of a series of trade marks which was filed before 1 October 2009.

Collective and Certification Marks

[5.175]

29 Filing of regulations for collective and certification marks; Schedules 1 & 2 (Form TM35)

Where an application for registration of a collective or certification mark is filed, the applicant shall, within such period of not less than three months as the registrar may specify, file Form TM35 accompanied by a copy of the regulations governing the use of the mark.

[5.176]

30 Amendment of regulations of collective and certification marks; Schedule 1 paragraph 10 and Schedule 2 paragraph 11 (Forms TM36 & TM7)

(1) An application for the amendment of the regulations governing the use of a registered collective or certification mark shall be filed on Form TM36.

(2) Where it appears to be expedient to the registrar that the amended regulations should be made available to the public the registrar shall publish a notice in the Journal indicating where copies of the amended regulations may be inspected.

(3) Any person may, within two months of the date of publication of the notice under paragraph (2), make observations to the registrar on the amendments relating to the matters referred to in paragraph 6(1) of Schedule 1 to the Act in relation to a collective mark, or paragraph 7(1) of Schedule 2 to the Act in relation to a certification mark and the registrar shall send a copy of those observations to the proprietor.

(4) Any person may, within two months of the date on which the notice was published under paragraph (2), give notice to the registrar of opposition to the amendment on Form TM7 which shall include a statement of the grounds of opposition indicating why the amended regulations do not comply with the requirements of paragraph 6(1) of Schedule 1 to the Act, or, as the case may be, paragraph 7(1) of Schedule 2 to the Act.

(5) The registrar shall send a copy of Form TM7 to the proprietor and the procedure in rules 18 and 20 shall apply to the proceedings relating to the opposition to the amendment as they apply to proceedings relating to opposition to an application for registration, but with the following modifications—

- (a) any reference to—
  - (i) the applicant shall be construed as a reference to the proprietor,
  - (ii) an application for registration shall be construed as a reference to an application for the amendment of the regulations,
  - (iii) the person opposing the registration shall be construed as a reference to the person opposing the amendment of the regulations;
- (b) the relevant period, referred to in rule 18(1), shall for these purposes be the period of two months [beginning immediately after] the date upon which the registrar sent a copy of Form TM7 to the proprietor;
- (c) rules 18(3) to (6), 20(2) and (3) shall not apply.

NOTES

Para (5): words in square brackets substituted by the Trade Marks and Registered Designs (Amendment) Rules 2013, SI 2013/444, rr 2, 4, Sch 1.

[5.177]

31 Registration subject to disclaimer or limitation; section 13

Where the applicant for registration of a trade mark or the proprietor by notice in writing sent to the registrar—

- (a) disclaims any right to the exclusive use of any specified element of the trade mark; or
- (b) agrees that the rights conferred by the registration shall be subject to a specified territorial or other limitation,

the registrar shall make the appropriate entry in the register and publish such disclaimer or limitation.

[5.178]

32 Alteration of registered trade marks; section 44 (Forms TM25 & TM7)

(1) The proprietor of a registered trade mark may request the registrar on Form TM25 for such alteration of the mark as is permitted under section 44 and following such request the registrar may require evidence as to the circumstances in which the application is made.

(2) Where, upon the request of the proprietor, the registrar proposes to allow such alteration, the registrar shall publish the mark as altered in the Journal.

(3) Any person claiming to be affected by the alteration may, within two months of the date on which the mark as altered was published under paragraph (2), give notice to the registrar of objection to the alteration on Form TM7 which shall include a statement of the grounds of objection.

(4) The registrar shall send a copy of Form TM7 to the proprietor and the procedure in rules 18 and 20 shall apply to the proceedings relating to the objection to the alteration as they apply to proceedings relating to opposition to an application for registration, but with the following modifications—

- (a) any reference to—
  - (i) the applicant shall be construed as a reference to the proprietor,
  - (ii) an application for registration shall be construed as a reference to a request for alteration,
  - (iii) the person opposing the registration shall be construed as a reference to the person objecting to the alteration,
  - (iv) the opposition shall be construed as a reference to the objection;
- (b) the relevant period, referred to in rule 18(1), shall for these purposes be the period of two months [beginning immediately after] the date upon which the registrar sent a copy of Form TM7 to the proprietor;
- (c) rules 18(3) to (6), 20(2) and (3) shall not apply.

NOTES

Para (4): words in square brackets substituted by the Trade Marks and Registered Designs (Amendment) Rules 2013, SI 2013/444, rr 2, 4, Sch 1.

[5.179]

33 Surrender of registered trade mark; section 45 (Forms TM22 & TM23)

(1) Subject to paragraph (2), the proprietor may surrender a registered trade mark, by sending notice to the registrar—

- (a) on Form TM22 in respect of all the goods or services for which it is registered; or
- (b) on Form TM23, in respect only of those goods or services specified by the proprietor in the notice.

(2) A notice under paragraph (1) shall be of no effect unless the proprietor in that notice—

- (a) gives the name and address of any person having a registered interest in the mark; and
- (b) certifies that any such person—
  - (i) has been sent not less than three months' notice of the proprietor's intention to surrender the mark, or
  - (ii) is not affected or if affected consents to the surrender.

(3) The registrar shall, upon the surrender taking effect, make the appropriate entry in the register and publish the date of surrender on the Office website.

Renewal and Restoration

[5.180]

34 Reminder of renewal of registration; section 43

(1) Subject to paragraph (2) below, at any time not earlier than six months nor later than one month before the expiration of the last registration of a trade mark, the registrar shall (except where renewal has already been affected under rule 35) send to the registered proprietor notice of the approaching expiration and inform the proprietor at the same time that the registration may be renewed in the manner described in rule 35.

(2) If it appears to the registrar that a trade mark may be registered under section 40 at any time within six months before or at any time on or after the date on which renewal would be due (by reference to the date of application for registration), the registrar shall be taken to have complied with paragraph (1) if the registrar sends to the applicant notice to that effect within one month following the date of actual registration.

[5.181]

35 Renewal of registration; section 43 (Form TM11)

Renewal of registration shall be effected by filing a request for renewal on Form TM11 at any time within the period of six months ending on the date of the expiration of the registration.

[5.182]
36 Delayed renewal and removal of registration; section 43 (Form TM11)

(1) If on the expiration of the last registration of a trade mark the renewal fee has not been paid, the registrar shall publish that fact.

(2) If, within six months from the date of the expiration of the last registration, a request for renewal is filed on Form TM11 accompanied by the appropriate renewal fee and additional renewal fee, the registrar shall renew the registration without removing the mark from the register.

(3) Where no request for renewal is filed, the registrar shall, subject to rule 37, remove the mark from the register.

(4) Where a mark is due to be registered after the date on which it is due for renewal (by reference to the date of application for registration), the request for renewal shall be filed together with the renewal fee and additional renewal fee within six months after the date of actual registration.

(5) The removal of the registration of a trade mark shall be published on the Office website.

[5.183]
37 Restoration of registration; section 43 (Form TM13)

(1) Where the registrar has removed the mark from the register for failure to renew its registration in accordance with rule 36, the registrar may, following receipt of a request filed on Form TM13 within six months of the date of the removal of the mark accompanied by the appropriate renewal fee and appropriate restoration fee—

(a) restore the mark to the register; and
(b) renew its registration,

if, having regard to the circumstances of the failure to renew, the registrar is satisfied that it is just to do so.

(2) The restoration of the registration, including the date of restoration, shall be published on the Office website.

Revocation, Invalidation and Rectification

[5.184]
38 Application for revocation (on the grounds of non-use); section 46(1)(a) or (b) (Forms TM8(N) & TM26(N))

(1) An application to the registrar for revocation of a trade mark under section 46, on the grounds set out in section 46(1)(a) or (b), shall be made on Form TM26(N).

(2) The registrar shall send a copy of Form TM26(N) to the proprietor.

(3) The proprietor shall, within two months of the date on which he was sent a copy of Form TM26(N) by the registrar, file a Form TM8(N), which shall include a counter-statement.

(4) Where the proprietor fails to file evidence of use of the mark or evidence supporting the reasons for non-use of the mark within the period specified in paragraph (3) above the registrar shall specify a further period of not less than two months within which the evidence shall be filed.

(5) The registrar shall send a copy of Form TM8(N) and any evidence of use, or evidence supporting reasons for non-use, filed by the proprietor to the applicant.

(6) Where the proprietor fails to file a Form TM8(N) within the period specified in paragraph (3) the registration of the mark shall, unless the registrar directs otherwise, be revoked.

(7) Where the proprietor fails to file evidence within the period specified under paragraph (3) or any further period specified under paragraph (4), the registrar may treat the proprietor as not opposing the application and the registration of the mark shall, unless the registrar directs otherwise, be revoked.

(8) The registrar may, at any time, give leave to either party to file evidence upon such terms as the registrar thinks fit.

[5.185]
39 Application for revocation (on grounds other than non-use); section 46(1)(c) or (d) (Forms TM8 & TM26(O))

(1) An application to the registrar for revocation of a trade mark under section 46, on the grounds set out in section 46(1)(c) or (d), shall be made on Form TM26(O) and shall include a statement of the grounds on which the application is made and be accompanied by a statement of truth.

(2) The registrar shall send a copy of Form TM26(O) and the statement of the grounds on which the application is made to the proprietor.

(3) The proprietor shall, within two months of the date on which he was sent a copy of Form TM26(O) and the statement by the registrar, file a Form TM8 which shall include a counter-statement, otherwise the registrar may treat the proprietor as not opposing the application and the registration of the mark shall, unless the registrar directs otherwise, be revoked.

(4) The registrar shall send a copy of Form TM8 to the applicant.

[5.186]

40 Application for revocation (on grounds other than non-use): evidence rounds

(1) Where the [proprietor] has filed a Form TM8, the registrar shall specify the periods within which further evidence may be filed by the parties.

(2) Where the applicant files no further evidence in support of the application the applicant, shall, unless the registrar otherwise directs, be deemed to have withdrawn the application.

(3) The registrar shall notify the proprietor of any direction given under paragraph (2).

(4) The registrar may, at any time give leave to either party to file evidence upon such terms as the registrar thinks fit.

NOTES

Para (1): word in square brackets substituted by the Trade Marks (Amendment) Rules 2008, SI 2008/2300, r 2.

[5.187]

41 Application for invalidation: filing of application and counter-statement; section 47 (Forms TM8 & TM26(I))

(1) An application to the registrar for a declaration of invalidity under section 47 shall be filed on Form TM26(I) and shall include a statement of the grounds on which the application is made and be accompanied by a statement of truth.

(2) Where the application is based on a trade mark which has been registered, there shall be included in the statement of the grounds on which the application is made a representation of that mark and—

- (a) the details of the authority with which the mark is registered;
- (b) the registration number of that mark;
- (c) the goods and services in respect of which—
  - (i) that mark is registered, and
  - (ii) the application is based; and
- (d) where neither section 47(2A)(a) nor (b) applies to the mark, a statement detailing whether during the period referred to in section 47(2B)(a) it has been put to genuine use in relation to each of the goods and services in respect of which the application is based or whether there are proper reasons for non-use (for the purposes of rule 42 this is the "statement of use").

(3) Where the application is based on a trade mark in respect of which an application for registration has been made, there shall be included in the statement of the grounds on which the application is made a representation of that mark and those matters set out in paragraph (2)(a) to (c), with references to registration being construed as references to the application for registration.

(4) Where the application is based on an unregistered trade mark or other sign which the applicant claims to be protected by virtue of any rule of law (in particular, the law of passing off), there shall be included in the statement of the grounds on which the application is made a representation of that mark or sign and the goods and services in respect of which such protection is claimed.

(5) The registrar shall send a copy of Form TM26(I) and the statement of the grounds on which the application is made to the proprietor.

(6) The proprietor shall, within two months of the date on which a copy of Form TM26(I) and the statement was sent by the registrar, file a Form TM8, which shall include a counter-statement, otherwise the registrar may treat the proprietor as not opposing the application and registration of the mark shall, unless the registrar otherwise directs, be declared invalid.

(7) The registrar shall send a copy of Form TM8 to the applicant.

[5.188]

42 Application for invalidation: evidence rounds

(1) Where the proprietor has filed Form TM8, the registrar shall send notice to the applicant inviting the applicant to file evidence in support of the grounds on which the application is made and any submissions and to send a copy to all the other parties.

(2) The registrar shall specify the periods within which evidence and submissions may be filed by the parties.

(3) Where—

- (a) the application is based on an earlier trade mark of a kind falling within section 6(1)(c); or
- (b) the application or part of it is based on grounds other than those set out in section 5(1) or (2); or
- (c) the truth of a matter set out in the statement of use is either denied or not admitted by the proprietor,

the applicant shall file evidence supporting the application.

(4) Where the applicant files no evidence under paragraph (3), the applicant shall be deemed to have withdrawn the application to the extent that it is based on—

- (a) the matters in paragraph (3)(a) or (b); or

(b) an earlier trade mark which has been registered and is the subject of the statement of use referred to in paragraph (3)(c).

(5) The registrar may, at any time give leave to either party to file evidence upon such terms as the registrar thinks fit.

[5.189]

43 Setting aside cancellation of application or revocation or invalidation of registration; (Form TM29)

(1) This rule applies where—

(a) an application for registration is treated as abandoned under rule 18(2);

(b) the registration of a mark is revoked under rule 38(6) or rule 39(3); or

(c) the registration of a mark is declared invalid under rule 41(6),

and the applicant or the proprietor (as the case may be) claims that the decision of the registrar to treat the application as abandoned or revoke the registration of the mark or declare the mark invalid (as the case may be) ("the original decision") should be set aside on the grounds set out in paragraph (4).

(2) Where this rule applies, the applicant or the proprietor shall, within a period of six months [beginning immediately after] the date that the application was refused or the register was amended to reflect the revocation or the declaration of invalidity (as the case may be), file an application on Form TM29 to set aside the decision of the registrar and shall include evidence in support of the application and shall copy the form and the evidence to the other party to the original proceedings under the rules referred to in paragraph (1).

(3) Where the applicant or the proprietor demonstrates to the reasonable satisfaction of the registrar that the failure to file Form TM8 within the period specified in the rules referred to in paragraph (1) was due to a failure to receive Form TM7, Form TM26(N), Form TM26(O) or Form TM26(I) (as the case may be), the original decision may be set aside on such terms and conditions as the registrar thinks fit.

(4) In considering whether to set aside the original decision the matters to which the registrar must have regard include whether the person seeking to set aside the decision made an application to do so promptly upon becoming aware of the original decision and any prejudice which may be caused to the other party to the original proceedings if the original decision were to be set aside.

NOTES

Para (2): words in square brackets substituted by the Trade Marks and Registered Designs (Amendment) Rules 2013, SI 2013/444, rr 2, 4, Sch 1.

[5.190]

44 Procedure on application for rectification; section 64 (Form TM26(R))

(1) An application for rectification of an error or omission in the register under section 64(1) shall be made on Form TM26(R) together with:

(a) a statement of the grounds on which the application is made; and

(b) any evidence to support those grounds.

(2) Where any application is made under paragraph (1) by a person other than the proprietor of the registered trade mark the registrar—

(a) shall send a copy of the application and the statement, together with any evidence filed, to the proprietor; and

(b) may give such direction with regard to the filing of subsequent evidence and upon such terms as the registrar thinks fit.

[5.191]

45 Procedure for intervention

(1) Any person, other than the registered proprietor, claiming to have an interest in proceedings on an application under rule 38, 39, 41 or 44, may file an application to the registrar on Form TM27 for leave to intervene, stating the nature of the person's interest and the registrar may, after hearing the parties concerned if they request a hearing, refuse leave or grant leave upon such terms and conditions (including any undertaking as to costs) as the registrar thinks fit.

(2) Any person granted leave to intervene shall, subject to any terms and conditions imposed in respect of the intervention, be treated as a party to the proceedings for the purposes of the application of the provisions of rules 38 to 40, 41 and 42 or 44 (as appropriate) and rules 62 to 73.

The Register

[5.192]

46 Form of register; section 63(1)

The register required to be maintained by the registrar under section 63(1) need not be kept in documentary form.

[5.193]

47 Entry in register of particulars of registered trade marks; section 63(2) (Form TM24)

In addition to the entries in the register of registered trade marks required to be made by section 63(2)(a), there shall be entered in the register in respect of each trade mark the following particulars—

(a) the date of registration as determined in accordance with section 40(3) (that is to say, the date of the filing of the application for registration);
(b) the date of completion of the registration procedure;
(c) the priority date (if any) to be accorded pursuant to a claim to a right to priority made under section 35 or 36;
(d) the name and address of the proprietor;
(e) the address for service (if any) filed under rule 11;
(f) any disclaimer or limitation of rights under section 13(1)(a) or (b);
(g) any memorandum or statement of the effect of any memorandum relating to a trade mark of which the registrar has been notified on Form TM24;
(h) the goods or services in respect of which the mark is registered;
(i) where the mark is a collective or certification mark, that fact;
(j) where the mark is registered pursuant to section 5(5) with the consent of the proprietor of an earlier trade mark or other earlier right, that fact;
(k) where the mark is registered pursuant to a transformation application,
  (i) the number of the international registration, and
  (ii) either:—
    (aa) the date accorded to the international registration under Article 3(4), or
    (bb) the date of recordal of the request for extension to the United Kingdom of the international registration under Article 3*ter*,
  as the case may be, of the Madrid Protocol;
(l) where the mark arises from the conversion of a [European Union] trade mark or an application for a [European Union] trade mark, the number of any other registered trade mark from which the [European Union] trade mark or the application for a [European Union] trade mark claimed seniority and the earliest seniority date.

NOTES

Para (l): words in square brackets substituted by the European Union Trade Mark Regulations 2016, SI 2016/299, reg 15, Schedule, para 5, subject to transitional provisions and savings as noted to the Trade Marks Act 1994, s 5 at **[5.5]**.

[5.194]

48 Entry in register of particulars of registrable transactions; section 25

Upon application made to the registrar by such person as is mentioned in section 25(1)(a) or (b) there shall be entered in the register in respect of each trade mark the following particulars of registrable transactions together with the date on which the entry is made—

(a) in the case of an assignment of a registered trade mark or any right in it—
  (i) the name and address of the assignee,
  (ii) the date of the assignment, and
  (iii) where the assignment is in respect of any right in the mark, a description of the right assigned;
(b) in the case of the grant of a licence under a registered trade mark—
  (i) the name and address of the licensee,
  (ii) where the licence is an exclusive licence, that fact,
  (iii) where the licence is limited, a description of the limitation, and
  (iv) the duration of the licence if the same is or is ascertainable as a definite period;
(c) in the case of the grant of any security interest over a registered trade mark or any right in or under it—
  (i) the name and address of the grantee,
  (ii) the nature of the interest (whether fixed or floating), and
  (iii) the extent of the security and the right in or under the mark secured;
(d) in the case of the making by personal representatives of an assent in relation to a registered trade mark or any right in or under it—
  (i) the name and address of the person in whom the mark or any right in or under it vests by virtue of the assent, and
  (ii) the date of the assent;
(e) in the case of a court or other competent authority transferring a registered trade mark or any right in or under it—
  (i) the name and address of the transferee,
  (ii) the date of the order, and
  (iii) where the transfer is in respect of a right in the mark, a description of the right transferred; and

(f) in the case of any amendment of the registered particulars relating to a licence under a registered trade mark or a security interest over a registered trade mark or any right in or under it, particulars to reflect such amendment.

[5.195]

49 Application to register or give notice of transaction; sections 25 & 27(3) (Form TM16, TM24, TM50 & TM51)

(1) An application to register particulars of a transaction to which section 25 applies or to give notice to the registrar of particulars of a transaction to which section 27(3) applies shall be made—

(a) relating to an assignment or transaction other than a transaction referred to in sub-paragraphs (b) to (d) below, on Form TM16;

(b) relating to a grant of a licence, on Form TM50;

(c) relating to an amendment to, or termination of a licence, on Form TM51;

(d) relating to the grant, amendment or termination of any security interest, on Form TM24; and

(e) relating to the making by personal representatives of an assent or to an order of a court or other competent authority, on Form TM24.

(2) An application under paragraph (1) shall—

(a) where the transaction is an assignment, be signed by or on behalf of the parties to the assignment;

(b) where the transaction falls within sub-paragraphs (b), (c) or (d) of paragraph (1), be signed by or on behalf of the grantor of the licence or security interest,

or be accompanied by such documentary evidence as suffices to establish the transaction.

(3) Where an application to give notice to the registrar has been made of particulars relating to an application for registration of a trade mark, upon registration of the trade mark, the registrar shall enter those particulars in the register.

[5.196]

50 Public inspection of register; section 63(3)

(1) The register shall be open for public inspection at the Office during the hours of business of the Office as published in accordance with rule 80.

(2) Where any portion of the register is kept otherwise than in documentary form, the right of inspection is a right to inspect the material on the register.

[5.197]

51 Supply of certified copies etc; section 63(3) (Form TM31R)

The registrar shall supply a certified copy or extract or uncertified copy or extract, as requested on Form TM31R, of any entry in the register.

[5.198]

52 Request for change of name or address in register; section 64(4) (Form TM21)

The registrar shall, on a request made on Form TM21 by the proprietor of a registered trade mark or a licensee or any person having an interest in or charge on a registered trade mark which has been registered under rule 48 ("the applicant"), enter a change in the applicant's name or address as recorded in the register.

[5.199]

53 Removal of matter from register; sections 25(5)(b) and 64(5) (Form TM7)

(1) Where it appears to the registrar that any matter in the register has ceased to have effect, before removing it from the register—

(a) the registrar may publish in the Journal the fact that it is intended to remove that matter, and

(b) where any person appears to the registrar to be affected by the removal, notice of the intended removal shall be sent to that person.

(2) Within two months of the date on which the intention to remove the matter is published, or notice of the intended removal is sent, as the case may be—

(a) any person may file notice of opposition to the removal on form TM7; and

(b) the person to whom a notice is sent under paragraph (1)(b) may file in writing their objections, if any, to the removal,

and where such opposition or objections are made, rule 63 shall apply.

(3) If the registrar is satisfied after considering any objections or opposition to the removal that the matter has not ceased to have effect, the registrar shall not remove it.

(4) Where there has been no response to the registrar's notice the registrar may remove the matter and where representations objecting to the removal of the entry have been made the registrar may, if after considering the objections the registrar is of the view that the entry or any part of it has ceased to have effect, remove it or the appropriate part of it.

Change of Classification

[5.200]

54 Change of classification; sections 65(2) & 76(1)

(1) The registrar may at any time amend an entry in the register which relates to the classification of a registered trade mark so that it accords with the version of the Nice Classification that has effect at that time.

(2) Before making any amendment to the register under paragraph (1) the registrar shall give the proprietor of the mark written notice of the proposed amendments and shall at the same time advise the proprietor that—

(a) the proprietor may make written objections to the proposals, within two months of the date of the notice, stating the grounds of those objections; and

(b) if no written objections are received within the period specified the registrar shall publish the proposals and the proprietor shall not be entitled to make any objections to the proposals upon such publication.

(3) If the proprietor makes no written objections within the period specified in paragraph (2)(a) or at any time before the expiration of that period decides not to make any objections and gives the registrar written notice to this effect, the registrar shall as soon as practicable after the expiration of that period or upon receipt of the notice publish the proposals in the Journal.

(4) Where the proprietor makes written objections within the period specified in paragraph (2)(a), the registrar shall, as soon as practicable after having considered the objections, publish the proposals in the Journal or, where the registrar has amended the proposals, publish the proposals as amended in the Journal; and the registrar's decision shall be final and not subject to appeal.

[5.201]

55 Opposition to proposals; sections 65(3), (5) & 76(1) (Form TM7)

(1) Any person may, within two months of the date on which the proposals were published under rule 54, give notice to the registrar of opposition to the proposals on Form TM7 which shall include a statement of the grounds of opposition which shall, in particular, indicate why the proposed amendments would be contrary to section 65(3).

(2) If no notice of opposition under paragraph (1) is filed within the time specified, or where any opposition has been determined, the registrar shall make the amendments as proposed and shall enter in the register the date when they were made; and the registrar's decision shall be final and not subject to appeal.

Request for Information, Inspection of Documents and Confidentiality

[5.202]

56 Request for information; section 67(1) (Form TM31C)

A request for information relating to an application for registration or to a registered trade mark shall be made on Form TM31C

[5.203]

57 Information available before publication; section 67(2)

(1) Before publication of an application for registration the registrar shall make available for inspection by the public the application and any amendments made to it and any particulars contained in a notice given to the registrar under rule 49.

(2) Nothing in section 67(2) relating to publication of information shall be construed as preventing the publication of decisions on cases relating to trade marks decided by the registrar.

[5.204]

58 Inspection of documents; sections 67 & 76(1)

(1) Subject to paragraphs (2) and (3), the registrar shall permit all documents filed or kept at the Office in relation to a registered mark or, where an application for the registration of a trade mark has been published, in relation to that application, to be inspected.

(2) The registrar shall not be obliged to permit the inspection of any such document as is mentioned in paragraph (1) until the completion of any procedure, or the stage in the procedure which is relevant to the document in question, which the registrar is required or permitted to carry out under the Act or these Rules.

(3) The right of inspection under paragraph (1) does not apply to—

(a) any document prepared in the Office solely for its own use;

(b) any document sent to the Office, whether at its request or otherwise, for inspection and subsequent return to the sender;

(c) any request for information under rule 56;

(d) any document received by the Office which the registrar considers should be treated as confidential;

(e) any document in respect of which the registrar issues directions under rule 59 that it be treated as confidential.

(4) Nothing in paragraph (1) shall be construed as imposing on the registrar any duty of making available for public inspection—

(a) any document or part of a document which in the registrar's opinion disparages any person in a way likely to cause damage to that person; or

(b) any document or information filed at or sent to or by the Office before 31st October 1994; or

(c) any document or information filed at or sent to or by the Office after 31st October 1994 relating to an application for registration of a trade mark under the Trade Marks Act 1938.

(5) No appeal shall lie from a decision of the registrar under paragraph (4) not to make any document or part of a document available for public inspection.

[5.205]

59 Confidential documents

(1) Where a document (other than a form required by the registrar and published in accordance with rule 3) is filed at the Office and the person filing it requests at the time of filing that it or a specified part of it be treated as confidential, giving reasons for the request, the registrar may direct that it or part of it, as the case may be, be treated as confidential, and the document shall not be open to public inspection while the matter is being determined by the registrar.

(2) Where such direction has been given and not withdrawn, nothing in this rule shall be taken to authorise or require any person to be allowed to inspect the document or part of it to which the direction relates except by leave of the registrar.

(3) The registrar shall not withdraw any direction given under this rule without prior consultation with the person at whose request the direction was given, unless the registrar is satisfied that such prior consultation is not reasonably practical.

(4) The registrar may where the registrar considers that any document issued by the Office should be treated as confidential so direct, and upon such direction that document shall not be open to public inspection except by leave of the registrar.

(5) Where a direction is given under this rule for a document to be treated as confidential a record of the fact shall be filed with the document.

Agents

[5.206]

60 Proof of authorisation of agent may be required; section 82 (Form TM33)

(1) Where an agent has been authorised under section 82, the registrar may in a particular case require the personal signature or presence of the agent or the person authorising the agent to act as agent.

(2) Subject to paragraph (3), where a person appoints an agent for the first time or appoints one agent in substitution for another, the newly appointed agent shall file Form TM33.

(3) Where after a person has become a party to proceedings involving a third party before the registrar, the person appoints an agent for the first time or appoints one agent in substitution for another, the newly appointed agent shall file Form TM33P.

(4) Any act required or authorised by the Act in connection with the registration of a trade mark or any procedure relating to a trade mark may not be done by or to the newly appointed agent until on or after the date on which the newly appointed agent files Form TM33 or TM33P as appropriate.

(5) The registrar may by notice in writing require an agent to produce evidence of his authority under section 82.

[5.207]

61 Registrar may refuse to deal with certain agents; section 88

The registrar may refuse to recognise as agent in respect of any business under the Act—

(a) a person who has been convicted of an offence under section 84;

(b) an individual whose name has been erased from and not restored to, or who is suspended from, the register of trade mark agents on the ground of misconduct;

(c) a person who is found by the Secretary of State to have been guilty of such conduct as would, in the case of an individual registered in that register, render that person liable to have their name erased from it on the ground of misconduct;

(d) a partnership or body corporate of which one of the partners or directors is a person whom the registrar could refuse to recognise under paragraph (a), (b) or (c).

Proceedings Before and Decision of Registrar, Evidence and Costs

[5.208]

62 General powers of registrar in relation to proceedings

(1) Except where the Act or these Rules otherwise provide, the registrar may give such directions as to the management of any proceedings as the registrar thinks fit, and in particular may—

(a) require a document, information or evidence to be filed within such period as the registrar may specify;

(b) require a translation of any document;

(c) require a party or a party's legal representative to attend a hearing;
(d) hold a hearing by telephone or by using any other method of direct oral communication;
[(e) allow a statement of case to be amended, provided that—
(i) where an application is made to add grounds of opposition other than under subsections 5(1) or (2) of the Act, the application shall be made on Form TM7G; and
(ii) in the case of fast track oppositions the registrar may only permit a statement of case to be amended to add additional or alternative earlier registered or protected trade marks as additional grounds of opposition under subsections 5(1) or 5(2) of the Act, provided that the total number of earlier trade marks relied upon may not exceed three;]
(f) stay the whole, or any part, of the proceedings either generally or until a specified date or event;
[(g) consolidate proceedings provided that where a fast track opposition is consolidated with other non-fast track proceedings, it shall no longer be treated as a fast track opposition;]
(h) direct that part of any proceedings be dealt with as separate proceedings;
(i) exclude any evidence which the registrar considers to be inadmissible;
[(j) direct that with effect from the date specified in the direction opposition proceedings which have been commenced on Form TM7F as a fast track opposition but which do not satisfy the criteria for a fast track opposition may continue as if the opposition proceedings were an opposition to the registration commenced under Rule 17 on Form TM7].

(2) The registrar may control the evidence by giving directions as to—
(a) the issues on which evidence is required; and
(b) the way in which the evidence is to be placed before the registrar.

(3) When the registrar gives directions under any provision of these Rules, the registrar may—
(a) make them subject to conditions; and
(b) specify the consequences of failure to comply with the directions or a condition.

(4) The registrar may at any stage of any proceedings direct that the parties to the proceedings attend a case management conference or pre-hearing review.

[(5) In the case of a fast track opposition—
(a) proceedings shall be held orally only if the Office requests it or if either party to the proceedings requests it and the registrar considers that oral proceedings are necessary to deal with the case justly and at proportionate cost; and
(b) the parties shall be given at least fourteen days' notice beginning on the date on which the notice is sent, of the time when the oral proceedings are to take place unless each party to the proceedings consents to shorter notice.

(6) In the case of a fast track opposition, where no oral hearing is held, the registrar shall give the parties the opportunity to provide arguments in writing before reaching a decision that is adverse to either party.]

NOTES

Para (1): sub-paras (e), (g) substituted and sub-para (j) inserted, by the Trade Marks (Fast Track Opposition) (Amendment) Rules 2013, SI 2013/2235, r 2(1), (7)(a)–(c).

Paras (5), (6): added by SI 2013/2235, r 2(1), (7)(d).

[5.209]

63 Decisions of registrar to be taken after hearing

(1) Without prejudice to any provisions of the Act or these Rules requiring the registrar to hear any party to proceedings under the Act or these Rules, or to give such party an opportunity to be heard, the registrar shall, before taking any decision on any matter under the Act or these Rules which is or may be adverse to any party to any proceedings, give that party an opportunity to be heard.

(2) The registrar shall give that party at least fourteen days' notice, beginning on the date on which notice is sent, of the time when the party may be heard unless the party consents to shorter notice.

[(3) This Rule shall not apply to fast track opposition proceedings.]

NOTES

Para (3): added by the Trade Marks (Fast Track Opposition) (Amendment) Rules 2013, SI 2013/2235, r 2(1), (8).

[5.210]

64 Evidence in proceedings before the registrar; section 69

(1) Subject to rule 62(2) and as follows, evidence filed in any proceedings under the Act or these Rules may be given—
(a) by witness statement, affidavit, statutory declaration; or
(b) in any other form which would be admissible as evidence in proceedings before the court.

(2) A witness statement may only be given in evidence if it includes a statement of truth.

(3) The general rule is that evidence at hearings is to be by witness statement unless the registrar or any enactment requires otherwise.

(4) For the purposes of these Rules, a statement of truth—

(a) means a statement that the person making the statement believes that the facts stated in a particular document are true; and

(b) shall be dated and signed by—

(i) in the case of a witness statement, the maker of the statement,

(ii) in any other case, the party or legal representative of such party.

(5) In these Rules, a witness statement is a written statement signed by a person that contains the evidence which that person would be allowed to give orally.

(6) Under these Rules, evidence shall only be considered filed when—

(a) it has been received by the registrar; and

(b) it has been sent to all other parties to the proceedings.

[5.211]

65 Registrar to have power of an official referee; section 69

The registrar shall have the powers of an official referee of the Supreme Court as regards—

(a) the attendance of witnesses and their examination on oath; and

(b) the discovery and production of documents,

but the registrar shall have no power to punish summarily for contempt.

[5.212]

66 Hearings before registrar to be in public

(1) The hearing before the registrar of any dispute between two or more parties relating to any matter in connection with an application for the registration of a mark or a registered mark shall be in public unless the registrar, after consultation with those parties who appear in person or are represented at the hearing, otherwise directs.

(2) . . .

NOTES

Para (2): revoked by the Tribunals, Courts and Enforcement Act 2007 (Transitional and Consequential Provisions) Order 2008, SI 2008/2683, art 6(1), Sch 1, para 345.

[5.213]

67 Costs of proceedings; section 68

The registrar may, in any proceedings under the Act or these Rules, by order award to any party such costs as the registrar may consider reasonable, and direct how and by what parties they are to be paid.

[5.214]

68 Security for costs; section 68

(1) The registrar may require any person who is a party in any proceedings under the Act or these Rules to give security for costs in relation to those proceedings; and may also require security for the costs of any appeal from the registrar's decision.

(2) In default of such security being given, the registrar, in the case of the proceedings before the registrar, or in the case of an appeal, the person appointed under section 76 may treat the party in default as having withdrawn their application, opposition, objection or intervention, as the case may be.

[5.215]

69 Decision of registrar (Form TM5)

(1) The registrar shall send to each party to the proceedings written notice of any decision made in any proceedings before the registrar stating the reasons for that decision and for the purposes of any appeal against that decision, subject to paragraph (2), the date on which the notice is sent shall be taken to be the date of the decision.

(2) Where a statement of the reasons for the decision is not included in the notice sent under paragraph (1), any party may, within one month of the date on which the notice was sent to that party, request the registrar on Form TM5 to send a statement of the reasons for the decision and upon such request the registrar shall send such a statement, and the date on which that statement is sent shall be deemed to be the date of the registrar's decision for the purpose of any appeal against it.

Appeals

[5.216]

70 Decisions subject to appeal; section 76(1)

(1) Except as otherwise expressly provided by these Rules an appeal lies from any decision of the registrar made under these Rules relating to a dispute between two or more parties in connection with a trade mark, including a decision which terminates the proceedings as regards one of the parties or a decision awarding costs to any party ("a final decision") or a decision which is made at any point in the proceedings prior to a final decision ("an interim decision").

(2) An interim decision (including a decision refusing leave to appeal under this paragraph) may only be appealed against independently of any appeal against a final decision with the leave of the registrar.

[5.217]

71 Appeal to person appointed; section 76

(1) [Subject to paragraph (1A), notice] of appeal to the person appointed under section 76 shall be filed on Form TM55 which shall include the appellant's grounds of appeal and his case in support of the appeal.

[(1A) Where the appeal arises in proceedings between two or more parties, notice of appeal to the person appointed under section 76 shall be filed on Form TM55P, which shall include the appellant's grounds of appeal and his case in support of the appeal.]

[(2) Forms TM55 or TM55P shall be filed within the period of 28 days beginning immediately after the date of the registrar's decision which is the subject of the appeal ("the original decision").]

(3) The registrar shall send the notice and the statement to the person appointed.

(4) Where any person other than the appellant was a party to the proceedings before the registrar in which the original decision was made ("the respondent"), the registrar shall send to the respondent a copy of the notice and the statement and the respondent may, within the period of 21 days [beginning immediately after] the date on which the notice and statement was sent, file a notice responding to the notice of appeal.

(5) The respondent's notice shall specify any grounds on which the respondent considers the original decision should be maintained where these differ from or are additional to the grounds given by the registrar in the original decision.

(6) The registrar shall send a copy of the respondent's notice to the person appointed and a copy to the appellant.

NOTES

Para (1): words in square brackets substituted by the Trade Marks (Fast Track Opposition) (Amendment) Rules 2013, SI 2013/2235, r 2(1), (9)(a).

Para (1A): inserted by SI 2013/2235, r 2(1), (9)(b).

Para (2): substituted by SI 2013/2235, r 2(1), (9)(c).

Para (4): words in square brackets substituted by the Trade Marks and Registered Designs (Amendment) Rules 2013, SI 2013/444, rr 2, 4, Sch 1.

[5.218]

72 Determination whether appeal should be referred to court; section 76(3)

(1) Within 28 days of the date on which the notice of appeal is sent to the respondent by the registrar under rule 71(4);

- (a) the registrar; or
- (b) any person who was a party to the proceedings in which the decision appealed against was made,

may request that the person appointed refer the appeal to the court.

(2) Where the registrar requests that the appeal be referred to the court, the registrar shall send a copy of the request to each party to the proceedings.

(3) A request under paragraph (1)(b) shall be sent to the registrar following which the registrar shall send it to the person appointed and shall send a copy of the request to any other party to the proceedings.

(4) Within 28 days of the date on which a copy of a request is sent by the registrar under paragraph (2) or (3), the person to whom it is sent may make representations as to whether the appeal should be referred to the court.

(5) In any case where it appears to the person appointed that a point of general legal importance is involved in the appeal, the person appointed shall send to the registrar and to every party to the proceedings in which the decision appealed against was made, notice to that effect.

(6) Within 28 days of the date on which a notice is sent under paragraph (5), the person to whom it was sent may make representations as to whether the appeal should be referred to the court.

[5.219]

73 Hearing and determination of appeal; section 76(4)

(1) Where the person appointed does not refer the appeal to the court, the person appointed shall send written notice of the time and place appointed for the oral hearing of the appeal—

(a) where no person other than the appellant was a party to the proceedings in which the decision appealed against was made, to the registrar and to the appellant; and

(b) in any other case, to the registrar and to each person who was a party to those proceedings.

(2) The person appointed shall send the notice at least fourteen days before the time appointed for the oral hearing.

(3) If all the persons notified under paragraph (1) inform the person appointed that they do not wish to make oral representations then—

(a) the person appointed may hear and determine the case on the basis of any written representations; and

(b) the time and place appointed for the oral hearing may be vacated.

(4) Rules 62, 65, 67 and 68 shall apply to the person appointed and to proceedings before the person appointed as they apply to the registrar and to proceedings before the registrar.

(5) If there is an oral hearing of the appeal then rule 66 shall apply to the person appointed and to proceedings before the person appointed as it applies to the registrar and to proceedings before the registrar.

(6) A copy of the decision of the appointed person shall be sent, with a statement of the reasons for the decision, to the registrar and to each person who was a party to the appeal.

Correction of Irregularities, Calculation and Extension of Time

[5.220]

74 Correction of irregularities in procedure

(1) Subject to rule 77, the registrar may authorise the rectification of any irregularity in procedure (including the rectification of any document filed) connected with any proceeding or other matter before the registrar or the Office.

(2) Any rectification made under paragraph (1) shall be made—

(a) after giving the parties such notice; and

(b) subject to such conditions,

as the registrar may direct.

[5.221]

75 Interrupted day

(1) The registrar may certify any day as an interrupted day where—

(a) there is an event or circumstance causing an interruption in the normal operation of the Office; or

(b) there is a general interruption or subsequent dislocation in the postal services of the United Kingdom.

(2) Any certificate of the registrar made under paragraph (1) shall be displayed in the Office and published on the Office website.

(3) The registrar shall, where the time for doing anything under these Rules expires on an interrupted day, extend that time to the next following day not being an interrupted day (or an excluded day).

(4) In this rule—

"excluded day" means a day which is not a business day as specified in a direction given by the registrar under section 80; and

"interrupted day" means a day which has been certified as such under paragraph (1).

[5.222]

76 Delays in communication services

(1) The registrar shall extend any time limit in these Rules where the registrar is satisfied that the failure to do something under these Rules was wholly or mainly attributed to a delay in, or failure of, a communication service.

(2) Any extension under paragraph (1) shall be—

(a) made after giving the parties such notice; and

(b) subject to such conditions,

as the registrar may direct.

(3) In this rule "communication service" means a service by which documents may be sent and delivered and includes post, facsimile, email and courier.

[5.223]
77 Alteration of time limits (Form TM9)

(1) Subject to paragraphs (4) and (5), the registrar may, at the request of the person or party concerned or at the registrar's own initiative extend a time or period prescribed by these Rules or a time or period specified by the registrar for doing any act and any extension under this paragraph shall be made subject to such conditions as the registrar may direct.

(2) A request for extension under this rule may be made before or after the time or period in question has expired and shall be made—

(a) where the application for registration has not been published and the request for an extension [relates to a time or period other than one specified under rule 13 and] is made before the time or period in question has expired, in writing; and

(b) in any other case, on Form TM9.

(3) Where an extension under paragraph (1) is requested in relation to proceedings before the registrar, the party seeking the extension shall send a copy of the request to every other person who is a party to the proceedings.

(4) The registrar shall extend a flexible time limit, except a time or period which applies in relation to proceedings before the registrar or the filing of an appeal to the Appointed Person under rule 71, where—

(a) the request for extension is made before the end of the period of two months [beginning immediately after] the date the relevant time or period expired; and

(b) no previous request has been made under this paragraph.

(5) A time limit listed in Schedule 1 (whether it has already expired or not) may be extended under paragraph (1) if, and only if—

(a) the irregularity or prospective irregularity is attributable, wholly or in part, to a default, omission or other error by the registrar, the Office or the International Bureau; and

(b) it appears to the registrar that the irregularity should be rectified.

(6) In this rule—

"flexible time limit" means—

(a) a time or period prescribed by these Rules, except a time or period prescribed by the rules listed in Schedule 1, or

(b) a time or period specified by the registrar for doing any act or taking any proceedings; and

"proceedings before the registrar" means any dispute between two or more parties relating to a matter before the registrar in connection with a trade mark.

NOTES

Para (2): words in square brackets in sub-para (a) inserted by the Trade Marks and Trade Marks and Patents (Fees) (Amendment) Rules 2009, SI 2009/2089, rr 3, 13.

Para (4): words in square brackets substituted by the Trade Marks and Registered Designs (Amendment) Rules 2013, SI 2013/444, rr 2, 4, Sch 1.

Filing of Documents, Hours of Business, Trade Marks Journal and Translations

[5.224]
78 Filing of documents by electronic means

The registrar may permit as an alternative to the sending by post or delivery of the application, notice or other document in legible form the filing of the application, notice or other document by electronic means subject to such terms or conditions as the registrar may specify either generally by published notice or in any particular case by written notice to the person desiring to file any such documents by such means.

[5.225]
79 Electronic communications

(1) The delivery using electronic communications to any person by the registrar of any document is deemed to be effected, unless the registrar has otherwise specified, by transmitting an electronic communication containing the document to an address provided or made available to the registrar by that person as an address for the receipt of electronic communications; and unless the contrary is proved such delivery is deemed to be effected immediately upon the transmission of the communication.

(2) In this rule "electronic communication" has the same meaning as in the Electronic Communications Act 2000.

[5.226]
80 Directions on hours of business; section 80

Any directions given by the registrar under section 80 specifying the hours of business of the Office and business days of the Office shall be published on the Office website.

[5.227]

81 Trade Marks Journal; section 81

The registrar shall publish a journal, entitled "The Trade Marks Journal" containing such information as is required to be published in the Journal under these Rules and such other information as the registrar thinks fit.

[5.228]

82 Translations

(1) Where any document or part thereof which is in a language other than English is filed or sent to the registrar in pursuance of the Act or these Rules, the registrar may require that there be furnished a translation into English of the document or that part, verified to the satisfaction of the registrar as corresponding to the original text.

(2) The registrar may refuse to accept any translation which the registrar considers to be inaccurate in which event there shall be furnished another translation of the document in question verified in accordance with paragraph (1).

Transitional Provisions and Revocations

[5.229]

83 Revocation of previous rules and proceedings commenced under previous rules

(1) The instruments set out in Schedule 2 ("the previous rules") are revoked to the extent specified.

(2) Where immediately before these Rules come into force, any time or period prescribed by the previous rules has effect in relation to any act or proceeding and has not expired, the time or period prescribed by the previous rules and not by these Rules shall apply to that act or proceeding.

(3) Except as provided by paragraph (4) where a new step is to be taken on or after 1st October 2008 in relation to any proceedings commenced under the previous rules these Rules shall apply to such proceedings from that date.

(4) Subject to paragraph (5) where prior to the entry into force of these Rules-

(a) a Form TM8 and counter-statement have been filed in-

(i) opposition proceedings, or

(ii) proceedings for the revocation of a trade mark on the grounds set out in section 46(1)(c) or (d); or

(iii) invalidation proceedings; or

(b) an application for revocation of a trade mark on the grounds set out in section 46(1)(a) or (b) has been filed,

the previous rules shall apply with regard to the filing of any evidence in relation to those proceedings.

(5) Where proceedings as described in paragraph (4) are consolidated with proceedings commenced on or after 1st October 2008 these Rules shall apply with regard to the filing of any evidence in relation to those consolidated proceedings.

SCHEDULE 1
EXTENSION OF TIME LIMITS

Rule 77

[5.230]

rule 17(2) (filing notice of opposition)

rule 17(3) (filing notice of opposition: request for extension of time)

rule 18(1) (counter-statement in opposition proceedings)

rule 19(4) (responding to preliminary indication)

rule 25(2) (opposition to amendment after publication)

rule 30(4) (opposition to amendment of regulations of collective and certification marks)

rule 32(3) (opposition to alteration of mark)

rule 35 (renewal of registration)

rule 36(2) (delayed renewal)

rule 37(1) (restoration of registration)

rule 38(3) (counter-statement for revocation on grounds of non-use)

rule 39(3) (counter-statement for revocation on grounds other than non-use)

rule 41(6) (counter-statement for invalidity)

rule 43(2) (setting aside cancellation of application or revocation or invalidation of registration)

rule 53(2) (opposition to removal of matter from register)

rule 55(1) (opposition to proposals for change of classification)

rule 77(4) (period for making a retrospective request to extend a flexible time period).

SCHEDULE 2

(*Sch 2 contains revocations only.*)

TRADE MARKS (INTERNATIONAL REGISTRATION) ORDER 2008

(SI 2008/2206)

NOTES

Made: 13 August 2008.
Authority: Trade Marks Act 1994, s 54.
Commencement: 1 October 2008.

ARRANGEMENT OF ARTICLES

SCHEDULES

[5.231]
1 Citation and commencement

This Order may be cited as the Trade Marks (International Registration) Order 2008 and shall come into force on 1st October 2008.

[5.232]
2 Interpretation

In this Order—

"the Act" means the Trade Marks Act 1994 and "section" means a section of that Act;

"Common Regulations" means the regulations adopted under article 10 of the Madrid Protocol with effect from 1 April 1996 and as amended with effect from 1 April 2002;

"concurrent registered trade mark" means a trade mark as defined in Schedule 4, paragraph 2;

"date of the international registration" means the date of the international registration under Article 3(4) of the Madrid Protocol;

"international application" means an application by way of the Patent Office as office of origin to the International Bureau for registration of a trade mark in the International Register;

"International Register" means the register of trade marks maintained by the International Bureau for the purposes of the Madrid Protocol;

"international registration" means a registration of a trade mark in the International Register;

"protected international trade mark (UK)" means an international registration which is the subject of a request for extension and which is protected in accordance with section 38 as modified by Schedule 2, paragraph 6 and references to "protection" and "protected" shall be construed accordingly;

"request for extension" means a request for an extension of protection to the United Kingdom under Article 3*ter* (1) or (2) of the Madrid Protocol which has been notified by the International Bureau;

"the Relative Grounds Order" means the Trade Marks (Relative Grounds) Order 2007;

"supplementary register" means the register of international trade marks (UK) required to be maintained under section 63 as modified by Schedule 2, paragraph 8;

"the Trade Marks Rules" means the Trade Marks Rules 2008 and "trade marks rule" shall be construed accordingly.

[5.233]
3 International trade marks (UK)

(1) An international registration which is the subject of a request for extension shall be entitled to protection subject to the provisions of the Act, the Relative Grounds Order and the Trade Marks Rules as applied by this Order if the particulars of the request for extension were contained in an application for registration of a trade mark under the Act and such application would satisfy the requirements of the Act (including any imposed by the Trade Mark Rules).

(2) Subject to paragraph (3) a protected international trade mark (UK) shall be treated as if it were a trade mark registered under the Act and the holder shall have the same rights and remedies but shall be subject to the same conditions as the proprietor of a registered trade mark.

(3) The provisions of the Act (except those listed in Schedule 1, Part 1), the Relative Grounds Order and the Trade Marks Rules (except those listed in Schedule 1, Part 2) shall apply to international trade marks (UK) and requests for extension with the following modifications;

(a) references to a registered trade mark shall include references to a protected international trade mark (UK);

(b) references to a proprietor of a registered trade mark shall include references to the holder of a protected international trade mark (UK);

(c) references to an application for registration of a trade mark shall include references to a request for extension;

(d) references to an applicant for registration shall include references to the holder of an international registration in respect of which a request for extension has been made;

(e) references to registration of a trade mark shall include the conferring of protection on an international registration which is the subject of a request for extension;

(f) references to the goods or services for which a trade mark is registered shall include references to the goods or services in respect of which a protected international trade mark (UK) confers protection;

(g) references to the publication of the application include references to the publication of the notice of details of the international registration in the Journal;

(h) references to the register are to the supplementary register;

(i) the modifications set out in Schedule 2; and

(j) such further modifications as the context requires for the purpose of giving effect to those provisions as applied by this Order.

[5.234]
4 International applications originating in the United Kingdom

The provisions set out in Schedule 3 shall apply in relation to the making of applications for international registration by way of the Patent Office as office of origin.

[5.235]
5 Concurrent registrations and transformation applications

The provisions set out in Schedule 4 shall apply in relation to—

(a) the effects of international registration where a trade mark is also registered under the Act; and

(b) the transformation of an application for an international registration, or an international registration, into an application for registration of a trade mark under the Act.

[5.236]
6 Miscellaneous and General Provisions

The provisions set out in Schedule 5 shall apply.

[5.237]
7 Fees

The fees to be paid in respect of any matters arising under this Order shall be those specified in Schedule 6.

[5.238]
8 Revocations and transitional provisions

(1) The instruments set out in Schedule 7 are revoked ("the previous Orders").

(2) Where immediately before this Order comes into force any time period prescribed by the previous Orders has effect in relation to any act or proceeding and has not expired, the time or period prescribed by the previous Orders and not by this Order shall apply to that act or proceeding.

(3) Except as provided by paragraph (4), where a new step is to be taken on or after 1st October 2008 in relation to any proceedings commenced under the previous Orders this Order shall apply to such proceedings from that date.

(4) Subject to paragraph (5), where prior to the entry into force of this Order:

(a) A Form TM8 and counter-statement have been filed in

(i) opposition proceedings; or

(ii) proceedings for the revocation of a trade mark on the grounds set out in section 46(1)(c) or (d); or

(iii) invalidation proceedings; or

(b) an application for revocation of a trade mark on the grounds set out in section 46(1)(a) or (b) has been filed,

the previous Orders shall apply with regard to the filing of any evidence in relation to those proceedings.

(5) Where proceedings as described in paragraph (4) are consolidated with proceedings commenced on or after 1st October 2008 this Order shall apply with regard to the filing of any evidence in relation to those consolidated proceedings.

SCHEDULE 1
PROVISIONS OF THE ACT AND TRADE MARKS RULES WHICH DO NOT APPLY TO INTERNATIONAL TRADE MARKS (UK) OR REQUESTS FOR EXTENSION

Article 3(3)

PART 1

[5.239]

section 24(2)(b) (assignment or other transmission in relation to use of the trade mark in a particular manner or locality)

section 32(1), (2) and (4) (application for registration)

section 33(1) (date of filing)

section 34 (classification of trade marks)

section 39(2) (withdrawal, restriction or amendment of application)

section 40 (registration)

section 41 (registration: supplementary provisions)

section 42 (duration of registration)

section 43 (renewal of registration)

section 44 (alteration of registered trade mark)

section 45 (surrender of registered trade mark)

section 64(4) (change of name and address by proprietor or licensee)

section 65 (adaptation of entries to new classification)

section 79 (fees)

section 94 (falsification of register)

PART 2

[5.240]

trade marks rule 6 (claim to priority; sections 35 & 36)

trade marks rule 8 (application may relate to more than one class and shall specify the class (Form TM31C))

trade marks rule 9 (determination of classification)

trade marks rule 12(4)(a) (failure to provide an address for service)

trade marks rule 13 (deficiencies in application; section 32)

trade marks rule 46 (form of register; section 63(1))

trade marks rule 47 (entry in register of particulars of registered trade marks; section 63(2) (Form TM24))

trade marks rule 56 (request for information; s 67(1) (Form TM31C))

SCHEDULE 2
MODIFICATIONS TO PROVISIONS OF THE ACT APPLIED TO INTERNATIONAL TRADE MARKS (UK)

Article 3(3)(i)

[5.241]

1. (1) Section 25 (registration of transactions affecting registered trade mark) is modified as follows.

(2) Omit paragraph (a) of subsection (1) and substitute—

"(a) a person claiming to be entitled to any security interest (whether fixed or floating) over a protected international trade mark (UK) or any right in or under it, or".

(3) Omit paragraphs (a), (b) and (c) of subsection (2) and substitute—

"(a) a change to the ownership of a registration recorded by the International Bureau in the International Register pursuant to article 9 of the Madrid Protocol;

(b) the grant of a licence recorded by the International Bureau in the International Register pursuant to rule 20 *bis* of the Common Regulations;".

(4) After subsection (2)(e) insert—

"(f) any matter other than as is referred to in paragraphs (a) and (b) above that is recorded in the International Register pursuant to article 9 *bis* of the Madrid Protocol.".

(5) In subsection (3) omit "Until an application has been made for registration of the prescribed particulars of a registrable transaction" and substitute "Until an application for registration of a matter in the supplementary register pursuant to subsection (1) has been made or an application for registration of a registrable transaction in the International Register (in accordance with Article 9 *bis* of the Madrid Protocol and rule 20 *bis* of the Common Regulations) has been made".

(6) In subsection (4)(a) omit "the prescribed particulars of the transaction" and substitute "a transaction in the International Register (in accordance with Article 9 *bis* of the Madrid Protocol and rule 20 *bis* of the Common Regulations)".

2. In section 33 (date of filing), for subsection (1), substitute—

"33 (1) The date of filing of a request for extension shall be the date of the international registration except—

(a) where at the time protection is conferred on an international trade mark (UK) there is a concurrent registered trade mark, the date of filing shall be the date of filing of the registered trade mark; and

(b) where a request for extension is made in accordance with Article 3*ter* (2) of the Madrid Protocol, the date of filing shall be the date that the request for extension was recorded in the International Register.".

3. In section 35 (claim to priority of convention application), for subsection (5), substitute—

"(5) The manner of claiming priority shall be determined in accordance with the Madrid Protocol and the Common Regulations.".

4. In section 37 (examination of application) omit subsections (3) to (5) and substitute—

"(3) If it appears to the registrar that the requirements for registration are not met, the registrar shall give notice of provisional refusal to the International Bureau.

(4) Where the International Bureau notifies the registrar or the registrar considers that a particular term used to indicate any of the goods or services included in the international registration is—

(a) too vague for the purposes of classification; or

(b) incomprehensible or linguistically incorrect,

the registrar may give notice of provisional refusal to the International Bureau in respect of that term.

(5) Where a decision of the registrar has been notified to the International Bureau pursuant to subsection (3) or (4), the registrar shall give the holder of the international registration an opportunity, within such period as the registrar may specify, to make representations or amend the request for extension by limiting the goods and services.".

5. In section 38(2) (publication, opposition proceedings and observations) after "opposition to the registration" insert "in which event the registrar shall give notice of provisional refusal to the International Bureau".

6. After section 38, insert—

"38A Notices of provisional refusal

(1) A notice of provisional refusal must set out the matters required by Article 5 of the Madrid Protocol and Rule 17 of the Common Regulations.

(2) Except as provided in subsection (3), a notice of provisional refusal may not be given after the expiry of the relevant period.

(3) Where before the expiry of the relevant period the registrar has given notice to the International Bureau—

(a) that the period prescribed for the purposes of section 38(2) expires after the end of the relevant period; or

(b) that the period prescribed for the purposes of section 38(2) expires less than one month before the end of the relevant period;

a notice of provisional refusal may be given after the expiry of the relevant period provided that it is given before the end of the period of one month beginning immediately after the period prescribed for the purposes of section 38(2).

(4) Where the registrar sends the International Bureau a notice of provisional refusal, the registrar must notify the International Bureau as to the final decision (meaning a decision from which no appeal may be brought) on whether the refusal should be upheld.

(5) The relevant period is the period of 18 months [beginning immediately after] the date the International Bureau sent the registrar the request for extension.

38B Protection

(1) Where no notice of provisional refusal is given to the International Bureau following publication under section 38(1), the international registration which is the subject of the request for extension shall be protected as a protected international trade mark (UK) with effect from the first day immediately following the end of the period prescribed for the purposes of section 38(2).

(2) Where notice of provisional refusal is given following publication under section 38(1), the international registration which is the subject of the request for extension shall be protected as a protected international trade mark (UK) with effect from the date on which the registrar notifies the International Bureau that the final decision is that the provisional refusal should not be upheld in accordance with section 38A(4).

(3) The reference to the completion of the registration procedure in section 46(1) shall be construed as a reference to the conferring of protection on an international registration in accordance with this section.

(4) When an international registration becomes protected as a protected international trade mark (UK), the registrar shall—

(a) notify the International Bureau that the international registration is protected in the United Kingdom; and

(b) publish a notice specifying the number of the international registration in respect of that trade mark, the date on which protection is conferred and the date and place of publication of the request for extension under section 38(1) in relation to that trade mark.".

7. In section 39 (Withdrawal, restriction or amendment of application) for subsection (1) substitute—

"(1) The goods and services covered by a request for extension may be restricted at any time by the applicant provided that if the request for extension has been published, the restriction must also be published in the Journal . . .".

8. (1) Section 63 (the register) shall be modified as follows.

(2) For subsection (1) substitute—

"(1) The registrar shall maintain a register for the purpose of entering transactions under section 25(1) (as modified by paragraph 1 of Schedule 2 to the Trade Marks International Registration) Order 2008) and disclaimers and limitations relating to international trade marks (UK).".

(3) In subsection (3) for the words "shall be kept in such manner as may be prescribed" substitute "need not be kept in documentary form".

(4) After subsection (3) insert—

"(4) Following notification from the International Bureau under rule 28(2) of the Common Regulations the registrar may correct an error or omission in the information entered in the register required to be maintained under subsection (1).".

9. In section 67(2)(a) (Information about applications and registered trade marks) before "in such cases" insert "any information recorded in the International Register or".

NOTES

Para 6: in the Trade Marks Act 1994, s 38A(5) (as set out) words in square brackets substituted by the Trade Marks (International Registration) (Amendment) Order 2013, SI 2013/445, arts 2, 3, subject to transitional provisions in art 6 thereof.

Para 7: in the Trade Marks Act 1994, s 39(1) (as set out) words omitted revoked by the Trade Marks (International Registration) (Amendment) Order 2009, SI 2009/2464, arts 2, 3.

SCHEDULE 3
INTERNATIONAL APPLICATIONS ORIGINATING IN THE UNITED KINGDOM

Article 4

Application for international registration at the Patent Office

[5.242]

1. (1) An applicant for the registration of a trade mark, or the proprietor of a registered trade mark, may, subject to the provisions of this paragraph, apply by way of the Patent Office as office of origin for the international registration of the trade mark.

(2) For the purposes of this paragraph an applicant shall be—

(a) a British citizen, a British overseas territories citizen, a British overseas citizen, a British subject or a British protected person;

(b) an individual domiciled in the United Kingdom;

(c) a body incorporated under the law of a part of the United Kingdom; or

(d) a person who has a real and effective industrial or commercial establishment in the United Kingdom.

(3) Where the registrar has reasonable doubts about whether an applicant is eligible, the registrar—

(a) must inform the applicant of the reason for those doubts; and

(b) may require that applicant to file evidence in support of his eligibility.

(4) Where—

(a) the registrar has no doubts or is satisfied as to the applicant's eligibility; and

(b) the particulars appearing in the application for an international registration correspond with the particulars at that time in the basic application or, as the case may be, the basic registration,

the registrar must submit the application to the International Bureau.

(5) In this Schedule—

(a) "basic application" means an application for registration of a trade mark in the United Kingdom in respect of which application is made for international registration;

(b) "basic registration" means a trade mark registered in the United Kingdom in respect of which application is made for international registration.

Termination of basic application or basic registration

2. (1) This paragraph applies where the registrar submits an application to the International Bureau in accordance with paragraph 1 and the basic application or basic registration is terminated.

(2) Where, before the end of the relevant period, a basic application or basic registration is terminated, the registrar shall request that the International Bureau cancel the International Registration.

(3) A basic application is terminated where it is—

(a) not accepted;

(b) refused; or

(c) withdrawn (including deemed as such).

(4) A basic registration is terminated where the rights in the registered trade mark cease to have effect.

(5) Where a basic application or basic registration is terminated in respect of some only of the goods or services for which the trade mark is registered (or is sought to be registered), the request must relate only to those goods and services.

(6) The relevant period is the period of 5 years [beginning immediately after] the date of the international registration.

(7) But if during that period the registrar becomes aware of proceedings which may result in the termination of the basic application or basic registration, the registrar must notify the International Bureau accordingly, stating that no final decision has been made.

(8) On completion of the proceedings referred to in paragraph (7) the registrar must promptly notify the International Bureau of their outcome.

Division or merger of basic application or basic registration

3. (1) This paragraph applies where the registrar submits an application to the International Bureau in accordance with paragraph 1 and—

(a) the basic application is divided into two or more applications; or

(b) two or more basic applications or basic registrations are merged into a single application or registration.

(2) Where, before the end of the relevant period, a basic application is divided or two or more basic applications or basic registrations are merged, the registrar shall notify the International Bureau and shall indicate—

(a) the number of the international registration or, where the mark has not been registered, the number of the basic application;

(b) the name of the applicant or the holder of the relevant trade mark; and

(c) the number of each application resulting from the division or the number of the application or registration resulting from the merger.

(3) The relevant period is the period of 5 years [beginning immediately after] the date of the international registration.

NOTES

Paras 2, 3: words in square brackets substituted by the Trade Marks (International Registration) (Amendment) Order 2013, SI 2013/445, arts 2, 4, subject to transitional provisions in art 6 thereof.

SCHEDULE 4
TRANSFORMATION APPLICATIONS AND CONCURRENT REGISTRATIONS

Article 5

Transformation applications

[5.243]

1. (1) A transformation application is an application to register a trade mark under the Act where—

(a) the mark was the subject of an international registration and the international registration was the subject of a request for extension; and

(b) the international registration was cancelled at the request of the Office of origin under Article 6(4) of the Madrid Protocol.

(2) But an application shall only be treated as a transformation application where the goods and services cited in it are identical to some or all of the goods and services included in the international registration.

(3) Any application made under the Act which is a transformation application shall state that it is made by way of transformation.

(4) Such an application may only be made before the end of the period of three months [beginning immediately after] the date on which the international registration was cancelled.

(5) A transformation application may only be made by the person who was the holder of the international registration immediately before it was cancelled.

(6) Where on or before the date the transformation application was made, the trade mark is protected as an international trade mark (UK), the mark shall be registered under the Act; and it shall have the date of filing of the cancelled international trade mark (UK).

(7) Where on that date the trade mark is not so protected, the transformation application shall be treated as an application to register under the Act and it shall have the date of filing of the request for extension relating to that mark.

(8) Where in relation to the international registration a right of priority was claimed on the basis of a Convention application, the transformation application shall have the same right of priority.

Concurrent registrations

2. (1) This paragraph applies where at the time protection is conferred on an international trade mark (UK) there is a concurrent registered trade mark.

(2) A registration is concurrent where—

(a) the proprietor of the registered trade mark is the holder of the protected international trade mark (UK);

(b) the registered trade mark is the same as the protected international trade mark (UK);

(c) the goods and services in relation to which protection is conferred by the international trade mark (UK) include all those for which the registered trade mark is registered.

(3) The protected international trade mark (UK) shall be treated as being registered under the Act as of the date of registration of the registered trade mark.

(4) The priorities claimed in respect of the registered trade mark may also be claimed in respect of the international trade mark (UK).

(5) The provisions of this paragraph shall continue to apply after the registered trade mark lapses or is surrendered, but shall cease to apply if or to the extent that it is revoked or declared invalid.

(6) On the application of the holder of the protected international trade mark (UK) the registrar shall note the international registration in the register against the registered trade mark.

(7) For the purposes of paragraph (6), the holder of the international trade mark (UK) shall make an application to the registrar using Form TM28.

NOTES

Para 1: words in square brackets substituted by the Trade Marks (International Registration) (Amendment) Order 2013, SI 2013/445, arts 2, 5, subject to transitional provisions in art 6 thereof.

SCHEDULE 5
MISCELLANEOUS AND GENERAL PROVISIONS

Article 6

Correction of international registration

[5.244]

1. (1) Where the International Bureau notifies the registrar that it has corrected an international registration and the correction either—

(a) substantially affects the identity of the trade mark; or

(b) alters the goods or services covered by the international registration,

the registrar may treat the notification as a new request for extension.

(2) Where paragraph (1)(a) applies, any earlier request for protection shall be deemed to have been withdrawn and any resulting protection granted to the international trade mark (UK) shall be treated as having been declared invalid.

(3) Where paragraph (1)(b) applies and—

(a) the correction extends the goods and services covered by the request for extension, the new request for extension shall apply only to the additional goods and services; or

(b) the correction restricts the goods and services covered by the international registration, to the extent it relates to goods and service outside the restriction, an earlier request for protection shall be treated as having been withdrawn, and any resulting protection granted to the international trade mark (UK) shall be treated as having been declared invalid.

Assignment

2. (1) A protected international trade mark (UK) may only be assigned to an eligible person.

(2) An eligible person is—

(a) a national of any country which is a party to the Madrid Protocol;

(b) an individual domiciled in such a country;

(c) a body incorporated under the law of such a country; and

(d) a person who has a real and effective industrial or commercial establishment in such a country.

Judicial notice

3. (1) Judicial notice shall be taken of the following—

(a) the Madrid Protocol and the Common Regulations;

(b) copies issued by the International Bureau of entries in the International Register;

(c) copies of the periodical gazette published by the International Bureau in accordance with rule 32 of the Common Regulations.

(2) Any document mentioned in paragraph (1)(b) or (c) shall be admissible as evidence of any instrument or other act of the International Bureau so communicated.

(3) Where in relation to the international registration a right of priority was claimed on the basis of a Convention application, the transformation application shall have the same right of priority.

Revocation

4. Where the protection of a protected international trade mark (UK) is revoked or declared invalid to any extent, the registrar shall notify the International Bureau, and—

(a) in the case of a revocation, the rights of the proprietor shall be deemed to have ceased to exist to that extent as from—

(i) the date of the application for revocation, or

(ii) if the registrar or court is satisfied that the grounds for revocation existed at an earlier date, that date;

(b) in the case of a declaration of invalidity, the trade mark shall to that extent be deemed never to have been a protected international trade mark (UK).

Requests for Information

5. A request for information relating to a protected international trade mark (UK) must be made on Form TM31M.

Communication of information to the International Bureau

6. Notwithstanding any other enactment or rule of law, the registrar may communicate to the International Bureau any information which the United Kingdom is required to communicate by virtue of this Order or pursuant to the Madrid Protocol or Common Regulations.

Transmission of fees to the International Bureau

7. The registrar may accept for transmission to the International Bureau fees payable to the International Bureau in respect of an application for international registration originating in the United Kingdom or a renewal of such an international registration, subject to such terms and conditions as the registrar may specify, either generally by published notice, or in any particular case by written notice to the applicant desiring to make payment by such means.

SCHEDULE 6
FEES

Article 7

[5.245]

Matter in respect of which fee payable	*Amount*
Notice of opposition to the conferring of protection on an international registration (trade marks rule 17)	£200
[Notice of opposition to the conferring of protection on an international registration where the grounds of opposition are based solely on either or both of sub-sections 5(1) and (2) of the Trade Marks Act 1994	£100
Notice of fast track opposition to the conferring of protection on an international registration (trade marks rule 17A)	£100
Application to add grounds, other than under section 5(1) or 5(2) of the Act, to an opposition to the conferring of protection on an international registration (trade marks rule 62(1)(e))	£100]
Request for the revocation of a protected international trade mark (UK) (on grounds other than non-use) (trade marks rule 39)	£200
Request for the revocation of a protected international trade mark (UK) (on grounds of non-use) (trade marks rule 38)	£200
Request for the invalidation of a protected international trade mark (UK) (trade marks rule 41)	£200
Submission fee for an international application (Schedule 3, paragraph 1)	£40
Handling fee for the transmission by the Patent Office of fees payable to the International Bureau for renewal of an international registration (Schedule 5, paragraph 7)	£20
Request to the Registrar for a statement of reasons for his decision (trade mark rule 69(2))	£20
Request for an extension of time (trade marks rule 77(2))	[£100]
Request for information in relation to an international mark (UK)	£50
Filing of regulations governing the use of a certification or collective mark (trade mark rules 29)	£200
Request to amend regulations governing the use of a certification or collective mark (trade mark rules 30)	£100
Notice of opposition to the amendment of regulations relating to a certification or collective mark (trademark rules 30(4))	£200
[Request to enter details in the supplementary register relating to the grant, amendment or termination of any security interest (trade marks rule 49(1)(d))	£50]
[Appeal to the person appointed under section 76 in proceedings between two or more parties (trade marks rule 71(1A))	£250]

NOTES

Entries in first pair of square brackets inserted and final entry in square brackets added, by the Trade Marks (International Registration) (Amendment No 2) Order 2013, SI 2013/2237, art 2.

In entry "Request for an extension of time (trade marks rule 77(2))", sum in square brackets substituted by the Trade Marks (International Registration) (Amendment) Order 2009, SI 2009/2464, arts 2, 4.

Entry "Request to enter details in the supplementary register" in square brackets added by the Trade Marks (International Registration) (Amendment) Order 2010, SI 2010/32, arts 2, 3.

SCHEDULE 7

(Sch 7 contains revocations only.)

COUNCIL REGULATION

(40/94/EEC)

of 20 December 1993

on the Community trade mark

NOTES

Date of publication in OJ: OJ L11, 14.1.1994, p 1.

This Regulation has been repealed and codified by Regulation 207/2009/EC of the European Parliament and of the Council, at **[5.576]**, with effect from 13 April 2009. However, for reference purposes, this Regulation is reproduced here.

THE COUNCIL OF THE EUROPEAN UNION,

Having regard to the Treaty establishing the European Community, and in particular Article 235 thereof,

Having regard to the proposal from the Commission,[1]

Having regard to the opinion of the European Parliament,[2]

Having regard to the opinion of the Economic and Social Committee,[3]

Whereas it is desirable to promote throughout the Community a harmonious development of economic activities and a continuous and balanced expansion by completing an internal market which functions properly and offers conditions which are similar to those obtaining in a national market; whereas in order to create a market of this kind and make it increasingly a single market, not only must be barriers to free movement of goods and services be removed and arrangements be instituted which ensure that competition is not distorted, but, in addition, legal conditions must be created which enable undertakings to adapt their activities to the scale of the Community, whether in manufacturing and distributing goods or in providing services; whereas for those purposes, trade marks enabling the products and services of undertakings to be distinguished by identical means throughout the entire Community, regardless of frontiers, should feature amongst the legal instruments which undertakings have at their disposal;

Whereas action by the Community would appear to be necessary for the purpose of attaining the Community's said objectives; whereas such action involves the creation of Community arrangements for trade marks whereby undertakings can by means of one procedural system obtain Community trade marks to which uniform protection is given and which produce their effects throughout the entire area of the Community; whereas the principle of the unitary character of the Community trade mark thus stated will apply unless otherwise provided for in this Regulation;

Whereas the barrier of territoriality of the rights conferred on proprietors of trade marks by the laws of the Member States cannot be removed by approximation of laws; whereas in order to open up unrestricted economic activity in the whole of the common market for the benefit of undertakings, trade marks need to be created which are governed by a uniform Community law directly applicable in all Member States;

Whereas since the Treaty has not provided the specific powers to establish such a legal instrument, Article 235 of the Treaty should be applied;

Whereas the Community law relating to trade marks nevertheless does not replace the laws of the Member States on trade marks; whereas it would not in fact appear to be justified to require undertakings to apply for registration of their trade marks as Community trade marks; whereas national trade marks continue to be necessary for those undertakings which do not want protection of their trade marks at Community level;

Whereas the rights in a Community trade mark may not be obtained otherwise than by registration, and registration is to be refused in particular if the trade mark is not distinctive, if it is unlawful or if it conflicts with earlier rights;

Whereas the protection afforded by a Community trade mark, the function of which is in particular to guarantee the trade mark as an indication of origin, is absolute in the case of identity between the mark and the sign and the goods or services; whereas the protection applies also in cases of similarity between the mark and the sign and the goods or services; whereas an interpretation should be given of the concept of similarity in relation to the likelihood of confusion; whereas the likelihood of confusion, the appreciation of which depends on numerous elements and, in particular, on the recognition of the trade mark on the market, the association which can be made with the used or registered sign, the degree of similarity between the trade mark and the sign and between the goods or services identified, constitutes the specific condition for such protection;

Whereas it follows from the principle of free flow of goods that the proprietor of a Community trade mark must not be entitled to prohibit its use by a third party in relation to goods which have been put into circulation in the Community, under the trade mark, by him or with his consent, save where there exist legitimate reasons for the proprietor to oppose further commercialisation of the goods;

Whereas there is no justification for protecting Community trade marks or, as against them, any trade mark which has been registered before them, except where the trade marks are actually used;

Whereas a Community trade mark is to be regarded as an object of property which exists separately from the undertakings whose goods or services are designated by it; whereas accordingly, it must be capable of being transferred, subject to the overriding need to prevent the public being misled as a result of the transfer. It must also be capable of being charged as security in favour of a third party and of being the subject matter of licences;

Whereas administrative measures are necessary at Community level for implementing in relation to every trade mark the trade mark law created by this Regulation; whereas it is therefore essential, while retaining the Community's existing institutional structure and balance of powers, to establish an Office for Harmonisation in the Internal Market (trade marks and designs) which is independent in relation to technical matters and has legal, administrative and financial autonomy; whereas to this end it is necessary and appropriate that it should be a body of the Community having legal personality and exercising the implementing powers which are conferred on it by this Regulation, and that it should operate within the framework of Community law without detracting from the competencies exercised by the Community institutions;

Whereas it is necessary to ensure that parties who are affected by decisions made by the Office are protected by the law in a manner which is suited to the special character of trade mark law; whereas to that end provision is made for an appeal to lie from decisions of the examiners and of the various divisions of the Office; whereas if the department whose decision is contested does not rectify its decision it is to remit the appeal to a Board of Appeal of the Office, which is to decide on it; whereas decisions of the Boards of Appeal are, in turn, amenable to actions before the Court of Justice of the European Communities, which has jurisdiction to annul or to alter the contested decision;

Whereas under Council Decision 88/591/ECSC, EEC, Euratom of 24 October 1988 establishing a Court of First Instance of the European Communities,[4] *as amended by Decision 93/350/Euratom, ECSC, EEC of 8 June 1993,*[5] *that Court shall exercise at the first instance the jurisdiction conferred on the Court of Justice by the Treaties establishing the Communities—with particular regard to appeals lodged under the second subparagraph of Article 173 of the EC Treaty—and by the acts adopted in implementation thereof, save as otherwise provided in an act setting up a body governed by Community law; whereas the jurisdiction which this Regulation confers on the Court of Justice to cancel and reform decisions of the appeal courts shall accordingly be exercised at the first instance by the Court in accordance with the above Decision;*

Whereas in order to strengthen the protection of Community trade marks the Member States should designate, having regard to their own national system, as limited a number as possible of national courts of first and second instance having jurisdiction in matters of infringement and validity of Community trade marks;

Whereas decisions regarding the validity and infringement of Community trade marks must have effect and cover the entire area of the Community, as this is the only way of preventing inconsistent decisions on the part of the courts and the Office and of ensuring that the unitary character of Community trade marks is not undermined; whereas the rules contained in the Brussels Convention of Jurisdiction and the Enforcement of Judgments in Civil and Commercial Matters will apply to all actions at law relating to Community trade marks, save where this Regulation derogates from those rules;

Whereas contradictory judgments should be avoided in actions which involve the same acts and the same parties and which are brought on the basis of a Community trade mark and parallel national trade marks; whereas for this purpose, when the actions are brought in the same Member State, the way in which this is to be achieved is a matter for national procedural rules, which are not prejudiced by this Regulation, whilst when the actions are brought in different Member States, provisions modelled on the rules on lis pendens and related actions of the abovementioned Brussels Convention appear appropriate;

Whereas in order to guarantee the full autonomy and independence of the Office, it is considered necessary to grant it an autonomous budget whose revenue comes principally from fees paid by the users of the system; whereas however, the Community budgetary procedure remains applicable as far as any subsidies chargeable to general budget of the European Communities are concerned; whereas moreover, the auditing of accounts should be undertaken by the Court of Auditors;

Whereas implementing measures are required for the Regulation's application, particularly as regards the adoption and amendment of fees regulations and an Implementing Regulation; whereas such measures should be adopted by the Commission, assisted by a Committee composed of representatives of the Member States, in accordance with the procedural rules laid down in Article 2, procedure III(b), of Council Decision 87/373/EEC of 13 July 1987 laying down the procedures for the exercise of implementing powers conferred on the Commission,[6]

NOTES

1 OJ C351, 31.12.1980, p 1 and OJ C230, 31.8.1984, p 1.

2 OJ C307, 14.11.1983, p 46 and OJ C280, 28.10.1991, p 153.

3 OJ C310, 30.11.1981, p 22.

4 OJ L319, 25.11.1988, p 1 and corrigendum in OJ L241, 17.8.1989, p 4.

5 OJ L144, 16.6.1993, p 21.

6 OJ L97, 18.7.1987, p 33.

HAS ADOPTED THIS REGULATION—

TITLE I
GENERAL PROVISIONS

[5.246]
Article 1
Community trade mark
1. A trade mark for goods or services which is registered in accordance with the conditions contained in this Regulation and in the manner herein provided is hereinafter referred to as a 'Community trade mark'.
2. A Community trade mark shall have a unitary character. It shall have equal effect throughout the Community: it shall not be registered, transferred or surrendered or be the subject of a decision revoking the rights of the proprietor or declaring it invalid, nor shall its use be prohibited, save in respect of the whole Community. This principle shall apply unless otherwise provided in this Regulation.

NOTES
This Regulation has been repealed and codified by Regulation 207/2009/EC of the European Parliament and of the Council, at **[5.576]**, with effect from 13 April 2009. However, for reference purposes, this Regulation is reproduced here.

[5.247]
Article 2
Office
An Office for Harmonisation in the Internal Market (trade marks and designs), hereinafter referred to as 'the Office', is hereby established.

NOTES
Repealed as noted to Art 1, at **[5.246]**.

[5.248]
Article 3
Capacity to act
For the purpose of implementing this Regulation, companies or firms and other legal bodies shall be regarded as legal persons if, under the terms of the law governing them, they have the capacity in their own name to have rights and obligations of all kinds, to make contracts or accomplish other legal acts and to sue and be sued.

NOTES
Repealed as noted to Art 1, at **[5.246]**.

TITLE II
THE LAW RELATING TO TRADE MARKS

SECTION 1
DEFINITION OF A COMMUNITY TRADE MARK OBTAINING A COMMUNITY TRADE MARK

[5.249]
Article 4
Signs of which a Community trade mark may consist
A Community trade mark may consist of any signs capable of being represented graphically, particularly words, including personal names, designs, letters, numerals, the shape of goods or of their packaging, provided that such signs are capable of distinguishing the goods or services of one undertaking from those of other undertakings.

NOTES
Repealed as noted to Art 1, at **[5.246]**.

[5.250]
[Article 5
Persons who can be proprietors of Community trade marks
Any natural or legal person, including authorities established under public law, may be the proprietor of a Community trade mark.]

NOTES
Substituted by Council Regulation 422/2004/EC, Art 1(1).
Repealed as noted to Art 1, at **[5.246]**.

[5.251]
Article 6
Means whereby a Community trade mark is obtained
A Community trade mark shall be obtained by registration.

NOTES

Repealed as noted to Art 1, at **[5.246]**.

[5.252]

Article 7

Absolute grounds for refusal

1. The following shall not be registered—

(a) signs which do not conform to the requirements of Article 4;

(b) trade marks which are devoid of any distinctive character;

(c) trade marks which consist exclusively of signs or indications which may serve, in trade, to designate the kind, quality, quantity, intended purpose, value, geographical origin or the time of production of the goods or of rendering of the service, or other characteristics of the goods or service;

(d) trade marks which consist exclusively of signs or indications which have become customary in the current language or in the bona fide and established practices of the trade;

(e) signs which consist exclusively of—

(i) the shape which results from the nature of the goods themselves; or

(ii) the shape of goods which is necessary to obtain a technical result; or

(iii) the shape which gives substantial value to the goods;

(f) trade marks which are contrary to public policy or to accepted principles of morality;

(g) trade marks which are of such a nature as to deceive the public, for instance as to the nature, quality or geographical origin of the goods or service;

(h) trade marks which have not been authorised by the competent authorities and are to be refused pursuant to Article 6ter of the Paris Convention;

(i) trade marks which include badges, emblems or escutcheons other than those covered by Article 6ter of the Paris Convention and which are of particular public interest, unless the consent of the appropriate authorities to their registration has been given;

[(j) trade marks for wines which contain or consist of a geographical indication identifying wines or for spirits which contain or consist of a geographical indication identifying spirits with respect to such wines or spirits not having that origin;]

[(k) trade marks which contain or consist of a designation of origin or a geographical indication registered in accordance with Regulation (EEC) No 2081/92 when they correspond to one of the situations covered by Article 13 of the said Regulation and regarding the same type of product, on condition that the application for registration of the trade mark has been submitted after the date of filing with the Commission of the application for registration of the designation of origin or geographical indication.]

2. Paragraph 1 shall apply notwithstanding that the grounds of non-registrability obtain in only part of the Community.

3. Paragraph 1(b), (c) and (d) shall not apply if the trade mark has become distinctive in relation to the goods or services for which registration is requested in consequence of the use which has been made of it.

NOTES

Repealed as noted to Art 1, at **[5.246]**.

Para 1: sub-para (j) added by Council Regulation 3288/94/EC, Art 1(3); sub-para (k) added by Council Regulation 422/2004/EC, Art 1(2).

[5.253]

Article 8

Relative grounds for refusal

1. Upon opposition by the proprietor of an earlier trade mark, the trade mark applied for shall not be registered—

(a) if it is identical with the earlier trade mark and the goods or services for which registration is applied for are identical with the goods or services for which the earlier trade mark is protected;

(b) if because of its identity with or similarity to the earlier trade mark and the identity or similarity of the goods or services covered by the trade marks there exists a likelihood of confusion on the part of the public in the territory in which the earlier trade mark is protected; the likelihood of confusion includes the likelihood of association with the earlier trade mark.

2. For the purposes of paragraph 1, 'Earlier trade marks' means—

(a) trade marks of the following kinds with a date of application for registration which is earlier than the date of application for registration of the Community trade mark, taking account, where appropriate, of the priorities claimed in respect of those trade marks—

(i) Community trade marks;

(ii) trade marks registered in a Member State, or, in the case of Belgium, the Netherlands or Luxembourg, at the Benelux Trade Mark Office;

(iii) *trade marks registered under international arrangements which have effect in a Member State;*

[(iv) *trade marks registered under international arrangements which have effect in the Community;*]

(b) *applications for the trade marks referred to in subparagraph (a), subject to their registration;*

(c) *trade marks which, on the date of application for registration of the Community trade mark, or, where appropriate, of the priority claimed in respect of the application for registration of the Community trade mark, are well known in a Member State, in the sense in which the words 'well known' are used in Article 6bis of the Paris Convention.*

3. Upon opposition by the proprietor of the trade mark, a trade mark shall not be registered where an agent or representative of the proprietor of the trade mark applies for registration thereof in his own name without the proprietor's consent, unless the agent or representative justifies his action.

[4. Upon opposition by the proprietor of a non-registered trade mark or of another sign used in the course of trade of more than mere local significance, the trade mark applied for shall not be registered where and to the extent that, pursuant to the Community legislation or the law of the Member State governing that sign—]

(a) *rights to that sign were acquired prior to the date of application for registration of the Community trade mark, or the date of the priority claimed for the application for registration of the Community trade mark;*

(b) *that sign confers on its proprietor the right to prohibit the use of a subsequent trade mark.*

5. Furthermore, upon opposition by the proprietor of an earlier trade mark within the meaning of paragraph 2, the trade mark applied for shall not be registered where it is identical with or similar to the earlier trade mark and is to be registered for goods or services which are not similar to those for which the earlier trade mark is registered, where in the case of an earlier Community trade mark the trade mark has a reputation in the Community and, in the case of an earlier national trade mark, the trade mark has a reputation in the Member State concerned and where the use without due cause of the trade mark applied for would take unfair advantage of, or be detrimental to, the distinctive character or the repute of the earlier trade mark.

NOTES

Repealed as noted to Art 1, at **[5.246]**.

Para 2: sub-para (a)(iv) added by Council Regulation 1992/2003/EC, Art 1(1).

Para 4: words in square brackets substituted by Council Regulation 422/2004/EC, Art 1(3).

SECTION 2
EFFECTS OF COMMUNITY TRADE MARKS

[5.254]
Article 9
Rights conferred by a Community trade mark

1. A Community trade mark shall confer on the proprietor exclusive rights therein. The proprietor shall be entitled to prevent all third parties not having his consent from using in the course of trade—

(a) *any sign which is identical with the Community trade mark in relation to goods or services which are identical with those for which the Community trade mark is registered;*

(b) *any sign where, because of its identity with or similarity to the Community trade mark and the identity or similarity of the goods or services covered by the Community trade mark and the sign, there exists a likelihood of confusion on the part of the public; the likelihood of confusion includes the likelihood of association between the sign and the trade mark;*

(c) *any sign which is identical with or similar to the Community trade mark in relation to goods or services which are not similar to those for which the Community trade mark is registered, where the latter has a reputation in the Community and where use of that sign without due cause takes unfair advantage of, or is detrimental to, the distinctive character or the repute of the Community trade mark.*

2. The following, inter alia, may be prohibited under paragraph 1—

(a) *affixing the sign to the goods or to the packaging thereof;*

(b) *offering the goods, putting them on the market or stocking them for these purposes under that sign, or offering or supplying services thereunder;*

(c) *importing or exporting the goods under that sign;*

(d) *using the sign on business papers and in advertising.*

3. The rights conferred by a Community trade mark shall prevail against third parties from the date of publication of registration of the trade mark. Reasonable compensation may, however, be claimed in respect of matters arising after the date of publication of a Community trade mark application, which matters would, after publication of the registration of the trade mark, be prohibited by virtue of that publication. The court seized of the case may not decide upon the merits of the case until the registration has been published.

NOTES

Repealed as noted to Art 1, at **[5.246]**.

[5.255]

Article 10

Reproduction of Community trade marks in dictionaries

If the reproduction of a Community trade mark in a dictionary, encyclopaedia or similar reference work gives the impression that it constitutes the generic name of the goods or services for which the trade mark is registered, the publisher of the work shall, at the request of the proprietor of the Community trade mark, ensure that the reproduction of the trade mark at the latest in the next edition of the publication is accompanied by an indication that it is a registered trade mark.

NOTES

Repealed as noted to Art 1, at **[5.246]**.

[5.256]

Article 11

Prohibition on the use of a Community trade mark registered in the name of an agent or representative

Where a Community trade mark is registered in the name of the agent or representative of a person who is the proprietor of that trade mark, without the proprietor's authorisation, the latter shall be entitled to oppose the use of his mark by his agent or representative if he has not authorised such use, unless the agent or representative justifies his action.

NOTES

Repealed as noted to Art 1, at **[5.246]**.

[5.257]

Article 12

Limitation of the effects of a Community trade mark

A Community trade mark shall not entitle the proprietor to prohibit a third party from using in the course of trade—

- *(a) his own name or address;*
- *(b) indications concerning the kind, quality, quantity, intended purpose, value, geographical origin, the time of production of the goods or of rendering of the service, or other characteristics of the goods or service;*
- *(c) the trade mark where it is necessary to indicate the intended purpose of a product or service, in particular as accessories or spare parts,*

provided he uses them in accordance with honest practices in industrial or commercial matters.

NOTES

Repealed as noted to Art 1, at **[5.246]**.

[5.258]

Article 13

Exhaustion of the rights conferred by a Community trade mark

1. A Community trade mark shall not entitle the proprietor to prohibit its use in relation to goods which have been put on the market in the Community under that trade mark by the proprietor or with his consent.

2. Paragraph 1 shall not apply where there exist legitimate reasons for the proprietor to oppose further commercialisation of the goods, especially where the condition of the goods is changed or impaired after they have been put on the market.

NOTES

Repealed as noted to Art 1, at **[5.246]**.

[5.259]

Article 14

Complementary application of national law relating to infringement

1. The effects of Community trade marks shall be governed solely by the provisions of this Regulation. In other respects, infringement of a Community trade mark shall be governed by the national law relating to infringement of a national trade mark in accordance with the provisions of Title X.

2. This Regulation shall not prevent actions concerning a Community trade mark being brought under the law of Member States relating in particular to civil liability and unfair competition.

3. The rules of procedure to be applied shall be determined in accordance with the provisions of Title X.

NOTES

Repealed as noted to Art 1, at **[5.246]**.

SECTION 3

USE OF COMMUNITY TRADE MARKS

[5.260]

Article 15

Use of Community trade marks

1. If, within a period of five years following registration, the proprietor has not put the Community trade mark to genuine use in the Community in connection with the goods or services in respect of which it is registered, or if such use has been suspended during an uninterrupted period of five years, the Community trade mark shall be subject to the sanctions provided for in this Regulation, unless there are proper reasons for non-use.

2. The following shall also constitute use within the meaning of paragraph 1—

(a) use of the Community trade mark in a form differing in elements which do not alter the distinctive character of the mark in the form in which it was registered;

(b) affixing of the Community trade mark to goods or to the packaging thereof in the Community solely for export purposes.

3. Use of the Community trade mark with the consent of the proprietor shall be deemed to constitute use by the proprietor.

NOTES

Repealed as noted to Art 1, at **[5.246]**.

SECTION 4

COMMUNITY TRADE MARKS AS OBJECTS OF PROPERTY

[5.261]

Article 16

Dealing with Community trade marks as national trade marks

1. Unless Articles 17 to 24 provide otherwise, a Community trade mark as an object of property shall be dealt with in its entirety, and for the whole area of the Community, as a national trade mark registered in the Member State in which, according to the Register of Community trade marks,

(a) the proprietor has his seat or his domicile on the relevant date; or

(b) where subparagraph (a) does not apply, the proprietor has an establishment on the relevant date.

2. In cases which are not provided for by paragraph 1, the Member State referred to in that paragraph shall be the Member State in which the seat of the Office is situated.

3. If two or more persons are mentioned in the Register of Community trade marks as joint proprietors, paragraph 1 shall apply to the joint proprietor first mentioned; failing this, it shall apply to the subsequent joint proprietors in the order in which they are mentioned. Where paragraph 1 does not apply to any of the joint proprietors, paragraph 2 shall apply.

NOTES

Repealed as noted to Art 1, at **[5.246]**.

[5.262]

Article 17

Transfer

1. A Community trade mark may be transferred, separately from any transfer of the undertaking in respect of some or all of the goods or services for which it is registered.

2. A transfer of the whole of the undertaking shall include the transfer of the Community trade mark except where, in accordance with the law governing the transfer, there is agreement to the contrary or circumstances clearly dictate otherwise. This provision shall apply to the contractual obligation to transfer the undertaking.

3. Without prejudice to paragraph 2, an assignment of the Community trade mark shall be made in writing and shall require the signature of the parties to the contract, except when it is a result of a judgment; otherwise it shall be void.

4. Where it is clear from the transfer documents that because of the transfer the Community trade mark is likely to mislead the public concerning the nature, quality or geographical origin of the goods or services in respect of which it is registered, the Office shall not register the transfer unless the successor agrees to limit registration of the Community trade mark to goods or services in respect of which it is not likely to mislead.

5. On request of one of the parties a transfer shall be entered in the Register and published.

6. As long as the transfer has not been entered in the Register, the successor in title may not invoke the rights arising from the registration of the Community trade mark.

7. Where there are time limits to be observed vis-à-vis the Office, the successor in title may make the corresponding statements to the Office once the request for registration of the transfer has been received by the Office.

8. All documents which require notification to the proprietor of the Community trade mark in accordance with Article 77 shall be addressed to the person registered as proprietor.

NOTES

Repealed as noted to Art 1, at **[5.246]**.

[5.263]

Article 18

Transfer of a trade mark registered in the name of an agent

Where a Community trade mark is registered in the name of the agent or representative of a person who is the proprietor of that trade mark, without the proprietor's authorisation, the latter shall be entitled to demand the assignment in his favour of the said registration, unless such agent or representative justifies his action.

NOTES

Repealed as noted to Art 1, at **[5.246]**.

[5.264]

Article 19

Rights in rem

1. A Community trade mark may, independently of the undertaking, be given as security or be the subject of rights in rem.

2. On request of one of the parties, rights mentioned in paragraph 1 shall be entered in the Register and published.

NOTES

Repealed as noted to Art 1, at **[5.246]**.

[5.265]

Article 20

Levy of execution

1. A Community trade mark may be levied in execution.

2. As regards the procedure for levy of execution in respect of a Community trade mark, the courts and authorities of the Member States determined in accordance with Article 16 shall have exclusive jurisdiction.

3. On request of one the parties, levy of execution shall be entered in the Register and published.

NOTES

Repealed as noted to Art 1, at **[5.246]**.

[5.266]

[Article 21

Insolvency proceedings

1. The only insolvency proceedings in which a Community trade mark may be involved are those opened in the Member State in the territory of which the debtor has his centre of main interests.

However, where the debtor is an insurance undertaking or a credit institution as defined in Directives 2001/17/EC[1] and 2001/24/EC[2], respectively, the only insolvency proceedings in which a Community trademark may be involved are those opened in the Member State where that undertaking or institution has been authorised.

2. In the case of joint proprietorship of a Community trade mark, paragraph 1 shall apply to the share of the joint proprietor.

3. Where a Community trade mark is involved in insolvency proceedings, on request of the competent national authority an entry to this effect shall be made in the Register and published in the Community Trade Marks Bulletin referred to in Article 85.]

NOTES

Substituted by Council Regulation 422/2004/EC, Art 1(4).

Repealed as noted to Art 1, at **[5.246]**.

[1] Directive 2001/17/EC of the European Parliament and of the Council of 19 March 2001 on the reorganization and winding-up of insurance undertakings (OJ L110, 20.4.2001, p 28).

[2] Directive 2001/24/EC of the European Parliament and of the Council of 4 April 2001 on the reorganization and winding up of credit institutions (OJ L125, 5.5.2001, p 15).

[5.267]
Article 22
Licensing
1. A Community trade mark may be licensed for some or all of the goods or services for which it is registered and for the whole or part of the Community. A licence may be exclusive or non-exclusive.
2. The proprietor of a Community trade mark may invoke the rights conferred by that trade mark against a licensee who contravenes any provision in his licensing contract with regard to its duration, the form covered by the registration in which the trade mark may be used, the scope of the goods or services for which the licence is granted, the territory in which the trade mark may be affixed, or the quality of the goods manufactured or of the services provided by the licensee.
3. Without prejudice to the provisions of the licensing contract, the licensee may bring proceedings for infringement of a Community trade mark only if its proprietor consents thereto. However, the holder of an exclusive licence may bring such proceedings if the proprietor of the trade mark, after formal notice, does not himself bring infringement proceedings within an appropriate period.
4. A licensee shall, for the purpose of obtaining compensation for damage suffered by him, be entitled to intervene in infringement proceedings brought by the proprietor of the Community trade mark.
5. On request of one of the parties the grant or transfer of a licence in respect of a Community trade mark shall be entered in the Register and published.

NOTES
Repealed as noted to Art 1, at **[5.246]**.

[5.268]
Article 23
Effects vis-à-vis third parties
1. Legal acts referred to in Article 17, 19 and 22 concerning a Community trade mark shall only have effects vis-à-vis third parties in all the Member States after entry in the Register. Nevertheless, such an act, before it is so entered, shall have effect vis-à-vis third parties who have acquired rights in the trade mark after the date of that act but who knew of the act at the date on which the rights were acquired.
2. Paragraph 1 shall not apply in the case of a person who acquires the Community trade mark or a right concerning the Community trade mark by way of transfer of the whole of the undertaking or by any other universal succession.
3. The effects vis-à-vis third parties of the legal acts referred to in Article 20 shall be governed by the law of the Member State determined in accordance with Article 16.
4. Until such time as common rules for the Member States in the field of bankruptcy enter into force, the effects vis-à-vis third parties of bankruptcy or like proceedings shall be governed by the law of the Member State in which such proceedings are first brought within the meaning of national law or of conventions applicable in this field.

NOTES
Repealed as noted to Art 1, at **[5.246]**.

[5.269]
Article 24
The application for a Community trade mark as an object of property
Articles 16 to 23 shall apply to applications for Community trade marks.

NOTES
Repealed as noted to Art 1, at **[5.246]**.

TITLE III
APPLICATION FOR COMMUNITY TRADE MARKS

SECTION 1
Filing of Applications and the Conditions Which Govern Them

[5.270]
Article 25
Filing of applications
1. An application for a Community trade mark shall be filed, at the choice of the applicant,
(a) at the Office; or
(b) at the central industrial property office of a Member State or at the Benelux Trade Mark Office. An application filed in this way shall have the same effect as if it had been filed on the same date at the Office.

2. Where the application is filed at the central industrial property office of a Member State or at the Benelux Trade Mark Office, that office shall take all steps to forward the application to the Office within two weeks after filing. It may charge the applicant a fee which shall not exceed the administrative costs of receiving and forwarding the application.

[3. Applications referred to in paragraph 2 which reach the Office more than two months after filing shall be deemed to have been filed on the date on which the application reached the Office.]

4. Ten years after the entry into force of this Regulation, the Commission shall draw up a report on the operation of the system of filing applications for Community trade marks, together with any proposals for modifying this system.

NOTES

Repealed as noted to Art 1, at **[5.246]**.

Para 3: substituted by Council Regulation 422/2004/EC, Art 1(5).

[5.271]

Article 26

Conditions with which applications must comply

1. An application for a Community trade mark shall contain—

(a) a request for the registration of a Community trade mark;

(b) information identifying the applicant;

(c) a list of the goods or services in respect of which the registration is requested;

(d) a representation of the trade mark.

2. The application for a Community trade mark shall be subject to the payment of the application fee and, when appropriate, of one or more class fees.

3. An application for a Community trade mark must comply with the conditions laid down in the implementing Regulation referred to in [Article 157].

NOTES

Repealed as noted to Art 1, at **[5.246]**.

Para 3: words in square brackets substituted by Council Regulation 1992/2003/EC, Art 1(6).

[5.272]

Article 27

Date of filing

The date of filing of a Community trade mark application shall be the date on which documents containing the information specified in Article 26(1) are filed with the Office by the applicant or, if the application has been filed with the central office of a Member State or with the Benelux Trade Mark Office, with that office, subject to payment of the application fee within a period of one month of filing the abovementioned documents.

NOTES

Repealed as noted to Art 1, at **[5.246]**.

[5.273]

Article 28

Classification

Goods and services in respect of which Community trade marks are applied for shall be classified in conformity with the system of classification specified in the Implementing Regulation.

NOTES

Repealed as noted to Art 1, at **[5.246]**.

SECTION 2

PRIORITY

[5.274]

Article 29

Right of priority

[1. A person who has duly filed an application for a trade mark in or for any State party to the Paris Convention or to the Agreement establishing the World Trade Organisation, or his successors in title, shall enjoy, for the purpose of filing a Community trade mark application for the same trade mark in respect of goods or services which are identical with or contained within those for which the application has been filed, a right or priority during a period of six months from the date of filing of the first application.]

2. Every filing that is equivalent to a regular national filing under the national law of the State where it was made or under bilateral or multilateral agreements shall be recognised as giving rise to a right of priority.

3. By a regular national filing is meant any filing that is sufficient to establish the date on which the application was filed, whatever may be the outcome of the application.

4. A subsequent application for a trade mark which was the subject of a previous first application in respect of the same goods or services, and which is filed in or in respect of the same State shall be considered as the first application for the purposes of determining priority, provided that, at the date of filing of the subsequent application, the previous application has been withdrawn, abandoned or refused, without being open to public inspection and without leaving any rights outstanding, and has not served as a basis for claiming a right of priority. The previous application may not thereafter serve as a basis for claiming a right of priority.

[5. If the first filing has been made in a State which is not a party to the Paris Convention or to the Agreement establishing the World Trade Organisation, paragraphs 1 to 4 shall apply only in so far as that State, according to published findings, grants, on the basis of the first filing made at the Office and subject to conditions equivalent to those laid down in this Regulation, a right of priority having equivalent effect.]

NOTES

Repealed as noted to Art 1, at **[5.246]**.

Paras 1, 5: substituted by Council Regulation 3288/94/EC, Art 1(4), (5).

[5.275]

Article 30

Claiming priority

An applicant desiring to take advantage of the priority of a previous application shall file a declaration of priority and a copy of the previous application. If the language of the latter is not one of the languages of the Office, the applicant shall file a translation of the previous application in one of those languages.

NOTES

Repealed as noted to Art 1, at **[5.246]**.

[5.276]

Article 31

Effect of priority right

The right of priority shall have the effect that the date of priority shall count as the date of filing of the Community trade mark application for the purposes of establishing which rights take precedence.

NOTES

Repealed as noted to Art 1, at **[5.246]**.

[5.277]

Article 32

Equivalence of Community filing with national filing

A Community trade mark application which has been accorded a date of filing shall, in the Member States, be equivalent to a regular national filing, where appropriate with the priority claimed for the Community trade mark application.

NOTES

Repealed as noted to Art 1, at **[5.246]**.

SECTION 3
EXHIBITION PRIORITY

[5.278]

Article 33

Exhibition priority

1. If an applicant for a Community trade mark has displayed goods or services under the mark applied for, at an official or officially recognised international exhibition falling within the terms of the Convention on International Exhibitions signed at Paris on 22 November 1928 and last revised on 30 November 1972, he may, if he files the application within a period of six months from the date of the first display of the goods or services under the mark applied for, claim a right of priority from that date within the meaning of Article 31.

2. An applicant who wishes to claim priority pursuant to paragraph 1 must file evidence of the display of goods or services under the mark applied for under the conditions laid down in the Implementing Regulation.

3. An exhibition priority granted in a Member State or in a third country does not extend the period of priority laid down in Article 29.

NOTES

Repealed as noted to Art 1, at **[5.246]**.

SECTION 4
CLAIMING THE SENIORITY OF A NATIONAL TRADE MARK

[5.279]
Article 34
Claiming the seniority of a national trade mark

1. The proprietor of an earlier trade mark registered in a Member State, including a trade mark registered in the Benelux countries, or registered under international arrangements having effect in a Member State, who applies for an identical trade mark for registration as a Community trade mark for goods or services which are identical with or contained within those for which the earlier trade mark has been registered, may claim for the Community trade mark the seniority of the earlier trade mark in respect of the Member State in or for which it is registered.

2. Seniority shall have the sole effect under this Regulation that, where the proprietor of the Community trade mark surrenders the earlier trade mark or allows it to lapse, he shall be deemed to continue to have the same rights as he would have had if the earlier trade mark had continued to be registered.

3. The seniority claimed for the Community trade mark shall lapse if the earlier trade mark the seniority of which is claimed is declared to have been revoked or to be invalid or if it is surrendered prior to the registration of the Community trade mark.

NOTES

Repealed as noted to Art 1, at **[5.246]**.

[5.280]
Article 35
Claiming seniority after registration of the Community trade mark

[1. The proprietor of a Community trade mark who is the proprietor of an earlier identical trade mark registered in a Member State, including a trade mark registered in the Benelux countries or of an earlier identical trade mark, with an international registration effective in a Member State, for goods or services which are identical to those for which the earlier trade mark has been registered, or contained within them, may claim the seniority of the earlier trade mark in respect of the Member State in or for which it was registered.]

2. Article 34(2) and (3) shall apply.

NOTES

Repealed as noted to Art 1, at **[5.246]**.
Para 1: substituted by Council Regulation 422/2004/EC, Art 1(6).

TITLE IV
REGISTRATION PROCEDURE

SECTION 1
EXAMINATION OF APPLICATIONS

[5.281]
Article 36
Examination of the conditions of filing

1. The Office shall examine whether—

(a) the Community trade mark application satisfies the requirements for the accordance of a date of filing in accordance with Article 27;

[(b) the Community trade mark application complies with the conditions laid down in this Regulation and with the conditions laid down in the Implementing Regulation;]

(c) where appropriate, the class fees have been paid within the prescribed period.

2. Where the Community trade mark application does not satisfy the requirements referred to in paragraph 1, the Office shall request the applicant to remedy the deficiencies or the default on payment within the prescribed period.

3. If the deficiencies or the default on payment established pursuant to paragraph 1(a) are not remedied within this period, the application shall not be dealt with as a Community trade mark application. If the applicant complies with the Office's request, the Office shall accord as the date of filing of the application the date on which the deficiencies or the default on payment established are remedied.

4. If the deficiencies established pursuant to paragraph 1(b) are not remedied within the prescribed period, the Office shall refuse the application.

5. If the default on payment established pursuant to paragraph 1(c) is not remedied within the prescribed period, the application shall be deemed to be withdrawn unless it is clear which categories of goods or services the amount paid is intended to cover.

6. Failure to satisfy the requirements concerning the claim to priority shall result in loss of the right of priority for the application.

7. Failure to satisfy the requirements concerning the claiming of seniority of a national trade mark shall result in loss of that right for the application.

NOTES

Repealed as noted to Art 1, at **[5.246]**.

Para 1: sub-para (b) substituted by Council Regulation 422/2004/EC, Art 1(7).

Article 37 *(Repealed by Council Regulation 422/2004/EC, Art 1(8).)*

[5.282]
Article 38
Examination as to absolute grounds for refusal

1. Where, under Article 7, a trade mark is ineligible for registration in respect of some or all of the goods or services covered by the Community trade mark application, the application shall be refused as regards those goods or services.

2. Where the trade mark contains an element which is not distinctive, and where the inclusion of said element in the trade mark could give rise to doubts as to the scope of protection of the trade mark, the Office may request, as a condition for registration of said trade mark, that the applicant state that he disclaims any exclusive right to such element. Any disclaimer shall be published together with the application or the registration of the Community trade mark, as the case may be.

3. The application shall not be refused before the applicant has been allowed the opportunity of withdrawing or amending the application or of submitting his observations.

NOTES

Repealed as noted to Art 1, at **[5.246]**.

SECTION 2
SEARCH

[5.283]
[Article 39
Search

1. Once the Office has accorded a date of filing, it shall draw up a Community search report citing those earlier Community trade marks or Community trade mark applications discovered which may be invoked under Article 8 against the registration of the Community trade mark applied for.

2. Where, at the time of filing a Community trade mark application, the applicant requests that a search report also be prepared by the central industrial property offices of the Member States and where the appropriate search fee has been paid within the time-limit for the payment of the filing fee, the Office shall, as soon as a Community trade mark application has been accorded a date of filing, transmit a copy thereof to the central industrial property office of each Member State which has informed the Office of its decision to operate a search in its own register of trade marks in respect of Community trade mark applications.

3. Each of the central industrial property offices referred to in paragraph 2 shall communicate to the Office within two months as from the date on which it received the Community trade mark application a search report which shall either cite those earlier national trade marks or trade mark applications discovered which may be invoked under Article 8 against the registration of the Community trade mark applied for, or state that the search has revealed no such rights.

4. The search reports referred to in paragraph 3 shall be prepared on a standard form drawn up by the Office, after consulting the Administrative Board. The essential contents of this form shall be set out in the Implementing Regulation provided for in Article 157(1).

5. An amount shall be paid by the Office to each central industrial property office for each search report provided by that office in accordance with paragraph 3. The amount, which shall be the same for each office, shall be fixed by the Budget Committee by means of a decision adopted by a majority of three-quarters of the representatives of the Member States.

6. The Office shall transmit without delay to the applicant for the Community trade mark the Community search report and any requested national search reports received within the time limit laid down in paragraph 3.

7. Upon publication of the Community trade mark application, which may not take place before the expiry of a period of one month as from the date on which the Office transmits the search reports to the applicant, the Office shall inform the proprietors of any earlier Community trade marks or Community trade mark applications cited in the Community search report of the publication of the Community trade mark application.]

NOTES

Substituted by Council Regulation 422/2004/EC, Art 1(9).

Repealed as noted to Art 1, at **[5.246]**.

SECTION 3
PUBLICATION OF THE APPLICATION

[5.284]
[Article 40
Publication of the application
1. If the conditions which the application for a Community trade mark must satisfy have been fulfilled and if the period referred to in Article 39(7) has expired, the application shall be published to the extent that it has not been refused pursuant to Article 38.
2. Where, after publication, the application is refused under Article 38, the decision that it has been refused shall be published upon becoming final.]

NOTES
Substituted by Council Regulation 422/2004/EC, Art 1(10).
Repealed as noted to Art 1, at **[5.246]**.

SECTION 4
OBSERVATIONS BY THIRD PARTIES AND OPPOSITION

[5.285]
Article 41
Observations by third parties
1. Following the publication of the Community trade mark application, any natural or legal person and any group or body representing manufacturers, producers, suppliers of services, traders or consumers may submit to the Office written observations, explaining on which grounds under Article 7, in particular, the trade mark shall not be registered ex officio. They shall not be parties to the proceedings before the Office.
2. The observations referred to in paragraph 1 shall be communicated to the applicant who may comment on them.

NOTES
Repealed as noted to Art 1, at **[5.246]**.

[5.286]
Article 42
Opposition
1. Within a period of three months following the publication of a Community trade mark application, notice of opposition to registration of the trade mark may be given on the grounds that it may not be registered under Article 8—
(a) by the proprietors of earlier trade marks referred to in Article 8(2) as well as licensees authorised by the proprietors of those trade marks, in respect of Article 8(1) and (5);
(b) by the proprietors of trade marks referred to it Article 8(3);
(c) by the proprietors of earlier marks or signs referred to in Article 8(4) and by persons authorised under the relevant national law to exercise these rights.
2. Notice of opposition to registration of the trade mark may also be given, subject to the conditions laid down in paragraph 1, in the event of the publication of an amended application in accordance with the second sentence of Article 44(2).
3. Opposition must be expressed in writing and must specify the grounds on which it is made. It shall not be treated as duly entered until the opposition fee has been paid. Within a period fixed by the Office, the opponent may submit in support of his case facts, evidence and arguments.

NOTES
Repealed as noted to Art 1, at **[5.246]**.

[5.287]
Article 43
Examination of opposition
1. In the examination of the opposition the Office shall invite the parties, as often as necessary, to file observations, within a period set them by the Office, on communications from the other parties or issued by itself.
2. If the applicant so requests, the proprietor of an earlier Community trade mark who has given notice of opposition shall furnish proof that, during the period of five years preceding the date of publication of the Community trade mark application, the earlier Community trade mark has been put to genuine use in the Community in connection with the goods or services in respect of which it is registered and which he cites as justification for his opposition, or that there are proper reasons for non-use, provided the earlier Community trade mark has at that date been registered for not less than five years. In the absence of proof to this effect, the opposition shall be rejected. If the earlier Community trade mark has been used in relation to part only of the goods or services for which it is registered it shall, for the purposes of the examination of the opposition, be deemed to be registered in respect only of that part of the goods or services.

3. Paragraph 2 shall apply to earlier national trade marks referred to in Article 8(2) (a), by substituting use in the Member State in which the earlier national trade mark is protected for use in the Community.
4. The Office may, if it thinks fit, invite the parties to make a friendly settlement.
5. If examination of the opposition reveals that the trade mark may not be registered in respect of some or all of the goods or services for which the Community trade mark application has been made, the application shall be refused in respect of those goods or services. Otherwise the opposition shall be rejected.
6. The decision refusing the application shall be published upon becoming final.

NOTES

Repealed as noted to Art 1, at **[5.246]**.

[SECTION 5

WITHDRAWAL, RESTRICTION, AMENDMENT AND DIVISION OF THE APPLICATION]

NOTES

Title: substituted by Council Regulation 422/2004/EC, Art 1(11).

[5.288]

Article 44

Withdrawal, restriction and amendment of the application

1. The applicant may at any time withdraw his Community trade mark application or restrict the list of goods or services contained therein. Where the application has already been published, the withdrawal or restriction shall also be published.
2. In other respects, a Community trade mark application may be amended, upon request of the applicant, only by correcting the name and address of the applicant, errors of wording or of copying, or obvious mistakes, provided that such correction does not substantially change the trade mark or extend the list of goods or services. Where the amendments affect the representation of the trade mark or the list of goods or services and are made after publication of the application, the trade mark application shall be published as amended.

NOTES

Repealed as noted to Art 1, at **[5.246]**.

[5.289]

[Article 44a

Division of the application

1. The applicant may divide the application by declaring that some of the goods or services included in the original application will be the subject of one or more divisional applications. The goods or services in the divisional application shall not overlap with the goods or services which remain in the original application or those which are included in other divisional applications.
2. The declaration of division shall not be admissible—
(a) if, where an opposition has been entered against the original application, such a divisional application has the effect of introducing a division amongst the goods or services against which the opposition has been directed, until the decision of the Opposition Division has become final or the opposition proceedings are finally terminated otherwise;
(b) during the periods laid down in the Implementing Regulation.
3. The declaration of division must comply with the provisions set out in the Implementing Regulation.
4. The declaration of division shall be subject to a fee. The application shall be deemed not to have been made until the fee has been paid.
5. The division shall take effect on the date on which it is recorded in the files kept by the Office concerning the original application.
6. All requests and applications submitted and all fees paid with regard to the original application prior to the date on which the Office receives the declaration of division are deemed also to have been submitted or paid with regard to the divisional application or applications. The fees for the original application which have been duly paid prior to the date on which the declaration of division is received shall not be refunded.
7. The divisional application shall preserve the filing date and any priority date and seniority date of the original application.]

NOTES

Inserted by Council Regulation 422/2004/EC, Art 1(12).
Repealed as noted to Art 1, at **[5.246]**.

SECTION 6
REGISTRATION

[5.290]
Article 45
Registration

Where an application meets the requirements of this Regulation and where no notice of opposition has been given within the period referred to in Article 42(1) or where opposition has been rejected by a definitive decision, the trade mark shall be registered as a Community trade mark, provided that the registration fee has been paid within the period prescribed. If the fee is not paid within this period the application shall be deemed to be withdrawn.

NOTES

Repealed as noted to Art 1, at **[5.246]**.

[TITLE V
DURATION, RENEWAL, ALTERATION AND DIVISION OF COMMUNITY TRADE MARKS]

NOTES

Title: substituted by Council Regulation 422/2004/EC, Art 1(13).

[5.291]
Article 46
Duration of registration

Community trade marks shall be registered for a period of ten years from the date of filing of the application. Registration may be renewed in accordance with Article 47 for further periods of ten years.

NOTES

Repealed as noted to Art 1, at **[5.246]**.

[5.292]
Article 47
Renewal

1. Registration of the Community trade mark shall be renewed at the request of the proprietor of the trade mark or any person expressly authorised by him, provided that the fees have been paid.
2. The Office shall inform the proprietor of the Community trade mark, and any person having a registered right in respect of the Community trade mark, of the expire of the registration in good time before the said expiry. Failure to give such information shall not involve the responsibility of the Office.
3. The request for renewal shall be submitted within a period of six months ending on the last day of the month in which protection ends. The fees shall also be paid within this period. Failing this, the request may be submitted and the fees paid within a further period of six months following the day referred to in the first sentence, provided that an additional fee is paid within this further period.
4. Where the request is submitted or the fees paid in respect of only some of the goods or services for which the Community trade mark is registered, registration shall be renewed for those goods or services only.
5. Renewal shall take effect from the day following the date on which the existing registration expires. The renewal shall be registered.

NOTES

Repealed as noted to Art 1, at **[5.246]**.

[5.293]
Article 48
Alteration

1. The Community trade mark shall not be altered in the register during the period of registration or on renewal thereof.
2. Nevertheless, where the Community trade mark includes the name and address of the proprietor, any alteration thereof not substantially affecting the identity of the trade mark as originally registered may be registered at the request of the proprietor.
3. The publication of the registration of the alteration shall contain a representation of the Community trade mark as altered. Third parties whose rights may be affected by the alteration may challenge the registration thereof within a period of three months following publication.

NOTES

Repealed as noted to Art 1, at **[5.246]**.

[5.294]
[Article 48a
Division of the registration

1. The proprietor of the Community trade mark may divide the registration by declaring that some of the goods or services included in the original registration will be the subject of one or more divisional registrations. The goods or services in the divisional registration shall not overlap with the goods or services which remain in the original registration or those which are included in other divisional registrations.

2. The declaration of division shall not be admissible—

(a) if, where an application for revocation of rights or for a declaration of invalidity has been entered against the original registration, such a divisional declaration has the effect of introducing a division amongst the goods or services against which the application for revocation of rights or for a declaration of invalidity is directed, until the decision of the Cancellation Division has become final or the proceedings are finally terminated otherwise;

(b) if, where a counterclaim for revocation or for a declaration of invalidity has been entered in a case before a Community trade mark court, such a divisional declaration has the effect of introducing a division amongst the goods or services against which the counterclaim is directed, until the mention of the Community trade mark court's judgement is recorded in the Register pursuant to Article 96(6).

3. The declaration of division must comply with the provisions set out in the Implementing Regulation.

4. The declaration of division shall be subject to a fee. The declaration shall be deemed not to have been made until the fee has been paid.

5. The division shall take effect on the date on which it is entered in the Register.

6. All requests and applications submitted and all fees paid with regard to the original registration prior to the date on which the Office receives the declaration of division shall be deemed also to have been submitted or paid with regard to the divisional registration or registrations. The fees for the original registration which have been duly paid prior to the date on which the declaration of division is received shall not be refunded.

7. The divisional registration shall preserve the filing date and any priority date and seniority date of the original registration.]

NOTES

Inserted by Council Regulation 422/2004/EC, Art 1(14).
Repealed as noted to Art 1, at **[5.246]**.

TITLE VI
SURRENDER, REVOCATION AND INVALIDITY

SECTION 1
SURRENDER

[5.295]
Article 49
Surrender

1. A Community trade mark may be surrendered in respect of some or all of the goods or services for which it is registered.

2. The surrender shall be declared to the Office in writing by the proprietor of the trade mark. It shall not have effect until it has been entered in the Register.

3. Surrender shall be entered only with the agreement of the proprietor of a right entered in the Register. If a licence has been registered, surrender shall only be entered in the Register if the proprietor of the trade mark proves that he has informed the licensee of his intention to surrender; this entry shall be made on expiry of the period prescribed by the Implementing Regulation.

NOTES

Repealed as noted to Art 1, at **[5.246]**.

SECTION 2
GROUNDS FOR REVOCATION

[5.296]
Article 50
Grounds for revocation

1. The rights of the proprietor of the Community trade mark shall be declared to be revoked on application to the Office or on the basis of a counterclaim infringement proceedings—

(a) if, within a continuous period of five years, the trade mark has not been put to genuine use in the Community in connection with the goods or services in respect of which it is registered, and there are no proper reasons for non-use; however, no person may claim

that the proprietor's rights in a Community trade mark should be revoked where, during the interval between expiry of the five-year period and filing of the application or counterclaim, genuine use of the trade mark has been started or resumed; the commencement or resumption of use within a period of three months preceding the filing of the application or counterclaim which began at the earliest on expiry of the continuous period of five years of non-use shall, however, be disregarded where preparations for the commencement or resumption occur only after the proprietor becomes aware that the application or counterclaim may be filed;

(b) if, in consequence of acts or inactivity of the proprietor, the trade mark has become the common name in the trade for a product or service in respect of which it is registered;

(c) if, in consequence of the use made of it by the proprietor of the trade mark or with his consent in respect of the goods or services for which it is registered, the trade mark is liable to mislead the public, particularly as to the nature, quality or geographical origin of those goods or services;

(d) . . .

2. Where the grounds for revocation of rights exist in respect of only some of the goods or services for which the Community trade mark is registered, the rights of the proprietor shall be declared to be revoked in respect of those goods or services only.

NOTES

Repealed as noted to Art 1, at **[5.246]**.

Para 1: sub-para (d) repealed by Council Regulation 422/2004/EC, Art 1(15).

SECTION 3
GROUNDS FOR INVALIDITY

[5.297]

Article 51

Absolute grounds for invalidity

1. A Community trade mark shall be declared invalid on application to the Office or on the basis of a counterclaim in infringement proceedings,

[(a) where the Community trade mark has been registered contrary to the provisions of Article 7;]

(b) where the applicant was acting in bad faith when he filed the application for the trade mark.

2. Where the Community trade mark has been registered in breach of the provisions of Article 7(1) (b), (c) or (d), it may nevertheless not be declared invalid if, in consequence of the use which has been made of it, it has after registration acquired a distinctive character in relation to the goods or services for which it is registered.

3. Where the ground for invalidity exists in respect of only some of the goods or services for which the Community trade mark is registered, the trade mark shall be declared invalid as regards those goods or services only.

NOTES

Repealed as noted to Art 1, at **[5.246]**.

Para 1: sub-para (a) substituted by Council Regulation 422/2004/EC, Art 1(16).

[5.298]

Article 52

Relative grounds for invalidity

1. A Community trade mark shall be declared invalid on application to the Office or on the basis of a counterclaim in infringement proceedings—

(a) where there is an earlier trade mark as referred to in Article 8(2) and the conditions set out in paragraph 1 or paragraph 5 of that Article are fulfilled;

(b) where there is a trade mark as referred to in Article 8(3) and the conditions set out in that paragraph are fulfilled;

(c) where there is an earlier right as referred to in Article 8(4) and the conditions set out in that paragraph are fulfilled.

[2. A Community trade mark shall also be declared invalid on application to the Office or on the basis of a counterclaim in infringement proceedings where the use of such trade mark may be prohibited pursuant to another earlier right, and in particular—

(a) a right to a name;

(b) a right of personal portrayal;

(c) a copyright;

(d) an industrial property right

under the Community legislation or national law governing the protection.]

3. A Community trade mark may not be declared invalid where the proprietor of a right referred to in paragraphs 1 or 2 consents expressly to the registration of the Community trade mark before submission of the application for a declaration of invalidity or the counterclaim.

4. Where the proprietor of one of the rights referred to in paragraphs 1 or 2 has previously applied for a declaration that a Community trade mark is invalid or made a counterclaim in infringement proceedings, he may not submit a new application for a declaration of invalidity or lodge a counterclaim on the basis of another of the said rights which he could have invoked in support of his first application or counterclaim.

5. Article 51(3) shall apply.

NOTES

Repealed as noted to Art 1, at **[5.246]**.

Para 2: substituted by Council Regulation 422/2004/EC, Art 1(17).

[5.299]

Article 53

Limitation in consequence of acquiescence

1. Where the proprietor of a Community trade mark has acquiesced, for a period of five successive years, in the use of a later Community trade mark in the Community while being aware of such use, he shall no longer be entitled on the basis of the earlier trade mark either to apply for a declaration that the later trade mark is invalid or to oppose the use of the later trade mark in respect of the goods or services for which the later trade mark has been used, unless registration of the later Community trade mark was applied for in bad faith.

2. Where the proprietor of an earlier national trade mark as referred to in Article 8(2) or of another earlier sign referred to in Article 8(4) has acquiesced, for a period of five successive years, in the use of a later Community trade mark in the Member State in which the earlier trade mark or the other earlier sign is protected while being aware of such use, he shall no longer be entitled on the basis of the earlier trade mark or of the other earlier sign either to apply for a declaration that the later trade mark is invalid or to oppose the use of the later trade mark in respect of the goods or services for which the later trade mark has been used, unless registration of the later Community trade mark was applied for in bad faith.

3. In the cases referred to in paragraphs 1 and 2, the proprietor of a later Community trade mark shall not be entitled to oppose the use of the earlier right, even though that right may no longer be invoked against the later Community trade mark.

NOTES

Repealed as noted to Art 1, at **[5.246]**.

SECTION 4

CONSEQUENCES OF REVOCATION AND INVALIDITY

[5.300]

Article 54

Consequences of revocation and invalidity

1. The Community trade mark shall be deemed not to have had, as from the date of the application for revocation or of the counterclaim, the effects specified in this Regulation, to the extent that the rights of the proprietor have been revoked. An earlier date, on which one of the grounds for revocation occurred, may be fixed in the decision at the request of one of the parties.

2. The Community trade mark shall be deemed not to have had, as from the outset, the effects specified in this Regulation, to the extent that the trade mark has been declared invalid.

3. Subject to the national provisions relating either to claims for compensation for damage caused by negligence or lack of good faith on the part of the proprietor of the trade mark, or to unjust enrichment, the retroactive effect of revocation or invalidity of the trade mark shall not affect—

(a) any decision on infringement which has acquired the authority of a final decision and been enforced prior to the revocation or invalidity decision;

(b) any contract concluded prior to the revocation or invalidity decision, in so far as it has been performed before that decision; however, repayment, to an extent justified by the circumstances, of sums paid under the relevant contract, may be claimed on grounds of equity.

NOTES

Repealed as noted to Art 1, at **[5.246]**.

SECTION 5

PROCEEDINGS IN THE OFFICE IN RELATION TO REVOCATION OR INVALIDITY

[5.301]

Article 55

Application for revocation or for a declaration of invalidity

1. An application for revocation of the rights of the proprietor of a Community trade mark or for a declaration that the trade mark is invalid may be submitted to the Office—

(a) *where Articles 50 and 51 apply, by any natural or legal person and any group or body set up for the purpose of representing the interests of manufacturers, producers, suppliers of services, traders or consumers, which under the terms of the law governing it has the capacity in its own name to sue and be sued;*
(b) *where Article 52(1) applies, by the persons referred to in Article 42(1);*
(c) *where Article 52(2) applies, by the owners of the earlier rights referred to in that provision or by the persons who are entitled under the law of the Member State concerned to exercise the rights in question.*

2. The application shall be filed in a written reasoned statement. It shall not be deemed to have been filed until the fee has been paid.

3. An application for revocation or for a declaration of invalidity shall be inadmissible if an application relating to the same subject matter and cause of action, and involving the same parties, has been adjudicated on by a court in a Member State and has acquired the authority of a final decision.

NOTES

Repealed as noted to Art 1, at **[5.246]**.

[5.302]
Article 56
Examination of the application

1. In the examination of the application for revocation of rights or for a declaration of invalidity, the Office shall invite the parties, as often as necessary, to file observations, within a period to be fixed by the Office, on communications from the other parties or issued by itself.

2. If the proprietor of the Community trade mark so requests, the proprietor of an earlier Community trade mark, being a party to the invalidity proceedings, shall furnish proof that, during the period of five years preceding the date of the application for a declaration of invalidity, the earlier Community trade mark has been put to genuine use in the Community in connection with the goods or services in respect of which it is registered and which he cites as justification for his application, or that there are proper reasons for non-use, provided the earlier Community trade mark has at that date been registered for non-use, provided the earlier Community trade mark has at that date been registered for not less than five years. If, at the date on which the Community trade mark application was published, the earlier Community trade mark had been registered for not less than five years, the proprietor of the earlier Community trade mark shall furnish proof that, in addition, the conditions contained in Article 43(2) were satisfied at that date. In the absence of proof to this effect the application for a declaration of invalidity shall be rejected. If the earlier Community trade mark has been used in relation to part only of the goods or services for which it is registered it shall, for the purpose of the examination of the application for a declaration of invalidity, be deemed to be registered in respect only of that part of the goods or services.

3. Paragraph 2 shall apply to earlier national trade marks referred to in Article 8(2)(a), by substituting use in the Member State in which the earlier national trade mark is protected for use in the Community.

4. The Office may, if it thinks fit, invite the parties to make a friendly settlement.

5. If the examination of the application for revocation of rights or for a declaration of invalidity reveals that the trade mark should not have been registered in respect of some or all of the goods or services for which it is registered, the rights of the proprietor of the Community trade mark shall be revoked or it shall be declared invalid in respect of those goods or services. Otherwise the application for revocation of rights or for a declaration of invalidity shall be rejected.

[6. A record of the Office's decision on the application for revocation of rights or for a declaration of invalidity shall be entered in the Register once it has become final.]

NOTES

Repealed as noted to Art 1, at **[5.246]**.
Para 6: substituted by Council Regulation 422/2004/EC, Art 1(18).

TITLE VII
APPEALS

[5.303]
Article 57
Decisions subject to appeal

1. An appeal shall lie from decisions of the examiners, Opposition Divisions, Administration of Trade Marks and Legal Division and Cancellation Divisions. It shall have suspensive effect.

2. A decision which does not terminate proceedings as regards one of the parties can only be appealed together with the final decision, unless the decision allows separate appeal.

NOTES

Repealed as noted to Art 1, at **[5.246]**.

[5.304]
Article 58
Persons entitled to appeal and to be parties to appeal proceeding
Any party to proceedings adversely affected by a decision may appeal. Any other parties to the proceedings shall be parties to the appeal proceedings as of right.

NOTES
Repealed as noted to Art 1, at **[5.246]**.

[5.305]
Article 59
Time limit and form of appeal
Notice of appeal must be filed in writing at the Office within two months after the date of notification of the decision appealed from. The notice shall be deemed to have been filed only when the fee for appeal has been paid. Within four months after the date of notification of the decision, a written statement setting out the grounds of appeal must be filed.

NOTES
Repealed as noted to Art 1, at **[5.246]**.

[5.306]
[Article 60
Revision of decisions in ex parte cases
1. If the party which has lodged the appeal is the sole party to the procedure, and if the department whose decision is contested considers the appeal to be admissible and well founded, the department shall rectify its decision.
2. If the decision is not rectified within one month after receipt of the statement of grounds, the appeal shall be remitted to the Board of Appeal without delay, and without comment as to its merit.]

NOTES
Repealed as noted to Art 1, at **[5.246]**.
Substituted by Council Regulation 422/2004/EC, Art 1(19).

[5.307]
[Article 60a
Revision of decisions in inter partes cases
1. Where the party which has lodged the appeal is opposed by another party and if the department whose decision is contested considers the appeal to be admissible and well founded, it shall rectify its decision.
2. The decision may only be rectified if the department whose decision is contested notifies the other party of its intention to rectify it, and that party accepts it within two months of the date on which it received the notification.
3. If, within two months of receiving the notification referred to in paragraph 2, the other party does not accept that the contested decision is to be rectified and makes a declaration to that effect or does not make any declaration within the period laid down, the appeal shall be remitted to the Board of Appeal without delay, and without comment as to its merit.
4. However, if the department whose decision is contested does not consider the appeal to be admissible and well founded within one month after receipt of the statement of grounds, it shall, instead of taking the measures provided for in paragraphs 2 and 3, remit the appeal to the Board of Appeal without delay, and without comment as to its merit.]

NOTES
Repealed as noted to Art 1, at **[5.246]**.
Inserted by Council Regulation 422/2004/EC, Art 1(20).

[5.308]
Article 61
Examination of appeals
1. If the appeal is admissible, the Board of Appeal shall examine whether the appeal is allowable.
2. In the examination of the appeal, the Board of Appeal shall invite the parties, as often as necessary, to file observations, within a period to be fixed by the Board of Appeal, on communications from the other parties or issued by itself.

NOTES
Repealed as noted to Art 1, at **[5.246]**.

[5.309]
Article 62
Decisions in respect of appeals
1. Following the examination as to the allowability of the appeal, the Board of Appeal shall decide on the appeal. The Board of Appeal may either exercise any power within the competence of the department which was responsible for the decision appealed or remit the case to that department for further prosecution.
2. If the Board of Appeal remits the case for further prosecution to the department whose decision was appealed, that department shall be bound by the ratio decidendi of the Board of Appeal, in so far as the facts are the same.
3. The decisions of the Boards of Appeal shall take effect only as from the date of expiration of the period referred to in Article 63(5) or, if an action has been brought before the Court of Justice within that period, as from the date of rejection of such action.

NOTES
Repealed as noted to Art 1, at **[5.246]**.

[5.310]
Article 63
Actions before the Court of Justice
1. Actions may be brought before the Court of Justice against decisions of the Boards of Appeal on appeals.
2. The action may be brought on grounds of lack of competence, infringement of an essential procedural requirement, infringement of the Treaty, of this Regulation or of any rule of law relating to their application or misuse of power.
3. The Court of Justice has jurisdiction to annul or to alter the contested decision.
4. The action shall be open to any party to proceedings before the Board of Appeal adversely affected by its decision.
5. The action shall be brought before the Court of Justice within two months of the date of notification of the decision of the Board of Appeal.
6. The Office shall be required to take the necessary measures to comply with the judgment of the Court of Justice.

NOTES
Repealed as noted to Art 1, at **[5.246]**.

TITLE VIII
COMMUNITY COLLECTIVE MARKS

[5.311]
Article 64
Community collective marks
1. A Community collective mark shall be a Community trade mark which is described as such when the mark is applied for and is capable of distinguishing the goods or services of the members of the association which is the proprietor of the mark from those of other undertakings. Associations of manufacturers, producers, suppliers of services, or traders which, under the terms of the law governing them, have the capacity in their own name to have rights and obligations of all kinds, to make contracts or accomplish other legal acts and to sue and be sued, as well as legal persons governed by public law, may apply for Community collective marks.
2. In derogation from Article 7(1)(c), signs or indications which may serve, in trade, to designate the geographical origin of the goods or services may constitute Community collective marks within the meaning of paragraph 1. A collective mark shall not entitle the proprietor to prohibit a third party from using in the course of trade such signs or indications, provided he uses them in accordance with honest practices in industrial or commercial matters; in particular, such a mark may not be invoked against a third party who is entitled to use a geographical name.
3. The provisions of this Regulation shall apply to Community collective marks, unless Articles 65 to 72 provide otherwise.

NOTES
Repealed as noted to Art 1, at **[5.246]**.

[5.312]
Article 65
Regulations governing use of the mark
1. An applicant for a Community collective mark must submit regulations governing its use within the period prescribed.

2. The regulations governing use shall specify the persons authorised to use the mark, the conditions of membership of the association and, where they exist, the conditions of use of the mark including sanctions. The regulations governing use of a mark referred to in Article 64(2) must authorise any person whose goods or services originate in the geographical area concerned to become a member of the association which is the proprietor of the mark.

NOTES

Repealed as noted to Art 1, at **[5.246]**.

[5.313]

Article 66

Refusal of the application

1. In addition to the grounds for refusal of a Community trade mark application provided for in Articles 36 and 38, an application for a Community collective mark shall be refused where the provisions of Article 64 or 65 are not satisfied, or where the regulations governing use are contrary to public policy or to awaited principles of morality.

2. An application for a Community collective mark shall also be refused if the public is liable to be misled as regards the character or the significance of the mark, in particular if it is likely to be taken to be something other than a collective mark.

3. An application shall not be refused if the applicant, as a result of amendment of the regulations governing use, meets the requirements of paragraphs 1 and 2.

NOTES

Repealed as noted to Art 1, at **[5.246]**.

[5.314]

Article 67

Observations by third parties

Apart from the cases mentioned in Article 41, any person, group or body referred to in that Article may submit to the Office written observations based on the particular grounds on which the application for a Community collective mark should be refused under the terms of Article 66.

NOTES

Repealed as noted to Art 1, at **[5.246]**.

[5.315]

Article 68

Use of marks

Use of a Community collective mark by any person who has authority to use it shall satisfy the requirements of this Regulation, provided that the other conditions which this Regulation imposes with regard to the use of Community trade marks are fulfilled.

NOTES

Repealed as noted to Art 1, at **[5.246]**.

[5.316]

Article 69

Amendment of the regulations governing use of the mark

1. The proprietor of a Community collective mark must submit to the Office any amended regulations governing use.

2. The amendment shall not be mentioned in the Register if the amended regulations do not satisfy the requirements of Article 65 or involve one of the grounds for refusal referred to in Article 66.

3. Article 67 shall apply to amended regulations governing use.

4. For the purposes of applying this Regulation, amendments to the regulations governing use shall take effect only from the date of entry of the mention of the amendment in the Register.

NOTES

Repealed as noted to Art 1, at **[5.246]**.

[5.317]

Article 70

Persons who are entitled to bring an action for infringement

1. The provisions of Article 22(3) and (4) concerning the rights of licensees shall apply to every person who has authority to use a Community collective mark.

2. The proprietor of a Community collective mark shall be entitled to claim compensation on behalf of persons who have authority to use the mark where they have sustained damage in consequence of unauthorised use of the mark.

NOTES

Repealed as noted to Art 1, at **[5.246]**.

[5.318]
Article 71
Grounds for revocation
Apart from the grounds for revocation provided for in Article 50, the rights of the proprietor of a Community collective mark shall be revoked on application to the Office or on the basis of a counterclaim in infringement proceedings, if—

(a) the proprietor does not take reasonable steps to prevent the mark being used in a manner incompatible with the conditions of use, where these exist, laid down in the regulations governing use, amendments to which have, where appropriate, been mentioned in the Register;
(b) the manner in which the mark has been used by the proprietor has caused it to become liable to mislead the public in the manner referred to in Article 66(2);
(c) an amendment to the regulations governing use of the mark has been mentioned in the Register in breach of the provisions of Article 69(2), unless the proprietor of the mark, by further amending the regulations governing use, complies with the requirements of those provisions.

NOTES
Repealed as noted to Art 1, at **[5.246]**.

[5.319]
Article 72
Grounds for invalidity
Apart from the grounds for invalidity provided for in Articles 51 and 52, a Community collective mark which is registered in breach of the provisions of Article 66 shall be declared invalid on application to the Office or on the basis of a counterclaim in infringement proceedings, unless the proprietor of the mark, by amending the regulations governing use, complies with the requirements of those provisions.

NOTES
Repealed as noted to Art 1, at **[5.246]**.

TITLE IX
PROCEDURE

SECTION 1
GENERAL PROVISIONS

[5.320]
Article 73
Statement of reasons on which decisions are based
Decisions of the Office shall state the reasons on which they are based. They shall be based only on reasons or evidence on which the parties concerned have had on opportunity to present their comments.

NOTES
Repealed as noted to Art 1, at **[5.246]**.

[5.321]
Article 74
Examination of the facts by the Office of its own motion
1. In proceedings before it the Office shall examine the facts of its own motion; however, in proceedings relating to relative grounds for refusal of registration, the Office shall be restricted in this examination to the facts, evidence and arguments provided by the parties and the relief sought.
2. The Office may disregard facts or evidence which are not submitted in due time by the parties concerned.

NOTES
Repealed as noted to Art 1, at **[5.246]**.

[5.322]
Article 75
Oral proceedings
1. If the Office considers that oral proceedings would be expedient they shall be held either at the instance of the Office or at the request of any party to the proceedings.
2. Oral proceedings before the examiners, the Opposition Division and the Administration of Trade Marks and Legal Division shall not be public.

3. Oral proceedings, including delivery of the decision, shall be public before the Cancellation Division and the Boards of Appeal, in so far as the department before which the proceedings are taking place does not decide otherwise in cases where admission of the public could have serious and unjustified disadvantages, in particular for a party to the proceedings.

NOTES

Repealed as noted to Art 1, at **[5.246]**.

[5.323]
Article 76
Taking of evidence

1. In any proceedings before the Office, the means of giving or obtaining evidence shall include the following—

(a) hearing the parties;
(b) requests for information;
(c) the production of documents and items of evidence;
(d) hearing witnesses;
(e) opinions by experts;
(f) statements in writing sworn or affirmed or having a similar effect under the law of the State in which the statement is drawn up.

2. The relevant department may commission one of its members to examine the evidence adduced.

3. If the Office considers it necessary for a party, witness or expert to give evidence orally, it shall issue a summons to the person concerned to appear before it.

4. The parties shall be informed of the hearing of a witness or expert before the Office. They shall have the right to be present and to put questions to the witness or expert.

NOTES

Repealed as noted to Art 1, at **[5.246]**.

[5.324]
Article 77
Notification

The Office shall, as a matter of course, notify those concerned of decisions and summonses and of any notice or other communication from which a time limit is reckoned, or of which those concerned must be notified under other provisions of this Regulation or of the Implementing Regulation, or of which notification has been ordered by the President of the Office.

NOTES

Repealed as noted to Art 1, at **[5.246]**.

[5.325]
[Article 77a
Revocation of decisions

1. Where the Office has made an entry in the Register or taken a decision which contains an obvious procedural error attributable to the Office, it shall ensure that the entry is cancelled or the decision is revoked. Where there is only one party to the proceedings and the entry or the act affects its rights, cancellation or revocation shall be determined even if the error was not evident to the party.

2. Cancellation or revocation as referred to in paragraph 1 shall be determined, ex officio or at the request of one of the parties to the proceedings, by the department which made the entry or took the decision. Cancellation or revocation shall be determined within six months from the date on which the entry was made in the Register or the decision was taken, after consultation with the parties to the proceedings and any proprietor of rights to the Community trade mark in question that are entered in the Register.

3. This Article shall be without prejudice to the right of the parties to submit an appeal under Articles 57 and 63, or to the possibility, under the procedures and conditions laid down by the Implementing Regulation referred to in Article 157(1), of correcting any linguistic errors or errors of transcription and obvious errors in the Office's decisions or errors attributable to the Office in registering the trade mark or in publishing its registration.]

NOTES

Inserted by Council Regulation 422/2004/EC, Art 1(21).
Repealed as noted to Art 1, at **[5.246]**.

[5.326]
Article 78
Restitutio in integrum

1. The applicant for or proprietor of a Community trade mark or any other party to proceedings before the Office who, in spite of all due care required by the circumstances having been taken, was unable to observe a time limit vis-à-vis the Office shall, upon application, have his rights re-established if the non-observance in question has the direct consequence, by virtue of the provisions of this Regulation, of causing the loss of any right or means of redress.

2. The application must be filed in writing within two months from the removal of the cause of non-compliance with the time limit. The omitted act must be completed within this period. The application shall only be admissible within the year immediately following the expire of the unobserved time limit. In the case of non-submission of the request for renewal of registration or of non-payment of a renewal fee, the further period of six months provided in Article 47(3), third sentence, shall be deducted from the period of one year.

3. The application must state the grounds on which it is based and must set out the facts on which it relies. It shall not be deemed to be filed until the fee for re-establishment of rights has been paid.

4. The department competent to decide on the omitted act shall decide upon the application.

[5. This Article shall not be applicable to the time limits referred to in paragraph 2 of this Article, Article 42(1) and (3) and Article 78a.]

6. Where the applicant for or proprietor of a Community trade mark has his rights re-established, he may not invoke his rights vis-à vis a third party who, in good faith, has put goods on the market or supplied services under a sign which is identical with or similar to the Community trade mark in the course of the period between the loss of rights in the application or in the Community trade mark and publication of the mention of re-establishment of those rights.

7. A third party who may avail himself of the provisions of paragraph 6 may bring third party proceedings against the decision re-establishing the rights of the applicant for or proprietor of a Community trade mark within a period of two months as from the date of publication of the mention of re-establishment of those rights.

8. Nothing in this Article shall limit the right of a Member State to grant restitutio in integrum in respect of time limits provided for in this Regulation and to be observed vis-à-vis the authorities of such State.

NOTES

Repealed as noted to Art 1, at **[5.246]**.
Para 5: substituted by Council Regulation 422/2004/EC, Art 1(22).

[5.327]
[Article 78a
Continuation of proceedings

1. An applicant for or proprietor of a Community trade mark or any other party to proceedings before the Office who has omitted to observe a time limit vis-à-vis the Office may, upon request, obtain the continuation of proceedings, provided that at the time the request is made the omitted act has been carried out. The request for continuation of proceedings shall be admissible only if it is presented within two months following the expiry of the unobserved time limit. The request shall not be deemed to have been filed until the fee for continuation of the proceedings has been paid.

2. This Article shall not be applicable to the time limits laid down in Article 25(3), Article 27, Article 29(1), Article 33(1), Article 36(2), Article 42, Article 43, Article 47(3), Article 59, Article 60a, Article 63(5), Article 78, Article 108, or to the time limits laid down in this Article or the time limits laid down by the Implementing Regulation referred to in Article 157(1) for claiming priority within the meaning of Article 30, exhibition priority within the meaning of Article 33 or seniority within the meaning of Article 34 after the application has been filed.

3. The department competent to decide on the omitted act shall decide upon the application.

4. If the Office accepts the application, the consequences of having failed to observe the time limit shall be deemed not to have occurred.

5. If the Office rejects the application, the fee shall be refunded.]

NOTES

Inserted by Council Regulation 422/2004/EC, Art 1(23).
Repealed as noted to Art 1, at **[5.246]**.

[5.328]
Article 79
Reference to general principles

In the absence of procedural provisions in this Regulation, the Implementing Regulation, the fees regulations or the rules of procedure of the Boards of Appeal, the Office shall take into account the principles of procedural law generally recognised in the Member States.

NOTES

Repealed as noted to Art 1, at **[5.246]**.

[5.329]
Article 80
Termination of financial obligations

1. Rights of the Office to the payment of a fee shall be extinguished after four years from the end of the calendar year in which the fee fell due.

2. Rights against the Office for the refunding of fees or sums of money paid in excess of a fee shall be extinguished after four years from the end of the calendar year in which the right arose.

3. The period laid down in paragraphs 1 and 2 shall be interrupted in the case covered by paragraph 1 by a request for payment of the fee and in the case covered by paragraph 2 by a reasoned claim in writing. On interruption it shall begin again immediately and shall end at the latest six years after the end of the year in which it originally began, unless, in the meantime, judicial proceedings to enforce the right have begun in this case the period shall end at the earliest one year after the judgment has acquired the authority of a final decision.

NOTES

Repealed as noted to Art 1, at **[5.246]**.

SECTION 2
COSTS

[5.330]
Article 81
Costs

1. The losing party in opposition proceedings, proceedings for revocation, proceedings for a declaration of invalidity or appeal proceedings shall bear the fees incurred by the other party as well as all costs, without prejudice to Article 115(6), incurred by him essential to the proceedings, including travel and subsistence and the remuneration of an agent, adviser or advocate, within the limits of the scales set for each category of costs under the conditions laid down in the Implementing Regulation.

2. However, where each party succeeds on some and fails on other heads, or if reasons of equity so dictate, the Opposition Division, Cancellation Division or Board of Appeal shall decide a different apportionment of costs.

3. The party who terminates the proceedings by withdrawing the Community trade mark application, the opposition, the application for revocation of rights, the application for a declaration of invalidity or the appeal, or by not renewing registration of the Community trade mark or by surrendering the Community trade mark, shall bear the fees and the costs incurred by the other party as stipulated in paragraphs 1 and 2.

4. Where a case does not proceed to judgment the costs shall be at the discretion of the Opposition Division, Cancellation Division or Board of Appeal.

5. Where the parties conclude before the Opposition Division, Cancellation Division or Board of Appeal a settlement of costs differing from that provided for in the preceding paragraphs, the department concerned shall take note of that agreement.

[6. The Opposition Division or Cancellation Division or Board of Appeal shall fix the amount of the costs to be paid pursuant to the preceding paragraphs when the costs to be paid are limited to the fees paid to the Office and the representation costs. In all other cases, the registry of the Board of Appeal or a member of the staff of the Opposition Division or Cancellation Division shall fix the amount of the costs to be reimbursed on request. The request is admissible only within two months of the date on which the decision for which an application was made for the costs to be fixed became final. The amount so determined may be reviewed by a decision of the Opposition Division or Cancellation Division or Board of Appeal on a request filed within the prescribed period.]

NOTES

Repealed as noted to Art 1, at **[5.246]**.
Para 6: substituted by Council Regulation 422/2004/EC, Art 1(24).

[5.331]
Article 82
Enforcement of decisions fixing the amount of costs

1. Any final decision of the Office fixing the amount of costs shall be enforceable.

2. Enforcement shall be governed by the rules of civil procedure in force in the State in the territory of which it is carried out. The order for its enforcement shall be appended to the decision, without other formality than verification of the authenticity of the decision, by the national authority which the Government of each Member State shall designate for this purpose and shall make known to the Office and to the Court of Justice.

3. When these formalities have been completed on application by the party concerned, the latter may proceed to enforcement in accordance with the national law, by bringing the matter directly before the competent authority.

4. Enforcement may be suspended only by a decision of the Court of Justice. However, the courts of the country concerned shall have jurisdiction over complaints that enforcement is being carried out in an irregular manner.

NOTES

Repealed as noted to Art 1, at **[5.246]**.

SECTION 3

INFORMATION OF THE PUBLIC AND OF THE OFFICIAL AUTHORITIES OF THE MEMBER STATES

[5.332]

Article 83

Register of Community trade marks

The Office shall keep a register to the known as the Register of Community trade marks, which shall contain those particulars the registration or inclusion of which is provided for by this Regulation or by the Implementing Regulation. The Register shall be open to public inspection.

NOTES

Repealed as noted to Art 1, at **[5.246]**.

[5.333]

Article 84

Inspection of files

1. The files relating to Community trade mark applications which have not yet been published shall not be made available for inspection without the consent of the applicant.

2. Any person who can prove that the applicant for a Community trade mark has stated that after the trade mark has been registered he will invoke the rights under it against him may obtain inspection of the files prior to the publication of that application and without the consent of the applicant.

3. Subsequent to the publication of the Community trade mark application, the files relating to such application and the resulting trade mark may be inspected on request.

4. However, where the files are inspected pursuant to paragraphs 2 or 3, certain documents in the file may be withheld from inspection in accordance with the provisions of the Implementing Regulation.

NOTES

Repealed as noted to Art 1, at **[5.246]**.

[5.334]

Article 85

Periodical publications

The Office shall periodically publish—

- *(a) a Community Trade Marks Bulletin containing entries made in the Register of Community trade marks as well as other particulars the publication of which is prescribed by this Regulation or by the Implementing Regulation;*
- *(b) an Official Journal containing notices and information of a general character issued by the President of the Office, as well as any other information relevant to this Regulation or its implementation.*

NOTES

Repealed as noted to Art 1, at **[5.246]**.

[5.335]

Article 86

Administrative co-operation

Unless otherwise provided in this Regulation or in national laws, the Office and the courts or authorities of the Member States shall on request give assistance to each other by communicating information or opening files for inspection. Where the Office lays files open to inspection by courts, Public Prosecutors' Offices or central industrial property offices, the inspection shall not be subject to the restrictions laid down in Article 84.

NOTES

Repealed as noted to Art 1, at **[5.246]**.

[5.336]

Article 87

Exchange of publications

1. The offices and the central industrial property offices of the Member States shall dispatch to each other on request and for their own use one or more copies of the respective publications free of charge.

2. The Office may conclude agreements relating to the exchange or supply of publications.

NOTES

Repealed as noted to Art 1, at **[5.246]**.

SECTION 4
REPRESENTATION

[5.337]

Article 88

General principles of representation

1. Subject to the provisions of paragraph 2, no person shall be compelled to be represented before the Office.

2. Without prejudice to paragraph 3, second sentence, natural or legal persons not having either their domicile or their principal place of business or a real and effective industrial or commercial establishment in the Community must be represented before the Office in accordance with Article 89(1) in all proceedings established by this Regulation, other than in filing an application for a Community trade mark; the Implementing Regulation may permit other exceptions.

3. [Natural or legal persons having their domicile or principal place of business or a real and effective industrial or commercial establishment in the Community may be represented before the Office by an employee.] An employee of a legal person to which this paragraph applies may also represent other legal persons which have economic connections with the first legal person, even if those other legal persons have neither their domicile nor their principal place of business nor a real and effective industrial or commercial establishment within the Community.

[4. The Implementing Regulation shall specify whether and under what conditions an employee must file with the Office a signed authorisation for insertion on the file.]

NOTES

Repealed as noted to Art 1, at **[5.246]**.

Para 3: words in square brackets substituted by Council Regulation 422/2004/EC, Art 1(25)(a).

Para 4: added by Council Regulation 422/2004/EC, Art 1(25)(b).

[5.338]

Article 89

Professional representatives

1. Representation of natural or legal persons before the Office may only be undertaken by—

- *(a) any legal practitioner qualified in one of the Member States and having his place of business within the Community, to the extent that he is entitled, within the said State, to act as a representative in trade mark matters; or*
- *[(b) professional representatives whose names appear on the list maintained for this purpose by the Office. The Implementing Regulation shall specify whether and under what conditions the representatives before the Office must file with the Office a signed authorisation for insertion on the file.]*

Representatives acting before the Office must file with it a signed authorisation for insertion on the files, the details of which are set out in the Implementing Regulation.

2. Any natural person who fulfils the following conditions may be entered on the list of professional representatives—

- *(a) he must be a national of one of the Member States;*
- *(b) he must have his place of business or employment in the Community;*
- *[(c) he must be entitled to represent natural or legal persons in trade mark matters before the central industrial property office of a Member State.] Where, in that State, the entitlement is not conditional upon the requirement of special professional qualifications, persons applying to be entered on the list who act in trade mark matters before the central industrial property office of the said State must have habitually so acted for at least five years. However, persons whose professional qualification to represent natural or legal persons in trade mark matters before the central industrial property office of one of the Member States is officially recognised in accordance with the regulations laid down by such State shall not be subject to the condition of having exercised the profession.*

3. Entry shall be effected upon request, accompanied by a certificate furnished by the central industrial property office of the Member State concerned, which must indicate that the conditions laid down in paragraph 2 are fulfilled.

4. The President of the Office may grant exemption from—

- *(a) the requirement of paragraph 2(c), second sentence, if the applicant furnishes proof that he has acquired the requisite qualification in another way;*
- *(b) the requirement of paragraph 2(a) in special circumstances.*

5. The conditions under which a person may be removed from the list of professional representatives shall be laid down in the Implementing Regulation.

NOTES

Repealed as noted to Art 1, at **[5.246]**.
Para 1: sub-para (b) substituted by Council Regulation 422/2004/EC, Art 1(26)(a).
Para 2: words in square brackets in sub-para (c) substituted by Council Regulation 422/2004/EC, Art 1(26)(b).

TITLE X
JURISDICTION AND PROCEDURE IN LEGAL ACTIONS RELATING TO COMMUNITY TRADE MARKS

SECTION 1
APPLICATION OF THE CONVENTION ON JURISDICTION AND ENFORCEMENT

[5.339]
Article 90
Application of the Convention on Jurisdiction and Enforcement

1. Unless otherwise specified in this Regulation, the Convention on Jurisdiction and the Enforcement of Judgments in Civil and Commercial Matters, signed in Brussels on 27 September 1968, as amended by the Conventions on the Accession to that Convention of the States acceding to the European Communities, the whole of which Convention and of which Conventions of Accession are hereinafter referred to as the 'Convention on Jurisdiction and Enforcement', shall apply to proceedings relating to Community trade marks and applications for Community trade marks, as well as to proceedings relating to simultaneous and successive actions on the basis of Community trade marks and national trade marks.

2. In the case of proceedings in respect of the actions and claims referred to in Article 92—
- *(a) Articles 2, 4, 5(1), (3), (4) and (5) and Article 24 of the Convention on Jurisdiction and Enforcement shall not apply;*
- *(b) Articles 17 and 18 of that Convention shall apply subject to the limitations in Article 93(4) of this Regulation;*
- *(c) the provisions of Title II of that Convention which are applicable to persons domiciled in a Member State shall also be applicable to persons who do not have a domicile in any Member State but have an establishment therein.*

NOTES

Repealed as noted to Art 1, at **[5.246]**.

SECTION 2
DISPUTES CONCERNING THE INFRINGEMENT AND VALIDITY OF COMMUNITY TRADE MARKS

[5.340]
Article 91
Community trade mark courts

1. The Member States shall designate in their territories as limited a number as possible of national courts and tribunals of first and second instance, hereinafter referred to as 'Community trade mark courts', which shall perform the functions assigned to them by this Regulation.

2. Each Member State shall communicate to the Commission within three years of the entry into force of this Regulation a list of Community trade mark courts indicating their names and their territorial jurisdiction.

3. Any change made after communication of the list referred to in paragraph 2 in the number, names or territorial jurisdiction of the courts shall be notified without delay by the Member State concerned to the Commission.

4. The information referred to in paragraphs 2 and 3 shall be notified by the Commission to the Member States and published in the Official Journal of the European Communities.

5. As long as a Member State has not communicated the list as stipulated in paragraph 2, jurisdiction for any proceedings resulting from an action or application covered by Article 92, and for which the courts of that State have jurisdiction under Article 93, shall lie with that court of the State in question which would have jurisdiction ratione loci and ratione materiale in the case of proceedings relating to a national trade mark registered in that State.

NOTES

Repealed as noted to Art 1, at **[5.246]**.

[5.341]
Article 92
Jurisdiction over infringement and validity

The Community trade mark courts shall have exclusive jurisdiction—
- *(a) for all infringement actions and—if they are permitted under national law—actions in respect of threatened infringement relating to Community trade marks;*
- *(b) for actions for declaration of non-infringement, if they are permitted under national law;*

(c) *for all actions brought as a result of acts referred to in Article 9(3), second sentence;*
(d) *for counterclaims for revocation or for a declaration of invalidity of the Community trade mark pursuant to Article 96.*

NOTES

Repealed as noted to Art 1, at **[5.246]**.

[5.342]
Article 93
International jurisdiction

1. Subject to the provisions of this Regulation as well as to any provisions of the Convention on Jurisdiction and Enforcement applicable by virtue of Article 90, proceedings in respect of the actions and claims referred to in Article 92 shall be brought in the courts of the Member State in which the defendant is domiciled or, if he is not domiciled in any of the Member States, in which he has an establishment.

2. If the defendant is neither domiciled nor has an establishment in any of the Member States, such proceedings shall be brought in the courts of the Member State in which the plaintiff is domiciled or, if he is not domiciled in any of the Member States, in which he has an establishment.

3. If neither the defendant nor the plaintiff is so domiciled or has such an establishment, such proceedings shall be brought in the courts of the Member State where the Office has its seat.

4. Notwithstanding the provisions of paragraphs 1, 2 and 3—
(a) *Article 17 of the Convention on Jurisdiction and Enforcement shall apply if the parties agree that a different Community trade mark court shall have jurisdiction;*
(b) *Article 18 of that Convention shall apply if the defendant enters an appearance before a different Community trade mark court.*

5. Proceedings in respect of the actions and claims referred to in Article 92, with the exception of actions for a declaration of non-infringement of a Community trade mark, may also be brought in the courts of the Member State in which the act of infringement has been committed or threatened, or in which an act within the meaning of Article 9(3), second sentence, has been committed.

NOTES

Repealed as noted to Art 1, at **[5.246]**.

[5.343]
Article 94
Extent of jurisdiction

1. A Community trade mark court whose jurisdiction is based on Article 93(1) to (4) shall have jurisdiction in respect of—
— *acts of infringement committed or threatened within the territory of any of the Member States,*
— *acts within the meaning of Article 9(3), second sentence, committed within the territory of any of the Member States.*

2. A Community trade mark court whose jurisdiction is based on Article 93(5) shall have jurisdiction only in respect of acts committed or threatened within the territory of the Member State in which that court is situated.

NOTES

Repealed as noted to Art 1, at **[5.246]**.

[5.344]
Article 95
Presumption of validity—Defence as to the merits

1. The Community trade mark courts shall treat the Community trade mark as valid unless its validity is put in issue by the defendant with a counterclaim for revocation or for a declaration of invalidity.

2. The validity of a Community trade mark may not be put in issue in an action for a declaration of non-infringement.

3. In the actions referred to in Article 92(a) and (c) a plea relating to revocation or invalidity of the Community trade mark submitted otherwise than by way of a counterclaim shall be admissible in so far as the defendant claims that the rights of the proprietor of the Community trade mark could be revoked for lack of use or that Community trade mark could be declared invalid on account of an earlier right of the defendant.

NOTES

Repealed as noted to Art 1, at **[5.246]**.

[5.345]
Article 96
Counterclaims

1. A counterclaim for revocation or for a declaration of invalidity may only be based on the grounds for revocation or invalidity mentioned in this Regulation.
2. A Community trade mark court shall reject a counterclaim for revocation or for a declaration of invalidity if a decision taken by the Office relating to the same subject matter and cause of action and involving the same parties has already become final.
3. If the counterclaim is brought in a legal action to which the proprietor of the trade mark is not already a party, he shall be informed thereof and may be joined as a party to the action in accordance with the conditions set out in national law.
4. The Community trade mark court with which a counterclaim for revocation or for a declaration of invalidity of the Community trade mark has been filed shall inform the Office of the date on which the counterclaim was filed. The latter shall record this fact in the Register of Community trade marks.
[5. Article 56(2) to (5) shall apply.]
6. Where a Community trade mark court has given a judgment which has become final on a counterclaim for revocation or for invalidity of a Community trade mark, a copy of the judgment shall be sent to the Office. Any party may request information about such transmission. The Office shall mention the judgment in the Register of Community trade marks in accordance with the provisions of the Implementing Regulation.
7. The Community trade mark court hearing a counterclaim for revocation or for a declaration of invalidity may stay the proceedings on application by the proprietor of the Community trade mark and after hearing the other parties and may request the defendant to submit an application for revocation or for a declaration of invalidity to the Office within a time limit which it shall determine. If the application is not made within the time limit, the proceedings shall continue; the counterclaim shall be deemed withdrawn. Article 100(3) shall apply.

NOTES
Repealed as noted to Art 1, at **[5.246]**.
Para 5: substituted by Council Regulation 422/2004/EC, Art 1(27).

[5.346]
Article 97
Applicable law

1. The Community trade mark courts shall apply the provisions of this Regulation.
2. On all matters not covered by this Regulation a Community trade mark court shall apply its national law, including its private international law.
3. Unless otherwise provided in this Regulation, a Community trade mark court shall apply the rules of procedure governing the same type of action relating to a national trade mark in the Member State where it has its seat.

NOTES
Repealed as noted to Art 1, at **[5.246]**.

[5.347]
Article 98
Sanctions

1. Where a Community trade mark court finds that the defendant has infringed or threatened to infringe a Community trade mark, it shall, unless there are special reasons for not doing so, issue an order prohibiting the defendant from proceeding with the acts which infringed or would infringe the Community trade mark. It shall also take such measures in accordance with its national law as are aimed at ensuring that this prohibition is complied with.
2. In all other respects the Community trade mark court shall apply the law of the Member State to which the acts of infringement or threatened infringement were committed, including the private international law.

NOTES
Repealed as noted to Art 1, at **[5.246]**.

[5.348]
Article 99
Provisional and protective measures

1. Application may be made to the courts of a Member State, including Community trade mark courts, for such provisional, including protective, measures in respect of a Community trade mark or Community trade mark application as may be available under the law of that State in respect of a national trade mark, even if, under this Regulation, a Community trade mark court of another Member State has jurisdiction as to the substance of the matter.

2. A Community trade mark court whose jurisdiction is based on Article 93(1), (2), (3) or (4) shall have jurisdiction to grant provisional and protective measures which, subject to any necessary procedure for recognition and enforcement pursuant to Title III of the Convention on Jurisdiction and Enforcement, are applicable in the territory of any Member State. No other court shall have such jurisdiction.

NOTES

Repealed as noted to Art 1, at **[5.246]**.

[5.349]
Article 100
Specific rules on related actions

1. A Community trade mark court hearing an action referred to in Article 92, other than an action for a declaration of non-infringement shall, unless there are special grounds for continuing the hearing, of its own motion after hearing the parties or at the request of one of the parties and after hearing the other parties, stay the proceedings where the validity of the Community trade mark is already in issue before another Community trade mark court on account of a counterclaim or where an application for revocation or for a declaration of invalidity has already been filed at the Office.
2. The Office, when hearing an application for revocation or for a declaration of invalidity shall, unless there are special grounds for continuing the hearing, of its own motion after hearing the parties or at the request of one of the parties and after hearing the other parties, stay the proceedings where the validity of the Community trade mark is already in issue on account of a counterclaim before a Community trade mark court. However, if one of the parties to the proceedings before the Community trade mark court so requests, the court may, after hearing the other parties to these proceedings, stay the proceedings. The Office shall in this instance continue the proceedings pending before it.
3. Where the Community trade mark court stays the proceedings it may order provisional and protective measures for the duration of the stay.

NOTES

Repealed as noted to Art 1, at **[5.246]**.

[5.350]
Article 101
Jurisdiction of Community trade mark courts of second instance—Further appeal

1. An appeal to the Community trade mark courts of second instance shall lie from judgments of the Community trade mark courts of first instance in respect of proceedings arising from the actions and claims referred to in Article 92.
2. The conditions under which an appeal may be lodged with a Community trade mark court of second instance shall be determined by the national law of the Member State in which that court is located.
3. The national rules concerning further appeal shall be applicable in respect of judgments of Community trade mark courts of second instance.

NOTES

Repealed as noted to Art 1, at **[5.246]**.

SECTION 3

OTHER DISPUTES CONCERNING COMMUNITY TRADE MARKS

[5.351]
Article 102
Supplementary provisions on the jurisdiction of national courts other than Community trade mark courts

1. Within the Member State whose courts have jurisdiction under Article 90(1) those courts shall have jurisdiction for actions other than those referred to in Article 92, which would have jurisdiction ratione loci and ratione materiae in the case of actions relating to a national trade mark registered in that State.
2. Actions relating to a Community trade mark, other than those referred to in Article 92, for which no court has jurisdiction under Article 90(1) and paragraph 1 of this Article may be heard before the courts of the Member State in which the Office has its seat.

NOTES

Repealed as noted to Art 1, at **[5.246]**.

[5.352]
Article 103
Obligation of the national court

A national court which is dealing with an action relating to a Community trade mark, other than the action referred to in Article 92, shall treat the trade mark as valid.

NOTES

Repealed as noted to Art 1, at **[5.246]**.

SECTION 4
TRANSITIONAL PROVISION

[5.353]
Article 104
Transitional provision relating to the application of the Convention on Jurisdiction and Enforcement

The provisions of the Convention on Jurisdiction and Enforcement which are rendered applicable by the preceding Articles shall have effect in respect of any Member State solely in the text of the Convention which is in force in respect of that State at any given time.

NOTES

Repealed as noted to Art 1, at **[5.246]**.

TITLE XI
EFFECTS ON THE LAWS OF THE MEMBER STATES

SECTION 1
CIVIL ACTIONS ON THE BASIS OF MORE THAN ONE TRADE MARK

[5.354]
Article 105
Simultaneous and successive civil actions on the basis of Community trade marks and national trade marks

1. Where actions for infringement involving the same cause of action and between the same parties are brought in the courts of different Member States, one seized on the basis of a Community trade mark and the other seized on the basis of a national trade mark—

(a) the court other than the court first seized shall of its own motion decline jurisdiction in favour of that court where the trade marks concerned are identical and valid for identical goods or services. The court which would be required to decline jurisdiction may stay its proceedings if the jurisdiction of the other court is contested;

(b) the court other than the court first seized may stay its proceedings where the trade marks concerned are identical and valid for similar goods or services and where the trade marks concerned are similar and valid for identical or similar goods or services.

2. The court hearing an action for infringement on the basis of a Community trade mark shall reject the action if a final judgment on the merits has been given on the same cause of action and between the same parties on the basis of an identical national trade mark valid for identical goods or services.

3. The court hearing an action for infringement on the basis of a national trade mark shall reject the action if a final judgment on the merits has been given on the same cause of action and between the same parties on the basis of an identical Community trade mark valid for identical goods or services.

4. Paragraphs 1, 2 and 3 shall not apply in respect of provisional, including protective, measures.

NOTES

Repealed as noted to Art 1, at **[5.246]**.

SECTION 2
APPLICATION OF NATIONAL LAWS FOR THE PURPOSE OF PROHIBITING THE USE OF COMMUNITY TRADE MARKS

[5.355]
Article 106
Prohibition of use of Community trade marks

1. This Regulation shall, unless otherwise provided for, not affect the right existing under the laws of the Member States to invoke claims for infringement of earlier rights within the meaning of Article 8 or Article 52(2) in relation to the use of a later Community trade mark. Claims for infringement of earlier rights within the meaning of Article 8(2) and (4) may, however, no longer be invoked if the proprietor of the earlier right may no longer apply for a declaration that the Community trade mark is invalid in accordance with Article 53(2).

2. This Regulation shall, unless otherwise provided for, not affect the right to bring proceedings under the civil, administrative or criminal law of a Member Sate or under provisions of Community law for the purpose of prohibiting the use of a Community trade mark to the extent that the use of a national trade mark may be prohibited under the law of that Member State or under Community law.

NOTES

Repealed as noted to Art 1, at **[5.246]**.

[5.356]

Article 107

Prior rights applicable to particular localities

1. The proprietor of an earlier right which only applies to a particular locality may oppose the use of the Community trade mark in the territory where his right is protected in so far as the law of the Member State concerned so permits.

2. Paragraph 1 shall cease to apply if the proprietor of the earlier right has acquiesced in the use of the Community trade mark in the territory where his right is protected for a period of five successive years, being aware of such use, unless the Community trade mark was applied for in bad faith.

3. The proprietor of the Community trade mark shall not be entitled to oppose use of the right referred to in paragraph 1 even though that right may no longer be invoked against the Community trade mark.

NOTES

Repealed as noted to Art 1, at **[5.246]**.

SECTION 3

CONVERSION INTO A NATIONAL TRADE MARK APPLICATION

[5.357]

Article 108

Request for the application of national procedure

1. The applicant for or proprietor of a Community trade mark may request the conversion of his Community trade mark application or Community trade mark into a national trade mark application—

(a) to the extent that the Community trade mark application is refused, withdrawn, or deemed to be withdrawn;

(b) to the extent that the Community trade mark ceases to have effect.

2. Conversion shall not take place—

(a) where the rights of the proprietor of the Community trade mark have been revoked on the grounds of non-use, unless in the Member State for which conversion is requested the Community trade mark has been put to use which would be considered to be genuine use under the laws of that Member State;

(b) for the purpose of protection in a Member State in which, in accordance with the decision of the Office or of the national court, grounds for refusal of registration or grounds for revocation or invalidity apply to the Community trade mark application or Community trade mark.

3. The national trade mark application resulting from the conversion of a Community trade mark application or a Community trade mark shall enjoy in respect of the Member State concerned the date of filing or the date of priority of that application or trade mark and, where appropriate, the seniority of a trade mark of that State claimed under Article 34 or 35.

[4. In cases where a Community trade mark application is deemed to be withdrawn, the Office shall send to the applicant a communication fixing a period of three months from the date of that communication in which a request for conversion may be filed.

5. Where the Community trade mark application is withdrawn or the Community trade mark ceases to have effect as a result of a surrender being recorded or of failure to renew the registration, the request for conversion shall be filed within three months after the date on which the Community trade mark application has been withdrawn or on which the Community trade mark ceases to have effect.

6. Where the Community trade mark application is refused by decision of the Office or where the Community trade mark ceases to have effect as a result of a decision of the Office or of a Community trade mark court, the request for conversion shall be filed within three months after the date on which that decision acquired the authority of a final decision.]

7. The effect referred to in Article 32 shall lapse if the request is not filed in due time.

NOTES

Repealed as noted to Art 1, at **[5.246]**.

Paras 4–6: substituted by Council Regulation 422/2004/EC, Art 1(28).

[5.358]
Article 109
Submission, publication and transmission of the request for conversion
1. A request for conversion shall be filed with the Office and shall specify the Member States in which application of the procedure for registration of a national trade mark is desired. The request shall not be deemed to be filed until the conversion fee has been paid.
2. If the Community trade mark application has been published, receipt of any such request shall be recorded in the Register of Community trade marks and the request for conversion shall be published.
[3. The Office shall check whether the conversion requested fulfils the conditions set out in this Regulation, in particular Article 108(1), (2), (4), (5) and (6), and paragraph 1 of this Article, together with the formal conditions laid down in the Implementing Regulation. If these conditions are fulfilled, the Office shall transmit the request for conversion to the industrial property offices of the Member States specified therein.]

NOTES
Repealed as noted to Art 1, at **[5.246]**.
Para 3: substituted by Council Regulation 422/2004/EC, Art 1(29).

[5.359]
Article 110
Formal requirements for conversion
[1. Any central industrial property office to which the request for conversion is transmitted may obtain from the Office any additional information concerning the request enabling that office to make a decision regarding the national trade mark resulting from the conversion.]
2. A Community trade mark application or a Community trade mark transmitted in accordance with Article 109 shall not be subjected to formal requirements of national law which are different from or additional to those provided for in this Regulation or in the Implementing Regulation.
3. Any central industrial property office to which the request is transmitted may require that the applicant shall, within not less than two months—
- *(a) pay the national application fee;*
- *(b) file a translation in one of the official languages of the State in question of the request and of the documents accompanying it;*
- *(c) indicate an address for service in the State in question;*
- *(d) supply a representation of the trade mark in the number of copies specified by the State in question.*

NOTES
Repealed as noted to Art 1, at **[5.246]**.
Para 1: substituted by Council Regulation 422/2004/EC, Art 1(30).

TITLE XII
THE OFFICE

SECTION 1
GENERAL PROVISIONS

[5.360]
Article 111
Legal status
1. The Office shall be a body of the Community. It shall have legal personality.
2. In each of the Member States the Office shall enjoy the most extensive legal capacity accorded to legal persons under their laws; it may, in particular, acquire or dispose of movable and immovable property and may be a party to legal proceedings.
3. The Office shall be represented by its President.

NOTES
Repealed as noted to Art 1, at **[5.246]**.

[5.361]
Article 112
Staff
1. The Staff Regulations of officials of the European Communities, the Conditions of Employment of other servants of the European Communities, and the rules adopted by agreement between the Institutions of the European Communities for giving effect to those Staff Regulations and Conditions of Employment shall apply to the staff of the Office, without prejudice to the application of Article 131 to the members of the Boards of Appeal.
2. Without prejudice to Article 120, the powers conferred on each Institution by the Staff Regulations and by the Conditions of Employment of other servants shall be exercised by the Office in respect of its staff.

NOTES

Repealed as noted to Art 1, at **[5.246]**.

[5.362]
Article 113
Privileges and immunities

The Protocol on the Privileges and Immunities of the European Communities shall apply to the Office.

NOTES

Repealed as noted to Art 1, at **[5.246]**.

[5.363]
Article 114
Liability

1. The contractual liability of the Office shall be governed by the law applicable to the contract in question.

2. The Court of Justice shall be competent to give judgment pursuant to any arbitration clause contained in a contract concluded by the Office.

3. In the case of non-contractual liability, the Office shall, in accordance with the general principles common to the laws of the Member States, make good any damage caused by its departments or by its servants in the performance of their duties.

4. The Court of Justice shall have jurisdiction in disputes relating to compensation for the damage referred to in paragraph 3.

5. The personal liability of its servants towards the Office shall be governed by the provisions laid down in their Staff Regulations or in the Conditions of Employment applicable to them.

NOTES

Repealed as noted to Art 1, at **[5.246]**.

[5.364]
Article 115
Languages

1. The application for a Community trade mark shall be filed in one of the official languages of the European Community.

2. The languages of the Office shall be English, French, German, Italian and Spanish.

3. The applicant must indicate a second language which shall be a language of the Office the use of which he accepts as a possible language of proceedings for opposition, revocation or invalidity proceedings.

If the application was filed in a language which is not one of the languages of the Office, the Office shall arrange to have the application, as described in Article 26(1), translated into the language indicated by the applicant.

4. Where the applicant for a Community trade mark is the sole party to proceedings before the Office, the language of proceedings shall be the language used for filing the application for a Community trade mark. If the application was made in a language other than the languages of the Office, the Office may send written communications to the applicant in the second language indicated by the applicant in his application.

5. The notice of opposition and an application for revocation or invalidity shall be filed in one of the languages of the Office.

6. If the language chosen, in accordance with paragraph 5, for the notice of opposition or the application for revocation or invalidity is the language of the application for a trade mark or the second language indicated when the application was filed, that language shall be the language of the proceedings.

If the language chosen, in accordance with paragraph 5, for the notice of opposition or the application for revocation or invalidity is neither the language of the application for a trade mark nor the second language indicated when the application was filed, the opposing party or the party seeking revocation or invalidity shall be required to produce, at his own expense, a translation of his application either into the language of the application for a trade mark, provided that it is a language of the Office, or into the second language indicated when the application was filed. The translation shall be produced within the period prescribed in the implementing regulation. The language into which the application has been translated shall then become the language of the proceedings.

7. Parties to opposition, revocation, invalidity or appeal proceedings may agree that a different official language of the European Community is to be the language of the proceedings.

NOTES

Repealed as noted to Art 1, at **[5.246]**.

[5.365]
Article 116
Publication; entries in the Register

1. An application for a Community trade mark, as described in Article 26(1), and all other information the publication of which is prescribed by this Regulation or the implementing regulation, shall be published in all the official languages of the European Community.

2. All entries in the Register of Community trade marks shall be made in all the official languages of the European Community.

3. In cases of doubt, the text in the language of the Office in which the application for the Community trade mark was filed shall be authentic. If the application was filed in an official language of the European Community other than one of the languages of the Office, the text in the second language indicated by the applicant shall be authentic.

NOTES

Repealed as noted to Art 1, at **[5.246]**.

[5.366]
Article 117

The translation services required for the functioning of the Office shall be provided by the Translation Centre of the Bodies of the Union once this begins operation.

NOTES

Repealed as noted to Art 1, at **[5.246]**.

[5.367]
Article 118
Control of legality

1. The Commission shall check the legality of those acts of the President of the Office in respect of which Community law does not provide for any check on legality by another body and of acts of the Budget Committee attached to the Office pursuant to Article 133.

2. It shall require that any unlawful acts as referred to in paragraph 1 be altered or annulled.

3. Member States and any person directly and personally involved may refer to the Commission any act as referred to in paragraph 1, whether express or implied, for the Commission to examine the legality of that act. Referral shall be made to the Commission [within one month] of the day on which the party concerned first became aware of the act in question. The Commission shall take a decision [within three months]. If no decision has been taken within this period, the case shall be deemed to have been dismissed.

NOTES

Repealed as noted to Art 1, at **[5.246]**.
Para 3: words in square brackets substituted by Council Regulation 422/2004/EC, Art 1(31).

[5.368]
[Article 118a
Access to documents

1. Regulation (EC) No 1049/2001 of the European Parliament and of the Council of 30 May 2001 regarding access to European Parliament, Council and Commission documents[1] shall apply to documents held by the Office.

2. The Administrative Board shall adopt the practical arrangements for implementing Regulation (EC) No 1049/2001 within six months of entry into force of Regulation (EC) No 1653/2003 of 18 June 2003 amending Regulation (EC) No 40/94 on the Community trade mark.[2]

3. Decisions taken by the Office pursuant to Article 8 of Regulation (EC) No 1049/2001 may give rise to the lodging of a complaint to the Ombudsman or form the subject of an action before the Court of Justice of the European Communities under the conditions laid down in Articles 195 and 230 of the Treaty respectively.]

NOTES

Inserted by Council Regulation 1653/2003/EC, Art 1(1).
Repealed as noted to Art 1, at **[5.246]**.

[1] OJ L145, 31.5.2001, p 43.

[2] OJ L245, 29.9.2003, p 36.

SECTION 2
MANAGEMENT OF THE OFFICE

[5.369]
Article 119
Powers of the President
1. The Office shall be managed by the President.
2. To this end the President shall have in particular the following functions and powers—
(a) he shall take all necessary steps, including the adoption of internal administrative instructions and the publication of notices, to ensure the functioning of the Office;
(b) he may place before the Commission any proposal to amend this Regulation, the Implementing Regulation, the rules of procedure of the Boards of Appeal, the fees regulations and any other rules applying to Community trade marks after consulting the Administrative Board and, in the case of the fees regulations and the budgetary provisions of this Regulation, the Budget Committee;
(c) he shall draw up the estimates of the revenue and expenditure of the Office and shall implement the budget;
(d) he shall submit a management report to the Commission, the European Parliament and the Administrative Board each year;
(e) he shall exercise in respect of the staff the powers laid down in Article 112(2);
(f) he may delegate his powers.
3. The President shall be assisted by one or more Vice-Presidents. If the President is absent or indisposed the Vice-President or one of the Vice-Presidents shall take his place in accordance with the procedure laid down by the Administrative Board.

NOTES
Repealed as noted to Art 1, at **[5.246]**.

[5.370]
Article 120
Appointment of senior officials
1. The President of the Office shall be appointed by the Council from a list of at most three candidates, which shall be prepared by the Administrative Board. Power to dismiss the President shall lie with the Council, acting on a proposal from the Administrative Board.
2. The term of office of the President shall not exceed five years. This term of office shall be renewable.
3. The Vice-President or Vice-Presidents of the Office shall be appointed or dismissed as in paragraph 1, after consultation with the President.
4. The Council shall exercise disciplinary authority over the officials referred to in paragraphs 1 and 3 of this Article.

NOTES
Repealed as noted to Art 1, at **[5.246]**.

SECTION 3
ADMINISTRATIVE BOARD

[5.371]
Article 121
Creation and powers
1. An Administrative Board is hereby set up, attached to the Office. Without prejudice to the powers attributed to the Budget Committee in Section 5—budget and financial control—the Administrative Board shall have the powers defined below.
2. The Administrative Board shall draw up the lists of candidates provided for in Article 120.
3. It shall fix the date for the first filing of Community trade mark applications, pursuant to Article 143(3).
4. It shall advise the President on matters for which the Office is responsible.
5. It shall be consulted before adoption of the guidelines for examination in the Office and in the other cases provided for in this Regulation.
6. It may deliver opinions and requests for information to the President and to the Commission where it considers that this is necessary.

NOTES
Repealed as noted to Art 1, at **[5.246]**.

[5.372]
Article 122
Composition
1. The Administrative Board shall be composed of one representative of each Member State and one representative of the Commission and their alternates.

2. The members of the Administrative Board may, subject to the provisions of its rules of procedure, be assisted by advisers or experts.

NOTES

Repealed as noted to Art 1, at **[5.246]**.

[5.373]
Article 123
Chairmanship

1. The Administrative Board shall elect a chairman and a deputy chairman from among its members. The deputy chairman shall ex officio replace the chairman in the event of his being prevented from attending to his duties.

2. The duration of the terms of office of the chairman and the deputy chairman shall be three years. The terms of office shall be renewable.

NOTES

Repealed as noted to Art 1, at **[5.246]**.

[5.374]
Article 124
Meetings

1. Meetings of the Administrative Board shall be convened by its chairman.

2. The President of the Office shall take part in the deliberations, unless the Administrative Board decides otherwise.

3. The Administrative Board shall hold an ordinary meeting once a year; in addition, it shall meet on the initiative of its chairman or at the request of the Commission or of one-third of the Member States.

4. The Administrative Board shall adopt rules of procedure.

5. The Administrative Board shall take its decisions by a simple majority of the representatives of the Member States. However, a majority of three-quarters of the representatives of the Member States shall be required for the decisions which the Administrative Board is empowered to take under Article 120(1) and (3). In both cases each Member State shall have one vote.

6. The Administrative Board may invite observers to attend its meetings.

7. The Secretariat for the Administrative Board shall be provided by the Office.

NOTES

Repealed as noted to Art 1, at **[5.246]**.

SECTION 4
IMPLEMENTATION OF PROCEDURES

[5.375]
Article 125
Competence

For taking decisions in connection with the procedures laid down in this Regulation, the following shall be competent—

(a) Examiners;
(b) Opposition Divisions;
(c) an Administration of Trade Marks and Legal Division;
(d) Cancellation Divisions;
(e) Boards of Appeal.

NOTES

Repealed as noted to Art 1, at **[5.246]**.

[5.376]
Article 126
Examiners

An examiner shall be responsible for taking decisions on behalf of the Office in relation to an application for registration of a Community trade mark, including the matters referred to in Articles 36, 37, 38 and 66, except in so far as an Opposition Division is responsible.

NOTES

Repealed as noted to Art 1, at **[5.246]**.

[5.377]
Article 127
Opposition Divisions

1. An Opposition Division shall be responsible for taking decisions on an opposition to an application to register a Community trade mark.

[2. The decisions of the Opposition Divisions shall be taken by three-member groups. At least one member shall be legally qualified. In certain specific cases provided for in the Implementing Regulation, the decisions shall be taken by a single member.]

NOTES

Repealed as noted to Art 1, at **[5.246]**.
Para 2: substituted by Council Regulation 422/2004/EC, Art 1(32).

[5.378]
Article 128
Administration of Trade Marks and Legal Division

1. The Administration of Trade Marks and Legal Division shall be responsible for those decisions required by this Regulation which do not fall within the competence of an examiner, an Opposition Division or a Cancellation Division. It shall in particular be responsible for decisions in respect of entries in the Register of Community trade marks.
2. It shall also be responsible for keeping the list of professional representatives which is referred to in Article 89.
3. A decision of the Division shall be taken by one member.

NOTES

Repealed as noted to Art 1, at **[5.246]**.

[5.379]
Article 129
Cancellation Divisions

1. A Cancellation Division shall be responsible for taking decisions in relation to an application for the revocation or declaration of invalidity of a Community trade mark.
[2. The decisions of the Cancellation Divisions shall be taken by three-member groups. At least one member shall be legally qualified. In certain specific cases provided for in the Implementing Regulation, the decisions shall be taken by a single member.]

NOTES

Repealed as noted to Art 1, at **[5.246]**.
Para 2: substituted by Council Regulation 422/2004/EC, Art 1(33).

[5.380]
Article 130
Boards of Appeal

1. The Boards of Appeal shall be responsible for deciding on appeals from decisions of the examiners, Opposition Divisions, Administration of Trade Marks and Legal Division and Cancellation Divisions.
[2. The decisions of the Boards of Appeal shall be taken by three members, at least two of whom are legally qualified. In certain specific cases, decisions shall be taken by an enlarged Board chaired by the President of the Boards of Appeal or by a single member, who must be legally qualified.]
[3. In order to determine the special cases which fall under the jurisdiction of the enlarged Board, account should be taken of the legal difficulty or the importance of the case or of special circumstances which justify it. Such cases may be referred to the enlarged Board—
(a) by the authority of the Boards of Appeal set up in accordance with the rules of procedure of the Boards referred to in Article 157(3), or
(b) by the Board handling the case.
4. The composition of the enlarged Board and the rules on referrals to it shall be laid down pursuant to the rules of procedure of the Boards referred to in Article 157(3).
5. To determine which specific cases fall under the authority of a single member, account should be taken of the lack of difficulty of the legal or factual matters raised, the limited importance of the individual case or the absence of other specific circumstances. The decision to confer a case on one member in the cases referred to shall be adopted by the Board handling the case. Further details shall be laid down in the rules of procedure of the Boards referred to in Article 157(3).]

NOTES

Repealed as noted to Art 1, at **[5.246]**.
Para 2: substituted by Council Regulation 422/2004/EC, Art 1(34)(a).
Paras 3–5: added by Council Regulation 422/2004/EC, Art 1(34)(b).

[5.381]
[Article 131
Independence of the members of the Boards of Appeal

1. The President of the Boards of Appeal and the chairmen of the Boards shall be appointed, in accordance with the procedure laid down in Article 120 for the appointment of the President of the Office, for a term of five years. They may not be removed from office during this term, unless there are serious grounds for such removal and the Court of Justice, on application by the institution which appointed them, takes a decision to this effect. The term of office of the President of Boards of Appeal and the chairmen of the Boards may be renewed for additional five-year periods, or until retirement age if this age is reached during the new term of office.

The President of the Boards of Appeal shall, inter alia, have managerial and organisational powers, principally to—

(a) chair the authority of the Boards of Appeal responsible for laying down the rules and organising the work of the Boards, which authority is provided for in the rules of procedure of the Boards referred to in Article 157(3);

(b) ensure the implementation of the authority's decisions;

(c) allocate cases to a Board on the basis of objective criteria determined by the authority of the Boards of Appeal;

(d) forward to the President of the Office the Boards' expenditure requirements, with a view to drawing up the expenditure estimates.

The President of the Boards of Appeal shall chair the enlarged Board.

Further details shall be laid down in the rules of procedure of the Boards referred to in Article 157(3).

2. The members of the Boards of Appeal shall be appointed by the Administrative Board for a term of five years. Their term of office may be renewed for additional five-year periods, or until retirement age if that age is reached during the new term of office.

3. The members of the Boards of Appeal may not be removed from office unless there are serious grounds for such removal and the Court of Justice, after the case has been referred to it by the Administrative Board on the recommendation of the President of the Boards of Appeal, after consulting the chairman of the Board to which the member concerned belongs, takes a decision to this effect.

4. The President of the Boards of Appeal and the chairmen and members of the Boards of Appeal shall be independent. In their decisions they shall not be bound by any instructions.

5. The President of the Boards of Appeal and the chairmen and members of the Boards of Appeal may not be examiners or members of the Opposition Divisions, Administration of Trade Marks and Designs and Legal Division or Cancellation Divisions.]

NOTES

Substituted by Council Regulation 422/2004/EC, Art 1(35).
Repealed as noted to Art 1, at **[5.246]**.

[5.382]
Article 132
Exclusion and objection

1. Examiners and members of the Divisions set up within the Office or of the Boards of Appeal may not take part in any proceedings if they have any personal interest therein, or if they have previously been involved as representatives of one of the parties. Two of the three members of an Opposition Division shall not have taken part in examining the application. Members of the Cancellation Divisions may not take part in any proceedings if they have participated in the final decision on the case in the proceedings for registration or opposition proceedings. Members of the Boards of Appeal may not take part in appeal proceedings if they participated in the decision under appeal.

2. If, for one of the reasons mentioned in paragraph 1 or for any other reason, a member of a Division or of a Board of Appeal considers that he should not take part in any proceedings, he shall inform the Division or Board accordingly.

3. Examiners and members of the Divisions or of a Board of Appeal may be objected to by any party for one of the reasons mentioned in paragraph 1, or if suspected of partiality. An objection shall not be admissible if, while being aware of a reason for objection, the party has taken a procedural step. No objection may be based upon the nationality of examiners or members.

4. The Divisions and the Boards of Appeal shall decide as to the action to be taken in the cases specified in paragraphs 2 and 3 without the participation of the member concerned. For the purposes of taking this decision the member who withdraws or has been objected to shall be replaced in the Division or Board of Appeal by his alternate.

NOTES

Repealed as noted to Art 1, at **[5.246]**.

SECTION 5
BUDGET AND FINANCIAL CONTROL

[5.383]
Article 133
Budget Committee

1. A Budget Committee is hereby set up, attached to the Office. The Budget Committee shall have the powers assigned to it in this Section and in Article 39(4).

2. Articles 121(6), 122, 123 and 124(1) to (4), (6) and (7) shall apply to the Budget Committee mutatis mutandis.

3. The Budget Committee shall take its decisions by a simple majority of the representatives of the Member States. However, a majority of three-quarters of the representatives of the Member States shall be required for the decisions which the Budget Committee is empowered to take under Articles 39(4), 135(3) and 138. In both cases each Member State shall have one vote.

NOTES

Repealed as noted to Art 1, at **[5.246]**.

[5.384]

Article 134

Budget

1. Estimates of all the Office's revenue and expenditure shall be prepared for each financial year and shall be shown in the Office's budget, and each financial year shall correspond with the calendar year.

2. The revenue and expenditure shown in the budget shall be in balance.

[3. Revenue shall comprise, without prejudice to other types of income, total fees payable under the fees regulations, total fees payable under the Madrid Protocol referred to in Article 140 of this Regulation for an international registration designating the European Communities and other payments made to Contracting Parties to the Madrid Protocol, total fees payable under the Geneva Act referred to in Article 106c of Regulation (EC) No 6/2002 for an international registration designating the European Community and other payments made to Contracting Parties to the Geneva Act, and, to the extend necessary, a subsidy entered against a specific heading of the general budget of the European Communities, Commission section.]

NOTES

Repealed as noted to Art 1, at **[5.246]**.

Para 3: substituted by Council Regulation 1891/2006/EC, Art 1.

[5.385]

Article 135

Preparation of the budget

1. The President shall draw up each year an estimate of the Office's revenue and expenditure for the following year and shall send it to the Budget Committee not later than 31 March in each year, together with a list of posts.

2. Should the budget estimates provide for a Community subsidy, the Budget Committee all immediately forward the estimate to the Commission, which shall forward it to the budget authority of the Communities. The Commission may attach an opinion on the estimate along with an alternative estimate.

3. The Budget Committee shall adopt the budget, which shall include the Office's list of posts. Should the budget estimates contain a subsidy from the general budget of the Communities, the Office's budget shall, if necessary, be adjusted.

NOTES

Repealed as noted to Art 1, at **[5.246]**.

[5.386]

[Article 136

Audit and control

1. An internal audit function shall be set up within the Office, to be performed in compliance with the relevant international standards. The internal auditor, appointed by the President shall be responsible to him for verifying the proper operation of budget implementation systems and procedures of the Office.

2. The internal auditor shall advise the President on dealing with the risks, by issuing independent opinions on the quality of management and control systems and by issuing recommendations for improving the conditions of implementation of operations and promoting sound financial management.

3. The responsibility for putting in place internal control systems and procedures suitable for carrying out his tasks shall lie with the authorising officer.]

NOTES

Substituted by Council Regulation 1653/2003/EC, Art 1(2).

Repealed as noted to Art 1, at **[5.246]**.

[5.387]
Article 137
Auditing of accounts
1. Not later than 31 March in each year the President shall transmit to the Commission, the European Parliament, the Budget Committee and the Court of Auditors accounts of the Office's total revenue and expenditure for the preceding financial year. The Court of Auditors shall examine them in accordance with Article 188c of the Treaty.
2. The Budget Committee shall give a discharge to the President of the Office in respect of the implementation of the budget.

NOTES
Repealed as noted to Art 1, at **[5.246]**.

[5.388]
Article 138
Financial provisions
The Budget Committee shall, after consulting the Court of Auditors of the European Communities and the Commission, adopt internal financial provisions specifying, in particular, the procedure for establishing and implementing the Office's budget. As far as is compatible with the particular nature of the Office, the financial provisions shall be based on the financial regulations adopted for other bodies set up by the Community.

NOTES
Repealed as noted to Art 1, at **[5.246]**.

[5.389]
Article 139
Fees regulations
1. The fees regulations shall determine in particular the amounts of the fees and the ways in which they are to be paid.
2. The amounts of the fees shall be fixed at such a level as to ensure that the revenue in respect thereof is in principle sufficient for the budget of the Office to be balanced.
3. The fees regulations shall be adopted and amended in accordance with the procedure laid down in [Article 158].

NOTES
Repealed as noted to Art 1, at **[5.246]**.
Para 3: words in square brackets substituted by Council Regulation 1992/2003/EC, Art 1(7).

[TITLE XIII
INTERNATIONAL REGISTRATION OF MARKS

SECTION 1
GENERAL PROVISIONS

NOTES
Title XIII (Arts 140–156) inserted by Council Regulation 1992/2003/EC, Art 1(3).

[5.390]
Article 140
Application of provisions
Unless otherwise specified in this title, this Regulation and any regulations implementing this Regulation adopted pursuant to Article 158 shall apply to applications for international registrations under the Protocol relating to the Madrid Agreement concerning the international registration of marks, adopted at Madrid on 27 June 1989 (hereafter referred to as 'international applications' and 'the Madrid Protocol' respectively), based on an application for a Community trade mark or on a Community trade mark and to registrations of marks in the international register maintained by the International Bureau of the World Intellectual Property Organisation (hereafter referred to as 'international registrations' and 'the International Bureau', respectively) designating the European Community.]

NOTES
Title XIII (Arts 140–156) inserted by Council Regulation 1992/2003/EC, Art 1(3).
Repealed as noted to Art 1, at **[5.246]**.

[SECTION 2
International Registration On the Basis of Applications for a Community Trade Mark and of Community Trade Marks

[5.391]
Article 141
Filing of an international application
1. International applications pursuant to Article 3 of the Madrid Protocol based on an application for a Community trade mark or on a Community trade mark shall be filed at the Office.
2. Where an international application is filed before the mark on which the international registration is to be based has been registered as a Community trade mark, the applicant for the international registration must indicate whether the international registration is to be based on a Community trade mark application or registration. Where the international registration is to be based on a Community trade mark once it is registered, the international application shall be deemed to have been received at the Office on the date of registration of the Community trade mark.]

NOTES
Inserted as noted to Art 140, at **[5.390]**.
Repealed as noted to Art 1, at **[5.246]**.

[5.392]
[Article 142
Form and contents of the international application
1. The international application shall be filed in one of the official languages of the European Community, using a form provided by the Office. Unless otherwise specified by the applicant on that form when he files the international application, the Office shall correspond with the applicant in the language of filing in a standard form.
2. If the international application is filed in a language which is not one of the languages allowed under the Madrid Protocol, the applicant must indicate a second language from among those languages. This shall be the language in which the Office submits the international application to the International Bureau.
3. Where the international application is filed in a language other than one of the languages allowed under the Madrid Protocol for the filing of international applications, the applicant may provide a translation of the list of goods or services in the language in which the international application is to be submitted to the International Bureau pursuant to paragraph 2.
4. The Office shall forward the international application to the International Bureau as soon as possible.
5. The filing of an international application shall be subject to the payment of a fee to the Office. In the cases referred to in the second sentence of Article 141(2), the fee shall be due on the date of registration of the Community trade mark. The application shall be deemed not to have been filed until the required fee has been paid.
6. The international application must fulfil the relevant conditions laid down in the Implementing Regulation referred to in Article 157.]

NOTES
Inserted as noted to Art 140, at **[5.390]**.
Repealed as noted to Art 1, at **[5.246]**.

[5.393]
[Article 143
Recordal in the files and in the Register
1. The date and number of an international registration based on a Community trade mark application, shall be recorded in the files of that application. When the application results in a Community trade mark, the date and number of the international registration shall be entered in the register.
2. The date and number of an international registration based on a Community trade mark shall be entered in the Register.]

NOTES
Inserted as noted to Art 140, at **[5.390]**.
Repealed as noted to Art 1, at **[5.246]**.

[5.394]
[Article 144
Request for territorial extension subsequent to the international registration
A request for territorial extension made subsequent to the international registration pursuant to Article 3ter(2) of the Madrid Protocol may be filed through the intermediary of the Office. The request must be filed in the language in which the international application was filed pursuant to Article 142.]

NOTES
Inserted as noted to Art 140, at **[5.390]**.
Repealed as noted to Art 1, at **[5.246]**.

[5.395]
[Article 145
International fees
Any fees payable to the International Bureau under the Madrid Protocol shall be paid direct to the International Bureau.]

NOTES
Inserted as noted to Art 140, at **[5.390]**.
Repealed as noted to Art 1, at **[5.246]**.

[SECTION 3
INTERNATIONAL REGISTRATIONS DESIGNATING THE EUROPEAN COMMUNITY

[5.396]
Article 146
Effects of international registrations designating the European Community
1. An international registration designating the European Community shall, from the date of its registration pursuant to Article 3(4) of the Madrid Protocol or from the date of the subsequent designation of the European Community pursuant to Article 3ter(2) of the Madrid Protocol, have the same effect as an application for a Community trade mark.
2. If no refusal has been notified in accordance with Article 5(1) and (2) of the Madrid Protocol or if any such refusal has been withdrawn, the international registration of a mark designating the European Community shall, from the date referred to in paragraph 1, have the same effect as the registration of a mark as a Community trade mark.
3. For the purposes of applying Article 9(3), publication of the particulars of the international registration designating the European Community pursuant to Article 147(1) shall take the place of publication of a Community trade mark application, and publication pursuant to Article 147(2) shall take the place of publication of the registration of a Community trade mark.]

NOTES
Inserted as noted to Art 140, at **[5.390]**.
Repealed as noted to Art 1, at **[5.246]**.

[5.397]
[Article 147
Publication
1. The Office shall publish the date of registration of a mark designating the European Community pursuant to Article 3(4) of the Madrid Protocol or the date of the subsequent designation of the European Community pursuant to Article 3ter(2) of the Madrid Protocol, the language of filing of the international application and the second language indicated by the applicant, the number of the international registration and the date of publication of such registration in the Gazette published by the International Bureau, a reproduction of the mark and the numbers of the classes of the goods or services in respect of which protection is claimed.
2. If no refusal of protection of an international registration designating the European Community has been notified in accordance with Article 5(1) and (2) of the Madrid Protocol or if any such refusal has been withdrawn, the Office shall publish this fact, together with the number of the international registration and, where applicable, the date of publication of such registration in the Gazette published by the International Bureau.]

NOTES
Inserted as noted to Art 140, at **[5.390]**.
Repealed as noted to Art 1, at **[5.246]**.

[5.398]
[Article 148
Seniority
1. The applicant for an international registration designating the European Community may claim, in the international application, the seniority of an earlier trade mark registered in a Member State, including a trade mark registered in the Benelux countries, or registered under international arrangements having effect in a Member State, as provided for in Article 34.
2. The holder of an international registration designating the European Community may, as from the date of publication of the effects of such registration pursuant to Article 147(2), claim at the Office the seniority of an earlier trade mark registered in a Member State, including a trade mark

registered in the Benelux countries, or registered under international arrangements having effect in a Member State, as provided for in Article 35. The Office shall notify the International Bureau accordingly.]

NOTES

Inserted as noted to Art 140, at **[5.390]**.
Repealed as noted to Art 1, at **[5.246]**.

[5.399]

[Article 149

Examination as to absolute grounds for refusal

1. International registrations designating the European Community shall be subject to examination as to absolute grounds for refusal in the same way as applications for Community trade marks.

2. Protection of an international registration shall not be refused before the holder of the international registration has been allowed the opportunity to renounce or limit the protection in respect of the European Community or of submitting his observations.

3. Refusal of protection shall take the place of refusal of a Community trade mark application.

4. Where protection of an international registration is refused by a decision under this Article which has become final or where the holder of the international registration has renounced the protection in respect of the European Community pursuant to paragraph 2, the Office shall refund the holder of the international registration a part of the individual fee to be laid down in the implementing Regulation.]

NOTES

Inserted as noted to Art 140, at **[5.390]**.
Repealed as noted to Art 1, at **[5.246]**.

[5.400]

[Article 150

Search

1. Once the Office has received a notification of an international registration designating the European Community, it shall draw up a Community search report as provided for in Article 39(1).

2. As soon as the Office has received a notification of an international registration designating the European Community, the Office shall transmit a copy thereof to the central industrial property office of each Member State which has informed the Office of its decision to operate a search in its own register of trade marks as provided for in Article 39(2).

[3. Article 39(3)–(6) shall apply mutatis mutandis.]

4. The Office shall inform the proprietors of any earlier Community trade marks or Community trade mark applications cited in the Community search report of the publication of the international registration designating the European Community as provided for in Article 147(1).]

NOTES

Inserted as noted to Art 140, at **[5.390]**.
Repealed as noted to Art 1, at **[5.246]**.
Para 3: substituted by Council Regulation 422/2004/EC, Art 1(37).

[5.401]

[Article 151

Opposition

1. International registration designating the European Community shall be subject to opposition in the same way as published Community trade mark applications.

2. Notice of opposition shall be filed within a period of three months which shall begin six months following the date of the publication pursuant to Article 147(1). The opposition shall not be treated as duly entered until the opposition fee has been paid.

3. Refusal of protection shall take the place of refusal of a Community trade mark application.

4. Where protection of an international registration is refused by a decision under this Article which has become final or where the holder of the international registration has renounced the protection in respect of the European Community prior to a decision under this Article which has become final, the Office shall refund the holder of the international registration a part of the individual fee to be laid down in the implementing Regulation.]

NOTES

Inserted as noted to Art 140, at **[5.390]**.
Repealed as noted to Art 1, at **[5.246]**.

[5.402]
[Article 152
Replacement of a Community trade mark by an international registration
The Office shall, upon request, enter a notice in the Register that a Community trade mark is deemed to have been replaced by an international registration in accordance with Article 4bis of the Madrid Protocol.]

NOTES
Inserted as noted to Art 140, at **[5.390]**.
Repealed as noted to Art 1, at **[5.246]**.

[5.403]
[Article 153
Invalidation of the effects of an international registration
1. The effects of an international registration designating the European Community may be declared invalid.
2. The application for invalidation of the effects of an international registration designating the European Community shall take the place of an application for a declaration of revocation as provided for in Article 50 or for invalidation as provided for in Article 51 or Article 52.]

NOTES
Inserted as noted to Art 140, at **[5.390]**.
Repealed as noted to Art 1, at **[5.246]**.

[5.404]
[Article 154
Conversion of a designation of the European Community through an international registration into a national trade mark application or into a designation of Member States
1. Where a designation of the European Community through an international registration has been refused or ceases to have effect, the holder of the international registration may request the conversion of the designation of the European Community—
(a) into a national trade mark application pursuant to Articles 108 to 110 or
(b) into a designation of a Member State party to the Madrid Protocol or the Madrid Agreement concerning the international registration of marks, adopted at Madrid on 14 April 1891, as revised and amended (hereafter referred to as the Madrid Agreement), provided that on the date when conversion was requested it was possible to have designated that Member State directly under the Madrid Protocol or the Madrid Agreement. Articles 108 to 110 shall apply.
2. The national trade mark application or the designation of a Member State party to the Madrid Protocol or the Madrid Agreement resulting from the conversion of the designation of the European Community through an international registration shall enjoy, in respect of the Member State concerned, the date of the international registration pursuant to Article 3(4) of the Madrid Protocol or the date of the extension to the European Community pursuant to Article 3ter(2) of the Madrid Protocol if the latter was made subsequently to the international registration, or the date of priority of that registration and, where appropriate, the seniority of a trade mark of that State claimed under Article 148.
3. The request for conversion shall be published.]

NOTES
Inserted as noted to Art 140, at **[5.390]**.
Repealed as noted to Art 1, at **[5.246]**.

[5.405]
[Article 155
Use of a mark subject of an international registration
For the purposes of applying Article 15(1), Article 43(2), Article 50(1)(a) and Article 56(2), the date of publication pursuant to Article 147(2) shall take the place of the date of registration for the purpose of establishing the date as from which the mark which is the subject of an international registration designating the European Community must be put to genuine use in the Community.]

NOTES
Inserted as noted to Art 140, at **[5.390]**.
Repealed as noted to Art 1, at **[5.246]**.

[5.406]
[Article 156
Transformation
1. Subject to paragraph 2, the provisions applicable to Community trade mark applications shall apply mutatis mutandis to applications for transformation of an international registration into a Community trade mark application pursuant to Article 9 quinquies of the Madrid Protocol.

2. When the application for transformation relates to an international registration designating the European Community the particulars of which have been published pursuant to Article 147(2), Articles 38 to 43 shall not apply.]

NOTES

Inserted as noted to Art 140, at **[5.390]**.
Repealed as noted to Art 1, at **[5.246]**.

TITLE [XIV]
FINAL PROVISIONS

NOTES

Title renumbered as "Title XIV" by Council Regulation 1992/2003/EC, Art 1(4). For new Title XIII see note preceding Art 140, at **[5.390]**.

[5.407]
Article [157]
Community implementing provisions

1. The rules implementing this Regulation shall be adopted in an Implementing Regulation.

2. In addition to the fees provided for in the preceding Articles, fees shall be charged, in accordance with the detailed rules of application laid down in the Implementing Regulation, in the cases listed below—

1.
2. *late payment of the registration fee;*
3. *issue of a copy of the certificate of registration;*
4.
5. *registration of a licence or another right in respect of a Community trade mark;*
6. *registration of a licence or another right in respect of an application for a Community trade mark;*
7. *cancellation of the registration of a licence or another right;*
8. *alteration of a registered Community trade mark;*
9. *issue of an extract from the Register;*
10. *inspection of the files;*
11. *issue of copies of file documents;*
12. *issue of certified copies of the application;*
13. *communication of information in a file;*
14. *review of the determination of the procedural costs to be refunded.*

3. The Implementing Regulation and the rules of procedure of the Boards of Appeal shall be adopted and amended in accordance with the procedure laid down in [Article 158].

NOTES

Renumbered as "Article 157" by Council Regulation 1992/2003/EC, Art 1(5).
Repealed as noted to Art 1, at **[5.246]**.
Para 2: sub-paras 1, 4 repealed by Council Regulation 422/2004/EC, Art 1(38).
Para 3: words in square brackets substituted by Council Regulation 1992/2003/EC, Art 1(7).

[5.408]
[Article [158]
Establishment of a committee and procedure for the adoption of implementing regulations

1. The Commission shall be assisted by a committee referred to as the Committee on Fees, Implementation Rules and the Procedure of the Boards of Appeal of the Office for Harmonisation in the Internal Market (trade marks and designs).

2. Where reference is made to this Article, Articles 5 and 7 of Decision 1999/468/EC (118) shall apply.

The period laid down in Article 5(6) of Decision 1999/468/EC shall be set at three months.

3. The committee shall adopt its rules of procedure.]

NOTES

Substituted by Council Regulation 807/2003/EC, Annex III, para 48.
Renumbered as "Article 158" by Council Regulation 1992/2003/EC, Art 1(5).
Repealed as noted to Art 1, at **[5.246]**.

[5.409]
Article [159]
Compatibility with other Community legal provisions

This Regulation shall not affect Council Regulation (EEC) No 2081/92 on the protection of geographical indications and designations of origin for agricultural products and foodstuffs[1] of 14 July 1992, and in particular Article 14 thereof.

NOTES

Renumbered as "Article 159" by Council Regulation 1992/2003/EC, Art 1(6).
Repealed as noted to Art 1, at **[5.246]**.

[1] OJ L208, 24.7.1992, p 1.

[5.410]

[Article [159a]

Provisions relating to the enlargement of the Community

[1. As from the date of accession of Bulgaria, the Czech Republic, Estonia, Cyprus, Latvia, Lithuania, Hungary, Malta, Poland, Romania, Slovenia and Slovakia (hereinafter referred to as "new Member State(s)"), a Community trade mark registered or applied for pursuant to this Regulation before the respective date of accession shall be extended to the territory of those Member States in order to have equal effect throughout the Community.]

2. The registration of a Community trade mark which is under application at the date of accession may not be refused on the basis of any of the absolute grounds for refusal listed in Article 7(1), if these grounds became applicable merely because of the accession of a new Member State.

3. Where an application for the registration of a Community trade mark has been filed during the six months prior to the date of accession, notice of opposition may be given pursuant to Article 42 where an earlier trade mark or another earlier right within the meaning of Article 8 was acquired in a new Member State prior to accession, provided that it was acquired in good faith and that the filing date or, where applicable, the priority date or the date of acquisition in the new Member State of the earlier trade mark or other earlier right precedes the filing date or, where applicable, the priority date of the Community

4. A Community trade mark as referred to in paragraph 1 may not be declared invalid—

- *pursuant to Article 51 if the grounds for invalidity became applicable merely because of the accession of a new Member State,*
- *pursuant to Article 52(1) and (2) if the earlier national right was registered, applied for or acquired in a new Member State prior to the date of accession.*

5. The use of a Community trade mark as referred to in paragraph 1 may be prohibited pursuant to Articles 106 and 107, if the earlier trade mark or other earlier right was registered, applied for or acquired in good faith in the new Member State prior to the date of accession of that State; or, where applicable, has a priority date prior to the date of accession of that State.]

NOTES

Article inserted as Art 142A by AA5, Annex II(4)(C)(I).
Renumbered as "Article 159a" by Council Regulation 422/2004/EC, Art 1(36).
Repealed as noted to Art 1, at **[5.246]**.
Para 1: substituted by the Treaty concerning the accession of the Republic of Bulgaria and Romania, Annex III(1)(I).

[5.411]

Article [160]

Entry into force

1. This Regulation shall enter into force on the 60th day following that of its publication in the Official Journal of the European Communities.

2. The Member States shall within three years following entry into force of this Regulation take the necessary measures for the purpose of implementing Articles 91 and 110 hereof and shall forthwith inform the Commission of those measures.

3. Applications for Community trade marks may be filed at the Office from the date fixed by the Administrative Board on the recommendation of the President of the Office.

4. Applications for Community trade marks filed within three months before the date referred to in paragraph 3 shall be deemed to have been filed on that date.

This Regulation shall be binding in its entirety and directly applicable in all Member States.

NOTES

Renumbered as "Article 160" by Council Regulation 1992/2003/EC, Art 1(5).
Repealed as noted to Art 1 at **[5.246]**.

[5.412]

Statement by the Council and the Commission on the seat of the Office for Harmonisation in the Internal Market (trade marks and designs)[1]

'In adopting the Regulation on the Community Trade Mark, the Council and the Commission note—

- *that the representatives of the Governments of the Member States, meeting at Head of State and Government level on 29 October 1993, decided that the Office for Harmonisation in the Internal Market (trade marks and designs) should have its seat in Spain, in a town to be determined by the Spanish Government;*
- *that the Spanish Government has designated Alicante as the seat of the Office.'*

NOTES

Repealed as noted to Art 1 at **[5.246]**.

[1] Date of publication in OJ: OJ L11, 14.1.1994, p 36.

COMMISSION REGULATION

(2868/95/EC)

of 13 December 1995

implementing Council Regulation (EC) No 40/94 on the Community trade mark

NOTES

Date of publication in OJ: OJ L303, 15.12.1995, p 1.

THE COMMISSION OF THE EUROPEAN COMMUNITIES,

Having regard to the Treaty establishing the European Community,

Having regard to Council Regulation (EC) No 40/94 of 20 December 1993 on the Community trade mark[1] as amended by Regulation (EC) No 3288/94,[2] and in particular Article 140 thereof,

Whereas Regulation (EC) No 40/94 (hereinafter the 'Regulation') creates a new trade mark system allowing a trade mark having effect throughout the Community to be obtained on the basis of an application to the Office for Harmonisation in the Internal Market (trade marks and designs) ('the Office');

Whereas for this purpose, the Regulation contains the necessary provisions for a procedure leading to the registration of a Community trade mark, as well as for the administration of Community trade marks, for appeals against decisions of the Office and for proceedings for the revocation or invalidation of a Community trade mark;

Whereas Article 140 of the Regulation provides that the rules implementing the Regulation shall be adopted in an implementing regulation;

Whereas the implementing regulation is to be adopted in accordance with the procedure laid down in Article 141 of the Regulation;

Whereas this implementing regulation therefore lays down the rules necessary for implementing the provisions of the Regulation on the Community trade mark;

Whereas these rules should ensure the smooth and efficient operating of trade mark proceedings before the Office;

Whereas in accordance with Article 116(1) of the Regulation, all the elements of the application for a Community trade mark specified in its Article 26(1) as well as any other information the publication of which is prescribed by this implementing regulation should be published in all the official languages of the Community;

Whereas, however, it is not appropriate for the trade mark itself, names, addresses, dates and any other similar data to be translated and published in all the official languages of the Community;

Whereas the Office should make available standard forms for proceedings before the Office in all official languages of the Community;

Whereas the measures envisaged in this Regulation are in accordance with the opinion of the Committee established under Article 141 of the Regulation,

NOTES

[1] OJ L11, 14.1.1994, p 1.

[2] OJ L349, 31.12.1994, p 83.

HAS ADOPTED THIS REGULATION—

[5.413]
Article 1

The rules implementing the Regulation shall be as follows—

TITLE I
APPLICATION PROCEDURE

[5.414]
Rule 1
Content of the application

(1) The application for a Community trade mark shall contain—

(a) a request for registration of the mark as a Community trade mark,

[(b) the name, address and nationality of the applicant and the State in which he is domiciled or has his seat or an establishment. Names of natural persons shall be indicated by the persons family name and given name(s). Names of legal entities, as well as bodies falling under

Article 3 of the Regulation, shall be indicated by their official designation and include the legal form of the entity, which may be abbreviated in a customary manner. The telephone numbers, fax numbers, electronic mail address and details of other data communications links under which the applicant accepts to receive communications may be given. Only one address shall, in principle, be indicated for each applicant. Where several addresses are indicated, only the address mentioned first shall be taken into account, except where the applicant designates one of the addresses as an address for service;]

(c) a list of the goods and services for which the trade mark is to be registered, in accordance with Rule 2[, or a reference to the list of the goods and services of a previous Community trade mark application;]

(d) a representation of the mark in accordance with Rule 3;

(e) if the applicant has appointed a representative, his name and the address of his place of business in accordance with point (b); if the representative has more than one business address or if there are two or more representatives with different business addresses, the application shall indicate which address shall be used as an address for service; where such an indication is not made, only the first-mentioned address shall be taken into account as an address for service;

(f) where the priority of a previous application is claimed pursuant to Article 30 of the Regulation, a declaration to that effect, stating the date on which and the country in or for which the previous application was filed;

(g) where exhibition priority is claimed pursuant to Article 33 of the Regulation, a declaration to that effect, stating the name of the exhibition and the date of the first display of the goods or services;

(h) where the seniority of one or more earlier trade marks, registered in a Member State, including a trade mark registered in the Benelux countries or registered under international arrangements having effect in a Member State (hereinafter referred to as 'earlier registered trade marks, as referred to in Article 34 of the Regulation') is claimed pursuant to Article 34 of the Regulation, a declaration to that effect, stating the Member State or Member States in or for which the earlier mark is registered, the date from which the relevant registration was effective, the number of the relevant registration, and the goods and services for which the mark is registered;

(i) where applicable, a statement that the application is for registration of a Community collective mark pursuant to Article 64 of the Regulation;

(j) specification of the language in which the application has been filed, and of the second language pursuant to Article 115(3) of the Regulation;

[(k) the signature of the applicant or his representative in accordance with Rule 79;]

[(l) where applicable, the request of a search report referred to in Article 39(2) of the Regulation].

(2) The application for a Community collective mark may include the regulations governing its use.

(3) . . .

(4) If there is more than one applicant, the application may contain the appointment of one applicant or representative as common representative.

NOTES

Para (1): sub-paras (b), (k) substituted, words in square brackets in sub-para (c) added, and sub-para (l) added, by Commission Regulation 1041/2005/EC, Art 1(1).

Para (3): repealed by European Parliament and Council Regulation 2015/2424/EU, Art 2(1).

Rule 2 (*Repealed by European Parliament and Council Regulation 2015/2424/EU, Art 2(2).*)

[5.415]
Rule 3
Representation of the mark

(1) If the applicant does not wish to claim any special graphic feature or colour, the mark shall be reproduced in normal script, as for example, by typing the letters, numerals and signs in the application. The use of small letters and capital letters shall be permitted and shall be followed accordingly in publications of the mark and in the registration by the Office.

[(2) In cases other than those referred to in paragraph 1 and save where the application is filed by electronic means, the mark shall be reproduced on a sheet of paper separate from the sheet on which the text of the application appears. The sheet on which the mark is reproduced shall not exceed DIN A4 size (29,7 cm high, 21 cm wide) and the space used for the reproduction (type-area) shall not be larger than 26,2 cm × 17 cm. A margin of at least 2,5 cm shall be left on the left-hand side. Where it is not obvious, the correct position of the mark shall be indicated by adding the word "top" to each reproduction. The reproduction of the mark shall be of such quality as to enable it to be reduced or enlarged to a size not more than 8 cm wide by 16 cm high for publication in the Community Trade Mark Bulletin.]

(3) In cases to which paragraph 2 applies, the application shall contain an indication to that effect. The application may contain a description of the mark.

(4) Where registration of a three-dimensional mark is applied for, the application shall contain an indication to that effect. The representation shall consist of a photographic reproduction or a graphic representation of the mark. The representation may contain up to six different perspectives of the mark.

[(5) Where registration in colour is applied for, the representation of the mark under paragraph 2 shall consist of the colour reproduction of the mark. The colours making up the mark shall also be indicated in words and a reference to a recognized colour code may be added.

(6) Where registration of a sound mark is applied for, the representation of the trade mark shall consist of a graphical representation of the sound, in particular a musical notation; where the application is filed through electronic means, it may be accompanied by an electronic file containing the sound. The President of the Office shall determine the formats and maximum size of the electronic file.]

NOTES

Paras (2), (5), (6): substituted by Commission Regulation 1041/2005/EC, Art 1(2).

Rules 4, 5, 5a *(Repealed by European Parliament and Council Regulation 2015/2424/EU, Art 2(3)–(5) (rule 5a was originally inserted by Commission Regulation 1041/2005/EC, Art 1(4)).)*

[5.416]
Rule 6
Claiming priority

(1) Where the priority of one or more previous applications pursuant to Article 30 of the Regulation is claimed in the application, the applicant shall indicate the file number of the previous application and file a copy of it within three months from the filing date. The copy shall be certified to be an exact copy of the previous application by the authority which received the previous application, and shall be accompanied by a certificate issued by that authority stating the date of filing of the previous application. [If the previous application is a Community trade mark application, the Office shall *ex officio* include a copy of the previous application in the file of the Community trade mark application.]

(2) Where the applicant wishes to claim the priority of one or more previous applications pursuant to Article 30 of the Regulation subsequent to the filing of the application, the declaration of priority, stating the date on which and the country in or for which the previous application was made, shall be submitted within a period of two months from the filing date. The indications and evidence required under paragraph 1 shall be submitted to the Office within a period of three months from receipt of the declaration of priority.

(3) If the language of the previous application is not one of the languages of the Office, the Office shall require the applicant to file, within a period specified by the Office, which shall be not less than three months, a translation of the previous application into one of these languages.

(4) The President of the Office may determine that the evidence to be provided by the applicant may consist of less than is required under paragraph 1, provided that the information required is available to the Office from other sources.

NOTES

Para (1): words in square brackets added by Commission Regulation 1041/2005/EC, Art 1(5).

[5.417]
Rule 7
Exhibition priority

(1) Where the exhibition priority pursuant to Article 33 of the Regulation has been claimed in the application, the applicant shall, within three months from the filing date, file a certificate issued at the exhibition by the authority responsible for the protection of industrial property at the exhibition. This certificate shall declare that the mark was in fact used for the goods or services, and shall state the opening date of the exhibition and, where the first public use did not coincide with the opening date of the exhibition, the date of such first public use. The certificate must be accompanied by an identification of the actual use of the mark, duly certified by the abovementioned authority.

(2) Where the applicant wishes to claim an exhibition priority subsequently to the filing of the application, the declaration of priority, indicating the name of the exhibition and the date of the first display of the goods or services, shall be submitted within a period of two months from the filing date. The indications and evidence required under paragraph 1 shall be submitted to the Office within a period of three months from receipt of the declaration of priority.

[5.418]
Rule 8
Claiming the seniority of a national trade mark

(1) Where the seniority of one or more earlier registered trade marks, as referred to in Article 34 of the Regulation, has been claimed in the application, the applicant shall, within three months from the filing date, submit a copy of the relevant registration. The copy must be certified by the competent authority to be an exact copy of the relevant registration.

[(2) Where the applicant wishes to claim the seniority of one or more earlier registered trade marks as referred to in Article 34 of the Regulation, subsequent to the filing of the application, the declaration of seniority, indicating the Member State or Member States in or for which the mark is registered, the number and the filing date of the relevant registration, and the goods and services for which the mark is registered, shall be submitted within a period of two months from the filing date. The evidence required under paragraph 1 shall be submitted to the Office within a period of three months from receipt of the declaration of seniority.]

(3) The Office shall inform the Benelux Trade Mark Office or the central industrial property office of the Member State concerned of the effective claiming of seniority.

(4) The President of the Office may determine that the evidence to be provided by the applicant may consist of less than is required under paragraph 1, provided that the information required is available to the Office from other sources.

NOTES

Para (2): substituted by Commission Regulation 1041/2005/EC, Art 1(6).

[5.419]
Rule 9
Examination of requirements for a filing date and of formal requirements

(1) If the application fails to meet the requirements for according a filing date because—

(a) the application does not contain—

(i) a request for registration of the mark as a Community trade mark;

(ii) information identifying the applicant;

(iii) a list of the goods and services for which the mark is to be registered;

(iv) a representation of the trade mark; or

(b) the basic fee for the application has not been paid within one month of the filing of the application with the Office or, if the application has been filed with the central industrial property office of a Member State or with the Benelux Trade Mark Office, with that office,

the Office shall notify the applicant that a date of filing cannot be accorded in view of those deficiencies.

(2) If the deficiencies referred to under paragraph 1 are remedied within two months of receipt of the notification, the date on which all the deficiencies are remedied shall determine the date of filing. If the deficiencies are not remedied before the time limit expires, the application shall not be dealt with as a Community trade mark application. Any fees paid shall be refunded.

(3) Where, although a date of filing has been accorded, the examination reveals that—

(a) the requirements of [Rules 1 and 3 and Article 28 of the Regulation] or the other formal requirements governing applications laid down in the Regulation or in these Rules are not complied with;

(b) the full amount of the class fees payable under [Article 26(2) of the Regulation], read in conjunction with Commission Regulation (EC) No 2869/95[1] (hereinafter 'the Fees Regulation') has not been received by the Office;

(c) where priority has been claimed pursuant to Rules 6 and 7, either in the application itself or within two months after the date of filing, the other requirements of the said Rules are not complied with; or

(d) where seniority has been claimed pursuant to Rule 8, either in the application itself or within two months after the date of filing, the other requirements of Rule 8 are not complied with,

the Office shall invite the applicant to remedy the deficiencies noted within such period as it may specify.

(4) If the deficiencies referred to in paragraph 3(a) are not remedied before the time limit expires, the Office shall reject the application.

(5) If the outstanding class fees are not paid before the time limit expires, the application shall be deemed to have been withdrawn, unless it is clear which class or classes the amount paid is intended to cover. In the absence of other criteria to determine which classes are intended to be covered, the Office shall take the classes in the order of the classification. The application shall be deemed to have been withdrawn with regard to those classes for which the class fees have not been paid or have not been paid in full.

(6) If the deficiencies referred to in paragraph 3 concern the claim to priority, the right of priority for the application shall be lost.

(7) If the deficiencies referred to in paragraph 3 concern the claim to seniority, the right of seniority in respect of that application shall be lost.

(8) If the deficiencies referred to in paragraph 3 concern only some of the goods and services, the Office shall refuse the application, or the right of priority or the right of seniority shall be lost, only in so far as those goods and services are concerned.

NOTES

Para (3): words in square brackets substituted by European Parliament and Council Regulation 2015/2424/EU, Art 2(6).

[1] OJ L303, 15.12.1995, p 33.

[5.420]
[Rule 10
Searches by national offices
(1) If the request for a search report referred to in Article 39(2) of the Regulation is not made in the application for a Community trade mark, or if the search fee referred to in [Article 38(2) of the Regulation] is not paid within the time limit for paying the basic application fee, the application shall not be subjected to a search by the central industrial property offices.
(2) An international registration designating the European Community shall not be subjected to a search by the central industrial property offices if the request for a search report pursuant to Article 39(2) of the Regulation is not made to the Office within one month starting with the date on which the International Bureau notifies the international registration to the Office, or if the search fee is not paid within the same period.]

NOTES
Substituted by Commission Regulation 1041/2005/EC, Art 1(7).
Para (1): words in square brackets substituted by European Parliament and Council Regulation 2015/2424/EU, Art 2(6a).

[5.421]
Rule 11
Examination as to absolute grounds for refusal
(1) Where, pursuant to Article 7 of the Regulation, the trade mark may not be registered for all or any part of the goods or services applied for, the office shall notify the applicant of the grounds for refusing registration. The Office shall specify a period within which the applicant may withdraw or amend the application or submit his observations.
(2) . . .
(3) Where the applicant fails to overcome the ground for refusing registration or to comply with the condition laid down in paragraph 2 within the time limit, the Office shall refuse the application in whole or in part.

NOTES
Para (2): repealed by European Parliament and Council Regulation 2015/2424/EU, Art 2(7).

[5.422]
Rule 12
Publication of the application
The publication of the application shall contain—
(a) the applicant's name and address;
(b) where applicable, the name and business address of the representative appointed by the applicant other than a representative falling within the first sentence of Article 88(3) of the Regulation; if there is more than one representative with the same business address, only the name and business address of the first-named representative shall be published and it shall be followed by the words 'and others'; if there are two or more representatives with different business addresses, only the address for service determined pursuant to Rule 1(1)(e) shall be published; where an association of representatives is appointed under Rule 76(9), only the name and business address of the association shall be published;
[(c) the reproduction of the mark, together with the elements and descriptions referred to in Rule 3; where the reproduction of the mark is in colour or contains colours, the publication shall be in colour and shall indicate the colour or colours making up the mark, as well as, where applicable, the colour code indicated;]
(d) the list of goods and services, grouped according to the classes of the Nice classification, each group being preceded by the number of the class of that classification to which that group of goods or services belongs, and presented in the order of the classes of that classification;
(e) the date of filing and the file number;
(f) where applicable, particulars of the claim of priority pursuant to Article 30 of the Regulation;
(g) where applicable, particulars of the claim of exhibition priority pursuant to Article 33 of the Regulation;
(h) where applicable, particulars of the claim of seniority pursuant to Article 34 of the Regulation;
(i) where applicable, a statement that the mark has become distinctive in consequence of the use which has been made of it, pursuant to Article 7(3) of the Regulation;
(j) where applicable, a statement that the application is for a Community collective mark;
(k) . . .
(l) the language in which the application was filed and the second language which the applicant has indicated pursuant to Article 115(3) of the Regulation;
[(m) where applicable, a statement that the application results from a transformation of an international registration designating the European Community pursuant to Article 156 of the Regulation, together with the date of the international registration pursuant to

Article 3(4) of the Madrid Protocol or the date on which the territorial extension to the European Community made subsequently to the international registration pursuant to Article 3*ter* (2) of the Madrid Protocol was recorded and, where applicable, the date of priority of the international registration].

NOTES

Para (c) substituted by Commission Regulation 1041/2005/EC, Art 1(8).
Para (k): repealed by European Parliament and Council Regulation 2015/2424/EU, Art 2(8).
Para (m): added by Commission Regulation 782/2004/EC, Art 1(1).

[5.423]
Rule 13
Amendment of the application

(1) An application for amendment of the application under Article 44 of the Regulation shall contain—

(a) the file number of the application;
(b) the name and the address of the applicant in accordance with Rule 1(1)(b);
(c) . . .
(d) the indication of the element of the application to be corrected or amended, and that element in its corrected or amended version;
(e) where the amendment relates to the representation of the mark, a representation of the mark as amended, in accordance with Rule 3.

(2) . . .
(3) If the requirements governing the amendment of the application are not fulfilled, the Office shall communicate the deficiency to the applicant. If the deficiency is not remedied within a period to be specified by the Office, the Office shall reject the application for amendment.
(4) Where the amendment is published pursuant to Article 44(2) of the Regulation, Rules 15 to 22 shall apply *mutatis mutandis.*
(5) A single application for amendment may be made for the amendment of the same element in two or more applications of the same applicant. Where the application for amendment is subject to the payment of a fee, the required fee shall be paid in respect of each application to be amended.
(6) Paragraphs 1 to 5 shall apply *mutatis mutandis* for applications to correct the name or the business address of a representative appointed by the applicant. Such applications shall not be subject to the payment of a fee.

NOTES

Para (1): sub-para (c) repealed by Commission Regulation 1041/2005/EC, Art 1(9).
Para (2): repealed by Commission Regulation 1041/2005/EC, Art 1(9).

[5.424]
[Rule 13a
Division of the application

(1) A declaration of the division of the application pursuant to Article 44a of the Regulation shall contain—

(a) the file number of the application;
(b) the name and address of the applicant in accordance with Rule 1(1)(b);
(c) the list of goods and services which shall form the divisional application, or, where the division into more than one divisional application is sought, the list of goods and services for each divisional application;
(d) the list of goods and services which shall remain in the original application.

(2) Where the Office finds that the requirements laid down in paragraph 1 are not fulfilled or the list of goods and services which shall form the divisional application overlap with the goods and services which shall remain in the original application, it shall invite the applicant to remedy the deficiencies noted within such period as it may specify.

If the deficiencies are not remedied before the time limit expires, the Office shall refuse the declaration of division.

(3) The periods as referred to in Article 44a(2)(b) of the Regulation during which a declaration of division of the application is not admissible shall be—

(a) the period before a date of filing has been accorded;
(b) the period of three months following the publication of the application provided for in Article 42(1) of the Regulation;
(c) . . .

(4) Where the Office finds, that the declaration of division is inadmissible pursuant to Article 44a of the Regulation or pursuant to paragraph 3(a) and (b), it shall refuse the declaration of division.
(5) The Office shall establish a separate file for the divisional application, which shall consist of a complete copy of the file of the original application, including the declaration of division and the correspondence relating thereto. The Office shall assign a new application number to the divisional application.

(6) Where the declaration of division relates to an application which has already been published pursuant to Article 40 of the Regulation, the division shall be published in the Community Trade Marks Bulletin. The divisional application shall be published; the publication shall contain the indications and elements referred to in Rule 12. The publication does not open a new period for the filing of oppositions.]

NOTES

Inserted by Commission Regulation 1041/2005/EC, Art 1(10).
Para (3): sub-para (c) repealed by Commission Regulation 355/2009/EC, Art 2(1).

[5.425]
Rule 14
Correction of mistakes and errors in publications

(1) Where the publication of the application contains a mistake or error attributable to the Office, the Office shall correct the mistake or error acting of its own motion or at the request of the applicant.
(2) Where a request as referred to in paragraph 1 is made by the applicant, Rule 13 shall apply *mutatis mutandis*. The request shall not be subject to the payment of a fee.
(3) The corrections effected under this Rule shall be published.
(4) Article 42(2) of the Regulation and Rules 15 to 22 shall apply *mutatis mutandis* where the correction concerns the list of goods or services or the representation of the mark.

TITLE II
PROCEDURE FOR OPPOSITION AND PROOF OF USE

[5.426]
[Rule 15
Notice of opposition

(1) A notice of opposition may be entered on the basis of one or more earlier marks within the meaning of Article 8(2) of the Regulation (earlier marks) and one and/or more other earlier rights within the meaning of Article 8(4) of the Regulation (earlier rights), provided that the earlier marks or earlier rights all belong to the same proprietor or proprietors. If an earlier mark and/or an earlier right has more than one proprietor (co-ownership), the opposition may be filed by any or all of them.
(2) The notice of opposition shall contain—
- (a) the file number of the application against which opposition is entered and the name of the applicant for the Community trade mark;
- (b) a clear identification of the earlier mark or earlier right on which the opposition is based, namely—
  - (i) where the opposition is based on an earlier mark within the meaning of Article 8(2)(a) or (b) of the Regulation or where the opposition is based on Article 8(3) of the Regulation, the indication of the file number or registration number of the earlier mark, the indication whether the earlier mark is registered or an application for registration, as well as the indication of the Member States including, where applicable, the Benelux, in or for which the earlier mark is protected, or, if applicable, the indication that it is a Community trade mark;
  - (ii) where the opposition is based on a well-known mark within the meaning of Article 8(2)(c) of the Regulation, the indication of the Member State where the mark is well-known and either the indications referred to in point (i) or a representation of the mark;
  - (iii) where the opposition is based on an earlier right within the meaning of Article 8(4), an indication of its kind or nature, a representation of the earlier right, and an indication of whether this earlier right exists in the whole Community or in one or more Member States, and if so, an indication of the Member States;
- (c) the grounds on which the opposition is based, namely a statement to the effect that the respective requirements under Article 8(1), (3), (4) and (5) of the Regulation are fulfilled;
- (d) the filing date and, where available, the registration date and the priority date of the earlier mark, unless it is an unregistered well-known trade mark;
- (e) a representation of the earlier mark as registered or applied for; if the earlier mark is in colour, the representation shall be in colour;
- (f) the goods and services on which the opposition is based;
- (g) where the opposition is based on an earlier mark having a reputation within the meaning of Article 8(5) of the Regulation, an indication of the Member State in which, and the goods and services for which, the mark has a reputation;
- (h) as concerns the opposing party—
  - (i) the name and address of the opposing party in accordance with Rule 1(1)(b);
  - (ii) where the opposing party has appointed a representative, the name and business address of the representative in accordance with Rule 1(1)(e);

(iii) where the opposition is entered by a licensee or by a person who is entitled under the relevant national law to exercise an earlier right, a statement to that effect and indications concerning the authorisation or entitlement to file the opposition.

(3) The notice of opposition may contain—

(a) an indication of the goods and services against which the opposition is directed; in the absence of such an indication the opposition shall be considered to be directed against all of the goods and services of the opposed Community trade mark application;

(b) a reasoned statement setting out the main facts and arguments on which the opposition relies, and evidence to support the opposition.

(4) Where the opposition is based on more than one earlier mark or earlier right, paragraphs 2 and 3 shall apply for each of these rights.]

NOTES

Substituted, together with rr 16, 16a, 17–20, for original rr 15–20, by Commission Regulation 1041/2005/EC, Art 1(11).

[5.427]
[Rule 16
Use of languages in the notice of opposition

(1) The time limit referred to in Article 115(6) of the Regulation within which the opposing party has to file a translation of his opposition shall be one month from the expiry of the opposition period.

(2) Where the opposing party or the applicant, before the date on which the opposition proceedings are deemed to commence pursuant to Rule 18(1), informs the Office that the applicant and the opposing party have agreed on a different language for the opposition proceedings pursuant to Article 115(7) of the Regulation, the opposing party shall, where the notice of opposition has not been filed in that language, file a translation of the notice of opposition in that language within a period of one month from the said date. Where the translation is not filed or filed late, the language of the proceedings shall remain unchanged.]

NOTES

Substituted as noted to r 15 at **[5.426]**.

[5.428]
[Rule 16a
Information of the applicant

Any notice of opposition and any document submitted by the opposing party, as well as any communication addressed to one of the parties by the Office prior to the expiry of the period referred to in Rule 18 shall be sent by the Office to the other party for purposes of informing of the introduction of an opposition.]

NOTES

Substituted as noted to r 15 at **[5.426]**.

[5.429]
[Rule 17
Examination of admissibility

(1) If the opposition fee has not been paid within the opposition period, the opposition shall be deemed not to have been entered. If the opposition fee has been paid after the expiry of the opposition period, it shall be refunded to the opposing party.

(2) If the notice of opposition has not been filed within the opposition period, or if the notice of opposition does not clearly identify the application against which opposition is entered or the earlier mark or the earlier right on which the opposition is based in accordance with Rule 15(2)(a) and (b), or does not contain grounds for opposition in accordance with Rule 15(2)(c), and if those deficiencies have not been remedied before the expiry of the opposition period, the Office shall reject the opposition as inadmissible.

(3) Where the opposing party does not submit a translation as required under Rule 16(1), the opposition shall be rejected as inadmissible. Where the opposing party submits an incomplete translation, the part of the notice of opposition that has not been translated shall not be taken into account in the examination of admissibility.

(4) If the notice of opposition does not comply with the other provisions of Rule 15, the Office shall inform the opposing party accordingly and shall invite him to remedy the deficiencies noted within a period of two months. If the deficiencies are not remedied before the time limit expires, the Office shall reject the opposition as inadmissible.

(5) Any finding pursuant to paragraph 1 that the notice of opposition is deemed not to have been entered and any decision to reject an opposition as inadmissible under paragraphs 2, 3 and 4 shall be notified to the applicant.]

NOTES

Substituted as noted to r 15 at **[5.426]**.

[5.430]
[Rule 18
Commencement of opposition proceedings

(1) When the opposition is found admissible pursuant to Rule 17, the Office shall send a communication to the parties informing them that the opposition proceedings shall be deemed to commence two months after receipt of the communication. This period may be extended up to a total of 24 months if both parties submit requests for such an extension before the period expires.

(2) If, within the period referred to in paragraph 1, the application is withdrawn or restricted to goods and services against which the opposition is not directed, or the Office is informed about a settlement between the parties, or the application is rejected in parallel proceedings, the opposition proceedings shall be closed.

(3) If, within the period referred to in paragraph 1, the applicant restricts the application by deleting some of the goods and services against which the opposition is directed, the Office shall invite the opposing party to state, within such a period as it may specify, whether he maintains the opposition, and if so, against which of the remaining goods and services. If the opposing party withdraws the opposition in view of the restriction the opposition proceedings shall be closed.

(4) If before expiry of the period referred to in paragraph 1 the opposition proceedings are closed pursuant to paragraphs 2 or 3, no decision on costs shall be taken.

(5) If before expiry of the period referred to in paragraph 1 the opposition proceedings are closed following a withdrawal or restriction of the application or pursuant to paragraph 3, the opposition fee shall be refunded.]

NOTES

Substituted as noted to r 15 at **[5.426]**.

[5.431]
[Rule 19
Substantiation of the opposition

(1) The Office shall give the opposing party the opportunity to present the facts, evidence and arguments in support of his opposition or to complete any facts, evidence or arguments that have already been submitted pursuant to Rule 15(3), within a time limit specified by it and which shall be at least 2 months starting on the date on which the opposition proceedings shall be deemed to commence in accordance with Rule 18(1).

(2) Within the period referred to in paragraph 1, the opposing party shall also file proof of the existence, validity and scope of protection of his earlier mark or earlier right, as well as evidence proving his entitlement to file the opposition. In particular, the opposing party shall provide the following evidence—

- (a) if the opposition is based on a trade mark which is not a Community trade mark, evidence of its filing or registration, by submitting—
  - (i) if the trade mark is not yet registered, a copy of the relevant filing certificate or an equivalent document emanating from the administration with which the trade mark application was filed; or
  - (ii) if the trade mark is registered, a copy of the relevant registration certificate and, as the case may be, of the latest renewal certificate, showing that the term of protection of the trade mark extends beyond the time limit referred to in paragraph 1 and any extension thereof, or equivalent documents emanating from the administration by which the trade mark was registered;
- (b) if the opposition is based on a well-known mark within the meaning of Article 8(2)(c) of the Regulation, evidence showing that this mark is well-known in the relevant territory;
- (c) if the opposition is based on a mark with reputation within the meaning of Article 8(5) of the Regulation, in addition to the evidence referred to in point (a) of this paragraph, evidence showing that the mark has a reputation, as well as evidence or arguments showing that use without due cause of the trade mark applied for would take unfair advantage of, or be detrimental to, the distinctive character or the repute of the earlier trade mark;
- (d) if the opposition is based on an earlier right within the meaning of Article 8(4) of the Regulation, evidence of its acquisition, continued existence and scope of protection of that right;
- (e) if the opposition is based on Article 8(3) of the Regulation, evidence of the opposing party's proprietorship and of the nature of his relationship with the agent or representative.

(3) The information and evidence referred to in paragraphs 1 and 2 shall be in the language of the proceedings or accompanied by a translation. The translation shall be submitted within the time limit specified for submitting the original document.

(4) The Office shall not take into account written submissions or documents, or parts thereof, that have not been submitted, or that have not been translated into the language of the proceedings, within the time limit set by the Office.]

NOTES

Substituted as noted to r 15 at **[5.426]**.

[5.432]
[Rule 20
Examination of the opposition

(1) If until expiry of the period referred to in Rule 19(1) the opposing party has not proven the existence, validity and scope of protection of his earlier mark or earlier right, as well his entitlement to file the opposition, the opposition shall be rejected as unfounded.

(2) If the opposition is not rejected pursuant to paragraph 1, the Office shall communicate the submission of the opposing party to the applicant and shall invite him to file his observations within a period specified by the Office.

(3) If the applicant submits no observations, the Office shall base its ruling on the opposition on the evidence before it.

(4) The observations submitted by the applicant shall be communicated to the opposing party who shall be invited by the Office, if it considers it necessary to do so, to reply within a period specified by the Office.

(5) Rule 18(2) and (3) shall apply *mutatis mutandis* after the date on which the opposition proceedings are deemed to commence.

(6) In appropriate cases, the Office may invite the parties to limit their observations to particular issues, in which case it shall allow the party to raise the other issues at a later stage of the proceedings. In no case shall the Office be required to inform the parties which facts or evidence could be or have not been submitted.

(7) The Office may suspend opposition proceedings—

(a) where the opposition is based on an application for registration pursuant to Article 8(2)(b) of the Regulation until a final decision is taken in that proceeding;

(b) where the opposition is based on an application for registration for a geographical indication or designation of origin under Council Regulation (EEC) No 2081/92[1] until a final decision is taken in that proceeding; or

(c) where a suspension is appropriate under the circumstances.]

NOTES

Substituted as noted to r 15 at **[5.426]**.

[1] OJ L208, 24.7.1992, p 1.

[5.433]
Rule 21
Multiple oppositions

(1) Where a number of oppositions have been entered in respect of the same application for a Community trade mark, the Office may deal with them in one set of proceedings. The Office may subsequently decide to no longer deal with them in this way.

(2) If a preliminary examination of one or more oppositions reveals that the Community trade mark for which an application for registration has been filed is possibly not eligible for registration in respect of some or all of the goods or services for which registration is sought, the Office may suspend the other opposition proceedings. The Office shall inform the remaining opposing parties of any relevant decisions taken during those proceedings which are continued.

(3) Once a decision rejecting the application has become final, the oppositions on which a decision was deferred in accordance with paragraph 2 shall be deemed to have been disposed of and the opposing parties concerned shall be informed accordingly. Such disposition shall be considered to constitute a case which has not proceeded to judgment within the meaning of Article 81(4) of the Regulation.

(4) The Office shall refund 50% of the opposition fee paid by each opposing party whose opposition is deemed to have been disposed of in accordance with paragraphs 1, 2 and 3.

[5.434]
[Rule 22
Proof of use

(1) A request for proof of use pursuant to Article 43(2) or (3) of the Regulation shall be admissible only if the applicant submits such a request within the period specified by the Office pursuant to Rule 20(2).

(2) Where the opposing party has to furnish proof of use or show that there are proper reasons for non-use, the Office shall invite him to provide the proof required within such period as it shall specify. If the opposing party does not provide such proof before the time limit expires, the Office shall reject the opposition.

(3) The indications and evidence for the furnishing of proof of use shall consist of indications concerning the place, time, extent and nature of use of the opposing trade mark for the goods and services in respect of which it is registered and on which the opposition is based, and evidence in support of these indications in accordance with paragraph 4.

(4) The evidence shall be filed in accordance with Rules 79 and 79a and shall, in principle, be confined to the submission of supporting documents and items such as packages, labels, price lists, catalogues, invoices, photographs, newspaper advertisements, and statements in writing as referred to in Article 76(1)(f) of the Regulation.

(5) A request for proof of use may be made with or without submitting at the same time observations on the grounds on which the opposition is based. Such observations may be filed together with the observations in reply to the proof of use.
(6) Where the evidence supplied by the opposing party is not in the language of the opposition proceedings, the Office may require the opposing party to submit a translation of that evidence in that language, within a period specified by the Office.]

NOTES

Substituted by Commission Regulation 1041/2005/EC, Art 1(12).

TITLE III
REGISTRATION PROCEDURE

Rule 23 (*Repealed by European Parliament and Council Regulation 2015/2424/EU, Art 2(8a).*)

[5.435]
Rule 24
Certificate of registration
(1) The Office shall issue to the proprietor of the trade mark a certificate of registration which shall contain the entries in the Register provided for in [Article 87(2) of the Regulation] and a statement to the effect that those entries have been recorded in the Register.
[(2) The Office shall provide certified or uncertified copies of the certificate of registration, upon payment of a fee.]

NOTES

Para (1): words in square brackets substituted by European Parliament and Council Regulation 2015/2424/EU, Art 2(8b).
Para (2): substituted by Commission Regulation 1041/2005/EC, Art 1(13).

[5.436]
Rule 25
Alteration of the registration
(1) An application for alteration of the registration pursuant to Article 48(2) of the Regulation shall contain—
- (a) the registration number;
- (b) the name and the address of the proprietor of the mark in accordance with Rule 1(1)(b);
- (c) . . .
- (d) the indication of the element in the representation of the mark to be altered and that element in its altered version;
- (e) a representation of the mark as altered, in accordance with Rule 3.

(2) The application shall be deemed not to have been filed until the required fee has been paid. If the fee has not been paid or has not been paid in full, the Office shall inform the applicant accordingly.
(3) If the requirements governing the alteration of the registration are not fulfilled, the Office shall communicate the deficiency to the applicant. If the deficiency is not remedied within a period to be specified by the Office, the Office shall reject the application.
(4) Where the registration of the alteration is challenged pursuant to Article 48(3) of the Regulation, the provisions on opposition contained in the Regulation and in these Rules shall apply *mutatis mutandis*.
(5) A single application may be made for the alteration of the same element in two or more registrations of the same proprietor. The required fee shall be paid in respect of each registration to be altered.

NOTES

Para (1): sub-para (c) repealed by Commission Regulation 1041/2005/EC, Art 1(14).

[5.437]
[Rule 25a
Division of a registration
(1) A declaration of the division of a registration pursuant to Article 48a of the Regulation shall contain—
- (a) the registration number;
- (b) the name and address of the proprietor of the trade mark in accordance with Rule 1(1)(b);
- (c) the list of goods and services which shall form the divisional registration, or, where the division into more than one divisional registration is sought, the list of goods and services for each divisional registration;
- (d) the list of goods and services which shall remain in the original registration.

(2) Where the Office finds that the requirements laid down in paragraph 1 are not fulfilled or the list of goods and services which shall form the divisional registration overlap with the goods and services which shall remain in the original registration, it shall invite the applicant to remedy the deficiencies noted within such period as it may specify.

If the deficiencies are not remedied before the time limit expires, the Office shall refuse the declaration of division.
(3) Where the Office finds, that the declaration of division is inadmissible pursuant to Article 48a of the Regulation, it shall refuse the declaration of division.
(4) The Office shall establish a separate file for the divisional registration, which shall consist of a complete copy of the file of the original registration, including the declaration of division and the correspondence relating thereto. The Office shall assign a new registration number to the divisional registration.]

NOTES

Inserted by Commission Regulation 1041/2005/EC, Art 1(15).

[5.438]
Rule 26
Change of the name or address of the proprietor of the Community trade mark or of his registered representative
(1) A change of the name or address of the proprietor of the Community trade mark which is not an alteration of the Community trade mark pursuant to Article 48(2) of the Regulation and which is not the consequence of a whole or partial transfer of the registered mark shall, at the request of the proprietor, be recorded in the register.
(2) An application for the change of the name or address of the proprietor of the registered mark shall contain—
- (a) the registration number of the mark;
- (b) the name and the address of the proprietor of the mark as recorded in the register;
- (c) the indication of the name and address of the proprietor of the mark, as amended, in accordance with Rule 1(1)(e).
- (d) . . .

(3) The application shall not be subject to payment of a fee.
(4) A single application may be made for the change of the name or address in respect of two or more registrations of the same proprietor.
(5) If the requirements governing the recording of a change are not fulfilled, the Office shall communicate the deficiency to the applicant. If the deficiency is not remedied within a period to be specified by the Office, the Office shall reject the application.
(6) Paragraphs 1 to 5 shall apply *mutatis mutandis* to a change of the name or address of the registered representative.
(7) Paragraphs 1 to 6 shall apply *mutatis mutandis* to applications for Community trade marks. The change shall be recorded in the files kept by the Office on the Community trade mark application.

NOTES

Para (2): sub-para (d) repealed by Commission Regulation 1041/2005/EC, Art 1(16).

[5.439]
Rule 27
Correction of mistakes and errors in the register and in the publication of the registration
(1) Where the registration of the mark or the publication of the registration contains a mistake or error attributable to the Office, the Office shall correct the error or mistake of its own motion or at the request of the proprietor.
(2) Where such a request is made by the proprietor, Rule 26 shall apply *mutatis mutandis*. The request shall not be subject to payment of a fee.
(3) The Office shall publish the corrections made under this Rule.

[5.440]
Rule 28
Claiming seniority after registration of the Community trade mark
(1) An application pursuant to Article 35 of the Regulation to obtain the seniority of one or more earlier registered trade marks as referred to in Article 34 of the Regulation, shall contain—
- (a) the registration number of the Community trade mark;
- (b) the name and address of the proprietor of the Community trade mark in accordance with Rule 1(1)(b);
- (c) . . .
- [(d) an indication of the Member State or Member States in or for which the earlier mark is registered, the number and the filing date of the relevant registration, and the goods and services for which the earlier mark is registered;]
- (e) an indication of the goods and services in respect of which seniority is claimed;
- (f) a copy of the relevant registration; the copy must be certified as an exact copy of the relevant registration by the competent authority.

(2) If the requirements governing the claiming of seniority are nor fulfilled, the Office shall communicate the deficiency to the applicant. If the deficiency is not remedied within a period specified by the Office, the Office shall reject the application.

(3) The Office shall inform the Benelux Trade Mark Office or the central industrial property office of the Member State concerned of the effective claiming of seniority.

(4) The President of the Office may determine that the material to be provided by the applicant may consist of less than is required under paragraph 1(f), provided that the information required is available to the Office from other sources.

NOTES

Para (1): sub-para (c) repealed and sub-para (d) substituted by Commission Regulation 1041/2005/EC, Art 1(17).

Rules 29, 30 *((Title IV) Repealed by European Parliament and Council Regulation 2015/2424/EU, Art 2(9).)*

TITLE V
TRANSFER, LICENCES AND OTHER RIGHTS, CHANGES

[5.441]
Rule 31
Transfer

(1) An application for registration of a transfer under Article 17 of the Regulation shall contain—

(a) the registration number of the Community trade mark;
(b) particulars of the new proprietor in accordance with Rule 1(1)(b);
(c) where not all the registered goods or services are included in the transfer, particulars of the registered goods or services to which the transfer relates;
(d) documents duly establishing the transfer in accordance with Article 17(2) and (3) of the Regulation;

(2) The application may contain, where applicable, the name and business address of the representative of the new proprietor, to be set out in accordance with Rule 1(1)(e).

(3), (4) . . .

(5) It shall constitute sufficient proof of transfer under paragraph 1(d)—

(a) that the application for registration of the transfer is signed by the registered proprietor or his representative and by the successor in title or his representative; or,
(b) that the application, if submitted by the successor in title, is accompanied by a declaration, signed by the registered proprietor or his representative, that he agrees to the registration of the successor in title; or
(c) that the application is accompanied by a completed transfer form or document, as specified in Rule 83(1)(d), signed by the registered proprietor or his representative and by the successor in title or his representative.

(6) Where the conditions applicable to the registration of a transfer, as laid down in Article 17(1) to (4) of the Regulation, in paragraphs 1 to 4 above, and in other applicable Rules are not fulfilled, the Office shall notify the applicant of the deficiencies. If the deficiencies are not remedied within a period specified by the Office, it shall reject the application for registration of the transfer.

(7) A single application for registration of a transfer may be submitted for two or more marks, provided that the registered proprietor and the successor in title are the same in each case.

(8) Paragraphs 1 to 7 shall apply *mutatis mutandis* to applications for Community trade marks. The transfer shall be recorded in the files kept by the Office concerning the Community trade mark application.

NOTES

Paras (3), (4): repealed by Commission Regulation 1041/2005/EC, Art 1(19).

[5.442]
Rule 32
Partial Transfers

(1) Where the application for registration of a transfer relates only to some of the goods and services for which the mark is registered, the application shall contain an indication of the goods and services to which the partial transfer relates.

(2) The goods and services in the original registration shall be distributed between the remaining registration and the new registration so that the goods and services in the remaining registration and the new registration shall not overlap.

(3) Rule 31 shall apply *mutatis mutandis* to applications for registrations of a partial transfer.

[(4) The Office shall establish a separate file for the new registration, which shall consist of a complete copy of the file of the original registration, including the application for registration of the partial transfer and the correspondence relating thereto. The Office shall assign a new registration number to the new registration.]

(5) Any application made by the original proprietor pending with regard to the original registration shall be deemed to be pending with regard to the remaining registration and the new registration. Where such application is subject to the payment of fees and these fees have been paid by the original proprietor, the new proprietor shall not be liable to pay any additional fees with regard to such application.

NOTES

Para (4): substituted by Commission Regulation 1041/2005/EC, Art 1(20).

[5.443]
Rule 33
Registration of licences and other rights

[(1) Rule 31(1), (2), (5) and (7) shall apply *mutatis mutandis* to the registration of a licence, of a transfer of a licence, of a right *in rem*, of a transfer of a right *in rem*, of an enforcement measure or of insolvency proceedings, subject to the following—

(a) Rule 31(1)(c) shall not apply in respect of a request for registration of a right *in rem*, of a levy of execution or of insolvency proceedings;

(b) Rule 31(1)(d) and (5) shall not apply where the request was made by the proprietor of the Community trade mark.]

[(2) The application for registration of a licence, a transfer of a licence, a right *in rem*, a transfer of a right *in rem* or an enforcement measure shall not be deemed to have been filed until the required fee has been paid.]

(3) Where the conditions applicable to registration, as laid down in [Articles 19 to 22] of the Regulation, [in paragraph 1 of this Rule and in Rule 34(2)], and the other applicable Rules are not fulfilled, the Office shall notify the applicant of the irregularity. If the irregularity is not corrected within a period specified by the Office, it shall reject the application for registration.

[(4) Paragraphs 1 and 3 shall apply *mutatis mutandis* to applications for Community trade marks. Licences, rights *in rem*, insolvency proceedings and enforcement measures shall be recorded in the files kept by the Office concerning the Community trade mark application.]

NOTES

Paras (1), (2), (4): substituted by Commission Regulation 1041/2005/EC, Art 1(21)(a), (b), (d).
Para (3): words in square brackets substituted by Commission Regulation 1041/2005/EC, Art 1(21)(c).

[5.444]
[Rule 34
Special provisions for the registration of a licence

(1) The application for registration of a licence may contain a request to record the licence in the Register as one or more of the following—

(a) an exclusive licence;

(b) a sub-licence in case where the licence is granted by a licensee whose licence is recorded in the Register;

(c) a licence limited to only a part of the goods or services for which the mark is registered;

(d) a licence limited to part of the Community;

(e) a temporary licence.

(2) Where a request is made to record the licence as a licence pursuant to paragraph 1(c), (d) and (e), the application for registration of a licence shall indicate the goods and services and the part of the Community and the time period for which the licence is granted.]

NOTES

Substituted by Commission Regulation 1041/2005/EC, Art 1(22).

[5.445]
Rule 35
Cancellation or modification of the registration of licences and other rights

(1) A registration effected under Rule 33(1) shall be cancelled at the request of one of the persons concerned.

(2) The application shall contain—

(a) the registration number of the Community trade mark; and

(b) particulars of the right whose registration is to be cancelled.

[(3) The application for cancellation of a licence, a right *in rem* or an enforcement measure shall not be deemed to have been filed until the required fee has been paid.]

(4) The application shall be accompanied by documents showing that the registered right no longer exists or by a statement by the licensee or the holder of another right, to the effect that he consents to cancellation of the registration.

(5) Where the requirements for cancellation of the registration are not satisfied, the Office shall notify the applicant of the irregularity. If the irregularity is not corrected within a period specified by the Office, it shall reject the application for cancellation of the registration.

(6) Paragraphs 1, 2, 4 and 5 shall apply *mutatis mutandis* to a request for the modification of a registration effected under Rule 33(1).
(7) Paragraphs 1 to 6 shall apply *mutatis mutandis* to entries made in the files pursuant to Rule 33(4).

NOTES

Para (3): substituted by Commission Regulation 1041/2005/EC, Art 1(23).

TITLE VI
SURRENDER

[5.446]
Rule 36
Surrender

(1) A declaration of surrender pursuant to Article 49 of the Regulation shall contain—
- (a) the registration number of the Community trade mark;
- (b) the name and address of the proprietor in accordance with Rule 1(1)(b);
- (c) . . .
- (d) where surrender is declared only for some of the goods and services for which the mark is registered, the goods and services for which the surrender is declared or the goods and services for which the mark is to remain registered.

(2) Where a right of a third party relating to the Community trade mark is entered in the register, it shall be sufficient proof of his agreement to the surrender that a declaration of consent to the surrender is signed by the proprietor of that right or his representative. Where a licence has been registered, surrender shall be registered three months after the date on which the proprietor of the Community trade mark satisfies the Office that he has informed the licensee of his intention to surrender it. If the proprietor proves to the Office before the expiry of that period that the licensee has given his consent, the surrender shall be registered forthwith.
(3) If the requirements governing surrender are not fulfilled, the Office shall communicate the deficiencies to the declarant. If the deficiencies are not remedied within a period to be specified by the Office, the Office shall reject the entry of the surrender in the Register.

NOTES

Para (1): sub-para (c) repealed by Commission Regulation 1041/2005/EC, Art 1(24).

TITLE VII
REVOCATION AND INVALIDITY

[5.447]
Rule 37
Application for revocation or for a declaration of invalidity

An application to the Office for revocation or for a declaration of invalidity pursuant to Article 55 of the Regulation shall contain—
- (a) as concerns the registration in respect of which revocation or a declaration of invalidity is sought—
  - (i) the registration number of the Community trade mark in respect of which revocation or a declaration of invalidity is sought;
  - (ii) the name and address of the proprietor of the Community trade mark in respect of which revocation or a declaration of invalidity is sought;
  - (iii) a statement of the registered goods and services in respect of which revocation or a declaration of invalidity is sought;
- (b) as regards the grounds on which the application is based—
  - (i) in the case of an application pursuant to Article 50 or Article 51 of the Regulation, a statement of the grounds on which the application for revocation or a declaration of invalidity is based;
  - (ii) in the case of an application pursuant to Article 52(1) of the Regulation, particulars of the right on which the application for a declaration of invalidity is based and if necessary particulars showing that the applicant is entitled to adduce the earlier right as grounds for invalidity;
  - (iii) in the case of an application pursuant to Article 52(2) of the Regulation, particulars of the right on which the application for a declaration of invalidity is based and particulars showing that the applicant is the proprietor of an earlier right as referred to in Article 52(2) of the Regulation or that he is entitled under the national law applicable to lay claim to that right;
  - (iv) an indication of the facts, evidence and arguments presented in support of those grounds;
- (c) as concerns the applicant—
  - (i) his name and address in accordance with Rule 1(1)(b);

(ii) if the applicant has appointed a representative, the name and the business address of the representative, in accordance with Rule 1(1)(e).

[5.448]
Rule 38
Languages used in revocation or invalidity proceedings

[(1) The time limit referred to in Article 115(6) of the Regulation within which the applicant for revocation or a declaration of invalidity has to file a translation of his application shall be one month, starting with the date of the filing of his application, failing which the application shall be rejected as inadmissible.]

(2) Where the evidence in support of the application is not filed in the language of the revocation or invalidity proceedings, the applicant shall file a translation of that evidence into that language within a period of two months after the filing of such evidence.

(3) Where the applicant for revocation or for a declaration of invalidity or the proprietor of the Community trade mark inform the Office before the expiry of a period of two months from receipt by the Community trade mark proprietor of the communication referred to in Rule 40(1), that they have agreed on a different language of proceedings pursuant to Article 115(7) of the Regulation, the applicant shall, where the application was not filed in that language, file a translation of the application in that language within a period of one month from the said date. [Where the translation is not filed or filed late, the language of the proceedings shall remain unchanged.]

NOTES

Para (1): substituted by Commission Regulation 1041/2005/EC, Art 1(25)(a).
Para (3): words in square brackets added by Commission Regulation 1041/2005/EC, Art 1(25)(b).

[5.449]
[Rule 39
Rejection of the application for revocation or for declaration of invalidity as inadmissible

(1) Where the Office finds that the required fee has not been paid, it shall invite the applicant to pay the fee within a period specified by it. If the required fee is not paid within the period specified by the Office, the Office shall inform the applicant that the application for revocation or for declaration of invalidity is deemed not to have been filed. If the fee has been paid after expiry of the period specified, it shall be refunded to the applicant.

(2) Where the translation required under Rule 38(1) is not filed within the prescribed period, the Office shall reject the application for revocation or for declaration of invalidity as inadmissible.

(3) If the Office finds that the application does not comply with Rule 37, it shall invite the applicant to remedy the deficiencies found within such period as it may specify. If the deficiencies are not remedied before expiry of the time limit, the Office shall reject the application as inadmissible.

(4) Any decision to reject an application for revocation or declaration of invalidity under paragraph 2 or 3 shall be communicated to the applicant and the proprietor of the Community trade mark.]

NOTES

Substituted by Commission Regulation 1041/2005/EC, Art 1(26).

[5.450]
Rule 40
Examination of the application for revocation or for a declaration of invalidity

[(1) Every application for revocation or for declaration of invalidity which is deemed to have been filed shall be notified to the proprietor of the Community trade mark. When the Office has found the application admissible, it shall invite the proprietor of the Community trade mark to file his observations within such period as it may specify.]

(2) If the proprietor of the Community trade mark files no observations, the Office may decide on the revocation or invalidity on the basis of the evidence before it.

(3) Any observations filed by the proprietor of the Community trade mark shall be communicated to the applicant, who shall be requested by the Office, if it sees fit, to reply within a period specified by the Office.

[(4) Save where Rule 69 otherwise provides or allows, all observations filed by the parties shall be sent to the other party concerned.]

[(5) In the case of an application for revocation based on Article 50(1)(a) of the Regulation, the Office shall invite the proprietor of the Community trade mark to furnish proof of genuine use of the mark, within such period as it may specify. If the proof is not provided within the time limit set, the Community trade mark shall be revoked. Rule 22(2), (3) and (4) shall apply *mutatis mutandis*.]

[(6) If the applicant has to furnish proof of use or proof that there are proper reasons for non-use under Article 56(2) or (3) of the Regulation, the Office shall invite the applicant to furnish proof of genuine use of the mark, within such period as it may specify. If the proof is not provided within the time limit set, the application for declaration of invalidity shall be rejected. Rule 22(2), (3) and (4) shall apply *mutatis mutandis*.]

NOTES

Paras (1), (4), (5): substituted by Commission Regulation 1041/2005/EC, Art 1(27)(a)–(c).
Para (6): added by Commission Regulation 1041/2005/EC, Art 1(27)(d).

[5.451]
Rule 41
Multiple applications for revocation or for a declaration of invalidity

(1) Where a number of applications for revocation or for a declaration of invalidity have been filed relating to the same Community trade mark, the Office may deal with them in one set of proceedings. The Office may subsequently decide no longer to deal with them in this way.
(2) Rule 21(2), (3) and (4) shall apply *mutatis mutandis*.

TITLE VIII
COMMUNITY COLLECTIVE MARKS

[5.452]
Rule 42
Application of provisions

The provisions of these Rules shall apply to Community collective marks, subject to Rule 43.

[5.453]
Rule 43
Regulation governing Community collective marks

(1) Where the application for a Community collective trade mark does not contain the regulations governing its use pursuant to Article 65 of the Regulation, those regulations shall be submitted to the Office within a period of two months after the date of filing.
(2) The regulations governing Community collective marks shall specify—
- (a) the name of the applicant and his office address;
- (b) the object of the association or the object for which the legal person governed by public law is constituted;
- (c) the bodies authorised to represent the association or the said legal person;
- (d) the conditions for membership;
- (e) the persons authorised to use the mark;
- (f) where appropriate, the conditions governing use of the mark, including sanctions;
- (g) where appropriate, the authorisation referred to in the second sentence of Article 65(2) of the Regulation.

TITLE IX
CONVERSION

[5.454]
[Rule 44
Application for conversion

(1) An application for conversion of a Community trade mark application or a registered Community trade mark into a national trade mark application pursuant to Article 108 of the Regulation shall contain—
- (a) the name and the address of the applicant for conversion in accordance with Rule 1(1)(b);
- (b) the filing number of the Community trade mark application or the registration number of the Community trade mark;
- (c) the indication of the ground for conversion in accordance with Article 108(1)(a) or (b) of the Regulation;
- (d) the specification of the Member State or the Member States in respect of which conversion is requested;
- (e) where the request does not relate to all of the goods and services for which the application has been filed or for which the trade mark has been registered, the application shall contain an indication of the goods and services for which conversion is requested, and, where conversion is requested in respect of more than one Member State and the list of goods and services is not the same for all Member States, an indication of the respective goods and services for each Member State;
- (f) where conversion is requested pursuant to Article 108(6) of the Regulation, the application shall contain the indication of the date on which the decision of the national court has become final, and a copy of that decision; that copy may be submitted in the language in which the decision was given.

(2) The application for conversion shall be filed within the relevant period pursuant to Article 108(4), (5) or (6) of the Regulation. Where conversion is requested following a failure to renew the registration, the period of three months provided for in Article 108(5) of the Regulation shall begin to run on the day following the last day on which the request for renewal can be presented pursuant to Article 47(3) of the Regulation.]

NOTES

Substituted, together with r 45, by Commission Regulation 1041/2005/EC, Art 1(28).

[5.455]
[Rule 45
Examination of application for conversion

(1) Where the application for conversion does not comply with the requirements of Article 108(1) or (2) of the Regulation or has not been filed within the relevant period of three months or does not comply with Rule 44 or other Rules, the Office shall notify the applicant accordingly and specify a period within which he may amend the application or furnish any missing information or indications.

(2) Where the conversion fee has not been paid within the relevant period of three months, the Office shall inform the applicant that the application for conversion is deemed not to have been filed.

(3) Where the missing indications have not been furnished within the period specified by the Office, the Office shall reject the application for conversion.

Where Article 108(2) of the Regulation applies, the Office shall reject the application for conversion as inadmissible only with respect to those Member States for which conversion is excluded under that provision.

(4) If the Office or a Community trade mark court has refused the Community trade mark application or has declared the Community trade mark invalid on absolute grounds by reference to the language of a Member State, conversion shall be excluded under Article 108(2) of the Regulation for all the Member States in which that language is one of the official languages. If the Office or a Community trade mark court has refused the Community trade mark application or has declared the Community trade mark invalid on absolute grounds which are found to apply in the whole Community or on account of an earlier Community trade mark or other Community industrial property right, conversion is excluded under Article 108(2) of the Regulation for all Member States.]

NOTES

Substituted as noted to r 44, at **[5.454]**.

[5.456]
Rule 46
Publication of application for conversion

(1) Where the application for conversion relates to a Community trade mark application which has already been published in the Community Trade Mark Bulletin pursuant to Article 40 of the Regulation or where the application for conversion relates to a Community trade mark, the application for conversion shall be published in the Community Trade Marks Bulletin.

(2) The publication of the application for conversion shall contain—

- (a) the filing number or the registration number of the trade mark in respect of which conversion is requested;
- (b) a reference to the previous publication of the application or the registration in the Community Trade Marks Bulletin;
- (c) an indication of the Member State or Member States in respect of which conversion has been requested;
- (d) where the request does not relate to all of the goods and services for which the application has been filed or for which the trade mark has been registered, an indication of the goods and services for which conversion is requested;
- (e) where conversion is requested in respect of more than one Member State and the list of goods and services is not the same for all Member States, an indication of the respective goods and services for each Member State;
- (f) the date of the application for conversion.

[5.457]
[Rule 47
Transmission to central industrial property offices of the Member States

Where the application for conversion complies with the requirements of the Regulation and these Rules, the Office shall transmit the application for conversion and the data referred to in [Article 87(2) of the Regulation], to the central industrial property offices of the Member States, including the Benelux Trade Mark Office, for which the application has been found admissible. The Office shall inform the applicant of the date of transmission.]

NOTES

Substituted by Commission Regulation 1041/2005/EC, Art 1(29).
Words in square brackets substituted by European Parliament and Council Regulation 2015/2424/EU, Art 2(9a).

TITLE X
APPEALS

[5.458]
Rule 48
Content of the notice of appeal

(1) The notice of appeal shall contain—

(a) the name and address of the appellant in accordance with rule 1(1)(b);
(b) where the appellant has appointed a representative, the name and the business address of the representative in accordance with Rule 1(1)(e);
(c) a statement identifying the decision which is contested and the extent to which amendment or cancellation of the decision is requested.

(2) The notice of appeal shall be filed in the language of the proceedings in which the decision subject to the appeal was taken.

[5.459]
Rule 49
Rejection of the appeal as inadmissible

(1) If the appeal does not comply with Articles 57, 58 and 59 of the Regulation and Rule 48(1)(c) and (2), the Board of Appeal shall reject it as inadmissible, unless each deficiency has been remedied before the relevant time limit laid down in Article 59 of the Regulation has expired.
(2) If the Board of Appeal finds that the appeal does not comply with other provisions of the Regulation or other provisions of these Rules, in particular Rule 48(1)(a) and (b), it shall inform the appellant accordingly and shall request him to remedy the deficiencies noted within such period as it may specify. If the appeal is not corrected in good time, the Board of Appeal shall reject it as inadmissible.
(3) If the fee for appeal has been paid after expiry of the period for the filing of appeal pursuant to Article 59 of the Regulation, the appeal shall be deemed not to have been filed and the appeal fee shall be refunded to the appellant.

[5.460]
Rule 50
Examination of appeals

(1) Unless otherwise provided, the provisions relating to proceedings before the department which has made the decision against which the appeal is brought shall be applicable to appeal proceedings before the department which has made the decision against which the appeal is brought shall be applicable to appeal proceedings *mutatis mutandis*.

[In particular, when the appeal is directed against a decision taken in opposition proceedings, Article 78a of the Regulation shall not be applicable to the time limits fixed pursuant to Article 61(2) of the Regulation.

Where the appeal is directed against a decision of an Opposition Division, the Board shall limit its examination of the appeal to facts and evidence presented within the time limits set in or specified by the Opposition Division in accordance with the Regulation and these Rules, unless the Board considers that additional or supplementary facts and evidence should be taken into account pursuant to Article 74(2) of the Regulation.]

(2) The Board of Appeal's decision shall contain—

(a) a statement that it is delivered by the Board;
(b) the date when the decision was taken;
(c) the names of the Chairman and of the other members of the Board of Appeal taking part;
(d) the name of the competent employee of the registry;
(e) the names of the parties and of their representatives;
(f) a statement of the issues to be decided;
(g) a summary of the facts;
(h) the reasons;
(i) the order of the Board of Appeal, including, where necessary, a decision on costs.

(3) The decision shall be signed by the Chairman and the other members of the Board of Appeal and by the employee of the registry of the Board of Appeal.

NOTES

Para (1): words in square brackets added by Commission Regulation 1041/2005/EC, Art 1(30).

[5.461]
[Rule 51
Reimbursement of appeal fees
The appeal fee shall only be reimbursed by order of either of the following—

(a) the department whose decision has been impugned, where it grants revision pursuant to Article 60(1) or Article 60a of the Regulation;

(b) the Board of Appeal, where it allows the appeal and considers such reimbursement equitable by reason of a substantial procedural violation.]

NOTES
Substituted by Commission Regulation 1041/2005/EC, Art 1(31).

TITLE XI
GENERAL PROVISIONS

PART A
DECISIONS AND COMMUNICATIONS OF THE OFFICE

[5.462]
Rule 52
Form of decisions
(1) Decisions of the Office shall be in writing and shall state the reasons on which they are based. Where oral proceedings are held before the Office, the decision may be given orally. Subsequently, the decision in writing shall be notified to the parties.
(2) Decisions of the Office which are open to appeal shall be accompanied by a written communication indicating that notice of appeal must be filed in writing at the Office within two months of the date of notification of the decision from which appeal is to be made. The communications shall also draw the attention of the parties to the provisions laid down in Articles 57, 58 and 59 of the Regulation. The parties may not plead any failure to communicate the availability proceedings.

[5.463]
[Rule 53
Correction of errors in decisions
Where the Office becomes aware, of its own motion or at the instance of a party to the proceedings, of a linguistic error, error of transcription or obvious mistake in a decision, it shall ensure that error or mistake is corrected by the department or division responsible.]

NOTES
Substituted by Commission Regulation 1041/2005/EC, Art 1(32).

[5.464]
[Rule 53a
Revocation of a decision or entry in the Register
(1) Where the Office finds of its own motion or pursuant to corresponding information by the parties to the proceedings that a decision or entry in the Register is subject to revocation pursuant to Article 77a of the Regulation, it shall inform the party affected about the intended revocation.
(2) The affected party may submit observations on the intended revocation within a period specified by the Office.
(3) Where the affected party agrees to the intended revocation or where he does not submit any observations within the period, the Office shall revoke the decision or entry. If the affected party does not agree to the revocation, the Office shall take a decision on the revocation.
(4) Paragraphs 1, 2 and 3 shall apply *mutatis mutandis* if the revocation is likely to affect more than one party. In these cases the observations submitted by one of the parties pursuant to paragraph 3 shall always be communicated to the other party or parties with an invitation to submit observations.
(5) Where the revocation of a decision or an entry in the Register affects a decision or entry that has been published, the revocation shall also be published.
(6) Competence for revocation under paragraphs 1 to 4 shall lie with the department or unit which took the decision.]

NOTES
Inserted by Commission Regulation 1041/2005/EC, Art 1(33).

[5.465]
Rule 54
Noting of loss of rights

(1) If the Office finds that the loss of any rights results from the Regulation or these Rules without any decision having been taken, it shall communicate this to the person concerned in accordance with Article 77 of the Regulation, and shall draw his attention to the substance of paragraph 2 of this Rule.

(2) If the person concerned considers that the finding of the Office is inaccurate, he may, within two months after notification of the communication referred to in paragraph 1, apply for a decision on the matter by the Office. Such decision shall be given only if the Office disagrees with the person requesting it; otherwise the Office shall amend its finding and inform the person requesting the decision.

[5.466]
Rule 55
Signature, name, seal

(1) Any decision, communication or notice from the Office shall indicate the department or division of the Office as well as the name or the names of the official or officials responsible. They shall be signed by the official or officials, or, instead of a signature, carry a printed or stamped seal of the Office.

(2) The President of the Office may determine that other means of identifying the department or division of the Office and the name of the official or officials responsible or an identification other than a seal may be used where decisions, communications or notices are transmitted by telecopier or any other technical means of communication.

PART B
ORAL PROCEEDINGS AND TAKING OF EVIDENCE

[5.467]
Rule 56
Summons to oral proceedings

(1) The parties shall be summoned to oral proceedings provided for in Article 75 of the Regulation and their attention shall be drawn to paragraph 3 of this Rule. At least one month's notice of the summons shall be given unless the parties agree to a shorter period.

(2) When issuing the summons, the Office shall draw attention to the points which in its opinion need to be discussed in order for the decision to be taken.

(3) If a party who has been duly summoned to oral proceedings before the Office does not appear as summoned, the proceedings may continue without him.

[5.468]
Rule 57
Taking of evidence by the Office

(1) Where the Office considers it necessary to hear the oral evidence of parties, of witnesses or of experts or to carry out an inspection, it shall take a decision to that end, stating the means by which it intends to obtain evidence, the relevant facts to be proved and the date, time and place of hearing or inspection. If oral evidence of witnesses and experts is requested by a party, the decision of the Office shall determine the period of time within which the party filing the request must make known to the Office the names and addresses of the witnesses and experts whom the party wishes to be heard.

(2) The period of notice given in the summons of a party, witness or expert to give evidence shall be at least one month, unless they agree to a shorter period. The summons shall contain—

- (a) an extract from the decision mentioned in paragraph 1, indicating in particular the date, time and place of the hearing ordered and stating the facts regarding which the parties, witnesses and experts are to be heard;
- (b) the names of the parties to proceedings and particulars of the rights which the witnesses or experts may invoke under Rule 59(2) to (5).

[5.469]
Rule 58
Commissioning of experts

(1) The Office shall decide in what form the report made by an expert whom it appoints shall be submitted.

(2) The terms of reference of the expert shall include—

- (a) a precise description of his task;
- (b) the time limit laid down for the submission of the expert report;
- (c) the names of the parties to the proceedings;
- (d) particulars of the claims which he may invoke under Rule 59(2), (3) and (4).

(3) A copy of any written report shall be submitted to the parties.

(4) The parties may object to an expert on grounds of incompetence or on the same grounds as those on which objection may be made to an examiner or to a member of a Division or Board of Appeal pursuant to Article 132(1) and (3) of the Regulation. The department of the Office concerned shall rule on the objection.

[5.470]
Rule 59
Costs of taking of evidence

(1) The taking of evidence by the Office may be made conditional upon deposit with it, by the party who has requested the evidence to be taken, of a sum which shall be fixed by reference to an estimate of the costs.

(2) Witnesses and experts who are summoned by and appear before the Office shall be entitled to reimbursement of reasonable expenses for travel and subsistence. An advance for these expenses may be granted to them by the Office. The first sentence shall apply also to witnesses and experts who appear before the Office without being summoned by it and are heard as witnesses or experts.

(3) Witnesses entitled to reimbursement under paragraph 2 shall also be entitled to appropriate compensation for loss of earnings, and experts to fees for their work. These payments shall be made to the witnesses and experts after they have fulfilled their duties or tasks, where such witnesses and experts have been summoned by the Office of its own initiative.

[(4) The amounts and the advances for expenses to be paid pursuant to paragraphs 1, 2 and 3 shall be determined by the President of the Office and shall be published in the Official Journal of the Office. The amounts shall be calculated on the same basis as laid in the Staff Regulations of the Officials of the European Communities and Annex VII thereto.]

(5) Final liability for the amounts due or paid pursuant to paragraphs 1 to 4 shall lie with—

(a) the Office where the Office, at its own initiative, considered it necessary to hear the oral evidence of witnesses or experts; or

(b) the party concerned where that party requested the giving of oral evidence by witnesses or experts, subject to the decision on apportionment and fixing of costs pursuant to Articles 81 and 82 of the Regulation and Rule 94. Such party shall reimburse the Office for any advances duly paid.

NOTES

Para (4): substituted by Commission Regulation 1041/2005/EC, Art 1(34).

[5.471]
[Rule 60
Minutes of oral proceedings

(1) Minutes of oral proceedings or the taking of evidence shall be drawn up, containing—

(a) the date of the proceedings;

(b) the names of the competent officials of the Office, the parties, their representatives, and of the witnesses and experts who are present;

(c) the applications and requests made by the parties;

(d) the means of giving or obtaining evidence;

(e) where applicable, the orders or the decision issued by the Office.

(2) The minutes shall become part of the file of the relevant Community trade mark application or registration. The parties shall be provided with a copy of the minutes.

(3) Where witnesses, experts or parties are heard in accordance with Article 76(1)(a) or (d) of the Regulation or Rule 59(2), their statements shall be recorded.]

NOTES

Substituted by Commission Regulation 1041/2005/EC, Art 1(35).

PART C
NOTIFICATIONS

[5.472]
Rule 61
General provisions on notifications

[(1) In proceedings before the Office, notifications to be made by the Office shall take the form of transmitting the original document, an uncertified copy thereof or a computer print-out in accordance with Rule 55, or, as concerns documents emanating from the parties themselves, duplicates or uncertified copies.]

(2) Notifications shall be made—

(a) by post in accordance with Rule 62;

(b) by hand delivery in accordance with Rule 63;

(c) by deposit in a post box at the Office in accordance with Rule 64;

(d) by telecopier and other technical means in accordance with Rule 65;

(e) by public notification in accordance with Rule 66.

[(3) Where the addressee has indicated his telecopier number or contact details for communicating with him through other technical means, the Office shall have the choice between any of these means of notification and notification by post.]

NOTES

Para (1): substituted by Commission Regulation 1041/2005/EC, Art 1(36)(a).
Para (3): added by Commission Regulation 1041/2005/EC, Art 1(36)(b).

[5.473]
Rule 62
Notification by post

[(1) Decisions subject to a time limit for appeal, summonses and other documents as determined by the President of the Office shall be notified by registered letter with advice of delivery. All other notifications shall be by ordinary mail.]

(2) Notifications in respect of addresses having neither their domicile nor their principal place of business nor an establishment [in the European Economic Area] and who have not appointed a representative in accordance with Article 88(2) of the Regulation shall be effected by posting the document requiring notification by ordinary mail to the last address of the addressee known to the Office. . . .

(3) Where notification is effected by registered letter, whether or not with advice of delivery, this shall be deemed to be delivered to the addressee on the 10th day following that of its posting, unless the letter has failed to reach the addressee or has reached him at a later date. In the event of any dispute, it shall be for the Office to establish that the letter has reached its destination or to establish the date on which it was delivered to the addressee, as the case may be.

(4) Notification by registered letter, with or without advice of delivery, shall be deemed to have been effected even if the addressee refuses to accept the letter.

[(5) Notification by ordinary mail shall be deemed to have been effected on the tenth day following that of its posting.]

NOTES

Paras (1), (5): substituted by Commission Regulation 1041/2005/EC, Art 1(37)(a), (c).
Para (2): words in square brackets substituted by European Parliament and Council Regulation 2015/2424/EU, Art 2(10); words omitted repealed by Commission Regulation 1041/2005/EC, Art 1(37)(b).

[5.474]
Rule 63
Notification by hand delivery

Notification may be effected on the premises of the Office by hand delivery of the document to the addressee, who shall on delivery acknowledge its receipt.

[5.475]
Rule 64
Notification by deposit in a post box at the Office

Notification may also be effected to addressees who have been provided with a post box at the Office, by depositing the document therein. A written notification of deposit shall be inserted in the files. The date of deposit shall be recorded on the document. Notification shall be deemed to have taken place on the fifth day following deposit of the document in the post box at the Office.

[5.476]
Rule 65
Notification by telecopier and other technical means

(1) Notification by telecopier shall be effected by transmitting either the original or a copy, as provided for in Rule 61(1), of the document to be notified. [Notification shall be deemed to have been taken place on the date on which the communication was received by the telecopying device of the recipient.]

(2) Details of notification by other technical means of communication shall be determined by the President of the Office.

NOTES

Para (1): words in square brackets substituted by Commission Regulation 1041/2005/EC, Art 1(38).

[5.477]
Rule 66
Public notification

[(1) If the address of the addressee cannot be established or if after at least one attempt, notification in accordance with Rule 62 has proved impossible, notification shall be effected by public notice.]

(2) The President of the Office shall determine how the public notice is to be given and shall fix the beginning of the one-month period on the expiry of which the document shall be deemed to have been notified.

NOTES

Para (1): substituted by Commission Regulation 1041/2005/EC, Art 1(39).

[5.478]
Rule 67
Notification to representatives

(1) If a representative has been appointed or where the applicant first named in a common application is considered to be the common representative pursuant to Rule 75(1), notifications shall be addressed to that appointed or common representative.

(2) If several representatives have been appointed for a single interested party, notification to any one of them shall be sufficient, unless a specific address for service has been indicated in accordance with Rule 1(1)(e).

(3) If several interested parties have appointed a common representative, notification of a single document to the common representative shall be sufficient.

[5.479]
Rule 68
Irregularities in notification

Where a document has reached the addressee, if the Office is unable to prove that it has been duly notified, or if provisions relating to its notification have not been observed, the document shall be deemed to have been notified on the date established by the Office as the date of receipt.

[5.480]
Rule 69
Notification of documents in the case of several parties

Documents emanating from parties which contain substantive proposals, or a declaration of withdrawal of a substantive proposal, shall be notified to the other parties as a matter of course. Notification may be dispensed with where the document contains no new pleadings and the matter is ready for decision.

PART D
TIME LIMITS

[5.481]
Rule 70
Calculation of time limits

(1) Periods shall be laid down in terms of full years, months, weeks or days.

(2) Calculation shall start on the day following the day on which the relevant event occurred, the event being either a procedural step or the expiry of another period. Where that procedural step is a notification, the event considered shall be the receipt of the document notified, unless otherwise provided.

(3) Where a period is expressed as one year or a certain number of years, it shall expire in the relevant subsequent year in the month having the same name and on the day having the same number as the month and the day on which the said event occurred. Where the relevant month has no day with the same number the period shall expire on the last day of that month.

(4) Where a period is expressed as one month or a certain number of months, it shall expire in the relevant subsequent month on the day which has the same number as the day on which the said event occurred. Where the day on which the said event occurred was the last day of a month or where the relevant subsequent month has no day with the same number the period shall expire on the last day of that month.

(5) Where a period is expressed as one week or a certain number of weeks, it shall expire in the relevant subsequent week on the day having the same name as the day on which the said event occurred.

[5.482]
Rule 71
Duration of time limits

(1) Where the Regulation or these Rules provide for a period to be specified by the Office, such period shall, when the party concerned has its domicile or its principal place of business or an establishment [within the European Economic Area], be not less than one month, or, when those conditions are not fulfilled, not less than two months, and no more than six months. The Office may, when this is appropriate under the circumstances, grant an extension of a period specified if such extension is requested by the party concerned and the request is submitted before the original period expired.

(2) Where there are two or more parties, the Office may extend a period subject to the agreement of the other parties.

NOTES

Para (1): words in square brackets substituted by European Parliament and Council Regulation 2015/2424/EU, Art 2(11).

[5.483]
Rule 72
Expiry of time limits in special cases

(1) If a time limit expires on a day on which the Office is not open for receipt of documents or on which, for reasons other than those referred to in paragraph 2, ordinary mail is not delivered in the locality in which the Office is located, the time limit shall extend until the first day thereafter on which the Office is open for receipt of documents and on which ordinary mail is delivered. The days referred to in the first sentence shall be as determined by the President of the Office before the commencement of each calendar year.

[(2) If a time limit expires on a day on which there is a general interruption in the delivery of mail in the Member State where the Office is located, or, if and to the extent that the President of the Office has allowed communications to be sent by electronic means pursuant to Rule 82, on which there is an actual interruption of the Offices connection to these electronic means of communication, the time limit shall extend until the first day following that interruption on which the Office is open for the receipt of documents and on which ordinary mail is delivered. The duration of the period of interruption shall be determined by the President of the Office.]

(3) Paragraphs 1 and 2 shall apply *mutatis mutandis* to the time limits provided for in the Regulation or these Rules in the case of transactions to be carried out with the competent authority within the meaning of Article 25(1)(b) of the Regulation.

[(4) If an exceptional occurrence such as a natural disaster or strike interrupts or dislocates proper communication from the parties to the proceedings to the Office or vice versa, the President of the Office may determine that for parties of the proceedings having their residence or registered office in the State concerned or who have appointed a representative with a place of business in the State concerned, all time limits that otherwise would expire on or after the date of commencement of such occurrence, as determined by him, shall extend until a date to be determined by him. If the occurrence affects the seat of the Office, such determination of the President shall specify that it applies in respect of all parties to the proceedings.]

NOTES

Paras (2), (4): substituted by Commission Regulation 1041/2005/EC, Art 1(40), (41).

PART E
INTERRUPTION OF PROCEEDINGS

[5.484]
Rule 73
Interruption of proceedings

(1) Proceedings before the Office shall be interrupted—

(a) in the event of the death or legal incapacity of the applicant for or proprietor of a Community trade mark or of the person authorised by national law to act on his behalf. To the extent that the above events do not affect the authorisation of a representative appointed under Article 89 of the Regulation, proceedings shall be interrupted only on application by such representative;

(b) in the event of the applicant for or proprietor of a Community trade mark, as a result of some action taken against his property, being prevented for legal reasons from continuing the proceedings before the Office;

(c) in the event of the death or legal incapacity of the representative of an applicant for or proprietor of a Community trade mark or of his being prevented for legal reasons resulting from action taken against his property from continuing the proceedings before the Office.

(2) When, in the cases referred to in paragraph 1(a) and (b), the Office has been informed of the identity of the person authorised to continue the proceedings before the Office, the Office shall communicate to such person and to any interested third parties that the proceedings shall be resumed as from a date to be fixed by the Office.

(3) In the case referred to in paragraph 1(c), the proceedings shall be resumed when the Office has been informed of the appointment of a new representative of the applicant or when the Office has notified to the other parties the communication of the appointment of a new representative of the proprietor of the Community trade mark. If, three months after the beginning of the interruption of the proceedings, the Office has not been informed of the appointment of a new representative, it shall inform the applicant for or proprietor of the Community trade mark—

(a) where Article 88(2) of the Regulation is applicable, that the Community trade mark application will be deemed to be withdrawn if the information is not submitted within two months after this communication is notified; or

(b) where Article 88(2) of the Regulation is not applicable, that the proceedings will be resumed with the applicant for or proprietor of the Community trade mark as from the date on which this communication is notified.

(4) The time limits, other than the time limit for paying the renewal fees, in force as regards the applicant for or proprietor of the Community trade mark at the date of interruption of the proceedings, shall begin again as from the day on which the proceedings are resumed.

PART F
WAIVING OF ENFORCED RECOVERY PROCEDURES

[5.485]
Rule 74
Waiving of enforced recovery procedures
The President of the Office may waive action for the enforced recovery of any sum due where the sum to be recovered is minimal or where such recovery is too uncertain.

PART G
REPRESENTATION

[5.486]
Rule 75
Appointment of a common representative
(1) If there is more than one applicant and the application for a Community trade mark does not name a common representative, the applicant first named in the application shall be considered to be the common representative. However, if one of the applicants is obliged to appoint a professional representative, such representative shall he considered to be the common representative unless the applicant named first in the application has appointed a professional representative. The same shall apply *mutatis mutandis* to third parties acting in common in filing notice of opposition or applying for revocation or for a declaration of invalidity, and to joint proprietors of a Community trade mark.
(2) If, during the course of proceedings, transfer is made to more than one person, and such persons have not appointed a common representative, paragraph 1 shall apply. If such application is not possible, the Office shall require such persons to appoint a common representative within two months. If this request is not complied with, the Office shall appoint the common representative.

[5.487]
Rule 76
Authorisations
[(1) Legal practitioners and professional representatives entered on the list maintained by the Office pursuant to Article 89(2) of the Regulation shall file with the Office a signed authorisation for insertion in the files only if the Office expressly requires it, or where there are several parties to the proceedings in which the representative acts before the Office, if the other party expressly asks for it.
(2) . . .
(3) The authorisation may be filed in any official language of the Community. It may cover one or more applications or registered trade marks or may be in the form of a general authorisation authorising the representative to act in respect of all proceedings before the Office to which the person giving the authorisation is a party.
(4) Where it is required, pursuant to paragraphs 1 or 2, that a signed authorisation be filed, the Office shall specify a time limit within which such authorisation shall be filed. If the authorisation is not filed in due time, proceedings shall be continued with the represented person. Any procedural steps other than the filing of the application taken by the representative shall be deemed not to have been taken if the represented person does not approve them within a period specified by the Office. The application of Article 88(2) of the Regulation shall remain unaffected.]
(5) Paragraphs 1 to 3 shall apply *mutatis mutandis* to a document withdrawing an authorisation.
(6) Any representative who has ceased to he authorised shall continue to be regarded as the representative until the termination of his authorisation has been communicated to the Office.
(7) Subject to any provisions to the contrary contained therein, an authorisation shall not terminate *vis-à-vis* the Office upon the death of the person who gave it.
[(8) Where the appointment of a representative is communicated to the Office, the name and the business address of the representative shall be indicated in accordance with Rule 1(1)(e). Where a representative acts before the Office who has already been appointed, he shall indicate his name and preferably the identification number attributed to him by the Office. Where several representatives are appointed by the same party, they may, notwithstanding any provisions to the contrary in their authorisations, act either jointly or singly.
(9) The appointment or authorisation of an association of representatives shall be deemed to be an appointment or authorisation of any representative who practices within that association.]

NOTES
Paras (1), (3), (4), (8), (9): substituted, together with para (2), by Commission Regulation 1041/2005/EC, Art 1(42).
Para (2): substituted as noted above; repealed by European Parliament and Council Regulation 2015/2424/EU, Art 2(12).

[5.488]
Rule 77
Representation

Any notification or other communication addressed by the Office to the duly authorised representative shall have the same effect as if it had been addressed to the represented person. Any communication addressed to the Office by the duly authorised representative shall have the same effect as if it originated from the represented person.

[5.489]
Rule 78
Amendment of the list of professional representatives

(1) The entry of a professional representative in the list of professional representatives, as referred to in Article 89 of the Regulation, shall be deleted at his request.

(2) The entry of a professional representative shall be deleted automatically—

(a) in the event of the death or legal incapacity of the professional representative;

(b) where the professional representative is no longer a national of a [Member State of the European Economic Area], unless the President of the Office has granted an exemption under Article 89(4)(b) of the Regulation;

(c) where the professional representative no longer has his place of business or employment [in the European Economic Area];

(d) where the professional representative no longer possesses the entitlement referred to in the first sentence of Article 89(2)(c) of the Regulation.

(3) The entry of a professional representative shall be suspended of the Office's own motion where his entitlement to represent natural or legal persons before the central industrial property office of the [Member State of the European Economic Area] as referred to in the first sentence of Article 89(2)(c) has been suspended.

(4) A person whose entry has been deleted shall, upon request pursuant to Article 89(3) of the Regulation, be reinstated in the list of professional representatives if the conditions for deletion no longer exist.

(5) The Benelux Trade Mark Office and the central industrial property offices of the [Member States of the European Economic Area] concerned shall, where they are aware thereof, promptly inform the Office of any relevant events under paragraphs 2 and 3.

(6) The amendments of the list of professional representatives shall be published in the Official Journal of the Office.

NOTES

Paras (2), (3), (5): words in square brackets substituted by European Parliament and Council Regulation 2015/2424/EU, Art 2(13).

PART H
WRITTEN COMMUNICATIONS AND FORMS

[5.490]
Rule 79
Communication in writing or by other means

Applications for the registration of a Community trade mark as well as any other application provided for in the Regulation and all other communications addressed to the Office shall be submitted as follows—

[(a) by submitting a signed original of the document in question at the Office, such as by post, personal delivery, or by any other means;

(b) by transmitting a document by telecopier in accordance with Rule 80;]

(c) . . .

(d) by transmitting the contents of the communication by electronic means in accordance with Rule 82.

NOTES

Paras (a), (b) substituted and para (c) repealed by Commission Regulation 1041/2005/EC, Art 1(43).

[5.491]
[Rule 79a
Annexes to written communications

Where a document or an item of evidence is submitted in accordance with Rule 79 point (a) by a party in a proceeding before the Office involving more than one party to the proceedings, the document or item of evidence, as well as any annex to the document, shall be submitted in as many copies as the number of parties to the proceedings.]

NOTES

Inserted by Commission Regulation 1041/2005/EC, Art 1(44).

[5.492]
Rule 80
Communication by telecopier

[(1) Where an application for a Community trade mark is submitted to the Office by telecopier and the application contains a reproduction of the mark pursuant to Rule 3(2) which does not satisfy the requirements of that Rule, the required reproduction suitable for publication shall be submitted to the Office in accordance with Rule 79(a). Where the reproduction is received by the Office within a period of one month from the date of receipt of the telecopy, the reproduction shall be deemed to have been received by the Office on the date on which the telecopy was received.]

(2) Where a communication received by telecopier is incomplete or illegible, or where the Office has reasonable doubts as to the accuracy of the transmission, the Office shall inform the sender accordingly and shall invite him, within a period to be specified by the Office, to retransmit the original by telecopy or to submit the original in accordance with Rule 79(a). Where this request is complied with within the period specified, the date of the receipt of the retransmission or of the original shall be deemed to be the date of the receipt of the original communication, provided that where the deficiency concerns the granting of a filing date for an application to register a trade mark, the provisions on the filing date shall apply. Where the request is not complied with within the period specified, the communication shall be deemed not to have been received.

(3) Any communication submitted to the Office by telecopier shall be considered to be duly signed if the reproduction of the signature appears on the printout produced by the telecopier.

[Where the communication has been sent by telecopier electronically, the indication of the name of the sender shall be equivalent to the signature.]

(4) . . .

NOTES

Para (1): substituted by Commission Regulation 1041/2005/EC, Art 1(45)(a).
Para (3): words in square brackets added by Commission Regulation 1041/2005/EC, Art 1(45)(b).
Para (4): repealed by Commission Regulation 1041/2005/EC, Art 1(45)(c).

Rule 81 (*Repealed by Commission Regulation 1041/2005/EC, Art 1(46).*)

[5.493]
Rule 82
Communication by electronic means

[(1) The President of the Office shall determine whether, to what extent and under what technical conditions communications may be sent to the Office by electronic means.]

(2) Where a communication is sent by electronic means, Rule 80(2) shall apply *mutatis mutandis.*

(3) Where a communication is sent to the Office by electronic means, the indication of the name of the sender shall be deemed to be equivalent to the signature.

(4) . . .

NOTES

Para (1): substituted by Commission Regulation 1041/2005/EC, Art 1(47)(a).
Para (4): repealed by Commission Regulation 1041/2005/EC, Art 1(47)(b).

[5.494]
[Rule 83
Forms

The Office shall make available to the public free of charge forms for the purposes of—

(a) filing an application for a Community trade mark, including where appropriate a request for the search report;
(b) entering an opposition;
(c) applying for revocation or declaration of invalidity;
(d) applying for the registration of a transfer and the transfer form and transfer document provided for in Rule 31(5);
(e) applying for the registration of a licence;
(f) applying for the renewal of a Community trade mark;
(g) making an appeal;
(h) authorising a representative, in the form of an individual authorisation or a general authorisation;
(i) submitting an international application or a subsequent designation under the Madrid Protocol to the Office.

(2) Parties to the proceedings before the Office may also use

(a) forms established under the Trademark Law Treaty or pursuant to recommendations of the Assembly of the Paris Union for the Protection of Industrial Property;
(b) with the exception of the form referred to in point (i) of paragraph 1, forms with the same content and format.

(3) The Office shall make available the forms referred to in paragraph 1 in all the official languages for the Community.]

NOTES

Substituted by Commission Regulation 1041/2005/EC, Art 1(48). In relation to the second part of para (1)(a), commencing with the word 'including', the substitution has effect from 10 March 2008.

PART I
INFORMATION OF THE PUBLIC

Rule 84 (*Repealed by European Parliament and Council Regulation 2015/2424/EU, Art 2(14).*)

PART J
COMMUNITY TRADE MARKS BULLETIN AND OFFICIAL JOURNAL OF THE OFFICE

[5.495]
Rule 85
Community Trade Marks Bulletin

[(1) The *Community Trade Marks Bulletin* shall be published in the manner and frequency determined by the President of the Office.]

(2) The *Community Trade Marks Bulletin* shall contain publications of applications and of entries made in the Register as well as other particulars relating to applications or registrations of trade marks whose publication is prescribed by the Regulation or by these Rules.

(3) Where particulars whose publication is prescribed in the Regulation or in these Rules are published in the *Community Trade Marks Bulletin,* the date of issue shown on the Bulletin shall be taken as the date of publication of the particulars.

(4) To the extent that the entries regarding the registration of a trade mark contain no changes as compared to the publication of the application, the publication of such entries shall be made by way of a reference to the particulars contained in the publication of the application.

(5) The elements of the application for a Community trade mark, as set out in Article 26(1) of the Regulation as well as any other information the publication of which is prescribed in Rule 12 shall, where appropriate, be published in all the official languages of the Community.

(6) The Office shall take into account any translation submitted by the applicant. If the language of the application is not one of the languages of the Office, the translation into the second language indicated by the applicant shall be communicated to the applicant. The applicant may propose changes to the translation within a period to be specified by the Office. If the applicant does not respond within this period or if the Office considers the proposed changes to be inappropriate, the translation proposed by the Office shall be published.

NOTES

Para (1): substituted by Commission Regulation 1041/2005/EC, Art 1(50).

[5.496]
Rule 86
Official Journal of the Office

(1) The Official Journal of the Office shall be published in periodic editions. The Office may make available to the public editions of the Official Journal on CD-ROM or in any other machine-readable form.

(2) The Official Journal shall be published in the languages of the Office. The President of the Office may determine that certain items shall be published in all the official languages of the Community.

Rules 87–91 (*Rule 87, rr 88–91 (Part K) repealed by European Parliament and Council Regulation 2015/2424/EU, Art 2(15), (16).*)

PART L
ADMINISTRATIVE COOPERATION

[5.497]
Rule 92
Exchange of information and communications between the Office and the authorities of the Member States

(1) The Office and the central industrial property offices of the Member States shall, upon request, communicate to each other relevant information about the filing of applications for Community trade marks or national marks and about proceedings relating to such applications and the marks registered as a result thereof. Such communications shall not be subject to the restrictions provided for in Article 84 of the Regulation.

(2) Communications between the Office and the courts or authorities of the Member States which arise out of the application of the Regulation or these Rules shall be effected directly between these authorities. Such communication may also be effected through the central industrial property offices of the Member States.

(3) Expenditure in respect of communications under paragraphs 1 and 2 shall be chargeable to the authority making the communications, which shall be exempt from fees.

[5.498]
Rule 93
Inspection of files by or via courts or authorities of the Member States

(1) Inspection of files relating to Community trade marks applied for or registered Community trade marks by courts or authorities of the Member States be of the original documents or of copies thereof . . . .

(2) Courts or Public Prosecutors' Offices of the Member States may, in the course of proceedings before them, open files or copies thereof transmitted by the Office to inspection by third parties. Such inspection shall be subject to Article 84 of the Regulation. The Office shall not charge any fee for such inspection.

(3) The Office shall, at the time of transmission of the files or copies thereof to the courts or Public Prosecutors' Offices of the Member States, indicate the restrictions to which the inspection of files relating to Community trade marks applied for or registered Community trade marks is subject pursuant to Article 84 of the Regulation . . . .

NOTES

Paras (1), (3): words omitted repealed by European Parliament and Council Regulation 2015/2424/EU, Art 2(16a), (16b).

PART M
COSTS

[5.499]
Rule 94
Apportionment and fixing of costs

(1) Apportionment of costs pursuant to Article 81(1) and (2) of the Regulation shall be dealt with in the decision on the opposition, the decision on the application for revocation or for a declaration of invalidity of a Community trade mark, or the decision on the appeal.

(2) Apportionment of costs pursuant to Article 81(3) and (4) of the Regulation shall be dealt with in a decision on costs by the Opposition Division, the Cancellation Division or the Board of Appeal.

[(3) Where the amount of the costs has not been fixed pursuant to Article 81(6), first sentence, of the Regulation, the request for the fixing of costs shall be accompanied by a bill and supporting evidence. For the costs of representation referred to in paragraph 7(d) of this Rule, an assurance by the representative that the costs have been incurred shall be sufficient. For other costs, it shall be sufficient if their plausibility is established. Where the amount of the costs is fixed pursuant to Article 81(6), first sentence, of the Regulation, representation costs shall be awarded at the level laid down in paragraph 7(d) of this Rule and irrespective of whether they have been actually incurred.]

(4) The request provided for in [the third sentence of Article 81(6)] of the Regulation for a review of the decision of the registry on the fixing of costs, stating the reasons on which it is based, must be filed at the Office within one month after the date of notification of the awarding of costs. It shall not be deemed to be filed until the fee for reviewing the amount of the costs has been paid.

(5) The Opposition Division, the Cancellation Division or the Board of Appeal, as the case may be, shall take a decision on the request referred to in paragraph 4 without oral proceedings.

(6) The fees to be borne by the losing party pursuant to Article 81(1) of the Regulation shall be limited to the fees incurred by the other party for opposition, for an application for revocation or for a declaration of invalidity of the Community trade mark and for appeal.

[(7) Subject to paragraph 3 of this Rule, costs essential to the proceedings and actually incurred by the successful party shall be borne by the losing party in accordance with Article 81(1) of the Regulation on the basis of the following maximum rates—

- (a) where the party is not represented by a representative, travel and subsistence expenses of one party for one person for the outward and return journey between the place of residence or the place of business and the place where oral proceedings are held pursuant to Rule 56, as follows—
  - (i) the cost of the first-class rail-fare including usual transport supplements where the total distance by rail does not exceed 800 km;
  - (ii) the cost of the tourist-class air-fare where the total distance by rail exceeds 800 km or the route includes a sea-crossing;
  - (iii) subsistence expenses as laid down in Article 13 of Annex VII to the Staff Regulations of Officials of the European Communities;
- (b) travel expenses of representatives within the meaning of Article 89(1) of the Regulation, at the rates provided for in point (a)(i) and (ii) of this Rule;
- (c) travel expenses, subsistence expenses, compensation for loss of earnings and fees to which witnesses and experts are entitled to be reimbursed pursuant to Rule 59(2), (3) or (4), to the extent that final liability lies with a party to the proceedings pursuant to Rule 59(5)(b);
- (d) cost of representation, within the meaning of Article 89(1) of the Regulation,
  - (i) of the opposing party in opposition proceedings—EUR 300;

(ii) of the applicant in opposition proceedings—EUR 300;
(iii) of the applicant in proceedings relating to revocation or invalidity of a Community trade mark—EUR 450;
(iv) of the proprietor of the trade mark in proceedings relating to revocation or invalidity of a Community trade mark—EUR 450;
(v) of the appellant in appeal proceedings—EUR 550;
(vi) of the defendant in appeal proceedings—EUR 550;
(vii) where an oral proceedings have taken place to which the parties have been summoned pursuant to Rule 56, the amount referred to in the points (i) to (vi) shall be incremented by EUR 400;

(e) where there are several applicants or proprietors of the Community trade mark application or registration or where there are several opposing parties or applicants for revocation or declaration of invalidity who have filed the opposition or application for revocation or declaration of invalidity jointly, the losing party shall bear the costs referred to in point (a) for one such person only;

(f) where the successful party is represented by more than one representative within the meaning of Article 89(1) of the Regulation, the losing party shall bear the costs referred to in points (b) and (d) of this Rule for one such person only;

(g) the losing party shall not be obliged to reimburse the successful party for any costs, expenses and fees other than those referred to in points (a) to (f).]

NOTES

Paras (3), (7): substituted by Commission Regulation 1041/2005/EC, Art 1(53)(a), (c).

Para (4): words in square brackets substituted by Commission Regulation 1041/2005/EC, Art 1(53)(b).

PART N
LANGUAGES

[5.500]
Rule 95
Applications and declarations

Without prejudice to Article 115(5) of the Regulation—

(a) any application or declaration relating to a Community trade mark application may be filed in the language used for filing the application for a Community trade mark or in the second language indicated by the applicant in his application;

(b) any application or declaration relating to a registered Community trade mark may be filed in one of the languages of the Office. However, when the application is filed by using any of the forms provided by the Office pursuant to Rule 83, such forms may be used in any of the official languages of the Community, provided that the form is completed in one of the languages of the Office, as far as textual elements are concerned.

[5.501]
Rule 96
Written proceedings

(1) Without prejudice to Article 115(4) and (7) of the Regulation, and unless otherwise provided for in these Rules, in written proceedings before the Office any party may use any language of the Office. If the language chosen is not the language of the proceedings, the party shall supply a translation into that language within one month from the date of the submission of the original document. Where the applicant for a Community trade mark is the sole party to proceedings before the Office and the language used for the filing of the application for the Community trade mark is not one of the languages of the Office, the translation may also be filed in the second language indicated by the applicant in his application.

(2) Unless otherwise provided for in these Rules, documents to be used in proceedings before the Office may be filed in any official language of the Community. Where the language of such documents is not the language of the proceedings the Office may require that a translation be supplied, within a period specified by it, in that language or, at the choice of the party to the proceeding, in any language of the Office.

[5.502]
Rule 97
Oral proceedings

(1) Any party to oral proceedings before the Office may, in place of the language of proceedings, use one of the other official languages of the Community, on condition that he makes provision for interpretation into the language of proceedings. Where the oral proceedings are held in a proceeding concerning the application for registration of a trade mark, the applicant may use either the language of the application or the second language indicated by him.

(2) In oral proceedings concerning the application for registration of a trade mark, the staff of the Office may use either the language of the application or the second language indicated by the applicant. In all other oral proceedings, the staff of the Office may use, in place of the language of the proceedings, one of the other languages of the Office, on condition that the party or parties to the proceedings agree to such use.
(3) In the case of taking of evidence, any party to be heard, witness or expert who is unable to express himself adequately in the language of proceedings, may use any of the official languages of the Community. Should the taking of evidence be decided upon following a request by a party to the proceedings, parties to be heard, witnesses or experts who express themselves in languages other than the language of proceedings may be heard only if the party who made the request makes provision for interpretation into that language. In proceedings concerning the application for registration of a trade mark, in place of the language of the application, the second language indicated by the applicant may be used. In any proceedings with only one party the Office may on request of the party concerned permit derogations from the provisions in this paragraph.
(4) If the parties and Office so agree, any official language of the Community may be used in oral proceedings.
(5) The Office shall, if necessary, make provision at its own expense for interpretation into the language of proceedings, or, where appropriate, into its other languages, unless this interpretation is the responsibility of one of the parties to the proceedings.
(6) Statements by staff of the Office, by parties to the proceedings and by witnesses and experts, made in one of the languages of the Office during oral proceedings shall be entered in the minutes in the language employed. Statements made in any other language shall be entered in the language of proceedings. Amendments to the text of the application for or the registration of a Community trade mark shall be entered in the minutes in the language of proceedings.

[5.503]
[Rule 98
Translations
(1) When a translation of a document is to be filed, the translation shall identify the document to which it refers and reproduce the structure and contents of the original document. The Office may require the filing, within a period to be specified by it, of a certificate that the translation corresponds to the original text. The President of the Office shall determine the manner in which translations shall be certified.
(2) Save where the Regulation or these Rules provide otherwise, a document for which a translation is to be filed shall be deemed not to have been received by the Office—
- (a) where the translation is received by the Office after expiry of the relevant period for submitting the original document or the translation;
- (b) in the case of paragraph 1, where the certificate is not filed within the period specified.]

NOTES
Substituted by Commission Regulation 1041/2005/EC, Art 1(54).

[5.504]
Rule 99
Legal authenticity of translations
In the absence of evidence to the contrary, the Office may assume that a translation corresponds to the relevant original text.

PART O
ORGANISATION OF THE OFFICE

[5.505]
[Rule 100
Decisions taken by a single member
The cases in which pursuant to Article 127(2), or Article 129(2), of the Regulation a single member of the Opposition Division or of the Cancellation Division may take a decision shall be the following—
- (a) decisions on the apportionment of costs;
- (b) decisions to fix the amount of the costs to be paid pursuant to Article 81(6), first sentence, of the Regulation;
- (c) decisions to close the file or not to proceed to judgment;
- (d) decisions to reject an opposition as inadmissible before expiry of the period referred to in Rule 18(1);
- (e) decisions to stay proceedings;
- (f) decisions to join or separate multiple oppositions pursuant to Rule 21(1).]

NOTES
Substituted by Commission Regulation 1041/2005/EC, Art 1(55).

TITLE XII
RECIPROCITY

[5.506]
Rule 101
Publication of reciprocity

[(1) If necessary, the President of the Office shall request the Commission to enquire whether a State which is not party to the Paris Convention or to the Agreement establishing the World Trade Organization accords reciprocal treatment within the meaning of Article 29(5) of the Regulation.

(2) If the Commission determines that reciprocal treatment in accordance with paragraph 1 is accorded, it shall publish a communication to this effect in the *Official Journal of the European Union*.

(3) Article 29(5) of the Regulation shall apply from the date of publication in the *Official Journal of the European Union* of the communication referred to in paragraph 2, unless the communication states an earlier date from which it is applicable. It shall cease to apply from the date of publication in the *Official Journal of the European Union* of a communication of the Commission to the effect that reciprocal treatment is no longer accorded, unless the communication states an earlier date from which it is applicable.]

(4) Communications referred to in paragraphs 2 and 3 shall also be published in the Official Journal of the Office.

NOTES

Paras (1)–(3): substituted by Commission Regulation 1041/2005/EC, Art 1(56).

[TITLE XIII
PROCEDURES CONCERNING THE INTERNATIONAL REGISTRATION OF MARKS

PART A
INTERNATIONAL REGISTRATION ON THE BASIS OF APPLICATIONS FOR A COMMUNITY TRADE MARK AND OF COMMUNITY TRADE MARKS

[5.507]
Rule 102
Filing of an international application

(1) The form provided by the Office for the filing of an international application, as referred to in Article 142(1) of the Regulation, shall be an adaptation of the official form provided by the International Bureau of the World Intellectual Property Organisation (hereinafter "the International Bureau") having the same format but including such additional indications and elements as are required or may be appropriate pursuant to these Rules. Applicants may also use the official form provided by the International Bureau.

(2) Paragraph 1 shall apply *mutatis mutandis* for the form for a request for territorial extension subsequent to the international registration pursuant to Article 144 of the Regulation.

(3) The Office shall inform the applicant filing the international application of the date on which the documents making up the international application are received by the Office.

(4) Where the international application is filed in an official language of the European Community other than a language allowed under the Madrid Protocol for the filing of an international application and where the international application does not contain, or is not accompanied by, a translation of the list of goods and services and of any other text matter forming part of the international application in the language in which the application is to be submitted to the International Bureau pursuant to Article 142(2) of the Regulation, the applicant shall authorise the Office to include in the international application a translation of the said list of goods and services and other text matter in the language in which the application is to be submitted to the International Bureau pursuant to Article 142(2) of the Regulation. Where the translation has not yet been established in the course of the registration procedure for the Community trade mark application on which the international application is based, the Office shall without delay arrange for the translation.]

NOTES

Title XIII (rr 102–126) added by Commission Regulation 782/2004/EC, Art 1(4).

[5.508]
[Rule 103
Examination of international applications

(1) Where the Office receives an international application and the fee referred to in Article 142(5) of the Regulation for the international application has not been paid, the Office shall inform the applicant that the international application will be deemed not to have been filed until the fee has been paid.

(2) Where the examination of the international application reveals any of the following deficiencies, the Office shall invite the applicant to remedy those deficiencies within such period as it may specify—

(a) the international application is not filed on one of the forms referred to in Rule 102(1), and does not contain all the indications and information required by that form;

(b) the list of goods and services contained in the international application is not covered by the list of goods and services appearing in the basic Community trade mark application or basic Community trade mark;

(c) the mark which is subject to the international application is not identical to the mark as appearing in the basic Community trade mark application or basic Community trade mark;

(d) any indication in the international application as to the mark, other than a disclaimer pursuant to Article 38(2) of the Regulation or a colour claim, does not also appear in the basic Community trade mark application or basic Community trade mark;

(e) if colour is claimed in the international application as a distinctive feature of the mark, the basic Community trade mark application or basic Community trade mark is not in the same colour or colours; or

(f) according to the indications made in the international form, the applicant is not eligible to file an international application through the Office in accordance with Article 2(1)(ii) of the Madrid Protocol,

(3) Where the applicant has failed to authorise the Office to include a translation as provided for in Rule 102(4), or where it is otherwise unclear on which list of goods and services the international application shall be based, the Office shall invite the applicant to make the required indications within such a period as it may specify.

(4) If the deficiencies referred to in paragraph 2 are not remedied or the required indications referred to in paragraph 3 are not made within the time limit fixed by the Office, the Office will take a decision refusing to forward the international application to the International Bureau.]

NOTES

Added as noted to r 102, at **[5.507]**.

[5.509]

[Rule 104

Forwarding of the international application

The Office shall forward the international application to the International Bureau along with the certification provided for under Article 3(1) of the Madrid Protocol as soon as the international application meets the requirements laid down in Rules 102 and 103 as well as in Articles 141 and 142 of the Regulation.]

NOTES

Added as noted to r 102, at **[5.507]**.

[5.510]

[Rule 105

Subsequent designations

(1) The Office shall invite the applicant requesting the territorial extension subsequent to the international registration, as referred to in Article 144 of the Regulation, to remedy any of the following deficiencies within such time limit as it may specify—

(a) the request for territorial extension is not filed on one of the form referred to Rule 102(1) and (2) and does not contain all the indications and information required by that form;

(b) the request for territorial extension does not indicate the number of the international registration to which it relates;

(c) the list of goods and services is not covered by the list of goods and services contained in the international registration; or

(d) according to the indications made in the international form, the applicant requesting the territorial extension is not entitled to make a designation subsequent to the international registration through the Office in accordance with Articles 2(1)(ii) and Article 3*ter* (2) of the Madrid Protocol,

(2) If the deficiencies referred to in paragraph 1 are not remedied within the time limit fixed by the Office, the Office will take a decision refusing to forward the request for territorial extension made subsequently to the international registration to the International Bureau.

(3) The Office shall inform the applicant requesting the territorial extension of the date on which the request for territorial extension is received by the Office.

(4) The Office shall forward the request for territorial extension made subsequently to the international registration to the International Bureau as soon as the deficiencies referred to in paragraph 1 of this Rule have been remedied and the requirements of Article 144 of the Regulation are complied with.]

NOTES

Added as noted to r 102, at **[5.507]**.

[5.511]

[Rule 106

Dependence of the international registration on the basic application or registration

(1) The Office shall notify the International Bureau where, within a period of five years from the date of the international registration,

(a) the Community trade mark application on which the international registration was based has been withdrawn, is deemed to be withdrawn or has been refused by a final decision;

(b) the Community trade mark on which the international registration was based has ceased to have effect because it is surrendered, has not been renewed, has been revoked, or has been declared invalid by the Office by a final decision or, on the basis of a counterclaim in infringement proceedings, by a Community trade mark court;

(c) the Community trade mark application or the Community trade mark on which the international registration was based has been divided into two applications or registrations,

(2) The notification referred to in paragraph 1 shall include—

(a) the number of the international registration;

(b) the name of the holder of the international registration;

(c) the facts and decisions affecting the basic application or registration, as well as the effective date of those facts and decisions;

(d) in the case referred to in paragraph 1(a) or (b), the request to cancel the international registration;

(e) where the act referred to in paragraph 1(a) or (b) affects the basic application or basic registration only with respect to some of the goods and services, those goods and services, or the goods and services which are not affected;

(f) in the case referred to in paragraph 1(c), the number of each Community trade mark application or registration concerned.

(3) The Office shall notify the International Bureau where, at the end of a period of five years from the date of the international registration,

(a) an appeal is pending against a decision of an examiner to refuse the Community trade mark application on which the international registration was based pursuant to Article 38 of the Regulation;

(b) an opposition is pending against the Community trade mark application on which the international registration was based;

(c) an application for revocation or an application for declaration of invalidity is pending against the Community trade mark on which the international registration was based;

(d) mention has been made in the Register of Community Trade Marks that a counterclaim for revocation or for declaration of invalidity has been filed before a Community trade mark court against the Community trade mark on which the international registration was based, but no mention has yet been made in the Register of the decision of the Community trade mark court on the counterclaim;

(4) Once the proceedings referred to in paragraph 3 have been concluded by means of a final decision or an entry in the register, the Office shall notify the International Bureau accordingly with paragraph 2.

(5) Any reference in paragraphs 1 and 3 to a Community trade mark on which the international registration was based shall include a Community trade mark registration resulting from a Community trade mark application on which the international application was based.]

NOTES

Added as noted to r 102, at **[5.507]**.

[5.512]

[Rule 107

Renewals

The international registration shall be renewed directly at the International Bureau.]

NOTES

Added as noted to r 102, at **[5.507]**.

[PART B

INTERNATIONAL REGISTRATIONS DESIGNATING THE EUROPEAN COMMUNITY

[5.513]

Rule 108

Seniority claimed in an international application

(1) Where the seniority of one or more earlier registered trade marks, as referred to in Article 34 of the Regulation, has been claimed in an international application pursuant to Article 148(1) of the Regulation, the holder shall, within three months from the date on which the International Bureau notifies the international registration to the Office, submit a copy of the relevant registration to the Office. The copy must be certified by the competent authority to be an exact copy of the relevant registration.

(2) Where the holder of the international registration is obliged to be represented in proceedings before the Office pursuant to Article 88(2) of the Regulation, the communication as referred to in paragraph 1 shall contain the appointment of a representative within the meaning of Article 89(1) of the Regulation.

(3) The President of the Office may determine that the evidence to be provided by the holder may consist of less than is required under paragraph 1, provided that the information required is available to the Office from other sources.]

NOTES

Added as noted to r 102, at **[5.507]**.

[5.514]

[Rule 109

Examination of seniority claims

(1) Where the Office finds that the seniority claim under Rule 108(1) does not comply with Article 34 of the Regulation, or does not comply with the other requirements of Rule 108, it shall invite the holder to remedy the deficiencies within such period as it may specify.

(2) If the requirements referred to in paragraph 1 are not satisfied within the time limit, the right of seniority in respect of that international registration shall be lost. If the deficiencies concern only some of the goods and services, the right of seniority shall be lost only in so far as those goods and services are concerned.

(3) The Office shall inform the International Bureau of any declaration of a loss of the right of seniority pursuant to paragraph 2. It shall also inform the International Bureau of any withdrawal or restriction of the seniority claim.

(4) The Office shall inform the Benelux Trade Mark Office or the central industrial property office of the Member State concerned of the claiming of seniority, unless the right of seniority is declared lost pursuant to paragraph 2.]

NOTES

Added as noted to r 102, at **[5.507]**.

[5.515]

[Rule 110

Seniority claimed before the Office

(1) The holder of an international registration designating the European Community may claim, directly before the Office, the seniority of one or more earlier registered trade marks as referred to in Article 35 of the Regulation as from the date on which the Office has, pursuant to Article 147(2) of the Regulation, published the fact that no refusal for protection of the international registration designating the European Community has been notified or if any such refusal has been withdrawn, as provided for in Article 148(2) of the Regulation.

(2) Where seniority is claimed before the Office before the date referred to in paragraph 1, the seniority claim shall be deemed to have been received by the Office on the date referred to in paragraph 1.

(3) An application to claim seniority pursuant to Article 148(2) of the Regulation and paragraph 1 shall contain—

(a) an indication that the seniority claim is made for an international registration under the Madrid Protocol;

(b) the registration number of the international registration;

(c) the name and address of the holder of the international registration in accordance with Rule 1(1)(b);

(d) where the holder has appointed a representative, the name and the business address of the representative in accordance with Rule 1(1)(e);

(e) an indication of the Member State or Member States in or for which the earlier mark is registered, the date from which the relevant registration was effective, the number of the relevant registration, and the goods and services for which the earlier mark is registered;

(f) where seniority is claimed for less than all the goods and services contained in the earlier registration, the indication of the goods and services in respect of which seniority is claimed;

(g) a copy of the relevant registration; certified by the competent authority as being an exact copy;

(h) where the holder of the international registration is obliged to be represented in proceedings before the Office pursuant to Article 88(2) of the Regulation, the appointment of a representative within the meaning of Article 89(1) of the Regulation.

(4) If the requirements governing the claiming of seniority referred to in paragraph 3 are not fulfilled, the Office shall invite the holder of the international registration to remedy the deficiencies. If the deficiencies are not remedied within a period specified by the Office, the Office shall reject the application.

(5) Where the Office has accepted the application to claim seniority, it shall inform the International Bureau accordingly by communicating—

(a) the number of the international registration concerned,
(b) the name of the Member state or Member States in or for which the earlier mark is registered,
(c) the number of the relevant registration, and
(d) the date from which the relevant registration was effective.

(6) The Office shall inform the Benelux Trade Mark Office or the central industrial property office of the Member State concerned of the application to claim seniority once it has been accepted by the Office.

(7) The President of the Office may determine that the evidence to be provided by the holder of the international registration may consist of less than is required under paragraph 1(g), provided that the information required is available to the Office from other sources.]

NOTES

Added as noted to r 102, at **[5.507]**.

[5.516]
[Rule 111
Decisions affecting seniority claims

Where a seniority claim which has been made in accordance with Article 148(1) of the Regulation, or which has been communicated pursuant to Rule 110(5), has been withdrawn or cancelled by the Office, the Office shall inform the International Bureau accordingly.]

NOTES

Added as noted to r 102, at **[5.507]**.

[5.517]
[Rule 112
Examination as to absolute grounds for refusal

(1) Where, in the course of the examination pursuant to Article 149(1) of the Regulation, the Office finds that pursuant to Article 38(1) of the Regulation, the trade mark which is subject to the territorial extension to the European Community is ineligible for protection for all or any part of the goods or services for which it has been registered by the International Bureau, the Office shall issue an ex officio notification of provisional refusal pursuant to Article 5(1), and (2) of the Madrid Protocol and Rule 17(1) of the Common Regulations to the International Bureau. Where the holder of the international registration is obliged to be represented in proceedings before the Office pursuant to Article 88(1) of the Regulation, the notification shall contain an invitation to appoint a representative within the meaning of Article 89(1) of the Regulation. The notification of provisional refusal shall state the reasons on which it is based, and shall specify a time limit within which the holder of the international registration may submit his observations and, if appropriate, must appoint a representative. The time limit shall start on the day on which the Office issues the provisional refusal.

(2) . . .

(3) Where, in the course of the examination pursuant to Article 149(1) of the Regulation, the Office finds that the international registration designating the European Community does not contain the indication of a second language pursuant to Rule 126 of the present Regulation and Rule 9(5)(g) (ii) of the Common Regulations, the Office shall issue an ex officio notification of provisional refusal pursuant to Article 5(1), and (2) of the Madrid Protocol and Rule 17(1) of the Common Regulations to the International Bureau. Paragraph 1, second, third and fourth sentence, shall apply.

(4) Where the holder of the international registration fails to overcome the ground for refusing protection within the time limit or to comply with the condition laid down in paragraph 2 or, if appropriate, to appoint a representative or to indicate a second language, the Office will take a decision refusing the protection in whole or for a part of the goods and services for which the international registration is registered. The decision shall be subject to appeal in accordance with Article 57 to 63 of the Regulation.

(5) Where, until the start of the opposition period referred to in Article 151(2) of the Regulation, the Office has not issued an ex officio notification of provisional refusal pursuant to paragraph 1, the Office shall send a statement of grant of protection to the International Bureau, indicating that the examination of absolute grounds of refusal pursuant to Article 38 of the Regulation has been completed but that the international registration is still subject to oppositions or observations of third parties.]

NOTES

Added as noted to r 102, at **[5.507]**.

Para (2): repealed by European Parliament and Council Regulation 2015/2424/EU, Art 2(17).

[5.518]
[Rule 113
Notification of ex officio provisional refusals to the International Bureau

(1) The notification of ex officio provisional refusal of protection of the international registration in whole or in part, pursuant to Rule 112, shall be sent to the International Bureau and shall contain—

(a) the number of the international registration;
(b) all the grounds on which the provisional refusal is based together with a reference to the corresponding provisions of the Regulation;
(c) the indication that the provisional refusal of protection will be confirmed by a decision of the Office if the holder of the international registration does not overcome the grounds for refusal by submitting his observations to the Office within a time limit of two months from the date on which the Offices issues the provisional refusal;
(d) if the provisional refusal relates to only part of the goods and services, the indication of those goods and services.

(2) In respect of each notification of ex officio provisional refusal issued pursuant to paragraph 1, and provided that the time limit for entering an opposition has expired and that no provisional refusal based on an opposition has been issued pursuant to Rule 115(1), the Office shall inform the International Bureau as follows—

(a) where as the result of the proceedings before the Office the provisional refusal has been withdrawn, the fact that the mark is protected in the European Community;
(b) where a decision to refuse protection of the mark has become final, if applicable, following an appeal under Article 57 of the Regulation or an action under Article 63 of the Regulation, the Office shall inform the International Bureau that protection of the mark is refused in the European Community;
(c) where the refusal pursuant to subparagraph (a) or (b) concerns only part of the goods and services, the goods and services for which the mark is protected in the European Community.]

NOTES
Added as noted to r 102, at **[5.507]**.

[5.519]
[Rule 114
Opposition proceedings

(1) Where opposition is entered against an international registration designating the European Community pursuant to Article 151 of the Regulation, the notice of opposition shall contain—

(a) the number of the international registration against which opposition is entered;
(b) an indication of the goods and services listed in the international registration against which opposition is entered;
(c) the name of the holder of the international registration;
[(d) the indications and elements referred to in Rule 15(2)(b) to (h).]

(2) [Rules 15(1), (3) and (4) and 16 to 22 shall apply, subject to the following—]

(a) any reference to an application for registration of the Community trade mark shall be read as a reference to an international registration; (b) any reference to a withdrawal of the application for registration of the Community trade mark shall be read as a reference to the renunciation of the international registration in respect of the European Community;
(c) any reference to the applicant shall be read as a reference to the holder of the international registration.

(3) If the notice of opposition is filed before the expiry of the period of six months referred to in Article 151(2) of the Regulation, the notice of opposition shall be deemed to have been filed on the first day following the expiry of the period of six months. The application of Article 42(3) second sentence of the Regulation shall remain unaffected.

(4) Where the holder of the international registration is obliged to be represented in proceedings before the Office pursuant to Article 88(2) of the Regulation, and where he has not already appointed a representative within the meaning of Article 89(1) of the Regulation, the communication of the opposition to the holder of the international registration pursuant to Rule 19 shall contain the invitation to appoint a representative within the meaning of Article 89(1) of the Regulation within a period of two months from the date of notification of the communication.

Where the holder of the international registration fails to appoint a representative within this period, the Office will take a decision refusing the protection of the international registration.

(5) The opposition procedure shall be stayed if an ex officio provisional refusal of protection is or has been issued pursuant to Rule 112. When the ex officio provisional refusal leads to a decision to refuse protection of the mark which has become final, the Office shall not proceed to judgment and refund the opposition fee, and no decision on the apportionment of costs shall be taken.]

NOTES
Added as noted to r 102, at **[5.507]**.

Paras (1), (2): words in square brackets substituted by Commission Regulation 1041/2005/EC, Art 1(57).

[5.520]
[Rule 115
Notification of provisional refusals based on an opposition

(1) When an opposition against an international registration is entered at the Office pursuant to Article 151(2) of the Regulation, or is deemed to have been entered pursuant to Rule 114(3), the Office shall issue a notification of provisional refusal of protection based on an opposition to the International Bureau.

(2) The notification of provisional refusal of protection based on an opposition shall contain—
- (a) the number of the international registration;
- (b) the indication that the refusal is based on the fact that an opposition has been filed, together with a reference to the provisions of Article 8 of the Regulation on which the opposition relies;
- (c) the name and the address of the opposing party.

(3) Where the opposition is based on a trademark application or registration, the notification referred to in paragraph 2 shall contain the following indications—
- (i) the filing date, the registration date and, if any, the priority date,
- (ii) the filing number and, if different, the registration number,
- (iii) the name and address of the owner,
- (iv) a reproduction of the mark, and
- (v) the list of goods and services on which the opposition is based.

(4) If the provisional refusal relates to only part of the goods and services, the notification referred to in paragraph 2 shall indicate those goods and services.

(5) The Office shall inform the International Bureau as follows—
- (a) where as the result of the opposition proceeding the provisional refusal has been withdrawn, the fact that the mark is protected in the European Community;
- (b) where a decision to refuse protection of the mark has become final, if applicable, following an appeal under Article 57 of the Regulation or an action under Article 63 of the Regulation, the fact that protection of the mark is refused in the European Community;
- (c) where the refusal pursuant to subparagraph (a) or (b) concerns only part of the goods and services, the goods and services for which the mark is protected in the European Community.

(6) Where for one and the same international registration, more than one provisional refusal has been issued pursuant to Rule 112(1) . . . or paragraph 1 of this Rule, the communication referred to in paragraph 5 of this Rule shall relate to the total or partial refusal of protection of the mark as it results from all the procedures under Article 149 and 151 of the Regulation.]

NOTES

Added as noted to r 102, at **[5.507]**.

Para (6): reference omitted repealed by European Parliament and Council Regulation 2015/2424/EU, Art 2(17a).

[5.521]
[Rule 116
Statement of grant of protection

(1) Where the Office has not issued an ex officio notification of provisional refusal pursuant to Rule 112 and no opposition has been received by the Office within the opposition period referred to in Article 151(2) of the Regulation and the Office has not issued an ex officio notification of provisional refusal as a result of the third party observations filed, the Office shall send a further statement of grant of protection to the International Bureau, indicating that the mark is protected in the European Community.

(2) For the purposes of Article 146(2) of the Regulation, the further statement of grant of protection referred to in paragraph 1 shall have the same effect as a statement by the Office that a notice of refusal has been withdrawn.]

NOTES

Added as noted to r 102, at **[5.507]**.

[5.522]
[Rule 117
Notification of invalidation to the International Bureau

(1) Where, pursuant to Article 56 or 96 and Article 153 of the Regulation, the effects of an international registration designating the European Community have been declared invalid and where that decision has become final, the Office shall notify the International Bureau accordingly.

(2) The notification shall be dated and shall contain—
- (a) the indication that the invalidation has been pronounced by the Office, or the indication of the Community trade mark court which has pronounced the invalidation;

(b) the indication whether invalidation has been pronounced in the form of revocation of the rights of the holder of the international registration, of a declaration that the trade mark is invalid on absolute grounds, or of a declaration that the trade mark is invalid on relative grounds;
(c) the indication of the fact that the invalidation is no longer subject to appeal;
(d) the number of the international registration;
(e) the name of the holder of the international registration;
(f) if the invalidation does not concern all the goods and services, those goods and services in respect of which the invalidation has been pronounced or those in respect of which the invalidation has not been pronounced;
(g) the date on which the invalidation has been pronounced, together with the indication whether the invalidation is effective as of that date or ex tunc.]

NOTES

Added as noted to r 102, at **[5.507]**.

[5.523]
[Rule 118
Legal effect of registration of transfers

For the purposes of Article 17, and also in conjunction with Article 23(1) or (2) and Article 24, of the Regulation, recordal of a change in the ownership of the international registration on the International Register shall replace the entry of a transfer in the Register of Community Trade Marks.]

NOTES

Added as noted to r 102, at **[5.507]**.

[5.524]
[Rule 119
Legal effect of registration of licenses and other rights

For the purposes of Articles 19, 20, 21 and 22, and also in conjunction with Article 23 and Article 24, of the Regulation, recordal of a license or a restriction of the holder's right of disposal in respect of the international registration on the International Register shall replace the registration of a license, a right *in rem*, a levy of execution or insolvency proceedings in the Register of Community Trade Marks.]

NOTES

Added as noted to r 102, at **[5.507]**.

[5.525]
[Rule 120
Examination of requests for registrations of transfers, licenses or restrictions of the holder's right of disposal

(1) Where a request to register a change in ownership, a license or a restriction of the holder's right of disposal is filed through the Office by a person other than the holder of the international registration, the Office shall refuse to transmit the request to the International Bureau if the request is not accompanied by proof of the transfer, license or the restriction of the right of disposal.
(2) Where a request to register the amendment or cancellation of a license or the removal of a restriction of the holder's right of disposal is filed through the Office by the holder of the international registration, the Office will take a decision refusing to transmit the request to the International Bureau if the request is not accompanied by proof that the license no longer exists or has been amended, or that the restriction of the right of disposal has been removed.]

NOTES

Added as noted to r 102, at **[5.507]**.

[5.526]
[Rule 121
Collective marks

(1) Where the international registration indicates that it is based on a basic application or basic registration which relates to a collective mark, certification mark or guarantee mark, the international registration designating the European Community shall be dealt with as a Community collective mark.
(2) The holder of the international registration shall submit the regulations governing use of the mark as provided for in Article 65 of the Regulation and Rule 43 directly to the Office within a period of two months from the date on which the International Bureau notifies the international registration to the Office.
(3) A notification of ex officio provisional refusal pursuant to Rule 112 shall also be issued—

(a) if one of the grounds for refusal foreseen in Article 66(1) or (2), in conjunction paragraph 3 of that Article, of the Regulation exists;

(b) where the regulations governing use of the mark have not been submitted in accordance with paragraph 2.

Rules 112 . . . (3) and 113 shall apply.

(4) Notice of amendments to the regulations governing use of the mark pursuant to Article 69 of the Regulation shall be published in the Community Trade Marks Bulletin.]

NOTES

Added as noted to r 102, at **[5.507]**.

Para (3): reference omitted repealed by European Parliament and Council Regulation 2015/2424/EU, Art 2(17b).

[5.527]

[Rule 122

Conversion of an international registration into a national trade mark application

(1) An application for conversion of an international registration designating the European Community into a national trade mark application pursuant to Articles 108 and 154 of the Regulation shall contain—

(a) the registration number of the international registration;

(b) the date of the international registration or the date of the designation of the European Community made subsequently to the international registration pursuant to Article 3*ter* (2) of the Madrid Protocol and, where applicable, particulars of the claim to priority for the international registration pursuant to Article 154(2) of the Regulation and particulars of the claim to seniority pursuant to Articles 34, 35 and 148 of the Regulation;

[(c) the indications and elements referred to in Rule 44(1) (a), (c), (d), (e) and (f).]

(2) Where conversion is requested pursuant to Article 108(5) and 154 of the Regulation following a failure to renew the international registration designating the European Community, the application referred to in paragraph 1 shall contain an indication to that effect, and the date on which the protection has expired. The period of three months provided for in Article 108(5) of the Regulation shall begin to run on the day following the last day on which the renewal may still be effected pursuant to Article 7(4) of the Madrid Protocol;

(3) Rules 45, 46(2) (a) and (c), and 47 shall apply *mutatis mutandis*.]

NOTES

Added as noted to r 102, at **[5.507]**.

Para (1): sub-para (c) substituted by Commission Regulation 1041/2005/EC, Art 1(58).

[5.528]

[Rule 123

Conversion of an international registration into a designation of a Member State party to the Madrid Protocol or the Madrid Agreement

(1) An application for conversion of an international registration designating the European Community into a designation of a Member State party to the Madrid Protocol or the Madrid Agreement pursuant to Article 154 of the Regulation shall contain the indications and elements referred to in Rule 122(1) and (2).

(2) Rule 45 shall apply *mutatis mutandis*. The Office shall also reject the application for conversion where the conditions to designate the Member State which is a party to the Madrid Protocol or to the Madrid Agreement were not fulfilled both on the date of the designation of the European Community and the date on which the application for conversion was received or, pursuant to the second sentence of Article 109(1) of the Regulation, is deemed to have been received by the Office.

(3) Rule 46(2)(a) and (c) shall apply *mutatis mutandis*. The publication of the application for conversion shall also contain the indication that conversion has been requested into a designation of a Member State party to the Madrid Protocol or the Madrid Agreement pursuant to Article 154 of the Regulation.

(4) Where the application for conversion complies with the requirements of the Regulation and these Rules, the Office shall transmit it without delay to the International Bureau. The Office shall inform the holder of the international registration of the date of transmission.]

NOTES

Added as noted to r 102, at **[5.507]**.

[5.529]
[Rule 124
Transformation of an international registration designating the European Community into a Community trade mark application

(1) In order to be considered a transformation of an international registration which has been cancelled at the request of the office of origin by the International Bureau pursuant to Article 9 quinquies of the Madrid Protocol and in accordance with Article 156 of the Regulation, a Community trade mark application must contain an indication to that effect. That indication must be made on filing of the application.

(2) The application shall contain, in addition to the indications and elements referred to in Rule 1,
- (a) the indication of the number of the international registration which has been cancelled;
- (b) the date on which the international registration was cancelled by the International Bureau;
- (c) as appropriate, the date of the international registration pursuant to Article 3(4) of the Madrid Protocol or the date of recordal of the territorial extension to the European Community made subsequently to the international registration pursuant to Article 3*ter* (2) of the Madrid Protocol;
- (d) where applicable, the date of priority claimed in the international application as entered in the International Register kept by the International Bureau.

(3) Where, in the course of the examination in accordance with Rule 9(3), the Office finds that the application was not filed within three months from the date on which the international registration was cancelled by the International Bureau; or the goods and services for which the Community trade mark is to be registered are not contained in the list of goods and services for which the international registration was registered in respect of the European Community, the Office shall invite the applicant to remedy the deficiencies noted and in particular to restrict the list of goods and services to those goods and services which have been contained in the list of goods and services for which the international registration was registered in respect of the European Community, within such a period as it may specify.

(4) If the deficiencies referred to in paragraph 3 are not remedied within the time limit, the right to the date of the international registration or to the date of the territorial extension and, if any, to the date of the priority of the international registration shall be lost.

NOTES

Added as noted to r 102, at **[5.507]**.

[PART C
COMMUNICATIONS

[5.530]
Rule 125
Communications with the International Bureau and electronic forms

(1) Communications with the International Bureau shall be in a manner and format agreed on between the International Bureau and the Office, preferably by electronic means.

(2) Any reference to forms shall be construed as including forms made available in electronic format.]

NOTES

Added as noted to r 102, at **[5.507]**.

[5.531]
[Rule 126
Use of languages

For the purposes of applying the Regulation and these Rules to international registrations designating the European Community, the language of filing of the international application shall be the language of the proceedings within the meaning of Article 115(4) of the Regulation, and the second language indicated in the international application shall be the second language within the meaning of Article 115(3) of the Regulation.]

NOTES

Added as noted to r 102, at **[5.507]**.

[5.532]
Article 2
Transitional Provisions

(1) Any application for registration of a Community trade mark filed within three months prior to the date determined pursuant to Article 143(3) of the Regulation shall be marked by the Office with the filing date determined pursuant to that provision and with the actual date of receipt of the application.

(2) With regard to the application, the priority period of six months provided for in Articles 29 and 33 of the Regulation shall be calculated from the date determined pursuant to Article 143(3) of the Regulation.
(3) The Office may issue a receipt to the applicant prior to the date determined pursuant to Article 143(3) of the Regulation.
(4) The Office may examine the applications prior to the date determined pursuant to Article 143(3) of the Regulation and communicate with the applicant with a view to remedying any deficiencies prior to that date. Any decisions with regard to such applications may be taken only after that date.
(5) With regard to the application, the Office shall not carry out any search pursuant to Article 39(1) of the Regulation, regardless of whether or not a priority was claimed for such application pursuant to Articles 29 or 33 of the Regulation.
(6) Where the date of receipt of an application for the registration of a Community trade mark by the Office, by the central industrial property office of a Member State or by the Benelux Trade Mark Office is before the commencement of the three months period specified in Article 143(4) of the Regulation the application shall be deemed not to have been filed. The application shall be informed accordingly and the application shall be sent back to him.

[5.533]
Article 3
Entry into force
This Regulation shall enter into force on the seventh day following that of its publication in the *Official Journal of the European Communities.*

This Regulation shall be binding in its entirety and directly applicable in all Member States.

COMMISSION REGULATION

(216/96/EC)

of 5 February 1996

laying down the rules of procedure of the Boards of Appeal of the Office for Harmonization in the Internal Market (Trade Marks and Designs)

NOTES
Date of publication in OJ: OJ L28, 6.2.1996, p 11.

THE COMMISSION OF THE EUROPEAN COMMUNITIES,

Having regard to the Treaty establishing the European Community,

Having regard to Council Regulation (EC) No 40/94 of 20 December 1994 on the Community trade mark,[1] as amended by Regulation (EC) No 3288/94,[2] and in particular Article 140(3) thereof,

Whereas Regulation (EC) No 40/94 (hereinafter 'the Regulation') creates a new trade mark system allowing a trade mark having effect throughout the Community to be obtained on the basis of an application to the Office for Harmonization in the Internal Market (Trade Marks and Designs) ('the Office');

Whereas for this purpose the Regulation contains in particular the necessary provisions for a procedure leading to the registration of a Community trade marks, as well as for the administration of Community trade marks, for appeals against decisions of the Office and for proceedings in relation to revocation or invalidity of a Community trade mark;

Whereas under Article 130 of the Regulation, the Boards of Appeal are to be responsible for deciding on appeals from decisions of the examiners, the Opposition Divisions, the Administration of Trade Marks and Legal Division and the Cancellation Divisions;

Whereas Title VII of the Regulation contains basic principles regarding appeals against decisions of examiners, the Opposition Divisions, the Administration of Trade Marks and Legal Division and the Cancellation Divisions;

Whereas Title X of Commission Regulation (EC) No 2868/95 of 13 December 1995 implementing Council Regulation No 40/94 on the Community Trade Mark[3] contains implementing rules to Title VII of the Regulation;

Whereas this Regulation supplements those other rules, in particular as regards the organization of the Boards and the oral procedure;

Whereas before the beginning of each working year a scheme should be established for the distribution of business between the Boards of Appeal by an Authority established for that purpose; whereas to this end the said Authority should apply objective criteria such as classes of products and services or initial letters of the names of applicants;

Whereas to facilitate the handling and disposal of appeals, a rapporteur should be designated for each case, who should be responsible inter alia for preparing communications with the parties and drafting decisions;

Whereas the parties to proceedings before the Boards of Appeal may not be in a position or may not be willing to bring questions of general relevance to a pending case to the attention of the Boards of Appeal; whereas, therefore, the Boards of Appeal should have the power, of their own motion or pursuant to a request by the President, to invite the President of the Office, to submit comments on questions of general interest in relation to a case pending before the Boards of Appeal;

Whereas the measures provided for in this Regulation are in accordance with the opinion of the Committee established under Article 141 of the Regulation,

NOTES

[1] OJ L11, 14.1.1994, p 1.

[2] OJ L349, 31.12.1994, p 83.

[3] OJ L303, 15.12.1995, p 1.

HAS ADOPTED THIS REGULATION—

[5.534]
[Article 1
Presidium of the Boards of Appeal

1. The authority referred to in Articles 130 and 131 of the Regulation shall be the Presidium of the Boards of Appeal (referred to hereinafter as "the Presidium").

2. The Presidium shall comprise the President of the Boards of Appeal, who shall chair it, the chairmen of the Boards and Board members elected for each calendar year by and from among all the members of the Boards other than the President of the Boards of Appeal and the chairmen of the Boards. The number of Board members so elected shall be a quarter of the number of Board members, other than the President of the Boards of Appeal and the chairmen of the Boards, rounded up if necessary.

3. If the President of the Boards of Appeal is unable to act or if the post of President is vacant, the Presidium shall be chaired by—
   (a) the chairman of the Board having the longest service on the Boards of Appeal; or
   (b) where chairmen have the same length of service, by the eldest of those qualifying under the preceding subparagraph.

4. The Presidium may validly deliberate only if at least two-thirds of its members are present, including its chairman and two Board chairmen. Decisions of the Presidium shall be taken by a majority vote. In the event of a tie, the vote of the chairman shall be decisive.

5. Before the beginning of each calendar year, and without prejudice to Article 1(b), the Presidium shall decide on objective criteria for allocating cases among the Boards for the calendar year in question and shall designate the full and alternate members of each of the Boards for that year. Each member of the Boards of Appeal may be assigned to several Boards as a full or alternate member. These measures may be modified, as necessary, in the course of the calendar year in question. Decisions adopted by the Presidium pursuant to this paragraph shall be published in the Official Journal of the Office.

6. The Presidium shall also be competent to—
   (a) lay down such rules of a procedural nature as are necessary for the processing of cases brought before the Boards and such rules as are necessary on the organisation of the Boards' work;
   (b) rule on any conflict concerning the allocation of cases among the Boards of Appeal;
   (c) lay down its internal rules;
   (d) lay down practical instructions of a procedural nature for parties involved in proceedings before the Boards of Appeal, for example, with regard to the submission of written statements and to oral proceedings;
   (e) exercise any other powers as are conferred to it by the present Regulation.

7. The President of the Boards of Appeal shall consult the Presidium on the expenditure requirements of the Boards, which he shall communicate to the President of the Office with a view to drawing up the expenditure estimates and where he considers it appropriate, on any other question relating to the management of the Boards of Appeal.]

NOTES

Substituted by Commission Regulation 2082/2004/EC, Art 1(1).

[5.535]
[Article 1a
Grand Board

1. The enlarged Board set up by Article 130(3) of the Regulation shall be the Grand Board.

2. The Grand Board shall comprise nine members, including the President of the Boards of Appeal, who shall chair it, the chairmen of the Boards, the rapporteur designated prior to referral to the Grand Board, if applicable, and members drawn in rotation from a list comprising the names of all members of the Boards of Appeal other than the President of the Boards of Appeal and the chairmen of the Boards.

The Presidium shall draw up the list referred to in the first paragraph and establish the rules according to which members are drawn from that list on the basis of objective criteria. The list and such rules shall be published in the Official Journal of the Office. If a rapporteur has not been designated prior to referral to the Grand Board, the chairman of the Grand Board shall designate a rapporteur from among the members of the Grand Board.

3. If the President of the Boards of Appeal is unable to act or if the post of President is vacant, or in the event of exclusion or objection within the meaning of Article 132 of the Regulation, the Grand Board shall be chaired by—

(a) the chairman having the longest service on the Boards of Appeal; or

(b) where chairmen have the same length of service, by the eldest of those qualifying under the preceding subparagraph 4.

4. If another member of the Grand Board is unable to act or in the event of exclusion or objection within the meaning of Article 132 of the Regulation, he or she shall be replaced by the person highest on the list referred to in paragraph 2 of this Article.

5. The Grand Board may not hear cases and oral proceedings may not take place before it unless seven of its members are present, including its chairman and the rapporteur.

If the Grand Board hears a case in the presence of only eight of its members, the member with the least seniority in the Boards of Appeal shall not take part in the vote, unless that member is the chairman or the rapporteur, in which case the member with the next highest seniority to that of the chairman or rapporteur shall not vote.]

NOTES

Inserted, together with Arts 1b–1d, by Commission Regulation 2082/2004/EC, Art 1(2).

[5.536]
[Article 1b
Referral to the Grand Board

1. A Board may refer a case allocated to it to the Grand Board if it believes that this is justified by the legal difficulty or importance of the case or by special circumstances, for example, if Boards of Appeal have issued diverging decisions on a point of law raised by that case.

2. A Board shall refer a case allocated to it to the Grand Board if it believes that it must deviate from an interpretation of the relevant legislation given in an earlier decision of the Grand Board.

3. The Presidium may, on a proposal made by the President of the Boards of Appeal on his or her own initiative or at the request of a member of the Presidium, refer to the Grand Board a case allocated to a Board if it believes that this is justified by the legal difficulty or importance of the case or by special circumstances, for example, if Boards of Appeal have issued diverging decisions on a point of law raised by that case.

4. The Grand Board shall, without delay, refer the case back to the Board to which it was originally allocated if it believes that the conditions for the original referral are not met.

5. All decisions relating to referral to the Grand Board shall be reasoned and shall be communicated to the parties to the case.]

NOTES

Inserted as noted to Art 1a, at **[5.535]**.

[5.537]
[Article 1c
Decisions by a single member

1. The Presidium shall draw up an indicative list of the types of cases which the Boards may, unless special circumstances apply, devolve to a single member, such as decisions closing the proceedings following agreement between the parties, and decisions on the award of costs and the admissibility of the appeal.

The Presidium may also draw up a list of the types of cases which may not be devolved to a single member.

2. A Board may delegate to its chairman the decision to allocate to a single member cases falling within the types of cases defined by the Presidium in accordance with paragraph 1.

3. The decision to devolve the case upon a single member shall be communicated to the parties.

The member to whom the case has been devolved shall refer it to the Board if he finds that the conditions for devolution are no longer met.]

NOTES

Inserted as noted to Art 1a, at **[5.535]**.

[5.538]
[Article 1d
Referral of a case following a ruling of the Court of Justice

1. If, pursuant to Article 63(6) of the Regulation, the measures necessary to comply with a judgment of the Court of Justice annulling all or part of a decision of a Board of Appeal or of the Grand Board include re-examination by the Boards of Appeal of the case which was the subject of that decision, the Presidium shall decide if the case shall be referred to the Board which adopted that decision, or to another Board, or to the Grand Board.
2. If the case is referred to another Board, that Board shall not comprise members who were party to the contested decision. This provision shall not apply if the case is referred to the Grand Board.]

NOTES

Inserted as noted to Art 1a, at **[5.535]**.

[5.539]
Article 2
Replacement of members

1. Reasons for replacement by alternates shall in particular include leave, sickness, inescapable commitments and the grounds of exclusion set out in Article 132 of the Regulation.
2. Any member asking to be replaced by an alternate shall without delay inform the Chairman of the Board concerned of his unavailability.

[5.540]
Article 3
Exclusion and objection

1. If a Board has knowledge of a possible reason for exclusion or objection under Article 132(3) of the Regulation which does not originate from a member himself or from any party to the proceedings, the procedure of Article 132(4) of the Regulation shall be applied.
2. The member concerned shall be invited to present his comments as to whether there is a reason for exclusion or objection.
3. Before a decision is taken on the action to be taken pursuant to Article 132(4) of the Regulation, there shall be no further proceedings in the case.

[5.541]
Article 4
Rapporteurs

1. The Chairman of each Board shall for each appeal designate a member of his Board, or himself, as rapporteur.
2. The rapporteur shall carry out a preliminary study of the appeal. He may prepare communications to the parties subject to the direction of the Chairman of the Board. Communications shall be signed by the rapporteur on behalf of the Board.
[3.] The rapporteur shall draft decisions.

NOTES

Para 3: original para 3 repealed and original para 4 renumbered as such by Commission Regulation 2082/2004/EC, Art 1(3).

[5.542]
[Article 5
Registry

1. A Registry shall be set up at the Boards of Appeal, and shall, inter alia, be responsible, under the authority of the President of the Boards of Appeal, for the receipt, dispatch, safekeeping and notification of all documents relating to the proceedings before the Boards of Appeal, and for compilation of the relevant files.
2. The Registry shall be headed by a Registrar. The President of the Boards of Appeal shall appoint a Registry agent who shall perform the tasks of the Registrar when the latter is absent or unable to act or if the post of Registrar is vacant.
3. The Registrar shall, in particular, ensure that the deadlines and other formal conditions relating to the presentation of the appeal and of the statement of grounds are respected.

If an irregularity is detected which is liable to make the appeal inadmissible, the Registrar shall, without delay, send a reasoned opinion to the chairman of the Board concerned.
4. The minutes of oral proceedings and of the taking of evidence shall be drawn up by the Registrar or, if the President of the Boards of Appeal agrees, by such agent of the Boards of Appeal as the chairman of the Board concerned may designate.
5. The President of the Boards of Appeal may delegate to the Registrar the task of allocating cases to the Boards of Appeal in accordance with allocation criteria laid down by the Presidium.

The Presidium may, upon a proposal by the President of the Boards of Appeal, delegate to the Registry other tasks relating to the conduct of proceedings before the Boards of Appeal.]

NOTES

Substituted by Commission Regulation 2082/2004/EC, Art 1(4).

[5.543]
Article 6
Change in the composition of a Board

1. If the composition of a Board is changed after oral proceedings, the parties to the proceedings shall be informed that, at the request of any party, fresh oral proceedings shall be held before the Board in its new composition. Fresh oral proceedings shall also be held if so requested by the new member and if the other members of the Board have given their agreement.
2. The new member shall be bound to the same extent as the other members by an interim decision which has already been taken.
3. If, when a Board has already reached a final decision, a member is unable to act, he shall not be replaced by an alternate. If the Chairman is unable to act, then the member of the Board concerned having the longer service on the Board, or where members have the same length of service, the older member, shall sign the decision on behalf of the Chairman.

[5.544]
Article 7
Joinder of appeal proceedings

1. If several appeals are filed against a decision, those appeals shall be considered in the same proceedings.
2. If appeals are filed against separate decisions and all the appeals are designated to be examined by one Board having the same composition, that Board may deal with those appeals in joined proceedings with the consent of the parties.

[5.545]
[Article 8
Procedure

1. If the Registrar sends the chairman of a Board of Appeal an opinion on the admissibility of an appeal in accordance with Article 5(3), second paragraph, the chairman of the Board in question may either suspend the proceedings and request the Board to rule on the admissibility of the appeal, or reserve judgement on the admissibility of the appeal for the decision to end the proceedings before the Board of Appeal.
2. In inter partes proceedings, and without prejudice to Article 61(2) of the Regulation, the statement setting out the grounds of appeal and the response to it may be supplemented by a reply from the appellant, lodged within two months of the notification of the response, and a rejoinder by the defendant, lodged within two months of notification of the reply.
3. In inter partes proceedings, the defendant may, in his or her response, seek a decision annulling or altering the contested decision on a point not raised in the appeal. Such submissions shall cease to have effect should the appellant discontinue the proceedings.]

NOTES

Substituted by Commission Regulation 2082/2004/EC, Art 1(5).

[5.546]
Article 9
Oral proceedings

1. If oral proceedings are to take place, the Board shall ensure that the parties have provided all relevant information and documents before the hearing.
2. The Board may, when issuing the summons to attend oral proceedings, add a communication drawing attention to matters which seem to be of special significance, or to the fact that certain questions appear no longer to be contentious, or containing other observations that may help to concentrate on essentials during the oral proceedings.
3. The Board shall ensure that the case is ready for decision at the conclusion of the oral proceedings, unless there are special reasons to the contrary.

[5.547]
Article 10
Communications to the parties

If a Board deems it expedient to communicate with the parties regarding a possible appraisal of substantive or legal matters, such communication shall be made in such a way as not to imply that the Board is in any way bound by it.

[5.548]
Article 11
Comments on questions of general interest

The Board may, on its own initiative or at the written, reasoned request of the President of the Office, invite him to comment in writing or orally on questions of general interest which arise in the course of proceedings pending before it. The parties shall be entitled to submit their observations on the President's comments.

[5.549]
Article 12
Deliberations preceding decisions
The rapporteur shall submit to the other members of the Board a draft of the decision to be taken and shall set a reasonable time-limit within which to oppose it or to ask for changes. The Board shall meet to deliberate on the decision to be taken if it appears that the members of a Board are not all of the same opinion. Only members of the Board shall participate in the deliberations; the Chairman of the Board concerned may, however, authorize other officers such as registrars or interpreters to attend. Deliberations shall be secret.

[5.550]
Article 13
Order of voting
1. During the deliberations between members of a Board, the opinion of the rapporteur shall be heard first, and, if the rapporteur is not the Chairman, the Chairman last.
2. If voting is necessary, votes shall be taken in the same sequence, save that if the Chairman is also the rapporteur, be shall vote last. Abstentions shall not be permitted.

[5.551]
Article 14
Entry into force
This Regulation shall enter into force the third day following its publication in the *Official Journal of the European Communities*.

This Regulation shall be binding in its entirety and directly applicable in all Member States.

COUNCIL DECISION

(2003/793/EC)

of 27 October 2003

approving the accession of the European Community to the Protocol relating to the Madrid Agreement concerning the international registration of marks, adopted at Madrid on 27 June 1989

NOTES

Date of publication in OJ: OJ L296, 14.11.2003, p 20.

THE COUNCIL OF THE EUROPEAN UNION,

Having regard to the Treaty establishing the European Community, and in particular Article 308, in conjunction with Article 300(2), second sentence, and Article 300(3), first subparagraph, thereof,

Having regard to the proposal from the Commission,[1]

Having regard to the opinion of the European Parliament,[2]

Having regard to the opinion of the European Economic and Social Committee,[3]

Whereas—

(1) Council Regulation (EC) No 40/94 of 20 December 1993 on the Community trade mark,[4] which is based on Article 308 of the Treaty, is designed to create a market which functions properly and offers conditions which are similar to those obtaining in a national market. In order to create a market of this kind and make it increasingly a single market, the said Regulation created the Community trade mark system whereby undertakings can by means of one procedural system obtain Community trade marks to which uniform protection is given and which produce their effects throughout the entire area of the European Community.

(2) Following preparations initiated and carried out by the World Intellectual Property Organisation with the participation of the Member States which are members of the Madrid Union, the Member States which are not members of the Madrid Union and the European Community, the Diplomatic Conference for the conclusion of a Protocol relating to the Madrid Agreement concerning the international registration of marks adopted the Protocol relating to the Madrid Agreement concerning the international registration of marks (hereafter referred to as 'the Madrid Protocol') on 27 June 1989, at Madrid.

(3) The Madrid Protocol was adopted in order to introduce certain new features into the system of the international registration of marks existing under the Madrid Agreement concerning the international registration of marks of 14 April 1891 as amended (hereafter referred to as 'the Madrid Agreement').[5]

(4) The objectives of the Madrid Protocol are to ease the way for certain States, and in particular the Member States which are not currently parties thereto, to accede to the system of international registration of marks.

(5) As compared to the Madrid Agreement, the Madrid Protocol introduced, in its Article 14, as

one of the main innovations, the possibility that an intergovernmental organisation which has a regional office for the purpose of registering marks with effect in the territory of the organisation may become party to the Madrid Protocol.

(6) The possibility that an intergovernmental organisation which has a regional office for the purpose of registering marks may become a party to the Madrid Protocol was introduced in the Madrid Protocol in order to allow, in particular, for the European Community to accede to the said Protocol.

(7) The Madrid Protocol entered into force on 1 December 1995 and became operational on 1 April 1996 and the Community trade mark system also became operational on the latter date.

(8) The Community trade mark system and the international registration system as established by the Madrid Protocol are complementary. Therefore, in order to enable firms to profit from the advantages of the Community trade mark through the Madrid Protocol and vice versa, it is necessary to allow Community trade mark applicants and holders of such trade marks to apply for international protection of their trade marks through the filing of an international application under the Madrid Protocol and, conversely, holders of international registrations under the Madrid Protocol to apply for protection of their trade marks under the Community trade mark system.

(9) Moreover, the establishment of a link between the Community trade mark system and the international registration system under the Madrid Protocol would promote a harmonious development of economic activities, will eliminate distortions of competition, will be cost efficient and will increase the level of integration and functioning of the internal market. Therefore, the accession of the Community to the Madrid Protocol is necessary in order for the Community trade mark system to become more attractive.

(10) The European Commission should be authorised to represent the European Community in the Assembly of the Madrid Union after the accession of the Community to the Madrid Protocol. The European Community will not express a view in the Assembly in matters relating solely to the Madrid Agreement.

(11) The competence of the European Community to conclude or accede to international agreements or treaties does not derive only from explicit conferral by the Treaty but may also derive from other provisions of the Treaty and from acts adopted pursuant to those provisions by Community institutions.

(12) This Decision does not affect the right of the Member States to participate in the Assembly of the Madrid Union with regard to their national trade marks,

NOTES

1 OJ C293, 5.10.1996, p 11.

2 OJ C167, 2.6.1997, p 252.

3 OJ C89, 19.3.1997, p 14.

4 OJ L11, 14.1.1994, p 1. Regulation as last amended by Regulation (EC) No 1653/2003, (OJ L245, 29.9.2003, p 36).

5 The Madrid Agreement concerning the international registration of marks as revised last at Stockholm on 14 July 1967 and as amended on 2 October 1979.

HAS DECIDED AS FOLLOWS—

[5.552]
Article 1
The Protocol relating to the Madrid Agreement concerning the international registration of marks, adopted at Madrid on 27 June 1989 (hereafter referred to as the Madrid Protocol), is hereby approved on behalf of the Community with regard to matters within its competence.

The text of the Madrid Protocol is attached to this Decision.

[5.553]
Article 2
1. The President of the Council is hereby authorised to deposit the instrument of accession with the Director-General of the World Intellectual Property Organisation as from the date on which the Council has adopted the measures which are necessary for the establishment of a link between the Community trade mark and the Madrid Protocol.
2. The declarations and notification, which are attached to this Decision, shall be made in the instrument of accession.

[5.554]
Article 3
1. The Commission is hereby authorised to represent the European Community at the meetings of the Madrid Union Assembly held under the auspices of the World Intellectual Property Organisation.
2. On all matters within the sphere of competence of the Community with regard to the Community trade mark, the Commission shall negotiate in the Madrid Union Assembly on behalf of the Community in accordance with the following arrangements—

(a) the position which the Community may adopt within the Assembly shall be prepared by the relevant Council working party or, if this is not possible, at on-the-spot meetings convened in the course of the work within the framework of the World Intellectual Property Organisation;
(b) as regards decisions involving the amendment of Regulation (EC) No 40/94, or of any other act of the Council requiring unanimity, the Community position shall be adopted by the Council acting unanimously on a proposal from the Commission;
(c) as regards other decisions affecting the Community trade mark, the Community position shall be adopted by the Council acting by a qualified majority on a proposal from the Commission.

DIRECTIVE OF THE EUROPEAN PARLIAMENT AND OF THE COUNCIL

(2008/95/EC)

of 22 October 2008

to approximate the laws of the Member States relating to trade marks ('Trade Marks Directive')

(codified version)

(Text with EEA relevance)

NOTES

Date of publication in OJ: OJ L299, 8.11.2008, p 25.

Note: this Directive is repealed by European Parliament and Council Directive 2015/2436/EU, with effect from 15 January 2019; see Art 55 thereof at [5.845].

THE EUROPEAN PARLIAMENT AND THE COUNCIL OF THE EUROPEAN UNION,

Having regard to the Treaty establishing the European Community, and in particular Article 95 thereof,

Having regard to the proposal from the Commission,

Having regard to the opinion of the European Economic and Social Committee,[1]

Acting in accordance with the procedure laid down in Article 251 of the Treaty,[2]

Whereas:

(1) The content of Council Directive 89/104/EEC of 21 December 1988 to approximate the laws of the Member States relating to trade marks[3] *has been amended.*[4] *In the interests of clarity and rationality the said Directive should be codified.*

(2) The trade mark laws applicable in the Member States before the entry into force of Directive 89/104/EEC contained disparities which may have impeded the free movement of goods and freedom to provide services and may have distorted competition within the common market. It was therefore necessary to approximate the laws of the Member States in order to ensure the proper functioning of the internal market.

(3) It is important not to disregard the solutions and advantages which the Community trade mark system may afford to undertakings wishing to acquire trade marks.

(4) It does not appear to be necessary to undertake full-scale approximation of the trade mark laws of the Member States. It will be sufficient if approximation is limited to those national provisions of law which most directly affect the functioning of the internal market.

(5) This Directive should not deprive the Member States of the right to continue to protect trade marks acquired through use but should take them into account only in regard to the relationship between them and trade marks acquired by registration.

(6) Member States should also remain free to fix the provisions of procedure concerning the registration, the revocation and the invalidity of trade marks acquired by registration. They can, for example, determine the form of trade mark registration and invalidity procedures, decide whether earlier rights should be invoked either in the registration procedure or in the invalidity procedure or in both and, if they allow earlier rights to be invoked in the registration procedure, have an opposition procedure or an ex officio examination procedure or both. Member States should remain free to determine the effects of revocation or invalidity of trade marks.

(7) This Directive should not exclude the application to trade marks of provisions of law of the Member States other than trade mark law, such as the provisions relating to unfair competition, civil liability or consumer protection.

(8) Attainment of the objectives at which this approximation of laws is aiming requires that the conditions for obtaining and continuing to hold a registered trade mark be, in general, identical in all Member States. To this end, it is necessary to list examples of signs which may constitute a trade

mark, provided that such signs are capable of distinguishing the goods or services of one undertaking from those of other undertakings. The grounds for refusal or invalidity concerning the trade mark itself, for example, the absence of any distinctive character, or concerning conflicts between the trade mark and earlier rights, should be listed in an exhaustive manner, even if some of these grounds are listed as an option for the Member States which should therefore be able to maintain or introduce those grounds in their legislation. Member States should be able to maintain or introduce into their legislation grounds of refusal or invalidity linked to conditions for obtaining and continuing to hold a trade mark for which there is no provision of approximation, concerning, for example, the eligibility for the grant of a trade mark, the renewal of the trade mark or rules on fees, or related to the non-compliance with procedural rules.

(9) In order to reduce the total number of trade marks registered and protected in the Community and, consequently, the number of conflicts which arise between them, it is essential to require that registered trade marks must actually be used or, if not used, be subject to revocation. It is necessary to provide that a trade mark cannot be invalidated on the basis of the existence of a non-used earlier trade mark, while the Member States should remain free to apply the same principle in respect of the registration of a trade mark or to provide that a trade mark may not be successfully invoked in infringement proceedings if it is established as a result of a plea that the trade mark could be revoked. In all these cases it is up to the Member States to establish the applicable rules of procedure.

(10) It is fundamental, in order to facilitate the free movement of goods and services, to ensure that registered trade marks enjoy the same protection under the legal systems of all the Member States. This should not, however, prevent the Member States from granting at their option extensive protection to those trade marks which have a reputation.

(11) The protection afforded by the registered trade mark, the function of which is in particular to guarantee the trade mark as an indication of origin, should be absolute in the case of identity between the mark and the sign and the goods or services. The protection should apply also in the case of similarity between the mark and the sign and the goods or services. It is indispensable to give an interpretation of the concept of similarity in relation to the likelihood of confusion. The likelihood of confusion, the appreciation of which depends on numerous elements and, in particular, on the recognition of the trade mark on the market, the association which can be made with the used or registered sign, the degree of similarity between the trade mark and the sign and between the goods or services identified, should constitute the specific condition for such protection. The ways in which likelihood of confusion may be established, and in particular the onus of proof, should be a matter for national procedural rules which should not be prejudiced by this Directive.

(12) It is important, for reasons of legal certainty and without inequitably prejudicing the interests of a proprietor of an earlier trade mark, to provide that the latter may no longer request a declaration of invalidity nor may he oppose the use of a trade mark subsequent to his own of which he has knowingly tolerated the use for a substantial length of time, unless the application for the subsequent trade mark was made in bad faith.

(13) All Member States are bound by the Paris Convention for the Protection of Industrial Property. It is necessary that the provisions of this Directive should be entirely consistent with those of the said Convention. The obligations of the Member States resulting from that Convention should not be affected by this Directive. Where appropriate, the second paragraph of Article 307 of the Treaty should apply.

(14) This Directive should be without prejudice to the obligations of the Member States relating to the time limit for transposition into national law of Directive 89/104/EEC set out in Annex I, Part B,

NOTES

1 OJ C161, 13.7.2007, p 44.

2 Opinion of the European Parliament of 19 June 2007 (OJ C146 E, 12.6.2008, p 76) and Council Decision of 25 September 2008.

3 OJ L40, 11.2.1989, p 1.

4 See Annex I, Part A.

HAVE ADOPTED THIS DIRECTIVE:

[5.555]
Article 1
Scope

This Directive shall apply to every trade mark in respect of goods or services which is the subject of registration or of an application in a Member State for registration as an individual trade mark, a collective mark or a guarantee or certification mark, or which is the subject of a registration or an application for registration in the Benelux Office for Intellectual Property or of an international registration having effect in a Member State.

[5.556]
Article 2
Signs of which a trade mark may consist
A trade mark may consist of any signs capable of being represented graphically, particularly words, including personal names, designs, letters, numerals, the shape of goods or of their packaging, provided that such signs are capable of distinguishing the goods or services of one undertaking from those of other undertakings.

[5.557]
Article 3
Grounds for refusal or invalidity
1. The following shall not be registered or, if registered, shall be liable to be declared invalid:
- *(a) signs which cannot constitute a trade mark;*
- *(b) trade marks which are devoid of any distinctive character;*
- *(c) trade marks which consist exclusively of signs or indications which may serve, in trade, to designate the kind, quality, quantity, intended purpose, value, geographical origin, or the time of production of the goods or of rendering of the service, or other characteristics of the goods or services;*
- *(d) trade marks which consist exclusively of signs or indications which have become customary in the current language or in the bona fide and established practices of the trade;*
- *(e) signs which consist exclusively of:*
  - *(i) the shape which results from the nature of the goods themselves;*
  - *(ii) the shape of goods which is necessary to obtain a technical result;*
  - *(iii) the shape which gives substantial value to the goods;*
- *(f) trade marks which are contrary to public policy or to accepted principles of morality;*
- *(g) trade marks which are of such a nature as to deceive the public, for instance as to the nature, quality or geographical origin of the goods or service;*
- *(h) trade marks which have not been authorised by the competent authorities and are to be refused or invalidated pursuant to Article 6ter of the Paris Convention for the Protection of Industrial Property, hereinafter referred to as the "Paris Convention".*

2. Any Member State may provide that a trade mark shall not be registered or, if registered, shall be liable to be declared invalid where and to the extent that:
- *(a) the use of that trade mark may be prohibited pursuant to provisions of law other than trade mark law of the Member State concerned or of the Community;*
- *(b) the trade mark covers a sign of high symbolic value, in particular a religious symbol;*
- *(c) the trade mark includes badges, emblems and escutcheons other than those covered by Article 6ter of the Paris Convention and which are of public interest, unless the consent of the competent authority to their registration has been given in conformity with the legislation of the Member State;*
- *(d) the application for registration of the trade mark was made in bad faith by the applicant.*

3. A trade mark shall not be refused registration or be declared invalid in accordance with paragraph 1(b), (c) or (d) if, before the date of application for registration and following the use which has been made of it, it has acquired a distinctive character. Any Member State may in addition provide that this provision shall also apply where the distinctive character was acquired after the date of application for registration or after the date of registration.

4. Any Member State may provide that, by derogation from paragraphs 1, 2 and 3, the grounds of refusal of registration or invalidity in force in that State prior to the date of entry into force of the provisions necessary to comply with Directive 89/104/EEC, shall apply to trade marks for which application has been made prior to that date.

[5.558]
Article 4
Further grounds for refusal or invalidity concerning conflicts with earlier rights
1. A trade mark shall not be registered or, if registered, shall be liable to be declared invalid:
- *(a) if it is identical with an earlier trade mark, and the goods or services for which the trade mark is applied for or is registered are identical with the goods or services for which the earlier trade mark is protected;*
- *(b) if because of its identity with, or similarity to, the earlier trade mark and the identity or similarity of the goods or services covered by the trade marks, there exists a likelihood of confusion on the part of the public; the likelihood of confusion includes the likelihood of association with the earlier trade mark.*

2. "Earlier trade marks" within the meaning of paragraph 1 means:
- *(a) trade marks of the following kinds with a date of application for registration which is earlier than the date of application for registration of the trade mark, taking account, where appropriate, of the priorities claimed in respect of those trade marks;*
  - *(i) Community trade marks;*
  - *(ii) trade marks registered in the Member State or, in the case of Belgium, Luxembourg or the Netherlands, at the Benelux Office for Intellectual Property;*

(iii) trade marks registered under international arrangements which have effect in the Member State;

(b) Community trade marks which validly claim seniority, in accordance with Council Regulation (EC) No 40/94[1] of 20 December 1993 on the Community trade mark, from a trade mark referred to in (a)(ii) and (iii), even when the latter trade mark has been surrendered or allowed to lapse;

(c) applications for the trade marks referred to in points (a) and (b), subject to their registration;

(d) trade marks which, on the date of application for registration of the trade mark, or, where appropriate, of the priority claimed in respect of the application for registration of the trade mark, are well known in a Member State, in the sense in which the words "well known" are used in Article 6bis of the Paris Convention.

3. A trade mark shall furthermore not be registered or, if registered, shall be liable to be declared invalid if it is identical with, or similar to, an earlier Community trade mark within the meaning of paragraph 2 and is to be, or has been, registered for goods or services which are not similar to those for which the earlier Community trade mark is registered, where the earlier Community trade mark has a reputation in the Community and where the use of the later trade mark without due cause would take unfair advantage of, or be detrimental to, the distinctive character or the repute of the earlier Community trade mark.

4. Any Member State may, in addition, provide that a trade mark shall not be registered or, if registered, shall be liable to be declared invalid where, and to the extent that:

(a) the trade mark is identical with, or similar to, an earlier national trade mark within the meaning of paragraph 2 and is to be, or has been, registered for goods or services which are not similar to those for which the earlier trade mark is registered, where the earlier trade mark has a reputation in the Member State concerned and where the use of the later trade mark without due cause would take unfair advantage of, or be detrimental to, the distinctive character or the repute of the earlier trade mark;

(b) rights to a non-registered trade mark or to another sign used in the course of trade were acquired prior to the date of application for registration of the subsequent trade mark, or the date of the priority claimed for the application for registration of the subsequent trade mark, and that non-registered trade mark or other sign confers on its proprietor the right to prohibit the use of a subsequent trade mark;

(c) the use of the trade mark may be prohibited by virtue of an earlier right other than the rights referred to in paragraph 2 and point (b) of this paragraph and in particular:

(i) a right to a name;

(ii) a right of personal portrayal;

(iii) a copyright;

(iv) an industrial property right;

(d) the trade mark is identical with, or similar to, an earlier collective trade mark conferring a right which expired within a period of a maximum of three years preceding application;

(e) the trade mark is identical with, or similar to, an earlier guarantee or certification mark conferring a right which expired within a period preceding application the length of which is fixed by the Member State;

(f) the trade mark is identical with, or similar to, an earlier trade mark which was registered for identical or similar goods or services and conferred on them a right which has expired for failure to renew within a period of a maximum of two years preceding application, unless the proprietor of the earlier trade mark gave his agreement for the registration of the later mark or did not use his trade mark;

(g) the trade mark is liable to be confused with a mark which was in use abroad on the filing date of the application and which is still in use there, provided that at the date of the application the applicant was acting in bad faith.

5. The Member States may permit that in appropriate circumstances registration need not be refused or the trade mark need not be declared invalid where the proprietor of the earlier trade mark or other earlier right consents to the registration of the later trade mark.

6. Any Member State may provide that, by derogation from paragraphs 1 to 5, the grounds for refusal of registration or invalidity in force in that State prior to the date of the entry into force of the provisions necessary to comply with Directive 89/104/EEC, shall apply to trade marks for which application has been made prior to that date.

NOTES

[1] OJ L11, 14.1.1994, p 1.

[5.559]

Article 5

Rights conferred by a trade mark

1. The registered trade mark shall confer on the proprietor exclusive rights therein. The proprietor shall be entitled to prevent all third parties not having his consent from using in the course of trade:

Part 5 Trade Marks

(a) any sign which is identical with the trade mark in relation to goods or services which are identical with those for which the trade mark is registered;

(b) any sign where, because of its identity with, or similarity to, the trade mark and the identity or similarity of the goods or services covered by the trade mark and the sign, there exists a likelihood of confusion on the part of the public; the likelihood of confusion includes the likelihood of association between the sign and the trade mark.

2. Any Member State may also provide that the proprietor shall be entitled to prevent all third parties not having his consent from using in the course of trade any sign which is identical with, or similar to, the trade mark in relation to goods or services which are not similar to those for which the trade mark is registered, where the latter has a reputation in the Member State and where use of that sign without due cause takes unfair advantage of, or is detrimental to, the distinctive character or the repute of the trade mark.

3. The following, inter alia, may be prohibited under paragraphs 1 and 2:

(a) affixing the sign to the goods or to the packaging thereof;

(b) offering the goods, or putting them on the market or stocking them for these purposes under that sign, or offering or supplying services thereunder;

(c) importing or exporting the goods under the sign;

(d) using the sign on business papers and in advertising.

4. Where, under the law of the Member State, the use of a sign under the conditions referred to in paragraph 1(b) or paragraph 2 could not be prohibited before the date of entry into force of the provisions necessary to comply with Directive 89/104/EEC in the Member State concerned, the rights conferred by the trade mark may not be relied on to prevent the continued use of the sign.

5. Paragraphs 1 to 4 shall not affect provisions in any Member State relating to the protection against the use of a sign other than for the purposes of distinguishing goods or services, where use of that sign without due cause takes unfair advantage of, or is detrimental to, the distinctive character or the repute of the trade mark.

[5.560]
Article 6
Limitation of the effects of a trade mark

1. The trade mark shall not entitle the proprietor to prohibit a third party from using, in the course of trade:

(a) his own name or address;

(b) indications concerning the kind, quality, quantity, intended purpose, value, geographical origin, the time of production of goods or of rendering of the service, or other characteristics of goods or services;

(c) the trade mark where it is necessary to indicate the intended purpose of a product or service, in particular as accessories or spare parts;

provided he uses them in accordance with honest practices in industrial or commercial matters.

2. The trade mark shall not entitle the proprietor to prohibit a third party from using, in the course of trade, an earlier right which only applies in a particular locality if that right is recognised by the laws of the Member State in question and within the limits of the territory in which it is recognised.

[5.561]
Article 7
Exhaustion of the rights conferred by a trade mark

1. The trade mark shall not entitle the proprietor to prohibit its use in relation to goods which have been put on the market in the Community under that trade mark by the proprietor or with his consent.

2. Paragraph 1 shall not apply where there exist legitimate reasons for the proprietor to oppose further commercialisation of the goods, especially where the condition of the goods is changed or impaired after they have been put on the market.

[5.562]
Article 8
Licensing

1. A trade mark may be licensed for some or all of the goods or services for which it is registered and for the whole or part of the Member State concerned. A licence may be exclusive or non-exclusive.

2. The proprietor of a trade mark may invoke the rights conferred by that trade mark against a licensee who contravenes any provision in his licensing contract with regard to:

(a) its duration;

(b) the form covered by the registration in which the trade mark may be used;

(c) the scope of the goods or services for which the licence is granted;

(d) the territory in which the trade mark may be affixed; or

(e) the quality of the goods manufactured or of the services provided by the licensee.

[5.563]
Article 9
Limitation in consequence of acquiescence
1. Where, in a Member State, the proprietor of an earlier trade mark as referred to in Article 4(2) has acquiesced, for a period of five successive years, in the use of a later trade mark registered in that Member State while being aware of such use, he shall no longer be entitled on the basis of the earlier trade mark either to apply for a declaration that the later trade mark is invalid or to oppose the use of the later trade mark in respect of the goods or services for which the later trade mark has been used, unless registration of the later trade mark was applied for in bad faith.
2. Any Member State may provide that paragraph 1 shall apply mutatis mutandis to the proprietor of an earlier trade mark referred to in Article 4(4)(a) or another earlier right referred to in Article 4(4)(b) or (c).
3. In the cases referred to in paragraphs 1 and 2, the proprietor of a later registered trade mark shall not be entitled to oppose the use of the earlier right, even though that right may no longer be invoked against the later trade mark.

[5.564]
Article 10
Use of trade marks
1. If, within a period of five years following the date of the completion of the registration procedure, the proprietor has not put the trade mark to genuine use in the Member State in connection with the goods or services in respect of which it is registered, or if such use has been suspended during an uninterrupted period of five years, the trade mark shall be subject to the sanctions provided for in this Directive, unless there are proper reasons for non-use.
The following shall also constitute use within the meaning of the first subparagraph:
- *(a) use of the trade mark in a form differing in elements which do not alter the distinctive character of the mark in the form in which it was registered;*
- *(b) affixing of the trade mark to goods or to the packaging thereof in the Member State concerned solely for export purposes.*

2. Use of the trade mark with the consent of the proprietor or by any person who has authority to use a collective mark or a guarantee or certification mark shall be deemed to constitute use by the proprietor.
3. In relation to trade marks registered before the date of entry into force in the Member State concerned of the provisions necessary to comply with Directive 89/104/EEC:
- *(a) where a provision in force prior to that date attached sanctions to non-use of a trade mark during an uninterrupted period, the relevant period of five years mentioned in the first subparagraph of paragraph 1 shall be deemed to have begun to run at the same time as any period of non-use which is already running at that date;*
- *(b) where there was no use provision in force prior to that date, the periods of five years mentioned in the first subparagraph of paragraph 1 shall be deemed to run from that date at the earliest.*

[5.565]
Article 11
Sanctions for non-use of a trade mark in legal or administrative proceedings
1. A trade mark may not be declared invalid on the ground that there is an earlier conflicting trade mark if the latter does not fulfil the requirements of use set out in Article 10(1) and (2), or in Article 10(3), as the case may be.
2. Any Member State may provide that registration of a trade mark may not be refused on the ground that there is an earlier conflicting trade mark if the latter does not fulfil the requirements of use set out in Article 10(1) and (2) or in Article 10(3), as the case may be.
3. Without prejudice to the application of Article 12, where a counter-claim for revocation is made, any Member State may provide that a trade mark may not be successfully invoked in infringement proceedings if it is established as a result of a plea that the trade mark could be revoked pursuant to Article 12(1).
4. If the earlier trade mark has been used in relation to part only of the goods or services for which it is registered, it shall, for purposes of applying paragraphs 1, 2 and 3, be deemed to be registered in respect only of that part of the goods or services.

[5.566]
Article 12
Grounds for revocation
1. A trade mark shall be liable to revocation if, within a continuous period of five years, it has not been put to genuine use in the Member State in connection with the goods or services in respect of which it is registered, and there are no proper reasons for non-use.
However, no person may claim that the proprietor's rights in a trade mark should be revoked where, during the interval between expiry of the five-year period and filing of the application for revocation, genuine use of the trade mark has been started or resumed.

The commencement or resumption of use within a period of three months preceding the filing of the application for revocation which began at the earliest on expiry of the continuous period of five years of non-use shall be disregarded where preparations for the commencement or resumption occur only after the proprietor becomes aware that the application for revocation may be filed.

2. Without prejudice to paragraph 1, a trade mark shall be liable to revocation if, after the date on which it was registered:

(a) in consequence of acts or inactivity of the proprietor, it has become the common name in the trade for a product or service in respect of which it is registered;

(b) in consequence of the use made of it by the proprietor of the trade mark or with his consent in respect of the goods or services for which it is registered, it is liable to mislead the public, particularly as to the nature, quality or geographical origin of those goods or services.

[5.567]
Article 13
Grounds for refusal or revocation or invalidity relating to only some of the goods or services
Where grounds for refusal of registration or for revocation or invalidity of a trade mark exist in respect of only some of the goods or services for which that trade mark has been applied for or registered, refusal of registration or revocation or invalidity shall cover those goods or services only.

[5.568]
Article 14
Establishment a posteriori of invalidity or revocation of a trade mark
Where the seniority of an earlier trade mark which has been surrendered or allowed to lapse is claimed for a Community trade mark, the invalidity or revocation of the earlier trade mark may be established a posteriori.

[5.569]
Article 15
Special provisions in respect of collective marks, guarantee marks and certification marks
1. Without prejudice to Article 4, Member States whose laws authorise the registration of collective marks or of guarantee or certification marks may provide that such marks shall not be registered, or shall be revoked or declared invalid, on grounds additional to those specified in Articles 3 and 12 where the function of those marks so requires.

2. By way of derogation from Article 3(1)(c), Member States may provide that signs or indications which may serve, in trade, to designate the geographical origin of the goods or services may constitute collective, guarantee or certification marks. Such a mark does not entitle the proprietor to prohibit a third party from using in the course of trade such signs or indications, provided he uses them in accordance with honest practices in industrial or commercial matters; in particular, such a mark may not be invoked against a third party who is entitled to use a geographical name.

[5.570]
Article 16
Communication
Member States shall communicate to the Commission the text of the main provisions of national law adopted in the field governed by this Directive.

[5.571]
Article 17
Repeal
Directive 89/104/EEC, as amended by the Decision listed in Annex I, Part A, is repealed, without prejudice to the obligations of the Member States relating to the time limit for transposition into national law of that Directive, set out in Annex I, Part B.

References to the repealed Directive shall be construed as references to this Directive and shall be read in accordance with the correlation table in Annex II.

[5.572]
Article 18
Entry into force
This Directive shall enter into force on the 20th day following its publication in the Official Journal of the European Union.

[5.573]
Article 19
Addressees
This Directive is addressed to the Member States.

ANNEX I

PART A
REPEALED DIRECTIVE WITH ITS AMENDMENT

[5.574]

(referred to in Article 17)

Council Directive 89/104/EEC	*(OJ L40, 11.2.1989, p 1)*
Council Decision 92/10/EEC	*(OJ L6, 11.1.1992, p 35)*

PART B
TIME LIMIT FOR TRANSPOSITION INTO NATIONAL LAW

(referred to in Article 17)

Directive	*Time-limit for transposition*
89/104/EEC	*31 December 1992*

ANNEX II
CORRELATION TABLE

[5.575]

Directive 89/104/EEC	*This Directive*
Article 1	*Article 1*
Article 2	*Article 2*
Article 3(1)(a) to (d)	*Article 3(1)(a) to (d)*
Article 3(1)(e), introductory wording	*Article 3(1)(e), introductory wording*
Article 3(1)(e), first indent	*Article 3(1)(e)(i)*
Article 3(1)(e), second indent	*Article 3(1)(e)(ii)*
Article 3(1)(e), third indent	*Article 3(1)(e)(iii)*
Article 3(1)(f), (g) and (h)	*Article 3(1)(f), (g) and (h)*
Article 3(2), (3) and (4)	*Article 3(2), (3) and (4)*
Article 4	*Article 4*
Article 5	*Article 5*
Article 6	*Article 6*
Article 7	*Article 7*
Article 8	*Article 8*
Article 9	*Article 9*
Article 10(1)	*Article 10(1), first subparagraph*
Article 10(2)	*Article 10(1), second subparagraph*
Article 10(3)	*Article 10(2)*
Article 10(4)	*Article 10(3)*
Article 11	*Article 11*
Article 12(1), first sentence	*Article 12(1), first subparagraph*
Article 12(1), second sentence	*Article 12(1), second subparagraph*
Article 12(1), third sentence	*Article 12(1), third subparagraph*
Article 12(2)	*Article 12(2)*
Article 13	*Article 13*
Article 14	*Article 14*
Article 15	*Article 15*
Article 16(1) and (2)	—
Article 16(3)	*Article 16*
—	*Article 17*
—	*Article 18*
Article 17	*Article 19*
—	*Annex I*
—	*Annex II*

COUNCIL REGULATION

(207/2009/EC)

of 26 February 2009

on the [European Union trade mark]

(codified version)

(Text with EEA relevance)

NOTES

Date of publication in OJ: OJ L78, 24.3.2009, p 1.

This Regulation is repealed and codified by European Parliament and Council Regulation 2017/1001/EU on the European Union trade mark, as from 1 October 2017. See Arts 211, 212 thereof at [5.1059], [5.1060].

Title: words in square brackets substituted (for original words "Community trade mark") by European Parliament and Council Regulation 2015/2424/EU, Art 1(1).

General amendments: note that in addition to specific amendments made by European Parliament and Council Regulation 2015/2424/EU to this Regulation, which are noted to the affected provisions below (and to the Title above), a number of general amendments are made by Regulation 2015/2424/EU, Art 1(2)–(6) and the text of this Regulation should be read accordingly. Art 1(2)–(6) provides as follows:

> ***"Article 1***
>
> Regulation (EC) No 207/2009 is amended as follows:
>
> (2) The term 'Community trade mark' is replaced by 'European Union trade mark ("EU trade mark")' in Article 1(1); and elsewhere in the Regulation, it is replaced by 'EU trade mark' and any necessary grammatical changes are made.
>
> (3) Throughout the Regulation, the term 'Community trade mark court' is replaced by 'EU trade mark court' and any necessary grammatical changes are made.
>
> (4) The term 'Community collective mark' is replaced by 'European Union collective mark ("EU collective mark")' in Article 66(1); and elsewhere in the Regulation, it is replaced by 'EU collective mark' and any necessary grammatical changes are made.
>
> (5) Throughout the Regulation, except in the cases referred to in points (2), (3) and (4), the words 'Community', 'European Community' and 'European Communities' are replaced by 'Union' and any necessary grammatical changes are made.
>
> (6) Throughout the Regulation, the term 'President of the Office' and all references to that President are replaced by 'Executive Director of the Office' or 'Executive Director', as appropriate, and any necessary grammatical changes are made.".

THE COUNCIL OF THE EUROPEAN UNION,

Having regard to the Treaty establishing the European Community, and in particular Article 308 thereof,

Having regard to the proposal from the Commission,

Having regard to the opinion of the European Parliament,[1]

Whereas:

(1) Council Regulation (EC) No 40/94 of 20 December 1993 on the Community trade mark[2] *has been substantially amended several times.*[3] *In the interests of clarity and rationality the said Regulation should be codified.*

(2) It is desirable to promote throughout the Community a harmonious development of economic activities and a continuous and balanced expansion by completing an internal market which functions properly and offers conditions which are similar to those obtaining in a national market. In order to create a market of this kind and make it increasingly a single market, not only must barriers to free movement of goods and services be removed and arrangements be instituted which ensure that competition is not distorted, but, in addition, legal conditions must be created which enable undertakings to adapt their activities to the scale of the Community, whether in manufacturing and distributing goods or in providing services. For those purposes, trade marks enabling the products and services of undertakings to be distinguished by identical means throughout the entire Community, regardless of frontiers, should feature amongst the legal instruments which undertakings have at their disposal.

(3) For the purpose of pursuing the Community's said objectives it would appear necessary to provide for Community arrangements for trade marks whereby undertakings can by means of one procedural system obtain Community trade marks to which uniform protection is given and which produce their effects throughout the entire area of the Community. The principle of the unitary character of the Community trade mark thus stated should apply unless otherwise provided for in this Regulation.

(4) The barrier of territoriality of the rights conferred on proprietors of trade marks by the laws of the Member States cannot be removed by approximation of laws. In order to open up unrestricted economic activity in the whole of the internal market for the benefit of undertakings, trade marks should be created which are governed by a uniform Community law directly applicable in all Member States.

(5) Since the Treaty has not provided the specific powers to establish such a legal instrument, Article 308 of the Treaty should be applied.

(6) The Community law relating to trade marks nevertheless does not replace the laws of the Member States on trade marks. It would not in fact appear to be justified to require undertakings to apply for registration of their trade marks as Community trade marks. National trade marks continue to be necessary for those undertakings which do not want protection of their trade marks at Community level.

(7) The rights in a Community trade mark should not be obtained otherwise than by registration, and registration should be refused in particular if the trade mark is not distinctive, if it is unlawful or if it conflicts with earlier rights.

(8) The protection afforded by a Community trade mark, the function of which is in particular to guarantee the trade mark as an indication of origin, should be absolute in the case of identity between the mark and the sign and the goods or services. The protection should apply also in cases of similarity between the mark and the sign and the goods or services. An interpretation should be given of the concept of similarity in relation to the likelihood of confusion. The likelihood of confusion, the appreciation of which depends on numerous elements and, in particular, on the recognition of the trade mark on the market, the association which can be made with the used or registered sign, the degree of similarity between the trade mark and the sign and between the goods or services identified, should constitute the specific condition for such protection.

(9) It follows from the principle of free movement of goods that the proprietor of a Community trade mark must not be entitled to prohibit its use by a third party in relation to goods which have been put into circulation in the Community, under the trade mark, by him or with his consent, save where there exist legitimate reasons for the proprietor to oppose further commercialisation of the goods.

(10) There is no justification for protecting Community trade marks or, as against them, any trade mark which has been registered before them, except where the trade marks are actually used.

(11) A Community trade mark is to be regarded as an object of property which exists separately from the undertakings whose goods or services are designated by it. Accordingly, it should be capable of being transferred, subject to the overriding need to prevent the public being misled as a result of the transfer. It should also be capable of being charged as security in favour of a third party and of being the subject matter of licences.

(12) Administrative measures are necessary at Community level for implementing in relation to every trade mark the trade mark law created by this Regulation. It is therefore essential, while retaining the Community's existing institutional structure and balance of powers, to provide for an Office for Harmonisation in the Internal Market (trade marks and designs) which is independent in relation to technical matters and has legal, administrative and financial autonomy. To this end it is necessary and appropriate that that Office should be a body of the Community having legal personality and exercising the implementing powers which are conferred on it by this Regulation, and that it should operate within the framework of Community law without detracting from the competencies exercised by the Community institutions.

(13) It is necessary to ensure that parties who are affected by decisions made by the Office are protected by the law in a manner which is suited to the special character of trade mark law. To that end provision is made for an appeal to lie from decisions of the examiners and of the various divisions of the Office. If the department whose decision is contested does not rectify its decision it is to remit the appeal to a Board of Appeal of the Office, which is to decide on it. Decisions of the Boards of Appeal are, in turn, amenable to actions before the Court of Justice of the European Communities, which has jurisdiction to annul or to alter the contested decision.

(14) Under the first subparagraph of Article 225(1) of the EC Treaty the Court of First Instance of the European Communities has jurisdiction to hear and determine at first instance the actions referred to in particular in Article 230 of the EC Treaty with the exception of those assigned to a judicial panel and those reserved in the Statute to the Court of Justice. The jurisdiction which this Regulation confers on the Court of Justice to cancel and alter decisions of the Boards of Appeal should accordingly be exercised at first instance by the Court.

(15) In order to strengthen the protection of Community trade marks the Member States should designate, having regard to their own national system, as limited a number as possible of national courts of first and second instance having jurisdiction in matters of infringement and validity of Community trade marks.

(16) Decisions regarding the validity and infringement of Community trade marks must have effect and cover the entire area of the Community, as this is the only way of preventing inconsistent decisions on the part of the courts and the Office and of ensuring that the unitary character of Community trade marks is not undermined. The provisions of Council Regulation (EC) No 44/2001 of 22 December 2000 on jurisdiction and the recognition and enforcement of judgments in civil and commercial matters[4] should apply to all actions at law relating to Community trade marks, save where this Regulation derogates from those rules.

(17) Contradictory judgments should be avoided in actions which involve the same acts and the

same parties and which are brought on the basis of a Community trade mark and parallel national trade marks. For this purpose, when the actions are brought in the same Member State, the way in which this is to be achieved is a matter for national procedural rules, which are not prejudiced by this Regulation, whilst when the actions are brought in different Member States, provisions modelled on the rules on lis pendens and related actions of Regulation (EC) No 44/2001 appear appropriate.

(18) In order to guarantee the full autonomy and independence of the Office, it is considered necessary to grant it an autonomous budget whose revenue comes principally from fees paid by the users of the system. However, the Community budgetary procedure remains applicable as far as any subsidies chargeable to the general budget of the European Communities are concerned. Moreover, the auditing of accounts should be undertaken by the Court of Auditors.

(19) Measures necessary for the implementation of this Regulation should be adopted, particularly as regards fees regulations and an Implementing Regulation, in accordance with Council Decision 1999/468/EC of 28 June 1999 laying down the procedures for the exercise of implementing powers conferred on the Commission,[5]

NOTES

[1] OJ C146 E, 12.6.2008, p 79.

[2] OJ L11, 14.1.1994, p 1.

[3] See Annex I.

[4] OJ L12, 16.1.2001, p 1.

[5] OJ L184, 17.7.1999, p 23.

HAS ADOPTED THIS REGULATION:

TITLE I
GENERAL PROVISIONS

[5.576]
Article 1 Community trade mark

1. A trade mark for goods or services which is registered in accordance with the conditions contained in this Regulation and in the manner herein provided is hereinafter referred to as a "Community trade mark".

2. A Community trade mark shall have a unitary character. It shall have equal effect throughout the Community: it shall not be registered, transferred or surrendered or be the subject of a decision revoking the rights of the proprietor or declaring it invalid, nor shall its use be prohibited, save in respect of the whole Community. This principle shall apply unless otherwise provided in this Regulation.

NOTES

General amendments to this Regulation: see further the note "General amendments" in the introductory notes to this Regulation *ante*.

[5.577]
[Article 2
Office

1. A European Union Intellectual Property Office ("the Office") is hereby established.

2. All references in Union law to the Office for Harmonization in the Internal Market (trade marks and designs) shall be read as references to the Office.]

NOTES

Substituted by European Parliament and Council Regulation 2015/2424/EU, Art 1(7).

[5.578]
Article 3
Capacity to act

For the purpose of implementing this Regulation, companies or firms and other legal bodies shall be regarded as legal persons if, under the terms of the law governing them, they have the capacity in their own name to have rights and obligations of all kinds, to make contracts or accomplish other legal acts and to sue and be sued.

TITLE II
THE LAW RELATING TO TRADE MARKS
SECTION 1
DEFINITION OF A COMMUNITY TRADE MARK AND OBTAINING A COMMUNITY TRADE MARK

[5.579]
[Article 4
Signs of which an EU trade mark may consist
An EU trade mark may consist of any signs, in particular words, including personal names, or designs, letters, numerals, colours, the shape of goods or of the packaging of goods, or sounds, provided that such signs are capable of:
(a) distinguishing the goods or services of one undertaking from those of other undertakings; and
(b) being represented on the Register of European Union trade marks, ("the Register"), in a manner which enables the competent authorities and the public to determine the clear and precise subject matter of the protection afforded to its proprietor.]

NOTES
Substituted by European Parliament and Council Regulation 2015/2424/EU, Art 1(8).

[5.580]
Article 5
Persons who can be proprietors of Community trade marks
Any natural or legal person, including authorities established under public law, may be the proprietor of a Community trade mark.

NOTES
General amendments to this Regulation: see further the note "General amendments" in the introductory notes to this Regulation *ante*.

[5.581]
Article 6
Means whereby a Community trade mark is obtained
A Community trade mark shall be obtained by registration.

NOTES
General amendments to this Regulation: see further the note "General amendments" in the introductory notes to this Regulation *ante*.

[5.582]
Article 7
Absolute grounds for refusal
1. The following shall not be registered:
(a) signs which do not conform to the requirements of Article 4;
(b) trade marks which are devoid of any distinctive character;
(c) trade marks which consist exclusively of signs or indications which may serve, in trade, to designate the kind, quality, quantity, intended purpose, value, geographical origin or the time of production of the goods or of rendering of the service, or other characteristics of the goods or service;
(d) trade marks which consist exclusively of signs or indications which have become customary in the current language or in the bona fide and established practices of the trade;
[(e) signs which consist exclusively of:
(i) the shape, or another characteristic, which results from the nature of the goods themselves;
(ii) the shape, or another characteristic, of goods which is necessary to obtain a technical result;
(iii) the shape, or another characteristic, which gives substantial value to the goods;]
(f) trade marks which are contrary to public policy or to accepted principles of morality;
(g) trade marks which are of such a nature as to deceive the public, for instance as to the nature, quality or geographical origin of the goods or service;
(h) trade marks which have not been authorised by the competent authorities and are to be refused pursuant to Article 6ter of the Paris Convention for the Protection of Industrial Property, hereinafter referred to as the "Paris Convention";
(i) trade marks which include badges, emblems or escutcheons other than those covered by Article 6ter of the Paris Convention and which are of particular public interest, unless the consent of the competent authority to their registration has been given;

[(j) *trade marks which are excluded from registration, pursuant to Union legislation or national law or to international agreements to which the Union or the Member State concerned is party, providing for protection of designations of origin and geographical indications;*

(k) *trade marks which are excluded from registration pursuant to Union legislation or international agreements to which the Union is party, providing for protection of traditional terms for wine;*]

[(l) *trade marks which are excluded from registration pursuant to Union legislation or international agreements to which the Union is party, providing for protection of traditional specialities guaranteed;*

(m) *trade marks which consist of, or reproduce in their essential elements, an earlier plant variety denomination registered in accordance with Union legislation or national law, or international agreements to which the Union or the Member State concerned is a party, providing for protection of plant variety rights, and which are in respect of plant varieties of the same or closely related species.*]

2. Paragraph 1 shall apply notwithstanding that the grounds of non-registrability obtain in only part of the Community.

3. Paragraph 1(b), (c) and (d) shall not apply if the trade mark has become distinctive in relation to the goods or services for which registration is requested in consequence of the use which has been made of it.

NOTES

Para 1: points (e), (j), (k) substituted and points (l), (m) inserted by European Parliament and Council Regulation 2015/2424/EU, Art 1(9).

[5.583]

Article 8

Relative grounds for refusal

1. Upon opposition by the proprietor of an earlier trade mark, the trade mark applied for shall not be registered:

(a) *if it is identical with the earlier trade mark and the goods or services for which registration is applied for are identical with the goods or services for which the earlier trade mark is protected;*

(b) *if because of its identity with, or similarity to, the earlier trade mark and the identity or similarity of the goods or services covered by the trade marks there exists a likelihood of confusion on the part of the public in the territory in which the earlier trade mark is protected; the likelihood of confusion includes the likelihood of association with the earlier trade mark.*

2. For the purposes of paragraph 1, "earlier trade marks" means:

(a) *trade marks of the following kinds with a date of application for registration which is earlier than the date of application for registration of the Community trade mark, taking account, where appropriate, of the priorities claimed in respect of those trade marks:*

(i) *Community trade marks;*

(ii) *trade marks registered in a Member State, or, in the case of Belgium, the Netherlands or Luxembourg, at the Benelux Office for Intellectual Property;*

(iii) *trade marks registered under international arrangements which have effect in a Member State;*

(iv) *trade marks registered under international arrangements which have effect in the Community;*

(b) *applications for the trade marks referred to in subparagraph (a), subject to their registration;*

(c) *trade marks which, on the date of application for registration of the Community trade mark, or, where appropriate, of the priority claimed in respect of the application for registration of the Community trade mark, are well known in a Member State, in the sense in which the words "well known" are used in Article 6bis of the Paris Convention.*

3. Upon opposition by the proprietor of the trade mark, a trade mark shall not be registered where an agent or representative of the proprietor of the trade mark applies for registration thereof in his own name without the proprietor's consent, unless the agent or representative justifies his action.

4. Upon opposition by the proprietor of a non-registered trade mark or of another sign used in the course of trade of more than mere local significance, the trade mark applied for shall not be registered where and to the extent that, pursuant to the Community legislation or the law of the Member State governing that sign:

(a) *rights to that sign were acquired prior to the date of application for registration of the Community trade mark, or the date of the priority claimed for the application for registration of the Community trade mark;*

(b) *that sign confers on its proprietor the right to prohibit the use of a subsequent trade mark.*

[4a. Upon opposition by any person authorised under the relevant law to exercise the rights arising from a designation of origin or a geographical indication, the trade mark applied for shall not be registered where and to the extent that, pursuant to the Union legislation or national law providing for the protection of designations of origin or geographical indications:

(i) an application for a designation of origin or a geographical indication had already been submitted, in accordance with Union legislation or national law, prior to the date of application for registration of the EU trade mark or the date of the priority claimed for the application, subject to its subsequent registration;

(ii) that designation of origin or geographical indication confers the right to prohibit the use of a subsequent trade mark.]

[5. Upon opposition by the proprietor of a registered earlier trade mark within the meaning of paragraph 2, the trade mark applied for shall not be registered where it is identical with, or similar to, an earlier trade mark, irrespective of whether the goods or services for which it is applied are identical with, similar to or not similar to those for which the earlier trade mark is registered, where, in the case of an earlier EU trade mark, the trade mark has a reputation in the Union or, in the case of an earlier national trade mark, the trade mark has a reputation in the Member State concerned, and where the use without due cause of the trade mark applied for would take unfair advantage of, or be detrimental to, the distinctive character or the repute of the earlier trade mark.]

NOTES

General amendments to this Regulation: see further the note "General amendments" in the introductory notes to this Regulation *ante*.

Para 4a: inserted by European Parliament and Council Regulation 2015/2424/EU, Art 1(10)(a).

Para 5: substituted by European Parliament and Council Regulation 2015/2424/EU, Art 1(10)(b).

SECTION 2
EFFECTS OF COMMUNITY TRADE MARKS

[5.584]

[Article 9

Rights conferred by an EU trade mark

1. The registration of an EU trade mark shall confer on the proprietor exclusive rights therein.

2. Without prejudice to the rights of proprietors acquired before the filing date or the priority date of the EU trade mark, the proprietor of that EU trade mark shall be entitled to prevent all third parties not having his consent from using in the course of trade, in relation to goods or services, any sign where:

(a) the sign is identical with the EU trade mark and is used in relation to goods or services which are identical with those for which the EU trade mark is registered;

(b) the sign is identical with, or similar to, the EU trade mark and is used in relation to goods or services which are identical with, or similar to, the goods or services for which the EU trade mark is registered, if there exists a likelihood of confusion on the part of the public; the likelihood of confusion includes the likelihood of association between the sign and the trade mark;

(c) the sign is identical with, or similar to, the EU trade mark irrespective of whether it is used in relation to goods or services which are identical with, similar to or not similar to those for which the EU trade mark is registered, where the latter has a reputation in the Union and where use of that sign without due cause takes unfair advantage of, or is detrimental to, the distinctive character or the repute of the EU trade mark.

3. The following, in particular, may be prohibited under paragraph 2:

(a) affixing the sign to the goods or to the packaging thereof;

(b) offering the goods, putting them on the market, or stocking them for those purposes under the sign, or offering or supplying services thereunder;

(c) importing or exporting the goods under the sign;

(d) using the sign as a trade or company name or part of a trade or company name;

(e) using the sign on business papers and in advertising;

(f) using the sign in comparative advertising in a manner that is contrary to Directive 2006/114/EC of the European Parliament and of the Council.[1]

4. Without prejudice to the rights of proprietors acquired before the filing date or the priority date of the EU trade mark, the proprietor of that EU trade mark shall also be entitled to prevent all third parties from bringing goods, in the course of trade, into the Union without being released for free circulation there, where such goods, including packaging, come from third countries and bear without authorisation a trade mark which is identical with the EU trade mark registered in respect of such goods, or which cannot be distinguished in its essential aspects from that trade mark.

The entitlement of the proprietor of an EU trade mark pursuant to the first subparagraph shall lapse if, during the proceedings to determine whether the EU trade mark has been infringed, initiated in accordance with Regulation (EU) No 608/2013 of the European Parliament and of the Council[2] concerning customs enforcement of intellectual property rights, evidence is provided by the declarant or the holder of the goods that the proprietor of the EU trade mark is not entitled to prohibit the placing of the goods on the market in the country of final destination.]

NOTES

Substituted by European Parliament and Council Regulation 2015/2424/EU, Art 1(11).

* Directive 2006/114/EC of the European Parliament and of the Council of 12 December 2006 concerning misleading and comparative advertising (OJ L376, 27.12.2006, p 21).

** Regulation (EU) No 608/2013 of the European Parliament and of the Council of 12 June 2013 concerning customs enforcement of intellectual property rights and repealing Council Regulation (EC) No 1383/2003 (OJ L181, 29.6.2013, p 15).

[5.585]

[Article 9a

Right to prohibit preparatory acts in relation to the use of packaging or other means

Where the risk exists that the packaging, labels, tags, security or authenticity features or devices or any other means to which the mark is affixed could be used in relation to goods or services and such use would constitute an infringement of the rights of the proprietor of an EU trade mark under Article 9(2) and (3), the proprietor of that trade mark shall have the right to prohibit the following acts if carried out in the course of trade:

(a) *affixing a sign identical with, or similar to, the EU trade mark on packaging, labels, tags, security or authenticity features or devices or any other means to which the mark may be affixed;*

(b) *offering or placing on the market, or stocking for those purposes, or importing or exporting, packaging, labels, tags, security or authenticity features or devices or any other means to which the mark is affixed.]*

NOTES

Inserted by European Parliament and Council Regulation 2015/2424/EU, Art 1(12).

[5.586]

[Article 9b

Date from which rights against third parties prevail

1. The rights conferred by an EU trade mark shall prevail against third parties from the date of publication of the registration of the trade mark.

2. Reasonable compensation may be claimed in respect of acts occurring after the date of publication of an EU trade mark application, where those acts would, after publication of the registration of the trade mark, be prohibited by virtue of that publication.

3. A court seized of a case shall not decide upon the merits of that case until the registration has been published.]

NOTES

Inserted by European Parliament and Council Regulation 2015/2424/EU, Art 1(12).

[5.587]

Article 10

Reproduction of Community trade marks in dictionaries

If the reproduction of a Community trade mark in a dictionary, encyclopaedia or similar reference work gives the impression that it constitutes the generic name of the goods or services for which the trade mark is registered, the publisher of the work shall, at the request of the proprietor of the Community trade mark, ensure that the reproduction of the trade mark at the latest in the next edition of the publication is accompanied by an indication that it is a registered trade mark.

NOTES

General amendments to this Regulation: see further the note "General amendments" in the introductory notes to this Regulation *ante*.

[5.588]

Article 11

Prohibition on the use of a Community trade mark registered in the name of an agent or representative

Where a Community trade mark is registered in the name of the agent or representative of a person who is the proprietor of that trade mark, without the proprietor's authorisation, the latter shall be entitled to oppose the use of his mark by his agent or representative if he has not authorised such use, unless the agent or representative justifies his action.

NOTES

General amendments to this Regulation: see further the note "General amendments" in the introductory notes to this Regulation *ante*.

[5.589]
[Article 12
Limitation of the effects of an EU trade mark

1. An EU trade mark shall not entitle the proprietor to prohibit a third party from using, in the course of trade:

- *(a) the name or address of the third party, where that third party is a natural person;*
- *(b) signs or indications which are not distinctive or which concern the kind, quality, quantity, intended purpose, value, geographical origin, the time of production of goods or of rendering of the service, or other characteristics of the goods or services;*
- *(c) the EU trade mark for the purpose of identifying or referring to goods or services as those of the proprietor of that trade mark, in particular, where the use of that trade mark is necessary to indicate the intended purpose of a product or service, in particular as accessories or spare parts.*

2. Paragraph 1 shall only apply where the use made by the third party is in accordance with honest practices in industrial or commercial matters.]

NOTES

Substituted by European Parliament and Council Regulation 2015/2424/EU, Art 1(13).

[5.590]
Article 13
Exhaustion of the rights conferred by a Community trade mark

[1. An EU trade mark shall not entitle the proprietor to prohibit its use in relation to goods which have been put on the market in the European Economic Area under that trade mark by the proprietor or with his consent.]

2. Paragraph 1 shall not apply where there exist legitimate reasons for the proprietor to oppose further commercialisation of the goods, especially where the condition of the goods is changed or impaired after they have been put on the market.

NOTES

General amendments to this Regulation: see further the note "General amendments" in the introductory notes to this Regulation *ante*.

NOTES

Para 1: substituted by European Parliament and Council Regulation 2015/2424/EU, Art 1(14).

[5.591]
[Article 13a
Intervening right of the proprietor of a later registered trade mark as a defence in infringement proceedings

1. In infringement proceedings, the proprietor of an EU trade mark shall not be entitled to prohibit the use of a later registered EU trade mark where that later trade mark would not be declared invalid pursuant to Article 53(1), (3) or (4), 54(1) or (2), or 57(2) of this Regulation.

2. In infringement proceedings, the proprietor of an EU trade mark shall not be entitled to prohibit the use of a later registered national trade mark where that later registered national trade mark would not be declared invalid pursuant to Article 8, or Article 9(1) or (2), or 46(3) of Directive (EU) 2015/2436 of the European Parliament and of the Council.[1]

3. Where the proprietor of an EU trade mark is not entitled to prohibit the use of a later registered trade mark pursuant to paragraph 1 or 2, the proprietor of that later registered trade mark shall not be entitled to prohibit the use of that earlier EU trade mark in infringement proceedings.]

NOTES

Inserted by European Parliament and Council Regulation 2015/2424/EU, Art 1(15).

[1] Directive (EU) 2015/2436 of the European Parliament and of the Council of 16 December 2015 to approximate the laws of the Member States relating to trade marks (OJ L 336, 23.12.2015, p. 1)'.

[5.592]
Article 14
Complementary application of national law relating to infringement

1. The effects of Community trade marks shall be governed solely by the provisions of this Regulation. In other respects, infringement of a Community trade mark shall be governed by the national law relating to infringement of a national trade mark in accordance with the provisions of Title X.

2. This Regulation shall not prevent actions concerning a Community trade mark being brought under the law of Member States relating in particular to civil liability and unfair competition.

3. The rules of procedure to be applied shall be determined in accordance with the provisions of Title X.

NOTES

General amendments to this Regulation: see further the note "General amendments" in the introductory notes to this Regulation *ante*.

SECTION 3
USE OF COMMUNITY TRADE MARKS

[5.593]
Article 15
Use of Community trade marks

1. If, within a period of five years following registration, the proprietor has not put the Community trade mark to genuine use in the Community in connection with the goods or services in respect of which it is registered, or if such use has been suspended during an uninterrupted period of five years, the Community trade mark shall be subject to the sanctions provided for in this Regulation, unless there are proper reasons for non-use.

[The following shall also constitute use within the meaning of the first subparagraph:

(a) use of the EU trade mark in a form differing in elements which do not alter the distinctive character of the mark in the form in which it was registered, regardless of whether or not the trade mark in the form as used is also registered in the name of the proprietor;

(b) affixing of the EU trade mark to goods or to the packaging thereof in the Union solely for export purposes.]

2. Use of the Community trade mark with the consent of the proprietor shall be deemed to constitute use by the proprietor.

NOTES

General amendments to this Regulation: see further the note "General amendments" in the introductory notes to this Regulation *ante*.

Para 1: words in square brackets substituted by European Parliament and Council Regulation 2015/2424/EU, Art 1(16).

SECTION 4
COMMUNITY TRADE MARKS AS OBJECTS OF PROPERTY

[5.594]
Article 16
Dealing with Community trade marks as national trade marks

[1. Unless Articles 17 to 24 provide otherwise, an EU trade mark as an object of property shall be dealt with in its entirety, and for the whole area of the Union, as a national trade mark registered in the Member State in which, according to the Register—]

(a) the proprietor has his seat or his domicile on the relevant date;

(b) where point (a) does not apply, the proprietor has an establishment on the relevant date.

2. In cases which are not provided for by paragraph 1, the Member State referred to in that paragraph shall be the Member State in which the seat of the Office is situated.

3. If two or more persons are mentioned in the Register of Community trade marks as joint proprietors, paragraph 1 shall apply to the joint proprietor first mentioned; failing this, it shall apply to the subsequent joint proprietors in the order in which they are mentioned. Where paragraph 1 does not apply to any of the joint proprietors, paragraph 2 shall apply.

NOTES

General amendments to this Regulation: see further the note "General amendments" in the introductory notes to this Regulation *ante*.

Para 1: words in square brackets substituted by European Parliament and Council Regulation 2015/2424/EU, Art 1(17).

[5.595]
Article 17
Transfer

1. A Community trade mark may be transferred, separately from any transfer of the undertaking, in respect of some or all of the goods or services for which it is registered.

2. A transfer of the whole of the undertaking shall include the transfer of the Community trade mark except where, in accordance with the law governing the transfer, there is agreement to the contrary or circumstances clearly dictate otherwise. This provision shall apply to the contractual obligation to transfer the undertaking.

3. Without prejudice to paragraph 2, an assignment of the Community trade mark shall be made in writing and shall require the signature of the parties to the contract, except when it is a result of a judgment; otherwise it shall be void.

4. . . .

5. On request of one of the parties a transfer shall be entered in the Register and published.

[5a. An application for registration of a transfer shall contain information to identify the EU trade mark, the new proprietor, the goods and services to which the transfer relates, as well as documents duly establishing the transfer in accordance with paragraphs 2 and 3. The application may further contain, where applicable, information to identify the representative of the new proprietor.

5b. The Commission shall adopt implementing acts specifying:

(a) the details to be contained in the application for registration of a transfer;

(b) the kind of documentation required to establish a transfer, taking account of the agreements given by the registered proprietor and the successor in title;

(c) the details of how to process applications for partial transfers, ensuring that the goods and services in the remaining registration and the new registration do not overlap and that a separate file, including a new registration number, is established for the new registration.

Those implementing acts shall be adopted in accordance with the examination procedure referred to in Article 163(2).

5c. Where the conditions applicable to the registration of a transfer, as laid down in paragraphs 1 to 3, or in the implementing acts referred to in paragraph 5b, are not fulfilled, the Office shall notify the applicant of the deficiencies. If the deficiencies are not remedied within a period to be specified by the Office, it shall reject the application for registration of the transfer.

5d. A single application for registration of a transfer may be submitted for two or more trade marks, provided that the registered proprietor and the successor in title are the same in each case.

5e. Paragraphs 5a to 5d shall also apply to applications for EU trade marks.

5f. In the case of a partial transfer, any application made by the original proprietor pending with regard to the original registration shall be deemed to be pending with regard to the remaining registration and the new registration. Where such application is subject to the payment of fees and those fees have been paid by the original proprietor, the new proprietor shall not be liable to pay any additional fees with regard to such application.]

6. As long as the transfer has not been entered in the Register, the successor in title may not invoke the rights arising from the registration of the Community trade mark.

7. Where there are time limits to be observed vis-à-vis the Office, the successor in title may make the corresponding statements to the Office once the request for registration of the transfer has been received by the Office.

8. All documents which require notification to the proprietor of the Community trade mark in accordance with Article 79 shall be addressed to the person registered as proprietor.

NOTES

General amendments to this Regulation: see further the note "General amendments" in the introductory notes to this Regulation *ante*.

Para 4: repealed by European Parliament and Council Regulation 2015/2424/EU, Art 1(18)(a).

Paras 5a–5f: inserted by European Parliament and Council Regulation 2015/2424/EU, Art 1(18)(b).

[5.596]

[Article 18

Transfer of a trade mark registered in the name of an agent

1. Where an EU trade mark is registered in the name of the agent or representative of a person who is the proprietor of that trade mark, without the proprietor's authorisation, the latter shall be entitled to demand the assignment of the EU trade mark in his favour, unless such agent or representative justifies his action.

2. The proprietor may submit a request for assignment pursuant to paragraph 1 of this Article to the following:

(a) the Office, pursuant to Article 53(1)(b), instead of an application for a declaration of invalidity;

(b) a European Union trade mark court ("EU trade mark court") as referred to in Article 95, instead of a counterclaim for a declaration of invalidity based on Article 100(1).]

NOTES

Substituted by European Parliament and Council Regulation 2015/2424/EU, Art 1(19).

[5.597]

Article 19

Rights in rem

1. A Community trade mark may, independently of the undertaking, be given as security or be the subject of rights in rem.

[2. At the request of one of the parties, the rights referred to in paragraph 1 or the transfer of those rights shall be entered in the Register and published.]

[3. An entry in the Register effected pursuant to paragraph 2 shall be cancelled or modified at the request of one of the parties.]

NOTES

General amendments to this Regulation: see further the note "General amendments" in the introductory notes to this Regulation *ante*.

Para 2: substituted by European Parliament and Council Regulation 2015/2424/EU, Art 1(20)(a).
Para 3: added by European Parliament and Council Regulation 2015/2424/EU, Art 1(20)(b).

[5.598]
Article 20
Levy of execution

1. A Community trade mark may be levied in execution.

2. As regards the procedure for levy of execution in respect of a Community trade mark, the courts and authorities of the Member States determined in accordance with Article 16 shall have exclusive jurisdiction.

3. On request of one the parties, levy of execution shall be entered in the Register and published.

[4. An entry in the Register effected pursuant to paragraph 3 shall be cancelled or modified at the request of one of the parties.]

NOTES

General amendments to this Regulation: see further the note "General amendments" in the introductory notes to this Regulation *ante*.

Para 4: added by European Parliament and Council Regulation 2015/2424/EU, Art 1(21).

[5.599]
Article 21
Insolvency proceedings

1. The only insolvency proceedings in which a Community trade mark may be involved are those opened in the Member State in the territory of which the debtor has his centre of main interests.

However, where the debtor is an insurance undertaking or a credit institution as defined in Directive 2001/17/EC of the European Parliament and of the Council of 19 March 2001 on the reorganisation and winding-up of insurance undertakings[1] and Directive 2001/24/EC of the European Parliament and of the Council of 4 April 2001 on the reorganisation and winding up of credit institutions,[2] respectively, the only insolvency proceedings in which a Community trademark may be involved are those opened in the Member State where that undertaking or institution has been authorised.

2. In the case of joint proprietorship of a Community trade mark, paragraph 1 shall apply to the share of the joint proprietor.

3. Where a Community trade mark is involved in insolvency proceedings, on request of the competent national authority an entry to this effect shall be made in the Register and published in the Community Trade Marks Bulletin referred to in Article 89.

NOTES

General amendments to this Regulation: see further the note "General amendments" in the introductory notes to this Regulation *ante*.

1 OJ L110, 20.4.2001, p 28.

2 OJ L125, 5.5.2001, p 15.

[5.600]
Article 22
Licensing

1. A Community trade mark may be licensed for some or all of the goods or services for which it is registered and for the whole or part of the Community. A licence may be exclusive or non-exclusive.

2. The proprietor of a Community trade mark may invoke the rights conferred by that trade mark against a licensee who contravenes any provision in his licensing contract with regard to:

- *(a) its duration;*
- *(b) the form covered by the registration in which the trade mark may be used;*
- *(c) the scope of the goods or services for which the licence is granted;*
- *(d) the territory in which the trade mark may be affixed; or*
- *(e) the quality of the goods manufactured or of the services provided by the licensee.*

3. Without prejudice to the provisions of the licensing contract, the licensee may bring proceedings for infringement of a Community trade mark only if its proprietor consents thereto. However, the holder of an exclusive licence may bring such proceedings if the proprietor of the trade mark, after formal notice, does not himself bring infringement proceedings within an appropriate period.

4. A licensee shall, for the purpose of obtaining compensation for damage suffered by him, be entitled to intervene in infringement proceedings brought by the proprietor of the Community trade mark.

5. On request of one of the parties the grant or transfer of a licence in respect of a Community trade mark shall be entered in the Register and published.

[6. An entry in the Register effected pursuant to paragraph 5 shall be cancelled or modified at the request of one of the parties.]

NOTES

General amendments to this Regulation: see further the note "General amendments" in the introductory notes to this Regulation *ante*.

Para 6: added by European Parliament and Council Regulation 2015/2424/EU, Art 1(22).

[5.601]

[Article 22a

Procedure for entering licences and other rights in the Register

1. Article 17(5a) and (5b) and the rules adopted pursuant to it, and Article 17(5d) shall apply mutatis mutandis to the registration of a right in rem or transfer of a right in rem as referred to in Article 19(2), the levy of execution as referred to in Article 20(3), the involvement in insolvency proceedings as referred to in Article 21(3), as well as to the registration of a licence or transfer of a licence as referred to in Article 22(5), subject to the following:

- *(a) the requirement relating to the identification of goods and services to which the transfer relates shall not apply in respect of a request for registration of a right in rem, of a levy of execution or of insolvency proceedings;*
- *(b) the requirement relating to the documents proving the transfer shall not apply where the request is made by the proprietor of the EU trade mark.*

2. The application for registration of the rights referred to in paragraph 1 shall not be deemed to have been filed until the required fee has been paid.

3. The application for registration of a licence may contain a request to record a licence in the Register as one or more of the following:

- *(a) an exclusive licence;*
- *(b) a sub-licence in the event that the licence is granted by a licensee whose licence is recorded in the Register;*
- *(c) a licence limited to only part of the goods or services for which the mark is registered;*
- *(d) a licence limited to part of the Union;*
- *(e) a temporary licence.*

Where a request is made to record the licence as a licence listed in points (c), (d) and (e) of the first subparagraph, the application for registration of a licence shall indicate the goods and services, the part of the Union and the time period for which the licence is granted.

4. Where the conditions applicable to registration, as laid down in Articles 19 to 22, paragraphs 1 and 3 of this Article, and in the other applicable rules adopted pursuant to this Regulation, are not fulfilled, the Office shall notify the applicant of the deficiency. If the deficiency is not corrected within a period specified by the Office, it shall reject the application for registration.

5. Paragraphs 1 and 3 shall apply mutatis mutandis to applications for EU trade marks.]

NOTES

Inserted by European Parliament and Council Regulation 2015/2424/EU, Art 1(23).

[5.602]

Article 23

Effects** vis-à-vis **third parties

1. Legal acts referred to in Articles 17, 19 and 22 concerning a Community trade mark shall have effects vis-à-vis third parties in all the Member States only after entry in the Register. Nevertheless, such an act, before it is so entered, shall have effect vis-à-vis third parties who have acquired rights in the trade mark after the date of that act but who knew of the act at the date on which the rights were acquired.

2. Paragraph 1 shall not apply in the case of a person who acquires the Community trade mark or a right concerning the Community trade mark by way of transfer of the whole of the undertaking or by any other universal succession.

3. The effects vis-à-vis third parties of the legal acts referred to in Article 20 shall be governed by the law of the Member State determined in accordance with Article 16.

4. Until such time as common rules for the Member States in the field of bankruptcy enter into force, the effects vis-à-vis third parties of bankruptcy or like proceedings shall be governed by the law of the Member State in which such proceedings are first brought within the meaning of national law or of conventions applicable in this field.

NOTES

General amendments to this Regulation: see further the note "General amendments" in the introductory notes to this Regulation *ante*.

[5.603]

Article 24

The application for a Community trade mark as an object of property

Articles 16 to 23 shall apply to applications for Community trade marks.

NOTES

General amendments to this Regulation: see further the note "General amendments" in the introductory notes to this Regulation *ante*.

[5.604]

[Article 24a

Procedure for cancelling or modifying the entry in the Register of licences and other rights

1. A registration effected under Article 22a(1) shall be cancelled or modified at the request of one of the persons concerned.

2. The application shall contain the registration number of the EU trade mark concerned and the particulars of the right for which registration is requested to be cancelled or modified.

3. The application for cancellation of a licence, a right in rem or an enforcement measure shall not be deemed to have been filed until the required fee has been paid.

4. The application shall be accompanied by documents showing that the registered right no longer exists or that the licensee or the holder of another right consents to the cancellation or modification of the registration.

5. Where the requirements for cancellation or modification of the registration are not satisfied, the Office shall notify the applicant of the deficiency. If the deficiency is not corrected within a period to be specified by the Office, it shall reject the application for cancellation or modification of the registration.

6. Paragraphs 1 to 5 of this Article shall apply mutatis mutandis to entries made in the files pursuant to Article 22a(5).]

NOTES

Inserted by European Parliament and Council Regulation 2015/2424/EU, Art 1(24).

TITLE III
APPLICATION FOR COMMUNITY TRADE MARKS

SECTION 1
FILING OF APPLICATIONS AND THE CONDITIONS WHICH GOVERN THEM

[5.605]

[Article 25

Filing of applications

1. An application for an EU trade mark shall be filed at the Office.

2. The Office shall issue to the applicant, without delay, a receipt which shall include at least the file number, a representation, description or other identification of the mark, the nature and the number of the documents and the date of their receipt. That receipt may be issued by electronic means.]

NOTES

Substituted by European Parliament and Council Regulation 2015/2424/EU, Art 1(25).

[5.606]

Article 26

Conditions with which applications must comply

1. An application for a Community trade mark shall contain:

(a) a request for the registration of a Community trade mark;

(b) information identifying the applicant;

(c) a list of the goods or services in respect of which the registration is requested;

[(d) a representation of the mark, which satisfies the requirements set out in Article 4(b).]

[2. The application for an EU trade mark shall be subject to the payment of the application fee covering one class of goods or services and, where appropriate, of one or more class fees for each class of goods and services exceeding the first class and, where applicable, the search fee.

3. In addition to the requirements referred to in paragraphs 1 and 2, an application for an EU trade mark shall comply with the formal requirements laid down in this Regulation and in the implementing acts adopted pursuant to it. If those conditions provide for the trade mark to be represented electronically, the Executive Director may determine the formats and maximum size of such an electronic file.]

[4. The Commission shall adopt implementing acts specifying the details to be contained in the application. Those implementing acts shall be adopted in accordance with the examination procedure referred to in Article 163(2).]

NOTES

General amendments to this Regulation: see further the note "General amendments" in the introductory notes to this Regulation *ante*.

Para 1: point (d) substituted by European Parliament and Council Regulation 2015/2424/EU, Art 1(26)(a).

Paras 2, 3: substituted by European Parliament and Council Regulation 2015/2424/EU, Art 1(26)(b).

Para 4: added by European Parliament and Council Regulation 2015/2424/EU, Art 1(26)(c).

[5.607]
[Article 27
Date of filing
The date of filing of an EU trade mark application shall be the date on which the documents containing the information specified in Article 26(1) are filed with the Office by the applicant, subject to payment of the application fee within one month of filing those documents.]

NOTES

Substituted by European Parliament and Council Regulation 2015/2424/EU, Art 1(27).

[5.608]
[Article 28
Designation and classification of goods and services

1. Goods and services in respect of which trade mark registration is applied for shall be classified in conformity with the system of classification established by the Nice Agreement Concerning the International Classification of Goods and Services for the Purposes of the Registration of Marks of 15 June 1957 ("the Nice Classification").

2. The goods and services for which the protection of the trade mark is sought shall be identified by the applicant with sufficient clarity and precision to enable the competent authorities and economic operators, on that sole basis, to determine the extent of the protection sought.

3. For the purposes of paragraph 2, the general indications included in the class headings of the Nice Classification or other general terms may be used, provided that they comply with the requisite standards of clarity and precision set out in this Article.

4. The Office shall reject an application in respect of indications or terms which are unclear or imprecise, where the applicant does not suggest an acceptable wording within a period set by the Office to that effect.

5. The use of general terms, including the general indications of the class headings of the Nice Classification, shall be interpreted as including all the goods or services clearly covered by the literal meaning of the indication or term. The use of such terms or indications shall not be interpreted as comprising a claim to goods or services which cannot be so understood.

6. Where the applicant requests registration for more than one class, the applicant shall group the goods and services according to the classes of the Nice Classification, each group being preceded by the number of the class to which that group of goods or services belongs, and shall present them in the order of the classes.

7. Goods and services shall not be regarded as being similar to each other on the ground that they appear in the same class under the Nice Classification. Goods and services shall not be regarded as being dissimilar from each other on the ground that they appear in different classes under the Nice Classification.

8. Proprietors of EU trade marks applied for before 22 June 2012 which are registered in respect of the entire heading of a Nice class may declare that their intention on the date of filing had been to seek protection in respect of goods or services beyond those covered by the literal meaning of the heading of that class, provided that the goods or services so designated are included in the alphabetical list for that class in the edition of the Nice Classification in force at the date of filing.

The declaration shall be filed at the Office by 24 September 2016, and shall indicate, in a clear, precise and specific manner, the goods and services, other than those clearly covered by the literal meaning of the indications of the class heading, originally covered by the proprietor's intention. The Office shall take appropriate measures to amend the Register accordingly. The possibility to make a declaration in accordance with the first subparagraph of this paragraph shall be without prejudice to the application of Article 15, Article 42(2), Article 51(1)(a), and Article 57(2).

EU trade marks for which no declaration is filed within the period referred to in the second subparagraph shall be deemed to extend, as from the expiry of that period, only to goods or services clearly covered by the literal meaning of the indications included in the heading of the relevant class.

9. Where the register is amended, the exclusive rights conferred by the EU trade mark under Article 9 shall not prevent a third party from continuing to use a trade mark in relation to goods or services where and to the extent that the use of the trade mark for those goods or services:

(a) commenced before the register was amended; and

(b) did not infringe the proprietor's rights based on the literal meaning of the record of the goods and services in the register at that time.

In addition, the amendment of the list of goods or services recorded in the register shall not give the proprietor of the EU trade mark the right to oppose or to apply for a declaration of invalidity of a later trade mark where and to the extent that:

(a) the later trade mark was either in use, or an application had been made to register the trade mark, for goods or services before the register was amended; and

(b) the use of the trade mark in relation to those goods or services did not infringe, or would not have infringed, the proprietor's rights based on the literal meaning of the record of the goods and services in the register at that time.]

NOTES

Substituted by European Parliament and Council Regulation 2015/2424/EU, Art 1(28).

SECTION 2
PRIORITY

[5.609]
Article 29
Right of priority

1. A person who has duly filed an application for a trade mark in or in respect of any State party to the Paris Convention or to the Agreement establishing the World Trade Organisation, or his successors in title, shall enjoy, for the purpose of filing a Community trade mark application for the same trade mark in respect of goods or services which are identical with or contained within those for which the application has been filed, a right of priority during a period of six months from the date of filing of the first application.

2. Every filing that is equivalent to a regular national filing under the national law of the State where it was made or under bilateral or multilateral agreements shall be recognised as giving rise to a right of priority.

3. By a regular national filing is meant any filing that is sufficient to establish the date on which the application was filed, whatever may be the outcome of the application.

4. A subsequent application for a trade mark which was the subject of a previous first application in respect of the same goods or services and which is filed in or in respect of the same State shall be considered as the first application for the purposes of determining priority, provided that, at the date of filing of the subsequent application, the previous application has been withdrawn, abandoned or refused, without being open to public inspection and without leaving any rights outstanding, and has not served as a basis for claiming a right of priority. The previous application may not thereafter serve as a basis for claiming a right of priority.

5. If the first filing has been made in a State which is not a party to the Paris Convention or to the Agreement establishing the World Trade Organisation, paragraphs 1 to 4 shall apply only in so far as that State, according to published findings, grants, on the basis of the first filing made at the Office and subject to conditions equivalent to those laid down in this Regulation, a right of priority having equivalent effect.

[The Executive Director shall, where necessary, request the Commission to consider enquiring as to whether a State within the meaning of the first sentence accords that reciprocal treatment. If the Commission determines that reciprocal treatment in accordance with the first sentence is accorded, it shall publish a communication to that effect in the Official Journal of the European Union.]

[6. Paragraph 5 shall apply from the date of publication in the Official Journal of the European Union of the communication determining that reciprocal treatment is accorded, unless the communication states an earlier date from which it is applicable. It shall cease to apply from the date of publication in the Official Journal of the European Union of a communication of the Commission to the effect that reciprocal treatment is no longer accorded, unless the communication states an earlier date from which it is applicable.

7. Communications as referred to in paragraphs 5 and 6 shall also be published in the Official Journal of the Office.]

NOTES

General amendments to this Regulation: see further the note "General amendments" in the introductory notes to this Regulation *ante*.

Para 5: words in square brackets added by European Parliament and Council Regulation 2015/2424/EU, Art 1(29)(a).

Paras 6, 7: added by European Parliament and Council Regulation 2015/2424/EU, Art 1(29)(b).

[5.610]
[Article 30
Claiming priority

1. Priority claims shall be filed together with the EU trade mark application and shall include the date, number and country of the previous application. The documentation in support of priority claims shall be filed within three months of the filing date.

2. The Commission shall adopt implementing acts specifying the kind of documentation to be filed for claiming the priority of a previous application in accordance with paragraph 1 of this Article. Those implementing acts shall be adopted in accordance with the examination procedure referred to in Article 163(2).

3. The Executive Director may determine that the documentation to be provided by the applicant in support of the priority claim may consist of less than what is required under the specifications adopted in accordance with paragraph 2, provided that the information required is available to the Office from other sources.]

NOTES

Substituted by European Parliament and Council Regulation 2015/2424/EU, Art 1(30).

[5.611]
Article 31
Effect of priority right

The right of priority shall have the effect that the date of priority shall count as the date of filing of the Community trade mark application for the purposes of establishing which rights take precedence.

NOTES

General amendments to this Regulation: see further the note "General amendments" in the introductory notes to this Regulation *ante*.

[5.612]
Article 32
Equivalence of Community filing with national filing

A Community trade mark application which has been accorded a date of filing shall, in the Member States, be equivalent to a regular national filing, where appropriate with the priority claimed for the Community trade mark application.

NOTES

General amendments to this Regulation: see further the note "General amendments" in the introductory notes to this Regulation *ante*.

SECTION 3
EXHIBITION PRIORITY

[5.613]
Article 33
Exhibition priority

1. If an applicant for a Community trade mark has displayed goods or services under the mark applied for, at an official or officially recognised international exhibition falling within the terms of the Convention on International Exhibitions signed at Paris on 22 November 1928 and last revised on 30 November 1972, he may, if he files the application within a period of six months from the date of the first display of the goods or services under the mark applied for, claim a right of priority from that date within the meaning of Article 31.
[The priority claim shall be filed together with the EU trade mark application.]
[2. An applicant who wishes to claim priority pursuant to paragraph 1 shall file evidence of the display of goods or services under the mark applied for within three months of the filing date.]
3. An exhibition priority granted in a Member State or in a third country does not extend the period of priority laid down in Article 29.
[4. The Commission shall adopt implementing acts specifying the type and details of evidence to be filed for claiming an exhibition priority in accordance with paragraph 2 of this Article. Those implementing acts shall be adopted in accordance with the examination procedure referred to in Article 163(2).]

NOTES

General amendments to this Regulation: see further the note "General amendments" in the introductory notes to this Regulation *ante*.

Para 1: words in square brackets added by European Parliament and Council Regulation 2015/2424/EU, Art 1(31)(a).

Para 2: substituted by European Parliament and Council Regulation 2015/2424/EU, Art 1(31)(b).

Para 4: added by European Parliament and Council Regulation 2015/2424/EU, Art 1(31)(c).

SECTION 4
CLAIMING THE SENIORITY OF A NATIONAL TRADE MARK

[5.614]
Article 34
Claiming the seniority of a national trade mark

1. The proprietor of an earlier trade mark registered in a Member State, including a trade mark registered in the Benelux countries, or registered under international arrangements having effect in a Member State, who applies for an identical trade mark for registration as a Community trade mark for goods or services which are identical with or contained within those for which the earlier trade mark has been registered, may claim for the Community trade mark the seniority of the earlier trade mark in respect of the Member State in or for which it is registered.
[1a. Seniority claims shall either be filed together with the EU trade mark application or within two months of the filing date of the application, and shall include the Member State or Member States in or for which the mark is registered, the number and the filing date of the relevant

registration, and the goods and services for which the mark is registered. Where the seniority of one or more registered earlier trade marks is claimed in the application, the documentation in support of the seniority claim shall be filed within three months of the filing date. Where the applicant wishes to claim the seniority subsequent to the filing of the application, the documentation in support of the seniority claim shall be submitted to the Office within three months of receipt of the seniority claim.]

2. Seniority shall have the sole effect under this Regulation that, where the proprietor of the Community trade mark surrenders the earlier trade mark or allows it to lapse, he shall be deemed to continue to have the same rights as he would have had if the earlier trade mark had continued to be registered.

[3. The seniority claimed for the EU trade mark shall lapse where the earlier trade mark the seniority of which is claimed is declared to be invalid or revoked. Where the earlier trade mark is revoked, the seniority shall lapse provided that the revocation takes effect prior to the filing date or priority date of that EU trade mark.]

[4. The Office shall inform the Benelux Office for Intellectual Property or the central industrial property office of the Member State concerned of the effective claiming of seniority.

5. The Commission shall adopt implementing acts specifying the kind of documentation to be filed for claiming the seniority of a national trade mark or a trade mark registered under international agreements having effect in a Member State in accordance with paragraph 1a of this Article. Those implementing acts shall be adopted in accordance with the examination procedure referred to in Article 163(2).

6. The Executive Director may determine that the documentation to be provided by the applicant in support of the seniority claim may consist of less than what is required under the specifications adopted in accordance with paragraph 5, provided that the information required is available to the Office from other sources.]

NOTES

General amendments to this Regulation: see further the note "General amendments" in the introductory notes to this Regulation *ante*.

Para 1a: inserted by European Parliament and Council Regulation 2015/2424/EU, Art 1(32)(a).

Para 3: substituted by European Parliament and Council Regulation 2015/2424/EU, Art 1(32)(b).

Paras 4–6: added by European Parliament and Council Regulation 2015/2424/EU, Art 1(32)(c).

[5.615]

Article 35

Claiming seniority after registration of the Community trade mark

1. The proprietor of a Community trade mark who is the proprietor of an earlier identical trade mark registered in a Member State, including a trade mark registered in the Benelux countries or of an earlier identical trade mark, with an international registration effective in a Member State, for goods or services which are identical to those for which the earlier trade mark has been registered, or contained within them, may claim the seniority of the earlier trade mark in respect of the Member State in or for which it was registered.

[2. Seniority claims filed pursuant to paragraph 1 of this Article shall include the registration number of the EU trade mark, the name and address of its proprietor, the Member State or Member States in or for which the earlier mark is registered, the number and the filing date of the relevant registration, the goods and services for which the mark is registered and those in respect of which seniority is claimed, and supporting documentation as provided for in the rules adopted pursuant to Article 34(5).]

[3. If the requirements governing the claiming of seniority are not fulfilled, the Office shall communicate the deficiency to the proprietor of the EU trade mark. If the deficiency is not remedied within a period to be specified by the Office, the Office shall reject the claim.

4. Article 34(2), (3), (4) and (6) shall apply.]

NOTES

General amendments to this Regulation: see further the note "General amendments" in the introductory notes to this Regulation *ante*.

Para 2: substituted by European Parliament and Council Regulation 2015/2424/EU, Art 1(33)(a).

Paras 3, 4: added by European Parliament and Council Regulation 2015/2424/EU, Art 1(33)(b).

TITLE IV
REGISTRATION PROCEDURE

SECTION 1
EXAMINATION OF APPLICATIONS

[5.616]

Article 36

Examination of the conditions of filing

1. The Office shall examine whether:

(a) the Community trade mark application satisfies the requirements for the accordance of a date of filing in accordance with Article 27;
[(b) the EU trade mark application complies with the conditions and requirements referred to in Article 26(3);];
(c) where appropriate, the class fees have been paid within the prescribed period.

2. Where the Community trade mark application does not satisfy the requirements referred to in paragraph 1, the Office shall request the applicant to remedy the deficiencies or the default on payment [within two months of the receipt of the notification].

3. If the deficiencies or the default on payment established pursuant to paragraph 1(a) are not remedied within this period, the application shall not be dealt with as a Community trade mark application. If the applicant complies with the Office's request, the Office shall accord as the date of filing of the application the date on which the deficiencies or the default on payment established are remedied.

4. If the deficiencies established pursuant to paragraph 1(b) are not remedied within the prescribed period, the Office shall refuse the application.

5. If the default on payment established pursuant to paragraph 1(c) is not remedied within the prescribed period, the application shall be deemed to be withdrawn unless it is clear which categories of goods or services the amount paid is intended to cover. [In the absence of other criteria to determine which classes are intended to be covered, the Office shall take the classes in the order of the classification. The application shall be deemed to have been withdrawn with regard to those classes for which the class fees have not been paid or have not been paid in full.]

6. Failure to satisfy the requirements concerning the claim to priority shall result in loss of the right of priority for the application.

7. Failure to satisfy the requirements concerning the claiming of seniority of a national trade mark shall result in loss of that right for the application.

[8. Where failure to satisfy the requirements referred to in paragraph 1(b) and (c) concerns only some of the goods or services, the Office shall refuse the application, or the right of priority or the right of seniority shall be lost, only in so far as those goods and services are concerned.]

NOTES

General amendments to this Regulation: see further the note "General amendments" in the introductory notes to this Regulation *ante*.

Para 1: point (b) substituted by European Parliament and Council Regulation 2015/2424/EU, Art 1(34)(a).

Para 2: words in square brackets substituted by European Parliament and Council Regulation 2015/2424/EU, Art 1(34)(b).

Para 5: words in square brackets inserted by European Parliament and Council Regulation 2015/2424/EU, Art 1(34)(c).

Para 8: added by European Parliament and Council Regulation 2015/2424/EU, Art 1(34)(d).

[5.617]
Article 37
Examination as to absolute grounds for refusal

1. Where, under Article 7, a trade mark is ineligible for registration in respect of some or all of the goods or services covered by the Community trade mark application, the application shall be refused as regards those goods or services.

2. . . .

[(3) The application shall not be refused before the applicant has been allowed the opportunity to withdraw or amend the application or to submit his observations. To this effect, the Office shall notify the applicant of the grounds for refusing registration and shall specify a period within which he may withdraw or amend the application or submit his observations. Where the applicant fails to overcome the grounds for refusing registration, the Office shall refuse registration in whole or in part.]

NOTES

General amendments to this Regulation: see further the note "General amendments" in the introductory notes to this Regulation *ante*.

Para 2: repealed by European Parliament and Council Regulation 2015/2424/EU, Art 1(35)(a).

Para 3: substituted by European Parliament and Council Regulation 2015/2424/EU, Art 1(35)(b).

SECTION 2
SEARCH

[5.618]
[Article 38
Search report

1. The Office shall, at the request of the applicant for the EU trade mark when filing the application, draw up a European Union search report ("EU search report") citing those earlier EU trade marks or EU trade mark applications discovered which may be invoked under Article 8 against the registration of the EU trade mark applied for.

2. Where, at the time of filing an EU trade mark application, the applicant requests that a search report be prepared by the central industrial property offices of the Member States and where the appropriate search fee has been paid within the time limit for the payment of the filing fee, the

Office shall transmit without delay a copy of the EU trade mark application to the central industrial property office of each Member State which has informed the Office of its decision to operate a search in its own register of trade marks in respect of EU trade mark applications.
3. Each of the central industrial property offices of the Member States referred to in paragraph 2 of this Article shall communicate a search report which shall either cite any earlier national trade marks, national trade mark applications or trade marks registered under international agreements, having effect in the Member State or Member States concerned, which have been discovered and which may be invoked under Article 8 against the registration of the EU trade mark applied for, or state that the search has revealed no such rights.
4. The Office, after consulting the Management Board provided for in Article 124 ("the Management Board"), shall establish the contents and modalities for the reports.
5. The Office shall pay an amount to each central industrial property office for each search report provided by the office in accordance with paragraph 3. The amount, which shall be the same for each office, shall be fixed by the Budget Committee by means of a decision adopted by a majority of three quarters of the representatives of the Member States.
6. The Office shall transmit to the applicant for the EU trade mark the EU search report requested and any requested national search reports received.
7. Upon publication of the EU trade mark application, the Office shall inform the proprietors of any earlier EU trade marks, or EU trade mark applications cited in the EU search report of the publication of the EU trade mark application. The latter shall apply irrespective of whether the applicant has requested to receive the EU search report, unless the proprietor of an earlier registration or application requests not to receive the notification.]

NOTES

Substituted by European Parliament and Council Regulation 2015/2424/EU, Art 1(36).

SECTION 3
PUBLICATION OF THE APPLICATION

[5.619]
Article 39
Publication of the application

[1. If the conditions which the application for an EU trade mark is required to satisfy have been fulfilled, the application shall be published for the purposes of Article 41 to the extent that it has not been refused pursuant to Article 37. The publication of the application shall be without prejudice to information already made available to the public otherwise in accordance with this Regulation or acts adopted pursuant to this Regulation.]
2. Where, after publication, the application is refused under Article 37, the decision that it has been refused shall be published upon becoming final.
[3. Where the publication of the application contains an error attributable to the Office, the Office shall of its own motion or at the request of the applicant correct the error and publish the correction.
The rules adopted pursuant to Article 43(3) shall apply mutatis mutandis where a correction is requested by the applicant.
4. Article 41(2) shall apply also where the correction concerns the list of goods or services or the representation of the mark.
5. The Commission shall adopt implementing acts laying down the details to be contained in the publication of the application. Those implementing acts shall be adopted in accordance with the examination procedure referred to in Article 163(2).]

NOTES

Para 1: substituted by European Parliament and Council Regulation 2015/2424/EU, Art 1(37)(a).
Paras 3–5: added by European Parliament and Council Regulation 2015/2424/EU, Art 1(37)(b).

SECTION 4
OBSERVATIONS BY THIRD PARTIES AND OPPOSITION

[5.620]
[Article 40
Observations by third parties

1. Any natural or legal person and any group or body representing manufacturers, producers, suppliers of services, traders or consumers may submit to the Office written observations, explaining on which grounds, under Articles 5 and 7, the trade mark should not be registered ex officio.
Persons and groups or bodies as referred to in the first subparagraph shall not be parties to the proceedings before the Office.
2. Third party observations shall be submitted before the end of the opposition period or, where an opposition against the trade mark has been filed, before the final decision on the opposition is taken.

3. The submission referred to in paragraph 1 shall be without prejudice to the right of the Office to re-open the examination of absolute grounds on its own initiative at any time before registration, where appropriate.

4. The observations referred to in paragraph 1 shall be communicated to the applicant who may comment on them.]

NOTES

Substituted by European Parliament and Council Regulation 2015/2424/EU, Art 1(38).

[5.621]

Article 41

Opposition

1. Within a period of three months following the publication of a Community trade mark application, notice of opposition to registration of the trade mark may be given on the grounds that it may not be registered under Article 8:

- *(a) by the proprietors of earlier trade marks referred to in Article 8(2) as well as licensees authorised by the proprietors of those trade marks, in respect of Article 8(1) and (5);*
- *(b) by the proprietors of trade marks referred to in Article 8(3);*
- *(c) by the proprietors of earlier marks or signs referred to in Article 8(4) and by persons authorised under the relevant national law to exercise these rights;*
- *[(d) by the persons authorised under the relevant Union legislation or national law to exercise the rights referred to in Article 8(4a).]*

2. Notice of opposition to registration of the trade mark may also be given, subject to the conditions laid down in paragraph 1, in the event of the publication of an amended application in accordance with the second sentence of Article 43(2).

[3. Opposition shall be expressed in writing, and shall specify the grounds on which it is made. It shall not be considered as duly entered until the opposition fee has been paid.]

[4. Within a period to be fixed by the Office, the opponent may submit facts, evidence and arguments in support of his case.]

NOTES

General amendments to this Regulation: see further the note "General amendments" in the introductory notes to this Regulation *ante*.

Para 1: point (d) added by European Parliament and Council Regulation 2015/2424/EU, Art 1(39)(a).

Para 3: substituted by European Parliament and Council Regulation 2015/2424/EU, Art 1(39)(b).

Para 4: added by European Parliament and Council Regulation 2015/2424/EU, Art 1(39)(c).

[5.622]

Article 42

Examination of opposition

1. In the examination of the opposition the Office shall invite the parties, as often as necessary, to file observations, within a period set them by the Office, on communications from the other parties or issued by itself.

[2. If the applicant so requests, the proprietor of an earlier EU trade mark who has given notice of opposition shall furnish proof that, during the five-year period preceding the date of filing or the date of priority of the EU trade mark application, the earlier EU trade mark has been put to genuine use in the Union in connection with the goods or services in respect of which it is registered and which he cites as justification for his opposition, or that there are proper reasons for non-use, provided the earlier EU trade mark has at that date been registered for not less than five years. In the absence of proof to this effect, the opposition shall be rejected. If the earlier EU trade mark has been used in relation to only part of the goods or services for which it is registered it shall, for the purposes of the examination of the opposition, be deemed to be registered in respect only of that part of the goods or services.]

3. Paragraph 2 shall apply to earlier national trade marks referred to in Article 8(2)(a), by substituting use in the Member State in which the earlier national trade mark is protected for use in the Community.

4. The Office may, if it thinks fit, invite the parties to make a friendly settlement.

5. If examination of the opposition reveals that the trade mark may not be registered in respect of some or all of the goods or services for which the Community trade mark application has been made, the application shall be refused in respect of those goods or services. Otherwise the opposition shall be rejected.

6. The decision refusing the application shall be published upon becoming final.

NOTES

General amendments to this Regulation: see further the note "General amendments" in the introductory notes to this Regulation *ante*.

Para 2: substituted by European Parliament and Council Regulation 2015/2424/EU, Art 1(40).

[5.623]
[Article 42a
Delegation of powers
The Commission shall be empowered to adopt delegated acts in accordance with Article 163a specifying the details of the procedure for filing and examining an opposition set out in Articles 41 and 42.]

NOTES
Inserted by European Parliament and Council Regulation 2015/2424/EU, Art 1(41).

SECTION 5
WITHDRAWAL, RESTRICTION, AMENDMENT AND DIVISION OF THE APPLICATION

[5.624]
Article 43
Withdrawal, restriction and amendment of the application
1. The applicant may at any time withdraw his Community trade mark application or restrict the list of goods or services contained therein. Where the application has already been published, the withdrawal or restriction shall also be published.
2. In other respects, a Community trade mark application may be amended, upon request of the applicant, only by correcting the name and address of the applicant, errors of wording or of copying, or obvious mistakes, provided that such correction does not substantially change the trade mark or extend the list of goods or services. Where the amendments affect the representation of the trade mark or the list of goods or services and are made after publication of the application, the trade mark application shall be published as amended.
[3. The Commission shall be empowered to adopt delegated acts in accordance with Article 163a specifying the details of the procedure governing the amendment of the application.]

NOTES
General amendments to this Regulation: see further the note "General amendments" in the introductory notes to this Regulation *ante*.
Para 3: added by European Parliament and Council Regulation 2015/2424/EU, Art 1(42).

[5.625]
Article 44
Division of the application
1. The applicant may divide the application by declaring that some of the goods or services included in the original application will be the subject of one or more divisional applications. The goods or services in the divisional application shall not overlap with the goods or services which remain in the original application or those which are included in other divisional applications.
2. The declaration of division shall not be admissible:
(a) if, where an opposition has been entered against the original application, such a divisional application has the effect of introducing a division amongst the goods or services against which the opposition has been directed, until the decision of the Opposition Division has become final or the opposition proceedings are finally terminated otherwise;
[(b) before the date of filing referred to in Article 27 has been accorded by the Office and during the opposition period provided for in Article 41(1).]
3. . . .
4. The declaration of division shall be subject to a fee. The declaration shall be deemed not to have been made until the fee has been paid.
[4a. Where the Office finds that the requirements laid down in paragraph 1 and in the rules adopted pursuant to paragraph 9(a) are not fulfilled, it shall invite the applicant to remedy the deficiencies within a period to be specified by the Office. If the deficiencies are not remedied before the time limit expires, the Office shall refuse the declaration of division.]
5. The division shall take effect on the date on which it is recorded in the files kept by the Office concerning the original application.
6. All requests and applications submitted and all fees paid with regard to the original application prior to the date on which the Office receives the declaration of division are deemed also to have been submitted or paid with regard to the divisional application or applications. The fees for the original application which have been duly paid prior to the date on which the declaration of division is received shall not be refunded.
7. The divisional application shall preserve the filing date and any priority date and seniority date of the original application.
[8. Where the declaration of division relates to an application which has already been published pursuant to Article 39, the division shall be published. The divisional application shall be published. The publication shall not open a new period for the filing of oppositions.
9. The Commission shall adopt implementing acts specifying:
(a) the details to be contained in a declaration of the division of an application made pursuant to paragraph 1;

(b) the details as to how to process a declaration of the division of an application, ensuring that a separate file, including a new application number, is established for the divisional application;

(c) the details to be contained in the publication of the divisional application pursuant to paragraph 8.

Those implementing acts shall be adopted in accordance with the examination procedure referred to in Article 163(2).]

NOTES

Para 2: point (b) substituted by European Parliament and Council Regulation 2015/2424/EU, Art 1(43)(a).
Para 3: repealed by European Parliament and Council Regulation 2015/2424/EU, Art 1(43)(b).
Para 4a: inserted by European Parliament and Council Regulation 2015/2424/EU, Art 1(43)(c).
Paras 8, 9: added by European Parliament and Council Regulation 2015/2424/EU, Art 1(43)(d).

SECTION 6
REGISTRATION

[5.626]
[Article 45
Registration

1. Where an application meets the requirements set out in this Regulation and where no notice of opposition has been given within the period referred to in Article 41(1) or where any opposition entered has been finally disposed of by withdrawal, rejection or other disposition, the trade mark and the particulars referred to in Article 87(2) shall be recorded in the Register. The registration shall be published.

2. The Office shall issue a certificate of registration. That certificate may be issued by electronic means. The Office shall provide certified or uncertified copies of the certificate subject to the payment of a fee, where those copies are issued other than by electronic means.

3. The Commission shall adopt implementing acts specifying the details to be contained in and the form of the certificate of registration referred to in paragraph 2 of this Article. Those implementing acts shall be adopted in accordance with the examination procedure referred to in Article 163(2).]

NOTES

Substituted by European Parliament and Council Regulation 2015/2424/EU, Art 1(44).

TITLE V
DURATION, RENEWAL, ALTERATION AND DIVISION OF COMMUNITY TRADE MARKS

[5.627]
Article 46
Duration of registration

Community trade marks shall be registered for a period of 10 years from the date of filing of the application. Registration may be renewed in accordance with Article 47 for further periods of 10 years.

NOTES

General amendments to this Regulation: see further the note "General amendments" in the introductory notes to this Regulation *ante*.

[5.628]
[Article 47
Renewal

1. Registration of the EU trade mark shall be renewed at the request of the proprietor of the EU trade mark or any person expressly authorised by him, provided that the fees have been paid.

2. The Office shall inform the proprietor of the EU trade mark, and any person having a registered right in respect of the EU trade mark, of the expiry of the registration at least six months before the said expiry. Failure to give such information shall not involve the responsibility of the Office and shall not affect the expiry of the registration.

3. The request for renewal shall be submitted in the six-month period prior to the expiry of the registration. The basic fee for the renewal, and where appropriate, one or more class fees for each class of goods or services exceeding the first one shall also be paid within this period. Failing this, the request may be submitted and the fees paid within a further period of six months following the expiry of registration, provided that an additional fee for late payment of the renewal fee or late submission of the request for renewal is paid within this further period.

4. The request for renewal shall include:

(a) the name of the person requesting renewal;

(b) the registration number of the EU trade mark to be renewed;

(c) if the renewal is requested for only part of the registered goods and services, an indication of those classes or those goods and services for which renewal is requested, or those

classes or those goods and services for which renewal is not requested, grouped according to the classes of the Nice classification, each group being preceded by the number of the class of that classification to which that group of goods or services belongs, and presented in the order of classes of that classification.

If the payment referred to in paragraph 3 is made, it shall be deemed to constitute a request for renewal provided that it contains all necessary indications to establish the purpose of the payment.

5. Where the request is submitted or the fees paid in respect of only some of the goods or services for which the EU trade mark is registered, registration shall be renewed for those goods or services only. Where the fees paid are insufficient to cover all the classes of goods and services for which renewal is requested, registration shall be renewed if it is clear which class or classes are to be covered. In the absence of other criteria, the Office shall take the classes into account in the order of classification.

6. Renewal shall take effect from the day following the date on which the existing registration expires. The renewal shall be registered.

7. Where the request for renewal is filed within the periods provided for in paragraph 3, but the other conditions governing renewal provided for in this Article are not satisfied, the Office shall inform the applicant of the deficiencies found.

8. Where a request for renewal is not submitted or is submitted after the expiry of the period provided for in paragraph 3, or where the fees are not paid or are paid only after the period in question has expired, or where the deficiencies referred to in paragraph 7 are not remedied within that period, the Office shall determine that the registration has expired and shall notify the proprietor of the EU trade mark accordingly. Where the determination has become final, the Office shall cancel the mark from the register. The cancellation shall take effect from the day following the date on which the existing registration expired. Where the renewal fees have been paid but the registration is not renewed, those fees shall be refunded.

9. A single request for renewal may be submitted for two or more marks, upon payment of the required fees for each of the marks, provided that the proprietors or the representatives are the same in each case.]

NOTES

Substituted by European Parliament and Council Regulation 2015/2424/EU, Art 1(45).

[5.629]

Article 48

Alteration

1. The Community trade mark shall not be altered in the Register during the period of registration or on renewal thereof.

2. Nevertheless, where the Community trade mark includes the name and address of the proprietor, any alteration thereof not substantially affecting the identity of the trade mark as originally registered may be registered at the request of the proprietor.

[3. The request for alteration shall include the element of the mark to be altered and that element in its altered version.

The Commission shall adopt implementing acts specifying the details to be contained in the request for alteration. Those implementing acts shall be adopted in accordance with the examination procedure referred to in Article 163(2).]

[4. The request shall be deemed not to have been filed until the required fee has been paid. If the fee has not been paid or has not been paid in full, the Office shall inform the applicant accordingly. A single request may be made for the alteration of the same element in two or more registrations of the same proprietor. The required fee shall be paid in respect of each registration to be altered. If the requirements governing the alteration of the registration are not fulfilled, the Office shall communicate the deficiency to the applicant. If the deficiency is not remedied within a period to be specified by the Office, the Office shall reject the request.

5. The publication of the registration of the alteration shall contain a representation of the EU trade mark as altered. Third parties whose rights may be affected by the alteration may challenge the registration thereof within the period of three months following publication. Articles 41 and 42, and rules adopted pursuant to Article 42a shall apply to the publication of the registration of the alteration.]

NOTES

General amendments to this Regulation: see further the note "General amendments" in the introductory notes to this Regulation *ante*.

Para 3: substituted by European Parliament and Council Regulation 2015/2424/EU, Art 1(46)(a).

Paras 4, 5: added by European Parliament and Council Regulation 2015/2424/EU, Art 1(46)(b).

[5.630]

[Article 48a

Change of the name or address

1. A change of the name or address of the proprietor of the EU trade mark which is not an alteration of the EU trade mark pursuant to Article 48(2) and which is not the consequence of a whole or partial transfer of the EU trade mark shall, at the request of the proprietor, be recorded in the Register.

The Commission shall adopt implementing acts specifying the details to be contained in a request for the change of name or address pursuant to the first subparagraph of this paragraph. Those implementing acts shall be adopted in accordance with the examination procedure referred to in Article 163(2).

2. A single request may be made for the change of the name or address in respect of two or more registrations of the same proprietor.

3. If the requirements governing the recording of a change are not fulfilled, the Office shall communicate the deficiency to the proprietor of the EU trade mark. If the deficiency is not remedied within a period to be specified by the Office, the Office shall reject the request.

4. Paragraphs 1 to 3 shall also apply to a change of the name or address of the registered representative.

5. Paragraphs 1 to 4 shall apply to applications for EU trade marks. The change shall be recorded in the files kept by the Office on the EU trade mark application.]

NOTES

Inserted by European Parliament and Council Regulation 2015/2424/EU, Art 1(47).

[5.631]

Article 49

Division of the registration

1. The proprietor of the Community trade mark may divide the registration by declaring that some of the goods or services included in the original registration will be the subject of one or more divisional registrations. The goods or services in the divisional registration shall not overlap with the goods or services which remain in the original registration or those which are included in other divisional registrations.

2. The declaration of division shall not be admissible:

(a) if, where an application for revocation of rights or for a declaration of invalidity has been entered at the Office against the original registration, such a divisional declaration has the effect of introducing a division amongst the goods or services against which the application for revocation of rights or for a declaration of invalidity is directed, until the decision of the Cancellation Division has become final or the proceedings are finally terminated otherwise;

(b) if, where a counterclaim for revocation or for a declaration of invalidity has been entered in a case before a Community trade mark court, such a divisional declaration has the effect of introducing a division amongst the goods or services against which the counterclaim is directed, until the mention of the Community trade mark court's judgment is recorded in the Register pursuant to Article 100(6).

[3. If the requirements laid down in paragraph 1 and pursuant to the implementing acts referred to in paragraph 8 are not fulfilled, or the list of goods and services which form the divisional registration overlap with the goods and services which remain in the original registration, the Office shall invite the proprietor of the EU trade mark to remedy the deficiencies within such period as it may specify. If the deficiencies are not remedied before the time period expires, the Office shall refuse the declaration of division.]

4. The declaration of division shall be subject to a fee. The declaration shall be deemed not to have been made until the fee has been paid.

5. The division shall take effect on the date on which it is entered in the Register.

6. All requests and applications submitted and all fees paid with regard to the original registration prior to the date on which the Office receives the declaration of division shall be deemed also to have been submitted or paid with regard to the divisional registration or registrations. The fees for the original registration which have been duly paid prior to the date on which the declaration of division is received shall not be refunded.

7. The divisional registration shall preserve the filing date and any priority date and seniority date of the original registration.

[8. The Commission shall adopt implementing acts specifying:

(a) the details to be contained in a declaration of the division of a registration pursuant to paragraph 1;

(b) the details as how to process a declaration of the division of a registration, ensuring that a separate file, including a new registration number, is established for the divisional registration.

Those implementing acts shall be adopted in accordance with the examination procedure referred to in Article 163(2).]

NOTES

General amendments to this Regulation: see further the note "General amendments" in the introductory notes to this Regulation *ante*.

Para 3: substituted by European Parliament and Council Regulation 2015/2424/EU, Art 1(48)(a).

Para 8: added by European Parliament and Council Regulation 2015/2424/EU, Art 1(48)(b).

TITLE VI
SURRENDER, REVOCATION AND INVALIDITY

SECTION 1
SURRENDER

[5.632]
Article 50
Surrender

1. A Community trade mark may be surrendered in respect of some or all of the goods or services for which it is registered.

[2. The surrender shall be declared to the Office in writing by the proprietor of the trade mark. It shall not have effect until it has been entered in the Register. The validity of the surrender of an EU trade mark which is declared to the Office subsequent to the submission of an application for revocation of that trade mark pursuant to Article 56(1) shall be conditional upon the final rejection or withdrawal of the application for revocation.

3. Surrender shall be entered only with the agreement of the proprietor of a right relating to the EU trade mark and which is entered in the Register. If a licence has been registered, surrender shall be entered in the Register only if the proprietor of the EU trade mark proves that he has informed the licensee of his intention to surrender. The entry of the surrender shall be made on expiry of the three-month period after the date on which the proprietor satisfies the Office that he has informed the licensee of his intention to surrender, or before the expiry of that period, as soon as he proves that the licensee has given his consent.]

[4. If the requirements governing surrender are not fulfilled, the Office shall communicate the deficiencies to the declarant. If the deficiencies are not remedied within a period to be specified by the Office, the Office shall reject the entry of surrender in the Register.

5. The Commission shall adopt implementing acts specifying the details to be contained in a declaration of surrender pursuant to paragraph 2 of this Article and the kind of documentation required to establish a third party's agreement pursuant to paragraph 3 of this Article. Those implementing acts shall be adopted in accordance with the examination procedure referred to in Article 163(2).]

NOTES

General amendments to this Regulation: see further the note "General amendments" in the introductory notes to this Regulation *ante*.

Paras 2, 3: substituted by European Parliament and Council Regulation 2015/2424/EU, Art 1(49)(a).

Paras 4, 5: added by European Parliament and Council Regulation 2015/2424/EU, Art 1(49)(b).

SECTION 2
GROUNDS FOR REVOCATION

[5.633]
Article 51
Grounds for revocation

1. The rights of the proprietor of the Community trade mark shall be declared to be revoked on application to the Office or on the basis of a counterclaim in infringement proceedings:

(a) if, within a continuous period of five years, the trade mark has not been put to genuine use in the Community in connection with the goods or services in respect of which it is registered, and there are no proper reasons for non-use; however, no person may claim that the proprietor's rights in a Community trade mark should be revoked where, during the interval between expiry of the five-year period and filing of the application or counterclaim, genuine use of the trade mark has been started or resumed; the commencement or resumption of use within a period of three months preceding the filing of the application or counterclaim which began at the earliest on expiry of the continuous period of five years of non-use shall, however, be disregarded where preparations for the commencement or resumption occur only after the proprietor becomes aware that the application or counterclaim may be filed;

(b) if, in consequence of acts or inactivity of the proprietor, the trade mark has become the common name in the trade for a product or service in respect of which it is registered;

(c) *if, in consequence of the use made of it by the proprietor of the trade mark or with his consent in respect of the goods or services for which it is registered, the trade mark is liable to mislead the public, particularly as to the nature, quality or geographical origin of those goods or services.*

2. Where the grounds for revocation of rights exist in respect of only some of the goods or services for which the Community trade mark is registered, the rights of the proprietor shall be declared to be revoked in respect of those goods or services only.

NOTES

General amendments to this Regulation: see further the note "General amendments" in the introductory notes to this Regulation *ante*.

SECTION 3
GROUNDS FOR INVALIDITY

[5.634]

Article 52

Absolute grounds for invalidity

1. A Community trade mark shall be declared invalid on application to the Office or on the basis of a counterclaim in infringement proceedings:

(a) *where the Community trade mark has been registered contrary to the provisions of Article 7;*

(b) *where the applicant was acting in bad faith when he filed the application for the trade mark.*

2. Where the Community trade mark has been registered in breach of the provisions of Article 7(1)(b), (c) or (d), it may nevertheless not be declared invalid if, in consequence of the use which has been made of it, it has after registration acquired a distinctive character in relation to the goods or services for which it is registered.

3. Where the ground for invalidity exists in respect of only some of the goods or services for which the Community trade mark is registered, the trade mark shall be declared invalid as regards those goods or services only.

NOTES

General amendments to this Regulation: see further the note "General amendments" in the introductory notes to this Regulation *ante*.

[5.635]

Article 53

Relative grounds for invalidity

1. A Community trade mark shall be declared invalid on application to the Office or on the basis of a counterclaim in infringement proceedings:

(a) *where there is an earlier trade mark as referred to in Article 8(2) and the conditions set out in paragraph 1 or paragraph 5 of that Article are fulfilled;*

(b) *where there is a trade mark as referred to in Article 8(3) and the conditions set out in that paragraph are fulfilled;*

(c) *where there is an earlier right as referred to in Article 8(4) and the conditions set out in that paragraph are fulfilled.*

[(d) *where there is an earlier designation of origin or geographical indication as referred to in Article 8(4a) and the conditions set out in that paragraph are fulfilled.*

All the conditions referred to in the first subparagraph shall be fulfilled at the filing date or the priority date of the EU trade mark.]

2. A Community trade mark shall also be declared invalid on application to the Office or on the basis of a counterclaim in infringement proceedings where the use of such trade mark may be prohibited pursuant to another earlier right under the Community legislation or national law governing its protection, and in particular:

(a) *a right to a name;*

(b) *a right of personal portrayal;*

(c) *a copyright;*

(d) *an industrial property right.*

3. A Community trade mark may not be declared invalid where the proprietor of a right referred to in paragraphs 1 or 2 consents expressly to the registration of the Community trade mark before submission of the application for a declaration of invalidity or the counterclaim.

4. Where the proprietor of one of the rights referred to in paragraphs 1 or 2 has previously applied for a declaration that a Community trade mark is invalid or made a counterclaim in infringement proceedings, he may not submit a new application for a declaration of invalidity or lodge a counterclaim on the basis of another of the said rights which he could have invoked in support of his first application or counterclaim.

5. Article 52(3) shall apply.

NOTES

General amendments to this Regulation: see further the note "General amendments" in the introductory notes to this Regulation *ante*.

Para 1: words in square brackets inserted by European Parliament and Council Regulation 2015/2424/EU, Art 1(50).

[5.636]

Article 54

Limitation in consequence of acquiescence

[1. Where the proprietor of an EU trade mark has acquiesced, for a period of five successive years, in the use of a later EU trade mark in the Union while being aware of such use, he shall no longer be entitled on the basis of the earlier trade mark to apply for a declaration that the later trade mark is invalid in respect of the goods or services for which the later trade mark has been used, unless registration of the later EU trade mark was applied for in bad faith.

2. Where the proprietor of an earlier national trade mark as referred to in Article 8(2) or of another earlier sign referred to in Article 8(4) has acquiesced, for a period of five successive years, in the use of a later EU trade mark in the Member State in which the earlier trade mark or the other earlier sign is protected while being aware of such use, he shall no longer be entitled on the basis of the earlier trade mark or of the other earlier sign to apply for a declaration that the later trade mark is invalid in respect of the goods or services for which the later trade mark has been used, unless registration of the later EU trade mark was applied for in bad faith.]

3. In the cases referred to in paragraphs 1 and 2, the proprietor of a later Community trade mark shall not be entitled to oppose the use of the earlier right, even though that right may no longer be invoked against the later Community trade mark.

NOTES

General amendments to this Regulation: see further the note "General amendments" in the introductory notes to this Regulation *ante*.

Paras 1, 2: substituted by European Parliament and Council Regulation 2015/2424/EU, Art 1(51).

SECTION 4

CONSEQUENCES OF REVOCATION AND INVALIDITY

[5.637]

Article 55

Consequences of revocation and invalidity

1. The Community trade mark shall be deemed not to have had, as from the date of the application for revocation or of the counterclaim, the effects specified in this Regulation, to the extent that the rights of the proprietor have been revoked. An earlier date, on which one of the grounds for revocation occurred, may be fixed in the decision at the request of one of the parties.

2. The Community trade mark shall be deemed not to have had, as from the outset, the effects specified in this Regulation, to the extent that the trade mark has been declared invalid.

3. Subject to the national provisions relating either to claims for compensation for damage caused by negligence or lack of good faith on the part of the proprietor of the trade mark, or to unjust enrichment, the retroactive effect of revocation or invalidity of the trade mark shall not affect:

- *(a) any decision on infringement which has acquired the authority of a final decision and been enforced prior to the revocation or invalidity decision;*
- *(b) any contract concluded prior to the revocation or invalidity decision, in so far as it has been performed before that decision; however, repayment, to an extent justified by the circumstances, of sums paid under the relevant contract, may be claimed on grounds of equity.*

NOTES

General amendments to this Regulation: see further the note "General amendments" in the introductory notes to this Regulation *ante*.

SECTION 5

PROCEEDINGS IN THE OFFICE IN RELATION TO REVOCATION OR INVALIDITY

[5.638]

Article 56

Application for revocation or for a declaration of invalidity

1. An application for revocation of the rights of the proprietor of a Community trade mark or for a declaration that the trade mark is invalid may be submitted to the Office:

- *(a) where Articles 51 and 52 apply, by any natural or legal person and any group or body set up for the purpose of representing the interests of manufacturers, producers, suppliers of services, traders or consumers, which under the terms of the law governing it has the capacity in its own name to sue and be sued;*
- *(b) where Article 53(1) applies, by the persons referred to in Article 41(1);*

(c) where Article 53(2) applies, by the owners of the earlier rights referred to in that provision or by the persons who are entitled [under Union legislation or the law of the Member State concerned] to exercise the rights in question.

2. The application shall be filed in a written reasoned statement. It shall not be deemed to have been filed until the fee has been paid.

[3. An application for revocation or for a declaration of invalidity shall be inadmissible where an application relating to the same subject matter and cause of action, and involving the same parties, has been adjudicated on its merits, either by the Office or by an EU trade mark court as referred to in Article 95, and the decision of the Office or that court on that application has acquired the authority of a final decision.]

NOTES

General amendments to this Regulation: see further the note "General amendments" in the introductory notes to this Regulation *ante*.

Para 1: words in square brackets in point (c) substituted by European Parliament and Council Regulation 2015/2424/EU, Art 1(52)(a).

Para 3: added by European Parliament and Council Regulation 2015/2424/EU, Art 1(52)(b).

[5.639]
Article 57
Examination of the application

1. On the examination of the application for revocation of rights or for a declaration of invalidity, the Office shall invite the parties, as often as necessary, to file observations, within a period to be fixed by the Office, on communications from the other parties or issued by itself.

[2. If the proprietor of the EU trade mark so requests, the proprietor of an earlier EU trade mark, being a party to the invalidity proceedings, shall furnish proof that, during the period of five years preceding the date of the application for a declaration of invalidity, the earlier EU trade mark has been put to genuine use in the Union in connection with the goods or services in respect of which it is registered and which the proprietor of that earlier trade mark cites as justification for his application, or that there are proper reasons for non-use, provided the earlier EU trade mark has at that date been registered for not less than five years. If, at the date on which the EU trade mark application was filed or at the priority date of the EU trade mark application, the earlier EU trade mark had been registered for not less than five years, the proprietor of the earlier EU trade mark shall furnish proof that, in addition, the conditions set out in Article 42(2) were satisfied at that date. In the absence of proof to this effect, the application for a declaration of invalidity shall be rejected. If the earlier EU trade mark has been used only in relation to part of the goods or services for which it is registered, it shall, for the purpose of the examination of the application for a declaration of invalidity, be deemed to be registered in respect of that part of the goods or services only.]

3. Paragraph 2 shall apply to earlier national trade marks referred to in Article 8(2)(a), by substituting use in the Member State in which the earlier national trade mark is protected for use in the Community.

4. The Office may, if it thinks fit, invite the parties to make a friendly settlement.

5. If the examination of the application for revocation of rights or for a declaration of invalidity reveals that the trade mark should not have been registered in respect of some or all of the goods or services for which it is registered, the rights of the proprietor of the Community trade mark shall be revoked or it shall be declared invalid in respect of those goods or services. Otherwise the application for revocation of rights or for a declaration of invalidity shall be rejected.

6. A record of the Office's decision on the application for revocation of rights or for a declaration of invalidity shall be entered in the Register once it has become final.

NOTES

General amendments to this Regulation: see further the note "General amendments" in the introductory notes to this Regulation *ante*.

Para 2: substituted by European Parliament and Council Regulation 2015/2424/EU, Art 1(53).

[5.640]
[Article 57a
Delegation of powers

The Commission shall be empowered to adopt delegated acts in accordance with Article 163a specifying the details of the procedures governing the revocation and declaration of invalidity of an EU trade mark as referred to in Articles 56 and 57, as well as the transfer of an EU trade mark registered in the name of an agent as referred to in Article 18.]

NOTES

Inserted by European Parliament and Council Regulation 2015/2424/EU, Art 1(54).

TITLE VII
APPEALS

[5.641]
Article 58
Decisions subject to appeal
[1. An appeal shall lie from decisions of any of the decision-making instances of the Office listed in points (a) to (d) of Article 130, and, where appropriate, point (f) of that Article. Those decisions shall take effect only as from the date of expiration of the appeal period referred to in Article 60. The filing of the appeal shall have suspensive effect.]
2. A decision which does not terminate proceedings as regards one of the parties can only be appealed together with the final decision, unless the decision allows separate appeal.

NOTES
Para 1: substituted by European Parliament and Council Regulation 2015/2424/EU, Art 1(55).

[5.642]
Article 59
Persons entitled to appeal and to be parties to appeal proceedings
Any party to proceedings adversely affected by a decision may appeal. Any other parties to the proceedings shall be parties to the appeal proceedings as of right.

[5.643]
[Article 60
Time limit and form of appeal
1. Notice of appeal shall be filed in writing at the Office within two months of the date of notification of the decision. The notice shall be deemed to have been filed only when the fee for appeal has been paid. It shall be filed in the language of the proceedings in which the decision subject to appeal was taken. Within four months of the date of notification of the decision, a written statement setting out the grounds of appeal shall be filed.
2. In inter partes proceedings, the defendant may, in his response, seek a decision annulling or altering the contested decision on a point not raised in the appeal. Such submissions shall cease to have effect should the appellant discontinue the proceedings.]

NOTES
Substituted by European Parliament and Council Regulation 2015/2424/EU, Art 1(56).

[5.644]
Article 61
Revision of decisions in ex parte cases
1. If the party which has lodged the appeal is the sole party to the procedure, and if the department whose decision is contested considers the appeal to be admissible and well founded, the department shall rectify its decision.
2. If the decision is not rectified within one month after receipt of the statement of grounds, the appeal shall be remitted to the Board of Appeal without delay, and without comment as to its merit.

Article 62 *(Repealed by European Parliament and Council Regulation 2015/2424/EU, Art 1(57).)*

[5.645]
Article 63
Examination of appeals
1. If the appeal is admissible, the Board of Appeal shall examine whether the appeal is allowable.
2. In the examination of the appeal, the Board of Appeal shall invite the parties, as often as necessary, to file observations, within a period to be fixed by the Board of Appeal, on communications from the other parties or issued by itself.

[5.646]
Article 64
Decisions in respect of appeals
1. Following the examination as to the allowability of the appeal, the Board of Appeal shall decide on the appeal. The Board of Appeal may either exercise any power within the competence of the department which was responsible for the decision appealed or remit the case to that department for further prosecution.
2. If the Board of Appeal remits the case for further prosecution to the department whose decision was appealed, that department shall be bound by the ratio decidendi of the Board of Appeal, in so far as the facts are the same.
[3. The decisions of the Board of Appeal shall take effect only as from the date of expiry of the period referred to in Article 65(5) or, if an action has been brought before the General Court within that period, as from the date of dismissal of such action or of any appeal filed with the Court of Justice against the decision of the General Court.]

NOTES

Para 3: substituted by European Parliament and Council Regulation 2015/2424/EU, Art 1(58).

[5.647]

Article 65

Actions before the Court of Justice

[1. Actions may be brought before the General Court against decisions of the Boards of Appeal in relation to appeals.]

2. The action may be brought on grounds of lack of competence, infringement of an essential procedural requirement, infringement of the Treaty, of this Regulation or of any rule of law relating to their application or misuse of power.

[3. The General Court shall have jurisdiction to annul or to alter the contested decision.]

4. The action shall be open to any party to proceedings before the Board of Appeal adversely affected by its decision.

[5. The action shall be brought before the General Court within two months of the date of notification of the decision of the Board of Appeal.

6. The Office shall take the necessary measures to comply with the judgment of the General Court or, in the event of an appeal against that judgment, the Court of Justice.]

NOTES

Paras 1, 3, 5, 6: substituted by European Parliament and Council Regulation 2015/2424/EU, Art 1(59).

[5.648]

[Article 65a

Delegation of powers

The Commission shall be empowered to adopt delegated acts in accordance with Article 163a specifying:

(a) the formal content of the notice of appeal referred to in Article 60 and the procedure for the filing and the examination of an appeal;

(b) the formal content and form of the Board of Appeal's decisions as referred to in Article 64;

(c) the reimbursement of the appeal fee as referred to in Article 60.]

NOTES

Inserted by European Parliament and Council Regulation 2015/2424/EU, Art 1(60).

TITLE VIII
[SPECIFIC PROVISIONS ON EUROPEAN UNION COLLECTIVE MARKS AND CERTIFICATION MARKS]

[SECTION 1
EU COLLECTIVE MARKS]

NOTES

Words in square brackets in title heading substituted and section heading inserted, by European Parliament and Council Regulation 2015/2424/EU, Art 1(61), (62).

[5.649]

Article 66

Community collective marks

1. A Community collective mark shall be a Community trade mark which is described as such when the mark is applied for and is capable of distinguishing the goods or services of the members of the association which is the proprietor of the mark from those of other undertakings. Associations of manufacturers, producers, suppliers of services, or traders which, under the terms of the law governing them, have the capacity in their own name to have rights and obligations of all kinds, to make contracts or accomplish other legal acts and to sue and be sued, as well as legal persons governed by public law, may apply for Community collective marks.

2. In derogation from Article 7(1)(c), signs or indications which may serve, in trade, to designate the geographical origin of the goods or services may constitute Community collective marks within the meaning of paragraph 1. A collective mark shall not entitle the proprietor to prohibit a third party from using in the course of trade such signs or indications, provided he uses them in accordance with honest practices in industrial or commercial matters; in particular, such a mark may not be invoked against a third party who is entitled to use a geographical name.

[3. Titles I to VII and IX to XIV shall apply to EU collective marks to the extent that this section does not provide otherwise.]

NOTES

General amendments to this Regulation: see further the note "General amendments" in the introductory notes to this Regulation *ante*.

Para 3: substituted by European Parliament and Council Regulation 2015/2424/EU, Art 1(63).

[5.650]
Article 67
Regulations governing use of the mark

[1. An applicant for an EU collective mark shall submit regulations governing its use within two months of the date of filing.]

2. The regulations governing use shall specify the persons authorised to use the mark, the conditions of membership of the association and, where they exist, the conditions of use of the mark, including sanctions. The regulations governing use of a mark referred to in Article 66(2) must authorise any person whose goods or services originate in the geographical area concerned to become a member of the association which is the proprietor of the mark.

[3. The Commission shall adopt implementing acts specifying the details to be contained in the regulations referred to in paragraph 2 of this Article. Those implementing acts shall be adopted in accordance with the examination procedure referred to in Article 163(2).]

NOTES

Para 1: substituted by European Parliament and Council Regulation 2015/2424/EU, Art 1(64)(a).

Para 3: added by European Parliament and Council Regulation 2015/2424/EU, Art 1(64)(b).

[5.651]
Article 68
Refusal of the application

1. In addition to the grounds for refusal of a Community trade mark application provided for in Articles 36 and 37, an application for a Community collective mark shall be refused where the provisions of Articles 66 or 67 are not satisfied, or where the regulations governing use are contrary to public policy or to accepted principles of morality.

2. An application for a Community collective mark shall also be refused if the public is liable to be misled as regards the character or the significance of the mark, in particular if it is likely to be taken to be something other than a collective mark.

3. An application shall not be refused if the applicant, as a result of amendment of the regulations governing use, meets the requirements of paragraphs 1 and 2.

NOTES

General amendments to this Regulation: see further the note "General amendments" in the introductory notes to this Regulation *ante*.

[5.652]
[Article 69
Observations by third parties

Where written observations on an EU collective mark are submitted to the Office pursuant to Article 40, those observations may also be based on the particular grounds on which the application for an EU collective mark should be refused pursuant to Article 68.]

NOTES

Substituted by European Parliament and Council Regulation 2015/2424/EU, Art 1(65).

[5.653]
Article 70
Use of marks

Use of a Community collective mark by any person who has authority to use it shall satisfy the requirements of this Regulation, provided that the other conditions which this Regulation imposes with regard to the use of Community trade marks are fulfilled.

NOTES

General amendments to this Regulation: see further the note "General amendments" in the introductory notes to this Regulation *ante*.

[5.654]
Article 71
Amendment of the regulations governing use of the mark

1. The proprietor of a Community collective mark must submit to the Office any amended regulations governing use.

2. The amendment shall not be mentioned in the Register if the amended regulations do not satisfy the requirements of Article 67 or involve one of the grounds for refusal referred to in Article 68.

[3. Written observations made in accordance with Article 69 may also be submitted with regard to amended regulations governing use.]

4. For the purposes of applying this Regulation, amendments to the regulations governing use shall take effect only from the date of entry of the mention of the amendment in the Register.

NOTES

General amendments to this Regulation: see further the note "General amendments" in the introductory notes to this Regulation *ante*.

Para 3: substituted by European Parliament and Council Regulation 2015/2424/EU, Art 1(66).

[5.655]

Article 72

Persons who are entitled to bring an action for infringement

1. The provisions of Article 22(3) and (4) concerning the rights of licensees shall apply to every person who has authority to use a Community collective mark.

2. The proprietor of a Community collective mark shall be entitled to claim compensation on behalf of persons who have authority to use the mark where they have sustained damage in consequence of unauthorised use of the mark.

NOTES

General amendments to this Regulation: see further the note "General amendments" in the introductory notes to this Regulation *ante*.

[5.656]

Article 73

Grounds for revocation

Apart from the grounds for revocation provided for in Article 51, the rights of the proprietor of a Community collective mark shall be revoked on application to the Office or on the basis of a counterclaim in infringement proceedings, if:

(a) the proprietor does not take reasonable steps to prevent the mark being used in a manner incompatible with the conditions of use, where these exist, laid down in the regulations governing use, amendments to which have, where appropriate, been mentioned in the Register;

(b) the manner in which the mark has been used by the proprietor has caused it to become liable to mislead the public in the manner referred to in Article 68(2);

(c) an amendment to the regulations governing use of the mark has been mentioned in the Register in breach of the provisions of Article 71(2), unless the proprietor of the mark, by further amending the regulations governing use, complies with the requirements of those provisions.

NOTES

General amendments to this Regulation: see further the note "General amendments" in the introductory notes to this Regulation *ante*.

[5.657]

Article 74

Grounds for invalidity

Apart from the grounds for invalidity provided for in Articles 52 and 53, a Community collective mark which is registered in breach of the provisions of Article 68 shall be declared invalid on application to the Office or on the basis of a counterclaim in infringement proceedings, unless the proprietor of the mark, by amending the regulations governing use, complies with the requirements of those provisions.

NOTES

General amendments to this Regulation: see further the note "General amendments" in the introductory notes to this Regulation *ante*.

[SECTION 2

EU CERTIFICATION MARKS

[5.658]

Article 74a

EU certification marks

1. An EU certification mark shall be an EU trade mark which is described as such when the mark is applied for and is capable of distinguishing goods or services which are certified by the proprietor of the mark in respect of material, mode of manufacture of goods or performance of services, quality, accuracy or other characteristics, with the exception of geographical origin, from goods and services which are not so certified.

2. Any natural or legal person, including institutions, authorities and bodies governed by public law, may apply for EU certification marks provided that such person does not carry on a business involving the supply of goods or services of the kind certified.

3. Titles I to VII and IX to XIV shall apply to EU certification marks to the extent that this Section does not provide otherwise.]

NOTES

Inserted, together with preceding section heading and Arts 74b–74k, by European Parliament and Council Regulation 2015/2424/EU, Art 1(67).

[5.659]

[Article 74b

Regulations governing use of the EU certification mark

1. An applicant for an EU certification mark shall submit regulations governing the use of the certification mark within two months of the date of filing.

2. The regulations governing use shall specify the persons authorised to use the mark, the characteristics to be certified by the mark, how the certifying body is to test those characteristics and to supervise the use of the mark. Those regulations shall also specify the conditions of use of the mark, including sanctions.

3. The Commission shall adopt implementing acts specifying the details to be contained in the regulations referred to in paragraph 2 of this Article. Those implementing acts shall be adopted in accordance with the examination procedure referred to in Article 163(2).]

NOTES

Inserted as noted to Art 74a at **[5.658]**.

[5.660]

[Article 74c

Refusal of the application

1. In addition to the grounds for refusal of an EU trade mark application provided for in Articles 36 and 37, an application for an EU certification mark shall be refused where the conditions set out in Articles 74a and 74b are not satisfied, or where the regulations governing use are contrary to public policy or to accepted principles of morality.

2. An application for an EU certification mark shall also be refused if the public is liable to be misled as regards the character or the significance of the mark, in particular if it is likely to be taken to be something other than a certification mark.

3. An application shall not be refused if the applicant, as a result of an amendment of the regulations governing use, meets the requirements of paragraphs 1 and 2.]

NOTES

Inserted as noted to Art 74a at **[5.658]**.

[5.661]

[Article 74d

Observations by third parties

Where written observations on an EU certification mark are submitted to the Office pursuant to Article 40, those observations may also be based on the particular grounds on which the application for an EU certification mark should be refused pursuant to Article 74c.]

NOTES

Inserted as noted to Art 74a at **[5.658]**.

[5.662]

[Article 74e

Use of the EU certification mark

Use of an EU certification mark by any person who has authority to use it according to the regulations governing use referred to in Article 74b shall satisfy the requirements of this Regulation, provided that the other conditions laid down in this Regulation with regard to the use of EU trade marks are fulfilled.]

NOTES

Inserted as noted to Art 74a at **[5.658]**.

[5.663]

[Article 74f

Amendment of the regulations governing use of the mark

1. The proprietor of an EU certification mark shall submit to the Office any amended regulations governing use.

2. Amendments shall not be mentioned in the Register where the regulations as amended do not satisfy the requirements of Article 74b or involve one of the grounds for refusal referred to in Article 74c.

3. Written observations in accordance with Article 74d may also be submitted with regard to amended regulations governing use.

4. For the purposes of this Regulation, amendments to the regulations governing use shall take effect only as from the date of entry of the mention of the amendment in the Register.]

NOTES

Inserted as noted to Art 74a at **[5.658]**.

[5.664]
[Article 74g
Transfer
By way of derogation from Article 17(1), an EU certification mark may only be transferred to a person who meets the requirements of Article 74a(2).]

NOTES

Inserted as noted to Art 74a at **[5.658]**.

[5.665]
[Article 74h
Persons who are entitled to bring an action for infringement
1. Only the proprietor of an EU certification mark, or any person specifically authorised by him to that effect, shall be entitled to bring an action for infringement.
2. The proprietor of an EU certification mark shall be entitled to claim compensation on behalf of persons who have authority to use the mark where they have sustained damage as a consequence of unauthorised use of the mark.]

NOTES

Inserted as noted to Art 74a at **[5.658]**.

[5.666]
[Article 74i
Grounds for revocation
In addition to the grounds for revocation provided for in Article 51, the rights of the proprietor of an EU certification mark shall be revoked on application to the Office or on the basis of a counterclaim in infringement proceedings, where any of the following conditions is fulfilled:

- *(a) the proprietor no longer complies with the requirements set out in Article 74a(2);*
- *(b) the proprietor does not take reasonable steps to prevent the mark being used in a manner that is incompatible with the conditions of use laid down in the regulations governing use, amendments to which have, where appropriate, been mentioned in the Register;*
- *(c) the manner in which the mark has been used by the proprietor has caused it to become liable to mislead the public in the manner referred to in Article 74c(2);*
- *(d) an amendment to the regulations governing use of the mark has been mentioned in the Register in breach of Article 74f(2), unless the proprietor of the mark, by further amending the regulations governing use, complies with the requirements of that Article.]*

NOTES

Inserted as noted to Art 74a at **[5.658]**.

[5.667]
[Article 74j
Grounds for invalidity
In addition to the grounds for invalidity provided for in Articles 52 and 53, an EU certification mark which is registered in breach of Article 74c shall be declared invalid on application to the Office or on the basis of a counterclaim in infringement proceedings, unless the proprietor of the mark, by amending the regulations governing use, complies with the requirements of Article 74c.]

NOTES

Inserted as noted to Art 74a at **[5.658]**.

[5.668]
[Article 74k
Conversion
Without prejudice to Article 112(2), conversion of an application for an EU certification mark or of a registered EU certification mark shall not take place where the national law of the Member State concerned does not provide for the registration of guarantee or certification marks pursuant to Article 28 of Directive (EU) 2015/2436 of the European Parliament and of the Council.]

NOTES

Inserted as noted to Art 74a at **[5.658]**.

TITLE IX
PROCEDURE

SECTION 1
GENERAL PROVISIONS

[5.669]
[Article 75
Decisions and communications of the Office
1. Decisions of the Office shall state the reasons on which they are based. They shall be based only on reasons or evidence on which the parties concerned have had an opportunity to present their comments. Where oral proceedings are held before the Office, the decision may be given orally. Subsequently, the decision shall be notified in writing to the parties.
2. Any decision, communication or notice from the Office shall indicate the department or division of the Office as well as the name or the names of the official or officials responsible. They shall be signed by that official or those officials, or, instead of a signature, carry a printed or stamped seal of the Office. The Executive Director may determine that other means of identifying the department or division of the Office and the name of the official or officials responsible, or an identification other than a seal, may be used where decisions, communications or notices from the Office are transmitted by telecopier or any other technical means of communication.
3. Decisions of the Office which are open to appeal shall be accompanied by a written communication indicating that any notice of appeal is to be filed in writing at the Office within two months of the date of notification of the decision in question. The communications shall also draw the attention of the parties to the provisions laid down in Articles 58, 59 and 60. The parties may not plead any failure on the part of the Office to communicate the availability of appeal proceedings.]

NOTES
Substituted by European Parliament and Council Regulation 2015/2424/EU, Art 1(68).

[5.670]
Article 76
Examination of the facts by the Office of its own motion
1. In proceedings before it the Office shall examine the facts of its own motion; however, in proceedings relating to relative grounds for refusal of registration, the Office shall be restricted in this examination to the facts, evidence and arguments provided by the parties and the relief sought. [In invalidity proceedings taken pursuant to Article 52, the Office shall limit its examination to the grounds and arguments submitted by the parties.]
2. The Office may disregard facts or evidence which are not submitted in due time by the parties concerned.

NOTES
Para 1: words in square brackets inserted by European Parliament and Council Regulation 2015/2424/EU, Art 1(69).

[5.671]
Article 77
Oral proceedings
1. If the Office considers that oral proceedings would be expedient they shall be held either at the instance of the Office or at the request of any party to the proceedings.
2. Oral proceedings before the examiners, the Opposition Division and the Administration of Trade Marks and Legal Division shall not be public.
3. Oral proceedings, including delivery of the decision, shall be public before the Cancellation Division and the Boards of Appeal, in so far as the department before which the proceedings are taking place does not decide otherwise in cases where admission of the public could have serious and unjustified disadvantages, in particular for a party to the proceedings.
[4. The Commission shall be empowered to adopt delegated acts in accordance with Article 163a specifying the detailed arrangements for oral proceedings, including the detailed arrangements for the use of languages in accordance with Article 119.]

NOTES
Para 4: added by European Parliament and Council Regulation 2015/2424/EU, Art 1(70).

[5.672]
Article 78
Taking of evidence
1. In any proceedings before the Office, the means of giving or obtaining evidence shall include the following:
(a) hearing the parties;
(b) requests for information;
(c) the production of documents and items of evidence;

(d) hearing witnesses;
(e) opinions by experts;
(f) statements in writing sworn or affirmed or having a similar effect under the law of the State in which the statement is drawn up.

2. The relevant department may commission one of its members to examine the evidence adduced.

3. If the Office considers it necessary for a party, witness or expert to give evidence orally, it shall issue a summons to the person concerned to appear before it. [The period of notice provided in such summons shall be at least one month, unless they agree to a shorter period.]

4. The parties shall be informed of the hearing of a witness or expert before the Office. They shall have the right to be present and to put questions to the witness or expert.

[5. The Executive Director shall determine the amounts of expenses to be paid, including advances, as regards the costs of taking of evidence as referred to in this Article.

6. The Commission shall be empowered to adopt delegated acts in accordance with Article 163a specifying the detailed arrangements for the taking of evidence.]

NOTES

Para 3: words in square brackets inserted by European Parliament and Council Regulation 2015/2424/EU, Art 1(71)(a).
Paras 5, 6: added by European Parliament and Council Regulation 2015/2424/EU, Art 1(71)(b).

[5.673]
[Article 79
Notification

1. The Office shall, as a matter of course, notify those concerned of decisions and summonses and of any notice or other communication from which a time limit is reckoned, or of which those concerned are to be notified under other provisions of this Regulation or of acts adopted pursuant to this Regulation, or of which notification has been ordered by the Executive Director.

2. The Executive Director may determine which documents other than decisions subject to a time limit for appeal and summonses shall be notified by registered letter with proof of delivery.

3. Notification may be effected by different means, including by electronic means. The details regarding electronic means shall be determined by the Executive Director.

4. Where notification is to be effected by public notice, the Executive Director shall determine how the public notice is to be given and shall fix the beginning of the one-month period on the expiry of which the document shall be deemed to have been notified.

5. The Commission shall be empowered to adopt delegated acts in accordance with Article 163a specifying the detailed arrangements for notification.]

NOTES

Substituted by European Parliament and Council Regulation 2015/2424/EU, Art 1(72).

[5.674]
[Article 79a
Notification of loss of rights

Where the Office finds that the loss of any rights results from this Regulation or acts adopted pursuant to this Regulation, without any decision having been taken, it shall communicate this to the person concerned in accordance with Article 79. The latter may apply for a decision on the matter within two months of notification of the communication, if he considers that the finding of the Office is incorrect. The Office shall adopt such a decision only where it disagrees with the person requesting it; otherwise the Office shall amend its finding and inform the person requesting the decision.]

NOTES

Inserted by European Parliament and Council Regulation 2015/2424/EU, Art 1(73).

[5.675]
[Article 79b
Communications to the Office

1. Communications addressed to the Office may be effected by electronic means. The Executive Director shall determine to what extent and under which technical conditions those communications may be submitted electronically.

2. The Commission shall be empowered to adopt delegated acts in accordance with Article 163a specifying the rules on the means of communication, including the electronic means of communication, to be used by the parties to proceedings before the Office and the forms to be made available by the Office.]

NOTES

Inserted by European Parliament and Council Regulation 2015/2424/EU, Art 1(73).

[5.676]
[Article 79c
Time limits
1. Time limits shall be laid down in terms of full years, months, weeks or days. Calculation shall start on the day following the day on which the relevant event occurred. The duration of time limits shall be no less than one month and no more than six months.
2. The Executive Director shall determine, before the commencement of each calendar year, the days on which the Office is not open for receipt of documents or on which ordinary post is not delivered in the locality in which the Office is located.
3. The Executive Director shall determine the duration of the period of interruption in the case of a general interruption in the delivery of post in the Member State where the Office is located or, in the case of an actual interruption of the Office's connection to admitted electronic means of communication.
4. If an exceptional occurrence, such as a natural disaster or strike, interrupts or interferes with proper communication from the parties to the proceedings to the Office or vice-versa, the Executive Director may determine that for parties to the proceedings having their residence or registered office in the Member State concerned or who have appointed a representative with a place of business in the Member State concerned, all time limits that otherwise would expire on or after the date of commencement of such occurrence, as determined by him, shall extend until a date to be determined by him. When determining that date, he shall assess when the exceptional occurrence comes to an end. If the occurrence affects the seat of the Office, such determination of the Executive Director shall specify that it applies in respect of all parties to the proceedings.
5. The Commission shall be empowered to adopt delegated acts in accordance with Article 163a specifying the details regarding the calculation and duration of time limits.]

NOTES
Inserted by European Parliament and Council Regulation 2015/2424/EU, Art 1(73).

[5.677]
[Article 79d
Correction of errors and manifest oversights
1. The Office shall correct any linguistic errors or errors of transcription and manifest oversights in its decisions, or technical errors attributable to it in registering a trade mark or in publishing the registration of its own motion or at the request of a party.
2. Where the correction of errors in the registration of a trade mark or the publication of the registration is requested by the proprietor, Article 48a shall apply mutatis mutandis.
3. Corrections of errors in the registration of a trade mark and in the publication of the registration shall be published by the Office.]

NOTES
Inserted by European Parliament and Council Regulation 2015/2424/EU, Art 1(73).

[5.678]
[Article 80
Revocation of decisions
1. Where the Office has made an entry in the Register or taken a decision which contains an obvious error attributable to the Office, it shall ensure that the entry is cancelled or the decision is revoked. Where there is only one party to the proceedings and the entry or the act affects its rights, cancellation or revocation shall be determined even if the error was not evident to the party.
2. Cancellation or revocation as referred to in paragraph 1 shall be determined, ex officio or at the request of one of the parties to the proceedings, by the department which made the entry or took the decision. The cancellation of the entry in the Register or the revocation of the decision shall be effected within one year of the date on which the entry was made in the Register or that decision was taken, after consultation with the parties to the proceedings and any proprietor of rights to the EU trade mark in question that are entered in the Register. The Office shall keep records of any such cancellation or revocation.
3. The Commission shall be empowered to adopt delegated acts in accordance with Article 163a specifying the procedure for the revocation of a decision or for the cancellation of an entry in the Register.
4. This Article shall be without prejudice to the right of the parties to submit an appeal under Articles 58 and 65, or to the possibility of correcting errors and manifest oversights under Article 79d. Where an appeal has been filed against a decision of the Office containing an error, the appeal proceedings shall become devoid of purpose upon revocation by the Office of its decision pursuant to paragraph 1 of this Article. In the latter case, the appeal fee shall be reimbursed to the appellant.]

NOTES
Substituted by European Parliament and Council Regulation 2015/2424/EU, Art 1(74).

[5.679]
Article 81
Restitutio in integrum

1. The applicant for or proprietor of a Community trade mark or any other party to proceedings before the Office who, in spite of all due care required by the circumstances having been taken, was unable to comply with a time limit vis-à-vis the Office shall, upon application, have his rights re-established if the obstacle to compliance has the direct consequence, by virtue of the provisions of this Regulation, of causing the loss of any right or means of redress.

2. The application must be filed in writing within two months from the removal of the obstacle to compliance with the time limit. The omitted act must be completed within this period. The application shall only be admissible within the year immediately following the expiry of the unobserved time limit. In the case of non-submission of the request for renewal of registration or of non-payment of a renewal fee, the further period of six months provided in Article 47(3), third sentence, shall be deducted from the period of one year.

3. The application must state the grounds on which it is based and must set out the facts on which it relies. It shall not be deemed to be filed until the fee for re-establishment of rights has been paid.

4. The department competent to decide on the omitted act shall decide upon the application.

5. This Article shall not be applicable to the time limits referred to in paragraph 2 of this Article, Article 41(1) and (3) and Article 82.

6. Where the applicant for or proprietor of a Community trade mark has his rights re-established, he may not invoke his rights vis-à-vis a third party who, in good faith, has put goods on the market or supplied services under a sign which is identical with, or similar to, the Community trade mark in the course of the period between the loss of rights in the application or in the Community trade mark and publication of the mention of re-establishment of those rights.

7. A third party who may avail himself of the provisions of paragraph 6 may bring third party proceedings against the decision re-establishing the rights of the applicant for or proprietor of a Community trade mark within a period of two months as from the date of publication of the mention of re-establishment of those rights.

8. Nothing in this Article shall limit the right of a Member State to grant restitutio in integrum in respect of time limits provided for in this Regulation and to be observed vis-à-vis the authorities of such State.

NOTES

General amendments to this Regulation: see further the note "General amendments" in the introductory notes to this Regulation *ante*.

[5.680]
Article 82
Continuation of proceedings

1. An applicant for or proprietor of a Community trade mark or any other party to proceedings before the Office who has omitted to observe a time limit vis-à-vis the Office may, upon request, obtain the continuation of proceedings, provided that at the time the request is made the omitted act has been carried out. The request for continuation of proceedings shall be admissible only if it is presented within two months following the expiry of the unobserved time limit. The request shall not be deemed to have been filed until the fee for continuation of the proceedings has been paid.

[2. This Article shall not apply to the time limits laid down in Article 27, Articles 29(1), 33(1), 36(2), 41(1) and (3), 47(3), Article 60, Articles 65(5) and 81(2), and Article 112, or to the time limits laid down in paragraph 1 of this Article or the time limit for claiming seniority pursuant to Article 34 after the application has been filed.]

3. The department competent to decide on the omitted act shall decide upon the application.

[4. If the Office accepts the application, the consequences of having failed to observe the time limit shall be deemed not to have occurred. If a decision has been taken between the expiry of that time limit and the request for the continuation of proceedings, the department competent to decide on the omitted act shall review the decision and, where completion of the omitted act itself is sufficient, take a different decision. If, following the review, the Office concludes that the original decision does not require to be altered, it shall confirm that decision in writing.]

5. If the Office rejects the application, the fee shall be refunded.

NOTES

General amendments to this Regulation: see further the note "General amendments" in the introductory notes to this Regulation *ante*.

Paras 2, 4: substituted by European Parliament and Council Regulation 2015/2424/EU, Art 1(75).

[5.681]
[Article 82a
Interruption of proceedings

1. Proceedings before the Office shall be interrupted:

(a) *in the event of the death or legal incapacity of the applicant for, or proprietor of, an EU trade mark or of the person authorised by national law to act on his behalf. To the extent that that death or incapacity does not affect the authorisation of a representative appointed under Article 93, proceedings shall be interrupted only on application by such representative;*

(b) *in the event of the applicant for, or proprietor of, an EU trade mark being prevented, for legal reasons resulting from action taken against his property, from continuing the proceedings before the Office;*

(c) *in the event of the death or legal incapacity of the representative of an applicant for, or proprietor of, an EU trade mark, or of that representative being prevented, for legal reasons resulting from action taken against his property, from continuing the proceedings before the Office.*

2. *Proceedings before the Office shall be resumed as soon as the identity of the person authorised to continue them has been established.*

3. *The Commission shall be empowered to adopt delegated acts in accordance with Article 163a specifying the detailed arrangements for the resumption of proceedings before the Office.]*

NOTES

Inserted by European Parliament and Council Regulation 2015/2424/EU, Art 1(76).

[5.682]

[Article 83

Reference to general principles

In the absence of procedural provisions in this Regulation or in acts adopted pursuant to this Regulation, the Office shall take into account the principles of procedural law generally recognised in the Member States.]

NOTES

Substituted by European Parliament and Council Regulation 2015/2424/EU, Art 1(77).

[5.683]

Article 84

Termination of financial obligations

1. *Rights of the Office to the payment of a fee shall be extinguished after four years from the end of the calendar year in which the fee fell due.*

2. *Rights against the Office for the refunding of fees or sums of money paid in excess of a fee shall be extinguished after four years from the end of the calendar year in which the right arose.*

3. *The period laid down in paragraphs 1 and 2 shall be interrupted, in the case covered by paragraph 1, by a request for payment of the fee, and in the case covered by paragraph 2, by a reasoned claim in writing. On interruption it shall begin again immediately and shall end at the latest six years after the end of the year in which it originally began, unless, in the meantime, judicial proceedings to enforce the right have begun; in this case the period shall end at the earliest one year after the judgment has acquired the authority of a final decision.*

SECTION 2

COSTS

[5.684]

Article 85

Costs

[1. The losing party in opposition proceedings, proceedings for revocation, proceedings for a declaration of invalidity or appeal proceedings shall bear the fees paid by the other party. Without prejudice to Article 119(6), the losing party shall also bear all costs incurred by the other party that are essential to the proceedings, including travel and subsistence and the remuneration of a representative within the meaning of Article 93(1), within the limits of the scales set for each category of costs in the implementing act to be adopted in accordance with paragraph 1a of this Article. The fees to be borne by the losing party shall be limited to the fees paid by the other party for opposition, for an application for revocation or for a declaration of invalidity of the EU trade mark and for appeal.]

[1a. The Commission shall adopt implementing acts specifying the maximum rates for costs essential to the proceedings and actually incurred by the successful party. Those implementing acts shall be adopted in accordance with the examination procedure referred to in Article 163(2).

When specifying such amounts with respect to travel and subsistence costs, the Commission shall take into account the distance between the place of residence or business of the party, representative or witness or expert and the place where the oral proceedings are held, the procedural stage at which the costs have been incurred, and, as far as costs of representation within the meaning of Article 93(1) are concerned, the need to ensure that the obligation to bear the costs

may not be misused for tactical reasons by the other party. Subsistence expenses shall be calculated in accordance with the Staff Regulations of Officials of the Union and the Conditions of Employment of Other Servants of the Union, laid down in Council Regulation (EEC, Euratom, ECSC) No 259/68.[1]
The losing party shall bear the costs for one opposing party only and, where applicable, one representative only.]
2. However, where each party succeeds on some and fails on other heads, or if reasons of equity so dictate, the Opposition Division, Cancellation Division or Board of Appeal shall decide a different apportionment of costs.
3. The party who terminates the proceedings by withdrawing the Community trade mark application, the opposition, the application for revocation of rights, the application for a declaration of invalidity or the appeal, or by not renewing registration of the Community trade mark or by surrendering the Community trade mark, shall bear the fees and the costs incurred by the other party as stipulated in paragraphs 1 and 2.
4. Where a case does not proceed to judgment the costs shall be at the discretion of the Opposition Division, Cancellation Division or Board of Appeal.
5. Where the parties conclude before the Opposition Division, Cancellation Division or Board of Appeal a settlement of costs differing from that provided for in the preceding paragraphs, the department concerned shall take note of that agreement.
[6. The Opposition Division or Cancellation Division or Board of Appeal shall fix the amount of the costs to be paid pursuant to paragraphs 1 to 5 of this Article when the costs to be paid are limited to the fees paid to the Office and the representation costs. In all other cases, the registry of the Board of Appeal or a member of the staff of the Opposition Division or Cancellation Division shall fix, on request, the amount of the costs to be reimbursed. The request shall be admissible only for the period of two months following the date on which the decision for which an application was made for the costs to be fixed becomes final and shall be accompanied by a bill and supporting evidence. For the costs of representation pursuant to Article 93(1), an assurance by the representative that the costs have been incurred shall be sufficient. For other costs, it shall be sufficient if their plausibility is established. Where the amount of the costs is fixed pursuant to the first sentence of this paragraph, representation costs shall be awarded at the level laid down in the act adopted pursuant to paragraph 1a of this Article and irrespective of whether they have been actually incurred.]
[7. The decision on the fixing of costs, stating the reasons on which it is based, may be reviewed by a decision of the Opposition Division or Cancellation Division or Board of Appeal on a request filed within one month of the date of notification of the awarding of costs. It shall not be deemed to be filed until the fee for reviewing the amount of the costs has been paid. The Opposition Division, the Cancellation Division or the Board of Appeal, as the case may be, shall take a decision on the request for a review of the decision on the fixing of costs without oral proceedings.]

NOTES

General amendments to this Regulation: see further the note "General amendments" in the introductory notes to this Regulation *ante*.

Para 1: substituted by European Parliament and Council Regulation 2015/2424/EU, Art 1(78)(a).

Para 1a: inserted by European Parliament and Council Regulation 2015/2424/EU, Art 1(78)(b).

Para 6: substituted by European Parliament and Council Regulation 2015/2424/EU, Art 1(78)(c).

Para 7: added by European Parliament and Council Regulation 2015/2424/EU, Art 1(78)(d).

[1] OJ L56, 4.3.1968, p 1.

[5.685]
Article 86
Enforcement of decisions fixing the amount of costs

1. Any final decision of the Office fixing the amount of costs shall be enforceable.
2. Enforcement shall be governed by the rules of civil procedure in force in the State in the territory of which it is carried out. [Each Member State shall designate a single authority responsible for verifying the authenticity of the decision referred to in paragraph 1 and shall communicate its contact details to the Office, the Court of Justice and the Commission. The order for the enforcement of the decision shall be appended to the decision by that authority, with the verification of the authenticity of the decision as the sole formality.]
3. When these formalities have been completed on application by the party concerned, the latter may proceed to enforcement in accordance with the national law, by bringing the matter directly before the competent authority.
4. Enforcement may be suspended only by a decision of the Court of Justice. However, the courts of the country concerned shall have jurisdiction over complaints that enforcement is being carried out in an irregular manner.

NOTES

Para 2: words in square brackets substituted by European Parliament and Council Regulation 2015/2424/EU, Art 1(79).

SECTION 3
INFORMATION WHICH MAY BE MADE AVAILABLE TO THE PUBLIC AND OF THE AUTHORITIES OF THE MEMBER STATES

[5.686]
[Article 87
Register of EU trade marks
1. The Office shall keep a Register of EU trade marks which it shall keep up to date.
2. The Register shall contain the following entries relating to EU trade mark applications and registrations:

(a) the date of filing the application;
(b) the file number of the application;
(c) the date of the publication of the application;
(d) the name and address of the applicant;
(e) the name and business address of the representative, other than a representative as referred to in the first sentence of Article 92(3);
(f) the representation of the mark, with indications as to its nature; and, where applicable, a description of the mark;
(g) an indication of the goods and services by their names;
(h) particulars of claims of priority pursuant to Article 30;
(i) particulars of claims of exhibition priority pursuant to Article 33;
(j) particulars of claims of seniority of a registered earlier trade mark as referred to in Article 34;
(k) a statement that the mark has become distinctive in consequence of the use which has been made of it, pursuant to Article 7(3);
(l) an indication that the mark is a collective mark;
(m) an indication that the mark is a certification mark;
(n) the language in which the application was filed and the second language which the applicant has indicated in his application, pursuant to Article 119(3);
(o) the date of registration of the mark in the Register and the registration number;
(p) a statement that the application is the result of a transformation of an international registration designating the Union, pursuant to Article 161 of this Regulation, together with the date of the international registration pursuant to Article 3(4) of the Madrid Protocol or the date on which the territorial extension to the Union made subsequent to the international registration pursuant to Article 3ter(2) of the Madrid Protocol was recorded and, where applicable, the date of priority of the international registration.

3. The Register shall also contain the following entries, each accompanied by the date of recording of such entry:

(a) changes in the name, address or nationality of the proprietor of an EU trade mark or a change in the State in which he is domiciled or has his seat or establishment;
(b) changes in the name or business address of the representative, other than a representative as referred to in the first sentence of Article 92(3);
(c) where a new representative is appointed, the name and business address of that representative;
(d) amendments and alterations of the mark, pursuant to Articles 43 and 48, and corrections of errors;
(e) notice of amendments to the regulations governing the use of the collective mark pursuant to Article 71;
(f) particulars of claims of seniority of a registered earlier trade mark as referred to in Article 34, pursuant to Article 35;
(g) total or partial transfers pursuant to Article 17;
(h) creation or transfer of a right in rem pursuant to Article 19, and the nature of the right in rem;
(i) levy of execution pursuant to Article 20 and insolvency proceedings pursuant to Article 21;
(j) the grant or transfer of a licence pursuant to Article 22 and, where applicable, the type of licence;
(k) renewal of a registration pursuant to Article 47, the date from which it takes effect and any restrictions pursuant to Article 47(4);
(l) a record of a determination of the expiry of a registration pursuant to Article 47;
(m) declarations of withdrawal or surrender by the proprietor of the mark pursuant to Articles 43 and 50 respectively;
(n) the date of submission and the particulars of an opposition pursuant to Article 41, of an application pursuant to Article 56, or a counterclaim pursuant to Article 100(4) for revocation, or for a declaration of invalidity, or of an appeal pursuant to Article 60;
(o) the date and content of a decision on an opposition, on an application or counterclaim pursuant to Article 57(6) or the third sentence of Article 100(6), or on an appeal pursuant to Article 64;
(p) a record of the receipt of a request for conversion pursuant to Article 113(2);

(q) *the cancellation of the representative recorded pursuant to point (e) of paragraph 2 of this Article;*
(r) *the cancellation of the seniority of a national mark;*
(s) *the modification to or cancellation from the Register of the items referred to in points (h), (i) and (j) of this paragraph;*
(t) *the replacement of the EU trade mark by an international registration pursuant to Article 157;*
(u) *the date and number of international registrations based on the EU trade mark application which has been registered as an EU trade mark pursuant to Article 148(1);*
(v) *the date and number of international registrations based on the EU trade mark pursuant to Article 148(2);*
(w) *the division of an application pursuant to Article 44 and the division of a registration pursuant to Article 49, together with the items referred to in paragraph 2 of this Article in respect of the divisional registration, as well as the list of goods and services of the original registration as amended;*
(x) *the revocation of a decision or an entry in the Register pursuant to Article 80, where the revocation concerns a decision or entry which has been published;*
(y) *notice of amendments to the regulations governing the use of the certification mark pursuant to Article 74f.*

4. The Executive Director may determine that items other than those referred to in paragraphs 2 and 3 of this Article are to be entered in the Register, subject to Article 123(4).

5. The Register may be maintained in electronic form. The Office shall collect, organise, make public and store the items referred to in paragraphs 2 and 3, including any personal data, for the purposes laid down in paragraph 9. The Office shall keep the register easily accessible for public inspection.

6. The proprietor of an EU trade mark shall be notified of any change in the Register.

7. The Office shall provide certified or uncertified extracts from the Register on request and on payment of a fee.

8. The processing of the data concerning the entries set out in paragraphs 2 and 3, including any personal data, shall take place for the purposes of:
(a) *administering the applications and/or registrations as described in this Regulation and acts adopted pursuant to it;*
(b) *maintaining a public register for inspection by, and the information of, public authorities and economic operators, in order to enable them to exercise the rights conferred on them by this Regulation and be informed about the existence of prior rights belonging to third parties; and*
(c) *producing reports and statistics enabling the Office to optimise its operations and improve the functioning of the system.*

9. All the data, including personal data, concerning the entries in paragraphs 2 and 3 shall be considered to be of public interest and may be accessed by any third party. For reasons of legal certainty, the entries in the Register shall be kept for an indefinite period of time.]

NOTES

Substituted by European Parliament and Council Regulation 2015/2424/EU, Art 1(80).

[5.687]

[Article 87a

Database

1. In addition to the obligation to keep a Register within the meaning of Article 87, the Office shall collect and store in an electronic database all the particulars provided by applicants or any other party to the proceedings under this Regulation or acts adopted pursuant to it.

2. The electronic database may include personal data, beyond those included in the Register pursuant to Article 87, to the extent that such particulars are required by this Regulation or acts adopted pursuant to it. The collection, storage and processing of such data shall serve the purposes of:
(a) *administering the applications and/or registrations as described in this Regulation and acts adopted pursuant to it;*
(b) *accessing the information necessary for conducting the relevant proceedings more easily and efficiently;*
(c) *communicating with the applicants and other parties to the proceedings;*
(d) *producing reports and statistics enabling the Office to optimise its operations and improve the functioning of the system.*

3. The Executive Director shall determine the conditions of access to the electronic database and the manner in which its contents, other than the personal data referred to in paragraph 2 of this Article but including those listed in Article 87, may be made available in machine-readable form, including the charge for such access.

4. Access to the personal data referred to in paragraph 2 shall be restricted and such data shall not be made publicly available unless the party concerned has given his express consent.

5. All data shall be kept indefinitely. However, the party concerned may request the removal of any personal data from the database after 18 months from the expiry of the trade mark or the closure of the relevant inter partes procedure. The party concerned shall have the right to obtain the correction of inaccurate or erroneous data at any time.]

NOTES

Inserted by European Parliament and Council Regulation 2015/2424/EU, Art 1(81).

[5.688]
Article 87b
Online access to decisions

1. The decisions of the Office shall be made available online for the information and consultation of the general public in the interest of transparency and predictability. Any party to the proceedings that led to the adoption of the decision may request the removal of any personal data included in the decision.

2. The Office may provide online access to judgments of national and Union courts related to its tasks in order to raise public awareness of intellectual property matters and promote convergence of practices. The Office shall respect the conditions of the initial publication with regard to personal data.]

NOTES

Inserted by European Parliament and Council Regulation 2015/2424/EU, Art 1(81).

[5.689]
Article 88
Inspection of files

1. The files relating to Community trade mark applications which have not yet been published shall not be made available for inspection without the consent of the applicant.

2. Any person who can prove that the applicant for a Community trade mark has stated that after the trade mark has been registered he will invoke the rights under it against him may obtain inspection of the files prior to the publication of that application and without the consent of the applicant.

3. Subsequent to the publication of the Community trade mark application, the files relating to such application and the resulting trade mark may be inspected on request.

[4. Where the files are inspected pursuant to paragraph 2 or 3 of this Article, documents relating to exclusion or objection pursuant to Article 137, draft decisions and opinions, and all other internal documents used for the preparation of decisions and opinions, as well as parts of the file which the party concerned showed a special interest in keeping confidential before the request for inspection of the files was made, unless inspection of such parts of the file is justified by overriding, legitimate interests of the party seeking inspection, may be withheld from inspection.]

[5. Inspection of the files of EU trade mark applications and of registered EU trade marks shall be of the original document, or of copies thereof, or of technical means of storage if the files are stored in this way. The Executive Director shall determine the means of inspection.

6. Where inspection of files takes place as provided for in paragraph 7, the request for inspection of the files shall not be deemed to have been made until the required fee has been paid. No fee shall be payable if inspection of technical means of storage takes place online.

7. Inspection of the files shall take place at the premises of the Office. On request, inspection of the files shall be effected by means of issuing copies of file documents. The issuing of such copies shall be conditional on the payment of a fee. The Office shall also issue on request certified or uncertified copies of the application for an EU trade mark upon payment of a fee.

8. The files kept by the Office relating to international registrations designating the Union may be inspected on request as from the date of publication referred to in Article 152(1), in accordance with the conditions laid down in paragraphs 1, 3 and 4 of this Article.

9. Subject to the restrictions provided for in paragraph 4, the Office may, on request, communicate information from any file of an EU trade mark applied for or of a registered EU trade mark, subject to payment of a fee. However, the Office may require the exercise of the option to obtain inspection of the file itself should it deem this to be appropriate in view of the quantity of information to be supplied.]

NOTES

General amendments to this Regulation: see further the note "General amendments" in the introductory notes to this Regulation *ante*.

Para 4: substituted by European Parliament and Council Regulation 2015/2424/EU, Art 1(82)(a).

Paras 5–9: added by European Parliament and Council Regulation 2015/2424/EU, Art 1(82)(b).

[5.690]
[Article 88a
Keeping of files
1. The Office shall keep the files of any procedure relating to an EU trade mark application or EU trade mark registration. The Executive Director shall determine the form in which those files shall be kept.
2. Where the files are kept in electronic format, the electronic files, or back-up copies thereof, shall be kept indefinitely. The original documents filed by parties to the proceedings, and forming the basis of such electronic files, shall be disposed of after a period following their reception by the Office, which shall be determined by the Executive Director.
3. Where and to the extent that files or parts of the files are kept in any form other than electronically, documents or items of evidence constituting part of such files shall be kept for at least five years from the end of the year in which the application is rejected or withdrawn or is deemed to be withdrawn, the registration of the EU trade mark expires completely pursuant to Article 47, the complete surrender of the EU trade mark is registered pursuant to Article 50, or the EU trade mark is completely removed from the Register pursuant to Article 57(6) or 100(6).]

NOTES
Inserted by European Parliament and Council Regulation 2015/2424/EU, Art 1(83).

[5.691]
[Article 89
Periodical publications
1. The Office shall periodically publish:
- *(a) a European Union Trade Marks Bulletin containing publications of applications and of entries made in the Register as well as other particulars relating to applications or registrations of EU trade marks the publication of which is required under this Regulation or by acts adopted pursuant to it;*
- *(b) an Official Journal of the Office containing notices and information of a general character issued by the Executive Director, as well as any other information relevant to this Regulation or its implementation.*

The publications referred to in points (a) and (b) of the first subparagraph may be effected by electronic means.
2. The European Union Trade Marks Bulletin shall be published in a manner and at a frequency to be determined by the Executive Director.
3. The Official Journal of the Office shall be published in the languages of the Office. However, the Executive Director may determine that certain items shall be published in the Official Journal of the Office in the official languages of the Union.
4. The Commission shall adopt implementing acts specifying:
- *(a) the date to be taken as the date of publication in the European Union Trade Marks Bulletin;*
- *(b) the manner of publication of entries regarding the registration of a trade mark which do not contain changes as compared to the publication of the application;*
- *(c) the forms in which editions of the Official Journal of the Office may be made available to the public.*

Those implementing acts shall be adopted in accordance with the examination procedure referred to in Article 163(2).]

NOTES
Substituted by European Parliament and Council Regulation 2015/2424/EU, Art 1(84).

[5.692]
Article 90
Administrative cooperation
[1.] Unless otherwise provided in this Regulation or in national laws, the Office and the courts or authorities of the Member States shall on request give assistance to each other by communicating information or opening files for inspection. Where the Office lays files open to inspection by courts, Public Prosecutors' Offices or central industrial property offices, the inspection shall not be subject to the restrictions laid down in Article 88.
[2. The Office shall not charge fees for the communication of information or the opening of files for inspection.
3. The Commission shall adopt implementing acts specifying the detailed arrangements as to how the Office and the authorities of the Member States are to exchange information between each other and open files for inspection, taking into account the restrictions to which the inspection of files relating to EU trade mark applications or registrations is subject, pursuant to Article 88, when it is opened to third parties. Those implementing acts shall be adopted in accordance with the examination procedure referred to in Article 163(2).]

NOTES
Para 1: existing provision numbered as such, by European Parliament and Council Regulation 2015/2424/EU, Art 1(85)(a).

Paras 2, 3: added by European Parliament and Council Regulation 2015/2424/EU, Art 1(85)(b).

[5.693]
Article 91
Exchange of publications

1. The Office and the central industrial property offices of the Member States shall despatch to each other on request and for their own use one or more copies of their respective publications free of charge.

2. The Office may conclude agreements relating to the exchange or supply of publications.

SECTION 4
REPRESENTATION

[5.694]
Article 92
General principles of representation

1. Subject to the provisions of paragraph 2, no person shall be compelled to be represented before the Office.

[2. Without prejudice to the second sentence of paragraph 3 of this Article, natural or legal persons having neither their domicile nor their principal place of business or a real and effective industrial or commercial establishment in the European Economic Area shall be represented before the Office in accordance with Article 93(1) in all proceedings provided for by this Regulation, other than the filing of an application for an EU trade mark.

3. Natural or legal persons having their domicile or principal place of business or a real and effective industrial or commercial establishment in the European Economic Area may be represented before the Office by an employee. An employee of a legal person to which this paragraph applies may also represent other legal persons which have economic connections with the first legal person, even if those other legal persons have neither their domicile nor their principal place of business nor a real and effective industrial or commercial establishment within the European Economic Area. Employees who represent persons, within the meaning of this paragraph, shall, at the request of the Office or, where appropriate, of the party to the proceedings, file with it a signed authorisation for insertion in the files.

4. Where there is more than one applicant or more than one third party acting in common, a common representative shall be appointed.]

NOTES

Paras 2–4: substituted by European Parliament and Council Regulation 2015/2424/EU, Art 1(86).

[5.695]
Article 93
Professional representatives

[1. Representation of natural or legal persons before the Office may only be undertaken by:

(a) a legal practitioner qualified in one of the Member States of the European Economic Area and having his place of business within the European Economic Area, to the extent that he is entitled, within the said Member State, to act as a representative in trade mark matters;

(b) professional representatives whose names appear on the list maintained for this purpose by the Office.

Representatives acting before the Office shall, at the request of the Office or, where appropriate, of the other party to the proceedings, file with it a signed authorisation for insertion on the files.

2. Any natural person who fulfils the following conditions may be entered on the list of professional representatives:

(a) being a national of one of the Member States of the European Economic Area;

(b) having his place of business or employment in the European Economic Area;

(c) being entitled to represent natural or legal persons in trade mark matters before the Benelux Office for Intellectual Property or before the central industrial property office of a Member State of the European Economic Area. Where, in the State concerned, the entitlement is not conditional upon the requirement of special professional qualifications, persons applying to be entered on the list who act in trade mark matters before the Benelux Office for Intellectual Property or those central industrial property offices shall have habitually so acted for at least five years. However, persons whose professional qualification to represent natural or legal persons in trade mark matters before the Benelux Office for Intellectual Property or those central industrial property offices is officially recognised in accordance with the regulations laid down by the State concerned shall not be required to have exercised the profession.]

3. Entry shall be effected upon request, accompanied by a certificate furnished by the central industrial property office of the Member State concerned, which must indicate that the conditions laid down in paragraph 2 are fulfilled.

[4. The Executive Director may grant an exemption from:

(a) the requirement in the second sentence of paragraph 2(c), if the applicant furnishes proof that he has acquired the requisite qualification in another way;

(b) the requirement set out in paragraph 2(a) in the case of highly qualified professionals, provided that the requirements set out in paragraphs 2(b) and (c) are fulfilled.

5. A person may be removed from the list of professional representatives at his request or when no longer in a capacity to represent. The amendments of the list of professional representatives shall be published in the Official Journal of the Office.]

NOTES

Paras 1, 2, 4, 5: substituted by European Parliament and Council Regulation 2015/2424/EU, Art 1(87).

[5.696]

[Article 93a

Delegation of powers

The Commission shall be empowered to adopt delegated acts in accordance with Article 163a specifying:

(a) the conditions and the procedure for the appointment of a common representative as referred to in Article 92(4);

(b) the conditions under which employees referred to in Article 92(3) and professional representatives referred to in Article 93(1) shall file with the Office a signed authorisation in order to undertake representation, and the content of that authorisation;

(c) the circumstances in which a person may be removed from the list of professional representatives referred to in Article 93(5).]

NOTES

Inserted by European Parliament and Council Regulation 2015/2424/EU, Art 1(88).

TITLE X
JURISDICTION AND PROCEDURE IN LEGAL ACTIONS RELATING TO COMMUNITY TRADE MARKS

SECTION 1
[APPLICATION OF UNION RULES ON JURISDICTION AND THE RECOGNITION AND ENFORCEMENT OF JUDGMENTS IN CIVIL AND COMMERCIAL MATTERS]

NOTES

Section heading: substituted by European Parliament and Council Regulation 2015/2424/EU, Art 1(89).

[5.697]

Article 94

[Application of Union rules on jurisdiction and the recognition and enforcement of judgments in civil and commercial matters]

1. Unless otherwise specified in this Regulation, [the Union rules on jurisdiction and the recognition and enforcement of judgments in civil and commercial matters] shall apply to proceedings relating to Community trade marks and applications for Community trade marks, as well as to proceedings relating to simultaneous and successive actions on the basis of Community trade marks and national trade marks.

2. In the case of proceedings in respect of the actions and claims referred to in Article 96:

(a) Articles 2 and 4, points 1, 3, 4 and 5 of Article 5 and Article 31 of Regulation (EC) No 44/2001 shall not apply;

(b) Articles 23 and 24 of Regulation (EC) No 44/2001 shall apply subject to the limitations in Article 97(4) of this Regulation;

(c) the provisions of Chapter II of Regulation (EC) No 44/2001 which are applicable to persons domiciled in a Member State shall also be applicable to persons who do not have a domicile in any Member State but have an establishment therein.

[3. References in this Regulation to Regulation (EC) No 44/2001 shall include, where appropriate, the Agreement between the European Community and the Kingdom of Denmark on jurisdiction and the recognition and enforcement of judgments in civil and commercial matters done on 19 October 2005.]

NOTES

General amendments to this Regulation: see further the note "General amendments" in the introductory notes to this Regulation *ante*.

Article heading: substituted by European Parliament and Council Regulation 2015/2424/EU, Art 1(90)(a).

Para 1: words in square brackets substituted by European Parliament and Council Regulation 2015/2424/EU, Art 1(90)(b).

Para 3: added by European Parliament and Council Regulation 2015/2424/EU, Art 1(90)(c).

SECTION 2

DISPUTES CONCERNING THE INFRINGEMENT AND VALIDITY OF COMMUNITY TRADE MARKS

[5.698]

Article 95

Community trade mark courts

1. The Member States shall designate in their territories as limited a number as possible of national courts and tribunals of first and second instance, hereinafter referred to as "Community trade mark courts", which shall perform the functions assigned to them by this Regulation.

2. Each Member State shall communicate to the Commission within three years of the entry into force of Regulation (EC) No 40/94 a list of Community trade mark courts indicating their names and their territorial jurisdiction.

3. Any change made after communication of the list referred to in paragraph 2 in the number, names or territorial jurisdiction of the courts shall be notified without delay by the Member State concerned to the Commission.

4. The information referred to in paragraphs 2 and 3 shall be notified by the Commission to the Member States and published in the Official Journal of the European Union.

5. As long as a Member State has not communicated the list as stipulated in paragraph 2, jurisdiction for any proceedings resulting from an action or application covered by Article 96, and for which the courts of that State have jurisdiction under Article 97, shall lie with that court of the State in question which would have jurisdiction ratione loci and ratione materiae in the case of proceedings relating to a national trade mark registered in that State.

NOTES

General amendments to this Regulation: see further the note "General amendments" in the introductory notes to this Regulation *ante*.

[5.699]

Article 96

Jurisdiction over infringement and validity

The Community trade mark courts shall have exclusive jurisdiction:

(a) for all infringement actions and — if they are permitted under national law — actions in respect of threatened infringement relating to Community trade marks;

(b) for actions for declaration of non-infringement, if they are permitted under national law;

(c) for all actions brought as a result of acts referred to in [Article 9b(2)];

(d) for counterclaims for revocation or for a declaration of invalidity of the Community trade mark pursuant to Article 100.

NOTES

General amendments to this Regulation: see further the note "General amendments" in the introductory notes to this Regulation *ante*.

Para (c): words in square brackets substituted by European Parliament and Council Regulation 2015/2424/EU, Art 1(91).

[5.700]

Article 97

International jurisdiction

1. Subject to the provisions of this Regulation as well as to any provisions of Regulation (EC) No 44/2001 applicable by virtue of Article 94, proceedings in respect of the actions and claims referred to in Article 96 shall be brought in the courts of the Member State in which the defendant is domiciled or, if he is not domiciled in any of the Member States, in which he has an establishment.

2. If the defendant is neither domiciled nor has an establishment in any of the Member States, such proceedings shall be brought in the courts of the Member State in which the plaintiff is domiciled or, if he is not domiciled in any of the Member States, in which he has an establishment.

3. If neither the defendant nor the plaintiff is so domiciled or has such an establishment, such proceedings shall be brought in the courts of the Member State where the Office has its seat.

4. Notwithstanding the provisions of paragraphs 1, 2 and 3:

(a) Article 23 of Regulation (EC) No 44/2001 shall apply if the parties agree that a different Community trade mark court shall have jurisdiction;

(b) Article 24 of Regulation (EC) No 44/2001 shall apply if the defendant enters an appearance before a different Community trade mark court.

5. Proceedings in respect of the actions and claims referred to in Article 96, with the exception of actions for a declaration of non-infringement of a Community trade mark, may also be brought in the courts of the Member State in which the act of infringement has been committed or threatened, or in which an act within the meaning of Article 9(3), second sentence, has been committed.

NOTES

General amendments to this Regulation: see further the note "General amendments" in the introductory notes to this Regulation *ante*.

[5.701]
Article 98
Extent of jurisdiction

1. A Community trade mark court whose jurisdiction is based on Article 97(1) to (4) shall have jurisdiction in respect of:

- *(a) acts of infringement committed or threatened within the territory of any of the Member States;*
- *(b) acts within the meaning of Article 9(3), second sentence, committed within the territory of any of the Member States.*

2. A Community trade mark court whose jurisdiction is based on Article 97(5) shall have jurisdiction only in respect of acts committed or threatened within the territory of the Member State in which that court is situated.

NOTES

General amendments to this Regulation: see further the note "General amendments" in the introductory notes to this Regulation *ante*.

[5.702]
Article 99
Presumption of validity — Defence as to the merits

1. The Community trade mark courts shall treat the Community trade mark as valid unless its validity is put in issue by the defendant with a counterclaim for revocation or for a declaration of invalidity.

2. The validity of a Community trade mark may not be put in issue in an action for a declaration of non-infringement.

[3. In the actions referred to in points (a) and (c) of Article 96, a plea relating to revocation of the EU trade mark submitted otherwise than by way of a counterclaim shall be admissible where the defendant claims that the EU trade mark could be revoked for lack of genuine use at the time the infringement action was brought.]

NOTES

General amendments to this Regulation: see further the note "General amendments" in the introductory notes to this Regulation *ante*.

Para 3: substituted by European Parliament and Council Regulation 2015/2424/EU, Art 1(92).

[5.703]
Article 100
Counterclaims

1. A counterclaim for revocation or for a declaration of invalidity may only be based on the grounds for revocation or invalidity mentioned in this Regulation.

2. A Community trade mark court shall reject a counterclaim for revocation or for a declaration of invalidity if a decision taken by the Office relating to the same subject matter and cause of action and involving the same parties has already become final.

3. If the counterclaim is brought in a legal action to which the proprietor of the trade mark is not already a party, he shall be informed thereof and may be joined as a party to the action in accordance with the conditions set out in national law.

[4. The EU trade mark court with which a counterclaim for revocation or for a declaration of invalidity of the EU trade mark has been filed shall not proceed with the examination of the counterclaim, until either the interested party or the court has informed the Office of the date on which the counterclaim was filed. The Office shall record that information in the Register. If an application for revocation or for a declaration of invalidity of the EU trade mark had already been filed before the Office before the counterclaim was filed, the court shall be informed thereof by the Office and stay the proceedings in accordance with Article 104(1) until the decision on the application is final or the application is withdrawn.]

5. Article 57(2) to (5) shall apply.

[6. Where an EU trade mark court has given a judgment which has become final on a counterclaim for revocation or for a declaration of invalidity of an EU trade mark, a copy of the judgment shall be sent to the Office without delay, either by the court or by any of the parties to the national proceedings. The Office or any other interested party may request information about such transmission. The Office shall mention the judgment in the Register and shall take the necessary measures to comply with its operative part.]

7. The Community trade mark court hearing a counterclaim for revocation or for a declaration of invalidity may stay the proceedings on application by the proprietor of the Community trade mark and after hearing the other parties and may request the defendant to submit an application for revocation or for a declaration of invalidity to the Office within a time limit which it shall determine. If the application is not made within the time limit, the proceedings shall continue; the counterclaim shall be deemed withdrawn. Article 104(3) shall apply.

NOTES

General amendments to this Regulation: see further the note "General amendments" in the introductory notes to this Regulation *ante*.

Paras 4, 6: substituted by European Parliament and Council Regulation 2015/2424/EU, Art 1(93).

[5.704]
Article 101
Applicable law

1. The Community trade mark courts shall apply the provisions of this Regulation.

[2. On all trade mark matters not covered by this Regulation, the relevant EU trade mark court shall apply the applicable national law.]

3. Unless otherwise provided in this Regulation, a Community trade mark court shall apply the rules of procedure governing the same type of action relating to a national trade mark in the Member State in which the court is located.

NOTES

General amendments to this Regulation: see further the note "General amendments" in the introductory notes to this Regulation *ante*.

Para 2: substituted by European Parliament and Council Regulation 2015/2424/EU, Art 1(94).

[5.705]
Article 102
Sanctions

1. Where a Community trade mark court finds that the defendant has infringed or threatened to infringe a Community trade mark, it shall, unless there are special reasons for not doing so, issue an order prohibiting the defendant from proceeding with the acts which infringed or would infringe the Community trade mark. It shall also take such measures in accordance with its national law as are aimed at ensuring that this prohibition is complied with.

[2. The EU trade mark court may also apply measures or orders available under the applicable law which it deems appropriate in the circumstances of the case.]

NOTES

General amendments to this Regulation: see further the note "General amendments" in the introductory notes to this Regulation *ante*.

Para 2: substituted by European Parliament and Council Regulation 2015/2424/EU, Art 1(95).

[5.706]
Article 103
Provisional and protective measures

1. Application may be made to the courts of a Member State, including Community trade mark courts, for such provisional, including protective, measures in respect of a Community trade mark or Community trade mark application as may be available under the law of that State in respect of a national trade mark, even if, under this Regulation, a Community trade mark court of another Member State has jurisdiction as to the substance of the matter.

2. A Community trade mark court whose jurisdiction is based on Article 97(1), (2), (3) or (4) shall have jurisdiction to grant provisional and protective measures which, subject to any necessary procedure for recognition and enforcement pursuant to Title III of Regulation (EC) No 44/2001, are applicable in the territory of any Member State. No other court shall have such jurisdiction.

NOTES

General amendments to this Regulation: see further the note "General amendments" in the introductory notes to this Regulation *ante*.

[5.707]
Article 104
Specific rules on related actions

1. A Community trade mark court hearing an action referred to in Article 96, other than an action for a declaration of non-infringement shall, unless there are special grounds for continuing the hearing, of its own motion after hearing the parties or at the request of one of the parties and after hearing the other parties, stay the proceedings where the validity of the Community trade mark is already in issue before another Community trade mark court on account of a counterclaim or where an application for revocation or for a declaration of invalidity has already been filed at the Office.

2. The Office, when hearing an application for revocation or for a declaration of invalidity shall, unless there are special grounds for continuing the hearing, of its own motion after hearing the parties or at the request of one of the parties and after hearing the other parties, stay the proceedings where the validity of the Community trade mark is already in issue on account of a counterclaim before a Community trade mark court. However, if one of the parties to the proceedings before the Community trade mark court so requests, the court may, after hearing the other parties to these proceedings, stay the proceedings. The Office shall in this instance continue the proceedings pending before it.

3. Where the Community trade mark court stays the proceedings it may order provisional and protective measures for the duration of the stay.

NOTES

General amendments to this Regulation: see further the note "General amendments" in the introductory notes to this Regulation *ante*.

[5.708]

Article 105

Jurisdiction of Community trade mark courts of second instance — Further appeal

1. An appeal to the Community trade mark courts of second instance shall lie from judgments of the Community trade mark courts of first instance in respect of proceedings arising from the actions and claims referred to in Article 96.

2. The conditions under which an appeal may be lodged with a Community trade mark court of second instance shall be determined by the national law of the Member State in which that court is located.

3. The national rules concerning further appeal shall be applicable in respect of judgments of Community trade mark courts of second instance.

NOTES

General amendments to this Regulation: see further the note "General amendments" in the introductory notes to this Regulation *ante*.

SECTION 3

OTHER DISPUTES CONCERNING COMMUNITY TRADE MARKS

[5.709]

Article 106

Supplementary provisions on the jurisdiction of national courts other than Community trade mark courts

1. Within the Member State whose courts have jurisdiction under Article 94(1) those courts shall have jurisdiction for actions other than those referred to in Article 96, which would have jurisdiction ratione loci and ratione materiae in the case of actions relating to a national trade mark registered in that State.

2. Actions relating to a Community trade mark, other than those referred to in Article 96, for which no court has jurisdiction under Article 94(1) and paragraph 1 of this Article may be heard before the courts of the Member State in which the Office has its seat.

NOTES

General amendments to this Regulation: see further the note "General amendments" in the introductory notes to this Regulation *ante*.

[5.710]

Article 107

Obligation of the national court

A national court which is dealing with an action relating to a Community trade mark, other than the action referred to in Article 96, shall treat the trade mark as valid.

NOTES

General amendments to this Regulation: see further the note "General amendments" in the introductory notes to this Regulation *ante*.

Article 108 (*Repealed by European Parliament and Council Regulation 2015/2424/EU, Art 1(96).*)

TITLE XI
EFFECTS ON THE LAWS OF THE MEMBER STATES

SECTION 1
CIVIL ACTIONS ON THE BASIS OF MORE THAN ONE TRADE MARK

[5.711]
Article 109
Simultaneous and successive civil actions on the basis of Community trade marks and national trade marks

1. Where actions for infringement involving the same cause of action and between the same parties are brought in the courts of different Member States, one seized on the basis of a Community trade mark and the other seized on the basis of a national trade mark:

- *(a) the court other than the court first seized shall of its own motion decline jurisdiction in favour of that court where the trade marks concerned are identical and valid for identical goods or services. The court which would be required to decline jurisdiction may stay its proceedings if the jurisdiction of the other court is contested;*
- *(b) the court other than the court first seized may stay its proceedings where the trade marks concerned are identical and valid for similar goods or services and where the trade marks concerned are similar and valid for identical or similar goods or services.*

2. The court hearing an action for infringement on the basis of a Community trade mark shall reject the action if a final judgment on the merits has been given on the same cause of action and between the same parties on the basis of an identical national trade mark valid for identical goods or services.

3. The court hearing an action for infringement on the basis of a national trade mark shall reject the action if a final judgment on the merits has been given on the same cause of action and between the same parties on the basis of an identical Community trade mark valid for identical goods or services.

4. Paragraphs 1, 2 and 3 shall not apply in respect of provisional, including protective, measures.

NOTES

General amendments to this Regulation: see further the note "General amendments" in the introductory notes to this Regulation *ante*.

SECTION 2
APPLICATION OF NATIONAL LAWS FOR THE PURPOSE OF PROHIBITING THE USE OF COMMUNITY TRADE MARKS

[5.712]
Article 110
Prohibition of use of Community trade marks

1. This Regulation shall, unless otherwise provided for, not affect the right existing under the laws of the Member States to invoke claims for infringement of earlier rights within the meaning of Article 8 or Article 53(2) in relation to the use of a later Community trade mark. Claims for infringement of earlier rights within the meaning of Article 8(2) and (4) may, however, no longer be invoked if the proprietor of the earlier right may no longer apply for a declaration that the Community trade mark is invalid in accordance with Article 54(2).

2. This Regulation shall, unless otherwise provided for, not affect the right to bring proceedings under the civil, administrative or criminal law of a Member Sate or under provisions of Community law for the purpose of prohibiting the use of a Community trade mark to the extent that the use of a national trade mark may be prohibited under the law of that Member State or under Community law.

NOTES

General amendments to this Regulation: see further the note "General amendments" in the introductory notes to this Regulation *ante*.

[5.713]
Article 111
Prior rights applicable to particular localities

1. The proprietor of an earlier right which only applies to a particular locality may oppose the use of the Community trade mark in the territory where his right is protected in so far as the law of the Member State concerned so permits.

2. Paragraph 1 shall cease to apply if the proprietor of the earlier right has acquiesced in the use of the Community trade mark in the territory where his right is protected for a period of five successive years, being aware of such use, unless the Community trade mark was applied for in bad faith.

3. The proprietor of the Community trade mark shall not be entitled to oppose use of the right referred to in paragraph 1 even though that right may no longer be invoked against the Community trade mark.

NOTES

General amendments to this Regulation: see further the note "General amendments" in the introductory notes to this Regulation *ante*.

SECTION 3

CONVERSION INTO A NATIONAL TRADE MARK APPLICATION

[5.714]

Article 112

Request for the application of national procedure

1. The applicant for or proprietor of a Community trade mark may request the conversion of his Community trade mark application or Community trade mark into a national trade mark application:

(a) to the extent that the Community trade mark application is refused, withdrawn, or deemed to be withdrawn;

(b) to the extent that the Community trade mark ceases to have effect.

2. Conversion shall not take place:

(a) where the rights of the proprietor of the Community trade mark have been revoked on the grounds of non-use, unless in the Member State for which conversion is requested the Community trade mark has been put to use which would be considered to be genuine use under the laws of that Member State;

(b) for the purpose of protection in a Member State in which, in accordance with the decision of the Office or of the national court, grounds for refusal of registration or grounds for revocation or invalidity apply to the Community trade mark application or Community trade mark.

3. The national trade mark application resulting from the conversion of a Community trade mark application or a Community trade mark shall enjoy in respect of the Member State concerned the date of filing or the date of priority of that application or trade mark and, where appropriate, the seniority of a trade mark of that State claimed under Articles 34 or 35.

4. In cases where a Community trade mark application is deemed to be withdrawn, the Office shall send to the applicant a communication fixing a period of three months from the date of that communication in which a request for conversion may be filed.

5. Where the Community trade mark application is withdrawn or the Community trade mark ceases to have effect as a result of a surrender being recorded or of failure to renew the registration, the request for conversion shall be filed within three months after the date on which the Community trade mark application has been withdrawn or on which the Community trade mark ceases to have effect.

6. Where the Community trade mark application is refused by decision of the Office or where the Community trade mark ceases to have effect as a result of a decision of the Office or of a Community trade mark court, the request for conversion shall be filed within three months after the date on which that decision acquired the authority of a final decision.

7. The effect referred to in Article 32 shall lapse if the request is not filed in due time.

NOTES

General amendments to this Regulation: see further the note "General amendments" in the introductory notes to this Regulation *ante*.

[5.715]

[Article 113

Submission, publication and transmission of the request for conversion

1. A request for conversion shall be filed with the Office within the relevant period pursuant to Article 112(4), (5) or (6), and shall include an indication of the grounds for conversion in accordance with Article 112(1)(a) or (b), the Member States in respect of which conversion is requested, and the goods and services subject to conversion. Where conversion is requested following a failure to renew the registration, the period of three months provided for in Article 112(5) shall begin to run on the day following the last day on which the request for renewal can be presented pursuant to Article 47(3). The request for conversion shall not be deemed to be filed until the conversion fee has been paid.

2. Where the request for conversion relates to an EU trade mark application which has already been published or where the request for conversion relates to an EU trade mark, receipt of any such request shall be recorded in the Register and the request for conversion shall be published.

3. The Office shall check whether the conversion requested fulfils the conditions set out in this Regulation, in particular Article 112(1), (2), (4), (5) and (6), and paragraph 1 of this Article, together with the formal conditions specified in the implementing act adopted pursuant to paragraph 6 of this Article. If the conditions governing the request are not fulfilled, the Office shall notify the applicant of the deficiencies. If the deficiencies are not remedied within a period to be specified by the Office, the Office shall reject the request for conversion. Where Article 112(2) applies, the Office shall reject the request for conversion as inadmissible only with respect to those

Member States for which conversion is excluded under that provision. Where the conversion fee has not been paid within the relevant period of three months pursuant to Article 112(4), (5) or (6), the Office shall inform the applicant that the request for conversion is deemed not to have been filed.
4. If the Office or an EU trade mark court has refused the EU trade mark application or has declared the EU trade mark invalid on absolute grounds by reference to the language of a Member State, conversion shall be excluded under Article 112(2) for all the Member States in which that language is one of the official languages. If the Office or an EU trade mark court has refused the EU trade mark application or has declared the EU trade mark invalid on absolute grounds which are found to apply throughout the Union or on account of an earlier EU trade mark or other Union industrial property right, conversion shall be excluded under Article 112(2) for all Member States.
5. Where the request for conversion complies with the requirements referred to in paragraph 3 of this Article, the Office shall transmit the request for conversion and the data referred to in Article 87(2) to the central industrial property offices of the Member States, including the Benelux Office for Intellectual Property, for which the request has been found admissible. The Office shall inform the applicant of the date of transmission.
6. The Commission shall adopt implementing acts specifying:
(a) the details to be contained in a request for conversion of an EU trade mark application or a registered EU trade mark into a national trade mark application pursuant to paragraph 1;
(b) the details which are to be contained in the publication of the request for conversion pursuant to paragraph 2.
Those implementing acts shall be adopted in accordance with the examination procedure referred to in Article 163(2).]

NOTES

Substituted by European Parliament and Council Regulation 2015/2424/EU, Art 1(97).

[5.716]
Article 114
Formal requirements for conversion

1. Any central industrial property office to which the request for conversion is transmitted may obtain from the Office any additional information concerning the request enabling that office to make a decision regarding the national trade mark resulting from the conversion.
[2. An EU trade mark application or a European Union trade mark transmitted in accordance with Article 113 shall not be subject to formal requirements of national law which are different from or additional to those provided for in this Regulation or in acts adopted pursuant to this Regulation.]
3. Any central industrial property office to which the request is transmitted may require that the applicant shall, within not less than two months:
(a) pay the national application fee;
(b) file a translation in one of the official languages of the State in question of the request and of the documents accompanying it;
(c) indicate an address for service in the State in question;
(d) supply a representation of the trade mark in the number of copies specified by the State in question.

NOTES

Para 2: substituted by European Parliament and Council Regulation 2015/2424/EU, Art 1(98).

TITLE XII
THE OFFICE

SECTION 1
GENERAL PROVISIONS

[5.717]
Article 115
Legal status

1. [The Office shall be an agency of the Union.] It shall have legal personality.
2. In each of the Member States the Office shall enjoy the most extensive legal capacity accorded to legal persons under their laws; it may, in particular, acquire or dispose of movable and immovable property and may be a party to legal proceedings.
3. The Office shall be represented by its President.

NOTES

Para 1: words in square brackets substituted by European Parliament and Council Regulation 2015/2424/EU, Art 1(99).

[5.718]
Article 116
Staff

1. The Staff Regulations of officials of the European Communities, hereinafter referred to as "the Staff Regulations", the Conditions of Employment of other servants of the European Communities, and the rules adopted by agreement between the Institutions of the European Communities for giving effect to those Staff Regulations and Conditions of Employment shall apply to the staff of the Office, without prejudice to the application of Article 136 to the members of the Boards of Appeal.

[2. Without prejudice to paragraph 1, the Office may make use of seconded national experts or other staff not employed by the Office. The Management Board shall adopt a decision laying down rules on the secondment to the Office of national experts.]

NOTES

Para 2: substituted by European Parliament and Council Regulation 2015/2424/EU, Art 1(100).

[5.719]
Article 117
Privileges and immunities

The Protocol on the Privileges and Immunities of the European Communities shall apply [to the Office and its staff].

NOTES

Words in square brackets substituted by European Parliament and Council Regulation 2015/2424/EU, Art 1(101).

[5.720]
Article 118
Liability

1. The contractual liability of the Office shall be governed by the law applicable to the contract in question.

2. The Court of Justice shall be competent to give judgment pursuant to any arbitration clause contained in a contract concluded by the Office.

3. In the case of non-contractual liability, the Office shall, in accordance with the general principles common to the laws of the Member States, make good any damage caused by its departments or by its servants in the performance of their duties.

4. The Court of Justice shall have jurisdiction in disputes relating to compensation for the damage referred to in paragraph 3.

5. The personal liability of its servants towards the Office shall be governed by the provisions laid down in their Staff Regulations or in the Conditions of Employment applicable to them.

[5.721]
Article 119
Languages

1. The application for a Community trade mark shall be filed in one of the official languages of the European Community.

2. The languages of the Office shall be English, French, German, Italian and Spanish.

3. The applicant must indicate a second language which shall be a language of the Office the use of which he accepts as a possible language of proceedings for opposition, revocation or invalidity proceedings.

If the application was filed in a language which is not one of the languages of the Office, the Office shall arrange to have the application, as described in Article 26(1), translated into the language indicated by the applicant.

4. Where the applicant for a Community trade mark is the sole party to proceedings before the Office, the language of proceedings shall be the language used for filing the application for a Community trade mark. If the application was made in a language other than the languages of the Office, the Office may send written communications to the applicant in the second language indicated by the applicant in his application.

[5. The notice of opposition and an application for revocation or a declaration of invalidity shall be filed in one of the languages of the Office.]

[5a. Without prejudice to paragraph 5:

(a) any application or declaration relating to an EU trade mark application may be filed in the language used for filing the application for that EU trade mark or in the second language indicated by the applicant in his application;

(b) any application or declaration relating to a registered EU trade mark may be filed in one of the languages of the Office.

However, when the application is filed by using any form provided by the Office as referred to in Article 79b(2), such forms may be used in any of the official languages of the Union, provided that the form is completed in one of the languages of the Office, as far as textual elements are concerned.]

6. If the language chosen, in accordance with paragraph 5, for the notice of opposition or the application for revocation or invalidity is the language of the application for a trade mark or the second language indicated when the application was filed, that language shall be the language of the proceedings.

If the language chosen, in accordance with paragraph 5, for the notice of opposition or the application for revocation or invalidity is neither the language of the application for a trade mark nor the second language indicated when the application was filed, the opposing party or the party seeking revocation or invalidity shall be required to produce, at his own expense, a translation of his application either into the language of the application for a trade mark, provided that it is a language of the Office, or into the second language indicated when the application was filed. [The translation shall be produced within one month of the expiry of the opposition period or of the date of filing an application for revocation or a declaration of invalidity.] The language into which the application has been translated shall then become the language of the proceedings.

7. Parties to opposition, revocation, invalidity or appeal proceedings may agree that a different official language of the European Community is to be the language of the proceedings.

[8. Without prejudice to paragraphs 4 and 7, and unless provided otherwise, in written proceedings before the Office any party may use any language of the Office. If the language chosen is not the language of the proceedings, the party shall supply a translation into that language within one month of the date of the submission of the original document. Where the applicant for an EU trade mark is the sole party to proceedings before the Office and the language used for the filing of the application for the EU trade mark is not one of the languages of the Office, the translation may also be filed in the second language indicated by the applicant in his application.

9. The Executive Director shall determine the manner in which translations are to be certified.

10. The Commission shall adopt implementing acts specifying:

(a) the extent to which supporting documents to be used in written proceedings before the Office may be filed in any language of the Union, and the need to supply a translation;

(b) the requisite standards of translations to be filed with the Office.

Those implementing acts shall be adopted in accordance with the examination procedure referred to Article 163(2).]

NOTES

General amendments to this Regulation: see further the note "General amendments" in the introductory notes to this Regulation *ante*.

Para 5: substituted by European Parliament and Council Regulation 2015/2424/EU, Art 1(102)(a).

Para 5a: inserted by European Parliament and Council Regulation 2015/2424/EU, Art 1(102)(b).

Para 6: words in square brackets substituted by European Parliament and Council Regulation 2015/2424/EU, Art 1(102)(c).

Paras 8–10: added by European Parliament and Council Regulation 2015/2424/EU, Art 1(102)(d).

[5.722]

Article 120

Publication and entries in the Register

1. An application for a Community trade mark, as described in Article 26(1), and all other information the publication of which is prescribed by this Regulation or [an act adopted pursuant to this Regulation], shall be published in all the official languages of the European Community.

2. All entries in the Register of Community trade marks shall be made in all the official languages of the European Community.

3. In cases of doubt, the text in the language of the Office in which the application for the Community trade mark was filed shall be authentic. If the application was filed in an official language of the European Community other than one of the languages of the Office, the text in the second language indicated by the applicant shall be authentic.

NOTES

General amendments to this Regulation: see further the note "General amendments" in the introductory notes to this Regulation *ante*.

Para 1: words in square brackets substituted by European Parliament and Council Regulation 2015/2424/EU, Art 1(103).

[5.723]

Article 121

The translation services required for the functioning of the Office shall be provided by the Translation Centre for the Bodies of the European Union.

Article 122 *(Repealed by European Parliament and Council Regulation 2015/2424/EU, Art 1(104).)*

[5.724]

[Article 123

Transparency

1. Regulation (EC) No 1049/2001 of the European Parliament and of the Council[1] shall apply to documents held by the Office.

2. The Management Board shall adopt detailed rules for applying Regulation (EC) No 1049/2001.

3. Decisions taken by the Office under Article 8 of Regulation (EC) No 1049/2001 may be challenged through the European Ombudsman or form the subject of an action before the Court of Justice of the European Union, under the conditions laid down in Articles 228 and 263 of the Treaty on the Functioning of the European Union respectively.

4. The processing of personal data by the Office shall be subject to Regulation (EC) No 45/2001 of the European Parliament and of the Council[2].]

NOTES

Substituted by European Parliament and Council Regulation 2015/2424/EU, Art 1(105).

[1] Regulation (EC) No 1049/2001 of the European Parliament and of the Council of 30 May 2001 regarding public access to European Parliament, Council and Commission documents (OJ L145, 31.5.2001, p 43).

[2] Regulation (EC) No 45/2001 of the European Parliament and of the Council of 18 December 2000 on the protection of individuals with regard to the processing of personal data by the Community institutions and bodies and on the free movement of such data (OJ L8, 12.1.2001, p 1).

[5.725]

[Article 123a

Security rules on the protection of classified and sensitive non-classified information

The Office shall apply the security principles contained in the Commission's security rules for protecting European Union Classified Information (EUCI) and sensitive non-classified information, as set out in Commission Decisions (EU, Euratom) 2015/443[1] and 2015/444[2]. The security principles shall cover, inter alia, provisions for the exchange, processing and storage of such information.]

NOTES

Inserted by European Parliament and Council Regulation 2015/2424/EU, Art 1(106).

[1] Commission Decision (EU, Euratom) 2015/443 of 13 March 2015 on Security in the Commission (OJ L72, 17.3.2015, p 41).

[2] Commission Decision (EU, Euratom) 2015/444 of 13 March 2015 on the security rules for protecting EU classified information (OJ L72, 17.3.2015, p 53).

[SECTION 1A

TASKS OF THE OFFICE AND COOPERATION TO PROMOTE CONVERGENCE

[5.726]

Article 123b

Tasks of the Office

1. The Office shall have the following tasks:

- *(a) administration and promotion of the EU trade mark system established in this Regulation;*
- *(b) administration and promotion of the European Union design system established in Council Regulation (EC) No 6/2002;[1]*
- *(c) promoting convergence of practices and tools in the fields of trade marks and designs, in cooperation with the central industrial property offices in the Member States, including the Benelux Office for Intellectual Property;*
- *(d) the tasks referred to in Regulation (EU) No 386/2012 of the European Parliament and of the Council;[2]*
- *(e) the tasks conferred on it under Directive 2012/28/EU of the European Parliament and of the Council.[3]*

2. The Office shall cooperate with institutions, authorities, bodies, industrial property offices, international and non-governmental organisations in relation to the tasks conferred on it in paragraph 1.

3. The Office may provide voluntary mediation services for the purpose of assisting parties in reaching a friendly settlement.]

NOTES

Inserted, together with preceding heading and Art 123c, by European Parliament and Council Regulation 2015/2424/EU, Art 1(107).

[1] Council Regulation (EC) No 6/2002 of 12 December 2001 on Community designs (OJ L3, 5.1.2002, p 1).

[2] Regulation (EU) No 386/2012 of the European Parliament and of the Council of 19 April 2012 on entrusting the Office for Harmonization in the Internal Market (Trade Marks and Designs) with tasks related to the enforcement of intellectual property rights, including the assembling of public and private-sector representatives as a European Observatory on Infringements of Intellectual Property Rights (OJ L129, 16.5.2012, p 1).

[3] Directive 2012/28/EU of the European Parliament and of the Council of 25 October 2012 on certain permitted uses of orphan works (OJ L299, 27.10.2012, p 5).

[5.727]
[Article 123c
Cooperation to promote convergence of practices and tools
1. The Office and the central industrial property offices of the Member States and the Benelux Office for Intellectual Property shall cooperate with each other to promote convergence of practices and tools in the field of trade marks and designs.
Without prejudice to paragraph 3, this cooperation shall in particular cover the following areas of activity:
- *(a) the development of common examination standards;*
- *(b) the creation of common or connected databases and portals for Union-wide consultation, search and classification purposes;*
- *(c) the continuous provision and exchange of data and information, including for the purposes of feeding of the databases and portals referred to in point (b);*
- *(d) the establishment of common standards and practices, with a view to ensuring interoperability between procedures and systems throughout the Union and enhancing their consistency, efficiency and effectiveness;*
- *(e) the sharing of information on industrial property rights and procedures, including mutual support to helpdesks and information centres;*
- *(f) the exchange of technical expertise and assistance in relation to the areas referred to in points (a) to (e).*

2. On the basis of a proposal by the Executive Director, the Management Board shall define and coordinate projects of interest to the Union and the Member States with regard to the areas referred to in paragraphs 1 and 6, and shall invite the central industrial property offices of the Member States and the Benelux Office for Intellectual Property to participate in those projects.
The project definition shall contain the specific obligations and responsibilities of each participating industrial property office of the Member States, the Benelux Office for Intellectual Property and the Office. The Office shall consult with user representatives in particular in the phases of definition of the projects and evaluation of their results.
3. The central industrial property offices of the Member States and the Benelux Office for Intellectual Property may opt out of, restrict or temporarily suspend their cooperation in the projects referred to in the first subparagraph of paragraph 2.
When making use of the possibilities provided for in the first subparagraph, the central industrial property offices of the Member States and the Benelux Office for Intellectual Property shall provide the Office with a written statement explaining the reasons for their decision.
4. Once having committed to participate in certain projects, the central industrial property offices of the Member States and the Benelux Office for Intellectual Property shall, without prejudice to paragraph 3, participate effectively in the projects referred to in paragraph 2 with a view to ensuring that they are developed, function, are interoperable and kept up to date.
5. The Office shall provide financial support to the projects referred to in paragraph 2 to the extent that is necessary in order to ensure, for the purposes of paragraph 4, the effective participation of the central industrial property offices of the Member States and the Benelux Office for Intellectual Property in those projects. That financial support may take the form of grants and in-kind contributions. The total amount of funding shall not exceed 15% of the yearly revenue of the Office. The beneficiaries of grants shall be the central industrial property offices of the Member States and the Benelux Office for Intellectual Property. Grants may be awarded without calls for proposals in accordance with the financial rules applicable to the Office and with the principles of grant procedures contained in Regulation (EU, Euratom) No 966/2012 of the European Parliament and of the Council[1] and in Commission Delegated Regulation (EU) No 1268/2012.[2]
6. The Office and the relevant competent authorities of the Member States shall cooperate with each other on a voluntary basis to promote the raising of awareness concerning the trade mark system and the fight against counterfeiting. Such cooperation shall include projects aiming, in particular, at the implementation of established standards and practices as well as at organising education and training activities. The financial support for those projects shall be part of the total amount of funding referred to in paragraph 5. Paragraphs 2 to 5 shall apply mutatis mutandis.]

NOTES

Inserted as noted to Art 123b at **[5.726]**.

1 Regulation (EU, Euratom) No 966/2012 of the European Parliament and of the Council of 25 October 2012 on the financial rules applicable to the general budget of the Union and repealing Council Regulation (EC, Euratom) No 1605/2002 (OJ L298, 26.10.2012, p 1).

2 Commission Delegated Regulation (EU) No 1268/2012 of 29 October 2012 on the rules of application of Regulation (EU, Euratom) No 966/2012 of the European Parliament and of the Council on the financial rules applicable to the general budget of the Union (OJ L362, 31.12.2012, p 1).

[SECTION 2
MANAGEMENT BOARD

[5.728]
Article 124
Functions of the Management Board

1. Without prejudice to the functions attributed to the Budget Committee in Section 5, the Management Board shall have the following functions:

(a) on the basis of a draft submitted by the Executive Director in accordance with Article 128(4)(c), adopting the annual work programme of the Office for the coming year, taking into account the opinion of the Commission, and forwarding the adopted annual work programme to the European Parliament, to the Council and to the Commission;
(b) on the basis of a draft submitted by the Executive Director in accordance with Article 128(4)(e) and taking into account the opinion of the Commission, adopting a multiannual strategic programme for the Office, including the Office's strategy for international cooperation, following an exchange of views between the Executive Director and the relevant committee in the European Parliament, and forwarding the adopted multiannual strategic programme to the European Parliament, to the Council and to the Commission;
(c) on the basis of a draft submitted by the Executive Director in accordance with Article 128(4)(g), adopting the annual report and forwarding the adopted annual report to the European Parliament, to the Council, to the Commission and to the Court of Auditors;
(d) on the basis of a draft submitted by the Executive Director in accordance with Article 128(4)(h), adopting the multiannual staff policy plan;
(e) exercising the powers conferred on it under Article 123c(2);
(f) exercising the powers conferred on it under Article 139(5);
(g) adopting rules on the prevention and management of conflicts of interest in the Office;
(h) in accordance with paragraph 2, exercising, with respect to the staff of the Office, the powers conferred by the Staff Regulations on the Appointing Authority and by the Conditions of Employment of Other Servants on the Authority Empowered to Conclude Contracts of Employment ("the appointing authority powers");
(i) adopting appropriate implementing rules to give effect to the Staff Regulations and the Conditions of Employment of Other Servants in accordance with Article 110 of the Staff Regulations;
(j) drawing up the list of candidates provided for in Article 129(2);
(k) ensuring adequate follow-up to the findings and recommendations stemming from the internal or external audit reports and evaluations referred to in Article 165a, as well as from investigations of the European Anti-fraud Office (OLAF);
(l) being consulted before adoption of the guidelines for examination in the Office and in the other cases provided for in this Regulation;
(m) providing opinions and requests for information to the Executive Director and to the Commission where it considers it necessary.

2. The Management Board shall adopt, in accordance with Article 110 of the Staff Regulations and Article 142 of the Conditions of Employment of Other Servants, a decision based on Article 2(1) of the Staff Regulations and on Article 6 of the Conditions of Employment of Other Servants, delegating the relevant appointing authority powers to the Executive Director and defining the conditions under which that delegation of appointing authority powers can be suspended.

The Executive Director shall be authorised to sub-delegate those powers.

Where exceptional circumstances so require, the Management Board may, by way of a decision, temporarily suspend the delegation of the appointing authority powers to the Executive Director and those sub-delegated by the latter, and exercise them itself or delegate them to one of its members or to a staff member other than the Executive Director.]

NOTES

Sections 2, 3 (arts 124–129) substituted by European Parliament and Council Regulation 2015/2424/EU, Art 1(108).

[5.729]
[Article 125
Composition of the Management Board

1. The Management Board shall be composed of one representative of each Member State, two representatives of the Commission and one representative of the European Parliament, and their respective alternates.

2. The members of the Management Board may, subject to its rules of procedure, be assisted by advisers or experts.]

NOTES

Substituted as noted to Art 124 at **[5.728]**.

[5.730]
[Article 126
Chairperson of the Management Board
1. The Management Board shall elect a chairperson and a deputy chairperson from among its members. The deputy chairperson shall ex officio replace the chairperson in the event of his being prevented from attending to his duties.
2. The duration of the terms of office of the chairperson and the deputy chairperson shall be four years. The terms of office shall be renewable once. If, however, their membership of the Management Board ends at any time during their term of office, their term of office shall automatically expire on that date also.]

NOTES
Substituted as noted to Art 124 at **[5.728]**.

[5.731]
[Article 127
Meetings
1. Meetings of the Management Board shall be convened by its chairperson.
2. The Executive Director shall take part in the deliberations, unless the Management Board decides otherwise.
3. The Management Board shall hold an ordinary meeting at least once a year. In addition, it shall meet on the initiative of its chairperson or at the request of the Commission or of one-third of the Member States.
4. The Management Board shall adopt rules of procedure.
5. The Management Board shall take its decisions by an absolute majority of its members. However, a majority of two-thirds of its members shall be required for the decisions which the Management Board is empowered to take under Article 124(1)(a) and (b), Article 126(1) and Article 129(2) and (4). In both cases each member shall have one vote.
6. The Management Board may invite observers to attend its meetings.
7. The secretariat for the Management Board shall be provided by the Office.]

NOTES
Substituted as noted to Art 124 at **[5.728]**.

[SECTION 3
EXECUTIVE DIRECTOR

[5.732]
Article 128
Functions of the Executive Director
1. The Office shall be managed by the Executive Director. The Executive Director shall be accountable to the Management Board.
2. Without prejudice to the powers of the Commission, the Management Board, and the Budget Committee, the Executive Director shall be independent in the performance of his duties and shall neither seek nor take instructions from a government or from any other body.
3. The Executive Director shall be the legal representative of the Office.
4. The Executive Director shall have in particular the following functions, which may be delegated:
- *(a) taking all necessary steps, including the adoption of internal administrative instructions and the publication of notices, to ensure the functioning of the Office;*
- *(b) implementing the decisions adopted by the Management Board;*
- *(c) preparing a draft annual work programme indicating estimated human and financial resources for each activity, and submitting it to the Management Board after consultation of the Commission;*
- *(d) submitting to the Management Board proposals pursuant to Article 123c(2);*
- *(e) preparing a draft multiannual strategic programme, including the Office's strategy for international cooperation, and submitting it to the Management Board after consultation of the Commission and following an exchange of views with the relevant committee in the European Parliament;*
- *(f) implementing the annual work programme and the multiannual strategic programme and reporting to the Management Board on their implementation;*
- *(g) preparing the annual report on the Office's activities and presenting it to the Management Board for approval;*
- *(h) preparing a draft multiannual staff policy plan and submitting it to the Management Board after consultation of the Commission;*
- *(i) preparing an action plan following-up on the conclusions of the internal or external audit reports and evaluations, as well as following up on the investigations of the OLAF, and reporting on progress twice a year to the Commission and to the Management Board;*

(j) *protecting the financial interests of the Union by the application of preventive measures against fraud, corruption and any other illegal activities, by effective checks and, if irregularities are detected, by recovering amounts wrongly paid and, where appropriate, by imposing effective, proportionate and dissuasive administrative and financial penalties;*

(k) *preparing an anti-fraud strategy for the Office and presenting it to the Budget Committee for approval;*

(l) *in order to ensure uniform application of the Regulation, referring, where appropriate, to the enlarged Board of Appeal ("the Grand Board") questions on a point of law, in particular if the Boards of Appeal have issued diverging decisions on the point;*

(m) *drawing up estimates of the revenue and expenditure of the Office and implementing the budget;*

(n) *exercising the powers entrusted to him in respect of staff by the Management Board under Article 124(1)(h);*

(o) *exercising the powers conferred on him under Articles 26(3), 29(5), 30(3), 75(2), 78(5), Articles 79, 79b, 79c, Articles 87(4), 87a(3), 88(5), Articles 88a, 89, Articles 93(4), 119(9), Article 144, Articles 144a(1) and 144b(2), and Article 144c in accordance with the criteria set out in this Regulation and in the acts adopted pursuant to this Regulation.*

5. The Executive Director shall be assisted by one or more Deputy Executive Directors. If the Executive Director is absent or indisposed, the Deputy Executive Director or one of the Deputy Executive Directors shall replace him in accordance with the procedure laid down by the Management Board.]

[5.733]
[Article 129
Appointment and removal of the Executive Director and extension of term of office

1. The Executive Director shall be engaged as a temporary agent of the Office under Article 2(a) of the Conditions of Employment of Other Servants.

2. The Executive Director shall be appointed by the Council by simple majority, from a list of candidates proposed by the Management Board, following an open and transparent selection procedure. Before being appointed, the candidate selected by the Management Board may be invited to make a statement before any competent European Parliament committee and to answer questions put by its members. For the purpose of concluding the contract with the Executive Director, the Office shall be represented by the chairperson of the Management Board.

The Executive Director may be removed from office only upon a decision of the Council acting on a proposal from the Management Board.

3. The term of office of the Executive Director shall be five years. By the end of that period, the Management Board shall undertake an assessment which takes into account an evaluation of the performance of the Executive Director and the Office's future tasks and challenges.

4. The Council, taking into account the assessment referred to in paragraph 3, may extend the term of office of the Executive Director once and for no more than five years.

5. An Executive Director whose term of office has been extended may not participate in another selection procedure for the same post at the end of his overall term of office.

6. The Deputy Executive Director or Deputy Executive Directors shall be appointed or removed from office as provided for in paragraph 2, after consultation of the Executive Director and, where applicable, the Executive Director-elect. The term of office of the Deputy Executive Director shall be five years. It may be extended once and for no more than five years by the Council, after consultation of the Executive Director.]

NOTES

Substituted as noted to Art 124 at **[5.728]**.

SECTION 4
IMPLEMENTATION OF PROCEDURES

[5.734]
Article 130
Competence

For taking decisions in connection with the procedures laid down in this Regulation, the following shall be competent:

(a) *examiners;*
(b) *Opposition Divisions;*
[(c) *a department in charge of the Register;]*
(d) *Cancellation Divisions;*
(e) *Boards of Appeal;*
[(f) *any other unit or person appointed by the Executive Director to that effect.]*

NOTES

Para (c) substituted and para (f) added by European Parliament and Council Regulation 2015/2424/EU, Art 1(109).

[5.735]
Article 131
Examiners
An examiner shall be responsible for taking decisions on behalf of the Office in relation to an application for registration of a Community trade mark, including the matters referred to in [Articles 36, 37, 68 and 74c], except in so far as an Opposition Division is responsible.

NOTES
General amendments to this Regulation: see further the note "General amendments" in the introductory notes to this Regulation *ante*.
Words in square brackets substituted by European Parliament and Council Regulation 2015/2424/EU, Art 1(110).

[5.736]
Article 132
Opposition Divisions
1. An Opposition Division shall be responsible for taking decisions on an opposition to an application to register a Community trade mark.
2. The decisions of the Opposition Divisions shall be taken by three-member groups. At least one member shall be legally qualified. [Decisions relating to costs or to procedures shall be taken by a single member.]
[The Commission shall adopt implementing acts specifying the exact types of decisions that are to be taken by a single member. Those implementing acts shall be adopted in accordance with the examination procedure referred to in Article 163(2).]

NOTES
General amendments to this Regulation: see further the note "General amendments" in the introductory notes to this Regulation *ante*.
Para 2: words in first pair of square brackets substituted and words in second pair of square brackets inserted, by European Parliament and Council Regulation 2015/2424/EU, Art 1(111).

[5.737]
[Article 133
Department in charge of the Register
1. The Department in charge of the Register shall be responsible for taking decisions in respect of entries in the Register.
2. It shall also be responsible for keeping the list of professional representatives referred to in Article 93(2).
3. The decisions of the Department shall be taken by a single member.]

NOTES
Substituted by European Parliament and Council Regulation 2015/2424/EU, Art 1(112).

[5.738]
Article 134
Cancellation Divisions
[1. A Cancellation Division shall be responsible for taking decisions in relation to:
(a) applications for the revocation or a declaration of invalidity of an EU trade mark;
(b) requests for the assignment of an EU trade mark as provided for in Article 18.]
2. The decisions of the Cancellation Divisions shall be taken by three-member groups. At least one member shall be legally qualified. [Decisions relating to costs or to procedures as specified in the acts adopted pursuant to Article 132(2) shall be taken by a single member.]

NOTES
Para 1: substituted by European Parliament and Council Regulation 2015/2424/EU, Art 1(113)(a).
Para 2: words in square brackets substituted by European Parliament and Council Regulation 2015/2424/EU, Art 1(113)(b).

[5.739]
[Article 134a
General Competence
Decisions required under this Regulation which do not fall within the competence of an examiner, an Opposition Division, a Cancellation Division or the Department in charge of the Register, shall be taken by any official or unit appointed by the Executive Director for that purpose.]

NOTES
Inserted by European Parliament and Council Regulation 2015/2424/EU, Art 1(114).

[5.740]
Article 135
Boards of Appeal
[1. The Boards of Appeal shall be responsible for deciding on appeals from decisions taken pursuant to Articles 131 to 134a.]

2. The decisions of the Boards of Appeal shall be taken by three members, at least two of whom are legally qualified. In certain specific cases, decisions shall be taken [by the Grand Board] chaired by the President of the Boards of Appeal or by a single member, who must be legally qualified.

[3. In order to determine the special cases which fall under the jurisdiction of the Grand Board, account should be taken of the legal difficulty or the importance of the case or of special circumstances which justify it. Such cases may be referred to the Grand Board:

(a) by the authority of the Boards of Appeal referred to in Article 136(4)(a); or

(b) by the Board handling the case.]

[4. The Grand Board shall also be responsible for giving reasoned opinions on questions of law referred to it by the Executive Director pursuant to Article 128(4)(l).]

5. To determine which specific cases fall under the authority of a single member, account should be taken of the lack of difficulty of the legal or factual matters raised, the limited importance of the individual case or the absence of other specific circumstances. The decision to confer a case on one member in the cases referred to shall be adopted by the Board handling the case. . . .

NOTES

Para 1: substituted by European Parliament and Council Regulation 2015/2424/EU, Art 1(115)(a).

Para 2: words in square brackets substituted by European Parliament and Council Regulation 2015/2424/EU, Art 1(115)(b).

Paras 3, 4: substituted by European Parliament and Council Regulation 2015/2424/EU, Art 1(115)(c), (d).

Para 5: words omitted repealed by European Parliament and Council Regulation 2015/2424/EU, Art 1(115)(e).

[5.741]

[Article 136

Independence of the members of the Boards of Appeal

1. The President of the Boards of Appeal and the chairpersons of the Boards shall be appointed, in accordance with the procedure laid down in Article 129 for the appointment of the Executive Director, for a term of five years. They shall not be removed from office during this term, unless there are serious grounds for such removal and the Court of Justice, on application by the institution which appointed them, takes a decision to this effect.

2. The term of office of the President of the Boards of Appeal may be extended once for one additional five-year period, or until retirement age if this age is reached during the new term of office, after a prior positive evaluation of his performance by the Management Board.

3. The term of office of the chairpersons of the Boards may be extended for additional five-year periods, or until retirement age if this age is reached during the new term of office, after a prior positive evaluation of their performance by the Management Board, and after consulting the President of the Boards of Appeal.

4. The President of the Boards of Appeal shall have the following managerial and organisational functions:

(a) chairing the Presidium of the Boards of Appeal ("the Presidium"), responsible for laying down the rules and organising the work of the Boards;

(b) ensuring the implementation of the decisions of the Presidium;

(c) allocating cases to a Board on the basis of objective criteria determined by the Presidium;

(d) forwarding to the Executive Director the Boards' expenditure requirements, with a view to drawing up the expenditure estimates.

The President of the Boards of Appeal shall chair the Grand Board.

5. The members of the Boards of Appeal shall be appointed by the Management Board for a term of five years. Their term of office may be extended for additional five-year periods, or until retirement age if that age is reached during the new term of office after a prior positive evaluation of their performance by the Management Board, and after consulting the President of the Boards of Appeal.

6. The members of the Boards of Appeal shall not be removed from office unless there are serious grounds for such removal and the Court of Justice, after the case has been referred to it by the Management Board on the recommendation of the President of the Boards of Appeal, and after consulting the chairperson of the Board to which the member concerned belongs, takes a decision to this effect.

7. The President of the Boards of Appeal and the chairpersons and members of the Boards of Appeal shall be independent. In their decisions, they shall not be bound by any instructions.

8. Decisions taken by the Grand Board on appeals or opinions on questions of law referred to it by the Executive Director pursuant to Article 135 shall be binding on the decision-making instances of the Office referred to in Article 130.

9. The President of the Boards of Appeal and the chairpersons and members of the Boards of Appeal shall not be examiners or members of the Opposition Divisions, the Department in charge of the Register or Cancellation Divisions.

NOTES

Substituted by European Parliament and Council Regulation 2015/2424/EU, Art 1(116).

[5.742]
[Article 136a
Presidium of the Boards of Appeal and Grand Board
1. The Presidium shall comprise the President of the Boards of Appeal, who shall chair it, the chairmen of the Boards and Board members elected for each calendar year by and from among all the members of the Boards other than the President of the Boards of Appeal and the chairmen of the Boards. The number of Board members so elected shall constitute a quarter of the number of Board members, other than the President of the Boards of Appeal and the chairmen of the Boards, and that number shall be rounded up if necessary.
2. The Grand Board referred to in Article 135(2) shall comprise nine members, including the President of the Boards of Appeal, the chairmen of the Boards, the rapporteur designated prior to referral to the Grand Board, if applicable, and members drawn in rotation from a list comprising the names of all members of the Boards of Appeal other than the President of the Boards of Appeal and the chairmen of the Boards.]

NOTES

Inserted by European Parliament and Council Regulation 2015/2424/EU, Art 1(117).

[5.743]
[Article 136b
Delegation of powers
The Commission shall be empowered to adopt delegated acts in accordance with Article 163a specifying the details concerning the organisation of the Boards of Appeal, including the setting up and the role of the Presidium, the composition of the Grand Board and the rules on referrals to it, and the conditions under which decisions are to be taken by a single member in accordance with Article 135(2) and (5).]

NOTES

Inserted by European Parliament and Council Regulation 2015/2424/EU, Art 1(118).

[5.744]
Article 137
Exclusion and objection
1. Examiners and members of the Divisions set up within the Office or of the Boards of Appeal may not take part in any proceedings if they have any personal interest therein, or if they have previously been involved as representatives of one of the parties. Two of the three members of an Opposition Division shall not have taken part in examining the application. Members of the Cancellation Divisions may not take part in any proceedings if they have participated in the final decision on the case in the proceedings for registration or opposition proceedings. Members of the Boards of Appeal may not take part in appeal proceedings if they participated in the decision under appeal.
2. If, for one of the reasons mentioned in paragraph 1 or for any other reason, a member of a Division or of a Board of Appeal considers that he should not take part in any proceedings, he shall inform the Division or Board accordingly.
3. Examiners and members of the Divisions or of a Board of Appeal may be objected to by any party for one of the reasons mentioned in paragraph 1, or if suspected of partiality. An objection shall not be admissible if, while being aware of a reason for objection, the party has taken a procedural step. No objection may be based upon the nationality of examiners or members.
4. The Divisions and the Boards of Appeal shall decide as to the action to be taken in the cases specified in paragraphs 2 and 3 without the participation of the member concerned. For the purposes of taking this decision the member who withdraws or has been objected to shall be replaced in the Division or Board of Appeal by his alternate.

[5.745]
[Article 137a
Mediation centre
1. For the purposes of Article 123b(3), the Office may establish a Mediation Centre ("the Centre").
2. Any natural or legal person may use the Centre's services on a voluntary basis with the aim of reaching a friendly settlement of disputes, based on this Regulation or Regulation (EC) No 6/2002, by mutual agreement.
3. The parties shall have recourse to mediation by means of a joint request. The request shall not be deemed to have been filed until the corresponding charge has been paid. The Executive Director shall fix the amount to be charged in accordance with Article 144(1).
4. In the case of disputes subject to the proceedings pending before the Opposition Divisions, Cancellation Divisions or before the Boards of Appeal of the Office a joint request for mediation may be presented at any time after the lodging of a notice of opposition, an application for revocation or an application for a declaration of invalidity or a notice of appeal against decisions of the Opposition or Cancellation Divisions.

5. The proceedings in question shall be suspended and the time periods, other than the time periods for the payment of the applicable fee, shall be interrupted as from the date of the filing of a joint request for mediation. The time periods shall continue as from the day on which the proceedings are resumed.

6. The parties shall be invited to jointly appoint, from the list referred to in paragraph 12, a mediator who has declared that he has a command of the language of the mediation in question. Where the parties do not appoint a mediator within 20 days of the invitation to do so, the mediation shall be deemed to have failed.

7. The parties shall agree together with the mediator on the detailed arrangements for the mediation in a mediation agreement.

8. The mediator shall conclude the mediation proceedings as soon as the parties reach a settlement agreement, or one of the parties declares that it wishes to end the mediation or the mediator establishes that the parties have failed to reach such an agreement.

9. The mediator shall inform the parties as well as the relevant instance of the Office as soon as the mediation proceedings have been concluded.

10. The discussions and negotiations conducted within the framework of mediation shall be confidential for all persons involved in the mediation, in particular for the mediator, the parties and their representatives. All documents and information submitted during the mediation shall be kept separately from, and shall not be part of, the file of any other proceedings before the Office.

11. The mediation shall be conducted in one of the official languages of the Union to be agreed upon by the parties. Where the mediation relates to disputes pending before the Office, the mediation shall be conducted in the language of the Office proceedings, unless otherwise agreed by the parties.

12. The Office shall establish a list of mediators who shall support parties in resolving disputes. The mediators shall be independent and possess relevant skills and experience. The list may include mediators who are employed by the Office, and mediators who are not so employed.

13. Mediators shall be impartial in the exercise of their duties and shall declare any real or perceived conflict of interest upon their designation. Members of the decision-making instances of the Office listed in Article 130 shall not take part in mediation concerning a case in which they have:

(a) had any prior involvement in the proceedings referred to mediation;

(b) any personal interest in those proceedings; or

(c) been previously involved as a representative of one of the parties.

14. Mediators shall not take part as members of the decision-making instances of the Office listed in Article 130 in proceedings resumed as a consequence of a mediation failure.

15. The Office may cooperate with other recognised national or international bodies dealing with mediation.]

NOTES

Inserted by European Parliament and Council Regulation 2015/2424/EU, Art 1(119).

SECTION 5

BUDGET AND FINANCIAL CONTROL

[5.746]

[Article 138

Budget Committee

1. The Budget Committee shall have the functions assigned to it in this Section.

2. Articles 125 and 126, Article 127(1) to (4), and (5), in so far as it relates to the election of the chairperson and deputy chairperson, (6) and (7) shall apply to the Budget Committee, mutatis mutandis.

3. The Budget Committee shall take its decisions by an absolute majority of its members. However, a majority of two-thirds of its members shall be required for the decisions which the Budget Committee is empowered to take under Article 140(3) and Article 143. In both cases each member shall have one vote.]

NOTES

Substituted by European Parliament and Council Regulation 2015/2424/EU, Art 1(120).

[5.747]

[Article 139

Budget

1. Estimates of all the Office's revenue and expenditure shall be prepared for each financial year and shall be shown in the Office's budget. Each financial year shall correspond to the calendar year.

2. The revenue and expenditure shown in the budget shall be in balance.

3. Revenue shall comprise, without prejudice to other types of income, total fees payable under Annex -I to this Regulation, total fees as provided for in Regulation (EC) No 6/2002, total fees payable, under the Madrid Protocol referred to in Article 145 of this Regulation, for an international registration designating the Union and other payments made to Contracting Parties to the Madrid Protocol, total fees payable, under the Geneva Act referred to in Article 106c of Regulation (EC) No 6/2002, for an international registration designating the Union and other payments made to Contracting Parties to the Geneva Act, and, to the extent necessary, a subsidy entered against a specific heading of the Commission section of the general budget of the Union.

4. Every year the Office shall offset the costs incurred by the central industrial property offices of the Member States, by the Benelux Office for Intellectual Property and by any other relevant authority to be nominated by a Member State, as the result of the specific tasks which they carry out as functional parts of the EU trade mark system in the context of the following services and procedures:

(a) opposition and invalidity proceedings before the central industrial property offices of the Member States and the Benelux Office for Intellectual Property involving EU trade marks;

(b) provision of information on the functioning of the EU trade mark system through helpdesks and information centres;

(c) enforcement of EU trade marks, including action taken pursuant to Article 9(4).

5. The overall offsetting of the costs identified in paragraph 4 shall correspond to 5% of the yearly revenue of the Office. Without prejudice to the third subparagraph of this paragraph, on a proposal by the Office and after having consulted the Budget Committee, the Management Board shall determine the distribution key on the basis of the following fair, equitable and relevant indicators:

(a) the annual number of EU trade mark applications originating from applicants in each Member State;

(b) the annual number of national trade mark applications in each Member State;

(c) the annual number of oppositions and applications for a declaration of invalidity submitted by proprietors of EU trade marks in each Member State;

(d) the annual number of cases brought before the EU trade mark courts designated by each Member State in accordance with Article 95.

For the purpose of substantiating the costs referred to in paragraph 4, Member States shall submit to the Office by 31 March of each year, statistical data demonstrating the figures referred to in points (a) to (d) of the first subparagraph of this paragraph for the preceding year, which shall be included in the proposal to be made to the Management Board.

On grounds of equity, the costs incurred by the bodies referred to in paragraph 4 in each Member State shall be deemed to correspond to at least 2% of the total offsetting provided for under this paragraph.

6. The obligation by the Office to offset the costs referred to in paragraph 4 and incurred in a given year shall only apply to the extent that no budgetary deficit occurs in that year.

7. In the event of a budgetary surplus, and without prejudice to paragraph 10, on a proposal by the Office and after having consulted the Budget Committee, the Management Board may increase the percentage laid down in paragraph 5 to a maximum of 10% of the yearly revenue of the Office.

8. Without prejudice to paragraphs 4 to 7 and paragraph 10 of this Article and to Articles 123b and 123c, where a substantive surplus is generated over five consecutive years, the Budget Committee, upon a proposal from the Office and in accordance with the annual work programme and multiannual strategic programme referred to in Article 124(1)(a) and (b), shall decide by a two-thirds majority on the transfer to the budget of the Union of a surplus generated from 23 March 2016.

9. The Office shall prepare on a biannual basis a report for the European Parliament, the Council and the Commission on its financial situation, including on the financial operations performed under Article 123c(5) and (6), and Article 139(5) and (7). On the basis of that report, the Commission shall review the financial situation of the Office.

10. The Office shall provide for a reserve fund covering one year of its operational expenditure to ensure the continuity of its operations and the execution of its tasks.]

NOTES

Substituted by European Parliament and Council Regulation 2015/2424/EU, Art 1(121).

[5.748]

Article 140

Preparation of the budget

1. The President shall draw up each year an estimate of the Office's revenue and expenditure for the following year and shall send it to the Budget Committee not later than 31 March in each year, together with a list of posts.

2. Should the budget estimates provide for a Community subsidy, the Budget Committee shall immediately forward the estimate to the Commission, which shall forward it to the budget authority of the Communities. The Commission may attach an opinion on the estimate along with an alternative estimate.

3. The Budget Committee shall adopt the budget, which shall include the Office's list of posts. Should the budget estimates contain a subsidy from the general budget of the Communities, the Office's budget shall, if necessary, be adjusted.

[5.749]
Article 141
Audit and control

1. An internal audit function shall be set up within the Office, to be performed in compliance with the relevant international standards. The internal auditor, appointed by the President, shall be responsible to him for verifying the proper operation of budget implementation systems and procedures of the Office.

2. The internal auditor shall advise the President on dealing with risks, by issuing independent opinions on the quality of management and control systems and by issuing recommendations for improving the conditions of implementation of operations and promoting sound financial management.

3. The responsibility for putting in place internal control systems and procedures suitable for carrying out his tasks shall lie with the authorising officer.

[5.750]
[Article 141a
Combating fraud

1. In order to facilitate combating fraud, corruption and other unlawful activities under Regulation (EU, Euratom) No 883/2013 of the European Parliament and of the Council[1], the Office shall accede to the Inter-institutional Agreement of 25 May 1999 concerning internal investigations by the European Anti-fraud Office (OLAF), and adopt the appropriate provisions applicable to all the employees of the Office using the template set out in the Annex to that Agreement.

2. The European Court of Auditors shall have the power of audit, on the basis of documents and on the spot, over all grant beneficiaries, contractors and subcontractors who have received Union funds from the Office.

3. OLAF may carry out investigations, including on-the-spot checks and inspections, in accordance with the provisions and procedures laid down in Regulation (EU, Euratom) No 883/2013 and Council Regulation (Euratom, EC) No 2185/96[2] with a view to establishing whether there has been fraud, corruption or any other illegal activity affecting the financial interests of the Union in connection with a grant or a contract funded by the Office.

4. Without prejudice to paragraphs 1, 2 and 3, cooperation agreements with third countries and international organisations, contracts, grant agreements and grant decisions of the Office shall contain provisions expressly empowering the European Court of Auditors and OLAF to conduct such audits and investigations, in accordance with their respective competences.

5. The Budget Committee shall adopt an anti-fraud strategy which is proportionate to the fraud risks having regard to the cost-benefit of the measures to be implemented.]

NOTES

Inserted by European Parliament and Council Regulation 2015/2424/EU, Art 1(122).

[1] Regulation (EU, Euratom) No 883/2013 of the European Parliament and of the Council of 11 September 2013 concerning investigations conducted by the European Anti-Fraud Office (OLAF) and repealing Regulation (EC) No 1073/1999 of the European Parliament and of the Council and Council Regulation (Euratom) No 1074/1999 (OJ L248, 18.9.2013, p 1).

[2] Council Regulation (Euratom, EC) No 2185/96 of 11 November 1996 concerning on-the-spot checks and inspections carried out by the Commission in order to protect the European Communities' financial interests against fraud and other irregularities (OJ L292, 15.11.1996, p 2).]

[5.751]
Article 142
Auditing of accounts

1. Not later than 31 March in each year the President shall transmit to the Commission, the European Parliament, the Budget Committee and the Court of Auditors accounts of the Office's total revenue and expenditure for the preceding financial year. The Court of Auditors shall examine them in accordance with Article 248 of the Treaty.

2. The Budget Committee shall give a discharge to the President of the Office in respect of the implementation of the budget.

[5.752]
Article 143
Financial provisions

The Budget Committee shall, after consulting the Court of Auditors of the European Communities and the Commission, adopt internal financial provisions specifying, in particular, the procedure for establishing and implementing the Office's budget. As far as is compatible with the particular nature of the Office, the financial provisions shall be based on the financial regulations adopted for other bodies set up by the Community.

[5.753]
[Article 144
Fees and charges and due date
1. The Executive Director shall lay down the amount to be charged for any services rendered by the Office other than those set out in Annex -I, as well as the amount to be charged for the European Union Trade Marks Bulletin, the Official Journal of the Office and any other publications issued by the Office. The amounts of charges shall be set in euros and shall be published in the Official Journal of the Office. The amount of each charge shall not exceed what is necessary to cover the costs of the specific service rendered by the Office.
2. Fees and charges in respect of which the due date is not specified in this Regulation shall be due on the date of receipt of the request for the service for which the fee or the charge is incurred.
With the consent of the Budget Committee, the Executive Director may determine which of the services mentioned in the first subparagraph are not to be dependent upon the advance payment of the corresponding fees or charges.]

NOTES

Substituted by European Parliament and Council Regulation 2015/2424/EU, Art 1(123).

[5.754]
[Article 144a
Payment of fees and charges
1. Fees and charges due to the Office shall be paid by payment or transfer to a bank account held by the Office.
With the consent of the Budget Committee, the Executive Director may establish which specific methods of payment other than those set out in the first subparagraph, in particular by means of deposits in current accounts held with the Office, may be used.
Determinations made pursuant to the second subparagraph shall be published in the Official Journal of the Office.
All payments, including by any other method of payment established pursuant to the second subparagraph, shall be made in euros.
2. Every payment shall indicate the name of the person making the payment and shall contain the necessary information to enable the Office to establish immediately the purpose of the payment. In particular, the following information shall be provided:
- *(a) when the application fee is paid, the purpose of the payment, namely "application fee";*
- *(b) when the opposition fee is paid, the file number of the application and the name of the applicant for the EU trade mark against which opposition is entered, and the purpose of the payment, namely "opposition fee";*
- *(c) when the revocation fee and the invalidity fee are paid, the registration number and the name of the proprietor of the EU trade mark against which the application is directed, and the purpose of the payment, namely "revocation fee" or "invalidity fee".*

3. If the purpose of the payment referred to in paragraph 2 cannot immediately be established, the Office shall require the person making the payment to notify it in writing of this purpose within such period as it may specify. If the person does not comply with this request in due time, the payment shall be considered not to have been made. The amount which has been paid shall be refunded.]

NOTES

Inserted by European Parliament and Council Regulation 2015/2424/EU, Art 1(124).

[5.755]
[Article 144b
Deemed date of payment
1. In the cases referred to in the first subparagraph of Article 144a(1), the date on which the payment shall be considered to have been made to the Office shall be the date on which the amount of the payment or of the transfer is actually entered in a bank account held by the Office.
2. Where the methods of payment referred to in the second subparagraph of Article 144a(1) may be used, the Executive Director shall establish the date on which such payments are to be considered to have been made.
3. Where, under paragraphs 1 and 2, payment of a fee is not considered to have been made until after the expiry of the period in which it was due, it shall be considered that this period has been observed if evidence is provided to the Office that the persons who made the payment in a Member State, within the period within which the payment should have been made, duly gave an order to a banking establishment to transfer the amount of the payment, and paid a surcharge of 10% of the relevant fee or fees, but not exceeding EUR 200. No surcharge shall be payable if the relevant order to the banking establishment has been given not later than 10 days before the expiry of the period for payment.

4. The Office may request the person who made the payment to produce evidence as to the date on which the order to the banking establishment as referred to in paragraph 3 was given and, where required, to pay the relevant surcharge within a period to be specified by it. If the person fails to comply with that request or if the evidence is insufficient, or if the required surcharge is not paid in due time, the period for payment shall be considered not to have been observed.]

NOTES

Inserted by European Parliament and Council Regulation 2015/2424/EU, Art 1(124).

[5.756]
[Article 144c
Insufficient payments and refund of insignificant amounts

1. A time limit for payment shall, in principle, be considered to have been observed only if the full amount of the fee has been paid in due time. If the fee is not paid in full, the amount which has been paid shall be refunded after the period for payment has expired.

2. The Office may, however, in so far as is possible within the time remaining before the end of the period, give the person making the payment the opportunity to pay the amount lacking or, where this is considered justified, overlook any small amounts lacking, without prejudice to the rights of the person making the payment.

3. With the consent of the Budget Committee, the Executive Director may waive action for the enforced recovery of any sum due where the sum to be recovered is minimal or where such recovery is too uncertain.

4. Where an excessive sum is paid to cover a fee or a charge, the excess shall not be refunded if the amount is insignificant and the party concerned has not expressly requested a refund.

With the consent of the Budget Committee the Executive Director may determine the amount below which an excessive sum paid to cover a fee or a charge shall not be refunded.

Determinations pursuant to the second subparagraph shall be published in the Official Journal of the Office.]

NOTES

Inserted by European Parliament and Council Regulation 2015/2424/EU, Art 1(124).

TITLE XIII
INTERNATIONAL REGISTRATION OF MARKS

SECTION 1
GENERAL PROVISIONS

[5.757]
Article 145
Application of provisions

Unless otherwise specified in this title, this Regulation and [the acts adopted pursuant to this Regulation] shall apply to applications for international registrations under the Protocol relating to the Madrid Agreement concerning the international registration of marks, adopted at Madrid on 27 June 1989 (hereafter referred to as "international applications" and "the Madrid Protocol" respectively), based on an application for a Community trade mark or on a Community trade mark and to registrations of marks in the international register maintained by the International Bureau of the World Intellectual Property Organisation (hereafter referred to as "international registrations" and "the International Bureau", respectively) designating the European Community.

NOTES

General amendments to this Regulation: see further the note "General amendments" in the introductory notes to this Regulation *ante*.

Words in square brackets substituted by European Parliament and Council Regulation 2015/2424/EU, Art 1(125).

SECTION 2
INTERNATIONAL REGISTRATION ON THE BASIS OF APPLICATIONS FOR A COMMUNITY TRADE MARK AND OF COMMUNITY TRADE MARKS

[5.758]
Article 146
Filing of an international application

1. International applications pursuant to Article 3 of the Madrid Protocol based on an application for a Community trade mark or on a Community trade mark shall be filed at the Office.

2. Where an international application is filed before the mark on which the international registration is to be based has been registered as a Community trade mark, the applicant for the international registration must indicate whether the international registration is to be based on a Community trade mark application or registration. Where the international registration is to be based on a Community trade mark once it is registered, the international application shall be deemed to have been received at the Office on the date of registration of the Community trade mark.

NOTES

General amendments to this Regulation: see further the note "General amendments" in the introductory notes to this Regulation *ante*.

[5.759]

Article 147

Form and contents of the international application

1. The international application shall be filed in one of the official languages of the European Community, using a form provided by the Office. [The Office shall inform the applicant filing the international application of the date on which the documents making up the international application are received by the Office.] Unless otherwise specified by the applicant on that form when he files the international application, the Office shall correspond with the applicant in the language of filing in a standard form.

2. If the international application is filed in a language which is not one of the languages allowed under the Madrid Protocol, the applicant must indicate a second language from among those languages. This shall be the language in which the Office submits the international application to the International Bureau.

[3. Where the international application is filed in a language other than one of the languages allowed under the Madrid Protocol for the filing of international applications, the applicant may provide a translation of the list of goods or services and of any other textual elements forming part of the international application in the language in which the international application is to be submitted to the International Bureau pursuant to paragraph 2. If the application is not accompanied by such translation, the applicant shall authorise the Office to include that translation in the international application. Where the translation has not yet been established in the course of the registration procedure for the EU trade mark application on which the international application is based, the Office shall, without delay, arrange for the translation.

4. The filing of an international application shall be subject to the payment of a fee to the Office. Where the international registration is to be based on an EU trade mark once it is registered, the fee shall be due on the date of registration of the EU trade mark. The application shall be deemed not to have been filed until the required fee has been paid. Where the fee has not been paid, the Office shall inform the applicant accordingly. In the event of electronic filing, the Office may authorise the International Bureau to collect the fee on its behalf.

5. Where the examination of the international application reveals any of the following deficiencies, the Office shall invite the applicant to remedy those deficiencies within such period as it may specify:

- *(a) the international application has not been filed using the form referred to in paragraph 1, and does not contain all the indications and information required by that form;*
- *(b) the list of goods and services contained in the international application is not covered by the list of goods and services appearing in the basic EU trade mark application or basic EU trade mark;*
- *(c) the mark which is subject to the international application is not identical with the mark as it appears in the basic EU trade mark application or basic EU trade mark;*
- *(d) an indication in the international application as to the trade mark, other than a disclaimer or a colour claim, does not also appear in the basic EU trade mark application or basic EU trade mark;*
- *(e) where colour is claimed in the international application as a distinctive feature of the mark, the basic EU trade mark application or basic EU trade mark is not in the same colour or colours; or*
- *(f) according to the indications made in the international form, the applicant is not eligible to file an international application through the Office in accordance with Article 2(1)(ii) of the Madrid Protocol.*

6. Where the applicant has failed to authorise the Office to include a translation as provided for in paragraph 3, or where it is otherwise unclear on which list of goods and services the international application is to be based, the Office shall invite the applicant to make the required indications within such period as it may specify.]

[7. If the deficiencies referred to in paragraph 5 are not remedied or the required indications referred to in paragraph 6 are not given within the period fixed by the Office, the Office shall refuse to forward the international application to the International Bureau.

8. The Office shall forward the international application to the International Bureau along with the certification provided for under Article 3(1) of the Madrid Protocol as soon as the international application meets the requirements laid down in this Article, the implementing act adopted pursuant to paragraph 9 of this Article, and in Article 146 of this Regulation.

9. The Commission shall adopt implementing acts specifying the exact form, including the elements thereof, to be used for the filing of an international application pursuant to paragraph 1. Those implementing acts shall be adopted in accordance with the examination procedure referred to in Article 163(2).]

NOTES

Para 1: words in square brackets inserted by European Parliament and Council Regulation 2015/2424/EU, Art 1(126)(a).
Paras 3–6: substituted by European Parliament and Council Regulation 2015/2424/EU, Art 1(126)(b).
Paras 7–9: added by European Parliament and Council Regulation 2015/2424/EU, Art 1(126)(c).

[5.760]
Article 148
Recordal in the files and in the Register

1. The date and number of an international registration based on a Community trade mark application, shall be recorded in the files of that application. When the application results in a Community trade mark, the date und number of the international registration shall be entered in the Register.

2. The date and number of an international registration based on a Community trade mark shall be entered in the Register.

NOTES

General amendments to this Regulation: see further the note "General amendments" in the introductory notes to this Regulation *ante*.

[5.761]
[Article 148a
Notification of the invalidity of the basic application or registration

1. Within a period of five years of the date of the international registration, the Office shall notify the International Bureau of any facts and decisions affecting the validity of the EU trade mark application or the EU trade mark registration on which the international registration was based.

2. The Commission shall adopt implementing acts specifying the individual facts and decisions subject to the notification obligation in accordance with Article 6(3) of the Madrid Protocol as well as the relevant point in time of such notifications. Those implementing acts shall be adopted in accordance with the examination procedure referred to in Article 163(2) of this Regulation.]

NOTES

Inserted by European Parliament and Council Regulation 2015/2424/EU, Art 1(127).

[5.762]
[Article 149
Request for territorial extension subsequent to international registration

1. A request for territorial extension made subsequent to an international registration pursuant to Article 3 ter(2) of the Madrid Protocol may be filed through the intermediary of the Office. The request shall be filed in the language in which the international application was filed pursuant to Article 147 of this Regulation. It shall include indications to substantiate the entitlement to make a designation in accordance with Article 2(1)(ii) and Article 3ter(2) of the Madrid Protocol. The Office shall inform the applicant requesting the territorial extension of the date on which the request for territorial extension was received.

2. The Commission shall adopt implementing acts specifying the detailed requirements regarding the request for territorial extension pursuant to paragraph 1 of this Article. Those implementing acts shall be adopted in accordance with the examination procedure referred to in Article 163(2).

3. Where the request for territorial extension made subsequent to the international registration does not comply with the requirements set out in paragraph 1 and in the implementing act adopted pursuant to paragraph 2, the Office shall invite the applicant to remedy the deficiencies found within such time limit as it may specify. If the deficiencies are not remedied within the time limit fixed by the Office, the Office shall refuse to forward the request to the International Bureau. The Office shall not refuse to forward the request to the International Bureau before the applicant has had the opportunity to correct any deficiency detected in the request.

4. The Office shall forward the request for territorial extension made subsequent to the international registration to the International Bureau as soon as the requirements referred to in paragraph 3 are complied with.]

NOTES

Substituted by European Parliament and Council Regulation 2015/2424/EU, Art 1(128).

[5.763]
Article 150
International fees

Any fees payable to the International Bureau under the Madrid Protocol shall be paid direct to the International Bureau.

SECTION 3
INTERNATIONAL REGISTRATIONS DESIGNATING THE EUROPEAN COMMUNITY

[5.764]
Article 151
Effects of international registrations designating the European Community
1. An international registration designating the European Community shall, from the date of its registration pursuant to Article 3(4) of the Madrid Protocol or from the date of the subsequent designation of the European Community pursuant to Article 3ter (2) of the Madrid Protocol, have the same effect as an application for a Community trade mark.
2. If no refusal has been notified in accordance with Article 5(1) and (2) of the Madrid Protocol or if any such refusal has been withdrawn, the international registration of a mark designating the European Community shall, from the date referred to in paragraph 1, have the same effect as the registration of a mark as a Community trade mark.
3. For the purposes of applying Article 9(3), publication of the particulars of the international registration designating the European Community pursuant to Article 152(1) shall take the place of publication of a Community trade mark application, and publication pursuant to Article 152(2) shall take the place of publication of the registration of a Community trade mark.

NOTES
General amendments to this Regulation: see further the note "General amendments" in the introductory notes to this Regulation *ante*.

[5.765]
Article 152
Publication
1. The Office shall publish the date of registration of a mark designating the European Community pursuant to Article 3(4) of the Madrid Protocol or the date of the subsequent designation of the European Community pursuant to Article 3ter (2) of the Madrid Protocol, the language of filing of the international application and the second language indicated by the applicant, the number of the international registration and the date of publication of such registration in the Gazette published by the International Bureau, a reproduction of the mark and the numbers of the classes of the goods or services in respect of which protection is claimed.
2. If no refusal of protection of an international registration designating the European Community has been notified in accordance with Article 5(1) and (2) of the Madrid Protocol or if any such refusal has been withdrawn, the Office shall publish this fact, together with the number of the international registration and, where applicable, the date of publication of such registration in the Gazette published by the International Bureau.

[5.766]
[Article 153
Seniority claimed in an international application
1. The applicant for an international registration designating the Union may claim, in the international application, the seniority of an earlier trade mark registered in a Member State, including a trade mark registered in the Benelux countries, or registered under international arrangements having effect in a Member State, as provided for in Article 34.
2. The documentation, as specified in the implementing act adopted pursuant to Article 34(5), in support of the seniority claim shall be submitted within three months of the date on which the International Bureau notifies the international registration to the Office. In this regard, Article 34(6) shall apply.
3. Where the holder of the international registration is obliged to be represented before the Office pursuant to Article 92(2), the communication as referred to in paragraph 2 of this Article shall contain the appointment of a representative within the meaning of Article 93(1).
4. Where the Office finds that the seniority claim under paragraph 1 of this Article does not comply with Article 34, or does not comply with the other requirements laid down in this Article, it shall invite the applicant to remedy the deficiencies. If the requirements referred to in the first sentence are not satisfied within the time limit specified by the Office, the right of seniority in respect of that international registration shall be lost. If the deficiencies concern only some of the goods and services, the right of seniority shall be lost only in so far as those goods and services are concerned.
5. The Office shall inform the International Bureau of any declaration of a loss of the right of seniority pursuant to paragraph 4. It shall also inform the International Bureau of any withdrawal or restriction of the seniority claim.
6. Article 34(4) shall apply, unless the right of seniority is declared lost pursuant to paragraph 4 of this Article.]

NOTES
Substituted by European Parliament and Council Regulation 2015/2424/EU, Art 1(129).

[5.767]
[Article 153a
Seniority claimed before the Office
1. The holder of an international registration designating the Union may, as from the date of publication of the effects of such registration pursuant to Article 152(2), claim at the Office the seniority of an earlier trade mark registered in a Member State, including a trade mark registered in the Benelux countries, or registered under international arrangements having effect in a Member State, as provided for in Article 35.
2. When the seniority is claimed before the date referred to in paragraph 1, the seniority claim shall be deemed to have been received by the Office on that date.
3. A seniority claim under paragraph 1 of this Article shall fulfil the requirements referred to in Article 35 and shall contain information to enable its examination against those requirements.
4. If the requirements governing the claiming of seniority referred to in paragraph 3 and specified in the implementing act adopted pursuant to paragraph 6 are not fulfilled, the Office shall invite the holder of the international registration to remedy the deficiencies. If the deficiencies are not remedied within a period to be specified by the Office, the Office shall reject the claim.
5. Where the Office has accepted the seniority claim, or where a seniority claim has been withdrawn or cancelled by the Office, the Office shall inform the International Bureau accordingly.
6. The Commission shall adopt implementing acts specifying the details to be contained in a seniority claim under paragraph 1 of this Article and the details of the information to be notified pursuant to paragraph 5 of this Article. Those implementing acts shall be adopted in accordance with the examination procedure referred to in Article 163(2).]

NOTES
Inserted by European Parliament and Council Regulation 2015/2424/EU, Art 1(130).

[5.768]
[Article 154
Designation of goods and services and examination as to absolute grounds for refusal
1. International registrations designating the Union shall be subject to examination as to their conformity with Article 28(2) to (4) and to absolute grounds for refusal in the same way as applications for EU trade marks.
2. Where an international registration designating the Union is found to be ineligible for protection pursuant to Article 28(4) or Article 37(1) of this Regulation for all or any part of the goods and services for which it has been registered by the International Bureau, the Office shall issue an ex officio provisional notification of refusal to the International Bureau, in accordance with Article 5(1) and (2) of the Madrid Protocol.
3. Where the holder of an international registration is obliged to be represented before the Office pursuant to Article 92(2), the notification referred to in paragraph 2 of this Article shall contain an invitation to appoint a representative within the meaning of Article 93(1).
4. The notification of provisional refusal shall state the reasons on which it is based, and shall specify a time period by which the holder of the international registration may submit his observations and, if appropriate, shall appoint a representative. The time period shall start on the day on which the Office issues the provisional refusal.
5. Where the Office finds that the international application designating the Union does not contain the indication of a second language pursuant to Article 161b of this Regulation, the Office shall issue an ex officio provisional notification of refusal to the International Bureau pursuant to Article 5(1) and (2) of the Madrid Protocol.
6. Where the holder of an international registration fails to overcome the ground for refusing protection within the time limit or, if appropriate, to appoint a representative or to indicate a second language, the Office shall refuse the protection in whole or for part of the goods and services for which the international registration is registered. The refusal of protection shall take the place of a refusal of an EU trade mark application. The decision shall be subject to appeal in accordance with Articles 58 to 65.
7. Where, as of the start of the opposition period referred to in Article 156(2), the Office has not issued an ex officio provisional notification of refusal pursuant to paragraph 2 of this Article, it shall send a statement to the International Bureau, indicating that the examination of absolute grounds of refusal pursuant to Article 37 has been completed but that the international registration is still subject to oppositions or observations of third parties. This interim statement shall be without prejudice to the right of the Office to re-open the examination of absolute grounds on its own initiative any time before the final statement of grant of protection has been issued.
8. The Commission shall adopt implementing acts specifying the details to be contained in the notification of ex officio provisional refusal of protection to be sent to the International Bureau and in the final communications to be sent to the International Bureau on the final grant or refusal of protection. Those implementing acts shall be adopted in accordance with the examination procedure referred to in Article 163(2).]

NOTES
Substituted by European Parliament and Council Regulation 2015/2424/EU, Art 1(131).

[5.769]
[Article 154a
Collective and certification marks
1. Where an international registration is based on a basic application or basic registration relating to a collective mark, certification mark or guarantee mark, the international registration designating the Union shall be dealt with as an EU collective mark or as an EU certification mark, whichever is applicable.
2. The holder of the international registration shall submit the regulations governing the use of the mark, as provided for in Articles 67 and 74b, directly to the Office within two months of the date on which the International Bureau notifies the international registration to the Office.
3. The Commission shall be empowered to adopt delegated acts in accordance with Article 163a specifying the details of the procedure concerning international registrations based on a basic application or basic registration relating to a collective mark, certification mark or guarantee mark.]

NOTES
Inserted by European Parliament and Council Regulation 2015/2424/EU, Art 1(132).

[5.770]
Article 155
Search
1. Once the Office has received a notification of an international registration designating the European Community, it shall draw up a Community search report as provided for in Article 38(1) [provided that a request for a search report, pursuant to Article 38(1), is made to the Office within one month of the date of notification.].
2. As soon as the Office has received a notification of an international registration designating the European Community, the Office shall transmit a copy thereof to the central industrial property office of each Member State which has informed the Office of its decision to operate a search in its own register of trade marks as provided for in Article 38(2) [provided that a request for a search report, pursuant to Article 38(2), is made to the Office within one month of the date of notification and the search fee is paid within the same period.].
3. Article 38(3) to (6) shall apply mutatis mutandis.
4. The Office shall inform the proprietors of any earlier Community trade marks or Community trade mark applications cited in the Community search report of the publication of the international registration designating the European Community as provided for in Article 152(1). [This shall apply whether or not the holder of the international registration has requested to receive the EU search report, unless the proprietor of an earlier registration or application requests not to receive the notification.]

NOTES
General amendments to this Regulation: see further the note "General amendments" in the introductory notes to this Regulation *ante*.
Paras 1, 2, 4: words in square brackets inserted by European Parliament and Council Regulation 2015/2424/EU, Art 1(133).

[5.771]
Article 156
Opposition
1. International registration designating the European Community shall be subject to opposition in the same way as published Community trade mark applications.
[2. Notice of opposition shall be filed within a period of three months which shall begin one month following the date of the publication pursuant to Article 152(1). The opposition shall not be considered as duly entered until the opposition fee has been paid.]
3. Refusal of protection shall take the place of refusal of a Community trade mark application.
[4. The Commission shall be empowered to adopt delegated acts in accordance with Article 163a specifying the procedure for the filing and examination of an opposition, including the necessary communications to be made to the International Bureau.]

NOTES
General amendments to this Regulation: see further the note "General amendments" in the introductory notes to this Regulation *ante*.
Paras 2, 4: substituted by European Parliament and Council Regulation 2015/2424/EU, Art 1(134).

[5.772]
Article 157
Replacement of a Community trade mark by an international registration
The Office shall, upon request, enter a notice in the Register that a Community trade mark is deemed to have been replaced by an international registration in accordance with Article 4bis of the Madrid Protocol.

NOTES

General amendments to this Regulation: see further the note "General amendments" in the introductory notes to this Regulation *ante*.

[5.773]

Article 158

Invalidation of the effects of an international registration

1. The effects of an international registration designating the European Community may be declared invalid.

2. The application for invalidation of the effects of an international registration designating the European Community shall take the place of an application for a declaration of revocation as provided for in Article 51 or for a declaration of invalidity as provided for in Article 52 or Article 53.

[3. Where pursuant to Article 57 or Article 100 of this Regulation and this Article, the effects of an international registration designating the Union have been declared invalid by means of a final decision, the Office shall notify the International Bureau in accordance with Article 5(6) of the Madrid Protocol.

4. The Commission shall adopt implementing acts specifying the details to be contained in the notification to be made to the International Bureau pursuant to paragraph 3 of this Article. Those implementing acts shall be adopted in accordance with the examination procedure referred to in Article 163(2).]

NOTES

Paras 3, 4: added by European Parliament and Council Regulation 2015/2424/EU, Art 1(135).

[5.774]

[Article 158a

Legal effect of registration of transfers

The recordal of a change in the ownership of an international registration on the International Register shall have the same effect as the entry of a transfer in the Register pursuant to Article 17.]

NOTES

Inserted by European Parliament and Council Regulation 2015/2424/EU, Art 1(136).

[5.775]

[Article 158b

Legal effect of registration of licences and other rights

The recordal of a licence or a restriction of the holder's right of disposal in respect of an international registration in the International Register shall have the same effect as the registration of a right in rem, a levy of execution, insolvency proceedings or a licence in the Register pursuant to Articles 19, 20, 21 and 22 respectively.]

NOTES

Inserted by European Parliament and Council Regulation 2015/2424/EU, Art 1(136).

[5.776]

[Article 158c

Examination of requests for registration of transfers, licences or restrictions of a holder's right of disposal

The Office shall transmit requests to register a change in ownership, a licence or a restriction of the holder's right of disposal, the amendment or cancellation of a licence or the removal of a restriction of the holder's right of disposal which have been filed with it to the International Bureau, if accompanied by appropriate proof of the transfer, licence, or the restriction of the right of disposal, or by proof that the licence no longer exists or that it has been amended, or that the restriction of the right of disposal has been removed.]

NOTES

Inserted by European Parliament and Council Regulation 2015/2424/EU, Art 1(136).

[5.777]

Article 159

Conversion of a designation of the European Community through an international registration into a national trade mark application or into a designation of Member States

1. Where a designation of the European Community through an international registration has been refused or ceases to have effect, the holder of the international registration may request the conversion of the designation of the European Community:

(a) into a national trade mark application pursuant to Articles 112, 113 and 114;

[(b) *into a designation of a Member State party to the Madrid Protocol, provided that on the date when conversion was requested it was possible to have designated that Member State directly under the Madrid Protocol. Articles 112, 113 and 114 of this Regulation shall apply.]*

[2. *The national trade mark application or the designation of a Member State party to the Madrid Protocol resulting from the conversion of the designation of the Union through an international registration shall enjoy, in respect of the Member State concerned, the date of the international registration pursuant to Article 3(4) of the Madrid Protocol or the date of the extension to the Union pursuant to Article 3ter(2) of the Madrid Protocol, if the latter was made subsequent to the international registration, or the date of priority of that registration and, where appropriate, the seniority of a trade mark of that State claimed under Article 153 of this Regulation.]*

3. *The request for conversion shall be published.*

[4. *The request for conversion of an international registration designating the Union into a national trade mark application shall include the information and indications referred to in Article 113(1).*

5. *Where conversion is requested pursuant to this Article and Article 112(5) of this Regulation following a failure to renew the international registration, the request referred to in paragraph 4 of this Article shall contain an indication to that effect and the date on which the protection expired. The period of three months provided for in Article 112(5) of this Regulation shall begin to run on the day following the last day on which the renewal may still be effected pursuant to Article 7(4) of the Madrid Protocol.*

6. *Article 113(3) and (5) shall apply to the request for conversion referred to in paragraph 4 of this Article mutatis mutandis.*

7. *The request for conversion of an international registration designating the Union into a designation of a Member State party to the Madrid Protocol shall include the indications and elements referred to in paragraphs 4 and 5.*

8. *Article 113(3) shall apply to the request for conversion referred to in paragraph 7 of this Article mutatis mutandis. The Office shall also reject the request for conversion where the conditions to designate the Member State which is a party to the Madrid Protocol or to the Madrid Agreement were fulfilled neither on the date of the designation of the Union nor on the date on which the application for conversion was received or, pursuant to the last sentence of Article 113(1), is deemed to have been received by the Office.*

9. *Where the request for conversion referred to in paragraph 7 complies with the requirements of this Regulation and rules adopted pursuant to it, the Office shall transmit the request without delay to the International Bureau. The Office shall inform the holder of the international registration of the date of transmission.*

10. *The Commission shall adopt implementing acts specifying:*

(a) *the details to be contained in the requests for conversion referred to in paragraphs 4 and 7;*

(b) *the details to be contained in the publication of the requests for conversion pursuant to paragraph 3.*

Those implementing acts shall be adopted in accordance with the examination procedure referred to in Article 163(2).]

NOTES

Para 1: point (b) substituted by European Parliament and Council Regulation 2015/2424/EU, Art 1(137)(a).

Para 2: substituted by European Parliament and Council Regulation 2015/2424/EU, Art 1(137)(b).

Paras 4–10: added by European Parliament and Council Regulation 2015/2424/EU, Art 1(137)(c).

[5.778]

Article 160

Use of a mark subject of an international registration

For the purposes of applying Article 15(1), Article 42(2), Article 51(1)(a) and Article 57(2), the date of publication pursuant to Article 152(2) shall take the place of the date of registration for the purpose of establishing the date as from which the mark which is the subject of an international registration designating the European Community must be put to genuine use in the Community.

[5.779]

Article 161

Transformation

1. Subject to paragraph 2, the provisions applicable to Community trade mark applications shall apply mutatis mutandis to applications for transformation of an international registration into a Community trade mark application pursuant to Article 9quinquies of the Madrid Protocol.

2. When the application for transformation relates to an international registration designating the European Community the particulars of which have been published pursuant to Article 152(2), Articles 37 to 42 shall not apply.

[3. In order to be considered a transformation of an international registration which has been cancelled at the request of the office of origin by the International Bureau pursuant to Article 9quinquies of the Madrid Protocol, an EU trade mark application shall contain an indication to that effect. That indication shall be made when filing the application.

4. Where, in the course of the examination in accordance with Article 36(1)(b), the Office finds that the application was not filed within three months of the date on which the international registration was cancelled by the International Bureau; or the goods and services for which the EU trade mark is to be registered are not contained in the list of goods and services for which the international registration was registered in respect of the Union, the Office shall invite the applicant to remedy the deficiencies.

5. If the deficiencies referred to in paragraph 4 are not remedied within the time period specified by the Office, the right to the date of the international registration or the territorial extension and, if any, of the priority of the international registration shall be lost.

6. The Commission shall adopt implementing acts specifying the details to be contained in an application for transformation pursuant to paragraph 3 of this Article. Those implementing acts shall be adopted in accordance with the examination procedure referred to in Article 163(2).]

NOTES

General amendments to this Regulation: see further the note "General amendments" in the introductory notes to this Regulation *ante*.

Paras 3–6: added by European Parliament and Council Regulation 2015/2424/EU, Art 1(138).

[5.780]

[Article 161a

Communication with the International Bureau

Communication with the International Bureau shall be in a manner and format agreed on between the International Bureau and the Office, and preferably be by electronic means. Any reference to forms shall be construed as including forms made available in electronic format.]

NOTES

Inserted by European Parliament and Council Regulation 2015/2424/EU, Art 1(139).

[5.781]

[Article 161b

Use of languages

For the purpose of applying this Regulation, and rules adopted pursuant to it, to international registrations designating the Union, the language of filing of the international application shall be the language of the proceedings within the meaning of Article 119(4), and the second language indicated in the international application shall be the second language within the meaning of Article 119(3).]

NOTES

Inserted by European Parliament and Council Regulation 2015/2424/EU, Art 1(139).

TITLE XIV
FINAL PROVISIONS

Article 162 *(Repealed by European Parliament and Council Regulation 2015/2424/EU, Art 1(140).)*

[5.782]

[Article 163

Committee Procedure

1. The Commission shall be assisted by a Committee on Implementation Rules. That committee shall be a committee within the meaning of Regulation (EU) No 182/2011 of the European Parliament and of the Council.[1]

2. Where reference is made to this paragraph, Article 5 of Regulation (EU) No 182/2011 shall apply.]

NOTES

Substituted by European Parliament and Council Regulation 2015/2424/EU, Art 1(141).

[1] Regulation (EU) No 182/2011 of the European Parliament and of the Council of 16 February 2011 laying down the rules and general principles concerning mechanisms for control by the Member States of the Commission's exercise of implementing powers (OJ L 55, 28.2.2011, p. 13).'.

[5.783]

[Article 163a

Exercise of the delegation

1. The power to adopt delegated acts is conferred on the Commission subject to the conditions laid down in this Article.

2. The delegation of power referred to in Article 42a, Article 43(3), Articles 57a and 65a, Article 77(4), 78(6), 79(5), 79b(2), 79c(5), 80(3), and 82a(3), Articles 93a and 136b, and Articles 154a(3) and 156(4) shall be conferred on the Commission for an indeterminate period of time from 23 March 2016. It is of particular importance that the Commission follow its usual practice and carry out consultations with experts, including Member States' experts, before adopting those delegated acts.

3. The delegation of power referred to in paragraph 2 may be revoked at any time by the European Parliament or by the Council. A decision to revoke shall put an end to the delegation of the power specified in that decision. It shall take effect the day following the publication of the decision in the Official Journal of the European Union or at a later date specified therein. It shall not affect the validity of any delegated acts already in force.

4. As soon as it adopts a delegated act, the Commission shall notify it simultaneously to the European Parliament and to the Council.

5. A delegated act adopted pursuant to Article 42a, Article 43(3), Articles 57a and 65a, Articles 77(4), 78(6), 79(5), 79b(2), 79c(5), 80(3), and 82a(3), Articles 93a and 136b, and Articles 154a(3) and 156(4) shall enter into force only if no objection has been expressed either by the European Parliament or the Council within a period of two months of notification of that act to the European Parliament and the Council or if, before the expiry of that period, the European Parliament and the Council have both informed the Commission that they will not object. That period shall be extended by 2 months at the initiative of the European Parliament or the Council.]

NOTES

Inserted by European Parliament and Council Regulation 2015/2424/EU, Art 1(142).

Article 164 *(Repealed by European Parliament and Council Regulation 2015/2424/EU, Art 1(143).)*

[5.784]

Article 165

Provisions relating to the enlargement of the Community

[1. As of the date of accession of Bulgaria, the Czech Republic, Estonia, Croatia, Cyprus, Latvia, Lithuania, Hungary, Malta, Poland, Romania, Slovenia and Slovakia (hereinafter referred to as "new Member State(s)"), a Community trade mark registered or applied for pursuant to this Regulation before their respective date of accession shall be extended to the territory of those Member States in order to have equal effect throughout the Community.]

2. The registration of a Community trade mark which is under application at the date of accession may not be refused on the basis of any of the absolute grounds for refusal listed in Article 7(1), if these grounds became applicable merely because of the accession of a new Member State.

3. Where an application for the registration of a Community trade mark has been filed during the six months prior to the date of accession, notice of opposition may be given pursuant to Article 41 where an earlier trade mark or another earlier right within the meaning of Article 8 was acquired in a new Member State prior to accession, provided that it was acquired in good faith and that the filing date or, where applicable, the priority date or the date of acquisition in the new Member State of the earlier trade mark or other earlier right precedes the filing date or, where applicable, the priority date of the Community trade mark applied for.

4. A Community trade mark as referred to in paragraph 1 may not be declared invalid:

(a) pursuant to Article 52 if the grounds for invalidity became applicable merely because of the accession of a new Member State;

(b) pursuant to Article 53(1) and (2) if the earlier national right was registered, applied for or acquired in a new Member State prior to the date of accession.

5. The use of a Community trade mark as referred to in paragraph 1 may be prohibited pursuant to Articles 110 and 111, if the earlier trade mark or other earlier right was registered, applied for or acquired in good faith in the new Member State prior to the date of accession of that State; or, where applicable, has a priority date prior to the date of accession of that State.

NOTES

General amendments to this Regulation: see further the note "General amendments" in the introductory notes to this Regulation *ante*.

Para 1: substituted by Art 15, Annex III.2.I of the Treaty between the Member States of the European Union and the Republic of Croatia concerning the accession of the Republic of Croatia to the European Union.

[5.785]

[Article 165a

Evaluation and review

1. By 24 March 2021, and every five years thereafter, the Commission shall evaluate the implementation of this Regulation.

2. The evaluation shall review the legal framework for cooperation between the Office and the central industrial property offices of the Member States and the Benelux Office for Intellectual Property, paying particular attention to the financing mechanism laid down in Article 123c. The

evaluation shall further assess the impact, effectiveness and efficiency of the Office and its working practices. The evaluation shall, in particular, address the possible need to modify the mandate of the Office, and the financial implications of any such modification.
3. The Commission shall forward the evaluation report together with its conclusions drawn on the basis of that report to the European Parliament, the Council and the Management Board. The findings of the evaluation shall be made public.
4. On the occasion of every second evaluation, there shall be an assessment of the results achieved by the Office having regard to its objectives, mandate and tasks.]

NOTES

Inserted by European Parliament and Council Regulation 2015/2424/EU, Art 1(144).

[5.786]
Article 166
Repeal

Regulation (EC) No 40/94, as amended by the instruments set out in Annex I, is repealed.

References to the repealed Regulation shall be construed as references to this Regulation and shall be read in accordance with the correlation table in Annex II.

[5.787]
Article 167
Entry into force

1. This Regulation shall enter into force on the 20th day following its publication in the Official Journal of the European Union.
2. The Member States shall within three years following entry into force of Regulation (EC) No 40/94 take the necessary measures for the purpose of implementing Articles 95 and 114.

This Regulation shall be binding in its entirety and directly applicable in all Member States.

[ANNEX -I

[5.788]
Amount of Fees

A. The fees to be paid to the Office under this Regulation shall be as follows (in EUR):

1. *Basic fee for the application for an individual EU trade mark (Article 26(2)):*
   EUR 1,000
2. *Basic fee for the application for an individual EU trade mark by electronic means (Article 26(2)):*
   EUR 850
3. *Fee for the second class of goods and services for an individual EU trade mark (Article 26(2)):*
   EUR 50
4. *Fee for each class of goods and services exceeding two for an individual EU trade mark (Article 26(2)):*
   EUR 150
5. *Basic fee for the application for an EU collective mark or an EU certification mark (Article 26(2) and Article 66(3) or Article 74a(3)):*
   EUR 1,800
6. *Basic fee for the application for an EU collective mark or an EU certification mark by electronic means (Article 26(2) and Article 66(3) or Article 74a(3)):*
   EUR 1,500
7. *Fee for the second class of goods and services for an EU collective mark or an EU certification mark: (Article 26(2) and Article 66(3) or Article 74a(3)):*
   EUR 50
8. *Fee for each class of goods and services exceeding two for an EU collective mark or an EU certification mark (Article 26(2) and 66(3) or Article 74a(3)):*
   EUR 150
9. *Search fee for an EU trade mark application (Article 38(2)) or for an international registration designating the Union (Article 38(2) and Article 155(2)): EUR 12 multiplied by the number of central industrial property offices referred to in Article 38(2); that amount, and the subsequent changes, shall be published by the Office in the Official Journal of the Office.*
10. *Opposition fee (Article 41(3)):*
    EUR 320
11. *Basic fee for the renewal of an individual EU trade mark (Article 47(3)):*
    EUR 1,000
12. *Basic fee for the renewal of an individual EU trade mark by electronic means (Article 47(3)):*
    EUR 850

13. *Fee for the renewal of the second class of goods and services for an individual EU trade mark (Article 47(3)):*
EUR 50
14. *Fee for the renewal of each class of goods and services exceeding two for an individual EU trade mark (Article 47(3)):*
EUR 150
15. *Basic fee for the renewal of an EU collective mark or an EU certification mark (Article 47(3) and Article 66(3) or Article 74a(3):*
EUR 1,800
16. *Basic fee for the renewal of an EU collective mark or an EU certification mark by electronic means (Article 47(3) and Article 66(3) or Article 74a(3)):*
EUR 1,500
17. *Fee for the renewal of the second class of goods and services for an EU collective mark or an EU certification mark (Article 47(3) and Article 66(3) or Article 74a(3)):*
EUR 50
18. *Fee for the renewal of each class of goods and services exceeding two for an EU collective mark or an EU certification mark (Article 47(3) and Article 66(3) or Article 74a(3)):*
EUR 150
19. *Additional fee for the late payment of the renewal fee or the late submission of the request for renewal (Article 47(3)): 25% of the belated renewal fee, subject to a maximum of EUR 1,500*
20. *Fee for the application for revocation or for a declaration of invalidity (Article 56(2)):*
EUR 630
21. *Appeal fee (Article 60(1)):*
EUR 720
22. *Fee for the application of restitutio in integrum (Article 81(3)):*
EUR 200
23. *Fee for the application for the conversion of an EU trade mark application or an EU trade mark (Article 113(1), also in conjunction with Article 159(1)):*
(a) *into a national trade mark application;*
(b) *into a designation of Member States under the Madrid Protocol:*

EUR 200

24. *Fee for continuation of proceedings (Article 82(1)):*
EUR 400
25. *Fee for the declaration of division of a registered EU trade mark (Article 49(4) or an application for an EU trade mark (Article 44(4)):*
EUR 250
26. *Fee for the application for the registration of a licence or another right in respect of a registered EU trade mark (before 1 October 2017, Rule 33(2) of Regulation (EC) No 2868/95; and from that date, Article 22a(2)) or an application for an EU trade mark (before 1 October 2017, Rule 33(2) of Regulation (EC) No 2868/95; and from that date, Article 22a(2)):*
(a) *grant of a licence;*
(b) *transfer of a licence;*
(c) *creation of a right in rem;*
(d) *transfer of a right in rem;*
(e) *levy of execution:*

EUR 200 per registration, but where multiple requests are submitted in the same application or at the same time, not to exceed a total of EUR 1,000

27. *Fee for the cancellation of the registration of a licence or other right (before 1 October 2017, Rule 35(3) of Regulation (EC) No 2868/95; and from that date, Article 24a(3)): EUR 200 per cancellation, but where multiple requests are submitted in the same application or at the same time, not to exceed a total of EUR 1,000*
28. *Fee for the alteration of a registered EU trade mark (Article 48(4)):*
EUR 200
29. *Fee for the issue of a copy of the application for an EU trade mark (Article 88(7)), a copy of the certificate of registration (Article (45(2)), or an extract from the register (Article 87(7)):*
(a) *uncertified copy or extract:*

EUR 10

(b) *certified copy or extract:*

EUR 30

30. *Fee for the inspection of the files (Article 88(6)):*
EUR 30
31. *Fee for the issue of copies of file documents (Article 88(7)):*
(a) *uncertified copy:*

EUR 10

(b) *certified copy:*

EUR 30
plus per page, exceeding 10
EUR 1

32. *Fee for the communication of information in a file (Article 88(9)):*
    EUR 10
33. *Fee for the review of the determination of the procedural costs to be refunded (before 1 October 2017, Rule 94(4) of Regulation (EC) No 2868/95; and from that date, Article 85(7)):*
    EUR 100
34. *Fee for the filing of an international application at the Office (before 1 October 2017, Article 147(5); and from that date, Article 147(4)):*
    EUR 300

B. Fees to be paid to the International Bureau

I. Individual fee for an international registration designating the Union

1. *The applicant for an international registration designating the Union shall be required to pay to the International Bureau an individual fee for the designation of the Union in accordance with Article 8(7) of the Madrid Protocol.*
2. *The holder of an international registration who files a request for territorial extension designating the Union made subsequent to the international registration shall be required to pay to the International Bureau an individual fee for the designation of the Union in accordance with Article 8(7) of the Madrid Protocol.*
3. *The amount of the fee under B.I.1 or B.I.2 shall be the equivalent in Swiss Francs, as established by the Director-General of the WIPO pursuant to Rule 35(2) of the Common Regulations under the Madrid Agreement and Protocol, of the following amounts:*
   (a) *for an individual trade mark: EUR 820 plus, where applicable, EUR 50 for the second class of goods and services and EUR 150 for each class of goods and services contained in the international registration exceeding two;*
   (b) *for a collective mark or a certification mark: EUR 1 400 plus, where applicable, EUR 50 for the second class of goods and services and EUR 150 for each class of goods or services exceeding two.*

II. Individual fee for a renewal of an international registration designating the Union

1. *The holder of an international registration designating the Union shall be required to pay to the International Bureau, as a part of the fees for a renewal of the international registration, an individual fee for the designation of the Union in accordance with Article 8(7) of the Madrid Protocol.*
2. *The amount of the fee referred to in B.II.1 shall be the equivalent in Swiss Francs, as established by the Director-General of the WIPO pursuant to Rule 35(2) of the Common Regulations under the Madrid Agreement and Protocol, of the following amounts:*
   (a) *for an individual trade mark: EUR 820 plus, where applicable, EUR 50 for the second class of goods and services and EUR 150 for each class of goods and services contained in the international registration exceeding two;*
   (b) *for a collective mark or a certification mark: EUR 1 400 plus, where applicable, EUR 50 for the second class of goods and services and EUR 150 for each class of goods and services contained in the international registration exceeding two.]*

NOTES

Annex -I inserted by European Parliament and Council Regulation 2015/2424/EU, Art 1(145), Annex.

ANNEX I
REPEALED REGULATION WITH LIST OF ITS SUCCESSIVE AMENDMENTS

[5.789]

(referred to in Article 166)

Council Regulation (EC) No 40/94
(OJ L11, 14.1.1994, p 1)

Council Regulation (EC) No 3288/94 (OJ L349, 31.12.1994, p 83)	
Council Regulation (EC) No 807/2003 (OJ L122, 16.5.2003, p 36)	*Only point 48 of Annex III*
Council Regulation (EC) No 1653/2003 (OJ L245, 29.9.2003, p 36)	
Council Regulation (EC) No 1992/2003	

(OJ L296, 14.11.2003, p 1)
Council Regulation (EC) No 422/2004
(OJ L70, 9.3.2004, p 1)
Council Regulation (EC) No 1891/2006 *Only Article 1*
(OJ L386, 29.12.2006, p 14)
Annex II, Part 4 (C)(I) of the 2003 Act of Accession
(OJ L236, 23.9.2003, p 342)
Annex III, Point 1.1 of the 2005 Act of Accession
(OJ L157, 21.6.2005, p 231)

ANNEX II
CORRELATION TABLE

[5.790]

Regulation 40/94/EC	*This Regulation*
Articles 1 to 14	*Articles 1 to 14*
Article 15(1)	*Article 15(1), first subparagraph*
Article 15(2), introductory words	*Article 15(1), second subparagraph, introductory words*
Article 15(2), point a	*Article 15(1), second subparagraph, point a*
Article 15(2), point b	*Article 15(1), second subparagraph, point b*
Article 15(3)	*Article 15(2)*
Articles 16 to 36	*Articles 16 to 36*
Article 37	—
Article 38	*Article 37*
Article 39	*Article 38*
Article 40	*Article 39*
Article 41	*Article 40*
Article 42	*Article 41*
Article 43	*Article 42*
Article 44	*Article 43*
Article 44a	*Article 44*
Articles 45 to 48	*Articles 45 to 48*
Article 48a	*Article 49*
Article 49	*Article 50*
Article 50	*Article 51*
Article 51	*Article 52*
Article 52	*Article 53*
Article 53	*Article 54*
Article 54	*Article 55*
Article 55	*Article 56*
Article 56	*Article 57*
Article 57	*Article 58*
Article 58	*Article 59*
Article 59	*Article 60*
Article 60	*Article 61*
Article 60a	*Article 62*
Article 61	*Article 63*
Article 62	*Article 64*
Article 63	*Article 65*
Article 64	*Article 66*
Article 65	*Article 67*
Article 66	*Article 68*
Article 67	*Article 69*

Regulation 40/94/EC	*This Regulation*
Article 68	*Article 70*
Article 69	*Article 71*
Article 70	*Article 72*
Article 71	*Article 73*
Article 72	*Article 74*
Article 73	*Article 75*
Article 74	*Article 76*
Article 75	*Article 77*
Article 76	*Article 78*
Article 77	*Article 79*
Article 77a	*Article 80*
Article 78	*Article 81*
Article 78a	*Article 82*
Article 79	*Article 83*
Article 80	*Article 84*
Article 81	*Article 85*
Article 82	*Article 86*
Article 83	*Article 87*
Article 84	*Article 88*
Article 85	*Article 89*
Article 86	*Article 90*
Article 87	*Article 91*
Article 88	*Article 92*
Article 89	*Article 93*
Article 90	*Article 94*
Article 91	*Article 95*
Article 92	*Article 96*
Article 93	*Article 97*
Article 94(1), introductory wording	*Article 98(1), introductory wording*
Article 94(1), first indent	*Article 98(1)(a)*
Article 94(1), second indent	*Article 98(1)(b)*
Article 94(2)	*Article 98(2)*
Article 95	*Article 99*
Article 96	*Article 100*
Article 97	*Article 101*
Article 98	*Article 102*
Article 99	*Article 103*
Article 100	*Article 104*
Article 101	*Article 105*
Article 102	*Article 106*
Article 103	*Article 107*
Article 104	*Article 108*
Article 105	*Article 109*
Article 106	*Article 110*
Article 107	*Article 111*
Article 108	*Article 112*
Article 109	*Article 113*
Article 110	*Article 114*
Article 111	*Article 115*
Article 112	*Article 116*
Article 113	*Article 117*

Regulation 40/94/EC	This Regulation
Article 114	Article 118
Article 115	Article 119
Article 116	Article 120
Article 117	Article 121
Article 118	Article 122
Article 118a	Article 123
Article 119	Article 124
Article 120	Article 125
Article 121(1) and (2)	Article 126(1) and (2)
Article 121(3)	—
Article 121(4)	Article 126(3)
Article 121(5)	Article 126(4)
Article 121(6)	Article 126(5)
Article 122	Article 127
Article 123	Article 128
Article 124	Article 129
Article 125	Article 130
Article 126	Article 131
Article 127	Article 132
Article 128	Article 133
Article 129	Article 134
Article 130	Article 135
Article 131	Article 136
Article 132	Article 137
Article 133	Article 138
Article 134	Article 139
Article 135	Article 140
Article 136	Article 141
Article 137	Article 142
Article 138	Article 143
Article 139	Article 144
Article 140	Article 145
Article 141	Article 146
Article 142	Article 147
Article 143	Article 148
Article 144	Article 149
Article 145	Article 150
Article 146	Article 151
Article 147	Article 152
Article 148	Article 153
Article 149	Article 154
Article 150	Article 155
Article 151	Article 156
Article 152	Article 157
Article 153	Article 158
Article 154	Article 159
Article 155	Article 160
Article 156	Article 161
Article 157(1)	Article 162(1)
Article 157(2), introductory wording	Article 162(2), introductory wording
Article 157(2)(2)	Article 162(2)(a)

Regulation 40/94/EC	*This Regulation*
Article 157(2)(3)	*Article 162(2)(b)*
Article 157(2)(5)	*Article 162(2)(c)*
Article 157(2)(6)	*Article 162(2)(d)*
Article 157(2)(7)	*Article 162(2)(e)*
Article 157(2)(8)	*Article 162(2)(f)*
Article 157(2)(9)	*Article 162(2)(g)*
Article 157(2)(10)	*Article 162(2)(h)*
Article 157(2)(11)	*Article 162(2)(i)*
Article 157(2)(12)	*Article 162(2)(j)*
Article 157(2)(13)	*Article 162(2)(k)*
Article 157(2)(14)	*Article 162(2)(l)*
Article 157(3)	*Article 162(3)*
Article 158	*Article 163*
Article 159	*Article 164*
Article 159a(1), (2) and (3)	*Article 165(1), (2) and (3)*
Article 159a(4), initial wording	*Article 165(4), initial wording*
Article 159a(4), first indent	*Article 165(4)(a)*
Article 159a(4), second indent	*Article 165(4)(b)*
Article 159a(5)	*Article 165(5)*
—	*Article 166*
Article 160(1)	*Article 167(1)*
Article 160(2)	*Article 167(2)*
Article 160(3) and (4)	—
—	*Annex I*
—	*Annex II*

DIRECTIVE OF THE EUROPEAN PARLIAMENT AND OF THE COUNCIL

(2015/2436/EU)

of 16 December 2015

to approximate the laws of the Member States relating to trade marks

(Recast)

(Text with EEA relevance)

NOTES

Date of publication in OJ: OJ L336, 23.12.2015, p 1.

THE EUROPEAN PARLIAMENT AND THE COUNCIL OF THE EUROPEAN UNION,

Having regard to the Treaty on the Functioning of the European Union, and in particular Article 114(1) thereof,

Having regard to the proposal from the European Commission,

After transmission of the draft legislative act to the national parliaments,

Having regard to the opinion of the European Economic and Social Committee,[1]

Acting in accordance with the ordinary legislative procedure,[2]

Whereas:

(1) A number of amendments should be made to Directive 2008/95/EC of the European Parliament and of the Council.[3] In the interests of clarity, that Directive should be recast.

(2) Directive 2008/95/EC has harmonised central provisions of substantive trade mark law which at the time of adoption were considered as most directly affecting the functioning of the internal market by impeding the free movement of goods and the freedom to provide services in the Union.

(3) Trade mark protection in the Member States coexists with protection available at Union level through European Union trade marks ('EU trade marks') which are unitary in character and valid throughout the Union as laid down in Council Regulation (EC) No 207/2009.[4] The coexistence and balance of trade mark systems at national and Union level in fact constitutes a cornerstone of the Union's approach to intellectual property protection.

(4) Further to the Commission's communication of 16 July 2008 on an industrial property rights strategy for Europe, the Commission carried out a comprehensive evaluation of the overall functioning of the trade mark system in Europe as a whole, covering Union and national levels and the interrelation between the two.

(5) In its conclusions of 25 May 2010 on the future revision of the trade mark system in the European Union, the Council called on the Commission to present proposals for the revision of Regulation (EC) No 207/2009 and Directive 2008/95/EC. The revision of that Directive should include measures to make it more consistent with Regulation (EC) No 207/2009, which would thus reduce the areas of divergence within the trade mark system in Europe as a whole, while maintaining national trade mark protection as an attractive option for applicants. In this context, the complementary relationship between the EU trade mark system and national trade mark systems should be ensured.

(6) The Commission concluded in its communication of 24 May 2011 entitled 'A single market for intellectual property rights' that in order to meet increased demands from stakeholders for faster, higher quality, more streamlined trade mark registration systems, which are also more consistent, user friendly, publicly accessible and technologically up to date, there is a necessity to modernise the trade mark system in the Union as a whole and adapt it to the internet era.

(7) Consultation and evaluation for the purpose of this Directive has revealed that, in spite of the previous partial harmonisation of national laws, there remain areas where further harmonisation could have a positive impact on competitiveness and growth.

(8) In order to serve the objective of fostering and creating a well-functioning internal market and to facilitate acquiring and protecting trade marks in the Union, to the benefit of the growth and the competitiveness of European businesses, in particular small and medium-sized enterprises, it is necessary to go beyond the limited scope of approximation achieved by Directive 2008/95/EC and extend approximation to other aspects of substantive trade mark law governing trade marks protected through registration pursuant to Regulation (EC) No 207/2009.

(9) For the purpose of making trade mark registrations throughout the Union easier to obtain and administer, it is essential to approximate not only provisions of substantive law but also procedural rules. Therefore, the principal procedural rules in the area of trade mark registration in the Member States and in the EU trade mark system should be aligned. As regards procedures under national law, it is sufficient to lay down general principles, leaving the Member States free to establish more specific rules.

(10) It is essential to ensure that registered trade marks enjoy the same protection under the legal systems of all the Member States. In line with the extensive protection granted to EU trade marks which have a reputation in the Union, extensive protection should also be granted at national level to all registered trade marks which have a reputation in the Member State concerned.

(11) This Directive should not deprive the Member States of the right to continue to protect trade marks acquired through use but should take them into account only with regard to their relationship with trade marks acquired by registration.

(12) Attainment of the objectives of this approximation of laws requires that the conditions for obtaining and continuing to hold a registered trade mark be, in general, identical in all Member States.

(13) To this end, it is necessary to list examples of signs which are capable of constituting a trade mark, provided that such signs are capable of distinguishing the goods or services of one undertaking from those of other undertakings. In order to fulfil the objectives of the registration system for trade marks, namely to ensure legal certainty and sound administration, it is also essential to require that the sign is capable of being represented in a manner which is clear, precise, self-contained, easily accessible, intelligible, durable and objective. A sign should therefore be permitted to be represented in any appropriate form using generally available technology, and thus not necessarily by graphic means, as long as the representation offers satisfactory guarantees to that effect.

(14) Furthermore, the grounds for refusal or invalidity concerning the trade mark itself, including the absence of any distinctive character, or concerning conflicts between the trade mark and earlier rights, should be listed in an exhaustive manner, even if some of those grounds are listed as an option for the Member States which should therefore be able to maintain or introduce them in their legislation.

(15) In order to ensure that the levels of protection afforded to geographical indications by Union legislation and national law are applied in a uniform and exhaustive manner in the examination of absolute and relative grounds for refusal throughout the Union, this Directive should include the same provisions in relation to geographical indications as contained in Regulation (EC) No 207/2009. Furthermore, it is appropriate to ensure that the scope of absolute grounds is extended to also cover protected traditional terms for wine and traditional specialties guaranteed.

(16) The protection afforded by the registered trade mark, the function of which is in particular to guarantee the trade mark as an indication of origin, should be absolute in the event of there being identity between the mark and the corresponding sign and the goods or services. The protection should apply also in the case of similarity between the mark and the sign and the goods or services. It is indispensable to give an interpretation of the concept of similarity in relation to the likelihood of confusion. The likelihood of confusion, the appreciation of which depends on numerous elements and, in particular, on the recognition of the trade mark on the market, the association which can be made with the used or registered sign, the degree of similarity between the trade mark and the sign and between the goods or services identified, should constitute the specific condition for such protection. The ways in which a likelihood of confusion can be established, and in particular the onus of proof in that regard, should be a matter for national procedural rules which should not be prejudiced by this Directive.

(17) In order to ensure legal certainty and full consistency with the principle of priority, under which a registered earlier trade mark takes precedence over later registered trade marks, it is necessary to provide that the enforcement of rights which are conferred by a trade mark should be without prejudice to the rights of proprietors acquired prior to the filing or priority date of the trade mark. Such an approach is in conformity with Article 16(1) of the Agreement on trade-related aspects of intellectual property rights of 15 April 1994 ('TRIPS Agreement').

(18) It is appropriate to provide that an infringement of a trade mark can only be established if there is a finding that the infringing mark or sign is used in the course of trade for the purposes of distinguishing goods or services. Use of the sign for purposes other than for distinguishing goods or services should be subject to the provisions of national law.

(19) The concept of infringement of a trade mark should also comprise the use of the sign as a trade name or similar designation, as long as such use is made for the purposes of distinguishing goods or services.

(20) In order to ensure legal certainty and full consistency with specific Union legislation, it is appropriate to provide that the proprietor of a trade mark should be entitled to prohibit a third party from using a sign in comparative advertising where such comparative advertising is contrary to Directive 2006/114/EC of the European Parliament and of the Council.[5]

(21) In order to strengthen trade mark protection and combat counterfeiting more effectively, and in line with international obligations of the Member States under the World Trade Organisation (WTO) framework, in particular Article V of the General Agreement on Tariffs and Trade on freedom of transit and, as regards generic medicines, the 'Declaration on the TRIPS Agreement and public health' adopted by the Doha WTO Ministerial Conference on 14 November 2001, the proprietor of a trade mark should be entitled to prevent third parties from bringing goods, in the course of trade, into the Member State where the trade mark is registered without being released for free circulation there, where such goods come from third countries and bear without authorisation a trade mark which is identical or essentially identical with the trade mark registered in respect of such goods.

(22) To this effect, it should be permissible for trade mark proprietors to prevent the entry of infringing goods and their placement in all customs situations, including, in particular transit, transhipment, warehousing, free zones, temporary storage, inward processing or temporary admission, also when such goods are not intended to be placed on the market of the Member State concerned. In performing customs controls, the customs authorities should make use of the powers and procedures laid down in Regulation (EU) No 608/2013 of the European Parliament and of the Council,[6] also at the request of the right holders. In particular, the customs authorities should carry out the relevant controls on the basis of risk analysis criteria.

(23) In order to reconcile the need to ensure the effective enforcement of trade mark rights with the necessity to avoid hampering the free flow of trade in legitimate goods, the entitlement of the proprietor of the trade mark should lapse where, during the subsequent proceedings initiated before the judicial or other authority competent to take a substantive decision on whether the registered trade mark has been infringed, the declarant or the holder of the goods is able to prove that the proprietor of the registered trade mark is not entitled to prohibit the placing of the goods on the market in the country of final destination.

(24) Article 28 of Regulation (EU) No 608/2013 provides that a right holder is to be liable for damages towards the holder of the goods where, inter alia, the goods in question are subsequently found not to infringe an intellectual property right.

(25) Appropriate measures should be taken with a view to ensuring the smooth transit of generic medicines. With respect to international non-proprietary names (INN) as globally recognised generic names for active substances in pharmaceutical preparations, it is vital to take due account of the existing limitations on the effect of trade mark rights. Consequently, the proprietor of a trade mark should not have the right to prevent a third party from bringing goods into a Member State where the trade mark is registered without being released for free circulation there based upon similarities between the INN for the active ingredient in the medicines and the trade mark.

(26) In order to enable proprietors of registered trade marks to combat counterfeiting more effectively, they should be entitled to prohibit the affixing of an infringing trade mark to goods, and certain preparatory acts carried out prior to such affixing.

(27) The exclusive rights conferred by a trade mark should not entitle the proprietor to prohibit the use of signs or indications by third parties which are used fairly and thus in accordance with honest practices in industrial and commercial matters. In order to create equal conditions for trade names and trade marks against the background that trade names are regularly granted unrestricted protection against later trade marks, such use should only be considered to include the use of the personal name of the third party. Such use should further permit the use of descriptive or non-distinctive signs or indications in general. Furthermore, the proprietor should not be entitled to prevent the fair and honest use of the mark for the purpose of identifying or referring to the goods or services as those of the proprietor. Use of a trade mark by third parties to draw the consumer's attention to the resale of genuine goods that were originally sold by, or with the consent of, the proprietor of the trade mark in the Union should be considered as being fair as long as it is at the same time in accordance with honest practices in industrial and commercial matters. Use of a trade mark by third parties for the purpose of artistic expression should be considered as being fair as long as it is at the same time in accordance with honest practices in industrial and commercial matters. Furthermore, this Directive should be applied in a way that ensures full respect for fundamental rights and freedoms, and in particular the freedom of expression.

(28) It follows from the principle of free movement of goods that the proprietor of a trade mark should not be entitled to prohibit its use by a third party in relation to goods which have been put into circulation in the Union, under the trade mark, by him or with his consent, unless the proprietor has legitimate reasons to oppose further commercialisation of the goods.

(29) It is important, for reasons of legal certainty to provide that, without prejudice to his interests as a proprietor of an earlier trade mark, the latter may no longer request a declaration of invalidity or oppose the use of a trade mark subsequent to his own trade mark, of which he has knowingly tolerated the use for a substantial length of time, unless the application for the subsequent trade mark was made in bad faith.

(30) In order to ensure legal certainty and safeguard legitimately acquired trade mark rights, it is appropriate and necessary to provide that, without prejudice to the principle that the later trade mark cannot be enforced against the earlier trade mark, proprietors of earlier trade marks should not be entitled to obtain refusal or invalidation or to oppose the use of a later trade mark if the later trade mark was acquired at a time when the earlier trade mark was liable to be declared invalid or revoked, for example because it had not yet acquired distinctiveness through use, or if the earlier trade mark could not be enforced against the later trade mark because the necessary conditions were not applicable, for example when the earlier mark had not yet obtained a reputation.

(31) Trade marks fulfil their purpose of distinguishing goods or services and allowing consumers to make informed choices only when they are actually used on the market. A requirement of use is also necessary in order to reduce the total number of trade marks registered and protected in the Union and, consequently, the number of conflicts which arise between them. It is therefore essential to require that registered trade marks actually be used in connection with the goods or services for which they are registered, or, if not used in that connection within five years of the date of the completion of the registration procedure, be liable to be revoked.

(32) Consequently, a registered trade mark should only be protected in so far as it is actually used and a registered earlier trade mark should not enable its proprietor to oppose or invalidate a later trade mark if that proprietor has not put his trade mark to genuine use. Furthermore, Member States should provide that a trade mark may not be successfully invoked in infringement proceedings if it is established, as a result of a plea, that the trade mark could be revoked or, when the action is brought against a later right, could have been revoked at the time when the later right was acquired.

(33) It is appropriate to provide that, where the seniority of a national mark or a trade mark registered under international arrangements having effect in the Member State has been claimed for an EU trade mark and the mark providing the basis for the seniority claim has thereafter been surrendered or allowed to lapse, the validity of that mark can still be challenged. Such a challenge should be limited to situations where the mark could have been declared invalid or revoked at the time it was removed from the register.

(34) For reasons of coherence and in order to facilitate the commercial exploitation of trade marks in the Union, the rules applicable to trade marks as objects of property should be aligned to the extent appropriate with those already in place for EU trade marks, and should include rules on assignment and transfer, licensing, rights *in rem* and levy of execution.

(35) Collective trade marks have proven a useful instrument for promoting goods or services with specific common properties. It is therefore appropriate to subject national collective trade marks to rules similar to the rules applicable to European Union collective marks.

(36) In order to improve and facilitate access to trade mark protection and to increase legal certainty and predictability, the procedure for the registration of trade marks in the Member States should be efficient and transparent and should follow rules similar to those applicable to EU trade marks.

(37) In order to ensure legal certainty with regard to the scope of trade mark rights and to facilitate access to trade mark protection, the designation and classification of goods and services covered by a trade mark application should follow the same rules in all Member States and should be aligned to those applicable to EU trade marks. In order to enable the competent authorities and

economic operators to determine the extent of the trade mark protection sought on the basis of the application alone, the designation of goods and services should be sufficiently clear and precise. The use of general terms should be interpreted as including only goods and services clearly covered by the literal meaning of a term. In the interest of clarity and legal certainty, the Member States' central industrial property offices and the Benelux Office for Intellectual Property should, in cooperation with each other, endeavour to compile a list reflecting their respective administrative practices with regard to the classification of goods and services.

(38) For the purpose of ensuring effective trade mark protection, Member States should make available an efficient administrative opposition procedure, allowing at least the proprietor of earlier trade mark rights and any person authorised under the relevant law to exercise the rights arising from a protected designation of origin or a geographical indication to oppose the registration of a trade mark application. Furthermore, in order to offer efficient means of revoking trademarks or declaring them invalid, Member States should provide for an administrative procedure for revocation or declaration of invalidity within the longer transposition period of seven years, after the entry into force of this Directive.

(39) It is desirable that Member States' central industrial property offices and the Benelux Office for Intellectual Property cooperate with each other and with the European Union Intellectual Property Office in all fields of trade mark registration and administration in order to promote convergence of practices and tools, such as the creation and updating of common or connected databases and portals for consultation and search purposes. The Member States should further ensure that their offices cooperate with each other and with the European Union Intellectual Property Office in all other areas of their activities which are relevant for the protection of trade marks in the Union.

(40) This Directive should not exclude the application to trade marks of provisions of law of the Member States other than trade mark law, such as provisions relating to unfair competition, civil liability or consumer protection.

(41) Member States are bound by the Paris Convention for the Protection of Industrial Property ('the Paris Convention') and the TRIPS Agreement. It is necessary that this Directive be entirely consistent with that Convention and that Agreement. The obligations of the Member States resulting from that Convention and that Agreement should not be affected by this Directive. Where appropriate, the second paragraph of Article 351 of the Treaty on the Functioning of the European Union should apply.

(42) Since the objectives of this Directive, namely to foster and create a well-functioning internal market and to facilitate the registration, administration and protection of trade marks in the Union to the benefit of growth and competitiveness, cannot be sufficiently achieved by the Member States but can rather, by reason of its scale and effects, be better achieved at Union level, the Union may adopt measures, in accordance with the principle of subsidiarity as set out in Article 5 of the Treaty on European Union. In accordance with the principle of proportionality as set out in that Article, this Directive does not go beyond what is necessary in order to achieve those objectives.

(43) Directive 95/46/EC of the European Parliament and of the Council[7] governs the processing of personal data carried out in the Member States in the context of this Directive.

(44) The European Data Protection Supervisor was consulted in accordance with Article 28(2) of Regulation (EC) No 45/2001 of the European Parliament and of the Council[8] and delivered an opinion on 11 July 2013.

(45) The obligation to transpose this Directive into national law should be confined to those provisions which represent a substantive amendment as compared with the earlier Directive. The obligation to transpose the provisions which are unchanged arises under the earlier Directive.

(46) This Directive should be without prejudice to the obligations of the Member States under Directive 2008/95/EC relating to the time limit for transposition of Council Directive 89/104/EEC[9] into national law as set out in Part B of Annex I to Directive 2008/95/EC,

NOTES

1 OJ C327, 12.11.2013, p 42.

2 Position of the European Parliament of 25 February 2014 (not yet published in the Official Journal) and position of the Council at first reading of 10 November 2015 (not yet published in the Official Journal). Position of the European Parliament of 15 December 2015.

3 Directive 2008/95/EC of the European Parliament and of the Council of 22 October 2008 to approximate the laws of the Member States relating to trade marks (OJ L299, 8.11.2008, p 25).

4 Council Regulation (EC) No 207/2009 of 26 February 2009 on the Community trade mark (OJ L78, 24.3.2009, p 1).

5 Directive 2006/114/EC of the European Parliament and of the Council of 12 December 2006 concerning misleading and comparative advertising (OJ L376, 27.12.2006, p 21).

6 Regulation (EU) No 608/2013 of the European Parliament and of the Council of 12 June 2013 concerning customs enforcement of intellectual property rights and repealing Council Regulation (EC) No 1383/2003 (OJ L181, 29.6.2013, p 15).

7 Directive 95/46/EC of the European Parliament and of the Council of 24 October 1995 on the protection of individuals with regard to the processing of personal data and on the free movement of such data (OJ L281, 23.11.1995, p 31).

8 Regulation (EC) No 45/2001 of the European Parliament and of the Council of 18 December 2000 on the protection of

individuals with regard to the processing of personal data by the Community institutions and bodies and on the free movement of such data (OJ L8, 12.1.2001, p 1).

9 First Council Directive 89/104/EEC of 21 December 1988 to approximate the laws of the Member States relating to trade marks (OJ L40, 11.2.1989, p 1).

HAVE ADOPTED THIS DIRECTIVE:

CHAPTER 1
GENERAL PROVISIONS

[5.791]
Article 1
Scope

This Directive applies to every trade mark in respect of goods or services which is the subject of registration or of an application for registration in a Member State as an individual trade mark, a guarantee or certification mark or a collective mark, or which is the subject of a registration or an application for registration in the Benelux Office for Intellectual Property or of an international registration having effect in a Member State.

[5.792]
Article 2
Definitions

For the purpose of this Directive, the following definitions apply:

(a) 'office' means the central industrial property office of the Member State or the Benelux Office for Intellectual Property, entrusted with the registration of trade marks;
(b) 'register' means the register of trade marks kept by an office.

CHAPTER 2
SUBSTANTIVE LAW ON TRADE MARKS

SECTION 1
SIGNS OF WHICH A TRADE MARK MAY CONSIST

[5.793]
Article 3
Signs of which a trade mark may consist

A trade mark may consist of any signs, in particular words, including personal names, or designs, letters, numerals, colours, the shape of goods or of the packaging of goods, or sounds, provided that such signs are capable of:

(a) distinguishing the goods or services of one undertaking from those of other undertakings; and
(b) being represented on the register in a manner which enables the competent authorities and the public to determine the clear and precise subject matter of the protection afforded to its proprietor.

SECTION 2
GROUNDS FOR REFUSAL OR INVALIDITY

[5.794]
Article 4
Absolute grounds for refusal or invalidity

1. The following shall not be registered or, if registered, shall be liable to be declared invalid:
(a) signs which cannot constitute a trade mark;
(b) trade marks which are devoid of any distinctive character;
(c) trade marks which consist exclusively of signs or indications which may serve, in trade, to designate the kind, quality, quantity, intended purpose, value, geographical origin, or the time of production of the goods or of rendering of the service, or other characteristics of the goods or services;
(d) trade marks which consist exclusively of signs or indications which have become customary in the current language or in the bona fide and established practices of the trade;
(e) signs which consist exclusively of:
(i) the shape, or another characteristic, which results from the nature of the goods themselves;
(ii) the shape, or another characteristic, of goods which is necessary to obtain a technical result;
(iii) the shape, or another characteristic, which gives substantial value to the goods;
(f) trade marks which are contrary to public policy or to accepted principles of morality;
(g) trade marks which are of such a nature as to deceive the public, for instance, as to the nature, quality or geographical origin of the goods or service;

(h) trade marks which have not been authorised by the competent authorities and are to be refused or invalidated pursuant to Article 6ter of the Paris Convention;

(i) trade marks which are excluded from registration pursuant to Union legislation or the national law of the Member State concerned, or to international agreements to which the Union or the Member State concerned is party, providing for protection of designations of origin and geographical indications;

(j) trade marks which are excluded from registration pursuant to Union legislation or international agreements to which the Union is party, providing for protection of traditional terms for wine;

(k) trade marks which are excluded from registration pursuant to Union legislation or international agreements to which the Union is party, providing for protection of traditional specialities guaranteed;

(l) trade marks which consist of, or reproduce in their essential elements, an earlier plant variety denomination registered in accordance with Union legislation or the national law of the Member State concerned, or international agreements to which the Union or the Member State concerned is party, providing protection for plant variety rights, and which are in respect of plant varieties of the same or closely related species.

2. A trade mark shall be liable to be declared invalid where the application for registration of the trade mark was made in bad faith by the applicant. Any Member State may also provide that such a trade mark is not to be registered.

3. Any Member State may provide that a trade mark is not to be registered or, if registered, is liable to be declared invalid where and to the extent that:

(a) the use of that trade mark may be prohibited pursuant to provisions of law other than trade mark law of the Member State concerned or of the Union;

(b) the trade mark includes a sign of high symbolic value, in particular a religious symbol;

(c) the trade mark includes badges, emblems and escutcheons other than those covered by Article 6ter of the Paris Convention and which are of public interest, unless the consent of the competent authority to their registration has been given in conformity with the law of the Member State.

4. A trade mark shall not be refused registration in accordance with paragraph 1(b), (c) or (d) if, before the date of application for registration, following the use which has been made of it, it has acquired a distinctive character. A trade mark shall not be declared invalid for the same reasons if, before the date of application for a declaration of invalidity, following the use which has been made of it, it has acquired a distinctive character.

5. Any Member State may provide that paragraph 4 is also to apply where the distinctive character was acquired after the date of application for registration but before the date of registration.

[5.795]

Article 5

Relative grounds for refusal or invalidity

1. A trade mark shall not be registered or, if registered, shall be liable to be declared invalid where:

(a) it is identical with an earlier trade mark, and the goods or services for which the trade mark is applied for or is registered are identical with the goods or services for which the earlier trade mark is protected;

(b) because of its identity with, or similarity to, the earlier trade mark and the identity or similarity of the goods or services covered by the trade marks, there exists a likelihood of confusion on the part of the public; the likelihood of confusion includes the likelihood of association with the earlier trade mark.

2. 'Earlier trade marks' within the meaning of paragraph 1 means:

(a) trade marks of the following kinds with a date of application for registration which is earlier than the date of application for registration of the trade mark, taking account, where appropriate, of the priorities claimed in respect of those trade marks:

(i) EU trade marks;

(ii) trade marks registered in the Member State concerned or, in the case of Belgium, Luxembourg or the Netherlands, at the Benelux Office for Intellectual Property;

(iii) trade marks registered under international arrangements which have effect in the Member State concerned;

(b) EU trade marks which validly claim seniority, in accordance with Regulation (EC) No 207/2009, of a trade mark referred to in points (a)(ii) and (iii), even when the latter trade mark has been surrendered or allowed to lapse;

(c) applications for the trade marks referred to in points (a) and (b), subject to their registration;

(d) trade marks which, on the date of application for registration of the trade mark, or, where appropriate, of the priority claimed in respect of the application for registration of the trade mark, are well known in the Member State concerned, in the sense in which the words 'well-known' are used in Article 6bis of the Paris Convention.

3. Furthermore, a trade mark shall not be registered or, if registered, shall be liable to be declared invalid where:

(a) it is identical with, or similar to, an earlier trade mark irrespective of whether the goods or services for which it is applied or registered are identical with, similar to or not similar to those for which the earlier trade mark is registered, where the earlier trade mark has a reputation in the Member State in respect of which registration is applied for or in which the trade mark is registered or, in the case of an EU trade mark, has a reputation in the Union and the use of the later trade mark without due cause would take unfair advantage of, or be detrimental to, the distinctive character or the repute of the earlier trade mark;

(b) an agent or representative of the proprietor of the trade mark applies for registration thereof in his own name without the proprietor's authorisation, unless the agent or representative justifies his action;

(c) and to the extent that, pursuant to Union legislation or the law of the Member State concerned providing for protection of designations of origin and geographical indications:

(i) an application for a designation of origin or a geographical indication had already been submitted in accordance with Union legislation or the law of the Member State concerned prior to the date of application for registration of the trade mark or the date of the priority claimed for the application, subject to its subsequent registration;

(ii) that designation of origin or geographical indication confers on the person authorised under the relevant law to exercise the rights arising therefrom the right to prohibit the use of a subsequent trade mark.

4. Any Member State may provide that a trade mark is not to be registered or, if registered, is liable to be declared invalid where, and to the extent that:

(a) rights to a non-registered trade mark or to another sign used in the course of trade were acquired prior to the date of application for registration of the subsequent trade mark, or the date of the priority claimed for the application for registration of the subsequent trade mark, and that non-registered trade mark or other sign confers on its proprietor the right to prohibit the use of a subsequent trade mark;

(b) the use of the trade mark may be prohibited by virtue of an earlier right, other than the rights referred to in paragraph 2 and point (a) of this paragraph, and in particular:

(i) a right to a name;

(ii) a right of personal portrayal;

(iii) a copyright;

(iv) an industrial property right;

(c) the trade mark is liable to be confused with an earlier trade mark protected abroad, provided that, at the date of the application, the applicant was acting in bad faith.

5. The Member States shall ensure that in appropriate circumstances there is no obligation to refuse registration or to declare a trade mark invalid where the proprietor of the earlier trade mark or other earlier right consents to the registration of the later trade mark.

6. Any Member State may provide that, by way of derogation from paragraphs 1 to 5, the grounds for refusal of registration or invalidity in force in that Member State prior to the date of the entry into force of the provisions necessary to comply with Directive 89/104/EEC are to apply to trade marks for which an application has been made prior to that date.

[5.796]
Article 6
Establishment a posteriori of invalidity or revocation of a trade mark

Where the seniority of a national trade mark or of a trade mark registered under international arrangements having effect in the Member State, which has been surrendered or allowed to lapse, is claimed for an EU trade mark, the invalidity or revocation of the trade mark providing the basis for the seniority claim may be established *a posteriori*, provided that the invalidity or revocation could have been declared at the time the mark was surrendered or allowed to lapse. In such a case, the seniority shall cease to produce its effects.

[5.797]
Article 7
Grounds for refusal or invalidity relating to only some of the goods or services

Where grounds for refusal of registration or for invalidity of a trade mark exist in respect of only some of the goods or services for which that trade mark has been applied or registered, refusal of registration or invalidity shall cover those goods or services only.

[5.798]
Article 8
Lack of distinctive character or of reputation of an earlier trade mark precluding a declaration of invalidity of a registered trade mark

An application for a declaration of invalidity on the basis of an earlier trade mark shall not succeed at the date of application for invalidation if it would not have been successful at the filing date or the priority date of the later trade mark for any of the following reasons:

(a) the earlier trade mark, liable to be declared invalid pursuant to Article 4(1)(b), (c) or (d), had not yet acquired a distinctive character as referred to in Article 4(4);

(b) the application for a declaration of invalidity is based on Article 5(1)(b) and the earlier trade mark had not yet become sufficiently distinctive to support a finding of likelihood of confusion within the meaning of Article 5(1)(b);

(c) the application for a declaration of invalidity is based on Article 5(3)(a) and the earlier trade mark had not yet acquired a reputation within the meaning of Article 5(3)(a).

[5.799]
Article 9
Preclusion of a declaration of invalidity due to acquiescence

1. Where, in a Member State, the proprietor of an earlier trade mark as referred to in Article 5(2) or Article 5(3)(a) has acquiesced, for a period of five successive years, in the use of a later trade mark registered in that Member State while being aware of such use, that proprietor shall no longer be entitled on the basis of the earlier trade mark to apply for a declaration that the later trade mark is invalid in respect of the goods or services for which the later trade mark has been used, unless registration of the later trade mark was applied for in bad faith.

2. Member States may provide that paragraph 1 of this Article is to apply to the proprietor of any other earlier right referred to in Article 5(4)(a) or (b).

3. In the cases referred to in paragraphs 1 and 2, the proprietor of a later registered trade mark shall not be entitled to oppose the use of the earlier right, even though that right may no longer be invoked against the later trade mark.

SECTION 3
RIGHTS CONFERRED AND LIMITATIONS

[5.800]
Article 10
Rights conferred by a trade mark

1. The registration of a trade mark shall confer on the proprietor exclusive rights therein.

2. Without prejudice to the rights of proprietors acquired before the filing date or the priority date of the registered trade mark, the proprietor of that registered trade mark shall be entitled to prevent all third parties not having his consent from using in the course of trade, in relation to goods or services, any sign where:

(a) the sign is identical with the trade mark and is used in relation to goods or services which are identical with those for which the trade mark is registered;

(b) the sign is identical with, or similar to, the trade mark and is used in relation to goods or services which are identical with, or similar to, the goods or services for which the trade mark is registered, if there exists a likelihood of confusion on the part of the public; the likelihood of confusion includes the likelihood of association between the sign and the trade mark;

(c) the sign is identical with, or similar to, the trade mark irrespective of whether it is used in relation to goods or services which are identical with, similar to, or not similar to, those for which the trade mark is registered, where the latter has a reputation in the Member State and where use of that sign without due cause takes unfair advantage of, or is detrimental to, the distinctive character or the repute of the trade mark.

3. The following, in particular, may be prohibited under paragraph 2:

(a) affixing the sign to the goods or to the packaging thereof;

(b) offering the goods or putting them on the market, or stocking them for those purposes, under the sign, or offering or supplying services thereunder;

(c) importing or exporting the goods under the sign;

(d) using the sign as a trade or company name or part of a trade or company name;

(e) using the sign on business papers and in advertising;

(f) using the sign in comparative advertising in a manner that is contrary to Directive 2006/114/EC.

4. Without prejudice to the rights of proprietors acquired before the filing date or the priority date of the registered trade mark, the proprietor of that registered trade mark shall also be entitled to prevent all third parties from bringing goods, in the course of trade, into the Member State where the trade mark is registered, without being released for free circulation there, where such goods, including the packaging thereof, come from third countries and bear without authorisation a trade mark which is identical with the trade mark registered in respect of such goods, or which cannot be distinguished in its essential aspects from that trade mark.

The entitlement of the trade mark proprietor pursuant to the first subparagraph shall lapse if, during the proceedings to determine whether the registered trade mark has been infringed, initiated in accordance with Regulation (EU) No 608/2013, evidence is provided by the declarant or the holder of the goods that the proprietor of the registered trade mark is not entitled to prohibit the placing of the goods on the market in the country of final destination.

5. Where, under the law of a Member State, the use of a sign under the conditions referred to in paragraph 2 (b) or (c) could not be prohibited before the date of entry into force of the provisions necessary to comply with Directive 89/104/EEC in the Member State concerned, the rights conferred by the trade mark may not be relied on to prevent the continued use of the sign.
6. Paragraphs 1, 2, 3 and 5 shall not affect provisions in any Member State relating to the protection against the use of a sign other than use for the purposes of distinguishing goods or services, where use of that sign without due cause takes unfair advantage of, or is detrimental to, the distinctive character or the repute of the trade mark.

[5.801]
Article 11
The right to prohibit preparatory acts in relation to the use of packaging or other means
Where the risk exists that the packaging, labels, tags, security or authenticity features or devices, or any other means to which the trade mark is affixed, could be used in relation to goods or services and that use would constitute an infringement of the rights of the proprietor of a trade mark under Article 10(2) and (3), the proprietor of that trade mark shall have the right to prohibit the following acts if carried out in the course of trade:
(a) affixing a sign identical with, or similar to, the trade mark on packaging, labels, tags, security or authenticity features or devices, or any other means to which the mark may be affixed;
(b) offering or placing on the market, or stocking for those purposes, or importing or exporting, packaging, labels, tags, security or authenticity features or devices, or any other means to which the mark is affixed.

[5.802]
Article 12
Reproduction of trade marks in dictionaries
If the reproduction of a trade mark in a dictionary, encyclopaedia or similar reference work, in print or electronic form, gives the impression that it constitutes the generic name of the goods or services for which the trade mark is registered, the publisher of the work shall, at the request of the proprietor of the trade mark, ensure that the reproduction of the trade mark is, without delay, and in the case of works in printed form at the latest in the next edition of the publication, accompanied by an indication that it is a registered trade mark.

[5.803]
Article 13
Prohibition of the use of a trade mark registered in the name of an agent or representative
1. Where a trade mark is registered in the name of the agent or representative of a person who is the proprietor of that trade mark, without the proprietor's consent, the latter shall be entitled to do either or both of the following:
(a) oppose the use of the trade mark by his agent or representative;
(b) demand the assignment of the trade mark in his favour.
2. Paragraph 1 shall not apply where the agent or representative justifies his action.

[5.804]
Article 14
Limitation of the effects of a trade mark
1. A trade mark shall not entitle the proprietor to prohibit a third party from using, in the course of trade:
(a) the name or address of the third party, where that third party is a natural person;
(b) signs or indications which are not distinctive or which concern the kind, quality, quantity, intended purpose, value, geographical origin, the time of production of goods or of rendering of the service, or other characteristics of goods or services;
(c) the trade mark for the purpose of identifying or referring to goods or services as those of the proprietor of that trade mark, in particular, where the use of the trade mark is necessary to indicate the intended purpose of a product or service, in particular as accessories or spare parts.
2. Paragraph 1 shall only apply where the use made by the third party is in accordance with honest practices in industrial or commercial matters.
3. A trade mark shall not entitle the proprietor to prohibit a third party from using, in the course of trade, an earlier right which only applies in a particular locality, if that right is recognised by the law of the Member State in question and the use of that right is within the limits of the territory in which it is recognised.

[5.805]
Article 15
Exhaustion of the rights conferred by a trade mark
1. A trade mark shall not entitle the proprietor to prohibit its use in relation to goods which have been put on the market in the Union under that trade mark by the proprietor or with the proprietor's consent.

2. Paragraph 1 shall not apply where there exist legitimate reasons for the proprietor to oppose further commercialisation of the goods, especially where the condition of the goods is changed or impaired after they have been put on the market.

[5.806]
Article 16
Use of trade marks

1. If, within a period of five years following the date of the completion of the registration procedure, the proprietor has not put the trade mark to genuine use in the Member State in connection with the goods or services in respect of which it is registered, or if such use has been suspended during a continuous five-year period, the trade mark shall be subject to the limits and sanctions provided for in Article 17, Article 19(1), Article 44(1) and (2), and Article 46(3) and (4), unless there are proper reasons for non-use.
2. Where a Member State provides for opposition proceedings following registration, the five-year period referred to in paragraph 1 shall be calculated from the date when the mark can no longer be opposed or, in the event that an opposition has been lodged, from the date when a decision terminating the opposition proceedings became final or the opposition was withdrawn.
3. With regard to trade marks registered under international arrangements and having effect in the Member State, the five-year period referred to in paragraph 1 shall be calculated from the date when the mark can no longer be rejected or opposed. Where an opposition has been lodged or when an objection on absolute or relative grounds has been notified, the period shall be calculated from the date when a decision terminating the opposition proceedings or a ruling on absolute or relative grounds for refusal became final or the opposition was withdrawn.
4. The date of commencement of the five-year period, as referred to in paragraphs 1 and 2, shall be entered in the register.
5. The following shall also constitute use within the meaning of paragraph 1:
   (a) use of the trade mark in a form differing in elements which do not alter the distinctive character of the mark in the form in which it was registered, regardless of whether or not the trade mark in the form as used is also registered in the name of the proprietor;
   (b) affixing of the trade mark to goods or to the packaging thereof in the Member State concerned solely for export purposes.
6. use of the trade mark with the consent of the proprietor shall be deemed to constitute use by the proprietor.

[5.807]
Article 17
Non-use as defence in infringement proceedings

The proprietor of a trade mark shall be entitled to prohibit the use of a sign only to the extent that the proprietor's rights are not liable to be revoked pursuant to Article 19 at the time the infringement action is brought. If the defendant so requests, the proprietor of the trade mark shall furnish proof that, during the five-year period preceding the date of bringing the action, the trade mark has been put to genuine use as provided in Article 16 in connection with the goods or services in respect of which it is registered and which are cited as justification for the action, or that there are proper reasons for non-use, provided that the registration procedure of the trade mark has at the date of bringing the action been completed for not less than five years.

[5.808]
Article 18
Intervening right of the proprietor of a later registered trade mark as defence in infringement proceedings

1. In infringement proceedings, the proprietor of a trade mark shall not be entitled to prohibit the use of a later registered mark where that later trade mark would not be declared invalid pursuant to Article 8, Article 9(1) or (2) or Article 46(3).
2. In infringement proceedings, the proprietor of a trade mark shall not be entitled to prohibit the use of a later registered EU trade mark where that later trade mark would not be declared invalid pursuant to Article 53(1), (3) or (4), 54(1) or (2) or 57(2) of Regulation (EC) No 207/2009.
3. Where the proprietor of a trade mark is not entitled to prohibit the use of a later registered trade mark pursuant to paragraph 1 or 2, the proprietor of that later registered trade mark shall not be entitled to prohibit the use of the earlier trade mark in infringement proceedings, even though that earlier right may no longer be invoked against the later trade mark.

SECTION 4
REVOCATION OF TRADE MARK RIGHTS

[5.809]
Article 19
Absence of genuine use as ground for revocation

1. A trade mark shall be liable to revocation if, within a continuous five-year period, it has not been put to genuine use in the Member State in connection with the goods or services in respect of which it is registered, and there are no proper reasons for non-use.

2. No person may claim that the proprietor's rights in a trade mark should be revoked where, during the interval between expiry of the five-year period and filing of the application for revocation, genuine use of the trade mark has been started or resumed.
3. The commencement or resumption of use within the three-month period preceding the filing of the application for revocation which began at the earliest on expiry of the continuous five-year period of non-use shall be disregarded where preparations for the commencement or resumption occur only after the proprietor becomes aware that the application for revocation may be filed.

[5.810]
Article 20
Trade mark having become generic or misleading indication as grounds for revocation
A trade mark shall be liable to revocation if, after the date on which it was registered:
(a) as a result of acts or inactivity of the proprietor, it has become the common name in the trade for a product or service in respect of which it is registered;
(b) as a result of the use made of it by the proprietor of the trade mark or with the proprietor's consent in respect of the goods or services for which it is registered, it is liable to mislead the public, particularly as to the nature, quality or geographical origin of those goods or services.

[5.811]
Article 21
Revocation relating to only some of the goods or services
Where grounds for revocation of a trade mark exist in respect of only some of the goods or services for which that trade mark has been registered, revocation shall cover those goods or services only.

SECTION 5
TRADE MARKS AS OBJECTS OF PROPERTY

[5.812]
Article 22
Transfer of registered trade marks
1. A trade mark may be transferred, separately from any transfer of the undertaking, in respect of some or all of the goods or services for which it is registered.
2. A transfer of the whole of the undertaking shall include the transfer of the trade mark except where there is agreement to the contrary or circumstances clearly dictate otherwise. This provision shall apply to the contractual obligation to transfer the undertaking.
3. Member States shall have procedures in place to allow for the recordal of transfers in their registers.

[5.813]
Article 23
Rights in rem
1. A trade mark may, independently of the undertaking, be given as security or be the subject of rights *in rem.*
2. Member States shall have procedures in place to allow for the recordal of rights *in rem* in their registers.

[5.814]
Article 24
Levy of execution
1. A trade mark may be levied in execution.
2. Member States shall have procedures in place to allow for the recordal of levy of execution in their registers.

[5.815]
Article 25
Licensing
1. A trade mark may be licensed for some or all of the goods or services for which it is registered and for the whole or part of the Member State concerned. A licence may be exclusive or non-exclusive.
2. The proprietor of a trade mark may invoke the rights conferred by that trade mark against a licensee who contravenes any provision in his licensing contract with regard to:
(a) its duration;
(b) the form covered by the registration in which the trade mark may be used;
(c) the scope of the goods or services for which the licence is granted;
(d) the territory in which the trade mark may be affixed; or
(e) the quality of the goods manufactured or of the services provided by the licensee.

3. Without prejudice to the provisions of the licensing contract, the licensee may bring proceedings for infringement of a trade mark only if its proprietor consents thereto. However, the holder of an exclusive licence may bring such proceedings if the proprietor of the trade mark, after formal notice, does not himself bring infringement proceedings within an appropriate period.
4. A licensee shall, for the purpose of obtaining compensation for damage suffered by him, be entitled to intervene in infringement proceedings brought by the proprietor of the trade mark.
5. Member States shall have procedures in place to allow for the recordal of licences in their registers.

[5.816]
Article 26
Applications for a trade mark as an object of property
Articles 22 to 25 shall apply to applications for trade marks.

SECTION 6
GUARANTEE OR CERTIFICATION MARKS AND COLLECTIVE MARKS

[5.817]
Article 27
Definitions
For the purposes of this Directive, the following definitions apply:

(a) 'guarantee or certification mark' means a trade mark which is described as such when the mark is applied for and is capable of distinguishing goods or services which are certified by the proprietor of the mark in respect of material, mode of manufacture of goods or performance of services, quality, accuracy or other characteristics, from goods and services which are not so certified;
(b) 'collective mark' means a trade mark which is described as such when the mark is applied for and is capable of distinguishing the goods or services of the members of an association which is the proprietor of the mark from the goods or services of other undertakings.

[5.818]
Article 28
Guarantee or certification marks
1. Member States may provide for the registration of guarantee or certification marks.
2. Any natural or legal person, including institutions, authorities and bodies governed by public law, may apply for guarantee or certification marks provided that such person does not carry on a business involving the supply of goods or services of the kind certified.
Member States may provide that a guarantee or certification mark is not to be registered unless the applicant is competent to certify the goods or services for which the mark is to be registered.
3. Member States may provide that guarantee or certification marks are not to be registered, or are to be revoked or declared invalid, on grounds other than those specified in Articles 4, 19 and 20, where the function of those marks so requires.
4. By way of derogation from Article 4(1)(c), Member States may provide that signs or indications which may serve, in trade, to designate the geographical origin of the goods or services may constitute guarantee or certification marks. Such a guarantee or certification mark shall not entitle the proprietor to prohibit a third party from using in the course of trade such signs or indications, provided that third party uses them in accordance with honest practices in industrial or commercial matters. In particular, such a mark may not be invoked against a third party who is entitled to use a geographical name.
5. The requirements laid down in Article 16 shall be satisfied where genuine use of a guarantee or certification mark in accordance with Article 16 is made by any person who has the authority to use it.

[5.819]
Article 29
Collective marks
1. Member States shall provide for the registration of collective marks.
2. Associations of manufacturers, producers, suppliers of services or traders, which, under the terms of the law governing them, have the capacity in their own name to have rights and obligations, to make contracts or accomplish other legal acts, and to sue and be sued, as well as legal persons governed by public law, may apply for collective marks.
3. By way of derogation from Article 4(1)(c), Member States may provide that signs or indications which may serve, in trade, to designate the geographical origin of the goods or services may constitute collective marks. Such a collective mark shall not entitle the proprietor to prohibit a third party from using, in the course of trade, such signs or indications, provided that third party uses them in accordance with honest practices in industrial or commercial matters. In particular, such a mark may not be invoked against a third party who is entitled to use a geographical name.

[5.820]
Article 30
Regulations governing use of a collective mark

1. An applicant for a collective mark shall submit the regulations governing its use to the office.
2. The regulations governing use shall specify at least the persons authorised to use the mark, the conditions of membership of the association and the conditions of use of the mark, including sanctions. The regulations governing use of a mark referred to in Article 29(3) shall authorise any person whose goods or services originate in the geographical area concerned to become a member of the association which is the proprietor of the mark, provided that the person fulfils all the other conditions of the regulations.

[5.821]
Article 31
Refusal of an application

1. In addition to the grounds for refusal of a trade mark application provided for in Article 4, where appropriate with the exception of Article 4(1)(c) concerning signs or indications which may serve, in trade, to designate the geographical origin of the goods or services, and Article 5,and without prejudice to the right of an office not to undertake examination *ex officio* of relative grounds, an application for a collective mark shall be refused where the provisions of point (b) of Article 27, Article 29 or Article 30 are not satisfied, or where the regulations governing use of that collective mark are contrary to public policy or to accepted principles of morality.
2. An application for a collective mark shall also be refused if the public is liable to be misled as regards the character or the significance of the mark, in particular if it is likely to be taken to be something other than a collective mark.
3. An application shall not be refused if the applicant, as a result of amendment of the regulations governing use of the collective mark, meets the requirements referred to in paragraphs 1 and 2.

[5.822]
Article 32
Use of collective marks

The requirements of Article 16 shall be satisfied where genuine use of a collective mark in accordance with that Article is made by any person who has authority to use it.

[5.823]
Article 33
Amendments to the regulations governing use of a collective mark

1. The proprietor of a collective mark shall submit to the office any amended regulations governing use.
2. Amendments to the regulations governing use shall be mentioned in the register unless the amended regulations do not satisfy the requirements of Article 30 or involve one of the grounds for refusal referred to in Article 31.
3. For the purposes of this Directive, amendments to the regulations governing use shall take effect only from the date of entry of the mention of those amendments in the register.

[5.824]
Article 34
Persons entitled to bring an action for infringement

1. Article 25(3) and (4) shall apply to every person who has the authority to use a collective mark.
2. The proprietor of a collective mark shall be entitled to claim compensation on behalf of persons who have authority to use the mark where those persons have sustained damage as a result of unauthorised use of the mark.

[5.825]
Article 35
Additional grounds for revocation

In addition to the grounds for revocation provided for in Articles 19 and 20, the rights of the proprietor of a collective mark shall be revoked on the following grounds:

(a) the proprietor does not take reasonable steps to prevent the mark being used in a manner that is incompatible with the conditions of use laid down in the regulations governing use, including any amendments thereto mentioned in the register;
(b) the manner in which the mark has been used by authorised persons has caused it to become liable to mislead the public in the manner referred to in Article 31(2);
(c) an amendment to the regulations governing use of the mark has been mentioned in the register in breach of Article 33(2), unless the proprietor of the mark, by further amending the regulations governing use, complies with the requirements of that Article.

[5.826]
Article 36
Additional grounds for invalidity

In addition to the grounds for invalidity provided for in Article 4, where appropriate with the exception of Article 4(1)(c) concerning signs or indications which may serve, in trade, to designate the geographical origin of the goods or services, and Article 5, a collective mark which is registered in breach of Article 31 shall be declared invalid unless the proprietor of the mark, by amending the regulations governing use, complies with the requirements of Article 31.

CHAPTER 3
PROCEDURES

SECTION 1
APPLICATION AND REGISTRATION

[5.827]
Article 37
Application requirements

1. An application for registration of a trade mark shall contain at least all of the following:
   (a) a request for registration;
   (b) information identifying the applicant;
   (c) a list of the goods or services in respect of which the registration is requested;
   (d) a representation of the trade mark, which satisfies the requirements set out in point (b) of Article 3.
2. The application for a trade mark shall be subject to the payment of a fee determined by the Member State concerned.

[5.828]
Article 38
Date of filing

1. The date of filing of a trade mark application shall be the date on which the documents containing the information specified in Article 37(1) are filed with the office by the applicant.
2. Member States may, in addition, provide that the accordance of the date of filing is to be subject to the payment of a fee as referred to in Article 37(2).

[5.829]
Article 39
Designation and classification of goods and services

1. The goods and services in respect of which trade mark registration is applied for shall be classified in conformity with the system of classification established by the Nice Agreement Concerning the International Classification of Goods and Services for the Purposes of the Registration of Marks of 15 June 1957 ('lsquo;the Nice Classification').
2. The goods and services for which protection is sought shall be identified by the applicant with sufficient clarity and precision to enable the competent authorities and economic operators, on that sole basis, to determine the extent of the protection sought.
3. For the purposes of paragraph 2, the general indications included in the class headings of the Nice Classification or other general terms may be used, provided that they comply with the requisite standards of clarity and precision set out in this Article.
4. The office shall reject an application in respect of indications or terms which are unclear or imprecise, where the applicant does not suggest an acceptable wording within a period set by the office to that effect.
5. The use of general terms, including the general indications of the class headings of the Nice Classification, shall be interpreted as including all the goods or services clearly covered by the literal meaning of the indication or term. The use of such terms or indications shall not be interpreted as comprising a claim to goods or services which cannot be so understood.
6. Where the applicant requests registration for more than one class, the applicant shall group the goods and services according to the classes of the Nice Classification, each group being preceded by the number of the class to which that group of goods or services belongs, and shall present them in the order of the classes.
7. Goods and services shall not be regarded as being similar to each other on the ground that they appear in the same class under the Nice Classification. Goods and services shall not be regarded as being dissimilar from each other on the ground that they appear in different classes under the Nice Classification.

[5.830]
Article 40
Observations by third parties

1. Member States may provide that prior to registration of a trade mark, any natural or legal person and any group or body representing manufacturers, producers, suppliers of services, traders or consumers may submit to the office written observations, explaining on which grounds the trade mark should not be registered *ex officio*.

Persons and groups or bodies, as referred to in the first subparagraph, shall not be parties to the proceedings before the office.

2. In addition to the grounds referred to in paragraph 1 of this Article, any natural or legal person and any group or body representing manufacturers, producers, suppliers of services, traders or consumers may submit to the office written observations based on the particular grounds on which the application for a collective mark should be refused under Article 31(1) and (2). This provision may be extended to cover certification and guarantee marks where regulated in Member States.

[5.831]
Article 41
Division of applications and registrations

The applicant or proprietor may divide a national trade mark application or registration into two or more separate applications or registrations by sending a declaration to the office and indicating for each divisional application or registration the goods or services covered by the original application or registration which are to be covered by the divisional applications or registrations.

[5.832]
Article 42
Class fees

Member States may provide that the application and renewal of a trade mark is to be subject to an additional fee for each class of goods and services beyond the first class.

SECTION 2
PROCEDURES FOR OPPOSITION, REVOCATION AND INVALIDITY

[5.833]
Article 43
Opposition procedure

1. Member States shall provide for an efficient and expeditious administrative procedure before their offices for opposing the registration of a trade mark application on the grounds provided for in Article 5.

2. The administrative procedure referred to in paragraph 1 of this Article shall at least provide that the proprietor of an earlier trade mark as referred to in Article 5(2) and Article 5(3)(a), and the person authorised under the relevant law to exercise the rights arising from a protected designation of origin or geographical indication as referred to in Article 5(3)(c) shall be entitled to file a notice of opposition. A notice of opposition may be filed on the basis of one or more earlier rights, provided that they all belong to the same proprietor, and on the basis of part or the totality of the goods or services in respect of which the earlier right is protected or applied for, and may be directed against part or the totality of the goods or services in respect of which the contested mark is applied for.

3. The parties shall be granted, at their joint request, a minimum of two months in the opposition proceedings in order to allow for the possibility of a friendly settlement between the opposing party and the applicant.

[5.834]
Article 44
Non-use as defence in opposition proceedings

1. In opposition proceedings pursuant to Article 43, where at the filing date or date of priority of the later trade mark, the five-year period within which the earlier trade mark must have been put to genuine use as provided for in Article 16 had expired, at the request of the applicant, the proprietor of the earlier trade mark who has given notice of opposition shall furnish proof that the earlier trade mark has been put to genuine use as provided for in Article 16 during the five-year period preceding the filing date or date of priority of the later trade mark, or that proper reasons for non-use existed. In the absence of proof to this effect, the opposition shall be rejected.

2. If the earlier trade mark has been used in relation to only part of the goods or services for which it is registered, it shall, for the purpose of the examination of the opposition as provided for in paragraph 1, be deemed to be registered in respect of that part of the goods or services only.

3. Paragraphs 1 and 2 of this Article shall also apply where the earlier trade mark is an EU trade mark. In such a case, the genuine use of the EU trade mark shall be determined in accordance with Article 15 of Regulation (EC) No 207/2009.

[5.835]

Article 45

Procedure for revocation or declaration of invalidity

1. Without prejudice to the right of the parties to appeal to the courts, Member States shall provide for an efficient and expeditious administrative procedure before their offices for the revocation or declaration of invalidity of a trade mark.

2. The administrative procedure for revocation shall provide that the trade mark is to be revoked on the grounds provided for in Articles 19 and 20.

3. The administrative procedure for invalidity shall provide that the trade mark is to be declared invalid at least on the following grounds:

(a) the trade mark should not have been registered because it does not comply with the requirements provided for in Article 4;

(b) the trade mark should not have been registered because of the existence of an earlier right within the meaning of Article 5(1) to (3).

4. The administrative procedure shall provide that at least the following are to be entitled to file an application for revocation or for a declaration of invalidity:

(a) in the case of paragraph 2 and paragraph 3(a), any natural or legal person and any group or body set up for the purpose of representing the interests of manufacturers, producers, suppliers of services, traders or consumers, and which, under the terms of the law governing it, has the capacity to sue in its own name and to be sued;

(b) in the case of paragraph 3(b) of this Article, the proprietor of an earlier trade mark as referred to in Article 5(2) and Article 5(3)(a), and the person authorised under the relevant law to exercise the rights arising from a protected designation of origin or geographical indication as referred to in Article 5(3)(c).

5. An application for revocation or for a declaration of invalidity may be directed against a part or the totality of the goods or services in respect of which the contested mark is registered.

6. An application for a declaration of invalidity may be filed on the basis of one or more earlier rights, provided they all belong to the same proprietor.

[5.836]

Article 46

Non-use as a defence in proceedings seeking a declaration of invalidity

1. In proceedings for a declaration of invalidity based on a registered trade mark with an earlier filing date or priority date, if the proprietor of the later trade mark so requests, the proprietor of the earlier trade mark shall furnish proof that, during the five-year period preceding the date of the application for a declaration of invalidity, the earlier trade mark has been put to genuine use, as provided for in Article 16, in connection with the goods or services in respect of which it is registered and which are cited as justification for the application, or that there are proper reasons for non-use, provided that the registration process of the earlier trade mark has at the date of the application for a declaration of invalidity been completed for not less than five years.

2. Where, at the filing date or date of priority of the later trade mark, the five-year period within which the earlier trade mark was to have been put to genuine use, as provided for in Article 16, had expired, the proprietor of the earlier trade mark shall, in addition to the proof required under paragraph 1 of this Article, furnish proof that the trade mark was put to genuine use during the five-year period preceding the filing date or date of priority, or that proper reasons for non-use existed.

3. In the absence of the proof referred to in paragraphs 1 and 2, an application for a declaration of invalidity on the basis of an earlier trade mark shall be rejected.

4. If the earlier trade mark has been used in accordance with Article 16 in relation to only part of the goods or services for which it is registered, it shall, for the purpose of the examination of the application for a declaration of invalidity, be deemed to be registered in respect of that part of the goods or services only.

5. Paragraphs 1 to 4 of this Article shall also apply where the earlier trade mark is an EU trade mark. In such a case, genuine use of the EU trade mark shall be determined in accordance with Article 15 of Regulation (EC) No 207/2009.

[5.837]

Article 47

Consequences of revocation and invalidity

1. A registered trade mark shall be deemed not to have had, as from the date of the application for revocation, the effects specified in this Directive, to the extent that the rights of the proprietor have been revoked. An earlier date, on which one of the grounds for revocation occurred, may be fixed in the decision on the application for revocation, at the request of one of the parties.

2. A registered trade mark shall be deemed not to have had, as from the outset, the effects specified in this Directive, to the extent that the trade mark has been declared invalid.

SECTION 3
DURATION AND RENEWAL OF REGISTRATION

[5.838]
Article 48
Duration of registration

1. Trade marks shall be registered for a period of 10 years from the date of filing of the application.
2. Registration may be renewed in accordance with Article 49 for further 10-year periods.

[5.839]
Article 49
Renewal

1. Registration of a trade mark shall be renewed at the request of the proprietor of the trade mark or any person authorised to do so by law or by contract, provided that the renewal fees have been paid. Member States may provide that receipt of payment of the renewal fees is to be deemed to constitute such a request.
2. The office shall inform the proprietor of the trade mark of the expiry of the registration at least six months before the said expiry. The office shall not be held liable if it fails to give such information.
3. The request for renewal shall be submitted and the renewal fees shall be paid within a period of at least six months immediately preceding the expiry of the registration. Failing that, the request may be submitted within a further period of six months immediately following the expiry of the registration or of the subsequent renewal thereof. The renewal fees and an additional fee shall be paid within that further period.
4. Where the request is submitted or the fees paid in respect of only some of the goods or services for which the trade mark is registered, registration shall be renewed for those goods or services only.
5. Renewal shall take effect from the day following the date on which the existing registration expires. The renewal shall be recorded in the register.

SECTION 4
COMMUNICATION WITH THE OFFICE

[5.840]
Article 50
Communication with the office

Parties to the proceedings or, where appointed, their representatives, shall designate an official address for all official communication with the office. Member States shall have the right to require that such an official address be situated in the European Economic Area.

CHAPTER 4
ADMINISTRATIVE COOPERATION

[5.841]
Article 51
Cooperation in the area of trade mark registration and administration

The offices shall be free to cooperate effectively with each other and with the European Union Intellectual Property Office in order to promote convergence of practices and tools in relation to the examination and registration of trade marks.

[5.842]
Article 52
Cooperation in other areas

The offices shall be free to cooperate effectively with each other and with the European Union Intellectual Property Office in all areas of their activities other than those referred to in Article 51 which are of relevance for the protection of trade marks in the Union.

CHAPTER 5
FINAL PROVISIONS

[5.843]
Article 53
Data protection

The processing of any personal data carried out in the Member States in the framework of this Directive shall be subject to national law implementing Directive 95/46/EC.

[5.844]
Article 54
Transposition

1. Member States shall bring into force the laws, regulations and administrative provisions necessary to comply with Articles 3 to 6, Articles 8 to 14, Articles 16, 17 and 18, Articles 22 to 39, Article 41, Articles 43 and 44 and Articles 46 to 50 by 14 January 2019. Member States shall bring into force the laws, regulations and administrative provisions to comply with Article 45 by 14 January 2023. They shall immediately communicate the text of those measures to the Commission.

When Member States adopt those measures, they shall contain a reference to this Directive or be accompanied by such a reference on the occasion of their official publication. They shall also include a statement that references in existing laws, regulations and administrative provisions to the Directive repealed by this Directive shall be construed as references to this Directive. Member States shall determine how such reference is to be made and how that statement is to be formulated.

2. Member States shall communicate to the Commission the text of the main provisions of national law which they adopt in the field covered by this Directive.

[5.845]
Article 55
Repeal

Directive 2008/95/EC is repealed with effect from 15 January 2019, without prejudice to the obligations of the Member States relating to the time limit for the transposition into national law of Directive 89/104/EEC set out in Part B of Annex I to Directive 2008/95/EC.

References to the repealed Directive shall be construed as references to this Directive and shall be read in accordance with the correlation table in the Annex.

[5.846]
Article 56
Entry into Force

This Directive shall enter into force on the twentieth day following that of its publication in the *Official Journal of the European Union*.

Articles 1, 7, 15, 19, 20 and 21 shall apply from 15 January 2019.

[5.847]
Article 57
Addressees

This Directive is addressed to the Member States.

ANNEX
CORRELATION TABLE

[5.848]

Directive 2008/95/EC	This Directive
Article 1	Article 1
—	Article 2
Article 2	Article 3
Article 3(1)(a) to (h)	Article 4(1)(a) to (h)
—	Article 4(1)(i) to (l)
Article 3(2)(a) to (c)	Article 4(3)(a) to (c)
Article 3(2)(d)	Article 4(2)
Article 3(3), first sentence	Article 4(4), first sentence
—	Article 4(4), second sentence
Article 3(3), second sentence	Article 4(5)
Article 3(4)	—
Article 4(1) and (2)	Article 5(1) and (2)
Article 4(3) and (4)(a)	Article 5(3)(a)
—	Article 5(3)(b)
—	Article 5(3)(c)
Article 4(4)(b) and (c)	Article 5(4)(a) and (b)
Article 4(4)(d) to (f)	—
Article 4(4)(g)	Article 5(4)(c)
Article 4(5) and (6)	Article 5(5) and (6)

Directive 2008/95/EC	This Directive
—	Article 8
Article 5(1), first sentence	Article 10(1)
Article 5(1), second sentence, introductory part	Article 10(2), introductory part of the sentence
Article 5(1)(a) and (b)	Article 10(2)(a) and (b)
Article 5(2)	Article 10(2)(c)
Article 5(3)(a) to (c)	Article 10(3)(a) to (c)
—	Article 10(3)(d)
Article 5(3)(d)	Article 10(3)(e)
—	Article 10(3)(f)
—	Article 10(4)
Article 5(4) and (5)	Article 10(5) and (6)
—	Article 11
—	Article 12
—	Article 13
Article 6(1)(a) to (c)	Article 14(1)(a) to (c), and (2)
Article 6(2)	Article 14(3)
Article 7	Article 15
Article 8(1) and (2)	Article 25(1) and (2)
—	Article 25(3) to (5)
Article 9	Article 9
Article 10(1), first subparagraph	Article 16(1)
—	Article 16(2) to (4)
Article 10(1), second subparagraph	Article 16(5)
Article 10(2)	Article 16(6)
Article 10(3)	—
Article 11(1)	Article 46(1) to (3)
Article 11(2)	Article 44(1)
Article 11(3)	Article 17
Article 11(4)	Articles 17, 44(2) and Article 46(4)
—	Article 18
Article 12(1), first subparagraph	Article 19(1)
Article 12(1), second subparagraph	Article 19(2)
Article 12(1), third subparagraph	Article 19(3)
Article 12(2)	Article 20
Article 13	Article 7 and Article 21
Article 14	Article 6
—	Articles 22 to 24
—	Article 26
—	Article 27
Article 15(1)	Article 28(1) and (3)
Article 15(2)	Article 28(4)
—	Article 28(2) and (5)
—	Articles 29 to 54(1)
Article 16	Article 54(2)
Article 17	Article 55
Article 18	Article 56
Article 19	Article 57

EUROPEAN PARLIAMENT AND COUNCIL REGULATION

(2017/1001/EU)

of 14 June 2017

on the European Union trade mark

(codification)

(Text with EEA relevance)

NOTES

Date of publication in OJ: OJ L154, 16.6.2017, p 1.

THE EUROPEAN PARLIAMENT AND THE COUNCIL OF THE EUROPEAN UNION,

Having regard to the Treaty on the Functioning of the European Union, and in particular the first paragraph of Article 118 thereof,

Having regard to the proposal from the European Commission,

After transmission of the draft legislative act to the national parliaments,

Acting in accordance with the ordinary legislative procedure,[1]

Whereas:

(1) Council Regulation (EC) No 207/2009[2] has been substantially amended several times. [3] In the interests of clarity and rationality, that Regulation should be codified.

(2) Council Regulation (EC) No 40/94,[4] which was codified in 2009 as Regulation (EC) No 207/2009, created a system of trade mark protection specific to the Union which provided for the protection of trade marks at the level of the Union, in parallel to the protection of trade marks available at the level of the Member States in accordance with the national trade mark systems, harmonised by Council Directive 89/104/EEC,[5] which was codified as Directive 2008/95/EC of the European Parliament and of the Council.[6]

(3) It is desirable to promote throughout the Union a harmonious development of economic activities and a continuous and balanced expansion by completing an internal market which functions properly and offers conditions which are similar to those obtaining in a national market. In order to establish a market of this kind and make it increasingly a single market, not only should barriers to free movement of goods and services be removed and arrangements be instituted which ensure that competition is not distorted, but, in addition, legal conditions should be laid down which enable undertakings to adapt their activities to the scale of the Union, whether in manufacturing and distributing goods or in providing services. For those purposes, trade marks enabling the products and services of undertakings to be distinguished by identical means throughout the entire Union, regardless of frontiers, should feature amongst the legal instruments which undertakings have at their disposal.

(4) For the purpose of pursuing the Union's said objectives it would appear necessary to provide for Union arrangements for trade marks whereby undertakings can by means of one procedural system obtain EU trade marks to which uniform protection is given and which produce their effects throughout the entire area of the Union. The principle of the unitary character of the EU trade mark thus stated should apply unless otherwise provided for in this Regulation.

(5) The barrier of territoriality of the rights conferred on proprietors of trade marks by the laws of the Member States cannot be removed by approximation of laws. In order to open up unrestricted economic activity in the whole of the internal market for the benefit of undertakings, it should be possible to register trade marks which are governed by a uniform Union law directly applicable in all Member States.

(6) The experience acquired since the establishment of the Community trade mark system has shown that undertakings from within the Union and from third countries have accepted the system which has become a successful and viable complement and alternative to the protection of trade marks at the level of the Member States.

(7) The Union law relating to trade marks nevertheless does not replace the laws of the Member States on trade marks. It would not in fact appear to be justified to require undertakings to apply for registration of their trade marks as EU trade marks.

(8) National trade marks continue to be necessary for those undertakings which do not want protection of their trade marks at Union level, or which are unable to obtain Union-wide protection while national protection does not face any obstacles. It should be left to each person seeking trade mark protection to decide whether the protection is sought only as a national trade mark in one or more Member States, or only as an EU trade mark, or both.

(9) The rights in an EU trade mark should not be obtained otherwise than by registration, and registration should be refused in particular if the trade mark is not distinctive, if it is unlawful or if it conflicts with earlier rights.

(10) A sign should be permitted to be represented in any appropriate form using generally available technology, and thus not necessarily by graphic means, as long as the representation is clear, precise, self-contained, easily accessible, intelligible, durable and objective.

(11) The protection afforded by an EU trade mark, the function of which is in particular to guarantee the trade mark as an indication of origin, should be absolute in the case of identity between the mark and the sign and the goods or services. The protection should apply also in cases of similarity between the mark and the sign and the goods or services. An interpretation should be given for the concept of similarity in relation to the likelihood of confusion. The likelihood of confusion, the appreciation of which depends on numerous elements and, in particular, on the recognition of the trade mark on the market, the association which can be made with the used or registered sign, the degree of similarity between the trade mark and the sign and between the goods or services identified, should constitute the specific condition for such protection.

(12) In order to ensure legal certainty and full consistency with the principle of priority, under which a registered earlier trade mark takes precedence over later registered trade marks, it is necessary to provide that the enforcement of rights conferred by an EU trade mark should be without prejudice to the rights of proprietors acquired prior to the filing or priority date of the EU trade mark. This is in conformity with Article 16(1) of the Agreement on trade-related aspects of intellectual property rights of 15 April 1994.

(13) Confusion as to the commercial source from which the goods or services emanate may occur when a company uses the same or a similar sign as a trade name in such a way that a link is established between the company bearing the name and the goods or services coming from that company. Infringement of an EU trade mark should therefore also comprise the use of the sign as a trade name or similar designation as long as the use is made for the purposes of distinguishing goods or services.

(14) In order to ensure legal certainty and full consistency with specific Union legislation, it is appropriate to provide that the proprietor of an EU trade mark should be entitled to prohibit a third party from using a sign in comparative advertising where such comparative advertising is contrary to Directive 2006/114/EC of the European Parliament and of the Council.[7]

(15) In order to ensure trade mark protection and combat counterfeiting effectively, and in line with international obligations of the Union under the framework of the World Trade Organisation (WTO), in particular Article V of the General Agreement on Tariffs and Trade (GATT) on freedom of transit and, as regards generic medicines, the 'Declaration on the TRIPS Agreement and public health' adopted by the Doha WTO Ministerial Conference on 14 November 2001, the proprietor of an EU trade mark should be entitled to prevent third parties from bringing goods, in the course of trade, into the Union without being released for free circulation there, where such goods come from third countries and bear without authorisation a trade mark which is identical or essentially identical with the EU trade mark registered in respect of such goods.

(16) To this effect, it should be permissible for EU trade mark proprietors to prevent the entry of infringing goods and their placement in all customs situations, including transit, transhipment, warehousing, free zones, temporary storage, inward processing or temporary admission, also when such goods are not intended to be placed on the market of the Union. In performing customs controls, the customs authorities should make use of the powers and procedures laid down in Regulation (EU) No 608/2013 of the European Parliament and the Council,[8] also at the request of the right holders. In particular, the customs authorities should carry out the relevant controls on the basis of risk analysis criteria.

(17) In order to reconcile the need to ensure the effective enforcement of trade mark rights with the necessity to avoid hampering the free flow of trade in legitimate goods, the entitlement of the proprietor of the EU trade mark should lapse where, during the subsequent proceedings initiated before the European Union trade mark court ('EU trade mark court') competent to take a substantive decision on whether the EU trade mark has been infringed, the declarant or the holder of the goods is able to prove that the proprietor of the EU trade mark is not entitled to prohibit the placing of the goods on the market in the country of final destination.

(18) Article 28 of Regulation (EU) No 608/2013 provides that a right holder is to be liable for damages towards the holder of the goods where, inter alia, the goods in question are subsequently found not to infringe an intellectual property right.

(19) Appropriate measures should be taken with a view to ensuring the smooth transit of generic medicines. With respect to international non-proprietary names (INN) as globally recognised generic names for active substances in pharmaceutical preparations, it is vital to take due account of the existing limitations on the effect of EU trade mark rights. Consequently, the proprietor of an EU trade mark should not have the right to prevent a third party from bringing goods into the Union without being released for free circulation there, based upon similarities between the INN for the active ingredient in the medicines and the trade mark.

(20) In order to enable proprietors of EU trade marks to combat counterfeiting effectively, they should be entitled to prohibit the affixing of an infringing mark to goods and preparatory acts carried out prior to the affixing.

(21) The exclusive rights conferred by an EU trade mark should not entitle the proprietor to prohibit the use of signs or indications by third parties which are used fairly and thus in accordance with honest practices in industrial and commercial matters. In order to ensure equal conditions for trade names and EU trade marks in the event of conflicts, given that trade names are regularly granted unrestricted protection against later trade marks, such use should be only considered to include the use of the personal name of the third party. It should further permit the use of descriptive or non-distinctive signs or indications in general. Furthermore, the proprietor should not be entitled to prevent the fair and honest use of the EU trade mark for the purpose of identifying or referring to the goods or services as those of the proprietor. Use of a trade mark by third parties to draw the consumer's attention to the resale of genuine goods that were originally sold by or with the consent of the proprietor of the EU trade mark in the Union should be considered as being fair as long as it is at the same time in accordance with honest practices in industrial and commercial matters. Use of a trade mark by third parties for the purpose of artistic expression should be considered as being fair as long as it is at the same time in accordance with honest practices in industrial and commercial matters. Furthermore, this Regulation should be applied in a way that ensures full respect for fundamental rights and freedoms, and in particular the freedom of expression.

(22) It follows from the principle of free movement of goods that it is essential that the proprietor of an EU trade mark not be entitled to prohibit its use by a third party in relation to goods which have been put into circulation in the European Economic Area, under the trade mark, by him or with his consent, save where there exist legitimate reasons for the proprietor to oppose further commercialisation of the goods.

(23) In order to ensure legal certainty and safeguard legitimately acquired trade mark rights, it is appropriate and necessary to lay down, without prejudice to the principle that the later trade mark cannot be enforced against the earlier trade mark, that proprietors of EU trade marks should not be entitled to oppose the use of a later trade mark if the later trade mark was acquired at a time when the earlier trade mark could not be enforced against the later trade mark.

(24) There is no justification for protecting EU trade marks or, as against them, any trade mark which has been registered before them, except where the trade marks are actually used.

(25) For reasons of equity and legal certainty, the use of an EU trade mark in a form that differs in elements which do not alter the distinctive character of that mark in the form in which it is registered should be sufficient to preserve the rights conferred regardless of whether the trade mark in the form as used is also registered.

(26) An EU trade mark is to be regarded as an object of property which exists separately from the undertakings whose goods or services are designated by it. Accordingly, it should be capable of being transferred, of being charged as security in favour of a third party and of being the subject matter of licences.

(27) Administrative measures are necessary at Union level for implementing in relation to every trade mark the trade mark law laid down by this Regulation. It is therefore essential, while retaining the Union's existing institutional structure and balance of powers, to provide for a European Union Intellectual Property Office ('the Office') which is independent in relation to technical matters and has legal, administrative and financial autonomy. To this end it is necessary and appropriate that the Office should be a body of the Union having legal personality and exercising the powers which are conferred on it by this Regulation, and that it should operate within the framework of Union law without detracting from the competences exercised by the Union institutions.

(28) EU trade mark protection is granted in relation to specific goods or services whose nature and number determine the extent of protection afforded to the trade mark proprietor. It is therefore essential to lay down rules for the designation and classification of goods and services in this Regulation and to ensure legal certainty and sound administration by requiring that the goods and services for which trade mark protection is sought are identified by the applicant with sufficient clarity and precision to enable the competent authorities and economic operators, on the basis of the application alone, to determine the extent of the protection applied for. The use of general terms should be interpreted as only including all goods and services clearly covered by the literal meaning of the term. Proprietors of EU trade marks, which because of the practice of the Office prior to 22 June 2012 were registered in respect of the entire heading of a class of the system of classification established by the Nice Agreement Concerning the International Classification of Goods and Services for the Purposes of the Registration of Marks of 15 June 1957, should be given the possibility to adapt their lists of goods and services in order to ensure that the content of the Register meets the requisite standard of clarity and precision in accordance with the case law of the Court of Justice of the European Union.

(29) In order to avoid unnecessary delays in registering an EU trade mark, it is appropriate to lay down a regime of optional EU and national trade mark searches that should be flexible in terms of user needs and preferences. The optional EU and national trade mark searches should be complemented by the making available of all-encompassing, fast and powerful search engines for the use of the public free of charge within the context of cooperation between the Office and the central industrial property offices of the Member States, including the Benelux Office for Intellectual Property.

(30) It is necessary to ensure that parties who are affected by decisions made by the Office are protected by the law in a manner which is suited to the special character of trade mark law. To that end, provision should be made for an appeal to lie from decisions of the various decision-making instances of the Office. A Board of Appeal of the Office should decide on the appeal. Decisions of the Boards of Appeal should, in turn, be amenable to actions before the General Court, which has jurisdiction to annul or to alter the contested decision.

(31) In order to ensure the protection of EU trade marks the Member States should designate, having regard to their own national system, as limited a number as possible of national courts of first and second instance having jurisdiction in matters of infringement and validity of EU trade marks.

(32) It is essential that decisions regarding the validity and infringement of EU trade marks have effect and cover the entire area of the Union, as this is the only way of preventing inconsistent decisions on the part of the courts and the Office and of ensuring that the unitary character of EU trade marks is not undermined. The provisions of Regulation (EU) No 1215/2012 of the European Parliament and of the Council[9] should apply to all actions at law relating to EU trade marks, save where this Regulation derogates from those rules.

(33) Contradictory judgments should be avoided in actions which involve the same acts and the same parties and which are brought on the basis of an EU trade mark and parallel national trade marks. For this purpose, when the actions are brought in the same Member State, the way in which this is to be achieved is a matter for national procedural rules, which are not prejudiced by this Regulation, whilst when the actions are brought in different Member States, provisions modelled on the rules on lis pendens and related actions of Regulation (EU) No 1215/2012 appear appropriate.

(34) With the aim of promoting convergence of practices and of developing common tools, it is necessary to establish an appropriate framework for cooperation between the Office and the industrial property offices of the Member States, including the Benelux Office for Intellectual Property, defining key areas of cooperation and enabling the Office to coordinate relevant common projects of interest to the Union and the Member States and to finance, up to a maximum amount, those projects. Those cooperation activities should be beneficial for undertakings using trade mark systems in Europe. For users of the Union regime laid down in this Regulation, the projects, particularly the databases for search and consultation purposes, should provide additional, inclusive, efficient tools that are free of charge to comply with the specific requirements arising from the unitary character of the EU trade mark.

(35) It is desirable to facilitate friendly, expeditious and efficient dispute resolution by entrusting the Office with the establishment of a mediation centre the services of which could be used by any person with the aim of achieving a friendly settlement of disputes relating to EU trade marks and Community designs by mutual agreement.

(36) The setting up of the EU trade mark system has resulted in increased financial burdens for the central industrial property offices and other authorities of the Member States. The additional costs are related to the handling of a higher number of opposition and invalidity proceedings involving EU trade marks or brought by proprietors of such trade marks; to the awareness-raising activities linked to the EU trade mark system; as well as to activities intended to ensure the enforcement of EU trade mark rights. It is, therefore, appropriate to ensure that the Office offset part of the costs incurred by Member States for the role they play in ensuring the smooth functioning of the EU trade mark system. The payment of such offsetting should be subject to the submission, by Member States, of relevant statistical data. The offsetting of costs should not be of such an extent that it would cause a budgetary deficit for the Office.

(37) In order to guarantee the full autonomy and independence of the Office, it is considered necessary to grant it an autonomous budget whose revenue comes principally from fees paid by the users of the system. However, the Union budgetary procedure remains applicable as far as any subsidies chargeable to the general budget of the Union are concerned. Moreover, the auditing of accounts should be undertaken by the Court of Auditors.

(38) In the interest of sound financial management, the accumulation by the Office of significant budgetary surpluses should be avoided. This should be without prejudice to the Office maintaining a financial reserve covering one year of its operational expenditure to ensure the continuity of its operations and the performance of its tasks. That reserve should only be used to ensure the continuity of the tasks of the Office as specified in this Regulation.

(39) Given the essential importance of the amounts of fees payable to the Office for the functioning of the EU trade mark system and its complementary relationship as regards national trade mark systems, it is necessary to set those fee amounts directly in this Regulation in the form of an annex. The amounts of the fees should be fixed at a level which ensures that: first, the revenue they produce is in principle sufficient for the budget of the Office to be balanced; second, there is coexistence and complementarity between the EU trade mark and the national trade mark systems, also taking into account the size of the market covered by the EU trade mark and the needs of small and medium-sized enterprises; and third, the rights of proprietors of an EU trade mark are enforced efficiently in the Member States.

(40) In order to ensure an effective, efficient and expeditious examination and registration of EU

trade mark applications by the Office using procedures which are transparent, thorough, fair and equitable, the power to adopt acts in accordance with Article 290 of the Treaty on the Functioning of the European Union (TFEU) should be delegated to the Commission in respect of specifying the details on the procedures for filing and examining an opposition and on the procedures governing the amendment of the application.

(41) In order to ensure that an EU trade mark can be revoked or declared invalid in an effective and efficient way by means of transparent, thorough, fair and equitable procedures, the power to adopt acts in accordance with Article 290 TFEU should be delegated to the Commission in respect of specifying the procedures for revocation and declaration of invalidity.

(42) In order to allow for an effective, efficient and complete review of decisions of the Office by the Boards of Appeal by means of a transparent, thorough, fair and equitable procedure which takes into account the principles laid down in this Regulation, the power to adopt acts in accordance with Article 290 TFEU should be delegated to the Commission in respect of specifying the formal content of the notice of appeal, the procedure for the filing and examination of an appeal, the formal content and form of the Board of Appeal's decisions, and the reimbursement of the appeal fees.

(43) In order to ensure a smooth, effective and efficient operation of the EU trade mark system, the power to adopt acts in accordance with Article 290 TFEU should be delegated to the Commission in respect of specifying the requirements as to the details on oral proceedings and the detailed arrangements for taking of evidence, the detailed arrangements for notification, the means of communication and the forms to be used by the parties to proceedings, the rules governing the calculation and duration of time limits, the procedures for the revocation of a decision or for cancellation of an entry in the Register, the detailed arrangements for the resumption of proceedings, and the details on representation before the Office.

(44) In order to ensure an effective and efficient organisation of the Boards of Appeal, the power to adopt acts in accordance with Article 290 TFEU should be delegated to the Commission in respect of specifying the details on the organisation of the Boards of Appeal.

(45) In order to ensure the effective and efficient registration of international trade marks in a manner that is fully consistent with the rules of the Protocol relating to the Madrid Agreement concerning the international registration of marks, adopted at Madrid on 27 June 1989 ('Madrid Protocol'), the power to adopt acts in accordance with Article 290 TFEU should be delegated to the Commission in respect of specifying the details on the procedures concerning the filing and examination of an opposition, including the necessary communications to be made to the World Intellectual Property Organisation (WIPO), and the details of the procedure concerning international registrations based on a basic application or basic registration relating to a collective mark, certification mark or guarantee mark.

(46) It is of particular importance that the Commission carry out appropriate consultations during its preparatory work, including at expert level, and that those consultations be conducted in accordance with the principles laid down in the Interinstitutional Agreement of 13 April 2016 on Better Law-Making.[10] In particular, to ensure equal participation in the preparation of delegated acts, the European Parliament and the Council receive all documents at the same time as Member States' experts, and their experts systematically have access to meetings of Commission expert groups dealing with the preparation of delegated acts.

(47) In order to ensure uniform conditions for the implementation of this Regulation, implementing powers should be conferred on the Commission in respect of specifying the details concerning applications, requests, certificates, claims, regulations, notifications and any other document under the relevant procedural requirements established by this Regulation, as well as in respect of maximum rates for costs essential to the proceedings and actually incurred, details concerning publications in the European Union Trade Marks Bulletin and the Official Journal of the Office, the detailed arrangements for exchange of information between the Office and national authorities, detailed arrangements concerning translations of supporting documents in written proceedings, exact types of decisions to be taken by a single member of the opposition or cancellation divisions, details of the notification obligation pursuant to the Madrid Protocol, and detailed requirements regarding the request for territorial extension subsequent to international registration. Those powers should be exercised in accordance with Regulation (EU) No 182/2011 of the European Parliament and of the Council.[11]

(48) Since the objectives of this Regulation cannot be sufficiently achieved by the Member States but can rather, by reason of its scale and effects, be better achieved at Union level, the Union may adopt measures, in accordance with the principle of subsidiarity as set out in Article 5 of the Treaty on European Union. In accordance with the principle of proportionality as set out in that Article, this Regulation does not go beyond what is necessary in order to achieve those objectives,

NOTES

[1] Position of the European Parliament of 27 April 2017 (not yet published in the Official Journal) and decision of the Council of 22 May 2017.

[2] Council Regulation (EC) No 207/2009 of 26 February 2009 on the European Union trade mark (OJ L78, 24.3.2009, p 1).

3 See Annex II.

4 Council Regulation (EC) No 40/94 of 20 December 1993 on the Community trade mark (OJ L11, 14.1.1994, p 1).

5 First Council Directive 89/104/EEC of 21 December 1988 to approximate the laws of the Member States relating to trade marks (OJ L40, 11.2.1989, p 1).

6 Directive 2008/95/EC of the European Parliament and of the Council of 22 October 2008 to approximate the laws of the Member States relating to trade marks (OJ L299, 8.11.2008, p 25).

7 Directive 2006/114/EC of the European Parliament and of the Council of 12 December 2006 concerning misleading and comparative advertising (OJ L376, 27.12.2006, p 21).

8 Regulation (EU) No 608/2013 of the European Parliament and of the Council of 12 June 2013 concerning customs enforcement of intellectual property rights and repealing Council Regulation (EC) No 1383/2003 (OJ L181, 29.6.2013, p 15).

9 Regulation (EU) No 1215/2012 of the European Parliament and of the Council of 12 December 2012 on jurisdiction and the recognition and enforcement of judgments in civil and commercial matters (OJ L351, 20.12.2012, p 1).

10 OJ L123, 12.5.2016, p 1.

11 Regulation (EU) No 182/2011 of the European Parliament and of the Council of 16 February 2011 laying down the rules and general principles concerning mechanisms for control by the Member States of the Commission's exercise of implementing powers (OJ L55, 28.2.2011, p 13).

HAVE ADOPTED THIS REGULATION:

CHAPTER I
GENERAL PROVISIONS

[5.849]
Article 1
EU trade mark

1. A trade mark for goods or services which is registered in accordance with the conditions contained in this Regulation and in the manner herein provided is hereinafter referred to as a 'European Union trade mark ("EU trade mark")'.

2. An EU trade mark shall have a unitary character. It shall have equal effect throughout the Union: it shall not be registered, transferred or surrendered or be the subject of a decision revoking the rights of the proprietor or declaring it invalid, nor shall its use be prohibited, save in respect of the whole Union. This principle shall apply unless otherwise provided for in this Regulation.

[5.850]
Article 2
Office

1. A European Union Intellectual Property Office ("the Office") is established.

2. All references in Union law to the Office for Harmonization in the Internal Market (Trade Marks and Designs) shall be read as references to the Office.

[5.851]
Article 3
Capacity to act

For the purpose of implementing this Regulation, companies or firms and other legal bodies shall be regarded as legal persons if, under the terms of the law governing them, they have the capacity in their own name to have rights and obligations of all kinds, to make contracts or accomplish other legal acts, and to sue and be sued.

CHAPTER II
THE LAW RELATING TO TRADE MARKS

SECTION 1
DEFINITION OF AN EU TRADE MARK AND OBTAINING AN EU TRADE MARK

[5.852]
Article 4
Signs of which an EU trade mark may consist

An EU trade mark may consist of any signs, in particular words, including personal names, or designs, letters, numerals, colours, the shape of goods or of the packaging of goods, or sounds, provided that such signs are capable of:

(a) distinguishing the goods or services of one undertaking from those of other undertakings; and

(b) being represented on the Register of European Union trade marks, ("the Register"), in a manner which enables the competent authorities and the public to determine the clear and precise subject matter of the protection afforded to its proprietor.

[5.853]
Article 5
Persons who can be proprietors of EU trade marks

Any natural or legal person, including authorities established under public law, may be the proprietor of an EU trade mark.

[5.854]
Article 6
Means whereby an EU trade mark is obtained

An EU trade mark shall be obtained by registration.

[5.855]
Article 7
Absolute grounds for refusal

1. The following shall not be registered:
 (a) signs which do not conform to the requirements of Article 4;
 (b) trade marks which are devoid of any distinctive character;
 (c) trade marks which consist exclusively of signs or indications which may serve, in trade, to designate the kind, quality, quantity, intended purpose, value, geographical origin or the time of production of the goods or of rendering of the service, or other characteristics of the goods or service;
 (d) trade marks which consist exclusively of signs or indications which have become customary in the current language or in the bona fide and established practices of the trade;
 (e) signs which consist exclusively of:
  (i) the shape, or another characteristic, which results from the nature of the goods themselves;
  (ii) the shape, or another characteristic, of goods which is necessary to obtain a technical result;
  (iii) the shape, or another characteristic, which gives substantial value to the goods;
 (f) trade marks which are contrary to public policy or to accepted principles of morality;
 (g) trade marks which are of such a nature as to deceive the public, for instance as to the nature, quality or geographical origin of the goods or service;
 (h) trade marks which have not been authorised by the competent authorities and are to be refused pursuant to Article 6*ter* of the Paris Convention for the Protection of Industrial Property ("Paris Convention");
 (i) trade marks which include badges, emblems or escutcheons other than those covered by Article 6*ter* of the Paris Convention and which are of particular public interest, unless the consent of the competent authority to their registration has been given;
 (j) trade marks which are excluded from registration, pursuant to Union legislation or national law or to international agreements to which the Union or the Member State concerned is party, providing for protection of designations of origin and geographical indications;
 (k) trade marks which are excluded from registration pursuant to Union legislation or international agreements to which the Union is party, providing for protection of traditional terms for wine;
 (l) trade marks which are excluded from registration pursuant to Union legislation or international agreements to which the Union is party, providing for protection of traditional specialities guaranteed;
 (m) trade marks which consist of, or reproduce in their essential elements, an earlier plant variety denomination registered in accordance with Union legislation or national law, or international agreements to which the Union or the Member State concerned is a party, providing for protection of plant variety rights, and which are in respect of plant varieties of the same or closely related species.

2. Paragraph 1 shall apply notwithstanding that the grounds of non-registrability obtain in only part of the Union.

3. Paragraph 1(b), (c) and (d) shall not apply if the trade mark has become distinctive in relation to the goods or services for which registration is requested as a consequence of the use which has been made of it.

[5.856]
Article 8
Relative grounds for refusal

1. Upon opposition by the proprietor of an earlier trade mark, the trade mark applied for shall not be registered:
 (a) if it is identical with the earlier trade mark and the goods or services for which registration is applied for are identical with the goods or services for which the earlier trade mark is protected;
 (b) if because of its identity with, or similarity to, the earlier trade mark and the identity or similarity of the goods or services covered by the trade marks there exists a likelihood of

confusion on the part of the public in the territory in which the earlier trade mark is protected; the likelihood of confusion includes the likelihood of association with the earlier trade mark.

2. For the purposes of paragraph 1, "earlier trade marks" means:

(a) trade marks of the following kinds with a date of application for registration which is earlier than the date of application for registration of the EU trade mark, taking account, where appropriate, of the priorities claimed in respect of those trade marks:

(i) EU trade marks;

(ii) trade marks registered in a Member State, or, in the case of Belgium, the Netherlands or Luxembourg, at the Benelux Office for Intellectual Property;

(iii) trade marks registered under international arrangements which have effect in a Member State;

(iv) trade marks registered under international arrangements which have effect in the Union;

(b) applications for the trade marks referred to in subparagraph (a), subject to their registration;

(c) trade marks which, on the date of application for registration of the EU trade mark, or, where appropriate, of the priority claimed in respect of the application for registration of the EU trade mark, are well known in a Member State, in the sense in which the words 'well known' are used in Article 6*bis* of the Paris Convention.

3. Upon opposition by the proprietor of the trade mark, a trade mark shall not be registered where an agent or representative of the proprietor of the trade mark applies for registration thereof in his own name without the proprietor's consent, unless the agent or representative justifies his action.

4. Upon opposition by the proprietor of a non-registered trade mark or of another sign used in the course of trade of more than mere local significance, the trade mark applied for shall not be registered where and to the extent that, pursuant to Union legislation or the law of the Member State governing that sign:

(a) rights to that sign were acquired prior to the date of application for registration of the EU trade mark, or the date of the priority claimed for the application for registration of the EU trade mark;

(b) that sign confers on its proprietor the right to prohibit the use of a subsequent trade mark.

5. Upon opposition by the proprietor of a registered earlier trade mark within the meaning of paragraph 2, the trade mark applied for shall not be registered where it is identical with, or similar to, an earlier trade mark, irrespective of whether the goods or services for which it is applied are identical with, similar to or not similar to those for which the earlier trade mark is registered, where, in the case of an earlier EU trade mark, the trade mark has a reputation in the Union or, in the case of an earlier national trade mark, the trade mark has a reputation in the Member State concerned, and where the use without due cause of the trade mark applied for would take unfair advantage of, or be detrimental to, the distinctive character or the repute of the earlier trade mark.

6. Upon opposition by any person authorised under the relevant law to exercise the rights arising from a designation of origin or a geographical indication, the trade mark applied for shall not be registered where and to the extent that, pursuant to the Union legislation or national law providing for the protection of designations of origin or geographical indications:

(i) an application for a designation of origin or a geographical indication had already been submitted, in accordance with Union legislation or national law, prior to the date of application for registration of the EU trade mark or the date of the priority claimed for the application, subject to its subsequent registration;

(ii) that designation of origin or geographical indication confers the right to prohibit the use of a subsequent trade mark.

SECTION 2
EFFECTS OF AN EU TRADE MARK

[5.857]
Article 9
Rights conferred by an EU trade mark

1. The registration of an EU trade mark shall confer on the proprietor exclusive rights therein.

2. Without prejudice to the rights of proprietors acquired before the filing date or the priority date of the EU trade mark, the proprietor of that EU trade mark shall be entitled to prevent all third parties not having his consent from using in the course of trade, in relation to goods or services, any sign where:

(a) the sign is identical with the EU trade mark and is used in relation to goods or services which are identical with those for which the EU trade mark is registered;

(b) the sign is identical with, or similar to, the EU trade mark and is used in relation to goods or services which are identical with, or similar to, the goods or services for which the EU trade mark is registered, if there exists a likelihood of confusion on the part of the public; the likelihood of confusion includes the likelihood of association between the sign and the trade mark;

(c) the sign is identical with, or similar to, the EU trade mark irrespective of whether it is used in relation to goods or services which are identical with, similar to or not similar to those for which the EU trade mark is registered, where the latter has a reputation in the Union and where use of that sign without due cause takes unfair advantage of, or is detrimental to, the distinctive character or the repute of the EU trade mark.

3. The following, in particular, may be prohibited under paragraph 2:

(a) affixing the sign to the goods or to the packaging of those goods;

(b) offering the goods, putting them on the market, or stocking them for those purposes under the sign, or offering or supplying services thereunder;

(c) importing or exporting the goods under the sign;

(d) using the sign as a trade or company name or part of a trade or company name;

(e) using the sign on business papers and in advertising;

(f) using the sign in comparative advertising in a manner that is contrary to Directive 2006/114/EC.

4. Without prejudice to the rights of proprietors acquired before the filing date or the priority date of the EU trade mark, the proprietor of that EU trade mark shall also be entitled to prevent all third parties from bringing goods, in the course of trade, into the Union without being released for free circulation there, where such goods, including packaging, come from third countries and bear without authorisation a trade mark which is identical with the EU trade mark registered in respect of such goods, or which cannot be distinguished in its essential aspects from that trade mark.

The entitlement of the proprietor of an EU trade mark pursuant to the first subparagraph shall lapse if, during the proceedings to determine whether the EU trade mark has been infringed, initiated in accordance with Regulation (EU) No 608/2013, evidence is provided by the declarant or the holder of the goods that the proprietor of the EU trade mark is not entitled to prohibit the placing of the goods on the market in the country of final destination.

[5.858]

Article 10

Right to prohibit preparatory acts in relation to the use of packaging or other means

Where the risk exists that the packaging, labels, tags, security or authenticity features or devices or any other means to which the mark is affixed could be used in relation to goods or services and such use would constitute an infringement of the rights of the proprietor of an EU trade mark under Article 9(2) and (3), the proprietor of that trade mark shall have the right to prohibit the following acts if carried out in the course of trade:

(a) affixing a sign identical with, or similar to, the EU trade mark on packaging, labels, tags, security or authenticity features or devices or any other means to which the mark may be affixed

(b) offering or placing on the market, or stocking for those purposes, or importing or exporting, packaging, labels, tags, security or authenticity features or devices or any other means to which the mark is affixed.

[5.859]

Article 11

Date from which rights against third parties prevail

1. The rights conferred by an EU trade mark shall prevail against third parties from the date of publication of the registration of the trade mark.

2. Reasonable compensation may be claimed in respect of acts occurring after the date of publication of an EU trade mark application, where those acts would, after publication of the registration of the trade mark, be prohibited by virtue of that publication.

3. A court seised of a case shall not decide upon the merits of that case until the registration has been published.

[5.860]

Article 12

Reproduction of an EU trade mark in a dictionary

If the reproduction of an EU trade mark in a dictionary, encyclopaedia or similar reference work gives the impression that it constitutes the generic name of the goods or services for which the trade mark is registered, the publisher of the work shall, at the request of the proprietor of the EU trade mark, ensure that the reproduction of the trade mark at the latest in the next edition of the publication is accompanied by an indication that it is a registered trade mark.

[5.861]

Article 13

Prohibition on the use of a EU trade mark registered in the name of an agent or representative

Where a EU trade mark is registered in the name of the agent or representative of a person who is the proprietor of that trade mark, without the proprietor's authorisation, the latter shall be entitled to oppose the use of his mark by his agent or representative if he has not authorised such use, unless the agent or representative justifies his action.

[5.862]
Article 14
Limitation of the effects of an EU trade mark

1. An EU trade mark shall not entitle the proprietor to prohibit a third party from using, in the course of trade:

(a) the name or address of the third party, where that third party is a natural person;
(b) signs or indications which are not distinctive or which concern the kind, quality, quantity, intended purpose, value, geographical origin, the time of production of goods or of rendering of the service, or other characteristics of the goods or services;
(c) the EU trade mark for the purpose of identifying or referring to goods or services as those of the proprietor of that trade mark, in particular, where the use of that trade mark is necessary to indicate the intended purpose of a product or service, in particular as accessories or spare parts.

2. Paragraph 1 shall only apply where the use made by the third party is in accordance with honest practices in industrial or commercial matters.

[5.863]
Article 15
Exhaustion of the rights conferred by a EU trade mark

1. An EU trade mark shall not entitle the proprietor to prohibit its use in relation to goods which have been put on the market in the European Economic Area under that trade mark by the proprietor or with his consent.

2. Paragraph 1 shall not apply where there exist legitimate reasons for the proprietor to oppose further commercialisation of the goods, especially where the condition of the goods is changed or impaired after they have been put on the market.

[5.864]
Article 16
Intervening right of the proprietor of a later registered trade mark as a defence in infringement proceedings

1. In infringement proceedings, the proprietor of an EU trade mark shall not be entitled to prohibit the use of a later registered EU trade mark where that later trade mark would not be declared invalid pursuant to Article 60(1), (3) or (4), Article 61(1) or (2), or Article 64(2) of this Regulation.

2. In infringement proceedings, the proprietor of an EU trade mark shall not be entitled to prohibit the use of a later registered national trade mark where that later registered national trade mark would not be declared invalid pursuant to Article 8 or Article 9(1) or (2), or Article 46(3) of Directive (EU) 2015/2436 of the European Parliament and of the Council.[1]

3. Where the proprietor of an EU trade mark is not entitled to prohibit the use of a later registered trade mark pursuant to paragraph 1 or 2, the proprietor of that later registered trade mark shall not be entitled to prohibit the use of that earlier EU trade mark in infringement proceedings.

NOTES

[1] Directive (EU) 2015/2436 of the European Parliament and of the Council of 16 December 2015 to approximate the laws of the Member States relating to trade marks (OJ L336, 23.12.2015, p 1).

[5.865]
Article 17
Complementary application of national law relating to infringement

1. The effects of EU trade marks shall be governed solely by the provisions of this Regulation. In other respects, infringement of an EU trade mark shall be governed by the national law relating to infringement of a national trade mark in accordance with the provisions of Chapter X.

2. This Regulation shall not prevent actions concerning an EU trade mark being brought under the law of Member States relating in particular to civil liability and unfair competition.

3. The rules of procedure to be applied shall be determined in accordance with the provisions of Chapter X.

SECTION 3
USE OF AN EU TRADE MARK

[5.866]
Article 18
Use of an EU trade mark

1. If, within a period of five years following registration, the proprietor has not put the EU trade mark to genuine use in the Union in connection with the goods or services in respect of which it is registered, or if such use has been suspended during an uninterrupted period of five years, the EU trade mark shall be subject to the sanctions provided for in this Regulation, unless there are proper reasons for non-use.

The following shall also constitute use within the meaning of the first subparagraph:

(a) use of the EU trade mark in a form differing in elements which do not alter the distinctive character of the mark in the form in which it was registered, regardless of whether or not the trade mark in the form as used is also registered in the name of the proprietor;
(b) affixing of the EU trade mark to goods or to the packaging thereof in the Union solely for export purposes.

2. Use of the EU trade mark with the consent of the proprietor shall be deemed to constitute use by the proprietor.

SECTION 4
EU TRADE MARKS AS OBJECTS OF PROPERTY

[5.867]
Article 19
Dealing with EU trade marks as national trade marks

1. Unless Articles 20 to 28 provide otherwise, an EU trade mark as an object of property shall be dealt with in its entirety, and for the whole area of the Union, as a national trade mark registered in the Member State in which, according to the Register:
(a) the proprietor has his seat or his domicile on the relevant date;
(b) where point (a) does not apply, the proprietor has an establishment on the relevant date.

2. In cases which are not provided for by paragraph 1, the Member State referred to in that paragraph shall be the Member State in which the seat of the Office is situated.

3. If two or more persons are mentioned in the Register as joint proprietors, paragraph 1 shall apply to the joint proprietor first mentioned; failing this, it shall apply to the subsequent joint proprietors in the order in which they are mentioned. Where paragraph 1 does not apply to any of the joint proprietors, paragraph 2 shall apply.

[5.868]
Article 20
Transfer

1. An EU trade mark may be transferred, separately from any transfer of the undertaking, in respect of some or all of the goods or services for which it is registered.

2. A transfer of the whole of the undertaking shall include the transfer of the EU trade mark except where, in accordance with the law governing the transfer, there is agreement to the contrary or circumstances clearly dictate otherwise. This provision shall apply to the contractual obligation to transfer the undertaking.

3. Without prejudice to paragraph 2, an assignment of the EU trade mark shall be made in writing and shall require the signature of the parties to the contract, except when it is a result of a judgment; otherwise it shall be void.

4. On request of one of the parties a transfer shall be entered in the Register and published.

5. An application for registration of a transfer shall contain information to identify the EU trade mark, the new proprietor, the goods and services to which the transfer relates, as well as documents duly establishing the transfer in accordance with paragraphs 2 and 3. The application may further contain, where applicable, information to identify the representative of the new proprietor.

6. The Commission shall adopt implementing acts specifying:
(a) the details to be contained in the application for registration of a transfer;
(b) the kind of documentation required to establish a transfer, taking account of the agreements given by the registered proprietor and the successor in title;
(c) the details of how to process applications for partial transfers, ensuring that the goods and services in the remaining registration and the new registration do not overlap and that a separate file, including a new registration number, is established for the new registration.

Those implementing acts shall be adopted in accordance with the examination procedure referred to in Article 207(2).

7. Where the conditions applicable to the registration of a transfer, as laid down in paragraphs 1, 2 and 3, or in the implementing acts referred to in paragraph 6, are not fulfilled, the Office shall notify the applicant of the deficiencies. If the deficiencies are not remedied within a period to be specified by the Office, it shall reject the application for registration of the transfer.

8. A single application for registration of a transfer may be submitted for two or more trade marks, provided that the registered proprietor and the successor in title are the same in each case.

9. Paragraphs 5 to 8 shall also apply to applications for EU trade marks.

10. In the case of a partial transfer, any application made by the original proprietor pending with regard to the original registration shall be deemed to be pending with regard to the remaining registration and the new registration. Where such application is subject to the payment of fees and those fees have been paid by the original proprietor, the new proprietor shall not be liable to pay any additional fees with regard to such application.

11. As long as the transfer has not been entered in the Register, the successor in title may not invoke the rights arising from the registration of the EU trade mark.

12. Where there are time limits to be observed vis-à-vis the Office, the successor in title may make the corresponding statements to the Office once the request for registration of the transfer has been received by the Office.

13. All documents which require notification to the proprietor of the EU trade mark in accordance with Article 98 shall be addressed to the person registered as proprietor.

[5.869]
Article 21
Transfer of a trade mark registered in the name of an agent

1. Where an EU trade mark is registered in the name of the agent or representative of a person who is the proprietor of that trade mark, without the proprietor's authorisation, the latter shall be entitled to demand the assignment of the EU trade mark in his favour, unless such agent or representative justifies his action.
2. The proprietor may submit a request for assignment pursuant to paragraph 1 of this Article to the following:
   (a) the Office, pursuant to Article 60(1)(b), instead of an application for a declaration of invalidity;
   (b) a European Union trade mark court ("EU trade mark court") as referred to in Article 123, instead of a counterclaim for a declaration of invalidity based on Article 128(1).

[5.870]
Article 22
Rights in rem

1. An EU trade mark may, independently of the undertaking, be given as security or be the subject of rights in rem.
2. At the request of one of the parties, the rights referred to in paragraph 1 or the transfer of those rights shall be entered in the Register and published.
3. An entry in the Register effected pursuant to paragraph 2 shall be cancelled or modified at the request of one of the parties.

[5.871]
Article 23
Levy of execution

1. An EU trade mark may be levied in execution.
2. As regards the procedure for levy of execution in respect of an EU trade mark, the courts and authorities of the Member States determined in accordance with Article 19 shall have exclusive jurisdiction.
3. On request of one the parties, the levy of execution shall be entered in the Register and published.
4. An entry in the Register effected pursuant to paragraph 3 shall be cancelled or modified at the request of one of the parties.

[5.872]
Article 24
Insolvency proceedings

1. The only insolvency proceedings in which an EU trade mark may be involved are those opened in the Member State in the territory of which the debtor has his centre of main interests.

However, where the debtor is an insurance undertaking or a credit institution as defined in Directive 2009/138/EC of the European Parliament and of the Council[1] and Directive 2001/24/EC of the European Parliament and of the Council,[2] respectively, the only insolvency proceedings in which an EU trade mark may be involved are those opened in the Member State where that undertaking or institution has been authorised.

2. In the case of joint proprietorship of an EU trade mark, paragraph 1 shall apply to the share of the joint proprietor.
3. Where an EU trade mark is involved in insolvency proceedings, on request of the competent national authority an entry to this effect shall be made in the Register and published in the European Union Trade Marks Bulletin referred to in Article 116.

NOTES

[1] Directive 2009/138/EC of the European Parliament and of the Council of 25 November 2009 on the taking-up and pursuit of the business of Insurance and Reinsurance (Solvency II) (OJ L335, 17.12.2009, p 1).

[2] Directive 2001/24/EC of the European Parliament and of the Council of 4 April 2001 on the reorganisation and winding up of credit institutions (OJ L125, 5.5.2001, p 15).

[5.873]
Article 25
Licensing

1. An EU trade mark may be licensed for some or all of the goods or services for which it is registered and for the whole or part of the Union. A licence may be exclusive or non-exclusive.
2. The proprietor of an EU trade mark may invoke the rights conferred by that trade mark against a licensee who contravenes any provision in his licensing contract with regard to:
   (a) its duration;
   (b) the form covered by the registration in which the trade mark may be used;

(c) the scope of the goods or services for which the licence is granted;
(d) the territory in which the trade mark may be affixed; or
(e) the quality of the goods manufactured or of the services provided by the licensee.

3. Without prejudice to the provisions of the licensing contract, the licensee may bring proceedings for infringement of an EU trade mark only if its proprietor consents thereto. However, the holder of an exclusive licence may bring such proceedings if the proprietor of the trade mark, after formal notice, does not himself bring infringement proceedings within an appropriate period.
4. A licensee shall, for the purpose of obtaining compensation for damage suffered by him, be entitled to intervene in infringement proceedings brought by the proprietor of the EU trade mark.
5. On request of one of the parties the grant or transfer of a licence in respect of an EU trade mark shall be entered in the Register and published.
6. An entry in the Register effected pursuant to paragraph 5 shall be cancelled or modified at the request of one of the parties.

[5.874]
Article 26
Procedure for entering licences and other rights in the Register

1. Article 20(5) and (6) and the rules adopted pursuant to it and Article 20(8) shall apply mutatis mutandis to the registration of a right in rem or transfer of a right in rem as referred to in Article 22(2), the levy of execution as referred to in Article 23(3), the involvement in insolvency proceedings as referred to in Article 24(3), as well as to the registration of a licence or transfer of a licence as referred to in Article 25(5), subject to the following:
(a) the requirement relating to the identification of goods and services to which the transfer relates shall not apply in respect of a request for registration of a right *in rem*, of a levy of execution or of insolvency proceedings;
(b) the requirement relating to the documents proving the transfer shall not apply where the request is made by the proprietor of the EU trade mark.

2. The application for registration of the rights referred to in paragraph 1 shall not be deemed to have been filed until the required fee has been paid.
3. The application for registration of a licence may contain a request to record a licence in the Register as one or more of the following:
(a) an exclusive licence;
(b) a sub-licence in the event that the licence is granted by a licensee whose licence is recorded in the Register;
(c) a licence limited to only part of the goods or services for which the mark is registered;
(d) a licence limited to part of the Union;
(e) a temporary licence.

Where a request is made to record the licence as a licence listed in points (c), (d) and (e) of the first subparagraph, the application for registration of a licence shall indicate the goods and services, the part of the Union and the time period for which the licence is granted.
4. Where the conditions applicable to registration, as laid down in Articles 22 to 25, in paragraphs 1 and 3 of this Article and in the other applicable rules adopted pursuant to this Regulation, are not fulfilled, the Office shall notify the applicant of the deficiency. If the deficiency is not corrected within a period specified by the Office, it shall reject the application for registration.
5. Paragraphs 1 and 3 shall apply mutatis mutandis to applications for EU trade marks.

[5.875]
Article 27
Effects vis-à-vis third parties

1. Legal acts referred to in Articles 20, 22 and 25 concerning an EU trade mark shall have effects vis-à-vis third parties in all the Member States only after entry in the Register. Nevertheless, such an act, before it is so entered, shall have effect vis-à-vis third parties who have acquired rights in the trade mark after the date of that act but who knew of the act at the date on which the rights were acquired.
2. Paragraph 1 shall not apply in the case of a person who acquires the EU trade mark or a right concerning the EU trade mark by way of transfer of the whole of the undertaking or by any other universal succession.
3. The effects vis-à-vis third parties of the legal acts referred to in Article 23 shall be governed by the law of the Member State determined in accordance with Article 19.
4. Until such time as common rules for the Member States in the field of bankruptcy enter into force, the effects vis-à-vis third parties of bankruptcy or similar proceedings shall be governed by the law of the Member State in which such proceedings are first brought within the meaning of national law or of conventions applicable in this field.

[5.876]
Article 28
The application for an EU trade mark as an object of property

Articles 19 to 27 shall apply to applications for EU trade marks.

[5.877]
Article 29
Procedure for cancelling or modifying the entry in the Register of licences and other rights
1. A registration effected under Article 26(1) shall be cancelled or modified at the request of one of the persons concerned.
2. The application shall contain the registration number of the EU trade mark concerned and the particulars of the right for which registration is requested to be cancelled or modified.
3. The application for cancellation of a licence, a right in rem or an enforcement measure shall not be deemed to have been filed until the required fee has been paid.
4. The application shall be accompanied by documents showing that the registered right no longer exists or that the licensee or the holder of another right consents to the cancellation or modification of the registration.
5. Where the requirements for cancellation or modification of the registration are not satisfied, the Office shall notify the applicant of the deficiency. If the deficiency is not corrected within a period to be specified by the Office, it shall reject the application for cancellation or modification of the registration.
6. Paragraphs 1 to 5 of this Article shall apply mutatis mutandis to entries made in the files pursuant to Article 26(5).

CHAPTER III
APPLICATION FOR EU TRADE MARKS

SECTION 1
FILING OF APPLICATIONS AND THE CONDITIONS WHICH GOVERN THEM

[5.878]
Article 30
Filing of applications
1. An application for an EU trade mark shall be filed at the Office.
2. The Office shall issue to the applicant, without delay, a receipt which shall include at least the file number, a representation, description or other identification of the mark, the nature and the number of the documents and the date of their receipt. That receipt may be issued by electronic means.

[5.879]
Article 31
Conditions with which applications must comply
1. An application for an EU trade mark shall contain:
(a) a request for the registration of an EU trade mark;
(b) information identifying the applicant;
(c) a list of the goods or services in respect of which the registration is requested;
(d) a representation of the mark, which satisfies the requirements set out in Article 4(b).
2. The application for an EU trade mark shall be subject to the payment of the application fee covering one class of goods or services and, where appropriate, of one or more class fees for each class of goods and services exceeding the first class and, where applicable, the search fee.
3. In addition to the requirements referred to in paragraphs 1 and 2, an application for an EU trade mark shall comply with the formal requirements laid down in this Regulation and in the implementing acts adopted pursuant to it. If those conditions provide for the trade mark to be represented electronically, the Executive Director may determine the formats and maximum size of such an electronic file.
4. The Commission shall adopt implementing acts specifying the details to be contained in the application. Those implementing acts shall be adopted in accordance with the examination procedure referred to in Article 207(2).

[5.880]
Article 32
Date of filing
The date of filing of an EU trade mark application shall be the date on which the documents containing the information specified in Article 31(1) are filed with the Office by the applicant, subject to payment of the application fee within one month of filing those documents.

[5.881]
Article 33
Designation and classification of goods and services
1. Goods and services in respect of which trade mark registration is applied for shall be classified in conformity with the system of classification established by the Nice Agreement Concerning the International Classification of Goods and Services for the Purposes of the Registration of Marks of 15 June 1957 ('the Nice Classification').

2. The goods and services for which the protection of the trade mark is sought shall be identified by the applicant with sufficient clarity and precision to enable the competent authorities and economic operators, on that sole basis, to determine the extent of the protection sought.
3. For the purposes of paragraph 2, the general indications included in the class headings of the Nice Classification or other general terms may be used, provided that they comply with the requisite standards of clarity and precision set out in this Article.
4. The Office shall reject an application in respect of indications or terms which are unclear or imprecise, where the applicant does not suggest an acceptable wording within a period set by the Office to that effect.
5. The use of general terms, including the general indications of the class headings of the Nice Classification, shall be interpreted as including all the goods or services clearly covered by the literal meaning of the indication or term. The use of such terms or indications shall not be interpreted as comprising a claim to goods or services which cannot be so understood.
6. Where the applicant requests registration for more than one class, the applicant shall group the goods and services according to the classes of the Nice Classification, each group being preceded by the number of the class to which that group of goods or services belongs, and shall present them in the order of the classes.
7. Goods and services shall not be regarded as being similar to each other on the ground that they appear in the same class under the Nice Classification. Goods and services shall not be regarded as being dissimilar from each other on the ground that they appear in different classes under the Nice Classification.
8. Proprietors of EU trade marks applied for before 22 June 2012 which are registered in respect of the entire heading of a Nice class may declare that their intention on the date of filing had been to seek protection in respect of goods or services beyond those covered by the literal meaning of the heading of that class, provided that the goods or services so designated are included in the alphabetical list for that class in the edition of the Nice Classification in force at the date of filing.
The declaration shall be filed at the Office by 24 September 2016, and shall indicate, in a clear, precise and specific manner, the goods and services, other than those clearly covered by the literal meaning of the indications of the class heading, originally covered by the proprietor's intention. The Office shall take appropriate measures to amend the Register accordingly. The possibility to make a declaration in accordance with the first subparagraph of this paragraph shall be without prejudice to the application of Article 18, Article 47(2), Article 58(1)(a), and Article 64(2).
EU trade marks for which no declaration is filed within the period referred to in the second subparagraph shall be deemed to extend, as from the expiry of that period, only to goods or services clearly covered by the literal meaning of the indications included in the heading of the relevant class.
9. Where the register is amended, the exclusive rights conferred by the EU trade mark under Article 9 shall not prevent a third party from continuing to use a trade mark in relation to goods or services where and to the extent that the use of the trade mark for those goods or services:
(a) commenced before the register was amended; and
(b) did not infringe the proprietor's rights based on the literal meaning of the record of the goods and services in the register at that time.

n addition, the amendment of the list of goods or services recorded in the register shall not give the proprietor of the EU trade mark the right to oppose or to apply for a declaration of invalidity of a later trade mark where and to the extent that:
(a) the later trade mark was either in use, or an application had been made to register the trade mark, for goods or services before the register was amended; and
(b) the use of the trade mark in relation to those goods or services did not infringe, or would not have infringed, the proprietor's rights based on the literal meaning of the record of the goods and services in the register at that time.

SECTION 2
PRIORITY

[5.882]
Article 34
Right of priority

1. A person who has duly filed an application for a trade mark in or in respect of any State party to the Paris Convention or to the Agreement establishing the World Trade Organisation, or his successors in title, shall enjoy, for the purpose of filing an EU trade mark application for the same trade mark in respect of goods or services which are identical with or contained within those for which the application has been filed, a right of priority during a period of six months from the date of filing of the first application.
2. Every filing that is equivalent to a regular national filing under the national law of the State where it was made or under bilateral or multilateral agreements shall be recognised as giving rise to a right of priority.
3. By a regular national filing is meant any filing that is sufficient to establish the date on which the application was filed, whatever may be the outcome of the application.

4. A subsequent application for a trade mark which was the subject of a previous first application in respect of the same goods or services and which is filed in or in respect of the same State shall be considered as the first application for the purposes of determining priority, provided that, at the date of filing of the subsequent application, the previous application has been withdrawn, abandoned or refused, without being open to public inspection and without leaving any rights outstanding, and has not served as a basis for claiming a right of priority. The previous application may not thereafter serve as a basis for claiming a right of priority.
5. If the first filing has been made in a State which is not a party to the Paris Convention or to the Agreement establishing the World Trade Organisation, paragraphs 1 to 4 shall apply only in so far as that State, according to published findings, grants, on the basis of the first filing made at the Office and subject to conditions equivalent to those laid down in this Regulation, a right of priority having equivalent effect. The Executive Director shall, where necessary, request the Commission to consider enquiring as to whether a State within the meaning of the first sentence accords that reciprocal treatment. If the Commission determines that reciprocal treatment in accordance with the first sentence is accorded, it shall publish a communication to that effect in the Official Journal of the European Union.
6. Paragraph 5 shall apply from the date of publication in the Official Journal of the European Union of the communication determining that reciprocal treatment is accorded, unless the communication states an earlier date from which it is applicable. It shall cease to apply from the date of publication in the Official Journal of the European Union of a communication of the Commission to the effect that reciprocal treatment is no longer accorded, unless the communication states an earlier date from which it is applicable.
7. Communications as referred to in paragraphs 5 and 6 shall also be published in the Official Journal of the Office.

[5.883]
Article 35
Claiming priority
1. Priority claims shall be filed together with the EU trade mark application and shall include the date, number and country of the previous application. The documentation in support of priority claims shall be filed within three months of the filing date.
2. The Commission shall adopt implementing acts specifying the kind of documentation to be filed for claiming the priority of a previous application in accordance with paragraph 1 of this Article. Those implementing acts shall be adopted in accordance with the examination procedure referred to in Article 207(2).
3. The Executive Director may determine that the documentation to be provided by the applicant in support of the priority claim may consist of less than what is required under the specifications adopted in accordance with paragraph 2, provided that the information required is available to the Office from other sources.

[5.884]
Article 36
Effect of priority right
The right of priority shall have the effect that the date of priority shall count as the date of filing of the EU trade mark application for the purposes of establishing which rights take precedence.

[5.885]
Article 37
Equivalence of Union filing with national filing
An EU trade mark application which has been accorded a date of filing shall, in the Member States, be equivalent to a regular national filing, where appropriate with the priority claimed for the EU trade mark application.

SECTION 3
EXHIBITION PRIORITY

[5.886]
Article 38
Exhibition priority
1. If an applicant for an EU trade mark has displayed goods or services under the mark applied for, at an official or officially recognised international exhibition falling within the terms of the Convention relating to international exhibitions signed at Paris on 22 November 1928 and last revised on 30 November 1972, he may, if he files the application within a period of six months of the date of the first display of the goods or services under the mark applied for, claim a right of priority from that date within the meaning of Article 36. The priority claim shall be filed together with the EU trade mark application.
2. An applicant who wishes to claim priority pursuant to paragraph 1 shall file evidence of the display of goods or services under the mark applied for within three months of the filing date.
3. An exhibition priority granted in a Member State or in a third country shall not extend the period of priority laid down in Article 34.

4. The Commission shall adopt implementing acts specifying the type and details of evidence to be filed for claiming an exhibition priority in accordance with paragraph 2 of this Article. Those implementing acts shall be adopted in accordance with the examination procedure referred to in Article 207(2).

SECTION 4
SENIORITY OF A NATIONAL TRADE MARK

[5.887]
Article 39
Claiming seniority of a national trade mark in an application for an EU trade mark or subsequent to the filing of the application

1. The proprietor of an earlier trade mark registered in a Member State, including a trade mark registered in the Benelux countries, or registered under international arrangements having effect in a Member State, who applies for an identical trade mark for registration as an EU trade mark for goods or services which are identical with or contained within those for which the earlier trade mark has been registered, may claim for the EU trade mark the seniority of the earlier trade mark in respect of the Member State in or for which it is registered.
2. Seniority claims shall either be filed together with the EU trade mark application or within two months of the filing date of the application, and shall include the Member State or Member States in or for which the mark is registered, the number and the filing date of the relevant registration, and the goods and services for which the mark is registered. Where the seniority of one or more registered earlier trade marks is claimed in the application, the documentation in support of the seniority claim shall be filed within three months of the filing date. Where the applicant wishes to claim the seniority subsequent to the filing of the application, the documentation in support of the seniority claim shall be submitted to the Office within three months of receipt of the seniority claim.
3. Seniority shall have the sole effect under this Regulation that, where the proprietor of the EU trade mark surrenders the earlier trade mark or allows it to lapse, he shall be deemed to continue to have the same rights as he would have had if the earlier trade mark had continued to be registered.
4. The seniority claimed for the EU trade mark shall lapse where the earlier trade mark the seniority of which is claimed is declared to be invalid or revoked. Where the earlier trade mark is revoked, the seniority shall lapse provided that the revocation takes effect prior to the filing date or priority date of that EU trade mark.
5. The Office shall inform the Benelux Office for Intellectual Property or the central industrial property office of the Member State concerned of the effective claiming of seniority.
6. The Commission shall adopt implementing acts specifying the kind of documentation to be filed for claiming the seniority of a national trade mark or a trade mark registered under international agreements having effect in a Member State in accordance with paragraph 2 of this Article. Those implementing acts shall be adopted in accordance with the examination procedure referred to in Article 207(2).
7. The Executive Director may determine that the documentation to be provided by the applicant in support of the seniority claim may consist of less than what is required under the specifications adopted in accordance with paragraph 6, provided that the information required is available to the Office from other sources.

[5.888]
Article 40
Claiming seniority of a national trade mark after registration of an EU trade mark

1. The proprietor of an EU trade mark who is the proprietor of an earlier identical trade mark registered in a Member State, including a trade mark registered in the Benelux countries or of an earlier identical trade mark, with an international registration effective in a Member State, for goods or services which are identical to those for which the earlier trade mark has been registered, or contained within them, may claim the seniority of the earlier trade mark in respect of the Member State in or for which it was registered.
2. Seniority claims filed pursuant to paragraph 1 of this Article shall include the registration number of the EU trade mark, the name and address of its proprietor, the Member State or Member States in or for which the earlier mark is registered, the number and the filing date of the relevant registration, the goods and services for which the mark is registered and those in respect of which seniority is claimed, and supporting documentation as provided for in the rules adopted pursuant to Article 39(6).
3. If the requirements governing the claiming of seniority are not fulfilled, the Office shall communicate the deficiency to the proprietor of the EU trade mark. If the deficiency is not remedied within a period to be specified by the Office, the Office shall reject the claim.
4. Article 39(3), (4), (5) and (7) shall apply.

CHAPTER IV
REGISTRATION PROCEDURE

SECTION 1
EXAMINATION OF APPLICATIONS

[5.889]
Article 41
Examination of the conditions of filing

1. The Office shall examine whether:
(a) the EU trade mark application satisfies the requirements for the accordance of a date of filing in accordance with Article 32;
(b) the EU trade mark application complies with the conditions and requirements referred to in Article 31(3);
(c) where appropriate, the class fees have been paid within the prescribed period.

2. Where the EU trade mark application does not satisfy the requirements referred to in paragraph 1, the Office shall request the applicant to remedy the deficiencies or the default on payment within two months of the receipt of the notification.
3. If the deficiencies or the default on payment established pursuant to paragraph 1(a) are not remedied within this period, the application shall not be dealt with as an EU trade mark application. If the applicant complies with the Office's request, the Office shall accord as the date of filing of the application the date on which the deficiencies or the default on payment established are remedied.
4. If the deficiencies established pursuant to paragraph 1(b) are not remedied within the prescribed period, the Office shall refuse the application.
5. If the default on payment established pursuant to paragraph 1(c) is not remedied within the prescribed period, the application shall be deemed to be withdrawn unless it is clear which categories of goods or services the amount paid is intended to cover. In the absence of other criteria to determine which classes are intended to be covered, the Office shall take the classes in the order of the classification. The application shall be deemed to have been withdrawn with regard to those classes for which the class fees have not been paid or have not been paid in full.
6. Failure to satisfy the requirements concerning the claim to priority shall result in loss of the right of priority for the application.
7. Failure to satisfy the requirements concerning the claiming of seniority of a national trade mark shall result in loss of that right for the application.
8. Where failure to satisfy the requirements referred to in paragraph 1(b) and (c) concerns only some of the goods or services, the Office shall refuse the application, or the right of priority or the right of seniority shall be lost, only in so far as those goods and services are concerned.

[5.890]
Article 42
Examination as to absolute grounds for refusal

1. Where, under Article 7, a trade mark is ineligible for registration in respect of some or all of the goods or services covered by the EU trade mark application, the application shall be refused as regards those goods or services.
2. The application shall not be refused before the applicant has been allowed the opportunity to withdraw or amend the application or to submit his observations. To this effect, the Office shall notify the applicant of the grounds for refusing registration and shall specify a period within which he may withdraw or amend the application or submit his observations. Where the applicant fails to overcome the grounds for refusing registration, the Office shall refuse registration in whole or in part.

SECTION 2
SEARCH

[5.891]
Article 43
Search report

1. The Office shall, at the request of the applicant for the EU trade mark when filing the application, draw up a European Union search report ('EU search report') citing those earlier EU trade marks or EU trade mark applications discovered which may be invoked under Article 8 against the registration of the EU trade mark applied for.
2. Where, at the time of filing an EU trade mark application, the applicant requests that a search report be prepared by the central industrial property offices of the Member States and where the appropriate search fee has been paid within the time limit for the payment of the filing fee, the Office shall transmit without delay a copy of the EU trade mark application to the central industrial property office of each Member State which has informed the Office of its decision to operate a search in its own register of trade marks in respect of EU trade mark applications.

3. Each of the central industrial property offices of the Member States referred to in paragraph 2 shall communicate a search report which shall either cite any earlier national trade marks, national trade mark applications or trade marks registered under international agreements, having effect in the Member State or Member States concerned, which have been discovered and which may be invoked under Article 8 against the registration of the EU trade mark applied for, or state that the search has revealed no such rights.
4. The Office, after consulting the Management Board provided for in Article 153 ('the Management Board'), shall establish the contents and modalities for the reports.
5. he Office shall pay an amount to each central industrial property office for each search report provided in accordance with paragraph 3. The amount, which shall be the same for each office, shall be fixed by the Budget Committee by means of a decision adopted by a majority of three quarters of the representatives of the Member States.
6. The Office shall transmit to the applicant for the EU trade mark the EU search report requested and any requested national search reports received.
7. Upon publication of the EU trade mark application, the Office shall inform the proprietors of any earlier EU trade marks or EU trade mark applications cited in the EU search report of the publication of the EU trade mark application. The latter shall apply irrespective of whether the applicant has requested to receive the EU search report, unless the proprietor of an earlier registration or application requests not to receive the notification.

SECTION 3
PUBLICATION OF THE APPLICATION

[5.892]
Article 44
Publication of the application

1. If the conditions which the application for an EU trade mark is required to satisfy have been fulfilled, the application shall be published for the purposes of Article 46 to the extent that it has not been refused pursuant to Article 42. The publication of the application shall be without prejudice to information already made available to the public otherwise in accordance with this Regulation or acts adopted pursuant to this Regulation.
2. Where, after publication, the application is refused pursuant to Article 42, the decision that it has been refused shall be published upon becoming final.
3. Where the publication of the application contains an error attributable to the Office, the Office shall of its own motion or at the request of the applicant correct the error and publish the correction. The rules adopted pursuant to Article 49(3) shall apply mutatis mutandis where a correction is requested by the applicant.
4. Article 46(2) shall also apply where the correction concerns the list of goods or services or the representation of the mark.
5. The Commission shall adopt implementing acts laying down the details to be contained in the publication of the application. Those implementing acts shall be adopted in accordance with the examination procedure referred to in Article 207(2).

SECTION 4
OBSERVATIONS BY THIRD PARTIES AND OPPOSITION

[5.893]
Article 45
Observations by third parties

1. Any natural or legal person and any group or body representing manufacturers, producers, suppliers of services, traders or consumers may submit to the Office written observations, explaining on which grounds, under Articles 5 and 7, the trade mark should not be registered *ex officio*.
Persons and groups or bodies as referred to in the first subparagraph shall not be parties to the proceedings before the Office.
2. Third party observations shall be submitted before the end of the opposition period or, where an opposition against the trade mark has been filed, before the final decision on the opposition is taken.
3. The submission referred to in paragraph 1 shall be without prejudice to the right of the Office to re-open the examination of absolute grounds on its own initiative at any time before registration, where appropriate.
4. The observations referred to in paragraph 1 shall be communicated to the applicant who may comment on them.

[5.894]
Article 46
Opposition

1. Within a period of three months following the publication of an EU trade mark application, notice of opposition to registration of the trade mark may be given on the grounds that it may not be registered under Article 8:

(a) by the proprietors of earlier trade marks referred to in Article 8(2) as well as licensees authorised by the proprietors of those trade marks, in respect of Article 8(1) and (5);
(b) by the proprietors of trade marks referred to in Article 8(3);
(c) by the proprietors of earlier marks or signs referred to in Article 8(4) and by persons authorised under the relevant national law to exercise these rights;
(d) by the persons authorised under the relevant Union legislation or national law to exercise the rights referred to in Article 8(6).

2. Notice of opposition to registration of the trade mark may also be given, subject to the conditions laid down in paragraph 1, in the event of the publication of an amended application in accordance with the second sentence of Article 49(2).

3. Opposition shall be expressed in writing, and shall specify the grounds on which it is made. It shall not be considered as duly entered until the opposition fee has been paid.

4. Within a period to be fixed by the Office, the opponent may submit facts, evidence and arguments in support of his case.

[5.895]
Article 47
Examination of opposition

1. In the examination of the opposition the Office shall invite the parties, as often as necessary, to file observations, within a period set by the Office, on communications from the other parties or issued by itself.

2. f the applicant so requests, the proprietor of an earlier EU trade mark who has given notice of opposition shall furnish proof that, during the five-year period preceding the date of filing or the date of priority of the EU trade mark application, the earlier EU trade mark has been put to genuine use in the Union in connection with the goods or services in respect of which it is registered and which he cites as justification for his opposition, or that there are proper reasons for non-use, provided that the earlier EU trade mark has at that date been registered for not less than five years. In the absence of proof to this effect, the opposition shall be rejected. If the earlier EU trade mark has been used in relation to only part of the goods or services for which it is registered it shall, for the purposes of the examination of the opposition, be deemed to be registered in respect only of that part of the goods or services.

3. Paragraph 2 shall apply to earlier national trade marks referred to in Article 8(2)(a), by substituting use in the Member State in which the earlier national trade mark is protected for use in the Union.

4. The Office may, if it thinks fit, invite the parties to make a friendly settlement.

5. If examination of the opposition reveals that the trade mark may not be registered in respect of some or all of the goods or services for which the EU trade mark application has been made, the application shall be refused in respect of those goods or services. Otherwise the opposition shall be rejected.

6. The decision refusing the application shall be published upon becoming final.

[5.896]
Article 48
Delegation of powers

The Commission is empowered to adopt delegated acts in accordance with Article 208 specifying the details of the procedure for filing and examining an opposition set out in Articles 46 and 47.

SECTION 5
WITHDRAWAL, RESTRICTION, AMENDMENT AND DIVISION OF THE APPLICATION

[5.897]
Article 49
Withdrawal, restriction and amendment of the application

1. The applicant may at any time withdraw his EU trade mark application or restrict the list of goods or services contained therein. Where the application has already been published, the withdrawal or restriction shall also be published.

2. In other respects, an EU trade mark application may be amended, upon request of the applicant, only by correcting the name and address of the applicant, errors of wording or of copying, or obvious mistakes, provided that such correction does not substantially change the trade mark or extend the list of goods or services. Where the amendments affect the representation of the trade mark or the list of goods or services and are made after publication of the application, the trade mark application shall be published as amended.

3. The Commission is empowered to adopt delegated acts in accordance with Article 208 specifying the details of the procedure governing the amendment of the application.

[5.898]
Article 50
Division of the application

1. The applicant may divide the application by declaring that some of the goods or services included in the original application will be the subject of one or more divisional applications. The goods or services in the divisional application shall not overlap with the goods or services which remain in the original application or those which are included in other divisional applications.
2. The declaration of division shall not be admissible:
   (a) if, where an opposition has been entered against the original application, such a divisional application has the effect of introducing a division amongst the goods or services against which the opposition has been directed, until the decision of the Opposition Division has become final or the opposition proceedings are finally terminated otherwise;
   (b) before the date of filing referred to in Article 32 has been accorded by the Office and during the opposition period provided for in Article 46(1).
3. The declaration of division shall be subject to a fee. The declaration shall be deemed not to have been made until the fee has been paid.
4. Where the Office finds that the requirements laid down in paragraph 1 and in the rules adopted pursuant to paragraph 9(a) are not fulfilled, it shall invite the applicant to remedy the deficiencies within a period to be specified by the Office. If the deficiencies are not remedied before the time limit expires, the Office shall refuse the declaration of division.
5. The division shall take effect on the date on which it is recorded in the files kept by the Office concerning the original application.
6. All requests and applications submitted and all fees paid with regard to the original application prior to the date on which the Office receives the declaration of division are deemed also to have been submitted or paid with regard to the divisional application or applications. The fees for the original application which have been duly paid prior to the date on which the declaration of division is received shall not be refunded.
7. The divisional application shall preserve the filing date and any priority date and seniority date of the original application.
8. Where the declaration of division relates to an application which has already been published pursuant to Article 44, the division shall be published. The divisional application shall be published. The publication shall not open a new period for the filing of oppositions.
9. The Commission shall adopt implementing acts specifying:
   (a) the details to be contained in a declaration of the division of an application made pursuant to paragraph 1;
   (b) the details as to how to process a declaration of the division of an application, ensuring that a separate file, including a new application number, is established for the divisional application;
   (c) the details to be contained in the publication of the divisional application pursuant to paragraph 8.

Those implementing acts shall be adopted in accordance with the examination procedure referred to in Article 207(2).

SECTION 6
REGISTRATION

[5.899]
Article 51
Registration

1. Where an application meets the requirements set out in this Regulation and where no notice of opposition has been given within the period referred to in Article 46(1) or where any opposition entered has been finally disposed of by withdrawal, rejection or other disposition, the trade mark and the particulars referred to in Article 111(2) shall be recorded in the Register. The registration shall be published.
2. The Office shall issue a certificate of registration. That certificate may be issued by electronic means. The Office shall provide certified or uncertified copies of the certificate subject to the payment of a fee, where those copies are issued other than by electronic means.
3. The Commission shall adopt implementing acts specifying the details to be contained in and the form of the certificate of registration referred to in paragraph 2 of this Article. Those implementing acts shall be adopted in accordance with the examination procedure referred to in Article 207(2).

CHAPTER V
DURATION, RENEWAL, ALTERATION AND DIVISION OF EU TRADE MARKS

[5.900]
Article 52
Duration of registration

EU trade marks shall be registered for a period of 10 years from the date of filing of the application. Registration may be renewed in accordance with Article 53 for further periods of 10 years.

[5.901]
Article 53
Renewal

1. Registration of the EU trade mark shall be renewed at the request of the proprietor of the EU trade mark or any person expressly authorised by him, provided that the fees have been paid.
2. The Office shall inform the proprietor of the EU trade mark, and any person having a registered right in respect of the EU trade mark, of the expiry of the registration at least six months before the said expiry. Failure to give such information shall not involve the responsibility of the Office and shall not affect the expiry of the registration.
3. The request for renewal shall be submitted in the six-month period prior to the expiry of the registration. The basic fee for the renewal, and where appropriate, one or more class fees for each class of goods or services exceeding the first one shall also be paid within this period. Failing this, the request may be submitted and the fees paid within a further period of six months following the expiry of registration, provided that an additional fee for late payment of the renewal fee or late submission of the request for renewal is paid within this further period.
4. The request for renewal shall include:
   (a) the name of the person requesting renewal;
   (b) the registration number of the EU trade mark to be renewed;
   (c) if the renewal is requested for only part of the registered goods and services, an indication of those classes or those goods and services for which renewal is requested, or those classes or those goods and services for which renewal is not requested, grouped according to the classes of the Nice classification, each group being preceded by the number of the class of that classification to which that group of goods or services belongs, and presented in the order of classes of that classification.

If the payment referred to in paragraph 3 is made, it shall be deemed to constitute a request for renewal provided that it contains all necessary indications to establish the purpose of the payment.
5. Where the request is submitted or the fees paid in respect of only some of the goods or services for which the EU trade mark is registered, registration shall be renewed for those goods or services only. Where the fees paid are insufficient to cover all the classes of goods and services for which renewal is requested, registration shall be renewed if it is clear which class or classes are to be covered. In the absence of other criteria, the Office shall take the classes into account in the order of classification.
6. Renewal shall take effect from the day following the date on which the existing registration expires. The renewal shall be registered.
7. Where the request for renewal is filed within the periods provided for in paragraph 3, but the other conditions governing renewal provided for in this Article are not satisfied, the Office shall inform the applicant of the deficiencies found.
8. Where a request for renewal is not submitted or is submitted after the expiry of the period provided for in paragraph 3, or where the fees are not paid or are paid only after the period in question has expired, or where the deficiencies referred to in paragraph 7 are not remedied within that period, the Office shall determine that the registration has expired and shall notify the proprietor of the EU trade mark accordingly. Where the determination has become final, the Office shall cancel the mark from the register. The cancellation shall take effect from the day following the date on which the existing registration expired. Where the renewal fees have been paid but the registration is not renewed, those fees shall be refunded.
9. A single request for renewal may be submitted for two or more marks, upon payment of the required fees for each of the marks, provided that the proprietors or the representatives are the same in each case.

[5.902]
Article 54
Alteration

1. The EU trade mark shall not be altered in the Register during the period of registration or on renewal thereof.
2. Nevertheless, where the EU trade mark includes the name and address of the proprietor, any alteration thereof not substantially affecting the identity of the trade mark as originally registered may be registered at the request of the proprietor.
3. The request for alteration shall include the element of the mark to be altered and that element in its altered version.

The Commission shall adopt implementing acts specifying the details to be contained in the request for alteration. Those implementing acts shall be adopted in accordance with the examination procedure referred to in Article 207(2).

4. The request shall be deemed not to have been filed until the required fee has been paid. If the fee has not been paid or has not been paid in full, the Office shall inform the applicant accordingly. A single request may be made for the alteration of the same element in two or more registrations of the same proprietor. The required fee shall be paid in respect of each registration to be altered. If the requirements governing the alteration of the registration are not fulfilled, the Office shall communicate the deficiency to the applicant. If the deficiency is not remedied within a period to be specified by the Office, the Office shall reject the request.

5. The publication of the registration of the alteration shall contain a representation of the EU trade mark as altered. Third parties whose rights may be affected by the alteration may challenge the registration thereof within the period of three months following publication. Articles 46 and 47 and rules adopted pursuant to Article 48 shall apply to the publication of the registration of the alteration.

[5.903]
[Article 55
Change of the name or address

1. A change of the name or address of the proprietor of the EU trade mark which is not an alteration of the EU trade mark pursuant to Article 54(2) and which is not the consequence of a whole or partial transfer of the EU trade mark shall, at the request of the proprietor, be recorded in the Register.

The Commission shall adopt implementing acts specifying the details to be contained in a request for the change of name or address pursuant to the first subparagraph of this paragraph. Those implementing acts shall be adopted in accordance with the examination procedure referred to in Article 207(2).

2. A single request may be made for the change of the name or address in respect of two or more registrations of the same proprietor.

3. If the requirements governing the recording of a change are not fulfilled, the Office shall communicate the deficiency to the proprietor of the EU trade mark. If the deficiency is not remedied within a period to be specified by the Office, the Office shall reject the request.

4. Paragraphs 1, 2 and 3 shall also apply to a change of the name or address of the registered representative.

5. Paragraphs 1 to 4 shall apply to applications for EU trade marks. The change shall be recorded in the files kept by the Office on the EU trade mark application.

[5.904]
Article 56
Division of the registration

1. The proprietor of the EU trade mark may divide the registration by declaring that some of the goods or services included in the original registration will be the subject of one or more divisional registrations. The goods or services in the divisional registration shall not overlap with the goods or services which remain in the original registration or those which are included in other divisional registrations.

2. The declaration of division shall not be admissible:

(a) if, where an application for revocation of rights or for a declaration of invalidity has been entered at the Office against the original registration, such a divisional declaration has the effect of introducing a division amongst the goods or services against which the application for revocation of rights or for a declaration of invalidity is directed, until the decision of the Cancellation Division has become final or the proceedings are finally terminated otherwise;

(b) if, where a counterclaim for revocation or for a declaration of invalidity has been entered in a case before an EU trade mark court, such a divisional declaration has the effect of introducing a division amongst the goods or services against which the counterclaim is directed, until the mention of the EU trade mark court's judgment is recorded in the Register pursuant to Article 128(6).

3. If the requirements laid down in paragraph 1 and pursuant to the implementing acts referred to in paragraph 8 are not fulfilled, or the list of goods and services which form the divisional registration overlap with the goods and services which remain in the original registration, the Office shall invite the proprietor of the EU trade mark to remedy the deficiencies within such period as it may specify. If the deficiencies are not remedied before the period expires, the Office shall refuse the declaration of division.

4. The declaration of division shall be subject to a fee. The declaration shall be deemed not to have been made until the fee has been paid.

5. The division shall take effect on the date on which it is entered in the Register.

6. All requests and applications submitted and all fees paid with regard to the original registration prior to the date on which the Office receives the declaration of division shall be deemed also to have been submitted or paid with regard to the divisional registration or registrations. The fees for the original registration which have been duly paid prior to the date on which the declaration of division is received shall not be refunded.
7. The divisional registration shall preserve the filing date and any priority date and seniority date of the original registration.
8. The Commission shall adopt implementing acts specifying:
(a) the details to be contained in a declaration of the division of a registration pursuant to paragraph 1;
(b) the details as how to process a declaration of the division of a registration, ensuring that a separate file, including a new registration number, is established for the divisional registration.
Those implementing acts shall be adopted in accordance with the examination procedure referred to in Article 207(2).

CHAPTER VI
SURRENDER, REVOCATION AND INVALIDITY

SECTION 1
SURRENDER

[5.905]
Article 57
Surrender
1. An EU trade mark may be surrendered in respect of some or all of the goods or services for which it is registered.
2. The surrender shall be declared to the Office in writing by the proprietor of the trade mark. It shall not have effect until it has been entered in the Register. The validity of the surrender of an EU trade mark which is declared to the Office subsequent to the submission of an application for revocation of that trade mark pursuant to Article 63(1) shall be conditional upon the final rejection or withdrawal of the application for revocation.
3. Surrender shall be entered only with the agreement of the proprietor of a right relating to the EU trade mark and which is entered in the Register. If a licence has been registered, surrender shall be entered in the Register only if the proprietor of the EU trade mark proves that he has informed the licensee of his intention to surrender. The entry of the surrender shall be made on expiry of the three-month period after the date on which the proprietor satisfies the Office that he has informed the licensee of his intention to surrender, or before the expiry of that period, as soon as he proves that the licensee has given his consent.
4. If the requirements governing surrender are not fulfilled, the Office shall communicate the deficiencies to the declarant. If the deficiencies are not remedied within a period to be specified by the Office, the Office shall reject the entry of surrender in the Register.
5. The Commission shall adopt implementing acts specifying the details to be contained in a declaration of surrender pursuant to paragraph 2 of this Article and the kind of documentation required to establish a third party's agreement pursuant to paragraph 3 of this Article. Those implementing acts shall be adopted in accordance with the examination procedure referred to in Article 207(2).

SECTION 2
GROUNDS FOR REVOCATION

[5.906]
Article 58
Grounds for revocation
1. The rights of the proprietor of the EU trade mark shall be declared to be revoked on application to the Office or on the basis of a counterclaim in infringement proceedings:
(a) if, within a continuous period of five years, the trade mark has not been put to genuine use in the Union in connection with the goods or services in respect of which it is registered, and there are no proper reasons for non-use; however, no person may claim that the proprietor's rights in an EU trade mark should be revoked where, during the interval between expiry of the five-year period and filing of the application or counterclaim, genuine use of the trade mark has been started or resumed; the commencement or resumption of use within a period of three months preceding the filing of the application or counterclaim which began at the earliest on expiry of the continuous period of five years of non-use shall, however, be disregarded where preparations for the commencement or resumption occur only after the proprietor becomes aware that the application or counterclaim may be filed;
(b) if, in consequence of acts or inactivity of the proprietor, the trade mark has become the common name in the trade for a product or service in respect of which it is registered;

(c) if, in consequence of the use made of the trade mark by the proprietor of the trade mark or with his consent in respect of the goods or services for which it is registered, the trade mark is liable to mislead the public, particularly as to the nature, quality or geographical origin of those goods or services.

2. Where the grounds for revocation of rights exist in respect of only some of the goods or services for which the EU trade mark is registered, the rights of the proprietor shall be declared to be revoked in respect of those goods or services only.

SECTION 3
GROUNDS FOR INVALIDITY

[5.907]
Article 59
Absolute grounds for invalidity

1. An EU trade mark shall be declared invalid on application to the Office or on the basis of a counterclaim in infringement proceedings:

(a) where the EU trade mark has been registered contrary to the provisions of Article 7;
(b) where the applicant was acting in bad faith when he filed the application for the trade mark.

2. Where the EU trade mark has been registered in breach of the provisions of Article 7(1)(b), (c) or (d), it may nevertheless not be declared invalid if, in consequence of the use which has been made of it, it has after registration acquired a distinctive character in relation to the goods or services for which it is registered.

3. Where the ground for invalidity exists in respect of only some of the goods or services for which the EU trade mark is registered, the trade mark shall be declared invalid as regards those goods or services only.

[5.908]
Article 60
Relative grounds for invalidity

1. An EU trade mark shall be declared invalid on application to the Office or on the basis of a counterclaim in infringement proceedings:

(a) where there is an earlier trade mark as referred to in Article 8(2) and the conditions set out in paragraph 1 or 5 of that Article are fulfilled;
(b) where there is a trade mark as referred to in Article 8(3) and the conditions set out in that paragraph are fulfilled;
(c) where there is an earlier right as referred to in Article 8(4) and the conditions set out in that paragraph are fulfilled;
(d) where there is an earlier designation of origin or geographical indication as referred to in Article 8(6) and the conditions set out in that paragraph are fulfilled.

All the conditions referred to in the first subparagraph shall be fulfilled at the filing date or the priority date of the EU trade mark.

2. An EU trade mark shall also be declared invalid on application to the Office or on the basis of a counterclaim in infringement proceedings where the use of such trade mark may be prohibited pursuant to another earlier right under the Union legislation or national law governing its protection, and in particular:

(a) a right to a name;
(b) a right of personal portrayal;
(c) a copyright;
(d) an industrial property right.

3. An EU trade mark may not be declared invalid where the proprietor of a right referred to in paragraph 1 or 2 consents expressly to the registration of the EU trade mark before submission of the application for a declaration of invalidity or the counterclaim.

4. Where the proprietor of one of the rights referred to in paragraph 1 or 2 has previously applied for a declaration that an EU trade mark is invalid or made a counterclaim in infringement proceedings, he may not submit a new application for a declaration of invalidity or lodge a counterclaim on the basis of another of the said rights which he could have invoked in support of his first application or counterclaim.

5. Article 59(3) shall apply.

[5.909]
Article 61
Limitation in consequence of acquiescence

1. Where the proprietor of an EU trade mark has acquiesced, for a period of five successive years, in the use of a later EU trade mark in the Union while being aware of such use, he shall no longer be entitled on the basis of the earlier trade mark to apply for a declaration that the later trade mark is invalid in respect of the goods or services for which the later trade mark has been used, unless registration of the later EU trade mark was applied for in bad faith.

2. Where the proprietor of an earlier national trade mark as referred to in Article 8(2) or of another earlier sign referred to in Article 8(4) has acquiesced, for a period of five successive years, in the use of a later EU trade mark in the Member State in which the earlier trade mark or the other earlier sign is protected while being aware of such use, he shall no longer be entitled on the basis of the earlier trade mark or of the other earlier sign to apply for a declaration that the later trade mark is invalid in respect of the goods or services for which the later trade mark has been used, unless registration of the later EU trade mark was applied for in bad faith.
3. In the cases referred to in paragraphs 1 and 2, the proprietor of a later EU trade mark shall not be entitled to oppose the use of the earlier right, even though that right may no longer be invoked against the later EU trade mark.

SECTION 4
CONSEQUENCES OF REVOCATION AND INVALIDITY

[5.910]
Article 62
Consequences of revocation and invalidity
1. The EU trade mark shall be deemed not to have had, as from the date of the application for revocation or of the counterclaim, the effects specified in this Regulation, to the extent that the rights of the proprietor have been revoked. An earlier date, on which one of the grounds for revocation occurred, may be fixed in the decision at the request of one of the parties.
2. The EU trade mark shall be deemed not to have had, as from the outset, the effects specified in this Regulation, to the extent that the trade mark has been declared invalid.
3. Subject to the national provisions relating either to claims for compensation for damage caused by negligence or lack of good faith on the part of the proprietor of the trade mark, or to unjust enrichment, the retroactive effect of revocation or invalidity of the trade mark shall not affect:
(a) any decision on infringement which has acquired the authority of a final decision and been enforced prior to the revocation or invalidity decision;
(b) any contract concluded prior to the revocation or invalidity decision, in so far as it has been performed before that decision; however, repayment, to an extent justified by the circumstances, of sums paid under the relevant contract may be claimed on grounds of equity.

SECTION 5
PROCEEDINGS IN THE OFFICE IN RELATION TO REVOCATION OR INVALIDITY

[5.911]
Article 63
Application for revocation or for a declaration of invalidity
1. An application for revocation of the rights of the proprietor of an EU trade mark or for a declaration that the trade mark is invalid may be submitted to the Office:
(a) where Articles 58 and 59 apply, by any natural or legal person and any group or body set up for the purpose of representing the interests of manufacturers, producers, suppliers of services, traders or consumers, which, under the terms of the law governing it, has the capacity in its own name to sue and be sued;
(b) where Article 60(1) applies, by the persons referred to in Article 46(1);
(c) where Article 60(2) applies, by the owners of the earlier rights referred to in that provision or by the persons who are entitled under Union legislation or the law of the Member State concerned to exercise the rights in question.
2. The application shall be filed in a written reasoned statement. It shall not be deemed to have been filed until the fee has been paid.
3. An application for revocation or for a declaration of invalidity shall be inadmissible where an application relating to the same subject matter and cause of action, and involving the same parties, has been adjudicated on its merits, either by the Office or by an EU trade mark court as referred to in Article 123, and the decision of the Office or that court on that application has acquired the authority of a final decision.

[5.912]
Article 64
Examination of the application
1. On the examination of the application for revocation of rights or for a declaration of invalidity, the Office shall invite the parties, as often as necessary, to file observations, within a period to be fixed by the Office, on communications from the other parties or issued by itself.
2. If the proprietor of the EU trade mark so requests, the proprietor of an earlier EU trade mark, being a party to the invalidity proceedings, shall furnish proof that, during the period of five years preceding the date of the application for a declaration of invalidity, the earlier EU trade mark has been put to genuine use in the Union in connection with the goods or services in respect of which it is registered and which the proprietor of that earlier trade mark cites as justification for his application, or that there are proper reasons for non-use, provided that the earlier EU trade mark has

at that date been registered for not less than five years. If, at the date on which the EU trade mark application was filed or at the priority date of the EU trade mark application, the earlier EU trade mark had been registered for not less than five years, the proprietor of the earlier EU trade mark shall furnish proof that, in addition, the conditions set out in Article 47(2) were satisfied at that date. In the absence of proof to this effect, the application for a declaration of invalidity shall be rejected. If the earlier EU trade mark has been used only in relation to part of the goods or services for which it is registered, it shall, for the purpose of the examination of the application for a declaration of invalidity, be deemed to be registered in respect of that part of the goods or services only.

3. Paragraph 2 shall apply to earlier national trade marks referred to in Article 8(2)(a), by substituting use in the Member State in which the earlier national trade mark is protected for use in the Union.

4. The Office may, if it thinks fit, invite the parties to make a friendly settlement.

5. If the examination of the application for revocation of rights or for a declaration of invalidity reveals that the trade mark should not have been registered in respect of some or all of the goods or services for which it is registered, the rights of the proprietor of the EU trade mark shall be revoked or it shall be declared invalid in respect of those goods or services. Otherwise the application for revocation of rights or for a declaration of invalidity shall be rejected.

6. A record of the Office's decision on the application for revocation of rights or for a declaration of invalidity shall be entered in the Register once it has become final.

[5.913]
Article 65
Delegation of powers

The Commission is empowered to adopt delegated acts in accordance with Article 208 specifying the details of the procedures governing the revocation and declaration of invalidity of an EU trade mark as referred to in Articles 63 and 64, as well as the transfer of an EU trade mark registered in the name of an agent as referred to in Article 21.

CHAPTER VII
APPEALS

[5.914]
Article 66
Decisions subject to appeal

1. An appeal shall lie from decisions of any of the decision-making instances of the Office listed in points (a) to (d) of Article 159, and, where appropriate, point (f) of that Article. Those decisions shall take effect only as from the date of expiration of the appeal period referred to in Article 68. The filing of the appeal shall have suspensive effect.

2. A decision which does not terminate proceedings as regards one of the parties can only be appealed together with the final decision, unless the decision allows separate appeal.

[5.915]
Article 67
Persons entitled to appeal and to be parties to appeal proceedings

Any party to proceedings adversely affected by a decision may appeal. Any other parties to the proceedings shall be parties to the appeal proceedings as of right.

[5.916]
Article 68
Time limit and form of appeal

1. Notice of appeal shall be filed in writing at the Office within two months of the date of notification of the decision. The notice shall be deemed to have been filed only when the fee for appeal has been paid. It shall be filed in the language of the proceedings in which the decision subject to appeal was taken. Within four months of the date of notification of the decision, a written statement setting out the grounds of appeal shall be filed.

2. In *inter partes* proceedings, the defendant may, in his response, seek a decision annulling or altering the contested decision on a point not raised in the appeal. Such submissions shall cease to have effect should the appellant discontinue the proceedings.

[5.917]
Article 69
Revision of decisions in ex parte cases

1. If the party which has lodged the appeal is the sole party to the procedure, and if the department whose decision is contested considers the appeal to be admissible and well founded, the department shall rectify its decision.

2. If the decision is not rectified within one month of receipt of the statement of grounds, the appeal shall be remitted to the Board of Appeal without delay, and without comment as to its merit.

[5.918]
Article 70
Examination of appeals

1. If the appeal is admissible, the Board of Appeal shall examine whether the appeal is allowable.
2. In the examination of the appeal, the Board of Appeal shall invite the parties, as often as necessary, to file observations, within a period to be fixed by the Board of Appeal, on communications from the other parties or issued by itself.

[5.919]
Article 71
Decisions in respect of appeals

1. Following the examination as to the allowability of the appeal, the Board of Appeal shall decide on the appeal. The Board of Appeal may either exercise any power within the competence of the department which was responsible for the decision appealed or remit the case to that department for further prosecution.
2. If the Board of Appeal remits the case for further prosecution to the department whose decision was appealed, that department shall be bound by the ratio decidendi of the Board of Appeal, in so far as the facts are the same.
3. The decisions of the Board of Appeal shall take effect only as from the date of expiry of the period referred to in Article 72(5) or, if an action has been brought before the General Court within that period, as from the date of dismissal of such action or of any appeal filed with the Court of Justice against the decision of the General Court.

[5.920]
Article 72
Actions before the Court of Justice

1. Actions may be brought before the General Court against decisions of the Boards of Appeal in relation to appeals.
2. The action may be brought on grounds of lack of competence, infringement of an essential procedural requirement, infringement of the TFEU, infringement of this Regulation or of any rule of law relating to their application or misuse of power.
3. The General Court shall have jurisdiction to annul or to alter the contested decision.
4. The action shall be open to any party to proceedings before the Board of Appeal adversely affected by its decision.
5. The action shall be brought before the General Court within two months of the date of notification of the decision of the Board of Appeal.
6. The Office shall take the necessary measures to comply with the judgment of the General Court or, in the event of an appeal against that judgment, the Court of Justice.

[5.921]
Article 73
Delegation of powers

The Commission is empowered to adopt delegated acts in accordance with Article 208 specifying:

(a) the formal content of the notice of appeal referred to in Article 68 and the procedure for the filing and the examination of an appeal;
(b) the formal content and form of the Board of Appeal's decisions as referred to in Article 71;
(c) the reimbursement of the appeal fee referred to in Article 68.

CHAPTER VIII
SPECIFIC PROVISIONS ON EUROPEAN UNION COLLECTIVE MARKS AND CERTIFICATION MARKS

SECTION 1
EU COLLECTIVE MARKS

[5.922]
Article 74
EU collective marks

1. A European Union collective mark ('EU collective mark') shall be an EU trade mark which is described as such when the mark is applied for and is capable of distinguishing the goods or services of the members of the association which is the proprietor of the mark from those of other undertakings. Associations of manufacturers, producers, suppliers of services, or traders which, under the terms of the law governing them, have the capacity in their own name to have rights and obligations of all kinds, to make contracts or accomplish other legal acts, and to sue and be sued, as well as legal persons governed by public law, may apply for EU collective marks.
2. By way of derogation from Article 7(1)(c), signs or indications which may serve, in trade, to designate the geographical origin of the goods or services may constitute EU collective marks within the meaning of paragraph 1. An EU collective mark shall not entitle the proprietor to prohibit

a third party from using in the course of trade such signs or indications, provided that he uses them in accordance with honest practices in industrial or commercial matters; in particular, such a mark shall not be invoked against a third party who is entitled to use a geographical name
3. Chapters I to VII and IX to XIV shall apply to EU collective marks to the extent that this section does not provide otherwise.

[5.923]
Article 75
Regulations governing use of an EU collective mark
1. An applicant for an EU collective mark shall submit regulations governing use within two months of the date of filing.
2. The regulations governing use shall specify the persons authorised to use the mark, the conditions of membership of the association and, where they exist, the conditions of use of the mark, including sanctions. The regulations governing use of a mark referred to in Article 74(2) shall authorise any person whose goods or services originate in the geographical area concerned to become a member of the association which is the proprietor of the mark.
3. The Commission shall adopt implementing acts specifying the details to be contained in the regulations referred to in paragraph 2 of this Article. Those implementing acts shall be adopted in accordance with the examination procedure referred to in Article 207(2).

[5.924]
Article 76
Refusal of the application
1. In addition to the grounds for refusal of an EU trade mark application provided for in Articles 41 and 42, an application for an EU collective mark shall be refused where the provisions of Articles 74 or 75 are not satisfied, or where the regulations governing use are contrary to public policy or to accepted principles of morality.
2. An application for an EU collective mark shall also be refused if the public is liable to be misled as regards the character or the significance of the mark, in particular if it is likely to be taken to be something other than a collective mark.
3. An application shall not be refused if the applicant, as a result of amendment of the regulations governing use, meets the requirements of paragraphs 1 and 2.

[5.925]
Article 77
Observations by third parties
Where written observations on an EU collective mark are submitted to the Office pursuant to Article 45, those observations may also be based on the particular grounds on which the application for an EU collective mark should be refused pursuant to Article 76.

[5.926]
Article 78
Use of marks
Use of an EU collective mark by any person who has authority to use it shall satisfy the requirements of this Regulation, provided that the other conditions which this Regulation imposes with regard to the use of EU trade marks are fulfilled.

[5.927]
Article 79
Amendment of the regulations governing use of the EU collective mark
1. The proprietor of an EU collective mark shall submit to the Office any amended regulations governing use.
2. The amendment shall not be mentioned in the Register if the amended regulations do not satisfy the requirements of Article 75 or involve one of the grounds for refusal referred to in Article 76.
3. Written observations made in accordance with Article 77 may also be submitted with regard to amended regulations governing use.
4. For the purposes of applying this Regulation, amendments to the regulations governing use shall take effect only from the date of entry of the mention of the amendment in the Register.

[5.928]
Article 80
Persons who are entitled to bring an action for infringement
1. The provisions of Article 25(3) and (4) concerning the rights of licensees shall apply to every person who has authority to use an EU collective mark.
2. The proprietor of an EU collective mark shall be entitled to claim compensation on behalf of persons who have authority to use the mark where they have sustained damage in consequence of unauthorised use of the mark.

[5.929]
Article 81
Grounds for revocation

Apart from the grounds for revocation provided for in Article 58, the rights of the proprietor of an EU collective mark shall be revoked on application to the Office or on the basis of a counterclaim in infringement proceedings, if:

(a) the proprietor does not take reasonable steps to prevent the mark being used in a manner incompatible with the conditions of use, where these exist, laid down in the regulations governing use, amendments to which have, where appropriate, been mentioned in the Register;

(b) the manner in which the mark has been used by the proprietor has caused it to become liable to mislead the public in the manner referred to in Article 76(2);

(c) an amendment to the regulations governing use of the mark has been mentioned in the Register in breach of the provisions of Article 79(2), unless the proprietor of the mark, by further amending the regulations governing use, complies with the requirements of those provisions.

[5.930]
Article 82
Grounds for invalidity

Apart from the grounds for invalidity provided for in Articles 59 and 60, an EU collective mark which is registered in breach of the provisions of Article 76 shall be declared invalid on application to the Office or on the basis of a counterclaim in infringement proceedings, unless the proprietor of the mark, by amending the regulations governing use, complies with the requirements of those provisions.

SECTION 2
EU CERTIFICATION MARKS

[5.931]
Article 83
EU certification marks

1. An EU certification mark shall be an EU trade mark which is described as such when the mark is applied for and is capable of distinguishing goods or services which are certified by the proprietor of the mark in respect of material, mode of manufacture of goods or performance of services, quality, accuracy or other characteristics, with the exception of geographical origin, from goods and services which are not so certified.

2. Any natural or legal person, including institutions, authorities and bodies governed by public law, may apply for EU certification marks provided that such person does not carry on a business involving the supply of goods or services of the kind certified.

3. Chapters I to VII and IX to XIV shall apply to EU certification marks to the extent that this Section does not provide otherwise.

[5.932]
Article 84
Regulations governing use of an EU certification mark

1. An applicant for an EU certification mark shall submit regulations governing the use of the EU certification mark within two months of the date of filing.

2. The regulations governing use shall specify the persons authorised to use the mark, the characteristics to be certified by the mark, how the certifying body is to test those characteristics and to supervise the use of the mark. Those regulations shall also specify the conditions of use of the mark, including sanctions.

3. The Commission shall adopt implementing acts specifying the details to be contained in the regulations referred to in paragraph 2 of this Article. Those implementing acts shall be adopted in accordance with the examination procedure referred to in Article 207(2).

[5.933]
Article 85
Refusal of the application

1. In addition to the grounds for refusal of an EU trade mark application provided for in Articles 41 and 42, an application for an EU certification mark shall be refused where the conditions set out in Articles 83 and 84 are not satisfied, or where the regulations governing use are contrary to public policy or to accepted principles of morality.

2. An application for an EU certification mark shall also be refused if the public is liable to be misled as regards the character or the significance of the mark, in particular if it is likely to be taken to be something other than a certification mark.

3. An application shall not be refused if the applicant, as a result of an amendment of the regulations governing use, meets the requirements of paragraphs 1 and 2.

[5.934]
Article 86
Observations by third parties

Where written observations on an EU certification mark are submitted to the Office pursuant to Article 45, those observations may also be based on the particular grounds on which the application for an EU certification mark should be refused pursuant to Article 85.

[5.935]
Article 87
Use of the EU certification mark

Use of an EU certification mark by any person who has authority to use it pursuant to the regulations governing use referred to in Article 84 shall satisfy the requirements of this Regulation, provided that the other conditions laid down in this Regulation with regard to the use of EU trade marks are fulfilled.

[5.936]
Article 88
Amendment of the regulations governing use of the mark

1. The proprietor of an EU certification mark shall submit to the Office any amended regulations governing use.
2. Amendments shall not be mentioned in the Register where the regulations as amended do not satisfy the requirements of Article 84 or involve one of the grounds for refusal referred to in Article 85.
3. Written observations in accordance with Article 86 may also be submitted with regard to amended regulations governing use.
4. For the purposes of this Regulation, amendments to the regulations governing use shall take effect only as from the date of entry of the mention of the amendment in the Register.

[5.937]
Article 89
Transfer

By way of derogation from Article 20(1), an EU certification mark may only be transferred to a person who meets the requirements of Article 83(2).

[5.938]
Article 90
Persons who are entitled to bring an action for infringement

1. Only the proprietor of an EU certification mark, or any person specifically authorised by him to that effect, shall be entitled to bring an action for infringement.
2. The proprietor of an EU certification mark shall be entitled to claim compensation on behalf of persons who have authority to use the mark where they have sustained damage as a consequence of unauthorised use of the mark.

[5.939]
Article 91
Grounds for revocation

In addition to the grounds for revocation provided for in Article 58, the rights of the proprietor of an EU certification mark shall be revoked on application to the Office or on the basis of a counterclaim in infringement proceedings, where any of the following conditions is fulfilled:

(a) the proprietor no longer complies with the requirements set out in Article 83(2);
(b) the proprietor does not take reasonable steps to prevent the EU certification mark being used in a manner that is incompatible with the conditions of use laid down in the regulations governing use, amendments to which have, where appropriate, been mentioned in the Register;
(c) the manner in which the EU certification mark has been used by the proprietor has caused it to become liable to mislead the public in the manner referred to in Article 85(2);
(d) an amendment to the regulations governing use of the EU certification mark has been mentioned in the Register in breach of Article 88(2), unless the proprietor of the mark, by further amending the regulations governing use, complies with the requirements of that Article.

[5.940]
Article 92
Grounds for invalidity

In addition to the grounds for invalidity provided for in Articles 59 and 60, an EU certification mark which is registered in breach of Article 85 shall be declared invalid on application to the Office or on the basis of a counterclaim in infringement proceedings, unless the proprietor of the EU certification mark, by amending the regulations governing use, complies with the requirements of Article 85.

[5.941]
Article 93
Conversion

Without prejudice to Article 139(2), conversion of an application for an EU certification mark or of a registered EU certification mark shall not take place where the national law of the Member State concerned does not provide for the registration of guarantee or certification marks pursuant to Article 28 of Directive (EU) 2015/2436.

CHAPTER IX
PROCEDURE

SECTION 1
GENERAL PROVISIONS

[5.942]
Article 94
Decisions and communications of the Office

1. Decisions of the Office shall state the reasons on which they are based. They shall be based only on reasons or evidence on which the parties concerned have had an opportunity to present their comments. Where oral proceedings are held before the Office, the decision may be given orally. Subsequently, the decision shall be notified in writing to the parties.

2. Any decision, communication or notice from the Office shall indicate the department or division of the Office as well as the name or the names of the official or officials responsible. They shall be signed by that official or those officials, or, instead of a signature, carry a printed or stamped seal of the Office. The Executive Director may determine that other means of identifying the department or division of the Office and the name of the official or officials responsible, or an identification other than a seal, may be used where decisions, communications or notices from the Office are transmitted by telecopier or any other technical means of communication.

3. Decisions of the Office which are open to appeal shall be accompanied by a written communication indicating that any notice of appeal is to be filed in writing at the Office within two months of the date of notification of the decision in question. The communications shall also draw the attention of the parties to the provisions laid down in Articles 66, 67 and 68. The parties may not plead any failure on the part of the Office to communicate the availability of appeal proceedings.

[5.943]
Article 95
Examination of the facts by the Office of its own motion

1. In proceedings before it the Office shall examine the facts of its own motion; however, in proceedings relating to relative grounds for refusal of registration, the Office shall be restricted in this examination to the facts, evidence and arguments provided by the parties and the relief sought. In invalidity proceedings pursuant to Article 59, the Office shall limit its examination to the grounds and arguments submitted by the parties.

2. The Office may disregard facts or evidence which are not submitted in due time by the parties concerned.

[5.944]
Article 96
Oral proceedings

1. If the Office considers that oral proceedings would be expedient they shall be held either at the instance of the Office or at the request of any party to the proceedings.

2. Oral proceedings before the examiners, the Opposition Division and the Department in charge of the Register shall not be public.

3. Oral proceedings, including delivery of the decision, shall be public before the Cancellation Division and the Boards of Appeal, in so far as the department before which the proceedings are taking place does not decide otherwise in cases where admission of the public could have serious and unjustified disadvantages, in particular for a party to the proceedings.

4. The Commission is empowered to adopt delegated acts in accordance with Article 208 specifying the detailed arrangements for oral proceedings, including the detailed arrangements for the use of languages in accordance with Article 146.

[5.945]
Article 97
Taking of evidence

1. In any proceedings before the Office, the means of giving or obtaining evidence shall include the following:

- (a) hearing the parties;
- (b) requests for information;
- (c) the production of documents and items of evidence;
- (d) hearing witnesses;

(e) opinions by experts;
(f) statements in writing sworn or affirmed or having a similar effect under the law of the State in which the statement is drawn up.

2. The relevant department may commission one of its members to examine the evidence adduced.
3. If the Office considers it necessary for a party, witness or expert to give evidence orally, it shall issue a summons to the person concerned to appear before it. The period of notice provided in such summons shall be at least one month, unless they agree to a shorter period.
4. The parties shall be informed of the hearing of a witness or expert before the Office. They shall have the right to be present and to put questions to the witness or expert.
5. The Executive Director shall determine the amounts of expenses to be paid, including advances, as regards the costs of taking of evidence as referred to in this Article.
6. The Commission is empowered to adopt delegated acts in accordance with Article 208 specifying the detailed arrangements for the taking of evidence.

[5.946]
Article 98
Notification

1. The Office shall, as a matter of course, notify those concerned of decisions and summonses and of any notice or other communication from which a time limit is reckoned, or of which those concerned are to be notified under other provisions of this Regulation or of acts adopted pursuant to this Regulation, or of which notification has been ordered by the Executive Director.
2. The Executive Director may determine which documents other than decisions subject to a time limit for appeal and summonses shall be notified by registered letter with proof of delivery.
3. Notification may be effected by different means, including by electronic means. The details regarding electronic means shall be determined by the Executive Director.
4. Where notification is to be effected by public notice, the Executive Director shall determine how the public notice is to be given and shall fix the beginning of the one-month period on the expiry of which the document shall be deemed to have been notified.
5. The Commission is empowered to adopt delegated acts in accordance with Article 208 specifying the detailed arrangements for notification.

[5.947]
Article 99
Notification of loss of rights

Where the Office finds that the loss of any rights results from this Regulation or acts adopted pursuant to this Regulation, without any decision having been taken, it shall communicate this to the person concerned in accordance with Article 98. The latter may apply for a decision on the matter within two months of notification of the communication, if he considers that the finding of the Office is incorrect. The Office shall adopt such a decision only where it disagrees with the person requesting it; otherwise the Office shall amend its finding and inform the person requesting the decision.

[5.948]
Article 100
Communications to the Office

1. Communications addressed to the Office may be effected by electronic means. The Executive Director shall determine to what extent and under which technical conditions those communications may be submitted electronically.
2. The Commission is empowered to adopt delegated acts in accordance with Article 208 specifying the rules on the means of communication, including the electronic means of communication, to be used by the parties to proceedings before the Office and the forms to be made available by the Office.

[5.949]
Article 101
Time limits

1. Time limits shall be laid down in terms of full years, months, weeks or days. Calculation shall start on the day following the day on which the relevant event occurred. The duration of time limits shall be no less than one month and no more than six months.
2. The Executive Director shall determine, before the commencement of each calendar year, the days on which the Office is not open for receipt of documents or on which ordinary post is not delivered in the locality in which the Office is located.
3. The Executive Director shall determine the duration of the period of interruption in the case of a general interruption in the delivery of post in the Member State where the Office is located or, in the case of an actual interruption of the Office's connection to admitted electronic means of communication.
4. If an exceptional occurrence, such as a natural disaster or strike, interrupts or interferes with proper communication from the parties to the proceedings to the Office or vice-versa, the Executive Director may determine that for parties to the proceedings having their residence or registered office

in the Member State concerned or who have appointed a representative with a place of business in the Member State concerned all time limits that otherwise would expire on or after the date of commencement of such occurrence, as determined by him, shall extend until a date to be determined by him. When determining that date, he shall assess when the exceptional occurrence comes to an end. If the occurrence affects the seat of the Office, such determination of the Executive Director shall specify that it applies in respect of all parties to the proceedings.
5. The Commission is empowered to adopt delegated acts in accordance with Article 208 specifying the details regarding the calculation and duration of time limits.

[5.950]
Article 102
Correction of errors and manifest oversights
1. The Office shall correct any linguistic errors or errors of transcription and manifest oversights in its decisions, or technical errors attributable to it in registering an EU trade mark or in publishing the registration of its own motion or at the request of a party.
2. Where the correction of errors in the registration of an EU trade mark or the publication of the registration is requested by the proprietor, Article 55 shall apply mutatis mutandis.
3. Corrections of errors in the registration of an EU trade mark and in the publication of the registration shall be published by the Office.

[5.951]
Article 103
Revocation of decisions
1. Where the Office has made an entry in the Register or taken a decision which contains an obvious error attributable to the Office, it shall ensure that the entry is cancelled or the decision is revoked. Where there is only one party to the proceedings and the entry or the act affects its rights, cancellation or revocation shall be determined even if the error was not evident to the party.
2. Cancellation or revocation as referred to in paragraph 1 shall be determined, ex officio or at the request of one of the parties to the proceedings, by the department which made the entry or took the decision. The cancellation of the entry in the Register or the revocation of the decision shall be effected within one year of the date on which the entry was made in the Register or that decision was taken, after consultation with the parties to the proceedings and any proprietor of rights to the EU trade mark in question that are entered in the Register. The Office shall keep records of any such cancellation or revocation.
3. The Commission is empowered to adopt delegated acts in accordance with Article 208 specifying the procedure for the revocation of a decision or for the cancellation of an entry in the Register.
4. This Article shall be without prejudice to the right of the parties to submit an appeal under Articles 66 and 72, or to the possibility of correcting errors and manifest oversights under Article 102. Where an appeal has been filed against a decision of the Office containing an error, the appeal proceedings shall become devoid of purpose upon revocation by the Office of its decision pursuant to paragraph 1 of this Article. In the latter case, the appeal fee shall be reimbursed to the appellant.

[5.952]
Article 104
Restitutio in integrum
1. The applicant for or proprietor of an EU trade mark or any other party to proceedings before the Office who, in spite of all due care required by the circumstances having been taken, was unable to comply with a time limit vis-à-vis the Office shall, upon application, have his rights re-established if the obstacle to compliance has the direct consequence, by virtue of the provisions of this Regulation, of causing the loss of any right or means of redress.
2. The application shall be filed in writing within two months of the removal of the obstacle to compliance with the time limit. The omitted act shall be completed within this period. The application shall only be admissible within the year immediately following the expiry of the unobserved time limit. In the case of non-submission of the request for renewal of registration or of non-payment of a renewal fee, the further period of six months provided in the third sentence of Article 53(3) shall be deducted from the period of one year.
3. The application shall state the grounds on which it is based and shall set out the facts on which it relies. It shall not be deemed to be filed until the fee for re-establishment of rights has been paid.
4. The department competent to decide on the omitted act shall decide upon the application.
5. This Article shall not be applicable to the time limits referred to in paragraph 2 of this Article, Article 46(1) and (3) and Article 105.
6. Where the applicant for or proprietor of an EU trade mark has his rights re-established, he may not invoke his rights vis-à-vis a third party who, in good faith, has put goods on the market or supplied services under a sign which is identical with, or similar to, the EU trade mark in the course of the period between the loss of rights in the application or in the EU trade mark and publication of the mention of re-establishment of those rights.

7. A third party who may avail himself of the provisions of paragraph 6 may bring third party proceedings against the decision re-establishing the rights of the applicant for or proprietor of an EU trade mark within a period of two months as from the date of publication of the mention of re-establishment of those rights.
8. Nothing in this Article shall limit the right of a Member State to grant restitutio in integrum in respect of time limits provided for in this Regulation and to be observed vis-à-vis the authorities of such State.

[5.953]
Article 105
Continuation of proceedings
1. An applicant for or proprietor of an EU trade mark or any other party to proceedings before the Office who has omitted to observe a time limit vis-à-vis the Office may, upon request, obtain the continuation of proceedings, provided that at the time the request is made the omitted act has been carried out. The request for continuation of proceedings shall be admissible only if it is submitted within two months of the expiry of the unobserved time limit. The request shall not be deemed to have been filed until the fee for continuation of the proceedings has been paid.
2. This Article shall not apply to the time limits laid down in Article 32, Article 34(1), Article 38(1), Article 41(2), Article 46(1) and (3), Article 53(3), Article 68, Article 72(5), Article 104(2) and Article 139, or to the time limits laid down in paragraph 1 of this Article or the time limit for claiming seniority pursuant to Article 39 after the application has been filed.
3. The department competent to decide on the omitted act shall decide upon the application.
4. If the Office accepts the application, the consequences of having failed to observe the time limit shall be deemed not to have occurred. If a decision has been taken between the expiry of that time limit and the request for the continuation of proceedings, the department competent to decide on the omitted act shall review the decision and, where completion of the omitted act itself is sufficient, take a different decision. If, following the review, the Office concludes that the original decision does not require to be altered, it shall confirm that decision in writing.
5. If the Office rejects the application, the fee shall be refunded.

[5.954]
Article 106
Interruption of proceedings
1. Proceedings before the Office shall be interrupted:
(a) in the event of the death or legal incapacity of the applicant for, or proprietor of, an EU trade mark or of the person authorised by national law to act on his behalf. To the extent that that death or incapacity does not affect the authorisation of a representative appointed under Article 120, proceedings shall be interrupted only on application by such representative;
(b) in the event of the applicant for, or proprietor of, an EU trade mark being prevented, for legal reasons resulting from action taken against his property, from continuing the proceedings before the Office;
(c) in the event of the death or legal incapacity of the representative of an applicant for, or proprietor of, an EU trade mark, or of that representative being prevented, for legal reasons resulting from action taken against his property, from continuing the proceedings before the Office.
2. Proceedings before the Office shall be resumed as soon as the identity of the person authorised to continue them has been established.
3. The Commission is empowered to adopt delegated acts in accordance with Article 208 specifying the detailed arrangements for the resumption of proceedings before the Office.

[5.955]
Article 107
Reference to general principles
In the absence of procedural provisions in this Regulation or in acts adopted pursuant to this Regulation, the Office shall take into account the principles of procedural law generally recognised in the Member States.

[5.956]
Article 108
Termination of financial obligations
1. Rights of the Office to the payment of a fee shall be extinguished after four years from the end of the calendar year in which the fee fell due.
2. Rights against the Office for the refunding of fees or sums of money paid in excess of a fee shall be extinguished after four years from the end of the calendar year in which the right arose.
3. The period laid down in paragraphs 1 and 2 shall be interrupted, in the case covered by paragraph 1, by a request for payment of the fee, and in the case covered by paragraph 2, by a reasoned claim in writing. On interruption it shall begin again immediately and shall end at the

latest six years after the end of the year in which it originally began, unless, in the meantime, judicial proceedings to enforce the right have begun; in this case the period shall end at the earliest one year after the judgment has acquired the authority of a final decision.

SECTION 2
COSTS

[5.957]
Article 109
Costs

1. The losing party in opposition proceedings, proceedings for revocation, proceedings for a declaration of invalidity or appeal proceedings shall bear the fees paid by the other party. Without prejudice to Article 146(7), the losing party shall also bear all costs incurred by the other party that are essential to the proceedings, including travel and subsistence and the remuneration of a representative within the meaning of Article 120(1), within the limits of the scales set for each category of costs in the implementing act to be adopted in accordance with paragraph 2 of this Article. The fees to be borne by the losing party shall be limited to the fees paid by the other party for opposition, for an application for revocation or for a declaration of invalidity of the EU trade mark and for appeal.

2. The Commission shall adopt implementing acts specifying the maximum rates for costs essential to the proceedings and actually incurred by the successful party. Those implementing acts shall be adopted in accordance with the examination procedure referred to in Article 207(2).

When specifying such amounts with respect to travel and subsistence costs, the Commission shall take into account the distance between the place of residence or business of the party, representative or witness or expert and the place where the oral proceedings are held, the procedural stage at which the costs have been incurred, and, as far as costs of representation within the meaning of Article 120(1) are concerned, the need to ensure that the obligation to bear the costs may not be misused for tactical reasons by the other party. Subsistence expenses shall be calculated in accordance with the Staff Regulations of Officials of the Union and the Conditions of Employment of Other Servants of the Union, laid down in Council Regulation (EEC, Euratom, ECSC) No 259/68[1] ('the Staff Regulations' and 'Conditions of Employment' respectively).

The losing party shall bear the costs for one opposing party only and, where applicable, one representative only.

3. However, where each party succeeds on some and fails on other heads, or if reasons of equity so dictate, the Opposition Division, Cancellation Division or Board of Appeal shall decide a different apportionment of costs.

4. The party who terminates the proceedings by withdrawing the EU trade mark application, the opposition, the application for revocation of rights, the application for a declaration of invalidity or the appeal, or by not renewing registration of the EU trade mark or by surrendering the EU trade mark, shall bear the fees and the costs incurred by the other party as stipulated in paragraphs 1 and 3.

5. Where a case does not proceed to judgment the costs shall be at the discretion of the Opposition Division, Cancellation Division or Board of Appeal.

6. Where the parties conclude before the Opposition Division, Cancellation Division or Board of Appeal a settlement of costs differing from that provided for in paragraphs 1 to 5, the department concerned shall take note of that agreement.

7. The Opposition Division or Cancellation Division or Board of Appeal shall fix the amount of the costs to be paid pursuant to paragraphs 1 to 6 of this Article when the costs to be paid are limited to the fees paid to the Office and the representation costs. In all other cases, the registry of the Board of Appeal or a member of the staff of the Opposition Division or Cancellation Division shall fix, on request, the amount of the costs to be reimbursed. The request shall be admissible only for the period of two months following the date on which the decision for which an application was made for the costs to be fixed becomes final and shall be accompanied by a bill and supporting evidence. For the costs of representation pursuant to Article 120(1), an assurance by the representative that the costs have been incurred shall be sufficient. For other costs, it shall be sufficient if their plausibility is established. Where the amount of the costs is fixed pursuant to the first sentence of this paragraph, representation costs shall be awarded at the level laid down in the implementing act adopted pursuant to paragraph 2 of this Article and irrespective of whether they have been actually incurred.

8. The decision on the fixing of costs, stating the reasons on which it is based, may be reviewed by a decision of the Opposition Division or Cancellation Division or Board of Appeal on a request filed within one month of the date of notification of the awarding of costs. It shall not be deemed to be filed until the fee for reviewing the amount of the costs has been paid. The Opposition Division, the Cancellation Division or the Board of Appeal, as the case may be, shall take a decision on the request for a review of the decision on the fixing of costs without oral proceedings.

NOTES

[1] OJ L56, 4.3.1968, p 1.

[5.958]
Article 110
Enforcement of decisions fixing the amount of costs

1. Any final decision of the Office fixing the amount of costs shall be enforceable.

2. Enforcement shall be governed by the rules of civil procedure in force in the State in the territory of which it is carried out. Each Member State shall designate a single authority responsible for verifying the authenticity of the decision referred to in paragraph 1 and shall communicate its contact details to the Office, the Court of Justice and the Commission. The order for the enforcement of the decision shall be appended to the decision by that authority, with the verification of the authenticity of the decision as the sole formality.

3. When these formalities have been completed on application by the party concerned, the latter may proceed to enforcement in accordance with the national law, by bringing the matter directly before the competent authority.

4. Enforcement may be suspended only by a decision of the Court of Justice. However, the courts of the country concerned shall have jurisdiction over complaints that enforcement is being carried out in an irregular manner.

SECTION 3
INFORMATION WHICH MAY BE MADE AVAILABLE TO THE PUBLIC AND OF THE AUTHORITIES OF THE MEMBER STATES

[5.959]
Article 111
Register of EU trade marks

1. The Office shall keep a Register of EU trade marks which it shall keep up to date.

2. The Register shall contain the following entries relating to EU trade mark applications and registrations:

(a) the date of filing the application;
(b) the file number of the application;
(c) the date of the publication of the application;
(d) the name and address of the applicant;
(e) the name and business address of the representative, other than a representative as referred to in the first sentence of Article 119(3);
(f) the representation of the mark, with indications as to its nature; and, where applicable, a description of the mark;
(g) an indication of the goods and services by their names;
(h) particulars of claims of priority pursuant to Article 35;
(i) particulars of claims of exhibition priority pursuant to Article 38;
(j) particulars of claims of seniority of a registered earlier trade mark as referred to in Article 39;
(k) a statement that the mark has become distinctive in consequence of the use which has been made of it, pursuant to Article 7(3);
(l) an indication that the mark is a collective mark;
(m) an indication that the mark is a certification mark;
(n) the language in which the application was filed and the second language which the applicant has indicated in his application, pursuant to Article 146(3);
(o) the date of registration of the mark in the Register and the registration number;
(p) a statement that the application is the result of a transformation of an international registration designating the Union, pursuant to Article 204 of this Regulation, together with the date of the international registration pursuant to Article 3(4) of the Madrid Protocol or the date on which the territorial extension to the Union made subsequent to the international registration pursuant to Article 3ter(2) of the Madrid Protocol was recorded and, where applicable, the date of priority of the international registration.

3. The Register shall also contain the following entries, each accompanied by the date of recording of such entry:

(a) changes in the name, address or nationality of the proprietor of an EU trade mark or a change in the State in which he is domiciled or has his seat or establishment;
(b) changes in the name or business address of the representative, other than a representative as referred to in the first sentence of Article 119(3);
(c) where a new representative is appointed, the name and business address of that representative;
(d) amendments and alterations of the mark, pursuant to Articles 49 and 54, and corrections of errors;
(e) notice of amendments to the regulations governing the use of the collective mark pursuant to Article 79;
(f) particulars of claims of seniority of a registered earlier trade mark as referred to in Article 39, pursuant to Article 40;
(g) total or partial transfers pursuant to Article 20;

(h) creation or transfer of a right *in rem* pursuant to Article 22, and the nature of the right *in rem;*
(i) levy of execution pursuant to Article 23 and insolvency proceedings pursuant to Article 24;
(j) the grant or transfer of a licence pursuant to Article 25 and, where applicable, the type of licence;
(k) renewal of a registration pursuant to Article 53, the date from which it takes effect and any restrictions pursuant to Article 53(4);
(l) a record of a determination of the expiry of a registration pursuant to Article 53;
(m) declarations of withdrawal or surrender by the proprietor of the mark pursuant to Articles 49 and 57 respectively;
(n) the date of submission and the particulars of an opposition pursuant to Article 46, of an application pursuant to Article 63, or a counterclaim pursuant to Article 128(4) for revocation or for a declaration of invalidity, or of an appeal pursuant to Article 68;
(o) the date and content of a decision on an opposition, on an application or counterclaim pursuant to Article 64(6) or the third sentence of Article 128(6), or on an appeal pursuant to Article 71;
(p) a record of the receipt of a request for conversion pursuant to Article 140(2);
(q) the cancellation of the representative recorded pursuant to point (e) of paragraph 2 of this Article;
(r) the cancellation of the seniority of a national mark;
(s) the modification to or cancellation from the Register of the items referred to in points (h), (i) and (j) of this paragraph;
(t) the replacement of the EU trade mark by an international registration pursuant to Article 197;
(u) the date and number of international registrations based on the EU trade mark application which has been registered as an EU trade mark pursuant to Article 185(1);
(v) the date and number of international registrations based on the EU trade mark pursuant to Article 185(2);
(w) the division of an application pursuant to Article 50 and the division of a registration pursuant to Article 56, together with the items referred to in paragraph 2 of this Article in respect of the divisional registration, as well as the list of goods and services of the original registration as amended;
(x) the revocation of a decision or an entry in the Register pursuant to Article 103, where the revocation concerns a decision or entry which has been published;
(y) notice of amendments to the regulations governing the use of the certification mark pursuant to Article 88.

4. The Executive Director may determine that items other than those referred to in paragraphs 2 and 3 of this Article are to be entered in the Register, subject to Article 149(4).
5. The Register may be maintained in electronic form. The Office shall collect, organise, make public and store the items referred to in paragraphs 2 and 3, including any personal data, for the purposes laid down in paragraph 8. The Office shall keep the register easily accessible for public inspection.
6. The proprietor of an EU trade mark shall be notified of any change in the Register.
7. The Office shall provide certified or uncertified extracts from the Register on request and on payment of a fee.
8. The processing of the data concerning the entries set out in paragraphs 2 and 3, including any personal data, shall take place for the purposes of:
(a) administering the applications and/or registrations as described in this Regulation and acts adopted pursuant to it;
(b) maintaining a public register for inspection by, and the information of, public authorities and economic operators, in order to enable them to exercise the rights conferred on them by this Regulation and be informed about the existence of prior rights belonging to third parties; and
(c) producing reports and statistics enabling the Office to optimise its operations and improve the functioning of the system.
9. All the data, including personal data, concerning the entries in paragraphs 2 and 3 shall be considered to be of public interest and may be accessed by any third party. For reasons of legal certainty, the entries in the Register shall be kept for an indefinite period of time.

[5.960]
Article 112
Database
1. In addition to the obligation to keep a Register within the meaning of Article 111, the Office shall collect and store in an electronic database all the particulars provided by applicants or any other party to the proceedings pursuant to this Regulation or acts adopted pursuant to it.
2. The electronic database may include personal data, beyond those included in the Register pursuant to Article 111, to the extent that such particulars are required by this Regulation or by acts adopted pursuant to it. The collection, storage and processing of such data shall serve the purposes of:

(a) administering the applications and/or registrations as described in this Regulation and in acts adopted pursuant to it;
(b) accessing the information necessary for conducting the relevant proceedings more easily and efficiently;
(c) communicating with the applicants and other parties to the proceedings;
(d) producing reports and statistics enabling the Office to optimise its operations and improve the functioning of the system.

3. The Executive Director shall determine the conditions of access to the electronic database and the manner in which its contents, other than the personal data referred to in paragraph 2 of this Article but including those listed in Article 111, may be made available in machine-readable form, including the charge for such access.

4. Access to the personal data referred to in paragraph 2 shall be restricted and such data shall not be made publicly available unless the party concerned has given his express consent.

5. All data shall be kept indefinitely. However, the party concerned may request the removal of any personal data from the database after 18 months from the expiry of the EU trade mark or the closure of the relevant inter partes procedure. The party concerned shall have the right to obtain the correction of inaccurate or erroneous data at any time.

[5.961]
Article 113
Online access to decisions

1. The decisions of the Office shall be made available online for the information and consultation of the general public in the interest of transparency and predictability. Any party to the proceedings that led to the adoption of the decision may request the removal of any personal data included in the decision.

2. The Office may provide online access to judgments of national and Union courts related to its tasks in order to raise public awareness of intellectual property matters and promote convergence of practices. The Office shall respect the conditions of the initial publication with regard to personal data.

[5.962]
Article 114
Inspection of files

1. The files relating to EU trade mark applications which have not yet been published shall not be made available for inspection without the consent of the applicant.

2. Any person who can prove that the applicant for an EU trade mark has stated that after the trade mark has been registered he will invoke the rights under it against him may obtain inspection of the files prior to the publication of that application and without the consent of the applicant.

3. Subsequent to the publication of the EU trade mark application, the files relating to such application and the resulting trade mark may be inspected on request.

4. Where the files are inspected pursuant to paragraph 2 or 3 of this Article, documents relating to exclusion or objection pursuant to Article 169, draft decisions and opinions, and all other internal documents used for the preparation of decisions and opinions, as well as parts of the file which the party concerned showed a special interest in keeping confidential before the request for inspection of the files was made, unless inspection of such parts of the file is justified by overriding, legitimate interests of the party seeking inspection, may be withheld from inspection.

5. Inspection of the files of EU trade mark applications and of registered EU trade marks shall be of the original document, or of copies thereof, or of technical means of storage if the files are stored in this way. The Executive Director shall determine the means of inspection.

6. Where inspection of files takes place as provided for in paragraph 7, the request for inspection of the files shall not be deemed to have been made until the required fee has been paid. No fee shall be payable if inspection of technical means of storage takes place online.

7. Inspection of the files shall take place at the premises of the Office. On request, inspection of the files shall be effected by means of issuing copies of file documents. The issuing of such copies shall be conditional on the payment of a fee. The Office shall also issue on request certified or uncertified copies of the application for an EU trade mark upon payment of a fee.

8. The files kept by the Office relating to international registrations designating the Union may be inspected on request as from the date of publication referred to in Article 190(1), in accordance with the conditions laid down in paragraphs 1, 3 and 4 of this Article.

9. Subject to the restrictions provided for in paragraph 4, the Office may, on request, communicate information from any file of an EU trade mark applied for or of a registered EU trade mark, subject to payment of a fee. However, the Office may require the exercise of the option to obtain inspection of the file itself should it deem this to be appropriate in view of the quantity of information to be supplied.

[5.963]
Article 115
Keeping of files

1. The Office shall keep the files of any procedure relating to an EU trade mark application or EU trade mark registration. The Executive Director shall determine the form in which those files shall be kept.
2. Where the files are kept in electronic format, the electronic files, or back-up copies thereof, shall be kept indefinitely. The original documents filed by parties to the proceedings, and forming the basis of such electronic files, shall be disposed of after a period following their reception by the Office, which shall be determined by the Executive Director.
3. Where and to the extent that files or parts of the files are kept in any form other than electronically, documents or items of evidence constituting part of such files shall be kept for at least five years from the end of the year in which the application is rejected or withdrawn or is deemed to be withdrawn, the registration of the EU trade mark expires completely pursuant to Article 53, the complete surrender of the EU trade mark is registered pursuant to Article 57, or the EU trade mark is completely removed from the Register pursuant to Article 64(6) or 128(6).

[5.964]
Article 116
Periodical publications

1. The Office shall periodically publish:
 (a) a European Union Trade Marks Bulletin containing publications of applications and of entries made in the Register as well as other particulars relating to applications or registrations of EU trade marks the publication of which is required under this Regulation or by acts adopted pursuant to it;
 (b) an Official Journal of the Office containing notices and information of a general character issued by the Executive Director, as well as any other information relevant to this Regulation or its implementation.

The publications referred to in points (a) and (b) of the first subparagraph may be effected by electronic means.
2. The European Union Trade Marks Bulletin shall be published in a manner and at a frequency to be determined by the Executive Director.
3. The Official Journal of the Office shall be published in the languages of the Office. However, the Executive Director may determine that certain items shall be published in the Official Journal of the Office in the official languages of the Union.
4. The Commission shall adopt implementing acts specifying:
 (a) the date to be taken as the date of publication in the European Union Trade Marks Bulletin;
 (b) the manner of publication of entries regarding the registration of a trade mark which do not contain changes as compared to the publication of the application;
 (c) the forms in which editions of the Official Journal of the Office may be made available to the public.

Those implementing acts shall be adopted in accordance with the examination procedure referred to in Article 207(2).

[5.965]
Article 117
Administrative cooperation

1. Unless otherwise provided in this Regulation or in national laws, the Office and the courts or authorities of the Member States shall on request give assistance to each other by communicating information or opening files for inspection. Where the Office lays files open to inspection by courts, Public Prosecutors' Offices or central industrial property offices, the inspection shall not be subject to the restrictions laid down in Article 114.
2. The Office shall not charge fees for the communication of information or the opening of files for inspection.
3. The Commission shall adopt implementing acts specifying the detailed arrangements as to how the Office and the authorities of the Member States are to exchange information between each other and open files for inspection, taking into account the restrictions to which the inspection of files relating to EU trade mark applications or registrations is subject, pursuant to Article 114, when it is opened to third parties. Those implementing acts shall be adopted in accordance with the examination procedure referred to in Article 207(2).

[5.966]
Article 118
Exchange of publications

1. The Office and the central industrial property offices of the Member States shall despatch to each other on request and for their own use one or more copies of their respective publications free of charge.
2. The Office may conclude agreements relating to the exchange or supply of publications.

SECTION 4
REPRESENTATION

[5.967]
Article 119
General principles of representation

1. Subject to the provisions of paragraph 2, no person shall be compelled to be represented before the Office.

2. Without prejudice to the second sentence of paragraph 3 of this Article, natural or legal persons having neither their domicile nor their principal place of business or a real and effective industrial or commercial establishment in the European Economic Area shall be represented before the Office in accordance with Article 120(1) in all proceedings provided for by this Regulation, other than the filing of an application for an EU trade mark.

3. Natural or legal persons having their domicile or principal place of business or a real and effective industrial or commercial establishment in the European Economic Area may be represented before the Office by an employee. An employee of a legal person to which this paragraph applies may also represent other legal persons which have economic connections with the first legal person, even if those other legal persons have neither their domicile nor their principal place of business nor a real and effective industrial or commercial establishment within the European Economic Area. Employees who represent persons, within the meaning of this paragraph, shall, at the request of the Office or, where appropriate, of the party to the proceedings, file with it a signed authorisation for insertion in the files.

4. Where there is more than one applicant or more than one third party acting in common, a common representative shall be appointed.

[5.968]
Article 120
Professional representatives

1. Representation of natural or legal persons before the Office may only be undertaken by:
(a) a legal practitioner qualified in one of the Member States of the European Economic Area and having his place of business within the European Economic Area, to the extent that he is entitled, within the said Member State, to act as a representative in trade mark matters;
(b) professional representatives whose names appear on the list maintained for this purpose by the Office.

Representatives acting before the Office shall, at the request of the Office or, where appropriate, of the other party to the proceedings, file with it a signed authorisation for insertion on the files.

2. Any natural person who fulfils the following conditions may be entered on the list of professional representatives:
(a) being a national of one of the Member States of the European Economic Area;
(b) having his place of business or employment in the European Economic Area;
(c) being entitled to represent natural or legal persons in trade mark matters before the Benelux Office for Intellectual Property or before the central industrial property office of a Member State of the European Economic Area. Where, in the State concerned, the entitlement is not conditional upon the requirement of special professional qualifications, persons applying to be entered on the list who act in trade mark matters before the Benelux Office for Intellectual Property or those central industrial property offices shall have habitually so acted for at least five years. However, persons whose professional qualification to represent natural or legal persons in trade mark matters before the Benelux Office for Intellectual Property or those central industrial property offices is officially recognised in accordance with the regulations laid down by the State concerned shall not be required to have exercised the profession.

3. Entry shall be effected upon request, accompanied by a certificate furnished by the central industrial property office of the Member State concerned, which must indicate that the conditions laid down in paragraph 2 are fulfilled.

4. The Executive Director may grant an exemption from:
(a) the requirement in the second sentence of paragraph 2(c), if the applicant furnishes proof that he has acquired the requisite qualification in another way;
(b) the requirement set out in paragraph 2(a) in the case of highly qualified professionals, provided that the requirements set out in paragraphs 2(b) and (c) are fulfilled.

5. A person may be removed from the list of professional representatives at his request or when no longer in a capacity to represent. The amendments of the list of professional representatives shall be published in the Official Journal of the Office.

[5.969]
Article 121
Delegation of powers

The Commission is empowered to adopt delegated acts in accordance with Article 208 specifying:
(a) the conditions and the procedure for the appointment of a common representative as referred to in Article 119(4);

(b) the conditions under which employees referred to in Article 119(3) and professional representatives referred to in Article 120(1) shall file with the Office a signed authorisation in order to undertake representation, and the content of that authorisation;
(c) the circumstances in which a person may be removed from the list of professional representatives referred to in Article 120(5).

CHAPTER X
JURISDICTION AND PROCEDURE IN LEGAL ACTIONS RELATING TO EU TRADE MARKS

SECTION 1
APPLICATION OF UNION RULES ON JURISDICTION AND THE RECOGNITION AND ENFORCEMENT OF JUDGMENTS IN CIVIL AND COMMERCIAL MATTERS

[5.970]
Article 122
Application of Union rules on jurisdiction and the recognition and enforcement of judgments in civil and commercial matters
1. Unless otherwise specified in this Regulation, the Union rules on jurisdiction and the recognition and enforcement of judgments in civil and commercial matters shall apply to proceedings relating to EU trade marks and applications for EU trade marks, as well as to proceedings relating to simultaneous and successive actions on the basis of EU trade marks and national trade marks.
2. In the case of proceedings in respect of the actions and claims referred to in Article 124:
(a) Articles 4 and 6, points 1, 2, 3 and 5 of Article 7 and Article 35 of Regulation (EU) No 1215/2012 shall not apply;
(b) Articles 25 and 26 of Regulation (EU) No 1215/2012 shall apply subject to the limitations in Article 125(4) of this Regulation;
(c) the provisions of Chapter II of Regulation (EU) No 1215/2012 which are applicable to persons domiciled in a Member State shall also be applicable to persons who do not have a domicile in any Member State but have an establishment therein.
3. References in this Regulation to Regulation (EU) No 1215/2012 shall include, where appropriate, the Agreement between the European Community and the Kingdom of Denmark on jurisdiction and the recognition and enforcement of judgments in civil and commercial matters done on 19 October 2005.

SECTION 2
DISPUTES CONCERNING THE INFRINGEMENT AND VALIDITY OF EU TRADE MARKS

[5.971]
Article 123
EU trade mark courts
1. The Member States shall designate in their territories as limited a number as possible of national courts and tribunals of first and second instance, which shall perform the functions assigned to them by this Regulation.
2. Any change made in the number, names or territorial jurisdiction of the courts included in the list of EU trade mark courts communicated by a Member State to the Commission in accordance with Article 95(2) of Regulation (EC) No 207/2009 shall be notified without delay by the Member State concerned to the Commission.
3. The information referred to in paragraph 2 shall be notified by the Commission to the Member States and published in the Official Journal of the European Union.

[5.972]
Article 124
Jurisdiction over infringement and validity
The EU trade mark courts shall have exclusive jurisdiction:
(a) for all infringement actions and — if they are permitted under national law — actions in respect of threatened infringement relating to EU trade marks;
(b) for actions for declaration of non-infringement, if they are permitted under national law;
(c) for all actions brought as a result of acts referred to in Article 11(2);
(d) for counterclaims for revocation or for a declaration of invalidity of the EU trade mark pursuant to Article 128.

[5.973]
Article 125
International jurisdiction

1. Subject to the provisions of this Regulation as well as to any provisions of Regulation (EU) No 1215/2012 applicable by virtue of Article 122, proceedings in respect of the actions and claims referred to in Article 124 shall be brought in the courts of the Member State in which the defendant is domiciled or, if he is not domiciled in any of the Member States, in which he has an establishment.
2. If the defendant is neither domiciled nor has an establishment in any of the Member States, such proceedings shall be brought in the courts of the Member State in which the plaintiff is domiciled or, if he is not domiciled in any of the Member States, in which he has an establishment.
3. If neither the defendant nor the plaintiff is so domiciled or has such an establishment, such proceedings shall be brought in the courts of the Member State where the Office has its seat.
4. Notwithstanding the provisions of paragraphs 1, 2 and 3:
   (a) Article 25 of Regulation (EU) No 1215/2012 shall apply if the parties agree that a different EU trade mark court shall have jurisdiction;
   (b) Article 26 of Regulation (EU) No 1215/2012 shall apply if the defendant enters an appearance before a different EU trade mark court.
5. Proceedings in respect of the actions and claims referred to in Article 124, with the exception of actions for a declaration of non-infringement of an EU trade mark, may also be brought in the courts of the Member State in which the act of infringement has been committed or threatened, or in which an act referred to in Article 11(2) has been committed.

[5.974]
Article 126
Extent of jurisdiction

1. An EU trade mark court whose jurisdiction is based on Article 125(1) to (4) shall have jurisdiction in respect of:
   (a) acts of infringement committed or threatened within the territory of any of the Member States;
   (b) acts referred to in Article 11(2) committed within the territory of any of the Member States.
2. An EU trade mark court whose jurisdiction is based on Article 125(5) shall have jurisdiction only in respect of acts committed or threatened within the territory of the Member State in which that court is situated.

[5.975]
Article 127
Presumption of validity — Defence as to the merits

1. The EU trade mark courts shall treat the EU trade mark as valid unless its validity is put in issue by the defendant with a counterclaim for revocation or for a declaration of invalidity.
2. The validity of an EU trade mark may not be put in issue in an action for a declaration of non-infringement.
3. In the actions referred to in points (a) and (c) of Article 124, a plea relating to revocation of the EU trade mark submitted otherwise than by way of a counterclaim shall be admissible where the defendant claims that the EU trade mark could be revoked for lack of genuine use at the time the infringement action was brought.

[5.976]
Article 128
Counterclaims

1. A counterclaim for revocation or for a declaration of invalidity may only be based on the grounds for revocation or invalidity mentioned in this Regulation.
2. An EU trade mark court shall reject a counterclaim for revocation or for a declaration of invalidity if a decision taken by the Office relating to the same subject matter and cause of action and involving the same parties has already become final.
3. If the counterclaim is brought in a legal action to which the proprietor of the trade mark is not already a party, he shall be informed thereof and may be joined as a party to the action in accordance with the conditions set out in national law.
4. The EU trade mark court with which a counterclaim for revocation or for a declaration of invalidity of the EU trade mark has been filed shall not proceed with the examination of the counterclaim, until either the interested party or the court has informed the Office of the date on which the counterclaim was filed. The Office shall record that information in the Register. If an application for revocation or for a declaration of invalidity of the EU trade mark had already been filed before the Office before the counterclaim was filed, the court shall be informed thereof by the Office and stay the proceedings in accordance with Article 132(1) until the decision on the application is final or the application is withdrawn.
5. Article 64(2) to (5) shall apply.

6. Where an EU trade mark court has given a judgment which has become final on a counterclaim for revocation or for a declaration of invalidity of an EU trade mark, a copy of the judgment shall be sent to the Office without delay, either by the court or by any of the parties to the national proceedings. The Office or any other interested party may request information about such transmission. The Office shall mention the judgment in the Register and shall take the necessary measures to comply with its operative part.
7. The EU trade mark court hearing a counterclaim for revocation or for a declaration of invalidity may stay the proceedings on application by the proprietor of the EU trade mark and after hearing the other parties and may request the defendant to submit an application for revocation or for a declaration of invalidity to the Office within a time limit which it shall determine. If the application is not made within the time limit, the proceedings shall continue; the counterclaim shall be deemed withdrawn. Article 132(3) shall apply.

[5.977]
Article 129
Applicable law
1. The EU trade mark courts shall apply the provisions of this Regulation.
2. On all trade mark matters not covered by this Regulation, the relevant EU trade mark court shall apply the applicable national law.
3. Unless otherwise provided for in this Regulation, an EU trade mark court shall apply the rules of procedure governing the same type of action relating to a national trade mark in the Member State in which the court is located.

[5.978]
Article 130
Sanctions
1. Where an EU trade mark court finds that the defendant has infringed or threatened to infringe an EU trade mark, it shall, unless there are special reasons for not doing so, issue an order prohibiting the defendant from proceeding with the acts which infringed or would infringe the EU trade mark. It shall also take such measures in accordance with its national law as are aimed at ensuring that this prohibition is complied with.
2. The EU trade mark court may also apply measures or orders available under the applicable law which it deems appropriate in the circumstances of the case.

[5.979]
Article 131
Provisional and protective measures
1. Application may be made to the courts of a Member State, including EU trade mark courts, for such provisional, including protective, measures in respect of an EU trade mark or EU trade mark application as may be available under the law of that State in respect of a national trade mark, even if, under this Regulation, an EU trade mark court of another Member State has jurisdiction as to the substance of the matter.
2. An EU trade mark court whose jurisdiction is based on Article 125(1), (2), (3) or (4) shall have jurisdiction to grant provisional and protective measures which, subject to any necessary procedure for recognition and enforcement pursuant to Chapter III of Regulation (EU) No 1215/2012, are applicable in the territory of any Member State. No other court shall have such jurisdiction.

[5.980]
Article 132
Specific rules on related actions
1. An EU trade mark court hearing an action referred to in Article 124 other than an action for a declaration of non-infringement shall, unless there are special grounds for continuing the hearing, of its own motion after hearing the parties or at the request of one of the parties and after hearing the other parties, stay the proceedings where the validity of the EU trade mark is already in issue before another EU trade mark court on account of a counterclaim or where an application for revocation or for a declaration of invalidity has already been filed at the Office.
2. The Office, when hearing an application for revocation or for a declaration of invalidity shall, unless there are special grounds for continuing the hearing, of its own motion after hearing the parties or at the request of one of the parties and after hearing the other parties, stay the proceedings where the validity of the EU trade mark is already in issue on account of a counterclaim before an EU trade mark court. However, if one of the parties to the proceedings before the EU trade mark court so requests, the court may, after hearing the other parties to these proceedings, stay the proceedings. The Office shall in this instance continue the proceedings pending before it.
3. Where the EU trade mark court stays the proceedings it may order provisional and protective measures for the duration of the stay.

[5.981]

Article 133

Jurisdiction of EU trade mark courts of second instance — Further appeal

1. An appeal to the EU trade mark courts of second instance shall lie from judgments of the EU trade mark courts of first instance in respect of proceedings arising from the actions and claims referred to in Article 124.

2. The conditions under which an appeal may be lodged with an EU trade mark court of second instance shall be determined by the national law of the Member State in which that court is located.

3. The national rules concerning further appeal shall be applicable in respect of judgments of EU trade mark courts of second instance.

SECTION 3
OTHER DISPUTES CONCERNING EU TRADE MARKS

[5.982]

Article 134

Supplementary provisions on the jurisdiction of national courts other than EU trade mark courts

1. Within the Member State whose courts have jurisdiction under Article 122(1) those courts shall have jurisdiction for actions other than those referred to in Article 124, which would have jurisdiction ratione loci and ratione materiae in the case of actions relating to a national trade mark registered in that State.

2. Actions relating to an EU trade mark, other than those referred to in Article 124, for which no court has jurisdiction under Article 122(1) and paragraph 1 of this Article may be heard before the courts of the Member State in which the Office has its seat.

[5.983]

Article 135

Obligation of the national court

A national court which is dealing with an action relating to an EU trade mark, other than the action referred to in Article 124, shall treat the EU trade mark as valid.

CHAPTER XI
EFFECTS ON THE LAWS OF THE MEMBER STATES

SECTION 1
CIVIL ACTIONS ON THE BASIS OF MORE THAN ONE TRADE MARK

[5.984]

Article 136

Simultaneous and successive civil actions on the basis of EU trade marks and national trade marks

1. Where actions for infringement involving the same cause of action and between the same parties are brought in the courts of different Member States, one seised on the basis of an EU trade mark and the other seised on the basis of a national trade mark:

(a) the court other than the court first seised shall of its own motion decline jurisdiction in favour of that court where the trade marks concerned are identical and valid for identical goods or services. The court which would be required to decline jurisdiction may stay its proceedings if the jurisdiction of the other court is contested;

(b) the court other than the court first seised may stay its proceedings where the trade marks concerned are identical and valid for similar goods or services and where the trade marks concerned are similar and valid for identical or similar goods or services.

2. The court hearing an action for infringement on the basis of an EU trade mark shall reject the action if a final judgment on the merits has been given on the same cause of action and between the same parties on the basis of an identical national trade mark valid for identical goods or services.

3. The court hearing an action for infringement on the basis of a national trade mark shall reject the action if a final judgment on the merits has been given on the same cause of action and between the same parties on the basis of an identical EU trade mark valid for identical goods or services.

4. Paragraphs 1, 2 and 3 shall not apply in respect of provisional, including protective, measures.

SECTION 2
APPLICATION OF NATIONAL LAWS FOR THE PURPOSE OF PROHIBITING THE USE OF EU TRADE MARKS

[5.985]

Article 137

Prohibition of use of EU trade marks

1. This Regulation shall, unless otherwise provided for, not affect the right existing under the laws of the Member States to invoke claims for infringement of earlier rights within the meaning of Article 8 or Article 60(2) in relation to the use of a later EU trade mark. Claims for infringement of

earlier rights within the meaning of Article 8(2) and (4) may, however, no longer be invoked if the proprietor of the earlier right may no longer apply for a declaration that the EU trade mark is invalid in accordance with Article 61(2).

2. This Regulation shall, unless otherwise provided for, not affect the right to bring proceedings under the civil, administrative or criminal law of a Member State or under provisions of Union law for the purpose of prohibiting the use of an EU trade mark to the extent that the use of a national trade mark may be prohibited under the law of that Member State or under Union law.

[5.986]
Article 138
Prior rights applicable to particular localities

1. The proprietor of an earlier right which only applies to a particular locality may oppose the use of the EU trade mark in the territory where his right is protected in so far as the law of the Member State concerned so permits.

2. Paragraph 1 shall cease to apply if the proprietor of the earlier right has acquiesced in the use of the EU trade mark in the territory where his right is protected for a period of five successive years, being aware of such use, unless the EU trade mark was applied for in bad faith.

3. The proprietor of the EU trade mark shall not be entitled to oppose use of the right referred to in paragraph 1 even though that right may no longer be invoked against the EU trade mark.

SECTION 3
CONVERSION INTO A NATIONAL TRADE MARK APPLICATION

[5.987]
Article 139
Request for the application of national procedure

1. The applicant for or proprietor of an EU trade mark may request the conversion of his EU trade mark application or EU trade mark into a national trade mark application:
   (a) to the extent that the EU trade mark application is refused, withdrawn, or deemed to be withdrawn;
   (b) to the extent that the EU trade mark ceases to have effect.

2. Conversion shall not take place:
   (a) where the rights of the proprietor of the EU trade mark have been revoked on the grounds of non-use, unless in the Member State for which conversion is requested the EU trade mark has been put to use which would be considered to be genuine use under the laws of that Member State;
   (b) for the purpose of protection in a Member State in which, in accordance with the decision of the Office or of the national court, grounds for refusal of registration or grounds for revocation or invalidity apply to the EU trade mark application or EU trade mark.

3. The national trade mark application resulting from the conversion of an EU trade mark application or an EU trade mark shall enjoy in respect of the Member State concerned the date of filing or the date of priority of that application or trade mark and, where appropriate, the seniority of a trade mark of that State claimed under Articles 39 or 40.

4. In cases where an EU trade mark application is deemed to be withdrawn, the Office shall send to the applicant a communication fixing a period of three months from the date of that communication in which a request for conversion may be filed.

5. Where the EU trade mark application is withdrawn or the EU trade mark ceases to have effect as a result of a surrender being recorded or of failure to renew the registration, the request for conversion shall be filed within three months of the date on which the EU trade mark application has been withdrawn or on which the EU trade mark ceases to have effect.

6. Where the EU trade mark application is refused by decision of the Office or where the EU trade mark ceases to have effect as a result of a decision of the Office or of an EU trade mark court, the request for conversion shall be filed within three months of the date on which that decision acquired the authority of a final decision.

7. The effect referred to in Article 37 shall lapse if the request is not filed in due time.

[5.988]
Article 140
Submission, publication and transmission of the request for conversion

1. A request for conversion shall be filed with the Office within the relevant period pursuant to Article 139(4), (5) or (6), and shall include an indication of the grounds for conversion in accordance with Article 139(1)(a) or (b), the Member States in respect of which conversion is requested, and the goods and services subject to conversion. Where conversion is requested following a failure to renew the registration, the period of three months provided for in Article 139(5) shall begin to run on the day following the last day on which the request for renewal can be presented pursuant to Article 53(3). The request for conversion shall not be deemed to be filed until the conversion fee has been paid.

2. Where the request for conversion relates to an EU trade mark application which has already been published or where the request for conversion relates to an EU trade mark, receipt of any such request shall be recorded in the Register and the request for conversion shall be published.
3. The Office shall check whether the conversion requested fulfils the conditions set out in this Regulation, in particular Article 139(1), (2), (4), (5) and (6), and paragraph 1 of this Article, together with the formal conditions specified in the implementing act adopted pursuant to paragraph 6 of this Article. If the conditions governing the request are not fulfilled, the Office shall notify the applicant of the deficiencies. If the deficiencies are not remedied within a period to be specified by the Office, the Office shall reject the request for conversion. Where Article 139(2) applies, the Office shall reject the request for conversion as inadmissible only with respect to those Member States for which conversion is excluded under that provision. Where the conversion fee has not been paid within the relevant period of three months pursuant to Article 139(4), (5) or (6), the Office shall inform the applicant that the request for conversion is deemed not to have been filed.
4. If the Office or an EU trade mark court has refused the EU trade mark application or has declared the EU trade mark invalid on absolute grounds by reference to the language of a Member State, conversion shall be excluded under Article 139(2) for all the Member States in which that language is one of the official languages. If the Office or an EU trade mark court has refused the EU trade mark application or has declared the EU trade mark invalid on absolute grounds which are found to apply throughout the Union or on account of an earlier EU trade mark or other Union industrial property right, conversion shall be excluded under Article 139(2) for all Member States.
5. Where the request for conversion complies with the requirements referred to in paragraph 3 of this Article, the Office shall transmit the request for conversion and the data referred to in Article 111(2) to the central industrial property offices of the Member States, including the Benelux Office for Intellectual Property, for which the request has been found admissible. The Office shall inform the applicant of the date of transmission.
6. The Commission shall adopt implementing acts specifying:
   (a) the details to be contained in a request for conversion of an EU trade mark application or a registered EU trade mark into a national trade mark application pursuant to paragraph 1;
   (b) the details which are to be contained in the publication of the request for conversion pursuant to paragraph 2.

Those implementing acts shall be adopted in accordance with the examination procedure referred to in Article 207(2).

[5.989]
Article 141
Formal requirements for conversion

1. Any central industrial property office to which the request for conversion is transmitted may obtain from the Office any additional information concerning the request enabling that office to make a decision regarding the national trade mark resulting from the conversion.
2. An EU trade mark application or an EU trade mark transmitted in accordance with Article 140 shall not be subject to formal requirements of national law which are different from or additional to those provided for in this Regulation or in acts adopted pursuant to this Regulation.
3. Any central industrial property office to which the request is transmitted may require that the applicant shall, within not less than two months:
   (a) pay the national application fee;
   (b) file a translation in one of the official languages of the State in question of the request and of the documents accompanying it;
   (c) indicate an address for service in the State in question;
   (d) supply a representation of the trade mark in the number of copies specified by the State in question.

CHAPTER XII
THE OFFICE

SECTION 1
General Provisions

[5.990]
Article 142
Legal status

1. The Office shall be an agency of the Union. It shall have legal personality.
2. In each of the Member States the Office shall enjoy the most extensive legal capacity accorded to legal persons under their laws; it may, in particular, acquire or dispose of movable and immovable property and may be a party to legal proceedings.
3. The Office shall be represented by its Executive Director.

[5.991]
Article 143
Staff

1. The Staff Regulations, the Conditions of Employment and the rules adopted by agreement between the institutions of the Union for giving effect to those Staff Regulations and Conditions of Employment shall apply to the staff of the Office, without prejudice to the application of Article 166 of this Regulation to the members of the Boards of Appeal.

2. Without prejudice to paragraph 1, the Office may make use of seconded national experts or other staff not employed by the Office. The Management Board shall adopt a decision laying down rules on the secondment to the Office of national experts.

[5.992]
Article 144
Privileges and immunities

The Protocol on the Privileges and Immunities of the Union shall apply to the Office and its staff.

[5.993]
Article 145
Liability

1. The contractual liability of the Office shall be governed by the law applicable to the contract in question.

2. The Court of Justice shall be competent to give judgment pursuant to any arbitration clause contained in a contract concluded by the Office.

3. In the case of non-contractual liability, the Office shall, in accordance with the general principles common to the laws of the Member States, make good any damage caused by its departments or by its servants in the performance of their duties.

4. The Court of Justice shall have jurisdiction in disputes relating to compensation for the damage referred to in paragraph 3.

5. The personal liability of its servants towards the Office shall be governed by the provisions laid down in the Staff Regulations or in the Conditions of Employment applicable to them.

[5.994]
Article 146
Languages

1. The application for an EU trade mark shall be filed in one of the official languages of the Union.

2. The languages of the Office shall be English, French, German, Italian and Spanish.

3. The applicant shall indicate a second language which shall be a language of the Office the use of which he accepts as a possible language of proceedings for opposition, revocation or invalidity proceedings. If the application was filed in a language which is not one of the languages of the Office, the Office shall arrange to have the application, as described in Article 31(1), translated into the language indicated by the applicant.

4. Where the applicant for an EU trade mark is the sole party to proceedings before the Office, the language of proceedings shall be the language used for filing the application for an EU trade mark. If the application was made in a language other than the languages of the Office, the Office may send written communications to the applicant in the second language indicated by the applicant in his application.

5. The notice of opposition and an application for revocation or a declaration of invalidity shall be filed in one of the languages of the Office.

6. Without prejudice to paragraph 5:

(a) any application or declaration relating to an EU trade mark application may be filed in the language used for filing the application for that EU trade mark or in the second language indicated by the applicant in his application;

(b) any application or declaration relating to a registered EU trade mark may be filed in one of the languages of the Office.

However, when the application is filed by using any form provided by the Office as referred to in Article 100(2), such forms may be used in any of the official languages of the Union, provided that the form is completed in one of the languages of the Office, as far as textual elements are concerned.

7. If the language chosen, in accordance with paragraph 5, for the notice of opposition or the application for revocation or invalidity is the language of the application for a trade mark or the second language indicated when the application was filed, that language shall be the language of the proceedings.

If the language chosen, in accordance with paragraph 5, for the notice of opposition or the application for revocation or invalidity is neither the language of the application for a trade mark nor the second language indicated when the application was filed, the opposing party or the party seeking revocation or invalidity shall be required to produce, at his own expense, a translation of his application either into the language of the application for a trade mark, provided that it is a language of the Office, or into the second language indicated when the application was filed. The translation shall be produced within one month of the expiry of the opposition period or of the date of filing an application for revocation or a declaration of invalidity. The language into which the application has been translated shall then become the language of the proceedings.

8. Parties to opposition, revocation, invalidity or appeal proceedings may agree that a different official language of the Union is to be the language of the proceedings.

9. Without prejudice to paragraphs 4 and 8, and unless provided otherwise, in written proceedings before the Office any party may use any language of the Office. If the language chosen is not the language of the proceedings, the party shall supply a translation into that language within one month of the date of the submission of the original document. Where the applicant for an EU trade mark is the sole party to proceedings before the Office and the language used for the filing of the application for the EU trade mark is not one of the languages of the Office, the translation may also be filed in the second language indicated by the applicant in his application.

10. The Executive Director shall determine the manner in which translations are to be certified.

11. The Commission shall adopt implementing acts specifying:

(a) the extent to which supporting documents to be used in written proceedings before the Office may be filed in any language of the Union, and the need to supply a translation;

(b) the requisite standards of translations to be filed with the Office.

Those implementing acts shall be adopted in accordance with the examination procedure referred to Article 207(2).

[5.995]
Article 147
Publication and entries in the Register

1. An application for an EU trade mark, as described in Article 31(1), and all other information the publication of which is prescribed by this Regulation or an act adopted pursuant to this Regulation, shall be published in all the official languages of the Union.

2. All entries in the Register shall be made in all the official languages of the Union.

3. In cases of doubt, the text in the language of the Office in which the application for the EU trade mark was filed shall be authentic. If the application was filed in an official language of the Union other than one of the languages of the Office, the text in the second language indicated by the applicant shall be authentic.

[5.996]
Article 148

The translation services required for the functioning of the Office shall be provided by the Translation Centre for the Bodies of the European Union.

[5.997]
Article 149
Transparency

1. Regulation (EC) No 1049/2001 of the European Parliament and of the Council[1] shall apply to documents held by the Office.

2. The Management Board shall adopt detailed rules for applying Regulation (EC) No 1049/2001.

3. Decisions taken by the Office under Article 8 of Regulation (EC) No 1049/2001 may be challenged through the European Ombudsman or form the subject of an action before the Court of Justice of the European Union, under the conditions laid down in Articles 228 and 263 TFEU respectively.

4. The processing of personal data by the Office shall be subject to Regulation (EC) No 45/2001 of the European Parliament and of the Council[2].

NOTES

[1] Regulation (EC) No 1049/2001 of the European Parliament and of the Council of 30 May 2001 regarding public access to European Parliament, Council and Commission documents (OJ L145, 31.5.2001, p 43).

[2] Regulation (EC) No 45/2001 of the European Parliament and of the Council of 18 December 2000 on the protection of individuals with regard to the processing of personal data by the Community institutions and bodies and on the free movement of such data (OJ L8, 12.1.2001, p 1).

[5.998]
Article 150
Security rules on the protection of classified and sensitive non-classified information

The Office shall apply the security principles contained in the Commission's security rules for protecting European Union Classified Information (EUCI) and sensitive non-classified information, as set out in Commission Decisions (EU, Euratom) 2015/443[1] and 2015/444[2]. The security principles shall cover, inter alia, provisions for the exchange, processing and storage of such information.

NOTES

[1] Commission Decision (EU, Euratom) 2015/443 of 13 March 2015 on Security in the Commission (OJ L72, 17.3.2015, p 41).

[2] Commission Decision (EU, Euratom) 2015/444 of 13 March 2015 on the security rules for protecting EU classified information (OJ L72, 17.3.2015, p 53).

SECTION 2
Tasks of the Office and cooperation to promote convergence

[5.999]
Article 151
Tasks of the Office

1. The Office shall have the following tasks:
 (a) administration and promotion of the EU trade mark system established in this Regulation;
 (b) administration and promotion of the European Union design system established in Council Regulation (EC) No 6/2002;[1]
 (c) promoting convergence of practices and tools in the fields of trade marks and designs, in cooperation with the central industrial property offices in the Member States, including the Benelux Office for Intellectual Property;
 (d) the tasks referred to in Regulation (EU) No 386/2012 of the European Parliament and of the Council;[2]
 (e) the tasks conferred on it under Directive 2012/28/EU of the European Parliament and of the Council.[3]

2. The Office shall cooperate with institutions, authorities, bodies, industrial property offices, international and non-governmental organisations in relation to the tasks conferred on it in paragraph 1.

3. The Office may provide voluntary mediation services for the purpose of assisting parties in reaching a friendly settlement.

NOTES

[1] Council Regulation (EC) No 6/2002 of 12 December 2001 on Community designs (OJ L3, 5.1.2002, p 1).

[2] Regulation (EU) No 386/2012 of the European Parliament and of the Council of 19 April 2012 on entrusting the Office for Harmonization in the Internal Market (Trade Marks and Designs) with tasks related to the enforcement of intellectual property rights, including the assembling of public and private-sector representatives as a European Observatory on Infringements of Intellectual Property Rights (OJ L129, 16.5.2012, p 1).

[3] Directive 2012/28/EU of the European Parliament and of the Council of 25 October 2012 on certain permitted uses of orphan works (OJ L299, 27.10.2012, p 5).

[5.1000]
Article 152
Cooperation to promote convergence of practices and tools

1. The Office and the central industrial property offices of the Member States and the Benelux Office for Intellectual Property shall cooperate with each other to promote convergence of practices and tools in the field of trade marks and designs.

Without prejudice to paragraph 3, this cooperation shall in particular cover the following areas of activity:
 (a) the development of common examination standards;
 (b) the creation of common or connected databases and portals for Union-wide consultation, search and classification purposes;
 (c) the continuous provision and exchange of data and information, including for the purposes of feeding of the databases and portals referred to in point (b);
 (d) the establishment of common standards and practices, with a view to ensuring interoperability between procedures and systems throughout the Union and enhancing their consistency, efficiency and effectiveness;
 (e) the sharing of information on industrial property rights and procedures, including mutual support to helpdesks and information centres;
 (f) the exchange of technical expertise and assistance in relation to the areas referred to in points (a) to (e).

2. On the basis of a proposal by the Executive Director, the Management Board shall define and coordinate projects of interest to the Union and the Member States with regard to the areas referred to in paragraphs 1 and 6, and shall invite the central industrial property offices of the Member States and the Benelux Office for Intellectual Property to participate in those projects.

The project definition shall contain the specific obligations and responsibilities of each participating industrial property office of the Member States, the Benelux Office for Intellectual Property and the Office. The Office shall consult with user representatives in particular in the phases of definition of the projects and evaluation of their results.

3. The central industrial property offices of the Member States and the Benelux Office for Intellectual Property may opt out of, restrict or temporarily suspend their cooperation in the projects referred to in the first subparagraph of paragraph 2.

When making use of the possibilities provided for in the first subparagraph, the central industrial property offices of the Member States and the Benelux Office for Intellectual Property shall provide the Office with a written statement explaining the reasons for their decision.

4. Once having committed to participate in certain projects, the central industrial property offices of the Member States and the Benelux Office for Intellectual Property shall, without prejudice to paragraph 3, participate effectively in the projects referred to in paragraph 2 with a view to ensuring that they are developed, function, are interoperable and kept up to date.
5. The Office shall provide financial support to the projects referred to in paragraph 2 to the extent that is necessary in order to ensure, for the purposes of paragraph 4, the effective participation of the central industrial property offices of the Member States and the Benelux Office for Intellectual Property in those projects. That financial support may take the form of grants and in-kind contributions. The total amount of funding shall not exceed 15% of the yearly revenue of the Office. The beneficiaries of grants shall be the central industrial property offices of the Member States and the Benelux Office for Intellectual Property. Grants may be awarded without calls for proposals in accordance with the financial rules applicable to the Office and with the principles of grant procedures contained in Regulation (EU, Euratom) No 966/2012 of the European Parliament and of the Council[1] and in Commission Delegated Regulation (EU) No 1268/2012.[2]
6. The Office and the relevant competent authorities of the Member States shall cooperate with each other on a voluntary basis to promote the raising of awareness concerning the trade mark system and the fight against counterfeiting. Such cooperation shall include projects aiming, in particular, at the implementation of established standards and practices as well as at organising education and training activities. The financial support for those projects shall be part of the total amount of funding referred to in paragraph 5. Paragraphs 2 to 5 shall apply *mutatis mutandis*.

NOTES

1 Regulation (EU, Euratom) No 966/2012 of the European Parliament and of the Council of 25 October 2012 on the financial rules applicable to the general budget of the Union and repealing Council Regulation (EC, Euratom) No 1605/2002 (OJ L298, 26.10.2012, p 1).

2 Commission Delegated Regulation (EU) No 1268/2012 of 29 October 2012 on the rules of application of Regulation (EU, Euratom) No 966/2012 of the European Parliament and of the Council on the financial rules applicable to the general budget of the Union (OJ L362, 31.12.2012, p 1).

SECTION 3
MANAGEMENT BOARD

[5.1001]
Article 153
Functions of the Management Board

1. Without prejudice to the functions attributed to the Budget Committee in Section 6, the Management Board shall have the following functions:

(a) on the basis of a draft submitted by the Executive Director in accordance with Article 157(4)(c), adopting the annual work programme of the Office for the coming year, taking into account the opinion of the Commission, and forwarding the adopted annual work programme to the European Parliament, to the Council and to the Commission;
(b) on the basis of a draft submitted by the Executive Director in accordance with Article 157(4)(e) and taking into account the opinion of the Commission, adopting a multiannual strategic programme for the Office, including the Office's strategy for international cooperation, following an exchange of views between the Executive Director and the relevant committee in the European Parliament, and forwarding the adopted multiannual strategic programme to the European Parliament, to the Council and to the Commission;
(c) on the basis of a draft submitted by the Executive Director in accordance with Article 157(4)(g), adopting the annual report and forwarding the adopted annual report to the European Parliament, to the Council, to the Commission and to the Court of Auditors;
(d) on the basis of a draft submitted by the Executive Director in accordance with Article 157(4)(h), adopting the multiannual staff policy plan;
(e) exercising the powers conferred on it under Article 152(2);
(f) exercising the powers conferred on it under Article 172(5);
(g) adopting rules on the prevention and management of conflicts of interest in the Office;
(h) in accordance with paragraph 2, exercising, with respect to the staff of the Office, the powers conferred by the Staff Regulations on the Appointing Authority and by the Conditions of Employment on the Authority Empowered to Conclude Contracts of Employment ('the appointing authority powers');
(i) adopting appropriate implementing rules to give effect to the Staff Regulations and the Conditions of Employment in accordance with Article 110 of the Staff Regulations;
(j) drawing up the list of candidates provided for in Article 158(2);
(k) ensuring adequate follow-up to the findings and recommendations stemming from the internal or external audit reports and evaluations referred to in Article 210, as well as from investigations of the European Anti-fraud Office (OLAF);
(l) being consulted before adoption of the guidelines for examination in the Office and in the other cases provided for in this Regulation;
(m) providing opinions and requests for information to the Executive Director and to the Commission where it considers it necessary.

2. The Management Board shall adopt, in accordance with Article 110 of the Staff Regulations and Article 142 of the Conditions of Employment, a decision based on Article 2(1) of the Staff Regulations and on Article 6 of the Conditions of Employment, delegating the relevant appointing authority powers to the Executive Director and defining the conditions under which that delegation of appointing authority powers can be suspended.
The Executive Director shall be authorised to sub-delegate those powers.
Where exceptional circumstances so require, the Management Board may, by way of a decision, temporarily suspend the delegation of the appointing authority powers to the Executive Director and those sub-delegated by the latter, and exercise them itself or delegate them to one of its members or to a staff member other than the Executive Director.

[5.1002]
Article 154
Composition of the Management Board
1. The Management Board shall be composed of one representative of each Member State, two representatives of the Commission and one representative of the European Parliament, and their respective alternates.
2. The members of the Management Board may, subject to its rules of procedure, be assisted by advisers or experts.

[5.1003]
Article 155
Chairperson of the Management Board
1. The Management Board shall elect a chairperson and a deputy chairperson from among its members. The deputy chairperson shall *ex officio* replace the chairperson in the event of his being prevented from attending to his duties.
2. The duration of the terms of office of the chairperson and the deputy chairperson shall be four years. The terms of office shall be renewable once. If, however, their membership of the Management Board ends at any time during their term of office, their term of office shall automatically expire on that date also.

[5.1004]
Article 156
Meetings
1. Meetings of the Management Board shall be convened by its chairperson.
2. The Executive Director shall take part in the deliberations, unless the Management Board decides otherwise.
3. The Management Board shall hold an ordinary meeting at least once a year. In addition, it shall meet on the initiative of its chairperson or at the request of the Commission or of one-third of the Member States.
4. The Management Board shall adopt rules of procedure.
5. The Management Board shall take its decisions by an absolute majority of its members. However, a majority of two-thirds of its members shall be required for the decisions which the Management Board is empowered to take under Article 153(1)(a) and (b), Article 155(1) and Article 158(2) and (4). In both cases each member shall have one vote.
6. The Management Board may invite observers to attend its meetings.
7. The secretariat for the Management Board shall be provided by the Office.

SECTION 4
EXECUTIVE DIRECTOR

[5.1005]
Article 157
Functions of the Executive Director
1. The Office shall be managed by the Executive Director. The Executive Director shall be accountable to the Management Board.
2. Without prejudice to the powers of the Commission, the Management Board, and the Budget Committee, the Executive Director shall be independent in the performance of his duties and shall neither seek nor take instructions from a government or from any other body.
3. The Executive Director shall be the legal representative of the Office.
4. The Executive Director shall have in particular the following functions, which may be delegated:
(a) taking all necessary steps, including the adoption of internal administrative instructions and the publication of notices, to ensure the functioning of the Office;
(b) implementing the decisions adopted by the Management Board;
(c) preparing a draft annual work programme indicating estimated human and financial resources for each activity, and submitting it to the Management Board after consultation of the Commission;
(d) submitting to the Management Board proposals pursuant to Article 152(2);

(e) preparing a draft multiannual strategic programme, including the Office's strategy for international cooperation, and submitting it to the Management Board after consultation of the Commission and following an exchange of views with the relevant committee in the European Parliament;
(f) implementing the annual work programme and the multiannual strategic programme and reporting to the Management Board on their implementation;
(g) preparing the annual report on the Office's activities and presenting it to the Management Board for approval;
(h) preparing a draft multiannual staff policy plan and submitting it to the Management Board after consultation of the Commission;
(i) preparing an action plan following-up on the conclusions of the internal or external audit reports and evaluations, as well as following up on the investigations of the OLAF, and reporting on progress twice a year to the Commission and to the Management Board;
(j) protecting the financial interests of the Union by the application of preventive measures against fraud, corruption and any other illegal activities, by effective checks and, if irregularities are detected, by recovering amounts wrongly paid and, where appropriate, by imposing effective, proportionate and dissuasive administrative and financial penalties;
(k) preparing an anti-fraud strategy for the Office and presenting it to the Budget Committee for approval;
(l) in order to ensure uniform application of the Regulation, referring, where appropriate, to the enlarged Board of Appeal ("the Grand Board") questions on a point of law, in particular if the Boards of Appeal have issued diverging decisions on the point;
(m) drawing up estimates of the revenue and expenditure of the Office and implementing the budget;
(n) exercising the powers entrusted to him in respect of staff by the Management Board under Article 153(1)(h);
(o) exercising the powers conferred on him under Articles 31(3), 34(5), 35(3), 94(2), 97(5), Articles 98, 100, 101, Articles 111(4), 112(3), 114(5), Articles 115, 116, Articles 120(4), 146(10), Article 178, Articles 179(1) and 180(2), and Article 181 in accordance with the criteria set out in this Regulation and in the acts adopted pursuant to this Regulation.

5. The Executive Director shall be assisted by one or more Deputy Executive Directors. If the Executive Director is absent or indisposed, the Deputy Executive Director or one of the Deputy Executive Directors shall replace him in accordance with the procedure laid down by the Management Board.

[5.1006]
Article 158
Appointment and removal of the Executive Director and extension of term of office

1. The Executive Director shall be engaged as a temporary agent of the Office under Article 2(a) of the Conditions of Employment of Other Servants.
2. The Executive Director shall be appointed by the Council by simple majority, from a list of candidates proposed by the Management Board, following an open and transparent selection procedure. Before being appointed, the candidate selected by the Management Board may be invited to make a statement before any competent European Parliament committee and to answer questions put by its members. For the purpose of concluding the contract with the Executive Director, the Office shall be represented by the chairperson of the Management Board.
The Executive Director may be removed from office only upon a decision of the Council acting on a proposal from the Management Board.
3. The term of office of the Executive Director shall be five years. By the end of that period, the Management Board shall undertake an assessment which takes into account an evaluation of the performance of the Executive Director and the Office's future tasks and challenges.
4. The Council, taking into account the assessment referred to in paragraph 3, may extend the term of office of the Executive Director once and for no more than five years.
5. An Executive Director whose term of office has been extended may not participate in another selection procedure for the same post at the end of his overall term of office.
6. The Deputy Executive Director or Deputy Executive Directors shall be appointed or removed from office as provided for in paragraph 2, after consultation of the Executive Director and, where applicable, the Executive Director-elect. The term of office of the Deputy Executive Director shall be five years. It may be extended once and for no more than five years by the Council, after consultation of the Executive Director.

SECTION 5
IMPLEMENTATION OF PROCEDURES

[5.1007]
Article 159
Competence

For taking decisions in connection with the procedures laid down in this Regulation, the following shall be competent:

(a) examiners;
(b) Opposition Divisions;
(c) a department in charge of the Register;
(d) Cancellation Divisions;
(e) Boards of Appeal;
(f) any other unit or person appointed by the Executive Director to that effect.

[5.1008]
Article 160
Examiners
An examiner shall be responsible for taking decisions on behalf of the Office in relation to an application for registration of an EU trade mark, including the matters referred to in Articles 41, 42, 76 and 85, except in so far as an Opposition Division is responsible.

[5.1009]
Article 161
Opposition Divisions
1. An Opposition Division shall be responsible for taking decisions on an opposition to an application to register an EU trade mark.
2. The decisions of the Opposition Divisions shall be taken by three-member groups. At least one member shall be legally qualified. Decisions relating to costs or to procedures shall be taken by a single member.
The Commission shall adopt implementing acts specifying the exact types of decisions that are to be taken by a single member. Those implementing acts shall be adopted in accordance with the examination procedure referred to in Article 207(2).

[5.1010]
Article 162
Department in charge of the Register
1. The Department in charge of the Register shall be responsible for taking decisions in respect of entries in the Register.
2. It shall also be responsible for keeping the list of professional representatives referred to in Article 120(2).
3. The decisions of the Department shall be taken by a single member.

[5.1011]
Article 163
Cancellation Divisions
1. A Cancellation Division shall be responsible for taking decisions in relation to:
(a) applications for the revocation or a declaration of invalidity of an EU trade mark;
(b) requests for the assignment of an EU trade mark as provided for in Article 21.
2. The decisions of the Cancellation Divisions shall be taken by three-member groups. At least one member shall be legally qualified. Decisions relating to costs or to procedures as specified in the acts adopted pursuant to Article 161(2) shall be taken by a single member.

[5.1012]
Article 164
General Competence
Decisions required under this Regulation which do not fall within the competence of an examiner, an Opposition Division, a Cancellation Division or the Department in charge of the Register, shall be taken by any official or unit appointed by the Executive Director for that purpose.

[5.1013]
Article 165
Boards of Appeal
1. The Boards of Appeal shall be responsible for deciding on appeals from decisions taken pursuant to Articles 160 to 164.
2. The decisions of the Boards of Appeal shall be taken by three members, at least two of whom are legally qualified. In certain specific cases, decisions shall be taken by the Grand Board chaired by the President of the Boards of Appeal or by a single member, who shall be legally qualified.
3. In order to determine the special cases which fall under the jurisdiction of the Grand Board, account should be taken of the legal difficulty or the importance of the case or of special circumstances which justify it. Such cases may be referred to the Grand Board:
(a) by the authority of the Boards of Appeal referred to in Article 166(4)(a); or
(b) by the Board handling the case.
4. The Grand Board shall also be responsible for giving reasoned opinions on questions of law referred to it by the Executive Director pursuant to Article 157(4)(l).

5. To determine which specific cases fall under the authority of a single member, account should be taken of the lack of difficulty of the legal or factual matters raised, the limited importance of the individual case or the absence of other specific circumstances. The decision to confer a case on one member in the cases referred to shall be adopted by the Board handling the case.

[5.1014]

Article 166

Independence of the members of the Boards of Appeal

1. The President of the Boards of Appeal and the chairpersons of the Boards shall be appointed, in accordance with the procedure laid down in Article 158 for the appointment of the Executive Director, for a term of five years. They shall not be removed from office during this term, unless there are serious grounds for such removal and the Court of Justice, on application by the institution which appointed them, takes a decision to this effect.

2. The term of office of the President of the Boards of Appeal may be extended once for one additional five-year period, or until retirement age if this age is reached during the new term of office, after a prior positive evaluation of his performance by the Management Board.

3. The term of office of the chairpersons of the Boards may be extended for additional five-year periods, or until retirement age if this age is reached during the new term of office, after a prior positive evaluation of their performance by the Management Board, and after consulting the President of the Boards of Appeal.

4. The President of the Boards of Appeal shall have the following managerial and organisational functions:

- (a) chairing the Presidium of the Boards of Appeal ('the Presidium'), responsible for laying down the rules and organising the work of the Boards;
- (b) ensuring the implementation of the decisions of the Presidium;
- (c) allocating cases to a Board on the basis of objective criteria determined by the Presidium;
- (d) forwarding to the Executive Director the Boards' expenditure requirements, with a view to drawing up the expenditure estimates.

The President of the Boards of Appeal shall chair the Grand Board.

5. The members of the Boards of Appeal shall be appointed by the Management Board for a term of five years. Their term of office may be extended for additional five-year periods, or until retirement age if that age is reached during the new term of office after a prior positive evaluation of their performance by the Management Board, and after consulting the President of the Boards of Appeal.

6. The members of the Boards of Appeal shall not be removed from office unless there are serious grounds for such removal and the Court of Justice, after the case has been referred to it by the Management Board on the recommendation of the President of the Boards of Appeal, and after consulting the chairperson of the Board to which the member concerned belongs, takes a decision to this effect.

7. The President of the Boards of Appeal and the chairpersons and members of the Boards of Appeal shall be independent. In their decisions, they shall not be bound by any instructions.

8. Decisions taken by the Grand Board on appeals or opinions on questions of law referred to it by the Executive Director pursuant to Article 165 shall be binding on the decision-making instances of the Office listed in Article 159.

9. The President of the Boards of Appeal and the chairpersons and members of the Boards of Appeal shall not be examiners or members of the Opposition Divisions, the Department in charge of the Register or Cancellation Divisions.

[5.1015]

Article 167

Presidium of the Boards of Appeal and Grand Board

1. The Presidium shall comprise the President of the Boards of Appeal, who shall chair it, the chairmen of the Boards and Board members elected for each calendar year by and from among all the members of the Boards other than the President of the Boards of Appeal and the chairmen of the Boards. The number of Board members so elected shall constitute a quarter of the number of Board members, other than the President of the Boards of Appeal and the chairmen of the Boards, and that number shall be rounded up if necessary.

2. The Grand Board referred to in Article 165(2) shall comprise nine members, including the President of the Boards of Appeal, the chairmen of the Boards, the rapporteur designated prior to referral to the Grand Board, if applicable, and members drawn in rotation from a list comprising the names of all members of the Boards of Appeal other than the President of the Boards of Appeal and the chairmen of the Boards.

[5.1016]
Article 168
Delegation of powers

The Commission is empowered to adopt delegated acts in accordance with Article 208 specifying the details concerning the organisation of the Boards of Appeal, including the setting up and the role of the Presidium, the composition of the Grand Board and the rules on referrals to it, and the conditions under which decisions are to be taken by a single member in accordance with Article 165(2) and (5).

[5.1017]
Article 169
Exclusion and objection

1. Examiners and members of the Divisions set up within the Office or of the Boards of Appeal may not take part in any proceedings if they have any personal interest therein, or if they have previously been involved as representatives of one of the parties. Two of the three members of an Opposition Division shall not have taken part in examining the application. Members of the Cancellation Divisions may not take part in any proceedings if they have participated in the final decision on the case in the proceedings for registration or opposition proceedings. Members of the Boards of Appeal may not take part in appeal proceedings if they participated in the decision under appeal.

2. If, for one of the reasons mentioned in paragraph 1 or for any other reason, a member of a Division or of a Board of Appeal considers that he should not take part in any proceedings, he shall inform the Division or Board accordingly.

3. Examiners and members of the Divisions or of a Board of Appeal may be objected to by any party for one of the reasons mentioned in paragraph 1, or if suspected of partiality. An objection shall not be admissible if, while being aware of a reason for objection, the party has taken a procedural step. No objection may be based upon the nationality of examiners or members.

4. The Divisions and the Boards of Appeal shall decide as to the action to be taken in the cases specified in paragraphs 2 and 3 without the participation of the member concerned. For the purposes of taking this decision the member who withdraws or has been objected to shall be replaced in the Division or Board of Appeal by his alternate.

[5.1018]
Article 170
Mediation centre

1. For the purposes of Article 151(3), the Office may establish a Mediation Centre ("the Centre").

2. Any natural or legal person may use the Centre's services on a voluntary basis with the aim of reaching a friendly settlement of disputes, based on this Regulation or Regulation (EC) No 6/2002, by mutual agreement.

3. The parties shall have recourse to mediation by means of a joint request. The request shall not be deemed to have been filed until the corresponding charge has been paid. The Executive Director shall fix the amount to be charged in accordance with Article 178(1).

4. In the case of disputes subject to the proceedings pending before the Opposition Divisions, Cancellation Divisions or before the Boards of Appeal of the Office a joint request for mediation may be presented at any time after the lodging of a notice of opposition, an application for revocation or an application for a declaration of invalidity or a notice of appeal against decisions of the Opposition or Cancellation Divisions.

5. The proceedings in question shall be suspended and the time periods, other than the time periods for the payment of the applicable fee, shall be interrupted as from the date of the filing of a joint request for mediation. The time periods shall continue as from the day on which the proceedings are resumed.

6. The parties shall be invited to jointly appoint, from the list referred to in paragraph 12, a mediator who has declared that he has a command of the language of the mediation in question. Where the parties do not appoint a mediator within 20 days of the invitation to do so, the mediation shall be deemed to have failed.

7. The parties shall agree together with the mediator on the detailed arrangements for the mediation in a mediation agreement.

8. The mediator shall conclude the mediation proceedings as soon as the parties reach a settlement agreement, or one of the parties declares that it wishes to end the mediation or the mediator establishes that the parties have failed to reach such an agreement.

9. The mediator shall inform the parties as well as the relevant instance of the Office as soon as the mediation proceedings have been concluded.

10. The discussions and negotiations conducted within the framework of mediation shall be confidential for all persons involved in the mediation, in particular for the mediator, the parties and their representatives. All documents and information submitted during the mediation shall be kept separately from, and shall not be part of, the file of any other proceedings before the Office.

11. The mediation shall be conducted in one of the official languages of the Union to be agreed upon by the parties. Where the mediation relates to disputes pending before the Office, the mediation shall be conducted in the language of the Office proceedings, unless otherwise agreed by the parties.

12. The Office shall establish a list of mediators who shall support parties in resolving disputes. The mediators shall be independent and possess relevant skills and experience. The list may include mediators who are employed by the Office, and mediators who are not so employed.

13. Mediators shall be impartial in the exercise of their duties and shall declare any real or perceived conflict of interest upon their designation. Members of the decision-making instances of the Office listed in Article 159 shall not take part in mediation concerning a case in which they have:

(a) had any prior involvement in the proceedings referred to mediation;
(b) any personal interest in those proceedings; or
(c) been previously involved as a representative of one of the parties.

14. Mediators shall not take part as members of the decision-making instances of the Office listed in Article 159 in proceedings resumed as a consequence of a mediation failure.

15. The Office may cooperate with other recognised national or international bodies dealing with mediation.

SECTION 6
BUDGET AND FINANCIAL CONTROL

[5.1019]
Article 171
Budget Committee

1. The Budget Committee shall have the functions assigned to it in this Section.

2. Articles 154 and 155, Article 156(1) to (4), and (5), in so far as it relates to the election of the chairperson and deputy chairperson, and Article 156(6) and (7) shall apply to the Budget Committee, mutatis mutandis.

3. The Budget Committee shall take its decisions by an absolute majority of its members. However, a majority of two-thirds of its members shall be required for the decisions which the Budget Committee is empowered to take under Article 173(3) and Article 177. In both cases each member shall have one vote.

[5.1020]
Article 172
Budget

1. Estimates of all the Office's revenue and expenditure shall be prepared for each financial year and shall be shown in the Office's budget. Each financial year shall correspond to the calendar year.

2. The revenue and expenditure shown in the budget shall be in balance.

3. Revenue shall comprise, without prejudice to other types of income, total fees payable under Annex I to this Regulation, total fees as provided for in Regulation (EC) No 6/2002, total fees payable, under the Madrid Protocol, for an international registration designating the Union, and other payments made to Contracting Parties to the Madrid Protocol, total fees payable, under the Geneva Act referred to in Article 106c of Regulation (EC) No 6/2002, for an international registration designating the Union and other payments made to Contracting Parties to the Geneva Act, and, to the extent necessary, a subsidy entered against a specific heading of the Commission section of the general budget of the Union.

4. Every year the Office shall offset the costs incurred by the central industrial property offices of the Member States, by the Benelux Office for Intellectual Property and by any other relevant authority to be nominated by a Member State, as the result of the specific tasks which they carry out as functional parts of the EU trade mark system in the context of the following services and procedures:

(a) opposition and invalidity proceedings before the central industrial property offices of the Member States and the Benelux Office for Intellectual Property involving EU trade marks;
(b) provision of information on the functioning of the EU trade mark system through helpdesks and information centres;
(c) enforcement of EU trade marks, including action taken pursuant to Article 9(4).

5. The overall offsetting of the costs identified in paragraph 4 shall correspond to 5 % of the yearly revenue of the Office. Without prejudice to the third subparagraph of this paragraph, on a proposal by the Office and after having consulted the Budget Committee, the Management Board shall determine the distribution key on the basis of the following fair, equitable and relevant indicators:

(a) the annual number of EU trade mark applications originating from applicants in each Member State;
(b) the annual number of national trade mark applications in each Member State;
(c) the annual number of oppositions and applications for a declaration of invalidity submitted by proprietors of EU trade marks in each Member State;

(d) the annual number of cases brought before the EU trade mark courts designated by each Member State in accordance with Article 123.

For the purpose of substantiating the costs referred to in paragraph 4, Member States shall submit to the Office by 31 March of each year, statistical data demonstrating the figures referred to in points (a) to (d) of the first subparagraph of this paragraph for the preceding year, which shall be included in the proposal to be made to the Management Board.

On grounds of equity, the costs incurred by the bodies referred to in paragraph 4 in each Member State shall be deemed to correspond to at least 2% of the total offsetting provided for under this paragraph.

6. The obligation by the Office to offset the costs referred to in paragraph 4 and incurred in a given year shall only apply to the extent that no budgetary deficit occurs in that year.

7. In the event of a budgetary surplus, and without prejudice to paragraph 10, on a proposal by the Office and after having consulted the Budget Committee, the Management Board may increase the percentage laid down in paragraph 5 to a maximum of 10% of the yearly revenue of the Office.

8. Without prejudice to paragraphs 4 to 7 and paragraph 10 of this Article and to Articles 151 and 152, where a substantive surplus is generated over five consecutive years, the Budget Committee, upon a proposal from the Office and in accordance with the annual work programme and multiannual strategic programme referred to in Article 153(1)(a) and (b), shall decide by a two-thirds majority on the transfer to the budget of the Union of a surplus generated from 23 March 2016.

9. The Office shall prepare on a biannual basis a report for the European Parliament, the Council and the Commission on its financial situation, including on the financial operations performed under Article 152(5) and (6), and paragraphs 5 and 7 of this Article. On the basis of that report, the Commission shall review the financial situation of the Office.

10. The Office shall provide for a reserve fund covering one year of its operational expenditure to ensure the continuity of its operations and the execution of its tasks.

[5.1021]
Article 173
Preparation of the budget

1. The Executive Director shall draw up each year an estimate of the Office's revenue and expenditure for the following year and shall send it to the Budget Committee not later than 31 March in each year, together with a list of posts.

2. Should the budget estimates provide for a Union subsidy, the Budget Committee shall immediately forward the estimate to the Commission, which shall forward it to the budget authority of the Union. The Commission may attach an opinion on the estimate along with an alternative estimate.

3. The Budget Committee shall adopt the budget, which shall include the Office's list of posts. Should the budget estimates contain a subsidy from the general budget of the Union, the Office's budget shall, if necessary, be adjusted.

[5.1022]
Article 174
Audit and control

1. An internal audit function shall be set up within the Office, to be performed in compliance with the relevant international standards. The internal auditor, appointed by the Executive Director, shall be responsible to him for verifying the proper operation of budget implementation systems and procedures of the Office.

2. The internal auditor shall advise the Executive Director on dealing with risks, by issuing independent opinions on the quality of management and control systems and by issuing recommendations for improving the conditions of implementation of operations and promoting sound financial management.

3. The responsibility for putting in place internal control systems and procedures suitable for carrying out his tasks shall lie with the authorising officer.

[5.1023]
Article 175
Combating fraud

1. In order to facilitate combating fraud, corruption and other unlawful activities under Regulation (EU, Euratom) No 883/2013 of the European Parliament and of the Council[1], the Office shall accede to the Inter-institutional Agreement of 25 May 1999 concerning internal investigations by the European Anti-fraud Office (OLAF), and adopt the appropriate provisions applicable to all the employees of the Office using the template set out in the Annex to that Agreement.

2. The European Court of Auditors shall have the power of audit, on the basis of documents and on the spot, over all grant beneficiaries, contractors and subcontractors who have received Union funds from the Office.

3. OLAF may carry out investigations, including on-the-spot checks and inspections, in accordance with the provisions and procedures laid down in Regulation (EU, Euratom) No 883/2013 and Council Regulation (Euratom, EC) No 2185/96[2] with a view to establishing whether there has been fraud, corruption or any other illegal activity affecting the financial interests of the Union in connection with a grant or a contract funded by the Office.
4. Without prejudice to paragraphs 1, 2 and 3, cooperation agreements with third countries and international organisations, contracts, grant agreements and grant decisions of the Office shall contain provisions expressly empowering the European Court of Auditors and OLAF to conduct such audits and investigations, in accordance with their respective competences.
5. The Budget Committee shall adopt an anti-fraud strategy which is proportionate to the fraud risks having regard to the cost-benefit of the measures to be implemented.

NOTES

[1] Regulation (EU, Euratom) No 883/2013 of the European Parliament and of the Council of 11 September 2013 concerning investigations conducted by the European Anti-Fraud Office (OLAF) and repealing Regulation (EC) No 1073/1999 of the European Parliament and of the Council and Council Regulation (Euratom) No 1074/1999 (OJ L248, 18.9.2013, p 1).

[2] Council Regulation (Euratom, EC) No 2185/96 of 11 November 1996 concerning on-the-spot checks and inspections carried out by the Commission in order to protect the European Communities' financial interests against fraud and other irregularities (OJ L292, 15.11.1996, p 2).]

[5.1024]
Article 176
Auditing of accounts

1. Not later than 31 March in each year the Executive Director shall transmit to the Commission, the European Parliament, the Budget Committee and the Court of Auditors accounts of the Office's total revenue and expenditure for the preceding financial year. The Court of Auditors shall examine them in accordance with Article 287 TFEU.
2. The Budget Committee shall give a discharge to the Executive Director in respect of the implementation of the budget.

[5.1025]
Article 177
Financial provisions

The Budget Committee shall, after consulting the Court of Auditors and the Commission, adopt internal financial provisions specifying, in particular, the procedure for establishing and implementing the Office's budget. As far as is compatible with the particular nature of the Office, the financial provisions shall be based on the financial regulations adopted for other bodies set up by the Union.

[5.1026]
Article 178
Fees and charges and due date

1. The Executive Director shall lay down the amount to be charged for any services rendered by the Office other than those set out in Annex I, as well as the amount to be charged for the European Union Trade Marks Bulletin, the Official Journal of the Office and any other publications issued by the Office. The amounts of charges shall be set in euros and shall be published in the Official Journal of the Office. The amount of each charge shall not exceed what is necessary to cover the costs of the specific service rendered by the Office.
2. Fees and charges in respect of which the due date is not specified in this Regulation shall be due on the date of receipt of the request for the service for which the fee or the charge is incurred.

With the consent of the Budget Committee, the Executive Director may determine which of the services mentioned in the first subparagraph are not to be dependent upon the advance payment of the corresponding fees or charges.

[5.1027]
Article 179
Payment of fees and charges

1. Fees and charges due to the Office shall be paid by payment or transfer to a bank account held by the Office.

With the consent of the Budget Committee, the Executive Director may establish which specific methods of payment other than those set out in the first subparagraph, in particular by means of deposits in current accounts held with the Office, may be used.

Determinations made pursuant to the second subparagraph shall be published in the Official Journal of the Office.

All payments, including by any other method of payment established pursuant to the second subparagraph, shall be made in euros.

2. Every payment shall indicate the name of the person making the payment and shall contain the necessary information to enable the Office to establish immediately the purpose of the payment. In particular, the following information shall be provided:
   (a) when the application fee is paid, the purpose of the payment, namely "application fee";

(b) when the opposition fee is paid, the file number of the application and the name of the applicant for the EU trade mark against which opposition is entered, and the purpose of the payment, namely "opposition fee";
(c) when the revocation fee and the invalidity fee are paid, the registration number and the name of the proprietor of the EU trade mark against which the application is directed, and the purpose of the payment, namely "revocation fee" or "invalidity fee".

3. If the purpose of the payment referred to in paragraph 2 cannot immediately be established, the Office shall require the person making the payment to notify it in writing of this purpose within such period as it may specify. If the person does not comply with this request in due time, the payment shall be considered not to have been made. The amount which has been paid shall be refunded.

[5.1028]
Article 180
Deemed date of payment

1. In the cases referred to in the first subparagraph of Article 179(1), the date on which the payment shall be considered to have been made to the Office shall be the date on which the amount of the payment or of the transfer is actually entered in a bank account held by the Office.
2. Where the methods of payment referred to in the second subparagraph of Article 179(1) may be used, the Executive Director shall establish the date on which such payments are to be considered to have been made.
3. Where, under paragraphs 1 and 2, payment of a fee is not considered to have been made until after the expiry of the period in which it was due, it shall be considered that this period has been observed if evidence is provided to the Office that the persons who made the payment in a Member State, within the period within which the payment should have been made, duly gave an order to a banking establishment to transfer the amount of the payment, and paid a surcharge of 10 % of the relevant fee or fees, but not exceeding EUR 200. No surcharge shall be payable if the relevant order to the banking establishment has been given not later than 10 days before the expiry of the period for payment.
4. The Office may request the person who made the payment to produce evidence as to the date on which the order to the banking establishment as referred to in paragraph 3 was given and, where required, to pay the relevant surcharge within a period to be specified by it. If the person fails to comply with that request or if the evidence is insufficient, or if the required surcharge is not paid in due time, the period for payment shall be considered not to have been observed.

[5.1029]
Article 181
Insufficient payments and refund of insignificant amounts

1. A time limit for payment shall, in principle, be considered to have been observed only if the full amount of the fee has been paid in due time. If the fee is not paid in full, the amount which has been paid shall be refunded after the period for payment has expired.
2. The Office may, however, in so far as is possible within the time remaining before the end of the period, give the person making the payment the opportunity to pay the amount lacking or, where this is considered justified, overlook any small amounts lacking, without prejudice to the rights of the person making the payment.
3. With the consent of the Budget Committee, the Executive Director may waive action for the enforced recovery of any sum due where the sum to be recovered is minimal or where such recovery is too uncertain.
4. Where an excessive sum is paid to cover a fee or a charge, the excess shall not be refunded if the amount is insignificant and the party concerned has not expressly requested a refund.

With the consent of the Budget Committee the Executive Director may determine the amount below which an excessive sum paid to cover a fee or a charge shall not be refunded.

Determinations pursuant to the second subparagraph shall be published in the Official Journal of the Office.

CHAPTER XIII
INTERNATIONAL REGISTRATION OF MARKS

SECTION 1
GENERAL PROVISIONS

[5.1030]
Article 182
Application of provisions

Unless otherwise specified in this chapter, this Regulation and the acts adopted pursuant to this Regulation shall apply to applications for international registrations under the Madrid Protocol ('international applications'), based on an application for an EU trade mark or on an EU trade mark and to registrations of marks in the international register maintained by the International Bureau of the World Intellectual Property Organisation ('international registrations' and 'the International Bureau', respectively) designating the Union.

SECTION 2
INTERNATIONAL REGISTRATION ON THE BASIS OF APPLICATIONS FOR AN EU TRADE MARK AND OF EU TRADE MARKS

[5.1031]
Article 183
Filing of an international application

1. International applications pursuant to Article 3 of the Madrid Protocol based on an application for an EU trade mark or on an EU trade mark shall be filed at the Office.
2. Where an international application is filed before the mark on which the international registration is to be based has been registered as an EU trade mark, the applicant for the international registration shall indicate whether the international registration is to be based on an EU trade mark application or registration. Where the international registration is to be based on an EU trade mark once it is registered, the international application shall be deemed to have been received at the Office on the date of registration of the EU trade mark.

[5.1032]
Article 184
Form and contents of the international application

1. The international application shall be filed in one of the official languages of the Union, using a form provided by the Office. The Office shall inform the applicant filing the international application of the date on which the documents making up the international application are received by the Office. Unless otherwise specified by the applicant on form when he files the international application, the Office shall correspond with the applicant in the language of filing in a standard form.
2. If the international application is filed in a language which is not one of the languages allowed under the Madrid Protocol, the applicant shall indicate a second language from among those languages. This shall be the language in which the Office submits the international application to the International Bureau.
3. Where the international application is filed in a language other than one of the languages allowed under the Madrid Protocol for the filing of international applications, the applicant may provide a translation of the list of goods or services and of any other textual elements forming part of the international application in the language in which the international application is to be submitted to the International Bureau pursuant to paragraph 2. If the application is not accompanied by such translation, the applicant shall authorise the Office to include that translation in the international application. Where the translation has not yet been established in the course of the registration procedure for the EU trade mark application on which the international application is based, the Office shall, without delay, arrange for the translation.
4. The filing of an international application shall be subject to the payment of a fee to the Office. Where the international registration is to be based on an EU trade mark once it is registered, the fee shall be due on the date of registration of the EU trade mark. The application shall be deemed not to have been filed until the required fee has been paid. Where the fee has not been paid, the Office shall inform the applicant accordingly. In the event of electronic filing, the Office may authorise the International Bureau to collect the fee on its behalf.
5. Where the examination of the international application reveals any of the following deficiencies, the Office shall invite the applicant to remedy those deficiencies within such period as it may specify:

(a) the international application has not been filed using the form referred to in paragraph 1, and does not contain all the indications and information required by that form;
(b) the list of goods and services contained in the international application is not covered by the list of goods and services appearing in the basic EU trade mark application or basic EU trade mark;
(c) the mark which is subject to the international application is not identical with the mark as it appears in the basic EU trade mark application or basic EU trade mark;
(d) an indication in the international application as to the trade mark, other than a disclaimer or a colour claim, does not also appear in the basic EU trade mark application or basic EU trade mark;
(e) where colour is claimed in the international application as a distinctive feature of the mark, the basic EU trade mark application or basic EU trade mark is not in the same colour or colours; or
(f) according to the indications made in the international form, the applicant is not eligible to file an international application through the Office in accordance with Article 2(1)(ii) of the Madrid Protocol.

6. Where the applicant has failed to authorise the Office to include a translation as provided for in paragraph 3, or where it is otherwise unclear on which list of goods and services the international application is to be based, the Office shall invite the applicant to make the required indications within such period as it may specify.
7. If the deficiencies referred to in paragraph 5 are not remedied or the required indications referred to in paragraph 6 are not given within the period fixed by the Office, the Office shall refuse to forward the international application to the International Bureau.
8. The Office shall forward the international application to the International Bureau along with the certification provided for under Article 3(1) of the Madrid Protocol as soon as the international application meets the requirements laid down in this Article, the implementing act adopted pursuant to paragraph 9 of this Article, and in Article 183 of this Regulation.
9. The Commission shall adopt implementing acts specifying the exact form, including the elements thereof, to be used for the filing of an international application pursuant to paragraph 1. Those implementing acts shall be adopted in accordance with the examination procedure referred to in Article 207(2).

[5.1033]
Article 185
Recordal in the files and in the Register
1. The date and number of an international registration based on an EU trade mark application shall be recorded in the files of that application. When the application results in an EU trade mark, the date and number of the international registration shall be entered in the Register.
2. The date and number of an international registration based on an EU trade mark shall be entered in the Register.

[5.1034]
Article 186
Notification of the invalidity of the basic application or registration
1. Within a period of five years of the date of the international registration, the Office shall notify the International Bureau of any facts and decisions affecting the validity of the EU trade mark application or the EU trade mark registration on which the international registration was based.
2. The Commission shall adopt implementing acts specifying the individual facts and decisions subject to the notification obligation in accordance with Article 6(3) of the Madrid Protocol as well as the relevant point in time of such notifications. Those implementing acts shall be adopted in accordance with the examination procedure referred to in Article 207(2) of this Regulation.

[5.1035]
Article 187
Request for territorial extension subsequent to international registration
1. A request for territorial extension made subsequent to an international registration pursuant to Article 3ter(2) of the Madrid Protocol may be filed through the intermediary of the Office. The request shall be filed in the language in which the international application was filed pursuant to Article 184 of this Regulation. It shall include indications to substantiate the entitlement to make a designation in accordance with Article 2(1)(ii) and Article 3ter(2) of the Madrid Protocol. The Office shall inform the applicant requesting the territorial extension of the date on which the request for territorial extension was received.
2. The Commission shall adopt implementing acts specifying the detailed requirements regarding the request for territorial extension pursuant to paragraph 1 of this Article. Those implementing acts shall be adopted in accordance with the examination procedure referred to in Article 207(2).
3. Where the request for territorial extension made subsequent to the international registration does not comply with the requirements set out in paragraph 1 and in the implementing act adopted pursuant to paragraph 2, the Office shall invite the applicant to remedy the deficiencies found within such time limit as it may specify. If the deficiencies are not remedied within the time limit fixed by the Office, the Office shall refuse to forward the request to the International Bureau. The Office shall not refuse to forward the request to the International Bureau before the applicant has had the opportunity to correct any deficiency detected in the request.
4. The Office shall forward the request for territorial extension made subsequent to the international registration to the International Bureau as soon as the requirements referred to in paragraph 3 are complied with.

[5.1036]
Article 188
International fees
Any fees payable to the International Bureau under the Madrid Protocol shall be paid direct to the International Bureau.

SECTION 3
INTERNATIONAL REGISTRATIONS DESIGNATING THE UNION

[5.1037]
Article 189
Effects of international registrations designating the Union

1. An international registration designating the Union shall, from the date of its registration pursuant to Article 3(4) of the Madrid Protocol or from the date of the subsequent designation of the Union pursuant to Article 3ter(2) of the Madrid Protocol, have the same effect as an application for an EU trade mark.

2. If no refusal has been notified in accordance with Article 5(1) and (2) of the Madrid Protocol or if any such refusal has been withdrawn, the international registration of a mark designating the Union shall, from the date referred to in paragraph 1, have the same effect as the registration of a mark as an EU trade mark.

3. For the purposes of applying Article 11 of this Regulation, publication of the particulars of the international registration designating the Union pursuant to Article 190(1) shall take the place of publication of an EU trade mark application, and publication pursuant to Article 190(2) shall take the place of publication of the registration of an EU trade mark.

[5.1038]
Article 190
Publication

1. The Office shall publish the date of registration of a mark designating the Union pursuant to Article 3(4) of the Madrid Protocol or the date of the subsequent designation of the Union pursuant to Article 3ter(2) of the Madrid Protocol, the language of filing of the international application and the second language indicated by the applicant, the number of the international registration and the date of publication of such registration in the Gazette published by the International Bureau, a reproduction of the mark and the numbers of the classes of the goods or services in respect of which protection is claimed.

2. If no refusal of protection of an international registration designating the Union has been notified in accordance with Article 5(1) and (2) of the Madrid Protocol or if any such refusal has been withdrawn, the Office shall publish this fact, together with the number of the international registration and, where applicable, the date of publication of such registration in the Gazette published by the International Bureau.

[5.1039]
Article 191
Seniority claimed in an international application

1. The applicant for an international registration designating the Union may claim, in the international application, the seniority of an earlier trade mark registered in a Member State, including a trade mark registered in the Benelux countries, or registered under international arrangements having effect in a Member State, as provided for in Article 39.

2. The documentation, as specified in the implementing act adopted pursuant to Article 39(6), in support of the seniority claim shall be submitted within three months of the date on which the International Bureau notifies the international registration to the Office. In this regard, Article 39(7) shall apply.

3. Where the holder of the international registration is obliged to be represented before the Office pursuant to Article 119(2), the communication as referred to in paragraph 2 of this Article shall contain the appointment of a representative within the meaning of Article 120(1).

4. Where the Office finds that the seniority claim under paragraph 1 of this Article does not comply with Article 39, or does not comply with the other requirements laid down in this Article, it shall invite the applicant to remedy the deficiencies. If the requirements referred to in the first sentence are not satisfied within the time limit specified by the Office, the right of seniority in respect of that international registration shall be lost. If the deficiencies concern only some of the goods and services, the right of seniority shall be lost only in so far as those goods and services are concerned.

5. The Office shall inform the International Bureau of any declaration of a loss of the right of seniority pursuant to paragraph 4. It shall also inform the International Bureau of any withdrawal or restriction of the seniority claim.

6. Article 39(5) shall apply, unless the right of seniority is declared lost pursuant to paragraph 4 of this Article.

[5.1040]
Article 192
Seniority claimed before the Office

1. The holder of an international registration designating the Union may, as from the date of publication of the effects of such registration pursuant to Article 190(2), claim at the Office the seniority of an earlier trade mark registered in a Member State, including a trade mark registered in the Benelux countries, or registered under international arrangements having effect in a Member State, as provided for in Article 40.

2. When the seniority is claimed before the date referred to in paragraph 1, the seniority claim shall be deemed to have been received by the Office on that date.
3. A seniority claim under paragraph 1 of this Article shall fulfil the requirements referred to in Article 40 and shall contain information to enable its examination against those requirements.
4. If the requirements governing the claiming of seniority referred to in paragraph 3 and specified in the implementing act adopted pursuant to paragraph 6 are not fulfilled, the Office shall invite the holder of the international registration to remedy the deficiencies. If the deficiencies are not remedied within a period to be specified by the Office, the Office shall reject the claim.
5. Where the Office has accepted the seniority claim, or where a seniority claim has been withdrawn or cancelled by the Office, the Office shall inform the International Bureau accordingly.
6. The Commission shall adopt implementing acts specifying the details to be contained in a seniority claim under paragraph 1 of this Article and the details of the information to be notified pursuant to paragraph 5 of this Article. Those implementing acts shall be adopted in accordance with the examination procedure referred to in Article 207(2).

[5.1041]
Article 193
Designation of goods and services and examination as to absolute grounds for refusal
1. International registrations designating the Union shall be subject to examination as to their conformity with Article 33(2), (3) and (4) and to absolute grounds for refusal in the same way as applications for EU trade marks.
2. Where an international registration designating the Union is found to be ineligible for protection pursuant to Article 33(4) or Article 42(1) of this Regulation for all or any part of the goods and services for which it has been registered by the International Bureau, the Office shall issue an ex officio provisional notification of refusal to the International Bureau, in accordance with Article 5(1) and (2) of the Madrid Protocol.
3. Where the holder of an international registration is obliged to be represented before the Office pursuant to Article 119(2), the notification referred to in paragraph 2 of this Article shall contain an invitation to appoint a representative within the meaning of Article 120(1).
4. The notification of provisional refusal shall state the reasons on which it is based, and shall specify a time period by which the holder of the international registration may submit his observations and, if appropriate, shall appoint a representative. The time period shall start on the day on which the Office issues the provisional refusal.
5. Where the Office finds that the international application designating the Union does not contain the indication of a second language pursuant to Article 206 of this Regulation, the Office shall issue an ex officio provisional notification of refusal to the International Bureau pursuant to Article 5(1) and (2) of the Madrid Protocol.
6. Where the holder of an international registration fails to overcome the ground for refusing protection within the time limit or, if appropriate, to appoint a representative or to indicate a second language, the Office shall refuse the protection in whole or for part of the goods and services for which the international registration is registered. The refusal of protection shall take the place of a refusal of an EU trade mark application. The decision shall be subject to appeal in accordance with Articles 66 to 72.
7. Where, as of the start of the opposition period referred to in Article 196(2), the Office has not issued an ex officio provisional notification of refusal pursuant to paragraph 2 of this Article, it shall send a statement to the International Bureau, indicating that the examination of absolute grounds of refusal pursuant to Article 42 has been completed but that the international registration is still subject to oppositions or observations of third parties. This interim statement shall be without prejudice to the right of the Office to re-open the examination of absolute grounds on its own initiative any time before the final statement of grant of protection has been issued.
8. The Commission shall adopt implementing acts specifying the details to be contained in the notification of ex officio provisional refusal of protection to be sent to the International Bureau and in the final communications to be sent to the International Bureau on the final grant or refusal of protection. Those implementing acts shall be adopted in accordance with the examination procedure referred to in Article 207(2).

[5.1042]
Article 194
Collective and certification marks
1. Where an international registration is based on a basic application or basic registration relating to a collective mark, certification mark or guarantee mark, the international registration designating the Union shall be dealt with as an EU collective mark or as an EU certification mark, whichever is applicable.
2. The holder of the international registration shall submit the regulations governing the use of the mark, as provided for in Articles 75 and 84, directly to the Office within two months of the date on which the International Bureau notifies the international registration to the Office.
3. The Commission is empowered to adopt delegated acts in accordance with Article 208 specifying the details of the procedure concerning international registrations based on a basic application or basic registration relating to a collective mark, certification mark or guarantee mark.

[5.1043]
Article 195
Search

1. Once the Office has received a notification of an international registration designating the Union, it shall draw up a Union search report as provided for in Article 43(1) provided that a request for a search report, pursuant to Article 43(1), is made to the Office within one month of the date of notification.
2. As soon as the Office has received a notification of an international registration designating the Union, the Office shall transmit a copy thereof to the central industrial property office of each Member State which has informed the Office of its decision to operate a search in its own register of trade marks as provided for in Article 43(2) provided that a request for a search report, pursuant to Article 43(2), is made to the Office within one month of the date of notification and the search fee is paid within the same period.
3. Article 43(3) to (6) shall apply mutatis mutandis.
4. The Office shall inform the proprietors of any earlier EU trade marks or EU trade mark applications cited in the Union search report of the publication of the international registration designating the Union as provided for in Article 190(1). This shall apply whether or not the holder of the international registration has requested to receive the EU search report, unless the proprietor of an earlier registration or application requests not to receive the notification.

[5.1044]
Article 196
Opposition

1. International registration designating the Union shall be subject to opposition in the same way as published EU trade mark applications.
2. Notice of opposition shall be filed within a period of three months which shall begin one month following the date of the publication pursuant to Article 190(1). The opposition shall not be considered as duly entered until the opposition fee has been paid.
3. Refusal of protection shall take the place of refusal of an EU trade mark application.
4. The Commission is empowered to adopt delegated acts in accordance with Article 208 specifying the procedure for the filing and examination of an opposition, including the necessary communications to be made to the International Bureau.

[5.1045]
Article 197
Replacement of an EU trade mark by an international registration

The Office shall, upon request, enter a notice in the Register that an EU trade mark is deemed to have been replaced by an international registration in accordance with Article 4bis of the Madrid Protocol.

[5.1046]
Article 198
Invalidation of the effects of an international registration

1. The effects of an international registration designating the Union may be declared invalid.
2. The application for invalidation of the effects of an international registration designating the Union shall take the place of an application for a declaration of revocation as provided for in Article 58 or for a declaration of invalidity as provided for in Article 59 or Article 60.
3. Where pursuant to Article 64 or Article 128 of this Regulation and this Article, the effects of an international registration designating the Union have been declared invalid by means of a final decision, the Office shall notify the International Bureau in accordance with Article 5(6) of the Madrid Protocol.
4. The Commission shall adopt implementing acts specifying the details to be contained in the notification to be made to the International Bureau pursuant to paragraph 3 of this Article. Those implementing acts shall be adopted in accordance with the examination procedure referred to in Article 207(2).

[5.1047]
Article 199
Legal effect of registration of transfers

The recordal of a change in the ownership of an international registration on the International Register shall have the same effect as the entry of a transfer in the Register pursuant to Article 20.

[5.1048]
Article 200
Legal effect of registration of licences and other rights

The recordal of a licence or a restriction of the holder's right of disposal in respect of an international registration in the International Register shall have the same effect as the registration of a right in rem, a levy of execution, insolvency proceedings or a licence in the Register pursuant to Articles 22, 23, 24 and 25 respectively.

[5.1049]
Article 201
Examination of requests for registration of transfers, licences or restrictions of a holder's right of disposal
The Office shall transmit requests to register a change in ownership, a licence or a restriction of the holder's right of disposal, the amendment or cancellation of a licence or the removal of a restriction of the holder's right of disposal which have been filed with it to the International Bureau, if accompanied by appropriate proof of the transfer, licence, or the restriction of the right of disposal, or by proof that the licence no longer exists or that it has been amended, or that the restriction of the right of disposal has been removed.

[5.1050]
Article 202
Conversion of a designation of the Union through an international registration into a national trade mark application or into a designation of Member States
1. Where a designation of the Union through an international registration has been refused or ceases to have effect, the holder of the international registration may request the conversion of the designation of the Union:
(a) into a national trade mark application pursuant to Articles 139, 140 and 141;
(b) into a designation of a Member State party to the Madrid Protocol, provided that on the date when conversion was requested it was possible to have designated that Member State directly under the Madrid Protocol. Articles 139, 140 and 141 of this Regulation shall apply.
2. The national trade mark application or the designation of a Member State party to the Madrid Protocol resulting from the conversion of the designation of the Union through an international registration shall enjoy, in respect of the Member State concerned, the date of the international registration pursuant to Article 3(4) of the Madrid Protocol or the date of the extension to the Union pursuant to Article 3ter(2) of the Madrid Protocol, if the latter was made subsequent to the international registration, or the date of priority of that registration and, where appropriate, the seniority of a trade mark of that State claimed under Article 191 of this Regulation.
3. The request for conversion shall be published.
4. The request for conversion of an international registration designating the Union into a national trade mark application shall include the information and indications referred to in Article 140(1).
5. Where conversion is requested pursuant to this Article and Article 139(5) of this Regulation following a failure to renew the international registration, the request referred to in paragraph 4 of this Article shall contain an indication to that effect and the date on which the protection expired. The period of three months provided for in Article 139(5) of this Regulation shall begin to run on the day following the last day on which the renewal may still be effected pursuant to Article 7(4) of the Madrid Protocol.
6. Article 140(3) and (5) shall apply to the request for conversion referred to in paragraph 4 of this Article mutatis mutandis.
7. The request for conversion of an international registration designating the Union into a designation of a Member State party to the Madrid Protocol shall include the indications and elements referred to in paragraphs 4 and 5.
8. Article 140(3) shall apply to the request for conversion referred to in paragraph 7 of this Article mutatis mutandis. The Office shall also reject the request for conversion where the conditions to designate the Member State which is a party to the Madrid Protocol or to the Madrid Agreement were fulfilled neither on the date of the designation of the Union nor on the date on which the application for conversion was received or, pursuant to the last sentence of Article 140(1), is deemed to have been received by the Office.
9. Where the request for conversion referred to in paragraph 7 complies with the requirements of this Regulation and rules adopted pursuant to it, the Office shall transmit the request without delay to the International Bureau. The Office shall inform the holder of the international registration of the date of transmission.
10. The Commission shall adopt implementing acts specifying
(a) the details to be contained in the requests for conversion referred to in paragraphs 4 and 7;
(b) the details to be contained in the publication of the requests for conversion pursuant to paragraph 3.
Those implementing acts shall be adopted in accordance with the examination procedure referred to in Article 207(2).

[5.1051]
Article 203
Use of a mark subject of an international registration
For the purposes of applying Article 18(1), Article 47(2), Article 58(1)(a) and Article 64(2), the date of publication pursuant to Article 190(2) shall take the place of the date of registration for the purpose of establishing the date as from which the mark which is the subject of an international registration designating the Union shall be put to genuine use in the Union.

[5.1052]
Article 204
Transformation

1. Subject to paragraph 2, the provisions applicable to EU trade mark applications shall apply mutatis mutandis to applications for transformation of an international registration into an EU trade mark application pursuant to Article 9quinquies of the Madrid Protocol.

2. When the application for transformation relates to an international registration designating the Union the particulars of which have been published pursuant to Article 190(2), Articles 42 to 47 shall not apply.

3. In order to be considered a transformation of an international registration which has been cancelled at the request of the office of origin by the International Bureau pursuant to Article 9quinquies of the Madrid Protocol, an EU trade mark application shall contain an indication to that effect. That indication shall be made when filing the application.

4. Where, in the course of the examination in accordance with Article 41(1)(b), the Office finds that the application was not filed within three months of the date on which the international registration was cancelled by the International Bureau, or the goods and services for which the EU trade mark is to be registered are not contained in the list of goods and services for which the international registration was registered in respect of the Union, the Office shall invite the applicant to remedy the deficiencies.

5. If the deficiencies referred to in paragraph 4 are not remedied within the time period specified by the Office, the right to the date of the international registration or the territorial extension and, if any, of the priority of the international registration shall be lost.

6. The Commission shall adopt implementing acts specifying the details to be contained in an application for transformation pursuant to paragraph 3 of this Article. Those implementing acts shall be adopted in accordance with the examination procedure referred to in Article 207(2).

[5.1053]
Article 205
Communication with the International Bureau

Communication with the International Bureau shall be in a manner and format agreed on between the International Bureau and the Office, and preferably be by electronic means. Any reference to forms shall be construed as including forms made available in electronic format.

[5.1054]
Article 206
Use of languages

For the purpose of applying this Regulation, and rules adopted pursuant to it, to international registrations designating the Union, the language of filing of the international application shall be the language of the proceedings within the meaning of Article 146(4), and the second language indicated in the international application shall be the second language within the meaning of Article 146(3).

CHAPTER XIV
FINAL PROVISIONS

[5.1055]
Article 207
Committee Procedure

1. The Commission shall be assisted by a Committee on Implementation Rules. That committee shall be a committee within the meaning of Regulation (EU) No 182/2011.

2. Where reference is made to this paragraph, Article 5 of Regulation (EU) No 182/2011 shall apply.

[5.1056]
Article 208
Exercise of the delegation

1. The power to adopt delegated acts is conferred on the Commission subject to the conditions laid down in this Article.

2. The power to adopt delegated acts referred to in Article 48, Article 49(3), Articles 65 and 73, Articles 96(4), 97(6), 98(5), 100(2), 101(5), 103(3), and 106(3), Articles 121 and 168, and Articles 194(3) and 196(4) shall be conferred on the Commission for an indeterminate period of time from 23 March 2016.

3. The delegation of power referred to in Article 48, Article 49(3), Articles 65 and 73, Articles 96(4), 97(6), 98(5), 100(2), 101(5), 103(3), and 106(3), Articles 121 and 168, and Articles 194(3) and 196(4) may be revoked at any time by the European Parliament or by the Council. A decision to revoke shall put an end to the delegation of the power specified in that decision. It shall take effect the day following the publication of the decision in the Official Journal of the European Union or at a later date specified therein. It shall not affect the validity of any delegated acts already in force.

4. Before adopting a delegated act, the Commission shall carry out consultations with experts, including experts designated by each Member State in accordance with the principles laid down in the Interinstitutional Agreement of 13 April 2016 on Better Law-Making.
5. As soon as it adopts a delegated act, the Commission shall notify it simultaneously to the European Parliament and to the Council.
6. A delegated act adopted pursuant to Article 48, Article 49(3), Articles 65 and 73, Articles 96(4), 97(6), 98(5), 100(2), 101(5), 103(3), and 106(3), Articles 121 and 168, and Articles 194(3) and 196(4) shall enter into force only if no objection has been expressed either by the European Parliament or by the Council within a period of two months of notification of that act to the European Parliament and the Council or if, before the expiry of that period, the European Parliament and the Council have both informed the Commission that they will not object. That period shall be extended by two months at the initiative of the European Parliament or of the Council.

[5.1057]
Article 209
Provisions relating to the enlargement of the Union
1. As of the date of accession of Bulgaria, the Czech Republic, Estonia, Croatia, Cyprus, Latvia, Lithuania, Hungary, Malta, Poland, Romania, Slovenia and Slovakia ('new Member State(s)'), an EU trade mark registered or applied for pursuant to this Regulation before their respective date of accession shall be extended to the territory of those Member States in order to have equal effect throughout the Union.
2. The registration of an EU trade mark which was under application at the date of accession may not be refused on the basis of any of the absolute grounds for refusal listed in Article 7(1), if these grounds became applicable merely because of the accession of a new Member State.
3. Where an application for the registration of an EU trade mark has been filed during the six months prior to the date of accession, notice of opposition may be given pursuant to Article 46 where an earlier trade mark or another earlier right within the meaning of Article 8 was acquired in a new Member State prior to accession, provided that it was acquired in good faith and that the filing date or, where applicable, the priority date or the date of acquisition in the new Member State of the earlier trade mark or other earlier right precedes the filing date or, where applicable, the priority date of the EU trade mark applied for.
4. An EU trade mark as referred to in paragraph 1 may not be declared invalid:
(a) pursuant to Article 59 if the grounds for invalidity became applicable merely because of the accession of a new Member State;
(b) pursuant to Article 60(1) and (2) if the earlier national right was registered, applied for or acquired in a new Member State prior to the date of accession.
5. The use of an EU trade mark as referred to in paragraph 1 may be prohibited pursuant to Articles 137 and 138, if the earlier trade mark or other earlier right was registered, applied for or acquired in good faith in the new Member State prior to the date of accession of that State; or, where applicable, has a priority date prior to the date of accession of that State.

[5.1058]
Article 210
Evaluation and review
1. By 24 March 2021, and every five years thereafter, the Commission shall evaluate the implementation of this Regulation.
2. The evaluation shall review the legal framework for cooperation between the Office and the central industrial property offices of the Member States and the Benelux Office for Intellectual Property, paying particular attention to the financing mechanism laid down in Article 152. The evaluation shall further assess the impact, effectiveness and efficiency of the Office and its working practices. The evaluation shall, in particular, address the possible need to modify the mandate of the Office, and the financial implications of any such modification.
3. The Commission shall forward the evaluation report together with its conclusions drawn on the basis of that report to the European Parliament, the Council and the Management Board. The findings of the evaluation shall be made public.
4. On the occasion of every second evaluation, there shall be an assessment of the results achieved by the Office having regard to its objectives, mandate and tasks.

[5.1059]
Article 211
Repeal
Regulation (EC) No 207/2009 is repealed.
References to the repealed Regulation shall be construed as references to this Regulation and shall be read in accordance with the correlation table in Annex III.

[5.1060]
Article 212
Entry into force
1. This Regulation shall enter into force on the twentieth day following that of its publication in the Official Journal of the European Union.
2. It shall apply from 1 October 2017.

This Regulation shall be binding in its entirety and directly applicable in all Member States.

ANNEX I

[5.1061]
Amount of Fees

A. The fees to be paid to the Office under this Regulation shall be as follows (in EUR):

1. Basic fee for the application for an individual EU trade mark (Article 31(2)):
   EUR 1,000
2. Basic fee for the application for an individual EU trade mark by electronic means (Article 31(2)):
   EUR 850
3. Fee for the second class of goods and services for an individual EU trade mark (Article 31(2)):
   EUR 50
4. Fee for each class of goods and services exceeding two for an individual EU trade mark (Article 31(2)):
   EUR 150
5. Basic fee for the application for an EU collective mark or an EU certification mark (Article 31(2) and Article 74(3) or Article 83(3)):
   EUR 1,800
6. Basic fee for the application for an EU collective mark or an EU certification mark by electronic means (Article 31(2) and Article 74(3) or Article 83(3)):
   EUR 1,500
7. Fee for the second class of goods and services for an EU collective mark or an EU certification mark: (Article 31(2) and Article 74(3) or Article 83(3)):
   EUR 50
8. Fee for each class of goods and services exceeding two for an EU collective mark or an EU certification mark (Article 31(2) and 74(3) or Article 83(3)):
   EUR 150
9. Search fee for an EU trade mark application (Article 43(2)) or for an international registration designating the Union (Article 43(2) and Article 195(2)):
   EUR 12 multiplied by the number of central industrial property offices referred to in Article 43(2); that amount, and the subsequent changes, shall be published by the Office in the Official Journal of the Office
10. Opposition fee (Article 46(3)):
    EUR 320
11. Basic fee for the renewal of an individual EU trade mark (Article 53(3)):
    EUR 1,000
12. Basic fee for the renewal of an individual EU trade mark by electronic means (Article 53(3)):
    EUR 850
13. Fee for the renewal of the second class of goods and services for an individual EU trade mark (Article 53(3)):
    EUR 50
14. Fee for the renewal of each class of goods and services exceeding two for an individual EU trade mark (Article 53(3)):
    EUR 150
15. Basic fee for the renewal of an EU collective mark or an EU certification mark (Article 53(3) and Article 74(3) or Article 83(3):
    EUR 1,800
16. Basic fee for the renewal of an EU collective mark or an EU certification mark by electronic means (Article 53(3) and Article 74(3) or Article 83(3)):
    EUR 1,500
17. Fee for the renewal of the second class of goods and services for an EU collective mark or an EU certification mark (Article 53(3) and Article 74(3) or Article 83(3)):
    EUR 50
18. Fee for the renewal of each class of goods and services exceeding two for an EU collective mark or an EU certification mark (Article 53(3) and Article 74(3) or Article 83(3)):
    EUR 150
19. Additional fee for the late payment of the renewal fee or the late submission of the request for renewal (Article 53(3)):

25% of the belated renewal fee, subject to a maximum of EUR 1 500

20. Fee for the application for revocation or for a declaration of invalidity (Article 63(2)):
EUR 630
21. Appeal fee (Article 68(1)):
EUR 720
22. Fee for the application of *restitutio in integrum* (Article 104(3)):
EUR 200
23. Fee for the application for the conversion of an EU trade mark application or an EU trade mark (Article 140(1), also in conjunction with Article 202(1)):
(a) into a national trade mark application;
(b) into a designation of Member States under the Madrid Protocol:

EUR 200

24. Fee for continuation of proceedings (Article 105(1)):
EUR 400
25. Fee for the declaration of division of a registered EU trade mark (Article 56(4) or an application for an EU trade mark (Article 50(3)):
EUR 250
26. Fee for the application for the registration of a licence or another right in respect of a registered EU trade mark (Article 26(2)) or an application for an EU trade mark (Article 26(2)):
(a) grant of a licence;
(b) transfer of a licence;
(c) creation of a right *in rem;*
(d) transfer of a right *in rem;*
(e) levy of execution:

EUR 200 per registration, but where multiple requests are submitted in the same application or at the same time, not to exceed a total of EUR 1,000

27. Fee for the cancellation of the registration of a licence or other right (Article 29(3)):
EUR 200 per cancellation, but where multiple requests are submitted in the same application or at the same time, not to exceed a total of EUR 1 000
28. Fee for the alteration of a registered EU trade mark (Article 54(4)):
EUR 200
29. Fee for the issue of a copy of the application for an EU trade mark (Article 114(7)), a copy of the certificate of registration (Article 51(2)), or an extract from the register (Article 111(7)):
(a) uncertified copy or extract:

EUR 10

(b) certified copy or extract:

EUR 30

30. Fee for the inspection of the files (Article 114(6)):
EUR 30
31. Fee for the issue of copies of file documents (Article 114(7)):
(a) uncertified copy:

EUR 10

(b) certified copy:

EUR 30

plus per page, exceeding 10

EUR 1

32. Fee for the communication of information in a file (Article 114(9)):
EUR 10
33. Fee for the review of the determination of the procedural costs to be refunded (Article 109(8)):
EUR 100
34. Fee for the filing of an international application at the Office (Article 184(4)):
EUR 300

B. Fees to be paid to the International Bureau

I. Individual fee for an international registration designating the Union

1. The applicant for an international registration designating the Union shall be required to pay to the International Bureau an individual fee for the designation of the Union in accordance with Article 8(7) of the Madrid Protocol.
2. The holder of an international registration who files a request for territorial extension designating the Union made subsequent to the international registration shall be required to pay to the International Bureau an individual fee for the designation of the Union in accordance with Article 8(7) of the Madrid Protocol.
3. The amount of the fee under points B.I.1 or B.I.2 shall be the equivalent in Swiss Francs, as established by the Director-General of the WIPO pursuant to Rule 35(2) of

the Common Regulations under the Madrid Agreement and Protocol, of the following amounts:

(a) for an individual trade mark: EUR 820 plus, where applicable, EUR 50 for the second class of goods and services and EUR 150 for each class of goods and services contained in the international registration exceeding two;

(b) for a collective mark or a certification mark: EUR 1 400 plus, where applicable, EUR 50 for the second class of goods and services and EUR 150 for each class of goods or services exceeding two.

II. Individual fee for a renewal of an international registration designating the Union

1. The holder of an international registration designating the Union shall be required to pay to the International Bureau, as a part of the fees for a renewal of the international registration, an individual fcc for thc designation of the Union in accordance with Article 8(7) of the Madrid Protocol.

2. he amount of the fee referred to in point B.II.1 shall be the equivalent in Swiss Francs, as established by the Director-General of the WIPO pursuant to Rule 35(2) of the Common Regulations under the Madrid Agreement and Protocol, of the following amounts:

(a) for an individual trade mark: EUR 820 plus, where applicable, EUR 50 for the second class of goods and services and EUR 150 for each class of goods and services contained in the international registration exceeding two;

(b) for a collective mark or a certification mark: EUR 1 400 plus, where applicable, EUR 50 for the second class of goods and services and EUR 150 for each class of goods and services contained in the international registration exceeding two.

ANNEX II
REPEALED REGULATION WITH LIST OF ITS SUCCESSIVE AMENDMENTS

[5.1062]

Council Regulation (EC) No 207/2009

(OJ L78, 24.3.2009, p 1)

Act of Accession of 2012, Annex III, point 2(I)

Regulation (EU) 2015/2424 of the European Parliament and of the Council (OJ L341, 24.12.2015, p 21) — Only Article 1

ANNEX III
CORRELATION TABLE

[5.1063]

Regulation (EC) No 207/2009	**This Regulation**
Articles 1 to 7	Articles 1 to 7
Article 8(1) to (4)	Article 8(1) to (4)
Article 8(4a)	Article 8(6)
Article 8(5)	Article 8(5)
Article 9	Article 9
Article 9a	Article 10
Article 9b	Article 11
Article 10	Article 12
Article 11	Article 13
Article 12	Article 14
Article 13	Article 15
Article 13a	Article 16
Article 14	Article 17
Article 15	Article 18
Article 16	Article 19
Article 17(1), (2) and (3)	Article 20(1), (2) and (3)
Article 17(5)	Article 20(4)
Article 17(5a)	Article 20(5)
Article 17(5b)	Article 20(6)
Article 17(5c)	Article 20(7)
Article 17(5d)	Article 20(8)

Part 5 Trade Marks

Regulation (EC) No 207/2009	This Regulation
Article 17(5e)	Article 20(9)
Article 17(5f)	Article 20(10)
Article 17(6)	Article 20(11)
Article 17(7)	Article 20(12)
Article 17(8)	Article 20(13)
Article 18	Article 21
Article 19	Article 22
Article 20	Article 23
Article 21	Article 24
Article 22	Article 25
Article 22a	Article 26
Article 23	Article 27
Article 24	Article 28
Article 24a	Article 29
Article 25	Article 30
Article 26	Article 31
Article 27	Article 32
Article 28	Article 33
Article 29	Article 34
Article 30	Article 35
Article 31	Article 36
Article 32	Article 37
Article 33	Article 38
Article 34(1)	Article 39(1)
Article 34(1a)	Article 39(2)
Article 34(2)	Article 39(3)
Article 34(3)	Article 39(4)
Article 34(4)	Article 39(5)
Article 34(5)	Article 39(6)
Article 34(6)	Article 39(7)
Article 35	Article 40
Article 36	Article 41
Article 37(1)	Article 42(1)
Article 37(3)	Article 42(2)
Article 38	Article 43
Article 39	Article 44
Article 40	Article 45
Article 41	Article 46
Article 42	Article 47
Article 42a	Article 48
Article 43	Article 49
Article 44(1) and (2)	Article 50(1) and (2)
Article 44(4)	Article 50(3)
Article 44(4a)	Article 50(4)
Article 44(5) to (9)	Article 50(5) to (9)
Article 45	Article 51
Article 46	Article 52
Article 47	Article 53
Article 48	Article 54
Article 48a	Article 55
Article 49	Article 56

Regulation (EC) No 207/2009	This Regulation
Article 50	Article 57
Article 51	Article 58
Article 52	Article 59
Article 53	Article 60
Article 54	Article 61
Article 55	Article 62
Article 56	Article 63
Article 57	Article 64
Article 57a	Article 65
Article 58	Article 66
Article 59	Article 67
Article 60	Article 68
Article 61	Article 69
Article 63	Article 70
Article 64	Article 71
Article 65	Article 72
Article 65a	Article 73
Article 66	Article 74
Article 67	Article 75
Article 68	Article 76
Article 69	Article 77
Article 70	Article 78
Article 71	Article 79
Article 72	Article 80
Article 73	Article 81
Article 74	Article 82
Article 74a	Article 83
Article 74b	Article 84
Article 74c	Article 85
Article 74d	Article 86
Article 74e	Article 87
Article 74f	Article 88
Article 74g	Article 89
Article 74h	Article 90
Article 74i	Article 91
Article 74j	Article 92
Article 74k	Article 93
Article 75	Article 94
Article 76	Article 95
Article 77	Article 96
Article 78	Article 97
Article 79	Article 98
Article 79a	Article 99
Article 79b	Article 100
Article 79c	Article 101
Article 79d	Article 102
Article 80	Article 103
Article 81	Article 104
Article 82	Article 105
Article 82a	Article 106
Article 83	Article 107

Regulation (EC) No 207/2009	This Regulation
Article 84	Article 108
Article 85(1)	Article 109(1)
Article 85(1a)	Article 109(2)
Article 85(2)	Article 109(3)
Article 85(3)	Article 109(4)
Article 85(4)	Article 109(5)
Article 85(5)	Article 109(6)
Article 85(6)	Article 109(7)
Article 85(7)	Article 109(8)
Article 86	Article 110
Article 87	Article 111
Article 87a	Article 112
Article 87b	Article 113
Article 88	Article 114
Article 88a	Article 115
Article 89	Article 116
Article 90	Article 117
Article 91	Article 118
Article 92	Article 119
Article 93	Article 120
Article 93a	Article 121
Article 94	Article 122
Article 95(1)	Article 123(1)
Article 95(2)	—
Article 95(3)	Article 123(2)
Article 95(4)	Article 123(3)
Article 95(5)	—
Article 96	Article 124
Article 97	Article 125
Article 98	Article 126
Article 99	Article 127
Article 100	Article 128
Article 101	Article 129
Article 102	Article 130
Article 103	Article 131
Article 104	Article 132
Article 105	Article 133
Article 106	Article 134
Article 107	Article 135
Article 109	Article 136
Article 110	Article 137
Article 111	Article 138
Article 112	Article 139
Article 113	Article 140
Article 114	Article 141
Article 115	Article 142
Article 116	Article 143
Article 117	Article 144
Article 118	Article 145
Article 119(1) to (5)	Article 146(1) to (5)
Article 119(5a)	Article 146(6)

Regulation (EC) No 207/2009	**This Regulation**
Article 119(6)	Article 146(7)
Article 119(7)	Article 146(8)
Article 119(8)	Article 146(9)
Article 119(9)	Article 146(10)
Article 119(10)	Article 146(11)
Article 120	Article 147
Article 121	Article 148
Article 123	Article 149
Article 123a	Article 150
Article 123b	Article 151
Article 123c	Article 152
Article 124	Article 153
Article 125	Article 154
Article 126	Article 155
Article 127	Article 156
Article 128	Article 157
Article 129	Article 158
Article 130	Article 159
Article 131	Article 160
Article 132	Article 161
Article 133	Article 162
Article 134	Article 163
Article 134a	Article 164
Article 135	Article 165
Article 136	Article 166
Article 136a	Article 167
Article 136b	Article 168
Article 137	Article 169
Article 137a	Article 170
Article 138	Article 171
Article 139	Article 172
Article 140	Article 173
Article 141	Article 174
Article 141a	Article 175
Article 142	Article 176
Article 143	Article 177
Article 144	Article 178
Article 144a	Article 179
Article 144b	Article 180
Article 144c	Article 181
Article 145	Article 182
Article 146	Article 183
Article 147	Article 184
Article 148	Article 185
Article 148a	Article 186
Article 149	Article 187
Article 150	Article 188
Article 151	Article 189
Article 152	Article 190
Article 153	Article 191
Article 153a	Article 192

Regulation (EC) No 207/2009	This Regulation
Article 154	Article 193
Article 154a	Article 194
Article 155	Article 195
Article 156	Article 196
Article 157	Article 197
Article 158	Article 198
Article 158a	Article 199
Article 158b	Article 200
Article 158c	Article 201
Article 159	Article 202
Article 160	Article 203
Article 161	Article 204
Article 161a	Article 205
Article 161b	Article 206
Article 163	Article 207
Article 163a(1)	Article 208(1)
Article 163a(2), first sentence	Article 208(2)
Article 163a(2), second sentence	Article 208(4)
Article 163a(3)	Article 208(3)
Article 163a(4)	Article 208(5)
Article 163a(5)	Article 208(6)
Article 165	Article 209
Article 165a	Article 210
Article 166	Article 211
Article 167	Article 212
Annex -I	Annex I
Annex I	Annex II
Annex II	Annex III

DRAFT COMMISSION IMPLEMENTING REGULATION

of 18.5.2017

laying down detailed rules for implementing certain provisions of Council Regulation (EC) No 207/2009 on the European Union trade mark

[5.1064]

NOTES

This draft Regulation is available at ec.europa.eu/info/law/better-regulation/initiatives/c-2017-3224

THE EUROPEAN COMMISSION,

Having regard to the Treaty on the Functioning of the European Union,

Having regard to Council Regulation (EC) No 207/2009 of 26 February 2009 on the European Union trade mark,[1] and in particular Article 17(5b), Article 26(4), Article 30(2), Article 33(4), Article 34(5), Article 39(5), Article 44(9), Article 45(3), the second subparagraph of Article 48(3), Article 48a(1), Article 49(8), Article 50(5), Article 67(3), Article 74b(3), the first subparagraph of Article 85(1a), Article 89(4), Article 90(3), Article 113(6), Article 119(10), the second subparagraph of Article 132(2), Article 147(9), Article 148a(2), Article 149(2), Article 153a(6), Article 154(8), Article 158(4), Article 159(10) and Article 161(6) thereof,

Whereas:

(1) Council Regulation (EC) No 40/94,[2] which was codified as Regulation (EC) No 207/2009, created a system specific to the Union for the protection of trade marks to be obtained at the level of the Union on the basis of an application to the European Union Intellectual Property Office ('the Office').

(2) Regulation (EU) 2015/2424 of the European Parliament and the Council[3] aligns the powers conferred upon the Commission under Regulation (EC) No 207/2009 to Articles 290 and 291 of the Treaty on the Functioning of the European Union. In order to conform with the new legal framework resulting from that alignment, certain rules should be adopted by means of implementing and delegated acts. The new rules should replace the existing rules which are laid down in Commission Regulation (EC) No 2868/95[4] and aim at implementing Regulation (EC) No 207/2009.

(3) In the interest of clarity, legal certainty and efficiency, and with a view to facilitating the filing of EU trade mark applications, it is of essential importance to specify, in a clear and exhaustive manner while avoiding unnecessary administrative burdens, the mandatory and optional particulars to be contained in an application for an EU trade mark.

(4) Regulation (EC) No 207/2009 no longer requires the representation of a mark to be graphic, as long as it enables the competent authorities and the public to determine with clarity and precision the subject matter of protection. It is therefore necessary, in order to ensure legal certainty, to clearly affirm that the precise subject matter of the exclusive right conferred by the registration is defined by the representation. The representation should, where appropriate, be complemented by an indication of the type of the mark concerned. It may be complemented by a description of the sign in appropriate cases. Such an indication or description should accord with the representation.

(5) Moreover, in order to ensure consistency in the process of filing an EU trade mark application and in order to enhance the effectiveness of clearance searches, it is appropriate to establish general principles to which the representation of every mark must conform, as well as lay down specific rules and requirements for the representation of certain types of trade mark, in accordance with the trade mark's specific nature and attributes.

(6) The introduction of technical alternatives to graphic representation, in line with new technologies, derives from the necessity of modernisation, bringing the registration process closer to technical developments. At the same time, the technical specifications for filing a representation of the trade mark, including representations filed electronically, should be laid down with a view to ensuring that the EU trade mark system remains interoperable with the system established by the Protocol relating to the Madrid Agreement concerning the international registration of marks, adopted at Madrid on 27 June 1989[5] (Madrid Protocol). In accordance with Regulation (EC) No 207/2009, and for the sake of increased flexibility and quicker adaptation to technological advances, it should be left to the Executive Director of the Office to lay down the technical specifications for marks filed electronically.

(7) It is appropriate to streamline proceedings so as to reduce administrative burdens in the filing and process of priority and seniority claims. It should therefore not be necessary any more to submit certified copies of the previous application or registration. Furthermore, the Office should no longer be required to include a copy of the prior trade mark application in the file in the case of a priority claim.

(8) Following the abolition of the requirement of a graphic representation of a trade mark, certain types of trade marks can be represented in electronic format and accordingly, their publication using conventional means is no longer suitable. In order to guarantee the publication of all the information concerning an application, which is required for reasons of transparency and legal certainty, access to the representation of the trade mark by way of a link to the Office's electronic register should be recognised as a valid form of representation of the sign for publication purposes.

(9) For the same reasons, it should also be permissible for the Office to issue certificates of registration in which the reproduction of the trade mark is substituted by an electronic link. Furthermore, for certificates issued after the registration, and to cater for requests made at a time when registration particulars may have changed, it is appropriate to provide for the possibility of issuing updated versions of the certificate, where relevant subsequent entries in the register are indicated.

(10) Practical experience in applying the former regime revealed the need of clarifying certain provisions, in particular in relation to partial transfers and partial surrenders, in order to ensure clarity and legal certainty.

(11) In order to ensure legal certainty, while keeping a certain level of flexibility, it is necessary to establish a minimum content of the regulations governing the use of EU Collective marks and of EU Certification marks submitted pursuant to Regulation (EC) No 207/2009, with the purpose of enabling market operators to avail themselves of this new type of trade mark protection.

(12) Maximum rates for representation costs incurred by the successful party to proceedings before the Office should be specified, taking into account the need to ensure that the obligation to bear the costs may not be misused inter alia for tactical reasons by the other party.

(13) For reasons of efficiency, electronic publications by the Office should be allowed.

(14) It is necessary to ensure an effective and efficient exchange of information between the Office and the authorities of the Member States in the context of administrative cooperation, taking appropriate account of the restrictions to which the inspection of files is subject.

(15) The requirements concerning requests for conversion should ensure a smooth and effective interface between the EU trade mark system and the national trade mark systems.

(16) In order to streamline proceedings before the Office, it should be possible to limit the submission of translations to those parts of documents that are relevant to the proceedings. For the same purpose, the Office should be authorised to require proof that a translation corresponds to the original only in the event of doubt.
(17) For reasons of efficiency, certain decisions of the Office in relation to oppositions or applications for the revocation or a declaration of invalidity of an EU trade mark should be taken by a single member.
(18) Due to the accession of the Union to the Madrid Protocol, it is necessary that the detailed requirements governing the procedures concerning the international registration of marks be entirely consistent with the rules of that Protocol.
(19) The detailed rules laid down in this Regulation relate to provisions of Regulation (EC) No 207/2009 that have been amended by Regulation (EU) 2015/2424 with effect from 1 October 2017. It is therefore necessary to defer the applicability of those rules until the same date. At the same time, certain proceedings initiated before that date should continue to be governed until their conclusion by specific provisions of Regulation (EC) No 2868/95.
(20) The measures provided for in this Regulation are in accordance with the opinion of the Committee on Implementation Rules,

NOTES

1 OJ L78, 24.3.2009, p 1.

2 Council Regulation (EC) No 40/94 of 20 December 1993 on the Community trade mark (OJ L11, 14.1.1994, p 1).

3 Regulation (EU) 2015/2424 of the European Parliament and of the Council of 16 December 2015 amending Council Regulation (EC) No 207/2009 on the Community trade mark and Commission Regulation (EC) No 2868/95 implementing Council Regulation (EC) No 40/94 on the Community trade mark, and repealing Commission Regulation (EC) No 2869/95 on the fees payable to the Office for Harmonization in the Internal Market (Trade Marks and Designs)(OJ L341, 24.12.2015, p 21).

4 Commission Regulation (EC) No 2868/95 of 13 December 1995 implementing Council Regulation (EC) No 40/94 on the Community trade mark (OJ L303, 15.12.1995, p 1).

5 OJ L296, 14.11.2003, p 22.

HAS ADOPTED THIS REGULATION:

TITLE I
GENERAL PROVISIONS

Article 1
Subject-matter

This Regulation lays down rules specifying:

(a) the details to be contained in an application for an EU trade mark to be filed at the European Union Intellectual Property Office ('the Office');
(b) the documentation required for claiming the priority of a previous application and for claiming seniority, and the evidence to be filed for claiming an exhibition priority;
(c) the details to be contained in the publication of an application for an EU trade mark;
(d) the content of a declaration of division of an application, how the Office has to process such a declaration, and the details to be contained in the publication of the divisional application;
(e) the content and form of the certificate of registration;
(f) the content of a declaration of division of a registration and how the Office has to process such a declaration;
(g) the details to be contained in requests for alteration and for the change of name or address;
(h) the content of an application for registration of a transfer, the documentation required to establish a transfer, and how to process applications for partial transfers;
(i) the details to be contained in a declaration of surrender and the required documentation to establish a third party's agreement;
(j) the details to be contained in the regulations governing use of an EU collective mark and those governing use of an EU certification mark;
(k) the maximum rates for costs essential to proceedings and actually incurred;
(l) certain details concerning publications in the European Union Trade Marks Bulletin and the Official Journal of the Office;
(m) the detailed arrangements as to how the Office and the authorities of the Member States are to exchange information between each other and open files for inspection;
(n) the details to be contained in requests for conversion and in the publication of a request for conversion;
(o) the extent to which supporting documents to be used in written proceedings before the Office may be filed in any official language of the Union, the need to supply a translation and the requisite standards of translations;
(p) the decisions to be taken by single members of the opposition and cancellation division;
(q) concerning the international registration of marks:

(i) the form to be used for the filing of an international application;
(ii) the facts and decisions of invalidity to be notified to the International Bureau and the relevant time of such notification;
(iii) the detailed requirements regarding requests for territorial extension subsequent to international registration;
(iv) the details to be contained in a seniority claim for an international registration and the details of the information to be notified to the International Bureau;
(v) the details to be contained in the notification of ex officio provisional refusal of protection to be sent to the International Bureau;
(vi) the details to be contained in the final grant or refusal of protection;
(vii) the details to be contained in the notification of invalidation;
(viii) the details to be contained in the requests for conversion of an international registration and in the publication of such requests;
(ix) the details to be contained in an application for transformation.

TITLE II
APPLICATION PROCEDURE

Article 2
Content of the application

1. The application for an EU trade mark shall contain:
(a) a request for registration of the trade mark as an EU trade mark;
(b) the name and address of the applicant and the State in which that applicant is domiciled or has a seat or an establishment. Names of natural persons shall be indicated by the person's family name(s) and given name(s). Names of legal entities, as well as bodies falling under Article 3 of Regulation (EC) No 207/2009, shall be indicated by their official designation and include the legal form of the entity, which may be abbreviated in a customary manner. The company's national identification number may also be specified if available. The Office may require the applicant to provide telephone numbers or other contact details for communication by electronic means as defined by the Executive Director. Only one address shall, in principle, be indicated for each applicant. Where several addresses are indicated, only the address mentioned first shall be taken into account, except where the applicant designates one of the addresses as an address for service. Where an identification number has already been given by the Office, it shall be sufficient for the applicant to indicate that number and the name of the applicant.
(c) a list of the goods or services for which the trade mark is to be registered, in accordance with Article 28(2) of Regulation (EC) No 207/2009. That list may be selected, in whole or in part, from a database of acceptable terms made available by the Office;
(d) a representation of the trade mark in accordance with Article 3 of this Regulation;
(e) where the applicant has appointed a representative, the name and business address of that representative or the identification number in accordance with point (b); where the representative has more than one business address or where there are two or more representatives with different business addresses, only the first-mentioned address shall be taken into account as an address for service unless the application indicates which address is to be used as an address for service;
(f) where the priority of a previous application is claimed pursuant to Article 30 of Regulation (EC) No 207/2009, a declaration to that effect, stating the date on which and the country in or for which the previous application was filed;
(g) where exhibition priority is claimed pursuant to Article 33 of Regulation (EC) No 207/2009, a declaration to that effect, stating the name of the exhibition and the date of the first display of the goods or services;
(h) where the seniority of one or more earlier trade marks, registered in a Member State, including a trade mark registered in the Benelux countries or registered under international arrangements having effect in a Member State, as referred to in Article 34(1) of Regulation (EC) No 207/2009), is claimed together with the application, a declaration to that effect, stating the Member State or Member States in or for which the earlier trade mark is registered, the date from which the relevant registration was effective, the number of the relevant registration, and the goods or services for which the trade mark is registered. Such declaration may also be made within the period referred to in Article 34(1a) of Regulation (EC) No 207/2009;
(i) where applicable, a statement that the application is for registration of an EU collective mark pursuant to Article 66 of Regulation (EC) No 207/2009 or for registration of an EU certification mark pursuant to Article 74a of Regulation (EC) No 207/2009;
(j) specification of the language in which the application has been filed, and of the second language pursuant to Article 119(3) of Regulation (EC) No 207/2009;
(k) the signature of the applicant or the applicant's representative in accordance with Article 63(1) of Commission Delegated Regulation (EU) . . . / . . . ;[6]

(l) where applicable, the request of a search report referred to in Article 38(1) or (2) of Regulation (EC) No 207/2009.

2. The application may include a claim that the sign has acquired distinctive character through use within the meaning of Article 7(3) of Regulation (EC) No 207/2009, as well as an indication of whether this claim is meant as a principal or subsidiary one. Such claim may also be made within the period referred to in Article 37(3), second sentence, of Regulation (EC) No 207/2009.

3. The application for an EU collective mark or an EU certification mark may include the regulations governing its use. Where such regulations are not included with the application, they shall be submitted within the period referred to in Article 67(1) and Article 74b(1) of Regulation (EC) No 207/2009.

4. If there is more than one applicant, the application may contain the appointment of one applicant or representative as common representative.

NOTES

6 Commission Delegated Regulation (EU) . . . / . . . of [. . .] supplementing Regulation (EC) No 207/2009 of 26 February 2009 on the European Union trade mark (OJ L, , p.).

Article 3
Representation of the trade mark

1. The trade mark shall be represented in any appropriate form using generally available technology, as long as it can be reproduced on the register in a clear, precise, self-contained, easily accessible, intelligible, durable and objective manner so as to enable the competent authorities and the public to determine with clarity and precision the subject-matter of the protection afforded to its proprietor.

2. The representation of the trade mark shall define the subject matter of the registration. Where the representation is accompanied by a description pursuant to paragraph 3(d), (e), (f)(ii), (h) or paragraph 4, such description shall accord with the representation and shall not extend its scope.

3. Where the application concerns any of the trade mark types listed in points (a) to (j), it shall contain an indication to that effect. Without prejudice to paragraphs 1 or 2, the type of the trade mark and its representation shall accord with each other as follows:

(a) in the case of a trade mark consisting exclusively of words or letters, numerals, other standard typographic characters or a combination thereof (word mark), the mark shall be represented by submitting a reproduction of the sign in standard script and layout, without any graphic feature or colour;

(b) in the case of a trade mark where non-standard characters, stylisation or layout, or a graphic feature or a colour are used (figurative mark), including marks that consist exclusively of figurative elements or of a combination of verbal and figurative elements, the mark shall be represented by submitting a reproduction of the sign showing all its elements and, where applicable, its colours;

(c) in the case of a trade mark consisting of, or extending to, a three-dimensional shape, including containers, packaging, the product itself or their appearance (shape mark), the mark shall be represented by submitting either a graphic reproduction of the shape, including computer-generated imaging, or a photographic reproduction. The graphic or photographic reproduction may contain different views. Where the representation is not provided electronically, it may contain up to six different views;

(d) in the case of a trade mark consisting of the specific way in which the mark is placed or affixed on the product (position mark), the mark shall be represented by submitting a reproduction which appropriately identifies the position of the mark and its size or proportion with respect to the relevant goods. The elements which do not form part of the subject-matter of the registration shall be visually disclaimed preferably by broken or dotted lines. The representation may be accompanied by a description detailing how the sign is affixed on the goods;

(e) in the case of a trade mark consisting exclusively of a set of elements which are repeated regularly (pattern mark), the mark shall be represented by submitting a reproduction showing the pattern of repetition. The representation may be accompanied by a description detailing how its elements are repeated regularly;

(f) in the case of a colour mark,

(i) where the trade mark consists exclusively of a single colour without contours, the mark shall be represented by submitting a reproduction of the colour and an indication of that colour by reference to a generally recognised colour code.

(ii) where the trade mark consists exclusively of a combination of colours without contours, the mark shall be represented by submitting a reproduction that shows the systematic arrangement of the colour combination in a uniform and predetermined manner and an indication of those colours by reference to a generally recognised colour code. A description detailing the systematic arrangement of the colours may also be added;

(g) in the case of a trade mark consisting exclusively of a sound or combination of sounds (sound mark), the mark shall be represented by submitting an audio file reproducing the sound or by an accurate representation of the sound in musical notation;
(h) in the case of a trade mark consisting of, or extending to, a movement or a change in the position of the elements of the mark (motion mark), the mark shall be represented by submitting a video file or by a series of sequential still images showing the movement or change of position. Where still images are used, they may be numbered or accompanied by a description explaining the sequence;
(i) in the case of a trade mark consisting of, or extending to, the combination of image and sound (multimedia mark), the mark shall be represented by submitting an audio-visual file containing the combination of the image and the sound;
(j) in the case of a trade mark consisting of elements with holographic characteristics (hologram mark), the mark shall be represented by submitting a video file or a graphic or photographic reproduction containing the views which are necessary to sufficiently identify the holographic effect in its entirety.

4. Where the trade mark is not covered by any of the types listed in paragraph 3, its representation shall comply with the standards set out in paragraph 1 and may be accompanied by a description.
5. Where the representation is provided electronically, the Executive Director of the Office shall determine the formats and size of the electronic file as well as any other relevant technical specifications.
6. Where the representation is not provided electronically, the trade mark shall be reproduced on a single sheet of paper separate from the sheet on which the text of the application appears. The single sheet on which the mark is reproduced shall contain all the relevant views or images and shall not exceed DIN A4 size (29,7 cm high, 21 cm wide). A margin of at least 2,5 cm shall be left all around.
7. Where the correct orientation of the mark is not obvious, it shall be indicated by adding the word 'top' to each reproduction.
8. The reproduction of the mark shall be of such quality as to enable it to be:
(a) reduced to a size of not less than 8 cm wide by 8 cm high; or
(b) enlarged to a size of not more than 8 cm wide by 8 cm high.
9. The filing of a sample or a specimen shall not constitute a proper representation of a trade mark.

Article 4
Claiming priority
1. Where the priority of one or more previous applications is claimed together with the application pursuant to Article 30 of Regulation (EC) No 207/2009, the applicant shall indicate the file number of the previous application and file a copy of it within three months from the filing date. That copy shall state the date of filing of the previous application.
2. Where the language of the previous application for which priority is claimed is not one of the languages of the Office, the applicant shall, if required by the Office, provide the Office with a translation of the previous application into the language of the Office used as the first or second language of the application, within a period specified by the Office.
3. Paragraphs 1 and 2 shall apply *mutatis mutandis* where the priority claim relates to one or more previous registrations.

Article 5
Exhibition priority
Where an exhibition priority is claimed together with the application pursuant to Article 33(1) of Regulation (EC) No 207/2009, the applicant shall, within three months from the filing date, file a certificate issued at the exhibition by the authority responsible for the protection of industrial property at the exhibition. That certificate shall attest that the mark was used for the goods or services covered by the application. It shall also state the opening date of the exhibition and the date of first public use, if different from the opening date of the exhibition. The certificate shall be accompanied by an identification of the actual use of the mark, duly certified by the authority.

Article 6
Claiming seniority of a national trade mark before registration of the EU trade mark
Where the seniority of an earlier registered trade mark, as referred to in Article 34(1) of Regulation (EC) No 207/2009, is claimed pursuant to Article 34(1a) of Regulation (EC) No 207/2009, the applicant shall submit a copy of the relevant registration within three months from the receipt of the seniority claim by the Office.

Article 7
Content of the publication of an application
The publication of the application shall contain:
(a) the applicant's name and address;

(b) where applicable, the name and business address of the representative appointed by the applicant other than a representative falling within the first sentence of Article 92(3) of Regulation (EC) No 207/2009. Where there is more than one representative with the same business address, only the name and business address of the first-named representative shall be published and it shall be followed by the words 'and others'. Where there are two or more representatives with different business addresses, only the address for service determined pursuant to Article 2(1)(e) of this Regulation shall be published. Where an association of representatives is appointed in accordance with Article 74(8) of Delegated Regulation (EU) . . . / . . . , only the name and business address of the association shall be published;

(c) the representation of the mark, together with the elements and descriptions referred to in Article 3 where applicable. Where the representation has been provided in the form of an electronic file, it shall be made accessible by means of a link to that file;

(d) the list of goods or services, grouped according to the classes of the Nice Classification, each group being preceded by the number of the class of that classification to which that group of goods or services belongs, and presented in the order of the classes of that classification;

(e) the date of filing and the file number;

(f) where applicable, particulars of the claim of priority filed by the applicant pursuant to Article 30 of Regulation (EC) No 207/2009;

(g) where applicable, particulars of the claim of exhibition priority filed by the applicant pursuant to Article 33 of Regulation (EC) No 207/2009;

(h) where applicable, particulars of the claim of seniority filed by the applicant pursuant to Article 34 of Regulation (EC) No 207/2009;

(i) where applicable, a statement pursuant to Article 7(3) of Regulation (EC) No 207/2009 that the mark has become distinctive in relation to the goods or services for which registration is requested in consequence of the use which has been made of it;

(j) where applicable, a statement that the application is for an EU collective mark or an EU certification mark;

(k) an indication of the language in which the application was filed and of the second language which the applicant has indicated pursuant to Article 119 (3) of Regulation (EC) No 207/2009;

(l) where applicable, a statement that the application results from a transformation of an international registration designating the Union pursuant to Article 161(2) of Regulation (EC) No 207/2009, together with the date of the international registration pursuant to Article 3(4) of the Madrid Protocol or the date on which thc territorial extension to the Union made subsequently to the international registration pursuant to Article 3 ter (2) of the Madrid Protocol was recorded in the international register and, where applicable, the priority date of the international registration.

Article 8
Division of the application

1. A declaration of the division of the application pursuant to Article 44 of Regulation (EC) No 207/2009 shall contain:

(a) the file number of the application;

(b) the name and address of the applicant in accordance with Article 2(1)(b) of this Regulation;

(c) the list of goods or services subject to the divisional application, or, where the division into more than one divisional application is sought, the list of goods or services for each divisional application;

(d) the list of goods or services which are to remain in the original application.

2. The Office shall establish a separate file for each divisional application, which shall consist of a complete copy of the file of the original application, including the declaration of division and the correspondence relating thereto. The Office shall assign a new application number to each divisional application.

3. The publication of each divisional application shall contain the indications and elements laid down in Article 7.

TITLE III
REGISTRATION PROCEDURE

Article 9
Certificate of registration

The certificate of registration issued in accordance with Article 45(2) of Regulation (EC) No 207/2009 shall contain the entries in the Register listed in Article 87(2) of Regulation (EC) No 207/2009 and a statement to the effect that those entries have been recorded in the Register. Where the representation of the mark is provided in the form of an electronic file, the relevant entry shall be made accessible by means of a link to that file. The certificate shall be complemented, where applicable, by an extract showing all entries to be recorded in the Register in accordance with Article 87(3) of Regulation (EC) No 207/2009 and a statement to the effect that those entries have been recorded in the Register.

Article 10
Content of the request for alteration of a registration

A request for alteration of the registration pursuant to Article 48(2) of Regulation (EC) No 207/2009 shall contain:

(a) the registration number of the EU trade mark;
(b) the name and the address of the proprietor of the EU trade mark in accordance with Article 2(1)(b) of this Regulation;
(c) an indication of the element in the representation of the EU trade mark to be altered and that element in its altered version in accordance with Article 48(3) of Regulation (EC) No 207/2009;
(d) a representation of the EU trade mark as altered, in accordance with Article 3 of this Regulation.

Article 11
Declaration of the division of a registration

1. A declaration of the division of a registration pursuant to Article 49(1) of Regulation (EC) No 207/2009 shall contain:

(a) the registration number of the EU trade mark;
(b) the name and address of the proprietor of the EU trade mark in accordance with Article 2(1)(b) of this Regulation;
(c) the list of goods or services which are to form the divisional registration, or, where the division into more than one divisional registration is sought, the list of goods or services for each divisional registration;
(d) the list of goods or services which are to remain in the original registration.

2. The Office shall establish a separate file for the divisional registration, which shall consist of a complete copy of the file of the original registration, including the declaration of division and the correspondence relating thereto. The Office shall assign a new registration number to the divisional registration.

Article 12
Content of a request for the change of the name or address of the proprietor of an EU trade mark or of the applicant for an EU trade mark

A request for the change of the name or address of the proprietor of a registered EU trade mark pursuant to Article 48a (1) of Regulation (EC) No 207/2009 shall contain:

(a) the registration number of the EU trade mark;
(b) the name and the address of the proprietor of the EU trade mark as recorded in the Register, unless an identification number has already been given by the Office to the proprietor, in which case it shall be sufficient for the applicant to indicate that number and the proprietor's name;
(c) the indication of the new name or address of the proprietor of the EU trade mark, in accordance with Article 2(1)(b) of this Regulation.

Points (b) and (c) of the first subparagraph shall apply *mutatis mutandis* for the purposes of a request for the change of the name or address of the applicant for an EU trade mark. Such a request shall also contain the application number.

TITLE IV
TRANSFER

Article 13
Application for registration of a transfer

1. An application for registration of a transfer under Article 17(5a) of Regulation (EC) No 207/2009 shall contain:

(a) the registration number of the EU trade mark;
(b) particulars of the new proprietor in accordance with Article 2(1)(b) of this Regulation;
(c) where not all the registered goods or services are included in the transfer, particulars of the registered goods or services to which the transfer relates;
(d) evidence duly establishing the transfer in accordance with Article 17(2) and (3) of Regulation (EC) No 207/2009;
(e) where applicable, the name and business address of the representative of the new proprietor, to be set out in accordance with Article 2(1)(e) of this Regulation;

2. Points (b) to (e) of paragraph 1 shall apply *mutatis mutandis* for the purposes of an application for the recording of a transfer of an EU trade mark application.

3. For the purposes of paragraph 1(d), any of the following shall constitute sufficient evidence of transfer:

(a) the signing of the application for registration of the transfer by the registered proprietor or a representative of that proprietor, and by the successor in title or a representative of that successor;

(b) where the application is submitted by the registered proprietor or a representative of that proprietor, a declaration signed by the successor in title or a representative of that successor that he agrees to the registration of the transfer;

(c) where the application for registration is submitted by the successor in title, a declaration, signed by the registered proprietor or a representative of that proprietor, that the registered proprietor agrees to the registration of the successor in title;

(d) the signing of a completed transfer form or document, as laid down in Article 65(1)(e) of Delegated Regulation (EU) . . . / . . . , by the registered proprietor or a representative of that proprietor and by the successor in title or a representative of that successor.

Article 14
Processing of applications for partial transfer

1. Where the application for registration of a transfer relates only to some of the goods or services for which the mark is registered, the applicant shall distribute the goods or services in the original registration between the remaining registration and the application for partial transfer so that the goods or services in the remaining registration and the new registration do not overlap.

2. The Office shall establish a separate file for the new registration, which shall consist of a complete copy of the file of the original registration, including the application for registration of the partial transfer and the correspondence relating thereto. The Office shall assign a new registration number to the new registration.

3. Paragraphs 1 and 2 shall apply *mutatis mutandis* for the purposes of an application for the recording of a transfer of an EU trade mark application. The Office shall assign a new application number to the new EU trade mark application.

TITLE V
SURRENDER

Article 15
Surrender

1. A declaration of surrender pursuant to Article 50(2) of Regulation (EC) No 207/2009 shall contain:

(a) the registration number of the EU trade mark;

(b) the name and address of the proprietor in accordance with Article 2(1)(b) of this Regulation;

(c) where surrender is declared only for some of the goods or services for which the mark is registered, an indication of the goods or services for which the mark is to remain registered.

2. Where a right of a third party relating to the EU trade mark is entered in the register, a declaration of consent to the surrender, signed by the proprietor of that right or a representative of that proprietor, shall be sufficient proof of the third party's agreement to the surrender.

TITLE VI
EU COLLECTIVE MARKS AND CERTIFICATION MARKS

Article 16
Content of regulations governing the use of EU collective marks

The regulations governing EU collective marks referred to in Article 67(1) of Regulation (EC) No 207/2009 shall specify:

(a) the name of the applicant;

(b) the object of the association or the object for which the legal person governed by public law is constituted;

(c) the bodies authorised to represent the association or the legal person governed by public law;

(d) in the case of an association, the conditions for membership;

(e) the representation of the EU collective mark;

(f) the persons authorised to use the EU collective mark;

(g) where appropriate, the conditions governing use of the EU collective mark, including sanctions;

(h) the goods or services covered by the EU collective mark including, where appropriate, any limitation introduced as a consequence of the application of Article 7(1)(j), (k) or (l) of Regulation (EC) No 207/2009;

(i) where appropriate, the authorisation referred to in the second sentence of Article 67(2) of Regulation (EC) No 207/2009.

Article 17
Content of regulations governing the use of EU certification marks
The regulations governing use of EU certification marks referred to in Article 74b of Regulation (EC) No 207/2009 shall specify:
(a) the name of the applicant;
(b) a declaration that the applicant complies with the requirements laid down in Article 74a(2) of Regulation (EC) No 207/2009;
(c) the representation of the EU certification mark;
(d) the goods or services covered by the EU certification mark;
(e) the characteristics of the goods or services to be certified by the EU certification mark, such as the material, mode of manufacture of goods or performance of services, quality or accuracy.
(f) the conditions governing the use of the EU certification mark, including sanctions;
(g) the persons authorised to use the EU certification mark;
(h) how the certifying body is to test those characteristics and to supervise the use of the EU certification mark.

TITLE VII
COSTS

Article 18
Maximum rates for costs
1. Costs referred to in the first subparagraph of Article 85(1a) of Regulation (EC) No 207/2009 shall be borne by the losing party on the basis of the following maximum rates:
(a) where the successful party is not represented, the travel and subsistence costs of that party for one person for the outward and return journey between the place of residence or the place of business and the place where oral proceedings are held pursuant to Article 49 of Delegated Regulation (EU) No . . . / . . . , as follows:
(i) the cost of the first-class rail-fare including usual transport supplements where the total distance by rail does not exceed 800 km or the cost of the tourist-class air-fare where the total distance by rail exceeds 800 km or the route includes a sea-crossing;
(ii) subsistence costs as laid down in Article 13 of Annex VII to the Staff Regulations of Officials of the Union and the Conditions of Employment of Other Servants of the Union, laid down in Council Regulation (EEC, Euratom, ECSC) No 259/68;[7]
(b) travel costs of representatives pursuant to Article 93(1) of Regulation (EC) No 207/2009, at the rates provided for in point (a)(i) of this paragraph;
(c) cost of representation, within the meaning of Article 93(1) of Regulation (EC) No 207/2009, incurred by the successful party, as follows:
(i) in opposition proceedings: EUR 300;
(ii) in proceedings relating to the revocation or invalidity of an EU trade mark: EUR 450;
(iii) in appeal proceedings: EUR 550;
(iv) where oral proceedings have taken place to which the parties have been summoned pursuant to Article 49 of Delegated Regulation (EU) . . . / . . . , the amount referred to in points (i), (ii) or (iii) increased by EUR 400.

2. Where there are several applicants or proprietors of the EU trade mark application or registration or where there are several opposing parties or applicants for revocation or declaration of invalidity who have filed the opposition or application for revocation or declaration of invalidity jointly, the losing party shall bear the costs referred to in paragraph 1(a) for one such person only.
3. Where the successful party is represented by more than one representative within the meaning of Article 93(1) of Regulation (EC) No 207/2009, the losing party shall bear the costs referred to in paragraph 1(b) and (c) of this Article for one such person only.
4. The losing party shall not be obliged to reimburse the successful party for any costs, expenses and fees relating to proceedings before the Office other than those referred to in paragraphs 1, 2 and 3.

NOTES
[7] OJ L56, 4.3.1968, p 1.

TITLE VIII
PERIODICAL PUBLICATIONS

Article 19
Periodical publications
1. Where particulars are published in the EU Trade Marks Bulletin in accordance with Regulation (EC) No 207/2009, Delegated Regulation (EU) . . . / . . . or this Regulation, the date of issue shown on the Bulletin shall be taken as the date of publication of the particulars.
2. To the extent that the entries regarding the registration of a trade mark contain no changes as compared to the publication of the application, the publication of such entries shall be made by way of a reference to the particulars contained in the publication of the application.
3. The Office may make editions of the Official Journal of the Office publicly available by electronic means.

TITLE IX
ADMINISTRATIVE COOPERATION

Article 20
Exchange of information between the Office and the authorities of the Member States
1. Without prejudice to Article 123c of Regulation (EC) No 207/2009, the Office and the central industrial property offices of the Member States, including the Benelux Office for Intellectual Property, shall, upon request, communicate to each other relevant information about the filing of applications for EU trade marks or national marks and about proceedings relating to such applications and the marks registered as a result thereof.
2. The Office and the courts or authorities of the Member States shall exchange information for the purposes of Regulation (EC) No 207/2009 directly or through the central industrial property offices of the Member States.
3. Expenditure in respect of communications under paragraphs 1 and 2 shall be chargeable to the authority making the communications. Such communications shall be exempt from fees.

Article 21
Opening of files for inspection
1. Inspection of files relating to EU trade mark applications or registered EU trade marks by courts or authorities of the Member States shall be of the original documents or of copies thereof, or of technical means of storage if the files are stored in this way.
2. The Office shall, at the time of transmission of files relating to EU trade marks applied for or registered, or copies thereof, to the courts or Public Prosecutors' Offices of the Member States, indicate the restrictions to which the inspection of those files is subject pursuant to Article 88 of Regulation (EC) No 207/2009.
3. Courts or Public Prosecutors' Offices of the Member States may, in the course of proceedings before them, open files or copies thereof transmitted to them by the Office to inspection by third parties. Such inspection shall be subject to Article 88 of Regulation (EC) No 207/2009.

TITLE X
CONVERSION

Article 22
Content of a request for conversion
A request for conversion of an EU trade mark application or a registered EU trade mark into a national trade mark application pursuant to Article 112 of Regulation (EC) No 207/2009 shall contain:
- (a) the name and the address of the applicant for conversion in accordance with Article 2(1)(b) of this Regulation;
- (b) the filing number of the EU trade mark application or the registration number of the EU trade mark;
- (c) an indication of the ground for conversion in accordance with Article 112(1)(a) or (b) of Regulation (EC) No 207/2009;
- (d) a specification of the Member State or the Member States in respect of which conversion is requested;
- (e) where the request does not relate to all of the goods or services for which the application has been filed or for which the EU trade mark has been registered, an indication of the goods or services for which conversion is requested, and, where conversion is requested in respect of more than one Member State and the list of goods or services is not the same for all Member States, an indication of the respective goods or services for each Member State;

(f) where conversion is requested, pursuant to Article 112(6) of Regulation (EC) No 207/2009, on the grounds that an EU trade mark has ceased to have effect as a result of a decision of an EU trade mark court, an indication of the date on which that decision became final, and a copy of the decision, which may be submitted in the language in which the decision was given.

Article 23
Content of the publication of a request for conversion

The publication of a request for conversion in accordance with Article 113(2) of Regulation (EC) No 207/2009 shall contain:

(a) the filing number or the registration number of the EU trade mark in respect of which conversion is requested;
(b) a reference to the previous publication of the request or to the registration in the EU Trade Marks Bulletin;
(c) an indication of the Member State or Member States in respect of which conversion has been requested;
(d) where the request does not relate to all of the goods or services for which the application has been filed or for which the EU trade mark has been registered, an indication of the goods or services for which conversion is requested;
(e) where conversion is requested in respect of more than one Member State and the list of goods or services is not the same for all Member States, an indication of the respective goods or services for each Member State;
(f) the date of the request for conversion.

TITLE XI
LANGUAGES

Article 24
Filing of supporting documents in written proceedings

Unless otherwise provided for in this Regulation or in Delegated Regulation (EU) . . . / . . . , supporting documents to be used in written proceedings before the Office may be filed in any official language of the Union. Where the language of such documents is not the language of the proceedings as determined in accordance with Article 119 of Regulation (EC) No 207/2009, the Office may, of its own motion or upon reasoned request by the other party, require that a translation be supplied, within a period specified by it, in that language.

Article 25
Standard of translations

1. Where a translation of a document is to be filed with the Office, the translation shall identify the document to which it refers and reproduce the structure and contents of the original document. Where a party has indicated that only parts of the document are relevant, the translation may be limited to those parts.

2. Unless otherwise provided for in Regulation (EC) No 207/2009, in Delegated Regulation (EU) . . . / . . . or in this Regulation, a document for which a translation is to be filed shall be deemed not to have been received by the Office in the following cases:

(a) where the translation is received by the Office after the expiry of the relevant period for submitting the original document or the translation;
(b) where the certificate referred to in Article 26 of this Regulation is not filed within the period specified by the Office.

Article 26
Legal authenticity of translations

In the absence of evidence or indications to the contrary, the Office shall assume that a translation corresponds to the relevant original text. In the event of doubt, the Office may require the filing, within a specific period, of a certificate that the translation corresponds to the original text.

TITLE XII
ORGANISATION OF THE OFFICE

Article 27
Decisions of an Opposition Division or a Cancellation Division taken by a single member

Pursuant to Article 132(2) or Article 134(2) of Regulation (EC) No 207/2009, a single member of an Opposition Division or of a Cancellation Division shall take the following types of decisions:

(a) decisions on the apportionment of costs;
(b) decisions to fix the amount of the costs to be paid pursuant to the first sentence of Article 85(6) of Regulation (EC) No 207/2009;

(c) decisions to discontinue the proceedings or decisions confirming that there is no need to proceed to a decision on merits;
(d) decisions to reject an opposition as inadmissible before expiry of the period referred to in Article 6(1) of Delegated Regulation (EU) . . . ;
(e) decisions to stay proceedings;
(f) decisions to join or separate multiple oppositions pursuant to Article 9(1) of Delegated Regulation (EU) . . . / . . . .

TITLE XIII
PROCEDURES CONCERNING THE INTERNATIONAL REGISTRATION OF MARKS

Article 28
Form to be used for the filing of an international application
The form made available by the Office for the filing of an international application, as referred to in Article 147(1) of Regulation (EC) No 207/2009 shall include all the elements of the official form provided by the International Bureau of the World Intellectual Property Organisation ("the International Bureau"). Applicants may also use the official form provided by the International Bureau.

Article 29
Facts and decisions on invalidity to be notified to the International Bureau
1. The Office shall notify the International Bureau within a period of five years from the date of the international registration in the following cases:
(a) where the EU trade mark application on which the international registration was based has been withdrawn, is deemed to be withdrawn or has been refused by a final decision, in respect of all or some of the goods or services listed in the international registration;
(b) where the EU trade mark on which the international registration was based has ceased to have effect because it is surrendered, has not been renewed, has been revoked, or has been declared invalid by the Office by a final decision or, on the basis of a counterclaim in infringement proceedings, by a EU trade mark court, in respect of all or some of the goods or services listed in the international registration;
(c) where the EU trade mark application or the EU trade mark on which the international registration was based has been divided into two applications or registrations.
2. The notification referred to in paragraph 1 shall include:
(a) the number of the international registration;
(b) the name of the holder of the international registration;
(c) the facts and decisions affecting the basic application or registration, as well as the effective date of those facts and decisions;
(d) in the case referred to in paragraph 1(a) or (b), the request to cancel the international registration;
(e) where the act referred to in paragraph 1(a) or (b) affects the basic application or basic registration only with respect to some of the goods or services, those goods or services, or the goods or services which are not affected;
(f) in the case referred to in paragraph 1(c), the number of each EU trade mark application or registration concerned.
3. The Office shall notify the International Bureau at the end of a period of five years from the date of the international registration in the following cases:
(a) where an appeal is pending against a decision of an examiner to refuse the EU trade mark application on which the international registration was based pursuant to Article 37 of Regulation (EC) No 207/2009;
(b) where an opposition is pending against the EU trade mark application on which the international registration was based;
(c) where an application for revocation or an application for declaration of invalidity is pending against the EU trade mark on which the international registration was based;
(d) where mention has been made in the Register of EU Trade Marks that a counterclaim for revocation or for declaration of invalidity has been filed before an EU trade mark court against the EU trade mark on which the international registration was based, but no mention has yet been made in the Register of the decision of the EU trade mark court on the counterclaim.
4. Once the proceedings referred to in paragraph 3 have been concluded by means of a final decision or an entry in the register, the Office shall notify the International Bureau in accordance with paragraph 2.
5. For the purposes of paragraphs 1 and 3, an EU trade mark on which the international registration was based shall include an EU trade mark registration resulting from an EU trade mark application on which the international application was based.

Article 30
Request for territorial extension subsequent to international registration

1. A request for territorial extension filed at the Office pursuant to Article 149(1) of Regulation (EC) No 207/2009 shall meet the following requirements:
   (a) it is filed using one of the forms referred to in Article 31 of this Regulation and contains all the indications and information required by the form used;
   (b) it indicates the number of the international registration to which it relates;
   (c) the list of goods or services is covered by the list of goods or services contained in the international registration;
   (d) the applicant is entitled, based on the indications made in the international form, to make a designation subsequent to the international registration through the Office in accordance with Article 2(1)(ii), and Article 3ter(2) of the Madrid Protocol.

2. Where a request for territorial extension does not meet all of the requirements laid down in paragraph 1, the Office shall invite the applicant to remedy the deficiencies within such time-limit as it may specify.

Article 31
Form to be used for a request for territorial extension

The form made available by the Office for a request for territorial extension subsequent to international registration, as referred to in Article 149(1) of Regulation (EC) No 207/2009 shall include all the elements of the official form provided by the International Bureau. Applicants may also use the official form provided by the International Bureau.

Article 32
Seniority claims before the Office

1. Without prejudice to Article 34(6) of Regulation (EC) No 207/2009, a seniority claim pursuant to Article 153a(1) of Regulation (EC) No 207/2009 shall contain:
   (a) the registration number of the international registration;
   (b) the name and address of the holder of the international registration in accordance with Article 2(1)(b) of this Regulation;
   (c) an indication of the Member State or Member States in or for which the earlier trade mark is registered;
   (d) the number and the filing date of the relevant registration;
   (e) an indication of the goods or services for which the earlier trade mark is registered and those in respect of which seniority is claimed;
   (f) a copy of the relevant registration certificate.

2. Where the holder of the international registration is obliged to be represented in proceedings before the Office pursuant to Article 92(2) of Regulation (EC) No 207/2009, the seniority claim shall contain the appointment of a representative within the meaning of Article 93(1) of Regulation (EC) No 207/2009.

3. Where the Office has accepted the seniority claim, it shall inform the International Bureau accordingly by communicating the following:
   (a) the number of the international registration concerned;
   (b) the name of the Member State or Member States in or for which the earlier trade mark is registered;
   (c) the number of the relevant registration;
   (d) the date from which the relevant registration was effective.

Article 33
Notification of ex officio provisional refusals to the International Bureau

1. The notification of an *ex officio* provisional refusal of protection of the international registration in whole or in part to be issued to the International Bureau pursuant to Article 154(2) and (5) of Regulation (EC) No 207/2009 shall, without prejudice to the requirements laid down in Article 154(3) and (4) of that Regulation, contain the following:
   (a) the number of the international registration;
   (b) a reference to the provisions of Regulation (EC) No 207/2009 which are relevant for the provisional refusal;
   (c) an indication that the provisional refusal of protection will be confirmed by a decision of the Office if the holder of the international registration does not overcome the grounds for refusal by submitting observations to the Office within a time limit of two months from the date on which the Offices issues the provisional refusal;
   (d) where the provisional refusal relates to only part of the goods or services, an indication of those goods or services.

2. In respect of each notification of an *ex officio* provisional refusal to the International Bureau, and provided that the time limit for entering an opposition has expired and that no notification of provisional refusal based on an opposition has been issued pursuant to Article 78(1) of Delegated Regulation (EU) . . . / . . . , the Office shall inform the International Bureau of the following:

(a) where as a result of the proceedings before the Office the provisional refusal has been withdrawn, the fact that the mark is protected in the Union;
(b) where a decision to refuse protection of the mark has become final, if applicable, following an appeal under Article 58 of Regulation (EC) No 207/2009 or an action under Article 65 of Regulation (EC) No 207/2009, the fact that protection of the mark is refused in the Union;
(c) where the refusal pursuant to point (b) concerns only part of the goods or services, the goods or services for which the mark is protected in the Union.

Article 34
Notification of invalidation of the effects of an international registration to the International Bureau
The notification referred to in Article 158(3) of Regulation (EC) No 207/2009 shall bear a date and shall contain:
(a) the indication that the invalidation has been pronounced by the Office, or the indication of the EU trade mark court which has pronounced the invalidation;
(b) an indication of whether invalidation has been pronounced in the form of revocation of the rights of the holder of the international registration, of a declaration that the trade mark is invalid on absolute grounds, or of a declaration that the trade mark is invalid on relative grounds;
(c) a statement to the effect that the invalidation is no longer subject to appeal;
(d) the number of the international registration;
(e) the name of the holder of the international registration;
(f) where the invalidation does not concern all the goods or services, an indication of the goods or services in respect of which the invalidation has been pronounced or those in respect of which the invalidation has not been pronounced;
(g) the date on which the invalidation has been pronounced, together with an indication of the date from when the invalidation is effective.

Article 35
Request for conversion of an international registration into a national trade mark application or into a designation of Member States
1. A request for conversion of an international registration designating the Union into a national trade mark application or into a designation of Member States pursuant to Articles 112 and 159 of Regulation (EC) No 207/2009 shall, without prejudice to the requirements laid down in Article 159(4) to (7) of that Regulation, contain:
(a) the registration number of the international registration;
(b) the date of the international registration or the date of the designation of the Union made subsequently to the international registration pursuant to Article 3ter(2) of the Madrid Protocol and, where applicable, particulars of the claim to priority for the international registration pursuant to Article 159(2) of Regulation (EC) No 207/2009, and particulars of the claim to seniority pursuant to Articles 34, 35 or 153 of Regulation (EC) No 207/2009;
(c) the indications and elements referred to in Article 113(1) of Regulation (EC) No 207/2009 and Article 22(a), (c) and (d) of this Regulation.
2. The publication of a request for conversion referred to in paragraph 1 shall contain the details laid down in Article 23.

Article 36
Transformation of an international registration designating the Union into an EU trade mark application
An application for transformation pursuant to Article 161(3) of Regulation (EC) No 207/2009 shall contain, in addition to the indications and elements referred to in Article 2 of this Regulation, the following:
(a) the number of the international registration which has been cancelled;
(b) the date on which the international registration was cancelled by the International Bureau;
(c) as appropriate, the date of the international registration pursuant to Article 3(4) of the Madrid Protocol or the date of recordal of the territorial extension to the Union made subsequently to the international registration pursuant to Article 3ter(2) of the Madrid Protocol;
(d) where applicable, the date of priority claimed in the international application as entered in the International Register kept by the International Bureau.

TITLE XIV
FINAL PROVISIONS

Article 37
Transitional measures
Notwithstanding Article 80 of Delegated Regulation (EU) . . . / . . . , the provisions of Regulation (EC) No 2868/95 shall continue to apply to ongoing proceedings where this Regulation does not apply in accordance with its Article 38, until such proceedings are concluded.

Article 38
Entry into force and application
1. This Regulation shall enter into force on the day following that of its publication in the Official Journal of the European Union.
2. It shall apply from 1 October 2017, subject to the following exceptions:
   (a) title II shall not apply to applications for an EU trade mark entered before the abovementioned date, as well as to international registrations for which the designation of the Union was made before that date;
   (b) Article 9 shall not apply to EU trade marks registered before the abovementioned date;
   (c) Article 10 shall not apply to requests for alteration entered before the abovementioned date;
   (d) Article 11 shall not apply to declarations of division entered before the abovementioned date;
   (e) Article 12 shall not apply to requests for the change of name or address entered before the abovementioned date;
   (f) title IV shall not apply to applications for registration of a transfer entered before the abovementioned date;
   (g) title V shall not apply to declarations of surrender entered before the abovementioned date;
   (h) title VI shall not apply to applications for EU collective marks or EU certification marks entered before the abovementioned date, as well as to international registrations for which the designation of the Union was made before that date;
   (i) title VII shall not apply to costs incurred in proceedings initiated before the abovementioned date;
   (j) title VIII shall not apply to publications made before the abovementioned date;
   (k) title IX shall not apply to requests for information or inspection entered before the abovementioned date;
   (l) title X shall not apply to requests for conversion entered before the abovementioned date;
   (m) title XI shall not apply to supporting documents or translations entered before the abovementioned date;
   (n) title XII shall not apply to decisions taken before the abovementioned date;
   (o) title XIII shall not apply to international applications, notifications of facts and decisions on invalidity of the EU trade mark application or registration on which the international registration was based, requests for territorial extension, seniority claims, notification of ex officio provisional refusals, notifications of invalidation of the effects of an international registration, requests for conversion for an international registration into a national trade mark application and applications for transformation of an international registration designating the Union into an EU trade mark application entered or made before the abovementioned date, as the case may be.
3. This Regulation shall be binding in its entirety and directly applicable in all Member States.

DRAFT COMMISSION DELEGATED REGULATION

of 18.5.2017

supplementing Council Regulation (EC) No 207/2009 on the European Union trade mark and repealing Commission Regulations (EC) No 2868/95 and (EC) No 216/96

[5.1065]

NOTES

This draft Regulation is available at ec.europa.eu/info/law/better-regulation/initiatives/c-2017-3212

EXPLANATORY MEMORANDUM

1.
CONTEXT OF THE DELEGATED ACT

The recent reform of the EU trade mark system aims to streamline procedures to apply and register an EU trade mark at the European Union Intellectual Property Office ('the Office'). It also aims to increase legal certainty by clarifying provisions and removing ambiguities. Under this reform, the powers conferred upon the Commission under Regulation (EC) No 207/2009 on the European Union trade mark ('the EU Trade Mark Regulation')[1] were aligned with Articles 290 and 291 of the Treaty on the Functioning of the European Union (TFEU). The delegated and implementing acts to be adopted on the basis of the new conferrals under the amended EU Trade Mark Regulation are to replace two existing regulations. These are Commission Regulation (EC) 2868/95 of 13 December 1995 implementing Council Regulation (EC) No 40/94 on the Community trade mark,[2] and Commission Regulation (EC) 216/96 of 5 February 1996 laying down the rules of procedure of the Boards of Appeal of the Office for Harmonisation in the Internal Market.[3]

NOTES

1 Council Regulation (EC) No 207/2009 of 26 February on the European Union trade mark (OJ L78, 24.3.2009, p 1), as amended by Regulation (EU) 2015/2424 of the European Parliament and of the Council of 16 December 2015 (OJ L341, 24.12.2015, p 21).

2 Commission Regulation (EC) No 2868/95 of 13 December 1995 implementing Council Regulation (EC) No 40/94 on the Community trade mark (OJ L303, 15.12.1995, p 1).

3 Commission Regulation (EC) No 216/96 of 5 February 1996 laying down the rules of procedure of the Boards of Appeal of the Office for Harmonization in the Internal Market (Trade Marks and Designs)(OJ L28, 6.2.1996, p 11).

2.
CONSULTATIONS PRIOR TO THE ADOPTION OF THE ACT

The preparation of this delegated act included a consultation of user associations and an exchange with experts of Member State national offices within the European Trade Mark and Design Network. The draft text of the present delegated act was published for feedback on the Commission's Better Regulation portal. The Commission held several meetings of the relevant expert group, during which the delegated provisions were discussed among Member State experts. Observers from the European Parliament and the Office also participated. This consultation process brought a broad consensus on the draft delegated regulation.

3.
LEGAL ELEMENTS OF THE DELEGATED ACT

The provisions adopted under this Regulation aim to enhance the level of transparency, effectiveness and efficiency in proceedings before the Office, and to adapt them to market reality and the everyday needs of users. To fulfil these main goals, the provisions of this Regulation provide a high level of clarity, legal certainty, flexibility, and simplification in comparison with the previous legal framework. They have also been modernised to take account of developments and innovations in communications technology.

3.1.
OPPOSITION PROCEEDINGS (ARTICLES 2, 5, 7 AND 8)

In relation to the procedure for filing and examining oppositions, this text presents, in a structured form, the requirements for admissibility and substantiation of an opposition on the consideration of the earlier marks or rights invoked. The text codifies the Office's practice, which has developed based on well-established case law. It also takes into account the extended relative grounds for refusal introduced by the EU Trade Mark Regulation.

A noteworthy contribution to the modernisation and simplification of opposition proceedings is introduced in the text. It is the possibility of relying on evidence accessible from online sources recognised by the Office as an alternative method for substantiating some of the earlier marks or rights invoked. The wording of the relevant provision (Article 7(2)) guarantees the reliability of evidence. It also provides for flexibility in future developments of existing tools or the availability of different online tools in the future. By presenting this option, the intention is to extend to national and international marks a practice that has previously worked very efficiently for EU trade marks.

The present text helps to make the structure of the opposition procedure clearer. It distinguishes between two types of opposition: those that are not substantiated from the outset because no evidence to that effect is provided or the evidence submitted within the time limit set for that purpose is manifestly insufficient or irrelevant (Article 8(1)); and those where relevant evidence is initially filed within the time limit (Article 8(2)). This distinction, based on defined criteria inferred from case law of the Court of Justice, improves legal certainty and transparency.

Moreover, this clear structure of the proceedings opens the way to another important contribution built upon relevant case law of the Court of Justice. This is the express conferral of discretionary powers to the Office when considering belated evidence submitted to substantiate the opposition (Article 8(5)). This results in greater predictability and flexibility. The application of this discretionary power should be reasoned and, for legal certainty, some of the factors to be considered are listed within this text.

At the same time, the text codifies the Office's practice developed in the light of the existing case law confirming the availability of discretion. Discretion can be used when examining belated evidence of use, either in opposition proceedings (Article 10(7)) or in proceedings for the revocation or declaration of invalidity of EU trade marks (Article 19(1)).

3.2.

PROCEEDINGS FOR REVOCATION AND DECLARATION OF INVALIDITY (ARTICLES 15, 16 AND 20)

As regards proceedings for revocation and declaration of invalidity of EU trade marks, the present text aligns the provisions applicable to such proceedings with those applicable to opposition proceedings. It retains only the differences justified by the different nature of the proceedings in question. In particular, the introduction of a list of admissibility requirements (Article 15) and of a new article on substantiation of these proceedings (Article 16) serves to underline the differences between these two procedural stages. This is recognised by Office practice and case law, including in proceedings for revocation and declaration of invalidity of EU trade marks and in proceedings to do away with ambiguous references contained in the previous law. That alignment with opposition proceedings will simplify the work of both users and examiners, who will no longer have to deal with two different sets of provisions. It will contribute to the goals of clarity, efficiency and increasing legal certainty.

The new assignment process under Article 18(2)(a) of the EU Trade Mark Regulation will follow the same procedural path as invalidity proceedings based on its Article 53(1)(b). Assignment will function in practice as an alternative remedy to invalidating a trade mark (Article 20). That measure simplifies proceedings and ensures high levels of effectiveness and efficiency. The present text also regulates the recording of the assignment in the Register after a decision granting it becomes final. This is required for reasons of legal certainty.

3.3.

APPEALS AND ORGANISATION OF THE BOARDS OF APPEAL (ARTICLES 21 TO 48)

The Office's 'first' instances (in particular examiners, opposition and cancellation divisions, Register department) take decisions as regards the registration of an EU trade mark according to the rules laid down in the EU Trade Mark Regulation. Some of these decisions can affect parties adversely. The appeal procedure ensures that parties can request an independent, specialised and relatively inexpensive review of such decisions. To fulfil that important function, the rules on appeal proceedings must provide a particularly high level of legal certainty and predictability.

The present text builds upon the current implementing regulations, the relevant case law of the Court of Justice, and the best practice developed by the Boards of Appeal over the past decade. It specifies the provisions of the EU Trade Mark Regulation. It improves the transparency, legal certainty and efficiency of appeal proceedings, and user-friendliness, in the following respects:

- First, the text brings together in one single and comprehensive text the provisions that are currently spread across three different legal texts. These are the Regulation implementing the Regulation on the Community trade mark, the Regulation on the rules of procedure of the Boards of Appeal and (to a lesser extent) the decisions of the Boards of Appeal on their organisation.
- Second, the text:
  - *clarifies* the current implementing rules where necessary (e.g. with respect to the respective tasks of a Board's chairperson and rapporteur);
  - *modernises* them in line with the case law of the Court of Justice (e.g. with respect to the admissibility of evidence filed after the expiry of the relevant time limit) and with best practices of the Boards (e.g. re-opening of the examination of a trade mark application on absolute grounds); and
  - where needed, *adapts* them to the changes made in the EU Trade Mark Regulation (e.g. abrogation of revision in *inter partes* cases or the Executive Director's requests for the Grand Board's reasoned opinion on questions on a point in law).

  Other provisions clarify the procedure for allocating an appeal case, the content of the appellant's statement of grounds and of the defendant's response, and the scope of examination of an appeal.
- *Third*, the text creates the procedural framework for the defendant's 'cross-appeal' under the second paragraph of Article 60 of the EU Trade Mark Regulation as amended. This improves legal certainty and transparency.

- *Lastly*, the text is carefully interlinked with the general rules on proceedings before the Office. These are also applicable in appeal proceedings unless specific rules justified by the particular nature of the appeal proceedings apply. This avoids unnecessary duplication of procedural provisions applicable before the Office and limits the corresponding risk of confusion, misinterpretations and 'accidental', thus unjustified, divergences.

3.4.
Language regime (Article 7(4), 10(6) and 13(1))

As regards the language regime (including translations) applicable to the evidence submitted in all proceedings before the Office, the new text introduces a language regime (including translations) depending on the kind of evidence of substantiation involved. Evidence of substantiation can be in the form of certificates of filing, registration and renewal or provisions of relevant law. Such evidence has to be submitted in the language of the proceedings or its translation within the time limit set for the submission of the original. However, for other evidence, the general provisions set out in Article 24 of Implementing Regulation (EU) . . . / . . . would apply. In this case, their translation into the language of the proceedings will have to be supplied only if the Office so requires and within the period that it determines for the said purpose. This brings the translation requirements for this second set of evidence in line with the regime currently applicable to proof of use. This new system reduces the burden (including cost) on the parties involved and speeds up the treatment of the file, resulting in user-friendly, streamlined proceedings.

3.5.
Suspension of proceedings (Article 71)

For the purposes of clarity and harmonisation, a single provision on suspensions applicable to opposition, revocation, declaration of invalidity and appeal proceedings has been introduced. It replaces the former structure of parallel articles in their corresponding titles. For reasons of legal certainty, this new provision identifies the situations where granting a suspension is subject, or not, to the Office's discretion. In suspension requests signed by both parties, limiting the total maximum period for which proceedings may be suspended or requesting a supporting justification for requesting an extension aims to make proceedings more effective. It will also address delaying tactics of parties whilst allowing for a reasonable period of time for negotiations to take place.

3.6.
Taking of evidence (Article 55)

The revised provisions on the 'taking of evidence' are meant to apply to all proceedings before the Office. They also aim at improving clarity and harmonisation. In particular, a legal footing is added for the basic structure and format of written evidence submitted. The relevant new provision (Article 55) has a direct impact on the clear identification of the evidence and arguments raised by the party and on the assurance of expeditious proceedings. This improves the efficiency and effectiveness of proceedings and brings legal certainty. It also aims to prevent abuse where massive amounts of unstructured evidence are used to 'swamp' a party.

3.7.
Notification and communication (Article 56 to 66)

Finally, means of notification and communication have been reordered and updated to take account of the reality of the market, and especially that electronic communication is the means that is most used by users. Thus, a broad definition of 'electronic means' is provided. It introduces the flexibility needed to encompass future means where submissions are made other than on paper. Those forms of notification that do not correspond to the current practice of the Office or that have become obsolete, namely 'by a letter box at the Office' and 'hand delivery', have been deleted for reasons of clarity and legal certainty. This serves to eradicate functionally redundant forms of communication. In line with the EU Trade Mark Regulation, technical specifications of electronic communications are to be drawn up by the Executive Director in order to maintain legal certainty. This also ensures the flexibility required to respond to the constant development of technology. As a result, the text aims to achieve a balance between the needs of the vast majority of users moving toward the electronic media provided by the Office and toward electronic communications in general, and the needs of users who prefer more traditional media. Some of the major benefits provided by these provisions are efficiency, flexibility, certainty and modernisation.

MADRID AGREEMENT CONCERNING THE INTERNATIONAL REGISTRATION OF MARKS

(14 April 1891)

(as revised at Brussels on 14 December 1900, at Washington on 2 June 1911, at The Hague on 6 November 1925, at London on 2 June 1934, at Nice on 15 June 1957, and at Stockholm on 14 July 1967, and as amended on 28 September 1979)

NOTES

This is a provisional English translation prepared by the International Bureau of the World Intellectual Property Organisation (WIPO). Articles have been given titles to facilitate their identification. There are no titles in the signed, French text.

[5.1066]
Article 1
[Establishment of a Special Union. Filing of Marks at International Bureau. Definition of Country of Origin]

(1) The countries to which this Agreement applies constitute a Special Union for the international registration of marks.

(2) Nationals of any of the contracting countries may, in all the other countries party to this Agreement, secure protection for their marks applicable to goods or services, registered in the country of origin, by filing the said marks at the International Bureau of Intellectual Property (hereinafter designated as "the International Bureau") referred to in the Convention establishing the World Intellectual Property Organisation (hereinafter designated as "the Organisation"), through the intermediary of the Office of the said country of origin.

(3) Shall be considered the country of origin the country of the Special Union where the applicant has a real and effective industrial or commercial establishment; if he has no such establishment in a country of the Special Union, the country of the Special Union where he has his domicile; if he has no domicile within the Special Union but is a national of a country of the Special Union, the country of which he is a national.

[5.1067]
Article 2
[Reference to Article 3 of Paris Convention (Same Treatment for Certain Categories of Persons as for Nationals of Countries of the Union)]

Nationals of countries not having acceded to this Agreement who, within the territory of the Special Union constituted by the said Agreement, satisfy the conditions specified in Article 3 of the Paris Convention for the Protection of Industrial Property shall be treated in the same manner as nationals of the contracting countries.

[5.1068]
Article 3
[Contents of Application for International Registration]

(1) Every application for international registration must be presented on the form prescribed by the Regulations; the Office of the country of origin of the mark shall certify that the particulars appearing in such application correspond to the particulars in the national register, and shall mention the dates and numbers of the filing and registration of the mark in the country of origin and also the date of the application for international registration.

(2) The applicant must indicate the goods or services in respect of which protection of the mark is claimed and also, if possible, the corresponding class or classes according to the classification established by the Nice Agreement concerning the International Classification of Goods and Services for the Purposes of the Registration of Marks. If the applicant does not give such indication, the International Bureau shall classify the goods or services in the appropriate classes of the said classification. The indication of classes given by the applicant shall be subject to control by the International Bureau, which shall exercise the said control in association with the national Office. In the event of disagreement between the national Office and the International Bureau, the opinion of the latter shall prevail.

(3) If the applicant claims colour as a distinctive feature of his mark, he shall be required—

1. to state the fact, and to file with his application a notice specifying the colour or the combination of colours claimed;
2. to append to his application copies in colour of the said mark, which shall be attached to the notification given by the International Bureau. The number of such copies shall be fixed by the Regulations.

(4) The International Bureau shall register immediately the marks filed in accordance with Article 1. The registration shall bear the date of the application for international registration in the country of origin, provided that the application has been received by the International Bureau within a period of two months from that date. If the application has not been received within that period, the International Bureau shall record it as at the date on which it received the said

application. The International Bureau shall notify such registration without delay to the Offices concerned. Registered marks shall be published in a periodical journal issued by the International Bureau, on the basis of the particulars contained in the application for registration. In the case of marks comprising a figurative element or a special form of writing, the Regulations shall determine whether a printing block must be supplied by the applicant.

(5) With a view to the publicity to be given in the contracting countries to registered marks, each Office shall receive from the International Bureau a number of copies of the said publication free of charge and a number of copies at a reduced price, in proportion to the number of units mentioned in Article 16(4)(a) of the Paris Convention for the Protection of Industrial Property, under the conditions fixed by the Regulations. Such publicity shall be deemed in all the contracting countries to be sufficient, and no other publicity may be required of the applicant.

[5.1069]
Article 3bis
["Territorial Limitation"]

(1) Any contracting country may, at any time, notify the Director General of the Organisation (hereinafter designated as "the Director General") in writing that the protection resulting from the international registration shall extend to that country only at the express request of the proprietor of the mark.

(2) Such notification shall not take effect until six months after the date of the communication thereof by the Director General to the other contracting countries.

[5.1070]
Article 3ter
[Request for "Territorial Extension"]

(1) Any request for extension of the protection resulting from the international registration to a country which has availed itself of the right provided for in Article 3*bis* must be specially mentioned in the application referred to in Article 3(1).

(2) Any request for territorial extension made subsequently to the international registration must be presented through the intermediary of the Office of the country of origin on a form prescribed by the Regulations. It shall be immediately registered by the International Bureau, which shall notify it without delay to the Office or Offices concerned. It shall be published in the periodical journal issued by the International Bureau. Such territorial extension shall be effective from the date on which it has been recorded in the International Register; it shall cease to be valid on the expiration of the international registration of the mark to which it relates.

[5.1071]
Article 4
[Effects of International Registration]

(1) From the date of the registration so effected at the International Bureau in accordance with the provisions of Articles 3 and 3*ter*, the protection of the mark in each of the contracting countries concerned shall be the same as if the mark had been filed therein direct. The indication of classes of goods or services provided for in Article 3 shall not bind the contracting countries with regard to the determination of the scope of the protection of the mark.

(2) Every mark which has been the subject of an international registration shall enjoy the right of priority provided for by Article 4 of the Paris Convention for the Protection of Industrial Property, without requiring compliance with the formalities prescribed in Section D of that Article.

[5.1072]
Article 4bis
[Substitution of International Registration for Earlier National Registrations]

(1) When a mark already filed in one or more of the contracting countries is later registered by the International Bureau in the name of the same proprietor or his successor in title, the international registration shall be deemed to have replaced the earlier national registrations, without prejudice to any rights acquired by reason of such earlier registrations.

(2) The national Office shall, upon request, be required to take note in its registers of the international registration.

[5.1073]
Article 5
[Refusal by National Offices]

(1) In countries where the legislation so authorises, Offices notified by the International Bureau of the registration of a mark or of a request for extension of protection made in accordance with Article 3*ter* shall have the right to declare that protection cannot be granted to such mark in their territory. Any such refusal can be based only on the grounds which would apply, under the Paris Convention for the Protection of Industrial Property, in the case of a mark filed for national registration. However, protection may not be refused, even partially, by reason only that national legislation would not permit registration except in a limited number of classes or for a limited number of goods or services.

(2) Offices wishing to exercise such right must give notice of their refusal to the International Bureau, together with a statement of all grounds, within the period prescribed by their domestic law and, at the latest, before the expiration of one year from the date of the international registration of the mark or of the request for extension of protection made in accordance with Article 3*ter*.

(3) The International Bureau shall, without delay, transmit to the Office of the country of origin and to the proprietor of the mark, or to his agent if an agent has been mentioned to the Bureau by the said Office, one of the copies of the declaration of refusal so notified. The interested party shall have the same remedies as if the mark had been filed by him direct in the country where protection is refused.

(4) The grounds for refusing a mark shall be communicated by the International Bureau to any interested party who may so request.

(5) Offices which, within the aforesaid maximum period of one year, have not communicated to the International Bureau any provisional or final decision of refusal with regard to the registration of a mark or a request for extension of protection shall lose the benefit of the right provided for in paragraph (1) of this Article with respect to the mark in question.

(6) Invalidation of an international mark may not be pronounced by the competent authorities without the proprietor of the mark having, in good time, been afforded the opportunity of defending his rights. Invalidation shall be notified to the International Bureau.

[5.1074]
Article 5bis
[Documentary Evidence of Legitimacy of Use of Certain Elements of Mark]

Documentary evidence of the legitimacy of the use of certain elements incorporated in a mark, such as armorial bearings, escutcheons, portraits, honorary distinctions, titles, trade names, names of persons other than the name of the applicant, or other like inscriptions, which might be required by the Offices of the contracting countries shall be exempt from any legalisation or certification other than that of the Office of the country of origin.

[5.1075]
Article 5ter
[Copies of Entries in International Register. Searches for Anticipation. Extracts from International Register]

(1) The International Bureau shall issue to any person applying therefor, subject to a fee fixed by the Regulations, a copy of the entries in the Register relating to a specific mark.

(2) The International Bureau may also, upon payment, undertake searches for anticipation among international marks.

(3) Extracts from the International Register requested with a view to their production in one of the contracting countries shall be exempt from all legalisation.

[5.1076]
Article 6
[Period of Validity of International Registration, Independence of International Registration. Termination of Protection in Country of Origin]

(1) Registration of a mark at the International Bureau is effected for twenty years, with the possibility of renewal under the conditions specified in Article 7.

(2) Upon expiration of a period of five years from the date of the international registration, such registration shall become independent of the national mark registered earlier in the country of origin, subject to the following provisions.

(3) The protection resulting from the international registration, whether or not it has been the subject of a transfer, may no longer be invoked, in whole or in part, if, within five years from the date of the international registration, the national mark, registered earlier in the country of origin in accordance with Article 1, no longer enjoys, in whole or in part, legal protection in that country. This provision shall also apply when legal protection has later ceased as the result of an action begun before the expiration of the period of five years.

(4) In the case of voluntary or ex officio cancellation, the Office of the country of origin shall request the cancellation of the mark at the International Bureau, and the latter shall effect the cancellation. In the case of judicial action, the said Office shall send to the International Bureau, ex officio or at the request of the plaintiff, a copy of the complaint or any other documentary evidence that an action has begun, and also of the final decision of the court; the Bureau shall enter notice thereof in the International Register.

[5.1077]
Article 7
[Renewal of International Registration]

(1) Any registration may be renewed for a period of twenty years from the expiration of the preceding period, by payment only of the basic fee and, where necessary, of the supplementary and complementary fees provided for in Article 8(2).

(2) Renewal may not include any change in relation to the previous registration in its latest form.

(3) The first renewal effected under the provisions of the Nice Act of 15 June 1957, or of this Act, shall include an indication of the classes of the International Classification to which the registration relates.

(4) Six months before the expiration of the term of protection, the International Bureau shall, by sending an unofficial notice, remind the proprietor of the mark and his agent of the exact date of expiration.

(5) Subject to the payment of a surcharge fixed by the Regulations, a period of grace of six months shall be granted for renewal of the international registration.

[5.1078]
Article 8
[National Fee. International Fee. Division of Excess Receipts, Supplementary Fees, and Complementary Fees]

(1) The Office of the country of origin may fix, at its own discretion, and collect, for its own benefit, a national fee which it may require from the proprietor of the mark in respect of which international registration or renewal is applied for.

(2) Registration of a mark at the International Bureau shall be subject to the advance payment of an international fee which shall include—

(a) a basic fee;
(b) a supplementary fee for each class of the International Classification, beyond three, into which the goods or services to which the mark is applied will fall;
(c) a complementary fee for any request for extension of protection under Article 3*ter*.

(3) However, the supplementary fee specified in paragraph (2)(b) may, without prejudice to the date of registration, be paid within a period fixed by the Regulations if the number of classes of goods or services has been fixed or disputed by the International Bureau. If, upon expiration of the said period, the supplementary fee has not been paid or the list of goods or services has not been reduced to the required extent by the applicant, the application for international registration shall be deemed to have been abandoned.

(4) The annual returns from the various receipts from international registration, with the exception of those provided for under (b) and (c) of paragraph (2), shall be divided equally among the countries party to this Act by the International Bureau, after deduction of the expenses and charges necessitated by the implementation of the said Act. If, at the time this Act enters into force, a country has not yet ratified or acceded to the said Act, it shall be entitled, until the date on which its ratification or accession becomes effective, to a share of the excess receipts calculated on the basis of that earlier Act which is applicable to it.

(5) The amounts derived from the supplementary fees provided for in paragraph (2)(b) shall be divided at the expiration of each year among the countries party to this Act or to the Nice Act of June 15, 1957, in proportion to the number of marks for which protection has been applied for in each of them during that year, this number being multiplied, in the case of countries which make a preliminary examination, by a coefficient which shall be determined by the Regulations. If, at the time this Act enters into force, a country has not yet ratified or acceded to the said Act, it shall be entitled, until the date on which its ratification or accession becomes effective, to a share of the amounts calculated on the basis of the Nice Act.

(6) The amounts derived from the complementary fees provided for in paragraph (2)(c) shall be divided according to the requirements of paragraph (5) among the countries availing themselves of the right provided for in Article 3*bis*. If, at the time this Act enters into force, a country has not yet ratified or acceded to the said Act, it shall be entitled, until the date on which its ratification or accession becomes effective, to a share of the amounts calculated on the basis of the Nice Act.

[5.1079]
Article 8bis
[Renunciation in Respect of One or More Countries]

The person in whose name the international registration stands may at any time renounce protection in one or more of the contracting countries by means of a declaration filed with the Office of his own country, for communication to the International Bureau, which shall notify accordingly the countries in respect of which renunciation has been made. Renunciation shall not be subject to any fee.

[5.1080]
Article 9
[Changes in National Registers also Affecting International Registration. Reduction of List of Goods and Services Mentioned in International Registration. Additions to that List. Substitutions in that List]

(1) The Office of the country of the person in whose name the international registration stands shall likewise notify the International Bureau of all annulments, cancellations, renunciations, transfers, and other changes made in the entry of the mark in the national register, if such changes also affect the international registration.

(2) The Bureau shall record those changes in the International Register, shall notify them in turn to the Offices of the contracting countries, and shall publish them in its journal.

(3) A similar procedure shall be followed when the person in whose name the international registration stands requests a reduction of the list of goods or services to which the registration applies.
(4) Such transactions may be subject to a fee, which shall be fixed by the Regulations.
(5) The subsequent addition of new goods or services to the said list can be obtained only by filing a new application as prescribed in Article 3.
(6) The substitution of one of the goods or services for another shall be treated as an addition.

[5.1081]
Article 9bis
[Transfer of International Mark Entailing Change in Country of Proprietor]
(1) When a mark registered in the International Register is transferred to a person established in a contracting country other than the country of the person in whose name the international registration stands, the transfer shall be notified to the International Bureau by the Officc of the latter country. The International Bureau shall record the transfer, shall notify the other Offices thereof, and shall publish it in its journal. If the transfer has been effected before the expiration of a period of five years from the international registration, the International Bureau shall seek the consent of the Office of the country of the new proprietor, and shall publish, if possible, the date and registration number of the mark in the country of the new proprietor.
(2) No transfer of a mark registered in the International Register for the benefit of a person who is not entitled to file an international mark shall be recorded.
(3) When it has not been possible to record a transfer in the International Register, either because the country of the new proprietor has refused its consent or because the said transfer has been made for the benefit of a person who is not entitled to apply for international registration, the Office of the country of the former proprietor shall have the right to demand that the International Bureau cancel the mark in its Register.

[5.1082]
Article 9ter
[Assignment of International Mark for Part Only of Registered Goods or Services or for Certain Contracting Countries. Reference to Article 6quater of Paris Convention (Assignment of Mark)]
(1) If the assignment of an international mark for part only of the registered goods or services is notified to the International Bureau, the Bureau shall record it in its Register. Each of the contracting countries shall have the right to refuse to recognise the validity of such assignment if the goods or services included in the part so assigned are similar to those in respect of which the mark remains registered for the benefit of the assignor.
(2) The International Bureau shall likewise record the assignment of an international mark in respect of one or several of the contracting countries only.
(3) If, in the above cases, a change occurs in the country of the proprietor, the Office of the country to which the new proprietor belongs shall, if the international mark has been transferred before the expiration of a period of five years from the international registration, give its consent as required by Article 9*bis*.
(4) The provisions of the foregoing paragraphs shall apply subject to Article 6*quater* of the Paris Convention for the Protection of Industrial Property.

[5.1083]
Article 9quater
[Common Office for Several Contracting Countries. Request by Several Contracting Countries to be Treated as a Single Country]
(1) If several countries of the Special Union agree to effect the unification of their domestic legislations on marks, they may notify the Director General—
  (a) that a common Office shall be substituted for the national Office of each of them, and
  (b) that the whole of their respective territories shall be deemed to be a single country for the purposes of the application of all or part of the provisions preceding this Article.
(2) Such notification shall not take effect until six months after the date of the communication thereof by the Director General to the other contracting countries.

[5.1084]
Article 10
[Assembly of the Special Union]
(1)
  (a) The Special Union shall have an Assembly consisting of those countries which have ratified or acceded to this Act.
  (b) The Government of each country shall be represented by one delegate, who may be assisted by alternate delegates, advisors, and experts.
  (c) The expenses of each delegation shall be borne by the Government which has appointed it, except for the travel expenses and the subsistence allowance of one delegate for each member country, which shall be paid from the funds of the Special Union.

(2)

(a) The Assembly shall—
(i) deal with all matters concerning the maintenance and development of the Special Union and the implementation of this Agreement;
(ii) give directions to the International Bureau concerning the preparation for conferences of revision, due account being taken of any comments made by those countries of the Special Union which have not ratified or acceded to this Act;
(iii) modify the Regulations, including the fixation of the amounts of the fees referred to in Article 8(2) and other fees relating to international registration;
(iv) review and approve the reports and activities of the Director General concerning the Special Union, and give him all necessary instructions concerning matters within the competence of the Special Union;
(v) determine the program and adopt the biennal budget of the Special Union, and approve its final accounts;
(vi) adopt the financial regulations of the Special Union;
(vii) establish such committees of experts and working groups as it may deem necessary to achieve the objectives of the Special Union;
(viii) determine which countries not members of the Special Union and which intergovernmental and international non-governmental organisations shall be admitted to its meetings as observers;
(ix) adopt amendments to Articles 10 to 13;
(x) take any other appropriate action designed to further the objectives of the Special Union;
(xi) perform such other functions as are appropriate under this Agreement.

(b) With respect to matters which are of interest also to other Unions administered by the Organisation, the Assembly shall make its decisions after having heard the advice of the Coordination Committee of the Organisation.

(3)
(a) Each country member of the Assembly shall have one vote.
(b) One-half of the countries members of the Assembly shall constitute a quorum.
(c) Notwithstanding the provisions of subparagraph (b), if, in any session, the number of countries represented is less than one-half but equal to or more than one-third of the countries members of the Assembly, the Assembly may make decisions but, with the exception of decisions concerning its own procedure, all such decisions shall take effect only if the conditions set forth hereinafter are fulfilled. The International Bureau shall communicate the said decisions to the countries members of the Assembly which were not represented and shall invite them to express in writing their vote or abstention within a period of three months from the date of the communication. If, at the expiration of this period, the number of countries having thus expressed their vote or abstention attains the number of countries which was lacking for attaining the quorum in the session itself, such decisions shall take effect provided that at the same time the required majority still obtains.
(d) Subject to the provisions of Article 13(2), the decisions of the Assembly shall require two-thirds of the votes cast.
(e) Abstentions shall not be considered as votes.
(f) A delegate may represent, and vote in the name of, one country only.
(g) Countries of the Special Union not members of the Assembly shall be admitted to the meetings of the latter as observers.

(4)
(a) The Assembly shall meet once in every second calendar year in ordinary session upon convocation by the Director General and, in the absence of exceptional circumstances, during the same period and at the same place as the General Assembly of the Organisation.
(b) The Assembly shall meet in extraordinary session upon convocation by the Director General, at the request of one-fourth of the countries members of the Assembly.
(c) The agenda of each session shall be prepared by the Director General.

(5) The Assembly shall adopt its own rules of procedure.

[5.1085]
Article 11
[International Bureau]

(1)
(a) International registration and related duties, as well as all other administrative tasks concerning the Special Union, shall be performed by the International Bureau.
(b) In particular, the International Bureau shall prepare the meetings and provide the secretariat of the Assembly and of such committees of experts and working groups as may have been established by the Assembly.
(c) The Director General shall be the chief executive of the Special Union and shall represent the Special Union.

(2) The Director General and any staff member designated by him shall participate, without the right to vote, in all meetings of the Assembly and of such committees of experts or working groups as may have been established by the Assembly. The Director General, or a staff member designated by him, shall be ex officio secretary of those bodies.

(3)

(a) The International Bureau shall, in accordance with the directions of the Assembly, make the preparations for the conferences of revision of the provisions of the Agreement other than Articles 10 to 13.

(b) The International Bureau may consult with intergovernmental and international non-governmental organisations concerning preparations for conferences of revision.

(c) The Director General and persons designated by him shall take part, without the right to vote, in the discussions at those conferences.

(4) The International Bureau shall carry out any other tasks assigned to it.

[5.1086]
Article 12
[Finances]

(1)

(a) The Special Union shall have a budget.

(b) The budget of the Special Union shall include the income and expenses proper to the Special Union, its contribution to the budget of expenses common to the Unions, and, where applicable, the sum made available to the budget of the Conference of the Organisation.

(c) Expenses not attributable exclusively to the Special Union but also to one or more other Unions administered by the Organisation shall be considered as expenses common to the Unions. The share of the Special Union in such common expenses shall be in proportion to the interest the Special Union has in them.

(2) The budget of the Special Union shall be established with due regard to the requirements of coordination with the budgets of the other Unions administered by the Organisation.

(3) The budget of the Special Union shall be financed from the following sources—

(i) international registration fees and other fees and charges due for other services rendered by the International Bureau in relation to the Special Union;

(ii) sale of, or royalties on, the publications of the International Bureau concerning the Special Union;

(iii) gifts, bequests, and subventions;

(iv) rents, interests, and other miscellaneous income.

(4)

(a) The amounts of the fees referred to in Article 8(2) and other fees relating to international registration shall be fixed by the Assembly on the proposal of the Director General.

(b) The amounts of such fees shall be so fixed that the revenues of the Special Union from fees, other than the supplementary and complementary fees referred to in Article 8(2)(b) and (c), and other sources shall be at least sufficient to cover the expenses of the International Bureau concerning the Special Union.

(c) If the budget is not adopted before the beginning of a new financial period, it shall be at the same level as the budget of the previous year, as provided in the financial regulations.

(5) Subject to the provisions of paragraph (4)(a), the amount of fees and charges due for other services rendered by the International Bureau in relation to the Special Union shall be established, and shall be reported to the Assembly, by the Director General.

(6)

(a) The Special Union shall have a working capital fund which shall be constituted by a single payment made by each country of the Special Union. If the fund becomes insufficient, the Assembly shall decide to increase it.

(b) The amount of the initial payment of each country to the said fund or of its participation in the increase thereof shall be a proportion of the contribution of that country as a member of the Paris Union for the Protection of Industrial Property to the budget of the said Union for the year in which the fund is established or the decision to increase it is made.

(c) The proportion and the terms of payment shall be fixed by the Assembly on the proposal of the Director General and after it has heard the advice of the Coordination Committee of the Organisation.

(d) As long as the Assembly authorises the use of the reserve fund of the Special Union as a working capital fund, the Assembly may suspend the application of the provisions of subparagraphs (a), (b), and (c).

(7)

(a) In the headquarters agreement concluded with the country on the territory of which the Organisation has its headquarters, it shall be provided that, whenever the working capital fund is insufficient, such country shall grant advances. The amount of those advances and the conditions on which they are granted shall be the subject of separate agreements, in each case, between such country and the Organisation.

(b) The country referred to in subparagraph (a) and the Organisation shall each have the right to denounce the obligation to grant advances, by written notification. Denunciation shall take effect three years after the end of the year in which it has been notified.

(8) The auditing of the accounts shall be effected by one or more of tile countries of the Special Union or by external auditors, as provided in the financial regulations. They shall be designated, with their agreement, by the Assembly.

[5.1087]
Article 13
[Amendment of Articles 10 to 13]

(1) Proposals for the amendment of Articles 10, 11, 12, and the present Article, may be initiated by any country member of the Assembly, or by the Director General. Such proposals shall be communicated by the Director General to the member countries of the Assembly at least six months in advance of their consideration by the Assembly.

(2) Amendments to the Articles referred to in paragraph (1) shall be adopted by the Assembly. Adoption shall require three-fourths of the votes cast, provided that any amendment to Article 10, and to the present paragraph, shall require four-fifths of the votes cast.

(3) Any amendment to the Articles referred to in paragraph (1) shall enter into force one month after written notifications of acceptance, effected in accordance with their respective constitutional processes, have been received by the Director General from three-fourths of the countries members of the Assembly at the time it adopted the amendment. Any amendment to the said Articles thus accepted shall bind all the countries which are members of the Assembly at the time the amendment enters into force, or which become members thereof at a subsequent date.

[5.1088]
Article 14
[Ratification and Accession. Entry into Force. Accession to Earlier Acts. Reference to Article 24 of Paris Convention (Territories)]

(1) Any country of the Special Union which has signed this Act may ratify it, and, if it has not signed it, may accede to it.

(2)

(a) Any country outside the Special Union which is party to the Paris Convention for the Protection of Industrial Property may accede to this Act and thereby become a member of the Special Union.

(b) As soon as the International Bureau is informed that such a country has acceded to this Act, it shall address to the Office of that country, in accordance with Article 3, a collective notification of the marks which, at that time, enjoy international protection.

(c) Such notification shall, of itself, ensure to the said marks the benefits of the foregoing provisions in the territory of the said country, and shall mark the commencement of the period of one year during which the Office concerned may make the declaration provided for in Article 5.

(d) However, any such country may, in acceding to this Act, declare that, except in the case of international marks which have already been the subject in that country of an earlier identical national registration still in force, and which shall be immediately recognised upon the request of the interested parties, application of this Act shall be limited to marks registered from the date on which its accession enters into force.

(e) Such declaration shall dispense the International Bureau from making the collective notification referred to above. The International Bureau shall notify only those marks in respect of which it receives, within a period of one year from the accession of the new country, a request, with the necessary particulars, to take advantage of the exception provided for in subparagraph (d).

(f) The International Bureau shall not make the collective notification to such countries as declare, in acceding to this Act, that they are availing themselves of the right provided for in Article 3*bis*. The said countries may also declare at the same time that the application of this Act shall be limited to marks registered from the day on which their accessions enter into force; however, such limitation shall not affect international marks which have already been the subject of an earlier identical national registration in those countries, and which could give rise to requests for extension of protection made and notified in accordance with Articles 3*ter* and 8(2)(c).

(g) Registrations of marks which have been the subject of one of the notifications provided for in this paragraph shall be regarded as replacing registration effected direct in the new contracting country before the date of entry into force of its accession.

(3) Instruments of ratification and accession shall be deposited with the Director General.

(4)

(a) With respect to the first five countries which have deposited their instruments of ratification or accession, this Act shall enter into force three months after the deposit of the fifth such instrument.

(b) With respect to any other country, this Act shall enter into force three months after the date on which its ratification or accession has been notified by the Director General, unless a subsequent date has been indicated in the instrument of ratification or accession. In the latter case, this Act shall enter into force with respect to that country on the date thus indicated.

(5) Ratification or accession shall automatically entail acceptance of all the clauses and admission to all the advantages of this Act.

(6) After the entry into force of this Act, a country may accede to the Nice Act of June 15, 1957, only in conjunction with ratification of, or accession to, this Act. Accession to Acts earlier than the Nice Act shall not be permitted, not even in conjunction with ratification of, or accession to, this Act.

(7) The provisions of Article 24 of the Paris Convention for the Protection of Industrial Property shall apply to this Agreement.

[5.1089]
Article 15
[Denunciation]

(1) This Agreement shall remain in force without limitation as to time.

(2) Any country may denounce this Act by notification addressed to the Director General. Such denunciation shall constitute also denunciation of all earlier Acts and shall affect only the country making it, the Agreement remaining in full force and effect as regards the other countries of the Special Union.

(3) Denunciation shall take effect one year after the day on which the Director General has received the notification.

(4) The right of denunciation provided for by this Article shall not be exercised by any country before the expiration of five years from the date upon which it becomes a member of the Special Union.

(5) International marks registered up to the date on which denunciation becomes effective, and not refused within the period of one year provided for in Article 5, shall continue, throughout the period of international protection, to enjoy the same protection as if they had been filed direct in the denouncing country.

[5.1090]
Article 16
[Application of Earlier Acts]

(1)

(a) This Act shall, as regards the relations between the countries of the Special Union by which it has been ratified or acceded to, replace, as from the day on which it enters into force with respect to them, the Madrid Agreement of 1891, in its texts earlier than this Act.

(b) However, any country of the Special Union which has ratified or acceded to this Act shall remain bound by the earlier texts which it has not previously denounced by virtue of Article 12(4) of the Nice Act of June 15, 1957, as regards its relations with countries which have not ratified or acceded to this Act.

(2) Countries outside the Special Union which become party to this Act shall apply it to international registrations effected at the International Bureau through the intermediary of the national Office of any country of the Special Union not party to this Act, provided that such registrations satisfy, with respect to the said countries, the requirements of this Act. With regard to international registrations effected at the International Bureau through the intermediary of the national Offices of the said countries outside the Special Union which become party to this Act, such countries recognise that the aforesaid country of the Special Union may demand compliance with the requirements of the most recent Act to which it is party.

[5.1091]
Article 17
[Signature, Languages, Depositary Functions]

(1)

(a) This Act shall be signed in a single copy in the French language and shall be deposited with the Government of Sweden.

(b) Official texts shall be established by the Director General, after consultation with the interested Governments, in such other languages as the Assembly may designate.

(2) This Act shall remain open for signature at Stockholm until January 13, 1968.

(3) The Director General shall transmit two copies, certified by the Government of Sweden, of the signed text of this Act to the Governments of all countries of the Special Union and, on request, to the Government of any other country.

(4) The Director General shall register this Act with the Secretariat of the United Nations.

(5) The Director General shall notify the Governments of all countries of the Special Union of signatures, deposits of instruments of ratification or accession and any declarations included in such instruments, entry into force of any provisions of this Act, notifications of denunciation, and notifications pursuant to Articles 3*bis*, 9*quater*, 13, 14(7), and 15(2).

[5.1092]
Article 18
[Transitional Provisions]

(1) Until the first Director General assumes office, references in this Act to the International Bureau of the Organisation or to the Director General shall be construed as references to the Bureau of the Union established by the Paris Convention for the Protection of Industrial Property or its Director, respectively.

(2) Countries of the Special Union not having ratified or acceded to this Act may, until five years after the entry into force of the Convention establishing the Organisation, exercise, if they so desire, the rights provided for under Articles 10 to 13 of this Act as if they were bound by those Articles. Any country desiring to exercise such rights shall give written notification to that effect to the Director General; such notification shall be effective from the date of its receipt. Such countries shall be deemed to be members of the Assembly until the expiration of the said period.

PROTOCOL RELATING TO THE MADRID AGREEMENT CONCERNING THE INTERNATIONAL REGISTRATION OF MARKS

(adopted at Madrid on 27 June 1989 and amended on 3 October 2006 and on 12 November 2007)

NOTES

The original source for this Protocol is the World Intellectual Property Organisation (WIPO).

[5.1093]
Article 1
Membership in the Madrid Union

The States party to this Protocol (hereinafter referred to as "the Contracting States"), even where they are not party to the Madrid Agreement Concerning the International Registration of Marks as revised at Stockholm in 1967 and as amended in 1979 (hereinafter referred to as "the Madrid (Stockholm) Agreement"), and the organisations referred to in Article 14(1)(b) which are party to this Protocol (hereinafter referred to as "the Contracting Organisations") shall be members of the same Union of which countries party to the Madrid (Stockholm) Agreement are members. Any reference in this Protocol to "Contracting Parties" shall be construed as a reference to both Contracting States and Contracting Organizations.

[5.1094]
Article 2
Securing Protection through International Registration

(1) Where an application for the registration of a mark has been filed with the Office of a Contracting Party, or where a mark has been registered in the register of the Office of a Contracting Party, the person in whose name that application (hereinafter referred to as "the basic application") or that registration (hereinafter referred to as "the basic registration") stands may, subject to the provisions of this Protocol, secure protection for his mark in the territory of the Contracting Parties, by obtaining the registration of that mark in the register of the International Bureau of the World Intellectual Property Organisation (hereinafter referred to as "the international registration," "the International Register," "the International Bureau" and "the Organisation," respectively), provided that—

- (i) where the basic application has been filed with the Office of a Contracting State or where the basic registration has been made by such an Office, the person in whose name that application or registration stands is a national of that Contracting State, or is domiciled, or has a real and effective industrial or commercial establishment, in the said Contracting State,
- (ii) where the basic application has been filed with the Office of a Contracting Organization or where the basic registration has been made by such an Office, the person in whose name that application or registration stands is a national of a State member of that Contracting Organization, or is domiciled, or has a real and effective industrial or commercial establishment, in the territory of the said Contracting Organization.

(2) The application for international registration (hereinafter referred to as "the international application") shall be filed with the International Bureau through the intermediary of the Office with which the basic application was filed or by which the basic registration was made (hereinafter referred to as "the Office of origin"), as the case may be.

(3) Any reference in this Protocol to an "Office" or an "Office of a Contracting Party" shall be construed as a reference to the office that is in charge, on behalf of a Contracting Party, of the registration of marks, and any reference in this Protocol to "marks" shall be construed as a reference to trademarks and service marks.

(4) For the purposes of this Protocol, "territory of a Contracting Party" means, where the Contracting Party is a State, the territory of that State and, where the Contracting Party is an intergovernmental organisation, the territory in which the constituting treaty of that intergovernmental organisation applies.

[5.1095]
Article 3
International Application

(1) Every international application under this Protocol shall be presented on the form prescribed by the Regulations. The Office of origin shall certify that the particulars appearing in the international application correspond to the particulars appearing, at the time of the certification, in the basic application or basic registration, as the case may be. Furthermore, the said Office shall indicate—

(i) in the case of a basic application, the date and number of that application,

(ii) in the case of a basic registration, the date and number of that registration as well as the date and number of the application from which the basic registration resulted.

The Office of origin shall also indicate the date of the international application.

(2) The applicant must indicate the goods and services in respect of which protection of the mark is claimed and also, if possible, the corresponding class or classes according to the classification established by the Nice Agreement Concerning the International Classification of Goods and Services for the Purposes of the Registration of Marks. If the applicant does not give such indication, the International Bureau shall classify the goods and services in the appropriate classes of the said classification. The indication of classes given by the applicant shall be subject to control by the International Bureau, which shall exercise the said control in association with the Office of origin. In the event of disagreement between the said Office and the International Bureau, the opinion of the latter shall prevail.

(3) If the applicant claims colour as a distinctive feature of his mark, he shall be required—

(i) to state the fact, and to file with his international application a notice specifying the colour or the combination of colours claimed;

(ii) to append to his international application copies in colour of the said mark, which shall be attached to the notifications given by the International Bureau; the number of such copies shall be fixed by the Regulations.

(4) The International Bureau shall register immediately the marks filed in accordance with Article 2. The international registration shall bear the date on which the international application was received in the Office of origin, provided that the international application has been received by the International Bureau within a period of two months from that date. If the international application has not been received within that period, the international registration shall bear the date on which the said international application was received by the International Bureau. The International Bureau shall notify the international registration without delay to the Offices concerned. Marks registered in the International Register shall be published in a periodical gazette issued by the International Bureau, on the basis of the particulars contained in the international application.

(5) With a view to the publicity to be given to marks registered in the International Register, each Office shall receive from the International Bureau a number of copies of the said gazette free of charge and a number of copies at a reduced price, under the conditions fixed by the Assembly referred to in Article 10 (hereinafter referred to as "the Assembly"). Such publicity shall be deemed to be sufficient for the purposes of all the Contracting Parties, and no other publicity may be required of the holder of the international registration.

[5.1096]
Article 3bis
Territorial Effect

The protection resulting from the international registration shall extend to any Contracting Party only at the request of the person who files the international application or who is the holder of the international registration. However, no such request can be made with respect to the Contracting Party whose Office is the Office of origin.

[5.1097]
Article 3ter
Request for "Territorial Extension"

(1) Any request for extension of the protection resulting from the international registration to any Contracting Party shall be specially mentioned in the international application.

(2) A request for territorial extension may also be made subsequently to the international registration. Any such request shall be presented on the form prescribed by the Regulations. It shall be immediately recorded by the International Bureau, which shall notify such recordal without delay to the Office or Offices concerned. Such recordal shall be published in the periodical gazette of the International Bureau. Such territorial extension shall be effective from the date on which it has been recorded in the International Register; it shall cease to be valid on the expiry of the international registration to which it relates.

[5.1098]
Article 4
Effects of International Registration

(1)

(a) From the date of the registration or recordal effected in accordance with the provisions of Articles 3 and 3*ter*, the protection of the mark in each of the Contracting Parties concerned shall be the same as if the mark had been deposited direct with the Office of that Contracting Party. If no refusal has been notified to the International Bureau in accordance with Article 5(1) and (2) or if a refusal notified in accordance with the said Article has been withdrawn subsequently, the protection of the mark in the Contracting Party concerned shall, as from the said date, be the same as if the mark had been registered by the Office of that Contracting Party.

(b) The indication of classes of goods and services provided for in Article 3 shall not bind the Contracting Parties with regard to the determination of the scope of the protection of the mark.

(2) Every international registration shall enjoy the right of priority provided for by Article 4 of the Paris Convention for the Protection of Industrial Property, without it being necessary to comply with the formalities prescribed in Section D of that Article.

[5.1099]
Article 4bis
Replacement of a National or Regional Registration by an International Registration

(1) Where a mark that is the subject of a national or regional registration in the Office of a Contracting Party is also the subject of an international registration and both registrations stand in the name of the same person, the international registration is deemed to replace the national or regional registration, without prejudice to any rights acquired by virtue of the latter, provided that—

(i) the protection resulting from the international registration extends to the said Contracting Party under Article 3*ter* (1) or (2),

(ii) all the goods and services listed in the national or regional registration are also listed in the international registration in respect of the said Contracting Party,

(iii) such extension takes effect after the date of the national or regional registration.

(2) The Office referred to in paragraph (1) shall, upon request, be required to take note in its register of the international registration.

[5.1100]
Article 5
Refusal and Invalidation of Effects of International Registration in Respect of Certain Contracting Parties

(1) Where the applicable legislation so authorises, any Office of a Contracting Party which has been notified by the International Bureau of an extension to that Contracting Party, under Article 3*ter* (1) or (2), of the protection resulting from the international registration shall have the right to declare in a notification of refusal that protection cannot be granted in the said Contracting Party to the mark which is the subject of such extension. Any such refusal can be based only on the grounds which would apply, under the Paris Convention for the Protection of Industrial Property, in the case of a mark deposited direct with the Office which notifies the refusal. However, protection may not be refused, even partially, by reason only that the applicable legislation would permit registration only in a limited number of classes or for a limited number of goods or services.

(2)

(a) Any Office wishing to exercise such right shall notify its refusal to the International Bureau, together with a statement of all grounds, within the period prescribed by the law applicable to that Office and at the latest, subject to subparagraphs (b) and (c), before the expiry of one year from the date on which the notification of the extension referred to in paragraph (1) has been sent to that Office by the International Bureau.

(b) Notwithstanding subparagraph (a), any Contracting Party may declare that, for international registrations made under this Protocol, the time limit of one year referred to in subparagraph (a) is replaced by 18 months.

(c) Such declaration may also specify that, when a refusal of protection may result from an opposition to the granting of protection, such refusal may be notified by the Office of the said Contracting Party to the International Bureau after the expiry of the 18-month time limit. Such an Office may, with respect to any given international registration, notify a refusal of protection after the expiry of the 18-month time limit, but only if—

(i) it has, before the expiry of the 18-month time limit, informed the International Bureau of the possibility that oppositions may be filed after the expiry of the 18-month time limit, and

(ii) the notification of the refusal based on an opposition is made within a time limit of one month from the expiry of the opposition period and, in any case, not later than seven months from the date on which the opposition period begins.

(d) Any declaration under subparagraphs (b) or (c) may be made in the instruments referred to in Article 14(2), and the effective date of the declaration shall be the same as the date of entry into force of this Protocol with respect to the State or intergovernmental organisation having made the declaration. Any such declaration may also be made later, in which case the declaration shall have effect three months after its receipt by the Director General of the Organisation (hereinafter referred to as "the Director General"), or at any later date indicated in the declaration, in respect of any international registration whose date is the same as or is later than the effective date of the declaration.

(e) Upon the expiry of a period of ten years from the entry into force of this Protocol, the Assembly shall examine the operation of the system established by subparagraphs (a) to (d). Thereafter, the provisions of the said subparagraphs may be modified by a unanimous decision of the Assembly.

(3) The International Bureau shall, without delay, transmit one of the copies of the notification of refusal to the holder of the international registration. The said holder shall have the same remedies as if the mark had been deposited by him direct with the Office which has notified its refusal. Where the International Bureau has received information under paragraph (2)(c)(i), it shall, without delay, transmit the said information to the holder of the international registration.

(4) The grounds for refusing a mark shall be communicated by the International Bureau to any interested party who may so request.

(5) Any Office which has not notified, with respect to a given international registration, any provisional or final refusal to the International Bureau in accordance with paragraphs (1) and (2) shall, with respect to that international registration, lose the benefit of the right provided for in paragraph (1).

(6) Invalidation, by the competent authorities of a Contracting Party, of the effects, in the territory of that Contracting Party, of an international registration may not be pronounced without the holder of such international registration having, in good time, been afforded the opportunity of defending his rights. Invalidation shall be notified to the International Bureau.

[5.1101]
Article 5bis
Documentary Evidence of Legitimacy of Use of Certain Elements of the Mark

Documentary evidence of the legitimacy of the use of certain elements incorporated in a mark, such as armorial bearings, escutcheons, portraits, honorary distinctions, titles, trade names, names of persons other than the name of the applicant, or other like inscriptions, which might be required by the Offices of the Contracting Parties shall be exempt from any legalisation as well as from any certification other than that of the Office of origin.

[5.1102]
Article 5ter
Copies of Entries in International Register; Searches for Anticipations; Extracts from International Register

(1) The International Bureau shall issue to any person applying therefor, upon the payment of a fee fixed by the Regulations, a copy of the entries in the International Register concerning a specific mark.

(2) The International Bureau may also, upon payment, undertake searches for anticipations among marks that are the subject of international registrations.

(3) Extracts from the International Register requested with a view to their production in one of the Contracting Parties shall be exempt from any legalisation.

[5.1103]
Article 6
Period of Validity of International Registration; Dependence and Independence of International Registration

(1) Registration of a mark at the International Bureau is effected for ten years, with the possibility of renewal under the conditions specified in Article 7.

(2) Upon expiry of a period of five years from the date of the international registration, such registration shall become independent of the basic application or the registration resulting therefrom, or of the basic registration, as the case may be, subject to the following provisions.

(3) The protection resulting from the international registration, whether or not it has been the subject of a transfer, may no longer be invoked if, before the expiry of five years from the date of the international registration, the basic application or the registration resulting therefrom, or the basic registration, as the case may be, has been withdrawn, has lapsed, has been renounced or has been the subject of a final decision of rejection, revocation, cancellation or invalidation, in respect of all or some of the goods and services listed in the international registration. The same applies if—

(i) an appeal against a decision refusing the effects of the basic application,

(ii) an action requesting the withdrawal of the basic application or the revocation, cancellation or invalidation of the registration resulting from the basic application or of the basic registration, or

(iii) an opposition to the basic application

results, after the expiry of the five-year period, in a final decision of rejection, revocation, cancellation or invalidation, or ordering the withdrawal, of the basic application, or the registration resulting therefrom, or the basic registration, as the case may be, provided that such appeal, action or opposition had begun before the expiry of the said period. The same also applies if the basic application is withdrawn, or the registration resulting from the basic application or the basic registration is renounced, after the expiry of the five-year period, provided that, at the time of the withdrawal or renunciation, the said application or registration was the subject of a proceeding referred to in item (i), (ii) or (iii) and that such proceeding had begun before the expiry of the said period.

(4) The Office of origin shall, as prescribed in the Regulations, notify the International Bureau of the facts and decisions relevant under paragraph (3), and the International Bureau shall, as prescribed in the Regulations, notify the interested parties and effect any publication accordingly. The Office of origin shall, where applicable, request the International Bureau to cancel, to the extent applicable, the international registration, and the International Bureau shall proceed accordingly.

[5.1104]
Article 7
Renewal of International Registration

(1) Any international registration may be renewed for a period of ten years from the expiry of the preceding period, by the mere payment of the basic fee and, subject to Article 8(7), of the supplementary and complementary fees provided for in Article 8(2).

(2) Renewal may not bring about any change in the international registration in its latest form.

(3) Six months before the expiry of the term of protection, the International Bureau shall, by sending an unofficial notice, remind the holder of the international registration and his representative, if any, of the exact date of expiry.

(4) Subject to the payment of a surcharge fixed by the Regulations, a period of grace of six months shall be allowed for renewal of the international registration.

[5.1105]
Article 8
Fees for International Application and Registration

(1) The Office of origin may fix, at its own discretion, and collect, for its own benefit, a fee which it may require from the applicant for international registration or from the holder of the international registration in connection with the filing of the international application or the renewal of the international registration.

(2) Registration of a mark at the International Bureau shall be subject to the advance payment of an international fee which shall, subject to the provisions of paragraph (7)(a), include,

- (i) a basic fee;
- (ii) a supplementary fee for each class of the International Classification, beyond three, into which the goods or services to which the mark is applied will fall;
- (iii) a complementary fee for any request for extension of protection under Article 3*ter*.

(3) However, the supplementary fee specified in paragraph (2)(ii) may, without prejudice to the date of the international registration, be paid within the period fixed by the Regulations if the number of classes of goods or services has been fixed or disputed by the International Bureau. If, upon expiry of the said period, the supplementary fee has not been paid or the list of goods or services has not been reduced to the required extent by the applicant, the international application shall be deemed to have been abandoned.

(4) The annual product of the various receipts from international registration, with the exception of the receipts derived from the fees mentioned in paragraph (2)(ii) and (2)(iii), shall be divided equally among the Contracting Parties by the International Bureau, after deduction of the expenses and charges necessitated by the implementation of this Protocol.

(5) The amounts derived from the supplementary fees provided for in paragraph (2)(ii) shall be divided, at the expiry of each year, among the interested Contracting Parties in proportion to the number of marks for which protection has been applied for in each of them during that year, this number being multiplied, in the case of Contracting Parties which make an examination, by a coefficient which shall be determined by the Regulations.

(6) The amounts derived from the complementary fees provided for in paragraph (2)(iii) shall be divided according to the same rules as those provided for in paragraph (5).

(7)

- (a) Any Contracting Party may declare that, in connection with each international registration in which it is mentioned under Article 3*ter*, and in connection with the renewal of any such international registration, it wants to receive, instead of a share in the revenue produced by the supplementary and complementary fees, a fee (hereinafter referred to as "the individual fee") whose amount shall be indicated in the declaration, and can be changed in further declarations, but may not be higher than the equivalent of the amount which the said Contracting Party's Office would be entitled to receive from an applicant for a ten-year registration, or from the holder of a registration for a ten-year renewal of that registration, of the mark in the register of the said Office, the said amount being diminished by the savings resulting from the international procedure. Where such an individual fee is payable,

(i) no supplementary fees referred to in paragraph (2)(ii) shall be payable if only Contracting Parties which have made a declaration under this subparagraph are mentioned under Article 3*ter*, and

(ii) no complementary fee referred to in paragraph (2)(iii) shall be payable in respect of any Contracting Party which has made a declaration under this subparagraph.

(b) Any declaration under subparagraph (a) may be made in the instruments referred to in Article 14(2), and the effective date of the declaration shall be the same as the date of entry into force of this Protocol with respect to the State or intergovernmental organisation having made the declaration. Any such declaration may also be made later, in which case the declaration shall have effect three months after its receipt by the Director General, or at any later date indicated in the declaration, in respcct of any international registration whose date is the same as or is later than the effective date of the declaration.

[5.1106]
Article 9
Recordal of Change in the Ownership of an International Registration

At the request of thc person in whose name the international registration stands, or at the request of an interested Office made ex officio or at the request of an interested person, the International Bureau shall record in the International Register any change in the ownership of that registration, in respect of all or some of the Contracting Parties in whose territories the said registration has effect and in respect of all or some of the goods and services listed in the registration, provided that the new holder is a person who, under Article 2(1), is entitled to file international applications.

[5.1107]
Article 9bis
Recordal of Certain Matters Concerning an International Registration

The International Bureau shall record in the International Register

(i) any change in the name or address of the holder of the international registration,

(ii) the appointment of a representative of the holder of the international registration and any other relevant fact concerning such representative,

(iii) any limitation, in respect of all or some of the Contracting Parties, of the goods and services listed in the international registration,

(iv) any renunciation, cancellation or invalidation of the international registration in respect of all or some of the Contracting Parties,

(v) any other relevant fact, identified in the Regulations, concerning the rights in a mark that is the subject of an international registration.

[5.1108]
Article 9ter
Fees for Certain Recordals

Any recordal under Article 9 or under Article 9*bis* may be subject to the payment of a fee.

[5.1109]
Article 9quater
Common Office of Several Contracting States

(1) If several Contracting States agree to effect the unification of their domestic legislations on marks, they may notify the Director General

(i) that a common Office shall be substituted for the national Office of each of them, and

(ii) that the whole of their respective territories shall be deemed to be a single State for the purposes of the application of all or part of the provisions preceding this Article as well as the provisions of Articles 9 *quinquies* and 9 *sexies*.

(2) Such notification shall not take effect until three months after the date of the communication thereof by the Director General to the other Contracting Parties.

[5.1110]
Article 9quinquies
Transformation of an International Registration into National or Regional Applications

Where, in the event that the international registration is cancelled at the request of the Office of origin under Article 6(4), in respect of all or some of the goods and services listed in the said registration, the person who was the holder of the international registration files an application for the registration of the same mark with the Office of any of the Contracting Parties in the territory of which the international registration had effect, that application shall be treated as if it had been filed on the date of the international registration according to Article 3(4) or on the date of recordal of the territorial extension according to Article 3*ter* (2) and, if the international registration enjoyed priority, shall enjoy the same priority, provided that

(i) such application is filed within three months from the date on which the international registration was cancelled,

(ii) the goods and services listed in the application are in fact covered by the list of goods and services contained in the international registration in respect of the Contracting Party concerned, and
(iii) such application complies with all the requirements of the applicable law, including the requirements concerning fees.

[5.1111]
Article 9sexies
Relations between States Party to both this Protocol and the Madrid (Stockholm) Agreement
(1)
(a) This Protocol alone shall be applicable as regards the mutual relations of States party to both this Protocol and the Madrid (Stockholm) Agreement.
(b) Notwithstanding subparagraph (a), a declaration made under Article 5(2)(b), Article 5(2)(c) or Article 8(7) of this Protocol, by a State party to both this Protocol and the Madrid (Stockholm) Agreement, shall have no effect in the relations with another State party to both this Protocol and the Madrid (Stockholm) Agreement.
(2) The Assembly shall, after the expiry of a period of three years from September 1, 2008, review the application of paragraph (1)(b) and may, at any time thereafter, either repeal it or restrict its scope, by a three-fourths majority. In the vote of the Assembly, only those States which are party to both the Madrid (Stockholm) Agreement and this Protocol shall have the right to participate.

[5.1112]
Article 10
Assembly
(1)
(a) The Contracting Parties shall be members of the same Assembly as the countries party to the Madrid (Stockholm) Agreement.
(b) Each Contracting Party shall be represented in that Assembly by one delegate, who may be assisted by alternate delegates, advisors, and experts.
(c) The expenses of each delegation shall be borne by the Contracting Party which has appointed it, except for the travel expenses and the subsistence allowance of one delegate for each Contracting Party, which shall be paid from the funds of the Union.
(2) The Assembly shall, in addition to the functions which it has under the Madrid (Stockholm) Agreement, also
(i) deal with all matters concerning the implementation of this Protocol;
(ii) give directions to the International Bureau concerning the preparation for conferences of revision of this Protocol, due account being taken of any comments made by those countries of the Union which are not party to this Protocol;
(iii) adopt and modify the provisions of the Regulations concerning the implementation of this Protocol;
(iv) perform such other functions as are appropriate under this Protocol.
(3)
(a) Each Contracting Party shall have one vote in the Assembly. On matters concerning only countries that are party to the Madrid (Stockholm) Agreement, Contracting Parties that are not party to the said Agreement shall not have the right to vote, whereas, on matters concerning only Contracting Parties, only the latter shall have the right to vote.
(b) One-half of the members of the Assembly which have the right to vote on a given matter shall constitute the quorum for the purposes of the vote on that matter.
(c) Notwithstanding the provisions of subparagraph (b), if, in any session, the number of the members of the Assembly having the right to vote on a given matter which are represented is less than one-half but equal to or more than one-third of the members of the Assembly having the right to vote on that matter, the Assembly may make decisions but, with the exception of decisions concerning its own procedure, all such decisions shall take effect only if the conditions set forth hereinafter are fulfilled. The International Bureau shall communicate the said decisions to the members of the Assembly having the right to vote on the said matter which were not represented and shall invite them to express in writing their vote or abstention within a period of three months from the date of the communication. If, at the expiry of this period, the number of such members having thus expressed their vote or abstention attains the number of the members which was lacking for attaining the quorum in the session itself, such decisions shall take effect provided that at the same time the required majority still obtains.
(d) Subject to the provisions of Articles 5(2)(e), 9 *sexies* (2), 12 and 13(2), the decisions of the Assembly shall require two-thirds of the votes cast.
(e) Abstentions shall not be considered as votes.
(f) A delegate may represent, and vote in the name of, one member of the Assembly only.

(4) In addition to meeting in ordinary sessions and extraordinary sessions as provided for by the Madrid (Stockholm) Agreement, the Assembly shall meet in extraordinary session upon convocation by the Director General, at the request of one-fourth of the members of the Assembly having the right to vote on the matters proposed to be included in the agenda of the session. The agenda of such an extraordinary session shall be prepared by the Director General.

[5.1113]
Article 11
International Bureau

(1) International registration and related duties, as well as all other administrative tasks, under or concerning this Protocol, shall be performed by the International Bureau.

(2)

- (a) The International Bureau shall, in accordance with the directions of the Assembly, make the preparations for the conferences of revision of this Protocol.
- (b) The International Bureau may consult with intergovernmental and international non-governmental organisations concerning preparations for such conferences of revision.
- (c) The Director General and persons designated by him shall take part, without the right to vote, in the discussions at such conferences of revision.

(3) The International Bureau shall carry out any other tasks assigned to it in relation to this Protocol.

[5.1114]
Article 12
Finances

As far as Contracting Parties are concerned, the finances of the Union shall be governed by the same provisions as those contained in Article 12 of the Madrid (Stockholm) Agreement, provided that any reference to Article 8 of the said Agreement shall be deemed to be a reference to Article 8 of this Protocol. Furthermore, for the purposes of Article 12(6)(b) of the said Agreement, Contracting Organizations shall, subject to a unanimous decision to the contrary by the Assembly, be considered to belong to contribution class I (one) under the Paris Convention for the Protection of Industrial Property.

[5.1115]
Article 13
Amendment of Certain Articles of the Protocol

(1) Proposals for the amendment of Articles 10, 11, 12, and the present Article, may be initiated by any Contracting Party, or by the Director General. Such proposals shall be communicated by the Director General to the Contracting Parties at least six months in advance of their consideration by the Assembly.

(2) Amendments to the Articles referred to in paragraph (1) shall be adopted by the Assembly. Adoption shall require three-fourths of the votes cast, provided that any amendment to Article 10, and to the present paragraph, shall require four-fifths of the votes cast.

(3) Any amendment to the Articles referred to in paragraph (1) shall enter into force one month after written notifications of acceptance, effected in accordance with their respective constitutional processes, have been received by the Director General from three-fourths of those States and intergovernmental organisations which, at the time the amendment was adopted, were members of the Assembly and had the right to vote on the amendment. Any amendment to the said Articles thus accepted shall bind all the States and intergovernmental organisations which are Contracting Parties at the time the amendment enters into force, or which become Contracting Parties at a subsequent date.

[5.1116]
Article 14
Becoming Party to the Protocol; Entry into Force

(1)

- (a) Any State that is a party to the Paris Convention for the Protection of Industrial Property may become party to this Protocol.
- (b) Furthermore, any intergovernmental organisation may also become party to this Protocol where the following conditions are fulfilled—
  - (i) at least one of the member States of that organisation is a party to the Paris Convention for the Protection of Industrial Property;
  - (ii) that organisation has a regional Office for the purposes of registering marks with effect in the territory of the organisation, provided that such Office is not the subject of a notification under Article 9*quater*.

(2) Any State or organisation referred to in paragraph (1) may sign this Protocol. Any such State or organisation may, if it has signed this Protocol, deposit an instrument of ratification, acceptance or approval of this Protocol or, if it has not signed this Protocol, deposit an instrument of accession to this Protocol.

(3) The instruments referred to in paragraph (2) shall be deposited with the Director General.

(4)

(a) This Protocol shall enter into force three months after four instruments of ratification, acceptance, approval or accession have been deposited, provided that at least one of those instruments has been deposited by a country party to the Madrid (Stockholm) Agreement and at least one other of those instruments has been deposited by a State not party to the Madrid (Stockholm) Agreement or by any of the organisations referred to in paragraph (1)(b).

(b) With respect to any other State or organisation referred to in paragraph (1), this Protocol shall enter into force three months after the date on which its ratification, acceptance, approval or accession has been notified by the Director General.

(5) Any State or organisation referred to in paragraph (1) may, when depositing its instrument of ratification, acceptance or approval of, or accession to, this Protocol, declare that the protection resulting from any international registration effected under this Protocol before the date of entry into force of this Protocol with respect to it cannot be extended to it.

[5.1117]
Article 15
Denunciation

(1) This Protocol shall remain in force without limitation as to time.

(2) Any Contracting Party may denounce this Protocol by notification addressed to the Director General.

(3) Denunciation shall take effect one year after the day on which the Director General has received the notification.

(4) The right of denunciation provided for by this Article shall not be exercised by any Contracting Party before the expiry of five years from the date upon which this Protocol entered into force with respect to that Contracting Party.

(5)

(a) Where a mark is the subject of an international registration having effect in the denouncing State or intergovernmental organisation at the date on which the denunciation becomes effective, the holder of such registration may file an application for the registration of the same mark with the Office of the denouncing State or intergovernmental organisation, which shall be treated as if it had been filed on the date of the international registration according to Article 3(4) or on the date of recordal of the territorial extension according to Article 3*ter* (2) and, if the international registration enjoyed priority, enjoy the same priority, provided that

(i) such application is filed within two years from the date on which the denunciation became effective,

(ii) the goods and services listed in the application are in fact covered by the list of goods and services contained in the international registration in respect of the denouncing State or intergovernmental organisation, and

(iii) such application complies with all the requirements of the applicable law, including the requirements concerning fees.

(b) The provisions of subparagraph (a) shall also apply in respect of any mark that is the subject of an international registration having effect in Contracting Parties other than the denouncing State or intergovernmental organisation at the date on which denunciation becomes effective and whose holder, because of the denunciation, is no longer entitled to file international applications under Article 2(1).

[5.1118]
Article 16
Signature; Languages; Depositary Functions

(1)

(a) This Protocol shall be signed in a single copy in the English, French and Spanish languages, and shall be deposited with the Director General when it ceases to be open for signature at Madrid. The texts in the three languages shall be equally authentic.

(b) Official texts of this Protocol shall be established by the Director General, after consultation with the interested governments and organisations, in the Arabic, Chinese, German, Italian, Japanese, Portuguese and Russian languages, and in such other languages as the Assembly may designate.

(2) This Protocol shall remain open for signature at Madrid until December 31, 1989.

(3) The Director General shall transmit two copies, certified by the Government of Spain, of the signed texts of this Protocol to all States and intergovernmental organisations that may become party to this Protocol.

(4) The Director General shall register this Protocol with the Secretariat of the United Nations.

(5) The Director General shall notify all States and international organisations that may become or are party to this Protocol of signatures, deposits of instruments of ratification, acceptance, approval or accession, the entry into force of this Protocol and any amendment thereto, any notification of denunciation and any declaration provided for in this Protocol.

COMMON REGULATIONS UNDER THE MADRID AGREEMENT CONCERNING THE INTERNATIONAL REGISTRATION OF MARKS AND THE PROTOCOL RELATING TO THAT AGREEMENT

(as in force on July 1, 2017)

NOTES

The original source for these Regulations is the World Intellectual Property Organisation (WIPO).

CHAPTER 1
GENERAL PROVISIONS

[5.1119]

Rule 1

Abbreviated Expressions

For the purposes of these Regulations,

(i) "Agreement" means the Madrid Agreement Concerning the International Registration of Marks of April 14, 1891, as revised at Stockholm on July 14, 1967, and amended on September 28, 1979;

(ii) "Protocol" means the Protocol Relating to the Madrid Agreement Concerning the International Registration of Marks, adopted at Madrid on June 27, 1989;

(iii) "Contracting Party" means any country party to the Agreement or any State or intergovernmental organization party to the Protocol;

(iv) "Contracting State" means a Contracting Party that is a State;

(v) "Contracting Organization" means a Contracting Party that is an intergovernmental organization;

(vi) "international registration" means the registration of a mark effected under the Agreement or the Protocol or both, as the case may be;

(vii) "international application" means an application for international registration filed under the Agreement or the Protocol or both, as the case may be;

(viii) "international application governed exclusively by the Agreement" means an international application whose Office of origin is the Office

— of a State bound by the Agreement but not by the Protocol, or

— of a State bound by both the Agreement and the Protocol, where only States are designated in the international application and all the designated States are bound by the Agreement but not by the Protocol;

(ix) "international application governed exclusively by the Protocol" means an international application whose Office of origin is the Office

— of a State bound by the Protocol but not by the Agreement, or

— of a Contracting Organization, or

— of a State bound by both the Agreement and the Protocol, where the international application does not contain the designation of any State bound by the Agreement but not by the Protocol;

(x) "international application governed by both the Agreement and the Protocol" means an international application whose Office of origin is the Office of a State bound by both the Agreement and the Protocol and which is based on a registration and contains the designations

— of at least one State bound by the Agreement but not by the Protocol, and

— of at least one State bound by the Protocol, whether or not that State is also bound by the Agreement or of at least one Contracting Organization;

(xi) "applicant" means the natural person or legal entity in whose name the international application is filed;

(xii) "legal entity" means a corporation, association or other group or organization which, under the law applicable to it, is capable of acquiring rights, assuming obligations and suing or being sued in a court of law;

(xiii) "basic application" means the application for the registration of a mark that has been filed with the Office of a Contracting Party and that constitutes the basis for the international application for the registration of that mark;

(xiv) "basic registration" means the registration of a mark that has been effected by the Office of a Contracting Party and that constitutes the basis for the international application for the registration of that mark;

(xv) "designation" means the request for extension of protection ("territorial extension") under Article 3*ter* (1) or (2) of the Agreement or under Article 3*ter* (1) or (2) of the Protocol, as the case may be; it also means such extension as recorded in the International Register;

(xvi) "designated Contracting Party" means a Contracting Party for which the extension of protection ("territorial extension") has been requested under Article 3*ter* (1) or (2) of the Agreement or under Article 3*ter* (1) or (2) of the Protocol, as the case may be, or in respect of which such extension has been recorded in the International Register;

(xvii) "Contracting Party designated under the Agreement" means a Contracting Party for which the extension of protection ("territorial extension") has been requested under Article 3*ter* (1) or (2) of the Agreement;

(xviii) "Contracting Party designated under the Protocol" means a Contracting Party for which the extension of protection ("territorial extension") has been requested under Article 3*ter* (1) or (2) of the Protocol;

(xix) "notification of provisional refusal" means a declaration by the Office of a designated Contracting Party, in accordance with Article 5(1) of the Agreement or Article 5(1) of the Protocol;

(xix*bis*) "invalidation" means a decision by the competent authority (whether administrative or judicial) of a designated Contracting Party revoking or cancelling the effects, in the territory of that Contracting Party, of an international registration with regard to all or some of the goods or services covered by the designation of the said Contracting Party;

(xx) "Gazette" means the periodical gazette referred to in Rule 32;

(xxi) "holder" means the natural person or legal entity in whose name the international registration is recorded in the International Register;

(xxii) "International Classification of Figurative Elements" means the Classification established by the Vienna Agreement Establishing an International Classification of the Figurative Elements of Marks of June 12, 1973;

(xxiii) "International Classification of Goods and Services" means the Classification established by the Nice Agreement Concerning the International Classification of Goods and Services for the Purposes of the Registration of Marks of June 15, 1957, as revised at Stockholm on July 14, 1967, and at Geneva on May 13, 1977;

(xxiv) "International Register" means the official collection of data concerning international registrations maintained by the International Bureau, which data the Agreement, the Protocol or the Regulations require or permit to be recorded, irrespective of the medium in which such data are stored;

(xxv) "Office" means the Office of a Contracting Party in charge of the registration of marks, or the common Office referred to in Article 9*quater* of the Agreement or Article 9*quater* of the Protocol, or both, as the case may be;

(xxvi) "Office of origin" means the Office of the country of origin defined in Article 1(3) of the Agreement or the Office of origin defined in Article 2(2) of the Protocol, or both, as the case may be;

(xxvi*bis*) "Contracting Party of the holder" means

— the Contracting Party whose Office is the Office of origin, or

— where a change of ownership has been recorded or in the case of State succession, the Contracting Party, or one of the Contracting Parties, in respect of which the holder fulfills the conditions, under Articles 1(2) and 2 of the Agreement or under Article 2 of the Protocol, to be the holder of an international registration;

(xxvii) "official form" means a form established by the International Bureau or any form having the same contents and format;

(xxviii) "prescribed fee" means the applicable fee set out in the Schedule of Fees;

(xxix) "Director General" means the Director General of the World Intellectual Property Organization;

(xxx) "International Bureau" means the International Bureau of the World Intellectual Property Organization.

(xxxi) "Administrative Instructions" means the Administrative Instructions referred to in Rule 41.

[5.1120]
Rule 1bis
Designations Governed by the Agreement and Designations Governed by the Protocol

(1) *[General Principle and Exceptions]* The designation of a Contracting Party shall be governed by the Agreement or by the Protocol depending on whether the Contracting Party has been designated under the Agreement or under the Protocol. However,

(i) where, with regard to a given international registration, the Agreement ceases to be applicable in the relations between the Contracting Party of the holder and a Contracting Party whose designation is governed by the Agreement, the designation of the latter shall become governed by the Protocol as of the date on which the Agreement so ceases to be applicable, insofar as, on that date, both the Contracting Party of the holder and the designated Contracting Party are parties to the Protocol, and

(ii) where, with regard to a given international registration, the Protocol ceases to be applicable in the relations between the Contracting Party of the holder and a Contracting Party whose designation is governed by the Protocol, the designation of the latter shall become governed by the Agreement as of the date on which the Protocol so ceases to be applicable, insofar as, on that date, both the Contracting Party of the holder and the designated Contracting Party are parties to the Agreement.

(2) *[Recording]* The International Bureau shall record in the International Register an indication of the treaty governing each designation.

[5.1121]
Rule 2
Communication with the International Bureau

Communications addressed to the International Bureau shall be effected as specified in the Administrative Instructions.

[5.1122]
Rule 3
Representation Before the International Bureau

(1) *[Representative; Number of Representatives]*

(a) The applicant or the holder may have a representative before the International Bureau.

(b) The applicant or the holder may have one representative only. Where the appointment indicates several representatives, only the one indicated first shall be considered to be a representative and be recorded as such.

(c) Where a partnership or firm composed of attorneys or patent or trademark agents has been indicated as representative to the International Bureau, it shall be regarded as one representative.

(2) *[Appointment of the Representative]*

(a) The appointment of a representative may be made in the international application, or in a subsequent designation or a request under Rule 25.

(b) The appointment of a representative may also be made in a separate communication which may relate to one or more specified international applications or international registrations of the same applicant or holder. The said communication shall be presented to the International Bureau

(i) by the applicant, the holder or the appointed representative, or

(ii) by the Office of the Contracting Party of the holder.

The communication shall be signed by the applicant or the holder, or by the Office through which it was presented.

(3) *[Irregular Appointment]*

(a) Where the International Bureau considers that the appointment of a representative under paragraph (2) is irregular, it shall notify accordingly the applicant or holder, the purported representative and, if the sender or transmitter is an Office, that Office.

(b) As long as the relevant requirements under paragraph (2) are not complied with, the International Bureau shall send all relevant communications to the applicant or holder himself.

(4) *[Recording and Notification of Appointment of a Representative; Effective Date of Appointment]*

(a) Where the International Bureau finds that the appointment of a representative complies with the applicable requirements, it shall record the fact that the applicant or holder has a representative, as well as the name and address of the representative, in the International Register. In such a case, the effective date of the appointment shall be the date on which the International Bureau received the international application, subsequent designation, request or separate communication in which the representative is appointed.

(b) The International Bureau shall notify the recording referred to in subparagraph (a) to both the applicant or holder and the representative. Where the appointment was made in a separate communication presented through an Office, the International Bureau shall also notify the recording to that Office.

(5) *[Effect of Appointment of a Representative]*

(a) Except where these Regulations expressly provide otherwise, the signature of a representative recorded under paragraph (4)(a) shall replace the signature of the applicant or holder.

(b) Except where these Regulations expressly require that an invitation, notification or other communication be addressed to both the applicant or holder and the representative, the International Bureau shall address to the representative recorded under paragraph (4)(a) any invitation, notification or other communication which, in the absence of a representative, would have to be sent to the applicant or holder; any invitation, notification or other communication so addressed to the said representative shall have the same effect as if it had been addressed to the applicant or holder.

(c) Any communication addressed to the International Bureau by the representative recorded under paragraph (4)(a) shall have the same effect as if it had been addressed to the said Bureau by the applicant or holder.

(6) *[Cancellation of Recording; Effective Date of Cancellation]*

(a) Any recording under paragraph (4)(a) shall be cancelled where cancellation is requested in a communication signed by the applicant, holder or representative. The recording shall be cancelled *ex officio* by the International Bureau where a new representative is appointed or, in case a change in ownership has been recorded, where no representative is appointed by the new holder of the international registration.

(b) Subject to subparagraph (c), the cancellation shall be effective from the date on which the International Bureau receives the corresponding communication.

(c) Where the cancellation is requested by the representative, it shall be effective from the earlier of the following:

(i) the date on which the International Bureau receives a communication appointing a new representative;

(ii) the date of the expiry of a period of two months counted from the receipt of the request of the representative that the recording be cancelled. Until the effective date of the cancellation, all communications referred to in paragraph (5)(b) shall be addressed by the International Bureau to both the applicant or holder and the representative.

(d) The International Bureau shall, upon receipt of a request for cancellation made by the representative, notify accordingly the applicant or holder, and add to the notification copies of all communications sent to the representative, or received by the International Bureau from the representative, during the six months preceding the date of the notification.

(e) The International Bureau shall, once the effective date of the cancellation is known, notify the cancellation and its effective date to the representative whose recording has been cancelled, to the applicant or holder and, where the appointment of the representative had been presented through an Office, to that Office.

[5.1123]
Rule 4
Calculation of Time Limits

(1) *[Periods Expressed in Years]* Any period expressed in years shall expire, in the relevant subsequent year, in the month having the same name and on the day having the same number as the month and the day of the event from which the period starts to run, except that, where the event occurred on February 29 and in the relevant subsequent year February ends on the 28th, the period shall expire on February 28.

(2) *[Periods Expressed in Months]* Any period expressed in months shall expire, in the relevant subsequent month, on the day which has the same number as the day of the event from which the period starts to run, except that, where the relevant subsequent month has no day with the same number, the period shall expire on the last day of that month.

(3) *[Periods Expressed in Days]* The calculation of any period expressed in days shall start with the day following the day on which the relevant event occurred and shall expire accordingly.

(4) *[Expiry on a Day on Which the International Bureau or an Office Is Not Open to the Public]* If a period expires on a day on which the International Bureau or the Office concerned is not open to the public, the period shall, notwithstanding paragraphs (1) to (3), expire on the first subsequent day on which the International Bureau or the Office concerned is open to the public.

(5) *[Indication of the Date of Expiry]* The International Bureau shall, in all cases in which it communicates a time limit, indicate the date of the expiry, according to paragraphs (1) to (3), of the said time limit.

[5.1124]
Rule 5
Irregularities in Postal and Delivery Services and in Communications Sent Electronically

(1) *[Communications Sent Through a Postal Service]* Failure by an interested party to meet a time limit for a communication addressed to the International Bureau and mailed through a postal service shall be excused if the interested party submits evidence showing, to the satisfaction of the International Bureau,

(i) that the communication was mailed at least five days prior to the expiry of the time limit, or, where the postal service was, on any of the ten days preceding the day of expiry of the time limit, interrupted on account of war, revolution, civil disorder, strike, natural calamity, or other like reason, that the communication was mailed not later than five days after postal service was resumed,

(ii) that the mailing of the communication was registered, or details of the mailing were recorded, by the postal service at the time of mailing, and

(iii) in cases where all classes of mail do not normally reach the International Bureau within two days of mailing, that the communication was mailed by a class of mail which normally reaches the International Bureau within two days of mailing or by airmail.

(2) *[Communications Sent Through a Delivery Service]* Failure by an interested party to meet a time limit for a communication addressed to the International Bureau and sent through a delivery service shall be excused if the interested party submits evidence showing, to the satisfaction of the International Bureau,

(i) that the communication was sent at least five days prior to the expiry of the time limit, or, where the delivery service was, on any of the ten days preceding the day of expiry of the time limit, interrupted on account of war, revolution, civil disorder, strike, natural calamity, or other like reason, that the communication was sent not later than five days after the delivery service was resumed, and

(ii) that details of the sending of the communication were recorded by the delivery service at the time of sending.

(3) *[Communication Sent Electronically]* Failure by an interested party to meet a time limit for a communication addressed to the International Bureau and submitted by electronic means shall be excused if the interested party submits evidence showing, to the satisfaction of the International Bureau, that the time limit was not met because of failure in the electronic communication with the International Bureau, or which affects the locality of the interested party owing to extraordinary circumstances beyond the control of the interested party, and that the communication was effected not later than five days after the electronic communication service was resumed.

(4) *[Limitation on Excuse]*Failure to meet a time limit shall be excused under this Rule only if the evidence referred to in paragraph (1), (2) or (3) and the communication or, where applicable, a duplicate thereof are received by the International Bureau not later than six months after the expiry of the time limit.

(5) *[International Application and Subsequent Designation]*Where the International Bureau receives an international application or a subsequent designation beyond the two-month period referred to in Article 3(4) of the Agreement, in Article 3(4) of the Protocol and in Rule 24(6)(b), and the Office concerned indicates that the late receipt resulted from circumstances referred to in paragraph (1), (2) or (3), paragraph (1), (2) or (3) and paragraph (4) shall apply.

[5.1125]
Rule 5bis
Continued Processing

(1) *[Request]*

(a) Where an applicant or holder has failed to comply with any of the time limits specified or referred to in Rules 11(2) and (3), 20bis(2), 24(5)(b), 26(2), 34(3)(c)(iii) and 39(1), the International Bureau shall, nevertheless, continue the processing of the international application, subsequent designation, payment or request concerned, if:

(i) a request to that effect, signed by the applicant or holder, is presented to the International Bureau on the official form; and

(ii) the request is received, the fee specified in the Schedule of Fees is paid and, together with the request, all of the requirements in respect of which the time limit concerned applied are complied with, within two months from the date of expiry of that time limit.

(b) A request not complying with items (i) and (ii) of subparagraph (a) shall not be considered as such and the applicant or holder shall be notified to that effect.

(2) *[Recording and Notification]* The International Bureau shall record in the International Register any continued processing and notify the applicant or holder accordingly.

[5.1126]
Rule 6
Languages

(1) *[International Application]* The international application shall be in English, French or Spanish according to what is prescribed by the Office of origin, it being understood that the Office of origin may allow applicants to choose between English, French and Spanish.

(2) *[Communications Other Than the International Application]* Any communication concerning an international application or an international registration shall, subject to Rule 17(2)(v) and (3), be

(i) in English, French or Spanish where such communication is addressed to the International Bureau by the applicant or holder, or by an Office;

(ii) in the language applicable under Rule 7(2) where the communication consists of the declaration of intention to use the mark annexed to the international application under Rule 9(5)(f) or to the subsequent designation under Rule 24(3)(b)(i);

(iii) in the language of the international application where the communication is a notification addressed by the International Bureau to an Office, unless that Office has notified the International Bureau that all such notifications are to be in English, or are to be in French or are to be in Spanish; where the notification addressed by the International Bureau concerns the recording in the International Register of an international registration, the notification shall indicate the language in which the relevant international application was received by the International Bureau;

(iv) in the language of the international application where the communication is a notification addressed by the International Bureau to the applicant or holder, unless that applicant or holder has expressed the wish that all such notifications be in English, or be in French or be in Spanish.

(3) *[Recording and Publication]*

(a) The recording in the International Register and the publication in the Gazette of the international registration and of any data to be both recorded and published under these Regulations in respect of the international registration shall be in English, French and Spanish. The recording and publication of the international registration shall indicate the language in which the international application was received by the International Bureau.

(b) Where a first subsequent designation is made in respect of an international registration that, under previous versions of this Rule, has been published only in French, or only in English and French, the International Bureau shall, together with the publication in the Gazette of that subsequent designation, either publish the international registration in English and Spanish and republish the international registration in French, or publish the international registration in Spanish and republish it in English and French, as the case may be. That subsequent designation shall be recorded in the International Register in English, French and Spanish.

(4) *[Translation]*

(a) The translations needed for the notifications under paragraph (2)(iii) and (iv), and recordings and publications under paragraph (3), shall be made by the International Bureau. The applicant or the holder, as the case may be, may annex to the international application, or to a request for the recording of a subsequent designation or of a change, a proposed translation of any text matter contained in the international application or the request. If the proposed translation is not considered by the International Bureau to be correct, it shall be corrected by the International Bureau after having invited the applicant or the holder to make, within one month from the invitation, observations on the proposed corrections.

(b) Notwithstanding subparagraph (a), the International Bureau shall not translate the mark. Where, in accordance with Rule 9(4)(b)(iii) or Rule 24(3)(c), the applicant or the holder gives a translation or translations of the mark, the International Bureau shall not check the correctness of any such translations.

[5.1127]
Rule 7
Notification of Certain Special Requirements

(1) [Deleted]

(2) *[Intention to Use the Mark]* Where a Contracting Party requires, as a Contracting Party designated under the Protocol, a declaration of intention to use the mark, it shall notify that requirement to the Director General. Where that Contracting Party requires the declaration to be signed by the applicant himself and to be made on a separate official form annexed to the international application, the notification shall contain a statement to that effect and shall specify the exact wording of the required declaration. Where the Contracting Party further requires the declaration to be in English, French or Spanish, the notification shall specify the required language.

(3) *[Notification]*

(a) Any notification referred to in paragraph (2) may be made at the time of the deposit by the Contracting Party of its instrument of ratification, acceptance or approval of, or accession to, the Protocol, and the effective date of the notification shall be the same as the date of entry into force of the Protocol with respect to the Contracting Party having made the notification. The notification may also be made later, in which case the notification shall have effect three months after its receipt by the Director General, or at any later date indicated in the notification, in respect of any international registration whose date is the same as or is later than the effective date of the notification.

(b) Any notification made under paragraph (2) may be withdrawn at any time. The notice of withdrawal shall be addressed to the Director General. The withdrawal shall have effect upon receipt of the notice of withdrawal by the Director General or at any later date indicated in the notice.

CHAPTER 2
INTERNATIONAL APPLICATIONS

[5.1128]
Rule 8
Several Applicants

(1) *[Two or More Applicants Applying Exclusively Under the Agreement or Applying Under Both the Agreement and the Protocol]* Two or more applicants may jointly file an international application governed exclusively by the Agreement or governed by both the Agreement and the Protocol if the basic registration is jointly owned by them and if the country of origin, as defined in Article 1(3) of the Agreement, is the same for each of them.

(2) *[Two or More Applicants Applying Exclusively Under the Protocol]* Two or more applicants may jointly file an international application governed exclusively by the Protocol if the basic application was jointly filed by them or the basic registration is jointly owned by them, and if each of them qualifies, in relation to the Contracting Party whose Office is the Office of origin, for filing an international application under Article 2(1) of the Protocol.

[5.1129]
Rule 9
Requirements Concerning the International Application

(1) *[Presentation]* The international application shall be presented to the International Bureau by the Office of origin.

(2) *[Form and Signature]*

(a) The international application shall be presented on the official form in one copy.

(b) The international application shall be signed by the Office of origin and, where the Office of origin so requires, also by the applicant. Where the Office of origin does not require the applicant to sign the international application but allows that the applicant also sign it, the applicant may do so.

(3) *[Fees]* The prescribed fees applicable to the international application shall be paid as provided for in Rules 10, 34 and 35.

(4) *[Contents of the International Application]*

(a) The international application shall contain or indicate

(i) the name of the applicant, given in accordance with the Administrative Instructions,

(ii) the address of the applicant, given in accordance with the Administrative Instructions,

(iii) the name and address of the representative, if any, given in accordance with the Administrative Instructions,

(iv) where the applicant wishes, under the Paris Convention for the Protection of Industrial Property, to take advantage of the priority of an earlier filing, a declaration claiming the priority of that earlier filing, together with an indication of the name of the Office where such filing was made and of the date and, where available, the number of that filing, and, where the earlier filing relates to less than all the goods and services listed in the international application, the indication of those goods and services to which the earlier filing relates,

(v) a reproduction of the mark that shall fit in the box provided on the official form; that reproduction shall be clear and shall, depending on whether the reproduction in the basic application or the basic registration is in black and white or in color, be in black and white or in color,

(vi) where the applicant wishes that the mark be considered as a mark in standard characters, a declaration to that effect,

(vii) where color is claimed as a distinctive feature of the mark in the basic application or basic registration, or where the applicant wishes to claim color as a distinctive feature of the mark and the mark contained in the basic application or basic registration is in color, an indication that color is claimed and an indication by words of the color or combination of colors claimed and, where the reproduction furnished under item (v) is in black and white, one reproduction of the mark in color,

(vii*bis*) where the mark that is the subject of the basic application or the basic registration consists of a color or a combination of colors as such, an indication to that effect,

(viii) where the basic application or the basic registration relates to a three-dimensional mark, the indication "three-dimensional mark,"

(ix) where the basic application or the basic registration relates to a sound mark, the indication "sound mark,"

(x) where the basic application or the basic registration relates to a collective mark or a certification mark or a guarantee mark, an indication to that effect,

(xi) where the basic application or the basic registration contains a description of the mark by words and the applicant wishes to include the description or the Office of origin requires the inclusion of the description, that same description; where the said description is in a language other than the language of the international application, it shall be given in the language of the international application,

(xii) where the mark consists of or contains matter in characters other than Latin characters or numbers expressed in numerals other than Arabic or Roman numerals, a transliteration of that matter in Latin characters and Arabic numerals; the transliteration into Latin characters shall follow the phonetics of the language of the international application,

(xiii) the names of the goods and services for which the international registration of the mark is sought, grouped in the appropriate classes of the International Classification of Goods and Services, each group preceded by the number of the class and presented in the order of the classes of that Classification; the goods and services shall be indicated in precise terms, preferably using the words appearing in the Alphabetical List of the said Classification; the international application may contain limitations of the list of goods and services in respect of one or more designated Contracting Parties; the limitation in respect of each Contracting Party may be different,

(xiv) the amount of the fees being paid and the method of payment, or instructions to debit the required amount of fees to an account opened with the International Bureau, and the identification of the party effecting the payment or giving the instructions, and

(xv) the designated Contracting Parties.

(b) The international application may also contain,

(i) where the applicant is a natural person, an indication of the State of which the applicant is a national;

(ii) where the applicant is a legal entity, indications concerning the legal nature of that legal entity and the State, and, where applicable, the territorial unit within that State, under the law of which the said legal entity has been organized;

(iii) where the mark consists of or contains a word or words that can be translated, a translation of that word or those words into English, French and Spanish, or in any one or two of those languages;

(iv) where the applicant claims color as a distinctive feature of the mark, an indication by words, in respect of each color, of the principal parts of the mark which are in that color;

(v) where the applicant wishes to disclaim protection for any element of the mark, an indication of that fact and of the element or elements for which protection is disclaimed.

(5) *[Additional Contents of an International Application]*

(a) An international application governed exclusively by the Agreement or by both the Agreement and the Protocol shall contain the number and date of the basic registration and shall indicate one of the following:

(i) that the applicant has a real and effective industrial or commercial establishment in the territory of the Contracting State whose Office is the Office of origin, or

(ii) where the applicant has no such establishment in any Contracting State of the Agreement, that he has a domicile in the territory of the State whose Office is the Office of origin, or

(iii) where the applicant has no such establishment or domicile in the territory of any Contracting State of the Agreement, that he is a national of the State whose Office is the Office of origin.

(b) An international application governed exclusively by the Protocol shall contain the number and date of the basic application or basic registration and shall indicate one or more of the following:

(i) where the Contracting Party whose Office is the Office of origin is a State, that the applicant is a national of that State;

(ii) where the Contracting Party whose Office is the Office of origin is an organization, the name of the Member State of that organization of which the applicant is a national;

(iii) that the applicant has a domicile in the territory of the Contracting Party whose Office is the Office of origin;

(iv) that the applicant has a real and effective industrial or commercial establishment in the territory of the Contracting Party whose Office is the Office of origin.

(c) Where the address of the applicant given in accordance with paragraph (4)(a)(ii) is not in the territory of the Contracting Party whose Office is the Office of origin and it has been indicated under subparagraph (a)(i) or (ii) or subparagraph (b)(iii) or (iv) that the applicant has a domicile or an establishment in the territory of that Contracting Party, that domicile or the address of that establishment shall be given in the international application.

(d) The international application shall contain a declaration by the Office of origin certifying

(i) the date on which the Office of origin received or, as provided for in Rule 11(1), is deemed to have received the request by the applicant to present the international application to the International Bureau,

(ii) that the applicant named in the international application is the same as the applicant named in the basic application or the holder named in the basic registration, as the case may be,

(iii) that any indication referred to in paragraph (4)(a)(vii*bis*) to (xi) and appearing in the international application appears also in the basic application or the basic registration, as the case may be,

(iv) that the mark that is the subject matter of the international application is the same as in the basic application or the basic registration, as the case may be,

(v) that, if color is claimed as a distinctive feature of the mark in the basic application or the basic registration, the same claim is included in the international application or that, if color is claimed as a distinctive feature of the mark in the international application without having being claimed in the basic application or basic registration, the mark in the basic application or basic registration is in fact in the color or combination of colors claimed, and

(vi) that the goods and services indicated in the international application are covered by the list of goods and services appearing in the basic application or basic registration, as the case may be.

(e) Where the international application is based on two or more basic applications or basic registrations, the declaration referred to in subparagraph (d) shall be deemed to apply to all those basic applications or basic registrations.

(f) Where the international application contains the designation of a Contracting Party that has made a notification under Rule 7(2), the international application shall also contain a declaration of intention to use the mark in the territory of that Contracting Party; the declaration shall be considered part of the designation of the Contracting Party requiring it and shall, as required by that Contracting Party,

(i) be signed by the applicant himself and be made on a separate official form annexed to the international application, or

(ii) be included in the international application.

(g) Where an international application contains the designation of a Contracting Organization, it may also contain the following indications:

(i) where the applicant wishes to claim, under the law of that Contracting Organization, the seniority of one or more earlier marks registered in, or for, a Member State of that Organization, a declaration to that effect, stating the Member State or Member States in or for which the earlier mark is registered, the date from which the relevant registration was effective, the number of the relevant registration and the goods and services for which the earlier mark is registered. Such indications shall be on an official form to be annexed to the international application;

(ii) where, under the law of that Contracting Organization, the applicant is required to indicate a second working language before the Office of that Contracting Organization, in addition to the language of the international application, an indication of that second language.

[5.1130]
Rule 10
Fees Concerning the International Application

(1) *[International Applications Governed Exclusively by the Agreement]* An international application governed exclusively by the Agreement shall be subject to the payment of the basic fee, the complementary fee and, where applicable, the supplementary fee, specified in item 1 of the Schedule of Fees. Those fees shall be paid in two instalments of ten years each. For the payment of the second instalment, Rule 30 shall apply.

(2) *[International Applications Governed Exclusively by the Protocol]* An international application governed exclusively by the Protocol shall be subject to the payment of the basic fee, the complementary fee and/or the individual fee and, where applicable, the supplementary fee, specified or referred to in item 2 of the Schedule of Fees. Those fees shall be paid for ten years.

(3) *[International Applications Governed by Both the Agreement and the Protocol]* An international application governed by both the Agreement and the Protocol shall be subject to the payment of the basic fee, the complementary fee and, where applicable, the individual fee and the supplementary fee, specified or referred to in item 3 of the Schedule of Fees. As far as the Contracting Parties designated under the Agreement are concerned, paragraph (1) shall apply. As far as the Contracting Parties designated under the Protocol are concerned, paragraph (2) shall apply.

[5.1131]
Rule 11
Irregularities Other Than Those Concerning the Classification of Goods and Services or Their Indication

(1) *[Premature Request to the Office of Origin]*

(a) Where the Office of origin received a request to present to the International Bureau an international application governed exclusively by the Agreement before the mark which is referred to in that request is registered in the register of the said Office, the said request shall be deemed to have been received by the Office of origin, for the purposes of Article 3(4) of the Agreement, on the date of the registration of the mark in the register of the said Office.

(b) Subject to subparagraph (c), where the Office of origin receives a request to present to the International Bureau an international application governed by both the Agreement and the Protocol before the mark which is referred to in that request is registered in the register of the said Office, the international application shall be treated as an international application governed exclusively by the Protocol, and the Office of origin shall delete the designation of any Contracting Party bound by the Agreement but not by the Protocol.

(c) Where the request referred to in subparagraph (b) is accompanied by an express request that the international application be treated as an international application governed by both the Agreement and the Protocol once the mark is registered in the register of the Office of origin, the said Office shall not delete the designation of any Contracting Party bound by the Agreement but not by the Protocol and the request to present the international application shall be deemed to have been received by the said Office, for the purposes of Article 3(4) of the Agreement and Article 3(4) of the Protocol, on the date of the registration of the mark in the register of the said Office.

(2) *[Irregularities to Be Remedied by the Applicant]*

(a) If the International Bureau considers that the international application contains irregularities other than those referred to in paragraphs (3), (4) and (6) and in Rules 12 and 13, it shall notify the applicant of the irregularity and at the same time inform the Office of origin.

(b) Such irregularities may be remedied by the applicant within three months from the date of the notification of the irregularity by the International Bureau. If an irregularity is not remedied within three months from the date of the notification of that irregularity by the International Bureau, the international application shall be considered abandoned and the International Bureau shall notify accordingly and at the same time the applicant and the Office of origin.

(3) *[Irregularity to Be Remedied by the Applicant or by the Office of Origin]*

(a) Notwithstanding paragraph (2), where the fees payable under Rule 10 have been paid to the International Bureau by the Office of origin and the International Bureau considers that the amount of the fees received is less than the amount required, it shall notify at the same time the Office of origin and the applicant. The notification shall specify the missing amount.

(b) The missing amount may be paid by the Office of origin or by the applicant within three months from the date of the notification by the International Bureau. If the missing amount is not paid within three months from the date of the notification of the irregularity by the International Bureau, the international application shall be considered abandoned and the International Bureau shall notify accordingly and at the same time the Office of origin and the applicant.

(4) *[Irregularities to Be Remedied by the Office of Origin]*

(a) If the International Bureau

(i) finds that the international application does not fulfill the requirements of Rule 2 or was not presented on the official form prescribed under Rule 9(2)(a),

(ii) finds that the international application contains any of the irregularities referred to in Rule 15(1),

(iii) considers that the international application contains irregularities relating to the entitlement of the applicant to file an international application,

(iv) considers that the international application contains irregularities relating to the declaration by the Office of origin referred to in Rule 9(5)(d),

(v) [Deleted]

(vi) finds that the international application is not signed by the Office of origin, or

(vii) finds that the international application does not contain the date and number of the basic application or basic registration, as the case may be, it shall notify the Office of origin and at the same time inform the applicant.

(b) Such irregularities may be remedied by the Office of origin within three months from the date of notification of the irregularity by the International Bureau. If an irregularity is not remedied within three months from the date of the notification of that irregularity by the International Bureau, the international application shall be considered abandoned and the International Bureau shall notify accordingly and at the same time the Office of origin and the applicant.

(5) *[Reimbursement of Fees]* Where, in accordance with paragraphs (2)(b), (3) or (4)(b), the international application is considered abandoned, the International Bureau shall refund any fees paid in respect of that application, after deduction of an amount corresponding to one-half of the basic fee referred to in items 1.1.1, 2.1.1 or 3.1.1 of the Schedule of Fees, to the party having paid those fees.

(6) *[Other Irregularity With Respect to the Designation of a Contracting Party Under the Protocol]*

(a) Where, in accordance with Article 3(4) of the Protocol, an international application is received by the International Bureau within a period of two months from the date of receipt of that international application by the Office of origin and the International Bureau considers that a declaration of intention to use the mark is required according to Rule 9(5)(f) but is missing or does not comply with the applicable requirements, the International Bureau shall promptly notify accordingly and at the same time the applicant and the Office of origin.

(b) The declaration of intention to use the mark shall be deemed to have been received by the International Bureau together with the international application if the missing or corrected declaration is received by the International Bureau within the period of two months referred to in subparagraph (a).

(c) Where subparagraph (a) applies and the Office referred to in the said subparagraph has, before the expiry of the 18-month time limit referred to in the same subparagraph, informed the International Bureau of the fact that the time limit for filing oppositions will expire within the 30 days preceding the expiry of the 18-month time limit and of the possibility that oppositions may be filed during those 30 days, a provisional refusal based on an opposition filed during the said 30 days may be notified to the International Bureau within one month from the date of filing of the opposition.

(7) *[International Application Not Considered as Such]* If the international application is presented direct to the International Bureau by the applicant or does not comply with the requirement applicable under Rule 6(1), the international application shall not be considered as such and shall be returned to the sender.

[5.1132]
Rule 12
Irregularities With Respect to the Classification of Goods and Services

(1) *[Proposal for Classification]*

(a) If the International Bureau considers that the requirements of Rule 9(4)(a)(xiii) are not complied with, it shall make a proposal of its own for the classification and grouping and shall send a notification of its proposal to the Office of origin and at the same time inform the applicant.

(b) The notification of the proposal shall also state the amount, if any, of the fees due as a consequence of the proposed classification and grouping.

(2) *[Opinion Differing From the Proposal]* The Office of origin may communicate to the International Bureau an opinion on the proposed classification and grouping within three months from the date of the notification of the proposal.

(3) *[Reminder of the Proposal]* If, within two months from the date of the notification referred to in paragraph (1)(a), the Office of origin has not communicated an opinion on the proposed classification and grouping, the International Bureau shall send to the Office of origin and to the applicant a communication reiterating the proposal. The sending of such a communication shall not affect the three-month period referred to in paragraph (2).

(4) *[Withdrawal of Proposal]* If, in the light of the opinion communicated under paragraph (2), the International Bureau withdraws its proposal, it shall notify the Office of origin accordingly and at the same time inform the applicant.

(5) *[Modification of Proposal]* If, in the light of the opinion communicated under paragraph (2), the International Bureau modifies its proposal, it shall notify the Office of origin and at the same time inform the applicant of such modification and of any consequent changes in the amount indicated under paragraph (1)(b).

(6) *[Confirmation of Proposal]* If, notwithstanding the opinion referred to in paragraph (2), the International Bureau confirms its proposal, it shall notify the Office of origin accordingly and at the same time inform the applicant.

(7) *[Fees]*

(a) If no opinion has been communicated to the International Bureau under paragraph (2), the amount referred to in paragraph (1)(b) shall be payable within four months from the date of the notification referred to in paragraph (1)(a), failing which the international application shall be considered abandoned and the International Bureau shall notify the Office of origin accordingly and at the same time inform the applicant.

(b) If an opinion has been communicated to the International Bureau under paragraph (2), the amount referred to in paragraph (1)(b) or, where applicable, paragraph (5) shall be payable within three months from the date of the communication by the International Bureau of the modification or confirmation of its proposal under paragraph (5) or (6), as the case may be, failing which the international application shall be considered abandoned and the International Bureau shall notify the Office of origin accordingly and at the same time inform the applicant.

(c) If an opinion has been communicated to the International Bureau under paragraph (2) and if, in the light of that opinion, the International Bureau withdraws its proposal in accordance with paragraph (4), the amount referred to in paragraph (1)(b) shall not be due.

(8) *[Reimbursement of Fees]* Where, in accordance with paragraph (7), the international application is considered abandoned, the International Bureau shall refund any fees paid in respect of that application, after deduction of an amount corresponding to one-half of the basic fee referred to in items 1.1.1, 2.1.1 or 3.1.1 of the Schedule of Fees, to the party having paid those fees.

(8*bis*) *[Examination of Limitations]* The International Bureau shall examine limitations contained in an international application, applying paragraphs (1)(a) and (2) to (6) mutatis mutandis. Where the International Bureau cannot group the goods and services listed in the limitation under the classes of the International Classification of Goods and Services listed in the international application concerned, as amended pursuant to paragraphs (1) to (6), as the case may be, it shall issue an irregularity. Where the irregularity is not remedied within three months from the date of the notification of the irregularity, the limitation shall be deemed not to contain the goods and services concerned.

(9) *[Classification in the Registration]* Subject to the conformity of the international application with the other applicable requirements, the mark shall be registered with the classification and grouping that the International Bureau considers to be correct.

[5.1133]
Rule 13
Irregularities With Respect to the Indication of Goods and Services

(1) *[Communication of Irregularity by the International Bureau to the Office of Origin]* If the International Bureau considers that any of the goods and services is indicated in the international application by a term that is too vague for the purposes of classification or is incomprehensible or is linguistically incorrect, it shall notify the Office of origin accordingly and at the same time inform the applicant. In the same notification, the International Bureau may suggest a substitute term, or the deletion of the term.

(2) *[Time Allowed to Remedy Irregularity]*

(a) The Office of origin may make a proposal for remedying the irregularity within three months from the date of the notification referred to in paragraph (1).

(b) If no proposal acceptable to the International Bureau for remedying the irregularity is made within the period indicated in subparagraph (a), the International Bureau shall include in the international registration the term as appearing in the international application, provided that the Office of origin has specified the class in which such term should be classified; the international registration shall contain an indication to the effect that, in the opinion of the International Bureau, the specified term is too vague for the purposes of classification or is incomprehensible or is linguistically incorrect, as the case may be. Where no class has been specified by the Office of origin, the International Bureau shall delete the said term *ex officio* and shall notify the Office of origin accordingly and at the same time inform the applicant.

CHAPTER 3
INTERNATIONAL REGISTRATIONS

[5.1134]
Rule 14
Registration of the Mark in the International Register

(1) *[Registration of the Mark in the International Register]* Where the International Bureau finds that the international application conforms to the applicable requirements, it shall register the mark in the International Register, notify the Offices of the designated Contracting Parties of the international registration and inform the Office of origin accordingly, and send a certificate to the holder. Where the Office of origin so wishes and has informed the International Bureau accordingly, the certificate shall be sent to the holder through the Office of origin.

(2) *[Contents of the Registration]* The international registration shall contain

(i) all the data contained in the international application, except any priority claim under Rule 9(4)(a)(iv) where the date of the earlier filing is more than six months before the date of the international registration,

(ii) the date of the international registration,

(iii) the number of the international registration,

(iv) where the mark can be classified according to the International Classification of Figurative Elements, and unless the international application contains a declaration to the effect that the applicant wishes that the mark be considered as a mark in standard characters, the relevant classification symbols of the said Classification as determined by the International Bureau,

(v) an indication, with respect to each designated Contracting Party, as to whether it is a Contracting Party designated under the Agreement or a Contracting Party designated under the Protocol.

(vi) indications annexed to the international application in accordance with Rule 9(5)(g)(i) concerning the Member State or Member States in or for which an earlier mark, for which seniority is claimed, is registered, the date from which the registration of that earlier mark was effective and the number of the relevant registration.

[5.1135]
Rule 15
Date of the International Registration

(1) *[Irregularities Affecting the Date of the International Registration]* Where the international application received by the International Bureau does not contain all of the following elements:

(i) indications allowing the identity of the applicant to be established and sufficient to contact the applicant or his representative, if any,

(ii) the Contracting Parties which are designated,

(iii) a reproduction of the mark,

(iv) the indication of the goods and services for which registration of the mark is sought, the international registration shall bear the date on which the last of the missing elements reached the International Bureau, provided that, where the last of the missing elements reaches the International Bureau within the two-month time limit referred to in Article 3(4) of the Agreement and Article 3(4) of the Protocol, the international registration shall bear the date on which the defective international application was received or, as provided in Rule 11(1), is deemed to have been received by the Office of origin.

(2) *[Date of the International Registration in Other Cases]* In any other case, the international registration shall bear the date determined in accordance with Article 3(4) of the Agreement and Article 3(4) of the Protocol.

CHAPTER 4 FACTS IN CONTRACTING PARTIES AFFECTING INTERNATIONAL REGISTRATIONS

[5.1136]

Rule 16 Possibility of Notification of a Provisional Refusal Based on an Opposition Under Article 5(2)(c) of the Protocol

(1) *[Information Relating to Possible Oppositions and Time Limit for Notifying Provisional Refusal Based on an Opposition]*

(a) Subject to Article 9 *sexies* (1)(b) of the Protocol, where a declaration has been made by a Contracting Party pursuant to Article 5(2)(b) and (c), first sentence, of the Protocol, the Office of that Contracting Party shall, where it has become apparent with regard to a given international registration designating that Contracting Party that the opposition period will expire too late for any provisional refusal based on an opposition to be notified to the International Bureau within the 18-month time limit referred to in Article 5(2)(b), inform the International Bureau of the number, and the name of the holder, of that international registration.

(b) Where, at the time of the communication of the information referred to in subparagraph (a), the dates on which the opposition period begins and ends are known, those dates shall be indicated in the communication. If such dates are not yet known at that time, they shall be communicated to the International Bureau as soon as they are known.[1]

(c) Where subparagraph (a) applies and the Office referred to in the said subparagraph has, before the expiry of the 18-month time limit referred to in the same subparagraph, informed the International Bureau of the fact that the time limit for filing oppositions will expire within the 30 days preceding the expiry of the 18-month time limit and of the possibility that oppositions may be filed during those 30 days, a provisional refusal based on an opposition filed during the said 30 days may be notified to the International Bureau within one month from the date of filing of the opposition.

(2) *[Recording and Transmittal of the Information]* The International Bureau shall record in the International Register the information received under paragraph (1) and shall transmit that information to the holder.

NOTES

[1] In adopting this provision, the Assembly of the Madrid Union understood that if the opposition period is extendable, the Office may communicate only the date the opposition period begins.

[5.1137]

Rule 17 Provisional Refusal

(1) *[Notification of Provisional Refusal]*

(a) A notification of provisional refusal may comprise a declaration stating the grounds on which the Office making the notification considers that protection cannot be granted in the Contracting Party concerned ("*ex officio* provisional refusal") or a declaration that protection cannot be granted in the Contracting Party concerned because an opposition has been filed ("provisional refusal based on an opposition") or both.

(b) A notification of provisional refusal shall relate to one international registration, shall be dated and shall be signed by the Office making it.

(2) *[Content of the Notification]* A notification of provisional refusal shall contain or indicate

(i) the Office making the notification,

(ii) the number of the international registration, preferably accompanied by other indications enabling the identity of the international registration to be confirmed, such as the verbal elements of the mark or the basic application or basic registration number,

(iii) [Deleted]

(iv) all the grounds on which the provisional refusal is based, together with a reference to the corresponding essential provisions of the law, (v) where the grounds on which the provisional refusal is based relate to a mark which has been the subject of an application or registration and with which the mark that is the subject of the international registration appears to be in conflict, the filing date and number, the priority date (if any), the registration date and number (if available), the name and address of the owner, and a reproduction, of the former mark, together with the list of all or the relevant goods and services in the application or registration of the former mark, it being understood that the said list may be in the language of the said application or registration,

(vi) either that the grounds on which the provisional refusal is based affect all the goods and services or an indication of the goods and services which are affected, or are not affected, by the provisional refusal,

(vii) the time limit, reasonable under the circumstances, for filing a request for review of, or appeal against, the *ex officio* provisional refusal or the provisional refusal based on an opposition and, as the case may be, for filing a response to the opposition, preferably with an indication of the date on which the said time limit expires, and the authority with which such request for review, appeal or response should be filed, with the indication, where applicable, that the request for review, the appeal or the response has to be filed through the intermediary of a representative whose address is within the territory of the Contracting Party whose Office has pronounced the refusal.

(3) *[Additional Requirements Concerning a Notification of Provisional Refusal Based on an Opposition]* Where the provisional refusal of protection is based on an opposition, or on an opposition and other grounds, the notification shall, in addition to complying with the requirements referred to in paragraph (2), contain an indication of that fact and the name and address of the opponent; however, notwithstanding paragraph (2)(v), the Office making the notification must, where the opposition is based on a mark which has been the subject of an application or registration, communicate the list of the goods and services on which the opposition is based and may, in addition, communicate the complete list of goods and services of that earlier application or registration, it being understood that the said lists may be in the language of the earlier application or registration.

(4) *[Recording; Transmittal of Copies of Notifications]* The International Bureau shall record the provisional refusal in the International Register together with the data contained in the notification, with an indication of the date on which the notification was sent or is regarded under Rule 18(1)(d) as having been sent to the International Bureau and shall transmit a copy thereof to the Office of origin, if that Office has informed the International Bureau that it wishes to receive such copies, and, at the same time, to the holder.

(5) *[Declarations Relating to the Possibility of Review]*

(a) [Deleted]

(b) [Deleted]

(c) [Deleted]

(d) The Office of a Contracting Party may, in a declaration, notify the Director General that, in accordance with the law of the said Contracting Party,

(i) any provisional refusal that has been notified to the International Bureau is subject to review by the said Office, whether or not such review has been requested by the holder, and

(ii) the decision taken on the said review may be the subject of a further review or appeal before the Office. Where this declaration applies and the Office is not in a position to communicate the said decision directly to the holder of the international registration concerned, the Office shall, notwithstanding the fact that all procedures before the said Office relating to the protection of the mark may not have been completed, send the statement referred to in Rule 18*ter* (2) or (3) to the International Bureau immediately following the said decision. Any further decision affecting the protection of the mark shall be sent to the International Bureau in accordance with Rule 18*ter* (4).

(e) The Office of a Contracting Party may, in a declaration, notify the Director General that, in accordance with the law of the said Contracting Party, any *ex officio* provisional refusal that has been notified to the International Bureau is not open to review before the said Office. Where this declaration applies, any *ex officio* notification of a provisional refusal by the said Office shall be deemed to include a statement in accordance with Rule 18*ter* (2)(ii) or (3).

(6) [Deleted]

[5.1138]
Rule 18
Irregular Notifications of Provisional Refusal

(1) *[Contracting Party Designated Under the Agreement]*

(a) A notification of provisional refusal communicated by the Office of a Contracting Party designated under the Agreement shall not be regarded as such by the International Bureau

(i) if it does not contain any international registration number, unless other indications contained in the notification permit the international registration to which the provisional refusal relates to be identified,

(ii) if it does not indicate any grounds for refusal, or

(iii) if it is sent too late to the International Bureau, that is, if it is sent after the expiry of one year from the date on which the recording of the international registration or the recording of the designation made subsequently to the international registration has been effected, it being understood that the said date is the same as the date of sending the notification of the international registration or of the designation made subsequently.

(b) Where subparagraph (a) applies, the International Bureau shall nevertheless transmit a copy of the notification to the holder, shall inform, at the same time, the holder and the Office that sent the notification that the notification of provisional refusal is not regarded as such by the International Bureau, and shall indicate the reasons therefor.

(c) If the notification

(i) is not signed on behalf of the Office which communicated it, or does not otherwise comply with the requirements of Rule 2 or with the requirement applicable under Rule 6(2),

(ii) does not contain, where applicable, the details of the mark with which the mark that is the subject of the international registration appears to be in conflict (Rule 17(2)(v) and (3)),

(iii) does not comply with the requirements of Rule 17(2)(vi),

(iv) does not comply with the requirements of Rule 17(2)(vii), or

(v) [Deleted]

(vi) does not contain, where applicable, the name and address of the opponent and the indication of the goods and services on which the opposition is based (Rule 17(3)),

the International Bureau shall, except where subparagraph (d) applies, nonetheless record the provisional refusal in the International Register. The International Bureau shall invite the Office that communicated the provisional refusal to send a rectified notification within two months from the invitation and shall transmit to the holder copies of the irregular notification and of the invitation sent to the Office concerned.

(d) Where the notification does not comply with the requirements of Rule 17(2)(vii), the provisional refusal shall not be recorded in the International Register. If however a rectified notification is sent within the time limit referred to in subparagraph (c), it shall be regarded, for the purposes of Article 5 of the Agreement, as having been sent to the International Bureau on the date on which the defective notification had been sent to it. If the notification is not so rectified, it shall not be regarded as a notification of provisional refusal. In the latter case, the International Bureau shall inform, at the same time, the holder and the Office that sent the notification that the notification of provisional refusal is not regarded as such by the International Bureau, and shall indicate the reasons therefor.

(e) Any rectified notification shall, where the applicable law so permits, indicate a new time limit, reasonable under the circumstances, for filing a request for review of, or appeal against, the *ex officio* provisional refusal or the provisional refusal based on an opposition and, as the case may be, for filing a response to the opposition, preferably with an indication of the date on which the said time limit expires.

(f) The International Bureau shall transmit a copy of any rectified notification to the holder.

(2) *[Contracting Party Designated Under the Protocol]*

(a) Paragraph (1) shall also apply in the case of a notification of provisional refusal communicated by the Office of a Contracting Party designated under the Protocol, it being understood that the time limit referred to in paragraph (1)(a)(iii) shall be the time limit applicable under Article 5(2)(a) or, subject to Article 9 *sexies* (1)(b) of the Protocol, under Article 5(2)(b) or (c)(ii) of the Protocol.

(b) Paragraph (1)(a) shall apply to determine whether the time limit before the expiry of which the Office of the Contracting Party concerned must give the International Bureau the information referred to in Article 5(2)(c)(i) of the Protocol has been complied with. If such information is given after the expiry of that time limit, it shall be regarded as not having been given and the International Bureau shall inform the Office concerned accordingly.

(c) Where the notification of provisional refusal based on an opposition is made under Article 5(2)(c)(ii) of the Protocol without the requirements of Article 5(2)(c)(i) of the Protocol having been complied with, it shall not be regarded as a notification of provisional refusal. In such a case, the International Bureau shall nevertheless transmit a copy of the notification to the holder, shall inform, at the same time, the holder and the Office that sent the notification that the notification of provisional refusal is not regarded as such by the International Bureau, and shall indicate the reasons therefor.

[5.1139]

Rule 18bis

Interim Status of a Mark in a Designated Contracting Party

(1) *[Ex Officio Examination Completed but Opposition or Observations by Third Parties Still Possible]*

(a) An Office which has not communicated a notification of provisional refusal may, within the period applicable under Article 5(2) of the Agreement or Article 5(2)(a) or (b) of the Protocol, send to the International Bureau a statement to the effect that the *ex officio* examination has been completed and that the Office has found no grounds for refusal but that the protection of the mark is still subject to opposition or observations by third parties, with an indication of the date by which such oppositions or observations may be filed.[1]

(b) An Office which has communicated a notification of provisional refusal may send to the International Bureau a statement to the effect that the *ex officio* examination has been completed but that the protection of the mark is still subject to opposition or observations by third parties, with an indication of the date by which such oppositions or observations may be filed.

(2) *[Recording, Information to the Holder and Transmittal of Copies]* The International Bureau shall record any statement received under this Rule in the International Register, inform the holder accordingly and, where the statement was communicated, or can be reproduced, in the form of a specific document, transmit a copy of that document to the holder.

NOTES

1 Interpretative statement endorsed by the Assembly of the Madrid Union: "The references in Rule 18*bis* to observations by third parties apply only to those Contracting Parties whose legislation provides for such observations."

[5.1140]
Rule 18ter
Final Disposition on Status of a Mark in a Designated Contracting Party

(1) *[Statement of Grant of Protection Where No Notification of Provisional Refusal Has Been Communicated]*[1] When, before the expiry of the period applicable under Article 5(2) of the Agreement or Article 5(2)(a), (b) or (c) of the Protocol, all procedures before an Office have been completed and there is no ground for that Office to refuse protection, that Office shall, as soon as possible and before the expiry of that period, send to the International Bureau a statement to the effect that protection is granted to the mark that is the subject of the international registration in the Contracting Party concerned.[2]

(2) *[Statement of Grant of Protection Following a Provisional Refusal]* Except where it sends a statement under paragraph (3), an Office which has communicated a notification of provisional refusal shall, once all procedures before the said Office relating to the protection of the mark have been completed, send to the International Bureau either

(i) a statement to the effect that the provisional refusal is withdrawn and that protection of the mark is granted, in the Contracting Party concerned, for all goods and services for which protection has been requested, or

(ii) a statement indicating the goods and services for which protection of the mark is granted in the Contracting Party concerned.

(3) *[Confirmation of Total Provisional Refusal]* An Office which has sent to the International Bureau a notification of a total provisional refusal shall, once all procedures before the said Office relating to the protection of the mark have been completed and the Office has decided to confirm refusal of the protection of the mark in the Contracting Party concerned for all goods and services, send to the International Bureau a statement to that effect.

(4) *[Further Decision]* Where, following the sending of a statement in accordance with either paragraph (2) or (3), a further decision affects the protection of the mark, the Office shall, to the extent that it is aware of that decision, send to the International Bureau a further statement indicating the goods and services for which the mark is protected in the Contracting Party concerned.[3]

(5) *[Recording, Information to the Holder and Transmittal of Copies]* The International Bureau shall record any statement received under this Rule in the International Register, inform the holder accordingly and, where the statement was communicated, or can be reproduced, in the form of a specific document, transmit a copy of that document to the holder.

NOTES

1 In adopting this provision, the Assembly of the Madrid Union understood that a statement of grant of protection could concern several international registrations and take the form of a list, communicated electronically or on paper, that permits identification of these international registrations.

2 In adopting paragraphs (1) and (2) of this rule, the Assembly of the Madrid Union understood that where Rule 34(3) applies, the grant of protection will be subject to the payment of the second part of the fee.

3 Interpretative statement endorsed by the Assembly of the Madrid Union: "The reference in Rule 18*ter* (4) to a further decision that affects the protection of the mark includes also the case where that further decision is taken by the Office, for example in the case of *restitutio in integrum*, notwithstanding the fact that the Office has already stated that the procedures before the Office have been completed."

[5.1141]
Rule 19
Invalidations in Designated Contracting Parties

(1) *[Contents of the Notification of Invalidation]* Where the effects of an international registration are invalidated in a designated Contracting Party under Article 5(6) of the Agreement or Article 5(6) of the Protocol and the invalidation is no longer subject to appeal, the Office of the Contracting Party whose competent authority has pronounced the invalidation shall notify the International Bureau accordingly. The notification shall contain or indicate

(i) the authority which pronounced the invalidation,

(ii) the fact that the invalidation is no longer subject to appeal,

(iii) the number of the international registration,
(iv) the name of the holder,
(v) if the invalidation does not concern all the goods and services, those in respect of which the invalidation has been pronounced or those in respect of which the invalidation has not been pronounced, and
(vi) the date on which the invalidation was pronounced and, where possible, its effective date.

(2) *[Recording of the Invalidation and Information to the Holder and the Office Concerned]*

(a) The International Bureau shall record the invalidation in the International Register, together with the data contained in the notification of invalidation, and shall inform accordingly the holder. The International Bureau shall also inform the Office that communicated the notification of invalidation of the date on which the invalidation was recorded in the International Register if that Office has requested to receive such information.

(b) The invalidation shall be recorded as of the date of receipt by the International Bureau of a notification complying with the applicable requirements.

[5.1142]
Rule 20
Restriction of the Holder's Right of Disposal

(1) *[Communication of Information]*

(a) The holder of an international registration or the Office of the Contracting Party of the holder may inform the International Bureau that the holder's right to dispose of the international registration has been restricted and, if appropriate, indicate the Contracting Parties concerned.

(b) The Office of any designated Contracting Party may inform the International Bureau that the holder's right of disposal has been restricted in respect of the international registration in the territory of that Contracting Party.

(c) Information given in accordance with subparagraph (a) or (b) shall consist of a summary statement of the main facts concerning the restriction.

(2) *[Partial or Total Removal of Restriction]* Where the International Bureau has been informed of a restriction of the holder's right of disposal in accordance with paragraph (1), the party that communicated the information shall also inform the International Bureau of any partial or total removal of that restriction.

(3) *[Recording]*

(a) The International Bureau shall record the information communicated under paragraphs (1) and (2) in the International Register and shall inform accordingly the holder, the Office of the Contracting Party of the holder and the Offices of the designated Contracting Parties concerned.

(b) The information communicated under paragraphs (1) and (2) shall be recorded as of the date of its receipt by the International Bureau, provided that the communication complies with the applicable requirements.

[5.1143]
Rule 20bis
Licenses

(1) *[Request for the Recording of a License]*

(a) A request for the recording of a license shall be presented to the International Bureau on the relevant official form by the holder or, if the Office admits such presentation, by the Office of the Contracting Party of the holder or the Office of a Contracting Party with respect to which the license is granted.

(b) The request shall indicate
(i) the number of the international registration concerned,
(ii) the name of the holder,
(iii) the name and address of the licensee, given in accordance with the Administrative Instructions,
(iv) the designated Contracting Parties with respect to which the license is granted,
(v) that the license is granted for all the goods and services covered by the international registration, or the goods and services for which the license is granted, grouped in the appropriate classes of the International Classification of Goods and Services.

(c) The request may also indicate
(i) where the licensee is a natural person, the State of which the licensee is a national,
(ii) where the licensee is a legal entity, the legal nature of that entity and the State and, where applicable, the territorial unit within that State, under the law of which the said legal entity has been organized,
(iii) that the license concerns only a part of the territory of a specified designated Contracting Party,
(iv) where the licensee has a representative, the name and address of the representative, given in accordance with the Administrative Instructions,
(v) where the license is an exclusive license or a sole license, that fact,[1]

(vi) where applicable, the duration of the license.

(d) The request shall be signed by the holder or by the Office through which it is presented.

(2) *[Irregular Request]*

(a) If the request for the recording of a license does not comply with the requirements of paragraph (1)(a), (b) and (d), the International Bureau shall notify that fact to the holder and, if the request was presented by an Office, to that Office.

(b) If the irregularity is not remedied within three months from the date of the notification of the irregularity by the International Bureau, the request shall be considered abandoned, and the International Bureau shall notify accordingly and at the same time the holder and, if the request was presented by an Office, that Office, and refund any fees paid, after deduction of an amount corresponding to one-half of the relevant fees referred to in item 7 of the Schedule of Fees, to the party having paid those fees.

(3) *[Recording and Notification]*

(a) Where the request complies with the requirements of paragraph (1)(a), (b) and (d), the International Bureau shall record the license in the International Register, together with the information contained in the request, shall notify accordingly the Offices of the designated Contracting Parties in respect of which the license is granted and shall inform at the same time the holder and, if the request was presented by an Office, that Office.

(b) The license shall be recorded as of the date of receipt by the International Bureau of a request complying with the applicable requirements.

(4) *[Amendment or Cancellation of the Recording of a License]* Paragraphs (1) to (3) shall apply *mutatis mutandis* to a request for the amendment or cancellation of the recording of a license.

(5) *[Declaration That the Recording of a Given License Has No Effect]*

(a) The Office of a designated Contracting Party which is notified by the International Bureau of the recording of a license in respect of that Contracting Party may declare that such recording has no effect in the said Contracting Party.

(b) The declaration referred to in subparagraph (a) shall indicate

(i) the reasons for which the recording of the license has no effect,

(ii) where the declaration does not affect all the goods and services to which the license relates, those which are affected by the declaration or those which are not affected by the declaration,

(iii) the corresponding essential provisions of the law, and

(iv) whether such declaration may be subject to review or appeal.

(c) The declaration referred to in subparagraph (a) shall be sent to the International Bureau before the expiry of 18 months from the date on which the notification referred to in paragraph (3) was sent to the Office concerned.

(d) The International Bureau shall record in the International Register any declaration made in accordance with subparagraph (c) and shall notify accordingly the party (holder or Office) that presented the request to record the license. The declaration shall be recorded as of the date of receipt by the International Bureau of a communication complying with the applicable requirements.

(e) Any final decision relating to a declaration made in accordance with subparagraph (c) shall be notified to the International Bureau which shall record it in the International Register and notify accordingly the party (holder or Office) that presented the request to record the license.

(6) *[Declaration That the Recording of Licenses in the International Register Has No Effect in a Contracting Party]*

(a) The Office of a Contracting Party the law of which does not provide for the recording of trademark licenses may notify the Director General that the recording of licenses in the International Register has no effect in that Contracting Party.

(b) The Office of a Contracting Party the law of which provides for the recording of trademark licenses may, before the date on which this Rule comes into force or the date on which the said Contracting Party becomes bound by the Agreement or the Protocol, notify the Director General that the recording of licenses in the International Register has no effect in that Contracting Party. Such notification may be withdrawn at any time.[2]

NOTES

[1] Interpretative statement endorsed by the Assembly of the Madrid Union:

"Where a request to record a license does not include the indication, provided for in Rule 20*bis* (1)(c)(v), that the license is exclusive or sole, it may be considered that the license is non-exclusive."

[2] Interpretative statement endorsed by the Assembly of the Madrid Union:

"Subparagraph (a) of Rule 20*bis* (6) deals with the case of a notification by a Contracting Party whose law does not provide for the recording of trademark licenses; such a notification may be made at any time; subparagraph (b) on the other hand deals with the case of a notification by a Contracting Party whose law does provide for the recording of trademark licenses but which is unable at present to give effect to the recording of a license in the International Register; this latter notification, which may be withdrawn at any time, may only be made before this Rule has come into force or before the Contracting Party has become bound by the Agreement or the Protocol."

[5.1144]

Rule 21

Replacement of a National or Regional Registration by an International Registration

(1) *[Notification]* Where, in accordance with Article 4*bis* (2) of the Agreement or Article 4*bis* (2) of the Protocol, the Office of a designated Contracting Party has taken note in its Register, following a request made direct by the holder with that Office, that a national or a regional registration has been replaced by an international registration, that Office shall notify the International Bureau accordingly. Such notification shall indicate

(i) the number of the international registration concerned,

(ii) where the replacement concerns only one or some of the goods and services listed in the international registration, those goods and services, and

(iii) the filing date and number, the registration date and number, and, if any, the priority date of the national or regional registration which has been replaced by the international registration. The notification may also include information relating to any other rights acquired by virtue of that national or regional registration, in a form agreed between the International Bureau and the Office concerned.

(2) *[Recording]*

(a) The International Bureau shall record the indications notified under paragraph (1) in the International Register and shall inform the holder accordingly.

(b) The indications notified under paragraph (1) shall be recorded as of the date of receipt by the International Bureau of a notification complying with the applicable requirements.

[5.1145]

Rule 21bis

Other Facts Concerning Seniority Claim

(1) *[Final Refusal of Seniority Claim]* Where a claim of seniority has been recorded in the International Register in respect of the designation of a Contracting Organization, the Office of that Organization shall notify the International Bureau of any final decision refusing, in whole or in part, the validity of such claim.

(2) *[Seniority Claimed Subsequent to the International Registration]* Where the holder of an international registration designating a Contracting Organization has, under the law of such Contracting Organization, claimed directly with the Office of that Organization the seniority of one or more earlier marks registered in, or for, a Member State of that Organization, and where such claim has been accepted by the Office concerned, that Office shall notify that fact to the International Bureau. Such notification shall indicate:

(i) the number of the international registration concerned, and

(ii) the Member State or Member States in or for which the earlier mark is registered, together with the date from which the registration of that earlier mark was effective and the number of the relevant registration.

(3) *[Other Decisions Affecting Seniority Claim]* The Office of a Contracting Organization shall notify the International Bureau of any further final decision, including withdrawal and cancellation, affecting a claim to seniority which has been recorded in the International Register.

(4) *[Recording in the International Register]* The International Bureau shall record in the International Register the information notified under paragraphs (1) to (3).

[5.1146]

Rule 22

Ceasing of Effect of the Basic Application, of the Registration Resulting Therefrom, or of the Basic Registration

(1) *[Notification Relating to Ceasing of Effect of the Basic Application, of the Registration Resulting Therefrom, or of the Basic Registration]*

(a) Where Article 6(3) and (4) of the Agreement or Article 6(3) and (4) of the Protocol, or both, apply, the Office of origin shall notify the International Bureau accordingly and shall indicate

(i) the number of the international registration,

(ii) the name of the holder,

(iii) the facts and decisions affecting the basic registration, or, where the international registration concerned is based on a basic application which has not resulted in a registration, the facts and decisions affecting the basic application, or, where the international registration is based on a basic application which has resulted in a registration, the facts and decisions affecting that registration, and the effective date of those facts and decisions, and

(iv) where the said facts and decisions affect the international registration only with respect to some of the goods and services, those goods and services which are affected by the facts and decisions or those which are not affected by the facts and decisions.

(b) Where a judicial action referred to in Article 6(4) of the Agreement, or a proceeding referred to in item (i), (ii) or (iii) of Article 6(3) of the Protocol, began before the expiry of the five-year period but has not, before the expiry of that period, resulted in the final decision referred to in Article 6(4) of the Agreement, or in the final decision referred to in the second sentence of Article 6(3) of the Protocol or in the withdrawal or renunciation referred to in the third sentence of Article 6(3) of the Protocol, the Office of origin shall, where it is aware thereof and as soon as possible after the expiry of the said period, notify the International Bureau accordingly.

(c) Once the judicial action or proceeding referred to in subparagraph (b) has resulted in the final decision referred to in Article 6(4) of the Agreement, in the final decision referred to in the second sentence of Article 6(3) of the Protocol or in the withdrawal or renunciation referred to in the third sentence of Article 6(3) of the Protocol, the Office of origin shall, where it is aware thereof, promptly notify the International Bureau accordingly and shall give the indications referred to in subparagraph (a)(i) to (iv).

(2) *[Recording and Transmittal of the Notification; Cancellation of the International Registration]*

(a) The International Bureau shall record any notification referred to in paragraph (1) in the International Register and shall transmit a copy of the notification to the Offices of the designated Contracting Parties and to the holder.

(b) Where any notification referred to in paragraph (1)(a) or (c) requests cancellation of the international registration and complies with the requirements of that paragraph, the International Bureau shall cancel, to the extent applicable, the international registration in the International Register.

(c) Where the international registration has been cancelled in the International Register in accordance with subparagraph (b), the International Bureau shall notify the Offices of the designated Contracting Parties and the holder of the following:

(i) the date on which the international registration was cancelled in the International Register;

(ii) where the cancellation concerns all goods and services, that fact;

(iii) where the cancellation concerns only some of the goods and services, the goods and services indicated under paragraph (1)(a)(iv).

[5.1147]
Rule 23
Division or Merger of the Basic Applications, of the Registrations Resulting Therefrom, or of the Basic Registrations

(1) *[Notification of the Division of the Basic Application or Merger of the Basic Applications]* Where, during the five-year period referred to in Article 6(3) of the Protocol, the basic application is divided into two or more applications, or several basic applications are merged into a single application, the Office of origin shall notify the International Bureau accordingly and shall indicate

(i) the number of the international registration or, if the international registration has not yet been effected, the number of the basic application,

(ii) the name of the holder or applicant,

(iii) the number of each application resulting from the division or the number of the application resulting from the merger.

(2) *[Recording and Notification by the International Bureau]* The International Bureau shall record the notification referred to in paragraph (1) in the International Register and shall notify the Offices of the designated Contracting Parties and, at the same time, the holder.

(3) *[Division or Merger of Registrations Resulting from Basic Applications or of Basic Registrations]* Paragraphs (1) and (2) shall apply, *mutatis mutandis*, to the division of any registration or merger of any registrations which resulted from the basic application or applications during the five-year period referred to in Article 6(3) of the Protocol and to the division of the basic registration or merger of the basic registrations during the five-year period referred to in Article 6(3) of the Agreement and in Article 6(3) of the Protocol.

CHAPTER 5
SUBSEQUENT DESIGNATIONS; CHANGES

[5.1148]
Rule 24
Designation Subsequent to the International Registration

(1) *[Entitlement]*

(a) A Contracting Party may be the subject of a designation made subsequent to the international registration (hereinafter referred to as “subsequent designation” where, at the time of that designation, the holder fulfills the conditions, under Article 1(2) and 2 of the Agreement or under Article 2 of the Protocol, to be the holder of an international registration.

(b) Where the Contracting Party of the holder is bound by the Agreement, the hold designate, under the Agreement, any Contracting Party that is bound by the Agree provided that the said Contracting Parties are not both bound also by the Protocol.

(c) Where the Contracting Party of the holder is bound by the Protocol, the holder designate, under the Protocol, any Contracting Party that is bound by the Protocol, whet or not the said Contracting Parties are both also bound by the Agreement.

(2) *[Presentation; Form and Signature]*

(a) A subsequent designation shall be presented to the International Bureau by the holder or by the Office of the Contracting Party of the holder; however,

(i) [Deleted]

(ii) where any of the Contracting Parties are designated under the Agreement, the subsequent designation must be presented by the Office of the Contracting Party of the holder;

(iii) where paragraph (7) applies, the subsequent designation resulting from conversion must be presented by the Office of the Contracting Organization.

(b) The subsequent designation shall be presented on the official form in one copy. Where it is presented by the holder, it shall be signed by the holder. Where it is presented by an Office, it shall be signed by that Office and, where the Office so requires, also by the holder. Where it is presented by an Office and that Office, without requiring that the holder also sign it, allows that the holder also sign it, the holder may do so.

(3) *[Contents]*

(a) Subject to paragraph (7)(b), the subsequent designation shall contain or indicate

(i) the number of the international registration concerned,

(ii) the name and address of the holder,

(iii) the Contracting Party that is designated,

(iv) where the subsequent designation is for all the goods and services listed in the international registration concerned, that fact, or, where the subsequent designation is for only part of the goods and services listed in the international registration concerned, those goods and services,

(v) the amount of the fees being paid and the method of payment, or instructions to debit the required amount of fees to an account opened with the International Bureau, and the identification of the party effecting the payment or giving the instructions, and,

(vi) where the subsequent designation is presented by an Office, the date on which it was received by that Office.

(b) Where the subsequent designation concerns a Contracting Party that has made a notification under Rule 7(2), that subsequent designation shall also contain a declaration of intention to use the mark in the territory of that Contracting Party; the declaration shall, as required by the said Contracting Party,

(i) be signed by the holder himself and be made on a separate official form annexed to the subsequent designation, or

(ii) be included in the subsequent designation.

(c) The subsequent designation may also contain

(i) the indications and translation or translations, as the case may be, referred to in Rule 9(4)(b),

(ii) a request that the subsequent designation take effect after the recording of a change or a cancellation in respect of the international registration concerned or after the renewal of the international registration,

(iii) where the subsequent designation concerns a Contracting Organization, the indications referred to in Rule 9(5)(g)(i), which shall be on a separate official form to be annexed to the subsequent designation, and in Rule 9(5)(g)(ii).

(d) Where the international registration is based on a basic application, a subsequent designation under the Agreement shall be accompanied by a declaration, signed by the Office of origin, certifying that the said application has resulted in a registration and indicating the date and number of that registration, unless such a declaration has already been received by the International Bureau.

(4) *[Fees]* The subsequent designation shall be subject to the payment of the fees specified or referred to in item 5 of the Schedule of Fees.

(5) *[Irregularities]*

(a) If the subsequent designation does not comply with the applicable requirements, and subject to paragraph (10), the International Bureau shall notify that fact to the holder and, if the subsequent designation was presented by an Office, that Office.

(b) If the irregularity is not remedied within three months from the date of the notification of the irregularity by the International Bureau, the subsequent designation shall be considered abandoned, and the International Bureau shall notify accordingly and at the same time the holder and, if the subsequent designation was presented by an Office, that Office, and refund any fees paid, after deduction of an amount corresponding to one-half of the basic fee referred to in item 5.1 of the Schedule of Fees, to the party having paid those fees.

(c) Notwithstanding subparagraphs (a) and (b), where the requirements of paragraph (1)(b) or (c) are not complied with in respect of one or more of the designated Contracting

Parties, the subsequent designation shall be deemed not to contain the designation of those Contracting Parties, and any complementary or individual fees already paid in respect of those Contracting Parties shall be reimbursed. Where the requirements of paragraph (1)(b) or (c) are complied with in respect of none of the designated Contracting Parties, subparagraph (b) shall apply.

(6) *[Date of Subsequent Designation]*

(a) A subsequent designation presented by the holder direct to the International Bureau shall, subject to subparagraph (c)(i), bear the date of its receipt by the International Bureau.

(b) A subsequent designation presented to the International Bureau by an Office shall, subject to subparagraph (c)(i), (d) and (e), bear the date on which it was received by that Office, provided that the said designation has been received by the International Bureau within a period of two months from that date. If the subsequent designation has not been received by the International Bureau within that period, it shall, subject to subparagraph (c)(i), (d) and (e), bear the date of its receipt by the International Bureau.

(c) Where the subsequent designation does not comply with the applicable requirements and the irregularity is remedied within three months from the date of the notification referred to in paragraph (5)(a),

(i) the subsequent designation shall, where the irregularity concerns any of the requirements referred to in paragraph (3)(a)(i), (iii) and (iv) and (b)(i), bear the date on which that designation is put in order, unless the said designation was presented to the International Bureau by an Office and the irregularity is remedied within the period of two months referred to in subparagraph (b); in the latter case, the subsequent designation shall bear the date on which it was received by the said Office;

(ii) the date applicable under subparagraph (a) or (b), as the case may be, shall not be affected by an irregularity concerning requirements other than those which are referred to in paragraph (3)(a)(i), (iii) and (iv) and (b)(i).

(d) Notwithstanding subparagraphs (a), (b) and (c), where the subsequent designation contains a request made in accordance with paragraph (3)(c)(ii), it may bear a date which is later than that resulting from subparagraph (a), (b) or (c).

(e) Where a subsequent designation results from conversion in accordance with paragraph (7), that subsequent designation shall bear the date on which the designation of the Contracting Organization was recorded in the International Register.

(7) *[Subsequent Designation Resulting From Conversion]*

(a) Where the designation of a Contracting Organization has been recorded in the International Register and to the extent that such designation has been withdrawn, refused or has ceased to have effect under the law of that Organization, the holder of the international registration concerned may request the conversion of the designation of the said Contracting Organization into the designation of any Member State of that Organization which is party to the Agreement and/or the Protocol.

(b) A request for conversion under subparagraph (a) shall indicate the elements referred to in paragraph (3)(a)(i) to (iii) and (v), together with:

(i) the Contracting Organization whose designation is to be converted, and

(ii) where the subsequent designation of a Contracting State resulting from conversion is for all the goods and services listed in respect of the designation of the Contracting Organization, that fact, or, where the designation of that Contracting State is for only part of the goods and services listed in the designation of that Contracting Organization, those goods and services.

(8) *[Recording and Notification]* Where the International Bureau finds that the subsequent designation conforms to the applicable requirements, it shall record it in the International Register and shall notify accordingly the Office of the Contracting Party that has been designated in the subsequent designation and at the same time inform the holder and, if the subsequent designation was presented by an Office, that Office.

(9) *[Refusal]* Rules 16 to 18*ter* shall apply *mutatis mutandis*.

(10) *[Subsequent Designation Not Considered as Such]* If the requirements of paragraph (2)(a) are not complied with, the subsequent designation shall not be considered as such and the International Bureau shall inform the sender accordingly.

[5.1149]
Rule 25
Request for Recording

(1) *[Presentation of the Request]*

(a) A request for recording shall be presented to the International Bureau on the relevant official form, in one copy, where the request relates to any of the following:

(i) a change in the ownership of the international registration in respect of all or some of the goods and services and all or some of the designated Contracting Parties;

(ii) a limitation of the list of goods and services in respect of all or some of the designated Contracting Parties;

(iii) a renunciation in respect of some of the designated Contracting Parties for all the goods and services;

(iv) a change in the name or address of the holder or, where the holder is a legal entity, an introduction of or a change in the indications concerning the legal nature of the holder and the State and, where applicable, the territorial unit within that State under the law of which the said legal entity has been organized;

(v) cancellation of the international registration in respect of all the designated Contracting Parties for all or some of the goods and services.

(b) Subject to subparagraph (c), the request shall be presented by the holder or by the Office of the Contracting Party of the holder; however, the request for the recording of a change in ownership may be presented through the Office of the Contracting Party, or of one of the Contracting Parties, indicated in the said request in accordance with paragraph (2)(a)(iv).

(c) The request for the recording of a renunciation or a cancellation may not be presented directly by the holder where the renunciation or cancellation affects any Contracting Party whose designation is, on the date of receipt of the request by the International Bureau, governed by the Agreement.

(d) Where the request is presented by the holder, it shall be signed by the holder. Where it is presented by an Office, it shall be signed by that Office and, where the Office so requires, also by the holder. Where it is presented by an Office and that Office, without requiring that the holder also sign it, allows that the holder also sign it, the holder may do so.

(2) *[Contents of the Request]*

(a) The request for the recording of a change or the request for the recording of a cancellation shall, in addition to the requested change or cancellation, contain or indicate

(i) the number of the international registration concerned,

(ii) the name of the holder, unless the change relates to the name or address of the representative,

(iii) in the case of a change in the ownership of the international registration, the name and address, given in accordance with the Administrative Instructions, of the natural person or legal entity mentioned in the request as the new holder of the international registration (hereinafter referred to as "the transferee"),

(iv) in the case of a change in the ownership of the international registration, the Contracting Party or Parties in respect of which the transferee fulfills the conditions, under Articles 1(2) and 2 of the Agreement or under Article 2 of the Protocol, to be the holder of an international registration,

(v) in the case of a change in the ownership of the international registration, where the address of the transferee given in accordance with item (iii) is not in the territory of the Contracting Party, or of one of the Contracting Parties, given in accordance with item (iv), and unless the transferee has indicated that he is a national of a Contracting State or of a State member of a Contracting Organization, the address of the establishment, or the domicile, of the transferee in the Contracting Party, or in one of the Contracting Parties, in respect of which the transferee fulfills the conditions to be the holder of an international registration,

(vi) in the case of a change in the ownership of the international registration that does not relate to all the goods and services and to all the designated Contracting Parties, the goods and services and the designated Contracting Parties to which the change in ownership relates, and

(vii) the amount of the fees being paid and the method of payment, or instructions to debit the required amount of fees to an account opened with the International Bureau, and the identification of the party effecting the payment or giving the instructions.

(b) The request for the recording of a change in the ownership of the international registration may also contain,

(i) where the transferee is a natural person, an indication of the State of which the transferee is a national;

(ii) where the transferee is a legal entity, indications concerning the legal nature of that legal entity and the State, and, where applicable, the territorial unit within that State, under the law of which the said legal entity has been organized.

(c) The request for recording of a change or a cancellation may also contain a request that it be recorded before, or after, the recording of another change or cancellation or a subsequent designation in respect of the international registration concerned or after the renewal of the international registration.

(d) The request for the recording of a limitation shall group the limited goods and services only under the corresponding numbers of the classes of the International Classification of Goods and Services appearing in the international registration or, where the limitation affects all the goods and services in one or more of those classes, indicate the classes to be deleted.

(3) *[Request Not Admissible]* A change in the ownership of an international registration may not be recorded in respect of a given designated Contracting Party if that Contracting Party

(i) is bound by the Agreement but not by the Protocol, and the Contracting Party indicated under paragraph (2)(a)(iv) is not bound by the Agreement, or none of the Contracting Parties indicated under that paragraph is bound by the Agreement;

(ii) is bound by the Protocol but not by the Agreement, and the Contracting Party indicated under paragraph (2)(a)(iv) is not bound by the Protocol, or none of the Contracting Parties indicated under that paragraph is bound by the Protocol.

(4) *[Several Transferees]* Where the request for the recording of a change in the ownership of the international registration mentions several transferees, that change may not be recorded in respect of a given designated Contracting Party if any of the transferees does not fulfill the conditions to be holder of the international registration in respect of that Contracting Party.

[5.1150]
Rule 26
Irregularities in Requests for Recording under Rule 25

(1) *[Irregular Request]* If a request under Rule 25(1)(a) does not comply with the applicable requirements, and subject to paragraph (3), the International Bureau shall notify that fact to the holder and, if the request was made by an Office, to that Office. For the purposes of this Rule, where the request is for the recording of a limitation, the International Bureau shall only examine whether the numbers of the classes indicated in the limitation appear in the international registration concerned.

(2) *[Time Allowed to Remedy Irregularity]* The irregularity may be remedied within three months from the date of the notification of the irregularity by the International Bureau. If the irregularity is not remedied within three months from the date of the notification of the irregularity by the International Bureau, the request shall be considered abandoned, and the International Bureau shall notify accordingly and at the same time the holder and, if the request under Rule 25(1)(a) was presented by an Office, that Office, and refund any fees paid, after deduction of an amount corresponding to one-half of the relevant fees referred to in item 7 of the Schedule of Fees, to the party having paid those fees.

(3) *[Requests Not Considered as Such]* If the requirements of Rule 25(1)(b) or (c) are not complied with, the request shall not be considered as such and the International Bureau shall inform the sender accordingly.

[5.1151]
Rule 27
Recording and Notification with respect to Rule 25; Merger of International Registrations; Declaration That a Change in Ownership or a Limitation Has No Effect

(1) *[Recording and Notification]*

(a) The International Bureau shall, provided that the request referred to in Rule 25(1)(a) is in order, promptly record the indications, the change or the cancellation in the International Register, shall notify accordingly the Offices of the designated Contracting Parties in which the recording has effect or, in the case of a cancellation, the Offices of all the designated Contracting Parties, and shall inform at the same time the holder and, if the request was presented by an Office, that Office. Where the recording relates to a change in ownership, the International Bureau shall also inform the former holder in the case of a total change in ownership and the holder of the part of the international registration which has been assigned or otherwise transferred in the case of a partial change in ownership. Where the request for the recording of a cancellation was presented by the holder or by an Office other than the Office of origin during the five-year period referred to in Article 6(3) of the Agreement and Article 6(3) of the Protocol, the International Bureau shall also inform the Office of origin.

(b) The indications, the change or the cancellation shall be recorded as of the date of receipt by the International Bureau of a request complying with the applicable requirements, except that, where a request has been made in accordance with Rule 25(2)(c), it may be recorded as of a later date.

(c) Notwithstanding subparagraph (b), where continued processing has been recorded under Rule 5bis, the change or cancellation shall be recorded in the International Register as of the date of expiry of the time limit specified in Rule 26(2), except that, where a request has been made in accordance with Rule 25(2)(c), it may be recorded as of a later date.

(2) [Deleted]

(3) *[Recording of Merger of International Registrations]* Where the same natural person or legal entity has been recorded as the holder of two or more international registrations resulting from a partial change in ownership, the registrations shall be merged at the request of the said person or entity, made either direct or through the Office of the Contracting Party of the holder. The International Bureau shall notify accordingly the Offices of the designated Contracting Parties affected by the change and shall inform at the same time the holder and, if the request was presented by an Office, that Office.

(4) *[Declaration That a Change in Ownership Has No Effect]*

(a) The Office of a designated Contracting Party which is notified, by the International Bureau, of a change in ownership affecting that Contracting Party may declare that the change in ownership has no effect in the said Contracting Party. The effect of such a declaration shall be that, with respect to the said Contracting Party, the international registration concerned shall remain in the name of the transferor.

(b) The declaration referred to in subparagraph (a) shall indicate

(i) the reasons for which the change in ownership has no effect,

(ii) the corresponding essential provisions of the law, and

(iii) whether such declaration may be subject to review or appeal.

(c) The declaration referred to in subparagraph (a) shall be sent to the International Bureau before the expiry of 18 months from the date on which the notification referred to in subparagraph (a) was sent to the Office concerned.

(d) The International Bureau shall record in the International Register any declaration made in accordance with subparagraph (c) and, as the case may be, record as a separate international registration that part of the international registration which has been the subject of the said declaration, and shall notify accordingly the party (holder or Office) that presented the request for the recording of a change in ownership and the new holder.

(e) Any final decision relating to a declaration made in accordance with subparagraph (c) shall be notified to the International Bureau which shall record it in the International Register and, as the case may be, modify the International Register accordingly, and shall notify accordingly the party (holder or Office) that presented the request for the recording of a change in ownership and the new holder.

(5) *[Declaration That a Limitation Has No Effect]*

(a) The Office of a designated Contracting Party which is notified by the International Bureau of a limitation of the list of goods and services affecting that Contracting Party may declare that the limitation has no effect in the said Contracting Party. The effect of such a declaration shall be that, with respect to the said Contracting Party, the limitation shall not apply to the goods and services affected by the declaration.

(b) The declaration referred to in subparagraph (a) shall indicate

(i) the reasons for which the limitation has no effect,

(ii) where the declaration does not affect all the goods and services to which the limitation relates, those which are affected by the declaration or those which are not affected by the declaration,

(iii) the corresponding essential provisions of the law, and

(iv) whether such declaration may be subject to review or appeal.

(c) The declaration referred to in subparagraph (a) shall be sent to the International Bureau before the expiry of 18 months from the date on which the notification referred to in subparagraph (a) was sent to the Office concerned.

(d) The International Bureau shall record in the International Register any declaration made in accordance with subparagraph (c) and shall notify accordingly the party (holder or Office) that presented the request to record the limitation.

(e) Any final decision relating to a declaration made in accordance with subparagraph (c) shall be notified to the International Bureau which shall record it in the International Register and notify accordingly the party (holder or Office) that presented the request to record the limitation.

[5.1152]
Rule 28
Corrections in the International Register

(1) *[Correction]* Where the International Bureau, acting *ex officio* or at the request of the holder or of an Office, considers that there is an error concerning an international registration in the International Register, it shall modify the Register accordingly.

(2) *[Notification]* The International Bureau shall notify accordingly the holder and, at the same time, the Offices of the designated Contracting Parties in which the correction has effect. In addition, where the Office that has requested the correction is not the Office of a designated Contracting Party in which the correction has effect, the International Bureau shall also inform that Office.

(3) *[Refusal Following a Correction]* Any Office referred to in paragraph (2) shall have the right to declare in a notification of provisional refusal addressed to the International Bureau that it considers that protection cannot, or can no longer, be granted to the international registration as corrected. Article 5 of the Agreement or Article 5 of the Protocol and Rules 16 to 18*ter* shall apply *mutatis mutandis*, it being understood that the period allowed for sending the said notification shall be counted from the date of sending the notification of the correction to the Office concerned.

(4) *[Time Limit for Correction]* Notwithstanding paragraph (1), an error which is attributable to an Office and the correction of which would affect the rights deriving from the international registration may be corrected only if a request for correction is received by the International Bureau within nine months from the date of publication of the entry in the International Register which is the subject of the correction.

CHAPTER 6
RENEWALS

[5.1153]
Rule 29
Unofficial Notice of Expiry

The fact that the unofficial notice referred to in Article 7(4) of the Agreement and Article 7(3) of the Protocol is not received shall not constitute an excuse for failure to comply with any time limit under Rule 30.

[5.1154]
Rule 30
Details Concerning Renewal

(1) *[Fees]*

(a) The international registration shall be renewed upon payment, at the latest on the date on which the renewal of the international registration is due, of
(i) the basic fee,
(ii) where applicable, the supplementary fee, and,
(iii) the complementary fee or individual fee, as the case may be, for each designated Contracting Party for which no statement of refusal under Rule 18ter or invalidation, in respect of all the goods and services concerned, is recorded in the International Register, as specified or referred to in item 6 of the Schedule of Fees. However, such payment may be made within six months from the date on which the renewal of the international registration is due, provided that the surcharge specified in item 6.5 of the Schedule of Fees is paid at the same time.

(b) If any payment made for the purposes of renewal is received by the International Bureau earlier than three months before the date on which the renewal of the international registration is due, it shall be considered as having been received three months before the date on which renewal is due.

(2) *[Further Details]*

(a) Where the holder does not wish to renew the international registration in respect of a designated Contracting Party for which no statement of refusal under Rule 18ter, in respect of all the goods and services concerned, is recorded in the International Register, payment of the required fees shall be accompanied by a statement by the holder that the renewal of the international registration is not to be recorded in the International Register in respect of that Contracting Party.

(b) Where the holder wishes to renew the international registration in respect of a designated Contracting Party notwithstanding the fact that a statement of refusal under Rule 18ter is recorded in the International Register for that Contracting Party in respect of all the goods and services concerned, payment of the required fees, including the complementary fee or individual fee, as the case may be, for that Contracting Party, shall be accompanied by a statement by the holder that the renewal of the international registration is to be recorded in the International Register in respect of that Contracting Party.

(c) The international registration shall not be renewed in respect of any designated Contracting Party in respect of which an invalidation has been recorded for all goods and services under Rule 19(2) or in respect of which a renunciation has been recorded under Rule 27(1)(a). The international registration shall not be renewed in respect of any designated Contracting Party for those goods and services in respect of which an invalidation of the effects of the international registration in that Contracting Party has been recorded under Rule 19(2) or in respect of which a limitation has been recorded under Rule 27(1)(a).

(d) Where a statement under Rule 18ter(2)(ii) or (4) is recorded in the International Register, the international registration shall not be renewed in respect of the designated Contracting Party concerned for the goods and services that are not included in that statement, unless payment of the required fees is accompanied by a statement by the holder that the international registration is to be renewed also for those goods and services.

(e) The fact that the international registration is not renewed under subparagraph (d) in respect of all the goods and services concerned, shall not be considered to constitute a change for the purposes of Article 7(2) of the Agreement or Article 7(2) of the Protocol. The fact that the international registration is not renewed in respect of all of the designated Contracting Parties shall not be considered to constitute a change for the purposes of Article 7(2) of the Agreement or Article 7(2) of the Protocol.

(3) *[Insufficient Fees]*

(a) If the amount of the fees received is less than the amount of the fees required for renewal, the International Bureau shall promptly notify at the same time both the holder and the representative, if any, accordingly. The notification shall specify the missing amount.

(b) If the amount of the fees received is, on the expiry of the period of six months referred to in paragraph (1)(a), less than the amount required under paragraph (1), the International Bureau shall not, subject to subparagraph (c), record the renewal, and shall reimburse the amount received to the party having paid it and notify accordingly the holder and the representative, if any.

(c) If the notification referred to in subparagraph (a) was sent during the three months preceding the expiry of the period of six months referred to in paragraph (1)(a) and if the amount of the fees received is, on the expiry of that period, less than the amount required under paragraph (1) but is at least 70% of that amount, the International Bureau shall proceed as provided in Rule 31(1) and (3). If the amount required is not fully paid within three months from the said notification, the International Bureau shall cancel the renewal, notify accordingly the holder, the representative, if any, and the Offices which had been notified of the renewal, and reimburse the amount received to the party having paid it.

(4) *[Period for Which Renewal Fees Are Paid]* The fees required for each renewal shall be paid for ten years, irrespective of the fact that the international registration contains, in the list of designated Contracting Parties, only Contracting Parties whose designation is governed by the Agreement, only Contracting Parties whose designation is governed by the Protocol, or both Contracting Parties whose designation is governed by the Agreement and Contracting Parties whose designation is governed by the Protocol. As regards payments under the Agreement, the payment for ten years shall be considered to be a payment for an instalment of ten years.

[5.1155]
Rule 31
Recording of the Renewal; Notification and Certificate

(1) *[Recording and Effective Date of the Renewal]* Renewal shall be recorded in the International Register with the date on which renewal was due, even if the fees required for renewal are paid within the period of grace referred to in Article 7(5) of the Agreement and in Article 7(4) of the Protocol.

(2) *[Renewal Date in the Case of Subsequent Designations]* The effective date of the renewal shall be the same for all designations contained in the international registration, irrespective of the date on which such designations were recorded in the International Register.

(3) *[Notification and Certificate]* The International Bureau shall notify the Offices of the designated Contracting Parties concerned of the renewal and shall send a certificate to the holder.

(4) *[Notification in Case of Non-Renewal]*

(a) Where an international registration is not renewed, the International Bureau shall notify accordingly the holder, the representative, if any, and the Offices of all of the Contracting Parties designated in that international registration.

(b) Where an international registration is not renewed in respect of a designated Contracting Party, the International Bureau shall notify the holder, the representative, if any, and the Office of that Contracting Party accordingly.

CHAPTER 7
GAZETTE AND DATA BASE

[5.1156]
Rule 32
Gazette

(1) *[Information Concerning International Registrations]*

(a) The International Bureau shall publish in the Gazette relevant data concerning
- (i) international registrations effected under Rule 14;
- (ii) information communicated under Rule 16(1);
- (iii) provisional refusals recorded under Rule 17(4), with an indication as to whether the refusal relates to all the goods and services or only some of them but without an indication of the goods and services concerned and without the grounds for refusal, and statements and information recorded under Rules 18*bis* (2) and 18*ter* (5);
- (iv) renewals recorded under Rule 31(1);
- (v) subsequent designations recorded under Rule 24(8);
- (vi) continuation of effects of international registrations under Rule 39;
- (vii) recordings under Rule 27;
- (viii) cancellations effected under Rule 22(2) or recorded under Rule 27(1) or Rule 34(3)(d);
- (ix) corrections effected under Rule 28;
- (x) invalidations recorded under Rule 19(2);
- (xi) information recorded under Rules 20, 20*bis*, 21, 21*bis*, 22(2)(a), 23, 27(3) and (4) and 40(3);
- (xii) international registrations which have not been renewed.

(b) The reproduction of the mark shall be published as it appears in the international application. Where the applicant has made the declaration referred to in Rule 9(4)(a)(vi), the publication shall indicate that fact.

(c) Where a color reproduction of the mark is furnished under Rule 9(4)(a)(v) or (vii), the Gazette shall contain both a reproduction of the mark in black and white and the reproduction in color.

(2) *[Information Concerning Particular Requirements and Certain Declarations of Contracting Parties]* The International Bureau shall publish in the Gazette

(i) any notification made under Rule 7 or Rule 20bis(6) and any declaration made under Rule 17(5)(d) or (e);

(ii) any declarations made under Article 5(2)(b) or Article 5(2)(b) and (c), first sentence, of the Protocol;

(iii) any declarations made under Article 8(7) of the Protocol;

(iv) any notification made under Rule 34(2)(b) or (3)(a);

(v) a list of the days on which the International Bureau is not scheduled to be open to the public during the current and the following calendar year.

(3) The Gazette shall be published on the website of the World Intellectual Property Organization.

[5.1157]
Rule 33
Electronic Data Base

(1) *[Contents of Data Base]* The data which are both recorded in the International Register and published in the Gazette under Rule 32 shall be entered in an electronic data base.

(2) *[Data Concerning Pending International Applications and Subsequent Designations]* If an international application or a designation under Rule 24 is not recorded in the International Register within three working days following the receipt by the International Bureau of the international application or designation, the International Bureau shall enter in the electronic data base, notwithstanding any irregularities that may exist in the international application or designation as received, all the data contained in the international application or designation.

(3) *[Access to Electronic Data Base]* The electronic data base shall be made accessible to the Offices of the Contracting Parties and, against payment of the prescribed fee, if any, to the public, by on-line access and through other appropriate means determined by the International Bureau. The cost of accessing shall be borne by the user. Data entered under paragraph (2) shall be accompanied by a warning to the effect that the International Bureau has not yet made a decision on the international application or on the designation under Rule 24.

CHAPTER 8
FEES

[5.1158]
Rule 34
Amounts and Payment of Fees

(1) *[Amounts of Fees]* The amounts of fees due under the Agreement, the Protocol or these Regulations, other than individual fees, are specified in the Schedule of Fees that is annexed to these Regulations and forms an integral part thereof.

(2) *[Payments]*

(a) The fees indicated in the Schedule of Fees may be paid to the International Bureau by the applicant or the holder, or, where the Office of the Contracting Party of the holder accepts to collect and forward such fees, and the applicant or the holder so wishes, by that Office.

(b) Any Contracting Party whose Office accepts to collect and forward fees shall notify that fact to the Director General.

(3) *[Individual Fee Payable in Two Parts]*

(a) A Contracting Party that makes or has made a declaration under Article 8(7) of the Protocol may notify the Director General that the individual fee to be paid in respect of a designation of that Contracting Party comprises two parts, the first part to be paid at the time of filing the international application or the subsequent designation of that Contracting Party and the second part to be paid at a later date which is determined in accordance with the law of that Contracting Party.

(b) Where subparagraph (a) applies, the references in items 2, 3 and 5 of the Schedule of Fees to an individual fee shall be construed as references to the first part of the individual fee.

(c) Where subparagraph (a) applies, the Office of the designated Contracting Party concerned shall notify the International Bureau when the payment of the second part of the individual fee becomes due. The notification shall indicate

(i) the number of the international registration concerned,

(ii) the name of the holder,

(iii) the date by which the second part of the individual fee must be paid,

(iv) where the amount of the second part of the individual fee is dependent on the number of classes of goods and services for which the mark is protected in the designated Contracting Party concerned, the number of such classes.

(d) The International Bureau shall transmit the notification to the holder. Where the second part of the individual fee is paid within the applicable period, the International Bureau shall record the payment in the International Register and notify the Office of the Contracting

Party concerned accordingly. Where the second part of the individual fee is not paid w. the applicable period, the International Bureau shall notify the Office of the Contract Party concerned, cancel the international registration in the International Register w. respect to the Contracting Party concerned and notify the holder accordingly.

(4) *[Modes of Payment of Fees to the International Bureau]* Fees shall be paid to the Internationa. Bureau as specified in the Administrative Instructions.

(5) *[Indications Accompanying the Payment]* At the time of the payment of any fee to the International Bureau, an indication must be given,

(i) before international registration, of the name of the applicant, the mark concerned and the purpose of the payment;

(ii) after international registration, of the name of the holder, the number of the international registration concerned and the purpose of the payment.

(6) *[Date of Payment]*

(a) Subject to Rule 30(1)(b) and to subparagraph (b), any fee shall be considered to have been paid to the International Bureau on the day on which the International Bureau receives the required amount.

(b) Where the required amount is available in an account opened with the International Bureau and that Bureau has received instructions from the holder of the account to debit it, the fee shall be considered to have been paid to the International Bureau on the day on which the International Bureau receives an international application, a subsequent designation, an instruction to debit the second part of an individual fee, a request for the recording of a change or an instruction to renew an international registration.

(7) *[Change in the Amount of the Fees]*

(a) Where the amount of the fees payable in respect of the filing of an international application is changed between, on the one hand, the date on which the request to present the international application to the International Bureau is received, or is deemed to have been received under Rule 11(1)(a) or (c), by the Office of origin and, on the other hand, the date of the receipt of the international application by the International Bureau, the fee that was valid on the first date shall be applicable.

(b) Where a designation under Rule 24 is presented by the Office of the Contracting Party of the holder and the amount of the fees payable in respect of that designation is changed between, on the one hand, the date of receipt, by the Office, of the request by the holder to present the said designation and, on the other hand, the date on which the designation is received by the International Bureau, the fee that was valid on the first date shall be applicable.

(c) Where paragraph (3)(a) applies, the amount of the second part of the individual fee which is valid on the later date referred to in that paragraph shall be applicable.

(d) Where the amount of the fees payable in respect of the renewal of an international registration is changed between the date of payment and the due date of the renewal, the fee that was valid on the date of payment, or on the date considered to be the date of payment under Rule 30(1)(b), shall be applicable. Where the payment is made after the due date, the fee that was valid on the due date shall be applicable.

(e) Where the amount of any fee other than the fees referred to in subparagraphs (a), (b), (c) and (d) is changed, the amount valid on the date on which the fee was received by the International Bureau shall be applicable.

[5.1159]
Rule 35
Currency of Payments

(1) *[Obligation to Use Swiss Currency]* All payments due under these Regulations shall be made to the International Bureau in Swiss currency irrespective of the fact that, where the fees are paid by an Office, that Office may have collected those fees in another currency.

(2) *[Establishment of the Amount of Individual Fees in Swiss Currency]*

(a) Where a Contracting Party makes a declaration under Article 8(7)(a) of the Protocol that it wants to receive an individual fee, the amount of the individual fee indicated to the International Bureau shall be expressed in the currency used by its Office.

(b) Where the fee is indicated in the declaration referred to in subparagraph (a) in a currency other than Swiss currency, the Director General shall, after consultation with the Office of the Contracting Party concerned, establish the amount of the individual fee in Swiss currency on the basis of the official exchange rate of the United Nations.

(c) Where, for more than three consecutive months, the official exchange rate of the United Nations between the Swiss currency and the other currency in which the amount of an individual fee has been indicated by a Contracting Party is higher or lower by at least 5% than the last exchange rate applied to establish the amount of the individual fee in Swiss currency, the Office of that Contracting Party may ask the Director General to establish a new amount of the individual fee in Swiss currency according to the official exchange rate of the United Nations prevailing on the day preceding the day on which the request is made. The Director General shall proceed accordingly. The new amount shall be applicable as from a date which shall be fixed by the Director General, provided that such date is between one and two months after the date of the publication of the said amount in the Gazette.

(d) Where, for more than three consecutive months, the official exchange rate of the United Nations between the Swiss currency and the other currency in which the amount of an individual fee has been indicated by a Contracting Party is lower by at least 10% than the last exchange rate applied to establish the amount of the individual fee in Swiss currency, the Director General shall establish a new amount of the individual fee in Swiss currency according to the current official exchange rate of the United Nations. The new amount shall be applicable as from a date which shall be fixed by the Director General, provided that such date is between one and two months after the date of the publication of the said amount in the Gazette.

[5.1160]
Rule 36
Exemption From Fees

Recording of the following shall be exempt from fees:

(i) the appointment of a representative, any change concerning a representative and the cancellation of the recording of a representative,

(ii) any change concerning the telephone and telefacsimile numbers, address for correspondence, electronic mail address and any other means of communication with the applicant or holder, as specified in the Administrative Instructions,

(iii) the cancellation of the international registration,

(iv) any renunciation under Rule 25(1)(a)(iii),

(v) any limitation effected in the international application itself under Rule 9(4)(a)(xiii) or in a subsequent designation under Rule 24(3)(a)(iv),

(vi) any request by an Office under Article 6(4), first sentence, of the Agreement or Article 6(4), first sentence, of the Protocol,

(vii) the existence of a judicial proceeding or of a final decision affecting the basic application, or the registration resulting therefrom, or the basic registration,

(viii) any refusal under Rule 17, Rule 24(9) or Rule 28(3), any statement under Rules 18*bis* or 18*ter* or any declaration under Rule 20*bis* (5) or Rule 27(4) or (5),

(ix) the invalidation of the international registration,

(x) information communicated under Rule 20,

(xi) any notification under Rule 21 or Rule 23,

(xii) any correction in the International Register.

[5.1161]
Rule 37
Distribution of Supplementary Fees and Complementary Fees

(1) The coefficient referred to in Article 8(5) and (6) of the Agreement and Article 8(5) and (6) of the Protocol shall be as follows:

for Contracting Parties which examine only for absolute grounds of refusal . . . . . . two

for Contracting Parties which also examine for prior rights:

(a) following opposition by third parties . . . . three

(b) *ex officio* . . . . four

(2) Coefficient four shall also be applied to Contracting Parties which carry out *ex officio* searches for prior rights with an indication of the most significant prior rights.

[5.1162]
Rule 38
Crediting of Individual Fees to the Accounts of the Contracting Parties Concerned

Any individual fee paid to the International Bureau in respect of a Contracting Party having made a declaration under Article 8(7)(a) of the Protocol shall be credited to the account of that Contracting Party with the International Bureau within the month following the month in the course of which the recording of the international registration, subsequent designation or renewal for which that fee has been paid was effected or the payment of the second part of the individual fee was recorded.

CHAPTER 9
MISCELLANEOUS

[5.1163]
Rule 39
Continuation of Effects of International Registrations in Certain Successor States

(1) Where any State ("the successor State") whose territory was, before the independence of that State, part of the territory of a Contracting Party ("the predecessor Contracting Party") has deposited with the Director General a declaration of continuation the effect of which is that the Agreement, the Protocol, or both the Agreement and the Protocol are applied by the successor State, the effects in the successor State of any international registration with a territorial extension to the predecessor Contracting Party which is effective from a date prior to the date fixed under paragraph (2) shall be subject to

(i) the filing with the International Bureau, within six months from the date of a notice addressed for that purpose by the International Bureau to the holder of the international registration concerned, of a request that such international registration continue its effects in the successor State, and

(ii) the payment to the International Bureau, within the same time limit, of a fee of 41 Swiss francs, which shall be transferred by the International Bureau to the Office of the successor State, and of a fee of 23 Swiss francs for the benefit of the International Bureau.

(2) The date referred to in paragraph (1) shall be the date notified by the successor State to the International Bureau for the purposes of this Rule, provided that such date may not be earlier than the date of independence of the successor State.

(3) The International Bureau shall, upon receipt of the request and the fees referred to in paragraph (1), notify the Office of the successor State and make the corresponding recording in the International Register.

(4) With respect to any international registration concerning which the Office of the successor State has received a notification under paragraph (3), that Office may only refuse protection if the applicable time limit referred to in Article 5(2) of the Agreement or in Article 5(2)(a), (b) or (c) of the Protocol has not expired with respect to the territorial extension to the predecessor Contracting Party and if the notification of refusal is received by the International Bureau within that time limit.

(5) This Rule shall not apply to the Russian Federation, nor to a State which has deposited with the Director General a declaration according to which it continues the legal personality of a Contracting Party.

[5.1164]
Rule 40
Entry into Force; Transitional Provisions

(1) *[Entry into Force]* These Regulations shall enter into force on April 1, 1996, and shall, as of that date, replace the Regulations under the Agreement as in force on March 31, 1996 (hereinafter referred to as "the Regulations under the Agreement").

(2) *[General Transitional Provisions]*

(a) Notwithstanding paragraph (1),

(i) an international application the request for presentation to the International Bureau of which was received, or is deemed to have been received under Rule 11(1)(a) or (c), by the Office of origin before April 1, 1996, shall, to the extent that it conforms to the requirements of the Regulations under the Agreement, be deemed to conform to the applicable requirements for the purposes of Rule 14;

(ii) a request for the recording of a change under Rule 20 of the Regulations under the Agreement sent by the Office of origin or by another interested Office to the International Bureau before April 1, 1996, or, where such date can be identified, whose date of receipt by the Office of origin or by another interested Office for presentation to the International Bureau is earlier than April 1, 1996, shall, to the extent that it conforms to the requirements of the Regulations under the Agreement, be deemed to conform to the applicable requirements for the purposes of Rule 24(7) or to be in order for the purposes of Rule 27;

(iii) an international application, or a request for the recording of a change under Rule 20 of the Regulations under the Agreement, that, before April 1, 1996, has been the subject of any action by the International Bureau under Rules 11, 12, 13 or 21 of the Regulations under the Agreement, shall continue to be processed by the International Bureau under the said Rules; the date of the resulting international registration or recording in the International Register shall be governed by Rule 15 or 22 of the Regulations under the Agreement;

(iv) a notification of refusal or a notification of invalidation sent by the Office of a designated Contracting Party before April 1, 1996, shall, to the extent that it conforms to the requirements of the Regulations under the Agreement, be deemed to conform to the applicable requirements for the purposes of Rule 17(4) and (5) or of Rule 19(2).

(b) For the purposes of Rule 34(7), the fees valid at any date before April 1, 1996, shall be the fees prescribed by Rule 32 of the Regulations under the Agreement.

(c) Notwithstanding Rule 10(1), where, in accordance with Rule 34(7)(a), the fees paid in respect of the filing of an international application are the fees prescribed for 20 years by Rule 32 of the Regulations under the Agreement, no second instalment shall be due.

(d) Where, in accordance with Rule 34(7)(b), the fees paid in respect of a subsequent designation are the fees prescribed by Rule 32 of the Regulations under the Agreement, paragraph (3) shall not apply.

(3) *[Transitional Provisions Applicable to International Registrations for Which Fees Have Been Paid for 20 Years]*

(a) Where an international registration for which the required fees had been paid for 20 years is the subject of a subsequent designation under Rule 24 and where the current term of protection of that international registration expires more than ten years after the effective date of the subsequent designation as determined in accordance with Rule 24(6), the provisions of subparagraphs (b) and (c) shall apply.

(b) Six months before the expiry of the first period of ten years of the current term of protection of the international registration, the International Bureau shall send to the holder and his representative, if any, a notice indicating the exact date of expiry of the first period of ten years and the Contracting Parties which were the subject of subsequent designations referred to in subparagraph (a). Rule 29 shall apply *mutatis mutandis*.

(c) Payment of complementary and individual fees corresponding to the fees referred to in Rule 30(1)(iii) shall be required for the second period of ten years in respect of the subsequent designations referred to in subparagraph (a). Rule 30(1) and (3) shall apply *mutatis mutandis*.

(d) The International Bureau shall record in the International Register the fact that payment has been made to the International Bureau for the second period of ten years. The date of recording shall be the date of expiry of the first period of ten years, even if the fees required are paid within the period of grace referred to in Article 7(5) of the Agreement and in Article 7(4) of the Protocol.

(e) The International Bureau shall notify the Offices of the designated Contracting Parties concerned of the fact that payment has or has not been made for the second period of ten years and shall at the same time inform the holder.

(4) *[Transitional Provisions Concerning Languages]*

(a) Rule 6 as in force before April 1, 2004, shall continue to apply to any international application filed before that date and to any international application governed exclusively by the Agreement filed between that date and August 31, 2008, inclusively, to any communication relating thereto and to any communication, recording in the International Register or publication in the Gazette relating to the international registration resulting therefrom, unless

(i) the international registration has been the subject of a subsequent designation under the Protocol between April 1, 2004, and August 31, 2008; or

(ii) the international registration is the subject of a subsequent designation on or after September 1, 2008; and

(iii) the subsequent designation is recorded in the International Register.

(b) For the purposes of this paragraph, an international application is deemed to be filed on the date on which the request to present the international application to the International Bureau is received, or deemed to have been received under Rule 11(1)(a) or (c), by the Office of origin, and an international registration is deemed to be the subject of a subsequent designation on the date on which the subsequent designation is presented to the International Bureau, if it is presented directly by the holder, or on the date on which the request for presentation of the subsequent designation is filed with the Office of the Contracting Party of the holder if it is presented through the latter.

(5) [Deleted]

[5.1165]
Rule 41
Administrative Instructions

(1) *[Establishment of Administrative Instructions; Matters Governed by Them]*

(a) The Director General shall establish Administrative Instructions. The Director General may modify them. Before establishing or modifying the Administrative Instructions, the Director General shall consult the Offices which have a direct interest in the proposed Administrative Instructions or their proposed modification.

(b) The Administrative Instructions shall deal with matters in respect of which these Regulations expressly refer to such Instructions and with details in respect of the application of these Regulations.

(2) *[Control by the Assembly]* The Assembly may invite the Director General to modify any provision of the Administrative Instructions, and the Director General shall proceed accordingly.

(3) *[Publication and Effective Date]*

(a) The Administrative Instructions and any modification thereof shall be published in the Gazette.

(b) Each publication shall specify the date on which the published provisions become effective. The dates may be different for different provisions, provided that no provision may be declared effective prior to its publication in the Gazette.

(4) *[Conflict with the Agreement, the Protocol or These Regulations]* In the case of conflict between, on the one hand, any provision of the Administrative Instructions and, on the other hand any provision of the Agreement, the Protocol or these Regulations, the latter shall prevail.

SCHEDULE OF FEES

[5.1166]

(in force on July 1, 2017)

1. International applications governed exclusively by the Agreement

		Swiss francs
The following fees shall be payable and shall cover 10 years—		
1.1	Basic fee (Article 8(2)(a) of the Agreement)—[1]	
	1.1.1 where no reproduction of the mark is in colour	653
	1.1.2 where any reproduction of the mark is in colour	903
1.2	Supplementary fee for each class of goods and services beyond three classes (Article 8(2)(b) of the Agreement)	100
1.3	Complementary fee for the designation of each designated Contracting State (Article 8(2)(c) of the Agreement)	100

2. International applications governed exclusively by the Protocol

		Swiss francs
The following fees shall be payable and shall cover 10 years—		
2.1	Basic fee (Article 8(2)(i) of the Protocol)—[1]	
	2.1.1 where no reproduction of the mark is in colour	653
	2.1.2 where any reproduction of the mark is in colour	903
2.2	Supplementary fee for each class of goods and services beyond three classes (Article 8(2)(ii) of the Protocol), except if only Contracting Parties in respect of which individual fees (see 2.4, below) are payable are designated (see Article 8(7)(a)(i) of the Protocol)	100
2.3	Complementary fee for the designation of each designated Contracting Party (Article 8(2)(iii) of the Protocol), except if the designated Contracting Party is a Contracting Party in respect of which an individual fee is payable (see 2.4 below) (see Article 8(7)(a)(ii) of the Protocol)	100
2.4	Individual fee for the designation of each designated Contracting Party in respect of which an individual fee (rather than a complementary fee) is payable (see Article 8(7)(a) of the Protocol) except where the designated Contracting Party is a State bound (also) by the Agreement and the Office of origin is the Office of a State bound (also) by the Agreement (in respect of such a Contracting Party, a complementary fee is payable): the amount of the individual fee is fixed by each Contracting Party concerned	

3. International applications governed by both the Agreement and the Protocol

		Swiss francs
The following fees shall be payable and shall cover 10 years—		
3.1	Basic fee—[1]	
	3.1.1 where no reproduction of the mark is in colour	653
	3.1.2 where any reproduction of the mark is in colour	903
3.2	Supplementary fee for each class of goods and services beyond three classes	100
3.3	Complementary fee for the designation of each designated Contracting Party in respect of which an individual fee is not payable (see 3.4, below)	100

3.4	Individual fee for the designation of each designated Contracting Party in respect of which an individual fee is payable (see Article 8(7)(a) of the Protocol), except where the designated Contracting Party is a State bound (also) by the Agreement and the Office of origin is the Office of a State bound (also) by the Agreement (in respect of such a Contracting Party, a complementary fee is payable): the amount of the individual fee is fixed by each Contracting Party concerned	

4. Irregularities with respect to the classification of goods and services

		Swiss francs
The following fees shall be payable (Rule 12(1)(b))—		
4.1	Where the goods and services are not grouped in classes	77 plus 4 per term in excess of 20
4.2	Where the classification, as appearing in the application, of one or more terms is incorrect provided that, where the total amount due under this item in respect of an international application is less than 150 Swiss francs, no fees shall be payable	20 plus 4 per incorrectly classified term

5. Designation subsequent to international registration

		Swiss francs
The following fees shall be payable and shall cover the period between the effective date of the designation and the expiry of the then current term of the international registration—		
5.1	Basic fee	300
5.2	Complementary fee for each designated Contracting Party indicated in the same request where an individual fee is not payable in respect of such designated Contracting Party (see 5.3, below)	100
5.3	Individual fee for the designation of each designated Contracting Party in respect of which an individual fee (rather than a complementary fee) is payable (see Article 8(7)(a) of the Protocol) except where the designated Contracting Party is a State bound (also) by the Agreement and the Office of the Contracting Party of the holder is the Office of a State bound (also) by the Agreement (in respect of such a Contracting Party, a complementary fee is payable): the amount of the individual fee is fixed by each Contracting Party concerned	

6. Renewal

		Swiss francs
The following fees shall be payable and shall cover 10 years—		
6.1	Basic fee	653
6.2	Supplementary fee, except if the renewal is made only for designated Contracting Parties in respect of which individual fees are payable (see 6.4, below)	100
6.3	Complementary fee for each designated Contracting Party in respect of which an individual fee is not payable (see 6.4, below)	100
6.4	Individual fcc for the designation of each designated Contracting Party in respect of which an individual fee (rather than a complementary fee) is payable (see Article 8(7)(a) of the Protocol) except where the designated Contracting Party is a State bound (also) by the Agreement and the Office of the Contracting Party of the holder is the Office of a State bound (also) by the Agreement (in respect of such a Contracting Party, a complementary fee is payable): the amount of the individual fee is fixed by each Contracting Party concerned	
6.5	Surcharge for the use of the period of grace	50% of the amount of the fee payable under item 6.1

7. Miscellaneous recordings

		Swiss francs
7.1	Total transfer of an international registration	177
7.2	Partial transfer (for some of the goods and services or for some of the Contracting Parties) of an international registration	177
7.3	Limitation requested by the holder subsequent to international registration, provided that, if the limitation affects more than one Contracting Party, it is the same for all	177
7.4	Change in the name and/or address of the holder and/or, where the holder is a legal entity, introduction of or change in the indications concerning the legal nature of the holder and the State and, where applicable, the territorial unit within that State under the law of which the said legal entity has been organized for one or more international registrations for which the same recording or change is requested in the same form	150
7.5	Recording of a licence in respect of an international registration or amendment of the recording of a licence	177
7.6	Request for a continued processing under Rule 5bis(1)	200

8. Information concerning international registrations

		Swiss francs
8.1	Establishing a certified extract from the International Register consisting of an analysis of the situation of an international registration (detailed certified extract)—	
	Up to three pages	155
	for each page after the third	10
8.2	Establishing a certified extract from the International Register consisting of a copy of all publications, and of all notifications of refusal, made with respect to an international registration (simple certified extract)—	
	up to three pages	77
	for each page after the third	2
8.3	A single attestation or information in writing—	
	for a single international registration	77
	for each additional international registration if the same information is requested in the same request	10
8.4	Reprint or photocopy of the publication of an international registration—	
	per page	5

9. Special services

The International Bureau is authorised to collect a fee, whose amount it shall itself fix, for operations to be performed urgently and for services not covered by this Schedule of Fees.

NOTES

1 For international applications filed by applicants whose country of origin is a Least Developed Country, in accordance with the list established by the United Nations, the basic fee is reduced to 10% of the prescribed amount (rounded to the nearest full figure). In such case, the basic fee will amount to 65 Swiss francs (where no reproduction of the mark is in colour) or to 90 Swiss francs (where any reproduction of the mark is in colour).

TRADEMARK LAW TREATY

(adopted at Geneva on October 27, 1994)

NOTES

The original source for this Treaty is the World Intellectual Property Organisation (WIPO). Entry into force: see Article 20(2).

[5.1167]
Article 1
Abbreviated Expressions

For the purposes of this Treaty, unless expressly stated otherwise—

(i) "Office" means the agency entrusted by a Contracting Party with the registration of marks;
(ii) "registration" means the registration of a mark by an Office;
(iii) "application" means an application for registration;
(iv) references to a "person" shall be construed as references to both a natural person and a legal entity;
(v) "holder" means the person whom the register of marks shows as the holder of the registration;
(vi) "register of marks" means the collection of data maintained by an Office, which includes the contents of all registrations and all data recorded in respect of all registrations, irrespective of the medium in which such data are stored;
(vii) "Paris Convention" means the Paris Convention for the Protection of Industrial Property, signed at Paris on March 20, 1883, as revised and amended;
(viii) "Nice Classification" means the classification established by the Nice Agreement Concerning the International Classification of Goods and Services for the Purposes of the Registration of Marks, signed at Nice on June 15, 1957, as revised and amended;
(ix) "Contracting Party" means any State or intergovernmental organisation party to this Treaty;
(x) references to an "instrument of ratification" shall be construed as including references to instruments of acceptance and approval;
(xi) "Organisation" means the World Intellectual Property Organisation;
(xii) "Director General" means the Director General of the Organisation;
(xiii) "Regulations" means the Regulations under this Treaty that are referred to in Article 17.

[5.1168]
Article 2
Marks to Which the Treaty Applies

(1) [*Nature of Marks*]
(a) This Treaty shall apply to marks consisting of visible signs, provided that only those Contracting Parties which accept for registration three-dimensional marks shall be obliged to apply this Treaty to such marks.
(b) This Treaty shall not apply to hologram marks and to marks not consisting of visible signs, in particular, sound marks and olfactory marks.

(2) [*Kinds of Marks*]
(a) This Treaty shall apply to marks relating to goods (trademarks) or services (service marks) or both goods and services.
(b) This Treaty shall not apply to collective marks, certification marks and guarantee marks.

[5.1169]
Article 3
Application

(1) [*Indications or Elements Contained in or Accompanying an Application; Fee*]
(a) Any Contracting Party may require that an application contain some or all of the following indications or elements—
(i) a request for registration;
(ii) the name and address of the applicant;
(iii) the name of a State of which the applicant is a national if he is the national of any State, the name of a State in which the applicant has his domicile, if any, and the name of a State in which the applicant has a real and effective industrial or commercial establishment, if any;
(iv) where the applicant is a legal entity, the legal nature of that legal entity and the State, and, where applicable, the territorial unit within that State, under the law of which the said legal entity has been organised;
(v) where the applicant has a representative, the name and address of that representative;
(vi) where an address for service is required under Article 4(2)(b), such address;
(vii) where the applicant wishes to take advantage of the priority of an earlier application, a declaration claiming the priority of that earlier application, together with indications and evidence in support of the declaration of priority that may be required pursuant to Article 4 of the Paris Convention;
(viii) where the applicant wishes to take advantage of any protection resulting from the display of goods and/or services in an exhibition, a declaration to that effect, together with indications in support of that declaration, as required by the law of the Contracting Party;

(ix) where the Office of the Contracting Party uses characters (letters and numbers) that it considers as being standard and where the applicant wishes that the mark be registered and published in standard characters, a statement to that effect;
(x) where the applicant wishes to claim colour as a distinctive feature of the mark, a statement to that effect as well as the name or names of the colour or colours claimed and an indication, in respect of each colour, of the principal parts of the mark which are in that colour;
(xi) where the mark is a three-dimensional mark, a statement to that effect;
(xii) one or more reproductions of the mark;
(xiii) a transliteration of the mark or of certain parts of the mark;
(xiv) a translation of the mark or of certain parts of the mark;
(xv) the names of the goods and/or services for which the registration is sought, grouped according to the classes of the Nice Classification, each group preceded by the number of the class of that Classification to which that group of goods or services belongs and presented in the order of the classes of the said Classification;
(xvi) a signature by the person specified in paragraph (4);
(xvii) a declaration of intention to use the mark, as required by the law of the Contracting Party.

(b) The applicant may file, instead of or in addition to the declaration of intention to use the mark referred to in subparagraph (a)(xvii), a declaration of actual use of the mark and evidence to that effect, as required by the law of the Contracting Party.
(c) Any Contracting Party may require that, in respect of the application, fees be paid to the Office.

(2) [*Presentation*] As regards the requirements concerning the presentation of the application, no Contracting Party shall refuse the application—
(i) where the application is presented in writing on paper, if it is presented, subject to paragraph (3), on a form corresponding to the application Form provided for in the Regulations,
(ii) where the Contracting Party allows the transmittal of communications to the Office by telefacsimile and the application is so transmitted, if the paper copy resulting from such transmittal corresponds, subject to paragraph (3), to the application Form referred to in item (i).

(3) [*Language*] Any Contracting Party may require that the application be in the language, or in one of the languages, admitted by the Office. Where the Office admits more than one language, the applicant may be required to comply with any other language requirement applicable with respect to the Office, provided that the application may not be required to be in more than one language.

(4) [*Signature*]
(a) The signature referred to in paragraph (1)(a)(xvi) may be the signature of the applicant or the signature of his representative.
(b) Notwithstanding subparagraph (a), any Contracting Party may require that the declarations referred to in paragraph (1)(a)(xvii) and (b) be signed by the applicant himself even if he has a representative.

(5) [*Single Application for Goods and/or Services in Several Classes*] One and the same application may relate to several goods and/or services, irrespective of whether they belong to one class or to several classes of the Nice Classification.

(6) [*Actual Use*] Any Contracting Party may require that, where a declaration of intention to use has been filed under paragraph (1)(a)(xvii), the applicant furnish to the Office within a time limit fixed in its law, subject to the minimum time limit prescribed in the Regulations, evidence of the actual use of the mark, as required by the said law.

(7) [*Prohibition of Other Requirements*] No Contracting Party may demand that requirements other than those referred to in paragraphs (1) to (4) and (6) be complied with in respect of the application. In particular, the following may not be required in respect of the application throughout its pendency—
(i) the furnishing of any certificate of, or extract from, a register of commerce;
(ii) an indication of the applicant's carrying on of an industrial or commercial activity, as well as the furnishing of evidence to that effect;
(iii) an indication of the applicant's carrying on of an activity corresponding to the goods and/or services listed in the application, as well as the furnishing of evidence to that effect;
(iv) the furnishing of evidence to the effect that the mark has been registered in the register of marks of another Contracting Party or of a State party to the Paris Convention which is not a Contracting Party, except where the applicant claims the application of Article 6 *quinquies* of the Paris Convention.

(8) [*Evidence*] Any Contracting Party may require that evidence be furnished to the Office in the course of the examination of the application where the Office may reasonably doubt the veracity of any indication or element contained in the application.

[5.1170]
Article 4
Representation; Address for Service

(1) [*Representatives Admitted to Practice*] Any Contracting Party may require that any person appointed as representative for the purposes of any procedure before the Office be a representative admitted to practice before the Office.

(2) [*Mandatory Representation; Address for Service*]

(a) Any Contracting Party may require that, for the purposes of any procedure before the Office, any person who has neither a domicile nor a real and effective industrial or commercial establishment on its territory be represented by a representative.

(b) Any Contracting Party may, to the extent that it does not require representation in accordance with subparagraph (a), require that, for the purposes of any procedure before the Office, any person who has neither a domicile nor a real and effective industrial or commercial establishment on its territory have an address for service on that territory.

(3) [*Power of Attorney*]

(a) Whenever a Contracting Party allows or requires an applicant, a holder or any other interested person to be represented by a representative before the Office, it may require that the representative be appointed in a separate communication (hereinafter referred to as "power of attorney") indicating the name of, and signed by, the applicant, the holder or the other person, as the case may be.

(b) The power of attorney may relate to one or more applications and/or registrations identified in the power of attorney or, subject to any exception indicated by the appointing person, to all existing and future applications and/or registrations of that person.

(c) The power of attorney may limit the powers of the representative to certain acts. Any Contracting Party may require that any power of attorney under which the representative has the right to withdraw an application or to surrender a registration contain an express indication to that effect.

(d) Where a communication is submitted to the Office by a person who refers to himself in the communication as a representative but where the Office is, at the time of the receipt of the communication, not in possession of the required power of attorney, the Contracting Party may require that the power of attorney be submitted to the Office within the time limit fixed by the Contracting Party, subject to the minimum time limit prescribed in the Regulations. Any Contracting Party may provide that, where the power of attorney has not been submitted to the Office within the time limit fixed by the Contracting Party, the communication by the said person shall have no effect.

(e) As regards the requirements concerning the presentation and contents of the power of attorney, no Contracting Party shall refuse the effects of the power of attorney—

(i) where the power of attorney is presented in writing on paper, if it is presented, subject to paragraph (4), on a form corresponding to the power of attorney Form provided for in the Regulations,

(ii) where the Contracting Party allows the transmittal of communications to the Office by telefacsimile and the power of attorney is so transmitted, if the paper copy resulting from such transmittal corresponds, subject to paragraph (4), to the power of attorney Form referred to in item (i).

(4) [*Language*] Any Contracting Party may require that the power of attorney be in the language, or in one of the languages, admitted by the Office.

(5) [*Reference to Power of Attorney*] Any Contracting Party may require that any communication made to the Office by a representative for the purposes of a procedure before the Office contain a reference to the power of attorney on the basis of which the representative acts.

(6) [*Prohibition of Other Requirements*] No Contracting Party may demand that requirements other than those referred to in paragraphs (3) to (5) be complied with in respect of the matters dealt with in those paragraphs.

(7) [*Evidence*] Any Contracting Party may require that evidence be furnished to the Office where the Office may reasonably doubt the veracity of any indication contained in any communication referred to in paragraphs (2) to (5).

[5.1171]
Article 5
Filing Date

(1) [*Permitted Requirements*]

(a) Subject to subparagraph (b) and paragraph (2), a Contracting Party shall accord as the filing date of an application the date on which the Office received the following indications and elements in the language required under Article 3(3)—

(i) an express or implicit indication that the registration of a mark is sought;

(ii) indications allowing the identity of the applicant to be established;

(iii) indications sufficient to contact the applicant or his representative if any, by mail;

(iv) a sufficiently clear reproduction of the mark whose registration is sought;

(v) the list of the goods and/or services for which the registration is sought;

(vi) where Article 3(1)(a)(xvii) or (b) applies, the declaration referred to in Article 3(1)(a)(xvii) or the declaration and evidence referred to in Article 3(1)(b), respectively, as required by the law of the Contracting Party, those declarations being, if so required by the said law, signed by the applicant himself even if he has a representative.

(b) Any Contracting Party may accord as the filing date of the application the date on which the Office received only some, rather than all, of the indications and elements referred to in subparagraph (a) or received them in a language other than the language required under Article 3(3).

(2) [*Permitted Additional Requirement*]

(a) A Contracting Party may provide that no filing date shall be accorded until the required fees are paid.

(b) A Contracting Party may apply the requirement referred to in sub-paragraph (a) only if it applied such requirement at the time of becoming party to this Treaty.

(3) [*Corrections and Time Limits*] The modalities of, and time limits for, corrections under paragraphs (1) and (2) shall be fixed in the Regulations.

(4) [*Prohibition of Other Requirements*] No Contracting Party may demand that requirements other than those referred to in paragraphs (1) and (2) be complied with in respect of the filing date.

[5.1172]
Article 6
Single Registration for Goods and/or Services in Several Classes

Where goods and/or services belonging to several classes of the Nice Classification have been included in one and the same application, such an application shall result in one and the same registration.

[5.1173]
Article 7
Division of Application and Registration

(1) [*Division of Application*]

(a) Any application listing several goods and/or services (hereinafter referred to as "initial application") may—

(i) at least until the decision by the Office on the registration of the mark,

(ii) during any opposition proceedings against the decision of the Office to register the mark,

(iii) during any appeal proceedings against the decision on the registration of the mark,

be divided by the applicant or at his request into two or more applications (hereinafter referred to as "divisional applications") by distributing among the latter the goods and/or services listed in the initial application. The divisional applications shall preserve the filing date of the initial application and the benefit of the right of priority, if any.

(b) Any Contracting Party shall, subject to subparagraph (a), be free to establish requirements for the division of an application, including the payment of fees.

(2) [*Division of Registration*] Paragraph (1) shall apply, *mutatis mutandis,* with respect to a division of a registration. Such a division shall be permitted—

(i) during any proceedings in which the validity of the registration is challenged before the Office by a third party,

(ii) during any appeal proceedings against a decision taken by the Office during the former proceedings.

provided that a Contracting Party may exclude the possibility of the division of registrations if its law allows third parties to oppose the registration of a mark before the mark is registered.

[5.1174]
Article 8
Signature

(1) [*Communication on Paper*] Where a communication to the Office of a Contracting Party is on paper and a signature is required, that Contracting Party—

(i) shall, subject to item (iii), accept a handwritten signature,

(ii) shall be free to allow, instead of a handwritten signature, the use of other forms of signature, such as a printed or stamped signature, or the use of a seal,

(iii) may, where the natural person who signs the communication is its national and such person's address is in its territory, require that a seal be used instead of a handwritten signature,

(iv) may, where a seal is used, require that the seal be accompanied by an indication in letters of the name of the natural person whose seal is used.

(2) [*Communication by Telefacsimile*]

(a) Where a Contracting Party allows the transmittal of communications to the Office by telefacsimile, it shall consider the communication signed if, on the printout produced by the telefacsimile, the reproduction of the signature, or the reproduction of the seal together with, where required under paragraph (1)(iv), the indication in letters of the name of the natural person whose seal is used, appears.

(b) The Contracting Party referred to in subparagraph (a) may require that the paper whose reproduction was transmitted by telefacsimile be filed with the Office within a certain period, subject to the minimum period prescribed in the Regulations.

(3) [*Communication by Electronic Means*] Where a Contracting Party allows the transmittal of communications to the Office by electronic means, it shall consider the communication signed if the latter identifies the sender of the communication by electronic means as prescribed by the Contracting Party.

(4) [*Prohibition of Requirement of Certification*] No Contracting Party may require the attestation, notarisation, authentication, legalisation or other certification of any signature or other means of self-identification referred to in the preceding paragraphs, except, if the law of the Contracting Party so provides, where the signature concerns the surrender of a registration.

[5.1175]
Article 9
Classification of Goods and/or Services

(1) [*Indications of Goods and/or Services*] Each registration and any publication effected by an Office which concerns an application or registration and which indicates goods and/or services shall indicate the goods and/or services by their names, grouped according to the classes of the Nice Classification, and each group shall be preceded by the number of the class of that Classification to which that group of goods or services belongs and shall be presented in the order of the classes of the said Classification.

(2) [*Goods or Services in the Same Class or in Different Classes*]

(a) Goods or services may not be considered as being similar to each other on the ground that, in any registration or publication by the Office, they appear in the same class of the Nice Classification.

(b) Goods or services may not be considered as being dissimilar from each other on the ground that, in any registration or publication by the Office, they appear in different classes of the Nice Classification.

[5.1176]
Article 10
Changes in Names or Addresses

(1) [*Changes in the Name or Address of the Holder*]

(a) Where there is no change in the person of the holder but there is a change in his name and/or address, each Contracting Party shall accept that a request for the recordal of the change by the Office in its register of marks be made in a communication signed by the holder or his representative and indicating the registration number of the registration concerned and the change to be recorded. As regards the requirements concerning the presentation of the request, no Contracting Party shall refuse the request—

(i) where the request is presented in writing on paper, if it is presented, subject to subparagraph (c), on a form corresponding to the request Form provided for in the Regulations,

(ii) where the Contracting Party allows the transmittal of communications to the Office by telefacsimile and the request is so transmitted, if the paper copy resulting from such transmittal corresponds, subject to subparagraph (c), to the request Form referred to in item (i).

(b) Any Contracting Party may require that the request indicate—

(i) the name and address of the holder;

(ii) where the holder has a representative, the name and address of that representative;

(iii) where the holder has an address for service, such address.

(c) Any Contracting Party may require that the request be in the language, or in one of the languages, admitted by the Office.

(d) Any Contracting Party may require that, in respect of the request, a fee be paid to the Office.

(e) A single request shall be sufficient even where the change relates to more than one registration, provided that the registration numbers of all registrations concerned are indicated in the request.

(2) [*Change in the Name or Address of the Applicant*] Paragraph (1) shall apply, *mutatis mutandis,* where the change concerns an application or applications, or both an application or applications and a registration or registrations, provided that, where the application number of any application concerned has not yet been issued or is not known to the applicant or his representative, the request otherwise identifies that application as prescribed in the Regulations.

(3) [*Change in the Name or Address of the Representative or in the Address for Service*] Paragraph (1) shall apply, *mutatis mutandis,* to any change in the name or address of the representative, if any, and to any change relating to the address for service, if any.

(4) [*Prohibition of Other Requirements*] No Contracting Party may demand that requirements other than those referred to in paragraphs (1) to (3) be complied with in respect of the request referred to in this Article. In particular, the furnishing of any certificate concerning the change may not be required.

(5) [*Evidence*] Any Contracting Party may require that evidence be furnished to the Office where the Office may reasonably doubt the veracity of any indication contained in the request.

[5.1177]
Article 11
Change in Ownership

(1)

(a) [*Change in the Ownership of a Registration*] Where there is a change in the person of the holder, each Contracting Party shall accept that a request for the recordal of the change by the Office in its register of marks be made in a communication signed by the holder or his representative, or by the person who acquired the ownership (hereinafter referred to as "new owner") or his representative, and indicating the registration number of the registration concerned and the change to be recorded. As regards the requirements concerning the presentation of the request, no Contracting Party shall refuse the request—

(i) where the request is presented in writing on paper, if it is presented, subject to paragraph (2)(a), on a form corresponding to the request Form provided for in the Regulations,

(ii) where the Contracting Party allows the transmittal of communications to the Office by telefacsimile and the request is so transmitted, if the paper copy resulting from such transmittal corresponds, subject to paragraph (2)(a), to the request Form referred to in item (i).

(b) Where the change in ownership results from a contract, any Contracting Party may require that the request indicate that fact and be accompanied, at the option of the requesting party, by one of the following—

(i) a copy of the contract, which copy may be required to be certified, by a notary public or any other competent public authority, as being in conformity with the original contract;

(ii) an extract of the contract showing the change in ownership, which extract may be required to be certified, by a notary public or any other competent public authority, as being a true extract of the contract;

(iii) an uncertified certificate of transfer drawn up in the form and with the content as prescribed in the Regulations and signed by both the holder and the new owner;

(iv) an uncertified transfer document drawn up in the form and with the content as prescribed in the Regulations and signed by both the holder and the new owner.

(c) Where the change in ownership results from a merger, any Contracting Party may require that the request indicate that fact and be accompanied by a copy of a document, which document originates from the competent authority and evidences the merger, such as a copy of an extract from a register of commerce, and that that copy be certified by the authority which issued the document or by a notary public or any other competent public authority, as being in conformity with the original document.

(d) Where there is a change in the person of one or more but not all of several co-holders and such change in ownership results from a contract or a merger, any Contracting Party may require that any co-holder in respect of which there is no change in ownership give his express consent to the change in ownership in a document signed by him.

(e) Where the change in ownership does not result from a contract or a merger but from another ground, for example, from operation of law or a court decision, any Contracting Party may require that the request indicate that fact and be accompanied by a copy of a document evidencing the change and that that copy be certified as being in conformity with the original document by the authority which issued the document or by a notary public or any other competent public authority.

(f) Any Contracting Party may require that the request indicate—

(i) the name and address of the holder;

(ii) the name and address of the new owner;

(iii) the name of a State of which the new owner is a national if he is the national of any State, the name of a State in which the new owner has his domicile, if any, and the name of a State in which the new owner has a real and effective industrial or commercial establishment, if any;

(iv) where the new owner is a legal entity, the legal nature of that legal entity and the State, and, where applicable, the territorial unit within that State, under the law of which the said legal entity has been organised;

(v) where the holder has a representative, the name and address of that representative;

(vi) where the holder has an address for service, such address;

(vii) where the new owner has a representative, the name and address of that representative;

(viii) where the new owner is required to have an address for service under Article 4(2)(b), such address.

(g) Any Contracting Party may require that, in respect of the request, a fee be paid to the Office.

(h) A single request shall be sufficient even where the change relates to more than one registration, provided that the holder and the new owner are the same for each registration and that the registration numbers of all registrations concerned are indicated in the request.

(i) Where the change of ownership does not affect all the goods and/or services listed in the holder's registration, and the applicable law allows the recording of such change, the Office shall create a separate registration referring to the goods and/or services in respect of which the ownership has changed.

(2) [*Language; Translation*]

(a) Any Contracting Party may require that the request, the certificate of transfer or the transfer document referred to in paragraph (1) be in the language, or in one of the languages, admitted by the Office.

(b) Any Contracting Party may require that, if the documents referred to in paragraph (1)(b)(i) and (ii), (c) and (e) are not in the language, or in one of the languages, admitted by the Office, the request be accompanied by a translation or a certified translation of the required document in the language, or in one of the languages, admitted by the Office.

(3) [*Change in the Ownership of an Application*] Paragraphs (1) and (2) shall apply, *mutatis mutandis,* where the change in ownership concerns an application or applications, or both an application or applications and a registration or registrations, provided that, where the application number of any application concerned has not yet been issued or is not known to the applicant or his representative, the request otherwise identifies that application as prescribed in the Regulations.

(4) [*Prohibition of Other Requirements*] No Contracting Party may demand that requirements other than those referred to in paragraphs (1) to (3) be complied with in respect of the request referred to in this Article. In particular, the following may not be required—

(i) subject to paragraph (1)(c), the furnishing of any certificate of, or extract from, a register of commerce;

(ii) an indication of the new owner's carrying on of an industrial or commercial activity, as well as the furnishing of evidence to that effect;

(iii) an indication of the new owner's carrying on of an activity corresponding to the goods and/or services affected by the change in ownership, as well as the furnishing of evidence to either effect;

(iv) an indication that the holder transferred, entirely or in part, his business or the relevant goodwill to the new owner, as well as the furnishing of evidence to either effect.

(5) [*Evidence*] Any Contracting Party may require that evidence, or further evidence where paragraph (1)(c) or (e) applies, be furnished to the Office where that Office may reasonably doubt the veracity of any indication contained in the request or in any document referred to in the present Article.

[5.1178]
Article 12
Correction of a Mistake

(1) [*Correction of a Mistake in Respect of a Registration*]

(a) Each Contracting Party shall accept that the request for the correction of a mistake which was made in the application or other request communicated to the Office and which mistake is reflected in its register of marks and/or any publication by the Office be made in a communication signed by the holder or his representative and indicating the registration number of the registration concerned, the mistake to be corrected and the correction to be entered. As regards the requirements concerning the presentation of the request, no Contracting Party shall refuse the request—

(i) where the request is presented in writing on paper, if it is presented, subject to subparagraph (c), on a form corresponding to the request Form provided for in the Regulations,

(ii) where the Contracting Party allows the transmittal of communications to the Office by telefacsimile and the request is so transmitted, if the paper copy resulting from such transmittal corresponds, subject to subparagraph (c), to the request Form referred to in item (i).

(b) Any Contracting Party may require that the request indicate—

(i) the name and address of the holder;

(ii) where the holder has a representative, the name and address of that representative;

(iii) where the holder has an address for service, such address.

(c) Any Contracting Party may require that the request be in the language, or in one of the languages, admitted by the Office.

(d) Any Contracting Party may require that, in respect of the request, a fee be paid to the Office.

(e) A single request shall be sufficient even where the correction relates to more than one registration of the same person, provided that the mistake and the requested correction are the same for each registration and that the registration numbers of all registrations concerned are indicated in the request.

(2) [*Correction of a Mistake in Respect of an Application*] Paragraph (1) shall apply, *mutatis mutandis,* where the mistake concerns an application or applications, or both an application or applications and a registration or registrations, provided that, where the application number of any application concerned has not yet been issued or is not known to the applicant or his representative, the request otherwise identifies that application as prescribed in the Regulations.

(3) [*Prohibition of Other Requirements*] No Contracting Party may demand that requirements other than those referred to in paragraphs (1) and (2) be complied with in respect of the request referred to in this Article.

(4) [*Evidence*] Any Contracting Party may require that evidence be furnished to the Office where the Office may reasonably doubt that the alleged mistake is in fact a mistake.

(5) [*Mistakes Made by the Office*] The Office of a Contracting Party shall correct its own mistakes, *ex officio* or upon request, for no fee.

(6) [*Uncorrectable Mistakes*] No Contracting Party shall be obliged to apply paragraphs (1), (2) and (5) to any mistake which cannot be corrected under its law.

[5.1179]
Article 13
Duration and Renewal of Registration

(1) [*Indications or Elements Contained in or Accompanying a Request for Renewal; Fee*]

(a) Any Contracting Party may require that the renewal of a registration be subject to the filing of a request and that such request contain some or all of the following indications—

(i) an indication that renewal is sought;

(ii) the name and address of the holder;

(iii) the registration number of the registration concerned;

(iv) at the option of the Contracting Party, the filing date of the application which resulted in the registration concerned or the registration date of the registration concerned;

(v) where the holder has a representative, the name and address of that representative;

(vi) where the holder has an address for service, such address;

(vii) where the Contracting Party allows the renewal of a registration to be made for some only of the goods and/or services which are recorded in the register of marks and such a renewal is requested, the names of the recorded goods and/or services for which the renewal is requested or the names of the recorded goods and/or services for which the renewal is not requested, grouped according to the classes of the Nice Classification, each group preceded by the number of the class of that Classification to which that group of goods or services belongs and presented in the order of the classes of the said Classification;

(viii) where a Contracting Party allows a request for renewal to be filed by a person other than the holder or his representative and the request is filed by such a person, the name and address of that person;

(ix) a signature by the holder or his representative or, where item (viii) applies, a signature by the person referred to in that item.

(b) Any Contracting Party may require that, in respect of the request for renewal, a fee be paid to the Office. Once the fee has been paid in respect of the initial period of the registration or of any renewal period, no further payment may be required for the maintenance of the registration in respect of that period. Fees associated with the furnishing of a declaration and/or evidence of use shall not be regarded, for the purposes of this subparagraph, as payments required for the maintenance of the registration and shall not be affected by this subparagraph.

(c) Any Contracting Party may require that the request for renewal be presented, and the corresponding fee referred to in subparagraph (b) be paid, to the Office within the period fixed by the law of the Contracting Party, subject to the minimum periods prescribed in the Regulations.

(2) [*Presentation*] As regards the requirements concerning the presentation of the request for renewal, no Contracting Party shall refuse the request—

(i) where the request is presented in writing on paper, if it is presented, subject to paragraph (3), on a form corresponding to the request Form provided for in the Regulations,

(ii) where the Contracting Party allows the transmittal of communications to the Office by telefacsimile and the request is so transmitted, if the paper copy resulting from such transmittal corresponds, subject to paragraph (3), to the request Form referred to in item (i).

(3) [*Language*] Any Contracting Party may require that the request for renewal be in the language, or in one of the languages, admitted by the Office.

(4) [*Prohibition of Other Requirements*] No Contracting Party may demand that requirements other than those referred to in paragraphs (1) to (3) be complied with in respect of the request for renewal. In particular, the following may not be required—

(i) any reproduction or other identification of the mark;
(ii) the furnishing of evidence to the effect that the mark has been registered, or that its registration has been renewed, in the register of marks of any other Contracting Party;
(iii) the furnishing of a declaration and/or evidence concerning use of the mark.

(5) [*Evidence*] Any Contracting Party may require that evidence be furnished to the Office in the course of the examination of the request for renewal where the Office may reasonably doubt the veracity of any indication or element contained in the request for renewal.

(6) [*Prohibition of Substantive Examination*] No Office of a Contracting Party may, for the purposes of effecting the renewal, examine the registration as to substance.

(7) [*Duration*] The duration of the initial period of the registration, and the duration of each renewal period, shall be 10 years.

[5.1180]
Article 14
Observations in Case of Intended Refusal
An application or a request under Articles 10 to 13 may not be refused totally or in part by an Office without giving the applicant or the requesting party, as the case may be, an opportunity to make observations on the intended refusal within a reasonable time limit.

[5.1181]
Article 15
Obligation to Comply with the Paris Convention
Any Contracting Party shall comply with the provisions of the Paris Convention which concern marks.

[5.1182]
Article 16
Service Marks
Any Contracting Party shall register service marks and apply to such marks the provisions of the Paris Convention which concern trademarks.

[5.1183]
Article 17
Regulations
(1) [*Content*]
(a) The Regulations annexed to this Treaty provide rules concerning—
(i) matters which this Treaty expressly provides to be "prescribed in the Regulations";
(ii) any details useful in the implementation of the provisions of this Treaty;
(iii) any administrative requirements, matters or procedures.
(b) The Regulations also contain Model International Forms.

(2) [*Conflict Between the Treaty and the Regulations*] In the case of conflict between the provisions of this Treaty and those of the Regulations, the former shall prevail.

NOTES
For the Regulations under the Trademark Law Treaty see **[5.746]**. The Model International Forms are not reproduced.

[5.1184]
Article 18
Revision; Protocols
(1) [*Revision*] This Treaty may be revised by a diplomatic conference.

(2) [*Protocols*] For the purposes of further developing the harmonisation of laws on marks, protocols may be adopted by a diplomatic conference insofar as those protocols do not contravene the provisions of this Treaty.

[5.1185]
Article 19
Becoming Party to the Treaty
(1) [*Eligibility*] The following entities may sign and, subject to paragraphs (2) and (3) and Article 20(1) and (3), become party to this Treaty—
(i) any State member of the Organisation in respect of which marks may be registered with its own Office;
(ii) any intergovernmental organisation which maintains an Office in which marks may be registered with effect in the territory in which the constituting treaty of the intergovernmental organisation applies, in all its member States or in those of its member States which are designated for such purpose in the relevant application, provided that all the member States of the intergovernmental organisation are members of the Organisation;
(iii) any State member of the Organisation in respect of which marks may be registered only through the Office of another specified State that is a member of the Organisation;

(iv) any State member of the Organisation in respect of which marks may be registered only through the Office maintained by an intergovernmental organisation of which that State is a member;
(v) any State member of the Organisation in respect of which marks may be registered only through an Office common to a group of States members of the Organisation.

(2) [*Ratification or Accession*] Any entity referred to in paragraph (1) may deposit—
(i) an instrument of ratification, if it has signed this Treaty,
(ii) an instrument of accession, if it has not signed this Treaty.

(3) [*Effective Date of Deposit*]
(a) Subject to subparagraph (b), the effective date of the deposit of an instrument of ratification or accession shall be—
(i) in the case of a State referred to in paragraph (1)(i), the date on which the instrument of that State is deposited;
(ii) in the case of an intergovernmental organisation, the date on which the instrument of that intergovernmental organisation is deposited;
(iii) in the case of a State referred to in paragraph (1)(iii), the date on which the following condition is fulfilled: the instrument of that State has been deposited and the instrument of the other, specified State has been deposited;
(iv) in the case of a State referred to in paragraph (1)(iv), the date applicable under (ii), above;
(v) in the case of a State member of a group of States referred to in paragraph (1)(v), the date on which the instruments of all the States members of the group have been deposited.
(b) Any instrument of ratification or accession (referred to in this subparagraph as "instrument") of a State may be accompanied by a declaration making it a condition to its being considered as deposited that the instrument of one other State or one intergovernmental organisation, or the instruments of two other States, or the instruments of one other State and one intergovernmental organisation, specified by name and eligible to become party to this Treaty, is or are also deposited. The instrument containing such a declaration shall be considered to have been deposited on the day on which the condition indicated in the declaration is fulfilled. However, when the deposit of any instrument specified in the declaration is, itself, accompanied by a declaration of the said kind, that instrument shall be considered as deposited on the day on which the condition specified in the latter declaration is fulfilled.
(c) Any declaration made under paragraph (b) may be withdrawn, in its entirety or in part, at any time. Any such withdrawal shall become effective on the date on which the notification of withdrawal is received by the Director General.

[5.1186]
Article 20
Effective Date of Ratifications and Accessions

(1) [*Instruments to Be Taken Into Consideration*] For the purposes of this Article, only instruments of ratification or accession that are deposited by entities referred to in Article 19(1) and that have an effective date according to Article 19(3) shall be taken into consideration.

(2) [*Entry Into Force of the Treat* y] This Treaty shall enter into force three months after five States have deposited their instruments of ratification or accession.

(3) [*Entry Into Force of Ratifications and Accessions Subsequent to the Entry Into Force of the Treaty*] Any entity not covered by paragraph (2) shall become bound by this Treaty three months after the date on which it has deposited its instrument of ratification or accession.

[5.1187]
Article 21
Reservations

(1) [*Special Kinds of Marks*] Any State or intergovernmental organisation may declare through a reservation that, notwithstanding Article 2(1)(a) and (2)(a), any of the provisions of Articles 3(1) and (2), 5, 7, 11 and 13 shall not apply to associated marks, defensive marks or derivative marks. Such reservation shall specify those of the aforementioned provisions to which the reservation relates.

(2) [*Modalities*] Any reservation under paragraph (1) shall be made in a declaration accompanying the instrument of ratification of, or accession to, this Treaty of the State or intergovernmental organisation making the reservation.

(3) [*Withdrawal*] Any reservation under paragraph (1) may be withdrawn at any time.

(4) [*Prohibition of Other Reservations*] No reservation to this Treaty other than the reservation allowed under paragraph (1) shall be permitted.

[5.1188]
Article 22
Transitional Provisions

(1) [*Single Application for Goods and Services in Several Classes; Division of Application*]

(a) Any State or intergovernmental organisation may declare that, notwithstanding Article 3(5), an application may be filed with the Office only in respect of goods or services which belong to one class of the Nice Classification.
(b) Any State or intergovernmental organisation may declare that, notwithstanding Article 6, where goods and/or services belonging to several classes of the Nice Classification have been included in one and the same application, such application shall result in two or more registrations in the register of marks, provided that each and every such registration shall bear a reference to all other such registrations resulting from the said application.
(c) Any State or intergovernmental organisation that has made a declaration under subparagraph (a) may declare that, notwithstanding Article 7(1), no application may be divided.

(2) [*Single Power of Attorney for More Than One Application and/or Registration*] Any State or intergovernmental organisation may declare that, notwithstanding Article 4(3)(b), a power of attorney may only relate to one application or one registration.

(3) [*Prohibition of Requirement of Certification of Signature of Power of Attorney and of Signature of Application*] Any State or intergovernmental organisation may declare that, notwithstanding Article 8(4), the signature of a power of attorney or the signature by the applicant of an application may be required to be the subject of an attestation, notarisation, authentication, legalisation or other certification.

(4) [*Single Request for More Than One Application and/or Registration in Respect of a Change in Name and/or Address, a Change in Ownership or a Correction of a Mistake*] Any State or intergovernmental organisation may declare that, notwithstanding Article 10(1)(e), (2) and (3), Article 11(1)(h) and (3) and Article 12(1)(e) and (2), a request for the recordal of a change in name and/or address, a request for the recordal of a change in ownership and a request for the correction of a mistake may only relate to one application or one registration.

(5) [*Furnishing, on the Occasion of Renewal, of Declaration and/or Evidence Concerning Use*] Any State or intergovernmental organisation may declare that, notwithstanding Article 13(4)(iii), it will require, on the occasion of renewal, the furnishing of a declaration and/or of evidence concerning use of the mark.

(6) [*Substantive Examination on the Occasion of Renewal*] Any State or intergovernmental organisation may declare that, notwithstanding Article 13(6), the Office may, on the occasion of the first renewal of a registration covering services, examine such registration as to substance, provided that such examination shall be limited to the elimination of multiple registrations based on applications filed during a period of six months following the entry into force of the law of such State or organisation that introduced, before the entry into force of this Treaty, the possibility of registering service marks.

(7) [*Common Provisions*]
(a) A State or an intergovernmental organisation may make a declaration under paragraphs (1) to (6) only if, at the time of depositing its instrument of ratification of, or accession to, this Treaty, the continued application of its law would, without such a declaration, be contrary to the relevant provisions of this Treaty.
(b) Any declaration under paragraphs (1) to (6) shall accompany the instrument of ratification of, or accession to, this Treaty of the State or intergovernmental organisation making the declaration.
(c) Any declaration made under paragraphs (1) to (6) may be withdrawn at any time.

(8) [*Loss of Effect of Declaration*]
(a) Subject to subparagraph (c), any declaration made under paragraphs (1) to (6) by a State regarded as a developing country in conformity with the established practice of the General Assembly of the United Nations, or by an intergovernmental organisation each member of which is such a State, shall lose its effect at the end of a period of eight years from the date of entry into force of this Treaty.
(b) Subject to subparagraph (c), any declaration made under paragraphs (1) to (6) by a State other than a State referred to in subparagraph (a), or by an intergovernmental organisation other than an intergovernmental organisation referred to in subparagraph (a), shall lose its effect at the end of a period of six years from the date of entry into force of this Treaty.
(c) Where a declaration made under paragraphs (1) to (6) has not been withdrawn under paragraph (7)(c), or has not lost its effect under subparagraph (a) or (b), before October 28, 2004, it shall lose its effect on October 28, 2004.

(9) [*Becoming Party to the Treaty*] Until December 31, 1999, any State which, on the date of the adoption of this Treaty, is a member of the International (Paris) Union for the Protection of Industrial Property without being a member of the Organisation may, notwithstanding Article 19(1)(i), become a party to this Treaty if marks may be registered with its own Office.

[5.1189]
Article 23
Denunciation of the Treaty

(1) [*Notification*] Any Contracting Party may denounce this Treaty by notification addressed to the Director General.

(2) [*Effective Date*] Denunciation shall take effect one year from the date on which the Director General has received the notification. It shall not affect the application of this Treaty to any application pending or any mark registered in respect of the denouncing Contracting Party at the time of the expiration of the said one-year period, provided that the denouncing Contracting Party may, after the expiration of the said one-year period, discontinue applying this Treaty to any registration as from the date on which that registration is due for renewal.

[5.1190]
Article 24
Languages of the Treaty; Signature

(1) [*Original Texts; Official Texts*]

(a) This Treaty shall be signed in a single original in the English, Arabic, Chinese, French, Russian and Spanish languages, all texts being equally authentic.

(b) At the request of a Contracting Party, an official text in a language not referred to in subparagraph (a) that is an official language of that Contracting Party shall be established by the Director General after consultation with the said Contracting Party and any other interested Contracting Party.

(2) [*Time Limit for Signature*] This Treaty shall remain open for signature at the headquarters of the Organisation for one year after its adoption.

[5.1191]
Article 25
Depositary

The Director General shall be the depositary of this Treaty.

REGULATIONS UNDER THE TRADEMARK LAW TREATY

(adopted at Geneva on October 27, 1994)

NOTES

The original source for these Regulations is the World Intellectual Property Organisation (WIPO).

[5.1192]
Rule 1
Abbreviated Expressions

(1) [*"Treaty"; "Article"*]

(a) In these Regulations, the word "Treaty" means the Trademark Law Treaty.

(b) In these Regulations, the word "Article" refers to the specified Article of the Treaty.

(2) [*Abbreviated Expressions Defined in the Treaty*] The abbreviated expressions defined in Article 1 for the purposes of the Treaty shall have the same meaning for the purposes of the Regulations.

[5.1193]
Rule 2
Manner of Indicating Names and Addresses

(1) [*Names*]

(a) Where the name of a person is to be indicated, any Contracting Party may require—

(i) where the person is a natural person, that the name to be indicated be the family or principal name and the given or secondary name or names of that person or that the name to be indicated be, at that person's option, the name or names customarily used by the said person;

(ii) where the person is a legal entity, that the name to be indicated be the full official designation of the legal entity.

(b) Where the name of a representative which is a firm or partnership is to be indicated, any Contracting Party shall accept as indication of the name the indication that the firm or partnership customarily uses.

(2) [*Addresses*]

(a) Where the address of a person is to be indicated, any Contracting Party may require that the address be indicated in such a way as to satisfy the customary requirements for prompt postal delivery at the indicated address and, in any case, consist of all the relevant administrative units up to, and including, the house or building number, if any.

(b) Where a communication to the Office of a Contracting Party is in the name of two or more persons with different addresses, that Contracting Party may require that such communication indicate a single address as the address for correspondence.

(c) The indication of an address may contain a telephone number and a telefacsimile number and, for the purposes of correspondence, an address different from the address indicated under subparagraph (a).

(d) Subparagraphs (a) and (c) shall apply, *mutatis mutandis,* to addresses for service.

(3) [*Script to Be Used*] Any Contracting Party may require that any indication referred to in paragraphs (1) and (2) be in the script used by the Office.

[5.1194]
Rule 3
Details Concerning the Application

(1) [*Standard Characters*] Where, pursuant to Article 3(1)(a)(ix), the application contains a statement to the effect that the applicant wishes that the mark be registered and published in the standard characters used by the Office of the Contracting Party, the Office shall register and publish that mark in such standard characters.

(2) [*Number of Reproductions*]

(a) Where the application does not contain a statement to the effect that the applicant wishes to claim colour as a distinctive feature of the mark, a Contracting Party may not require more than—

(i) five reproductions of the mark in black and white where the application may not, under the law of that Contracting Party, or does not contain a statement to the effect that the applicant wishes the mark to be registered and published in the standard characters used by the Office of the said Contracting Party;

(ii) one reproduction of the mark in black and white where the application contains a statement to the effect that the applicant wishes the mark to be registered and published in the standard characters used by the Office of that Contracting Party.

(b) Where the application contains a statement to the effect that the applicant wishes to claim colour as a distinctive feature of the mark, a Contracting Party may not require more than five reproductions of the mark in black and white and five reproductions of the mark in colour.

(3) [*Reproduction of a Three-Dimensional Mark*]

(a) Where, pursuant to Article 3(1)(a)(xi), the application contains a statement to the effect that the mark is a three-dimensional mark, the reproduction of the mark shall consist of a two-dimensional graphic or photographic reproduction.

(b) The reproduction furnished under subparagraph (a) may, at the option of the applicant, consist of one single view of the mark or of several different views of the mark.

(c) Where the Office considers that the reproduction of the mark furnished by the applicant under subparagraph (a) does not sufficiently show the particulars of the three-dimensional mark, it may invite the applicant to furnish, within a reasonable time limit fixed in the invitation, up to six different views of the mark and/or a description by words of that mark.

(d) Where the Office considers that the different views and/or the description of the mark referred to in subparagraph (c) still do not sufficiently show the particulars of the three-dimensional mark, it may invite the applicant to furnish, within a reasonable time limit fixed in the invitation, a specimen of the mark.

(e) Paragraph (2)(a)(i) and (b) shall apply *mutatis mutandis*.

(4) [*Transliteration of the Mark*] For the purposes of Article 3(1)(a)(xiii), where the mark consists of or contains matter in script other than the script used by the Office or numbers expressed in numerals other than numerals used by the Office, a transliteration of such matter in the script and numerals used by the Office may be required.

(5) [*Translation of the Mark*] For the purposes of Article 3(1)(a)(xiv), where the mark consists of or contains a word or words in a language other than the language, or one of the languages, admitted by the Office, a translation of that word or those words into that language or one of those languages may be required.

(6) [*Time Limit for Furnishing Evidence of Actual Use of the Mark*] The time limit referred to in Article 3(6) shall not be shorter than six months counted from the date of allowance of the application by the Office of the Contracting Party where that application was filed. The applicant or holder shall have the right to an extension of that time limit, subject to the conditions provided for by the law of that Contracting Party, by periods of at least six months each, up to a total extension of at least two years and a half.

[5.1195]
Rule 4
Details Concerning Representation

The time limit referred to in Article 4(3)(d) shall be counted from the date of receipt of the communication referred to in that Article by the Office of the Contracting Party concerned and shall not be less than one month where the address of the person on whose behalf the communication is made is on the territory of that Contracting Party and not less than two months where such an address is outside the territory of that Contracting Party.

[5.1196]
Rule 5
Details Concerning the Filing Date

(1) [*Procedure in Case of Non-Compliance with Requirements*] If the application does not, at the time of its receipt by the Office, comply with any of the applicable requirements of Article 5(1)(a) or (2)(a), the Office shall promptly invite the applicant to comply with such requirements within a time limit indicated in the invitation, which time limit shall be at least one month from the date of the invitation where the applicant's address is on the territory of the Contracting Party concerned and at least two months where the applicant's address is outside the territory of the Contracting Party concerned. Compliance with the invitation may be subject to the payment of a special fee. Even if the Office fails to send the said invitation, the said requirements remain unaffected.

(2) [*Filing Date in Case of Correction*] If, within the time limit indicated in the invitation, the applicant complies with the invitation referred to in paragraph (1) and pays any required special fee, the filing date shall be the date on which all the required indications and elements referred to in Article 5(1)(a) have been received by the Office and, where applicable, the required fee referred to in Article 5(2)(a) has been paid to the Office. Otherwise, the application shall be treated as if it had not been filed.

(3) [*Date of Receipt*] Each Contracting Party shall be free to determine the circumstances in which the receipt of a document or the payment of a fee shall be deemed to constitute receipt by or payment to the Office in cases in which the document was actually received by or payment was actually made to—

(i) a branch or sub-office of the Office,
(ii) a national Office on behalf of the Office of the Contracting Party, where the Contracting Party is an intergovernmental organisation referred to in Article 19(1)(ii),
(iii) an official postal service,
(iv) a delivery service, other than an official postal service, specified by the Contracting Party.

(4) [*Use of Telefacsimile*] Where a Contracting Party allows the filing of an application by telefacsimile and the application is filed by telefacsimile, the date of receipt of the telefacsimile by the Office of that Contracting Party shall constitute the date of receipt of the application, provided that the said Contracting Party may require that the original of such application reach the Office within a time limit which shall be at least one month from the day on which the telefacsimile was received by the said Office.

[5.1197]
Rule 6
Details Concerning the Signature

(1) [*Legal Entities*] Where a communication is signed on behalf of a legal entity, any Contracting Party may require that the signature, or the seal, of the natural person who signs or whose seal is used be accompanied by an indication in letters of the family or principal name and the given or secondary name or names of that person or, at the option of that person, of the name or names customarily used by the said person.

(2) [*Communication by Telefacsimile*] The period referred to in Article 8(2)(b) shall not be less than one month from the date of the receipt of a transmittal by telefacsimile.

(3) [*Date*] Any Contracting Party may require that a signature or seal be accompanied by an indication of the date on which the signing or sealing was effected. Where that indication is required but is not supplied, the date on which the signing or sealing is deemed to have been effected shall be the date on which the communication bearing the signature or seal was received by the Office or, if the Contracting Party so allows, a date earlier than the latter date.

[5.1198]
Rule 7
Manner of Identification of an Application Without Its Application Number

(1) [*Manner of Identification*] Where it is required that an application be identified by its application number but where such a number has not yet been issued or is not known to the applicant or his representative, that application shall be considered identified if the following is supplied—

(i) the provisional application number, if any, given by the Office, or
(ii) a copy of the application, or
(iii) a reproduction of the mark, accompanied by an indication of the date on which, to the best knowledge of the applicant or the representative, the application was received by the Office and an identification number given to the application by the applicant or the representative.

(2) [*Prohibition of Other Requirements*] No Contracting Party may demand that requirements other than those referred to in paragraph (1) be complied with in order for an application to be identified where its application number has not yet been issued or is not known to the applicant or his representative.

[5.1199]
Rule 8
Details Concerning Duration and Renewal

For the purposes of Article 13(1)(c), the period during which the request for renewal may be presented and the renewal fee may be paid shall start at least six months before the date on which the renewal is due and shall end at the earliest six months after that date. If the request for renewal is presented and/or the renewal fees are paid after the date on which the renewal is due, any Contracting Party may subject the renewal to the payment of a surcharge.

.EU ALTERNATIVE DISPUTE RESOLUTION RULES (THE "ADR RULES")

NOTES

The ADR Rules can be found at www.adr.eu.

Alternative dispute resolution proceedings for the resolution of disputes under Paragraph 22(1)(a) and (b) of Commission Regulation (EC) No 874/2004 of 28 April 2004 laying down public policy rules concerning the implementation and functions of the.eu Top Level Domain and principles governing registration shall be governed by these *ADR Rules* and the *Supplemental ADR Rules* of the *Provider* administering the *ADR Proceedings*, as far as available and posted on its web site. The interpretation and application of these ADR Rules will be done in the light of the EU legal framework which will prevail in case of conflict.

A GENERAL

1 DEFINITIONS

[5.1200]

In these ADR Rules:

ADR means an alternative dispute resolution.

ADR Proceeding is a proceeding initiated in accordance with the Procedural Rules.

Complaint means the document including all annexes prepared by the *Complainant* to initiate a cause of action under the *ADR Proceeding*.

Complainant means the *Party* initiating a *Complaint* concerning a.eu domain name registration or requesting to change the language of the *ADR Proceeding*.

Date of Commencement of an ADR Proceeding means a date on which all the following conditions are fulfilled:

(a) an administratively compliant *Complaint* has been properly filed with the *Provider*; and
(b) the appropriate fee for the *ADR Proceeding* is paid.

Domain Name Holder means a legal or natural person who holds an activated registration of a.eu domain name.

European Union Regulations refer to Regulation (EC) No 733/2002 of the European Parliament and of the Council of 22 April 2002 on the implementation of the.eu Top Level Domain[1] and Commission Regulation (EC) No 874/2004 of 28 April 2004 laying down public policy rules concerning the implementation and functions of the.eu Top Level Domain and principles governing registration[2] and any further regulation that would replace, amend or complete such rules and principles.

Registry means the entity entrusted by the European Commission with the organization, administration and management of the.eu designated in accordance with the procedure established in Article 3 of Regulation (EC) No 733/2002.

Mutual Jurisdiction means a court jurisdiction at the location of either

(a) the principal office of the *Registrar* (provided the *Respondent* has submitted in its *Registration Agreement* to that jurisdiction for court adjudication of disputes concerning or arising from the use of the domain name, and provided that the court thus designated is located within the European Union) or
(b) the *Respondent's* address as shown for the registration of the domain name in the *Registry*'s Whois database at the time the *Complaint* is submitted to the *Provider* or as received from *the Registry* by the *Complainant* if such information is not available in *the Registry*'s Whois database or
(c) the principal office of *the Registry* in case of *ADR Proceeding* s against *the Registry*.[3]

Panel means an *ADR* panel appointed by a *Provider* to decide a *Complaint* concerning a.eu domain name registration.

Panelist means an individual appointed by a *Provider* to be a member of a *Panel*.

Party means a *Complainant* or a *Respondent*; **Parties** means both of them.

Procedural Rules means these *ADR Rules*, *Provider's Supplemental ADR Rules* and *European Union Regulations*. In case of conflict between any of these rules, the European Union Regulations take precedence.

Provider means a dispute resolution service provider selected by *the Registry*.

Registrar means an entity with which the *Respondent* has registered a domain name that is the subject of a *Complaint*.

Registration Agreement means the agreement between a *Registrar* and a domain name holder.

Registration Policy means the.eu Domain Name Registration Policy issued by *the Registry*.

Respondent means the holder of a.eu domain name registration (or the holder's legal heirs or *the Registry* in case of an *ADR Proceeding* against *the Registry*) in respect of which a *Complaint* and/or a request to change the language of the *ADR Proceeding* is initiated.

Response means the document including all annexes filed by the *Respondent* responding to the allegations set forth in the *Complaint* in accordance with these *ADR Rules* and the *Supplemental ADR Rules*.

Sunrise Appeal Period means a 40 day period during which a *Complaint* against the *Registry's* decision to register a domain name within the Sunrise period can be filed as specified in the *Sunrise Rules*.

Sunrise Rules means the.eu *Registration Policy* and the Terms and Conditions for Domain Name Applications made during the Phased Registration Period issued by *the Registry.*

Supplemental ADR Rules means the rules adopted by the *Provider* administering *ADR Proceeding* s to supplement these *ADR Rules*.

Terms and Conditions mean the.eu Domain Name Registration Terms and Conditions issued by *the Registry.*

Time of Filing means a point in time when the following conditions are fulfilled:

(a) a *Complaint* or a request to change the language of the *ADR Proceeding* has been properly filed with the *Provider*; and

(b) the appropriate fee for the *ADR Proceeding* is received by the *Provider*.

Working days mean all days falling between Monday and Friday other than those which are public holidays in the country or the state where the Provider or either of the *Parties*, as the case may be, is subject to an obligation to adhere to a period of time as specified under these *ADR Rules*.

2 COMMUNICATIONS AND PERIODS OF TIME

(a) When forwarding a *Complaint* to the *Respondent*, it shall be the *Provider's* responsibility to employ reasonably available means calculated to achieve actual notice to the *Respondent*.

(b) The *Provider* shall discharge its obligation to achieve actual notice by (i) sending the *Complaint* or a notice with information how to access the *Complaint* (*eg* for the purposes of an on-line platform operated by the *Provider*) to the *Respondent* employing the means stipulated in (c) below to the address which the *Registry* has communicated to the *Provider* for the registered domain name holder or to *the Registry*'s seat in case of a *Complaint* against the *Registry's* decision; and (ii) in case the Respondent does not confirm receiving the electronic communication made pursuant to (i) above within five (5) days from sending the communication, by forwarding the above mentioned notice with information how to access the *Complaint* by registered postal or courier service, postage pre-paid and return receipt requested, to the address(es) specified in (i) above.

(c) Unless specified otherwise in these *ADR Rules*, any written communication to the *Complainant,* the *Respondent* or the *Provider* provided for under these *ADR Rules*, shall be made by the preferred means stated by the *Complainant* or *Respondent*, respectively, or in the absence of such specification:

  (1) electronically via the Internet, provided a record of its transmission is available; or
  (2) by telecopy or facsimile transmission, with a confirmation of transmission; or
  (3) by registered postal or courier service, postage pre-paid and return receipt requested.

(d) Either *Party* may update its contact details by notifying the *Provider* and *the Registry*.

(e) Except as otherwise provided in these *ADR Rules*, all communications provided for under these *ADR Rules* shall be deemed to have been received, in accordance with this provision:

  (1) if via the Internet, on the date that the communication was transmitted, provided that the date of transmission is verifiable; or
  (2) if delivered by facsimile transmission, on the date shown on the confirmation of transmission; or
  (3) if by registered postal or courier service, on the date marked on the receipt, or, if it is not possible to deliver the communication in this way, on the expiry of twelve (12) *days* from the handing over of the communication to a postal or courier service provider.

(f) It shall be the responsibility of the sender to retain records of the fact and circumstances of delivery, which shall be available for inspection by the *Provider* and for reporting purposes.

(g) A system log of data messages of the *Provider* shall be considered as valid records in the absence of any evidence of malfunction of the *Provider's* system.

(h) Except as otherwise provided in these *ADR Rules*, all time periods calculated under these ADR Rules begin on the earliest date that the communication is deemed to have been made in accordance with Paragraph A2(e).

(i) At the request of a *Party* filed before the expiration of the relevant period(s) of time, the *Provider* and, after its appointment, the *Panel*, may – in its sole discretion—extend the periods of time laid down in these *ADR Rules* which are applicable to the *Parties* in exceptional circumstances or upon agreement by both *Parties*. The *Provider* and, after its appointment, the *Panel*, shall decide on any such limited period of extension.

(j) No *Party* or anyone acting on its behalf may engage in any unilateral communication with the *Panel*. All communications between a *Party*, on the one hand, and the *Panel* or the *Provider* on the other shall be made to a case administrator appointed by the *Provider* by the means and in the manner prescribed in the *Provider's Supplemental ADR Rules*.

(k) Any communication in an *ADR Proceeding* initiated by

(1) a *Panel* to a *Party* shall be made through the *Provider*;

(2) a *Party* shall be made through the *Provider*;

(3) the *Provider* to any *Party* or by a *Party* on after the *Date of Commencement of an ADR Proceeding* shall be copied by the Provider to the other *Party* and the *Panel*.

(l) In the event a *Party* sending a communication receives notification of non-delivery of the communication, the *Party* shall promptly notify the *Provider* of the circumstances of the notification.

3 LANGUAGE OF PROCEEDINGS

(a) The language of the *ADR Proceeding* s must be one of the official EU languages. Unless otherwise agreed by the *Parties*, or specified otherwise in the *Registration Agreement*, the language of the *ADR Proceeding* shall be the language of the *Registration Agreement* for the disputed domain name. In the absence of an agreement between the *Parties*, the *Panel* may in its sole discretion, having regard to the circumstances of the *ADR Proceeding*, decide on the written request of a Complainant, filed before initiating a *Complaint*, that the language of the *ADR Proceeding* will be different than the language of the *Registration Agreement* for the disputed domain name.

(b) The procedure related to the request of a change of the language of the *ADR Proceeding* shall be as follows:

(1) The request shall be submitted to the *Provider* and shall:

(i) specify the information under Paragraphs B1 (b)(2), (b)(3), (b)(5), (b)(6), and (b)(7) of the *ADR Rules*;

(ii) specify the requested change of the language of *ADR Proceeding*;

(iii) specify the circumstances that would justify such a change of the language of an *ADR Proceeding*;

(iv) conclude with the statement under B1(b)(15) of the *ADR Rules*.

(2) The *Provider* will acknowledge receiving the request from the *Complainant*, subject to the receipt of the fees due hereunder, and, if applicable, shall notify *the Registry* of the *Time of Filing* in accordance with B1(e) of the *ADR Rules*, having the same consequences as under B1(e) of the *ADR Rules*.

(3) The *Provider* shall notify the *Respondent* of the request to change the language of the *ADR Proceeding* within five (5) *days* following receipt of the fees payable hereunder.

(4) The *Respondent* shall have a right to submit a response to the *Provider* within twelve (12) *days* of the date of notification of the request to change the language of the *ADR Proceeding*.

(5) The *Provider* will acknowledge receiving the response from the *Respondent* and will appoint a single *Panel* to decide the request. Paragraph B5 applies accordingly.

(6) The *Panel* shall issue a decision whether or not to allow the requested change of the language of the *ADR Proceeding* within twelve (12) *days* from the date of its appointment. The *Panel's* decision shall be final and not subject to appeal. The decision shall be communicated to the *Parties* without delay.

(7) In case the *Complainant* files the *Complaint* within thirty (30) *Working days* from receiving the decision under (b)(6) above, the *Time of Filing* of the request to change the language of the *ADR Proceeding* shall apply with respect to the *Complaint*, provided the appropriate fee is paid.

(c) All documents including communications made as part of the *ADR Proceeding* shall be made in the language of the *ADR Proceeding* or in different requested language if the *Complainant* proves in his submission that the *Respondent* has adequate knowledge of such different language. Notwithstanding anything mentioned above, the *Panel* may request the translation of any documents submitted in other languages than the *ADR Proceeding*. The *Panel* may disregard documents submitted in other languages than the language of the *ADR Proceeding* without requesting their translation. Any communication by the *Provider* which, from its content, cannot be regarded as amounting to procedural documents (such as cover letters with which the *Provider* sends procedural documents or automatic system notifications generated by the *Provider*'s application) shall be made in the language of the *ADR Proceeding* or in English.

(d) The *Provider* and, after its constitution, the *Panel* by itself or upon the request of a *Party*, may order that any documents submitted in languages other than the language of the *ADR Proceeding* be accompanied by a translation in whole or in part into the language of the *ADR Proceeding*.

4 SETTLEMENT OR OTHER GROUNDS FOR TERMINATION

(a) The *ADR Proceeding* will be understood to be concluded once the *Panel* has received confirmation from both *Parties* that an agreement has been entered into by the *Parties* concerning the object of the dispute.

(b) If the *Parties* wish to negotiate a settlement, the *Complainant* may request that the *Provider* or, after its constitution, the *Panel* suspend the *ADR Proceeding* for a limited period. The suspension period may be extended by the *Panel* upon the *Complainant*'s request. Any such suspension shall be without prejudice to the obligation of the *Panel* to forward its decision on the *Complaint* to the *Provider* within the time period specified in Paragraph B12(b) below. Resumption of the ADR Proceeding shall take place automatically upon receipt of a request thereto from either the *Respondent* or the *Complainant* or upon the expiration of such limited and specified time period.

(c) The *Panel* shall terminate the *ADR Proceeding* if it becomes aware that the dispute that is the subject of the *Complaint* has been finally decided by a court of competent jurisdiction or an alternative dispute resolution body.

(d) The *Panel* shall suspend *ADR Proceeding* (s) pursuant to Paragraphs B1(f), B2(e) and B3(d) below.

5 COURT PROCEEDINGS

The conduct of the *ADR Proceeding* shall not be prejudiced by any court proceeding, subject to Paragraph A4(c) above.

6 FEES

(a) The *Complainant* shall pay to the *Provider* an initial fixed fee, in accordance with the *Supplemental ADR Rules*. Until the *Provider* has received this initial fee, it is not obliged to take any action on the *Complaint*. If the *Provider* has not received the fee within ten (10) days of the date of notification of unpaid fees, the *Complaint* shall be deemed withdrawn and the *ADR Proceeding* cancelled.

(b) A *Complainant* initiating a request to change the language of the *ADR Proceeding* under Section A3 above or initiating a challenge to the withdrawal of Complaint due to its administrative deficiency under Paragraph B2(c) below shall pay to the *Provider* separate fees in accordance with the *Supplemental ADR Rules*. If the *Provider* has not received the fee within five (5) days of the date of notification of unpaid fees, the request shall be deemed as withdrawn.

(c) A *Respondent* electing under Paragraph B3(b)(4) to have the dispute decided by a three-member *Panel*, rather than single-member *Panel* elected by the *Complainant*, shall pay the *Provider* an additional fee specified in the *Supplemental ADR Rules*. In all other cases, the *Complainant* shall bear all of the *Provider's* fees.

(d) In exceptional circumstances, for example in the event an in-person hearing is held, the *Provider* shall request the *Party* or the *Parties* requesting such event respectively to pay additional fees, which, after its constitution, shall be established in consultation with the *Panel* before scheduling any such hearing.

(e) Subject to Paragraph B1(f) below, the fees paid are not reimbursable.

NOTES

1 OJ L113, 30.4.2002, p 1.

2 OJ L162, 30.4.2004, p 40.

3 OJ L12, 16.1.2001, p 1.

B CONDUCT OF THE PROCEEDINGS

1 THE COMPLAINT

[5.1201]

(a) Any person or entity may initiate an *ADR Proceeding* by submitting a *Complaint* in accordance with the *Procedural Rules* to any *Provider*. A *Complaint* may be filed:

(1) against a *Domain Name Holder* in respect of which domain name the *Complaint* is initiated; or

(2) against *the Registry*.

For the avoidance of doubt, until the domain name in respect of which the *Complaint* is initiated has been registered and activated, a party can initiate an *ADR Proceeding* only against *the Registry*.

(b) The *Complaint* shall:

(1) Request that the *Complaint* be submitted for a decision in an *ADR Proceeding* in accordance with the *Procedural Rules*;

(2) Provide the name, postal and e-mail addresses, and the telephone and fax numbers of the *Complainant* and of any representative authorized to act for the *Complainant* in the *ADR Proceeding*;

(3) Specify a preferred method for communication directed to the *Complainant* in the *ADR Proceeding* (including the person to be contacted, means of communication, and address information);

(4) Designate whether the *Complainant* elects to have the dispute decided by a single-member or a three-member *Panel* and, in the event the *Complainant* elects a three-member *Panel*, provide the names of three candidates to serve as one of the *Panelists* (these candidates may be drawn from the list of panelists of the *Provider* dealing with the proceedings); to the maximum extent practicable, such candidates should not have been involved in the past three (3) years in any prior *ADR Proceeding* where the *Complainant* was a *Party*;

(5) Provide the name of the *Respondent* and, in case of an ADR Proceeding against a *Domain Name Holder* provide all information (including any postal and e-mail addresses and telephone and fax numbers) known to the *Complainant* on how to contact the *Respondent* or any representative of the *Respondent*, including contact information based on pre-*Complaint* dealings, in sufficient detail to allow the *Provider* to send the *Complaint* to the *Respondent* as described in Paragraph A2(a);

(6) Specify the domain name(s) that is/are the subject of the *Complaint*;

(7) Identify the *Registrar(s)* with whom the domain name(s) is/are registered at the time the *Complaint* is filed (not applicable for *Complaint* s filed against the decision(s) of *the Registry* before the registration of the disputed domain name);

(8) In case the *Complaint* is filed against the decision(s) of *the Registry*, identify the disputed *Registry* decision(s) and whether or not the disputed decision deals with the registration of a domain name within the Sunrise Period.

(9) Specify the names in respect of which a right is recognized or established by the national law of a Member State and/or Community law. For each such name, describe exactly the type of right(s) claimed, specify the law or law(s) as well as the conditions under which the right is recognized and/or established.

(10) Describe, in accordance with these *ADR Rules*, the grounds on which the *Complaint* is made including, in particular,

(i) In case of an *ADR Proceeding* against the *Domain Name Holder* in respect of which domain name the *Complaint* is initiated:

(A) why the domain name is identical or confusingly similar to the name or names in respect of which a right or rights are recognized or established by national and/or Community law (as specified and described in accordance with Paragraph B 1 (b) (9)); and, either

(B) why the domain name has been registered by its holder without rights or legitimate interests in respect of the domain name that is the subject of the *Complaint*; or

(C) why the domain name should be considered as having been registered or being used in bad faith.

(ii) In case of an *ADR Proceeding* against *the Registry*, the reasons why a decision taken by *the Registry* conflicts with *European Union Regulations*.

(11) Specify, in accordance with these *ADR Rules*, the remedies sought (see Paragraph B11 (b) and (c) below);

(12) If the *Complainant* requests transfer of the domain name, provide evidence that the *Complainant* satisfies the general eligibility criteria for registration set out in Paragraph 4(2)(b) of Regulation (EC) No 733/2002;

(13) Identify any other legal proceedings that have been commenced or terminated in connection with or relating to any of the domain name(s) that is/are the subject of the *Complaint*;

(14) State that the *Complainant* will submit, with respect to any challenges to a decision in the *ADR Proceeding* revoking or transferring the domain name, to the jurisdiction of the courts in at least one specified *Mutual Jurisdiction* in accordance with Paragraph A1;

(15) Conclude with the following statement followed by the signature of the *Complainant* or its authorised representative; in case of electronic filing the signature must comply with requirements of the *Provider's* on-line platform:

"*Complainant* warrants that all information provided hereunder is complete and accurate.

Complainant agrees with the processing of his personal data by the *Provider* to the extent necessary for the due performance of the *Provider's* responsibilities hereunder. *Complainant* also agrees with the publication of the full decision (including personal details contained in the decision) issued in the *ADR Proceeding* initiated by this *Complaint* in the language of the *ADR Proceeding* and in an unofficial English translation secured by the *Provider*.

Complainant further agrees that its claims and remedies concerning the registration of the domain name, the dispute, or the dispute's resolution shall be solely against the domain name holder and hereby waives any and all claims and remedies against

(i) the *Provider*, as well as its directors, officers, employees, advisors and agents, except in the case of deliberate wrongdoing;

(ii) *Panelists*, except in the case of deliberate wrongdoing;

(iii) the *Registrar*, except in the case of deliberate wrongdoing; and

(iv) *the Registry*, as well as its directors, officers, employees, advisors, and agents, except in the case of deliberate wrongdoing."

(16) Annex any documentary or other evidence, including any evidence concerning the rights upon which the *Complaint* relies, together with a schedule indexing such evidence.

(17) Include any forms prescribed in the *Supplemental ADR Rules* and comply with any formal requirements contained in the *Supplemental ADR Rules*, including any word limit.

(c) The *Complaint* may relate to more than one domain name, provided that the *Parties* and the language of the *ADR Proceedings* are the same.

(d) The *Provider* will acknowledge receiving the *Complaint* from the *Complainant*, subject to the receipt of the fees due above.

(e) As soon as practicable after the *Time of Filing*, but in any event not later than five (5) *days* from the date of *Time of Filing* and before notifying the *Respondent* pursuant to Article B2 below, the *Provider* shall inform *the Registry* of the identity of the *Complainant* and the domain name(s) involved. Upon receiving information from the *Provider*, *the Registry* shall block the disputed domain name pursuant to eu Domain Name Registration *Terms and Conditions*.

(f) Any *ADR Proceeding* (s) against a *Domain Name Holder* with a later *Time of Filing* with respect to the same domain name(s) shall be suspended pending the outcome of the ADR Proceeding initiated by the *Complaint* with the earliest *Time of Filing*. If in such *ADR Proceeding* the *Panel* decides to grant the *Complainant* the remedies requested, all suspended *ADR Proceedings* will be terminated and any fees paid shall be reimbursed. If in the *ADR Proceeding* the *Panel* rejects the *Complaint*, the *Provider* shall activate the *Complaint* next in time to the *Time of Filing*. The *Provider* shall notify the respective *Complainant(s)* of the termination, activation, or continued suspension of their *Complaint(s)* in writing within five (5) days from the date the *Panel* decision related to the prior *Complaint* is issued.

(g) In case an *ADR Proceeding* is initiated against *the Registry* with a later *Time of Filing* than another *ADR Proceeding* against the *Registry* with respect to the same decision taken by the *Registry*, the *ADR Proceeding* against the *Registry* with a later *Time of Filing* shall be terminated and any fees paid shall be reimbursed.

(h) Nothing mentioned in Paragraph 15, (i) to (iv) above, prevents the *Complainant* from initiating an *ADR Proceeding* against *the Registry* where a decision taken by *the Registry* conflicts with *European Union Regulations*.

(i) In case of an *ADR Proceeding* against the *Registry*, any request of a *Complainant* for documents or other information related to the *Registry* decision challenged in the *ADR Proceeding* must be made directly to the *Registry* in accordance with the *Registration Policy*.

2 NOTIFICATION OF COMPLAINT

(a) The *Provider* shall review the *Complaint* for administrative compliance with the *Procedural Rules* and with Regulation (EC) No 733/2002 and, if in compliance, shall forward the *Complaint* (together with the explanatory cover sheet prescribed by the *Provider's Supplemental ADR Rules*) to the *Respondent*, in the manner prescribed by Paragraphs A2(a) and A2(b), within five (5) *Working days* following receipt of the fees to be paid by the *Complainant* in accordance with Paragraph A6.

(b) If the *Provider* finds the *Complaint* not to be in administrative compliance with the *Procedural Rules*, it shall promptly notify the *Complainant* of the nature of the deficiencies identified. If the deficiencies are capable of being corrected, the *Complainant* shall have seven (7) *days* within which to correct any such deficiencies and submit an amended *Complaint*, after which, if not corrected, the *Provider* shall inform the *Complainant* that the *ADR Proceeding* is deemed to be withdrawn due to administrative deficiency and without prejudice to submission of a different *Complaint* by the *Complainant*.

(c) A *Complainant* can challenge the withdrawal of its *Complaint* due to administrative deficiency pursuant to Paragraph B2(b) above. The procedure related to such a challenge shall be as follows:

(1) The request shall be submitted to the *Provider* within 5 days from receiving the information about the withdrawal and shall:
(i) specify the information under Paragraphs B1 (b)(2), B1 (b)(6) and B1 (b)(8) (if applicable) of the *ADR Rules*;
(ii) specify the requested cancellation of the withdrawal of the *Complaint* due to administrative deficiency;
(iii) specify the reasons of the requested cancellation;
(iv) conclude with the statement under B1(b)(15) of the *ADR Rules*.
(2) The *Provider* will acknowledge receiving the request from the *Complainant*, subject to the receipt of the fees due pursuant to Paragraph A6(a) above and will appoint a single *Panel* to decide the request. Paragraph B5 applies accordingly.
(3) The *Panel* shall issue a decision whether or not to allow the requested challenge within twelve (12) *days* from the date of its appointment. The *Panel's* decision shall be final and not subject to appeal. The decision shall be communicated to the *Complainant* without delay.

(d) The Provider shall immediately notify the Complainant, the Respondent, and the Registry of the Date of Commencement of an ADR Proceeding.
(e) The Provider shall suspend the ADR Proceeding until the procedures specified in Paragraphs B2(b) and B2(c) above are completed.

3 THE RESPONSE

(a) Within thirty (30) *Working days* of the date of delivery of the *Complaint* in accordance with Paragraph A2(b), the *Respondent* shall submit a *Response* to the *Provider*.
(b) The *Response* shalll:
(1) Provide the name, postal and e-mail addresses, and the telephone and fax numbers of the *Respondent* and of any representative authorized to act for the *Respondent* in the *ADR Proceeding*;
(2) Specify a preferred method for communication directed to the *Respondent* in the *ADR Proceeding* (including person to be contacted, medium, and address information);
(3) If the *Complainant* has elected a single-member *Panel* in the *Complaint* (see Paragraph B1(b)(3)), state whether the *Respondent* elects instead to have the dispute decided by a three-member *Panel*;
(4) If either *Complainant* or *Respondent* elects a three-member *Panel*, provide the names and contact details of three candidates to serve as one of the *Panelists* (these candidates may be drawn from any *Provider's* list of panelists; to the maximum extent practicable, such candidates should not have been involved in the past three (3) years in any prior *ADR Proceeding* where the *Respondent* was a *Party*;
(5) Identify any other legal proceedings that have been commenced or terminated in connection with or relating to any of the domain name(s) that is/are the subject of the *Complaint*;
(6) Describe, in accordance with these *ADR Rules*, the grounds on which the *Response* is made.
(7) Conclude with the following statement followed by the signature of the *Respondent* or its authorised representative; in case of electronic filing the signature must comply with requirements of the *Provider's* on-line platform:
"*Respondent* warrants that all information provided hereunder is complete and accurate.
Respondent agrees with the processing of his personal data by the *Provider* to the extent necessary for the due performance of the *Provider's* responsibilities hereunder.
Respondent also agrees with the publication of the full decision (including personal data contained in the decision) issued in this *ADR Proceeding* in the language of the *ADR Proceeding* and in an unofficial English translation secured by the *Provider.*
Respondent hereby waives any and all claims and remedies related to the current *ADR Proceeding* against
(i) the *Provider* as well as its directors, officers, employees, advisors and agents, except in the case of deliberate wrongdoing;
(ii) *Panelists*, except in the case of deliberate wrongdoing,
(iii) the *Registrar*, except in the case of deliberate wrongdoing and
(iv) *the Registry*, as well as its directors, officers, employees, and agents, except in the case of deliberate wrongdoing."
(8) Attach any documentary or other evidence, including any evidence concerning the rights upon which the *Respondent* relies, together with a schedule indexing such evidence.
(9) Include any forms prescribed in the *Supplemental ADR Rules* and comply with any formal requirements contained in the *Supplemental ADR Rules*, including any word limit.

(c) If the *Complainant* has elected to have the dispute decided by a single-member *Panel* and the *Respondent* elects a three-member *Panel*, the *Respondent* shall be required to pay a fee in accordance with Paragraph A6(b). This payment shall be made together with the submission of the *Response* to the *Provider*. In the event that the required payment is not made, the dispute shall be decided by a single-member *Panel*.

(d) The *Provider* shall confirm receipt of the *Response* to the *Respondent*. If the *Provider* finds the *Response* not to be in administrative compliance with the *Procedural Rules*, it shall promptly notify the *Respondent* of the nature of the deficiencies identified. If the deficiencies are capable of being remedied, the *Respondent* shall have seven (7) *days* within which to correct any such deficiencies and submit an amended *Response*, after which the *Response* shall be deemed not submitted by the *Respondent*. The *Provider* shall suspend the *ADR Proceeding* until either of the two actions happens first: (i) it receives the amended *Response* or (ii) the time period mentioned in this Paragraph expires.

(e) The *Provider* shall forward the administratively compliant *Response* to the *Complainant* without delay.

(f) If a *Respondent* does not submit a *Response* or submits solely an administratively deficient *Response*, the *Provider* shall notify the *Parties* of *Respondent*'s default. The *Provider* shall send to the *Panel* for its information and to the *Complainant* the administratively deficient *Response* submitted by the *Respondent*. The *Provider's* notification of the *Respondent*'s default shall be without prejudice to the *Respondent*'s right to have the dispute decided by a three member Panel pursuant to Paragraph B3(b)(4) above, provided the fees under Paragraph A.6(c) above have been paid.

(g) The *Respondent* can challenge the *Provider's* notification of the *Respondent's* default in a written submission to the *Provider* filed within five (5) days from receiving the notification of *Respondent's* default. The *Provider* shall acknowledge receiving the *Respondent's* challenge and shall forward the *Respondent's* challenge to the *Panel* within three (3) days from its receipt. The *Respondent's* challenge shall be considered by the *Panel* in its sole discretion as part of its decision making. If the *Panel* confirms that the *Response* is administratively deficient, the *Panel* may decide the dispute based upon the *Complaint* only.

(h) Nothing mentioned in Paragraph 7, (i) to (iv) above, prevents the *Respondent* from initiating an *ADR Proceeding* against a decision taken by *the Registry* which conflicts with *European Union Regulations*.

4 APPOINTMENT OF THE PANEL AND TIMING OF DECISION

(a) The *Panelists* shall be selected in accordance to the internal procedures of the *Providers*. They shall have appropriate expertise and shall be selected in an objective, transparent and non-discriminatory manner. Each *Provider* shall maintain and publish a publicly available list of panelists and their qualifications.

(b) If neither the *Complainant* nor the *Respondent* has elected a three-member *Panel* (Paragraphs B1(b)(3) and B3(b)(4)), the *Provider* shall appoint a single *Panelist* from its list of panelists.

(c) Unless it has already elected a three-member *Panel*, the *Complainant* shall submit to the *Provider*, within five (5) days of communication of a *Response* in which the *Respondent* elects a three-member *Panel*, the names and contact details of three candidates to serve as one of the *Panelists*. These candidates may be drawn from any *Provider's* list of panelists; to the maximum extent practicable, such candidates should not have been involved in the last three (3) years in any prior *ADR Proceeding* where the *Complainant* was a *Party*.

(d) In the event that either the *Complainant* or the *Respondent* elects a three-member *Panel*, the *Provider* shall appoint one *Panelist* from the list of candidates submitted by the *Complainant*, one *Panelist* from the list of candidates submitted by the *Respondent*, and one *Panelist* from its list of panelists. If either *Party* does not duly submit its list of candidates, the *Provider* shall appoint an additional *Panelist* from its list of Panelists.

(e) Once the entire *Panel* is appointed, the *Provider* shall notify the *Parties* of the identity of the *Panelists* appointed and the date by which, absent exceptional circumstances, the *Panel* shall forward its decision on the *Complaint* to the *Provider*.

5 IMPARTIALITY AND INDEPENDENCE

(a) The *Panelists* shall have no personal or economic interests in the results of the dispute, and they undertake to resolve the dispute under the principles of good faith, fairness and due diligence. The *Panelists* shall maintain the confidential character of the information disclosed to them during the *ADR Proceedings*.

(b) A *Panelist* shall be impartial and independent and shall have, before accepting appointment, disclosed to the *Provider* any circumstances giving rise to justifiable doubt as to the *Panelist's* impartiality or independence. If, at any stage during the *ADR Proceeding*, new circumstances arise that could give rise to justifiable doubt as to the impartiality or independence of a *Panelist*, that *Panelist* shall promptly disclose such circumstances to the *Provider*. In such event, the *Provider* shall have the sole discretion to appoint a substitute *Panelist*.

(c) Apart from the above, the *Parties* can also challenge the appointment of a *Panelist*. The *Party* that challenges a *Panelist* should explain to the *Provider* his reasons for the challenge. The challenge shall be filed within two (2) *days* from receiving the notice of the subject *Panelist's* appointment, or after having become aware of the circumstances giving rise to justifiable doubt in regard to the impartiality or independence of the *Panelist*.

(d) When a *Panelist* has been challenged by one *Party*, the other *Party* and/or the challenged *Panelist* will be entitled to submit a response. This right will be exercised within two (2) *days* after receiving the communication to which the previous Paragraph refers.

(e) The *Provider* will decide on the challenge, and its decision will be final and not subject to appeal.

6 TRANSMISSION OF THE FILE TO THE PANEL

The *Provider* shall forward the file to the *Panel* as soon as the *Panelist* is appointed in the case of a *Panel* consisting of a single member, or as soon as the last *Panelist* is appointed in the case of a three-member *Panel*.

7 GENERAL POWERS OF THE PANEL

(a) The *Panel* shall conduct the *ADR Proceeding* in such manner as it considers appropriate in accordance with the *Procedural Rules*. The Panel is not obliged, but is permitted in its sole discretion, to conduct its own investigations on the circumstances of the case.

(b) In all cases, the *Panel* shall ensure that the *Parties* are treated fairly and with equality.

(c) The *Panel* shall ensure that the *ADR Proceeding* takes place with due expedition.

(d) The *Panel* shall determine in its sole discretion the admissibility, relevance, materiality and weight of the evidence.

8 FURTHER STATEMENTS

In addition to the *Complaint* and the *Response*, the *Panel* may request or admit, in its sole discretion, further statements or documents from either of the *Parties*.

9 IN-PERSON HEARINGS

There shall be no in-person hearings (including hearings by teleconference, videoconference, and web conference). The decision will be handled based on documents or other types of written evidence unless the *Panel* determines, in its sole discretion and as a matter of exceptional circumstances, that such a hearing is necessary for rendering a decision on the *Complaint*.

10 DEFAULT

(a) In the event that a *Party* does not comply with any of the time periods established by these *ADR Rules* or the *Panel*, the *Panel* shall proceed to a decision on the *Complaint* and may consider this failure to comply as grounds to accept the claims of the other *Party*.

(b) Unless provided differently in these *ADR Rules*, if a *Party* does not comply with any provision of, or requirement under, these *ADR Rules*, the *Supplemental ADR Rules* or any request from the *Panel*, the *Panel* shall draw such inferences therefrom as it considers appropriate.

11 BASIS FOR DECISION

(a) A *Panel* shall decide a *Complaint* on the basis of the statements and documents submitted and in accordance with the *Procedural Rules*.

(b) The remedies available pursuant to an *ADR Proceeding* where the *Respondent* is the *Domain Name Holder* in respect of which domain name the *Complaint* was initiated shall be limited to the revocation of the disputed domain name(s) /or, if the *Complainant* satisfies the general eligibility criteria for registration set out in Paragraph 4(2)(b) of Regulation (EC) No 733/2002, the transfer of the disputed domain name(s) to the *Complainant*.

(c) The main remedy available pursuant to an ADR Proceeding where the *Respondent* is the *Registry* shall be the annulment of the disputed decision taken by the *Registry*. The *Panel* may decide in appropriate cases pursuant to the *Procedural Rules*, *Registration Policy*, *Sunrise Rules* and/or the *Terms and Conditions* that the domain name in question shall be transferred, revoked or attributed. However, with regard to any *Registry* decision relating to a prior right invoked during the phased registration period such measures of transfer and attribution will only be granted by the *Panel* if the *Complainant* is the next applicant in the queue for the domain name concerned and subject to the decision by the *Registry* that the *Complainant* satisfies all registration criteria set out in *the European Union Regulations* and to the subsequent activation by the *Registry* of the domain name in the name of the *Complainant* who is the next applicant in the queue.

(d) The *Panel* shall issue a decision granting the remedies requested under the *Procedural Rules* in the event that the *Complainant* proves

(1) in *ADR Proceeding* s where the *Respondent* is the holder of a.eu domain name registration in respect of which the *Complaint* was initiated that

(i) The domain name is identical or confusingly similar to a name in respect of which a right is recognized or established by the national law of a Member State and/or Community law and; either

(ii) The domain name has been registered by the *Respondent* without rights or legitimate interest in the name; or

(iii) The domain name has been registered or is being used in bad faith.

(2) in ADR Proceedings where the Respondent is the Registry that the decision taken by the Registry conflicts with the European Union Regulations.

(e) Any of the following circumstances, in particular but without limitation, if found by the *Panel* to be proved based on its evaluation of all evidence presented, shall demonstrate the *Respondent's* rights or legitimate interests to the domain name for purposes of Paragraph B11(d)(1)(ii):

(1) prior to any notice of the dispute, the *Respondent* has used the domain name or a name corresponding to the domain name in connection with the offering of goods or services or has made demonstrable preparation to do so;

(2) the *Respondent*, being an undertaking, organization or natural person, has been commonly known by the domain name, even in the absence of a right recognized or established by national and/or Community law;

(3) the *Respondent* is making a legitimate and non-commercial or fair use of the domain name, without intent to mislead consumers or harm the reputation of a name in which a right is recognized or established by national law and/or Community law.

(f) For purposes of Paragraph B11(d)(1)(iii), the following circumstances, in particular but without limitation, if found by the *Panel* to be present, may be evidence of the registration or use of a domain name in bad faith:

(1) circumstances indicating that the domain name was registered or acquired primarily for the purpose of selling, renting, or otherwise transferring the domain name to the holder of a name, in respect of which a right is recognized or established by national and/or Community law, or to a public body; or

(2) the domain name has been registered in order to prevent the holder of such a name in respect of which a right is recognized or established by national and/or Community law, or a public body, from reflecting this name in a corresponding domain name, provided that:

(i) the *Respondent* has engaged in a pattern of such conduct; or

(ii) the domain name has not been used in a relevant way for at least two years from the date of registration; or

(iii) there are circumstances where, at the time the *ADR Proceeding* was initiated, the *Respondent* has declared its intention to use the domain name, in respect of which a right is recognized or established by national and/or Community law or which corresponds to the name of a public body, in a relevant way but failed to do so within six months of the day on which the *ADR Proceeding* was initiated;

(3) the domain name was registered primarily for the purpose of disrupting the professional activities of a competitor; or

(4) the domain name was intentionally used to attract Internet users, for commercial gain to the *Respondent's* website or other on-line location, by creating a likelihood of confusion with a name on which a right is recognized or established, by national and/or Community law, or it is a name of a public body, such likelihood arising as to the source, sponsorship, affiliation or endorsement of the website or location or of a product or service on the website or location of the Respondent; or

(5) the domain name is a personal name for which no demonstrable link exists between the *Respondent* and the domain name registered.

12 DECISION-MAKING AND FORM OF DECISIONS

(a) The decisions of the *Panelists* will be final, not subject to appeal, and compulsory for the *Parties*, without detriment to the right of the *Parties* to initiate a court proceeding in a *Mutual Jurisdiction* which will have consequences to the implementation of the decision as described in the *Terms and Conditions*.

(b) The *Panel* shall forward its decision on the *Complaint* to the *Provider* within one month of the *Provider's* receipt of administratively compliant *Response* or the lapse of the time period for its submission.

(c) In the case of a three-member *Panel*, the *Panel's* decision shall be made by simple majority.

(d) The *Panel's* decision shall be in writing, provide the reasons on which it is based, indicate the date on which it was rendered and identify the name(s) of the *Panelist(s)*. If the *Panel* decides that the disputed domain name be revoked or transferred to the *Complainant*, it shall state that the decision shall be implemented by *the Registry* within thirty (30) days after the notification of the decision to the *Parties*, unless the *Respondent* initiates court proceedings in a *Mutual Jurisdiction* (see Paragraphs B12(a) and B14).

(e) *Panel* decisions shall comply with formal requirements set forth in the *Provider's Supplemental ADR Rules*.

(f) If the *Panel* concludes that the dispute is not within the scope of the Regulation (EC) No 874/2004, it shall so state.

(g) If the *Complainant* has

(1) proved that the domain name is identical or confusingly similar to a name in respect of which a right is recognized or established by a Member State's national law and/or Community law or to a name of a public body; and;

(2) failed to prove the *Respondent's* lack of rights and legitimate interests, as specified in Paragraph B11(d)(1)(ii) of these *ADR Rules*; and

(3) relied on Paragraph B11(f)(2)(iii) of these *ADR Rules* to prove bad faith; and

(4) failed to prove bad faith on any other grounds;

the *Panel* shall issue an interim decision setting out its findings on issues (1) to (4) above and shall suspend the proceedings until a date six months after the *Time of Filing*. In such an event (and should the *Respondent* not submit evidence of relevant use by the postponed date and the *Complainant* prove the remaining elements required by Paragraph B11(f)(2)(iii)), the *Panel* shall decide whether or not to grant to the *Complainant* the requested remedy. Under all other circumstances, the *Panel* shall proceed to a decision without reference to Paragraph B11(f)(2)(iii).

All evidence submitted by the *Respondent* must be accompanied by a declaration of completeness and accuracy and be given to the *Complainant*. The *Complainant* shall have a right to submit a response to the *Respondent*'s evidence within fifteen (15) days from receiving the evidence.

(h) If after considering the submissions the *Panel* finds that the *Complaint* was initiated in bad faith, the *Panel* shall declare in its decision that the *Complaint* was brought in bad faith and constitutes an abuse of administrative proceeding.

(i) Each *Panel* decision shall contain a brief summary in English in accordance with guidelines prepared by the *Provider*.

13 COMMUNICATION OF DECISION TO PARTIES

(a) Within three (3) *Working days* after receiving the final decision from the *Panel*, the *Provider* shall communicate the full text of the decision to each *Party*, the concerned *Registrar(s)* and to *the Registry*.

(b) The *Provider* shall publish the full decision on a publicly accessible web site.

14 IMPLEMENTATION OF DECISION

The implementation of the decision shall follow the *Terms and Conditions*.

C CONCLUDING PROVISIONS

1 EXCLUSION OF LIABILITY

[5.1202]

Except in the case of deliberate wrongdoing, neither the *Provider* nor a *Panelist* shall be liable to a *Party* for any act or omission in connection with any *ADR Proceeding* under these *ADR Rules*.

2 AMENDMENTS

The version of these *ADR Rules* in effect at the time of the submission of the *Complaint* to the *Provider* shall apply to the *ADR Proceeding* commenced thereby. The *Provider* may amend these *ADR Rules* at any time after receiving the prior written approval of *the Registry*.

3 EFFECTIVE DATE

These *ADR Rules* apply to all *Complaints* filed on or after 1 February 2010.

SUPPLEMENTAL ADR RULES OF THE ARBITRATION COURT ATTACHED TO THE ECONOMIC CHAMBER OF THE CZECH REPUBLIC AND AGRICULTURAL CHAMBER OF THE CZECH REPUBLIC

NOTES

The ADR Supplemental Rules can be found at www.adr.eu. © Arbitration Court attached to the Economic Chamber of the Czech Republic and Agricultural Chamber of the Czech Republic (Czech Arbitration Court), 2006.

A GENERAL

1 SCOPE

[5.1203]

(a) **Relationship to ADR Rules and EU legislation**. These *Supplemental ADR Rules* are to be read and used in connection with the. *eu Dispute Resolution Rules*, adopted by the Registry (the "*ADR Rules*") and with the Regulations (EC) No 733/2002 and No 874/2004 and with any other applicable EU legislation. These supplemental rules may not derogate from either the *ADR Rules* or the *European Union Regulations*.

(b) **Version of Supplemental Rules**. The version of these *Supplemental ADR Rules* in effect on the date of the submission of the *Complaint* shall apply to the administrative proceeding commenced thereby.

2 DEFINITIONS

Provider means the Arbitration Court attached to the Economic Chamber of the Czech Republic and Agricultural Chamber of the Czech Republic.

Any other term defined in the *ADR Rules* shall have the same meaning when used in these *Supplemental ADR Rules*.

3 FEES AND PAYMENT INSTRUCTIONS

The fees applicable for administrative procedures and obligatory payment instructions are specified in Annex A hereto and posted on the Provider's website. The Provider may grant discounts on the applicable fees in justified cases. The conditions for obtaining discounts shall be published on the Provider's website.

4 COMMUNICATION INSTRUCTIONS

The *Parties* shall be required to adhere to communication instructions contained in Annex C hereto.

5 TIME PERIODS

The expiration of any given time period occurs at midnight (24.00) of the final day of that respective time period. When the last day of a deadline prescribed by the *ADR Rules* and/or *ADR Supplemental Rules* is not a *Working Day*, the time period shall be extended automatically to include the next *Working Day* following the last day of the deadline.

B CONDUCT OF THE PROCEEDINGS

1 SUBMISSION OF COMPLAINT

(a) The *Complaint* must include all elements listed in Paragraph B1(b) of the *ADR Rules*.

(b) **Complaint Form**. In accordance with Paragraph B1(b)(17) of the *ADR Rules*, the *Complainant* shall be required to prepare its *Complaint* using the *Complaint Form* included in the list of Forms contained in Annex B hereto and posted on the *Provider's* website.

(c) **Number of Copies**. When a hard-copy submission is to be made to the *Provider* by a *Party*, it shall be submitted in three (3) copies together with one (1) original of such submission.

2 APPOINTMENT OF CASE ADMINISTRATOR

(a) **Notification**. The *Provider* shall advise the *Parties* of the name and contact details of a member of its staff who shall be the *Case Administrator* and who shall be responsible for all administrative matters relating to the dispute and communications to the *ADR Panel*.

(b) **Responsibilities**. *The Case Administrator* may provide administrative assistance to the *Panel* or *Panelist(s)*, but shall have no authority to decide matters of a substantive nature concerning the dispute.

3 SUBMISSION OF RESPONSE

(a) The *Response* must include all elements listed in Paragraph B3(b) of the *ADR Rules*.

(b) *Response Form*. In accordance with Paragraph B3(b)(9) of the *ADR Rules*, the *Respondent* shall be required to prepare its *Response* using the *Response Form* included in the list of Forms contained in Annex B hereto and posted on the *Provider's* web site.

4 PANELIST APPOINTMENT PROCEDURES

(a) **Party Candidates**. Where a Party is required to submit the names of three (3) candidates for consideration for appointment by the *Provider* as a *Panelist* (ie, in accordance with paragraphs B1(b)(4), B3(b)(4) and B4(c) of the *ADR Rules*), that *Party* shall provide the names and contact details of its three candidates in the order of its preference. In appointing a *Panelist*, the *Provider* shall, subject to availability, respect the order of preference indicated by a *Party*.

(b) **Presiding Panelist**. The *Panelist* appointed in accordance with Paragraph B4(d) of the *ADR Rules* from the *Provider's* list of Panelists shall be the *Presiding Panelist*, coordinating the *Panel*.

(c) **Respondent Default**. Where the *Respondent* does not submit a *Response* or does not submit the payment provided for in Paragraph B3(c) of the *ADR Rules* by the deadline specified by the *Provider*, the *Provider* shall proceed to appoint the *Panel*.

5 DECLARATION

In accordance with Paragraph B5 of the *ADR Rules*, prior to appointment as a *Panelist*, a candidate shall be required to submit to the *Provider* a *Declaration of Independence and Impartiality* using the form included in the list of Forms contained in Annex B hereto and posted on the *Provider's* web site.

6 FORMS

In addition to the Form Complaint in relation to the Complaint (Section B1(b) above) and Form Response in relation to the *Response* (Section B3(b) above) the *Parties* shall be required to use for their other communication during the *ADR Proceeding* form documents set out in Annex B hereto and posted on the *Provider's* web site.

7 IN-PERSON HEARINGS

In case the *Panel* determines, in its sole discretion, that an in-person hearing is necessary, the hearing will be carried out by teleconference, videoconference, or web conference at the CHAT address of the *Provider* if both Parties agree with the use of such technology; otherwise, the hearing will be carried out in-person at the location specified by the *Panel*. The *Panel* will give the *Parties* seven (7) days notice that the aforementioned hearing will be held, including the date, time and electronic place or physical location where it will take place.

8 PANEL DECISION

The Panel decision will meet the requirements set forth in Article B13 of the *ADR Rules* and will comply with all formal requirements contained in these *Supplemental ADR Rules*, with the exception of the limit of number of pages pursuant to Paragraph 11 below where the *Panel* will exercise its discretion. A model decision is included in the list of Forms contained in Annex B hereto and posted in the *Provider's* website.

9 CORRECTION OF CLERICAL MISTAKES

Within seven (7) days of receiving the decision, a *Party* may, by written notice to the *Panel* and the other *Party*, request the *Panel* to correct in the decision any errors in computation, any clerical or typographical errors, or any errors of a similar nature. Any such corrections shall be given in writing to the *Parties* and shall become a part of the decision.

The *Panel* may correct any errors on its own initiative of the type referred to in the preceding Paragraph within seven (7) days of the date of the decision being rendered.

10 PUBLICATION OF THE DECISION

The Provider shall inform the Parties, the Registry and the concerned Registrar(s) of the Panel's decision. The concerned Registrar(s) shall be informed of the Panel's decision through its publication. The *Provider* shall publish the full decision on his website, listing at least the following:

(a) The Domain Name which is in dispute and is the subject of a Complaint;
(b) The case number;
(c) The Complainant and the Respondent.

The decision shall be published in the language of the ADR Proceeding. With respect to ADR Proceedings which are not conducted in English, the Provider shall also publish accompanying unofficial English translations of selected ADR decisions.

11 WORD LIMITS

Panelists shall exercise reasonable efforts to adhere the following guidelines as to length of the decisions:

(a) The word limit under Paragraph B1(b)(10) of the *ADR Rules* shall be 5,000 words.
(b) The word limit under Paragraph B3(b)(6) of the *ADR Rules* shall be 5,000 words.
(c) The word limit under Paragraph B12(e) of the *ADR Rules* shall be 5,000 words.

C CONCLUDING PROVISIONS

1 AMENDMENTS

Subject to the *ADR Rules*, the *Provider* may amend these *Supplemental ADR Rules* in its sole discretion.

2 EFFECTIVE DATE

These *Supplemental ADR Rules* apply to all cases filed on or after 1 February 2010.

3 LIST OF ANNEXES

Annex A: Fee Schedule;

Annex B: List of Forms;

Annex C: Communication Instructions.

NOTES

The Annexes to the Supplemental ADR Rules are not reproduced here.

COMMON COMMUNICATION ON THE COMMON PRACTICE ON THE GENERAL INDICATIONS OF THE NICE CLASS HEADINGS (CP1)

v1.2, 28 October 2015

NOTES

Reproduced with the kind permission of the European Union Intellectual Property Office (EUIPO)

[5.1204]

On 19/06/2012 the Court delivered its ruling in Case C-307/10 "IP Translator", giving the following answers to the referred questions:

(1) – Directive 2008/95 must be interpreted as meaning that it requires the goods and services for which the protection of the trade mark is sought to be identified by the applicant with sufficient clarity and precision to enable the competent authorities and economic operators, on that basis alone, to determine the extent of the protection conferred by the trade mark;

(2) – Directive 2008/95 must be interpreted as meaning that it does not preclude the use of the general indications of the class headings of the Nice Classification to identify the goods and services for which the protection of the trade mark is sought, provided that such identification is sufficiently clear and precise;

(3) – an applicant for a national trade mark who uses all the general indications of a particular class heading of the Nice Classification to identify the goods or services for which the protection of the trade mark is sought must specify whether its application for registration is intended to cover all the goods or services included in the alphabetical list of that class or only some of those goods or services. If the application concerns only some of those goods or services, the applicant is required to specify which of the goods or services in that class are intended to be covered.

This Judgment has an influence on the practice of all Trade Mark Offices of the European Union and in the interest of establishing certainty within the trademark system and for its users, calls for convergence on the interpretation of the general indications of the Nice class headings. Without prejudice to the fact that each Office is bound by its national legislation, national court decisions and, in some cases, previous communications, it is recognised by all that it is only through collaboration in implementing this Judgment in a harmonised manner will there be legal certainty both for the competent authorities and the economic operators.

As regards the first question, the Trade Mark Offices of the European Union are working together to establish a common understanding of the requirements necessary to achieve clarity and precision in the identification of goods and services in an application for registration and to develop a common set of criteria which will be subject of a subsequent common communication.

As concerns the second question, the Trade Mark Offices of the European Union have already reviewed all general indications of the Nice class headings in order to determine which indications are sufficiently clear and precise. This review has determined that the 5 general indications detailed below are not clear and precise, and consequently cannot be accepted without further specification. The remaining general indications are considered acceptable. Further, the reasons why each of the 5 non-acceptable general indications of the Nice class headings are not found clear and precise have been agreed.

Implementation* will take place within 3 months of the date of publication of this Common communication. In exceptional cases this period can be extended for another 3 months.

The Offices have agreed that the judgment should not have a retrospective effect requiring that the register be changed ex officio with respect to registrations that contain one or more of these non-acceptable 5 general indications prior to the implementation of this communication.

Tools such as TMclass are available to assist in searching for and identifying acceptable terms.

As regards the third question, the "Common Communication on the Implementation of 'IP Translator'" provides an overview on how Trade Mark Offices of the European Union deal with specific topics relating to the implementation of the said Judgement.

The Trade Mark Offices of the European Union reiterate their commitment to continue to collaborate in the context of the Convergence Programme, further increasing transparency and predictability for the benefit of examiners and users alike.

EUROPEAN TRADE MARK AND DESIGN NETWORK

NOTES

* An overview of definite implementation dates in each office is annexed.

List of implementing offices: AT, BG, BX, CY, CZ, DE, DK, EE, ES, FI, FR, GR, HR, HU, IE, IT, LV, LT, MT, NO, OHIM, PL, PT, RO, SE, SI, SK, UK

ACCEPTABLE AND NON-ACCEPTABLE GENERAL INDICATIONS OF THE NICE CLASS HEADINGS

[5.1205]

The general indications are the expressions that appear in the class headings between semicolons; for example, Class 13 is made up of 4 general indications: "Firearms;", "ammunition and projectiles;", "explosives;" and "fireworks".

The 204 general indications of the Nice class headings were examined with respect to the requisites of clarity and precision. Of these, 5 were considered to lack the clarity and precision to specify the scope of protection that they would give, and consequently cannot be accepted without further specification. These are set out below, highlighted in bold.

- Cl. 7 – **Machines** and machine tools
- Cl. 37 – **Repair**
- Cl. 37 – **Installation services**
- Cl. 40 – **Treatment of materials**
- Cl. 45 – **Personal and social services rendered by others to meet the needs of individuals**

In some cases, a part of a general indication may be considered to be sufficiently clear and precise if used on its own, for example, in the general indication "Machines and machine tools", the description 'machine tools' on its own would be acceptable because it describes a specific type of goods. Where this applies, the part of the general indication is shown in grey. However this does not apply to the phrase ", not included in other classes".

The reasons why each of the 5 general indications of the Nice class headings are not clear and precise are expressed below.

- Cl. 7 – **Machines** and machine tools – In light of the need for clarity and precision, the term "machines" does not provide a clear indication of what machines are covered. Machines can have different characteristics or different purposes, they may require very different levels of technical capabilities and know-how to be produced and / or used, could be targeting different consumers, be sold through different sales channels, and therefore relate to different market sectors.
- Cl. 37 – **Repair** – In light of the need for clarity and precision, this term does not provide a clear indication of the services being provided, as it simply states that these are repair services, and not what is to be repaired. As the goods to be repaired may have different characteristics, the repair services will be carried out by service providers with different levels of technical capabilities and know-how, and may relate to different market sectors.
- Cl. 37 – **Installation services** – In light of the need for clarity and precision, this term does not provide a clear indication of the services being provided, as it simply states that these are installation services, and not what is to be installed. As the goods to be installed may have different characteristics, the installation services will be carried out by service providers with different levels of technical capabilities and know-how, and may relate to different market sectors.
- Cl. 40 – **Treatment of materials** – In light of the need for clarity and precision, this term does not give a clear indication of the services being provided. The nature of the treatment is unclear, as are the materials to be treated. These services cover a wide range of activities performed by different service providers on materials of different characteristics requiring very different levels of technical capabilities and know-how, and may relate to different market sectors.
- Cl. 45 – **Personal and social services rendered by others to meet the needs of individuals** – In light of the need for clarity and precision, this term does not give a clear indication of the services being provided. These services cover a wide range of activities performed by different service providers requiring very different levels of skill and know-how, and may relate to different market sectors.

OVERVIEW OF IMPLEMENTATION DATES OF THE COMMON PRACTICE ON ACCEPTABLE AND NON-ACCEPTABLE GENERAL INDICATIONS OF THE NICE CLASS HEADINGS

[5.1206]

National Office	Implementation date
AT	01.01.2014
BG	20.02.2014

National Office	Implementation date
BX	20.11.2013
CY	20.11.2013
CZ	01.05.2014
DE	01.02.2014
DK	01.01.2014
EE	20.02.2014
ES	20.02.2014
FI	01.01.2014
FR	21.11.2013
GR	01.05.2014
HR	01.01.2014
HU	20.02.2014
IE	16.01.2013
IT	20.05.2014
LV	01.01.2014
LT	20.02.2014
MT	20.02.2014
NO	01.02.2014
OHIM	02.12.2013
PL	20.11.2013
PT	21.11.2013
RO	01.02.2014
SE	01.01.2014
SI	01.12.2013
SK	20.11.2013
UK	05.08.2013

COMMON COMMUNICATION ON THE IMPLEMENTATION OF 'IP TRANSLATOR'

(v1.3, 24 September 2016)

NOTES

Reproduced with the kind permission of the European Union Intellectual Property Office (EUIPO)

[5.1207]

On 19/06/2012 the Court delivered its ruling in Case C-307/10 "IP Translator", giving the following answers to the referred questions:

(1) – Directive 2008/95 must be interpreted as meaning that it requires the goods and services for which the protection of the trade mark is sought to be identified by the applicant with sufficient clarity and precision to enable the competent authorities and economic operators, on that basis alone, to determine the extent of the protection conferred by the trade mark;

(2) – Directive 2008/95 must be interpreted as meaning that it does not preclude the use of the general indications of the class headings of the Nice Classification to identify the goods and services for which the protection of the trade mark is sought, provided that such identification is sufficiently clear and precise;

(3) – an applicant for a national trade mark who uses all the general indications of a particular class heading of the Nice Classification to identify the goods or services for which the protection of the trade mark is sought must specify whether its application for registration is intended to cover all the goods or services included in the alphabetical list of that class or only some of those goods or services. If the application concerns only some of those goods or services, the applicant is required to specify which of the goods or services in that class are intended to be covered.

This Judgment has an influence on the practice of all Trade Mark Offices of the European Union and calls for convergence on the interpretation of the general indications of the Nice Class Headings. Without prejudice to the fact that each Office is bound by its national legislation, national court decisions and, in some cases, previous communications, there is a willingness and a need to collaborate with a view to implementing this Judgment in a harmonised manner in order to provide legal certainty both for the competent authorities and the economic operators.

As regards the first question, the Trade Mark Offices of the European Union are working together to establish a common understanding of the requirements of clarity and precision in the designation of goods and services and to develop a common set of principles to be applied to their respective classification practices.

As concerns the second question, the Trade Mark Offices of the European Union are working together to determine which of the general indications of the Nice Class Headings are acceptable for classification, pursuant to the above criteria of clarity and precision. This will result in a harmonised approach on the acceptance for classification of each of them. As soon as this agreement is finalized, it will be communicated accordingly.

As regards the third question, the Trade Mark Offices of the European Union have created an overview (see Annex) that provides full transparency on how each Office deals with specific topics relating to the implementation of the Court's ruling. The overview addresses the following topics:

- It reflects how each Office interprets the scope of protection of its own trade marks containing entire Nice Class Headings filed before and after the "IP Translator" Judgment. (Table 1, Table 2)
- It contains information about how each Office reflects in its register, publications and certificates the intention of the applicant with respect to Nice Class Headings and the alphabetical list. (Table 3)
- Each National Office informs how it interprets the scope of protection of CTMs containing an entire Nice Class Heading, filed before and after the IPT judgment. (Table 4)
- EUIPO informs how it interprets the scope of protection of national trade marks containing an entire Nice Class Heading, filed before and after the IPT judgment. (Table 5)
- Trade marks filed after "IP Translator" containing the entire class heading: How can the applicant obtain protection for the full alphabetical list? (Table 6)

The Trade Mark Offices of the European Union reiterate their commitment to continue to collaborate in the context of the Convergence Programme, with the purpose of further increasing transparency and predictability for the benefit of examiners and users alike.

A first concrete aim is a harmonised list of acceptable goods and services. It will be presented in a visual hierarchical structure, which will allow the user to easily locate descriptions of goods and services that match the desired level of protection. This will be implemented into classification tools such as TMClass.

Whilst the hierarchical structure serves administrative purposes only and does not have any legal consequences the result is a comprehensive and dynamic classification tool that, by containing commonly acceptable terminology, offers more certainty to the user when constructing specifications of goods and services. This will help applicants to comply with the requisites of clarity and precision set forth in the "IP Translator" Judgment.

EUROPEAN TRADE MARK AND DESIGN NETWORK

LIST OF OFFICES: AT, BG, BX, CY, CZ, DE, DK, EE, ES, EUIPO, FI, FR, GR, HR, HU, IE, IT, LV, LT, MT, NO,* PL, PT, RO, SE, SI, SK, UK

NOTES

* observer

TABLE 1
TRADE MARKS FILED BEFORE "IP TRANSLATOR" CONTAINING ENTIRE NICE CLASS HEADINGS INTERPRETATION BY THE OFFICE OF THE SCOPE OF PROTECTION OF THE CLASS HEADINGS OF ITS OWN TRADE MARKS

National Office	Class Headings cover the entire class	Class Headings terms are to be interpreted literally (means what it says)	Class headings cover the literal meaning of the class headings plus the alphabetical list of the edition of Nice at the time of filing
AT		X	
BG	X		
BX		X	
CY		X	

National Office	Class Headings cover the entire class	Class Headings terms are to be interpreted literally (means what it says)	Class headings cover the literal meaning of the class headings plus the alphabetical list of the edition of Nice at the time of filing
CZ		X	
DE		X	
DK		X	
EE		X	
ES		X	
EUIPO		X	
FI	X		
FR		X	
GR	X		
HR		X	
HU			X
IE		X	
IT	X		
LV		X	
LT			X
MT	X		
NO		X	
PL		X	
PT		X	
RO			X
SE		X	
SI		X	
SK		X	
UK		X	

TABLE 2

TRADE MARKS FILED AFTER "IP TRANSLATOR" CONTAINING ENTIRE NICE CLASS HEADINGS INTERPRETATION BY THE OFFICE OF THE SCOPE OF PROTECTION OF ITS OWN TRADE MARKS

National Office	Class Headings cover the entire class	Class Headings terms are to be interpreted literally (means what it says)	Class headings cover the literal meaning of the class headings plus the alphabetical list of the edition of Nice at the time of filing
AT		X	
BG		X	
BX		X	
CY		X	
CZ		X	
DE		X	
DK		X	
EE		X	
ES		X	
EUIPO		X	
FI		X	
FR		X	
GR		X	

National Office	Class Headings cover the entire class	Class Headings terms are to be interpreted literally (means what it says)	Class headings cover the literal meaning of the class headings plus the alphabetical list of the edition of Nice at the time of filing
HR		X	
HU			X
IE		X	
IT		X (from 20.5.2014)	X (from 3.5.2013)
LV		X	
LT			X
MT		X	
NO		X	
PL		X	
PT		X	
RO			X
SE		X	
SI		X	
SK		X	
UK		X	

TABLE 3
TRADE MARKS FILED AFTER "IP TRANSLATOR" CONTAINING ENTIRE NICE CLASS HEADINGS HOW DOES THE OFFICE REFLECT THE APPLICANT'S INTENTION WITH RESPECT TO THE CLASS HEADINGS AND/OR THE ALPHABETICAL LIST

National Office	All goods and services applied for or registered will be listed individually	A general reference to the applicable edition of the alphabetical list will be available
AT	X	
BG	X	
BX	X (in the publications, certificates and register)	X (in the application)
CY	X	
CZ	X	
DE	X	
DK	X	
EE	X	
ES	X	
EUIPO	X	
FI	X (from 1.1.2014)	X (until 31.12.2013)
FR	X	
GR		X
HR	X	
HU		X
IE	X	
IT	X (from 20.5.2014)	X (from 3.5.2013)
LV	X	
LT	X	
MT	X	
NO	X	
PL	X	
PT	X	
RO		X

National Office	All goods and services applied for or registered will be listed individually	A general reference to the applicable edition of the alphabetical list will be available
SE	X	
SI	X	
SK	X	
UK	X	

TABLE 4
HOW WILL THE SCOPE OF PROTECTION OF CTMS CONTAINING GENERAL INDICATIONS OF THE NICE CLASS HEADINGS BE INTERPRETED

National Office	For CTMs filed before "IP TRANSLATOR"			For CTMs filed after "IP TRANSLATOR"		
	Terms of the class headings are to be interpreted literally	Class headings cover all goods or services in the class	Class headings cover the literal sense of the class headings terms plus the alphabetical list valid at the time of filing	Terms of the class headings are to be interpreted literally	Class headings cover all goods or services in the class	Class headings cover the literal sense of the class headings terms plus the alphabetical list valid at the time of filing
AT	X			X		
BG		X		X		
BX	X			X		
CY	X			X		
CZ	X			X		
DE	X			X		
DK	X			X		
EE	X			X		
ES	X			X		
EUIPO	X			X		
FI			X	X		
FR	X			X		
GR		X		X		
HR	X			X		
HU			X	X		
IE	X			X		
IT		X		X		
LV	X			X		
LT			X	X		
MT		X		X		
PL	X			X		
PT	X			X		
RO			X	X		
SE	X			X		
SI	X			X		
SK	X			X		
UK	X			X		

TABLE 5
EUIPO INTERPRETATION OF THE SCOPE OF PROTECTION OF NATIONAL TMS CONTAINING GENERAL INDICATIONS OF THE NICE CLASS HEADINGS

For trade marks filed <u>before</u> "IP TRANSLATOR"	For trade marks filed <u>after</u> "IP TRANSLATOR"
EUIPO will accept the filing practice of all EU Trade Mark Offices. National trade marks have the scope of protection awarded by the National Office **<u>unless the National Office interprets the Class Headings to cover all goods and services in the Class</u>**. In this case, the National trade mark containing Nice Class headings will be interpreted as covering the class heading on a 'literal' basis plus the alphabetical list of the Nice edition in force at the time of filing.	**Terms are to be interpreted literally**

TABLE 6
"TRADE MARKS FILED AFTER "IP TRANSLATOR" CONTAINING THE ENTIRE CLASS HEADING: HOW CAN THE APPLICANT OBTAIN PROTECTION FOR THE FULL ALPHABETICAL LIST?"

National Office	By completing a declaration	By means of an electronic tickbox	By listing each of the terms individually
AT			X
BG	X		X
BX	X		
CY			X
CZ			X
DE			X
DK			X
EE			X
ES			X
EUIPO			X
FI	X (until 31.12.2013)		X (from 1.1.2014)
FR			X
GR	X		
HR			X
HU	X	X	
IE			X
IT	X (from 3.5.2013)		X (from 20.5.2014)
LV			X
LT	X		X
MT			X
NO			X
PL			X
PT			X
RO	X		
SE			X
SI			X
SK			X
UK			X

COMMON COMMUNICATION ON THE COMMON PRACTICE OF THE SCOPE OF PROTECTION OF BLACK AND WHITE ("B&W") MARKS

Principles of the common practice Convergence Programme CP4 Scope of protection of B&W marks

15 April 2014

NOTES

1. PROGRAMME BACKGROUND

[5.1208]

Despite growth in world wide trade mark and design activity in recent years, efforts to achieve convergence in the way offices around the world operate have only yielded modest results. Within Europe there is still a long way to go to iron out the inconsistencies among the EU IP offices. The OHIM Strategic Plan identifies this as one of its main challenges to address.

With this in mind, the Convergence Programme was established in June 2011. It reflects the shared determination of national offices, OHIM and users, to move towards a new era among EU IP offices with the progressive creation of a European interoperable and collaborative network contributing to a stronger IP environment in Europe.

The vision of this Programme is ***"To establish and communicate clarity, legal certainty, quality and usability for both applicant and office."*** This goal will be achieved by working together to harmonise practices and will bring considerable benefits to both users and IP Offices.

In the first wave the following five projects were launched under the umbrella of the Convergence Programme:

- **CP 1. Harmonisation of Classification**
- **CP 2. Convergence of Class Headings**
- **CP 3. Absolute Grounds – Figurative Marks**
- **CP 4. Scope of Protection of B&W Marks**
- **CP 5. Relative Grounds – Likelihood of Confusion**

This document focuses on the common practice of the fourth project: CP 4. Scope of Protection of B&W Marks

2. PROJECT BACKGROUND

[5.1209]

At the moment of initiation of the project, there was a division between the national offices regarding the scope of protection which should be given to trade marks registered in B&W. Some national offices applied the "B&W-covers-all" approach under which trade marks in B&W have protection for all colours and colour combinations, thus maximum protection, colour-wise. Other offices applied the "what you see is what you get" approach which gives protection to the mark as it is registered, meaning that trade marks which are filed in B&W are only protected as such.

The different practices and interpretations as regards B&W trade marks cause confusion for applicants applying for a mark in multiple offices, as it may not be interpreted the same way in all jurisdictions. This can lead to legal unpredictability in cases of priority, opposition decisions and use, where the conflicting trade marks are registered or seek registration in offices with different practices, since it is not clear which of the two interpretations will then be followed. Given that situation, the offices have seen the need for harmonisation concerning the scope of protection of B&W marks and have considered that a common practice would be beneficial for the users and for themselves.

There are four key deliverables in this project and each of them addresses a different issue, namely the following:

(1) A **common practice including a common approach** described in a document and translated into all EU languages.
(2) A common **communication strategy** for this practice.
(3) An **action plan to put in place** the common practice.
(4) An analysis of the needs to address the **past practice.**

These project deliverables will be created and agreed upon by the national offices and OHIM taking into consideration comments from user associations.

The first working group meeting took place on February 2012 in Alicante to determine the general lines of action, the project scope and the project methodology.

3. OBJECTIVE OF THIS DOCUMENT

[5.1210]

This document will be the reference for OHIM, national offices and BOIP, user associations, applicants, and representatives on the common practice as regards B&W trade marks. It will be widely available and easily accessible, providing a **clear and comprehensive explanation of the principles on which the common practice will be based**. In a next step, following the agreed project methodology, these principles will be applied to each particular case. However, there can be exceptions to these principles.

4. THE PROJECT SCOPE

[5.1211]
The **scope** of the project is:

"This project will converge the practice regarding a ***trade mark filed in B&W and/or greyscale****, and*

(a) *determine whether the* ***same mark in colour is considered identical*** *with respect to:*
 i. ***Priority claims***
 ii. ***Relative grounds for refusal***
(b) *determine whether* ***use*** *of the same mark in colour is considered use of the trade mark registered in B&W (considering also trade marks registered in colour but used in B&W)"*

The following items are **out of the scope** of the project:

- Determine whether a mark in B&W is considered identical to a trade mark filed in colour, with respect to priority claims and relative grounds for refusal (reverse question).
- The assessment of similarities between colours.
- Marks registered in B&W that have acquired distinctiveness in a specific colour due to extensive use.
- Colour marks *per se*.

As agreed during the kick-off meeting in February 2012, **the project will not deal with infringement issues**.

By reorganising and giving structure to the project scope it is possible to identify four different objectives:

- To converge the practice on whether a trade mark registered in B&W and/or greyscale is considered identical to the same mark in colour as regards **priority claims**.
- To converge the practice on whether a trade mark registered in B&W and/or greyscale is considered identical to the same mark in colour as regards **relative grounds for refusal**.
- To converge the practice on whether **use of a mark in colour** is considered use of the **same trade mark registered in B&W**.
- To converge the practice on whether **use of a mark in B&W** is considered use of the **same trade mark registered in colour**.

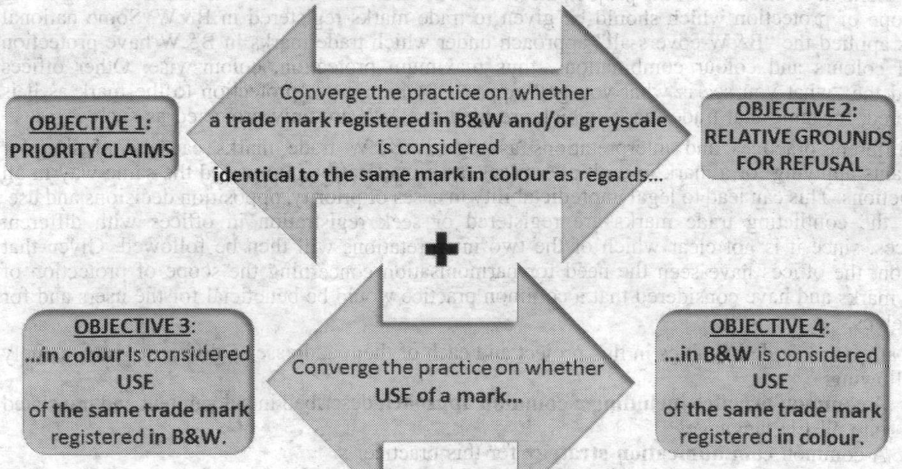

5. THE COMMON PRACTICE

5.1. THE CONCEPT OF IDENTITY

[5.1212]
In the context of the interpretation of Article 8(1)(a) CTMR (which corresponds to Article 4(1)(a) of the Directive), the Court states in its Judgment C-291/00 'LTJ Diffusion' that **"a sign is** identical **with a trade mark only where it reproduces, without any modification or addition, all the**

elements constituting the trade mark or where, viewed as a whole, it contains differences so insignificant that they may go unnoticed by an average consumer." (para 54)

In the context of seniorities, the Court gives the same definition of identity as in *LTJ Diffusion* in its Judgment T103/11 'JUSTING', (para 16), indicating that the condition that the signs must be identical must be interpreted restrictively because of the consequences attached to such identity (paras 17–18).

In addition to that, in its Judgment T 378/11 'MEDINET', the Court also states that **"A concept which is used in different provisions of a legal measure, must, for reasons of coherence and legal certainty, and particularly if it is to be interpreted strictly, be presumed to mean the same thing, irrespective of the provision in which it appears."**

In view of the above:

- The concept of identity applicable to relative grounds for refusal and to priorities must be interpreted in the same way.
- The criterion of identity between the signs must be interpreted strictly: either the two signs should be the same in all respects or they contain differences so insignificant that they may go unnoticed by an average consumer.
- As a consequence, two signs would be identical if the differences between a B&W and a coloured version of the same sign would only be noticed by an average consumer upon side by side examination.

5.1.1 What are "insignificant differences"?

An "insignificant difference" could be defined as follows:

An insignificant difference between two marks is a difference that a reasonably observant consumer will perceive only upon side by side examination **of the marks.**

5.1.2 Practical examples

(**Editor's Note:** *the colour logos are not reproduced in this work. Please refer to the original.*)

5.2. PRIORITY

The principles of priority were first established in the Paris Convention for the Protection of Industrial Property of March 20, 1883. They have been revised several times and last amended in 1979 and ratified by many Contracting States.

Articles 4 (A)(2) of the Paris Convention states that "*Any filing that is equivalent to a regular national filing under the domestic legislation (. . .) shall be recognized as giving rise to the right of priority*".

The priority right is limited in time. It is triggered by the first filing of a trade mark and may be claimed during six months following the first filing, provided the country of first filing was a party to the Paris Convention or to the WTO, or a country with a reciprocity agreement

Sometimes the differences in colour that can exist are due to technical reasons (printer, scanner, etc.), since up to some years ago it was only possible to issue a priority document in B&W because colour printers or colour copiers did not exist. The document was therefore received in B&W irrespective of the colour in which the mark was originally registered. As this is not the case anymore, the difference between marks filed in colour and marks filed in B&W acquires more relevance.

A priority mark filed in B&W can contain a colour claim or not. The following possibilities exist:

- No colour claim whatsoever is present
- Specific colours (other than B&W and greyscales) are claimed
- The colour claim expressly states the colours black and white only
- The colour claim expressly states black, white and grey (the mark is in greyscale)
- The colour claim states that the mark is intended to cover all colours

For this reason, with regards to priority the marks need to be the same in the strictest possible meaning, and the examiner will object if there is any difference in the appearance of the marks. Therefore, and notwithstanding the technological differences or the colour claims, **a trade mark registered in B&W is not considered identical to the same sign in colour as regards priority claims. However, if the differences in colour are so insignificant that they may go unnoticed by the average consumer, the signs will be considered identical.**[1]

As a result of the aforementioned, the following practical implications can be drawn with respect to priorities:

– If the priority mark has no colour claim and is depicted in greyscale, it will be identical to the same mark with a colour claim stating "greyscale", unless it contains "significant differences"
– If the priority mark has no colour claim and is depicted in B&W, it will be identical to the same mark with a colour claim stating "black and white", unless it contains "significant differences".

On the contrary,

– If the priority mark contains a colour claim "black and white" and the application is filed in colour (other than the colours black and white) the marks will not be identical and thus the priority claim will not be accepted, unless the differences are insignificant.

NOTES

[1] In relation to International Trade Mark Applications, the application form requires that where priority is claimed from a B&W mark containing a colour claim, the later mark be reproduced using the colours as claimed.

5.3. RELATIVE GROUNDS FOR REFUSAL

According to Article 4(1)(a) of the Directive 2008/95/EC of The European Parliament and of The Council of 22 October 2008 to approximate the laws of the Member States relating to trade marks, "*A trade mark shall not be registered or, if registered, shall be liable to be declared invalid:*

(a) ***If it is identical with an earlier trade mark****, and the goods or services for which the trade mark is applied for or is registered are identical with the goods or services for which the earlier trade mark is protected."*

In accordance with Judgment C-291/00 'LTJ Diffusion', the national offices and OHIM agreed on the following conclusion:

The differences between a B&W and a coloured version of the same sign will normally be noticed by the average consumer. Only under exceptional circumstances, namely where these differences are so insignificant that they may go unnoticed by an average consumer, will the signs be considered identical.

Therefore, it is not necessary to find a strict conformity between the signs. However, the difference in colour must be negligible and hardly noticeable by an average consumer, for the signs to be considered identical. The fact that the signs are not identical is without prejudice to a possible similarity between the signs which could lead to likelihood of confusion. Similarity, however, is outside the scope of this project.

5.4. USE

In general terms, Art.10.1 (a) of the *Directive 2008/95/EC of The European Parliament and of The Council of 22 October 2008 to approximate the laws of the Member States relating to trade marks* states that:

"The following shall also constitute ***use*** *within the meaning of the first subparagraph:*

(a) *use of the trade mark in a form* ***differing in elements which do not alter the distinctive character of the mark*** *in the form in which it was registered"*

According to this article, use of the mark in a form different from the one registered still constitutes use of the trade mark as long as it does not alter the distinctive character of the trade mark. This provision allows the proprietor of the mark to make variations in the sign as long as these variations do not alter its distinctive character.

Therefore, it is not necessary to find a strict conformity between the sign as it is used and the sign as it has been registered.

As regards specifically alterations in colour, the main question that needs to be addressed is whether the mark as used alters this distinctive character of the registered mark, i.e. whether use of the mark in colour, while being registered in B&W (and the reverse question), constitutes an alteration of the registered form. These questions have to be answered on a case-by-case basis using the criteria below.

For the purposes of **USE**, a change only in colour **does not alter the distinctive character of the trade mark** as long as:

- The **word/figurative elements coincide** and are the **main distinctive elements**.
- The **contrast of shades is respected**.
- Colour or combination of colours does **not have distinctive character in itself**.
- Colour is **not one of the main contributors to the overall distinctiveness** of the mark.

This goes in line with the MAD case (Judgment of 24/05/2012, T-152/11, 'MAD', paras 41, 45), where the Court considers that use of a mark in a different form is acceptable, as long as the arrangement of the verbal/figurative elements stays the same, the word/figurative elements coincide, are the main distinctive elements and the contrast of shades is respected.

5.5. GREYSCALE

It would be too difficult to make a distinction between grey consisting of black and white pixels, and the colour grey, making dependent the sort of protection on the type of grey.

a) Priority

A trade mark registered in greyscale is not considered identical to the same mark in colour as regards priority claims.

A trade mark registered in B&W should only be considered identical to the same mark in greyscale if the differences in the contrast of shades are so insignificant that they may go unnoticed by an average consumer.

b) Relative grounds for refusal

The differences between a greyscale and a coloured version of the same mark will normally be noticed by the average consumer.

Only under exceptional circumstances, namely where these differences are so insignificant that they may go unnoticed by an average consumer, will the marks be considered identical.

c) Use

For the purposes of **USE**, a change only in colour **does not alter the distinctive character of the trade mark** as long as:

- The **word/figurative elements coincide** and are the **main distinctive elements**.
- The **contrast of shades is respected.**
- Colour or combination of colours does **not have distinctive character in itself**.
- Colour is **not one of the main contributors to the overall distinctiveness** of the mark.

6. OFFICES WITH LEGAL CONSTRAINTS

[5.1213]
The Swedish, Danish and Norwegian national offices, acknowledging and supporting the work carried out by the working group, opt out of implementation of the common practice due to legal constraints, and submit the following statements:

6.1 SWEDEN

"The Swedish office has not formally participated in the working group but submitted comments to the working documents throughout the project. The Swedish office fully supports the strive towards a common practice and endorses the principles behind the common practice as presented in the current document. Due to legal constraints that imply that B&W or greyscale marks cover all colours, the Swedish office is currently not in a position to implement the common practice. The legal constraints emanate from the preparatory work in SOU 1958:10, p107, which is still valid in Sweden."

6.2 DENMARK

"The DKPTO has participated in the working group in CP4 and fully supports the continued effort to converge the practices of the EU offices in the area of trademarks. However, due to legal constraints in national law that imply that B&W marks cannot be interpreted as simply consisting of the colours black and white, and as the practice described in the "common practice" will have retroactive effect, the DKPTO is not at present in a position to implement this practice."

6.3 NORWAY

"The Norwegian office has participated in the project and fully supports the continued effort to converge the practices of the European offices in the area of trade marks. However, under our national law, marks in B&W have protection for all colours when assessing likelihood of confusion. Due to this legal constraint, the Norwegian office is not at present in a position to implement the part of the common practice on relative grounds which concerns likelihood of confusion."

COMMON COMMUNICATION ON THE COMMON PRACTICE OF RELATIVE GROUNDS OF REFUSAL – LIKELIHOOD OF CONFUSION (IMPACT OF NON-DISTINCTIVE/WEAK COMPONENTS)

Principles of the common practice Convergence Programme
CP5 Relative Grounds — Likelihood of Confusion (Impact of non-distinctive/weak components)

2 October 2014

NOTES

1. PROGRAMME BACKGROUND

[5.1214]
Despite the growth in world-wide trade mark and design activity in recent years, efforts to achieve

convergence in the way offices around the world operate have only yielded modest results. Within Europe there is still a long way to go to iron out the inconsistencies among the EU IP offices. The OHIM Strategic Plan identifies this as one of the main challenges to address.

With this in mind the Convergence Programme was established in June 2011. It reflects the shared determination of national offices, the OHIM and users, to move towards a new era among EU IP offices with the progressive creation of a European interoperable and collaborative network contributing to a stronger IP environment in Europe.

The vision of this Programme is ***"To establish and communicate clarity, legal certainty, quality and usability for both applicant and office."*** This goal will be achieved by working together to harmonise practices and will bring considerable benefits to both users and IP Offices.

In the first wave the following five projects were launched under the umbrella of the Convergence Programme:

- **CP 1. Harmonisation of Classification**
- **CP 2. Convergence of Class Headings**
- **CP 3. Absolute Grounds – Figurative Marks**
- **CP 4. Scope of Protection of B&W Marks**
- **CP 5. Relative Grounds – Likelihood of Confusion**

This document focuses on the common practice of the fifth project: CP 5. Relative Grounds – Likelihood of Confusion

2. PROJECT BACKGROUND

[5.1215]

At the time of initiation of the project, there was a division among OHIM, BOIP and the national offices regarding the different interpretations on the assessment and consequences of dealing with non-distinctive/weak components of marks in the examination of relative grounds for refusal (likelihood of confusion).

In particular there were different practices and interpretations regarding what importance, if any, should be attached to the fact that an earlier and later mark, covering identical goods and/or services, coincide in a component that has no (or low) distinctiveness. These different practices and interpretations led to different outcomes when assessing likelihood of confusion even though the facts of the case were the same (the marks and the relevant goods and services at issue).

Such differences led to unpredictability and legal uncertainty in the examination of relative grounds. Consequently, the offices saw the need for harmonisation and considered that a common practice would be beneficial for the users and for themselves.

The aim of this project is to **converge the approach regarding the impact** of **non-distinctive/weak components of the marks at issue, which has to be taken into account for the assessment of likelihood of confusion.**

There are four key deliverables in this project each of which addresses a different issue:

(1) A **common practice including a common approach** to be set out in a document and translated into all EU languages.
(2) A common **communication strategy** for this practice.
(3) An **action plan to implement** the common practice.
(4) An analysis of the needs to address the **past practice**.

These project deliverables are created and agreed upon by the national offices and OHIM taking into consideration the comments of the user associations.

The present document is the first of the four deliverables

The first working group meeting took place in February 2012 in Alicante to determine the general lines of action, the project scope and the project methodology. Subsequent meetings were held in October 2012, June 2013 and October 2013 during which the objectives of the project were thoroughly discussed by the Work Package Group, and agreement on the principles for the common practice was reached. Also, several presentations on the project were given during the Liaison meeting and the ABBC meeting.

3. OBJECTIVE OF THIS DOCUMENT

[5.1216]

This document is the reference for IP offices, user associations, applicants, opponents and representatives on the common practice as regards non-distinctive/weak components of marks for the purpose of assessing likelihood of confusion, assuming that the goods and/or services are identical. It will be made widely available and will be easily accessible, providing a **clear and comprehensive explanation of the principles on which the common practice will be based**. These principles will be generally applied, and are aimed at covering the large majority of cases. Since likelihood of confusion must be assessed on a case-by-case basis, the common principles serve as guidance in order to ensure that different offices come to a similar, predictable conclusion when the same marks and grounds are involved.

4. THE PROJECT SCOPE

[5.1217]
The **scope** of the project reads:

> *"This project will converge the practice regarding* ***non-distinctive/weak components of marks*** *for the purpose of* ***assessing likelihood of confusion (LOC)****, assuming that the* ***goods and/or services are identical.*** *In particular it will:*
>
> - *Define* ***what marks are subject to assessment of distinctiveness:*** *the earlier mark (and/or parts thereof) and/or the later mark (and/or parts thereof);*
> - *Determine the* ***criteria to assess the distinctiveness*** *of the mark (and/or parts thereof);*
> - *Determine the impact on LOC when the* ***common components have a low degree of distinctiveness***
> - *Determine the impact on LOC when the* ***common components have no distinctiveness."***

The eleventh recital of the Directive 2008/95/EC of the European Parliament and of the Council of 22 October 2008, to approximate the laws of the Member States relating to trade marks (the "Directive"), states that the appreciation of likelihood of confusion depends on numerous elements and, as the case-law has repeatedly asserted, it must be appreciated **globally**, taking into account all factors relevant to the circumstances of the case (e.g. see, Judgments C-251/95 'Sabel' para 22 and C-342/97, 'Lloyd Schuhfabrik Meyer', para 18).

In the Judgment C-251/95, 'Sabel', the Court states that:

> "global appreciation of the visual, aural or conceptual similarity of the marks in question, must be based on the overall impression given by the marks, bearing in mind, in particular, their distinctive and dominant components."

As already mentioned, the project analyses the **impact of the non-distinctive/weak components** of the marks at issue as one of the factors to be taken into account for the assessment of likelihood of confusion.

Although **there are many factors** that may have an impact in the **global appreciation of likelihood of confusion**, such as the dominant components, the degree of attention of the relevant public, coexistence, situation of the market, family of marks, etc., it is not the objective of this project to determine which are all the factors, nor the criteria for their assessment, nor the interdependency between them. Consequently, the project does not deal with the overall assessment of likelihood of confusion, but with one of its essential parts.

The following are out of the scope of the project:

- *The assessment of enhanced distinctiveness and/or acquired distinctiveness through use and/or reputation: for the purpose of this project, it is assumed that there is no evidence and/or claim and/or previous knowledge that any of the marks are reputed or have an enhanced distinctiveness acquired through use.*
- *Agreement on the factors that are considered when assessing the likelihood of confusion.*
- *Agreement on the interdependencies between the assessment of distinctiveness and all the other factors that are considered when assessing the likelihood of confusion.*
- *Language issues: It is considered for the sake of the project that marks which contain word elements with no (or low) distinctiveness in English will be considered as having no (or low) distinctiveness in all languages and are understood by the national offices.*

It is possible to identify four different objectives, as represented in the following figure:

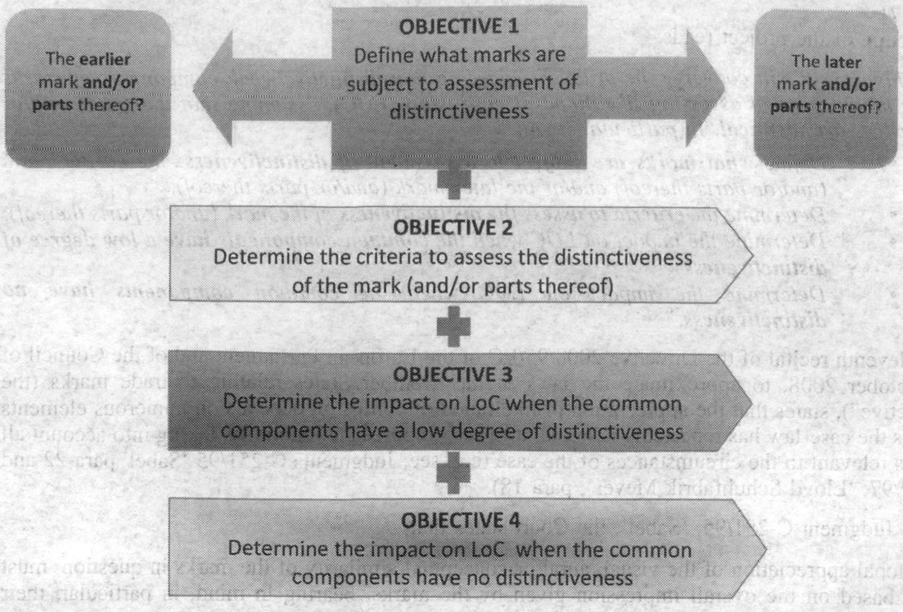

Objectives of the project.

Several approaches are followed for the examination of likelihood of confusion, wherein the distinctiveness of the components may be assessed at different stages. Regardless of the performed approach, the practical outcome regarding the impact of the non-distinctive/weak components of the marks at issue will remain unaffected.

5. THE COMMON PRACTICE

5.1. ASSESSMENT OF DISTINCTIVENESS: THE EARLIER MARK AND/OR PARTS THEREOF, AND/OR THE LATER MARK AND/OR PARTS THEREOF (OBJECTIVE 1)

[5.1218]
When evaluating likelihood of confusion:

- The distinctiveness of the earlier mark as a whole is assessed.
- The distinctiveness of all components of the **earlier** mark and of the **later** mark is also assessed, prioritising the coinciding components.

Nonetheless, when assessing the distinctiveness of the earlier mark as a whole, account must be taken of the fact that in accordance with the Judgment of the Court C-196/11P, *F1-LIVE*, when assessing likelihood of confusion the validity of earlier registered marks may not be called into question (para 40). Therefore, "it is necessary to **acknowledge a certain degree of distinctiveness** of an earlier national mark on which an opposition against the registration of a Community trade mark is based." (para 47).

5.2. CRITERIA TO ASSESS THE DISTINCTIVENESS OF THE MARK (AND/OR PARTS THEREOF)(OBJECTIVE 2)

In interpreting the provisions contained in both Articles 4(1)(b) and 5(1)(b) of the Directive the Court in its Judgment C-342/97, 'Lloyd Schuhfabrik Meyer', states that:

> "in determining the **distinctive character of a mark** and, accordingly, in assessing whether it is highly distinctive, the national court must make an overall assessment of the greater or lesser capacity of the mark to identify the goods or services for which it has been registered as coming from a particular undertaking, and thus to distinguish those goods or services from those of other undertakings" (para 22).

Accordingly, and due to the lesser capacity of a weak mark to perform its essential function within the market, its scope of protection considering its non (or low) distinctive components should be narrow.

When assessing the distinctiveness of the marks in relative grounds the same criteria that are used to determine distinctiveness as in absolute grounds apply. However, in relative grounds these criteria are used not only to determine whether a minimum threshold of distinctiveness is met but also to consider the varying degrees of distinctiveness.

5.3. IMPACT ON LIKELIHOOD OF CONFUSION WHEN THE COMMON COMPONENTS HAVE A LOW DEGREE OF DISTINCTIVENESS (OBJECTIVE 3).

- When marks share an element with low distinctiveness, the assessment of LOC will focus on the impact of the non-coinciding components on the overall impression of the marks. It will take into account the similarities/differences and distinctiveness of the non-coinciding components.
- A coincidence in an element with a low degree of distinctiveness will not normally **on its own** lead to LOC.

However, there may be LOC if:

- The other components are of a lower (or equally low) degree of distinctiveness or are of insignificant visual impact and the overall impression of the marks is similar.

OR

- The overall impression of the marks is highly similar or identical.

Examples:

* For the purpose of this project, all the other factors which may be relevant for the global appreciation of likelihood of confusion are deemed not to affect the outcome. Also, it is considered that the goods and services are identical.

(**Editor's Note:** *the colour logos are not reproduced in this work. Please refer to the original.*)

5.4. IMPACT ON LIKELIHOOD OF CONFUSION WHEN THE COMMON COMPONENTS HAVE NO DISTINCTIVENESS (OBJECTIVE 4).

- When marks share a component with no distinctiveness, the assessment of LOC will focus on the impact of the non-coinciding components on the overall impression of the marks. It will take into account the similarities/differences and distinctiveness of the non-coinciding components.
- A coincidence only in non-distinctive components **does not lead to LOC.**
- When marks also contain other figurative and/or word elements which are similar, **there will be LOC,** if the overall impression of the marks is highly similar or identical.

Examples:

* For the purpose of this project, all the other factors which may be relevant for the global appreciation of likelihood of confusion are deemed not to affect the outcome. Also, it is considered that the goods and services are identical.

(**Editor's Note:** *the colour logos are not reproduced in this work. Please refer to the original.*)

COMMUNICATION NO 1/2016 OF THE PRESIDENT OF THE OFFICE

concerning the implementation of Article 28 EUTMR

8 February 2016

NOTES

THE PRESIDENT OF THE OFFICE FOR HARMONIZATION IN THE INTERNAL MARKET (TRADE MARKS AND DESIGNS),

Having regard to Council Regulation (EC) No 207/2009 of 26 February 2009 on the Community trade mark (CTMR),

Having regard to Commission Regulation (EC) No 2868/95 of 13 December 1995 implementing Council Regulation (EC) No 40/94 on the EU trade mark (CTMIR),

Having regard to Regulation (EU) No 2015/2424 of 16 December 2015 of the European Parliament and of the Council amending Council Regulation (EC) No 207/2009 on the Community trade mark and Commission Regulation (EC) No 2868/95 implementing Council Regulation (EC) No 40/94 on the Community trade mark and repealing Commission Regulation (EC) No 2869/95 on the fees payable to the Office for Harmonization in the Internal Market (Trade Marks and Designs) (the Amending Regulation),

Whereas:

(1) Communication No 2/12 of the President of 20 June 2012 concerning the use of class headings in lists of goods and services for Community trade mark applications and registrations established the practice of the Office as regards the scope of protection of class headings in applications and registrations filed before, and after, the entry into force of that Communication in the light of the Court's judgment of 19/06/2012 in case C-307/10, IP Translator, EU:C:2012:361.

(2) Upon entry into force of the Amending Regulation, Article 28(1) to (7) of Council Regulation No 207/2009, as amended (EUTMR), will lay down the requirements for designating and classifying goods and services, including the conditions for, and the consequences of, the use of class headings.

(3) Article 28(8) EUTMR allows for a transitional period during which proprietors of EU trade marks applied for before 22 June 2012 and registered for the entire heading of a Nice class may declare that their intention on the date of filing had been to seek protection for goods and services beyond those covered by the literal meaning of that heading.

(4) Pursuant to Article 124(2)(a) CTMR, the President of the Office will take all necessary steps, including the adoption of internal administrative instructions and the publication of notices, to ensure the functioning of the Office.

(5) In the absence of more detailed implementing rules and in view of the need to give effect to Article 28 EUTMR, it is necessary to specify the procedure for its implementation, explain how it will be applied and determine its impact on future and existing registrations,

HAS ADOPTED THE FOLLOWING COMMUNICATION:1.

SCOPE OF ARTICLE 28 EUTMR

[5.1219]
Article 28(1) to (7) EUTMR lays down the requirements for designating and classifying goods and services, including the conditions for, and the consequences of, the use of the class headings of the Nice Classification.

In accordance with Article 28(3) EUTMR, the Office will accept the use of general indications included in the class headings of the Nice Classification or other general terms, provided that they comply with the requisite standards of clarity and precision set out in Article 28 EUTMR. This provision applies directly to the designation of goods and services in all EU trade mark applications filed as from the entry into force of the EUTMR.

In accordance with Article 28(5) EUTMR, the use of class headings of the Nice classification and other general terms shall be interpreted as including all the goods or services clearly covered by the literal meaning of the general indication or term. Article 28(5) EUTMR applies as from the date of entry into force of the EUTMR and extends to all marks filed **after** 21 June 2012, as well as to applications that were filed **on or before** that date but are still not registered at the date of entry into force of the EUTMR.

Further guidance on the rules governing the designation and classification of goods and services are given in the Guidelines of the Office, Part B, Examination, Section 3, Classification.

Article 28(8) EUTMR introduces a transitional period during which proprietors of EU trade marks applied for before 22 June 2012 and registered for the entire heading of a Nice class may declare that their intention on the date of filing was to seek protection for goods and services beyond those covered by the literal meaning of the heading of that class, provided that the goods or services so designated are included in the alphabetical list for that class of the edition of the Nice Classification in force at the date of filing.

Declarations made pursuant to Article 28(8) EUTMR (declarations) are subject to the conditions specified in this Communication.2.

ELIGIBLE REGISTRATIONS

[5.1220]
Declarations may only be made for EU trade marks that were filed before 22 June 2012, and continue to be registered for the entire heading of at least one Nice class.

In accordance with Articles 145 and 151 CTMR, the provisions of Article 28(8) EUTMR also extend to protected international registrations that designated, or subsequently designated the EU before 22 June 2012, and that continue to be in force for the entire class heading of at least one Nice class.

The existence of additional goods and services in the specification, either in the same or in another class, does not preclude the application of Article 28(8) EUTMR to the class that includes the entire heading, provided that the language used does not limit or in any way disclaim the general indications of the Nice class heading.3.

TIME LIMIT

[5.1221]
Declarations must be submitted to the Office within the period laid down in the Amending Regulation, that is, between 23 March 2016 and 24 September 2016 inclusive.4.

FORM

[5.1222]
In accordance with Rule 79 CTMIR, applications to record a declaration in the Register must be filed in writing.

In order to ensure that declarations concerning EU trade marks are handled efficiently, the Office has created a specific online form. It can be found in the User Area of the Office's website under 'Online forms — online Recordal application — Recordal — EUTM Recordal - Declaration under Art.28(8)' (the form).

The form contains a text box for indicating the goods and services claimed in accordance with Section 8 below.

The text box should be completed by indicating the class number followed by the names of the goods and services to be added. The individual goods and services should be separated by commas (to separate items within a similar category or expression) and/or semi-colons (to separate expressions), as the case may be. The different classes should be listed on a new line using a paragraph break.

The use of the online form is highly recommended as it may considerably decrease the likelihood of formality deficiencies. Applicants who opt for other means of communication must ensure that their application complies with the requirements of this Communication.

For international registrations designating, or subsequently designating the EU, declarations should be filed using the ordinary Recordal application form.5.

LANGUAGE

[5.1223]
In accordance with Rule 95(b) CTMIR, declarations for EU trade marks filed directly must be filed in one of the five languages of the Office, namely English, French, German, Italian or Spanish.

Any language version of the form identified in Section 4 above may be used, provided that it is completed in one of the languages of the Office, in particular as concerns the list of goods and services.

Declarations for international registrations designating or subsequently designating the EU must be filed in the language of the international application.6.

APPLICANTS AND REPRESENTATIVES

[5.1224]
Declarations must be submitted to the Office by the proprietor(s) of the EU trade mark, or the holder of the international registration designating the EU, or their duly appointed representative before the Office.

The standard rules on mandatory representation apply (see Article 92(2) CTMR).

When the proprietor appoints a representative, they must indicate the representative's name and Office ID number. If the representative has not yet been assigned an ID number, the business address must be indicated. The Office may request authorisation in accordance with Articles 92(3) and 93(1) CTMR, in particular if the declaration is submitted by a representative different from the representative on file.7.

MANDATORY INDICATIONS

[5.1225]
By analogy to Rule 36(1) CTMIR, declarations must contain the following information:

(a) the registration number of the EU trade mark, or international registration designating the EU;
(b) the proprietor's name and/or the proprietor's Office ID number;
(c) an indication of each of the goods and services the proprietor wishes to add, in accordance with Sections 4 and 8.

Pursuant to Rule 79 CTMIR, the claim must be signed by the EU trade mark proprietor or their duly appointed representative.

In accordance with Rules 80 and 82 CTMIR, if the declaration is submitted by telecopier (fax) or by electronic means, the indication of the sender's name is deemed to be equivalent to a signature.8.

CONTENT OF THE DECLARATION

[5.1226]
In accordance with Article 28(8) EUTMR, the goods and services designated must be indicated in the proprietor's declaration in a clear, precise and specific manner.

The declaration must only include goods and/or services that:

(i) are contained in the alphabetical list for the class in question of the edition of the Nice Classification in force at the date of filing, and
(ii) are not clearly covered by the literal meaning of the general indications of the corresponding class heading.

In particular, the Office will object to:

- claims for the entire alphabetical list;

- the use of unclear, imprecise or unspecific expressions;
- declarations for goods and services that are clearly covered by the literal meaning of the class heading;
- declarations for goods or services not contained in the alphabetical list in question.

In order to assist proprietors in identifying goods and services that go beyond the literal meaning of the general indications of the class headings, the Office has compiled a non-exhaustive list of examples of such goods and services in Annex I of this Communication. This list is purely a guide that identifies the goods and services that the Office considers are clearly not covered by the literal meaning of the headings. Declarations relating to any of the goods or services included in this list for the corresponding class and edition will not be objected to by the Office on the ground of being covered by the literal meaning of the general indications.9.

FEES

[5.1227]
Declarations are not subject to a fee.10.

EXAMINATION BY THE OFFICE

[5.1228]
The Office will examine whether the declaration complies with the requirements of Article 28(8) EUTMR and with Sections 2 to 8 of this Communication. If the declaration does not comply with these requirements, the Office will issue a deficiency letter stating the reasons why the claim is unacceptable and set a deadline of two months for the proprietor to remedy the deficiency. Rule 71 CTMIR sets down the applicable rules on time limits.

In the absence of a response, or if the deficiency is not overcome, the declaration will be rejected, wholly or in part.

In accordance with Articles 58 to 60 and 135 CTMR the proprietor may file an appeal against this decision.11.

REGISTRATION AND PUBLICATION

[5.1229]
If the declaration complies with the requirements of Article 28(8) EUTMR and Sections 2 to 8 above, the Office will amend the Register and inform the proprietor accordingly.

The declaration will be published in the EUTM Bulletin, in Part C.3.2.

The publication will contain the following data:
- the EU trade mark registration number;
- the list of goods and services after the Article 28(8) EUTMR declaration;
- the date and number of the entry of the Article 28(8) EUTMR declaration (i.e. the date when the Register was amended);
- the date the entry is published in the EUTM Bulletin;
- the indication 'Art. 28(8)' under INID code 580.

In the case of international registrations designating or subsequently designating the EU, the Office will send the International Bureau statements under Rule 18*ter*(4) of the Common Regulations.12.

TRACEABILITY

[5.1230]
In the interest of legal certainty, and in order to enable the competent authorities and economic operators to keep track of additions made by virtue of Article 28(8) EUTMR, in particular for the purposes of applying Article 28(9) EUTMR, acceptable declarations will be entered in the Register and can be found as follows:
- through the Office's online database (eSearch Plus) under the 'Publications' section for the mark concerned, identified by the description 'Partial Surrender/Article 28(8) declaration': upon clicking, the relevant publication will open in the CTM Bulletin under Part C.3.2, 'Partial Surrender/Article 28(8) declaration', with the indication 'Art. 28(8)' under INID code 580 (date on which the Register is amended);
- through the Office's online database (eSearch Plus) under the 'Recordals' section for the mark concerned, identified as being Recordal type 'Declaration under Art. 28(8) EUTMR';

For international registrations designating the EU:
- the International Bureau will record and publish the pertinent information in the International Register and inform the holders of the concerned international registrations;13.

EFFECT

[5.1231]
As from the end of the period referred to in Section 3, all the marks referred to in Section 2 for which

no acceptable declaration has been filed will be deemed to protect only the goods or services clearly covered by the literal meaning of the indications included in the heading of the relevant class.

During the transitional period referred to in Section 3 above, Communication No 2/12 of 20 June 2012 of the President of the Office will continue to apply.

Declarations filed within the period referred to in Section 3 above will take effect from the date of their entry in the Register. Until registration is effected, the previous paragraph applies.14.

LIMITATIONS OF RIGHTS

[5.1232]
Where the declaration is accepted and the Register is amended, Article 28(9) EUTMR will apply.

Consequently, the amendment of the list of goods and services of the earlier EU trade mark or international registration designating the EU, pursuant to Article 28(8) EUTMR, shall not give the proprietor the right to prevent the use by third parties of any of the goods or services so added, provided that use commenced before the Register was amended and did not infringe on the proprietor's rights on the basis of the literal meaning of the goods and services in the Register at that time.

Nor will the proprietor have the right to oppose or to apply for a declaration of invalidity of a later trade mark if that later trade mark was in use or had been applied for prior to the Register being amended and the use in relation to those goods or services did not infringe, or would not have infringed, the proprietor's rights based on the literal meaning of the goods or services recorded in the Register at that time.

Further details on how Article 28(9) EUTMR is applied are given in the Guidelines of the Office, Part C, Opposition, Section 2, Double Identity and Likelihood of Confusion, Chapter 2, Comparison of Goods and Services.15.

RELATIONSHIP WITH OTHER PROVISIONS

[5.1233]
Article 28(8) EUTMR is an exceptional, transitional arrangement that allows proprietors to amend the wording of their specifications in the interest of legal certainty, by expressly identifying goods and services that they originally intended to include in their specifications, but which were not clearly reflected in the Register as they fell outside the natural and usual meaning of the class heading concerned.

Proprietors are advised to carefully consider the declaration they wish to make under Article 28(8) EUTMR bearing in mind, in particular, that any such addition of goods and services (i) is made without prejudice to Article 15, Article 42(2) and Article 51(1)(a) CTMR, with regard to the obligation to put said goods and services to genuine use and (ii) will be subject to the sanctions of Article 28(9) EUTMR.

Therefore, declarations made pursuant to Article 28(8) EUTMR should not be confused with, or be considered as an alternative to, partial surrenders within the meaning of Article 50 CTMR, which are, and will remain, available to proprietors after the end of the transitional period.

In particular, declarations under Article 28(8) EUTMR should not be used to restrict lists containing class headings to specific goods or services covered by their literal meaning, or to replace a general indication with more precise terms. In such cases proprietors should make use of partial surrenders under Article 50 CTMR using the 'Online forms — online Recordal application — Recordal — EUTM Recordal — Partial Surrender'.16.

ENTRY INTO FORCE

[5.1234]
This Communication enters into force on the date of entry into force of the Amending Regulation, that is, 23 March 2016. It will be published in the Official Journal of the Office.

Communication No 2/12 of the President of 20 June 2012, concerning the use of class headings in lists of goods and services for Community trade mark applications and registrations, is repealed:

- as of 23 March 2016, as far as it concerns EU trade marks filed after 21 June 2012, and EU trade marks filed before 22 June 2012 but not yet registered at the time of entry into force of the EUTMR (paragraphs I to V and IV to XI of that Communication);
- as of 25 September 2016, for marks filed before 22 June 2012 and registered for the entire heading of a Nice class at the time of entry into force of the EUTMR, for which no declaration is filed;
- as of the date of entry in the Register for the declaration of those marks for which an acceptable declaration is filed within the period referred to in Section 3 above.

António Campinos

President

DECLARATIONS UNDER ARTICLE 28(8) EUTMR: FREQUENTLY ASKED QUESTIONS

Updated 09/09/2016

NOTES

FREQUENTLY ASKED QUESTIONS

[5.1235]

1. Who can make a declaration under Article 28(8) EUTMR?

Proprietors of EU trade marks, or international registrations designating the EU, filed or designated before 22/06/2012 and registered before the entry into force of Regulation 2015/2424 of 16 December 2015 amending Council Regulation (EC) No 207/2009 of 26 February 2009 on the EU trade mark that contain the entire heading of a Nice Class.

2. Will trade mark owners be informed about the need to amend?

The EUIPO will not individually inform trade mark owners about the possibility of filing a declaration under Article 28(8) EUTMR, but the President of the Office has issued a Communication explaining in detail which marks are affected and what steps owners can take should they wish to amend their specifications.

3. Do all trade mark owners have to make a declaration for trade marks that were filed before 22/06/2012 and which contain an entire class heading?

Trade mark proprietors/holders are not required to confirm whether they wish to cover the items listed in their trade mark or amend their specification. Rather, they may wish to declare that their intention at the date of filing was to seek protection for goods or services beyond those covered by the literal meaning of the class heading, provided that they are included in the alphabetical list for that class in the edition of the Nice Classification in force at the date of filing, and then the Register will be amended accordingly.

In other words, if you have an EU trade mark (or an international registration designating the EU) that complies with the requirements of Article 28(8) EUTMR, but all you wish to protect can be understood to fall within the literal meaning of the class heading, you do not need to take any action. If you would like to make a declaration for goods or services that are included in the alphabetical list but are not covered by the literal meaning of the heading, you will need to take into account the limitations of the effects of the amendment, as laid down in Article 28(9) EUTMR.

4. I have a trade mark for an entire class heading that was filed after 22/06/2012. Can I make a declaration under Article 28(8) EUTMR?

No. Pursuant to the wording of Article 28(8) EUTMR, trade marks filed on or after 22/06/2012 are not eligible.

5. My trade mark was filed before 22/06/2012 for an entire class heading but it is not yet registered. Can I make a declaration under Article 28(8) EUTMR?

No. Pursuant to the wording of Article 28(8) EUTMR, declarations can only be made for **registered** trade marks.

Applicants for EU marks that are not yet registered can amend their specification of goods and services under Article 43 EUTMR. However, this must be done before the entry into force of the amending Regulation. After the entry into force of the amending Regulation, Article 28(5) EUTMR will apply to all pending applications.

6. Do I need to appoint a representative?

Proprietors/holders that have their domicile or place of business in the EEA (European Economic Area) need not appoint a representative.

For all other proprietors/holders, the general rules on representation apply (see the Guidelines, Part A, General Rules, Section 5, Professional Representation).

7. When can the declaration be made?

Article 28(8) EUTMR declarations must be made between 23 March 2016 and 24 September 2016 inclusive.

8. Can the six-month period be extended?

The six-month period for making the declaration cannot be extended. However, as the closing date falls on 24/09/2016 (i.e. a Saturday) and, pursuant to Rule 72 EUTMIR, the deadline is automatically extended for the receipt of documents until the first working day of the Office.

9. Does the provision cover national and international trade marks as well as EU trade marks?

Article 28(8) EUTMR applies to EU trade marks (CTMs) and international registrations designating the EU.

Article 28(8) EUTMR does not apply to national offices, but Article 39(5) of Directive (EU) 2015/2436 of the European Parliament and of the Council does apply. The latter will oblige all EU Member States to interpret class headings literally. In those Member States where the previous policy was to interpret them as covering the entire alphabetical list this may lead to establishing a transitional mechanism, such as Article 28(8) EUTMR. In any event, this is for the Member States concerned to decide within the period they have for transposing the Directive (until 15 January 2019).

10. Which form should I use?

The Office has created a new online Recordal application form, under 'EUTM Recordal' subtype 'Declaration under Art. 28(8)'. The form will be available from 23 March 2016, and can be accessed here. Users need to log in to make the online request.

Proprietors/holders wishing to file on paper should use the normal Recordal Application form.

Only one form may be filed per EU trade mark.

11. In which language can I file my declaration?

Any language version of this form may be used, provided that it is completed in one of the five official languages of the Office, namely, English, French, German, Italian or Spanish in the case of EU trade marks, or in the case of IRs designating or subsequently designating the EU in the language of the international applications (English, French or Spanish).

12. Is there a fee for making an Article 28(8) EUTMR declaration?

No. These entries in the register are free of charge.

13. Is it possible to modify general indications that are considered to be unclear or imprecise (e.g. the 11 general indications)?

Under Article 28(8) EUTMR, it will only be possible to specify the goods and services that go beyond the literal meaning of the class heading of that class, provided that those goods and services are included in the alphabetical list for the class of the edition of the Nice Classification in force at the date of filing.

Proprietors should not use Article 28(8) EUTMR to clarify general indications lacking in clarity and precision (see the Guidelines, Part B, Examination, Section 3, Classification, paragraph 4.2). Article 28(3) EUTMR does not apply retroactively and such indications will be afforded their natural and usual meaning in proceedings before the Office.

Proprietors may, however, amend general indications lacking in clarity and precision by specifying the goods or services covered by the literal meaning, as usual, under Article 50 EUTMR using the recordal type 'Partial Surrender' (for more information see the Guidelines, Part E, Register Operations, Section 1, Changes in a Registration, paragraph 1.3.5, Partial Surrender.)

14. What criteria will be applied to determine whether an expression is clear and precise?

Declarations can only be made for specific goods or services contained within the alphabetical list and not covered by the literal meaning of the class heading for the class of the edition of the Nice Classification in force at the date of filing. All goods and services contained within the alphabetical list are deemed to be sufficiently clear and precise.

15. Will the Office accept all declarations?

No. In particular, the Office will object to:

- generic expressions claiming, for instance, the entire alphabetical list;
- the use of unclear, imprecise or unspecific expressions (e.g. 'all goods in Class X' or 'all goods not clearly covered by the literal meaning');
- declarations for goods and services that are deemed to be clearly covered by the literal meaning of the class heading;
- declarations for goods or services not contained in the alphabetical list in question.

In such cases, the Office will issue a deficiency letter stating the reasons why the claim is unacceptable and set a deadline of two months for the proprietor to remedy the deficiency. In accordance with Rule 71 EUTMIR, the deadline may be extended.

16. In the event that a mark has been limited as such, or as the result of an opposition, or cancellation action, will proprietors/holders be able to amend their list of goods and services under Article 28(8) EUTMR?

If the class heading is limited in any way, the Office cannot accept a declaration under Article 28(8) EUTMR. The trade mark must continue to contain the entire class heading in order for an Article 28(8) declaration to be acceptable.

Oppositions or cancellation actions resulting in a mark being partially rejected must have been worded in such a way that it is clear which goods/services are no longer covered by the mark.

17. Will there be a possibility of opposition or cancellation proceedings against the goods and services included in an Article 28(8) EUTMR declaration?

Under current practice, as defined in Communication No 2/12 of the President of the Office, marks filed on or before 21/06/2012 covering all the general indications of a particular class heading of the Nice Classification are interpreted as covering all the goods and services included in the alphabetical list of the particular class concerned in the edition in force at the time when the filing was made.

The transitional period, during which proprietors can declare that their intention at the time of filing was to cover specific goods and services of the alphabetical list not covered by the literal meaning, is an opportunity for proprietors to clarify the exact scope of their goods and services. It is not considered to be an extension of the scope of goods and services, but rather a clarification based on the assumption that these goods and services already formed part of the scope of the registration even though they were not stated explicitly.

The exact wording of Article 28(8) EUTMR makes it clear that the possibility of making such a declaration is without prejudice to use requirements. That provision, however, does not foresee the possibility of filing an opposition or cancellation against the declaration. Nor does this situation fall under Rule 14 CTMIR, which is only applicable to the publication of applications. It is clear, therefore, that the intention of the legislator was that no new opposition period should be opened.

Six months after the entry into force of the amending Regulation, and where no declaration under Article 28(8) EUTMR has been made, those marks will be deemed to cover only goods and services clearly covered by the literal meaning of the indications included in the class heading of the relevant class.

18. I have a CTM on which an international application is based. Can I make a declaration?

Yes, providing your CTM fulfils the requirements of Article 28(8) EUTMR (i.e. filed before 22/06/2012 and registered for an entire class heading of the Nice Classification). The Office will not forward the declaration to WIPO as it is not considered to be a 'ceasing of effect'. According to the Office's interpretation, the scope of protection is not reduced, only clarified. The declaration will not have any immediate effect in the designated territories, which will continue to interpret the heading in accordance with their respective national laws.

19. Will the Office provide an exhaustive list of terms clearly not covered by the literal meaning of the class headings?

As an Annex to the Communication of the President on the implementation of Article 28 EUTMR, the Office has provided users with a non-exhaustive list of examples of goods and services clearly not covered by the literal meaning of the general indications of the Nice class headings. This list is purely for guidance. Declarations relating to any of the goods or services included in this list for the corresponding class and edition will not be objected to by the Office on the ground of being covered by the literal meaning of the general indications.

20. Can I make a declaration for goods or services not included in the list of examples?

Yes. The list is purely for guidance purposes. It is a non-exhaustive list containing examples of terms clearly not covered by the literal meaning, but there may be others for which there is reasonable doubt as to whether or not they are covered by the literal meaning of the class heading. Pursuant to Article 28(8) EUTMR, the Office will not object to the inclusion of terms not clearly covered by the headings in the specification. An example would be *computer software, recorded* or *computer programs [downloadable software].* Computer software was not included as such in the class heading of Class 9 in the editions of the Nice Classification that were in force before 01/01/2012. While it could be interpreted as being covered by the literal meaning of one of the indications of the heading, namely *data processing equipment and computers*, the Office will not object to its inclusion in a declaration under Article 28(8) EUTMR, since there is reasonable doubt (i.e. it is not clearly covered by the class heading).

Further examples of terms that would be accepted as, even if they were considered to be covered, there is room for reasonable doubt are *diagnostic preparations for medical purposes* in Class 5 or *personnel recruitment* in Class 35.

21. If my mark fulfils all the requirements for making an Article 28(8) EUTMR declaration and I choose to make one, what are the consequences?

The Office will examine the declaration to ensure that it fulfils all the requirements. If the declaration is accepted and the register is amended, Article 28(9) EUTMR will apply.

Pursuant to Article 28(8) EUTMR, amending the list of goods and services of the earlier EU trade mark (or international registration designating the EU) will not give the proprietor the right to prevent third parties from using any of the added goods or services, on the understanding that the use commenced before the register was amended and did not infringe the proprietor's rights on the basis of the literal meaning of the goods and services in the register at that time.

Furthermore, the proprietor will not have the right to oppose or apply for a declaration of invalidity of a later trade mark if that later trade mark was in use or had been applied for prior to the register being amended, and that the use in relation to those goods or services did not infringe, or would not have infringed, the proprietor's rights based on the literal meaning of the goods or services recorded in the register at that time.

22. If my mark fulfils all the requirements for making an Article 28(8) EUTMR declaration but I choose not to make one, what are the consequences?

Under Article 28(8) EUTMR, if no declaration has been made within six months of the entry into force of the amending Regulation, those marks will be deemed to cover only goods and services clearly covered by the literal meaning of the indications included in the class heading of the relevant class.

23. How can I see if a declaration under Article 28(8) EUTMR has been recorded in the register?

Under Article 28(8) EUTMR, acceptable declarations will be recorded in the register and published in the EUTM Bulletin in Part C.3.2. These changes will also be reflected in eSearch plus. Acceptable declarations can be found as follows:

- through the Office's online database (eSearch plus) under the 'Publications' section for the mark concerned, and identified by the description 'Partial Surrender/Article 28(8) declaration'. Upon clicking, the relevant publication will open in the EUTM Bulletin under Part C.3.2 'Partial Surrender/Article 28(8) declaration', with the indication 'Art. 28(8)' under INID code 580 (date that the register is amended).
- through the Office's online database (eSearch plus) under the 'Recordals' section for the mark concerned, identified as being recordal type 'Declaration under Art. 28(8) EUTMR'.

The Office is looking at ways of reflecting such entries clearly in the list of goods and services on its website. This requires IT developments and may take some time.

24. How will the Office deal with oppositions when the ground for opposition is a national trade mark registration whose list of goods contains the class heading of the class?

Table 5 of the Common Communication on the Implementation of 'IP Translator' explains how the Office interprets the scope of protection of national trade marks containing general indications of the Nice class headings.

25. How do I know if I have all the general indications of a class heading?

WIPO's website on the Nice Classification contains all the editions and versions of the Nice Classification since it was established, as well as an indication of the class headings for each edition/version.

The existence of additional goods and services in the specification, either in the same or in another class, does not preclude the application of Article 28(8) EUTMR to the class that includes the entire heading, provided that the language used does not limit or in any way disclaim the general indications of the heading. For example, a limitation in the class heading of Class 25, *Clothing; footwear; headgear* to *except shirts* would preclude the application of Article 28(8) EUTMR, because the general indication *clothing* has been limited.

26. Which Nice Classification should I use for my declaration?

The wording of Article 28(8) requires that the declaration be made for goods and services that appear in the alphabetical list of the Nice Classification. The Nice Classification has to be the one which was in force at the time the trade mark was filed. It can be anything from the 6th edition to the 10th edition which was in force at the time of filing the trade mark.

27. Can I make a declaration for goods or services that are not contained in the alphabetical list in force at the time of filing?

No. The goods and services have to be contained in the alphabetical list that was in force at the time of filing.

28. Will the Office make all language versions of the Nice Classification available for all the editions concerned?

The Office will not be making the Nice Classification available in all language versions because this is already available at the WIPO website, at least in English and French. The Office cannot provide translations of the Nice Classification into the other languages of the Office because OHIM is not competent for providing those translations. It is recommended to visit the WIPO website, and if the translations to the desired languages are not available, it is advised to contact the national office which is competent for translating the Nice Classifications into those languages.

29. Can I file multiple declarations under Article 28(8) EUTMR for the same mark?

In principle, a single declaration should be filed for each mark. However, the proprietor may submit a new declaration providing the six-month period is still in progress.

30. I have an International Registration designating the European Union. Can I file a declaration?

Yes. Declarations for international registrations that designated or subsequently designated the EU before 22 June 2012 and that contain the entire class heading and continue to be protected for the entire class heading may file a declaration under Article 28(8). Nonetheless, they cannot do that using the e-filing form mentioned earlier, and must use instead the PDF form for recordal applications available on the Office's website and file it in the language of the international registration.

31. For IRs designating the EU, what date is to be taken into account for determining the registration date of the mark?

The date to take into account is the date of second republication of the mark. Declarations under Article 28(8) would only be admissible in respect of IRs designating the EU before 22/06/2012 which have been the object of a **second republication** by the Office by 23/03/2016.

32. How will the declaration be communicated to the World Intellectual Property Office?

The Office will use the mechanism of further decision under rule 18ter(4) of the Common Regulation under the Madrid Agreement Concerning the International Registration of Marks and the Protocols Related to that Agreement. The Office will be communicating the further decision to the International Bureau which in return will take the necessary steps to record that decision in its register and to publish the statement in its gazette.

33. I have the entire class heading as well as additional goods. Can I file a declaration?

Yes. The Office has interpreted the wording of Article 28(8) to mean that the trade mark *covers* the entire class heading. Therefore, it can contain the entire class heading and additional goods or services provided that they do not limit the class heading.

34. I do not have the entire class heading, but I have some general indications. Can I file a declaration?

No. The wording of Article 28(8) refers to the entire class heading. The Office will allow declarations for trade marks that have the entire class heading and that continue to be registered for the entire class heading. In the case of having only some general indications, the Office will not accept a declaration for that trade mark.

35. I have the entire class heading but it is has a limitation. Can I file a declaration?

No because there is a limitation which affects the entire list of goods and services and the entire specification is affected by a limitation - and therefore the class heading is also limited. If the class heading is limited the Office cannot accept a declaration under Article 28(8). The trade mark must continue to contain the entire class heading in order for an Article 28(8) declaration to be acceptable.

36. I have the entire class heading of class 35. Can I file a declaration under Article 28(8) for "retail services in connection with . . . "?

No. Retail services as such did not appear on the alphabetical list until the 2013 version of the 10th edition. Nor are they considered to be covered by the literal meaning.

37. Where can I find more information?

Information on the change in practice can be found in Communication No 1/2016 of the President of the Office.

Please also visit our website for more information on the Legal Reform.

PART 6
PLANT VARIETIES PROTECTION

PLANT VARIETIES AND SEEDS ACT 1964

(1964 c 14)

An Act to provide for the granting of proprietary rights to persons who breed or discover plant varieties and for the issue of compulsory licences in respect thereof; to establish a tribunal to hear appeals and other proceedings relating to the rights, and to exclude certain agreements relating to the rights from Part I of the Restrictive Trade Practices Act 1956; to confer power to regulate, and to amend in other respects the law relating to, transactions in seeds and seed potatoes, including provision for the testing of seeds and seed potatoes, the establishment of an index of names of varieties and the imposition of restrictions as respects the introduction of new varieties; to control the import of seeds and seed potatoes; to authorise measures to prevent injurious cross-pollination; and for connected purposes

[12 March 1964]

ARRANGEMENT OF SECTIONS

NOTES

Transfer of functions in relation to Wales: as to the transfer of functions under this Act from Ministers of the Crown to the National Assembly for Wales, see the National Assembly for Wales (Transfer of Functions) Order 1999, SI 1999/672.

1–15 *((Pt I) Ss 1–15 repealed by the Plant Varieties Act 1997, s 52, Sch 4.)*

PART II
SEEDS AND SEED POTATOES

Regulation of sales

[6.1]
16 Seeds regulations

(1) The Minister, after consultation with representatives of such interests as appear to him to be concerned, may by statutory instrument make such regulations as appear to him to be necessary or expedient for the purpose—

(a) of ensuring that reliable and adequate information is afforded as to the nature, condition and quality of seeds which are sold or are for sale,

(b) of preventing the sale of seeds which are deleterious, and of preventing the sale of seeds which have not been tested for purity and germination, or which are of a variety the performance of which has not been subjected to trials,

(c) of preventing the spread of plant disease by [means] of seeds,

(d) of regulating the descriptions under which seeds are sold, and

(e) of prescribing anything which, under this Part of this Act, is authorised or required to be prescribed,

and regulations under this section shall be known as seeds regulations.

[(1A) Seeds regulations may further make provision for regulating the marketing, or the importation or exportation, of seeds or any related activities (whether by reference to officially published lists of permitted varieties or otherwise), and may in that connection include provision—

(a) for the registration or licensing of persons engaged in the seeds industry or related activities,

(b) for ensuring that seeds on any official list remain true to variety,

(c) for the keeping and inspection of records and the giving of information,

(d) for conferring rights of appeal to the Tribunal,

(e) for excluding, extending or modifying, in relation to or in connection with any provision of the regulations, the operation of any provision made by the following sections of this Part of this Act or of Part IV of this Act, and for the charging of fees.]

(2) Seeds regulations may include provisions as to the packets, bags, trays or other containers in which seeds may be sold or delivered to purchasers, and requirements as to the marking of such containers.

(3) Seeds regulations may in particular—

(a) require information to be given in the prescribed manner (which may include the giving of it on any label, container or package) as regards seeds which are sold or offered or exposed for sale and, in particular, require the seller of any seeds to deliver a statement containing the prescribed particulars to the purchaser within the time limited by the regulations,

(b) require any of the particulars contained in a statement to be delivered to a purchaser or other person under seeds regulations to be particulars ascertained on a test of the seeds,

(c) prohibit the selling, or the offering or exposing for sale, of seeds which contain more than a prescribed proportion of weed seeds, or of weed seeds of a prescribed kind,

(d) prohibit persons from using, in relation to seeds which are sold, or are offered or exposed for sale, a prescribed name or designation or description except where the seeds have been grown or selected under the prescribed conditions,

(e) require persons who deal in seeds to supply the Minister with information as to, and to keep records of,—

  (i) transactions in seeds,

  (ii) statutory statements given or received by them, and other statements or invoices given or received by them in connection with the sale of seeds,

  (iii) processes or treatments applied to seeds, and

  (iv) the results of tests of seeds,

  and authorise officers of the Minister and other persons to call for production of the records,

(f) where persons who deal in seeds also grow seeds, require those persons to supply the Minister with information as to, and to keep records of—

  (i) [areas] sown, and

  (ii) the yields of the crops,

  and authorise officers of the Minister and other persons to call for production of the records,

(g) regulate the procedure to be observed at, and the conduct of, official testing stations, and other establishments at which tests may be carried out for the purposes of the regulations,

(h) regulate the manner in which any tests are to be made for the purposes of this Part of this Act,

(i) provide for the licensing by the Minister of establishments for the testing of seeds, other than official testing stations, and authorise the Minister to charge a fee for, and to attach conditions to, any such licence, and to make the conditions enforceable by withdrawal of the licence or by making a breach of any of the conditions an offence against seeds regulations.

(4) In prescribing the manner in which samples are to be taken for the purposes of any provision in this Part of this Act or for the purposes of seeds regulations, the regulations—

(a) may impose conditions as to the persons authorised to take samples and the places where they may be taken,

(b) may require the person taking a sample to give part of it to the owner of the seeds or to some other person, may prescribe the manner in which the sample is to be divided into parts and may impose duties as respects the marking or labelling and the preservation of the parts of the sample, and

(c) may provide for the identification, by the labelling or marking of their container or by some other method, of seeds from which a sample has been taken.

(5) Seeds regulations—

(a) may exempt, or authorise the Minister to exempt, any person or class of persons, or persons generally, from compliance with any of the provisions of the regulations, and may provide that the exemptions are to be, or may be made, subject to conditions, and

(b) may contain such transitional provisions consequent on the repeal of the Seeds Act 1920 by this Act as may appear to the Minister to be expedient.

[(5A) In determining any fees to be charged under seeds regulations the Minister may have regard to the costs incurred by him in connection with the enforcement of the regulations.]

(6) A statutory instrument containing regulations under this section shall be subject to annulment in pursuance of a resolution of either House of Parliament.

(7) If any person—

(a) in a statutory statement includes anything which is false in a material particular, or

(b) contravenes any provision contained in seeds regulations [he shall be liable on summary conviction to a fine not exceeding [level 5 on the standard scale]].

[(8) The Ministers acting jointly may make seeds regulations for the whole of Great Britain.]

NOTES

Sub-s (1): word in square brackets substituted by the European Communities Act 1972, s 4, Sch 4, para 5(1), (2).

Sub-s (1A): inserted by the European Communities Act 1972, s 4, Sch 4, para 5(1), (2).

Sub-s (3): word in square brackets in para (f) substituted by the Plant Varieties and Seeds Act 1964 (Amendment) Regulations 1977, SI 1977/1112, reg 2.

Sub-s (5A): inserted by the Agriculture Act 1986, s 2.

Sub-s (7): in para (b) words in first (outer) pair of square brackets substituted by the European Communities Act 1972, s 4, Sch 4, para 5(1), (2)(a); words in second (inner) pair of square brackets substituted by virtue of the Criminal Justice Act 1982, s 46.

Sub-s (8): substituted by the European Communities Act 1972, s 4, Sch 4, para 5(1)–(3).

Seeds Act 1920: repealed by s 31 of, and Sch 6 to, this Act.

Regulations: the Seeds (National Lists of Varieties) (Fees) Regulations 1994, SI 1994/676; the Seed Potatoes (Fees) Regulations 1998, SI 1998/1228; the Seeds (National Lists of Varieties) (Fees) Regulations 1999, SI 1999/1090; the Seed Marketing Regulations 2011, SI 2011/463; the Seed Marketing (Wales) Regulations 2012, SI 2012/245; the Seeds and Vegetable Plant Material (Nomenclature Changes) Regulations 2014, SI 2014/487; the Seeds and Vegetable Plant Material (Nomenclature Changes) (Wales) Regulations 2014, SI 2014/519; the Seed Potatoes (England) Regulations 2015, SI 2015/1953; the Seed Potatoes (Wales) Regulations 2016, SI 2016/106; the Oil and Fibre Plant Seed (Scotland) Regulations 2004, SSI 2004/317; the Cereal Seed (Scotland) Regulations 2005, SSI 2005/328; the Fodder Plant Seed (Scotland) Regulations 2005, SSI 2005/329; the Beet Seed (Scotland) (No 2) Regulations 2010, SSI 2010/148; the Seed Potatoes (Scotland) Regulations 2015, SSI 2015/395; the Seed Potatoes (Fees) (Scotland) Regulations 2015, SSI 2015/396; the Seed (Licensing and Enforcement etc) (Scotland) Regulations 2016, SSI 2016/68; the Seed (Fees) (Scotland) Regulations 2016, SSI 2016/69.

[6.2]

17 Civil liabilities of sellers of seeds

(1) If and so far as seeds regulations provide that a statutory statement shall constitute a statutory warranty for the purposes of this section, the statutory statement, when received by the purchaser, shall, notwithstanding any contract or notice to the contrary, have effect as a written warranty by the seller that the particulars contained in the statutory statement are correct.

(2) If and so far as seeds regulations apply this subsection to the particulars in a statutory statement and prescribe limits of variation in relation to those particulars, those particulars shall, for the purposes of any legal proceedings on a contract for the sale of the seeds to which the statutory statement relates, be deemed to be true except so far as there is a mis-statement in the statutory particulars which exceeds the limits of variation so prescribed.

(3) If and so far as seeds regulations apply this subsection to the particulars in a statutory statement, the particulars in the statutory statement shall, for the purposes of any legal proceedings on a contract for the sale of the seeds to which the statutory statement relates, be deemed to be true unless it is made to appear on a test carried out at an official testing station, and made on a sample taken in the manner, and within the period, prescribed by seeds regulations, that the particulars were untrue.

(4) Where a purchaser intends to obtain a test of seeds for the purposes of subsection (3) of this section, the seller of the seeds shall be given written notice of the purchaser's intention not more than the prescribed period after delivery to the purchaser of the seeds under the sale, and seeds

regulations shall prescribe a procedure for taking a sample of seeds to be tested for the purposes of that subsection which will afford to the seller of the seeds or his agent an opportunity of being present when the sample is taken, and of obtaining part of the sample.

(5) A contravention of seeds regulations shall not affect the validity of a contract for the sale of seeds, or the right to enforce such a contract.

(6) In Scotland, a contract for the sale of seeds may not be treated as repudiated by reason only of a breach of a written warranty having effect by virtue of subsection (1) of this section.

[6.3]
18 Defences in proceedings for offences against seeds regulations

(1) If and so far as seeds regulations for the purposes of this section prescribe limits of variation in relation to the particulars in a statutory statement, it shall be a defence to proceedings under this Act for including in a statutory statement any false particulars to prove that the mis-statements in the particulars alleged to be false do not exceed the limits of variation so prescribed.

(2) Subject to the provisions of this section, it shall be a defence—

(a) to proceedings under this Part of this Act for including false particulars in a statutory statement,
(b) to proceedings under this Part of this Act [for any other offence]
(c) . . .

to prove—

(i) that the accused took all reasonable precautions against committing an offence of the kind alleged and had not at the time of the alleged offence any reason to suspect that an offence was being committed by him, and
(ii) where the accused obtained the seeds to which the alleged offence relates from some other person, that on demand by or on behalf of the prosecutor the accused gave all the information in his power with respect to the name and address of that other person, and with respect to any statutory statement or other document in his possession or power relating to the seeds, and the contract of sale.

(3) If in any such proceedings as are mentioned in subsection (2)(a) of this section any of the particulars alleged to be false are particulars which, by seeds regulations, are to be particulars ascertained by means of a test made in accordance with the regulations, the defence under subsection (2) of this section shall not be available unless it is proved—

(a) that those particulars were ascertained on such a test and that the test was made not earlier than the date, if any, prescribed by seeds regulations for the purpose, or
(b) that—
  (i) the accused purchased the seeds from another person who, in connection with the sale, duly delivered to the accused a statutory statement giving particulars of the seeds which were the same as the particulars alleged to be false, and
  (ii) the accused had not reason to believe that paragraph (a) of this subsection did not apply in relation to those particulars.

NOTES

Sub-s (2): words in square brackets in para (b) substituted, and para (c) repealed, by the European Communities Act 1972, s 4, Sch 4, para 5(1), (2).

[6.4]
19 Presumption as respects statutory statements under seeds regulations

For the purposes of this Part of this Act and of any seeds regulations, any statutory statement made as respects seeds which are in distinct portions shall be presumed to be made both as respects the seeds as a whole and also as respects each portion taken separately.

20–23A *(Repealed by the European Communities Act 1972, s 4, Sch 3, Pt III (s 23A originally inserted by the Agricultural (Miscellaneous Provisions) Act 1968, s 43(2), Sch 7).)*

Official testing stations

[6.5]
24 Official testing stations and certificates of test

(1) Subject to this section, the Minister of Agriculture, Fisheries and Food and the Secretary of State shall respectively continue to maintain the official seed testing stations established for England and Wales and for Scotland under the Seeds Act 1920.

(2) The Ministers may unite in establishing and maintaining, on such terms as may be agreed between them, a common official seed testing station for the whole of Great Britain.

(3) Either or both of the Ministers may at any time alter the arrangements made by them for official seed testing stations for England and Wales and for Scotland respectively, and any official seed testing station established by either or both of them may be established in conjunction with any other bodies or persons.

(4) The Minister or Ministers concerned may, subject to the approval of the Treasury, authorise the charging of fees for the services given at an official seed testing station.

(5) A certificate of the result of a test at an official seed testing station of a sample taken by an authorised officer for the purposes of this Part of this Act shall be in the form prescribed by seeds regulations.

(6) A certificate of the result of a test at an official seed testing station of a sample taken for the purposes of this Act, and purporting to be issued by an officer of an official seed testing station,—

(a) if the sample was taken by an authorised officer, shall, if a copy of the certificate has been served on the accused with the summons or complaint, be sufficient evidence of the facts stated in the certificate in any proceedings for an offence under this Part of this Act, and

(b) if the sample was taken by a person other than an authorised officer in order to obtain the test for the purposes of section 17(3) of this Act, shall be sufficient evidence of the facts stated in the certificate in any such legal proceedings as are mentioned in that subsection,

unless, in either case, either party to the proceedings requires that the person under whose direction the test was made be called as a witness; and in that event, in the case of proceedings in Scotland, the evidence of that person shall be sufficient evidence of the facts stated in the certificate.

(7) In any proceedings for an offence under this Part of this Act in which a copy of a certificate of the result of a test has been served with the summons or complaint in pursuance of paragraph (a) of the last foregoing subsection, the accused, unless the court otherwise directs, shall not be entitled to require that the person under whose direction the test was made be called as a witness unless he has, at least three clear days before the day on which the summons is returnable or, in Scotland, the case proceeds to trial, given notice to the prosecutor that he intends to do so.

NOTES

Seeds Act 1920: repealed by s 31(1) of, and Sch 6 to, this Act.

Regulations: the Seed (Licensing and Enforcement etc) (Scotland) Regulations 2016, SSI 2016/68.

Supplemental

[6.6]

25 Powers of entry

(1) The powers of entry conferred by subsections (3) and (4) of this section may be exercised for the purpose of exercising—

(a) the further powers conferred by subsections (5) and (6) of this section, or

(b) any powers of calling for, inspecting or taking copies of records or other documents conferred by seeds regulations,

or for the purpose of ascertaining whether there is, or has been, on or in connection with the premises (including any vehicle or vessel) any contravention of any provision contained in this Part of this Act or in seeds regulations.

(2) This section shall not authorise entry into any premises which are used exclusively as a private dwelling.

(3) Any person duly authorised by the Minister in that behalf may, on production if so required of his authority, at all reasonable hours enter any premises which he has reasonable cause to believe to be used for any purpose of a business in the course of which seeds are sold, whether the sale is by wholesale or retail, and whether the person conducting it acts as principal or agent.

(4) Any person duly authorised by the Minister in that behalf may, on production if so required of his authority, at all reasonable hours enter any premises on which he has reasonable cause to believe that there are any seed potatoes which have been sold and which are to be delivered, or are in the course of delivery, to the purchaser, and the power of entry under this subsection may be exercised when the seed potatoes are in transit in the course of delivery to the purchaser, and in particular when they are in any vehicle or vessel in the course of delivery.

(5) A person may, on any premises (including any vehicle or vessel) which he has power under this section to enter for the purpose of exercising the powers conferred by this subsection, examine any seeds which he finds there and may without payment take samples of any seeds so found.

(6) The owner of any seeds which are offered or exposed for sale, or are stored for purposes of sale, or any person authorised to sell those seeds, may be required by a person duly authorised by the Minister in that behalf to deliver to him such a statement, if any, as the person selling them would by seeds regulations be obliged to deliver to a purchaser of those seeds, and to deliver it within the time prescribed for such a statement.

(7) If any person fails to comply with a requirement under subsection (6) of this section he shall be liable on summary conviction [to a fine not exceeding [level 3 on the standard scale]] and references in this Part of this Act to a statutory statement shall include references to a statement delivered under subsection (6) of this section.

(8) This section shall apply as respects—

(a) all kinds of seeds in respect of which an offence may under any circumstances be committed under seeds regulations as for the time being in force . . .

(b) . . .

(9) A person who obstructs or impedes any person acting in the exercise of the powers conferred by this section shall be liable on summary conviction to a fine not exceeding [level 3 on the standard scale].

Part 6 Plant Varieties Protection

NOTES

Sub-s (7): words in first (outer) pair of square brackets substituted by the European Communities Act 1972, s 4, Sch 4, para 5(1), (2); words in second (inner) pair of square brackets substituted by virtue of the Criminal Justice Act 1982, s 46.

Sub-s (8): words omitted repealed by the European Communities Act 1972, s 4, Sch 3, Pt III.

Sub-s (9): words in square brackets substituted, in relation to England and Wales, by virtue of the Criminal Justice Act 1982, ss 39, 46, Sch 3, and in relation to Scotland, by the Criminal Procedure (Consequential Provisions) (Scotland) Act 1995, s 3(2), Sch 2, Pt III.

Modified, in relation to seed potatoes by the Seed Potatoes (England) Regulations 2015, SI 2015/1953, reg 24(1)–(4), (6) and the Seed Potatoes (Wales) Regulations 2016, SI 2016/106, reg 24(1)–(4), (6).

[6.7]

26 Use of samples in criminal proceedings

(1) Evidence shall not be adduced in proceedings for an offence under this Part of this Act respecting a sample taken by an authorised officer unless the sample was taken in the manner prescribed by seeds regulations.

(2) Seeds regulations shall provide for the sample being divided into at least two parts, and for one of the parts being given to the owner of the seeds or to such other person as may be prescribed by seeds regulations, and shall provide for a third part of the sample to be retained for production in all cases where use of it may be made by the court under this section.

(3) A certificate in the form prescribed by seeds regulations purporting to be issued by an authorised officer and stating that a sample was taken in the prescribed manner shall be sufficient evidence of the facts stated in the certificate.

(4) If part of a sample taken by an authorised officer is sent to the chief officer of an official testing station, it shall be so sent as soon as practicable after the sample is taken, and the person to whom any other part of the sample is given shall be informed before the first-mentioned part is sent.

(5) A copy of a certificate issued by an official testing station stating the result of a test of part of a sample taken by an authorised officer shall be sent to the person to whom any other part of the sample is given.

(6) In any proceedings for an offence under this Part of this Act in respect of seeds which have been sampled by an authorised officer, the summons shall not be made returnable, and, in Scotland, the case shall not proceed to trial, less than fourteen days from the day on which the summons or complaint is served, and a copy of any certificate of an official testing station which the prosecutor intends to adduce as evidence shall be served with the summons or complaint.

(7) In proceedings for including in a statutory statement false particulars concerning matters which are under seeds regulations to be ascertained, for the purpose of the statement, by a test of the seeds, if any sample of the seeds has been taken by an authorised officer, the third part of that sample required by seeds regulations to be retained as mentioned in subsection (2) of this section shall be produced at the hearing.

(8) The court may, if it thinks fit, on the request of either party, cause the part so produced to be sent to the chief officer of an official testing station, who shall transmit to the court a certificate of the result of a test of that part of the sample.

(9) If, in a case where an appeal is brought, no action has been taken under the last foregoing subsection the provisions of that subsection shall apply also to the court by which the appeal is heard.

(10) . . .

NOTES

Sub-s (10): repealed by the Statute Law (Repeals) Act 2004.

Modified, in relation to seed potatoes by the Seed Potatoes (England) Regulations 2015, SI 2015/1953, reg 24(1), (5) and the Seed Potatoes (Wales) Regulations 2016, SI 2016/106, reg 24(1), (5).

Regulations: the Seed (Licensing and Enforcement etc) (Scotland) Regulations 2016, SSI 2016/68.

[6.8]

27 Tampering with samples

(1) If any person—

- (a) tampers with any seeds so as to procure that a sample taken in the manner prescribed by seeds regulations for any purpose does not correctly represent the bulk of the seeds, or
- (b) tampers with any sample so taken, or
- (c) with intent to deceive sends, or causes or allows to be sent to any official testing station or licensed testing establishment, to be tested for any purpose, a sample of seeds which to his knowledge does not correctly represent the bulk of the seeds,

he shall be liable on summary conviction to a fine not exceeding [level 5 on the standard scale] or to imprisonment for a term not exceeding *three months*, or to both.

(2) In this section "licensed testing establishment" means an establishment licensed under seeds regulations for the testing of seeds.

NOTES

Sub-s (1): words in square brackets substituted, in relation to England and Wales, by virtue of the Criminal Justice Act 1982, ss 39, 46, Sch 3, and in relation to Scotland, by the Criminal Procedure (Consequential Provisions) (Scotland) Act 1995, s 3(2),

Sch 2, Pt III; for the words in italics there are substituted the words "51 weeks" by the Criminal Justice Act 2003, s 280(2), (3), Sch 26, para 18, as from a day to be appointed.

[6.9]

28 Institution of criminal proceedings

(1) Notwithstanding anything in [section 127(1) of the Magistrates' Courts Act 1980] or section 23 of the Summary Jurisdiction (Scotland) Act 1954 (time limit for proceedings), where a part of a sample has been tested at an official testing station proceedings for including in a statutory statement false particulars concerning the matters which are under seeds regulations to be ascertained, for the purposes of the statement, by a test of the seeds, being proceedings relating to the seeds from which the sample was taken, may be brought at any time not more than six months from the time when the sample was taken.

(2) If at any time before a test is begun at an official testing station to ascertain whether a part of a sample of seeds is of a specified variety or type, and not more than six months after the sample was taken, the person to whom any other part of the sample was given, or any other person, is notified in writing by an authorised officer that it is intended so to test the seeds and that, after the test, proceedings may be brought against that person for including in a statutory statement a false statement that seeds were of a specified variety or type, then notwithstanding anything in [the said section 127(1)] or 23, any such proceedings relating to the seeds from which the sample was taken may be brought against the person so notified at any time not more than two years from the time when the sample was taken.

A certificate purporting to be issued by an authorised officer and stating that a person was so notified shall be sufficient evidence of that fact.

[(2A) Notwithstanding anything in section 127(1) of the Magistrates' Courts Act 1980 or section 136 of the Criminal Procedure (Scotland) Act 1995, proceedings for contravening a provision contained in seeds regulations may be brought at any time not more than one year from the time when the contravention occurred.]

(3) Proceedings for an offence under this Part of this Act relating to a statutory statement which has been delivered to a purchaser of seeds, or relating to seeds which have been sold and delivered to the purchaser, may be brought before a court having jurisdiction at the place of delivery of the statement or seeds.

NOTES

Sub-ss (1), (2): words in square brackets substituted by the Magistrates' Courts Act 1980, s 154, Sch 7, paras 43, 44.

Sub-s (2A): inserted by the Plant Varieties Act 1997, s 47.

[6.10]

29 Application of Part II to seed potatoes

(1) This Part of this Act applies to seed potatoes [to any other vegetative propagating material and to silvicultural planting material] as it applies to seeds, and accordingly, except where the context otherwise requires, references in this Part of this Act to seeds include references to seed potatoes [to any other vegetative propagating material and to silvicultural planting material].

[(2) The [appropriate authority] may establish and maintain an official seed testing station for silvicultural propagating and planting material, and seeds regulations may confer on [appropriate authority] any functions the regulations may confer on a Minister, and [the appropriate authority] may charge or authorise the charging of fees for services given at any such station or in connection with any such functions; and accordingly—

(a) references in this Part of this Act to an authorised officer shall include an officer of [appropriate authority]; and

(b) in section 25 above the references in subsections (3), (4) and (6) to a person duly authorised by the Minister shall include a person duly authorised by [the appropriate authority].

[Any expenses incurred or fees received by the Commissioners by virtue of this subsection shall be defrayed, or as the case may be treated, in accordance with section 41 of the Forestry Act 1967.]

(3) In relation to matters concerning silvicultural propagating or planting material or concerning the [appropriate authority], "the Minister" shall in this Part of this Act mean, in relation to Wales and Monmouthshire, the Secretary of State, and the reference in section 16(8) to the Ministers shall be construed accordingly.]

[(4) In this section "appropriate authority" means—

(a) in relation to Wales, the Welsh Ministers;

(b) in all other respects, the Forestry Commissioners.]

NOTES

Sub-s (1): words in square brackets inserted by the European Communities Act 1972, s 4, Sch 4, para 5(1), (4).

Sub-s (2): added, together with sub-s (3), by the European Communities Act 1972, s 4, Sch 4, para 5(1), (4); words in first, second, third, fourth and fifth pairs of square brackets substituted by the Natural Resources Body for Wales (Functions) Order 2013, SI 2013/755, art 4(1), Sch 2, Pt 1, para 29(1), (2); words in final pair of square brackets substituted by the Scotland Act 1998 (Cross-Border Public Authorities) (Forestry Commissioners) Order 2000, SI 2000/746, art 2, Schedule, para 2.

Sub-s (3): added as noted to sub-s (2) above; words in square brackets substituted by SI 2013/755, art 4(1), Sch 2, Pt 1, para 29(1), (3).

Sub-s (4): added by SI 2013/755, art 4(1), Sch 2, Pt 1, para 29(1), (4).

[6.11]

30 Interpretation of Part II

(1) In this Part of this Act, unless the context otherwise requires,—

"authorised officer" means an officer of the Minister or a person authorised by the Minister to execute this Part of this Act;

"official testing station" means an official seed testing station maintained . . . under this Part of this Act;

"seeds" includes agricultural and horticultural seeds, vegetable seeds, flower seeds, seeds of grasses, whether used for agricultural purposes or other purposes, and seeds of trees;

"statutory statement" means a statement given in pursuance of seeds regulations, whether the statement be in the form of a notice or other document, or in the form of particulars given on any label or container or package, or in any other form, and includes a statement delivered under section 25(6) of this Act.

(2) In this Part of this Act references to a contravention of any provision contained in this Act or in seeds regulations include references to a failure to comply with such a provision, and references to a contravention of any provision contained in seeds regulations include references to anything which, by the regulations, is expressed to be an offence against a provision contained in the regulations and also include references to any failure to comply with a condition subject to which an exemption is granted by or under seeds regulations.

(3) In this Part of this Act any reference to an offence under this Part of this Act includes, unless the context otherwise requires, a reference to a contravention of any provision contained in seeds regulations.

NOTES

Sub-s (1): words omitted repealed by the European Communities Act 1972, s 4, Sch 4, para 5(1), (4).

[6.12]

31 Repeals and consequential amendment

(1) The enactments mentioned in Schedule 6 to this Act (which include certain enactments which were obsolete before the passing of this Act) shall . . . be repealed to the extent specified in the third column of that Schedule.

(2) . . .

NOTES

Sub-s (1): words omitted repealed by the Statute Law (Repeals) Act 2004.
Sub-s (2): repealed by the Trade Descriptions Act 1968, s 41(2), Sch 2.

PART III
CONTROL OF IMPORTS AND PREVENTION OF CROSS-POLLINATION

32 (*Repealed by the European Communities Act 1972, s 4, Sch 3, Pt III.*)

[6.13]

33 Measures to prevent injurious cross-pollination affecting crops of seeds

(1) This section shall have effect for the purpose of maintaining the purity of seed of any types and varieties of plants of any species of the genus Allium, Beta or Brassica.

(2) The Minister may by order bring this section into force in an area in any part of Great Britain in which persons are engaged in growing crops of seeds of any type or variety of plant mentioned in subsection (1) of this section if he is satisfied that in that area satisfactory arrangements (whether legally enforceable or not) have been made for locating such crops so as to isolate them from crops or plants which might cause injurious cross-pollination.

(3) An order under this section—

(a) shall be made after consultation with the persons responsible for the arrangements mentioned in subsection (2) of this section, and with persons representative of such other interests as appear to the Minister to be concerned, and

(b) shall be made by statutory instrument and may be varied or revoked by a subsequent order so made.

(4) An order under this section—

(a) shall state which of the types and varieties of plants mentioned in subsection (1) of this section are protected by the order, and

(b) shall specify the kinds of crops and plants which are to be controlled in the area to which the order relates, and

(c) may relate to more than one area and, if so, may make different provision under paragraphs (a) and (b) of this subsection in respect of the different areas to which it relates;

and in this section, in relation to an area to which an order under this section relates—

(i) "protected crop" means a crop of a type or variety of plant which is protected by the order in that area, being a crop grown for the purpose of producing seeds, and

(ii) "controlled crops or plants" means crops, grown for any purpose, of the types or varieties of plants which are protected by the order in that area, and such additional kinds of crops or plants, whether grown or self-sown and whether of those or any other types or varieties, as may be specified in the order for the purposes of this definition in that area.

(5) If in an area where this section is in force controlled crops or plants are growing and, on an application made in accordance with Schedule 7 to this Act, the Minister is satisfied—

(a) that they are causing or may cause injurious cross-pollination in a protected crop which is being grown in the area, and

(b) in the case of controlled crops or plants which are not self-sown, that the person growing them did not give to the persons responsible for the arrangements mentioned in subsection (2) of this section such notice of his intention to grow those crops or plants to the flowering stage as would have enabled them to take any appropriate steps for altering the arrangements,

the Minister may serve a notice on the occupier of the land where the controlled crops or plants are growing requiring him to take such steps as may be specified in the notice for the purpose of preventing any of the controlled crops or plants from causing or continuing to cause injurious cross-pollination in the protected crop.

(6) If the person served with a notice under this section does not comply with any requirement in the notice, the Minister may enter and do what that person has failed to do or, if in the opinion of the Minister that would no longer serve the purpose for which the notice was served, may take such other action as appears to the Minister appropriate for that purpose; and where, when the default occurs, further obligations remain under the notice, the Minister may also take such action as appears to him appropriate to meet the purposes for which those further obligations were imposed.

The Minister may recover from the person on whom the notice was served a sum equal to the reasonable cost incurred by the Minister in taking any action under this subsection.

(7) Without prejudice to the power of proceeding under the last foregoing subsection, a person who unreasonably fails to comply with any requirement in a notice under this section shall be liable on summary conviction [to a fine not exceeding level 3 on the standard scale].

(8) A person duly authorised by the Minister may, on production if so required of his authority, at all reasonable hours enter on any land (but not into any dwellinghouse) in an area where this section is in force for the purpose of ascertaining whether controlled crops or plants are growing on the land or of inspecting and taking samples of any controlled crops or plants growing on the land.

(9) A notice under this section or Schedule 7 to this Act may be served by leaving it at, or sending it by post addressed to, the last known address of the person on whom it is to be served, and if it is not practicable after reasonable inquiry to ascertain his name and address, the notice may be served by addressing it to him as "the occupier" of the land and affixing it or a copy of it to some conspicuous object on the land.

(10) A person who obstructs or impedes a person acting in the exercise of the powers conferred by subsection (6) or subsection (8) of this section shall be liable on summary conviction to a fine not exceeding [level 1 on the standard scale].

(11) In this section, and in the said Schedule—

"the occupier" means, in the case of unoccupied land, the person entitled to occupy the land;

"protected crop" and "controlled crops or plants" have the meanings respectively assigned by subsection (4) of this section.

NOTES

Sub-s (7): enhanced penalties were abolished by the Criminal Justice Act 1982, s 32, and the higher penalty previously applicable is now the relevant penalty for the purposes of that section on any summary conviction for this offence, by virtue of the 1982 Act, ss 38, 46.

Sub-s (10): words in square brackets substituted by virtue of the Criminal Justice Act 1982, s 46.

PART IV
GENERAL

[6.14]

34 The gazette

(1) The Ministers shall from time to time publish a gazette (in this Act referred to as "the gazette"), and shall use the gazette as one of the means of publishing notice of matters to be published under this Act [or Part I of the Plant Varieties Act 1997].

(2) It shall be no defence in civil or criminal proceedings to show that at any time a person did not know of an entry in the register under [section 18 of the Plant Varieties Act 1997] . . . if before that time notice of that entry . . . has been published in the gazette.

NOTES

Sub-s (1): words in square brackets added by the Plant Varieties Act 1997, s 51(1)(a).

Sub-s (2): words in square brackets substituted by the Plant Varieties Act 1997, s 51(1)(b); words omitted repealed by the European Communities Act 1972, s 4, Sch 3, Pt III.

[6.15]
35 General provisions as to offences

(1) Where an offence punishable under this Act committed by a body corporate is proved to have been committed with the consent or connivance of, or to be attributable to any neglect on the part of, any director, manager, secretary or other similar officer of the body corporate, or any person who was purporting to act in any such capacity, he, as well as the body corporate, shall be guilty of that offence and shall be liable to be proceeded against and punished accordingly.

(2) Proceedings for any offence punishable under this Act may (without prejudice to any jurisdiction exercisable apart from this subsection) be taken against a person before the appropriate court in Great Britain having jurisdiction in the place where that person is for the time being.

[6.16]
36 Supplemental provisions as to regulations

Regulations under this Act—

(a) may make different provision for different types or classes of plant varieties, for different seasons of the year and for other different circumstances, and

(b) may contain such supplemental, incidental and transitional provisions as may appear to the Minister or Ministers making the regulations to be expedient.

[6.17]
37 Departmental expenses and payments into Exchequer

(1) There shall be paid out of moneys provided by Parliament—

(a)–(c) . . .

(d) (so far as not falling under the foregoing paragraphs) any expenses incurred by a Minister in the execution of this Act, and

(e) any increase attributable to this Act in the sums payable out of money so provided under the Superannuation Acts 1834 to 1960.

(2) Any fees received by virtue of this Act by a Minister . . . shall be paid into the Exchequer.

NOTES

Words omitted repealed by the Plant Varieties Act 1997, s 52, Sch 4.

Superannuation Acts 1834 to 1960: see now the Superannuation Act 1972.

[6.18]
38 Interpretation

(1) In this Act—

. . .

"the Minister" means [(subject to section 29(3))], as respects England and Wales, the Minister of Agriculture, Fisheries and Food and, as respects Scotland, the Secretary of State; and "the Ministers" means, except as otherwise expressly provided, [the Minister, the Secretary of State for Scotland and the Secretary of State for Wales] acting jointly;

. . .

["the Tribunal" means the Plant Varieties and Seeds Tribunal;]

. . .

(2) References in this Act to seeds are references to seeds for sowing.

(3) Any reference in this Act to any other enactment shall, except so far as the context otherwise requires, be construed as a reference to that enactment as amended or applied by or under any other enactment, including this Act.

NOTES

Sub-s (1): definitions omitted repealed, and definition "the Tribunal" substituted, by the Plant Varieties Act 1997, ss 51(2), 52, Sch 4; in definition "the Minister" words in first pair of square brackets inserted by the European Communities Act 1972, s 4, Sch 4, para 5(1), (4), words in second pair of square brackets substituted by the Transfer of Functions (Wales) (No 1) Order 1978, SI 1978/272, art 11, Sch 5.

[6.19]
39 Extension of Act to Northern Ireland

(1) This Act, so far as not expressly extended to Northern Ireland by any provision contained in this Act or by any Order in Council under the next following subsection, shall not extend to Northern Ireland; . . .

(2) Her Majesty may, by an Order in Council made under this subsection in pursuance of resolutions passed by the two Houses of the Parliament of Northern Ireland, direct that—

(a) . . .

(b) any of the provisions of Part II or this Part of this Act specified in the Order,

shall (whether as originally enacted or as they have effect by virtue of any Order in Council under the next following section) extend to Northern Ireland; and any such Order in Council may be varied or revoked by a subsequent Order in Council made under this subsection in pursuance of such resolutions as aforesaid.

(3) While any of the provisions of this Act extend to Northern Ireland by virtue of an Order in Council under subsection (2) of this section, they shall (without prejudice to the validity of anything previously done under this Act)—

(a) have effect as if—

(i) any reference to Great Britain were a reference to the United Kingdom; and

[(ii) any power expressed to be exercisable by "the Ministers" were exercisable by them only with the consent of the Northern Ireland Department of Agriculture and Rural Development; and]

(b) . . .

(4) While any provisions of this Act extend to Northern Ireland by virtue of an Order in Council under subsection (2) of this section, they shall have effect subject to such exceptions, adaptations and modifications as may be specified in the Order; and in the application of those provisions to Northern Ireland any reference to any enactment of the Parliament of Northern Ireland shall be construed as a reference to that enactment as amended by any Act of that Parliament, whether passed before or after this Act, and to any enactment of that Parliament passed after this Act and re-enacting the said enactment with or without modification.

(5) If the Parliament of Northern Ireland pass legislation amending or repealing the Seeds Act 1920, Her Majesty may by Order in Council made under this subsection direct that that legislation (and any related enactments forming part of the law of Northern Ireland), and any provisions in Part II or this Part of this Act, shall have effect subject to such exceptions, adaptations and modifications as may appear to Her Majesty to be expedient for the purpose of securing that the two systems of legislation operate, to such extent as may be specified, as a single system; and any such Order in Council may be varied or revoked by a subsequent Order in Council under this subsection.

(6) An Order in Council under subsection (2) or subsection (5) of this section may contain such transitional and other consequential provisions as appear to Her Majesty to be expedient.

NOTES

Sub-s (1): words omitted repealed by the Northern Ireland Constitution Act 1973, s 41(1), Sch 6, Pt I.

Sub-s (2): para (a) repealed by the Plant Varieties Act 1997, s 52, Sch 4.

Sub-s (3): para (a)(ii) substituted by the Northern Ireland Act 1998 (Modification of Enactments) Order 2002, SI 2002/2843, art 5; para (b) repealed by the Plant Varieties Act 1997, s 52, Sch 4.

Seeds Act 1920: repealed by s 31(1) of, and Sch 6 to, this Act.

Orders in Council: the Plant Varieties and Seeds (Northern Ireland) Order 1964, SI 1964/1574, the Plant Varieties and Seeds (Northern Ireland) Order 1973, SI 1973/609.

[6.20]

40 Extension of Act to Isle of Man and Channel Islands

Her Majesty may by Order in Council direct that any of the provisions of this Act specified in the Order shall (whether as originally enacted or as they have effect by virtue of any Order in Council under the last foregoing section) extend, subject to such exceptions, adaptations and modifications as may be specified in the Order, to the Isle of Man or any of the Channel Islands; and any such Order in Council may contain such transitional and other consequential provisions as appear to Her Majesty to be expedient, and may be varied or revoked by a subsequent Order in Council.

NOTES

Orders in Council: the Plant Varieties and Seeds (Isle of Man) Order 2016, SI 2016/758.

[6.21]

41 Short title and commencement

(1) This Act may be cited as the Plant Varieties and Seeds Act 1964.

(2) . . .

NOTES

Sub-s (2): repealed by the Statute Law (Repeals) Act 2004.

Orders: the Plant Varieties and Seeds Act 1964 (Commencement No 1) Order 1966, SI 1966/276; the Plant Varieties and Seeds Act 1964 (Commencement No 2) Order 1968, SI 1968/206; the Plant Varieties and Seeds Act 1964 (Commencement No 3) Order 1973, SI 1973/928; and the Plant Varieties and Seeds Act 1964 (Commencement No 4) Order 1978, SI 1978/1002.

SCHEDULES

SCHEDULES 1–6

(Schs 1–4 repealed by the Plant Varieties Act 1997, s 52, Sch 4; Sch 5 repealed by the European Communities Act 1972, s 4, Sch 3, Pt III; Sch 6 contains repeals.)

SEVENTH SCHEDULE
CROSS-POLLINATION INJURING PROTECTED CROPS

Section 33

[6.22]

1. An application under section 33 of this Act seeking the issue of a notice under that section shall be in writing.

2. Before deciding whether to issue a notice in accordance with the application the Minister shall serve a notice on the occupier of the land giving him particulars of the application, and of his right to make representations in accordance with the next following paragraph.

3. The Minister shall, if requested within such time as may be specified in the notice under paragraph 2 above, afford to the applicant, and to the occupier of the land, an opportunity of appearing before and making representations to a person appointed by the Minister for the purpose.

4. In deciding whether to issue a notice in accordance with the application, and in deciding the terms of any such notice, the Minister shall have regard—

(a) to the need to maintain, in the interests of the public, the purity of the seed in question,

(b) to the degree to which the injurious cross-pollination will or may diminish the value of the protected crop or disturb arrangements made for the purpose of maintaining the purity of the seed in question, and

(c) to the value, if any, of the controlled crops or plants and the inconvenience or disturbance involved in complying with a notice.

PLANT VARIETIES ACT 1997

(1997 c 66)

An Act to make provision about rights in relation to plant varieties; to make provision about the Plant Varieties and Seeds Tribunal; to extend the time limit for institution of proceedings for contravention of seeds regulations; and for connected purposes

[27 November 1997]

PART I
PLANT VARIETIES

PART I
PLANT VARIETIES

Preliminary

[6.23]

1 Plant breeders' rights

(1) Rights, to be known as plant breeders' rights, may be granted in accordance with this Part of this Act.

Part 6 Plant Varieties Protection

(2) Plant breeders' rights may subsist in varieties of all plant genera and species.

(3) For the purposes of this Act, "variety" means a plant grouping within a single botanical taxon of the lowest known rank, which grouping, irrespective of whether the conditions for the grant of plant breeders' rights (which are laid down in section 4 below) are met, can be—

- (a) defined by the expression of the characteristics resulting from a given genotype or combination of genotypes,
- (b) distinguished from any other plant grouping by the expression of at least one of those characteristics, and
- (c) considered as a unit with regard to its suitability for being propagated unchanged.

[6.24]
2 The Plant Variety Rights Office

(1) The office known as the Plant Variety Rights Office shall continue in being for the purposes of this Part of this Act under the immediate control of an officer appointed by the Ministers and known as the Controller of Plant Variety Rights ("the Controller").

(2) Schedule 1 to this Act (which makes further provision about the Plant Variety Rights Office) shall have effect.

Grant of plant breeders' rights

[6.25]
3 Grant on application

(1) Subject to this Part of this Act, plant breeders' rights shall be granted to an applicant by the Controller on being satisfied that the conditions laid down in section 4 below are met.

(2) The Controller may by notice require an applicant for the grant of plant breeders' rights to provide him, within such time as may be specified in the notice, with such information, documents, plant or other material, facilities or test or trial results relevant to the carrying out of his function under subsection (1) above as may be so specified.

(3) If an applicant fails to comply with a notice under subsection (2) above within the period specified in the notice, the Controller may refuse the application.

[6.26]
4 Conditions for the grant of rights

(1) The conditions which must be met in relation to an application for the grant of plant breeders' rights are—

- (a) that the variety to which the application relates is a qualifying variety, and
- (b) that the person by whom the application is made is the person entitled to the grant of plant breeders' rights in respect of the variety to which it relates.

(2) For the purposes of subsection (1) above, a variety is a qualifying variety if it is—

- (a) distinct,
- (b) uniform,
- (c) stable, and
- (d) new;

and Part I of Schedule 2 to this Act has effect for the purpose of determining whether these criteria are met.

(3) Subject to subsections (4) and (5) below, the person entitled to the grant of plant breeders' rights in respect of a variety is the person who breeds it, or discovers and develops it, or his successor in title.

(4) If a person breeds a variety, or discovers and develops it, in the course of his employment, then, subject to agreement to the contrary, his employer, or his employer's successor in title, is the person entitled to the grant of plant breeders' rights in respect of it.

(5) Part II of Schedule 2 to this Act shall have effect as respects priorities between two or more persons who have independently bred, or discovered and developed, a variety.

(6) In this section and Schedule 2 to this Act, references to the discovery of a variety are to the discovery of a variety, whether growing in the wild or occurring as a genetic variant, whether artificially induced or not.

[6.27]
5 Rights in relation to application period

(1) If an application for plant breeders' rights is granted, the holder of the rights shall be entitled to reasonable compensation for anything done during the application period which, if done after the grant of the rights, would constitute an infringement of them.

(2) In subsection (1) above, "application period", in relation to a grant of plant breeders' rights, means the period—

- (a) beginning with the day on which details of the application for the grant of the rights are published in the gazette, and
- (b) ending with the grant of the rights.

Scope of plant breeders' rights

[6.28]

6 Protected variety

(1) Plant breeders' rights shall have effect to entitle the holder to prevent anyone doing any of the following acts as respects the propagating material of the protected variety without his authority, namely—

(a) production or reproduction (multiplication),
(b) conditioning for the purpose of propagation,
(c) offering for sale,
(d) selling or other marketing,
(e) exporting,
(f) importing,
(g) stocking for any of the purposes mentioned in paragraphs (a) to (f) above, and
(h) any other act prescribed for the purposes of this provision.

(2) The holder of plant breeders' rights may give authority for the purposes of subsection (1) above with or without conditions or limitations.

(3) The rights conferred on the holder of plant breeders' rights by subsections (1) and (2) above shall also apply as respects harvested material obtained through the unauthorised use of propagating material of the protected variety, unless he has had a reasonable opportunity before the harvested material is obtained to exercise his rights in relation to the unauthorised use of the propagating material.

(4) In the case of a variety of a prescribed description, the rights conferred on the holder of plant breeders' rights by subsections (1) and (2) above shall also apply as respects any product which—

(a) is made directly from harvested material in relation to which subsection (3) above applies, and
(b) is of a prescribed description,

unless subsection (5) below applies.

(5) This subsection applies if, before the product was made, any act mentioned in subsection (1) above was done as respects the harvested material from which the product was made and either—

(a) the act was done with the authority of the holder of the plant breeders' rights, or
(b) the holder of those rights had a reasonable opportunity to exercise them in relation to the doing of the act.

(6) In this section—

(a) "prescribed" means prescribed by regulations made by the Ministers, and
(b) references to harvested material include entire plants and parts of plants.

[6.29]

7 Dependent varieties

(1) The holder of plant breeders' rights shall have, in relation to any variety which is dependent on the protected variety, the same rights as he has under section 6 above in relation to the protected variety.

(2) For the purposes of this section, one variety is dependent on another if—

(a) its nature is such that repeated production of the variety is not possible without repeated use of the other variety, or
(b) it is essentially derived from the other variety and the other variety is not itself essentially derived from a third variety.

(3) For the purposes of subsection (2) above, a variety shall be deemed to be essentially derived from another variety ("the initial variety") if—

(a) it is predominantly derived from—
    (i) the initial variety, or
    (ii) a variety that is itself predominantly derived from the initial variety,

    while retaining the expression of the essential characteristics resulting from the genotype or combination of genotypes of the initial variety,
(b) it is clearly distinguishable from the initial variety by one or more characteristics which are capable of a precise description, and
(c) except for the differences which result from the act of derivation, it conforms to the initial variety in the expression of the essential characteristics that result from the genotype or combination of genotypes of the initial variety.

(4) For the purposes of subsection (3) above, derivation may, for example, be by—

(a) the selection of—
    (i) a natural or induced mutant,
    (ii) a somaclonal variant, or
    (iii) a variant individual from plants of the initial variety,
(b) backcrossing, or
(c) transformation by genetic engineering.

(5) Subsection (1) above shall not apply where the existence of the dependent variety was common knowledge immediately before the coming into force of this Act.

Part 6 Plant Varieties Protection

Exceptions

[6.30]

8 General exceptions

Plant breeders' rights shall not extend to any act done—

(a) for private and non-commercial purposes,

(b) for experimental purposes, or

(c) for the purpose of breeding another variety.

[6.31]

9 Farm saved seed

(1) Subject to subsection (2) below, plant breeders' rights shall not extend to the use by a farmer for propagating purposes in the field, on his own holding, of the product of the harvest which he has obtained by planting on his own holding propagating material of—

(a) the protected variety, or

(b) a variety which is essentially derived from the protected variety.

(2) Subsection (1) above only applies if the material is of a variety which is of a species or group specified for the purposes of this subsection by order made by the Ministers.

(3) If a farmer's use of material is excepted from plant breeders' rights by subsection (1) above, he shall, at the time of the use, become liable to pay the holder of the rights equitable remuneration, which shall be sensibly lower than the amount charged for the production of propagating material of the same variety in the same area with the holder's authority.

(4) Subsection (3) above shall not apply to a farmer who is considered to be a small farmer for the purposes of Article 14(3) third indent of the Council Regulation.

(5) . . .

(6) The Ministers may by order provide that, on such date after 30th June 2001 as may be specified in the order, subsection (5) above shall cease to have effect in relation to a variety so specified, or varieties of a species or group so specified.

(7) The Ministers may by regulations—

(a) make provision enabling—

(i) holders of plant breeders' rights to require farmers or seed processors, and

(ii) farmers or seed processors to require holders of plant breeders' rights,

to supply such information as may be specified in the regulations, being information the supply of which the Ministers consider necessary for the purposes of this section,

(b) make provision restricting the circumstances in which the product of a harvest of a variety which is subject to plant breeders' rights may be moved, for the purpose of being processed for planting, from the holding on which it was obtained, and

(c) make provision for the purpose of enabling the Ministers to monitor the operation of any provision of this section or regulations under this section.

(8) Regulations under subsection (7)(a) above may include provision imposing obligations of confidence in relation to information supplied by virtue of the regulations.

(9) Subsections (3) and (4) of section 7 above shall apply for the purposes of subsection (1)(b) above as they apply for the purposes of subsection (2) of that section.

(10) For the purposes of subsection (3) above, remuneration shall be taken to be sensibly lower if it would be taken to be sensibly lower within the meaning of Article 14(3) fourth indent of the Council Regulation.

(11) In this section, references to a farmer's own holding are to any land which he actually exploits for plant growing, whether as his property or otherwise managed under his own responsibility and on his own account.

(12) The Ministers may by order amend this section as they think fit for the purpose of securing that it corresponds with the provisions for the time being of the law relating to Community plant variety rights about farm saved seed.

NOTES

Sub-s (5): repealed in relation to England by the Plant Breeders' Rights (Discontinuation of Prior Use Exemption) Order 2005, SI 2005/2726, art 2 and in relation to Wales by the Plant Breeders' Rights (Discontinuation of Prior Use Exemption) (Wales) Order 2006, SI 2006/1261, art 2.

Orders: the Plant Breeders' Rights (Farm Saved Seed) (Specification of Species and Groups) Order 1998, SI 1998/1025; the Plant Breeders' Rights (Discontinuation of Prior Use Exemption) (Scotland) Order 2005, SSI 2005/460; the Plant Breeders' Rights (Discontinuation of Prior Use Exemption) Order 2005, SI 2005/2726; the Plant Breeders' Rights (Discontinuation of Prior Use Exemption) (Wales) Order 2006, SI 2006/1261.

Regulations: the Plant Breeders' Rights (Farm Saved Seed) (Specified Information) Regulations 1998, SI 1998/1026.

[6.32]

10 Exhaustion of rights

(1) Plant breeders' rights shall not extend to any act concerning material of a variety if the material—

(a) has been sold or otherwise marketed in the United Kingdom by, or with the consent of, the holder of the rights, or

(b) is derived from material which has been so sold or otherwise marketed.

(2) Subsection (1) above shall not apply where the act involves—
(a) further propagation of the variety, or
(b) the export of material which enables propagation of the variety to a non-qualifying country, otherwise than for the purposes of final consumption.

(3) For the purposes of subsection (2)(b) above, a non-qualifying country is one which does not provide for the protection of varieties of the genus or species to which the variety belongs.

(4) In this section, "material", in relation to a variety, means—
(a) any kind of propagating material of the variety,
(b) harvested material of the variety, including entire plants and parts of plants, and
(c) any product made directly from material falling within paragraph (b) above.

Duration and transmission of plant breeders' rights

[6.33]

11 Duration

(1) A grant of plant breeders' rights shall have effect—
(a) in the case of potatoes, trees and vines, for 30 years from the date of the grant, and
(b) in other cases, for 25 years from that date.

(2) The Ministers may by regulations provide that, in relation to varieties of a species or group specified in the regulations, subsection (1) above shall have effect with the substitution in paragraph (a) or (b), as the case may be, of such longer period, not exceeding—
(a) in the case of paragraph (a), 35 years, and
(b) in the case of paragraph (b), 30 years,
as may be so specified.

(3) The period for which a grant of plant breeders' rights has effect shall not be affected by the fact it becomes impossible to invoke the rights—
(a) because of Article 92(2) of the Council Regulation (effect of subsequent grant of Community plant variety right), or
(b) because of suspension under section 23 below.

[6.34]

12 Transmission

Plant breeders' rights shall be assignable like other kinds of proprietary rights, but in any case rights under section 6 above and rights under section 7 above may not be assigned separately.

Remedies for infringement

[6.35]

13 Remedies for infringement

(1) Plant breeders' rights shall be actionable at the suit of the holder of the rights.

(2) In any proceedings for the infringement of plant breeders' rights, all such relief by way of damages, injunction, interdict, account or otherwise shall be available as is available in any corresponding proceedings in respect of infringements of other proprietary rights.

[6.36]

14 Presumptions in proceedings relating to harvested material

(1) This section applies to any proceedings for the infringement of plant breeders' rights as respects harvested material.

(2) If, in any proceedings to which this section applies, the holder of the plant breeders' rights proves, in relation to any of the material to which the proceedings relate—
(a) that it has been the subject of an information notice given to the defendant by or on behalf of the holder, and
(b) that the defendant has not, within the prescribed time after the service of the notice, supplied the holder with the information about it requested in the notice,
then, as regards the material in relation to which the holder proves that to be the case, the presumptions mentioned in subsection (3) below shall apply, unless the contrary is proved or the defendant shows that he had a reasonable excuse for not supplying the information.

(3) The presumptions are—
(a) that the material was obtained through unauthorised use of propagating material, and
(b) that the holder did not have a reasonable opportunity before the material was obtained to exercise his rights in relation to the unauthorised use of the propagating material.

(4) The reference in subsection (2) above to an information notice is to a notice which—
(a) is in the prescribed form,
(b) specifies the material to which it relates,
(c) contains, in relation to that material, a request for the supply of the prescribed, but no other, information, and
(d) contains such other particulars as may be prescribed.

(5) In this section, "prescribed" means prescribed by regulations made by the Ministers.

NOTES

Regulations: the Plant Breeders' Rights (Information Notices) Regulations 1998, SI 1998/1024.

[6.37]
15 Presumptions in proceedings relating to products made from harvested material

(1) This section applies to any proceedings for the infringement of plant breeders' rights as respects any product made directly from harvested material.

(2) If, in any proceedings to which this section applies, the holder of the plant breeders' rights proves, in relation to any product to which the proceedings relate—

(a) that it has been the subject of an information notice given to the defendant by or on behalf of the holder, and

(b) that the defendant has not, within the prescribed time after the service of the notice, supplied the holder with the information about it requested in the notice,

then, as regards the product in relation to which the holder proves that to be the case, the presumptions mentioned in subsection (3) below shall apply, unless the contrary is proved or the defendant shows that he had a reasonable excuse for not supplying the information.

(3) The presumptions are—

(a) that the harvested material from which the product was made was obtained through unauthorised use of propagating material,

(b) that the holder did not have a reasonable opportunity before the harvested material was obtained to exercise his rights in relation to the unauthorised use of the propagating material, and

(c) that no relevant act was done, before the product was made, as respects the harvested material from which it was made.

(4) An act is relevant for the purposes of subsection (3)(c) above if it is mentioned in section 6(1) above and is—

(a) done with the authority of the holder, or

(b) one in relation to the doing of which he has a reasonable opportunity to exercise his rights.

(5) The reference in subsection (2) above to an information notice is to a notice which—

(a) is in the prescribed form,

(b) specifies the product to which it relates,

(c) contains, in relation to that product, a request for the supply of the prescribed, but no other, information, and

(d) contains such other particulars as may be prescribed.

(6) In this section, "prescribed" means prescribed by regulations made by the Ministers.

Duties of holder of plant breeders' rights

[6.38]
16 Maintenance of protected variety

(1) The holder of any plant breeders' rights shall ensure that, throughout the period for which the grant of the rights has effect, he is in a position to produce to the Controller propagating material which is capable of producing the protected variety.

(2) The holder of any plant breeders' rights shall give to the Controller, within such time as he may specify, all such information and facilities as he may request for the purpose of satisfying himself that the holder is fulfilling his duty under subsection (1) above.

(3) The facilities to be given under subsection (2) above include facilities for the inspection by or on behalf of the Controller of the measures taken for the preservation of the protected variety.

[6.39]
17 Compulsory licences

(1) Subject to subsections (2) and (3) below, if the Controller is satisfied on application that the holder of any plant breeders' rights—

(a) has unreasonably refused to grant a licence to the applicant, or

(b) has imposed or put forward unreasonable terms in granting, or offering to grant, a licence to the applicant,

he may grant to the applicant in the form of a licence under this section any such rights as might have been granted by the holder.

(2) The Controller shall not grant an application for a licence under this section unless he is satisfied—

(a) that it is necessary to do so for the purpose of securing that the variety to which the application relates—

(i) is available to the public at reasonable prices,

(ii) is widely distributed, or

(iii) is maintained in quality,

(b) that the applicant is financially and otherwise in a position to exploit in a competent and businesslike manner the rights to be conferred on him, and

(c) that the applicant intends so to exploit those rights.

(3) A licence under this section shall not be an exclusive licence.

(4) A licence under this section shall be on such terms as the Controller thinks fit and, in particular, may include—

(a) terms as to the remuneration payable to the holder of the plant breeders' rights, and

(b) terms obliging the holder of the plant breeders' rights to make propagating material available to the holder of the licence.

(5) In deciding on what terms to grant an application for a licence under this section, the Controller shall have regard to the desirability of securing—

(a) that the variety to which the application relates—

(i) is available to the public at reasonable prices,

(ii) is widely distributed, and

(iii) is maintained in quality, and

(b) that there is reasonable remuneration for the holder of the plant breeders' rights to which the application relates.

(6) An application for a licence under this section may be granted whether or not the holder of the plant breeders' rights to which the application relates has granted licences to the applicant or any other person.

(7) If and so far as any agreement purports to bind any person not to apply for a licence under this section, it shall be void.

(8) If—

(a) a licence under this section is granted as respects a variety of a species or group in relation to which a period is specified for the purposes of this provision by regulations made by the Ministers, and

(b) the grant takes place before a period of that length has passed since the date of grant of the plant breeders' rights to which the licence relates,

the licence shall not have effect until a period of that length has passed since that date.

(9) The Controller may, at any time, on the application of any person, extend, limit or in any other respect vary a licence under this section, or revoke it.

NOTES

Regulations: the Plant Breeders' Rights Regulations 1998, SI 1998/1027.

Naming of protected varieties

[6.40]

18 Selection and registration of names

(1) The Ministers may by regulations—

(a) make provision for the selection of names for varieties which are the subject of applications for the grant of plant breeders' rights,

(b) make provision about change of name in relation to varieties in respect of which plant breeders' rights have been granted, and

(c) make provision for the keeping of a register of the names of varieties in respect of which plant breeders' rights have been granted.

(2) Regulations under subsection (1) above may, in particular—

(a) make provision enabling the Controller to require an applicant for the grant of plant breeders' rights to select a name for the variety to which the application relates,

(b) make provision enabling the Controller to require the holder of plant breeders' rights to select a different name for the protected variety,

(c) prescribe classes of variety for the purposes of the regulations,

(d) prescribe grounds on which the registration of a proposed name may be refused,

(e) prescribe the circumstances in which representations may be made regarding any decision as to the name to be registered in respect of any variety,

(f) make provision enabling the Controller—

(i) to refuse an application for the grant of plant breeders' rights, or

(ii) to terminate the period for which a grant of plant breeders' rights has effect,

if the applicant or holder fails to comply with a requirement imposed under the regulations,

(g) make provision for the publication or service of notices of decisions which the Controller proposes to take, and

(h) prescribe the times at which, and the circumstances in which, the register may be inspected by members of the public.

(3) The Controller shall publish notice of all entries made in the register, including alterations, corrections and erasures—

(a) in the gazette, and

(b) in such other manner as appears to the Controller to be convenient for the publication of these to all concerned.

(4) For the purposes of subsection (1) above, the variety in respect of which plant breeders' rights are granted is the protected variety.

NOTES

Regulations: the Plant Breeders' Rights Regulations 1998, SI 1998/1027; the Plant Breeders' Rights (Naming and Fees) Regulations 2006, SI 2006/648.

[6.41]
19 Duty to use registered name
(1) Where a name is registered under section 18 above in respect of a variety, a person may not use any other name in selling, offering for sale or otherwise marketing propagating material of the variety.
(2) Subsection (1) above shall have effect in relation to any variety from the date on which plant breeders' rights in respect of that variety are granted, and shall continue to apply after the period for which the grant of those rights has effect.
(3) Subsection (1) above shall not preclude the use of any trade mark or trade name (whether registered under the Trade Marks Act 1994 or not) if—
(a) that mark or name and the registered name are juxtaposed, and
(b) the registered name is easily recognisable.
(4) A person who contravenes subsection (1) above shall be liable on summary conviction to a fine not exceeding level 3 on the standard scale.
(5) In any proceedings for an offence under subsection (4) above, it shall be a defence to prove that the accused took all reasonable precautions against committing the offence and had not at the time of the offence any reason to suspect that he was committing an offence.

[6.42]
20 Improper use of registered name
(1) If any person uses the registered name of a protected variety in offering for sale, selling or otherwise marketing material of a different variety within the same class, the use of the name shall be a wrong actionable in proceedings by the holder of the rights.
(2) Subsection (1) above shall also apply to the use of a name so nearly resembling the registered name as to be likely to deceive or cause confusion.
(3) In any proceedings under this section, it shall be a defence to a claim for damages to prove that the defendant took all reasonable precautions against committing the wrong and had not, when using the name, any reason to suspect that it was wrongful.
(4) In this section—
"class" means a class prescribed for the purposes of regulations under section 18(1) above,
"registered name", in relation to a protected variety, means the name registered in respect of it under section 18 above.

Termination and suspension of plant breeders' rights

[6.43]
21 Nullity
(1) The Controller shall declare the grant of plant breeders' rights null and void if it is established—
(a) that when the rights were granted the protected variety did not meet the criterion specified in paragraph (a) or (d) of section 4(2) above,
(b) where the grant of the rights was essentially based upon information and documents furnished by the applicant, that when the rights were granted the protected variety did not meet the criterion specified in paragraph (b) or (c) of that provision, or
(c) that the person to whom the rights were granted was not the person entitled to the grant of the rights and the rights have not subsequently been transferred to him, or his successor in title.
(2) If, because of paragraph 6 of Schedule 2 to this Act, priority is established for an application for the grant of plant breeders' rights after such rights have been granted in pursuance of an application against which priority is established, subsection (1)(c) above shall only apply to the grant if the Controller decides that the application for which priority is established should be granted.
(3) Where the grant of plant breeders' rights is declared null and void under this section, it shall be deemed never to have had effect.

[6.44]
22 Cancellation
(1) The Controller may terminate the period for which a grant of plant breeders' rights has effect if—
(a) he is satisfied that the protected variety no longer meets the criterion specified in paragraph (b) or (c) of section 4(2) above,
(b) it appears to him that the holder of the rights is no longer in a position to provide him with the propagating material mentioned in section 16(1) above,
(c) he is satisfied that the holder of the rights has failed to comply with a request under section 16(2) above, or
(d) on application by the holder of the rights, he is satisfied that the rights may properly be surrendered.
(2) Before determining an application under subsection (1)(d) above, the Controller shall—
(a) give notice of the application in the manner prescribed by regulations made by the Ministers, and

(b) follow the procedure so prescribed for hearing any person on whom the right to object is conferred by such regulations.

(3) If the Controller is satisfied, not only that the protected variety no longer meets the criterion specified in paragraph (b) or (c) of section 4(2) above, but also that it ceased to do so at some earlier date, he may make the termination retrospective to that date.

NOTES

Regulations: the Plant Breeders' Rights Regulations 1998, SI 1998/1027.

[6.45]

23 Suspension

(1) The Controller may suspend the exercise of any plant breeders' rights if, on application by the holder of a licence under section 17 above, he is satisfied that the holder of the rights is in breach of any obligation imposed on him by the licence.

(2) The Controller shall terminate a suspension under subsection (1) above if, on application by the holder of the plant breeders' rights concerned, he is satisfied that the holder is no longer in breach of the obligation whose breach led to the suspension.

(3) Subsection (1) above is without prejudice to the remedies available to the holder of a licence under section 17 above by the taking of proceedings in any court.

Proceedings before the Controller

[6.46]

24 Right to be heard: general

The Ministers shall by regulations make provision for any decision of the Controller against which an appeal lies to the Tribunal to be made only after an opportunity of making representations to him, and of being heard by him or by a person appointed by him for the purpose, has been afforded—

(a) to the person entitled to appeal to the Tribunal against that decision, and

(b) to persons of such other descriptions as may be prescribed by the regulations.

NOTES

Regulations: the Plant Breeders' Rights Regulations 1998, SI 1998/1027.

[6.47]

25 Right to be heard: applications for compulsory licences

(1) This section applies to an application for the grant of a licence under section 17 above if the holder of the plant breeders' rights to which the application relates is, or includes, or is represented by, a society or other organisation falling within subsection (2) below.

(2) A society or other organisation falls within this subsection if it has as its main object, or one of its main objects, the negotiation or granting of licences to exercise plant breeders' rights, either as the holder of the rights or as agent for holders.

(3) If—

(a) any organisation or person applies to the Controller for an opportunity of making representations concerning an application to which this section applies, and

(b) the Controller is satisfied that the conditions mentioned in subsection (4) below are met,

he shall afford to the organisation or person by whom the application under this subsection is made an opportunity of making representations to him and of being heard by him or by a person appointed by him for the purpose.

(4) The conditions referred to in subsection (3) above are—

(a) that the organisation or person has a substantial interest in the application for a licence under section 17 above,

(b) that that application involves issues which may affect other applicants for licences under that section, and

(c) where the application under subsection (3) above is made by an organisation, that the organisation is reasonably representative of the class of persons which it claims to represent.

(5) The rights conferred by this section are in addition to any rights which may be conferred under section 24 above.

[6.48]

26 Appeals to the Tribunal

(1) An appeal shall lie to the Tribunal against the following decisions of the Controller—

(a) a decision to allow or refuse an application for the grant of plant breeders' rights,

(b) any decision preliminary to the determination of such an application as to the conditions laid down in section 4 above,

(c) a decision to allow or refuse an application under section 17(1) or (9) above,

(d) any decision under section 21 or 22(1)(a), (b) or (c) above,

(e) a decision to refuse an application under section 22(1)(d) above, and

(f) a decision to allow or refuse an application under section 23(1) or (2) above.

(2) The Ministers may by regulations confer a right of appeal to the Tribunal against—

(a) a decision of the Controller to refuse an application under section 25(3)(a) above, or
(b) any decision of the Controller under regulations made under section 18 above or section 28 or 29 below.

NOTES

Regulations: the Plant Breeders' Rights Regulations 1998, SI 1998/1027.

Discharge of the Controller's functions

[6.49]

27 Ministerial guidance

The Controller shall, in exercising his functions, act under the general direction of the Ministers, except in relation to the taking of a decision from which an appeal lies to the Tribunal.

[6.50]

28 Regulations

(1) The Ministers may by regulations make such provision as they think fit as respects the manner in which the Controller is to discharge his functions under this Part of this Act, in particular as respects applications for the grant of plant breeders' rights and other applications to the Controller under this Part of this Act.

(2) Regulations under subsection (1) above may, in particular—
(a) make provision for restricting the making of repeated applications on the same subject,
(b) prescribe the circumstances in which representations may be made regarding any decision on an application or in connection with the charging of fees,
(c) make provision as to the keeping of registers and records by the Controller and their rectification, and prescribe the circumstances in which they may be inspected by members of the public,
(d) make provision for the publication or service of notice of applications and of the Controller's decisions,
(e) prescribe the manner of dealing with objections to applications.

NOTES

Regulations: the Plant Breeders' Rights Regulations 1998, SI 1998/1027; the Plant Breeders' Rights (Naming and Fees) Regulations 2006, SI 2006/648.

[6.51]

29 Fees

(1) The Ministers may make regulations as respects the charging of fees by the Controller, including periodical fees payable by persons holding plant breeders' rights.

(2) Regulations under subsection (1) above may authorise the Controller—
(a) in the case of a failure to pay any fees payable in connection with any application to him under this Part of this Act, to refuse the application, and
(b) in the case of a failure by a holder of plant breeders' rights to pay any fees payable in connection with those rights, to terminate the period for which the grant of those rights has effect;

and may provide for the restoration of the application or the rights if the failure to pay fees is made good.

NOTES

Regulations: the Plant Breeders' Rights (Fees) Regulations 1998, SI 1998/1021; the Plant Breeders' Rights (Naming and Fees) Regulations 2006, SI 2006/648.

[6.52]

30 Use of outsiders

The Controller may use the services of persons who are not appointed as officers or servants of the Plant Variety Rights Office—
(a) in carrying out the tests and trials which he considers expedient for the purposes of this Part of this Act, and
(b) in assessing the results of any tests and trials (whether carried out by him or not) which he considers relevant for those purposes.

False information and representations as to rights

[6.53]

31 False information

(1) If any information to which this section applies is false in a material particular and the person giving the information knows that it is false or gives it recklessly, he shall be guilty of an offence and liable on summary conviction to a fine not exceeding level 3 on the standard scale.

(2) The information to which this section applies is—
(a) information given in an application to the Controller for a decision against which an appeal lies to the Tribunal,

(b) information given by or on behalf of the applicant in connection with such an application, and

(c) information given in pursuance of a request under section 16(2) above.

[6.54]

32 False representations as to rights

(1) If, in relation to any variety, a person falsely represents that he is entitled to exercise plant breeders' rights, or any rights derived from such rights, and he knows that the representation is false, or makes it recklessly, he shall be guilty of an offence and liable on summary conviction to a fine not exceeding level 3 on the standard scale.

(2) It is immaterial for the purposes of subsection (1) above whether or not the variety to which the representation relates is the subject of plant breeders' rights.

Miscellaneous

33 (*Repealed by Competition Act 1998 (Transitional, Consequential and Supplemental Provisions) Order 2000, SI 2000/311, art 33.*)

[6.55]

34 Disclosure of information obtained under section 14 or 15

(1) If the holder of plant breeders' rights obtains information pursuant to a notice given for the purposes of section 14 or 15 above, he shall owe an obligation of confidence in respect of the information to the person who supplied it.

(2) Subsection (1) above shall not have effect to restrict disclosure of information—

(a) for the purposes of, or in connection with, establishing whether plant breeders' rights have been infringed, or

(b) for the purposes of, or in connection with, any proceedings for the infringement of plant breeders' rights.

[6.56]

35 Reference collections of plant material

(1) The Controller may establish and maintain reference collections of plant material.

(2) The Controller may by means of grants of such amounts as he may determine defray or contribute towards the expenses incurred by any other person in maintaining any reference collection of plant material.

General

[6.57]

36 Offences by bodies corporate, etc

(1) Where an offence under this Part of this Act committed by a body corporate is proved to have been committed with the consent or connivance of, or to be attributable to any neglect on the part of, any director, manager, secretary or other similar officer of the body corporate, or any person who was purporting to act in any such capacity, he, as well as the body corporate, shall be guilty of the offence and liable to be proceeded against and punished accordingly.

(2) Where an offence under this Part of this Act committed by a Scottish partnership is proved to have been committed with the consent or connivance of, or to be attributable to any neglect on the part of, a partner, he, as well as the partnership, shall be guilty of the offence and liable to be proceeded against and punished accordingly.

[6.58]

37 Jurisdiction in relation to offences

(1) Proceedings for an offence under this Part of this Act may be taken against a person before the appropriate court in the United Kingdom having jurisdiction in the place where that person is for the time being.

(2) Subsection (1) above is without prejudice to any jurisdiction exercisable apart from that subsection.

[6.59]

38 Interpretation of Part I

(1) In this Part of this Act—

"the Council Regulation" means Council Regulation (EC) No 2100/94 of 27th July 1994 on Community plant variety rights, and references to particular provisions of the Council Regulation shall be construed as references to those provisions, or provisions of any [EU] instrument replacing them, as amended from time to time;

"gazette" means the gazette published under section 34 of the Plant Varieties and Seeds Act 1964;

"name" includes any designation;

"protected variety", in relation to any plant breeders' rights, means the variety which was the basis of the application for the grant of the rights;

"variety" has the meaning given by section 1(3) above.

Part 6 Plant Varieties Protection

(2) In this Part of this Act references to an applicant for the grant of plant breeders' rights, or to the holder of plant breeders' rights, include, where the context allows, references to his predecessors in title or his successors in title.

(3) For the purposes of this Part of this Act, the existence of a variety shall be taken to be a matter of common knowledge if—

(a) it is, or has been, the subject of a plant variety right under any jurisdiction,

(b) it is, or has been, entered in an official register of plant varieties under any jurisdiction, or

(c) it is the subject of an application which subsequently leads to its falling within paragraph (a) or (b) above.

(4) Otherwise, common knowledge may be established for those purposes by reference, for example, to—

(a) plant varieties already in cultivation or exploited for commercial purposes,

(b) plant varieties included in a recognised commercial or botanical reference collection, or

(c) plant varieties of which there are precise descriptions in any publication.

NOTES

Sub-s (1): in definition "the Council Regulation" reference to "EU" in square brackets substituted by the Treaty of Lisbon (Changes in Terminology) Order 2011, SI 2011/1043, art 6(1)(d).

[6.60]
39 Application of Part I to the Crown

(1) If—

(a) any servant or agent of the Crown infringes any plant breeders' rights or makes himself liable to civil proceedings under section 20 above, and

(b) the infringement or wrong is committed with the authority of the Crown,

civil proceedings in respect of the infringement or wrong shall lie against the Crown.

(2) Except as provided by subsection (1) above, no proceedings shall lie against the Crown by virtue of the Crown Proceedings Act 1947 in respect of the infringement of plant breeders' rights or any wrong under section 20 above.

(3) This section shall have effect as if contained in Part I of the Crown Proceedings Act 1947.

[6.61]
40 Application of Part I to existing rights

(1) Subject to the following provisions of this section, this Part of this Act applies in relation to existing rights as it applies in relation to plant breeders' rights granted under this Part of this Act.

(2) Section 5 above shall not apply in relation to existing rights.

(3) Section 11 above shall only apply to existing rights if the effect is to extend the period for which the rights are exercisable.

(4) In this section, "existing rights" means plant breeders' rights granted under Part I of the Plant Varieties and Seeds Act 1964 which are exercisable on the coming into force of this Part of this Act.

NOTES

Plant Varieties and Seeds Act 1964, Pt I: repealed by s 52 of, and Sch 4 to, this Act.

Transition

[6.62]
41 Varieties of recent creation

(1) This section applies where, before the end of the period of 12 months beginning with the day on which this Part of this Act comes into force, an application for the grant of plant breeders' rights is made in respect of a variety—

(a) which was in existence on the coming into force of this Part of this Act,

(b) which is of a species or group which was not, immediately before the coming into force of this Part of this Act, prescribed by a scheme under Part I of the Plant Varieties and Seeds Act 1964 (grant of plant breeders' rights), and

(c) to which paragraph 4(2) of Schedule 2 to this Act does not apply.

(2) The variety to which the application relates shall, for the purposes of section 4(2) above, be deemed to be new if no sale or other disposal of propagating or harvested material of the variety for the purposes of exploiting the variety has, with the consent of the applicant, taken place earlier than 4 years, or, in the case of trees or vines, 6 years, before the day on which this Part of this Act comes into force.

(3) Paragraph 4(4) and (10) of Schedule 2 to this Act shall also apply for the purposes of subsection (2) above.

(4) If plant breeders' rights are granted by virtue of this section, the period for which the grant of those rights has effect shall be reduced by the period before the application since the first date on which a sale or other disposal of propagating or harvested material of the variety for the purposes of exploiting the variety took place in the United Kingdom with the consent of the applicant, less one year.

NOTES

Plant Variety and Seeds Act 1964, Pt I: repealed by s 52 of, and Sch 4 to, this Act.

PART II
THE PLANT VARIETIES AND SEEDS TRIBUNAL

[6.63]

42 The Tribunal

(1) There shall continue to be a tribunal known as the Plant Varieties and Seeds Tribunal ("the Tribunal").

(2) Schedule 3 to this Act (which makes provision about the Tribunal) shall have effect.

NOTES

The Plant Varieties and Seeds Tribunal: as to the transfer of functions in relation to the Plant Varieties and Seeds Tribunal, in consequence of provision made by the Scotland Act 1998, see the Scotland Act 1998 (Cross-Border Public Authorities) (Adaptation of Functions etc) Order 1999, SI 1999/1747, arts 3–5, Sch 8, subject to savings and transitional provisions.

[6.64]

43 Jurisdiction under arbitration agreements

(1) The Tribunal shall hear and determine any matters agreed to be referred to the Tribunal by any arbitration agreement relating to the infringement of plant breeders' rights, or to matters which include the infringement of plant breeders' rights.

(2) The fees payable to the Tribunal for acting under any arbitration agreement shall be such as the Tribunal may determine.

(3) Nothing in section 4 of the Arbitration (Scotland) Act 1894 (power to name oversman) shall be taken as applying to the Tribunal.

(4) In the application of this section to England and Wales or Northern Ireland, "arbitration agreement" has the same meaning as in Part I of the Arbitration Act 1996.

[6.65]

44 Statutory jurisdiction: regulations

The Ministers may, as respects appeals to the Tribunal under their statutory jurisdiction, by regulations—

(a) make provision for determining in which part of the United Kingdom an appeal is to be heard,

(b) make provision authorising persons other than the person by whom an appeal is made and the authority whose decision is appealed against to appear and be heard as parties to the appeal,

(c) make provision for suspending, or authorising or requiring the suspension of, the operation of a decision pending final determination of an appeal against it, or

(d) make provision for the publication of notices or the taking of other steps for securing that the persons affected by the suspension of the operation of a decision appealed against will be informed of its suspension.

NOTES

Regulations: the Plant Breeders' Rights Regulations 1998, SI 1998/1027.

[6.66]

45 Appeals from the Tribunal

(1) In relation to any decision of the Tribunal on an appeal under their statutory jurisdiction, section 11 of the Tribunals and Inquiries Act 1992 (appeal on point of law) shall apply as if the Tribunal were included among the tribunals mentioned in subsection (1) of that section.

(2) Subject to any right of appeal by virtue of subsection (1) above, any decision of the Tribunal on an appeal under their statutory jurisdiction shall be final and conclusive.

[6.67]

46 Interpretation of Part II

In this Part of this Act, references to the statutory jurisdiction of the Tribunal are to any jurisdiction of the Tribunal under Part I of this Act, Part II of the Plant Varieties and Seeds Act 1964 or the Seeds Act (Northern Ireland) 1965.

PART III
MISCELLANEOUS AND GENERAL

47 (*Inserts the Plant Varieties and Seeds Act 1964, s 28(2A) at* **[6.9]**.)

General

[6.68]

48 Regulations and orders

(1) Any regulations or order under this Act made by the Ministers—

Part 6 Plant Varieties Protection

(a) may make different provision for different cases or circumstances, and
(b) may contain such supplemental, incidental and transitional provisions as appear to the Ministers to be expedient.

(2) Any regulations or order under this Act made by the Ministers shall be made by statutory instrument.

(3) A statutory instrument containing any regulations or order under this Act made by the Ministers, other than an order under section 9(12) above, shall be subject to annulment in pursuance of a resolution of either House of Parliament.

(4) No order shall be made under section 9(12) above unless a draft of the order has been laid before and approved by resolution of each House of Parliament.

(5) Before making any regulations or order under this Act, the Ministers shall consult such organisations as appear to them to be representative of persons likely to be substantially affected by the regulations or order.

(6) Nothing in this section applies to an order under section 54(3) below.

[6.69]
49 General interpretation

(1) In this Act—

"the Controller" has the meaning given by section 2(1) above;

"the Ministers" means the Minister of Agriculture, Fisheries and Food, the Secretary of State for Scotland, the Secretary of State for Wales and the Secretary of State for Northern Ireland acting jointly; and

"the Tribunal" has the meaning given by section 42 above.

(2) In this Act, references to plant breeders' rights include rights under section 7 above.

NOTES

Transfer of functions in relation to Wales, Scotland and Northern Ireland: see the relevant notes preceding s 1 at **[6.23]**.

[6.70]
50 Receipts

Any fees received by virtue of this Act by the Controller or the Tribunal shall be paid into the Consolidated Fund.

51 (*Amends the Plant Varieties and Seeds Act 1964, ss 34(1), (2), 38 at* **[6.14]**, **[6.18]**, *the Parliamentary Commissioner Act 1967, Sch 4, the Trade Descriptions Act 1968, s 2(4) and the Tribunals and Inquiries Act 1992, Sch 1.*)

[6.71]
52 Repeals

The enactments mentioned in Schedule 4 to this Act are hereby repealed to the extent specified in the third column of that Schedule.

[6.72]
53 Extent

(1) This Act, except section 47 above, extends to Northern Ireland.

(2) Her Majesty may by Order in Council direct that any of the provisions of this Act shall, subject to such modifications as appear to Her Majesty to be appropriate, extend to any of the Channel Islands or the Isle of Man.

(3) An Order in Council under subsection (2) above may contain such transitional and consequential provisions as appear to Her Majesty to be expedient.

NOTES

Orders in Council: the Plant Varieties and Seeds (Isle of Man) Order 2016, SI 2016/758.

[6.73]
54 Short title and commencement

(1) This Act may be cited as the Plant Varieties Act 1997.

(2) This section and sections 49 and 53 above shall come into force on the day on which this Act is passed.

(3) The remaining provisions of this Act shall come into force on such day as the Ministers may by order made by statutory instrument appoint; and different days may be so appointed for different purposes.

(4) An order under subsection (3) above may contain such transitional provisions and savings as appear to the Ministers to be expedient.

NOTES

Orders: the Plant Varieties Act 1997 (Commencement) Order 1998, SI 1998/1028.

SCHEDULES

SCHEDULE 1
THE PLANT VARIETY RIGHTS OFFICE

Section 2

Staff

[6.74]

1. The Ministers may appoint a deputy controller and such other officers and servants to act in the Plant Variety Rights Office as the Ministers may determine.

Remuneration

2. There shall be paid to the Controller and any other officers or servants appointed under paragraph 1 above such remuneration and allowances as the Ministers may with the consent of the Minister for the Civil Service determine.

Authority of officers

3. Any act or thing directed to be done by or to the Controller may be done by or to any officer authorised by the Ministers.

Proof of documents

4. Prima facie evidence, or in Scotland sufficient evidence, of any document issued by the Controller may be given in all legal proceedings by the production of a copy or extract certified to be a true copy or extract by an officer appointed under paragraph 1 above and authorised to give a certificate under this paragraph.

5. Any document purporting to be certified in accordance with paragraph 4 above shall, unless the contrary is proved, be deemed to have been duly certified without proof of the official character or handwriting of the person appearing to have certified the document.

SCHEDULE 2
CONDITIONS FOR THE GRANT OF PLANT BREEDERS' RIGHTS

Section 4

PART I
CRITERIA FOR GRANT OF RIGHTS

Distinctness

[6.75]

1. The variety shall be deemed to be distinct if it is clearly distinguishable by one or more characteristics which are capable of a precise description from any other variety whose existence is a matter of common knowledge at the time of the application.

Uniformity

2. The variety shall be deemed to be uniform if, subject to the variation that may be expected from the particular features of its propagation, it is sufficiently uniform in those characteristics which are included in the examination for distinctness.

Stability

3. The variety shall be deemed to be stable if those characteristics which are included in the examination for distinctness, as well as any others used for the variety description, remain unchanged after repeated propagation or, in the case of a particular cycle of propagation, at the end of each such cycle.

Novelty

4. (1) The variety shall be deemed to be new if sub-paragraphs (2) and (3) below apply.

(2) This sub-paragraph applies if no sale or other disposal of propagating or harvested material of the variety for the purposes of exploiting the variety has, with the consent of the applicant, taken place in the United Kingdom earlier than one year before the date of the application.

(3) This sub-paragraph applies if no sale or other disposal of propagating or harvested material of the variety for the purposes of exploiting the variety has, with the consent of the applicant, taken place elsewhere than in the United Kingdom earlier than 4 years, or, in the case of trees or vines, 6 years, before the date of the application.

(4) For the purposes of sub-paragraphs (2) and (3) above, there shall be disregarded any sale or other disposal to which sub-paragraph (5), (6), (8) or (9) below applies.

(5) This sub-paragraph applies to any sale or other disposal of a stock of material of the variety to a person who at the time of the sale or other disposal is, or who subsequently becomes, the person entitled to the grant of plant breeders' rights in respect of the variety.

(6) This sub-paragraph applies to—

(a) any sale or other disposal of propagating material of the variety to a person as part of qualifying arrangements, and

(b) any sale or other disposal to the applicant, by a person who uses propagating material of the variety under any such arrangements, of the material produced directly or indirectly from the use.

(7) For the purposes of sub-paragraph (6) above, qualifying arrangements are arrangements under which—

(a) a person uses propagating material of the variety under the applicant's control for the purpose of increasing the applicant's stock, or of carrying out tests or trials, and

(b) the whole of the material produced, directly or indirectly, from the material becomes or remains the property of the applicant.

(8) This sub-paragraph applies to any sale or other disposal of material of the variety, other than propagating material, produced in the course of—

(a) the breeding of the variety,

(b) increasing the applicant's stock of material of the variety, or

(c) carrying out tests or trials of the variety,

which does not involve identifying the variety from which the material is produced.

(9) This sub-paragraph applies to any disposal of material of the variety, otherwise than by way of sale, at an exhibition or for the purposes of display at an exhibition.

(10) For the purposes of sub-paragraphs (2) and (3) above, any sale or other disposal of propagating or harvested material of a variety for the purposes of exploiting the variety shall, if the variety is related to another variety, be treated as being also a sale or other disposal of propagating or harvested material of the other variety for the purposes of exploiting that variety.

(11) For the purposes of sub-paragraph (10) above, a variety is related to another if its nature is such that repeated production of the variety is not possible without repeated use of the other variety.

PART II
PRIORITIES BETWEEN APPLICANTS FOR RIGHTS

[6.76]

5. (1) If a variety is bred, or discovered and developed, by two or more persons independently, the first of those persons, and any successors in title of theirs, to apply for the grant of plant breeders' rights in respect of it shall be the person entitled to the grant.

(2) As between persons making applications for the grant of plant breeders' rights in respect of the same variety on the same date, the one who was first in a position to make an application for the grant of plant breeders' rights in respect of that variety, or who would have been first in that position if this Part of this Act had always been in force, shall be the person entitled to the grant.

6. (1) If the following conditions are met, an application for the grant of plant breeders' rights shall be treated for the purposes of paragraphs 1, 4 and 5 above as made, not on the date on which it is in fact made, but on the earlier date mentioned in sub-paragraph (7) below.

(2) The first condition is that, in the 12 months immediately preceding the application under this Part of this Act, the applicant has duly made a parallel application under the law of—

(a) the [European Union],

(b) any other intergovernmental organisation, or any State, which is, and was at the time of the application, a member of the Union as defined by Article 1(xi) of the Convention, or

(c) any country or territory which is, and was at the time of the application, designated for the purposes of this provision by order made by the Ministers.

(3) The second condition is that the applicant has not duly made such a parallel application earlier than 12 months before the application under this Part of this Act.

(4) The third condition is that the application under this Part of this Act includes a claim to priority under this paragraph by reference to the parallel application.

(5) The fourth condition is that the application by reference to which priority is claimed has not been withdrawn or refused when the application under this Part of this Act is made.

(6) The fifth condition is that, within 3 months from the date of the application under this Part of this Act, the applicant submits to the Controller a copy of the documents constituting the parallel application, certified as a true copy by the authority to whom it is made.

(7) The earlier date referred to in sub-paragraph (1) above is the date of the parallel application mentioned in sub-paragraph (2) above.

(8) If more than one parallel application has been duly made as mentioned in sub-paragraph (2) above, the references in sub-paragraphs (4) to (7) above to the parallel application shall be construed as references to the earlier, or earliest, of the applications.

(9) In this paragraph—

(a) "the Convention" means the International Convention for the Protection of New Varieties of Plants done on 2nd December 1961 and revised at Geneva on 10th November 1972, 23rd October 1978 and 19th March 1991, and

(b) references to a parallel application, in relation to an application for the grant of plant breeders' rights, are to an application for the grant of plant variety rights in respect of the variety to which the application under this Part of this Act relates.

7. (1) Any priority which an application for the grant of plant breeders' rights enjoys by virtue of paragraph 6 above shall be forfeited if the applicant does not, before the end of the relevant period, satisfy all the requirements which are to be satisfied by an applicant before plant breeders' rights can be granted to him.

(2) For the purposes of sub-paragraph (1) above, the relevant period is the period of 2 years beginning with the day after the last day on which the applicant could have claimed priority under paragraph 6 above for his application.

(3) Where—

(a) an application for the grant of plant breeders' rights enjoys priority by virtue of paragraph 6 above, and

(b) the application by reference to which it enjoys priority is withdrawn or refused before the applicant has satisfied all the requirements which are to be satisfied by an applicant before plant breeders' rights can be granted to him,

sub-paragraph (1) above shall have effect with the substitution for "the relevant period" of "such period as the Controller may specify".

NOTES

Para 2: words in square brackets substituted by the Treaty of Lisbon (Changes in Terminology) Order 2011, SI 2011/1043, art 4(1).

SCHEDULE 3
THE PLANT VARIETIES AND SEEDS TRIBUNAL

Section 42

Constitution of the Tribunal

[6.77]

1. In any case, the jurisdiction of the Tribunal shall be exercised by—

(a) the relevant chairman,

(b) a member of the panel constituted under paragraph 7(1)(a) below, and

(c) a member of the panel constituted under paragraph 7(1)(b) below;

and references to the Tribunal in this Act or the Plant Varieties and Seeds Act 1964 shall be construed accordingly.

Chairman

2. (1) The Lord Chancellor shall appoint a person to be chairman of the Tribunal for the purpose of proceedings brought before them in England and Wales.

(2) A person may only be appointed under this paragraph if he has a seven year general qualification, within the meaning of section 71 of the Courts and Legal Services Act 1990.

3. (1) The Lord President of the Court of Session shall appoint a person to be chairman of the Tribunal for the purpose of proceedings brought before them in Scotland.

(2) A person may only be appointed under this paragraph if he is an advocate or solicitor in Scotland of at least 7 years' standing.

4. (1) The [Northern Ireland Judicial Appointments Commission] shall appoint a person to be chairman of the Tribunal for the purpose of proceedings brought before them in Northern Ireland.

(2) A person may only be appointed under this paragraph if he is a member of the Bar of Northern Ireland or [solicitor of the Court of Judicature of Northern Ireland] of at least 7 years' standing.

5. (1) Subject to sub-paragraph (2) below, a person's appointment under paragraph 2, 3 or 4 above shall be for such term as the appointing authority may determine before the person's appointment.

[(1A) For an appointment under paragraph 4 above, the term mentioned in sub-paragraph (1) above is to be determined with the agreement of the [Department of Justice].]

(2) No appointment of a person under paragraph 2, 3 or 4 above shall be such as to extend beyond the day on which he attains the age of 70.

(3) A person who ceases to hold office under paragraph 2, 3 or 4 above shall be eligible for re-appointment.

(4) A person may resign his appointment under paragraph 2, 3 or 4 above by notice in writing to the appointing authority.

(5) The appointing authority may revoke a person's appointment under [paragraph 2 or 3] above if satisfied that the person is unfit to continue in office or incapable of discharging his duties.

[(5A) Where the appointing authority is the Lord Chancellor, the power conferred by sub-paragraph (5) may be exercised only with the concurrence of the Lord Chief Justice of England and Wales.]

(6) Sub-paragraph (2) above is subject to section 26(4) to (6) of the Judicial Pensions and Retirement Act 1993 (power to authorise continuance in office up to the age of 75).

6. (1) In the case of the temporary absence or inability to act of a person appointed under paragraph 2, 3 or 4 above, the appointing authority may appoint another person to act as deputy for that person.

(2) A person may only be appointed to act as deputy for a person appointed under paragraph 2, 3 or 4 above if he has the qualification required for appointment under that paragraph.

(3) A person appointed under sub-paragraph (1) above shall, when acting as deputy for a person appointed under paragraph 2, 3 or 4 above, have all the functions of that person.

The two panels

7. (1) The Ministers shall draw up and from time to time revise—

(a) a panel of persons who have wide general knowledge in the field of agriculture, of horticulture or of forestry, and

(b) a panel of persons who have specialised knowledge of particular species or groups of plants or of the seeds industry.

(2) The power to revise the panels drawn up under this paragraph shall include power to terminate a person's membership of either of them, and shall accordingly to that extent be subject to section 7 of the Tribunals and Inquiries Act 1992 [(which makes it necessary to obtain the concurrence of the Lord Chancellor and certain judicial office holders to dismissals in certain cases)].

Selection from the panels

8. (1) The members of the panels who are to deal with any case shall be selected as follows—

(a) the Ministers may select a member or members to deal with that particular case or class or group of cases, or

(b) the Ministers may select for a class or group of cases members from amongst whom members to deal with any particular case shall be selected, and the selection from amongst those members of a member or members to deal with the particular case shall then be made either by the Ministers, or, if they so direct, by the relevant chairman.

(2) The member from the panel constituted under paragraph 7(1)(b) above shall be selected for his knowledge of the subject matter of a particular case or class or group of cases.

Sittings of the Tribunal

9. The Tribunal may, for the purpose of hearing proceedings brought before them in any part of the United Kingdom, sit anywhere in the United Kingdom.

Decisions of the Tribunal

10. (1) Any decision of the Tribunal in exercise of their jurisdiction shall be taken, in the event of a difference between members dealing with the case, by the votes of the majority.

(2) If, after the commencement of the hearing of any proceedings before the Tribunal, one of the three members of the Tribunal becomes incapable of continuing to hear the proceedings on account of sickness or for any other reason, the proceedings may, with the consent of all parties to the proceedings, be continued before the remaining two members of the Tribunal and heard and determined accordingly.

(3) If, in the case of proceedings continued under sub-paragraph (2) above, the two members differ in opinion, the case shall, on the application of any party to the proceedings, be re-argued and determined by the Tribunal as ordinarily constituted.

(4) A decision of the Tribunal shall not be questioned on the ground that a member was not validly appointed or selected.

Costs

11. (1) In any proceedings brought before the Tribunal in England and Wales or Northern Ireland under their statutory jurisdiction, the Tribunal may order any party to the proceedings to pay to any other party to the proceedings—

(a) a specified sum in respect of the costs incurred in the proceedings by the second-mentioned party, or

(b) the taxed amount of those costs.

(2) In the case of an order under sub-paragraph (1) above relating to proceedings brought in England and Wales, any costs required by the order to be taxed may be taxed in the county court according to such of the scales prescribed by [rules of court] for proceedings in the county court as may be directed by the order or, if the order gives no direction, by the county court.

(3) In the case of any order under sub-paragraph (1) above relating to proceedings brought in Northern Ireland, any costs required by the order to be taxed may be taxed by the taxing master of the Supreme Court of Judicature of Northern Ireland according to such of the scales provided for equity suits or proceedings in the county courts under the County Courts (Northern Ireland) Order 1980 as may be directed by the order or, if the order gives no direction, by the taxing master.

12. In any proceedings brought before the Tribunal in Scotland under their statutory jurisdiction, the Tribunal may order any party to the proceedings to pay to any other party to the proceedings any expenses incurred in the proceedings by the second-mentioned party and may tax or settle the amount of any expenses to be paid under any such order or direct in what manner they are to be taxed.

Rules

13. (1) The Lord Chancellor may make rules as to the procedure in connection with proceedings brought before the Tribunal in exercise of their statutory jurisdiction and as to the fees chargeable in respect of those proceedings, and the rules may in particular make provision—

(a) as to the circumstances in which the Tribunal need not sit, or are not to sit, in public,

(b) as to the form of any decision of the Tribunal,

(c) as to the time within which any proceedings are to be instituted,

(d) as to the evidence which may be required or admitted in any proceedings,

(e) as to the examination of the parties, and of witnesses, on oath or affirmation in any proceedings,

(f) as to the procedure for securing the attendance of witnesses and the production of documents in any proceedings.

(2) Rules under sub-paragraph (1) above shall be made by statutory instrument which shall be subject to annulment in pursuance of a resolution of either House of Parliament.

Remuneration of Tribunal members

14. The Ministers may pay to members of the Tribunal such remuneration and allowances as the Ministers may determine.

Officers and servants

15. (1) The Ministers may appoint such officers and servants of the Tribunal as the Ministers may determine.

(2) There shall be paid to the officers and servants appointed under this paragraph such remuneration and allowances as the Ministers may determine.

Interpretation

16. In this Schedule—

"appointing authority" means—

(a) in relation to an appointment under paragraph 2 above, the Lord Chancellor,

(b) in relation to an appointment under paragraph 3 above, the Lord President of the Court of Session, and

(c) in relation to an appointment under paragraph 4 above, the [Northern Ireland Judicial Appointments Commission]; and

"relevant chairman" means—

(a) in relation to proceedings brought before the Tribunal in England and Wales, the person appointed under paragraph 2 above,

(b) in relation to proceedings brought before the Tribunal in Scotland, the person appointed under paragraph 3 above, and

(c) in relation to proceedings brought before the Tribunal in Northern Ireland, the person appointed under paragraph 4 above.

NOTES

Para 4: words in square brackets in sub-para (1) substituted by the Northern Ireland Act 2009, s 2(3), Sch 4, para 27(1), (2); words in square brackets in sub-para (2) substituted by the Constitutional Reform Act 2005, s 59(5), Sch 11, Pt 3, para 5.

Para 5: sub-para (1A) inserted by the Northern Ireland Act 2009, s 2(3), Sch 4, para 27(1), (3); words in square brackets in sub-para (1A) substituted by the Department of Justice Act (Northern Ireland) 2010, s 1(5), Schedule, para 11; words in square brackets in sub-para (5) substituted and sub-para (5A) inserted by the Constitutional Reform Act 2005, s 15(1), Sch 4, Pt 1, para 269(1), (3).

Para 7: words in square brackets in sub-para (2) substituted by the Constitutional Reform Act 2005, s 15(1), Sch 4, Pt 1, para 269(1), (4).

Para 11: words in square brackets in sub-para (2) substituted by the Crime and Courts Act 2013, s 17(5), Sch 9, Pt 3, para 120.

Para 16: in definition "appointing authority" words in square brackets substituted by the Northern Ireland Act 2009, s 2(3), Sch 4, para 27(1), (4).

Rules: the Plant Varieties and Seeds Tribunal Rules 1974, SI 1974/1136, which were made under the Plant Varieties and Seeds Act 1964, s 10(5) (repealed by s 52 of, and Sch 4 to, this Act), are thought to have effect under this Part of this Schedule by virtue of the Interpretation Act 1978, s 17(2)(b).

SCHEDULE 4

(Sch 4 contains repeals which, in so far as relevant to this work, have been incorporated at the appropriate place.)

PLANT VARIETIES AND SEEDS TRIBUNAL RULES 1974

(SI 1974/1136)

NOTES

Made: 26 June 1974.

Authority: the Plant Varieties and Seeds Act 1964, Sch 4, para 9(2) (repealed): by virtue of the Interpretation Act 1978, s 17(2)(b), these rules are now thought to have effect under the Plant Varieties Act 1997, Sch 3, para 13.

Commencement: 1 August 1974.

ARRANGEMENT OF RULES

Preliminary

SCHEDULES

Preliminary

[6.78]

1 Citation and commencement

These Rules may be cited as the Plant Varieties and Seeds Tribunal Rules 1974 and shall come into operation on 1st August 1974.

[6.79]
2 Interpretation

(1) In these Rules, unless the context otherwise requires—

"the Act" means the Plant Varieties and Seeds Act 1964;

"the chairman" means the chairman of the tribunal [appointed in accordance with paragraph 2, 3 or 4 of Schedule 3 to the Plant Varieties Act 1997], as the case may be;

"the Controller" means the Controller of Plant Variety Rights;

"the Part I regulations" means the Plant Breeders' Rights Regulations 1969;

"the Part II regulations" means [the Forest Reproductive Material (Great Britain) Regulations 2002], the Seeds (National Lists of Varieties) Regulations 1973 and the Seeds (Registration and Licensing) Regulations 1974;

"respondent authority" means—

(a) in relation to an appeal under [the Forest Reproductive Material (Great Britain) Regulations 2002][—

(i) the Forestry Commissioners, where the appeal is made against their decision;

(ii) the Welsh Ministers, where the appeal is made against their decision;]

(b) in relation to an appeal under the Seeds (National Lists of Varieties) Regulations 1973, the Minister of Agriculture, Fisheries and Food, the Secretary of State for Scotland and the Secretary of State concerned with agriculture in Northern Ireland; and

(c) in relation to an appeal under the Seeds (Registration and Licensing) Regulations 1974, the Minister of Agriculture, Fisheries and Food or the Secretary of State, as the case may be;

"the secretary" means the secretary of the tribunal;

"the tribunal" means the Plant Varieties and Seeds Tribunal established by section 10 of and Schedule 4 to the Act as respectively amended by paragraph 5(5) of Schedule 4 to the European Communities Act 1972;

expressions defined in the Part I regulations or in the Part II regulations shall have the same meaning in these Rules;

a form referred to by number means the form so numbered in Schedule 1 to these Rules or a form substantially to the like effect.

(2) Unless the context otherwise requires, any reference in these Rules to any regulation or enactment shall be construed as a reference to that regulation or enactment, as amended, extended or applied by any other regulation or enactment.

(3) The Interpretation Act 1889 shall apply to the interpretation of these Rules as it applies to the interpretation of an Act of Parliament.

NOTES

Para (1): in definition "the chairman" words in square brackets substituted by the Constitutional Reform Act 2005, s 15(1), Sch 4, Pt 1, para 80; in definitions "the Part II Regulations" and "respondent authority" words in first pair of square brackets substituted for original words "the Forest Reproductive Material Regulations 1973", in relation to England and Wales, by the Plant Varieties and Seeds Tribunal (Amendment) (England and Wales) Rules 2002, SI 2002/3198, r 2(1), (2); words in second pair of square brackets substituted by the Natural Resources Body for Wales (Functions) Order 2013, SI 2013/755, art 4(2), Sch 4, paras 5, 6.

Minister of Agriculture, Fisheries and Food: functions of the Minister under the relevant regulations, so far as exercisable in relation to Wales, were transferred to the Secretary of State by virtue of the Transfer of Functions (Wales) (No 1) Order 1978, SI 1978/272, and then to the National Assembly for Wales by the National Assembly for Wales (Transfer of Functions) Order 1999, SI 1999/672 (subject to the provisions of art 2(b)–(f) thereof). As to the transfer of the functions of the Minister of Agriculture, Fisheries and Food to the Secretary of State, see the Minister of Agriculture, Fisheries and Food (Dissolution) Order 2002, SI 2002/794.

Plant Varieties and Seeds Act 1964: Pt I of the Act was repealed and replaced by the Plant Varieties Act 1997, s 52, Sch 4. Pt II of the 1964 Act is unrepealed.

Interpretation Act 1889: repealed and replaced by the Interpretation Act 1978.

Plants Breeders' Rights Regulations 1969: SI 1969/1021 (revoked); see now the Plant Breeders' Rights Regulations 1998, SI 1998/1027.

Seeds (National Lists of Varieties) Regulations 1973: SI 1973/994 (revoked); see now the Seeds (National Lists of Varieties) Regulations 2001, SI 2001/3510.

Seeds (Registration and Licensing) Regulations 1974: SI 1974/760 (revoked).

Appeals From Controller

[6.80]
3 Notice of appeal

An appeal under Part I of the Act or under the Part I regulations against any decision of the Controller shall be instituted by the appellant serving on the secretary within 28 days of the Controller's giving notice of his decision in pursuance of the Part I regulations a notice of appeal in Form 1, which shall be accompanied by all documents referred to therein.

[6.81]

4 Notices to appellant and persons entitled to be heard

(1) On receiving a notice of appeal the secretary shall serve a copy on the Controller, who shall on receiving the notice, or, where there is more than one appeal against the same decision, the first notice, supply the secretary with—

- (a) a copy of the notice of his decision, including the reasons for it;
- (b) a list containing the names and addresses of the persons entitled under the Part I regulations to appear and be heard as parties to any appeal against the decision;
- (c) a copy of any representations made to the Controller and any written evidence or other documents given or supplied in the course of the proceedings before him;
- (d) a factual summary of the oral evidence at any hearing before the Controller or any person appointed by him; and
- (e) a list of all plants and plant material relevant to the decision which are in the Controller's possession or under his control, stating where such plants and material are available for inspection by the tribunal and by any person entitled to appear and be heard as a party to any appeal against the decision.

(2) On receiving from the Controller the names and addresses of the persons entitled to appear and be heard, the secretary shall—

- (a) serve on every appellant—
  - (i) a notice in Form 2;
  - (ii) a list of the documents and plants or plant material supplied or made available by the Controller in accordance with sub-paragraphs (c), (d) and (e) of paragraph (1) of this rule, stating where such documents, plants and plant material may be inspected; and
- (b) serve on all persons, other than the appellant, entitled to appear and be heard as parties to the appeal—
  - (i) a notice in Form 3;
  - (ii) a list of the documents and plants or plant material mentioned in sub-paragraph (a)(ii) above, stating where such documents, plants and plant material may be inspected;
  - (iii) a copy of the notice of appeal, stating where the documents supplied with it may be inspected.

[6.82]

5 Notice of intention to appear

(1) Any person entitled under the Part I regulations to appear and be heard as a party to an appeal may, within 28 days of receiving notice from the secretary under rule 4(2)(b), serve on the secretary a notice in Form 4 of his intention to appear, and the secretary shall serve a copy of the notice on the appellant, the Controller, and every other person entitled to appear and be heard.

(2) If the Controller intends to appear on the hearing of an appeal, he shall notify the secretary within 28 days of receiving a copy of the relevant notice of appeal and the secretary shall notify the appellant and every other person entitled to appear and be heard as a party to the appeal of the Controller's intention.

[6.83]

6 Inspection and copies of evidence

(1) The appellant and any person who has given notice under rule 5(1) of his intention to appear shall be entitled, on serving notice on the secretary in Form 5, and on payment of the prescribed fee, to inspect any document (including the summary of oral evidence) and any plants or plant material supplied or made available by the Controller or by any party to the appeal, and to be supplied with copies of any such document.

(2) If the Controller has given notice under rule 5(2) of his intention to appear on the hearing of the appeal, he shall, on giving notice in that behalf to the secretary, be entitled to inspect any document and any plants or plant material supplied or made available by any party to the appeal and to be supplied with copies of any such document.

[6.84]

7 Date and place of hearing

(1) As soon as may be after the members of the tribunal to hear the appeal have been selected, the chairman shall fix a date, time and place for the hearing, and the secretary shall serve not less than 28 days' notice thereof on the appellant, the Controller and on every person who has given notice under rule 5(1) of his intention to appear.

(2) Where more than one appeal against the same decision falls to be heard by the same members of the tribunal, the chairman may direct that the appeals shall be heard at the same time.

(3) The chairman may alter the date, time or place of the hearing if it appears to him necessary or desirable to do so to avoid hardship or inconvenience to any party or for any other reason appearing to the chairman to be sufficient.

[6.85]
8 Withdrawal of appeal and default of appearance

(1) An appellant who wishes to withdraw his appeal may do so by serving notice in writing on the secretary at any time before the hearing and on receiving such a notice the secretary shall forthwith notify the Controller, all persons entitled to appear and be heard as parties to the appeal and any other person who is appealing against the same decision.

(2) An appellant who without good cause fails to attend a hearing at the place and time fixed shall be deemed to have withdrawn his appeal.

(3) If, on the withdrawal of an appeal, it appears to the chairman that the case may be a proper one for the award of costs (or, in Scotland, expenses) in accordance with paragraph 9(1) or paragraph 9(4) of Schedule 4 to the Act, he shall cause the tribunal to be convened for the purpose of determining whether costs or expenses should be awarded; and the secretary shall serve not less than seven days' notice of the date, time and place appointed for that purpose on all persons on whom notice of the hearing was served in pursuance of rule 7(1).

NOTES

Para 9(1) or (4) of Sch 4 to the Act: see now the Plant Varieties Act 1997, Sch 3, paras 11, 12.

[6.86]
9 Attendance of witnesses

(1) The attendance of witnesses before the tribunal, with or without documents, may be secured by a notice in Form 6 signed by the chairman and served by the secretary on the person to whom it is addressed.

(2) The appellant, any person who has given notice under rule 5(1), and the Controller if he has notified the secretary under rule 5(2) of his intention to appear, may apply for the issue of a notice under paragraph (1) of this rule by serving on the secretary a notice in Form 7.

[6.87]
10 Tribunal to sit in public

(1) The tribunal shall sit in public unless it appears to them that there are exceptional reasons which make it desirable that the hearing or any part of it should take place in private.

(2) . . .

NOTES

Para (2): revoked by the Tribunals, Courts and Enforcement Act 2007 (Transitional and Consequential Provisions) Order 2008, SI 2008/2683, art 6(1), Sch 1, para 3.

[6.88]
11 Representation and procedure at hearing

(1) The Controller, the appellant and any other person entitled to appear and be heard may do so in person, by counsel or solicitor, or by a representative appointed in writing.

(2) At the hearing the appellant or, if more than one, such of the appellants as the tribunal may direct shall begin and the other parties shall be heard in such order as the tribunal may determine.

(3) Subject to the provisions of these Rules and to any direction given by the chairman, the procedure at the hearing shall be such as the tribunal may direct.

[6.89]
12 Evidence

(1) Subject to paragraph (4) of this rule, every party appearing before the tribunal may give evidence and call witnesses, and shall be entitled to cross-examine any other witness and re-examine his own witnesses after cross-examination.

(2) The tribunal may consider any representations submitted to the Controller in the course of the proceedings before him and any other written evidence or documents given or supplied in the course of those proceedings and may inspect any plants or plant material made available by the Controller or, subject to paragraph (4) of this rule, by any person entitled to appear and be heard.

(3) The tribunal may call a witness who may, after giving evidence, be cross-examined by any party.

(4) The tribunal may refuse to consider any documents or to inspect any plants or plant material not submitted with or sufficiently described in any notice of appeal or in a notice under rule 5(1) or statement under rule 17(1) and may refuse to hear any witness (other than a party to the appeal) who has not been named in any such notice or statement.

(5) The tribunal may require any witness to give evidence on oath or affirmation, to be administered by the chairman.

(6) The tribunal shall not be bound to reject any evidence on the ground only that it would be inadmissible in a court of law.

[6.90]
13 Adjournments

The tribunal may adjourn any hearing to enable any plant to be grown or tested or for any other reason appearing to the tribunal to be sufficient.

[6.91]
14 Decision of tribunal

(1) The decision of the tribunal shall be given in writing, together with a statement of the tribunal's reasons for their decision.

(2) The chairman may correct any clerical mistake in the written record of the tribunal's decision.

(3) The secretary shall serve a copy of the tribunal's decision and reasons on the appellant, the Controller and on every person who was entitled to appear and be heard as a party to the appeal.

Appeals From Ministers and From the Forestry Commissioners

[6.92]
15 Notice of appeal

An appeal under the Part II regulations against a decision of a respondent authority shall be instituted by the appellant serving on the secretary within 28 days of the respondent authority's giving notice of its decision a notice of appeal in Form 8, which shall be accompanied by the documents referred to therein.

[6.93]
16 Parties

(1) The appellant and the respondent authority shall be parties to an appeal under the Part II regulations.

(2) Any person who was under the Part II regulations entitled to make representations to, or to be heard by, the respondent authority in the proceedings in respect of which the decision was given, and who availed himself of that opportunity, shall be entitled to appear and be heard as a party to an appeal against the decision of the respondent authority.

[6.94]
17 Respondent authority's statement, etc

(1) On receiving notice of appeal under rule 15 the secretary shall serve a copy on the respondent authority which shall within 28 days supply the secretary with a copy of its decision and of the reasons for it, together with two copies of a statement in Form 9.

(2) On receiving the respondent authority's statement, the secretary shall serve a copy on the appellant together with a notice in Form 10.

(3) Where any person is entitled under rule 16(2) to appear and be heard as a party to any appeal—

- (a) the respondent authority shall, when supplying a statement under paragraph (1) of this rule, supply the secretary with a list containing the names and addresses of the persons so entitled;
- (b) the secretary shall serve on each such person a notice in Form 3 together with a copy of the notice of appeal and of the respondent authority's statement;
- (c) rule 5(1) shall apply in relation to each such person as it applies in relation to a person entitled to appear under the Part I regulations as if for the reference therein to rule 4(2)(b) there were substituted a reference to sub-paragraph (b) of this paragraph.

(4) The respondent authority shall, on giving notice in that behalf to the secretary, be entitled to inspect any document and any plants or plant material or [basic material or forest reproductive material] supplied or made available by any party to the appeal and to be supplied with copies of any such document.

NOTES

Para (4): words in square brackets substituted for original words "basic material", in relation to England and Wales, by the Plant Varieties and Seeds Tribunal (Amendment) (England and Wales) Rules 2002, SI 2002/3198, r 2(1), (3).

[6.95]
18 Application of rules

Rules 3, 4, 5(2) and 6(2) shall not apply to appeals from a respondent authority but in all other respects these rules shall, subject to rule 17(3)(c), apply to such appeals as if for references to the Controller there were substituted references to the respondent authority, as if the references in rules 6(1), 12(2) and 12(4) to plants or plant material included a reference to [basic material or forest reproductive material] and as if in rule 9(2) the words "if he has notified the secretary under rule 5(2) of his intention to appear" were omitted.

NOTES

Words in square brackets substituted for original words "basic material", in relation to England and Wales, by the Plant Varieties and Seeds Tribunal (Amendment) (England and Wales) Rules 2002, SI 2002/3198, r 2(1), (4).

Supplemental

[6.96]
19

(1) Every document required or authorised by these Rules to be served on any person shall be deemed to have been duly served if it is delivered to him personally or delivered or sent by post to his proper address.

(2) Any document required or authorised to be served on an incorporated body or company shall be duly served if it is served on the secretary or clerk of the body or company.

(3) For the purpose of these Rules, the proper address of a person shall, in the case of a secretary or clerk of any incorporated body or company, be that of the registered or principal office of the body or company and shall in any other case be his last known address.

(4) If any person on whom any document is required to be served cannot be found, or has died and has no known personal representative, or if for any other reason service on that person cannot be readily effected in accordance with these Rules, the chairman may dispense with service or may make an order for substituted service on such other person or in such form (whether by advertisement in a newspaper or otherwise) as the chairman may think fit.

[6.97]
20 Extension of time

The time appointed by these Rules for doing any act or taking any step in connection with any proceedings may be extended by the chairman on such terms and conditions, if any, as appear to him to be just.

[6.98]
21 Interlocutory applications

An application to the tribunal or the chairman to exercise any power under rules 13, 14, 19(4) and 20 shall, if not made in the course of a hearing, be made in writing to the secretary, who shall serve a copy of the application on each of the following persons not being the applicant, that is to say, the appellant, the Controller and every person who has given notice under rule 5(1) of his intention to appear.

[6.99]
22 Failure to comply with rules

Failure to comply with any requirement of these Rules shall not render the proceedings or anything done in pursuance thereof invalid unless the chairman or the tribunal so directs.

[6.100]
23 Fees

The fees specified in Schedule 2 to these Rules shall be payable to the secretary in respect of the matters mentioned in that Schedule and shall be paid when the relevant notice or application is served on or made to the secretary by cheque or postal order.

24 (*Revokes the Plant Variety Rights Tribunal Rules 1965, SI 1965/1623.*)

SCHEDULE 1

Rule 3

FORM 1

[6.101]
Ref No

To be inserted by Secretary

Plant Varieties and Seeds Tribunal
Notice of Appeal from Controller

To the Secretary of the Plant Varieties and Seeds Tribunal.

1. I, ... [*block capitals*]
of . . . . [*address*]
hereby give notice of appeal against the decision of the Controller of Plant Variety Rights of which I received notice dated

2. The decision was that—

3. My grounds of appeal are—

4. In support of my case, I intend—

*(a) to give evidence myself;

*(b) to call the following witnesses—

(i) who gave evidence before the Controller;

(ii) who did not give evidence before the Controller;

*(c) to rely on the following documents—

(i) which I attach;

(ii) which I will produce at the hearing, copies of which I attach;

(iii) copies of which I attach, the original documents being in the possession of:

*(d) to refer to the following plants or plant material which are now at . . . . [*address*] where they may be inspected by any party giving due notice through the secretary of the tribunal.

* *Strike out any which is inapplicable*

5. I enclose a cheque/postal order* in respect of the fees payable by me.

* *Strike out any which is inapplicable*

Date . . . . Signed . . . . (1)

(1) If signed by any person other than the appellant himself, he should state in what capacity or by what authority he signs.

FORM 2

Rule 4(2)

[6.102]
Ref No

To be inserted by Secretary

Plant Varieties and Seeds Tribunal
Notice to Appellant (Appeal from Controller)

1. A copy of your notice of appeal (Ref No) dated , has been served on the Controller of Plant Variety Rights and on the following persons who are entitled under Regulation 14(2) of the Plant Breeders' Rights Regulations 1969 to appear and be heard as parties to the appeal:

. . . .

. . . . [*address*]

. . . .

. . . . [*address*]

2. The Controller has supplied the tribunal with a factual summary of the oral evidence of the following persons:—

3. He has also supplied or made available to the tribunal the documents and the plants and plant material, shown in the attached list.

4. On completing the attached form (Form 5) and on paying the appropriate fees, you will be entitled to inspect any document and any plants or plant material supplied by the Controller or by any party to the appeal, and to be supplied with a copy of any such document.

5. You will be informed if the Controller or any of the persons whose names are shown in paragraph I of this notice notifies the tribunal of his intention to appear and be heard, or submits or makes available any document or plants or plant material, or applies to inspect any plants or plant material mentioned in paragraph 4(d) of your notice of appeal.

6. Attached is a copy of the schedule of fees payable.

Date . . . . Signed: . . . .

Secretary of the Tribunal.

FORM 3

Rules 4(2) and 17(3)

[6.103]
Ref No

To be inserted by Secretary

Plant Varieties and Seeds Tribunal
Notice to Person Entitled to Appear and be Heard

1. This notice is served on you . . . . as a person entitled under [Regulation 14(2) of the Plant Breeders' Rights Regulations 1969] [Rule 16(2) of the Plant Varieties and Seeds Tribunal Rules 1974] to appear and to be heard as a party to an appeal against the decision of the [*here insert "Controller of Plant Variety Rights" or the name of the relevant respondent authority*] of which a notice was served on you dated

2. A notice of appeal (Ref No) has been received from . . . . a copy of which is enclosed with this notice. [A copy of the respondent authority's statement is also enclosed.]

3. If you wish to appear and be heard, you should complete the attached form (Form 4) and return it within 28 days of receiving this notice together with the appropriate fee to the secretary of the tribunal at . . . . [*address*]. You will then be given notice of the date, time and place of the hearing of the appeal, when these have been fixed.

The tribunal may exclude any evidence or refuse to inspect any [plants or plant material] [basic material or forest reproductive material] not submitted with or sufficiently described in a notice in Form 4, and may refuse to hear any witness, other than a party to the appeal, who has not been named in such a notice.

[4. The Controller has supplied the tribunal with a factual summary of the oral evidence of the following persons:—

5. He has also supplied or made available to the tribunal the written evidence, and the plants and plant material shown in the attached list]

6. On completing the attached form (Form 5) and on paying the appropriate fees you will be entitled to inspect any document and any [plants or plant material] [basic material or forest reproductive material] supplied or made available by [the Controller or by] any party to the appeal, and to be supplied with a copy of any such document.

7. Attached is a copy of the schedule of fees payable.

Date . . . . Signed: . . . .

Secretary of the Tribunal.

NOTES

Paras 3, 6: words "basic material or forest reproductive material" in square brackets substituted for original words "basic material", in relation to England and Wales, by the Plant Varieties and Seeds Tribunal (Amendment) (England and Wales) Rules 2002, SI 2002/3198, r 2(1), (5)(a).

FORM 4

Rule 5(1)

[6.104]
Ref No

To be inserted by Secretary

Plant Varieties and Seeds Tribunal
Notice of Intention to Appear

To the Secretary of the Plant Varieties and Seeds Tribunal

1. I, ... [*block capitals*]
of . . . . [address]
hereby give notice of my intention to appear at the hearing of the appeal of . . . . a copy of the notice of which (bearing the reference number) was sent to me on 19

2. I intend

*(a) to support the decision of the Controller [*or* respondent authority]

*(b) to support this appeal against the decision of the Controller [*or* respondent authority]

for the following reasons:—

* *Strike out whichever is inapplicable*

3. In support of my case, I intend—

*(a) to give evidence myself;

*(b) to call the following witnesses—

(i) who gave evidence before the Controller [or respondent authority]:

(ii) who did not give evidence before the Controller [or respondent authority]

*(c) to rely on the following documents

(i) which I attach;

(ii) which I will produce at the hearing, copies of which I attach;

(iii) copies of which I attach, the original documents being in the possession of:

*(d) to refer to the following plants or plant material [or [basic material or forest reproductive material]] which are [*or* is] now at . . . . [address] where they [*or* it] may be inspected by any party giving due notice through the secretary of the tribunal.

* *Strike out whichever is inapplicable*

4. I enclose a cheque/postal order* in respect of the fees payable by me.

* *Strike out whichever is inapplicable*

Date . . . . Signed . . . . (1)

(1) If signed by any person other than the person entitled to appear as a party, he should state in what capacity or by what authority he signs.

NOTES

Para 3: words "basic material or forest reproductive material" in square brackets substituted for original words "basic material", in relation to England and Wales, by the Plant Varieties and Seeds Tribunal (Amendment) (England and Wales) Rules 2002, SI 2002/3198, r 2(1), (5)(b).

FORM 5

Rule 6(1)

[6.105]
Ref No

To be inserted by Secretary

Plant Varieties and Seeds Tribunal
Application to Inspect Evidence

To the Secretary of the Plant Varieties and Seeds Tribunal

1. I, ... [*block capitals*]
of . . . . [*address*]

*(having served a notice of appeal dated)

*(having received a notice in Form 3 (bearing the reference number)
in the appeal of . . . . [*name of appellant*] and having completed a notice in Form 4 of my intention to appear at the hearing of the appeal)

hereby apply

*(a) to inspect the documents supplied or submitted to the tribunal in this case;

*(b) to inspect the following plants or plant material [*or* [basic material or forest reproductive material]] at the place named:

Plants or plant material

[*or* [basic material or forest reproductive material]] to be inspected:
Now at:

(c) to be supplied with . . . . [*number*] copies of the following documents:—

* *Strike out any which is inapplicable*

*2. I wish to carry out this inspection at . . . . [*name of place*] . . . . *(on) *(between) the following dates:—

* *Strike out any which is inapplicable*

3. I enclose a cheque/postal order* in respect of the fees payable by me.

* *Strike out whichever is inapplicable*

Date . . . . Signed . . . . (1)

(1) If signed by any person other than the person entitled to appear as a party, he should state in what capacity or by what authority he signs.

NOTES

Para 1: words "basic material or forest reproductive material" in square brackets in both places they occur substituted for original words "basic material", in relation to England and Wales, by the Plant Varieties and Seeds Tribunal (Amendment) (England and Wales) Rules 2002, SI 2002/3198, r 2(1), (5)(c).

FORM 6

Rule 9(1)

[6.106]
Ref No

To be inserted by Secretary

Plant Varieties and Seeds Tribunal
Notice to Secure Attendance of Witness
Plant Varieties and Seeds Act 1964

In the matter of the appeal by . . . . against the decision of the . . . .
(1) dated

TAKE NOTICE THAT, on application of . . . .
you . . . . of . . . . [*address*]
are required by the tribunal to attend the hearing of the appeal at . . . .
. . . . on . . . . at the hour of . . . .
in the . . . . noon and to give evidence when called.

*(And you are also to bring with you and produce at the aforesaid place and time the following documents:—)

* *Strike out if inapplicable*

Date . . . . Signed . . . .

Part 6 Plant Varieties Protection

(Chairman).

(1) Here insert "Controller of Plant Variety Rights" or the name of the relevant respondent authority.

FORM 7

Rule 9(2)

[6.107]
Ref No

To be inserted by Secretary

Plant Varieties and Seeds Tribunal
Application to Secure Attendance of Witness

To the Secretary of the Plant Varieties and Seeds Tribunal

In the matter of the appeal by . . . .
against the decision of the . . . . (1), dated
19 (Ref No)

1. I hereby request the chairman of the tribunal to order the service of a notice, to secure the attendance of . . . . [*block capitals*] of . . . . [*address*] as a witness at the hearing of this appeal* (and requiring him to bring and produce in evidence the following documents. . . . .)

* *Strike out if inapplicable*

2. I make this application

   *(a) as appellant;

   *(b) as Controller of Plant Variety Rights;

   *(c) as the respondent authority:

   *(d) as a person entitled to appear and be heard at the hearing of the appeal, and have informed the tribunal of my intention to appear in a notice in Form 4 dated 19 .

* *Strike out if inapplicable*

3. My reasons for making this application are that—(2)

* *Strike out whichever is inapplicable*

4. I enclose a cheque/postal order* in respect of the fees payable by me.

* *Strike out whichever is inapplicable*

Date . . . . Signed . . . . (3)

(1) Here insert "Controller of Plant Variety Rights" or the name of the relevant respondent authority.

(2) Mention, in particular, your reason for thinking that the witness will not attend (or not produce the documents) without the service of a notice.

(3) If signed by any person other than the person applying, he should state in what capacity or by what authority he signs.

FORM 8

Rule 15

[6.108]
Ref No

To be inserted by Secretary

Plant Varieties and Seeds Tribunal
Notice of Appeal from the [Ministers] [Minister] [Forestry Commissioners] under regulation . . . . of the . . . . Regulations 197 .

To the Secretary of the Plant Varieties and Seeds Tribunal

1. I, ... [*block capitals*] of . . . . [*address*] hereby give notice of appeal against—

*(a) the [refusal] [*or* decision] of the Ministers to—

(i) [add a plant variety to] [*or* remove a plant variety from] a National List;

(ii) renew the period during which a plant variety may remain on a National List;

(iii) remove from the National List Record the name of a person responsible for the maintenance of a plant variety;

(iv) enter in a National List a plant variety which has been entered in a list of a Member State corresponding to a National List;

*(b) the decision of the Minister to—

(i) [refuse to register] [*or* revoke the registration of] a person as a seed merchant, seed packer or seed processor;

(ii) prohibit the marketing by a person of seeds of a particular category, kind or variety;

[*(c) the decision of [(the Forestry Commissioners) (or the Welsh Ministers)]—

(i) not to approve basic material;

(ii) to approve basic material in the form of clones or clonal mixtures subject to qualifications as to duration of approval or level of production;

(iii) to withdraw or amend approval of basic material;

(iv) not to issue a Master Certificate;

(v) not to enter a person's name in the Register of Suppliers;

(vi) to remove a supplier's name from the Register of Suppliers or impose conditions upon his continued registration;

(vii) not to grant a licence to market forest reproductive material;

(viii) that testing techniques used to obtain assessments necessary to provide the information required under regulation 19(2) of the Forest Reproductive Material Regulations 2002 are not, to the Commissioners' satisfaction, internationally accepted techniques;

(ix) in respect of the following requirements of the Forest Reproductive Material Regulations 2002 in:

(aa) Schedule 4, paragraphs (1)(d) and 2(d) not to approve verification test methodology;

(bb) Schedule 5, paragraph 1(d)(ii) not to approve a statistical design, and

(cc) Schedule 5, paragraph 1(e)(i) not to approve a statistical methodology as being one that is internationally recognised].

2. My grounds of appeal are—

3. In support of my case I intend—

*(a) to give evidence myself;

*(b) to call the following witnesses:—

*(c) to rely on the following documents—

(i) which I attach;

(ii) which I will produce at the hearing, copies of which I attach;

(iii) copies of which I attach, the original documents being in the possession of: . . . .

*(d) to refer to the following [plants or plant material] [[(or basic material or forest reproductive material)]] which are [*or* is] now at . . . . [*address*] where they [*or* it] may be inspected by the respondent authority on giving due notice through the secretary of the tribunal.

4. I enclose a cheque/postal order* in respect of the fees payable by me.

Date . . . . Signed. . . . . (1)

(1) If signed by any person other than the appellant himself, he should state in what capacity or by what authority he signs.

* *Strike out any which is inapplicable*

NOTES

Para 1: sub-para (c) substituted, in relation to England and Wales, by the Plant Varieties and Seeds Tribunal (Amendment) (England and Wales) Rules 2002, SI 2002/3198, r 2(1), (6)(a); words in square brackets substituted by the Natural Resources Body for Wales (Functions) Order 2013, SI 2013/755, art 4(2), Sch 4, paras 5, 7. The original sub-para (c) read as follows—

"*(c) the decision of the Forestry Commissioners to—

(i) refuse to register basic material submitted for registration in the National Register;

(ii) remove basic material from the National Register".

Para 3: words "(or basic material or forest reproductive material)" in square brackets substituted for original words "(or basic material)", in relation to England and Wales, by SI 2002/3198, r 2(1), (6)(b).

FORM 9

Rule 17(1)

[6.109]
Ref No

To be inserted by Secretary

Plant Varieties and Seeds Tribunal
Statement by Respondent Authority in Reply to Appeal under Regulation . . . . of the . . . . Regulations 197

To the Secretary of the Plant Varieties and Seeds Tribunal

1. The. . . . .
having received notice of appeal dated . . . . (Ref No)
by . . . . against . . . .
. . . .
[here insert the ground[s] of appeal specified in the notice of appeal]

state[s] that they [*or* he] intend[s] to resist the appeal on the following grounds:—

[2. Attached is a list containing the names and addresses of the persons entitled to appear and be heard as a party to the appeal.]

3. In support of the respondent authority's case, it is proposed to—

*(a) call the following witnesses:

*(b) rely on the following documents—

(i) which are attached;

(ii) which will be produced at the hearing of the appeal, copies of which are attached;

(iii) copies of which are attached, the original documents being in the possession of:

*(c) refer to the following plants or plant material [*or* [basic material or forest reproductive material]] which are [*or* is] now at . . . . [*address*]

where they [*or* it] may be inspected by the appellant on giving due notice through the secretary of the tribunal.

Signed for and on behalf of the . . . .
Rank and Department [*or as appropriate*]

Address. . . . .

Date. . . . .

* *Strike out any which is inapplicable*

NOTES

Para 3: "basic material or forest reproductive material" in square brackets substituted for original words "basic material", in relation to England and Wales, by the Plant Varieties and Seeds Tribunal (Amendment) (England and Wales) Rules 2002, SI 2002/3198, r 2(1), (7)(a).

FORM 10

Rule 17(2)

[6.110]
Ref No

To be inserted by Secretary

Plant Varieties and Seeds Tribunal
Notice to Appellant
(Appeal against respondent authority)

1. A copy of your notice of appeal (Ref No) dated . . . . has been served on the . . . . (the respondent authority).
2. A copy of the respondent authority's statement is enclosed.
3. Copies of your notice of appeal and of the respondent authority's statement have been served on the following persons who are entitled under rule 16(2) of the Plant Varieties and Seeds Tribunal Rules 1974 to appear and be heard as parties to the appeal:—

. . . .

. . . . [*address*]

. . . .

. . . . [*address*]

4. On completing the attached form (Form 5) and on paying the appropriate fees, you will be entitled to inspect any document and any [plants or plant material] [[basic material or forest reproductive material]] supplied by the respondent authority or by any other party to the appeal and to be supplied with a copy of any such document.
5. You will be informed if the respondent authority or any of the persons whose names are shown in paragraph 1 of this notice notifies the tribunal of his intention to appear and be heard, or submits or makes available any document or plants or plant material or [basic material or forest reproductive material], or applies to inspect any plants or plant material or [basic material or forest reproductive material] mentioned in paragraph 3(d) of your notice of appeal.
6. Attached is a copy of the schedule of fees payable.

Date. . . . . Signed. . . . .

Secretary of the Tribunal

NOTES

Paras 4, 5: words "basic material or forest reproductive material" in square brackets wherever they occur substituted for original words "basic material", in relation to England and Wales, by the Plant Varieties and Seeds Tribunal (Amendment) (England and Wales) Rules 2002, SI 2002/3198, r 2(1), (7)(b).

SCHEDULE 2
FEES

[6.111]

No of Fee	*Description of Proceeding*	*Amount of Fee*
		£
1.	On giving notice of appeal under rule 3 or rule 15	10.00
2.	On giving notice under rule 5(1) of intention to appear	2.00
3.	On applying under rule 6(1)—	
	(a) to inspect documents supplied or submitted to the tribunal	0.50
	(b) to inspect any plants or plant material or [basic material or forest reproductive material]—	
	(i) in the custody of the Controller or of the respondent authority	2.00
	(ii) in the custody of any other person	1.00
	(c) for copies of documents—	
	(i) foolscap (or A4 ISO) or smaller, per page	0.10
	(ii) larger pages, per page	0.20
4.	On applying under rule 9 for a notice to secure the attendance of a witness, for each witness	1.00
5.	On making an interlocutory application (except in the course of a hearing) to the tribunal or the chairman	2.00

NOTES

Item 3: words "basic material or forest reproductive material" in square brackets substituted for original words "basic material", in relation to England and Wales, by the Plant Varieties and Seeds Tribunal (Amendment) (England and Wales) Rules 2002, SI 2002/3198, r 2(1), (8).

PLANT VARIETY RIGHTS OFFICE (EXTENSION OF FUNCTIONS) REGULATIONS 1995

(SI 1995/2655)

NOTES

Made: 29 September 1995.
Authority: European Communities Act 1972, s 2(2).
Commencement: 1 November 1995.

Introductory

[6.112]

1 Title, commencement and interpretation

(1) These Regulations may be cited as the Plant Variety Rights Office (Extension of Functions) Regulations 1995 and shall come into force on 1st November 1995.

(2) In these Regulations—

"Community Office" means the Community Plant Variety Office established by Council Regulation (EC) No 2100/94;

"National Office" means the Plant Variety Rights Office established by section 11 of the Plant Varieties and Seeds Act 1964.

NOTES

Plant Varieties and Seeds Act 1964: Pt I of that Act was repealed by the Plant Varieties Act 1997, s 52, Sch 4. The Plant Variety Rights Office is continued in being by s 2 of that Act.

Council Regulation (EC) No 2100/94: OJ L227, 1.9.94, p 1.

[6.113]

2 Functions which may be entrusted to the National Office by the Community Office

The National Office shall have power to carry out such functions as may be entrusted to it by the Community Office in accordance with Articles 30(4) and 55(1) of Council Regulation (EC) No 2100/94.

NOTES

Council Regulation (EC) No 2100/94: OJ L227, 1.9.94, p 1.

PATENTS AND PLANT VARIETY RIGHTS (COMPULSORY LICENSING) REGULATIONS 2002

(SI 2002/247)

NOTES

Made: 7 February 2002.
Authority: European Communities Act 1972, s 2(2).
Commencement: 1 March 2002.

ARRANGEMENT OF REGULATIONS

PART I
INTRODUCTORY

[6.114]

1 Citation, commencement and extent

(1) These Regulations may be cited as the Patents and Plant Variety Rights (Compulsory Licensing) Regulations 2002 and shall come into force on 1st March 2002.

(2) These Regulations extend to England, Wales, Scotland and Northern Ireland.

[6.115]

2 Interpretation

(1) In these Regulations—

"the 1977 Act" means the Patents Act 1977;

"the 1997 Act" means the Plant Varieties Act 1997;

"biotechnological invention" has the meaning given by section 130 of the 1977 Act;

"Breeders' regulations" means the Plant Breeders' Regulations as extended and applied by regulation 23, unless and until the Ministers exercise their powers under sections 24, 26(2)(a), 28, 29, 44 and 48(1) of the 1997 Act as extended by regulation 21, at which time "Breeders' regulations" shall refer to the regulations so made and in force;

"Community plant variety right" means a right granted by the Community Plant Variety Office under the Council Regulation;

"Comptroller General of Patents" means the Comptroller-General of Patents, Designs and Trade Marks appointed under section 63(1) of the Patents and Designs Act 1907;

"compulsory patent licence" means a licence ordered to be granted by the controllers under regulation 6;

"compulsory plant variety licence" means a licence granted by the controllers under regulation 13;

"Controller of Plant Variety Rights" means the officer appointed under section 2(1) of the 1997 Act;

"controllers" means the Controller of Plant Variety Rights and the Comptroller General of Patents acting jointly in accordance with the provisions of these Regulations;

"Council Regulation" means Council Regulation (EC) No 2100/94 of 27th July 1994 on Community plant variety rights as amended by Council Regulation (EC) No 2506/95 of 25th October 1995;

"court" means—

(a) in England, Wales and Northern Ireland, the Patents Court of the High Court,

(b) in Scotland, the Court of Session;

"Ministers" has the meaning given by section 49 of the 1997 Act;

"new plant variety" means the plant variety produced, or to be produced as the case may be, by using an invention protected by a patent;

"patent" has the meaning given by section 130 of the 1977 Act;

["Patents (Fees) Rules" means the Patents (Fees) Rules 2007;]

["Patents Rules" means the Patents Rules 2007;]

"plant breeders' fee" means the fee payable under the Plant Breeders' (Fees) Regulations as extended and applied by regulation 25, unless and until the Ministers exercise their powers to make regulations under sections 29 and 48(1) of the 1997 Act as extended by regulation 21 and prescribe a fee, at which time "plant breeders' fee" shall mean that fee in respect of applications under these Regulations;

"Plant Breeders' (Fees) Regulations" mean the Plant Breeders' Rights (Fees) Regulations 1998 in force immediately before the coming into force of these Regulations;

"Plant Breeders' Regulations" means the Plant Breeders' Rights Regulations 1998 in force immediately before the coming into force of these Regulations;

"plant breeders' rights" means rights granted by the Controller of Plant Variety Rights under section 3 of the 1997 Act and existing rights as defined by section 40(4) of the 1997 Act;

"plant variety" has the meaning given by paragraph 11 of Schedule A2 to the 1977 Act;

"prescribed fee" means the fee payable under the Patents (Fees) Rules as extended and applied by regulation 24, unless and until the Secretary of State exercises her powers to make rules under section 123 of the 1977 Act as extended by regulation 20 and prescribes a fee, at which time "prescribed fee" shall mean that fee in respect of applications under these Regulations;

"rules" means the Patents Rules as extended and applied by regulation 22, unless and until the Secretary of State exercises her powers under section 123 of the 1977 Act as extended by regulation 20, at which time "rules" shall refer to the rules so made and in force;

"Tribunal" means the Plant Varieties and Seeds Tribunal referred to in section 42 of the 1997 Act; and

"UK" means England, Wales, Scotland and Northern Ireland.

(2) Any reference to a numbered regulation is a reference to the regulation so numbered in these Regulations and any reference to a numbered paragraph is a reference to the paragraph so numbered in the regulation in which the reference occurs.

NOTES

Para (1): definitions "Patents (Fees) Rules" and "Patents Rules" substituted by the Patents (Compulsory Licensing and Supplementary Protection Certificates) Regulations 2007, SI 2007/3293, reg 3(1), (2).

PART II
COMPULSORY PATENT LICENCES

[6.116]

3 Applications

(1) Where a person cannot acquire or exploit plant breeders' rights or a Community plant variety right in a new variety without infringing a prior patent, he may apply in accordance with rules to the Comptroller General of Patents for a licence under the patent and on such application shall pay the prescribed fee.

(2) An application under paragraph (1) shall be accompanied by particulars which seek to demonstrate that—

(a) the applicant cannot acquire or exploit plant breeders' rights or a Community plant variety right without infringing a prior patent,

(b) the applicant has applied unsuccessfully to the proprietor of the prior patent concerned for a licence to use that patent to acquire or exploit plant breeders' rights or a Community plant variety right, and

(c) the new plant variety, in which the applicant wishes to acquire or exploit the plant breeders' rights or Community plant variety right, constitutes significant technical progress of considerable economic interest in relation to the invention protected by the patent.

(3) If and so far as any agreement purports to bind any person not to apply for a licence under paragraph (1), it shall be void.

[6.117]
4 Proceedings before controllers

On receipt by the Comptroller General of Patents of an application under regulation 3(1) and payment of the prescribed fee, the controllers shall consider and process the application in accordance with rules.

[6.118]
5

(1) The proprietor of the patent concerned or any other person wishing to oppose an application under regulation 3(1) may, in accordance with rules, give to the Comptroller General of Patents notice of opposition and on giving such notice shall pay the prescribed fee.

(2) On receipt of a notice of opposition under paragraph (1) and payment of the prescribed fee, the controllers, in deciding whether to grant an application under regulation 3(1), shall consider and process any opposition in accordance with rules.

[6.119]
6 Grant

Where, having considered the application made under regulation 3(1), the controllers are satisfied that—

(a) the applicant cannot acquire or exploit plant breeders' rights or a Community plant variety right without infringing a prior patent,
(b) the applicant has applied unsuccessfully to the proprietor of the patent concerned for a licence to use the prior patent to acquire or exploit plant breeders' rights or a Community plant variety right, and
(c) the new plant variety, in which the applicant wishes to acquire or exploit the plant breeders' rights or Community plant variety right, constitutes significant technical progress of considerable economic interest in relation to the invention protected by the patent,

the controllers shall order the grant to the applicant (or, where the applicant is a government department, shall order the grant to any person specified in the application) of a licence to use the invention protected by the prior patent in so far as the licence is necessary for the exploitation of the new plant variety on the conditions set out in regulation 7 and on such other terms as the controllers think fit.

[6.120]
7 Conditions

(1) A compulsory patent licence shall—

(a) not be exclusive,
(b) entitle the proprietor of the patent concerned to an appropriate royalty, and
(c) entitle the proprietor of the patent concerned to a cross licence on reasonable terms to use the new plant variety.

(2) Where the controllers order the grant of a compulsory patent licence to a person who has been granted plant breeders' rights in the new plant variety, the proprietor of the patent concerned may request, a cross licence on reasonable terms of the plant breeders' rights to use the new plant variety in respect of which the compulsory patent licence has been granted and, on such request, the controllers shall order the grant of such a cross licence to that proprietor (or, where the proprietor of the patent is a government department, to any person specified in the request).

(3) Where the controllers order the grant of a compulsory patent licence to a person who has yet to acquire plant breeders' rights in the new plant variety, the proprietor of the patent concerned may request a cross licence on reasonable terms of the plant breeders' rights to use the new plant variety in respect of which the compulsory patent licence has been granted and, on such request, the controllers shall order the grant of such a cross licence to that proprietor (or, where the proprietor of the patent is a government department, to any person specified in the request), and the cross licence shall come into effect on the grant to the holder of the compulsory patent licence of plant breeders' rights in the new plant variety.

(4) Where the controllers order the grant of a compulsory patent licence to a person who has been granted a Community plant variety right in the new plant variety, if the proprietor of the patent wishes, the compulsory patent licence shall be subject to the grant to the proprietor of the patent concerned (or, where the proprietor of the patent is a government department, to any person the proprietor specifies) of a cross licence of the Community plant variety right on reasonable terms to use in the UK the new plant variety in respect of which the compulsory patent licence has been granted.

(5) Where the controllers order the grant of a compulsory patent licence to a person who has yet to acquire a Community plant variety right in the new plant variety, the order for grant shall, if the proprietor of the patent wishes, include a condition that, on the grant of the Community plant variety right to such person in the new plant variety in respect of which the compulsory patent

licence has been granted, the proprietor of the patent concerned (or, where the proprietor of the patent is a government department, such person as the proprietor specifies) shall be granted a cross licence on reasonable terms to use in the UK the new plant variety in respect of which the compulsory patent licence has been granted.

[6.121]
8 Variation

(1) On application at any time by a party to the Comptroller General of Patents in accordance with rules, the controllers may extend, limit or in any other respect vary an order for grant of a—

(a) compulsory patent licence, or
(b) cross licence under regulation 7(2) or 7(3),

and extend, limit or in any other respect vary the licence granted under the order.

(2) On receipt of an application under paragraph (1), the controllers shall consider and process the application in accordance with rules.

[6.122]
9 Revocation

(1) A party may, at any time, apply to the Comptroller General of Patents in accordance with rules to revoke an order for grant of—

(a) a compulsory patent licence, or
(b) cross licence under regulation 7(2) or 7(3),

if the circumstances which led to the order for grant have ceased to exist or are unlikely to recur.

(2) On receipt by the Comptroller General of Patents of an application under paragraph (1), the controllers shall consider and process the application in accordance with rules and if the controllers are satisfied that the circumstances which led to an order for grant of a—

(a) compulsory patent licence, or
(b) cross licence under regulation 7(2) or 7(3),

have ceased to exist or are unlikely to recur, the controllers may revoke the order and terminate the licence granted under the order, subject to such terms and conditions as they think necessary for the protection of the legitimate interests of the holder of the compulsory patent licence or the cross licence ordered to be granted under regulation 7(2) or 7(3).

[6.123]
10

In regulations 8 and 9, "party" means the proprietor of the patent concerned or the applicant, as the case may be, in an application under regulation 3(1) or their respective successors in title.

PART III
COMPULSORY PLANT VARIETY LICENCES

[6.124]
11 Applications

(1) Where a proprietor of a patent for a biotechnological invention cannot exploit a biotechnological invention protected by the patent without infringing prior plant breeders' rights, he may apply in accordance with Breeders' regulations to the Controller of Plant Variety Rights for a licence and on such application shall pay the plant breeders' fee.

(2) An application under paragraph (1) shall be accompanied by particulars which seek to demonstrate that—

(a) the proprietor of the patent for a biotechnological invention cannot exploit the biotechnological invention protected by the patent without infringing prior plant breeders' rights,
(b) the proprietor of the patent has unsuccessfully applied to the holder of the prior plant breeders' rights for a licence, and
(c) the biotechnological invention protected by the patent constitutes significant technical progress of considerable economic interest in relation to the plant variety protected by the prior plant breeders' rights.

(3) If and so far as any agreement purports to bind any person not to apply for a licence under paragraph (1), it shall be void.

[6.125]
12 Proceedings before controllers

(1) On receipt by the Controller of Plant Varieties of an application under regulation 11(1) and payment of the appropriate plant breeders' fee, the controllers shall consider and process the application in accordance with Breeders' regulations.

(2) In proceedings before them in relation to an application under regulation 11(1), 16(1) or 16(2) the controllers, in addition to any powers conferred by Breeders' regulations, may give such directions as they think fit with regard to the subsequent procedure.

(3) Any person entitled under Breeders' regulations to make written or oral representations on an application under regulation 11(1), 16(1) or 16(2) shall do so in accordance with Breeders' regulations and shall pay the appropriate plant breeders' fee.

[6.126]
13 Grant

Where, having considered the application under regulation 11(1), the controllers are satisfied that—

(a) the proprietor of a patent for a biotechnological invention cannot exploit the biotechnological invention protected by the patent without infringing prior plant breeders' rights,
(b) the proprietor of the patent has unsuccessfully applied to the holder of the prior plant breeders' rights for a licence, and
(c) the biotechnological invention protected by the patent constitutes significant technical progress of considerable economic interest in relation to the plant variety protected by the prior plant breeders' rights,

the controllers shall grant to the proprietor of the patent for the biotechnological invention (or, where the proprietor is a government department, to any person specified in the application) a licence to use the plant variety protected by prior plant breeders rights on the conditions set out in regulation 14 and on such other terms as the controllers see fit.

[6.127]
14 Conditions

(1) A compulsory plant variety licence shall—

(a) not be exclusive,
(b) entitle the holder of the plant breeders' rights concerned to an appropriate royalty, and
(c) entitle the holder of the plant breeders' rights concerned to a cross licence on reasonable terms to use the biotechnological invention protected by the patent.

(2) Where the controllers grant a compulsory plant variety licence to a proprietor of a patent for a biotechnological invention, the holder of the plant breeders' rights concerned may request the grant of a cross licence on reasonable terms to use the biotechnological invention protected by the patent and, on such request, the controllers shall grant such cross licence to the holder of plant breeders' rights (or, where the holder is a government department, to any person specified in the request).

[6.128]
15 Community plant variety rights: cross licences of patents

(1) Where the Community Plant Variety Office has granted—

(a) on the grounds specified in Article 12(3) of Directive 98/44/EC of the European Parliament and of the Council on the legal protection of biotechnological inventions, and
(b) under Article 29 of Council Regulation,

a compulsory exploitation right in respect of a Community plant variety right to a proprietor of a biotechnological invention protected by a patent, who could not otherwise exploit in the UK the biotechnological invention protected by the patent without infringing a Community plant variety right, the holder of the Community plant variety right concerned may, in accordance with rules, apply to the Comptroller General of Patents for a cross licence of the biotechnological invention protected by the patent and on such application shall pay the prescribed fee.

(2) On receipt of an application under paragraph (1) and payment of the prescribed fee, the Comptroller General shall consider and process the application in accordance with rules.

(3) Where the holder of the Community plant variety right concerned has paid the prescribed fee and demonstrates in his application to the satisfaction of the Comptroller General of Patents that—

(a) he has a Community plant variety right, and
(b) the Community Plant Variety Office has granted, under Article 29 of Council Regulation, a compulsory exploitation right in respect of it which allows a proprietor of a patent for a biotechnological invention to exploit in the UK the biotechnological invention protected by the patent,

the Comptroller General of Patents shall order the grant of a cross licence on reasonable terms to the holder of the Community plant variety right concerned (or, where the holder is a government department, to any person specified in the application) to use in the UK the biotechnological invention protected by the patent.

[6.129]
16 Variation and revocation

(1) Any person may at any time apply to the Controller of Plant Variety Rights in accordance with Breeders' regulations to extend, limit or in any other respect vary a compulsory plant variety licence or cross licence granted under regulation 14(2) and, on making such application shall pay the appropriate plant breeders' fee, and on receipt by the Controller of Plant Varieties of the application

and the fee, the controllers shall consider and process the application and may extend, limit or in any other respect vary the compulsory plant variety licence or cross licence granted under regulation 14(2).

(2) Any person may at any time apply to the Controller of Plant Variety Rights in accordance with Breeders' regulations to revoke the grant of a compulsory plant variety licence or a cross licence under regulation 14(2) if the circumstances which led to the grant of the compulsory patent licence or the cross licence under regulation 14(2) have ceased to exist or are unlikely to recur and, on making such application, the applicant shall pay the appropriate plant breeders' fee.

(3) On receipt of an application under paragraph (2) and payment of the appropriate plant breeders' fee, the controllers shall consider and process the application in accordance with Breeders' regulations and if the controllers are satisfied that the circumstances which led to the grant of the compulsory plant variety licence or the cross licence under regulation 14(2) have ceased to exist or are unlikely to recur, the controllers may revoke the grant of the compulsory plant variety licence or the cross licence under regulation 14(2), subject to such terms and conditions as they think necessary for the protection of the legitimate interests of the holder of the compulsory plant variety licence or cross licence granted under regulation 14(2).

(4) On the application of any party at any time in accordance with rules, the Comptroller General of Patents may, having considered and processed the application in accordance with rules, extend, limit or in any other respect vary an order for grant of a cross licence under regulation 15(3) and extend, limit or in any other respect vary the licence granted under the order accordingly.

(5) A party may at any time apply to the Comptroller General of Patents in accordance with rules for an order to revoke a cross licence ordered to be granted under regulation 15(3), if the circumstances which led to an order for grant of the cross licence under regulation 15(3) have ceased to exist or are unlikely to recur.

(6) On receipt of an application under paragraph (5), the Comptroller General of Patents shall consider and process the application in accordance with rules and if the Comptroller General is satisfied that the circumstances which led to an order for grant of a cross licence under regulation 15(3) have ceased to exist or are unlikely to recur, the Comptroller General of Patents may revoke the order and terminate the licence granted under the order, subject to such terms and conditions as they think necessary for the protection of the legitimate interests of the holder of the cross licence.

(7) In paragraphs (4), (5) and (6), "party" means the proprietor of the patent concerned or the applicant, as the case may be, in an application under regulation 15(1) or their respective successors in title.

PART IV
APPEALS AND GENERAL PROVISIONS

[6.130]
17 Appeals

(1) An appeal lies from a decision of the controllers or Comptroller General of Patents under these Regulations.

(2) Where a decision of the controllers relates to a compulsory patent licence or cross licence ordered to be granted under regulation 7(2) or 7(3), or where a decision of the Comptroller General of Patents relates to a cross licence ordered to be granted under regulation 15(3), an appeal may be brought to the court.

(3) Where a decision of the controllers relates to a compulsory plant variety licence or cross licence of a patent for a biotechnological invention granted under regulation 14(2), an appeal may be brought to the Tribunal as if the decision of the controllers were one made by the Controller of Plant Variety Rights under section 17, and referred to in section 26(1)(c), of the 1997 Act and section 45 of the 1997 Act shall apply accordingly.

[6.131]
18

The Secretary of State shall draw up and from time to time revise a panel of persons who have specialised knowledge of biotechnological inventions.

[6.132]
19

(1) Subject to paragraph (2), appeals to the Tribunal under regulation 17(3) shall be governed by the provisions of Part II of the 1997 Act and Breeders' regulations.

(2) The provisions of Schedule 3 to the 1997 Act shall apply to appeals under regulation 17(3) with the following modifications—

- (a) paragraph 1(b) of Schedule 3 shall be treated as if it referred to a member of the panel constituted under regulation 18; and
- (b) the panels referred to in paragraph 8(1) of Schedule 3 to the 1997 Act shall be treated as including the panel constituted under regulation 18.

[6.133]
20 Extension of powers to make rules and regulations

The power of the Secretary of State to make rules under section 123 of the 1977 Act shall be extended so as to permit her to make rules regulating the business of the Patent Office in respect of—

(a) applications for the grant of licences under regulations 3(1) and 15(1),
(b) applications under regulations 8 and 16(4) for variation and under regulations 9 and 16(5) for revocation of compulsory patent licences and cross licences,
(c) proceedings before the controllers or the Comptroller General of Patents as the case may be in relation to applications in sub-paragraphs (a) and (b),
(d) fees, and
(e) other matters related to or arising under these Regulations,

and section 124 of the 1977 Act shall apply accordingly.

[6.134]
21

The powers of the Ministers to make regulations under sections 24, 26(2)(a), 28, 29, 44, and 48(1) of the 1997 Act shall be extended so as to permit them to make regulations in respect of—

(a) applications for the grant of licences under regulation 11(1),
(b) applications under regulation 16(1) for variation and under regulation 16(2) for revocation of compulsory plant variety licences and cross licences,
(c) proceedings before the controllers in relation to applications in sub-paragraphs (a) and (b),
(d) appeals from the decisions of the controllers in relation to such applications,
(e) fees, and
(f) other matters related to or arising under these Regulations,

and section 48(2) to (5) of the 1997 Act shall apply accordingly.

[6.135]
22 Application of existing rules and regulations

(1) Subject to the exercise by the Secretary of State of her powers under section 123 of the 1977 Act as extended by regulation 20, the Patents Rules in respect of—

(a) applications for the grant and revocation of compulsory licences under section 48(1) of the 1977 Act including forms,
(b) proceedings before the Comptroller General of Patents in relation to—
  (i) the grant of such applications, and
  (ii) the revocation of compulsory licences granted under section 48(1) of the 1977 Act, and
(c) other matters provided for in the Patents Rules related to applications and proceedings in respect of such compulsory licences,

shall, subject to paragraph (2), extend and apply to and be taken to make corresponding provision in respect of applications for the grant of licences under regulation 3(1), proceedings before the controllers in relation to the grant of such applications, the variation or revocation of compulsory patent licences and cross licences under regulations 7(2), 7(3) and 15(3), and other matters related to or arising under these Regulations.

(2) For the purposes of paragraph (1), the Patents Rules shall have effect as if a reference to the Comptroller General of Patents in the Patents Rules were to the controllers, other than . . . in relation to an application under regulation 15(1), and with any other necessary modifications.

NOTES

Para (2): words omitted revoked by the Patents (Compulsory Licensing and Supplementary Protection Certificates) Regulations 2007, SI 2007/3293, reg 3(1), (3).

[6.136]
23

Subject to the exercise by the Ministers of their powers under sections 24, 26(2)(a), 28, 29, 44 and 48(1) of the 1997 Act as extended by regulation 21, the Plant Breeders' Regulations in respect of—

(a) applications for the grant, variation and revocation of compulsory licences under section 17(1) of the 1997 Act,
(b) proceedings before the Controller of Plant Variety Rights in relation to—
  (i) the grant of such applications, and
  (ii) the variation or revocation of compulsory licences granted under section 17(1) of the 1997 Act,
(c) appeals to the Tribunal, and
(d) other matters provided for in the Plant Breeders' Regulations related to applications and proceedings in respect of such compulsory licences,

shall, subject to paragraphs (2) and (3), extend and apply to and be taken to make corresponding provision in respect of applications under regulation 11(1), proceedings before the controllers in relation to such applications, the variation or revocation of compulsory plant variety licences and cross licences granted under regulation 14(2), appeals to the Tribunal and other matters related to or arising under these Regulations.

(2) For the purposes of paragraph (1), the Plant Breeders' Regulations shall have effect as if a reference to the Controller of Plant Variety Rights in the regulations were to the controllers and with any other necessary modifications.

(3) Regulation 10 of the Plant Breeders' Regulations shall not extend and apply to and shall not be taken to make corresponding provision in these Regulations.

[6.137]
24

Subject to the exercise by the Secretary of State of her powers under section 123 of the 1977 Act as extended by regulation 20, the Patents (Fees) Rules in respect of—

(a) making an application for the grant of compulsory licences under section 48(1) of the 1977 Act, and
(b) giving a notice of opposition to an application made under section 48,

shall extend and apply to and be taken to make corresponding provision in respect of an application for a licence under regulation 3(1) or 15(1), and giving a notice of opposition under regulation 5(1).

[6.138]
25

Subject to the exercise by the Ministers of their powers under sections 29 and 48(1) of the 1997 Act as extended by regulation 21, the Plant Breeders' (Fees) Regulations in respect of—

(a) applications for the grant of compulsory licences under section 17(1) of the 1997 Act,
(b) applications to extend, limit, vary or revoke such licences,
(c) making representations in writing to the Controller, and
(d) attending to be heard by the Controller,

shall extend and apply to and be taken to make corresponding provision in respect of an application for a licence under regulation 11(1), applications to extend, limit, vary or revoke compulsory plant variety licences and cross licences granted under regulation 14(2), and proceedings before the controllers referred to in regulation 12.

[6.139]
26 Application of 1977 and 1997 Acts

(1) Subject to paragraphs (2) and (3), the provisions of the 1977 Act in respect of—

(a) proceedings before the Comptroller General of Patents,
(b) decisions of the Comptroller General of Patents including orders for grant of compulsory licences,
(c) legal proceedings in respect of appeals from the Comptroller General of Patents, and
(d) other matters,

as and to the extent they relate to compulsory licences under section 48(1), shall extend and apply to and be taken to make corresponding provision in the UK in respect of proceedings before the controllers, decisions of the controllers including orders for the grant, variation and revocation, of compulsory patent licences and cross licences ordered to be granted under regulations 7(2), 7(3) and 15(3), legal proceedings in respect of appeals from the controllers and other matters related to compulsory patent licences and cross licences ordered to be granted under regulations 7(2), 7(3) and 15(3) arising under these Regulations.

(2) An application for a licence under regulation 3(1) is additional to any application an applicant may make under section 48 of the 1977 Act but the provisions of sections 48, 48A, 48B, 49, 50 and 52 do not extend and apply to and shall not be taken to make corresponding provision in respect of compulsory patent licences and cross licences ordered to be granted under these Regulations.

(3) For the purposes of paragraph (1), the provisions of the 1977 Act shall have effect as if a reference to the Comptroller General of Patents were to the controllers, other than in relation to applications under regulations 15(1), 16(3) and 16(4), and with any other necessary modifications.

[6.140]
27

(1) Subject to regulation 19(2) and paragraphs (2) and (3) of this regulation, the provisions of the 1997 Act in respect of—

(a) proceedings before the Controller of Plant Variety Rights,
(b) decisions of the Controller of Plant Variety Rights in relation to compulsory licences,
(c) appeals from the Controller of Plant Variety Rights to the Tribunal,
(d) appeals from the Tribunal, and
(e) other matters,

as and to the extent they relate to compulsory licences under section 17(1), shall extend and apply to and be taken to make corresponding provision in respect of proceedings before the controllers, decisions of the controllers including the grant, variation and revocation of compulsory plant variety licences and cross licences granted under regulation 14(2), appeals from the controllers and other matters related to compulsory plant variety licences and cross licences granted under regulation 14(2) arising under these Regulations.

(2) An application for a licence under regulation 11(1) is additional to any application an applicant may make under section 17 of the 1997 Act but the provisions of sections 17 and 23 of the 1997 Act do not extend and apply to and shall not be taken to make corresponding provision in respect of compulsory plant variety licences and cross licences under these Regulations.

(3) For the purposes of paragraph (1), the provisions of the 1997 Act shall have effect as if a reference to the Controller of Plant Variety Rights were to the controllers and with any other necessary modifications.

COUNCIL REGULATION

(2100/94/EC)

of 27 July 1994

on Community plant variety rights

NOTES

Date of publication in OJ: OJ L227, 1.9.1994, p 1.

THE COUNCIL OF THE EUROPEAN UNION,

Having regard to the Treaty establishing the European Community, and in particular Article 235 thereof,

Having regard to the proposal from the Commission,[1]

Having regard to the opinion of the European Parliament,[2]

Having regard to the opinion of the Economic and Social Committee,[3]

Whereas plant varieties pose specific problems as regards the industrial property régime which may be applicable;

Whereas industrial property regimes for plant varieties have not been harmonised at Community level and therefore continue to be regulated by the legislation of the Member States, the content of which is not uniform;

Whereas in such circumstances it is appropriate to create a Community regime which, although co-existing with national regimes, allows for the grant of industrial property rights valid throughout the Community;

Whereas it is appropriate that the implementation and application of this Community regime should not be carried out by the authorities of the Member States but by a Community Office with legal personality, the 'Community Plan Variety Office';

Whereas the system must also have regard to developments in plant breeding techniques including biotechnology; whereas in order to stimulate the breeding and development of new varieties, there should be improved protection compared with the present situation for all plant breeders without, however, unjustifiably impairing access to protection generally or in the case of certain breeding techniques;

Whereas varieties of all botanical genera and species should be protectable;

Whereas protectable varieties must comply with internationally recognised requirements, ie distinctness, uniformity, stability and novelty, and also be designated by a prescribed variety denomination;

Whereas it is important to provide for a definition of a plant variety, in order to ensure the proper functioning of the system;

Whereas this definition is not intended to alter definitions which may have been established in the field of intellectual property rights, especially the patent field, nor to interfere with or exclude from application laws governing the protectability of products, including plants and plant material, or processes under such other industrial property rights;

Whereas it is however highly desirable to have a common definition in both fields; whereas therefore appropriate efforts at international level should be supported to reach such a common definition;

Whereas for the grant of Community plant variety rights an assessment of important characteristics relating to the variety is necessary; whereas, however, these characteristics need not necessarily relate to their economic importance;

Whereas the system must also clarify to whom the right to Community plant variety protection pertains; whereas in some cases it would be to several persons in common, not just to one; whereas the formal entitlement to make applications must be regulated;

Whereas the system must also define the term 'holder' used in this Regulation; whereas that term 'holder' without further specification is used in this Regulation including in its Article 29(5), it is intended to be within the meaning of Article 13(1) thereof;

Whereas, since the effect of a Community plant variety right should be uniform throughout the Community, commercial transactions subject to the holder's agreement must be precisely delimited; whereas the scope of protection should be extended, compared with most national systems, to certain material of the variety to take account of trade via countries outside the Community without protection; whereas, however, the introduction of the principle of exhaustion of rights must ensure that the protection is not excessive;

Whereas in order to stimulate plant breeding, the system basically confirms the internationally accepted rule of free access to protected varieties for the development therefrom, and exploitation, of new varieties;

Whereas in certain cases where the new variety, although distinct, is essentially derived from the initial variety, a certain form of dependency from the holder of the latter one should be created;

Whereas, the exercise of Community plant variety rights must be subjected to restrictions laid down in provisions adopted in the public interest;

Whereas this includes safeguarding agricultural production; whereas that purpose requires an authorisation for farmers to use the product of the harvest for propagation under certain conditions;

Whereas it must be ensured that the conditions are laid down at Community level;

Whereas compulsory licensing should also be provided for under certain circumstances in the public interest, which may include the need to supply the market with material offering specified features, or to maintain the incentive for continued breeding of improved varieties;

Whereas the use of prescribed variety denominations should be made obligatory;

Whereas the Community plant variety right should in principle have a life of at least 25 years and in the case of vine and tree species, at least 30 years; whereas other grounds for termination must be specified;

Whereas a Community plant variety right is an object of the holder's property and its role in relation to the non-harmonised legal provisions of the Member States, particularly of civil law, must therefore be clarified; whereas this applies also to the settlement of infringements and the enforcement of entitlement to Community plant variety rights;

Whereas, it is necessary to ensure that the full application of the principles of the Community plant variety rights system is not impaired by the effects of other systems; whereas for this purpose certain rules, in conformity with Member States' existing international commitments, are required concerning the relationship to other industrial property rights;

Whereas it is indispensable to examine whether and to what extent the conditions for the protection accorded in other industrial property systems, such as patents, should be adapted or otherwise modified for consistency with the Community plant variety rights system; whereas this, where necessary, should be laid down in balanced rules by additional Community law;

Whereas the duties and powers of the Community Plant Variety Office, including its Boards of Appeal, relating to the grant, termination or verification of Community plant variety rights and publications are as far as possible to be modelled on rules developed for other systems, as are also the Office's structure and Rules of Procedure, the collaboration with the Commission and Member States particularly through an Administrative Council, the involvement of Examination Offices in technical examination and moreover the necessary budgetary measures;

Whereas the Office should be advised and supervised by the aforementioned Administrative Council, composed of representatives of Member States and the Commission;

Whereas the Treaty does not provide, for the adoption of this Regulation, powers other than those of Article 235;

Whereas this Regulation takes into account existing international conventions such as the International Convention for the Protection of New Varieties of Plants (UPOV Convention), the Convention of the Grant of European Patents (European Patent Convention) or the Agreement on trade-related aspects of intellectual property rights, including trade in counterfeit goods; whereas it consequently implements the ban on patenting plant varieties only to the extent that the European Patent Convention so requires, ie to plant varieties as such;

Whereas this Regulation should be re-examined for amendment as necessary in the light of future developments in the aforementioned Conventions,

NOTES

1 OJ C244, 28.9.1990, p 1 and OJ C113, 23.4.1993, p 7.

2 OJ C305, 23.11.1992, p 55 and OJ C67, 16.3.1992, p 148.

3 OJ C60, 8.3.1991, p 45.

HAS ADOPTED THIS REGULATION—

PART ONE
GENERAL PROVISIONS

[6.141]
Article 1
Community plant variety rights

A system of Community plant variety rights is hereby established as the sole and exclusive form of Community industrial property rights for plant varieties.

[6.142]
Article 2
Uniform effect of Community plant variety rights
Community plant variety rights shall have uniform effect within the territory of the Community and may not be granted, transferred or terminated in respect of the abovementioned territory otherwise than on a uniform basis.

[6.143]
Article 3
National property rights for plant varieties
This Regulation shall be without prejudice to the right of the Member States to grant national property rights for plant varieties, subject to the provisions of Article 92(1).

[6.144]
Article 4
Community Office
For the purpose of the implementation of this Regulation a Community Plant Variety Office, hereinafter referred to as 'the Office', is hereby established.

PART TWO
SUBSTANTIVE LAW

CHAPTER I
CONDITIONS GOVERNING THE GRANT OF COMMUNITY PLANT VARIETY RIGHTS

[6.145]
Article 5
Object of Community plant variety rights
1. Varieties of all botanical genera and species, including, inter alia, hybrids between genera or species, may form the object of Community plant variety rights.
2. For the purpose of this Regulation, 'variety' shall be taken to mean a plant grouping within a single botanical taxon of the lowest known rank, which grouping, irrespective of whether the conditions for the grant of a plant variety right are fully met, can be—
— defined by the expression of the characteristics that results from a given genotype or combination of genotypes,
— distinguished from any other plant grouping by the expression of at least one of the said characteristics, and
— considered as a unit with regard to its suitability for being propagated unchanged.
3. A plant grouping consists of entire plants or parts of plants as far as such parts are capable of producing entire plants, both referred to hereinafter as 'variety constituents'.
4. The expression of the characteristics referred to in paragraph 2, first indent, may be either invariable or variable between variety constituents of the same kind provided that also the level of variation results from the genotype or combination of genotypes.

[6.146]
Article 6
Protectable varieties
Community plant variety rights shall be granted for varieties that are—
(a) distinct;
(b) uniform;
(c) stable; and
(d) new.
Moreover, the variety must be designated by a denomination in accordance with the provisions of Article 63.

[6.147]
Article 7
Distinctness
1. A variety shall be deemed to be distinct if it is clearly distinguishable by reference to the expression of the characteristics that results from a particular genotype or combination of genotypes, from any other variety whose existence is a matter of common knowledge on the date of application determined pursuant to Article 51.
2. The existence of another variety shall in particular be deemed to be a matter of common knowledge if on the date of application determined pursuant to Article 51—
(a) it was the object of a plant variety right or entered in an official register of plant varieties, in the Community or any State, or in any intergovernmental organisation with relevant competence;
(b) an application for the granting of a plant variety right in its respect or for its entering in such an official register was filed, provided the application has led to the granting or entering in the meantime.

The implementing rules pursuant to Article 114 may specify further cases as examples which shall be deemed to be a matter of common knowledge.

[6.148]
Article 8
Uniformity
A variety shall be deemed to be uniform if, subject to the variation that may be expected from the particular features of its propagation, it is sufficiently uniform in the expression of those characteristics which are included in the examination for distinctness, as well as any others used for the variety description.

[6.149]
Article 9
Stability
A variety shall be deemed to be stable if the expression of the characteristics which are included in the examination for distinctness as well as any others used for the variety description, remain unchanged after repeated propagation or, in the case of a particular cycle of propagation, at the end of each such cycle.

[6.150]
Article 10
Novelty
1. A variety shall be deemed to be new if, at the date of application determined pursuant to Article 51, variety constituents or harvested material of the variety have not been sold or otherwise disposed of to others, by or with the consent of the breeder within the meaning of Article 11, for purposes of exploitation of the variety—

(a) earlier than one year before the abovementioned date, within the territory of the Community;

(b) earlier than four years or, in the case of trees or of vines, earlier than six years before the said date, outside the territory of the Community.

2. The disposal of variety constituents to an official body for statutory purposes, or to others on the basis of a contractual or other legal relationship solely for production, reproduction, multiplication, conditioning or storage, shall not be deemed to be a disposal to others within the meaning of paragraph 1, provided that the breeder preserves the exclusive right of disposal of these and other variety constituents, and no further disposal is made. However, such disposal of variety constituents shall be deemed to be a disposal in terms of paragraph 1 if these constituents are repeatedly used in the production of a hybrid variety and if there is disposal of variety constituents or harvested material of the hybrid variety.

Likewise, the disposal of variety constituents by one company or firm within the meaning of the second paragraph of Article 58 of the Treaty to another of such companies or firms shall not be deemed to be a disposal to others, if one of them belongs entirely to the other or if both belong entirely to a third such company or firm, provided no further disposal is made. This provision shall not apply in respect of cooperative societies.

3. The disposal of variety constituents or harvested material of the variety, which have been produced from plants grown for the purposes specified in Article 15(b) and (c) and which are not used for further reproduction or multiplication, shall not be deemed to be exploitation of the variety, unless reference is made to the variety for purposes of that disposal.

Likewise, no account shall be taken of any disposal to others, if it either was due to, or in consequence of the fact that the breeder had displayed the variety at an official or officially recognised exhibition within the meaning of the Convention on International Exhibitions, or at an exhibition in a Member State which was officially recognised as equivalent by that Member State.

CHAPTER II
PERSONS ENTITLED

[6.151]
Article 11
Entitlement to Community plant variety rights
1. The person who bred, or discovered and developed the variety, or his successor in title, both—the person and his successor—referred to hereinafter as 'the breeder', shall be entitled to the Community plant variety right.

2. If two or more persons bred, or discovered and developed the variety jointly, entitlement shall be vested jointly in them or their respective successors in title. This provision shall also apply to two or more persons in cases where one or more of them discovered the variety and the other or the others developed it.

3. Entitlement shall also be invested jointly in the breeder and any other person or persons, if the breeder and the other person or persons have agreed to joint entitlement by written declaration.

4. If the breeder is an employee, the entitlement to the Community plant variety right shall be determined in accordance with the national law applicable to the employment relationship in the context of which the variety was bred, or discovered and developed.

5. Where entitlement to a Community plant variety right is vested jointly in two or more persons pursuant to paragraphs 2 to 4, one or more of them may empower the others by written declaration to such effect to claim entitlement thereto.

[6.152]
[Article 12
Entitlement to file an application for a Community plant variety right
An application for a Community plant variety right may be filed by any natural or legal person, or any body ranking as a legal person under the law applicable to that body.
An application may be filed jointly by two or more such persons.]

NOTES
Substituted by Council Regulation 15/2008/EC, Art 1(1).

CHAPTER III
EFFECTS OF COMMUNITY PLANT VARIETY RIGHTS

[6.153]
Article 13
Rights of the holder of a Community plant variety right and prohibited acts
1. A Community plant variety right shall have the effect that the holder or holders of the Community plant variety right, hereinafter referred to as 'the holder', shall be entitled to effect the acts set out in paragraph 2.
2. Without prejudice to the provisions of Articles 15 and 16, the following acts in respect of variety constituents, or harvested material of the protected variety, both referred to hereinafter as 'material', shall require the authorisation of the holder—
(a) production or reproduction (multiplication);
(b) conditioning for the purpose of propagation;
(c) offering for sale;
(d) selling or other marketing;
(e) exporting from the Community;
(f) importing to the Community;
(g) stocking for any of the purposes mentioned in (a) to (f).
The holder may make his authorisation subject to conditions and limitations.
3. The provisions of paragraph 2 shall apply in respect of harvested material only if this was obtained through the unauthorised use of variety constituents of the protected variety, and unless the holder has had reasonable opportunity to exercise his right in relation to the said variety constituents.
4. In the implementing rules pursuant to Article 114, it may be provided that in specific cases the provisions of paragraph 2 of this Article shall also apply in respect of products obtained directly from material of the protected variety. They may apply only if such products were obtained through the unauthorised use of material of the protected variety, and unless the holder has had reasonable opportunity to exercise his right in relation to the said material. To the extent that the provisions of paragraph 2 apply to products directly obtained, they shall also be considered to be 'material'.
5. The provisions of paragraphs 1 to 4 shall also apply in relation to—
(a) varieties which are essentially derived from the variety in respect of which the Community plant variety right has been granted, where this variety is not itself an essentially derived variety;
(b) varieties which are not distinct in accordance with the provisions of Article 7 from the protected variety; and
(c) varieties whose production requires the repeated use of the protected variety.
6. For the purposes of paragraph 5(a), a variety shall be deemed to be essentially derived from another variety, referred to hereinafter as 'the initial variety' when—
(a) it is predominantly derived from the initial variety, or from a variety that is itself predominantly derived from the initial variety;
(b) it is distinct in accordance with the provisions of Article 7 from the initial variety; and
(c) except for the differences which result from the act of derivation, it conforms essentially to the initial variety in the expression of the characteristics that results from the genotype or combination of genotypes of the initial variety.
7. The implementing rules pursuant to Article 114 may specify possible acts of derivation which come at least under the provisions of paragraph 6.
8. Without prejudice to Article 14 and 29, the exercise of the rights conferred by Community plant variety rights may not violate any provisions adopted on the grounds of public morality, public policy or public security, the protection of health and life of humans, animals or plants, the protection of the environment, the protection of industrial or commercial property, or the safeguarding of competition, of trade or of agricultural production.

[6.154]
Article 14
Derogation from Community plant variety right

1. Notwithstanding Article 13(2), and for the purposes of safeguarding agricultural production, farmers are authorised to use for propagating purposes in the field, on their own holding the product of the harvest which they have obtained by planting, on their own holding, propagating material of a variety other than a hybrid or synthetic variety, which is covered by a Community plant variety right.

2. The provisions of paragraph 1 shall only apply to agricultural plant species of—

(a) Fodder plants—
Cicer arietinum L—Chickpea milkvetch
Lupinus luteus L—Yellow lupin
Medicago sativa L—Lucerne
Pisum sativum L (partim)—Field pea
Trifolium alexandrinum L—Berseem/Egyptian clover
Trifolium resupinatum L—Persian clover
Vicia faba—Field bean
Vicia sativa L—Common vetch
and, in the case of Portugal, Lolium multiflorum lam—Italian rye-grass

(b) Cereals—
Avena sativa—Oats
Hordeum vulgare L—Barley
Oryza sativa L—Rice
Phalaris canariensis L—Canary grass
Secale cereale L—Rye
X Triticosecale Wittm—Triticale
Triticium aestivum L emend Fiori et Paol—Wheat
Triticum durum Desf—Durum wheat
Triticum spelta L—Spelt wheat

(c) Potatoes—
Solanum tuberosum—Potatoes

(d) Oil and fibre plants—
Brassica napus L (partim)—Swede rape
Brassica rapa L (partim)—Turnip rape
Linum usitatissimum—linseed with the exclusion of flax.

3. Conditions to give effect to the derogation provided for in paragraph 1 and to safeguard the legitimate interests of the breeder and of the farmer, shall be established, before the entry into force of this Regulation, in implementing rules pursuant to Article 114, on the basis of the following criteria—

— there shall be no quantitative restriction of the level of the farmer's holding to the extent necessary for the requirements of the holding,
— the product of the harvest may be processed for planting, either by the farmer himself or through services supplied to him, without prejudice to certain restrictions which Member States may establish regarding the organisation of the processing of the said product of the harvest, in particular in order to ensure identity of the product entered for processing with that resulting from processing,
— small farmers shall not be required to pay any remuneration to the holder; small farmers shall be considered to be—
— in the case of those of the plant species referred to in paragraph 2 of this Article to which Council Regulation (EEC) No 1765/92 of 30 June 1992 establishing a support system for producers of certain arable crops[1] applies, farmers who do not grow plants on an area bigger than the area which would be needed to produce 92 tonnes of cereals; for the calculation of the area, Article 8(2) of the aforesaid Regulation shall apply,
— in the case of other plant species referred to in paragraph 2 of this Article, farmers who meet comparable appropriate criteria,
— other farmers shall be required to pay an equitable remuneration to the holder, which shall be sensibly lower than the amount charged for the licensed production of propagating material of the same variety in the same area; the actual level of this equitable remuneration may be subject to variation over time, taking into account the extent to which use will be made of the derogation provided for in paragraph 1 in respect of the variety concerned,
— monitoring compliance with the provisions of this Article or the provisions adopted pursuant to this Article shall be a matter of exclusive responsibility of holders; in organising that monitoring, they may not provide for assistance from official bodies,
— relevant information shall be provided to the holders on their request, by farmers and by suppliers of processing services; relevant information may equally be provided by official bodies involved in the monitoring of agricultural production, if such information has been

obtained through ordinary performance of their tasks, without additional burden or costs. These provisions are without prejudice, in respect of personal data, to Community and national legislation on the protection of individuals with regard to the processing and free movement of personal data.

NOTES

[1] OJ L181, 1.7.1992, p 12. Regulation as last amended by Regulation (EEC) No 1552/93 (OJ L154, 25.6.1993, p 19).

[6.155]
Article 15
Limitation of the effects of Community plant variety rights

The Community plant variety rights shall not extend to—

(a) acts done privately and for non-commercial purposes;
(b) acts done for experimental purposes;
(c) acts done for the purpose of breeding, or discovering and developing other varieties;
(d) acts referred to in Article 13(2) to (4), in respect of such other varieties, except where the provisions of Article 13(5) apply, or where the other variety or the material of this variety comes under the protection of a property right which does not contain a comparable provision; and
(e) acts whose prohibition would violate the provisions laid down in Articles 13(8), 14 or 29.

[6.156]
Article 16
Exhaustion of Community plant variety rights

The Community plant variety right shall not extend to acts concerning any material of the protected variety, or of a variety covered by the provisions of Article 13(5), which has been disposed of to others by the holder or with his consent, in any part of the Community, or any material derived from the said material, unless such acts—

(a) involve further propagation of the variety in question, except where such propagation was intended when the material was disposed of; or
(b) involve an export of variety constituents into a third country which does not protect varieties of the plant genus or species to which the variety belongs, except where the exported materials is for final consumption purposes.

[6.157]
Article 17
Use of variety denominations

1. Any person who, within the territory of the Community, offers or disposes of to others for commercial purposes variety constituents of a protected variety, or a variety covered by the provisions of Article 13(5), must use the variety denomination designated pursuant to Article 63; where it is used in writing, the variety denomination shall be readily distinguishable and clearly legible. If a trade mark, trade name or similar indication is associated with the designated denomination, this denomination must be easily recognisable as such.
2. Any person effecting such acts in respect of any other material of the variety, must inform of that denomination in accordance with other provisions in law or if a request is made by an authority, by the purchaser or by any other person having a legitimate interest.
3. Paragraphs 1 and 2 shall apply even after the termination of the Community plant variety right.

[6.158]
Article 18
Limitation of the use of variety denominations

1. The holder may not use any right granted in respect of a designation that is identical with the variety denomination to hamper the free use of that denomination in connection with the variety, even after the termination of the Community plant variety right.
2. A third party may use a right granted in respect of a designation that is identical with the variety denomination to hamper the free use of that denomination only if that right was granted before the variety denomination was designated pursuant to Article 63.
3. Where a variety is protected by a Community plant variety right or, in a Member State or in a Member of the International Union for the Protection of New Varieties of Plants by a national property right, neither its designated denomination or any designation which might be confused with it can be used, within the territory of the Community, in connection with another variety of the same botanical species or a species regarded as related pursuant to the publication made in accordance with Article 63(5), or for material of such variety.

CHAPTER IV
DURATION AND TERMINATION OF COMMUNITY PLANT VARIETY RIGHTS

[6.159]
Article 19
Duration of Community plant variety rights

1. The term of the Community plant variety right shall run until the end of the 25th calendar year or, in the case of varieties of vine and tree species, until the end of the 30th calendar year, following the year of grant.
2. The Council, acting by qualified majority on proposal from the Commission, may, in respect of specific genera or species, provide for an extension of these terms up to a further five years.
3. A Community plant variety right shall lapse before the expiry of the terms laid down in paragraph 1 or pursuant to paragraph 2, if the holder surrenders it by sending a written declaration to such effect to the Office, and with effect from the day following the day on which the declaration is received by the Office.

[6.160]
Article 20
Nullity of Community plant variety rights

1. The Office shall declare the Community plant variety right null and void if it is established—
   (a) that the conditions laid down in Articles 7 or 10 were not complied with at the time of the Community plant variety right; or
   (b) that where the grant of the Community plant variety right has been essentially based upon information and documents furnished by the applicant, the conditions laid down in Articles 8 and 9 were not complied with at the time of the grant of the right; or
   (c) that the right has been granted to a person who is not entitled to it, unless it is transferred to the person who is so entitled.
2. Where the Community plant variety right is declared null and void, it shall be deemed not to have had, as from the outset, the effects specified in this Regulation.

[6.161]
Article 21
Cancellation of Community plant variety rights

1. The Office shall cancel the Community plant variety right with effect in futurum if it is established that the conditions laid down in Article 8 or 9 are no longer complied with. If it is established that these conditions were already no longer complied with from a point in time prior to cancellation, cancellation may be made effective as from that juncture.
2. The Office may cancel a Community plant variety right with effect in futurum if the holder, after being requested to do so, and within a time limit specified by the Office—
   (a) has not fulfilled an obligation pursuant to Article 64(3); or
   (b) in the case referred to in Article 66, does not propose another suitable variety denomination; or
   (c) fails to pay such fees as may be payable to keep the Community plant variety right in force; or
   (d) either as the initial holder or as a successor in title as a result of a transfer pursuant to Article 23, no longer satisfies the conditions laid down in Articles 12 and 82.

CHAPTER V
COMMUNITY PLANT VARIETY RIGHTS AS OBJECTS OF PROPERTY

[6.162]
Article 22
Assimilation with national laws

1. Save where otherwise provided in Articles 23 to 29, a Community plant variety right as an object of property shall be regarded in all respects, and for the entire territory of the Community, as a corresponding property right in the Member State in which—
   (a) according to the entry in the Register of Community Plant Variety Rights, the holder was domiciled or had his seat or an establishment on the relevant date; or
   (b) if the conditions laid down in subparagraph (a) are not fulfilled, the first-mentioned procedural representative of the holder, as indicated in the said Register, was domiciled or had his seat or an establishment on the date of registration.
2. Where the conditions laid down in paragraph 1 are not fulfilled, the Member State referred to in paragraph 1 shall be the Member State in which the seat of the Office is located.
3. Where domiciles, seats or establishments in two or more Member States are entered in respect of the holder or the procedural representatives in the Register referred to in paragraph 1, the first-mentioned domicile or seat shall apply for the purposes of paragraph 1.
4. Where two or more persons are entered in the Register referred to in paragraph 1 as joint holders, the relevant holder for the purposes of applying paragraph 1(a) shall be the first joint holder taken in order of entry in the Register who fulfils the conditions. Where none of the joint holders fulfils the conditions laid down in paragraph 1(a), paragraph 2 shall be applicable.

[6.163]
Article 23
Transfer

1. A Community plant variety right may be the object of a transfer to one or more successors in title.

2. Transfer of a Community plant variety right by assignment can be made only to successors who comply with the conditions laid down in Article 12 and 82. It shall be made in writing and shall require the signature of the parties to the contract, except when it is a result of a judgement or of any other acts terminating court proceedings. Otherwise it shall be void.

3. Save as otherwise provided in Article 100, a transfer shall have no bearing on the rights acquired by third parties before the date of transfer.

4. A transfer shall not take effect for the Office and may not be cited *vis-à-vis* third parties unless documentary evidence thereof as provided for in the implementing rules is provided and until it has been entered in the Register of Community Plant Variety Rights. A transfer that has not yet been entered in the Register may, however, be cited *vis-à-vis* third parties who have acquired rights after the date of transfer but who knew of the transfer at the date on which they acquired those rights.

[6.164]
Article 24
Levy of execution

A Community plant variety right may be levied in execution and be the subject of provisional, including protective, measures within the meaning of Article 24 of the Convention on Jurisdiction and the Enforcement of Judgments in Civil and Commercial Matters, signed in Lugano on 16 September 1988, hereinafter referred to as the 'Lugano Convention'.

[6.165]
Article 25
Bankruptcy or like proceedings

Until such time as common rules for the Member States in this field enter into force, the only Member State in which a Community plant variety right may be involved in bankruptcy or like proceedings shall be that in which such proceedings are first brought within the meaning of national law or of conventions applicable in this field.

[6.166]
Article 26
The application for a Community plant variety right as an object of property

Articles 22 to 25 shall apply to applications for Community plant variety rights. Concerning such applications, the references made in those Articles to the Register of Community Plant Variety Rights shall be regarded as references to the Register of Application for Community Plant Variety Rights.

[6.167]
Article 27
Contractual exploitation rights

1. Community plant variety rights may form in full or in part the subject of contractually granted exploitation rights. Exploitation rights may be exclusive or non-exclusive.

2. The holder may invoke the rights conferred by the Community plant variety right against a person enjoying the right of exploitation who contravenes any of the conditions or limitations attached to his exploitation right pursuant to paragraph 1.

[6.168]
Article 28
Joint holdership

Articles 22 to 27 shall apply *mutatis mutandis* in the event of joint holdership of a Community plant variety right in proportion to the respective share held, where such shares have been determined.

[6.169]
[Article 29
Compulsory licensing

1. Compulsory licences shall be granted to one or more persons by the Office, on application by that person or those persons, but only on grounds of public interest and after consulting the Administrative Council referred to in Article 36.

2. On application by a Member State, by the Commission or by an organisation set up at Community level and registered by the Commission, a compulsory licence may be granted, either to a category of persons satisfying specific requirements, or to anyone in one or more Member States or throughout the Community. It may be granted only on grounds of public interest and with the approval of the Administrative Council.

3. The Office shall, when granting the compulsory licence pursuant to paragraphs 1, 2, 5 or 5a, stipulate the type of acts covered and specify the reasonable conditions pertaining thereto as well as the specific requirements referred to in paragraph 2. The reasonable conditions shall take into

account the interests of any holder of plant variety rights who would be affected by the grant of the compulsory licence. The reasonable conditions may include a possible time limitation, the payment of an appropriate royalty as equitable remuneration to the holder and may impose certain obligations on the holder, the fulfilment of which are necessary to make use of the compulsory licence.

4. On the expiry of each one-year period after the grant of the compulsory licence pursuant to paragraphs 1, 2, 5 or 5a, and within the possible time limitation set out in paragraph 3, any of the parties to proceedings may request that the decision on the grant of the compulsory licence be cancelled or amended. The sole grounds for such a request shall be that the circumstances determining the decision taken have in the meantime undergone change.

5. On application, a compulsory licence shall be granted to the holder in respect of an essentially derived variety if the criteria set out in paragraph 1 are met. The reasonable conditions referred to in paragraph 3 shall include the payment of an appropriate royalty as equitable remuneration to the holder of the initial variety.

5a. On application, a compulsory licence for the nonexclusive use of a protected plant variety pursuant to Article 12(2) of Directive 98/44/EC shall be granted to the holder of a patent for a biotechnological invention, subject to payment of an appropriate royalty as equitable remuneration, provided that the patent holder demonstrates that—

(i) he/she has applied unsuccessfully to the holder of the plant variety right to obtain a contractual licence; and

(ii) the invention constitutes significant technical progress of considerable economic interest compared with the protected plant variety.

Where, in order to enable him/her to acquire or exploit his/her plant variety right, a holder has been granted a compulsory licence in accordance with Article 12(1) of Directive 98/44/EC for the non-exclusive use of a patented invention, a non-exclusive cross-licence on reasonable terms to exploit the variety shall be granted, on application, to the holder of the patent for that invention,

The territorial scope of the licence or cross-licence referred to in this paragraph shall be limited to the part or parts of the Community covered by the patent.

6. The implementing rules pursuant to Article 114 may specify certain other examples of licences in the public interest referred to in paragraphs 1, 2 and 5a, and moreover lay down details for the implementation of paragraphs 1 to 5a.

7. Compulsory licences may not be granted by Member States in respect of a Community plant variety right.]

NOTES

Substituted by Council Regulation 873/2004/EC, Art 1.

PART THREE
THE COMMUNITY PLANT VARIETY OFFICE

CHAPTER I
GENERAL PROVISIONS

[6.170]
Article 30
Legal status, sub-offices

1. The Office shall be a body of the Community. It shall have legal personality.

2. In each of the Member States, the Office shall enjoy the most extensive legal capacity accorded to legal persons under their laws. It may, in particular, acquire or dispose of movable and immovable property and may be a party to legal proceedings.

3. The Office shall be represented by its President.

4. With the consent of the Administrative Council referred to in Article 36, the Office may entrust national agencies with the exercise of specific administrative functions of the Office or establish its own sub-offices for that purpose in the Member States, subject to their consent.

[6.171]
Article 31
Staff

1. The Staff Regulations of Officials of the European Communities, the Conditions of Employment of Other Servants of the European Communities and the rules adopted jointly by the institutions of the European Communities for purposes of the application of those Staff Regulations and Conditions of Employment shall apply to the staff of the Office, without prejudice to the application of Article 47 to the members of the Board of Appeal.

2. Without prejudice to Article 43, the powers conferred on the appointing authority by the Staff Regulations, and by the Conditions of Employment of Other Servants, shall be exercised by the Office in respect of its own staff.

[6.172]
Article 32
Privileges and immunities

The Protocol on the Privileges and Immunities of the European Communities shall apply to the Office.

[6.173]
Article 33
Liability

1. The contractual liability of the Office shall be governed by the law applicable to the contract in question.
2. The Court of Justice of the European Communities shall have jurisdiction to give judgment pursuant to any arbitration clause contained in a contract concluded by the Office.
3. In the case of non-contractual liability, the Office shall, in accordance with the general principles common to the laws of the Member States, make good any damage caused by its departments or by its servants in the performance of their duties.
4. The Court of Justice shall have jurisdiction in disputes relating to compensation for the damage referred to in paragraph 3.
5. The personal liability of its servants towards the Office shall be governed by the provisions laid down in the Staff Regulations or Conditions of Employment applicable to them.

[6.174]
[Article 33a
Access to documents

1. Regulation (EC) No 1049/2001 of the European Parliament and of the Council of 30 May 2001 regarding public access to European Parliament, Council and Commission documents[1] shall apply to documents held by the Office.
2. The Administrative Council shall adopt the practical arrangements for implementing Regulation (EC) No 1049/2001 within six months of entry into force of Council Regulation (EC) No 1650/2003 of 18 June 2003 amending Regulation (EC) No 2100/94 on Community plant variety rights.[2]
3. Decisions taken by the Office pursuant to Article 8 of Regulation (EC) No 1049/2001 may form the subject of a complaint to the Ombudsman or of an action before the Court of Justice, under the conditions laid down in Articles 195 and 230 of the Treaty respectively.]

NOTES

Inserted by Council Regulation 1650/2003/EC, Art 1(1).

[1] OJ L145, 31.5.2001, p 43.

[2] OJ L245, 29.9.2003, p 28.

[6.175]
Article 34
Languages

1. The provisions laid down in Regulation No 1 of 15 April 1958 determining the languages to be used in the European Economic Community,[1] shall apply regarding the Office.
2. Applications to the Office, the documents required to process such applications and all other papers submitted shall be filed in one of the official languages of the European Communities.
3. Parties to proceedings before the Office as specified in the implementing rules pursuant to Article 114, shall be entitled, to conduct written and oral proceedings in any official language of the European Communities with translation and, in the case of hearings, simultaneous interpretation, at least into any other of the official languages of the European Communities chosen by any other party to proceedings. The exercise of these rights does not imply specific charges for the parties to proceedings.
4. The translation services required for the functioning of the Office are in principle provided by the Translation Centre of the Bodies of the Union.

NOTES

[1] OJ 17, 6.10.1958, p 385/58. Regulation as last amended by the 1985 Act of Accession.

[6.176]
Article 35
Decisions of the Office

1. Decisions of the Office shall, provided they do not have to be made by the Board of Appeal pursuant to Article 72, be taken by or under the authority of the President of the Office.
2. Subject to paragraph 1, decisions pursuant to Articles 20, 21, 29, 59, 61, 62, 63, 66 or 100(2) shall be taken by a Committee of three members of the Office's staff. The qualifications of the members of such Committee, the powers of individual members in the preparatory phase of the

decisions, the voting conditions and the role of the President in respect of such Committee shall be determined in the implementing rules pursuant to Article 114. Otherwise, the members of such Committee, in making their decisions, shall not be bound by any instructions.
3. Decisions of the President, other than those specified in paragraph 2, if not taken by the President, may be taken by a member of the Office's staff to whom the power to do so has been delegated pursuant to Article 42(2)(h).

CHAPTER II
THE ADMINISTRATIVE COUNCIL

[6.177]
Article 36
Creation and powers
1. An Administrative Council is hereby set up, attached to the Office. In addition to the powers assigned to the Administrative Council by other provisions of this Regulation, or by the provisions referred to in Articles 113 and 114, it shall have the powers in relation to the Office defined below—
(a) It shall advise on matters for which the Office is responsible, or issue general guidelines in this respect.
(b) It shall examine the management report of the President, and shall moreover monitor the Office's activities, on the basis of that examination and any other information obtained.
(c) It shall, on a proposal from the Office, either determine the number of Committees referred to in Article 35, the work allocation and the duration of their respective function, or issue general guidelines in this respect.
(d) It may establish rules on working methods of the Office.
(e) It may issue test guidelines pursuant to Article 56(2).
2. Moreover the Administrative Council—
— may deliver opinions to, and require information from the Office or the Commission, where it considers that this is necessary,
— may forward to the Commission, with or without amendments, the drafts placed before it pursuant to Article 42(2)(g), or its own draft amendments to this Regulation, to the provisions referred to in Articles 113 and 114 or to any other rules relating to Community plant variety rights,
— shall be consulted pursuant to Articles 113(4) and 114(2),
— shall carry out its functions relating the Office's budget pursuant to Articles 109, 111 and 112.

[6.178]
Article 37
Composition
1. The Administrative Council shall be composed of one representative of each Member State and one representative of the Commission and their alternates.
2. The members of the Administrative Council may, subject to the provisions of its rules of procedure, be assisted by advisers or experts.

[6.179]
Article 38
Chairmanship
1. The Administrative Council shall elect a Chairman and a Deputy Chairman from among its members. The Deputy Chairman shall ex officio replace the Chairman in the event of him being prevented from attending to his duties.
2. The terms of office of the Chairman or Deputy Chairman shall expire when their respective membership of the Administrative Council ceases. Without prejudice to this provision, the duration of the terms of office of the Chairman or Deputy Chairman shall be three years, unless another Chairman or Deputy Chairman have been elected before the end of this period. The terms of office shall be renewable.

[6.180]
Article 39
Meetings
1. Meetings of the Administrative Council shall be convened by its Chairman.
2. The President of the Office shall take part in the deliberations, unless the Administrative Council decides otherwise. He shall not have the right to vote.
3. The Administrative Council shall hold an ordinary meeting once a year; in addition, it shall meet on the initiative of its Chairman or at the request of the Commission or of one-third of the Member States.
4. It shall adopt rules of procedure, and may set up, in accordance with these rules, Committees placed under its authority.
5. The Administrative Council may invite observers to attend its meetings.
6. The secretariat for the Administrative Council shall be provided by the Office.

[6.181]
Article 40
Place of meetings

The Administrative Council shall meet at the seat of the Commission, or at the location of the Office or of an Examination Office. The details shall be determined in the rules of procedure.

[6.182]
Article 41
Voting

1. The Administrative Council shall take its decisions, other than those referred to in paragraph 2, by a simple majority of the representatives of the Member States.
2. The majority of three quarters of the representatives of the Member States shall be required for the decisions which the Administrative Council is empowered to take under Articles . . . 29, 36(1)(a), (b), (d) and (e), 43, 47, 109(3) and 112.
3. Each Member State shall have one vote.
4. The decisions of the Administrative Council shall have no binding force within the meaning of Article 189 of the Treaty.

NOTES

Para 2: words omitted repealed by Council Regulation 15/2008/EC, Art 1(2).

CHAPTER III
MANAGEMENT OF THE OFFICE

[6.183]
Article 42
Functions and powers of the President

1. The Office shall be managed by the President.
2. To this end, the President shall have, in particular, the following functions and powers—
   (a) The President shall take all necessary steps, including the adoption of internal administrative instructions and the publications of notices, to ensure the functioning of the Office in accordance with the provisions of this Regulation, with those referred to in Articles 113 and 114, or with the rules established, or guidelines issued, by the Administrative Council pursuant to Article 36(1).
   (b) He shall submit a management report to the Commission and Administrative Council each year.
   (c) He shall exercise in respect of the staff the powers laid down in Article 31(2).
   (d) He shall submit proposals as referred to in Article 36(1)(c) and 47(2).
   (e) He shall draw up estimates of the revenue and expenditure of the Office pursuant to Article 109(1), and shall implement the budget pursuant to Article 110.
   (f) He shall supply information as required by the Administrative Council pursuant to Article 36(2), first indent.
   (g) He may place before the Administrative Council draft amendments to this Regulation, to the provisions referred to in Articles 113 and 114 or to any other rules relating to Community plant variety rights.
   (h) He may delegate his powers to other members of the Office's staff, and subject to the provisions referred to in Articles 113 and 114.
3. The President shall be assisted by one or more Vice-Presidents. If the President is absent or indisposed, the Vice-President or one of the Vice-Presidents shall take his place in accordance with the procedure laid down in the rules established, or the guidelines issued, by the Administrative Council pursuant to Article 36(1).

[6.184]
Article 43
Appointment of senior officials

1. The President of the Office shall be appointed by the Council from a list of candidates which shall be proposed by the Commission after obtaining the opinion of the Administrative Council. Power to dismiss the President shall lie with the Council, acting on a proposal from the Commission after obtaining the opinion of the Administrative Council.
2. The term of office of the President shall not exceed five years. This term of office shall be renewable.
3. The Vice-President or Vice-Presidents of the Office shall be appointed or dismissed as in paragraphs 1 and 2, after consultation of the President.
4. The Council shall exercise disciplinary authority over the officials referred to in paragraphs 1 and 3.

[6.185]
Article 44
Control of legality

1. The Commission shall control the legality of those acts of the President in respect of which Community law does not provide for any control on legality by another body, and of the acts of the Administrative Council relating to the Office's budget.
2. The Commission shall require that any unlawful act referred to in paragraph 1 be altered or annulled.
3. Member States, any member of the Administrative Council or any other persons directly and personally involved may refer to the Commission any act referred to in paragraph 1, whether express or implied, to examine the legality of that act. Referral shall be made to the Commission within two months of the day on which the party concerned became aware of the act in question. The Commission shall take and communicate a decision within two months.

CHAPTER IV
THE BOARDS OF APPEAL

[6.186]
Article 45
Establishment and powers

1. There shall be established within the Office one or more Boards of Appeal.
2. The Board or Boards of Appeal shall be responsible for deciding on appeals from the decisions referred to in Article 67.
3. The Board or Boards of Appeal shall be convened as necessary. The number of Boards of Appeal and the work allocation shall be determined in the implementing rules pursuant to Article 114.

[6.187]
Article 46
Composition of the Boards of Appeal

1. A Board of Appeal shall consist of a Chairman and two other members.
2. The Chairman shall select for each case the other members and their respective alternates from the list of qualified members established pursuant to Article 47(2).
3. Where the Board of Appeal considers that the nature of the appeal so requires, it may call up to two further members from the aforesaid list for that case.
4. The qualifications required for the members of each Board of Appeal, the powers of individual members in the preparatory phase of the decisions and the voting conditions shall be determined in the implementing rules pursuant to Article 114.

[6.188]
Article 47
Independence of the members of the Boards of Appeal

1. The Chairmen of the Boards of Appeal and their respective alternates shall be appointed by the Council from a list of candidates for each chairman and each alternate which shall be proposed by the Commission after obtaining the opinion of the Administrative Council. The term of office shall be five years. It shall be renewable.
2. The other members of the Boards of Appeal shall be those selected pursuant to Article 46(2), from a list of qualified members established on a proposal from the Office, for a term of five years, by the Administrative Council. The list shall be established for a term of five years. This shall be renewable for whole or part of the list.
3. The members of the Board of Appeal shall be independent. In making their decisions they shall not be bound by any instructions.
4. The members of the Boards of Appeal may not be members of the Committees referred to in Article 35 nor perform any other duties in the Office. The function of the members of the Boards of Appeal may be a part-time function.
5. The members of the Boards of Appeal may not be removed from office nor from the list respectively, during the respective term, unless there are serious grounds for such removal and the Court of Justice of the European Communities, on application by the Commission after obtaining the opinion of the Administrative Council takes a decision to this effect.

[6.189]
Article 48
Exclusion and objection

1. Members of the Boards of Appeal may not take part in any appeal proceedings if they have any personal interest therein, or if they have previously been involved as representatives of one of the parties to proceedings, or if they participated in the decision under appeal.
2. If, for one of the reasons mentioned in paragraph 1 or for any other reason, a member of a Board of Appeal considers that he should not take part in any appeal proceedings, he shall inform the Board of Appeal accordingly.

3. Members of the Boards of Appeal may be objected to by any party to the appeal proceedings for one of the reasons mentioned in paragraph 1, or if suspected of partiality. An objection shall not be admissible if, while being aware of a reason for objecting, the party to the appeal proceedings has taken a procedural step. No objection may be based on the nationality of members.
4. The Boards of Appeal shall decide as to the action to be taken in the cases specified in paragraphs 2 and 3 without the participation of the member concerned. For the purposes of taking this decision, the member who withdraws or has been objected to shall be replaced in the Board of Appeal by his alternate.

PART FOUR
PROCEEDINGS BEFORE THE OFFICE

CHAPTER I
APPLICATIONS

[6.190]
Article 49
Filing of applications

1. An application for a Community plant variety right shall be filed at the choice of the applicant—
   (a) at the Office directly; or
   (b) at one of the sub-offices or national agencies, established or entrusted, pursuant to Article 30(4), subject to the applicant forwarding an information on this filing to the Office directly within two weeks after filing.

Details on the manner in which the information referred to in (b) above must be forwarded, may be laid down in the implementing rules pursuant to Article 114. The omission of forwarding information on an application to the Office pursuant to (b) above, does not affect the validity of the application if the application has reached the Office within one month after filing at the sub-office or national agency.

2. Where the application is filed at one of the national agencies referred to in paragraph 1(b), the national agency shall take all steps to forward the application to the Office within two weeks after filing. National agencies may charge the applicant a fee which shall not exceed the administrative costs of receiving and forwarding the application.

[6.191]
Article 50
Conditions governing applications

1. The application for a Community plant variety right must contain at least the following—
   (a) a request for the grant of a Community plant variety right;
   (b) identification of the botanical taxon;
   (c) information identifying the applicant or, where appropriate, the joint applicants;
   (d) the name of the breeder and an assurance that, to the best of the applicants knowledge, no further persons have been involved in the breeding, or discovery and development, of the variety; if the applicant is not the breeder, or not the only breeder, he shall provide the relevant documentary evidence as to how the entitlement to the Community plant variety right came into his possession;
   (e) a provisional designation for the variety;
   (f) a technical description of the variety;
   (g) the geographic origin of the variety;
   (h) the credentials of any procedural representative;
   (i) details of any previous commercialisation of the variety;
   (j) details of any other application made in respect of the variety.
2. Details of the conditions referred to in paragraph 1, including the provision of further information, may be laid down in the implementing rules pursuant to Article 114.
3. An application shall propose a variety denomination which may accompany the application.

[6.192]
Article 51
Date of application

The date of application for a Community plant variety right shall be the date on which a valid application was received by the Office pursuant to Article 49(1)(a) or by a sub-office or national agency pursuant to Article 49(1)(b), provided it complies with Article 50(1) and subject to payment of the fees due pursuant to Article 83 within a time limit specified by the Office.

[6.193]
Article 52
The right of priority

1. The right of priority of an application shall be determined by the date of receipt of the application. Where applications have the same date of application, the priorities thereof shall be determined according to the order in which they were received, if this can be established. Otherwise they shall have the same priority.

2. If the applicant or his predecessor in title has already applied for a property right for the variety in a Member State or in a Member of the International Union for the Protection of New Varieties of Plants, and the date of application is within 12 months of the filing of the earlier application, the applicant shall enjoy a right of priority for the earlier application as regards the application for the Community plant variety right, provided the earlier application still exists on the date of application.

3. The right of priority shall have the effect that the date on which the earlier application was filed shall count as the date of application for the Community plant variety right for the purposes of Articles 7, 10 and 11.

[4. Paragraphs 2 and 3 shall also apply in respect of earlier applications that were filed in another State.]

5. Any claim for a right of priority earlier than that provided for in paragraph 2 shall lapse if the applicant does not submit to the Office within three months of the date of application copies of the earlier application that have been certified by the authorities responsible for such application. If the earlier application has not been made in one of the official languages of the European Communities, the Office may require, in addition, a translation of the earlier application in one of these languages.

NOTES

Para 4: substituted by Council Regulation 15/2008/EC, Art 1(3).

CHAPTER II
EXAMINATION

[6.194]
Article 53
Formal examination of application

1. The Office shall examine whether—
   (a) the application has effectively been filed pursuant to Article 49;
   (b) the application complies with the conditions laid down in Article 50 and the conditions laid down in the implementing rules pursuant to that Article;
   (c) where appropriate, a claim for priority complies with the provision laid down in Article 52(2), (4) and (5); and
   (d) the fees due pursuant to Article 83 have been paid within a time limit specified by the Office.

2. If the application, although complying with the conditions referred to in Article 51, does not comply with other conditions laid down in Article 50, the Office shall give the applicant an opportunity to correct any deficiencies that may have been identified.

3. If the application does not comply with the conditions referred to in Article 51, the Office shall inform the applicant thereof, or, where this is not possible, publish the information pursuant to Article 89.

[6.195]
Article 54
Substantive examination

1. The Office shall examine whether the variety may be the object of a Community plant variety right pursuant to Article 5, whether the variety is new pursuant to Article 10, whether the applicant is entitled to file an application pursuant to Article 12 and whether the conditions laid down in Article 82 are complied with. The Office shall also examine whether the proposed variety denomination is suitable pursuant to Article 63. For such purposes, it may avail itself of the services of other bodies.

2. The first applicant shall be deemed to be entitled to the Community plant variety right pursuant to Article 11. This shall not apply if, before a decision on the application is taken, the Office is aware, or it is shown by a final judgment delivered with regard to a claim for entitlement pursuant to Article 98(4), that entitlement is not or is not solely vested in the first applicant. Where the identity of the sole or other person entitled has been determined, the person or persons may enter the proceedings as applicant or applicants.

[6.196]
Article 55
Technical examination

1. Where the Office has not discovered any impediment to the grant of a Community plant variety right on the basis of the examination pursuant to Articles 53 and 54, it shall arrange for the technical examination relating to compliance with the conditions laid down in Articles 7, 8 and 9 to be carried

out by the competent office or offices in at least one of the Member States entrusted w[ith] responsibility for the technical examination of varieties of the species concerned by [the] Administrative Council, hereafter referred to as the 'Examination Office or Offices'.

2. Where no Examination Office is available, the Office may, with the consent of th[e] Administrative Council, entrust other appropriate agencies with responsibility therefore or establish its own sub-offices for the same purposes. For the purpose of the provisions of this Chapter, such agencies or sub-offices shall be considered as Examination Offices. They may avail themselves of facilities made available by the applicant.

3. The Office shall forward to the Examination Offices copies of the application as required under the implementing rules pursuant to Article 114.

4. The Office shall determine, through general rules or through requests in individual cases, when, where and in what quantities and qualities the material for the technical examination and reference samples are to be submitted.

5. Where the applicant makes a claim for priority pursuant to Article 52(2) or (4), he shall submit the necessary material and any further documents required within two years of the date of application pursuant to Article 51. If the earlier application is withdrawn or refused before the expiry of two years, the Office may require the applicant to submit the material or any further documents within a specified time limit.

[6.197]
Article 56
The conduct of technical examinations

1. Unless a different manner of technical examination relating to compliance with the conditions laid down in Articles 7 to 9 has been arranged, the Examination Offices shall, for the purposes of the technical examination, grow the variety or undertake any other investigations required.

2. The conduct of any technical examinations shall be in accordance with test guidelines issued by the Administrative Council and any instructions given by the Office.

3. For the purposes of the technical examination, the Examination Offices may, with the approval of the Office, avail themselves of the services of other technically qualified bodies and take into account the available findings of such bodies.

4. Each Examination Office shall begin the technical examination, unless the Office has otherwise provided, no later than on the date on which a technical examination would have begun on the basis of an application for a national property right filed on the date on which the application sent by the Office was received by the Examination Office.

5. In the case of Article 55(5), each Examination Office shall begin the technical examination, unless the Office has otherwise provided, no later than on the date on which an examination would have begun on the basis of an application for a national property right, provided the necessary material and any further documents required were submitted at that date.

6. The Administrative Council may determine that the technical examination for varieties of vine and tree species may begin at a later date.

[6.198]
Article 57
Examination reports

1. The Examination Office shall, at the request of the Office or if it deems the results of the technical examination to be adequate to evaluate the variety, send the Office an examination report, and, where it considers that the conditions laid down in Articles 7 to 9 are complied with, a description of the variety.

2. The Office shall communicate the results of the technical examinations and the variety description to the applicant and shall give him an opportunity to comment thereon.

3. Where the Office does not consider the examination report to constitute a sufficient basis for decision, it may provide of its own motion, after consultation of the applicant, or on request of the applicant for complementary examination. For the purposes of assessment of the results, any complementary examination carried out until a decision taken pursuant to Articles 61 and 62 becomes final shall be considered to be part of the examination referred to in Article 56(1).

4. The results of the technical examination shall be subject to the exclusive rights of disposal of the Office and may only otherwise be used by the Examination Offices in so far as this is approved by the Office.

[6.199]
Article 58
Costs of technical examinations

The Office shall pay the Examination Offices a fee in accordance with the implementing rules pursuant to Article 114.

[6.200]
Article 59
Objections to grant of right

1. Any person may lodge with the Office a written objection to the grant of a Community plant variety right.

Objectors shall be party to the proceedings for grant of the Community plant variety right in ition to the applicant. Without prejudice to Article 88, objectors shall have access to the cuments, including the results of the technical examination and the variety description as referred in Article 57(2).

. Objections may be based only on the contention that—

(a) the conditions laid down in Articles 7 to 11 are not complied with;

(b) there is an impediment under Article 63(3) or (4) to a proposed variety denomination.

4. Objections may be lodged—

(a) at any time after the application and prior to a decision pursuant to Articles 61 or 62, in the case of paragraph 3(a) hereof;

(b) within three months of the publication of the proposed variety denomination pursuant to Article 89, in the case of objections under paragraph 3(b) hereof.

5. The decisions on objections may be taken together with the decisions pursuant to Articles 61, 62 or 63.

[6.201]
Article 60
Priority of a new application in the case of objections

Where an objection on the grounds that the conditions laid down in Article 11 are not met leads to the withdrawal or refusal of the application for a Community plant variety right and if the objector files an application for a Community plant variety right within one month following the withdrawal or within one month of the date on which the refusal becomes final in respect of the same variety, he may require that the date of the withdrawn or refused application be deemed to be the date of his application.

CHAPTER III
DECISIONS

[6.202]
Article 61
Refusal

1. The Office shall refuse applications for a Community plant variety right if and as soon as it establishes that the applicant—

(a) has not remedied any deficiencies within the meaning of Article 53 which he was given an opportunity to correct within the time limit notified to him;

(b) has not complied with a rule or request pursuant to Article 55(4) or (5) within the time limit laid down, unless the Office has consented to non-submission; or

(c) has not proposed a variety denomination which is suitable pursuant to Article 63.

2. The Office shall also refuse applications for a Community plant variety right if—

(a) it establishes that the conditions it is required to verify pursuant to Article 54 have not been fulfilled; or

(b) it reaches the opinion on the basis of the examination reports pursuant to Article 57, that the conditions laid down in Articles 7, 8 and 9 have not been fulfilled.

[6.203]
Article 62
Grant

If the Office is of the opinion that the findings of the examination are sufficient to decide on the application and there are no impediments pursuant to Articles 59 and 61, it shall grant the Community plant variety right. The decision shall include an official description of the variety.

[6.204]
Article 63
Variety denomination

1. Where a Community plant variety right is granted, the Office shall approve, for the variety in question, the variety denomination proposed by the applicant pursuant to Article 50(3), if it considers, on the basis of the examination made pursuant to the second sentence of Article 54(1), that this denomination is suitable.

2. A variety denomination is suitable, if there is no impediment pursuant to paragraphs 3 or 4 of this Article.

3. There is an impediment for the designation of a variety denomination where—

(a) its use in the territory of the Community is precluded by the prior right of a third party;

(b) it may commonly cause its users difficulties as regards recognition or reproduction;

(c) it is identical or may be confused with a variety denomination under which another variety of the same or of a closely related species is entered in an official register of plant varieties or under which material of another variety has been marketed in a Member State or in a Member of the International Unit for the Protection of New Varieties of Plants, unless the other variety no longer remains in existence and its denomination has acquired no special significance;

(d) it is identical or may be confused with other designations which are commonly used for the marketing of goods or which have to be kept free under other legislation;
(e) it is liable to give offence in one of the Member States or is contrary to public policy;
(f) it is liable to mislead or to cause confusion concerning the characteristics, the value or the identity of the variety, or the identity of the breeder or any other party to proceedings.

4. There is another impediment where, in the case of a variety which has already been entered—
(a) in one of the Member States; or
(b) in a Member of the International Union for the Protection of New Varieties of Plants; or
(c) in another State for which it has been established in a Community act that varieties are evaluated there under rules which are equivalent to those laid down in the Directives on common catalogues;

in an official register of plant varieties or material thereof and has been marketed there for commercial purposes, and the proposed variety denomination differs from that which has been registered or used there, unless the latter one is the object of an impediment pursuant to paragraph 3.

5. The Office shall publish the species which it considers 'closely related' within the meaning of paragraph 3(c).

CHAPTER IV
THE MAINTENANCE OF COMMUNITY PLANT VARIETY RIGHTS

[6.205]
Article 64
Technical verification

1. The Office shall verify the continuing existence unaltered of the protected varieties.
2. For this purpose, a technical verification shall be carried out pursuant to Articles 55 and 56.
3. The holder shall be required to provide all the information necessary to assess the continuing existence unaltered of the variety to the Office and to the Examination Offices to which technical verification of the variety has been entrusted. He shall be required, in accordance with the instructions given by the Office, to submit material of the variety and to permit to verify whether appropriate measures have been taken to ensure the continuing existence unaltered of the variety.

[6.206]
Article 65
Report on the technical verification

1. At the request of the Office, or if it establishes that the variety is not uniform or stable, the Examination Office entrusted with the technical verification shall send the Office a report on its findings.
2. If any deficiencies pursuant to paragraph 1 have been found during the technical verification, the Office shall inform the holder of the results of the technical verification and shall give him an opportunity to comment thereon.

[6.207]
Article 66
Amendment of the variety denomination

1. The Office shall amend a variety denomination designated pursuant to Article 63 if it establishes that the denomination does not satisfy, or no longer satisfies, the conditions laid down in Article 63 and in the event of a prior conflicting right of a third party, if the holder agrees to the amendment or the holder or any other person required to use the variety denomination has been prohibited, by a final judgment, for this reason from using the variety denomination.
2. The Office shall give the holder an opportunity to propose an amended variety denomination and shall proceed in accordance with Article 63.
3. Objections may be lodged against the proposed amended variety denomination in accordance with Article 59(3)(b).

CHAPTER V
APPEALS

[6.208]
Article 67
Decisions subject to appeal

1. An appeal shall lie from decisions of the Office which have been taken pursuant to Articles 20, 21, 59, 61, 62, 63 and 66, as well as on decisions related to fees pursuant to Article 83, to costs pursuant to Article 85, to the entering or deletion of information in the Register pursuant to Article 87 and to the public inspection pursuant to Article 88.
2. An appeal lodged pursuant to paragraph 1 shall have suspensory effect. The Office may, however, if it considers that circumstances so require, order that the contested decision not be suspended.
3. An appeal may lie from decisions of the Office pursuant to Articles 29 and 100(2), unless a [direct action] is [brought] pursuant to Article 74. The appeal shall not have suspensory effect.

4. An appeal against a decision which does not terminate proceedings as regards one of the parties may only be made in conjunction with an appeal against the final decision, unless the decision provides for separate appeal.

NOTES

Para 3: words in square brackets substituted by Council Regulation 2506/95/EC, Art 1(1).

[6.209]
Article 68
Persons entitled to appeal and to be parties to appeal proceedings

Any natural or legal person may appeal, subject to Article 82, against a decision, addressed to that person, or against a decision which, although in the form of a decision addressed to another person, is of direct and individual concern to the former. The parties to proceedings may, and the Office shall, be party to the appeal proceedings.

[6.210]
Article 69
Time limit and form

Notice of appeal shall be filed in writing at the Office within two months of the service of the decision where addressed to the appealing person, or, in the absence thereof, within two months of the publication of the decision, and a written statement setting out the grounds of appeal shall be filed within four months after the aforesaid service or publication.

[6.211]
Article 70
Interlocutory revision

1. If the body of the Office which has prepared the decision considers the appeal to be admissible and well founded, the Office shall rectify the decision. This shall not apply where the appellant is opposed by another party to the appeal proceedings.
2. If the decision is not rectified within one month after receipt of the statement of grounds, for the appeal, the Office shall forthwith—
— decide whether it will take an action pursuant to Article 67(2), second sentence, and
— remit the appeal to the Board of Appeal.

[6.212]
Article 71
Examination of appeals

1. If the appeal is admissible, the Board of Appeal shall examine whether the appeal is well-founded.
2. When examining the appeal, the Board of Appeal shall as often as necessary invite the parties to the appeal proceedings to file observations on notifications issued by itself or on communications from the other parties to the appeal proceedings within specified time limits. Parties to the appeal proceedings shall be entitled to make oral representations.

[6.213]
Article 72
Decision on appeal

The Board of Appeal shall decide on the appeal on the basis of the examination carried out pursuant to Article 71. The Board of Appeal may exercise any power which lies within the competence of the Office, or it may remit the case to the competent body of the Office for further action. The latter one shall, in so far as the facts are the same, be bound by the ratio decidendi of the Board of Appeal.

[6.214]
[Article 73
Appeals against decisions of the Boards of Appeal

1. Actions may be brought before the Court of Justice against decisions of the Boards of Appeal on appeals.
2. The action may be brought on grounds of lack of competence, infringement of an essential procedural requirement, infringement of the Treaty, of this Regulation or of any rule of law relating to their application, or misuse of power.
3. The Court of Justice shall have jurisdiction to annul or to alter the contested decision.
4. The action shall be open to any party to appeal proceedings which has been unsuccessful, in whole or in part, in its submissions.
5. The action shall be brought before the Court of Justice within two months of the date of service of the decision of the Board of Appeal.
6. The Office shall be required to take the necessary measures to comply with the judgment of the Court of Justice.]

NOTES

Substituted by Council Regulation 2506/95/EC, Art 1(2).

[6.215]
Article 74
[Direct action]
1. [A direct action may be brought before the Court of Justice against] decisions of the Office pursuant to Articles 29 and 100(2).
2. The provisions laid down in Article 73 shall apply *mutatis mutandis*.

NOTES
Heading: substituted by Council Regulation 2506/95/EC, Art 1(3).
Para 1: words in square brackets substituted by Council Regulation 2506/95/EC, Art 1(3).

CHAPTER VI
MISCELLANEOUS CONDITIONS GOVERNING PROCEEDINGS

[6.216]
Article 75
Statement of grounds on which decisions are based, right of audience
Decisions of the Office shall be accompanied by statements of the grounds on which they are based. They shall be based only on grounds or evidence on which the parties to proceedings have had an opportunity to present their comments orally or in writing.

[6.217]
Article 76
Examination of the facts by the Office of its own motion
In proceedings before it the Office shall make investigations on the facts of its own motion, to the extent that they come under the examination pursuant to Articles 54 and 55. It shall disregard facts or items of evidence which have not been submitted within the time limit set by the Office.

[6.218]
Article 77
Oral proceedings
1. Oral proceedings shall be held either on the initiative of the Office itself or at the request of any of the parties to proceedings.
2. Without prejudice to paragraph 3, oral proceedings before the Office shall not be public.
3. Oral proceedings before the Board of Appeal including delivery of the decision, shall be public in so far as the Board of Appeal before which the proceedings are taking place does not decide otherwise in circumstances where serious and unwarranted disadvantages could arise from admitting the public, particularly for any of the parties to the appeal proceedings.

[6.219]
Article 78
Taking of evidence
1. In any proceedings before the Office, the means of giving or obtaining evidence may include the following—
(a) hearing the parties to proceedings;
(b) requests for information;
(c) the production of documents or other evidence;
(d) hearing the witnesses;
(e) opinions by experts;
(f) inspection;
(g) sworn affidavits.
2. Where the Office decides through a collective body, that body may commission one of its members to examine the evidence adduced.
3. If the Office considers it necessary that a party to proceedings, witness or expert give evidence orally, it shall either—
(a) issue a summons requiring the relevant person to appear before it; or
(b) request the competent judicial or other authority in the country of domicile of the relevant person to take the evidence as provided for in Article 91(2).
4. A party to proceedings, witness or expert who is summoned before the Office may request it to allow his evidence to be heard by the competent judicial or other authority in his country of domicile. On receipt of such a request or in the case that no reaction was given to the summons, the Office may, in accordance with Article 91(2), request the competent judicial or other authority to hear the evidence of that person.
5. If a party to proceedings, witness or expert gives evidence before the Office, the Office may, if it considers it advisable that the evidence be given under oath or otherwise in binding form, request the competent judicial or other authority in the country of domicile of the relevant person to hear his evidence under the requisite conditions.

6. When the Office requests a competent judicial or other authority to take evidence, it may request it to take the evidence in binding form and to permit a member of the Office to attend the hearing and question the party to proceedings, witness or expert either through that judicial or other authority or directly.

[6.220]
Article 79
Service
The Office shall of its own motion effect service of all decisions and summonses, and of notifications and communications, from which a time limit is reckoned, or which are required to be served either in pursuance of other provisions of this Regulation or by provisions adopted pursuant to this Regulation or by order of the President of the Office. Service may be effected through the competent variety offices of the Member States.

[6.221]
Article 80
Restitutio in integrum
1. Where, in spite of having taken all due care in the particular circumstances, the applicant for a Community plant variety right or the holder or any other party to proceedings before the Office has been unable to observe a time limit *vis-à-vis* the Office, his rights shall, upon application, be restored if his failure to respect the time limit has resulted directly, by virtue of this Regulation, in the loss of any right or means of redress.
2. Applications shall be filed in writing within two months after the cause of non-compliance when the time limit has ceased to operate. The act omitted shall be completed within this period. Applications shall be admissible only within the period of one year following the expiry of the time limit which has not been observed.
3. An application shall be accompanied by a statement of the grounds on which it is based and the facts on which it relies.
4. The provisions of this Article shall not apply to the time limits referred to in paragraph 2 nor to the time limits specified in Article 52(2), (4) and (5).
5. Any person who, in a Member State, has in good faith used or made effective and genuine arrangements to use a variety which is the subject of a published application for grant of a Community plant variety right, or of a Community plant variety right that has been granted, in the course of a period between the loss of rights pursuant to paragraph 1 in respect of the application or of a Community plant variety right that has been granted and the restoration of those rights, may without payment continue such use in the course of his business or for the needs thereof.

[6.222]
Article 81
General principles
1. In the absence of procedural provisions in this Regulation or in provisions adopted pursuant to this Regulation, the Office shall apply the principles of procedural law which are generally recognised in the Member States.
2. Article 48 shall apply *mutatis mutandis* to the staff of the Office in so far as it is involved in decisions of the kind referred to in Article 67, and to the staff of the Examination Offices, in so far as it participates in measures for the preparation of such decisions.

[6.223]
Article 82
Procedural representative
Persons who are not domiciled or do not have a seat or an establishment within the territory of the Community may participate as party to proceedings before the Office only if they have designated a procedural representative who is domiciled or has his seat or an establishment within the territory of the Community.

CHAPTER VII
FEES, SETTLEMENT OF COSTS

[6.224]
Article 83
Fees
1. The Office shall charge fees for its official acts provided for under this Regulation as well as for each year of the duration of a Community plant variety right, pursuant to the fees regulations adopted in accordance with Article 113.
2. If fees due in respect of the official acts set out in Article 113(2) or of other official acts referred to in the fees regulations, which are only to be carried out on application, are not paid, the application shall be deemed not to have been filled or the appeal not to have been lodged if the acts necessary for the payment of the fees have not been effected within one month of the date on which the Office served a new request for payment of fees and indicated in so doing these consequences of failure to pay.

3. If certain information provided by the applicant for grant of a Community plant variety right can only be verified by a technical examination which goes beyond the framework established for the technical examination of varieties of the taxon concerned, the fees for the technical examination may be increased, after having heard the person liable to pay the fees, up to the amount of the expenditure actually incurred.
4. In the case of a successful appeal, the appeal fees or, in case of a partial success, the corresponding part of the appeal fees, shall be refunded. However, the refund can be fully or partly refused if the success of the appeal is based on facts which were not available at the time of the original decision.

[6.225]
Article 84
Termination of financial obligations
1. The Office's right to require payment of fees shall lapse after four years from the end of the calendar year in which the fees became due for payment.
2. Rights against the Office for the refunding of fees or of sums overcharged by the Office shall lapse after four years from the end of the calendar year in which the rights arose.
3. A request for payment of a fee shall have the effect of interrupting the time limit specified in paragraph 1, and a written and reasoned claim for refund shall have the effect of interrupting the time limit specified in paragraph 2. After interruption the time limit shall begin to run again immediately and shall terminate at the latest six years after the end of the calendar year in which it originally commenced, unless judicial proceedings to enforce the right have been instituted in the meantime; in that case the time limit shall end not earlier than one year after the judgment has acquired the authority of a final decision.

[6.226]
Article 85
Apportionment of costs
1. The losing party to proceedings for revocation or cancellation of a Community plant variety right, or to appeal proceedings shall bear the costs incurred by the other party to proceedings as well as all costs incurred by him essential to the proceedings, including travel and subsistence and the remuneration of an agent, adviser or advocate, within the limits of the scales set for each category of costs under the conditions laid down in the implementing rules pursuant to Article 114.
2. However, where each party to proceedings succeeds on some and fails on other heads, or if reasons of equity so dictate, the Office or Board of Appeal shall decide a different apportionment of costs.
3. The party to proceedings who terminates the proceedings by withdrawing the application for a Community plant variety right, the application for revocation or cancellation of rights, or the appeal, or by surrendering the Community plant variety rights, shall bear the costs incurred by the other party to proceedings as stipulated in paragraphs 1 and 2.
4. Where the parties to proceedings conclude before the Office, or Board of Appeal a settlement of costs differing from that provided for in the preceding paragraphs, note shall be taken of that agreement.
5. On request, the Office or Board of Appeal shall determine the amount of the costs to be paid pursuant to the preceding paragraphs.

[6.227]
Article 86
Enforcement of decisions which determine the amount of costs
1. Final decisions of the Office which determine the amount of costs shall be enforceable.
2. Enforcement shall be governed by the rules of civil procedure applicable in the Member State in which it takes place. Subject only to verification that the relevant document is authentic, the enforcement clause or endorsement shall be appended by the national authority appointed for that purpose by the Government of each Member State; the Governments shall inform the Office and the Court of Justice of the European Communities of the identity of each such national authority.
3. When, upon application by the party seeking enforcement, these formalities have been completed, it shall be entitled to proceed to endorsement under national law by bringing the matter directly before the competent body.
4. Enforcement shall not be suspended except by decision of the Court of Justice of the European Communities. Control as to the regularity of enforcement measures shall, however, reside with the national courts.

CHAPTER VIII
REGISTERS

[6.228]
Article 87
Establishment of the Registers
1. The Office shall keep a Register of Applications for Community Plant Variety Rights which shall contain the following particulars—

(a) applications for a Community plant variety right together with a statement of the taxon and the provisional designation of the variety, the date of application and the name and address of the applicant, of the breeder and of any procedural representative concerned;
(b) any cases of termination of proceedings concerning applications for a Community plant variety right together with the information set out in subparagraph (a);
(c) proposals for variety denominations;
(d) changes in the identity of the applicant or his procedural representative;
(e) on request, any levy of execution as referred to in Articles 24 and 26.

2. The Office shall keep a Register of Community Plant Variety Rights wherein, after grant of a Community plant variety right, the following particulars shall be entered—
(a) the species and variety denomination of the variety;
(b) the official description of the variety or a reference to documents in the Office's possession in which the official description of the variety is contained as integrating part of the Register;
(c) in the case of varieties for which material with specific components has to be used repeatedly for the production of material, a reference to such components;
(d) the name and address of the holder, of the breeder and of any procedural representative concerned;
(e) the date on which the Community plant variety right begins and ends, together with the reasons for the termination of right;
(f) on request, any contractual exclusive exploitation right or compulsory exploitation right, including the name and address of the person enjoying the right of exploitation;
(g) on request, any levy of execution as referred to in Article 24;
(h) where the holder of an initial variety and the breeder of a variety essentially derived from the initial variety both so request, the identification of the varieties as initial and essentially derived including the variety denominations and the names of the parties concerned. A request from one of the parties concerned only shall suffice if he has obtained either a non-contentious acknowledgement by the other party pursuant to Article 99 or a final decision or a final judgment pursuant to the provisions of this Regulation which contain an identification of the varieties concerned as initial and essentially derived.

3. Any other particular or any condition for the entering in both Registers may be specified in the implementing rules pursuant to Article 114.

4. The Office may of its own motion and upon consultation with the holder adapt the official variety description in respect of the number and type of characteristics or of the specified expressions of those characteristics, when necessary, in the light of the current principles governing the description of varieties of the taxon concerned, in order to render the description of the variety comparable with the descriptions of other varieties of the taxon concerned.

[6.229]
Article 88
Public inspection

1. The Registers mentioned in Article 87 shall be open to public inspection.

2. In case of a legitimate interest, the following shall be open to public inspection, in accordance with the conditions set up in the implementing rules pursuant to Article 114—
(a) documents relating to applications for grant of a Community plant variety right;
(b) documents relating to Community plant variety rights already granted;
(c) the growing of varieties for the purposes of their technical examination;
(d) the growing of varieties for the purpose of verifying their continuing existence.

3. In the case of varieties for which material with specific components has to be used repeatedly for the production of material, at the request of the applicant for a Community plant variety right, all data relating to components, including their cultivation, shall be withheld from inspection. Such a request for withholding from inspection may not be filed once the decision on the application for grant of a Community plant variety right has been taken.

4. Materials submitted or obtained in connection with examinations under Articles 55(4), 56 and 64 may not be given to other parties by the competent authorities under this Regulation unless the person entitled gives his consent or such transfer is required in connection with the cooperation covered by this Regulation for the purposes of the examination or by virtue of legal provisions.

[6.230]
Article 89
Periodical publications

The Office shall at least every two months, issue a publication containing the information entered into the Registers pursuant to Article 87(1) and (2)(a), (d), (e), (f), (g) and (h), and not yet published. The Office shall also publish an annual report, containing information which the Office regards as expedient, but at least a list of valid Community plant variety rights, their holders, the dates of grant and expiry and the approved variety denominations. Details of these publications shall be specified by the Administrative Council.

[6.231]
Article 90
Exchange of information and of publications
1. The Office and the competent variety offices of the Member States shall, on request and without prejudice to the conditions set up for the sending of results of technical examinations, dispatch to each other for their own use, free of charge, one or more copies of their respective publications and any other useful information relating to property rights applied for or granted.
2. The data referred to in Article 88(3) shall be excluded from information, unless—
(a) the information is necessary for the conduct of the examinations pursuant to Articles 55 and 64; or
(b) the applicant for a Community plant variety right or the holder gives his consent.

[6.232]
Article 91
Administrative and legal cooperation
1. Unless otherwise provided in this Regulation or in national law, the Office, Examination Offices referred to in Article 55(1) and the courts or authorities of the Member States shall on request give assistance to each other by communicating information or opening files related to the variety, and samples or growing thereof for inspection. Where the Office and the Examination Offices lay files, samples or growing thereof open to inspection by courts or public prosecutors' offices, the inspection shall not be subject to the restrictions laid down in Article 88, and the inspection given by the Examination Offices shall not be subject to a decision of the Office pursuant to that Article.
2. Upon receipt of letters rogatory from the Office, the courts or other competent authorities of the Member States shall undertake on behalf of that Office and within the limits of their jurisdiction, any necessary enquiries or other related measures.

PART FIVE
IMPACT ON OTHER LAWS

[6.233]
Article 92
Cumulative protection prohibited
1. Any variety which is the subject matter of a Community plant variety right shall not be the subject of a national plant variety right or any patent for that variety. Any rights granted contrary to the first sentence shall be ineffective.
2. Where the holder has been granted another right as referred to in paragraph 1 for the same variety prior to grant of the Community plant variety right, he shall be unable to invoke the rights conferred by such protection for the variety for as long as the Community plant variety right remains effective.

[6.234]
Article 93
Application of national law
Claims under Community plant variety rights shall be subject to limitations imposed by the law of the Member States only as expressly referred to in this Regulation.

PART SIX
CIVIL LAW CLAIMS, INFRINGEMENTS, JURISDICTION

[6.235]
Article 94
Infringement
1. Whosoever—
(a) effects one of the acts set out in Article 13(2) without being entitled to do so, in respect of a variety for which a Community plant variety right has been granted; or
(b) omits the correct usage of a variety denomination as referred to in Article 17(1) or omits the relevant information as referred to in Article 17(2); or
(c) contrary to Article 18(3) uses the variety denomination of a variety for which a Community plant variety right has been granted or a designation that may be confused with it;

may be sued by the holder to enjoin such infringement or to pay reasonable compensation or both.
2. Whosoever acts intentionally or negligently shall moreover be liable to compensate the holder for any further damage resulting from the act in question. In cases of slight negligence, such claims may be reduced according to the degree of such slight negligence, but not however to the extent that they are less than the advantage derived therefrom by the person who committed the infringement.

Part 6 Plant Varieties Protection

.236]
ticle 95
cts prior to grant of Community plant variety rights
he holder may require reasonable compensation from any person who has, in the time between publication of the application for a Community plant variety right and grant thereof, effected an act that he would be prohibited from performing subsequent thereto.

[6.237]
Article 96
Prescription
Claims pursuant to Articles 94 and 95 shall be time barred after three years from the time at which the Community plant variety right has finally been granted and the holder has knowledge of the act and of the identity of the party liable or, in the absence of such knowledge, after 30 years from the termination of the act concerned.

[6.238]
Article 97
Supplementary application of national law regarding infringement
1. Where the party liable pursuant to Article 94 has, by virtue of the infringement, made any gain at the expense of the holder or of a person entitled to exploitation rights, the courts competent pursuant to Articles 101 or 102 shall apply their national law, including their private international law, as regards restitution.
2. Paragraph 1 shall also apply as regards other claims that may arise in respect of the performance or omission of acts pursuant to Article 95 in the time between publication of the application for grant of a Community plant variety right and the disposal of the request.
3. In all other respects the effects of Community plant variety rights shall be determined solely in accordance with this Regulation.

[6.239]
Article 98
Claiming entitlement to a Community plant variety right
1. If a Community plant variety right has been granted to a person who is not [illegible] Article 11, the person entitled to it may, without prejudice to any other remedy which [illegible] to him under the laws of the Member States, claim to have the Community plant variety right transferred to him.
2. Where a person is entitled to only part of a Community plant variety right, that person may, in accordance with paragraph 1, claim to be made a joint holder.
3. Claims pursuant to paragraphs 1 and 2 may be invoked only within a period of up to five years of publication of the grant of the Community plant variety right. This provision shall not apply if the holder knew, at the time it was granted to or acquired by him, that he was not entitled to such rights or that entitlement thereto was not vested solely in him.
4. The person entitled shall be eligible *mutatis mutandis* to pursue claims pursuant to paragraphs 1 and 2 in respect of an application for grant of a Community plant variety right filed by a person who was not entitled to it or whom the entitlement was not vested solely.

[6.240]
Article 99
Obtaining identification of a variety
The holder of an initial variety and the breeder of a variety essentially derived from the initial variety shall be entitled to obtain an acknowledgement of the identification of the varieties concerned as initial and essentially derived.

[6.241]
Article 100
Consequences of a change in holdership of a Community plant variety right
1. In the event of a complete change in the holdership of a Community plant variety right in consequence of a final judgment delivered pursuant to Articles 101 or 102 for the purposes of claiming entitlement under Article 98(1), any exploitation or other rights shall lapse with the entry of the person entitled in the Register of Community Plant Variety Rights.
2. Where the holder or a person enjoying the right of exploitation has effected one of the acts set out in Article 13(2) or has made effective and genuine arrangements to do so prior to the commencement of the proceedings pursuant to Articles 101 or 102, he may continue or perform such acts provided he requests a non-exclusive exploitation right from the new holder entered in the Register of Community Plant Variety Rights. Such requests must be made within the time limit laid down in the implementing rules. The exploitation right may be granted by the Office in the absence of an agreement between the parties. Article 29(3) to (7) shall apply *mutatis mutandis*.
3. Paragraph 2 shall not apply where the holder or persons enjoying the right of exploitation acted in bad faith when they effected the acts or began to make the arrangements.

[6.242]
Article 101
Jurisdiction and procedure in legal actions relating to civil law claims

1. The Lugano Convention as well as the complementary provisions of this Article and of Articles 102 to 106 of this Regulation shall apply to proceedings relating to actions in respect of the claims referred to in Articles 94 to 100.

2. Proceedings of the type referred to in paragraph 1 shall be brought in the courts—
   (a) of the Member State or another Contracting Party to the Lugano Convention in which the defendant is domiciled or has his seat or, in the absence of such, has an establishment; or
   (b) if this condition is not met in any of the Member States or Contracting Parties, of the Member State in which the plaintiff is domiciled or has his seat or, in the absence of such, has an establishment; or
   (c) if this condition is also not met in any of the Member States, of the Member States in which the seat of the Office is located.

The competent courts shall have jurisdiction in respect of infringements alleged to have been committed in any of the Member States.

3. Proceedings relating to actions in respect of claims for infringement may also be brought in the courts for the place where the harmful event occurred. In such cases, the court shall have jurisdiction only in respect of infringements alleged to have been committed in the territory of the Member State to which it belongs.

4. The legal processes and the competent courts shall be those that operate under the laws of the State determined pursuant to paragraphs 2 or 3.

[6.243]
Article 102
Supplementary provisions

1. Actions for claiming entitlement pursuant to Article 98 of this Regulation shall not be considered to fall under the provisions of Article 5(3) and (4) of the Lugano Convention.

2. Notwithstanding Article 101 of this Regulation, Articles 5(1), 17 and 18 of the Lugano Convention shall apply.

3. For the purposes of applying Articles 101 and 102 of this Regulation, the domicile or seat of a party shall be determined pursuant to Articles 52 and 53 of the Lugano Convention.

[6.244]
Article 103
Rules of procedure applicable

Where jurisdiction lies with national courts pursuant to Articles 101 and 102, the rules of procedure of the relevant State governing the same type of action relating to corresponding national property rights shall apply without prejudice to Articles 104 and 105.

[6.245]
Article 104
Entitlement to bring an action for infringement

1. Actions for infringement may be brought by the holder. Persons enjoying exploitation rights may bring such actions unless that has been expressly excluded by agreement with the holder in the case of an exclusive exploitation right or by the Office pursuant to Articles 29 or 100(2).

2. Any person enjoying exploitation rights shall, for the purpose of obtaining compensation for damage suffered by him, be entitled to intervene in an infringement action brought by the holder.

[6.246]
Article 105
Obligation of national courts or other bodies

A national court or other body hearing an action relating to a Community plant variety right shall treat the Community plant variety right as valid.

[6.247]
Article 106
Stay of proceedings

1. Where an action relates to claims pursuant to Article 98(4) and the decision depends upon the protectability of the variety pursuant to Article 6, this decision may not be given before the Office has decided on the application for a Community plant variety right.

2. Where an action relates to a Community plant variety right that has been granted and in respect of which proceedings for revocation or cancellation pursuant to Articles 20 or 21 have been initiated, the proceedings may be stayed in so far as the decision depends upon the validity of the Community plant variety right.

[6.248]
Article 107
Penalties for infringement of Community plant variety rights
Member States shall take all appropriate measures to ensure that the same provisions are made applicable to penalise infringements of Community plant variety rights as apply in the matter of infringements of corresponding national rights.

PART SEVEN
BUDGET, FINANCIAL CONTROL, COMMUNITY IMPLEMENTING RULES

[6.249]
Article 108
Budget
1. Estimates of all the Office's revenue and expenditure shall be prepared for each financial year and shall be shown in the Office's budget, and each financial year shall correspond with the calendar year.
2. The revenue and expenditure shown in the budget shall be in balance.
3. Revenue shall comprise, without prejudice to other types of income, total fees payable pursuant to Article 83 under the fees regulations referred to in Article 113, and, to the extent necessary, a subsidy from the general budget of the European Communities.
4. Expenditure shall comprise, without prejudice to other types of expenditure, the fixed costs of the Office and the costs arising from the Office's normal functioning, including sums payable to the Examination Offices.

[6.250]
Article 109
Preparation of the budget
1. The President shall draw up each year an estimate of the Office's revenue and expenditure for the following year and shall transmit it to the Administrative Council not later than 31 March each year, together with a list of posts and, where the estimate provides for a subsidy referred to in Article 108(3), prefaced by an explanatory statement.
2. Should the estimate provide for a subsidy referred to in Article 108(3), the Administrative Council shall immediately forward the estimate to the Commission, together with the list of posts and the explanatory statement, and may attach its opinion. The Commission shall forward them to the budget authority of the Communities and may attach an opinion along with an alternative estimate.
3. The Administrative Council shall adopt the budget, which shall include the Office's list of posts. Should the estimate contain a subsidy referred to in Article 108(3), the budget shall, if necessary, be adjusted to the appropriations in the general budget of the European Communities.

[6.251]
Article 110
Implementation of the budget
The President shall implement the Office's budget.

[6.252]
Article 111
[Audit and control]
[1. An internal audit function shall be set up within the Office, to be performed in compliance with the relevant international standards. The internal auditor, appointed by the President, shall be responsible to him for verifying the proper operation of budget implementation systems and procedures of the Office.

The internal auditor shall advise the President on dealing with risks, by issuing independent opinions on the quality of management and control systems and by issuing recommendations for improving the conditions of implementation of operations and promoting sound financial management.

The responsibility for putting in place internal control systems and procedures suitable for carrying out his tasks shall lie with the authorising officer.]
2. Not later than 31 March each year the President shall transmit to the Commission, the Administrative Council and the Court of Auditors of the European Communities accounts of the Office's total revenue and expenditure for the preceding financial year. The Court of Auditors shall examine them in accordance with relevant provisions applicable to the general budget of the European Communities.
3. The Administrative Council shall give a discharge to the President of the Office in respect to the implementation of the budget.

NOTES
Article title and para 1 substituted by Council Regulation 1650/2003/EC, Art 1(2).

[6.253]

Article 112

Financial provisions

The Administrative Council shall, after consulting the Court of Auditors, adopt internal financial provisions specifying, in particular, the procedure for establishing and implementing the Office's budget. The financial provisions must, as far as possible, correspond to the provisions of the Financial Regulation applicable to the general budget of the European Communities and depart from them only when the specific requirements of the individual operation of the Office so dictate.

[6.254]

Article 113

Fees regulations

1. The fees regulations shall determine in particular the matters for which fees pursuant to Article 83(1) are due, the amounts of the fees and the way in which they are to be paid.

2. Fees shall be charged for at least in respect of the following matters for—

(a) the processing of applications for grant of a Community plant variety right; this fee shall cover—

— the formal examination, (Article 53),

— the substantive examination (Article 54),

— the examination of the variety denomination (Article 63),

— the decision (Articles 61, 62)

— the related publishing (Article 89);

(b) the arranging and carrying out of the technical examination;

(c) the processing of an appeal including the decision;

(d) each year of the duration of a Community plant variety right.

3.—

(a) Without prejudice to (b) and (c), the amounts of the fees shall be fixed at such a level as to ensure that the revenue in respect thereof is in principle sufficient for the budget of the Office to be balanced.

(b) However, the subsidy referred to in Article 108(3) may cover, for a transitional period ending on 31 December of the fourth year from the date laid down in Article 118(2), the expenditure relating to the initial running phase of the Office. In accordance with the procedure laid down in Article 115, this period may be extended, if necessary, for no more than one year.

(c) Moreover, during the abovementioned transitional period only, the subsidy referred to in Article 108(3) may also cover certain expenditure of the Office relating to certain activities other than the processing of applications, the arranging and carrying out of the technical examinations and the processing of appeals. These activities shall be specified, at the latest one year after the adoption of this Regulation, in implementing rules pursuant to Article 114.

4. The fees regulations shall be adopted in accordance with the procedure laid down in Article 115, after consultation of the Administrative Council on the draft of the measures to be taken.

[6.255]

Article 114

Other implementing rules

1. Detailed implementing rules shall be adopted for the purpose of applying this Regulation. They shall in particular include provisions—

— defining the relationship between the Office and the Examination Offices, agencies or its own sub-offices referred to in Articles 30(4) and 55(1) and (2),

— on matters referred to in Articles 36(1) and 42(2),

— on the procedure of the Boards of Appeal.

2. Without prejudice to Articles 112 and 113, all the implementing rules referred to in this Regulation shall be adopted in accordance with the procedure laid down in Article 115, after consultation of the Administrative Council on the draft of the measures to be taken.

[6.256]

[Article 115

Procedure

1. The Commission shall be assisted by a committee.

2. Where reference is made to this Article, Articles 5 and 7 of Decision 1999/468/EC[1] shall apply. The period laid down in Article 5(6) of Decision 1999/468/EC shall be set at three months.

3. The committee shall adopt its rules of procedure.]

NOTES

Substituted by Council Regulation 807/2003/EC, Art 49.

[1] OJ L184, 17.7.1999, p 23.

PART EIGHT
TRANSITIONAL AND FINAL PROVISIONS

[6.257]
Article 116
Derogations

1. Notwithstanding Article 10(1)(a) and without prejudice to the provisions of Article 10(2) and (3), a variety shall be deemed to be new also in cases where variety constituents or harvested material thereof have not been sold or otherwise disposed of to others, by or with the consent of the breeder, within the territory of the Community for purposes of exploitation of the variety, earlier than four years, in the case of trees or of vines earlier than six years, before the entry into force of this Regulation, if the date of application is within one year of that date.

2. The provision of paragraph 1 shall apply to such varieties also in cases where a national plant variety right was granted in one or more Member States before the entry into force of this Regulation.

3. Notwithstanding Articles 55 and 56, the technical examination of these varieties shall be carried out to the extent possible by the Office on the basis of the available findings resulting from any proceedings for the grant of a national plant variety right, in agreement with the authority before which these proceedings were held.

4. In the case of a Community plant variety right granted pursuant to paragraphs 1 or 2—

— Article 13(5)(a) shall not apply in relation to essentially derived varieties, the existence of which was a matter of common knowledge in the Community before the date of entry into force of this Regulation.

— Article 14(3), fourth indent shall not apply to farmers who continue to use an established variety in accordance with the authorisation of Article 14(1) if, before the entry into force of this Regulation, they have already used the variety for the purposes described in Article 14(1) without payment of a remuneration; this provision shall apply until 30 June of the seventh year following that of the entry into force of this Regulation. Before that date the Commission shall submit a report on the situation of the established varieties dealing with each variety individually. That period may be extended, in the implementing provisions adopted pursuant to Article 114, in so far as the Commission's report justifies it.

— without prejudice to the rights conferred by national protection, the provisions of Article 16 shall apply *mutatis mutandis* to acts concerning material disposed of to others by the breeder or with his consent prior to the date of entry into force of this Regulation, and effected by person who, prior to that date, have already effected such acts or have made effective and genuine arrangements to do so.

If such earlier acts have involved further propagation which was intended within the meaning of Article 16(a), the authorisation of the holder shall be required for any further propagation after the expiry of the second year, in the case of varieties of vine and tree species after the expiry of the fourth year, following the date of entry into force of this Regulation.

Notwithstanding Article 19, the duration of the Community plant variety right shall be reduced by the longest period—

— during which variety constituents or harvested material thereof have been sold or otherwise disposed of to others, by or with the consent of the breeder, within the territory of the Community for purposes of exploitation of the variety, as established in the findings resulting from the procedure for the grant of the Community plant variety right, in the case of paragraph 1,

— during which any national plant variety right or rights have been effective, in the case of paragraph 2,

but not more than by five years.

[6.258]
Article 117
Transitional provisions

The Office shall be set up in good time to assume fully the tasks incumbent upon it pursuant to this Regulation as from 27 April 1995.

[6.259]
Article 118
Entry into force

1. This Regulation shall enter into force on the day of its publication in the *Official Journal of the European Communities*.

2. Articles 1, 2, 3, 5 to 29 and 49 to 106 shall apply from 27 April 1995.

This Regulation shall be binding in its entirety and directly applicable in all Member States.

COMMISSION REGULATION

(1768/95/EC)

of 24 July 1995

implementing rules on the agricultural exemption provided for in Article 14(3) of Council Regulation (EC) No 2100/94 on Community plant variety rights

NOTES

Date of publication in OJ: OJ L173, 25.7.1995, p 14.

THE COMMISSION OF THE EUROPEAN COMMUNITIES,

Having regard to the Treaty establishing the European Community,

Having regard to Council Regulation (EC) No 2100/94 of 27 July 1994 on Community plant variety rights (the basic Regulation),[1] and in particular Article 14(3) thereof,

Whereas Article 14 of the basic Regulation provides for a derogation from Community plant variety right for the purposes of safeguarding agricultural production (agricultural exemption);

Whereas the conditions to give effect to this derogation and to safeguard the legitimate interests of the breeder and of the farmer shall be established in implementing rules, on the basis of criteria laid down in Article 14(3) of the basic Regulation;

Whereas this Regulation establishes those conditions in specifying, in particular, the obligations of farmers, processors and holders resulting from the aforesaid criteria;

Whereas these obligations relate essentially to the payment, by farmers, of an equitable remuneration to the holder for the use made of the derogation, to the supply of information, to the safeguarding of the identity of the product of the harvest entered for processing with that resulting from processing as well as to the monitoring of compliance with the provisions on the derogation;

Whereas, also, the definition of 'small farmers' who shall not be required to pay a remuneration to the holder for the use made of the derogation, is completed in particular in respect of farmers growing certain fodder plants and potatoes;

Whereas the Commission will thoroughly monitor, throughout the Community, the effects which the definition of 'small farmers' as laid down in the basic Regulation and, in particular concerning the implications of set aside and – in the case of potatoes – the maximum size of the area, in this Regulation may produce with regard to the role of the remuneration as specified in Article 5(3) of this Regulation, and where necessary, make the appropriate proposals or take the appropriate steps with a view to establishing Community-wide coherence in respect of the ratio between the use of licensed propagating material and that of the product of the harvest under the derogation provided for in Article 14 of the basic Regulation;

Whereas, however, it has not yet been possible to assess the extent to which use has been made of comparable derogations under the current legislations of Member States, in relation with the amounts currently charged for the licensed production of propagating material of varieties protected under the aforesaid legislations of Member States;

Whereas, therefore, the Commission can at present not properly define, within the scope of the discretion left to the Community legislator under Article 14(3) of the basic Regulation, the level of the equitable remuneration which must be sensibly lower than the amount charged for the licensed production of propagating material;

Whereas, however, the initial level as well as the system for subsequent adaptations should be specified as soon as possible and not later than 1 July 1997;

Whereas, moreover, this Regulation aims at specifying the connection between the Community plant variety right and the rights which derive from the provisions of Article 14 of the basic Regulation, on one hand, and that between the authorization granted to the farmer and his holding, on the other hand;

Whereas, finally, the consequences of not fulfilling obligations which derive from the provisions concerned should be clarified;

Whereas the Administrative Council has been consulted;

Whereas the provisions provided for in this Regulation are in accordance with the opinion of the Standing Committee on Plant Variety Rights,

NOTES

[1] OJ No L227, 1.9.1994, p 1.

HAS ADOPTED THIS REGULATION—

Part 6 Plant Varieties Protection

CHAPTER I
GENERAL PROVISIONS

[6.260]
Article 1
Scope

1. This Regulation establishes the implementing rules on the conditions to give effect to the derogation provided for in Article 14(1) of the basic Regulation.
2. The conditions shall apply to the rights and their exercise, and to the obligations and their fulfilment, of the holder within the meaning of Article 13(1) of the basic Regulation, as well as to the authorization and its use, and to the obligations and their fulfilment, of the farmer, to the extent that such rights, authorization and obligations derive from the provisions of Article 14 of the basic Regulation. They shall also apply in respect of rights, authorization and obligations which derive from the provisions of Article 14(3) of the basic Regulation for others.
3. Unless otherwise specified in this Regulation, the details relating to the exercise of the rights, to the use of the authorizations or to the fulfilment of the obligations shall be governed by the law of the Member State, including its international private law, in which the farmer's holding on which the derogation is used, is located.

[6.261]
Article 2
Safeguarding interests

1. The conditions referred to in Article 1 shall be implemented both by the holder, representing the breeder, and by the farmer in such a way as to safeguard the legitimate interests of each other.
2. The legitimate interests shall not be considered to be safeguarded if one or more of these interests are adversely affected without account being taken of the need to maintain a reasonable balance between all of them, or of the need for proportionality between the purpose of the relevant condition and the actual effect of the implementation thereof.

CHAPTER 2
THE HOLDER AND THE FARMER

[6.262]
Article 3
The holder

1. The rights and obligations of the holder which derive from the provisions of Article 14 of the basic Regulation, as specified in this Regulation, other than the right on an already quantifiable payment of the equitable remuneration referred to in Article 5, may not be the object of a transfer to others. However, they shall be included in the rights and obligations which are concerned by a transfer of the Community plant variety right in accordance with the provisions of Article 23 of the basic Regulation.
2. Rights referred to in paragraph 1 may be invoked by individual holders, collectively by several holders or by an organization of holders which is established in the Community at Community, national, regional or local level. An organization of holders may act only for its members, and only for those thereof which have given the respective mandate in writing to the organization. It shall act either through one or more of its representatives or through auditors accredited by it, within the limits of their respective mandates.
3. A representative of the holder or of an organization of holders as well as an accredited auditor shall:
   (a) be domiciled or shall have his seat or an establishment within the territory of the Community, and
   (b) be authorized by the holder or the organization in writing, and
   (c) provide evidence for the conditions laid down in (a) and (b), either through reference to relevant information published by holders or communicated by holders to organizations of farmers, or otherwise, and produce, on request, a copy of the written authorization referred to in (b), to any farmer against whom he invokes the rights.

[6.263]
Article 4
The farmer

1. The authorization and obligations of the farmer which derive from the provisions of Article 14 of the basic Regulation, as specified in this regulation or in provisions adopted pursuant to this Regulation, may not be the object of a transfer to others. However, they shall be included in the rights and obligations which are concerned by a transfer of the holding of the farmer, unless, in respect of the obligation to pay the equitable remuneration referred to in Article 5, otherwise agreed in the act of transfer of the holding. The transfer of the authorization and obligations shall take effect at the same time at which the transfer of the holding takes effect.

2. An 'own holding' within the meaning of Article 14(1) of the basic Regulation shall be considered to be any holding or part thereof which the farmer actually exploits for plant growing, whether as his property or otherwise managed under his own responsibility and on his own account, in particular in the case of leaseholds. The disposal of a holding or part thereof for the purpose of exploitation by others shall be regarded as transfer within the meaning of paragraph 1.
3. The person or persons to whom the holding concerned belongs as property at the time at which the fulfilment of an obligation is claimed, shall be deemed to be the farmer, unless they provide the proof that another person is the farmer who must fulfil the obligation, in accordance with the provisions of paragraphs 1 and 2.

CHAPTER 3
REMUNERATION

[6.264]
Article 5
Level of remuneration

1. The level of the equitable remuneration to be paid to the holder pursuant to Article 14(3), fourth indent of the basic Regulation may form the object of a contract between the holder and the farmer concerned.
2. Where such contract has not been concluded or does not apply, the level of remuneration shall be sensibly lower than the amount charged for the licensed production of propagating material of the lowest category qualified for official certification, of the same variety in the same area.

If no licensed production of propagating material of the variety concerned has taken place in the area in which the holding of the farmer is located, and if there is no uniform level of the aforesaid amount throughout the Community, the level of remuneration shall be sensibly lower than the amount which is normally included, for the above purpose, in the price at which propagating material of the lowest category qualified for official certification, of that variety is sold in that area, provided that it is not higher than the aforesaid amount charged in the area in which that propagating material has been produced.
3. The level of remuneration shall be considered to be sensibly lower within the meaning of Article 14(3), fourth indent of the basic Regulation as specified in paragraph 2 above, if it does not exceed the one necessary to establish or to stabilize, as an economic factor determining the extent to which use is made of the derogation, a reasonably balanced ratio between the use of licensed propagating material and the planting of the product of the harvest of the respective varieties covered by a Community plant variety right. Such ratio shall be considered to be reasonably balanced, if it ensures that the holder obtains, as a whole, a legitimate compensation for the total use of his variety.
[4. Where in the case of paragraph 2 the level of remuneration is the subject of agreements between organisations of holders and of farmers, with or without participation of organisations of processors, which are established in the Community at Community, national or regional level respectively, the agreed levels shall be used as guidelines for the determination of the remuneration to be paid in the area and for the species concerned, if these levels and the conditions thereof have been notified to the Commission in writing by authorised representatives of the relevant organisations and if on that basis the agreed levels and conditions thereof have been published in the *Official Gazette* issued by the Community Plant Variety Office.
5. Where in the case of paragraph 2 an agreement as referred to in paragraph 4 does not apply, the remuneration to be paid shall be 50% of the amounts charged for the licensed production of propagating material as specified in paragraph 2.

However, if a Member State has notified the Commission before 1 January 1999 of the imminent conclusion of an agreement as referred to in paragraph 4 between the relevant organisations established at national or regional level, the remuneration to be paid in the area and for the species concerned shall be 40% instead of 50% as specified above, but only in respect of the use of the agricultural exemption made prior to the implementation of such agreement and not later than 1 April 1999.
6. Where in the case of paragraph 5 the farmer has made use, in the relevant period, of the agricultural exemption at a ratio of more than 55 % of the total material of the relevant variety used for his production, the level of the remuneration to be paid in the area and for the species concerned shall be the one which would apply in respect of such a variety if it was protected in the relevant Member State under its national system of plant variety rights, if a national system exists which has established such level, and provided that that level is more than 50% of the amounts charged for the licensed production of propagating material as specified in paragraph 2. In the absence of such level under the national scheme, the provisions of paragraph 5 shall apply irrespective of the ratio of use.
7. By 1 January 2003 at the latest, the provisions of paragraph 5, first subparagraph, and of paragraph 6 shall be reviewed in the light of experiences gained under this Regulation and of developments of the ratio referred to in paragraph 3, with a view to their possible adaptation, by 1 July 2003, as may be necessary to establish or to stabilise the reasonably balanced ratio, stipulated in the aforesaid paragraph, in the whole or part of the Community.]

NOTES

Paras 4–7: added by Commission Regulation 2605/98/EC, Art 1.

[6.265]
Article 6
Individual obligation to payment

1. Without prejudice to the provisions of paragraph 2, the individual obligation of a farmer to pay the equitable remuneration shall come to existence at the time when he actually makes use of the product of the harvest for propagating purposes in the field.

The holder may determine the date and the manner of payment. However, he shall not determine a date of payment which is earlier than the date on which the obligation has come to existence.

2. In the case of a Community plant variety right granted pursuant to Article 116 of the basic Regulation, the individual obligation of a farmer entitled to invoke the provisions of Article 116(4) second indent of the basic Regulation shall come to existence at the time when he actually makes use of the product of the harvest for propagating purposes in the field after 30 June 2001.

[6.266]
Article 7
Small farmers

1. An area on which plants are grown within the meaning of Article 14(3) third indent of the basic Regulation shall be an area which has been planted for regular cultivation and harvesting. In particular, forest land, permanent pastures established for a duration of more than five years, permanent natural green land and assimilated cases as determined in the Standing Committee on Plant Variety Rights shall not be considered to be areas on which plants are grown.

2. Areas of the holding of the farmer on which plants have been grown, but which are land set aside, on a temporary or permanent basis, in the marketing year starting on 1 July and ending on 30 June of the subsequent calendar year ('the marketing year'), in which the payment of the remuneration would be due, shall be considered to be areas on which plants are still grown, if subsidies or compensatory payments are granted by the Community or by the Member State concerned in respect of that set aside.

3. Without prejudice to the provisions laid down in Article 14(3), third indent, first sub-indent of the Basic Regulation, small farmers in the case of other plant species (Article 14(3), third indent, second sub-indent of the Basic Regulation) shall be considered to be farmers who

(a) in the case of fodder plants coming under that latter provision: irrespective of the area on which they grow plants other than those fodder plants, do not grow those fodder plants for a duration of not more than five years on an area bigger than the area which would be needed to produce 92 tonnes of cereals per harvest,

(b) in the case of potatoes: irrespective of the area on which they grow plants other than potatoes, do not grow potatoes on an area bigger than the area which would be needed to produce 185 tonnes of potatoes per harvest.

4. The calculation of the areas referred to in paragraphs 1, 2 and 3 shall be made, for the territory of each Member State,

— in the case of plant species to which Council Regulation (EEC) No 1765/92[1] applies, and in the case of fodder plants other than those already coming under the provisions thereof, in accordance with the provisions of that Regulation, and in particular Articles 3 and 4 thereof, or with provisions adopted pursuant to that Regulation, and

— in the case of potatoes, on the basis of the average yield per hectare established in the Member State concerned, in accordance with the statistical information delivered pursuant to Council Regulation (EEC) No 959/93[2] concerning statistical information to be supplied by Member States on crop products other than cereals.

5. A farmer who claims to be a 'small farmer' shall, in the case of dispute, provide the proof that the requirements for this category of farmers are met. However, the requirements for a 'small producer' within the meaning of Article 8(1) and (2) of Council Regulation (EEC) No 1765/92 shall not be applicable for that purpose, unless the holder agrees to the contrary.

NOTES

[1] OJ No L181, 1.7.1992, p 12.

[2] OJ No L98, 24.4.1993, p 1.

CHAPTER 4
INFORMATION

[6.267]
Article 8
Information by the farmer

1. The details of the relevant information to be provided by the farmer to the holder pursuant to Article 14(3), sixth indent of the basic Regulation may form the object of a contract between the holder and the farmer concerned.

2. Where such contract has not been concluded or does not apply, the farmer shall, without prejudice to information requirements under other Community legislation or under legislation of Member States, on request of the holder, be required to provide a statement of relevant information to the holder. The following items shall be considered to be relevant:

(a) the name of the farmer, the place of his domicile and the address of his holding,

(b) the fact whether the farmer has made use of the product of the harvest belonging to one or more varieties of the holder for planting in the field or fields of his holding,

(c) if the farmer has made such use, the amount of the product of the harvest belonging to the variety or varieties concerned, which has been used by the farmer in accordance with Article 14(1) of the basic Regulation,

(d) under the same condition, the name and address of the person or persons who have supplied a service of processing the relevant product of the harvest for him for planting,

(e) if the information obtained under (b), (c) or (d) cannot be confirmed in accordance with the provisions of Article 14, the amount of licensed propagating material of the varieties concerned used as well as the name and address of the supplier or suppliers thereof, and

(f) in the case of a farmer invoking the provisions of Article 116(4) second indent of the Basic Regulation, whether he has already used the variety concerned for the purpose described in Article 14(1) of the Basic Regulation without payment of a remuneration, and if so, since when.

3. The information under paragraph 2(b), (c), (d) and (e) shall refer to the current marketing year, and to one or more of the three preceding marketing years for which the farmer had not previously provided relevant information on request made by the holder in accordance with the provisions of paragraphs 4 or 5.

However, the first marketing year to which the information refers, shall be not earlier than the one in which the first of such requests for information was made in respect of the variety or varieties and the farmer concerned, or, alternatively, in which the farmer acquired propagating material of the variety or varieties concerned, if this was accompanied by information at least on the filing of the application for the grant of a Community plant variety right or on the grant of such right as well as on possible conditions relating to the use of that propagating material.

In the case of varieties coming under the provisions of Article 116 of the Basic Regulation and in respect of farmers entitled to invoke the provisions of Article 116(4), second indent of the basic Regulation, the first marketing year shall be 2001/02.

4. In his request, the holder shall specify his name and address, the variety or varieties in respect of which he is interested in information, as well as the reference or references to the relevant Community plant variety right or rights. If required by the farmer, the request shall be made in writing, and evidence for holdership shall be provided. Without prejudice to the provisions of paragraph 5, the request shall be made directly to the farmer concerned.

5. A request which has not been made directly to the farmer concerned, shall be considered to comply with the provisions of paragraph 4, third sentence, if it is sent to farmers through the following bodies or persons, with their prior agreement respectively:

- organizations of farmers or cooperatives, concerning all farmers who are members of such organization or cooperative, or,
- processors, concerning all farmers to whom they have supplied a service of processing the relevant product of the harvest for planting, in the current marketing year and in the three preceding marketing years, starting in the marketing year as specified in paragraph 3, or,
- suppliers of licensed propagating material of varieties of the holder, concerning all farmers to whom they have supplied such propagating material in the current marketing year and in the three preceding marketing years, starting in the marketing year as specified in paragraph 3.

6. For a request made in accordance with the provisions of paragraph 5, the specification of individual farmers is not required. The organizations, cooperatives, processors or suppliers may be authorized by the farmers concerned to forward the required information to the holder.

[6.268]
Article 9
Information by the processor

1. The details of the relevant information to be provided by the processor to the holder pursuant to Article 14(3), sixth indent of the basic Regulation may form the object of a contract between the holder and the processor concerned.

2. Where such contract has not been concluded or does not apply, the processor shall, without prejudice to information requirements under other Community legislation or under legislation of Member States, on request of the holder, be required to provide a statement of relevant information to the holder. The following items shall be considered to be relevant:

(a) the name of the processor, the place of his domicile and the name and address registered for his business;

(b) the fact whether the processor has supplied a service of processing the product of the harvest belonging to one or more varieties of the holder for planting, where the variety or varieties were declared or otherwise known to the processor;

(c) if the processor has supplied such service, the amount of the product of the harvest belonging to the variety or varieties concerned, which has been processed for planting, by the processor, and the total amount resulting from that processing;

(d) the dates and places of the processing referred to in (c); and (e) the name and address of the person or persons to whom he has supplied the service of processing referred to in (c), and the respective amounts.

3. The information under paragraph 2(b), (c), (d) and (e) shall refer to the current marketing year and to one or more of the three preceding marketing years for which the holder has not yet made an earlier request in accordance with the provisions of paragraphs 4 or 5; however, the first marketing year to which the information refers, shall be the one in which the first of such requests was made in respect of the variety or varieties and the processor concerned.

4. The provisions of Article 8(4) shall apply *mutatis mutandis*.

5. A request which has not been made directly to the processor concerned, shall be considered to comply with the provisions of Article 8(4), third sentence, if it is sent to processors through the following bodies or persons, with their prior agreement respectively:

— organizations of processors in the Community which are established at Community, national, regional or local level, concerning all processors who are members of, or represented in, such organization,

— farmers, concerning all processors who have supplied a service of processing the relevant product of the harvest to them for planting, in the current marketing year and in the three preceding marketing years, starting in the marketing year as specified in paragraph 3.

6. For a request made in accordance with the provisions of paragraph 5, the specification of individual processors is not required. The organizations or farmers may be authorized by the processors concerned to forward the required information to the holder.

[6.269]
Article 10
Information by the holder

1. The details of the information to be provided by the holder to the farmer pursuant to Article 14(3), fourth indent of the basic Regulation may form the object of a contract between the farmer and the holder concerned.

2. Where such contract has not been concluded or does not apply, the holder shall, without prejudice to information requirements under other Community legislation or under legislation of Member States, on request of the farmer from whom the holder has claimed the payment of the remuneration referred to in Article 5, be required to provide a statement of relevant information to the farmer. The following items shall be considered to be relevant:

— the amount charged for the licensed production of propagating material of the lowest category qualified for official certification, of the same variety in the area in which the holding of the farmer is located, or,

— if no licensed production of propagating material of the variety concerned has taken place in the are a in which the holding of the farmer is located, and if there is no uniform level of the aforesaid amount throughout the Community, the amount which is normally included, for the above purpose, in the price at which propagating material of the lowest category qualified for official certification, of that variety is sold in that area, as well as the aforesaid amount charged in the area in which that propagating material has been produced.

[6.270]
Article 11
Information by official bodies

1. A request for information on the actual use of material, by planting, of specific species or varieties, or on the results of such use, which a holder addresses to an official body, must be made in writing. In this request, the holder shall specify his name and address, the variety or varieties in respect of which he is interested in information and the type of information he seeks. He also shall provide evidence for his holdership.

2. The official body may, without prejudice to the provisions of Article 12, withhold the requested information only, if

— it is not involved in the monitoring of agricultural production, or

— it is not allowed, under Community rules or rules of Member States governing the general discretion applicable in respect of activities of official bodies, to provide such information to holders, or

— it is under its discretion, pursuant to the Community legislation or the legislation of Member States under which the information has been collected, to withhold such information, or

— the requested information is not or no longer available, or

— such information cannot be obtained through ordinary performance of the tasks of the official body, or

— such information can only be obtained with additional burden or costs, or

— such information relates specifically to material which does not belong to varieties of the holder.

The official bodies concerned shall inform the Commission on the manner in which they exercise the discretion referred to in the third indent above.

3. In providing the information, the official body shall not differenciate between holders. The official body may provide the requested information in making copies available to the holder, which have been produced from documents containing information additional to that relating to material belonging to varieties of the holder, provided that it is ensured that any possibility to identify individuals protected under the provisions referred to in Article 12 has been removed.

4. If the official body takes the decision to withhold the requested information, it shall inform the requesting holder thereof in writing and indicate the reason for this decision.

[6.271]
Article 12
Protection of personal data

1. Any person who is providing or receiving information under the provisions of Articles 8, 9, 10 or 11 shall be subject, in respect of personal data, to the provisions of Community legislation or of legislation of Member States on the protection of individuals with regard to the processing and free movement of personal data.

2. Any person receiving information under the provisions of Articles 8, 9, 10 or 11 shall not, without prior consent of the person who has supplied the information, pass any of this information to another person or use it for any purpose other than for the exercise of the Community plant variety right or for the use of the authorization provided for in Article 14 of the Basic Regulation, respectively.

CHAPTER 5
OTHER OBLIGATIONS

[6.272]
Article 13
Obligations in the case of processing outside the holding of the farmer

1. Without prejudice to the restrictions which Member States may have established pursuant to Article 14(3) second indent of the basic Regulation, the product of the harvest of a variety which is covered by a Community plant variety right shall not, without the prior consent of the holder, be moved from the holding on which it was obtained, for the purpose of being processed for planting, unless the farmer:

(a) has implemented appropriate measures to ensure identity of the product entered for processing with that resulting from processing; and

(b) makes sure that the actual processing is carried out by a processor for the supply of services of processing the product of the harvest for planting, who has:

— either been registered under legislation of the Member State concerned adopted on the grounds of public interest, or has undertaken to the farmer to notify this activity, as far as varieties covered by a Community plant variety right are concerned, to the competent body established, designated or authorized in the Member State for that purpose, either by an official body or by an organization of holders, farmers or processors, for subsequent inclusion in a list established by the said competent body, and

— has undertaken to the farmer to also implement appropriate measures to ensure identity of the product entered by the farmer for processing with that resulting from processing.

2. For the purpose of the listing of processors as specified in paragraph 1, Member States may lay down requirements of qualification to be met by processors.

3. The registers and the lists referred to in paragraph 1 shall be published or be made available to organisations of holders, farmers and processors respectively.

4. The lists referred to in paragraph 1 shall be established not later than 1 July 1997.

CHAPTER 6
MONITORING BY THE HOLDER

[6.273]
Article 14
Monitoring of farmers

1. For the purpose of monitoring, by the holder, compliance with the provisions of Article 14 of the basic Regulation as specified in this Regulation, as far as the fulfilment of obligations of the farmer is concerned, the farmer shall, on request of the holder:

(a) provide evidence supporting his statements of information under Article 8, through disclosure of available relevant documents such as invoices, used labels, or any other appropriate device such as that required pursuant Article 13(1) (a), relating to:

— the supply of services of processing the product of the harvest of a variety of the holder for planting, by any third person, or

— in the case of Articles 8(2)(e), the supply of propagating material of a variety of the holder, or
— through the demonstration of land or storage facilities.

(b) make available or accessible the proof required under Article 4(3) or 7(5).

2. Without prejudice to other Community legislation or to legislation of Member States, farmers shall be required to conserve any of such document or device referred to in paragraph 1 for at least the period of time specified in Article 8(3), provided that, in the case of used labels, the information by which the propagating material referred to in Article 8(3) second subparagraph was accompanied included the advice for the conservation of the label relating to that material.

[6.274]
Article 15
Monitoring of processors

1. For the purpose of monitoring, by the holder, compliance with the provisions of Article 14 of the basic Regulation as specified in this Regulation, as far as the fulfilment of obligations of the processor is concerned, the processor shall, on request of the holder, provide evidence supporting his statements of information under Article 9, through disclosure of available relevant documents such as invoices, devices suitable for the identification of material, or any other appropriate device such as that required pursuant to Article 13(1) (b), second indent, or samples of processed material, relating to his supply of services of processing the product of the harvest of a variety of the holder to farmers for planting, or through the demonstration of processing or storage facilities.

2. Without prejudice to other Community legislation or to legislation of Member States, processors shall be required to conserve any of such document or device referred to in paragraph 1 for at least the period of time specified in Article 9(3).

[6.275]
Article 16
Manner of monitoring

1. The monitoring shall be carried out by the holder. He may make appropriate arrangements to ensure assistance from organizations of farmers, processors, cooperatives or other circles of the agricultural community.

2. Conditions relating to the methods of monitoring laid down in agreements between organizations of holders and of farmers or processors, which are established in the Community at Community, national, regional or local level respectively, shall be used as guidelines, if these agreements have been notified to the Commission in writing by authorized representatives of the relevant organizations and published in the 'Official Gazette' issued by the Community Plant Variety Office.

CHAPTER 7
INFRINGEMENT AND SPECIAL CIVIL LAW CLAIMS

[6.276]
Article 17
Infringement

The holder may invoke the rights conferred by the Community plant variety right against a person who contravenes any of the conditions or limitations attached to the derogation pursuant to Article 14 of the basic Regulation as specified in this Regulation.

[6.277]
Article 18
Special civil law claims

1. A person referred to in Article 17 may be sued by the holder to fulfil his obligations pursuant to Article 14(3) of the basic Regulation as specified in this Regulation.

2. If such person has repeatedly and intentionally not complied with his obligation pursuant to Article 14(3) 4th indent of the basic Regulation, in respect of one or more varieties of the same holder, the liability to compensate the holder for any further damage pursuant to Article 94(2) of the basic Regulation shall cover at least a lump sum calculated on the basis of the quadruple average amount charged for the licensed production of a corresponding quantity of propagating material of protected varieties of the plant species concerned in the same area, without prejudice to the compensation of any higher damage.

CHAPTER 8
FINAL PROVISIONS

[6.278]
Article 19
Entry into force

This Regulation shall enter into force on the day of its publication in the *Official Journal of the European Communities*.

This Regulation shall be binding in its entirety and directly applicable in all Member States.

COMMISSION REGULATION

(874/2009/EC)

of 17 September 2009

establishing implementing rules for the application of Council Regulation (EC) No 2100/94 as regards proceedings before the Community Plant Variety Office (recast)

NOTES

Date of publication in OJ: OJ L251, 24.9.2009, p 3.

THE COMMISSION OF THE EUROPEAN COMMUNITIES,

Having regard to the Treaty establishing the European Community,

Having regard to Council Regulation (EC) No 2100/94 of 27 July 1994 on Community plant variety rights,[1] and in particular Article 114 thereof,

Whereas:

(1) Commission Regulation (EC) No 1239/95 of 31 May 1995 establishing implementing rules for the application of Council Regulation (EC) No 2100/94 as regards proceedings before the Community Plant Variety Office[2] has been substantially amended several times.[3] Since further amendments are to be made, it should be recast in the interests of clarity.

(2) Regulation (EC) No 2100/94 (the basic Regulation) creates a new Community system of plant variety rights, whereby a plant variety right is valid throughout the Community.

(3) Such a system should be carried out in an effective manner by the Community Plant Variety Office (the Office), which is assisted by Examination Offices in conducting the technical examination of the plant varieties concerned and which may avail itself of the services of designated national agencies or one of its own sub-offices established for that purpose. In that regard, it is indispensable to define the relationship between the Office and its own sub-offices, the Examination Offices and national agencies.

(4) A fee for the conduct of the technical examination should be paid by the Office to the Examination Offices on the basis of full recovery of costs incurred. Uniform methods for the calculation of the costs should be established by the Administrative Council.

(5) Decisions of the Office may be appealed against before its Board of Appeal. Provisions on the procedure of the Board of Appeal should be adopted. Further Boards of Appeal may be established, if necessary, by the Administrative Council.

(6) Examination reports made under the responsibility of authorities of a Member State or a third country which is a member of the International Union for the Protection of New Varieties of Plants (UPOV) should be considered a sufficient basis for decision.

(7) The use of electronic means for the filing of applications, objections or appeals and the service of documents by the Office should be permitted. Moreover, the Office should be given the possibility to issue certificates for Community plant variety rights in electronic form. Publication of information regarding Community plant variety rights should also be possible by electronic means. Finally, the electronic storage of files relating to proceedings should be allowed.

(8) The President of the Office should be empowered to determine all necessary details with respect to the use of electronic means of communication or storage.

(9) Certain provisions of Articles 23, 29, 34, 35, 36, 42, 45, 46, 49, 50, 58, 81, 85, 87, 88 and 100 of the basic Regulation already explicitly provide that detailed rules shall or may be drawn up for their implementation. Other detailed rules should be drawn up for the same purpose if clarification is required.

(10) The entry into effect of a transfer of a Community plant variety right or a transfer of an entitlement thereto should be defined in the rules relating to the entries in the Registers.

(11) The Administrative Council of the Community Plant Variety Office has been consulted.

(12) The rules provided for in this Regulation are in accordance with the opinion of the Standing Committee on Plant Variety Rights,

NOTES

[1] OJ L227, 1.9.1994, p 1.

[2] OJ L121, 1.6.1995, p 37.

[3] See Annex II.

HAS ADOPTED THIS REGULATION:

Part 6 Plant Varieties Protection

TITLE I
PARTIES TO PROCEEDINGS, OFFICE AND EXAMINATION OFFICES

CHAPTER I
PARTIES TO PROCEEDINGS

[6.279]
Article 1
Parties to proceedings

1. The following persons may be party to proceedings before the Community Plant Variety Office, hereinafter referred to as 'the Office':
   (a) the applicant for a Community plant variety right;
   (b) the objector referred to in Article 59(2) of Regulation (EC) No 2100/94, hereinafter referred to as 'the basic Regulation';
   (c) the holder or holders of the Community plant variety right, hereinafter referred to as 'the holder';
   (d) any person whose application or request is a prerequisite for a decision to be taken by the Office.

2. The Office may allow participation in the proceedings by any person other than those referred to in paragraph 1 who is directly and individually concerned, upon written request.

3. Any natural or legal person as well as any body qualifying as a legal person under the law applicable to that body shall be considered a person within the meaning of paragraphs 1 and 2.

[6.280]
Article 2
Designation of parties to proceedings

[1. Parties to proceedings shall be designated by their name, address and email address, where an email address is used by the party concerned.

2. Natural persons shall be indicated by their family name and given names. Legal persons as well as companies or firms shall be indicated by their official designations, as recorded in the respective Member State or third country.]

3. Addresses shall contain all the relevant administrative information, including the name of the State in which the party to proceedings is resident or where his seat or establishment is located. Only one address should preferably be indicated for each party to proceedings; where several addresses are indicated, only the address mentioned first shall be taken into account, except where the party to proceedings designates one of the other addresses as an address for service.

The President of the Office shall determine the details concerning the address including any relevant details of other data communication links.

4. Where a party to proceedings is a legal person, it shall also be designated by the name and address of the natural person legally representing the party to proceedings by virtue of the relevant national legislation. The provisions of paragraph 2 shall apply *mutatis mutandis* to such natural person.

The Office may permit derogations from the provisions of the first sentence of the first subparagraph.

5. Where the Commission or a Member State is party to proceedings, it shall communicate a representative for each proceeding in which it takes part.

NOTES

Paras 1, 2: substituted by Commission Implementing Regulation 2016/1448/EU, Art 1(1).

[6.281]
Article 3
Languages of parties to proceedings

1. A language, being an official language of the European Union, chosen by a party to proceedings for use in the document first submitted to the Office and signed for the purpose of submission shall be used by the party to proceedings until a final decision is delivered by the Office.

[A successor in title as referred to in Article 23(1) of the basic Regulation may however request that another official language of the European Union be used during future proceedings, provided that such request is submitted upon the entry of the transfer of a Community plant variety right into the Register of Community Plant Variety Rights.]

2. If a party to proceedings files a document signed for that purpose by him in any other official language of the European Union than that to be used pursuant to paragraph 1, the document shall be deemed to have been received when the Office holds a translation thereof, provided by other services. The Office may permit derogations from this requirement.

3. If, in oral proceedings, a party uses a language other than the official language of the European Union used by the competent members of the staff of the Office, by other parties to proceedings, or by both, being the language to be used by him, he shall make provision for simultaneous

interpretation into that official language. If no such provision is made, oral proceedings may continue in the languages used by the competent members of the staff of the Office and by other parties to the proceedings.

NOTES

Para 1: words in square brackets inserted by Commission Implementing Regulation 2016/1448/EU, Art 1(2).

[6.282]
Article 4
Languages in oral proceedings and in the taking of evidence

1. Any party to proceedings and any witness or expert who gives evidence in oral proceedings may use any of the official languages of the European Union Communities.

[2. Should the taking of evidence referred to in paragraph 1 be allowed at the request of a party to proceedings, then, should a party to proceedings, a witness or expert be unable to express himself adequately in any of the official languages of the European Union, he may be heard only if the party who made the request makes provision for interpretation into the official language of the European Union used by all parties to proceedings or by the members of the staff of the Office.

Parties to the proceedings, a witness or expert, and the members of the staff of the Office or the Board of Appeal may agree that during the oral proceedings only one of the official languages of the European Union shall be used.

The Office may allow derogations from the first subparagraph.]

3. Statements made by the members of the staff of the Office, by parties to proceedings, witnesses or experts in one of the official languages of the European Union during oral proceedings or taking of evidence shall be entered in the minutes in the language used. Statements made in any other language shall be entered in the language used by the members of the staff of the Office.

NOTES

Para 2: substituted by Commission Implementing Regulation 2016/1448/EU, Art 1(3).

[6.283]
Article 5
Translation of documents of parties to proceedings

[1. Where a party to proceedings files a document in a language other than any official language of the European Union, the Office may require from that party a translation of that document into one of the official languages of the European Union used by that party or by the members of the staff of the Office or of the Board of Appeal.

2. Where a translation of a document is filed by a party to proceedings, the Office may require the filing, within such time as it may specify, of a certificate that the translation corresponds to the original text. The translations of lengthy documents may be confined to extracts or summaries. The Office or the Board of Appeal may however, either at their own motion or at the request of a party to the proceeding, at any time require a more extensive or complete translation of such documents.

Parties to proceedings and the members of the staff of the Office or of the Board of Appeal may agree to have a translation of a document in only one of the official languages of the European Union.]

3. Failure to file the translation referred to in paragraph 1 and the certificate referred to in paragraph 2 shall lead to the document being deemed not to have been received.

NOTES

Paras 1, 2: substituted by Commission Implementing Regulation 2016/1448/EU, Art 1(4).

CHAPTER II
THE OFFICE

SECTION 1
COMMITTEES OF THE OFFICE

[6.284]
Article 6
Qualification of members of the Committees

1. The Committees referred to in Article 35(2) of the basic Regulation shall, at the discretion of the President of the Office, be composed of technical or legally qualified members, or both.

2. A technical member shall hold a degree, or shall be qualified by recognised experience, in the field of plant science.

[3. A legally qualified member shall be a graduate in law with recognised experience in the field of intellectual property, plant variety rights or plant variety registration.]

NOTES

Para 3: substituted by Commission Implementing Regulation 2016/1448/EU, Art 1(5).

[6.285]
Article 7
Decisions of the Committee

1. A Committee shall, besides taking the decisions referred to in Article 35(2) of the basic Regulation, deal with:

— the non-suspension of a decision pursuant to Article 67(2) of the basic Regulation,
— interlocutory revision pursuant to Article 70 of the basic Regulation,
— the *restitutio in integrum* pursuant to Article 80 of the basic Regulation, and
— the award of costs pursuant to Article 85(2) of the basic Regulation and Article 75 of this Regulation.

2. A decision of the Committee shall be taken by a majority of its members.

[6.286]
Article 8
Power of individual members of the Committees

1. The Committee shall designate one of its members as rapporteur on its behalf.
2. The rapporteur may in particular:

(a) perform the duties under Article 25 and monitor the submission of reports by the Examination Offices, referred to in Articles 13 and 14;
(b) pursue the procedure within the Office, including the communication of any deficiencies to be remedied by a party to proceedings and the setting of time limits; and
(c) ensure a close consultation and exchange of information with the parties to the proceedings.

[6.287]
Article 9
Role of the President

The President of the Office shall ensure the consistency of decisions taken under his authority. He shall in particular lay down the conditions under which decisions on objections lodged pursuant to Article 59 of the basic Regulation, and also decisions pursuant to Articles 61, 62, 63 or 66 of that Regulation, are taken.

[6.288]
[Article 10
Consultations

Members of the staff of the Office may use, free of charge, the premises of national agencies referred to in Article 30(4) of the basic Regulation and those of Examination Offices and agencies referred to in Article 13 and Article 14, respectively, of this Regulation, for holding periodical consultation days with parties to proceedings and third persons.]

NOTES

Substituted by Commission Implementing Regulation 2016/1448/EU, Art 1(6).

SECTION 2
BOARDS OF APPEAL

[6.289]
Article 11
Boards of Appeal

1. For the purpose of deciding on appeals from the decisions referred to in Article 67 of the basic Regulation, a Board of Appeal is established. If necessary, the Administrative Council may, on a proposal from the Office, establish more Boards of Appeal. In that event, it shall determine the allocation of work between the Boards of Appeal thus established.
2. Each Board of Appeal shall consist of technical and legally qualified members. Article 6(2) and (3) shall apply *mutatis mutandis*. The chairman shall be a legally qualified member.
3. The examination of an appeal shall be assigned by the chairman of the Board of Appeal to one of its members as rapporteur. Such assignment may include, where appropriate, the taking of evidence.
4. Decisions of the Board of Appeal shall be taken by a majority of its members.
[5. The Chairman and the members of the Board of Appeal shall receive remuneration for the performance of their assignments. That remuneration shall be determined by the Administrative Council of the Office and be based on a proposal by the President of the Office.]

NOTES

Para 5: added by Commission Implementing Regulation 2016/1448/EU, Art 1(7).

[6.290]
Article 12
Registry attached to a Board of Appeal

1. The President of the Office shall attach a registry to the Board of Appeal; members of the staff of the Office shall be excluded from the registry if they have participated in proceedings relating to the decisions under appeal.

2. The employees of the registry shall in particular be responsible for:
— drawing up the minutes of oral proceedings and taking evidence pursuant to Article 63 of this Regulation,
— apportioning costs pursuant to Article 85(5) of the basic Regulation and Article 76 of this Regulation, and
— confirming any settlement of costs referred to in Article 77 of this Regulation.

CHAPTER III
EXAMINATION OFFICES

[6.291]
Article 13
Designation of an Examination Office referred to in Article 55(1) of the basic Regulation

[1. Where the Administrative Council entrusts the competent office in a Member State with responsibility for the technical examination for certain genera or species, the President of the Office shall notify such office, hereinafter referred to as "the Examination Office", of that fact, hereinafter referred to as "the designation of an Examination Office". That designation shall take effect on the day of that notification. This provision shall apply *mutatis mutandis* to the amendment or cancellation of the designation of an Examination Office, subject to Article 15(6) of this Regulation.]

[1a. The Administrative Council may make the designation of an Examination Office, or an extension of the scope of an existing designation of an Examination Office subject to compliance with the relevant requirements, guidelines and procedures of the Office.

Should an Examination Office make use of technically qualified bodies referred to in Article 56(3) of the basic Regulation, the Examination Office shall ensure compliance with the relevant requirements, guidelines and procedures of the Office.

The Office shall conduct an audit to check whether the Examination Office complies with the relevant requirements, guidelines and procedures of the Office. Following an audit, the Office shall draw up an audit report.

The Administrative Council shall base its decision on the designation of an Examination Office on the audit report drawn up by the Office.

1b. For the extension of the scope of an existing designation of an Examination Office initiated by the Office, the Administrative Council may, in the absence of an audit report, base its decision on a report drawn up by the Office in which compliance with the relevant requirements, guidelines and procedures of the Office is assessed.

For the extension of the scope of an existing designation of an Examination Office initiated by an Examination Office, the Administrative Council shall base its decision on an audit report drawn up by the Office.

1c. Based on an audit report, the Administrative Council may decide to cancel, or reduce the scope of, an existing designation of an Examination Office.

Based on a request by an Examination Office, to which the Office agrees, the scope of an existing designation of an Examination Office may be reduced. The Office shall implement the reduction in the agreement referred to in Article 15(1).]

2. A member of the staff of the Examination Office taking part in a technical examination shall not be allowed to make any unauthorised use of, or disclose to any unauthorised person, any facts, documents and information coming to their knowledge in the course of or in connection with the technical examination. They shall continue to be bound by this obligation after the termination of the technical examination concerned, after leaving the service and after the cancellation of the designation of the Examination Office concerned.

3. Paragraph 2 shall apply *mutatis mutandis* to material of the plant variety which has been made available to the Examination Office by the applicant.

[The Office may develop guiding principles concerning the use by Examination Offices of plant material that has been submitted for distinctiveness, uniformity and stability testing in the framework of applications for a Community plant variety right. Such guiding principles may include conditions under which such plant material may be transferred between Examination Offices.]

4. The Office shall monitor compliance with paragraphs 2 and 3 and shall decide on the exclusion of or objections raised to members of the staff of Examination Offices in accordance with Article 81(2) of the basic Regulation.

NOTES

Para 1: substituted by Commission Implementing Regulation 2016/1448/EU, Art 1(8)(a).
Paras 1a–1c: inserted by Commission Implementing Regulation 2016/1448/EU, Art 1(8)(b).

Para 3: words in square brackets inserted by Commission Implementing Regulation 2016/1448/EU, Art 1(8)(c).

[6.292]
Article 14
[Designation of an agency or establishment of a sub-office referred to in Article 55(2) of the basic Regulation]

[1. Where the Office intends to entrust an agency with responsibility for the technical examination of varieties in accordance with Article 55(2) of the basic Regulation, hereinafter referred to as "the designation of an agency", it shall transmit an explanatory statement on the technical suitability of that agency as an Examination Office to the Administrative Council for consent. Article 13(1a), (1b) and (1c) shall apply *mutatis mutandis*.]

2. Where the Office intends to establish its own sub-office for the technical examination of varieties in accordance with Article 55(2) of the basic Regulation, it shall transmit an explanatory statement on the technical and economic appropriateness of establishing such a sub-office for that purpose and on the siting of such sub-office to the Administrative Council for consent.

[3. Where the Administrative Council gives its consent to the explanatory statements referred to in paragraphs 1 and 2, the President of the Office shall notify the designation of an agency to the agency concerned, or shall publish the establishment of a sub-office in the *Official Journal of the European Union*. Such designation or establishment may be cancelled only with the consent of the Administrative Council. Article 13(2) and (3) shall apply *mutatis mutandis* to the members of the staff of the agency referred to in paragraph 1 of this Article.]

NOTES

Heading: substituted by Commission Implementing Regulation 2016/1448/EU, Art 1(9)(a).
Para 1: substituted by Commission Implementing Regulation 2016/1448/EU, Art 1(9)(b).
Para 3: substituted by Commission Implementing Regulation 2016/1448/EU, Art 1(9)(c).

[6.293]
Article 15
Procedure for designation

[1. The designation of an Examination Office or agency shall take effect by a written agreement between the Office and the Examination Office or agency, providing for the performance by the Examination Office or agency of the technical examination of plant varieties for certain genera and species and for the payment by the Office of the fee referred to in Article 58 of the basic Regulation. In the case of a sub-office referred to in Article 14(2) of this Regulation, the establishment shall be by internal rules on working methods issued by the Office.

2. The effect of the written agreement referred to in paragraph 1 shall be such that acts performed after the signing of that agreement or to be performed by members of the staff of the Examination Office in accordance therewith shall be considered, as far as third parties are concerned, to be acts of the Office.]

3. Where the Examination Office intends to avail itself of the services of other technically qualified bodies in accordance with Article 56(3) of the basic Regulation, such bodies shall be named in the written agreement with the Office. Article 81(2) of the basic Regulation and Article 13(2) and (3) of this Regulation shall apply *mutatis mutandis* to the staff members concerned, who shall sign a written undertaking to observe confidentiality.

4. The Office shall pay the Examination Office a fee for the conduct of the technical examination, on the basis of full recovery of costs incurred. The Administrative Council shall determine uniform methods for calculating the costs and the uniform constituents of the costs, which shall apply to all designated Examination Offices.

[5. An Examination Office shall periodically submit to the Office on request a breakdown of the costs of the technical examinations performed and of the maintenance of the necessary reference collections. In the circumstances set out in paragraph 3, a separate auditing report of the bodies shall be submitted to the Office by the Examination Office.

In the circumstances set out in paragraph 3, the Examination Office shall take into account costs incurred by such a body. The Office shall lay down the format of breakdown of the costs. If, after two requests from the Office, the Examination Office fails to provide the Office with the breakdown of the costs within the deadline established by the Office, the fee referred to in paragraph 4 may be reduced by 20%.

6. Any cancellation or amendment of the designation of an Examination Office or agency may not take effect prior to the day on which the revocation of the written agreement referred to in paragraph 1 takes effect.]

NOTES

Paras 1, 2: substituted by Commission Implementing Regulation 2016/1448/EU, Art 1(10)(a).
Paras 5, 6: substituted by Commission Implementing Regulation 2016/1448/EU, Art 1(10)(b).

TITLE II
SPECIFIC PROCEEDINGS BEFORE THE OFFICE

CHAPTER I
APPLICATION FOR A COMMUNITY PLANT VARIETY RIGHT

SECTION 1
ACTION OF THE APPLICANT

[6.294]
Article 16
Filing of the application

1. An application for a Community plant variety right shall be filed at the Office, at the national agencies designated or the sub-offices established pursuant to Article 30(4) of the basic Regulation.

Where the application is filed at the Office it may be filed in paper format or by electronic means. Where it is filed at the national agencies or sub-offices it shall be filed in paper format in duplicate.

2. The information sent to the Office in accordance with Article 49(1)(b) of the basic Regulation shall contain:

— particulars for identifying the applicant and, where appropriate, his procedural representative,
— the national agency or sub-office at which the application for a Community plant variety right was filed, and
— the provisional designation of the variety concerned.

3. The Office shall make available the following forms free of charge:

(a) an application form and a technical questionnaire, for the purposes of filing an application for a Community plant variety right;
(b) a form for forwarding the information referred to in paragraph 2, indicating the consequences of any failure of the forwarding.

4. The applicant shall fill in and sign the forms provided for in paragraph 3. Where the application is submitted by electronic means it shall comply with the second subparagraph of Article 57(3) as regards the signature.

[6.295]
Article 17
Receipt of the application

[1. Where a national agency or sub-office exercising the specific administrative functions referred to in Article 30(4) of the basic Regulation receives an application, it shall, by electronic means, send to the Office a confirmation of receipt and forward the application in accordance with Article 49(2) of the basic Regulation. The confirmation of receipt shall include the file number of the national agency or sub-office, the nature and the number of forwarded documents and the date of receipt at the national agency or sub-office. The national agency or sub-office shall transmit to the applicant a copy of the confirmation of receipt sent to the Office, by electronic or other means.

2. Where the Office receives an application from the applicant directly or via a national agency or sub-office, it shall, without prejudice to other provisions, mark the documents making up the application with a file number and the date of receipt at the Office and issue a confirmation of receipt to the applicant. That confirmation shall include the file number of the Office, the nature and the number of documents received, the date of receipt at the Office and the date of application within the meaning of Article 51 of the basic Regulation. A copy of the confirmation of receipt shall be transmitted to the national agency or sub-office via which the Office has received the application.]

3. If the Office receives an application via a sub-office or national agency more than one month after its filing by the applicant, the 'date of application' within the meaning of Article 51 of the basic Regulation may not be earlier than the date of receipt at the Office, unless the Office establishes on the basis of sufficient documentary evidence that the applicant has forwarded an information to it in accordance with Article 49(1)(b) of the basic Regulation and Article 16(2) of this Regulation.

NOTES

Paras 1, 2: substituted by Commission Implementing Regulation 2016/1448/EU, Art 1(11).

[6.296]
Article 18
Conditions laid down in Article 50(1) of the basic Regulation

1. If the Office finds that the application does not comply with the conditions laid down in Article 50(1) of the basic Regulation, it shall notify to the applicant the deficiencies it has found, stating that only such date as sufficient information remedying those deficiencies is received shall be treated as the date of application for the purposes of Article 51 of that Regulation.

Part 6 Plant Varieties Protection

2. An application complies with the condition laid down in Article 50(1)(i) of the basic Regulation only if date and country of any first disposal within the meaning of Article 10(1) of that Regulation are indicated, or if, in the absence of such disposal a declaration is made that no such disposal has occurred.

[3. An application complies with the condition laid down in Article 50(1)(j) of the basic Regulation only if the date and the country given in any earlier application for the variety are, to the best of the applicant's knowledge, indicated in respect of:

— an application for a property right in respect of the variety, in a Member State or a member of the International Union for the Protection of New Varieties of Plants ("UPOV"); and
— an application for official acceptance of the variety for certification and marketing where official acceptance includes an official description of the variety.]

NOTES

Para 3: substituted by Commission Implementing Regulation 2016/1448/EU, Art 1(12).

[6.297]

Article 19

Conditions referred to in Article 50(2) of the basic Regulation

1. If the Office finds that the application does not comply with the provisions of paragraphs 2, 3 and 4 of this Article or with Article 16 of this Regulation, it shall apply Article 17(2) hereof, but shall require the applicant to remedy the deficiencies it has found within such time limit as it may specify. Where those deficiencies are not remedied in good time the Office shall without delay refuse the application, pursuant to Article 61(1)(a) of the basic Regulation.

[2. The applicant shall provide the following information in the application form or in the technical questionnaire referred to in Article 16(3)(a), where relevant:

(a) the identity and the contact details of the applicant, his designation as a party to proceedings referred to in Article 2 and, where appropriate, the name and address of the procedural representative;
(b) where the applicant is not the breeder, the name and address of the breeder and his entitlement to apply for the Community plant variety right;
(c) the scientific name of the genus, species or subspecies to which the variety belongs, and the common name;
(d) the variety denomination or, in the absence thereof, the provisional designation;
(e) the location in which the variety was bred or discovered and developed, and the maintenance and the propagation of the variety, including information on the characteristics, the cultivation of any other variety or varieties the material of which has to be used repeatedly for the production of the variety. For material to be used repeatedly for the production of the variety, the applicant may provide the information concerning such material, if he requests so, in the form provided by the Office pursuant to Article 86;
(f) the characteristics of the variety, including the state of expression for certain characteristics based on the technical questionnaire referred to in Article 16(3)(a);
(g) where appropriate, similar varieties and differences from those varieties, which, in the applicant's opinion, are relevant for the technical examination;
(h) additional information that may help distinguishing the variety, including representative colour photos of the variety and other information on the plant material to be examined during the technical examination;
(i) where appropriate, characteristics that have been genetically modified, where the variety concerned represents a genetically modified organism within the meaning of Article 2(2) of Directive 2001/18/EC of the European Parliament and of the Council;[1]
(j) the date of any sale or first disposal to others, of varietal constituents or harvested material of the variety, to exploit the variety within the territory of the European Union or in one or more third countries, or to assess whether a variety is new as referred to in Article 10 of the basic Regulation, or a declaration that such sale or first disposal has not yet occurred;
(k) the designation of the authority applied to and the file number of the applications referred to in Article 18(3) of this Regulation;
(l) existing national or regional plant variety rights that have been granted to the variety;
(m) whether an application for the variety concerned has been submitted for listing or registration or a decision has been taken pursuant to Article 5 of Council Directive 68/193/EEC,[2] Article 10 of Council Directive 2002/53/EC,[3] Article 10 of Council Directive 2002/55/EC[4] and Article 5 of Commission Implementing Directive 2014/97/EU.[5]]

3. The Office may call for any necessary information and documentation, and, if necessary, sufficient drawings or photographs for the conduct of the technical examination within such time limit as it shall specify.

4. Where the variety concerned represents a genetically modified organism within the meaning of Article 2(2) of Directive 2001/18/EC, the Office may require the applicant to transmit a copy of the written attestation of the responsible authorities stating that a technical examination of the variety under Articles 55 and 56 of the basic Regulation does not pose risks to the environment according to the norms of that Directive.

NOTES

Para 2: substituted by Commission Implementing Regulation 2016/1448/EU, Art 1(13).

1 Directive 2001/18/EC of the European Parliament and of the Council of 12 March 2001 on the deliberate release into the environment of genetically modified organisms and repealing Council Directive 90/220/EEC (OJ L106, 17.4.2001, p 1).

2 Council Directive 68/193/EEC of 9 April 1968 on the marketing of material for the vegetative propagation of the vine (OJ L93, 17.4.1968, p 15).

3 Council Directive 2002/53/EC of 13 June 2002 on the common catalogue of varieties of agricultural plant species (OJ L193, 20.7.2002, p 1).

4 Council Directive 2002/55/EC of 13 June 2002 on the marketing of vegetable seed (OJ L193, 20.7.2002, p 33).

5 Commission Implementing Directive 2014/97/EU of 15 October 2014 implementing Council Directive 2008/90/EC as regards the registration of suppliers and of varieties and the common list of varieties (OJ L298, 16.10.2014, p 16).

[6.298]
Article 20
Claiming priority

If the applicant claims a right of priority for an application within the meaning of Article 52(2) of the basic Regulation, which is not the earliest of those to be indicated pursuant to the first indent of Article 18(3) of this Regulation, the Office shall state that a priority date can only be given to such earlier application. Where the Office has issued a receipt including the date of filing of an application which is not the earliest of those to be indicated, the priority date notified shall be considered void.

[6.299]
Article 21
Entitlement to a Community plant variety right during proceedings

1. When the commencement of an action against the applicant in respect of a claim referred to in Article 98(4) of the basic Regulation has been entered in the Register of Applications for Community plant variety rights, the Office may stay the application proceedings. The Office may set a date on which it intends to continue the proceedings pending before it.
2. When a final decision in, or any other termination of, the action referred to in paragraph 1 has been entered in the Register of Applications for Community plant variety rights, the Office shall resume proceedings. It may resume them at an earlier date, but not prior to the date already set pursuant to paragraph 1.
3. Where entitlement to a Community plant variety right is validly transferred to another person for the purposes of the Office, that person may pursue the application of the first applicant as if it were his own, provided that he gives notice to this effect to the Office within one month of the entry of final judgment in the Register of Applications for Community plant variety rights. Fees due pursuant to Article 83 of the basic Regulation and already paid by the first applicant shall be deemed to have been paid by the subsequent applicant.

SECTION 2
CONDUCT OF THE TECHNICAL EXAMINATION

[6.300]
Article 22
Decision on test guidelines

1. Upon proposal of the President of the Office, the Administrative Council shall take a decision as to test guidelines. The date of the decision and the species concerned by it shall be published in the Official Gazette referred to in Article 87.
2. In the absence of a decision of the Administrative Council as to test guidelines, the President of the Office may take a provisional decision thereon. The provisional decision shall lapse on the date of the decision of the Administrative Council. Where the provisional decision of the President of the Office deviates from the decision of the Administrative Council, a technical examination started prior to the decision of the Administrative Council shall not be affected The Administrative Council may decide otherwise, if circumstances so dictate.
[3. In the absence of a decision of the Administrative Council, or a provisional decision of the President of the Office as referred to in paragraph 2, as to test guidelines established by the Office, the guidelines per genera and species of the UPOV shall apply. In the absence of such guidelines, national guidelines developed by a competent authority in charge of the technical examination of a plant variety may be used, provided that the President of the Office agrees to such use. The competent authority shall submit those guidelines to the Office, and the Office shall publish them on its website.]

NOTES

Para 3: added by Commission Implementing Regulation 2016/1448/EU, Art 1(14).

[6.301]
Article 23
Powers vested in the President of the Office

1. Where the Administrative Council takes a decision on test guidelines, it shall include a power whereby the President of the Office may insert additional characteristics and their expressions in respect of a variety.

2. . . .

NOTES

Para 2: repealed by Commission Implementing Regulation 2016/1448/EU, Art 1(15).

[6.302]
Article 24
Notification by the Office of the Examination Office

[In accordance with Article 55(3) of the basic Regulation, the Office shall transmit to the Examination Office the following documents relating to the variety in electronic format:]

(a) the application form, the technical questionnaire and each additional document submitted by the applicant containing information needed for the conduct of the technical examination;
(b) the forms filled out by the applicant pursuant to Article 86 of this Regulation;
(c) documents relating to an objection based on the contention that the conditions laid down in Articles 7, 8 and 9 of the basic Regulation have not been met.

NOTES

Words in square brackets substituted by Commission Implementing Regulation 2016/1448/EU, Art 1(16).

[6.303]
Article 25
Cooperation between the Office and the Examination Office

The staff of the Examination Office responsible for the technical examination and the rapporteur designated in accordance with Article 8(1) shall cooperate in all phases of a technical examination. Cooperation shall cover at least the following aspects:

(a) the monitoring of the conduct of the technical examination, including the inspection of the locations of the test plots and the methods used for the tests by the rapporteur;
(b) without prejudice to other investigations by the Office, information from the Examination Office about details of any previous disposal of the variety; and
(c) the submission by the Examination Office to the Office of interim reports on each growing period.

[6.304]
Article 26
Form of the examination reports

1. The examination report referred to in Article 57 of the basic Regulation shall be signed by the responsible member of the staff of the Examination Office and shall expressly acknowledge the exclusive rights of disposal of the Office under Article 57(4) of that Regulation.

2. The provisions of paragraph 1 shall apply *mutatis mutandis* to any interim reports to be submitted to the Office. The Examination Office shall issue a copy of each interim report direct to the applicant.

[6.305]
Article 27
Other examination reports

1. An examination report on the results of any technical examination which has been carried out or is in the process of being carried out for official purposes in a Member State by one of the offices responsible for the species concerned pursuant to Article 55(1) of the basic Regulation may be considered by the Office to constitute a sufficient basis for decision, provided that:

(a) the material submitted for the technical examination has complied, in quantity and quality, with any standards that may have been laid down pursuant to Article 55(4) of the basic Regulation;
[(b) the technical examination has been carried out in a manner consistent with the designation by the Administrative Council pursuant to Article 55(1) of the basic Regulation and with the requirements referred to in Article 13(1a) of this Regulation and has been conducted in accordance with the test guidelines issued and any general instructions given, pursuant to Article 56(2) of the basic Regulation and Articles 22 and 23 of this Regulation;]
(c) the Office has had the opportunity to monitor the conduct of the technical examination concerned; and
(d) where the final report is not immediately available, the interim reports on each growing period are submitted to the Office prior to the examination report.

2. Where the Office does not consider the examination report referred to in paragraph 1 to constitute a sufficient basis for a decision, it may follow the procedure laid down in Article 55 of the basic Regulation, after consulting the applicant and the Examination Office concerned.
3. The Office and each competent national plant variety office in a Member State shall give administrative assistance to the other by making available, upon request, any examination reports on a variety, for the purpose of assessing distinctiveness, uniformity and stability of that variety. A specific amount shall be charged by the Office or the competent national plant variety office for the submission of such a report, such amount being agreed by the offices concerned.
[4. An examination report on the results of a technical examination that has been carried out or is in the process of being carried out for official purposes in a third country or in the territory of a regional organisation that is a member of the UPOV or that is a party to the Agreement on Trade-Related Aspects of Intellectual Property Rights ("TRIPS"), may be considered by the Office to constitute a sufficient basis for decision, provided that the technical examination complies with the conditions laid down in a written agreement between the Office and the competent authority of such third country or regional organisation. Such conditions shall at least include:
(a) conditions relating to the material, as referred to in point (a) of paragraph 1;
(b) the condition that the technical examination has been conducted in accordance with the test guidelines issued, or general instructions given, pursuant to Article 56(2) of the basic Regulation and Article 22 of this Regulation;
(c) the condition that the Office has had the opportunity to assess the suitability of facilities for carrying out a technical examination for the species concerned in that third country or in the territory of that regional organisation;
(d) conditions relating to the availability of reports, as laid down in point (d) of paragraph 1;
(e) the condition that the third country has adequate experience in testing the genera or species concerned; and
(f) the condition that the written agreement is concluded with the consent of the Administrative Council.]
[5. The Office may request a competent authority of a third country or of a regional organisation that is a member of the UPOV or is a party to TRIPS to perform the technical examination, provided that a written agreement has been signed between the Office and that competent authority and provided that one of the following conditions applies:
(a) there is no possibility to realise the technical examination for the specific species in an Examination Office in the European Union, and an examination report on the results of a technical examination, referred to in paragraph 4, is not available or is not expected to become available;
(b) an examination report on the results of a technical examination referred to in paragraph 4 is expected to be made available but the conditions established under paragraph 4 to conduct the technical examination are not fulfilled.
6. The written agreement referred to in paragraph 5 shall be concluded with the consent of the Administrative Council, based on the following conditions:
(a) conditions relating to the material, as referred to in point (a) of paragraph 1;
(b) the condition that the technical examination will be conducted in accordance with the test guidelines issued, or general instructions given, pursuant to Article 56(2) of the basic Regulation and Article 22 of this Regulation;
(c) the condition that the Office has had the opportunity to assess the suitability of facilities for carrying out a technical examination for the species concerned in that third country or in the territory of that regional organisation and to monitor the technical examination concerned;
(d) conditions relating to the availability of reports, as laid down in point (d) of paragraph 1;
(e) the condition that the third country has adequate experience in testing the genera or species concerned.]

NOTES

Para 1: point (b) substituted by Commission Implementing Regulation 2016/1448/EU, Art 1(17)(a).
Para 4: substituted by Commission Implementing Regulation 2016/1448/EU, Art 1(17)(b).
Paras 5, 6: added by Commission Implementing Regulation 2016/1448/EU, Art 1(17)(c).

SECTION 3
VARIETY DENOMINATION

[6.306]
Article 28
Proposal for a variety denomination
The proposal for a variety denomination shall be signed and shall be filed at the Office . . .
The Office shall make available, free of charge, a form for the purposes of proposing a variety denomination.
Where the proposal for a variety denomination is submitted by electronic means it shall comply with the second subparagraph of Article 57(3) of this Regulation as regards the signature.

NOTES

Words omitted repealed by Commission Implementing Regulation 2016/1448/EU, Art 1(18).

[6.307]
Article 29
Examination of a proposal

1. Where the proposal does not accompany the application for a Community plant variety right or where a proposed variety denomination cannot be approved by the Office, the Office shall without delay communicate this to the applicant, shall require him to submit a proposal or a new proposal and shall indicate the consequences of failure to do so.

2. Where the Office establishes at the time of receipt of the results of the technical examination pursuant to Article 57(1) of the basic Regulation that the applicant has not submitted any proposal for a variety denomination, it shall without delay refuse the application for a Community plant variety right in accordance with Article 61(1)(c) of that Regulation.

[6.308]
Article 30
Guidelines for variety denomination

The Administrative Council shall adopt guidelines establishing uniform and definitive criteria for determining impediments to the generic designation of a variety denomination referred to in Article 63(3) and (4) of the basic Regulation.

CHAPTER II
OBJECTION

[6.309]
Article 31
Filing of objections

1. Objections under Article 59 of the basic Regulation shall contain:
   (a) the name of the applicant and the file number of the application to which the objection is lodged;
   (b) the designation of the objector as a party to proceedings as set out in Article 2 of this Regulation;
   (c) if the objector has appointed a procedural representative, his name and address;
   (d) a statement on the contention referred to in Article 59(3) of the basic Regulation on which the objection is based, and on particulars, items of evidence and arguments presented in support of the objection.

2. If several objections in respect of the same application for a Community plant variety right are filed, the Office may deal with those objections in one set of proceedings.

[6.310]
Article 32
Rejection of objections

1. If the Office finds that the objection does not comply with Article 59(1) and (3) of the basic Regulation or Article 31(1)(d) of this Regulation or that it does not provide sufficient identification of the application against which objection is lodged, it shall reject the objection as inadmissible unless such deficiencies have been remedied within such time limit as it may specify.

2. If the Office notes that the objection does not comply with other provisions of the basic Regulation or of this Regulation, it shall reject the objection as inadmissible unless such deficiencies have been remedied prior to the expiry of the objection periods.

CHAPTER III
MAINTENANCE OF COMMUNITY PLANT VARIETY RIGHTS

[6.311]
Article 33
Obligations of the holder under Article 64(3) of the basic Regulation

1. The holder shall permit inspection of material of the variety concerned and of the location where the identity of the variety is preserved, in order to furnish the information necessary for assessing the continuance of the variety in its unaltered state, pursuant to Article 64(3) of the basic Regulation.

2. The holder shall be required to keep written records in order to facilitate verification of appropriate measures referred to in Article 64(3) of the basic Regulation.

[6.312]
Article 34
Technical verification of the protected variety
Without prejudice to Article 87(4) of the basic Regulation, a technical verification of the protected variety shall be conducted in accordance with the test guidelines duly applied when the Community plant variety right was granted in respect of that variety. Articles 22 and 24 to 27 of this Regulation shall apply *mutatis mutandis* to the Office, the Examination Office and to the holder.

[6.313]
Article 35
Other material to be used for a technical verification
When the holder has submitted material of the variety in accordance with Article 64(3) of the basic Regulation, the Examination Office may, with the consent of the Office, verify the submitted material by inspecting other material which has been taken from holdings where material is produced by the holder, or with his consent, or taken from material being marketed by him, or with his consent, or taken by official bodies in a Member State by virtue of their powers.

[6.314]
Article 36
Amendments of the variety denominations
1. Where the variety denomination has to be amended in accordance with Article 66 of the basic Regulation, the Office shall communicate the grounds thereof to the holder, shall set up a time limit within which the holder must submit a suitable proposal for an amended variety denomination, and shall state that, should he fail to do so, the Community plant variety right may be cancelled pursuant to Article 21 of that Regulation.
2. Where the proposal for an amended variety denomination cannot be approved by the Office, the Office shall without delay inform the holder, shall again set a time limit within which the holder must submit a suitable proposal, and shall state that, should he fail to comply, the Community plant variety right may be cancelled pursuant to Article 21 of the basic Regulation.
3. Articles 31 and 32 of this Regulation shall apply *mutatis mutandis* to an objection lodged pursuant to Article 66(3) of the basic Regulation.
4. Where the proposal for an amendment of a variety denomination is submitted by electronic means it shall comply with the second subparagraph of Article 57(3) as regards the signature.

CHAPTER IV
COMMUNITY LICENCES TO BE GRANTED BY THE OFFICE

SECTION 1
COMPULSORY LICENCES PURSUANT TO ARTICLE 29 OF THE BASIC REGULATION

[6.315]
Article 37
Applications for a compulsory licence
1. The application for a compulsory licence pursuant to Article 29(1), (2) and (5) of the basic Regulation shall contain:
(a) the designation of the applicant and the opposing holder of the variety concerned as parties to proceedings;
(b) the variety denomination and the plant species of the variety or varieties concerned;
(c) a proposal for the type of acts to be covered by the compulsory licence;
(d) a statement setting out the public interest concerned, including details of facts, items of evidence and arguments presented in support of the public interest claimed;
(e) in the case of an application referred to in Article 29(2) of the basic Regulation, a proposal for the category of persons to which the compulsory licence shall be granted, including, as the case may be, the specific requirements related to that category of persons;
(f) a proposal for an equitable remuneration and the basis for calculating the remuneration.
2. The application for a compulsory licence referred to in Article 29(5a) of the basic Regulation shall contain:
(a) the designation of the applicant holding a patent right and the opposing holder of the variety concerned as parties to proceedings;
(b) the variety denomination and the plant species of the variety or varieties concerned;
[(c) an electronic copy of the patent certificate(s) showing the number and claims of the patent for a biotechnological invention and the granting authority or authorities of the patent;]
(d) a proposal for the type of acts to be covered by the compulsory licence;
(e) a proposal for an equitable remuneration and the basis for calculating the remuneration;
(f) a statement setting out why the biotechnological invention constitutes significant technical progress of considerable economic interest compared with the protected variety, including details of facts, items of evidence and arguments in support of the claim;
(g) a proposal for the territorial scope of the licence, which may not exceed the territorial scope of the patent referred to in point (c).

Part 6 Plant Varieties Protection

3. The application for a cross-licence referred to in the second subparagraph of Article 29(5a) of the basic Regulation shall contain:
   (a) the designation of the applicant holding a patent right and the opposing holder of the variety concerned as parties to proceedings;
   (b) the variety denomination and the plant species of the variety or varieties concerned;
   [(c) an electronic copy of the patent certificate(s) showing the number and claims of the patent for a biotechnological invention and the granting authority or authorities of the patent;]
   (d) an official document showing that a compulsory licence for a patented biotechnological invention has been granted to the holder of the plant variety right;
   (e) a proposal for the type of acts to be covered by the cross-licence;
   (f) a proposal for an equitable remuneration and the basis for calculating the remuneration;
   (g) a proposal for the territorial scope of the cross-licence, which may not exceed the territorial scope of the patent referred to in point (c).

4. The application for a compulsory licence shall be accompanied by documents evidencing that the applicant has applied unsuccessfully to obtain a contractual licence from the holder of the plant variety right. Should the Commission or a Member State be the applicant for a compulsory licence pursuant to Article 29(2) of the basic Regulation, the Office may waive this condition in the case of *force majeure*.

5. A request for a contractual licence shall be considered unsuccessful within the meaning of paragraph 4 if:
   (a) the opposing holder has not given a final reply to the person seeking such right within a reasonable period; or
   (b) the opposing holder has refused to grant a contractual licence to the person seeking it; or
   (c) the opposing holder has offered a licence to the person seeking it, on obviously unreasonable fundamental terms including those relating to the royalty to be paid, or on terms which, seen as a whole, are obviously unreasonable.

NOTES

Para 2: point (c) substituted by Commission Implementing Regulation 2016/1448/EU, Art 1(19)(a).
Para 3: point (c) substituted by Commission Implementing Regulation 2016/1448/EU, Art 1(19)(b).

[6.316]
Article 38
Examination of the application for a compulsory licence

1. Oral proceedings and the taking of evidence shall in principle be held together in one hearing.
2. Requests for further hearings shall be inadmissible except for those requests based on circumstances which have undergone change during or after the hearing.
3. Before taking a decision, the Office shall invite the parties concerned to come to an amicable settlement on a contractual licence. If appropriate, the Office shall make a proposal for such an amicable settlement.

[6.317]
Article 39
Tenure of a Community plant variety right during the proceedings

1. If the commencement of an action in respect of a claim referred to in Article 98(1) of the basic Regulation against the holder has been entered in the Register of Community Plant Variety Rights, the Office may suspend the proceedings on the grant of a compulsory licence. It shall not resume them prior to the entry in the same Register of the final judgment upon, or any other termination of, such action.
2. If a transfer of the Community plant variety right is binding on the Office, the new holder shall enter the proceedings as a party thereto, upon request of the applicant, if that applicant has unsuccessfully requested the new holder to grant him a licence within two months of receipt of communication from the Office that the name of the new holder has been entered in the Register of Community Plant Variety Rights. A request from the applicant shall be accompanied by sufficient documentary evidence of his vain attempt and, if appropriate, of the conduct of the new holder.
3. In the case of an application referred to in Article 29(2) of the basic Regulation, the new holder shall enter the proceedings as a party thereto. Paragraph 1 of this Article shall not apply.

[6.318]
Article 40
Contents of the decision on the application

The written decision shall be signed by the President of the Office. The decision shall contain:
   (a) a statement that the decision is delivered by the Office;
   (b) the date when the decision was taken;
   (c) the names of the members of the committee having taken part in the proceedings;
   (d) the names of the parties to the proceedings and of their procedural representatives;
   (e) the reference to the opinion of the Administrative Council;
   (f) a statement of the issues to be decided;
   (g) a summary of the facts;

(h) the grounds on which the decision is based;
(i) the order of the Office; if need be, the order shall include the stipulated acts covered by the compulsory licence, the specific conditions pertaining thereto and the category of persons, including where appropriate the specific requirements relating to that category.

[6.319]
Article 41
Grant of a compulsory licence

1. The decision to grant a compulsory licence pursuant to Article 29(1), (2) and (5) of the basic Regulation shall contain a statement setting out the public interest involved.
2. The following grounds may in particular constitute a public interest:
(a) the protection of life or health of humans, animals or plants;
(b) the need to supply the market with material offering specific features;
(c) the need to maintain the incentive for continued breeding of improved varieties.
3. The decision to grant a compulsory licence pursuant to Article 29(5a) of the basic Regulation shall contain a statement setting out the reasons why the invention constitutes significant technical progress of considerable economic interest. The following grounds may in particular constitute reasons why the invention constitutes significant technical progress of considerable economic interest compared to the protected plant variety:
(a) improvement of cultural techniques;
(b) improvement of the environment;
(c) improvement of techniques to facilitate the use of genetic biodiversity;
(d) improvement of quality;
(e) improvement of yield;
(f) improvement of resistance;
(g) improvement of adaptation to specific climatological and/or environmental conditions.
4. The compulsory licence shall be non-exclusive.
5. The compulsory licence may not be transferred otherwise than together with that part of an enterprise which makes use of the compulsory licence, or, in the circumstances set out in Article 29(5) of the basic Regulation, together with the assignment of the rights of an essentially derived variety.

[6.320]
Article 42
Conditions pertaining to the person to whom a compulsory licence is granted

1. Without prejudice to the other conditions referred to in Article 29(3) of the basic Regulation, the person to whom the compulsory licence is granted shall have the appropriate financial and technical capacity to make use of the compulsory licence.
2. Compliance with the conditions pertaining to the compulsory licence and laid down in the decision thereon shall be considered a 'circumstance' within the meaning of Article 29(4) of the basic Regulation.
3. The Office shall provide that the person to whom a compulsory licence is granted may not bring a legal action for infringement of a Community plant variety right unless the holder has refused or neglected to do so within two months after being so requested.

[6.321]
Article 43
Category of persons satisfying specific requirements pursuant to Article 29(2) of the basic Regulation

1. Any person intending to make use of a compulsory licence who comes under the category of persons satisfying specific requirements referred to in Article 29(2) of the basic Regulation shall declare his intention to the Office and to the holder by registered letter with advice of delivery. The declaration shall include:
(a) the name and address of that person as laid down for parties to proceedings pursuant to Article 2 of this Regulation;
(b) a statement on the facts meeting the specific requirements;
(c) a statement setting out the acts to be effected; and
(d) an assurance that that person has the appropriate financial resources as well as information about his technical capacity, to make use of the compulsory licence.
2. Upon request, the Office shall enter a person in the Register of Community Plant Variety Rights if such person has fulfilled the conditions relating to the declaration referred to in paragraph 1. Such person shall not be entitled to make use of the compulsory licence prior to the entry. The entry shall be communicated to that person and the holder.
3. Article 42(3) shall apply *mutatis mutandis* to a person entered in the Register of Community Plant Variety Rights pursuant to paragraph 2 of this Article. Any judgment, or other termination, of the legal action in respect of the act of infringement shall apply to the other persons entered or to be entered.

4. The entry referred to in paragraph 2 may be deleted on the sole ground that the specific requirements laid down in the decision on the grant of a compulsory licence or the financial and technical capacities established pursuant to paragraph 2 have undergone change more than one year after the grant of the compulsory licence and within any time limit stipulated in that grant. The deletion of the entry shall be communicated to the person entered and the holder.

SECTION 2
EXPLOITATION RIGHTS PURSUANT TO ARTICLE 100(2) OF THE BASIC REGULATION

[6.322]
Article 44
Exploitation rights pursuant to Article 100(2) of the basic Regulation

1. A request for a contractual non-exclusive exploitation right from a new holder, as referred to in Article 100(2) of the basic Regulation, shall be made, in the case of the former holder within two months, or in the case of a person having enjoyed an exploitation right within four months, of receipt of notification from the Office that the name of the new holder has been entered in the Register of Community Plant Variety Rights.

2. An application for an exploitation right to be granted pursuant to Article 100(2) of the basic Regulation shall be accompanied by documents supporting the unsuccessful request referred to in paragraph 1 of this Article. The provisions of Article 37(1)(a), (b), (c) and (5), Article 38, Article 39(3), Article 40 except letter (f), Article 41(3) and (4) and Article 42 of this Regulation shall apply *mutatis mutandis*.

TITLE III
PROCEEDINGS BEFORE THE BOARD OF APPEAL

[6.323]
Article 45
Contents of the notice of appeal

The notice of appeal shall contain:

[(a) the designation of the appellant as a party to appeal proceedings in accordance with Article 2, and, where the appellant has appointed a procedural representative, the name and address of the representative;]

(b) the file number of the decision against which the appeal is lodged and a statement as to the extent to which amendment or cancellation of the decision is sought.

NOTES

Point (a): substituted by Commission Implementing Regulation 2016/1448/EU, Art 1(20).

[6.324]
Article 46
Receipt of the notice of appeal

Where the Office receives a notice of appeal, it shall mark it with a file number of the appeal proceedings and the date of receipt at the Office and shall notify the appellant of the time limit for setting out the grounds of the appeal; any omission of such notice may not be pleaded.

[6.325]
Article 47
Participation as a party to the appeal proceedings

1. The Office shall promptly transmit a copy of the notice of appeal marked with the file number and the date of its receipt to the parties to proceedings having participated in the proceedings before the Office.

2. The parties to proceedings referred to in paragraph 1 may intervene as parties to the appeal proceedings within two months of transmission of a copy of the notice of appeal.

[6.326]
Article 48
Role of the Office

1. The body of the Office referred to in Article 70(1) of the basic Regulation and the chairman of the Board of Appeal shall ensure by internal preparatory measures that the Board of Appeal can examine the case immediately after its remittal; the chairman shall in particular select the two other members in accordance with Article 46(2) of that Regulation and shall designate a rapporteur, prior to the remittal of the case.

2. Prior to the remittal of the case, the body of the Office referred to in Article 70(1) of the basic Regulation shall promptly transmit a copy of the documents received by a party to the appeal proceedings to the other parties to the appeal proceedings.

3. The President of the Office shall provide for the publication of the information referred to in Article 89, prior to the remittal of the case.

[6.327]
Article 49
Rejection of the appeal as inadmissible
1. If the appeal does not comply with the provisions of the basic Regulation and in particular Articles 67, 68 and 69 thereof or those of this Regulation and in particular Article 45 thereof, the Board of Appeal shall so inform the appellant and shall require him to remedy the deficiencies found, if possible, within such period as it may specify. If the appeal is not rectified in good time, the Board of Appeal shall reject it as inadmissible.
2. Where an appeal is lodged against a decision of the Office against which an action under Article 74 of the basic Regulation is likewise lodged, the Board of Appeal shall forthwith submit the appeal as an action to the Court of Justice of the European Communities, with the consent of the appellant; if the appellant does not consent, it shall reject the appeal as inadmissible. In the case of the submission of an appeal to the Court of Justice, such an appeal shall be deemed to have been lodged with the Court of Justice as at the date of receipt at the Office under Article 46 of this Regulation.

[6.328]
Article 50
Oral proceedings
1. After the remittal of the case, the chairman of the Board of Appeal shall, without delay, summon the parties to the appeal proceedings to oral proceedings as provided for in Article 77 of the basic Regulation and shall draw their attention to the contents of Article 59(2) of this Regulation.
2. The oral proceedings and the taking of evidence shall in principle be held in one hearing.
3. Requests for further hearings shall be inadmissible except for requests based on circumstances which have undergone change during or after the hearing.

[6.329]
Article 51
Examination of appeals
Unless otherwise provided, the provisions relating to proceedings before the Office shall apply to appeal proceedings *mutatis mutandis*; parties to proceedings shall in that regard be treated as parties to appeal proceedings.

[6.330]
[Article 51a
Several appeals
1. If several appeals are filed against a decision, those appeals may be considered in the same proceedings.
2. If appeals filed against decisions are to be examined by the Board having the same composition, that Board may deal with those appeals in joint proceedings.]

NOTES
Inserted by Commission Implementing Regulation 2016/1448/EU, Art 1(21).

[6.331]
Article 52
Decision on the appeal
1. Within three months after closure of the oral proceedings, the decision on the appeal shall be forwarded in writing, by any means provided for in Article 64(3), to the parties to the appeal proceedings.
2. The decision shall be signed by the chairman of the Board of Appeal and by the rapporteur designated pursuant to Article 48(1). The decision shall contain:
(a) a statement that the decision is delivered by the Board of Appeal;
(b) the date when the decision was taken;
(c) the names of the chairman and of the other members of the Board of Appeal having taken part in the appeal proceedings;
(d) the names of the parties to the appeal proceedings and their procedural representatives;
(e) a statement of the issues to be decided;
(f) a summary of the facts;
(g) the grounds on which the decision is based;
(h) the order of the Board of Appeal, including, where necessary, a decision as to the award of costs or the refund of fees.
3. The written decision of the Board of Appeal shall be accompanied by a statement that further appeal is possible, together with the time limit for lodging such further appeal. The parties to the appeal proceedings may not plead the omission of that statement.

TITLE IV
GENERAL PROVISIONS RELATING TO PROCEEDINGS

CHAPTER I
DECISIONS, COMMUNICATIONS AND DOCUMENTS

[6.332]
Article 53
Decisions

1. Any decision of the Office is to be signed by and to state the name of the member of staff duly authorised by the President of the Office in accordance with Article 35 of the basic Regulation.
2. Where oral proceedings are held before the Office, the decisions may be given orally. Subsequently, the decision in writing shall be served on the parties to proceedings in accordance with Article 64.
3. Decisions of the Office which are open to appeal under Article 67 of the basic Regulation or to direct action under Article 74 thereof shall be accompanied by a statement of that appeal or direct action if possible, together with the time limits provided for lodging such appeal or direct action. The parties to proceedings may not plead the omission of that statement.
4. Linguistic errors, errors of transcription and patent mistakes in decisions of the Office shall be corrected.
[5. The Office shall cancel the entry in the Register of Community Plant Variety Rights or revoke the decision that contains an obvious procedural error attributable to negligence.]

NOTES
Para 5: inserted by Commission Implementing Regulation 2016/1448/EU, Art 1(22).

[6.333]
[Article 53a
Proceedings for nullity and cancellation

1. Proceedings on nullity and cancellations as referred to in Articles 20 and 21, respectively, of the basic Regulation may be opened by the Office when there are serious doubts as regards the validity of the title. Such proceedings may be initiated by the Office on its own motion or upon request.
2. A request to the Office to open the proceedings on nullity or cancellation, as referred to in Articles 20 and 21, respectively, of the basic Regulation, shall be accompanied by evidence and facts raising serious doubts as to the validity of the title and shall contain:
   (a) as regards the registration in respect of which nullity or cancellation is sought:
      (i) the registration number of the Community plant variety right;
      (ii) the name and address of the holder of the Community plant variety right;
   (b) as regards the grounds on which the request is based:
      (i) a statement of the grounds on which the request to open the proceedings on nullity or cancellation is based;
      (ii) an indication of the facts, evidence and arguments presented in support of those grounds;
   (c) the name and address of the person making the request and, where he has appointed a procedural representative, the name and address of that representative.
3. Any decision of the Office to reject a request as referred to in paragraph 2 shall be communicated to the person who made the request and the holder of the Community plant variety right.
4. The Office shall not take into account written submissions or documents, or parts thereof, that have not been submitted within the time limit set by the Office.
5. Any decision of the Office to declare null and void or cancel a Community plant variety right shall be published in the Official Gazette referred to in Article 87.]

NOTES
Inserted by Commission Implementing Regulation 2016/1448/EU, Art 1(23).

[6.334]
Article 54
Certificate for a Community plant variety right

1. Where the Office grants a Community plant variety right, it shall issue, together with the decision thereon, a certificate for the Community plant variety right as evidence of the grant.
[That certificate shall be delivered by the Office, in the form of a digital document, to the holder of the right or his procedural representative.]
2. The Office shall issue the certificate for the Community plant variety right in whichever official language or languages of the European Union is requested by the holder.
3. On request, the Office may issue a copy to the person entitled if it establishes that the original certificate has been lost or destroyed.

NOTES

Para 1: words in square brackets inserted by Commission Implementing Regulation 2016/1448/EU, Art 1(24).

[6.335]
Article 55
Communications

Unless otherwise provided, any communication by the Office or an Examination Office shall include the name of the competent member of the staff.

[6.336]
Article 56
Right of audience

1. If the Office finds that a decision may not be adopted in the terms sought, it shall communicate the deficiencies noted to the party to the proceedings and shall require him to remedy those deficiencies within such time limit as it may specify. If the deficiencies noted and communicated are not remedied in good time, the Office shall proceed to take its decision.
2. If the Office receives observations from a party to proceedings, it shall communicate those observations to the other parties to the proceedings and shall require them, if it considers it necessary, to reply within such time limit as it may specify. If a reply is not received in good time, the Office shall disregard any document received later.

[6.337]
Article 57
Documents filed by parties to proceedings

1. Any documents filed by a party to proceedings shall be submitted by post, personal delivery or electronic means.
The details concerning electronic submissions shall be determined by the President of the Office.
2. The date of receipt of any document filed by parties to proceedings shall be deemed to be the date on which a document is in fact received on the premises or in the case of a document filed by electronic means, when the document is received electronically by the Office.
3. With the exception of annexed documents, any documents filed by parties to proceedings must be signed by them or their procedural representative.

[Where a document is submitted to the Office by electronic means, the indication of the name of the sender and the electronic authentication, consisting of a successful submission of login and password, shall be deemed to be equivalent to the signature.]

4. If a document has not duly been signed, or where a document received is incomplete or illegible, or where the Office has doubts as to the accuracy of the document, the Office shall inform the sender accordingly and shall invite him to submit the original of the document signed in accordance with paragraph 3, or to retransmit a copy of the original, within a time limit of one month.

Where the request is complied with within the period specified, the date of receipt of the signed document or of the retransmission shall be deemed to be the date of the receipt of the first document. Where the request is not complied with within the period specified, the document shall be deemed not to have been received.

[5. Such document submitted by a party to proceedings must be communicated by electronic means or on paper to the other parties and to the Examination Office concerned.

In case of paper submissions, documents relating to the proceedings, to two or more applications for a Community plant variety right or to an exploitation right, shall be filed in a sufficient number of copies. Missing copies shall be provided at the expense of the party concerned.]

NOTES

Para 3: words in square brackets substituted by Commission Implementing Regulation 2016/1448/EU, Art 1(25)(a).
Para 5: substituted by Commission Implementing Regulation 2016/1448/EU, Art 1(25)(b).

[6.338]
Article 58
Documentary evidence

[1. Evidence of final judgments and decisions, other than those of the Office, or other documentary evidence to be submitted by a party to proceedings, may be furnished by submitting a digital document or uncertified copy.]
2. Where the Office has doubts as to the authenticity of the evidence referred to in paragraph 1, it may require submission of the original or a certified copy.

NOTES

Para 1: substituted by Commission Implementing Regulation 2016/1448/EU, Art 1(26).

CHAPTER II
ORAL PROCEEDINGS AND TAKING OF EVIDENCE

[6.339]
Article 59
Summons to oral proceedings

1. The parties to proceedings shall be summoned to oral proceedings provided for in Article 77 of the basic Regulation and their attention shall be drawn to paragraph 2 hereof. At least one month's notice of the summons dispatched to the parties to proceedings shall be given unless the parties to proceedings and the Office agree on a shorter period.
2. If a party to proceedings who has duly been summoned to oral proceedings before the Office does not appear as summoned, the proceedings may continue without him.

[6.340]
Article 60
Taking of evidence by the Office

1. Where the Office considers it necessary to hear the oral evidence of parties to proceedings or of witnesses or experts, or to carry out an inspection, it shall take a decision to that effect, stating the means by which it intends to obtain evidence, the relevant facts to be proved and the date, time and place of hearing or inspection. If oral evidence from witnesses and experts is requested by a party to proceedings, the decision of the Office shall state the period of time within which the party to proceedings filing the request must make known to the Office the names and addresses of the witnesses and experts whom the party to proceedings wishes to be heard.
2. At least one month's notice of a summons dispatched to a party to proceedings, witness or expert to give evidence shall be given unless the Office and they agree to a shorter period. The summons shall contain:
   (a) an extract from the decision referred to in paragraph 1, indicating in particular the date, time and place of the investigation ordered and setting out the facts regarding which parties to proceedings, witnesses and experts are to be heard;
   (b) the names of the parties to proceedings and particulars of the rights which the witnesses or experts may invoke under the provisions of Article 62(2), (3) and (4);
   (c) a statement that the party to proceedings, witness or expert may ask to be heard by the competent judicial or other authority in his country of domicile and a request that he inform the Office within a time limit to be fixed by the Office whether he is prepared to appear before it.
3. Before a party to proceedings, a witness or an expert may be heard, he shall be informed that the Office may request the competent judicial or other authority in his country of domicile to re-examine his evidence on oath or in some other binding form.
4. The parties to proceedings shall be informed of the hearing of a witness or expert before a competent judicial or other authority. They shall have the right to be present and to put questions to the testifying parties to proceedings, witnesses and experts, either through the intermediary of the authority or direct.

[6.341]
Article 61
Commissioning of experts

1. The Office shall decide in what form the report to be made by an expert whom it appoints shall be submitted.
2. The mandate of the expert shall contain:
   (a) a precise description of his task;
   (b) the time limit laid down for the submission of the report;
   (c) the names of the parties to the proceedings;
   (d) particulars of the rights which he may invoke under Article 62(2), (3) and (4).
3. For the purposes of the expert's report, the Office may require the Examination Office having conducted the technical examination of the variety concerned to make available material in accordance with instructions given. If necessary, the Office may also require material from parties to proceedings or third persons.
4. The parties to proceedings shall be provided with a copy and, where appropriate, a translation of any written report.
5. The parties to proceedings may object to an expert. Articles 48(3) and 81(2) of the basic Regulation shall apply *mutatis mutandis*.
6. Article 13(2) and (3) shall apply *mutatis mutandis* to the expert appointed by the Office. When appointing the expert, the Office shall inform him of the requirement of confidentiality.

[6.342]
Article 62
Costs of taking evidence

1. The taking of evidence may be made conditional upon deposit with the Office, by the party to proceedings who requested that such evidence be taken, of a sum to be quantified by the Office by reference to an estimate of the costs.

[2. Witnesses and experts who are summoned by and appear before the Office shall be entitled to appropriate reimbursement of expenses for travel and subsistence. An advance may be granted to them by the Office.]

3. Witnesses entitled to reimbursement under paragraph 2 shall also be entitled to appropriate compensation for loss of earnings, and experts unless members of the staff of the Examination Offices, to fees for their work. Those payments shall be made to the witnesses after the taking of evidence and to the experts after they have fulfilled their duties or tasks.

4. Payments of amounts due pursuant to paragraphs 2 and 3 and in accordance with the details and scales laid down in Annex I shall be made by the Office.

[The party that requested oral evidence by witnesses or experts shall reimburse the costs of that evidence to the Office, subject to the decision on apportionment and fixing costs pursuant to Article 52.]

NOTES

Para 2: substituted by Commission Implementing Regulation 2016/1448/EU, Art 1(27)(a).

Para 4: words in square brackets inserted by Commission Implementing Regulation 2016/1448/EU, Art 1(27)(b).

[6.343]

Article 63

Minutes of oral proceedings and of taking of evidence

1. Minutes of oral proceedings and of the taking of evidence shall record the essentials of the oral proceedings or of the taking of evidence, the relevant statements made by the parties to proceedings, the testimony of the parties to proceedings, witnesses or experts and the result of any inspection. [They shall also contain the names of the officials of the Office, the parties, their procedural representatives, and of the witnesses and experts who were present.]

2. The minutes of the testimony of a witness, expert or party to proceedings shall be read out or submitted to him so that he may examine them. It shall be noted in the minutes that this formality has been carried out and that the person who gave the testimony approved the minutes. Where his approval is not given, his objections shall be noted.

[3. The minutes shall be signed by the person who drew them up and by the person who conducted the oral proceedings or took the evidence.]

4. The parties to proceedings shall be provided with a copy and, where appropriate, a translation of the minutes.

NOTES

Para 1: words in square brackets inserted by Commission Implementing Regulation 2016/1448/EU, Art 1(28)(a).

Para 3: substituted by Commission Implementing Regulation 2016/1448/EU, Art 1(28)(b).

CHAPTER III
SERVICE

[6.344]

Article 64

General provisions on service

[1. In proceedings before the Office, any service of documents to be made by the Office on a party to proceedings shall take the form of a digital document, an uncertified copy, a print-out or the original document. Documents emanating from other parties to proceedings may be served in the form of uncertified copies.]

2. If a procedural representative has been appointed by one or more parties to proceedings, service shall be made on him in accordance with the provisions of paragraph 1.

[3. Service shall be made by one or more of the following means:

(a) by electronic means or any other technical means in accordance with Article 64a;

(b) by post in accordance with Article 65;

(c) by delivery by hand in accordance with Article 66;

(d) by public notice in accordance with Article 67.

4. Documents or copies thereof containing actions for which service is provided for in Article 79 of the basic Regulation shall be served by electronic means to be determined by the President of the Office or by postal means by recorded delivery with advice of delivery served.]

NOTES

Para 1: substituted by Commission Implementing Regulation 2016/1448/EU, Art 1(29)(a).

Paras 3, 4: substituted by Commission Implementing Regulation 2016/1448/EU, Art 1(29)(b).

[6.345]

[Article 64a

Service by electronic means or other technical means

1. Service by electronic means shall be made by transmitting a digital copy of the document to be notified. Service shall be deemed to have taken place on the date on which the communication was received by the recipient. The President of the Office shall determine the details of service by electronic means.

2. Where service is made by electronic means, a party to proceedings, including his procedural representative, shall provide an electronic address to the Office for all official communication.
3. The President of the Office shall determine the details of service by other technical means of communication.]

NOTES

Inserted by Commission Implementing Regulation 2016/1448/EU, Art 1(30).

[6.346]
Article 65
Service by post

1. Service on addressees not having their domicile or their seat or establishment within the Community and who have not appointed a procedural representative in accordance with Article 82 of the basic Regulation shall be effected by posting the documents to be served by ordinary letter to the addressee's last address known to the Office. Service shall be deemed to have been effected by posting even if the letter is returned as undeliverable.
2. Where service is effected by registered letter, whether or not with advice of delivery, this shall be deemed to have been delivered to the addressee on the tenth day following its posting, unless the letter has failed to reach the addressee or has reached him on a later day; in the event of any dispute, it shall be for the Office to establish that the letter has reached its destination or to establish the date on which the letter was delivered to the addressee, as the case may be.
3. Service by registered letter, whether or not with advice of delivery, shall be deemed to have been effected even if the addressee refuses to accept the letter or to acknowledge receipt thereof.
4. Where service by post is not covered by paragraphs 1, 2 and 3, the law of the State on the territory of which the service is made shall apply.

[6.347]
Article 66
Service by hand delivery

On the premises of the Office, service of a document may be effected by delivery by hand to the addressee, who shall on delivery acknowledge its receipt. Service shall be deemed to have taken place even if the addressee refuses to accept the document or to acknowledge receipt thereof.

[6.348]
[Article 66a
Service to procedural representatives

1. Where a procedural representative has been appointed, or where the applicant first named in a joint application pursuant to Article 73(5) is considered to be the procedural representative, notifications shall be addressed to the procedural representative.
2. Where several procedural representatives have been appointed for a single party, notification to any one of those representatives shall be sufficient, unless a specific address for service has been indicated.
3. Where several parties have appointed a common procedural representative, notification of the relevant documents to that representative shall be sufficient.]

NOTES

Inserted by Commission Implementing Regulation 2016/1448/EU, Art 1(31).

[6.349]
Article 67
Public notice

If the address of the addressee cannot be established, or if service in accordance with Article 64(4) has proved to be impossible even after a second attempt by the Office, service shall be effected by public notice, to be issued in the periodical publication referred to in Article 89 of the basic Regulation. [The President of the Office shall determine details as to the issue of a public notice and shall determine the period within which the relevant document shall be deemed to have been notified.]

NOTES

Words in square brackets substituted by Commission Implementing Regulation 2016/1448/EU, Art 1(32).

[6.350]
Article 68
Irregularities in service

If the Office is unable to prove that a document which has reached the addressee has been duly served, or if provisions relating to its service have not been observed, the document shall be deemed to have been served on the date established by the Office as the date of receipt.

CHAPTER IV
TIME LIMITS AND INTERRUPTION OF PROCEEDINGS

[6.351]
Article 69
Computation of time limits

1. Time limits shall be laid down in terms of full years, months, weeks or days.
2. Time limits shall run from the day following the day on which the relevant event occurred, the event being either an action or the expiry of another time limit. Unless otherwise provided, the event considered shall be the receipt of the document served, where the action consists in service.
3. Notwithstanding the provisions of paragraph 2, the time limits shall run from the 15th day following the day of publication of a relevant action, where the action is either the public notice referred to in Article 67, a decision of the Office unless served to the relevant person, or any action of a party to proceedings to be published.
4. When a time limit is expressed as one year or a certain number of years, it shall expire in the relevant subsequent year in the month having the same name and on the day having the same number as the month and the day on which the said event occurred; where the relevant subscqucnt month has no day bearing the same number the time limit shall expire on the last day of that month.
5. When a time limit is expressed as one month or a certain number of months, it shall expire in the relevant subsequent month on the day which has the same number as the day on which the said event occurred; where the relevant subsequent month has no day bearing the same number the period shall expire on the last day of that month.
6. Where a time limit is expressed as one week or a certain number of weeks, it shall expire in the relevant subsequent week on the day having the same name as the day on which the said event occurred.

[6.352]
Article 70
Duration of time limits

Where either the basic Regulation or this Regulation specifies a time limit to be determined by the Office, such a time limit shall be not less than one month and not more than three months. In certain special cases, the time limit may be extended by up to six months upon a request presented before the expiry of such time limit.

[6.353]
Article 71
Extension of time limits

1. If a time limit expires on a day on which the Office is not open for receipt of documents or on which, for reasons other than those referred to in paragraph 2, ordinary mail is not delivered in the locality in which the Office is situated, the time limit shall extend until the first day thereafter on which the Office is open for receipt of documents and on which ordinary mail is delivered. [The days referred to in the first sentence shall be as stated by the President of the Office before the commencement of each calendar year and shall be published in the Official Gazette referred to in Article 87.]
2. If a time limit expires on a day on which there is a general interruption or a subsequent dislocation in the delivery of mail in a Member State or between a Member State and the Office, the time limit shall be extended until the first day following the end of the period of dislocation or interruption in the delivery of mail for parties to proceedings having their domicile or seat or establishment in the Member State concerned or having appointed procedural representatives with a seat in that State. Should the Member State concerned be the State in which the Office is located, this provision shall apply to all parties to proceedings. The duration of the period of interruption or dislocation shall be as stated and communicated by the President of the Office.

[As regards documents submitted by electronic means, the first subparagraph shall apply *mutatis mutandis* where there is an interruption of the connection of the Office or of one of the parties to the proceedings to the electronic means of communication. Parties to the proceedings shall demonstrate the interruption of the connection with the electronic provider.]
3. Paragraphs 1 and 2 shall apply *mutatis mutandis* to the national agencies, or the sub-offices designated, pursuant to Article 30(4) of the basic Regulation as well as to the Examination Offices.

NOTES

Para 1: words in square brackets substituted by Commission Implementing Regulation 2016/1448/EU, Art 1(33)(a).
Para 2: words in square brackets substituted by Commission Implementing Regulation 2016/1448/EU, Art 1(33)(b).

[6.354]
Article 72
Interruption of proceedings

1. Proceedings before the Office shall be interrupted:

Part 6 Plant Varieties Protection

(a) in the event of the death or legal incapacity of the applicant for, or holder of, a Community plant variety right or of the applicant for an exploitation right to be granted by the Office or of the person entitled to enjoy such exploitation right, or of the procedural representative of any of those parties; or
(b) in the event of a supervening legal impediment to such person's continuation of proceedings before the Office, due to some action taken against his property.

2. When the necessary particulars in respect of the identity of the person authorised to continue proceedings as party thereto or procedural representative have been entered in the relevant register, the Office shall inform such person and the other parties that the proceedings shall be resumed as from the date to be determined by the Office.
3. The time limits in force shall begin afresh as from the day on which proceedings are resumed.
4. The interruption of proceedings shall not affect the pursuit of the technical examination or verification of the variety concerned by an Examination Office where the relevant fees have already been paid to the Office.

CHAPTER V
PROCEDURAL REPRESENTATIVES

[6.355]
Article 73
Designation of a procedural representative
1. Any designation of a procedural representative shall be communicated to the Office. The communication shall contain the name and address of the procedural representative; Article 2(2) and (3) shall apply *mutatis mutandis*.
2. Without prejudice to Article 2(4), the communication referred to in paragraph 1 shall also identify as such any employee of the party to proceedings. An employee may not be designated as a procedural representative within the meaning of Article 82 of the basic Regulation.
3. Failure to comply with the provisions of paragraphs 1 and 2 shall lead to the communication being deemed not to have been received.
4. A procedural representative whose mandate has ended shall continue to be considered as procedural representative until the termination of his mandate has been communicated to the Office. Subject to any provisions to the contrary contained therein, a mandate shall however, terminate vis-à-vis the Office upon the death of the person who conferred it.
[5. Two or more parties to proceedings acting in common shall appoint one procedural representative and notify the Office thereof. Where they have not notified a procedural representative to the Office, the party to the proceedings first named in an application for a Community plan variety right or for an exploitation right to be granted by the Office or in an objection shall be deemed to be appointed as the procedural representative of the other party or parties to the proceedings.]
[6. Paragraph 5 shall apply where, in the course of proceedings, a transfer of a Community plant variety right is made to more than one person and where such persons have appointed more than one procedural representative.]

NOTES
Para 5: substituted by Commission Implementing Regulation 2016/1448/EU, Art 1(34)(a).
Para 6: added by Commission Implementing Regulation 2016/1448/EU, Art 1(34)(b).

[6.356]
Article 74
Credentials of procedural representatives
1. Where the appointment of a procedural representative is notified to the Office, the necessary signed credentials shall be presented for inclusion in the files within such period as the Office may specify unless otherwise provided. If the credentials are not filed in due time, any procedural step taken by the procedural representative shall be deemed not to have been taken.
[2. Credentials may cover one or more proceedings. General credentials enabling a procedural representative to act in all the proceedings of the party giving the credentials may be filed. A single document embodying the general credentials shall be sufficient.]
3. The President of the Office may determine the contents of, and make available, forms for credentials, including the general credentials referred to in paragraph 2, free of charge.
[4. The entry of a procedural representative in the Register of Applications for Community Plant Variety Rights shall be deleted:
(a) in the event of the death or legal incapacity of the procedural representative;
(b) where the procedural representative is no longer domiciled or no longer has his seat or establishment within the European Union;
(c) where the procedural representative is no longer appointed by the party to the proceedings and the party has informed the Office accordingly.]

NOTES
Para 2: substituted by Commission Implementing Regulation 2016/1448/EU, Art 1(35)(a).

Para 4: added by Commission Implementing Regulation 2016/1448/EU, Art 1(35)(b).

CHAPTER VI
APPORTIONMENT AND DETERMINATION OF COSTS

[6.357]
Article 75
Awards of costs

1. A decision as to costs shall be dealt with in the decision on the revocation or cancellation of a Community plant variety right, or the decision on the appeal.
2. In the case of an award of costs pursuant to Article 85(1) of the basic Regulation, the Office shall set out that award in the statement of the grounds of the decision on the revocation or cancellation of a Community plant variety right, or the decision on the appeal. The parties to proceedings may not plead the omission of that indication.

[6.358]
Article 76
Determination of costs

1. A request for the determination of costs shall be admissible only if the decision has been taken in respect of which the determination of costs is required and if, in the event of an appeal against such decision, the Board of Appeal has decided upon that appeal. A bill of costs, with supporting documents, shall be attached to the request.
2. Costs may be determined once their credibility is established.
3. Where one party to proceedings incurs the costs of another party to the proceedings, it shall not be required to reimburse any costs other than those referred to in paragraph 4. Where the successful party to proceedings is represented by more than one agent, adviser or advocate, the losing party shall bear the costs referred to in paragraph 4 for one such person only.
4. The costs essential to proceedings shall cover:
 (a) costs of witnesses and experts paid by the Office to the witness or expert concerned;
 (b) expenses for travel and subsistence of a party to proceedings and an agent, adviser or advocate duly designated as a procedural representative before the Office, within the relevant scales applicable to witnesses and experts laid down in Annex I;
 (c) remuneration of an agent, adviser or advocate duly designated as the procedural representative of a party to proceedings before the Office, within the scales laid down in Annex I.

[6.359]
Article 77
Settlement of costs

In the event of a settlement of costs referred to in Article 85(4) of the basic Regulation, the Office shall confirm such settlement in a communication to the parties to the proceedings. Where such communication confirms also a settlement as to the amount of costs to be paid, a request for the determination of costs shall be inadmissible.

TITLE V
INFORMATION GIVEN TO THE PUBLIC

CHAPTER I
REGISTERS, PUBLIC INSPECTION AND PUBLICATIONS

SECTION 1
THE REGISTERS

[6.360]
Article 78
Entries related to proceedings and to Community plant variety rights, to be entered in the Registers

1. The following 'other particulars' referred to in Article 87(3) of the basic Regulation shall be entered in the Register of Applications for Community Plant Variety Rights:
 (a) date of publication where such publication is a relevant event for the computation of time limits;
 (b) any objection, together with its date, the name and address of the objector and those of his procedural representative;
 [(c) a particular claim regarding priority pursuant to Article 20 of this Regulation (date and place of the earlier application);]
 (d) any institution of actions in respect of claims referred to in Article 98(4) and Article 99 of the basic Regulation as to entitlement to the Community plant variety right, and the final decision in, or of any other termination of, any such action;

[(e) the giving of the right deriving from an application for a Community plant variety right as a security or as the object of any other rights in rem.]

2. The following 'other particulars' referred to in Article 87(3) of the basic Regulation shall be entered in the Register of Community Plant Variety Rights, upon request:

(a) the giving of a Community plant variety right as a security or as the object of any other rights *in rem*; or

(b) any institution of actions in respect of claims referred to in Article 98(1) and (2) and Article 99 of the basic Regulation and relating to the Community plant variety right, and the final decision in, or of any other termination of, any such action.

3. The President of the Office shall decide upon the details of the entries to be made and may decide upon further particulars to be entered in the Registers for the purpose of the management of the Office.

The President of the Office shall determine the form of Registers. The Registers may be maintained in the form of an electronic database.

NOTES

Para 1: point (c) substituted and point (e) inserted by Commission Implementing Regulation 2016/1448/EU, Art 1(36).

[6.361]
Article 79
Entry of transfer of a Community plant variety right

1. Any transfer of Community plant variety rights shall be entered in the Register of Community Plant Variety Rights on production of documentary evidence of the transfer, or of official documents confirming the transfer, or of such extracts from those documents as suffice to establish the transfer. The Office shall retain a copy of those pieces of documentary evidence in its files.

The President of the Office shall determine the form in and the conditions under which those pieces of documentary evidence are to be retained in the files of the Office.

2. The entry of a transfer may be refused only in the event of failure to comply with the conditions laid down in paragraph 1 and in Article 23 of the basic Regulation.

3. Paragraphs 1 and 2 shall apply to any transfer of an entitlement to a Community plant variety right for which an application has been entered in the Register of Applications for Community Plant Variety Rights. The reference to the Register of Community Plant Variety Rights shall be understood as a reference to the Register of Applications for Community Plant Variety Rights.

[6.362]
Article 80
Conditions for entries in the Registers

Without prejudice to other provisions of the basic Regulation or of this Regulation, a request for an entry or a deletion of an entry in the Registers may be made by any interested person. The request shall be made in writing, accompanied by supporting documents.

[6.363]
Article 81
Conditions for specific entries in the Registers

1. Where a Community plant variety right applied for or granted is concerned by bankruptcy or like proceedings, an entry to this effect shall be made, free of charge, in the Register for Community Plant Variety Rights at the request of the competent national authority. This entry shall also be deleted at the request of the competent national authority, free of charge.

[2. Paragraph 1 shall apply *mutatis mutandis* to the institution of actions in respect of claims referred to in Articles 98 and 99 of the basic Regulation, and the final decision not subject to any appeal in, or of any other termination of, any such action.

3. Where varieties are identified as initial or essentially derived, respectively, a request for entry by all the parties to the proceedings may be made jointly or separately. A request from only one party to the proceedings shall be accompanied by documentary evidence of the elements referred to in Article 87(2)(h) of the basic Regulation to replace the request of the other party. Such documentary evidence shall include the identification of the varieties concerned as initial and essentially derived, and the non-contentious acknowledgement by the other party or the final judgement.]

4. Where the entry of a contractual exclusive exploitation right or of a Community plant variety right given as security or as the subject of rights *in rem* is requested, such request shall be accompanied by sufficient documentary evidence.

NOTES

Paras 2, 3: substituted by Commission Implementing Regulation 2016/1448/EU, Art 1(37).

[6.364]
Article 82
Public inspection of the Registers

1. The Registers shall be open for public inspection on the premises of the Office.

Access to the Registers and the documents held therein shall be granted under the same terms and conditions as apply to the access to documents held by the Office within the meaning of Article 84.
2. On-the-spot inspection of the Registers shall be free of charge.
The production and delivery of extracts from the Registers in any form that requires the processing or manipulating of data other than the mere reproduction of a document or parts thereof shall be subject to the payment of a fee.
[3. The President of the Office may provide for public inspection of the Registers on the premises of national agencies or sub-offices involved in the exercise of specific administrative functions, pursuant to Article 30(4) of the basic Regulation.]

NOTES

Para 3: substituted by Commission Implementing Regulation 2016/1448/EU, Art 1(38).

SECTION 2
KEEPING OF DOCUMENTS, PUBLIC INSPECTION OF DOCUMENTS AND VARIETIES GROWN

[6.365]
Article 83
Keeping of the files

[1. Documents relating to proceedings shall be kept in electronic format in electronic files, a file number being attached to such proceedings, except for those documents relating to the exclusion of, or objection to, members of the Board of Appeal, or to the staff of the Office or the Examination Office concerned, which shall be kept separately.
2. The Office shall keep an electronic copy of the file referred in paragraph 1 ("file copy") which shall be considered the true and complete copy of the file. The Examination Office shall keep a copy of the additional documents relating to such proceedings (examination copy).]
3. The original documents filed by parties to the proceedings which form the basis of any electronic files may be disposed of after a period following their reception by the Office.
4. The President of the Office shall determine the details as to the form in which the files are to be kept, the period during which files are to be kept and the period referred to in paragraph 3.

NOTES

Paras 1, 2: substituted by Commission Implementing Regulation 2016/1448/EU, Art 1(39).

[6.366]
Article 84
Access to documents held by the Office

1. The Administrative Council shall adopt the practical arrangements for access to the documents held by the Office, including the Registers.
2. The Administrative Council shall adopt the categories of documents of the Office that are to be made directly accessible to the public by way of publication, including publication by electronic means.

[6.367]
Article 85
Inspection of the growing of the varieties

1. A request for inspection of the growing of the varieties shall be addressed in writing to the Office. With the consent of the Office, access to the test plots shall be arranged by the Examination Office.
2. Without prejudice to Article 88(3) of the basic Regulation, general access to the test plots by visitors shall not be affected by the provisions of this Regulation, provided that all grown varieties are coded, that appropriate measures against any removal of material are taken by the Examination Office entrusted and are approved by the Office, and that all necessary steps are taken to safeguard the rights of the applicant for, or holder of, a Community plant variety right.
3. The President of the Office may lay down the details of the procedure for the inspection of the growing of the varieties, and may review the safeguards to be provided under paragraph 2.

[6.368]
Article 86
Confidential information

For the purpose of keeping information confidential, the Office shall make available, free of charge, forms to be used by the applicant for a Community plant variety right in order to request the withholding of all data relating to components as referred to in Article 88(3) of the basic Regulation.

SECTION 3
PUBLICATIONS

[6.369]
Article 87
Official Gazette

1. The publication to be issued at least every two months pursuant to Article 89 of the basic Regulation shall be called the Official Gazette of the Community Plant Variety Office (hereinafter the Official Gazette).
2. The Official Gazette shall also contain the information entered in the Registers pursuant to Article 78(1)(c) and (d), Article 78(2) and Article 79.
3. The President of the Office shall determine the manner in which the Official Gazette is published.

[6.370]
Article 88
Publication of applications for exploitation rights to be granted by the Office and decisions thereon

The date of receipt of an application for an exploitation right to be granted by the Office and of delivery of the decision on such application, the names and addresses of the parties to proceedings and the form of order sought, or decided upon, shall be published in the Official Gazette. In the case of a decision to grant a compulsory licence, the contents of such decision shall likewise be published.

[6.371]
Article 89
Publication of appeals and decisions thereon

The date of receipt of a notice of appeal and of delivery of the decision on such appeal, the names and addresses of the parties to the appeal proceedings and the form of order sought, or decided upon, shall be published in the Official Gazette.

CHAPTER II
ADMINISTRATIVE AND LEGAL COOPERATION

[6.372]
Article 90
Communication of information

1. Information to be exchanged in accordance with Article 90 of the basic Regulation shall be communicated directly between the authorities referred to in that provision.
2. The communication of information referred to in Article 91(1) of the basic Regulation by or to the Office may be effected through the competent plant variety offices of the Member States, free of charge.
3. Paragraph 2 shall apply *mutatis mutandis* to the communication of information referred to in Article 91(1) of the basic Regulation effected to or by the Examination Office. The Office shall receive a copy of such communication.

[6.373]
Article 91
Inspection by or via courts or public prosecutors' offices of the Member States

1. The inspection of files under Article 91(1) of the basic Regulation shall be of copies of the files issued by the Office exclusively for that purpose.
2. Courts or public prosecutors' offices of the Member States may, in the course of proceedings before them, lay the documents transmitted by the Office open to inspection by third parties. Such inspection shall be subject to Article 88 of the basic Regulation; the Office shall not charge any fee for it.
[3. At the time of transmission of the files to the courts or public prosecutor's offices of the Member States, the Office shall indicate the restrictions to which the inspection of documents relating to applications for, or to grants of Community plant variety rights is subject pursuant to Articles 33a and 88 of the basic Regulation.]

NOTES
Para 3: substituted by Commission Implementing Regulation 2016/1448/EU, Art 1(40).

[6.374]
Article 92
Procedure for letters rogatory

1. Each Member State shall designate a central authority which will undertake to receive letters rogatory issued by the Office and to transmit them to the court or authority competent to execute them.

2. The Office shall draw up letters rogatory in the language of the competent court or authority or shall attach to such letters a translation into that language.
3. Subject to paragraphs 4 and 5, the competent court or authority shall apply its own law as to the procedures to be followed in executing such requests. In particular, it shall apply suitable coercive measures in accordance with its law.
4. The Office shall be informed of the time when, and the place where, the enquiry or other legal measures is to take place and shall inform the parties to proceedings, witnesses and experts concerned.
5. If so requested by the Office, the competent court or authority shall permit the attendance of the staff of the Office concerned and allow them to question any person giving evidence, either directly or through the competent court or authority.
6. The execution of letters rogatory shall not give rise to any charge of fees or to costs of any kind. Nevertheless, the Member State in which letters rogatory are executed shall have the right to require the Office to reimburse any fees paid to experts and interpreters and the costs arising from the procedure under paragraph 5.

TITLE VI
FINAL PROVISIONS

[6.375]
Article 93
Regulation (EC) No 1239/95 is repealed.
References to the repealed Regulation shall be construed as references to this Regulation and shall be read in accordance with the correlation table in Annex III.

[6.376]
Article 94
Entry into force
This Regulation shall enter into force on the 20th day following its publication in the *Official Journal of the European Union*.
This Regulation shall be binding in its entirety and directly applicable in all Member States.

ANNEX I

[6.377]
1. The compensation payable to witnesses and experts in respect of travel and subsistence expenses provided for in Article 62(2) shall be calculated as follows:

1.1. Travel expenses:
For the outward and return journey between the domicile or seat and the place where oral proceedings are held or where evidence is taken:
(a) the cost of the first-class rail transport including usual transport supplements shall be paid where the total distance by the shortest rail route does not exceed 800 km;
(b) the cost of the tourist-class air transport shall be paid where the total distance by the shortest rail route exceeds 800 km or the shortest route requires a sea-crossing.

1.2. Subsistence expenses shall be paid equal to the daily subsistence allowance of officials as laid down in Article 13 of Annex VII to the Staff Regulations of Officials of the European Communities.

1.3. When a witness or expert is summoned to proceedings at the Office he shall receive with the summons a travel order containing details of those amounts payable under points 1.1 and 1.2, together with a request form covering an advance on expenses. Before an advance can be paid to a witness or expert his entitlement must be certified by the member of the staff of the Office who ordered the evidence to be taken or, in the case of appeal proceedings, the chairman of the responsible Board of Appeal. The request form must therefore be returned to the Office for certification.

2. The compensation payable to witnesses in respect of loss of earnings provided for in Article 62(3) shall be calculated as follows:

2.1. If a witness is required to be absent for a total period of 12 hours or less, the compensation for loss of earnings shall be equal to one sixtieth of the basic monthly salary of an employee of the Office at the lowest step of grade AD 12.

2.2. If a witness is required to be absent for a total period of more than 12 hours, he shall be entitled to payment of further compensation equal to one sixtieth of the basic salary referred to in point 2.1 in respect of each further period of 12 hours which is commenced.

3. The fees payable to experts provided for in Article 62(3) shall be determined, case by case, taking into account a proposal by the expert concerned. The Office may decide to invite the parties to proceedings to submit their comments on the amount proposed. [Fees may be paid to an expert only if he produces evidence by supporting documents that he is not a member of the staff of an Examination Office or a technical qualified body.]

4. Payments to witnesses or experts for loss of earnings or fees under points 2 and 3 shall be made following certification of the entitlement of the witness or expert concerned by the member of the staff of the Office who ordered the evidence to be taken or, in the case of the appeal proceedings, the chairman of the responsible Boards of Appeal.

5. The remuneration of an agent, adviser or advocate acting as a representative of a party to proceedings as provided for in Article 76(3) and Article 76(4)(c) shall be borne by the other party to proceedings on the basis of the following maximum rates:

(a) in the case of appeal proceedings except for the taking of evidence which involves the examination of witnesses, opinions by experts or inspection: EUR [550];

(b) in the case of taking of evidence in appeal proceedings which involves the examination of witnesses, opinions by experts or inspection: EUR [400];

[(c) in the case of proceedings for nullity or cancellation of a Community plant variety right: EUR 450.]

NOTES

Point 3: words in square brackets substituted by Commission Implementing Regulation 2016/1448/EU, Art 1(41), Annex, para (1).

Point 5: figures and words in square brackets substituted by Commission Implementing Regulation 2016/1448/EU, Art 1(41), Annex, para (2).

ANNEX II
REPEALED REGULATION WITH LIST OF ITS SUCCESSIVE AMENDMENTS

[6.378]

Commission Regulation (EC) No 1239/95	(OJ L121, 1.6.1995, p 37)
Commission Regulation (EC) No 448/96	(OJ L62, 13.3.1996, p 3)
Commission Regulation (EC) No 2181/2002	(OJ L331, 7.12.2002, p 14)
Commission Regulation (EC) No 1002/2005	(OJ L170, 1.7.2005, p 7)
Commission Regulation (EC) No 355/2008	(OJ L110, 22.4.2008, p 3)

ANNEX III
CORRELATION TABLE

[6.379]

Regulation (EC) No 1239/95	This Regulation
Articles 1 to 14	Articles 1 to 14
Article 15(1), (2) and (3)	Article 15(1), (2) and (3)
Article 15(4)	—
Article 15(5) and (6)	Article 15(5) and (6)
Articles 16 to 26	Articles 16 to 26
Article 27(1), first to fourth indents	Article 27(1) (a) to (d)
Article 27(2) and (3)	Article 27(2) and (3)
Article 27(4), first to fourth indents	Article 27(4) (a) to (d)
Articles 28 to 40	Articles 28 to 40
Article 41, first sentence	Article 41(1)
Article 41(1) to (4)	Article 41(2) to (5)
Articles 42 to 64	Articles 42 to 64
Article 65(2) to (5)	Article 65(1) to (4)
Articles 66 to 92	Articles 66 to 92
Article 93(1)	Article 15(4)
Article 93(2) and (3)	—
Article 94	—
—	Article 93
Article 95	Article 94
Annex	Annex I
—	Annexes II and III

INTERNATIONAL CONVENTION FOR THE PROTECTION OF NEW VARIETIES OF PLANTS (UPOV CONVENTION)

of December 2, 1961, as revised at Geneva on November 10, 1972, on October 23, 1978, and on March 19, 1991

NOTES

CHAPTER I
DEFINITIONS

[6.380]
Article 1
Definitions

For the purposes of this Act—

(i) "this Convention" means the present (1991) Act of the International Convention for the Protection of New Varieties of Plants;

(ii) "Act of 1961/1972" means the International Convention for the Protection of New Varieties of Plants of December 2, 1961, as amended by the Additional Act of November 10, 1972;

(iii) "Act of 1978" means the Act of October 23, 1978, of the International Convention for the Protection of New Varieties of Plants;

(iv) "breeder" means
- — the person who bred, or discovered and developed, a variety,
- — the person who is the employer of the aforementioned person or who has commissioned the latter's work, where the laws of the relevant Contracting Party so provide, or
- — the successor in title of the first or second aforementioned person, as the case may be;

(v) "breeder's right" means the right of the breeder provided for in this Convention;

(vi) "variety" means a plant grouping within a single botanical taxon of the lowest known rank, which grouping, irrespective of whether the conditions for the grant of a breeder's right are fully met, can be
- — defined by the expression of the characteristics resulting from a given genotype or combination of genotypes,
- — distinguished from any other plant grouping by the expression of at least one of the said characteristics and
- — considered as a unit with regard to its suitability for being propagated unchanged;

(vii) "Contracting Party" means a State or an intergovernmental organisation party to this Convention;

(viii) "territory," in relation to a Contracting Party, means, where the Contracting Party is a State, the territory of that State and, where the Contracting Party is an intergovernmental organisation, the territory in which the constituting treaty of that intergovernmental organisation applies;

(ix) "authority" means the authority referred to in Article 30(1)(ii);

(x) "Union" means the Union for the Protection of New Varieties of Plants founded by the Act of 1961 and further mentioned in the Act of 1972, the Act of 1978 and in this Convention;

(xi) "member of the Union" means a State party to the Act of 1961/1972 or the Act of 1978, or a Contracting Party.

CHAPTER II
GENERAL OBLIGATIONS OF THE CONTRACTING PARTIES

[6.381]
Article 2
Basic Obligation of the Contracting Parties

Each Contracting Party shall grant and protect breeders' rights.

[6.382]
Article 3
Genera and Species to be Protected

(1) [*States already members of the Union*] Each Contracting Party which is bound by the Act of 1961/1972 or the Act of 1978 shall apply the provisions of this Convention,

(i) at the date on which it becomes bound by this Convention, to all plant genera and species to which it applies, on the said date, the provisions of the Act of 1961/1972 or the Act of 1978 and,

(ii) at the latest by the expiration of a period of five years after the said date, to all plant genera and species.

(2) [*New members of the Union*] Each Contracting Party which is not bound by the Act of 1961/1972 or the Act of 1978 shall apply the provisions of this Convention,

(i) at the date on which it becomes bound by this Convention, to at least 15 plant genera or species and,

(ii) at the latest by the expiration of a period of 10 years from the said date, to all plant genera and species.

[6.383]
Article 4
National Treatment

(1) [*Treatment*] Without prejudice to the rights specified in this Convention, nationals of a Contracting Party as well as natural persons resident and legal entities having their registered offices within the territory of a Contracting Party shall, insofar as the grant and protection of breeders' rights are concerned, enjoy within the territory of each other Contracting Party the same treatment as is accorded or may hereafter be accorded by the laws of each such other Contracting Party to its own nationals, provided that the said nationals, natural persons or legal entities comply with the conditions and formalities imposed on the nationals of the said other Contracting Party.

(2) [*"Nationals"*] For the purposes of the preceding paragraph, "nationals" means, where the Contracting Party is a State, the nationals of that State and, where the Contracting Party is an intergovernmental organisation, the nationals of the States which are members of that organisation.

CHAPTER III
CONDITIONS FOR THE GRANT OF THE BREEDER'S RIGHT

[6.384]
Article 5
Conditions of Protection

(1) [*Criteria to be satisfied*] The breeder's right shall be granted where the variety is

(i) new,
(ii) distinct,
(iii) uniform and
(iv) stable.

(2) [*Other conditions*] The grant of the breeder's right shall not be subject to any further or different conditions, provided that the variety is designated by a denomination in accordance with the provisions of Article 20, that the applicant complies with the formalities provided for by the law of the Contracting Party with whose authority the application has been filed and that he pays the required fees.

[6.385]
Article 6
Novelty

(1) [*Criteria*] The variety shall be deemed to be new if, at the date of filing of the application for a breeder's right, propagating or harvested material of the variety has not been sold or otherwise disposed of to others, by or with the consent of the breeder, for purposes of exploitation of the variety

(i) in the territory of the Contracting Party in which the application has been filed earlier than one year before that date and

(ii) in a territory other than that of the Contracting Party in which the application has been filed earlier than four years or, in the case of trees or of vines, earlier than six years before the said date.

(2) [*Varieties of recent creation*] Where a Contracting Party applies this Convention to a plant genus or species to which it did not previously apply this Convention or an earlier Act, it may consider a variety of recent creation existing at the date of such extension of protection to satisfy the condition of novelty defined in paragraph (1) even where the sale or disposal to others described in that paragraph took place earlier than the time limits defined in that paragraph.

(3) [*"Territory" in certain cases*] For the purposes of paragraph (1), all the Contracting Parties which are member States of one and the same intergovernmental organisation may act jointly, where the regulations of that organisation so require, to assimilate acts done on the territories of the States members of that organisation to acts done on their own territories and, should they do so, shall notify the Secretary-General accordingly.

[6.386]
Article 7
Distinctness

The variety shall be deemed to be distinct if it is clearly distinguishable from any other variety whose existence is a matter of common knowledge at the time of the filing of the application. In particular, the filing of an application for the granting of a breeder's right or for the entering of another variety in an official register of varieties, in any country, shall be deemed to render that other variety a matter of common knowledge from the date of the application, provided that the application leads to the granting of a breeder's right or to the entering of the said other variety in the official register of varieties, as the case may be.

[6.387]
Article 8
Uniformity

The variety shall be deemed to be uniform if, subject to the variation that may be expected from the particular features of its propagation, it is sufficiently uniform in its relevant characteristics.

[6.388]
Article 9
Stability

The variety shall be deemed to be stable if its relevant characteristics remain unchanged after repeated propagation or, in the case of a particular cycle of propagation, at the end of each such cycle.

CHAPTER IV
APPLICATION FOR THE GRANT OF THE BREEDER'S RIGHT

[6.389]
Article 10
Filing of Applications

(1) [*Place of first application*] The breeder may choose the Contracting Party with whose authority he wishes to file his first application for a breeder's right.

(2) [*Time of subsequent applications*] The breeder may apply to the authorities of other Contracting Parties for the grant of breeders' rights without waiting for the grant to him of a breeder's right by the authority of the Contracting Party with which the first application was filed.

(3) [*Independence of protection*] No Contracting Party shall refuse to grant a breeder's right or limit its duration on the ground that protection for the same variety has not been applied for, has been refused or has expired in any other State or intergovernmental organisation.

[6.390]
Article 11
Right of Priority

(1) [*The right; its period*] Any breeder who has duly filed an application for the protection of a variety in one of the Contracting Parties (the "first application") shall, for the purpose of filing an application for the grant of a breeder's right for the same variety with the authority of any other Contracting Party (the "subsequent application"), enjoy a right of priority for a period of twelve months. This period shall be computed from the date of filing of the first application. The day of filing shall not be included in the latter period.

(2) [*Claiming the right*] In order to benefit from the right of priority, the breeder shall, in the subsequent application, claim the priority of the first application. The authority with which the subsequent application has been filed may require the breeder to furnish, within a period of not less than three months from the filing date of the subsequent application, a copy of the documents which constitute the first application, certified to be a true copy by the authority with which that application was filed, and samples or other evidence that the variety which is the subject matter of both applications is the same.

(3) [*Documents and material*] The breeder shall be allowed a period of two years after the expiration of the period of priority or, where the first application is rejected or withdrawn, an appropriate time after such rejection or withdrawal, in which to furnish, to the authority of the Contracting Party with which he has filed the subsequent application, any necessary information, document or material required for the purpose of the examination under Article 12, as required by the laws of that Contracting Party.

(4) [*Events occurring during the period*] Events occurring within the period provided for in paragraph (1), such as the filing of another application or the publication or use of the variety that is the subject of the first application, shall not constitute a ground for rejecting the subsequent application. Such events shall also not give rise to any third-party right.

[6.391]
Article 12
Examination of the Application
Any decision to grant a breeder's right shall require an examination for compliance with the conditions under Article 5 to Article 9. In the course of the examination, the authority may grow the variety or carry out other necessary tests, cause the growing of the variety or the carrying out of other necessary tests, or take into account the results of growing tests or other trials which have already been carried out. For the purposes of examination, the authority may require the breeder to furnish all the necessary information, documents or material.

[6.392]
Article 13
Provisional Protection
Each Contracting Party shall provide measures designed to safeguard the interests of the breeder during the period between the filing or the publication of the application for the grant of a breeder's right and the grant of that right. Such measures shall have the effect that the holder of a breeder's right shall at least be entitled to equitable remuneration from any person who, during the said period, has carried out acts which, once the right is granted, require the breeder's authorisation as provided in Article 14. A Contracting Party may provide that the said measures shall only take effect in relation to persons whom the breeder has notified of the filing of the application.

CHAPTER V
THE RIGHTS OF THE BREEDER

[6.393]
Article 14
Scope of the Breeder's Right
(1) [*Acts in respect of the propagating material*]
(a) Subject to Article 15 and Article 16, the following acts in respect of the propagating material of the protected variety shall require the authorisation of the breeder—
(i) production or reproduction (multiplication),
(ii) conditioning for the purpose of propagation,
(iii) offering for sale,
(iv) selling or other marketing,
(v) exporting,
(vi) importing,
(vii) stocking for any of the purposes mentioned in (i) to (vi), above.
(b) The breeder may make his authorisation subject to conditions and limitations.
(2) [*Acts in respect of the harvested material*] Subject to Article 15 and Article 16, the acts referred to in items paragraph (1)(a)(i) to paragraph (1)(a)(vii) in respect of harvested material, including entire plants and parts of plants, obtained through the unauthorised use of propagating material of the protected variety shall require the authorisation of the breeder, unless the breeder has had reasonable opportunity to exercise his right in relation to the said propagating material.
(3) [*Acts in respect of certain products*] Each Contracting Party may provide that, subject to Article 15 and Article 16, the acts referred to in items paragraph (1)(a)(i) to paragraph (1)(a)(vii) in respect of products made directly from harvested material of the protected variety falling within the provisions of paragraph (2) through the unauthorised use of the said harvested material shall require the authorisation of the breeder, unless the breeder has had reasonable opportunity to exercise his right in relation to the said harvested material.
(4) [*Possible additional acts*] Each Contracting Party may provide that, subject to Article 15 and Article 16, acts other than those referred to in items paragraph (1)(a)(i) to paragraph (1)(a)(vii) shall also require the authorisation of the breeder.
(5) [*Essentially derived and certain other varieties*]
(a) The provisions of paragraph (1) to paragraph (4) shall also apply in relation to
(i) varieties which are essentially derived from the protected variety, where the protected variety is not itself an essentially derived variety,
(ii) varieties which are not clearly distinguishable in accordance with Article 7 from the protected variety and
(iii) varieties whose production requires the repeated use of the protected variety.
(b) For the purposes of subparagraph (a)(i), a variety shall be deemed to be essentially derived from another variety ("the initial variety") when
(i) it is predominantly derived from the initial variety, or from a variety that is itself predominantly derived from the initial variety, while retaining the expression of the essential characteristics that result from the genotype or combination of genotypes of the initial variety,
(ii) it is clearly distinguishable from the initial variety and
(iii) except for the differences which result from the act of derivation, it conforms to the initial variety in the expression of the essential characteristics that result from the genotype or combination of genotypes of the initial variety.

(c) Essentially derived varieties may be obtained for example by the selection of a natural or induced mutant, or of a somaclonal variant, the selection of a variant individual from plants of the initial variety, backcrossing, or transformation by genetic engineering.

[6.394]
Article 15
Exceptions to the Breeder's Right

(1) [*Compulsory exceptions*] The breeder's right shall not extend to
(i) acts done privately and for non-commercial purposes,
(ii) acts done for experimental purposes and
(iii) acts done for the purpose of breeding other varieties, and, except where the provisions of Article 14(5) apply, acts referred to in Article 14(1) to Article 14(4) in respect of such other varieties.

(2) [*Optional exception*] Notwithstanding Article 14, each Contracting Party may, within reasonable limits and subject to the safeguarding of the legitimate interests of the breeder, restrict the breeder's right in relation to any variety in order to permit farmers to use for propagating purposes, on their own holdings, the product of the harvest which they have obtained by planting, on their own holdings, the protected variety or a variety covered by Article 14(5)(a)(i) or Article 14(5)(a)(ii).

[6.395]
Article 16
Exhaustion of the Breeder's Right

(1) [*Exhaustion of right*] The breeder's right shall not extend to acts concerning any material of the protected variety, or of a variety covered by the provisions of Article 14(5), which has been sold or otherwise marketed by the breeder or with his consent in the territory of the Contracting Party concerned, or any material derived from the said material, unless such acts
(i) involve further propagation of the variety in question or
(ii) involve an export of material of the variety, which enables the propagation of the variety, into a country which does not protect varieties of the plant genus or species to which the variety belongs, except where the exported material is for final consumption purposes.

(2) [*Meaning of "material"*] For the purposes of paragraph (1), "material" means, in relation to a variety,
(i) propagating material of any kind,
(ii) harvested material, including entire plants and parts of plants, and
(iii) any product made directly from the harvested material.

(3) [*"Territory" in certain cases*] For the purposes of paragraph (1), all the Contracting Parties which are member States of one and the same intergovernmental organisation may act jointly, where the regulations of that organisation so require, to assimilate acts done on the territories of the States members of that organisation to acts done on their own territories and, should they do so, shall notify the Secretary-General accordingly.

[6.396]
Article 17
Restrictions on the Exercise of the Breeder's Right

(1) [*Public interest*] Except where expressly provided in this Convention, no Contracting Party may restrict the free exercise of a breeder's right for reasons other than of public interest.

(2) [*Equitable remuneration*] When any such restriction has the effect of authorising a third party to perform any act for which the breeder's authorisation is required, the Contracting Party concerned shall take all measures necessary to ensure that the breeder receives equitable remuneration.

[6.397]
Article 18
Measures Regulating Commerce

The breeder's right shall be independent of any measure taken by a Contracting Party to regulate within its territory the production, certification and marketing of material of varieties or the importing or exporting of such material. In any case, such measures shall not affect the application of the provisions of this Convention.

[6.398]
Article 19
Duration of the Breeder's Right

(1) [*Period of protection*] The breeder's right shall be granted for a fixed period.

(2) [*Minimum period*] The said period shall not be shorter than 20 years from the date of the grant of the breeder's right. For trees and vines, the said period shall not be shorter than 25 years from the said date.

CHAPTER VI
VARIETY DENOMINATION

[6.399]
Article 20
Variety Denomination

(1) [*Designation of varieties by denominations; use of the denomination*]

(a) The variety shall be designated by a denomination which will be its generic designation.

(b) Each Contracting Party shall ensure that, subject to paragraph (4), no rights in the designation registered as the denomination of the variety shall hamper the free use of the denomination in connection with the variety, even after the expiration of the breeder's right.

(2) [*Characteristics of the denomination*] The denomination must enable the variety to be identified. It may not consist solely of figures except where this is an established practice for designating varieties. It must not be liable to mislead or to cause confusion concerning the characteristics, value or identity of the variety or the identity of the breeder. In particular, it must be different from every denomination which designates, in the territory of any Contracting Party, an existing variety of the same plant species or of a closely related species.

(3) [*Registration of the denomination*] The denomination of the variety shall be submitted by the breeder to the authority. If it is found that the denomination does not satisfy the requirements of paragraph (2), the authority shall refuse to register it and shall require the breeder to propose another denomination within a prescribed period. The denomination shall be registered by the authority at the same time as the breeder's right is granted.

(4) [*Prior rights of third persons*] Prior rights of third persons shall not be affected. If, by reason of a prior right, the use of the denomination of a variety is forbidden to a person who, in accordance with the provisions of paragraph (7), is obliged to use it, the authority shall require the breeder to submit another denomination for the variety.

(5) [*Same denomination in all Contracting Parties*] A variety must be submitted to all Contracting Parties under the same denomination. The authority of each Contracting Party shall register the denomination so submitted, unless it considers the denomination unsuitable within its territory. In the latter case, it shall require the breeder to submit another denomination.

(6) [*Information among the authorities of Contracting Parties*] The authority of a Contracting Party shall ensure that the authorities of all the other Contracting Parties are informed of matters concerning variety denominations, in particular the submission, registration and cancellation of denominations. Any authority may address its observations, if any, on the registration of a denomination to the authority which communicated that denomination.

(7) [*Obligation to use the denomination*] Any person who, within the territory of one of the Contracting Parties, offers for sale or markets propagating material of a variety protected within the said territory shall be obliged to use the denomination of that variety, even after the expiration of the breeder's right in that variety, except where, in accordance with the provisions of paragraph (4), prior rights prevent such use.

(8) [*Indications used in association with denominations*] When a variety is offered for sale or marketed, it shall be permitted to associate a trademark, trade name or other similar indication with a registered variety denomination. If such an indication is so associated, the denomination must nevertheless be easily recognisable.

CHAPTER VII
NULLITY AND CANCELLATION OF THE BREEDER'S RIGHT

[6.400]
Article 21
Nullity of the Breeder's Right

(1) [*Reasons of nullity*] Each Contracting Party shall declare a breeder's right granted by it null and void when it is established

(i) that the conditions laid down in Article 6 or Article 7 were not complied with at the time of the grant of the breeder's right,

(ii) that, where the grant of the breeder's right has been essentially based upon information and documents furnished by the breeder, the conditions laid down in Article 8 or Article 9 were not complied with at the time of the grant of the breeder's right, or

(iii) that the breeder's right has been granted to a person who is not entitled to it, unless it is transferred to the person who is so entitled.

(2) [*Exclusion of other reasons*] No breeder's right shall be declared null and void for reasons other than those referred to in paragraph (1).

[6.401]
Article 22
Cancellation of the Breeder's Right

(1) [*Reasons for cancellation*]

(a) Each Contracting Party may cancel a breeder's right granted by it if it is established that the conditions laid down in Article 8 or Article 9 are no longer fulfilled.

(b) Furthermore, each Contracting Party may cancel a breeder's right granted by it if, after being requested to do so and within a prescribed period,
  (i) the breeder does not provide the authority with the information, documents or material deemed necessary for verifying the maintenance of the variety,
  (ii) the breeder fails to pay such fees as may be payable to keep his right in force, or
  (iii) the breeder does not propose, where the denomination of the variety is cancelled after the grant of the right, another suitable denomination.

(2) [*Exclusion of other reasons*] No breeder's right shall be cancelled for reasons other than those referred to in paragraph (1).

CHAPTER VIII
THE UNION

[6.402]
Article 23
Members
The Contracting Parties shall be members of the Union.

[6.403]
Article 24
Legal Status and Seat
(1) [*Legal personality*] The Union has legal personality.
(2) [*Legal capacity*] The Union enjoys on the territory of each Contracting Party, in conformity with the laws applicable in the said territory, such legal capacity as may be necessary for the fulfilment of the objectives of the Union and for the exercise of its functions.
(3) [*Seat*] The seat of the Union and its permanent organs are at Geneva.
(4) [*Headquarters agreement*] The Union has a headquarters agreement with the Swiss Confederation.

[6.404]
Article 25
Organs
The permanent organs of the Union are the Council and the Office of the Union.

[6.405]
Article 26
The Council
(1) [*Composition*] The Council shall consist of the representatives of the members of the Union. Each member of the Union shall appoint one representative to the Council and one alternate. Representatives or alternates may be accompanied by assistants or advisers.
(2) [*Officers*] The Council shall elect a President and a first Vice-President from among its members. It may elect other Vice-Presidents. The first Vice-President shall take the place of the President if the latter is unable to officiate. The President shall hold office for three years.
(3) [*Sessions*] The Council shall meet upon convocation by its President. An ordinary session of the Council shall be held annually. In addition, the President may convene the Council at his discretion; he shall convene it, within a period of three months, if one-third of the members of the Union so request.
(4) [*Observers*] States not members of the Union may be invited as observers to meetings of the Council. Other observers, as well as experts, may also be invited to such meetings.
(5) [*Tasks*] The tasks of the Council shall be to—
  (i) study appropriate measures to safeguard the interests and to encourage the development of the Union;
  (ii) establish its rules of procedure;
  (iii) appoint the Secretary-General and, if it finds it necessary, a Vice Secretary-General and determine the terms of appointment of each;
  (iv) examine an annual report on the activities of the Union and lay down the programme for its future work;
  (v) give to the Secretary-General all necessary directions for the accomplishment of the tasks of the Union;
  (vi) establish the administrative and financial regulations of the Union;
  (vii) examine and approve the budget of the Union and fix the contribution of each member of the Union;
  (viii) examine and approve the accounts presented by the Secretary-General;
  (ix) fix the date and place of the conferences referred to in Article 38 and take the measures necessary for their preparation; and
  (x) in general, take all necessary decisions to ensure the efficient functioning of the Union.
(6) [*Votes*]
  (a) Each member of the Union that is a State shall have one vote in the Council.

(b) Any Contracting Party that is an intergovernmental organisation may, in matters within its competence, exercise the rights to vote of its member States that are members of the Union. Such an intergovernmental organisation shall not exercise the rights to vote of its member States if its member States exercise their right to vote, and vice versa.

(7) [*Majorities*] Any decision of the Council shall require a simple majority of the votes cast, provided that any decision of the Council under paragraph (5)(ii), paragraph (5)(vi) and paragraph (5)(vii) and under Article 28(3), Article 29(5)(b) and Article 38(1) shall require three-fourths of the votes cast. Abstentions shall not be considered as votes.

[6.406]
Article 27
The Office of the Union

(1) [*Tasks and direction of the Office*] The Office of the Union shall carry out all the duties and tasks entrusted to it by the Council. It shall be under the direction of the Secretary-General.

(2) [*Duties of the Secretary-General*] The Secretary-General shall be responsible to the Council; he shall be responsible for carrying out the decisions of the Council. He shall submit the budget of the Union for the approval of the Council and shall be responsible for its implementation. He shall make reports to the Council on his administration and the activities and financial position of the Union.

(3) [*Staff*] Subject to the provisions of Article 26(5)(iii), the conditions of appointment and employment of the staff necessary for the efficient performance of the tasks of the Office of the Union shall be fixed in the administrative and financial regulations.

[6.407]
Article 28
Languages

(1) [*Languages of the Office*] The English, French, German and Spanish languages shall be used by the Office of the Union in carrying out its duties.

(2) [*Languages in certain meetings*] Meetings of the Council and of revision conferences shall be held in the four languages.

(3) [*Further languages*] The Council may decide that further languages shall be used.

[6.408]
Article 29
Finances

(1) [*Income*] The expenses of the Union shall be met from
  (i) the annual contributions of the States members of the Union,
  (ii) payments received for services rendered,
  (iii) miscellaneous receipts.

(2) [*Contributions: units*]
  (a) The share of each State member of the Union in the total amount of the annual contributions shall be determined by reference to the total expenditure to be met from the contributions of the States members of the Union and to the number of contribution units applicable to it under paragraph (3). The said share shall be computed according to paragraph (4).
  (b) The number of contribution units shall be expressed in whole numbers or fractions thereof, provided that no fraction shall be smaller than one-fifth.

(3) [*Contributions: share of each member*]
  (a) The number of contribution units applicable to any member of the Union which is party to the Act of 1961/1972 or the Act of 1978 on the date on which it becomes bound by this Convention shall be the same as the number applicable to it immediately before the said date.
  (b) Any other State member of the Union shall, on joining the Union, indicate, in a declaration addressed to the Secretary-General, the number of contribution units applicable to it.
  (c) Any State member of the Union may, at any time, indicate, in a declaration addressed to the Secretary-General, a number of contribution units different from the number applicable to it under subparagraph (a) or subparagraph (b). Such declaration, if made during the first six months of a calendar year, shall take effect from the beginning of the subsequent calendar year; otherwise, it shall take effect from the beginning of the second calendar year which follows the year in which the declaration was made.

(4) [*Contributions: computation of shares*]
  (a) For each budgetary period, the amount corresponding to one contribution unit shall be obtained by dividing the total amount of the expenditure to be met in that period from the contributions of the States members of the Union by the total number of units applicable to those States members of the Union.
  (b) The amount of the contribution of each State member of the Union shall be obtained by multiplying the amount corresponding to one contribution unit by the number of contribution units applicable to that State member of the Union.

(5) [*Arrears in contributions*]

(a) A State member of the Union which is in arrears in the payment of its contributions may not, subject to subparagraph (b), exercise its right to vote in the Council if the amount of its arrears equals or exceeds the amount of the contribution due from it for the preceding full year. The suspension of the right to vote shall not relieve such State member of the Union of its obligations under this Convention and shall not deprive it of any other rights thereunder.

(b) The Council may allow the said State member of the Union to continue to exercise its right to vote if, and as long as, the Council is satisfied that the delay in payment is due to exceptional and unavoidable circumstances.

(6) [*Auditing of the accounts*] The auditing of the accounts of the Union shall be effected by a State member of the Union as provided in the administrative and financial regulations. Such State member of the Union shall be designated, with its agreement, by the Council.

(7) [*Contributions of intergovernmental organisations*] Any Contracting Party which is an intergovernmental organisation shall not be obliged to pay contributions. If, nevertheless, it chooses to pay contributions, the provisions of paragraph (1) to paragraph (4) shall be applied accordingly.

CHAPTER IX
IMPLEMENTATION OF THE CONVENTION; OTHER AGREEMENTS

[6.409]
Article 30
Implementation of the Convention

(1) [*Measures of implementation*] Each Contracting Party shall adopt all measures necessary for the implementation of this Convention; in particular, it shall—

(i) provide for appropriate legal remedies for the effective enforcement of breeders' rights;
(ii) maintain an authority entrusted with the task of granting breeders' rights or entrust the said task to an authority maintained by another Contracting Party;
(iii) ensure that the public is informed through the regular publication of information concerning
— applications for and grants of breeders' rights, and
— proposed and approved denominations.

(2) [*Conformity of laws*] It shall be understood that, on depositing its instrument of ratification, acceptance, approval or accession, as the case may be, each State or intergovernmental organisation must be in a position, under its laws, to give effect to the provisions of this Convention.

[6.410]
Article 31
Relations Between Contracting Parties and States Bound by Earlier Acts

(1) [*Relations between States bound by this Convention*] Between States members of the Union which are bound both by this Convention and any earlier Act of the Convention, only this Convention shall apply.

(2) [*Possible relations with States not bound by this Convention*] Any State member of the Union not bound by this Convention may declare, in a notification addressed to the Secretary-General, that, in its relations with each member of the Union bound only by this Convention, it will apply the latest Act by which it is bound. As from the expiration of one month after the date of such notification and until the State member of the Union making the declaration becomes bound by this Convention, the said member of the Union shall apply the latest Act by which it is bound in its relations with each of the members of the Union bound only by this Convention, whereas the latter shall apply this Convention in respect of the former.

[6.411]
Article 32
Special Agreements

Members of the Union reserve the right to conclude among themselves special agreements for the protection of varieties, insofar as such agreements do not contravene the provisions of this Convention.

CHAPTER X
FINAL PROVISIONS

[6.412]
Article 33
Signature

This Convention shall be open for signature by any State which is a member of the Union at the date of its adoption. It shall remain open for signature until March 31, 1992.

[6.413]
Article 34
Ratification, Acceptance or Approval; Accession

(1) [*States and certain intergovernmental organisations*]

(a) Any State may, as provided in this Article, become party to this Convention.
(b) Any intergovernmental organisation may, as provided in this Article, become party to this Convention if it
 (i) has competence in respect of matters governed by this Convention,
 (ii) has its own legislation providing for the grant and protection of breeders' rights binding on all its member States and
 (iii) has been duly authorised, in accordance with its internal procedures, to accede to this Convention.

(2) [*Instrument of adherence*] Any State which has signed this Convention shall become party to this Convention by depositing an instrument of ratification, acceptance or approval of this Convention. Any State which has not signed this Convention and any intergovernmental organisation shall become party to this Convention by depositing an instrument of accession to this Convention. Instruments of ratification, acceptance, approval or accession shall be deposited with the Secretary-General.

(3) [*Advice of the Council*] Any State which is not a member of the Union and any intergovernmental organisation shall, before depositing its instrument of accession, ask the Council to advise it in respect of the conformity of its laws with the provisions of this Convention. If the decision embodying the advice is positive, the instrument of accession may be deposited.

[6.414]
Article 35
Reservations

(1) [*Principle*] Subject to paragraph (2), no reservations to this Convention are permitted.

(2) [*Possible exception*]
 (a) Notwithstanding the provisions of Article 3(1), any State which, at the time of becoming party to this Convention, is a party to the Act of 1978 and which, as far as varieties reproduced asexually are concerned, provides for protection by an industrial property title other than a breeder's right shall have the right to continue to do so without applying this Convention to those varieties.
 (b) Any State making use of the said right shall, at the time of depositing its instrument of ratification, acceptance, approval or accession, as the case may be, notify the Secretary-General accordingly. The same State may, at any time, withdraw the said notification.

[6.415]
Article 36
Communications Concerning Legislation and the Genera and Species Protected; Information to be Published

(1) [*Initial notification*] When depositing its instrument of ratification, acceptance or approval of or accession to this Convention, as the case may be, any State or intergovernmental organisation shall notify the Secretary-General of
 (i) its legislation governing breeder's rights and
 (ii) the list of plant genera and species to which, on the date on which it will become bound by this Convention, it will apply the provisions of this Convention.

(2) [*Notification of changes*] Each Contracting Party shall promptly notify the Secretary-General of
 (i) any changes in its legislation governing breeders' rights and
 (ii) any extension of the application of this Convention to additional plant genera and species.

(3) [*Publication of the information*] The Secretary-General shall, on the basis of communications received from each Contracting Party concerned, publish information on
 (i) the legislation governing breeders' rights and any changes in that legislation, and
 (ii) the list of plant genera and species referred to in paragraph (1)(ii) and any extension referred to in paragraph (2)(ii).

[6.416]
Article 37
Entry into Force; Closing of Earlier Acts

(1) [*Initial entry into force*] This Convention shall enter into force one month after five States have deposited their instruments of ratification, acceptance, approval or accession, as the case may be, provided that at least three of the said instruments have been deposited by States party to the Act of 1961/1972 or the Act of 1978.

(2) [*Subsequent entry into force*] Any State not covered by paragraph (1) or any intergovernmental organisation shall become bound by this Convention one month after the date on which it has deposited its instrument of ratification, acceptance, approval or accession, as the case may be.

(3) [*Closing of the 1978 Act*] No instrument of accession to the Act of 1978 may be deposited after the entry into force of this Convention according to paragraph (1), except that any State that, in conformity with the established practice of the General Assembly of the United Nations, is

regarded as a developing country may deposit such an instrument until December 31, 1995, and that any other State may deposit such an instrument until December 31, 1993, even if this Convention enters into force before that date.

[6.417]
Article 38
Revision of the Convention

(1) [*Conference*] This Convention may be revised by a conference of the members of the Union. The convocation of such conference shall be decided by the Council.

(2) [*Quorum and majority*] The proceedings of a conference shall be effective only if at least half of the States members of the Union are represented at it. A majority of three-quarters of the States members of the Union present and voting at the conference shall be required for the adoption of any revision.

[6.418]
Article 39
Denunciation

(1) [*Notifications*] Any Contracting Party may denounce this Convention by notification addressed to the Secretary-General. The Secretary-General shall promptly notify all members of the Union of the receipt of that notification.

(2) [*Earlier Acts*] Notification of the denunciation of this Convention shall be deemed also to constitute notification of the denunciation of any earlier Act by which the Contracting Party denouncing this Convention is bound.

(3) [*Effective date*] The denunciation shall take effect at the end of the calendar year following the year in which the notification was received by the Secretary-General.

(4) [*Acquired rights*] The denunciation shall not affect any rights acquired in a variety by reason of this Convention or any earlier Act prior to the date on which the denunciation becomes effective.

[6.419]
Article 40
Preservation of Existing Rights

This Convention shall not limit existing breeders' rights under the laws of Contracting Parties or by reason of any earlier Act or any agreement other than this Convention concluded between members of the Union.

[6.420]
Article 41
Original and Official Texts of the Convention

(1) [*Original*] This Convention shall be signed in a single original in the English, French and German languages, the French text prevailing in case of any discrepancy among the various texts. The original shall be deposited with the Secretary-General.

(2) [*Official texts*] The Secretary-General shall, after consultation with the interested Governments, establish official texts of this Convention in the Arabic, Dutch, Italian, Japanese and Spanish languages and such other languages as the Council may designate.

[6.421]
Article 42
Depositary Functions

(1) [*Transmittal of copies*] The Secretary-General shall transmit certified copies of this Convention to all States and intergovernmental organisations which were represented in the Diplomatic Conference that adopted this Convention and, on request, to any other State or intergovernmental organisation.

(2) [*Registration*] The Secretary-General shall register this Convention with the Secretariat of the United Nations.

[6.422]
Resolution on Article 14(5)

The Diplomatic Conference for the Revision of the International Convention for the Protection of New Varieties of Plants held from March 4 to 19, 1991, requests the Secretary-General of UPOV to start work immediately after the Conference on the establishment of draft standard guidelines, for adoption by the Council of UPOV, on essentially derived varieties.

Recommendation Relating to Article 15(2)

The Diplomatic Conference recommends that the provisions laid down in Article 15(2) of the International Convention for the Protection of New Varieties of Plants of December 2, 1961, as Revised at Geneva on November 10, 1972, on October 23, 1978, and on March 19, 1991, should not be read so as to be intended to open the possibility of extending the practice commonly called "farmer's privilege" to sectors of agricultural or horticultural production in which such a privilege is not a common practice on the territory of the Contracting Party concerned.

Common Statement Relating to Article 34

The Diplomatic Conference noted and accepted a declaration by the Delegation of Denmark and a declaration by the Delegation of the Netherlands according to which the Convention adopted by the Diplomatic Conference will not, upon its ratification, acceptance, approval or accession by Denmark or the Netherlands, be automatically applicable, in the case of Denmark, in Greenland and the Faroe Islands and, in the case of the Netherlands, in Aruba and the Netherlands Antilles. The said Convention will only apply in the said territories if and when Denmark or the Netherlands, as the case may be, expressly so notifies the Secretary-General.

PART 7
OTHER UK LEGISLATION

HUMAN RIGHTS ACT 1998

(1998 c 42)

An Act to give further effect to rights and freedoms guaranteed under the European Convention on Human Rights; to make provision with respect to holders of certain judicial offices who become judges of the European Court of Human Rights; and for connected purposes

[9 November 1998]

ARRANGEMENT OF SECTIONS

Introduction

[7.1]

1 The Convention Rights

(1) In this Act "the Convention rights" means the rights and fundamental freedoms set out in—
- (a) Articles 2 to 12 and 14 of the Convention,
- (b) Articles 1 to 3 of the First Protocol, and
- (c) [Article 1 of the Thirteenth Protocol],

as read with Articles 16 to 18 of the Convention.

Part 7 Other UK legislation

(2) Those Articles are to have effect for the purposes of this Act subject to any designated derogation or reservation (as to which see sections 14 and 15).
(3) The Articles are set out in Schedule 1.
(4) The [Secretary of State] may by order make such amendments to this Act as he considers appropriate to reflect the effect, in relation to the United Kingdom, of a protocol.
(5) In subsection (4) "protocol" means a protocol to the Convention—
(a) which the United Kingdom has ratified; or
(b) which the United Kingdom has signed with a view to ratification.
(6) No amendment may be made by an order under subsection (4) so as to come into force before the protocol concerned is in force in relation to the United Kingdom.

NOTES

Sub-s (1): words in square brackets in para (c) substituted by the Human Rights Act 1998 (Amendment) Order 2004, SI 2004/1574, art 2(1).

Sub-s (4): words in square brackets substituted by the Secretary of State for Constitutional Affairs Order 2003, SI 2003/1887, art 9, Sch 2, para 10(1).

[7.2]
2 Interpretation of Convention rights
(1) A court or tribunal determining a question which has arisen in connection with a Convention right must take into account any—
(a) judgment, decision, declaration or advisory opinion of the European Court of Human Rights,
(b) opinion of the Commission given in a report adopted under Article 31 of the Convention,
(c) decision of the Commission in connection with Article 26 or 27(2) of the Convention, or
(d) decision of the Committee of Ministers taken under Article 46 of the Convention,
whenever made or given, so far as, in the opinion of the court or tribunal, it is relevant to the proceedings in which that question has arisen.
(2) Evidence of any judgment, decision, declaration or opinion of which account may have to be taken under this section is to be given in proceedings before any court or tribunal in such manner as may be provided by rules.
(3) In this section "rules" means rules of court or, in the case of proceedings before a tribunal, rules made for the purposes of this section—
(a) by . . . [the Lord Chancellor or] the Secretary of State, in relation to any proceedings outside Scotland;
(b) by the Secretary of State, in relation to proceedings in Scotland; or
(c) by a Northern Ireland department, in relation to proceedings before a tribunal in Northern Ireland—
(i) which deals with transferred matters; and
(ii) for which no rules made under paragraph (a) are in force.

NOTES

Sub-s (3): words omitted from para (a) repealed by the Secretary of State for Constitutional Affairs Order 2003, SI 2003/1887, art 9, Sch 2, para 10(2); words in square brackets in para (a) inserted by the Transfer of Functions (Lord Chancellor and Secretary of State) Order 2005, SI 2005/3429, art 8, Schedule, para 3.

Rules: the Act of Adjournal (Criminal Procedure Rules Amendment No 2) (Human Rights Act 1998) 2000, SSI 2000/315; the Act of Sederunt (Rules of the Court of Session Amendment No 6) (Human Rights Act 1998) 2000, SSI 2000/316.

Legislation

[7.3]
3 Interpretation of legislation
(1) So far as it is possible to do so, primary legislation and subordinate legislation must be read and given effect in a way which is compatible with the Convention rights.
(2) This section—
(a) applies to primary legislation and subordinate legislation whenever enacted;
(b) does not affect the validity, continuing operation or enforcement of any incompatible primary legislation; and
(c) does not affect the validity, continuing operation or enforcement of any incompatible subordinate legislation if (disregarding any possibility of revocation) primary legislation prevents removal of the incompatibility.

[7.4]
4 Declaration of incompatibility
(1) Subsection (2) applies in any proceedings in which a court determines whether a provision of primary legislation is compatible with a Convention right.
(2) If the court is satisfied that the provision is incompatible with a Convention right, it may make a declaration of that incompatibility.
(3) Subsection (4) applies in any proceedings in which a court determines whether a provision of subordinate legislation, made in the exercise of a power conferred by primary legislation, is compatible with a Convention right.

(4) If the court is satisfied—
(a) that the provision is incompatible with a Convention right, and
(b) that (disregarding any possibility of revocation) the primary legislation concerned prevents removal of the incompatibility,

it may make a declaration of that incompatibility.

(5) In this section "court" means—
[(a) the Supreme Court;]
(b) the Judicial Committee of the Privy Council;
(c) the [Court Martial Appeal Court];
(d) in Scotland, the High Court of Justiciary sitting otherwise than as a trial court or the Court of Session;
(e) in England and Wales or Northern Ireland, the High Court or the Court of Appeal;
[(f) the Court of Protection, in any matter being dealt with by the President of the Family Division, the [Chancellor of the High Court] or a puisne judge of the High Court.]

(6) A declaration under this section ("a declaration of incompatibility")—
(a) does not affect the validity, continuing operation or enforcement of the provision in respect of which it is given; and
(b) is not binding on the parties to the proceedings in which it is made.

NOTES

Sub-s (5): para (a) substituted by the Constitutional Reform Act 2005, s 40(4), Sch 9, Pt 1, para 66(1), (2); words in square brackets in para (c) substituted by the Armed Forces Act 2006, s 378(1), Sch 16, para 156; para (f) added by the Mental Capacity Act 2005, s 67(1), Sch 6, para 43; words in square brackets in para (f) substituted by the Crime and Courts Act 2013, s 21(4), Sch 14, Pt 3, para 5(5).

[7.5]

5 Right of Crown to intervene

(1) Where a court is considering whether to make a declaration of incompatibility, the Crown is entitled to notice in accordance with rules of court.

(2) In any case to which subsection (1) applies—
(a) a Minister of the Crown (or a person nominated by him),
(b) a member of the Scottish Executive,
(c) a Northern Ireland Minister,
(d) a Northern Ireland department,

is entitled, on giving notice in accordance with rules of court, to be joined as a party to the proceedings.

(3) Notice under subsection (2) may be given at any time during the proceedings.

(4) A person who has been made a party to criminal proceedings (other than in Scotland) as the result of a notice under subsection (2) may, with leave, appeal to the [Supreme Court] against any declaration of incompatibility made in the proceedings.

(5) In subsection (4)—
"criminal proceedings" includes all proceedings before the [Court Martial Appeal Court]; and
"leave" means leave granted by the court making the declaration of incompatibility or by the [Supreme Court].

NOTES

Sub-s (4): words in square brackets substituted by the Constitutional Reform Act 2005, s 40(4), Sch 9, Pt 1, para 66(1), (3).

Sub-s (5): words in square brackets in definition "criminal proceedings" substituted by the Armed Forces Act 2006, s 378(1), Sch 16, para 157; words in square brackets in definition "leave" substituted by the Constitutional Reform Act 2005, s 40(4), Sch 9, Pt 1, para 66(1), (3).

Transfer of functions: the function under sub-s (2) shall be exercisable by the National Assembly for Wales concurrently with any Minister of the Crown by whom it is exercisable, in so far as it relates to any proceedings in which a court is considering whether to make a declaration of incompatibility within the meaning of s 4 of this Act, in respect of subordinate legislation made by the National Assembly, and subordinate legislation made, in relation to Wales, by a Minister of the Crown in the exercise of a function which is exercisable by the National Assembly: see the National Assembly for Wales (Transfer of Functions) (No 2) Order 2000, SI 2000/1830, art 2.

Rules: the Act of Adjournal (Criminal Procedure Rules Amendment No 2) (Human Rights Act 1998) 2000, SSI 2000/315; the Act of Sederunt (Rules of the Court of Session Amendment No 6) (Human Rights Act 1998) 2000, SSI 2000/316.

Public authorities

[7.6]

6 Acts of public authorities

(1) It is unlawful for a public authority to act in a way which is incompatible with a Convention right.

(2) Subsection (1) does not apply to an act if—
(a) as the result of one or more provisions of primary legislation, the authority could not have acted differently; or
(b) in the case of one or more provisions of, or made under, primary legislation which cannot be read or given effect in a way which is compatible with the Convention rights, the authority was acting so as to give effect to or enforce those provisions.

(3) In this section "public authority" includes—

(a) a court or tribunal, and
(b) any person certain of whose functions are functions of a public nature,
but does not include either House of Parliament or a person exercising functions in connection with proceedings in Parliament.
(4) . . .
(5) In relation to a particular act, a person is not a public authority by virtue only of subsection (3)(b) if the nature of the act is private.
(6) "An act" includes a failure to act but does not include a failure to—
(a) introduce in, or lay before, Parliament a proposal for legislation; or
(b) make any primary legislation or remedial order.

NOTES
Sub-s (4): repealed by the Constitutional Reform Act 2005, ss 40(4), 146, Sch 9, Pt 1, para 66(1), (4), Sch 18, Pt 5.

[7.7]
7 Proceedings
(1) A person who claims that a public authority has acted (or proposes to act) in a way which is made unlawful by section 6(1) may—
(a) bring proceedings against the authority under this Act in the appropriate court or tribunal, or
(b) rely on the Convention right or rights concerned in any legal proceedings,
but only if he is (or would be) a victim of the unlawful act.
(2) In subsection (1)(a) "appropriate court or tribunal" means such court or tribunal as may be determined in accordance with rules; and proceedings against an authority include a counterclaim or similar proceeding.
(3) If the proceedings are brought on an application for judicial review, the applicant is to be taken to have a sufficient interest in relation to the unlawful act only if he is, or would be, a victim of that act.
(4) If the proceedings are made by way of a petition for judicial review in Scotland, the applicant shall be taken to have title and interest to sue in relation to the unlawful act only if he is, or would be, a victim of that act.
(5) Proceedings under subsection (1)(a) must be brought before the end of—
(a) the period of one year beginning with the date on which the act complained of took place; or
(b) such longer period as the court or tribunal considers equitable having regard to all the circumstances,
but that is subject to any rule imposing a stricter time limit in relation to the procedure in question.
(6) In subsection (1)(b) "legal proceedings" includes—
(a) proceedings brought by or at the instigation of a public authority; and
(b) an appeal against the decision of a court or tribunal.
(7) For the purposes of this section, a person is a victim of an unlawful act only if he would be a victim for the purposes of Article 34 of the Convention if proceedings were brought in the European Court of Human Rights in respect of that act.
(8) Nothing in this Act creates a criminal offence.
(9) In this section "rules" means—
(a) in relation to proceedings before a court or tribunal outside Scotland, rules made by . . . [the Lord Chancellor or] the Secretary of State for the purposes of this section or rules of court,
(b) in relation to proceedings before a court or tribunal in Scotland, rules made by the Secretary of State for those purposes,
(c) in relation to proceedings before a tribunal in Northern Ireland—
(i) which deals with transferred matters; and
(ii) for which no rules made under paragraph (a) are in force,
rules made by a Northern Ireland department for those purposes,
and includes provision made by order under section 1 of the Courts and Legal Services Act 1990.
(10) In making rules, regard must be had to section 9.
(11) The Minister who has power to make rules in relation to a particular tribunal may, to the extent he considers it necessary to ensure that the tribunal can provide an appropriate remedy in relation to an act (or proposed act) of a public authority which is (or would be) unlawful as a result of section 6(1), by order add to—
(a) the relief or remedies which the tribunal may grant; or
(b) the grounds on which it may grant any of them.
(12) An order made under subsection (11) may contain such incidental, supplemental, consequential or transitional provision as the Minister making it considers appropriate.
(13) "The Minister" includes the Northern Ireland department concerned.

NOTES
Sub-s (9): words omitted from para (a) repealed by the Secretary of State for Constitutional Affairs Order 2003, SI 2003/1887, art 9, Sch 2, para 10(2); in para (a) words in square brackets inserted by the Transfer of Functions (Lord Chancellor and Secretary of State) Order 2005, SI 2005/3429, art 8, Schedule, para 3.

Rules: the Human Rights Act 1998 (Jurisdiction) (Scotland) Rules 2000, SSI 2000/301; the Proscribed Organisations Appeal Commission (Human Rights Act 1998 Proceedings) Rules 2006, SI 2006/2290.

[7.8]
8 Judicial remedies

(1) In relation to any act (or proposed act) of a public authority which the court finds is (or would be) unlawful, it may grant such relief or remedy, or make such order, within its powers as it considers just and appropriate.

(2) But damages may be awarded only by a court which has power to award damages, or to order the payment of compensation, in civil proceedings.

(3) No award of damages is to be made unless, taking account of all the circumstances of the case, including—

(a) any other relief or remedy granted, or order made, in relation to the act in question (by that or any other court), and

(b) the consequences of any decision (of that or any other court) in respect of that act,

the court is satisfied that the award is necessary to afford just satisfaction to the person in whose favour it is made.

(4) In determining—

(a) whether to award damages, or

(b) the amount of an award,

the court must take into account the principles applied by the European Court of Human Rights in relation to the award of compensation under Article 41 of the Convention.

(5) A public authority against which damages are awarded is to be treated—

(a) in Scotland, for the purposes of section 3 of the Law Reform (Miscellaneous Provisions) (Scotland) Act 1940 as if the award were made in an action of damages in which the authority has been found liable in respect of loss or damage to the person to whom the award is made;

(b) for the purposes of the Civil Liability (Contribution) Act 1978 as liable in respect of damage suffered by the person to whom the award is made.

(6) In this section—

"court" includes a tribunal;

"damages" means damages for an unlawful act of a public authority; and

"unlawful" means unlawful under section 6(1).

[7.9]
9 Judicial acts

(1) Proceedings under section 7(1)(a) in respect of a judicial act may be brought only—

(a) by exercising a right of appeal;

(b) on an application (in Scotland a petition) for judicial review; or

(c) in such other forum as may be prescribed by rules.

(2) That does not affect any rule of law which prevents a court from being the subject of judicial review.

(3) In proceedings under this Act in respect of a judicial act done in good faith, damages may not be awarded otherwise than to compensate a person to the extent required by Article 5(5) of the Convention.

(4) An award of damages permitted by subsection (3) is to be made against the Crown; but no award may be made unless the appropriate person, if not a party to the proceedings, is joined.

(5) In this section—

"appropriate person" means the Minister responsible for the court concerned, or a person or government department nominated by him;

"court" includes a tribunal;

"judge" includes a member of a tribunal, a justice of the peace [(or, in Northern Ireland, a lay magistrate)] and a clerk or other officer entitled to exercise the jurisdiction of a court;

"judicial act" means a judicial act of a court and includes an act done on the instructions, or on behalf, of a judge; and

"rules" has the same meaning as in section 7(9).

NOTES

Sub-s (5): in definition "judge" words in square brackets inserted by the Justice (Northern Ireland) Act 2002, s 10(6), Sch 4, para 39.

Rules: the Human Rights Act 1998 (Jurisdiction) (Scotland) Rules 2000, SSI 2000/301.

Remedial action

[7.10]
10 Power to take remedial action

(1) This section applies if—

(a) a provision of legislation has been declared under section 4 to be incompatible with a Convention right and, if an appeal lies—

(i) all persons who may appeal have stated in writing that they do not intend to do so;

(ii) the time for bringing an appeal has expired and no appeal has been brought within that time; or

(iii) an appeal brought within that time has been determined or abandoned; or

(b) it appears to a Minister of the Crown or Her Majesty in Council that, having regard to a finding of the European Court of Human Rights made after the coming into force of this section in proceedings against the United Kingdom, a provision of legislation is incompatible with an obligation of the United Kingdom arising from the Convention.

(2) If a Minister of the Crown considers that there are compelling reasons for proceeding under this section, he may by order make such amendments to the legislation as he considers necessary to remove the incompatibility.

(3) If, in the case of subordinate legislation, a Minister of the Crown considers—

(a) that it is necessary to amend the primary legislation under which the subordinate legislation in question was made, in order to enable the incompatibility to be removed, and

(b) that there are compelling reasons for proceeding under this section,

he may by order make such amendments to the primary legislation as he considers necessary.

(4) This section also applies where the provision in question is in subordinate legislation and has been quashed, or declared invalid, by reason of incompatibility with a Convention right and the Minister proposes to proceed under paragraph 2(b) of Schedule 2.

(5) If the legislation is an Order in Council, the power conferred by subsection (2) or (3) is exercisable by Her Majesty in Council.

(6) In this section "legislation" does not include a Measure of the Church Assembly or of the General Synod of the Church of England.

(7) Schedule 2 makes further provision about remedial orders.

NOTES

Orders: the Marriage Act 1949 (Remedial) Order 2007, SI 2007/438; the Terrorism Act 2000 (Remedial) Order 2011, SI 2011/631; the Asylum and Immigration (Treatment of Claimants, etc) Act 2004 (Remedial) Order 2011, SI 2011/1158; the Sexual Offences Act 2003 (Remedial) Order 2012, SI 2012/1883.

Other rights and proceedings

[7.11]

11 Safeguard for existing human rights

A person's reliance on a Convention right does not restrict—

(a) any other right or freedom conferred on him by or under any law having effect in any part of the United Kingdom; or

(b) his right to make any claim or bring any proceedings which he could make or bring apart from sections 7 to 9.

[7.12]

12 Freedom of expression

(1) This section applies if a court is considering whether to grant any relief which, if granted, might affect the exercise of the Convention right to freedom of expression.

(2) If the person against whom the application for relief is made ("the respondent") is neither present nor represented, no such relief is to be granted unless the court is satisfied—

(a) that the applicant has taken all practicable steps to notify the respondent; or

(b) that there are compelling reasons why the respondent should not be notified.

(3) No such relief is to be granted so as to restrain publication before trial unless the court is satisfied that the applicant is likely to establish that publication should not be allowed.

(4) The court must have particular regard to the importance of the Convention right to freedom of expression and, where the proceedings relate to material which the respondent claims, or which appears to the court, to be journalistic, literary or artistic material (or to conduct connected with such material), to—

(a) the extent to which—

(i) the material has, or is about to, become available to the public; or

(ii) it is, or would be, in the public interest for the material to be published;

(b) any relevant privacy code.

(5) In this section—

"court" includes a tribunal; and

"relief" includes any remedy or order (other than in criminal proceedings).

[7.13]

13 Freedom of thought, conscience and religion

(1) If a court's determination of any question arising under this Act might affect the exercise by a religious organisation (itself or its members collectively) of the Convention right to freedom of thought, conscience and religion, it must have particular regard to the importance of that right.

(2) In this section "court" includes a tribunal.

Derogations and reservations

[7.14]

14 Derogations

(1) In this Act "designated derogation" means . . . any derogation by the United Kingdom from an Article of the Convention, or of any protocol to the Convention, which is designated for the purposes of this Act in an order made by the [Secretary of State].

(2) . . .

(3) If a designated derogation is amended or replaced it ceases to be a designated derogation.

(4) But subsection (3) does not prevent the [Secretary of State] from exercising his power under subsection (1) . . . to make a fresh designation order in respect of the Article concerned.

(5) The [Secretary of State] must by order make such amendments to Schedule 3 as he considers appropriate to reflect—

(a) any designation order; or

(b) the effect of subsection (3).

(6) A designation order may be made in anticipation of the making by the United Kingdom of a proposed derogation.

NOTES

Sub-s (1): words omitted repealed by the Human Rights Act (Amendment) Order 2001, SI 2001/1216, art 2; words in square brackets substituted by the Secretary of State for Constitutional Affairs Order 2003, SI 2003/1887, art 9, Sch 2, para 10(1).

Sub-s (2): repealed by SI 2001/1216, art 2(b).

Sub-s (4): words in square brackets substituted by SI 2003/1887, art 9, Sch 2, para 10(1); words omitted repealed by SI 2001/1216, art 2(c).

Sub-s (5): words in square brackets substituted by SI 2003/1887, art 9, Sch 2, para 10(1).

Orders: the Human Rights Act 1998 (Designated Derogation) Order 2001, SI 2001/3644.

[7.15]

15 Reservations

(1) In this Act "designated reservation" means—

(a) the United Kingdom's reservation to Article 2 of the First Protocol to the Convention; and

(b) any other reservation by the United Kingdom to an Article of the Convention, or of any protocol to the Convention, which is designated for the purposes of this Act in an order made by the [Secretary of State].

(2) The text of the reservation referred to in subsection (1)(a) is set out in Part II of Schedule 3.

(3) If a designated reservation is withdrawn wholly or in part it ceases to be a designated reservation.

(4) But subsection (3) does not prevent the [Secretary of State] from exercising his power under subsection (1)(b) to make a fresh designation order in respect of the Article concerned.

(5) The [Secretary of State] must by order make such amendments to this Act as he considers appropriate to reflect—

(a) any designation order; or

(b) the effect of subsection (3).

NOTES

Sub-ss (1), (4), (5): words in square brackets substituted by the Secretary of State for Constitutional Affairs Order 2003, SI 2003/1887, art 9, Sch 2, para 10(1).

[7.16]

16 Period for which designated derogations have effect

(1) If it has not already been withdrawn by the United Kingdom, a designated derogation ceases to have effect for the purposes of this Act . . . , at the end of the period of five years beginning with the date on which the order designating it was made.

(2) At any time before the period—

(a) fixed by subsection (1) . . . , or

(b) extended by an order under this subsection,

comes to an end, the [Secretary of State] may by order extend it by a further period of five years.

(3) An order under section 14(1) . . . ceases to have effect at the end of the period for consideration, unless a resolution has been passed by each House approving the order.

(4) Subsection (3) does not affect—

(a) anything done in reliance on the order; or

(b) the power to make a fresh order under section 14(1) . . .

(5) In subsection (3) "period for consideration" means the period of forty days beginning with the day on which the order was made.

(6) In calculating the period for consideration, no account is to be taken of any time during which—

(a) Parliament is dissolved or prorogued; or

(b) both Houses are adjourned for more than four days.

(7) If a designated derogation is withdrawn by the United Kingdom, the [Secretary of State] must by order make such amendments to this Act as he considers are required to reflect that withdrawal.

NOTES

Sub-s (1): words omitted repealed by the Human Rights Act (Amendment) Order 2001, SI 2001/1216, art 3(a).

Sub-s (2): words omitted repealed by SI 2001/1216, art 3(b); words in square brackets substituted by the Secretary of State for Constitutional Affairs Order 2003, SI 2003/1887, art 9, Sch 2, para 10(1).

Sub-s (3): words omitted repealed SI 2001/1216, art 3(c).

Sub-s (4): words omitted repealed SI 2001/1216, art 3(d).

Sub-s (7): words in square brackets substituted by SI 2003/1887, art 9, Sch 2, para 10(1).

[7.17]

17 Periodic review of designated reservations

(1) The appropriate Minister must review the designated reservation referred to in section 15(1)(a)—

(a) before the end of the period of five years beginning with the date on which section 1(2) came into force; and

(b) if that designation is still in force, before the end of the period of five years beginning with the date on which the last report relating to it was laid under subsection (3).

(2) The appropriate Minister must review each of the other designated reservations (if any)—

(a) before the end of the period of five years beginning with the date on which the order designating the reservation first came into force; and

(b) if the designation is still in force, before the end of the period of five years beginning with the date on which the last report relating to it was laid under subsection (3).

(3) The Minister conducting a review under this section must prepare a report on the result of the review and lay a copy of it before each House of Parliament.

Judges of the European Court of Human Rights

[7.18]

18 Appointment to European Court of Human Rights

(1) In this section "judicial office" means the office of—

(a) Lord Justice of Appeal, Justice of the High Court or Circuit judge, in England and Wales;

(b) judge of the Court of Session or sheriff, in Scotland;

(c) Lord Justice of Appeal, judge of the High Court or county court judge, in Northern Ireland.

(2) The holder of a judicial office may become a judge of the European Court of Human Rights ("the Court") without being required to relinquish his office.

(3) But he is not required to perform the duties of his judicial office while he is a judge of the Court.

(4) In respect of any period during which he is a judge of the Court—

(a) a Lord Justice of Appeal or Justice of the High Court is not to count as a judge of the relevant court for the purposes of section 2(1) or 4(1) of the [Senior Courts Act 1981] (maximum number of judges) nor as a judge of the [Senior Courts] for the purposes of section 12(1) to (6) of that Act (salaries etc);

(b) a judge of the Court of Session is not to count as a judge of that court for the purposes of section 1(1) of the Court of Session Act 1988 (maximum number of judges) or of section 9(1)(c) of the Administration of Justice Act 1973 ("the 1973 Act") (salaries etc);

(c) a Lord Justice of Appeal or judge of the High Court in Northern Ireland is not to count as a judge of the relevant court for the purposes of section 2(1) or 3(1) of the Judicature (Northern Ireland) Act 1978 (maximum number of judges) nor as a judge of the [Court of Judicature] of Northern Ireland for the purposes of section 9(1)(d) of the 1973 Act (salaries etc);

(d) a Circuit judge is not to count as such for the purposes of section 18 of the Courts Act 1971 (salaries etc);

(e) a sheriff is not to count as such for the purposes of section 14 of the Sheriff Courts (Scotland) Act 1907 (salaries etc);

(f) a county court judge of Northern Ireland is not to count as such for the purposes of section 106 of the County Courts Act (Northern Ireland) 1959 (salaries etc).

(5) If a sheriff principal is appointed a judge of the Court, section 11(1) of the Sheriff Courts (Scotland) Act 1971 (temporary appointment of sheriff principal) applies, while he holds that appointment, as if his office is vacant.

(6) Schedule 4 makes provision about judicial pensions in relation to the holder of a judicial office who serves as a judge of the Court.

(7) The Lord Chancellor or the Secretary of State may by order make such transitional provision (including, in particular, provision for a temporary increase in the maximum number of judges) as he considers appropriate in relation to any holder of a judicial office who has completed his service as a judge of the Court.

[(7A) The following paragraphs apply to the making of an order under subsection (7) in relation to any holder of a judicial office listed in subsection (1)(a)—

(a) before deciding what transitional provision it is appropriate to make, the person making the order must consult the Lord Chief Justice of England and Wales;

(b) before making the order, that person must consult the Lord Chief Justice of England and Wales.

(7B) The following paragraphs apply to the making of an order under subsection (7) in relation to any holder of a judicial office listed in subsection (1)(c)—

(a) before deciding what transitional provision it is appropriate to make, the person making the order must consult the Lord Chief Justice of Northern Ireland;

(b) before making the order, that person must consult the Lord Chief Justice of Northern Ireland.

(7C) The Lord Chief Justice of England and Wales may nominate a judicial office holder (within the meaning of section 109(4) of the Constitutional Reform Act 2005) to exercise his functions under this section.

(7D) The Lord Chief Justice of Northern Ireland may nominate any of the following to exercise his functions under this section—

(a) the holder of one of the offices listed in Schedule 1 to the Justice (Northern Ireland) Act 2002;

(b) a Lord Justice of Appeal (as defined in section 88 of that Act).]

NOTES

Sub-s (4): words in square brackets in paras (a), (c) substituted by the Constitutional Reform Act 2005, s 59(5), Sch 11, Pt 1, para 1(2), Pt 2, para 4(1), (3), Pt 3, para 6(1), (3).

Sub-ss (7A)–(7D): added by the Constitutional Reform Act 2005, s 15(1), Sch 4, Pt 1, para 278.

Orders: the Judicial Pensions (European Court of Human Rights) Order 1998, SI 1998/2768.

Parliamentary procedure

[7.19]

19 Statements of compatibility

(1) A Minister of the Crown in charge of a Bill in either House of Parliament must, before Second Reading of the Bill—

(a) make a statement to the effect that in his view the provisions of the Bill are compatible with the Convention rights ("a statement of compatibility"); or

(b) make a statement to the effect that although he is unable to make a statement of compatibility the government nevertheless wishes the House to proceed with the Bill.

(2) The statement must be in writing and be published in such manner as the Minister making it considers appropriate.

Supplemental

[7.20]

20 Orders etc under this Act

(1) Any power of a Minister of the Crown to make an order under this Act is exercisable by statutory instrument.

(2) The power of . . . [the Lord Chancellor or] the Secretary of State to make rules (other than rules of court) under section 2(3) or 7(9) is exercisable by statutory instrument.

(3) Any statutory instrument made under section 14, 15 or 16(7) must be laid before Parliament.

(4) No order may be made by . . . [the Lord Chancellor or] the Secretary of State under section 1(4), 7(11) or 16(2) unless a draft of the order has been laid before, and approved by, each House of Parliament.

(5) Any statutory instrument made under section 18(7) or Schedule 4, or to which subsection (2) applies, shall be subject to annulment in pursuance of a resolution of either House of Parliament.

(6) The power of a Northern Ireland department to make—

(a) rules under section 2(3)(c) or 7(9)(c), or

(b) an order under section 7(11),

is exercisable by statutory rule for the purposes of the Statutory Rules (Northern Ireland) Order 1979.

(7) Any rules made under section 2(3)(c) or 7(9)(c) shall be subject to negative resolution; and section 41(6) of the Interpretation Act (Northern Ireland) 1954 (meaning of "subject to negative resolution") shall apply as if the power to make the rules were conferred by an Act of the Northern Ireland Assembly.

(8) No order may be made by a Northern Ireland department under section 7(11) unless a draft of the order has been laid before, and approved by, the Northern Ireland Assembly.

NOTES

Sub-ss (2), (4): words omitted repealed by the Secretary of State for Constitutional Affairs Order 2003, SI 2003/1887, art 9, Sch 2, para 10(2); words in square brackets inserted by the Transfer of Functions (Lord Chancellor and Secretary of State) Order 2005, SI 2005/3429, art 8, Schedule, para 3.

[7.21]

21 Interpretation, etc

(1) In this Act—

"amend" includes repeal and apply (with or without modifications);

"the appropriate Minister" means the Minister of the Crown having charge of the appropriate authorised government department (within the meaning of the Crown Proceedings Act 1947);

"the Commission" means the European Commission of Human Rights;

"the Convention" means the Convention for the Protection of Human Rights and Fundamental Freedoms, agreed by the Council of Europe at Rome on 4th November 1950 as it has effect for the time being in relation to the United Kingdom;

"declaration of incompatibility" means a declaration under section 4;

"Minister of the Crown" has the same meaning as in the Ministers of the Crown Act 1975;

"Northern Ireland Minister" includes the First Minister and the deputy First Minister in Northern Ireland;

"primary legislation" means any—

(a) public general Act;
(b) local and personal Act;
(c) private Act;
(d) Measure of the Church Assembly;
(e) Measure of the General Synod of the Church of England;
(f) Order in Council—
  (i) made in exercise of Her Majesty's Royal Prerogative;
  (ii) made under section 38(1)(a) of the Northern Ireland Constitution Act 1973 or the corresponding provision of the Northern Ireland Act 1998; or
  (iii) amending an Act of a kind mentioned in paragraph (a), (b) or (c);

and includes an order or other instrument made under primary legislation (otherwise than by the [Welsh Ministers, the First Minister for Wales, the Counsel General to the Welsh Assembly Government], a member of the Scottish Executive, a Northern Ireland Minister or a Northern Ireland department) to the extent to which it operates to bring one or more provisions of that legislation into force or amends any primary legislation;

"the First Protocol" means the protocol to the Convention agreed at Paris on 20th March 1952;

. . .

"the Eleventh Protocol" means the protocol to the Convention (restructuring the control machinery established by the Convention) agreed at Strasbourg on 11th May 1994;

["the Thirteenth Protocol" means the protocol to the Convention (concerning the abolition of the death penalty in all circumstances) agreed at Vilnius on 3rd May 2002;]

"remedial order" means an order under section 10;

"subordinate legislation" means any—

(a) Order in Council other than one—
  (i) made in exercise of Her Majesty's Royal Prerogative;
  (ii) made under section 38(1)(a) of the Northern Ireland Constitution Act 1973 or the corresponding provision of the Northern Ireland Act 1998; or
  (iii) amending an Act of a kind mentioned in the definition of primary legislation;

[(ba) Measure of the National Assembly for Wales;
(bb) Act of the National Assembly for Wales;]
(b) Act of the Scottish Parliament;
(c) Act of the Parliament of Northern Ireland;
(d) Measure of the Assembly established under section 1 of the Northern Ireland Assembly Act 1973;
(e) Act of the Northern Ireland Assembly;
(f) order, rules, regulations, scheme, warrant, byelaw or other instrument made under primary legislation (except to the extent to which it operates to bring one or more provisions of that legislation into force or amends any primary legislation);
(g) order, rules, regulations, scheme, warrant, byelaw or other instrument made under legislation mentioned in paragraph (b), (c), (d) or (e) or made under an Order in Council applying only to Northern Ireland;
(h) order, rules, regulations, scheme, warrant, byelaw or other instrument made by a member of the Scottish Executive[, Welsh Ministers, the First Minister for Wales, the Counsel General to the Welsh Assembly Government], a Northern Ireland Minister or a Northern Ireland department in exercise of prerogative or other executive functions of Her Majesty which are exercisable by such a person on behalf of Her Majesty;

"transferred matters" has the same meaning as in the Northern Ireland Act 1998; and

"tribunal" means any tribunal in which legal proceedings may be brought.

(2) The references in paragraphs (b) and (c) of section 2(1) to Articles are to Articles of the Convention as they had effect immediately before the coming into force of the Eleventh Protocol.

(3) The reference in paragraph (d) of section 2(1) to Article 46 includes a reference to Articles 32 and 54 of the Convention as they had effect immediately before the coming into force of the Eleventh Protocol.

(4) The references in section 2(1) to a report or decision of the Commission or a decision of the Committee of Ministers include references to a report or decision made as provided by paragraphs 3, 4 and 6 of Article 5 of the Eleventh Protocol (transitional provisions).
(5) . . .

NOTES

Sub-s (1): in definition "primary legislation" words in square brackets substituted, in definition "subordinate legislation" paras (ba), (bb) inserted and words in square brackets in para (h) inserted, by the Government of Wales Act 2006, s 160(1), Sch 10, para 56(1), (2); definition "the Sixth Protocol" omitted repealed and definition "the Thirteenth Protocol" inserted by the Human Rights Act 1998 (Amendment) Order 2004, SI 2004/1574, art 2(2).

Sub-s (5): repealed by the Armed Forces Act 2006, s 378(2), Sch 17.

[7.22]
22 Short title, commencement, application and extent
(1) This Act may be cited as the Human Rights Act 1998.
(2) Sections 18, 20 and 21(5) and this section come into force on the passing of this Act.
(3) The other provisions of this Act come into force on such day as the Secretary of State may by order appoint; and different days may be appointed for different purposes.
(4) Paragraph (b) of subsection (1) of section 7 applies to proceedings brought by or at the instigation of a public authority whenever the act in question took place; but otherwise that subsection does not apply to an act taking place before the coming into force of that section.
(5) This Act binds the Crown.
(6) This Act extends to Northern Ireland.
(7) . . .

NOTES

Sub-s (7): repealed by the Armed Forces Act 2006, s 378(2), Sch 17.

Orders: the Human Rights Act 1998 (Commencement) Order 1998, SI 1998/2882; the Human Rights Act 1998 (Commencement No 2) Order 2000, SI 2000/1851.

SCHEDULE 1
THE ARTICLES

Section 1(3)

PART I
THE CONVENTION RIGHTS AND FREEDOMS

[7.23]
Article 2 Right to life
1. Everyone's right to life shall be protected by law. No one shall be deprived of his life intentionally save in the execution of a sentence of a court following his conviction of a crime for which this penalty is provided by law.
2. Deprivation of life shall not be regarded as inflicted in contravention of this Article when it results from the use of force which is no more than absolutely necessary—
(a) in defence of any person from unlawful violence;
(b) in order to effect a lawful arrest or to prevent the escape of a person lawfully detained;
(c) in action lawfully taken for the purpose of quelling a riot or insurrection.

Article 3 Prohibition of torture
No one shall be subjected to torture or to inhuman or degrading treatment or punishment.

Article 4 Prohibition of slavery and forced labour
1. No one shall be held in slavery or servitude.
2. No one shall be required to perform forced or compulsory labour.
3. For the purpose of this Article the term "forced or compulsory labour" shall not include—
(a) any work required to be done in the ordinary course of detention imposed according to the provisions of Article 5 of this Convention or during conditional release from such detention;
(b) any service of a military character or, in case of conscientious objectors in countries where they are recognised, service exacted instead of compulsory military service;
(c) any service exacted in case of an emergency or calamity threatening the life or well-being of the community;
(d) any work or service which forms part of normal civic obligations.

Article 5 Right to liberty and security
1. Everyone has the right to liberty and security of person. No one shall be deprived of his liberty save in the following cases and in accordance with a procedure prescribed by law—
(a) the lawful detention of a person after conviction by a competent court;
(b) the lawful arrest or detention of a person for non-compliance with the lawful order of a court or in order to secure the fulfilment of any obligation prescribed by law;

(c) the lawful arrest or detention of a person effected for the purpose of bringing him before the competent legal authority on reasonable suspicion of having committed an offence or when it is reasonably considered necessary to prevent his committing an offence or fleeing after having done so;
(d) the detention of a minor by lawful order for the purpose of educational supervision or his lawful detention for the purpose of bringing him before the competent legal authority;
(e) the lawful detention of persons for the prevention of the spreading of infectious diseases, of persons of unsound mind, alcoholics or drug addicts or vagrants;
(f) the lawful arrest or detention of a person to prevent his effecting an unauthorised entry into the country or of a person against whom action is being taken with a view to deportation or extradition.

2. Everyone who is arrested shall be informed promptly, in a language which he understands, of the reasons for his arrest and of any charge against him.

3. Everyone arrested or detained in accordance with the provisions of paragraph 1(c) of this Article shall be brought promptly before a judge or other officer authorised by law to exercise judicial power and shall be entitled to trial within a reasonable time or to release pending trial. Release may be conditioned by guarantees to appear for trial.

4. Everyone who is deprived of his liberty by arrest or detention shall be entitled to take proceedings by which the lawfulness of his detention shall be decided speedily by a court and his release ordered if the detention is not lawful.

5. Everyone who has been the victim of arrest or detention in contravention of the provisions of this Article shall have an enforceable right to compensation.

Article 6 Right to a fair trial

1. In the determination of his civil rights and obligations or of any criminal charge against him, everyone is entitled to a fair and public hearing within a reasonable time by an independent and impartial tribunal established by law. Judgment shall be pronounced publicly but the press and public may be excluded from all or part of the trial in the interest of morals, public order or national security in a democratic society, where the interests of juveniles or the protection of the private life of the parties so require, or to the extent strictly necessary in the opinion of the court in special circumstances where publicity would prejudice the interests of justice.

2. Everyone charged with a criminal offence shall be presumed innocent until proved guilty according to law.

3. Everyone charged with a criminal offence has the following minimum rights—
(a) to be informed promptly, in a language which he understands and in detail, of the nature and cause of the accusation against him;
(b) to have adequate time and facilities for the preparation of his defence;
(c) to defend himself in person or through legal assistance of his own choosing or, if he has not sufficient means to pay for legal assistance, to be given it free when the interests of justice so require;
(d) to examine or have examined witnesses against him and to obtain the attendance and examination of witnesses on his behalf under the same conditions as witnesses against him;
(e) to have the free assistance of an interpreter if he cannot understand or speak the language used in court.

Article 7 No punishment without law

1. No one shall be held guilty of any criminal offence on account of any act or omission which did not constitute a criminal offence under national or international law at the time when it was committed. Nor shall a heavier penalty be imposed than the one that was applicable at the time the criminal offence was committed.

2. This Article shall not prejudice the trial and punishment of any person for any act or omission which, at the time when it was committed, was criminal according to the general principles of law recognised by civilised nations.

Article 8 Right to respect for private and family life

1. Everyone has the right to respect for his private and family life, his home and his correspondence.

2. There shall be no interference by a public authority with the exercise of this right except such as is in accordance with the law and is necessary in a democratic society in the interests of national security, public safety or the economic well-being of the country, for the prevention of disorder or crime, for the protection of health or morals, or for the protection of the rights and freedoms of others.

Article 9 Freedom of thought, conscience and religion

1. Everyone has the right to freedom of thought, conscience and religion; this right includes freedom to change his religion or belief and freedom, either alone or in community with others and in public or private, to manifest his religion or belief, in worship, teaching, practice and observance.

2. Freedom to manifest one's religion or beliefs shall be subject only to such limitations as are prescribed by law and are necessary in a democratic society in the interests of public safety, for the protection of public order, health or morals, or for the protection of the rights and freedoms of others.

Article 10 Freedom of expression

1. Everyone has the right to freedom of expression. This right shall include freedom to hold opinions and to receive and impart information and ideas without interference by public authority and regardless of frontiers. This Article shall not prevent States from requiring the licensing of broadcasting, television or cinema enterprises.

2. The exercise of these freedoms, since it carries with it duties and responsibilities, may be subject to such formalities, conditions, restrictions or penalties as are prescribed by law and are necessary in a democratic society, in the interests of national security, territorial integrity or public safety, for the prevention of disorder or crime, for the protection of health or morals, for the protection of the reputation or rights of others, for preventing the disclosure of information received in confidence, or for maintaining the authority and impartiality of the judiciary.

Article 11 Freedom of assembly and association

1. Everyone has the right to freedom of peaceful assembly and to freedom of association with others, including the right to form and to join trade unions for the protection of his interests.

2. No restrictions shall be placed on the exercise of these rights other than such as are prescribed by law and are necessary in a democratic society in the interests of national security or public safety, for the prevention of disorder or crime, for the protection of health or morals or for the protection of the rights and freedoms of others. This Article shall not prevent the imposition of lawful restrictions on the exercise of these rights by members of the armed forces, of the police or of the administration of the State.

Article 12 Right to marry

Men and women of marriageable age have the right to marry and to found a family, according to the national laws governing the exercise of this right.

Article 14 Prohibition of discrimination

The enjoyment of the rights and freedoms set forth in this Convention shall be secured without discrimination on any ground such as sex, race, colour, language, religion, political or other opinion, national or social origin, association with a national minority, property, birth or other status.

Article 16 Restrictions on political activity of aliens

Nothing in Articles 10, 11 and 14 shall be regarded as preventing the High Contracting Parties from imposing restrictions on the political activity of aliens.

Article 17 Prohibition of abuse of rights

Nothing in this Convention may be interpreted as implying for any State, group or person any right to engage in any activity or perform any act aimed at the destruction of any of the rights and freedoms set forth herein or at their limitation to a greater extent than is provided for in the Convention.

Article 18 Limitation on use of restrictions on rights

The restrictions permitted under this Convention to the said rights and freedoms shall not be applied for any purpose other than those for which they have been prescribed.

PART II
THE FIRST PROTOCOL

[7.24]

Article 1 Protection of property

Every natural or legal person is entitled to the peaceful enjoyment of his possessions. No one shall be deprived of his possessions except in the public interest and subject to the conditions provided for by law and by the general principles of international law.

The preceding provisions shall not, however, in any way impair the right of a State to enforce such laws as it deems necessary to control the use of property in accordance with the general interest or to secure the payment of taxes or other contributions or penalties.

Article 2 Right to education

No person shall be denied the right to education. In the exercise of any functions which it assumes in relation to education and to teaching, the State shall respect the right of parents to ensure such education and teaching in conformity with their own religious and philosophical convictions.

Article 3 Right to free elections

The High Contracting Parties undertake to hold free elections at reasonable intervals by secret ballot, under conditions which will ensure the free expression of the opinion of the people in the choice of the legislature.

[PART 3
ARTICLE 1 OF THE THIRTEENTH PROTOCOL

Abolition of the death penalty

[7.25]

The death penalty shall be abolished. No one shall be condemned to such penalty or executed.]

NOTES

Substituted by the Human Rights Act 1998 (Amendment) Order 2004, SI 2004/1574, art 2(3).

SCHEDULE 2
REMEDIAL ORDERS

Section 10

Orders

[7.26]

1. (1) A remedial order may—

(a) contain such incidental, supplemental, consequential or transitional provision as the person making it considers appropriate;

(b) be made so as to have effect from a date earlier than that on which it is made;

(c) make provision for the delegation of specific functions;

(d) make different provision for different cases.

(2) The power conferred by sub-paragraph (1)(a) includes—

(a) power to amend primary legislation (including primary legislation other than that which contains the incompatible provision); and

(b) power to amend or revoke subordinate legislation (including subordinate legislation other than that which contains the incompatible provision).

(3) A remedial order may be made so as to have the same extent as the legislation which it affects.

(4) No person is to be guilty of an offence solely as a result of the retrospective effect of a remedial order.

Procedure

2. No remedial order may be made unless—

(a) a draft of the order has been approved by a resolution of each House of Parliament made after the end of the period of 60 days beginning with the day on which the draft was laid; or

(b) it is declared in the order that it appears to the person making it that, because of the urgency of the matter, it is necessary to make the order without a draft being so approved.

Orders laid in draft

3. (1) No draft may be laid under paragraph 2(a) unless—

(a) the person proposing to make the order has laid before Parliament a document which contains a draft of the proposed order and the required information; and

(b) the period of 60 days, beginning with the day on which the document required by this sub-paragraph was laid, has ended.

(2) If representations have been made during that period, the draft laid under paragraph 2(a) must be accompanied by a statement containing—

(a) a summary of the representations; and

(b) if, as a result of the representations, the proposed order has been changed, details of the changes.

Urgent cases

4. (1) If a remedial order ("the original order") is made without being approved in draft, the person making it must lay it before Parliament, accompanied by the required information, after it is made.

(2) If representations have been made during the period of 60 days beginning with the day on which the original order was made, the person making it must (after the end of that period) lay before Parliament a statement containing—

(a) a summary of the representations; and

(b) if, as a result of the representations, he considers it appropriate to make changes to the original order, details of the changes.

(3) If sub-paragraph (2)(b) applies, the person making the statement must—

(a) make a further remedial order replacing the original order; and
(b) lay the replacement order before Parliament.

(4) If, at the end of the period of 120 days beginning with the day on which the original order was made, a resolution has not been passed by each House approving the original or replacement order, the order ceases to have effect (but without that affecting anything previously done under either order or the power to make a fresh remedial order).

Definitions

5. In this Schedule—

"representations" means representations about a remedial order (or proposed remedial order) made to the person making (or proposing to make) it and includes any relevant Parliamentary report or resolution; and

"required information" means—

(a) an explanation of the incompatibility which the order (or proposed order) seeks to remove, including particulars of the relevant declaration, finding or order; and
(b) a statement of the reasons for proceeding under section 10 and for making an order in those terms.

Calculating periods

6. In calculating any period for the purposes of this Schedule, no account is to be taken of any time during which—

(a) Parliament is dissolved or prorogued; or
(b) both Houses are adjourned for more than four days.

[**7.** (1) This paragraph applies in relation to—

(a) any remedial order made, and any draft of such under an order proposed to be made,—
 (i) by the Scottish Ministers; or
 (ii) within devolved competence (within the meaning of the Scotland Act 1998) by Her Majesty in Council; and
(b) any document or statement to be laid in connection with such an order (or proposed order).

(2) This Schedule has effect in relation to any such order (or proposed order), document or statement subject to the following modifications.

(3) Any reference to Parliament, each House of Parliament or both Houses of Parliament shall be construed as a reference to the Scottish Parliament.

(4) Paragraph 6 docs not apply and instead, in calculating the period for the purposes of this Schedule, no account is to be taken of any time during which the Scottish Parliament is dissolved or is in recess for more than four days.]

NOTES

Para 7: added by the Scotland Act 1998 (Consequential Modifications) Order 2000, SI 2000/2040, art 2(1), Schedule, Pt I, para 21

Orders: the Marriage Act 1949 (Remedial) Order 2007, SI 2007/438; the Asylum and Immigration (Treatment of Claimants, etc) Act 2004 (Remedial) Order 2011, SI 2011/1158; the Sexual Offences Act 2003 (Remedial) Order 2012, SI 2012/1883.

SCHEDULE 3
DEROGATION AND RESERVATION

Sections 14 and 15

PART I

(*Original Sch 3, Pt I repealed by the Human Rights Act (Amendment) Order 2001, SI 2001/1216; new Sch 3, Pt I inserted by the Human Rights Act (Amendment No 2) Order 2001, SI 2001/4032, art 2, Schedule and repealed by the Human Rights Act 1998 (Amendment) Order 2005, SI 2005/1071, art 2.*)

PART II
RESERVATION

[7.27]

At the time of signing the present (First) Protocol, I declare that, in view of certain provisions of the Education Acts in the United Kingdom, the principle affirmed in the second sentence of Article 2 is accepted by the United Kingdom only so far as it is compatible with the provision of efficient instruction and training, and the avoidance of unreasonable public expenditure.

Dated 20 March 1952. Made by the United Kingdom Permanent Representative to the Council of Europe.

SCHEDULE 4
JUDICIAL PENSIONS

Section 18(6)

Duty to make orders about pensions

[7.28]

1. (1) The appropriate Minister must by order make provision with respect to pensions payable to or in respect of any holder of a judicial office who serves as an ECHR judge.

(2) A pensions order must include such provision as the Minister making it considers is necessary to secure that—

(a) an ECHR judge who was, immediately before his appointment as an ECHR judge, a member of a judicial pension scheme is entitled to remain as a member of that scheme;

(b) the terms on which he remains a member of the scheme are those which would have been applicable had he not been appointed as an ECHR judge; and

(c) entitlement to benefits payable in accordance with the scheme continues to be determined as if, while serving as an ECHR judge, his salary was that which would (but for section 18(4)) have been payable to him in respect of his continuing service as the holder of his judicial office.

Contributions

2. A pensions order may, in particular, make provision—

(a) for any contributions which are payable by a person who remains a member of a scheme as a result of the order, and which would otherwise be payable by deduction from his salary, to be made otherwise than by deduction from his salary as an ECHR judge; and

(b) for such contributions to be collected in such manner as may be determined by the administrators of the scheme.

Amendments of other enactments

3. A pensions order may amend any provision of, or made under, a pensions Act in such manner and to such extent as the Minister making the order considers necessary or expedient to ensure the proper administration of any scheme to which it relates.

Definitions

4. In this Schedule—

"appropriate Minister" means—

(a) in relation to any judicial office whose jurisdiction is exercisable exclusively in relation to Scotland, the Secretary of State; and

(b) otherwise, the Lord Chancellor;

"ECHR judge" means the holder of a judicial office who is serving as a judge of the Court;

"judicial pension scheme" means a scheme established by and in accordance with a pensions Act;

"pensions Act" means—

(a) the County Courts Act (Northern Ireland) 1959;

(b) the Sheriffs' Pensions (Scotland) Act 1961;

(c) the Judicial Pensions Act 1981; or

(d) the Judicial Pensions and Retirement Act 1993;

[(e) the Public Service Pensions Act 2013;] and

"pensions order" means an order made under paragraph 1.

NOTES

Para 4: in definition "pensions Act" para (e) added by the Public Service Pensions Act 2013, s 27, Sch 8, para 26.

Orders: the Judicial Pensions (European Court of Human Rights) Order 1998, SI 1998/2768.

LONDON OLYMPIC GAMES AND PARALYMPIC GAMES ACT 2006

(2006 c 12)

ARRANGEMENT OF SECTIONS

Introductory

An Act to make provision in connection with the Olympic Games and Paralympic Games that are to take place in London in the year 2012; to amend the Olympic Symbol etc (Protection) Act 1995; and for connected purposes.

[30 March 2006]

Introductory

[7.29]

1 Interpretation of principal terms

(1) In this Act "the London Olympics" means—

(a) the Games of the Thirtieth Olympiad that are to take place in 2012, and
(b) the Paralympic Games that are to take place in that year.

(2) A reference in this Act to the London Olympics includes a reference to any event which forms part of the Games specified in subsection (1)(a) or (b) including, in particular—

(a) an event, other than a sporting event, held in accordance with the Host City Contract, and
(b) an event which is to take place outside London.

(3) In this Act—

(a) "the British Olympic Association" means the company limited by guarantee registered with that name,
(b) "London Olympic event" means an event (whether or not a sporting event and whether or not held in London) held as part of the London Olympics,
(c) "the London Olympics period" means the period which—
  (i) begins four weeks before the day of the opening ceremony of the Games of the Thirtieth Olympiad that are to take place in 2012, and
  (ii) ends with the fifth day after the day of the closing ceremony of the Paralympic Games 2012,
(d) "the London Organising Committee" means the organising committee formed in accordance with section 2 of the Host City Contract as the company limited by guarantee registered as the London Organising Committee of the Olympic Games Limited (LOCOG),
(e) "the Host City Contract" means the Host City Contract, for the Games of the Thirtieth Olympiad that are to take place in 2012, signed at Singapore on 6th July 2005 and entered into by—
  (i) the International Olympic Committee,
  (ii) the Mayor of London (representing London), and
  (iii) the British Olympic Association,

Part 7 Other UK legislation

(f) "the Paralympic Games" means the events known by that name and to be organised by the London Organising Committee in accordance with section 60 of the Host City Contract, and
(g) "the Olympic Charter" means the Olympic Charter of the International Olympic Committee.

[7.30]

2 Alteration of Olympic documents

(1) If the Secretary of State [. . .] thinks that a reference in this Act to an Olympic document has ceased to be accurate by reason of the amendment or substitution of that document, he may by order amend the reference.

(2) In subsection (1) "Olympic document" means a document referred to in section 1.

(3) An order under subsection (1)—

(a) may include consequential or incidental provision,
(b) shall be made by statutory instrument,
(c) shall be subject to annulment in pursuance of a resolution of either House of Parliament, and
(d) may not be made unless the Secretary of State [. . .] has consulted the London Organising Committee.

NOTES

Sub-ss (1), (3): words omitted from square brackets inserted by the Transfer of Functions (Olympics and Paralympics) Order 2007, SI 2007/2129, arts 3(1), (2)(d), 5, Schedule, para 6(1)(a) and repealed by the Secretary of State for Culture, Olympics, Media and Sport Order 2010, SI 2010/1551, art 11, Schedule, para 8(1)(a).

The Olympic Delivery Authority

3–8 (*Repealed by the Olympic Delivery Authority (Dissolution) Order 2014, SI 2014/3184, art 2(2), Schedule, paras 1, 2(a)–(f).*)

[7.31]

9 Dissolution

(1) The Secretary of State [. . .] may by order make provision for the dissolution of the Authority.

(2) An order under this section may, in particular—

(a) provide for the transfer of property, rights or liabilities of the Authority to—
 (i) the Secretary of State, or
 (ii) any other person;
(b) make provision enabling a person to receive anything transferred under paragraph (a) (and that provision shall have effect despite any other enactment or instrument);
(c) establish a body corporate;
(d) make consequential, incidental or transitional provision which may, in particular—
 (i) provide for anything done by or in relation to the Authority to have effect as if done by or in relation to another person;
 (ii) permit anything (which may include legal proceedings) which is in the process of being done by or in relation to the Authority when a transfer takes effect, to be continued by or in relation to another person;
 (iii) provide for a reference to the Authority in an instrument or other document to be treated as a reference to another person;
 (iv) amend an enactment.

(3) Before making an order under this section the Secretary of State [. . .] shall consult—

(a) the Mayor of London, and
(b) such other persons as the Secretary of State [. . .] thinks appropriate.

(4) The Secretary of State [. . .] may not make an order under this section providing for the transfer of property, rights or liabilities to a person unless the person has consented to the transfer.

(5) An order under this section—

(a) may transfer rights and liabilities relating to employees, but
(b) shall not affect the operation of the Transfer of Undertakings (Protection of Employment) Regulations 1981 (SI 1981/1794).

(6) The Secretary of State [. . .] may not make an order by virtue of subsection (5)(a) unless satisfied that sufficient notice has been given to enable compliance with any applicable requirement of those regulations.

(7) An order under this section—

(a) shall be made by statutory instrument, and
(b) shall not be made unless a draft has been laid before Parliament.

NOTES

Sub-ss (1), (3), (4), (6): words omitted from square brackets inserted by the Transfer of Functions (Olympics and Paralympics) Order 2007, SI 2007/2129, arts 3(1), (2)(d), 5, Schedule, para 6(1)(d) and repealed by the Secretary of State for Culture, Olympics, Media and Sport Order 2010, SI 2010/1551, art 11, Schedule, para 8(1)(d).

Orders: the Olympic Delivery Authority (Dissolution) Order 2014, SI 2014/3184.

10–18 (*Ceased to have effect on 14 September 2012, in accordance with s 40(6) of this Act at* **[7.50]**.)

Advertising

[7.32]

19 Advertising regulations

(1) The Secretary of State [. . .] shall make regulations about advertising in the vicinity of London Olympic events.

(2) In making the regulations the Secretary of State [. . .]—

(a) shall aim to secure compliance with obligations imposed on any person by the Host City Contract,

(b) shall have regard to any requests or guidance from the International Olympic Committee, and

(c) shall also have regard to amenity and public safety.

(3) The regulations shall specify, or provide criteria for determining—

(a) the places in respect of advertising in which the regulations apply,

(b) the nature of the advertising in respect of which the regulations apply, and

(c) what is, or is not, to be treated for the purposes of the regulations as advertising in the vicinity of a place.

(4) The regulations may apply in respect of advertising of any kind including, in particular—

(a) advertising of a non-commercial nature, and

(b) announcements or notices of any kind.

(5) The regulations may apply in respect of advertising in any form including, in particular—

(a) the distribution or provision of documents or articles,

(b) the display or projection of words, images, lights or sounds, and

(c) things done with or in relation to material which has or may have purposes or uses other than as an advertisement.

(6) The regulations shall specify, or provide criteria for determining, the period of time during which they apply; and—

(a) the regulations shall apply only for such time as the Secretary of State [. . .] considers necessary for the purpose of securing compliance with obligations imposed on any person by the Host City Contract, and

(b) the regulations may apply during different periods in respect of different places.

(7) The regulations shall permit, subject to any specified conditions, advertising undertaken or controlled by—

(a) any person specified in the regulations as appearing to the Secretary of State [. . .] to have responsibility in accordance with the Host City Contract for the control of advertising in relation to the London Olympics ("a responsible body"), or

(b) any person authorised by a responsible body (whether or not subject to terms and conditions and whether or not in accordance with a sponsorship or other commercial agreement).

(8) The regulations—

(a) may prohibit action of a specified kind or in specified circumstances,

(b) may impose obligations on persons who—

(i) take action in relation to an advertisement, or

(ii) have an interest in or responsibility for a product or service to which an advertisement relates,

(c) may impose obligations on persons who own, occupy or have responsibility for the management of land, premises or other property,

(d) may, in particular, impose on a person an obligation to take steps to ensure—

(i) that other persons do not take action of a particular kind;

(ii) that a situation is not permitted to continue, and

(e) shall have effect despite any consent or permission granted (whether before or after the commencement of the regulations) by any landowner, local authority or other person.

NOTES

Sub-ss (1), (2), (6), (7): words omitted from square brackets inserted by the Transfer of Functions (Olympics and Paralympics) Order 2007, SI 2007/2129, arts 3(1), (2)(d), 5, Schedule, para 6(1)(e) and repealed by the Secretary of State for Culture, Olympics, Media and Sport Order 2010, SI 2010/1551, art 11, Schedule, para 8(1)(e).

[7.33]

20 Regulations: supplemental

(1) Regulations under section 19—

(a) may, to a specified extent or for specified purposes, disapply or modify specified enactments relating to planning or the control of advertising,

(b) may apply (with or without modifications) or make provision similar to any enactment (including, but not limited to, provisions of Chapter III of Part VIII of the Town and Country Planning Act 1990 (c 8) (control of advertising) and regulations under that Chapter)),

(c) may provide for exceptions (in addition to those referred to in section 19(7)) which may be expressed by reference to the nature of advertising, its purpose, the circumstances of its display or any other matter (which may include the consent of a specified person),
(d) may make provision for application, with any specified modifications or exceptions, to the Crown,
(e) may make provision which applies generally or only for specified purposes or in specified circumstances,
(f) may make different provision for different purposes or circumstances, and
(g) may apply in relation to advertising whether or not it consists of the result or continuation of activity carried out before the regulations come into force.

(2) Regulations under section 19—
(a) shall be made by statutory instrument, and
(b) may not be made unless a draft has been laid before and approved by resolution of each House of Parliament.

[(2A) But if, in relation to regulations under section 19 other than the first regulations, the Secretary of State considers that by reason of urgency it is necessary that they be made without being approved in draft—
(a) subsection (2)(b) does not apply to the regulations, and
(b) the regulations are instead subject to annulment in pursuance of a resolution of either House of Parliament.]

(3) Before making regulations under section 19 the Secretary of State [. . .] shall consult—
(a) such authorities, with responsibilities for planning in respect of places to which the regulations apply or may apply, as he thinks appropriate,
(b) one or more persons who appear to the Secretary of State [. . .] to represent interests within the advertising industry which are likely to be affected by the regulations,
(c) such other persons, who appear to the Secretary of State [. . .] to represent interests likely to be affected by the regulations, as he thinks appropriate,
(d) . . .
(e) the London Organising Committee.

(4) If regulations under section 19 would be treated as a hybrid instrument for the purposes of the standing orders of either House of Parliament, they shall proceed in that House as if they were not a hybrid instrument.

NOTES

Sub-s (2A): inserted by the London Olympic Games and Paralympic Games (Amendment) Act 2011, s 2(1).

Sub-s (3): words omitted from square brackets inserted by the Transfer of Functions (Olympics and Paralympics) Order 2007, SI 2007/2129, arts 3(1), (2)(d), 5, Schedule, para 6(1)(f) and repealed by the Secretary of State for Culture, Olympics, Media and Sport Order 2010, SI 2010/1551, art 11, Schedule, para 8(1)(f); para (d) repealed by the Olympic Delivery Authority (Dissolution) Order 2014, SI 2014/3184, art 2(2), Schedule, paras 1, 3.

[7.34]

21 Offence

(1) A person commits an offence if he contravenes regulations under section 19.

(2) It shall be a defence for a person charged with an offence under subsection (1) to prove that the contravention of the regulations occurred—
(a) without his knowledge, or
(b) despite his taking all reasonable steps to prevent it from occurring or (where he became aware of it after its commencement) from continuing.

(3) A person guilty of an offence under subsection (1) shall be liable—
(a) on conviction on indictment, to a fine, or
(b) on summary conviction, to a fine not exceeding £20,000.

(4) . . .

NOTES

Sub-s (4): repealed by the London Olympic Games and Paralympic Games (Amendment) Act 2011, s 1(1).

[7.35]

22 Enforcement: power of entry

(1) A constable . . . may—
(a) enter land or premises on which they reasonably believe a contravention of regulations under section 19 is occurring (whether by reason of advertising on that land or premises or by the use of that land or premises to cause an advertisement to appear elsewhere);
(b) remove, destroy, conceal or erase any infringing article;
(c) when entering land under paragraph (a), be accompanied by one or more persons for the purpose of taking action under paragraph (b);
(d) use, or authorise the use of, reasonable force for the purpose of taking action under this subsection.

(2) The power to enter land or premises may be exercised only at a time that a constable . . . thinks reasonable having regard to the nature and circumstances of the contravention of regulations under section 19.

(3) Before entering land or premises a constable . . . must take reasonable steps to—
(a) establish the identity of an owner, occupier or person responsible for the management of the land or premises or of any infringing article on the land or premises, and
(b) give any owner, occupier or responsible person identified under paragraph (a) such opportunity as seems reasonable to the constable . . . in the circumstances of the case to end the contravention of the regulations (whether by removing, destroying or concealing any infringing article or otherwise).

(4) The power to enter premises may be exercised in relation to a dwelling only in accordance with a warrant issued by a justice of the peace; and a justice of the peace may issue a warrant only if satisfied on the application of a constable . . . that—
(a) there are reasonable grounds to believe a contravention of regulations under section 19 is occurring in the dwelling or on land that can reasonably be entered only through the dwelling,
(b) the constable . . . has complied with subsection (3),
(c) the constable . . . has taken reasonable steps to give notice to persons likely to be interested of his intention to apply for a warrant, and
(d) that it is reasonable in the circumstances of the case to issue a warrant.

(5) The power to remove an article may be exercised only if the constable . . . thinks it necessary for the purpose of—
(a) ending the contravention of regulations under section 19,
(b) preventing a future contravention of the regulations, [or]
(c) enabling the article to be used as evidence in proceedings for an offence under section 21, . . .
(d) . . .

(6) . . .

(7) Having exercised a power under this section a constable . . . —
(a) shall take reasonable steps to leave the land or premises secure, and
(b) shall comply with any provision of regulations under section 19 about informing specified persons of what the constable . . . has done.

(8) Regulations under section 19 shall include provision enabling a person whose property is damaged in the course of the exercise or purported exercise of a power under this section (other than a person responsible for a contravention of the regulations or for the management of an infringing article) to obtain compensation from [a local policing body] [or a police authority]; and the regulations may, in particular, include provision—
(a) conferring jurisdiction on a court or tribunal;
(b) about appeals.

(9) A [local policing body] [or a police authority] may recover from a person responsible for the contravention of the regulations, as if it were a debt, the reasonable costs of taking action under this section.

(10) In this section—

. . .

"infringing article" means—
(a) an advertisement which contravenes regulations under section 19, and
(b) any other thing[, or an animal,] that constitutes a contravention of regulations under section 19 or is being used in connection with a contravention of the regulations.

NOTES

Sub-ss (1)–(4): words omitted repealed by the Olympic Delivery Authority (Dissolution) Order 2014, SI 2014/3184, art 2(2), Schedule, paras 1, 4(a).

Sub-s (5): first words omitted repealed by SI 2014/3184, art 2(2), Schedule, paras 1, 4(a); in para (b) word in square brackets inserted and para (d) and word immediately preceding it repealed by the London Olympic Games and Paralympic Games (Amendment) Act 2011, s 1(2).

Sub-s (6): repealed by SI 2014/3184, art 2(2), Schedule, paras 1, 4(b).

Sub-s (7): words omitted repealed by SI 2014/3184, art 2(2), Schedule, paras 1, 4(a).

Sub-ss (8), (9): words in first pair of square brackets inserted by the Police Reform and Social Responsibility Act 2011, s 99, Sch 16, Pt 3, paras 354, 356; words in second pair of square brackets substituted by SI 2014/3184, art 2(2), Schedule, paras 1, 4(c).

Sub-s (10): definition "enforcement officer" repealed by SI 2014/3184, art 2(2), Schedule, paras 1, 4(d); in definition "infringing article" words in square brackets inserted by the London Olympic Games and Paralympic Games (Amendment) Act 2011, s 1(4).

23 *(Repealed by the Olympic Delivery Authority (Dissolution) Order 2014, SI 2014/3184, art 2(2), Schedule, paras 1, 2(g).)*

[7.36]

24 Local planning authorities

(1) The Secretary of State [. . .] may by order require a specified local planning authority who grant advertising consent to a person to notify him of the effect of—
(a) section 19(8)(e), and
(b) any regulations under section 19.

(2) In subsection (1) "advertising consent" means consent of such kind as the order shall specify.
(3) An order under subsection (1)—
 (a) shall be made by statutory instrument, and
 (b) shall be subject to annulment in pursuance of a resolution of either House of Parliament.

NOTES

Sub-s (1): words omitted from square brackets inserted by the Transfer of Functions (Olympics and Paralympics) Order 2007, SI 2007/2129, arts 3(1), (2)(d), 5, Schedule, para 6(1)(h) and repealed by the Secretary of State for Culture, Olympics, Media and Sport Order 2010, SI 2010/1551, art 11, Schedule, para 8(1)(h).

Trading

[7.37]

25 Street trading, &c

(1) The Secretary of State [. . .] shall make regulations about trading in the vicinity of London Olympic events.
(2) In making the regulations the Secretary of State [. . .]—
 (a) shall aim to secure compliance with obligations imposed on any person by the Host City Contract,
 (b) shall have regard to any requests or guidance from the International Olympic Committee, and
 (c) shall also have regard to amenity and public safety (including in each case the need to avoid congestion).
(3) The regulations shall specify, or provide criteria for determining—
 (a) the places in respect of which the regulations apply,
 (b) the nature of the trading in respect of which the regulations apply, and
 (c) what is, or is not, to be treated for the purposes of the regulations as trading in the vicinity of a place.
(4) The regulations may apply only in respect of trading which takes place—
 (a) on a highway, or
 (b) in another place—
  (i) to which the public have access (whether generally or only for the purpose of the trading), and
  (ii) which is not in any building other than one designed or generally used for the parking of cars.
(5) The regulations shall specify, or provide criteria for determining, the period of time during which they apply; and—
 (a) the regulations shall apply only for such time as the Secretary of State [. . .] considers necessary for the purpose of securing compliance with obligations imposed on any person by the Host City Contract, and
 (b) the regulations may apply during different periods in respect of different places.
(6)–(8) . . .

NOTES

Sub-ss (1), (2), (5): words omitted from square brackets inserted by the Transfer of Functions (Olympics and Paralympics) Order 2007, SI 2007/2129, arts 3(1), (2)(d), 5, Schedule, para 6(1)(i) and repealed by the Secretary of State for Culture, Olympics, Media and Sport Order 2010, SI 2010/1551, art 11, Schedule, para 8(1)(i).

Sub-ss (6)–(8): repealed by the Olympic Delivery Authority (Dissolution) Order 2014, SI 2014/3184, art 2(2), Schedule, paras 1, 2(h).

[7.38]

26 Section 25: supplemental

(1) Regulations under section 25—
 (a) may, to a specified extent or for specified purposes, disapply or modify specified enactments relating to trading . . . ,
 (b) may apply (with or without modifications) or make provision similar to any enactment (which may include provision conferring a right of appeal in respect of the refusal of an authorisation),
 (c) may provide for exceptions which may be expressed by reference to the nature of trading, its circumstances, the application of profits or any other matter (which may include the consent of a specified person),
 (d) may make provision which applies generally or only for specified purposes or in specified circumstances, and
 (e) may make different provision for different purposes or circumstances.
(2) Regulations under section 25—
 (a) shall be made by statutory instrument, and
 (b) may not be made unless a draft has been laid before and approved by resolution of each House of Parliament.
[(2A) But if, in relation to regulations under section 25 other than the first regulations, the Secretary of State considers that by reason of urgency it is necessary that they be made without being approved in draft—

(a) subsection (2)(b) does not apply to the regulations, and
(b) the regulations are instead subject to annulment in pursuance of a resolution of either House of Parliament.]

(3) Before making regulations under section 25 the Secretary of State [. . .] shall consult—
(a) such authorities, with responsibilities for the licensing of trading in respect of places to which the regulations apply or may apply, as he thinks appropriate,
(b) such persons, who appear to the Secretary of State [. . .] to represent interests likely to be affected by the regulations, as he thinks appropriate,
(c) . . .
(d) the London Organising Committee.

(4) Regulations under section 25 shall have effect despite any licence granted (whether before or after the commencement of the regulations)—
(a) by any landowner, local authority or other person, or
(b) by or by virtue of any enactment, Charter or other document.

(5) If regulations under section 25 would be treated as a hybrid instrument for the purposes of the standing orders of either House of Parliament, they shall proceed in that House as if they were not a hybrid instrument.

(6) In section 25 and this section "licence" includes any kind of consent, certificate, permission or authority (by whatever name).

NOTES

Sub-s (1): words omitted repealed by the Olympic Delivery Authority (Dissolution) Order 2014, SI 2014/3184, art 2(2), Schedule, paras 1, 5(a).

Sub-s (2A): inserted by the London Olympic Games and Paralympic Games (Amendment) Act 2011, s 2(3).

Sub-s (3): words omitted from square brackets inserted by the Transfer of Functions (Olympics and Paralympics) Order 2007, SI 2007/2129, arts 3(1), (2)(d), 5, Schedule, para 6(1)(j) and repealed by the Secretary of State for Culture, Olympics, Media and Sport Order 2010, SI 2010/1551, art 11, Schedule, para 8(1)(j); para (c) repealed by SI 2014/3184, art 2(2), Schedule, paras 1, 5(b).

[7.39]

27 Offence

(1) A person commits an offence if he contravenes regulations under section 25.

(2) A person guilty of an offence under subsection (1) shall be liable—
(a) on conviction on indictment, to a fine, or
(b) on summary conviction, to a fine not exceeding £20,000.

[7.40]

28 Enforcement: power of entry

(1) A constable . . . may—
(a) enter land or premises on which they reasonably believe a contravention of regulations under section 25 is occurring;
(b) remove any infringing article;
(c) when entering land under paragraph (a), be accompanied by one or more persons for the purpose of taking action under paragraph (b);
(d) use, or authorise the use of, reasonable force for the purpose of taking action under this subsection.

(2) The power to remove an article may be exercised only if the constable . . . thinks it necessary for the purpose of—
(a) ending the contravention of regulations under section 25,
(b) preventing a future contravention of the regulations, [or]
(c) enabling the article to be used as evidence in proceedings for an offence under section 27, . . .
(d) . . .

(3) . . .

(4) . . .

(5) Having exercised a power under this section a constable . . . —
(a) shall take reasonable steps to leave the land or premises secure, and
(b) shall comply with any provision of regulations under section 25 about informing specified persons of what the constable . . . has done.

(6) Regulations under section 25 shall include provision enabling a person whose property is damaged in the course of the exercise or purported exercise of a power under this section (other than a person responsible for a contravention of the regulations) to obtain compensation from [a local policing body] [or a police authority]; and the regulations may, in particular, include provision—
(a) conferring jurisdiction on a court or tribunal;
(b) about appeals.

(7) A [local policing body] [or a police authority] may recover from a person responsible for the contravention of regulations under section 25, as if it were a debt, the reasonable costs of taking action under this section.

(8) In this section—

. . .

"infringing article" means

(a) an article [or animal] that is being offered for trade in contravention of regulations under section 25 or is otherwise being used in connection with a contravention of the regulations, and

(b) anything (other than a vehicle) containing an article [or animal] to which paragraph (a) applies.

NOTES

Sub-s (1): words omitted repealed by the Olympic Delivery Authority (Dissolution) Order 2014, SI 2014/3184, art 2(2), Schedule, paras 1, 6(a).

Sub-s (2): first words omitted repealed by SI 2014/3184, art 2(2), Schedule, paras 1, 6(a); in para (b) word in square brackets inserted and para (d) and word immediately preceding it repealed by the London Olympic Games and Paralympic Games (Amendment) Act 2011, s 1(5).

Sub-s (3): repealed by the London Olympic Games and Paralympic Games (Amendment) Act 2011, s 1(6).

Sub-s (4): repealed by SI 2014/3184, art 2(2), Schedule, paras 1, 6(b).

Sub-s (5): words omitted repealed by SI 2014/3184, art 2(2), Schedule, paras 1, 6(a).

Sub-ss (6), (7): words in first pair of square brackets inserted by the Police Reform and Social Responsibility Act 2011, s 99, Sch 16, Pt 3, paras 354, 357; words in second pair of square brackets substituted by SI 2014/3184, art 2(2), Schedule, paras 1, 6(c).

Sub-s (8): definition "enforcement officer" (omitted) repealed by SI 2014/3184, art 2(2), Schedule, paras 1, 6(d); in definition "infringing article" words in square brackets inserted by the London Olympic Games and Paralympic Games (Amendment) Act 2011, s 1(8).

29 *(Repealed by the Olympic Delivery Authority (Dissolution) Order 2014, SI 2014/3184, art 2(2), Schedule, paras 1, 2(i).)*

[7.41]

30 Other authorities

(1) The Secretary of State [. . .] may by order require specified persons to give information about the effect or likely effect of regulations under section 25 to persons falling within a specified class.

(2) In particular, the order may require a person who grants a consent, certificate, permission or authority (by whatever name) to inform the recipient of the effect of section 26(4).

(3) An order under this section—

(a) shall be made by statutory instrument, and

(b) shall be subject to annulment in pursuance of a resolution of either House of Parliament.

NOTES

Sub-s (1): words omitted from square brackets inserted by the Transfer of Functions (Olympics and Paralympics) Order 2007, SI 2007/2129, arts 3(1), (2)(d), 5, Schedule, para 6(1)(l) and repealed by the Secretary of State for Culture, Olympics, Media and Sport Order 2010, SI 2010/1551, art 11, Schedule, para 8(1)(l).

[7.42]

31 Sale of tickets

(1) A person commits an offence if he sells an Olympic ticket—

(a) in a public place or in the course of a business, and

(b) otherwise than in accordance with a written authorisation issued by the London Organising Committee.

(2) For the purposes of subsection (1)—

(a) "Olympic ticket" means anything which is or purports to be a ticket for one or more London Olympic events,

(b) a reference to selling a ticket includes a reference to—

(i) offering to sell a ticket,

(ii) exposing a ticket for sale,

(iii) advertising that a ticket is available for purchase, and

(iv) giving, or offering to give, a ticket to a person who pays or agrees to pay for some other goods or services, and

(c) a person shall (without prejudice to the generality of subsection (1)(a)) be treated as acting in the course of a business if he does anything as a result of which he makes a profit or aims to make a profit.

(3) A person does not commit an offence under subsection (1) by advertising that a ticket is available for purchase if—

(a) the sale of the ticket if purchased would be in the course of a business only by reason of subsection (2)(c), and

(b) the person does not know, and could not reasonably be expected to discover, that subsection (2)(c) would apply to the sale.

(4) A person does not commit an offence under subsection (1) (whether actual or inchoate) only by virtue of making facilities available in connection with electronic communication or the storage of electronic data.

(5) Where a person who provides services for electronic communication or for the storage of electronic data discovers that they are being used in connection with the commission of an offence under subsection (1), the defence in subsection (4) does not apply in respect of continued provision of the services after the shortest time reasonably required to withdraw them.
(6) A person guilty of an offence under subsection (1) shall be liable on summary conviction to a fine not exceeding [£20,000].
(7) Section 32(2)(b) of the Police and Criminal Evidence Act 1984 (c 60) (power to search premises) shall, in its application to the offence under subsection (1) above, permit the searching of a vehicle which a constable reasonably thinks was used in connection with the offence.
(8) Subsection (9) applies where a person in Scotland is arrested in connection with the commission of an offence under subsection (1).
(9) For the purposes of recovering evidence relating to the offence, a constable in Scotland may without warrant enter and search—
(a) premises in which the person was when arrested or immediately before he was arrested, and
(b) a vehicle which the constable reasonably believes is being used or was used in connection with the offence.
(10) Subsection (9) is without prejudice to any power of entry or search which is otherwise exercisable by a constable in Scotland.
(11) The London Organising Committee shall make arrangements for the grant of authorisations under subsection (1)(b); and the arrangements may, in particular—
(a) make provision about charges;
(b) enable the Committee to exercise unfettered discretion.
(12) In this section a reference to a London Olympic event includes a reference to an event held by way of a pre-Olympic event in accordance with arrangements made by the London Organising Committee in pursuance of paragraph 7 of the Bye-Law to Rule 49 of the Olympic Charter.

NOTES
Sub-s (6): sum in square brackets substituted by the London Olympic Games and Paralympic Games (Amendment) Act 2011, s 3(1), in relation to offences committed after 14 February 2012, see ss 3(2), 10(1) thereof.

31A–31E (*Inserted by the London Olympic Games and Paralympic Games (Amendment) Act 2011, s 1(9) and repealed by the Olympic Delivery Authority (Dissolution) Order 2014, SI 2014/3184, art 2(2), Schedule, paras 1, 2(j)–(n).*)

Miscellaneous

[7.43]
32 Olympic Symbol etc (Protection) Act 1995
Schedule 3 (which amends the Olympic Symbol etc (Protection) Act 1995 (c 32)) shall have effect.
33 (*Repealed by s 40(8) of this Act at* **[7.50]**.)

[7.44]
34 Greater London Authority: powers
(1) The Greater London Authority may do anything—
(a) for the purpose of complying with an obligation of thc Mayor of London under the Host City Contract (whether before, during or after the London Olympics),
(b) for a purpose connected with preparing for or managing the London Olympics, or
(c) for a purpose connected with anything done in accordance with paragraph (a) or (b).
(2) In particular, the Greater London Authority may—
(a) arrange for the construction, improvement or adaptation of premises or facilities of any description;
(b) arrange for the provision of services of any description;
(c) undertake works of any description;
(d) acquire land or other property;
(e) enter into agreements;
(f) act jointly or cooperate with any person (whether or not having functions under the Host City Contract);
(g) give financial or other assistance to persons in respect of activity connected with the London Olympics (whether or not the activity is undertaken in pursuance of an agreement with the Authority);
(h) take action in respect of places outside London.
(3) In exercising the function under subsection (1) the Authority shall have regard to the desirability of consulting and cooperating with—
(a) the Secretary of State,
[(aa) . . .]
(b) the British Olympic Association,
(c) the London Organising Committee, and

(d) other persons with experience or knowledge which might be useful in relation to preparing for or managing the London Olympics.

(4) In exercising the function under subsection (1) the Authority shall have regard to the desirability of maximising the benefits to be derived after the London Olympics from things done in preparation for them.

(5) . . .

NOTES

Sub-s (3): para (aa) inserted by the Transfer of Functions (Olympics and Paralympics) Order 2007, SI 2007/2129, arts 3(1), (2)(d), 5, Schedule, para 6(2) and repealed by the Secretary of State for Culture, Olympics, Media and Sport Order 2010, SI 2010/1551, art 11, Schedule, para 8(2).

Sub-s (5): repealed by the Localism Act 2011, s 237, Sch 25, Pt 32.

[7.45]

35 Section 34: supplemental

(1) Financial assistance under section 34(2)(g) may be given on terms or conditions (which may, in particular, include terms or conditions for repayment with or without interest).

(2) The Greater London Authority may accept contributions towards expenditure in connection with the London Olympics.

(3) The Secretary of State [. . .] may, after the conclusion of the London Olympics, repeal section 34 and this section by order made by statutory instrument; and the order may—

(a) include savings (which may include provision saving, to such extent as may be specified and whether or not subject to modifications, the effect of a provision of the Greater London Authority Act 1999 or another primary or subordinate enactment in so far as it applies in relation to section 34);

(b) include transitional provision (which may include provision relating to the effect of a provision of an enactment in so far as it applies in relation to section 34);

(c) include provision for the transfer of property, rights or liabilities (which may, in particular, include provision for transfer—

(i) to the Secretary of State or to any other person whether or not exercising functions of a public nature;

(ii) on terms and conditions, whether as to payment or otherwise;

(iii) of liabilities whether arising under the Host City Contract or otherwise;

(iv) of rights or liabilities in relation to legal proceedings);

(d) include provision of any other kind relating to the management, control or treatment of anything constructed or done in accordance with section 34(1);

(e) include incidental or consequential provision;

(f) make provision having effect generally or only for specified cases or purposes;

(g) make different provision for different cases or purposes.

(4) Before making an order under subsection (3) the Secretary of State [. . .] shall consult the Mayor of London.

(5) An order under subsection (3) shall be subject to annulment in pursuance of a resolution of either House of Parliament.

NOTES

Sub-ss (3), (4): words omitted from square brackets inserted by the Transfer of Functions (Olympics and Paralympics) Order 2007, SI 2007/2129, arts 3(1), (2)(d), 5, Schedule, para 6(1)(m) and repealed by the Secretary of State for Culture, Olympics, Media and Sport Order 2010, SI 2010/1551, art 11, Schedule, para 8(1)(m).

[7.46]

36 Regional development agencies

(1), (2) . . .

(3) In relation to the purchase of land by a regional development agency for the purpose of preparing for the London Olympics (whether or not by virtue of subsection (1) and whether or not the purchase has another purpose also)— . . .

(a), (b) . . .

(c) no enactment regulating the use of commons, open spaces or allotments shall prevent or restrict the use of the land for construction, other works or any other purpose (but this paragraph does not disapply a requirement for planning permission), and

(d) . . .

(4), (5) . . .

NOTES

Sub-ss (1), (2), (3)(a), (b), (d), (4), (5): repealed by the Public Bodies Act 2011, s 30(3), Sch 6.

Sub-s (3)(c): repealed by the Public Bodies Act 2011, s 30(3), Sch 6, as from a day to be appointed.

General

[7.47]

37 Scotland

(1) In its application to Scotland, this Act has effect subject to the following modifications.

(2) "Enactment", except in section 9(2)(d)(iv), includes an enactment contained in, or in an instrument under, an Act of the Scottish Parliament.

(3) "Local authority" means a council constituted under section 2 of the Local Government etc (Scotland) Act 1994 (c 39).

(4) "Local planning authority" means a planning authority for the purposes of the Town and Country Planning (Scotland) Act 1997 (c 8).

(5) "Police authority" includes a joint police board constituted under an amalgamation scheme made under section 19 of the Police (Scotland) Act 1967 (c 77).

(6) . . .

(7) References to a highway are to be read as if they were references to a road within the meaning of the Roads (Scotland) Act 1984 (c 54).

(8) In sections 19 to 30—

(a) references to the Secretary of State [. . .] are to be read as if they were references to the Scottish Ministers, and

(b) references [(other than in sections 20 and 26)] to a resolution of either House of Parliament are to be read as if they were references to a resolution of the Scottish Parliament.

(9) In section 20(1)(b), the reference to Chapter III of Part VIII of the Town and Country Planning Act 1990 (c 8) is to be read as if it were a reference to Chapter 3 of Part 7 of the Town and Country Planning (Scotland) Act 1997.

[(9A) Sections 20 and 26 are to have effect as if, in each case, for subsections (2) and (2A) there were substituted—

"(2) Regulations under that section are subject to the affirmative procedure.

(2A) But if, in relation to regulations under that section other than the first regulations, the Scottish Ministers consider that by reason of urgency it is necessary that they be made without being approved in draft—

(a) subsection (2) does not apply to the regulations, and

(b) the regulations are instead subject to the negative procedure."]

(10) In section 22(4)—

(a) the references to a justice of the peace are to be read as if they were references to a sheriff, and

(b) the reference to the application of a constable . . . is to be read as if it were a reference to the application of a procurator fiscal.

(11) . . .

[(12) In section 22, subsection (6) has effect as if there were substituted for it—

"(6) An article that is held by a constable (having been removed by or delivered to the constable) shall be returned when retention is no longer justified by a matter specified in subsection (5)(a) to (c), unless—

(a) in the case of a perishable article, the article has ceased to be usable for trade, or

(b) the court orders the article to be forfeited under Part 2 of the Proceeds of Crime (Scotland) Act 1995.

(6A) Subject to subsection (6), the article shall be treated as if acquired by the constable in the course of the investigation of an offence.

. . ."

(13) In section 28, subsection (4) has effect as if there were substituted for it

"(4) An article that is held by a constable (having been removed by or delivered to the constable) shall be returned when retention is no longer justified by a matter specified in subsection (2)(a) to (c), unless—

(a) in the case of a perishable article, the article has ceased to be usable for trade, or

(b) the court orders the article to be forfeited under Part 2 of the Proceeds of Crime (Scotland) Act 1995.

(4A) Subject to subsection (4), the article shall be treated as if acquired by the constable in the course of the investigation of an offence.

. . ."

(14)–(16) . . .]

NOTES

Sub-ss (6), (11): repealed by the London Olympic Games and Paralympic Games (Amendment) Act 2011, s 1(10).

Sub-s (8): in para (a) words omitted from square brackets inserted by the Transfer of Functions (Olympics and Paralympics) Order 2007, SI 2007/2129, arts 3(1), (2)(d), 5, Schedule, para 6(1)(o) and repealed by the Secretary of State for Culture, Olympics, Media and Sport Order 2010, SI 2010/1551, art 11, Schedule, para 8(1)(o); in para (b) words in square brackets inserted by the London Olympic Games and Paralympic Games (Amendment) Act 2011, s 2(5).

Sub-s (9A): inserted by the London Olympic Games and Paralympic Games (Amendment) Act 2011, s 2(6).

Sub-s (10): words omitted repealed by the Olympic Delivery Authority (Dissolution) Order 2014, SI 2014/3184, art 2(2), Schedule, paras 1, 7(a).

Sub-ss (12), (13): inserted by the London Olympic Games and Paralympic Games (Amendment) Act 2011, s 1(11); words omitted repealed by SI 2014/3184, art 2(2), Schedule, paras 1, 7(b), (c).

Sub-ss (14)–(16): inserted by the London Olympic Games and Paralympic Games (Amendment) Act 2011, s 1(11) and repealed by SI 2014/3184, art 2(2), Schedule, paras 1, 7(d).

[7.48]
38 Northern Ireland

In its application to Northern Ireland this Act has effect as if—

(a) references to an enactment included references to Northern Ireland legislation,
(b) references to a police authority were references to the Northern Ireland Policing Board,
(c) references to a justice of the peace were references to a lay magistrate,
(d) references to a local planning authority were references to the Department of the Environment in Northern Ireland,
(e) references to a highway were references to a road (within the meaning of the Roads (Northern Ireland) Order 1980 (SI 1980/1085 (NI 11)),
(f) references to a local authority were references to a district council,
(g) . . .
(h) the reference in section 31(5) to section 32(2)(b) of the Police and Criminal Evidence Act 1984 (c 60) were a reference to Article 34(2)(b) of the Police and Criminal Evidence (Northern Ireland) Order 1989 (SI 1989/1341 (NI 12)), and
(i) for section 39 there were substituted—

"39 Offences: arrest

In Article 26(2) of the Police and Criminal Evidence (Northern Ireland) Order 1989 (arrestable offences) at the end add—

"(r) offences under section 21(1), 27(1) or 31(1) of the London Olympic Games and Paralympic Games Act 2006 (unauthorised advertising, trading and ticket sales)."."

NOTES

Para (g): repealed by the London Olympic Games and Paralympic Games (Amendment) Act 2011, s 1(12).

[7.49]
39 Offences: arrest

(1) (*Amends the Police and Criminal Evidence Act 1984, Sch 1A.*)

(2) A constable in Scotland may arrest without warrant a person who the constable reasonably believes is committing or has committed an offence under section 21(1), 27(1) or 31(1).

(3) Subsection (2) is without prejudice to any power of arrest which is otherwise exercisable by a constable in Scotland.

[7.50]
40 Commencement and duration

(1) The following provisions of this Act shall come into force on Royal Assent—

(a) section 1,
(b) sections 3 to 5 and Schedule 1,
(c) section 32 and paragraphs 1 to 11 of Schedule 3,
(d) section 33 and Schedule 4,
(e) sections 34 and 35(1) and (2),
(f) section 36(3)(a) and (d),
(g) section 37, and
(h) section 38.

(2) The other preceding provisions of this Act (including paragraphs 12 to 14 of Schedule 3) shall come into force in accordance with provision made by order of the Secretary of State [. . .].

(3) But the following provisions of this Act, so far as they extend to Scotland, shall come into force in accordance with provision made by order of the Scottish Ministers—

(a) sections 19 to 31, and
(b) section 39(2) and (3).

(4) An order under subsection (2) or (3)—

(a) may make provision generally or only for specified purposes,
(b) may make different provision for different purposes,
(c) may include transitional or incidental provision, and
(d) shall be made by statutory instrument.

(5) Despite subsection (1)(c), for the purposes of criminal proceedings under a provision of the Olympic Symbol etc (Protection) Act 1995 (c 32) in respect of anything done before the end of the period of two months beginning with the date on which this Act receives Royal Assent, no account shall be taken of any amendment made of that Act by Schedule 3 to this Act.

(6) Sections 10 to 18 (including any power to make orders or give directions) shall cease to have effect at the end of the London Olympics period.

(7) Paragraph 14 of Schedule 3, which inserts new sections 12A and 12B into the Olympic Symbol etc (Protection) Act 1995, shall have effect in relation to things arriving in the United Kingdom during the period—

(a) beginning with the day specified under subsection (2) above for the commencement of paragraph 14 of Schedule 3, and
(b) ending with 31st December 2012.

(8) Section 33 and Schedule 4 shall cease to have effect at the end of 31st December 2012.

(9) In respect of section 36(3)—
(a) paragraph (a) shall have effect in relation to compulsory purchase orders made on or after 1st October 2005,
(b) an order bringing paragraph (b) into force on a date ("the commencement date")—
(i) may provide for paragraph (b) to have effect in relation to purchases (whether compulsory or voluntary) completed before, on or after the commencement date, but
(ii) must include provision modifying section 295 of the Housing Act 1985 in its application by virtue of section 36(3)(b) so that extinguishment of rights and easements takes effect, in the case of a purchase completed before the commencement date, on the commencement date,
(c) an order bringing paragraph (c) into force on a date ("the commencement date")—
(i) may provide for paragraph (c) to have effect in relation to purchases (whether compulsory or voluntary) completed on or after 1st October 2005, but
(ii) shall not affect the lawfulness of anything done before the commencement date, and
(d) paragraph (d) shall be treated as having taken effect on 1st October 2005.

NOTES

Sub-s (2): words omitted from square brackets inserted by the Transfer of Functions (Olympics and Paralympics) Order 2007, SI 2007/2129, arts 3(1), (2)(d), 5, Schedule, para 6(1)(p) and repealed by the Secretary of State for Culture, Olympics, Media and Sport Order 2010, SI 2010/1551, art 11, Schedule, para 8(1)(p).

Orders: the London Olympic Games and Paralympic Games Act 2006 (Commencement No 1) Order 2006, SI 2006/1118; the London Olympic Games and Paralympic Games Act 2006 (Commencement No 2) Order 2007, SI 2007/1064; the London Olympic Games and Paralympic Games Act 2006 (Commencement No 3) Order 2009, SI 2009/2577; the London Olympic Games and Paralympic Games Act 2006 (Commencement) (Scotland) Order 2006, SSI 2006/611.

[7.51]
41 Extent and application

(1) The following provisions of this Act extend only to England and Wales—
(a) . . .
(b) . . .
(c) sections 10 to 18, and
(d) sections 34 to 36.

(2) The remaining provisions of this Act extend to—
(a) England and Wales,
(b) Scotland, and
(c) Northern Ireland.

(3) The provisions specified in subsection (1) (except section 36) shall apply only in relation to—
(a) places in England, and
(b) things done in or in respect of England.

(4) In their application to things done in Wales, sections 19 to 30 shall have effect as if—
(a) a reference to the Secretary of State [. . .] were a reference to the National Assembly for Wales, and
(b) a reference to a resolution of each or either House of Parliament were a reference to a resolution of the National Assembly for Wales.

(5) Section 31 shall apply in respect of anything done whether in the United Kingdom or elsewhere.

NOTES

Sub-ss (1): paras (a), (b) repealed by the Olympic Delivery Authority (Dissolution) Order 2014, SI 2014/3184, art 2(2), Schedule, paras 1, 2(o).

Sub-s (4): words omitted from square brackets inserted by the Transfer of Functions (Olympics and Paralympics) Order 2007, SI 2007/2129, arts 3(1), (2)(d), 5, Schedule, para 6(1)(q) and repealed by the Secretary of State for Culture, Olympics, Media and Sport Order 2010, SI 2010/1551, art 11, Schedule, para 8(1)(q).

[7.52]
42 Short title

This Act may be cited as the London Olympic Games and Paralympic Games Act 2006.

SCHEDULES 1, 2

(Schs 1, 2 repealed by the Olympic Delivery Authority (Dissolution) Order 2014, SI 2014/3184, art 2(2), Schedule, paras 1, 2(p), (q).)

SCHEDULE 3
OLYMPIC SYMBOL PROTECTION

Section 32

[7.53]

1–10. *(Para 1 introduces the amendments to the Olympic Symbol etc (Protection) Act 1995; para 2 inserts s 1(2A) to the 1995 Act; para 3 amends ss 3, 4 of the 1995 Act; para 4 substitutes s 4(1)–(10) of the 1995 Act; para 5 amends s 5 of the 1995 Act; para 6 inserts s 5A to the 1995 Act; paras 7–9 amend s 18 of the 1995 Act; para 10 amends s 7 of the 1995 Act.)*

Penalties

11. (1) In respect of an offence under section 8 (infringement marketing of goods) committed during the period specified in sub-paragraph (2), the reference in section 8(5)(a) (maximum fine on summary conviction) to the statutory maximum shall be taken as a reference to £20,000.

(2) The period referred to in sub-paragraph (1)—

(a) begins at the end of the period of two months beginning with the date on which this Act receives Royal Assent, and

(b) ends with 31st December 2012.

Enforcement

12. (1) *(Inserts the Olympic Symbol etc (Protection) Act 1995, s 8A.)*

(2) The London Organising Committee may—

(a) make arrangements with a local weights and measures authority for the exercise of the authority's power under section 8 of the Olympic Symbol etc (Protection) Act 1995 (as inserted by sub-paragraph (1));

(b) may make payments to a local weights and measures authority in respect of expenses incurred in the exercise of that power.

13, 14. *(Para 13 inserts the Olympic Symbol etc (Protection) Act 1995, s 8B; para 14 inserted ss 12A, 12B to the 1995 Act, and is now spent in accordance with s 40(7) at* **[7.50]***.)*

SCHEDULE 4

(Repealed by s 40(8) of this Act at **[7.50]***.)*

INTELLECTUAL PROPERTY ACT 2014

(2014 c 18)

An Act to make provision about intellectual property.

[14 May 2014]

1–19 *((Pts 1, 2) Ss 1–5, 10(7), (8), 11(2) amend the Copyright, Designs and Patents Act 1988 at* **[2.7]** *et seq; ss 6–9, 10(1)–(6), 11(1), (3), 12–14 amend the Registered Designs Act 1949 at* **[3.1]** *et seq; ss 15–19 amend the Patents Act 1977 at* **[1.1]** *et seq; s 10(9)–(11) amends legislation outside the scope of this work.)*

PART 3
MISCELLANEOUS

20 *(Inserts the Freedom of Information Act 2000, s 22A (outside the scope of this work).)*

[7.54]

21 Reporting duty

(1) The Secretary of State must, before the end of the period of 6 months beginning with the end of each financial year, lay before Parliament a report setting out—

(a) the Secretary of State's opinion of the extent to which during that year—

(i) the activities of the Patent Office have contributed to the promotion of innovation and of economic growth in the United Kingdom, and

(ii) legislation relating to intellectual property has been effective in facilitating innovation and economic growth in the United Kingdom, and

(b) how the promotion of innovation and of economic growth in the United Kingdom was taken into account in the case of any legislation relating to intellectual property that was passed or made during that year.

(2) The reference to the activities of the Patent Office is a reference to—

(a) the activities of the comptroller-general of patents, designs and trade marks, and

(b) the activities of the officers and clerks of the Patent Office.

(3) The references to legislation relating to intellectual property do not include a reference to legislation relating to plant breeders' rights or rights under section 7 of the Plant Varieties Act 1997.

(4) "Financial year" means a period of 12 months ending with 31 March.

(5) "Legislation" includes—

(a) subordinate legislation within the meaning of the Interpretation Act 1978, and

(b) legislation of the European Union.

NOTES

Commencement: 1 October 2014.

22 (*Amends the Copyright, Designs and Patents Act 1988 at* **[2.7]** *et seq.*)

PART 4
GENERAL

[7.55]

23 Power to make consequential or transitional provision etc

(1) The Secretary of State may by order made by statutory instrument—

(a) make provision in consequence of a provision of this Act;

(b) make transitional, transitory or saving provision in connection with the commencement of a provision of this Act or of provision made under paragraph (a).

(2) An order under this section may amend, repeal, revoke or otherwise modify an enactment.

(3) The power conferred by this section is not restricted by any other provision of this Act.

(4) In this section, "enactment" includes—

(a) an enactment contained in subordinate legislation (within the meaning of the Interpretation Act 1978), and

(b) an enactment contained in, or in an instrument made under, an Act of the Scottish Parliament, an Act or Measure of the National Assembly for Wales or Northern Ireland legislation,

and references to an enactment include a reference to an enactment passed or made after the passing of this Act.

(5) A statutory instrument which contains an order under this section containing (whether alone or with other provision) provision that amends or repeals a provision of an Act of Parliament may not be made unless a draft of the instrument has been laid before, and approved by a resolution of, each House of Parliament.

(6) Subject to that, a statutory instrument which contains an order under this section containing (whether alone or with other provision) provision under subsection (1)(a) is subject to annulment in pursuance of a resolution of either House of Parliament.

NOTES

Commencement: 1 August 2014.

Orders: the Intellectual Property Act 2014 (Commencement No 3 and Transitional Provisions) Order 2014, SI 2014/2330; the Intellectual Property Act 2014 (Commencement No 5 and Saving Provisions) Order 2016, SI 2016/1139.

[7.56]

24 Commencement, extent and short title

(1) The preceding provisions of this Act come into force on such day as the Secretary of State may by order made by statutory instrument appoint.

(2) An order under this section may appoint different days for different purposes.

(3) An amendment or repeal made by this Act has the same extent as the enactment being amended or repealed.

(4) Section 21 extends to England and Wales, Scotland and Northern Ireland.

(5) Section 23 extends to England and Wales, Scotland, Northern Ireland and the Isle of Man.

(6) This Act may be cited as the Intellectual Property Act 2014.

NOTES

Commencement: 14 May 2014.

Orders: the Intellectual Property Act 2014 (Commencement No 1) Order 2014, SI 2014/1715; the Intellectual Property Act 2014 (Commencement No 2) Order 2014, SI 2014/2069; the Intellectual Property Act 2014 (Commencement No 3 and Transitional Provisions) Order 2014, SI 2014/2330; the Intellectual Property Act 2014 (Commencement No 4) Order 2015, SI 2015/165; the Intellectual Property Act 2014 (Commencement No 5 and Saving Provisions) Order 2016, SI 2016/1139.

SCHEDULE

(*The Schedule contains amendments to the Patents Act 1977 at* **[1.1]** *et seq.*)

GOODS INFRINGING INTELLECTUAL PROPERTY RIGHTS (CUSTOMS) REGULATIONS 2004

(SI 2004/1473)

NOTES

Made: 4 June 2004.
Authority: European Communities Act 1972, s 2(2).
Commencement: 1 July 2004.

[7.57]
1 Citation and commencement

These Regulations may be cited as the Goods Infringing Intellectual Property Rights (Customs) Regulations 2004 and shall come into force on 1st July 2004.

[7.58]
2 Interpretation

(1) In these Regulations—

"the 1979 Act" means the Customs and Excise Management Act 1979;

"application" means an application under Article 5 of the Council Regulation;

"the Commissioners" means the Commissioners of Customs and Excise;

. . .

"the Council Regulation" means Council Regulation (EC) No 1383/2003 concerning customs action against goods suspected of infringing certain intellectual property rights and the measures to be taken against goods found to have infringed such rights;

"the customs and excise Acts" has the meaning given in section 1(1) of the 1979 Act;

"database rights" has the meaning given in regulation 13 of the Copyright and Rights in Databases Regulations 1997;

"decision" means a decision granting an application in accordance with Article 8 of the Council Regulation;

"declarant" has the meaning given in Article 4(18) of Council Regulation (EEC) No 2913/1992 establishing the Community Customs Code;

. . .

"goods infringing an intellectual property right" has the meaning given in Article 2(1) of the Council Regulation and related expressions shall be construed accordingly;

. . .

"publication rights" has the meaning given in regulation 16 of the Copyright and Related Rights Regulations 1996;

. . .

"right-holder" has the meaning given in Article 2(2) of the Council Regulation;

. . .

"working days" has the meaning given in Article 3(1) of Council Regulation (EEC, Euratom) No 1182/1971 determining the rules applicable to periods, dates and time limits.

(2) For the purposes of these Regulations, any reference in the Council Regulation to "copyright or related right" is to be construed as a reference to "copyright, rights in performances, publication rights or database rights".

(3) These Regulations shall apply to goods which fall to be treated by virtue of [Article 2] of the Council Regulation as being goods infringing an intellectual property right; but these Regulations shall not apply to any goods in relation to which the Council Regulation does not apply by virtue of [Article 3] thereof.

NOTES

Para (1): definitions omitted revoked by the Goods Infringing Intellectual Property Rights (Customs) (Amendment) (No 2) Regulations 2010, SI 2010/992, regs 2, 3.

Para (3): words in square brackets substituted by SI 2010/992, regs 2, 4.

3, 4 (*Reg 3 revoked by the Goods Infringing Intellectual Property Rights (Customs) (Amendment) Regulations 2010, SI 2010/324, reg 2(1); reg 4 revoked by the Goods Infringing Intellectual Property Rights (Customs) (Amendment) (No 2) Regulations 2010, SI 2010/992, regs 2, 5.*)

[7.59]

5 Decision to cease to have effect

A decision shall have no further effect where—

(a) any change, following the making of the application, which takes place in the ownership or authorised use of the intellectual property right specified in the application, is not communicated in writing to the Commissioners; or

(b) the intellectual property right specified in the application expires.

6 *(Revoked by the Goods Infringing Intellectual Property Rights (Customs) (Amendment) (No 2) Regulations 2010, SI 2010/992, regs 2, 5.)*

[7.60]

[7 Simplified procedure

(1) The Commissioners may treat as abandoned for destruction goods which have been suspended from release or detained by virtue of [Article 9 of the Council Regulation] where the right-holder has informed the Commissioners in writing within the specified period that those goods infringe an intellectual property right and either of the following conditions applies—

(a) the right-holder has provided the Commissioners with the written agreement of the declarant, the holder or the owner of the goods ("the interested parties") that the goods may [be] destroyed; or

(b) none of the interested parties has specifically opposed the destruction of the goods within the specified period.

(2) The Commissioners may not treat the goods as abandoned for destruction where one interested party has given its written agreement as mentioned in regulation 7(1)(a), but either or both of the other interested parties has specifically opposed destruction within the specified period.

(3) The Commissioners may, at their discretion, accept the written agreement mentioned in regulation 7(1)(a) directly from the interested party.

(4) Where goods are treated as abandoned for destruction by virtue of paragraph (1)—

(a) the right-holder must bear the expense and the responsibility for the destruction of the goods, unless otherwise specified by the Commissioners; and

(b) the Commissioners must retain a sample of the goods in such conditions that it can be used if required as evidence in legal proceedings.

(5) The specified period means ten working days from receipt of the notification to the right-holder provided for in [Article 9 of the Council Regulation], or three working days in the case of perishable goods. The Commissioners may, at their discretion, extend this period by a further ten working days.

(6) A reference in this regulation to the Commissioners is to be construed as a reference to the Secretary of State.]

NOTES

Substituted by the Goods Infringing Intellectual Property Rights (Customs) (Amendment) Regulations 2010, SI 2010/324, reg 2(2).

Para (1): words in first pair of square brackets substituted and word in second pair of square brackets inserted by the Goods Infringing Intellectual Property Rights (Customs) (Amendment) (No 2) Regulations 2010, SI 2010/992, regs 2, 6.

Para (5): words in square brackets substituted by SI 2010/992, regs 2, 7.

8, 9 *(Revoked by the Goods Infringing Intellectual Property Rights (Customs) (Amendment) Regulations 2010, SI 2010/324, reg 2(1).)*

[7.61]

10 Relationship with other powers

Nothing in these Regulations shall be taken to affect—

(a) any power of the Commissioners conferred otherwise than by any provision of these Regulations to suspend the release of, or detain, any goods; or

(b) the power of any court to grant any relief, including any power to make an order by way of interim relief.

[7.62]

11 Misuse of information by a right-holder

(1) Where the Commissioners have reasonable grounds for believing that there has been a misuse of information by a right-holder the Commissioners may suspend the decision in force at the time of the misuse of information, in relation to a relevant intellectual property right, for the remainder of its period of validity.

(2) Where the Commissioners have reasonable grounds for believing that there has been a further misuse of information within three years of a previous misuse of information by that right-holder the Commissioners may—

(a) suspend the decision in force at the time of the further misuse of information, in relation to a relevant intellectual property right, for the remainder of its period of validity; and

(b) for a period of up to one year from its expiry, refuse to renew the decision in force at the time of the further misuse of information, or to accept a new application, in relation to a relevant intellectual property right.

(3) In this regulation—

(a) "misuse of information" means the use of information supplied to a right-holder pursuant to the first sub-paragraph of Article 9(3) of the Council Regulation other than for the purposes specified in Articles 10, 11 and 13(1) of the Council Regulation, or pursuant to an enactment or order of a court, and related expressions shall be construed accordingly;

(b) "relevant intellectual property right" means any intellectual property right in relation to a suspected infringement of which information was supplied to a right-holder pursuant to the first sub-paragraph of Article 9(3) of the Council Regulation, and in relation to which the Commissioners have reasonable grounds for believing that there has been a misuse of that information.

12, 13 (*Reg 12 amends the Copyright, Designs and Patents Act 1988, s 111 at* **[2.147]***; reg 13 amends the Trade Marks Act 1994, s 89 at* **[5.89]***.*)

[7.63]
14 Revocations

The Regulations listed in the Schedule are hereby revoked.

SCHEDULE

(*The Schedule revokes the Trade Marks (EC Measures Relating to Counterfeit Goods) Regulations 1995, SI 1995/1444, the Goods Infringing Intellectual Property Rights (Customs) Regulations 1999, SI 1999/1601, the Goods Infringing Intellectual Property Rights (Consequential Provisions) Regulations 1999, SI 1999/1618, and the Goods Infringing Intellectual Property Rights (Customs) Regulations 2003, SI 2003/2316.*)

INTELLECTUAL PROPERTY (ENFORCEMENT, ETC) REGULATIONS 2006

(SI 2006/1028)

NOTES

Made: 5 April 2006.
Authority: European Communities Act 1972, s 2(2).
Commencement: 29 April 2006.

[7.64]
1 Citation and commencement

These Regulations may be cited as the Intellectual Property (Enforcement, etc) Regulations 2006 and shall come into force on 29th April 2006.

[7.65]
2 Amendments of legislation

(1) Schedule 1 (amendments to the Registered Designs Act 1949) shall have effect.

(2) Schedule 2 (amendments to other primary legislation) shall have effect.

(3) Schedule 3 (amendments to secondary legislation) shall have effect.

(4) Thc enactments set out in Schedule 4 (repeals) shall be repealed or revoked to the extent specified.

[7.66]
3 Assessment of damages

(1) Where in an action for infringement of an intellectual property right the defendant knew, or had reasonable grounds to know, that he engaged in infringing activity, the damages awarded to the claimant shall be appropriate to the actual prejudice he suffered as a result of the infringement.

(2) When awarding such damages—

(a) all appropriate aspects shall be taken into account, including in particular—

(i) the negative economic consequences, including any lost profits, which the claimant has suffered, and any unfair profits made by the defendant; and

(ii) elements other than economic factors, including the moral prejudice caused to the claimant by the infringement; or

(b) where appropriate, they may be awarded on the basis of the royalties or fees which would have been due had the defendant obtained a licence.

(3) This regulation does not affect the operation of any enactment or rule of law relating to remedies for the infringement of intellectual property rights except to the extent that it is inconsistent with the provisions of this regulation.

(4) In the application of this regulation to—

(a) Scotland, "claimant" includes pursuer; "defendant" includes defender; and "enactment" includes an enactment comprised in, or an instrument made under, an Act of the Scottish Parliament; and

(b) Northern Ireland, "claimant" includes plaintiff.

[7.67]

4 Order in Scotland for disclosure of information

(1) This regulation applies to proceedings in Scotland concerning an infringement of an intellectual property right.

(2) The pursuer may apply to the court for an order that information regarding the origin and distribution networks of goods or services which infringe an intellectual property right shall be disclosed to him by the relevant person.

(3) The court may only order the information to be disclosed where it considers it just and proportionate having regard to the rights and privileges of the relevant person and others; such an order may be subject to such conditions as the court thinks fit.

(4) The relevant person is—

(a) the alleged infringer,

(b) any person who—

(i) was found in possession of the infringing goods on a commercial scale,

(ii) was found to be using the infringing services on a commercial scale, or

(iii) was found to be providing services on a commercial scale, which are used in activities which infringe an intellectual property right, or

(c) any person who has been identified by a person specified in sub-paragraph (b) as being involved in—

(i) the production, manufacture or distribution of the infringing goods, or

(ii) the provision of the infringing services.

(5) For the purposes of paragraph (3), the court may order the disclosure of any of the following types of information—

(a) the names and addresses of—

(i) each producer, manufacturer, distributor or supplier of the infringing goods or services;

(ii) any person who previously possessed the infringing goods; and

(iii) the intended wholesaler and retailer of the infringing goods or services; and

(b) information relating to—

(i) the quantities of infringing goods or the amount of infringing services provided, produced, manufactured, delivered, received or ordered; and

(ii) the price paid for the infringing goods or infringing services in question.

(6) Nothing in this regulation affects—

(a) any right of the pursuer to receive information under any other enactment (including an enactment comprised in, or an instrument made under, an Act of the Scottish Parliament) or rule of law; and

(b) any other power of the court.

(7) For the purposes of this regulation and regulation 5, "court" means the Court of Session or the sheriff.

[7.68]

5 Order in Scotland for publication of judgments

In Scotland, where the court finds that an intellectual property right has been infringed, the court may, at the request of the pursuer, order appropriate measures for the dissemination and publication of the judgment to be taken at the defender's expense.

SCHEDULES

SCHEDULE 1

(*Sch 1 inserts the Registered Designs Act 1949, ss 15A–15C at* **[3.32]–[3.34]**, *24A–24G at* **[3.42]–[3.48]**, *amends ss 26, 46 at* **[3.50]**, **[3.77]**, *and substitutes s 45 at* **[3.76]**.)

SCHEDULE 2
AMENDMENTS TO OTHER PRIMARY LEGISLATION

Regulation 2(2)

Amendment of the Patents Act 1977

1–4. (*Para 1 introduces the amendments to the Patents Act 1977; para 2 amends s 62 of that Act at* **[1.69]**; *paras 3 amends s 63 of that Act at* **[1.70]**; *para 4 amends s 68 of that Act at* **[1.75]**.)

[7.69]
5. (1) (*Amends s 130(1) of the 1977 Act.*)

(2) Sub-paragraph (1) does not apply to an application for a patent to which article 20, 21 or 22 of the Regulatory Reform (Patents) Order 2004 applies.

6–18. (*Para 6 introduces the amendments to the Copyright, Designs and Patents Act 1988; para 7 amends s 114 of that Act at* **[2.150]**; *para 8 amends s 172A of that Act at* **[2.229]**; *para 9 amends s 179 of that Act at* **[2.236]**; *para 10 inserts s 197A to that Act at* **[2.277]**; *para 11 amends s 204 of that Act at* **[2.285]**; *para 12 amends s 211 of that Act at* **[2.309]**; *para 13 amends s 212 of that Act at* **[2.310]**; *para 14 amends s 231 of that Act at* **[2.330]**; *para 15 introduces the amendments to the Trade Marks Act 1994; para 16 amends s 19 of that Act at* **[5.20]**; *para 17 amends s 25 of that Act at* **[5.26]**; *para 18 amends s 55 of that Act at* **[5.56]**.)

SCHEDULES 3 AND 4

(*Sch 3 amends the Duration of Copyright and Rights in Performances Regulations 1995, reg 2 at* **[2.475]**, *amends the Copyright and Related Rights Regulations 1996, regs 2, 16 at* **[2.502]**, **[2.505]** *and inserts regs 17A, 17B to the 1996 Regulations at* **[2.507]**, **[2.508]**, *substitutes the Copyright and Rights in Databases Regulations 1997, reg 23 at* **[2.538]**, *amends the Community Design Regulations 2005, reg 1 at* **[3.99]** *and inserts regs 1A–1D, 5A to the 2005 Regulations at* **[3.100]**–**[3.103]**, **[3.108]**; *Sch 4 contains repeals only.*)

LEGAL SERVICES ACT 2007 (LICENSING AUTHORITY) (NO 2) ORDER 2014

(SI 2014/3077)

NOTES

Made: 17 November 2014.
Authority: Legal Services Act 2007, Sch 10, para 15(1)(a).
Commencement: 1 January 2015.

[7.70]
1 Citation and commencement

This Order may be cited as the Legal Services Act 2007 (Licensing Authority) (No 2) Order 2014 and comes into force on 1st January 2015.

NOTES

Commencement: 1 January 2015.

[7.71]
2 Designation of the Chartered Institute of Patent Attorneys as a licensing authority

The Chartered Institute of Patent Attorneys is designated as a licensing authority in relation to—

(a) the exercise of a right of audience;
(b) the conduct of litigation;
(c) reserved instrument activities; and
(d) the administration of oaths.

NOTES

Commencement: 1 January 2015.

[7.72]
3 Designation of the Institute of Trade Mark Attorneys as a licensing authority

The Institute of Trade Mark Attorneys is designated as a licensing authority in relation to—

(a) the exercise of a right of audience;
(b) the conduct of litigation;
(c) reserved instrument activities; and
(d) the administration of oaths.

NOTES

Commencement: 1 January 2015.

COMPANY, LIMITED LIABILITY PARTNERSHIP AND BUSINESS NAMES (SENSITIVE WORDS AND EXPRESSIONS) REGULATIONS 2014

(SI 2014/3140)

NOTES

26 November 2014.

Companies Act 2006, ss 55(1), 56(1)(b), 1194(1), 1195(1)(b), 1292(1).

Commencement: 31 January 2015.

[7.73]

1 Citation and commencement

These Regulations may be cited as the Company, Limited Liability Partnership and Business Names (Sensitive Words and Expressions) Regulations 2014 and come into force on 31st January 2015.

NOTES

Commencement: 31 January 2015.

[7.74]

2 Interpretation

(1) In these Regulations "the 2006 Act" means the Companies Act 2006.

(2) Any reference in these Regulations to section 55 or 88 of the 2006 Act includes a reference to that section as applied by regulation 8 or 17 of the Limited Liability Partnerships (Application of Companies Act 2006) Regulations 2009.

NOTES

Commencement: 31 January 2015.

[7.75]

3 Specified words and expressions to which sections 55 and 1194 of the 2006 Act apply

The following words and expressions are specified for the purposes of sections 55(1) and 1194(1) of the 2006 Act—

(a) the words and expressions set out in Part 1 of Schedule 1;

(b) the plural and possessive forms of those words and expressions, and, where relevant, the feminine form; and

(c) in the case of the words and expressions set out in Part 1 of Schedule 1 which are marked with an asterisk, the grammatically mutated forms of those words and expressions.

NOTES

Commencement: 31 January 2015.

[7.76]

4 Specified words and expressions to which section 55 of the 2006 Act applies

The following words and expressions are specified for the purposes of section 55(1) of the 2006 Act—

(a) the words and expressions set out in Part 2 of Schedule 1;

(b) the plural and possessive forms of those words and expressions, and, where relevant, the feminine form; and

(c) in the case of the words and expressions set out in Part 2 of Schedule 1 which are marked with an asterisk, the grammatically mutated forms of those words and expressions.

NOTES

Commencement: 31 January 2015.

[7.77]

5 Applications where situation of registered office or principal place of business is irrelevant

In connection with an application for the approval of the Secretary of State under section 55 or 1194 of the 2006 Act in relation to a name that includes a word or expression specified in column (1) of Part 1 of Schedule 2, the applicant must seek the view of the Government department or other body set out opposite that word or expression in column (2) of Part 1 of Schedule 2.

NOTES

Commencement: 31 January 2015.

[7.78]

6 Applications where situation of registered office or principal place of business is relevant

In connection with an application for the approval of the Secretary of State under section 55 or 1194 of the 2006 Act in relation to a name that includes a word or expression specified in column (1) of Part 2 of Schedule 2, the applicant must seek the view of a Government department or other body as follows—

(a) in the case of—
  (i) a company or limited liability partnership that has already been registered, whose registered office is situated in England and Wales;
  (ii) a proposed company or limited liability partnership that has not yet been registered under the 2006 Act, whose registered office is to be situated in England and Wales;
  (iii) a business, whose principal place of business is or is to be situated in England; and
  (iv) an overseas company (see section 1044 of the 2006 Act),

  the Government department or other body set out in column (2) of Part 2 of Schedule 2 opposite that word or expression;

(b) in the case of—
  (i) a company or limited liability partnership that has already been registered, that is a Welsh company or Welsh LLP (see section 88 of the 2006 Act);
  (ii) a proposed company or limited liability partnership that has not yet been registered, that is to be a Welsh company or Welsh LLP; and
  (iii) a business, whose principal place of business is or is to be situated in Wales,

  the Government department or other body set out in column (3) of Part 2 of Schedule 2 opposite that word or expression;

(c) in the case of—
  (i) a company or limited liability partnership that has already been registered, whose registered office is situated in Scotland;
  (ii) a proposed company or limited liability partnership that has not yet been registered, whose registered office is to be situated in Scotland; and
  (iii) a business, whose principal place of business is or is to be situated in Scotland,

  the Government department or other body set out in column (4) of Part 2 of Schedule 2 opposite that word or expression; and

(d) in the case of—
  (i) a company or limited liability partnership that has already been registered, whose registered office is situated in Northern Ireland;
  (ii) a proposed company or limited liability partnership that has not yet been registered, whose registered office is to be situated in Northern Ireland; and
  (iii) a business, whose principal place of business is or is to be situated in Northern Ireland,

  the Government department or other body set out in column (5) of Part 2 of Schedule 2 opposite that word or expression.

NOTES

Commencement: 31 January 2015.

7 *(Revokes the Company, Limited Liability Partnership and Business Names (Sensitive Words and Expressions) Regulations 2009, SI 2009/2615.)*

SCHEDULE 1
SPECIFIED WORDS AND EXPRESSIONS

Regulations 3 and 4

PART 1
WORDS AND EXPRESSIONS SPECIFIED FOR THE PURPOSES OF SECTIONS 55(1) AND 1194(1) OF THE 2006 ACT

[7.79]

Accredit

Accreditation

Accredited

Accrediting

Adjudicator

Association

Assurance

Assurer
Audit office
Auditor General
*Banc
Bank
Banking
Benevolent
*Breatannach
*Breatainn
*Brenhinol
*Brenin
*Brenhiniaeth
Britain
British
Chamber of commerce
Charitable
Charity
Charter
Chartered
Child maintenance
Child support
*Coimisean
*Comhairle
*Comisiwn
Commission
Co-operative
Council
*Cyngor
Dental
Dentistry
*Diùc
*Dug
Duke
Ei Fawrhydi
England
English
Federation
Friendly Society
Foundation
Fund
Government
*Gwasanaeth iechyd
Health centre
Health service
Health visitor
His Majesty
HPSS
HSC
Inspectorate
Institute
Institution
Insurance

Insurer
Judicial appointment
King
Licensing
*Llywodraeth
Medical centre
Midwife
Midwifery
*Mòrachd
Mutual
NHS
Northern Ireland
Northern Irish
Nurse
Nursing
Oifis sgrùdaidh
*Oilthigh
Ombudsman
*Ombwdsmon
*Parlamaid
Parliament
Parliamentarian
Parliamentary
Patent
Patentee
Police
Polytechnic
Post office
*Prifysgol
Prince
*Prionnsa
*Prydain
*Prydeinig
Queen
Reassurance
Reassurer
Registrar
Regulator
Reinsurance
Reinsurer
*Riaghaltas
*Rìgh
Rìoghachd Aonaichte
Rìoghail
Rìoghalachd
Royal
Royalty
Scotland
Scottish
Senedd
Sheffield
Siambr fasnach

Social service
Society
Special school
Standards
Stock exchange
Swyddfa archwilio
*Teyrnas Gyfunol
*Teyrnas Unedig
Trade union
Tribunal
Trust
*Tywysog
Underwrite
Underwriting
University
Wales
Welsh
Windsor

NOTES

Commencement: 31 January 2015.

PART 2
WORDS AND EXPRESSIONS SPECIFIED FOR THE PURPOSES OF SECTION 55(1) OF THE 2006 ACT

[7.80]

Alba
Albannach
Na h-Alba
*Cymru
*Cymraeg
*Cymreig

NOTES

Commencement: 31 January 2015.

SCHEDULE 2
LIST OF GOVERNMENT DEPARTMENTS AND OTHER BODIES WHOSE VIEWS MUST BE SOUGHT

Regulations 5 and 6

PART 1
APPLICATIONS WHERE SITUATION OF REGISTERED OFFICE OR PRINCIPAL PLACE OF BUSINESS IS IRRELEVANT

[7.81]

Column (1)	*Column (2)*
Word or expression specified under regulation 3	Specified Government department or other body whose view must be sought
Accredit	[Department for Business, Energy and Industrial Strategy]
Accreditation	[Department for Business, Energy and Industrial Strategy]
Accredited	[Department for Business, Energy and Industrial Strategy]

Accrediting	[Department for Business, Energy and Industrial Strategy]
Assurance	Financial Conduct Authority
Assurer	Financial Conduct Authority
Banc	Financial Conduct Authority
Bank	Financial Conduct Authority
Banking	Financial Conduct Authority
Brenhinol	The Welsh Assembly Government
Brenin	The Welsh Assembly Government
Brenhiniaeth	The Welsh Assembly Government
Child maintenance	Department for Work and Pensions
Child support	Department for Work and Pensions
Dental	General Dental Council
Dentistry	General Dental Council
Diùc	The Scottish Government
Dug	The Welsh Assembly Government
Ei Fawrhydi	The Welsh Assembly Government
Friendly Society	Financial Conduct Authority
Fund	Financial Conduct Authority
Gwasanaeth iechyd	The Welsh Assembly Government
Health visitor	Nursing & Midwifery Council
HPSS	Department of Health, Social Services and Public Safety
HSC	Department of Health, Social Services and Public Safety
Insurance	Financial Conduct Authority
Insurer	Financial Conduct Authority
Judicial appointment	Ministry of Justice
Llywodraeth	The Welsh Assembly Government
Medical centre	Department of Health, Social Services and Public Safety
Midwife	Nursing & Midwifery Council
Midwifery	Nursing & Midwifery Council
Mòrachd	The Scottish Government
Mutual	Financial Conduct Authority
NHS	Department of Health
Nurse	Nursing & Midwifery Council
Nursing	Nursing & Midwifery Council
Oifis sgrùdaidh	Audit Scotland
Oilthigh	The Scottish Government
Parlamaid	The Scottish Parliamentary Corporate Body
Parliament	The Corporate Officer of the House of Lords and The Corporate Officer of the House of Commons
Parliamentarian	The Corporate Officer of the House of Lords and The Corporate Officer of the House of Commons
Parliamentary	The Corporate Officer of the House of Lords and The Corporate Officer of the House of Commons
Patent	The Patent Office
Patentee	The Patent Office
Polytechnic	[Department for Education]
Prifysgol	The Welsh Assembly Government
Prionnsa	The Scottish Government
Reassurance	Financial Conduct Authority
Reassurer	Financial Conduct Authority
Reinsurance	Financial Conduct Authority
Reinsurer	Financial Conduct Authority

Riaghaltas	The Scottish Government
Rìgh	The Scottish Government
Rìoghail	The Scottish Government
Rìoghalachd	The Scottish Government
Senedd	The National Assembly for Wales
Sheffield	The Company of Cutlers in Hallamshire
Swyddfa archwilio	Auditor General for Wales
Tywysog	The Welsh Assembly Government
Underwrite	Financial Conduct Authority
Underwriting	Financial Conduct Authority

NOTES

Commencement: 31 January 2015.

In column (1), words in square brackets in entries "Accredit", "Accreditation", "Accredited", "Accrediting" and "Polytechnic" substituted by the Secretaries of State for Business, Energy and Industrial Strategy, for International Trade and for Exiting the European Union and the Transfer of Functions (Education and Skills) Order 2016, SI 2016/992, art 14, Schedule, Pt 2, para 51(1), (2).

PART 2
APPLICATIONS WHERE SITUATION OF REGISTERED OFFICE OR PRINCIPAL PLACE OF BUSINESS IS RELEVANT

[7.82]

Column (1)	*Column (2)*	*Column (3)*	*Column (4)*	*Column (5)*
Word or expression specified under regulation 3	*Specified Government department or other body whose view must be sought*			
	under regulation 6(a)	*under regulation 6(b)*	*under regulation 6(c)*	*under regulation 6(d)*
Audit office	Comptroller & Auditor General	Auditor General for Wales	Audit Scotland	Northern Ireland Audit Office
Charitable Charity	The Charity Commission	The Charity Commission	Office of the Scottish Charity Regulator	The Charity Commission
Duke	Ministry of Justice	The Welsh Assembly Government	The Scottish Government	Ministry of Justice
His Majesty				
King				
Prince				
Queen				
Royal				
Royalty				
Windsor				
Health centre	Department of Health	The Welsh Assembly Government	The Scottish Government	Department of Health, Social Services and Public Safety
Health service				
Police	The Home Office	The Home Office	The Scottish Government	Department of Justice in Northern Ireland
Special school	Department for Education	The Welsh Assembly Government	The Scottish Government	Department of Education
University	[Department for Education]	The Welsh Assembly Government	The Scottish Government	Department for Employment and Learning

NOTES

Commencement: 31 January 2015.

In entry relating to "University" in column (2) words in square brackets substituted by the Secretaries of State for Business, Energy and Industrial Strategy, for International Trade and for Exiting the European Union and the Transfer of Functions (Education and Skills) Order 2016, SI 2016/992, art 14, Schedule, Pt 2, para 51(1), (3).

COMPANY, LIMITED LIABILITY PARTNERSHIP AND BUSINESS (NAMES AND TRADING DISCLOSURES) REGULATIONS 2015

(SI 2015/17)

NOTES

Made: 7 January 2015.

Authority: Companies Act 2006, ss 54(1)(c), 56(1)(a), (5), 57(1)(a), (2), (5), 60(1)(b), 65(1), (2), (4), 66(2), (3), (4), (6), 82, 84, 1193(1)(c), 1195(1)(a), (5), 1197(1), (2), (3), 1292(1), (2), 1294, 1296.

Commencement: 31 January 2015.

PART 1 INTRODUCTORY

[7.83]

1 Citation, commencement and interpretation

(1) These Regulations may be cited as the Company, Limited Liability Partnership and Business (Names and Trading Disclosures) Regulations 2015 and come into force on 31st January 2015.

(2) In these Regulations, "the Act" means the Companies Act 2006.

NOTES

Commencement: 31 January 2015.

PART 2 COMPANY NAMES

[7.84]

2 Permitted characters

(1) This regulation sets out the characters, signs, symbols (including accents and other diacritical marks) and punctuation that may be used in the name of a company registered under the Act ("the permitted characters").

(2) The following permitted characters may be used in any part of the name—

(a) any character, character with an accent or other diacritical mark, sign or symbol set out in table 1 in Schedule 1;

(b) 0, 1, 2, 3, 4, 5, 6, 7, 8 or 9;

(c) full stop, comma, colon, semi-colon or hyphen; and

(d) any other punctuation referred to in column 1 of table 2 in Schedule 1 but only in one of the forms set out opposite that punctuation in column 2 of that table.

(3) The signs and symbols set out in table 3 in Schedule 1 arc permitted characters that may be used but not as one of the first three permitted characters of the name.

(4) The name must not consist of more than 160 permitted characters.

(5) For the purposes of computing the number of permitted characters in paragraph (4) of this regulation (but not in paragraph (3) of this regulation), any blank space between one permitted character and another in the name shall be counted as though it was a permitted character.

NOTES

Commencement: 31 January 2015.

[7.85]

3 Exemption from requirement as to use of "limited"

(1) A private company limited by guarantee is exempt from section 59 of the Act (requirement to have name ending with "limited" or permitted alternative) so long as it meets the following two conditions.

(2) The first condition is that the objects of that company are the promotion or regulation of commerce, art, science, education, religion, charity or any profession, and anything incidental or conducive to any of those objects.

(3) The second condition is that the company's articles—

(a) require its income to be applied in promoting its objects;

(b) prohibit the payment of dividends, or any return of capital, to its members; and

(c) require all the assets that would otherwise be available to its members generally to be transferred on its winding up either—
   (i) to another body with objects similar to its own; or
   (ii) to another body the objects of which are the promotion of charity and anything incidental or conducive thereto,

(whether or not the body is a member of the company).

NOTES

Commencement: 31 January 2015.

[7.86]

4 Inappropriate indication of company type or legal form: generally applicable provisions

(1) A company must not be registered under the Act by a name that includes, otherwise than at the end of the name, an expression or abbreviation specified in inverted commas in paragraph 3(a) to (f) of Schedule 2 (or any expression or abbreviation specified as similar).

(2) A company must not be registered under the Act by a name that includes in any part of the name an expression or abbreviation specified in inverted commas in paragraph 3(g) or (h) of Schedule 2 (or any expression or abbreviation specified as similar) unless that company is a RTE company within the meaning of section 4A of the Leasehold Reform, Housing and Urban Development Act 1993.

(3) A company must not be registered under the Act by a name that includes in any part of the name an expression or abbreviation specified in inverted commas in paragraph 3(i) or (j) of Schedule 2 (or any expression or abbreviation specified as similar) unless that company is a RTM company within the meaning of section 73 of the Commonhold and Leasehold Reform Act 2002.

(4) A company must not be registered under the Act by a name that includes in any part of the name an expression or abbreviation specified in inverted commas in paragraph 3(k) to (x) of Schedule 2 (or any expression or abbreviation specified as similar).

(5) A company must not be registered under the Act by a name that includes immediately before an expression or abbreviation specified in inverted commas in paragraph 3(a) to (j) of Schedule 2 an abbreviation specified in inverted commas in paragraph 3(y) of that Schedule (or any abbreviation specified as similar).

(6) Paragraph (1) is subject to regulations 5(b) and 6(b).

NOTES

Commencement: 31 January 2015.

[7.87]

5 Inappropriate indication of company type or legal form: company exempt from requirement to have name ending in "limited"

A company which is exempt from section 59 of the Act (requirement to have name ending with "limited" or permitted alternative) under section 60 of the Act must not be registered under the Act by a name that concludes with—

(a) a word specified in inverted commas in paragraph 1(c) or (d) of Schedule 2 (or any word specified as similar); or
(b) an expression or abbreviation specified in inverted commas in paragraph 3(a) to (f) or (y) of Schedule 2 (or any expression or abbreviation specified as similar).

NOTES

Commencement: 31 January 2015.

[7.88]

6 Inappropriate indication of company type or legal form: unlimited company

An unlimited company must not be registered under the Act by a name that concludes with—

(a) a word or abbreviation specified in inverted commas in paragraph 1(a) or (b) of Schedule 2 (or any word or abbreviation specified as similar); or
(b) an expression or abbreviation specified in inverted commas in paragraph 3(a) to (f) or (y) of Schedule 2 (or any expression or abbreviation specified as similar).

NOTES

Commencement: 31 January 2015.

[7.89]

7 Name not to be the same as another in the registrar's index of company names

For the purposes of section 66 of the Act (determining whether a name to be registered under the Act is the same as another name appearing in the registrar's index of company names) Schedule 3 has effect for setting out—

(a) the matters that are to be disregarded; and
(b) the words, expressions, signs and symbols that are to be regarded as the same.

NOTES

Commencement: 31 January 2015.

[7.90]

8 Consent to registration of a name which is the same as another in the registrar's index of company names

(1) A company may be registered under the Act by a proposed same name if the conditions in paragraph (2) are met.

(2) The conditions are—

(a) the company or other body whose name already appears in the registrar's index of company names ("Body X") consents to the proposed same name being the name of a company ("Company Y");

(b) Company Y forms, or is to form, part of the same group as Body X; and

(c) Company Y provides to the registrar a copy of a statement made by Body X indicating—

(i) the consent of Body X as referred to in sub-paragraph (a); and

(ii) that Company Y forms, or is to form, part of the same group as Body X.

(3) If the proposed same name is to be taken by a company which has not yet been incorporated, the copy of such statement must be provided to the registrar instead by the person who delivers to the registrar the application for registration of the company (and the reference in paragraph (1) to the conditions in paragraph (2) shall be read accordingly).

(4) The registrar may accept the statement referred to in paragraph (2)(c) as sufficient evidence that the conditions referred to in paragraph (2)(a) and (b) have been met.

(5) If the consent referred to in paragraph (2)(a) is given by Body X, a subsequent withdrawal of that consent does not affect the registration of Company Y by that proposed same name.

(6) In this regulation—

(a) "group" has the meaning given in section 474(1) of the Act; and

(b) "proposed same name" means a name which is, due to the application of regulation 8 and Schedule 3, considered the same as a name appearing in the registrar's index of company names and differs from that name appearing in the index by any of the matters set out in inverted commas in paragraph 5 of Schedule 3.

NOTES

Commencement: 31 January 2015.

[7.91]

9 Names with connection to Public Authorities

(1) Each of the persons and bodies set out in column (1) of Schedule 4 is specified for the purposes of section 54 of the Act.

(2) In connection with an application for the approval of the Secretary of State under section 54 of the Act in relation to a name that would be likely to give the impression of a connection with a public authority set out in column (1) of Schedule 4 the applicant must seek the view of the Government department or other body set out opposite that public authority in column (2) of Schedule 4.

NOTES

Commencement: 31 January 2015.

[7.92]

10 Interpretation

In this Part—

(a) "expression or abbreviation specified as similar" has the meaning given in paragraph 4 of Schedule 2 and "abbreviation specified as similar" has the meaning that would be given to it in that paragraph if that paragraph made no reference to "expressions";

(b) "permitted characters" has the meaning given in regulation 2(1);

(c) "word or abbreviation specified as similar" has the meaning given in paragraph 2 of Schedule 2; and

(d) "word specified as similar" has the meaning given in paragraph 2 of Schedule 2.

NOTES

Commencement: 31 January 2015.

PART 3
LIMITED LIABILITY PARTNERSHIP NAMES

[7.93]
11 Application to Limited Liability Partnerships

(1) In regulation 9 of these Regulations, any reference to section 54 of the Act includes a reference to that section as applied by regulation 8 of the Limited Liability Partnerships (Application of Companies Act 2006) Regulations 2009.

(2) . . .

NOTES

Commencement: 31 January 2015.

Para (2): amends legislation outside the scope of this work.

PART 4
OVERSEAS COMPANY NAMES

[7.94]
12 Interpretation and permitted characters

Regulations 2 and 10 apply to the name of an overseas company which is registered by that company under Part 34 of the Act (overseas companies) as they apply to the name of a company formed and registered under the Act.

NOTES

Commencement: 31 January 2015.

[7.95]
13 Inappropriate indication of company type or legal form

(1) An overseas company must not be registered under the Act by a name that concludes with a word or abbreviation specified in inverted commas in paragraph 1(a) or (b) of Schedule 2 (or any word or abbreviation specified as similar) unless the liability of the members of the company is limited by its constitution.

(2) An overseas company must not be registered under the Act by a name that concludes with a word specified in inverted commas in paragraph 1(c) or (d) of Schedule 2 (or any word specified as similar) unless the liability of the members of the company is not limited by its constitution.

(3) An overseas company must not be registered under the Act by a name that includes in any part of the name an expression or abbreviation specified in inverted commas in paragraph 3 of Schedule 2 (or any expression or abbreviation specified as similar).

NOTES

Commencement: 31 January 2015.

[7.96]
14 Name not to be the same as another in the registrar's index of company names

Regulation 7 applies to the name of an overseas company which is registered by that company under Part 34 of the Act as it applies to the name of a company formed and registered under the Act.

NOTES

Commencement: 31 January 2015.

[7.97]
15 Consent to registration of a name which is the same as another in the registrar's index of company names

(1) Regulation 8 applies to the proposed same name of an overseas company as it applies to the proposed same name of a company formed and registered under the Act.

(2) In this regulation "proposed same name" has the same meaning as in regulation 8.

NOTES

Commencement: 31 January 2015.

PART 5
BUSINESS NAMES

[7.98]
16 "Limited" and permitted alternatives

(1) A person must not carry on business in the United Kingdom under a name that concludes with any word or abbreviation set out in inverted commas in paragraph 1(a) or (b) of Schedule 2 unless that person is—

(a) a company or an overseas company registered in the United Kingdom by that name;
(b) an overseas company incorporated with that name;
(c) a society registered under the Co-operative and Community Benefit Societies Act 2014 or the Industrial and Provident Societies Act (Northern Ireland) 1969 by that name;
(d) an incorporated friendly society (as defined in section 116 of the Friendly Societies Act 1992) which has that name; or
(e) a company to which section 1040 of the Act (companies authorised to register under the Companies Act 2006) applies which has that name.

(2) A person must not carry on business in the United Kingdom under a name that concludes with any word or abbreviation specified as similar to any word or abbreviation set out in inverted commas in paragraph 1(a) or (b) of Schedule 2.

NOTES

Commencement: 31 January 2015.

[7.99]

17 Other indications of legal form

(1) A person must not carry on business in the United Kingdom under a name that includes any expression or abbreviation set out in inverted commas in paragraph 3 of Schedule 2 unless that person is such a company, partnership, grouping or organisation as is indicated in that expression or abbreviation.

(2) A person must not carry on business in the United Kingdom under a name that includes any expression or abbreviation specified as similar to any expression or abbreviation set out in inverted commas in paragraph 3 of Schedule 2.

NOTES

Commencement: 31 January 2015.

[7.100]

18 Names with connection to Public Authorities

(1) Each of the persons and bodies set out in column (1) of Schedule 4 is specified for the purposes of section 1193 of the Act.

(2) In connection with an application for the approval of the Secretary of State under section 1193 of the Act in relation to a name that would be likely to give the impression of a connection with a public authority set out in column (1) of Schedule 4 the applicant must seek the view of the Government department or other body set out opposite that public authority in column (2) of Schedule 4.

NOTES

Commencement: 31 January 2015.

[7.101]

19 Savings and Transitional provisions

(1) Regulation 17 does not apply to the carrying on of a business under a name by a person who—
(a) carried on that business under that name immediately before these Regulations came into force; and
(b) continues to carry it on under that name,
if it was lawful for the business to be carried on under that name immediately before these Regulations came into force.

(2) Regulation 17 does not apply to the carrying on of a business under a name by a person to whom the business is transferred on or after the date on which these Regulations came into force—
(a) where that person continues to carry on the business under that name; and
(b) where it was lawful for the business to be carried on under that name immediately before the transfer,
during the period of 12 months beginning with the date of the transfer.

(3) Regulation 18 does not apply to the carrying on of a business by a person who—
(a) carried on the business immediately before the date on which these Regulations came into force, and
(b) continues to carry it on under the name that immediately before that date was its lawful business name.

(4) Regulation 18 does not apply in relation to the carrying on of the business under that name during the period of twelve months beginning with the date of the transfer where—
(a) a business is transferred to a person on or after the date on which these Regulations came into force, and
(b) that person carries on the business under the name that was its lawful business name immediately before the transfer,

(5) In this regulation "lawful business name", in relation to a business, means a name under which the business was carried on without contravening the provisions of Chapter 1 of Part 41 of the Act.

NOTES

Commencement: 31 January 2015.

PART 6
TRADING DISCLOSURES

[7.102]

20 Legibility of displays and disclosures

Any display or disclosure of information required by this Part must be in characters that can be read with the naked eye.

NOTES

Commencement: 31 January 2015.

[7.103]

21 Requirement to display registered name at registered office and inspection place

(1) A company shall display its registered name at—
- (a) its registered office; and
- (b) any inspection place.

(2) But paragraph (1) docs not apply to any company which has at all times since its incorporation been dormant.

(3) Paragraph (1) shall also not apply to the registered office or an inspection place of a company where—
- (a) in respect of that company, a liquidator, administrator or administrative receiver has been appointed; and
- (b) the registered office or inspection place is also a place of business of that liquidator, administrator or administrative receiver.

NOTES

Commencement: 31 January 2015.

[7.104]

22 Requirement to display registered name at other business locations

(1) This regulation applies to a location other than a company's registered office or any inspection place.

(2) A company shall display its registered name at any such location at which it carries on business.

(3) But paragraph (2) shall not apply to a location which is primarily used for living accommodation.

(4) Paragraph (2) shall also not apply to any location at which business is carried on by a company where—
- (a) in respect of that company, a liquidator, administrator or administrative receiver has been appointed; and
- (b) the location is also a place of business of that liquidator, administrator or administrative receiver.

(5) Paragraph (2) shall also not apply to any location at which business is carried on by a company of which every director who is an individual is a relevant director.

(6) In this regulation—
- (a) "administrative receiver" has the meaning given—
  - (i) in England and Wales or Scotland, by section 251 of the Insolvency Act 1986, and
  - (ii) in Northern Ireland, by Article 5 of the Insolvency (Northern Ireland) Order 1989;
- (b) "credit reference agency" has the meaning given in section 243(7) of the Act;
- (c) "protected information" has the meaning given in section 240 of the Act; and
- (d) "relevant director" means an individual in respect of whom the registrar is required by regulations made pursuant to section 243(4) of the Act to refrain from disclosing protected information to a credit reference agency.

NOTES

Commencement: 31 January 2015.

[7.105]

23 Manner of display of registered name

(1) This regulation applies where a company is required to display its registered name at any office, place or location.

(2) Where that office, place or location is shared by no more than five companies, the registered name—

(a) shall be so positioned that it may be easily seen by any visitor to that office, place or location; and

(b) shall be displayed continuously.

(3) Where any such office, place or location is shared by six or more companies, each such company must ensure that either—

(a) its registered name is displayed for at least fifteen continuous seconds at least once every three minutes; or

(b) its registered name is available for inspection on a register by any visitor to that office, place or location.

NOTES

Commencement: 31 January 2015.

[7.106]

24 Registered name to appear in communications

(1) Every company shall disclose its registered name on—

(a) its business letters, notices and other official publications;

(b) its bills of exchange, promissory notes, endorsements and order forms;

(c) cheques purporting to be signed by or on behalf of the company;

(d) orders for money, goods or services purporting to be signed by or on behalf of the company;

(e) its bills of parcels, invoices and other demands for payment, receipts and letters of credit;

(f) its applications for licences to carry on a trade or activity; and

(g) all other forms of its business correspondence and documentation.

(2) Every company shall disclose its registered name on its websites.

NOTES

Commencement: 31 January 2015.

[7.107]

25 Further particulars to appear in business letters, order forms and websites

(1) Every company shall disclose the particulars set out in paragraph (2) on—

(a) its business letters;

(b) its order forms; and

(c) its websites.

(2) The particulars are—

(a) the part of the United Kingdom in which the company is registered;

(b) the company's registered number;

(c) the address of the company's registered office;

(d) in the case of a limited company exempt from the obligation to use the word "limited" as part of its registered name under section 60 of the Act, the fact that it is a limited company;

(e) in the case of a community interest company which is not a public company, the fact that it is a limited company; and

(f) in the case of an investment company within the meaning of section 833 of the Act, the fact that it is such a company.

(3) If, in the case of a company having a share capital, there is a disclosure as to the amount of share capital on—

(a) its business letters;

(b) its order forms; or

(c) its websites,

that disclosure must be as to paid up share capital.

NOTES

Commencement: 31 January 2015.

[7.108]

26 Disclosure of names of directors

(1) Where a company's business letter includes the name of any director of that company, other than in the text or as a signatory, the letter must disclose the name of every director of that company.

(2) In paragraph (1), "name" has the following meanings—

(a) in the case of a director who is an individual, "name" has the meaning given in section 163(2) of the Act; and

(b) in the case of a director who is a body corporate or a firm that is a legal person under the law by which it is governed, "name" means corporate name or firm name.

NOTES

Commencement: 31 January 2015.

[7.109]

27 Disclosures relating to registered office and inspection place

(1) A company shall disclose—

(a) the address of its registered office;

(b) any inspection place; and

(c) the type of company records which are kept at that office or place,

to any person it deals with in the course of business who makes a written request to the company for that information.

(2) The company shall send a written response to that person within five working days of the receipt of that request.

NOTES

Commencement: 31 January 2015.

[7.110]

28 Offence

(1) Where a company fails, without reasonable excuse, to comply with any requirement in regulations 20 to 27, an offence is committed by—

(a) the company; and

(b) every officer of the company who is in default.

(2) A person guilty of an offence under paragraph (1) is liable on summary conviction to—

(a) a fine not exceeding level 3 on the standard scale; and

(b) for continued contravention, a daily default fine not exceeding one-tenth of level 3 on the standard scale.

(3) For the purposes of this regulation a shadow director is to be treated as an officer of the company.

NOTES

Commencement: 31 January 2015.

[7.111]

29 Interpretation

In this Part—

(a) "company record" means—

(i) any register, index, accounting records, agreement, memorandum, minutes or other document required by the Companies Acts to be kept by a company; and

(ii) any register kept by a company of its debenture holders;

(b) "inspection place" means any location, other than a company's registered office, at which a company keeps available for inspection any company record which it is required under the Companies Acts to keep available for inspection;

(c) a reference to any type of document is a reference to a document of that type in hard copy, electronic or any other form; and

(d) in relation to a company, a reference to "its websites" includes a reference to any part of a website relating to that company which that company has caused or authorised to appear.

NOTES

Commencement: 31 January 2015.

30 (*(Pt 7) Introduces Sch 6; outside the scope of this work.*)

SCHEDULE 1
CHARACTERS, SIGNS, SYMBOLS (INCLUDING ACCENTS AND OTHER DIACRITICAL MARKS) AND PUNCTUATION

Regulation 2

[7.112]

Characters, signs and symbols				
A	À	Á	Â	Ã
Ä	Å	Ā	Ă	Ą
Ǻ	Æ	Ǽ	B	C
Ç	Ć	Ĉ	Ċ	Č
D	Þ	Ď	Đ	E
È	É	Ê	Ë	Ē
Ĕ	Ė	Ę	Ě	F
G	Ĝ	Ğ	Ġ	Ģ
H	Ĥ	Ħ	I	Ì
Í	Î	Ï	Ĩ	Ī
Ĭ	Į	İ	J	Ĵ
K	Ķ	L	Ĺ	Ļ
Ľ	Ŀ	Ł	M	N
Ñ	Ń	Ņ	Ň	Ŋ
O	Ò	Ó	Ô	Õ
Ö	Ø	Ō	Ŏ	Ő
Ǿ	Œ	P	Q	R
Ŕ	Ŗ	Ř	S	Ś
Ŝ	Ş	Š	T	Ţ
Ť	Ŧ	U	Ù	Ú
Û	Ü	Ũ	Ū	Ŭ
Ů	Ű	Ų	V	W
Ŵ	Ẁ	Ẃ	Ẅ	X
Y	Ỳ	Ý	Ŷ	Ÿ
Z	Ź	Ż	Ž	&
@	£	$	€	¥

Table 2	
Column 1 (type of punctuation)	*Column 2 (punctuation mark)*
Apostrophe	‘
	’
Bracket	(
	)
	[
	]
	{
	}
	<
	>
Exclamation mark	!
Guillemet	«
	»
Inverted comma	“
	”
	″
Question mark	?
Solidus	\
	/

Table 3: Signs and symbols
*
=
#
%
+

NOTES

Commencement: 31 January 2015.

SCHEDULE 2
SPECIFIED WORDS, EXPRESSIONS AND ABBREVIATIONS

Regulations 4 to 6, 10, 13, 16 and 17

[7.113]

1 The words and abbreviations specified are—

(a) "LIMITED" or (with or without full stops) the abbreviation "LTD";
(b) "CYFYNGEDIG" or (with or without full stops) the abbreviation "CYF";
(c) "UNLIMITED"; and
(d) "ANGHYFYNGEDIG".

2 The words and abbreviations specified as similar to the words and abbreviations set out in inverted commas in paragraph 1(a) and (b) and the words specified as similar to the words set out in inverted commas in paragraph 1(c) and (d) are any in which—

(a) one or more permitted characters has been omitted;
(b) one or more permitted characters has been added; or
(c) each of one or more permitted characters has been substituted by one or more other permitted characters,

in such a way as to be likely to mislead the public as to the legal form of a company or business if included in the registered name of the company or in a business name.

3 The expressions and abbreviations specified are—

(a) "PUBLIC LIMITED COMPANY" or (with or without full stops) the abbreviation "PLC";
(b) "CWMNI CYFYNGEDIG CYHOEDDUS" or (with or without full stops) the abbreviation "CCC";
(c) "COMMUNITY INTEREST COMPANY" or (with or without full stops) the abbreviation "CIC";
(d) "CWMNI BUDDIANT CYMUNEDOL" or (with or without full stops) the abbreviation "CBC";
(e) "COMMUNITY INTEREST PUBLIC LIMITED COMPANY" or (with or without full stops) the abbreviation "COMMUNITY INTEREST PLC";
(f) "CWMNI BUDDIANT CYMUNEDOL CYHOEDDUS CYFYNGEDIG" or (with or without full stops) the abbreviation "CWMNI BUDDIANT CYMUNEDOL CCC";
(g) "RIGHT TO ENFRANCHISEMENT" or (with or without full stops) the abbreviation "RTE";
(h) "HAWL I RYDDFREINIAD";
(i) "RIGHT TO MANAGE" or (with or without full stops) the abbreviation "RTM";
(j) "CWMNI RTM CYFYNGEDIG";
(k) "EUROPEAN ECONOMIC INTEREST GROUPING" or (with or without full stops) the abbreviation "EEIG";
(l) "INVESTMENT COMPANY WITH VARIABLE CAPITAL";
(m) "CWMNI BUDDSODDI Â CHYFALAF NEWIDIOL";
(n) "LIMITED PARTNERSHIP";
(o) "PARTNERIAETH CYFYNGEDIG";
(p) "LIMITED LIABILITY PARTNERSHIP";
(q) "PARTNERIAETH ATEBOLRWYDD CYFYNGEDIG";
(r) "OPEN-ENDED INVESTMENT COMPANY";
(s) "CWMNI BUDDSODDIAD PENAGORED";
(t) "CHARITABLE INCORPORATED ORGANISATION";
(u) "SEFYDLIAD ELUSENNOL CORFFOREDIG";
(v) "INDUSTRIAL AND PROVIDENT SOCIETY";
(w) "CO-OPERATIVE SOCIETY"
(x) "COMMUNITY BENEFIT SOCIETY"; and
(y) the following abbreviations (with or without full stops) of the expressions specified in sub-paragraphs (n), (o), (p), (q), (t) and (u) respectively, namely "LP", "PC", "LLP", "PAC", "CIO" and "SEC".

4 The expressions and abbreviations specified as similar to the expressions and abbreviations set out in inverted commas in paragraph 3 are any in which—

(a) one or more permitted characters has been omitted;
(b) one or more permitted characters has been added; or
(c) each of one or more permitted characters has been substituted by one or more other permitted characters,

in such a way as to be likely to mislead the public as to the legal form of a company or business if included in the registered name of the company or in a business name.

NOTES

Commencement: 31 January 2015.

SCHEDULE 3
NAME SAME AS ANOTHER IN THE REGISTRAR'S INDEX OF COMPANY NAMES

Regulations 7 and 8

[7.114]

1 In determining whether a name is the same as another name appearing in the registrar's index of company names the provisions in this Schedule are to be applied in the order set out in the Schedule.

2 Regard each permitted character set out in column 1 of the table to this paragraph as the same as a corresponding permitted character, or combination of permitted characters, in column 2.

(The full text of this form is currently unavailable. Please see the original.)

3 Taking the name remaining after the application of paragraph 2, disregard any word, expression or abbreviation set out in inverted commas in Schedule 2 where it appears at the end of the name.

4 (1) Taking the name remaining after the application of paragraphs 2 and 3, regard each of the words, expressions, signs and symbols set out in inverted commas in any of the paragraphs of sub-paragraph (2) ("relevant matters") as the same as the other relevant matters set out in that paragraph where each relevant matter—

(a) is preceded by and followed by a blank space; or
(b) where the relevant matter is at the beginning of the name, where it is followed by a blank space.

(2) The words, expressions, signs and symbols are—

(a) "AND" and "&";
(b) "PLUS" and "+";
(c) "0", "ZERO" and "O";
(d) "1" and "ONE";
(e) "2", "TWO", "TO" and "TOO";
(f) "3" and "THREE";
(g) "4", "FOUR" and "FOR";
(h) "5" and "FIVE";
(i) "6" and "SIX";
(j) "7" and "SEVEN";
(k) "8" and "EIGHT";
(l) "9" and "NINE";
(m) "£" and "POUND";
(n) "€" and "EURO";
(o) "$" and "DOLLAR";
(p) "¥" and "YEN";
(q) "%", "PER CENT", "PERCENT", "PER CENTUM" and "PERCENTUM"; and
(r) "@" and "AT".

5 (1) Taking the name remaining after the application of paragraphs 2 to 4, disregard at the end of the name the matters set out in inverted commas in sub-paragraph (2) (or any combination of such matters) where the matter (or combination) is preceded by a blank space or by the following punctuation or symbol in inverted commas—

(a) a full stop; or
(b) "@".

(2) The matters are—

(a) "& CO";
(b) "& COMPANY";
(c) "AND CO";
(d) "AND COMPANY";
(e) "BIZ";
(f) "CO";
(g) "CO UK";

(h) "CO.UK";
(i) "COM";
(j) "COMPANY";
(k) "EU";
(l) "GB";
(m) "GREAT BRITAIN";
(n) "NET";
(o) "NI";
(p) "NORTHERN IRELAND";
(q) "ORG";
(r) "ORG UK";
(s) "ORG.UK";
(t) "UK";
(u) "UNITED KINGDOM";
(v) "WALES";
(w) "& CWMNI";
(x) "A'R CWMNI";
(y) "CWMNI";
(z) "CYM";
(aa) "CYMRU";
(bb) "DU";
(cc) "PF";
(dd) "PRYDAIN FAWR"; and
(ee) "Y DEYRNAS UNEDIG".

(3) The matters in sub-paragraph (2) include any matter in inverted commas that is preceded by and followed by brackets set out in column 2 of table 2 in Schedule 1.

6 Taking the name remaining after the application of paragraphs 2 to 5, disregard the following matters in any part of the name—
(a) any punctuation set out in regulation 2(2)(c) or in column 2 of table 2 in Schedule 1; and
(b) the following words and symbols set out in inverted commas—
(i) "*";
(ii) "="; and
(iii) "#".

7 Taking the name remaining after the application of paragraphs 2 to 6, disregard the letter "S" at the end of the name.

8 (1) Taking the name remaining after the application of paragraphs 2 to 7, disregard any permitted character after the first 60 permitted characters of the name.

(2) For the purposes of computing the number of permitted characters in this paragraph, any blank space between one permitted character and another in the name shall be counted as though it was a permitted character.

9 Taking the name remaining after the application of paragraphs 2 to 8, disregard the following matters or any combination of the following matters set out in inverted commas where they appear at the beginning of the name—
(a) "@";
(b) "THE" (but only where followed by a blank space); and
(c) "WWW".

10 Taking the name remaining after the application of paragraphs 2 to 9, disregard blank spaces between permitted characters.

NOTES

Commencement: 31 January 2015.

SCHEDULE 4
SPECIFIED "PUBLIC AUTHORITIES" AND LIST OF GOVERNMENT DEPARTMENTS AND OTHER BODIES WHOSE VIEWS MUST BE SOUGHT

Regulations 9 and 18

[7.115]

Column (1)	*Column (2)*
Public authority	***Government department or other body whose view must be sought***
Accounts Commission for Scotland	Accounts Commission for Scotland
Audit Commission for Local Authorities and the National Health Service in England	Audit Commission for Local Authorities and the National Health Service in England

Audit Scotland	Audit Scotland
Auditor General for Scotland	Auditor General For Scotland
Auditor General for Wales (known in Welsh as "Archwilydd Cyffredinol Cymru")	Auditor General for Wales (known in Welsh as "Archwilydd Cyffredinol Cymru")
Comptroller and Auditor General	Comptroller and Auditor General
Comptroller and Auditor General for Northern Ireland	Comptroller and Auditor General for Northern Ireland
Financial Reporting Council	Financial Reporting Council
Financial Conduct Authority	Financial Conduct Authority
Health and Safety Executive	Health and Safety Executive
House of Commons	The Corporate Officer of the House of Commons
House of Lords	The Corporate Officer of the House of Lords
Law Commission	Ministry of Justice
National Assembly for Wales (known in Welsh as "Cynulliad Cenedlaethol Cymru")	National Assembly for Wales Commission (known in Welsh as "Comisiwn Cynulliad Cenedlaethol Cymru")
National Assembly for Wales Commission (known in Welsh as "Comisiwn Cynulliad Cenedlaethol Cymru")	National Assembly for Wales Commission (known in Welsh as "Comisiwn Cynulliad Cenedlaethol Cymru")
Northern Ireland Assembly	Northern Ireland Assembly Commission
Northern Ireland Assembly Commission	Northern Ireland Assembly Commission
Northern Ireland Audit Office	Northern Ireland Audit Office
Office for Nuclear Regulation	Office for Nuclear Regulation
Prudential Regulation Authority	[the Governor and Company of the Bank of England]
Regional Agency for Public Health and Social Well-being.	Regional Agency for Public Health and Social Well-being.
Regional Health and Social Care Board	Regional Health and Social Care Board
Scottish Law Commission	Scottish Law Commission
The Governor and Company of the Bank of England	The Governor and Company of the Bank of England
The Pensions Advisory Service	Department for Work and Pensions
The Scottish Parliament	The Scottish Parliamentary Corporate Body
The Scottish Parliamentary Corporate Body	The Scottish Parliamentary Corporate Body
Wales Audit Office (known in Welsh as "Swyddfa Archwilio Cymru")	Wales Audit Office (known in Welsh as "Swyddfa Archwilio Cymru")

NOTES

Commencement: 31 January 2015.

Table: in entry relating to "Prudential Regulation Authority" in column 2 words in square brackets substituted by the Bank of England and Financial Services (Consequential Amendments) Regulations 2017, SI 2017/80, reg 2, Schedule, Pt 2, para 44.

SCHEDULES 5, 6

(Schs 5, 6 contain amendments to legislation outside the scope of this work.)

PART 8
OTHER EU MATERIALS

DIRECTIVE OF THE EUROPEAN PARLIAMENT AND OF THE COUNCIL

(96/9/EC)

of 11 March 1996

on the legal protection of databases ('Database Directive')

NOTES

Date of publication in OJ: OJ L77, 27.3.96, p 20.

THE EUROPEAN PARLIAMENT AND THE COUNCIL OF THE EUROPEAN UNION,

Having regard to the Treaty establishing the European Community, and in particular Article 57(2), 66 and 100a thereof,

Having regard to the proposal from the Commission,[1]

Having regard to the opinion of the Economic and Social Committee,[2]

Acting in accordance with the procedure laid down in Article 189b of the Treaty,[3]

(1) Whereas databases are at present not sufficiently protected in all Member States by existing legislation; whereas such protection, where it exists, has different attributes;

(2) Whereas such differences in the legal protection of databases offered by the legislation of the Member States have direct negative effects on the functioning of the internal market as regards databases and in particular on the freedom of natural and legal persons to provide on-line database goods and services on the basis of harmonised legal arrangements throughout the Community; whereas such differences could well become more pronounced as Member States introduce new legislation in this field, which is now taking on an increasingly international dimension;

(3) Whereas existing differences distorting the functioning of the internal market need to be removed and new ones prevented from arising, while differences not adversely affecting the functioning of the internal market or the development of an information market within the Community need not be removed or prevented from arising;

(4) Whereas copyright protection for databases exists in varying forms in the Member States according to legislation or case-law, and whereas, if differences in legislation in the scope and conditions of protection remain between the Member States, such unharmonised intellectual property rights can have the effect of preventing the free movement of goods or services within the Community;

(5) Whereas copyright remains an appropriate form of exclusive right for authors who have created databases;

(6) Whereas, nevertheless, in the absence of a harmonised system of unfair-competition legislation or of case-law, other measures are required in addition to prevent the unauthorised extraction and/or re-utilisation of the contents of a database;

(7) Whereas the making of databases requires the investment of considerable human, technical and financial resources while such databases can be copied or accessed at a fraction of the cost needed to design them independently;

(8) Whereas the unauthorised extraction and/or re-utilisation of the contents of a database constitute acts which can have serious economic and technical consequences;

(9) Whereas databases are a vital tool in the development of an information market within the Community; whereas this tool will also be of use in many other fields;

(10) Whereas the exponential growth, in the Community and worldwide, in the amount of information generated and processed annually in all sectors of commerce and industry calls for investment in all the Member States in advanced information processing systems;

(11) Whereas there is at present a very great imbalance in the level of investment in the database sector both as between the Member States and between the Community and the world's largest database-producing third countries;

(12) Whereas such an investment in modern information storage and processing systems will not take place within the Community unless a stable and uniform legal protection regime is introduced for the protection of the rights of makers of databases;

(13) Whereas this Directive protects collections, sometimes called 'compilations', of works, data or other materials which are arranged, stored and accessed by means which include electronic, electromagnetic or electro-optical processes or analogous processes;

(14) Whereas protection under this Directive should be extended to cover non-electronic databases;

(15) Whereas the criteria used to determine whether a database should be protected by copyright should be defined to the fact that the selection or the arrangement of the contents of the database is

the author's own intellectual creation; whereas such protection should cover the structure of the database;

(16) Whereas no criterion other than originality in the sense of the author's intellectual creation should be applied to determine the eligibility of the database for copyright protection, and in particular no aesthetic or qualitative criteria should be applied;

(17) Whereas the term 'database' should be understood to include literary, artistic, musical or other collections of works or collections of other material such as texts, sound, images, numbers, facts, and data; whereas it should cover collections of independent works, data or other materials which are systematically or methodically arranged and can be individually accessed; whereas this means that a recording or an audiovisual, cinematographic, literary or musical work as such does not fall within the scope of this Directive;

(18) Whereas this Directive is without prejudice to the freedom of authors to decide whether, or in what manner, they will allow their works to be included in a database, in particular whether or not the authorisation given is exclusive; whereas the protection of databases by the *sui generis* right is without prejudice to existing rights over their contents, and whereas in particular where an author or the holder of a related right permits some of his works or subject matter to be included in a database pursuant to a non-exclusive agreement a third party may make use of those works or subject matter subject to the required consent of the author or of the holder of the related right without the *sui generis* right of the maker of the database being invoked to prevent him doing so, on condition that those works or subject matter are neither extracted from the database nor re-utilised on the basis thereof;

(19) Whereas, as a rule, the compilation of several recordings of musical performances on a CD does not come within the scope of this Directive, both because, as a compilation, it does not meet the conditions for copyright protection and because it does not represent a substantial enough investment to be eligible under the *sui generis* right;

(20) Whereas protection under this Directive may also apply to the materials necessary for the operation or consultation of certain databases such as thesaurus and indexation systems;

(21) Whereas the protection provided for in this Directive relates to databases in which works, data or other materials have been arranged systematically or methodically; whereas it is not necessary for those materials to have been physically stored in an organised manner;

(22) Whereas electronic databases within the meaning of this Directive may also include devices such as CD-ROM and CD-i;

(23) Whereas the term 'database' should not be taken to extend to computer programs used in the making or operation of a database, which are protected by Council Directive 91/250/EEC of 14 May 1991 on the legal protection of computer programs;[4]

(24) Whereas the rental and lending of databases in the field of copyright and related rights are governed exclusively by Council Directive 92/100/EEC of 19 November 1992 on rental right and lending right and on certain rights related to copyright in the field of intellectual property;[5]

(25) Whereas the term of copyright is already governed by Council Directive 93/98/EEC of 29 October 1993 harmonising the term of protection of copyright and certain related rights;[6]

(26) Whereas works protected by copyright and subject matter protected by related rights, which are incorporated into a database, remain nevertheless protected by the respective exclusive rights and may not be incorporated into, or extracted from, the database without the permission of the rightholder or his successors in title;

(27) Whereas copyright in such works and related rights in subject matter thus incorporated into a database are in no way affected by the existence of a separate right in the selection or arrangement of these works and subject matter in a database;

(28) Whereas the moral rights of the natural person who created the database belong to the author and should be exercised according to the legislation of the Member States and the provisions of the Berne Convention for the Protection of Literary and Artistic Works; whereas such moral rights remain outside the scope of this Directive;

(29) Whereas the arrangements applicable to databases created by employees are left to the discretion of the Member States; whereas, therefore nothing in this Directive prevents Member States from stipulating in their legislation that where a database is created by an employee in the execution of his duties or following the instructions given by his employer, the employer exclusively shall be entitled to exercise all economic rights in the database so created, unless otherwise provided by contract;

(30) Whereas the author's exclusive rights should include the right to determine the way in which his work is exploited and by whom, and in particular to control the distribution of his work to unauthorised persons;

(31) Whereas the copyright protection of databases includes making databases available by means other than the distribution of copies;

(32) Whereas Member States are required to ensure that their national provisions are at least

materially equivalent in the case of such acts subject to restrictions as are provided for by this Directive;

(33) Whereas the question of exhaustion of the right of distribution does not arise in the case of on-line databases, which come within the field of provision of services; whereas this also applies with regard to a material copy of such a database made by the user of such a service with the consent of the rightholder; whereas, unlike CD-ROM or CD-i, where the intellectual property is incorporated in a material medium, namely an item of goods, every on-line service is in fact an act which will have to be subject to authorisation where the copyright so provides;

(34) Whereas, nevertheless, once the rightholder has chosen to make available a copy of the database to a user, whether by an on-line service or by other means of distribution, that lawful user must be able to access and use the database for the purposes and in the way set out in the agreement with the rightholder, even if such access and use necessitate performance of otherwise restricted acts;

(35) Whereas a list should be drawn up of exceptions to restricted acts, taking into account the fact that copyright as covered by this Directive applies only to the selection or arrangements of the contents of a database; whereas Member States should be given the option of providing for such exceptions in certain cases; whereas, however, this option should be exercised in accordance with the Berne Convention and to the extent that the exceptions relate to the structure of the database; whereas a distinction should be drawn between exceptions for private use and exceptions for reproduction for private purposes, which concerns provisions under national legislation of some Member States on levies on blank media or recording equipment;

(36) Whereas the term 'scientific research' within the meaning of this Directive covers both the natural sciences and the human sciences;

(37) Whereas Article 10(1) of the Berne Convention is not affected by this Directive;

(38) Whereas the increasing use of digital recording technology exposes the database maker to the risk that the contents of his database may be copied and rearranged electronically, without his authorisation, to produce a database of identical content which, however, does not infringe any copyright in the arrangement of his database;

(39) Whereas, in addition to aiming to protect the copyright in the original selection or arrangement of the contents of a database, this Directive seeks to safeguard the position of makers of databases against misappropriation of the results of the financial and professional investment made in obtaining and collection the contents by protecting the whole or substantial parts of a database against certain acts by a user or competitor;

(40) Whereas the object of this *sui generis* right is to ensure protection of any investment in obtaining, verifying or presenting the contents of a database for the limited duration of the right; whereas such investment may consist in the deployment of financial resources and/or the expending of time, effort and energy;

(41) Whereas the objective of the *sui generis* right is to give the maker of a database the option of preventing the unauthorised extraction and/or re-utilisation of all or a substantial part of the contents of that database; whereas the maker of a database is the person who takes the initiative and the risk of investing; whereas this excludes subcontractors in particular from the definition of maker;

(42) Whereas the special right to prevent unauthorised extraction and/or re-utilisation relates to acts by the user which go beyond his legitimate rights and thereby harm the investment; whereas the right to prohibit extraction and/or re-utilisation of all or a substantial part of the contents relates not only to the manufacture of a parasitical competing product but also to any user who, through his acts, causes significant detriment, evaluated qualitatively or quantitatively, to the investment;

(43) Whereas, in the case of on-line transmission, the right to prohibit re-utilisation is not exhausted either as regards the database or as regards a material copy of the database or of part thereof made by the addressee of the transmission with the consent of the rightholder;

(44) Whereas, when on-screen display of the contents of a database necessitates the permanent or temporary transfer of all or a substantial part of such contents to another medium, that act should be subject to authorisation by the rightholder;

(45) Whereas the right to prevent unauthorised extraction and/or re-utilisation does not in any way constitute an extension of copyright protection to mere facts or data;

(46) Whereas the existence of a right to prevent the unauthorised extraction and/or re-utilisation of the whole or a substantial part of works, data or materials from a database should not give rise to the creation of a new right in the works, data or materials themselves;

(47) Whereas, in the interests of competition between suppliers of information products and services, protection by the *sui generis* right must not be afforded in such a way as to facilitate abuses of a dominant position, in particular as regards the creation and distribution of new products and services which have an intellectual, documentary, technical, economic or commercial added value; whereas, therefore, the provisions of this Directive are without prejudice to the application of Community or national competition rules;

(48) Whereas the objective of this Directive, which is to afford an appropriate and uniform level

of protection of databases as a means to secure the remuneration of the maker of the database, is different from the aim of Directive 95/46/EC of the European Parliament and of the Council of 24 October 1995 on the protection of individuals with regard to the processing of personal data and on the free movement of such data,[7] which is to guarantee free circulation of personal data on the basis of harmonised rules designed to protect fundamental rights, notably the right to privacy which is recognised in Article 8 of the European Convention for the Protection of Human Rights and Fundamental Freedoms; whereas the provisions of this Directive are without prejudice to data protection legislation;

(49) Whereas, notwithstanding the right to prevent extraction and/or re-utilisation of all or a substantial part of a database, it should be laid down that the maker of a database or rightholder may not prevent a lawful user of the database from extracting and re-utilising insubstantial parts; whereas, however, that user may not unreasonably prejudice either the legitimate interests of the holder of the *sui generis* right or the holder of copyright or a related right in respect of the works or subject matter contained in the database;

(50) Whereas the Member States should be given the option of providing for exceptions to the right to prevent the unauthorised extraction and/or re-utilisation of a substantial part of the contents of a database in the case of extraction for private purposes, for the purposes of illustration for teaching or scientific research, or where extraction and/or re-utilisation are/is carried out in the interests of public security or for the purposes of an administrative or judicial procedure; whereas such operations must not prejudice the exclusive rights of the maker to exploit the database and their purpose must not be commercial;

(51) Whereas the Member States, where they avail themselves of the option to permit a lawful user of a database to extract a substantial part of the contents for the purposes of illustration for teaching or scientific research, may limit that permission to certain categories of teaching or scientific research institution;

(52) Whereas those Member States which have specific rules providing for a right comparable to the *sui generis* right provided for in this Directive should be permitted to retain, as far as the new right is concerned, the exceptions traditionally specified by such rules;

(53) Whereas the burden of proof regarding the date of completion of the making of a database lies with the maker of the database;

(54) Whereas the burden of proof that the criteria exist for concluding that a substantial modification of the contents of a database is to be regarded as a substantial new investment lies with the maker of the database resulting from such investment;

(55) Whereas a substantial new investment involving a new term of protection may include a substantial verification of the contents of the database;

(56) Whereas the right to prevent unauthorised extraction and/or re-utilisation in respect of a database should apply to databases whose makers are nationals or habitual residents of third countries or to those produced by legal persons not established in a Member State, within the meaning of the Treaty, only if such third countries offer comparable protection to databases produced by nationals of a Member State or persons who have their habitual residence in the territory of the Community;

(57) Whereas, in addition to remedies provided under the legislation of the Member States for infringements of copyright or other rights, Member States should provide for appropriate remedies against unauthorised extraction and/or re-utilisation of the contents of a database;

(58) Whereas, in addition to the protection given under this Directive to the structure of the database by copyright, and to its contents against unauthorised extraction and/or re-utilisation under the *sui generis* right, other legal provisions in the Member States relevant to the supply of database goods and services continue to apply;

(59) Whereas this Directive is without prejudice to the application to databases composed of audiovisual works of any rules recognised by a Member State's legislation concerning the broadcasting of audiovisual programmes;

(60) Whereas some Member States currently protect under copyright arrangements databases which do not meet the criteria for eligibility for copyright protection laid down in this Directive; whereas, even if the databases concerned are eligible for protection under the right laid down in this Directive to prevent unauthorised extraction and/or re-utilisation of their contents, the term of protection under that right is considerably shorter than that which they enjoy under the national arrangements currently in force; whereas harmonisation of the criteria for determining whether a database is to be protected by copyright may not have the effect of reducing the term of protection currently enjoyed by the rightholders concerned; whereas a derogation should be laid down to that effect; whereas the effects of such derogation must be confined to the territories of the Member States concerned,

NOTES

[1] OJ C156, 23.6.92, p 4 and OJ C308, 15.11.93, p 1.

[2] OJ C19, 25.1.93, p 3.

[3] Opinion of the European Parliament of 23 June 1993, OJ C194, 19.7.93, p 144, Common Position of the Council of 10 July 1995, OJ C288, 30.10.95, p 14, Decision of the European Parliament of 14 December 1995, OJ C17, 22.1.96, and Council Decision of 26 February 1996.

[4] OJ L122, 17.5.91, p 42, as amended by OJ L290, 24.11.93, p 9.

[5] OJ L346, 27.11.92, p 61.

[6] OJ L290, 24.11.93, p 9.

[7] OJ L281, 23.11.95, p 31.

HAVE ADOPTED THIS DIRECTIVE—

CHAPTER I
SCOPE

[8.1]
Article 1
Scope

1. This Directive concerns the legal protection of databases in any form.
2. For the purposes of this Directive, 'database' shall mean a collection of independent works, data or other materials arranged in a systematic or methodical way and individually accessible by electronic or other means.
3. Protection under this Directive shall not apply to computer programs used in the making or operation of databases accessible by electronic means.

[8.2]
Article 2
Limitations on the scope

This Directive shall apply without prejudice to Community provisions relating to—

(a) the legal protection of computer programs;
(b) rental right, lending right and certain rights related to copyright in the field of intellectual property;
(c) the term of protection of copyright and certain related rights.

CHAPTER II
COPYRIGHT

[8.3]
Article 3
Object of protection

1. In accordance with this Directive, databases which, by reason of the selection or arrangement of their contents, constitute the author's own intellectual creation shall be protected as such by copyright. No other criteria shall be applied to determine their eligibility for that protection.
2. The copyright protection of databases provided for by this Directive shall not extend to their contents and shall be without prejudice to any rights subsisting in those contents themselves.

[8.4]
Article 4
Database authorship

1. The author of a database shall be the natural person or group of natural persons who created the base or, where the legislation of the Member States so permits, the legal person designated as the rightholder by that legislation.
2. Where collective works are recognised by the legislation of a Member State, the economic rights shall be owned by the person holding the copyright.
3. In respect of a database created by a group of natural persons jointly, the exclusive rights shall be owned jointly.

[8.5]
Article 5
Restricted acts

In respect of the expression of the database which is protectable by copyright, the author of a database shall have the exclusive right to carry out or to authorise—

(a) temporary or permanent reproduction by any means and in any form, in whole or in part;
(b) translation, adaptation, arrangement and any other alteration;
(c) any form of distribution to the public of the database or of copies thereof. The first sale in the Community of a copy of the database by the rightholder or with his consent shall exhaust the right to control resale of that copy within the Community;
(d) any communication, display or performance to the public;
(e) any reproduction, distribution, communication, display or performance to the public of the results of the acts referred to in (b).

[8.6]
Article 6
Exceptions to restricted acts

1. The performance by the lawful user of a database or of a copy thereof of any of the acts listed in Article 5 which is necessary for the purposes of access to the contents of the databases and normal use of the contents by the lawful user shall not require the authorisation of the author of the database. Where the lawful user is authorised to use only part of the database, this provision shall apply only to that part.

2. Member States shall have the option of providing for limitations on the rights set out in Article 5 in the following cases—

(a) in the case of reproduction for private purposes of a non-electronic database;

(b) where there is use for the sole purpose of illustration for teaching or scientific research, as long as the source is indicated and to the extent justified by the non-commercial purpose to be achieved;

(c) where there is use for the purposes of public security of for the purposes of an administrative or judicial procedure;

(d) where other exceptions to copyright which are traditionally authorised under national law are involved, without prejudice to points (a), (b) and (c).

3. In accordance with the Berne Convention for the protection of Literary and Artistic Works, this Article may not be interpreted in such a way as to allow its application to be used in a manner which unreasonably prejudices the rightholder's legitimate interests or conflicts with normal exploitation of the database.

CHAPTER III
SUI GENERIS RIGHT

[8.7]
Article 7
Object of protection

1. Member States shall provide for a right for the maker of a database which shows that there has been qualitatively and/or quantitatively a substantial investment in either the obtaining, verification or presentation of the contents to prevent extraction and/or re-utilisation of the whole or of a substantial part, evaluated qualitatively and/or quantitatively, of the contents of that database.

2. For the purposes of this Chapter—

(a) 'extraction' shall mean the permanent or temporary transfer of all or a substantial part of the contents of a database to another medium by any means or in any form;

(b) 're-utilisation' shall mean any form of making available to the public all or a substantial part of the contents of a database by the distribution of copies, by renting, by on-line or other forms of transmission. The first sale of a copy of a database within the Community by the rightholder or with his consent shall exhaust the right to control resale of that copy within the Community;

Public lending is not an act of extraction or re-utilisation.

3. The right referred to in paragraph 1 may be transferred, assigned or granted under contractual licence.

4. The right provided for in paragraph 1 shall apply irrespective of the eligibility of that database for protection by copyright or by other rights. Moreover, it shall apply irrespective of eligibility of the contents of that database for protection by copyright or by other rights. Protection of databases under the right provided for in paragraph 1 shall be without prejudice to rights existing in respect of their contents.

5. The repeated and systematic extraction and/or re-utilisation of insubstantial parts of the contents of the database implying acts which conflict with a normal exploitation of that database or which unreasonably prejudice the legitimate interests of the maker of the database shall not be permitted.

[8.8]
Article 8
Rights and obligations of lawful users

1. The maker of a database which is made available to the public in whatever manner may not prevent a lawful user of the database from extracting and/or re-utilising insubstantial parts of its contents, evaluated qualitatively and/or quantitatively, for any purposes whatsoever. Where the lawful user is authorised to extract and/or re-utilise only part of the database, this paragraph shall apply only to that part.

2. A lawful user of a database which is made available to the public in whatever manner may not perform acts which conflict with normal exploitation of the database or unreasonably prejudice the legitimate interests of the maker of the database.

3. A lawful user of a database which is made available to the public in any manner may not cause prejudice to the holder of a copyright or related right in respect of the works or subject matter contained in the database.

[8.9]
Article 9
Exceptions to the sui generis right
Member States may stipulate that lawful users of a database which is made available to the public in whatever manner may, without the authorisation of its maker, extract or re-utilise a substantial part of its contents—
(a) in the case of extraction for private purposes of the contents of a non-electronic database;
(b) in the case of extraction for the purposes of illustration for teaching or scientific research, as long as the source is indicated and to the extent justified by the non-commercial purpose to be achieved;
(c) in the case of extraction and/or re-utilisation for the purposes of public security or an administrative or judicial procedure.

[8.10]
Article 10
Term of protection
1. The right provided for in Article 7 shall run from the date of completion of the making of the database. It shall expire fifteen years from the first of January of the year following the date of completion.
2. In the case of a database which is made available to the public in whatever manner before expiry of the period provided for in paragraph 1, the term of protection by that right shall expire fifteen years from the first of January of the year following the date when the database was first made available to the public.
3. Any substantial change, evaluated qualitatively or quantitatively, to the contents of a database, including any substantial change resulting from the accumulation of successive additions, deletions or alterations, which would result in the database being considered to be a substantial new investment, evaluated qualitatively or quantitatively, shall qualify the database resulting from that investment for its own term of protection.

[8.11]
Article 11
Beneficiaries of protection under the sui generis right
1. The right provided for in Article 7 shall apply to database whose makers or rightholders are nationals of a Member State or who have their habitual residence in the territory of the Community.
2. Paragraph 1 shall also apply to companies and firms formed in accordance with the law of a Member State and having their registered office, central administration or principal place of business within the Community; however, where such a company or firm has only its registered office in the territory of the Community, its operations must be genuinely linked on an ongoing basis with the economy of a Member State.
3. Agreements extending the right provided for in Article 7 to databases made in third countries and falling outside the provisions of paragraphs 1 and 2 shall be concluded by the Council acting on a proposal from the Commission. The term of any protection extended to databases by virtue of that procedure shall not exceed that available pursuant to Article 10.

CHAPTER IV
COMMON PROVISIONS

[8.12]
Article 12
Remedies
Member States shall provide appropriate remedies in respect of infringements of the rights provided for in this Directive.

[8.13]
Article 13
Continued application of other legal provisions
This Directive shall be without prejudice to provisions concerning in particular copyright, rights related to copyright or any other rights or obligations subsisting in the data, works or other materials incorporated into a database, patent rights, trade marks, design rights, the protection of national treasures, laws on restrictive practices and unfair competition, trade secrets, security, confidentiality, data protection and privacy, access to public documents, and the law of contract.

[8.14]
Article 14
Application over time
1. Protection pursuant to this Directive as regards copyright shall also be available in respect of databases created prior to the date referred to Article 16(1) which on that date fulfil the requirements laid down in this Directive as regards copyright protection of databases.

2. Notwithstanding paragraph 1, where a database protected under copyright arrangements in a Member State on the date of publication of this Directive does not fulfil the eligibility criteria for copyright protection laid down in Article 3(1), this Directive shall not result in any curtailing in that Member State of the remaining term of protection afforded under those arrangements.
3. Protection pursuant to the provisions of this Directive as regards the right provided for in Article 7 shall also be available in respect of databases the making of which was completed not more than fifteen years prior to the date referred to in Article 16(1) and which on that date fulfil the requirements laid down in Article 7.
4. The protection provided for in paragraphs 1 and 3 shall be without prejudice to any acts concluded and rights acquired before the date referred to in those paragraphs.
5. In the case of a database the making of which was completed not more than fifteen years prior to the date referred to in Article 16(1), the term of protection by the right provided for in Article 7 shall expire fifteen years from the first of January following that date.

[8.15]
Article 15
Binding nature of certain provisions
Any contractual provision contrary to Articles 6(1) and 8 shall be null and void.

[8.16]
Article 16
Final provisions
1. Member States shall bring into force the laws, regulations and administrative provisions necessary to comply with this Directive before 1 January 1998.

When Member States adopt these provisions, they shall contain a reference to this Directive or shall be accompanied by such reference on the occasion of their official publication. The methods of making such reference shall be laid down by Member States.
2. Member States shall communicate to the Commission the text of the provisions of domestic law which they adopt in the field governed by this Directive.
3. Not later than at the end of the third year after the date referred to in paragraph 1, and every three years thereafter, the Commission shall submit to the European Parliament, the Council and the Economic and Social Committee a report on the application of this Directive, in which, inter alia, on the basis of specific information supplied by the Member States, it shall examine in particular the application of the *sui generis* right, including Articles 8 and 9, and shall verify especially whether the application of this right has led to abuse of a dominant position or other interference with free competition which would justify appropriate measures being taken, including the establishment of non-voluntary licensing arrangements. Where necessary, it shall submit proposals for adjustment of this Directive in line with developments in the area of databases.

[8.17]
Article 17
This Directive is addressed to the Member States.

DIRECTIVE OF THE EUROPEAN PARLIAMENT AND OF THE COUNCIL

(98/44/EC)
of 6 July 1998

on the legal protection of biotechnological inventions ('Biotech Directive')

NOTES
Date of publication in OJ: OJ L213, 30.7.98, p 13.

THE EUROPEAN PARLIAMENT AND THE COUNCIL OF THE EUROPEAN UNION,

Having regard to the Treaty establishing the European Community, and in particular Article 100a thereof,

Having regard to the proposal from the Commission,[1]

Having regard to the opinion of the Economic and Social Committee,[2]

Acting in accordance with the procedure laid down in Article 189b of the Treaty,[3]

Whereas biotechnology and genetic engineering are playing an increasingly important role in a broad range of industries and the protection of biotechnological inventions will certainly be of fundamental importance for the Community's industrial development;

Whereas, in particular in the field of genetic engineering, research and development require a considerable amount of high-risk investment and therefore only adequate legal protection can make them profitable;

Whereas effective and harmonised protection throughout the Member States is essential in order to maintain and encourage investment in the field of biotechnology;

Whereas following the European Parliament's rejection of the joint text, approved by the Conciliation Committee, for a European Parliament and Council Directive on the legal protection of biotechnological inventions,[4] the European Parliament and the Council have determined that the legal protection of biotechnological inventions requires clarification;

Whereas differences exist in the legal protection of biotechnological inventions offered by the laws and practices of the different Member States; whereas such differences could create barriers to trade and hence impede the proper functioning of the internal market;

Whereas such differences could well become greater as Member States adopt new and different legislation and administrative practices, or whereas national case-law interpreting such legislation develops differently;

Whereas uncoordinated development of national laws on the legal protection of biotechnological inventions in the Community could lead to further disincentives to trade, to the detriment of the industrial development of such inventions and of the smooth operation of the internal market;

Whereas legal protection of biotechnological inventions does not necessitate the creation of a separate body of law in place of the rules of national patent law; whereas the rules of national patent law remain the essential basis for the legal protection of biotechnological inventions given that they must be adapted or added to in certain specific respects in order to take adequate account of technological developments involving biological material which also fulfil the requirements for patentability;

Whereas in certain cases, such as the exclusion from patentability of plant and animal varieties and of essentially biological processes for the production of plants and animals, certain concepts in national laws based upon international patent and plant variety conventions have created uncertainty regarding the protection of biotechnological and certain microbiological inventions; whereas harmonisation is necessary to clarify the said uncertainty;

Whereas regard should be had to the potential of the development of biotechnology for the environment and in particular the utility of this technology for the development of methods of cultivation which are less polluting and more economical in their use of ground; whereas the patent system should be used to encourage research into, and the application of, such processes;

Whereas the development of biotechnology is important to developing countries, both in the field of health and combating major epidemics and endemic diseases and in that of combating hunger in the world; whereas the patent system should likewise be used to encourage research in these fields; whereas international procedures for the dissemination of such technology in the Third World and to the benefit of the population groups concerned should be promoted;

Whereas the Agreement on Trade-Related Aspects of Intellectual Property Rights (TRIPs)[5] signed by the European Community and the Member States, has entered into force and provides that patent protection must be guaranteed for products and processes in all areas of technology;

Whereas the Community's legal framework for the protection of biotechnological inventions can be limited to laying down certain principles as they apply to the patentability of biological material as such, such principles being intended in particular to determine the difference between inventions and discoveries with regard to the patentability of certain elements of human origin, to the scope of protection conferred by a patent on a biotechnological invention, to the right to use a deposit mechanism in addition to written descriptions and lastly to the option of obtaining non-exclusive compulsory licences in respect of interdependence between plant varieties and inventions, and conversely;

Whereas a patent for invention does not authorise the holder to implement that invention, but merely entitles him to prohibit third parties from exploiting it for industrial and commercial purposes; whereas, consequently, substantive patent law cannot serve to replace or render superfluous national, European or international law which may impose restrictions or prohibitions or which concerns the monitoring of research and of the use or commercialisation of its results, notably from the point of view of the requirements of public health, safety, environmental protection, animal welfare, the preservation of genetic diversity and compliance with certain ethical standards;

Whereas no prohibition or exclusion exists in national or European patent law (Munich Convention) which precludes a priori the patentability of biological matter;

Whereas patent law must be applied so as to respect the fundamental principles safeguarding the dignity and integrity of the person; whereas it is important to assert the principle that the human body, at any stage in its formation or development, including germ cells, and the simple discovery of one of its elements or one of its products, including the sequence or partial sequence of a human gene, cannot be patented; whereas these principles are in line with the criteria of patentability proper to patent law, whereby a mere discovery cannot be patented;

Whereas significant progress in the treatment of diseases has already been made thanks to the existence of medicinal products derived from elements isolated from the human body and/or otherwise produced, such medicinal products resulting from technical processes aimed at obtaining elements similar in structure to those existing naturally in the human body and whereas, consequently, research aimed at obtaining and isolating such elements valuable to medicinal production should be encouraged by means of the patent system;

Whereas, since the patent system provides insufficient incentive for encouraging research into and production of biotechnological medicines which are needed to combat rare or 'orphan' diseases, the Community and the Member States have a duty to respond adequately to this problem;

Whereas account has been taken of Opinion No 8 of the Group of Advisers on the Ethical Implications of Biotechnology to the European Commission;

Whereas, therefore, it should be made clear that an invention based on an element isolated from the human body or otherwise produced by means of a technical process, which is susceptible of industrial application, is not excluded from patentability, even where the structure of that element is identical to that of a natural element, given that the rights conferred by the patent do not extend to the human body and its elements in their natural environment;

Whereas such an element isolated from the human body or otherwise produced is not excluded from patentability since it is, for example, the result of technical processes used to identify, purify and classify it and to reproduce it outside the human body, techniques which human beings alone are capable of putting into practice and which nature is incapable of accomplishing by itself;

Whereas the discussion on the patentability of sequences or partial sequences of genes is controversial; whereas, according to this Directive, the granting of a patent for inventions which concern such sequences or partial sequences should be subject to the same criteria of patentability as in all other areas of technology: novelty, inventive step and industrial application; whereas the industrial application of a sequence or partial sequence must be disclosed in the patent application as filed;

Whereas a mere DNA sequence without indication of a function does not contain any technical information and is therefore not a patentable invention;

Whereas, in order to comply with the industrial application criterion it is necessary in cases where a sequence or partial sequence of a gene is used to produce a protein or part of a protein, to specify which protein or part of a protein is produced or what function it performs;

Whereas, for the purposes of interpreting rights conferred by a patent, when sequences overlap only in parts which are not essential to the invention, each sequence will be considered as an independent sequence in patent law terms;

Whereas if an invention is based on biological material of human origin or if it uses such material, where a patent application is filed, the person from whose body the material is taken must have had an opportunity of expressing free and informed consent thereto, in accordance with national law;

Whereas if an invention is based on biological material of plant or animal origin or if it uses such material, the patent application should, where appropriate, include information on the geographical origin of such material, if known; whereas this is without prejudice to the processing of patent applications or the validity of rights arising from granted patents;

Whereas this Directive does not in any way affect the basis of current patent law, according to which a patent may be granted for any new application of a patented product;

Whereas this Directive is without prejudice to the exclusion of plant and animal varieties from patentability; whereas on the other hand inventions which concern plants or animals are patentable provided that the application of the invention is not technically confined to a single plant or animal variety;

Whereas the concept 'plant variety' is defined by the legislation protecting new varieties, pursuant to which a variety is defined by its whole genome and therefore possesses individuality and is clearly distinguishable from other varieties;

Whereas a plant grouping which is characterised by a particular gene (and not its whole genome) is not covered by the protection of new varieties and is therefore not excluded from patentability even if it comprises new varieties of plants;

Whereas, however, if an invention consists only in genetically modifying a particular plant variety, and if a new plant variety is bred, it will still be excluded from patentability even if the genetic modification is the result not of an essentially biological process but of a biotechnological process;

Whereas it is necessary to define for the purposes of this Directive when a process for the breeding of plants and animals is essentially biological;

Whereas this Directive shall be without prejudice to concepts of invention and discovery, as developed by national, European or international patent law;

Whereas this Directive shall be without prejudice to the provisions of national patent law whereby processes for treatment of the human or animal body by surgery or therapy and diagnostic methods practised on the human or animal body are excluded from patentability;

Whereas the TRIPs Agreement provides for the possibility that members of the World Trade Organisation may exclude from patentability inventions, the prevention within their territory of the commercial exploitation of which is necessary to protect ordre public or morality, including to protect human, animal or plant life or health or to avoid serious prejudice to the environment, provided that such exclusion is not made merely because the exploitation is prohibited by their law;

Whereas the principle whereby inventions must be excluded from patentability where their commercial exploitation offends against ordre public or morality must also be stressed in this Directive;

Whereas the operative part of this Directive should also include an illustrative list of inventions excluded from patentability so as to provide national courts and patent offices with a general guide to interpreting the reference to ordre public and morality; whereas this list obviously cannot presume to be exhaustive; whereas processes, the use of which offend against human dignity, such as processes to produce chimeras from germ cells or totipotent cells of humans and animals, are obviously also excluded from patentability;

Whereas ordre public and morality correspond in particular to ethical or moral principles recognised in a Member State, respect for which is particularly important in the field of biotechnology in view of the potential scope of inventions in this field and their inherent relationship to living matter; whereas such ethical or moral principles supplement the standard legal examinations under patent law regardless of the technical field of the invention;

Whereas there is a consensus within the Community that interventions in the human germ line and the cloning of human beings offends against ordre public and morality; whereas it is therefore important to exclude unequivocally from patentability processes for modifying the germ line genetic identity of human beings and processes for cloning human beings;

Whereas a process for cloning human beings may be defined as any process, including techniques of embryo splitting, designed to create a human being with the same nuclear genetic information as another living or deceased human being;

Whereas, moreover, uses of human embryos for industrial or commercial purposes must also be excluded from patentability; whereas in any case such exclusion does not affect inventions for therapeutic or diagnostic purposes which are applied to the human embryo and are useful to it;

Whereas pursuant to Article F(2) of the Treaty on European Union, the Union is to respect fundamental rights, as guaranteed by the European Convention for the Protection of Human Rights and Fundamental Freedoms signed in Rome on 4 November 1950 and as they result from the constitutional traditions common to the Member States, as general principles of Community law;

Whereas the Commission's European Group on Ethics in Science and New Technologies evaluates all ethical aspects of biotechnology; whereas it should be pointed out in this connection that that Group may be consulted only where biotechnology is to be evaluated at the level of basic ethical principles, including where it is consulted on patent law;

Whereas processes for modifying the genetic identity of animals which are likely to cause them suffering without any substantial medical benefit in terms of research, prevention, diagnosis or therapy to man or animal, and also animals resulting from such processes, must be excluded from patentability;

Whereas, in view of the fact that the function of a patent is to reward the inventor for his creative efforts by granting an exclusive but time-bound right, and thereby encourage inventive activities, the holder of the patent should be entitled to prohibit the use of patented self-reproducing material in situations analogous to those where it would be permitted to prohibit the use of patented, non-self-reproducing products, that is to say the production of the patented product itself;

Whereas it is necessary to provide for a first derogation from the rights of the holder of the patent when the propagating material incorporating the protected invention is sold to a farmer for farming purposes by the holder of the patent or with his consent; whereas that initial derogation must authorise the farmer to use the product of his harvest for further multiplication or propagation on his own farm; whereas the extent and the conditions of that derogation must be limited in accordance with the extent and conditions set out in Council Regulation (EC) No 2100/94 of 27 July 1994 on Community plant variety rights;[6]

Whereas only the fee envisaged under Community law relating to plant variety rights as a condition for applying the derogation from Community plant variety rights can be required of the farmer;

Whereas, however, the holder of the patent may defend his rights against a farmer abusing the derogation or against a breeder who has developed a plant variety incorporating the protected invention if the latter fails to adhere to his commitments;

Whereas a second derogation from the rights of the holder of the patent must authorise the farmer to use protected livestock for agricultural purposes;

Whereas the extent and the conditions of that second derogation must be determined by national laws, regulations and practices, since there is no Community legislation on animal variety rights;

Whereas, in the field of exploitation of new plant characteristics resulting from genetic engineering, guaranteed access must, on payment of a fee, be granted in the form of a compulsory licence where, in relation to the genus or species concerned, the plant variety represents significant technical progress of considerable economic interest compared to the invention claimed in the patent;

Whereas, in the field of the use of new plant characteristics resulting from new plant varieties in genetic engineering, guaranteed access must, on payment of a fee, be granted in the form of a compulsory licence where the invention represents significant technical progress of considerable economic interest;

Whereas Article 34 of the TRIPs Agreement contains detailed provisions on the burden of proof which is binding on all Member States; whereas, therefore, a provision in this Directive is not necessary;

Whereas following Decision 93/626/EEC[7] the Community is party to the Convention on Biological Diversity of 5 June 1992; whereas, in this regard, Member States must give particular weight to Article 3 and Article 8(j), the second sentence of Article 16(2) and Article 16(5) of the Convention when bringing into force the laws, regulations and administrative provisions necessary to comply with this Directive;

Whereas the Third Conference of the Parties to the Biodiversity Convention, which took place in November 1996, noted in Decision III/17 that 'further work is required to help develop a common appreciation of the relationship between intellectual property rights and the relevant provisions of the TRIPs Agreement and the Convention on Biological Diversity, in particular on issues relating to technology transfer and conservation and sustainable use of biological diversity and the fair and equitable sharing of benefits arising out of the use of genetic resources, including the protection of knowledge, innovations and practices of indigenous and local communities embodying traditional lifestyles relevant for the conservation and sustainable use of biological diversity',

NOTES

1 OJ C296, 8.10.1996, p 4 and OJ C311, 11.10.1997, p 12.

2 OJ C295, 7.10.1996, p 11.

3 Opinion of the European Parliament of 16 July 1997 (OJ C286, 22.9.1997, p 87). Council Common Position of 26 February 1998 (OJ C110, 8.4.1998, p 17) and Decision of the European Parliament of 12 May 1998 (OJ C167, 1.6.1998). Council Decision of 16 June 1998.

4 OJ C68, 20.3.1995, p 26.

5 OJ L336, 23.12.1994, p 213.

6 OJ L227, 1.9.1994, p 1. Regulation as amended by Regulation 2506/95/EC (OJ L258, 28.10.1995, p 3).

7 OJ L309, 31.12.1993, p 1.

HAVE ADOPTED THIS DIRECTIVE—

CHAPTER I
PATENTABILITY

[8.18]
Article 1

1. Member States shall protect biotechnological inventions under national patent law. They shall, if necessary, adjust their national patent law to take account of the provisions of this Directive.
2. This Directive shall be without prejudice to the obligations of the Member States pursuant to international agreements, and in particular the TRIPs Agreement and the Convention on Biological Diversity.

[8.19]
Article 2

1. For the purposes of this Directive,
   (a) 'biological material' means any material containing genetic information and capable of reproducing itself or being reproduced in a biological system;
   (b) 'microbiological process' means any process involving or performed upon or resulting in microbiological material.
2. A process for the production of plants or animals is essentially biological if it consists entirely of natural phenomena such as crossing or selection.
3. The concept of 'plant variety' is defined by Article 5 of Regulation (EC) No 2100/94.

[8.20]
Article 3

1. For the purposes of this Directive, inventions which are new, which involve an inventive step and which are susceptible of industrial application shall be patentable even if they concern a product consisting of or containing biological material or a process by means of which biological material is produced, processed or used.
2. Biological material which is isolated from its natural environment or produced by means of a technical process may be the subject of an invention even if it previously occurred in nature.

[8.21]
Article 4

1. The following shall not be patentable—
   (a) plant and animal varieties;
   (b) essentially biological processes for the production of plants or animals.
2. Inventions which concern plants or animals shall be patentable if the technical feasibility of the invention is not confined to a particular plant or animal variety.
3. Paragraph 1(b) shall be without prejudice to the patentability of inventions which concern a microbiological or other technical process or a product obtained by means of such a process.

[8.22]
Article 5

1. The human body, at the various stages of its formation and development, and the simple discovery of one of its elements, including the sequence or partial sequence of a gene, cannot constitute patentable inventions.

2. An element isolated from the human body or otherwise produced by means of a technical process, including the sequence or partial sequence of a gene, may constitute a patentable invention, even if the structure of that element is identical to that of a natural element.
3. The industrial application of a sequence or a partial sequence of a gene must be disclosed in the patent application.

[8.23]
Article 6
1. Inventions shall be considered unpatentable where their commercial exploitation would be contrary to ordre public or morality; however, exploitation shall not be deemed to be so contrary merely because it is prohibited by law or regulation.
2. On the basis of paragraph 1, the following, in particular, shall be considered unpatentable—
(a) processes for cloning human beings;
(b) processes for modifying the germ line genetic identity of human beings;
(c) uses of human embryos for industrial or commercial purposes;
(d) processes for modifying the genetic identity of animals which are likely to cause them suffering without any substantial medical benefit to man or animal, and also animals resulting from such processes.

[8.24]
Article 7
The Commission's European Group on Ethics in Science and New Technologies evaluates all ethical aspects of biotechnology.

CHAPTER II
SCOPE OF PROTECTION

[8.25]
Article 8
1. The protection conferred by a patent on a biological material possessing specific characteristics as a result of the invention shall extend to any biological material derived from that biological material through propagation or multiplication in an identical or divergent form and possessing those same characteristics.
2. The protection conferred by a patent on a process that enables a biological material to be produced possessing specific characteristics as a result of the invention shall extend to biological material directly obtained through that process and to any other biological material derived from the directly obtained biological material through propagation or multiplication in an identical or divergent form and possessing those same characteristics.

[8.26]
Article 9
The protection conferred by a patent on a product containing or consisting of genetic information shall extend to all material, save as provided in Article 5(1), in which the product in incorporated and in which the genetic information is contained and performs its function.

[8.27]
Article 10
The protection referred to in Articles 8 and 9 shall not extend to biological material obtained from the propagation or multiplication of biological material placed on the market in the territory of a Member State by the holder of the patent or with his consent, where the multiplication or propagation necessarily results from the application for which the biological material was marketed, provided that the material obtained is not subsequently used for other propagation or multiplication.

[8.28]
Article 11
1. By way of derogation from Articles 8 and 9, the sale or other form of commercialisation of plant propagating material to a farmer by the holder of the patent or with his consent for agricultural use implies authorisation for the farmer to use the product of his harvest for propagation or multiplication by him on his own farm, the extent and conditions of this derogation corresponding to those under Article 14 of Regulation (EC) No 2100/94.
2. By way of derogation from Articles 8 and 9, the sale or any other form of commercialisation of breeding stock or other animal reproductive material to a farmer by the holder of the patent or with his consent implies authorisation for the farmer to use the protected livestock for an agricultural purpose. This includes making the animal or other animal reproductive material available for the purposes of pursuing his agricultural activity but not sale within the framework or for the purpose of a commercial reproduction activity.
3. The extent and the conditions of the derogation provided for in paragraph 2 shall be determined by national laws, regulations and practices.

CHAPTER III
COMPULSORY CROSS-LICENSING

[8.29]
Article 12

1. Where a breeder cannot acquire or exploit a plant variety right without infringing a prior patent, he may apply for a compulsory licence for non-exclusive use of the invention protected by the patent inasmuch as the licence is necessary for the exploitation of the plant variety to be protected, subject to payment of an appropriate royalty. Member States shall provide that, where such a licence is granted, the holder of the patent will be entitled to a cross-licence on reasonable terms to use the protected variety.

2. Where the holder of a patent concerning a biotechnological invention cannot exploit it without infringing a prior plant variety right, he may apply for a compulsory licence for non-exclusive use of the plant variety protected by that right, subject to payment of an appropriate royalty. Member States shall provide that, where such a licence is granted, the holder of the variety right will be entitled to a cross-licence on reasonable terms to use the protected invention.

3. Applicants for the licences referred to in paragraphs 1 and 2 must demonstrate that—
   (a) they have applied unsuccessfully to the holder of the patent or of the plant variety right to obtain a contractual licence;
   (b) the plant variety or the invention constitutes significant technical progress of considerable economic interest compared with the invention claimed in the patent or the protected plant variety.

4. Each Member State shall designate the authority or authorities responsible for granting the licence. Where a licence for a plant variety can be granted only by the Community Plant Variety Office, Article 29 of Regulation (EC) No 2100/94 shall apply.

CHAPTER IV
DEPOSIT, ACCESS AND RE-DEPOSIT OF A BIOLOGICAL MATERIAL

[8.30]
Article 13

1. Where an invention involves the use of or concerns biological material which is not available to the public and which cannot be described in a patent application in such a manner as to enable the invention to be reproduced by a person skilled in the art, the description shall be considered inadequate for the purposes of patent law unless—
   (a) the biological material has been deposited no later than the date on which the patent application was filed with a recognised depositary institution. At least the international depositary authorities which acquired this status by virtue of Article 7 of the Budapest Treaty of 28 April 1977 on the international recognition of the deposit of micro-organisms for the purposes of patent procedure, hereinafter referred to as the 'Budapest Treaty', shall be recognised;
   (b) the application as filed contains such relevant information as is available to the applicant on the characteristics of the biological material deposited;
   (c) the patent application states the name of the depository institution and the accession number.

2. Access to the deposited biological material shall be provided through the supply of a sample—
   (a) up to the first publication of the patent application, only to those persons who are authorised under national patent law;
   (b) between the first publication of the application and the granting of the patent, to anyone requesting it or, if the applicant so requests, only to an independent expert;
   (c) after the patent has been granted, and notwithstanding revocation or cancellation of the patent, to anyone requesting it.

3. The sample shall be supplied only if the person requesting it undertakes, for the term during which the patent is in force—
   (a) not to make it or any material derived from it available to third parties; and
   (b) not to use it or any material derived from it except for experimental purposes, unless the applicant for or proprietor of the patent, as applicable, expressly waives such an undertaking.

4. At the applicant's request, where an application is refused or withdrawn, access to the deposited material shall be limited to an independent expert for 20 years from the date on which the patent application was filed. In that case, paragraph 3 shall apply.

5. The applicant's requests referred to in point (b) of paragraph 2 and in paragraph 4 may only be made up to the date on which the technical preparations for publishing the patent application are deemed to have been completed.

[8.31]
Article 14

1. If the biological material deposited in accordance with Article 13 ceases to be available from the recognised depositary institution, a new deposit of the material shall be permitted on the same terms as those laid down in the Budapest Treaty.

2. Any new deposit shall be accompanied by a statement signed by the depositor certifying that the newly deposited biological material is the same as that originally deposited.

CHAPTER V
FINAL PROVISIONS

[8.32]
Article 15

1. Member States shall bring into force the laws, regulations and administrative provisions necessary to comply with this Directive not later than 30 July 2000. They shall forthwith inform the Commission thereof.

When Member States adopt these measures, they shall contain a reference to this Directive or shall be accompanied by such reference on the occasion of their official publication. The methods of making such reference shall be laid down by Member States.

2. Member States shall communicate to the Commission the text of the provisions of national law which they adopt in the field covered by this Directive.

[8.33]
Article 16

The Commission shall send the European Parliament and the Council—

(a) every five years as from the date specified in Article 15(1) a report on any problems encountered with regard to the relationship between this Directive and international agreements on the protection of human rights to which the Member States have acceded;

(b) within two years of entry into force of this Directive, a report assessing the implications for basic genetic engineering research of failure to publish, or late publication of, papers on subjects which could be patentable;

(c) annually as from the date specified in Article 15(1), a report on the development and implications of patent law in the field of biotechnology and genetic engineering.

[8.34]
Article 17

This Directive shall enter into force on the day of its publication in the Official Journal of the European Communities.

[8.35]
Article 18

This Directive is addressed to the Member States.

DIRECTIVE OF THE EUROPEAN PARLIAMENT AND OF THE COUNCIL

(98/71/EC)

of 13 October 1998

on the legal protection of designs

NOTES

Date of publication in OJ: OJ L289, 28.10.98, p 28.

THE EUROPEAN PARLIAMENT AND THE COUNCIL OF THE EUROPEAN UNION,

Having regard to the Treaty establishing the European Community and in particular Article 100a thereof,

Having regard to the proposal by the Commission,[1]

Having regard to the opinion of the Economic and Social Committee,[2]

Acting in accordance with the procedure laid down in Article 189b of the Treaty,[3] in the light of the joint text approved by the Conciliation Committee on 29 July 1998,

Whereas the objectives of the Community, as laid down in the Treaty, include laying the foundations of an ever closer union among the peoples of Europe, fostering closer relations between Member States of the Community, and ensuring the economic and social progress of the Community countries by common action to eliminate the barriers which divide Europe; whereas to that end the Treaty provides for the establishment of an internal market characterised by the abolition of obstacles to the free movement of goods and also for the institution of a system

Part 8 Other EU Materials

ensuring that competition in the internal market is not distorted; whereas an approximation of the laws of the Member States on the legal protection of designs would further those objectives;

Whereas the differences in the legal protection of designs offered by the legislation of the Member States directly affect the establishment and functioning of the internal market as regards goods embodying designs; whereas such differences can distort competition within the internal market;

Whereas it is therefore necessary for the smooth functioning of the internal market to approximate the design protection laws of the Member States;

Whereas in doing so, it is important to take into consideration the solutions and the advantages with which the Community design system will provide undertakings wishing to acquire design rights;

Whereas it is unnecessary to undertake a full-scale approximation of the design laws of the Member States, and it will be sufficient if approximation is limited to those national provisions of law which most directly affect the functioning of the internal market; whereas provisions on sanctions, remedies and enforcement should be left to national law; whereas the objectives of this limited approximation cannot be sufficiently achieved by the Member States acting alone;

Whereas Member States should accordingly remain free to fix the procedural provisions concerning registration, renewal and invalidation of design rights and provisions concerning the effects of such invalidity;

Whereas this Directive does not exclude the application to designs of national or Community legislation providing for protection other than that conferred by registration or publication as design, such as legislation relating to unregistered design rights, trade marks, patents and utility models, unfair competition or civil liability;

Whereas in the absence of harmonisation of copyright law, it is important to establish the principle of cumulation of protection under specific registered design protection law and under copyright law, whilst leaving Member States free to establish the extent of copyright protection and the conditions under which such protection is conferred;

Whereas the attainment of the objectives of the internal market requires that the conditions for obtaining a registered design right be identical in all the Member States; whereas to that end it is necessary to give a unitary definition of the notion of design and of the requirements as to novelty and individual character with which registered design rights must comply;

Whereas it is essential, in order to facilitate the free movement of goods, to ensure in principle that registered design rights confer upon the right holder equivalent protection in all Member States;

Whereas protection is conferred by way of registration upon the right holder for those design features of a product, in whole or in part, which are shown visibly in an application and made available to the public by way of publication or consultation of the relevant file;

Whereas protection should not be extended to those component parts which are not visible during normal use of a product, or to those features of such part which are not visible when the part is mounted, or which would not, in themselves, fulfil the requirements as to novelty and individual character; whereas features of design which are excluded from protection for these reasons should not be taken into consideration for the purpose of assessing whether other features of the design fulfil the requirements for protection;

Whereas the assessment as to whether a design has individual character should be based on whether the overall impression produced on an informed user viewing the design clearly differs from that produced on him by the existing design corpus, taking into consideration the nature of the product to which the design is applied or in which it is incorporated, and in particular the industrial sector to which it belongs and the degree of freedom of the designer in developing the design;

Whereas technological innovation should not be hampered by granting design protection to features dictated solely by a technical function; whereas it is understood that this does not entail that a design must have an aesthetic quality; whereas, likewise, the interoperability of products of different makes should not be hindered by extending protection to the design of mechanical fittings; whereas features of a design which are excluded from protection for these reasons should not be taken into consideration for the purpose of assessing whether other features of the design fulfil the requirements for protection;

Whereas the mechanical fittings of modular products may nevertheless constitute an important element of the innovative characteristics of modular products and present a major marketing asset and therefore should be eligible for protection;

Whereas a design right shall not subsist in a design which is contrary to public policy or to accepted principles of morality; whereas this Directive does not constitute a harmonisation of national concepts of public policy or accepted principles of morality;

Whereas it is fundamental for the smooth functioning of the internal market to unify the term of protection afforded by registered design rights;

Whereas the provisions of this Directive are without prejudice to the application of the competition rules under Articles 85 and 86 of the Treaty;

Whereas the rapid adoption of this Directive has become a matter of urgency for a number of industrial sectors; whereas full-scale approximation of the laws of the Member States on the use of protected designs for the purpose of permitting the repair of a complex product so as to restore its original appearance, where the product incorporating the design or to which the design is applied constitutes a component part of a complex product upon whose appearance the protected design is dependent, cannot be introduced at the present stage; whereas the lack of full-scale approximation of the laws of the Member States on the use of protected designs for such repair of a complex product should not constitute an obstacle to the approximation of those other national provisions of design law which most directly affect the functioning of the internal market; whereas for this reason Member States should in the meantime maintain in force any provisions in conformity with the Treaty relating to the use of the design of a component part used for the purpose of the repair of a complex product so as to restore its original appearance, or, if they introduce any new provisions relating to such use, the purpose of these provisions should be only to liberalise the market in such parts; whereas those Member States which, on the date of entry into force of this Directive, do not provide for protection for designs of component parts are not required to introduce registration of designs for such parts; whereas three years after the implementation date the Commission should submit an analysis of the consequences of the provisions of this Directive for Community industry, for consumers, for competition and for the functioning of the internal market; whereas, in respect of component parts of complex products, the analysis should, in particular, consider harmonisation on the basis of possible options, including a remuneration system and a limited term of exclusivity; whereas, at the latest one year after the submission of its analysis, the Commission should, after consultation with the parties most affected, propose to the European Parliament and the Council any changes to this Directive needed to complete the internal market in respect of component parts of complex products, and any other changes which it considers necessary;

Whereas the transitional provision in Article 14 concerning the design of a component part used for the purpose of the repair of a complex product so as to restore its original appearance is in no case to be construed as constituting an obstacle to the free movement of a product which constitutes such a component part;

Whereas the substantive grounds for refusal of registration in those Member States which provide for substantive examination of applications prior to registration, and the substantive grounds for the invalidation of registered design rights in all the Member States, must be exhaustively enumerated,

NOTES

1 OJ C345, 23.12.1993, p 14 and OJ C142, 14.5.1996, p 7.

2 OJ C388, 31.12.1994, p 9 and OJ C110, 2.5.1995, p 12.

3 Opinion of the European Parliament of 12 October 1995 (OJ C287, 30.10.1995, p 157), common position of the Council of 17 June 1997 (OJ C237, 4.8.1997, p 1), Decision of the European Parliament of 22 October 1997 (OJ C339, 10.11.1997, p 52). Decision of the European Parliament of 15 September 1998. Decision of the Council of 24 September 1998.

HAVE ADOPTED THIS DIRECTIVE—

[8.36]
Article 1
Definitions

For the purpose of this Directive—

(a) 'design' means the appearance of the whole or a part of a product resulting from the features of, in particular, the lines, contours, colours, shape, texture and/or materials of the product itself and/or its ornamentation;
(b) 'product' means any industrial or handicraft item, including inter alia parts intended to be assembled into a complex product, packaging, get-up, graphic symbols and typographic typefaces, but excluding computer programs;
(c) 'complex product' means a product which is composed of multiple components which can be replaced permitting disassembly and reassembly of the product.

[8.37]
Article 2
Scope of application

1. This Directive shall apply to—
(a) design rights registered with the central industrial property offices of the Member States;
(b) design rights registered at the Benelux Design Office;
(c) design rights registered under international arrangements which have effect in a Member State;
(d) applications for design rights referred to under (a), (b) and (c).

2. For the purpose of this Directive, design registration shall also comprise the publication following filing of the design with the industrial property office of a Member State in which such publication has the effect of bringing a design right into existence.

[8.38]
Article 3
Protection requirements

1. Member States shall protect designs by registration, and shall confer exclusive rights upon their holders in accordance with the provisions of this Directive.
2. A design shall be protected by a design right to the extent that it is new and has individual character.
3. A design applied to or incorporated in a product which constitutes a component part of a complex product shall only be considered to be new and to have individual character—
   (a) if the component part, once it has been incorporated into the complex product, remains visible during normal use of the latter, and
   (b) to the extent that those visible features of the component part fulfil in themselves the requirements as to novelty and individual character.
4. 'Normal use' within the meaning of paragraph (3)(a) shall mean use by the end user, excluding maintenance, servicing or repair work.

[8.39]
Article 4
Novelty

A design shall be considered new if no identical design has been made available to the public before the date of filing of the application for registration or, if priority is claimed, the date of priority. Designs shall be deemed to be identical if their features differ only in immaterial details.

[8.40]
Article 5
Individual character

1. A design shall be considered to have individual character if the overall impression it produces on the informed user differs from the overall impression produced on such a user by any design which has been made available to the public before the date of filing of the application for registration or, if priority is claimed, the date of priority.
2. In assessing individual character, the degree of freedom of the designer in developing the design shall be taken into consideration.

[8.41]
Article 6
Disclosure

1. For the purpose of applying Articles 4 and 5, a design shall be deemed to have been made available to the public if it has been published following registration or otherwise, or exhibited, used in trade or otherwise disclosed, except where these events could not reasonably have become known in the normal course of business to the circles specialised in the sector concerned, operating within the Community, before the date of filing of the application for registration or, if priority is claimed, the date of priority. The design shall not, however, be deemed to have been made available to the public for the sole reason that it has been disclosed to a third person under explicit or implicit conditions of confidentiality.
2. A disclosure shall not be taken into consideration for the purpose of applying Articles 4 and 5 if a design for which protection is claimed under a registered design right of a Member State has been made available to the public—
   (a) by the designer, his successor in title, or a third person as a result of information provided or action taken by the designer, or his successor in title; and
   (b) during the 12-month period preceding the date of filing of the application or, if priority is claimed, the date of priority.
3. Paragraph 2 shall also apply if the design has been made available to the public as a consequence of an abuse in relation to the designer or his successor in title.

[8.42]
Article 7
Designs dictated by their technical function and designs of interconnections

1. A design right shall not subsist in features of appearance of a product which are solely dictated by its technical function.
2. A design right shall not subsist in features of appearance of a product which must necessarily be reproduced in their exact form and dimensions in order to permit the product in which the design is incorporated or to which it is applied to be mechanically connected to or placed in, around or against another product so that either product may perform its function.
3. Notwithstanding paragraph 2, a design right shall, under the conditions set out in Articles 4 and 5, subsist in a design serving the purpose of allowing multiple assembly or connection of mutually interchangeable products within a modular system.

[8.43]
Article 8
Designs contrary to public policy or morality

A design right shall not subsist in a design which is contrary to public policy or to accepted principles of morality.

[8.44]
Article 9
Scope of protection

1. The scope of the protection conferred by a design right shall include any design which does not produce on the informed user a different overall impression.
2. In assessing the scope of protection, the degree of freedom of the designer in developing his design shall be taken into consideration.

[8.45]
Article 10
Term of protection

Upon registration, a design which meets the requirements of Article 3(2) shall be protected by a design right for one or more periods of five years from the date of filing of the application. The right holder may have the term of protection renewed for one or more periods of five years each, up to a total term of 25 years from the date of filing.

[8.46]
Article 11
Invalidity or refusal of registration

1. A design shall be refused registration, or, if the design has been registered, the design right shall be declared invalid—
    (a) if the design is not a design within the meaning of Article 1(a); or
    (b) if it does not fulfil the requirements of Articles 3 to 8; or
    (c) if the applicant for or the holder of the design right is not entitled to it under the law of the Member State concerned; or
    (d) if the design is in conflict with a prior design which has been made available to the public after the date of filing of the application or, if priority is claimed, the date of priority, and which is protected from a date prior to the said date by a registered Community design or an application for a registered Community design or by a design right of the Member State concerned, or by an application for such a right.
2. Any Member State may provide that a design shall be refused registration, or, if the design has been registered, that the design right shall be declared invalid—
    (a) if a distinctive sign is used in a subsequent design, and Community law or the law of the Member State concerned governing that sign confers on the right holder of the sign the right to prohibit such use; or
    (b) if the design constitutes an unauthorised use of a work protected under the copyright law of the Member State concerned; or
    (c) if the design constitutes an improper use of any of the items listed in Article 6b of the Paris Convention for the Protection of Industrial Property, or of badges, emblems and escutcheons other than those covered by Article 6b of the said Convention which are of particular public interest in the Member State concerned.
3. The ground provided for in paragraph 1(c) may be invoked solely by the person who is entitled to the design right under the law of the Member State concerned.
4. The grounds provided for in paragraph 1(d) and in paragraph 2(a) and (b) may be invoked solely by the applicant for or the holder of the conflicting right.
5. The ground provided for in paragraph 2(c) may be invoked solely by the person or entity concerned by the use.
6. Paragraphs 4 and 5 shall be without prejudice to the freedom of Member States to provide that the grounds provided for in paragraphs 1(d) and 2(c) may also be invoked by the appropriate authority of the Member State in question on its own initiative.
7. When a design has been refused registration or a design right has been declared invalid pursuant to paragraph 1(b) or to paragraph 2, the design may be registered or the design right maintained in an amended form, if in that form it complies with the requirements for protection and the identity of the design is retained. Registration or maintenance in an amended form may include registration accompanied by a partial disclaimer by the holder of the design right or entry in the design Register of a court decision declaring the partial invalidity of the design right.
8. Any Member State may provide that, by way of derogation from paragraphs 1 to 7, the grounds for refusal of registration or for invalidation in force in that State prior to the date on which the provisions necessary to comply with this Directive enter into force shall apply to design applications which have been made prior to that date and to resulting registrations.
9. A design right may be declared invalid even after it has lapsed or has been surrendered.

[8.47]
Article 12
Rights conferred by the design right

1. The registration of a design shall confer on its holder the exclusive right to use it and to prevent any third party not having his consent from using it. The aforementioned use shall cover, in particular, the making, offering, putting on the market, importing, exporting or using of a product in which the design is incorporated or to which it is applied, or stocking such a product for those purposes.

2. Where, under the law of a Member State, acts referred to in paragraph 1 could not be prevented before the date on which the provisions necessary to comply with this Directive entered into force, the rights conferred by the design right may not be invoked to prevent continuation of such acts by any person who had begun such acts prior to that date.

[8.48]
Article 13
Limitation of the rights conferred by the design right

1. The rights conferred by a design right upon registration shall not be exercised in respect of—
   (a) acts done privately and for non-commercial purposes;
   (b) acts done for experimental purposes;
   (c) acts of reproduction for the purposes of making citations or of teaching, provided that such acts are compatible with fair trade practice and do not unduly prejudice the normal exploitation of the design, and that mention is made of the source.

2. In addition, the rights conferred by a design right upon registration shall not be exercised in respect of—
   (a) the equipment on ships and aircraft registered in another country when these temporarily enter the territory of the Member State concerned;
   (b) the importation in the Member State concerned of spare parts and accessories for the purpose of repairing such craft;
   (c) the execution of repairs on such craft.

[8.49]
Article 14
Transitional provision

Until such time as amendments to this Directive are adopted on a proposal from the Commission in accordance with the provisions of Article 18, Member States shall maintain in force their existing legal provisions relating to the use of the design of a component part used for the purpose of the repair of a complex product so as to restore its original appearance and shall introduce changes to those provisions only if the purpose is to liberalise the market for such parts.

[8.50]
Article 15
Exhaustion of rights

The rights conferred by a design right upon registration shall not extend to acts relating to a product in which a design included within the scope of protection of the design right is incorporated or to which it is applied, when the product has been put on the market in the Community by the holder of the design right or with his consent.

[8.51]
Article 16
Relationship to other forms of protection

The provisions of this Directive shall be without prejudice to any provisions of Community law or of the law of the Member State concerned relating to unregistered design rights, trade marks or other distinctive signs, patents and utility models, typefaces, civil liability or unfair competition.

[8.52]
Article 17
Relationship to copyright

A design protected by a design right registered in or in respect of a Member State in accordance with this Directive shall also be eligible for protection under the law of copyright of that State as from the date on which the design was created or fixed in any form. The extent to which, and the conditions under which, such a protection is conferred, including the level of originality required, shall be determined by each Member State.

[8.53]
Article 18
Revision

Three years after the implementation date specified in Article 19, the Commission shall submit an analysis of the consequences of the provisions of this Directive for Community industry, in particular the industrial sectors which are most affected, particularly manufacturers of complex products and component parts, for consumers, for competition and for the functioning of the internal market. At the latest one year later the Commission shall propose to the European Parliament and the Council any changes to this Directive needed to complete the internal market in respect of component parts of complex products and any other changes which it considers necessary in light of its consultations with the parties most affected.

[8.54]
Article 19
Implementation

1. Member States shall bring into force the laws, regulations or administrative provisions necessary to comply with this Directive not later than 28 October 2001.

When Member States adopt these provisions, they shall contain a reference to this Directive or shall be accompanied by such reference on the occasion of their official publication. The methods of making such reference shall be laid down by Member States.

2. Member States shall communicate to the Commission the provisions of national law which they adopt in the field governed by this Directive.

[8.55]
Article 20
Entry into force

This Directive shall enter into force on the 20th day following its publication in the Official Journal of the European Communities.

[8.56]
Article 21
Addressees

This Directive is addressed to the Member States.

STATEMENT BY THE COMMISSION

[8.57]
The Commission shares the European Parliament's concern about combating counterfeiting.

The Commission's intention is to present before the end of the year a Green Paper regarding piracy and counterfeiting in the internal market.

The Commission will include in this Green Paper Parliament's idea of creating an obligation for counterfeiters to provide holders of design rights with information on their illegal acts.

STATEMENT BY THE COMMISSION REGARDING ARTICLE 18

[8.58]
Immediately following the date of adoption of the Directive, and without prejudice to Article 18, the Commission proposes to launch a consultation exercise involving manufacturers of complex products and of component parts in the motor vehicles sector. The aim of this consultation will be to arrive at a voluntary agreement between the parties involved on the protection of designs in cases where the product incorporating the design or to which the design is applied constitutes a component part of a complex product upon whose appearance the protected design is dependent.

The Commission will coordinate the consultation exercise and will report regularly to the Parliament and the Council on its progress. The consulted parties will be invited by the Commission to consider a range of possible options on which to base a voluntary agreement, including a remuneration system and a system based on a limited period of design protection.

DIRECTIVE OF THE EUROPEAN PARLIAMENT AND OF THE COUNCIL

(98/84/EC)

of 20 November 1998

on the legal protection of services based on, or consisting of, conditional access ('Conditional Access Directive')

NOTES

Date of publication in OJ: OJ L320, 28.11.98, p 54.

THE EUROPEAN PARLIAMENT AND THE COUNCIL OF THE EUROPEAN UNION,

Having regard to the Treaty establishing the European Community, and in particular Articles 57(2), 66 and 100a thereof,

Having regard to the proposal from the Commission,[1]

Having regard to the opinion of the Economic and Social Committee,[2]

Acting in accordance with the procedure laid down in Article 189b of the Treaty,[3]

Whereas the objectives of the Community as laid down in the Treaty include creating an ever closer union among the peoples of Europe and ensuring economic and social progress, by eliminating the barriers which divide them;

Whereas the cross-border provision of broadcasting and information society services may contribute, from the individual point of view, to the full effectiveness of freedom of expression as a fundamental right and, from the collective point of view, to the achievement of the objectives laid down in the Treaty;

Whereas the Treaty provides for the free movement of all services which are normally provided for remuneration; whereas this right, as applied to broadcasting and information society services, is also a specific manifestation in Community law of a more general principle, namely freedom of expression as enshrined in Article 10 of the European Convention for the Protection of Human Rights and Fundamental Freedoms; whereas that Article explicitly recognises the right of citizens to receive and impart information regardless of frontiers and whereas any restriction of that right must be based on due consideration of other legitimate interests deserving of legal protection;

Whereas the Commission undertook a wide-ranging consultation based on the Green Paper 'Legal Protection of Encrypted Services in the Internal Market'; whereas the results of that consultation confirmed the need for a Community legal instrument ensuring the legal protection of all those services whose remuneration relies on conditional access;

Whereas the European Parliament, in its Resolution of 13 May 1997 on the Green Paper,[4] called on the Commission to present a proposal for a Directive covering all encoded services in respect of which encoding is used to ensure payment of a fee, and agreed that this should include information society services provided at a distance by electronic means and at the individual request of a service receiver, as well as broadcasting services;

Whereas the opportunities offered by digital technologies provide the potential for increasing consumer choice and contributing to cultural pluralism, by developing an even wider range of services within the meaning of Articles 59 and 60 of the Treaty; whereas the viability of those services will often depend on the use of conditional access in order to obtain the remuneration of the service provider; whereas, accordingly, the legal protection of service providers against illicit devices which allow access to these services free of charge seems necessary in order to ensure the economic viability of the services;

Whereas the importance of this issue was recognised by the Commission Communication on 'A European Initiative in Electronic Commerce';

Whereas, in accordance with Article 7a of the Treaty, the internal market is to comprise an area without internal frontiers in which the free movement of services and goods is ensured; whereas Article 128(4) of the Treaty requires the Community to take cultural aspects into account in its action under other provisions of the Treaty; whereas by virtue of Article 130(3) of the Treaty, the Community must, through the policies and activities it pursues, contribute to creating the conditions necessary for the competitiveness of its industry;

Whereas this Directive is without prejudice to possible future Community or national provisions meant to ensure that a number of broadcasting services, recognised as being of public interest, are not based on conditional access;

Whereas this Directive is without prejudice to the cultural aspects of any further Community action concerning new services;

Whereas the disparity between national rules concerning the legal protection of services based on, or consisting of, conditional access is liable to create obstacles to the free movement of services and goods;

Whereas the application of the Treaty is not sufficient to remove these internal market obstacles; whereas those obstacles should therefore be removed by providing for an equivalent level of protection between Member States; whereas this implies an approximation of the national rules relating to the commercial activities which concern illicit devices;

Whereas it seems necessary to ensure that Member States provide appropriate legal protection against the placing on the market, for direct or indirect financial gain, of an illicit device which enables or facilitates without authority the circumvention of any technological measures designed to protect the remuneration of a legally provided service;

Whereas those commercial activities which concern illicit devices include commercial communications covering all forms of advertising, direct marketing, sponsorship, sales promotion and public relations promoting such products and services;

Whereas those commercial activities are detrimental to consumers who are misled about the origin of illicit devices; whereas a high level of consumer protection is needed in order to fight against this kind of consumer fraud; whereas Article 129a(1) of the Treaty provides that the Community should contribute to the achievement of a high level of consumer protection by the measures it adopts pursuant to Article 100a thereof;

Whereas, therefore, the legal framework for the creation of a single audiovisual area laid down in Council Directive 89/552/EEC of 3 October 1989 on the coordination of certain provisions laid down by law, regulation or administrative action in Member States concerning the pursuit of television broadcasting activities[5] should be supplemented with reference to conditional access techniques as laid down in this Directive, in order, not least, to ensure equal treatment of the suppliers of cross-border broadcasts, regardless of their place of establishment;

Whereas, in accordance with the Council Resolution of 29 June 1995 on the effective uniform application of Community law and on the penalties applicable for breaches of Community law in the internal market,[6] Member States are required to take action to ensure that Community law is duly applied with the same effectiveness and thoroughness as national law;

Whereas, in accordance with Article 5 of the Treaty, Member States are required to take all appropriate measures to guarantee the application and effectiveness of Community law, in particular by ensuring that the sanctions chosen are effective, dissuasive and proportionate and the remedies appropriate;

Whereas the approximation of the laws, regulations and administrative provisions of the Member States should be limited to what is needed in order to achieve the objectives of the internal market, in accordance with the principle of proportionality as set out in the third paragraph of Article 3b of the Treaty;

Whereas the distribution of illicit devices includes transfer by any means and putting such devices on the market for circulation inside or outside the Community;

Whereas this Directive is without prejudice to the application of any national provisions which may prohibit the private possession of illicit devices, to the application of Community competition rules and to the application of Community rules concerning intellectual property rights;

Whereas national law concerning sanctions and remedies for infringing commercial activities may provide that the activities have to be carried out in the knowledge or with reasonable grounds for knowing that the devices in question were illicit;

Whereas the sanctions and remedies provided for under this Directive are without prejudice to any other sanction or remedy for which provision may be made under national law, such as preventive measures in general or seizure of illicit devices; whereas Member States are not obliged to provide criminal sanctions for infringing activities covered by this Directive; whereas Member States' provisions for actions for damages are to be in conformity with their national legislative and judicial systems;

Whereas this Directive is without prejudice to the application of national rules which do not fall within the field herein coordinated, such as those adopted for the protection of minors, including those in compliance with Directive 89/552/EEC, or national provisions concerned with public policy or public security,

NOTES

1 OJ C314, 16.10.1997, p 7 and OJ C203, 30.6.1998, p 12.

2 OJ C129, 27.4.1998, p 16.

3 Opinion of the European Parliament of 30 April 1998 (OJ C152, 18.5.1998, p 59), Council Common Position of 29 June 1998 (OJ C262, 19.8.1998, p 34) and Decision of the European Parliament of 8 October 1998 (OJ C328, 26.10.1998). Council Decision of 9 November 1998.

4 OJ C167, 2.6.1997, p 31.

5 OJ L298, 17.10.1989, p 23. Directive as amended by Directive 97/36/EC of the European Parliament and of the Council (OJ L202, 30.7.1997, p 60).

6 OJ C188, 22.7.1995, p 1.

HAVE ADOPTED THIS DIRECTIVE—

[8.59]
Article 1
Scope

The objective of this Directive is to approximate provisions in the Member States concerning measures against illicit devices which give unauthorised access to protected services.

[8.60]
Article 2
Definitions

For the purposes of this Directive—

(a) 'protected service' shall mean any of the following services, where provided against remuneration and on the basis of conditional access—
- television broadcasting, as defined in Article 1(a) of Directive 89/552/EEC,
- radio broadcasting, meaning any transmission by wire or over the air, including by satellite, of radio programmes intended for reception by the public,
- information society services within the meaning of Article 1(2) of Directive 98/34/EC of the European Parliament and of the Council of 22 June 1998 laying down a procedure for the provision of information in the field of technical standards and regulations and of rules on information society services,[1]

or the provision of conditional access to the above services considered as a service in its own right;

(b) 'conditional access' shall mean any technical measure and/or arrangement whereby access to the protected service in an intelligible form is made conditional upon prior individual authorisation;

(c) 'conditional access device' shall mean any equipment or software designed or adapted to give access to a protected service in an intelligible form;

(d) 'associated service' shall mean the installation, maintenance or replacement of conditional access devices, as well as the provision of commercial communication services in relation to them or to protected services;

(e) 'illicit device' shall mean any equipment or software designed or adapted to give access to a protected service in an intelligible form without the authorisation of the service provider;

(f) 'field coordinated by this Directive' shall mean any provision relating to the infringing activities specified in Article 4.

NOTES

[1] OJ L204, 21.7.1998, p 37. Directive as amended by Directive 98/48/EC (OJ L217, 5.8.1998, p 18).

[8.61]
Article 3
Internal market principles

1. Each Member State shall take the measures necessary to prohibit on its territory the activities listed in Article 4, and to provide for the sanctions and remedies laid down in Article 5.

2. Without prejudice to paragraph 1, Member States may not—

(a) restrict the provision of protected services, or associated services, which originate in another Member State; or

(b) restrict the free movement of conditional access devices;

for reasons falling within the field coordinated by this Directive.

[8.62]
Article 4
Infringing activities

Member States shall prohibit on their territory all of the following activities—

(a) the manufacture, import, distribution, sale, rental or possession for commercial purposes of illicit devices;

(b) the installation, maintenance or replacement for commercial purposes of an illicit device;

(c) the use of commercial communications to promote illicit devices.

[8.63]
Article 5
Sanctions and remedies

1. The sanctions shall be effective, dissuasive and proportionate to the potential impact of the infringing activity.

2. Member States shall take the necessary measures to ensure that providers of protected services whose interests are affected by an infringing activity as specified in Article 4, carried out on their territory, have access to appropriate remedies, including bringing an action for damages and obtaining an injunction or other preventive measure, and where appropriate, applying for disposal outside commercial channels of illicit devices.

[8.64]
Article 6
Implementation

1. Member States shall bring into force the laws, regulations and administrative provisions necessary to comply with this Directive by 28 May 2000. They shall notify them to the Commission forthwith.

When Member States adopt such measures, they shall contain a reference to this Directive or shall be accompanied by such reference at the time of their official publication. The methods of making such reference shall be laid down by Member States.

2. Member States shall communicate to the Commission the text of the provisions of national law which they adopt in the field coordinated by this Directive.

[8.65]
Article 7
Reports

Not later than three years after the entry into force of this Directive, and every two years thereafter, the Commission shall present a report to the European Parliament, the Council and the Economic and Social Committee concerning the implementation of this Directive accompanied, where appropriate, by proposals, in particular as regards the definitions under Article 2, for adapting it in light of technical and economic developments and of the consultations carried out by the Commission.

[8.66]
Article 8
Entry into force
This Directive shall enter into force on the day of its publication in the Official Journal of the European Communities.

[8.67]
Article 9
Addressees
This Directive is addressed to the Member States.

DIRECTIVE OF THE EUROPEAN PARLIAMENT AND OF THE COUNCIL

(2001/29/EC)

of 22 May 2001

on the harmonisation of certain aspects of copyright and related rights in the information society ('InfoSoc Directive')

NOTES

Date of publication in OJ: OJ L167, 22.6.2001, p 10.
This Directive is reproduced as corrected by the corrigendum published in OJ L6, 10.1.2002, p 70.

THE EUROPEAN PARLIAMENT AND THE COUNCIL OF THE EUROPEAN UNION,

Having regard to the Treaty establishing the European Community, and in particular Articles 47(2), 55 and 95 thereof,

Having regard to the proposal from the Commission,[1]

Having regard to the opinion of the Economic and Social Committee,[2]

Acting in accordance with the procedure laid down in Article 251 of the Treaty,[3]

Whereas—

(1) The Treaty provides for the establishment of an internal market and the institution of a system ensuring that competition in the internal market is not distorted. Harmonisation of the laws of the Member States on copyright and related rights contributes to the achievement of these objectives.

(2) The European Council, meeting at Corfu on 24 and 25 June 1994, stressed the need to create a general and flexible legal framework at Community level in order to foster the development of the information society in Europe. This requires, *inter alia*, the existence of an internal market for new products and services. Important Community legislation to ensure such a regulatory framework is already in place or its adoption is well under way. Copyright and related rights play an important role in this context as they protect and stimulate the development and marketing of new products and services and the creation and exploitation of their creative content.

(3) The proposed harmonisation will help to implement the four freedoms of the internal market and relates to compliance with the fundamental principles of law and especially of property, including intellectual property, and freedom of expression and the public interest.

(4) A harmonised legal framework on copyright and related rights, through increased legal certainty and while providing for a high level of protection of intellectual property, will foster substantial investment in creativity and innovation, including network infrastructure, and lead in turn to growth and increased competitiveness of European industry, both in the area of content provision and information technology and more generally across a wide range of industrial and cultural sectors. This will safeguard employment and encourage new job creation.

(5) Technological development has multiplied and diversified the vectors for creation, production and exploitation. While no new concepts for the protection of intellectual property are needed, the current law on copyright and related rights should be adapted and supplemented to respond adequately to economic realities such as new forms of exploitation.

(6) Without harmonisation at Community level, legislative activities at national level which have already been initiated in a number of Member States in order to respond to the technological challenges might result in significant differences in protection and thereby in restrictions on the free movement of services and products incorporating, or based on, intellectual property, leading to a refragmentation of the internal market and legislative inconsistency. The impact of such legislative differences and uncertainties will become more significant with the further development of the information society, which has already greatly increased transborder exploitation of intellectual property. This development will and should further increase. Significant legal differences and uncertainties in protection may hinder economies of scale for new products and services containing copyright and related rights.

(7) The Community legal framework for the protection of copyright and related rights must, therefore, also be adapted and supplemented as far as is necessary for the smooth functioning of the internal market. To that end, those national provisions on copyright and related rights which vary considerably from one Member State to another or which cause legal uncertainties hindering the smooth functioning of the internal market and the proper development of the information society in Europe should be adjusted, and inconsistent national responses to the technological developments should be avoided, whilst differences not adversely affecting the functioning of the internal market need not be removed or prevented.

(8) The various social, societal and cultural implications of the information society require that account be taken of the specific features of the content of products and services.

(9) Any harmonisation of copyright and related rights must take as a basis a high level of protection, since such rights are crucial to intellectual creation. Their protection helps to ensure the maintenance and development of creativity in the interests of authors, performers, producers, consumers, culture, industry and the public at large. Intellectual property has therefore been recognised as an integral part of property.

(10) If authors or performers are to continue their creative and artistic work, they have to receive an appropriate reward for the use of their work, as must producers in order to be able to finance this work. The investment required to produce products such as phonograms, films or multimedia products, and services such as "on-demand" services, is considerable. Adequate legal protection of intellectual property rights is necessary in order to guarantee the availability of such a reward and provide the opportunity for satisfactory returns on this investment.

(11) A rigorous, effective system for the protection of copyright and related rights is one of the main ways of ensuring that European cultural creativity and production receive the necessary resources and of safeguarding the independence and dignity of artistic creators and performers.

(12) Adequate protection of copyright works and subject-matter of related rights is also of great importance from a cultural standpoint. Article 151 of the Treaty requires the Community to take cultural aspects into account in its action.

(13) A common search for, and consistent application at European level of, technical measures to protect works and other subject-matter and to provide the necessary information on rights are essential insofar as the ultimate aim of these measures is to give effect to the principles and guarantees laid down in law.

(14) This Directive should seek to promote learning and culture by protecting works and other subject-matter while permitting exceptions or limitations in the public interest for the purpose of education and teaching.

(15) The Diplomatic Conference held under the auspices of the World Intellectual Property Organisation (WIPO) in December 1996 led to the adoption of two new Treaties, the 'WIPO Copyright Treaty' and the 'WIPO Performances and Phonograms Treaty', dealing respectively with the protection of authors and the protection of performers and phonogram producers. Those Treaties update the international protection for copyright and related rights significantly, not least with regard to the so-called 'digital agenda', and improve the means to fight piracy world-wide. The Community and a majority of Member States have already signed the Treaties and the process of making arrangements for the ratification of the Treaties by the Community and the Member States is under way. This Directive also serves to implement a number of the new international obligations.

(16) Liability for activities in the network environment concerns not only copyright and related rights but also other areas, such as defamation, misleading advertising, or infringement of trademarks, and is addressed horizontally in Directive 2000/31/EC of the European Parliament and of the Council of 8 June 2000 on certain legal aspects of information society services, in particular electronic commerce, in the internal market ('Directive on electronic commerce'),[4] which clarifies and harmonises various legal issues relating to information society services including electronic commerce. This Directive should be implemented within a timescale similar to that for the implementation of the Directive on electronic commerce, since that Directive provides a harmonised framework of principles and provisions relevant *inter alia* to important parts of this Directive. This Directive is without prejudice to provisions relating to liability in that Directive.

(17) It is necessary, especially in the light of the requirements arising out of the digital environment, to ensure that collecting societies achieve a higher level of rationalisation and transparency with regard to compliance with competition rules.

(18) This Directive is without prejudice to the arrangements in the Member States concerning the management of rights such as extended collective licences.

(19) The moral rights of rightholders should be exercised according to the legislation of the Member States and the provisions of the Berne Convention for the Protection of Literary and Artistic Works, of the WIPO Copyright Treaty and of the WIPO Performances and Phonograms Treaty. Such moral rights remain outside the scope of this Directive.

(20) This Directive is based on principles and rules already laid down in the Directives currently in force in this area, in particular Directives 91/250/EEC,[5] 92/100/EEC,[6] 93/83/EEC,[7] 93/98/EEC[8]

and 96/9/EC,[9] and it develops those principles and rules and places them in the context of the information society. The provisions of this Directive should be without prejudice to the provisions of those Directives, unless otherwise provided in this Directive.

(21) This Directive should define the scope of the acts covered by the reproduction right with regard to the different beneficiaries. This should be done in conformity with the acquis communautaire. A broad definition of these acts is needed to ensure legal certainty within the internal market.

(22) The objective of proper support for the dissemination of culture must not be achieved by sacrificing strict protection of rights or by tolerating illegal forms of distribution of counterfeited or pirated works.

(23) This Directive should harmonise further the author's right of communication to the public. This right should be understood in a broad sense covering all communication to the public not present at the place where the communication originates. This right should cover any such transmission or retransmission of a work to the public by wire or wireless means, including broadcasting. This right should not cover any other acts.

(24) The right to make available to the public subject-matter referred to in Article 3(2) should be understood as covering all acts of making available such subject-matter to members of the public not present at the place where the act of making available originates, and as not covering any other acts.

(25) The legal uncertainty regarding the nature and the level of protection of acts of on-demand transmission of copyright works and subject-matter protected by related rights over networks should be overcome by providing for harmonised protection at Community level. It should be made clear that all rightholders recognised by this Directive should have an exclusive right to make available to the public copyright works or any other subject-matter by way of interactive on-demand transmissions. Such interactive on-demand transmissions are characterised by the fact that members of the public may access them from a place and at a time individually chosen by them.

(26) With regard to the making available in on-demand services by broadcasters of their radio or television productions incorporating music from commercial phonograms as an integral part thereof, collective licensing arrangements are to be encouraged in order to facilitate the clearance of the rights concerned.

(27) The mere provision of physical facilities for enabling or making a communication does not in itself amount to communication within the meaning of this Directive.

(28) Copyright protection under this Directive includes the exclusive right to control distribution of the work incorporated in a tangible article. The first sale in the Community of the original of a work or copies thereof by the rightholder or with his consent exhausts the right to control resale of that object in the Community. This right should not be exhausted in respect of the original or of copies thereof sold by the rightholder or with his consent outside the Community. Rental and lending rights for authors have been established in Directive 92/100/EEC. The distribution right provided for in this Directive is without prejudice to the provisions relating to the rental and lending rights contained in Chapter I of that Directive.

(29) The question of exhaustion does not arise in the case of services and on-line services in particular. This also applies with regard to a material copy of a work or other subject-matter made by a user of such a service with the consent of the rightholder. Therefore, the same applies to rental and lending of the original and copies of works or other subject-matter which are services by nature. Unlike CD-ROM or CD-I, where the intellectual property is incorporated in a material medium, namely an item of goods, every on-line service is in fact an act which should be subject to authorisation where the copyright or related right so provides.

(30) The rights referred to in this Directive may be transferred, assigned or subject to the granting of contractual licences, without prejudice to the relevant national legislation on copyright and related rights.

(31) A fair balance of rights and interests between the different categories of rightholders, as well as between the different categories of rightholders and users of protected subject-matter must be safeguarded. The existing exceptions and limitations to the rights as set out by the Member States have to be reassessed in the light of the new electronic environment. Existing differences in the exceptions and limitations to certain restricted acts have direct negative effects on the functioning of the internal market of copyright and related rights. Such differences could well become more pronounced in view of the further development of transborder exploitation of works and cross-border activities. In order to ensure the proper functioning of the internal market, such exceptions and limitations should be defined more harmoniously. The degree of their harmonisation should be based on their impact on the smooth functioning of the internal market.

(32) This Directive provides for an exhaustive enumeration of exceptions and limitations to the reproduction right and the right of communication to the public. Some exceptions or limitations only apply to the reproduction right, where appropriate. This list takes due account of the different legal traditions in Member States, while, at the same time, aiming to ensure a functioning internal market. Member States should arrive at a coherent application of these exceptions and limitations, which will be assessed when reviewing implementing legislation in the future.

(33) The exclusive right of reproduction should be subject to an exception to allow certain acts of temporary reproduction, which are transient or incidental reproductions, forming an integral and essential part of a technological process and carried out for the sole purpose of enabling either efficient transmission in a network between third parties by an intermediary, or a lawful use of a work or other subject-matter to be made. The acts of reproduction concerned should have no separate economic value on their own. To the extent that they meet these conditions, this exception should include acts which enable browsing as well as acts of caching to take place, including those which enable transmission systems to function efficiently, provided that the intermediary does not modify the information and does not interfere with the lawful use of technology, widely recognised and used by industry, to obtain data on the use of the information. A use should be considered lawful where it is authorised by the rightholder or not restricted by law.

(34) Member States should be given the option of providing for certain exceptions or limitations for cases such as educational and scientific purposes, for the benefit of public institutions such as libraries and archives, for purposes of news reporting, for quotations, for use by people with disabilities, for public security uses and for uses in administrative and judicial proceedings.

(35) In certain cases of exceptions or limitations, rightholders should receive fair compensation to compensate them adequately for the use made of their protected works or other subject-matter. When determining the form, detailed arrangements and possible level of such fair compensation, account should be taken of the particular circumstances of each case. When evaluating these circumstances, a valuable criterion would be the possible harm to the rightholders resulting from the act in question. In cases where rightholders have already received payment in some other form, for instance as part of a licence fee, no specific or separate payment may be due. The level of fair compensation should take full account of the degree of use of technological protection measures referred to in this Directive. In certain situations where the prejudice to the rightholder would be minimal, no obligation for payment may arise.

(36) The Member States may provide for fair compensation for rightholders also when applying the optional provisions on exceptions or limitations which do not require such compensation.

(37) Existing national schemes on reprography, where they exist, do not create major barriers to the internal market. Member States should be allowed to provide for an exception or limitation in respect of reprography.

(38) Member States should be allowed to provide for an exception or limitation to the reproduction right for certain types of reproduction of audio, visual and audiovisual material for private use, accompanied by fair compensation. This may include the introduction or continuation of remuneration schemes to compensate for the prejudice to rightholders. Although differences between those remuneration schemes affect the functioning of the internal market, those differences, with respect to analogue private reproduction, should not have a significant impact on the development of the information society. Digital private copying is likely to be more widespread and have a greater economic impact. Due account should therefore be taken of the differences between digital and analogue private copying and a distinction should be made in certain respects between them.

(39) When applying the exception or limitation on private copying, Member States should take due account of technological and economic developments, in particular with respect to digital private copying and remuneration schemes, when effective technological protection measures are available. Such exceptions or limitations should not inhibit the use of technological measures or their enforcement against circumvention.

(40) Member States may provide for an exception or limitation for the benefit of certain non-profit making establishments, such as publicly accessible libraries and equivalent institutions, as well as archives. However, this should be limited to certain special cases covered by the reproduction right. Such an exception or limitation should not cover uses made in the context of on-line delivery of protected works or other subject-matter. This Directive should be without prejudice to the Member States' option to derogate from the exclusive public lending right in accordance with Article 5 of Directive 92/100/EEC. Therefore, specific contracts or licences should be promoted which, without creating imbalances, favour such establishments and the disseminative purposes they serve.

(41) When applying the exception or limitation in respect of ephemeral recordings made by broadcasting organisations it is understood that a broadcaster's own facilities include those of a person acting on behalf of and under the responsibility of the broadcasting organisation.

(42) When applying the exception or limitation for non-commercial educational and scientific research purposes, including distance learning, the non-commercial nature of the activity in question should be determined by that activity as such. The organisational structure and the means of funding of the establishment concerned are not the decisive factors in this respect.

(43) It is in any case important for the Member States to adopt all necessary measures to facilitate access to works by persons suffering from a disability which constitutes an obstacle to the use of the works themselves, and to pay particular attention to accessible formats.

(44) When applying the exceptions and limitations provided for in this Directive, they should be

exercised in accordance with international obligations. Such exceptions and limitations may not be applied in a way which prejudices the legitimate interests of the rightholder or which conflicts with the normal exploitation of his work or other subject-matter. The provision of such exceptions or limitations by Member States should, in particular, duly reflect the increased economic impact that such exceptions or limitations may have in the context of the new electronic environment. Therefore, the scope of certain exceptions or limitations may have to be even more limited when it comes to certain new uses of copyright works and other subject-matter.

(45) The exceptions and limitations referred to in Article 5(2), (3) and (4) should not, however, prevent the definition of contractual relations designed to ensure fair compensation for the rightholders insofar as permitted by national law.

(46) Recourse to mediation could help users and rightholders to settle disputes. The Commission, in cooperation with the Member States within the Contact Committee, should undertake a study to consider new legal ways of settling disputes concerning copyright and related rights.

(47) Technological development will allow rightholders to make use of technological measures designed to prevent or restrict acts not authorised by the rightholders of any copyright, rights related to copyright or the *sui generis* right in databases. The danger, however, exists that illegal activities might be carried out in order to enable or facilitate the circumvention of the technical protection provided by these measures. In order to avoid fragmented legal approaches that could potentially hinder the functioning of the internal market, there is a need to provide for harmonised legal protection against circumvention of effective technological measures and against provision of devices and products or services to this effect.

(48) Such legal protection should be provided in respect of technological measures that effectively restrict acts not authorised by the rightholders of any copyright, rights related to copyright or the *sui generis* right in databases without, however, preventing the normal operation of electronic equipment and its technological development. Such legal protection implies no obligation to design devices, products, components or services to correspond to technological measures, so long as such device, product, component or service does not otherwise fall under the prohibition of Article 6. Such legal protection should respect proportionality and should not prohibit those devices or activities which have a commercially significant purpose or use other than to circumvent the technical protection. In particular, this protection should not hinder research into cryptography.

(49) The legal protection of technological measures is without prejudice to the application of any national provisions which may prohibit the private possession of devices, products or components for the circumvention of technological measures.

(50) Such a harmonised legal protection does not affect the specific provisions on protection provided for by Directive 91/250/EEC. In particular, it should not apply to the protection of technological measures used in connection with computer programs, which is exclusively addressed in that Directive. It should neither inhibit nor prevent the development or use of any means of circumventing a technological measure that is necessary to enable acts to be undertaken in accordance with the terms of Article 5(3) or Article 6 of Directive 91/250/EEC. Articles 5 and 6 of that Directive exclusively determine exceptions to the exclusive rights applicable to computer programs.

(51) The legal protection of technological measures applies without prejudice to public policy, as reflected in Article 5, or public security. Member States should promote voluntary measures taken by rightholders, including the conclusion and implementation of agreements between rightholders and other parties concerned, to accommodate achieving the objectives of certain exceptions or limitations provided for in national law in accordance with this Directive. In the absence of such voluntary measures or agreements within a reasonable period of time, Member States should take appropriate measures to ensure that rightholders provide beneficiaries of such exceptions or limitations with appropriate means of benefiting from them, by modifying an implemented technological measure or by other means. However, in order to prevent abuse of such measures taken by right-holders, including within the framework of agreements, or taken by a Member State, any technological measures applied in implementation of such measures should enjoy legal protection.

(52) When implementing an exception or limitation for private copying in accordance with Article 5(2)(b), Member States should likewise promote the use of voluntary measures to accommodate achieving the objectives of such exception or limitation. If, within a reasonable period of time, no such voluntary measures to make reproduction for private use possible have been taken, Member States may take measures to enable beneficiaries of the exception or limitation concerned to benefit from it. Voluntary measures taken by right-holders, including agreements between rightholders and other parties concerned, as well as measures taken by Member States, do not prevent rightholders from using technological measures which are consistent with the exceptions or limitations on private copying in national law in accordance with Article 5(2)(b), taking account of the condition of fair compensation under that provision and the possible differentiation between various conditions of use in accordance with Article 5(5), such as controlling the number of reproductions. In order to prevent abuse of such measures, any technological measures applied in their implementation should enjoy legal protection.

(53) The protection of technological measures should ensure a secure environment for the

provision of interactive on-demand services, in such a way that members of the public may access works or other subject-matter from a place and at a time individually chosen by them. Where such services are governed by contractual arrangements, the first and second subparagraphs of Article 6(4) should not apply. Non-interactive forms of online use should remain subject to those provisions.

(54) Important progress has been made in the international standardisation of technical systems of identification of works and protected subject-matter in digital format. In an increasingly networked environment, differences between technological measures could lead to an incompatibility of systems within the Community. Compatibility and interoperability of the different systems should be encouraged. It would be highly desirable to encourage the development of global systems.

(55) Technological development will facilitate the distribution of works, notably on networks, and this will entail the need for rightholders to identify better the work or other subject-matter, the author or any other rightholder, and to provide information about the terms and conditions of use of the work or other subject-matter in order to render easier the management of rights attached to them. Rightholders should be encouraged to use markings indicating, in addition to the information referred to above, *inter alia* their authorisation when putting works or other subject-matter on networks.

(56) There is, however, the danger that illegal activities might be carried out in order to remove or alter the electronic copyright-management information attached to it, or otherwise to distribute, import for distribution, broadcast, communicate to the public or make available to the public works or other protected subject-matter from which such information has been removed without authority. In order to avoid fragmented legal approaches that could potentially hinder the functioning of the internal market, there is a need to provide for harmonised legal protection against any of these activities.

(57) Any such rights-management information systems referred to above may, depending on their design, at the same time process personal data about the consumption patterns of protected subject matter by individuals and allow for tracing of on-line behaviour. These technical means, in their technical functions, should incorporate privacy safeguards in accordance with Directive 95/46/EC of the European Parliament and of the Council of 24 October 1995 on the protection of individuals with regard to the processing of personal data and the free movement of such data.[10]

(58) Member States should provide for effective sanctions and remedies for infringements of rights and obligations as set out in this Directive. They should take all the measures necessary to ensure that those sanctions and remedies are applied. The sanctions thus provided for should be effective, proportionate and dissuasive and should include the possibility of seeking damages and/or injunctive relief and, where appropriate, of applying for seizure of infringing material.

(59) In the digital environment, in particular, the services of intermediaries may increasingly be used by third parties for infringing activities. In many cases such intermediaries are best placed to bring such infringing activities to an end. Therefore, without prejudice to any other sanctions and remedies available, rightholders should have the possibility of applying for an injunction against an intermediary who carries a third party's infringement of a protected work or other subject-matter in a network. This possibility should be available even where the acts carried out by the intermediary are exempted under Article 5. The conditions and modalities relating to such injunctions should be left to the national law of the Member States.

(60) The protection provided under this Directive should be without prejudice to national or Community legal provisions in other areas, such as industrial property, data protection, conditional access, access to public documents, and the rule of media exploitation chronology, which may affect the protection of copyright or related rights.

(61) In order to comply with the WIPO Performances and Phonograms Treaty, Directives 92/100/EEC and 93/ 98/EEC should be amended,

NOTES

1 OJ C108, 7.4.98, p 6 and OJ C180, 25.6.99, p 6.

2 OJ C407, 28.12.98, p 30.

3 Opinion of the European Parliament of 10 February 1999 (OJ C150, 28.5.99, p 171), Council Common Position of 28 September 2000 (OJ C344, 1.12.2000, p 1) and Decision of the European Parliament of 14 February 2001 (not yet published in the Official Journal). Council Decision of 9 April 2001.

4 OJ L178, 17.7.2000, p 1.

5 Council Directive 91/250/EEC of 14 May 1991 on the legal protection of computer programs (OJ L122, 17.5.1991, p 42). Directive as amended by Directive 93/98/EEC.

6 Council Directive 92/100/EEC of 19 November 1992 on rental right and lending right and on certain rights related to copyright in the field of intellectual property (OJ L346, 27.11.92, p 61). Directive as amended by Directive 93/98/EEC.

7 Council Directive 93/83/EEC of 27 September 1993 on the coordination of certain rules concerning copyright and rights related to copyright applicable to satellite broadcasting and cable retransmission (OJ L248, 6.10.93, p 15).

8 Council Directive 93/98/EEC of 29 October 1993 harmonising the term of protection of copyright and certain related rights (OJ L290, 24.11.93, p 9).

[9] Directive 96/9/EC of the European Parliament and of the Council of 11 March 1996 on the legal protection of databases (OJ L77, 27.3.1996, p 20).

[10] OJ L281, 23.11.95, p 31.

HAVE ADOPTED THIS DIRECTIVE—

CHAPTER I
OBJECTIVE AND SCOPE

[8.68]
Article 1
Scope

1. This Directive concerns the legal protection of copyright and related rights in the framework of the internal market, with particular emphasis on the information society.

2. Except in the cases referred to in Article 11, this Directive shall leave intact and shall in no way affect existing Community provisions relating to—

(a) the legal protection of computer programs;

(b) rental right, lending right and certain rights related to copyright in the field of intellectual property;

(c) copyright and related rights applicable to broadcasting of programmes by satellite and cable retransmission;

(d) the term of protection of copyright and certain related rights;

(e) the legal protection of databases.

CHAPTER II
RIGHTS AND EXCEPTIONS

[8.69]
Article 2
Reproduction right

Member States shall provide for the exclusive right to authorise or prohibit direct or indirect, temporary or permanent reproduction by any means and in any form, in whole or in part—

(a) for authors, of their works;

(b) for performers, of fixations of their performances;

(c) for phonogram producers, of their phonograms;

(d) for the producers of the first fixations of films, in respect of the original and copies of their films;

(e) for broadcasting organisations, of fixations of their broadcasts, whether those broadcasts are transmitted by wire or over the air, including by cable or satellite.

[8.70]
Article 3
Right of communication to the public of works and right of making available to the public other subject-matter

1. Member States shall provide authors with the exclusive right to authorise or prohibit any communication to the public of their works, by wire or wireless means, including the making available to the public of their works in such a way that members of the public may access them from a place and at a time individually chosen by them.

2. Member States shall provide for the exclusive right to authorise or prohibit the making available to the public, by wire or wireless means, in such a way that members of the public may access them from a place and at a time individually chosen by them—

(a) for performers, of fixations of their performances;

(b) for phonogram producers, of their phonograms;

(c) for the producers of the first fixations of films, of the original and copies of their films;

(d) for broadcasting organisations, of fixations of their broadcasts, whether these broadcasts are transmitted by wire or over the air, including by cable or satellite.

3. The rights referred to in paragraphs 1 and 2 shall not be exhausted by any act of communication to the public or making available to the public as set out in this Article.

[8.71]
Article 4
Distribution right

1. Member States shall provide for authors, in respect of the original of their works or of copies thereof, the exclusive right to authorise or prohibit any form of distribution to the public by sale or otherwise.

2. The distribution right shall not be exhausted within the Community in respect of the original or copies of the work, except where the first sale or other transfer of ownership in the Community of that object is made by the rightholder or with his consent.

[8.72]
Article 5
Exceptions and limitations

1. Temporary acts of reproduction referred to in Article 2, which are transient or incidental, which are an integral and essential part of a technological process and the sole purpose of which is to enable—

(a) a transmission in a network between third parties by an intermediary, or
(b) a lawful use

of a work or other subject-matter to be made, and which have no independent economic significance, shall be exempted from the reproduction right provided for in Article 2.

2. Member States may provide for exceptions or limitations to the reproduction right provided for in Article 2 in the following cases—

(a) in respect of reproductions on paper or any similar medium, effected by the use of any kind of photographic technique or by some other process having similar effects, with the exception of sheet music, provided that the right-holders receive fair compensation;
(b) in respect of reproductions on any medium made by a natural person for private use and for ends that are neither directly nor indirectly commercial, on condition that the rightholders receive fair compensation which takes account of the application or non-application of technological measures referred to in Article 6 to the work or subject-matter concerned;
(c) in respect of specific acts of reproduction made by publicly accessible libraries, educational establishments or museums, or by archives, which are not for direct or indirect economic or commercial advantage;
(d) in respect of ephemeral recordings of works made by broadcasting organisations by means of their own facilities and for their own broadcasts; the preservation of these recordings in official archives may, on the grounds of their exceptional documentary character, be permitted;
(e) in respect of reproductions of broadcasts made by social institutions pursuing non-commercial purposes, such as hospitals or prisons, on condition that the rightholders receive fair compensation.

3. Member States may provide for exceptions or limitations to the rights provided for in Articles 2 and 3 in the following cases—

(a) use for the sole purpose of illustration for teaching or scientific research, as long as the source, including the author's name, is indicated, unless this turns out to be impossible and to the extent justified by the non-commercial purpose to be achieved;
(b) uses, for the benefit of people with a disability, which are directly related to the disability and of a non-commercial nature, to the extent required by the specific disability;
(c) reproduction by the press, communication to the public or making available of published articles on current economic, political or religious topics or of broadcast works or other subject-matter of the same character, in cases where such use is not expressly reserved, and as long as the source, including the author's name, is indicated, or use of works or other subject-matter in connection with the reporting of current events, to the extent justified by the informatory purpose and as long as the source, including the author's name, is indicated, unless this turns out to be impossible;
(d) quotations for purposes such as criticism or review, provided that they relate to a work or other subject-matter which has already been lawfully made available to the public, that, unless this turns out to be impossible, the source, including the author's name, is indicated, and that their use is in accordance with fair practice, and to the extent required by the specific purpose;
(e) use for the purposes of public security or to ensure the proper performance or reporting of administrative, parliamentary or judicial proceedings;
(f) use of political speeches as well as extracts of public lectures or similar works or subject-matter to the extent justified by the informatory purpose and provided that the source, including the author's name, is indicated, except where this turns out to be impossible;
(g) use during religious celebrations or official celebrations organised by a public authority;
(h) use of works, such as works of architecture or sculpture, made to be located permanently in public places;
(i) incidental inclusion of a work or other subject-matter in other material;
(j) use for the purpose of advertising the public exhibition or sale of artistic works, to the extent necessary to promote the event, excluding any other commercial use;
(k) use for the purpose of caricature, parody or pastiche;
(l) use in connection with the demonstration or repair of equipment;
(m) use of an artistic work in the form of a building or a drawing or plan of a building for the purposes of reconstructing the building;
(n) use by communication or making available, for the purpose of research or private study, to individual members of the public by dedicated terminals on the premises of establishments referred to in paragraph 2(c) of works and other subject-matter not subject to purchase or licensing terms which are contained in their collections;

(o) use in certain other cases of minor importance where exceptions or limitations already exist under national law, provided that they only concern analogue uses and do not affect the free circulation of goods and services within the Community, without prejudice to the other exceptions and limitations contained in this Article.

4. Where the Member States may provide for an exception or limitation to the right of reproduction pursuant to paragraphs 2 and 3, they may provide similarly for an exception or limitation to the right of distribution as referred to in Article 4 to the extent justified by the purpose of the authorised act of reproduction.

5. The exceptions and limitations provided for in paragraphs 1, 2, 3 and 4 shall only be applied in certain special cases which do not conflict with a normal exploitation of the work or other subject-matter and do not unreasonably prejudice the legitimate interests of the rightholder.

CHAPTER III
PROTECTION OF TECHNOLOGICAL MEASURES AND RIGHTS-MANAGEMENT INFORMATION

[8.73]
Article 6
Obligations as to technological measures

1. Member States shall provide adequate legal protection against the circumvention of any effective technological measures, which the person concerned carries out in the knowledge, or with reasonable grounds to know, that he or she is pursuing that objective.

2. Member States shall provide adequate legal protection against the manufacture, import, distribution, sale, rental, advertisement for sale or rental, or possession for commercial purposes of devices, products or components or the provision of services which—

(a) are promoted, advertised or marketed for the purpose of circumvention of, or

(b) have only a limited commercially significant purpose or use other than to circumvent, or

(c) are primarily designed, produced, adapted or performed for the purpose of enabling or facilitating the circumvention of,

any effective technological measures.

3. For the purposes of this Directive, the expression "technological measures" means any technology, device or component that, in the normal course of its operation, is designed to prevent or restrict acts, in respect of works or other subject-matter, which are not authorised by the rightholder of any copyright or any right related to copyright as provided for by law or the *sui generis* right provided for in Chapter III of Directive 96/9/EC. Technological measures shall be deemed "effective" where the use of a protected work or other subject-matter is controlled by the rightholders through application of an access control or protection process, such as encryption, scrambling or other transformation of the work or other subject-matter or a copy control mechanism, which achieves the protection objective.

4. Notwithstanding the legal protection provided for in paragraph 1, in the absence of voluntary measures taken by rightholders, including agreements between rightholders and other parties concerned, Member States shall take appropriate measures to ensure that rightholders make available to the beneficiary of an exception or limitation provided for in national law in accordance with Article 5(2)(a), (2)(c), (2)(d), (2)(e), (3)(a), (3)(b) or (3)(e) the means of benefiting from that exception or limitation, to the extent necessary to benefit from that exception or limitation and where that beneficiary has legal access to the protected work or subject-matter concerned.

A Member State may also take such measures in respect of a beneficiary of an exception or limitation provided for in accordance with Article 5(2)(b), unless reproduction for private use has already been made possible by rightholders to the extent necessary to benefit from the exception or limitation concerned and in accordance with the provisions of Article 5(2)(b) and (5), without preventing rightholders from adopting adequate measures regarding the number of reproductions in accordance with these provisions.

The technological measures applied voluntarily by rightholders, including those applied in implementation of voluntary agreements, and technological measures applied in implementation of the measures taken by Member States, shall enjoy the legal protection provided for in paragraph 1.

The provisions of the first and second subparagraphs shall not apply to works or other subject-matter made available to the public on agreed contractual terms in such a way that members of the public may access them from a place and at a time individually chosen by them.

When this Article is applied in the context of Directives 92/100/EEC and 96/9/EC, this paragraph shall apply *mutatis mutandis*.

[8.74]
Article 7
Obligations concerning rights-management information

1. Member States shall provide for adequate legal protection against any person knowingly performing without authority any of the following acts—

(a) the removal or alteration of any electronic rights-management information;

(b) the distribution, importation for distribution, broadcasting, communication or making available to the public of works or other subject-matter protected under this Directive or under Chapter III of Directive 96/9/EC from which electronic rights-management information has been removed or altered without authority,

if such person knows, or has reasonable grounds to know, that by so doing he is inducing, enabling, facilitating or concealing an infringement of any copyright or any rights related to copyright as provided by law, or of the *sui generis* right provided for in Chapter III of Directive 96/9/EC.

2. For the purposes of this Directive, the expression "rights-management information" means any information provided by rightholders which identifies the work or other subject-matter referred to in this Directive or covered by the *sui generis* right provided for in Chapter III of Directive 96/9/EC, the author or any other rightholder, or information about the terms and conditions of use of the work or other subject-matter, and any numbers or codes that represent such information.

The first subparagraph shall apply when any of these items of information is associated with a copy of, or appears in connection with the communication to the public of, a work or other subject-matter referred to in this Directive or covered by the *sui generis* right provided for in Chapter III of Directive 96/9/EC.

CHAPTER IV
COMMON PROVISIONS

[8.75]
Article 8
Sanctions and remedies

1. Member States shall provide appropriate sanctions and remedies in respect of infringements of the rights and obligations set out in this Directive and shall take all the measures necessary to ensure that those sanctions and remedies are applied. The sanctions thus provided for shall be effective, proportionate and dissuasive.

2. Each Member State shall take the measures necessary to ensure that rightholders whose interests are affected by an infringing activity carried out on its territory can bring an action for damages and/or apply for an injunction and, where appropriate, for the seizure of infringing material as well as of devices, products or components referred to in Article 6(2).

3. Member States shall ensure that rightholders are in a position to apply for an injunction against intermediaries whose services are used by a third party to infringe a copyright or related right.

[8.76]
Article 9
Continued application of other legal provisions

This Directive shall be without prejudice to provisions concerning in particular patent rights, trade marks, design rights, utility models, topographies of semiconductor products, type faces, conditional access, access to cable of broadcasting services, protection of national treasures, legal deposit requirements, laws on restrictive practices and unfair competition, trade secrets, security, confidentiality, data protection and privacy, access to public documents, the law of contract.

[8.77]
Article 10
Application over time

1. The provisions of this Directive shall apply in respect of all works and other subject-matter referred to in this Directive which are, on 22 December 2002, protected by the Member States' legislation in the field of copyright and related rights, or which meet the criteria for protection under the provisions of this Directive or the provisions referred to in Article 1(2).

2. This Directive shall apply without prejudice to any acts concluded and rights acquired before 22 December 2002.

Article 11 (*Repeals Directive 92/100/EEC, Art 7, and amends Art 10 of that Directive, and amends Directive 93/98/EEC, Art 3.*)

[8.78]
Article 12
Final provisions

1. Not later than 22 December 2004 and every three years thereafter, the Commission shall submit to the European Parliament, the Council and the Economic and Social Committee a report on the application of this Directive, in which, *inter alia*, on the basis of specific information supplied by the Member States, it shall examine in particular the application of Articles 5, 6 and 8 in the light of the development of the digital market. In the case of Article 6, it shall examine in particular whether that Article confers a sufficient level of protection and whether acts which are permitted by law are being adversely affected by the use of effective technological measures. Where necessary, in particular to ensure the functioning of the internal market pursuant to Article 14 of the Treaty, it shall submit proposals for amendments to this Directive.

2. Protection of rights related to copyright under this Directive shall leave intact and shall in no way affect the protection of copyright.

3. A contact committee is hereby established. It shall be composed of representatives of the competent authorities of the Member States. It shall be chaired by a representative of the Commission and shall meet either on the initiative of the chairman or at the request of the delegation of a Member State.
4. The tasks of the committee shall be as follows—
(a) to examine the impact of this Directive on the functioning of the internal market, and to highlight any difficulties;
(b) to organise consultations on all questions deriving from the application of this Directive;
(c) to facilitate the exchange of information on relevant developments in legislation and case-law, as well as relevant economic, social, cultural and technological developments;
(d) to act as a forum for the assessment of the digital market in works and other items, including private copying and the use of technological measures.

[8.79]
Article 13
Implementation
1. Member States shall bring into force the laws, regulations and administrative provisions necessary to comply with this Directive before 22 December 2002. They shall forthwith inform the Commission thereof.
When Member States adopt these measures, they shall contain a reference to this Directive or shall be accompanied by such reference on the occasion of their official publication. The methods of making such reference shall be laid down by Member States.
2. Member States shall communicate to the Commission the text of the provisions of domestic law which they adopt in the field governed by this Directive.

[8.80]
Article 14
Entry into force
This Directive shall enter into force on the day of its publication in the *Official Journal of the European Communities*.

[8.81]
Article 15
Addressees
This Directive is addressed to the Member States.

DIRECTIVE OF THE EUROPEAN PARLIAMENT AND OF THE COUNCIL

(2001/84/EC)

of 27 September 2001

on the resale right for the benefit of the author of an original work of art ('Resale Rights Directive')

NOTES
Date of publication in OJ: OJ L272, 13.10.2001, p 32.

THE EUROPEAN PARLIAMENT AND THE COUNCIL OF THE EUROPEAN UNION,
Having regard to the Treaty establishing the European Community, and in particular Article 95 thereof,
Having regard to the proposal from the Commission,[1]
Having regard to the opinion of the Economic and Social Committee,[2]
Acting in accordance with the procedure laid down in Article 251 of the Treaty,[3] and in the light of the joint text approved by the Conciliation Committee on 6 June 2001,
Whereas—

(1) In the field of copyright, the resale right is an unassignable and inalienable right, enjoyed by the author of an original work of graphic or plastic art, to an economic interest in successive sales of the work concerned.

(2) The resale right is a right of a productive character which enables the author/artist to receive consideration for successive transfers of the work. The subject-matter of the resale right is the physical work, namely the medium in which the protected work is incorporated.

(3) The resale right is intended to ensure that authors of graphic and plastic works of art share in the economic success of their original works of art. It helps to redress the balance between the economic situation of authors of graphic and plastic works of art and that of other creators who benefit from successive exploitations of their works.

(4) The resale right forms an integral part of copyright and is an essential prerogative for authors. The imposition of such a right in all Member States meets the need for providing creators with an adequate and standard level of protection.

(5) Under Article 151(4) of the Treaty the Community is to take cultural aspects into account in its action under other provisions of the Treaty.

(6) The Berne Convention for the Protection of Literary and Artistic Works provides that the resale right is available only if legislation in the country to which the author belongs so permits. The right is therefore optional and subject to the rule of reciprocity. It follows from the case-law of the Court of Justice of the European Communities on the application of the principle of non-discrimination laid down in Article 12 of the Treaty, as shown in the judgment of 20 October 1993 in Joined Cases C-92/92 and C-326/92 Phil Collins and Others,[4] that domestic provisions containing reciprocity clauses cannot be relied upon in order to deny nationals of other Member States rights conferred on national authors. The application of such clauses in the Community context runs counter to the principle of equal treatment resulting from the prohibition of any discrimination on grounds of nationality.

(7) The process of internationalisation of the Community market in modern and contemporary art, which is now being speeded up by the effects of the new economy, in a regulatory context in which few States outside the EU recognise the resale right, makes it essential for the European Community, in the external sphere, to open negotiations with a view to making Article 14b of the Berne Convention compulsory.

(8) The fact that this international market exists, combined with the lack of a resale right in several Member States and the current disparity as regards national systems which recognise that right, make it essential to lay down transitional provisions as regards both entry into force and the substantive regulation of the right, which will preserve the competitiveness of the European market.

(9) The resale right is currently provided for by the domestic legislation of a majority of Member States. Such laws, where they exist, display certain differences, notably as regards the works covered, those entitled to receive royalties, the rate applied, the transactions subject to payment of a royalty, and the basis on which these are calculated. The application or non-application of such a right has a significant impact on the competitive environment within the internal market, since the existence or absence of an obligation to pay on the basis of the resale right is an element which must be taken into account by each individual wishing to sell a work of art. This right is therefore a factor which contributes to the creation of distortions of competition as well as displacement of sales within the Community.

(10) Such disparities with regard to the existence of the resale right and its application by the Member States have a direct negative impact on the proper functioning of the internal market in works of art as provided for by Article 14 of the Treaty. In such a situation Article 95 of the Treaty constitutes the appropriate legal basis.

(11) The objectives of the Community as set out in the Treaty include laying the foundations of an ever closer union among the peoples of Europe, promoting closer relations between the Member States belonging to the Community, and ensuring their economic and social progress by common action to eliminate the barriers which divide Europe. To that end the Treaty provides for the establishment of an internal market which presupposes the abolition of obstacles to the free movement of goods, freedom to provide services and freedom of establishment, and for the introduction of a system ensuring that competition in the common market is not distorted. Harmonisation of Member States' laws on the resale right contributes to the attainment of these objectives.

(12) The Sixth Council Directive (77/388/EEC) of 17 May 1977 on the harmonisation of the laws of the Member States relating to turnover taxes – common system of value added tax: uniform basis of assessment,[5] progressively introduces a Community system of taxation applicable *inter alia* to works of art. Measures confined to the tax field are not sufficient to guarantee the harmonious functioning of the art market. This objective cannot be attained without harmonisation in the field of the resale right.

(13) Existing differences between laws should be eliminated where they have a distorting effect on the functioning of the internal market, and the emergence of any new differences of that kind should be prevented. There is no need to eliminate, or prevent the emergence of, differences which cannot be expected to affect the functioning of the internal market.

(14) A precondition of the proper functioning of the internal market is the existence of conditions of competition which are not distorted. The existence of differences between national provisions on the resale right creates distortions of competition and displacement of sales within the Community and leads to unequal treatment between artists depending on where their works are sold. The issue under consideration has therefore transnational aspects which cannot be satisfactorily regulated by action by Member States. A lack of Community action would conflict with the requirement of the Treaty to correct distortions of competition and unequal treatment.

(15) In view of the scale of divergences between national provisions it is therefore necessary to adopt harmonising measures to deal with disparities between the laws of the Member States in areas

where such disparities are liable to create or maintain distorted conditions of competition. It is not however necessary to harmonise every provision of the Member States' laws on the resale right and, in order to leave as much scope for national decision as possible, it is sufficient to limit the harmonisation exercise to those domestic provisions that have the most direct impact on the functioning of the internal market.

(16) This Directive complies therefore, in its entirety, with the principles of subsidiarity and proportionality as laid down in Article 5 of the Treaty.

(17) Pursuant to Council Directive 93/98/EEC of 29 October 1993 harmonising the term of protection of copyright and certain related rights,[6] the term of copyright runs for 70 years after the author's death. The same period should be laid down for the resale right. Consequently, only the originals of works of modern and contemporary art may fall within the scope of the resale right. However, in order to allow the legal systems of Member States which do not, at the time of the adoption of this Directive, apply a resale right for the benefit of artists to incorporate this right into their respective legal systems and, moreover, to enable the economic operators in those Member States to adapt gradually to the aforementioned right whilst maintaining their economic viability, the Member States concerned should be allowed a limited transitional period during which they may choose not to apply the resale right for the benefit of those entitled under the artist after his death.

(18) The scope of the resale right should be extended to all acts of resale, with the exception of those effected directly between persons acting in their private capacity without the participation of an art market professional. This right should not extend to acts of resale by persons acting in their private capacity to museums which are not for profit and which are open to the public. With regard to the particular situation of art galleries which acquire works directly from the author, Member States should be allowed the option of exempting from the resale right acts of resale of those works which take place within three years of that acquisition. The interests of the artist should also be taken into account by limiting this exemption to such acts of resale where the resale price does not exceed EUR 10,000.

(19) It should be made clear that the harmonisation brought about by this Directive does not apply to original manuscripts of writers and composers.

(20) Effective rules should be laid down based on experience already gained at national level with the resale right. It is appropriate to calculate the royalty as a percentage of the sale price and not of the increase in value of works whose original value has increased.

(21) The categories of works of art subject to the resale right should be harmonised.

(22) The non-application of royalties below the minimum threshold may help to avoid disproportionately high collection and administration costs compared with the profit for the artist. However, in accordance with the principle of subsidiarity, the Member States should be allowed to establish national thresholds lower than the Community threshold, so as to promote the interests of new artists. Given the small amounts involved, this derogation is not likely to have a significant effect on the proper functioning of the internal market.

(23) The rates set by the different Member States for the application of the resale right vary considerably at present. The effective functioning of the internal market in works of modern and contemporary art requires the fixing of uniform rates to the widest possible extent.

(24) It is desirable to establish, with the intention of reconciling the various interests involved in the market for original works of art, a system consisting of a tapering scale of rates for several price bands. It is important to reduce the risk of sales relocating and of the circumvention of the Community rules on the resale right.

(25) The person by whom the royalty is payable should, in principle, be the seller. Member States should be given the option to provide for derogations from this principle in respect of liability for payment. The seller is the person or undertaking on whose behalf the sale is concluded.

(26) Provision should be made for the possibility of periodic adjustment of the threshold and rates. To this end, it is appropriate to entrust to the Commission the task of drawing up periodic reports on the actual application of the resale right in the Member States and on the impact on the art market in the Community and, where appropriate, of making proposals relating to the amendment of this Directive.

(27) The persons entitled to receive royalties must be specified, due regard being had to the principle of subsidiarity. It is not appropriate to take action through this Directive in relation to Member States' laws of succession. However, those entitled under the author must be able to benefit fully from the resale right after his death, at least following the expiry of the transitional period referred to above.

(28) The Member States are responsible for regulating the exercise of the resale right, particularly with regard to the way this is managed. In this respect management by a collecting society is one possibility. Member States should ensure that collecting societies operate in a transparent and efficient manner. Member States must also ensure that amounts intended for authors who are nationals of other Member States are in fact collected and distributed. This Directive is without prejudice to arrangements in Member States for collection and distribution.

(29) Enjoyment of the resale right should be restricted to Community nationals as well as to foreign authors whose countries afford such protection to authors who are nationals of Member States. A Member State should have the option of extending enjoyment of this right to foreign authors who have their habitual residence in that Member State.

(30) Appropriate procedures for monitoring transactions should be introduced so as to ensure by practical means that the resale right is effectively applied by Member States. This implies also a right on the part of the author or his authorised representative to obtain any necessary information from the natural or legal person liable for payment of royalties. Member States which provide for collective management of the resale right may also provide that the bodies responsible for that collective management should alone be entitled to obtain information,

NOTES

1 OJ C178, 21.6.1996, p 16 and OJ C125, 23.4.1998, p 8.

2 OJ C75, 10.3.1997, p 17.

3 Opinion of the European Parliament of 9 April 1997 (OJ C132, 28.4.1997, p 88), confirmed on 27 October 1999, Council Common Position of 19 June 2000 (OJ C300, 20.10.2000, p 1) and Decision of the European Parliament of 13 December 2000 (OJ C232, 17.8.2001, p 173). Decision of the European Parliament of 3 July 2001 and Decision of the Council of 19 July 2001.

4 [1993] ECR I-5145.

5 OJ L145, 13.6.1977, p 1. Directive as last amended by Directive 1999/85/EC (OJ L277, 28.10.1999, p 34).

6 OJ L290, 24.11.1993, p 9.

HAVE ADOPTED THIS DIRECTIVE—

CHAPTER I
SCOPE

[8.82]
Article 1
Subject matter of the resale right

1. Member States shall provide, for the benefit of the author of an original work of art, a resale right, to be defined as an inalienable right, which cannot be waived, even in advance, to receive a royalty based on the sale price obtained for any resale of the work, subsequent to the first transfer of the work by the author.
2. The right referred to in paragraph 1 shall apply to all acts of resale involving as sellers, buyers or intermediaries art market professionals, such as salesrooms, art galleries and, in general, any dealers in works of art.
3. Member States may provide that the right referred to in paragraph 1 shall not apply to acts of resale where the seller has acquired the work directly from the author less than three years before that resale and where the resale price does not exceed EUR 10,000.
4. The royalty shall be payable by the seller. Member States may provide that one of the natural or legal persons referred to in paragraph 2 other than the seller shall alone be liable or shall share liability with the seller for payment of the royalty.

[8.83]
Article 2
Works of art to which the resale right relates

1. For the purposes of this Directive, 'original work of art' means works of graphic or plastic art such as pictures, collages, paintings, drawings, engravings, prints, lithographs, sculptures, tapestries, ceramics, glassware and photographs, provided they are made by the artist himself or are copies considered to be original works of art.
2. Copies of works of art covered by this Directive, which have been made in limited numbers by the artist himself or under his authority, shall be considered to be original works of art for the purposes of this Directive. Such copies will normally have been numbered, signed or otherwise duly authorised by the artist.

CHAPTER II
PARTICULAR PROVISIONS

[8.84]
Article 3
Threshold

1. It shall be for the Member States to set a minimum sale price from which the sales referred to in Article 1 shall be subject to resale right.
2. This minimum sale price may not under any circumstances exceed EUR 3,000.

[8.85]
Article 4
Rates

1. The royalty provided for in Article 1 shall be set at the following rates—
   (a) 4% for the portion of the sale price up to EUR 50,000;
   (b) 3% for the portion of the sale price from EUR 50,000.01 to EUR 200,000;
   (c) 1% for the portion of the sale price from EUR 200,000.01 to EUR 350,000;
   (d) 0.5% for the portion of the sale price from EUR 350,000.01 to EUR 500,000;
   (e) 0.25% for the portion of the sale price exceeding EUR 500,000.

   However, the total amount of the royalty may not exceed EUR 12,500.
2. By way of derogation from paragraph 1, Member States may apply a rate of 5% for the portion of the sale price referred to in paragraph 1(a).
3. If the minimum sale price set should be lower than EUR 3,000, the Member State shall also determine the rate applicable to the portion of the sale price up to EUR 3,000; this rate may not be lower than 4%.

[8.86]
Article 5
Calculation basis

The sale prices referred to in Articles 3 and 4 are net of tax.

[8.87]
Article 6
Persons entitled to receive royalties

1. The royalty provided for under Article 1 shall be payable to the author of the work and, subject to Article 8(2), after his death to those entitled under him/her.
2. Member States may provide for compulsory or optional collective management of the royalty provided for under Article 1.

[8.88]
Article 7
Third-country nationals entitled to receive royalties

1. Member States shall provide that authors who are nationals of third countries and, subject to Article 8(2), their successors in title shall enjoy the resale right in accordance with this Directive and the legislation of the Member State concerned only if legislation in the country of which the author or his/her successor in title is a national permits resale right protection in that country for authors from the Member States and their successors in title.
2. On the basis of information provided by the Member States, the Commission shall publish as soon as possible an indicative list of those third countries which fulfil the condition set out in paragraph 1. This list shall be kept up to date.
3. Any Member State may treat authors who are not nationals of a Member State but who have their habitual residence in that Member State in the same way as its own nationals for the purpose of resale right protection.

[8.89]
Article 8
Term of protection of the resale right

1. The term of protection of the resale right shall correspond to that laid down in Article 1 of Directive 93/98/EEC.
2. By way of derogation from paragraph 1, those Member States which do not apply the resale right on (the entry into force date referred to in Article 13), shall not be required, for a period expiring not later than 1 January 2010, to apply the resale right for the benefit of those entitled under the artist after his/her death.
3. A Member State to which paragraph 2 applies may have up to two more years, if necessary to enable the economic operators in that Member State to adapt gradually to the resale right system while maintaining their economic viability, before it is required to apply the resale right for the benefit of those entitled under the artist after his/her death. At least 12 months before the end of the period referred to in paragraph 2, the Member State concerned shall inform the Commission giving its reasons, so that the Commission can give an opinion, after appropriate consultations, within three months following the receipt of such information. If the Member State does not follow the opinion of the Commission, it shall within one month inform the Commission and justify its decision. The notification and justification of the Member State and the opinion of the Commission shall be published in the *Official Journal of the European Communities* and forwarded to the European Parliament.
4. In the event of the successful conclusion, within the periods referred to in Article 8(2) and (3), of international negotiations aimed at extending the resale right at international level, the Commission shall submit appropriate proposals.

[8.90]
Article 9
Right to obtain information
The Member States shall provide that for a period of three years after the resale, the persons entitled under Article 6 may require from any art market professional mentioned in Article 1(2) to furnish any information that may be necessary in order to secure payment of royalties in respect of the resale.

CHAPTER III
FINAL PROVISIONS

[8.91]
Article 10
Application in time
This Directive shall apply in respect of all original works of art as defined in Article 2 which, on 1 January 2006, are still protected by the legislation of the Member States in the field of copyright or meet the criteria for protection under the provisions of this Directive at that date.

[8.92]
Article 11
Revision clause
1. The Commission shall submit to the European Parliament, the Council and the Economic and Social Committee not later than 1 January 2009 and every four years thereafter a report on the implementation and the effect of this Directive, paying particular attention to the competitiveness of the market in modern and contemporary art in the Community, especially as regards the position of the Community in relation to relevant markets that do not apply the resale right and the fostering of artistic creativity and the management procedures in the Member States. It shall examine in particular its impact on the internal market and the effect of the introduction of the resale right in those Member States that did not apply the right in national law prior to the entry into force of this Directive. Where appropriate, the Commission shall submit proposals for adapting the minimum threshold and the rates of royalty to take account of changes in the sector, proposals relating to the maximum amount laid down in Article 4(1) and any other proposal it may deem necessary in order to enhance the effectiveness of this Directive.
2. A Contact Committee is hereby established. It shall be composed of representatives of the competent authorities of the Member States. It shall be chaired by a representative of the Commission and shall meet either on the initiative of the Chairman or at the request of the delegation of a Member State.
3. The task of the Committee shall be as follows—
— to organise consultations on all questions deriving from application of this Directive,
— to facilitate the exchange of information between the Commission and the Member States on relevant developments in the art market in the Community.

[8.93]
Article 12
Implementation
1. Member States shall bring into force the laws, regulations and administrative provisions necessary to comply with this Directive before 1 January 2006. They shall forthwith inform the Commission thereof.

When Member States adopt these measures, they shall contain a reference to this Directive or shall be accompanied by such reference on the occasion of their official publication. The methods of making such a reference shall be laid down by the Member States.
2. Member States shall communicate to the Commission the provisions of national law which they adopt in the field covered by this Directive.

[8.94]
Article 13
Entry into force
This Directive shall enter into force on the day of its publication in the *Official Journal of the European Communities*.

[8.95]
Article 14
Addressees
This Directive is addressed to the Member States.

COUNCIL DIRECTIVE

(2003/49/EC)

of 3 June 2003

on a common system of taxation applicable to interest and royalty payments made between associated companies of different Member States ('Interest and Royalties Directive')

NOTES

Date of publication in OJ: OJ L157, 26.6.2003, p 49.

THE COUNCIL OF THE EUROPEAN UNION,

Having regard to the Treaty establishing the European Community, and in particular Article 94 thereof,

Having regard to the proposal from the Commission,[1]

Having regard to the opinion of the European Parliament,[2]

Having regard to the opinion of the European Economic and Social Committee,[3]

Whereas—

(1) In a Single Market having the characteristics of a domestic market, transactions between companies of different Member States should not be subject to less favourable tax conditions than those applicable to the same transactions carried out between companies of the same Member State.

(2) This requirement is not currently met as regards interest and royalty payments; national tax laws coupled, where applicable, with bilateral or multilateral agreements may not always ensure that double taxation is eliminated, and their application often entails burdensome administrative formalities and cash-flow problems for the companies concerned.

(3) It is necessary to ensure that interest and royalty payments are subject to tax once in a Member State.

(4) The abolition of taxation on interest and royalty payments in the Member State where they arise, whether collected by deduction at source or by assessment, is the most appropriate means of eliminating the aforementioned formalities and problems and of ensuring the equality of tax treatment as between national and crossborder transactions; it is particularly necessary to abolish such taxes in respect of such payments made between associated companies of different Member States as well as between permanent establishments of such companies.

(5) The arrangements should only apply to the amount, if any, of interest or royalty payments which would have been agreed by the payer and the beneficial owner in the absence of a special relationship.

(6) It is moreover necessary not to preclude Member States from taking appropriate measures to combat fraud or abuse.

(7) Greece and Portugal should, for budgetary reasons, be allowed a transitional period in order that they can gradually decrease the taxes, whether collected by deduction at source or by assessment, on interest and royalty payments, until they are able to apply the provisions of Article 1.

(8) Spain, which has launched a plan for boosting the Spanish technological potential, for budgetary reasons should be allowed during a transitional period not to apply the provisions of Article 1 on royalty payments.

(9) It is necessary for the Commission to report to the Council on the operation of the Directive three years after the date by which it must be transposed, in particular with a view to extending its coverage to other companies or undertakings and reviewing the scope of the definition of interest and royalties in pursuance of the necessary convergence of the provisions dealing with interest and royalties in national legislation and in bilateral or multilateral double-taxation treaties.

(10) Since the objective of the proposed action, namely setting up a common system of taxation applicable to interest and royalty payments of associated companies of different Member States cannot be sufficiently achieved by the Member States and can therefore be better achieved at Community level, the Community may adopt measures, in accordance with the principle of subsidiarity as set out in Article 5 of the Treaty. In accordance with the principle of proportionality, as set out in that Article, this Directive does not go beyond what is necessary in order to achieve that objective,

NOTES

1 OJ C123, 22.4.1998, p 9.

2 OJ C313, 12.10.1998, p 151.

3 OJ C284, 14.9.1998, p 50.

HAS ADOPTED THIS DIRECTIVE—

Part 8 Other EU Materials

[8.96]

Article 1

Scope and procedure

1. Interest or royalty payments arising in a Member State shall be exempt from any taxes imposed on those payments in that State, whether by deduction at source or by assessment, provided that the beneficial owner of the interest or royalties is a company of another Member State or a permanent establishment situated in another Member State of a company of a Member State.

2. A payment made by a company of a Member State or by a permanent establishment situated in another Member State shall be deemed to arise in that Member State, hereafter referred to as the 'source State'.

3. A permanent establishment shall be treated as the payer of interest or royalties only insofar as those payments represent a tax-deductible expense for the permanent establishment in the Member State in which it is situated.

4. A company of a Member State shall be treated as the beneficial owner of interest or royalties only if it receives those payments for its own benefit and not as an intermediary, such as an agent, trustee or authorised signatory, for some other person.

5. A permanent establishment shall be treated as the beneficial owner of interest or royalties—

(a) if the debt-claim, right or use of information in respect of which interest or royalty payments arise is effectively connected with that permanent establishment; and

(b) if the interest or royalty payments represent income in respect of which that permanent establishment is subject in the Member State in which it is situated to one of the taxes mentioned in Article 3(a)(iii) or in the case of Belgium to the 'impôt des non-résidents/belasting der niet-verblijfhouders' or in the case of Spain to the 'Impuesto sobre la Renta de no Residentes' or to a tax which is identical or substantially similar and which is imposed after the date of entry into force of this Directive in addition to, or in place of, those existing taxes.

6. Where a permanent establishment of a company of a Member State is treated as the payer, or as the beneficial owner, of interest or royalties, no other part of the company shall be treated as the payer, or as the beneficial owner, of that interest or those royalties for the purposes of this Article.

7. This Article shall apply only if the company which is the payer, or the company whose permanent establishment is treated as the payer, of interest or royalties is an associated company of the company which is the beneficial owner, or whose permanent establishment is treated as the beneficial owner, of that interest or those royalties.

8. This Article shall not apply where interest or royalties are paid by or to a permanent establishment situated in a third State of a company of a Member State and the business of the company is wholly or partly carried on through that permanent establishment.

9. Nothing in this Article shall prevent a Member State from taking interest or royalties received by its companies, by permanent establishments of its companies or by permanent establishments situated in that State into account when applying its tax law.

10. A Member State shall have the option of not applying this Directive to a company of another Member State or to a permanent establishment of a company of another Member State in circumstances where the conditions set out in Article 3(b) have not been maintained for an uninterrupted period of at least two years.

11. The source State may require that fulfilment of the requirements laid down in this Article and in Article 3 be substantiated at the time of payment of the interest or royalties by an attestation. If fulfilment of the requirements laid down in this Article has not been attested at the time of payment, the Member State shall be free to require deduction of tax at source.

12. The source State may make it a condition for exemption under this Directive that it has issued a decision currently granting the exemption following an attestation certifying the fulfilment of the requirements laid down in this Article and in Article 3. A decision on exemption shall be given within three months at most after the attestation and such supporting information as the source State may reasonably ask for have been provided, and shall be valid for a period of at least one year after it has been issued.

13. For the purposes of paragraphs 11 and 12, the attestation to be given shall, in respect of each contract for the payment, be valid for at least one year but for not more than three years from the date of issue and shall contain the following information—

(a) proof of the receiving company's residence for tax purposes and, where necessary, the existence of a permanent establishment certified by the tax authority of the Member State in which the receiving company is resident for tax purposes or in which the permanent establishment is situated;

(b) beneficial ownership by the receiving company in accordance with paragraph 4 or the existence of conditions in accordance with paragraph 5 where a permanent establishment is the recipient of the payment;

(c) fulfilment of the requirements in accordance with Article 3(a)(iii) in the case of the receiving company;

(d) a minimum holding or the criterion of a minimum holding of voting rights in accordance with Article 3(b);

(e) the period for which the holding referred to in (d) has existed.

Member States may request in addition the legal justification for the payments under the contract (eg loan agreement or licensing contract).

14. If the requirements for exemption cease to be fulfilled, the receiving company or permanent establishment shall immediately inform the paying company or permanent establishment and, if the source State so requires, the competent authority of that State.

15. If the paying company or permanent establishment has withheld tax at source to be exempted under this Article, a claim may be made for repayment of that tax at source. The Member State may require the information specified in paragraph 13. The application for repayment must be submitted within the period laid down. That period shall last for at least two years from the date when the interest or royalties are paid.

16. The source State shall repay the excess tax withheld at source within one year following due receipt of the application and such supporting information as it may reasonably ask for. If the tax withheld at source has not been refunded within that period, the receiving company or permanent establishment shall be entitled on expiry of the year in question to interest on the tax which is refunded at a rate corresponding to the national interest rate to be applied in comparable cases under the domestic law of the source State.

[8.97]
Article 2
Definition of interest and royalties

For the purposes of this Directive—

(a) the term 'interest' means income from debt-claims of every kind, whether or not secured by mortgage and whether or not carrying a right to participate in the debtor's profits, and in particular, income from securities and income from bonds or debentures, including premiums and prizes attaching to such securities, bonds or debentures; penalty charges for late payment shall not be regarded as interest;

(b) the term 'royalties' means payments of any kind received as a consideration for the use of, or the right to use, any copyright of literary, artistic or scientific work, including cinematograph films and software, any patent, trade mark, design or model, plan, secret formula or process, or for information concerning industrial, commercial or scientific experience; payments for the use of, or the right to use, industrial, commercial or scientific equipment shall be regarded as royalties.

[8.98]
Article 3
Definition of company, associated company and permanent establishment

For the purposes of this Directive—

(a) the term 'company of a Member State' means any company—

(i) taking one of the forms listed in the Annex hereto; and

(ii) which in accordance with the tax laws of a Member State is considered to be resident in that Member State and is not, within the meaning of a Double Taxation Convention on Income concluded with a third state, considered to be resident for tax purposes outside the Community; and

(iii) which is subject to one of the following taxes without being exempt, or to a tax which is identical or substantially similar and which is imposed after the date of entry into force of this Directive in addition to, or in place of, those existing taxes—

— impôt des sociétés/vennootschapsbelasting in Belgium,
— selskabsskat in Denmark,
— Körperschaftsteuer in Germany,
— Φόρος εισοδήματος νομικών προσώπων in Greece,
— impuesto sobre sociedades in Spain,
— impôt sur les sociétés in France,
[— porez na dobit in Croatia,]
— corporation tax in Ireland,
— imposta sul reddito delle persone giuridiche in Italy,
— impôt sur le revenu des collectivités in Luxembourg,
— vennootschapsbelasting in the Netherlands,
— Körperschaftsteuer in Austria,
— imposto sobre o rendimento da pessoas colectivas in Portugal,
— yhteisöjen tulovero/inkomstskatten för samfund in Finland,
— statlig inkomstskatt in Sweden,
— corporation tax in the United Kingdom;
[— Daň z příjmů právnických osob in the Czech Republic,
— Tulumaks in Estonia,
— φόρος εισοδήματος in Cyprus,
— Uzņēmumu ienākuma nodoklis in Latvia,
— Pelno mokestis in Lithuania,

— Társasági adó in Hungary,
— Taxxa fuq l-income in Malta,
— Podatek dochodowy od osób prawnych in Poland,
— Davek od dobička pravnih oseb in Slovenia,
— Daň z príjmov právnických osôb in Slovakia',]
[— корпоративен данък in Bulgaria,
— impozit pe profit, impozitul pe veniturile obţinute din România de nerezidenţi in Romania.]

(b) a company is an 'associated company' of a second company if, at least—
(i) the first company has a direct minimum holding of 25% in the capital of the second company, or
(ii) the second company has a direct minimum holding of 25% in the capital of the first company, or
(iii) a third company has a direct minimum holding of 25% both in the capital of the first company and in the capital of the second company.

Holdings must involve only companies resident in Community territory.

However, Member States shall have the option of replacing the criterion of a minimum holding in the capital with that of a minimum holding of voting rights;

(c) the term 'permanent establishment' means a fixed place of business situated in a Member State through which the business of a company of another Member State is wholly or partly carried on.

NOTES

Para (a): entry in first pair of square brackets inserted by Council Directive 2013/13/EU, Art 1, Annex, para 2(a); entry in second pair of square brackets added by Council Directive 2004/66/EC, Art 1, Annex, V(3)(a); entry in third pair of square brackets added by Council Directive 2006/98/EC, Art 1, Annex, para 9(a).

[8.99]
Article 4
Exclusion of payments as interest or royalties

1. The source State shall not be obliged to ensure the benefits of this Directive in the following cases—
(a) payments which are treated as a distribution of profits or as a repayment of capital under the law of the source State;
(b) payments from debt-claims which carry a right to participate in the debtor's profits;
(c) payments from debt-claims which entitle the creditor to exchange his right to interest for a right to participate in the debtor's profits;
(d) payments from debt-claims which contain no provision for repayment of the principal amount or where the repayment is due more than 50 years after the date of issue.

2. Where, by reason of a special relationship between the payer and the beneficial owner of interest or royalties, or between one of them and some other person, the amount of the interest or royalties exceeds the amount which would have been agreed by the payer and the beneficial owner in the absence of such a relationship, the provisions of this Directive shall apply only to the latter amount, if any.

[8.100]
Article 5
Fraud and abuse

1. This Directive shall not preclude the application of domestic or agreement-based provisions required for the prevention of fraud or abuse.

2. Member States may, in the case of transactions for which the principal motive or one of the principal motives is tax evasion, tax avoidance or abuse, withdraw the benefits of this Directive or refuse to apply this Directive.

[8.101]
[Article 6
Transitional rules for the Czech Republic, Greece, Spain, Latvia, Lithuania, Poland, Portugal and Slovakia

1. Greece, Latvia, Poland and Portugal shall be authorised not to apply the provisions of Article 1 until the date of application referred to in Article 17(2) and (3) of Council Directive 2003/48/EC of 3 June 2003 on taxation of savings income in the form of interest payments. During a transitional period of eight years starting on the aforementioned date, the rate of tax on payments of interest or royalties made to an associated company of another Member State or to a permanent establishment situated in another Member State of an associated company of a Member State must not exceed 10% during the first four years and 5% during the final four years.

Lithuania shall be authorised not to apply the provisions of Article 1 until the date of application referred to in Article 17(2) and (3) of Directive 2003/48/EC. During a transitional period of six years starting on the aforementioned date, the rate of tax on payments of royalties made to an associated company of another Member State or to a permanent establishment situated in another Member State of an associated company of a Member State must not exceed 10%. During the first four years of the six-year transitional period, the rate of tax on payments of interest made to an associated company of another Member State or to a permanent establishment situated in another Member State must not exceed 10%; and for the following two years, the rate of tax on such payments of interest must not exceed 5%.

Spain and the Czech Republic shall be authorised, for royalty payments only, not to apply the provisions of Article 1 until the date of application referred to in Article 17(2) and (3) of Directive 2003/48/EC. During a transitional period of six years starting on the aforementioned date, the rate of tax on payments of royalties made to an associated company of another Member State or to a permanent establishment situated in another Member State of an associated company of a Member State must not exceed 10%. Slovakia shall be authorised, for royalty payments only, not to apply the provisions of Article 1 during a transitional period of two years starting on 1 May 2004.

These transitional rules shall, however, remain subject to the continued application of any rate of tax lower than those referred to in the first, second and third subparagraphs provided by bilateral agreements concluded between the Czech Republic, Greece, Spain, Latvia, Lithuania, Poland, Portugal or Slovakia and other Member States. Before the end of any of the transitional periods mentioned in this paragraph the Council may decide unanimously, on a proposal from the Commission, on a possible extension of the said transitional periods.

2. Where a company of a Member State, or a permanent establishment situated in that Member State of a company of a Member State:

— receives interest or royalties from an associated company of Greece, Latvia, Lithuania, Poland or Portugal,
— receives royalties from an associated company of the Czech Republic, Spain or Slovakia,
— receives interest or royalties from a permanent establishment situated in Greece, Latvia, Lithuania, Poland or Portugal, of an associated company of a Member State, or
— receives royalties from a permanent establishment situated in the Czech Republic, Spain or Slovakia, of an associated company of a Member State,

the first Member State shall allow an amount equal to the tax paid in the Czech Republic, Greece, Spain, Latvia, Lithuania, Poland, Portugal, or Slovakia in accordance with paragraph 1 on that income as a deduction from the tax on the income of the company or permanent establishment which received that income.

3. The deduction provided for in paragraph 2 need not exceed the lower of:

(a) the tax payable in the Czech Republic, Greece, Spain, Latvia, Lithuania, Poland, Portugal or Slovakia, on such income on the basis of paragraph 1,

or

(b) that part of the tax on the income of the company or permanent establishment which received the interest or royalties, as computed before the deduction is given, which is attributable to those payments under the domestic law of the Member State of which it is a company or in which the permanent establishment is situated.]

NOTES

Substituted by Council Directive 2004/76/EC, Art 1.

[8.102]
Article 7
Implementation

1. Member States shall bring into force the laws, regulations and administrative provisions necessary to comply with this Directive not later than 1 January 2004. They shall forthwith inform the Commission thereof.

When Member States adopt these measures, they shall contain a reference to this Directive or shall be accompanied by such reference on the occasion of their official publication. The methods of making such a reference shall be laid down by the Member States.

2. Member States shall communicate to the Commission the text of the main provisions of national law which they adopt in the field covered by this Directive, together with a table showing how the provisions of this Directive correspond to the national provisions adopted.

[8.103]
Article 8
Review

By 31 December 2006, the Commission shall report to the Council on the operation of this Directive, in particular with a view to extending its coverage to companies or undertakings other than those referred to in Article 3 and the Annex.

[8.104]
Article 9
Delimitation clause

This Directive shall not affect the application of domestic or agreement-based provisions which go beyond the provisions of this Directive and are designed to eliminate or mitigate the double taxation of interest and royalties.

[8.105]
Article 10
Entry into force
This Directive shall enter into force on the day of its publication in the *Official Journal of the European Union*.

[8.106]
Article 11
Addressees
This Directive is addressed to the Member States.

ANNEX
LIST OF COMPANIES COVERED BY ARTICLE 3(A) OF THE DIRECTIVE

[8.107]
(a) Companies under Belgian law known as: 'naamloze vennootschap/société anonyme, commanditaire vennootschap op aandelen/société en commandite par actions, besloten vennootschap met beperkte aansprakelijkheid/société privée à responsabilité limitée' and those public law bodies that operate under private law;

[(aa) companies under Bulgarian law known as: "събирателното дружество", "командитното дружество", "дружеството с ограничена отговорност", "акционерното дружество", "командитното дружество с акции", "кооперации", "кооперативни съюзи", "държавни предприятия" constituted under Bulgarian law and carrying on commercial activities;

(ab) companies under Romanian law known as: "societăţi pe acţiuni", "societăţi în comandită pe acţiuni", "societăţi cu răspundere limitată".]

(b) companies under Danish law known as: 'aktieselskab' and 'anpartsselskab';

(c) companies under German law known as: 'Aktiengesellschaft, Kommanditgesellschaft auf Aktien, Gesellschaft mit beschränkter Haftung' and 'bergrechtliche Gewerkschaft';

(d) companies under Greek law known as: 'ανώνυμη εταιρία';

(e) companies under Spanish law known as: 'sociedad anónima, sociedad comanditaria por acciones, sociedad de responsabilidad limitada' and those public law bodies which operate under private law;

(f) companies under French law known as: 'société anonyme, société en commandite par actions, société à responsabilité limitée' and industrial and commercial public establishments and undertakings;

(g) companies in Irish law known as public companies limited by shares or by guarantee, private companies limited by shares or by guarantee, bodies registered under the Industrial and Provident Societies Acts or building societies registered under the Building Societies Acts;

(h) companies under Italian law known as: 'società per azioni, società in accomandita per azioni, società a responsabilità limitata' and public and private entities carrying on industrial and commercial activities;

(i) companies under Luxembourg law known as: 'société anonyme, société en commandite par actions and société à responsabilité limitée';

(j) companies under Dutch law known as: 'naamloze vennootschap' and 'besloten vennootschap met beperkte aansprakelijkheid';

(k) companies under Austrian law known as: 'Aktiengesellschaft' and 'Gesellschaft mit beschränkter Haftung';

(l) commercial companies or civil law companies having a commercial form, cooperatives and public undertakings incorporated in accordance with Portuguese law;

(m) companies under Finnish law known as: 'osakeyhtiö/aktiebolag, osuuskunta/andelslag, säästöpankki/sparbank' and 'vakuutusyhtiö/försäkringsbolag';

(n) companies under Swedish law known as: 'aktiebolag' and 'försäkringsaktiebolag';

(o) companies incorporated under the law of the United Kingdom.

[(p) companies under Czech law known as: "akciová společnost", "společnost s ručením omezeným", "veřejná obchodní společnost", "komanditní společnost", "družstvo";

(q) companies under Estonian law known as: "täisühing", "usaldusühing", "osaühing", "aktsiaselts", "tulundusühistu";

(r) companies under Cypriot law known as: companies in accordance with the Company's Law, Public Corporate Bodies as well as any other Body which is considered as a company in accordance with the Income tax Laws;

(s) companies under Latvian law known as: "akciju sabiedrība", "sabiedrība ar ierobežotu atbildību";

(t) companies incorporated under the law of Lithuania;

(u) companies under Hungarian law known as: "közkereseti társaság", "betéti társaság", "közös vállalat", "korlátolt felelősségű társaság", "részvénytársaság", "egyesülés", "közhasznú társaság", "szövetkezet";

(v) companies under Maltese law known as: "Kumpaniji ta' Responsabilita' Limitata", "Soċjetajiet in akkomandita li l-kapital tagħhom maqsum f'azzjonijiet";

(w) companies under Polish law known as: "spółka akcyjna", "spółka z ograniczoną odpowiedzialnością";

(x) companies under Slovenian law known as: "delniška družba", "komanditna delniška družba", "komanditna družba", "družba z omejeno odgovornostjo", "družba z neomejeno odgovornostjo";

(y) companies under Slovak law known as: "akciová spoločnos", "spoločnosť s ručcním obmedzeným", "komanditná spoločnos", "verejná obchodná spoločnos", "družstvo".]

[(z) companies under Croatian law known as: "dioničko društvo", "društvo s ograničenom odgovornošću", and other companies constituted under Croatian law subject to Croatian profit tax.]

NOTES

Paras (aa), (ab) inserted by Council Directive 2006/98/EC, Art 1, Annex, para 9(b).
Paras (p)–(y): added by Council Directive 2004/66/EC, Art 1, Annex, V(3)(b).
Para (z): added by Council Directive 2013/13/EU, Art 1, Annex, para 2(b).

COUNCIL REGULATION

(1383/2003/EC)

of 22 July 2003

concerning customs action against goods suspected of infringing certain intellectual property rights and the measures to be taken against goods found to have infringed such rights ('EU Customs Regulation')

NOTES

Date of publication in OJ: OJ L196, 2.8.2003, p 7.
This regulation has been repealed by Regulation 608/2013/EU of the European Parliament and of the Council, at **[8.636]**, with effect from 1 January 2014, subject to a transitional provision in Art 39 thereof at **[8.674]**.

THE COUNCIL OF THE EUROPEAN UNION,

Having regard to the Treaty establishing the European Community, and in particular Article 133 thereof,

Having regard to the proposal from the Commission,

Whereas—

(1) To improve the working of the system concerning the entry into the Community and the export and re-export from the Community of goods infringing certain intellectual property rights introduced by Council Regulation (EC) No 3295/94 of 22 December 1994 laying down measures to prohibit the release for free circulation, export, re-export or entry for a suspensive procedure of counterfeit and pirated goods,[1] *conclusions should be drawn from experience of its application. In the interests of clarity, Regulation (EC) No 3295/94 should be repealed and replaced.*

(2) The marketing of counterfeit and pirated goods, and indeed all goods infringing intellectual property rights, does considerable damage to law-abiding manufacturers and traders and to right-holders, as well as deceiving and in some cases endangering the health and safety of consumers. Such goods should, in so far as is possible, be kept off the market and measures adopted to deal effectively with this unlawful activity without impeding the freedom of legitimate trade. This objective is consistent with efforts under way at international level.

(3) In cases where counterfeit goods, pirated goods and, more generally, goods infringing an intellectual property right originate in or come from third countries, their introduction into the Community customs territory, including their transhipment, release for free circulation in

the Community, placing under a suspensive procedure and placing in a free zone or warehouse, should be prohibited and a procedure set up to enable the customs authorities to enforce this prohibition as effectively as possible.

(4) Customs authorities should also be able to take action against counterfeit goods, pirated goods and goods infringing certain intellectual property rights which are in the process of being exported, re-exported or leaving the Community customs territory.

(5) Action by the customs authorities should involve, for the period necessary to determine whether suspect goods are indeed counterfeit goods, pirated goods or goods infringing certain intellectual property rights, suspending release for free circulation, export and re-export or, in the case of goods placed under a suspensive procedure, placed in a free zone or a free warehouse, in the process of being re-exported with notification, introduced into the customs territory or leaving that territory, detaining those goods.

(6) The particulars of the application for action, such as its period of validity and form, need to be defined and harmonised in all Member States. The same applies to the conditions governing the acceptance of applications by the customs authorities and the service designated to receive, process and register them.

(7) Even where no application has yet been lodged or approved, the Member States should be authorised to detain the goods for a certain period to allow right-holders to lodge an application for action with the customs authorities.

(8) Proceedings initiated to determine whether an intellectual property right has been infringed under national law will be conducted with reference to the criteria used to establish whether goods produced in that Member State infringe intellectual property rights. This Regulation does not affect the Member States' provisions on the competence of the courts or judicial procedures.

(9) To make the Regulation easier to apply for customs administrations and right-holders alike, provision should also be made for a more flexible procedure allowing goods infringing certain intellectual property rights to be destroyed without there being any obligation to initiate proceedings to establish whether an intellectual property right has been infringed under national law.

(10) It is necessary to lay down the measures applicable to goods which have been found to be counterfeit, pirated or generally to infringe certain intellectual property rights. Those measures should not only deprive those responsible for trading in such goods of the economic benefits of the transaction and penalise them but should also constitute an effective deterrent to further transactions of the same kind.

(11) To avoid disrupting the clearance of goods carried in travellers' personal baggage, it is appropriate, except where certain material indications suggest commercial traffic is involved, to exclude from the scope of this Regulation goods that may be counterfeit, pirated or infringe certain intellectual property rights when imported from third countries within the limits of the duty-free allowance accorded by Community rules.

(12) In the interests of this Regulation's effectiveness, it is important to ensure the uniform application of the common rules it lays down and to reinforce mutual assistance between the Member States and between the Member States and the Commission, in particular by recourse to Council Regulation (EC) No 515/97 of 13 March 1997 on mutual assistance between the administrative authorities of the Member States and co-operation between the latter and the Commission to ensure the correct application of the law on customs and agricultural matters.[2]

(13) In the light of the experience gained in the implementation of this Regulation, inter alia, consideration should be given to the possibility of increasing the number of intellectual property rights covered.

(14) The measures necessary for the implementation of this Regulation should be adopted in accordance with Council Decision 1999/468/EC of 28 June 1999 laying down the procedures for the exercise of implementing powers conferred on the Commission.[3]

(15) Regulation (EC) No 3295/94 should be repealed,

NOTES

1 OJ L341, 30.12.1994, p 8. Regulation as last amended by Regulation (EC) No 806/2003 (OJ L122, 16.5.2003, p 1).

2 OJ L82, 22.3.1997, p 1. Regulation as last amended by Regulation (EC) No 807/2003 (OJ L122, 16.5.2003, p 36).

3 OJ L184, 17.7.1999, p 23.

HAS ADOPTED THIS REGULATION—

CHAPTER I
SUBJECT MATTER AND SCOPE

[8.108]
Article 1

1. This Regulation sets out the conditions for action by the customs authorities when goods are suspected of infringing an intellectual property right in the following situations—

(a) when they are entered for release for free circulation, export or re-export in accordance with Article 61 of Council Regulation (EC) No 2913/92 of 12 October 1992 establishing the Community Customs Code;[1]

(b) when they are found during checks on goods entering or leaving the Community customs territory in accordance with Articles 37 and 183 of Regulation (EEC) No 2913/92, placed under a suspensive procedure within the meaning of Article 84(1)(a) of that Regulation, in the process of being re-exported subject to notification under Article 182(2) of that Regulation or placed in a free zone or free warehouse within the meaning of Article 166 of that Regulation.

2. This Regulation also fixes the measures to be taken by the competent authorities when the goods referred to in paragraph 1 are found to infringe intellectual property rights.

NOTES

This regulation has been repealed by Regulation 608/2013/EU of the European Parliament and of the Council, at **[8.636]**, with effect from 1 January 2014, subject to a transitional provision in Art 39 thereof at **[8.674]**.

1 OJ L302, 19.10.1992, p 1. Regulation as last amended by Regulation (EC) No 2700/2000, of the European Parliament and of the Council (OJ L311, 12.12.2000, p 17).

[8.109]

Article 2

1. For the purposes of this Regulation, "goods infringing an intellectual property right" means—

(a) "counterfeit goods", namely—

(i) goods, including packaging, bearing without authorisation a trademark identical to the trademark validly registered in respect of the same type of goods, or which cannot be distinguished in its essential aspects from such a trademark, and which thereby infringes the trademarkholder's rights under Community law, as provided for by Council Regulation (EC) No 40/94 of 20 December 1993 on the Community trademark[1] *or the law of the Member State in which the application for action by the customs authorities is made;*

(ii) any trademark symbol (including a logo, label, sticker, brochure, instructions for use or guarantee document bearing such a symbol), even if presented separately, on the same conditions as the goods referred to in point (i);

(iii) packaging materials bearing the trademarks of counterfeit goods, presented separately, on the same conditions as the goods referred to in point (i);

(b) "pirated goods", namely goods which are or contain copies made without the consent of the holder of a copyright or related right or design right, regardless of whether it is registered in national law, or of a person authorised by the right-holder in the country of production in cases where the making of those copies would constitute an infringement of that right under Council Regulation (EC) No 6/2002 of 12 December 2001 on Community designs[2] *or the law of the Member State in which the application for customs action is made;*

(c) goods which, in the Member State in which the application for customs action is made, infringe—

(i) a patent under that Member State's law;

(ii) a supplementary protection certificate of the kind provided for in Council Regulation (EEC) No 1768/92[3] *or Regulation (EC) No 1610/ 96 of the European Parliament and of the Council;*[4]

(iii) a national plant variety right under the law of that Member State or a Community plant variety right of the kind provided for in Council Regulation (EC) No 2100/94;[5]

(iv) designations of origin or geographical indications under the law of that Member State or Council Regulations (EEC) No 2081/92[6] *and (EC) No 1493/1999;*[7]

(v) geographical designations of the kind provided for in Council Regulation (EEC) No 1576/89.[8]

2. For the purposes of this Regulation, "right-holder" means—

(a) the holder of a trademark, copyright or related right, design right, patent, supplementary protection certificate, plant variety right, protected designation of origin, protected geographical indication and, more generally, any right referred to in paragraph 1; or

(b) any other person authorised to use any of the intellectual property rights mentioned in point (a), or a representative of the right-holder or authorised user.

3. Any mould or matrix which is specifically designed or adapted for the manufacture of goods infringing an intellectual property right shall be treated as goods of that kind if the use of such moulds or matrices infringes the right-holder's rights under Community law or the law of the Member State in which the application for action by the customs authorities is made.

NOTES

Repealed as noted to Art 1 at **[8.108]**.

1 OJ L11, 14.1.1994, p 1. Regulation as last amended by Regulation (EC) No 807/2003.

2 OJ L3, 5.1.2002, p 1.

3 OJ L182, 2.7.1992, p 1.

4 OJ L198, 8.8.1996, p 30.

5 OJ L227, 1.9.1994, p 1. Regulation as last amended by Regulation (EC) No 807/2003.

6 OJ L208, 24.7.1992, p 1. Regulation as last amended by Regulation (EC) No 806/2003.

7 OJ L179, 14.7.1999, p 1. Regulation as last amended by Regulation (EC) No 806/2003.

8 OJ L160, 12.6.1989, p 1. Regulation as last amended by Regulation (EC) No 3378/94 of the European Parliament and of the Council (OJ L366, 31.12.1994, p 1).

[8.110]
Article 3

1. This Regulation shall not apply to goods bearing a trademark with the consent of the holder of that trademark or to goods bearing a protected designation of origin or a protected geographical indication or which are protected by a patent or a supplementary protection certificate, by a copyright or related right or by a design right or a plant variety right and which have been manufactured with the consent of the right-holder but are placed in one of the situations referred to in Article 1(1) without the latter's consent.

It shall similarly not apply to goods referred to in the first subparagraph and which have been manufactured or are protected by another intellectual property right referred to in Article 2(1) under conditions other than those agreed with the right-holder.

2. Where a traveller's personal baggage contains goods of a non-commercial nature within the limits of the duty-free allowance and there are no material indications to suggest the goods are part of commercial traffic, Member States shall consider such goods to be outside the scope of this Regulation.

NOTES

Repealed as noted to Art 1 at **[8.108]**.

CHAPTER II
APPLICATIONS FOR ACTION BY THE CUSTOMS AUTHORITIES

SECTION 1
MEASURES PRIOR TO AN APPLICATION FOR ACTION BY THE CUSTOMS AUTHORITIES

[8.111]
Article 4

1. Where the customs authorities, in the course of action in one of the situations referred to in Article 1(1) and before an application has been lodged by a right-holder or granted, have sufficient grounds for suspecting that goods infringe an intellectual property right, they may suspend the release of the goods or detain them for a period of three working days from the moment of receipt of the notification by the right-holder and by the declarant or holder of the goods, if the latter are known, in order to enable the right-holder to submit an application for action in accordance with Article 5.

2. In accordance with the rules in force in the Member State concerned, the customs authorities may, without divulging any information other than the actual or supposed number of items and their nature and before informing the right-holder of the possible infringement, ask the right-holder to provide them with any information they may need to confirm their suspicions.

NOTES

Repealed as noted to Art 1 at **[8.108]**.

SECTION 2
THE LODGING AND PROCESSING OF APPLICATIONS FOR CUSTOMS ACTION

[8.112]
Article 5

1. In each Member State a right-holder may apply in writing to the competent customs department for action by the customs authorities when goods are found in one of the situations referred to in Article 1(1) (application for action).

2. Each Member State shall designate the customs department competent to receive and process applications for action.

3. Where electronic data interchange systems exist, the Member States shall encourage right-holders to lodge applications electronically.

4. Where the applicant is the right-holder of a Community trademark or a Community design right, a Community plant variety right or a designation of origin or geographical indication or a geographical designation protected by the Community, an application may, in addition to requesting action by the customs authorities of the Member State in which it is lodged, request action by the customs authorities of one or more other Member States.

5. The application for action shall be made out on a form established in accordance with the procedure referred to in Article 21(2); it must contain all the information needed to enable the goods in question to be readily recognised by the customs authorities, and in particular—

(i) an accurate and detailed technical description of the goods;
(ii) any specific information the right-holder may have concerning the type or pattern of fraud;
(iii) the name and address of the contact person appointed by the right-holder.

The application for action must also contain the declaration required of the applicant by Article 6 and proof that the applicant holds the right for the goods in question.

In the situation described in paragraph 4 the application for action shall indicate the Member State or States in which customs action is requested as well as the names and addresses of the right-holder in each of the Member States concerned.

By way of indication and where known, right-holders should also forward any other information they may have, such as—

(a) the pre-tax value of the original goods on the legitimate market in the country in which the application for action is lodged;
(b) the location of the goods or their intended destination;
(c) particulars identifying the consignment or packages;
(d) the scheduled arrival or departure date of the goods;
(e) the means of transport used;
(f) the identity of the importer, exporter or holder of the goods;
(g) the country or countries of production and the routes used by traffickers;
(h) the technical differences, if known, between the authentic and suspect goods.

6. Details may also be required which are specific to the type of intellectual property right referred to in the application for action.

7. On receiving an application for action, the competent customs department shall process that application and notify the applicant in writing of its decision within 30 working days of its receipt.

The right-holder shall not be charged a fee to cover the administrative costs occasioned by the processing of the application.

8. Where the application does not contain the mandatory information listed in paragraph 5, the competent customs department may decide not to process the application for action; in that event it shall provide reasons for its decision and include information on the appeal procedure. The application can only be re-submitted when duly completed.

NOTES

Repealed as noted to Art 1 at **[8.108]**.

[8.113]
Article 6

1. Applications for action shall be accompanied by a declaration from the right-holder, which may be submitted either in writing or electronically, in accordance with national legislation, accepting liability towards the persons involved in a situation referred to in Article 1(1) in the event that a procedure initiated pursuant to Article 9(1) is discontinued owing to an act or omission by the right-holder or in the event that the goods in question are subsequently found not to infringe an intellectual property right.

In that declaration the right-holder shall also agree to bear all costs incurred under this Regulation in keeping goods under customs control pursuant to Article 9 and, where applicable, Article 11.

2. Where an application is submitted under Article 5(4), the right-holder shall agree in the declaration to provide and pay for any translation necessary; this declaration shall be valid in every Member State in which the decision granting the application applies.

NOTES

Repealed as noted to Art 1 at **[8.108]**.

[8.114]
Article 7

Articles 5 and 6 shall apply mutatis mutandis to requests for an extension.

NOTES

Repealed as noted to Art 1 at **[8.108]**.

SECTION 3
ACCEPTANCE OF THE APPLICATION FOR ACTION

[8.115]
Article 8
1. When granting an application for action, the competent customs department shall specify the period during which the customs authorities are to take action. That period shall not exceed one year. On expiry of the period in question, and subject to the prior discharge of any debt owed by the right-holder under this Regulation, the department which took the initial decision may, at the right-holder's request, extend that period.

The right-holder shall notify the competent customs department referred to in Article 5(2), if his right ceases to be validly registered or expires.

2. The decision granting the right-holder's application for action shall immediately be forwarded to those customs offices of the Member State or States likely to be concerned by the goods alleged in the application to infringe an intellectual property right.

When an application for action submitted in accordance with Article 5(4) is granted, the period during which the customs authorities are to take action shall be set at one year; on expiry of the period in question, the department which processed the initial application shall, on the right-holder's written application, extend that period. The first indent of Article 250 of Regulation (EEC) No 2913/92 shall apply mutatis mutandis to the decision granting that application and to decisions extending or repealing it.

Where an application for action is granted, it is for the applicant to forward that decision, with any other information and any translations that may be necessary, to the competent customs department of the Member State or States in which the applicant has requested customs action. However, with the applicant's consent, the decision may be forwarded directly by the customs department which has taken the decision.

At the request of the customs authorities of the Member States concerned, the applicant shall provide any additional information necessary for the implementation of the decision.

3. The period referred to in the second subparagraph of paragraph 2 shall run from the date of adoption of the decision granting the application. The decision will not enter into force in the recipient Member State or States until it has been forwarded in accordance with the third subparagraph of paragraph 2 and the right-holder has fulfilled the formalities referred to in Article 6.

The decision shall then be sent immediately to the national customs offices likely to have to deal with the goods suspected of infringing intellectual property rights.

This paragraph shall apply mutatis mutandis to a decision extending the initial decision.

NOTES
Repealed as noted to Art 1 at **[8.108]**.

CHAPTER III
CONDITIONS GOVERNING ACTION BY THE CUSTOMS AUTHORITIES AND BY THE AUTHORITY COMPETENT TO DECIDE ON THE CASE

[8.116]
Article 9
1. Where a customs office to which the decision granting an application by the right-holder has been forwarded pursuant to Article 8 is satisfied, after consulting the applicant where necessary, that goods in one of the situations referred to in Article 1(1) are suspected of infringing an intellectual property right covered by that decision, it shall suspend release of the goods or detain them.

The customs office shall immediately inform the competent customs department which processed the application.

2. The competent customs department or customs office referred to in paragraph 1 shall inform the right-holder and the declarant or holder of the goods within the meaning of Article 38 of Regulation (EEC) No 2913/92 of its action and is authorised to inform them of the actual or estimated quantity and the actual or supposed nature of the goods whose release has been suspended or which have been detained, without being bound by the communication of that information to notify the authority competent to take a substantive decision.

3. With a view to establishing whether an intellectual property right has been infringed under national law, and in accordance with national provisions on the protection of personal data, commercial and industrial secrecy and professional and administrative confidentiality, the customs office or department which processed the application shall inform the right-holder, at his request and if known, of the names and addresses of the consignee, the consignor, the declarant or the holder of the goods and the origin and provenance of goods suspected of infringing an intellectual property right.

The customs office shall give the applicant and the persons involved in any of the situations referred to in Article 1(1) the opportunity to inspect goods whose release has been suspended or which have been detained.

When examining goods, the customs office may take samples and, according to the rules in force in the Member State concerned, hand them over or send them to the right-holder, at his express request, strictly for the purposes of analysis and to facilitate the subsequent procedure. Where circumstances allow, subject to the requirements of Article 11(1) second indent where applicable, samples must be returned on completion of the technical analysis and, where applicable, before goods are released or their detention is ended. Any analysis of these samples shall be carried out under the sole responsibility of the right-holder.

NOTES

Repealed as noted to Art 1 at **[8.108]**.

[8.117]

Article 10

The law in force in the Member State within the territory of which the goods are placed in one of the situations referred to in Article 1(1) shall apply when deciding whether an intellectual property right has been infringed under national law.

That law shall also apply to the immediate notification of the customs department or office referred to in Article 9(1) that the procedure provided for in Article 13 has been initiated, unless the procedure was initiated by that department or office.

NOTES

Repealed as noted to Art 1 at **[8.108]**.

[8.118]

Article 11

1. Where customs authorities have detained or suspended the release of goods which are suspected of infringing an intellectual property right in one of the situations covered by Article 1(1), the Member States may provide, in accordance with their national legislation, for a simplified procedure, to be used with the rightholder's agreement, which enables customs authorities to have such goods abandoned for destruction under customs control, without there being any need to determine whether an intellectual property right has been infringed under national law. To this end, Member States shall, in accordance with their national legislation, apply the following conditions—

- *that the right-holder inform the customs authorities in writing within 10 working days, or three working days in the case of perishable goods, of receipt of the notification provided for in Article 9, that the goods concerned by the procedure infringe an intellectual property right referred to in Article 2(1) and provide those authorities with the written agreement of the declarant, the holder or the owner of the goods to abandon the goods for destruction. With the agreement of the customs authorities, this information may be provided directly to customs by the declarant, the holder or the owner of the goods. This agreement shall be presumed to be accepted when the declarant, the holder or the owner of the goods has not specifically opposed destruction within the prescribed period. This period may be extended by a further ten working days where circumstances warrant it;*
- *that destruction be carried out, unless otherwise specified in national legislation, at the expense and under the responsibility of the right-holder, and be systematically preceded by the taking of samples for keeping by the customs authorities in such conditions that they constitute evidence admissible in legal proceedings in the Member State in which they might be needed.*

2. In all other cases, for example where the declarant, holder or owner objects to or contests the destruction of the goods, the procedure laid down in Article 13 shall apply.

NOTES

Repealed as noted to Art 1 at **[8.108]**.

[8.119]

Article 12

A right-holder receiving the particulars cited in the first subparagraph of Article 9(3) shall use that information only for the purposes specified in Articles 10, 11 and 13(1).

Any other use, not permitted by the national legislation of the Member State where the situation arose, may, on the basis of the law of the Member State in which the goods in question are located, cause the right-holder to incur civil liability and lead to the suspension of the application for action, for the period of validity remaining before renewal, in the Member State in which the events have taken place.

In the event of a further breach of this rule, the competent customs department may refuse to renew the application. In the case of an application of the kind provided for in Article 5(4), it must also notify the other Member States indicated on the form.

NOTES

Repealed as noted to Art 1 at **[8.108]**.

[8.120]

Article 13

1. If, within 10 working days of receipt of the notification of suspension of release or of detention, the customs office referred to in Article 9(1) has not been notified that proceedings have been initiated to determine whether an intellectual property right has been infringed under national law in accordance with Article 10 or has not received the right-holder's agreement provided for in Article 11(1) where applicable, release of the goods shall be granted, or their detention shall be ended, as appropriate, subject to completion of all customs formalities.

This period may be extended by a maximum of 10 working days in appropriate cases.

2. In the case of perishable goods suspected of infringing an intellectual property right, the period referred to in paragraph 1 shall be three working days. That period may not be extended.

NOTES

Repealed as noted to Art 1 at **[8.108]**.

[8.121]

Article 14

1. In the case of goods suspected of infringing design rights, patents, supplementary protection certificates or plant variety rights, the declarant, owner, importer, holder or consignee of the goods shall be able to obtain the release of the goods or an end to their detention on provision of a security, provided that—

(a) the customs office or department referred to in Article 9(1) has been notified, in accordance with Article 13(1), that a procedure has been initiated within the period provided for in Article 13(1) to establish whether an intellectual property right has been infringed under national law;

(b) the authority empowered for this purpose has not authorised precautionary measures before the expiry of the time limit laid down in Article 13(1);

(c) all customs formalities have been completed.

2. The security provided for in paragraph 1 must be sufficient to protect the interests of the right-holder.

Payment of the security shall not affect the other legal remedies available to the right-holder.

Where the procedure to determine whether an intellectual property right has been infringed under national law has been initiated other than on the initiative of the holder of a design right, patent, supplementary protection certificate or plant variety right, the security shall be released if the person initiating the said procedure does not exercise his right to institute legal proceedings within 20 working days of the date on which he receives notification of the suspension of release or detention.

Where the second subparagraph of Article 13(1) applies, this period may be extended to a maximum of 30 working days.

NOTES

Repealed as noted to Art 1 at **[8.108]**.

[8.122]

Article 15

The conditions of storage of the goods during the period of suspension of release or detention shall be determined by each Member State but shall not give rise to costs for the customs administrations.

NOTES

Repealed as noted to Art 1 at **[8.108]**.

CHAPTER IV
PROVISIONS APPLICABLE TO GOODS FOUND TO INFRINGE AN INTELLECTUAL PROPERTY RIGHT

[8.123]

Article 16

Goods found to infringe an intellectual property right at the end of the procedure provided for in Article 9 shall not be—

— allowed to enter into the Community customs territory,
— released for free circulation,
— removed from the Community customs territory,
— exported,
— re-exported,
— placed under a suspensive procedure or
— placed in a free zone or free warehouse.

NOTES

Repealed as noted to Art 1 at **[8.108]**.

[8.124]

Article 17

1. Without prejudice to the other legal remedies open to the right-holder, Member States shall adopt the measures necessary to allow the competent authorities—

- *(a) in accordance with the relevant provisions of national law, to destroy goods found to infringe an intellectual property right or dispose of them outside commercial channels in such a way as to preclude injury to the right-holder, without compensation of any sort and, unless otherwise specified in national legislation, at no cost to the exchequer;*
- *(b) to take, in respect of such goods, any other measures effectively depriving the persons concerned of any economic gains from the transaction.*

Save in exceptional cases, simply removing the trademarks which have been affixed to counterfeit goods without authorisation shall not be regarded as effectively depriving the persons concerned of any economic gains from the transaction.

2. Goods found to infringe an intellectual property right may be forfeited to the exchequer. In that event, paragraph 1(a) shall apply.

NOTES

Repealed as noted to Art 1 at **[8.108]**.

CHAPTER V
PENALTIES

[8.125]

Article 18

Each Member State shall introduce penalties to apply in cases of violation of this Regulation. Such penalties must be effective, proportionate and dissuasive.

NOTES

Repealed as noted to Art 1 at **[8.108]**.

CHAPTER VI
LIABILITY OF THE CUSTOMS AUTHORITIES AND THE RIGHT-HOLDER

[8.126]

Article 19

1. Save as provided by the law of the Member State in which an application is lodged or, in the case of an application under Article 5(4), by the law of the Member State in which goods infringing an intellectual property right are not detected by a customs office, the acceptance of an application shall not entitle the right-holder to compensation in the event that such goods are not detected by a customs office and are released or no action is taken to detain them in accordance with Article 9(1).

2. The exercise by a customs office or by another duly empowered authority of the powers conferred on them in order to fight against goods infringing an intellectual property right shall not render them liable towards the persons involved in the situations referred to in Article 1(1) or the persons affected by the measures provided for in Article 4 for damages suffered by them as a result of the authority's intervention, except where provided for by the law of the Member State in which the application is made or, in the case of an application under Article 5(4), by the law of the Member State in which loss or damage is incurred.

3. A right-holder's civil liability shall be governed by the law of the Member State in which the goods in question were placed in one of the situations referred to in Article 1(1).

NOTES

Repealed as noted to Art 1 at **[8.108]**.

CHAPTER VII
FINAL PROVISIONS

[8.127]

Article 20

The measures necessary for the application of this Regulation shall be adopted in accordance with the procedure referred to in Article 21(2).

NOTES

Repealed as noted to Art 1 at **[8.108]**.

[8.128]
Article 21
1. The Commission shall be assisted by the Customs Code Committee.
2. Where reference is made to this paragraph, Articles 4 and 7 of Decision 1999/468/EC shall apply.
The period laid down in Article 4(3) of Decision 1999/468/EC shall be set at three months.

NOTES
Repealed as noted to Art 1 at **[8.108]**.

[8.129]
Article 22
Member States shall communicate all relevant information on the application of this Regulation to the Commission.
The Commission shall forward this information to the other Member States.
The provisions of Regulation (EC) No 515/97 shall apply mutatis mutandis.
The details of the information procedure shall be drawn up under the implementing provisions in accordance with the procedure referred to in Article 21(2).

NOTES
Repealed as noted to Art 1 at **[8.108]**.

[8.130]
Article 23
On the basis of the information referred to in Article 22, the Commission shall report annually to the Council on the application of this Regulation. This report may, where appropriate, be accompanied by a proposal to amend the Regulation.

NOTES
Repealed as noted to Art 1 at **[8.108]**.

[8.131]
Article 24
Regulation (EC) No 3295/94 is repealed with effect from 1 July 2004.
References to the repealed Regulation shall be construed as references to this Regulation.

NOTES
Repealed as noted to Art 1 at **[8.108]**.

[8.132]
Article 25
This Regulation shall enter into force on the seventh day following that of its publication in the Official Journal of the European Union.
It shall apply with effect from 1 July 2004.
This Regulation shall be binding in its entirety and directly applicable in all Member States.

NOTES
Repealed as noted to Art 1 at **[8.108]**.

DIRECTIVE OF THE EUROPEAN PARLIAMENT AND OF THE COUNCIL

(2004/48/EC)

of 29 April 2004

on the enforcement of intellectual property rights

(Text with EEA relevance)

NOTES
Date of publication in OJ: this Directive originally appeared in OJ L157, 30.4.2004, p 45. Note that a corrigendum was published in OJ L195, 2.6.2004, p 16; that corrigendum set out the whole of the Directive (with changes incorporated) and it is the version from that corrigendum that is reproduced here.

THE EUROPEAN PARLIAMENT AND THE COUNCIL OF THE EUROPEAN UNION,

Having regard to the Treaty establishing the European Community, and in particular Article 95 thereof,

Having regard to the proposal from the Commission,

Having regard to the opinion of the European Economic and Social Committee,[1]
After consulting the Committee of the Regions,
Acting in accordance with the procedure laid down in Article 251 of the Treaty,[2]
Whereas—

(1) The achievement of the internal market entails eliminating restrictions on freedom of movement and distortions of competition, while creating an environment conducive to innovation and investment. In this context, the protection of intellectual property is an essential element for the success of the internal market. The protection of intellectual property is important not only for promoting innovation and creativity, but also for developing employment and improving competitiveness.

(2) The protection of intellectual property should allow the inventor or creator to derive a legitimate profit from his/her invention or creation. It should also allow the widest possible dissemination of works, ideas and new know-how. At the same time, it should not hamper freedom of expression, the free movement of information, or the protection of personal data, including on the Internet.

(3) However, without effective means of enforcing intellectual property rights, innovation and creativity are discouraged and investment diminished. It is therefore necessary to ensure that the substantive law on intellectual property, which is nowadays largely part of the acquis communautaire, is applied effectively in the Community. In this respect, the means of enforcing intellectual property rights are of paramount importance for the success of the Internal Market.

(4) At international level, all Member States, as well as the Community itself as regards matters within its competence, are bound by the Agreement on trade-related aspects of intellectual property (the TRIPS Agreement), approved, as part of the multilateral negotiations of the Uruguay Round, by Council Decision 94/800/EC[3] and concluded in the framework of the World Trade Organisation.

(5) The TRIPS Agreement contains, in particular, provisions on the means of enforcing intellectual property rights, which are common standards applicable at international level and implemented in all Member States. This Directive should not affect Member States' international obligations, including those under the TRIPS Agreement.

(6) There are also international conventions to which all Member States are parties and which also contain provisions on the means of enforcing intellectual property rights. These include, in particular, the Paris Convention for the Protection of Industrial Property, the Berne Convention for the Protection of Literary and Artistic Works, and the Rome Convention for the Protection of Performers, Producers of Phonograms and Broadcasting Organisations.

(7) It emerges from the consultations held by the Commission on this question that, in the Member States, and despite the TRIPS Agreement, there are still major disparities as regards the means of enforcing intellectual property rights. For instance, the arrangements for applying provisional measures, which are used in particular to preserve evidence, the calculation of damages, or the arrangements for applying injunctions, vary widely from one Member State to another. In some Member States, there are no measures, procedures and remedies such as the right of information and the recall, at the infringer's expense, of the infringing goods placed on the market.

(8) The disparities between the systems of the Member States as regards the means of enforcing intellectual property rights are prejudicial to the proper functioning of the Internal Market and make it impossible to ensure that intellectual property rights enjoy an equivalent level of protection throughout the Community. This situation does not promote free movement within the internal market or create an environment conducive to healthy competition.

(9) The current disparities also lead to a weakening of the substantive law on intellectual property and to a fragmentation of the internal market in this field. This causes a loss of confidence in the internal market in business circles, with a consequent reduction in investment in innovation and creation. Infringements of intellectual property rights appear to be increasingly linked to organised crime. Increasing use of the Internet enables pirated products to be distributed instantly around the globe. Effective enforcement of the substantive law on intellectual property should be ensured by specific action at Community level. Approximation of the legislation of the Member States in this field is therefore an essential prerequisite for the proper functioning of the internal market.

(10) The objective of this Directive is to approximate legislative systems so as to ensure a high, equivalent and homogeneous level of protection in the internal market.

(11) This Directive does not aim to establish harmonised rules for judicial cooperation, jurisdiction, the recognition and enforcement of decisions in civil and commercial matters, or deal with applicable law. There are Community instruments which govern such matters in general terms and are, in principle, equally applicable to intellectual property.

(12) This Directive should not affect the application of the rules of competition, and in particular Articles 81 and 82 of the Treaty. The measures provided for in this Directive should not be used to restrict competition unduly in a manner contrary to the Treaty.

(13) It is necessary to define the scope of this Directive as widely as possible in order to

encompass all the intellectual property rights covered by Community provisions in this field and/or by the national law of the Member State concerned. Nevertheless, that requirement does not affect the possibility, on the part of those Member States which so wish, to extend, for internal purposes, the provisions of this Directive to include acts involving unfair competition, including parasitic copies, or similar activities.

(14) The measures provided for in Articles 6(2), 8(1) and 9(2) need to be applied only in respect of acts carried out on a commercial scale. This is without prejudice to the possibility for Member States to apply those measures also in respect of other acts. Acts carried out on a commercial scale are those carried out for direct or indirect economic or commercial advantage; this would normally exclude acts carried out by end-consumers acting in good faith.

(15) This Directive should not affect substantive law on intellectual property, Directive 95/46/EC of 24 October 1995 of the European Parliament and of the Council on the protection of individuals with regard to the processing of personal data and on the free movement of such data,[4] Directive 1999/93/EC of the European Parliament and of the Council of 13 December 1999 on a Community framework for electronic signatures[5] and Directive 2000/31/EC of the European Parliament and of the Council of 8 June 2000 on certain legal aspects of information society services, in particular electronic commerce, in the internal market.[6]

(16) The provisions of this Directive should be without prejudice to the particular provisions for the enforcement of rights and on exceptions in the domain of copyright and related rights set out in Community instruments and notably those found in Council Directive 91/250/EEC of 14 May 1991 on the legal protection of computer programs[7] or in Directive 2001/29/EC of the European Parliament and of the Council of 22 May 2001 on the harmonisation of certain aspects of copyright and related rights in the information society.[8]

(17) The measures, procedures and remedies provided for in this Directive should be determined in each case in such a manner as to take due account of the specific characteristics of that case, including the specific features of each intellectual property right and, where appropriate, the intentional or unintentional character of the infringement.

(18) The persons entitled to request application of those measures, procedures and remedies should be not only the rightholders but also persons who have a direct interest and legal standing in so far as permitted by and in accordance with the applicable law, which may include professional organisations in charge of the management of those rights or for the defence of the collective and individual interests for which they are responsible.

(19) Since copyright exists from the creation of a work and does not require formal registration, it is appropriate to adopt the rule laid down in Article 15 of the Berne Convention, which establishes the presumption whereby the author of a literary or artistic work is regarded as such if his/her name appears on the work. A similar presumption should be applied to the owners of related rights since it is often the holder of a related right, such as a phonogram producer, who will seek to defend rights and engage in fighting acts of piracy.

(20) Given that evidence is an element of paramount importance for establishing the infringement of intellectual property rights, it is appropriate to ensure that effective means of presenting, obtaining and preserving evidence are available. The procedures should have regard to the rights of the defence and provide the necessary guarantees, including the protection of confidential information. For infringements committed on a commercial scale it is also important that the courts may order access, where appropriate, to banking, financial or commercial documents under the control of the alleged infringer.

(21) Other measures designed to ensure a high level of protection exist in certain Member States and should be made available in all the Member States. This is the case with the right of information, which allows precise information to be obtained on the origin of the infringing goods or services, the distribution channels and the identity of any third parties involved in the infringement.

(22) It is also essential to provide for provisional measures for the immediate termination of infringements, without awaiting a decision on thc substancc of thc casc, while observing the rights of the defence, ensuring the proportionality of the provisional measures as appropriate to the characteristics of the case in question and providing the guarantees needed to cover the costs and the injury caused to the defendant by an unjustified request. Such measures are particularly justified where any delay would cause irreparable harm to the holder of an intellectual property right.

(23) Without prejudice to any other measures, procedures and remedies available, rightholders should have the possibility of applying for an injunction against an intermediary whose services are being used by a third party to infringe the rightholder's industrial property right. The conditions and procedures relating to such injunctions should be left to the national law of the Member States. As far as infringements of copyright and related rights are concerned, a comprehensive level of harmonisation is already provided for in Directive 2001/29/EC. Article 8(3) of Directive 2001/29/EC should therefore not be affected by this Directive.

(24) Depending on the particular case, and if justified by the circumstances, the measures, procedures and remedies to be provided for should include prohibitory measures aimed at preventing further infringements of intellectual property rights. Moreover there should be corrective measures,

where appropriate at the expense of the infringer, such as the recall and definitive removal from the channels of commerce, or destruction, of the infringing goods and, in appropriate cases, of the materials and implements principally used in the creation or manufacture of these goods. These corrective measures should take account of the interests of third parties including, in particular, consumers and private parties acting in good faith.

(25) Where an infringement is committed unintentionally and without negligence and where the corrective measures or injunctions provided for by this Directive would be disproportionate, Member States should have the option of providing for the possibility, in appropriate cases, of pecuniary compensation being awarded to the injured party as an alternative measure. However, where the commercial use of counterfeit goods or the supply of services would constitute an infringement of law other than intellectual property law or would be likely to harm consumers, such use or supply should remain prohibited.

(26) With a view to compensating for the prejudice suffered as a result of an infringement committed by an infringer who engaged in an activity in the knowledge, or with reasonable grounds for knowing, that it would give rise to such an infringement, the amount of damages awarded to the rightholder should take account of all appropriate aspects, such as loss of earnings incurred by the rightholder, or unfair profits made by the infringer and, where appropriate, any moral prejudice caused to the rightholder. As an alternative, for example where it would be difficult to determine the amount of the actual prejudice suffered, the amount of the damages might be derived from elements such as the royalties or fees which would have been due if the infringer had requested authorisation to use the intellectual property right in question. The aim is not to introduce an obligation to provide for punitive damages but to allow for compensation based on an objective criterion while taking account of the expenses incurred by the rightholder, such as the costs of identification and research.

(27) To act as a supplementary deterrent to future infringers and to contribute to the awareness of the public at large, it is useful to publicise decisions in intellectual property infringement cases.

(28) In addition to the civil and administrative measures, procedures and remedies provided for under this Directive, criminal sanctions also constitute, in appropriate cases, a means of ensuring the enforcement of intellectual property rights.

(29) Industry should take an active part in the fight against piracy and counterfeiting. The development of codes of conduct in the circles directly affected is a supplementary means of bolstering the regulatory framework. The Member States, in collaboration with the Commission, should encourage the development of codes of conduct in general. Monitoring of the manufacture of optical discs, particularly by means of an identification code embedded in discs produced in the Community, helps to limit infringements of intellectual property rights in this sector, which suffers from piracy on a large scale. However, these technical protection measures should not be misused to protect markets and prevent parallel imports.

(30) In order to facilitate the uniform application of this Directive, it is appropriate to provide for systems of cooperation and the exchange of information between Member States, on the one hand, and between the Member States and the Commission on the other, in particular by creating a network of correspondents designated by the Member States and by providing regular reports assessing the application of this Directive and the effectiveness of the measures taken by the various national bodies.

(31) Since, for the reasons already described, the objective of this Directive can best be achieved at Community level, the Community may adopt measures, in accordance with the principle of subsidiarity as set out in Article 5 of the Treaty. In accordance with the principle of proportionality as set out in that Article, this Directive does not go beyond what is necessary in order to achieve that objective.

(32) This Directive respects the fundamental rights and observes the principles recognised in particular by the Charter of Fundamental Rights of the European Union. In particular, this Directive seeks to ensure full respect for intellectual property, in accordance with Article 17(2) of that Charter,

NOTES

1 OJ C32, 5.2.2004, p 15.

2 Opinion of the European Parliament of 9 March 2004 (not yet published in the Official Journal) and Council Decision of 26 April 2004.

3 OJ L336, 23.12.1994, p 1.

4 OJ L281, 23.11.1995, p 31. Directive as amended by Regulation (EC) No 1882/2003 (OJ L284, 31.10.2003, p 1).

5 OJ L13, 19.1.2000, p 12.

6 OJ L178, 17.7.2000, p 1.

7 OJ L122, 17.5.1991, p 42. Directive as amended by Directive 93/98/EEC (OJ L290, 24.11.1993, p 9).

8 OJ L167, 22.6.2001, p 10.

HAVE ADOPTED THIS DIRECTIVE—

CHAPTER I
OBJECTIVE AND SCOPE

[8.133]
Article 1
Subject matter
This Directive concerns the measures, procedures and remedies necessary to ensure the enforcement of intellectual property rights. For the purposes of this Directive, the term "intellectual property rights" includes industrial property rights.

[8.134]
Article 2
Scope
1. Without prejudice to the means which are or may be provided for in Community or national legislation, in so far as those means may be more favourable for rightholders, the measures, procedures and remedies provided for by this Directive shall apply, in accordance with Article 3, to any infringement of intellectual property rights as provided for by Community law and/or by the national law of the Member State concerned.
2. This Directive shall be without prejudice to the specific provisions on the enforcement of rights and on exceptions contained in Community legislation concerning copyright and rights related to copyright, notably those found in Directive 91/250/EEC and, in particular, Article 7 thereof or in Directive 2001/29/EC and, in particular, Articles 2 to 6 and Article 8 thereof.
3. This Directive shall not affect—
(a) the Community provisions governing the substantive law on intellectual property, Directive 95/46/EC, Directive 1999/93/EC or Directive 2000/31/EC, in general, and Articles 12 to 15 of Directive 2000/31/EC in particular;
(b) Member States' international obligations and notably the TRIPS Agreement, including those relating to criminal procedures and penalties;
(c) any national provisions in Member States relating to criminal procedures or penalties in respect of infringement of intellectual property rights.

CHAPTER II
MEASURES, PROCEDURES AND REMEDIES

SECTION 1
GENERAL PROVISIONS

[8.135]
Article 3
General obligation
1. Member States shall provide for the measures, procedures and remedies necessary to ensure the enforcement of the intellectual property rights covered by this Directive. Those measures, procedures and remedies shall be fair and equitable and shall not be unnecessarily complicated or costly, or entail unreasonable time-limits or unwarranted delays.
2. Those measures, procedures and remedies shall also be effective, proportionate and dissuasive and shall be applied in such a manner as to avoid the creation of barriers to legitimate trade and to provide for safeguards against their abuse.

[8.136]
Article 4
Persons entitled to apply for the application of the measures, procedures and remedies
Member States shall recognise as persons entitled to seek application of the measures, procedures and remedies referred to in this chapter—
(a) the holders of intellectual property rights, in accordance with the provisions of the applicable law;
(b) all other persons authorised to use those rights, in particular licensees, in so far as permitted by and in accordance with the provisions of the applicable law;
(c) intellectual property collective rights-management bodies which are regularly recognised as having a right to represent holders of intellectual property rights, in so far as permitted by and in accordance with the provisions of the applicable law;
(d) professional defence bodies which are regularly recognised as having a right to represent holders of intellectual property rights, in so far as permitted by and in accordance with the provisions of the applicable law.

[8.137]
Article 5
Presumption of authorship or ownership
For the purposes of applying the measures, procedures and remedies provided for in this Directive,

(a) for the author of a literary or artistic work, in the absence of proof to the contrary, to be regarded as such, and consequently to be entitled to institute infringement proceedings, it shall be sufficient for his/her name to appear on the work in the usual manner;

(b) the provision under (a) shall apply *mutatis mutandis* to the holders of rights related to copyright with regard to their protected subject matter.

SECTION 2
EVIDENCE

[8.138]
Article 6
Evidence

1. Member States shall ensure that, on application by a party which has presented reasonably available evidence sufficient to support its claims, and has, in substantiating those claims, specified evidence which lies in the control of the opposing party, the competent judicial authorities may order that such evidence be presented by the opposing party, subject to the protection of confidential information. For the purposes of this paragraph, Member States may provide that a reasonable sample of a substantial number of copies of a work or any other protected object be considered by the competent judicial authorities to constitute reasonable evidence.

2. Under the same conditions, in the case of an infringement committed on a commercial scale Member States shall take such measures as are necessary to enable the competent judicial authorities to order, where appropriate, on application by a party, the communication of banking, financial or commercial documents under the control of the opposing party, subject to the protection of confidential information.

[8.139]
Article 7
Measures for preserving evidence

1. Member States shall ensure that, even before the commencement of proceedings on the merits of the case, the competent judicial authorities may, on application by a party who has presented reasonably available evidence to support his/her claims that his/her intellectual property right has been infringed or is about to be infringed, order prompt and effective provisional measures to preserve relevant evidence in respect of the alleged infringement, subject to the protection of confidential information. Such measures may include the detailed description, with or without the taking of samples, or the physical seizure of the infringing goods, and, in appropriate cases, the materials and implements used in the production and/or distribution of these goods and the documents relating thereto. Those measures shall be taken, if necessary without the other party having been heard, in particular where any delay is likely to cause irreparable harm to the rightholder or where there is a demonstrable risk of evidence being destroyed.

Where measures to preserve evidence are adopted without the other party having been heard, the parties affected shall be given notice, without delay after the execution of the measures at the latest. A review, including a right to be heard, shall take place upon request of the parties affected with a view to deciding, within a reasonable period after the notification of the measures, whether the measures shall be modified, revoked or confirmed.

2. Member States shall ensure that the measures to preserve evidence may be subject to the lodging by the applicant of adequate security or an equivalent assurance intended to ensure compensation for any prejudice suffered by the defendant as provided for in paragraph 4.

3. Member States shall ensure that the measures to preserve evidence are revoked or otherwise cease to have effect, upon request of the defendant, without prejudice to the damages which may be claimed, if the applicant does not institute, within a reasonable period, proceedings leading to a decision on the merits of the case before the competent judicial authority, the period to be determined by the judicial authority ordering the measures where the law of a Member State so permits or, in the absence of such determination, within a period not exceeding 20 working days or 31 calendar days, whichever is the longer.

4. Where the measures to preserve evidence are revoked, or where they lapse due to any act or omission by the applicant, or where it is subsequently found that there has been no infringement or threat of infringement of an intellectual property right, the judicial authorities shall have the authority to order the applicant, upon request of the defendant, to provide the defendant appropriate compensation for any injury caused by those measures.

5. Member States may take measures to protect witnesses' identity.

SECTION 3
RIGHT OF INFORMATION

[8.140]
Article 8
Right of information

1. Member States shall ensure that, in the context of proceedings concerning an infringement of an intellectual property right and in response to a justified and proportionate request of the claimant, the competent judicial authorities may order that information on the origin and distribution networks of the goods or services which infringe an intellectual property right be provided by the infringer and/or any other person who—
   (a) was found in possession of the infringing goods on a commercial scale;
   (b) was found to be using the infringing services on a commercial scale;
   (c) was found to be providing on a commercial scale services used in infringing activities; or
   (d) was indicated by the person referred to in point (a), (b) or (c) as being involved in the production, manufacture or distribution of the goods or the provision of the services.
2. The information referred to in paragraph 1 shall, as appropriate, comprise—
   (a) the names and addresses of the producers, manufacturers, distributors, suppliers and other previous holders of the goods or services, as well as the intended wholesalers and retailers;
   (b) information on the quantities produced, manufactured, delivered, received or ordered, as well as the price obtained for the goods or services in question.
3. Paragraphs 1 and 2 shall apply without prejudice to other statutory provisions which—
   (a) grant the rightholder rights to receive fuller information;
   (b) govern the use in civil or criminal proceedings of the information communicated pursuant to this Article;
   (c) govern responsibility for misuse of the right of information; or
   (d) afford an opportunity for refusing to provide information which would force the person referred to in paragraph 1 to admit to his/her own participation or that of his/her close relatives in an infringement of an intellectual property right; or
   (e) govern the protection of confidentiality of information sources or the processing of personal data.

SECTION 4
PROVISIONAL AND PRECAUTIONARY MEASURES

[8.141]
Article 9
Provisional and precautionary measures

1. Member States shall ensure that the judicial authorities may, at the request of the applicant—
   (a) issue against the alleged infringer an interlocutory injunction intended to prevent any imminent infringement of an intellectual property right, or to forbid, on a provisional basis and subject, where appropriate, to a recurring penalty payment where provided for by national law, the continuation of the alleged infringements of that right, or to make such continuation subject to the lodging of guarantees intended to ensure the compensation of the rightholder; an interlocutory injunction may also be issued, under the same conditions, against an intermediary whose services are being used by a third party to infringe an intellectual property right; injunctions against intermediaries whose services are used by a third party to infringe a copyright or a related right are covered by Directive 2001/29/EC;
   (b) order the seizure or delivery up of the goods suspected of infringing an intellectual property right so as to prevent their entry into or movement within the channels of commerce.
2. In the case of an infringement committed on a commercial scale, the Member States shall ensure that, if the injured party demonstrates circumstances likely to endanger the recovery of damages, the judicial authorities may order the precautionary seizure of the movable and immovable property of the alleged infringer, including the blocking of his/her bank accounts and other assets. To that end, the competent authorities may order the communication of bank, financial or commercial documents, or appropriate access to the relevant information.
3. The judicial authorities shall, in respect of the measures referred to in paragraphs 1 and 2, have the authority to require the applicant to provide any reasonably available evidence in order to satisfy themselves with a sufficient degree of certainty that the applicant is the rightholder and that the applicant's right is being infringed, or that such infringement is imminent.
4. Member States shall ensure that the provisional measures referred to in paragraphs 1 and 2 may, in appropriate cases, be taken without the defendant having been heard, in particular where any delay would cause irreparable harm to the rightholder. In that event, the parties shall be so informed without delay after the execution of the measures at the latest.

A review, including a right to be heard, shall take place upon request of the defendant with a view to deciding, within a reasonable time after notification of the measures, whether those measures shall be modified, revoked or confirmed.

5. Member States shall ensure that the provisional measures referred to in paragraphs 1 and 2 are revoked or otherwise cease to have effect, upon request of the defendant, if the applicant does not institute, within a reasonable period, proceedings leading to a decision on the merits of the case before the competent judicial authority, the period to be determined by the judicial authority ordering the measures where the law of a Member State so permits or, in the absence of such determination, within a period not exceeding 20 working days or 31 calendar days, whichever is the longer.

6. The competent judicial authorities may make the provisional measures referred to in paragraphs 1 and 2 subject to the lodging by the applicant of adequate security or an equivalent assurance intended to ensure compensation for any prejudice suffered by the defendant as provided for in paragraph 7.

7. Where the provisional measures are revoked or where they lapse due to any act or omission by the applicant, or where it is subsequently found that there has been no infringement or threat of infringement of an intellectual property right, the judicial authorities shall have the authority to order the applicant, upon request of the defendant, to provide the defendant appropriate compensation for any injury caused by those measures.

SECTION 5
MEASURES RESULTING FROM A DECISION ON THE MERITS OF THE CASE

[8.142]
Article 10
Corrective measures

1. Without prejudice to any damages due to the rightholder by reason of the infringement, and without compensation of any sort, Member States shall ensure that the competent judicial authorities may order, at the request of the applicant, that appropriate measures be taken with regard to goods that they have found to be infringing an intellectual property right and, in appropriate cases, with regard to materials and implements principally used in the creation or manufacture of those goods. Such measures shall include—

(a) recall from the channels of commerce;
(b) definitive removal from the channels of commerce; or
(c) destruction.

2. The judicial authorities shall order that those measures be carried out at the expense of the infringer, unless particular reasons are invoked for not doing so.

3. In considering a request for corrective measures, the need for proportionality between the seriousness of the infringement and the remedies ordered as well as the interests of third parties shall be taken into account.

[8.143]
Article 11
Injunctions

Member States shall ensure that, where a judicial decision is taken finding an infringement of an intellectual property right, the judicial authorities may issue against the infringer an injunction aimed at prohibiting the continuation of the infringement. Where provided for by national law, non-compliance with an injunction shall, where appropriate, be subject to a recurring penalty payment, with a view to ensuring compliance. Member States shall also ensure that rightholders are in a position to apply for an injunction against intermediaries whose services are used by a third party to infringe an intellectual property right, without prejudice to Article 8(3) of Directive 2001/29/EC.

[8.144]
Article 12
Alternative measures

Member States may provide that, in appropriate cases and at the request of the person liable to be subject to the measures provided for in this section, the competent judicial authorities may order pecuniary compensation to be paid to the injured party instead of applying the measures provided for in this section if that person acted unintentionally and without negligence, if execution of the measures in question would cause him/her disproportionate harm and if pecuniary compensation to the injured party appears reasonably satisfactory.

SECTION 6
DAMAGES AND LEGAL COSTS

[8.145]
Article 13
Damages

1. Member States shall ensure that the competent judicial authorities, on application of the injured party, order the infringer who knowingly, or with reasonable grounds to know, engaged in an infringing activity, to pay the rightholder damages appropriate to the actual prejudice suffered by him/her as a result of the infringement.

When the judicial authorities set the damages—

(a) they shall take into account all appropriate aspects, such as the negative economic consequences, including lost profits, which the injured party has suffered, any unfair profits made by the infringer and, in appropriate cases, elements other than economic factors, such as the moral prejudice caused to the rightholder by the infringement;

or

(b) as an alternative to (a), they may, in appropriate cases, set the damages as a lump sum on the basis of elements such as at least the amount of royalties or fees which would have been due if the infringer had requested authorisation to use the intellectual property right in question.

2. Where the infringer did not knowingly, or with reasonable grounds know, engage in infringing activity, Member States may lay down that the judicial authorities may order the recovery of profits or the payment of damages, which may be pre-established.

[8.146]
Article 14
Legal costs

Member States shall cnsure that reasonable and proportionate legal costs and other expenses incurred by the successful party shall, as a general rule, be borne by the unsuccessful party, unless equity does not allow this.

SECTION 7
PUBLICITY MEASURES

[8.147]
Article 15
Publication of judicial decisions

Member States shall ensure that, in legal proceedings instituted for infringement of an intellectual property right, the judicial authorities may order, at the request of the applicant and at the expense of the infringer, appropriate measures for the dissemination of the information concerning the decision, including displaying the decision and publishing it in full or in part. Member States may provide for other additional publicity measures which are appropriate to the particular circumstances, including prominent advertising.

CHAPTER III
SANCTIONS BY MEMBER STATES

[8.148]
Article 16
Sanctions by Member States

Without prejudice to the civil and administrative measures, procedures and remedies laid down by this Directive, Member States may apply other appropriate sanctions in cases where intellectual property rights have been infringed.

CHAPTER IV
CODES OF CONDUCT AND ADMINISTRATIVE COOPERATION

[8.149]
Article 17
Codes of conduct

Member States shall encourage—

(a) the development by trade or professional associations or organisations of codes of conduct at Community level aimed at contributing towards the enforcement of the intellectual property rights, particularly by recommending the use on optical discs of a code enabling the identification of the origin of their manufacture;

(b) the submission to the Commission of draft codes of conduct at national and Community level and of any evaluations of the application of these codes of conduct.

[8.150]
Article 18
Assessment

1. Three years after the date laid down in Article 20(1), each Member State shall submit to the Commission a report on the implementation of this Directive.

On the basis of those reports, the Commission shall draw up a report on the application of this Directive, including an assessment of the effectiveness of the measures taken, as well as an evaluation of its impact on innovation and the development of the information society. That report shall then be transmitted to the European Parliament, the Council and the European Economic and Social Committee. It shall be accompanied, if necessary and in the light of developments in the Community legal order, by proposals for amendments to this Directive.

2. Member States shall provide the Commission with all the aid and assistance it may need when drawing up the report referred to in the second subparagraph of paragraph 1.

[8.151]
Article 19
Exchange of information and correspondents

For the purpose of promoting cooperation, including the exchange of information, among Member States and between Member States and the Commission, each Member State shall designate one or more national correspondents for any question relating to the implementation of the measures provided for by this Directive. It shall communicate the details of the national correspondent(s) to the other Member States and to the Commission.

CHAPTER V
FINAL PROVISIONS

[8.152]
Article 20
Implementation

1. Member States shall bring into force the laws, regulations and administrative provisions necessary to comply with this Directive by 29 April 2006. They shall forthwith inform the Commission thereof.

When Member States adopt these measures, they shall contain a reference to this Directive or shall be accompanied by such reference on the occasion of their official publication. The methods of making such reference shall be laid down by Member States.

2. Member States shall communicate to the Commission the texts of the provisions of national law which they adopt in the field governed by this Directive.

[8.153]
Article 21
Entry into force

This Directive shall enter into force on the 20th day following that of its publication in the *Official Journal of the European Union*.

[8.154]
Article 22
Addressees

This Directive is addressed to the Member States.

COMMISSION REGULATION

(772/2004/EC)

of 7 April 2004

on the application of Article 81(3) of the Treaty to categories of technology transfer agreements ('Technology Transfer Block Exemption')

(Text with EEA relevance)

NOTES

Date of publication in OJ: OJ L123, 27.4.2004, p 11.

THE COMMISSION OF THE EUROPEAN COMMUNITIES,

Having regard to the Treaty establishing the European Community,

Having regard to Council Regulation No 19/65/EEC of 2 March 1965 on application of Article 85(3) of the Treaty to certain categories of agreements and concerted practices,[1] and in particular Article 1 thereof,

Having published a draft of this Regulation,[2]

After consulting the Advisory Committee on Restrictive Practices and Dominant Positions,
Whereas—

(1) Regulation No 19/65/EEC empowers the Commission to apply Article 81(3) of the Treaty by Regulation to certain categories of technology transfer agreements and corresponding concerted practices to which only two undertakings are party which fall within Article 81(1).

(2) Pursuant to Regulation No 19/65/EEC, the Commission has, in particular, adopted Regulation (EC) No 240/96 of 31 January 1996 on the application of Article 85(3) of the Treaty to certain categories of technology transfer agreements.[3]

(3) On 20 December 2001 the Commission published an evaluation report on the transfer of technology block exemption Regulation (EC) No 240/96.[4] This generated a public debate on the application of Regulation (EC) No 240/96 and on the application in general of Article 81(1) and (3) of the Treaty to technology transfer agreements. The response to the evaluation report from Member States and third parties has been generally in favour of reform of Community competition policy on technology transfer agreements. It is therefore appropriate to repeal Regulation (EC) No 240/96.

(4) This Regulation should meet the two requirements of ensuring effective competition and providing adequate legal security for undertakings. The pursuit of these objectives should take account of the need to simplify the regulatory framework and its application. It is appropriate to move away from the approach of listing exempted clauses and to place greater emphasis on defining the categories of agreements which are exempted up to a certain level of market power and on specifying the restrictions or clauses which are not to be contained in such agreements. This is consistent with an economics-based approach which assesses the impact of agreements on the relevant market. It is also consistent with such an approach to make a distinction between agreements between competitors and agreements between non-competitors.

(5) Technology transfer agreements concern the licensing of technology. Such agreements will usually improve economic efficiency and be pro-competitive as they can reduce duplication of research and development, strengthen the incentive for the initial research and development, spur incremental innovation, facilitate diffusion and generate product market competition.

(6) The likelihood that such efficiency-enhancing and procompetitive effects will outweigh any anti-competitive effects due to restrictions contained in technology transfer agreements depends on the degree of market power of the undertakings concerned and, therefore, on the extent to which those undertakings face competition from undertakings owning substitute technologies or undertakings producing substitute products.

(7) This Regulation should only deal with agreements where the licensor permits the licensee to exploit the licensed technology, possibly after further research and development by the licensee, for the production of goods or services. It should not deal with licensing agreements for the purpose of subcontracting research and development. It should also not deal with licensing agreements to set up technology pools, that is to say, agreements for the pooling of technologies with the purpose of licensing the created package of intellectual property rights to third parties.

(8) For the application of Article 81(3) by regulation, it is not necessary to define those technology transfer agreements that are capable of falling within Article 81(1). In the individual assessment of agreements pursuant to Article 81(1), account has to be taken of several factors, and in particular the structure and the dynamics of the relevant technology and product markets.

(9) The benefit of the block exemption established by this Regulation should be limited to those agreements which can be assumed with sufficient certainty to satisfy the conditions of Article 81(3). In order to attain the benefits and objectives of technology transfer, the benefit of this Regulation should also apply to provisions contained in technology transfer agreements that do not constitute the primary object of such agreements, but are directly related to the application of the licensed technology.

(10) For technology transfer agreements between competitors it can be presumed that, where the combined share of the relevant markets accounted for by the parties does not exceed 20% and the agreements do not contain certain severely anti-competitive restraints, they generally lead to an improvement in production or distribution and allow consumers a fair share of the resulting benefits.

(11) For technology transfer agreements between non-competitors it can be presumed that, where the individual share of the relevant markets accounted for by each of the parties does not exceed 30% and the agreements do not contain certain severely anti-competitive restraints, they generally lead to an improvement in production or distribution and allow consumers a fair share of the resulting benefits.

(12) There can be no presumption that above these market-share thresholds technology transfer agreements do fall within the scope of Article 81(1). For instance, an exclusive licensing agreement between non-competing undertakings does often not fall within the scope of Article 81(1). There can also be no presumption that, above these market-share thresholds, technology transfer agreements falling within the scope of Article 81(1) will not satisfy the conditions for exemption. However, it can also not be presumed that they will usually give rise to objective advantages of such a character and size as to compensate for the disadvantages which they create for competition.

(13) This Regulation should not exempt technology transfer agreements containing restrictions which are not indispensable to the improvement of production or distribution. In particular, technology transfer agreements containing certain severely anti-competitive restraints such as the fixing of prices charged to third parties should be excluded from the benefit of the block exemption established by this Regulation irrespective of the market shares of the undertakings concerned. In the case of such hardcore restrictions the whole agreement should be excluded from the benefit of the block exemption.

(14) In order to protect incentives to innovate and the appropriate application of intellectual property rights, certain restrictions should be excluded from the block exemption. In particular exclusive grant back obligations for severable improvements should be excluded. Where such a restriction is included in a licence agreement only the restriction in question should be excluded from the benefit of the block exemption.

(15) The market-share thresholds, the non-exemption of technology transfer agreements containing severely anticompetitive restraints and the excluded restrictions provided for in this Regulation will normally ensure that the agreements to which the block exemption applies do not enable the participating undertakings to eliminate competition in respect of a substantial part of the products in question.

(16) In particular cases in which the agreements falling under this Regulation nevertheless have effects incompatible with Article 81(3), the Commission should be able to withdraw the benefit of the block exemption. This may occur in particular where the incentives to innovate are reduced or where access to markets is hindered.

(17) Council Regulation (EC) No 1/2003 of 16 December 2002 on the implementation of the rules on competition laid down in Articles 81 and 82 of the Treaty[5] empowers the competent authorities of Member States to withdraw the benefit of the block exemption in respect of technology transfer agreements having effects incompatible with Article 81(3), where such effects are felt in their respective territory, or in a part thereof, and where such territory has the characteristics of a distinct geographic market. Member States must ensure that the exercise of this power of withdrawal does not prejudice the uniform application throughout the common market of the Community competition rules or the full effect of the measures adopted in implementation of those rules.

(18) In order to strengthen supervision of parallel networks of technology transfer agreements which have similar restrictive effects and which cover more than 50% of a given market, the Commission should be able to declare this Regulation inapplicable to technology transfer agreements containing specific restraints relating to the market concerned, thereby restoring the full application of Article 81 to such agreements.

(19) This Regulation should cover only technology transfer agreements between a licensor and a licensee. It should cover such agreements even if conditions are stipulated for more than one level of trade, by, for instance, requiring the licensee to set up a particular distribution system and specifying the obligations the licensee must or may impose on resellers of the products produced under the licence. However, such conditions and obligations should comply with the competition rules applicable to supply and distribution agreements. Supply and distribution agreements concluded between a licensee and its buyers should not be exempted by this Regulation.

(20) This Regulation is without prejudice to the application of Article 82 of the Treaty,

NOTES

[1] OJ 36, 6.3.1965, p 533/65. Regulation as last amended by Regulation (EC) No 1/2003 (OJ L1, 4.1.2003, p 1).

[2] OJ C235, 1.10.2003, p 10.

[3] OJ L31, 9.2.1996, p 2. Regulation as amended by the 2003 Act of Accession.

[4] COM(2001) 786 final.

[5] OJ L1, 4.1.2003, p 1. Regulation as amended by Regulation (EC) No 411/2004 (OJ L68, 6.3.2004, p 1).

HAS ADOPTED THIS REGULATION—

[8.155]
Article 1
Definitions

1. For the purposes of this Regulation, the following definitions shall apply—
   (a) 'agreement' means an agreement, a decision of an association of undertakings or a concerted practice;
   (b) 'technology transfer agreement' means a patent licensing agreement, a know-how licensing agreement, a software copyright licensing agreement or a mixed patent, knowhow or software copyright licensing agreement, including any such agreement containing provisions which relate to the sale and purchase of products or which relate to the licensing of other intellectual property rights or the assignment of intellectual property rights, provided that those provisions do not constitute the primary object of the agreement and are directly related to the production of the contract products; assignments of patents, know-how, software copyright or a combination thereof where part of the risk associated

with the exploitation of the technology remains with the assignor, in particular where the sum payable in consideration of the assignment is dependent on the turnover obtained by the assignee in respect of products produced with the assigned technology, the quantity of such products produced or the number of operations carried out employing the technology, shall also be deemed to be technology transfer agreements;

(c) 'reciprocal agreement' means a technology transfer agreement where two undertakings grant each other, in the same or separate contracts, a patent licence, a know-how licence, a software copyright licence or a mixed patent, know-how or software copyright licence and where these licences concern competing technologies or can be used for the production of competing products;

(d) 'non-reciprocal agreement' means a technology transfer agreement where one undertaking grants another undertaking a patent licence, a know-how licence, a software copyright licence or a mixed patent, know-how or software copyright licence, or where two undertakings grant each other such a licence but where these licences do not concern competing technologies and cannot be used for the production of competing products;

(e) 'product' means a good or a service, including both intermediary goods and services and final goods and services;

(f) 'contract products' means products produced with the licensed technology;

(g) 'intellectual property rights' includes industrial property rights, know-how, copyright and neighbouring rights;

(h) 'patents' means patents, patent applications, utility models, applications for registration of utility models, designs, topographies of semiconductor products, supplementary protection certificates for medicinal products or other products for which such supplementary protection certificates may be obtained and plant breeder's certificates;

(i) 'know-how' means a package of non-patented practical information, resulting from experience and testing, which is—

(i) secret, that is to say, not generally known or easily accessible,

(ii) substantial, that is to say, significant and useful for the production of the contract products, and

(iii) identified, that is to say, described in a sufficiently comprehensive manner so as to make it possible to verify that it fulfils the criteria of secrecy and substantiality;

(j) 'competing undertakings' means undertakings which compete on the relevant technology market and/or the relevant product market, that is to say—

(i) competing undertakings on the relevant technology market, being undertakings which license out competing technologies without infringing each others' intellectual property rights (actual competitors on the technology market); the relevant technology market includes technologies which are regarded by the licensees as interchangeable with or substitutable for the licensed technology, by reason of the technologies' characteristics, their royalties and their intended use,

(ii) competing undertakings on the relevant product market, being undertakings which, in the absence of the technology transfer agreement, are both active on the relevant product and geographic market(s) on which the contract products are sold without infringing each others' intellectual property rights (actual competitors on the product market) or would, on realistic grounds, undertake the necessary additional investments or other necessary switching costs so that they could timely enter, without infringing each others' intellectual property rights, the(se) relevant product and geographic market(s) in response to a small and permanent increase in relative prices (potential competitors on the product market); the relevant product market comprises products which are regarded by the buyers as interchangeable with or substitutable for the contract products, by reason of the products' characteristics, their prices and their intended use;

(k) 'selective distribution system' means a distribution system where the licensor undertakes to license the production of the contract products only to licensees selected on the basis of specified criteria and where these licensees undertake not to sell the contract products to unauthorised distributors;

(l) 'exclusive territory' means a territory in which only one undertaking is allowed to produce the contract products with the licensed technology, without prejudice to the possibility of allowing within that territory another licensee to produce the contract products only for a particular customer where this second licence was granted in order to create an alternative source of supply for that customer;

(m) 'exclusive customer group' means a group of customers to which only one undertaking is allowed actively to sell the contract products produced with the licensed technology;

(n) 'severable improvement' means an improvement that can be exploited without infringing the licensed technology.

2. The terms 'undertaking', 'licensor' and 'licensee' shall include their respective connected undertakings.

'Connected undertakings' means—

(a) undertakings in which a party to the agreement, directly or indirectly—

(i) has the power to exercise more than half the voting rights, or

(ii) has the power to appoint more than half the members of the supervisory board, board of management or bodies legally representing the undertaking, or
(iii) has the right to manage the undertaking's affairs;

(b) undertakings which directly or indirectly have, over a party to the agreement, the rights or powers listed in (a);

(c) undertakings in which an undertaking referred to in (b) has, directly or indirectly, the rights or powers listed in (a);

(d) undertakings in which a party to the agreement together with one or more of the undertakings referred to in (a), (b) or (c), or in which two or more of the latter undertakings, jointly have the rights or powers listed in (a);

(e) undertakings in which the rights or the powers listed in (a) are jointly held by—
(i) parties to the agreement or their respective connected undertakings referred to in (a) to (d), or
(ii) one or more of the parties to the agreement or one or more of their connected undertakings referred to in (a) to (d) and one or more third parties.

[8.156]
Article 2
Exemption

Pursuant to Article 81(3) of the Treaty and subject to the provisions of this Regulation, it is hereby declared that Article 81(1) of the Treaty shall not apply to technology transfer agreements entered into between two undertakings permitting the production of contract products. This exemption shall apply to the extent that such agreements contain restrictions of competition falling within the scope of Article 81(1). The exemption shall apply for as long as the intellectual property right in the licensed technology has not expired, lapsed or been declared invalid or, in the case of know-how, for as long as the know-how remains secret, except in the event where the know-how becomes publicly known as a result of action by the licensee, in which case the exemption shall apply for the duration of the agreement.

[8.157]
Article 3
Market-share thresholds

1. Where the undertakings party to the agreement are competing undertakings, the exemption provided for in Article 2 shall apply on condition that the combined market share of the parties does not exceed 20% on the affected relevant technology and product market.

2. Where the undertakings party to the agreement are not competing undertakings, the exemption provided for in Article 2 shall apply on condition that the market share of each of the parties does not exceed 30% on the affected relevant technology and product market.

3. For the purposes of paragraphs 1 and 2, the market share of a party on the relevant technology market(s) is defined in terms of the presence of the licensed technology on the relevant product market(s). A licensor's market share on the relevant technology market shall be the combined market share on the relevant product market of the contract products produced by the licensor and its licensees.

[8.158]
Article 4
Hardcore restrictions

1. Where the undertakings party to the agreement are competing undertakings, the exemption provided for in Article 2 shall not apply to agreements which, directly or indirectly, in isolation or in combination with other factors under the control of the parties, have as their object—

(a) the restriction of a party's ability to determine its prices when selling products to third parties;

(b) the limitation of output, except limitations on the output of contract products imposed on the licensee in a non-reciprocal agreement or imposed on only one of the licensees in a reciprocal agreement;

(c) the allocation of markets or customers except—
(i) the obligation on the licensee(s) to produce with the licensed technology only within one or more technical fields of use or one or more product markets,
(ii) the obligation on the licensor and/or the licensee, in a non-reciprocal agreement, not to produce with the licensed technology within one or more technical fields of use or one or more product markets or one or more exclusive territories reserved for the other party,
(iii) the obligation on the licensor not to license the technology to another licensee in a particular territory,
(iv) the restriction, in a non-reciprocal agreement, of active and/or passive sales by the licensee and/or the licensor into the exclusive territory or to the exclusive customer group reserved for the other party,
(v) the restriction, in a non-reciprocal agreement, of active sales by the licensee into the exclusive territory or to the exclusive customer group allocated by the licensor to

another licensee provided the latter was not a competing undertaking of the licensor at the time of the conclusion of its own licence,

(vi) the obligation on the licensee to produce the contract products only for its own use provided that the licensee is not restricted in selling the contract products actively and passively as spare parts for its own products,

(vii) the obligation on the licensee, in a non-reciprocal agreement, to produce the contract products only for a particular customer, where the licence was granted in order to create an alternative source of supply for that customer;

(d) the restriction of the licensee's ability to exploit its own technology or the restriction of the ability of any of the parties to the agreement to carry out research and development, unless such latter restriction is indispensable to prevent the disclosure of the licensed know-how to third parties.

2. Where the undertakings party to the agreement are not competing undertakings, the exemption provided for in Article 2 shall not apply to agreements which, directly or indirectly, in isolation or in combination with other factors under the control of the parties, have as their object—

(a) the restriction of a party's ability to determine its prices when selling products to third parties, without prejudice to the possibility of imposing a maximum sale price or recommending a sale price, provided that it does not amount to a fixed or minimum sale price as a result of pressure from, or incentives offered by, any of the parties;

(b) the restriction of the territory into which, or of the customers to whom, the licensee may passively sell the contract products, except—

(i) the restriction of passive sales into an exclusive territory or to an exclusive customer group reserved for the licensor,

(ii) the restriction of passive sales into an exclusive territory or to an exclusive customer group allocated by the licensor to another licensee during the first two years that this other licensee is selling the contract products in that territory or to that customer group,

(iii) the obligation to produce the contract products only for its own use provided that the licensee is not restricted in selling the contract products actively and passively as spare parts for its own products,

(iv) the obligation to produce the contract products only for a particular customer, where the licence was granted in order to create an alternative source of supply for that customer,

(v) the restriction of sales to end-users by a licensee operating at the wholesale level of trade,

(vi) the restriction of sales to unauthorised distributors by the members of a selective distribution system;

(c) the restriction of active or passive sales to end-users by a licensee which is a member of a selective distribution system and which operates at the retail level, without prejudice to the possibility of prohibiting a member of the system from operating out of an unauthorised place of establishment.

3. Where the undertakings party to the agreement are not competing undertakings at the time of the conclusion of the agreement but become competing undertakings afterwards, paragraph 2 and not paragraph 1 shall apply for the full life of the agreement unless the agreement is subsequently amended in any material respect.

[8.159]
Article 5
Excluded restrictions

1. The exemption provided for in Article 2 shall not apply to any of the following obligations contained in technology transfer agreements—

(a) any direct or indirect obligation on the licensee to grant an exclusive licence to the licensor or to a third party designated by the licensor in respect of its own severable improvements to or its own new applications of the licensed technology;

(b) any direct or indirect obligation on the licensee to assign, in whole or in part, to the licensor or to a third party designated by the licensor, rights to its own severable improvements to or its own new applications of the licensed technology;

(c) any direct or indirect obligation on the licensee not to challenge the validity of intellectual property rights which the licensor holds in the common market, without prejudice to the possibility of providing for termination of the technology transfer agreement in the event that the licensee challenges the validity of one or more of the licensed intellectual property rights.

2. Where the undertakings party to the agreement are not competing undertakings, the exemption provided for in Article 2 shall not apply to any direct or indirect obligation limiting the licensee's ability to exploit its own technology or limiting the ability of any of the parties to the agreement to carry out research and development, unless such latter restriction is indispensable to prevent the disclosure of the licensed know-how to third parties.

[8.160]
Article 6
Withdrawal in individual cases

1. The Commission may withdraw the benefit of this Regulation, pursuant to Article 29(1) of Regulation (EC) No 1/2003, where it finds in any particular case that a technology transfer agreement to which the exemption provided for in Article 2 applies nevertheless has effects which are incompatible with Article 81(3) of the Treaty, and in particular where—

(a) access of third parties' technologies to the market is restricted, for instance by the cumulative effect of parallel networks of similar restrictive agreements prohibiting licensees from using third parties' technologies;

(b) access of potential licensees to the market is restricted, for instance by the cumulative effect of parallel networks of similar restrictive agreements prohibiting licensors from licensing to other licensees;

(c) without any objectively valid reason, the parties do not exploit the licensed technology.

2. Where, in any particular case, a technology transfer agreement to which the exemption provided for in Article 2 applies has effects which are incompatible with Article 81(3) of the Treaty in the territory of a Member State, or in a part thereof, which has all the characteristics of a distinct geographic market, the competition authority of that Member State may withdraw the benefit of this Regulation, pursuant to Article 29(2) of Regulation (EC) No 1/2003, in respect of that territory, under the same circumstances as those set out in paragraph 1 of this Article.

[8.161]
Article 7
Non-application of this Regulation

1. Pursuant to Article 1a of Regulation No 19/65/EEC, the Commission may by regulation declare that, where parallel networks of similar technology transfer agreements cover more than 50% of a relevant market, this Regulation is not to apply to technology transfer agreements containing specific restraints relating to that market.

2. A regulation pursuant to paragraph 1 shall not become applicable earlier than six months following its adoption.

[8.162]
Article 8
Application of the market-share thresholds

1. For the purposes of applying the market-share thresholds provided for in Article 3 the rules set out in this paragraph shall apply.

The market share shall be calculated on the basis of market sales value data. If market sales value data are not available, estimates based on other reliable market information, including market sales volumes, may be used to establish the market share of the undertaking concerned.

The market share shall be calculated on the basis of data relating to the preceding calendar year.

The market share held by the undertakings referred to in point (e) of the second subparagraph of Article 1(2) shall be apportioned equally to each undertaking having the rights or the powers listed in point (a) of the second subparagraph of Article 1(2).

2. If the market share referred to in Article 3(1) or (2) is initially not more than 20% respectively 30% but subsequently rises above those levels, the exemption provided for in Article 2 shall continue to apply for a period of two consecutive calendar years following the year in which the 20% threshold or 30% threshold was first exceeded.

[8.163]
Article 9
Repeal

Regulation (EC) No 240/96 is repealed.

References to the repealed Regulation shall be construed as references to this Regulation.

[8.164]
Article 10
Transitional period

The prohibition laid down in Article 81(1) of the Treaty shall not apply during the period from 1 May 2004 to 31 March 2006 in respect of agreements already in force on 30 April 2004 which do not satisfy the conditions for exemption provided for in this Regulation but which, on 30 April 2004, satisfied the conditions for exemption provided for in Regulation (EC) No 240/96.

[8.165]
Article 11
Period of validity

This Regulation shall enter into force on 1 May 2004.

It shall expire on 30 April 2014.

This Regulation shall be binding in its entirety and directly applicable in all Member States.

DIRECTIVE OF THE EUROPEAN PARLIAMENT AND OF THE COUNCIL

(2006/114/EC)

of 12 December 2006

concerning misleading and comparative advertising

(codified version)

(Text with EEA relevance)

NOTES

Date of publication in OJ: OJ L376, 27.12.2006, p 21.

THE EUROPEAN PARLIAMENT AND THE COUNCIL OF THE EUROPEAN UNION,

Having regard to the Treaty establishing the European Community, and in particular Article 95 thereof,

Having regard to the proposal from the Commission,

Having regard to the opinion of the European Economic and Social Committee,[1]

Acting in accordance with the procedure laid down in Article 251 of the Treaty,[2]

Whereas:

(1) Council Directive 84/450/EEC of 10 September 1984 concerning misleading and comparative advertising[3] has been substantially amended several times.[4] In the interests of clarity and rationality the said Directive should be codified.

(2) The laws against misleading advertising in force in the Member States differ widely. Since advertising reaches beyond the frontiers of individual Member States, it has a direct effect on the smooth functioning of the internal market.

(3) Misleading and unlawful comparative advertising can lead to distortion of competition within the internal market.

(4) Advertising, whether or not it induces a contract, affects the economic welfare of consumers and traders.

(5) The differences between the laws of the Member States on advertising which misleads business hinder the execution of advertising campaigns beyond national boundaries and thus affect the free circulation of goods and provision of services.

(6) The completion of the internal market means a wide range of choice. Given that consumers and traders can and must make the best possible use of thc internal market, and that advertising is a very important means of creating genuine outlets for all goods and services throughout the Community, the basic provisions governing the form and content of comparative advertising should be uniform and the conditions of the use of comparative advertising in the Member States should be harmonised. If these conditions are met, this will help demonstrate objectively the merits of the various comparable products. Comparative advertising can also stimulate competition between suppliers of goods and services to the consumer's advantage.

(7) Minimum and objective criteria for determining whether advertising is misleading should be established.

(8) Comparative advertising, when it compares material, relevant, verifiable and representative features and is not misleading, may be a legitimate means of informing consumers of their advantage. It is desirable to provide a broad concept of comparative advertising to cover all modes of comparative advertising.

(9) Conditions of permitted comparative advertising, as far as the comparison is concerned, should be established in order to determine which practices relating to comparative advertising may distort competition, be detrimental to competitors and have an adverse effect on consumer choice. Such conditions of permitted advertising should include criteria of objective comparison of the features of goods and services.

(10) The international conventions on copyright as well as the national provisions on contractual and non-contractual liability should apply when the results of comparative tests carried out by third parties are referred to or reproduced in comparative advertising.

(11) The conditions of comparative advertising should be cumulative and respected in their entirety. In accordance with the Treaty, the choice of forms and methods for the implementation of these conditions should be left to the Member States, insofar as those forms and methods are not already determined by this Directive.

(12) These conditions should include, in particular, consideration of the provisions resulting from Council Regulation (EC) No 510/2006 of 20 March 2006 on the protection of geographical indications and designations of origin for agricultural products and foodstuffs,[5] and in particular

Article 13 thereof, and of the other Community provisions adopted in the agricultural sphere.

(13) Article 5 of First Council Directive 89/104/EEC of 21 December 1988 to approximate the laws of the Member States relating to trade marks[6] confers exclusive rights on the proprietor of a registered trade mark, including the right to prevent all third parties from using, in the course of trade, any sign which is identical to, or similar to, the trade mark in relation to identical goods or services or even, where appropriate, other goods.

(14) It may, however, be indispensable, in order to make comparative advertising effective, to identify the goods or services of a competitor, making reference to a trade mark or trade name of which the latter is the proprietor.

(15) Such use of another's trade mark, trade name or other distinguishing marks does not breach this exclusive right in cases where it complies with the conditions laid down by this Directive, the intended target being solely to distinguish between them and thus to highlight differences objectively.

(16) Persons or organisations regarded under national law as having a legitimate interest in the matter should have facilities for initiating proceedings against misleading and unlawful comparative advertising, either before a court or before an administrative authority which is competent to decide upon complaints or to initiate appropriate legal proceedings.

(17) The courts or administrative authorities should have powers enabling them to order or obtain the cessation of misleading and unlawful comparative advertising. In certain cases it may be desirable to prohibit misleading and unlawful comparative advertising even before it is published. However, this in no way implies that Member States are under an obligation to introduce rules requiring the systematic prior vetting of advertising.

(18) The voluntary control exercised by self-regulatory bodies to eliminate misleading or unlawful comparative advertising may avoid recourse to administrative or judicial action and ought therefore to be encouraged.

(19) While it is for national law to determine the burden of proof, it is appropriate to enable courts and administrative authorities to require traders to produce evidence as to the accuracy of factual claims they have made.

(20) Regulating comparative advertising is necessary for the smooth functioning of the internal market. Action at Community level is therefore required. The adoption of a Directive is the appropriate instrument because it lays down uniform general principles while allowing the Member States to choose the form and appropriate method by which to attain these objectives. It is in accordance with the principle of subsidiarity.

(21) This Directive should be without prejudice to the obligations of the Member States relating to the time-limits for transposition into national law and application of the Directives as set out in Part B of Annex I,

NOTES

1 Opinion of 26 October 2006 (not yet published in the Official Journal).

2 Opinion of the European Parliament of 12 October 2006 (not yet published in the Official Journal) and Council Decision of 30 November 2006.

3 OJ L250, 19.9.1984, p 17. Directive as last amended by Directive 2005/29/EC of the European Parliament and of the Council (OJ L149, 11.6.2005, p 22).

4 See Annex I, Part A.

5 OJ L93, 31.3.2006, p 12.

6 OJ L40, 11.2.1989, p 1. Directive as amended by Decision 92/10/EEC (OJ L6, 11.1.1992, p 35).

HAVE ADOPTED THIS DIRECTIVE:

[8.166]
Article 1
The purpose of this Directive is to protect traders against misleading advertising and the unfair consequences thereof and to lay down the conditions under which comparative advertising is permitted.

[8.167]
Article 2
For the purposes of this Directive:

(a) "advertising" means the making of a representation in any form in connection with a trade, business, craft or profession in order to promote the supply of goods or services, including immovable property, rights and obligations;

(b) "misleading advertising" means any advertising which in any way, including its presentation, deceives or is likely to deceive the persons to whom it is addressed or whom it reaches and which, by reason of its deceptive nature, is likely to affect their economic behaviour or which, for those reasons, injures or is likely to injure a competitor;

(c) "comparative advertising" means any advertising which explicitly or by implication identifies a competitor or goods or services offered by a competitor;

(d) "trader" means any natural or legal person who is acting for purposes relating to his trade, craft, business or profession and anyone acting in the name of or on behalf of a trader;

(e) "code owner" means any entity, including a trader or group of traders, which is responsible for the formulation and revision of a code of conduct and/or for monitoring compliance with the code by those who have undertaken to be bound by it.

[8.168]

Article 3

In determining whether advertising is misleading, account shall be taken of all its features, and in particular of any information it contains concerning:

(a) the characteristics of goods or services, such as their availability, nature, execution, composition, method and date of manufacture or provision, fitness for purpose, uses, quantity, specification, geographical or commercial origin or the results to be expected from their use, or the results and material features of tests or checks carried out on the goods or services;

(b) the price or the manner in which the price is calculated, and the conditions on which the goods are supplied or the services provided;

(c) the nature, attributes and rights of the advertiser, such as his identity and assets, his qualifications and ownership of industrial, commercial or intellectual property rights or his awards and distinctions.

[8.169]

Article 4

Comparative advertising shall, as far as the comparison is concerned, be permitted when the following conditions are met:

(a) it is not misleading within the meaning of Articles 2(b), 3 and 8(1) of this Directive or Articles 6 and 7 of Directive 2005/29/EC of the European Parliament and of the Council of 11 May 2005 concerning unfair business-to-consumer commercial practices in the internal market ("Unfair Commercial Practices Directive");[1]

(b) it compares goods or services meeting the same needs or intended for the same purpose;

(c) it objectively compares one or more material, relevant, verifiable and representative features of those goods and services, which may include price;

(d) it does not discredit or denigrate the trade marks, trade names, other distinguishing marks, goods, services, activities or circumstances of a competitor;

(e) for products with designation of origin, it relates in each case to products with the same designation;

(f) it does not take unfair advantage of the reputation of a trade mark, trade name or other distinguishing marks of a competitor or of the designation of origin of competing products;

(g) it does not present goods or services as imitations or replicas of goods or services bearing a protected trade mark or trade name;

(h) it does not create confusion among traders, between the advertiser and a competitor or between the advertiser's trade marks, trade names, other distinguishing marks, goods or services and those of a competitor.

NOTES

[1] OJ L149, 11.6.2005, p 22.

[8.170]

Article 5

1. Member States shall ensure that adequate and effective means exist to combat misleading advertising and enforce compliance with the provisions on comparative advertising in the interests of traders and competitors.

Such means shall include legal provisions under which persons or organisations regarded under national law as having a legitimate interest in combating misleading advertising or regulating comparative advertising may:

(a) take legal action against such advertising;

or

(b) bring such advertising before an administrative authority competent either to decide on complaints or to initiate appropriate legal proceedings.

2. It shall be for each Member State to decide which of the facilities referred to in the second subparagraph of paragraph 1 shall be available and whether to enable the courts or administrative authorities to require prior recourse to other established means of dealing with complaints, including those referred to in Article 6.

It shall be for each Member State to decide:

(a) whether these legal facilities may be directed separately or jointly against a number of traders from the same economic sector;

and

(b) whether these legal facilities may be directed against a code owner where the relevant code promotes non-compliance with legal requirements.

3. Under the provisions referred to in paragraphs 1 and 2, Member States shall confer upon the courts or administrative authorities powers enabling them, in cases where they deem such measures to be necessary taking into account all the interests involved and in particular the public interest:

(a) to order the cessation of, or to institute appropriate legal proceedings for an order for the cessation of, misleading advertising or unlawful comparative advertising;

or

(b) if the misleading advertising or unlawful comparative advertising has not yet been published but publication is imminent, to order the prohibition of, or to institute appropriate legal proceedings for an order for the prohibition of, such publication.

The first subparagraph shall apply even where there is no proof of actual loss or damage or of intention or negligence on the part of the advertiser.

Member States shall make provision for the measures referred to in the first subparagraph to be taken under an accelerated procedure either with interim effect or with definitive effect, at the Member States' discretion.

4. Member States may confer upon the courts or administrative authorities powers enabling them, with a view to eliminating the continuing effects of misleading advertising or unlawful comparative advertising, the cessation of which has been ordered by a final decision:

(a) to require publication of that decision in full or in part and in such form as they deem adequate;

(b) to require in addition the publication of a corrective statement.

5. The administrative authorities referred to in point (b) of the second subparagraph of paragraph 1 must:

(a) be composed so as not to cast doubt on their impartiality;

(b) have adequate powers, where they decide on complaints, to monitor and enforce the observance of their decisions effectively;

(c) normally give reasons for their decisions.

6. Where the powers referred to in paragraphs 3 and 4 are exercised exclusively by an administrative authority, reasons for its decisions shall always be given. In this case, provision must be made for procedures whereby improper or unreasonable exercise of its powers by the administrative authority or improper or unreasonable failure to exercise the said powers can be the subject of judicial review.

[8.171]
Article 6

This Directive does not exclude the voluntary control, which Member States may encourage, of misleading or comparative advertising by self-regulatory bodies and recourse to such bodies by the persons or organisations referred to in the second subparagraph of Article 5(1) on condition that proceedings before such bodies are additional to the court or administrative proceedings referred to in that Article.

[8.172]
Article 7

Member States shall confer upon the courts or administrative authorities powers enabling them in the civil or administrative proceedings referred to in Article 5:

(a) to require the advertiser to furnish evidence as to the accuracy of factual claims in advertising if, taking into account the legitimate interest of the advertiser and any other party to the proceedings, such a requirement appears appropriate on the basis of the circumstances of the particular case and in the case of comparative advertising to require the advertiser to furnish such evidence in a short period of time;

and

(b) to consider factual claims as inaccurate if the evidence demanded in accordance with point (a) is not furnished or is deemed insufficient by the court or administrative authority.

[8.173]
Article 8

1. This Directive shall not preclude Member States from retaining or adopting provisions with a view to ensuring more extensive protection, with regard to misleading advertising, for traders and competitors.

The first subparagraph shall not apply to comparative advertising as far as the comparison is concerned.

2. The provisions of this Directive shall apply without prejudice to Community provisions on advertising for specific products and/or services or to restrictions or prohibitions on advertising in particular media.

3. The provisions of this Directive concerning comparative advertising shall not oblige Member States which, in compliance with the provisions of the Treaty, maintain or introduce advertising bans regarding certain goods or services, whether imposed directly or by a body or

organisation responsible, under the law of the Member States, for regulating the exercise of a commercial, industrial, craft or professional activity, to permit comparative advertising regarding those goods or services. Where these bans are limited to particular media, this Directive shall apply to the media not covered by these bans.

4. Nothing in this Directive shall prevent Member States, in compliance with the provisions of the Treaty, from maintaining or introducing bans or limitations on the use of comparisons in the advertising of professional services, whether imposed directly or by a body or organisation responsible, under the law of the Member States, for regulating the exercise of a professional activity.

[8.174]
Article 9
Member States shall communicate to the Commission the text of the main provisions of national law which they adopt in the field covered by this Directive.

[8.175]
Article 10
Directive 84/450/EEC is hereby repealed, without prejudice to the obligations of the Member States relating to the time-limits for transposition into national law and application of the Directives, as set out in Part B of Annex I.

References made to the repealed Directive shall be construed as being made to this Directive and should be read in accordance with the correlation table set out in Annex II.

[8.176]
Article 11
This Directive shall enter into force on 12 December 2007.

[8.177]
Article 12
This Directive is addressed to the Member States.

ANNEX I

PART A
REPEALED DIRECTIVE WITH ITS SUCCESSIVE AMENDMENTS

[8.178]

Council Directive 84/450/EEC (OJ L250, 19.9.1984, p 17)	
Directive 97/55/EC of the European Parliament and of the Council (OJ L290, 23.10.1997, p 18)	
Directive 2005/29/EC of the European Parliament and of the Council (OJ L149, 11.6.2005, p 22)	only Article 14

PART B
LIST OF TIME-LIMITS FOR TRANSPOSITION INTO NATIONAL LAW AND APPLICATION

(referred to in Article 10)

Directive	**Time-limit for transposition**	**Date of application**
84/450/EEC	1 October 1986	—
97/55/EC	23 April 2000	—
2005/29/EC	12 June 2007	12 December 2007

ANNEX II
CORRELATION TABLE

[8.179]

Directive 84/450/EEC	*This Directive*
Article 1	Article 1
Article 2, introductory words	Article 2, introductory words
Article 2, point 1	Article 2(a)
Article 2, point 2	Article 2(b)
Article 2, point 2a	Article 2(c)
Article 2, point 3	Article 2(d)
Article 2, point 4	Article 2(e)

Directive 84/450/EEC	*This Directive*
Article 3	Article 3
Article 3a(1)	Article 4
Article 4(1), first subparagraph, first sentence	Article 5(1), first subparagraph
Article 4(1), first subparagraph, second sentence	Article 5(1), second subparagraph
Article 4(1), second subparagraph	Article 5(2), first subparagraph
Article 4(1), third subparagraph	Article 5(2), second subparagraph
Article 4(2), first subparagraph, introductory words	Article 5(3), first subparagraph, introductory words
Article 4(2), first subparagraph, first indent	Article 5(3), first subparagraph, point (a)
Article 4(2), first subparagraph, second indent	Article 5(3), first subparagraph, point (b)
Article 4(2), first subparagraph, final words	Article 5(3), second subparagraph
Article 4(2), second subparagraph, introductory words	Article 5(3), third subparagraph
Article 4(2), second subparagraph, first indent	Article 5(3), third subparagraph
Article 4(2), second subparagraph, second indent	Article 5(3), third subparagraph
Article 4(2), second subparagraph, final words	Article 5(3), third subparagraph
Article 4(2), third subparagraph, introductory words	Article 5(4), introductory words
Article 4(2), third subparagraph, first indent	Article 5(4), point (a)
Article 4(2), third subparagraph, second indent	Article 5(4), point (b)
Article 4(3), first subparagraph	Article 5(5)
Article 4(3), second subparagraph	Article 5(6)
Article 5	Article 6
Article 6	Article 7
Article 7(1)	Article 8(1), first subparagraph
Article 7(2)	Article 8(1), second subparagraph
Article 7(3)	Article 8(2)
Article 7(4)	Article 8(3)
Article 7(5)	Article 8(4)
Article 8, first subparagraph	—
Article 8, second subparagraph	Article 9
—	Article 10
—	Article 11
Article 9	Article 12
—	Annex I
—	Annex II

DIRECTIVE OF THE EUROPEAN PARLIAMENT AND OF THE COUNCIL

(2005/29/EC)

of 11 May 2005

concerning unfair business-to-consumer commercial practices in the internal market and amending Council Directive 84/450/EEC, Directives 97/7/EC, 98/27/EC and 2002/65/EC of the European Parliament and of the Council and Regulation (EC) No 2006/2004 of the European Parliament and of the Council ('Unfair Commercial Practices Directive')

(Text with EEA relevance)

NOTES

Date of publication in OJ: OJ L149, 11.6.2005, p 22.

Part 8 Other EU Materials

THE EUROPEAN PARLIAMENT AND THE COUNCIL OF THE EUROPEAN UNION,

Having regard to the Treaty establishing the European Community, and in particular Article 95 thereof,

Having regard to the proposal from the Commission,

Having regard to the opinion of the European Economic and Social Committee,[1]

Acting in accordance with the procedure laid down in Article 251 of the Treaty,[2]

Whereas:

(1) Article 153(1) and (3)(a) of the Treaty provides that the Community is to contribute to the attainment of a high level of consumer protection by the measures it adopts pursuant to Article 95 thereof.

(2) In accordance with Article 14(2) of the Treaty, the internal market comprises an area without internal frontiers in which the free movement of goods and services and freedom of establishment are ensured. The development of fair commercial practices within the area without internal frontiers is vital for the promotion of the development of cross-border activities.

(3) The laws of the Member States relating to unfair commercial practices show marked differences which can generate appreciable distortions of competition and obstacles to the smooth functioning of the internal market. In the field of advertising, Council Directive 84/450/EEC of 10 September 1984 concerning misleading and comparative advertising[3] establishes minimum criteria for harmonising legislation on misleading advertising, but does not prevent the Member States from retaining or adopting measures which provide more extensive protection for consumers. As a result, Member States' provisions on misleading advertising diverge significantly.

(4) These disparities cause uncertainty as to which national rules apply to unfair commercial practices harming consumers' economic interests and create many barriers affecting business and consumers. These barriers increase the cost to business of exercising internal market freedoms, in particular when businesses wish to engage in cross border marketing, advertising campaigns and sales promotions. Such barriers also make consumers uncertain of their rights and undermine their confidence in the internal market.

(5) In the absence of uniform rules at Community level, obstacles to the free movement of services and goods across borders or the freedom of establishment could be justified in the light of the case-law of the Court of Justice of the European Communities as long as they seek to protect recognised public interest objectives and are proportionate to those objectives. In view of the Community's objectives, as set out in the provisions of the Treaty and in secondary Community law relating to freedom of movement, and in accordance with the Commission's policy on commercial communications as indicated in the Communication from the Commission entitled "The follow-up to the Green Paper on Commercial Communications in the Internal Market", such obstacles should be eliminated. These obstacles can only be eliminated by establishing uniform rules at Community level which establish a high level of consumer protection and by clarifying certain legal concepts at Community level to the extent necessary for the proper functioning of the internal market and to meet the requirement of legal certainty.

(6) This Directive therefore approximates the laws of the Member States on unfair commercial practices, including unfair advertising, which directly harm consumers' economic interests and thereby indirectly harm the economic interests of legitimate competitors. In line with the principle of proportionality, this Directive protects consumers from the consequences of such unfair commercial practices where they are material but recognises that in some cases the impact on consumers may be negligible. It neither covers nor affects the national laws on unfair commercial practices which harm only competitors' economic interests or which relate to a transaction between traders; taking full account of the principle of subsidiarity, Member States will continue to be able to regulate such practices, in conformity with Community law, if they choose to do so. Nor does this Directive cover or affect the provisions of Directive 84/450/EEC on advertising which misleads business but which is not misleading for consumers and on comparative advertising. Further, this Directive does not affect accepted advertising and marketing practices, such as legitimate product placement, brand differentiation or the offering of incentives which may legitimately affect consumers' perceptions of products and influence their behaviour without impairing the consumer's ability to make an informed decision.

(7) This Directive addresses commercial practices directly related to influencing consumers' transactional decisions in relation to products. It does not address commercial practices carried out primarily for other purposes, including for example commercial communication aimed at investors, such as annual reports and corporate promotional literature. It does not address legal requirements related to taste and decency which vary widely among the Member States. Commercial practices such as, for example, commercial solicitation in the streets, may be undesirable in Member States for cultural reasons. Member States should accordingly be able to continue to ban commercial practices in their territory, in conformity with Community law, for reasons of taste and decency even where such practices do not limit consumers' freedom of choice. Full account should be taken of the context of the individual case concerned in applying this Directive, in particular the general clauses thereof.

(8) This Directive directly protects consumer economic interests from unfair business-to-

consumer commercial practices. Thereby, it also indirectly protects legitimate businesses from their competitors who do not play by the rules in this Directive and thus guarantees fair competition in fields coordinated by it. It is understood that there are other commercial practices which, although not harming consumers, may hurt competitors and business customers. The Commission should carefully examine the need for Community action in the field of unfair competition beyond the remit of this Directive and, if necessary, make a legislative proposal to cover these other aspects of unfair competition.

(9) This Directive is without prejudice to individual actions brought by those who have been harmed by an unfair commercial practice. It is also without prejudice to Community and national rules on contract law, on intellectual property rights, on the health and safety aspects of products, on conditions of establishment and authorisation regimes, including those rules which, in conformity with Community law, relate to gambling activities, and to Community competition rules and the national provisions implementing them. The Member States will thus be able to retain or introduce restrictions and prohibitions of commercial practices on grounds of the protection of the health and safety of consumers in their territory wherever the trader is based, for example in relation to alcohol, tobacco or pharmaceuticals. Financial services and immovable property, by reason of their complexity and inherent serious risks, necessitate detailed requirements, including positive obligations on traders. For this reason, in the field of financial services and immovable property, this Directive is without prejudice to the right of Member States to go beyond its provisions to protect the economic interests of consumers. It is not appropriate to regulate here the certification and indication of the standard of fineness of articles of precious metal.

(10) It is necessary to ensure that the relationship between this Directive and existing Community law is coherent, particularly where detailed provisions on unfair commercial practices apply to specific sectors. This Directive therefore amends Directive 84/450/EEC, Directive 97/7/EC of the European Parliament and of the Council of 20 May 1997 on the protection of consumers in respect of distance contracts,[4] Directive 98/27/EC of the European Parliament and of the Council of 19 May 1998 on injunctions for the protection of consumers' interests[5] and Directive 2002/65/EC of the European Parliament and of the Council of 23 September 2002 concerning the distance marketing of consumer financial services.[6] This Directive accordingly applies only in so far as there are no specific Community law provisions regulating specific aspects of unfair commercial practices, such as information requirements and rules on the way the information is presented to the consumer. It provides protection for consumers where there is no specific sectoral legislation at Community level and prohibits traders from creating a false impression of the nature of products. This is particularly important for complex products with high levels of risk to consumers, such as certain financial services products. This Directive consequently complements the Community acquis, which is applicable to commercial practices harming consumers' economic interests.

(11) The high level of convergence achieved by the approximation of national provisions through this Directive creates a high common level of consumer protection. This Directive establishes a single general prohibition of those unfair commercial practices distorting consumers' economic behaviour. It also sets rules on aggressive commercial practices, which are currently not regulated at Community level.

(12) Harmonisation will considerably increase legal certainty for both consumers and business. Both consumers and business will be able to rely on a single regulatory framework based on clearly defined legal concepts regulating all aspects of unfair commercial practices across the EU. The effect will be to eliminate the barriers stemming from the fragmentation of the rules on unfair commercial practices harming consumer economic interests and to enable the internal market to be achieved in this area.

(13) In order to achieve the Community's objectives through the removal of internal market barriers, it is necessary to replace Member States' existing, divergent general clauses and legal principles. The single, common general prohibition established by this Directive therefore covers unfair commercial practices distorting consumers' economic behaviour. In order to support consumer confidence the general prohibition should apply equally to unfair commercial practices which occur outside any contractual relationship between a trader and a consumer or following the conclusion of a contract and during its execution. The general prohibition is elaborated by rules on the two types of commercial practices which are by far the most common, namely misleading commercial practices and aggressive commercial practices.

(14) It is desirable that misleading commercial practices cover those practices, including misleading advertising, which by deceiving the consumer prevent him from making an informed and thus efficient choice. In conformity with the laws and practices of Member States on misleading advertising, this Directive classifies misleading practices into misleading actions and misleading omissions. In respect of omissions, this Directive sets out a limited number of key items of information which the consumer needs to make an informed transactional decision. Such information will not have to be disclosed in all advertisements, but only where the trader makes an invitation to purchase, which is a concept clearly defined in this Directive. The full harmonisation approach adopted in this Directive does not preclude the Member States from specifying in national law the main characteristics of particular products such as, for example, collectors' items or electrical goods, the omission of which would be material when an invitation to purchase is made. It is not the

intention of this Directive to reduce consumer choice by prohibiting the promotion of products which look similar to other products unless this similarity confuses consumers as to the commercial origin of the product and is therefore misleading. This Directive should be without prejudice to existing Community law which expressly affords Member States the choice between several regulatory options for the protection of consumers in the field of commercial practices. In particular, this Directive should be without prejudice to Article 13(3) of Directive 2002/58/EC of the European Parliament and of the Council of 12 July 2002 concerning the processing of personal data and the protection of privacy in the electronic communications sector.[7]

(15) Where Community law sets out information requirements in relation to commercial communication, advertising and marketing that information is considered as material under this Directive. Member States will be able to retain or add information requirements relating to contract law and having contract law consequences where this is allowed by the minimum clauses in the existing Community law instruments. A non-exhaustive list of such information requirements in the acquis is contained in Annex II. Given the full harmonisation introduced by this Directive only the information required in Community law is considered as material for the purpose of Article 7(5) thereof. Where Member States have introduced information requirements over and above what is specified in Community law, on the basis of minimum clauses, the omission of that extra information will not constitute a misleading omission under this Directive. By contrast Member States will be able, when allowed by the minimum clauses in Community law, to maintain or introduce more stringent provisions in conformity with Community law so as to ensure a higher level of protection of consumers' individual contractual rights.

(16) The provisions on aggressive commercial practices should cover those practices which significantly impair the consumer's freedom of choice. Those are practices using harassment, coercion, including the use of physical force, and undue influence.

(17) It is desirable that those commercial practices which are in all circumstances unfair be identified to provide greater legal certainty. Annex I therefore contains the full list of all such practices. These are the only commercial practices which can be deemed to be unfair without a case-by-case assessment against the provisions of Articles 5 to 9. The list may only be modified by revision of the Directive.

(18) It is appropriate to protect all consumers from unfair commercial practices; however the Court of Justice has found it necessary in adjudicating on advertising cases since the enactment of Directive 84/450/EEC to examine the effect on a notional, typical consumer. In line with the principle of proportionality, and to permit the effective application of the protections contained in it, this Directive takes as a benchmark the average consumer, who is reasonably well-informed and reasonably observant and circumspect, taking into account social, cultural and linguistic factors, as interpreted by the Court of Justice, but also contains provisions aimed at preventing the exploitation of consumers whose characteristics make them particularly vulnerable to unfair commercial practices. Where a commercial practice is specifically aimed at a particular group of consumers, such as children, it is desirable that the impact of the commercial practice be assessed from the perspective of the average member of that group. It is therefore appropriate to include in the list of practices which are in all circumstances unfair a provision which, without imposing an outright ban on advertising directed at children, protects them from direct exhortations to purchase. The average consumer test is not a statistical test. National courts and authorities will have to exercise their own faculty of judgement, having regard to the case-law of the Court of Justice, to determine the typical reaction of the average consumer in a given case.

(19) Where certain characteristics such as age, physical or mental infirmity or credulity make consumers particularly susceptible to a commercial practice or to the underlying product and the economic behaviour only of such consumers is likely to be distorted by the practice in a way that the trader can reasonably foresee, it is appropriate to ensure that they are adequately protected by assessing the practice from the perspective of the average member of that group.

(20) It is appropriate to provide a role for codes of conduct, which enable traders to apply the principles of this Directive effectively in specific economic fields. In sectors where there are specific mandatory requirements regulating the behaviour of traders, it is appropriate that these will also provide evidence as to the requirements of professional diligence in that sector. The control exercised by code owners at national or Community level to eliminate unfair commercial practices may avoid the need for recourse to administrative or judicial action and should therefore be encouraged. With the aim of pursuing a high level of consumer protection, consumers' organisations could be informed and involved in the drafting of codes of conduct.

(21) Persons or organisations regarded under national law as having a legitimate interest in the matter must have legal remedies for initiating proceedings against unfair commercial practices, either before a court or before an administrative authority which is competent to decide upon complaints or to initiate appropriate legal proceedings. While it is for national law to determine the burden of proof, it is appropriate to enable courts and administrative authorities to require traders to produce evidence as to the accuracy of factual claims they have made.

(22) It is necessary that Member States lay down penalties for infringements of the provisions

of this Directive and they must ensure that these are enforced. The penalties must be effective, proportionate and dissuasive.

(23) Since the objectives of this Directive, namely to eliminate the barriers to the functioning of the internal market represented by national laws on unfair commercial practices and to provide a high common level of consumer protection, by approximating the laws, regulations and administrative provisions of the Member States on unfair commercial practices, cannot be sufficiently achieved by the Member States and can therefore be better achieved at Community level, the Community may adopt measures, in accordance with the principle of subsidiarity as set out in Article 5 of the Treaty. In accordance with the principle of proportionality, as set out in that Article, this Directive does not go beyond what is necessary in order to eliminate the internal market barriers and achieve a high common level of consumer protection.

(24) It is appropriate to review this Directive to ensure that barriers to the internal market have been addressed and a high level of consumer protection achieved. The review could lead to a Commission proposal to amend this Directive, which may include a limited extension to the derogation in Article 3(5), and/or amendments to other consumer protection legislation reflecting the Commission's Consumer Policy Strategy commitment to review the existing acquis in order to achieve a high, common level of consumer protection.

(25) This Directive respects the fundamental rights and observes the principles recognised in particular by the Charter of Fundamental Rights of the European Union,

NOTES

1 OJ C108, 30.4.2004, p 81.

2 Opinion of the European Parliament of 20 April 2004 (OJ C104 E, 30.4.2004, p 260), Council Common Position of 15 November 2004 (OJ C38 E, 15.2.2005, p 1), Position of the European Parliament of 24 February 2005 (not yet published in the Official Journal) and Council Decision of 12 April 2005.

3 OJ L250, 19.9.1984, p 17. Directive as amended by Directive 97/55/EC of the European Parliament and of the Council (OJ L290, 23.10.1997, p 18).

4 OJ L144, 4.6.1997, p 19. Directive as amended by Directive 2002/65/EC (OJ L271, 9.10.2002, p 16).

5 OJ L166, 11.6.1998, p 51. Directive as last amended by Directive 2002/65/EC.

6 OJ L271, 9.10.2002, p 16.

7 OJ L201, 31.7.2002, p 37.

HAVE ADOPTED THIS DIRECTIVE—

CHAPTER 1
GENERAL PROVISIONS

[8.180]
Article 1
Purpose

The purpose of this Directive is to contribute to the proper functioning of the internal market and achieve a high level of consumer protection by approximating the laws, regulations and administrative provisions of the Member States on unfair commercial practices harming consumers' economic interests.

[8.181]
Article 2
Definitions

For the purposes of this Directive:

(a) "consumer" means any natural person who, in commercial practices covered by this Directive, is acting for purposes which are outside his trade, business, craft or profession;

(b) "trader" means any natural or legal person who, in commercial practices covered by this Directive, is acting for purposes relating to his trade, business, craft or profession and anyone acting in the name of or on behalf of a trader;

(c) "product" means any goods or service including immovable property, rights and obligations;

(d) "business-to-consumer commercial practices" (hereinafter also referred to as commercial practices) means any act, omission, course of conduct or representation, commercial communication including advertising and marketing, by a trader, directly connected with the promotion, sale or supply of a product to consumers;

(e) "to materially distort the economic behaviour of consumers" means using a commercial practice to appreciably impair the consumer's ability to make an informed decision, thereby causing the consumer to take a transactional decision that he would not have taken otherwise;

(f) "code of conduct" means an agreement or set of rules not imposed by law, regulation or administrative provision of a Member State which defines the behaviour of traders who undertake to be bound by the code in relation to one or more particular commercial practices or business sectors;

(g) "code owner" means any entity, including a trader or group of traders, which is responsible for the formulation and revision of a code of conduct and/or for monitoring compliance with the code by those who have undertaken to be bound by it;

(h) "professional diligence" means the standard of special skill and care which a trader may reasonably be expected to exercise towards consumers, commensurate with honest market practice and/or the general principle of good faith in the trader's field of activity;

(i) "invitation to purchase" means a commercial communication which indicates characteristics of the product and the price in a way appropriate to the means of the commercial communication used and thereby enables the consumer to make a purchase;

(j) "undue influence" means exploiting a position of power in relation to the consumer so as to apply pressure, even without using or threatening to use physical force, in a way which significantly limits the consumer's ability to make an informed decision;

(k) "transactional decision" means any decision taken by a consumer concerning whether, how and on what terms to purchase, make payment in whole or in part for, retain or dispose of a product or to exercise a contractual right in relation to the product, whether the consumer decides to act or to refrain from acting;

(l) "regulated profession" means a professional activity or a group of professional activities, access to which or the pursuit of which, or one of the modes of pursuing which, is conditional, directly or indirectly, upon possession of specific professional qualifications, pursuant to laws, regulations or administrative provisions.

[8.182]
Article 3
Scope

1. This Directive shall apply to unfair business-to-consumer commercial practices, as laid down in Article 5, before, during and after a commercial transaction in relation to a product.

2. This Directive is without prejudice to contract law and, in particular, to the rules on the validity, formation or effect of a contract.

3. This Directive is without prejudice to Community or national rules relating to the health and safety aspects of products.

4. In the case of conflict between the provisions of this Directive and other Community rules regulating specific aspects of unfair commercial practices, the latter shall prevail and apply to those specific aspects.

5. For a period of six years from 12 June 2007, Member States shall be able to continue to apply national provisions within the field approximated by this Directive which are more restrictive or prescriptive than this Directive and which implement directives containing minimum harmonisation clauses. These measures must be essential to ensure that consumers are adequately protected against unfair commercial practices and must be proportionate to the attainment of this objective. The review referred to in Article 18 may, if considered appropriate, include a proposal to prolong this derogation for a further limited period.

6. Member States shall notify the Commission without delay of any national provisions applied on the basis of paragraph 5.

7. This Directive is without prejudice to the rules determining the jurisdiction of the courts.

8. This Directive is without prejudice to any conditions of establishment or of authorisation regimes, or to the deontological codes of conduct or other specific rules governing regulated professions in order to uphold high standards of integrity on the part of the professional, which Member States may, in conformity with Community law, impose on professionals.

9. In relation to "financial services", as defined in Directive 2002/65/EC, and immovable property, Member States may impose requirements which are more restrictive or prescriptive than this Directive in the field which it approximates.

10. This Directive shall not apply to the application of the laws, regulations and administrative provisions of Member States relating to the certification and indication of the standard of fineness of articles of precious metal.

[8.183]
Article 4
Internal market

Member States shall neither restrict the freedom to provide services nor restrict the free movement of goods for reasons falling within the field approximated by this Directive.

CHAPTER 2
UNFAIR COMMERCIAL PRACTICES

[8.184]
Article 5
Prohibition of unfair commercial practices

1. Unfair commercial practices shall be prohibited.
2. A commercial practice shall be unfair if:
   (a) it is contrary to the requirements of professional diligence, and
   (b) it materially distorts or is likely to materially distort the economic behaviour with regard to the product of the average consumer whom it reaches or to whom it is addressed, or of the average member of the group when a commercial practice is directed to a particular group of consumers.
3. Commercial practices which are likely to materially distort the economic behaviour only of a clearly identifiable group of consumers who are particularly vulnerable to the practice or the underlying product because of their mental or physical infirmity, age or credulity in a way which the trader could reasonably be expected to foresee, shall be assessed from the perspective of the average member of that group. This is without prejudice to the common and legitimate advertising practice of making exaggerated statements or statements which are not meant to be taken literally.
4. In particular, commercial practices shall be unfair which:
   (a) are misleading as set out in Articles 6 and 7, or
   (b) are aggressive as set out in Articles 8 and 9.
5. Annex I contains the list of those commercial practices which shall in all circumstances be regarded as unfair. The same single list shall apply in all Member States and may only be modified by revision of this Directive.

SECTION 1
MISLEADING COMMERCIAL PRACTICES

[8.185]
Article 6
Misleading actions

1. A commercial practice shall be regarded as misleading if it contains false information and is therefore untruthful or in any way, including overall presentation, deceives or is likely to deceive the average consumer, even if the information is factually correct, in relation to one or more of the following elements, and in either case causes or is likely to cause him to take a transactional decision that he would not have taken otherwise:
   (a) the existence or nature of the product;
   (b) the main characteristics of the product, such as its availability, benefits, risks, execution, composition, accessories, after-sale customer assistance and complaint handling, method and date of manufacture or provision, delivery, fitness for purpose, usage, quantity, specification, geographical or commercial origin or the results to be expected from its use, or the results and material features of tests or checks carried out on the product;
   (c) the extent of the trader's commitments, the motives for the commercial practice and the nature of the sales process, any statement or symbol in relation to direct or indirect sponsorship or approval of the trader or the product;
   (d) the price or the manner in which the price is calculated, or the existence of a specific price advantage;
   (e) the need for a service, part, replacement or repair;
   (f) the nature, attributes and rights of the trader or his agent, such as his identity and assets, his qualifications, status, approval, affiliation or connection and ownership of industrial, commercial or intellectual property rights or his awards and distinctions;
   (g) the consumer's rights, including the right to replacement or reimbursement under Directive 1999/44/EC of the European Parliament and of the Council of 25 May 1999 on certain aspects of the sale of consumer goods and associated guarantees,[1] or the risks he may face.
2. A commercial practice shall also be regarded as misleading if, in its factual context, taking account of all its features and circumstances, it causes or is likely to cause the average consumer to take a transactional decision that he would not have taken otherwise, and it involves:
   (a) any marketing of a product, including comparative advertising, which creates confusion with any products, trade marks, trade names or other distinguishing marks of a competitor;
   (b) non-compliance by the trader with commitments contained in codes of conduct by which the trader has undertaken to be bound, where:
      (i) the commitment is not aspirational but is firm and is capable of being verified, and
      (ii) the trader indicates in a commercial practice that he is bound by the code.

NOTES

[1] OJ L 171, 7.7.1999, p 12.

[8.186]
Article 7
Misleading omissions

1. A commercial practice shall be regarded as misleading if, in its factual context, taking account of all its features and circumstances and the limitations of the communication medium, it omits material information that the average consumer needs, according to the context, to take an informed transactional decision and thereby causes or is likely to cause the average consumer to take a transactional decision that he would not have taken otherwise.

2. It shall also be regarded as a misleading omission when, taking account of the matters described in paragraph 1, a trader hides or provides in an unclear, unintelligible, ambiguous or untimely manner such material information as referred to in that paragraph or fails to identify the commercial intent of the commercial practice if not already apparent from the context, and where, in either case, this causes or is likely to cause the average consumer to take a transactional decision that he would not have taken otherwise.

3. Where the medium used to communicate the commercial practice imposes limitations of space or time, these limitations and any measures taken by the trader to make the information available to consumers by other means shall be taken into account in deciding whether information has been omitted.

4. In the case of an invitation to purchase, the following information shall be regarded as material, if not already apparent from the context:
   (a) the main characteristics of the product, to an extent appropriate to the medium and the product;
   (b) the geographical address and the identity of the trader, such as his trading name and, where applicable, the geographical address and the identity of the trader on whose behalf he is acting;
   (c) the price inclusive of taxes, or where the nature of the product means that the price cannot reasonably be calculated in advance, the manner in which the price is calculated, as well as, where appropriate, all additional freight, delivery or postal charges or, where these charges cannot reasonably be calculated in advance, the fact that such additional charges may be payable;
   (d) the arrangements for payment, delivery, performance and the complaint handling policy, if they depart from the requirements of professional diligence;
   (e) for products and transactions involving a right of withdrawal or cancellation, the existence of such a right.

5. Information requirements established by Community law in relation to commercial communication including advertising or marketing, a non-exhaustive list of which is contained in Annex II, shall be regarded as material.

SECTION 2
AGGRESSIVE COMMERCIAL PRACTICES

[8.187]
Article 8
Aggressive commercial practices

A commercial practice shall be regarded as aggressive if, in its factual context, taking account of all its features and circumstances, by harassment, coercion, including the use of physical force, or undue influence, it significantly impairs or is likely to significantly impair the average consumer's freedom of choice or conduct with regard to the product and thereby causes him or is likely to cause him to take a transactional decision that he would not have taken otherwise.

[8.188]
Article 9
Use of harassment, coercion and undue influence

In determining whether a commercial practice uses harassment, coercion, including the use of physical force, or undue influence, account shall be taken of:
   (a) its timing, location, nature or persistence;
   (b) the use of threatening or abusive language or behaviour;
   (c) the exploitation by the trader of any specific misfortune or circumstance of such gravity as to impair the consumer's judgement, of which the trader is aware, to influence the consumer's decision with regard to the product;
   (d) any onerous or disproportionate non-contractual barriers imposed by the trader where a consumer wishes to exercise rights under the contract, including rights to terminate a contract or to switch to another product or another trader;
   (e) any threat to take any action that cannot legally be taken.

CHAPTER 3
CODES OF CONDUCT

[8.189]
Article 10
Codes of conduct

This Directive does not exclude the control, which Member States may encourage, of unfair commercial practices by code owners and recourse to such bodies by the persons or organisations referred to in Article 11 if proceedings before such bodies are in addition to the court or administrative proceedings referred to in that Article.

Recourse to such control bodies shall never be deemed the equivalent of foregoing a means of judicial or administrative recourse as provided for in Article 11.

CHAPTER 4
FINAL PROVISIONS

[8.190]
Article 11
Enforcement

1. Member States shall ensure that adequate and effective means exist to combat unfair commercial practices in order to enforce compliance with the provisions of this Directive in the interest of consumers.

Such means shall include legal provisions under which persons or organisations regarded under national law as having a legitimate interest in combating unfair commercial practices, including competitors, may:

(a) take legal action against such unfair commercial practices; and/or
(b) bring such unfair commercial practices before an administrative authority competent either to decide on complaints or to initiate appropriate legal proceedings.

It shall be for each Member State to decide which of these facilities shall be available and whether to enable the courts or administrative authorities to require prior recourse to other established means of dealing with complaints, including those referred to in Article 10. These facilities shall be available regardless of whether the consumers affected are in the territory of the Member State where the trader is located or in another Member State.

It shall be for each Member State to decide:

(a) whether these legal facilities may be directed separately or jointly against a number of traders from the same economic sector; and
(b) whether these legal facilities may be directed against a code owner where the relevant code promotes non-compliance with legal requirements.

2. Under the legal provisions referred to in paragraph 1, Member States shall confer upon the courts or administrative authorities powers enabling them, in cases where they deem such measures to be necessary taking into account all the interests involved and in particular the public interest:

(a) to order the cessation of, or to institute appropriate legal proceedings for an order for the cessation of, unfair commercial practices; or
(b) if the unfair commercial practice has not yet been carried out but is imminent, to order the prohibition of the practice, or to institute appropriate legal proceedings for an order for the prohibition of the practice,

even without proof of actual loss or damage or of intention or negligence on the part of the trader.

Member States shall also make provision for the measures referred to in the first subparagraph to be taken under an accelerated procedure:

— either with interim effect, or
— with definitive effect,

on the understanding that it is for each Member State to decide which of the two options to select.

Furthermore, Member States may confer upon the courts or administrative authorities powers enabling them, with a view to eliminating the continuing effects of unfair commercial practices the cessation of which has been ordered by a final decision:

(a) to require publication of that decision in full or in part and in such form as they deem adequate;
(b) to require in addition the publication of a corrective statement.

3. The administrative authorities referred to in paragraph 1 must:

(a) be composed so as not to cast doubt on their impartiality;
(b) have adequate powers, where they decide on complaints, to monitor and enforce the observance of their decisions effectively;
(c) normally give reasons for their decisions.

Where the powers referred to in paragraph 2 are exercised exclusively by an administrative authority, reasons for its decisions shall always be given. Furthermore, in this case, provision must be made for procedures whereby improper or unreasonable exercise of its powers by the administrative authority or improper or unreasonable failure to exercise the said powers can be the subject of judicial review.

[8.191]
Article 12
Courts and administrative authorities: substantiation of claims

Member States shall confer upon the courts or administrative authorities powers enabling them in the civil or administrative proceedings provided for in Article 11:

(a) to require the trader to furnish evidence as to the accuracy of factual claims in relation to a commercial practice if, taking into account the legitimate interest of the trader and any other party to the proceedings, such a requirement appears appropriate on the basis of the circumstances of the particular case; and

(b) to consider factual claims as inaccurate if the evidence demanded in accordance with (a) is not furnished or is deemed insufficient by the court or administrative authority.

[8.192]
Article 13
Penalties

Member States shall lay down penalties for infringements of national provisions adopted in application of this Directive and shall take all necessary measures to ensure that these are enforced. These penalties must be effective, proportionate and dissuasive.

Articles 14–16 (*Art 14 substitutes Directive 84/450/EEC, Arts 1, 3a, and amends Arts 2, 4, 7 of that Directive (all repealed); Art 15 substitutes Directive 97/7/EC, Art 9 and Directive 2002/65/EC, Art 9; Art 16 amends Directive 98/27/EC and Regulation 2006/2004/EC.*)

[8.193]
Article 17
Information

Member States shall take appropriate measures to inform consumers of the national law transposing this Directive and shall, where appropriate, encourage traders and code owners to inform consumers of their codes of conduct.

[8.194]
Article 18
Review

1. By 12 June 2011 the Commission shall submit to the European Parliament and the Council a comprehensive report on the application of this Directive, in particular of Articles 3(9) and 4 and Annex I, on the scope for further harmonisation and simplification of Community law relating to consumer protection, and, having regard to Article 3(5), on any measures that need to be taken at Community level to ensure that appropriate levels of consumer protection are maintained. The report shall be accompanied, if necessary, by a proposal to revise this Directive or other relevant parts of Community law.

2. The European Parliament and the Council shall endeavour to act, in accordance with the Treaty, within two years of the presentation by the Commission of any proposal submitted under paragraph 1.

[8.195]
Article 19
Transposition

Member States shall adopt and publish the laws, regulations and administrative provisions necessary to comply with this Directive by 12 June 2007. They shall forthwith inform the Commission thereof and inform the Commission of any subsequent amendments without delay. They shall apply those measures by 12 December 2007. When Member States adopt those measures, they shall contain a reference to this Directive or be accompanied by such a reference on the occasion of their official publication. Member States shall determine how such reference is to be made.

[8.196]
Article 20
Entry into force

This Directive shall enter into force on the day following its publication in the Official Journal of the European Union.

[8.197]
Article 21
Addressees

This Directive is addressed to the Member States.

ANNEX I
COMMERCIAL PRACTICES WHICH ARE IN ALL CIRCUMSTANCES CONSIDERED UNFAIR

MISLEADING COMMERCIAL PRACTICES

[8.198]

1. Claiming to be a signatory to a code of conduct when the trader is not.

2. Displaying a trust mark, quality mark or equivalent without having obtained the necessary authorisation.

3. Claiming that a code of conduct has an endorsement from a public or other body which it does not have.

4. Claiming that a trader (including his commercial practices) or a product has been approved, endorsed or authorised by a public or private body when he/it has not or making such a claim without complying with the terms of the approval, endorsement or authorisation.

5. Making an invitation to purchase products at a specified price without disclosing the existence of any reasonable grounds the trader may have for believing that he will not be able to offer for supply or to procure another trader to supply, those products or equivalent products at that price for a period that is, and in quantities that are, reasonable having regard to the product, the scale of advertising of the product and the price offered (bait advertising).

6. Making an invitation to purchase products at a specified price and then:
   (a) refusing to show the advertised item to consumers; or
   (b) refusing to take orders for it or deliver it within a reasonable time; or
   (c) demonstrating a defective sample of it,

with the intention of promoting a different product (bait and switch)

7. Falsely stating that a product will only be available for a very limited time, or that it will only be available on particular terms for a very limited time, in order to elicit an immediate decision and deprive consumers of sufficient opportunity or time to make an informed choice.

8. Undertaking to provide after-sales service to consumers with whom the trader has communicated prior to a transaction in a language which is not an official language of the Member State where the trader is located and then making such service available only in another language without clearly disclosing this to the consumer before the consumer is committed to the transaction.

9. Stating or otherwise creating the impression that a product can legally be sold when it cannot.

10. Presenting rights given to consumers in law as a distinctive feature of the trader's offer.

11. Using editorial content in the media to promote a product where a trader has paid for the promotion without making that clear in the content or by images or sounds clearly identifiable by the consumer (advertorial). This is without prejudice to Council Directive 89/552/EEC.[1]

12. Making a materially inaccurate claim concerning the nature and extent of the risk to the personal security of the consumer or his family if the consumer does not purchase the product.

13. Promoting a product similar to a product made by a particular manufacturer in such a manner as deliberately to mislead the consumer into believing that the product is made by that same manufacturer when it is not.

14. Establishing, operating or promoting a pyramid promotional scheme where a consumer gives consideration for the opportunity to receive compensation that is derived primarily from the introduction of other consumers into the scheme rather than from the sale or consumption of products.

15. Claiming that the trader is about to cease trading or move premises when he is not.

16. Claiming that products are able to facilitate winning in games of chance.

17. Falsely claiming that a product is able to cure illnesses, dysfunction or malformations.

18. Passing on materially inaccurate information on market conditions or on the possibility of finding the product with the intention of inducing the consumer to acquire the product at conditions less favourable than normal market conditions.

19. Claiming in a commercial practice to offer a competition or prize promotion without awarding the prizes described or a reasonable equivalent.

20. Describing a product as "gratis", "free", "without charge" or similar if the consumer has to pay anything other than the unavoidable cost of responding to the commercial practice and collecting or paying for delivery of the item.

21. Including in marketing material an invoice or similar document seeking payment which gives the consumer the impression that he has already ordered the marketed product when he has not.

22. Falsely claiming or creating the impression that the trader is not acting for purposes relating to his trade, business, craft or profession, or falsely representing oneself as a consumer.

23. Creating the false impression that after-sales service in relation to a product is available in a Member State other than the one in which the product is sold.

AGGRESSIVE COMMERCIAL PRACTICES

24. Creating the impression that the consumer cannot leave the premises until a contract is formed.

25. Conducting personal visits to the consumer's home ignoring the consumer's request to leave or not to return except in circumstances and to the extent justified, under national law, to enforce a contractual obligation.

26. Making persistent and unwanted solicitations by telephone, fax, e-mail or other remote media except in circumstances and to the extent justified under national law to enforce a contractual obligation. This is without prejudice to Article 10 of Directive 97/7/EC and Directives 95/46/EC[2] and 2002/58/EC.

27. Requiring a consumer who wishes to claim on an insurance policy to produce documents which could not reasonably be considered relevant as to whether the claim was valid, or failing systematically to respond to pertinent correspondence, in order to dissuade a consumer from exercising his contractual rights.

28. Including in an advertisement a direct exhortation to children to buy advertised products or persuade their parents or other adults to buy advertised products for them. This provision is without prejudice to Article 16 of Directive 89/552/EEC on television broadcasting.

29. Demanding immediate or deferred payment for or the return or safekeeping of products supplied by the trader, but not solicited by the consumer except where the product is a substitute supplied in conformity with Article 7(3) of Directive 97/7/EC (inertia selling).

30. Explicitly informing a consumer that if he does not buy the product or service, the trader's job or livelihood will be in jeopardy.

31. Creating the false impression that the consumer has already won, will win, or will on doing a particular act win, a prize or other equivalent benefit, when in fact either:

— there is no prize or other equivalent benefit, or
— taking any action in relation to claiming the prize or other equivalent benefit is subject to the consumer paying money or incurring a cost.

NOTES

[1] Council Directive 89/552/EEC of 3 October 1989 on the coordination of certain provisions laid down by Law, Regulation or Administrative Action in Member States concerning the pursuit of television broadcasting activities (OJ L 298, 17.10.1989, p 23). Directive as amended by Directive 97/36/EC of the European Parliament and of the Council (OJ L 202, 30.7.1997, p 60).

[2] Directive 95/46/EC of the European Parliament and of the Council of 24 October 1995 on the protection of individuals with regard to the processing of personal data and on the free movement of such data (OJ L 281, 23.11.1995, p 31). Directive as amended by Regulation (EC) No 1882/2003 (OJ L 284, 31.10.2003, p 1).

ANNEX II
COMMUNITY LAW PROVISIONS SETTING OUT RULES FOR ADVERTISING AND COMMERCIAL COMMUNICATION

[8.199]
Articles 4 and 5 of Directive 97/7/EC

Article 3 of Council Directive 90/314/EEC of 13 June 1990 on package travel, package holidays and package tours[1]

Article 3(3) of Directive 94/47/EC of the European Parliament and of the Council of 26 October 1994 on the protection of purchasers in respect of certain aspects of contracts relating to the purchase of a right to use immovable properties on a timeshare basis[2]

Article 3(4) of Directive 98/6/EC of the European Parliament and of the Council of 16 February 1998 on consumer protection in the indication of the prices of products offered to consumers[3]

Articles 86 to 100 of Directive 2001/83/EC of the European Parliament and of the Council of 6 November 2001 on the Community code relating to medicinal products for human use[4]

Articles 5 and 6 of Directive 2000/31/EC of the European Parliament and of the Council of 8 June 2000 on certain legal aspects of information society services, in particular electronic commerce, in the Internal Market (Directive on electronic commerce)[5]

Article 1(d) of Directive 98/7/EC of the European Parliament and of the Council of 16 February 1998 amending Council Directive 87/102/EEC for the approximation of the laws, regulations and administrative provisions of the Member States concerning consumer credit[6]

Articles 3 and 4 of Directive 2002/65/EC

Article 1(9) of Directive 2001/107/EC of the European Parliament and of the Council of 21 January 2002 amending Council Directive 85/611/EEC on the coordination of laws, regulations and administrative provisions relating to undertakings for collective investment in transferable securities (UCITS) with a view to regulating management companies and simplified prospectuses[7]

Articles 12 and 13 of Directive 2002/92/EC of the European Parliament and of the Council of 9 December 2002 on insurance mediation[8]

Article 36 of Directive 2002/83/EC of the European Parliament and of the Council of 5 November 2002 concerning life assurance[9]

Article 19 of Directive 2004/39/EC of the European Parliament and of the Council of 21 April 2004 on markets in financial instruments[10]

Articles 31 and 43 of Council Directive 92/49/EEC of 18 June 1992 on the coordination of laws, regulations and administrative provisions relating to direct insurance other than life assurance[11] (third non-life insurance Directive)

Articles 5, 7 and 8 of Directive 2003/71/EC of the European Parliament and of the Council of 4 November 2003 on the prospectus to be published when securities are offered to the public or admitted to trading[12]

NOTES

1 OJ L158, 23.6.1990, p 59.

2 OJ L280, 29.10.1994, p 83.

3 OJ L80, 18.3.1998, p 27.

4 OJ L311, 28.11.2001, p 67. Directive as last amended by Directive 2004/27/EC (OJ L136, 30.4.2004, p 34).

5 OJ L178, 17.7.2000, p 1.

6 OJ L101, 1.4.1998, p 17.

7 OJ L41, 13.2.2002, p 20.

8 OJ L9, 15.1.2003, p 3.

9 OJ L345, 19.12.2002, p 1. Directive as amended by Council Directive 2004/66/EC (OJ L168, 1.5.2004, p 35).

10 OJ L145, 30.4.2004, p 1.

11 OJ L228, 11.8.1992, p 1. Directive as last amended by Directive 2002/87/EC of the European Parliament and of the Council (OJ L35, 11.2.2003, p 1).

12 OJ L345, 31.12.2003, p 64.

COUNCIL REGULATION

(834/2007/EC)

of 28 June 2007

on organic production and labelling of organic products and repealing Regulation (EEC) No 2092/91

NOTES

Date of publication in OJ: OJ L189, 20.7.2007, p 1.

THE COUNCIL OF THE EUROPEAN UNION,

Having regard to the Treaty establishing the European Community, and in particular Article 37 thereof,

Having regard to the proposal from the Commission,

Having regard to the opinion of the European Parliament,[1]

Whereas:

(1) Organic production is an overall system of farm management and food production that

combines best environmental practices, a high level of biodiversity, the preservation of natural resources, the application of high animal welfare standards and a production method in line with the preference of certain consumers for products produced using natural substances and processes. The organic production method thus plays a dual societal role, where it on the one hand provides for a specific market responding to a consumer demand for organic products, and on the other hand delivers public goods contributing to the protection of the environment and animal welfare, as well as to rural development.

(2) The share of the organic agricultural sector is on the increase in most Member States. Growth in consumer demand in recent years is particularly remarkable. Recent reforms of the common agricultural policy, with its emphasis on market-orientation and the supply of quality products to meet consumer demands, are likely to further stimulate the market in organic produce. Against this background the legislation on organic production plays an increasingly important role in the agricultural policy framework and is closely related to developments in the agricultural markets.

(3) The Community legal framework governing the sector of organic production should pursue the objective of ensuring fair competition and a proper functioning of the internal market in organic products, and of maintaining and justifying consumer confidence in products labelled as organic. It should further aim at providing conditions under which this sector can progress in line with production and market developments.

(4) The Communication from the Commission to the Council and the European Parliament on a European Action Plan for Organic Food and Farming proposes to improve and reinforce the Community's organic farming standards and import and inspection requirements. In its conclusions of 18 October 2004, the Council called on the Commission to review the Community legal framework in this field with a view to ensure simplification and overall coherence and in particular to establish principles encouraging harmonisation of standards and, where possible, to reduce the level of detail.

(5) It is therefore appropriate to define more explicitly the objectives, principles and rules applicable to organic production, in order to contribute to transparency and consumer confidence as well as to a harmonised perception of the concept of organic production.

(6) To that end, Council Regulation (EEC) No 2092/91 of 24 June 1991 on organic production of agricultural products and indications referring thereto on agricultural products and foodstuffs [2] should be repealed and replaced by a new regulation.

(7) A general Community framework of organic production rules should be established with regard to plant, livestock, and aquaculture production, including rules for the collection of wild plants and seaweeds, rules on conversion, as well as rules on the production of processed food, including wine, and feed and organic yeast. The Commission should authorise the use of products and substances and decide on methods to be used in organic farming and in the processing of organic food.

(8) The development of organic production should be facilitated further, in particular by fostering the use of new techniques and substances better suited to organic production.

(9) Genetically modified organisms (GMOs) and products produced from or by GMOs are incompatible with the concept of organic production and consumers' perception of organic products. They should therefore not be used in organic farming or in the processing of organic products.

(10) The aim is to have the lowest possible presence of GMOs in organic products. The existing labelling thresholds represent ceilings which are exclusively linked to the adventitious and technically unavoidable presence of GMOs.

(11) Organic farming should primarily rely on renewable resources within locally organised agricultural systems. In order to minimise the use of non-renewable resources, wastes and by-products of plant and animal origin should be recycled to return nutrients to the land.

(12) Organic plant production should contribute to maintaining and enhancing soil fertility as well as to preventing soil erosion. Plants should preferably be fed through the soil eco-system and not through soluble fertilisers added to the soil.

(13) The essential elements of the organic plant production management system are soil fertility management, choice of species and varieties, multiannual crop rotation, recycling organic materials and cultivation techniques. Additional fertilisers, soil conditioners and plant protection products should only be used if they are compatible with the objectives and principles of organic production.

(14) Livestock production is fundamental to the organisation of agricultural production on organic holdings in so far as it provides the necessary organic matter and nutrients for cultivated land and accordingly contributes towards soil improvement and the development of sustainable agriculture.

(15) In order to avoid environmental pollution, in particular of natural resources such as the soil and water, organic production of livestock should in principle provide for a close relationship between such production and the land, suitable multiannual rotation systems and the feeding of livestock with organic-farming crop products produced on the holding itself or on neighbouring organic holdings.

(16) As organic stock farming is a land-related activity animals should have, whenever possible, access to open air or grazing areas.

(17) Organic stock farming should respect high animal welfare standards and meet animals' species-specific behavioural needs while animal-health management should be based on disease prevention. In this respect, particular attention should be paid to housing conditions, husbandry practices and stocking densities. Moreover, the choice of breeds should take account of their capacity to adapt to local conditions. The implementing rules for livestock production and aquaculture production should at least ensure compliance with the provisions of the European Convention for the Protection of Animals kept for Farming purposes and the subsequent recommendations by its standing committee (T-AP).

(18) The organic livestock production system should aim at completing the production cycles of the different livestock species with organically reared animals. It should therefore encourage the increase of the gene pool of organic animals, improve self reliance and thus ensure the development of the sector.

(19) Organic processed products should be produced by the use of processing methods which guarantee that the organic integrity and vital qualities of the product are maintained through all stages of the production chain.

(20) Processed food should be labelled as organic only where all or almost all the ingredients of agricultural origin are organic. However, special labelling provisions should be laid down for processed foods which include agricultural ingredients that cannot be obtained organically, as it is the case for products of hunting and fishing. Moreover, for the purpose of consumer information, transparency in the market and to stimulate the use of organic ingredients, it should also be made possible to refer to organic production in the ingredients list under certain conditions.

(21) It is appropriate to provide for flexibility as regards the application of production rules, so as to make it possible to adapt organic standards and requirements to local climatic or geographic conditions, specific husbandry practices and stages of development. This should allow for the application of exceptional rules, but only within the limits of specific conditions laid down in Community legislation.

(22) It is important to maintain consumer confidence in organic products. Exceptions from the requirements applicable to organic production should therefore be strictly limited to cases where the application of exceptional rules is deemed to be justified.

(23) For the sake of consumer protection and fair competition, the terms used to indicate organic products should be protected from being used on non-organic products throughout the Community and independently of the language used. The protection should also apply to the usual derivatives or diminutives of those terms, whether they are used alone or combined.

(24) In order to create clarity for consumers throughout the Community market, the EU-logo should be made obligatory for all organic pre-packaged food produced within the Community. It should otherwise be possible to use the EUlogo on a voluntary basis in the case of non pre-packaged organic products produced within the Community or any organic products imported from third countries.

(25) It is however considered appropriate to limit the use of the EU-logo to products which contain only, or almost only, organic ingredients in order not to mislead consumers as to the organic nature of the entire product. It should therefore not be allowed to use it in the labelling of in-conversion products or processed foodstuffs of which less than 95% of its ingredients of agricultural origin are organic.

(26) The EU-logo should under no circumstances prevent the simultaneous use of national or private logos.

(27) Moreover, for the sake of avoiding deceptive practices and any possible confusion amongst consumers on the Community or non-Community origin of the product, whenever the EU-logo is used, consumers should be informed about the place were the agricultural raw materials of which the product is composed have been farmed.

(28) The Community rules should promote a harmonised concept of organic production. The competent authorities, control authorities and control bodies should refrain from any conduct that might create obstacles to the free movement of compliant products that have been certified by an authority or body located in another Member State. They should in particular not impose any additional controls or financial burdens.

(29) For the sake of consistency with Community legislation in other fields, in the case of plant and livestock production, Member States should be allowed to apply within their own territories, national production rules which are stricter than the Community organic production rules, provided that these national rules also apply to non-organic production and are otherwise in conformity with Community law.

(30) The use of GMOs in organic production is prohibited. For the sake of clarity and coherence, it should not be possible to label a product as organic where it has to be labelled as containing GMOs, consisting of GMOs or produced from GMOs.

(31) In order to ensure that organic products are produced in accordance with the requirements laid down under the Community legal framework on organic production, activities performed by operators at all stages of production, preparation and distribution of organic products should be submitted to a control system set up and managed in conformity with the rules laid down in Regulation (EC) No 882/2004 of the European Parliament and of the Council of 29 April 2004 on official controls performed to ensure the verification of compliance with feed and food law, animal health and animal welfare rules.[3]

(32) It might in some cases appear disproportionate to apply notification and control requirements to certain types of retail operators, such as those who sell products directly to the final consumer or user. It is therefore appropriate to allow Member States to exempt such operators from these requirements. However, in order to avoid fraud it is necessary to exclude from the exemption those retail operators who produce, prepare or store products other than in connection with the point of sale, or who import organic products or who have contracted out the aforesaid activities to a third party.

(33) Organic products imported into the European Community should be allowed to be placed on the Community market as organic, where they have been produced in accordance with production rules and subject to control arrangements that are in compliance with or equivalent to those laid down in Community legislation. In addition, the products imported under an equivalent system should be covered by a certificate issued by the competent authority, or recognised control authority or body of the third country concerned.

(34) The assessment of equivalency with regard to imported products should take into account the international standards laid down in Codex Alimentarius.

(35) It is considered appropriate to maintain the list of third countries recognised by the Commission as having production standards and control arrangement which are equivalent to those provided for in Community legislation. For third countries which are not included in that list, the Commission should set up a list of control authorities and control bodies recognised as being competent for the task of ensuring controls and certification in third countries concerned.

(36) Relevant statistical information should be collected in order to obtain reliable data needed for the implementation and follow-up of this Regulation and as a tool for producers, market operators and policy makers. The statistical information needed should be defined within the context of the Community Statistical Programme.

(37) This Regulation should apply from a date which gives the Commission sufficient time to adopt the measures necessary for its implementation.

(38) The measures necessary for the implementation of this Regulation should be adopted in accordance with Council Decision 1999/468/EC of 28 June 1999 laying down the procedures for the exercise of implementing powers conferred on the Commission.[4]

(39) The dynamic evolution of the organic sector, certain highly sensitive issues linked to the organic production method and the need to ensure a smooth functioning of the internal market and control system makes it appropriate to provide for a future review of the Community rules on organic farming, taking into account the experience gained from the application of these rules.

(40) Pending the adoption of detailed Community production rules for certain animal species and aquatic plants and micro-algae, Member States should have the possibility to provide for the application of national standards or, in the absence thereof, private standards accepted or recognised by the Member States,

NOTES

1 Opinion delivered on 22 May 2007 (not yet published in the Official Journal).

2 OJ L198, 22.7.1991, p 1. Regulation as last amended by Commission Regulation (EC) No 394/2007 (OJ L98, 13.4.2007, p 3).

3 OJ L165, 30.4.2004, p 1. Corrected by OJ L191, 28.5.2004, p 1.

4 OJ L184, 17.7.1999, p 23. Decision as amended by Decision 2006/512/EC (OJ L200, 22.7.2006, p 11).

HAS ADOPTED THIS REGULATION:

TITLE I
AIM, SCOPE AND DEFINITIONS

[8.200]
Article 1
Aim and scope

1. This Regulation provides the basis for the sustainable development of organic production while ensuring the effective functioning of the internal market, guaranteeing fair competition, ensuring consumer confidence and protecting consumer interests.

It establishes common objectives and principles to underpin the rules set out under this Regulation concerning:

(a) all stages of production, preparation and distribution of organic products and their control;

(b) the use of indications referring to organic production in labelling and advertising.

2. This Regulation shall apply to the following products originating from agriculture, including aquaculture, where such products are placed on the market or are intended to be placed on the market:

(a) live or unprocessed agricultural products;
(b) processed agricultural products for use as food;
(c) feed;
(d) vegetative propagating material and seeds for cultivation.

The products of hunting and fishing of wild animals shall not be considered as organic production.

This Regulation shall also apply to yeasts used as food or feed.

3. This Regulation shall apply to any operator involved in activities, at any stage of production, preparation and distribution, relating to the products set out in paragraph 2.

However, mass catering operations shall not be subject to this Regulation. Member States may apply national rules or, in the absence thereof, private standards, on labelling and control of products originating from mass catering operations, in so far as the said rules comply with Community Law.

4. This Regulation shall apply without prejudice to other community provisions or national provisions, in conformity with Community law concerning products specified in this Article, such as provisions governing the production, preparation, marketing, labelling and control, including legislation on foodstuffs and animal nutrition.

[8.201]

Article 2

Definitions

For the purposes of this Regulation, the following definitions shall apply:

(a) 'organic production' means the use of the production method compliant with the rules established in this Regulation, at all stages of production, preparation and distribution;
(b) 'stages of production, preparation and distribution' means any stage from and including the primary production of an organic product up to and including its storage, processing, transport, sale or supply to the final consumer, and where relevant labelling, advertising, import, export and subcontracting activities;
(c) 'organic' means coming from or related to organic production;
(d) 'operator' means the natural or legal persons responsible for ensuring that the requirements of this Regulation are met within the organic business under their control;
(e) 'plant production' means production of agricultural crop products including harvesting of wild plant products for commercial purposes;
(f) 'livestock production' means the production of domestic or domesticated terrestrial animals (including insects);
(g) the definition of 'aquaculture' is that given in Council Regulation (EC) No 1198/2006 of 27 July 2006 on the European Fisheries Fund;[1]
(h) 'conversion' means the transition from non organic to organic farming within a given period of time, during which the provisions concerning the organic production have been applied;
(i) 'preparation' means the operations of preserving and/or processing of organic products, including slaughter and cutting for livestock products, and also packaging, labelling and/or alterations made to the labelling concerning the organic production method;
(j) the definitions of 'food', 'feed' and 'placing on the market' are those given in Regulation (EC) No 178/2002 of the European Parliament and of the Council of 28 January 2002 laying down the general principles and requirements of food law, establishing the European Food Safety Authority and laying down procedures in matters of food safety;[2]
(k) 'labelling' means any terms, words, particulars, trade marks, brand name, pictorial matter or symbol relating to and placed on any packaging, document, notice, label, board, ring or collar accompanying or referring to a product;
(l) the definition of 'pre-packaged foodstuff' is that given in Article 1(3)(b) of Directive 2000/13/EC of the European Parliament and of the Council of 20 March 2000 on the approximation of the laws of the Member States relating to the labelling, presentation and advertising of foodstuffs;[3]
(m) 'advertising' means any representation to the public, by any means other than a label, that is intended or is likely to influence and shape attitude, beliefs and behaviours in order to promote directly or indirectly the sale of organic products;
(n) 'competent authority' means the central authority of a Member State competent for the organisation of official controls in the field of organic production in accordance with the provisions set out under this Regulation, or any other authority on which that competence has been conferred to; it shall also include, where appropriate, the corresponding authority of a third country;
(o) 'control authority' means a public administrative organisation of a Member State to which the competent authority has conferred, in whole or in part, its competence for the

inspection and certification in the field of organic production in accordance with the provisions set out under this Regulation; it shall also include, where appropriate, the corresponding authority of a third country or the corresponding authority operating in a third country;

(p) 'control body' means an independent private third party carrying out inspection and certification in the field of organic production in accordance with the provisions set out under this Regulation; it shall also include, where appropriate, the corresponding body of a third country or the corresponding body operating in a third country;

(q) 'mark of conformity' means the assertion of conformity to a particular set of standards or other normative documents in the form of a mark;

(r) the definition of 'ingredients' is that given in Article 6(4) of Directive 2000/13/EC;

(s) the definition of 'plant protection products' is that given in Council Directive 91/414/EEC of 15 July 1991 concerning the placing of plant protection products on the market;[4]

(t) the definition of 'Genetically modified organism (GMO)' is that given in Directive 2001/18/EC of the European Parliament and of the Council of 12 March 2001 on the deliberate release into the environment of genetically modified organisms and repealing Council Directive 90/220/EEC[5] and which is not obtained through the techniques of genetic modifications listed in Annex I.B of that Directive;

(u) 'produced from GMOs' means derived in whole or in part from GMOs but not containing or consisting of GMOs;

(v) 'produced by GMOs' means derived by using a GMO as the last living organism in the production process, but not containing or consisting of GMOs nor produced from GMOs;

(w) the definition of 'feed additives' is that given in Regulation (EC) No 1831/2003 of the European Parliament and of the Council of 22 September 2003 on additives for use in animal nutrition;[6]

(x) 'equivalent', in describing different systems or measures, means that they are capable of meeting the same objectives and principles by applying rules which ensure the same level of assurance of conformity;

(y) 'processing aid' means any substance not consumed as a food ingredient by itself, intentionally used in the processing of raw materials, foods or their ingredients, to fulfil a certain technological purpose during treatment or processing and which may result in the unintentional but technically unavoidable presence of residues of the substance or its derivatives in the final product, provided that these residues do not present any health risk and do not have any technological effect on the finished product;

(z) the definition of 'ionising radiation' is that given in Council Directive 96/29/Euratom of 13 May 1996 laying down basic safety standards for the protection of the health of workers and the general public against the dangers arising from ionising radiation[7] and as restricted by Article 1(2) of Directive 1999/2/EC of the European Parliament and of the Council of 22 February 1999 on the approximation of the laws of the Member States concerning foods and food ingredients treated with ionising radiation.[8]

(aa) 'mass catering operations' means the preparation of organic products in restaurants, hospitals, canteens and other similar food business at the point of sale or delivery to the final consumer.

NOTES

1 OJ L223, 15.8.2006, p 1.

2 OJ L31, 1.2.2002, p 1. Regulation as last amended by Commission Regulation (EC) No 575/2006 (OJ L100, 8.4.2006, p 3).

3 OJ L109, 6.5.2000, p 29. Directive as last amended by Commission Directive 2006/142/EC (OJ L368, 23.12.2006, p 110).

4 OJ L230, 19.8.1991, p 1. Directive as last amended by Commission Directive 2007/31/EC (OJ L140, 1.6.2007, p 44).

5 OJ L106, 17.4.2001, p 1. Regulation as last amended by Regulation (EC) No 1830/2003 (OJ L268, 18.10.2003, p 24).

6 OJ L268, 18.10.2003, p 29. Regulation as amended by Commission Regulation (EC) No 378/2005 (OJ L59, 5.3.2005, p 8).

7 OJ L 159, 29.6.1996, p. 1.

8 OJ L 66, 13.3.1999, p. 16. Directive as amended by Regulation (EC) No 1882/2003 (OJ L 284, 31.10.2003, p. 1).

TITLE II
OBJECTIVES AND PRINCIPLES FOR ORGANIC PRODUCTION

[8.202]
Article 3
Objectives

Organic production shall pursue the following general objectives:

(a) establish a sustainable management system for agriculture that:

(i) respects nature's systems and cycles and sustains and enhances the health of soil, water, plants and animals and the balance between them;

(ii) contributes to a high level of biological diversity;

(iii) makes responsible use of energy and the natural resources, such as water, soil, organic matter and air;
(iv) respects high animal welfare standards and in particular meets animals' species-specific behavioural needs;

(b) aim at producing products of high quality;
(c) aim at producing a wide variety of foods and other agricultural products that respond to consumers' demand for goods produced by the use of processes that do not harm the environment, human health, plant health or animal health and welfare.

[8.203]
Article 4
Overall principles

Organic production shall be based on the following principles:

(a) the appropriate design and management of biological processes based on ecological systems using natural resources which are internal to the system by methods that:
(i) use living organisms and mechanical production methods;
(ii) practice land-related crop cultivation and livestock production or practice aquaculture which complies with the principle of sustainable exploitation of fisheries;
(iii) exclude the use of GMOs and products produced from or by GMOs with the exception of veterinary medicinal products;
(iv) are based on risk assessment, and the use of precautionary and preventive measures, when appropriate;

(b) the restriction of the use of external inputs. Where external inputs are required or the appropriate management practices and methods referred to in paragraph (a) do not exist, these shall be limited to:
(i) inputs from organic production;
(ii) natural or naturally-derived substances;
(iii) low solubility mineral fertilisers;

(c) the strict limitation of the use of chemically synthesised inputs to exceptional cases these being:
(i) where the appropriate management practices do not exist; and
(ii) the external inputs referred to in paragraph (b) are not available on the market; or
(iii) where the use of external inputs referred to in paragraph (b) contributes to unacceptable environmental impacts;

(d) the adaptation, where necessary, and within the framework of this Regulation, of the rules of organic production taking account of sanitary status, regional differences in climate and local conditions, stages of development and specific husbandry practices.

[8.204]
Article 5
Specific principles applicable to farming

In addition to the overall principles set out in Article 4, organic farming shall be based on the following specific principles:

(a) the maintenance and enhancement of soil life and natural soil fertility, soil stability and soil biodiversity preventing and combating soil compaction and soil erosion, and the nourishing of plants primarily through the soil ecosystem;
(b) the minimisation of the use of non-renewable resources and off-farm inputs;
(c) the recycling of wastes and by-products of plant and animal origin as input in plant and livestock production;
(d) taking account of the local or regional ecological balance when taking production decisions;
(e) the maintenance of animal health by encouraging the natural immunological defence of the animal, as well as the selection of appropriate breeds and husbandry practices;
(f) the maintenance of plant health by preventative measures, such as the choice of appropriate species and varieties resistant to pests and diseases, appropriate crop rotations, mechanical and physical methods and the protection of natural enemies of pests;
(g) the practice of site-adapted and land-related livestock production;
(h) the observance of a high level of animal welfare respecting species-specific needs;
(i) the production of products of organic livestock from animals that have been raised on organic holdings since birth or hatching and throughout their life;
(j) the choice of breeds having regard to the capacity of animals to adapt to local conditions, their vitality and their resistance to disease or health problems;
(k) the feeding of livestock with organic feed composed of agricultural ingredients from organic farming and of natural non-agricultural substances;
(l) the application of animal husbandry practices, which enhance the immune system and strengthen the natural defence against diseases, in particular including regular exercise and access to open air areas and pastureland where appropriate;
(m) the exclusion of rearing artificially induced polyploid animals;

(n) the maintenance of the biodiversity of natural aquatic ecosystems, the continuing health of the aquatic environment and the quality of surrounding aquatic and terrestrial ecosystems in aquaculture production;

(o) the feeding of aquatic organisms with feed from sustainable exploitation of fisheries as defined in Article 3 of Council Regulation (EC) No 2371/2002 of 20 December 2002 on the conservation and sustainable exploitation of fisheries resources under the Common Fisheries Policy[1] or with organic feed composed of agricultural ingredients from organic farming and of natural non-agricultural substances.

NOTES

[1] OJ L358, 31.12.2002, p 59.

[8.205]
Article 6
Specific principles applicable to processing of organic food

In addition to the overall principles set out in Article 4, the production of processed organic food shall be based on the following specific principles:

(a) the production of organic food from organic agricultural ingredients, except where an ingredient is not available on the market in organic form;

(b) the restriction of the use of food additives, of non organic ingredients with mainly technological and sensory functions and of micronutrients and processing aids, so that they are used to a minimum extent and only in case of essential technological need or for particular nutritional purposes;

(c) the exclusion of substances and processing methods that might be misleading regarding the true nature of the product;

(d) the processing of food with care, preferably with the use of biological, mechanical and physical methods.

[8.206]
Article 7
Specific principles applicable to processing of organic feed

In addition to the overall principles set out in Article 4, the production of processed organic feed shall be based on the following specific principles:

(a) the production of organic feed from organic feed materials, except where a feed material is not available on the market in organic form;

(b) the restriction of the use of feed additives and processing aids to a minimum extent and only in case of essential technological or zootechnical needs or for particular nutritional purposes;

(c) the exclusion of substances and processing methods that might be misleading as to the true nature of the product;

(d) the processing of feed with care, preferably with the use of biological, mechanical and physical methods.

TITLE III
PRODUCTION RULES

CHAPTER 1
GENERAL PRODUCTION RULES

[8.207]
Article 8
General requirements

Operators shall comply with the production rules set out in this Title and with the implementing rules provided for in Article 38(a).

[8.208]
Article 9
Prohibition on the use of GMOs

1. GMOs and products produced from or by GMOs shall not be used as food, feed, processing aids, plant protection products, fertilisers, soil conditioners, seeds, vegetative propagating material, micro-organisms and animals in organic production.

2. For the purpose of the prohibition referred to in paragraph 1 concerning GMOs or products produced from GMOs for food and feed, operators may rely on the labels accompanying a product or any other accompanying document, affixed or provided pursuant to Directive 2001/18/EC, Regulation (EC) 1829/2003 of the European Parliament and the Council of 22 September 2003 on genetically modified food and feed[1] or Regulation (EC) 1830/2003 concerning the traceability and labelling of genetically modified organisms and the traceability of food and feed products produced from genetically modified organisms.

Operators may assume that no GMOs or products produced from GMOs have been used in the manufacture of purchased food and feed products when the latter are not labelled, or accompanied by a document, pursuant to those Regulations, unless they have obtained other information indicating that labelling of the products in question is not in conformity with those Regulations.

3. For the purpose of the prohibition referred to in paragraph 1, with regard to products not being food or feed, or products produced by GMOs, operators using such non-organic products purchased from third parties shall require the vendor to confirm that the products supplied have not been produced from or by GMOs.

4. The Commission shall decide on measures implementing the prohibition on the use of GMOs and products produced from or by GMOs in accordance with the procedure referred to in Article 37(2).

NOTES

1 OJ L268, 18.10.2003, p 1. Regulation as amended by Commission Regulation (EC) No 1981/2006 (OJ L368, 23.12.2006, p 99).

[8.209]
Article 10
Prohibition on the use of ionising radiation

The use of ionising radiation for the treatment of organic food or feed, or of raw materials used in organic food or feed is prohibited.

CHAPTER 2
FARM PRODUCTION

[8.210]
Article 11
General farm production rules

The entire agricultural holding shall be managed in compliance with the requirements applicable to organic production.

However, in accordance with specific conditions to be laid down in accordance with the procedure referred to in Article 37(2), a holding may be split up into clearly separated units or aquaculture production sites which are not all managed under organic production. As regards animals, different species shall be involved. As regards aquaculture the same species may be involved, provided that there is adequate separation between the production sites. As regards plants, different varieties that can be easily differentiated shall be involved.

Where, in accordance with the second subparagraph, not all units of a holding are used for organic production, the operator shall keep the land, animals, and products used for, or produced by, the organic units separate from those used for, or produced by, the non-organic units and keep adequate records to show the separation.

[8.211]
Article 12
Plant production rules

1. In addition to the general farm production rules laid down in Article 11, the following rules shall apply to organic plant production:

(a) organic plant production shall use tillage and cultivation practices that maintain or increase soil organic matter, enhance soil stability and soil biodiversity, and prevent soil compaction and soil erosion;

(b) the fertility and biological activity of the soil shall be maintained and increased by multiannual crop rotation including legumes and other green manure crops, and by the application of livestock manure or organic material, both preferably composted, from organic production;

(c) the use of biodynamic preparations is allowed;

(d) in addition, fertilisers and soil conditioners may only be used if they have been authorised for use in organic production under Article 16;

(e) mineral nitrogen fertilisers shall not be used;

(f) all plant production techniques used shall prevent or minimise any contribution to the contamination of the environment;

(g) the prevention of damage caused by pests, diseases and weeds shall rely primarily on the protection by natural enemies, the choice of species and varieties, crop rotation, cultivation techniques and thermal processes;

(h) in the case of an established threat to a crop, plant protection products may only be used if they have been authorised for use in organic production under Article 16;

(i) for the production of products other than seed and vegetative propagating material only organically produced seed and propagating material shall be used. To this end, the mother plant in the case of seeds and the parent plant in the case of vegetative propagating material shall have been produced in accordance with the rules laid down in this Regulation for at least one generation, or, in the case of perennial crops, two growing seasons;

(j) products for cleaning and disinfection in plant production shall be used only if they have been authorised for use in organic production under Article 16.

2. The collection of wild plants and parts thereof, growing naturally in natural areas, forests and agricultural areas is considered an organic production method provided that:

(a) those areas have not, for a period of at least three years before the collection, received treatment with products other than those authorised for use in organic production under Article 16;

(b) the collection does not affect the stability of the natural habitat or the maintenance of the species in the collection area.

3. The measures necessary for the implementation of the production rules contained in this Article shall be adopted in accordance with the procedure referred to in Article 37(2).

[8.212]
Article 13
Production rules for seaweed

1. The collection of wild seaweeds and parts thereof, growing naturally in the sea, is considered as an organic production method provided that:

(a) the growing areas are of high ecological quality as defined by Directive 2000/60/EC of the European Parliament and of the Council of 23 October 2000 establishing a framework for Community action in the field of water policy[1] and, pending its implementation, of a quality equivalent to designated waters under Directive 2006/113/EC of the European Parliament and of the Council of 12 December 2006 on the quality required of shellfish waters,[2] and are not unsuitable from a health point of view. Pending more detailed rules to be introduced in implementing legislation, wild edible seaweeds shall not be collected in areas which would not meet the criteria for Class A or Class B areas as defined in Annex II of Regulation (EC) No 854/2004 of the European Parliament and of the Council of 29 April 2004 laying down specific rules for the organisation of official controls on products of animal origin intended for human consumption;[3]

(b) the collection does not affect the long term stability of the natural habitat or the maintenance of the species in the collection area.

2. The farming of seaweeds shall take place in coastal areas with environmental and health characteristics at least equivalent to those outlined in paragraph 1 in order to be considered organic. In addition to this:

(a) sustainable practices shall be used in all stages of production, from collection of juvenile seaweed to harvesting;

(b) to ensure that a wide gene-pool is maintained, the collection of juvenile seaweed in the wild should take place on a regular basis to supplement indoor culture stock;

(c) fertilisers shall not be used except in indoor facilities and only if they have been authorised for use in organic production for this purpose under Article 16.

3. The measures necessary for the implementation of production rules contained in this Article shall be adopted in accordance with the procedure referred to in Article 37(2).

NOTES

[1] OJ L327, 22.12.2000, p 1. Directive as amended by Decision No 2455/2001/EC (OJ L331, 15.12.2001, p 1).

[2] OJ L376, 27.12.2006, p 14.

[3] OJ L139, 30.4.2004, p 206. Corrected version in OJ L226, 25.6.2004, p 83.

[8.213]
Article 14
Livestock production rules

1. In addition to the general farm production rules laid down in Article 11, the following rules shall apply to livestock production:

(a) with regard to the origin of the animals:

(i) organic livestock shall be born and raised on organic holdings;

(ii) for breeding purposes, non-organically raised animals may be brought onto a holding under specific conditions. Such animals and their products may be deemed organic after compliance with the conversion period referred to in Article 17(1)(c);

(iii) animals existing on the holding at the beginning of the conversion period and their products may be deemed organic after compliance with the conversion period referred to in Article 17(1)(c);

(b) with regard to husbandry practices and housing conditions:

(i) personnel keeping animals shall possess the necessary basic knowledge and skills as regards the health and the welfare needs of the animals;

(ii) husbandry practices, including stocking densities, and housing conditions shall ensure that the developmental, physiological and ethological needs of animals are met;

(iii) the livestock shall have permanent access to open air areas, preferably pasture, whenever weather conditions and the state of the ground allow this unless restrictions and obligations related to the protection of human and animal health are imposed on the basis of Community legislation;

(iv) the number of livestock shall be limited with a view to minimising overgrazing, poaching of soil, erosion, or pollution caused by animals or by the spreading of their manure;

(v) organic livestock shall be kept separate from other livestock. However, grazing of common land by organic animals and of organic land by non-organic animals is permitted under certain restrictive conditions;

(vi) tethering or isolation of livestock shall be prohibited, unless for individual animals for a limited period of time, and in so far as this is justified for safety, welfare or veterinary reasons;

(vii) duration of transport of livestock shall be minimised;

(viii) any suffering, including mutilation, shall be kept to a minimum during the entire life of the animal, including at the time of slaughter;

(ix) apiaries shall be placed in areas which ensure nectar and pollen sources consisting essentially of organically produced crops or, as appropriate, of spontaneous vegetation or non-organically managed forests or crops that are only treated with low environmental impact methods. Apiaries shall be kept at sufficient distance from sources that may lead to the contamination of beekeeping products or to the poor health of the bees;

(x) hives and materials used in beekeeping shall be mainly made of natural materials;

(xi) the destruction of bees in the combs as a method associated with the harvesting of beekeeping products is prohibited;

(c) with regard to breeding:

(i) reproduction shall use natural methods. Artificial insemination is however allowed;

(ii) reproduction shall not be induced by treatment with hormones or similar substances, unless as a form of veterinary therapeutic treatment in case of an individual animal;

(iii) other forms of artificial reproduction, such as cloning and embryo transfer, shall not be used;

(iv) appropriate breeds shall be chosen. The choice of breeds shall also contribute to the prevention of any suffering and to avoiding the need for the mutilation of animals;

(d) with regard to feed:

(i) primarily obtaining feed for livestock from the holding where the animals are kept or from other organic holdings in the same region;

(ii) livestock shall be fed with organic feed that meets the animal's nutritional requirements at the various stages of its development. A part of the ration may contain feed from holdings which are in conversion to organic farming;

(iii) with the exception of bees, livestock shall have permanent access to pasture or roughage;

(iv) non organic feed materials from plant origin, feed materials from animal and mineral origin, feed additives, certain products used in animal nutrition and processing aids shall be used only if they have been authorised for use in organic production under Article 16;

(v) growth promoters and synthetic amino-acids shall not be used;

(vi) suckling mammals shall be fed with natural, preferably maternal, milk;

(e) with regard to disease prevention and veterinary treatment:

(i) disease prevention shall be based on breed and strain selection, husbandry management practices, high quality feed and exercise, appropriate stocking density and adequate and appropriate housing maintained in hygienic conditions;

(ii) disease shall be treated immediately to avoid suffering to the animal; chemically synthesised allopathic veterinary medicinal products including antibiotics may be used where necessary and under strict conditions, when the use of phytotherapeutic, homeopathic and other products is inappropriate. In particular restrictions with respect to courses of treatment and withdrawal periods shall be defined;

(iii) the use of immunological veterinary medicines is allowed;

(iv) treatments related to the protection of human and animal health imposed on the basis of Community legislation shall be allowed;

(f) with regard to cleaning and disinfection, products for cleaning and disinfection in livestock buildings and installations, shall be used only if they have been authorised for use in organic production under Article 16.

2. The measures and conditions necessary for the implementation of the production rules contained in this Article shall be adopted in accordance with the procedure referred to in Article 37(2).

[8.214]
Article 15
Production rules for aquaculture animals

1. In addition to the general farm production rules laid down in Article 11, the following rules shall apply to aquaculture animal production:

(a) with regard to the origin of the aquaculture animals:
  (i) organic aquaculture shall be based on the rearing of young stock originating from organic broodstock and organic holdings;
  (ii) when young stock from organic broodstock or holdings are not available, non-organically produced animals may be brought onto a holding under specific conditions;
(b) with regard to husbandry practices:
  (i) personnel keeping animals shall possess the necessary basic knowledge and skills as regards the health and the welfare needs of the animals;
  (ii) husbandry practices, including feeding, design of installations, stocking densities and water quality shall ensure that the developmental, physiological and behavioural needs of animals are met;
  (iii) husbandry practices shall minimise negative environmental impact from the holding, including the escape of farmed stock;
  (iv) organic animals shall be kept separate from other aquaculture animals;
  (v) transport shall ensure that the welfare of animals is maintained;
  (vi) any suffering of the animals including the time of slaughtering shall be kept to a minimum;
(c) with regard to breeding:
  (i) artificial induction of polyploidy, artificial hybridisation, cloning and production of monosex strains, except by hand sorting, shall not be used;
  (ii) the appropriate strains shall be chosen;
  (iii) species-specific conditions for broodstock management, breeding and juvenile production shall be established;
(d) with regard to feed for fish and crustaceans:
  (i) animals shall be fed with feed that meets the animal's nutritional requirements at the various stages of its development;
  (ii) the plant fraction of feed shall originate from organic production and the feed fraction derived from aquatic animals shall originate from sustainable exploitation of fisheries;
  (iii) in the case of non-organic feed materials from plant origin, feed materials from animal and mineral origin, feed additives, certain products used in animal nutrition and processing aids shall be used only if they have been authorised for use in organic production under Article 16;
  (iv) growth promoters and synthetic amino-acids shall not be used;
(e) with regard to bivalve molluscs and other species which are not fed by man but feed on natural plankton:
  (i) such filter-feeding animals shall receive all their nutritional requirements from nature except in the case of juveniles reared in hatcheries and nurseries;
  (ii) they shall be grown in waters which meet the criteria for Class A or Class B areas as defined in Annex II of Regulation (EC) No 854/2004;
  (iii) the growing areas shall be of high ecological quality as defined by Directive 2000/60/EC and, pending its implementation of a quality equivalent to designated waters under Directive 2006/113/EC;
(f) with regard to disease prevention and veterinary treatment:
  (i) disease prevention shall be based on keeping the animals in optimal conditions by appropriate siting, optimal design of the holdings, the application of good husbandry and management practices, including regular cleaning and disinfection of premises, high quality feed, appropriate stocking density, and breed and strain selection;
  (ii) disease shall be treated immediately to avoid suffering to the animal; chemically synthesised allopathic veterinary medicinal products including antibiotics may be used where necessary and under strict conditions, when the use of phytotherapeutic, homeopathic and other products is inappropriate. In particular restrictions with respect to courses of treatment and withdrawal periods shall be defined;
  (iii) the use of immunological veterinary medicines is allowed;
  (iv) treatments related to the protection of human and animal health imposed on the basis of Community legislation shall be allowed.
(g) With regard to cleaning and disinfection, products for cleaning and disinfection in ponds, cages, buildings and installations, shall be used only if they have been authorised for use in organic production under Article 16.

2. The measures and conditions necessary for the implementation of the production rules contained in this Article shall be adopted in accordance with the procedure referred to in Article 37(2).

[8.215]
Article 16
Products and substances used in farming and criteria for their authorisation

1. The Commission shall, in accordance with the procedure referred to in Article 37(2), authorise for use in organic production and include in a restricted list the products and substances, which may be used in organic farming for the following purposes:

(a) as plant protection products;
(b) as fertilisers and soil conditioners;
(c) as non-organic feed materials from plant origin, feed material from animal and mineral origin and certain substances used in animal nutrition;
(d) as feed additives and processing aids;
(e) as products for cleaning and disinfection of ponds, cages, buildings and installations for animal production;
(f) as products for cleaning and disinfection of buildings and installations used for plant production, including storage on an agricultural holding.

Products and substances contained in the restricted list may only be used in so far as the corresponding use is authorised in general agriculture in the Member States concerned in accordance with the relevant Community provisions or national provisions in conformity with Community law.

2. The authorisation of the products and substances referred to in paragraph 1 is subject to the objectives and principles laid down in Title II and the following general and specific criteria which shall be evaluated as a whole:

(a) their use is necessary for sustained production and essential for its intended use;
(b) all products and substances shall be of plant, animal, microbial or mineral origin except where products or substances from such sources are not available in sufficient quantities or qualities or if alternatives are not available;
(c) in the case of products referred to in paragraph 1(a), the following shall apply:
  (i) their use is essential for the control of a harmful organism or a particular disease for which other biological, physical or breeding alternatives or cultivation practices or other effective management practices are not available;
  (ii) if products are not of plant, animal, microbial or mineral origin and are not identical to their natural form, they may be authorised only if their conditions for use preclude any direct contact with the edible parts of the crop;
(d) in the case of products referred to in paragraph 1(b), their use is essential for obtaining or maintaining the fertility of the soil or to fulfil specific nutrition requirements of crops, or specific soil-conditioning purposes;
(e) in the case of products referred to in paragraph 1(c) and (d), the following shall apply:
  (i) they are necessary to maintain animal health, animal welfare and vitality and contribute to an appropriate diet fulfilling the physiological and behavioural needs of the species concerned or it would be impossible to produce or preserve such feed without having recourse to such substances;
  (ii) feed of mineral origin, trace elements, vitamins or provitamins shall be of natural origin. In case these substances are unavailable, chemically well-defined analogic substances may be authorised for use in organic production.

3.
(a) The Commission may, in accordance with the procedure referred to in Article 37(2), lay down conditions and limits as regards the agricultural products to which the products and substances referred to in paragraph 1 can be applied to, the application method, the dosage, the time limits for use and the contact with agricultural products and, if necessary, decide on the withdrawal of these products and substances.
(b) Where a Member State considers that a product or substance should be added to, or withdrawn from the list referred to in paragraph 1, or that the specifications of use mentioned in subparagraph (a) should be amended, the Member State shall ensure that a dossier giving the reasons for the inclusion, withdrawal or amendments is sent officially to the Commission and to the Member States.
Requests for amendment or withdrawal, as well as decisions thereon, shall be published.
(c) Products and substances used before adoption of this Regulation for purposes corresponding to those laid down in paragraph 1 of this Article, may continue to be used after said adoption. The Commission may in any case withdraw such products or substances in accordance with Article 37(2).

4. Member States may regulate, within their territory, the use of products and substances in organic farming for purposes different than those mentioned in paragraph 1 provided their use is subject to objectives and principles laid down in Title II and the general and specific criteria set out in paragraph 2, and in so far as it respects Community law. The Member State concerned shall inform other Member States and the Commission of such national rules.

5. The use of products and substances not covered under paragraph 1 and 4, and subject to the objectives and principles laid down in Title II and the general criteria in this Article, shall be allowed in organic farming.

[8.216]
Article 17
Conversion

1. The following rules shall apply to a farm on which organic production is started:
   (a) the conversion period shall start at the earliest when the operator has notified his activity to the competent authorities and subjected his holding to the control system in accordance with Article 28(1);
   (b) during the conversion period all rules established by this Regulation shall apply;
   (c) conversion periods specific to the type of crop or animal production shall be defined;
   (d) on a holding or unit partly under organic production and partly in conversion to organic production, the operator shall keep the organically produced and in-conversion products separate and the animals separate or readily separable and keep adequate records to show the separation;
   (e) in order to determine the conversion period referred to above, a period immediately preceding the date of the start of the conversion period, may be taken into account, in so far as certain conditions concur;
   (f) animals and animal products produced during the conversion period referred to in subparagraph (c) shall not be marketed with the indications referred to in Articles 23 and 24 used in the labelling and advertising of products.
2. The measures and conditions necessary for the implementation of the rules contained in this Article, and in particular the periods referred to in paragraph 1(c) to (f) shall be defined in accordance with the procedure referred to in Article 37(2).

CHAPTER 3
PRODUCTION OF PROCESSED FEED

[8.217]
Article 18
General rules on the production of processed feed

1. Production of processed organic feed shall be kept separate in time or space from production of processed non organic feed.
2. Organic feed materials, or feed materials from production in conversion, shall not enter simultaneously with the same feed materials produced by non organic means into the composition of the organic feed product.
3. Any feed materials used or processed in organic production shall not have been processed with the aid of chemically synthesised solvents.
4. Substances and techniques that reconstitute properties that are lost in the processing and storage of organic feed, that correct the results of negligence in the processing or that otherwise may be misleading as to the true nature of these products shall not be used.
5. The measures and conditions necessary for the implementation of the production rules contained in this Article shall be adopted in accordance with the procedure referred to in Article 37(2).

CHAPTER 4
PRODUCTION OF PROCESSED FOOD

[8.218]
Article 19
General rules on the production of processed food

1. The preparation of processed organic food shall be kept separate in time or space from non-organic food.
2. The following conditions shall apply to the composition of organic processed food:
   (a) the product shall be produced mainly from ingredients of agricultural origin; in order to determine whether a product is produced mainly from ingredients of agricultural origin added water and cooking salt shall not be taken into account;
   (b) only additives, processing aids, flavourings, water, salt, preparations of micro-organisms and enzymes, minerals, trace elements, vitamins, as well as amino acids and other micronutrients in foodstuffs for particular nutritional uses may be used, and only in so far as they have been authorised for use in organic production in accordance with Article 21;
   (c) non-organic agricultural ingredients may be used only if they have been authorised for use in organic production in accordance with Article 21 or have been provisionally authorised by a Member State;
   (d) an organic ingredient shall not be present together with the same ingredient in non-organic form or an ingredient in conversion;
   (e) food produced from in-conversion crops shall contain only one crop ingredient of agricultural origin.
3. Substances and techniques that reconstitute properties that are lost in the processing and storage of organic food, that correct the results of negligence in the processing of these products or that otherwise may be misleading as to the true nature of these products shall not be used.

The measures necessary for the implementation of the production rules contained in this Article, and in particular regarding processing methods and the conditions for the provisional authorisation by Member States mentioned in paragraph 2(c), shall be adopted in accordance with the procedure referred to in Article 37(2).

[8.219]
Article 20
General rules on the production of organic yeast

1. For the production of organic yeast only organically produced substrates shall be used. Other products and substances may only be used in so far as they have been authorised for use in organic production in accordance with Article 21.
2. Organic yeast shall not be present in organic food or feed together with non-organic yeast.
3. Detailed production rules may be laid down in accordance with the procedure referred to in Article 37(2).

[8.220]
Article 21
Criteria for certain products and substances in processing

1. The authorisation of products and substances for use in organic production and their inclusion in a restricted list of the products and substances referred to in Article 19(2)(b) and (c) shall be subject to the objectives and principles laid down in Title II and the following criteria, which shall be evaluated as a whole:
   (i) alternatives authorised in accordance with this chapter are not available;
   (ii) without having recourse to them, it would be impossible to produce or preserve the food or to fulfil given dietary requirements provided for on the basis of the Community legislation.

In addition, the products and substances referred to in Article 19(2)(b) are to be found in nature and may have undergone only mechanical, physical, biological, enzymatic or microbial processes, except where such products and substances from such sources are not available in sufficient quantities or qualities on the market.

2. The Commission shall, in accordance with the procedure referred to in Article 37(2), decide on the authorisation of the products and substances and their inclusion in the restricted list referred to in paragraph 1 of this Article and lay down specific conditions and limits for their use, and, if necessary, on the withdrawal of products.

Where a Member State considers that a product or substance should be added to, or withdrawn from the list referred to in paragraph 1, or that the specifications of use mentioned in this paragraph should be amended, the Member State shall ensure that a dossier giving the reasons for the inclusion, withdrawal or amendments is sent officially to the Commission and to the Member States.

Requests for amendment or withdrawal, as well as decisions thereon, shall be published.

Products and substances used before adoption of this Regulation and falling under Article 19(2)(b) and (c) may continue to be used after the said adoption. The Commission may, in any case, withdraw such products or substances in accordance with Article 37(2).

CHAPTER 5
FLEXIBILITY

[8.221]
Article 22
Exceptional production rules

1. The Commission may, in accordance with the procedure referred to in Article 37(2) and the conditions set out in paragraph 2 of this Article and subject to the objectives and principles laid down in Title II, provide for the granting of exceptions from the production rules laid down in Chapters 1 to 4.
2. Exceptions as referred to in paragraph 1 shall be kept to a minimum and, where appropriate, limited in time and may only be provided for in the following cases:
   (a) where they are necessary in order to ensure that organic production can be initiated or maintained on holdings confronted with climatic, geographical or structural constraints;
   (b) where it is necessary in order to ensure access to feed, seed and vegetative propagating material, live animals and other farm inputs, where such inputs are not available on the market in organic form;
   (c) where it is necessary in order to ensure access to ingredients of agricultural origin, where such ingredients are not available on the market in organic form;
   (d) where they are necessary in order to solve specific problems related to the management of organic livestock;
   (e) where they are necessary with regard to the use of specific products and substances in the processing referred to in Article 19(2)(b) in order to ensure production of well established food products in organic form;
   (f) where temporary measures are necessary in order to allow organic production to continue or recommence in the case of catastrophic circumstances;

(g) where it is necessary to use food additives and other substances as set out in Article 19(2)(b) or feed additives and other substances as set out in Article 16(1)(d) and such substances are not available on the market other than produced by GMOs;

(h) where the use of food additives and other substances as set out in Article 19(2)(b) or feed additives as set out in Article 16(1)(d) is required on the basis of Community law or national law.

3. The Commission may in accordance with the procedure referred to in Article 37(2) lay down specific conditions for the application of exceptions provided for under paragraph 1.

TITLE IV
LABELLING

[8.222]
Article 23
Use of terms referring to organic production

1. For the purposes of this Regulation a product shall be regarded as bearing terms referring to the organic production method where, in the labelling, advertising material or commercial documents, such a product, its ingredients or feed materials are described in terms suggesting to the purchaser that the product, its ingredients or feed materials have been obtained in accordance with the rules laid down in this Regulation. In particular, the terms listed in the Annex, their derivatives or diminutives, such as 'bio' and 'eco', alone or combined, may be used throughout the Community and in any Community language for the labelling and advertising of products which satisfy the requirements set out under or pursuant to this Regulation.

In the labelling and advertising of live or unprocessed agricultural products terms referring to the organic production method may be used only where, in addition, all the ingredients of that product have also been produced in accordance with the requirements laid down in this Regulation.

2. The terms referred to in paragraph 1 shall not be used anywhere in the Community and in any Community language for the labelling, advertising and commercial documents of a product which does not satisfy the requirements set out under this Regulation, unless they are not applied to agricultural products in food or feed or clearly have no connection with organic production.

Furthermore, any terms, including terms used in trademarks, or practices used in labelling or advertising liable to mislead the consumer or user by suggesting that a product or its ingredients satisfy the requirements set out under this Regulation shall not be used.

3. The terms referred to in paragraph 1 shall not be used for a product for which it has to be indicated in the labelling or advertising that it contains GMOs, consists of GMOs or is produced from GMOs according to Community provisions.

4. As regards processed food, the terms referred to in paragraph 1 may be used:

(a) in the sales description, provided that:

(i) the processed food complies with Article 19;

(ii) at least 95% by weight, of its ingredients of agricultural origin are organic;

(b) only in the list of ingredients, provided that the food complies with Article 19(1), 19(2)(a), 19(2)(b) and 19(2)(d);

(c) in the list of ingredients and in the same visual field as the sales description, provided that:

(i) the main ingredient is a product of hunting or fishing;

(ii) it contains other ingredients of agricultural origin that are all organic;

(iii) the food complies with Article 19(1), 19(2)(a), 19(2)(b) and 19(2)(d).

The list of ingredients shall indicate which ingredients are organic.

In the case where points (b) and (c) of this paragraph apply, the references to the organic production method may only appear in relation to the organic ingredients and the list of ingredients shall include an indication of the total percentage of organic ingredients in proportion to the total quantity of ingredients of agricultural origin.

The terms and the indication of percentage referred to in the previous subparagraph shall appear in the same colour, identical size and style of lettering as the other indications in the list of ingredients.

5. Member States shall take the measures necessary to ensure compliance with this Article.

6. The Commission may in accordance with the procedure referred to in Article 37(2) adapt the list of terms set out in the Annex.

[8.223]
Article 24
Compulsory indications

1. Where terms as referred to in Article 23(1) are used:

(a) the code number referred to in Article 27(10) of the control authority or control body to which the operator who has carried out the most recent production or preparation operation is subject, shall also appear in the labelling;

(b) the Community logo referred to in Article 25(1) as regards pre-packaged food shall also appear on the packaging;

(c) where the Community logo is used, an indication of the place where the agricultural raw materials of which the product is composed have been farmed, shall also appear in the same visual field as the logo and shall take one of the following forms, as appropriate:
- 'EU Agriculture', where the agricultural raw material has been farmed in the EU,
- 'non-EU Agriculture', where the agricultural raw material has been farmed in third countries,
- 'EU/non-EU Agriculture', where part of the agricultural raw materials has been farmed in the Community and a part of it has been farmed in a third country.

The abovementioned indication 'EU' or 'non-EU' may be replaced or supplemented by a country in the case where all agricultural raw materials of which the product is composed have been farmed in that country.

For the abovementioned 'EU' or 'non-EU' indication, small quantities by weight of ingredients may be disregarded provided that the total quantity of the disregarded ingredients does not exceed 2% of the total quantity by weight of raw materials of agricultural origin.

The abovementioned 'EU' or 'non-EU' indication shall not appear in a colour, size and style of lettering more prominent than the sales description of the product.

The use of the Community logo as referred to in Article 25(1) and the indication referred to in the first subparagraph shall be optional for products imported from third countries. However, where the Community logo as referred to in Article 25(1) appears in the labelling, the indication referred to in the first subparagraph shall also appear in the labelling.

2. The indications referred to in paragraph 1 shall be marked in a conspicuous place in such a way as to be easily visible, clearly legible and indelible.

3. The Commission shall, in accordance with the procedure referred to in Article 37(2), lay down specific criteria as regards the presentation, composition and size of the indications referred to in paragraph 1(a) and (c).

[8.224]
Article 25
Organic production logos

1. The Community organic production logo may be used in the labelling, presentation and advertising of products which satisfy the requirements set out under this Regulation.

The Community logo shall not be used in the case of inconversion products and food as referred to in Article 23(4)(b) and (c).

2. National and private logos may be used in the labelling, presentation and advertising of products which satisfy the requirements set out under this Regulation.

3. The Commission shall, in accordance with the procedure referred to in Article 37(2), lay down specific criteria as regards presentation, composition, size and design of the Community logo.

[8.225]
Article 26
Specific labelling requirements

The Commission shall in accordance with the procedure referred to in Article 37(2) establish specific labelling and composition requirements applicable to:

(a) organic feed;
(b) in-conversion products of plant origin;
(c) vegetative propagating material and seeds for cultivation.

TITLE V
CONTROLS

[8.226]
Article 27
Control system

1. Member States shall set up a system of controls and designate one or more competent authorities responsible for controls in respect of the obligations established by this Regulation in conformity with Regulation (EC) No 882/2004.

2. In addition to the conditions laid down in Regulation (EC) No 882/2004, the control system set up under this Regulation shall comprise at least the application of precautionary and control measures to be adopted by the Commission in accordance with the procedure referred to in Article 37(2).

3. In the context of this Regulation the nature and frequency of the controls shall be determined on the basis of an assessment of the risk of occurrence of irregularities and infringements as regards compliance with the requirements laid down in this Regulation. In any case, all operators with the exception of wholesalers dealing only with pre-packaged products and operators selling to the final consumer or user as described in Article 28(2), shall be subject to a verification of compliance at least once a year.

4. The competent authority may:

(a) confer its control competences to one or more other control authorities. Control authorities shall offer adequate guarantees of objectivity and impartiality, and have at their disposal the qualified staff and resources necessary to carry out their functions;
(b) delegate control tasks to one or more control bodies. In that case, the Member States shall designate authorities responsible for the approval and supervision of such bodies.

5. The competent authority may delegate control tasks to a particular control body only if the conditions laid down in Article 5(2) of Regulation (EC) No 882/2004 are satisfied, and in particular where:
(a) there is an accurate description of the tasks that the control body may carry out and of the conditions under which it may carry them out;
(b) there is proof that the control body:
(i) has the expertise, equipment and infrastructure required to carry out the tasks delegated to it;
(iii) has a sufficient number of suitable qualified and experienced staff; and
(iii) is impartial and free from any conflict of interest as regards the exercise of the tasks delegated to it;
(c) the control body is accredited to the most recently notified version, by a publication in the C series of the *Official Journal of the European Union*, of European Standard EN 45011 or ISO Guide 65 (General requirements for bodies operating product certification systems), and is approved by the competent authorities;
(d) the control body communicates the results of the controls carried out to the competent authority on a regular basis and whenever the competent authority so requests. If the results of the controls indicate non-compliance or point to the likelihood of non-compliance, the control body shall immediately inform the competent authority;
(e) there is an effective coordination between the delegating competent authority and the control body.

6. In addition to the provisions of paragraph 5, the competent authority shall take into account the following criteria whilst approving a control body:
(a) the standard control procedure to be followed, containing a detailed description of the control measures and precautions that the body undertakes to impose on operators subject to its control;
(b) the measures that the control body intends to apply where irregularities and/or infringements are found.

7. The competent authorities may not delegate the following tasks to the control bodies;
(a) the supervision and audit of other control bodies;
(b) the competence to grant exceptions, as referred to in Article 22, unless this is provided for in the specific conditions laid down by the Commission in accordance with Article 22(3).

8. In accordance with Article 5(3) of Regulation (EC) No 882/ 2004, competent authorities delegating control tasks to control bodies shall organise audits or inspections of control bodies as necessary. If, as a result of an audit or an inspection, it appears that such bodies are failing to carry out properly the tasks delegated to them, the delegating competent authority may withdraw the delegation. It shall withdraw it without delay if the control body fails to take appropriate and timely remedial action.

9. In addition to the provisions of paragraph 8, the competent authority shall:
(a) ensure that the controls carried out by the control body are objective and independent;
(b) verify the effectiveness of its controls;
(c) take cognisance of any irregularities or infringements found and corrective measures applied;
(d) withdraw approval of that body where it fails to satisfy the requirements referred to in (a) and (b) or no longer fulfils the criteria indicated in paragraph 5, 6 or fails to satisfy the requirements laid down in paragraphs 11, 12 and 14.

10. Member States shall attribute a code number to each control authority or control body performing control tasks as referred to in paragraph 4.

11. Control authorities and control bodies shall give the competent authorities access to their offices and facilities and provide any information and assistance deemed necessary by the competent authorities for the fulfilment of their obligations according to this Article.

12. The control authorities and control bodies shall ensure that at least the precautionary and control measures referred to in paragraph 2 are applied to operators subject to their control.

13. Member States shall ensure that the control system as set up allows for the traceability of each product at all stages of production, preparation and distribution in accordance with Article 18 of Regulation (EC) No 178/2002, in particular, in order to give consumers guarantees that organic products have been produced in compliance with the requirements set out in this Regulation.

14. By 31 January each year at the latest the control authorities and control bodies shall transmit to the competent authorities a list of the operators which were subject to their controls on 31 December of the previous year. A summary report of the control activities carried out during the previous year shall be provided by 31 March each year.

[8.227]
Article 28
Adherence to the control system

1. Any operator who produces, prepares, stores, or imports from a third country products in the meaning of Article 1(2) or who places such products on the market shall, prior to placing on the market of any products as organic or in conversion to organic:
   (a) notify his activity to the competent authorities of the Member State where the activity is carried out;
   (b) submit his undertaking to the control system referred to in Article 27.

The first subparagraph shall apply also to exporters who export products produced in compliance with the production rules laid down in this Regulation.

Where an operator contracts out any of the activities to a third party, that operator shall nonetheless be subject to the requirements referred to in points (a) and (b), and the subcontracted activities shall be subject to the control system.

2. Member States may exempt from the application of this Article operators who sell products directly to the final consumer or user provided they do not produce, prepare, store other than in connection with the point of sale or import such products from a third country or have not contracted out such activities to a third party.

3. Member States shall designate an authority or approve a body for the reception of such notifications.

4. Member States shall ensure that any operator who complies with the rules of this Regulation, and who pays a reasonable fee as a contribution to the control expenses, is entitled to be covered by the control system.

5. The control authorities and control bodies shall keep an updated list containing the names and addresses of operators under their control. This list shall be made available to the interested parties.

6. The Commission, in accordance with the procedure referred to in Article 37(2), shall adopt implementing rules to provide details of the notification and submission procedure referred to in paragraph 1 of this Article in particular with regard to the information included in the notification referred to in paragraph 1(a) of this Article.

[8.228]
Article 29
Documentary evidence

1. The control authorities and the control bodies referred to in Article 27(4) shall provide documentary evidence to any such operator who is subject to their controls and who in the sphere of his activities, meets the requirements laid down in this Regulation. The documentary evidence shall at least permit the identification of the operator and the type or range of products as well as the period of validity.

2. The operator shall verify the documentary evidence of his suppliers.

3. The form of the documentary evidence referred to in paragraph 1 shall be drawn up in accordance with the procedure referred to in Article 37(2), taking into account the advantages of electronic certification.

[8.229]
Article 30
Measures in case of infringements and irregularities

1. Where an irregularity is found as regards compliance with the requirements laid down in this Regulation, the control authority or control body shall ensure that no reference to the organic production method is made in the labelling and advertising of the entire lot or production run affected by this irregularity, where this would be proportionate to the relevance of the requirement that has been violated and to the nature and particular circumstances of the irregular activities.

Where a severe infringement or an infringement with prolonged effect is found, the control authority or control body shall prohibit the operator concerned from marketing products which refer to the organic production method in the labelling and advertising for a period to be agreed with the competent authority of the Member State.

2. Information on cases of irregularities or infringements affecting the organic status of a product shall be immediately communicated between the control bodies, control authorities, competent authorities and Member States concerned and, where appropriate, to the Commission.

The level of communication shall depend on the severity and the extent of the irregularity or infringement found.

The Commission may, in accordance with the procedure referred to in Article 37(2), lay down specifications regarding the form and modalities of such communications.

[8.230]
Article 31
Exchange of information

Upon a request duly justified by the necessity to guarantee that a product has been produced in accordance with this Regulation, the competent authorities, control authorities and the control bodies shall exchange relevant information on the results of their controls with other competent authorities, control authorities and control bodies. They may also exchange such information on their own initiative.

TITLE VI
TRADE WITH THIRD COUNTRIES

[8.231]
Article 32
Import of compliant products

1. A product imported from a third country may be placed on the Community market as organic provided that:
   (a) the product complies with the provisions set out in Titles II, III and IV as well as with the implementing rules affecting its production adopted pursuant to this Regulation;
   (b) all operators, including the exporters, have been subject to control by a control authority or control body recognised in accordance with paragraph 2;
   (c) the operators concerned shall be able to provide at any time, to the importers or the national authorities, documentary evidence as referred to in Article 29, permitting the identification of the operator who carried out the last operation and the verification of compliance by that operator with points (a) and (b), issued by the control authority or control body referred to in point (b).

2. The Commission shall, in accordance with the procedure referred to in Article 37(2), recognise the control authorities and control bodies referred to in paragraph 1(b) of this Article, including control authorities and control bodies as referred to in Article 27, which are competent to carry out controls and to issue the documentary evidence referred to in paragraph 1(c) of this Article in third countries, and establish a list of these control authorities and control bodies.

The control bodies shall be accredited to the most recently notified version, by a publication in the C series of the *Official Journal of the European Union*, of European Standard EN 45011 or ISO Guide 65 (General requirements for bodies operating product certification systems). The control bodies shall undergo regular on-the-spot evaluation, surveillance and multiannual reassessment of their activities by the accreditation body.

When examining requests for recognition, the Commission shall invite the control authority or control body to supply all the necessary information. The Commission may also entrust experts with the task of examining on-the-spot the rules of production and the control activities carried out in the third country by the control authority or control body concerned.

The recognised control bodies or control authorities shall provide the assessment reports issued by the accreditation body or, as appropriate, the competent authority on the regular on-the-spot evaluation, surveillance and multiannual re-assessment of their activities.

Based on the assessment reports, the Commission assisted by the Member States shall ensure appropriate supervision of the recognised control authorities and control bodies by regularly reviewing their recognition. The nature of the supervision shall be determined on the basis of an assessment of the risk of the occurrence of irregularities or infringements of the provisions set out in this Regulation.

[8.232]
Article 33
Import of products providing equivalent guarantees

1. A product imported from a third country may also be placed on the Community market as organic provided that:
   (a) the product has been produced in accordance with production rules equivalent to those referred to in Titles III and IV;
   (b) the operators have been subject to control measures of equivalent effectiveness to those referred to in Title V and such control measures have been permanently and effectively applied;
   (c) the operators at all stages of production, preparation and distribution in the third country have submitted their activities to a control system recognised in accordance with paragraph 2 or to a control authority or control body recognised in accordance with paragraph 3;
   (d) the product is covered by a certificate of inspection issued by the competent authorities, control authorities or control bodies of the third country recognised in accordance with paragraph 2, or by a control authority or control body recognised in accordance with paragraph 3, which confirms that the product satisfies the conditions set out in this paragraph.

The original of the certificate referred to in this paragraph shall accompany the goods to the premises of the first consignee; thereafter the importer must keep the certificate at the disposal of the control authority or the control body for not less than two years.

2. The Commission may, in accordance with the procedure referred to in Article 37(2), recognise the third countries whose system of production complies with principles and production rules equivalent to those laid down in Titles II, III and IV and whose control measures are of equivalent effectiveness to those laid down in Title V, and establish a list of these countries. The assessment of equivalency shall take into account *Codex Alimentarius* guidelines CAC/GL 32.

When examining requests for recognition, the Commission shall invite the third country to supply all the necessary information. The Commission may entrust experts with the task of examining on-the-spot the rules of production and the control measures of the third country concerned.

By 31 March of each year, the recognised third countries shall send a concise annual report to the Commission regarding the implementation and the enforcement of the control measures established in the third country.

Based on the information in these annual reports, the Commission assisted by the Member States ensures appropriate supervision of the recognised third countries by regularly reviewing their recognition. The nature of the supervision shall be determined on the basis of an assessment of the risk of the occurrence of irregularities or infringements of the provisions set out in this Regulation.

3. For products not imported under Article 32 and not imported from a third country which is recognised under paragraph 2 of this Article, the Commission may, in accordance with the procedure referred to in Article 37(2), recognise the control authorities and control bodies, including control authorities and control bodies as referred to in Article 27, competent to carry out controls and issue certificates in third countries for the purpose of paragraph 1, and establish a list of these control authorities and control bodies. The assessment of equivalency shall take into account *Codex Alimentarius* guidelines CAC/GL 32.

The Commission shall examine any request for recognition lodged by a control authority or control body in a third country.

When examining requests for recognition, the Commission shall invite the control authority or control body to supply all the necessary information. The control body or the control authority shall undergo regular on-the-spot evaluation, surveillance and multiannual re-assessment of their activities by an accreditation body or, as appropriate, by a competent authority. The Commission may also entrust experts with the task of examining on-the-spot the rules of production and the control measures carried out in the third country by the control authority or control body concerned.

The recognised control bodies or control authorities shall provide the assessment reports issued by the accreditation body or, as appropriate, the competent authority on the regular on-the-spot evaluation, surveillance and multiannual re-assessment of their activities.

Based on these assessment reports, the Commission assisted by the Member States shall ensure appropriate supervision of recognised control authorities and control bodies by regularly reviewing their recognition. The nature of the supervision shall be determined on the basis of an assessment of the risk of the occurrence of irregularities or infringements of the provisions set out in this Regulation.

TITLE VII
FINAL AND TRANSITIONAL RULES

[8.233]
Article 34
Free movement of organic products

1. Competent authorities, control authorities and control bodies may not, on grounds relating to the method of production, to the labelling or to the presentation of that method, prohibit or restrict the marketing of organic products controlled by another control authority or control body located in another Member State, in so far as those products meet the requirements of this Regulation. In particular, no additional controls or financial burdens in addition to those foreseen in Title V of this Regulation may be imposed.

2. Member States may apply stricter rules within their territory to organic plant and livestock production, where these rules are also applicable to non-organic production and provided that they are in conformity with Community law and do not prohibit or restrict the marketing of organic products produced outside the territory of the Member State concerned.

[8.234]
Article 35
Transmission of information to the Commission

Members States shall regularly transmit the following information to the Commission:

(a) the names and addresses of the competent authorities and where appropriate their code numbers and their marks of conformity;
(b) lists of control authorities and bodies and their code numbers and, where appropriate, their marks of conformity. The Commission shall publish regularly the list of control authorities and bodies.

[8.235]
Article 36
Statistical information

Member States shall transmit to the Commission the statistical information necessary for the implementation and follow-up of this Regulation. This statistical information shall be defined within the context of the Community Statistical Programme.

[8.236]
Article 37
Committee on organic production

1. The Commission shall be assisted by a regulatory Committee on organic production.
2. Where reference is made to this paragraph, Articles 5 and 7 of Decision 1999/468/EC shall apply. The period provided for in Article 5(6) of Decision 1999/468/EC shall be set at three months.

[8.237]
Article 38
Implementing rules

The Commission shall, in accordance with the procedure referred to in Article 37(2), and subject to the objectives and principles laid down in Title II, adopt detailed rules for the application of this Regulation. These shall include in particular the following:

(a) detailed rules as regards the production rules laid down in Title III, in particular as regards the specific requirements and conditions to be respected by operators;
(b) detailed rules as regards the labelling rules laid down in Title IV;
(c) detailed rules as regards the control system established under Title V, in particular as regards minimum control requirements, supervision and audit, the specific criteria for delegation of tasks to private control bodies the criteria for approval and withdrawal of such bodies and the documentary evidence referred to in Article 29;
(d) detailed rules as regards the rules on imports from third countries laid down in Title VI, in particular as regards the criteria and procedures to be followed with regard to the recognition under Article 32 and 33 of third countries and control bodies, including the publication of lists of recognised third countries and control bodies, and as regards the certificate referred to in Article 33(1) point (d) taking into account the advantages of electronic certification;
(e) detailed rules as regards the free movement of organic products laid down in Article 34 and the transmission of information to the Commission in Article 35.

[8.238]
Article 39
Repeal of Regulation (EEC) No 2092/91

1. Regulation (EEC) No 2092/91 is hereby repealed as from 1 January 2009.
2. References to the repealed Regulation (EEC) No 2092/91 shall be construed as references to this Regulation.

[8.239]
Article 40
Transitional measures

Where necessary, measures to facilitate the transition from the rules established by Regulation (EEC) No 2092/91 to this Regulation shall be adopted in accordance with the procedure referred to in Article 37(2).

[8.240]
Article 41
Report to the Council

1. By 31 December 2011, the Commission shall submit a report to the Council.
2. The report shall, in particular, review the experience gained from the application of this Regulation and consider in particular the following issues:

(a) the scope of this Regulation, in particular as regards organic food prepared by mass caterers;
(b) the prohibition on the use of GMOs, including the availability of products not produced by GMOs, the vendor declaration, the feasibility of specific tolerance thresholds and their impact on the organic sector;
(c) the functioning of the internal market and controls system, assessing in particular that the established practices do not lead to unfair competition or barriers to the production and marketing of organic products.

3. The Commission shall, if appropriate, accompany the report with relevant proposals.

[8.241]
Article 42
Entry into force and application
This Regulation shall enter into force on the seventh day following its publication in the *Official Journal of the European Union*.
For certain animal species, certain aquatic plants and certain micro algae, where the detailed production rules are not laid down, the rules provided for labelling in Article 23 and for the controls in Title V shall apply. Pending the inclusion of detailed production rules, national rules or, in the absence thereof, private standards accepted or recognised by the Member States shall apply.
It shall apply as from 1 January 2009.
[However, Article 24(1)(b) and (c) shall apply as from 1 July 2010.]
This Regulation shall be binding in its entirety and directly applicable in all Member States.

NOTES
Words in square brackets inserted by Council Regulation 967/2008/EC, Art 1.

ANNEX
TERMS REFERRED TO IN ARTICLE 23(1)

[8.242]

BG: биологичен.
ES: ecológico, biológico.
CS: ekologické, biologické.
DA: økologisk.
DE: ökologisch, biologisch.
ET: mahe, ökoloogiline.
EL: βιολογικό.
EN: organic.
FR: biologique.
GA: orgánach.
[HR: ekološki.]
IT: biologico.
LV: bioloģisks, ekoloģisks.
LT: ekologiškas.
LU: biologesch.
HU: ökológiai.
MT: organiku.
NL: biologisch.
PL: ekologiczne.
PT: biológico.
RO: ecologic.
SK: ekologické, biologické.
SL: ekološki.
FI: luonnonmukainen.
SV: ekologisk.

NOTES
Entry in square brackets added by Council Regulation 517/2013/EU, Art 1, Annex.

COUNCIL DECISION

(2007/845/JHA)

of 6 December 2007

concerning cooperation between Asset Recovery Offices of the Member States in the field of tracing and identification of proceeds from, or other property related to, crime

NOTES
Date of publication in OJ: OJ L332, 18.12.2007, p 103.

THE COUNCIL OF THE EUROPEAN UNION,

Having regard to the Treaty on European Union, and in particular Articles 30(1)(a) and (b) and 34(2)(c) thereof,

Having regard to the initiative of the Kingdom of Belgium, the Republic of Austria and the Republic of Finland,

Having regard to the opinion of the European Parliament,[1]

Whereas:

(1) The main motive for cross-border organised crime is financial gain. This financial gain is a stimulus for committing further crime to achieve even more profit. Accordingly, law enforcement services should have the necessary skills to investigate and analyse financial trails of criminal activity. To combat organised crime effectively, information that can lead to the tracing and seizure of proceeds from crime and other property belonging to criminals has to be exchanged rapidly between the Member States of the European Union.

(2) The Council adopted Framework Decision 2003/577/JHA of 22 July 2003 on the execution in the European Union of orders freezing property or evidence[2] and Framework Decision 2005/212/JHA of 24 February 2005 on Confiscation of Crime-Related Proceeds, Instrumentalities and Property,[3] dealing with certain aspects of judicial cooperation in criminal matters in the field of the freezing and confiscation of the proceeds from, instrumentalities of, and other property related to, crime.

(3) Close cooperation is necessary between the relevant authorities of the Member States involved in the tracing of illicit proceeds and other property that may become liable to confiscation and provision should be made allowing for direct communication between those authorities.

(4) To that end, Member States should have national Asset Recovery Offices in place which are competent in these fields, and should ensure that these offices can exchange information rapidly.

(5) The Camden Assets Recovery Inter-Agency Network (CARIN) established at The Hague on 22–23 September 2004 by Austria, Belgium, Germany, Ireland, Netherlands and the United Kingdom already constitutes a global network of practitioners and experts with the intention of enhancing mutual knowledge on methods and techniques in the area of cross-border identification, freezing, seizure and confiscation of the proceeds from, and other property related to, crime. This Decision should complete the CARIN by providing a legal basis for the exchange of information between Asset Recovery Offices of all the Member States.

(6) In its Communication to the Council and the European Parliament 'The Hague Programme: Ten Priorities for the next five years', the Commission advocated strengthening tools to address the financial aspects of organised crime, *inter alia*, by promoting the establishment of criminal asset intelligence units in Member States.

(7) Cooperation between the Asset Recovery Offices and between the Asset Recovery Offices and other authorities charged with the facilitation of the tracing and identification of proceeds of crime should take place on the basis of the procedures and time limits provided for in Council Framework Decision 2006/960/JHA of 18 December 2006 on simplifying the exchange of information and intelligence between law enforcement authorities of the Member States of the European Union,[4] including the grounds for refusal contained therein.

(8) This Decision should be without prejudice to the cooperation arrangements under Council Decision 2000/642/JHA of 17 October 2000 concerning arrangements for cooperation between financial intelligence units of the Member States in exchanging information[5] and to existing arrangements for police cooperation,

NOTES

1 Opinion of 12 December 2006 (not yet published in the Official Journal).

2 OJ L196, 2.8.2003, p 45.

3 OJ L68, 15.3.2005, p 49.

4 OJ L386, 29.12.2006, p 89.

5 OJ L271, 24.10.2000, p 4.

HAS DECIDED AS FOLLOWS:

[8.243]
Article 1
Asset Recovery Offices

1. Each Member State shall set up or designate a national Asset Recovery Office, for the purposes of the facilitation of the tracing and identification of proceeds of crime and other crime related property which may become the object of a freezing, seizure or confiscation order made by a competent judicial authority in the course of criminal or, as far as possible under the national law of the Member State concerned, civil proceedings.

2. Without prejudice to paragraph 1, a Member State may, in conformity with its national law, set up or designate two Asset Recovery Offices. Where a Member State has more than two authorities charged with the facilitation of the tracing and identification of proceeds of crime, it shall nominate a maximum of two of its Asset Recovery Offices as contact point(s).
3. Member States shall indicate the authorities which are the national Asset Recovery Offices within the meaning of this Article. They shall notify this information and any subsequent changes to the General Secretariat of the Council in writing. This notification shall not preclude other authorities which are charged with the facilitation of the tracing and identification of proceeds of crime from exchanging information under Articles 3 and 4 with an Asset Recovery Office of another Member State.

[8.244]
Article 2
Cooperation between Asset Recovery Offices
1. Member States shall ensure that their Asset Recovery Offices cooperate with each other for the purposes set out in Article 1(1), by exchanging information and best practices, both upon request and spontaneously.
2. Member States shall ensure that this cooperation is not hampered by the status of the Asset Recovery Offices under national law, regardless of whether they form part of an administrative, law enforcement or a judicial authority.

[8.245]
Article 3
Exchange of information between Asset Recovery Offices on request
1. An Asset Recovery Office of a Member State or other authorities in a Member State charged with the facilitation of the tracing and identification of proceeds of crime may make a request to an Asset Recovery Office of another Member State for information for the purposes set out in Article 1(1). To that end it shall rely on Framework Decision 2006/960/JHA and on the rules adopted in implementation thereof.
2. When filling out the form provided for under Framework Decision 2006/960/JHA, the requesting Asset Recovery Office shall specify the object of and the reasons for the request and the nature of the proceedings. It shall also provide details on property targeted or sought (bank accounts, real estate, cars, yachts and other high value items) and/or the natural or legal persons presumed to be involved (e.g. names, addresses, dates and places of birth, date of registration, shareholders, headquarters). Such details shall be as precise as possible.

[8.246]
Article 4
Spontaneous exchange of information between Asset Recovery Offices
1. Asset Recovery Offices or other authorities charged with the facilitation of the tracing and identification of proceeds of crime may, within the limits of the applicable national law and without a request to that effect, exchange information which they consider necessary for the execution of the tasks of another Asset Recovery Office in pursuance of purpose set out in Article 1(1).
2. Article 3 shall apply to the exchange of information under this Article *mutatis mutandis*.

[8.247]
Article 5
Data protection
1. Each Member State shall ensure that the established rules on data protection are applied also within the procedure on exchange of information provided for by this Decision.
2. The use of information which has been exchanged directly or bilaterally under this Decision shall be subject to the national data protection provisions of the receiving Member State, where the information shall be subject to the same data protection rules as if they had been gathered in the receiving Member State. The personal data processed in the context of the application of this Decision shall be protected in accordance with the Council of Europe Convention of 28 January 1981 for the Protection of Individuals with regard to Automatic Processing of Personal Data, and, for those Member States which have ratified it, the Additional Protocol of 8 November 2001 to that Convention, regarding Supervisory Authorities and Transborder Data Flows. The principles of Recommendation No R(87) 15 of the Council of Europe Regulating the Use of Personal Data in the Police Sector should also be taken into account when law enforcement authorities handle personal data obtained under this Decision.

[8.248]
Article 6
Exchange of best practices
Member States shall ensure that the Asset Recovery Offices shall exchange best practices concerning ways to improve the effectiveness of Member States' efforts in tracing and identifying proceeds from, and other property related to, crime which may become the object of a freezing, seizure or confiscation order by a competent judicial authority.

[8.249]
Article 7
Relationship to existing arrangements for cooperation
This Decision shall be without prejudice to the obligations resulting from European Union instruments on mutual legal assistance or on mutual recognition of decisions regarding criminal matters, from bilateral or multilateral agreements or arrangements between the Member States and third countries on mutual legal assistance and from Decision 2000/642/JHA and Framework Decision 2006/960/JHA.

[8.250]
Article 8
Implementation
1. The Member States shall ensure that they are able to cooperate fully in accordance with the provisions of this Decision by 18 December 2008. By the same date Member States shall transmit to the General Secretariat of the Council and to the Commission the text of any provisions of their national law enabling them to comply with the obligations imposed on them under this Decision.
2. So long as the Member States have not yet implemented Framework Decision 2006/960/JHA, references to that Framework Decision in this Decision shall be understood as references to the applicable instruments on police cooperation between the Member States.
3. By 18 December 2010 the Council shall assess Member States' compliance with this Decision on the basis of a report made by the Commission.

[8.251]
Article 9
Application
This Decision shall take effect on the date of its publication in the *Official Journal of the European Union.*

COMMISSION REGULATION

(889/2008/EC)

of 5 September 2008

laying down detailed rules for the implementation of Council Regulation (EC) No 834/2007 on organic production and labelling of organic products with regard to organic production, labelling and control

NOTES
Date of publication in OJ: OJ L250, 18.9.2008, p 1.

THE COMMISSION OF THE EUROPEAN COMMUNITIES,

Having regard to the Treaty establishing the European Community,

Having regard to Council Regulation (EC) No 834/2007 of 28 June 2007 on organic production and labelling of organic products and repealing Regulation (EEC) No 2092/91,[1] and in particular Article 9(4), the second paragraph of Article 11 Articles 12(3), 14(2), 16(3)(c), 17(2) and 18(5), the second subparagraph of Article 19(3), Articles 21(2), 22(1), 24(3), 25(3), 26, 28(6), 29(3) and 38(a), (b), (c) and (e), and Article 40 thereof,

Whereas:

(1) Regulation (EC) No 834/2007, and in particular Titles III, IV and V thereof, lay down basic requirements with regard to production, labelling and control of organic products in the plant and livestock sector. Detailed rules for the implementation of those requirements should be laid down.

(2) The evolution of new detailed production rules on certain animal species, organic aquaculture, seaweed and yeasts used as food or feed on community level will require more time and therefore should be elaborated in a subsequent procedure. It is therefore appropriate to exclude those products from the scope of this Regulation. However, as regards certain livestock species, aquaculture products and seaweed, the Community rules provided for production, controls and labelling should apply *mutatis mutandis* to those products, in accordance with Article 42 of Regulation (EC) No 834/2007.

(3) Certain definitions should be laid down in order to avoid ambiguities and to guarantee the uniform application of the organic production rules.

(4) Organic plant production is based on nourishing the plants primarily through the soil ecosystem. Therefore hydroponic cultivation, where plants grow with their roots in an inert medium feed with soluble minerals and nutrients, should not be allowed.

(5) Organic plant production involves varied cultivation practices and limited use of fertilisers and conditioners of low solubility, therefore these practices should be specified. In particular, conditions for the use of certain non-synthetic products should be laid down.

(6) The use of pesticides, which may have detrimental effects on the environment or result in the presence of residues in agricultural products, should be significantly restricted. Preference should be given to the application of preventive measures in pest, disease and weed control. In addition, conditions for the use of certain plant protection products should be laid down.

(7) For the purpose of organic farming, the use of certain plant protection products, fertilisers, soil conditioners, as well as certain non-organic feed materials, feed additives and feed processing aids and certain products used for cleaning and disinfection was allowed under Council Regulation (EEC) No 2092/91[2] under well-defined conditions. For the sake of ensuring the continuity of organic farming the products and substances in question should, in accordance with the provisions laid down in Article 16(3)(c) of Regulation (EC) No 834/2007, continue to be allowed. Moreover, for the sake of clarity, it is appropriate to list in the Annexes to this Regulation the products and substances which had been allowed under Regulation (EEC) No 2092/91. Other products and substances may be added to these lists in the future under a different legal basis, namely Article 16(1) of Regulation (EC) No 834/2007. It is therefore appropriate to identify the distinct status of each category of products and substances by means of a symbol in the list.

(8) The holistic approach of organic farming requires a livestock production related to the land, where the produced manure is used to nourish the crop production. Since livestock farming always implies the management of agricultural land, provision should be made to prohibit landless livestock production. In organic livestock production the choice of breeds should take account of their capacity to adapt to local conditions, their vitality and their resistance to disease and a wide biological diversity should be encouraged.

(9) Under certain circumstances operators may face difficulties in obtaining organic breeding animals from a reduced gene pool, which would hamper the development of the sector. Therefore the possibility of bringing a limited number of non-organic animals onto a farm for breeding purposes should be provided for.

(10) Organic stock farming should ensure that specific behavioural needs of animals are met. In this regard, housing for all species of livestock should satisfy the needs of the animals concerned as regards ventilation, light, space and comfort and sufficient area should accordingly be provided to permit ample freedom of movement for each animal and to develop the animal's natural social behaviour. Specific housing conditions and husbandry practices with regard to certain animals, including bees, should be laid down. These specific housing conditions should serve a high level of animal welfare, which is a priority in organic livestock farming and therefore may go beyond Community welfare standards which apply to farming in general. Organic husbandry practices should prevent poultry from being reared too quickly. Therefore specific provisions to avoid intensive rearing methods should be laid down. In particular poultry shall either be reared until they reach a minimum age or else shall come from slow-growing poultry strains, so that in either case there is no incentive to use intensive rearing methods.

(11) In most cases, livestock should have permanent access to open air areas for grazing, weather conditions permitting, and such open air areas should in principle be organised under an appropriate system of rotation.

(12) In order to avoid environmental pollution of natural resources such as soil and water by nutrients, an upper limit for the use of manure per hectare and for keeping livestock per hectare should be set. This limit should be related to the nitrogen content of the manure.

(13) Mutilations which lead to stress, harm, disease or the suffering of animals should be banned. However, specific operations essential to certain types of production and for the sake of security for animals and human beings may be permitted under restricted conditions.

(14) Livestock should be fed on grass, fodder and feedingstuffs produced in accordance with the rules of organic farming, preferably coming from the own holding, by taking into account their physiological needs. In addition, in order to provide for the basic nutritional requirements of livestock, certain minerals, trace elements and vitamins may need to be used under well-defined conditions.

(15) Since the existing regional differences in the possibility for organic ruminants to obtain the necessary essential vitamins A, D and E through their feed rations, as regards climate and available sources of feed, are expected to persist, the use of such vitamins for ruminants should be allowed.

(16) Animal-health management should mainly be based on prevention of disease. In addition specific cleaning and disinfection measures should be applied.

(17) The preventive use of chemically-synthesised allopathic medicinal products is not permitted in organic farming. However, in the event of a sickness or injury of an animal requiring an immediate treatment, the use of chemically-synthesised allopathic medicinal products should be limited to a strict minimum. Furthermore, in order to guarantee the integrity of organic production for consumers it should be possible to take restrictive measures such as doubling the withdrawal period after use of chemically synthesised allopathic medicinal products.

(18) Specific rules for disease prevention and veterinary treatment in beekeeping should be laid down.

(19) Provision should be made to require operators producing feed or food to take account of appropriate procedures based on a systematic identification of critical processing steps in order to ensure that the produced processed products comply with the organic production rules.

(20) Certain non-organic products and substances are needed in order to ensure the production of certain processed organic food and feed. The harmonization of wine processing rules on Community level will require more time. Therefore the mentioned products should be excluded for wine processing until, in a subsequent procedure, specific rules are laid down.

(21) For the purpose of processing organic food, the use of certain ingredients of non-agricultural origin, certain food processing aid and certain non-organic ingredients of agricultural origin was allowed under Regulation (EEC) No 2092/91 under well-defined conditions. For the sake of ensuring the continuity of organic farming the products and substances in question should, in accordance with the provisions laid down in Article 21(2) of Regulation (EC) No 834/2007, continue to be allowed. Moreover, for the sake of clarity, it is appropriate to list in the Annexes to this Regulation the products and substances which had been allowed under Regulation (EEC) No 2092/91. Other products and substances may be added to these lists in the future under a different legal basis, namely Article 21(2) of Regulation (EC) No 834/2007. It is therefore appropriate to identify the distinct status of each category of products and substances by means of a symbol in the list.

(22) Under certain conditions organic products and non-organic products can be collected and transported simultaneously. In order to duly separate organic from non-organic products during handling and to avoid any commingling specific provisions should be laid down.

(23) The conversion to the organic production method requires certain periods of adaptation of all means in use. Depending on the previous farm production, specific time periods for the various production sectors should be laid down.

(24) In accordance with Article 22 of Regulation (EC) No 834/ 2007, specific conditions for the application of exceptions provided for in that Article should be laid down. It is appropriate to set out such conditions with regard to the non availability of organic animals, feed, beeswax, seeds and seed potatoes and organic ingredients as well as to specific problems related to the livestock management and in the case of catastrophic circumstances.

(25) Geographical and structural differences in agriculture and climatic constraints may hamper the development of organic production in certain regions and therefore call for exceptions for certain practices as regards the characteristics of livestock buildings and installations. Therefore tethering of animals should, under well-defined conditions, be allowed in holdings which, due to their geographical location and structural constraints, in particular with regard to mountainous areas, are of small size, and only where it is not possible to keep the cattle in groups appropriate to their behavioural needs.

(26) For the purpose of ensuring the development of an incipient organic livestock sector, several temporary derogations as regards tethering of animals, housing conditions for animals and stocking densities were granted under Regulation (EEC) No 2092/91. These derogations should, on a transitional basis, be maintained until their expiry date, in order not to disrupt the organic livestock sector.

(27) Considering the importance of pollination of the organic beekeeping sector it should be possible to grant exceptions permitting the parallel production of organic and non-organic beekeeping unit on the same farm.

(28) Under certain circumstances, farmers may experience difficulty in securing supplies of organically reared livestock and organic feedingstuffs and therefore authorisation should be granted for a limited number of non-organically produced farm input to be used in restricted quantities.

(29) Major efforts have been undertaken by producers involved in organic production for the development of the production of organic seeds and vegetative materials in order to establish a broad choice of plant varieties of plant species for which organic seeds and vegetative propagating material is available. However, currently for many species there is still not enough organic seed and vegetative propagating material available and, in those cases, the use of non-organic seed and vegetative propagating material should be allowed.

(30) In order to help operators to find organic seed and seed potatoes, each Member State should ensure that a database is set up that contains the varieties of which organic seed and seed potatoes are available on the market.

(31) The management of adult bovine animals may endanger the keeper and other persons handling the animals. Therefore provision should be made to allow for exceptions to be granted during the final fattening phase of mammals, in particular with regard to bovine animals.

(32) Catastrophic circumstances or widespread animal or plant diseases may have serious effects on the organic production in the regions concerned. Appropriate measures need to be taken to ensure the maintenance of farming or even the reestablishment of farming. Therefore the supply of non-organic animals, or non-organic feed should be made possible for a limited period in the affected areas.

(33) In accordance with Articles 24(3) and 25(3) of Regulation (EC) No 834/2007, specific criteria as regards the presentation, composition, size and design of the Community logo, as well as the presentation and composition of the code number of the control authority or control body and of the indication of the place where the agricultural product has been farmed should be laid down.

(34) In accordance with Article 26 of Regulation (EC) No 834/2007, specific requirements for the labelling of organic feed should be laid down taking into account the varieties and composition of feed and the horizontal labelling provisions applicable to feed.

(35) In addition to the control system based on the Regulation (EC) No 882/2004 of the European Parliament and of the Council of 29 April 2004 on official controls performed to ensure the verification of compliance with feed and food law, animal health and animal welfare rules[3] specific control measures should be laid down. In particular, detailed requirements with regard to all stages of production, preparation and distribution related to organic products.

(36) Notifications of information by the Member States to the Commission must enable it to use the information sent directly and as effectively as possible for the management of statistical information and referential data. To achieve this objective, all information to be made available or to be communicated between the Member States and the Commission should be sent electronically or in digital form.

(37) Exchanges of information and documents between the Commission and the Member States, and the provision and notification of information from the Member States to the Commission are generally carried out electronically or in digital form. In order to improve the way such exchanges of information under organic production rules are dealt with and to extend their use, it is necessary to adapt the existing computer systems or set up new ones. Provision should be made for this to be done by the Commission and implemented after informing the Member States via the Committee on organic production.

(38) The conditions under which information is processed by these computer systems and the form and content of documents which have to be communicated under Regulation (EC) No 834/2007 have to be adjusted frequently in line with changes to the applicable rules or management requirements. Uniform presentation of the documents to be sent in by the Member States is also necessary. To achieve these objectives and to simplify procedures and ensure that the computer systems concerned can be made operational immediately, the form and content of the documents should be laid down on the basis of models or questionnaires, which should be adapted and updated by the Commission after informing the Committee on organic production.

(39) Transitional measures should be laid down, for certain provisions established under Regulation (EEC) No 2092/91, in order not to jeopardize the continuity of the organic production.

(40) Commission Regulation (EEC) No 207/93 of 29 January 1993 defining the content of Annex VI to Regulation (EEC) No 2092/91 on organic production of agricultural products and indications referring thereto on agricultural products and foodstuffs and laying down detailed rules for implementing the provisions of Article 5(4) thereto[4] Commission Regulation (EC) No 1452/2003 of 14 August 2003 maintaining the derogation provided for in Article 6(3)(a) of Council Regulation (EEC) No 2092/91 with regard to certain species of seed and vegetative propagating material and laying down procedural rules and criteria relating to that derogation[5] and Commission Regulation (EC) No 223/2003 of 5 February 2003 on labelling requirements related to the organic production method for feedingstuffs, compound feedingstuffs and feed materials and amending Council Regulation (EEC) No 2092/91[6] should be repealed and replaced by a new Regulation.

(41) Regulation (EEC) No 2092/91 is repealed by Regulation (EC) No 834/2007 with effect from 1 January 2009. However, many of its provisions should, with some adaptation, continue to apply and should therefore be adopted in the framework of this Regulation. For the sake of clarity it is appropriate to set out the correlation between those provisions of Regulation (EEC) No 2092/91 and the provisions of this Regulation.

(42) The measures provided for in this Regulation are in accordance with the opinion of the regulatory Committee on organic production,

NOTES

[1] OJ L189, 20.7.2007, p 1.

[2] OJ L198, 22.7.1991, p 1.

[3] OJ L165, 30.4.2004, p 1. Corrected by OJ L191, 28.5.2004, p 1.

[4] OJ L25, 2.2.1993, p 5.

[5] OJ L206, 15.8.2003, p 17.

[6] OJ L31, 6.2.2003, p 3.

HAS ADOPTED THIS REGULATION:

TITLE I
INTRODUCTORY PROVISIONS

[8.252]
Article 1
Subject matter and scope

1. This Regulation lays down specific rules on organic production, labelling and control in respect of products referred to in Article 1(2) of Regulation (EC) No 834/2007.

[2. This Regulation shall not apply to:

(a) livestock species other than those referred to in Article 7; and

(b) to aquaculture animals other than those referred to in Article 25a.

However, Title II, Title III and Title IV shall apply mutatis mutandis to such products until detailed production rules for those products are laid down on the basis of Regulation (EC) No 834/2007.]

NOTES

Para 2: substituted by Commission Regulation 710/2009/EC, Art 1(1).

[8.253]
Article 2
Definitions

In addition to the definitions laid down in Article 2 of Regulation (EC) No 834/2007, the following definitions shall apply for the purposes of this Regulation:

(a) 'non-organic': means not coming from or not related to a production in accordance to Regulation (EC) No 834/2007 and this Regulation;

(b) 'veterinary medicinal products': means products as defined in Article 1(2) of Directive 2001/82/EC of the European Parliament and of the Council[1] concerning the Community code relating to veterinary medicinal products

(c) 'importer': means the natural or legal person within the community who presents a consignment for release for free circulation into the Community, either in person, or through a representative;

(d) 'first consignee' means the natural or legal person to whom the imported consignment is delivered and who will receive it for further preparation and/or marketing;

(e) 'holding' means all the production units operated under a single management for the purpose of producing agricultural products;

[(f) 'production unit' means all assets to be used for a production sector such as production premises, land parcels, pasturages, open air areas, livestock buildings, fish ponds, containment systems for seaweed or aquaculture animals, shore or seabed concessions, the premises for the storage of crops, crop products, seaweed products, animal products, raw materials and any other input relevant for this specific production sector;]

(g) 'hydroponic production' means the method of growing plants with their roots in a mineral nutrient solution only or in an inert medium, such as perlite, gravel or mineral wool to which a nutrient solution is added;

(h) 'veterinary treatment' means all courses of a curative or preventive treatment against one occurrence of a specific disease;

(i) 'in-conversion feedingstuffs' means feedingstuffs produced during the conversion period to organic production, with the exclusion of those harvested in the 12 months following the beginning of the conversion as referred to in Article 17(1)(a) of Regulation (EC) No 834/2007.

[(j) "closed recirculation aquaculture facility" means a facility where aquaculture takes place within an enclosed environment on land or on a vessel involving the recirculation of water, and depending on permanent external energy input to stabilize the environment for the aquaculture animals;

(k) "energy from renewable sources" means renewable non-fossil energy sources: wind, solar, geothermal, wave, tidal, hydropower, landfill gas, sewage treatment plant gas and biogases;

(l) "hatchery" means a place of breeding, hatching and rearing through the early life stages of aquaculture animals, finfish and shellfish in particular;

(m) "nursery" means a place where an intermediate farming system, between the hatchery and grow-out stages is applied. The nursery stage is completed within the first third of the production cycle with the exception of species undergoing a smoltification process;

(n) "pollution" in the framework of aquaculture and seaweed production means the direct or indirect introduction into the aquatic environment of substances or energy as defined in Directive 2008/56/EC of the European Parliament and of the Council[2] and in Directive 2000/60/EC of the European Parliament and of the Council,[3] in the waters where they respectively apply;

(o) "polyculture" in the framework of aquaculture and seaweed production, means the rearing of two or more species usually from different trophic levels in the same culture unit;

(p) "production cycle" in the framework of aquaculture and seaweed production, means the lifespan of an aquaculture animal or seaweed from the earliest life stage to harvesting;

(q) "locally grown species" in the framework of aquaculture and seaweed production, means those which are neither alien nor locally absent species under Council Regulation (EC) No 708/2007.[4] Those species listed in Annex IV of Regulation (EC) No 708/2007 may be considered as locally grown species.

(r) "stocking density" in the framework of aquaculture, means the live weight of animals per cubic metre of water at any time during the grow-out phase and in the case of flatfish and shrimp the weight per square metre of surface.]

[(s) "control file" means all the information and documents transmitted, for the purposes of the control system, to the competent authorities of the Member State or to control authorities and control bodies by an operator subject to the control system as referred to in Article 28 of Regulation (EC) No 834/2007, including all the relevant information and documents relating to that operator or the activities of that operator held by competent authorities, control authorities and control bodies, with the exception of information or documents that have no bearing on the operation of the control system.]

[(t) "preserving" means any action, different from farming and harvesting, that is carried out on products, but which does not qualify as processing as defined in point (u), including all actions referred to in point (n) of Article 2(1) of Regulation (EC) No 852/2004 of the European Parliament and of the Council[5] and excluding packaging or labelling of the product;

(u) "processing" means any action referred to in point (m) of Article 2(1) of Regulation (EC) No 852/2004, including the use of substances referred to in Article 19(2)(b) of Regulation (EC) No 834/2007. Packaging or labelling operations shall not be considered as processing.]

NOTES

Para (f) substituted and paras (j)–(r) added by Commission Regulation 710/2009/EC, Art 1(1).
Para (s): added by Commission Regulation 392/2013/EU, Art 1(1).
Paras (t), (u): added by Commission Implementing Regulation 2016/1842/EU, Art 2(1).

1 OJ L311, 28.11.2001, p 1.
2 OJ L164, 25.6.2008, p 19.
3 OJ L327, 22.12.2000, p 1.
4 OJ L168, 28.6.2007, p 1.
5 Regulation (EC) No 852/2004 of the European Parliament and of the Council of 29 April 2004 on the hygiene of foodstuffs (OJ L139, 30.4.2004, p 1)..

TITLE II
[RULES ON PRODUCTION, PRESERVATION, PROCESSING, PACKAGING, TRANSPORT AND STORAGE OF ORGANIC PRODUCTS]

NOTES

Title heading: words in square brackets substituted by Commission Implementing Regulation 2016/1842/EU, Art 2(2).

CHAPTER 1
PLANT PRODUCTION

[8.254]
Article 3
Soil management and fertilisation

1. Where the nutritional needs of plants cannot be met by measures provided for in Article 12(1)(a), (b) and (c) of Regulation (EC) No 834/2007, only fertilisers and soil conditioners referred to in Annex I to this Regulation may be used in organic production and only to the extent necessary. Operators shall keep documentary evidence of the need to use the product.

2. The total amount of livestock manure, as defined in Council Directive 91/676/EEC[1] concerning the protection of waters against pollution caused by nitrates from agricultural sources, applied on the holding may not exceed 170 kg of nitrogen per year/hectare of agricultural area used. This limit shall only apply to the use of farmyard manure, dried farmyard manure and dehydrated poultry manure, composted animal excrements, including poultry manure, composted farmyard manure and liquid animal excrements.

3. Organic-production holdings may establish written cooperation agreements exclusively with other holdings and enterprises which comply with the organic production rules, with the intention of spreading surplus manure from organic production. The maximum limit as referred to in paragraph 2, shall be calculated on the basis of all of the organic-production units involved in such cooperation.

4. Appropriate preparations of micro-organisms may be used to improve the overall condition of the soil or the availability of nutrients in the soil or in the crops.

5. For compost activation appropriate plant-based preparations or preparations of micro-organisms may be used.

NOTES

[1] OJ L375, 31.12.1991, p 1.

[8.255]
Article 4
Prohibition of hydroponic production
Hydroponic production is prohibited.

[8.256]
Article 5
Pest, disease and weed management
1. Where plants cannot be adequately protected from pests and diseases by measures provided for in Article 12 (1)(a), (b), (c) and (g) of Regulation (EC) No 834/2007, only products referred to in Annex II to this Regulation may be used in organic production. Operators shall keep documentary evidence of the need to use the product.
2. For products used in traps and dispensers, except pheromone dispensers, the traps and/or dispensers, shall prevent the substances from being released into the environment and prevent contact between the substances and the crops being cultivated. The traps shall be collected after use and disposed off safely.

[8.257]
Article 6
Specific rules on mushroom production
For production of mushrooms, substrates may be used, if they are composed only of the following components:
(a) farmyard manure and animal excrements:
 (i) either from holdings producing according to the organic production method;
 (ii) or referred to in Annex I, only when the product referred to in point (i) is not available; and when they do not exceed 25% of the weight of total components of the substrate, excluding the covering material and any added water, before composting;
(b) products of agricultural origin, other than those referred to in point (a), from holdings producing according to organic production method;
(c) peat not chemically treated;
(d) wood, not treated with chemical products after felling;
(e) mineral products referred to in Annex I, water and soil.

[CHAPTER 1A
SEAWEED PRODUCTION

[8.258]
[Article 6a
Scope
This Chapter lays down detailed production rules for seaweed.
For the purposes of this Chapter "seaweed" includes multi-cellular marine algae, phytoplankton and micro-algae.]

NOTES

Chapter 1a (Arts 6a–6e) inserted by Commission Regulation 710/2009/EC, Art 1(3).
Article 6a substituted by Commission Implementing Regulation 2016/673/EU, Art 1(1).

[8.259]
[Article 6b
Suitability of aquatic medium and sustainable management plan
1. Operations shall be situated in locations that are not subject to contamination by products or substances not authorised for organic production, or pollutants that would compromise the organic nature of the products.
2. Organic and non-organic production units shall be separated adequately. Such separation measures shall be based on the natural situation, separate water distribution systems, distances, the tidal flow, the upstream and the downstream location of the organic production unit. Member State authorities may designate locations or areas which they consider to be unsuitable for organic aquaculture or seaweed harvesting and may also set up minimum separation distances between organic and non-organic production units.
Where minimum separation distances are set Member States shall provide this information to operators, other Member States and the Commission.
3. An environmental assessment proportionate to the production unit shall be required for all new operations applying for organic production and producing more than 20 tonnes of aquaculture products per year to ascertain the conditions of the production unit and its immediate environment and likely effects of its operation. The operator shall provide the environmental assessment to the

control body or control authority. The content of the environmental assessment shall be based on Annex IV to Council Directive 85/337/EEC[1]. If the unit has already been subject to an equivalent assessment, then its use shall be permitted for this purpose.

4. The operator shall provide a sustainable management plan proportionate to the production unit for aquaculture and seaweed harvesting.

The plan shall be updated annually and shall detail the environmental effects of the operation, the environmental monitoring to be undertaken, and list measures to be taken to minimise negative impacts on the surrounding aquatic and terrestrial environments, including, where applicable, nutrient discharge into the environment per production cycle or per annum. The plan shall record the surveillance and repair of technical equipment.

5. Aquaculture and seaweed business operators shall by preference use renewable energy sources and re-cycle materials and shall draw up as part of the sustainable management plan a waste reduction schedule to be put in place at the commencement of operations. Where possible, the use of residual heat shall be limited to energy from renewable sources.

6. For seaweed harvesting a once-off biomass estimate shall be undertaken at the outset.]

NOTES

Inserted as noted to Art 6a at **[8.258]**.

[1] OJ L175, 5.7.1985, p 40.

[8.260]
[Article 6c
Sustainable harvesting of wild seaweed

1. Documentary accounts shall be maintained in the unit or premises and shall enable the operator to identify and the control authority or control body to verify that the harvesters have supplied only wild seaweed produced in accordance with Regulation (EC) No 834/2007.

2. Harvesting shall be carried out in such a way that the amounts harvested do not cause a significant impact on the state of the aquatic environment. Measures shall be taken to ensure that seaweed can regenerate, such as harvest technique, minimum sizes, ages, reproductive cycles or size of remaining seaweed.

3. If seaweed is harvested from a shared or common harvest area, documentary evidence shall be available that the total harvest complies with this Regulation.

4. With respect to Article 73b(2)(b) and (c), these records must provide evidence of sustainable management and of no long-term impact on the harvesting areas.]

NOTES

Inserted as noted to Art 6a at **[8.258]**.

[8.261]
[Article 6d
Seaweed Cultivation

1. Seaweed culture at sea shall only utilise nutrients naturally occurring in the environment, or from organic aquaculture animal production, preferably located nearby as part of a polyculture system.

2. In facilities on land where external nutrient sources are used the nutrient levels in the effluent water shall be verifiably the same, or lower, than the inflowing water. Only nutrients of plant or mineral origin and as listed in Annex I may be used.

3. Culture density or operational intensity shall be recorded and shall maintain the integrity of the aquatic environment by ensuring that the maximum quantity of seaweed which can be supported without negative effects on the environment is not exceeded.

4. Ropes and other equipment used for growing seaweed shall be re-used or recycled where possible.]

NOTES

Inserted as noted to Art 6a at **[8.258]**.

[8.262]
[Article 6e
Antifouling measures and cleaning of production equipment and facilities

1. Bio-fouling organisms shall be removed only by physical means or by hand and where appropriate returned to the sea at a distance from the farm.

2. Cleaning of equipment and facilities shall be carried out by physical or mechanical measures. Where this is not satisfactory only substances as listed in Annex VII, Section 2 may be used.]

NOTES

Inserted as noted to Art 6a at **[8.258]**.

CHAPTER 2
LIVESTOCK PRODUCTION

[8.263]
Article 7
Scope

This Chapter lays down detailed production rules for the following species: bovine including *bubalus* and bison, equidae, porcine, ovine, caprine, poultry (species as mentioned in Annex III) and bees.

SECTION 1
ORIGIN OF ANIMALS

[8.264]
Article 8
Origin of organic animals

1. In the choice of breeds or strains, account shall be taken of the capacity of animals to adapt to local conditions, their vitality and their resistance to disease. In addition, breeds or strains of animals shall be selected to avoid specific diseases or health problems associated with some breeds or strains used in intensive production, such as porcine stress syndrome, PSE Syndrome (pale-soft-exudative), sudden death, spontaneous abortion and difficult births requiring caesarean operations. Preference is to be given to indigenous breeds and strains.
2. For bees, preference shall be given to the use of *Apis mellifera* and their local ecotypes.

[8.265]
Article 9
Origin of non-organic animals

1. In accordance with Article 14(1)(a)(ii) of Regulation (EC) No 834/2007, non-organic animals may be brought onto a holding for breeding purposes, only when organic animals are not available in sufficient number and subject to the conditions provided for in paragraphs 2 to 5 of this Article.
2. Non-organic young mammals, when a herd or flock is constituted for the first time, shall be reared in accordance with the organic production rules immediately after they are weaned. Moreover, the following restrictions shall apply at the date on which the animals enter the herd:
   (a) buffalo, calves and foals shall be less than six months old;
   (b) lambs and kids shall be less than 60 days old;
   (c) piglets shall weigh less than 35 kg.
3. Non-organic adult male and nulliparous female mammals, for the renewal of a herd or flock, shall be reared subsequently in accordance with the organic production rules. Moreover, the number of female mammals is subject to the following restrictions per year:
   (a) up to a maximum of 10% of adult equine or bovine, including *bubalus* and bison species, livestock and 20% of the adult porcine, ovine and caprine livestock, as female animals;
   (b) for units with less than 10 equine or bovine animals, or with less than five porcine, ovine or caprine animals any renewal as mentioned above shall be limited to a maximum of one animal per year.

   This provision of this paragraph will be reviewed in 2012 with a view to phase it out.
4. The percentages referred to in paragraph 3 may be increased up to 40%, subject to prior authorisation by the competent authority, in the following special cases:
   (a) when a major extension to the farm is undertaken;
   (b) when a breed is changed;
   (c) when a new livestock specialisation is initiated;
   (d) when breeds are in danger of being lost to farming as laid down in Annex IV to Commission Regulation (EC) No 1974/2006[1] and in that case animals of those breeds must not necessarily be nulliparous.
5. For the renovation of apiaries, 10% per year of the queen bees and swarms may be replaced by non-organic queen bees and swarms in the organic production unit provided that the queen bees and swarms are placed in hives with combs or comb foundations coming from organic production units.

NOTES

[1] OJ L368, 23.12.2006, p 15.

SECTION 2
LIVESTOCK HOUSING AND HUSBANDRY PRACTICES

[8.266]
Article 10
Rules pertaining to housing conditions

1. Insulation, heating and ventilation of the building shall ensure that air circulation, dust level, temperature, relative air humidity and gas concentration, are kept within limits which are not harmful to the animals. The building shall permit plentiful natural ventilation and light to enter.

2. Housing for livestock shall not be mandatory in areas with appropriate climatic conditions to enable animals to live outdoors.
3. The stocking density in buildings shall provide for the comfort, the well being and the species-specific needs of the animals which, in particular, shall depend on the species, the breed and the age of the animals. It shall also take account of the behavioural needs of the animals, which depend in particular on the size of the group and the animals' sex. The density shall ensure the animals' welfare by providing them with sufficient space to stand naturally, lie down easily, turn round, groom themselves, assume all natural postures and make all natural movements such as stretching and wing flapping.
4. The minimum surface for indoor and outdoor areas, and other characteristics of housing for different species and categories of animals, are laid down in Annex III.

[8.267]
Article 11
Specific housing conditions and husbandry practices for mammals
1. Livestock housing shall have smooth, but not slippery floors. At least half of the indoor surface area as specified in Annex III shall be solid, that is, not of slatted or of grid construction.
2. The housing shall be provided with a comfortable, clean and dry laying/rest area of sufficient size, consisting of a solid construction which is not slatted. Ample dry bedding strewn with litter material shall be provided in the rest area. The litter shall comprise straw or other suitable natural material. The litter may be improved and enriched with any mineral product listed in Annex I.
3. Notwithstanding Article 3(3) of Council Directive 91/629/ EEC[1] the housing of calves in individual boxes shall be forbidden after the age of one week.
4. Notwithstanding Article 3(8) of Council Directive 91/630/ EEC[2] sows shall be kept in groups, except in the last stages of pregnancy and during the suckling period.
5. Piglets shall not be kept on flat decks or in piglet cages.
6. Exercise areas shall permit dunging and rooting by porcine animals. For the purposes of rooting different substrates can be used.

NOTES

[1] OJ L340, 11.12.1991, p 28.

[2] OJ L340, 11.12.1991, p 33.

[8.268]
Article 12
Specific housing conditions and husbandry practices for poultry
1. Poultry shall not be kept in cages.
2. Water fowl shall have access to a stream, pond, lake or a pool whenever the weather and hygienic conditions permit in order to respect their species-specific needs and animal welfare requirements.
3. Buildings for all poultry shall meet the following conditions:
(a) at least one third of the floor area shall be solid, that is, not of slatted or of grid construction, and covered with a litter material such as straw, wood shavings, sand or turf;
(b) in poultry houses for laying hens, a sufficiently large part of the floor area available to the hens shall be available for the collection of bird droppings;
(c) they shall have perches of a size and number commensurate with the size of the group and of the birds as laid down in Annex III.
(d) they shall have exit/entry pop-holes of a size adequate for the birds, and these pop-holes shall have a combined length of at least 4 m per 100 m^2 area of the house available to the birds;
(e) each poultry house shall not contain more than:
  (i) 4 800 chickens,
  (ii) 3 000 laying hens,
  (iii) 5 200 guinea fowl,
  (iv) 4 000 female Muscovy or Peking ducks or 3 200 male Muscovy or Peking ducks or other ducks,
  (v) 2 500 capons, geese or turkeys;
(f) the total usable area of poultry houses for meat production on any single unit, shall not exceed 1 600 m^2;
(g) poultry houses shall be constructed in a manner allowing all birds easy access to open air area.
4. Natural light may be supplemented by artificial means to provide a maximum of 16 hours light per day with a continuous nocturnal rest period without artificial light of at least eight hours.
5. To prevent the use of intensive rearing methods, poultry shall either be reared until they reach a minimum age or else shall come from slow-growing poultry strains. Where slow-growing poultry strains are not used by the operator the following minimum age at slaughter shall be:
(a) 81 days for chickens,
(b) 150 days for capons,
(c) 49 days for Peking ducks,

(d) 70 days for female Muscovy ducks,
(e) 84 days for male Muscovy ducks,
(f) 92 days for Mallard ducks,
(g) 94 days for guinea fowl,
(h) 140 days for male turkeys and roasting geese and
(i) 100 days for female turkeys.

The competent authority shall define the criteria of slow-growing strains or draw up a list thereof and provide this information to operators, other Member States and the Commission.

[8.269]
Article 13
Specific requirements and housing conditions in beekeeping

1. The siting of the apiaries shall be such that, within a radius of 3 km from the apiary site, nectar and pollen sources consist essentially of organically produced crops and/or spontaneous vegetation and/or crops treated with low environmental impact methods equivalent to those as described in Article 36 of Council Regulation (EC) No 1698/2005[1] or in Article 22 of Council Regulation 1257/1999[2] which cannot affect the qualification of beekeeping production as being organic. The above mentioned requirements do not apply where flowering is not taking place, or the hives are dormant.
2. The Member States may designate regions or areas where beekeeping complying with organic production rules is not practicable.
3. The hives shall be made basically of natural materials presenting no risk of contamination to the environment or the apiculture products.
4. The bees wax for new foundations shall come from organic production units.
5. Without prejudice to Article 25, only natural products such as propolis, wax and plant oils can be used in the hives.
6. The use of chemical synthetic repellents is prohibited during honey extractions operations.
7. The use of brood combs is prohibited for honey extraction.

NOTES

1 OJ L277, 21.10.2005, p 1.

2 OJ L160, 26.6.1999, p 80.

[8.270]
Article 14
Access to open air areas

1. Open air areas may be partially covered.
2. In accordance with Article 14(1)(b)(iii) of Regulation (EC) No 834/2007 herbivores shall have access to pasturage for grazing whenever conditions allow.
3. In cases where herbivores have access to pasturage during the grazing period and where the winter-housing system gives freedom of movement to the animals, the obligation to provide open air areas during the winter months may be waived.
4. Notwithstanding paragraph 2, bulls over one year old shall have access to pasturage or an open air area.
5. Poultry shall have access to an open air area for at least one third of their life.
6. Open air areas for poultry shall be mainly covered with vegetation and be provided with protective facilities and permit fowl to have easy access to adequate numbers of drinking and feeding troughs.
7. Where poultry are kept indoors due to restrictions or obligations imposed on the basis of Community legislation, they shall permanently have access to sufficient quantities of roughage and suitable material in order to meet their ethological needs.

[8.271]
Article 15
Stocking density

1. The total stocking density shall be such as not to exceed the limit of 170 kg of nitrogen per year and hectare of agricultural area as referred to in Article 3(2).
2. To determine the appropriate density of livestock referred to above, the competent authority shall set out the livestock units equivalent to the above limit, taking as a guideline, the figures laid down in Annex IV or the relevant national provisions adopted pursuant to Directive 91/676/EEC.

[8.272]
Article 16
Prohibition of landless livestock production

Landless livestock production, by which the operator of the livestock does not manage agricultural land and/or has not established a written cooperation agreement with another operator according to Article 3(3), is prohibited.

[8.273]
Article 17
Simultaneous production of organic and non-organic livestock

1. Non organic livestock may be present on the holding provided they are reared on units where the buildings and parcels are separated clearly from the units producing in accordance with the organic production rules and a different species is involved.
2. Non-organic livestock may use organic pasturage for a limited period of time each year, provided that such animals come from a farming system as defined in paragraph 3(b) and that organic animals are not present at the same time on that pasture.
3. Organic animals may be grazed on common land, providing that:
   (a) the land has not been treated with products not authorised for organic production for at least three years;
   (b) any non-organic animals which use the land concerned are derived from a farming system equivalent to those as described in Article 36 of Regulation (EC) No 1698/2005 or in Article 22 of Regulation 1257/1999;
   (c) any livestock products from organic animals, whilst using this land, shall not be regarded as being from organic-production, unless adequate segregation from non-organic animals can be proved.
4. During the period of transhumance animals may graze on non-organic land when they are being moved on foot from one grazing area to another. The uptake of non-organic feed, in the form of grass and other vegetation on which the animals graze, during this period shall not exceed 10% of the total feed ration per year. This figure shall be calculated as a percentage of the dry matter of feedingstuffs from agricultural origin.
5. Operators shall keep documentary evidence of the use of provisions referred to in this Article.

[8.274]
Article 18
Management of animals

1. Operations such as attaching elastic bands to the tails of sheep, tail-docking, cutting of teeth, trimming of beaks and dehorning shall not be carried out routinely in organic farming. However, some of these operations may be authorised by the competent authority for reasons of safety or if they are intended to improve the health, welfare or hygiene of the livestock on a case-by-case basis.

Any suffering to the animals shall be reduced to a minimum by applying adequate anaesthesia and/or analgesia and by carrying out the operation only at the most appropriate age by qualified personnel.
2. Physical castration is allowed in order to maintain the quality of products and traditional production practices but only under the conditions set out in the second subparagraph of paragraph 1.
3. Mutilation such as clipping the wings of queen bees is prohibited.
4. Loading and unloading of animals shall be carried out without the use of any type of electrical stimulation to coerce the animals. The use of allopathic tranquillisers, prior to or during transport, is prohibited.

SECTION 3
FEED

[8.275]
[Article 19
Feed from own holding and other sources

1. In case of herbivores, except during the period each year when the animals are under transhumance subject to Article 17(4), at least 60% of the feed shall come from the farm unit itself or in case this is not feasible, be produced in cooperation with other organic farms in the same region.
2. In case of pigs and poultry, at least 20% of the feed shall come from the farm unit itself or in case this is not feasible, be produced in the same region in cooperation with other organic farms or feed business operators.
3. In the case of bees, at the end of the production season hives shall be left with sufficient reserves of honey and pollen to survive the winter.

The feeding of bee colonies shall only be permitted where the survival of the hives is endangered due to climatic conditions. Feeding shall be with organic honey, organic sugar syrups, or organic sugar.]

NOTES

Substituted by Commission Regulation (EU) 505/2012, Art 1(1).

[8.276]
Article 20
Feed meeting animals' nutritional requirements

1. All young mammals shall be fed on maternal milk in preference to natural milk, for a minimum period of three months for bovines including *bubalus* and bison species and equidae, 45 days for sheep and goats and 40 days for pigs.
2. Rearing systems for herbivores are to be based on maximum use of grazing pasturage according to the availability of pastures in the different periods of the year. At least 60% of the dry matter in daily rations of herbivores shall consist of roughage, fresh or dried fodder, or silage. A reduction to 50% for animals in dairy production for a maximum period of three months in early lactation is allowed.
3. Roughage, fresh or dried fodder, or silage shall be added to the daily ration for pigs and poultry.
4. The keeping of livestock in conditions, or on a diet, which may encourage anaemia, is prohibited.
5. Fattening practices shall be reversible at any stage of the rearing process. Force-feeding is forbidden.

[8.277]
Article 21
In-conversion feed

[1. Up to 30% of the feed formula of rations on average may comprise in-conversion feedingstuffs. When the in-conversion feedingstuffs come from a unit of the holding itself, this percentage may be increased to 100%.]
[2. Up to 20% of the total average amount of feedingstuffs fed to livestock may originate from the grazing or harvesting of permanent pastures, perennial forage parcels or protein crops, sown under organic management on lands in their first year of conversion, provided that they are part of the holding itself and have not been part of an organic production unit of that holding in the last five years. When both in-conversion feedingstuffs and feedingstuffs from parcels in their first year of conversion are being used, the total combined percentage of such feedingstuffs shall not exceed the maximum percentages fixed in paragraph 1.]
3. The figures in paragraph 1 and 2 shall be calculated annually as a percentage of the dry matter of feedingstuffs of plant origin.

NOTES

Para 1: substituted by Commission Regulation 1254/2008/EC, Art 2.
Para 2: substituted by Commission Regulation 710/2009/EC, Art 1(4).

[8.278]
[Article 22
Use of certain products and substances in feed

For the purposes of Article 14(1)(d)(iv) of Regulation (EC) No 834/2007 only the following substances may be used in the processing of organic feed and feeding organic animals:
- (a) non-organic feed materials of plant or animal origin, or other feed materials that are listed in Section 2 of Annex V, provided that:
  - (i) they are produced or prepared without chemical solvents; and
  - (ii) the restrictions laid down in Article 43 or Article 47(c) are complied with;
- (b) non-organic spices, herbs, and molasses, provided that:
  - (i) their organic form is not available;
  - (ii) they are produced or prepared without chemical solvents; and
  - (iii) their use is limited to 1% of the feed ration of a given species, calculated annually as a percentage of the dry matter of feed from agricultural origin;
- (c) organic feed materials of animal origin;
- (d) feed materials of mineral origin that are listed in Section 1 of Annex V;
- (e) products from sustainable fisheries, provided that:
  - (i) they are produced or prepared without chemical solvents;
  - (ii) their use is restricted to non-herbivores; and
  - (iii) the use of fish protein hydrolysate is restricted solely to young animals;
- (f) salt as sea salt, coarse rock salt;
- (g) feed additives listed in Annex VI.]

NOTES

Substituted by Commission Regulation 505/2012/EU, Art 1(2).

SECTION 4
DISEASE PREVENTION AND VETERINARY TREATMENT

[8.279]
Article 23
Disease prevention

1. The use of chemically synthesised allopathic veterinary medicinal products or antibiotics for preventive treatment is prohibited, without prejudice to Article 24(3).
2. The use of substances to promote growth or production (including antibiotics, coccidiostatics and other artificial aids for growth promotion purposes) and the use of hormones or similar substances to control reproduction or for other purposes (e.g. induction or synchronisation of oestrus), is prohibited.
3. Where livestock is obtained from non-organic units, special measures such as screening tests or quarantine periods may apply, depending on local circumstances.
4. Housing, pens, equipment and utensils shall be properly cleaned and disinfected to prevent cross-infection and the build-up of disease carrying organisms. Faeces, urine and uneaten or spilt feed shall be removed as often as necessary to minimise smell and to avoid attracting insects or rodents.

For the purpose of Article 14(1)(f) of Regulation (EC) No 834/2007, only products listed in Annex VII may be used for cleaning and disinfection of livestock buildings installations and utensils. Rodenticides (to be used only in traps), and the products listed in Annex II, can be used for the elimination of insects and other pests in buildings and other installations where livestock is kept.
5. Buildings shall be emptied of livestock between each batch of poultry reared. The buildings and fittings shall be cleaned and disinfected during this time. In addition, when the rearing of each batch of poultry has been completed, runs shall be left empty to allow vegetation to grow back. Member States shall establish the period for which runs must be empty. The operator shall keep documentary evidence of the application of this period. These requirements shall not apply where poultry is not reared in batches, is not kept in runs and is free to roam, throughout the day.

[8.280]
Article 24
Veterinary treatment

1. Where despite preventive measures to ensure animal health as laid down in Article 14(1)(e)(i) of Regulation (EC) No 834/ 2007 animals become sick or injured they shall be treated immediately, if necessary in isolation and in suitable housing.
[2. Phytotherapeutic and homeopathic products, trace elements and products listed in Section 1 of Annex V and in Section 3 of Annex VI shall be used in preference to chemically-synthesised allopathic veterinary treatment or antibiotics, provided that their therapeutic effect is effective for the species of animal, and the condition for which the treatment is intended.]
3. If the use of measures referred to in paragraph 1 and 2 is not effective in combating illness or injury, and if treatment is essential to avoid suffering or distress of the animal, chemically-synthesised allopathic veterinary medicinal products or antibiotics may be used under the responsibility of a veterinarian.
4. With the exception of vaccinations, treatments for parasites and compulsory eradication schemes where an animal or group of animals receive more than three courses of treatments with chemically-synthesised allopathic veterinary medicinal products or antibiotics within 12 months, or more than one course of treatment if their productive lifecycle is less than one year, the livestock concerned, or produce derived from them, may not be sold as organic products, and the livestock shall undergo the conversion periods laid down in Article 38(1).

Records of documented evidence of the occurrence of such circumstances shall be kept for the control body or control authority.
5. The withdrawal period between the last administration of an allopathic veterinary medicinal product to an animal under normal conditions of use, and the production of organically produced foodstuffs from such animals, is to be twice the legal withdrawal period as referred to in Article 11 of Directive 2001/82/EC or, in a case in which this period is not specified, 48 hours.

NOTES

Para 2: substituted by Commission Regulation 354/2014/EU, Art 2(1).

[8.281]
Article 25
Specific rules on disease prevention and veterinary treatment in beekeeping

1. For the purposes of protecting frames, hives and combs, in particular from pests, only rodenticides (to be used only in traps), and appropriate products listed in Annex II, are permitted.
2. Physical treatments for disinfection of apiaries such as steam or direct flame are permitted.
3. The practice of destroying the male brood is permitted only to isolate the infestation of *Varroa destructor.*
4. If despite all preventive measures, the colonies become sick or infested, they shall be treated immediately and, if necessary, the colonies can be placed in isolation apiaries.

5. Veterinary medicinal products may be used in organic beekeeping in so far as the corresponding use is authorised in the Member State in accordance with the relevant Community provisions or national provisions in conformity with Community law.
6. Formic acid, lactic acid, acetic acid and oxalic acid as well as menthol, thymol, eucalyptol or camphor may be used in cases of infestation with *Varroa destructor*.
7. If a treatment is applied with chemically synthesised allopathic products, during such a period, the colonies treated shall be placed in isolation apiaries and all the wax shall be replaced with wax coming from organic beekeeping. Subsequently, the conversion period of one year laid down in Article 38(3) will apply to those colonies.
8. The requirements laid down in paragraph 7 shall not apply to products listed in paragraph 6.

[CHAPTER 2A
AQUACULTURE ANIMAL PRODUCTION

SECTION 1
GENERAL RULES

[8.282]
Article 25a
Scope
This Chapter lays down detailed production rules for species of fish, crustaceans, echinoderms and molluscs as covered by Annex XIIIa.
It applies mutatis mutandis to zooplankton, micro-crustaceans, rotifers, worms and other aquatic feed animals.]

NOTES
Chapter 2a (Arts 25a–25t) inserted by Commission Regulation 710/2009/EC, Art 1(5).

[8.283]
[Article 25b
Suitability of aquatic medium and sustainable management plan
1. The provisions of Article 6b(1) to (5) shall apply to this Chapter.
2. Defensive and preventive measures taken against predators under Council Directive 92/43/EEC[1] and national rules shall be recorded in the sustainable management plan.
3. Verifiable coordination shall take place with the neighbouring operators in drawing up their management plans where applicable.
4. For aquaculture animal production in fishponds, tanks or raceways, farms shall be equipped with either natural-filter beds, settlement ponds, biological filters or mechanical filters to collect waste nutrients or use seaweeds and/or animals (bivalves and algae) which contribute to improving the quality of the effluent. Effluent monitoring shall be carried out at regular intervals where appropriate.]

NOTES
Inserted as noted to Art 25a at **[8.282]**.

[1] OJ L 206, 22.7.1992, p. 7.

[8.284]
[Article 25c
Simultaneous production of organic and non-organic aquaculture animals
1. The competent authority may permit hatcheries and nurseries to rear both organic and non-organic juveniles in the same holding provided there is clear physical separation between the units and a separate water distribution system exists.
2. In case of grow-out production, the competent authority may permit organic and non-organic aquaculture animal production units on the same holding provided Article 6b(2) of this Regulation is complied with and where different production phases and different handling periods of the aquaculture animals are involved.
3. Operators shall keep documentary evidence of the use of provisions referred to in this Article.]

NOTES
Inserted as noted to Art 25a at **[8.282]**.

[SECTION 2
ORIGIN OF AQUACULTURE ANIMALS

[8.285]
Article 25d
Origin of organic aquaculture animals
1. Locally grown species shall be used and breeding shall aim to give strains which are more adapted to farming conditions, good health and good utilisation of feed resources. Documentary evidence of their origin and treatment shall be provided for the control body or control authority.

2. Species shall be chosen which can be farmed without causing significant damage to wild stocks.]

NOTES

Inserted as noted to Art 25a at **[8.282]**.

[8.286]
[Article 25e
Origin and management of non-organic aquaculture animals

1. For breeding purposes or for improving genetic stock and when organic aquaculture animals are not available, wild caught or non-organic aquaculture animals may be brought into a holding. Such animals shall be kept under organic management for at least three months before they may be used for breeding.
2. For on-growing purposes and when organic aquaculture juvenile animals are not available non-organic aquaculture juveniles may be brought into a holding. At least the latter two thirds of the duration of the production cycle shall be managed under organic management.
[3. The maximum percentage of non-organic aquaculture juveniles introduced to the farm shall be 80% by 31 December 2011, 50% by 31 December 2014 and 0% by 31 December 2016.]
[4. For on-growing purposes the collection of wild aquaculture juveniles is specifically restricted to the following cases:
  (a) natural influx of fish or crustacean larvae and juveniles when filling ponds, containment systems and enclosures;
  (b) European glass eel, provided that an approved eel management plan is in place for the location and artificial reproduction of eel remains unsolved;
  (c) the collection of wild fry of species other than European eel for on-growing in traditional extensive aquaculture farming inside wetlands, such as brackish water ponds, tidal areas and costal lagoons, closed by levees and banks, provided that:
    (i) the restocking is in line with management measures approved by the relevant authorities in charge of the management of the fish stocks in question to ensure the sustainable exploitation of the species concerned, and
    (ii) the fish are fed exclusively with feed naturally available in the environment.]]

NOTES

Inserted as noted to Art 25a at **[8.282]**.
Para 3: substituted by Commission Implementing Regulation 2016/673/EU, Art 1(2).
Para 4: substituted by Commission Regulation 1358/2014/EU, Art 1(1).

[SECTION 3
AQUACULTURE HUSBANDRY PRACTICES

[8.287]
Article 25f
General aquaculture husbandry rules

1. The husbandry environment of the aquaculture animals shall be designed in such a way that, in accordance with their species specific needs, the aquaculture animals shall:
  (a) have sufficient space for their wellbeing;
  (b) be kept in water of good quality with sufficient oxygen levels, and
  (c) be kept in temperature and light conditions in accordance with the requirements of the species and having regard to the geographic location;
  (d) in the case of freshwater fish the bottom type shall be as close as possible to natural conditions;
  (e) in the case of carp the bottom shall be natural earth.

[2. Stocking density and husbandry practices are set out in Annex XIIIa by species or group of species. In considering the effects of stocking density and husbandry practices on the welfare of farmed fish, the condition of the fish (such as fin damage, other injuries, growth rate, behaviour expressed and overall health) and the water quality shall be monitored.]
3. The design and construction of aquatic containment systems shall provide flow rates and physiochemical parameters that safeguard the animals' health and welfare and provide for their behavioural needs.
4. Containment systems shall be designed, located and operated to minimize the risk of escape incidents.
5. If fish or crustaceans escape, appropriate action must be taken to reduce the impact on the local ecosystem, including recapture, where appropriate. Documentary evidence shall be maintained.]

NOTES

Inserted as noted to Art 25a at **[8.282]**.
Para 2: substituted by Commission Regulation 1358/2014/EU, Art 1(2).

[8.288]
[Article 25g
Specific rules for aquatic containment systems

1. Closed recirculation aquaculture animal production facilities are prohibited, with the exception of hatcheries and nurseries or for the production of species used for organic feed organisms.
2. Rearing units on land shall meet the following conditions:
   (a) for flow-through systems it shall be possible to monitor and control the flow rate and water quality of both in-flowing and out-flowing water;
   (b) at least five percent of the perimeter ("land-water interface") area shall have natural vegetation.
3. Containment systems at sea shall:
   (a) be located where water flow, depth and water-body exchange rates are adequate to minimize the impact on the seabed and the surrounding water body;
   (b) shall have suitable cage design, construction and maintenance with regard to their exposure to the operating environment.
4. Artificial heating or cooling of water shall only be permitted in hatcheries and nurseries. Natural borehole water may be used to heat or cool water at all stages of production.]

NOTES

Inserted as noted to Art 25a at **[8.282]**.

[8.289]
[Article 25h
Management of aquaculture animals

1. Handling of aquaculture animals shall be minimised, undertaken with the greatest care and proper equipment and protocols used to avoid stress and physical damage associated with handling procedures. Broodstock shall be handled in a manner to minimize physical damage and stress and under anaesthesia where appropriate. Grading operations shall be kept to a minimum and as required to ensure fish welfare.
2. The following restrictions shall apply to the use of artificial light:
   (a) for prolonging natural day-length it shall not exceed a maximum that respects the ethological needs, geographical conditions and general health of farmed animals, this maximum shall not exceed 16 hours per day, except for reproductive purposes;
   (b) Abrupt changes in light intensity shall be avoided at the changeover time by the use of dimmable lights or background lighting.
3. Aeration is permitted to ensure animal welfare and health, under the condition that mechanical aerators are preferably powered by renewable energy sources.

All such use is to be recorded in the aquaculture production record.

4. The use of oxygen is only permitted for uses linked to animal health requirements and critical periods of production or transport, in the following cases:
   (a) exceptional cases of temperature rise or drop in atmospheric pressure or accidental pollution,
   (b) occasional stock management procedures such as sampling and sorting,
   (c) in order to assure the survival of the farm stock.

Documentary evidence shall be maintained.

5. Slaughter techniques shall render fish immediately unconscious and insensible to pain. Differences in harvesting sizes, species, and production sites must be taken into account when considering optimal slaughtering methods.]

NOTES

Inserted as noted to Art 25a at **[8.282]**.

[SECTION 4
BREEDING

[8.290]
Article 25i
Prohibition of hormones

The use of hormones and hormone derivates is prohibited.]

NOTES

Inserted as noted to Art 25a at **[8.282]**.

[SECTION 5

FEED FOR FISH, CRUSTACEANS AND ECHINODERMES

[8.291]
Article 25j
General rules on feeds

Feeding regimes shall be designed with the following priorities:

(a) animal health;

(b) high product quality, including the nutritional composition which shall ensure high quality of the final edible product;

(c) low environmental impact.]

NOTES

Inserted as noted to Art 25a at **[8.282]**.

[8.292]
[Article 25k
Specific rules on feeds for carnivorous aquaculture animals

1. Feed for carnivorous aquaculture animals shall be sourced with the following priorities:

(a) organic feed products of aquaculture origin;

(b) fish meal and fish oil from organic aquaculture trimmings;

(c) fish meal and fish oil and ingredients of fish origin derived from trimmings of fish already caught for human consumption in sustainable fisheries;

[(d) organic feed materials of plant or animal origin];

[(e) feed products derived from whole fish caught in fisheries certified as sustainable under a scheme recognised by the competent authority in line with the principles laid down in Regulation (EU) No 1380/2013 of the European Parliament and of the Council.[1]]

2. . . .

3. The feed ration may comprise a maximum of 60% organic plant products.

4. Astaxanthin derived primarily from organic sources, such as organic crustacean shells may be used in the feed ration for salmon and trout within the limit of their physiological needs. If organic sources are not available natural sources of astaxanthin (such as Phaffia yeast) may be used.

[5. Histidine produced through fermentation may be used in the feed ration for salmonid fish when the feed sources listed in paragraph 1 do not provide a sufficient amount of histidine to meet the dietary needs of the fish and prevent the formation of cataracts.]]

NOTES

Inserted as noted to Art 25a at **[8.282]**.

Para 1: sub-para (d) substituted by Commission Regulation 505/2012/EU, Art 1(4); sub-para (e) added by Commission Regulation 1358/2014/EU, Art 1(3).

Para 2: repealed by Commission Regulation 1358/2014/EU, Art 1(4).

Para 5: added by Commission Regulation 1358/2014/EU, Art 1(5).

[1] Regulation (EU) No 1380/2013 of the European Parliament and of the Council of 11 December 2013 on the Common Fisheries Policy, amending Council Regulations (EC) No 1954/2003 and (EC) No 1224/2009 and repealing Council Regulations (EC) No 2371/2002 and (EC) No 639/2004 and Council Decision 2004/585/EC (OJ L354, 28.12.2013, p 22).

[8.293]
[Article 25l
Specific rules on feeds for certain aquaculture animals

[1. In the grow-out stages, aquaculture animals as referred to in Annex XIIIa, Section 6, Section 7 and Section 9 shall be fed with feed naturally available in ponds and lakes.]

2. Where natural feed resources are not available in sufficient quantities as referred to in paragraph 1, organic feed of plant origin, preferably grown on the farm itself or seaweed may be used. Operators shall keep documentary evidence of the need to use additional feed.

[3. Where natural feed is supplemented according to paragraph 2—

(a) the feed ration of siamese catfish (Pangasius spp.) as referred to in Section 9 of Annex XIIIa may comprise a maximum of 10 % fishmeal or fish oil derived from sustainable fisheries;

(b) the feed ration of shrimps as referred to in Section 7 of Annex XIIIa may comprise a maximum of 25% fishmeal and 10% fish oil derived from sustainable fisheries. In order to secure the quantitative dietary needs of shrimps, organic cholesterol may be used to supplement their diets; where organic cholesterol is not available, non-organic cholesterol derived from wool, shellfish or other sources may be used.]]

NOTES

Inserted as noted to Art 25a at **[8.282]**.

Para 1: substituted by Commission Implementing Regulation 2017/838/EU, Art 1.

Para 3: substituted by Commission Regulation 1358/2014/EU, Art 1(6).

[8.294]
[Article 25la
Specific rules on feeds for organic juveniles
In the larval rearing of organic juveniles, conventional phytoplankton and zooplankton may be used as feed.]

NOTES
Inserted by Commission Regulation 1358/2014/EU, Art 1(7).

[8.295]
[Article 25m
Products and substances as referred to in Article 15(1)(d)(iii) of Regulation (EC) No 834/2007
[1. Feed materials of mineral origin may be used in organic aquaculture only if listed in Section 1 of Annex V.]
2. Feed additives, certain products used in animal nutrition and processing aids may be used if listed in Annex VI and the restrictions laid down therein are complied with.]

NOTES
Inserted as noted to Art 25a at **[8.282]**.
Para 1: substituted by Commission Implementing Regulation 505/2012/EU, Art 1(5).

[SECTION 6
SPECIFIC RULES FOR MOLLUSCS

[8.296]
Article 25n
Growing area
1. Bivalve mollusc farming may be carried out in the same area of water as organic finfish and seaweed farming in a polyculture system to be documented in the sustainable management plan. Bivalve molluscs may also be grown together with gastropod molluscs, such as periwinkles, in polyculture.
2. Organic bivalve mollusc production shall take place within areas delimited by posts, floats or other clear markers and shall, as appropriate, be restrained by net bags, cages or other man made means.
3. Organic shellfish farms shall minimise risks to species of conservation interest. If predator nets are used their design shall not permit diving birds to be harmed.]

NOTES
Inserted as noted to Art 25a at **[8.282]**.

[8.297]
[Article 25o
Sourcing of seed
1. Provided that there is no significant damage to the environment and if permitted by local legislation, wild seed from outside the boundaries of the production unit can be used in the case of bivalve shellfish provided it comes from:
(a) settlement beds which are unlikely to survive winter weather or are surplus to requirements, or
(b) natural settlement of shellfish seed on collectors.

Records shall be kept of how, where and when wild seed was collected to allow traceability back to the collection area.

[However, the maximum percentage of seed from non- organic bivalve shellfish hatcheries that may be introduced to the organic production units shall be 80% by 31 December 2011, 50% by 31 December 2014 and 0% by 31 December 2016.]
2. For the cupped oyster, Crassostrea gigas, preference shall be given to stock which is selectively bred to reduce spawning in the wild.]

NOTES
Inserted as noted to Art 25a at **[8.282]**.
Para 1: words in square brackets substituted by Commission Implementing Regulation 2016/673/EU, Art 1(3).

[8.298]
[Article 25p
Management
1. Production shall use a stocking density not in excess of that used for non-organic shellfish in the locality. Sorting, thinning and stocking density adjustments shall be made according to the biomass and to ensure animal welfare and high product quality.
2. Biofouling organisms shall be removed by physical means or by hand and where appropriate returned to the sea away from shellfish farms. Shellfish may be treated once during the production cycle with a lime solution to control competing fouling organisms.]

NOTES

Inserted as noted to Art 25a at **[8.282]**.

[8.299]
[Article 25q
Cultivation rules

1. Cultivation on mussel ropes and other methods listed in Annex XIIIa, Section 8 may be eligible for organic production.

2. Bottom cultivation of molluscs is only permitted where no significant environmental impact is caused at the collection and growing sites. The evidence of minimal environmental impact shall be supported by a survey and report on the exploited area to be provided by the operator to the control body or control authority. The report shall be added as a separate chapter to the sustainable management plan.]

NOTES

Inserted as noted to Art 25a at **[8.282]**.

[8.300]
[Article 25r
Specific cultivation rules for oysters

Cultivation in bags on trestles is permitted. These or other structures in which the oysters are contained shall be set out so as to avoid the formation of a total barrier along the shoreline. Stock shall be positioned carefully on the beds in relation to tidal flow to optimise production. Production shall meet the criteria listed in the Annex XIIIa, Section 8.]

NOTES

Inserted as noted to Art 25a at **[8.282]**.

[SECTION 7
DISEASE PREVENTION AND VETERINARY TREATMENT

[8.301]
Article 25s
General rules on disease prevention

1. The animal health management plan in conformity with Article 9 of Directive 2006/88/EC shall detail biosecurity and disease prevention practices including a written agreement for health counselling, proportionate to the production unit, with qualified aquaculture animal health services who shall visit the farm at a frequency of not less than once per year and not less than once every two years in the case of bivalve shellfish.

2. Holding systems, equipment and utensils shall be properly cleaned and disinfected. Only products listed in Annex VII, Sections 2.1 to 2.2 may be used.

3. With regard to fallowing:
   (a) The competent authority shall determine whether fallowing is necessary and the appropriate duration which shall be applied and documented after each production cycle in open water containment systems at sea. Fallowing is also recommended for other production methods using tanks, fishponds, and cages;
   (b) it shall not be mandatory for bivalve mollusc cultivation;
   (c) during fallowing the cage or other structure used for aquaculture animal production is emptied, disinfected and left empty before being used again.

4. Where appropriate, uneaten fish-feed, faeces and dead animals shall be removed promptly to avoid any risk of significant environmental damage as regards water status quality, minimize disease risks, and to avoid attracting insects or rodents.

5. Ultraviolet light and ozone may be used only in hatcheries and nurseries.

[6. For biological control of ectoparasites, preference shall be given to the use of cleaner fish and to the use of freshwater, marine water and sodium chloride solutions.]]

NOTES

Inserted as noted to Art 25a at **[8.282]**.
Para 6: substituted by Commission Regulation 1358/2014/EU, Art 1(8).

[8.302]
[Article 25t
Veterinary treatments

1. When despite preventive measures to ensure animal health, according to Article 15(1)(f)(i) of Regulation (EC) No 834/2007, a health problem arises, veterinary treatments may be used in the following order of preference:
   (a) substances from plants, animals or minerals in a homoeopathic dilution;
   (b) plants and their extracts not having anaesthetic effects, and

(c) substances such as: trace elements, metals, natural immunostimulants or authorised probiotics.

2. The use of allopathic treatments is limited to two courses of treatment per year, with the exception of vaccinations and compulsory eradication schemes. However, in the cases of a production cycle of less than a year a limit of one allopathic treatment applies. If the mentioned limits for allopathic treatments are exceeded the concerned aquaculture animals can not be sold as organic products.

3. The use of parasite treatments, not including compulsory control schemes operated by Member States, shall be limited to twice per year or once per year where the production cycle is less than 18 months.

4. The withdrawal period for allopathic veterinary treatments and parasite treatments according to paragraph 3 including treatments under compulsory control and eradication schemes shall be twice the legal withdrawal period as referred to in Article 11 of Directive 2001/82/EC or in a case in which this period in not specified 48 hours.

5. Whenever veterinary medicinal products are used, such use is to be declared to the control body or the control authority before the animals are marketed as organic. Treated stock shall be clearly identifiable.]

NOTES

Inserted as noted to Art 25a at **[8.282]**.

CHAPTER 3
[PRESERVED AND PROCESSED PRODUCTS]

NOTES

Chapter heading: words in square brackets substituted by Commission Implementing Regulation 2016/1842/EU, Art 2(3).

[8.303]

[Article 26

Rules for preserving products and for the production of processed feed and food

1. Operators preserving products or producing processed feed or food shall establish and update appropriate procedures based on a systematic identification of critical processing steps.

The application of those procedures shall guarantee at all times that preserved or processed products comply with the organic production rules.

2. Operators shall comply with and implement the procedures referred to in paragraph 1. In particular, operators shall:

(a) take precautionary measures to avoid the risk of contamination by unauthorised substances or products;

(b) implement suitable cleaning measures, monitor their effectiveness and record those measures;

(c) guarantee that non-organic products are not placed on the market with an indication referring to the organic production method.

3. Where non-organic products are also prepared or stored in the preparation unit concerned, the operator shall:

(a) carry out the operations continuously until the complete run has been dealt with, separated by place or time from similar operations carried out on non-organic products;

(b) store organic products, before and after the operations, separate by place or time from non-organic products;

(c) inform the control authority or control body of the operations referred to in points (a) and (b) and keep available an updated register of all operations and quantities processed;

(d) take the necessary measures to ensure identification of lots and to avoid mixtures or exchanges with non-organic products;

(e) carry out operations on organic products only after suitable cleaning of the production equipment.

4. Additives, processing aids and other substances and ingredients used for processing feed or food and any processing practice applied, such as smoking, shall respect the principles of good manufacturing practice.]

NOTES

Substituted by Commission Implementing Regulation 2016/1842/EU, Art 2(4).

[8.304]

Article 27

Use of certain products and substances in processing of food

1. [For the purposes of Article 19(2)(b) of Regulation (EC) No 834/2007, only the following substances can be used in the processing of organic food, with the exception of products of the wine sector, for which the provisions of Chapter 3a shall apply:]

(a) substances listed in Annex VIII to this Regulation;

(b) preparations of micro-organisms and enzymes normally used in food processing [however, enzymes to be used as food additives have to be listed in Annex VIII, Section A];
(c) substances, and products as defined in Articles 1(2)(b)(i) and 1(2)(c) of Council Directive 88/388/EEC[1] labelled as natural flavouring substances or natural flavouring preparations, according to Articles 9(1)(d) and (2) of that Directive.
(d) colours for stamping meat and eggshells in accordance with, respectively, Article 2(8) and Article 2(9) of European Parliament and Council Directive 94/36/EC;[2]
(e) drinking water and salt (with sodium chloride or potassium chloride as basic components) generally used in food processing;
(f) minerals (trace elements included), vitamins, aminoacids, and micronutrients, only authorised as far their use is legally required in the foodstuffs in which they are incorporated.

2. For the purpose of the calculation referred to in Article 23 (4)(a)(ii) of Regulation (EC) No 834/2007,
(a) food additives listed in Annex VIII and marked with an asterisk in the column of the additive code number, shall be calculated as ingredients of agricultural origin;
(b) preparations and substances referred to in paragraph (1)(b), (c), (d), (e) and (f) of this Article and substances not marked with an asterisk in the column of the additive code number shall not be calculated as ingredients of agricultural origin.
[(c) yeast and yeast products shall be calculated as ingredients of agricultural origin as of 31 December 2013.]

3. The use of the following substances listed in Annex VIII shall be re-examined before 31 December 2010:
(a) Sodium nitrite and potassium nitrate in Section A with a view to withdrawing these additives;
(b) Sulphur dioxide and potassium metabisulphite in Section A;
(c) Hydrochloric acid in Section B for the processing of Gouda, Edam and Maasdammer cheeses, Boerenkaas, Friese, and Leidse Nagelkaas.

The re-examination referred to in point (a) shall take account of the efforts made by Member States to find safe alternatives to nitrites/nitrates and in establishing educational programmes in alternative processing methods and hygiene for organic meat processors/manufacturers.

[4. For the traditional decorative colouring of the shell of boiled eggs produced with the intention to place them on the market at a given period of the year, the competent authority may authorise for the period referred to above, the use of natural colours and natural coating substances. The authorisation may comprise synthetic forms of iron oxides and iron hydroxides until 31 December 2013. Authorisations shall be notified to the Commission and the Member States.]

NOTES

Para 1: words in first pair of square brackets substituted by Commission Regulation 203/2012/EU, Art 1(1)(a); words in square brackets in para (b) added by Commission Regulation 1254/2008/EC, Art 3(a).

Para 2: sub-para (c) added by Commission Regulation 1254/2008/EC, Art 3(b).

Para 4: added by Commission Regulation 1254/2008/EC, Art 3(c).

[1] OJ L184, 15.7.1988, p 61.

[2] OJ L237, 10.9.1994, p 13.

[8.305]
[Article 27a

For the purpose of the application of Article 20(1) of Regulation (EC) No 834/2007, the following substances may be used in the production, confection and formulation of yeast:
(a) substances listed in Annex VIII, Section C to this Regulation;
(b) products and substances referred to in Article 27(1)(b) and (e) of this Regulation.]

NOTES

Inserted by Commission Regulation 1254/2008/EC, Art 4.

[8.306]
Article 28
Use of certain non-organic ingredients of agricultural origin in processing food

For the purpose of Article 19(2)(c) of Regulation (EC) No 834/2007, non-organic agricultural ingredients listed in Annex IX to this Regulation can be used in the processing of organic food.

[8.307]
Article 29
Authorisation of non-organic food ingredients of agricultural origin by Member State

1. Where an ingredient of agricultural origin is not included in Annex IX to this Regulation, that ingredient may only be used under the following conditions:

(a) the operator has notified to the competent authority of the Member State all the requisite evidence showing that the ingredient concerned is not produced in sufficient quantity in the Community in accordance with the organic production rules or cannot be imported from third countries;

(b) the competent authority of the Member State has provisionally authorised, the use for a maximum period of 12 months after having verified that the operator has undertaken the necessary contacts with suppliers in the Community to ensure himself of the unavailability of the ingredients concerned with the required quality requirements;

(c) no decision has been taken, in accordance with the provisions of paragraphs 3 or 4 that a granted authorisation with regard to the ingredient concerned shall be withdrawn.

The Member State may prolong the authorisation provided for in point (b) a maximum of three times for 12 months each.

2. Where an authorisation as referred to in paragraph 1 has been granted, the Member State shall immediately notify to the other Member States and to the Commission, the following information:

(a) the date of the authorisation and in case of a prolonged authorisation, the date of the first authorisation;

(b) the name, address, telephone, and where relevant, fax and e-mail of the holder of the authorisation; the name and address of the contact point of the authority which granted the authorisation;

(c) the name and, where necessary, the precise description and quality requirements of the ingredient of agricultural origin concerned;

(d) the type of products for the preparation of which the requested ingredient is necessary;

(e) the quantities that are required and the justification for those quantities;

(f) the reasons for, and expected period of, the shortage;

(g) the date on which the Member State sends this notification to the other Member States and the Commission. The Commission and/or Member States may make this information available to the public.

3. Where a Member State submits comments to the Commission and to the Member State which granted the authorisation, which show that supplies are available during the period of the shortage, the Member State shall consider withdrawal of the authorisation or reducing the envisaged period of validity, and shall inform the Commission and the other Member States of the measures it has taken or will take, within 15 working days from the date of receipt of the information.

4. At the request of a Member State or at the Commission's initiative, the matter shall be submitted for examination to the Committee set up in accordance with Article 37 of Regulation (EC) No 834/2007. It may be decided, in accordance with the procedure laid down in paragraph 2 of that Article, that a previously granted authorisation shall be withdrawn or its period of validity amended, or where appropriate, that the ingredient concerned shall be included in Annex IX to this Regulation.

5. In case of an extension as referred to in the second subparagraph of paragraph 1, the procedures of paragraphs 2 and 3 shall apply.

[8.308]
[Article 29a
Specific provisions for seaweed

1. If the final product is fresh seaweed, flushing of freshly harvested seaweed shall use seawater. If the final product is dehydrated seaweed, potable water may also be used for flushing. Salt may be used for removal of moisture.

2. The use of direct flames which come in direct contact with the seaweed shall be prohibited for drying. If ropes or other equipment are used in the drying process they shall be free of anti-fouling treatments and cleaning or disinfection substances except where a product is listed in Annex VII for this use.]

NOTES

Inserted by Commission Regulation 710/2009/EC, Art 1(6).

[CHAPTER 3A
SPECIFIC RULES FOR THE MAKING OF WINE

[8.309]
Article 29b
Scope

1. This Chapter lays down specific rules for the organic production of the products of the wine sector as referred to in Article 1(1)(l) of Council Regulation (EC) No 1234/2007.[1]

2. Commission Regulations (EC) No 606/2009[2] (EC) No 607/2009[3] shall apply, save as explicitly provided otherwise in this Chapter.]

NOTES

Chapter 3a (Arts 29b–29d) inserted by Commission Regulation 203/2012/EU, Art 1(1)(b).

[1] OJ L 299, 16.11.2007, p. 1

2 OJ L 193, 24.7.2009, p. 1.

3 OJ L 193, 24.7.2009, p. 60.

[8.310]
[Article 29c
Use of certain products and substances

1. For the purposes of Article 19(2)(a) of Regulation (EC) No 834/2007, products of the wine sector shall be produced from organic raw material.
2. For the purposes of Article 19(2)(b) of Regulation (EC) No 834/2007, only products and substances listed in Annex VIIIa to this Regulation can be used for the making of products of the wine sector, including during the processes and oenological practices, subject to the conditions and restrictions laid down in Regulation (EC) No 1234/2007 and Regulation (EC) No 606/2009 and in particular in Annex I A to that Regulation.
3. Products and substances listed in Annex VIIIa to this Regulation and marked with an asterisk, derived from organic raw material, shall be used if available.]

NOTES

Inserted as noted to Art 29b at **[8.309]**.

[8.311]
[Article 29d
Oenological practices and restrictions

1. Without prejudice to Article 29c and to specific prohibitions and restrictions provided for in paragraphs 2 to 5 of this Article, only oenological practices, processes and treatments, including the restrictions provided for in Article 120c and 120d of Regulation (EC) No 1234/2007 and in Articles 3, 5 to 9 and 11 to 14 of Regulation (EC) No 606/2009 and in their Annexes, used before 1 August 2010 are permitted.
2. The use of the following oenological practices, processes and treatments is prohibited:
   (a) partial concentration through cooling according to point (c) of Section B.1 of Annex XVa to Regulation (EC) No 1234/2007;
   (b) elimination of sulphur dioxide by physical processes according to point 8 of Annex I A to Regulation (EC) No 606/2009;
   (c) electrodialysis treatment to ensure the tartaric stabilisation of the wine according to point 36 of Annex I A to Regulation (EC) No 606/2009;
   (d) partial dealcoholisation of wine according to point 40 of Annex I A to Regulation (EC) No 606/2009;
   (e) treatment with cation exchangers to ensure the tartaric stabilisation of the wine according to point 43 of Annex I A to Regulation (EC) No 606/2009.
3. The use of the following oenological practices, processes and treatments is permitted under the following conditions:
   (a) for heat treatments according to point 2 of Annex I A to Regulation (EC) No 606/2009, the temperature shall not exceed 70°C;
   (b) for centrifuging and filtration with or without an inert filtering agent according to point 3 of Annex I A to Regulation (EC) No 606/2009, the size of the pores shall be not smaller than 0,2 micrometer.
4. The use of the following oenological practices, processes and treatments shall be re-examined by the Commission before [1 August 2018] with a view to phase out or to further restrict those practices:
   (a) heat treatments as referred to in point 2 of Annex I A to Regulation (EC) No 606/2009;
   (b) use of ion exchange resins as referred to in point 20 of Annex I A to Regulation (EC) No 606/2009;
   (c) reverse osmosis according to point (b) of Section B.1 of Annex XVa to Regulation (EC) No 1234/2007.
5. Any amendment introduced after 1 August 2010, as regards the oenological practice, processes and treatments provided for in Regulation (EC) No 1234/2007 or Regulation (EC) No 606/2009, may be applicable in the organic production of wine only after the adoption of the measures necessary for the implementation of the production rules provided for in Article 19(3) of Regulation (EC) No 834/2007 and, if required, an evaluation process according to Article 21 of that Regulation.]

NOTES

Inserted as noted to Art 29b at **[8.309]**.

Words in square brackets substituted by Commission Implementing Regulation 2016/673/EU, Art 1(4).

CHAPTER 4
COLLECTION, PACKAGING, TRANSPORT AND STORAGE OF PRODUCTS

[8.312]
Article 30
Collection of products and transport to preparation units

Operators may carry out simultaneous collection of organic and non-organic products, only where appropriate measures are taken to prevent any possible mixture or exchange with non-organic products and to ensure the identification of the organic products. The operator shall keep the information relating to collection days, hours, circuit and date and time of reception of the products available to the control body or control authority.

[8.313]
Article 31
Packaging and transport of products to other operators or units

1. Operators shall ensure that organic products are transported to other units, including wholesalers and retailers, only in appropriate packaging, containers or vehicles closed in such a manner that substitution of the content cannot be achieved without manipulation or damage of the seal and provided with a label stating, without prejudice to any other indications required by law:
   (a) the name and address of the operator and, where different, of the owner or seller of the product;
   (b) the name of the product or a description of the compound feedingstuff accompanied by a reference to the organic production method;
   (c) the name and/or the code number of the control body or authority to which the operator is subject; and
   (d) where relevant, the lot identification mark according to a marking system either approved at national level or agreed with the control body or authority and which permits to link the lot with the accounts referred to in Article 66.

The information referred to in points (a) to (d) of the first subparagraph may also be presented on an accompanying document, if such a document can be undeniably linked with the packaging, container or vehicular transport of the product. This accompanying document shall include information on the supplier and/or the transporter.

2. The closing of packaging, containers or vehicles shall not be required where:
   (a) transportation is direct between an operator and another operator who are both subject to the organic control system, and
   (b) the products are accompanied by a document giving the information required under paragraph 1, and
   (c) both the expediting and the receiving operators shall keep documentary records of such transport operations available for the control body or control authority of such transport operations.

[8.314]
Article 32
Special rules for transporting feed to other production/preparation units or storage premises

In addition to the provisions of Article 31, when transporting feed to other production or preparation units or storage premises, operators shall ensure that the following conditions are met:
   (a) during transport, organically-produced feed, in-conversion feed, and non-organic feed shall be effectively physically separated;
   (b) the vehicles and/or containers which have transported non-organic products are used to transport organic products provided that:
      (i) suitable cleaning measures, the effectiveness of which has been checked, have been carried out before commencing the transport of organic products; operators shall record these operations,
      (ii) all appropriate measures are implemented, depending on the risks evaluated in accordance with Article 88 (3) and, where necessary, operators shall guarantee that non-organic products cannot be placed on the market with an indication referring to organic production,
      (iii) the operator shall keep documentary records of such transport operations available for the control body or control authority;
   (c) the transport of finished organic feed shall be separated physically or in time from the transport of other finished products;
   (d) during transport, the quantity of products at the start and each individual quantity delivered in the course of a delivery round shall be recorded.

[8.315]
[Article 32a
Transport of live fish

1. Live fish shall be transported in suitable tanks with clean water which meets their physiological needs in terms of temperature and dissolved oxygen.

2. Before transport of organic fish and fish products, tanks shall be thoroughly cleaned, disinfected and rinsed.
3. Precautions shall be taken to reduce stress. During transport, the density shall not reach a level which is detrimental to the species.
4. Documentary evidence shall be maintained for paragraphs 1 to 3.]

NOTES

Inserted by Commission Regulation 710/2009/EC, Art 1(7).

[8.316]
Article 33
Reception of products from other units and other operators

On receipt of an organic product, the operator shall check the closing of the packaging or container where it is required and the presence of the indications provided to in Article 31.
The operator shall crosscheck the information on the label referred to in Article 31 with the information on the accompanying documents. The result of these verifications shall be explicitly mentioned in the documentary accounts referred to in Article 66.

[8.317]
Article 34
Special rules for the reception of products from a third country

Organic products shall be imported from a third country in appropriate packaging or containers, closed in a manner preventing substitution of the content and provided with identification of the exporter and with any other marks and numbers serving to identify the lot and with the certificate of control for import from third countries as appropriate.
On receipt of an organic product, imported from a third country, the first consignee shall check the closing of the packaging or container and, in the case of products imported in accordance with Article 33 of Regulation (EC) No 834/2007, shall check that the certificate mentioned in that Article covers the type of product contained in the consignment. The result of this verification shall be explicitly mentioned in the documentary accounts referred to in Article 66 of this Regulation.

[8.318]
Article 35
Storage of products

1. For the storage of products, areas shall be managed in such a way as to ensure identification of lots and to avoid any mixing with or contamination by products and/or substances not in compliance with the organic production rules. Organic products shall be clearly identifiable at all times.
[2. In case of organic plant, seaweed, livestock and aquaculture animal production units, storage of input products other than those authorised under this Regulation is prohibited in the production unit.
3. The storage of allopathic veterinary medicinal products and antibiotics is permitted on holdings provided that they have been prescribed by a veterinarian in connection with treatment as referred to in Articles 14(1)(e)(ii) or 15(1)(f)(ii) of Regulation (EC) No 834/2007, that they are stored in a supervised location and that they are entered in the livestock record as referred to in Article 76 of this Regulation, or as appropriate, in the aquaculture production records as referred to in Article 79b of this Regulation.]
4. In case where operators handle both non-organic products and organic products and the latter are stored in storage facilities in which also other agricultural products or foodstuffs are stored:
- (a) the organic products shall be kept separate from the other agricultural products and/or foodstuffs;
- (b) every measure shall be taken to ensure identification of consignments and to avoid mixtures or exchanges with non-organic products;
- (c) suitable cleaning measures, the effectiveness of which has been checked, have been carried out before the storage of organic products; operators shall record these operations.

NOTES

Paras 2, 3: substituted by Commission Regulation 710/2009/EC, Art 1(8).

CHAPTER 5
CONVERSION RULES

[8.319]
Article 36
Plant and plant products

1. For plants and plant products to be considered organic, the production rules as referred to in Articles 9, 10, 11 and 12 of Regulation (EC) No 834/2007 and Chapter 1 of this Regulation and where applicable the exceptional production rules in Chapter 6 of this Regulation must have been

applied on the parcels during a conversion period of at least two years before sowing, or, in the case of grassland or perennial forage, at least two years before its use as feed from organic farming, or, in the case of perennial crops other than forage, at least three years before the first harvest of organic products.

2. The competent authority may decide to recognise retroactively as being part of the conversion period any previous period in which:

(a) the land parcels were subject of measures defined in a programme implemented pursuant to Regulations (EC) No 1257/99, (EC) No 1698/2005, or in another official programme, provided that the measures concerned ensure that products not authorised for organic production have not been used on those parcels, or

(b) the parcels were natural or agricultural areas which were not treated with products not authorised for organic production.

The period referred to in point (b) of the first subparagraph can be taken into consideration retroactively only where satisfactory proof has been furnished to the competent authority allowing it to satisfy itself that the conditions were met for a period of at least three years.

3. The competent authority may decide, in certain cases, where the land had been contaminated with products not authorised for organic production, to extend the conversion period beyond the period referred to in paragraph 1.

4. In the case of parcels which have already been converted to or were in the process of conversion to organic farming, and which are treated with a product not authorised for organic production, the Member State may shorten the conversion period referred to in paragraph 1 in the following two cases:

(a) parcels treated with a product not authorised for organic production as part of a compulsory disease or pest control measure imposed by the competent authority of the Member State;

(b) parcels treated with a product not authorised for organic production as part of scientific tests approved by the competent authority of the Member State.

In the cases provided for in points (a) and (b) of the first subparagraph, the length of the conversion period shall be fixed taking into account of the following factors:

(a) the process of degradation of the product concerned shall guarantee, at the end of the conversion period, an insignificant level of residues in the soil and, in the case of a perennial crop, in the plant;

(b) the harvest following the treatment may not be sold with reference to organic production methods.

The Member State concerned shall inform the other Member States and the Commission of its decision to require compulsory measures.

[8.320]
[Article 36a
Seaweed

1. The conversion period for a seaweed harvesting site shall be six months.

2. The conversion period for a seaweed cultivation unit shall be the longer of six months or one full production cycle.]

NOTES

Inserted by Commission Regulation 710/2009/EC, Art 1(9).

[8.321]
Article 37
Specific conversion rules for land associated with organic livestock production

1. The conversion rules as referred to in Article 36 of this Regulation shall apply to the whole area of the production unit on which animal feed is produced.

2. Notwithstanding the provisions in paragraph 1, the conversion period may be reduced to one year for pasturages and open air areas used by non-herbivore species. This period may be reduced to six months where the land concerned has not during the last year, received treatments with products not authorised for organic production.

[8.322]
Article 38
Livestock and livestock products

1. Where non-organic livestock has been brought onto a holding in accordance with Article 14(1)(a)(ii) of Regulation (EC) No 834/2007 and Article 9 and/or Article 42 of this Regulation and if livestock products are to be sold as organic products, the production rules as referred to in Articles 9, 10, 11 and 14 of Regulation (EC) No 834/2007 and in Chapter 2 of Title II and where applicable in Article 42 of this Regulation must have been applied for at least:

(a) 12 months in the case of equidae and bovines, including *bubalus* and bison species, for meat production, and in any case at least three quarters of their lifetime;

(b) six months in the case of small ruminants and pigs and animals for milk production;

(c) 10 weeks for poultry for meat production, brought in before they are three days old;

(d) six weeks in the case of poultry for egg production.

2. Where non-organic animals exist on a holding at the beginning of the conversion period in accordance with Article 14(1)(a)(iii) of Regulation (EC) No 834/2007 their products may be deemed organic if there is simultaneous conversion of the complete production unit, including livestock, pasturage and/or any land used for animal feed. The total combined conversion period for both existing animals and their offspring, pasturage and/or any land used for animal feed, may be reduced to 24 months, if the animals are mainly fed with products from the production unit.
3. Beekeeping products can be sold with references to the organic production method only when the organic production rules have been complied with for at least one year.
4. The conversion period for apiaries does not apply in the case of application of Article 9(5) of this Regulation.
5. During the conversion period the wax shall be replaced with wax coming from organic beekeeping.

[8.323]
[Article 38a
Aquaculture animal production
1. The following conversion periods for aquaculture production units shall apply for the following types of aquaculture facilities including the existing aquaculture animals:
- (a) for facilities that cannot be drained, cleaned and disinfected, a conversion period of 24 months;
- (b) for facilities that have been drained, or fallowed, a conversion period of 12 months;
- (c) for facilities that have been drained, cleaned and disinfected a conversion period of six months;
- (d) for open water facilities including those farming bivalve molluscs, a three month conversion period.

2. The competent authority may decide to recognize retroactively as being part of the conversion period any previously documented period in which the facilities were not treated or exposed to products not authorized for organic production.]

NOTES
Inserted by Commission Regulation 710/2009/EC, Art 1(10).

CHAPTER 6
EXCEPTIONAL PRODUCTION RULES

SECTION 1
EXCEPTIONAL PRODUCTION RULES RELATED TO CLIMATIC, GEOGRAPHICAL OR STRUCTURAL CONSTRAINTS IN ACCORDANCE WITH ARTICLE 22(2)(A) OF REGULATION (EC) NO 834/2007

[8.324]
Article 39
Tethering of animals
Where the conditions laid down in Article 22(2)(a) of Regulation (EC) No 834/2007 apply, competent authorities may authorise cattle in small holdings to be tethered if it is not possible to keep the cattle in groups appropriate to their behaviour requirements, provided they have access to pastures during the grazing period according to Article 14(2), and at least twice a week access to open air areas when grazing is not possible.

[8.325]
Article 40
Parallel production
1. Where the conditions laid down in Article 22(2)(a) of Regulation (EC) No 834/2007 apply, a producer may run organic and non-organic production units in the same area:
- (a) in the case of the production of perennial crops, which require a cultivation period of at least three years, where varieties cannot be easily differentiated, provided the following conditions are met:
  - (i) the production in question forms part of a conversion plan in respect of which the producer gives a firm undertaking and which provides for the beginning of the conversion of the last part of the area concerned to organic production in the shortest possible period which may not in any event exceed a maximum of five years;
  - (ii) appropriate measures have been taken to ensure the permanent separation of the products obtained from each unit concerned;
  - (iii) the control authority or control body is notified of the harvest of each of the products concerned at least 48 hours in advance;
  - (iv) upon completion of the harvest, the producer informs the control authority or control body of the exact quantities harvested on the units concerned and of the measures applied to separate the products;

(v) the conversion plan and the control measures referred to in Chapter 1 and 2 of Title IV have been approved by the competent authority; this approval shall be confirmed each year after the start of the conversion plan;

(b) in the case of areas intended for agricultural research or formal education agreed by the Member States' competent authorities and provided the conditions set out in point (a)(ii)(iii)(iv) and the relevant part of point (v) are met;

(c) in the case of production of seed, vegetative propagating material and transplants and provided the conditions set out in point (a)(ii)(iii)(iv) and the relevant part of point (v) are met;

(d) in the case of grassland exclusively used for grazing.

2. The competent authority may authorise holdings carrying out agricultural research or formal education to rear organic and non-organic livestock of the same species, where the following conditions are met:

(a) appropriate measures, notified in advance to the control authority or control body, have been taken in order to guarantee the permanent separation between livestock, livestock products, manure and feedingstuffs of each of the units;

(b) the producer informs the control authority or control body in advance of any delivery or selling of the livestock or livestock products;

(c) the operator informs the control authority or control body of the exact quantities produced in the units together with all characteristics permitting the identification of the products and confirms that the measures taken to separate the products have been applied.

[8.326]
Article 41
Management of beekeeping units for the purpose of pollination

Where the conditions laid down in Article 22(2)(a) of Regulation (EC) No 834/2007 apply, for the purpose of pollination actions an operator may run organic and non-organic beekeeping units on the same holding, provided that all the requirements of the organic production rules are fulfilled, with the exception of the provisions for the siting of the apiaries. In that case the product cannot be sold as organic.

The operator shall keep documentary evidence of the use of this provision.

SECTION 2
EXCEPTIONAL PRODUCTION RULES RELATED TO NON-AVAILABILITY OF ORGANIC FARM INPUTS IN ACCORDANCE WITH ARTICLE 22(2)(B) OF REGULATION (EC) NO 834/2007

[8.327]
Article 42
Use of non-organic animals

Where the conditions laid down in Article 22(2)(b) of Regulation (EC) No 834/2007 apply, and with prior authorisation of the competent authority,

(a) when a flock is constituted for the first time, renewed or reconstituted and organically reared poultry are not available in sufficient numbers, non-organically reared poultry may be brought into an organic poultry production unit, provided that the pullets for the production of eggs and poultry for meat production are less than three days old;

(b) non-organically reared pullets for egg production of not more than 18 weeks may be brought into an organic livestock unit until [31 December 2017], when organically reared pullets are not available and provided that the relevant provisions laid down in Section 3 and 4 of Chapter 2 are complied with.

NOTES

Words in square brackets in para (b) substituted by Commission Regulation 836/2014/EU, Art 1(1).

[8.328]
[Article 43
Use of non-organic protein feed of plant and animal origin for livestock

Where the conditions laid down in Article 22(2)(b) of Regulation (EC) No 834/2007 apply and where farmers are unable to obtain protein feed exclusively from organic production, the use of a limited proportion of non-organic protein feed is allowed for porcine and poultry species.

[The maximum percentage of non-organic protein feed authorised per period of 12 months for those species shall be 5% for calendar years 2015, 2016 and 2017.]

The figures shall be calculated annually as a percentage of the dry matter of feed from agricultural origin.

The operator shall keep documentary evidence of the need for the use of this provision.]

NOTES

Substituted by Commission Regulation 505/2012/EU, Art 1(7).
Words in square brackets substituted by Commission Regulation 836/2014/EU, Art 1(2).

[8.329]

Article 44

Use of non-organic beeswax

In the case of new installations or during the conversion period, non-organic beeswax may be used only

(a) where beeswax from organic beekeeping is not available on the market;

(b) where it is proven free of contamination by substances not authorised for organic production; and

(c) provided that it comes from the cap.

[8.330]

Article 45

Use of seed or vegetative propagating material not obtained by the organic production method

1. Where the conditions laid down in Article 22(2)(b) of Regulation (EC) No 834/2007 apply,

(a) seed and vegetative propagating material from a production unit in conversion to organic farming may be used,

(b) where point (a) is not applicable, Member States may authorise the use of non-organic seed or vegetative propagating material if not available from organic production. However, for the use of non-organic seed and seed potatoes the following paragraphs (2) to (9) apply.

2. Non-organic seed and seed potatoes may be used, provided that the seed or seed potatoes are not treated with plant protection products, other than those authorised for treatment of seed in accordance with Article 5(1), unless chemical treatment is prescribed in accordance with Council Directive 2000/29/EC[1] for phytosanitary purposes by the competent authority of the Member State for all varieties of a given species in the area where the seed or seed potatoes are to be used.

3. Species for which it is established that organically produced seed or seed potatoes are available in sufficient quantities and for a significant number of varieties in all parts of the Community are set out in Annex X.

The species listed in Annex X may not be subject of authorisations pursuant to paragraph 1(b), unless these are justified by one of the purposes referred to in paragraph 5(d).

4. Member States may delegate the responsibility for granting the authorisation referred to in paragraph 1(b) to another public administration under their supervision or to the control authorities or control bodies referred to in Article 27 of Regulation (EC) No 834/2007.

5. Authorisation to use seed or seed potatoes not obtained by the organic production method may only be granted in the following cases:

(a) where no variety of the species which the user wants to obtain is registered in the database referred to in Article 48;

(b) where no supplier, meaning an operator who markets seed or seed potatoes to other operators, is able to deliver the seed or seed potatoes before sowing or planting in situations where the user has ordered the seed or seed potatoes in reasonable time;

(c) where the variety which the user wants to obtain is not registered in the database referred to in Article 48, and the user is able to demonstrate that none of the registered alternatives of the same species are appropriate and that the authorisation therefore is significant for his production;

(d) where it is justified for use in research, test in small-scale field trials or for variety conservation purposes agreed by the competent authority of the Member State.

6. The authorisation shall be granted before the sowing of the crop.

7. The authorisation shall be granted only to individual users for one season at a time and the authority or body responsible for the authorisations shall register the quantities of seed or seed potatoes authorised.

8. By way of derogation from paragraph 7, the competent authority of the Member State may grant to all users a general authorisation:

(a) for a given species when and in so far as the condition laid down in paragraph 5(a) is fulfilled;

(b) for a given variety when and in so far as the conditions laid down in paragraph 5(c) are fulfilled.

The authorisations referred to in the first subparagraph shall be clearly indicated in the database referred to in Article 48.

9. Authorisation may only be granted during periods for which the database is updated in accordance with Article 49(3).

NOTES

[1] OJ L169, 10.7.2000, p 1.

SECTION 3
EXCEPTIONAL PRODUCTION RULES RELATED TO SPECIFIC MANAGEMENT PROBLEMS INORGANIC LIVESTOCK IN ACCORDANCE WITH ARTICLE 22(2)(D) OF REGULATION (EC) NO 834/2007

[8.331]
Article 46
Specific management problems in organic livestock
The final fattening phase of adult bovines for meat production may take place indoors, provided that this indoors period does not exceed one fifth of their lifetime and in any case for a maximum period of three months.

[SECTION 3A
EXCEPTIONAL PRODUCTION RULES WITH REGARD TO THE USE OF SPECIFIC PRODUCTS AND SUBSTANCES IN THE PROCESSING IN ACCORDANCE WITH ARTICLE 22(2)(E) OF REGULATION (EC) NO 834/2007

[8.332]
Article 46a
Addition of non-organic yeast extract
Where the conditions laid down in Article 22(2)(e) of Regulation (EC) No 834/2007 apply, the addition of up to 5% non-organic yeast extract or autolysate to the substrate (calculated in dry matter) is allowed for the production of organic yeast, where operators are unable to obtain yeast extract or autolysate from organic production.

The availability of organic yeast extract or autolysate shall be re-examined by 31 December 2013 with a view to withdrawing this provision.]

NOTES
Inserted, together with preceding cross-heading, by Commission Regulation 1254/2008/EC, Art 5.

SECTION 4
EXCEPTIONAL PRODUCTION RULES RELATED TO CATASTROPHIC CIRCUMSTANCES IN ACCORDANCE WITH ARTICLE 22(2)(F) OF REGULATION (EC) NO 834/2007

[8.333]
Article 47
Catastrophic circumstances
The competent authority may authorise on a temporary basis:

[(a) in the case of high mortality of animals caused by health or catastrophic circumstances, the renewal or reconstitution of the herd or flock with non-organic animals, when organically reared animals are not available and provided that the respective conversion period are applied to the non-organic animals;]

(b) in case of high mortality of bees caused by health or catastrophic circumstances, the reconstitution of the apiaries with non-organic bees, when organic apiaries are not available;

(c) the use of non-organic feedingstuffs for a limited period and in relation to a specific area by individual operators, when forage production is lost or when restrictions are imposed, in particular as a result of exceptional meteorological conditions, the outbreak of infectious diseases, the contamination with toxic substances, or as a consequence of fires;

(d) the feeding of bees with organic honey, organic sugar or organic sugar syrup in case of long lasting exceptional weather conditions or catastrophic circumstances, which hamper the nectar or honeydew production.

[(e) the use of sulphur dioxide up to the maximum content to be fixed in accordance with the Annex I B to Regulation (EC) No 606/2009 if the exceptional climatic conditions of a given harvest year deteriorate the sanitary status of organic grapes in a specific geographical area because of severe bacterial attacks or fungal attacks, which oblige the winemaker to use more sulphur dioxide than in previous years to obtain a comparable final product];

[(f) in the case of high mortality of aquaculture animals caused by circumstances listed in Article 57(1)(a) to (d) of Regulation (EU) No 508/2014 of the European Parliament and of the Council,[1] the renewal or reconstitution of the aquaculture stock with non-organic aquaculture animals, when organically reared animals are not available and provided that at least the latter two thirds of the duration of the production cycle are managed under organic management.]

[Upon approval by the competent authority, the individual operators shall keep documentary evidence of the use of the above exceptions. Member States shall inform each other and the Commission on the exceptions they have granted under points (c) and (e) of the first paragraph.]

NOTES
Para (a) substituted and para (f) inserted by Commission Implementing Regulation 2016/673/EU, Art 1(5); para (e) inserted and words in final pair of square brackets substituted by Commission Regulation 203/2012/EU, Art 1(1)(c).

1 Regulation (EU) No 508/2014 of the European Parliament and of the Council of 15 May 2014 on the European Maritime and Fisheries Fund and repealing Council Regulations (EC) No 2328/2003, (EC) No 861/2006, (EC) No 1198/2006 and (EC) No 791/2007 and Regulation (EU) No 1255/2011 of the European Parliament and of the Council (OJ L149, 20.5.2014, p 1).]

CHAPTER 7
SEED DATA BASE

[8.334]
Article 48
Database

1. Each Member State shall ensure that a computerised database is established for the listing of the varieties for which seed or seed potatoes obtained by the organic production method are available on its territory.
2. The database shall be managed either by the competent authority of the Member State or by an authority or body designated for this purpose by the Member State, hereinafter referred to as 'manager of the database'. Member States may also designate an authority or a private body in another country.
3. Each Member State shall inform the Commission and the other Member States of the authority or private body designated to manage the database.

[8.335]
Article 49
Registration

1. Varieties for which seed or seed potatoes produced by the organic production method are available shall be registered in the database referred to in Article 48 at the request of the supplier.
2. Any variety which has not been registered in the database shall be considered as unavailable with regard to Article 45(5).
3. Each Member State shall decide in which period of the year the database has to be regularly updated for each species or group of species cultivated on its territory. The database shall hold information with regard to that decision.

[8.336]
Article 50
Conditions for registration

1. For registration, the supplier shall:
 (a) demonstrate that he or the last operator, in cases where the supplier is only dealing with pre-packaged seed or seed potatoes, has been subject to the control system referred to in Article 27 of Regulation (EC) No 834/2007;
 (b) demonstrate that the seed or seed potatoes to be placed on the market comply with the general requirements applicable to seed and seed potatoes;
 (c) make available all the information required under Article 51 of this Regulation, and undertake to update this information at the request of the manager of the database or whenever such updating is necessary to ensure that the information remains reliable.
2. The manager of the database may, with the approval by the competent authority of the Member State, refuse a supplier's application for registration or delete a previously accepted registration if the supplier does not comply with the requirements set out in paragraph 1.

[8.337]
Article 51
Registered information

1. For each registered variety and for each supplier, the database referred to in Article 48 shall contain at least the following information:
 (a) the scientific name of the species and the variety denomination;
 (b) the name and contact details of the supplier or his representative;
 (c) the area where the supplier can deliver the seed or seed potatoes to the user in the usual time needed for the delivery;
 (d) the country or region in which the variety is tested and approved for the purpose of the common catalogues of varieties of agricultural plant species and vegetable species as defined in Council Directives 2002/53/EC on the common catalogue of varieties of agricultural plant species[1] and 2002/55/EC on the marketing of vegetable seed;[2]
 (e) the date from which the seed or seed potatoes will be available;
 (f) the name and/or code number of the control authority or control body in charge of the control of the operator as referred to in Article 27 of Regulation (EC) No 834/2007.
2. The supplier shall immediately inform the manager of the database if any of the registered varieties are no longer available. The amendments shall be recorded in the database.
3. Besides the information specified in paragraph 1, the database shall contain a list of the species listed in Annex X.

NOTES

[1] OJ L193, 20.7.2002, p 1.

[2] OJ L193, 20.7.2002, p 33.

[8.338]
Article 52
Access to information

1. The information in the database referred to in Article 48 shall be available through the Internet, free of cost, to the users of seed or seed potatoes and to the public. Member States may decide that any user who has notified its activity in accordance with Article 28(1)(a) of Regulation (EC) No 834/2007 may obtain, on request, an extract of data concerning one or several groups of species from the database manager.

2. The Member States shall ensure that all users referred to in paragraph 1 are informed, at least once a year, about the system and how to obtain the information in the database.

[8.339]
Article 53
Registration fee

Each registration may be subject to the levying of a fee, which shall represent the cost of inserting and maintaining the information in the database referred to in Article 48. The competent authority of the Member State shall approve the amount of the fee charged by the manager of the database.

[8.340]
Article 54
Annual report

1. The authorities or bodies designated to grant authorisations in accordance with Article 45 shall register all authorisations, and shall make this information available in a report to the competent authority of the Member State and to the manager of the database.

The report shall contain, for each species concerned by an authorisation according to Article 45(5), the following information:

(a) the scientific name of the species and the variety denomination;
(b) the justification for the authorisation indicated by a reference to Article 45(5)(a), (b), (c) or (d);
(c) the total number of authorisations;
(d) the total quantity of seed or seed potatoes involved;
(e) the chemical treatment for phytosanitary purposes, as referred to in Article 45(2).

2. For authorisations according to Article 45(8) the report shall contain the information referred to in point (a) of the second subparagraph of paragraph 1 of this Article and the period for which the authorisations were in force.

[8.341]
Article 55
Summary report

The competent authority of the Member State shall, before 31 March each year, collect the reports and send a summary report covering all authorisations of the Member State from the previous calendar year to the Commission and to the other Member States. The report shall cover the information specified in Article 54. The information shall be published in the database referred to in Article 48. The competent authority may delegate the task of collecting the reports to the manager of the database.

[8.342]
Article 56
Information upon request

Upon request from a Member State or the Commission, detailed information on authorisations granted in individual cases shall be made available to other Member States or to the Commission.

TITLE III
LABELLING

CHAPTER 1
[ORGANIC PRODUCTION LOGO OF THE EUROPEAN UNION]

[8.343]
[Article 57
Organic logo of the EU

In accordance with Article 25(3) of Regulation (EC) No 834/2007, the organic production logo of the European Union (hereinafter "Organic logo of the EU") shall follow the model set out in Part A of Annex XI to this Regulation.

[For the purpose of labelling, the organic logo of the EU shall only be used if the product concerned is produced in accordance with the requirements of Regulation (EC) No 834/2007, of Commission Regulation (EC) No 1235/2008[1] and of this Regulation, by operators who comply with the requirements of the control system referred to in Articles 27, 28, 29, 32 and 33 of Regulation (EC) No 834/2007.]]

NOTES

Chapter heading: substituted by Commission Regulation 271/2010/EU, Art 1(1).

Art 57 substituted by Commission Regulation 271/2010/EU, Art 1(1); words in square brackets substituted by Commission Regulation 344/2011/EU, Art 1(1).

[1] OJ 334, 12.12.2008, p 25.

[8.344]
Article 58
Conditions for the use of the code number and place of origin

1. The indication of the code number of the control authority or control body referred to in Article 24(1)(a) of Regulation (EC) 834/2007 shall,

(a) start with the acronym identifying the Member State or the third country, as referred to in the international standard for the two letter country codes under ISO 3166 (*Codes for the representation of names of countries and their subdivisions*);

[(b) include a term which establishes a link with the organic production method, as referred to in Article 23(1) of Regulation (EC) No 834/2007 in accordance with Part B(2) of Annex XI to this Regulation;

(c) include a reference number to be decided by the Commission or by the competent authority of the Member States in accordance with Part B(3) of Annex XI to this Regulation; and

(d) be placed in the same visual field as the Organic logo of the EU, where the Organic logo of the EU is used in the labelling.]

2. The indication of the place where the agricultural raw materials of which the products is composed have been farmed, as referred to in Article 24(1)(c) of Regulation (EC) 834/2007, shall be placed immediately below the code number referred to in paragraph 1.

NOTES

Para 1: sub-paras (b)–(d) substituted by Commission Regulation 271/2010/EU, Art 1(3).

CHAPTER 2
SPECIFIC LABELLING REQUIREMENTS FOR FEED

[8.345]
[Article 59
Scope, use of trade marks and sales descriptions

This Chapter shall not apply to pet food and feed for fur animals.

The trade marks and sales descriptions bearing an indication referred to in Article 23(1) of Regulation (EC) No 834/2007 may be used only if all ingredients of plant or animal origin are from the organic production method and at least 95% of the product's dry matter is comprised of such ingredients.]

NOTES

Substituted, together with Art 60, by Commission Regulation 505/2012/EU, Art 1(8).

[8.346]
[Article 60
Indications on processed feed

1. The terms referred to in Article 23(1) of Regulation (EC) No 834/2007 and the Organic logo of the EU may be used on processed feed provided that all the following requirements are complied with:

(a) the processed feed complies with the provisions of Regulation (EC) No 834/2007 and in particular with Article 14(1)(d)(iv) and (v) for livestock or with Article 15(1)(d) for aquaculture animals and Article 18 thereof;

(b) the processed feed complies with the provisions of this Regulation and in particular with Articles 22 and 26 thereof;

(c) all ingredients of plant or animal origin contained in the processed feed are from the organic production method;

(d) at least 95% of the product's dry matter is comprised of organic agricultural products.

2. Subject to the requirements laid down in points (a) and (b) of paragraph 1, the following statement is permitted in the case of products comprising variable quantities of feed materials from the organic production method and/or feed materials from products in conversion to organic farming and/or products as referred to in Article 22 of this Regulation:

"may be used in organic production in accordance with Regulations (EC) No 834/2007 and (EC) No 889/2008".]

NOTES

Substituted as noted to Art 59 at **[8.345]**.

[8.347]
Article 61
Conditions for the use of indications on processed feed

1. The indication provided for in Article 60 shall be:
   (a) separate from the wording referred to in Article 5 of Council Directive 79/373/EEC[1] or in Article 5(1) of Council Directive 96/25/EC;[2]
   (b) presented in a colour, format or character font that does not draw more attention to it than to the description or name of the animal feedingstuff referred to in Article 5(1)(a) of Directive 79/373/EEC or in Article 5(1)(b) of Directive 96/ 25/EC respectively;
   (c) accompanied, in the same field of vision, by an indication by weight of dry matter referring:
      (i) to the percentage of feed material(s) from the organic production method;
      (ii) to the percentage of feed material(s) from products in conversion to organic farming;
      (iii) to the percentage of feed material(s) not covered by points (i) and (ii);
      (iv) to the total percentage of animal feed of agricultural origin;
   (d) accompanied by a list of names of feed materials from the organic production method;
   (e) accompanied by a list of names of feed materials from products in conversion to organic production.

2. The indication provided for in Article 60 may be also accompanied by a reference to the requirement to use the feedingstuffs in accordance with Articles 21 and 22.

NOTES

1 OJ L86, 6.4.1979, p 30.

2 OJ L125, 23.5.1996, p 35.

CHAPTER 3
OTHER SPECIFIC LABELLING REQUIREMENTS

[8.348]
Article 62
In-conversion products of plant origin

In-conversion products of plant origin may bear the indication 'product under conversion to organic farming' provided that:
   (a) a conversion period of at least 12 months before the harvest has been complied with;
   (b) the indication shall appear in a colour, size and style of lettering which is not more prominent than the sales description of the product, the entire indication shall have the same size of letters;
   (c) the product contains only one crop ingredient of agricultural origin;
   (d) the indication is linked to the code number of the control body or control authority as referred to in Article 27(10) of Regulation 834/2007.

TITLE IV
CONTROLS

CHAPTER 1
MINIMUM CONTROL REQUIREMENTS

[8.349]
Article 63
Control arrangements and undertaking by the operator

1. When the control arrangements are first implemented, the operator shall draw up and subsequently maintain:
   (a) a full description of the unit and/or premises and/or activity;
   (b) all the practical measures to be taken at the level of the unit and/or premises and/or activity to ensure compliance with the organic production rules;
   (c) the precautionary measures to be taken in order to reduce the risk of contamination by unauthorised products or substances and the cleaning measures to be taken in storage places and throughout the operator's production chain.
   [(d) the specific characteristics of the production method used, where the operator intends to request documentary evidence in accordance with Article 68(2).]

Where appropriate, the description and measures provided for in the first subparagraph may be part of a quality system as set up by the operator.

2. The description and the measures referred to in paragraph 1 shall be contained in a declaration, signed by the responsible operator. In addition, this declaration shall include an undertaking by the operator:

(a) to perform the operations in accordance with the organic production rules;
(b) to accept, in the event of infringement or irregularities, the enforcement of the measures of the organic production rules;
(c) to undertake to inform in writing the buyers of the product in order to ensure that the indications referring to the organic production method are removed from this production.
[(d) to accept, in cases where the operator and/or the subcontractors of that operator are checked by different control authorities or control bodies in accordance with the control system set up by Member State concerned, the exchange of information between those authorities or bodies;
(e) to accept, in cases where the operator and/or the subcontractors of that operator change their control authority or control body, the transmission of their control files to the subsequent control authority or control body;
(f) to accept, in cases where the operator withdraws from the control system, to inform without delay the relevant competent authority and control authority or control body;
(g) to accept, in cases where the operator withdraws from the control system, that the control file is kept for a period of at least five years;
(h) to accept to inform the relevant control authority or authorities or control body or bodies without delay of any irregularity or infringement affecting the organic status of their product or organic products received from other operators or subcontractors.]

The declaration provided for in the first subparagraph shall be verified by the control body or control authority that issues a report identifying the possible deficiencies and non-compliances with the organic production rules. The operator shall countersign this report and take the necessary corrective measures.

3. For the application of Article 28(1) of Regulation (EC) No 834/2007 the operator shall notify the following information to the competent authority:
(a) Name and address of operator;
(b) Location of premises and, where appropriate, parcels (land register data) where operations are carried out;
(c) Nature of operations and products;
(d) Undertaking by the operator to carry out the operation in accordance with the provision laid down in Regulation (EC) No 834/2007 and this Regulation;
(e) In the case of an agricultural holding, the date on which the producer ceased to apply products not authorised for organic production on the parcels concerned;
(f) The name of the approved body to which the operator entrusted control of his undertaking, where the Member State has implemented the control system by approving such bodies.

NOTES

Para 1: sub-para (d) added by Commission Regulation 126/2012/EU, Art 1(1).

Para 2: sub-paras (d)–(h) added by Commission Regulation 392/2013/EU, Art 1(2), as from 1 January 2014, subject to Art 2 thereof, which provides that sub-paras (d)–(h) shall also apply to operators who signed the declaration referred to in para 2 before that date.

[8.350]
Article 64
Modification of control arrangements

The operator responsible shall notify any change in the description or of the measures referred to in Article 63 and in the initial control arrangements set out in Articles 70, 74, 80, 82, 86 and 88 to the control authority or control body in due time.

[8.351]
Article 65
Control visits

1. The control authority or control body shall carry out at least once a year a physical inspection of all operators.

[2. The control authority or control body shall take and analyse samples for detecting of products not authorised for organic production, for checking production techniques not in conformity with the organic production rules or for detecting possible contamination by products not authorised for organic production. The number of samples to be taken and analysed by the control authority or control body every year shall correspond to at least 5% of the number of operators under its control. The selection of the operators where samples have to be taken shall be based on the general evaluation of the risk of non-compliance with the organic production rules. This general evaluation shall take into account all stages of production, preparation and distribution.

The control authority or control body shall take and analyse samples in each case where the use of products or techniques not authorised for organic production is suspected. In such cases no minimum number of samples to be taken and analysed shall apply.

Samples may also be taken and analysed by the control authority or control body in any other case for detecting of products not authorised for organic production, for checking production techniques not in conformity with the organic production rules or for detecting possible contamination by products not authorised for organic production.]

3. A control report shall be drawn up after each visit, countersigned by the operator of the unit or his representative.
4. Moreover, the control authority or control body shall carry out random control visits, primarily unannounced, based on the general evaluation of the risk of non-compliance with the organic production rules, taking into account at least the results of previous controls, the quantity of products concerned and the risk for exchange of products.

NOTES

Para 2: substituted by Commission Regulation 392/2013/EU, Art 1(3).

[8.352]
Article 66
Documentary accounts

1. Stock and financial records shall be kept in the unit or premises and shall enable the operator to identify and the control authority or control body to verify:
   (a) the supplier and, where different, the seller, or the exporter of the products;
   (b) the nature and the quantities of organic products delivered to the unit and, where relevant, of all materials bought and the use of such materials, and, where relevant, the composition of the compound feedingstuffs;
   (c) the nature and the quantities of organic products held in storage at the premises;
   (d) the nature, the quantities and the consignees and, where different, the buyers, other than the final consumers, of any products which have left the unit or the first consignee's premises or storage facilities;
   (e) in case of operators who do not store or physically handle such organic products, the nature and the quantities of organic products bought and sold, and the suppliers, and where different, the sellers or the exporters and the buyers, and where different, the consignees.
2. The documentary accounts shall also comprise the results of the verification at reception of organic products and any other information required by the control authority or control body for the purpose of proper control. The data in the accounts shall be documented with appropriate justification documents. The accounts shall demonstrate the balance between the input and the output.
3. Where an operator runs several production units in the same area, the units for non organic products, together with storage premises for input products must also be subject to the minimum control requirements.

[8.353]
Article 67
Access to facilities

1. The operator shall:
   (a) give the control authority or control body, for control purposes, access to all parts of the unit and all premises, as well as to the accounts and relevant supporting documents;
   (b) provide the control authority or control body with any information reasonably necessary for the purposes of the control;
   (c) submit, when requested by the control authority or control body, the results of its own quality assurance programmes.
2. In addition to the requirements set out in paragraph 1, importers and first consignees shall submit the information on imported consignments referred to in Article 84.

[8.354]
[Article 68
Documentary evidence

1. For the purpose of the application of Article 29(1) of Regulation (EC) No 834/2007 the control authorities and control bodies shall use the model of the documentary evidence set out in Annex XII to this Regulation.

[In case of electronic certification as referred to in Article 29(3) of Regulation (EC) No 834/2007, the signature in box 8 of the documentary evidence shall not be required if the authenticity of the documentary evidence is otherwise shown by a tamper-proof electronic method.]

2. If an operator subject to the controls of the control authorities and control bodies as referred to in paragraph 1 so requests within a time period to be indicated by those control authorities and control bodies, the control authorities and control bodies shall provide complementary documentary evidence confirming the specific characteristics of the production method used by means of the model set out in Annex XIIa.

Applications for complementary documentary evidence shall contain in box 2 of the model set out in Annex XIIa the relevant entry listed in Annex XIIb.]

NOTES

Substituted by Commission Regulation 126/2012/EU, Art 1(2).
Para 1: words in square brackets added by Commission Regulation 392/2013/EU, Art 1(4).

[8.355]
Article 69
Vendor declaration

For the purpose of the application of Article 9(3) of Regulation (EC) No 834/2007 the vendor declaration that products supplied have not been produced from or by GMOs may follow the model set out in Annex XIII to this Regulation.

CHAPTER 2
SPECIFIC CONTROL REQUIREMENTS FOR PLANTS AND PLANT PRODUCTS FROM FARM PRODUCTION OR COLLECTION

[8.356]
Article 70
Control arrangements

1. The full description of the unit referred to in Article 63(1)(a) shall:
   (a) be drawn up even where the operator limits his activity to the collection of wild plants;
   (b) indicate the storage and production premises and land parcels and/or collection areas and, where applicable, premises where certain processing and/or packaging operations take place; and
   (c) specify the date of the last application on the parcels and/or collection areas concerned of products, the use of which is not compatible with the organic production rules.

2. In case of collection of wild plants, the practical measures referred to in Article 63(1)(b) shall include any guarantees given by third parties which the operator can provide to ensure that the provisions of Article 12(2) of Regulation (EC) No 834/2007 are complied with.

[8.357]
Article 71
Communications

Each year, before the date indicated by the control authority or control body, the operator shall notify the control authority or control body of its schedule of production of crop products, giving a breakdown by parcel.

[8.358]
Article 72
Plant production records

Plant production records shall be compiled in the form of a register and kept available to the control authorities or bodies at all times at the premises of the holding. In addition to Article 71 such records shall provide at least the following information:
   (a) as regards the use of fertiliser: date of application, type and amount of fertiliser, parcels concerned;
   (b) as regards the use of plant protection products: reason and date of treatment, type of product, method of treatment;
   (c) as regards purchase of farm inputs: date, type and amount of purchased product;
   (d) as regards harvest: date, type and amount of organic or in conversion crop production.

[8.359]
Article 73
Several production units run by the same operator

Where an operator runs several production units in the same area, the units producing non-organic crops, together with storage premises for farm input products shall also be subject to the general and the specific control requirements laid down in Chapter 1 and this Chapter of this Title.

[CHAPTER 2A
SPECIFIC CONTROL REQUIREMENTS FOR SEAWEED

[8.360]
Article 73a
Control arrangements for seaweed

When the control system applying specifically to seaweed is first implemented, the full description of the site referred to in Article 63(1)(a) shall include:
   (a) a full description of the installations on land and at sea;
   (b) the environmental assessment as outlined in Article 6b(3) where applicable;
   (c) the sustainable management plan as outlined in Article 6b(4) where applicable;
   (d) for wild seaweed a full description and a map of shore and sea collection areas and land areas where post collection activities take place shall be drawn up.]

NOTES

Chapter 2a (Arts 73a, 73b) inserted by Commission Regulation 710/2009/EC, Art 1(14).

[8.361]
[Article 73b
Seaweed Production Records

1. Seaweed production records shall be compiled in the form of a register by the operator and kept available for the control authorities or control bodies at all times at the premises of the holding. It shall provide at least the following information:
   (a) list of species, date and quantity harvested;
   (b) date of application, type and amount of fertiliser used.
2. For collection of wild seaweeds the register shall also contain:
   (a) history of harvesting activity for each species in named beds;
   (b) harvest estimate (volumes) per season;
   (c) sources of possible pollution for harvest beds;
   (d) sustainable annual yield for each bed.]

NOTES

Inserted as noted to Art 73a at **[8.360]**.

CHAPTER 3
CONTROL REQUIREMENTS FOR LIVESTOCK AND LIVESTOCK PRODUCTS PRODUCED BY ANIMAL HUSBANDRY

[8.362]
Article 74
Control arrangements

1. When the control system applying specifically to livestock production is first implemented, the full description of the unit referred to in Article 63(1)(a) shall include:
   (a) a full description of the livestock buildings, pasturage, open air areas, etc., and, where applicable, the premises for the storage, packaging and processing of livestock, livestock products, raw materials and inputs;
   (b) a full description of the installations for the storage of livestock manure.
2. The practical measures referred to in Article 63(1)(b) shall include:
   (a) a plan for spreading manure agreed with the control body or authority, together with a full description of the areas given over to crop production;
   (b) where appropriate, as regards the spreading of manure, the written arrangements with other holdings as referred to in Article 3(3) complying with the provisions of the organic production rules;
   (c) a management plan for the organic-production livestock unit.

[8.363]
Article 75
Identification of livestock

The livestock shall be identified permanently using techniques adapted to each species, individually in the case of large mammals and individually or by batch in the case of poultry and small mammals.

[8.364]
Article 76
Livestock records

Livestock records shall be compiled in the form of a register and kept available to the control authorities or bodies at all times at the premises of the holding. Such records shall provide a full description of the herd or flock management system comprising at least the following information:
   (a) as regards animals arriving at the holding: origin and date of arrival, conversion period, identification mark and veterinary record;
   (b) as regards livestock leaving the holding: age, number of heads, weight in case of slaughter, identification mark and destination;
   (c) details of any animals lost and reasons thereof;
   (d) as regards feed: type, including feed supplements, proportions of various ingredients of rations and periods of access to free-range areas, periods of transhumance where restrictions apply;
   (e) as regards disease prevention and treatment and veterinary care: date of treatment, details of the diagnosis, the posology; type of treatment product, the indication of the active pharmacological substances involved method of treatment and veterinary prescription for veterinary care with reasons and withdrawal periods applying before livestock products can be marketed labelled as organic.

[8.365]
Article 77
Control measures on veterinary medicinal products for livestock
Whenever veterinary medicinal products are used the information according to Article 76(e) is to be declared to the control authority or body before the livestock or livestock products are marketed as organically produced. Livestock treated shall be clearly identified, individually in the case of large animals; individually, or by batch, or by hive, in the case of poultry, small animals and bees.

[8.366]
Article 78
Specific control measures on beekeeping
1. A map on an appropriate scale listing the location of hives shall be provided to the control authority or control body by the beekeeper. Where no areas are identified in accordance with Article 13(2), the beekeeper shall provide the control authority or control body with appropriate documentation and evidence, including suitable analyses if necessary, that the areas accessible to his colonies meet the conditions required in this Regulation.
2. The following information shall be entered in the register of the apiary with regard to the use of feeding: type of product, dates, quantities and hives where it is used.
3. Whenever veterinary medicinal products are to be used, the type of product, including the indication of the active pharmacological substance, together with details of the diagnosis, the posology, the method of administration, the duration of the treatment and the legal withdrawal period shall be recorded clearly and declared to the control body or authority before the products are marketed as organically produced.
4. The zone where the apiary is situated shall be registered together with the identification of the hives. The control body or authority shall be informed of the moving of apiaries by a deadline agreed on with the control authority or body.
5. Particular care shall be taken to ensure adequate extraction, processing and storage of beekeeping products. All the measures to comply with this requirement shall be recorded.
6. The removals of the supers and the honey extraction operations shall be entered in the register of the apiary.

[8.367]
Article 79
Several production units run by the same operator
Where an operator manages several production units, as provided for in Articles 17(1), 40 and 41, the units which produce non-organic livestock or non-organic livestock products shall also be subject to the control system as laid down in Chapter 1 and this Chapter of this Title.

[CHAPTER 3A
SPECIFIC CONTROL REQUIREMENTS FOR AQUACULTURE ANIMAL PRODUCTION

[8.368]
Article 79a
Control arrangements for aquaculture animal production
When the control system applying specifically to aquaculture animal production is first implemented, the full description of the unit referred to in Article 63(1)(a) shall include:
(a) a full description of the installations on land and at sea;
(b) the environmental assessment as outlined in Article 6b(3) where applicable;
(c) the sustainable management plan as outlined in Article 6b(4) where applicable;
(d) in the case of molluscs a summary of the special chapter of the sustainable management plan as required by Article 25q(2).]

NOTES
Chapter 3a (Arts 79a–79d) inserted by Commission Regulation 710/2009/EC, Art 1(15).

[8.369]
[Article 79b
Aquaculture animal production records
The following information shall be provided by the operator in the form of a register which shall be kept up to date and made available for the control authorities or control bodies at all times at the premises of the holding:
(a) the origin, date of arrival and conversion period of animals arriving at the holding;
(b) the number of lots, the age, weight and destination of animals leaving the holding;
(c) records of escapes of fish;
(d) for fish the type and quantity of feed and in the case of carp and related species a documentary record of the use additional feed;
(e) veterinary treatments giving details of the purpose, date of application, method of application, type of product and withdrawal period;
(f) disease prevention measures giving details of fallowing, cleaning and water treatment.]

NOTES

Inserted as noted to Art 79a at **[8.368]**.

[8.370]
[Article 79c
Specific control visits for bivalve molluscs

For bivalve mollusc production inspection visits shall take place before and during maximum biomass production.]

NOTES

Inserted as noted to Art 79a at**[8.368]**.

[8.371]
[Article 79d
Several production units run by the same operator

When an operator manages several production units as provided for in Articles 25c, the units which produce non-organic aquaculture animals shall also be subject to the control system as laid down in Chapter 1 and this Chapter.]

NOTES

Inserted as noted to Art 79a at **[8.368]**.

CHAPTER 4
[CONTROL REQUIREMENTS FOR UNITS FOR PREPARATION OF PLANT, SEAWEED, LIVESTOCK AND AQUACULTURE ANIMAL PRODUCTS AND FOODSTUFFS COMPOSED THEREOF]

[8.372]
Article 80
Control arrangements

In the case of a unit involved in the preparation for its own account or for account of a third party, and including in particular units involved in packaging and/or re-packaging of such products or units involved in labelling and/or re-labelling of such products, the full description of the unit referred to in Article 63(1)(a) shall show the facilities used for the reception, the processing, packaging, labelling and storage of agricultural products before and after the operations concerning them, as well as the procedures for the transport of the products.

NOTES

Chapter heading substituted by Commission Regulation 710/2009/EC, Art 1(16).

CHAPTER 5
[CONTROL REQUIREMENTS FOR IMPORTS OF ORGANIC PRODUCTS FROM THIRD COUNTRIES]

[8.373]
Article 81
Scope

This Chapter applies to any operator involved, as importer and/or as first consignee, in the import and/or reception, for its own account or for account of another operator, of organic products.

NOTES

Chapter heading substituted by Commission Regulation 710/2009/EC, Art 1(17).

[8.374]
Article 82
Control arrangements

1. In the case of the importer, the full description of the unit referred to in Article 63(1)(a) shall include the importer's premises and of his import activities, indicating the points of entry of the products into the Community and any other facilities the importer intends to use for the storage of the imported products pending their delivery to the first consignee.

In addition, the declaration referred to in Article 63(2) shall include an undertaking by the importer to ensure that any facilities that the importer will use for storage of products are submitted to control, to be carried out either by the control body or control authority or, when these storage facilities are situated in another Member State or region, by a control body or authority approved for control in that Member State or region.

2. In the case of the first consignee, the full description of the unit referred to in Article 63(1)(a) shall show the facilities used for the reception and storage.

3. Where the importer and the first consignee are the same legal person and operate in one single unit, the reports referred to in the second subparagraph of Article 63(2) may be formalised within one single report.

[8.375]
Article 83
Documentary accounts
The importer and the first consignee shall keep separate stock and financial records, unless where they are operating in one single unit.
On request of the control authority or control body, any details on the transport arrangements from the exporter in the third country to the first consignee and, from the first consignee's premises or storage facilities to the consignees within the Community shall be provided.

[8.376]
Article 84
Information on imported consignments
The importer shall, in due time, inform the control body or control authority of each consignment to be imported into the Community, providing:
(a) the name and address of the first consignee;
(b) any details the control body or authority may reasonably require,
(i) in case of products imported in accordance with Article 32 of Regulation (EC) No 834/2007, the documentary evidence referred to in that Article;
(ii) in case of products imported in accordance with Article 33 of Regulation (EC) No 834/2007, a copy of the certificate of inspection referred to in that Article.

On the request of the control body or control authority of the importer, the latter shall forward the information referred to in the first paragraph to the control body or control authority of the first consignee.
[The importer shall transmit the information referred to in the first and second paragraphs by using the electronic Trade Control and Expert System (TRACES) established by Commission Decision 2003/24/EC.[1]]

NOTES
Words in square brackets inserted by Commission Implementing Regulation 2016/1842/EU, Art 2(5).
[1] Commission Decision 2003/24/EC of 30 December 2002 concerning the development of an integrated computerised veterinary system (OJ L8, 14.1.2003, p 44)..

[8.377]
Article 85
Control visits
The control authority or control body shall check the documentary accounts referred to in Article 83 of this Regulation and the certificate referred to in Article 33(1)(d) of Regulation (EC) No 834/2007 or the documentary evidence referred to in Article 32(1)(c) of the latter Regulation.
Where the importer performs the import operations by different units or premises, he shall make available on request the reports referred to in the second subparagraph of Article 63(2) of this Regulation for each of these facilities.

CHAPTER 6
CONTROL REQUIREMENTS FOR UNITS INVOLVED IN THE PRODUCTION, PREPARATION OR IMPORT OF ORGANIC PRODUCTS AND WHICH HAVE CONTRACTED OUT TO THIRD PARTIES IN PART OR IN TOTAL THE ACTUAL OPERATIONS CONCERNED

[8.378]
Article 86
Control arrangements
With regard to the operations, which are contracted out to third parties, the full description of the unit referred to in Article 63(1)(a) shall include:
(a) a list of the subcontractors with a description of their activities and an indication of the control bodies or authorities to which they are subject;
(b) written agreement by the subcontractors that their holding will be subject to the control regime of Title V of Regulation (EC) No 834/2007;
(c) all the practical measures, including inter alia an appropriate system of documentary accounts, to be taken at the level of the unit to ensure that the products the operator places on the market can be traced to, as appropriate, their suppliers, sellers, consignees and buyers.

CHAPTER 7
CONTROL REQUIREMENTS FOR UNITS PREPARING FEED

[8.379]
Article 87
Scope

This Chapter applies to any unit involved in the preparation of products referred to in Article 1(2)(c) of Regulation (EC) No 834/2007 on its own account or on behalf of a third party.

[8.380]
Article 88
Control arrangements

1. The full description of the unit referred to in Article 63(1)(a) shall indicate:
   (a) the facilities used for the reception, preparation and storage of the products intended for animal feed before and after the operations concerning them;
   (b) the facilities used for the storage of other products used to prepare feedingstuffs;
   (c) the facilities used to store products for cleaning and disinfection;
   (d) where necessary, the description of the compound feedingstuff that the operator intends to produce, in accordance with Article 5(1)(a) of Directive 79/373/EEC, and the livestock species or class for which the compound feedingstuff is intended;
   (e) where necessary, the name of the feed materials that the operator intends to prepare.
2. The measures to be taken by operators, as referred to in Article 63(1)(b), to guarantee compliance with the organic production rules shall include the indications of measures referred to in Article 26.
3. The control authority or control body shall use these measures to carry out a general evaluation of the risks attendant on each preparation unit and to draw up a control plan. This control plan shall provide for a minimum number of random samples depending on the potential risks.

[8.381]
Article 89
Documentary accounts

For the purposes of proper control of the operations, the documentary accounts referred to in Article 66 shall include information on the origin, nature and quantities of feed materials, additives, sales and finished products.

[8.382]
Article 90
Control visits

The control visit referred to in Article 65 shall comprise a full physical inspection of all premises. Moreover, the control authority or control body shall make targeted visits based on a general evaluation of the potential risks of non-compliance with the organic production rules.
The control body or authority shall pay particular attention to the critical control points pointed out for the operator, with a view to establishing whether the surveillance and checking operations are carried out correctly.
All the premises used by the operator for the conduct of his activities may be checked as frequently as the attendant risks warrant.

CHAPTER 8
INFRINGEMENTS AND EXCHANGE OF INFORMATION

[8.383]
Article 91
Measures in case of suspicion of infringements and irregularities

1. Where an operator considers or suspects that a product which he has produced, prepared, imported or that he has received from another operator, is not in compliance with organic production rules, he shall initiate procedures either to withdraw from this product any reference to the organic production method or to separate and identify the product. He may only put it into processing or packaging or on the market after elimination of that doubt, unless it is placed on the market without indication referring to the organic production method. In case of such doubt, the operator shall immediately inform the control body or authority. The control authority or control body may require that the product cannot be placed on the market with indications referring to the organic production method until it is satisfied, by the information received from the operator or from other sources, that the doubt has been eliminated.
2. Where a control authority or control body has a substantiated suspicion that an operator intends to place on the market a product not in compliance with the organic production rules but bearing a reference to the organic production method, this control authority or control body can require that the operator may provisionally not market the product with this reference for a time period to be set by that control authority or control body. Before taking such a decision, the control authority or

control body shall allow the operator to comment. This decision shall be supplemented by the obligation to withdraw from this product any reference to the organic production method if the control authority or control body is sure that the product does not fulfil the requirements of organic production.

However, if the suspicion is not confirmed within the said time period, the decision referred to in the first subparagraph shall be cancelled not later than the expiry of that time period. The operator shall cooperate fully with the control body or authority in resolving the suspicion.

3. Member States shall take whatever measures and sanctions are required to prevent fraudulent use of the indications referred to in Title IV of Regulation (EC) No 834/2007 and Title III and/or Annex XI of this Regulation.

[8.384]

[Article 92

Exchange of information between control authorities, control bodies and competent authorities

1. Where the operator and/or the subcontractors of that operator are checked by different control authorities or control bodies, the control authorities or control bodies shall exchange the relevant information on the operations under their control.

2. Where operators and/or their subcontractors change their control authority or control body, the change shall be notified without delay to the competent authority by the control authorities or control bodies concerned.

The previous control authority or control body shall hand over the relevant elements of the control file of the operator concerned and the reports referred to in the second subparagraph of Article 63(2) to the subsequent control authority or control body.

The new control authority or control body shall ensure that non-conformities noted in the report of the previous control authority or control body have been or are being addressed by the operator.

3. Where the operator withdraws from the control system, the control authority or control body of that operator shall, without delay, inform the competent authority.

4. Where a control authority or control body finds irregularities or infringements affecting the organic status of products, it shall without delay inform the competent authority of the Member State which designated or approved it in accordance with Article 27 of Regulation (EC) No 834/2007.

That competent authority may require, on its own initiative, also any other information on irregularities or infringements.

In case of irregularities or infringements found with regard to products under the control of other control authorities or control bodies, it shall also inform those authorities or bodies without delay.

5. Member States shall take the appropriate measures and establish documented procedures to enable exchange of information between all control authorities they have designated and/or all control bodies they have approved in accordance with Article 27 of Regulation (EC) No 834/2007, including procedures for the exchange of information for the purpose of verifying documentary evidence referred to in Article 29(1) of that Regulation.

6. Member States shall take the appropriate measures and establish documented procedures in order to ensure that information on the results of inspections and visits as referred to in Article 65 of this Regulation is communicated to the paying agency in accordance with the needs of that paying agency as provided for in Article 33(1) of Commission Regulation (EU) No 65/2011.[1]]

NOTES

Arts 92, 92a, 92b substituted (for Art 92 as originally enacted and Art 92a as inserted by Commission Regulation 426/2011/EU, Art 1) by Commission Regulation 392/2013/EU, Art 1(5).

[1] OJ L25, 28.1.2011, p 8.

[8.385]

[Article 92a

Exchange of information between different Member States and the Commission

1. Where a Member State finds irregularities or infringements relating to the application of this Regulation with regard to a product coming from another Member State and bearing indications as referred to in Title IV of Regulation (EC) No 834/2007 and in Title III and/or Annex XI to this Regulation, it shall notify the Member State which designated the control authority or approved the control body, the other Member States and the Commission without delay via the system referred to in Article 94(1) of this Regulation.

2. Where a Member State finds irregularities or infringements as regards compliance of the products imported in accordance with Article 33(2) or (3) of Regulation (EC) No 834/2007 with the requirements laid down in that Regulation or Regulation (EC) No 1235/2008, it shall notify the other Member States and the Commission without delay via the system referred to in Article 94(1) of this Regulation.

3. Where a Member State finds irregularities or infringements as regards compliance of the products imported in accordance with Article 19 of Regulation (EC) No 1235/2008 with the requirements laid down in that Regulation and Regulation (EC) No 834/2007, it shall notify the

Member State which issued the authorisation, the other Member States and the Commission without delay via the system referred to in Article 94(1) of this Regulation. The notification shall be sent to the other Member States and to the Commission in case the irregularity or infringement is found with regard to products for which the Member State itself issued the authorisation referred to in Article 19 of Regulation (EC) No 1235/2008.

4. The Member State which receives a notification relating to non-compliant products in accordance with paragraph 1 or 3 or the Member State which issued the authorisation referred to in Article 19 of Regulation (EC) No 1235/2008 for a product for which an irregularity or infringement was found, shall investigate the origin of the irregularities or infringements. It shall take appropriate action immediately.

It shall inform the Member State which sent the notification, the other Member States and the Commission of the result of the investigation and of the action taken by replying to the original notification via the system referred to in Article 94(1). The reply shall be sent within 30 calendar days from the date of the original notification.

5. The Member State which sent the original notification may ask the replying Member State for additional information, if needed. In any case, after receiving a reply or additional information from a notified Member State, the Member State which sent the original notification shall make the necessary entries and updates in the system referred to in Article 94(1).]

NOTES

Substituted as noted to Art 92 at **[8.384]**.

[8.386]
[Article 92b
Publication of information

Member States shall make available to the public, in an appropriate manner including publication on the internet, the updated lists referred to in Article 28(5) of Regulation (EC) No 834/2007 containing updated documentary evidence related to each operator, as provided for in Article 29(1) of that Regulation and using the model set out in Annex XII to this Regulation. The Member States shall duly observe the requirements of the protection of personal data as laid down in Directive 95/46/EC of the European Parliament and of the Council.[1]]

NOTES

Substituted as noted to Art 92 at **[8.384]**.

[1] OJ L281, 23.11.1995, p 3.

[CHAPTER 9
SUPERVISION BY COMPETENT AUTHORITIES

[8.387]
Article 92c
Supervisory activities relating to control bodies

1. The supervisory activities by competent authorities delegating control tasks to control bodies in accordance with Article 27(4)(b) of Regulation (EC) No 834/2007 shall focus on the evaluation of the operational performance of those control bodies, taking into account the results of the work of the national accreditation body as referred to in Article 2(11) of Regulation (EC) No 765/2008 of the European Parliament and of the Council.[1]

Those supervisory activities shall include an assessment of the internal procedures of the control bodies for the controls, the management and examination of control files in the light of the obligations established by Regulation (EC) No 834/2007 and the verification of handling of non-conformities and the handling of appeals and complaints.

2. The competent authorities shall require control bodies to submit documentation on their risk analysis procedure.

The risk analysis procedure shall be designed in such a way that:

(a) the result of the risk analysis provides the basis for determining the intensity of the unannounced or announced annual inspections and visits;
(b) additional random control visits carried out in accordance with Article 65(4) of at least 10% of operators under contract in accordance with the risk category are performed;
(c) at least 10% of all inspections and visits carried out in accordance with Article 65(1) and (4) are unannounced;
(d) the selection of operators to be submitted to unannounced inspections and visits is determined on the basis of the risk analysis and that these are planned according to the level of risk.

3. Competent authorities delegating control tasks to control bodies shall verify that the staff of the control bodies has sufficient knowledge, including knowledge of the risk elements affecting the organic status of products, qualifications, training and experience with respect to organic production in general and with the relevant Union rules in particular and that appropriate rules on rotation of inspectors are in force.
4. Competent authorities shall have documented procedures for the delegation of tasks to control bodies in accordance with Article 27(5) of Regulation (EC) No 834/2007 and for the supervision in accordance with this Article, detailing the information to be submitted by control bodies.]

NOTES

Chapter 9 (Arts 92c–92f) inserted by Commission Regulation 392/2013/EU, Art 1(6).

[1] OJ L218, 13.8.2008, p 30.

[8.388]
[Article 92d
Catalogue of measures in case of irregularities and infringements

Competent authorities shall adopt and communicate to control bodies that have been delegated control tasks, a catalogue at least listing infringements and irregularities affecting the organic status of products and corresponding measures to be applied by control bodies in case of infringements or irregularities by operators under their control who are involved in organic production.

Competent authorities may include other relevant information in the catalogue on their own initiative.]

NOTES

Inserted as noted to Art 92c at **[8.387]**.

[8.389]
[Article 92e
Annual inspection of control bodies

Competent authorities shall organise an annual inspection of the control bodies that have been delegated control tasks in accordance with Article 27(4)(b) of Regulation (EC) No 834/2007. For the purposes of the annual inspection, the competent authority shall take into account the results of the work of the national accreditation body as referred to in Article 2(11) of Regulation (EC) No 765/2008. During the annual inspection, the competent authority shall, in particular, verify:

(a) the compliance with the control body's standard control procedure as submitted by the control body to the competent authority in accordance with Article 27(6)(a) of Regulation (EC) No 834/2007;
(b) that the control body has a sufficient number of suitable qualified and experienced staff in accordance with Article 27(5)(b) of Regulation (EC) No 834/2007 and that training concerning risks affecting the organic status of products has been implemented;
(c) that the control body has and follows documented procedures and templates for:
    (i) the annual risk analysis in accordance with Article 27(3) of Regulation (EC) No 834/2007;
    (ii) preparing a risk-based sampling strategy, conducting sampling and laboratory analysis;
    (iii) information exchange with other control bodies and with the competent authority;
    (iv) initial and follow-up controls of operators under their control;
    (v) the application and follow-up to the catalogue of measures to be applied in case of infringements or irregularities;
    (vi) observing the requirements of the protection of personal data for the operators under its control as laid down by the Member States where that competent authority operates and in accordance with Directive 95/46/EC.]

NOTES

Inserted as noted to Art 92c at **[8.387]**.

[8.390]
[Article 92f
Organic data in the multi-annual national control plan and annual report

Member States shall ensure that their multi-annual national control plans referred to in Article 41 of Regulation (EC) No 882/2004 cover the supervision of controls performed on the organic production in accordance with this Regulation and to include the specific data on that supervision, hereinafter referred to as "the organic data", in the annual report referred to in Article 44 of Regulation (EC) No 882/2004. The organic data shall cover the topics listed in Annex XIIIb to this Regulation.

The organic data shall be based on information on the controls performed by the control bodies and/or control authorities and on audits performed by the competent authority.

The data shall be presented according to the templates provided for in Annex XIIIc to this Regulation as from 2015 for the year 2014.

Member States may insert the organic data as an organic chapter of their national control plan and their annual report.]

NOTES

Inserted as noted to Art 92c at **[8.387]**.

TITLE V
TRANSMISSION OF INFORMATION TO THE COMMISSION, TRANSITIONAL AND FINAL PROVISIONS

CHAPTER 1
TRANSMISSION OF INFORMATION TO THE COMMISSION

[8.391]
Article 93
Statistical information

1. Member States shall provide the Commission with the annual statistical information on organic production referred to in Article 36 of Regulation (EC) No 834/2007 by using the computer system enabling electronic exchanges of documents and information made available by the Commission (Eurostat) before 1 July each year.

2. The statistical information referred to in paragraph 1 shall comprise, in particular the following data:

(a) the number of organic producers, processors, importers and exporters;
(b) the organic crop production and crop area under conversion and under organic production;
(c) the organic livestock numbers and the organic animal products;
(d) the data on organic industrial production by type of activities.
[(e) the number of organic aquaculture animal production units,
(f) the volume of organic aquaculture animal production,
(g) optionally, the number of organic seaweed units and the volume of organic seaweed production.]

3. For the transmission of the statistical information referred to in paragraphs 1 and 2, Member States shall use the Single Entry point provided by the Commission (Eurostat).

4. The provisions relating to the characteristics of statistical data and metadata shall be defined within the context of the Community Statistical Programme on the basis of models or questionnaires made available via the system referred to in paragraph 1.

NOTES

Para 2: sub-paras (e)–(g) added by Commission Regulation 710/2009/EC, Art 1(18).

[8.392]
Article 94
Other information

1. Member States shall provide the Commission with the following information by using the computer system enabling electronic exchanges of documents and information made available by the Commission (DG Agriculture and rural development) for information other than statistical information:

(a) by 30 June 2017, the information referred to in Article 35(a) of Regulation (EC) No 834/2007, including email address and internet address, and afterwards any changes thereto;
(b) by 30 June 2017, the information referred to in Article 35(b) of Regulation (EC) No 834/2007, including address, email address and internet address, and afterwards any changes thereto;]
(c) before 1 July each year, all other information required or needed in accordance with this Regulation.
[(d) within one month from their approval, the exceptions granted by the Member States under points (c) and (e) of the first paragraph of Article 47];
[(e) by 30 June 2017, the name, address, email address and internet address of the relevant Member State's competent authorities as defined in point (6) of Article 2 of Regulation (EC) No 1235/2008, and afterwards any changes thereto.]

2. The data shall be communicated, entered and updated in the system referred to in paragraph 1 under the responsibility of the competent authority as referred to in Article 35 of Regulation (EC) No 834/2007, by the authority itself or by the body to which that function has been delegated.

3. The provisions relating to the characteristics of data and metadata shall be defined on the basis of models or questionnaires made available via the system referred to in paragraph 1.

NOTES

Para 1: sub-paras (a), (b) substituted and sub-para (e) added by Commission Implementing Regulation 2016/1842/EU, Art 2(6).

sub-para (d) added by Commission Regulation 203/2012/EU, Art 1(2)(a).

CHAPTER 2
TRANSITIONAL AND FINAL PROVISIONS

[8.393]
Article 95
Transitional measures

1. For a transitional period expiring on 31 December 2010, cattle may be tethered in buildings already existing before 24 August 2000, provided that regular exercise is provided and rearing takes place in line with animal welfare requirements with comfortably littered areas as well as individual management and provided that the competent authority has authorised this measure. The competent authority may continue authorising this measure upon request of individual operators for its application in a limited period ending before the 31 December 2013, under the additional condition that the controls visits referred to in Article 65(1) are carried out at least twice a year.
2. The competent authority may authorise, for a transitional period expiring on 31 December 2010, the exceptions concerning housing conditions and stocking density granted to livestock producing holdings on the basis of the derogation provided for in part B, paragraph 8.5.1 of Annex I to Regulation (EEC) No 2092/91. The operators benefiting from this extension shall present a plan to the control authority or control body, containing the description of arrangements which are intended to ensure compliance with the provisions of the organic production rules by the end of the transitional period. The competent authority may continue authorising this measure upon request of individual operators for its application in a limited period ending before the 31 December 2013, under the additional condition that the controls visits referred to in Article 65(1) are carried out at least twice a year.
3. For a transition period expiring 31 December 2010 the final fattening phase of sheep and pigs for meat production as laid down under point 8.3.4 of Annex I.B of Regulation (EEC) No 2092/91 may take place indoors under the condition that the controls visits referred to in Article 65(1) are carried out at least twice a year.
4. The castration of piglets may be carried out without the application of anaesthesia and/or analgesia during a transition period expiring on 31 December 2011.
5. Pending the inclusion of detailed processing rules for pet food, national rules or in the absence thereof, private standards accepted or recognised by the Member States shall apply.
[6. For the purpose of Article 12(1)(j) of Regulation (EC) No 834/2007 and pending the inclusion of specific substances according to Article 16(1)(f) of that Regulation, only products authorised by the competent authority may be used.]
7. Authorisations of non-organic ingredients of agricultural origin granted by Member States under Regulation (EEC) No 207/93 may be deemed granted as under this Regulation. However, authorisations granted in accordance with Article 3(6) of the former Regulation shall expire on 31 December 2009.
8. For a transitional period expiring on the 1 July 2010, the operators may continue to use in the labelling the provisions as laid down in Regulation (EEC) No 2092/91 for:
- (i) the system for calculation the percentage of organic ingredients of food;
- (ii) the code number and/or the name of the control body or control authority.

[9. Stocks of products produced, packaged and labelled before 1 July 2010 in accordance with either Regulation (EEC) No 2092/91 or Regulation (EC) No 834/2007 may continue to be brought on the market bearing terms referring to organic production until stocks are exhausted.
10. Packaging material in accordance with either Regulation (EEC) No 2092/91 or Regulation (EC) No 834/2007 may continue to be used for products placed on the market bearing terms referring to organic production until 1 July 2012, where the product otherwise complies with the requirements of Regulation (EC) No 834/2007.]
[10a. As regards products of the wine sector, the transitional period referred to in paragraph 8 shall expire on 31 July 2012.

Stocks of wines produced until 31 July 2012 in accordance with either Regulation (EEC) No 2092/91 or Regulation (EC) No 834/2007 may continue to be brought on the market until stocks are exhausted, and subject to the following labelling requirements:
- (a) the Community organic production logo as referred to in Article 25(1) of Regulation (EC) No 834/2007, called from 1 July 2010 the "Organic logo of the EU" may be used provided that the wine-making process complies with Chapter 3a of Title II of this Regulation;
- (b) operators using "Organic logo of the EU" shall keep recorded evidence, for a period of at least five years after they placed on the market that wine obtained from organic grapes, including of the corresponding quantities of wine in litres, per wine category and per year;
- (c) where the evidence referred to in point (b) of this paragraph is not available, such wine may be labelled as "wine made from organic grapes", provided that it complies with the requirements of this Regulation except those provided for in Chapter 3a of Title II thereof;
- (d) wine labelled as "wine made from organic grapes" cannot bear the "Organic logo of the EU".]

[(11) The competent authority may authorise for a period expiring on [1 January 2015], those aquaculture animal and seaweed production units which are established and produce under nationally accepted organic rules before entry into force of this Regulation, to keep their organic status while adapting to the rules of this Regulation, provided there is no undue pollution of the waters with substances not allowed in organic production. Operators benefiting from this measure shall notify the facilities, fishponds, cages or seaweed lots which are concerned to the competent authority.]

NOTES

Para 6: substituted by Commission Regulation 710/2009/EC, Art 1(19).

Paras 9, 10: substituted by Commission Regulation 271/2010/EU, Art 1(4).

Para 10a: inserted by Commission Regulation 344/2011/EU, Art 1(4); substituted by Commission Regulation 203/2012/EU, Art 1(2)(b).

Para 11: added by Commission Regulation 710/2009/EC, Art 1(20); words in square brackets substituted by Commission Regulation 1030/2013/EU, Art 1.

[8.394]
Article 96
Repeal

Regulations (EEC) No 207/93, (EC) No 223/2003 and (EC) No 1452/2003 are repealed.

References to the repealed Regulations and to Regulation (EEC) No 2092/91 shall be construed as references to this Regulation and shall be read in accordance with the correlation table in Annex XIV.

[8.395]
Article 97
Entry into force and application

This Regulation shall enter into force on the seventh day following that of its publication in the *Official Journal of the European Union*.

It shall apply as from 1 January 2009.

However, paragraph 2(a) of Article 27 and Article 58 shall apply as of 1 July 2010.

This Regulation shall be binding in its entirety and directly applicable in all Member States.

ANNEX I
[FERTILIZERS, SOIL CONDITIONERS AND NUTRIENTS REFERRED TO IN ARTICLE 3(1) AND ARTICLE 6D(2)]

[8.396]

Note:

A: authorised under Regulation (EEC) No 2092/91 and carried over by Article 16(3)(c) of Regulation (EC) No 834/2007

B: authorised under Regulation (EC) No 834/2007

[Authorisation	Name Compound products or products containing only materials listed hereunder	Description, compositional requirements, conditions for use
A	Farmyard manure	Products comprising a mixture of animal excrements and vegetable matter (animal bedding). Factory farming origin forbidden]
A	Dried farmyard manure and dehydrated poultry manure	Factory farming origin forbidden
A	Composted animal excrements, including poultry manure and composted farmyard manure included	Factory farming origin forbidden
A	Liquid animal excrements	Use after controlled fermentation and/or appropriate dilution Factory farming origin forbidden
A	Composted or fermented household waste	Product obtained from source separated household waste, which has been submitted to composting or to anaerobic fermentation for biogas production Only vegetable and animal household waste Only when produced in a closed and monitored collection system, accepted by the Member State

[Authorisation	**Name Compound products or products containing only materials listed hereunder**	**Description, compositional requirements, conditions for use**
		Maximum concentrations in mg/kg of dry matter: cadmium: 0,7; copper: 70; nickel: 25; lead: 45; zinc: 200; mercury: 0,4; chromium (total): 70; chromium (VI): 0
A	Peat	Use limited to horticulture (market gardening, floriculture, arboriculture, nursery)
A	Mushroom culture wastes	The initial composition of the substrate shall be limited to products of this Annex
A	Dejecta of worms (vermicompost) and insects	
A	Guano	
A	Composted or fermented mixture of vegetable matter	Product obtained from mixtures of vegetable matter, which have been submitted to composting or to anaerobic fermentation for biogas production
A	Products or by-products of animal origin as below: blood meal hoof meal horn meal bone meal or degelatinized bone meal fish meal fish meal feather, hair and 'chiquette' meal wool fur hair dairy products	[For fur: maximum concentration in mg/kg of dry matter of chromium (VI): 0]
A	Products and by-products of plant origin for fertilisers	Examples: oilseed cake meal, cocoa husks, malt culms
A	Seaweeds and seaweed products	As far as directly obtained by: (i) physical processes including dehydration, freezing and grinding (ii) extraction with water or aqueous acid and/or alkaline solution (iii) fermentation
A	Sawdust and wood chips	Wood not chemically treated after felling
A	Composted bark	Wood not chemically treated after felling
A	Wood ash	From wood not chemically treated after felling
A	Soft ground rock phosphate	Product as specified in point 7 of Annex IA.2. to Regulation (EC) No 2003/2003 of the European Parliament and of the Council[1] relating to fertilisers, 7 Cadmium content less than or equal to 90 mg/kg of $P_2 0_5$
A	Aluminium-calcium phosphate	Product as specified in point 6 of Annex IA.2. of Regulation 2003/2003, Cadmium content less than or equal to 90 mg/kg of $P_2 0_5$ Use limited to basic soils (pH > 7,5)
A	Basic slag	Products as specified in point 1 of Annex IA.2. of Regulation 2003/2003

Part 8 Other EU Materials

[Authorisation	Name Compound products or products containing only materials listed hereunder	Description, compositional requirements, conditions for use
A	Crude potassium salt or kainit	Products as specified in point 1 of Annex IA.3. of Regulation 2003/2003
A	Potassium sulphate, possibly containing magnesium salt	Product obtained from crude potassium salt by a physical extraction process, containing possibly also magnesium salts
A	Stillage and stillage extract	Ammonium stillage excluded
A	Calcium carbonate (chalk, marl, ground limestone, Breton ameliorant, (maerl), phosphate chalk)	Only of natural origin
A	Magnesium and calcium carbonate	Only of natural origin e.g. magnesian chalk, ground magnesium, limestone
A	Magnesium sulphate (kieserite)	Only of natural origin
A	Calcium chloride solution	Foliar treatment of apple trees, after identification of deficit of calcium
A	Calcium sulphate (gypsum)	Products as specified in point 1 of Annex ID. of Regulation 2003/2003 Only of natural origin
A	Industrial lime from sugar production	By-product of sugar production from sugar beet
A	Industrial lime from vacuum salt production	By-product of the vacuum salt production from brine found in mountains
A	Elemental sulphur	Products as specified in Annex ID.3 of Regulation 2003/2003
A	Trace elements	Inorganic micronutrients listed in part E of Annex I to Regulation 2003/2003
A	Sodium chloride	Only mined salt
A	Stone meal and clays	

NOTES

Annex heading, table heading, and words in square brackets in table substituted by Commission Regulation 710/2009/EC, Art 1(21), Annex, para 1.

[1] OJ L304, 21.11.2003, p 1.

[ANNEX II
PESTICIDES — PRODUCTS REFERRED TO IN ARTICLE 5(1)

[8.397]

All the substances listed in this Annex have to comply at least with the conditions for use as specified in the Annex to Commission Implementing Regulation (EU) No 540/2011.[1] More restrictive conditions for use for organic production are specified in the second column of each table.

[1] Commission Implementing Regulation (EU) No 540/2011 of 25 May 2011 implementing Regulation (EC) No 1107/2009 of the European Parliament and of the Council as regards the list of approved active substances (OJ L153, 11.6.2011, p 1).

1. Substances of plant or animal origin

Name	Description, compositional requirement, conditions for use
Azadirachtin extracted from *Azadirachta indica* (Neem tree)	

Name	Description, compositional requirement, conditions for use
Basic substances	Only those basic substances within the meaning of Article 23(1) of Regulation (EC) No 1107/2009 of the European Parliament and of the Council[1] that are covered by the definition of "foodstuff" in Article 2 of Regulation (EC) No 178/2002 of the European Parliament and of the Council[2] and have plant or animal origin. Substances not to be used as herbicides, but only for the control of pests and diseases.
Beeswax	Only as pruning agent/wound protectant.
Hydrolysed proteins excluding gelatine	
Laminarin	Kelp shall be either grown organically in accordance with Article 6d or harvested in a sustainable way in accordance with Article 6c.
Pheromones	Only in traps and dispensers.
Plant oils	All uses authorised, except herbicide.
Pyrethrins extracted from *Chrysanthemum cinerariaefolium*	
Pyrethroids (only deltamethrin or lambdacyhalothrin)	Only in traps with specific attractants; only against *Bactrocera oleae* and *Ceratitis capitata Wied*.
Quassia extracted from *Quassia amara*	Only as insecticide, repellent.
Repellents by smell of animal or plant origin/ sheep fat	Only on non-edible parts of the crop and where crop material is not ingested by sheep or goats.

[1] Regulation (EC) No 1107/2009 of the European Parliament and of the Council of 21 October 2009 concerning the placing of plant protection products on the market (OJ L309, 24.11.2009, p 1).

[2] Regulation (EC) No 178/2002 of the European Parliament and of the Council of 28 January 2002 laying down the general principles and requirements of food law, establishing the European Food Safety Authority and laying down procedures in matters of food safety (OJ L31, 1.2.2002, p 1).

2. **Micro-organisms or substances produced by micro-organisms**

Name	Description, compositional requirement, conditions for use
Micro-organisms	Not from GMO origin.
Spinosad	

3. **Substances other than those mentioned in Sections 1 and 2**

Name	Description, compositional requirement, conditions or restrictions to use
Aluminium silicate (Kaolin)	
Calcium hydroxide	When used as fungicide, only in fruit trees, including nurseries, to control *Nectria galligena*.
Carbon dioxide	
Copper compounds in the form of: copper hydroxide, copper oxychloride, copper oxide, Bordeaux mixture, and tribasic copper sulphate	Up to 6 kg copper per ha per year. For perennial crops, by way of derogation from the first paragraph, Member States may provide that the 6 kg copper limit can be exceeded in a given year provided that the average quantity actually used over a 5-year period consisting of that year and of the 4 preceding years does not exceed 6 kg.
Ethylene	
Fatty acids	All uses authorised, except herbicide.
Ferric phosphate (iron (III) orthophosphate)	Preparations to be surface-spread between cultivated plants.
Kieselgur (diatomaceous earth)	
Lime sulphur (calcium polysulphide)	

Name	Description, compositional requirement, conditions or restrictions to use
Paraffin oil	
Potassium hydrogen carbonate (aka potassium bicarbonate)	
Quartz sand	
Sulphur]	

NOTES

Annex II substituted by Commission Implementing Regulation 2016/673/EU, Art 1(6), Annex I.

ANNEX III
MINIMUM SURFACE AREAS INDOORS AND OUTDOORS AND OTHER CHARACTERISTICS OF HOUSING IN THE DIFFERENT SPECIES AND TYPES OF PRODUCTION REFERRED TO IN ARTICLE 10(4)

[8.398]

1. **Bovines, equidae, ovine, caprine and porcine**

	Indoors area (net area available to animals)		Outdoors area (exercise area, excluding pasturage)
	Live weight minimum (kg)	M^2/head	M^2/head
Breeding and fattening bovine and equidae	up to 100	1,5	1,1
	up to 200	2,5	1,9
	up to 350	4,0	3
	over 350	5 with a minimum of 1 m^2/100 kg	3,7 with a minimum of 0,75 m^2/100 kg
Dairy cows		6	4,5
Bulls for breeding		10	30
Sheep and goats		1,5 sheep/goat	2,5
		0,35 lamb/kid	0,5
Farrowing sows with piglets up to 40 days		7,5 sow	2,5
Fattening pigs	up to 50	0,8	0,6
	up to 85	1,1	0,8
	up to 110	1,3	1
	[Over 110 kg	1,5	1,2]
Piglets	over 40 days and up to 30 kg	0,6	0,4
Brood pigs		2,5 female	1,9
		6 male If pens are used for natural service: 10 m^2/boar	8,0

2. **Poultry**

	Indoors area (net area available to animals)			Outdoors area (m^2 of area available in rotation/head)
	No animals/m^2	cm perch/ animal	nest	
Laying hens	6	18	7 laying hens per nest or in case of common nest 120 cm^2/bird	4, provided that the limit of 170 kg of N/ha/year is not exceeded

	Indoors area (net area available to animals)			Outdoors area (m^2 of area available in rotation/head)
	No animals/m^2	cm perch/ animal	nest	
Fattening poultry (in fixed housing)	10 with a maximum of 21 kg liveweight/m^2	20 (for guinea fowl only)		4 broilers and guinea fowl 4,5 ducks 10 turkey 15 geese In all the species mentioned above the limit of 170 kg of N/ha/year is not exceeded
Fattening poultry in mobile housing	16[1] in mobile poultry houses with a maximum of 30 kg liveweight/m^2			2,5, provided that the limit of 170 kg of N/ha/year is not exceeded

NOTES

Entry relating to "fattening pigs": words in square brackets inserted by Commission Regulation 710/2009/EC, Art 1(21), Annex, para 2.

[1] Only in the case of mobile houses not exceeding 150 m^2 floor space.

ANNEX IV
MAXIMUM NUMBER OF ANIMALS PER HECTARE REFERRED TO IN ARTICLE 15(2)

[8.399]

Class or species	Maximum number of animals per ha equivalent to 170 kg N/ha/year
Equines over six months old	2
Calves for fattening	5
Other bovine animals less than one year old	5
Male bovine animals from one to less than two years old	3,3
Female bovine animals from one to less than two years old	3,3
Male bovine animals two years old or over	2
Breeding heifers	2,5
Heifers for fattening	2,5
Dairy cows	2
Cull dairy cows	2
Other cows	2,5
Female breeding rabbits	100
Ewes	13,3
Goats	13,3
Piglets	74
Breeding sows	6,5
Pigs for fattening	14
Other pigs	14
Table chickens	580
Laying hens	230

[ANNEX V
FEED MATERIALS AS REFERRED TO IN ARTICLE 22(D), ARTICLE 24(2) AND ARTICLE 25M(1)

[8.400]

[1. FEED MATERIALS OF MINERAL ORIGIN

A	Calcareous marine shells	
A	Maerl	
A	Lithotamn	
A	Calcium gluconate	
A	Calcium carbonate	
A	Defluorinated monocalciumphosphate	
A	Defluorinated dicalciumphosphate	
A	Magnesium oxide (anhydrous magnesia)	
A	Magnesium sulphate	
A	Magnesium chloride	
A	Magnesium carbonate	
A	Calcium magnesium phosphate	
A	Magnesium phosphate	
A	Monosodium phosphate	
A	Calcium sodium phosphate	
A	Sodium chloride	
A	Sodium bicarbonate	
A	Sodium carbonate	
A	Sodium sulphate	
A	Potassium chloride]	

2. OTHER FEED MATERIALS

Fermentation (by-)products from microorganisms the cells of which have been inactivated or killed:

A	Saccharomyces cerevisiae	
A	Saccharomyces carlsbergiensis	]

NOTES

Substituted, together with Annex VI, by Commission Regulation 505/2012/EU, Art 1(9), Annex.

Section 1: substituted by Commission Regulation 354/2014/EU, Art 2(2), Annex, point 3.

[ANNEX VI
FEED ADDITIVES USED IN ANIMAL NUTRITION REFERRED TO IN ARTICLE 22(G), ARTICLE 24(2) AND ARTICLE 25M(2)

[8.401]

Feed additives listed in this Annex must be approved under Regulation (EC) No 1831/2003 of the European Parliament and of the Council.[1]

1. TECHNOLOGICAL ADDITIVES

(a) *Preservatives*

ID number or Functional groups	Substance	Description, conditions for use
E 200	Sorbic acid	
E 236	Formic acid	
E 237	Sodium formate	
E 260	Acetic acid	
E 270	Lactic acid	
E 280	Propionic acid	
E 330	Citric acid	

(b) *Antioxidants*

ID number or Functional groups	Substance	Description, conditions for use
1b306(i)	Tocopherol extracts from vegetable oils	
1b306(ii)	Tocopherol-rich extracts from vegetable oils (delta rich)	

(c) *Emulsifiers, stabilisers, thickeners and gelling agents*

ID number or Functional groups	Substance	Description, conditions for use
E 322	Lecithins	Only when derived from organic raw material. Use restricted to aquaculture animal feed.

(d) *Binders and anti-caking agents*

ID number or Functional groups	Substance	Description, conditions for use
E 535	Sodium ferrocyanide	Maximum dose rate of 20 mg/kg NaCl calculated as ferrocyanide anion
E 551b	Colloidal silica	
E 551c	Kieselgur (diatomaceous earth, purified)	
1m558i	Bentonite	
E 559	Kaolinitic clays, free of asbestos	
E 560	Natural mixtures of stearites and chlorite	
E 561	Vermiculite	
E 562	Sepiolite	
E 566	Natrolite-Phonolite	
1g568	Clinoptilolite of sedimentary origin	
E 599	Perlite	

(e) *Silage additives*

ID number or Functional groups	Substance	Description, conditions for use
1k	Enzymes and micro-organisms	Use restricted to production of silage when weather conditions do not allow for adequate fermentation.

2. SENSORY ADDITIVES

ID number or Functional groups	Substance	Description, conditions for use
2b	Flavouring compounds	Only extracts from agricultural products

3. NUTRITIONAL ADDITIVES

(a) *Vitamins, pro-vitamins and chemically well-defined substances having similar effect*

ID number or Functional groups	Substance	Description, conditions for use
3a	Vitamins and provitamins	Derived from agricultural products If derived synthetically, only those identical to vitamins derived from agricultural products may be used for monogastric animals and aquaculture animals. If derived synthetically, only vitamins A, D and E identical to vitamins derived from agricultural products may be used for ruminants, the use is subject to prior authorisation of the Member States based on the assessment of the possibility for organic ruminants to obtain the necessary quantities of the said vitamins through their feed rations

(b) *Compounds of trace elements*

ID number or Functional groups	Substance	Description, conditions for use
E1 Iron	Ferric oxide Ferrous carbonate Ferrous sulphate, heptahydrate Ferrous sulphate, monohydrate	
3b201 3b202 3b203	Potassium iodide Calcium iodate, anhydrous Coated granulated calcium iodate anhydrous	
3b301 3b302 3b303 3b304 3b305	Cobalt(II) acetate tetrahydrate Cobalt(II) carbonate Cobalt(II) carbonate hydroxide (2:3) monohydrate Coated granulated cobalt(II) carbonate Cobalt(II) sulphate heptahydrate	
E4 Copper	Basic cupric carbonate, monohydrate Cupric oxide Cupric sulphate, pentahydrate	
3b409	Dicopper chloride trihydroxide (TBCC)	
E5 Manganese	Manganous oxide Manganous sulfate, monohydrate Manganous carbonate	
E6 Zinc	Zinc oxide Zinc sulphate monohydrate Zinc sulphate heptahydrate	
3b609	Zinc chloride hydroxide monohydrate (TBZC)	
E7 Molybdenum	Sodium molybdate	
E8 Selenium	Sodium selenite Sodium selenate	
3b8.10, 3b8.11, 3b8.12, 3b813 and 3b817	Selenised yeast inactivated	

4. ZOOTECHNICAL ADDITIVES

ID number or Functional groups	Substance	Description, conditions for use
4a, 4b, 4c and 4d	Enzymes and microorganism in the category of "Zootechnical additives"]	

NOTES

Substituted as noted to Annex V at **[8.400]**; Annex VI further substituted by Commission Implementing Regulation 2016/673/EU, Art 1(7), Annex II.

1 Regulation (EC) No 1831/2003 of the European Parliament and of the Council of 22 September 2003 on additives for use in animal nutrition (OJ L268, 18.10.2003, p 29).

[ANNEX VII
PRODUCTS FOR CLEANING AND DISINFECTION

[8.402]

1. Products for cleaning and disinfection of buildings and installations for livestock production referred to in Article 23(4):
- — Potassium and sodium soap
- — Water and steam
- — Milk of lime
- — Lime
- — Quicklime
- — Sodium hypochlorite (e.g. as liquid bleach)
- — Caustic soda
- — Caustic potash
- — Hydrogen peroxide
- — Natural essences of plants
- — Citric, peracetic acid, formic, lactic, oxalic and acetic acid
- — Alcohol
- — Nitric acid (dairy equipment)
- — Phosporic acid (dairy equipment)
- — Formaldehyde
- — Cleaning and disinfection products for teats and milking facilities
- — Sodium carbonate

[2. Products for cleaning and disinfection for aquaculture animals and seaweed production referred to in Articles 6e(2), 25s(2) and 29a.

2.1. Subject to compliance with relevant Union and national provisions as referred to in Article 16(1) of Regulation (EC) No 834/2007, and in particular with Regulation (EU) No 528/2012 of the European Parliament and of the Council,[1] products used for cleaning and disinfection of equipment and facilities in the absence of aquaculture animals may contain the following active substances:
- — ozone
- — sodium hypochlorite
- — calcium hypochlorite
- — calcium hydroxide
- — calcium oxide
- — caustic soda
- — alcohol
- — copper sulphate: only until 31 December 2015
- — potassium permanganate
- — tea seed cake made of natural camelia seed (use restricted to shrimp production)
- — mixtures of potassium peroxomonosulphate and sodium chloride producing hypochlorous acid.

2.2. Subject to compliance with relevant Union and national provisions as referred to in Article 16(1) of Regulation (EC) No 834/2007, and in particular with Regulation (EU) No 528/2012 and Directive 2001/82/EC of the European Parliament and of the Council,[2] products used for cleaning and disinfection of equipment and facilities in the presence as well as in the absence of aquaculture animals may contain the following active substances:
- — limestone (calcium carbonate) for pH control
- — dolomite for pH correction (use restricted to shrimp production)
- — sodium chloride
- — hydrogen peroxide
- — sodium percarbonate
- — organic acids (acetic acid, lactic acid, citric acid)
- — humic acid

— peroxyacetic acids
— peracetic and peroctanoic acids
— iodophores (only in the presence of eggs).]]

NOTES

Substituted by Commission Regulation 710/2009/EC, Art 1(21), Annex, para 5.
Point 2: substituted by Commission Regulation 1358/2014/EU, Art 1(9), Annex, para 1.

[1] Regulation (EU) No 528/2012 of the European Parliament and of the Council of 22 May 2012 concerning the making available on the market and use of biocidal products (OJ L167, 27.6.2012, p 1).

[2] Directive 2001/82/EC of the European Parliament and of the Council of 6 November 2001 on the Community code relating to veterinary medicinal products (OJ L311, 28.11.2001, p 1).

ANNEX VIII
[CERTAIN PRODUCTS AND SUBSTANCES FOR USE IN PRODUCTION OF PROCESSED ORGANIC FOOD, YEAST AND YEAST PRODUCTS REFERRED TO IN ARTICLE 27(1)(A) AND ARTICLE 27A(A)]

[8.403]

. . .

SECTION A — FOOD ADDITIVES, INCLUDING CARRIERS

For the purpose of the calculation referred to in Article 23(4)(a)(ii) of Regulation (EC) No 834/2007, food additives marked with an asterisk in the column of the code number, shall be calculated as ingredients of agricultural origin.

. . .	Code	Name	Preparation of foodstuffs of		Specific conditions
			plant origin	animal origin	
. . .	E 153	Vegetable carbon		X	Ashy goat cheese Morbier cheese
. . .	E 160b*	Annatto, Bixin, Norbixin		X	Red Leicester cheese Double Gloucester cheese Cheddar Mimolette cheese
. . .	E 170	Calcium carbonate	X	X	Shall not be used for colouring or calcium enrichment of products
. . .	[E 220	Sulphur dioxide	X	X (only for mead)	In fruit wines(*) and mead with and without added sugar):100 mg(**)
	E 224	Potassium metabisulphite	X	X (only for mead)	In fruit wines(*) and mead with and without added sugar):100 mg(**).
					(*) In this context, 'fruit wine' is defined as wine made from fruits other than grapes (including cider and perry). (**) Maximum levels available from all sources, expressed as SO2 in mg/l.]
[. . .	E 223	Sodium metabisulphite		X	Crustaceans[2]]
. . .	E 250 or	Sodium nitrite		X	For meat products:[1]
	E 252	Potassium nitrate		X	For E 250: indicative ingoing amount expressed as $NaNO_2$: 80 mg/kg For E 252: indicative ingoing amount expressed as NaNO: 80 mg/kg For E 250: maximum residual amount expressed as NaNO: 50 mg/kg

. . .	Code	Name	Preparation of foodstuffs of		Specific conditions
			plant origin	animal origin	
					For E 252: maximum residual amount expressed as NaNO: 50 mg/kg
. . .	E 270	Lactic acid	X	X	
. . .	E 290	Carbon dioxide	X	X	
. . .	E 296	Malic acid	X		
. . .	E 300	Ascorbic acid	X	X	Meat products[2]
. . .	E 301	Sodium ascorbate		X	Meat products[2] in connection with nitrates and nitrites
. . .	[E 306*	Tocopherol-rich extract	X	X	Anti-oxidant]
. . .	[E 322*	Lecithins	X	X	Milk products[2] Only when derived from organic material (as from 1 January 2019)]
. . .	E 325	Sodium lactate		X	Milk-based and meat products
. . .	[E 330	Citric acid	X	X]	
. . .	[E 331	Sodium citrate	X	X]	
. . .	E 333	Calcium citrates	X		
. . .	[E 334	Tartaric acid (L(+)–)	X (only for mead)		
. . .	E 335	Sodium tartrates	X		
. . .	E 336	Potassium tartrates	X		
. . .	E 341 (i)	Monocalciumphosphate	X		Raising agent for self raising flour
[. . .	E 392*	Extracts of rosemary	X	X	Only when derived from organic production]
. . .	E 400	Alginic acid	X	X	Milk-based products[2]
. . .	E 401	Sodium alginate	X	X	Milk-based products[2]
. . .	E 402	Potassium alginate	X	X	Milk-based products[2]
. . .	E 406	Agar	X	X	Milk-based and meat products[2]
. . .	E 407	Carrageenan	X	X	Milk-based products[2]
. . .	E 410*	Locust bean gum	X	X	
. . .	E 412*	Guar gum	X	X	
. . .	E 414*	Arabic gum	X	X	
	[E 418	Gellan gum	X	X	High-acyl form only]
. . .	E 415	Xanthan gum	X	X	
. . .	[E 422	Glycerol	X		From plant origin. For plant extracts and flavourings]
. . .	E 440 (i)*	Pectin	X	X	Milk-based products[2]
. . .	E 464	Hydroxypropyl methyl cellulose	X	X	Encapsulation material for capsules
. . .	[E 500	Sodium carbonate	X	X]	
. . .	E 501	Potassium carbonates	X		

. . .	Code	Name	Preparation of foodstuffs of		Specific conditions
			plant origin	animal origin	
. . .	E 503	Ammonium carbonates	X		
. . .	E 504	Magnesium carbonates	X		
. . .	E 509	Calcium chloride		X	Milk coagulation
. . .	E 516	Calcium sulphate	X		Carrier
. . .	[E 524	Sodium hydroxide	X		Surface treatment of "Laugengebäck" and regulation of acidity in organic flavourings]
. . .	[E 551	Silicon dioxide gel or colloidal solution	X		For herbs and spices in dried powdered form Flavourings and propolis]
. . .	E 553b	Talc	X	X	Coating agent for meat products
. . .	[E 901	Beeswax	X		As a glazing agent for confectionary only. Beeswax from organic beekeeping]
	[E 903	Carnauba wax	X		As a glazing agent for confectionary only. Only when derived from organic raw material]
. . .	E 938	Argon	X	X	
. . .	E 939	Helium	X	X	
. . .	E 941	Nitrogen	X	X	
. . .	E 948	Oxygen	X	X	
. . .	[E 968	Erythritol	X	X	Only when derived from organic production without using ion exchange technology]
1	This additive can only be used, if it has been demonstrated to the satisfaction of the competent authority that no technological alternative, giving the same guarantees and/or allowing to maintain the specific features of the product, is available.				
2	The restriction concerns only animal products.				

SECTION B — PROCESSING AIDS AND OTHER PRODUCTS, WHICH MAY BE USED FOR PROCESSING OF INGREDIENTS OF AGRICULTURAL ORIGIN FROM ORGANIC PRODUCTION

. . .

. . .	Name	Preparation of foodstuffs of plant origin	Preparation of foodstuffs of animal origin	Specific conditions
. . .	Water	X	X	Drinking water within the meaning of Council Directive 98/83/EC
. . .	Calcium chloride	X		Coagulation agent
. . .	Calcium carbonate	X		
. . .	Calcium hydroxide	X		
. . .	Calcium sulphate	X		Coagulation agent
. . .	Magnesium chloride (or nigari)	X		Coagulation agent
. . .	Potassium carbonate	X		Drying of grapes
. . .	[Sodium carbonate	X	X]	

. . .	Name	Preparation of foodstuffs of plant origin	Preparation of foodstuffs of animal origin	Specific conditions
. . .	Lactic acid		X	For the regulation of the pH of the brine bath in cheese production[1]
. . .	[Citric acid	X	X]	
. . .	[Sodium hydroxide	X		For sugar(s) production. For oil production excluding olive oil production]
. . .	Sulphuric acid	X	X	Gelatine production[1] Sugar(s) production[2]
. . .	Hydrochloric acid		X	Gelatine production For the regulation of the pH of the brine bath in the processing of Gouda-, Edam and Maasdammer cheeses, Boerenkaas, Friese and Leidse Nagelkaas
. . .	Ammonium hydroxide		X	Gelatine production
. . .	Hydrogen peroxide		X	Gelatine production
. . .	Carbon dioxide	X	X	
. . .	Nitrogen	X	X	
. . .	Ethanol	X	X	Solvent
. . .	Tannic acid	X		Filtration aid
. . .	Egg white albumen	X		
. . .	Casein	X		
. . .	Gelatin	X		
. . .	Isinglass	X		
. . .	[Vegetable oils	X	X	Greasing, releasing or anti-foaming agent Only when derived from organic production]
. . .	Silicon dioxide gel or colloidal solution	X		
. . .	Activated carbon	X		
. . .	Talc	X		In compliance with the specific purity criteria for food additive E 553b
. . .	[Bentonite	X	X	Sticking agent for mead[1]]
. . .	Celluose	X	X	Gelatine production[1]
. . .	Diatomaceous earth	X	X	Gelatine production[1]
. . .	Perlite	X	X	Gelatine production[1]
. . .	Hazelnut shells	X		
. . .	Rice meal	X		
. . .	[Beeswax	X		Releasing agent Beeswax from organic beekeeping]
. . .	Carnauba wax	X		Releasing agent Only when derived from organic raw material]

. . .	Name	Preparation of foodstuffs of plant origin	Preparation of foodstuffs of animal origin	Specific conditions
	[Acetic acid/vinegar		X	Only when derived from organic production. For fish processing, only from biotechnological source, except if produced by or from GMO]
	[Thiamin hydrochloride	X	X	Only for use in processing of fruit wines, including cider and perry and mead]
	[Diammonium phosphate	X	X	Only for use in processing of fruit wines, including cider and perry and mead]
	[Wood fibre	X	X	The source of timber should be restricted to certified, sustainably harvested wood. Wood used must not contain toxic components (post-harvest treatment, naturally occurring toxins or toxins from micro-organisms)]
1	The restriction concerns only animal products.			
2	The restriction concerns only plant products.			

[SECTION C — PROCESSING AIDS FOR THE PRODUCTION OF YEAST AND YEAST PRODUCTS

Name	Primary yeast	Yeast confections/ formulations	Specific conditions
Calcium chloride	X		
Carbon dioxide	X	X	
Citric acid	X		For the regulation of the pH in yeast production
Lactic acid	X		For the regulation of the pH in yeast production
Nitrogen	X	X	
Oxygen	X	X	
[Potato starch	X	X	For filtering Only when derived from organic production]
Sodium carbonate	X	X	For the regulation of the pH
[Vegetable oils	X	X	Greasing, releasing or anti-foaming agent Only when derived from organic production]]

NOTES

Heading substituted by Commission Regulation 1254/2008/EC, Art 5.

Section A: entries relating to "E 223 Sodium metabisulphite" and "E 330 Citric acid" inserted by Commission Regulation 710/2009/EC, Art 1(21), Annex, para 6; entry relating to "E 392 Extracts of rosemary" inserted by Commission Regulation 344/2011/EU, Art 1(3) and substituted by Commission Regulation 505/2012/EU, Art 2; words omitted repealed and all other words in square brackets substituted or inserted by Commission Implementing Regulation 2016/673/EU, Art 1(8), Annex III, points (1), (2).

Section B: words omitted repealed and words in square brackets substituted or inserted by Commission Implementing Regulation 2016/673/EU, Art 1(8), Annex III, points (1), (3).

Section C: added by Commission Regulation 1254/2008/EC, Art 6, Annex; entries relating to "potato starch" and "vegetable oils" substituted by Commission Implementing Regulation 2016/673/EU, Art 1(8), Annex III, point (4).

[ANNEX VIIIA
PRODUCTS AND SUBSTANCES AUTHORISED FOR USE OR ADDITION IN ORGANIC PRODUCTS OF THE WINE SECTOR REFERRED TO IN ARTICLE 29C

[8.404]

Type of treatment in accordance with Annex I A to Regulation (EC) No 606/2009	Name of products or substances	Specific conditions, restrictions within the limits and conditions set out in Regulation (EC) No 1234/2007 and Regulation (EC) No 606/2009
Point 1: Use for aeration or oxygenation	—Air —Gaseous oxygen	
Point 3: Centrifuging and filtration	—Perlite —Cellulose —Diatomeceous earth	Use only as an inert filtering agent
Point 4: Use in order to create an inert atmosphere and to handle the product shielded from the air	—Nitrogen —Carbon dioxide —Argon	
Points 5, 15 and 21: Use	—Yeasts[1]	
Point 6: Use	—Di-ammonium phosphate —Thiamine hydrochloride	
Point 7: Use	—Sulphur dioxide —Potassium bisulphite or potassium metabisulphite	(a) The maximum sulphur dioxide content shall not exceed 100 milligrams per litre for red wines as referred to in point 1(a) of Part A of Annex I B to Regulation (EC) No 606/2009 and with a residual sugar level lower than 2 grams per litre;
		(b) The maximum sulphur dioxide content shall not exceed 150 milligrams per litre for white and rosé wines as referred to in point 1(b) of Part A of Annex I B to Regulation (EC) No 606/2009 and with a residual sugar level lower than 2 grams per litre;
		(c) For all other wines, the maximum sulphur dioxide content applied in accordance with Annex I B to Regulation (EC) No 606/2009 on 1 August 2010, shall be reduced by 30 milligrams per litre.
Point 9: Use	—Charcoal for oenological use	

Type of treatment in accordance with Annex I A to Regulation (EC) No 606/2009	Name of products or substances	Specific conditions, restrictions within the limits and conditions set out in Regulation (EC) No 1234/2007 and Regulation (EC) No 606/2009
Point 10: Clarification	—Edible gelatine[2] —Plant proteins from wheat or peas[2] —Isinglass[2] —Egg white albumin[2] —Tannins[2]	
	—Casein —Potassium caseinate —Silicon dioxide —Bentonite —Pectolytic enzymes	
Point 12: Use for acidification purposes	—Lactic acid —L(+)Tartaric acid	
Point 13: Use for deacidification purposes	— L(+)Tartaric acid —Calcium carbonate —Neutral potassium tartrate —Potassium bicarbonate	
Point 14: Addition	—Aleppo pine resin	
Point 17: Use	—Lactic bacteria	
Point 19: Addition	—L-Ascorbic acid	
Point 22: Use for bubbling	—Nitrogen	
Point 23: Addition	—Carbon dioxide	
Point 24: Addition for wine stabilisation purposes	—Citric acid	
Point 25: Addition	—Tannins[2]	
Point 27: Addition	—Meta-tartaric acid	
Point 28: Use	—Acacia gum[2] (= gum arabic)	
Point 30: Use	—Potassium bitartrate	
Point 31: Use	—Cupric citrate	
Point 31: Use	—Copper sulphate	Authorised until 31 July 2015
Point 38: Use	—Oak chips	

Type of treatment in accordance with Annex I A to Regulation (EC) No 606/2009	Name of products or substances	Specific conditions, restrictions within the limits and conditions set out in Regulation (EC) No 1234/2007 and Regulation (EC) No 606/2009
Point 39: Use	—Potassium alginate	
Type of treatment in accordance with Annex III, point A(2)(b) to Regulation (EC) No 606/2009	—Calcium sulphate	Only for "vino generoso" or "vino generoso de licor"

[1] For the individual yeast strains: if available, derived from organic raw material.

[2] Derived from organic raw material if available.]

NOTES

Inserted by Commission Regulation 203/2012/EU, Art 1(3), Annex.

ANNEX IX
INGREDIENTS OF AGRICULTURAL ORIGIN WHICH HAVE NOT BEEN PRODUCED ORGANICALLY REFERRED TO IN ARTICLE 28

[8.405]

1. UNPROCESSED VEGETABLE PRODUCTS AS WELL AS PRODUCTS DERIVED THEREFROM BY PROCESSES

1.1. **Edible fruits, nuts and seeds:**

— acorns	*Quercus* spp.
— cola nuts	*Cola acuminate*
— gooseberries	*Ribes uva-crispa*
— maracujas (passion fruit)	*Passiflora edulis*
— raspberries (dried)	*Rubus idaeus*
— red currants (dried)	*Ribes rubrum*

1.2. **Edible spices and herbs:**

— pepper (Peruvian)	*Schinus molle* L.
— horseradish seeds	*Armoracia rusticana*
— lesser galangal	*Alpinia officinarum*
— safflower flowers	*Carthamus tinctorius*
— watercress herb	*Nasturtium officinale*

1.3. **Miscellaneous:**
Algae, including seaweed, permitted in non-organic foodstuffs preparation

2. VEGETABLE PRODUCTS

2.1. **Fats and oils whether or not refined, but not chemically modified, derived from plants other than:**

— cocoa	*Theobroma cacao*
— coconut	*Cocos nucifera*
— olive	*Olea europaea*
— sunflower	*Helianthus annuus*
— palm	*Elaeis guineensis*
— rape	*Brassica napus, rapa*
— safflower	*Carthamus tinctorius*
— sesame	*Sesamum indicum*
— soya	*Glycine max*

2.2. **The following sugars, starches and other products from cereals and tubers:**
- — fructose
- — rice paper
- — unleavened bread paper
- — starch from rice and waxy maize, not chemically modified

2.3. **Miscellaneous:**
- — pea protein *Pisum* spp.
- — rum, only obtained from cane sugar juice
- — kirsch prepared on the basis of fruits and flavourings as referred to in Article 27(1)(c).

3. ANIMAL PRODUCTS

aquatic organisms, not originating from aquaculture, and permitted in no-organic foodstuffs preparation
- — gelatin
- — whey powder '*herasuola*'
- — casings

ANNEX X
SPECIES FOR WHICH ORGANICALLY PRODUCED SEED OR SEED POTATOES ARE AVAILABLE IN SUFFICIENT QUANTITIES AND FOR A SIGNIFICANT NUMBER OF VARIETIES IN ALL PARTS OF THE COMMUNITY REFERRED TO IN ARTICLE 45(3)

[8.406]

NOTES

Note that there is no text in the original version of this Annex in the Official Journal.

[ANNEX XI

A.
ORGANIC LOGO OF THE EU, REFERRED TO IN ARTICLE 57

[8.407]

1. The Organic logo of the EU shall comply with the model below:

2. The reference colour in Pantone is Green Pantone No 376 and Green (50% Cyan + 100% Yellow), when a four-colour process is used.

3. The Organic logo of the EU can also be used in black and white as shown, only where it is not practicable to apply it in colour:

4. If the background colour of the packaging or label is dark, the symbols may be used in negative format, using the background colour of the packaging or label.

5. If a symbol is used in colour on a coloured background, which makes it difficult to see, a delimiting outer line around the symbol can be used to improve contrast with the background colours.

6. In certain specific situations where there are indications in a single colour on the packaging, the Organic logo of the EU may be used in the same colour.

7. The Organic logo of the EU must have a height of at least 9 mm and a width of at least 13.5 mm; the proportion ratio height/width shall always be 1:1.5. Exceptionally the minimum size may be reduced to a height of 6 mm for very small packages.

8. The Organic logo of the EU may be associated with graphical or textual elements referring to organic farming, under the condition that they do not modify or change the nature of the Organic logo of the EU, nor any of the indications mentioned at Article 58. When associated to national or private logos using a green colour different from the reference colour mentioned in point 2, the Organic logo of the EU may be used in that non-reference colour.

9. . . .

B.
CODE NUMBERS REFERRED TO IN ARTICLE 58

The general format of the code numbers is as follows:
AB-CDE-999

Where:

1. 'AB' is the ISO code as specified in Article 58(1)(a) for the country where the controls take place; and

2. 'CDE' is a term, indicated in three letters to be decided by the Commission or each Member State, like 'bio' or 'öko' or 'org' or 'eko' establishing a link with the organic production method as specified in Article 58(1)(b); and

3. '999' is the reference number, indicated in maximum three digits, to be attributed, as specified in Article 58(1)(c) by:
  (a) each Member State's competent authority to the Control Authorities or Control Bodies to which they have delegated control tasks in accordance with Article 27 of Regulation (EC) No 834/2007;
  (b) the Commission, to:
    (i) the Control Authorities and Control Bodies referred to in Article 3(2)(a) of Commission Regulation (EC) No 1235/2008[1] and listed in Annex I to that Regulation;
    (ii) the third countries' competent authorities or Control Bodies referred to in Article 7(2)(f) of Regulation (EC) No 1235/2008 and listed in Annex III to that Regulation;
    (iii) the Control Authorities and Control Bodies referred to in Article 10(2)(a) of Regulation (EC) No 1235/2008, and listed in Annex IV to that Regulation;
  (c) each Member State's competent authority to the Control Authority or Control Body which has been authorised until 31 December 2012 for issuing the certificate of inspection in accordance with Article 19(1) fourth subparagraph of Regulation (EC) No 1235/2008 (import authorisations), upon proposal of the Commission.

The Commission shall make the code numbers available to the public by any appropriate technical means, including publication on the Internet.]

NOTES

Substituted by Commission Regulation 271/2010/EU, Art 1, para 5.
Pt A: para 9 repealed by Commission Regulation 344/2011/EU, Art 1(4).
Note that the first image above appears in colour in the Official Journal.

[1] OJ L334, 12.12.2008, p 25.

[ANNEX XII
MODEL OF DOCUMENTARY EVIDENCE TO THE OPERATOR ACCORDING TO ARTICLE 29(1) OF REGULATION (EC) NO 834/2007 REFERRED TO IN [ARTICLE 68(1)] OF THIS REGULATION

[8.408]

Documentary evidence to the operator according to Article 29(1) of Regulation (EC) No 834/2007 1. Document Number:	
2. Name and address of operator: main activity (producer, processor, importer, etc.):	3. Name, address and code number of control body/authority:
4. Product groups/Activity:	5. Defined as:

Documentary evidence to the operator according to Article 29(1) of Regulation (EC) No 834/2007	
— Plant and plant products: — Seaweed and seaweed products: — Livestock and livestock products: — Aquaculture animals and aquaculture animal products: — Processed products:	organic production, in-conversion products; and also non-organic production where parallel production/processing pursuant to Article 11 of Regulation (EC) No 834/2007 occurs
6. Validity period: Plant products from . . . . to . . . . Seaweed products from . . . . to . . . . Livestock products from . . . . to . . . . Aquaculture animal products from . . . . to . . . . Processed products from . . . . to	7. Date of control(s):
8. This document has been issued on the basis of Article 29(1) of Regulation (EC) No 834/2007 and of Regulation (EC) No 889/2008. The declared operator has submitted his activities under control, and meets the requirements laid down in the named Regulations. Date, place: Signature on behalf of the issuing control body/authority:]	

NOTES

Substituted by Commission Regulation 710/2009/EC, Art 1(21), Annex, para 7.

Title: words in square brackets substituted by Commission Regulation 126/2012/EU, Art 1(3).

[ANNEX XIIA
MODEL OF COMPLEMENTARY DOCUMENTARY EVIDENCE TO THE OPERATOR ACCORDING TO ARTICLE 29(1) OF REGULATION (EC) NO 834/2007 REFERRED TO IN ARTICLE 68(2) OF THIS REGULATION

[8.409]

Complementary documentary evidence to the operator according to Article 29(1) of Regulation (EC) No 834/2007

1.1 Number of the document:

1.2 Reference to the documentary evidence provided in accordance with Article 29(1) of Regulation (EC) No 834/2007: (1)

2. Specific characteristics of the production method used by the operator, referred to in Article 68(2) of Regulation (EC) No 889/2008: (2)

3. This document has been issued on the basis of Article 29(1) of Regulation (EC) No 834/2007 and Article 68(2) of Regulation (EC) No 889/2008. The declared operator has submitted his activities under control, and meets the requirements laid down in those Regulations.

Date, place:

Signature and stamp on behalf of the issuing control body/authority:

(1) Insert number of the documentary evidence provided in accordance with Article 68(1) of, and Annex XII to, this Regulation.

(2) Insert the relevant entry set out in Annex XIIb to this Regulation.]

NOTES

Inserted, together with Annex XIIb, by Commission Regulation 126/2012/EU, Art 1(4), Annex I.

[ANNEX XIIB

[8.410]

Entry referred to in the second subparagraph of Article 68(2):

— In Bulgarian : Животински продукти, произведени без използване на антибиотици
— In Spanish : Productos animales producidos sin utilizar antibióticos
— In Czech : Živočišné produkty vyprodukované bez použití antibiotik
— In Danish : Animalske produkter, der er produceret uden brug af antibiotika
— In German : Ohne Anwendung von Antibiotika erzeugte tierische Erzeugnisse
— In Estonian : Loomsed tooted, mille tootmisel ei ole kasutatud antibiootikume
— In Greek : Ζωικά προϊόντα που παράγονται χωρίς τη χρήση αντιβιοτικών
— In English : Animal products produced without the use of antibiotics
— In French : produits animaux obtenus sans recourir aux antibiotiques
[— In Croatian : Proizvodi životinjskog podrijetla dobiveni bez uporabe antibiotika]
— In Italian : Prodotti animali ottenuti senza l'uso di antibiotici
— In Latvian : Dzīvnieku izcelsmes produkti, kuru ražošanā nav izmantotas antibiotikas
— In Lithuanian : nenaudojant antibiotikų pagaminti gyvūniniai produktai
— In Hungarian : Antibiotikumok alkalmazása nélkül előállított állati eredetű termékek
— In Maltese : Il-prodotti tal-annimali prodotti mingħajr l-użu tal-antibijotiċi
— In Dutch : Zonder het gebruik van antibiotica geproduceerde dierlijke producten
— In Polish : Produkty zwierzęce wytwarzane bez użycia antybiotyków
— In Portuguese : Produtos de origem animal produzidos sem utilização de antibióticos
— In Romanian : Produse de origine animală obținute a se recurge la antibiotice
— In Slovak : Výrobky živočíšneho pôvodu vyrobené bez použitia antibiotík
— In Slovenian : Živalski proizvodi, proizvedeni brez uporabe antibiotikov
— In Finnish : Eläintuotteet, joiden tuotannossa ei ole käytetty antibiootteja
— In Swedish : Animaliska produkter som produceras utan antibiotika]

NOTES

Inserted as noted to Annex XIIa at **[8.409]**.
Entry in square brackets added by Commission Regulation 519/2013/EU, Art 1, Annex.

ANNEX XIII
MODEL OF A VENDOR DECLARATION REFERRED TO IN ARTICLE 69

[8.411]

Vendor declaration according to Article 9(3) of Council Regulation (EC) No 834/2007	
Name, address of vendor:	
Identification (e.g. lot or stock number):	Product name:
Components: (Specify all components existing in the product/used the last in the production process)	
I declare that this product was manufactured neither 'from' nor 'by' GMOs as those terms are used in Articles 2 and 9 of Council Regulation (EC) No 834/2007. I do not have any information which could suggest that this statement is inaccurate. Thus, I declare that the above named product complies with Article 9 of Regulation (EC) No 834/2007 regarding the prohibition on the use of GMOs. I undertake to inform our customer and its control body/authority immediately if this declaration is withdrawn or modified, or if any information comes to light which would undermine its accuracy. I authorise the control body or control authority, as defined in Article 2 of Council Regulation (EC) No 834/2007, which supervises our customer to examine the accuracy of this declaration and if necessary to take samples for analytic proof. I also accept that this task may be carried out by an independent institution which has been appointed in writing by the control body. The undersigned takes responsibility for the accuracy of this declaration.	
Country, place, date, signature of vendor:	Company stamp of vendor (*if appropriate*):

[ANNEX XIIIA

SECTION 1

[8.412]
Organic production of salmonids in fresh water:

Brown trout *(Salmo trutta)* — Rainbow trout *(Oncorhynchus mykiss)* — American brook trout *(Salvelinus fontinalis)* — Salmon *(Salmo salar)* — Charr *(Salvelinus alpinus)* — Grayling *(Thymallus thymallus)* — American lake trout (or grey trout) *(Salvelinus namaycush)* — Huchen *(Hucho hucho)*

Production system	Ongrowing farm systems must be fed from open systems. The flow rate must ensure a minimum of 60% oxygen saturation for stock and must ensure their comfort and the elimination of farming effluent.
Maximum stocking density	Salmonid species not listed below 15 kg/m^3 Salmon 20 kg/m^3 Brown trout and Rainbow trout 25 kg/m^3 [Arctic charr 25 kg/m^3]

SECTION 2

Organic production of salmonids in sea water:

Salmon *(Salmo salar)*, Brown trout *(Salmo trutta)* — Rainbow trout *(Oncorhynchus mykiss)*

Maximum stocking density	10 kg/m^3 in net pens

SECTION 3

Organic production of cod *(Gadus morhua)* and other Gadidae, sea bass *(Dicentrarchus labrax)*, sea bream *(Sparus aurata)*, meagre *(Argyrosomus regius)*, turbot *(Psetta maxima [= Scopthalmus maximux])*, red porgy *(Pagrus pagrus [= Sparus pagrus])*, red drum *(Sciaenops ocellatus)* and other Sparidae, and spinefeet (*Siganus* spp.)

Production system	**In open water containment systems (net pens/cages) with minimum sea current speed to provide optimum fish welfare or in open systems on land.**
Maximum stocking density	For fish other than turbot: 15 kg/m^3 For turbot: 25 kg/m^2

SECTION 4

Organic production of sea bass, sea bream, meagre, mullets (*Liza, Mugil)* and eel (*Anguilla spp.*) in earth ponds of tidal areas and costal lagoons

Containment system	Traditional salt pans transformed into aquaculture production units and similar earth ponds in tidal areas
Production system	There shall be adequate renewal of water to ensure the welfare of the species, At least 50% of the dikes must have plant cover Wetland based depuration ponds required
Maximum stocking density	4 kg/m^3

SECTION 5

Organic production of Sturgeon in fresh water:

Species concerned: *Acipenser* family

Production system	Water flow in each rearing unit shall be sufficient to ensure animal welfare Effluent water to be of equivalent quality to incoming water

Maximum stocking density	30 kg/m^3

SECTION 6

Organic production of fish in inland waters:

Species concerned: Carp family (*Cyprinidae*) and other associated species in the context of polyculture, including perch, pike, catfish, coregonids, sturgeon.

Production system	In fishponds which shall periodically be fully drained and in lakes. Lakes must be devoted exclusively to organic production, including the growing of crops on dry areas. The fishery capture area must be equipped with a clean water inlet and of a size to provide optimal comfort for the fish. The fish must be stored in clean water after harvest. Organic and mineral fertilisation of the ponds and lakes shall be carried out in compliance with Annex I to Regulation (EC) No 889/2008 with a maximum application of 20 kg Nitrogen/ha. Treatments involving synthetic chemicals for the control of hydrophytes and plant coverage present in production waters are prohibited. Areas of natural vegetation shall be maintained around inland water units as a buffer zone for external land areas not involved in the farming operation in accordance with the rules of organic aquaculture. For grow-out 'polyculture' shall be used on condition that the criteria laid down in the present specifications for the other species of lakes fish are duly adhered to.
Farming yield	The total production of species is limited to 1,500 kg of fish per hectare per year.

SECTION 7

Organic production of penaeid shrimps and freshwater prawns (*Macrobrachium* spp.):

Establishment of production unit/s	Location to be in sterile clay areas to minimise environmental impact of pond construction. Ponds to be built with the natural pre-existing clay. Mangrove destruction is not permitted.
Conversion time	Six months per pond, corresponding to the normal lifespan of a farmed shrimp.
Broodstock origin	A minimum of half the broodstock shall be domesticated after three years operating The remainder is to be pathogen free wild broodstock originating from sustainable fisheries. A compulsory screening to be implemented on the first and second generation prior to introducing to the farm.
Eyestalk ablation	Is prohibited.
Maximum on farm stocking densities and production limits	Seeding: maximum 22 post larvae/m^2 Maximum instantaneous biomass: 240 g/m^2

[SECTION 7A

Organic production of crayfish:

Species concerned: *Astacus astacus, Pacifastacus leniusculus.*

Maximum stocking density:	For small-sized crayfish (< 20 mm): 100 individuals per m^2. For crayfish of intermediate size (20–50 mm): 30 individuals per m^2. For adult crayfish (> 50 mm): 10 individuals per m^2, provided that adequate hiding places are available.]

SECTION 8

Molluscs and echinoderms:

Production systems	Long-lines, rafts, bottom culture, net bags, cages, trays, lantern nets, bouchot poles and other containment systems. For mussel cultivation on rafts the number of drop-ropes shall not exceed one per square meter of surface area. The maximum drop-rope length shall not exceed 20 metres. Thinning-out of drop-ropes shall not take place during the production cycle, however sub-division of drop ropes shall be permitted without increasing stocking density at the outset.

SECTION 9

Tropical fresh water fish: milkfish *(Chanos chanos)*, tilapia (*Oreochromis* spp.), siamese catfish (*Pangasius* spp.):

Production systems	Ponds and net cages
Maximum stocking density	Pangasius: 10 kg/m^3 Oreochromis: 20 kg/m^3

SECTION 10

Other aquaculture animal species: none]

NOTES

Inserted by Commission Regulation 710/2009/EC, Art 1(21), Annex, para 8.
Section 1: words in square brackets substituted by Commission Regulation 1358/2014/EU, Art 1(9), Annex, para 2(a).
Section 7a: inserted by Commission Regulation 1358/2014/EU, Art 1(9), Annex, para 2(b).

[ANNEX XIIIB
TOPICS TO BE COVERED BY THE NATIONAL COMPETENT AUTHORITY IN THE ORGANIC DATA REFERRED TO IN ARTICLE 92F

[8.413]

1. Information on the competent authority for the organic production
   — which body is the competent authority
   — resources available to the competent authority
   — description of audits performed by the competent authority (how, by whom)
   — documented procedure of the competent authority

2. Description of the control system for organic production
   — system of control bodies and/or control authorities
   — registered operators covered by the control system — minimum annual inspection
   — how is the risk based approach applied

3. Information on control bodies/authorities
   — list of control bodies/authorities
   — tasks delegated to the control bodies/conferred to control authorities
   — supervision of delegated control bodies (by whom and how)
   — coordination of activities in case of more than one control body/authority
   — training of staff performing the controls
   — announced/unannounced inspections and visits]

NOTES

Inserted, together with Annex XIIIc, by Commission Regulation 392/2013/EU, Art 1(6).

[ANNEX XIIIC
TEMPLATES FOR THE ORGANIC DATA REFERRED TO UNDER ARTICLE 92F

[8.414]

Report on official controls in the organic sector

Country:

Year:

1) Information on controls of operators:

Code number of control body or control authority	Number of registered operators per control body or control authority	Number of registered operators						Number of annual inspections						Number of additional risk based visits						Total number of inspections/visits					
		Agricultural Producers *	Aquaculture animal production units	Processors **	Importers	Exporters	Other operators ***	Agricultural Producers *	Aquaculture animal production units	Processors **	Importers	Exporters	Other operators ***	Agricultural Producers *	Aquaculture animal production units	Processors **	Importers	Exporters	Other operators ***	Agricultural Producers *	Aquaculture animal production units	Processors **	Importers	Exporters	Other operators ***
MS-BIO-01																									
MS-BIO-02																									
MS-BIO- . . .																									
Total																									

* Agricultural producers include agricultural producers only, producers that are also processors, producers that are also importers, other mixed producers not elsewhere classified (n.e.c.).

** Processors include processors only, processors that are also importers, other mixed processors n.e.c.

*** Other operators include traders (wholesalers, retailers), other operators n.e.c.

Code number of control body or control authority or Name of Competent Authority	Number of registered operators						Number of samples analysed						Number of samples indicating breach of Regulations (EC) No 834/2007 and (EC) No 1235/2008					
	Agricultural Producers *	Aquaculture animal production units	Processors **	Importers	Exporters	Other operators ***	Agricultural Producers *	Aquaculture animal production units	Processors **	Importers	Exporters	Other operators ***	Agricultural Producers *	Aquaculture animal production units	Processors **	Importers	Exporters	Other operators ***
MS-BIO-01																		
MS-BIO-02																		
MS-BIO- . . .																		
Total																		

* Agricultural producers include agricultural producers only, producers that are also processors, producers that are also importers, other mixed producers not elsewhere classified (n.e.c.).

** Processors include processors only, processors that are also importers, other mixed processors n.e.c.

*** Other operators include traders (wholesalers, retailers), other operators n.e.c.

Code number of control body or control authority	Number of registered operators						Number of irregularities or infringements found[1]						Number of measures applied on the lot or the production run[2]						Number of measures applied on the operator[3]					
	Agricultural Producers *	Aquaculture animal production units	Processors **	Importers	Exporters	Other operators ***	Agricultural Producers *	Aquaculture animal production units	Processors **	Importers	Exporters	Other operators ***	Agricultural Producers *	Aquaculture animal production units	Processors **	Importers	Exporters	Other operators ***	Agricultural Producers *	Aquaculture animal production units	Processors **	Importers	Exporters	Other operators ***
MS-BIO-01																								
MS-BIO-02																								
MS-BIO- . . .																								
Total																								

* Agricultural producers include agricultural producers only, producers that are also processors, producers that are also importers, other mixed producers not elsewhere classified (n.e.c.).

** Processors include processors only, processors that are also importers, other mixed processors n.e.c.

*** Other operators include traders (wholesalers, retailers), other operators n.e.c.

1 Only irregularities and infringements which affect the organic status of products and/or have resulted in a measure being applied are included.

2 Where an irregularity is found as regards compliance with the requirements laid down in this Regulation, the control authority or control body shall ensure that no reference to the organic production method is made in the labelling and advertising of the entire lot or production run affected by this irregularity, where this would be proportionate to the relevance of the requirement that has been violated and to the nature and particular circumstances of the irregular activities (as referred to in first subparagraph of Article 30(1) of Regulation (EC) No 834/2007).

3 Where a severe infringement or an infringement with prolonged effect is found, the control authority or control body shall prohibit the operator concerned from marketing products which refer to the organic production method in the labelling and advertising for a period to be agreed with the competent authority of the Member State (as referred to in second subparagraph of Article 30(1) of Regulation (EC) No 834/2007).

2) Information on supervision and audits:

Code number of control body or control authority	Number of registered operators per control body or control authority	Number of registered operators						Document review and office audit[1] (Number of operator files checked)						Number of review audits[2]						Number witness audits[3]					
		Agricultural Producers *	Aquaculture animal production units	Processors **	Importers	Exporters	Other operators ***	Agricultural Producers *	Aquaculture animal production units	Processors **	Importers	Exporters	Other operators ***	Agricultural Producers *	Aquaculture animal production units	Processors **	Importers	Exporters	Other operators ***	Agricultural Producers *	Aquaculture animal production units	Processors **	Importers	Exporters	Other operators ***
MS-BIO-01																									
MS-BIO-02																									
MS-BIO- . . .																									
Total																									

* Agricultural producers include agricultural producers only, producers that are also processors, producers that are also importers, other mixed producers not elsewhere classified (n.e.c.).

** Processors include processors only, processors that are also importers, other mixed processors n.e.c.

*** Other operators include traders (wholesalers, retailers), other operators n.e.c.

1 Document review of the relevant general documents describing the structure, functioning and quality management of the control body. Office audit of the control body, including checking of operator files and verification of handling of non-conformities and complaints, including the minimum control frequency, the use of risk based approach, unannounced and follow-up visits, the sampling policy and the exchange of information with other control bodies and control authorities.

2 Review audit: inspection of an operator by the competent authority to verify compliance with the operating procedures of the control body and to verify its effectiveness.

3 Witness audit: observation by the competent authority of an inspection by an inspector of the control body.

3) Conclusions on the control system for the organic production:

Code number of control body or control authority	Withdrawal of the approval			Actions taken to ensure effective operation of the control system for the organic production (enforcement)
	Yes/No	From (date)	To (date)	
MS-BIO-01				
MS-BIO-02				
MS-BIO- . . .				

Statement of overall performance of the control system for the organic production:]

NOTES

Inserted as noted to Annex XIIIb at **[8.413]**.

ANNEX XIV
CORRELATION TABLE REFERRED TO IN ARTICLE 96

[8.415]

Regulation (EEC) No 2092/91	(1) Regulation (EC) No 207/93 (2) Regulation (EC) No 223/2003 (3) Regulation (EC) No 1452/2003	This Regulation
—		Article 1
—		Article 2(a)
Article 4(15)		Article 2(b)
Annex III, C (first indent)		Article 2(c)
Annex III, C (second indent)		Article 2(d)
—		Article 2(e)
—		Article 2(f)
—		Article 2(g)
—		Article 2(h)
Article 4(24)		Article 2(i)
—		Article 3(1)
Annex I.B, 7.1 and 7.2		Article 3(2)
Annex I.B, 7.4		Article 3(3)
Annex I.A, 2.4		Article 3(4)
Annex I.A, 2.3		Article 3(5)
—		Article 4
Article 6(1), Annex I.A, 3		Article 5
Annex I.A, 5		Article 6
Annex I.B and C (titles)		Article 7
Annex I.B, 3.1		Article 8(1)
Annex I.C, 3.1		Article 8(2)
Annex I.B, 3.4, 3.8, 3.9, 3.10, 3.11		Article 9(1) to (4)
Annex I.C, 3.6		Article 9(5)
Annex I.B, 8.1.1		Article 10(1)
Annex I.B, 8.2.1		Article 10(2)
Annex I.B, 8.2.2		Article 10(3)
Annex I.B, 8.2.3		Article 10(4)
Annex I.B, 8.3.5		Article 11(1)
Annex I.B, 8.3.6		Article 11(2)
Annex I.B, 8.3.7		Article 11(3)
Annex I.B, 8.3.8		Article 11(4), (5)
Annex I.B, 6.1.9, 8.4.1 to 8.4.5		Article 12(1) to (4)
Annex I.B, 6.1.9		Article 12(5)
Annex I.C, 4, 8.1 to 8.5		Article 13
Annex I.B, 8.1.2		Article 14
Annex I.B, 7.1, 7.2		Article 15
Annex I.B, 1.2		Article 16
Annex I.B, 1.6		Article 17(1)
Annex I.B, 1.7		Article 17(2)
Annex I.B, 1.8		Article 17(3)
Annex I.B, 4.10		Article 17(4)
Annex I.B, 6.1.2		Article 18(1)
Annex I.B, 6.1.3		Article 18(2)

Regulation (EEC) No 2092/91	**(1) Regulation (EC) No 207/93** **(2) Regulation (EC) No 223/2003** **(3) Regulation (EC) No 1452/2003**	**This Regulation**
Annex I.C, 7.2		Article 18(3)
Annex I.B, 6.2.1		Article 18(4)
Annex I.B, 4.3		Article 19(1)
Annex I.C, 5.1, 5.2		Article 19(2) to (4)
Annex I.B, 4.1, 4.5, 4.7 and 4.11		Article 20
Annex I.B, 4.4		Article 21
Article 7		Article 22
Annex I.B, 3.13, 5.4, 8.2.5 and 8.4.6		Article 23
Annex I.B, 5.3, 5.4, 5.7 and 5.8		Article 24
Annex I.C, 6		Article 25
Annex III, E.3 and B		Article 26
Article 5(3) and Annex VI, part A and B		Article 27
Article 5(3)		Article 28
Article 5(3) (1):	Article 3	Article 29
Annex III, B.3		Article 30
Annex III.7		Article 31
Annex III, E.5		Article 32
Annex III.7a		Article 33
Annex III, C.6		Article 34
Annex III.8 and A.2.5		Article 35
Annex I.A, 1.1 to 1.4		Article 36
Annex I.B, 2.1.2		Article 37
Annex I.B, 2.1.1, 2.2.1, 2.3 and Annex I.C, 2.1, 2.3		Article 38
Annex I.B, 6.1.6		Article 39
Annex III, A1.3 and b		Article 40
Annex I.C, 1.3		Article 41
Annex I.B, 3.4 (first indent and 3.6(b))		Article 42
Annex I.B, 4.8		Article 43
Annex I.C, 8.3		Article 44
Article 6(3)		Article 45
	(3): Article 1(1), (2)	Article 45(1), (2)
	(3): Article 3(a)	Article 45(1)
	(3): Article 4	Article 45(3)
	(3): Article 5(1)	Article 45(4)
	(3): Article 5(2)	Article 45(5)
	(3): Article 5(3)	Article 45(6)
	(3): Article 5(4)	Article 45(7)
	(3): Article 5(5)	Article 45(8)
Annex I.B, 8.3.4		Article 46
Annex I.B, 3.6(a)		Article 47(1)
Annex I.B, 4.9		Article 47(2)
Annex I.C, 3.5		Article 47(3)
	(3): Article 6	Article 48

Regulation (EEC) No 2092/91	(1) Regulation (EC) No 207/93 (2) Regulation (EC) No 223/2003 (3) Regulation (EC) No 1452/2003	This Regulation
	(3): Article 7	Article 49
	(3): Article 8(1)	Article 50(1)
	(3): Article 8(2)	Article 50(2)
	(3): Article 9(1)	Article 51(1)
	(3): Article 9(2), (3)	Article 51(2)
		Article 51(3)
	(3): Article 10	Article 52
	(3): Article 11	Article 53
	(3): Article 12(1)	Article 54(1)
	(3): Article 12(2)	Article 54(2)
	(3): Article 13	Article 55
	(3): Article 14	Article 56
		Article 57
		Article 58
	(2): Article 1 and Article 5	Article 59
	(2): Article 5 and 3	Article 60
	(2): Article 4	Article 61
Article 5(5)		Article 62
Annex III.3		Article 63
Annex III.4		Article 64
Annex III.5		Article 65
Annex III.6		Article 66
Annex III.10		
Article 67		
—		Article 68
—		Article 69
Annex III, A.1.		Article 70
Annex III, A.1.2.		Article 71
—		Article 72
Annex III, A.1.3		Article 73
Annex III, A.2.1		Article 74
Annex III, A.2.2		Article 75
Annex III, A.2.3		Article 76
Annex I.B, 5.6		Article 77
Annex I.C, 5.5, 6.7, 7.7, 7.8		Article 78
Annex III, A.2.4		Article 79
Annex III, B.1		Article 80
Annex III, C		Article 81
Annex III, C.1		Article 82
Annex III, C.2		Article 83
Annex III, C.3		Article 84
Annex III, C.5		Article 85
Annex III, D		Article 86
Annex III, E		Article 87
Annex III, E.1		Article 88
Annex III, E.2		Article 89
Annex III, E.4		Article 90

Regulation (EEC) No 2092/91	(1) Regulation (EC) No 207/93 (2) Regulation (EC) No 223/2003 (3) Regulation (EC) No 1452/2003	This Regulation
Annex III, 9		Article 91
Annex III, 11		Article 92
		Article 93
		Article 94
Annex I.B, 6.1.5		Article 95(1)
Annex I.B, 8.5.1		Article 95(2)
—		Article 95(3)-(8)
—		Article 95
—		Article 96
—		Article 97
Annex II, part A		Annex I
Annex II, part B		Annex II
Annex VIII		Annex III
Annex VII		Annex IV
Annex II, part C		Annex V
Annex II, part D		Annex VI
Annex II, part E		Annex VII
Annex VI, part A and B		Annex VIII
Annex VI, part C		Annex IX
—		Annex X
—		Annex XI
—		Annex XIII
—		Annex IX

COMMISSION REGULATION

(607/2009/EC)

of 14 July 2009

laying down certain detailed rules for the implementation of Council Regulation (EC) No 479/2008 as regards protected designations of origin and geographical indications, traditional terms, labelling and presentation of certain wine sector products

THE COMMISSION OF THE EUROPEAN COMMUNITIES,

Having regard to the Treaty establishing the European Community,

Having regard to Council Regulation (EC) No 479/2008 of 29 April 2008 on the common organisation of the market in wine, amending Regulations (EC) No 1493/1999, (EC) No 1782/2003, (EC) No 1290/2005, (EC) No 3/2008 and repealing Regulations (EEC) No 2392/86 and (EC) No 1493/1999,[1] and in particular Articles 52, 56, 63 and 126(a) thereof,

Whereas:

(1) Chapter IV of Title III of Regulation (EC) No 479/2008 lays down the general rules for protecting the designations of origin and geographical indications of certain wine sector products.

(2) To ensure that Community-registered designations of origin and geographical indications meet the conditions laid down in Regulation (EC) No 479/2008, applications should be examined by the national authorities of the Member State concerned, in the context of a preliminary national objection procedure. Subsequent checks should be carried out to ensure that applications meet the conditions laid down by this Regulation, that the approach is uniform across the Member States and that registrations of designations of origin and geographical indications do not harm third parties. Consequently, the detailed implementing rules on application, examination, objection and cancellation procedures for the designations of origin and geographical indications of certain wine sector products should be established.

(3) The conditions in which a natural or legal person may apply for registration should be defined. Particular attention should be paid to defining the area concerned, taking into account the production zone and the characteristics of the product. Any producer established in the demarcated geographical area should be able to use the registered name provided the conditions laid down in the product specification are met. The demarcation of the area should be detailed, precise and unambiguous so that producers, the competent authorities and the control bodies can ascertain whether operations are being carried out within the demarcated geographical area.

(4) Specific rules should be established concerning the registration of designations of origin and geographical indications.

(5) The fact of restricting the packaging of a wine sector product with a designation of origin or a geographical indication, or operations connected with the presentation of the product, to a defined geographical area constitutes a restriction on the free movement of goods and freedom to provide services. In the light of the case-law of the Court of Justice, such restrictions may be imposed only if they are necessary, proportionate and suitable to protecting the reputation of the designation of origin or geographical indication. Any restriction should be duly justified from the point of view of the free movement of goods and the freedom to provide services.

(6) Provisions should be made concerning the condition relating to the production in the demarcated area. Indeed, a limited number of derogations exists in the Community.

(7) The details bearing out the link with the characteristics of the geographical area and their influence on the final product should also be defined.

(8) Entry in a Community register of designations of origin and geographical indications should also provide those involved in the trade and consumers with information. In order to ensure that it is accessible to all, it should be available electronically.

(9) In order to preserve the particular character of wines with protected designations of origin and geographical indications and to approximate the legislation of the Member States with a view to establishing a level playing field for competition within the Community, a Community legal framework governing checks on such wines, with which the specific provisions adopted by the Member States must comply, should be laid down. Such checks should make it possible to improve the traceability of the products in question and to specify the aspects which checks must cover. In order to prevent distortions of competition, checks should be carried out on an ongoing basis by independent bodies.

(10) In order to ensure that Regulation (EC) No 479/2008 is implemented in a consistent manner, models should be drawn up for applications, objections, amendments and cancellations.

(11) Chapter V of Title III of Regulation (EC) No 479/2008 lays down the general rules regarding the use of protected traditional terms in connection with certain wine sector products.

(12) The use, regulation and protection of certain terms (other than designations of origin and geographical indications) to describe wine sector products is a long-established practice in the Community. Such traditional terms evoke in the minds of consumers a production or ageing method or a quality, colour or type of place or a particular event linked to the history of the wine. So as to ensure fair competition and avoid misleading consumers, a common framework should be laid down regarding the definition, the recognition, protection and use of such traditional terms.

(13) The use of traditional terms on third countries' products is allowed provided they fulfil the same or equivalent conditions to those required from Member States in order to ensure that consumers are not misled. Furthermore, given that several third countries do not have the same level of centralised rules as the community legal system, some requirements for 'representative professional organisations' of third countries should be laid down to ensure the same guarantees as those provided for in the Community rules.

(14) Chapter VI of Title III of Regulation (EC) No 479/2008 lays down the general rules for the labelling and presentation of certain wine sector products.

(15) Certain rules on the labelling of foodstuffs are laid down in First Council Directive 89/104/EEC,[2] Council Directive 89/396/EEC of 14 June 1989 on indications or marks identifying the lot to which a foodstuff belongs,[3] Directive 2000/13/EC of the European Parliament and of the Council[4] and Directive 2007/45/EC of the European Parliament and of the Council of 5 September 2007 laying down rules on nominal quantities for prepacked products.[5] Those rules also apply to wine sector products, except where expressly excluded by the Directives concerned.

(16) Regulation (EC) No 479/2008 harmonises the labelling for all wine sector products and allows the use of terms other than those expressly covered by Community legislation, provided that they are accurate.

(17) Regulation (EC) No 479/2008 provides for conditions to be laid down for the use of certain terms referring, among others, to the provenance, bottler, producer, importer, etc. For some of these terms, Community rules are necessary for the smooth functioning of the internal market. Such rules should, in general, be based on existing provisions. For other terms, the Member States should lay down the rules for wine produced in their territory — which should be compatible with Community law — so as to allow for those rules to be adopted as close as possible to the

producer. The transparency of such rules should nevertheless be assured.

(18) To assist consumers, certain mandatory information should be grouped in a single visual field on the container, tolerance limits should be set for the indication of the actual alcoholic strength and account should be taken of the specific character of the products concerned.

(19) The existing rules on the use of indications or marks on labelling identifying the lot to which a foodstuff belongs have proved useful and should therefore be retained.

(20) Terms referring to the organic production of grapes are governed solely by Council Regulation (EC) No 834/2007 of 28 June 2007 on organic production and labelling of organic products[6] and apply to all wine sector products.

(21) The use of lead-based capsules to cover the closing devices of containers holding products covered by Regulation (EC) No 479/2008 should continue to be banned, in order to avoid any risk, firstly, of contamination, in particular by accidental contact with such capsules and, secondly, of environmental pollution from waste containing lead from such capsules.

(22) In the interests of product traceability and transparency, new rules on 'indication of provenance' should be introduced.

(23) The use of indications relating to wine grape varieties and vintage year for wines without designation of origin and geographical indications require specific implementing rules.

(24) The use of certain types of bottle for certain products is a long-established practice in the Community and third countries. Such bottles can evoke certain characteristics or a certain origin of products in the minds of consumers due to their long-established use. Such bottles types should therefore be reserved for the wines in question.

(25) The rules for labelling third-country wine sector products circulating on the Community market should also be harmonised as far as possible with the approach laid down for Community wine sector products in order to avoid misleading consumers and unfair competition for producers. However, consideration should be given to the differences in production conditions, winemaking traditions and legislation in third countries.

(26) In view of the differences between products covered by this Regulation and their markets, and the expectations of consumers, the rules should be differentiated according to the products concerned, in particular as far as certain optional particulars used for wines without protected designation of origin and geographical indication which nevertheless bear wine grapes varieties' names and vintage years if they conform with a certification accreditation (so-called 'varietal wines'). Therefore, in order to distinguish, within the category of wines without PDO/PGI, those which fall under the sub-category 'varietal wines' from those which do not benefit from this openness, specific rules on the use of optional particulars, should be established on one hand for wines with protected designations of origin and geographical indications, and on the other hand for wines without protected designation of origin and geographical indication, bearing in mind that also covers 'varietal wines'.

(27) Measures to ease the transition from the previous wine sector legislation to this Regulation (notably Council Regulation (EC) No 1493/1999 of 17 May 1999 on the common organisation of the market in wine)[7] should be adopted, so as to avoid unnecessary burdens on operators. In order to allow economic operators established in the Community and in third countries to comply with the labelling requirements, a transitional adaptation period should be granted. Therefore, provisions should be enacted to ensure that products labelled in accordance with the existing rules may continue to be marketed during a transitional period.

(28) Due to administrative burdens, certain Member States are not able to introduce the laws, regulation, or administrative provisions necessary to comply with Article 38 of Regulation (EC) No 479/2008 by 1 August 2009. In order to ensure that economic operators and competent authorities are not prejudiced by this deadline, a transitional period should be granted and transitional provisions should be established.

(29) The provisions of this Regulation should be without prejudice to any specific rules negotiated under agreements with third countries concluded under the procedure provided for in Article 133 of the Treaty.

(30) The new detailed rules for the implementation of Chapters IV, V and VI of Title III of Regulation (EC) No 479/2008 should replace the existing legislation, implementing Regulation (EC) No 1493/1999. Commission Regulation (EC) No 1607/2000 of 24 July 2000 laying down detailed rules for implementing Regulation (EC) No 1493/1999 on the common organisation of the market in wine in particular the Title relating to quality wine produced in specified regions[8] and Commission Regulation (EC) No 753/2002 of 29 April 2002 laying down certain rules for applying Council Regulation (EC) No 1493/1999 as regards the description, designation, presentation and protection of certain wine sector products[9] should therefore be repealed.

(31) Article 128 of Regulation (EC) No 479/2008 repeals the existing Council legislation in the wine sector, including that dealing with aspects covered by this Regulation. In order to avoid any trade difficulties, to allow a smooth transition for the economic operators and a reasonable period for

Member States to adopt a number of implementing measures, transitional periods need to be established.

(32) The detailed rules provided for in this Regulation should apply as from the same date as that on which Chapters IV, V and VI of Title III of Regulation (EC) No 479/2008 apply.

(33) The measures provided for in this Regulation are in accordance with the opinion of the Management Committee for the Common Organisation of Agricultural Markets,

NOTES

1 OJ L148, 6.6.2008, p 1.

2 OJ L40, 11.2.1989, p 1.

3 OJ L186, 30.6.1989, p 21.

4 OJ L109, 6.5.2000, p 29.

5 OJ L247, 21.9.2007, p 17.

6 OJ L189, 20.7.2007, p 1.

7 OJ L179, 14.7.1999, p 1.

8 OJ L185, 25.7.2000, p 17.

9 OJ L118, 4.5.2002, p 1.

HAS ADOPTED THIS REGULATION:

CHAPTER I
INTRODUCTORY PROVISIONS

[8.416]
Article 1
Subject matter

This Regulation lays down detailed rules for the implementation of Title III of Regulation (EC) No 479/2008 as regards in particular:

(a) the provisions contained in Chapter IV of that Title which relate to protected designations of origin and geographical indications of the products referred to in Article 33(1) of Regulation (EC) No 479/2008;

(b) the provisions contained in Chapter V of that Title which relate to the traditional terms of the products referred to in Article 33(1) of Regulation (EC) No 479/2008;

(c) the provisions contained in Chapter VI of that Title which relate to the labelling and presentation of certain wine sector products.

CHAPTER II
PROTECTED DESIGNATIONS OF ORIGIN AND GEOGRAPHICAL INDICATIONS

SECTION 1
APPLICATION FOR PROTECTION

[8.417]
Article 2
Applicant

1. A single producer may be an applicant within the meaning of Article 37(1) of Regulation (EC) No 479/2008 if it is shown that:

(a) the person in question is the only producer in the demarcated geographical area; and

(b) where the relevant demarcated geographical area is surrounded by areas with designations of origin or geographical indications, this relevant area possesses features which are substantially different from those of the surrounding demarcated areas or characteristics of the product differ from those of the products obtained in the surrounding demarcated areas.

2. A Member State or third country, or the respective authorities thereof shall not be an applicant within the meaning of Article 37 of Regulation (EC) No 479/2008.

[8.418]
[Article 3
Application for protection

An application for the protection of a designation of origin or of a geographical indication shall comprise the documents required in Articles 118c and 118d of Regulation (EC) No 1234/2007, the product specification and the single document.

The application and the single document shall be communicated to the Commission in accordance with Article 70a(1) of this Regulation.]

NOTES

Substituted by Commission Regulation 670/2011/EU, Art 1(3).

[8.419]
Article 4
Name

1. The name to be protected shall be registered only in the language(s) used to describe the product in question in the demarcated geographical area.
2. The name shall be registered with its original spelling(s).

[8.420]
Article 5
Demarcation of the geographical area

The area shall be demarcated in a detailed, precise and unambiguous manner.

[8.421]
Article 6
Production in the demarcated geographical area

1. For the purpose of application of Article 34(1)(a)(iii) and (b)(iii) of Regulation (EC) No 479/2008 and of this Article'*production*' covers all the operations involved, from the harvesting of the grapes to the completion of the wine-making process, with the exception of any post-production processes.
2. For products with a protected geographical indication, the portion of grapes, of up to 15 %, which may originate outside the demarcated geographical area as provided for in Article 34(1)(b)(ii) of Regulation (EC) No 479/2008, shall come from the Member State or third country concerned in which the demarcated area lies.
3. By way of derogation from Article 34(1)(a)(ii) of Regulation (EC) No 479/2008, Annex III, Part B, paragraph 3 of Commission Regulation (EC) No 606/2009[1] on wine-making practices and restrictions applies.
4. By way of derogation from Article 34(1)(a)(iii) and (1)(b)(iii) of Regulation (EC) No 479/2008, and on condition that the product specification so provides, a product with a protected designation of origin or geographical indication may be made into wine either:
   (a) in an area in the immediate proximity of the demarcated area concerned; or
   (b) in an area located within the same administrative unit or within a neighbouring administrative unit, in conformity with national rules; or
   (c) in the case of a trans-border designation of origin or geographical indication, or where an agreement on control measures exists between two or more Member States or between one or more Member State(s) and one or more third country(-ies), a product with a protected designation of origin or geographical indication may be made into wine in an area situated in the immediate proximity of the demarcated area in question.

By way of derogation from Article 34(1)(b)(iii) of Regulation (EC) No 479/2008, and on condition that the product specification so provides, wines with a protected geographical indication may continue to be made into wine beyond the immediate proximity of the demarcated area in question until 31 December 2012.

By way of derogation from Article 34(1)(a)(iii) of Regulation (EC) No 479/2008, and on condition that the product specification so provides, a product may be made into sparkling wine or semi-sparkling wine with a protected designation of origin beyond the immediate proximity of the demarcated area in question if this practice was in use prior to 1 March 1986.

NOTES

[1] See page 1 of this Official Journal.

[8.422]
Article 7
Link

1. The details bearing out the geographical link referred to in Article 35(2)(g) of Regulation (EC) No 479/2008 shall explain to what extent the features of the demarcated geographical area influence the final product.
In case of applications covering different categories of grapevine products, the details bearing out the link shall be demonstrated for each of the grapevine products concerned.
2. In the case of a designation of origin, the product specification shall set out:
   (a) details of the geographical area, and in particular natural and human factors, relevant to the link;
   (b) details of the quality or characteristics of the product essentially or exclusively attributable to the geographical environment;
   (c) a description of the causal interaction between the details referred to in point (a) and those referred to in point (b).
3. In the case of a geographical indication, the product specification shall set out:
   (a) details of the geographical area relevant to the link;
   (b) details of the quality, reputation or other specific characteristics of the product attributable to its geographical origin;

(c) a description of the causal interaction between the details referred to in point (a) and those referred to in point (b).

4. The product specification for a geographical indication shall state whether it is based on a specific quality or reputation or other characteristics linked to its geographical origin.

[8.423]
Article 8
Packaging in the demarcated geographical area

If a product specification indicates that packaging of the product must take place within the demarcated geographical area or in an area in the immediate proximity of the demarcated area in question, in accordance with a requirement referred to in Article 35(2)(h) of Regulation (EC) No 479/2008, justification for this requirement shall be given in respect of the product concerned.

SECTION 2
COMMISSION EXAMINATION PROCEDURE

[8.424]
[Article 9
Filing of the application

1. The date of submission of an application to the Commission shall be the date on which the application is received by the Commission.

2. The Commission shall confirm receipt of the application to the competent authorities of the Member State or those of the third country or the applicant established in the third country in question and shall attribute a file number to the application.

The confirmation of receipt shall include at least the following:

(a) the file number;
(b) the name to be registered;
(c) the date of receipt of the request.]

NOTES

Substituted by Commission Regulation 670/2011/EU, Art 1(2).

[8.425]
Article 10
Submission of a trans-border application

1. In the case of a trans-border request, a joint application may be submitted for a name designating a trans-border geographical area by more than one group of producers representing that area.

2. Where only Member States are concerned, the preliminary national procedure referred to in Article 38 of Regulation (EC) No 479/2008 applies in all the Member States concerned.

For the purposes of application of Article 38(5) of Regulation (EC) No 479/2008, a trans-border application shall be forwarded to the Commission by one Member State on behalf of the others, and shall include an authorisation from each of the other Member States concerned authorising the Member State forwarding the application to act on its behalf.

3. Where a trans-border application involves only third countries, the application shall be forwarded to the Commission either by one of the applicant groups on behalf of the others or by one of the third countries on behalf of the others and shall include:

(a) the elements proving that the conditions laid down in Articles 34 and 35 of Regulation (EC) No 479/2008 are fulfilled;
(b) the proof of protection in the third countries concerned; and
(c) an authorisation as referred to in paragraph 2 from each of the other third countries concerned.

4. Where a trans-border application involves at least one Member State and at least one third country, the preliminary national procedure referred to in Article 38 of Regulation (EC) No 479/2008 applies in all the Member States concerned. The application shall be forwarded to the Commission by one of the Member States or third countries or by one of the third-country applicant groups and shall include:

(a) the elements proving that the conditions laid down in Articles 34 and 35 of Regulation (EC) No 479/2008 are fulfilled;
(b) the proof of protection in the third countries concerned; and
(c) an authorisation as referred to in paragraph 2 from each of the other Member States or third countries concerned.

5. The Member State, third countries or groups of producers established in third countries which forwards to the Commission a trans-border application as referred to in paragraphs 2, 3 and 4 of this Article, becomes the consignee of any notification or decision issued by the Commission.

[8.426]

[Article 11

Admissibility of the application

1. An application shall be admissible when the single document is duly completed and the supporting documents are enclosed. The single document shall be considered to be duly completed when all the mandatory fields, as presented in the information systems referred to in Article 70a, have been filled in.

In this case, the application shall be considered admissible on the date on which it is received by the Commission. The applicant shall be informed.

This date shall be made known to the public.

2. If the application has not been completed or has been partially completed, or if the supporting documents referred to in paragraph 1 have not been submitted at the same time as the application or some are missing, the application shall be inadmissible.

3. Where the application is inadmissible, the competent authorities of the Member State or those of the third country or the applicant established in the third country in question shall be informed of the reasons for its inadmissibility and that they are entitled to submit another application duly completed.]

NOTES

Substituted by Commission Regulation 670/2011/EU, Art 1(3).

[8.427]

Article 12

Scrutiny of the conditions of validity

[1. If an admissible application does not meet the requirements laid down in Articles 118b and 118c of Regulation (EC) No 1234/2007, the Commission shall inform the Member State or authorities of the third country or the applicant established in the third country in question of the grounds for refusal, setting a deadline of at least 2 months for the withdrawal or amendment of the application or for the submission of comments.]

2. If the obstacles to registration are not remedied by the Member State or third-country authorities or the applicant established in the third country in question within the deadline, the Commission shall reject the application in accordance with Article 39(3) of Regulation (EC) No 479/2008.

3. Any decision to reject the designation of origin or geographical indication concerned shall be taken by the Commission on the basis of the documents and information available to it. Such decision on rejection shall be notified to the Member State or the third-country authorities or the applicant established in the third country in question.

NOTES

Para 1: substituted by Commission Regulation 670/2011/EU, Art 1(4).

SECTION 3
OBJECTION PROCEDURES

[8.428]

Article 13

National objection procedure in case of trans-border applications

For the purposes of Article 38(3) of Regulation (EC) No 479/2008 where a trans-border application involves only Member States or at least one Member State and at least one third country, the objection procedure shall be applied in all the Member States concerned.

[8.429]

[Article 14

Submission of objections under Community procedure

1. The objections referred to in Article 118h of Regulation (EC) No 1234/2007 shall be communicated in accordance with Article 70a(1) of this Regulation. The date of submission of an objection to the Commission shall be the date on which the objection is received by the Commission. This date shall be made known to the authorities and persons concerned by the present Regulation.

2. The Commission shall confirm receipt of the objection and assign a file number to the objection.

The confirmation of receipt shall include at least the following:

(a) the file number;

(b) the date of receipt of the objection.]

NOTES

Substituted by Commission Regulation 670/2011/EU, Art 1(5).

[8.430]
Article 15
Admissibility under Community procedure

1. For the purposes of determining whether an objection is admissible, in accordance with Article 40 of Regulation (EC) No 479/2008, the Commission shall verify that the objection mentions the prior right(s) claimed and the ground(s) for the objection and was received by the Commission within the deadline.

2. If the objection is based on the existence of an earlier trademark of reputation and renown, in accordance with Article 43(2) of Regulation (EC) No 479/2008, the objection shall be accompanied by proof of the filing, registration or use of that earlier trademark, such as the certificate of registration or proof of its use, and proof of its reputation and renown.

3. Any duly substantiated objection shall contain details of the facts, evidence and comments submitted in support of the objection, accompanied by the relevant supporting documents.

The information and evidence to be produced in support of the use of an earlier trademark shall comprise particulars of the location, duration, extent and nature of the use made of the earlier trademark, and of its reputation and renown.

4. If the details of the prior right(s) claimed, ground(s), facts, evidence or comments, or the supporting documents, as referred to in paragraphs 1 to 3, have not been produced at the same time as the objection or if some are missing, the Commission shall inform the opponent accordingly and shall invite him to remedy the deficiencies noted within a period of two months. If the deficiencies are not remedied before the time limit expires, the Commission shall reject the objection as inadmissible. The decision on inadmissibility shall be notified to the objector and to the Member State or the third-country authorities or the applicant established in the third country in question.

5. An objection that is deemed admissible shall be notified to the Member State or the third-country authorities or the applicant established in the third country in question.

[8.431]
Article 16
Scrutiny of an objection under Community procedure

1. If the Commission has not rejected the objection in accordance with Article 15(4), it shall communicate the objection to the Member State or the third-country authorities or the applicant established in the third country in question and shall invite him to file observations within two months from the issuance date of such communication. Any observations received within this two months period shall be communicated to the objector.

In the course of the scrutiny of an objection, the Commission shall request the parties to submit comments, if appropriate, within a period of two months from the issuance date of such request, on the communications received from the other parties.

2. If the Member State or the third-country authorities or the applicant established in the third country in question or the objector files no observations in response, or does not respect the time periods, the Commission gives a ruling on the opposition.

3. Any decision to reject or register the designation of origin or geographical indication concerned shall be taken by the Commission on the basis of the evidence available to it. The decision on rejection shall be notified to the objector and to the Member State or the third-country authorities or the applicant established in the third country in question.

4. In the event of multiple objectors, following a preliminary examination of one or more such objections, it may not be possible to accept the application for registration; in such cases, the Commission may suspend the other objection procedures. The Commission shall inform the other objectors of any decision affecting them which was taken in the course of the procedure.

Where an application is rejected, objection procedures which have been suspended shall be deemed to be closed and the objectors concerned shall be duly informed.

SECTION 4
PROTECTION

[8.432]
Article 17
Decision on protection

1. Unless applications for protection of designations of origin or geographical indications are rejected pursuant to Articles 11, 12, 16 and 28, the Commission shall decide to protect the designations of origin or geographical indications.

2. Decisions on protection taken pursuant to Article 41 of Regulation (EC) No 479/2008 shall be published in the *Official Journal of the European Union*.

[8.433]
[Article 18
Register

1. A "register of protected designations of origin and protected geographical indications", hereinafter "the Register", is established and kept updated by the Commission in accordance with Article 118n of Regulation (EC) No 1234/2007. It is established in the electronic database "E-Bacchus" on the basis of the decisions granting protection to the designations in question.

2. A designation of origin or geographical indication that has been accepted shall be recorded in the Register.

In the case of names registered under Article 118s(1) of Regulation (EC) No 1234/2007, the Commission shall enter in the Register the data provided for in paragraph 3 of this Article.

3. The Commission shall enter the following data in the Register:
- (a) the protected designation;
- (b) the file number;
- (c) a record of the fact that the name is protected as either a geographical indication or designation of origin;
- (d) the name of the country or countries of origin;
- (e) the date of registration;
- (f) the reference to the legal instrument protecting the name;
- (g) the reference to the single document.

4. The register shall be made available to the public.]

NOTES

Substituted by Commission Regulation 670/2011/EU, Art 1(6).

[8.434]
Article 19
Protection

1. Protection of a designation of origin or geographical indication shall run from the date on which it is entered in the Register.

2. In the event of unlawful use of a protected designation of origin or geographical indication, the competent authorities of the Member States shall on their own initiative, pursuant to Article 45(4) of Regulation (EC) No 479/2008, or at the request of a party, take the steps necessary to stop such unlawful use and to prevent any marketing or export of the products at issue.

3. The protection of a designation of origin or geographical indication shall apply to the whole denomination including its constitutive elements provided they are distinctive in themselves. A non-distinctive or generic element of a protected designation of origin or geographical indication shall not be protected.

SECTION 5
AMENDMENTS AND CANCELLATION

[8.435]
Article 20
Amendment to the product specification or single document

[1. An application for approval of amendments to the product specification submitted by an applicant as referred to in Article 118e of Regulation (EC) No 1234/2007 of a protected designation of origin or geographical indication shall be communicated in accordance with Article 70a(1) of this Regulation.

2. An application for the approval of the amendment of a product specification under Article 118q(1) of Regulation (EC) No 1234/2007 shall be admissible if the information required under Article 118c(2) of that Regulation and the request duly drawn up have been communicated to the Commission.

3. For the purposes of applying the first sentence of Article 118q(2) of Regulation (EC) No 1234/2007, Articles 9 to 18 of this Regulation shall apply *mutandis mutadis*.]

4. An amendment is considered to be minor if:
- (a) it does not relate the essential characteristics of the product;
- (b) it does not alter the link;
- (c) it does not include a change in the name or any part of the name of the product;
- (d) it does not affect the demarcated geographical area;
- (e) it does not entail any further restrictions on the marketing of the product.

5. Where the application for approval of amendments to the product specification is submitted by an applicant other than the initial applicant, the commission shall communicate the application to the initial applicant.

6. Where the Commission decides to accept an amendment to the product specification that affects or comprises an amendment to the information recorded in the Register, it shall delete the original data from the Register and enter the new data with effect from the date on which the relevant decision takes effect.

NOTES

Paras 1–3: substituted by Commission Regulation 670/2011/EU, Art 1(7).

[8.436]
[Article 21
Submission of a request for cancellation

1. A request for cancellation submitted in accordance with Article 118r of Regulation (EC) No 1234/2007 shall be communicated in accordance with Article 70a(1) of this Regulation. The date of submission of request for cancellation to the Commission shall be the date on which the request is received by the Commission. This date shall be made known to the public.
2. The Commission shall confirm receipt of the request and assign a file number to the request. The confirmation of receipt shall include at least the following:
   (a) the file number;
   (b) the date of receipt of the request.
3. Paragraphs 1 and 2 do not apply when the cancellation is initiated by the Commission.]

NOTES

Substituted by Commission Regulation 670/2011/EU, Art 1(8).

[8.437]
Article 22
Admissibility

1. For the purposes of determining whether a request of cancellation is admissible, in accordance with Article 50 of Regulation (EC) No 479/2008, the Commission shall verify that the request:
   (a) mentions the legitimate interest, the reasons and justification of the author of the request of cancellation;
   (b) explains the ground for cancellation; and
   (c) refers to a statement from the Member State or third country where the residence or registered office of the author of the request is located supporting the request for cancellation.
2. Any request for cancellation shall contain details of the facts, evidence and comments submitted in support of the cancellation, accompanied by the relevant supporting documents.
3. If detailed information concerning the grounds, facts, evidence and comments, as well as the supporting documents referred to in paragraphs 1 and 2, have not been produced at the same time as the request of cancellation, the Commission shall inform the author of the request of cancellation accordingly and shall invite him to remedy the deficiencies noted within a period of two months. If the deficiencies are not remedied before the time limit expires, the Commission shall reject the request as inadmissible. The decision on inadmissibility shall be notified to the author of the request of cancellation and to the Member State or the third-country authorities or the author of the request of cancellation established in the third country in question.
4. Any request of cancellation that is deemed admissible, as well as a Commission own-initiative cancellation procedure, shall be notified to the Member State or the third-country authorities or the applicants established in the third country whose designation of origin or geographical indication is affected by the cancellation.
[5. The communications to the Commission referred to in paragraph 3 shall be carried out in accordance with Article 70a(1).]

NOTES

Para 5: added by Commission Regulation 670/2011/EU, Art 1(9).

[8.438]
Article 23
Scrutiny of a cancellation

1. If the Commission has not rejected the request of cancellation in accordance with Article 22(3), it shall communicate the cancellation to the Member State or the third-country authorities or the producers concerned established in the third country in question and shall invite him to file observations within two months from the issuance date of such communication. Any observations received within this two months period shall be communicated, where applicable, to the author of the request of cancellation.

In the course of the scrutiny of a cancellation, the Commission shall request the parties to submit comments, if appropriate, within a period of two months from the issuance date of such request, on the communications received from the other parties.

[The communications to the Commission referred to in the first and second subparagraphs shall be carried out in accordance with Article 70a(1).]

2. If the Member State or the third-country authorities or the applicant established in the third country in question or the author of a request of cancellation files no observations in response, or does not respect the time periods, the Commission decides upon the cancellation.

3. Any decision to cancel the designation of origin or geographical indication concerned shall be taken by the Commission on the basis of the evidence available to it. It shall consider whether compliance with the product specification for a wine sector product covered by a protected designation of origin or geographical indication is no longer possible or can no longer be guaranteed, particularly if the conditions laid down in Article 35 of Regulation (EC) No 479/2008 are no longer fulfilled or may no longer be fulfilled in the near future.

Such decision on cancellation shall be notified to the author of the request of cancellation and to the Member State or the third-country authorities or the applicant established in the third country in question.

4. In the event of multiple requests of cancellation, following a preliminary examination of one or more such requests of cancellation, it may not be possible to accept to continue to protect a designation or origin or geographical indication, in which case the Commission may suspend the other cancellation procedures. In this case the Commission shall inform the other authors of the requests of cancellation of any decision affecting them which was taken in the course of the procedure.

Where a protected designation of origin or geographical indication is cancelled, cancellation procedures which have been suspended shall be deemed to be closed and the authors of the request of cancellation concerned shall be duly informed.

5. When a cancellation takes effect, the Commission shall delete the name from the Register.

NOTES

Para 1: words in square brackets added by Commission Regulation 670/2011/EU, Art 1(10).

SECTION 6
CHECKS

[8.439]
[Article 24
Notification of operators

Each operator wishing to participate in all or part of the production or packaging of a product with a protected designation of origin or geographical indication shall be notified to the competent control authority referred to in Article 118o of Regulation (EC) No 1234/2007.]

NOTES

Substituted by Commission Regulation 401/2010/EU, Art 1(2).

[8.440]
Article 25
Annual verification

1. The annual verification carried out by the competent control authority as referred to in Article 48(1) of Regulation (EC) No 479/2008 shall consist of:

(a) an organoleptic and analytical testing for products covered by a designation of origin;

(b) either analytical testing only or both organoleptic and analytical testing for products covered by a geographical indication; and

(c) a check on the conditions set out in the product specification.

[The annual verification shall be conducted in the Member State in which production took place in accordance with the product specification and shall be carried out either through:

(a) random checks based on a risk analysis; or

(b) sampling; or

(c) systematically[; or

(d) a combination of any of the above.]

In the case of random checks, Member States shall select the minimum number of operators to be subjected to those checks.

In the case of sampling, Member States shall ensure that by their number, nature and frequency of controls, they are representative of the whole of the demarcated geographical area concerned and correspond to the volume of wine-sector products marketed or held with a view to their marketing.

2. The testing referred to in paragraph 1, first subparagraph, points (a) and (b) shall be performed on anonymous samples, demonstrate that the product tested complies with the characteristics and qualities described in the product specification for the relevant designation of origin or geographical indication, and be carried out at any stage in the production process, including even the packaging stage, or later. Each sample taken shall be representative of the relevant wines held by the operator.

3. For the purposes of checking compliance with the product specification referred to in paragraph 1, first subparagraph, point (c), the control authority shall check:

(a) the premises of operators, consisting in checking that the operators are actually able to meet the conditions laid down in the product specification; and

(b) the products at any stage of the production process, including the packaging stage, on the basis of an inspection plan which is drawn up in advance by the control authority and of which operators are aware, covering every stage of production of the product.

4. The annual verification shall ensure that a product cannot use the protected designation of origin or geographical indication relating to it unless:

[(a) the results of the testing referred to in paragraph 1, first subparagraph, points (a) and (b) and in paragraph 2 prove that the product in question complies with the conditions in the specification and possesses all the appropriate characteristics of the designation of origin or geographical indication concerned;]

(b) the other conditions listed in the product specification are met in accordance with the procedures laid down in paragraph 3.

5. Any product failing to meet the conditions set out in this Article may be placed on the market, but without the relevant designation of origin or geographical indication, provided that the other legal requirements are satisfied.

6. In the case of a protected trans-border designation of origin or geographical indication, the verification may be performed by a control authority of either of the Member States affected by this designation of origin or geographical indication.

7. In the case where annual verification is carried out at the packaging stage of the product in the territory of a Member State which is not the Member State where the production took place, Article 84 of Commission Regulation (EC) No 555/2008[1] applies.

8. Paragraphs 1 to 7 apply to wines bearing a designation of origin or a geographical indication, whose designation of origin or geographical indication concerned meet the requirements as referred to in Article 38(5) of Regulation (EC) No 479/2008.

NOTES

Para 1: words in square brackets substituted and words omitted repealed by Commission Regulation 401/2010/EU, Art 1(3)(a).

Para 4: sub-para (a) substituted by Commission Regulation 401/2010/EU, Art 1(3)(b).

[1] OJ L170, 30.6.2008, p 1.

[8.441]
Article 26
Analytical and organoleptic testing

The analytical and organoleptic testing referred to in the first subparagraph of paragraph 1 under (a) and (b) of Article 25 consists of:

(a) an analysis of the wine in question measuring the following characteristic properties:

(i) determined on the basis of a physical and chemical analysis:

— total and actual alcoholic strength,

— total sugars expressed in terms of fructose and glucose (including any sucrose, in the case of semi-sparkling and sparkling wines),

— total acidity,

— volatile acidity,

— total sulphur dioxide.

(ii) determined on the basis of an additional analysis:

— carbon dioxide (semi-sparkling and sparkling wines, excess pressure in bar at 20°C),

— any other characteristic properties provided for in Member States legislation or product specifications of protected designations of origin and geographical indications concerned;

(b) an organoleptic test covering visual appearance, odour and taste.

[8.442]
Article 27
Checks on products originating in third countries

If third country's wines benefit from the protection of a protected designation of origin or geographical indication, the third country concerned shall send the Commission, at its request, information on the competent authorities referred to in Article 48(2) of Regulation (EC) No 479/2008 and on the aspects covered by the check, as well as proof that the wine in question fulfils the conditions of the relevant designation of origin or geographical indication.

SECTION 7
CONVERSION INTO A GEOGRAPHICAL INDICATION

[8.443]
Article 28
Request

1. A Member State or third country authority or the applicant established in the third country in question may request the conversion of a protected designation of origin into a protected geographical indication if the compliance with the product specification of a protected designation of origin is no longer possible or can no longer be guaranteed.

[The application shall be communicated in accordance with Article 70a(1). The date of submission of an application for conversion to the Commission shall be the date on which the application is received by the Commission.]

2. If the request for conversion into a geographical indication does not meet the requirements laid down in Articles 34 and 35 of Regulation (EC) No 479/2008, the Commission shall inform the Member State or the third-country authorities or the applicant established in the third country in question of the grounds for refusal, and shall invite him to withdrew or amend the request or submit comments within a period of two months.

3. If the obstacles to the conversion into a geographical indication are not remedied by the Member State or third-country authorities or the applicant established in the third country in question before the time limit expires, the Commission shall reject the request.

4. Any decision to reject the conversion request shall be taken by the Commission on the basis of the documents and information available to it. Such decision on rejection shall be notified to the Member State or the third-country authorities or the applicant established in the third country in question.

5. Articles 40 and 49(1) of Regulation (EC) No 479/2008 shall not apply.

NOTES

Para 1: words in square brackets substituted by Commission Regulation 670/2011/EU, Art 1(11).

CHAPTER III
TRADITIONAL TERMS

SECTION 1
APPLICATION

[8.444]
Article 29
Applicants

1. Competent authorities of Member States or third countries or representative professional organisations established in third countries may submit to the Commission an application for protection of traditional terms within the meaning of Article 54(1) of Regulation (EC) No 479/2008.

2. '*Representative professional organisation*' shall mean any producer organisation or association of producer organisations having adopted the same rules, operating in a given or more wine designation of origin or geographical indication area(s) where it includes in its membership at least two thirds of the producers in the designation of origin or geographical indication area(s) in which it operates and accounts for at least two thirds of that areas' production. A representative professional organisation may lodge an application for protection only for wines which it produces.

[8.445]
[Article 30
Application for protection

1. The application for protection of a traditional term shall be communicated by the competent authorities of the Member States or those of the third countries or by the representative trade organisations in accordance with Article 70a(1). The application shall be accompanied by the legislation of the Member States or rules applicable to wine producers in third countries governing the use of the term in question and the reference to that legislation or those rules.

2. In the case of a request submitted by a representative trade organisation established in a third country, the applicant shall communicate to the Commission the information regarding the representative trade organisation and its members, in accordance with Article 70a(1). The Commission shall make this information public.]

NOTES

Substituted by Commission Regulation 670/2011/EU, Art 1(12).

[8.446]
Article 31
Language

1. The term to be protected shall be either:
   (a) in the official language(s), regional language(s) of the Member State or third country where the term originates; or
   (b) in the language used in commerce for this term.

The term used in a certain language shall refer to specific products referred to in Article 33(1) of Regulation (EC) No 479/2008.

2. The term shall be registered with its original spelling(s).

[8.447]
[Article 32
Rules on traditional terms of third countries

1. The definition of traditional terms provided for in Article 118u(1) of Regulation (EC) No 1234/2007 shall apply *mutatis mutandis* to terms traditionally used in third countries for wine products covered by geographical indications or names of origin under the legislation of those third countries.

2. Wines originating in third countries whose labels bear traditional indications other than the traditional terms listed in the electronic database "E-Bacchus" may use these traditional indications on wine labels in accordance with the rules applicable in the third countries concerned, including those emanating from representative professional organisations.]

NOTES

Substituted by Commission Regulation 538/2011/EU, Art 1(2).

SECTION 2
EXAMINATION PROCEDURE

[8.448]
[Article 33
Filing of the application

1. The date of submission of an application to the Commission shall be the date on which the application is received by the Commission.

2. The Commission shall confirm receipt of the application to the authorities of the Member State or of the third country or the applicant established in the third country in question and shall attribute a file number to the application.

The confirmation of receipt shall include at least the following:

(a) the file number;
(b) the traditional term;
(c) the date of receipt of the request.]

NOTES

Substituted by Commission Regulation 670/2011/EU, Art 1(13).

[8.449]
[Article 34
Admissibility

1. An application shall be admissible where the application form is duly filled in and the documents required in accordance with the provisions of Article 30 are enclosed with the application. The application form shall be considered to be duly filled in when all the mandatory fields, as presented in the information systems referred to in Article 70a, have been filled in.

In this case, the application shall be considered admissible on the date on which it is received by the Commission. The applicant shall be informed.

This date shall be made known to the public.

2. If the form has not been completed or has only been partially completed, or if the documents referred to in paragraph 1 were not submitted at the same time as the application or some are missing, the application shall be inadmissible.

3. Where the application is inadmissible, the authorities of the Member State or those of the third country or the applicant established in the third country in question shall be informed of the reasons for its inadmissibility and that they are entitled to submit another application duly completed.]

NOTES

Substituted by Commission Regulation 670/2011/EU, Art 1(14).

[8.450]
Article 35
Conditions of validity

1. The recognition of a traditional term shall be accepted if:

(a) it fulfils the definition as laid down in Article 54(1)(a) or (b) of Regulation (EC) No 479/2008 and the conditions laid down in Article 31 of this Regulation;
(b) the term exclusively consists of either:
  (i) a name traditionally used in commerce in a large part of the territory of the Community or of the third country concerned, to distinguish specific categories of grapevine products referred to in Article 33(1) of Regulation (EC) No 479/2008; or
  (ii) a reputed name traditionally used in commerce in at least the territory of the Member State or third country concerned, to distinguish specific categories of grapevine products referred to in Article 33(1) of Regulation (EC) No 479/2008;
(c) the term shall:

(i) not be generic;
(ii) be defined and regulated in the Member State's legislation; or
(iii) be subject to conditions of use as provided for by rules applicable to wine producers in the third country concerned, including those emanating from representative professional organisations.

2. For the purpose of paragraph (1), point (b), traditional use means:
(a) at least five years in case of terms filed in language(s) referred to in Article 31(a) of this Regulation;
(b) at least 15 years in case of terms filed in a language referred to in Article 31(b) of this Regulation.

3. For the purpose of paragraph (1), point (c)(i), 'generic' means the name of a traditional term although it relates to a specific production method or ageing method, or the quality, colour, type of place, or a particular linked to the history of a grapevine product, has become the common name of the grapevine product in question in the Community.

4. The condition listed in paragraph 1(b) of this Article does not apply to traditional terms referred to in Article 54(1)(a) to Regulation (EC) No 479/2008.

[8.451]
Article 36
Grounds for refusal

1. If an application for a traditional term does not meet the definition laid down in Article 54(1) of Regulation (EC) No 479/2008 and the requirements laid down in Articles 31 and 35, the Commission shall inform the applicant of the grounds for refusal, setting a deadline of two months from the issuance date of such communication, for the withdrawal or amendment of the application or for the submission of comments.

The Commission shall decide on the protection based on the information available to it.

2. If the obstacles are not remedied by the applicant within the deadline referred to in paragraph 1, the Commission shall reject the application. Any decision to reject the traditional term concerned shall be taken by the Commission on the basis of the documents and information available to it. Such decision on rejection shall be notified to the applicant.

SECTION 3
OBJECTION PROCEDURES

[8.452]
Article 37
Submission of a request of objection

1. Within two months from the date of publication provided for in the first sub-paragraph of Article 33, any Member State or third country, or any natural or legal person having a legitimate interest may object to the proposed recognition by lodging a request of objection.

[2. The objection shall be communicated in accordance with Article 70a(1). The date of submission of an objection to the Commission shall be the date on which the application is received by the Commission.

3. The Commission shall confirm receipt of the objection and assign a file number to the objection.

The confirmation of receipt shall include at least the following:
(a) the file number;
(b) the date of receipt of the objection.]

NOTES

Paras 2, 3: substituted by Commission Regulation 670/2011/EU, Art 1(15).

[8.453]
Article 38
Admissibility

1. For the purposes of determining whether an objection is admissible, the Commission shall verify that the request of objection mentions the prior right(s) claimed and the ground(s) for the objection and was received by the Commission within the deadline provided for in the first paragraph of Article 37.

2. If the objection is based on the existence of an earlier trademark of reputation and renown, in accordance with Article 41(2), the request of objection shall be accompanied by proof of the filing, registration or use of that earlier trademark, such as the certificate of registration and proof of its reputation and renown.

3. Any duly substantiated request of objection shall contain details of the facts, evidence and comments submitted in support of the objection, accompanied by the relevant supporting documents.

The information and evidence to be produced in support of the use of an earlier trademark shall comprise particulars of the location, duration, extent and nature of the use made of the earlier trademark, and of its reputation and renown.

4. If the details of the prior right(s) claimed, ground(s), facts, evidence or comments, or the supporting documents, as referred to in paragraphs 1 to 3, have not been produced at the same time as the request of objection or if some are missing, the Commission shall inform the opponent accordingly and shall invite him to remedy the deficiencies noted within a period of two months. If the deficiencies are not remedied before the time limit expires, the Commission shall reject the request as inadmissible. The decision on inadmissibility shall be notified to the objector and to the Member State or the third-country authorities or the representative professional organisation established in the third country in question.

5. Any request of objection that is deemed admissible shall be notified to the Member State or the third-country authorities or the representative professional organisation in the third country in question.

[8.454]
Article 39
Scrutiny of an objection

1. If the Commission has not rejected the request of opposition in accordance with Article 38(4), it shall communicate the objection to the Member State or the third-country authorities or the representative professional organisation established in the third country in question and shall invite him to file observations within two months from the issuance date of such communication. Any observations received within this two months period shall be communicated to the objector.

In the course of its scrutiny of an objection, the Commission shall request the parties to submit comments, if appropriate, within a period of two months from the issuance date of such request, on the communications received from the other parties.

2. If the Member State or the third-country authorities or the representative professional organisation established in the third country in question or the objector files no observations in response, or does not respect the time periods, the Commission gives ruling on the opposition.

3. Any decision to reject or recognise the traditional term concerned shall be taken by the Commission on the basis of the evidence available to it. It shall consider whether the conditions referred to in Article 40(1), or laid down in Articles 41(3) or 42 are not fulfilled. The decision on rejection shall be notified to the objector and to the Member State or the third-country authorities or the representative professional organisation established in the third country in question.

4. In the event of multiple requests of objection, following a preliminary examination of one or more such requests of objection, it may not be possible to accept the application for recognition; in such cases, the Commission may suspend the other objection procedures. The Commission shall inform the other objectors of any decision affecting them which was taken in the course of the procedure.

Where an application is rejected, objection procedures which have been suspended shall be deemed to be closed and the objectors concerned shall be duly informed.

SECTION 4
PROTECTION

[8.455]
[Article 40
General protection

1. If a traditional term for which protection is requested meets the conditions set out in Article 118u(1) of Regulation (EC) No 1234/2007 and in Articles 31 and 35 of this Regulation and is not rejected by virtue of Articles 36, 38 and 39 of this Regulation, the traditional term is listed and defined in the "E-Bacchus" database, in accordance with Article 118u(2) of Regulation (EC) No 1234/2007 on the basis of the information communicated to the Commission in accordance with Article 70a(1) of this Regulation, mentioning the following:

(a) the language referred to in Article 31(1);
(b) the grapevine product category or categories concerned by the protection;
(c) a reference to the national legislation of the Member State or third country in which the traditional term is defined and regulated, or to the rules applicable to wine producers in the third country, including those originating from representative trade organisations, in the absence of national legislation in those third countries;
(d) a summary of the definition or conditions of use;
(e) the name of the country or countries of origin;
(f) the date of inclusion in the electronic database "E-Bacchus".

2. The traditional terms listed in the electronic database "E-Bacchus", shall be protected only in the language and for the categories of grape vine products claimed in the application, against:

(a) any misuse even if the protected term is accompanied by an expression such as "style", "type", "method", "as produced in", "imitation", "flavour", "like" or similar;
(b) any other false or misleading indication as to the nature, characteristics or essential qualities of the product, on the inner or outer packaging, advertising material or documents relating to it;
(c) any other practice liable to mislead the consumer, in particular to give the impression that the wine qualifies for the protected traditional term.

3. The traditional terms listed in the electronic database "E-Bacchus" shall be made known to the public.]

NOTES

Substituted by Commission Regulation 670/2011/EU, Art 1(16).

[8.456]
Article 41
Relationship with trademarks

[1. Where a traditional term is protected under this Regulation, the registration of a trademark, the use of which would contravene Article 40(2), shall be assessed in accordance with Directive 2008/95/EC of the European Parliament and of the Council[1] or Council Regulation (EC) No 207/2009.[2]

Trademarks registered in breach of the first subparagraph shall be declared invalid upon request in accordance with the applicable procedures as specified by Directive 2008/95/EC or Regulation (EC) No 207/2009.]

2. A trademark, which corresponds to one of the situations referred to in Article 40 of this Regulation, and which has been applied for, registered or established by use, if that possibility is provided for by the legislation concerned, in the territory of the Community before 4 May 2002 or before the date of submission of the application for protection of the traditional term to the Commission, may continue to be used and renewed notwithstanding the protection of the traditional term.

In such cases the use of the traditional term shall be permitted alongside the relevant trademark.

3. A name shall not be protected as a traditional term, where in the light of a trademark's reputation and renown, such protection is liable to mislead the consumer as to the true identity, nature, characteristic or quality of the wine.

NOTES

Para 1: substituted by Commission Regulation 538/2011/EU, Art 1(4).

[1] OJ L299, 8.11.2008, p 25.

[2] OJ L11, 14.1.1994, p 1.

[8.457]
Article 42
Homonyms

[1. A term, for which an application is lodged and which is wholly or partially homonymous with that of a traditional term already protected under this Chapter shall be protected with due regard to local and traditional usage and the risk of confusion.

A homonymous term which misleads consumers as to the nature, quality or the true origin of the products shall not be registered even if the term is accurate.

[The use of a protected homonymous term shall be subject to there being a sufficient distinction in practice between the homonym protected subsequently and the traditional term listed in the electronic database "E-Bacchus", having regard to the need to treat the producers concerned in an equitable manner and not to mislead the consumer.]]

2. Paragraph 1 shall apply mutatis mutandis for traditional terms protected before 1 August 2009, which are partially homonymous with a protected designation of origin or geographical indication or a wine grape variety name or its synonym listed in Annex XV.

NOTES

Para 1: substituted by Commission Regulation 538/2011/EU, Art 1(5); words in square brackets substituted by Commission Regulation 670/2011/EU, Art 1(17).

[8.458]
[Article 42a
Modification

An applicant as referred to in Article 29 may apply for an approval of a modification of a traditional term, the language indicated, the wine or wines concerned or of the summary of the definition or conditions of use of the traditional term concerned.

Articles 33 to 39 apply *mutatis mutandis* to applications for modification.]

NOTES

Inserted by Commission Regulation 538/2011/EU, Art 1(6).

[8.459]
Article 43
Enforcement of the protection

For the purposes of the application of Article 55 of Regulation (EC) No 479/2008, in case of illegal use of protected traditional terms, competent national authorities, on their own initiative or at the request of a party, take all measures to stop the marketing, including any export, of the products concerned.

SECTION 5
CANCELLATION PROCEDURE

[8.460]
Article 44
Grounds of cancellation

The grounds for cancelling a traditional term shall be that it no longer meets the definition laid down in Article 54(1) of Regulation (EC) No 479/2008 or the requirements laid down in Articles 31, 35, 40(2), 41(3) or 42.

[8.461]
[Article 45
Submission of a request for cancellation

1. A duly substantiated request for cancellation may be communicated to the Commission by a Member State, a third country or a natural or legal person having a legitimate interest in accordance with Article 70a(1). The date of submission of a request to the Commission shall be the date on which the request is received by the Commission. This date shall be made known to the public.

2. The Commission shall confirm receipt of the request and assign a file number to the request. The confirmation of receipt shall include at least the following:

(a) the file number;

(b) the date of receipt of the request.

3. Paragraphs 1 and 2 do not apply when the cancellation is initiated by the Commission.]

NOTES

Substituted by Commission Regulation 670/2011/EU, Art 1(18).

[8.462]
Article 46
Admissibility

1. For the purposes of determining whether a request of cancellation is admissible, the Commission shall verify that the request:

(a) mentions the legitimate interest of the author of the request of cancellation;

(b) the ground(s) for cancellation; and

(c) refers to a statement from the Member State or third country where the residence or registered office of the author of the request is located explaining the legitimate interest, reasons and justification of the author of the cancellation.

2. Any request for cancellation shall contain details of the facts, evidence and comments submitted in support of the cancellation, accompanied by the relevant supporting documents.

3. If detailed information concerning the grounds, facts, evidence and comments, as well as the supporting documents referred to in paragraphs 1 and 2, have not been produced at the same time as the request of cancellation, the Commission shall inform the author of the request of cancellation accordingly and shall invite him to remedy the deficiencies noted within a period of two months. If the deficiencies are not remedied before the time limit expires, the Commission shall reject the request as inadmissible. The decision on inadmissibility shall be notified to the author of the request of cancellation and to the Member State or the third-country authorities or the author of the request of cancellation established in the third country in question.

4. Any request of cancellation that is deemed admissible, including Commission own-initiative cancellation procedure, shall be notified to the Member State or the third-country authorities or the author of the request of cancellation established in the third country whose traditional term is affected by the cancellation.

[8.463]
Article 47
Scrutiny of a cancellation

1. If the Commission has not rejected the request of cancellation in accordance with Article 46(3), it shall communicate the request of cancellation to the Member State or the third-country authorities or the applicant established in the third country in question and shall invite him to file observations within two months from the issuance date of such communication. Any observations received within this two months period shall be communicated to the author of the request of cancellation.

In the course of the scrutiny of a cancellation, the Commission shall request the parties to submit comments, if appropriate, within a period of two months from the issuance date of such request, on the communications received from the other parties.

2. If the Member State or the third-country authorities or the applicant established in the third country in question or the author of a request of cancellation files no observations in response, or does not respect the time periods, the Commission gives ruling on the cancellation.
3. Any decision to cancel the traditional term concerned shall be taken by the Commission on the basis of the evidence available to it. It shall consider whether the conditions referred to in Article 44 are no longer fulfilled.

Such decision on cancellation shall be notified to the author of the request of cancellation and to the Member State or the third-country authorities in question.
4. In the event of multiple requests of cancellation, following a preliminary examination of one or more such requests of cancellation, it may not be possible to accept to continue to protect a traditional term, in which case the Commission may suspend the other cancellation procedures. In this case the Commission shall inform the other authors of the request of cancellation of any decision affecting them which was taken in the course of the procedure.

Where a traditional term is cancelled, cancellation procedures which have been suspended shall be deemed to be closed and the authors of the request of cancellation concerned shall be duly informed.
[5. When a cancellation takes effect, the Commission shall remove the name concerned from the list set out in the electronic database "E-Bacchus".]

NOTES

Para 5: substituted by Commission Regulation 670/2011/EU, Art 1(19).

SECTION 6
EXISTING PROTECTED TRADITIONAL TERMS

[8.464]
Article 48
Existing protected traditional terms

Traditional terms, which are protected in accordance with Articles 24, 28 and 29 of Regulation (EC) No 753/2002, shall automatically be protected under this Regulation, provided:

(a) a summary of the definition or the conditions of use was submitted to the Commission by 1 May 2009;
(b) Member States or third countries have not ceased to protect certain traditional terms.

CHAPTER IV
LABELLING AND PRESENTATION

[8.465]
Article 49
Common rule to all labelling particulars

Save as otherwise provided for in this Regulation, the labelling of the products referred to in paragraphs 1 to 11, 13, 15 and 16 of Annex IV to Regulation (EC) No 479/2008 (hereinafter 'products') may not be supplemented by any particulars other than those provided for in Article 58 and those regulated in Article 59(1) and 60(1) of that Regulation, unless they satisfy the requirements of Article 2(1)(a) of Directive 2000/13/EC.

SECTION 1
COMPULSORY PARTICULARS

[8.466]
Article 50
Presentation of the compulsory particulars

1. Compulsory particulars referred to in Article 58 of Regulation (EC) No 479/2008 as well as those listed in Article 59 thereof shall appear in the same field of vision on the container, in such a way as to be simultaneously readable without having to turn the container.

However, the compulsory particulars of the lot number and those referred to in Articles 51 and 56(4) of this Regulation may appear outside the visual field in which the other compulsory particulars appear.
2. The compulsory particulars referred to in paragraph 1 and those applicable by virtue of the legal instruments mentioned in Article 58 of Regulation (EC) No 479/2008 shall be presented in indelible characters and shall be clearly distinguishable from surrounding text or graphics.

[8.467]
[Article 51
Application of certain horizontal rules

1. For the purposes of indicating the ingredients as referred to in Article 6(3a) of Directive 2000/13/EC, the terms concerning sulphites/sulfites, milk and milk-based products and eggs and egg-based products that must be used are those listed in part A of Annex X.
2. The terms referred to in paragraph 1 may be accompanied, as applicable, by one of the pictograms shown in part B of Annex X.]

NOTES

Substituted by Commission Regulation 579/2012/EU, Art 1(1).

[8.468]
Article 52
Marketing and export

1. Products whose label or presentation does not conform to the corresponding conditions as laid down in this Regulation cannot be marketed in the Community or exported.
2. By way of derogation from Chapters V and VI of Regulation (EC) No 479/2008, where the products concerned are to be exported, Member States may allow that particulars, which conflict with labelling rules as provided for by Community legislation, appear on the label of wines for export, when they are required by the legislation of the third country concerned. These particulars may appear in languages other than the official Community languages.

[8.469]
Article 53
Prohibition of lead-based capsules or foil

The closing devices for products as referred to in Article 49 shall not be enclosed in lead-based capsules or foil.

[8.470]
Article 54
Actual alcoholic strength

1. The actual alcoholic strength by volume referred to in Article 59(1)(c) to Regulation (EC) No 479/2008 shall be indicated in percentage units or half units.

The figure shall be followed by '*% vol*' and may be preceded by '*actual alcoholic strength*', '*actual alcohol*' or '*alc*'.

Without prejudice to the tolerances set for the reference analysis method used, the strength shown may not differ by more than 0,5 % vol from that given by analysis. However, the alcoholic strength of products with protected designations of origin or geographical indications stored in bottles for more than three years, sparkling wines, quality sparkling wines, aerated sparkling wines, semi-sparkling wines, aerated semi-sparkling wines, liqueur wines and wines of overripe grapes, without prejudice to the tolerances set for the reference analysis method used, may not differ by more than 0,8 % vol from that given by analysis.
2. The actual alcoholic strength shall appear on the label in characters at least 5 mm high if the nominal volume is over 100 cl, at least 3 mm high if it is equal to or less than 100 cl but more than 20 cl and 2 mm high if it is 20 cl or less.
[3. In case of partially fermented grape must or new wine still in fermentation, the actual and/or total alcoholic strength by volume shall appear on the label. When the total alcoholic strength by volume appears on the label, the figures shall be followed by "% vol" and may be preceded by words "total alcoholic strength" or "total alcohol".]

NOTES

Para 3: added by Commission Regulation 538/2011/EU, Art 1(8).

[8.471]
Article 55
Indication of the provenance

1. The indication of provenance as referred to in Article 59(1)(d) of Regulation (EC) No 479/2008, shall be indicated as follows:
   (a) for wines referred to in paragraphs 1, 2, 3, 7 to 9, 15 and 16 of Annex IV to Regulation (EC) No 479/2008, without protected designation of origin or geographical indication, one of the following:
      (i) the words '*wine of* (. . .)', '*produced in* (. . .)', or '*product of* (. . .)', or expressed in equivalent terms, supplemented by the name of the Member State or third country where the grapes are harvested and turned into wine in that territory;
      In the case of a trans-border wine produced from certain wine grapes varieties as referred to in Article 60(2)(c) of Regulation (EC) No 479/2008, only the name of one or more Member State(s) or third countrie(s) may be mentioned.
      (ii) either the words '*European Community wine*', or expressed in equivalent terms, or '*blend of wines from different countries of the European Community*' in the case of wine resulting from a blending of wines originating in a number of Member States, or
      the words '*blend of wines from different countries outside the European Community*' or '*blend from* (. . .)' citing the names of the third countries in question, in the case if wine resulting from a blending of wines originating in a number of third countries;

(iii) either the words '*European Community wine*', or expressed in equivalent terms, or '*wine obtained in (. . .) from grapes harvested in* (. . .)', supplemented by the names of the Member States concerned in the case of wines produced in a Member State from grapes harvested in another Member State, or the words '*wine obtained in (. . .) from grapes harvested in* (. . .)' citing the names of the third countries in question, for wines made in a third country from grapes harvested in another third country;

(b) for wines referred to in paragraph 4, 5 and 6 to Annex IV of Regulation (EC) No 479/2008, without protected designation of origin or geographical indication, one of the following:

(i) the words '*wine of* (. . .)', '*produced in* (. . .)', '*product of* (. . .)' or '*sekt of* (. . .)', or expressed in equivalent terms, supplemented by the name of the Member State or third country where the grapes are harvested and turned into wine in that territory;

(ii) the words '*produced in* (. . .)', or expressed in equivalent terms, supplemented by the name of the Member State where the second fermentation takes place;

(c) for wines with protected designation of origin or geographical indication, the words '*wine of* (. . .)', '*produced in* (. . .)' or '*product of* (. . .)', or expressed in equivalent terms, supplemented by the name of the Member State or third country where the grapes are harvested and turned into wine in that territory.

In the case of a trans-border protected designation of origin or geographical indication, only the name of one or more Member State(s) or third countrie(s) shall be mentioned.

This paragraph is without prejudice to Articles 56 and 67.

2. The indication of provenance as referred to in Article 59(1)(d) of Regulation (EC) No 479/2008, on labels of grape must, grape must in fermentation, concentrated grape must or new wine still in fermentation shall be indicated as follows:

(a) '*must of* (. . .)' or '*must produced in* (. . .)' or expressed in equivalent terms, supplemented by the name of the Member State, an individual country forming part of the Member State where the product is produced;

(b) '*blend made from the produce of two or more European Community* countries' in case of coupage of products produced in two or more Member States;

(c) '*must obtained in (. . .) from grapes harvested in* (. . .)' in case of grape must which has not been made in the Member State where the grapes used were harvested.

3. In the case of United Kingdom, the name of the Member State may be replaced by the name of an individual country forming part of United Kingdom.

[8.472]

Article 56

Indication of the bottler, producer, importer and vendor

1. For the purposes of the application of Article 59(1)(e) and (f) of Regulation (EC) No 479/2008 and of this Article:

[(a) '*bottler*' means a natural or legal person or a group of such persons established in the European Union and carrying out bottling or having bottling carried out on their behalf.]

(b) '*bottling*' means putting the product concerned in containers of a capacity *not* exceeding 60 litres for subsequent sale;

(c) '*producer*' means a natural or legal person or a group of such persons by whom or on whose behalf the processing of the grapes, grape musts and wine into sparkling wines, aerated sparkling wine, quality sparkling wine or quality aromatic sparkling wines is carried out;

(d) '*importer*' means a natural or legal person or group of such persons established within the Community assuming responsibility for bringing into circulation non-Community goods within the meaning of Article 4(8) of Council Regulation (EEC) No 2913/92;[1]

(e) '*vendor*' means a natural or legal person or a group of such persons, not covered by the definition of producer, purchasing and then putting sparkling wines, aerated sparkling wine, quality sparkling wine or quality aromatic sparkling wines into circulation;

[(f) '*address*' means the indications of the local administrative area and the Member State or third country in which the head office of the bottler, producer, vendor or importer is situated.]

2. The name and address of the bottler shall be supplemented either,

(a) by the words '*bottler*' or '*bottled by* (. . .)'; or

(b) by terms, whose conditions of use are defined by Member States, where bottling of wines with protected designation of origin or geographical indication takes place:

(i) on the producer's holding; or

(ii) on the premises of a producer group; or

(iii) in an enterprise located in the demarcated geographical area or in the immediate proximity of the demarcated geographical area concerned.

In case of contract bottling, the indication of the bottler shall be supplemented by the words '*bottled for* (. . .)' or, where the name, address of the person who has carried out the bottling on behalf of a third party are indicated, by the words '*bottled for (. . .) by* (. . .)'.

Where bottling takes place in another place than that of the bottler, the particulars referred to in this paragraph shall be accompanied by a reference to the exact place where the operation took place and, if it is carried out in another Member State, the name of that State.
In case of containers other than bottles, the words '*packager*' and'*packaged by* (. . .)' shall replace the words '*bottler*' and '*bottled by* (. . .)' respectively, except when the language used does not indicate by itself such a difference.

[These requirements do not apply where bottling is carried out in a place of immediate proximity to that of the bottler.]

[3. The name and address of the producer or vendor shall be supplemented by the terms "*producer*" or "*produced by*" and "*vendor*" or "*sold by*", or equivalent.

Member States may decide to:

(a) make compulsory the indication of the producer;

[(b) to authorise the replacement of the words "*producer*" or "*produced by*" by the words listed in Annex Xa to this Regulation.]]

4. The *name* and address of the importer shall be preceded by the words '*importer*' or '*imported by* (. . .)'.

5. The indications referred to in paragraphs 2, 3 and 4 can be grouped together, if they concern the same natural or legal person.
One of these indications may be replaced by a code determined by the Member State in which the bottler, producer, importer or vendor has its head office. The code shall be supplemented by a reference to the Member State in question. The name and address of another natural or legal person involved in the commercial distribution other than the bottler, producer, importer or vendor indicated by a code shall also appear on the wine label of the product concerned.

6. Where the name or the address of the bottler, producer, importer or vendor consists of or contains a protected designation of origin or geographical indication, it shall appear on the label:

(a) in characters which are no more than half the size of those used either for the protected designation of origin or geographical indications or for the designation of the category of the grapevine product concerned; or

(b) by using a code as provided for in paragraph 5, second sub-paragraph.

Member States may decide which option applies to products produced in their territories.

NOTES

Para 1: sub-paras (a), (f) substituted by Commission Regulation 401/2010/EU, Art 1(4).

Para 2: words in square brackets added by Commission Regulation 538/2011/EU, Art 1(9)(a).

Para 3: substituted by Commission Regulation 538/2011/EU, Art 1(9)(b); sub-para (b) substituted by Commission Regulation 1185/2012/EU, Art 1(1).

[1] OJ L302, 19.10.1992, p 1.

[8.473]
Article 57
Indication of the holding

1. The terms referring to a holding listed in Annex XIII, other than the indication of the name of the bottler, producer or vendor, shall be reserved for wines with protected designation of origin or geographical indication provided that:

(a) the wine is made exclusively from grapes harvested in vineyards exploited by that holding;

(b) the winemaking is entirely carried out on that holding;

(c) Member States regulate the use of their respective terms listed in Annex XIII. Third countries establish the rules on use applicable to their respective terms listed in Annex XIII, including those emanating from representative professional organisations.

2. The name of a holding may be used by other operators involved in the marketing of the product only where the holding in question agrees to that use.

[8.474]
Article 58
Indication of the sugar content

1. The terms listed in Part A of Annex XIV to this Regulation indicating the sugar content shall appear on the label of the products provided for in Article 59(1)(g) of Regulation (EC) No 479/2008.

2. If the sugar content of the products, expressed in terms of fructose and glucose (including any sucrose), justifies the use of two of the terms listed in Part A of Annex XIV, only one of those two terms shall be chosen.

3. Without prejudice to the conditions of use described in Part A of Annex XIV, the sugar content may not differ by more than 3 grams per litre from what appears on the product label.

[8.475]
Article 58
Derogations

In accordance with Article 59(3)(b) to Regulation (EC) No 479/2008, the terms '*protected designation of origin*' may be omitted for wines bearing the following protected designations of origin, provided this possibility is regulated in the Member State legislation or in the rules applicable in the third country concerned, including those emanating from representative professional organisations:

(a)	Cyprus:	Κουμανδαρία (Commandaria);
(b)	Greece:	Σάμος (Samos);
(c)	Spain:	Cava, Jerez, Xérès or Sherry, Manzanilla;
(d)	France:	Champagne;
(e)	Italy:	Asti, Marsala, Franciacorta;
(f)	Portugal:	Madeira or Madère, Port or Porto.

[8.476]
Article 60
Specific rules for aerated sparkling wine, aerated semi-sparkling wine and quality sparkling wine

1. The terms '*aerated sparkling wine*' and '*aerated semi-sparkling wine*' as referred to in Annex IV to Regulation (EC) No 479/2008 shall be supplemented in characters of the same type and size by the words '*obtained by adding carbon dioxide*' or '*obtained by adding carbon anhydride*', except when the language used indicates by itself that carbon dioxide has been added.

The words '*obtained by adding carbon dioxide*' or '*obtained by adding carbon anhydride*' shall be indicated even where Article 59(2) of Regulation (EC) No 479/2008 applies.

2. For quality sparkling wines, the reference to the category of the grapevine product may be omitted for wines whose labels include the term '*Sekt*'.

SECTION 2
OPTIONAL PARTICULARS

[8.477]
Article 61
Vintage year

1. The vintage year referred to in Article 60(1)(a) of Regulation (EC) No 479/2008 may appear on the labels of products as referred to in Article 49 provided that at least 85 % of the grapes used to make the products have been harvested in the year in question. This does not include:

(a) any quantity of products used in sweetening, '*expedition liqueur*' or '*tirage liqueur*'; or
(b) any quantity of product as referred to in Annex IV(3)(e) and (f) to Regulation (EC) No 479/2008.

2. For products traditionally obtained from grapes harvested in January or February, the vintage year to appear on the label of wines shall be that of the previous calendar year.

3. Products without protected designation of origin or geographical indication shall also comply with the requirements laid down in paragraphs 1 and 2 of this Article and in Article 63.

[8.478]
Article 62
Name of wine grape variety

1. The names of the wine grape varieties or their synonyms referred to in Article 60(1)(b) of Regulation (EC) No 479/2008 used for the production of products as referred to in Article 49 of this Regulation may appear on the labels of the products concerned under the conditions laid down in points (a) and (b) of this Article.

(a) For wines produced in the European Community, the names of the wine grape varieties or their synonyms shall be those mentioned in the wine grape varieties classification as referred to in Article 24(1) of Regulation (EC) No 479/2008.

For Member States exempted from the classification obligation as provided for in Article 24(2) of Regulation (EC) No 479/2008, the names of the wine grape varieties or synonyms shall be mentioned in the 'International list of vine varieties and their synonyms' managed by the International Organisation of Vine and Wine (OIV).

(b) For wines originating in third countries, the conditions of use of the names of the wine grape varieties or their synonyms shall conform with the rules applicable to wine producers in the third country concerned, including those emanating from representative professional organisations and the names of the wine grape varieties or their synonyms are mentioned in at least one of the following lists:
   (i) the International Organisation of Vine and Wine (OIV);
   (ii) the Union for the Protection of Plant Varieties (UPOV);
   (iii) the International Board for Plant Genetic Resources (IBPGR).

(c) For products with protected designation of origin or geographical indication or with a geographical indication of a third country, the names of the wine grape varieties or their synonyms may be mentioned:
   (i) if only one wine grape variety or its synonym is named, at least 85 % of the products have been made from that variety, not including:
      — any quantity of products used in sweetening, '*expedition liqueur*' or '*tirage liqueur*'; or
      — any quantity of product as referred to in Annex IV(3)(e) and (f) to Regulation (EC) No 479/2008;
   (ii) if two or more wine grape varieties or their synonyms are named, 100 % of the products concerned have been made from these varieties, not including:
      — any quantity of products used in sweetening, '*expedition liqueur*' or '*tirage liqueur*'; or
      — any quantity of product as referred to in Annex IV(3)(e) and (f) of Regulation (EC) No 479/2008.

   In the case referred to in point (ii), the wine grape varieties must appear in descending order of the proportion used and in characters of the same size.

(d) For products without protected designation of origin or geographical indication, the names of the wine grape varieties or their synonyms may be mentioned provided the requirements laid down in points (a) or (b), and (c) of paragraph 1 and in Article 63 are fulfilled.

2. In the case of sparkling wines and quality sparkling wines, the wine grape variety names used to supplement the description of the product, namely, '*pinot blanc*', '*pinot noir*', '*pinot meunier*' or '*pinot gris*' and the equivalent names in the other Community languages, may be replaced by the synonym '*pinot*'.

3. By way of derogation from Article 42(3) of Regulation (EC) No 479/2008, the wine grape variety names and their synonyms listed in Part A of Annex XV to this Regulation, that consist of or contain a protected designation of origin or geographical indication may only appear on the label of a product with protected designation of origin or geographical indication or geographical indication of a third country if they were authorised under Community rules in force on 11 May 2002 or on the date of accession of Member States, whichever is later.

4. The wine grape variety names and their synonyms listed in Part B of Annex XV to this Regulation, that partially contain a protected designation of origin or geographical indication and directly refers to the geographical element of the protected designation of origin or geographical indication in question, may only appear on the label of a product with protected designation of origin or geographical indication or geographical indication of a third country.

[8.479]

Article 63

Specific rules on wine grape varieties and vintage years for wines without protected designation of origin or geographical indication.

[1. Member States shall designate the competent authority or authorities responsible for ensuring certification as provided for in Article 118z(2)(a) of Regulation (EC) No 1234/2007, in accordance with the criteria laid down in Article 4 of Regulation (EC) No 882/2004 of the European Parliament and of the Council[1]

Each Member State shall communicate to the Commission the following details before 1 October 2011, as well as any amendments to those details in accordance with Article 70a(1) of this Regulation:

(a) the name, address and contact points, including e-mail addresses, of the authority or authorities responsible for the application of this Article;
(b) where applicable, the name, address and contact points, including e-mail addresses, of all the bodies authorised by an authority for the application of this Article;
(c) the measures they have taken to implement this Article, where those measures are of specific value for the purposes of cooperation between Member States as referred to in Regulation (EC) No 555/2008;
(d) the wine grape varieties concerned by the application of Articles 118z(2) and 120a of Regulation (EC) No 1234/2007.

The Commission shall draw up and keep up-to-date a list containing the names and addresses of the competent authorities and authorised bodies, as well as the authorised wine grape varieties, based on information communicated by the Member States. The Commission shall make this list known to the public.]

2. Certification of wine, at any stage of the production, including during the conditioning of the wine, shall be ensured either by:

(a) the competent authority or authorities referred to in paragraph 1; or,

(b) one or more control bodies within the meaning of point 5 of the second subparagraph of Article 2 of Regulation (EC) No 882/2004 operating as a product certification body in accordance with the criteria laid down in Article 5 of that Regulation.

The authority or authorities referred to in paragraph 1 shall offer adequate guarantees of objectivity and impartiality, and have at their disposal the qualified staff and resources needed to carry out their tasks.

The certification bodies referred to in point (b) of the first subparagraph shall comply with, and from 1 May 2010 be accredited in accordance with, the European standard EN 45011 or ISO/IEC Guide 65 (General requirements for bodies operating product certification systems).

[The costs of the certification shall be borne by the operators subject to it, save where Member States decide otherwise.]

3. The Certification procedure as provided for in Article 60(2)(a) of Regulation (EC) No 479/2008 shall ensure administrative evidence to support the veracity of the wine grape variety(-ies) or the vintage year shown on the label of the wine(s) concerned.

In addition, producing Member States may decide on:

(a) an organoleptic test of the wine relating to the odour and the taste with the view to verifying that the essential characteristic of the wine is due to the wine grape variety(-ies) used may be carried out and shall concern anonymous samples;

(b) an analytical test in case of a wine made from a single wine grape variety.

The certification procedure shall be carried out by competent authority(-ies) or control body(-ies) as referred to in paragraphs 1 and 2 in the Member State in which production took place.

The certification shall be carried out either through:

(a) random checks based on a risk analysis;

(b) sampling; or

(c) systematically.

In the case of random checks, they shall be based on a control pl of production of the product. The control plan shall be known by the operators. Member States shall select randomly the minimum number of operators to be subjected to this check.

In the case of sampling, Member States shall ensure that by their number, nature and frequency controls, they are representative of the whole of their territory and correspond to the volume of wine-sector products marketed or held with a view to their marketing.

Random checks may be combined with sampling.

4. As regards Article 60(2)(a) of Regulation (EC) No 479/2008, producing Member States shall ensure that producers of the wines in question are approved by the Member State where the production takes place.

5. As regards control, including traceability, producing Member States shall ensure that Title V of Regulation (EC) No 555/2008 and Regulation (EC) No 606/2009 apply.

6. In case of a trans-border wine as referred to in Article 60(2)(c) of Regulation (EC) No 479/2008, certification can be carried out by either one of the authority(-ies) of the Member States concerned.

7. For wines produced in accordance with Article 60(2) of Regulation (EC) No 479/2008, Member States may decide to use the terms '*varietal wine*' supplemented by the name(s) of:

(a) the Member State(s) concerned;

(b) the wine grape variety(-ies).

For wines without protected designation of origin, protected geographical indication or geographical indication produced in third countries which bear on labels the name of one or more wine grape varieties or the vintage year, third countries may decide to use the terms '*varietal wine*' supplemented by the name(s) of the third country(ies) concerned.

In the case of the indication of the name(s) of the Member State(s) or third country(ies), Article 55 of this Regulation shall not apply.

[In the case of United Kingdom, the name of the Member State may be replaced by the name of an individual country forming part of United Kingdom.]

8. Paragraphs 1 to 6 shall apply for products produced from grapes harvested as from and including 2009.

NOTES

Para 1: substituted by Commission Regulation 670/2011/EU, Art 1(20).

Para 2: words in square brackets substituted by Commission Regulation 401/2010/EU, Art 1(5)(a).

Para 7: words in square brackets added by Commission Regulation 401/2010/EU, Art 1(5)(b).

[1] OJ L165, 30.4.2004, p 1.

Part 8 Other EU Materials

[8.480]
Article 64
Indication of the sugar content

1. Save as otherwise provided for in Article 58 of this Regulation, the sugar content expressed as fructose and glucose as provided for in Part B of Annex XIV to this Regulation, may appear on the label of the products as referred to in Article 60(1)(c) of Regulation (EC) No 479/2008.

2. If the sugar content of the products justifies the use of two of the terms listed in Part B of Annex XIV to this Regulation, only one of those two terms shall be chosen.

3. Without prejudice to the conditions of use described in Part B of Annex XIV to this Regulation, the sugar content may not differ by more than 1 gram per litre from what appears on the product label.

[4. Paragraph 1 shall not apply to products referred to in paragraphs 3, 8 and 9 of Annex XIb to Regulation (EC) No 1234/2007 provided that the conditions of the use of the indication of the sugar content are regulated by the Member State or established in rules applicable in the third country concerned, including, in the case of third countries, rules emanating from representative professional organisations.]

NOTES

Para 4: substituted by Commission Regulation 401/2010/EU, Art 1(6).

[8.481]
Article 65
Indication of the Community symbols

1. The Community symbols referred to in Article 60(1)(e) of Regulation (EC) No 479/2008 may appear on labels of wines as laid down in Annex V to Commission Regulation (EC) No 1898/2006.[1] Notwithstanding Article 59, the indications '*PROTECTED DESIGNATION OF ORIGIN*' and '*PROTECTED GEOGRAPHICAL INDICATION*' within the symbols may be replaced by the equivalent terms in another official language of the Community as laid down in the aforesaid Annex.

2. Where the Community symbols or the indications referred to in Article 60(1)(e) of Regulation (EC) No 479/2008 appear on the label of a product, they shall be accompanied by the corresponding protected designation of origin or geographical indication.

NOTES

[1] OJ L369, 23.12.2006, p 1.

[8.482]
Article 66
Terms referring to certain production methods

1. In Accordance with Article 60(1)(f) of Regulation (EC) No 479/2008, wines marketed in the Community may bear indications referring to certain production methods, among others, those which are laid down in paragraphs 2, 3, 4, 5 and 6 of this Article.

2. The indications listed in Annex XVI are the only terms which may be used to describe a wine with protected designations of origin or geographical indications or with a geographical indication of a third country that has been fermented, matured or aged in a wood container. Member States and third countries may, however, establish other indications equivalent to those laid down in Annex XVI for such wines.

Use of one of the indications referred to in the first subparagraph shall be permitted where the wine has been aged in a wood container in accordance with the national rules in force, even when the ageing process continues in another type of container.

The indications referred to in the first subparagraph may not be used to describe a wine that has been produced with the aid of oak chips, even in association with the use of a wood container or wood containers.

3. The expression '*bottle-fermented*' may be used only to describe sparkling wines with protected designations of origin or geographical indication of a third country or quality sparkling wines provided that:

- (a) the product was made sparkling by a second alcoholic fermentation in a bottle;
- (b) the length of the production process, including ageing in the undertaking where the product was made, calculated from the start of the fermentation process designed to make the cuvée sparkling, has not been less than nine months;
- (c) the process of fermentation designed to make the *cuvée* sparkling and the presence of the cuvée on the lees lasted at least 90 days; and
- (d) the product was separated from the lees by filtering in accordance with the racking method or by disgorging.

4. The expressions '*bottle-fermented by the traditional method*' or '*traditional method*' or '*classical method*' or '*classical traditional method*' may be used only to describe sparkling wines with protected designations of origin or with a geographical indication of a third country or quality sparkling wines provided the product:

- (a) was made sparkling by a second alcoholic fermentation in the bottle;

(b) stayed without interruption in contact with the lees for at least nine months in the same undertaking from the time when the cuvée was constituted;
(c) was separated from the lees by disgorging.

5. The expression '*Crémant*' may only be used for white or '*rosé*' quality sparkling wines with protected designations of origin or with a geographical indication of a third country provided:
(a) the grapes shall be harvested manually;
(b) the wine is made from must obtained by pressing whole or destemmed grapes. The quantity of must obtained shall not exceed 100 litres for every150 kg of grapes;
(c) the maximum sulphur dioxide content does not exceed 150 mg/l;
(d) the sugar content is less than 50 g/l;
(e) the wine complies with the requirements laid down in paragraph 4; and
(f) without prejudice to Article 67, the term '*Crémant*' shall be indicated on labels of quality sparkling wines in combination with the name of the geographical unit underlying the demarcated area of the protected designation of origin or the a geographical indication of a third country in question.

Points (a) and (f) does not apply to producers who own trademarks containing the term '*crémant*' registered before 1 March 1986.

6. References to the organic production of grapes are governed by Council Regulation (EC) No 834/2007.[1]

NOTES

[1] OJ L189, 20.7.2007, p 1.

[8.483]
Article 67
Name of a smaller or larger geographical unit than the area underlying the designation of origin or geographical indication and geographical area references

1. As regards Article 60(1)(g) to Regulation (EC) No 479/2008 and without prejudice to Articles 55 and 56 of this Regulation, the name of a geographical unit and geographical area references may only appear on labels of wines with protected designation of origin or geographical indication or with a geographical indication of a third country.

2. [For the use of the name of a smaller geographical unit than the area underlying the designation of origin or geographical indication the area of the geographical unit in question shall be well defined. Member States may establish rules concerning the use of these geographical units. At least 85% of the grapes from which the wine has been produced shall originate in that smaller geographical unit. This does not include:
(a) any quantity of products used in sweetening, "*expedition liqueur*" or "*tirage liqueur*"; or
(b) any quantity of product as referred to in Annex XIb (3) points (e) and (f) of Regulation (EC) No 1234/2007.

The remaining 15% of the grapes shall originate in the geographical demarcated area of the designation of origin or geographical indication concerned.]

Member States may decide, in the case of registered trademarks or trademarks established by use before 11 May 2002 which contain or consist of a name of a smaller geographical unit than the area underlying the designation of origin or geographical indication and geographical area references of the Member States concerned, not to apply the requirements laid down in the third and fourthsentences of the first subparagraph.

3. The name of a smaller or larger geographical unit than the area underlying the designation of origin or geographical indication or a geographical area references shall consist of:
(a) a locality or group of localities;
(b) a local administrative area or part thereof;
(c) a wine-growing sub-region or part thereof;
(d) an administrative area.

NOTES

Para 2: words in square brackets substituted by Commission Regulation 401/2010/EU, Art 1(7).

SECTION 3
RULES ON CERTAIN SPECIFIC BOTTLE SHAPES AND CLOSURES AND ADDITIONAL PROVISIONS LAID DOWN BY THE PRODUCER MEMBER STATES

[8.484]
Article 68
Conditions of use of certain specific bottle shapes

To qualify for inclusion in the list of specific types of bottle set out in Annex XVII, a bottle type shall meet the following requirements:
(a) it shall have been exclusively, genuinely and traditionally used for the last 25 years for a wine with a particular protected designation of origin or geographical indication; and
(b) its use shall evoke for consumers a wine with a particular protected designation of origin or geographical indication.

Annex XVII indicates the conditions governing the use of the recognised specific types of bottles.

[8.485]
[Article 69
Rules on presentation for certain products

1. Sparkling wine, quality sparkling wine and quality aromatic sparkling wine produced in the European Union shall be marketed or exported in "sparkling wine"-type glass bottles closed with:
   (a) for bottles with a nominal volume more than 0,20 litres: a mushroom-shaped stopper made of cork or other material permitted to come into contact with foodstuffs, held in place by a fastening, covered, if necessary, by a cap and sheathed in foil completely covering the stopper and all or part of the neck of the bottle;
   (b) for bottles with a nominal volume content not exceeding 0,20 litres: any other suitable closure.

Other products produced in the Union shall not be marketed or exported in either "sparkling wine"-type glass bottles or with a closure as described in point (a) of the first subparagraph.

2. By way of derogation from the second subparagraph of paragraph 1, Member States may decide that the following products may be marketed or exported in "sparkling wine"-type glass bottles and/or with a closure as described in point (a) of the first subparagraph of paragraph 1:
   (a) products traditionally bottled in such bottles and which:
      (i) are listed in Article 113d(1)(a) of Regulation (EC) No 1234/2007;
      (ii) are listed in points 7, 8 and 9 of Annex XIb to Regulation (EC) No 1234/2007;
      (iii) are listed in Council Regulation (EEC) No 1601/1991;[1] or
      (iv) have an actual alcoholic strength by volume no greater than 1,2 % vol;
   (b) products other than those referred to in point (a) provided that they do not mislead consumers with regard to the real nature of the product.]

NOTES

Substituted by Commission Regulation 538/2011/EU, Art 1(10).

[1] OJ L149, 14.6.1991, p 1.

[8.486]
Article 70
Additional provisions laid down by the producer Member States relating to labelling and presentation

1. For wines with protected designation of origin or geographical indication produced on their territory, the particulars referred to in Articles 61, 62 and 64 to 67 may be rendered compulsory, prohibited or limited as regards their use by introducing conditions stricter than those laid down in this Chapter through the corresponding product specifications of those wines.

2. As regards wines without protected designation of origin or geographical indication produced on their territory, Member States may render compulsory the particulars referred to in Articles 64 and 66.

3. For control purposes, Member States may decide to define and regulate other particulars than those listed in Articles 59(1) and 60(1) of Regulation (EC) No 479/2008 for wines produced in their territories.

4. For control purposes, Member States may decide to render applicable Article 58, 59 and 60 of Regulation (EC) No 479/2008 for wines bottled in their territories but not marketed or exported yet.

CHAPTER V
GENERAL, TRANSITIONAL AND FINAL PROVISIONS

[8.487]
[Article 70a
Method applicable to communications between the Commission, the Member States, third countries and other operators

1. As regards the present paragraph, the documents and information required for the implementation of this Regulation shall be communicated to the Commission in accordance with the following method:
   (a) for the competent authorities of Member States, through the intermediary of the information system made available to them by the Commission in accordance with the provisions of Regulation (EC) No 792/2009;
   (b) for the competent authorities and representative trade organisations of third countries, as well as natural or legal persons who have a legitimate interest under this Regulation, through electronic means, using the methods and forms made available to them by the Commission and made accessible under the conditions specified in Annex XVIII to this Regulation.

However, paper-based communication is also possible, using those forms.

The filing of an application and the content of the communications is a matter for the competent authorities designated by the third countries, or the representative trade organisations, or the legal or natural persons that are involved, as the case may be.

2. Information shall be communicated and made available by the Commission to the authorities and persons affected by this Regulation and, where applicable, to the public, through the information systems put in place by the Commission.

The authorities and persons affected by this Regulation may contact the Commission, in accordance with Annex XIX, in order to obtain information on the practicalities of accessing the information systems, of communication and of making information available.

3. Article 5(2) and Articles 6, 7 and 8 of Regulation (EC) No 792/2009 apply *mutatis mutandis* to the communication and making available of information, referred to in paragraph 1(b) and paragraph 2 of this Article.

4. As regards the implementation of paragraph 1(b), the rights to access the information systems for the competent authorities and the representative trade organisations of third countries, as well as for natural or legal persons who have a legitimate interest under this Regulation, shall be assigned by those responsible for the information systems in the Commission.

Those who are responsible for the information systems in the Commission shall approve access rights, as appropriate, on the basis of:

(a) information regarding the competent authorities designated by the third country with their contact points and e-mail addresses, held by the Commission under international agreements or communicated to the Commission in accordance with these agreements;

(b) an official request from a third country specifying information regarding the authorities responsible for the communication of the documents and information required for the implementation of paragraph 1(b), as well as the contact points and e-mail addresses of the authorities concerned;

(c) a request from a representative trade organisation in a third country or a legal or natural person, with proof of identity, evidence of its legitimate interest and an e-mail address.

After access rights have been approved, they shall be activated by those responsible for the information systems in the Commission.]

NOTES

Added, together with Art 70b, by Commission Regulation 670/2011/EU, Art 1(21).

[8.488]

[Article 70b

Communication and provision of information regarding the authorities responsible for examining applications at national level

1. Member States shall communicate to the Commission before 1 October 2011, in accordance with Article 70a(1), the name, address and contact points, including e-mail addresses of the authorities responsible for the implementation of Article 118f(2) of Regulation (EC) No 1234/2007 as well as any changes to these details.

2. The Commission shall draw up and maintain a list containing the names and addresses of the competent authorities of the Member States or third countries on the basis of information communicated by the Member States in accordance with paragraph 1 or by third countries in accordance with international agreements concluded with the EU. The Commission shall make this list known to the public.]

NOTES

Added as noted to Art 70a at **[8.487]**.

[8.489]

Article 71

Wine names protected under Regulation (EC) No 1493/1999

[1. The documents referred to in Article 118s(2) of Regulation (EC) No 1234/2007, hereinafter "the file" and the amendments to a product specification referred to in Article 73(1)(c) and (d) and 73(2) of this Regulation, shall be sent by the Member States in accordance with Article 70a(1) of this Regulation in accordance with the following rules and procedures:

(a) the Commission shall confirm receipt of the file or of the amendment, as indicated in Article 9 of this Regulation;

(b) the file or amendment shall be considered as admissible on the date on which it is received by the Commission, under the conditions set out in Article 11 of this Regulation and provided that they are received by the Commission at the latest on 31 December 2011;

(c) the Commission shall confirm the registration of the designation of origin or the geographical indication in question in the register in accordance with Article 18 of this Regulation, with any amendments, and assigns it a file number;

(d) the Commission shall examine the validity of the application file, taking account where applicable of the amendments received, in accordance with the time-limit laid down in Article 12(1) of this Regulation.

2. The Commission may decide to withdraw the designation of origin or geographical indication concerned in accordance with Article 118s(4) of Regulation (EC) No 1234/2007 on the basis of the documents available to it under Article 118s(2) of that Regulation.]

[3. By way of derogation from Article 2(2) of this Regulation, in respect of the transmission of the technical files as referred to in point (a) of Article 118s(2) of Regulation (EC) No 1234/2007 the authorities of the Member States may be considered as applicants for the purpose of the application of point (b) of Article 118c(1) of that Regulation.]

NOTES

Paras 1, 2: substituted by Commission Regulation 670/2011/EU, Art 1(22).
Para 3: added by Commission Regulation 538/2011/EU, Art 1(11).

[8.490]
Article 72
Temporary labelling

1. By way of derogation from Article 65 of this Regulation, wines bearing a designation of origin or a geographical indication, whose designation of origin or geographical indication concerned meet the requirements as referred to in Article 38(5) of Regulation (EC) No 479/2008, shall be labelled in accordance with the provisions laid down in Chapter IV of this Regulation.
2. Where the Commission decides not to confer protection to a designation of origin or geographical indication pursuant to Article 41 of Regulation (EC) No 479/2008, wines labelled in accordance with paragraph 1 of this Article shall be withdrawn from the market or re-labelled in accordance with Chapter IV of this Regulation.

[8.491]
[Article 73
Transitional provisions

1. The procedure set out in Article 118s of Regulation (EC) No 1234/2007 shall apply in the following cases:
   (a) for any wine designation submitted to a Member State as a designation of origin or geographical indication and approved by that Member State before 1 August 2009;
   (b) for any wine designation submitted to a Member State as a designation of origin or geographical indication before 1 August 2009, and approved by that Member State before 31 December 2011;
   (c) for any modification to the product specification submitted to a Member State before 1 August 2009 and sent to the Commission by that Member State before 31 December 2011;
   (d) for any minor modification to the product specification submitted to a Member State on or after 1 August 2009 and sent to the Commission by that Member State before 31 December 2011.
2. The procedure set out in Article 118q of Regulation (EC) No 1234/2007 does not apply to amendments to a product specification submitted to a Member State on or after 1 August 2009 and sent to the Commission by that Member State before 30 June 2014, where these amendments are concerned exclusively with bringing the product specification sent to the Commission under Article 118s(2) of Regulation (EC) No 1234/2007 into compliance with Article 118c of Regulation (EC) No 1234/2007 of this Regulation.
3. Wines placed on the market or labelled before 31 December 2010 that comply with the relevant provisions applicable before 1 August 2009 may be marketed until stocks are exhausted.]

NOTES

Substituted by Commission Regulation 670/2011/EU, Art 1(23).

[8.492]
Article 74
Repeal

Regulations (EC) No 1607/2000 and (EC) No 753/2002 are hereby repealed.

[8.493]
Article 75
Entry into force

This Regulation shall enter into force on the seventh day following its publication in the *Official Journal of the European Union*.
It shall apply from 1 August 2009.
This Regulation shall be binding in its entirety and directly applicable in all Member States.

ANNEXES I–IX

(*Repealed, together with Annexes XI, XII, by Commission Regulation 670/2011/EU, Art 1(24).*)

[ANNEX X

PART A
TERMS REFERRED TO IN ARTICLE 51(1)

[8.494]

Language	Terms concerning sulphites/sulfites	Terms concerning eggs and egg-based products	Terms concerning milk and milk-based products
in Bulgarian	*"сулфити"* or *"серен диоксид"*	*"яйце"*, *"яйчен протеин"*, *"яйчен продукт"*, *"яйчен лизозим"* or *"яйчен албумин"*	*"мляко"*, *"млечни продукти"*, *"млечен казеин"* or *"млечен протеин"*
in Spanish	*"sulfitos"* or *"dióxido de azufre"*	*"huevo"*, *"proteína de huevo"*, *"ovoproducto"*, *"lisozima de huevo"* or *"ovoalbúmina"*	*"leche"*, *"productos lácteos"*, *"caseína de leche"* or *"proteína de leche"*
in Czech	*"siřičitany"* or *"oxid siřičitý"*	*"vejce"*, *"vaječná bílkovina"*, *"výrobky z vajec"*, *"vaječný lysozym"* or *"vaječný albumin"*	*"mléko"*, *"výrobky z mléka"*, *"mléčný kasein"* or *"mléčná bílkovina"*
in Danish	*"sulfitter"* or *"svovldioxid"*.	*"æg"*, *"ægprotein"*, *"ægprodukt"*, *"æglysozym"*, or *"ægalbumin"*	*"mælk"*, *"mælkeprodukt"*, *"mælkecasein"* or *"mælkeprotein"*,
in German	*"Sulfite"* or *"Schwefeldioxid"*	*"Ei"*, *"Eiprotein"*, *"Eiprodukt"*, *"Lysozym aus Ei"* or *"Albumin aus Ei"*	*"Milch"*, *"Milcherzeugnis"*, *"Kasein aus Milch"* or *"Milchprotein"*
in Estonian	*"sulfitid"* or *"vääveldioksiid"*	*"muna"*, *"munaproteiin"*, *"munatooted"*, *"munalüsosüüm"* or *"munaalbumiin"* . . .	*"piim"*, *"piimatooted"*, *"piimakaseiin"* or *"piimaproteiin"*
in Greek	"θειώδη", "διοξείδιο του θείου" or "ανυδρίτης του θειώδους οξέος"	"αυγό", "πρωτεΐνη αυγού", "προϊόν αυγού", "λυσοζύμη αυγού" or "αλβουμίνη αυγού"	"γάλα", "προϊόντα γάλακτος", "καζεΐνη γάλακτος" or "πρωτεΐνη γάλακτος"
in English	*'sulphites'*, *'sulfites'*, *'sulphur dioxide'* or *'sulfur dioxide'*	*'egg'*, *'egg protein'*, *'egg product'*, *'egg lysozyme'* or *'egg albumin'*	*'milk'*, *'milk products'*, *'milk casein'* or *'milk protein'*
in French	*"sulfites"* or *"anhydride sulfureux"*	*"oeuf"*, *"protéine de l'oeuf"*, *"produit de l'oeuf"*, *"lysozyme de l'oeuf"* or *"albumine de l'oeuf"*	*"lait"*, *"produits du lait"*, *"caséine du lait"* or *"protéine du lait"*
[in Croatian	*"sulfiti"* ili *"sumporov dioksid"*	*"jaje"*, *"bjelančevine iz jaja"*, *"proizvodi od jaja"*, *"lizozim iz jaja"* ili *"albumin iz jaja"*;	*"mlijeko"*, *"mliječni proizvodi"*, *"kazein iz mlijeka"* ili *"mliječne bjelančevine"*.]

Language	Terms concerning sulphites/sulfites	Terms concerning eggs and egg-based products	Terms concerning milk and milk-based products
in Italian	*"solfiti"*, or *"anidride solforosa"*	*"uovo"*, *"proteina dell'uovo"*, *"derivati dell'uovo"*, *"lisozima da uovo"* or *"ovoalbumina"*	*"latte"*, *"derivati del latte"*, *"caseina del latte"* or *"proteina del latte"*
in Latvian	*"sulfīti"* or *"sēra dioksīds"*	*"olas"*, *"olu olbaltumviela"*, *"olu produkts"*, *"olu lizocīms"* or *"olu albumīns"*	*"piens"*, *"piena produkts"*, *"piena kazeīns"* or *"piena olbaltumviela"*
in Lithuanian	*"sulfitai"* or *"sieros dioksidas"*	*"kiaušiniai"*, *"kiaušinių baltymai"*, *"kiaušinių produktai"*, *"kiaušinių lizocimas"* or *"kiaušinių albuminas"*	*"pienas"*, *„pieno produktai"*, *"pieno kazeinas"* or *"pieno baltymai"*
in Hungarian	*"szulfitok"* or *"kén-dioxid"*	*"tojás"*, *"tojásból származó fehérje"*, *"tojástermék"*, *"tojásból származó lizozim"* or *"tojásból származó albumin"*	*"tej"*, *"tejtermékek"*, *"tejkazein"* or *"tejfehérje"*
in Maltese	*"sulfiti"*, or *"diossidu tal-kubrit"*	*"bajd"*, *"proteina tal-bajd"*, *"prodott tal-bajd"*, *"liżożima tal-bajd"* or *"albumina tal-bajd"*	*"ħalib"*, *"prodotti tal-ħalib"*, *"kaseina tal-ħalib"* or *"proteina tal-ħalib"*
in Dutch	*"sulfieten"* or *"zwaveldioxide"*	*"ei"*, *"eiproteïne"*, *"eiderivaat"*, *"eilysozym"* or *"eialbumine"*	*"melk"*, *"melkderivaat"*, *"melkcaseïne"* or *"melkproteïnen"*
in Polish	*"siarczyny"*, *"dwutlenek siarki"* or *"ditlenek siarki"*	*"jajo"*, *"białko jaja"*,*"produkty z jaj"*,*"lizozym z jaja"* or *"albuminę z jaja"*	*"mleko"*, *"produkty mleczne"*, *"kazeinę z mleka"* or *"białko mleka"*
in Portuguese	*"sulfitos"* or *"dióxido de enxofre"*	*"ovo"*, *"proteína de ovo"*, *"produto de ovo"*,*"lisozima de ovo"* or *"albumina de ovo"*	*"leite"*,*"produtos de leite"*, *"caseína de leite"* or *"proteína de leite"*
in Romanian	*"sulfii"* or *"dioxid de sulf"*	*"ouă"*, *"proteine din ouă"*, *"produse din ouă"*, *"lizozimă din ouă"* or *"albumină din ouă"*	*"lapte"*, *"produse din lapte"*, *"cazeină din lapte"* or *"proteine din lapte"*
in Slovak	*"siričitany"* or *"oxid siričitý"*	*"vajce"*, *"vaječná bielkovina"*, *"výrobok z vajec"*, *"vaječný lyzozým"* or *"vaječný albumín"*	*"mlieko"*, *"výrobky z mlieka"*, *"mliečne výrobky"*, *"mliečny kazeín"* or *"mliečna bielkovina"*
in Slovene	*"ulfiti"* or *"žveplov dioksid"*	*"jajce"*, *"jajčne beljakovine"*, *"proizvod iz jajc"*, *"jajčni lizocim"* or *"jajčni albumin"*	*"mleko"*, *"proizvod iz mleka"*, *"mlečni kazein"* or *"mlečne beljakovine"*

Language	Terms concerning sulphites/sulfites	Terms concerning eggs and egg-based products	Terms concerning milk and milk-based products
in Finnish	*"sulfiittia"*, *"sulfiitteja"* or *"rikkidioksidia"*	*"kananmunaa"*, *"kananmunaproteiinia"*, *"kananmunatuotetta"*, *"lysotsyymiä (kananmunasta)"* or *"kananmuna-albumiinia"*	*"maitoa"*, *"maitotuotteita"*, *"kaseiinia (maidosta)"* or *"maitoproteiinia"*
in Swedish	*"sulfiter"* or *"svaveldioxid"*	*"ägg"*, *"äggprotein"*, *"äggprodukt"*, *"ägglysozym"* or *"äggalbumin"*	*"mjölk"*, *"mjölkprodukter"*, *"mjölkkasein"* or *"mjölkprotein"*

PART B
PICTOGRAMS REFERRED TO IN ARTICLE 51(2)]

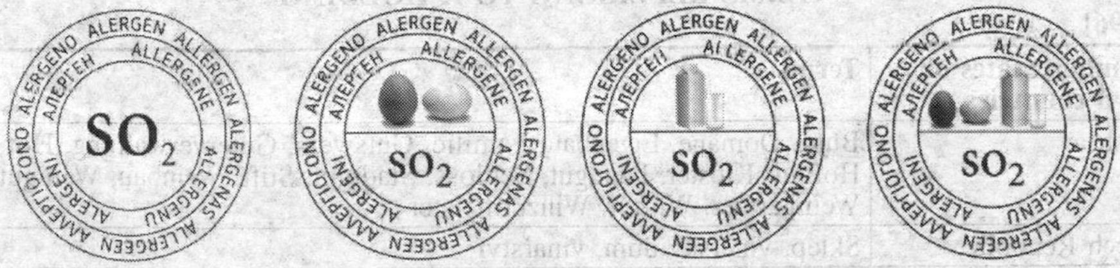

NOTES

Substituted by Commission Regulation 579/2012/EU, Art 1(2), Annex.

Part A: entry in square brackets added by Commission Regulation 519/2013/EU, Art 1, Annex, para 5.K.(3).

[ANNEX XA
WORDS REFERRED TO IN ARTICLE 56(3)(B)

[8.495]

Language	Words authorised instead of 'producer'	Words authorised instead of 'produced by'
BG	"преработвател"	"преработено от"
ES	*"elaborador"*	*"elaborado por"*
CS	*"zpracovatel"* or *"vinař"*	*"zpracováno v"* or *"vyrobeno v"*
DA	*"forarbejdningsvirksomhed"* or *"vinproducent"*	*"forarbejdet af"*
DE	*"Verarbeiter"*	*"verarbeitet von"* or *"versektet durch"*
ET	*"töötleja"*	*"töödelnud"*
EL	"οινοποιός"	"οινοποιήθηκε από",
EN	*"processor"* or *"winemaker"*	*"processed by"* or *"made by"*
FR	*"élaborateur"*	*"élaboré par"*
IT	*"elaboratore"* or *"spumantizzatore"*	*"elaborato da"* or *"spumantizzato da"*
LV	*"izgatavotājs"*	*"vīndaris"* or *"ražojis"*
LT	*"perdirbėjas"*	*"perdirbo"*
HU	*"feldolgozó:"*	*"feldolgozta:"*
MT	*"proċessur"*	*"ipproċessat minn"*
NL	*"verwerker"* or *"bereider"*	*"verwerkt door"* or *"bereid door"*
PL	*"przetwórca"* or *"wytwórca"*	*"przetworzone przez"* or *"wytworzone przez"*

Language	Words authorised instead of 'producer'	Words authorised instead of 'produced by'
PT	*"elaborador"* or *"preparador"*	*"elaborado por"* or *"preparado por"*
RO	*"elaborator"*	*"elaborat de"*
SI	*"pridelovalec"*	*"prideluje"*
SK	*"spracovateľ"*	*"spracúva"*
FI	*"valmistaja"*	*"valmistanut"*
SV	*"bearbetningsföretag"*	*"bearbetat av"*]

NOTES

Added by Commission Regulation 1185/2012/EU, Art 1(2), Annex.

ANNEXES XI, XII

(*Repealed by Commission Regulation 538/2011/EU, Art 1(14).*)

ANNEX XIII
TERMS REFERRING TO A HOLDING

[8.496]

Member States or third countries	Terms
Austria	Burg, Domäne, Eigenbau, Familie, Gutswein, Güterverwaltung, Hof, Hofgut, Kloster, Landgut, Schloss, Stadtgut, Stift, Weinbau, Weingut, Weingärtner, Winzer, Winzermeister
Czech Republic	Sklep, vinařský dům, vinařství
Germany	Burg, Domäne, Kloster, Schloss, Stift, Weinbau, Weingärtner, Weingut, Winzer
France	Abbaye, Bastide, Campagne, Chapelle, Château, Clos, Commanderie, Cru, Domaine, Mas, Manoir, Mont, Monastère, Monopole, Moulin, Prieuré, Tour
Greece	Αγρέπαυλη (Agrepavlis), Αμπελι (Ampeli), Αμπελώνας(-ες) (Ampelonas-(es)), Αρχοντικό (Archontiko), Κάστρο (Kastro), Κτήμα (Ktima), Μετόχι (Metochi), Μοναστήρι (Monastiri), Ορεινό Κτήμα (Orino Ktima), Πύργος (Pyrgos)
Italy	abbazia, abtei, ansitz, burg, castello, kloster, rocca, schlofl, stift, torre, villa
Cyprus	Αμπελώνας (-ες) (Ampelonas (-es), Κτήμα (Ktima), Μοναστήρι (Monastiri), Μονή (Moni)
Portugal	Casa, Herdade, Paço, Palácio, Quinta, Solar
Slovakia	Kaštieľ, Kúria, Pivnica, Vinárstvo, Usadlosť
Slovenia	Klet, Kmetija, Posestvo, Vinska klet

ANNEX XIV
INDICATION OF THE SUGAR CONTENT

[8.497]

Terms	Conditions of use
PART A — LIST OF TERMS TO BE USED FOR SPARKLING WINE, AERATED SPARKLING WINE, QUALITY SPARKLING WINE OR QUALITY AROMATIC SPARKLING WINE	
brut nature, naturherb, bruto natural, pas dosé, dosage zéro, natūralusis briutas, īsts bruts, přírodně tvrdé, popolnoma suho, dosaggio zero, брют натюр, brut natur	If its sugar content is less than 3 grams per litre; these terms may be used only for products to which no sugar has been added after the secondary fermentation.
extra brut, extra herb, ekstra briutas, ekstra brut, ekstra bruts, zvláště tvrdé, extra bruto, izredno suho, ekstra wytrawne, екстра брют	If its sugar content is between 0 and 6 grams per litre.
brut, herb, briutas, bruts, tvrdé, bruto, zelo suho, bardzo wytrawne, брют	If its sugar content is less than 12 grams per litre.

Terms	Conditions of use
extra dry, extra trocken, extra seco, labai sausas, ekstra kuiv, ekstra sausais, különlegesen száraz, wytrawne, suho, zvláště suché, extra suché, екстра сухо, extra sec, ekstra tør	If its sugar content is between 12 and 17 grams per litre.
sec, trocken, secco, asciutto, dry, tør, ξηρός, seco, torr, kuiva, sausas, kuiv, sausais, száraz, półwytrawne, polsuho, suché, сухо	If its sugar content is between 17 and 32 grams per litre.
demi-sec, halbtrocken, abboccato, medium dry, halvtør, ημίξηρος, semi seco, meio seco, halvtorr, puolikuiva, pusiau sausas, poolkuiv, pussausais, félszáraz, półsłodkie, polsladko, polosuché, polosladké, полусухо	If its sugar content is between 32 and 50 grams per litre.
doux, mild, dolce, sweet, sød, γλυκός, dulce, doce, söt, makea, saldus, magus, édes, ħelu, słodkie, sladko, sladké, сладко, dulce, saldais	If its sugar content is greater than 50 grams per litre.

PART B — LIST OF TERMS TO BE USED FOR OTHER PRODUCTS THAN THOSE LISTED IN PART A	
сухо, seco, suché, tør, trocken, kuiv, ξηρός, dry, sec, secco, asciuttto, sausais, sausas, száraz, droog, wytrawne, seco, sec, suho, kuiva	If its sugar content does not exceed: — 4 grams per litre, or — 9 grams per litre, provided that the total acidity expressed as grams of tartaric acid per litre is not more than 2 grams below the residual sugar content.
полусухо, semiseco, polosuché, halvtør, halbtrocken, poolkuiv, ημίξηρος, medium dry, demi-sec, abboccato, pussausais, pusiau sausas, félszáraz, halfdroog, półwytrawne, meio seco, adamado, demisec, polsuho, puolikuiva, halvtorrt	If its sugar content exceeds the maximum set at above but not exceeds: — 12 grams per litre, or — 18 grams per litre, provided that the total acidity expressed as grams of tartaric acid per litre is not more than 10 grams below the residual sugar content.
полусладко, semidulce, polosladké, halvsød, lieblich, poolmagus, ημίγλυκος, medium, medium sweet, moelleux, amabile, pussaldais, pusiau saldus, félédes, halfzoet, półsłodkie, meio doce, demidulce, polsladko, puolimakea, halvsött	If its sugar content is higher than the maximum set at above but not more than 45 grams per litre.
сладко, dulce, sladké, sød, süss, magus, γλυκός, sweet, doux, dolce, saldais, saldus, édes, ħelu, zoet, słodkie, doce, dulce, sladko, makea, sött.	If its sugar content is of at least 45 grams per litre.

[ANNEX XV
LIST OF WINE GRAPE VARIETIES AND THEIR SYNONYMS THAT MAY APPEAR ON THE LABELLING OF WINES

PART A: LIST OF WINE GRAPE VARIETIES AND THEIR SYNONYMS THAT MAY APPEAR ON THE LABELLING OF WINES IN ACCORDANCE WITH ARTICLE 62(3)

[8.498]

	Name of a protected designation of origin or geographical indication	Variety name or its synonyms	Countries that may use the variety name or one of its synonyms[1]
1	Alba (IT)	**Albarossa**	Italy°
2	Alicante (ES)	**Alicante Bouschet**	**Greece°, Italy°, Portugal°, Algeria°, Tunisia°, United States°, Cyprus°, South Africa, [Croatia]** *N.B.: The name "Alicante" may not be used on its own to designate wine.*

Part 8 Other EU Materials

	Name of a protected designation of origin or geographical indication	Variety name or its synonyms	Countries that may use the variety name or one of its synonyms[1]
3		**Alicante Branco**	**Portugal°**
4		**Alicante Henri Bouschet**	**France°, Serbia and Montenegro** (6)
5		**Alicante**	**Italy°**
6		Alikant Buse	Serbia and Montenegro (4)
7	Avola (IT)	Nero d'Avola	Italy
8	Bohotin (RO)	**Busuioacă de Bohotin**	**Romania**
9	Borba (PT)	**Borba**	**Spain°**
10	Bourgogne (FR)	Blauburgunder	Former Yugoslav Republic of Macedonia (13-**20**-30), Austria (**18**-20), Canada (20–30), Chile (20–30), Italy (20–30), Switzerland
11		**Blauer Burgunder**	**Austria** (10–13), Serbia and Montenegro (**17**-30)
12		**Blauer Frühburgunder**	**Germany** (24)
13		**Blauer Spätburgunder**	**Germany** (30), Former Yugoslav Republic of Macedonia (10-**20**-30), Austria (10-**11**), Bulgaria (30), Canada (10–30), Chile (10–30), Romania (30), Italy (10–30)
14		**Burgund Mare**	**Romania** (35, 27, 39, 41)
[14A		Bourgogne (FR) Borgonja istarska	Croatia]
15		**Burgundac beli**	**Serbia and Montenegro** (34)
[15A		Bourgogne (FR) Burgundac bijeli	Croatia]
. . .		. . .	. . .
17		**Burgundac crni**	**[Croatia], Serbia and Montenegro** (11–30)
18		**Burgundac sivi**	Croatia°, **Serbia and Montenegro°**
19		**Burgundec bel**	**Former Yugoslav Republic of Macedonia°**
20		**Burgundec crn**	**Former Yugoslav Republic of Macedonia** (10-13-30)
21		**Burgundec siv**	**Former Yugoslav Republic of Macedonia°**
22		**Early Burgundy**	**United States°**
23		Fehér Burgundi, Burgundi	Hungary (31)
24		Frühburgunder	Germany (**12**), **Netherlands°**
25		Grauburgunder	Germany, Bulgaria, Hungary°, Romania (26)
26		Grauer Burgunder	Canada, Romania (25), Germany, **Austria**
27		Grossburgunder	Romania (37, **14**, 40, 42)
28		Kisburgundi kék	Hungary (30)
29		**Nagyburgundi**	Hungary°
30		Spätburgunder	Former Yugoslav Republic of Macedonia (10-13-**20**), Serbia and Montenegro (11-**17**), Bulgaria (13), Canada (10–13), Chile, Hungary (29), Moldavia°, Romania (13), Italy (10–13), **United Kingdom**, Germany (**13**)

	Name of a protected designation of origin or geographical indication	**Variety name or its synonyms**	**Countries that may use the variety name or one of its synonyms[1]**
31		Weißburgunder	South Africa (33), Canada, Chile (32), Hungary (23), Germany (**32**, 33), Austria (**32**), United Kingdom°, Italy
32		**Weißer Burgunder**	**Germany** (31, 33), **Austria** (31), Chile (31), Slovenia, Italy
33		**Weissburgunder**	South Africa (31), Germany (31, **32**), United Kingdom, Italy, **Switzerland**°
34		Weisser Burgunder	Serbia and Montenegro (**15**)
35	Calabria (IT)	Calabrese	**Italy**
36	Cotnari (RO)	**Grasă de Cotnari**	**Romania**
37	Franken (DE)	**Blaufränkisch**	Czech Republic (**39**), Austria°, Germany, Slovenia (**Modra frankinja**, Frankinja), Hungary, Romania (**14**, 27, 39, 41)
38		**Frâncuşă**	**Romania**
39		**Frankovka**	**[Croatia], Czech Republic** (37), Slovakia (**40**), Romania (**14**, 27, 38, 41)
40		**Frankovka modrá**	**Slovakia** (39)
41		**Kékfrankos**	Hungary, Romania (37, **14**, 27, 39)
42	Friuli (IT)	Friulano	Italy
43	Graciosa (PT)	**Graciosa**	**Portugal**°
44	Мелник (BU) *Melnik*	**Мелник** *Melnik*	**Bulgaria**
45	Montepulciano (IT)	**Montepulciano**	**Italy**°
46	Moravské (CZ)	Cabernet Moravia	**Czech Republic**°
47		Moravia dulce	**Spain**°
48		Moravia agria	**Spain**°
49		**Muškat moravský**	**Czech Republic**°, **Slovakia**
50	Odobeşti (RO)	**Galbenă de Odobeşti**	**Romania**
51	Porto (PT)	**Portoghese**	**Italy**°
52	Rioja (ES)	**Torrontés riojano**	**Argentina**°
53	Sardegna (IT)	Barbera Sarda	Italy
54	Sciacca (IT)	Sciaccarello	France

NOTES

Words in square brackets in entries numbered 2, 17, 39 inserted, entries 14A, 15A inserted and entry 16 repealed, by Commission Regulation 753/2013/EU, Art 1(2), Annex, para 1.

1 For the states concerned, the derogations provided for in this Annex are authorised only in the case of wines bearing a protected designation of origin or geographical indication produced with the varieties concerned.

PART B: LIST OF WINE GRAPE VARIETIES AND THEIR SYNONYMS THAT MAY APPEAR ON THE LABELLING OF WINES IN ACCORDANCE WITH ARTICLE 62(4)

	Name of a protected designation of origin or geographical indication	**Variety name or its synonyms**	**Countries that may use the variety name or one of its synonyms[1]**
1	Mount Athos — Agioritikos (GR)	**Agiorgitiko**	**Greece**°, Cyprus°
2	Aglianico del Taburno (IT)	**Aglianico**	**Italy**°, **Greece**°, **Malta**°, **United States**
[2A	Aglianico del Taburno (IT)	**Aglianico crni**	**Croatia**]
3	Aglianico del Vulture (IT)	**Aglianicone**	**Italy**°

	Name of a protected designation of origin or geographical indication	Variety name or its synonyms	Countries that may use the variety name or one of its synonyms[1]
4	Aleatico di Gradoli (IT) Aleatico di Puglia (IT)	**Aleatico**	**Italy, Australia, United States**
5	Ansonica Costa dell'Argentario (IT)	**Ansonica**	**Italy, Australia**
6	Conca de Barbera (ES)	**Barbera Bianca**	**Italy°**
7		**Barbera**	**South Africa°, Argentina°, Australia°, Croatia°, Mexico°, Slovenia°, Uruguay°, United States°, Greece°, Italy°, Malta°**
8		**Barbera Sarda**	**Italy°**
9	Malvasia di Castelnuovo Don Bosco (IT) Bosco Eliceo (IT)	**Bosco**	**Italy°**
10	Brachetto d'Acqui (IT)	**Brachetto**	**Italy, Australia**
11	Etyek-Buda (HU)	**Budai**	**Hungary°**
12	Cesanese del Piglio (IT) Cesanese di Olevano Romano (IT) Cesanese di Affile (IT)	**Cesanese**	**Italy, Australia**
13	Cortese di Gavi (IT) Cortese dell'Alto Monferrato (IT)	**Cortese**	**Italy, Australia, United States**
14	Duna (HU)	**Duna gyöngye**	**Hungary**
15	Dunajskostredský (SK)	**Dunaj**	**Slovakia**
16	Côte de Duras (FR)	**Durasa**	**Italy**
17	Korinthos-Korinthiakos (GR)	**Corinto Nero**	**Italy°**
18		**Korinthiaki**	**Greece°**
19	Fiano di Avellino (IT)	**Fiano**	**Italy, Australia, United States**
20	Fortana del Taro (IT)	**Fortana**	**Italy, Australia**
21	Freisa d'Asti (IT) Freisa di Chieri (IT)	**Freisa**	**Italy, Australia, United States**
22	Greco di Bianco (IT) Greco di Tufo (IT)	**Greco**	**Italy, Australia**
23	Grignolino d'Asti (IT) Grignolino del Monferrato Casalese (IT)	**Grignolino**	**Italy, Australia, United States**
24	Izsáki Arany Sárfehér (HU)	**Izsáki Sáfeher**	**Hungary**
25	Lacrima di Morro d'Alba (IT)	**Lacrima**	**Italy, Australia**
26	Lambrusco Grasparossa di Castelvetro	**Lambrusco grasparossa**	**Italy**
27		**Lambrusco**	**Italy, Australia[2], United States**
28	Lambrusco di Sorbara (IT)		
29	Lambrusco Mantovano (IT)		
30	Lambrusco Salamino di Santa Croce (IT)		
31		**Lambrusco Salamino**	**Italy**
32	Colli Maceratesi	Maceratino	**Italy, Australia**
33	Nebbiolo d'Alba (IT)	**Nebbiolo**	**Italy, Australia, United States[, Croatia]**

	Name of a protected designation of origin or geographical indication	Variety name or its synonyms	Countries that may use the variety name or one of its synonyms[1]
34	Colli Orientali del Friuli Picolit (IT)	**Picolit**	**Italy**
35		**Pikolit**	**Slovenia**
36	Colli Bolognesi Classico Pignoletto (IT)	**Pignoletto**	**Italy, Australia**
37	Primitivo di Manduria	**Primitivo**	**Italy, Australia, United States[, Croatia]**
38	Rheingau (DE)	**Rajnai rizling**	**Hungary** (41)
39	Rheinhessen (DE)	Rajnski rizling	Serbia and Montenegro [, Croatia] (40-41-**46**)
40		Renski rizling	Serbia and Montenegro (39-43-**46**), **Slovenia**° (45)
41		Rheinriesling	Bulgaria°, Austria, Germany (43), Hungary (**38**), Czech Republic (**49**), Italy (43), Greece, Portugal, Slovenia
42		Rhine Riesling	South Africa°, Australia°, Chile (44), Moldavia°, New Zealand°, **Cyprus, Hungary**°
43		Riesling renano	Germany (41), Serbia and Montenegro (39-40-**46**), **Italy** (41)
44		**Riesling Renano**	Chile (42), **Malta**°
45		Radgonska ranina	**Slovenia[, Croatia]**
46		**Rizling rajnski**	**Serbia and Montenegro** (39-40-43)
47		**Rizling Rajnski**	**Former Yugoslav Republic of Macedonia°, Croatia**°
48		**Rizling rýnsky**	**Slovakia**°
49		**Ryzlink rýnský**	**Czech Republic** (41)
50	Rossese di Dolceacqua (IT)	**Rossese**	**Italy, Australia**
51	Sangiovese di Romagna (IT)	**Sangiovese**	**Italy, Australia, United States[, Croatia]**
52	Štajerska Slovenija (SV)	Štajerska belina	**Slovenia[, Croatia]**
[52A	Štajerska Slovenija (SV)	Štajerka	**Croatia]**
53	Teroldego Rotaliano (IT)	Teroldego	**Italy, Australia, United States**
54	Vinho Verde (PT)	**Verdea**	**Italy**°
55		**Verdeca**	**Italy**
56		**Verdese**	**Italy**°
57	Verdicchio dei Castelli di Jesi (IT) Verdicchio di Matelica (IT)	**Verdicchio**	**Italy, Australia**
[58	Vermentino di Gallura (IT) Vermentino di Sardegna (IT)	**Vermentino**	**Italy, Australia, United States of America[, Croatia]]**
59	Vernaccia di San Gimignano (IT) Vernaccia di Oristano (IT) Vernaccia di Serrapetrona (IT)	**Vernaccia**	**Italy, Australia**
60	Zala (HU)	**Zalagyöngye**	**Hungary**

(*) *LEGEND:*

— terms in italic: reference to the synonym for the wine grape variety

Name of a protected designation of origin or geographical indication	Variety name or its synonyms	Countries that may use the variety name or one of its synonyms[1]

— "o" no synonym

— terms in bold: column 3: name of the wine grape variety

column 4: country where the name corresponds to a variety and reference to the variety

— terms not in bold: column 3: name of the synonym of a vine variety

column 4: name of country using the synonym of a vine variety]

NOTES

Substituted by Commission Regulation 401/2010/EU, Art 1(9), Annex.

Rows 2A, 52A inserted and word in square brackets in rows 33, 37, 39, 45, 51, 52, 58 inserted by Commission Regulation 753/2013/EU, Art 1(2), Annex, para 2.

Row 58 substituted by Commission Regulation 428/2012/EU, Art 1.

1 For the states concerned, the derogations provided for in this Annex are authorised only in the case of wines bearing a protected designation of origin or geographical indication produced with the varieties concerned.

2 Use authorised in accordance with the provisions of Article 22(4) of the Agreement of 1 December 2008 between the Euopean Community and Australia on trade in wine (OJ L28, 30.1.2009, p 3).

ANNEX XVI
INDICATIONS AUTHORISED FOR USE ON WINE LABELLING PURSUANT TO ARTICLE 66(2)

[8.499]

barrel fermented	barrel matured	barrel aged
[. . .]-cask fermented	[. . .]-cask matured	[. . .]-cask aged
[indicate the type of wood]	*[indicate the type of wood]*	*[indicate the type of wood]*
cask fermented	cask matured	cask aged

ANNEX XVII
RESERVATION OF CERTAIN SPECIFIC TYPES OF BOTTLE

[8.500]

1. **'Flûte d'Alsace':**
   (a) type: a glass bottle consisting of a straight cylindrical body with a long neck, with approximately the following proportions:
   — total height/diameter at base =5:1,
   — height of the cylindrical body = total height/3;
   (b) the wines for which this type of bottle is reserved, in the case of wines produced from grapes harvested in French territory, are the following wines with designations of origin:
   — 'Alsace' or 'vin d'Alsace', 'Alsace Grand Cru',
   — 'Crépy',
   — 'Château-Grillet',
   — 'Côtes de Provence', red and rosé,
   — 'Cassis',
   — 'Jurançon', 'Jurançon sec',
   — 'Béarn', 'Béarn-Bellocq', rosé,
   — 'Tavel', rosé.

   However, the restriction on the use of bottles of this type shall apply only to wines produced from grapes harvested in French territory.

2. **'Bocksbeutel' or 'Cantil':**
   (a) type: short-necked glass bottle, pot-bellied but flattened in shape; the base and the cross-section of the bottle at the point of greatest convexity are ellipsoidal:
   — the ratio between the long and short axes of the ellipsoidal cross-section = 2:1,
   — the ratio of the height of the convex body to the cylindrical neck of the bottle = 2.5:1;
   (b) wines for which this type of bottle is reserved:
   (i) German wines with designations of origin of:
   — Franken,
   — Baden:
   — originating in Taubertal and Schüpfergrund,
   — originating in the following parts of the local administrative area of Baden-Baden: Neuweier, Steinbach, Umweg and Varnhalt;

(ii) Italian wines with designations of origin of:
— Santa Maddalena (St. Magdalener),
— Valle Isarco (Eisacktaler), made from the Sylvaner and Müller-Thurgau varieties,
— Terlaner, made from the Pinot bianco variety,
— Bozner Leiten,
— Alto Adige (Südtiroler), made from the Riesling, Müller-Thurgau, Pinot nero, Moscato giallo, Sylvaner, Lagrein, Pinot blanco (Weissburgunder) and Moscato rosa (Rosenmuskateller) varieties,
— Greco di Bianco,
— Trentino, made from the Moscato variety;

(iii) Greek wines:
— Agioritiko,
— Rombola Kephalonias,
— wines from the island of Kefalonia,
— wines from the island of Paros,
— wines with protected geographical indication from Peloponnese;

(iv) Portuguese wines:
— rosé wines and only those other wines with designations of origin and geographical indications which can be proven to have already been correctly and traditionally presented in 'cantil'-type bottles before they were classified as wines with designations of origin and geographical indications.

3. 'Clavelin':

(a) type: a short-necked glass bottle containing 0,62 litres, consisting of a cylindrical body with broad shoulders, giving the bottle a squat appearance, with approximately the following proportions:
— total height/diameter at base = 2,75,
— height of the cylindrical part = total height/2;

(b) wines for which this type of bottle is reserved:
— French wines with protected designations of origin of:
— Côte du Jura,
— Arbois,
— L'Etoile,
— Château Chalon.

4. 'Tokaj':

(a) type: a straight, long-necked, colourless glass bottle consisting of a cylindrical body with the following proportions:
— height of cylindrical body / total height = 1:2,7,
— total height / diameter at base = 1:3,6,
— capacity: 500 ml; 375 ml, 250 ml, 100 ml or 187,5 ml (in case of exporting to a third country),
— a seal made of the material of the bottle referring to the wine region or the producer may be placed on the bottle;

(b) wines for which this type of bottle is reserved:
Hungarian and Slovak wines with protected designations of origin of:
[— Tokaj,]
Vinohradnícka oblasť Tokaj.]
supplemented by one of the following traditional terms:
— aszú/výber,
— aszúeszencia/esencia výberova,
— eszencia/esencia,
— máslas/mášláš,
— fordítás/forditáš,
— szamorodni/samorodné.

However, the restriction on the use of bottles of this type shall apply only to wines produced from grapes harvested in Hungarian or Slovakian territory.

NOTES

Point 4: words in square brackets in para (b) substituted by Commission Regulation 401/2010/EU, Art 1(10).

[ANNEX XVIII
ACCESS TO THE METHODS AND ELECTRONIC FORMS REFERRED TO IN ARTICLE 70A(1)(B)

[8.501]
The methods and electronic forms referred to in Article 70a(1)(b) are freely accessible through the "E-Bacchus" electronic database by the Commission through its information systems:

http://ec.europa.eu/agriculture/markets/wine/e-bacchus/]

NOTES
Added by Commission Regulation 670/2011/EU, Art 1(25), Annex I.

[ANNEX XIX
PRACTICALITIES OF COMMUNICATION AND MAKING INFORMATION AVAILABLE REFERRED TO IN ARTICLE 70A(2)

[8.502]
In order to obtain information as to the practicalities of accessing information systems, of communications and of making information available, the authorities and persons affected by this Regulation should contact the Commission at the following address:

Functional mailbox: AGRI-CONTACT-EBACCHUS@ec.europa.eu]

NOTES
Added by Commission Regulation 670/2011/EU, Art 1(25), Annex II.

COUNCIL OF THE EUROPEAN UNION RESOLUTION

of 1 March 2010 on the enforcement of intellectual property rights in the internal market

2999th COMPETITIVENESS Council meeting Brussels, 1 March 2010

[8.503]

The Council adopted the following conclusions:
"THE COUNCIL OF THE EUROPEAN UNION,

1. WELCOMING the Commission Communication of 11 September 2009 on enhancing the enforcement of intellectual property rights in the internal market;

2. RECALLING its Resolution of 25 September 2008 on a comprehensive European anticounterfeiting and anti-piracy plan;

3. RECALLING the Commission Communication of 16 July 2008 on an industrial property rights strategy for Europe;

4. CONSIDERING the Community instruments adopted to combat the infringement of intellectual property rights, particularly Directive 2004/48/EC on the enforcement of intellectual property rights, Regulation (EC) No 1383/2003 concerning customs action against goods suspected of infringing certain intellectual property rights and the measures to be taken against goods found to have infringed such rights, Directive 2001/29/EC on the harmonisation of certain aspects of copyright and related rights in the information society and Directive 2009/24/EC on the legal protection of computer programs;

5. CONSIDERING its Conclusions of 20 November 2008 on the development of legal offers of online cultural and creative content and the prevention and combating of piracy in the digital environment;

6. CONSIDERING its Conclusions of 22 May 2008 on a European approach to media literacy in the digital environment and its Conclusions of 27 November 2009 on media literacy in the digital environment;

7. CONSIDERING Directive 2000/31/EC of the European Parliament and of the Council of 8 June 2000 on certain legal aspects of information society services, in particular electronic commerce, in the Internal Market ("Directive on electronic commerce");

8. CONSIDERING Directive 2009/140/EC of the European Parliament and of the Council of 25 November 2009 amending Directives 2002/21/EC on a common regulatory framework for electronic communications networks and services, 2002/19/EC on access to, and interconnection of, electronic communications networks and associated facilities, and 2002/20/EC on the authorisation of electronic communications networks and services;

9. RECALLING its Resolution of 23 October 2009 on a reinforced strategy for customs cooperation;

10. RECALLING its Resolution of 16 March 2009 on the European Union Customs Action Plan to combat IPR infringements for the years 2009–2012;

11. RECALLING its Decision 2009/371/JHA of 6 April 2009 establishing the European Police Office (Europol);

12. RECALLING its Decision 2002/187/JHA of 28 February 2002 setting up Eurojust with a view of reinforcing the fight against serious crime;

13. RECALLING its Conclusions of 24 September 2009 on "Making the internal market work better";[1]

14. CONSIDERING Commission Recommendation 2009/524/EC of 29 June 2009 on measures to improve the functioning of the single market;

15. CONSIDERING the ongoing international activities aimed at supporting the fight against counterfeiting and piracy, including in particular the negotiation on the Anti-counterfeiting Trade Agreement;[2]

16. EMPHASISING the importance of protecting intellectual property rights, which are fundamental to promoting culture and diversity, and for drawing full benefit from the research, innovation and creative activity of European undertakings, especially small and medium-sized enterprises, in order to support growth and jobs in the European Union and make Europe more competitive in the world;

17. STRESSING that the European Union has been called upon, in this respect, to continue its efforts to make the system for protecting intellectual property rights more efficient in order to more effectively combat infringements of intellectual property rights;

18. REITERATING its ambition to establish a consistent, high level of enforcement across the internal market, avoiding the creation of barriers to legitimate trade, and providing legal certainty while safeguarding consumers' and users' interests;

19. EMPHASISING that in the field of copyright and related rights, piracy in cultural and creative goods in a rapidly developing digital environment is damaging the legal marketing of the media, hampering the arrival of competitive business models of legal supply of cultural and creative content, calling into question the adequate remuneration of right holders and holding back the dynamism of the European cultural industry that provides access to legal, diverse and high quality cultural supply;

20. RECOGNISES the shared responsibility of the Commission and the Member States to make the internal market work more effectively, particularly in the field of the protection of intellectual property;

21. RECOGNISES the importance of developing new competitive business models enlarging the legal offer of cultural and creative content and at the same time preventing and combating piracy as necessary means for fostering economic growth, employment and cultural diversity; Therefore, efforts to encourage creation of and access to online content and services in the European Union should be increased and, to that effect, robust solutions, which are practical, balanced and attractive for both users and right holders alike, need to be found;

22. ACKNOWLEDGES the importance of developing multi-agency administrative cooperation in the field of intellectual property rights enforcement and INVITES the Commission, in close collaboration and coordination with the competent authorities or institutions of Member States, to further analyse existing national administrative arrangements;

23. RECOGNISES the need for evidence-based and outcome-oriented policy making and in this context welcomes the recent creation and work of the European Observatory on Counterfeiting and Piracy;

24. INVITES the Commission to elaborate further on the scope of competences, tasks and role of the Observatory, supporting its activity through existing institutional structures. The Observatory will act through the plenary or through working groups on an ad hoc basis and will make full use of available national expertise, such as in particular the national correspondents designated by Member States pursuant to Article 19 of Directive 2004/48/EC;

25. AGREES with the principal lines of action put forward by the Commission and encourages national authorities, right holders, consumer organisations and other stakeholders from all sectors, to actively participate in, and contribute to the work of the Observatory;

26. CALLS UPON Member States to develop national anti-counterfeiting and anti-piracy strategies and to establish transparent coordination structures in this field;

27. RECOGNISES the importance of reliable and comparable data on counterfeiting and piracy and INVITES the Commission, the Member States and industry to provide the Observatory with available information and to jointly develop and agree, in the context of the Observatory, on plans to collect further information. and to jointly develop a common methodology for collecting data;

28. NOTES the importance of public awareness in relation to the impact of counterfeiting and piracy on society and on the economy, in particular the potential danger of counterfeits and pirated products for health and safety as well as for European competitiveness, creation, innovation and jobs, and encourages the Commission, the Member States and stakeholders, including consumers, to analyse and implement effective awareness campaigns. The financial implications will be assessed by the Observatory in cooperation with the Commission in order to define appropriate funding resources. The campaigns will focus on specific target audiences such as consumers and young people;

29. STRESSES, in the context of the establishment and functioning of the internal market, the importance of using all appropriate means with a view to ensuring efficient enforcement of intellectual property rights throughout the Union in accordance with the Union acquis in force;
30. INVITES the Commission, in accordance with Article 18 of Directive 2004/48/EC and in close collaboration with the Member States, to analyse the application of that Directive, including an assessment of the effectiveness of the measures taken, and, if necessary, propose appropriate amendments to ensure a better protection of intellectual property rights;
31. NOTES the importance of simplifying the cross-border enforcement of judicial decisions in order to ensure an effective intellectual property rights protection; in this respect, asks the Commission and the Member States to consider how to support the review of the Brussels I Regulation;[3]
32. INVITES the Commission to analyse the opportunity of submitting an amended proposal for a Directive on criminal measures aimed at combating counterfeiting and piracy. This analysis must include an assessment of the extent to which action is essential to ensure the effective implementation of a Union policy in an area which has been subject to harmonisation measures, as well as an examination of the impact, costs and benefits of any new measures;
33. REQUESTS the Observatory to facilitate regular experts' meetings, involving representatives from public authorities, private sector bodies and consumer organisations, to promote successful and proportional solutions against counterfeiting and piracy. The Observatory will pay special attention to the compilation of best practices in public and private sectors and codes of conduct in private sectors. In its Annual Report, the Observatory should take into account the conclusions of the experts' meetings and relevant round tables;
34. PROMOTES the use, within the limits of data protection law, of the European network for administrative cooperation referred to in the Council Resolution of 25 September 2008 with a view to ensuring rapid exchanges of information and mutual assistance among the authorities engaged in the field of the enforcement of intellectual property rights;
35. INVITES the Observatory to publish each year a comprehensive Annual Report covering the scope, scale and principal characteristics of counterfeiting and piracy as well as its impact on the internal market. This report will be prepared with the relevant information provided by the authorities of the Member States, the Commission and the private sector, within the limits of data protection law;
36. INVITES the Observatory to extend the study of causes, consequences and the effects of violations of intellectual property rights on innovation, competitiveness, the labour market, healthcare, security, creativity and cultural diversity in the internal market and to explore the need for the implementation of European Union level training programmes for those involved in combating counterfeiting and piracy;
37. INVITES the Commission to assess, in close cooperation with Member States, how best to enhance coordination, cooperation, information exchange and mutual assistance between all national and European authorities involved in combating counterfeiting and piracy with the cooperation of the economic operators;
38. URGES Member States and the Commission to explore how to make best use of the experience and knowledge readily available in the European Union and in national intellectual property offices to examine the possibilities for providing information to right holders, in particular small and medium-sized enterprises, through the strengthening of existing and the possible creation of new portals or helpdesks, in order to enable them to effectively and efficiently protect their intellectual property;
39. WELCOMES the Commission's new and innovative approach to facilitate dialogues amongst stakeholders, aimed at jointly agreed voluntary measures to reduce counterfeiting and piracy in compliance with the legal framework;
40. ENCOURAGES the Commission, the Member States and the relevant stakeholders to pursue ongoing dialogues and to resolutely seek agreements on voluntary practical measures aimed at reducing counterfeiting and piracy in the internal market, both online and offline;
41. INVITES the Member States to communicate to the Commission any existing agreements referred to in the previous point and ENCOURAGES the Commission to analyse, in cooperation with Member States and economic operators, the efficacy of these agreements in the fight against counterfeiting in the internal market in order to state the existing best practices;
42. INVITES the Commission, within the limits of European Union competence, in cases where stakeholders' dialogues are unable to reach agreed solutions, to review the situation in cooperation with Member States and to come forward with proposals for an appropriate followup, including proposals for legislation, if necessary and appropriate;
43. INVITES the Member States and the Commission to act towards promoting appropriate and effective levels of protection of intellectual property in both bilateral and multilateral international agreements with due regard to the Union acquis."

NOTES

1 Council document 13024/09.

2 The Commission will continue to inform the Member States and the Council, as well as the European Parliament and

relevant stakeholders as appropriate.

[3] Council Regulation (EC) No 44/2001 of 22 December 2000 on jurisdiction and the recognition and enforcement of judgments in civil and commercial matters, OJ L12, 16.1.2001, p 1.

REGULATION OF THE EUROPEAN PARLIAMENT AND OF THE COUNCIL

(1007/2011/EU)

of 27 September 2011

on textile fibre names and related labelling and marking of the fibre composition of textile products and repealing Council Directive 73/44/EEC and Directives 96/73/EC and 2008/121/EC of the European Parliament and of the Council

(Text with EEA relevance)

NOTES

Date of publication in OJ: OJ L272, 18.10.2011, p 1.

This Regulation is reproduced as corrected by the Corrigendum published in OJ L243, 18.9.2015, p 13.

THE EUROPEAN PARLIAMENT AND THE COUNCIL OF THE EUROPEAN UNION,

Having regard to the Treaty on the Functioning of the European Union, and in particular Article 114 thereof,

Having regard to the proposal from the European Commission,

Having regard to the opinion of the European Economic and Social Committee,[1]

Acting in accordance with the ordinary legislative procedure,[2]

Whereas:

(1) Council Directive 73/44/EEC of 26 February 1973 on the approximation of the laws of the Member States relating to the quantitative analysis of ternary fibre mixtures,[3] Directive 96/73/EC of the European Parliament and of the Council of 16 December 1996 on certain methods for the quantitative analysis of binary textile fibre mixtures[4] and Directive 2008/121/EC of the European Parliament and of the Council of 14 January 2009 on textile names[5] have been amended several times. Since further amendments are to be made, those acts should be replaced by a single legal instrument, in the interest of clarity.

(2) The legal acts of the Union on textile fibre names and related labelling and marking of fibre composition of textile products are very technical in their content, with detailed provisions that need to be adapted regularly. In order to avoid the need for Member States to transpose the technical amendments into national legislation and thus reduce the administrative burden for national authorities and in order to allow for a faster adoption of new textile fibre names to be used simultaneously throughout the Union, a regulation seems to be the most appropriate legal instrument to carry out the legislative simplification.

(3) In order to eliminate potential obstacles to the proper functioning of the internal market caused by Member States' diverging provisions with regard to textile fibre names and related labelling and marking of fibre composition of textile products, it is necessary to harmonise the names of textile fibres and the indications appearing on labels, markings and documents which accompany textile products at the various stages of their production, processing and distribution.

(4) The labelling and marking requirements laid down in this Regulation should not apply in cases where textile products are contracted out to persons working in their own homes or to independent firms that carry out work from materials supplied to them without the property therein being transferred for consideration or where customised textile products are made up by self-employed tailors. However, those exemptions should be limited to the transactions between those persons working in their own homes or independent firms and the persons contracting out work to them, and between self-employed tailors and consumers.

(5) This Regulation lays down harmonised provisions with regard to certain aspects of textile labelling and marking, in particular textile fibre names. Other labelling and marking may exist, provided that it does not cover the same scope as this Regulation and that it is compatible with the Treaties.

(6) It is appropriate to lay down rules enabling manufacturers to ask for the inclusion of a new textile fibre name in the Annexes to this Regulation.

(7) Provision should also be made in respect of certain products which are not made exclusively of textile materials but have a textile content which constitutes an essential part of the product or to which attention is specifically drawn by the economic operator.

(8) It is appropriate to lay down rules concerning the labelling or marking of certain textile products which contain non-textile parts of animal origin. This Regulation should, in particular, set

out the requirement to indicate the presence of non-textile parts of animal origin on the labelling or marking of textile products containing such parts, in order to enable consumers to make informed choices. The labelling or marking should not be misleading.

(9) The tolerance in respect of 'extraneous fibres', which are not to be stated on the labels and markings, should apply both to pure products and to mixtures.

(10) Labelling or marking of the fibre composition should be compulsory to ensure that correct and uniform information is made available to all consumers in the Union. However, this Regulation should not prevent economic operators from indicating, in addition, the presence of small quantities of fibres requiring particular attention to keep the original quality of the textile product. Where it is technically difficult to specify the fibre composition of a textile product at the time of its manufacture, it should be possible to state, on the label or marking, only those fibres which are known at the time of manufacture provided that they account for a certain percentage of the finished product.

(11) In order to avoid differences in practice among the Member States, it is necessary to lay down the exact methods of labelling or marking for certain textile products consisting of two or more components, and also to specify the components of textile products that need not be taken into account for the purposes of labelling, marking and analysis.

(12) Textile products subject only to the requirements of inclusive labelling, and those sold by the metre or in cut lengths, should be made available on the market in such a way that the consumer can fully acquaint himself with the information affixed to the overall packaging or the roll.

(13) The use of textile fibre names or descriptions of fibre compositions which enjoy particular prestige among users and consumers should be made subject to certain conditions. Furthermore, in order to provide information to users and consumers, it is appropriate that the textile fibre names are related to the characteristics of the fibre.

(14) The market surveillance in Member States of products covered by this Regulation is subject to Regulation (EC) No 765/2008 of the European Parliament and of the Council of 9 July 2008 setting out the requirements for accreditation and market surveillance relating to the marketing of products[6] and Directive 2001/95/EC of the European Parliament and of the Council of 3 December 2001 on general product safety.[7]

(15) It is necessary to lay down methods for the sampling and analysis of textile products in order to exclude any possibility of objections to the methods used. The methods used for official tests carried out in the Member States to determine the fibre composition of textile products composed of binary and ternary fibre mixtures should be uniform, as regards both the pre-treatment of the sample and its quantitative analysis. In order to simplify this Regulation and adapt the uniform methods set out therein to technical progress, it is appropriate that those methods be turned into harmonised standards. To that end, the Commission should manage the transition from the current system, which is based on the methods set out in this Regulation, to a harmonised standard-based system. The use of uniform methods of analysis of textile products composed of binary and ternary fibre mixtures will facilitate the free movement of those products, and thereby improve the functioning of the internal market.

(16) In the case of binary textile fibre mixtures for which there is no uniform method of analysis at Union level, the laboratory responsible for the test should be allowed to determine the composition of such mixtures, indicating in the analysis report the result obtained, the method used and its degree of accuracy.

(17) This Regulation should set out the agreed allowances to be applied to the anhydrous mass of each fibre during the determination by analysis of the fibre content of textile products, and should give two different agreed allowances for calculating the composition of carded or combed fibres containing wool and/or animal hair. Since it cannot always be established whether a product is carded or combed, and consequently inconsistent results can arise from the application of the tolerances during checks on the conformity of textile products carried out in the Union, the laboratories carrying out those checks should be authorised to apply a single agreed allowance in doubtful cases.

(18) Rules should be laid down in respect of products exempt from the general labelling and marking requirements set out in this Regulation, in particular with respect to disposable products or products for which only inclusive labelling is required.

(19) Misleading commercial practices, involving the provision of false information that would cause consumers to take a transactional decision that they would not have taken otherwise, are prohibited by Directive 2005/29/EC of the European Parliament and of the Council of 11 May 2005 concerning unfair business-to-consumer commercial practices in the internal market[8] and are covered by Regulation (EC) No 2006/2004 of the European Parliament and of the Council of 27 October 2004 on cooperation between national authorities responsible for the enforcement of consumer protection law.[9]

(20) Consumer protection requires transparent and consistent trade rules, including as regards indications of origin. When such indications are used, they should enable consumers to be fully

aware of the origin of the products they purchase, so as to protect them against fraudulent, inaccurate or misleading claims of origin.

(21) The European textiles sector is affected by counterfeiting, which poses problems in terms of consumer protection and information. Member States should pay particular attention to the implementation of horizontal Union legislation and measures regarding counterfeit products in the field of textile products, for example Council Regulation (EC) No 1383/2003 of 22 July 2003 concerning customs action against goods suspected of infringing certain intellectual property rights and the measures to be taken against goods found to have infringed such rights.[10]

(22) It is appropriate to establish a procedure for the inclusion of new textile fibre names in the Annexes to this Regulation. This Regulation should thus set out requirements regarding applications by manufacturers or other persons acting on their behalf for new textile fibre names to be added to those Annexes.

(23) It is necessary that manufacturers, or other persons acting on their behalf, who wish to add a new textile fibre name to the Annexes to this Regulation, include in the technical file to be submitted with their application available scientific information concerning possible allergic reactions or other adverse effects of the new textile fibre on human health, including results of tests conducted to that effect in compliance with relevant Union legislation.

(24) The power to adopt acts in accordance with Article 290 of the Treaty on the Functioning of the European Union should be delegated to the Commission in respect of the adoption of technical criteria and procedural rules for the authorisation of higher tolerances, the amendment of Annexes II, IV, V, VI, VII, VIII and IX in order to adapt them to technical progress and the amendment of Annex I in order to include new textile fibre names in the list set out in that Annex. It is of particular importance that the Commission carry out appropriate consultations during its preparatory work, including at expert level. The Commission, when preparing and drawing up delegated acts, should ensure a simultaneous, timely and appropriate transmission of relevant documents to the European Parliament and to the Council.

(25) Since the objectives of this Regulation cannot be sufficiently achieved by the Member States and can therefore, by reason of its scale, be better achieved at Union level, the Union may adopt measures, in accordance with the principle of subsidiarity as set out in Article 5 of the Treaty on European Union. In accordance with the principle of proportionality, as set out in that Article, this Regulation does not go beyond what is necessary in order to achieve those objectives.

(26) In order to eliminate possible obstacles to the proper functioning of the internal market caused by divergent provisions or practices of Member States, and in order to keep pace with the development of electronic commerce and future challenges in the market for textile products, the harmonisation or standardisation of other aspects of textile labelling should be examined. To that end, the Commission is invited to submit a report to the European Parliament and to the Council regarding possible new labelling requirements to be introduced at Union level with a view to facilitating the free movement of textile products in the internal market and to achieving a high level of consumer protection throughout the Union. That report should examine in particular consumer views relating to the amount of information that should be supplied on the label of textile products, and investigate which means other than labelling may be used to provide additional information to consumers. The report should be based on an extended consultation of relevant stakeholders, including consumers, and should take into account existing related European and international standards. The report should examine, in particular: the scope and features of possible harmonised rules on the indication of origin, taking into account the results of developments on potential horizontal country-of-origin rules; the added value to the consumer of possible labelling requirements relating to care instructions, size, hazardous substances, flammability and environmental performance of the textile products; the use of language-independent symbols or codes for identifying the textile fibres contained in a textile product, enabling the consumer to understand easily the composition and, in particular, the use of natural or synthetic fibres; social labelling and electronic labelling; as well as the inclusion of an identification number on the label to obtain additional on-demand information, especially via the Internet, about the product and the manufacturer. The report should be accompanied, where appropriate, by legislative proposals.

(27) The Commission should carry out a study to evaluate whether there is a causal link between allergic reactions and chemical substances or mixtures used in textile products. On the basis of that study, the Commission should, where appropriate, submit legislative proposals in the context of existing Union legislation.

(28) Directives 73/44/EEC, 96/73/EC and 2008/121/EC should be repealed,

NOTES

1 OJ C255, 22.9.2010, p 37.

2 Position of the European Parliament of 18 May 2010 (OJ C161 E, 31.5.2011, p 179) and position of the Council at first reading of 6 December 2010 (OJ C50 E, 17.2.2011, p 1). Position of the European Parliament of 11 May 2011 (not yet published in the Official Journal) and decision of the Council of 19 July 2011.

3 OJ L83, 30.3.1973, p 1.

4 OJ L32, 3.2.1997, p 1.

[5] OJ L19, 23.1.2009, p 29.
[6] OJ L218, 13.8.2008, p 30.
[7] OJ L11, 15.1.2002, p 4.
[8] OJ L149, 11.6.2005, p 22.
[9] OJ L364, 9.12.2004, p 1.
[10] OJ L196, 2.8.2003, p 7.

HAVE ADOPTED THIS REGULATION:

CHAPTER 1
GENERAL PROVISIONS

[8.504]
Article 1
Subject matter

This Regulation lays down rules concerning the use of textile fibre names and related labelling and marking of fibre composition of textile products, rules concerning the labelling or marking of textile products containing non-textile parts of animal origin and rules concerning the determination of the fibre composition of textile products by quantitative analysis of binary and ternary textile fibre mixtures, with a view to improving the functioning of the internal market and to providing accurate information to consumers.

[8.505]
Article 2
Scope

1. This Regulation shall apply to textile products when made available on the Union market and to the products referred to in paragraph 2.
2. For the purposes of this Regulation, the following products shall be treated in the same way as textile products:
   (a) products containing at least 80% by weight of textile fibres;
   (b) furniture, umbrella and sunshade coverings containing at least 80% by weight of textile components;
   (c) the textile components of:
      (i) the upper layer of multi-layer floor coverings;
      (ii) mattress coverings;
      (iii) coverings of camping goods;
   provided such textile components constitute at least 80% by weight of such upper layers or coverings;
   (d) textiles incorporated in other products and forming an integral part thereof, where their composition is specified.
3. This Regulation shall not apply to textile products which are contracted out to persons working in their own homes or to independent firms that carry out work from materials supplied without the property therein being transferred for consideration.
4. This Regulation shall not apply to customised textile products made up by self-employed tailors.

[8.506]
Article 3
Definitions

1. For the purposes of this Regulation, the following definitions shall apply:
   (a) 'textile product' means any raw, semi-worked, worked, semi-manufactured, manufactured, semi-made-up or made-up product which is exclusively composed of textile fibres, regardless of the mixing or assembly process employed;
   (b) 'textile fibre' means either of the following:
      (i) a unit of matter characterised by its flexibility, fineness and high ratio of length to maximum transverse dimension, which render it suitable for textile applications;
      (ii) a flexible strip or tube, of which the apparent width does not exceed 5 mm, including strips cut from wider strips or films, produced from the substances used for the manufacture of the fibres listed in Table 2 of Annex I and suitable for textile applications;
   (c) 'apparent width' means the width of the strip or tube when folded, flattened, compressed or twisted, or the average width where the width is not uniform;
   (d) 'textile component' means a part of a textile product with an identifiable fibre content;
   (e) 'extraneous fibres' means fibres other than those stated on the label or marking;
   (f) 'lining' means a separate component used in making up garments and other products, consisting of a single layer or multiple layers of textile material held in place along one or more of the edges;

(g) 'labelling' means affixing the required information to the textile product by way of attaching a label;

(h) 'marking' means indicating the required information directly on the textile product by way of sewing, embroidering, printing, embossing or any other technology of application;

(i) 'inclusive labelling' means the use of a single label for several textile products or components;

(j) 'disposable product' means a textile product designed to be used only once or for a limited time, and the normal use of which is not intended for subsequent use for the same or a similar purpose;

(k) 'agreed allowance' means the value of moisture regain to be used in the calculation of the percentage of fibre components on a clean, dry mass basis, with adjustment by conventional factors.

2. For the purposes of this Regulation, the definitions of 'making available on the market', 'placing on the market', 'manufacturer', 'importer', 'distributor', 'economic operators', 'harmonised standard', 'market surveillance' and 'market surveillance authority' set out in Article 2 of Regulation (EC) No 765/2008 shall apply.

[8.507]
Article 4
General requirement on the making available on the market of textile products

Textile products shall only be made available on the market provided that such products are labelled, marked or accompanied with commercial documents in compliance with this Regulation.

CHAPTER 2
TEXTILE FIBRE NAMES AND RELATED LABELLING AND MARKING REQUIREMENTS

[8.508]
Article 5
Textile fibre names

1. Only the textile fibre names listed in Annex I shall be used for the description of fibre compositions on labels and markings of textile products.

2. Use of the names listed in Annex I shall be reserved for textile fibres the nature of which corresponds to the description set out in that Annex.

The names listed in Annex I shall not be used for other fibres, whether on their own or as a root or as an adjective.

The term 'silk' shall not be used to indicate the shape or particular presentation in continuous filament yarn of textile fibres.

[8.509]
Article 6
Applications for new textile fibre names

Any manufacturer or any person acting on a manufacturer's behalf may apply to the Commission to add a new textile fibre name to the list set out in Annex I.

The application shall include a technical file compiled in accordance with Annex II.

[8.510]
Article 7
Pure textile products

1. Only textile products exclusively composed of the same fibre may be labelled or marked as '100%', 'pure' or 'all'.

Those or similar terms shall not be used for other textile products.

2. Without prejudice to Article 8(3), a textile product containing no more than 2% by weight of extraneous fibres may also be treated as exclusively composed of the same fibre, provided this quantity is justified as being technically unavoidable in good manufacturing practice and is not added as a matter of routine.

A textile product which has undergone a carding process may also be treated as exclusively composed of the same fibre if it contains no more than 5% by weight of extraneous fibres, provided this quantity is justified as being technically unavoidable in good manufacturing practice and is not added as a matter of routine.

[8.511]
Article 8
Fleece wool or virgin wool products

1. A textile product may be labelled or marked by one of the names set out in Annex III provided it is composed exclusively of a wool fibre which has not previously been incorporated in a finished product, which has not been subjected to any spinning and/or felting processes other than those required in the manufacture of that product, and which has not been damaged by treatment or use.

2. By way of derogation from paragraph 1, the names listed in Annex III may be used to describe wool contained in a textile fibre mixture if all the following conditions are met:

(a) all the wool contained in that mixture satisfies the requirements defined in paragraph 1;
(b) such wool accounts for not less than 25% of the total weight of the mixture;
(c) in the case of a scribbled mixture, the wool is mixed with only one other fibre.

The full percentage composition of such mixture shall be given.

3. The extraneous fibres in the products referred to in paragraphs 1 and 2, including wool products which have undergone a carding process, shall not exceed 0.3% by weight, shall be justified as being technically unavoidable in good manufacturing practice and shall not be added as a matter of routine.

[8.512]
Article 9
Multi-fibre textile products

1. A textile product shall be labelled or marked with the name and percentage by weight of all constituent fibres in descending order.

2. By way of derogation from paragraph 1, and without prejudice to Article 7(2), a fibre which accounts for up to 5% of the total weight of the textile product, or fibres which collectively account for up to 15% of the total weight of the textile product, may, where they cannot easily be stated at the time of the manufacture, be designated by the term 'other fibres', immediately preceded or followed by their total percentage by weight.

3. Products having a pure cotton warp and a pure flax weft, in which the percentage of flax accounts for at least 40% of the total weight of the unsized fabric may be given the name 'cotton linen union' which must be accompanied by the composition specification 'pure cotton warp — pure flax (or linen) weft'.

4. Without prejudice to Article 5(1), for textile products the composition of which is hard to state at the time of their manufacture, the term 'mixed fibres' or the term 'unspecified textile composition' may be used on the label or marking.

5. By way of derogation from paragraph 1 of this Article, fibres not yet listed in Annex I may be designated by the term 'other fibres', immediately preceded or followed by their total percentage by weight.

[8.513]
Article 10
Decorative fibres and fibres with antistatic effect

1. Visible, isolable fibres which are purely decorative and do not exceed 7% of the weight of the finished product do not have to be taken into account in the fibre compositions provided for in Articles 7 and 9.

2. Metallic fibres and other fibres which are incorporated in order to obtain an antistatic effect and which do not exceed 2% of the weight of the finished product do not have to be taken into account in the fibre compositions provided for in Articles 7 and 9.

3. In the case of the products referred to in Article 9(3), the percentages provided for in paragraphs 1 and 2 of this Article shall be calculated on the weight of the warp and that of the weft separately.

[8.514]
Article 11
Multi-component textile products

1. Any textile product containing two or more textile components which have different textile fibre contents shall bear a label or marking stating the textile fibre content of each component.

2. The labelling or marking referred to in paragraph 1 shall not be compulsory for textile components when the following two conditions are fulfilled:

(a) those components are not main linings; and
(b) those components represent less than 30% of the total weight of the textile product.

3. Where two or more textile products have the same fibre content and normally form a single unit, they may bear only one label or marking.

[8.515]
Article 12
Textile products containing non-textile parts of animal origin

1. The presence of non-textile parts of animal origin in textile products shall be indicated by using the phrase 'Contains non-textile parts of animal origin' on the labelling or marking of products containing such parts whenever they are made available on the market.

2. The labelling or marking shall not be misleading and shall be carried out in such a way that the consumer can easily understand.

[8.516]
Article 13
Labelling and marking of textile products listed in Annex IV

The fibre composition of textile products listed in Annex IV shall be indicated in accordance with the labelling and marking provisions set out in that Annex.

[8.517]
Article 14
Labels and markings

1. Textile products shall be labelled or marked to give an indication of their fibre composition whenever they are made available on the market.

The labelling and marking of textile products shall be durable, easily legible, visible and accessible and, in the case of a label, securely attached.

2. Without prejudice to paragraph 1, labels or markings may be replaced or supplemented by accompanying commercial documents when the products are being supplied to economic operators within the supply chain, or when they are delivered in performance of an order placed by any contracting authority as defined in Article 1 of Directive 2004/18/EC of the European Parliament and of the Council of 31 March 2004 on the coordination of procedures for the award of public works contracts, public supply contracts and public service contracts.[1]

3. The textile fibre names and descriptions of fibre compositions referred to in Articles 5, 7, 8 and 9 shall be clearly indicated in the accompanying commercial documents referred to in paragraph 2 of this Article.

Abbreviations shall not be used with the exception of a mechanised processing code, or where the abbreviations are defined in international standards, provided that they are explained in the same commercial document.

NOTES

[1] OJ L134, 30.4.2004, p 114.

[8.518]
Article 15
Obligation to supply the label or marking

1. When placing a textile product on the market, the manufacturer shall ensure the supply of the label or marking and the accuracy of the information contained therein. If the manufacturer is not established in the Union, the importer shall ensure the supply of the label or marking and the accuracy of the information contained therein.

2. A distributor shall be considered a manufacturer for the purposes of this Regulation where he places a product on the market under his name or trademark, attaches the label himself or modifies the content of the label.

3. When making a textile product available on the market, the distributor shall ensure that textile products bear the appropriate labelling or marking prescribed by this Regulation.

4. The economic operators referred to in paragraphs 1, 2 and 3 shall ensure that any information supplied when textile products are made available on the market cannot be confused with the textile fibre names and the descriptions of fibre compositions, as laid down by this Regulation.

[8.519]
Article 16
The use of textile fibre names and fibre composition descriptions

1. When making a textile product available on the market, the textile fibre composition descriptions referred to in Articles 5, 7, 8 and 9 shall be indicated in catalogues and trade literature, on packaging, labels and markings in a manner that is easily legible, visible, clear and in print which is uniform as regards its size, style and font. This information shall be clearly visible to the consumer before the purchase, including in cases where the purchase is made by electronic means.

2. Trade marks or the name of the undertaking may be given immediately before or after textile fibre composition descriptions referred to in Articles 5, 7, 8 and 9.

However, where a trade mark or a name of an undertaking contains, on its own or as a root or as an adjective, one of the textile fibre names listed in Annex I or a name liable to be confused therewith, such trade mark or name shall be given immediately before or after the textile fibre composition descriptions referred to in Articles 5, 7, 8 and 9.

Other information shall be always displayed separately.

3. The labelling or marking shall be provided in the official language or languages of the Member State on the territory of which the textile products are made available to the consumer, unless the Member State concerned provides otherwise.

In the case of bobbins, reels, skeins, balls or other small quantities of sewing, mending and embroidery yarns, the first subparagraph shall apply to the inclusive labelling referred to in Article 17(3). Whenever these products are individually sold, they may be labelled or marked in any of the official languages of the institutions of the Union, provided they are also inclusively labelled.

[8.520]
Article 17
Derogations

1. The rules laid down in Articles 11, 14, 15 and 16 shall be subject to the derogations provided for in paragraphs 2, 3 and 4 of this Article.

2. The indication of textile fibre names or fibre composition on the labels and markings of textile products listed in Annex V is not required.

However, where a trade mark or name of an undertaking contains, on its own or as a root or as an adjective, one of the names listed in Annex I or a name liable to be confused therewith, Articles 11, 14, 15 and 16 shall apply.

3. Where textile products listed in Annex VI are of the same type and fibre composition, they may be made available on the market together with an inclusive labelling.

4. The fibre composition of textile products sold by the metre may be shown on the length or roll made available on the market.

5. The textile products referred to in paragraphs 3 and 4 shall be made available on the market in such a way that the fibre composition of those products is made known to each purchaser in the supply chain, including the consumer.

CHAPTER 3
MARKET SURVEILLANCE

[8.521]
Article 18
Market surveillance checks

Market surveillance authorities shall carry out checks on the conformity of the fibre composition of textile products with the supplied information related to the fibre composition of those products in accordance with this Regulation.

[8.522]
Article 19
Determination of fibre composition

1. For the purpose of determining the fibre composition of textile products, the checks referred to in Article 18 shall be carried out in accordance with the methods set out in Annex VIII or with the harmonised standards to be introduced in that Annex.

2. In the determination of fibre compositions set out in Articles 7, 8 and 9, the items listed in Annex VII shall not be taken into account.

3. The fibre compositions set out in Articles 7, 8 and 9 shall be determined by applying to the anhydrous mass of each fibre the appropriate agreed allowance laid down in Annex IX, after having removed the items set out in Annex VII.

4. The laboratories responsible for the testing of textile mixtures for which there is no uniform method of analysis at Union level shall determine the fibre composition of such mixtures, indicating in the analysis report the result obtained, the method used and its degree of accuracy.

[8.523]
Article 20
Tolerances

1. For the purposes of establishing the fibre composition of textile products, the tolerances laid down in paragraphs 2, 3 and 4 shall apply.

2. Without prejudice to Article 8(3), the presence of extraneous fibres in the fibre composition to be provided in accordance with Article 9 does not need to be indicated if the percentage of those fibres does not reach the following values:

(a) 2% of the total weight of the textile product, provided this quantity is justified as being technically unavoidable in good manufacturing practice and is not added as a matter of routine; or

(b) 5% of the total weight in the case of textile products which have undergone a carding process, provided this quantity is justified as being technically unavoidable in good manufacturing practice and is not added as a matter of routine.

3. A manufacturing tolerance of 3% shall be permitted between the stated fibre composition to be provided in accordance with Article 9 and the percentages obtained from analysis carried out in accordance with Article 19, in relation to the total weight of fibres shown on the label or marking. Such tolerance shall also apply to the following:

(a) fibres which may be designated by the term 'other fibres' in accordance with Article 9;

(b) the percentage of wool referred to in point (b) of Article 8(2).

For the purposes of the analysis, the tolerances shall be calculated separately. The total weight to be taken into account in calculating the tolerance referred to in this paragraph shall be that of the fibres of the finished product less the weight of any extraneous fibres found when applying the tolerance referred to in paragraph 2 of this Article.

4. The cumulative application of the tolerances referred to in paragraphs 2 and 3 shall be permitted only if any extraneous fibres found by analysis, when applying the tolerance referred to in paragraph 2, prove to be of the same chemical type as one or more of the fibres shown on the label or marking.

5. In the case of particular textile products for which the manufacturing process requires tolerances higher than those laid down in paragraphs 2 and 3, the Commission may authorise higher tolerances.

Prior to placing the textile product on the market, the manufacturer shall submit a request for authorisation by the Commission providing sufficient reasons for and evidence of the exceptional manufacturing circumstances. The authorisation may only be granted in exceptional cases and where adequate justification is provided by the manufacturer.

If appropriate, the Commission shall adopt, by means of delegated acts in accordance with Article 22, technical criteria and procedural rules for the application of this paragraph.

CHAPTER 4
FINAL PROVISIONS

[8.524]
Article 21
Delegated acts

1. The Commission shall be empowered to adopt delegated acts in accordance with Article 22 concerning the adoption of technical criteria and procedural rules for the application of Article 20(5), amendments to Annexes II, IV, V, VI, VII, VIII and IX, in order to take account of technical progress, and amendments to Annex I in order to include, pursuant to Article 6, new textile fibre names in the list set out in that Annex.
2. When adopting such delegated acts, the Commission shall act in accordance with the provisions of this Regulation.

[8.525]
Article 22
Exercise of the delegation

1. The power to adopt delegated acts is conferred on the Commission subject to the conditions laid down in this Article.
2. The power to adopt delegated acts referred to in Article 20(5) and Article 21 shall be conferred on the Commission for a period of five years from 7 November 2011. The Commission shall draw up a report in respect of the delegation of power not later than nine months before the end of the five-year period. The delegation of power shall be tacitly extended for periods of an identical duration, unless the European Parliament or the Council opposes such extension not later than three months before the end of each period.
3. The delegation of power referred to in Article 20(5) and Article 21 may be revoked at any time by the European Parliament or by the Council. A decision to revoke shall put an end to the delegation of the power specified in that decision. It shall take effect the day following its publication in the *Official Journal of the European Union* or at a later date specified therein. It shall not affect the validity of any delegated acts already in force.
4. As soon as it adopts a delegated act, the Commission shall notify it simultaneously to the European Parliament and to the Council.
5. A delegated act adopted pursuant to Article 20(5) and Article 21 shall enter into force only if no objection has been expressed either by the European Parliament or the Council within a period of two months of notification of that act to the European Parliament and to the Council or if, before the expiry of that period, the European Parliament and the Council have both informed the Commission that they will not object. That period shall be extended by two months at the initiative of the European Parliament or of the Council.

[8.526]
Article 23
Reporting

By 8 November 2014, the Commission shall submit a report to the European Parliament and to the Council on the application of this Regulation, with an emphasis on the requests for and adoption of new textile fibre names and submit, where appropriate, a legislative proposal.

[8.527]
Article 24
Review

1. By 30 September 2013, the Commission shall submit a report to the European Parliament and to the Council regarding possible new labelling requirements to be introduced at Union level with a view to providing consumers with accurate, relevant, intelligible and comparable information on the characteristics of textile products.
2. The report shall be based on a consultation of relevant stakeholders and shall take into account existing related European and international standards.
3. The report shall be accompanied, where appropriate, by legislative proposals, and shall examine, inter alia, the following issues:
   (a) an origin labelling scheme aimed at providing consumers with accurate information on the country of origin and additional information ensuring full traceability of textile products, taking into account the results of developments on potential horizontal country-of-origin rules;
   (b) a harmonised care labelling system;
   (c) a Union-wide uniform size labelling system for relevant textile products;

Part 8 Other EU Materials

(d) an indication of allergenic substances;
(e) electronic labelling and other new technologies, and the use of language-independent symbols or codes for the identification of fibres.

[8.528]
Article 25
Study on hazardous substances
By 30 September 2013, the Commission shall carry out a study to evaluate whether there is a causal link between allergic reactions and chemical substances or mixtures used in textile products. On the basis of that study, the Commission shall, where appropriate, submit legislative proposals in the context of existing Union legislation.

[8.529]
Article 26
Transitional provision
Textile products which comply with Directive 2008/121/EC and which are placed on the market before 8 May 2012 may continue to be made available on the market until 9 November 2014.

[8.530]
Article 27
Repeal
Directives 73/44/EEC, 96/73/EC and 2008/121/EC are hereby repealed with effect from 8 May 2012.

References to the repealed Directives shall be construed as references to this Regulation and shall be read in accordance with the correlation tables in Annex X.

[8.531]
Article 28
Entry into force
This Regulation shall enter into force on the 20th day following its publication in the *Official Journal of the European Union*.

It shall apply from 8 May 2012.

This Regulation shall be binding in its entirety and directly applicable in all Member States.

ANNEX I
LIST OF TEXTILE FIBRE NAMES

(referred to in Article 5)

[8.532]

TABLE 1

Number	Name	Fibre description
1	wool	fibre from sheep's or lambs' fleeces (*Ovis aries*) or a mixture of fibres from sheep's or lambs' fleeces and the hairs of animals listed in number 2
2	alpaca, llama, camel, cashmere, mohair, angora, vicuna, yak, guanaco, cashgora, beaver, otter, followed or not by the word 'wool' or 'hair'	hair of the following animals: alpaca, llama, camel, kashmir goat, angora goat, angora rabbit, vicuna, yak, guanaco, cashgora goat, beaver, otter
3	animal or horschair, with or without an indication of the kind of animal (e.g. cattle hair, common goat hair, horsehair)	hair of the various animals not mentioned under number 1 or 2
4	Silk	fibre obtained exclusively from silk-secreting insects
5	cotton	fibre obtained from the bolls of the cotton plant (*Gossypium*)
6	kapok	fibre obtained from the inside of the kapok fruit (*Ceiba pentandra*)
7	flax (or linen)	fibre obtained from the bast of the flax plant (*Linum usitatissimum*)
8	true hemp	fibre obtained from the bast of hemp (*Cannabis sativa*)

Number	Name	Fibre description
9	Jute	fibre obtained from the bast of *Corchorus olitorius* and *Corchorus capsularis*. For the purposes of this Regulation, bast fibres obtained from the following species shall be treated in the same way as jute: *Hibiscus cannabinus, Hibiscus sabdariffa, Abutilon avicennae, Urena lobata, Urena sinuata*
10	abaca (Manila hemp)	fibre obtained from the sheathing leaf of *Musa textilis*
11	Alfa	fibre obtained from the leaves of *Stipa tenacissima*
12	coir (coconut)	fibre obtained from the fruit of *Cocos nucifera*
13	broom	fibre obtained from the bast of *Cytisus scoparius and/or Spartium Junceum*
14	ramie	fibre obtained from the bast of *Boehmeria nivea and Boehmeria tenacissima*
15	sisal	fibre obtained from the leaves of *Agave sisalana*
16	sunn	fibre from the bast of *Crotalaria juncea*
17	henequen	fibre from the bast of *Agave fourcroydes*
18	maguey	fibre from the bast of *Agave cantala*

TABLE 2

Number	Name	Fibre description
19	acetate	cellulose acetate fibre wherein less than 92% but at least 74% of the hydroxyl groups are acetylated
20	alginate	fibre obtained from metallic salts of alginic acid
21	cupro	regenerated cellulose fibre obtained by the cuprammonium process
22	modal	a regenerated cellulose fibre obtained by a modified viscose process having a high breaking force and high wet modulus. The breaking force (B_C) in the conditioned state and the force (B_M) required to produce an elongation of 5% in the wet state are: $$B_C(cN) \geq 1.3\sqrt{T} + 2T$$ $$B_M(cN) \geq 1.5\sqrt{T}$$ where T is the mean linear density in decitex
23	protein	fibre obtained from natural protein substances regenerated and stabilised through the action of chemical agents
24	triacetate	cellulose acetate fibre wherein at least 92% of the hydroxyl groups are acetylated
25	viscose	regenerated cellulose fibre obtained by the viscose process for filament and discontinuous fibre
26	acrylic	fibre formed of linear macromolecules comprising at least 85% (by mass) in the chain of the acrylonitrilic pattern
27	chlorofibre	fibre formed of linear macromolecules having in their chain more than 50% by mass of chlorinated vinyl or chlorinated vinylidene monomeric units
28	fluorofibre	fibre formed of linear macromolecules made from fluorocarbon aliphatic monomers
29	modacrylic	fibre formed of linear macromolecules having in the chain more than 50% and less than 85% (by mass) of the acrylonitrilic pattern
30	polyamide or nylon	fibre formed from synthetic linear macromolecules having in the chain recurring amide linkages of which at least 85% are joined to aliphatic or cycloaliphatic units

Number	Name	Fibre description
31	aramid	fibre formed from synthetic linear macromolecules made up of aromatic groups joined by amide or imide linkages, of which at least 85% are joined directly to two aromatic rings and with the number of imide linkages, if present, not exceeding the number of amide linkages
32	polyimide	fibre formed from synthetic linear macromolecules having in the chain recurring imide units
33	lyocell	a regenerated cellulose fibre obtained by dissolution, and an organic solvent (mixture of organic chemicals and water) spinning process, without formation of derivatives
34	polylactide	fibre formed of linear macromolecules having in the chain at least 85% (by mass) of lactic acid ester units derived from naturally occurring sugars, and which has a melting temperature of at least 135 °C
35	polyester	fibre formed of linear macromolecules comprising at least 85% (by mass) in the chain of an ester of a diol and terephthalic acid
36	polyethylene	fibre formed of un-substituted aliphatic saturated hydrocarbon linear macromolecules
37	polypropylene	fibre formed of an aliphatic saturated hydrocarbon linear macromolecule where one carbon atom in two carries a methyl side chain in an isotactic disposition and without further substitution
38	polycarbamide	fibre formed of linear macromolecules having in the chain the recurring ureylene (NH-CO-NH) functional group
39	polyurethane	fibre formed of linear macromolecules composed of chains with the recurring urethane functional group
40	vinylal	fibre formed of linear macromolecules whose chain is constituted by poly(vinyl alcohol) with differing levels of acetalisation
41	trivinyl	fibre formed of acrylonitrile terpolymer, a chlorinated vinyl monomer and a third vinyl monomer, none of which represents as much as 50% of the total mass
42	elastodiene	elastofibre composed of natural or synthetic polyisoprene, or composed of one or more dienes polymerised with or without one or more vinyl monomers, and which, when stretched to three times its original length and released, recovers rapidly and substantially to its initial length
43	elastane	elastofibre composed of at least 85% (by mass) of a segmented polyurethane, and which, when stretched to three times its original length and released, recovers rapidly and substantially to its initial length
44	glass fibre	fibre made of glass
45	elastomultiester	fibre formed by interaction of two or more chemically distinct linear macromolecules in two or more distinct phases (of which none exceeds 85% by mass) which contains ester groups as the dominant functional unit (at least 85%) and which, after suitable treatment when stretched to one and half times its original length and released, recovers rapidly and substantially to its initial length
46	elastolefin	fibre composed of at least 95% (by mass) of macromolecules partially cross-linked, made up from ethylene and at least one other olefin and which, when stretched to one and a half times its original length and released, recovers rapidly and substantially to its initial length
47	melamine	fibre formed of at least 85% by mass of cross-linked macromolecules made up of melamine derivatives

Number	Name	Fibre description
48	name corresponding to the material of which the fibres are composed, e.g. metal (metallic, metallised), asbestos, paper, followed or not by the word 'yarn' or 'fibre'	fibres obtained from miscellaneous or new materials not listed above
[49	Polypropylene/ polyamide bicomponent	a bicomponent fibre composed of between 10 % and 25 % by mass of polyamide fibrils embedded in polypropylene matrix]

NOTES

Entry in square brackets added by Commission Delegated Regulation 286/2012/EU, Art 1, Annex, para (1).

ANNEX II
MINIMUM REQUIREMENTS REGARDING A TECHNICAL FILE TO BE INCLUDED IN THE APPLICATION FOR A NEW TEXTILE FIBRE NAME

(referred to in Article 6)

[8.533]

A technical file to be attached to an application for the inclusion of a new textile fibre name in the list set out in Annex I, as provided for in Article 6, shall contain at least the following information:

(1) Proposed name of the textile fibre:
The name proposed shall be related to the chemical composition and shall provide information about the characteristics of the fibre, if appropriate. The name proposed shall be free of any intellectual property rights and shall not be linked to the manufacturer.

(2) Proposed definition of the textile fibre:
The characteristics mentioned in the definition of the new textile fibre, such as elasticity, shall be verifiable via testing methods to be provided with the technical file along with the experimental results of analyses.

(3) Identification of the textile fibre: chemical formula, differences from existing textile fibres, together with, where relevant, detailed data such as melting point, density, refractive index, burning behaviour and FTIR spectrum.

(4) Proposed agreed allowance to be used in the calculation of fibre composition.

(5) Sufficiently developed identification and quantification methods, including experimental data:
The applicant shall evaluate the possibility to use the methods listed in Annex VIII or the harmonised standards to be introduced in that Annex to analyse the most expected commercial mixtures of the new textile fibre with other textile fibres and shall propose at least one of those methods. For those methods or harmonised standards where the textile fibre can be considered as an insoluble component, the applicant shall evaluate the mass correction factors of the new textile fibre. All the experimental data shall be submitted with the application.
If methods listed in this Regulation are not suitable, the applicant shall provide adequate reasoning and propose a new method.
The application shall contain all the experimental data for the methods proposed. Data on the accuracy, robustness and repeatability of the methods shall be provided with the file.

(6) Available scientific information concerning possible allergic reactions or other adverse effects of the new textile fibre on human health, including results of tests conducted to that effect in compliance with relevant Union legislation.

(7) Additional information to support the application: production process, consumer relevance.

The manufacturer or any person acting on the manufacturer's behalf shall provide representative samples of the new pure textile fibre and the relevant textile fibre mixtures necessary to conduct the validation of the proposed identification and quantification methods. The Commission may request additional samples of relevant fibre mixtures from the manufacturer or the person acting on the manufacturer's behalf.

ANNEX III
NAMES REFERRED TO IN ARTICLE 8(1)

[8.534]

— in Bulgarian: 'необработена вълна'

— in Spanish: 'lana virgen' or 'lana de esquilado'

— in Czech: 'střižní vlna'

— in Danish: 'ren, ny uld'

— in German: 'Schurwolle'

— in Estonian: 'uus vill'

— in Greek: 'παρθένο μαλλί'

— in English: 'fleece wool' or 'virgin wool'

— in French: 'laine vierge' or 'laine de tonte'

[— in Croatian : "runska vuna"]

— in Irish: 'olann lomra'

— in Italian: 'lana vergine' or 'lana di tosa'

— in Latvian: 'pirmlietojuma vilna' or 'cirptā vilna'

— in Lithuanian: 'natūralioji vilna'

— in Hungarian: 'élőgyapjú'

— in Maltese: 'suf verġni'

— in Dutch: 'scheerwol'

— in Polish: 'żywa wełna'

— in Portuguese: 'lã virgem'

— in Romanian: 'lână virgină'

— in Slovak: 'strižná vlna'

— in Slovene: 'runska volna'

— in Finnish: 'uusi villa'

— in Swedish: 'ny ull'

NOTES

Words in square brackets added by Council Regulation 517/2013/EU, Art 1, para 1(a), Annex.

ANNEX IV
SPECIAL PROVISIONS FOR THE LABELLING AND MARKING OF CERTAIN TEXTILE PRODUCTS

(referred to in Article 13)

[8.535]

Products	Labelling and marking provisions
1. The following corsetry products:	The fibre composition shall be indicated on the label and marking by stating the composition of the whole product or, either inclusively or separately, that of the components listed respectively:
(a) Brassières	the outside and the inside fabric of the surface of the cups and back
(b) Corsets and girdles	the front, the rear and side panels
(c) Corselets	the outside and inside fabric of the surface of cups, the front and rear stiffening panels and the side panels
2. Other corsetry products not listed above	The fibre composition shall be indicated by stating the composition of the whole product or, either inclusively or separately, the composition of the various components of the products. Such labelling shall not be compulsory for components representing less than 10% of the total weight of the product
3. All corsetry products	The separate labelling and marking of the various parts of corsetry products shall be carried out in such a way that the consumer can easily understand to which part of the product the information on the label or marking refers

Products	Labelling and marking provisions
4. Etch-printed textiles	The fibre composition shall be given for the product as a whole and may be indicated by stating, separately, the composition of the base fabric and that of the etched parts. Those components shall be mentioned by name
5. Embroidered textiles	The fibre composition shall be given for the product as a whole and may be indicated by stating, separately, the composition of the base fabric and that of the embroidery yarn. Those components shall be mentioned by name. Such labelling or marking is compulsory only for the embroidered parts which amount to at least 10% of the surface area of the product
6. Yarns consisting of a core and a cover made up of different fibres and made available on the market as such to the consumer	The fibre composition shall be given for the product as a whole and may be indicated by stating the composition of the core and the cover separately. Those components shall be mentioned by name
7. Velvet and plush textiles, or textiles resembling velvet or plush	The fibre composition shall be given for the whole product and, where the product comprises a distinct backing and a use-surface composed of different fibres, may be stated separately for those components. Those components shall be mentioned by name
8. Floor coverings and carpets of which the backing and the use-surface are composed of different fibres	The fibre composition may be stated for the use-surface alone. The use-surface must be mentioned by name

ANNEX V
TEXTILE PRODUCTS FOR WHICH LABELLING OR MARKING IS NOT MANDATORY

(referred to in Article 17(2))

[8.536]

1. Sleeve-supporting armbands
2. Watch straps of textile materials
3. Labels and badges
4. Stuffed pan-holders of textile materials
5. Coffee cosy covers
6. Tea cosy covers
7. Sleeve protectors
8. Muffs other than in pile fabric
9. Artificial flowers
10. Pin cushions
11. Painted canvas
12. Textile products for base and underlying fabrics and stiffenings
13. Old made-up textile products, where explicitly stated to be such
14. Gaiters
15. Packaging, not new and sold as such
16. Fancy goods and saddlery, of textile materials
17. Travel goods of textile materials
18. Hand-embroidered tapestries, finished or unfinished, and materials for their production, including embroidery yarns, sold separately from the canvas and specially presented for use in such tapestries
19. Slide fasteners

20. Buttons and buckles covered with textile materials

21. Book covers of textile materials

22. Toys

23. Textile parts of footwear

24. Table mats having several components and a surface area of not more than $500cm^2$

25. Oven gloves and cloths

26. Egg cosy covers

27. Make-up cases

28. Tobacco pouches of textile fabric

29. Spectacle, cigarette and cigar, lighter and comb cases of textile fabric

30. Covers for mobile telephones and portable media players with a surface of not more than $160cm^2$

31. Protective requisites for sports with the exception of gloves

32. Toilet cases

33. Shoe-cleaning cases

34. Funeral products

35. Disposable products, with the exception of wadding

36. Textile products subject to the rules of the European Pharmacopoeia and covered by a reference to those rules, non-disposable bandages for medical and orthopaedic use and orthopaedic textile products in general

37. Textile products including cordage, ropes and string, subject to item 12 of Annex VI, normally intended:
   (a) for use as equipment components in the manufacture and processing of goods;
   (b) for incorporation in machines, installations (eg. for heating, air conditioning or lighting), domestic and other appliances, vehicles and other means of transport, or for their operation, maintenance or equipment, other than tarpaulin covers and textile motor vehicle accessories sold separately from the vehicle

38. Textile products for protection and safety purposes such as safety belts, parachutes, life-jackets, emergency chutes, fire-fighting devices, bulletproof waistcoats and special protective garments (eg protection against fire, chemical substances or other safety hazards)

39. Air-supported structures (eg sports halls, exhibition stands or storage facilities), provided that details of the performances and technical specifications of these products are supplied

40. Sails

41. Animal clothing

42. Flags and banners

ANNEX VI
TEXTILE PRODUCTS FOR WHICH INCLUSIVE LABELLING IS SUFFICIENT

(referred to in Article 17(3))

[8.537]
1. Floorcloths
2. Cleaning cloths
3. Edgings and trimmings
4. Passementerie
5. Belts
6. Braces
7. Suspenders and garters
8. Shoe and boot laces
9. Ribbons

10. Elastic

11. New packaging sold as such

12. Packing string and agricultural twine; string, cordage and ropes other than those falling within item 37 of Annex V*

13. Table mats

14. Handkerchiefs

15. Bun nets and hair nets

16. Ties and bow ties for children

17. Bibs, washgloves and face flannels

18. Sewing, mending and embroidery yarns presented for retail sale in small quantities with a net weight of 1 gram or less

19. Tape for curtains and blinds and shutters

NOTES

* For the products falling within this item and sold in cut lengths, the inclusive labelling shall be that of the reel. The cordage and ropes falling within this item include those used in mountaineering and water sports.

ANNEX VII
ITEMS NOT TO BE TAKEN INTO ACCOUNT FOR THE DETERMINATION OF FIBRE COMPOSITION

(referred to in Article 19(2))

[8.538]

Products	Items excluded
(a) All textile products	(i) Non-textile parts, selvedges, labels and badges, edgings and trimmings not forming an integral part of the product, buttons and buckles covered with textile materials, accessories, decorations, non-elastic ribbons, elastic threads and bands added at specific and limited points of the product and, subject to the conditions specified in Article 10, visible, isolable fibres which are purely decorative and fibres with antistatic effect (ii) Fatty substances, binders, weightings, sizings and dressings, impregnating products, additional dyeing and printing products and other textile processing products
(b) Floor coverings and carpets	All components other than the use-surface
(c) Upholstery fabrics	Binding and filling warps and wefts which do not form part of the use-surface
(d) Hangings and curtains	Binding and filling warps and wefts which do not form part of the right side of the fabric
(e) Socks	Additional elastic yarns used in the cuff and the stiffening and reinforcement yarns of the toe and the heel
(f) Tights	Additional elastic yarns used in the belt and the stiffening and reinforcement yarns of the toe and the heel
(g) Textile products other than those under points (b) to (f)	Base or underlying fabrics, stiffenings and reinforcements, inter-linings and canvas backings, stitching and assembly threads unless they replace the warp and/or weft of the fabric, fillings not having an insulating function and, subject to Article 11(2), linings For the purposes of this provision; (i) the base or underlying material of textile products which serve as a backing for the use-surface, in particular in blankets and double fabrics, and the backings of velvet or plush fabrics and kindred products shall not be regarded as backings to be removed; (ii) 'stiffenings and reinforcements' mean the yarns or materials added at specific and limited points of the textile products to strengthen them or to give them stiffness or thickness

ANNEX VIII
METHODS FOR THE QUANTITATIVE ANALYSIS OF BINARY AND TERNARY TEXTILE FIBRE MIXTURES

(referred to in Article 19(1))

CHAPTER 1

[8.539]

I. **Preparation of laboratory test samples and test specimens to determine the fibre composition of textile products**

1. FIELD OF APPLICATION

This Chapter gives procedures for obtaining laboratory test samples of a suitable size for pre-treatment for quantitative analysis (ie of a mass not exceeding 100 g) from laboratory bulk samples, and for selecting test specimens from the laboratory test samples that have been pre-treated to remove non-fibrous matter.[1]

2. DEFINITIONS

2.1. Bulk source

The quantity of material which is assessed on the basis of one series of test results. This may comprise, for example, all the material in one delivery of cloth; all the cloth woven from a particular beam; a consignment of yarn, a bale or a group of bales of raw fibre.

2.2. Laboratory bulk sample

The portion of the bulk source taken to be representative of the whole, and which is available to the laboratory. The size and nature of the laboratory bulk sample shall be sufficient to adequately overcome the variability of the bulk source and to facilitate ease of handling in the laboratory.[2]

2.3. Laboratory test sample

That portion of the laboratory bulk sample that is subjected to pre-treatment to remove non-fibrous matter, and from which test specimens are taken. The size and nature of the laboratory test sample shall be sufficient to overcome adequately the variability of the laboratory bulk sample.[3]

2.4. Test specimen

The portion of material required to give an individual test result, and selected from the laboratory test sample.

3. PRINCIPLE

The laboratory test sample is selected so that it is representative of the laboratory bulk sample. The test specimens are taken from the laboratory test sample in such a way that each of them is representative of the laboratory test sample.

4. SAMPLING FROM LOOSE FIBRES

4.1. Unorientated fibres

Obtain the laboratory test sample by selecting tufts at random from the laboratory bulk sample. Mix thoroughly the whole of the laboratory test sample by means of a laboratory carder.[4] Subject the web or mixture, including loose fibres and fibres adhering to the equipment used for mixing, to pre-treatment. Then select test specimens, in proportion to the respective masses, from the web or mixture, from the loose fibres and from the fibres adhering to the equipment.

If the card web remains intact after pre-treatment, select the test specimens in the manner described in 4.2. If the card web is disturbed by the pre-treatment, select each test specimen by removing at random at least 16 small tufts of suitable and approximately equal size and then combine them.

4.2. Orientated fibres (cards, webs, slivers, rovings)

From randomly selected parts of the laboratory bulk sample cut not less than 10 cross-sections each of mass approximately 1 g. Subject the laboratory test sample so formed to the pre-treatment. Recombine the cross-sections by laying them side by side and obtain the test specimen by cutting through them so as to take a portion of each of the 10 lengths.

5. SAMPLING YARN

5.1. Yarn in packages or in banks

Sample all the packages in the bulk laboratory sample.

Withdraw the appropriate continuous equal lengths from each package either by winding skeins of the same number of turns on a wrap-reel,[5] or by some other means. Unite the lengths side by side either as a single skein or as a tow to form the laboratory test sample, ensuring that there are equal lengths from each package in the skein or tow.

Subject the laboratory test sample to the pre-treatment.

Take test specimens from the laboratory test sample by cutting a bunch of threads of equal length from the skein or tow, taking care to see that the bunch contains all the threads in the sample.

If the tex of the yarn is t and the number of packages selected from the laboratory bulk sample is n, then to obtain a test sample of 10 g, the length of yarn to be withdrawn from each package is 10^6/nt cm.

If nt is high, i.e. more than 2,000, wind a heavier skein and cut it across in two places to make a tow of suitable mass. The ends of any sample in the form of a tow shall be securely tied before pre-treatment and test specimens taken from a place remote from the tie bands.

5.2. Yarn on warp

Take the laboratory test sample by cutting a length from the end of the warp, not less than 20 cm long and comprising all the yarns in the warp except the selvedge yarns, which are rejected. Tie the bunch of threads together near one end. If the sample is too large for pre-treatment as a whole divide it into two or more portions, each tied together for pre-treatment, and reunite the portions after each has been pre-treated separately. Take a test specimen by cutting a suitable length from the laboratory test sample from the end remote from the tie band, and comprising all the threads in the warp. For warp of N threads of text, the length of a specimen of mass 1 g is 10^5/Nt cm.

6. SAMPLING FABRIC

6.1. From a laboratory bulk sample consisting of a single cutting representative of the cloth

Cut a diagonal strip from one corner to the other and remove the selvedges. This strip is the laboratory test sample. To obtain a laboratory test sample of x g, the strip area shall be x10^4/G cm^2, where G is the mass of the cloth in g/m^2.

Subject the laboratory test sample to the pre-treatment and then cut the strip transversely into four equal lengths and superimpose them. Take test specimens from any part of the layered material by cutting through all the layers so that each specimen contains an equal length of each layer.

If the fabric has a woven design, make the width of the laboratory test sample, measured parallel to the warp direction, not less than one warp repeat of the design. If, with this condition satisfied, the laboratory test sample is too large to be treated as a whole, cut it into equal parts, pre-treat them separately, and superimpose these parts before selection of the test specimen, taking care that corresponding parts of the design do not coincide.

6.2. From a laboratory bulk sample consisting of several cuttings

Treat each cutting as described in 6.1, and give each result separately.

7. SAMPLING MADE-UP AND FINISHED PRODUCTS

The bulk laboratory sample is normally a complete made-up or finished product or representative fraction of one.

Where appropriate determine the percentage of the various parts of the product not having the same fibre content, in order to check compliance with Article 11.

Select a laboratory test sample representative of the part of the made-up or finished product, whose composition must be shown by the label. If the product has several labels, select laboratory test samples representative of each part corresponding to a given label.

If the product whose composition is to be determined is not uniform, it may be necessary to select laboratory test samples from each of the parts of the product and to determine the relative proportions of the various parts in relation to the whole product in question.

Then calculate the percentages taking into account the relative proportions of the sampled parts.

Subject the laboratory test samples to the pre-treatment.

Then select test specimens representative of the pre-treated laboratory test samples.

II. Introduction to the methods for the quantitative analysis of textile fibre mixtures

Methods for the quantitative analysis of fibre mixtures are based on two main processes, the manual separation and the chemical separation of fibres.

The method of manual separation shall be used whenever possible since it generally gives more accurate results than the chemical method. It can be used for all textiles whose component fibres do not form an intimate mixture, as for example in the case of yarns composed of several elements each of which is made up of only one type of fibre, or fabrics in which the fibre of the warp is of a different kind to that of the weft, or knitted fabrics capable of being unravelled made up of yarns of different types.

In general, the methods of chemical quantitative analysis are based on the selective solution of the individual components. After the removal of a component the insoluble residue is weighed, and the proportion of the soluble component is calculated from the loss in mass. This first part of the Annex gives the information common to the analyses by this method of all fibre mixtures dealt with in the

Annex, whatever their composition. It shall thus be used in conjunction with the succeeding individual sections of the Annex, which contain the detailed procedures applicable to particular fibre mixtures. Occasionally, an analysis is based on a principle other than selective solution; in such cases full details are given in the appropriate section.

Mixtures of fibres during processing and, to a lesser extent, finished textiles may contain non-fibrous matter, such as fats, waxes or dressings, or water-soluble matter, either occurring naturally or added to facilitate processing. Non-fibrous matter must be removed before analysis. For this reason a method for removing oils, fats, waxes and water-soluble matter is also given.

In addition, textiles may contain resins or other matter added to confer special properties. Such matter, including dyestuffs in exceptional cases, may interfere with the action of the reagent on the soluble component and/or it may be partially or completely removed by the reagent. This type of added matter may thus cause errors and shall be removed before the sample is analysed. If it is impossible to remove such added matter the methods for quantitative chemical analysis given in this Annex are no longer applicable.

Dye in dyed fabrics is considered to be an integral part of the fibre and is not removed.

Analyses are conducted on the basis of dry mass and a procedure is given for determining dry mass.

The result is obtained by applying to the dry mass of each fibre the agreed allowances listed in Annex IX.

Before proceeding with any analysis, all the fibres present in the mixture shall have been identified. In some methods, the insoluble component of a mixture may be partially dissolved in the reagent used to dissolve the soluble component(s).

Where possible, reagents have been chosen that have little or no effect on the insoluble fibres. If loss in mass is known to occur during the analysis, the result shall be corrected; correction factors for this purpose are given. These factors have been determined in several laboratories by treating, with the appropriate reagent as specified in the method of analysis, fibres cleaned by the pre treatment.

These correction factors apply only to undegraded fibres and different correction factors may be necessary if the fibres have been degraded before or during processing. The procedures given apply to single determinations.

At least two determinations on separate test specimens shall be made, both in the case of manual separation and in the case of chemical separation.

For confirmation, unless technically impossible, it is recommended to use alternative procedures whereby the constituent that was the residue in the standard method is dissolved out first.

NOTES

1 In some cases it is necessary to pre-treat the individual test specimen.

2 For made-up and finished articles see point 7.

3 See point 1.

4 The laboratory carder may be replaced by a fibre blender, or the fibres may be mixed by the method of 'tufts and rejects'.

5 If the packages can be mounted in a convenient creel a number can be wound simultaneously.

CHAPTER 2
METHODS FOR QUANTITATIVE ANALYSIS OF CERTAIN BINARY TEXTILE FIBRE MIXTURES

[8.540]

I. General information common to the methods given for the quantitative chemical analysis of textile fibre mixtures

I.1. FIELD OF APPLICATION

The field of application for each method specifies to which fibres the method is applicable.

I.2. PRINCIPLE

After the identification of the components of a mixture, the non-fibrous material is removed by suitable pre-treatment and then one of the components, usually by selective solution.[1] The insoluble residue is weighed and the proportion of soluble component calculated from the loss in mass. Except where this presents technical difficulties, it is preferable to dissolve the fibre present in the greater proportion, thus obtaining the fibre present in the smaller proportion as residue.

I.3. MATERIALS AND EQUIPMENT

I.3.1. Apparatus

I.3.1.1. Filter crucibles and weighing bottles large enough to contain such crucibles, or any other apparatus giving identical results.

I.3.1.2. Vacuum flask.

I.3.1.3. Desiccator containing self-indicating silica gel.

I.3.1.4. Ventilated oven for drying specimens at 105 ± 3 °C.

I.3.1.5. Analytical balance, accurate to 0.0002 g.

I.3.1.6. Soxhlet extractor or other apparatus giving identical results.

I.3.2. Reagents.

I.3.2.1. Light petroleum, redistilled, boiling range 40 to 60 °C.

I.3.2.2. Other reagents are specified in the appropriate section of each method.

I.3.2.3. Distilled or deionised water.

I.3.2.4. Acetone.

I.3.2.5. Orthophosphoric acid.

I.3.2.6. Urea.

I.3.2.7. Sodium bicarbonate.
All reagents used shall be chemically pure.

I.4. CONDITIONING AND TESTING ATMOSPHERE
Because dry masses are determined, it is unnecessary to condition the specimen or to conduct analyses in a conditioned atmosphere.

I.5. LABORATORY TEST SAMPLE
Take a laboratory test sample that is representative of the laboratory bulk sample and sufficient to provide all the specimens, each of at least 1 g, that are required.

I.6. PRE-TREATMENT OF LABORATORY TEST SAMPLE[2]
Where a substance not to be taken into account in the percentage calculations (see Article 19) is present, it shall first be removed by a suitable method that does not affect any of the fibre constituents.
For this purpose, non-fibrous matter which can be extracted with light petroleum and water is removed by treating the laboratory test sample in a Soxhlet extractor with light petroleum for 1 hour at a minimum rate of six cycles per hour. Allow the light petroleum to evaporate from the sample, which is then extracted by direct treatment consisting in soaking the laboratory test sample in water at room temperature for 1 hour and then soaking it in water at 65 ± 5 °C for a further hour, agitating the liquor from time to time. Use a liquor-laboratory test sample ratio of 100:1. Remove the excess water from the sample by squeezing, suction or centrifuging and then allow the sample to become air-dry.
In the case of elastolefin or fibre mixtures containing elastolefin and other fibres (wool, animal hair, silk, cotton, flax (or linen) true hemp, jute, abaca, alfa, coir, broom, ramie, sisal, cupro, modal, protein, viscose, acrylic, polyamide or nylon, polyester, elastomultiester) the procedure just described shall be slightly modified, in that light petroleum ether shall be replaced by acetone.
In the case of binary fibre mixtures containing elastolefin and acetate the following procedure shall apply as pre-treatment. Extract the laboratory test sample for 10 minutes at 80 °C with a solution containing 25 g/l of 50% orthophosphoric acid and 50 g/l of urea. Use a liquor-laboratory test sample ratio of 100:1. Wash laboratory test sample in water, then drain and wash it in a 0.1% sodium bicarbonate solution, finally wash it carefully in water.
Where non-fibrous matter cannot be extracted with light petroleum and water, it shall be removed by substituting for the water method described above a suitable method that does not substantially alter any of the fibre constituents. However, for some unbleached, natural vegetable fibres (e.g. jute, coir) it is to be noted that normal pre-treatment with light petroleum and water does not remove all the natural non-fibrous substances; nevertheless additional pre-treatment is not applied unless the sample contains finishes insoluble in both light petroleum and water.
Analysis reports shall include full details of the methods of pre-treatment used.

I.7. TEST PROCEDURE

I.7.1. General instructions

I.7.1.1. Drying

Conduct all drying operations for not less than 4 hours and not more than 16 hours at 105 ± 3 °C in a ventilated oven with the oven door closed throughout. If the drying period is less than 14 hours, the specimen must be weighed to check that its mass has become constant. The mass may be considered to have become constant if, after a further drying period of 60 minutes, its variation is less than 0.05%.

Avoid handling crucibles and weighing bottles, specimens or residues with bare hands during the drying, cooling and weighing operations.

Dry specimens in a weighing bottle with its cover beside it. After drying, stopper the weighing bottle before removing it from the oven, and transfer it quickly to the desiccator.

Dry the filter crucible in a weighing bottle with its cover beside it in the oven. After drying, close the weighing bottle and transfer it quickly to the desiccator.

Where apparatus other than a filter crucible is used, drying operations in the oven shall be conducted in such a way as to enable the dry mass of the fibres to be determined without loss.

I.7.1.2. Cooling

Conduct all cooling operations in the desiccator, the latter placed beside the balance, until complete cooling of the weighing bottles is attained, and in any case for not less than 2 hours.

I.7.1.3. Weighing

After cooling, complete the weighing of the weighing bottle within 2 minutes of its removal from the desiccator. Weigh to an accuracy of 0.0002 g.

I.7.2. Procedure

Take from the pre-treated laboratory test sample a test specimen weighing at least 1 g. Cut yarn or cloth into lengths of about 10 mm, dissected as much as possible. Dry the specimen in a weighing bottle, cool it in the desiccator and weigh it. Transfer the specimen to the glass vessel specified in the appropriate section of the relevant Union method, reweigh the weighing bottle immediately and obtain the dry mass of the specimen by difference. Complete the test as specified in the appropriate section of the applicable method. Examine the residue microscopically to check that the treatment has in fact completely removed the soluble fibre.

I.8. CALCULATION AND EXPRESSION OF RESULTS

Express the mass of the insoluble component as a percentage of the total mass of fibre in the mixture. The percentage of soluble component is obtained by difference. Calculate the results on the basis of clean, dry mass, adjusted by (a) the agreed allowances and (b) the correction factors necessary to take account of loss of matter during pre-treatment and analysis. Calculations shall be made by applying the formula given in I.8.2.

I.8.1. Calculation of percentage of insoluble component on clean, dry mass basis, disregarding loss of fibre mass during pre-treatment:

$$P_1\% = \frac{100rd}{m}$$

where

$P_1\%$ is the percentage of clean, dry insoluble component,

m is the dry mass of the test specimen after pre-treatment,

r is the dry mass of the residue,

d is the correction factor for loss in mass of the insoluble component in the reagent during the analysis. Suitable values for 'd' are given in the relevant section of each method.

Of course, these values for 'd' are the normal values applicable to chemically undegraded fibres.

I.8.2. Calculation of percentage of insoluble component on clean, dry mass basis, with adjustment by conventional factors and, where appropriate, correction factors for loss of mass during pre-treatment:

$$P_{1A}\% = \frac{100P_1\left(1+\frac{(a_1+b_1)}{100}\right)}{P_1\left(1+\frac{(a_1+b_1)}{100}\right)+(100-P_1)\left(1+\frac{(a_2+b_2)}{100}\right)}$$

where

$P_{1A}\%$ is the percentage of insoluble component adjusted by agreed allowances and for loss in mass during pre-treatment,

P_1 is the percentage of clean dry insoluble component as calculated from the formula shown in I.8.1,

a_1 is the agreed allowance for the insoluble component (see Annex IX),

a_2 is the agreed allowance for the soluble component (see Annex IX),
b_1 is the percentage loss of insoluble component caused by pre-treatment,
b_2 is the percentage loss of soluble component caused by pre-treatment.
The percentage of the second component is $P_{2A}\% = 100 - P_{1A}\%$.

Where a special pre-treatment has been used, the values of b_1 and b_2 shall be determined, if possible, by submitting each of the pure fibre constituents to the pre-treatment applied in the analysis. Pure fibres are those free from all non-fibrous material except that which they normally contain (either naturally or because of the manufacturing process), in the state (unbleached, bleached) in which they are found in the material to be analysed.

Where no clean separate constituent fibres used in the manufacture of the material to be analysed are available, average values of b1 and b2 as obtained from tests performed on clean fibres similar to those in the mixture under examination, shall be used.

If normal pre-treatment by extraction with light petroleum and water is applied, correction factors b1 and b2 may generally be ignored, except in the case of unbleached cotton, unbleached flax (or linen) and unbleached hemp, where the loss due to the pre-treatment is conventionally taken as 4%, and in the case of polypropylene, where it is taken as 1%.

In the case of other fibres, losses due to the pre-treatment are conventionally disregarded in calculations.

II. Method of quantitative analysis by manual separation

II.1. FIELD OF APPLICATION

This method is applicable to textile fibres of all types provided they do not form an intimate mixture and that it is possible to separate them by hand.

II.2. PRINCIPLE

After identification of the constituents of the textile, the non-fibrous material is removed by suitable pre-treatment and then the fibres are separated by hand, dried and weighed in order to calculate the proportion of each fibre in the mixture.

II.3. APPARATUS

II.3.1. Weighing bottle or any other apparatus giving identical results.

II.3.2. Desiccator containing self-indicating silica gel.

II.3.3. Ventilated oven for drying specimens at 105 ± 3 °C.

II.3.4. Analytical balance, accurate to 0.0002 g.

II.3.5. Soxhlet extractor, or other apparatus giving an identical result.

II.3.6. Needle.

II.3.7. Twist tester or similar apparatus.

II.4. REAGENTS

II.4.1. Light petroleum, redistilled, boiling range 40 to 60 °C.

II.4.2. Distilled or deionised water.

II.4.3. Acetone.

II.4.4. Orthophosphoric acid.

II.4.5. Urea.

II.4.6. Sodium bicarbonate.

All reagents used shall be chemically pure.

II.5. CONDITIONING AND TESTING ATMOSPHERE

See I.4.

II.6. LABORATORY TEST SAMPLE

See I.5.

II.7. PRE-TREATMENT OF LABORATORY TEST SAMPLE

See I.6.

II.8. PROCEDURE

II.8.1. Analysis of yarn

Select from the pre-treatment laboratory test sample a specimen of mass not less than 1 g. For a very fine yarn, the analysis may be made on a minimum length of 30 m, whatever its mass.

Cut the yarn into pieces of a suitable length and separate the fibre types by means of a needle and, if necessary, a twist tester. The fibre types so obtained are placed in pre-weighed weighing bottles and dried at 105 ± 3 °C until a constant mass is obtained, as described in I.7.1 and I.7.2.

II.8.2. Analysis of cloth

Select from the pre-treated laboratory test sample, well away from all selvedges, a specimen of mass not less than 1 g, with edges carefully trimmed to avoid fraying and running parallel with weft or warp yarns, or in the case of knitted fabrics in the line of wales and courses. Separate the different fibre types, collect them in pre-weighed weighing bottles and proceed as described in II.8.1.

II.9. CALCULATION AND EXPRESSION OF RESULTS

Express the mass of each fibre constituent as a percentage of the total mass of the fibres in the mixture. Calculate the results on the basis of clean, dry mass, adjusted by (a) the agreed allowances and (b) the correction factors necessary to take account of loss of matter during pre-treatment.

II.9.1. Calculation of percentage masses of clean, dry fibre, disregarding loss of fibre mass during pre-treatment:

$$P_1\% = \frac{100m_1}{m_1 + m_2} = \frac{100}{1 + \frac{m_2}{m_1}}$$

$P_1\%$ is the percentage of the first clean, dry component,
m_1 is the clean, dry mass of the first component,
m_2 is the clean, dry mass of the second component.

II.9.2. For calculation of the percentage of each component with adjustment by agreed allowances and, where appropriate, by correction factors for loss of matter during pre-treatment, see I.8.2.

III.1. PRECISION OF THE METHODS

The precision indicated in individual methods relates to the reproducibility.

The reproducibility refers to the reliability, i.e. the closeness of agreement between experimental values obtained by operators in different laboratories or at different times using the same method and obtaining individual results on specimens of an identical consistent mixture.

The reproducibility is expressed by confidence limits of the results for a confidence level of 95%.

Therefore, the difference between two results in a series of analyses made in different laboratories would, given a normal and correct application of the method to an identical and consistent mixture, exceed the confidence limit only in five cases out of 100.

III.2. TEST REPORT

III.2.1. State that the analysis was conducted in accordance with this method.

III.2.2. Give details of any special pre-treatment (see I.6).

III.2.3. Give the individual results and the arithmetic mean, each to an accuracy of 0.1.

IV. **Special methods**
[8.541]

[SUMMARY TABLE

Method	**Field of application (*)**		**Reagent**
	Insoluble component	**Soluble component**	
1.	Acetate	Certain other fibres	Acetone
2.	Certain protein fibres	Certain other fibres	Hypochlorite
3.	Viscose, cupro or certain types of modal	Certain other fibres	Formic acid and zinc chloride
4.	Polyamide or nylon	Certain other fibres	Formic acid, 80 % m/m
5.	Acetate	Certain other fibres	Benzyl alcohol
6.	Triacetate or polylactide	Certain other fibres	Dichloromethane
7.	Certain cellulose fibres	Certain other fibres	Sulphuric acid, 75 % m/m
8.	Acrylics, certain modacrylics or certain chlorofibres	Certain other fibres	Dimethylformamide

Method	Field of application (*)		Reagent
	Insoluble component	**Soluble component**	
9.	Certain chlorofibres	Certain other fibres	Carbon disulphide/acetone, 55,5/44,5 v/v
10.	Acetate	Certain other fibres	Glacial acetic acid
11.	Silk, polyamide or nylon	Certain other fibres	Sulphuric acid, 75 % m/m
12.	Jute	Certain animal fibres	Nitrogen content method
13.	Polypropylene	Certain other fibres	Xylene
14.	Certain fibres	Certain other fibres	Concentrated sulphuric acid method
15.	Chlorofibres, certain modacrylics, certain elastanes, acetates, triacetates	Certain other fibres	Cyclohexanone
16.	Melamine	Certain other fibres	Hot formic acid 90 % m/m
(*) Detailed list of fibres under each method]			

NOTES

Table: substituted by Commission Delegated Regulation 286/2012/EU, Art 1, Annex, para (2)(a).

1 Method 12 is an exception. It is based on a determination of the content of a constituent substance of one of the two components.

2 See Chapter 1.1.

METHOD NO 1
ACETATE AND CERTAIN OTHER FIBRES

(Acetone method)

[8.542]

1. FIELD OF APPLICATION

This method is applicable, after removal of non-fibrous matter, to binary fibre mixtures of:

1. acetate (19)

with

[2. wool (1), animal hair (2 and 3), silk (4), cotton (5), flax (7) true hemp (8), jute (9), abaca (10), alfa (11), coir (12), broom (13), ramie (14), sisal (15), cupro (21), modal (22), protein (23), viscose (25), acrylic (26), polyamide or nylon (30), polyester (35), polypropylene (37), elastomultiester (45), elastolefin (46), melamine (47) and polypropylene/polyamide bicomponent (49).

In no circumstances is the method applicable to acetate fibres which have been deacetylated on the surface.]

2. PRINCIPLE

The acetate is dissolved out from a known dry mass of the mixture, with acetone. The residue is collected, washed, dried and weighed; its mass, corrected if necessary, is expressed as a percentage of the dry mass of the mixture. The percentage of dry acetate is found by difference.

3. APPARATUS AND REAGENTS (additional to those specified in the general instructions)

3.1. Apparatus

Glass-stoppered conical flasks of at least 200 ml capacity.

3.2. Reagent

Acetone.

4. TEST PROCEDURE

Follow the procedure described in the general instructions and proceed as follows:

To the test specimen contained in a glass-stoppered conical flask of at least 200 ml capacity, add 100 ml of acetone per gram of test specimen, shake the flask, stand it for 30 minutes at room temperature, stirring from time to time, and then decant the liquid through the weighed filter crucible.

Repeat the treatment twice more (making three extractions in all), but for periods of 15 minutes only, so that the total time of treatment in acetone is 1 hour. Transfer the residue to the filter crucible. Wash the residue in the filter crucible with acetone and drain with suction. Refill the crucible with acetone and allow to drain under gravity.

Finally, drain the crucible with suction, dry the crucible and residue, and cool and weigh them.

5. CALCULATION AND EXPRESSION OF RESULTS

Calculate the results as described in the general instructions. The value of 'd' is 1.00, except for melamine, for which 'd' – 1.01.

6. PRECISION

On a homogeneous mixture of textile materials, the confidence limits of results obtained by this method are not greater than ± 1 for a confidence level of 95%.

NOTES

Point 1: para 2 substituted by Commission Delegated Regulation 286/2012/EU, Art 1, Annex, para (2)(b).

METHOD NO 2

CERTAIN PROTEIN FIBRES AND CERTAIN OTHER FIBRES

(Method using hypochlorite)

[8.543]

1. FIELD OF APPLICATION

This method is applicable, after removal of non-fibrous matter, to binary fibre mixtures of:

1. certain protein fibres, namely: wool (1), animal hair (2 and 3), silk (4), protein (23) with

[2. cotton (5), cupro (21), viscose (25), acrylic (26), chlorofibres (27), polyamide or nylon (30), polyester (35), polypropylene (37), elastane (43), glass fibre (44) elastomultiester (45), elastolefin (46), melamine (47) and polypropylene/polyamide bicomponent (49).

If different protein fibres are present, the method gives the total of their amounts but not their individual quantities.]

2. PRINCIPLE

The protein fibre is dissolved out from a known dry mass of the mixture, with a hypochlorite solution. The residue is collected, washed, dried and weighed; its mass, corrected if necessary, is expressed as a percentage of the dry mass of the mixture. The percentage of dry protein fibre is found by difference.

Either lithium hypochlorite or sodium hypochlorite can be used for the preparation of the hypochlorite solution.

Lithium hypochlorite is recommended in cases involving a small number of analyses or for analyses conducted at fairly lengthy intervals. This is because the percentage of hypochlorite in solid lithium hypochlorite — unlike that in sodium hypochlorite — is virtually constant. If the percentage of hypochlorite is known, hypochlorite content need not be checked iodometrically for each analysis, since a constant weighed portion of lithium hypochlorite can be employed.

3. APPARATUS AND REAGENTS (other than those specified in the general instructions)

3.1. Apparatus

(a) Erlenmeyer flask with ground-glass stopper, 250 ml.

(b) Thermostat, adjustable to 20 ± 2 °C.

3.2. Reagents

(a) Hypochlorite reagent

(i) Lithium hypochlorite solution

This consists of a freshly prepared solution containing 35 ± 2 g/l of active chlorine (approximately 1 M), to which 5 ± 0.5 g/l of previously dissolved sodium hydroxide is added. To prepare, dissolve 100 grams of lithium hypochlorite containing 35% active chlorine (or 115 grams containing 30% active chlorine) in approximately 700 ml of distilled water, add 5 grams of sodium hydroxide dissolved in approximately 200 ml of distilled water and make up to 1 litre with distilled water. The solution which has been freshly prepared need not be checked iodometrically.

(ii) Sodium hypochlorite solution

This consists of a freshly prepared solution containing 35 ± 2 g/l of active chlorine (approximately 1 M) to which 5 ± 0.5 g/l of previously dissolved sodium hydroxide is added.

Check the active chlorine content of the solution iodometrically before each analysis.

(b) Acetic acid, dilute solution

Dilute 5 ml of glacial acetic acid to 1 litre with water.

4. TEST PROCEDURE

Follow the procedure described in the general instructions and proceed as follows: mix approximately 1 gram of the test specimen with approximately 100 ml of the hypochlorite solution (lithium or sodium hypochlorite) in the 250 ml flask and agitate thoroughly in order to wet out the test specimen.

Then heat the flask for 40 minutes in a thermostat at 20 °C and agitate continuously, or at least at regular intervals. Since the dissolution of the wool proceeds exothermically, the reaction heat of this method must be distributed and removed. Otherwise, considerable errors may be caused by the incipient dissolution of the non-soluble fibres.

After 40 minutes, filter the flask contents through a weighed glass-filter crucible and transfer any residual fibres into the filter crucible by rinsing the flask with a little hypochlorite reagent. Drain the crucible with suction and wash the residue successively with water, dilute acetic acid, and finally water, draining the crucible with suction after each addition. Do not apply suction until each washing liquor has drained under gravity.

Finally, drain the crucible with suction, dry the crucible with the residue, and cool and weigh them.

5. CALCULATION AND EXPRESSION OF RESULTS

Calculate the results as described in the general instructions. The value of 'd' is 1.00, except for cotton, viscose, modal and melamine for which 'd' = 1.01, and unbleached cotton, for which 'd' = 1.03.

6. PRECISION

On homogeneous mixtures of textile materials, the confidence limits for results obtained by this method are not greater than ± 1 for a confidence level of 95%.

NOTES

Point 1: para 2 substituted by Commission Delegated Regulation 286/2012/EU, Art 1, Annex, para (2)(c).

METHOD NO 3

[VISCOSE, CUPRO OR CERTAIN TYPES OF MODAL AND CERTAIN OTHER FIBRES

(Method using formic acid and zinc chloride)]

[8.544]

1. FIELD OF APPLICATION

This method is applicable, after removal of non-fibrous matter, to binary fibre mixtures of:

1. viscose (25) or cupro (21), including certain types of modal fibre (22)

with

[2. cotton (5), polypropylene (37), elastolefin (46) and melamine (47).

If a modal fibre is found to be present, a preliminary test shall be carried out to see whether it is soluble in the reagent.

This method is not applicable to mixtures in which the cotton has suffered extensive chemical degradation nor when the viscose or cupro is rendered incompletely soluble by the presence of certain dyes or finishes that cannot be removed completely.]

2. PRINCIPLE

The viscose, cupro or modal fibre is dissolved from a known dry mass of the mixture, with a reagent consisting of formic acid and zinc chloride. The residue is collected, washed, dried and weighed; its corrected mass is expressed as a percentage of the dry mass of the mixture. The percentage of dry viscose, cupro or modal fibre is found by difference.

3. APPARATUS AND REAGENTS (other than those specified in the general instructions)

3.1. Apparatus

(a) Glass-stoppered conical flasks of at least 200 ml capacity.

(b) Apparatus for maintaining flasks at 40 ± 2 °C.

3.2. Reagents

(a) Solution containing 20 g of fused anhydrous zinc chloride and 68 g of anhydrous formic acid made up to 100 g with water (namely 20 parts by mass of fused anhydrous zinc chloride to 80 parts by mass of 85% m/m formic acid).

Note:

Attention is drawn, in this respect, to point I.3.2.2, which lays down that all reagents used shall be chemically pure; in addition, it is essential to use only fused anhydrous zinc chloride.

(b) Ammonium hydroxide solution: dilute 20 ml of a concentrated ammonia solution (relative density at 20 °C: 0.880) to 1 litre with water.

4. TEST PROCEDURE

Follow the procedure described in the general instructions and proceed as follows: place the specimen immediately in the flask, pre-heated to 40 °C. Add 100 ml of the solution of formic acid and zinc chloride, pre-heated to 40 °C per gram of specimen. Insert the stopper and shake the flask vigorously. Keep the flask and its contents at a constant temperature of 40 °C for 2.5 hours, shaking the flask at hourly intervals.

Filter the contents of the flask through the weighed filter crucible and with the help of the reagent transfer to the crucible any fibres remaining in the flask. Rinse with 20 ml of reagent pre-heated to 40 °C.

Wash crucible and residue thoroughly with water at 40 °C. Rinse the fibrous residue in approximately 100 ml of cold ammonia solution (3.2(b)) ensuring that this residue remains wholly immersed in the solution for 10 minutes;[1] then rinse thoroughly with cold water.

Do not apply suction until each washing liquor has drained under gravity.

Finally, drain the remaining liquid with suction, dry the crucible and residue, and cool and weigh them.

[5. CALCULATION AND EXPRESSION OF RESULTS

Calculate the results as described in the general instructions. The value of "d" is 1,00, except for cotton, for which "d" = 1,02 and for melamine, for which "d" = 1,01.]

6. PRECISION

On a homogeneous mixture of textile materials, the confidence limits of results obtained by this method are not greater than ± 2 for a confidence level of 95%.

NOTES

Title: substituted by Commission Delegated Regulation 286/2012/EU, Art 1, Annex, para (2)(d)(i).

Point 1: para 2 substituted by Commission Delegated Regulation 286/2012/EU, Art 1, Annex, para (2)(d)(ii).

Point 5: substituted by Commission Delegated Regulation 286/2012/EU, Art 1, Annex, para (2)(d)(iii).

1 To ensure that the fibrous residue is immersed in the ammonia solution for 10 minutes, one may, for example, use a filter crucible adaptor fitted with a tap by which the flow of the ammonia solution can be regulated.

METHOD NO 4
POLYAMIDE OR NYLON, AND CERTAIN OTHER FIBRES

(Method using 80% m/m formic acid)

[8.545]

1. FIELD OF APPLICATION

This method is applicable, after removal of non-fibrous matter, to binary fibre mixtures of:

1. polyamide or nylon (30)

with

2. wool (1), animal hair (2 and 3), cotton (5), cupro (21), modal (22), viscose (25), acrylic (26), chlorofibre (27), polyester (35), polypropylene (37), glass fibre (44), elastomultiester (45), elastolefin (46) and melamine (47).

As mentioned above, this method is also applicable to mixtures with wool, but when the wool content exceeds 25%, method No 2 shall be applied (dissolving wool in a solution of alkaline sodium hypochlorite or lithium hypochlorite).

2. PRINCIPLE

The polyamide or nylon fibre is dissolved out from a known dry mass of the mixture, with formic acid. The residue is collected, washed, dried and weighed; its mass, corrected if necessary, is expressed as a percentage of the dry mass of the mixture. The percentage of dry polyamide or nylon is found by difference.

3. APPARATUS AND REAGENTS (other than those specified in the general instructions)

3.1. Apparatus

Glass-stoppered conical flask of at least 200 ml capacity.

3.2. Reagents

(a) Formic acid (80% m/m, relative density at 20 °C: 1.186). Dilute 880 ml of 90% m/m formic acid (relative density at 20 °C: 1.204) to 1 litre with water. Alternatively, dilute 780 ml of 98 to 100% m/m formic acid (relative density at 20 °C: 1.220) to 1 litre with water.

The concentration is not critical within the range 77 to 83% m/m formic acid.

(b) Ammonia, dilute solution: dilute 80 ml of concentrated ammonia solution (relative density at 20 °C: 0.880) to 1 litre with water.

4. TEST PROCEDURE

Follow the procedure described in the general instructions and proceed as follows: to the specimen contained in the conical flask of at least 200 ml capacity, add 100 ml of formic acid per gram of specimen. Insert the stopper, shake the flask to wet out the specimen. Stand the flask for 15 minutes at room temperature, shaking it at intervals. Filter the contents of the flask through the weighed filter crucible and transfer any residual fibres to the crucible by washing out the flask with a little formic acid reagent.

Drain the crucible with suction and wash the residue on the filter successively with formic acid reagent, hot water, dilute ammonia solution, and finally cold water, draining the crucible with suction after each addition. Do not apply suction until each washing liquor has drained under gravity.

Finally, drain the crucible with suction, dry the crucible and residue, and cool and weigh them.

5. CALCULATION AND EXPRESSION OF RESULTS

Calculate the results as described in the general instructions. The value of 'd' is 1.00, except for melamine, for which 'd' = 1.01.

6. PRECISION

On a homogeneous mixture of textile materials, the confidence limits of results obtained by this method are not greater than ± 1 for a confidence level of 95%.

METHOD NO 5
[ACETATE AND CERTAIN OTHER FIBRES
(Method using benzyl alcohol)]

[8.546]

1. FIELD OF APPLICATION

This method is applicable, after removal of non-fibrous matter, to binary fibre mixtures of:

1. acetate (19)

with

[2. triacetate (24), polypropylene (37), elastolefin (46), melamine (47) and polypropylene/polyamide bicomponent (49).]

2. PRINCIPLE

The acetate fibre is dissolved out from a known dry mass of the mixture, with benzyl alcohol at 52 ± 2 °C.

The residue is collected, washed, dried and weighed; its mass is expressed as a percentage of the dry mass of the mixture. The percentage of dry acetate is found by difference.

3. APPARATUS AND REAGENTS (other than those specified in the general instructions)

3.1. Apparatus

(a) Glass-stoppered conical flask of at least 200 ml capacity.
(b) Mechanical shaker.
(c) Thermostat or other apparatus for keeping the flask at a temperature of 52 ± 2 °C.

3.2. Reagents

(a) Benzyl alcohol.
(b) Ethanol.

4. TEST PROCEDURE

Follow the procedure described in the general instructions and proceed as follows:

To the specimen contained in the conical flask, add 100 ml of benzyl alcohol per gram of specimen. Insert the stopper, secure the flask to the shaker so that it is immersed in the water-bath, kept at 52 ± 2 °C, and shake for 20 minutes at this temperature.

(Instead of using a mechanical shaker, the flask may be shaken vigorously by hand).

Decant the liquid through the weighed filter crucible. Add a further dose of benzyl alcohol in the flask and shake as before at 52 ± 2 °C for 20 minutes.

Decant the liquid through the crucible. Repeat the cycle of operations a third time.

Finally pour the liquid and the residue into the crucible; wash any remaining fibres from the flask into the crucible with an extra quantity of benzyl alcohol at 52 ± 2 °C. Drain the crucible thoroughly.

Transfer the fibres into a flask, rinse with ethanol and after shaking manually decant through the filter crucible.

Repeat this rinsing operation two or three times. Transfer the residue into the crucible and drain thoroughly. Dry the crucible and the residue and cool and weigh them.

5. CALCULATION AND EXPRESSION OF RESULTS

Calculate the results as described in the general instructions. The value of 'd' is 1.00, except for melamine, for which 'd' = 1.01.

6. PRECISION

On a homogeneous mixture of textile materials, the confidence limits of results obtained by this method are not greater than ± 1 for a confidence level of 95%.

NOTES

Title: substituted by Commission Delegated Regulation 286/2012/EU, Art 1, Annex, para (2)(e)(i).

Point 1: para 2 substituted by Commission Delegated Regulation 286/2012/EU, Art 1, Annex, para (2)(e)(ii).

METHOD NO 6
[TRIACETATES OR POLYLACTIDE AND CERTAIN OTHER FIBRES
(Method using dichloromethane)]

[8.547]

1. FIELD OF APPLICATION

This method is applicable, after removal of non-fibrous matter, to binary fibre mixtures of:

1. triacetate (24) or polylactide (34)

with

[2. wool (1), animal hair (2 and 3), silk (4), cotton (5), cupro (21), modal (22), viscose (25), acrylic (26), polyamide or nylon (30), polyester (35), polypropylene (37), glass fibre (44) elastomultiester (45), elastolefin (46), melamine (47) and polypropylene/polyamide bicomponent (49).

Note:

Triacetate fibres which have received a finish leading to partial hydrolysis cease to be completely soluble in the reagent. In such cases, the method is not applicable.]

2. PRINCIPLE

The triacetate or polylactide fibres are dissolved out from a known dry mass of the mixture, with dichloromethane. The residue is collected, washed, dried and weighed; its mass, corrected if necessary, is expressed as a percentage of the dry mass of the mixture. The percentage of dry triacetate or polylactide is found by difference.

3. APPARATUS AND REAGENTS (other than those specified in the general instructions)

3.1. Apparatus

Glass-stoppered conical flask of at least 200 ml capacity.

3.2. Reagent

Dichloromethane.

4. TEST PROCEDURE

Follow the procedure described in the general instructions and proceed as follows:

To the test specimen contained in the 200 ml glass-stoppered conical flask, add 100 ml of dichloromethane per gram of the test specimen, insert the stopper, shake the flask to wet out the test specimen and stand for 30 minutes at room temperature, shaking the flask every 10 minutes. Decant the liquid through the weighed filter crucible. Add 60 ml of dichloromethane to the flask containing the residue, shake manually and filter the contents of the flask through the filter crucible. Transfer the residual fibres to the crucible by washing out the flask with a little more dichloromethane. Drain the crucible with suction to remove excess liquid, refill the crucible with dichloromethane and allow it to drain under gravity.

Finally, apply suction to eliminate excess liquid, then treat the residue with boiling water to eliminate all the solvent, apply suction, dry the crucible and residue, cool and weigh them.

5. CALCULATION AND EXPRESSION OF RESULTS

Calculate the results as described in the general instructions. The value of 'd' is 1.00, except in the case of polyester, elastomultiester, elastolefin and melamine for which the value of 'd' is 1.01.

6. PRECISION

On a homogeneous mixture of textile materials, the confidence limits of results obtained by this method are not greater than ± 1 for a confidence level of 95%.

NOTES

Title: substituted by Commission Delegated Regulation 286/2012/EU, Art 1, Annex, para (2)(f)(i).

Point 1: para 2 substituted by Commission Delegated Regulation 286/2012/EU, Art 1, Annex, para (2)(f)(ii).

METHOD NO 7
[CERTAIN CELLULOSE FIBRES AND CERTAIN OTHER FIBRES
(Method using 75% m/m sulphuric acid)]

[8.548]

1. FIELD OF APPLICATION

This method is applicable, after removal of non-fibrous matter, to binary fibre mixtures of:

1. cotton (5), flax (or linen) (7), true hemp (8), ramie (14), cupro (21), modal (22), viscose (25)

with

[2. polyester (35), polypropylene (37), elastomultiester (45), elastolefin (46) and polypropylene/polyamide bicomponent (49).]

2. PRINCIPLE

The cellulose fibre is dissolved out from a known dry mass of the mixture, with 75% m/m sulphuric acid. The residue is collected, washed, dried and weighed; its mass is expressed as a percentage of the dry mass of the mixture. The proportion of dry cellulose fibre is found by difference.

3. APPARATUS AND REAGENTS (other than those specified in the general instructions)

3.1. Apparatus
(a) Glass-stoppered conical flask of at least 500 ml capacity.
(b) Thermostat or other apparatus for maintaining the flask at 50 ± 5 °C.

3.2. Reagents
(a) Sulphuric acid, 75 ± 2% m/m
Prepare by adding carefully, while cooling, 700 ml of sulphuric acid (relative density at 20 °C: 1.84) to 350 ml of distilled water.
After the solution has cooled to room temperature, dilute to 1 litre with water.
(b) Ammonia, dilute solution
Dilute 80 ml of ammonia solution (relative density at 20 °C: 0.880) to 1 litre with water.

4. TEST PROCEDURE
Follow the procedure described in the general instructions and proceed as follows:
To the specimen contained in the glass-stoppered conical flask of at least 500 ml capacity, add 200 ml of 75% sulphuric acid per gram of specimen, insert the stopper and carefully shake the flask to wet out the specimen.
Maintain the flask at 50 ± 5 °C for 1 hour, shaking it at regular intervals of approximately 10 minutes. Filter the contents of the flask through the weighed filter crucible by means of suction. Transfer any residual fibres by washing out the flask with a little 75% sulphuric acid. Drain the crucible with suction and wash the residue on the filter once by filling the crucible with a fresh portion of sulphuric acid. Do not apply suction until the acid has drained under gravity.
Wash the residue successively several times with cold water, twice with dilute ammonia solution, and then thoroughly with cold water, draining the crucible with suction after each addition. Do not apply suction until each washing liquor has drained under gravity. Finally, drain the remaining liquid from the crucible with suction, dry the crucible and residue, and cool and weigh them.

[5. CALCULATION AND EXPRESSION OF RESULTS
Calculate the results as described in the general instructions. The value of "d" is 1,00, except for polypropylene/polyamide bicomponent, for which the value of "d" is 1,01.]

6. PRECISION
On a homogeneous mixture of textile materials, the confidence limits of results obtained by this method are not greater than ± 1 for a confidence level of 95%.

NOTES
Title: substituted by Commission Delegated Regulation 286/2012/EU, Art 1, Annex, para (2)(g)(i).
Point 1: para 2 substituted by Commission Delegated Regulation 286/2012/EU, Art 1, Annex, para (2)(g)(ii).
Point 5: substituted by Commission Delegated Regulation 286/2012/EU, Art 1, Annex, para (2)(g)(iii).

METHOD NO 8
ACRYLICS, CERTAIN MODACRYLICS OR CERTAIN CHLOROFIBRES AND CERTAIN OTHER FIBRES

(Method using dimethylformamide)

[8.549]
1. FIELD OF APPLICATION
This method is applicable, after removal of non-fibrous matter, to binary fibre mixtures of:
1. acrylics (26), certain modacrylics (29), or certain chlorofibres (27)[1]
with
[2. wool (1), animal hair (2 and 3), silk (4), cotton (5), cupro (21), modal (22), viscose (25), polyamide or nylon (30), polyester (35), polypropylene (37), elastomultiester (45), elastolefin (46), melamine (47) and polypropylene/polyamide bicomponent (49).
It is equally applicable to acrylics, and certain modacrylics, treated with pre-metallised dyes, but not to those dyed with afterchrome dyes.]

2. PRINCIPLE
The acrylic, modacrylic or chlorofibre is dissolved out from a known dry mass of the mixture, with dimethylformamide heated in a water-bath at boiling point. The residue is collected, washed, dried and weighed. Its mass, corrected if necessary, is expressed as a percentage of the dry mass of the mixture and the percentage of dry acrylic, modacrylic or chlorofibre is found by difference.

3. APPARATUS AND REAGENTS (other than those specified in the general instructions)

3.1. Apparatus
(a) Glass-stoppered conical flask of at least 200 ml capacity.
(b) Water bath at boiling point.

3.2. Reagent
Dimethylformamide (boiling point 153 ± 1 °C) not containing more than 0.1% water.
This reagent is toxic and the use of a hood is thus recommended.

4. TEST PROCEDURE
Follow the procedure described in the general instructions and proceed as follows:
To the specimen contained in the glass-stoppered conical flask of at least 200 ml capacity, add per gram of specimen 80 ml of dimethylformamide, pre-heated in the water-bath at boiling point, insert the stopper, shake the flask to wet out the specimen and heat in the water-bath at boiling point for 1 hour. Shake the flask and its contents gently by hand five times during this period.
Decant the liquid through the weighed filter crucible, retaining the fibres in the flask. Add a further 60 ml of dimethylformamide to the flask and heat for a further 30 minutes, shaking the flask and contents gently by hand twice during this period.
Filter the contents of the flask through the filter crucible by means of suction.
Transfer any residual fibre to the crucible by washing out the beaker with dimethylformamide.
Drain the crucible with suction. Wash the residue with about 1 litre of hot water at 70–80 °C, filling the crucible each time.
After each addition of water, apply suction briefly but not until the water has drained under gravity. If the washing liquor drains through the crucible too slowly slight suction may be applied.
Finally dry the crucible with the residue, cool and weigh them.

5. CALCULATION AND EXPRESSION OF RESULTS
Calculate the results as described in the general instructions. The value of 'd' is 1.00, except in the case of wool, cotton, cupro, modal, polyester, elastomultiester and melamine, for which the value of 'd' is 1.01.

6. PRECISION
On a homogeneous mixture of textile materials, the confidence limits of results obtained by this method are not greater than ± 1 for a confidence level of 95%.

NOTES
Point 1: para 2 substituted by Commission Delegated Regulation 286/2012/EU, Art 1, Annex, para (2)(h).

[1] The solubility of such modacrylics or chlorofibres in the reagent shall be checked before carrying out the analysis.

METHOD NO 9
CERTAIN CHLOROFIBRES AND CERTAIN OTHER FIBRES

(Method using 55.5/44.5% v/v mixture of carbon disulphide and acetone)

[8.550]

1. FIELD OF APPLICATION
This method is applicable, after removal of non-fibrous matter, to binary fibre mixtures of:
1. certain chlorofibres (27), namely certain polyvinyl chloride fibres, whether after-chlorinated or not[1]

with

[2. wool (1), animal hair (2 and 3), silk (4), cotton (5), cupro (21), modal (22), viscose (25), acrylic (26), polyamide or nylon (30), polyester (35), polypropylene (37), glass fibre (44), elastomultiester (45), melamine (47) and polypropylene/polyamide bicomponent (49).

When the wool or silk content of the mixture exceeds 25%, method No 2 shall be used.
When the polyamide or nylon content of the mixture exceeds 25%, method No 4 shall be used.]

2. PRINCIPLE
The chlorofibre is dissolved out from a known dry mass of the mixture, with an azeotropic mixture of carbon disulphide and acetone. The residue is collected, washed, dried and weighed; its mass, corrected if necessary, is expressed as a percentage of the dry mass of the mixture. The percentage of dry polyvinyl chloride fibre is found by difference.

3. APPARATUS AND REAGENTS (other than those specified in the general instructions)

3.1. Apparatus
(a) Glass-stoppered conical flask of at least 200 ml capacity.
(b) Mechanical shaker.

3.2. Reagents

(a) Azeotropic mixture of carbon disulphide and acetone (55.5% by volume carbon disulphide to 44.5% acetone). As this reagent is toxic, the use of a hood is recommended.

(b) Ethanol (92% by volume) or methanol.

4. TEST PROCEDURE

Follow the procedure described in the general instructions and proceed as follows:

To the specimen contained in the glass-stoppered conical flask of at least 200 ml capacity, add 100 ml of the azeotropic mixture per gram of specimen. Seal the flask securely, and shake the flask on a mechanical shaker, or vigorously by hand, for 20 minutes at room temperature. Decant the supernatant liquid through the weighed filter crucible.

Repeat the treatment with 100 ml of fresh reagent. Continue this cycle of operations until no polymer deposit is left on a watch glass when a drop of the extraction liquid is evaporated. Transfer the residue to the filter crucible using more reagent, apply suction to remove the liquid, and rinse the crucible and residue with 20 ml of alcohol and then three times with water. Allow the washing liquor to drain under gravity before draining with suction. Dry the crucible and residue and cool and weigh them.

Note:

With certain mixtures having a high chlorofibre content there may be substantial shrinkage of the specimen during the drying procedure, as a result of which the dissolution of chlorofibre by the solvent is retarded.

This does not, however, affect the ultimate dissolution of the chlorofibre in the solvent.

5. CALCULATION AND EXPRESSION OF RESULTS

Calculate the results as described in the general instructions. The value of 'd' is 1.00, except for melamine, for which 'd' = 1.01.

6. PRECISION

On a homogeneous mixture of textile materials, the confidence limits of the results obtained by this method are not greater than ± 1 for a confidence level of 95%.

NOTES

Point 1: para 2 substituted by Commission Delegated Regulation 286/2012/EU, Art 1, Annex, para (2)(i).

[1] Before carrying out the analysis, the solubility of the polyvinyl chloride fibres in the reagent shall be checked.

METHOD NO 10
[ACETATE AND CERTAIN OTHER FIBRES

(Method using glacial acetic acid)]

[8.551]

1. FIELD OF APPLICATION

This method is applicable, after removal of non-fibrous matter, to binary fibre mixtures of:

1. acetate (19)

with

[2. certain chlorofibres (27) namely polyvinyl chloride fibres, whether after-chlorinated or not, polypropylene (37), elastolefin (46), melamine (47) and polypropylene/polyamide bicomponent (49).]

2. PRINCIPLE

The acetate fibre is dissolved out from a known dry mass of the mixture, with glacial acetic acid. The residue is collected, washed, dried and weighed; its mass, corrected if necessary, is expressed as a percentage of the dry mass of the mixture. The percentage of dry acetate is found by difference.

3. APPARATUS AND REAGENTS (other than those specified in the general instructions)

3.1. Apparatus

(a) Glass-stoppered conical flask of at least 200 ml capacity.

(b) Mechanical shaker.

3.2. Reagent

Glacial acetic acid (over 99%). This reagent shall be handled with care since it is highly caustic.

4. TEST PROCEDURE

Follow the procedure described in the general instructions and proceed as follows:

To the specimen contained in the glass-stoppered conical flask of at least 200 ml capacity, add 100 ml glacial acetic acid per gram of specimen. Seal the flask securely and shake on the mechanical shaker, or vigorously by hand, for 20 minutes at room temperature. Decant the supernatant liquid through the weighed filter crucible. Repeat this treatment twice, using 100 ml of fresh reagent each time, making three extractions in all.

Transfer the residue to the filter crucible, drain with suction to remove the liquid and rinse the crucible and the residue with 50 ml of glacial acetic acid, and then three times with water. After each rinse, allow the liquid to drain under gravity before applying suction. Dry the crucible and residue, and cool and weigh them.

5. CALCULATION AND EXPRESSION OF RESULTS
Calculate the results as described in the general instructions. The value of 'd' is 1.00.

6. PRECISION
On a homogeneous mixture of textile materials, the confidence limits of the results obtained by this method are not greater than ± 1 for a confidence level of 95%.

NOTES
Title: substituted by Commission Delegated Regulation 286/2012/EU, Art 1, Annex, para (2)(j)(i).
Point 1: para 2 substituted by Commission Delegated Regulation 286/2012/EU, Art 1, Annex, para (2)(j)(ii).

METHOD NO 11
[SILK OR POLYAMIDE AND CERTAIN OTHER FIBRES

(Method using 75% m/m sulphuric acid)]

[8.552]

[1. FIELD OF APPLICATION
This method is applicable, after removal of non-fibrous matter, to binary fibre mixtures of:
1. silk (4) or polyamide or nylon (30)

with

2. wool (1), animal hair (2 and 3), polypropylene (37), elastolefin (46), melamine (47) and polypropylene/polyamide bicomponent (49).]

[2. PRINCIPLE
The silk or polyamide or nylon fibre is dissolved out from a known dry mass of the mixture, with 75 % m/m sulphuric acid[1]
The residue is collected, washed, dried and weighed. Its mass, corrected if necessary, is expressed as a percentage of the dry mass of the mixture. The percentage of the dry silk or polyamide or nylon is found by difference.]

3. APPARATUS AND REAGENTS (other than those specified in the general instructions)

3.1. Apparatus
Glass-stoppered conical flask of at least 200 ml capacity.

3.2. Reagents
(a) Sulphuric acid (75 ± 2% m/m)
Prepare by adding carefully, while cooling, 700 ml sulphuric acid (relative density at 20 °C: 1.84) to 350 ml distilled water.
After cooling to room temperature, dilute the solution to 1 litre with water.
(b) Sulphuric acid, dilute solution: add 100 ml sulphuric acid (relative density at 20 °C: 1.84) slowly to 1.900 ml distilled water.
(c) Ammonia, dilute solution: dilute 200 ml concentrated ammonia (relative density at 20 °C: 0.880) to 1 litre with water.

[4. TEST PROCEDURE
Follow the procedure described in the general instructions and proceed as follows:
To the specimen contained in a glass-stoppered conical flask of at least 200 ml capacity, add 100 ml of 75 % m/m sulphuric acid per gram of specimen and insert the stopper. Shake vigorously and stand for 30 minutes at room temperature. Shake again and stand for 30 minutes. Shake a last time and filter the contents of the flask through the weighed filter crucible. Wash any remaining fibres from the flask with the 75 % sulphuric acid reagent. Wash the residue on the crucible successively with 50 ml of the dilute sulphuric acid reagent, 50 ml water and 50 ml of the dilute ammonia solution. Each time allow the fibres to remain in contact with the liquid for about 10 minutes before applying suction. Finally rinse with water, leaving the fibres in contact with the water for about 30 minutes. Drain the crucible with suction, dry the crucible and residue, and cool and weigh them.
In the case of binary mixtures of polyamide with polypropylene/polyamide bicomponent, after filtering fibres through the weighed filter crucible and before applying the described washing procedure, wash twice the residue on the filter crucible with 50 ml of 75 % sulphuric acid reagent each time.

[5. CALCULATION AND EXPRESSION OF RESULTS
Calculate the results as described in the general instructions. The value of "d" is 1,00, except for wool, for which "d" = 0,985, for polypropylene/polyamide bicomponent, for which "d" = 1,005 and for melamine, for which "d" = 1,01.

6. PRECISION

On a homogeneous mixture of textile materials, the confidence limits of results obtained by this method are not greater than ± 1 for a confidence level of 95 %, except for binary mixtures of polyamide with polypropylene/polyamide bicomponent for which the confidence limits of results are not greater than ± 2.]

NOTES

Title: substituted by Commission Delegated Regulation 286/2012/EU, Art 1, Annex, para (2)(k)(i).
Point 1: substituted by Commission Delegated Regulation 286/2012/EU, Art 1, Annex, para (2)(k)(ii).
Point 2: substituted by Commission Delegated Regulation 286/2012/EU, Art 1, Annex, para (2)(k)(iii).
Point 4: substituted by Commission Delegated Regulation 286/2012/EU, Art 1, Annex, para (2)(k)(iv).
Points 5, 6: substituted by Commission Delegated Regulation 286/2012/EU, Art 1, Annex, para (2)(k)(v).

[1] Wild silks, such as tussah silk, are not completely soluble in 75% m/m sulphuric acid.

METHOD NO 12
JUTE AND CERTAIN ANIMAL FIBRES

(Method by determining nitrogen content)

[8.553]

1. FIELD OF APPLICATION

This method is applicable, after removal of non-fibrous matter, to binary fibre mixtures of:

1. jute (9)

with

2. certain animal fibres.

The animal-fibre component may consist solely of hair (2 and 3) or wool (1) or of any mixture of the two. This method is not applicable to textile mixtures containing non-fibrous matter (dyes, finishes, etc.) with a nitrogen base.

2. PRINCIPLE

The nitrogen content of the mixture is determined, and from this and the known or assumed nitrogen contents of the two components, the proportion of each component is calculated.

3. APPARATUS AND REAGENTS (other than those specified in the general instructions)

3.1. Apparatus

(a) Kjeldahl digestion flask, 200–300 ml capacity.
(b) Kjeldahl distillation apparatus with steam injection.
(c) Titration apparatus, allowing precision of 0.05 ml.

3.2. Reagents

(a) Toluene.
(b) Methanol.
(c) Sulphuric acid, relative density at 20 °C: 1.84.[1]
(d) Potassium sulphate.[1]
(e) Selenium dioxide.[1]
(f) Sodium hydroxide solution (400 g/litre). Dissolve 400 g of sodium hydroxide in 400–500 ml of water and dilute to 1 litre with water.
(g) Mixed indicator. Dissolve 0.1 g of methyl red in 95 ml of ethanol and 5 ml of water, and mix with 0.5 g of bromocresol green dissolved in 475 ml of ethanol and 25 ml of water.
(h) Boric acid solution. Dissolve 20 g of boric acid in 1 litre of water.
(i) Sulphuric acid, 0.02N (standard volumetric solution).

4. PRE-TREATMENT OF TEST SAMPLE

The following pre-treatment is substituted for the pre-treatment described in the general instructions:

Extract the air-dry laboratory test sample in a Soxhlet apparatus with a mixture of 1 volume of toluene and 3 volumes of methanol for 4 hours at a minimum rate of 5 cycles per hour. Allow the solvent to evaporate from the sample in air, and remove the last traces in an oven at 105 ± 3 °C. Then extract the sample in water (50 ml per g of sample) by boiling under reflux for 30 minutes. Filter, return the sample to the flask, and repeat the extraction with an identical volume of water. Filter, remove excess water from the sample by squeezing, suction, or centrifuging and then allow the sample to become air-dry.

Note:

The toxic effects of toluene and methanol shall be borne in mind and full precautions shall be taken in their use.

5. TEST PROCEDURE

5.1. General instructions

Follow the procedure described in the general instructions as regards the selection, drying and weighing of the specimen.

5.2. Detailed procedure

Transfer the specimen to a Kjeldahl digestion flask. To the specimen weighing at least 1 g contained in the digestion flask, add, in the following order, 2.5 g potassium sulphate, 0.1–0.2 g selenium dioxide and 10 ml sulphuric acid (relative density at 20 °C: 1.84). Heat the flask, gently at first, until the whole of the fibre is destroyed, and then heat it more vigorously until the solution becomes clear and almost colourless. Heat it for a further 15 minutes. Allow the flask to cool, dilute the contents carefully with 10–20 ml water, cool, transfer the contents quantitatively to a 200 ml graduated flask and make up to volume with water to form the digest solution. Place about 20 ml of boric acid solution in a 100 ml conical flask and place the flask under the condenser of the Kjeldahl distillation apparatus so that the delivery tube dips just below the surface of the boric acid solution. Transfer exactly 10 ml of digest solution to the distillation flask, add not less than 5 ml of sodium hydroxide solution to the funnel, lift the stopper slightly and allow the sodium hydroxide solution to run slowly into the flask. If the digest solution and sodium hydroxide solution remain as two separate layers, mix them by gentle agitation. Heat the distillation flask gently and pass it into steam from the generator. Collect about 20 ml of distillate, lower the conical flask so that the tip of the delivery tube of the condenser is about 20 mm above the surface of the liquid and distil for 1 minute more. Rinse the tip of the delivery tube with water, catching the washings in the conical flask. Remove the conical flask and replace it with another conical flask containing roughly 10 ml of boric acid solution and collect about 10 ml distillate.

Titrate the two distillates separately with 0.02 N sulphuric acid, use the mixed indicator. Record the total titre for the two distillates. If the titre for the second distillate is more than 0.2 ml, repeat the test and start the distillation again using a fresh aliquot of digest solution. Carry out a blank determination, i.e. digestion and distillation using the reagents only.

6. CALCULATION AND EXPRESSION OF RESULTS

6.1. Calculate the percentage nitrogen content in the dry specimen as follows:

$$A\% = \frac{28(V-b)N}{W}$$

where

A = percentage nitrogen in the clean dry specimen,

V = total volume in ml of standard sulphuric acid used in the determination,

b = total volume in ml of standard sulphuric acid used in the blank determination,

N = normality of standard sulphuric acid,

W = dry mass (g) of specimen.

6.2. Using the values of 0.22% for the nitrogen content of jute and 16.2% for the nitrogen content of animal fibre, both percentages being expressed on the dry mass of the fibre, calculate the composition of the mixture as follows:

$$PA\% = \frac{A-0.22}{16.2-0.22} \times 100$$

where

PA% = percentage of animal fibre in the clean dry specimen.

7. PRECISION

On a homogeneous mixture of textile materials, the confidence limits of results obtained by this method are not greater than ± 1 for a confidence level of 95%.

NOTES

[1] These reagents should be nitrogen-free.

METHOD NO 13

POLYPROPYLENE FIBRES AND CERTAIN OTHER FIBRES

(Xylene method)

[8.554]

1. FIELD OF APPLICATION

This method is applicable, after removal of non-fibrous matter, to binary fibre mixtures of:

1. polypropylene fibres (37)

with

2. wool (1), animal hair (2 and 3), silk (4), cotton (5), acetate (19), cupro (21), modal (22), triacetate (24), viscose (25), acrylic (26), polyamide or nylon (30), polyester (35), glass fibre (44), elastomultiester (45) and melamine (47).

2. PRINCIPLE

The polypropylene fibre is dissolved out from a known dry mass of the mixture with boiling xylene. The residue is collected, washed, dried and weighed; its mass, corrected if necessary, is expressed as a percentage of the dry mass of the mixture. The percentage of polypropylene is found by difference.

3. APPARATUS AND REAGENTS (other than those specified in the general instructions)

3.1. Apparatus

(a) Glass-stoppered conical flask of at least 200 ml capacity.
(b) Reflux condenser (suitable for liquids of high boiling point), fitting the conical flask (a).
(c) Heating mantle at boiling point of xylene.

3.2. Reagent

Xylene distilling between 137 and 142 °C.

Note:

Xylene is highly flammable and has a toxic vapour. Suitable precautions must be taken in its use.

4. TEST PROCEDURE

Follow the procedure described in the general instructions then proceed as follows:

To the specimen contained in the conical flask (3.1(a)), add 100 ml of xylene (3.2) per gram of specimen. Attach the condenser (3.1(b)), bring the contents to the boil and maintain at boiling point for 3 minutes.

Immediately decant the hot liquid through the weighed filter crucible (see Note 1). Repeat this treatment twice more, each time using a fresh 50 ml portion of solvent.

Wash the residue remaining in the flask successively with 30 ml of boiling xylene (twice), then with 75 ml of light petroleum (I.3.2.1 of general instructions) (twice). After the second wash with light petroleum, filter the contents of the flask through the crucible, transfer any residual fibres to the crucible with the aid of a small quantity of light petroleum and allow the solvent to evaporate. Dry the crucible and residue, cool and weigh them.

Notes:

1. The filter crucible through which the xylene is to be decanted must be pre-heated.
2. After the treatment with boiling xylene, ensure that the flask containing the residue is cooled sufficiently before the light petroleum is introduced.
3. In order to reduce the fire and toxicity hazards to the operator, a hot extraction apparatus using the appropriate procedures, giving identical results, may be used.

5. CALCULATION AND EXPRESSION OF RESULTS

Calculate the results as described in the general instructions. The value of ‘d’ is 1.00, except for melamine, for which ‘d’ = 1.01.

6. PRECISION

On a homogeneous mixture of textile materials, the confidence limits of results obtained by this method are not greater than ± 1 for a confidence level of 95%.

NOTES

[1] See for example the apparatus described in Melliand Textilberichte 56 (1975), pp. 643 645.

METHOD NO 14
[CERTAIN FIBRES AND OTHER FIBRES
(Method using concentrated sulphuric acid)]

[8.555]

1. FIELD OF APPLICATION

This method is applicable, after removal of non-fibrous matter, to binary fibre mixtures of:

1. cotton (5), acetate (19), cupro (21), modal (22), triacetate (24), viscose (25), certain acrylics (26), certain modacrylics (29), polyamide or nylon (30), polyester (35) and elastomultiester (45)

with

[2. chlorofibres (27) based on homopolymers of vinyl chloride, whether after-chlorinated or not, polypropylene (37), elastolefin (46), melamine (47) and polypropylene/polyamide bicomponent (49).

The modacrylics concerned are those which give a limpid solution when immersed in concentrated sulphuric acid (relative density 1,84 at 20 °C).

This method can be used in place of methods No 8 and 9.]

[2. PRINCIPLE

The constituent other than the chlorofibre, polypropylene, elastolefin, melamine or polypropylene/ polyamide bicomponent (i.e. the fibres mentioned in paragraph 1.1) is dissolved out from a known dry mass of the mixture with concentrated sulphuric acid (relative density 1,84 at 20 °C). The residue, consisting of the chlorofibre, polypropylene, elastolefin, melamine or polypropylene/polyamide bicomponent is collected, washed, dried and weighed; its mass, corrected if necessary, is expressed as a percentage of the dry mass of the mixture. The percentage of the second constituents is obtained by difference.]

3. APPARATUS AND REAGENTS (other than those specified in the general instructions)

3.1. Apparatus

(a) Glass-stoppered conical flask of at least 200 ml capacity.

(b) Glass rod with flattened end.

3.2. Reagents

(a) Sulphuric acid, concentrated (relative density at 20 °C: 1.84).

(b) Sulphuric acid, approximately 50% (m/m) aqueous solution.

Prepare by adding carefully, while cooling, 400 ml of sulphuric acid (relative density at 20 °C: 1.84) to 500 ml of distilled or deionised water. After cooling to room temperature, dilute the solution to one litre with water.

(c) Ammonia, dilute solution.

Dilute 60 ml of concentrated ammonia solution (relative density at 20 °C: 0.880) to one litre with distilled water.

4. TEST PROCEDURE

Follow the procedure described in the general instructions, then proceed as follows:

To the test specimen contained in the flask (3.1(a)) add 100 ml of sulphuric acid (3.2(a)) per gram of specimen.

Allow the contents of the flask to remain at room temperature for 10 minutes and during that time stir the test specimen occasionally by means of the glass rod. If a woven or knitted fabric is being treated, wedge it between the wall of the flask and the glass rod and exert a light pressure in order to separate the material dissolved by the sulphuric acid.

Decant the liquid through the weighed filter crucible. Add to the flask a fresh portion of 100 ml of sulphuric acid (3.2(a)) and repeat the same operation. Transfer the contents of the flask to the filter crucible and transfer the fibrous residue there with the aid of the glass rod. If necessary, add a little concentrated sulphuric acid (3.2(a)) to the flask in order to remove any fibres adhering to the wall. Drain the filter crucible with suction; remove the filtrate by emptying or changing the filter-flask, wash the residue in the crucible successively with 50% sulphuric acid solution (3.2(b)), distilled or deionised water (I.3.2.3 of the general instructions), ammonia solution (3.2(c)) and finally wash thoroughly with distilled or deionised water, draining the crucible with suction after each addition. (Do not apply suction during the washing operation, but only after the liquid has drained off by gravity.) Dry the crucible and residue, cool and weigh them.

[5. CALCULATION AND EXPRESSION OF RESULTS

Calculate the results as described in the general instructions. The value of "d" is 1,00, except for melamine and polypropylene/polyamide bicomponent, for which the value of "d" is 1,01.]

6. PRECISION

On a homogeneous mixture of textile materials, the confidence limits of results obtained by this method are not greater than ± 1 for a confidence level of 95%.

NOTES

Title: substituted by Commission Delegated Regulation 286/2012/EU, Art 1, Annex, para (2)(l)(i).

Point 1: para 2 substituted by Commission Delegated Regulation 286/2012/EU, Art 1, Annex, para (2)(l)(ii).

Point 2: substituted by Commission Delegated Regulation 286/2012/EU, Art 1, Annex, para (2)(l)(iii).

Point 5: substituted by Commission Delegated Regulation 286/2012/EU, Art 1, Annex, para (2)(l)(iv).

METHOD NO 15
CHLOROFIBRES, CERTAIN MODACRYLICS, CERTAIN ELASTANES, ACETATES, TRIACETATES AND CERTAIN OTHER FIBRES
(Method using cyclohexanone)

[8.556]

1. FIELD OF APPLICATION

This method is applicable, after removal of non-fibrous matter, to binary fibre mixtures of:

1. acetate (19), triacetate (24), chlorofibre (27), certain modacrylics (29), certain elastanes (43)

with

2. wool (1), animal hair (2 and 3), silk (4), cotton (5), cupro (21), modal (22), viscose (25), polyamide or nylon (30), acrylic (26), glass fibre (44) and melamine (47).

Where modacrylics or elastanes are present a preliminary test must first be carried out to determine whether the fibre is completely soluble in the reagent.

It is also possible to analyse mixtures containing chlorofibres by using method No 9 or 14.

2. PRINCIPLE

The acetate and triacetate fibres, chlorofibres, certain modacrylics, and certain elastanes are dissolved out from a known dry mass with cyclohexanone at a temperature close to boiling point. The residue is collected, washed, dried and weighed; its mass, corrected if necessary, is expressed as a percentage of the dry mass of the mixture. The percentage of chlorofibre, modacrylic, elastane, acetate and triacetate is found by difference.

3. APPARATUS AND REAGENTS (other than those specified in the general instructions)

3.1. Apparatus

(a) Hot extraction apparatus suitable for use in the test procedure in point 4 (see figure: this is a variant of the apparatus described in Melliand Textilberichte 56 (1975) pp. 643–645).
(b) Filter crucible to contain the test specimen.
(c) Porous baffle (porosity grade 1).
(d) Reflux condenser that can be adapted to the distillation flask.
(e) Heating device.

3.2. Reagents

(a) Cyclohexanone, boiling point 156 °C.
(b) Ethyl alcohol, 50% by volume.

Note:

Cyclohexanone is flammable and toxic. Suitable precautions must be taken in its use.

4. TEST PROCEDURE

Follow the procedure described in the general instructions and then proceed as follows:

Pour into the distillation flask 100 ml of cyclohexanone per gram of material, insert the extraction container in which the filter crucible, containing the specimen and the porous baffle, slightly inclined, have previously been placed. Insert the reflux condenser. Bring to the boil and continue extraction for 60 minutes at a minimum rate of 12 cycles per hour.

After extraction and cooling remove the extraction container, take out the filter crucible and remove the porous baffle. Wash the contents of the filter crucible three or four times with 50% ethyl alcohol heated to about 60 °C and subsequently with 1 litre of water at 60 °C.

Do not apply suction during or between the washing operations. Allow the liquid to drain under gravity and then apply suction.

Finally, dry the crucible with the residue, cool and weigh them.

5. CALCULATION AND EXPRESSION OF RESULTS

Calculate the results as described in the general instructions. The value of 'd' is 1.00 except in the case of silk and melamine for which 'd' = 1.01, and acrylic, for which 'd' = 0.98.

6. PRECISION

On homogeneous mixtures of textile fibres, the confidence limits of results obtained by this method are not greater than ± 1 for a confidence level of 95%.

Figure referred to in point 3.1(a) of method No 15

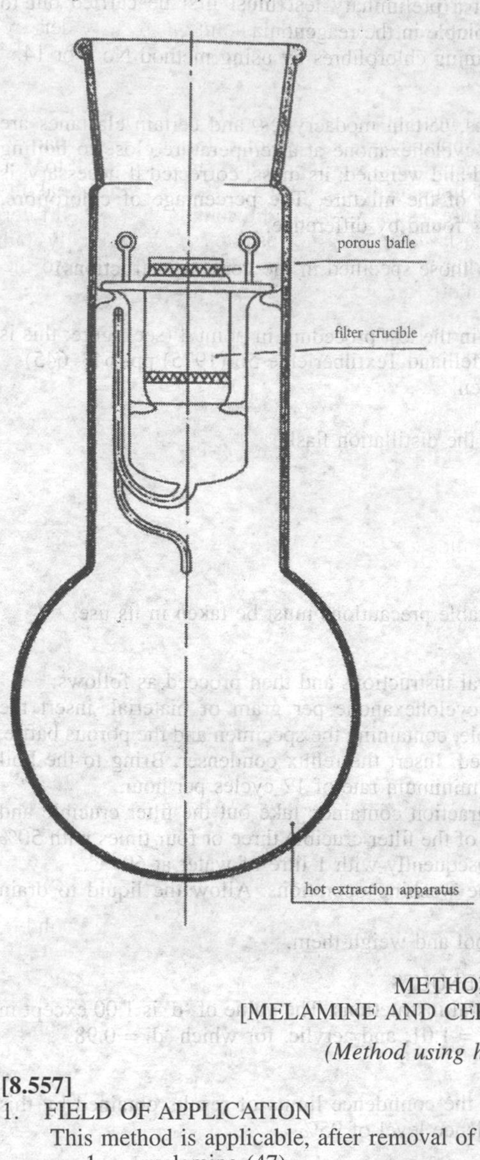

METHOD NO 16

[MELAMINE AND CERTAIN OTHER FIBRES

(Method using hot formic acid)]

[8.557]

1. FIELD OF APPLICATION

This method is applicable, after removal of non-fibrous matter, to binary fibre mixtures of:

1. melamine (47)

with

[2. cotton (5), aramid (31) and polypropylene (37).]

2. PRINCIPLE

The melamine is dissolved out from a known dry mass of the mixture with hot formic acid (90% m/m).

The residue is collected, washed, dried and weighed; its mass, corrected if necessary, is expressed as a percentage of the dry mass of the mixture. The percentage of the second constituents is obtained by difference.

Note:

Keep strictly the recommended temperature range because the solubility of melamine is very much dependent on temperature.

3. APPARATUS AND REAGENTS (other than those specified in the general instructions)

3.1. Apparatus

(a) Glass-stoppered conical flask of at least 200 ml capacity.

(b) Shaking water bath or other apparatus to shake and maintain the flask at 90 ± 2 °C.

3.2. Reagents

(a) Formic acid (90% m/m, relative density at 20 °C: 1.204). Dilute 890 ml of 98 to 100% m/m formic acid (relative density at 20 °C: 1.220) to 1 litre with water.
Hot formic acid is very corrosive and must be handled with care.

(b) Ammonia, dilute solution: dilute 80 ml of concentrated ammonia solution (relative density at 20 °C: 0.880) to 1 litre with water.

4. TEST PROCEDURE

Follow the procedure described in the general instructions, then proceed as follows:

To the test specimen contained in the glass-stoppered conical flask of at least 200 ml capacity, add 100 ml of formic acid per gram of specimen. Insert the stopper and shake the flask to wet out the specimen. Maintain the flask in a shaking water bath at 90 ± 2 °C for 1 hour, shaking it vigorously. Cool the flask to room temperature. Decant the liquid through the weighed filter crucible. Add 50 ml of formic acid to the flask containing the residue, shake manually and filter the contents of the flask through the filter crucible. Transfer any residual fibres to the crucible by washing out the flask with a little more formic acid reagent. Drain the crucible with suction and wash the residue with formic acid reagent, hot water, dilute ammonia solution, and finally cold water, draining the crucible with suction after each addition. Do not apply suction until each washing liquor has drained under gravity. Finally, drain the crucible with suction, dry the crucible and residue, and cool and weigh them.

5. CALCULATION AND EXPRESSION OF RESULTS

Calculate the results as described in the general instructions. The value of 'd' is 1.02.

6. PRECISION

On a homogeneous mixture of textile materials, the confidence limits of results obtained by this method are not greater than ± 2 for a confidence level of 95%.

NOTES

Title: substituted by Commission Delegated Regulation 286/2012/EU, Art 1, Annex, para (2)(m)(i).

Point 1: para 2 substituted by Commission Delegated Regulation 286/2012/EU, Art 1, Annex, para (2)(m)(ii).

CHAPTER 3
QUANTITATIVE ANALYSIS OF TERNARY TEXTILE FIBRE MIXTURES

INTRODUCTION

[8.558]

In general, the methods of quantitative chemical analysis are based on the selective solution of the individual components. There are four possible variants of this method:

1. Using two different test specimens, a component (a) is dissolved from the first test specimen, and another component (b) from the second test specimen. The insoluble residues of each specimen are weighed and the percentage of each of the two soluble components is calculated from the respective losses in mass. The percentage of the third component (c) is calculated by difference.
2. Using two different test specimens, a component (a) is dissolved from the first test specimen and two components (a and b) from the second test specimen. The insoluble residue of the first test specimen is weighed and the percentage of the component (a) is calculated from the loss in mass. The insoluble residue of the second test specimen is weighed; it corresponds to component (c). The percentage of the third component (b) is calculated by difference.
3. Using two different test specimens, two components (a and b) are dissolved from the first test specimen and two components (b and c) from the second test specimen. The insoluble residues correspond to the two components (c) and (a) respectively. The percentage of the third component (b) is calculated by difference.
4. Using only one test specimen, after removal of one of the components, the insoluble residue formed by the two other fibres is weighed and the percentage of the soluble component is calculated from the loss in mass. One of the two fibres of the residue is dissolved, the insoluble component is weighed and the percentage of the second soluble component is calculated from the loss in mass.

Where a choice is possible, it is advisable to use one of the first three variants.

Where chemical analysis is used, the expert responsible for the analysis must take care to select methods employing solvents which dissolve only the correct fibre(s), leaving the other fibre(s) intact.

By way of example, a table is given in Section V which contains a certain number of ternary fibre mixtures, together with methods for analysing binary fibre mixtures which can, in principle, be used for analysing these ternary fibre mixtures.

In order to reduce the possibility of error to a minimum, it is recommended that, whenever possible, chemical analysis using at least two of the four abovementioned variants shall be made.

Before proceeding with any analysis, all the fibres present in the mixture must be identified. In some chemical methods, the insoluble component of a mixture may be partially dissolved in the reagent used to dissolve the soluble component(s). Wherever possible, reagents have been chosen that have little or no effect on the insoluble fibres. If a loss in mass is known to occur during the analysis, the result shall be corrected; correction factors are given for this purpose. These factors have been determined in several laboratories by treating, with the appropriate reagent as specified in the method of analysis, fibres cleaned by the pre-treatment. These correction factors apply only to undergraded fibres and different correction factors may be necessary if the fibres have been degraded before or during processing. If the fourth variant, in which a textile fibre is subjected to the successive action of two different solvents, must be used, correction factors must be applied for possible losses in mass undergone by the fibre in the two treatments. At least two determinations shall be made, both in the case of manual separation and in the case of chemical separation.

I. General information on methods for the quantitative chemical analysis of ternary fibre mixtures

Information common to the methods given for the quantitative chemical analysis of ternary fibre mixtures.

I.1. FIELD OF APPLICATION

The field of application of each method for analysing binary fibre mixtures specifies to which fibres the method is applicable (see Chapter 2 relating to methods for quantitative analysis of certain binary textile fibre mixtures).

I.2. PRINCIPLE

After the identification of the components of a mixture, the non-fibrous material is removed by suitable pre-treatment and then one or more of the four variants of the process of selective solution described in the introduction is applied. Except where this presents technical difficulties, it is preferable to dissolve the major fibre component so as to obtain the minor fibre component as final residue.

I.3. MATERIALS AND EQUIPMENT

I.3.1. Apparatus

I.3.1.1. Filter crucibles and weighing bottles large enough to contain such crucibles, or any other apparatus giving identical results.

I.3.1.2. Vacuum flask.

I.3.1.3. Desiccator containing self-indicating silica gel.

I.3.1.4. Ventilated oven for drying specimens at 105 ± 3 °C.

I.3.1.5. Analytical balance, accurate to 0.0002 g.

I.3.1.6. Soxhlet extractor or other apparatus giving identical results.

I.3.2. Reagents

I.3.2.1. Light petroleum, redistilled, boiling range 40 to 60 °C.

I.3.2.2. Other reagents are specified in the appropriate sections of each method.

I.3.2.3. Distilled or deionised water.

I.3.2.4. Acetone.

I.3.2.5. Orthophosphoric acid.

I.3.2.6. Urea.

I.3.2.7. Sodium bicarbonate.

All reagents used shall be chemically pure.

I.4. CONDITIONING AND TESTING ATMOSPHERE

Because dry masses are determined, it is unnecessary to condition the specimen or to conduct analyses in a conditioned atmosphere.

I.5. LABORATORY TEST SAMPLE

Take a laboratory test sample that is representative of the laboratory bulk sample and sufficient to provide all the specimens, each of at least 1 g, that are required.

I.6. PRE-TREATMENT OF LABORATORY TEST SAMPLE[1]

Where a substance not to be taken into account in the percentage calculations (see Article 19) is present, it shall first be removed by a suitable method that does not affect any of the fibre constituents.

For this purpose, non-fibrous matter which can be extracted with light petroleum and water is removed by treating the laboratory test sample in a Soxhlet extractor with light petroleum for 1 hour at a minimum rate of six cycles per hour. Allow the light petroleum to evaporate from the laboratory test sample, which is then extracted by direct treatment consisting in soaking the laboratory test sample in water at room temperature for 1 hour and then soaking it in water at 65 ± 5 °C for a further hour, agitating the liquor from time to time. Use a liquor: laboratory test sample ratio of 100:1. Remove the excess water from the laboratory test sample by squeezing, suction or centrifuging and then allow the laboratory test sample to become air-dry.

In the case of elastolefin or fibre mixtures containing elastolefin and other fibres (wool, animal hair, silk, cotton, flax (or linen), true hemp, jute, abaca, alfa, coir, broom, ramie, sisal, cupro, modal, protein, viscose, acrylic, polyamide or nylon, polyester, elastomultiester) the procedure just described shall be slightly modified, in fact light petroleum ether shall be replaced by acetone.

Where non-fibrous matter cannot be extracted with light petroleum and water, it shall be removed by substituting for the water method described above a suitable method that does not substantially alter any of the fibre constituents. However, for some unbleached, natural vegetable fibres (e.g. jute, coir) it is to be noted that normal pre-treatment with light petroleum and water does not remove all the natural non-fibrous substances; nevertheless additional pre-treatment is not applied unless the sample contains finishes insoluble in both light petroleum and water.

Analysis reports shall include full details of the methods of pre-treatment used.

I.7. TEST PROCEDURE

I.7.1. General instructions

I.7.1.1. Drying

Conduct all drying operations for not less than 4 hours and not more than 16 hours at 105 ± 3 °C in a ventilated oven with the oven door closed throughout. If the drying period is less than 14 hours, the specimen must be checkweighed to determine whether its mass is constant. The mass may be considered as constant if, after a further drying period of 60 minutes, its variation is less than 0.05%.

Avoid handling crucibles and weighing bottles, specimens or residues with bare hands during the drying, cooling and weighing operations.

Dry specimens in a weighing bottle with its cover beside it. After drying, stopper the weighing bottle before removing it from the oven, and transfer it quickly to the desiccator.

Dry the filter crucible in a weighing bottle with its cover beside it in the oven. After drying, close the weighing bottle and transfer it quickly to the desiccator.

Where apparatus other than a filter crucible is used, drying operations shall be conducted in the oven so as to determine the dry mass of the fibres without loss.

I.7.1.2. Cooling

Conduct all cooling operations in the desiccator, placed beside the balance, until the cooling of the weighing bottles is complete, and in any case for not less than 2 hours.

I.7.1.3. Weighing

After cooling, complete the weighing of the weighing bottle within 2 minutes of its removal from the desiccator; weigh to an accuracy of 0.0002 g.

I.7.2. Procedure

Take from the pre-treated laboratory test sample a test specimen of at least 1 g (in mass). Cut yarn or cloth into lengths of about 10 mm, dissected as much as possible. Dry the specimen in a weighing bottle, cool it in the desiccator and weigh it. Transfer the specimen to the glass vessel specified in the appropriate section of the Union method, reweigh the weighing bottle immediately and obtain the dry mass of the specimen by difference; complete the test as specified in the appropriate section of the applicable method. Examine the residue microscopically to check that the treatment has in fact completely removed the soluble fibre(s).

I.8. CALCULATION AND EXPRESSION OF RESULTS

Express the mass of each component as a percentage of the total mass of fibre in the mixture. Calculate the results on the basis of dean dry mass, adjusted by (a) the agreed allowances and (b) the correction factors necessary to take account of loss of non-fibrous matter during pre-treatment and analysis.

I.8.1. Calculation of percentages of mass of clean dry fibres disregarding loss of fibre mass during pre-treatment.

I.8.1.1. - VARIANT 1 -

Formulae to be applied where a component of the mixture is removed from one specimen and another component from a second specimen:

$$P_1\% = \left[\frac{d_2}{d_1} - d_2 \times \frac{r_1}{m_1} + \frac{r_2}{m_2} \times \left(1 - \frac{d_2}{d_1}\right)\right] \times 100$$

$$P_2\% = \left[\frac{d_4}{d_3} - d_4 \times \frac{r_2}{m_2} + \frac{r_1}{m_1} \times \left(1 - \frac{d_4}{d_3}\right)\right] \times 100$$

$$P_3\% = 100 - (P_1\% + P_2\%)$$

$P_1\%$ is the percentage of the first clean dry component (component in the first specimen dissolved in the first reagent),
$P_2\%$ is the percentage of the second clean dry component (component in the second specimen dissolved in the second reagent),
$P_3\%$ is the percentage of the third clean dry component (component undissolved in both specimens),
m_1 is the dry mass of the first specimen after pre-treatment,
m_2 is the dry mass of the second specimen after pre-treatment,
r_1 is the dry mass of the residue after removal of the first component from the first specimen in the first reagent,
r_2 is the dry mass of the residue after removal of the second component from the second specimen in the second reagent,
d_1 is the correction factor for loss in mass in the first reagent, of the second component undissolved in the first specimen;[2]
d_2 is the correction factor for loss in mass in the first reagent, of the third component undissolved in the first specimen,
d_3 is the correction factor for loss in mass in the second reagent, of the first component undissolved in the second specimen,
d_4 is the correction factor for loss in mass in the second reagent, of the third component undissolved in the second specimen.

I.8.1.2. - VARIANT 2 -

Formulae to be applied where a component (a) is removed from the first test specimen, leaving as residue the other two components (b + c), and two components (a + b) are removed from the second test specimen, leaving as residue the third component (c):

$$P_1\% = 100 - (P_2\% + P_3\%)$$

$$P_2\% = 100 \times \frac{d_1 r_1}{m_1} - \frac{d_1}{d_2} \times P_3\%$$

$$P_3\% = \frac{d_4 r_2}{m_2} \times 100$$

$P_1\%$ is the percentage of the first clean dry component (component in the first specimen dissolved in the first reagent),
$P_2\%$ is the percentage of the second clean dry component (component soluble, at the same time as the first component of the second specimen, in the second reagent),
$P_3\%$ is the percentage of the third clean dry component (component undissolved in both specimens),
m_1 is the dry mass of the first specimen after pre-treatment,
m_2 is the dry mass of the second specimen after pre-treatment,
r_1 is the dry mass of the residue after removal of the first component from the first specimen in the first reagent,
r_2 is the dry mass of the residue after removal of the first and second components from the second specimen in the second reagent,
d_1 is the correction factor for loss in mass in the first reagent, of the second component undissolved in the first specimen,
d_2 is the correction factor for loss in mass in the first reagent, of the third component undissolved in the first specimen,
d_4 is the correction factor for loss in mass in the second reagent, of the third component undissolved in the second specimen.

I.8.1.3. - VARIANT 3 -

Formulae to be applied where two components (a + b) are removed from a specimen, leaving as residue the third component (c), then two components (b + c) are removed from another specimen, leaving as residue the first component (a):

$$P_1\% = \frac{d_3 r_2}{m_2} \times 100$$

$$P_2\% = 100 - (P_1\% + P_3\%)$$

$$P_3\% = \frac{d_2 r_1}{m_1} \times 100$$

$P_1\%$ is the percentage of the first clean dry component (component dissolved by the reagent),
$P_2\%$ is the percentage of the second clean dry component (component dissolved by the reagent),
$P_3\%$ is the percentage of the third clean dry component (component dissolved in the second specimen by the reagent),
m_1 is the dry mass of the first specimen after pre-treatment,
m_2 is the dry mass of the second specimen after pre-treatment,
r_1 is the dry mass of the residue after the removal of the first and second components from the first specimen with the first reagent,
r_2 is the dry mass of the residue after the removal of the second and third components from the second specimen with the second reagent,
d_2 is the correction factor for loss in mass in the first reagent of the third component undissolved in the first specimen,
d_3 is the correction factor for loss in mass in the second reagent of the first component undissolved in the second specimen.

I.8.1.4. - VARIANT 4 -

Formulae to be applied where two components are successively removed from the mixture using the same specimen:

$$P_1\% = 100 - (P_2\% + P_3\%)$$

$$P_2\% = \frac{d_1 r_1}{m} \times 100 - \frac{d_1}{d_2} \times P_3\%$$

$$P_3\% = \frac{d_3 r_2}{m} \times 100$$

$P_1\%$ is the percentage of the first clean dry component (first soluble component),
$P_2\%$ is the percentage of the second clean dry component (second soluble component),
$P_3\%$ is the percentage of the third clean dry component (insoluble component),
m is the dry mass of the specimen after pre-treatment,
r_1 is the dry mass of the residue after elimination of the first component by the first reagent,
r_2 is the dry mass of the residue after elimination of the first and second component by the first and second reagents,
d_1 is the correction factor for loss in mass of the second component in the first reagent,
d_2 is the correction factor for loss in mass of the third component in the first reagent,
d_3 is the correction factor for loss in mass of the third component in the first and second reagents.[3]

I.8.2. Calculation of the percentage of each component with adjustment by agreed allowances and, where appropriate, correction factors for losses in mass during pre-treatment operations: Given:

$$A = 1 + \frac{a_1 + b_1}{100} \quad B = 1 + \frac{a_2 + b_2}{100} \quad C = 1 + \frac{a_3 + b_3}{100}$$

then:

Part 8 Other EU Materials

$$P_1A\% = \frac{P_1A}{P_1A + P_2B + P_3C} \times 100$$

$$P_2A\% = \frac{P_2B}{P_1A + P_2B + P_3C} \times 100$$

$$P_3A\% = \frac{P_3C}{P_1A + P_2B + P_3C} \times 100$$

P_1 A% is the percentage of the first clean dry component, including moisture content and loss in mass during pre-treatment,
P_2 A% is the percentage of the second clean dry component, including moisture content and loss in mass during pre-treatment,
P_3 A% is the percentage of the third clean dry component, including moisture content and loss in mass during pre-treatment,
P_1 is the percentage of the first clean dry component obtained by one of the formulae given in I.8.1,
P_2 is the percentage of the second clean dry component obtained by one of the formulae given in I.8.1,
P_3 is the percentage of the third clean dry component obtained by one of the formulae given in I.8.1,
a_1 is the agreed allowance of the first component,
a_2 is the agreed allowance of the second component,
a_3 is the agreed allowance of the third component,
b_1 is the percentage of loss in mass of the first component during pre-treatment,
b_2 is the percentage of loss in mass of the second component during pre-treatment,
b_3 is the percentage of loss in mass of the third component during pre-treatment.

Where a special pre-treatment is used the values b_1, b_2 and b_3 shall be determined, if possible, by submitting each of the pure fibre constituents to the pre-treatment applied in the analysis. Pure fibres are those free from all non-fibrous material except those which they normally contain (either naturally or because of the manufacturing process), in the state (unbleached, bleached) in which they are found in the material to be analysed.

Where no clean separate constituent fibres used in the manufacture of the material to be analysed are available, average values of b_1, b_2 and b_3 as obtained from tests performed on clean fibres similar to those in the mixture under examination, must be used.

If normal pre-treatment by extraction with light petroleum and water is applied, correction factors b_1, b_2 and b_3 may generally be ignored, except in the case of unbleached cotton, unbleached flax (or linen) and unbleached hemp where the loss due to pre-treatment is usually accepted as 4% and in the case of polypropylene as 1%.

In the case of other fibres, losses due to pre-treatment are usually disregarded in calculations.

I.8.3. Note:

Calculation examples are given in Section IV.

NOTES

1 See Chapter 1.1.

2 The values of d are indicated in Chapter 2 of this Annex relating to the various methods of analysing binary mixtures.

3 Wherever possible d 3 should be determined in advance by experimental methods.

II. Method of quantitative analysis by manual separation of ternary fibre mixtures

II.1. FIELD OF APPLICATION

This method is applicable to textile fibres of all types provided they do not form an intimate mixture and that it is possible to separate them by hand.

II.2. PRINCIPLE

After identification of the textile components, the non-fibrous matter is removed by a suitable pre-treatment and then the fibres are separated by hand, dried and weighed in order to calculate the proportion of each fibre in the mixture.

II.3. APPARATUS

II.3.1. Weighing bottles or other apparatus giving identical results.

II.3.2. Desiccator containing self-indicating silica gel.

II.3.3. Ventilated oven for drying specimens at 105 ± 3 °C.

II.3.4. Analytical balance accurate to 0.0002 g.

II.3.5. Soxhlet extractor, or other apparatus giving identical results.

II.3.6. Needle.

II.3.7. Twist tester or similar apparatus.

II.4. REAGENTS

II.4.1. Light petroleum, redistilled, boiling range 40 to 60 °C.

II.4.2. Distilled or deionised water.

II.5. CONDITIONING AND TESTING ATMOSPHERE

See I.4.

II.6. LABORATORY TEST SAMPLE

See I.5.

II.7. PRE-TREATMENT OF LABORATORY TEST SAMPLES

See I.6.

II.8. PROCEDURE

II.8.1. Analysis of yarn

Take from the pre-treated laboratory test sample a specimen of mass not less than 1 g. For a very fine yarn, the analysis may be made on a minimum length of 30 m, whatever its mass. Cut the yarn into pieces of a suitable length and separate the fibre types by means of a needle and, if necessary, a twist tester. The fibre types so obtained are placed in pre-weighed weighing bottles and dried at 105 ± 3 °C to constant mass, as described in I.7.1 and I.7.2.

II.8.2. Analysis of cloth

Take from the pre-treated laboratory test sample a specimen of mass not less than 1 g, not including a selvedge with edges carefully trimmed to avoid fraying and running parallel with weft or warp yarns, or in the case of knitted fabrics in the line of the wales and courses. Separate the different types of fibres and collect them in pre-weighed weighing bottles and proceed as described in II.8.1.

II.9. CALCULATION AND EXPRESSION OF RESULTS

Express the mass of each component fibre as a percentage of the total mass of the fibres in the mixture. Calculate the results on the basis of clean dry mass, adjusted by (a) the agreed allowances and (b) the correction factors necessary to take account of losses in mass during pre-treatment operations.

II.9.1. Calculation of percentage masses of clean dry fibre, disregarding loss in fibre mass during pre-treatment:

$$P_1\% = \frac{100m_1}{m_1 + m_2 + m_3} = \frac{100}{1 + \dfrac{m_2 + m_3}{m_1}}$$

$$P_2\% = \frac{100m_2}{m_1 + m_2 + m_3} = \frac{100}{1 + \dfrac{m_1 + m_3}{m_2}}$$

$$P_3\% = 100 - (P_1\% + P_2\%)$$

$P_1\%$ is the percentage of the first clean dry component,
$P_2\%$ is the percentage of the second clean dry component,
$P_3\%$ is the percentage of the third clean dry component,
m_1 is the clean dry mass of the first component,
m_2 is the clean dry mass of the second component,
m_3 is the clean dry mass of the third component.

II.9.2. For calculation of the percentage of each component with adjustment by agreed allowances and, where appropriate, by correction factors for losses in mass during pre-treatment: see I.8.2.

III. Method of quantitative analysis of ternary fibre mixtures by a combination of manual separation and chemical separation

Wherever possible, manual separation shall be used, taking account of the proportions of components separated before proceeding to any chemical treatment of each of the separate components.

III.1. PRECISION OF THE METHODS

The precision indicated in each method of analysis of binary fibre mixtures relates to the reproducibility (see Chapter 2 relating to methods for quantitative analysis of certain binary textile fibre mixtures).

Reproducibility refers to the reliability, i.e. the closeness of agreement between experimental values obtained by operators in different laboratories or at different times using the same method and obtaining individual results on specimens of an identical homogeneous mixture.

Reproducibility is expressed by confidence limits of the results for a confidence level of 95%.

By this is meant that the difference between two results in a series of analyses made in different laboratories would, given a normal and correct application of the method to an identical and homogeneous mixture, exceed the confidence limit only in five cases out of 100.

To determine the precision of the analysis of a ternary fibre mixture the values indicated in the methods for the analysis of binary fibre mixtures which have been used to analyse the ternary fibre mixture are applied in the usual way.

Given that in the four variants of the quantitative chemical analysis of ternary fibre mixtures, provision is made for two dissolutions (using two separate specimens for the first three variants and a single specimen for the fourth variant) and, assuming that E 1 and E 2 denote the precision of the two methods for analysing binary fibre mixtures, the precision of the results for each component is shown in the following table:

Component fibre	**Variants**		
	1	**2 and 3**	**4**
a	E_1	E_1	E_1
b	E_2	$E_1 + E_2$	$E_1 + E_2$
c	$E_1 + E_2$	E_2	$E_1 + E_2$

If the fourth variant is used, the degree of precision may be found to be lower than that calculated by the method indicated above, owing to possible action of the first reagent on the residue consisting of components b and c, which would be difficult to evaluate.

III.2. TEST REPORT

III.2.1. Indicate the variant(s) used to carry out the analysis, the methods, reagents and correction factors.

III.2.2. Give details of any special pre-treatments (see I.6).

III.2.3. Give the individual results and the arithmetic mean, each to the first decimal place.

III.2.4. Wherever possible, state the precision of the method for each component, calculated according to the table in Section III.1.

IV. Examples of the calculation of percentages of the components of certain ternary fibre mixtures using some of the variants described in point I.8.1.

Consider the case of a fibre mixture which gave the following components when qualitatively analysed for raw material composition: 1. carded wool; 2. nylon (polyamide); 3. unbleached cotton.

VARIANT No 1

Using this variant, that is using two different specimens and removing one component (a = wool) by dissolution from the first specimen and a second component (b = polyamide) from the second specimen, the following results can be obtained:

1. Dry mass of the first specimen after pre-treatment is (m_1) = 1.6000 g
2. Dry mass of the residue after treatment with alkaline sodium hypochlorite (polyamide + cotton) (r_1) = 1.4166 g
3. Dry mass of the second specimen after pre-treatment (m_2) = 1.8000g
4. Dry mass of the residue after treatment with formic acid (wool + cotton) (r_2) = 0.9000g

Treatment with alkaline sodium hypochlorite does not entail any loss in mass of polyamide, while unbleached cotton loses 3%, therefore d_1 = 1.00 and d_2 = 1.03.

Treatment with formic acid does not entail any loss in mass for wool or unbleached cotton, therefore d_3 and d_4 = 1.00.

If the values obtained by chemical analysis and the correction factors are substituted in the formula under I.8.1.1, the following result is obtained:

P_1% (wool) = [1.03/1.00 – 1.03 × 1.4166/1,6000 + (0.9000/1.8000) × (1 – 1.03/1.00)] ×100 = 10.30

P_2% (polyamide) = [1.00/1.00 – 1.00 × 0.9000/1.8000 + (1.4166/1.6000) × (1 – 1.00/1.00)] × 100 = 50.00

P_3% (cotton) = 100 – (10.30 + 50.00) = 39.70

The percentages of the various clean dry fibres in the mixture are as follows:

wool	10.30%
polyamide	50.00%
cotton	39.70%

These percentages must be corrected according to the formulae under I.8.2, in order to take account of the agreed allowances and the correction factors for any losses in mass after pre-treatment.

As indicated in Annex IX, the agreed allowances are as follows: carded wool 17.00%, polyamide 6.25%, cotton 8.50%, also unbleached cotton shows a loss in mass of 4%, after pre-treatment with light petroleum and water.

Therefore:

P_1 A% (wool) = 10.30 × [1 + (17.00 + 0.0)/100] / [10.30 × (1 + (17.00 + 0.0)/100) + 50.00 × (1 + (6.25 + 0.0)/100) + 39.70 × (1 + (8.50 + 4.0)/100)] × 100 = 10.97

P_2 A% (polyamide) = 50.0 × [(1 + (6.25 + 0.0)/100)/109.8385] × 100 = 48.37

P_3 A% (cotton) = 100 – (10.97 + 48.37) = 40.66

The raw material composition of the yarn is therefore as follows: polyamide

polyamide	48.4%
cotton	40.6%
wool	11.0%
	100.0%

VARIANT No 4

Consider the case of a fibre mixture which when qualitatively analysed gave the following components: carded wool, viscose, unbleached cotton.

Suppose that using variant 4, that is successively removing two components from the mixture of one single specimen, the following results are obtained:

1. Dry mass of the specimen after pre-treatment (m) = 1.6000 g
2. Dry mass of the residue after treatment with alkaline sodium hypochlorite (viscose + cotton) (r_1) = 1.4166 g
3. Dry mass of the residue after the second treatment of the residue r 1 with zinc chloride/formic acid (cotton) (r_2) = 0.6630 g

Treatment with alkaline sodium hypochlorite does not entail any loss in mass of viscose, while unbleached cotton loses 3%, therefore d_1 =1.00 and d^2 = 1.03.

As a result of treatment with formic acid-zinc chloride, the mass of cotton increases by 4%, so that d_3 = 1.03 × 0.96 = 0.9888, rounded to 0.99, (d_3 being the correction factor for the respective loss or increase in mass of the third component in the first and second reagents).

If the values obtained by chemical analysis and the correction factors are substituted in the formulae given in I.8.1.4, the following result is obtained:

P_2% (viscose) = 1.00 × (1.4166/1,6000) × 100 – (1.00/1.03) × 41.02 = 48.71%

P_3% (cotton) = 0.99 × (0.6630/1.6000) × 100 = 41.02%

P_1% (wool) = 100 – (48.71 + 41.02) = 10.27%

As has already been indicated for Variant 1, these percentages must be corrected by the formulae indicated in point I.8.2.

P_1 A% (wool) = 10.27 × [1 + (17.0 + 0.0)/100)]/[10.27 × (1 + (17.00 + 0.0)/100) +48.71 × (1 + (13 + 0.0)/100) + 41.02 × (1 + (8.5 + 4.0)/100)] × 100 = 10.61%

P_2 A% (viscose) = 48.71 × [1 + (13 + 0.0)/100] / 113.2057 × 100 = 48.62%

P_3 A% (cotton) = 100 – (10.61 + 48.62) = 40.77%

The raw material composition of the mixture is therefore as follows: viscose

viscose	48.6%
cotton	40.8%
wool	10.6%
	—
	100.0%

V. Table of typical ternary fibre mixtures which may be analysed using Union methods of analysis of binary fibre mixtures (for illustration purposes)

Mixture No	Component fibres			Variant	Number of method used and reagent for binary fibre mixtures
	Component 1	Component 2	Component 3		
1.	wool or hair	viscose, cupro or certain types of modal	cotton	1 and/or 4	2. (hypochlorite) and 3. (zinc chloride/formic acid)
2.	wool or hair	polyamide or nylon	cotton, viscose, cupro or modal	1 and/or 4	2. (hypochlorite) and 4. (formic acid, 80% m/m)
3.	wool, hair or silk	certain other fibres	viscose, cupro modal or cotton	1 and/or 4	2. (hypochlorite) and 9. (carbon disulphide/acetone 55.5/44.5% v/v)
4.	wool or hair	polyamide or nylon	polyester, polypropylene, acrylic or glass fibre	1 and/or 4	2. (hypochlorite) and 4. (formic acid, 80% m/m)
5.	wool, hair or silk	certain other fibres	polyester, acrylic, polyamide or nylon or glass fibre	1 and/or 4	2. (hypochlorite) and 9. (carbon disulphide/acetone 55.5/44.5% v/v)
6.	silk	wool or hair	polyester	2	11. (sulphuric acid 75% m/m) and 2. (hypochlorite)
7.	polyamide or nylon	acrylic or certain other fibres	cotton, viscose, cupro or modal	1 and/or 4	4. (formic acid 80% m/m) and 8. (dimethylformamide)
8.	certain chlorofibres	polyamide or nylon	cotton, viscose, cupro or modal	1 and/or 4	8. (dimethylformamide) and 4. (formic acid, 80% m/m) or 9. (carbon disulphide/acetone, 55.5/44.5% v/v) and 4. (formic acid, 80% m/m)
9.	acrylic	polyamide or nylon	polyester	1 and/or 4	8. (dimethylformamide) and 4. (formic acid, 80% m/m)
10.	acetate	polyamide or nylon or certain other fibres	viscose, cotton, cupro or modal	4	1. (acetone) and 4. (formic acid, 80% m/m)
11.	certain chlorofibres	acrylic or certain other fibres	polyamide or nylon	2 and/or 4	9. (carbon disulphide/acetone 55.5/44.5% v/v) and 8. (dimethylformamide)
12.	certain chlorofibres	polyamide or nylon	acrylic	1 and/or 4	9. (carbon disulphide/acetone 55.5/44.5% v/v) and 4. (formic acid, 80%m/m)
13.	polyamide or nylon	viscose, cupro, modal or cotton	polyester	4	4. (formic acid, 80% m/m) and 7. (sulphuric acid, 75% m/m)
14.	acetate	viscose, cupro, modal or cotton	polyester	4	1. (acetone) and 7 (sulphuric acid, 75% m/m)
15.	acrylic	viscose, cupro, modal or cotton	polyester	4	8. (dimethylformamide) and 7. (sulphuric acid, 75% m/m)

Mixture No	Component fibres			Variant	Number of method used and reagent for binary fibre mixtures
	Component 1	Component 2	Component 3		
16.	acetate	wool, hair or silk	cotton, viscose, cupro, modal, polyamide or nylon, polyester, acrylic	4	1. (acetone) and 2. (hypochlorite)
17.	triacetate	wool, hair or silk	cotton, viscose, cupro, modal, polyamide or nylon, polyester, acrylic	4	6. (dichloromethane) and 2. (hypochlorite)
18.	acrylic	wool, hair or silk	polyester	1 and/or 4	8. (dimethylformamide) and 2. (hypochlorite)
19.	acrylic	silk	wool or hair	4	8. (dimethylformamide) and 11. (sulphuric acid 75% m/m)
20.	acrylic	wool or hair silk	cotton, viscose, cupro or modal	1 and/or 4	8. (dimethylformamide) and 2. (hypochlorite)
21.	wool, hair or silk	cotton, viscose, modal, cupro	polyester	4	2. (hypochlorite) and 7. (sulphuric acid 75% m/m)
22.	viscose, cupro or certain types of modal	cotton	polyester	2 and/or 4	3. (zinc chloride/formic acid) and 7. (sulphuric acid 75% m/m)
23.	acrylic	viscose, cupro or certain types of modal	cotton	4	8. (dimethylformamide) and 3 (zinc chloride/formic acid)
24.	certain chlorofibres	viscose, cupro or certain types of modal	cotton	1 and/or 4	9. (carbon disulphide/acetone, 55.5/44.5% v/v) and 3. (zinc chloride/ formic acid) or 8. (dimethylformamide) and 3. (zinc chloride/formic acid)
25.	acetate	viscose, cupro or certain types of modal	cotton	4	1. (acetone) and 3. (zinc chloride/formic acid)
26.	triacetate	viscose, cupro or certain types of modal	cotton	4	6. (dichloromethane) and 3. (zinc chloride/formic acid)
27.	acetate	silk	wool or hair	4	1. (acetone) and 11. (sulphuric acid 75% m/m)
28.	triacetate	silk	wool or hair	4	6. (dichloromethane) and 11. (sulphuric acid 75% m/m)
29.	acetate	acrylic	cotton, viscose, cupro or modal	4	1. (acetone) and 8. (dimethylformamide)
30.	triacetate	acrylic	cotton, viscose, cupro or modal	4	6. (dichloromethane) and 8. (dimethylformamide)

Mixture No	Component fibres			Variant	Number of method used and reagent for binary fibre mixtures
	Component 1	Component 2	Component 3		
31.	triacetate	polyamide or nylon	cotton, viscose, cupro or modal	4	6. (dichloromethane) and 4. (formic acid 80% m/m)
32.	triacetate	cotton, viscose, cupro or modal	polyester	4	6. (dichloromethane) and 7. (sulphuric acid 75% m/m)
33.	acetate	polyamide or nylon	polyester or acrylic	4	1. (acetone) and 4. (formic acid 80% m/m)
34.	acetate	acrylic	polyester	4	1. (acetone) and 8. (dimethylformamide)
35.	certain chlorofibres	cotton, viscose, cupro or modal	polyester	4	8. (dimethylformamide) and 7. (sulphuric acid 75% m/m) or 9 (carbon disulphide/acetone, 55.5/44.5% v/v) and 7. (sulphuric acid 75% m/m)
36.	cotton	polyester	elastolefin	2 and/or 4	7. (sulphuric acid 75% m/m) and 14. (concentrated sulphuric acid)
37.	certain modacrylics	polyester	melamine	2 and/or 4	8. (dimethylformamide) and 14. (concentrated sulphuric acid)

ANNEX IX
AGREED ALLOWANCES USED TO CALCULATE THE MASS OF FIBRES CONTAINED IN A TEXTILE PRODUCT

(referred to in Article 19(3)) Fibre No

[8.559]

Fibre No	Fibres	Percentages
1–2	Wool and animal hair:	
	combed fibres	18.25
	carded fibres	17.00[1]
3	Animal hair:	
	combed fibres	18.25
	carded fibres	17.00[1]
	Horsehair:	
	combed fibres	16.00
	carded fibres	15.00
4	Silk	11.00
5	Cotton:	
	normal fibres	8.50
	mercerised fibres	10.50
6	Kapok	10.90
7	Flax (or linen)	12.00
8	True hemp	12.00
9	Jute	17.00
10	Abaca	14.00
11	Alfa	14.00
12	Coir	13.00
13	Broom	14.00
14	Ramie (bleached fibre)	8.50
15	Sisal	14.00
16	Sunn	12.00
17	Henequen	14.00
18	Maguey	14.00
19	Acetate	9.00
20	Alginate	20.00
21	Cupro	13.00
22	Modal	13.00
23	Protein	17.00
24	Triacetate	7.00
25	Viscose	13.00
26	Acrylic	2.00
27	Chlorofibre	2.00
28	Fluorofibre	0.00
29	Modacrylic	2.00
30	Polyamide or nylon:	
	discontinuous fibre	6.25
	filament	5.75
31	Aramid	8.00
32	Polyimide	3.50
33	Lyocell	13.00
34	Polylactide	1.50
35	Polyester	1.50
36	Polyethylene	1.50
37	Polypropylene	2.00

Fibre No	Fibres	Percentages
38	Polycarbamide	2.00
39	Polyurethane:	
	discontinuous fibre	3.50
	filament	3.00
40	Vinylal	5.00
41	Trivinyl	3.00
42	Elastodiene	1.00
43	Elastane	1.50
44	Glass fibre:	
	with an average diameter of over 5 μm	2.00
	with an average diameter of 5 μm or less	3.00
45	Elastomultiester	1.50
46	Elastolefin	1.50
47	Melamine	7.00
48	Metal fibre	2.00
	Metallised fibre	2.00
	Asbestos	2.00
	Paper yarn	13.75
[49	Polypropylene/polyamide bicomponent	1.00]

NOTES

Entry in square brackets added by Commission Delegated Regulation 286/2012/EU, Art 1, Annex, para (3).

[1] The agreed allowances of 17.00% shall also be applied where it is impossible to ascertain whether the textile product containing wool and/or animal hair is combed or carded.

ANNEX X
CORRELATION TABLES

[8.560]

Directive 2008/121/EC	This Regulation
Article 1(1)	Article 4
Article 1(2)(a)-(c)	—
Article 1(2)(d)	Article 2(3)
Article 2(1)	Article 3(1)
Article 2(2) introductory wording	Article 2(2) introductory wording
Article 2(2)(a)	Article 2(2)(a)
Article 2(2)(b)	Article 2(2)(b) and (c)
Article 2(2)(c)	Article 2(2)(d)
Article 3	Article 5
Article 4	Article 7
Article 5	Article 8
Article 6(1) and (2)	—
Article 6(3)	Article 9(3)
Article 6(4)	Article 9(4)
Article 6(5)	Article 20
Article 7	Article 10
Article 8(1) first sentence	Article 14(1)
Article 8(1) second sentence	Article 14(2)
Article 8(2)	Article 14(3)
Article 8(3) first subparagraph	Article 16(1)
Article 8(3) second and third subparagraph	Article 16(2)
Article 8(4)	Article 16(3)
Article 8(5)	—
Article 9(1)	Article 11(1) and (2)

Directive 2008/121/EC	This Regulation
Article 9(2)	Article 11(3)
Article 9(3)	Article 13 and Annex IV
Article 10(1)(a)	Article 17(2)
Article 10(1)(b)	Article 17(3)
Article 10(1)(c)	Article 17(4)
Article 10(2)	Article 17(5)
Article 11	Article 15(4)
Article 12	Article 19(2) and Annex VII
Article 13(1)	Article 19(1)
Article 13(2)	—
Article 14(1)	—
Article 14(2)	—
Article 15	Article 21
Article 16	—
Article 17	—
Article 18	—
Article 19	—
Article 20	—
Annex I	Annex I
Annex II	Annex III
Annex III	Annex V
Annex III point 36	Article 3(1)(j)
Annex IV	Annex VI
Annex V	Annex IX
Annex VI	—
Annex VII	—

Directive 96/73/EC	This Regulation
Article 1	Article 1
Article 2	Annex VIII Chapter 1 Section I (2)
Article 3	Article 19(1)
Article 4	Article 19(4)
Article 5	Article 21
Article 6	—
Article 7	—
Article 8	—
Article 9	—
Annex I	Annex VIII Chapter 1 Section I
Annex II	Annex VIII Chapter 1 Section II and Chapter 2
Annex III	—
Annex IV	—

Directive 73/44/EEC	This Regulation
Article 1	Article 1
Article 2	Annex VIII Chapter 1 Section I
Article 3	Article 19(1)
Article 4	Article 19(4)
Article 5	Article 21
Article 6	—
Article 7	—

Directive 73/44/EEC	This Regulation
Annex I	Annex VIII Chapter 3 introduction and Sections I to III
Annex II	Annex VIII Chapter 3 Section IV
Annex III	Annex VIII Chapter 3 Section V

[STATEMENT BY THE EUROPEAN PARLIAMENT AND THE COUNCIL

[8.561]
The European Parliament and the Council are mindful of the importance of providing accurate information to consumers, in particular when products are marked with an indication of origin, so as to protect them against fraudulent, inaccurate or misleading claims. The use of new technologies, such as electronic labelling, including radio frequency identification, may be a useful tool to provide such information while keeping pace with technical development. The European Parliament and the Council invite the Commission, when drawing up the report pursuant to Article 24 of the Regulation, to consider their impact on possible new labelling requirements, including with a view to improve the traceability of products.]

NOTES
Added by Addendum (OJ L272 18.10.2011, p 1).

EUROPEAN PARLIAMENT AND COUNCIL REGULATION

(1151/2012/EU)

of 21 November 2012

on quality schemes for agricultural products and foodstuffs

NOTES
Date of publication in OJ: L343, 14.12.2012, p 1.

THE EUROPEAN PARLIAMENT AND THE COUNCIL OF THE EUROPEAN UNION,

Having regard to the Treaty on the Functioning of the European Union, and in particular Article 43(2) and the first paragraph of Article 118 thereof,

Having regard to the proposal from the European Commission,

After transmission of the draft legislative act to the national parliaments,

Having regard to the opinion of the European Economic and Social Committee,[1]

Having regard to the opinion of the Committee of the Regions,[2]

Acting in accordance with the ordinary legislative procedure,[3]

Whereas:

(1) The quality and diversity of the Union's agricultural, fisheries and aquaculture production is one of its important strengths, giving a competitive advantage to the Union's producers and making a major contribution to its living cultural and gastronomic heritage. This is due to the skills and determination of Union farmers and producers who have kept traditions alive while taking into account the developments of new production methods and material.

(2) Citizens and consumers in the Union increasingly demand quality as well as traditional products. They are also concerned to maintain the diversity of the agricultural production in the Union. This generates a demand for agricultural products or foodstuffs with identifiable specific characteristics, in particular those linked to their geographical origin.

(3) Producers can only continue to produce a diverse range of quality products if they are rewarded fairly for their effort. This requires that they are able to communicate to buyers and consumers the characteristics of their product under conditions of fair competition. It also requires them to be able to correctly identify their products on the marketplace.

(4) Operating quality schemes for producers which reward them for their efforts to produce a diverse range of quality products can benefit the rural economy. This is particularly the case in less favoured areas, in mountain areas and in the most remote regions, where the farming sector accounts for a significant part of the economy and production costs are high. In this way quality schemes are able to contribute to and complement rural development policy as well as market and income support policies of the common agricultural policy (CAP). In particular, they may contribute to areas in which the farming sector is of greater economic importance and, especially, to disadvantaged areas.

(5) The Europe 2020 policy priorities as set out in the Commission Communication entitled 'Europe 2020: A strategy for smart, sustainable and inclusive growth', include the aims of achieving a competitive economy based on knowledge and innovation and fostering a high-employment economy delivering social and territorial cohesion. Agricultural product quality policy should

therefore provide producers with the right tools to better identify and promote those of their products that have specific characteristics while protecting those producers against unfair practices.

(6) The set of complementary measures envisaged should respect the principles of subsidiarity and proportionality.

(7) Agricultural product quality policy measures are laid down in Council Regulation (EEC) No 1601/91 of 10 June 1991 laying down general rules on the definition, description and presentation of aromatized wines, aromatized wine-based drinks and aromatized wine-product cocktails;[4] Council Directive 2001/110/EC of 20 December 2001 relating to honey[5] and in particular in Article 2 thereof, Council Regulation (EC) No 247/2006 of 30 January 2006 laying down specific measures for agriculture in the outermost regions of the Union[6] and in particular in Article 14 thereof; Council Regulation (EC) No 509/2006 of 20 March 2006 on agricultural products and foodstuffs as traditional specialities guaranteed;[7] Council Regulation (EC) No 510/2006 of 20 March 2006 on the protection of geographical indications and designations of origin for agricultural products and foodstuffs;[8] Council Regulation (EC) No 1234/2007 of 22 October 2007 establishing a common organisation of agricultural markets and on specific provisions for certain agricultural products (Single CMO Regulation)[9] and in particular in Part II, Title II, Chapter I, Section I and in Section Ia, Subsection I thereof; Council Regulation (EC) No 834/2007 of 28 June 2007 on organic production and labelling of organic products;[10] and Regulation (EC) No 110/2008 of the European Parliament and of the Council of 15 January 2008 on the definition, description, presentation, labelling and the protection of geographical indications of spirit drinks.[11]

(8) The labelling of agricultural products and foodstuffs should be subject to the general rules laid down in Directive 2000/13/EC of the European Parliament and of the Council of 20 March 2000 on the approximation of the laws of the Member States relating to the labelling, presentation and advertising of foodstuffs,[12] and in particular the provisions aimed at preventing labelling that may confuse or mislead consumers.

(9) The Communication from the Commission to the European Parliament, the Council, the European Economic and Social Committee and the Committee of the Regions on agricultural product quality policy identified the achievement of a greater overall coherence and consistency of agricultural product quality policy as a priority.

(10) The geographical indications scheme for agricultural products and foodstuffs and the traditional specialities guaranteed scheme have certain common objectives and provisions.

(11) The Union has for some time been pursuing an approach that aims to simplify the regulatory framework of the CAP. This approach should also be applied to regulations in the field of agricultural product quality policy, without, in so doing, calling into question the specific characteristics of those products.

(12) Some regulations that form part of the agricultural product quality policy have been reviewed recently but are not yet fully implemented. As a result, they should not be included in this Regulation. However, they may be incorporated at a later stage, once the legislation has been fully implemented.

(13) In the light of the aforementioned considerations, the following provisions should be amalgamated into a single legal framework comprising the new or updated provisions of Regulations (EC) No 509/2006 and (EC) No 510/2006 and those provisions of Regulations (EC) No 509/2006 and (EC) No 510/2006 that are maintained.

(14) In the interests of clarity and transparency, Regulations (EC) No 509/2006 and (EC) No 510/2006 should therefore be repealed and replaced by this Regulation.

(15) The scope of this Regulation should be limited to the agricultural products intended for human consumption listed in Annex I to the Treaty and to a list of products outside the scope of that Annex that are closely linked to agricultural production or to the rural economy.

(16) The rules provided for in this Regulation should apply without affecting existing Union legislation on wines, aromatised wines, spirit drinks, product of organic farming, or outermost regions.

(17) The scope for designations of origin and geographical indications should be limited to products for which an intrinsic link exists between product or foodstuff characteristics and geographical origin. The inclusion in the current scheme of only certain types of chocolate as confectionery products is an anomaly that should be corrected.

(18) The specific objectives of protecting designations of origin and geographical indications are securing a fair return for farmers and producers for the qualities and characteristics of a given product, or of its mode of production, and providing clear information on products with specific characteristics linked to geographical origin, thereby enabling consumers to make more informed purchasing choices.

(19) Ensuring uniform respect throughout the Union for the intellectual property rights related to names protected in the Union is a priority that can be achieved more effectively at Union level.

(20) A Union framework that protects designations of origin and geographical indications by providing for their inclusion on a register facilitates the development of those instruments, since the

resulting, more uniform, approach ensures fair competition between the producers of products bearing such indications and enhances the credibility of the products in the consumers' eyes. Provision should be made for the development of designations of origin and geographical indications at Union level and for promoting the creation of mechanisms for their protection in third countries in the framework of the World Trade Organisation (WTO) or multilateral and bilateral agreements, thereby contributing to the recognition of the quality of products and of their model of production as a factor that adds value.

(21) In the light of the experience gained from the implementation of Council Regulation (EEC) No 2081/92 of 14 July 1992 on the protection of geographical indications and designations of origin for agricultural products and foodstuffs[13] and Regulation (EC) No 510/2006, there is a need to address certain issues, to clarify and simplify some rules and to streamline the procedures of this scheme.

(22) In the light of existing practice, the two different instruments for identifying the link between the product and its geographical origin, namely the protected designation of origin and the protected geographical indication, should be further defined and maintained. Without changing the concept of those instruments, some modifications to the definitions should be adopted in order to better take into account the definition of geographical indications laid down in the Agreement on Trade-Related Aspects of Intellectual Property Rights and to make them simpler and clearer for operators to understand.

(23) An agricultural product or foodstuff bearing such a geographical description should meet certain conditions set out in a specification, such as specific requirements aimed at protecting the natural resources or landscape of the production area or improving the welfare of farm animals.

(24) To qualify for protection in the territories of Member States, designations of origin and geographical indications should be registered only at Union level. With effect from the date of application for such registration at Union level, Member States should be able to grant transitional protection at national level without affecting intra-Union or international trade. The protection afforded by this Regulation upon registration, should be equally available to designations of origin and geographical indications of third countries that meet the corresponding criteria and that are protected in their country of origin.

(25) The registration procedure at Union level should enable any natural or legal person with a legitimate interest from a Member State, other than the Member State of the application, or from a third country, to exercise their rights by notifying their opposition.

(26) Entry in the register of protected designations of origin and protected geographical indications should also provide information to consumers and to those involved in trade.

(27) The Union negotiates international agreements, including those concerning the protection of designations of origin and geographical indications, with its trade partners. In order to facilitate the provision to the public of information about the names so protected, and in particular to ensure protection and control of the use to which those names are put, the names may be entered in the register of protected designations of origin and protected geographical indications. Unless specifically identified as designations of origin in such international agreements, the names should be entered in the register as protected geographical indications.

(28) In view of their specific nature, special provisions concerning labelling should be adopted in respect of protected designations of origin and protected geographical indications that require producers to use the appropriate Union symbols or indications on packaging. In the case of Union names, the use of such symbols or indications should be made obligatory in order to make this category of products, and the guarantees attached to them, better known to consumers and in order to permit easier identification of these products on the market, thereby facilitating checks. Taking into account the requirements of the WTO, the use of such symbols or indications should be made voluntary for third-country geographical indications and designations of origin.

(29) Protection should be granted to names included in the register with the aim of ensuring that they are used fairly and in order to prevent practices liable to mislead consumers. In addition, the means of ensuring that geographical indications and designations of origin are protected should be clarified, particularly as regards the role of producer groups and competent authorities of Member States.

(30) Provision should be made for specific derogations that permit, for transitional periods, the use of a registered name alongside other names. Those derogations should be simplified and clarified. In certain cases, in order to overcome temporary difficulties and with the long-term objective of ensuring that all producers comply with the specifications, those derogations may be granted for a period of up to 10 years.

(31) The scope of the protection granted under this Regulation should be clarified, in particular with regard to those limitations on registration of new trade marks set out in Directive 2008/95/EC of the European Parliament and of the Council of 22 October 2008 to approximate the laws of the Member States relating to trade marks[14] that conflict with the registration of protected designations of origin and protected geographical indications as is already the case for the registration of new trade marks at Union level. Such clarification is also necessary with regard to the holders of prior

rights in intellectual property, in particular those concerning trade marks and homonymous names registered as protected designations of origin or as protected geographical indications.

(32) Protection of designations of origin and geographical indications should be extended to the misuse, imitation and evocation of the registered names on goods as well as on services in order to ensure a high level of protection and to align that protection with that which applies to the wine sector. When protected designations of origin or protected geographical indications are used as ingredients, the Commission Communication entitled 'Guidelines on the labelling of foodstuffs using protected designations of origin (PDOs) or protected geographical indications (PGIs) as ingredients' should be taken into account.

(33) The names already registered under Regulation (EC) No 510/2006 on 3 January 2013 should continue to be protected under this Regulation and they should be automatically included in the register.

(34) The specific objective of the scheme for traditional specialities guaranteed is to help the producers of traditional products to communicate to consumers the value-adding attributes of their product. However, as only a few names have been registered, the current scheme for traditional specialities guaranteed has failed to realise its potential. Current provisions should therefore be improved, clarified and sharpened in order to make the scheme more understandable, operational and attractive to potential applicants.

(35) The current scheme provides the option to register a name for identification purposes without reservation of the name in the Union. As this option has not been well understood by stakeholders and since the function of identifying traditional products can be better achieved at Member State or regional level in application of the principle of subsidiarity, this option should be discontinued. In the light of experience, the scheme should only deal with the reservation of names across the Union.

(36) To ensure that names of genuine traditional products are registered under the scheme, the criteria and conditions for registration of a name should be adapted, in particular those concerning the definition of 'traditional', which should cover products that have been produced for a significant period of time.

(37) To ensure that traditional specialities guaranteed comply with their specification and are consistent, producers organised into groups should themselves define the product in a specification. The option of registering a name as a traditional speciality guaranteed should be open to third-country producers.

(38) To qualify for reservation, traditional specialities guaranteed should be registered at Union level. The entry in the register should also provide information to consumers and to those involved in the trade.

(39) In order to avoid creating unfair conditions of competition, any producer, including a third-country producer, should be able to use a registered name of a traditional speciality guaranteed, provided that the product concerned complies with the requirements of the relevant specification and the producer is covered by a system of controls. For traditional specialities guaranteed produced within the Union, the Union symbol should be indicated on the labelling and it should be possible to associate it with the indication 'traditional speciality guaranteed'.

(40) In order to protect registered names from misuse, or from practices that might mislead consumers, their use should be reserved.

(41) For those names already registered under Regulation (EC) No 509/2006 that, on 3 January 2013, would otherwise not be covered by the scope of this Regulation, the terms of use laid down in Regulation (EC) No 509/2006 should continue to apply for a transitional period.

(42) A procedure should be introduced for registering names that are registered without reservation of name pursuant to Regulation (EC) No 509/2006, enabling them to be registered with reservation of name.

(43) Provision should also be made for transitional measures applicable to registration applications received by the Commission before 3 January 2013.

(44) A second tier of quality systems, based on quality terms which add value, which can be communicated on the internal market and which are to be applied voluntarily, should be introduced. Those optional quality terms should refer to specific horizontal characteristics, with regard to one or more categories of products, farming methods or processing attributes which apply in specific areas. The optional quality term 'mountain product' has met the conditions up to now and will add value to the product on the market. In order to facilitate the application of Directive 2000/13/EC where the labelling of foodstuffs may give rise to consumer confusion in relation to optional quality terms, including in particular 'mountain products', the Commission may adopt guidelines.

(45) In order to provide mountain producers with an effective tool to better market their product and to reduce the actual risks of consumer confusion as to the mountain provenance of products in the market place, provision should be made for the definition at Union level of an optional quality term for mountain products. The definition of mountain areas should build on the general classification criteria employed to identify a mountain area in Council Regulation (EC)

No 1257/1999 of 17 May 1999 on support for rural development from the European Agricultural Guidance and Guarantee Fund (EAGGF).[15]

(46) The added value of the geographical indications and traditional specialities guaranteed is based on consumer trust. It is only credible if accompanied by effective verification and controls. Those quality schemes should be subject to a monitoring system of official controls, in line with the principles set out in Regulation (EC) No 882/2004 of the European Parliament and of the Council of 29 April 2004 on official controls performed to ensure the verification of compliance with feed and food law, animal health and animal welfare rules,[16] and should include a system of checks at all stages of production, processing and distribution. In order to help Member States to better apply provisions of Regulation (EC) No 882/2004 for the controls of geographical indications and traditional specialities guaranteed, references to the most relevant articles should be mentioned in this Regulation.

(47) To guarantee to the consumer the specific characteristics of geographical indications and traditional specialities guaranteed, operators should be subject to a system that verifies compliance with the product specification.

(48) In order to ensure that they are impartial and effective, the competent authorities should meet a number of operational criteria. Provisions on delegating some competences of performing specific control tasks to control bodies should be envisaged.

(49) European standards (EN standards) developed by the European Committee for Standardisation (CEN) and international standards developed by the International Organisation for Standardisation (ISO) should be used for the accreditation of the control bodies as well as by those bodies for their operations. The accreditation of those bodies should take place in accordance with Regulation (EC) No 765/2008 of the European Parliament and of the Council of 9 July 2008 setting out the requirements for accreditation and market surveillance relating to the marketing of products.[17]

(50) Information on control activities for geographical indications and traditional specialities guaranteed should be included in the multiannual national control plans and annual report prepared by the Member States in accordance with Regulation (EC) No 882/2004.

(51) Member States should be authorised to charge a fee to cover the costs incurred.

(52) Existing rules concerning the continued use of names that are generic should be clarified so that generic terms that are similar to or form part of a name or term that is protected or reserved should retain their generic status.

(53) The date for establishing the seniority of a trade mark and of a designation of origin or a geographical indication should be that of the date of application of the trade mark for registration in the Union or in the Member States and the date of application for protection of a designation of origin or a geographical indication to the Commission.

(54) The provisions dealing with the refusal or coexistence of a designation of origin or a geographical indication on the ground of conflict with a prior trade mark should continue to apply.

(55) The criteria by which subsequent trade marks should be refused or, if registered, invalidated on the ground that they conflict with a prior designation of origin or geographical indication should correspond to the scope of protection of designation of origin or a geographical indication laid down.

(56) The provisions of systems establishing intellectual property rights, and particularly of those established by the quality scheme for designations of origin and geographical indications or those established under trade mark law, should not be affected by the reservation of names and the establishment of indications and symbols pursuant to the quality schemes for traditional specialities guaranteed and for optional quality terms.

(57) The role of groups should be clarified and recognised. Groups play an essential role in the application process for the registration of names of designations of origin and geographical indications and traditional specialities guaranteed, as well as in the amendment of specifications and cancellation requests. The group can also develop activities related to the surveillance of the enforcement of the protection of the registered names, the compliance of the production with the product specification, the information and promotion of the registered name as well as, in general, any activity aimed at improving the value of the registered names and effectiveness of the quality schemes. Moreover, it should monitor the position of the products on the market. Nevertheless, these activities should not facilitate nor lead to anti-competitive conduct incompatible with Articles 101 and 102 of the Treaty.

(58) To ensure that registered names of designations of origin and geographical indications and traditional specialities guaranteed meet the conditions laid down by this Regulation, applications should be examined by the national authorities of the Member State concerned, in compliance with minimum common provisions, including a national opposition procedure. The Commission should subsequently scrutinise applications to ensure that there are no manifest errors and that Union law and the interests of stakeholders outside the Member State of application have been taken into account.

(59) Registration as designations of origin, geographical indications and traditional specialities

guaranteed should be open to names that relate to products originating in third countries and that satisfy the conditions laid down by this Regulation.

(60) The symbols, indications and abbreviations identifying participation in a quality scheme, and the rights therein pertaining to the Union, should be protected in the Union as well as in third countries with the aim of ensuring that they are used on genuine products and that consumers are not misled as to the qualities of products. Furthermore, in order for the protection to be effective, the Commission should have recourse to reasonable budget resources on a centralised basis within the framework of Council Regulation (EC) No 1698/2005 of 20 September 2005 on support for rural development by the European Agricultural Fund for Rural Development (EAFRD)[18] and in accordance with Article 5 of Council Regulation (EC) No 1290/2005 of 21 June 2005 on the financing of the common agricultural policy.[19]

(61) The registration procedure for protected designations of origin, protected geographical indications and traditional specialities guaranteed, including the scrutiny and the opposition periods, should be shortened and improved, in particular as regards decision making. The Commission, in certain circumstances acting with the assistance of Member States, should be responsible for decision-making on registration. Procedures should be laid down to allow the amendment of product specifications after registration and the cancellation of registered names, in particular if the product no longer complies with the corresponding product specification or if a name is no longer used in the market place.

(62) In order to facilitate cross-border applications for joint registration of protected designations of origin, protected geographical indications or traditional specialities guaranteed, provision should be made for appropriate procedures.

(63) In order to supplement or amend certain non-essential elements of this Regulation, the power to adopt acts in accordance with Article 290 of the Treaty should be delegated to the Commission in respect of supplementing the list of products set out in Annex I to this Regulation; establishing the restrictions and derogations with regard to the sourcing of feed in the case of a designation of origin; establishing restrictions and derogations with regard to the slaughtering of live animals or with regard to the sourcing of raw materials; laying down rules which limit the information contained in the product specification; establishing the Union symbols; laying down additional transitional rules in order to protect the rights and legitimate interests of producers or stakeholders concerned; laying down further details on the eligibility criteria for the names of traditional specialities guaranteed; laying down detailed rules relating to the criteria for optional quality terms; reserving an additional optional quality term, laying down its conditions of use and amending those conditions; laying down derogations to the use of the term 'mountain product' and establishing the methods of production, and other criteria relevant for the application of that optional quality term, in particular, laying down the conditions under which raw materials or feedstuffs are permitted to come from outside the mountain areas; laying down additional rules for determining the generic status of terms in the Union; laying down rules for determining the use of the name of a plant variety or of an animal breed; defining the rules for carrying out the national objection procedure for joint applications concerning more than one national territory; and for complementing the rules of the application process, the opposition process, the amendment application process and the cancellation process in general. It is of particular importance that the Commission carry out appropriate consultations during its preparatory work, including at expert level. The Commission, when preparing and drawing up delegated acts, should ensure a simultaneous, timely and appropriate transmission of relevant documents to the European Parliament and to the Council.

(64) In order to ensure uniform conditions for the implementation of this Regulation, implementing powers should be conferred on the Commission as regards laying down rules on the form of the product specification; laying down detailed rules on the form and content of the register of protected designations of origin and protected geographical indications; defining the technical characteristics of the Union symbols and indications as well as the rules on their use on products, including the appropriate linguistic versions to be used; granting and extending transitional periods for temporary derogations for use of protected designations of origin and protected geographical indication; laying down detailed rules on the form and content of the register of traditional specialities guaranteed; laying down rules for the protection of traditional specialities guaranteed; laying down all measures relating to forms, procedures and other technical details for the application of Title IV; laying down rules for the use of optional quality terms; laying down rules for the uniform protection of indications, abbreviations and symbols referring to the quality schemes; laying down detailed rules on the procedure, form and presentation of applications for registration and of oppositions; rejecting the application; deciding on the registration of a name if an agreement has not been reached; laying down detailed rules on the procedure, form and presentation of an amendment application; cancelling the registration of a protected designation of origin, a protected geographical indication or a traditional speciality guaranteed; and laying down detailed rules on the procedure and form of the cancellation process and on the presentation of the requests for cancellation. Those powers should be exercised in accordance with Regulation (EU) No 182/2011 of the European Parliament and of the Council of 16 February 2011 laying down the rules and general principles concerning mechanisms for control by Member States of the Commission's exercise of implementing powers.[20]

(65) In respect of establishing and maintaining registers of protected designations of origin, protected geographical indications and traditional specialties guaranteed, recognised under this scheme; defining the means by which the name and address of product certification bodies are to be made public; and registering a name if there is no notice of opposition or no admissible reasoned statement of opposition or in the case there is one the agreement has been reached, the Commission should be empowered to adopt implementing acts without applying Regulation (EU) No 182/2011,

NOTES

[1] OJ C218, 23.7.2011, p 114.

[2] OJ C192, 1.7.2011, p 28.

[3] Position of the European Parliament of 13 September 2012 (not yet published in the Official Journal) and decision of the Council of 13 November 2012.

[4] OJ L149, 14.6.1991, p 1.

[5] OJ L10, 12.1.2002, p 47.

[6] OJ L42, 14.2.2006, p 1.

[7] OJ L93, 31.3.2006, p 1.

[8] OJ L93, 31.3.2006, p 12.

[9] OJ L299, 16.11.2007, p 1.

[10] OJ L189, 20.7.2007, p 1.

[11] OJ L39, 13.2.2008, p 16.

[12] OJ L109, 6.5.2000, p 29.

[13] OJ L208, 24.7.1992, p 1.

[14] OJ L299, 8.11.2008, p 25.

[15] OJ L160, 26.6.1999, p 80.

[16] OJ L165, 30.4.2004, p 1.

[17] OJ L218, 13.8.2008, p 30.

[18] OJ L277, 21.10.2005, p 1.

[19] OJ L209, 11.8.2005, p 1.

[20] OJ L55, 28.2.2011, p 13.

HAVE ADOPTED THIS REGULATION:

TITLE I
GENERAL PROVISIONS

[8.562]
Article 1
Objectives

1. This Regulation aims to help producers of agricultural products and foodstuffs to communicate the product characteristics and farming attributes of those products and foodstuffs to buyers and consumers, thereby ensuring:

(a) fair competition for farmers and producers of agricultural products and foodstuffs having value-adding characteristics and attributes;
(b) the availability to consumers of reliable information pertaining to such products;
(c) respect for intellectual property rights; and
(d) the integrity of the internal market.

The measures set out in this Regulation are intended to support agricultural and processing activities and the farming systems associated with high quality products, thereby contributing to the achievement of rural development policy objectives.

2. This Regulation establishes quality schemes which provide the basis for the identification and, where appropriate, protection of names and terms that, in particular, indicate or describe agricultural products with:

(a) value-adding characteristics; or
(b) value-adding attributes as a result of the farming or processing methods used in their production, or of the place of their production or marketing.

[8.563]
Article 2
Scope

1. This Regulation covers agricultural products intended for human consumption listed in Annex I to the Treaty and other agricultural products and foodstuffs listed in Annex I to this Regulation.
In order to take into account international commitments or new production methods or material, the Commission shall be empowered to adopt delegated acts, in accordance with Article 56, supplementing the list of products set out in Annex I to this Regulation. Such products shall be closely linked to agricultural products or to the rural economy.

2. This Regulation shall not apply to spirit drinks, aromatised wines or grapevine products as defined in Annex XIb to Regulation (EC) No 1234/2007, with the exception of wine-vinegars.
3. This Regulation shall apply without prejudice to other specific Union provisions relating to the placing of products on the market and, in particular, to the single common organisation of the markets, and to food labelling.
4. Directive 98/34/EC of the European Parliament and of the Council of 22 June 1998 laying down a procedure for the provision of information in the field of technical standards and regulations and of rules on Information Society services[1] shall not apply to the quality schemes established by this Regulation.

NOTES

[1] OJ L204, 21.7.1998, p 37.

[8.564]
Article 3
Definitions

For the purposes of this Regulation the following definitions shall apply:

(1) 'quality schemes' means the schemes established under Titles II, III and IV;
(2) 'group' means any association, irrespective of its legal form, mainly composed of producers or processors working with the same product;
(3) 'traditional' means proven usage on the domestic market for a period that allows transmission between generations; this period is to be at least 30 years;
(4) 'labelling' means any words, particulars, trade marks, brand name, pictorial matter or symbol relating to a foodstuff and placed on any packaging, document, notice, label, ring or collar accompanying or referring to such foodstuff;
(5) 'specific character' in relation to a product means the characteristic production attributes which distinguish a product clearly from other similar products of the same category;
(6) 'generic terms' means the names of products which, although relating to the place, region or country where the product was originally produced or marketed, have become the common name of a product in the Union;
(7) 'production step' means production, processing or preparation;
(8) 'processed products' means foodstuffs resulting from the processing of unprocessed products. Processed products may contain ingredients that are necessary for their manufacture or to give them specific characteristics.

TITLE II
PROTECTED DESIGNATIONS OF ORIGIN AND PROTECTED GEOGRAPHICAL INDICATIONS

[8.565]
Article 4
Objective

A scheme for protected designations of origin and protected geographical indications is established in order to help producers of products linked to a geographical area by:

(a) securing fair returns for the qualities of their products;
(b) ensuring uniform protection of the names as an intellectual property right in the territory of the Union;
(c) providing clear information on the value-adding attributes of the product to consumers.

[8.566]
Article 5
Requirements for designations of origin and geographical indications

1. For the purpose of this Regulation, 'designation of origin' is a name which identifies a product:
(a) originating in a specific place, region or, in exceptional cases, a country;
(b) whose quality or characteristics are essentially or exclusively due to a particular geographical environment with its inherent natural and human factors; and
(c) the production steps of which all take place in the defined geographical area.

2. For the purpose of this Regulation, 'geographical indication' is a name which identifies a product:
(a) originating in a specific place, region or country;
(b) whose given quality, reputation or other characteristic is essentially attributable to its geographical origin; and
(c) at least one of the production steps of which take place in the defined geographical area.

3. Notwithstanding paragraph 1, certain names shall be treated as designations of origin even though the raw materials for the products concerned come from a geographical area larger than, or different from, the defined geographical area, provided that:
(a) the production area of the raw materials is defined;
(b) special conditions for the production of the raw materials exist;

(c) there are control arrangements to ensure that the conditions referred to in point (b) are adhered to; and

(d) the designations of origin in question were recognised as designations of origin in the country of origin before 1 May 2004.

Only live animals, meat and milk may be considered as raw materials for the purposes of this paragraph.

4. In order to take into account the specific character of production of products of animal origin, the Commission shall be empowered to adopt delegated acts, in accordance with Article 56, concerning restrictions and derogations with regard to the sourcing of feed in the case of a designation of origin.

In addition, in order to take into account the specific character of certain products or areas, the Commission shall be empowered to adopt delegated acts in accordance with Article 56, concerning restrictions and derogations with regard to the slaughtering of live animals or with regard to the sourcing of raw materials.

These restrictions and derogations shall, based on objective criteria, take into account quality or usage and recognised know-how or natural factors.

[8.567]

Article 6

Generic nature, conflicts with names of plant varieties and animal breeds, with homonyms and trade marks

1. Generic terms shall not be registered as protected designations of origin or protected geographical indications.

2. A name may not be registered as a designation of origin or geographical indication where it conflicts with a name of a plant variety or an animal breed and is likely to mislead the consumer as to the true origin of the product.

3. A name proposed for registration that is wholly or partially homonymous with a name already entered in the register established under Article 11 may not be registered unless there is sufficient distinction in practice between the conditions of local and traditional usage and presentation of the homonym registered subsequently and the name already entered in the register, taking into account the need to ensure equitable treatment of the producers concerned and that consumers are not misled.

A homonymous name which misleads the consumer into believing that products come from another territory shall not be registered even if the name is accurate as far as the actual territory, region or place of origin of the products in question is concerned.

4. A name proposed for registration as a designation of origin or geographical indication shall not be registered where, in the light of a trade mark's reputation and renown and the length of time it has been used, registration of the name proposed as the designation of origin or geographical indication would be liable to mislead the consumer as to the true identity of the product.

[8.568]

Article 7

Product specification

1. A protected designation of origin or a protected geographical indication shall comply with a specification which shall include at least:

(a) the name to be protected as a designation of origin or geographical indication, as it is used, whether in trade or in common language, and only in the languages which are or were historically used to describe the specific product in the defined geographical area;

(b) a description of the product, including the raw materials, if appropriate, as well as the principal physical, chemical, microbiological or organoleptic characteristics of the product;

(c) the definition of the geographical area delimited with regard to the link referred to in point (f)(i) or (ii) of this paragraph, and, where appropriate, details indicating compliance with the requirements of Article 5(3);

(d) evidence that the product originates in the defined geographical area referred to in Article 5(1) or (2);

(e) a description of the method of obtaining the product and, where appropriate, the authentic and unvarying local methods as well as information concerning packaging, if the applicant group so determines and gives sufficient product-specific justification as to why the packaging must take place in the defined geographical area to safeguard quality, to ensure the origin or to ensure control, taking into account Union law, in particular that on the free movement of goods and the free provision of services;

(f) details establishing the following:

(i) the link between the quality or characteristics of the product and the geographical environment referred to in Article 5(1); or

(ii) where appropriate, the link between a given quality, the reputation or other characteristic of the product and the geographical origin referred to in Article 5(2);

(g) the name and address of the authorities or, if available, the name and address of bodies verifying compliance with the provisions of the product specification pursuant to Article 37 and their specific tasks;

(h) any specific labelling rule for the product in question.

2. In order to ensure that product specifications provide relevant and succinct information, the Commission shall be empowered to adopt delegated acts, in accordance with Article 56, laying down rules which limit the information contained in the specification referred to in paragraph 1 of this Article, where such a limitation is necessary to avoid excessively voluminous applications for registration.

The Commission may adopt implementing acts laying down rules on the form of the specification. Those implementing acts shall be adopted in accordance with the examination procedure referred to in Article 57(2).

[8.569]
Article 8
Content of application for registration

1. An application for registration of a designation of origin or geographical indication pursuant to Article 49(2) or (5) shall include at least:

(a) the name and address of the applicant group and of the authorities or, if available, bodies verifying compliance with the provisions of the product specification;
(b) the product specification provided for in Article 7;
(c) a single document setting out the following:
  (i) the main points of the product specification: the name, a description of the product, including, where appropriate, specific rules concerning packaging and labelling, and a concise definition of the geographical area;
  (ii) a description of the link between the product and the geographical environment or geographical origin referred to in Article 5(1) or (2), as the case may be, including, where appropriate, the specific elements of the product description or production method justifying the link.

An application as referred to in Article 49(5) shall, in addition, include proof that the name of the product is protected in its country of origin.

2. An application dossier referred to in Article 49(4) shall comprise:

(a) the name and address of the applicant group;
(b) the single document referred to in point (c) of paragraph 1 of this Article;
(c) a declaration by the Member State that it considers that the application lodged by the applicant group and qualifying for the favourable decision meets the conditions of this Regulation and the provisions adopted pursuant thereto;
(d) the publication reference of the product specification.

[8.570]
Article 9
Transitional national protection

A Member State may, on a transitional basis only, grant protection to a name under this Regulation at national level, with effect from the date on which an application is lodged with the Commission.

Such national protection shall cease on the date on which either a decision on registration under this Regulation is taken or the application is withdrawn.

Where a name is not registered under this Regulation, the consequences of such national protection shall be the sole responsibility of the Member State concerned.

The measures taken by Member States under the first paragraph shall produce effects at national level only, and they shall have no effect on intra-Union or international trade.

[8.571]
Article 10
Grounds for opposition

1. A reasoned statement of opposition as referred to in Article 51(2) shall be admissible only if it is received by the Commission within the time limit set out in that paragraph and if it:

(a) shows that the conditions referred to in Article 5 and Article 7(1) are not complied with;
(b) shows that the registration of the name proposed would be contrary to Article 6(2), (3) or (4);
(c) shows that the registration of the name proposed would jeopardise the existence of an entirely or partly identical name or of a trade mark or the existence of products which have been legally on the market for at least five years preceding the date of the publication provided for in point (a) of Article 50(2); or
(d) gives details from which it can be concluded that the name for which registration is requested is a generic term.

2. The grounds for opposition shall be assessed in relation to the territory of the Union.

[8.572]
Article 11
Register of protected designations of origin and protected geographical indications

1. The Commission shall adopt implementing acts, without applying the procedure referred to in Article 57(2), establishing and maintaining a publicly accessible updated register of protected designations of origin and protected geographical indications recognised under this scheme.

2. Geographical indications pertaining to products of third countries that are protected in the Union under an international agreement to which the Union is a contracting party may be entered in the register. Unless specifically identified in the said agreement as protected designations of origin under this Regulation, such names shall be entered in the register as protected geographical indications.

3. The Commission may adopt implementing acts laying down detailed rules on the form and content of the register. Those implementing acts shall be adopted in accordance with the examination procedure referred to in Article 57(2).

4. The Commission shall make public and regularly update the list of the international agreements referred to in paragraph 2 as well as the list of geographical indications protected under those agreements.

[8.573]

Article 12

Names, symbols and indications

1. Protected designations of origin and protected geographical indications may be used by any operator marketing a product conforming to the corresponding specification.

2. Union symbols designed to publicise protected designations of origin and protected geographical indications shall be established.

3. In the case of products originating in the Union that are marketed under a protected designation of origin or a protected geographical indication registered in accordance with the procedures laid down in this Regulation, the Union symbols associated with them shall appear on the labelling. In addition, the registered name of the product should appear in the same field of vision. The indications 'protected designation of origin' or 'protected geographical indication' or the corresponding abbreviations 'PDO' or 'PGI' may appear on the labelling.

4. In addition, the following may also appear on the labelling: depictions of the geographical area of origin, as referred to in Article 5, and text, graphics or symbols referring to the Member State and/or region in which that geographical area of origin is located.

5. Without prejudice to Directive 2000/13/EC, the collective geographical marks referred to in Article 15 of Directive 2008/95/EC may be used on labels, together with the protected designation of origin or protected geographical indication.

6. In the case of products originating in third countries marketed under a name entered in the register, the indications referred to in paragraph 3 or the Union symbols associated with them may appear on the labelling.

7. In order to ensure that the appropriate information is communicated to the consumer, the Commission shall be empowered to adopt delegated acts, in accordance with Article 56, establishing the Union symbols.

The Commission may adopt implementing acts defining the technical characteristics of the Union symbols and indications as well as the rules of their use on the products marketed under a protected designation of origin or a protected geographical indication, including rules concerning the appropriate linguistic versions to be used. Those implementing acts shall be adopted in accordance with the examination procedure referred to in Article 57(2).

[8.574]

Article 13

Protection

1. Registered names shall be protected against:

(a) any direct or indirect commercial use of a registered name in respect of products not covered by the registration where those products are comparable to the products registered under that name or where using the name exploits the reputation of the protected name, including when those products are used as an ingredient;

(b) any misuse, imitation or evocation, even if the true origin of the products or services is indicated or if the protected name is translated or accompanied by an expression such as 'style', 'type', 'method', 'as produced in', 'imitation' or similar, including when those products are used as an ingredient;

(c) any other false or misleading indication as to the provenance, origin, nature or essential qualities of the product that is used on the inner or outer packaging, advertising material or documents relating to the product concerned, and the packing of the product in a container liable to convey a false impression as to its origin;

(d) any other practice liable to mislead the consumer as to the true origin of the product.

Where a protected designation of origin or a protected geographical indication contains within it the name of a product which is considered to be generic, the use of that generic name shall not be considered to be contrary to points (a) or (b) of the first subparagraph.

2. Protected designations of origin and protected geographical indications shall not become generic.

3. Member States shall take appropriate administrative and judicial steps to prevent or stop the unlawful use of protected designations of origin and protected geographical indications, as referred to in paragraph 1, that are produced or marketed in that Member State.

To that end Member States shall designate the authorities that are responsible for taking these steps in accordance with procedures determined by each individual Member State.

These authorities shall offer adequate guarantees of objectivity and impartiality, and shall have at their disposal the qualified staff and resources necessary to carry out their functions.

[8.575]

Article 14

Relations between trade marks, designations of origin and geographical indications

1. Where a designation of origin or a geographical indication is registered under this Regulation, the registration of a trade mark the use of which would contravene Article 13(1) and which relates to a product of the same type shall be refused if the application for registration of the trade mark is submitted after the date of submission of the registration application in respect of the designation of origin or the geographical indication to the Commission.

Trade marks registered in breach of the first subparagraph shall be invalidated.

The provisions of this paragraph shall apply notwithstanding the provisions of Directive 2008/95/EC.

2. Without prejudice to Article 6(4), a trade mark the use of which contravenes Article 13(1) which has been applied for, registered, or established by use if that possibility is provided for by the legislation concerned, in good faith within the territory of the Union, before the date on which the application for protection of the designation of origin or geographical indication is submitted to the Commission, may continue to be used and renewed for that product notwithstanding the registration of a designation of origin or geographical indication, provided that no grounds for its invalidity or revocation exist under Council Regulation (EC) No 207/2009 of 26 February 2009 on the Community trade mark[1] or under Directive 2008/95/EC. In such cases, the use of the protected designation of origin or protected geographical indication shall be permitted as well as use of the relevant trade marks.

NOTES

[1] OJ L78, 24.3.2009, p 1.

[8.576]

Article 15

Transitional periods for use of protected designations of origin and protected geographical indications

1. Without prejudice to Article 14, the Commission may adopt implementing acts granting a transitional period of up to five years to enable products originating in a Member State or a third country the designation of which consists of or contains a name that contravenes Article 13(1) to continue to use the designation under which it was marketed on condition that an admissible statement of opposition under Article 49(3) or Article 51 shows that:

(a) the registration of the name would jeopardise the existence of an entirely or partly identical name; or

(b) such products have been legally marketed with that name in the territory concerned for at least five years preceding the date of the publication provided for point (a) of Article 50(2).

Those implementing acts shall be adopted in accordance with the examination procedure referred to in Article 57(2).

2. Without prejudice to Article 14, the Commission may adopt implementing acts extending the transitional period mentioned in paragraph 1 of this Article to 15 years in duly justified cases where it is shown that:

(a) the designation referred to in paragraph 1 of this Article has been in legal use consistently and fairly for at least 25 years before the application for registration was submitted to the Commission;

(b) the purpose of using the designation referred to in paragraph 1 of this Article has not, at any time, been to profit from the reputation of the registered name and it is shown that the consumer has not been nor could have been misled as to the true origin of the product.

Those implementing acts shall be adopted in accordance with the examination procedure referred to in Article 57(2).

3. When using a designation referred to in paragraphs 1 and 2, the indication of country of origin shall clearly and visibly appear on the labelling.

4. To overcome temporary difficulties with the long-term objective of ensuring that all producers in the area concerned comply with the specification, a Member State may grant a transitional period of up to 10 years, with effect from the date on which the application is lodged with the Commission, on condition that the operators concerned have legally marketed the products in question, using the names concerned continuously for at least the five years prior to the lodging of the application to the authorities of the Member State and have made that point in the national opposition procedure referred to in Article 49(3).

The first subparagraph shall apply *mutatis mutandis* to a protected geographical indication or protected designation of origin referring to a geographical area situated in a third country, with the exception of the opposition procedure.

Such transitional periods shall be indicated in the application dossier referred to in Article 8(2).

[8.577]
Article 16
Transitional provisions

1. Names entered in the register provided for in Article 7(6) of Regulation (EC) No 510/2006 shall automatically be entered in the register referred to in Article 11 of this Regulation. The corresponding specifications shall be deemed to be the specifications referred to in Article 7 of this Regulation. Any specific transitional provisions associated with such registrations shall continue to apply.
2. In order to protect the rights and legitimate interests of producers or stakeholders concerned, the Commission shall be empowered to adopt delegated acts, in accordance with Article 56, concerning additional transitional rules.
3. This Regulation shall apply without prejudice to any right of coexistence recognised under Regulation (EC) No 510/2006 in respect of designations of origin and geographical indications, on the one hand, and trade marks, on the other.

TITLE III
TRADITIONAL SPECIALITIES GUARANTEED

[8.578]
Article 17
Objective

A scheme for traditional specialities guaranteed is established to safeguard traditional methods of production and recipes by helping producers of traditional product in marketing and communicating the value-adding attributes of their traditional recipes and products to consumers.

[8.579]
Article 18
Criteria

1. A name shall be eligible for registration as a traditional speciality guaranteed where it describes a specific product or foodstuff that:
   (a) results from a mode of production, processing or composition corresponding to traditional practice for that product or foodstuff; or
   (b) is produced from raw materials or ingredients that are those traditionally used.
2. For a name to be registered as a traditional speciality guaranteed, it shall:
   (a) have been traditionally used to refer to the specific product; or
   (b) identify the traditional character or specific character of the product.
3. If it is demonstrated in the opposition procedure under Article 51 that the name is also used in another Member State or in a third country, in order to distinguish comparable products or products that share an identical or similar name, the decision on registration taken in accordance with Article 52(3) may provide that the name of the traditional speciality guaranteed is to be accompanied by the claim 'made following the tradition of' immediately followed by the name of a country or a region thereof.
4. A name may not be registered if it refers only to claims of a general nature used for a set of products, or to claims provided for by particular Union legislation.
5. In order to ensure the smooth functioning of the scheme, the Commission shall be empowered to adopt delegated acts, in accordance with Article 56, concerning further details of the eligibility criteria laid down in this Article.

[8.580]
Article 19
Product specification

1. A traditional speciality guaranteed shall comply with a specification which shall comprise:
   (a) the name proposed for registration, in the appropriate language versions;
   (b) a description of the product including its main physical, chemical, microbiological or organoleptic characteristics, showing the product's specific character;
   (c) a description of the production method that the producers must follow, including, where appropriate, the nature and characteristics of the raw materials or ingredients used, and the method by which the product is prepared; and
   (d) the key elements establishing the product's traditional character.
2. In order to ensure that product specifications provide relevant and succinct information, the Commission shall be empowered to adopt delegated acts, in accordance with Article 56, laying down rules which limit the information contained in the specification referred to in paragraph 1 of this Article, where such a limitation is necessary to avoid excessively voluminous applications for registration.

The Commission may adopt implementing acts laying down rules on the form of the specification. Those implementing acts shall be adopted in accordance with the examination procedure referred to in Article 57(2).

[8.581]
Article 20
Content of application for registration

1. An application for registration of a name as a traditional speciality guaranteed referred to in Article 49(2) or (5) shall comprise:
   (a) the name and address of the applicant group;
   (b) the product specification as provided for in Article 19.
2. An application dossier referred to in Article 49(4) shall comprise:
   (a) the elements referred to in paragraph 1 of this Article; and
   (b) a declaration by the Member State that it considers that the application lodged by the group and qualifying for the favourable decision meets the conditions of this Regulation and the provisions adopted pursuant thereto.

[8.582]
Article 21
Grounds for opposition

1. A reasoned statement of opposition as referred to in Article 51(2) shall be admissible only if it is received by the Commission before expiry of the time limit and if it:
   (a) gives duly substantiated reasons why the proposed registration is incompatible with the terms of this Regulation; or
   (b) shows that use of the name is lawful, renowned and economically significant for similar agricultural products or foodstuffs.
2. The criteria referred to in point (b) of paragraph 1 shall be assessed in relation to the territory of the Union.

[8.583]
Article 22
Register of traditional specialities guaranteed

1. The Commission shall adopt implementing acts, without applying the procedure referred to in Article 57(2), establishing and maintaining a publicly accessible updated register of traditional specialties guaranteed recognised under this scheme.
2. The Commission may adopt implementing acts laying down detailed rules on the form and content of the register. Those implementing acts shall be adopted in accordance with the examination procedure referred to in Article 57(2).

[8.584]
Article 23
Names, symbol and indication

1. A name registered as a traditional speciality guaranteed may be used by any operator marketing a product that conforms to the corresponding specification.
2. A Union symbol shall be established in order to publicise the traditional specialities guaranteed.
3. In the case of the products originating in the Union that are marketed under a traditional speciality guaranteed that is registered in accordance with this Regulation, the symbol referred to in paragraph 2 shall, without prejudice to paragraph 4, appear on the labelling. In addition, the name of the product should appear in the same field of vision. The indication 'traditional speciality guaranteed' or the corresponding abbreviation 'TSG' may also appear on the labelling.

The symbol shall be optional on the labelling of traditional specialities guaranteed which are produced outside the Union.

4. In order to ensure that the appropriate information is communicated to the consumer, the Commission shall be empowered to adopt delegated acts, in accordance with Article 56, establishing the Union symbol.

The Commission may adopt implementing acts defining the technical characteristics of the Union symbol and indication, as well as the rules of their use on the products bearing the name of a traditional speciality guaranteed, including as to the appropriate linguistic versions to be used. Those implementing acts shall be adopted in accordance with the examination procedure referred to in Article 57(2).

[8.585]
Article 24
Restriction on use of registered names

1. Registered names shall be protected against any misuse, imitation or evocation, or against any other practice liable to mislead the consumer.
2. Member States shall ensure that sales descriptions used at national level do not give rise to confusion with names that are registered.
3. The Commission may adopt implementing acts laying down rules for the protection of traditional specialities guaranteed. Those implementing acts shall be adopted in accordance with the examination procedure referred to in Article 57(2).

[8.586]
Article 25
Transitional provisions

1. Names registered in accordance with Article 13(2) of Regulation (EC) No 509/2006 shall be automatically entered in the register referred to in Article 22 of this Regulation. The corresponding specifications shall be deemed to be the specifications referred to in Article 19 of this Regulation. Any specific transitional provisions associated with such registrations shall continue to apply.

2. Names registered in accordance with the requirements laid down in Article 13(1) of Regulation (EC) No 509/2006, including those registered pursuant to applications referred to in the second subparagraph of Article 58(1) of this Regulation, may continue to be used under the conditions provided for in Regulation (EC) No 509/2006 until 4 January 2023 unless Member States use the procedure set out in Article 26 of this Regulation.

3. In order to protect the rights and legitimate interests of producers or stakeholders concerned, the Commission shall be empowered to adopt delegated acts, in accordance with Article 56, laying down additional transitional rules.

[8.587]
Article 26
Simplified procedure

1. At the request of a group, a Member State may submit, no later than 4 January 2016, to the Commission names of traditional specialities guaranteed that are registered in accordance with Article 13(1) of Regulation (EC) No 509/2006 and that comply with this Regulation.

Before submitting a name, the Member State shall initiate an opposition procedure as defined in Article 49(3) and (4).

If it is demonstrated in the course of this procedure that the name is also used in reference to comparable products or products that share an identical or similar name, the name may be complemented by a term identifying its traditional or specific character.

A group from a third country may submit such names to the Commission, either directly or through the authorities of the third country.

2. The Commission shall publish the names referred to in paragraph 1 together with the specifications for each such name in the *Official Journal of the European Union* within two months from reception.

3. Articles 51 and 52 shall apply.

4. Once the opposition procedure has finished, the Commission shall, where appropriate, adjust the entries in the register set out in Article 22. The corresponding specifications shall be deemed to be the specifications referred to in Article 19.

TITLE IV
OPTIONAL QUALITY TERMS

[8.588]
Article 27
Objective

A scheme for optional quality terms is established in order to facilitate the communication within the internal market of the value-adding characteristics or attributes of agricultural products by the producers thereof.

[8.589]
Article 28
National Rules

Member States may maintain national rules on optional quality terms which are not covered by this Regulation, provided that such rules comply with Union law.

[8.590]
Article 29
Optional quality terms

1. Optional quality terms shall satisfy the following criteria:
   (a) the term relates to a characteristic of one or more categories of products, or to a farming or processing attribute which applies in specific areas;
   (b) the use of the term adds value to the product as compared to products of a similar type; and
   (c) the term has a European dimension.

2. Optional quality terms that describe technical product qualities with the purpose of putting into effect compulsory marketing standards and are not intended to inform consumers about those product qualities shall be excluded from this scheme.

3. Optional quality terms shall exclude optional reserved terms which support and complement specific marketing standards determined on a sectoral or product category basis.

4. In order to take into account the specific character of certain sectors as well as consumer expectations, the Commission shall be empowered to adopt delegated acts, in accordance with Article 56, laying down detailed rules relating to the criteria referred to in paragraph 1 of this Article.

5. The Commission may adopt implementing acts laying down all measures related to forms, procedures or other technical details, necessary for the application of this Title. Those implementing acts shall be adopted in accordance with the examination procedure referred to in Article 57(2).
6. When adopting delegated and implementing acts in accordance with paragraphs 4 and 5 of this Article, the Commission shall take account of any relevant international standards.

[8.591]
Article 30
Reservation and amendment
1. In order to take account of the expectations of consumers, developments in scientific and technical knowledge, the market situation, and developments in marketing standards and in international standards, the Commission shall be empowered to adopt delegated acts, in accordance with Article 56, reserving an additional optional quality term and laying down its conditions of use.
2. In duly justified cases and in order to take into account the appropriate use of the additional optional quality term, the Commission shall be empowered to adopt delegated acts, in accordance with Article 56, laying down amendments to the conditions of use referred to in paragraph 1 of this Article.

[8.592]
Article 31
Mountain product
1. The term 'mountain product' is established as an optional quality term.
This term shall only be used to describe products intended for human consumption listed in Annex I to the Treaty in respect of which:
(a) both the raw materials and the feedstuffs for farm animals come essentially from mountain areas;
(b) in the case of processed products, the processing also takes place in mountain areas.
2. For the purposes of this Article, mountain areas within the Union are those delimited pursuant to Article 18(1) of Regulation (EC) No 1257/1999. For third-country products, mountain areas include areas officially designated as mountain areas by the third country or that meet criteria equivalent to those set out in Article 18(1) of Regulation (EC) No 1257/1999.
3. In duly justified cases and in order to take into account natural constraints affecting agricultural production in mountain areas, the Commission shall be empowered to adopt delegated acts, in accordance with Article 56, laying down derogations from the conditions of use referred to in paragraph 1 of this Article. In particular, the Commission shall be empowered to adopt a delegated act laying down the conditions under which raw materials or feedstuffs are permitted to come from outside the mountain areas, the conditions under which the processing of products is permitted to take place outside of the mountain areas in a geographical area to be defined, and the definition of that geographical area.
4. In order to take into account natural constraints affecting agricultural production in mountain areas, the Commission shall be empowered to adopt delegated acts, in accordance with Article 56, concerning the establishment of the methods of production, and other criteria relevant for the application of the optional quality term established in paragraph 1 of this Article.

[8.593]
Article 32
Product of island farming
No later than 4 January 2014 the Commission shall present a report to the European Parliament and to the Council on the case for a new term, 'product of island farming'. The term may only be used to describe the products intended for human consumption that are listed in Annex I to the Treaty the raw materials of which come from islands. In addition, for the term to be applied to processed products, processing must also take place on islands in cases where this substantially affects the particular characteristics of the final product.

That report shall, if necessary, be accompanied by appropriate legislative proposals to reserve an optional quality term 'product of island farming'.

[8.594]
Article 33
Restrictions on use
1. An optional quality term may only be used to describe products that comply with the corresponding conditions of use.
2. The Commission may adopt implementing acts laying down rules for the use of optional quality terms. Those implementing acts shall be adopted in accordance with the examination procedure referred to in Article 57(2).

[8.595]
Article 34
Monitoring
Member States shall undertake checks, based on a risk analysis, to ensure compliance with the requirements of this Title and, in the event of breach, shall apply appropriate administrative penalties.

TITLE V
COMMON PROVISIONS

CHAPTER I
OFFICIAL CONTROLS OF PROTECTED DESIGNATIONS OF ORIGIN, PROTECTED GEOGRAPHICAL INDICATIONS AND TRADITIONAL SPECIALITIES GUARANTEED

[8.596]
Article 35
Scope
The provisions of this Chapter shall apply in respect of the quality schemes set out in Title II and Title III.

[8.597]
Article 36
Designation of competent authority
1. In accordance with Regulation (EC) No 882/2004, Member States shall designate the competent authority or authorities responsible for official controls carried out to verify compliance with the legal requirements related to the quality schemes established by this Regulation.

Procedures and requirements of Regulation (EC) No 882/2004 shall apply *mutatis mutandis* to the official controls carried out to verify compliance with the legal requirement related to the quality schemes for all products covered by Annex I to this Regulation.
2. The competent authorities referred to in paragraph 1 shall offer adequate guarantees of objectivity and impartiality, and shall have at their disposal the qualified staff and resources necessary to carry out their functions.
3. Official controls shall cover:
(a) verification that a product complies with the corresponding product specification; and
(b) monitoring of the use of registered names to describe product placed on the market, in conformity with Article 13 for names registered under Title II and in conformity with Article 24 for names registered under Title III.

[8.598]
Article 37
Verification of compliance with product specification
1. In respect of protected designations of origin, protected geographical indications and traditional specialities guaranteed that designate products originating within the Union, verification of compliance with the product specification, before placing the product on the market, shall be carried out by:
(a) one or more of the competent authorities as referred to in Article 36 of this Regulation; and/or
(b) one or more of the control bodies within the meaning of point (5) of Article 2 of Regulation (EC) No 882/2004 operating as a product certification body.

The costs of such verification of compliance with the specifications may be borne by the operators that are subject to those controls. The Member States may also contribute to these costs.
2. In respect of designations of origin, geographical indications and traditional specialities guaranteed that designate products originating in a third country, the verification of compliance with the specifications before placing the product on the market shall be carried out by:
(a) one or more of the public authorities designated by the third country; and/or
(b) one or more of the product certification bodies.
3. Member States shall make public the name and address of the authorities and bodies referred to paragraph 1 of this Article, and update that information periodically.

The Commission shall make public the name and address of the authorities and bodies referred to in paragraph 2 of this Article and update that information periodically.
4. The Commission may adopt implementing acts, without applying the procedure referred to in Article 57(2), defining the means by which the name and address of product certification bodies referred to in paragraphs 1 and 2 of this Article shall be made public.

[8.599]
Article 38
Surveillance of the use of the name in the market place
Member States shall inform the Commission of the names and addresses of the competent authorities referred to in Article 36. The Commission shall make public the names and addresses of those authorities.

Member States shall carry out checks, based on a risk analysis, to ensure compliance with the requirements of this Regulation and, in the event of breaches, Member States shall take all necessary measures.

[8.600]
Article 39
Delegation by competent authorities to control bodies

1. Competent authorities may delegate, in accordance with Article 5 of Regulation (EC) No 882/2004, specific tasks related to official controls of the quality schemes to one or more control bodies.
2. Such control bodies shall be accredited in accordance with European Standard EN 45011 or ISO/IEC Guide 65 (General requirements for bodies operating product certification systems).
3. Accreditation referred to in paragraph 2 of this Article may only be performed by:
   (a) a national accreditation body in the Union in accordance with the provisions of Regulation (EC) No 765/2008; or
   (b) an accreditation body outside the Union that is a signatory of a multilateral recognition arrangement under the auspices of the International Accreditation Forum.

[8.601]
Article 40
Planning and reporting of control activities

1. Member States shall ensure that activities for the control of obligations under this Chapter are specifically included in a separate section within the multi-annual national control plans in accordance with Articles 41, 42 and 43 of Regulation (EC) No 882/2004.
2. The annual reports concerning the control of the obligations established by this Regulation shall include a separate section comprising the information laid down in Article 44 of Regulation (EC) No 882/2004.

CHAPTER II
EXCEPTIONS FOR CERTAIN PRIOR USES

[8.602]
Article 41
Generic terms

1. Without prejudice to Article 13, this Regulation shall not affect the use of terms that are generic in the Union, even if the generic term is part of a name that is protected under a quality scheme.
2. To establish whether or not a term has become generic, account shall be taken of all relevant factors, in particular:
   (a) the existing situation in areas of consumption;
   (b) the relevant national or Union legal acts.
3. In order to fully protect the rights of interested parties, the Commission shall be empowered to adopt delegated acts, in accordance with Article 56, laying down additional rules for determining the generic status of terms referred to in paragraph 1 of this Article.

[8.603]
Article 42
Plant varieties and animal breeds

1. This Regulation shall not prevent the placing on the market of products the labelling of which includes a name or term protected or reserved under a quality scheme described in Title II, Title III, or Title IV that contains or comprises the name of a plant variety or animal breed, provided that the following conditions are met:
   (a) the product in question comprises or is derived from the variety or breed indicated;
   (b) consumers are not misled;
   (c) the usage of the name of the variety or breed name constitutes fair competition;
   (d) the usage does not exploit the reputation of the protected term; and
   (e) in the case of the quality scheme described in Title II, production and marketing of the product had spread beyond its area of origin prior to the date of application for registration of the geographical indication.
2. In order to further clarify the extent of rights and freedoms of food business operators to use the name of a plant variety or of an animal breed referred to in paragraph 1 of this Article, the Commission shall be empowered to adopt delegated acts, in accordance with Article 56, concerning rules for determining the use of such names.

[8.604]
Article 43
Relation to intellectual property

The quality schemes described in Titles III and IV shall apply without prejudice to Union rules or to those of Member States governing intellectual property, and in particular to those concerning designations of origin and geographical indications and trade marks, and rights granted under those rules.

CHAPTER III
QUALITY SCHEME INDICATIONS AND SYMBOLS AND ROLE OF PRODUCERS

[8.605]
Article 44
Protection of indications and symbols

1. Indications, abbreviations and symbols referring to the quality schemes may only be used in connection with products produced in conformity with the rules of the quality scheme to which they apply. This applies in particular to the following indications, abbreviations and symbols:
   (a) 'protected designation of origin', 'protected geographical indication', 'geographical indication', 'PDO', 'PGI', and the associated symbols, as provided for in Title II;
   (b) 'traditional speciality guaranteed', 'TSG', and the associated symbol, as provided for in Title III;
   (c) 'mountain product', as provided for in Title IV.

2. In accordance with Article 5 of Regulation (EC) No 1290/2005, the European Agricultural Fund for Rural Development (EAFRD) may, on the initiative of the Commission or on its behalf, finance, on a centralised basis, administrative support concerning the development, preparatory work, monitoring, administrative and legal support, legal defence, registration fees, renewal fees, trade mark watching fees, litigation fees and any other related measure required to protect the use of the indications, abbreviations and symbols referring to the quality schemes from misuse, imitation, evocation or any other practice liable to mislead the consumer, within the Union and in third countries.

3. The Commission shall adopt implementing acts laying down rules for the uniform protection of the indications, abbreviations and symbols referred to in paragraph 1 of this Article. Those implementing acts shall be adopted in accordance with the examination procedure referred to in Article 57(2).

[8.606]
Article 45
Role of groups

1. Without prejudice to specific provisions on producer organisations and inter-branch organisations as laid down in Regulation (EC) No 1234/2007, a group is entitled to:
   (a) contribute to ensuring that the quality, reputation and authenticity of their products are guaranteed on the market by monitoring the use of the name in trade and, if necessary, by informing competent authorities as referred to in Article 36, or any other competent authority within the framework of Article 13(3);
   (b) take action to ensure adequate legal protection of the protected designation of origin or protected geographical indication and of the intellectual property rights that are directly connected with them;
   (c) develop information and promotion activities aiming at communicating the value-adding attributes of the product to consumers;
   (d) develop activities related to ensuring compliance of a product with its specification;
   (e) take action to improve the performance of the scheme, including developing economic expertise, carrying out economic analyses, disseminating economic information on the scheme and providing advice to producers;
   (f) take measures to enhance the value of products and, where necessary, take steps to prevent or counter any measures which are, or risk being, detrimental to the image of those products.

2. Member States may encourage the formation and functioning of groups on their territories by administrative means. Moreover, Member States shall communicate to the Commission the name and address of the groups referred to in point 2 of Article 3. The Commission shall make this information public.

[8.607]
Article 46
Right to use the schemes

1. Member States shall ensure that any operator complying with the rules of a quality scheme set out in Titles II and III is entitled to be covered by the verification of compliance established pursuant to Article 37.

2. Operators who prepare and store a product marketed under the traditional speciality guaranteed, protected designation of origin or protected geographical indication schemes or who place such products on the market shall also be subject to the controls laid down in Chapter I of this Title.

3. Member States shall ensure that operators willing to adhere to the rules of a quality scheme set out in Titles III and IV are able to do so and do not face obstacles to participation that are discriminatory or otherwise not objectively founded.

[8.608]
Article 47
Fees

Without prejudice to Regulation (EC) No 882/2004 and in particular the provisions of Chapter VI of Title II thereof, Member States may charge a fee to cover their costs of managing the quality schemes, including those incurred in processing applications, statements of opposition, applications for amendments and requests for cancellations provided for in this Regulation.

CHAPTER IV
APPLICATION AND REGISTRATION PROCESSES FOR DESIGNATIONS OF ORIGIN, GEOGRAPHICAL INDICATIONS, AND TRADITIONAL SPECIALITIES GUARANTEED

[8.609]
Article 48
Scope of application processes

The provisions of this Chapter shall apply in respect of the quality schemes set out in Title II and Title III.

[8.610]
Article 49
Application for registration of names

1. Applications for registration of names under the quality schemes referred to in Article 48 may only be submitted by groups who work with the products with the name to be registered. In the case of a 'protected designations of origin' or 'protected geographical indications' name that designates a trans-border geographical area or in the case of a 'traditional specialities guaranteed' name, several groups from different Member States or third countries may lodge a joint application for registration.

A single natural or legal person may be treated as a group where it is shown that both of the following conditions are fulfilled:

(a) the person concerned is the only producer willing to submit an application;
(b) with regard to protected designations of origin and protected geographical indications, the defined geographical area possesses characteristics which differ appreciably from those of neighbouring areas or the characteristics of the product are different from those produced in neighbouring areas.

2. Where the application under the scheme set out in Title II relates to a geographical area in a Member State, or where an application under the scheme set out in Title III is prepared by a group established in a Member State, the application shall be addressed to the authorities of that Member State.

The Member State shall scrutinise the application by appropriate means in order to check that it is justified and meets the conditions of the respective scheme.

3. As part of the scrutiny referred to in the second subparagraph of paragraph 2 of this Article, the Member State shall initiate a national opposition procedure that ensures adequate publication of the application and that provides for a reasonable period within which any natural or legal person having a legitimate interest and established or resident on its territory may lodge an opposition to the application.

The Member State shall examine the admissibility of oppositions received under the scheme set out in Title II in the light of the criteria referred to in Article 10(1), or the admissibility of oppositions received under the scheme set out in Title III in the light of the criteria referred to in Article 21(1).

4. If, after assessment of any opposition received, the Member State considers that the requirements of this Regulation are met, it may take a favourable decision and lodge an application dossier with the Commission. It shall in such case inform the Commission of admissible oppositions received from a natural or legal person that have legally marketed the products in question, using the names concerned continuously for at least five years preceding the date of the publication referred to in paragraph 3.

The Member State shall ensure that its favourable decision is made public and that any natural or legal person having a legitimate interest has an opportunity to appeal.

The Member State shall ensure that the version of the product specification on which its favourable decision is based, is published, and shall provide electronic access to the product specification.

With reference to protected designations of origin and protected geographical indications, the Member State shall also ensure adequate publication of the version of the product specification on which the Commission takes its decision pursuant to Article 50(2).

5. Where the application under the scheme set out in Title II relates to a geographical area in a third country, or where an application under the scheme set out in Title III is prepared by a group established in a third country, the application shall be lodged with the Commission, either directly or via the authorities of the third country concerned.

6. The documents referred to in this Article which are sent to the Commission shall be in one of the official languages of the Union.

7. In order to facilitate the application process, the Commission shall be empowered to adopt delegated acts, in accordance with Article 56, defining the rules for carrying out the national objection procedure for joint applications concerning more than one national territory and complementing the rules of the application process.

The Commission may adopt implementing acts laying down detailed rules on procedures, form and presentation of applications, including for applications concerning more than one national territory. Those implementing acts shall be adopted in accordance with the examination procedure referred to in Article 57(2).

[8.611]
Article 50
Scrutiny by the Commission and publication for opposition

1. The Commission shall scrutinise by appropriate means any application that it receives pursuant to Article 49, in order to check that it is justified and that it meets the conditions of the respective scheme. This scrutiny should not exceed a period of six months. Where this period is exceeded, the Commission shall indicate in writing to the applicant the reasons for the delay.

The Commission shall, at least each month, make public the list of names for which registration applications have been submitted to it, as well as their date of submission.

2. Where, based on the scrutiny carried out pursuant to the first subparagraph of paragraph 1, the Commission considers that the conditions laid down in this Regulation are fulfilled, it shall publish in the *Official Journal of the European Union*:

(a) for applications under the scheme set out in Title II, the single document and the reference to the publication of the product specification;
(b) for applications under the scheme set out in Title III, the specification.

[8.612]
Article 51
Opposition procedure

1. Within three months from the date of publication in the *Official Journal of the European Union*, the authorities of a Member State or of a third country, or a natural or legal person having a legitimate interest and established in a third country may lodge a notice of opposition with the Commission.

Any natural or legal person having a legitimate interest, established or resident in a Member State other than that from which the application was submitted, may lodge a notice of opposition with the Member State in which it is established within a time limit permitting an opposition to be lodged pursuant to the first subparagraph.

A notice of opposition shall contain a declaration that the application might infringe the conditions laid down in this Regulation. A notice of opposition that does not contain this declaration is void.

The Commission shall forward the notice of opposition to the authority or body that lodged the application without delay.

2. If a notice of opposition is lodged with the Commission and is followed within two months by a reasoned statement of opposition, the Commission shall check the admissibility of this reasoned statement of opposition.

3. Within two months after the receipt of an admissible reasoned statement of opposition, the Commission shall invite the authority or person that lodged the opposition and the authority or body that lodged the application to engage in appropriate consultations for a reasonable period that shall not exceed three months.

The authority or person that lodged the opposition and the authority or body that lodged the application shall start such appropriate consultations without undue delay. They shall provide each other with the relevant information to assess whether the application for registration complies with the conditions of this Regulation. If no agreement is reached, this information shall also be provided to the Commission.

At any time during these three months, the Commission may, at the request of the applicant extend the deadline for the consultations by a maximum of three months.

4. Where, following the appropriate consultations referred to in paragraph 3 of this Article, the details published in accordance with Article 50(2) have been substantially amended, the Commission shall repeat the scrutiny referred to in Article 50.

5. The notice of opposition, the reasoned statement of opposition and the related documents which are sent to the Commission in accordance with paragraphs 1 to 4 of this Article shall be in one of the official languages of the Union.

6. In order to establish clear procedures and deadlines for opposition, the Commission shall be empowered to adopt delegated acts, in accordance with Article 56, complementing the rules of the opposition procedure.

The Commission may adopt implementing acts laying down detailed rules on procedures, form and presentation of the oppositions. Those implementing acts shall be adopted in accordance with the examination procedure referred to in Article 57(2).

[8.613]
Article 52
Decision on registration

1. Where, on the basis of the information available to the Commission from the scrutiny carried out pursuant to the first subparagraph of Article 50(1), the Commission considers that the conditions for registration are not fulfilled, it shall adopt implementing acts rejecting the application. Those implementing acts shall be adopted in accordance with the examination procedure referred to in Article 57(2).
2. If the Commission receives no notice of opposition or no admissible reasoned statement of opposition under Article 51, it shall adopt implementing acts, without applying the procedure referred to in Article 57(2), registering the name.
3. If the Commission receives an admissible reasoned statement of opposition, it shall, following the appropriate consultations referred to in Article 51(3), and taking into account the results thereof, either:
   - (a) if an agreement has been reached, register the name by means of implementing acts adopted without applying the procedure referred to in Article 57(2), and, if necessary, amend the information published pursuant to Article 50(2) provided such amendments are not substantial; or
   - (b) if an agreement has not been reached, adopt implementing acts deciding on the registration. Those implementing acts shall be adopted in accordance with the examination procedure referred to in Article 57(2).
4. Acts of registration and decisions on rejection shall be published in the *Official Journal of the European Union*.

[8.614]
Article 53
Amendment to a product specification

1. A group having a legitimate interest may apply for approval of an amendment to a product specification.

Applications shall describe and give reasons for the amendments requested.

2. Where the amendment involves one or more amendments to the specification that are not minor, the amendment application shall follow the procedure laid down in Articles 49 to 52.

However, if the proposed amendments are minor, the Commission shall approve or reject the application. In the event of the approval of amendments implying a modification of the elements referred to in Article 50(2), the Commission shall publish those elements in the *Official Journal of the European Union*.

For an amendment to be regarded as minor in the case of the quality scheme described in Title II, it shall not:
- (a) relate to the essential characteristics of the product;
- (b) alter the link referred to in point (f)(i) or (ii) of Article 7(1);
- (c) include a change to the name, or to any part of the name of the product;
- (d) affect the defined geographical area; or
- (e) represent an increase in restrictions on trade in the product or its raw materials.

For an amendment to be regarded as minor in the case of the quality scheme described in Title III, it shall not:
- (a) relate to the essential characteristics of the product;
- (b) introduce essential changes to the production method; or
- (c) include a change to the name, or to any part of the name of the product.

The scrutiny of the application shall focus on the proposed amendment.

3. In order to facilitate the administrative process of an amendment application, including where the amendment does not involve any change to the single document and where it concerns a temporary change in the specification resulting from the imposition of obligatory sanitary or phytosanitary measures by the public authorities, the Commission shall be empowered to adopt delegated acts, in accordance with Article 56, complementing the rules of the amendment application process.

The Commission may adopt implementing acts laying down detailed rules on procedures, form and presentation of an amendment application. Those implementing acts shall be adopted in accordance with the examination procedure referred to in Article 57(2).

[8.615]
Article 54
Cancellation

1. The Commission may, on its own initiative or at the request of any natural or legal person having a legitimate interest, adopt implementing acts to cancel the registration of a protected designation of origin or of a protected geographical indication or of a traditional speciality guaranteed in the following cases:
   - (a) where compliance with the conditions of the specification is not ensured;

(b) where no product is placed on the market under the traditional speciality guaranteed, the protected designation of origin or the protected geographical indication for at least seven years.

The Commission may, at the request of the producers of product marketed under the registered name, cancel the corresponding registration.

Those implementing acts shall be adopted in accordance with the examination procedure referred to in Article 57(2).

2. In order to ensure legal certainty that all parties have the opportunity to defend their rights and legitimate interests, the Commission shall be empowered to adopt delegated acts, in accordance with Article 56 complementing the rules regarding the cancellation process.

The Commission may adopt implementing acts laying down detailed rules on procedures and form of the cancellation process, as well as on the presentation of the requests referred to in paragraph 1 of this Article. Those implementing acts shall be adopted in accordance with the examination procedure referred to in Article 57(2).

TITLE VI
PROCEDURAL AND FINAL PROVISIONS

CHAPTER I
LOCAL FARMING AND DIRECT SALES

[8.616]
Article 55
Reporting on local farming and direct sales

No later than 4 January 2014 the Commission shall present a report to the European Parliament and to the Council on the case for a new local farming and direct sales labelling scheme to assist producers in marketing their produce locally. That report shall focus on the ability of the farmer to add value to his produce through the new label, and should take into account other criteria, such as the possibilities of reducing carbon emissions and waste through short production and distribution chains.

That report shall, if necessary, be accompanied by appropriate legislative proposals on the creation of a local farming and direct sales labelling scheme.

CHAPTER II
PROCEDURAL RULES

[8.617]
Article 56
Exercise of the delegation

1. The power to adopt the delegated acts is conferred on the Commission subject to the conditions laid down in this Article.

2. The power to adopt delegated acts referred to in the second subparagraph of Article 2(1), Article 5(4), the first subparagraph of Article 7(2), the first subparagraph of Article 12(5), Article 16(2), Article 18(5), the first subparagraph of Article 19(2), the first subparagraph of Article 23(4), Article 25(3), Article 29(4), Article 30, Article 31(3) and (4), Article 41(3), Article 42(2), the first subparagraph of Article 49(7), the first subparagraph of Article 51(6), the first subparagraph of Article 53(3) and the first subparagraph of Article 54(2) shall be conferred on the Commission for a period of five years from 3 January 2013. The Commission shall draw up a report in respect of the delegation of power not later than nine months before the end of the five-year period. The delegation of power shall be tacitly extended for periods of an identical duration, unless the European Parliament or the Council opposes such extension not later than three months before the end of each period.

3. The delegation of power referred to in the second subparagraph of Article 2(1), Article 5(4), the first subparagraph of Article 7(2), the first subparagraph of Article 12(5), Article 16(2), Article 18(5), the first subparagraph of Article 19(2), the first subparagraph of Article 23(4), Article 25(3), Article 29(4), Article 30, Article 31(3) and (4), Article 41(3), Article 42(2), the first subparagraph of Article 49(7), the first subparagraph of Article 51(6), the first subparagraph of Article 53(3) and the first subparagraph of Article 54(2) may be revoked at any time by the European Parliament or by the Council. A decision to revoke shall put an end to the delegation of the power specified in that decision. It shall take effect the day following the publication of the decision in the *Official Journal of the European Union* or at a later date specified therein. It shall not affect the validity of any delegated acts already in force.

4. As soon as it adopts a delegated act, the Commission shall notify it simultaneously to the European Parliament and to the Council.

5. A delegated act adopted pursuant to the second subparagraph of Article 2(1), Article 5(4), the first subparagraph of Article 7(2), the first subparagraph of Article 12(5), Article 16(2), Article 18(5), the first subparagraph of Article 19(2), the first subparagraph of Article 23(4), Article 25(3), Article 29(4), Article 30, Article 31(3) and (4), Article 41(3), Article 42(2), the first subparagraph of Article 49(7), the first subparagraph of Article 51(6), the first subparagraph of

Article 53(3) and the first subparagraph of Article 54(2) shall enter into force only if no objection has been expressed either by the European Parliament or the Council within a period of two months of notification of that act to the European Parliament and the Council or if, before the expiry of that period, the European Parliament and the Council have both informed the Commission that they will not object. That period shall be extended by two months at the initiative of the European Parliament or of the Council.

[8.618]
Article 57
Committee procedure

1. The Commission shall be assisted by the Agricultural Product Quality Policy Committee. That committee shall be a committee within the meaning of Regulation (EU) No 182/2011.
2. Where reference is made to this paragraph, Article 5 of Regulation (EU) No 182/2011 shall apply.

Where the committee delivers no opinion, the Commission shall not adopt the draft implementing act and the third subparagraph of Article 5(4) of Regulation (EU) No 182/2011 shall apply.

CHAPTER III
REPEAL AND FINAL PROVISIONS

[8.619]
Article 58
Repeal

1. Regulations (EC) No 509/2006 and (EC) No 510/2006 are hereby repealed.

However, Article 13 of Regulation (EC) No 509/2006 shall continue to apply in respect of applications concerning products falling outside the scope of Title III of this Regulation, received by the Commission prior to the date of entry into force of this Regulation.
2. References to the repealed Regulations shall be construed as references to this Regulation and be read in accordance with the correlation table in Annex II to this Regulation.

[8.620]
Article 59
Entry into force

This Regulation shall enter into force on the twentieth day following that of its publication in the *Official Journal of the European Union*.

However, Article 12(3) and Article 23(3) shall apply from 4 January 2016, without prejudice to products already placed on the market before that date.

This Regulation shall be binding in its entirety and directly applicable in all Member States.

ANNEX I
AGRICULTURAL PRODUCTS AND FOODSTUFFS REFERRED TO IN ARTICLE 2(1)

[8.621]

I. Designations of Origin and Geographical indications

— beer,
— chocolate and derived products,
— bread, pastry, cakes, confectionery, biscuits and other baker's wares,
— beverages made from plant extracts,
— pasta,
— salt,
— natural gums and resins,
— mustard paste,
— hay,
— essential oils,
— cork,
— cochineal,
— flowers and ornamental plants,
— cotton,
— wool,
— wicker,
— scutched flax,
— leather,
— fur,
— feather.

II. Traditional specialities guaranteed

— prepared meals,
— beer,
— chocolate and derived products,

— bread, pastry, cakes, confectionery, biscuits and other baker's wares,
— beverages made from plant extracts,
— pasta,
— salt.

ANNEX II
CORRELATION TABLE REFERRED TO IN ARTICLE 58(2)

[8.622]

Regulation (EC) No 509/2006	This Regulation
Article 1(1)	Article 2(1)
Article 1(2)	Article 2(3)
Article 1(3)	Article 2(4)
Article 2(1), point (a)	Article 3, point (5)
Article 2(1), point (b)	Article 3, point (3)
Article 2(1), point (c)	—
Article 2(1), point (d)	Article 3, point (2)
Article 2(2), first to third subparagraph	—
Article 2(2), fourth subparagraph	—
Article 3	Article 22(1)
Article 4(1), first subparagraph	Article 18(1)
Article 4(2)	Article 18(2)
Article 4(3), first subparagraph	—
Article 4(3), second subparagraph	Article 18(4)
Article 5(1)	Article 43
Article 5(2)	Article 42(1)
Article 6(1)	Article 19(1)
Article 6(1), point (a)	Article 19(1), point (a)
Article 6(1), point (b)	Article 19(1), point (b)
Article 6(1), point (c)	Article 19(1), point (c)
Article 6(1), point (d)	—
Article 6(1), point (e)	Article 19(1), point (d)
Article 6(1), point (f)	—
Article 7(1) and (2)	Article 49(1)
Article 7(3), points (a) and (b)	Article 20(1), points (a) and (b)
Article 7(3), point (c)	—
Article 7(3), point (d)	—
Article 7(4)	Article 49(2)
Article 7(5)	Article 49(3)
Article 7(6), points (a), (b) and (c)	Article 49(4)
Article 7(6), point (d)	Article 20(2)
Article 7(7)	Article 49(5)
Article 7(8)	Article 49(6)
Article 8(1)	Article 50(1)
Article 8(2), first subparagraph	Article 50(2), point (b)
Article 8(2), second subparagraph	Article 52(1)
Article 9(1) and (2)	Article 51(1)
Article 9(3)	Article 21(1) and (2)
Article 9(4)	Article 52(2)
Article 9(5)	Article 52(3) and (4)
Article 9(6)	Article 51(5)
Article 10	Article 54
Article 11	Article 53
Article 12	Article 23
Article 13(1)	—

Regulation (EC) No 509/2006	This Regulation
Article 13(2)	—
Article 13(3)	—
Article 14(1)	Article 36(1)
Article 14(2)	Article 46(1)
Article 14(3)	Article 37(3), second subparagraph
Article 15(1)	Article 37(1)
Article 15(2)	Article 37(2)
Article 15(3)	Article 39(2)
Article 15(4)	Article 36(2)
Article 16	—
Article 17(1) and (2)	Article 24(1)
Article 17(3)	Article 24(2)
Article 18	Article 57
Article 19(1), point (a)	—
Article 19(1), point (b)	Article 49(7), second subparagraph
Article 19(1), point (c)	Article 49(7), first subparagraph
Article 19(1), point (d)	Article 22(2)
Article 19(1), point (e)	Article 51(6)
Article 19(1), point (f)	Article 54(1)
Article 19(1), point (g)	Article 23(4)
Article 19(1), point (h)	—
Article 19(1), point (i)	—
Article 19(2)	Article 25(1)
Article 19(3), point (a)	—
Article 19(3), point (b)	Article 25(2)
Article 20	Article 47
Article 21	Article 58
Article 22	Article 59
Annex I	Annex I (Part II)

Regulation (EC) No 510/2006	This Regulation
Article 1(1)	Article 2(1) and (2)
Article 1(2)	Article 2(3)
Article 1(3)	Article 2(4)
Article 2	Article 5
Article 3(1), first subparagraph	Article 6(1)
Article 3(1), second and third subparagraph	Article 41(1), (2) and (3)
Article 3(2), (3) and (4)	Article 6(2), (3) and (4)
Article 4	Article 7
Article 5(1)	Article 3, point (2), and Article 49(1)
Article 5(2)	Article 49(1)
Article 5(3)	Article 8(1)
Article 5(4)	Article 49(2)
Article 5(5)	Article 49(3)
Article 5(6)	Article 9
Article 5(7)	Article 8(2)
Article 5(8)	—
Article 5(9), first subparagraph	—
Article 5(9), second subparagraph	Article 49(5)
Article 5(10)	Article 49(6)
Article 5(11)	—

Regulation (EC) No 510/2006	**This Regulation**
Article 6(1), first subparagraph	Article 50(1)
Article 6(2), first subparagraph	Article 50(2), point (a)
Article 6(2), second subparagraph	Article 52(1)
Article 7(1)	Article 51(1), first subparagraph
Article 7(2)	Article 51(1), second subparagraph
Article 7(3)	Article 10
Article 7(4)	Article 52(2) and (4)
Article 7(5)	Article 51(3) and Article 52(3) and (4)
Article 7(6)	Article 11
Article 7(7)	Article 51(5)
Article 8	Article 12
Article 9	Article 53
Article 10(1)	Article 36(1)
Article 10(2)	Article 46(1)
Article 10(3)	Article 37(3), second subparagraph
Article 11(1)	Article 37(1)
Article 11(2)	Article 37(2)
Article 11(3)	Article 39(2)
Article 11(4)	Article 36(2)
Article 12	Article 54
Article 13(1)	Article 13(1)
Article 13(2)	Article 13(2)
Article 13(3)	Article 15(1)
Article 13(4)	Article 15(2)
Article 14	Article 14
Article 15	Article 57
Article 16, point (a)	Article 5(4), second subparagraph
Article 16, point (b)	—
Article 16, point (c)	—
Article 16, point (d)	Article 49(7)
Article 16, point (e)	—
Article 16, point (f)	Article 51(6)
Article 16, point (g)	Article 12(7)
Article 16, point (h)	—
Article 16, point (i)	Article 11(3)
Article 16, point (j)	—
Article 16, point (k)	Article 54(2)
Article 17	Article 16
Article 18	Article 47
Article 19	Article 58
Article 20	Article 59
Annex I and Annex II	Annex I (Part I)

DIRECTIVE OF THE EUROPEAN PARLIAMENT AND OF THE COUNCIL

(2012/28/EU)

of 25 October 2012

on certain permitted uses of orphan works

NOTES

Date of publication in OJ: OJ L299, 27.10.2012, p 5.

THE EUROPEAN PARLIAMENT AND THE COUNCIL OF THE EUROPEAN UNION,

Having regard to the Treaty on the Functioning of the European Union, and in particular Articles 53(1), 62 and 114 thereof,

Having regard to the proposal from the European Commission,

After transmission of the draft legislative act to the national parliaments,

Having regard to the opinion of the European Economic and Social Committee,[1]

Acting in accordance with the ordinary legislative procedure,[2]

Whereas:

(1) Publicly accessible libraries, educational establishments and museums, as well as archives, film or audio heritage institutions and public-service broadcasting organisations, established in the Member States, are engaged in large-scale digitisation of their collections or archives in order to create European Digital Libraries. They contribute to the preservation and dissemination of European cultural heritage, which is also important for the creation of European Digital Libraries, such as Europeana. Technologies for mass digitisation of print materials and for search and indexing enhance the research value of the libraries' collections. Creating large online libraries facilitates electronic search and discovery tools which open up new sources of discovery for researchers and academics who would otherwise have to content themselves with more traditional and analogue search methods.

(2) The need to promote free movement of knowledge and innovation in the internal market is an important component of the Europe 2020 Strategy, as set out in the Communication from the Commission entitled 'Europe 2020: A strategy for smart, sustainable and inclusive growth', which includes as one of its flagship initiatives the development of a Digital Agenda for Europe.

(3) Creating a legal framework to facilitate the digitisation and dissemination of works and other subject-matter which are protected by copyright or related rights and for which no rightholder is identified or for which the rightholder, even if identified, is not located — so-called orphan works — is a key action of the Digital Agenda for Europe, as set out in the Communication from the Commission entitled 'A Digital Agenda for Europe'. This Directive targets the specific problem of the legal determination of orphan work status and its consequences in terms of the permitted users and permitted uses of works or phonograms considered to be orphan works.

(4) This Directive is without prejudice to specific solutions being developed in the Member States to address larger mass digitisation issues, such as in the case of so-called 'out-of-commerce' works. Such solutions take into account the specificities of different types of content and different users and build upon the consensus of the relevant stakeholders. This approach has also been followed in the Memorandum of Understanding on key principles on the digitisation and making available of out-of-commerce works, signed on 20 September 2011 by representatives of European libraries, authors, publishers and collecting societies and witnessed by the Commission. This Directive is without prejudice to that Memorandum of Understanding, which calls on Member States and the Commission to ensure that voluntary agreements concluded between users, rightholders and collective rights management organisations to licence the use of out-of-commerce works on the basis of the principles contained therein benefit from the requisite legal certainty in a national and cross-border context.

(5) Copyright is the economic foundation for the creative industry, since it stimulates innovation, creation, investment and production. Mass digitisation and dissemination of works is therefore a means of protecting Europe's cultural heritage. Copyright is an important tool for ensuring that the creative sector is rewarded for its work.

(6) The rightholders' exclusive rights of reproduction of their works and other protected subject-matter and of making them available to the public, as harmonised under Directive 2001/29/EC of the European Parliament and of the Council of 22 May 2001 on the harmonisation of certain aspects of copyright and related rights in the information society,[3] necessitate the prior consent of rightholders to the digitisation and the making available to the public of a work or other protected subject-matter.

(7) In the case of orphan works, it is not possible to obtain such prior consent to the carrying-out of acts of reproduction or of making available to the public.

(8) Different approaches in the Member States to the recognition of orphan work status can

present obstacles to the functioning of the internal market and the use of, and cross-border access to, orphan works. Such different approaches can also result in restrictions on the free movement of goods and services which incorporate cultural content. Therefore, ensuring the mutual recognition of such status is appropriate, since it will allow access to orphan works in all Member States.

(9) In particular, a common approach to determining the orphan work status and the permitted uses of orphan works is necessary in order to ensure legal certainty in the internal market with respect to the use of orphan works by publicly accessible libraries, educational establishments and museums, as well as by archives, film or audio heritage institutions and public-service broadcasting organisations.

(10) Cinematographic or audiovisual works and phonograms in the archives of public-service broadcasting organisations and produced by them include orphan works. Taking into account the special position of broadcasters as producers of phonograms and audiovisual material and the need to adopt measures to limit the phenomenon of orphan works in the future, it is appropriate to set a cut-off date for the application of this Directive to works and phonograms in the archives of broadcasting organisations.

(11) Cinematographic and audiovisual works and phonograms contained in the archives of public-service broadcasting organisations and produced by them, should for the purposes of this Directive be regarded as including cinematographic and audiovisual works and phonograms which are commissioned by such organisations for the exclusive exploitation by them or other co-producing public-service broadcasting organisations. Cinematographic and audiovisual works and phonograms contained in the archives of public-service broadcasting organisations which have not been produced or commissioned by such organisations, but which those organisations have been authorised to use under a licensing agreement, should not fall within the scope of this Directive.

(12) For reasons of international comity, this Directive should apply only to works and phonograms that are first published in the territory of a Member State or, in the absence of publication, first broadcast in the territory of a Member State or, in the absence of publication or broadcast, made publicly accessible by the beneficiaries of this Directive with the consent of the rightholders. In the latter case, this Directive should only apply provided that it is reasonable to assume that the rightholders would not oppose the use allowed by this Directive.

(13) Before a work or phonogram can be considered an orphan work, a diligent search for the rightholders in the work or phonogram, including rightholders in works and other protected subject-matter that are embedded or incorporated in the work or phonogram, should be carried out in good faith. Member States should be permitted to provide that such diligent search may be carried out by the organisations referred to in this Directive or by other organisations. Such other organisations may charge for the service of carrying out a diligent search.

(14) It is appropriate to provide for a harmonised approach concerning such diligent search in order to ensure a high level of protection of copyright and related rights in the Union. A diligent search should involve the consultation of sources that supply information on the works and other protected subject-matter as determined, in accordance with this Directive, by the Member State where the diligent search has to be carried out. In so doing, Member States could refer to the diligent search guidelines agreed in the context of the High Level Working Group on Digital Libraries established as part of the i2010 digital library initiative.

(15) In order to avoid duplication of search efforts, a diligent search should be carried out in the Member State where the work or phonogram was first published or, in cases where no publication has taken place, where it was first broadcast. The diligent search in respect of cinematographic or audiovisual works the producer of which has his headquarters or habitual residence in a Member State should be carried out in that Member State. In the case of cinematographic or audiovisual works which are co-produced by producers established in different Member States, the diligent search should be carried out in each of those Member States. With regard to works and phonograms which have neither been published nor broadcast but which have been made publicly accessible by the beneficiaries of this Directive with the consent of the rightholders, the diligent search should be carried out in the Member State where the organisation that made the work or phonogram publicly accessible with the consent of the rightholder is established. Diligent searches for the rightholders in works and other protected subject-matter that are embedded or incorporated in a work or phonogram should be carried out in the Member State where the diligent search for the work or phonogram containing the embedded or incorporated work or other protected subject-matter is carried out. Sources of information available in other countries should also be consulted if there is evidence to suggest that relevant information on rightholders is to be found in those other countries. The carrying-out of diligent searches may generate various kinds of information, such as a search record and the result of the search. The search record should be kept on file in order for the relevant organisation to be able to substantiate that the search was diligent.

(16) Member States should ensure that the organisations concerned keep records of their diligent searches and that the results of such searches, consisting in particular of any finding that a work or phonogram is to be considered an orphan work within the meaning of this Directive, as well as information on the change of status and on the use which those organisations make of orphan works, are collected and made available to the public at large, in particular through the recording of the

relevant information in an online database. Considering in particular the pan-European dimension, and in order to avoid duplication of efforts, it is appropriate to make provision for the creation of a single online database for the Union containing such information and for making it available to the public at large in a transparent manner. This can enable both the organisations which are carrying out diligent searches and the rightholders easily to access such information. The database could also play an important role in preventing and bringing to an end possible copyright infringements, particularly in the case of changes to the orphan work status of the works and phonograms. Under Regulation (EU) No 386/2012,[4] the Office for Harmonization in the Internal Market ('the Office') is entrusted with certain tasks and activities, financed by making use of its own budgetary means, aimed at facilitating and supporting the activities of national authorities, the private sector and the Union institutions in the fight against, including the prevention of, infringement of intellectual property rights.

In particular, pursuant to point (g) of Article 2(1) of that Regulation, those tasks include providing mechanisms which help to improve the online exchange of relevant information between the Member States' authorities concerned and fostering cooperation between those authorities. It is therefore appropriate to rely on the Office to establish and manage the European database containing information related to orphan works referred to in this Directive.

(17) There can be several rightholders in respect of a particular work or phonogram, and works and phonograms can themselves include other works or protected subject-matter. This Directive should not affect the rights of identified and located rightholders. If at least one rightholder has been identified and located, a work or phonogram should not be considered an orphan work. The beneficiaries of this Directive should only be permitted to use a work or phonogram one or more of the rightholders in which are not identified or not located, if they are authorised to carry out the acts of reproduction and of making available to the public covered by Articles 2 and 3 respectively of Directive 2001/29/EC by those rightholders that have been identified and located, including the rightholders of works and other protected subject-matter which are embedded or incorporated in the works or phonograms. Rightholders that have been identified and located can give this authorisation only in relation to the rights that they themselves hold, either because the rights are their own rights or because the rights were transferred to them, and should not be able to authorise under this Directive any use on behalf of rightholders that have not been identified and located. Correspondingly, when previously non-identified or non-located rightholders come forward in order to claim their rights in the work or phonogram, the lawful use of the work or phonogram by the beneficiaries can continue only if those rightholders give their authorisation to do so under Directive 2001/29/EC in relation to the rights that they hold.

(18) Rightholders should be entitled to put an end to the orphan work status in the event that they come forward to claim their rights in the work or other protected subject-matter. Rightholders that put an end to the orphan work status of a work or other protected subject-matter should receive fair compensation for the use that has been made of their works or other protected subject-matter under this Directive, to be determined by the Member State where the organisation that uses an orphan work is established. Member States should be free to determine the circumstances under which the payment of such compensation may be organised, including the point in time at which the payment is due. For the purposes of determining the possible level of fair compensation, due account should be taken, inter alia, of Member States' cultural promotion objectives, of the non-commercial nature of the use made by the organisations in question in order to achieve aims related to their public-interest missions, such as promoting learning and disseminating culture, and of the possible harm to rightholders.

(19) If a work or phonogram has been wrongly found to be an orphan work, following a search which was not diligent, the remedies for copyright infringement in Member States' legislation, provided for in accordance with the relevant national provisions and Union law, remain available.

(20) In order to promote learning and the dissemination of culture, Member States should provide for an exception or limitation in addition to those provided for in Article 5 of Directive 2001/29/EC. That exception or limitation should permit certain organisations, as referred to in point (c) of Article 5(2) of Directive 2001/29/EC and film or audio heritage institutions which operate on a non-profit making basis, as well as public-service broadcasting organisations, to reproduce and make available to the public, within the meaning of that Directive, orphan works, provided that such use fulfils their public interest missions, in particular the preservation of, the restoration of, and the provision of cultural and educational access to, their collections, including their digital collections. Film or audio heritage institutions should, for the purposes of this Directive, cover organisations designated by Member States to collect, catalogue, preserve and restore films and other audiovisual works or phonograms forming part of their cultural heritage. Public-service broadcasters should, for the purposes of this Directive, cover broadcasters with a public-service remit as conferred, defined and organised by each Member State. The exception or limitation established by this Directive to permit the use of orphan works is without prejudice to the exceptions and limitations provided for in Article 5 of Directive 2001/29/EC. It can be applied only in certain special cases which do not conflict with the normal exploitation of the work or other protected subject-matter and do not unreasonably prejudice the legitimate interests of the rightholder.

(21) In order to incentivise digitisation, the beneficiaries of this Directive should be allowed to

generate revenues in relation to their use of orphan works under this Directive in order to achieve aims related to their public-interest missions, including in the context of public-private partnership agreements.

(22) Contractual arrangements may play a role in fostering the digitisation of European cultural heritage, it being understood that publicly accessible libraries, educational establishments and museums, as well as archives, film or audio heritage institutions and public-service broadcasting organisations, should be allowed, with a view to undertaking the uses permitted under this Directive, to conclude agreements with commercial partners for the digitisation and making available to the public of orphan works. Those agreements may include financial contributions by such partners. Such agreements should not impose any restrictions on the beneficiaries of this Directive as to their use of orphan works and should not grant the commercial partner any rights to use, or control the use of, the orphan works.

(23) In order to foster access by the Union's citizens to Europe's cultural heritage, it is also necessary to ensure that orphan works which have been digitised and made available to the public in one Member State may also be made available to the public in other Member States. Publicly accessible libraries, educational establishments and museums, as well as archives, film or audio heritage institutions and public-service broadcasting organisations that use an orphan work in order to achieve their public-interest missions should be able to make the orphan work available to the public in other Member States.

(24) This Directive is without prejudice to the arrangements in the Member States concerning the management of rights such as extended collective licences, legal presumptions of representation or transfer, collective management or similar arrangements or a combination of them, including for mass digitisation.

(25) Since the objective of this Directive, namely ensuring legal certainty with respect to the use of orphan works, cannot be sufficiently achieved by the Member States and can therefore, by reason of the need for uniformity of the rules governing the use of orphan works, be better achieved at Union level, the Union may adopt measures, in accordance with the principle of subsidiarity as set out in Article 5 of the Treaty on European Union. In accordance with the principle of proportionality, as set out in that Article, this Directive does not go beyond what is necessary in order to achieve that objective,

NOTES

[1] OJ C376, 22.12.2011, p 66.

[2] Position of the European Parliament of 13 September 2012 (not yet published in the Official Journal) and decision of the Council of 4 October 2012.

[3] OJ L167, 22.6.2001, p 10.

[4] Regulation (EU) No 386/2012 of the European Parliament and of the Council of 19 April 2012 on entrusting the Office for Harmonization in the Internal Market (Trade Marks and Designs) with tasks related to the enforcement of intellectual property rights, including the assembling of public and private-sector representatives as a European Observatory on Infringements of Intellectual Property Rights (OJ L129, 16.5.2012, p 1).

HAVE ADOPTED THIS DIRECTIVE—

[8.623]

Article 1

Subject-matter and scope

1. This Directive concerns certain uses made of orphan works by publicly accessible libraries, educational establishments and museums, as well as by archives, film or audio heritage institutions and public-service broadcasting organisations, established in the Member States, in order to achieve aims related to their public-interest missions.

2. This Directive applies to:

(a) works published in the form of books, journals, newspapers, magazines or other writings contained in the collections of publicly accessible libraries, educational establishments or museums as well as in the collections of archives or of film or audio heritage institutions;

(b) cinematographic or audiovisual works and phonograms contained in the collections of publicly accessible libraries, educational establishments or museums as well as in the collections of archives or of film or audio heritage institutions; and

(c) cinematographic or audiovisual works and phonograms produced by public-service broadcasting organisations up to and including 31 December 2002 and contained in their archives;

which are protected by copyright or related rights and which are first published in a Member State or, in the absence of publication, first broadcast in a Member State.

3. This Directive also applies to works and phonograms referred to in paragraph 2 which have never been published or broadcast but which have been made publicly accessible by the organisations referred to in paragraph 1 with the consent of the rightholders, provided that it is reasonable to assume that the rightholders would not oppose the uses referred to in Article 6. Member States may limit the application of this paragraph to works and phonograms which have been deposited with those organisations before 29 October 2014.

4. This Directive shall also apply to works and other protected subject-matter that are embedded or incorporated in, or constitute an integral part of, the works or phonograms referred to in paragraphs 2 and 3.
5. This Directive does not interfere with any arrangements concerning the management of rights at national level.

[8.624]
Article 2
Orphan works
1. A work or a phonogram shall be considered an orphan work if none of the rightholders in that work or phonogram is identified or, even if one or more of them is identified, none is located despite a diligent search for the rightholders having been carried out and recorded in accordance with Article 3.
2. Where there is more than one rightholder in a work or phonogram, and not all of them have been identified or, even if identified, located after a diligent search has been carried out and recorded in accordance with Article 3, the work or phonogram may be used in accordance with this Directive provided that the rightholders that have been identified and located have, in relation to the rights they hold, authorised the organisations referred to in Article 1(1) to carry out the acts of reproduction and making available to the public covered respectively by Articles 2 and 3 of Directive 2001/29/EC.
3. Paragraph 2 shall be without prejudice to the rights in the work or phonogram of rightholders that have been identified and located.
4. Article 5 shall apply *mutatis mutandis* to the rightholders that have not been identified and located in the works referred to in paragraph 2.
5. This Directive shall be without prejudice to national provisions on anonymous or pseudonymous works.

[8.625]
Article 3
Diligent search
1. For the purposes of establishing whether a work or phonogram is an orphan work, the organisations referred to in Article 1(1) shall ensure that a diligent search is carried out in good faith in respect of each work or other protected subject-matter, by consulting the appropriate sources for the category of works and other protected subject-matter in question. The diligent search shall be carried out prior to the use of the work or phonogram.
2. The sources that are appropriate for each category of works or phonogram in question shall be determined by each Member State, in consultation with rightholders and users, and shall include at least the relevant sources listed in the Annex.
3. A diligent search shall be carried out in the Member State of first publication or, in the absence of publication, first broadcast, except in the case of cinematographic or audiovisual works the producer of which has his headquarters or habitual residence in a Member State, in which case the diligent search shall be carried out in the Member State of his headquarters or habitual residence.
In the case referred to in Article 1(3), the diligent search shall be carried out in the Member State where the organisation that made the work or phonogram publicly accessible with the consent of the rightholder is established.
4. If there is evidence to suggest that relevant information on rightholders is to be found in other countries, sources of information available in those other countries shall also be consulted.
5. Member States shall ensure that the organisations referred to in Article 1(1) maintain records of their diligent searches and that those organisations provide the following information to the competent national authorities:
(a) the results of the diligent searches that the organisations have carried out and which have led to the conclusion that a work or a phonogram is considered an orphan work;
(b) the use that the organisations make of orphan works in accordance with this Directive;
(c) any change, pursuant to Article 5, of the orphan work status of works and phonograms that the organisations use;
(d) the relevant contact information of the organisation concerned.
6. Member States shall take the necessary measures to ensure that the information referred to in paragraph 5 is recorded in a single publicly accessible online database established and managed by the Office for Harmonization in the Internal Market ('the Office') in accordance with Regulation (EU) No 386/2012. To that end, they shall forward that information to the Office without delay upon receiving it from the organisations referred to in Article 1(1).

[8.626]
Article 4
Mutual recognition of orphan work status
A work or phonogram which is considered an orphan work according to Article 2 in a Member State shall be considered an orphan work in all Member States. That work or phonogram may be used and accessed in accordance with this Directive in all Member States. This also applies

to works and phonograms referred to in Article 2(2) in so far as the rights of the non-identified or non-located rightholders are concerned.

[8.627]
Article 5
End of orphan work status

Member States shall ensure that a rightholder in a work or phonogram considered to be an orphan work has, at any time, the possibility of putting an end to the orphan work status in so far as his rights are concerned.

[8.628]
Article 6
Permitted uses of orphan works

1. Member States shall provide for an exception or limitation to the right of reproduction and the right of making available to the public provided for respectively in Articles 2 and 3 of Directive 2001/29/EC to ensure that the organisations referred to in Article 1(1) are permitted to use orphan works contained in their collections in the following ways:

(a) by making the orphan work available to the public, within the meaning of Article 3 of Directive 2001/29/EC;

(b) by acts of reproduction, within the meaning of Article 2 of Directive 2001/29/EC, for the purposes of digitisation, making available, indexing, cataloguing, preservation or restoration.

2. The organisations referred to in Article 1(1) shall use an orphan work in accordance with paragraph 1 of this Article only in order to achieve aims related to their public-interest missions, in particular the preservation of, the restoration of, and the provision of cultural and educational access to, works and phonograms contained in their collection. The organisations may generate revenues in the course of such uses, for the exclusive purpose of covering their costs of digitising orphan works and making them available to the public.

3. Member States shall ensure that the organisations referred to in Article 1(1) indicate the name of identified authors and other rightholders in any use of an orphan work.

4. This Directive is without prejudice to the freedom of contract of such organisations in the pursuit of their public-interest missions, particularly in respect of public-private partnership agreements.

5. Member States shall provide that a fair compensation is due to rightholders that put an end to the orphan work status of their works or other protected subject-matter for the use that has been made by the organisations referred to in Article 1(1) of such works and other protected subject-matter in accordance with paragraph 1 of this Article. Member States shall be free to determine the circumstances under which the payment of such compensation may be organised. The level of the compensation shall be determined, within the limits imposed by Union law, by the law of the Member State in which the organisation which uses the orphan work in question is established.

[8.629]
Article 7
Continued application of other legal provisions

This Directive shall be without prejudice to provisions concerning, in particular, patent rights, trade marks, design rights, utility models, the topographies of semi-conductor products, type faces, conditional access, access to cable of broadcasting services, the protection of national treasures, legal deposit requirements, laws on restrictive practices and unfair competition, trade secrets, security, confidentiality, data protection and privacy, access to public documents, the law of contract, and rules on the freedom of the press and freedom of expression in the media.

[8.630]
Article 8
Application in time

1. This Directive shall apply in respect of all works and phonograms referred to in Article 1 which are protected by the Member States' legislation in the field of copyright on or after 29 October 2014.

2. This Directive shall apply without prejudice to any acts concluded and rights acquired before 29 October 2014.

[8.631]
Article 9
Transposition

1. Member States shall bring into force the laws, regulations and administrative provisions necessary to comply with this Directive by 29 October 2014. They shall forthwith communicate to the Commission the text of those provisions.

When Member States adopt those provisions, they shall contain a reference to this Directive or shall be accompanied by such a reference on the occasion of their official publication. The methods of making such reference shall be laid down by Member States.

2. Member States shall communicate to the Commission the text of the main provisions of national law which they adopt in the field covered by this Directive.

[8.632]
Article 10
Review clause
The Commission shall keep under constant review the development of rights information sources and shall by 29 October 2015, and at annual intervals thereafter, submit a report concerning the possible inclusion in the scope of application of this Directive of publishers and of works or other protected subject-matter not currently included in its scope, and in particular stand-alone photographs and other images.

By 29 October 2015, the Commission shall submit to the European Parliament, the Council and the European Economic and Social Committee a report on the application of this Directive, in the light of the development of digital libraries.

When necessary, in particular to ensure the functioning of the internal market, the Commission shall submit proposals for amendment of this Directive.

A Member State that has valid reasons to consider that the implementation of this Directive hinders one of the national arrangements concerning the management of rights referred to in Article 1(5) may bring the matter to the attention of the Commission together with all relevant evidence. The Commission shall take such evidence into account when drawing up the report referred to in the second paragraph of this Article and when assessing whether it is necessary to submit proposals for amendment of this Directive.

[8.633]
Article 11
Entry into force
This Directive shall enter into force on the day following that of its publication in the *Official Journal of the European Union*.

[8.634]
Article 12
Addressees
This Directive is addressed to the Member States.

ANNEX

[8.635]
The sources referred to in Article 3(2) include the following:

(1) for published books:
- (a) legal deposit, library catalogues and authority files maintained by libraries and other institutions;
- (b) the publishers' and authors' associations in the respective country;
- (c) existing databases and registries, WATCH (Writers, Artists and their Copyright Holders), the ISBN (International Standard Book Number) and databases listing books in print;
- (d) the databases of the relevant collecting societies, in particular reproduction rights organisations;
- (e) sources that integrate multiple databases and registries, including VIAF (Virtual International Authority Files) and ARROW (Accessible Registries of Rights Information and Orphan Works);

(2) for newspapers, magazines, journals and periodicals:
- (a) the ISSN (International Standard Serial Number) for periodical publications;
- (b) indexes and catalogues from library holdings and collections;
- (c) legal deposit;
- (d) the publishers' associations and the authors' and journalists' associations in the respective country;
- (e) the databases of relevant collecting societies including reproduction rights organisations;

(3) for visual works, including fine art, photography, illustration, design, architecture, sketches of the latter works and other such works that are contained in books, journals, newspapers and magazines or other works:
- (a) the sources referred to in points (1) and (2);
- (b) the databases of the relevant collecting societies, in particular for visual arts, and including reproduction rights organisations;
- (c) the databases of picture agencies, where applicable;

(4) for audiovisual works and phonograms:
- (a) legal deposit;
- (b) the producers' associations in the respective country;
- (c) databases of film or audio heritage institutions and national libraries;

(d) databases with relevant standards and identifiers such as ISAN (International Standard Audiovisual Number) for audiovisual material, ISWC (International Standard Music Work Code) for musical works and ISRC (International Standard Recording Code) for phonograms;
(e) the databases of the relevant collecting societies, in particular for authors, performers, phonogram producers and audiovisual producers;
(f) credits and other information appearing on the work's packaging;
(g) databases of other relevant associations representing a specific category of rightholders.

REGULATION OF THE EUROPEAN PARLIAMENT AND OF THE COUNCIL

(608/2013/EU)

of 12 June 2013

concerning customs enforcement of intellectual property rights and repealing Council Regulation (EC) No 1383/2003

THE EUROPEAN PARLIAMENT AND THE COUNCIL OF THE EUROPEAN UNION,

Having regard to the Treaty on the Functioning of the European Union, and in particular Article 207 thereof,

Having regard to the proposal from the European Commission,

After transmission of the draft legislative act to the national parliaments,

Acting in accordance with the ordinary legislative procedure,[1]

Whereas:

(1) The Council requested, in its Resolution of 25 September 2008 on a comprehensive European anti-counterfeiting and anti-piracy plan, that Council Regulation (EC) No 1383/2003 of 22 July 2003 concerning customs action against goods suspected of infringing certain intellectual property rights and the measures to be taken against goods found to have infringed such rights,[2] be reviewed.

(2) The marketing of goods infringing intellectual property rights does considerable damage to right-holders, users or groups of producers, and to law-abiding manufacturers and traders. Such marketing could also be deceiving consumers, and could in some cases be endangering their health and safety. Such goods should, in so far as is possible, be kept off the Union market and measures should be adopted to deal with such unlawful marketing without impeding legitimate trade.

(3) The review of Regulation (EC) No 1383/2003 showed that, in the light of economic, commercial and legal developments, certain improvements to the legal framework are necessary to strengthen the enforcement of intellectual property rights by customs authorities, as well as to ensure appropriate legal certainty.

(4) The customs authorities should be competent to enforce intellectual property rights with regard to goods, which, in accordance with Union customs legislation, are liable to customs supervision or customs control, and to carry out adequate controls on such goods with a view to preventing operations in breach of intellectual property rights laws. Enforcing intellectual property rights at the border, wherever the goods are, or should have been, under customs supervision or customs control is an efficient way to quickly and effectively provide legal protection to the right-holder as well as the users and groups of producers. Where the release of goods is suspended or goods are detained by customs authorities at the border, only one legal proceeding should be required, whereas several separate proceedings should be required for the same level of enforcement for goods found on the market, which have been disaggregated and delivered to retailers. An exception should be made for goods released for free circulation under the end-use regime, as such goods remain under customs supervision, even though they have been released for free circulation. This Regulation should not apply to goods carried by passengers in their personal luggage provided that those goods are for their own personal use and there are no indications that commercial traffic is involved.

(5) Regulation (EC) No 1383/2003 does not cover certain intellectual property rights and certain infringements are excluded from its scope. In order to strengthen the enforcement of intellectual property rights, customs intervention should be extended to other types of infringements not covered by Regulation (EC) No 1383/2003. This Regulation should therefore, in addition to the rights already covered by Regulation (EC) No 1383/2003, also include trade names in so far as they are protected as exclusive property rights under national law, topographies of semiconductor products and utility models and devices which are primarily designed, produced or adapted for the purpose of enabling or facilitating the circumvention of technological measures.

(6) Infringements resulting from so-called illegal parallel trade and overruns are excluded from the scope of Regulation (EC) No 1383/2003. Goods subject to illegal parallel trade, namely goods that have been manufactured with the consent of the right-holder but placed on the market for the

first time in the European Economic Area without his consent, and overruns, namely goods that are manufactured by a person duly authorised by a right-holder to manufacture a certain quantity of goods, in excess of the quantities agreed between that person and the right-holder, are manufactured as genuine goods and it is therefore not appropriate that customs authorities focus their efforts on such goods. Illegal parallel trade and overruns should therefore also be excluded from the scope of this Regulation.

(7) Member States should, in cooperation with the Commission, provide appropriate training for customs officials, in order to ensure the correct implementation of this Regulation.

(8) This Regulation, when fully implemented, will further contribute to an internal market which ensures right-holders a more effective protection, fuels creativity and innovation and provides consumers with reliable and high-quality products, which should in turn strengthen cross-border transactions between consumers, businesses and traders.

(9) Member States face increasingly limited resources in the field of customs. Therefore, the promotion of risk management technologies and strategies to maximise resources available to customs authorities should be supported.

(10) This Regulation solely contains procedural rules for customs authorities. Accordingly, this Regulation does not set out any criteria for ascertaining the existence of an infringement of an intellectual property right.

(11) Under the 'Declaration on the TRIPS Agreement and Public Health' adopted by the Doha WTO Ministerial Conference on 14 November 2001, the Agreement on Trade-Related Aspects of Intellectual Property Rights (TRIPS Agreement) can and should be interpreted and implemented in a manner supportive of WTO Members' right to protect public health and, in particular, to promote access to medicines for all. Consequently, in line with the Union's international commitments and its development cooperation policy, with regard to medicines, the passage of which across the customs territory of the Union, with or without transhipment, warehousing, breaking bulk, or changes in the mode or means of transport, is only a portion of a complete journey beginning and terminating beyond the territory of the Union, customs authorities should, when assessing a risk of infringement of intellectual property rights, take account of any substantial likelihood of diversion of such medicines onto the market of the Union.

(12) This Regulation should not affect the provisions on the competence of courts, in particular, those of Regulation (EU) No 1215/2012 of the European Parliament and of the Council of 12 December 2012 on jurisdiction and the recognition and enforcement of judgments in civil and commercial matters.[3]

(13) Persons, users, bodies or groups of producers, who are in a position to initiate legal proceedings in their own name with respect to a possible infringement of an intellectual property right, should be entitled to submit an application.

(14) In order to ensure that intellectual property rights are enforced throughout the Union, it is appropriate to allow persons or entities seeking enforcement of Union-wide rights to apply to the customs authorities of a single Member State. Such applicants should be able to request that those authorities decide that action be taken to enforce the intellectual property right both in their own Member State and in any other Member State.

(15) In order to ensure the swift enforcement of intellectual property rights, it should be provided that, where the customs authorities suspect, on the basis of reasonable indications, that goods under their supervision infringe intellectual property rights, they may suspend the release of or detain the goods whether at their own initiative or upon application, in order to enable a person or entity entitled to submit an application to initiate proceedings for determining whether an intellectual property right has been infringed.

(16) Regulation (EC) No 1383/2003 allowed Member States to provide for a procedure allowing the destruction of certain goods without there being any obligation to initiate proceedings to establish whether an intellectual property right has been infringed. As recognised in the European Parliament Resolution of 18 December 2008 on the impact of counterfeiting on international trade,[4] such procedure has proved very successful in the Member States where it has been available. Therefore, the procedure should be made compulsory with regard to all infringements of intellectual property rights and should be applied, where the declarant or the holder of the goods agrees to destruction. Furthermore, the procedure should provide that customs authorities may deem that the declarant or the holder of the goods has agreed to the destruction of the goods where he has not explicitly opposed destruction within the prescribed period.

(17) In order to reduce the administrative burden and costs to a minimum, a specific procedure should be introduced for small consignments of counterfeit and pirated goods, which should allow for such goods to be destroyed without the explicit agreement of the applicant in each case. However, a general request made by the applicant in the application should be required in order for that procedure to be applied. Furthermore, customs authorities should have the possibility to require that the applicant covers the costs incurred by the application of that procedure.

(18) For further legal certainty, it is appropriate to modify the timelines for suspending the release of or detaining goods suspected of infringing an intellectual property right and the conditions

in which information about detained goods is to be passed on to persons and entities concerned by customs authorities, as provided for in Regulation (EC) No 1383/2003.

(19) Taking into account the provisional and preventive character of the measures adopted by the customs authorities when applying this Regulation and the conflicting interests of the parties affected by the measures, some aspects of the procedures should be adapted to ensure the smooth application of this Regulation, whilst respecting the rights of the concerned parties. Thus, with respect to the various notifications envisaged by this Regulation, the customs authorities should notify the relevant person, on the basis of the documents concerning the customs treatment or of the situation in which the goods are placed. Furthermore, since the procedure for destruction of goods implies that both the declarant or the holder of the goods and the holder of the decision should communicate their possible objections to destruction in parallel, it should be ensured that the holder of the decision is given the possibility to react to a potential objection to destruction by the declarant or the holder of the goods. It should therefore be ensured that the declarant or the holder of the goods is notified of the suspension of the release of the goods or their detention before, or on the same day as, the holder of the decision.

(20) Customs authorities and the Commission are encouraged to cooperate with the European Observatory on Infringements of Intellectual Property Rights in the framework of their respective competences.

(21) With a view to eliminating international trade in goods infringing intellectual property rights, the TRIPS Agreement provides that WTO Members are to promote the exchange of information between customs authorities on such trade. Accordingly, it should be possible for the Commission and the customs authorities of the Member States to share information on suspected breaches of intellectual property rights with the relevant authorities of third countries, including on goods which are in transit through the territory of the Union and originate in or are destined for those third countries.

(22) In the interest of efficiency, the provisions of Council Regulation (EC) No 515/97 of 13 March 1997 on mutual assistance between the administrative authorities of the Member States and cooperation between the latter and the Commission to ensure the correct application of the law on customs or agricultural matters,[5] should apply.

(23) The liability of the customs authorities should be governed by the legislation of the Member States, though the granting by the customs authorities of an application should not entitle the holder of the decision to compensation in the event that goods suspected of infringing an intellectual property right are not detected by the customs authorities and are released or no action is taken to detain them.

(24) Given that customs authorities take action upon application, it is appropriate to provide that the holder of the decision should reimburse all the costs incurred by the customs authorities in taking action to enforce his intellectual property rights. Nevertheless, this should not preclude the holder of the decision from seeking compensation from the infringer or other persons that might be considered liable under the legislation of the Member State where the goods were found. Such persons might include intermediaries, where applicable. Costs and damages incurred by persons other than customs authorities as a result of a customs action, where the release of goods is suspended or the goods are detained on the basis of a claim of a third party based on intellectual property, should be governed by the specific legislation applicable in each particular case.

(25) This Regulation introduces the possibility for customs authorities to allow goods which are to be destroyed to be moved, under customs supervision, between different places within the customs territory of the Union. Customs authorities may furthermore decide to release such goods for free circulation with a view to further recycling or disposal outside commercial channels including for awareness-raising, training and educational purposes.

(26) Customs enforcement of intellectual property rights entails the exchange of data on decisions relating to applications. Such processing of data covers also personal data and should be carried out in accordance with Union law, as set out in Directive 95/46/EC of the European Parliament and of the Council of 24 October 1995 on the protection of individuals with regard to the processing of personal data and on the free movement of such data[6] and Regulation (EC) No 45/2001 of the European Parliament and of the Council of 18 December 2000 on the protection of individuals with regard to the processing of personal data by Community institutions and bodies and on the free movement of such data.[7]

(27) The exchange of information relating to decisions on applications and to customs actions should be made via a central electronic database. The entity which will control and manage that database and the entities in charge of ensuring the security of the processing of the data contained in the database should be defined. Introducing any type of possible interoperability or exchange should first and foremost comply with the purpose limitation principle, namely that data should be used for the purpose for which the database has been established, and no further exchange or interconnection should be allowed other than for that purpose.

(28) In order to ensure that the definition of small consignments can be adapted if it proves to be impractical, taking into account the need to ensure the effective operation of the procedure, or

where necessary to avoid any circumvention of this procedure as regards the composition of consignments, the power to adopt acts in accordance with Article 290 of the Treaty on the Functioning of the European Union should be delegated to the Commission in respect of amending the non-essential elements of the definition of small consignments, namely the specific quantities set out in that definition. It is of particular importance that the Commission carry out appropriate consultations during its preparatory work, including at expert level. The Commission, when preparing and drawing up delegated acts, should ensure a simultaneous, timely and appropriate transmission of relevant documents to the European Parliament and to the Council.

(29) In order to ensure uniform conditions for the implementation of the provisions concerning defining the elements of the practical arrangements for the exchange of data with third countries and the provisions concerning the forms for the application and for requesting the extension of the period during which customs authorities are to take action, implementing powers should be conferred on the Commission, namely to define those elements of the practical arrangements and to establish standard forms. Those powers should be exercised in accordance with Regulation (EU) No 182/2011 of the European Parliament and of the Council of 16 February 2011 laying down the rules and general principles concerning mechanisms for control by Member States of the Commission's exercise of implementing powers.[8] For establishing the standard forms, although the subject of the provisions of this Regulation to be implemented falls within the scope of the common commercial policy, given the nature and impacts of those implementing acts, the advisory procedure should be used for their adoption, because all details of what information to include in the forms follows directly from the text of this Regulation. Those implementing acts will therefore only establish the format and structure of the form and will have no further implications for the common commercial policy of the Union.

(30) Regulation (EC) No 1383/2003 should be repealed.

(31) The European Data Protection Supervisor was consulted in accordance with Article 28(2) of Regulation (EC) No 45/2001 and delivered an opinion on 12 October 2011,[9]

NOTES

1 Position of the European Parliament of 3 July 2012 (not yet published in the Official Journal) and position of the Council at first reading of 16 May 2013 (not yet published in the Official Journal). Position of the European Parliament of 11 June 2013 (not yet published in the Official Journal).

2 OJ L196, 2.8.2003, p 7.

3 OJ L351, 20.12.2012, p 1.

4 OJ C45 E, 23.2.2010, p 47.

5 OJ L82, 22.3.1997, p 1.

6 OJ L281, 23.11.1995, p 31.

7 OJ L8, 12.1.2001, p 1.

8 OJ L55, 28.2.2011, p 13.

9 OJ C363, 13.12.2011, p 3.

HAVE ADOPTED THIS REGULATION:

CHAPTER I
SUBJECT MATTER, SCOPE AND DEFINITIONS

[8.636]

Article 1

Subject matter and scope

1. This Regulation sets out the conditions and procedures for action by the customs authorities where goods suspected of infringing an intellectual property right are, or should have been, subject to customs supervision or customs control within the customs territory of the Union in accordance with Council Regulation (EEC) No 2913/92 of 12 October 1992 establishing the Community Customs Code,[1] particularly goods in the following situations:

(a) when declared for release for free circulation, export or re-export;

(b) when entering or leaving the customs territory of the Union;

(c) when placed under a suspensive procedure or in a free zone or free warehouse.

2. In respect of the goods subject to customs supervision or customs control, and without prejudice to Articles 17 and 18, the customs authorities shall carry out adequate customs controls and shall take proportionate identification measures as provided for in Article 13(1) and Article 72 of Regulation (EEC) No 2913/92 in accordance with risk analysis criteria with a view to preventing acts in breach of intellectual property laws applicable in the territory of the Union and in order to cooperate with third countries on the enforcement of intellectual property rights.

3. This Regulation shall not apply to goods that have been released for free circulation under the end-use regime.

4. This Regulation shall not apply to goods of a non-commercial nature contained in travellers' personal luggage.

5. This Regulation shall not apply to goods that have been manufactured with the consent of the right-holder or to goods manufactured, by a person duly authorised by a right-holder to manufacture a certain quantity of goods, in excess of the quantities agreed between that person and the right-holder.
6. This Regulation shall not affect national or Union law on intellectual property or the laws of the Member States in relation to criminal procedures.

NOTES

[1] OJ L302, 19.10.1992, p 1.

[8.637]
Article 2
Definitions

For the purposes of this Regulation:

(1) 'intellectual property right' means:
   (a) a trade mark;
   (b) a design;
   (c) a copyright or any related right as provided for by national or Union law;
   (d) a geographical indication;
   (e) a patent as provided for by national or Union law;
   (f) a supplementary protection certificate for medicinal products as provided for in Regulation (EC) No 469/2009 of the European Parliament and of the Council of 6 May 2009 concerning the supplementary protection certificate for medicinal products;[1]
   (g) a supplementary protection certificate for plant protection products as provided for in Regulation (EC) No 1610/96 of the European Parliament and of the Council of 23 July 1996 concerning the creation of a supplementary protection certificate for plant protection products;[2]
   (h) a Community plant variety right as provided for in Council Regulation (EC) No 2100/94 of 27 July 1994 on Community plant variety rights;[3]
   (i) a plant variety right as provided for by national law;
   (j) a topography of semiconductor product as provided for by national or Union law;
   (k) a utility model in so far as it is protected as an intellectual property right by national or Union law;
   (l) a trade name in so far as it is protected as an exclusive intellectual property right by national or Union law;

(2) 'trade mark' means:
   (a) a Community trade mark as provided for in Council Regulation (EC) No 207/2009 of 26 February 2009 on the Community trade mark;[4]
   (b) a trade mark registered in a Member State, or, in the case of Belgium, Luxembourg or the Netherlands, at the Benelux Office for Intellectual Property;
   (c) a trade mark registered under international arrangements which has effect in a Member State or in the Union;

(3) 'design' means:
   (a) a Community design as provided for in Council Regulation (EC) No 6/2002 of 12 December 2001 on Community designs;[5]
   (b) a design registered in a Member State, or, in the case of Belgium, Luxembourg or the Netherlands, at the Benelux Office for Intellectual Property;
   (c) a design registered under international arrangements which has effect in a Member State or in the Union;

(4) 'geographical indication' means:
   (a) a geographical indication or designation of origin protected for agricultural products and foodstuff as provided for in Regulation (EU) No 1151/2012 of the European Parliament and of the Council of 21 November 2012 on quality schemes for agricultural products and foodstuffs;[6]
   (b) a designation of origin or geographical indication for wine as provided for in Council Regulation (EC) No 1234/2007 of 22 October 2007 establishing a common organisation of agricultural markets and on specific provisions for certain agricultural products (Single CMO Regulation);[7]
   (c) a geographical designation for aromatised drinks based on wine products as provided for in Council Regulation (EEC) No 1601/91 of 10 June 1991 laying down general rules on the definition, description and presentation of aromatized wines, aromatized wine-based drinks and aromatized wine-product cocktails;[8]
   (d) a geographical indication of spirit drinks as provided for in Regulation (EC) No 110/2008 of the European Parliament and of the Council of 15 January 2008 on the definition, description, presentation, labelling and the protection of geographical indications of spirit drinks;[9]

(e) a geographical indication for products not falling under points (a) to (d) in so far as it is established as an exclusive intellectual property right by national or Union law;
(f) a geographical indication as provided for in Agreements between the Union and third countries and as such listed in those Agreements;

(5) 'counterfeit goods' means:
(a) goods which are the subject of an act infringing a trade mark in the Member State where they are found and bear without authorisation a sign which is identical to the trade mark validly registered in respect of the same type of goods, or which cannot be distinguished in its essential aspects from such a trade mark;
(b) goods which are the subject of an act infringing a geographical indication in the Member State where they are found and, bear or are described by, a name or term protected in respect of that geographical indication;
(c) any packaging, label, sticker, brochure, operating instructions, warranty document or other similar item, even if presented separately, which is the subject of an act infringing a trade mark or a geographical indication, which includes a sign, name or term which is identical to a validly registered trade mark or protected geographical indication, or which cannot be distinguished in its essential aspects from such a trade mark or geographical indication, and which can be used for the same type of goods as that for which the trade mark or geographical indication has been registered;

(6) 'pirated goods' means goods which are the subject of an act infringing a copyright or related right or a design in the Member State where the goods are found and which are, or contain copies, made without the consent of the holder of a copyright or related right or a design, or of a person authorised by that holder in the country of production;

(7) 'goods suspected of infringing an intellectual property right' means goods with regard to which there are reasonable indications that, in the Member State where those goods are found, they are prima facie:
(a) goods which are the subject of an act infringing an intellectual property right in that Member State;
(b) devices, products or components which are primarily designed, produced or adapted for the purpose of enabling or facilitating the circumvention of any technology, device or component that, in the normal course of its operation, prevents or restricts acts in respect of works which are not authorised by the holder of any copyright or any right related to copyright and which relate to an act infringing those rights in that Member State;
(c) any mould or matrix which is specifically designed or adapted for the manufacture of goods infringing an intellectual property right, if such moulds or matrices relate to an act infringing an intellectual property right in that Member State;

(8) 'right-holder' means the holder of an intellectual property right;

(9) 'application' means a request made to the competent customs department for customs authorities to take action with respect to goods suspected of infringing an intellectual property right;

(10) 'national application' means an application requesting the customs authorities of a Member State to take action in that Member State;

(11) 'Union application' means an application submitted in one Member State and requesting the customs authorities of that Member State and of one or more other Member States to take action in their respective Member States;

(12) 'applicant' means the person or entity in whose name an application is submitted;

(13) 'holder of the decision' means the holder of a decision granting an application;

(14) 'holder of the goods' means the person who is the owner of the goods suspected of infringing an intellectual property right or who has a similar right of disposal, or physical control, over such goods;

(15) 'declarant' means the declarant as defined in point (18) of Article 4 of Regulation (EEC) No 2913/92;

(16) 'destruction' means the physical destruction, recycling or disposal of goods outside commercial channels, in such a way as to preclude damage to the holder of the decision;

(17) 'customs territory of the Union' means the customs territory of the Community as defined in Article 3 of Regulation (EEC) No 2913/92;

(18) 'release of the goods' means the release of the goods as defined in point (20) of Article 4 of Regulation (EEC) No 2913/92;

(19) 'small consignment' means a postal or express courier consignment, which:
(a) contains three units or less;
or
(b) has a gross weight of less than two kilograms.

For the purpose of point (a), 'units' means goods as classified under the Combined Nomenclature in accordance with Annex I to Council Regulation (EEC) No 2658/87 of 23 July 1987 on the tariff and statistical nomenclature and on the Common Customs Tariff[10] if unpackaged, or the package of such goods intended for retail sale to the ultimate consumer.

For the purpose of this definition, separate goods falling in the same Combined Nomenclature code shall be considered as different units and goods presented as sets classified in one Combined Nomenclature code shall be considered as one unit;

(20) 'perishable goods' means goods considered by customs authorities to deteriorate by being kept for up to 20 days from the date of their suspension of release or detention;

(21) 'exclusive licence' means a licence (whether general or limited) authorising the licensee to the exclusion of all other persons, including the person granting the licence, to use an intellectual property right in the manner authorised by the licence.

NOTES

1 OJ L152, 16.6.2009, p 1.

2 OJ L198, 8.8.1996, p 30.

3 OJ L227, 1.9.1994, p 1.

4 OJ L78, 24.3.2009, p 1.

5 OJ L3, 5.1.2002, p 1.

6 OJ L343, 14.12.2012, p 1.

7 OJ L299, 16.11.2007, p 1.

8 OJ L149, 14.6.1991, p 1.

9 OJ L39, 13.2.2008, p 16.

10 OJ L256, 7.9.1987, p 1.

CHAPTER II
APPLICATIONS

SECTION 1
SUBMISSION OF APPLICATIONS

[8.638]

Article 3

Entitlement to submit an application

The following persons and entities shall, to the extent they are entitled to initiate proceedings, in order to determine whether an intellectual property right has been infringed, in the Member State or Member States where the customs authorities are requested to take action, be entitled to submit:

(1) a national or a Union application:

(a) right-holders;

(b) intellectual property collective rights management bodies as referred to in point (c) of Article 4(1) of Directive 2004/48/EC of the European Parliament and of the Council of 29 April 2004 on the enforcement of intellectual property rights;[1]

(c) professional defence bodies as referred to in point (d) of Article 4(1) of Directive 2004/48/EC;

(d) groups within the meaning of point (2) of Article 3, and Article 49(1) of Regulation (EU) No 1151/2012, groups of producers within the meaning of Article 118e of Regulation (EC) No 1234/2007 or similar groups of producers provided for in Union law governing geographical indications representing producers of products with a geographical indication or representatives of such groups, in particular Regulations (EEC) No 1601/91 and (EC) No 110/2008 and operators entitled to use a geographical indication as well as inspection bodies or authorities competent for such a geographical indication;

(2) a national application:

(a) persons or entities authorised to use intellectual property rights, which have been authorised formally by the right-holder to initiate proceedings in order to determine whether the intellectual property right has been infringed;

(b) groups of producers provided for in the legislation of the Member States governing geographical indications representing producers of products with geographical indications or representatives of such groups and operators entitled to use a geographical indication, as well as inspection bodies or authorities competent for such a geographical indication;

(3) a Union application: holders of exclusive licenses covering the entire territory of two or more Member States, where those licence holders have been authorised formally in those Member States by the right-holder to initiate proceedings in order to determine whether the intellectual property right has been infringed.

NOTES

1 OJ L157, 30.4.2004, p 45.

[8.639]
Article 4
Intellectual property rights covered by Union applications

A Union application may be submitted only with respect to intellectual property rights based on Union law producing effects throughout the Union.

[8.640]
Article 5
Submission of applications

1. Each Member State shall designate the customs department competent to receive and process applications ('competent customs department'). The Member State shall inform the Commission accordingly and the Commission shall make public a list of competent customs departments designated by the Member States.

2. Applications shall be submitted to the competent customs department. The applications shall be completed using the form referred to in Article 6 and shall contain the information required therein.

3. Where an application is submitted after notification by the customs authorities of the suspension of the release or detention of the goods in accordance with Article 18(3), that application shall comply with the following:

(a) it is submitted to the competent customs department within four working days of the notification of the suspension of the release or detention of the goods;

(b) it is a national application;

(c) it contains the information referred to in Article 6(3). The applicant may, however, omit the information referred to in point (g), (h) or (i) of that paragraph.

4. Except in the circumstances referred to in point (3) of Article 3, only one national application and one Union application may be submitted per Member State for the same intellectual property right protected in that Member State. In the circumstances referred to in point (3) of Article 3, more than one Union application shall be allowed.

5. Where a Union application is granted for a Member State already covered by another Union application granted to the same applicant and for the same intellectual property right, the customs authorities of that Member State shall take action on the basis of the Union application first granted. They shall inform the competent customs department of the Member State where any subsequent Union application was granted, which shall, amend or revoke the decision granting that subsequent Union application.

6. Where computerised systems are available for the purpose of receiving and processing applications, applications as well as attachments shall be submitted using electronic data-processing techniques. Member States and the Commission shall develop, maintain and employ such systems in accordance with the multi-annual strategic plan referred to in Article 8(2) of Decision No 70/2008/EC of the European Parliament and of the Council of 15 January 2008 on a paperless customs environment for customs and trade.[1]

NOTES

[1] OJ L23, 26.1.2008, p 21.

[8.641]
Article 6
Application form

1. The Commission shall establish an application form by means of implementing acts. Those implementing acts shall be adopted in accordance with the advisory procedure referred to in Article 34(2).

2. The application form shall specify the information that has to be provided to the data subject pursuant to Regulation (EC) No 45/2001 and national laws implementing Directive 95/46/EC.

3. The Commission shall ensure that the following information is required of the applicant in the application form:

(a) details concerning the applicant;

(b) the status, within the meaning of Article 3, of the applicant;

(c) documents providing evidence to satisfy the competent customs department that the applicant is entitled to submit the application;

(d) where the applicant submits the application by means of a representative, details of the person representing him and evidence of that person's powers to act as representative, in accordance with the legislation of the Member State in which the application is submitted;

(e) the intellectual property right or rights to be enforced;

(f) in the case of a Union application, the Member States in which customs action is requested;

(g) specific and technical data on the authentic goods, including markings such as bar-coding and images where appropriate;

(h) the information needed to enable the customs authorities to readily identify the goods in question;

(i) information relevant to the customs authorities' analysis and assessment of the risk of infringement of the intellectual property right or the intellectual property rights concerned, such as the authorised distributors;
(j) whether information provided in accordance with point (g), (h) or (i) of this paragraph is to be marked for restricted handling in accordance with Article 31(5);
(k) the details of any representative designated by the applicant to take charge of legal and technical matters;
(l) an undertaking by the applicant to notify the competent customs department of any of the situations laid down in Article 15;
(m) an undertaking by the applicant to forward and update any information relevant to the customs authorities' analysis and assessment of the risk of infringement of the intellectual property right(s) concerned;
(n) an undertaking by the applicant to assume liability under the conditions laid down in Article 28;
(o) an undertaking by the applicant to bear the costs referred to in Article 29 under the conditions laid down in that Article;
(p) an agreement by the applicant that the data provided by him may be processed by the Commission and by the Member States;
(q) whether the applicant requests the use of the procedure referred to in Article 26 and, where requested by the customs authorities, agrees to cover the costs related to destruction of goods under that procedure.

SECTION 2
DECISIONS ON APPLICATIONS

[8.642]
Article 7
Processing of incomplete applications
1. Where, on receipt of an application, the competent customs department considers that the application does not contain all the information required by Article 6(3), the competent customs department shall request the applicant to supply the missing information within 10 working days of notification of the request.

In such cases, the time-limit referred to in Article 9(1) shall be suspended until the relevant information is received.
2. Where the applicant does not provide the missing information within the period referred to in the first subparagraph of paragraph 1, the competent customs department shall reject the application.

[8.643]
Article 8
Fees
The applicant shall not be charged a fee to cover the administrative costs resulting from the processing of the application.

[8.644]
Article 9
Notification of decisions granting or rejecting applications
1. The competent customs department shall notify the applicant of its decision granting or rejecting the application within 30 working days of the receipt of the application. In the event of rejection, the competent customs department shall provide reasons for its decision and include information on the appeal procedure.
2. If the applicant has been notified of the suspension of the release or the detention of the goods by the customs authorities before the submission of an application, the competent customs department shall notify the applicant of its decision granting or rejecting the application within two working days of the receipt of the application.

[8.645]
Article 10
Decisions concerning applications
1. A decision granting a national application and any decision revoking or amending it shall take effect in the Member State in which the national application was submitted from the day following the date of adoption.
A decision extending the period during which customs authorities are to take action shall take effect in the Member State in which the national application was submitted on the day following the date of expiry of the period to be extended.
2. A decision granting a Union application and any decision revoking or amending it shall take effect as follows:
(a) in the Member State in which the application was submitted, on the day following the date of adoption;

(b) in all other Member States where action by the customs authorities is requested, on the day following the date on which the customs authorities are notified in accordance with Article 14(2), provided that the holder of the decision has fulfilled his obligations under Article 29(3) with regard to translation costs.

A decision extending the period during which customs authorities are to take action shall take effect in the Member State in which the Union application was submitted and in all other Member States where action by the customs authorities is requested the day following the date of expiry of the period to be extended.

[8.646]
Article 11
Period during which the customs authorities are to take action

1. When granting an application, the competent customs department shall specify the period during which the customs authorities are to take action.

That period shall begin on the day the decision granting the application takes effect, pursuant to Article 10, and shall not exceed one year from the day following the date of adoption.

2. Where an application submitted after notification by the customs authorities of the suspension of the release or detention of the goods in accordance with Article 18(3) does not contain the information referred to in point (g), (h) or (i) of Article 6(3), it shall be granted only for the suspension of the release or detention of those goods, unless that information is provided within 10 working days after the notification of the suspension of the release or detention of the goods.

3. Where an intellectual property right ceases to have effect or where the applicant ceases for other reasons to be entitled to submit an application, no action shall be taken by the customs authorities. The decision granting the application shall be revoked or amended accordingly by the competent customs department that granted the decision.

[8.647]
Article 12
Extension of the period during which the customs authorities are to take action

1. On expiry of the period during which the customs authorities are to take action, and subject to the prior discharge by the holder of the decision of any debt owed to the customs authorities under this Regulation, the competent customs department which adopted the initial decision may, at the request of the holder of the decision, extend that period.

2. Where the request for extension of the period during which the customs authorities are to take action is received by the competent customs department less than 30 working days before the expiry of the period to be extended, it may refuse that request.

3. The competent customs department shall notify its decision on the extension to the holder of the decision within 30 working days of the receipt of the request referred to in paragraph 1. The competent customs department shall specify the period during which the customs authorities are to take action.

4. The extended period during which the customs authorities are to take action shall run from the day following the date of expiry of the previous period and shall not exceed one year.

5. Where an intellectual property right ceases to have effect or where the applicant ceases for other reasons to be entitled to submit an application, no action shall be taken by the customs authorities. The decision granting the extension shall be revoked or amended accordingly by the competent customs department that granted the decision.

6. The holder of the decision shall not be charged a fee to cover the administrative costs resulting from the processing of the request for extension.

7. The Commission shall establish an extension request form by means of implementing acts. Those implementing acts shall be adopted in accordance with the advisory procedure referred to in Article 34(2).

[8.648]
Article 13
Amending the decision with regard to intellectual property rights.

The competent customs department that adopted the decision granting the application may, at the request of the holder of that decision, modify the list of intellectual property rights in that decision.

Where a new intellectual property right is added, the request shall contain the information referred to in points (c), (e), (g), (h) and (i) of Article 6(3).

In the case of a decision granting a Union application, any modification consisting of the addition of intellectual property rights shall be limited to intellectual property rights covered by Article 4.

[8.649]
Article 14
Notification obligations of the competent customs department

1. The competent customs department to which a national application has been submitted shall forward the following decisions to the customs offices of its Member State, immediately after their adoption:

(a) decisions granting the application;
(b) decisions revoking decisions granting the application;

(c) decisions amending decisions granting the application;
(d) decisions extending the period during which the customs authorities are to take action.

2. The competent customs department to which a Union application has been submitted shall forward the following decisions to the competent customs department of the Member State or Member States indicated in the Union application, immediately after their adoption:

(a) decisions granting the application;
(b) decisions revoking decisions granting the application;
(c) decisions amending decisions granting the application;
(d) decisions extending the period during which the customs authorities are to take action.

The competent customs department of the Member State or Member States indicated in the Union application shall immediately after receiving those decisions forward them to their customs offices.

3. The competent customs department of the Member State or Member States indicated in the Union application may request the competent customs department that adopted the decision granting the application to provide them with additional information deemed necessary for the implementation of that decision.

4. The competent customs department shall forward its decision suspending the actions of the customs authorities under point (b) of Article 16(1) and Article 16(2) to the customs offices of its Member State, immediately after its adoption.

[8.650]
Article 15
Notification obligations of the holder of the decision

The holder of the decision shall immediately notify the competent customs department that granted the application of any of the following:

(a) an intellectual property right covered by the application ceases to have effect;
(b) the holder of the decision ceases for other reasons to be entitled to submit the application;
(c) modifications to the information referred to in Article 6(3).

[8.651]
Article 16
Failure of the holder of the decision to fulfil his obligations

1. Where the holder of the decision uses the information provided by the customs authorities for purposes other than those provided for in Article 21, the competent customs department of the Member State where the information was provided or misused may:

(a) revoke any decision adopted by it granting a national application to that holder of the decision, and refuse to extend the period during which the customs authorities are to take action;
(b) suspend in their territory, during the period during which the customs authorities are to take action, any decision granting a Union application to that holder of the decision.

2. The competent customs department may decide to suspend the actions of the customs authorities until the expiry of the period during which those authorities are to take action, where the holder of the decision:

(a) does not fulfil the notification obligations set out in Article 15;
(b) does not fulfil the obligation on returning samples set out in Article 19(3);
(c) does not fulfil the obligations on costs and translation set out in Article 29(1) and (3);
(d) without valid reason does not initiate proceedings as provided for in Article 23(3) or Article 26(9).

In the case of a Union application, the decision to suspend the actions of the customs authorities shall have effect only in the Member State where such decision is taken.

CHAPTER III
ACTION BY THE CUSTOMS AUTHORITIES

SECTION 1
SUSPENSION OF THE RELEASE OR DETENTION OF GOODS SUSPECTED OF INFRINGING AN INTELLECTUAL PROPERTY RIGHT

[8.652]
Article 17
Suspension of the release or detention of the goods following the grant of an application

1. Where the customs authorities identify goods suspected of infringing an intellectual property right covered by a decision granting an application, they shall suspend the release of the goods or detain them.

2. Before suspending the release of or detaining the goods, the customs authorities may ask the holder of the decision to provide them with any relevant information with respect to the goods. The customs authorities may also provide the holder of the decision with information about the actual or estimated quantity of goods, their actual or presumed nature and images thereof, as appropriate.

3. The customs authorities shall notify the declarant or the holder of the goods of the suspension of the release of the goods or the detention of the goods within one working day of that suspension or detention.

Where the customs authorities opt to notify the holder of the goods and two or more persons are considered to be the holder of the goods, the customs authorities shall not be obliged to notify more than one of those persons.

The customs authorities shall notify the holder of the decision of the suspension of the release of the goods or the detention on the same day as, or promptly after, the declarant or the holder of the goods is notified.

The notifications shall include information on the procedure set out in Article 23.

4. The customs authorities shall inform the holder of the decision and the declarant or the holder of the goods of the actual or estimated quantity and the actual or presumed nature of the goods, including available images thereof, as appropriate, whose release has been suspended or which have been detained. The customs authorities shall also, upon request and where available to them, inform the holder of the decision of the names and addresses of the consignee, the consignor and the declarant or the holder of the goods, of the customs procedure and of the origin, provenance and destination of the goods whose release has been suspended or which have been detained.

[8.653]
Article 18
Suspension of the release or detention of the goods before the grant of an application

1. Where the customs authorities identify goods suspected of infringing an intellectual property right, which are not covered by a decision granting an application, they may, except for in the case of perishable goods, suspend the release of those goods or detain them.

2. Before suspending the release of or detaining the goods suspected of infringing an intellectual property right, the customs authorities may, without disclosing any information other than the actual or estimated quantity of goods, their actual or presumed nature and images thereof, as appropriate, request any person or entity potentially entitled to submit an application concerning the alleged infringement of the intellectual property rights to provide them with any relevant information.

3. The customs authorities shall notify the declarant or the holder of the goods of the suspension of the release of the goods or their detention within one working day of that suspension or detention.

Where the customs authorities opt to notify the holder of the goods and two or more persons are considered to be the holder of the goods, the customs authorities shall not be obliged to notify more than one of those persons.

The customs authorities shall notify persons or entities entitled to submit an application concerning the alleged infringement of the intellectual property rights, of the suspension of the release of the goods or their detention on the same day as, or promptly after, the declarant or the holder of the goods is notified.

The customs authorities may consult the competent public authorities in order to identify the persons or entities entitled to submit an application.

The notifications shall include information on the procedure set out in Article 23.

4. The customs authorities shall grant the release of the goods or put an end to their detention immediately after completion of all customs formalities in the following cases:

(a) where they have not identified any person or entity entitled to submit an application concerning the alleged infringement of intellectual property rights within one working day from the suspension of the release or the detention of the goods;

(b) where they have not received an application in accordance with Article 5(3), or where they have rejected such an application.

5. Where an application has been granted, the customs authorities shall, upon request and where available to them, inform the holder of the decision of the names and addresses of the consignee, the consignor and the declarant or the holder of the goods, of the customs procedure and of the origin, provenance and destination of the goods whose release has been suspended or which have been detained.

[8.654]
Article 19
Inspection and sampling of goods whose release has been suspended or which have been detained

1. The customs authorities shall give the holder of the decision and the declarant or the holder of the goods the opportunity to inspect the goods whose release has been suspended or which have been detained.

2. The customs authorities may take samples that are representative of the goods. They may provide or send such samples to the holder of the decision, at the holder's request and strictly for the purposes of analysis and to facilitate the subsequent procedure in relation to counterfeit and pirated goods. Any analysis of those samples shall be carried out under the sole responsibility of the holder of the decision.

3. The holder of the decision shall, unless circumstances do not allow, return the samples referred to in paragraph 2 to the customs authorities on completion of the analysis, at the latest before the goods are released or their detention is ended.

[8.655]
Article 20
Conditions for storage
The conditions of storage of goods during a period of suspension of release or detention shall be determined by the customs authorities.

[8.656]
Article 21
Permitted use of certain information by the holder of the decision
Where the holder of the decision has received the information referred to in Article 17(4), Article 18(5), Article 19 or Article 26(8), he may disclose or use that information only for the following purposes:
(a) to initiate proceedings to determine whether an intellectual property right has been infringed and in the course of such proceedings;
(b) in connection with criminal investigations related to the infringement of an intellectual property right and undertaken by public authorities in the Member State where the goods are found;
(c) to initiate criminal proceedings and in the course of such proceedings;
(d) to seek compensation from the infringer or other persons;
(e) to agree with the declarant or the holder of the goods that the goods be destroyed in accordance with Article 23(1);
(f) to agree with the declarant or the holder of the goods of the amount of the guarantee referred to in point (a) of Article 24(2).

[8.657]
Article 22
Sharing of information and data between customs authorities
1. Without prejudice to applicable provisions on data protection in the Union and for the purpose of contributing to eliminating international trade in goods infringing intellectual property rights, the Commission and the customs authorities of the Member States may share certain data and information available to them with the relevant authorities in third countries according to the practical arrangements referred to in paragraph 3.
2. The data and information referred to in paragraph 1 shall be exchanged to swiftly enable effective enforcement against shipments of goods infringing an intellectual property right. Such data and information may relate to seizures, trends and general risk information, including on goods which are in transit through the territory of the Union and which have originated in or are destined for the territory of third countries concerned. Such data and information may include, where appropriate, the following:
(a) nature and quantity of goods;
(b) suspected intellectual property right infringed;
(c) origin, provenance and destination of the goods;
(d) information on movements of means of transport, in particular:
  (i) name of vessel or registration of means of transport;
  (ii) reference numbers of freight bill or other transport document;
  (iii) number of containers;
  (iv) weight of load;
  (v) description and/or coding of goods;
  (vi) reservation number;
  (vii) seal number;
  (viii) place of first loading;
  (ix) place of final unloading;
  (x) places of transhipment;
  (xi) expected date of arrival at place of final unloading;
(e) information on movements of containers, in particular:
  (i) container number;
  (ii) container loading status;
  (iii) date of movement;
  (iv) type of movement (loaded, unloaded, transhipped, entered, left, etc.);
  (v) name of vessel or registration of means of transport;
  (vi) number of voyage/journey;
  (vii) place;
  (viii) freight bill or other transport document.

3. The Commission shall adopt implementing acts defining the elements of the necessary practical arrangements concerning the exchange of data and information referred to in paragraphs 1 and 2 of this Article. Those implementing acts shall be adopted in accordance with the examination procedure referred to in Article 34(3).

SECTION 2
DESTRUCTION OF GOODS, INITIATION OF PROCEEDINGS AND EARLY RELEASE OF GOODS

[8.658]
Article 23
Destruction of goods and initiation of proceedings

1. Goods suspected of infringing an intellectual property right may be destroyed under customs control, without there being any need to determine whether an intellectual property right has been infringed under the law of the Member State where the goods are found, where all of the following conditions are fulfilled:

(a) the holder of the decision has confirmed in writing to the customs authorities, within 10 working days, or three working days in the case of perishable goods, of notification of the suspension of the release or the detention of the goods, that, in his conviction, an intellectual property right has been infringed;

(b) the holder of the decision has confirmed in writing to the customs authorities, within 10 working days, or three working days in the case of perishable goods, of notification of the suspension of the release or the detention of the goods, his agreement to the destruction of the goods;

(c) the declarant or the holder of the goods has confirmed in writing to the customs authorities, within 10 working days, or three working days in the case of perishable goods, of notification of the suspension of the release or the detention of the goods, his agreement to the destruction of the goods. Where the declarant or the holder of the goods has not confirmed his agreement to the destruction of the goods nor notified his opposition thereto to the customs authorities, within those deadlines, the customs authorities may deem the declarant or the holder of the goods to have confirmed his agreement to the destruction of those goods.

The customs authorities shall grant the release of the goods or put an end to their detention, immediately after completion of all customs formalities, where within the periods referred to in points (a) and (b) of the first subparagraph, they have not received both the written confirmation from the holder of the decision that, in his conviction, an intellectual property right has been infringed and his agreement to destruction, unless those authorities have been duly informed about the initiation of proceedings to determine whether an intellectual property right has been infringed.

2. The destruction of the goods shall be carried out under customs control and under the responsibility of the holder of the decision, unless otherwise specified in the national law of the Member State where the goods are destroyed. Samples may be taken by competent authorities prior to the destruction of the goods. Samples taken prior to destruction may be used for educational purposes.

3. Where the declarant or the holder of the goods has not confirmed his agreement to the destruction in writing and where the declarant or the holder of the goods has not been deemed to have confirmed his agreement to the destruction, in accordance with point (c) of the first subparagraph of paragraph 1 within the periods referred to therein, the customs authorities shall immediately notify the holder of the decision thereof. The holder of the decision shall, within 10 working days, or three working days in the case of perishable goods, of notification of the suspension of the release or the detention of the goods, initiate proceedings to determine whether an intellectual property right has been infringed.

4. Except in the case of perishable goods the customs authorities may extend the period referred to in paragraph 3 by a maximum of 10 working days upon a duly justified request by the holder of the decision in appropriate cases.

5. The customs authorities shall grant the release of the goods or put an end to their detention, immediately after completion of all customs formalities, where, within the periods referred to in paragraphs 3 and 4, they have not been duly informed, in accordance with paragraph 3, on the initiation of proceedings to determine whether an intellectual property right has been infringed.

[8.659]
Article 24
Early release of goods

1. Where the customs authorities have been notified of the initiation of proceedings to determine whether a design, patent, utility model, topography of semiconductor product or plant variety has been infringed, the declarant or the holder of the goods may request the customs authorities to release the goods or put an end to their detention before the completion of those proceedings.

2. The customs authorities shall release the goods or put an end to their detention only where all the following conditions are fulfilled:

(a) the declarant or the holder of the goods has provided a guarantee that is of an amount sufficient to protect the interests of the holder of the decision;
(b) the authority competent to determine whether an intellectual property right has been infringed has not authorised precautionary measures;
(c) all customs formalities have been completed.

3. The provision of the guarantee referred to in point (a) of paragraph 2 shall not affect the other legal remedies available to the holder of the decision.

[8.660]
Article 25
Goods for destruction

1. Goods to be destroyed under Article 23 or 26 shall not be:
(a) released for free circulation, unless customs authorities, with the agreement of the holder of the decision, decide that it is necessary in the event that the goods are to be recycled or disposed of outside commercial channels, including for awareness-raising, training and educational purposes. The conditions under which the goods can be released for free circulation shall be determined by the customs authorities;
(b) brought out of the customs territory of the Union;
(c) exported;
(d) re-exported;
(e) placed under a suspensive procedure;
(f) placed in a free zone or free warehouse.

2. The customs authorities may allow the goods referred to in paragraph 1 to be moved under customs supervision between different places within the customs territory of the Union with a view to their destruction under customs control.

[8.661]
Article 26
Procedure for the destruction of goods in small consignments

1. This Article shall apply to goods where all of the following conditions are fulfilled:
(a) the goods are suspected of being counterfeit or pirated goods;
(b) the goods are not perishable goods;
(c) the goods are covered by a decision granting an application;
(d) the holder of the decision has requested the use of the procedure set out in this Article in the application;
(e) the goods are transported in small consignments.

2. When the procedure set out in this Article is applied, Article 17(3) and (4) and Article 19(2) and (3) shall not apply.

3. The customs authorities shall notify the declarant or the holder of the goods of the suspension of the release of the goods or their detention within one working day of the suspension of the release or of the detention of the goods. The notification of the suspension of the release or the detention of the goods shall include the following information:
(a) that the customs authorities intend to destroy the goods;
(b) the rights of the declarant or the holder of the goods under paragraphs 4, 5 and 6.

4. The declarant or the holder of the goods shall be given the opportunity to express his point of view within 10 working days of notification of the suspension of the release or the detention of the goods.

5. The goods concerned may be destroyed where, within 10 working days of notification of the suspension of the release or the detention of the goods, the declarant or the holder of the goods has confirmed to the customs authorities his agreement to the destruction of the goods.

6. Where the declarant or the holder of the goods has not confirmed his agreement to the destruction of the goods nor notified his opposition thereto to the customs authorities, within the period referred to in paragraph 5, the customs authorities may deem the declarant or the holder of the goods to have confirmed his agreement to the destruction of the goods.

7. The destruction shall be carried out under customs control. The customs authorities shall, upon request and as appropriate, provide the holder of the decision with information about the actual or estimated quantity of destroyed goods and their nature.

8. Where the declarant or the holder of the goods has not confirmed his agreement to the destruction of the goods and where the declarant or the holder of the goods has not been deemed to have confirmed such agreement, in accordance with paragraph 6, the customs authorities shall immediately notify the holder of the decision thereof and of the quantity of goods and their nature, including images thereof, where appropriate. The customs authorities shall also, upon request and where available to them, inform the holder of the decision of the names and addresses of the consignee, the consignor and the declarant or the holder of the goods, of the customs procedure and of the origin, provenance and destination of the goods whose release has been suspended or which have been detained.

9. The customs authorities shall grant the release of the goods or put an end to their detention immediately after completion of all customs formalities where they have not received information from the holder of the decision on the initiation of proceedings to determine whether an intellectual property right has been infringed within 10 working days of the notification referred to in paragraph 8.

10. The Commission shall be empowered to adopt delegated acts in accordance with Article 35 concerning the amendment of quantities in the definition of small consignments in the event that the definition is found to be impractical in the light of the need to ensure the effective operation of the procedure set out in this Article, or where necessary in order to avoid any circumvention of this procedure as regards the composition of consignments.

CHAPTER IV
LIABILITY, COSTS AND PENALTIES

[8.662]
Article 27
Liability of the customs authorities

Without prejudice to national law, the decision granting an application shall not entitle the holder of that decision to compensation in the event that goods suspected of infringing an intellectual property right are not detected by a customs office and are released, or no action is taken to detain them.

[8.663]
Article 28
Liability of the holder of the decision

Where a procedure duly initiated pursuant to this Regulation is discontinued owing to an act or omission on the part of the holder of the decision, where samples taken pursuant to Article 19(2) are either not returned or are damaged and beyond use owing to an act or omission on the part of the holder of the decision, or where the goods in question are subsequently found not to infringe an intellectual property right, the holder of the decision shall be liable towards any holder of the goods or declarant, who has suffered damage in that regard, in accordance with specific applicable legislation.

[8.664]
Article 29
Costs

1. Where requested by the customs authorities, the holder of the decision shall reimburse the costs incurred by the customs authorities, or other parties acting on behalf of customs authorities, from the moment of detention or suspension of the release of the goods, including storage and handling of the goods, in accordance with Article 17(1), Article 18(1) and Article 19(2) and (3), and when using corrective measures such as destruction of goods in accordance with Articles 23 and 26.

The holder of a decision to whom the suspension of release or detention of goods has been notified shall, upon request, be given information by the customs authorities on where and how those goods are being stored and on the estimated costs of storage referred to in this paragraph. The information on estimated costs may be expressed in terms of time, products, volume, weight or service depending on the circumstances of storage and the nature of the goods.

2. This Article shall be without prejudice to the right of the holder of the decision to seek compensation from the infringer or other persons in accordance with the legislation applicable.

3. The holder of a decision granting a Union application shall provide and pay for any translation required by the competent customs department or customs authorities which are to take action concerning the goods suspected of infringing an intellectual property right.

[8.665]
Article 30
Penalties

The Member States shall ensure that the holders of decisions comply with the obligations set out in this Regulation, including, where appropriate, by laying down provisions establishing penalties. The penalties provided for shall be effective, proportionate and dissuasive.

The Member States shall notify those provisions and any subsequent amendment affecting them to the Commission without delay.

CHAPTER V
EXCHANGE OF INFORMATION

[8.666]
Article 31
Exchange of data on decisions relating to applications and detentions between the Member States and the Commission

1. The competent customs departments shall notify without delay the Commission of the following:

(a) decisions granting applications, including the application and its attachments;
(b) decisions extending the period during which the customs authorities are to take action or decisions revoking the decision granting the application or amending it;
(c) the suspension of a decision granting the application.

2. Without prejudice to point (g) of Article 24 of Regulation (EC) No 515/97, where the release of the goods is suspended or the goods are detained, the customs authorities shall transmit to the Commission any relevant information, except personal data, including information on the quantity and type of the goods, value, intellectual property rights, customs procedures, countries of provenance, origin and destination, and transport routes and means.

3. The transmission of the information referred to in paragraphs 1 and 2 of this Article and all exchanges of data on decisions concerning applications as referred to in Article 14 between customs authorities of the Member States shall be made via a central database of the Commission. The information and data shall be stored in that database.

4. For the purposes of ensuring processing of the information referred to in paragraphs 1 to 3 of this Article, the central database referred to in paragraph 3 shall be established in an electronic form. The central database shall contain the information, including personal data, referred to in Article 6(3), Article 14 and this Article.

5. The customs authorities of the Member States and the Commission shall have access to the information contained in the central database as appropriate for the fulfilment of their legal responsibilities in applying this Regulation. The access to information marked for restricted handling in accordance with Article 6(3) is restricted to the customs authorities of the Member States where action is requested. Upon justified request by the Commission, the customs authorities of the Member States may give access to the Commission to such information where it is strictly necessary for the application of this Regulation.

6. The customs authorities shall introduce into the central database information related to the applications submitted to the competent customs department. The customs authorities which have introduced information into the central database shall, where necessary, amend, supplement, correct or delete such information. Each customs authority that has introduced information in the central database shall be responsible for the accuracy, adequacy and relevancy of this information.

7. The Commission shall establish and maintain adequate technical and organisational arrangements for the reliable and secure operation of the central database. The customs authorities of each Member State shall establish and maintain adequate technical and organisational arrangements to ensure the confidentiality and security of processing with respect to the processing operations carried out by their customs authorities and with respect to terminals of the central database located on the territory of that Member State.

[8.667]
Article 32
Establishment of a central database

The Commission shall establish the central database referred to in Article 31. That database shall be operational as soon as possible and not later than 1 January 2015.

[8.668]
Article 33
Data protection provisions

1. The processing of personal data in the central database of the Commission shall be carried out in accordance with Regulation (EC) No 45/2001 and under the supervision of the European Data Protection Supervisor.

2. Processing of personal data by the competent authorities in the Member States shall be carried out in accordance with Directive 95/46/EC and under the supervision of the public independent authority of the Member State referred to in Article 28 of that Directive.

3. Personal data shall be collected and used solely for the purposes of this Regulation. Personal data so collected shall be accurate and shall be kept up to date.

4. Each customs authority that has introduced personal data into the central database shall be the controller with respect to the processing of this data.

5. A data subject shall have a right of access to the personal data relating to him or her that are processed through the central database and, where appropriate, the right to the rectification, erasure or blocking of personal data in accordance with Regulation (EC) No 45/2001 or the national laws implementing Directive 95/46/EC.

6. All requests for the exercise of the right of access, rectification, erasure or blocking shall be submitted to and processed by the customs authorities. Where a data subject has submitted a request for the exercise of that right to the Commission, the Commission shall forward such request to the customs authorities concerned.

7. Personal data shall not be kept longer than six months from the date the relevant decision granting the application has been revoked or the relevant period during which the customs authorities are to take action has expired.

8. Where the holder of the decision has initiated proceedings in accordance with Article 23(3) or Article 26(9) and has notified the customs authorities of the initiation of such proceedings, personal data shall be kept for six months after proceedings have determined in a final way whether an intellectual property right has been infringed.

CHAPTER VI
COMMITTEE, DELEGATION AND FINAL PROVISIONS

[8.669]
Article 34
Committee procedure
1. The Commission shall be assisted by the Customs Code Committee established by Articles 247a and 248a of Regulation (EEC) No 2913/92. That committee shall be a committee within the meaning of Regulation (EU) No 182/2011.
2. Where reference is made to this paragraph, Article 4 of Regulation (EU) No 182/2011 shall apply.
3. Where reference is made to this paragraph, Article 5 of Regulation (EU) No 182/2011 shall apply.

[8.670]
Article 35
Exercise of the delegation
1. The power to adopt delegated acts is conferred on the Commission subject to the conditions laid down in this Article.
2. The power to adopt delegated acts referred to in Article 26(10) shall be conferred on the Commission for an indeterminate period of time from 19 July 2013.
3. The delegation of power referred to in Article 26(10) may be revoked at any time by the European Parliament or by the Council. A decision to revoke shall put an end to the delegation of the power specified in that decision. It shall take effect the day following the publication of the decision in the *Official Journal of the European Union* or at a later date specified therein. It shall not affect the validity of any delegated acts already in force.
4. As soon as it adopts a delegated act, the Commission shall notify it simultaneously to the European Parliament and to the Council.
5. A delegated act adopted pursuant to Article 26(10) shall enter into force only if no objection has been expressed either by the European Parliament or the Council within a period of two months of notification of that act to the European Parliament and the Council or if, before the expiry of that period the European Parliament and the Council have both informed the Commission that they will not object. That period shall be extended by two months on the initiative of the European Parliament or of the Council.

[8.671]
Article 36
Mutual administrative assistance
The provisions of Regulation (EC) No 515/97 shall apply *mutatis mutandis* to this Regulation.

[8.672]
Article 37
Reporting
By 31 December 2016, the Commission shall submit to the European Parliament and to the Council a report on the implementation of this Regulation. If necessary, that report shall be accompanied by appropriate recommendations.

That report shall refer to any relevant incidents concerning medicines in transit across the customs territory of the Union that might occur under this Regulation, including an assessment of its potential impact on the Union commitments on access to medicines under the 'Declaration on the TRIPS Agreement and Public Health' adopted by the Doha WTO Ministerial Conference on 14 November 2001, and the measures taken to address any situation creating adverse effects in that regard.

[8.673]
Article 38
Repeal
Regulation (EC) No 1383/2003 is repealed with effect from 1 January 2014.

References to the repealed Regulation shall be construed as references to this Regulation and shall be read in accordance with the correlation table set out in the Annex.

[8.674]

Article 39

Transitional provisions

Applications granted in accordance with Regulation (EC) No 1383/2003 shall remain valid for the period specified in the decision granting the application during which the customs authorities are to take action and shall not be extended.

[8.675]

Article 40

Entry into force and application

1. This Regulation shall enter into force on the twentieth day following that of its publication in the *Official Journal of the European Union*.

2. It shall apply from 1 January 2014, with the exception of:
   (a) Article 6, Article 12(7) and Article 22(3), which shall apply from 19 July 2013;
   (b) Article 31(1) and (3) to (7) and Article 33, which shall apply from the date on which the central database referred to in Article 32 is in place. The Commission shall make that date public.

This Regulation shall be binding in its entirety and directly applicable in all Member States.

ANNEX
CORRELATION TABLE

[8.676]

Regulation (EC) No 1383/2003	This Regulation
Article 1	Article 1
Article 2	Article 2
Article 3	Article 1
Article 4	Article 18
Article 5	Articles 3 to 9
Article 6	Articles 6 and 29
Article 7	Article 12
Article 8	Articles 10, 11, 12, 14 and 15
Article 9	Articles 17 and 19
Article 10	—
Article 11	Article 23
Article 12	Articles 16 and 21
Article 13	Article 23
Article 14	Article 24
Article 15	Article 20
Article 16	Article 25
Article 17	—
Article 18	Article 30
Article 19	Articles 27 and 28
Article 20	Articles 6, 12, 22 and 26
Article 21	Article 34
Article 22	Articles 31 and 36
Article 23	—
Article 24	Article 38
Article 25	Article 40

COMMISSION IMPLEMENTING REGULATION

(1352/2013/EU)

of 4 December 2013

establishing the forms provided for in Regulation (EU) No 608/2013 of the European Parliament and of the Council concerning customs enforcement of intellectual property rights

NOTES

Date of publication in OJ: OJ L341, 18.12.2013, p 10.

THE EUROPEAN COMMISSION,

Having regard to the Treaty on the Functioning of the European Union,

Having regard to Regulation (EU) No 608/2013 of the European Parliament and of the Council of 12 June 2013 concerning customs enforcement of intellectual property rights and repealing Council Regulation (EC) No 1383/2003,[1] and in particular Article 6(1) and Article 12(7) thereof,

After consulting the European Data Protection Supervisor,

Whereas:

(1) Regulation (EU) No 608/2013 sets out the conditions and procedures for action by the customs authorities where goods suspected of infringing an intellectual property right are, or should have been, subject to customs supervision or customs controls in accordance with Council Regulation (EEC) No 2913/92.[2]

(2) In accordance with Regulation (EU) No 608/2013 persons and entities duly entitled may submit an application to the competent customs department requesting that customs authorities take action on those goods (application) and may also request the extension of the period during which the customs authorities are to take action in accordance with a previously granted application (extension request).

(3) In order to ensure uniform conditions for the application and for the extension request, standard forms should be established.

(4) Those standard forms should replace those provided for in Commission Regulation (EC) No 1891/2004[3] implementing Council Regulation (EC) No 1383/2003,[4] which is to be repealed by Regulation (EU) No 608/2013.

(5) Regulation (EC) No 1891/2004 should therefore be repealed.

(6) Regulation (EU) No 608/2013 shall apply from 1 January 2014 and, therefore, this Regulation should also be applicable from the same date.

(7) The measures provided for in this Regulation are in accordance with the opinion of the Customs Code Committee, referred to in Article 34(1) of Regulation (EU) No 608/2013,

NOTES

1 OJ L181, 29.6.2013, p 15.

2 Council Regulation (EEC) No 2913/92 of 12 October 1992 establishing the Community Customs Code (OJ L302, 19.10.1992, p 1.).

3 Commission Regulation (EC) No 1891/2004 of 21 October 2004 laying down provisions for the implementation of Council Regulation (EC) No 1383/2003 concerning customs action against goods suspected of infringing certain intellectual property rights and the measures to be taken against goods found to have infringed such rights (OJ L328, 30.10.2004, p 16.).

4 Council Regulation (EC) No 1383/2003 of 22 July 2003 concerning customs action against goods suspected of infringing certain intellectual property rights and the measures to be taken against goods found to have infringed such rights (OJ L196, 2.8.2003, p 7).

HAS ADOPTED THIS REGULATION:

[8.677]

Article 1

1. The application requesting that customs authorities take action with respect to goods suspected of infringing an intellectual property right (application) referred to in Article 6 of Regulation (EU) No 608/2013 shall be made by using the form set out in Annex I to this Regulation.

2. The request for extension of the period during which the customs authorities are to take action (extension request) referred to in Article 12 of Regulation (EU) No 608/2013 shall be made by using the form set out in Annex II to this Regulation.

3. The forms set out in Annexes I and II shall be completed in accordance with the notes on completion set out in Annex III.

[8.678]

Article 2

Without prejudice to Article 5(6) of Regulation (EU) No 608/2013, the forms set out in Annexes I and II to this Regulation may, where necessary, be completed legibly by hand.

Those forms shall contain no erasures, overwritten words or other alterations and shall be made up of two copies.

The handwritten forms shall be completed in ink and block capitals.

[8.679]

Article 3

Regulation (EC) No 1891/2004 is repealed.

[8.680]

Article 4

This Regulation shall enter into force on the twentieth day following that of its publication in the *Official Journal of the European Union*.

It shall apply from 1 January 2014.

This Regulation shall be binding in its entirety and directly applicable in all Member States.

ANNEX I

[8.681]
EUROPEAN UNION – APPLICATION FOR ACTION

EUROPEAN UNION – APPLICATION FOR ACTION

1

COPY FOR THE COMPETENT CUSTOMS DEPARTMENT

1. Applicant
Name*:
Address*:
Town*:
Postal Code:
Country*:
EORI-No:
TIN No:
National registration No:
Telephone: (+)
Mobile: (+)
Fax: (+)
Email:
Website:

For official use
Date of receipt

Registration number of application

INTELLECTUAL PROPERTY RIGHTS

APPLICATION FOR ACTION BY CUSTOMS AUTHORITIES

under Article 6 of Regulation (EU) No 608/2013

2*. Union application ☐
National application ☐

3*. Status of applicant
☐ Right-holder
☐ Person or entity authorised to use the IP right
☐ IP collective rights management body
☐ Professional defence body
☐ Group of producers of products with a Geographical Indication or representative of such group
☐ Operator entitled to use a Geographical Indication
☐ Inspection body or authority competent for a Geographical Indication
☐ Exclusive license holder covering two or more Member States

4. Representative submitting the application in the name of the applicant
Company:
Name*:
Address*:
Town*:
Postal Code:
Country*:
Telephone: (+)
Mobile: (+)
Fax: (+)

☐ Evidence of the representatives power to act is enclosed

1

5*. Type of right to which the application refers
☐ National trademark (NTM)
☐ Community trademark (CTM)
☐ International registered trademark (ITM)
☐ Registered national design (ND)
☐ Registered Community design (CDR)
☐ International registered design (ICD)
Unregistered Community design (CDU)
☐ Copyright and related right (NCPR)
☐ Trade name (NTN)
☐ Topography of semiconductor product (NTSP)
☐ Patent as provided for by national law (NPT)
☐ Patent as provided for by Union law (UPT)
☐ Utility model (NUM)

Geographical Indication/Designation of origin:
☐ for agricultural products and foodstuff (CGIP)
☐ for wine (CGIW)
☐ for aromatised drinks based on wine products (CGIA)
☐ for spirit drinks (CGIS)
☐ for other products (NGI)
☐ as listed in Agreements between the Union and third countries (CGIL)

Plant variety right:
☐ national (NPVR)
☐ Community (CPVR)

Supplementary protection certificate:
☐ for medicinal products (SPCM)
☐ for plant protection products (SPCP)

6*. Member State or, in the case of a Union application, Member States in which customs action is requested

☐ ALL MEMBER STATES ☐ BE ☐ BG ☐ CZ ☐ DK ☐ DE ☐ EE ☐ IE ☐ EL ☐ ES ☐ FR ☐ HR ☐ IT ☐ CY ☐ LV
☐ LT ☐ LU ☐ HU ☐ MT ☐ NL ☐ AT ☐ PL ☐ PT ☐ RO ☐ SI ☐ SK ☐ FI ☐ SE ☐ UK

7. Representative for legal matters
Company:
Name*:
Address*:
Town*:
Postal Code:
Country*:
Telephone: (+)
Mobile: (+)
Fax: (+)
Email:
Website:

8. Representative for technical matters
Company:
Name*:
Address*:
Town*:
Postal Code:
Country*:
Telephone: (+)
Mobile: (+)
Fax: (+)
Email:
Website:

9. In case of a Union application, the details of the designated representatives for legal and technical matters are included in annex no ......

10. Small consignment procedure
☐ I request the use of the procedure in Article 26 of Regulation (EU) No 608/2013 and, where requested by the customs authorities, agree to cover the costs related to the destruction of goods under this procedure.

* these are mandatory fields and shall be filled in   1   (+) at least one of these fields shall be filled in

11*. List of rights to which the application refers

No	Type of right	Registration number	Date of registration	Expiry date	List of goods to which the right refers

For further rights see annex no …… ☐ Restricted handling

Authentic goods

12. Goods details* ☐ Restricted handling

IP right no:

Goods description*:

CN tariff number:

Customs value:

European average market value:

National market value: ☐ See enclosed annex no ……

13. Goods distinctive features* ☐ Restricted handling

Position on the goods*:

Description*:

☐ See enclosed annex no ……

14. Place of production* ☐ Restricted handling

Country:

Company:

Address:

Town: ☐ See enclosed annex no ……

15. Involved companies* ☐ Restricted handling

Role:

Name*:

Address:

Town: ☐ See enclosed annex no ……

16. Traders* ☐ Restricted handling

☐ See enclosed annex no ……

17. Goods clearance details and distribution information ☐ Restricted handling

☐ See enclosed annex no ……

18. Packages ☐ Restricted handling

Kind of packages:

Number of items per package:

Description (incl. distinctive features):

☐ See enclosed annex no ……

19. Accompanying documents ☐ Restricted handling

Type of document:

Description:

☐ See enclosed annex no ……

2

Part 8 Other EU Materials

Infringing goods

20. Goods details ☐ Restricted handling
IP right no:
Goods description:

CN tariff number:
Minimum value: ☐ See enclosed annex no ……

21. Goods distinctive features ☐ Restricted handling
Position on the goods:
Description:

☐ See enclosed annex no ……

22. Place of production ☐ Restricted handling
Country:
Company:
Address:
Town:

☐ See enclosed annex no ……

23. Involved companies ☐ Restricted handling
Role:
Name:
Address:
Town:

☐ See enclosed annex no ……

24. Traders ☐ Restricted handling

☐ See enclosed annex no ……

25. Goods distribution information ☐ Restricted handling

☐ See enclosed annex no ……

26. Packages ☐ Restricted handling
Kind of packages:
Number of items per package:
Description (incl. distinctive features):

☐ See enclosed annex no ……

27. Accompanying documents ☐ Restricted handling
Type of document:
Description:

☐ See enclosed annex no ……

28. Additional information ☐ Restricted handling

☐

☐ See enclosed annex no ......

29. Undertakings

By signing I undertake to:

- notify immediately the competent customs department that granted this application of any change in the information provided by me within this application or attachments in accordance with Article 15 of Regulation (EU) No 608/2013.
- forward to the competent customs department that granted this application any update on the information as referred to in point (g), (h) or (i) of Article 6(3) of Regulation (EU) No 608/2013 that are relevant to customs authorities' analysis and assessment of the risk of infringement of the intellectual property right(s) included in this application.
- assume liability under the conditions laid down in Article 28 of Regulation (EU) No 608/2013 and bear the costs as referred to in Article 29 of Regulation (EU) No 608/2013.

I agree that all the data submitted with this application may be processed by the European Commission and by the Member States.

30. Signature*

Date (DD/MM/YYYY) Applicant's signature

Place Name (Block capitals)

For official use

Decision by customs authorities (within the meaning of Section 2 of Regulation (EU) No 608/2013)

☐ The application is completely granted.

☐ The application has been partially granted (for the granted rights see attached list).

Date of adoption (DD/MM/YYYY) Signature and stamp Competent customs department

Expiry date of the application:

Any request for extension of the period that customs authorities are to take action should be received by the competent customs department at the latest 30 working days before the expiry date.

☐ The application has been rejected.

A reasoned decision stating the grounds for partial or complete rejection and information concerning the appeal procedure are attached.

Date (DD/MM/YYYY) Signature and stamp Competent customs department

Personal data protection and the central database for the processing of applications for action.

Where the European Commission processes personal data contained in this application for action Regulation (EC) No 45/2001 of the European Parliament and of the Council on the protection of individuals with regard to the processing of personal data by the Community Institutions and bodies and on the free movement of such data will apply. Where the competent customs authority of a Member State processes personal data contained in this application for action the national provisions implementing Directive 95/46/EC will apply.

The purpose of the processing of personal data of the application for action is the enforcement of intellectual property rights by customs authorities in the Union in accordance with Regulation (EU) No 608/2013 of the European Parliament and of the Council of 12 June 2013 concerning customs enforcement of intellectual property rights.

The controller with respect to the processing of the data in the central database is the national competent customs department where the application has been submitted. The list of competent customs departments is published on the website of the Commission:
http://ec.europa.eu/taxation_customs/customs/customs_controls/counterfeit_piracy/right_holders/index_en.htm
.

The access to all personal data of this application is granted through UserID/Password to customs authorities in the Member States and the Commission.

Personal data forming part of the information that falls under restricted handling will only be accessible by customs authorities of the Member States as indicated in box 6 of the application through UserID/Password.

In accordance with Article 22 of Regulation (EU) No 608/2013, without prejudice to applicable provisions on data protection in the Union and for the purpose of contributing to eliminating international trade in goods infringing intellectual property rights, the Commission and the customs authorities of the Member States may share personal data and information contained in the application with the relevant authorities in third countries.

Replies to data fields marked with an * and to at least one of the fields marked "+" are obligatory to be filled in. In case of failure to fill in these obligatory data, the application shall be rejected.

The data subject has a right of access to the personal data relating to him or her that will be processed through the central database and, where appropriate, the right to rectify, erase or block personal data in accordance with Regulation (EC) No 45/2001 or the national laws Implementing Directive 95/46/EC.

All requests for the exercise of the right of access, rectification, erasure or blocking shall be submitted to and processed by the competent customs department where the application was submitted.

The legal basis for processing the personal data for the enforcement of intellectual property rights is Regulation (EU) No 608/2013 of the European Parliament and of the Council of 12 June 2013 concerning customs enforcement of intellectual property rights.

Personal data shall not be stored longer than six months from the date the decision granting the application has been revoked or the relevant period during which customs authorities are to take action has expired. That period shall be specified by the competent customs department when granting the application and shall not exceed one year from the day following the date of adoption of the decision granting the application. However, where customs authorities have been notified of proceedings initiated to determine a possible infringement of goods under the application, personal data shall be kept for six months after the proceedings have been concluded.

Complaints, in case of conflict, can be addressed to the relevant national data protection authority. The contact details of the national data protection authorities are available on the web-site of the European Commission, Directorate General for Justice (http://ec.europa.eu/justice/data-protection/bodies/authorities/eu/index_en.htm#h2-1). Where the complaint concerns processing of personal data by the European Commission, it should be addressed to the European Data Protection Supervisor (http://www.edps.europa.eu/EDPSWEB/).

5

NOTES

* these are mandatory fields and shall be filled in

(+) at least one of these fields shall be filled in

EUROPEAN UNION – APPLICATION FOR ACTION

2

COPY FOR THE APPLICANT

1. Applicant
Name*:
Address*:
Town*:
Postal Code:
Country*:
EORI-No:
TIN No:
National registration No:
Telephone: (+)
Mobile: (+)
Fax: (+)
Email:
Website:

For official use
Date of receipt

Registration number of application

INTELLECTUAL PROPERTY RIGHTS

APPLICATION FOR ACTION BY CUSTOMS AUTHORITIES

under Article 6 of Regulation (EU) No 608/2013

2*. Union application ☐
National application ☐

3*. Status of applicant
☐ Right-holder
☐ Person or entity authorised to use the IP right
☐ IP collective rights management body
☐ Professional defence body
☐ Group of producers of products with a Geographical Indication or representative of such group
☐ Operator entitled to use a Geographical Indication
☐ Inspection body or authority competent for a Geographical Indication
☐ Exclusive license holder covering two or more Member States

4. Representative submitting the application in the name of the applicant
Company:
Name*:
Address*:
Town*:
Postal Code:
Country*:
Telephone: (+)
Mobile: (+)
Fax: (+)

☐ Evidence of the representatives power to act is enclosed

2

5*. Type of right to which the application refers
☐ National trademark (NTM)
☐ Community trademark (CTM)
☐ International registered trademark (ITM)
☐ Registered national design (ND)
☐ Registered Community design (CDR)
☐ International registered design (ICD)
Unregistered Community design (CDU)
☐ Copyright and related right (NCPR)
☐ Trade name (NTN)
☐ Topography of semiconductor product (NTSP)
☐ Patent as provided for by national law (NPT)
☐ Patent as provided for by Union law (UPT)
☐ Utility model (NUM)

Geographical Indication/Designation of origin:
☐ for agricultural products and foodstuff (CGIP)
☐ for wine (CGIW)
☐ for aromatised drinks based on wine products (CGIA)
☐ for spirit drinks (CGIS)
☐ for other products (NGI)
☐ as listed in Agreements between the Union and third countries (CGIL)

Plant variety right:
☐ national (NPVR)
☐ Community (CPVR)

Supplementary protection certificate:
☐ for medicinal products (SPCM)
☐ for plant protection products (SPCP)

6*. Member State or, in the case of a Union application, Member States in which customs action is requested

☐ ALL MEMBER STATES ☐ BE ☐ BG ☐ CZ ☐ DK ☐ DE ☐ EE ☐ IE ☐ EL ☐ ES ☐ FR ☐ HR ☐ IT ☐ CY ☐ LV
☐ LT ☐ LU ☐ HU ☐ MT ☐ NL ☐ AT ☐ PL ☐ PT ☐ RO ☐ SI ☐ SK ☐ FI ☐ SE ☐ UK

7. Representative for legal matters
Company:
Name*:
Address*:
Town*:
Postal Code:
Country*:
Telephone: (+)
Mobile: (+)
Fax: (+)
Email:
Website:

8. Representative for technical matters
Company:
Name*:
Address*:
Town*:
Postal Code:
Country*:
Telephone: (+)
Mobile: (+)
Fax: (+)
Email:
Website:

9. In case of a Union application, the details of the designated representatives for legal and technical matters are included in annex no ......

10. Small consignment procedure

☐ I request the use of the procedure in Article 26 of Regulation (EU) No 608/2013 and, where requested by the customs authorities, agree to cover the costs related to the destruction of goods under this procedure.

* these are mandatory fields and shall be filled in 1 (+) at least one of these fields shall be filled in

11*. List of rights to which the application refers					
No	Type of right	Registration number	Date of registration	Expiry date	List of goods to which the right refers

For further rights see annex no …… ☐ Restricted handling

Authentic goods

12. Goods details* ☐ Restricted handling

IP right no:

Goods description*:

CN tariff number:

Customs value:

European average market value:

National market value: ☐ See enclosed annex no ……

13. Goods distinctive features* ☐ Restricted handling

Position on the goods*:

Description*:

☐ See enclosed annex no ……

14. Place of production* ☐ Restricted handling

Country:

Company:

Address:

Town: ☐ See enclosed annex no ……

15. Involved companies* ☐ Restricted handling

Role:

Name*:

Address:

Town: ☐ See enclosed annex no ……

16. Traders* ☐ Restricted handling

☐ See enclosed annex no ……

17. Goods clearance details and distribution information ☐ Restricted handling

☐ See enclosed annex no ……

18. Packages ☐ Restricted handling

Kind of packages:

Number of items per package:

Description (incl. distinctive features):

☐ See enclosed annex no ……

19. Accompanying documents ☐ Restricted handling

Type of document:

Description:

☐ See enclosed annex no ……

Infringing goods	
20. Goods details IP right no: Goods description: CN tariff number: Minimum value:	☐ Restricted handling ☐ See enclosed annex no ……
21. Goods distinctive features Position on the goods: Description:	☐ Restricted handling ☐ See enclosed annex no ……
22. Place of production Country: Company: Address: Town:	☐ Restricted handling ☐ See enclosed annex no ……
23. Involved companies Role: Name: Address: Town:	☐ Restricted handling ☐ See enclosed annex no ……
24. Traders	☐ Restricted handling ☐ See enclosed annex no ……
25. Goods distribution information	☐ Restricted handling ☐ See enclosed annex no ……
26. Packages Kind of packages: Number of items per package: Description (incl. distinctive features):	☐ Restricted handling ☐ See enclosed annex no ……
27. Accompanying documents Type of document: Description:	☐ Restricted handling ☐ See enclosed annex no ……

3

28. Additional information ☐ Restricted handling

☐

☐ See enclosed annex no ......

29. Undertakings

By signing I undertake to:

• notify immediately the competent customs department that granted this application of any change in the information provided by me within this application or attachments in accordance with Article 15 of Regulation (EU) No 608/2013.

• forward to the competent customs department that granted this application any update on the information as referred to in point (g), (h) or (i) of Article 6(3) of Regulation (EU) No 608/2013 that are relevant to customs authorities' analysis and assessment of the risk of infringement of the intellectual property right(s) included in this application.

• assume liability under the conditions laid down in Article 28 of Regulation (EU) No 608/2013 and bear the costs as referred to in Article 29 of Regulation (EU) No 608/2013.

I agree that all the data submitted with this application may be processed by the European Commission and by the Member States.

30. Signature*

Date (DD/MM/YYYY) Applicant's signature

Place Name (Block capitals)

For official use

Decision by customs authorities (within the meaning of Section 2 of Regulation (EU) No 608/2013)

☐ The application is completely granted.

☐ The application has been partially granted (for the granted rights see attached list).

Date of adoption (DD/MM/YYYY) Signature and stamp Competent customs department

Expiry date of the application:

Any request for extension of the period that customs authorities are to take action should be received by the competent customs department at the latest 30 working days before the expiry date.

☐ The application has been rejected.

A reasoned decision stating the grounds for partial or complete rejection and information concerning the appeal procedure are attached.

Date (DD/MM/YYYY) Signature and stamp Competent customs department

Personal data protection and the central database for the processing of applications for action.

Where the European Commission processes personal data contained in this application for action Regulation (EC) No 45/2001 of the European Parliament and of the Council on the protection of individuals with regard to the processing of personal data by the Community Institutions and bodies and on the free movement of such data will apply. Where the competent customs authority of a Member State processes personal data contained in this application for action the national provisions implementing Directive 95/46/EC will apply.
The purpose of the processing of personal data of the application for action is the enforcement of intellectual property rights by customs authorities in the Union in accordance with Regulation (EU) No 608/2013 of the European Parliament and of the Council of 12 June 2013 concerning customs enforcement of intellectual property rights.
The controller with respect to the processing of the data in the central database is the national competent customs department where the application has been submitted. The list of competent customs departments is published on the website of the Commission:
http://ec.europa.eu/taxation_customs/customs/customs_controls/counterfeit_piracy/right_holders/index_en.htm
.

The access to all personal data of this application is granted through UserID/Password to customs authorities in the Member States and the Commission.
Personal data forming part of the information that falls under restricted handling will only be accessible by customs authorities of the Member States as indicated in box 6 of the application through UserID/Password.
In accordance with Article 22 of Regulation (EU) No 608/2013, without prejudice to applicable provisions on data protection in the Union and for the purpose of contributing to eliminating international trade in goods infringing intellectual property rights, the Commission and the customs authorities of the Member States may share personal data and information contained in the application with the relevant authorities in third countries.
Replies to data fields marked with an * and to at least one of the fields marked "+" are obligatory to be filled in. In case of failure to fill in these obligatory data, the application shall be rejected.
The data subject has a right of access to the personal data relating to him or her that will be processed through the central database and, where appropriate, the right to rectify, erase or block personal data in accordance with Regulation (EC) No 45/2001 or the national laws implementing Directive 95/46/EC.
All requests for the exercise of the right of access, rectification, erasure or blocking shall be submitted to and processed by the competent customs department where the application was submitted.
The legal basis for processing the personal data for the enforcement of intellectual property rights is Regulation (EU) No 608/2013 of the European Parliament and of the Council of 12 June 2013 concerning customs enforcement of intellectual property rights.
Personal data shall not be stored longer than six months from the date the decision granting the application has been revoked or the relevant period during which customs authorities are to take action has expired. That period shall be specified by the competent customs department when granting the application and shall not exceed one year from the day following the date of adoption of the decision granting the application. However, where customs authorities have been notified of proceedings initiated to determine a possible infringement of goods under the application, personal data shall be kept for six months after the proceedings have been concluded.
Complaints, in case of conflict, can be addressed to the relevant national data protection authority. The contact details of the national data protection authorities are available on the web-site of the European Commission, Directorate General for Justice (http://ec.europa.eu/justice/data-protection/bodies/authorities/eu/index_en.htm#h2-1). Where the complaint concerns processing of personal data by the European Commission, it should be addressed to the European Data Protection Supervisor (http://www.edps.europa.eu/EDPSWEB/).

5

NOTES

* these are mandatory fields and shall be filled in

(+) at least one of these fields shall be filled in

ANNEX II

[8.682]
EUROPEAN UNION – REQUEST FOR EXTENSION

EUROPEAN UNION – REQUEST FOR EXTENSION

1

1 Holder of the decision
Name*:
Address*:
Town*:
Postal Code:
Country*:
Telephone: (+)
Mobile: (+)
Fax: (+)
Email:

For official use
Date of receipt

INTELLECTUAL PROPERTY RIGHTS

REQUEST FOR EXTENSION OF THE PERIOD FOR ACTION

under Article 12 of Regulation (EU) No 608/2013

COPY FOR THE COMPETENT CUSTOMS DEPARTMENT

2*. I request the extension of the period during which the customs authorities are to take action in respect of the following application

Registration number of application: /

☐ I confirm, that there are no changes in the information concerning the application for action and its annexes.

☐ I provide the following information concerning the application for action.

1

See enclosed annex no ……

Any request for extension of the period that customs authorities are to take action should be received by the competent customs department at the latest 30 working days before the expiry date.

3 Signature*

Date (DD/MM/YYYY) Signature of the holder of the decision

Place Name (Block capitals)

For official use
Decision by customs authorities (within the meaning of Section 2 of Regulation (EU) 608/2013)

☐ The request for extension is completely granted.

☐ The request for extension has been partially granted (for the granted rights see attached list).

Date (DD/MM/YYYY) Signature and stamp Competent customs department

Expiry date of the application:

☐ The request for extension has been rejected.

A reasoned decision stating the grounds for partial or complete rejection and information concerning the appeal procedure are attached.

Date (DD/MM/YYYY) Signature and stamp Competent customs department

* these are mandatory fields and shall be filled in 1 (+) at least one of these fields shall be filled in

Personal data protection and the central database for the processing of applications for action.

Where the European Commission processes personal data contained in this extension request Regulation (EC) No 45/2001 of the European Parliament and of the Council on the protection of individuals with regard to the processing of personal data by the Community Institutions and bodies and on the free movement of such data will apply. Where the competent customs authority of a Member State processes personal data contained in this extension request the national provisions implementing Directive 95/46/EC will apply.
The purpose of the processing of personal data of the application for action is the enforcement of intellectual property rights by customs authorities in the Union in accordance with Regulation (EU) No 608/2013 of the European Parliament and of the Council of 12 June 2013 concerning customs enforcement of intellectual property rights.
The controller with respect to the processing of the data in the central database is the national competent customs department where the application has been submitted. The list of competent customs departments is published on the website of the Commission:
http://ec.europa.eu/taxation_customs/customs/customs_controls/counterfeit_piracy/right_holders/index_en.htm
.
The access to all personal data of the application is granted through UserID/Password to customs authorities in the Member States and the Commission.
Personal data forming part of the information that falls under restricted handling will only be accessible by customs authorities of the Member States as indicated in box 6 of the application through UserID/Password.
In accordance with Article 22 of Regulation (EU) No 608/2013, without prejudice to applicable provisions on data protection in the Union and for the purpose of contributing to eliminating international trade in goods infringing intellectual property rights, the Commission and the customs authorities of the Member States may share personal data and information contained in the application with the relevant authorities in third countries.
Replies to data fields marked with an * are obligatory to be filled in. In case of failure to fill in these obligatory data, the extension request shall be rejected.
The data subject has a right of access to the personal data relating to him or her that will be processed through the central database and, where appropriate, the right to rectify, erase or block personal data in accordance with Regulation (EC) No 45/2001 or the national laws implementing Directive 95/46/EC.
All requests for the exercise of the right of access, rectification, erasure or blocking shall be submitted to and processed by the competent customs department where the application was submitted.
The legal basis for processing the personal data for the enforcement of intellectual property rights is Regulation (EU) No 608/2013 of the European Parliament and of the Council of 12 June 2013 concerning customs enforcement of intellectual property rights.
Personal data shall not be stored longer than six months from the date the decision granting the application has been revoked or the relevant period during which customs authorities are to take action has expired. That period shall be specified by the competent customs department when granting the extension request and shall not exceed one year from the day following the date of adoption of the decision granting the extension request. However, where customs authorities have been notified of proceedings initiated to determine a possible infringement of goods under the application, personal data shall be kept for six months after the proceedings have been concluded.
Complaints, in case of conflict, can be addressed to the relevant national data protection authority. The contact details of the national data protection authorities are available on the web-site of the European Commission, Directorate General for Justice (http://ec.europa.eu/justice/data-protection/bodies/authorities/eu/index_en.htm#h2-1). Where the complaint concerns processing of personal data by the European Commission, it should be addressed to the European Data Protection Supervisor (http://www.edps.europa.eu/EDPSWEB/).

2

NOTES

* these are mandatory fields and shall be filled in

(+) at least one of these fields shall be filled in

EUROPEAN UNION – REQUEST FOR EXTENSION

2

COPY FOR THE APPLICANT

1. Holder of the decision
Name*:
Address*:
Town*:
Postal Code:
Country*:
Telephone: (+)
Mobile: (+)
Fax: (+)
Email:

For official use
Date of receipt

INTELLECTUAL PROPERTY RIGHTS

REQUEST FOR EXTENSION OF THE PERIOD FOR ACTION

under Article 12 of Regulation (EU) No 608/2013

2*. I request the extension of the period during which the customs authorities are to take action in respect of the following application

Registration number of application: /

☐ I confirm, that there are no changes in the information concerning the application for action and its annexes.

☐ I provide the following information concerning the application for action.

2

See enclosed annex no ......

Any request for extension of the period that customs authorities are to take action should be received by the competent customs department at the latest 30 working days before the expiry date.

3. Signature*
Date (DD/MM/YYYY) Signature of the holder of the decision

Place Name (Block capitals)

For official use
Decision by customs authorities (within the meaning of Section 2 of Regulation (EU) 608/2013)

☐ The request for extension is completely granted.

☐ The request for extension has been partially granted (for the granted rights see attached list).

Date (DD/MM/YYYY) Signature and stamp Competent customs department

Expiry date of the application:

☐ The request for extension has been rejected.

A reasoned decision stating the grounds for partial or complete rejection and information concerning the appeal procedure are attached.

Date (DD/MM/YYYY) Signature and stamp Competent customs department

* these are mandatory fields and shall be filled in 1 (+) at least one of these fields shall be filled in

Personal data protection and the central database for the processing of applications for action.

Where the European Commission processes personal data contained in this extension request Regulation (EC) No 45/2001 of the European Parliament and of the Council on the protection of individuals with regard to the processing of personal data by the Community Institutions and bodies and on the free movement of such data will apply. Where the competent customs authority of a Member State processes personal data contained in this extension request the national provisions implementing Directive 95/46/EC will apply.
The purpose of the processing of personal data of the application for action is the enforcement of intellectual property rights by customs authorities in the Union in accordance with Regulation (EU) No 608/2013 of the European Parliament and of the Council of 12 June 2013 concerning customs enforcement of intellectual property rights.
The controller with respect to the processing of the data in the central database is the national competent customs department where the application has been submitted. The list of competent customs departments is published on the website of the Commission:
http://ec.europa.eu/taxation_customs/customs/customs_controls/counterfeit_piracy/right_holders/index_en.htm

The access to all personal data of the application is granted through UserID/Password to customs authorities in the Member States and the Commission.
Personal data forming part of the information that falls under restricted handling will only be accessible by customs authorities of the Member States as indicated in box 6 of the application through UserID/Password.
In accordance with Article 22 of Regulation (EU) No 608/2013, without prejudice to applicable provisions on data protection in the Union and for the purpose of contributing to eliminating international trade in goods infringing intellectual property rights, the Commission and the customs authorities of the Member States may share personal data and information contained in the application with the relevant authorities in third countries.
Replies to data fields marked with an * are obligatory to be filled in. In case of failure to fill in these obligatory data, the extension request shall be rejected.
The data subject has a right of access to the personal data relating to him or her that will be processed through the central database and, where appropriate, the right to rectify, erase or block personal data in accordance with Regulation (EC) No 45/2001 or the national laws implementing Directive 95/46/EC.
All requests for the exercise of the right of access, rectification, erasure or blocking shall be submitted to and processed by the competent customs department where the application was submitted.
The legal basis for processing the personal data for the enforcement of intellectual property rights is Regulation (EU) No 608/2013 of the European Parliament and of the Council of 12 June 2013 concerning customs enforcement of intellectual property rights.
Personal data shall not be stored longer than six months from the date the decision granting the application has been revoked or the relevant period during which customs authorities are to take action has expired. That period shall be specified by the competent customs department when granting the extension request and shall not exceed one year from the day following the date of adoption of the decision granting the extension request. However, where customs authorities have been notified of proceedings initiated to determine a possible infringement of goods under the application, personal data shall be kept for six months after the proceedings have been concluded.
Complaints, in case of conflict, can be addressed to the relevant national data protection authority. The contact details of the national data protection authorities are available on the web-site of the European Commission, Directorate General for Justice (http://ec.europa.eu/justice/data-protection/bodies/authorities/eu/index_en.htm#h2-1). Where the complaint concerns processing of personal data by the European Commission, it should be addressed to the European Data Protection Supervisor (http://www.edps.europa.eu/EDPSWEB/).

2

NOTES

* these are mandatory fields and shall be filled in

(+) at least one of these fields shall be filled in

ANNEX III
NOTES ON COMPLETION

[8.683]

I. SPECIFICATIONS OF THE BOXES OF THE APPLICATION FOR ACTION FORM SET OUT IN ANNEX I TO BE FILLED IN BY THE APPLICANT

Fields in the form marked with an asterisk (*) are mandatory fields and shall be filled in.

Where in a box one or more fields are marked with a plus sign (+) at least one of those fields shall be filled in.

No data shall be entered in the boxes marked 'for official use'.

Box 1: Applicant

Details concerning the applicant shall be entered in this box. It shall contain information on the name and complete address of the applicant and his telephone, mobile telephone or fax number. The applicant may, where appropriate, enter his Taxpayer Identification Number, any other national registration number and his Economic Operator Registration and Identification Number (EORI-No), which is a number, unique throughout the Union, assigned by a customs authority in a Member State to economic operators involved in customs activities. The applicant may also enter, where appropriate, his e-mail address and his website address.

Box 2: Union/National application

The appropriate box shall be ticked to indicate whether the application is a National or a Union application, as referred to in points (10) and (11) of Article 2 of Regulation (EU) No 608/2013.

Box 3: Status of the applicant

The appropriate box shall be ticked to indicate the status of the applicant within the meaning of Article 3 of Regulation (EU) No 608/2013. The application shall include documents providing evidence to satisfy the competent customs department that the applicant is entitled to submit an application.

Box 4: Representative submitting the application in the name of the applicant

Where the application is submitted by the applicant by means of a representative, details concerning that representative shall be entered in this box. The application shall include evidence of his powers to act as a representative in accordance with the legislation of the Member State in which the application is submitted and the corresponding box shall be ticked.

Box 5: Type of right to which the application refers

The type(s) of the intellectual property rights (IPR) to be enforced shall be indicated by ticking the appropriate box.

Box 6: Member State or, in the case of a Union application, Member States in which customs action is requested

The Member State or, in the case of a Union application, Member States in which customs action is requested shall be indicated by ticking the appropriate box.

Box 7: Representative for legal matters

The details of the representative designated by the applicant to take charge of legal matters shall be indicated in this box.

Box 8: Representative for technical matters

In case the representative for technical matters is different from the representative indicated in box 7, the details of the representative for technical matters shall be indicated in this box.

Box 9: Details of the designated representatives for legal and technical matters in case of a Union application

In case of a Union application, the details of the representative or representatives designated by the applicant to take charge of technical and legal matters in the Member States indicated in box 6 shall be provided in a separate annex which shall contain the elements of information requested in boxes 7 and 8. In case a representative has been designated for more than one Member State, it shall be clearly indicated for which Member States he has been designated.

Box 10: Small consignment procedure

Where the applicant wishes to request the use of the procedure for destruction of goods in small consignments set out in Article 26 of Regulation (EU) No 608/2013, this box shall be ticked.

Box 11: List of rights to which the application refers

Information on the right or rights to be enforced shall be entered in this box.

In the column 'No', sequential numbers shall be entered for each of the intellectual property rights to which the application refers.

In the column 'Type of right', the type of IPR shall be indicated by using the appropriate abbreviations which appear in box 5 in brackets.
In the column 'list of goods to which the right refers', the type of goods which are covered by the relevant IPR and with regard to which the applicant wishes to request customs enforcement shall be entered.

Sub-box 'Restricted handling' in boxes 12–28
Where the applicant wishes to request that information provided by him in boxes 12–28 be the subject of restricted handling within the meaning of Article 31(5) of Regulation (EU) No 608/2013, this sub-box shall be ticked.

Page 2: Information on authentic goods in boxes 12–19
The applicant shall enter in boxes 12–19, as appropriate, specific and technical data on the authentic goods, information needed to enable the customs authorities to readily identify goods suspected of infringing IPR and information relevant to the customs authorities' analysis and assessment of the risk of infringement of the IPR(s) concerned.

Box 12: Goods details
Box 12 shall contain a description of the authentic goods, including get-up and graphic symbols, their Combined Nomenclature code and their value in the EU internal market. The applicant, where appropriate, shall provide images of those goods. The information shall be arranged per different type of goods or different assortment of goods.

Box 13: Goods distinctive features
Box 13 shall contain information on the typical features of the authentic goods, such as markings, labels, security threads, holograms, buttons, hangtags and bar-coding, indicating the exact position of the features on the goods and their appearance.

Box 14: Place of production
Box 14 shall contain information on the place of production of the authentic goods.

Box 15: Involved companies
Box 15 shall contain information on authorised importers, suppliers, manufacturers, carriers, consignees or exporters. The information shall be arranged per different type of goods.

Box 16: Traders
Box 16 shall contain information on persons or entities authorised to trade in products involving the use of the IPR(s) for which enforcement is sought. The information shall refer to name, address and registration numbers, such as EORI number, of those persons or entities. Likewise, the information shall comprise information on how licensees may demonstrate their authorisation to use the IPR(s) in question.

Box 17: Goods clearance details and distribution information
Box 17 shall contain information on channels of distribution of the authentic goods, such as information related to central warehouses, dispatch departments, means of transport, transport routes and delivery, and on customs procedures and offices where the clearance of the authentic goods is carried out.

Box 18: Packages
This box shall contain information on the packaging of the authentic goods, such as information on the following:
(a) the kind of packages, indicated by using the relevant codes as given in Annex 38 to Commission Regulation (EEC) No 2454/93;[1]
(b) typical features of the packages (for instance, markings, labels, security threads, holograms, buttons, hangtags and bar-coding), including the exact position of the features in the package;
(c) special package designs (colour, shape);
(d) where appropriate, images of those goods.

Box 19: Accompanying documents
Box 19 shall contain information on documents accompanying the authentic goods, such as brochures, operating instructions, warranty documents or other similar items.

Page 3: Information on infringing goods in boxes 20–27
The applicant shall enter in boxes 20–27, as appropriate, information relevant to the customs authorities' analysis and assessment of the risk of infringement of the IPR(s) concerned.

Box 20: Goods details
Box 20 shall contain a description of goods suspected of infringing an intellectual property right (infringing goods), including get-up and graphic symbols. The applicant, where appropriate, shall provide images of those goods. The information shall be arranged per different type of goods or different assortment of goods.

Box 21: Goods distinctive features

Box 21 shall contain information on the typical features of the suspected infringing goods, such as markings, labels, security threads, holograms, buttons, hangtags and bar-coding, indicating the exact position of the features on the goods and their appearance.

Box 22: Place of production

Box 22 shall contain information on the known or suspected place of origin, provenance and delivery of the infringing goods.

Box 23: Involved companies

Box 23 shall contain information on importers, suppliers, manufacturers, carriers, consignees or exporters who are suspected of being involved in infringements of the relevant intellectual property rights.

Box 24: Traders

Box 24 shall contain information on persons or entities not authorised to trade in products involving the use of the IPR(s) for which enforcement is sought and who have been trading the products in the Union in the past.

Box 25: Goods distribution information

Box 25 shall contain information on channels of distribution of the infringing goods, such as information related to warehouses, dispatch departments, means of transport, transport routes and places of delivery, and on customs procedures and offices where the clearance of the infringing goods is carried out.

Box 26: Packages

This box shall contain information on the packaging of the suspected infringing goods, such as information on the following:

(a) the kind of packages, indicated by using the relevant codes as given in Annex 38 to Regulation (EEC) No 2454/93;
(b) typical features of the packages (for instance, markings, labels, holograms, buttons, hangtags and bar-coding), including the exact position of the features in the package;
(c) special package designs (colour, shape);
(d) where appropriate, images of those goods.

Box 27: Accompanying documents

Box 27 shall contain information on documents accompanying the suspected infringing goods, such as brochures, operating instructions, warranty documents or other similar items.

Box 28: Additional information

The applicant may provide in box 28 any additional information relevant to the customs authorities' analysis and assessment of the risk of infringement of the IPR(s) concerned such as specific information concerning planned deliveries of suspected infringing goods, including specific and detailed information on means of transport, containers and persons involved.

Box 29: Undertakings

Do not amend the wording, or enter data in this box.

Box 30: Signature

In box 30, the applicant or the representative of the applicant indicated in box 4 shall enter the place and date of completion of the application and shall sign. The signatory's name shall be given in block capitals.

II. SPECIFICATIONS OF THE BOXES OF THE REQUEST FOR EXTENSION FORM SET OUT IN ANNEX II TO BE FILLED IN BY THE HOLDER OF THE DECISION

Fields in the form marked with an asterisk (*) are mandatory fields and shall be filled in.

In boxes where fields are marked with a plus (+) at least one of these fields shall be filled in.

Do not enter data in the boxes marked 'for official use'.

Box 1: Details concerning the holder of the decision

Details concerning the holder of the decision shall be entered in this box.

Box 2: Extension request

The application registration number including the first two digits representing the iso/alpha-2 code of the Member State that granted the application shall be entered in this box. The holder of the decision shall indicate whether he is requesting modifications to the information contained in the application by ticking the appropriate box.

Box 3: Signature

In box 3, the holder of the decision or the representative of the holder of the decision shall enter the place and date of completion of the request and shall sign. The signatory's name shall be given in block capitals.

NOTES

[1] Commission Regulation (EEC) No 2454/93 of 2 July 1993 laying down provisions for the implementation of Council Regulation (EEC) No 2913/92 establishing the Community Customs Code (OJ L253, 11.10.1993, p 1).

DIRECTIVE OF THE EUROPEAN PARLIAMENT AND OF THE COUNCIL

(2014/40/EU)

of 3 April 2014

on the approximation of the laws, regulations and administrative provisions of the Member States concerning the manufacture, presentation and sale of tobacco and related products and repealing Directive 2001/37/EC

(Text with EEA relevance)

NOTES

Date of publication in OJ: OJ L127, 29.4.2014, p 1.

This Directive is reproduced as corrected by the Corrigendum published in OJ L150, 17.6.2015, p 24.

THE EUROPEAN PARLIAMENT AND THE COUNCIL OF THE EUROPEAN UNION,

Having regard to the Treaty on the Functioning of the European Union, and in particular Articles 53(1), 62 and 114 thereof,

Having regard to the proposal from the European Commission,

After transmission of the draft legislative act to the national parliaments,

Having regard to the opinion of the European Economic and Social Committee,[1]

Having regard to the opinion of the Committee of the Regions,[2]

Acting in accordance with the ordinary legislative procedure,[3]

Whereas:

(1) Directive 2001/37/EC of the European Parliament and of the Council[4] lays down rules at Union level concerning tobacco products. In order to reflect scientific, market and international developments, substantial changes to that Directive would be needed and it should therefore be repealed and replaced by a new Directive.

(2) In its reports of 2005 and 2007 on the application of Directive 2001/37/EC the Commission identified areas in which further action was considered useful for the smooth functioning of the internal market. In 2008 and 2010 the Scientific Committee on Emerging and Newly Identified Health Risks (SCENIHR) provided scientific advice to the Commission on smokeless tobacco products and tobacco additives. In 2010 a broad stakeholder consultation took place, which was followed by targeted stakeholder consultations and accompanied by studies by external consultants. Member States were consulted throughout the process. The European Parliament and the Council repeatedly called on the Commission to review and update Directive 2001/37/EC.

(3) In certain areas covered by Directive 2001/37/EC, Member States are legally or in practice prevented from effectively adapting their legislation to new developments. This is in particular relevant for the labelling rules, where Member States have not been permitted to increase the size of the health warnings, change their location on an individual packet ('unit packet') or replace misleading warnings on the tar, nicotine and carbon monoxide (TNCO) emission levels.

(4) In other areas there are still substantial differences between the Member States' laws, regulations and administrative provisions on the manufacture, presentation and sale of tobacco and related products which present obstacles to the smooth functioning of the internal market. In the light of scientific, market and international developments these discrepancies are expected to increase. This also applies to electronic cigarettes and refill containers for electronic cigarettes ('refill containers'), herbal products for smoking, ingredients and emissions from tobacco products, certain aspects of labelling and packaging and to cross-border distance sales of tobacco products.

(5) Those obstacles should be eliminated and, to this end, the rules on the manufacture, presentation and sale of tobacco and related products should be further approximated.

(6) The size of the internal market in tobacco and related products, the increasing tendency of manufacturers of tobacco products to concentrate production for the entire Union in only a small number of production plants within the Union and the resulting significant cross-border trade of tobacco and related products calls for stronger legislative action at Union rather than national level to achieve the smooth functioning of the internal market.

(7) Legislative action at Union level is also necessary in order to implement the WHO

Framework Convention on Tobacco Control ('FCTC') of May 2003, the provisions of which are binding on the Union and its Member States. The FCTC provisions on the regulation of the contents of tobacco products, the regulation of tobacco product disclosures, the packaging and labelling of tobacco products, advertising and illicit trade in tobacco products are particularly relevant. The Parties to the FCTC, including the Union and its Member States, adopted a set of guidelines for the implementation of FCTC provisions by consensus during various Conferences.

(8) In accordance with Article 114(3) of the Treaty of the Functioning of the European Union (TFEU), a high level of health protection should be taken as a base for legislative proposals and, in particular, any new developments based on scientific facts should be taken into account. Tobacco products are not ordinary commodities and in view of the particularly harmful effects of tobacco on human health, health protection should be given high importance, in particular, to reduce smoking prevalence among young people.

(9) It is necessary to establish a number of new definitions in order to ensure that this Directive is uniformly applied by Member States. Where different obligations imposed by this Directive apply to different product categories and the relevant product falls into more than one of those categories (e.g. pipe, roll your-own tobacco), the stricter obligations should apply.

(10) Directive 2001/37/EC established maximum limits for tar, nicotine and carbon monoxide yields of cigarettes that should also be applicable to cigarettes which are exported from the Union. Those maximum limits and that approach remain valid.

(11) For measuring the tar, nicotine and carbon monoxide yields of cigarettes (hereinafter referred to as 'emission levels'), reference should be made to the relevant, internationally recognised ISO standards. The verification process should be protected from tobacco industry influence by using independent laboratories, including State laboratories. Member States should be able to use laboratories situated in other Member States of the Union. For other emissions from tobacco products, there are no internationally agreed standards or tests for quantifying maximum levels. The ongoing efforts at international level to develop such standards or tests should be encouraged.

(12) As regards establishing maximum emission levels, it could be necessary and appropriate at a later date to reduce the emission levels for tar, nicotine and carbon monoxide or to establish maximum levels for other emissions from tobacco products, taking into consideration their toxicity or addictiveness.

(13) In order to carry out their regulatory tasks, Member States and the Commission require comprehensive information on the ingredients and emissions from tobacco products to assess the attractiveness, addictiveness and toxicity of tobacco products and the health risks associated with the consumption of such products. To this end, the existing reporting obligations for ingredients and emissions should be strengthened. Additional enhanced reporting obligations should be provided for in respect of additives included in a priority list in order to assess, inter alia their toxicity, addictiveness and carcinogenic, mutagenic or reprotoxic properties ('CMR properties'), including in combusted form. The burden of such enhanced reporting obligations for SMEs should be limited to the extent possible. Such reporting obligations are consistent with the obligation placed on the Union to ensure a high level of protection for human health.

(14) The use of differing reporting formats, as is currently the case, makes it difficult for manufacturers and importers to fulfil their reporting obligations and burdensome for the Member States and the Commission to compare, analyse and draw conclusions from the information received. Therefore, there should be a common mandatory format for the reporting of ingredients and emissions. The greatest possible transparency of product information should be ensured for the general public, whilst ensuring that appropriate account is taken of the trade secrets of the manufacturers of tobacco products. Existing systems for the reporting of ingredients should be taken into account.

(15) The lack of a harmonised approach to regulating the ingredients of tobacco products affects the smooth functioning of the internal market and has a negative impact on the free movement of goods across the Union. Some Member States have adopted legislation or entered into binding agreements with the industry allowing or prohibiting certain ingredients. As a result, some ingredients are regulated in certain Member States, but not in others. Member States also take differing approaches as regards additives in the filters of cigarettes as well as additives colouring the tobacco smoke. Without harmonisation, the obstacles to the smooth functioning of the internal market are expected to increase in the coming years, taking into account the implementation of the FCTC and the relevant FCTC guidelines throughout the Union and in the light of experience gained in other jurisdictions outside the Union. The FCTC guidelines in relation to the regulation of the contents of tobacco products and regulation of tobacco product disclosures call in particular for the removal of ingredients that increase palatability, create the impression that tobacco products have health benefits, are associated with energy and vitality or have colouring properties.

(16) The likelihood of diverging regulation is further increased by concerns over tobacco products having a characterising flavour other than one of tobacco, which could facilitate initiation of tobacco consumption or affect consumption patterns. Measures introducing unjustified differences of treatment between different types of flavoured cigarettes should be avoided. However, products with characterising flavour with a higher sales volume should be phased out over an extended time

period to allow consumers adequate time to switch to other products.

(17) The prohibition of tobacco products with characterising flavours does not preclude the use of individual additives outright, but it does oblige manufacturers to reduce the additive or the combination of additives to such an extent that the additives no longer result in a characterising flavour. The use of additives necessary for the manufacture of tobacco products, for example sugar to replace sugar that is lost during the curing process, should be allowed, as long as they do not result in a characterising flavour or increase the addictiveness, toxicity or CMR properties of the product. An independent European advisory panel should assist in such decision making. The application of this Directive should not lead to discrimination between different tobacco varieties, nor should it prevent product differentiation.

(18) Certain additives are used to create the impression that tobacco products have health benefits, present reduced health risks or increase mental alertness and physical performance. These additives, as well as additives that have CMR properties in unburnt form, should be prohibited in order to ensure uniform rules throughout the Union and a high level of protection of human health. Additives that increase addictiveness and toxicity should also be prohibited.

(19) Considering this Directive's focus on young people, tobacco products other than cigarettes and roll-your-own tobacco, should be granted an exemption from certain requirements relating to ingredients as long as there is no substantial change of circumstances in terms of sales volumes or consumption patterns of young people.

(20) Given the general prohibition of the sale of tobacco for oral use in the Union, the responsibility for regulating the ingredients of tobacco for oral use, which requires in-depth knowledge of the specific characteristics of this product and of its patterns of consumption, should, in accordance with the principle of subsidiarity, remain with Sweden, where the sale of this product is permitted pursuant to Article 151 of the Act of Accession of Austria, Finland and Sweden.

(21) In line with the purposes of this Directive, namely to facilitate the smooth functioning of the internal market for tobacco and related products, taking as a base a high level of health protection, especially for young people, and in line with Council Recommendation 2003/54/EC,[5] Member States should be encouraged to prevent sales of such products to children and adolescents, by adopting appropriate measures that lay down and enforce age limits.

(22) Disparities still exist between national provisions regarding the labelling of tobacco products, in particular with regard to the use of combined health warnings consisting of a picture and a text, information on cessation services and promotional elements in and on unit packets.

(23) Such disparities are liable to constitute a barrier to trade and to impede the smooth functioning of the internal market in tobacco products, and should, therefore, be eliminated. Also, it is possible that consumers in some Member States are better informed about the health risks of tobacco products than consumers in other Member States. Without further action at Union level, the existing disparities are likely to increase in the coming years.

(24) Adaptation of the provisions on labelling is also necessary to align the rules that apply at Union level to international developments. For example, the FCTC guidelines on the packaging and labelling of tobacco products call for large picture warnings on both principal display areas, mandatory cessation information and strict rules on misleading information. The provisions on misleading information will complement the general ban on misleading business to consumer commercial practices laid down in Directive 2005/29/EC of the European Parliament and of the Council.[6]

Member States that use tax stamps or national identification marks for fiscal purposes on the packaging of tobacco products may, in some cases, have to provide for these stamps and marks to be repositioned in order to allow for the combined health warnings to be at the top of the principal display areas, in line with this Directive and the FCTC guidelines. Transitional arrangements should be put in place to allow Member States to maintain tax stamps or national identification marks used for fiscal purposes at the top of unit packets for a certain period after transposition of this Directive.

(25) The labelling provisions should also be adapted to new scientific evidence. For example, the indication of the emission levels for tar, nicotine and carbon monoxide on unit packets of cigarettes has proven to be misleading as it leads consumers to believe that certain cigarettes are less harmful than others. Evidence also suggests that large combined health warnings comprised of a text warning and a corresponding colour photograph are more effective than warnings consisting only of text. As a consequence, combined health warnings should become mandatory throughout the Union and cover significant and visible parts of the surface of unit packets. Minimum dimensions should be set for all health warnings to ensure their visibility and effectiveness.

(26) For tobacco products for smoking, other than cigarettes and roll-your-own tobacco products, which are mainly consumed by older consumers and small groups of the population, it should be possible to continue to grant an exemption from certain labelling requirements as long as there is no substantial change of circumstances in terms of sales volumes or consumption patterns of young people. The labelling of these other tobacco products should follow rules that are specific to them. The visibility of health warnings on smokeless tobacco products should be ensured. Health warnings should, therefore, be placed on the two main surfaces of the packaging of smokeless

tobacco products. As regards waterpipe tobacco, which is often perceived as less harmful than traditional tobacco products for smoking, the full labelling regime should apply in order to avoid consumers being misled.

(27) Tobacco products or their packaging could mislead consumers, in particular young people, where they suggest that these products are less harmful. This is, for example, the case if certain words or features are used, such as the words 'low-tar', 'light', 'ultra-light', 'mild', 'natural', 'organic', 'without additives', 'without flavours' or 'slim', or certain names, pictures, and figurative or other signs. Other misleading elements might include, but are not limited to, inserts or other additional material such as adhesive labels, stickers, onserts, scratch-offs and sleeves or relate to the shape of the tobacco product itself. Certain packaging and tobacco products could also mislead consumers by suggesting benefits in terms of weight loss, sex appeal, social status, social life or qualities such as femininity, masculinity or elegance. Likewise, the size and appearance of individual cigarettes could mislead consumers by creating the impression that they are less harmful. Neither the unit packets of tobacco products nor their outside packaging should include printed vouchers, discount offers, reference to free distribution, two-for-one or other similar offers that could suggest economic advantages to consumers thereby inciting them to buy those tobacco products.

(28) In order to ensure the integrity and the visibility of health warnings and maximise their efficacy, provisions should be made regarding the dimensions of the health warnings as well as regarding certain aspects of the appearance of the unit packets of tobacco products, including the shape and opening mechanism. When prescribing a cuboid shape for a unit packet, rounded or bevelled edges should be considered acceptable, provided the health warning covers a surface area that is equivalent to that on a unit packet without such edges. Member States apply different rules on the minimum number of cigarettes per unit packet. Those rules should be aligned in order to ensure free circulation of the products concerned.

(29) Considerable volumes of illicit products, which do not fulfil the requirements laid down in Directive 2001/37/EC, are placed on the market and there are indications that these volumes might increase. Such illicit products undermine the free circulation of compliant products and the protection provided for by tobacco control legislation. In addition, the FCTC requires the Union to combat illicit tobacco products, including those illegally imported into the Union, as part of a comprehensive Union policy on tobacco control. Provision should, therefore, be made for unit packets of tobacco products to be marked with a unique identifier and security features and for their movements to be recorded so that such products can be tracked and traced throughout the Union and their compliance with this Directive can be monitored and better enforced. In addition, provision should be made for the introduction of security features that will facilitate the verification of whether or not tobacco products are authentic.

(30) An interoperable tracking and tracing system and security features should be developed at Union level. For an initial period only cigarettes and roll-your-own tobacco should be subjected to the tracking and tracing system and the security features. This would allow manufacturers of other tobacco products to benefit from the experience gained prior to the tracking and tracing system and security features becoming applicable to those other products.

(31) In order to ensure independence and transparency of the tracking and tracing system, manufacturers of tobacco products should conclude data storage contracts with independent third parties. The Commission should approve the suitability of those independent third parties and an independent external auditor should monitor their activities. The data related to the tracking and tracing system should be kept separate from other company related data and should be under the control of, and accessible at all times by, the competent authorities from Member States and the Commission.

(32) Council Directive 89/622/EEC[7] prohibited the sale in the Member States of certain types of tobacco for oral use. Directive 2001/37/EC reaffirmed that prohibition. Article 151 of the Act of Accession of Austria, Finland and Sweden grants Sweden a derogation from the prohibition. The prohibition of the sale of tobacco for oral use should be maintained in order to prevent the introduction in the Union (apart from Sweden) of a product that is addictive and has adverse health effects. For other smokeless tobacco products that are not produced for the mass market, strict provisions on labelling and certain provisions relating to their ingredients are considered sufficient to contain their expansion in the market beyond their traditional use.

(33) Cross-border distance sales of tobacco products could facilitate access to tobacco products that do not comply with this Directive. There is also an increased risk that young people would get access to tobacco products. Consequently, there is a risk that tobacco control legislation would be undermined. Member States should, therefore, be allowed to prohibit cross-border distance sales. Where cross-border distance sales are not prohibited, common rules on the registration of retail outlets engaging in such sales are appropriate to ensure the effectiveness of this Directive. Member States should, in accordance with Article 4(3) of the Treaty on European Union (TEU) cooperate with each other in order to facilitate the implementation of this Directive, in particular with respect to measures taken as regards cross-border distance sales of tobacco products.

(34) All tobacco products have the potential to cause mortality, morbidity and disability. Accordingly, their manufacture, distribution and consumption should be regulated. It is, therefore,

important to monitor developments as regards novel tobacco products. Manufacturers and importers should be obliged to submit a notification of novel tobacco products, without prejudice to the power of the Member States to ban or to authorise such novel products.

(35) In order to ensure a level playing field, novel tobacco products, that are tobacco products as defined in this Directive, should comply with the requirements of this Directive.

(36) Electronic cigarettes and refill containers should be regulated by this Directive, unless they are – due to their presentation or function – subject to Directive 2001/83/EC of the European Parliament and of the Council[8] or to Council Directive 93/42/EEC.[9] Diverging legislation and practices as regards these products, including on safety requirements, exist between Member States, hence, action at Union level is required to improve the smooth functioning of the internal market. A high level of public health protection should be taken into account when regulating these products. In order to enable Member States to carry out their surveillance and control tasks, manufacturers and importers of electronic cigarettes and refill containers should be required to submit a notification of the relevant products before they are placed on the market.

(37) Member States should ensure that electronic cigarettes and refill containers comply with the requirements of this Directive. Where the manufacturer of the relevant product is not established in the Union, the importer of that product should bear the responsibilities relating to the compliance of those products with this Directive.

(38) Nicotine-containing liquid should only be allowed to be placed on the market under this Directive, where the nicotine concentration does not exceed 20 mg/ml. This concentration allows for a delivery of nicotine that is comparable to the permitted dose of nicotine derived from a standard cigarette during the time needed to smoke such a cigarette. In order to limit the risks associated with nicotine, maximum sizes for refill containers, tanks and cartridges should be set.

(39) Only electronic cigarettes that deliver nicotine doses at consistent levels should be allowed to be placed on the market under this Directive. Delivery of nicotine doses at consistent levels under normal conditions of use is necessary for health protection, safety and quality purposes, including to avoid the risk of accidental consumption of high doses.

(40) Electronic cigarettes and refill containers could create a health risk when in the hands of children. Therefore, it is necessary to ensure that such products are child- and tamperproof, including by means of child-proof labelling, fastenings and opening mechanisms.

(41) In view of the fact that nicotine is a toxic substance and considering the potential health and safety risks, including to persons for whom the product is not intended, nicotine-containing liquid should only be placed on the market in electronic cigarettes or in refill containers that meet certain safety and quality requirements. It is important to ensure that electronic cigarettes do not break or leak during use and refill.

(42) The labelling and packaging of these products should display sufficient and appropriate information on their safe use, in order to protect human health and safety, should carry appropriate health warnings and should not include any misleading elements or features.

(43) Disparities between national laws and practices on advertising and sponsorship concerning electronic cigarettes present an obstacle to the free movement of goods and the freedom to provide services and create an appreciable risk of distortion of competition. Without further action at Union level, those disparities are likely to increase over the coming years, also taking into account the growing market for electronic cigarettes and refill containers. Therefore, it is necessary to approximate the national provisions on advertising and sponsorship of those products having cross-border effects, taking as a base a high level of protection of human health. Electronic cigarettes can develop into a gateway to nicotine addiction and ultimately traditional tobacco consumption, as they mimic and normalize the action of smoking. For this reason, it is appropriate to adopt a restrictive approach to advertising electronic cigarettes and refill containers.

(44) In order to perform their regulatory tasks, the Commission and Member States need comprehensive information on market developments as regards electronic cigarettes and refill containers. To this end manufacturers and importers of these products should be subject to reporting obligations on sales volumes, preference of various consumer groups and mode of sales. It should be ensured that this information is made available to the general public, taking the need to protect trade secrets duly into account.

(45) In order to ensure appropriate market surveillance by Member States, it is necessary that manufacturers, importers and distributors operate an appropriate system for monitoring and recording suspected adverse effects and inform the competent authorities about such effects so that appropriate action can be taken. It is warranted to provide for a safeguard clause that would allow Member States to take action to address serious risks to public health.

(46) In the context of an emerging market for electronic cigarettes, it is possible that, although complying with this Directive, specific electronic cigarettes or refill containers, or a type of electronic cigarette or refill container, placed on the market could pose an unforeseen risk to human health. It is therefore advisable to provide for a procedure to address this risk, which should include the possibility for a Member State to adopt provisional appropriate measures. Such provisional appropriate measures could involve the prohibition of the placing on the market of specific electronic

cigarettes or refill containers, or of a type of electronic cigarette or refill container. In this context, the Commission should be empowered to adopt delegated acts in order to prohibit the placing on the market of specific electronic cigarettes or refill containers, or of a type of electronic cigarette or refill container. The Commission should be empowered to do so, when at least three Member States have prohibited the products concerned on duly justified grounds and it is necessary to extend this prohibition to all Member States in order to ensure the smooth functioning of the internal market for products complying with this Directive but not presenting the same health risks. The Commission should report on the potential risks associated with refillable electronic cigarettes by 20 May 2016.

(47) This Directive does not harmonise all aspects of electronic cigarettes or refill containers. For example, the responsibility for adopting rules on flavours remains with the Member States. It could be useful for Member States to consider allowing the placing on the market of flavoured products. In doing so, they should be mindful of the potential attractiveness of such products for young people and non smokers. Any prohibition of such flavoured products would need to be justified and notification thereof submitted in accordance with Directive 98/34/EC of the European Parliament and of the Council.[10]

(48) Moreover, this Directive does not harmonise the rules on smoke-free environments, or on domestic sales arrangements or domestic advertising, or brand stretching, nor does it introduce an age limit for electronic cigarettes or refill containers. In any case, the presentation and advertising of those products should not lead to the promotion of tobacco consumption or give rise to confusion with tobacco products. Member States are free to regulate such matters within the remit of their own jurisdiction and are encouraged to do so.

(49) The regulation of herbal products for smoking differs between Member States and these products are often perceived as harmless or less harmful despite the health risk caused by their combustion. In many cases consumers do not know the content of these products. In order to ensure the smooth functioning of the internal market and improve information to consumers, common labelling rules and ingredients reporting for these products should be introduced at Union level.

(50) In order to ensure uniform conditions for the implementation of this Directive implementing powers should be conferred on the Commission concerning the laying down and updating of a priority list of additives for enhanced reporting, the laying down and updating of the format for the reporting of ingredients and for the dissemination of that information, determining whether a tobacco product has a characterising flavour or has increased levels of toxicity, addictiveness or CMR properties, the methodology for determining whether a tobacco product has a characterising flavour, the procedures for the establishment and operation of an independent advisory panel for determining tobacco products with characterising flavours, the precise position of health warnings on pouches of roll-your-own tobacco, the technical specifications for the layout, design, and shape of combined health warnings, the technical standards for the establishment and operation of the tracking and tracing system, for ensuring the compatibility of the systems for the unique identifiers and for the security features, as well as establishing a common format for notification of electronic cigarettes and refill containers and the technical standards for the refill mechanisms for such products. Those implementing powers should be exercised in accordance with Regulation (EU) No 182/2011 of the European Parliament and of the Council.[11]

(51) In order to ensure that this Directive is fully operational and to adapt it to technical, scientific and international developments in tobacco manufacture, consumption and regulation, the power to adopt acts in accordance with Article 290 TFEU should be delegated to the Commission in respect of adopting and adapting maximum emission levels and methods for measuring those emissions, setting maximum levels for additives that result in a characterising flavour or that increase toxicity or addictiveness, withdrawing certain exemptions granted to tobacco products other than cigarettes and roll-your-own tobacco, adapting the health warnings, establishing and adapting the picture library, defining the key elements of the data storage contracts to be concluded for the purposes of the tracking and tracing system, and extending measures adopted by Member States to the entire Union concerning specific electronic cigarettes or refill containers or a type of electronic cigarette or refill container. It is of particular importance that the Commission carry out appropriate consultations during its preparatory work, including at expert level. The Commission, when preparing and drawing up delegated acts, should ensure a simultaneous, timely and appropriate transmission of relevant documents to the European Parliament and to the Council.

(52) The Commission should monitor the developments as regards the implementation and impact of this Directive and submit a report by 21 May 2021, and when necessary thereafter, in order to assess whether amendments to this Directive are necessary. The report should include information on the surfaces of unit packets of tobacco products that are not governed by this Directive, market developments concerning novel tobacco products, market developments that amount to a substantial change of circumstances, market developments concerning, and the consumer perception of, slim cigarettes, of waterpipe tobacco and of electronic cigarettes and refill containers.

The Commission should prepare a report regarding the feasibility, benefits and impact of a European system for the regulation of ingredients in tobacco products, including the feasibility and benefits of establishing a list of ingredients at Union level that can be used, or present in or added to tobacco products (so-called 'positive list'). In preparing that report, the Commission should evaluate, inter alia, the available scientific evidence on the toxic and addictive effects of ingredients.

(53) Tobacco and related products which comply with this Directive should benefit from the free movement of goods. However, in light of the different degrees of harmonisation achieved by this Directive, the Member States should, under certain conditions, retain the power to impose further requirements in certain respects in order to protect public health. This is the case in relation to the presentation and the packaging, including colours, of tobacco products other than health warnings, for which this Directive provides a first set of basic common rules. Accordingly, Member States could, for example, introduce provisions providing for further standardisation of the packaging of tobacco products, provided that those provisions are compatible with the TFEU, with WTO obligations and do not affect the full application of this Directive.

(54) Moreover, in order to take into account possible future market developments, Member States should also be allowed to prohibit a certain category of tobacco or related products, on grounds relating to the specific situation in the Member State concerned and provided the provisions are justified by the need to protect public health, taking into account the high level of protection achieved through this Directive. Member States should notify such stricter national provisions to the Commission.

(55) A Member State should remain free to maintain or introduce national laws applying to all products placed on its national market for aspects not regulated by this Directive, provided they are compatible with the TFEU and do not jeopardise the full application of this Directive. Accordingly and under those conditions, a Member State could, inter alia, regulate or ban paraphernalia used for tobacco products (including waterpipes) and for herbal products for smoking as well as regulate or ban products resembling in appearance a type of tobacco or related product. Prior notification is required for national technical regulations pursuant to Directive 98/34/EC.

(56) Member States should ensure that personal data are only processed in accordance with the rules and safeguards laid down in Directive 95/46/EC of the European Parliament and of the Council.[12]

(57) This Directive is without prejudice to Union laws governing the use and labelling of genetically modified organisms.

(58) In accordance with the Joint Political Declaration of 28 September 2011 of Member States and the Commission on explanatory documents,[13] Member States have undertaken to accompany, in justified cases, the notification of their transposition measures with one or more documents explaining the relationship between the components of a directive and the corresponding parts of national transposition instruments. With regard to this Directive, the legislator considers the transmission of such documents to be justified.

(59) The obligation to respect the fundamental rights and legal principles enshrined in the Charter of Fundamental Rights of the European Union is not changed by this Directive. Several fundamental rights are affected by this Directive. It is therefore necessary to ensure that the obligations imposed on manufacturers, importers and distributors of tobacco and related products not only guarantee a high level of health and consumer protection, but also protect all other fundamental rights and are proportionate with respect to the smooth functioning of the internal market. The application of this Directive should respect Union law and relevant international obligations.

(60) Since the objectives of this Directive, namely to approximate the laws, regulations and administrative provisions of the Member States concerning the manufacture, presentation and sale of tobacco and related products, cannot be sufficiently achieved by the Member States, but can rather, by reason of their scale and effects, be better achieved at Union level, the Union may adopt measures, in accordance with the principle of subsidiarity as set out in Article 5 TEU. In accordance with the principle of proportionality, as set out in that Article, this Directive does not go beyond what is necessary in order to achieve those objectives,

NOTES

1 OJ C327, 12.11.2013, p 65.

2 OJ C280, 27.9.2013, p 57.

3 Position of the European Parliament of 26 February 2014 (not yet published in the Official Journal) and decision of the Council of 14 March 2014.

4 Directive 2001/37/EC of the European Parliament and of the Council of 5 June 2001 on the approximation of the laws, regulations and administrative provisions of the Member States concerning the manufacture, presentation and sale of tobacco products (OJ L194, 18.7.2001, p 26).

5 Council Recommendation 2003/54/EC of 2 December 2002 on the prevention of smoking and on initiatives to improve tobacco control (OJ L22, 25.1.2003, p 31).

6 Directive 2005/29/EC of the European Parliament and of the Council of 11 May 2005 concerning unfair business-to-consumer commercial practices in the internal market and amending Council Directive 84/450/EEC, Directives 97/7/EC, 98/27/EC and 2002/65/EC of the European Parliament and of the Council and Regulation (EC) No 2006/2004 of the European Parliament and of the Council ('Unfair Commercial Practices Directive') (OJ L149, 11.6.2005, p 22).

7 Council Directive 89/622/EEC of 13 November 1989 on the approximation of the laws, regulations and administrative provisions of the Member States concerning the labelling of tobacco products and the prohibition of the marketing of

certain types of tobacco for oral use (OJ L359, 8.12.1989, p 1).

[8] Directive 2001/83/EC of the European Parliament and of the Council of 6 November 2001 on the Community code relating to medicinal products for human use (OJ L311, 28.11.2001, p 67).

[9] Council Directive 93/42/EEC of 14 June 1993 concerning medical devices (OJ L169, 12.7.1993, p 1).

[10] Directive 98/34/EC of the European Parliament and of the Council of 22 June 1998 laying down a procedure for the provision of information in the field of technical standards and regulations and of rules on Information Society services (OJ L204, 21.7.1998, p 37).

[11] Regulation (EU) No 182/2011 of the European Parliament and of the Council of 16 February 2011 laying down the rules and general principles concerning mechanisms for control by Member States of the Commission's exercise of implementing powers (OJ L55, 28.2.2011, p 13).

[12] Directive 95/46/EC of the European Parliament and of the Council of 24 October 1995 on the protection of individuals with regard to the processing of personal data and on the free movement of such data (OJ L281, 23.11.1995, p 31).

[13] OJ C369, 17.12.2011, p 14.

HAVE ADOPTED THIS DIRECTIVE:

TITLE I
COMMON PROVISIONS

[8.684]
Article 1
Subject matter

The objective of this Directive is to approximate the laws, regulations and administrative provisions of the Member States concerning:

(a) the ingredients and emissions of tobacco products and related reporting obligations, including the maximum emission levels for tar, nicotine and carbon monoxide for cigarettes;
(b) certain aspects of the labelling and packaging of tobacco products including the health warnings to appear on unit packets of tobacco products and any outside packaging as well as traceability and security features that are applied to tobacco products to ensure their compliance with this Directive;
(c) the prohibition on the placing on the market of tobacco for oral use;
(d) cross-border distance sales of tobacco products;
(e) the obligation to submit a notification of novel tobacco products;
(f) the placing on the market and the labelling of certain products, which are related to tobacco products, namely electronic cigarettes and refill containers, and herbal products for smoking;

in order to facilitate the smooth functioning of the internal market for tobacco and related products, taking as a base a high level of protection of human health, especially for young people, and to meet the obligations of the Union under the WHO Framework Convention for Tobacco Control ('FCTC').

[8.685]
Article 2
Definitions

For the purposes of this Directive, the following definitions shall apply:

(1) 'tobacco' means leaves and other natural processed or unprocessed parts of tobacco plants, including expanded and reconstituted tobacco;
(2) 'pipe tobacco' means tobacco that can be consumed via a combustion process and exclusively intended for use in a pipe;
(3) 'roll-your-own tobacco' means tobacco which can be used for making cigarettes by consumers or retail outlets;
(4) 'tobacco products' means products that can be consumed and consist, even partly, of tobacco, whether genetically modified or not;
(5) 'smokeless tobacco product' means a tobacco product not involving a combustion process, including chewing tobacco, nasal tobacco and tobacco for oral use;
(6) 'chewing tobacco' means a smokeless tobacco product exclusively intended for the purpose of chewing;
(7) 'nasal tobacco' means a smokeless tobacco product that can be consumed via the nose;
(8) 'tobacco for oral use' means all tobacco products for oral use, except those intended to be inhaled or chewed, made wholly or partly of tobacco, in powder or in particulate form or in any combination of those forms, particularly those presented in sachet portions or porous sachets;
(9) 'tobacco products for smoking' means tobacco products other than a smokeless tobacco product;
(10) 'cigarette' means a roll of tobacco that can be consumed via a combustion process and is further defined in Article 3(1) of Council Directive 2011/64/EU;[1]
(11) 'cigar' means a roll of tobacco that can be consumed via a combustion process and is further defined in Article 4(1) of Directive 2011/64/EU;

(12) 'cigarillo' means a small type of cigar and is further defined in Article 8(1) of Council Directive 2007/74/EC;[2]

(13) 'waterpipe tobacco' means a tobacco product that can be consumed via a waterpipe. For the purpose of this Directive, waterpipe tobacco is deemed to be a tobacco product for smoking. If a product can be used both via waterpipes and as roll-your-own tobacco, it shall be deemed to be roll-your-own tobacco;

(14) 'novel tobacco product' means a tobacco product which:

(a) does not fall into any of the following categories: cigarettes, roll-your-own tobacco, pipe tobacco, waterpipe tobacco, cigars, cigarillos, chewing tobacco, nasal tobacco or tobacco for oral use; and

(b) is placed on the market after 19 May 2014;

(15) 'herbal product for smoking' means a product based on plants, herbs or fruits which contains no tobacco and that can be consumed via a combustion process;

(16) 'electronic cigarette' means a product that can be used for consumption of nicotine-containing vapour via a mouth piece, or any component of that product, including a cartridge, a tank and the device without cartridge or tank. Electronic cigarettes can be disposable or refillable by means of a refill container and a tank, or rechargeable with single use cartridges;

(17) 'refill container' means a receptacle that contains a nicotine-containing liquid, which can be used to refill an electronic cigarette;

(18) 'ingredient' means tobacco, an additive, as well as any substance or element present in a finished tobacco product or related products, including paper, filter, ink, capsules and adhesives;

(19) 'nicotine' means nicotinic alkaloids;

(20) 'tar' means the raw anhydrous nicotine-free condensate of smoke;

(21) 'emissions' means substances that are released when a tobacco or related product is consumed as intended, such as substances found in smoke, or substances released during the process of using smokeless tobacco products;

(22) 'maximum level' or 'maximum emission level' means the maximum content or emission, including zero, of a substance in a tobacco product measured in milligrams;

(23) 'additive' means a substance, other than tobacco, that is added to a tobacco product, a unit packet or to any outside packaging;

(24) 'flavouring' means an additive that imparts smell and/or taste;

(25) 'characterising flavour' means a clearly noticeable smell or taste other than one of tobacco, resulting from an additive or a combination of additives, including, but not limited to, fruit, spice, herbs, alcohol, candy, menthol or vanilla, which is noticeable before or during the consumption of the tobacco product;

(26) 'addictiveness' means the pharmacological potential of a substance to cause addiction, a state which affects an individual's ability to control his or her behaviour, typically by instilling a reward or a relief from withdrawal symptoms, or both;

(27) 'toxicity' means the degree to which a substance can cause harmful effects in the human organism, including effects occurring over time, usually through repeated or continuous consumption or exposure;

(28) 'substantial change of circumstances' means an increase of the sales volumes by product category by at least 10% in at least five Member States based on sales data transmitted in accordance with Article 5(6) or an increase of the level of prevalence of use in the under 25 years of age consumer group by at least five percentage points in at least five Member States for the respective product category based on the Special Eurobarometer 385 report of May 2012 or equivalent prevalence studies; in any case, a substantial change of circumstances is deemed not to have occurred if the sales volume of the product category at retail level does not exceed 2.5% of total sales of tobacco products at Union level;

(29) 'outside packaging' means any packaging in which tobacco or related products are placed on the market and which includes a unit packet or an aggregation of unit packets; transparent wrappers are not regarded as outside packaging;

(30) 'unit packet' means the smallest individual packaging of a tobacco or related product that is placed on the market;

(31) 'pouch' means a unit packet of roll-your own tobacco, either in the form of a rectangular pocket with a flap that covers the opening or in the form of a standing pouch;

(32) 'health warning' means a warning concerning the adverse effects on human health of a product or other undesired consequences of its consumption, including text warnings, combined health warnings, general warnings and information messages, as provided for in this Directive;

(33) 'combined health warning' means a health warning consisting of a combination of a text warning and a corresponding photograph or illustration, as provided for in this Directive;

(34) 'cross-border distance sales' means distance sales to consumers where, at the time the consumer orders the product from a retail outlet, the consumer is located in a Member State other than the Member State or the third country where that retail outlet is established; a retail outlet is deemed to be established in a Member State:

(a) in the case of a natural person: if he or she has his or her place of business in that Member State;

(b) in other cases: if the retail outlet has its statutory seat, central administration or place of business, including a branch, agency or any other establishment, in that Member State;

(35) 'consumer' means a natural person who is acting for purposes which are outside his or her trade, business, craft or profession;

(36) 'age verification system' means a computing system that unambiguously confirms the consumer's age electronically in accordance with national requirements;

(37) 'manufacturer' means any natural or legal person who manufactures a product or has a product designed or manufactured, and markets that product under their name or trademark;

(38) 'import of tobacco or related products' means the entry into the territory of the Union of such products unless the products are placed under a customs suspensive procedure or arrangement upon their entry into the Union, as well as their release from a customs suspensive procedure or arrangement;

(39) 'importer of tobacco or related products' means the owner of, or a person having the right of disposal over, tobacco or related products that have been brought into the territory of the Union;

(40) 'placing on the market' means to make products, irrespective of their place of manufacture, available to consumers located in the Union, with or without payment, including by means of distance sale; in the case of cross-border distance sales the product is deemed to be placed on the market in the Member State where the consumer is located;

(41) 'retail outlet' means any outlet where tobacco products are placed on the market including by a natural person.

NOTES

1 Council Directive 2011/64/EU of 21 June 2011 on the structure and rates of excise duty applied to manufactured tobacco (OJ L176, 5.7.2011, p 24).

2 Council Directive 2007/74/EC of 20 December 2007 on the exemption from value added tax and excise duty of goods imported by persons travelling from third countries (OJ L346, 29.12.2007, p 6).

TITLE II
TOBACCO PRODUCTS

CHAPTER I
INGREDIENTS AND EMISSIONS

[8.686]
Article 3
Maximum emission levels for tar, nicotine, carbon monoxide and other substances

1. The emission levels from cigarettes placed on the market or manufactured in the Member States ('maximum emission levels') shall not be greater than:

(a) 10 mg of tar per cigarette;
(b) 1 mg of nicotine per cigarette;
(c) 10 mg of carbon monoxide per cigarette.

2. The Commission shall be empowered to adopt delegated acts in accordance with Article 27 to decrease the maximum emission levels laid down in paragraph 1, where this is necessary based on internationally agreed standards.

3. Member States shall notify the Commission of any maximum emission levels they set for emissions from cigarettes other than the emissions referred to in paragraph 1 and for emissions from tobacco products other than cigarettes.

4. The Commission shall adopt delegated acts in accordance with Article 27 to integrate standards agreed by the parties to the FCTC or by the WHO relating to maximum emission levels for emissions from cigarettes other than the emissions referred to in paragraph 1 and for emissions from tobacco products other than cigarettes into Union law.

[8.687]
Article 4
Measurement methods

1. The tar, nicotine and carbon monoxide emissions from cigarettes shall be measured on the basis of ISO standard 4387 for tar, ISO standard 10315 for nicotine, and ISO standard 8454 for carbon monoxide.

The accuracy of the tar, nicotine and carbon monoxide measurements shall be determined in accordance with ISO standard 8243.

2. The measurements referred to in paragraph 1 shall be verified by laboratories which are approved and monitored by the competent authorities of the Member States.

Those laboratories shall not be owned or controlled directly or indirectly by the tobacco industry. Member States shall communicate to the Commission a list of approved laboratories, specifying the criteria used for approval and the methods of monitoring applied, and shall update that list whenever any change is made. The Commission shall make those lists of approved laboratories publicly available.

3. The Commission shall be empowered to adopt delegated acts in accordance with Article 27 to adapt the methods of measurement of the tar, nicotine and carbon monoxide emissions, where this is necessary, based on scientific and technical developments or internationally agreed standards.

4. Member States shall notify the Commission of any measurement methods they use for emissions from cigarettes other than the emissions referred to in paragraph 3 and for emissions from tobacco products other than cigarettes.

5. The Commission shall adopt delegated acts in accordance with Article 27 to integrate standards agreed by the parties to the FCTC or by the WHO for measurement methods into Union law.

6. Member States may charge manufacturers and importers of tobacco products proportionate fees for the verification of the measurements referred to in paragraph 1 of this Article.

[8.688]

Article 5

Reporting of ingredients and emissions

1. Member States shall require manufacturers and importers of tobacco products to submit to their competent authorities the following information by brand name and type:

(a) a list of all ingredients, and quantities thereof, used in the manufacture of the tobacco products, in descending order of the weight of each ingredient included in the tobacco products;

(b) the emission levels referred to in Article 3(1) and (4);

(c) where available, information on other emissions and their levels.

For products already placed on the market that information shall be provided by 20 November 2016.

Manufacturers or importers shall also inform the competent authorities of the Member States concerned, if the composition of a product is modified in a way that affects the information provided under this Article.

For a new or modified tobacco product the information required under this Article shall be submitted prior to the placing on the market of those products.

2. The list of ingredients referred to in point (a) of paragraph 1 shall be accompanied by a statement setting out the reasons for the inclusion of such ingredients in the tobacco products concerned. That list shall also indicate the status of the ingredients, including whether they have been registered under Regulation (EC) No 1907/2006 of the European Parliament and of the Council[1] as well as their classification under Regulation (EC) No 1272/2008 of the European Parliament and of the Council.[2]

3. The list referred to in point (a) of paragraph 1 shall also be accompanied by the relevant toxicological data regarding the ingredients in burnt or unburnt form, as appropriate, referring in particular to their effects on the health of consumers and taking into account, inter alia, any addictive effects.

Furthermore, for cigarettes and roll-your-own tobacco, a technical document setting out a general description of the additives used and their properties, shall be submitted by the manufacturer or importer.

Other than for tar, nicotine and carbon monoxide and for emissions referred to in Article 4(4), manufacturers and importers shall indicate the methods of measurement of emissions used. Member States may also require manufacturers or importers to carry out studies as may be prescribed by the competent authorities in order to assess the effects of ingredients on health, taking into account, inter alia, their addictiveness and toxicity.

4. Member States shall ensure that the information submitted in accordance with paragraph 1 of this Article and of Article 6 is made publicly available on a website. The Member States shall take the need to protect trade secrets duly into account when making that information publicly available. Member States shall require manufacturers and importers to specify, when submitting the information pursuant to paragraph 1 of this Article and Article 6, the information which they consider to constitute trade secrets.

5. The Commission shall, by means of implementing acts, lay down and, if necessary, update the format for the submission and the making available of information referred to in paragraphs 1 and 6 of this Article and Article 6. Those implementing acts shall be adopted in accordance with the examination procedure referred to in Article 25(2).

6. Member States shall require manufacturers and importers to submit internal and external studies available to them on market research and preferences of various consumer groups, including young people and current smokers, relating to ingredients and emissions, as well as executive summaries of any market surveys they carry out when launching new products. Member States shall also require manufacturers and importers to report their sales volumes per brand and type, reported in sticks or kilograms, and per Member State on a yearly basis starting from 1 January 2015. Member States shall provide any other sales volume data that is available to them.

7. All data and information to be provided to and by Member States under this Article and under Article 6 shall be provided in electronic form. Member States shall store the information electronically and shall ensure that the Commission and other Member States have access to that information for the purposes of applying this Directive. Member States and the Commission shall ensure that trade secrets and other confidential information are treated in a confidential manner.
8. Member States may charge manufacturers and importers of tobacco products proportionate fees for receiving, storing, handling, analysing and publishing the information submitted to them pursuant to this Article.

NOTES

1 Regulation (EC) No 1907/2006 of the European Parliament and of the Council of 18 December 2006 concerning the Registration, Evaluation, Authorisation and Restriction of Chemicals (REACH), establishing a European Chemicals Agency, amending Directive 1999/45/EC and repealing Council Regulation (EEC) No 793/93 and Commission Regulation (EC) No 1488/94 as well as Council Directive 76/769/EEC and Commission Directives 91/155/EEC, 93/67/EEC, 93/105/EC and 2000/21/EC (OJ L396, 30.12.2006, p 1).

2 Regulation (EC) No 1272/2008 of the European Parliament and of the Council of 16 December 2008 on classification, labelling and packaging of substances and mixtures, amending and repealing Directives 67/548/EEC and 1999/45/EC, and amending Regulation (EC) No 1907/2006 (OJ L353, 31.12.2008, p 1).

[8.689]
Article 6
Priority list of additives and enhanced reporting obligations

1. In addition to the reporting obligations laid down in Article 5, enhanced reporting obligations shall apply to certain additives contained in cigarettes and roll-your-own tobacco that are included in a priority list. The Commission shall adopt implementing acts laying down and subsequently updating such a priority list of additives. This list shall contain additives:

(a) for which initial indications, research, or regulation in other jurisdictions exist suggesting that they have onc of the properties set out in points (a) to (d) of paragraph 2 of this Article; and

(b) which are amongst the most commonly used additives by weight or number according to the reporting of ingredients pursuant to paragraphs 1 and 3 of Article 5.

Those implementing acts shall be adopted in accordance with the examination procedure referred to in Article 25(2). A first list of additives shall be adopted by 20 May 2016 and shall contain at least 15 additives.

2. Member States shall require manufacturers and importers of cigarettes and roll-your-own tobacco containing an additive that is included in the priority list provided for in paragraph 1, to carry out comprehensive studies, which shall examine for each additive whether it:

(a) contributes to the toxicity or addictiveness of the products concerned, and whether this has the effect of increasing the toxicity or addictiveness of any of the products concerned to a significant or measurable degree;

(b) results in a characterising flavour;

(c) facilitates inhalation or nicotine uptake; or

(d) leads to the formation of substances that have CMR properties, the quantities thereof, and whether this has the effect of increasing the CMR properties in any of the products concerned to a significant or measurable degree.

3. Those studies shall take into account the intended use of the products concerned and examine in particular the emissions resulting from the combustion process involving the additive concerned. The studies shall also examine the interaction of that additive with other ingredients contained in the products concerned. Manufacturers or importers using the same additive in their tobacco products may carry out a joint study when using that additive in a comparable product composition.

4. Manufacturers or importers shall establish a report on the results of these studies. That report shall include an executive summary, and a comprehensive overview compiling the available scientific literature on that additive and summarising internal data on the effects of the additive.

Manufacturers or importers shall submit these reports to the Commission and a copy thereof to the competent authorities of those Member States where a tobacco product containing this additive is placed on the market at the latest 18 months after the additive concerned has been included in the priority list pursuant to paragraph 1. The Commission and the Member States concerned may also request supplementary information from manufacturers or importers regarding the additive concerned. This supplementary information shall form part of the report.

The Commission and the Member States concerned may require these reports to be peer reviewed by an independent scientific body, in particular as regards their comprehensiveness, methodology and conclusions. The information received shall assist the Commission and Member States in taking the decisions pursuant to Article 7. The Member States and the Commission may charge manufacturers and importers of tobacco products proportionate fees for those peer reviews.

5. Small and medium-sized enterprises as defined in Commission Recommendation 2003/361/EC[1] shall be exempted from the obligations pursuant to this Article, if a report on that additive is prepared by another manufacturer or importer.

NOTES

[1] Commission Recommendation 2003/361/EC of 6 May 2003 concerning the definition of micro, small and medium-sized enterprises (OJ L124, 20.5.2003, p 36).

[8.690]
Article 7
Regulation of ingredients

1. Member States shall prohibit the placing on the market of tobacco products with a characterising flavour.

Member States shall not prohibit the use of additives which are essential for the manufacture of tobacco products, for example sugar to replace sugar that is lost during the curing process, provided those additives do not result in a product with a characterising flavour and do not increase to a significant or measureable degree the addictiveness, toxicity or the CMR properties of the tobacco product.

Member States shall notify the Commission of the measures taken pursuant to this paragraph.

2. The Commission shall, at the request of a Member State, or may, on its own initiative, determine by means of implementing acts whether a tobacco product falls within the scope of paragraph 1. Those implementing acts shall be adopted in accordance with the examination procedure referred to in Article 25(2).

3. The Commission shall adopt implementing acts laying down uniform rules for the procedures for determining whether a tobacco product falls within the scope of paragraph 1. Those implementing acts shall be adopted in accordance with the examination procedure referred to in Article 25(2).

4. An independent advisory panel shall be established at Union level. Member States and the Commission may consult this panel before adopting a measure pursuant to paragraphs 1 and 2 of this Article. The Commission shall adopt implementing acts laying down the procedures for the establishment and operation of this panel.

Those implementing acts shall be adopted in accordance with the examination procedure referred to in Article 25(2).

5. Where the content level or concentration of certain additives or the combination thereof has resulted in prohibitions pursuant to paragraph 1 of this Article in at least three Member States, the Commission shall be empowered to adopt delegated acts in accordance with Article 27 to set maximum content levels for those additives or combination of additives that result in the characterising flavour.

6. Member States shall prohibit the placing on the market of tobacco products containing the following additives:
- (a) vitamins or other additives that create the impression that a tobacco product has a health benefit or presents reduced health risks;
- (b) caffeine or taurine or other additives and stimulant compounds that are associated with energy and vitality;
- (c) additives having colouring properties for emissions;
- (d) for tobacco products for smoking, additives that facilitate inhalation or nicotine uptake; and
- (e) additives that have CMR properties in unburnt form.

7. Member States shall prohibit the placing on the market of tobacco products containing flavourings in any of their components such as filters, papers, packages, capsules or any technical features allowing modification of the smell or taste of the tobacco products concerned or their smoke intensity. Filters, papers and capsules shall not contain tobacco or nicotine.

8. Member States shall ensure that the provisions and conditions laid down in Regulation (EC) No 1907/2006 are applied to tobacco products as appropriate.

9. Member States shall, on the basis of scientific evidence, prohibit the placing on the market of tobacco products containing additives in quantities that increase the toxic or addictive effect, or the CMR properties of a tobacco product at the stage of consumption to a significant or measureable degree.

Member States shall notify to the Commission the measures they have taken pursuant to this paragraph.

10. The Commission shall, at the request of a Member State, or may, on its own initiative, determine by means of an implementing act whether a tobacco product falls within the scope of paragraph 9. Those implementing acts shall be adopted in accordance with the examination procedure referred to in Article 25(2) and shall be based on the latest scientific evidence.

11. Where an additive or a certain quantity thereof has been shown to amplify the toxic or addictive effect of a tobacco product, and where this has resulted in prohibitions pursuant to paragraph (9) of this Article in at least three Member States, the Commission shall be empowered to adopt delegated acts in accordance with Article 27 to set maximum content levels for those additives. In this case, the maximum content level shall be set at the lowest maximum level that led to one of the national prohibitions referred to in this paragraph.

12. Tobacco products other than cigarettes and roll-your-own tobacco shall be exempted from the prohibitions laid down in paragraphs 1 and 7. The Commission shall adopt delegated acts in accordance with Article 27 to withdraw that exemption for a particular product category, if there is a substantial change of circumstances as established in a Commission report.
13. The Member States and the Commission may charge proportionate fees to manufacturers and importers of tobacco products for assessing whether a tobacco product has a characterising flavour, whether prohibited additives or flavourings are used and whether a tobacco product contains additives in quantities that increase to a significant and measurable degree the toxic or addictive effect or the CMR properties of the tobacco product concerned.
14. In the case of tobacco products with a characterising flavour whose Union-wide sales volumes represent 3% or more in a particular product category, the provisions of this Article shall apply from 20 May 2020.
15. This Article shall not apply to tobacco for oral use.

CHAPTER II
LABELLING AND PACKAGING

[8.691]
Article 8
General provisions

1. Each unit packet of a tobacco product and any outside packaging shall carry the health warnings provided for in this Chapter in the official language or languages of the Member State where the product is placed on the market.
2. Health warnings shall cover the entire surface of the unit packet or outside packaging that is reserved for them and they shall not be commented on, paraphrased or referred to in any form.
3. Member States shall ensure that the health warnings on a unit packet and any outside packaging are irremovably printed, indelible and fully visible, including not being partially or totally hidden or interrupted by tax stamps, price marks, security features, wrappers, jackets, boxes, or other items, when tobacco products are placed on the market. On unit packets of tobacco products other than cigarettes and roll-your-own tobacco in pouches, the health warnings may be affixed by means of stickers, provided that such stickers are irremovable. The health warnings shall remain intact when opening the unit packet other than packets with a flip-top lid, where the health warnings may be split when opening the packet, but only in a manner that ensures the graphical integrity and visibility of the text, photographs and cessation information.
4. The health warnings shall in no way hide or interrupt the tax stamps, price marks, tracking and tracing marks, or security features on unit packets.
5. The dimensions of the health warnings provided for in Articles 9, 10, 11 and 12 shall be calculated in relation to the surface concerned when the packet is closed.
6. Health warnings shall be surrounded by a black border of a width of 1 mm inside the surface area that is reserved for these warnings, except for health warnings pursuant to Article 11.
7. When adapting a health warning pursuant to Articles 9(5), 10(3) and 12(3), the Commission shall ensure that it is factual or that Member States shall have a choice of two warnings, one of which is factual.
8. Images of unit packets and any outside packaging targeting consumers in the Union shall comply with the provisions of this chapter.

[8.692]
Article 9
General warnings and information messages on tobacco products for smoking

1. Each unit packet and any outside packaging of tobacco products for smoking shall carry one of the following general warnings:

 'Smoking kills – quit now'

or

 'Smoking kills'

Member States shall determine which of the general warnings referred to in the first subparagraph is to be used.

2. Each unit packet and any outside packaging of tobacco products for smoking shall carry the following information message:

 'Tobacco smoke contains over 70 substances known to cause cancer.'

3. For cigarette packets and roll-your-own tobacco in cuboid packets the general warning shall appear on the bottom part of one of the lateral surfaces of the unit packets, and the information message shall appear on the bottom part of the other lateral surface. These health warnings shall have a width of not less than 20 mm.

For packets in the form of a shoulder box with a hinged lid that result in the lateral surfaces being split into two when the packet is open, the general warning and the information message shall appear in their entirety on the larger parts of those split surfaces. The general warning shall also appear on the inside of the top surface that is visible when the packet is open.

The lateral surfaces of this type of packet shall have a height of not less than 16 mm.

For roll-your-own tobacco marketed in pouches the general warning and the information message shall appear on the surfaces that ensure the full visibility of those health warnings. For roll-your-own tobacco in cylindrical packets the general warning shall appear on the outside surface of the lid and the information message on the inside surface of the lid.

Both the general warning and the information message shall cover 50% of the surfaces on which they are printed.

4. The general warning and information message referred to in paragraphs 1 and 2 shall be:

(a) printed in black Helvetica bold type on a white background. In order to accommodate language requirements, Member States may determine the font size, provided that the font size specified in national law ensures that the relevant text occupies the greatest possible proportion of the surface reserved for these health warnings; and

(b) at the centre of the surface reserved for them, and on cuboid packets and any outside packaging they shall be parallel to the lateral edge of the unit packet or of the outside packaging.

5. The Commission shall be empowered to adopt delegated acts in accordance with Article 27 to adapt the wording of the information message laid down in paragraph 2 to scientific and market developments.

6. The Commission shall, by means of implementing acts, determine the precise position of the general warning and the information message on roll-your-own tobacco marketed in pouches, taking into account the different shapes of pouches.

Those implementing acts shall be adopted in accordance with the examination procedure referred to in Article 25(2).

[8.693]

Article 10

Combined health warnings for tobacco products for smoking

1. Each unit packet and any outside packaging of tobacco products for smoking shall carry combined health warnings. The combined health warnings shall:

(a) contain one of the text warnings listed in Annex I and a corresponding colour photograph specified in the picture library in Annex II;

(b) include smoking cessation information such as telephone numbers, e-mail addresses or Internet sites intending to inform consumers about the programmes that are available to support persons who want to stop smoking;

(c) cover 65% of both the external front and back surface of the unit packet and any outside packaging. Cylindrical packets shall display two combined health warnings, equidistant from each other, each covering 65% of their respective half of the curved surface;

(d) show the same text warning and corresponding colour photograph on both sides of the unit packets and any outside packaging;

(e) appear at the top edge of a unit packet and any outside packaging, and be positioned in the same direction as any other information appearing on that surface of the packaging. Transitional exemptions from that obligation on the position of the combined health warning may apply in Member States where tax stamps or national identification marks used for fiscal purposes remain mandatory, as follows:

(i) in those cases, where the tax stamp or national identification mark used for fiscal purposes is affixed at the top edge of a unit packet made of carton material, the combined health warning that is to appear on the back surface may be positioned directly below the tax stamp or national identification mark;

(ii) where a unit packet is made of soft material, Member States may allow for a rectangular area to be reserved for the tax stamp or national identification mark used for fiscal purposes of a height not exceeding 13 mm between the top edge of the packet and the top end of the combined health warnings.

The exemptions referred to in points (i) and (ii) shall apply for a period of three years from 20 May 2016. Brand names or logos shall not be positioned above the health warnings;

(f) be reproduced in accordance with the format, layout, design and proportions specified by the Commission pursuant to paragraph 4;

(g) in the case of unit packets of cigarettes, respect the following dimensions:

(i) height: not less than 44 mm;

(ii) width: not less than 52 mm.

2. The combined health warnings are grouped into three sets as set out in Annex II and each set shall be used in a given year and rotated on an annual basis. Member States shall ensure that each combined health warning available for use in a given year is displayed to the extent possible in equal numbers on each brand of tobacco products.

3. The Commission shall be empowered to adopt delegated acts in accordance with Article 27 to:

(a) adapt the text warnings listed in Annex I taking into account scientific and market developments;

(b) establish and adapt the picture library referred to in point (a) of paragraph 1 of this Article taking into account scientific and market developments.

4. The Commission shall by means of implementing acts define the technical specifications for the layout, design and shape of the combined health warnings, taking into account the different packet shapes.

Those implementing acts shall be adopted in accordance with the examination procedure referred to in Article 25(2).

[8.694]
Article 11
Labelling of tobacco products for smoking other than cigarettes, roll-your-own tobacco and waterpipe tobacco

1. Member States may exempt tobacco products for smoking other than cigarettes, roll-your-own tobacco and waterpipe tobacco from the obligations to carry the information message laid down in Article 9(2) and the combined health warnings laid down in Article 10. In that event, and in addition to the general warning provided for in Article 9(1), each unit packet and any outside packaging of such products shall carry one of the text warnings listed in Annex I. The general warning specified in Article 9(1) shall include a reference to the cessation services referred to in Article 10(1)(b).

The general warning shall appear on the most visible surface of the unit packet and any outside packaging.

Member States shall ensure that each text warning is displayed to the extent possible in equal numbers on each brand of these products. The text warnings shall appear on the next most visible surface of the unit packet and any outside packaging.

For unit packets with a hinged lid, the next most visible surface is the one that becomes visible when the packet is open.

2. The general warning referred to in paragraph 1 shall cover 30% of the relevant surface of the unit packet and any outside packaging. That proportion shall be increased to 32% for Member States with two official languages and to 35% for Member States with more than two official languages.

3. The text warning referred to in paragraph 1 shall cover 40% of the relevant surface of the unit packet and any outside packaging. That proportion shall be increased to 45% for Member States with two official languages and 50% for Member States with more than two official languages.

4. Where the health warnings referred to in paragraph 1 are to appear on a surface exceeding 150 cm^2, the warnings shall cover an area of 45 cm^2. That area shall be increased to 48 cm^2 for Member States with two official languages and 52.5 cm^2 for Member States with more than two official languages.

5. The health warnings referred to in paragraph 1 shall comply with the requirements specified in Article 9(4). The text of the health warnings shall be parallel to the main text on the surface reserved for these warnings.

The health warnings shall be surrounded by a black border of a width of not less than 3 mm and not more than 4 mm. This border shall appear outside the surface reserved for the health warnings.

6. The Commission shall adopt delegated acts in accordance with Article 27, to withdraw the possibility of granting exemptions for any of the particular product categories referred to in paragraph 1 if there is a substantial change of circumstances as established in a Commission report for the product category concerned.

[8.695]
Article 12
Labelling of smokeless tobacco products

1. Each unit packet and any outside packaging of smokeless tobacco products shall carry the following health warning:

'This tobacco product damages your health and is addictive.'

2. The health warning laid down in paragraph 1 shall comply with the requirements specified in Article 9(4). The text of the health warnings shall be parallel to the main text on the surface reserved for these warnings.

In addition, it shall:

(a) appear on the two largest surfaces of the unit packet and any outside packaging;
(b) cover 30% of the surfaces of the unit packet and any outside packaging. That proportion shall be increased to 32% for Member States with two official languages and 35% for Member States with more than two official languages.

3. The Commission shall be empowered to adopt delegated acts in accordance with Article 27 to adapt the wording of the health warning laid down in paragraph 1 to scientific developments.

[8.696]
Article 13
Product presentation

1. The labelling of unit packets and any outside packaging and the tobacco product itself shall not include any element or feature that:

(a) promotes a tobacco product or encourages its consumption by creating an erroneous impression about its characteristics, health effects, risks or emissions; labels shall not include any information about the nicotine, tar or carbon monoxide content of the tobacco product;

(b) suggests that a particular tobacco product is less harmful than others or aims to reduce the effect of some harmful components of smoke or has vitalising, energetic, healing, rejuvenating, natural, organic properties or has other health or lifestyle benefits;
(c) refers to taste, smell, any flavourings or other additives or the absence thereof;
(d) resembles a food or a cosmetic product;
(e) suggests that a certain tobacco product has improved biodegradability or other environmental advantages.

2. The unit packets and any outside packaging shall not suggest economic advantages by including printed vouchers, offering discounts, free distribution, two-for-one or other similar offers.
3. The elements and features that are prohibited pursuant to paragraphs 1 and 2 may include but are not limited to texts, symbols, names, trademarks, figurative or other signs.

[8.697]
Article 14
Appearance and content of unit packets

1. Unit packets of cigarettes shall have a cuboid shape. Unit packets of roll-your-own tobacco shall have a cuboid or cylindrical shape, or the form of a pouch. A unit packet of cigarettes shall include at least 20 cigarettes. A unit packet of roll-your-own tobacco shall contain tobacco weighing not less than 30 g.
2. A unit packet of cigarettes may consist of carton or soft material and shall not have an opening that can be re-closed or re-sealed after it is first opened, other than the flip-top lid and shoulder box with a hinged lid. For packets with a flip-top lid and hinged lid, the lid shall be hinged only at the back of the unit packet.

[8.698]
Article 15
Traceability

1. Member States shall ensure that all unit packets of tobacco products are marked with a unique identifier. In order to ensure the integrity of the unique identifier, it shall be irremovably printed or affixed, indelible and not hidden or interrupted in any form, including through tax stamps or price marks, or by the opening of the unit packet. In the case of tobacco products that are manufactured outside of the Union, the obligations laid down in this Article apply only to those that are destined for, or placed on, the Union market.
2. The unique identifier shall allow the following to be determined:
(a) the date and place of manufacturing;
(b) the manufacturing facility;
(c) the machine used to manufacture the tobacco products;
(d) the production shift or time of manufacture;
(e) the product description;
(f) the intended market of retail sale;
(g) the intended shipment route;
(h) where applicable, the importer into the Union;
(i) the actual shipment route from manufacturing to the first retail outlet, including all warehouses used as well as the shipment date, shipment destination, point of departure and consignee;
(j) the identity of all purchasers from manufacturing to the first retail outlet; and
(k) the invoice, order number and payment records of all purchasers from manufacturing to the first retail outlet.

3. The information referred to in points (a), (b), (c), (d), (e), (f), (g) and, where applicable, (h) of paragraph 2 shall form part of the unique identifier.
4. Member States shall ensure that the information mentioned in points (i), (j) and (k) of paragraph 2 is electronically accessible by means of a link to the unique identifier.
5. Member States shall ensure that all economic operators involved in the trade of tobacco products, from the manufacturer to the last economic operator before the first retail outlet, record the entry of all unit packets into their possession, as well as all intermediate movements and the final exit of the unit packets from their possession. This obligation may be complied with by the marking and recording of aggregated packaging such as cartons, mastercases or pallets, provided that the tracking and tracing of all unit packets remains possible.
6. Member States shall ensure that all natural and legal persons engaged in the supply chain of tobacco products maintain complete and accurate records of all relevant transactions.
7. Member States shall ensure that the manufacturers of tobacco products provide all economic operators involved in the trade of tobacco products, from the manufacturer to the last economic operator before the first retail outlet, including importers, warehouses and transporting companies, with the equipment that is necessary for the recording of the tobacco products purchased, sold, stored, transported or otherwise handled. That equipment shall be able to read and transmit the recorded data electronically to a data storage facility pursuant to paragraph 8.

8. Member States shall ensure that manufacturers and importers of tobacco products conclude data storage contracts with an independent third party, for the purpose of hosting the data storage facility for all relevant data. The data storage facility shall be physically located on the territory of the Union. The suitability of the third party, in particular its independence and technical capacities, as well as the data storage contract, shall be approved by the Commission.

The third party's activities shall be monitored by an external auditor, who is proposed and paid by the tobacco manufacturer and approved by the Commission. The external auditor shall submit an annual report to the competent authorities and to the Commission, assessing in particular any irregularities in relation to access.

Member States shall ensure that the Commission, the competent authorities of the Member States, and the external auditor have full access to the data storage facilities. In duly justified cases the Commission or the Member States may grant manufacturers or importers access to the stored data, provided that commercially sensitive information remains adequately protected in conformity with the relevant Union and national law.

9. Recorded data shall not be modified or deleted by an economic operator involved in the trade of tobacco products.

10. Member States shall ensure that personal data are only processed in accordance with the rules and safeguards laid down in Directive 95/46/EC.

11. The Commission shall, by means of implementing acts:

(a) determine the technical standards for the establishment and the operation of the tracking and tracing system as provided for in this Article, including the marking with a unique identifier, the recording, transmitting, processing and storing of data and access to stored data;

(b) determine the technical standards for ensuring that the systems used for the unique identifier and the related functions are fully compatible with each other across the Union.

Those implementing acts shall be adopted in accordance with the examination procedure referred to in Article 25(2).

12. The Commission shall be empowered to adopt delegated acts in accordance with Article 27 to define the key elements of the data storage contracts referred to in paragraph 8 of this Article, such as duration, renewability, expertise required or confidentiality, including the regular monitoring and evaluation of those contracts.

13. Paragraphs 1 to 10 shall apply to cigarettes and roll-your-own tobacco from 20 May 2019 and to tobacco products other than cigarettes and roll-your-own tobacco from 20 May 2024.

[8.699]
Article 16
Security feature

1. In addition to the unique identifier referred to in Article 15, Member States shall require that all unit packets of tobacco products, which are placed on the market, carry a tamper proof security feature, composed of visible and invisible elements. The security feature shall be irremovably printed or affixed, indelible and not hidden or interrupted in any form, including through tax stamps and price marks, or other elements imposed by legislation.

Member States requiring tax stamps or national identification marks used for fiscal purposes may allow that they are used for the security feature provided that the tax stamps or national identification marks fulfil all of the technical standards and functions required under this Article.

2. The Commission shall, by means of implementing acts, define the technical standards for the security feature and their possible rotation and adapt them to scientific, market and technical developments.

Those implementing acts shall be adopted in accordance with the examination procedure referred to in Article 25(2).

3. Paragraph 1 shall apply to cigarettes and roll-your-own tobacco from 20 May 2019 and to tobacco products other than cigarettes and roll-your-own tobacco from 20 May 2024.

CHAPTER III
TOBACCO FOR ORAL USE, CROSS-BORDER DISTANCE SALES OF TOBACCO PRODUCTS AND NOVEL TOBACCO PRODUCTS

[8.700]
Article 17
Tobacco for oral use

Member States shall prohibit the placing on the market of tobacco for oral use, without prejudice to Article 151 of the Act of Accession of Austria, Finland and Sweden.

[8.701]
Article 18
Cross-border distance sales of tobacco products

1. Member States may prohibit cross-border distance sales of tobacco products to consumers. Member States shall cooperate to prevent such sales. Retail outlets engaging in cross-border distance sales of tobacco products may not supply such products to consumers in Member States

where such sales have been prohibited. Member States which do not prohibit such sales shall require retail outlets intending to engage in cross-border distance sales to consumers located in the Union to register with the competent authorities in the Member State, where the retail outlet is established, and in the Member State, where the actual or potential consumers are located. Retail outlets established outside the Union shall be required to register with the competent authorities in the Member State where the actual or potential consumers are located. All retail outlets intending to engage in cross-border distance sales shall submit at least the following information to the competent authorities when registering:

(a) name or corporate name and permanent address of the place of activity from where the tobacco products will be supplied;

(b) the starting date of the activity of offering tobacco products for cross-border distance sales to consumers by means of Information Society services, as defined in point 2 of Article 1 of Directive 98/34/EC;

(c) the address of the website or websites used for that purpose and all relevant information necessary to identify the website.

2. The competent authorities of the Member States shall ensure that consumers have access to the list of all retail outlets registered with them. When making that list available, Member States shall ensure that the rules and safeguards laid down in Directive 95/46/EC are complied with. Retail outlets may only start placing tobacco products on the market via cross-border distance sales when they have received confirmation of their registration with the relevant competent authority.

3. The Member States of destination of tobacco products sold via cross-border distance sales may require that the supplying retail outlet nominates a natural person to be responsible for verifying — before the tobacco products reach the consumer — that they comply with the national provisions adopted pursuant to this Directive in the Member State of destination, if such verification is necessary in order to ensure compliance and facilitate enforcement.

4. Retail outlets engaged in cross-border distance sales shall operate an age verification system, which verifies, at the time of sale, that the purchasing consumer complies with minimum age requirements provided for under the national law of the Member State of destination. The retail outlet or natural person nominated pursuant to paragraph 3 shall provide to the competent authorities of that Member State a description of the details and functioning of the age verification system.

5. Retail outlets shall only process personal data of the consumer in accordance with Directive 95/46/EC and those data shall not be disclosed to the manufacturer of tobacco products or companies forming part of the same group of companies or to other third parties. Personal data shall not be used or transferred for purposes other than the actual purchase. This also applies if the retail outlet forms part of a manufacturer of tobacco products.

[8.702]
Article 19
Notification of novel tobacco products

1. Member Stes shall require manufacturers and importers of novel tobacco products to submit a notification to the competent authorities of Member States of any such product they intend to place on the national market concerned. The notification shall be submitted in electronic form six months before the intended placing on the market. It shall be accompanied by a detailed description of the novel tobacco product concerned as well as instructions for its use and information on ingredients and emissions in accordance with Article 5. The manufacturers and importers submitting a notification of a novel tobacco product shall also provide the competent authorities with:

(a) available scientific studies on toxicity, addictiveness and attractiveness of the novel tobacco product, in particular as regards its ingredients and emissions;

(b) available studies, executive summaries thereof and market research on the preferences of various consumer groups, including young people and current smokers;

(c) other available and relevant information, including a risk/benefit analysis of the product, its expected effects on cessation of tobacco consumption, its expected effects on initiation of tobacco consumption and predicted consumer perception.

2. Member States shall require manufacturers and importers of novel tobacco products to transmit to their competent authorities any new or updated information on the studies, research and other information referred to in points (a) to (c) of paragraph 1. Member States may require manufacturers or importers of novel tobacco products to carry out additional tests or submit additional information. Member States shall make all information received pursuant to this Article available to the Commission.

3. Member States may introduce a system for the authorisation of novel tobacco products. Member States may charge manufacturers and importers proportionate fees for that authorisation.

4. Novel tobacco products placed on the market shall respect the requirements of this Directive. Which of the provisions of this Directive apply to novel tobacco products depends on whether those products fall under the definition of a smokeless tobacco product or of a tobacco product for smoking.

TITLE III
ELECTRONIC CIGARETTES AND HERBAL PRODUCTS FOR SMOKING

[8.703]
Article 20
Electronic cigarettes

1. The Member States shall ensure that electronic cigarettes and refill containers are only placed on the market if they comply with this Directive and with all other relevant Union legislation.

This Directive does not apply to electronic cigarettes and refill containers that are subject to an authorisation requirement under Directive 2001/83/EC or to the requirements set out in Directive 93/42/EEC.

2. Manufacturers and importers of electronic cigarettes and refill containers shall submit a notification to the competent authorities of the Member States of any such products which they intend to place on the market. The notification shall be submitted in electronic form six months before the intended placing on the market. For electronic cigarettes and refill containers already placed on the market on 20 May 2016, the notification shall be submitted within six months of that date. A new notification shall be submitted for each substantial modification of the product.

The notification shall, depending on whether the product is an electronic cigarette or a refill container, contain the following information:

(a) the name and contact details of the manufacturer, a responsible legal or natural person within the Union, and, if applicable, the importer into the Union;
(b) a list of all ingredients contained in, and emissions resulting from the use of, the product, by brand name and type, including quantities thereof;
(c) toxicological data regarding the product's ingredients and emissions, including when heated, referring in particular to their effects on the health of consumers when inhaled and taking into account, inter alia, any addictive effect;
(d) information on the nicotine doses and uptake when consumed under normal or reasonably foreseeable conditions;
(e) a description of the components of the product; including, where applicable, the opening and refill mechanism of the electronic cigarette or refill containers;
(f) a description of the production process, including whether it involves series production, and a declaration that the production process ensures conformity with the requirements of this Article;
(g) a declaration that the manufacturer and importer bear full responsibility for the quality and safety of the product, when placed on the market and used under normal or reasonably foreseeable conditions.

Where Member States consider that the information submitted is incomplete, they shall be entitled to request the completion of the information concerned.

Member States may charge manufacturers and importers proportionate fees for receiving, storing, handling and analysing the information submitted to them.

3. Member States shall ensure that:

(a) nicotine-containing liquid is only placed on the market in dedicated refill containers not exceeding a volume of 10 ml, in disposable electronic cigarettes or in single use cartridges and that the cartridges or tanks do not exceed a volume of 2 ml;
(b) the nicotine-containing liquid does not contain nicotine in excess of 20 mg/ml;
(c) the nicotine-containing liquid does not contain additives listed in Article 7(6);
(d) only ingredients of high purity are used in the manufacture of the nicotine-containing liquid. Substances other than the ingredients referred to in point (b) of the second subparagraph of paragraph 2 of this Article are only present in the nicotine-containing liquid in trace levels, if such traces are technically unavoidable during manufacture;
(e) except for nicotine, only ingredients are used in the nicotine-containing liquid that do not pose a risk to human health in heated or unheated form;
(f) electronic cigarettes deliver the nicotine doses at consistent levels under normal conditions of use;
(g) electronic cigarettes and refill containers are child- and tamper-proof, are protected against breakage and leakage and have a mechanism that ensures refilling without leakage.

4. Member States shall ensure that:

(a) unit packets of electronic cigarettes and refill containers include a leaflet with information on:
 (i) instructions for use and storage of the product, including a reference that the product is not recommended for use by young people and non-smokers;
 (ii) contra-indications;
 (iii) warnings for specific risk groups;
 (iv) possible adverse effects;
 (v) addictiveness and toxicity; and
 (vi) contact details of the manufacturer or importer and a legal or natural contact person within the Union;
(b) unit packets and any outside packaging of electronic cigarettes and refill containers:

(i) include a list of all ingredients contained in the product in descending order of the weight, and an indication of the nicotine content of the product and the delivery per dose, the batch number and a recommendation to keep the product out of reach of children;

(ii) without prejudice to point (i) of this point, do not include elements or features referred to in Article 13, with the exception of Article 13(1)(a) and (c) concerning information on the nicotine content and on flavourings; and

(iii) carry one of the following health warnings:

'This product contains nicotine which is a highly addictive substance. It is not recommended for use by non-smokers'.

or

'This product contains nicotine which is a highly addictive substance.'

Member States shall determine which of these health warnings is to be used;

(c) health warnings comply with the requirements specified in Article 12(2).

5. Member States shall ensure that:

(a) commercial communications in Information Society services, in the press and other printed publications, with the aim or direct or indirect effect of promoting electronic cigarettes and refill containers are prohibited, except for publications that are intended exclusively for professionals in the trade of electronic cigarettes or refill containers and for publications which are printed and published in third countries, where those publications are not principally intended for the Union market;

(b) commercial communications on the radio, with the aim or direct or indirect effect of promoting electronic cigarettes and refill containers, are prohibited;

(c) any form of public or private contribution to radio programmes with the aim or direct or indirect effect of promoting electronic cigarettes and refill containers is prohibited;

(d) any form of public or private contribution to any event, activity or individual person with the aim or direct or indirect effect of promoting electronic cigarettes and refill containers and involving or taking place in several Member States or otherwise having cross-border effects is prohibited;

(e) audiovisual commercial communications to which Directive 2010/13/EU of the European Parliament and of the Council[1] applies, are prohibited for electronic cigarettes and refill containers.

6. Article 18 of this Directive shall apply to cross-border distance sales of electronic cigarettes and refill containers.

7. Member States shall require manufacturers and importers of electronic cigarettes and refill containers to submit, annually, to the competent authorities:

(i) comprehensive data on sales volumes, by brand name and type of the product;

(ii) information on the preferences of various consumer groups, including young people, non-smokers and the main types of current users;

(iii) the mode of sale of the products; and

(iv) executive summaries of any market surveys carried out in respect of the above, including an English translation thereof.

Member States shall monitor the market developments concerning electronic cigarettes and refill containers, including any evidence that their use is a gateway to nicotine addiction and ultimately traditional tobacco consumption among young people and non-smokers.

8. Member States shall ensure that the information received pursuant to paragraph 2 is made publicly available on a website. The Member States shall take the need to protect trade secrets duly into account when making that information publicly available.

Member States shall, upon request, make all information received pursuant to this Article available to the Commission and other Member States. The Member States and the Commission shall ensure that trade secrets and other confidential information are treated in a confidential manner.

9. Member States shall require manufacturers, importers and distributers of electronic cigarettes and refill containers to establish and maintain a system for collecting information about all of the suspected adverse effects on human health of these products.

Should any of these economic operators consider or have reason to believe that electronic cigarettes or refill containers, which are in their possession and are intended to be placed on the market or are placed on the market, are not safe or are not of good quality or are otherwise not in conformity with this Directive, that economic operator shall immediately take the corrective action necessary to bring the product concerned into conformity with this Directive, to withdraw or to recall it, as appropriate. In such cases the economic operator shall also be required to immediately inform the market surveillance authorities of the Member States in which the product is made available or is intended to be made available, giving details, in particular, of the risk to human health and safety and of any corrective action taken, and of the results of such corrective action.

Member States may also request additional information from the economic operators, for example on the safety and quality aspects or any adverse effects of electronic cigarettes or refill containers.

10. The Commission shall submit a report to the European Parliament and the Council on the potential risks to public health associated with the use of refillable electronic cigarettes by 20 May 2016 and whenever appropriate thereafter.

11. In the case of electronic cigarettes and refill containers that comply with the requirements of this Article, where a competent authority ascertains or has reasonable grounds to believe that specific electronic cigarettes or refill containers, or a type of electronic cigarette or refill container, could present a serious risk to human health, it may take appropriate provisional measures. It shall immediately inform the Commission and the competent authorities of other Member States of the measures taken and shall communicate any supporting data. The Commission shall determine, as soon as possible after having received that information, whether the provisional measure is justified. The Commission shall inform the Member State concerned of its conclusions to enable the Member State to take appropriate follow-up measures.
Where, in application of the first subparagraph of this paragraph, the placing on the market of specific electronic cigarettes or refill containers, or a type of electronic cigarette or refill container has been prohibited on duly justified grounds in at least three Member States, the Commission shall be empowered to adopt delegated acts in accordance with Article 27 to extend such a prohibition to all Member States, if such an extension is justified and proportionate.
12. The Commission shall be empowered to adopt delegated acts in accordance with Article 27 to adapt the wording of the health warning in paragraph 4(b) of this Article. When adapting that health warning, the Commission shall ensure that it is factual.
13. The Commission shall, by means of an implementing act, lay down a common format for the notification provided for in paragraph 2 and technical standards for the refill mechanism provided for in paragraph 3(g).
These implementing acts shall be adopted in accordance with the examination procedure referred to in Article 25(2).

NOTES

1 Directive 2010/13/EU of the European Parliament and of the Council of 10 March 2010 on the coordination of certain provisions laid down by law, regulation or administrative action in Member States concerning the provision of audiovisual media services (Audiovisual Media Services Directive) (OJ L95, 15.4.2010, p 1).

[8.704]
Article 21
Herbal products for smoking

1. Each unit packet and any outside packaging of herbal products for smoking shall carry the following health warning:

'Smoking this product damages your health.'

2. The health warning shall be printed on the front and back external surface of the unit packet and on any outside packaging.
3. The health warning shall comply with the requirements set out in Article 9(4). It shall cover 30% of the area of the corresponding surface of the unit packet and of any outside packaging. That proportion shall be increased to 32% for Member States with two official languages and to 35% for Member States with more than two official languages.
4. Unit packets and any outside packaging of herbal products for smoking shall not include any of the elements or features set out in Article 13(1)(a), (b) and (d) and shall not state that the product is free of additives or flavourings.

[8.705]
Article 22
Reporting of ingredients of herbal products for smoking

1. Member States shall require manufacturers and importers of herbal products for smoking to submit to their competent authorities a list of all ingredients, and quantities thereof that are used in the manufacture of such products by brand name and type. Manufacturers or importers shall also inform the competent authorities of the Member States concerned when the composition of a product is modified in a way that affects the information submitted pursuant to this Article. The information required under this Article shall be submitted prior to the placing on the market of a new or modified herbal product for smoking.
2. Member States shall ensure that the information submitted in accordance with paragraph 1 is made publicly available on a website. The Member States shall take the need to protect trade secrets duly into account when making that information publicly available. Economic operators shall specify exactly which information they consider to constitute a trade secret.

TITLE IV
FINAL PROVISIONS

[8.706]
Article 23
Cooperation and enforcement

1. Member States shall ensure that manufacturers and importers of tobacco and related products provide the Commission and the competent authorities of the Member States with complete and correct information requested pursuant to this Directive and within the time limits set out herein. The obligation to provide the requested information shall lie primarily with the manufacturer, if the

manufacturer is established in the Union. The obligation to provide the requested information shall lie primarily with the importer, if the manufacturer is established outside the Union and the importer is established inside the Union. The obligation to provide the requested information shall lie jointly with the manufacturer and the importer if both are established outside the Union.

2. Member States shall ensure that tobacco and related products which do not comply with this Directive, including the implementing and delegated acts provided for therein, are not placed on the market. Member States shall ensure that tobacco and related products are not placed on the market if the reporting obligations set out in this Directive are not complied with.

3. Member States shall lay down rules on penalties applicable to infringements of the national provisions adopted pursuant to this Directive and shall take all measures that are necessary to ensure that these penalties are enforced. The penalties provided for shall be effective, proportionate and dissuasive. Any financial administrative penalty that may be imposed as a result of an intentional infringement may be such as to offset the economic advantage sought through the infringement.

4. The competent authorities of the Member States shall cooperate with each other and with the Commission to ensure the correct application and due enforcement of this Directive and shall transmit to each other all information necessary with a view to applying this Directive in a uniform manner.

[8.707]
Article 24
Free movement

1. Member States may not, for considerations relating to aspects regulated by this Directive, and subject to paragraphs 2 and 3 of this Article, prohibit or restrict the placing on the market of tobacco or related products which comply with this Directive.

2. This Directive shall not affect the right of a Member State to maintain or introduce further requirements, applicable to all products placed on its market, in relation to the standardisation of the packaging of tobacco products, where it is justified on grounds of public health, taking into account the high level of protection of human health achieved through this Directive. Such measures shall be proportionate and may not constitute a means of arbitrary discrimination or a disguised restriction on trade between Member States. Those measures shall be notified to the Commission together with the grounds for maintaining or introducing them.

3. A Member State may also prohibit a certain category of tobacco or related products, on grounds relating to the specific situation in that Member State and provided the provisions are justified by the need to protect public health, taking into account the high level of protection of human health achieved through this Directive. Such national provisions shall be notified to the Commission together with the grounds for introducing them. The Commission shall, within six months of the date of receiving the notification provided for in this paragraph, approve or reject the national provisions after having verified, taking into account the high level of protection of human health achieved through this Directive, whether or not they are justified, necessary and proportionate to their aim and whether or not they are a means of arbitrary discrimination or a disguised restriction on trade between the Member States. In the absence of a decision by the Commission within the period of six months, the national provisions shall be deemed to be approved.

[8.708]
Article 25
Committee procedure

1. The Commission shall be assisted by a committee. That committee shall be a committee within the meaning of Regulation (EU) No 182/2011.

2. Where reference is made to this paragraph, Article 5 of Regulation (EU) No 182/2011 shall apply.

3. Where the opinion of the committee is to be obtained by written procedure, that procedure shall be terminated without result when, within the time-limit for delivery of the opinion, the chair of the committee so decides or a simple majority of committee members so requests.

4. Where the Committee delivers no opinion, the Commission shall not adopt the draft implementing act and the third subparagraph of Article 5(4) of Regulation (EU) No 182/2011 shall apply.

[8.709]
Article 26
Competent authorities

Member States shall designate the competent authorities that shall be responsible for the implementation and enforcement of the obligations provided for in this Directive within three months of 20 May 2016. Member States shall inform the Commission about the identity of the designated authorities without delay. The Commission shall publish that information in the *Official Journal of the European Union*.

[8.710]
Article 27
Exercise of the delegation

1. The power to adopt delegated acts is conferred on the Commission subject to the conditions laid down in this Article.
2. The power to adopt delegated acts referred to in Articles 3(2) and (4), 4(3) and (5), 7(5), (11) and (12), 9(5), 10(3), 11(6), 12(3), 15(12), 20(11) and (12) shall be conferred on the Commission for a period of five years from 19 May 2014. The Commission shall draw up a report in respect of the delegation of power not later than nine months before the end of the five-year period. The delegation of power shall be tacitly extended for periods of an identical duration, unless the European Parliament or the Council opposes such extension not later than three months before the end of each period.
3. The delegation of powers referred to in Articles 3(2) and(4), 4(3) and (5), 7(5), (11) and (12), 9(5), 10(3), 11(6), 12(3), 15(12), 20(11) and (12) may be revoked at any time by the European Parliament or by the Council. A decision to revoke shall put an end to the delegation of the power specified in that decision. It shall take effect the day following the publication of the decision in the *Official Journal of the European Union* or at a later date specified therein. It shall not affect the validity of any delegated acts already in force.
4. As soon as it adopts a delegated act, the Commission shall notify it simultaneously to the European Parliament and to the Council.
5. A delegated act adopted pursuant to Articles 3(2) and (4), 4(3) and (5), 7(5), (11) and (12), 9(5), 10(3), 11(6), 12(3), 15(12), 20(11) and (12) shall enter into force only if no objection has been expressed either by the European Parliament or the Council within a period of two months of notification of that act to the European Parliament and the Council or if, before the expiry of that period, the European Parliament and the Council have both informed the Commission that they will not object. That period shall be extended by two months at the initiative of the European Parliament or of the Council.

[8.711]
Article 28
Report

1. No later than five years from 20 May 2016, and whenever necessary thereafter, the Commission shall submit to the European Parliament, the Council, the European Economic and Social Committee and the Committee of the Regions a report on the application of this Directive. When drafting the report, the Commission shall be assisted by scientific and technical experts in order to have all the necessary information at its disposal.
2. In the report, the Commission shall indicate, in particular, the elements of the Directive which should be reviewed or adapted in the light of scientific and technical developments, including the development of internationally agreed rules and standards on tobacco and related products. The Commission shall pay special attention to:

(a) the experience gained with respect to the design of package surfaces not governed by this Directive taking into account national, international, legal, economic and scientific developments;
(b) market developments concerning novel tobacco products considering, inter alia, notifications received under Article 19;
(c) market developments which constitute a substantial change of circumstances;
(d) the feasibility, benefits and possible impact of a European system for the regulation of the ingredients used in tobacco products, including the establishment, at Union level, of a list of ingredients that may be used or present in, or added to tobacco products, taking into account, inter alia, the information collected in accordance with Articles 5 and 6;
(e) market developments concerning cigarettes with a diameter of less than 7.5 mm, and consumer perception of their harmfulness as well as the misleading character of such cigarettes;
(f) the feasibility, benefits and possible impact of a Union database containing information on ingredients and emissions from tobacco products collected in accordance with Articles 5 and 6;
(g) market developments concerning electronic cigarettes and refill containers considering, amongst others, information collected in accordance with Article 20, including on the initiation of consumption such products by young people and non-smokers and the impact of such products on cessation efforts as well as measures taken by Member States regarding flavours;
(h) market developments and consumer preferences as regards waterpipe tobacco, with a particular focus on its flavours.

The Member States shall assist the Commission and provide all available information for carrying out the assessment and preparing the report.

3. The report shall be followed-up by proposals for amending this Directive, which the Commission deem necessary to adapt it — to the extent necessary for the smooth functioning of the internal market — to developments in the field of tobacco and related products, and to take into account new developments based on scientific facts and developments concerning internationally agreed standards for tobacco and related products.

[8.712]
Article 29
Transposition
1. Member States shall bring into force the laws, regulations and administrative provisions necessary to comply with this Directive by 20 May 2016. They shall forthwith communicate to the Commission the text of those provisions.
The Member States shall apply those measures from 20 May 2016, without prejudice to Articles 7(14), 10(1)(e), 15(13) and 16(3).
2. When Member States adopt these provisions, they shall contain a reference to this Directive or be accompanied by such reference on the occasion of their official publication. They shall also include a statement that references in existing laws, regulations and administrative provisions to the Directive repealed by this Directive shall be construed as references to this Directive. The Member States shall determine how such reference is to be made and how that statement is to be formulated.
3. Member States shall communicate to the Commission the text of the main provisions of national law which they adopt in the field covered by this Directive.

[8.713]
Article 30
Transitional provision
Member States may allow the following products, which are not in compliance with this Directive, to be placed on the market until 20 May 2017:
- (a) tobacco products manufactured or released for free circulation and labelled in accordance with Directive 2001/37/EC before 20 May 2016;
- (b) electronic cigarettes or refill containers manufactured or released for free circulation before 20 November 2016;
- (c) herbal products for smoking manufactured or released for free circulation before 20 May 2016.

[8.714]
Article 31
Repeal
Directive 2001/37/EC is repealed with effect from 20 May 2016, without prejudice to the obligations of the Member States relating to the time-limits for the transposition into national law of that Directive.
References to the repealed Directive shall be construed as references to this Directive and read in accordance with the correlation table in Annex III to this Directive.

[8.715]
Article 32
Entry into force
This Directive shall enter into force on the twentieth day following that of its publication in the *Official Journal of the European Union*.

[8.716]
Article 33
Addressees
This Directive is addressed to the Member States.

ANNEX I
LIST OF TEXT WARNINGS

(referred to in Article 10 and Article 11(1))

[8.717]
(1) Smoking causes 9 out of 10 lung cancers

(2) Smoking causes mouth and throat cancer

(3) Smoking damages your lungs

(4) Smoking causes heart attacks

(5) Smoking causes strokes and disability

(6) Smoking clogs your arteries

(7) Smoking increases the risk of blindness

(8) Smoking damages your teeth and gums

(9) Smoking can kill your unborn child

(10) Your smoke harms your children, family and friends

(11) Smokers' children are more likely to start smoking

(12) Quit smoking – stay alive for those close to you

(13) Smoking reduces fertility

(14) Smoking increases the risk of impotence

ANNEX II

(*Annex II (as substituted by Commission Delegated Directive 2014/109/EU, Art 1, Annex) is not reproduced in this Handbook. It contains a picture library of combined health warnings; see further Art 10 at* **[8.693]**.)

ANNEX III
CORRELATION TABLE

[8.718]

Directive 2001/37/EC	**This Directive**
Article 1	Article 1
Article 2	Article 2
Article 3(1)	Article 3(1)
Article 3(2) and (3)	—
Article 4(1)	Article 4(1)
Article 4(2)	Article 4(2)
Article 4(3) to (5)	—
Article 5(1)	—
Article 5(2) point (a)	Article 9(1)
Article 5(2) point (b)	Article 10(1) point (a) and 10(2), Article 11(1)
Article 5(3)	Article 10(1)
Article 5(4)	Article 12
Article 5(5) first subparagraph	Article 9(3) fifth subparagraph Article 11(2) and (3) Article 12(2) point (b)
Article 5(5) second subparagraph	Article 11(4)
Article 5(6) point (a)	Article 9(4) point (a)
Article 5(6) point (b)	—
Article 5(6) point (c)	Article 9(4) point(b)
Article 5(6) point (d)	Article 8(6) and Article 11(5) second subparagraph
Article 5(6) point (e)	Article 8(1)
Article 5(7)	Article 8(3) and (4)
Article 5(8)	—
Article 5(9) first subparagraph	Article 15(1) and (2)
Article 5(9) second subparagraph	Article 15(11)
Article 6 (1) first subparagraph	Article 5(1) first subparagraph
Article 6 (1) second subparagraph	Article 5(2) and (3)
Article 6 (1) third subparagraph	—
Article 6(2)	Article 5(4)
Article 6(3) and (4)	—
Article 7	Article 13(1) point (b)
Article 8	Article 17
Article 9(1)	Article 4(3)

Directive 2001/37/EC	This Directive
Article 9(2)	Article 10(2) and (3) point (a)
Article 9(3)	Article 16(2)
Article 10(1)	Article 25(1)
Article 10(2) and (3)	Article 25(2)
Article 11 first and second subparagraphs	Article 28(1) first and second subparagraphs
Article 11 third subparagraph	Article 28(2) first subparagraph
Article 11 fourth subparagraph	Article 28(3)
Article 12	—
Article 13(1)	Article 24(1)
Article 13(2)	Article 24(2)
Article 13(3)	
Article 14(1) first subparagraph	Article 29(1) first subparagraph
Article 14(1) second subparagraph	Article 29(2)
Article 14(2) and (3)	Article 30 point (a)
Article 14(4)	Article 29(3)
Article 15	Article 31
Article 16	Article 32
Article 17	Article 33
Annex I (List of additional health warnings)	Annex I (List of text warnings)
Annex II (Time-limits for transposition and implementation of repealed Directives)	—
Annex III (Correlation table)	Annex III (Correlation table)

REGULATION OF THE EUROPEAN PARLIAMENT AND OF THE COUNCIL

(251/2014/EU)

of 26 February 2014

on the definition, description, presentation, labelling and the protection of geographical indications of aromatised wine products and repealing Council Regulation (EEC) No 1601/91

NOTES

Date of publication in OJ: OJ L84, 20.3.2014, p 14.
This Regulation is reproduced as corrected by the corrigendum published in OJ L105, 8.4.2014, p 12.

THE EUROPEAN PARLIAMENT AND THE COUNCIL OF THE EUROPEAN UNION,

Having regard to the Treaty on the Functioning of the European Union, and in particular Article 43(2) and Article 114 thereof,

Having regard to the proposal from the European Commission,

After transmission of the draft legislative act to the national Parliaments,

Having regard to the opinion of the European Economic and Social Committee,[1]

Acting in accordance with the ordinary legislative procedure,[2]

Whereas:

(1) Council Regulation (EEC) No 1601/91[3] and Commission Regulation (EC) No 122/94[4] have proved successful in regulating aromatised wines, aromatised wine-based drinks and aromatised wine-product cocktails ('aromatised wine products'). However, in the light of technologic innovation, market developments and evolving consumer expectations it is necessary to update the rules applicable to the definition, description, presentation, labelling and protection of geographical indications of certain aromatised wine products, while taking into account traditional production methods.

(2) Further amendments are needed as a consequence of the entry into force of the Lisbon Treaty, in order to align the powers conferred upon the Commission pursuant to Regulation (EEC) No 1601/91 to Articles 290 and 291 of the Treaty on the Functioning of the European Union (TFEU). In view of the scope of those amendments, it is appropriate to repeal Regulation (EEC) No 1601/91 and to replace it with this Regulation. Regulation (EC) No 122/94 introduced rules on flavouring and addition of alcohol applicable to some aromatised wine products, and in order to ensure clarity, those

Part 8 Other EU Materials

rules should be incorporated into this Regulation.

(3) Regulation (EU) No 1169/2011 of the European Parliament and of the Council[5] applies to the presentation and labelling of aromatised wine products, save as otherwise provided for in this Regulation.

(4) Aromatised wine products are important for consumers, producers and the agricultural sector in the Union. The measures applicable to aromatised wine products should contribute to the attainment of a high level of consumer protection, the prevention of deceptive practices and the attainment of market transparency and fair competition. By doing so, the measures will safeguard the reputation that the Union's aromatised wine products have achieved in the internal market and on the world market by continuing to take into account the traditional practices used in the production of aromatised wine products as well as increased demand for consumer protection and information. Technological innovation should also be taken into account in respect of the products for which such innovation serves to improve quality, without affecting the traditional character of the aromatised wine products concerned.

(5) The production of aromatised wine products constitutes a major outlet for the agricultural sector of the Union, which should be emphasised by the regulatory framework.

(6) In the interest of consumers, this Regulation should apply to all aromatised wine products placed on the market in the Union, whether produced in the Member States or in third countries. In order to maintain and improve the reputation of the Union's aromatised wine products on the world market, the rules provided for in this Regulation should also apply to aromatised wine products produced in the Union for export.

(7) To ensure clarity and transparency in Union law governing aromatised wine products, it is necessary to clearly define the products covered by that law, the criteria for the production, description, presentation and labelling of aromatised wine products and in particular, the sales denomination. Specific rules on the voluntary indication of the provenance supplementing those laid down in Regulation (EU) No 1169/2011 should also be laid down. By laying down such rules, all stages in the production chain are regulated and consumers are protected and properly informed.

(8) The definitions of aromatised wine products should continue to respect traditional quality practices but should be updated and improved in the light of technological developments.

(9) Aromatised wine products should be produced in accordance with certain rules and restrictions, which guarantee that consumer expectations as regards quality and production methods are met. In order to meet the international standards in this field, the production methods should be established and the Commission should as a general rule take into account the standards recommended and published by the International Organisation of Vine and Wine (OIV).

(10) Regulation (EC) No 1333/2008 of the European Parliament and of the Council[6] and Regulation (EC) No 1334/2008 of the European Parliament and of the Council[7] should apply to aromatised wine products.

(11) Moreover, the ethyl alcohol used for the production of aromatised wine products should be exclusively of agricultural origin, so as to meet consumer expectations and conform to traditional quality practices. This will also ensure an outlet for basic agricultural products.

(12) Given the importance and complexity of the aromatised wine products sector, it is appropriate to lay down specific rules on the description and presentation of aromatised wine products supplementing the labelling provisions laid down in Regulation (EU) No 1169/2011. Those specific rules should also prevent the misuse of sales denominations of aromatised wine products in the case of products which do not meet the requirements set out in this Regulation.

(13) With a view to facilitating consumers' understanding, it should be possible to supplement the sales denominations laid down in this Regulation with the customary name of the product within the meaning of Regulation (EU) No 1169/2011.

(14) Council Regulation (EC) No 834/2007[8] applies, inter alia, to processed agricultural products for use as food, which includes aromatised wine products. Accordingly, aromatised wine products which meet the requirements laid down in that Regulation and the acts adopted pursuant to it may be placed on the market as organic aromatised wine products.

(15) In applying a quality policy and in order to allow a high level of quality of aromatised wine products with a geographical indication, Member States should be allowed to adopt stricter rules than those laid down in this Regulation on the production, description, presentation and labelling of aromatised wine products with a geographical indication that are produced in their own territory, in so far as such rules are compatible with Union law.

(16) Given that Regulation (EC) No 110/2008 of the European Parliament and of the Council,[9] Regulation (EU) No 1151/2012 of the European Parliament and of the Council,[10] and the provisions on geographical indications in Regulation (EU) No 1308/2013 of the European Parliament and of the Council[11] do not apply to aromatised wine products, specific rules on protection of geographical indications for aromatised wine products should be laid down. Geographical indications should be used to identify aromatised wine products as originating in the territory of a country, or a region or locality in that territory, where a given quality, reputation or other characteristic of the aromatised

wine product is essentially attributable to its geographical origin and such geographical indications should be registered by the Commission.

(17) A procedure for the registration, compliance, alteration and possible cancellation of third country and Union geographical indications should be laid down in this Regulation.

(18) Member State authorities should be responsible for ensuring compliance with this Regulation, and arrangements should be made for the Commission to be able to monitor and verify such compliance.

(19) In order to supplement or amend certain non-essential elements of this Regulation, the power to adopt acts in accordance with Article 290 of the TFEU should be delegated to the Commission in respect of the establishment of production processes for obtaining aromatised wine products; criteria for the demarcation of geographical areas and rules, restrictions and derogations related to production in such areas; the conditions under which a product specification may include additional requirements; the determination of the cases in which a single producer may apply for the protection of a geographical indication and the restrictions governing the type of applicant that may apply for such protection; the establishment of the conditions to be complied with in respect of an application for the protection of a geographical indication, scrutiny by the Commission, the objection procedure and procedures for amendment and cancellation of geographical indications; the establishment of the conditions applicable to trans-border applications; the setting of the date for the submission of an application or a request, the date from which the protection applies and the date on which an amendment to a protection applies; the establishment of the conditions relating to amendments to product specifications, including the conditions when an amendment is considered minor and the conditions relating to the applications for, and approval of, amendments, which do not involve any change to the single document; the restrictions regarding the protected name; the nature and type of information to be notified in the exchange of information between Member States and the Commission, the methods of notification, the rules related to the access rights to information or information systems made available and the modalities of publication of the information. It is of particular importance that the Commission carry out appropriate consultations during its preparatory work, including at expert level. The Commission, when preparing and drawing up delegated acts, should ensure a simultaneous, timely and appropriate transmission of relevant documents to the European Parliament and to the Council.

(20) In order to ensure uniform conditions for the implementation of this Regulation with regard to the methods of analysis for determining the composition of aromatised wine products; decisions on conferring protection on geographical indications and on rejecting applications for such protection; decisions on cancelling the protection of geographical indications and of existing geographical designations; decisions on approval of application for amendments in the case of minor amendments to the product specifications; the information to be provided in the product specification with regard to the definition of geographical indication; the means of making decisions on protection or rejection of geographical indications available to the public; relating to the submission of trans-border applications; checks and verifications to be carried out by Member States; the procedure, including admissibility, for the examination of applications for protection or for the approval of an amendment of a geographical indication, and the procedure, including admissibility, for requests for objection, cancellation or conversion and the submission of information relating to existing geographical designations; administrative and physical checks to be carried out by Member States; and rules on providing the information necessary for the application of the provision concerning the exchange of information between Member States and the Commission, the arrangements for the management of the information to be notified, the content, form, timing, frequency and deadlines of the notifications and arrangements for transmitting or making information and documents available to the Member States, the competent authorities in third countries, or the public; implementing power should be conferred on the Commission. Those implementing powers should be exercised in accordance with Regulation (EU) No 182/2011 of the European Parliament and of the Council.[12]

(21) The Commission should, by means of implementing acts and, given their special nature, acting without applying Regulation (EU) No 182/2011, publish the single document in the *Official Journal of the European Union*, decide whether to reject an application for protection of a geographical indication on grounds of inadmissibility and establish and maintain a register of geographical indications protected under this Regulation, including the listing of existing geographical designations in that register or their removal from the register.

(22) The transition from the rules provided for in Regulation (EEC) No 1601/91 to those laid down in this Regulation could give rise to difficulties which are not dealt with in this Regulation. For that purpose, the power to adopt the necessary transitional measures should be delegated to the Commission.

(23) Sufficient time and appropriate arrangements should be allowed to facilitate a smooth transition from the rules provided for in Regulation (EEC) No 1601/91 to the rules laid down in this Regulation. In any event the marketing of existing stocks should be allowed after the application of this Regulation, until those stocks are exhausted.

(24) Since the objectives of this Regulation, namely the establishment of the rules on the

definition, description, presentation and labelling of aromatised wine products and rules on the protection of geographical indications of aromatised wine products, cannot be sufficiently achieved by the Member States but can rather, by reason of its scale and effects, be better achieved at Union level, the Union may adopt measures, in accordance with the principle of subsidiarity as set out in Article 5 of the Treaty on European Union. In accordance with the principle of proportionality, as set out in that Article, this Regulation does not go beyond what is necessary in order to achieve those objectives,

NOTES

1 OJ C43, 15.2.2012, p 67.

2 Position of the European Parliament of 14 January 2014 (not yet published in the Official Journal) and decision of the Council of 17 February 2014.

3 Council Regulation (EEC) No 1601/91 of 10 June 1991 laying down general rules on the definition, description and presentation of aromatised wines, aromatised wine-based drinks and aromatised wine-product cocktails (OJ L149, 14.6.1991, p 1).

4 Commission Regulation (EC) No 122/94 of 25 January 1994 laying down certain detailed rules for the application of Council Regulation (EEC) No 1601/91 on the definition, description and presentation of aromatized wines, aromatized wine-based drinks, and aromatized wine-product cocktails (OJ L21, 26.1.1994, p 7).

5 Regulation (EU) No 1169/2011 of the European Parliament and of the Council of 25 October 2011 on the provision of food information to consumers, amending Regulations (EC) No 1924/2006 and (EC) No 1925/2006 of the European Parliament and of the Council, and repealing Commission Directive 87/250/EEC, Council Directive 90/496/EEC, Commission Directive 1999/10/EC, Directive 2000/13/EC of the European Parliament and of the Council, Commission Directives 2002/67/EC and 2008/5/EC and Commission Regulation (EC) No 608/2004 (OJ L304, 22.11.2011, p 18).

6 Regulation (EC) No 1333/2008 of the European Parliament and of the Council of 16 December 2008 on food additives (OJ L354, 31.12.2008, p 16).

7 Regulation (EC) No 1334/2008 of the European Parliament and of the Council of 16 December 2008 on flavourings and certain food ingredients with flavouring properties for use in and on foods and amending Council Regulation (EEC) No 1601/91, Regulations (EC) No 2232/96 and (EC) No 110/2008 and Directive 2000/13/EC (OJ L354, 31.12.2008, p 34).

8 Council Regulation (EC) No 834/2007 of 28 June 2007 on organic production and labelling of organic products and repealing Regulation (EEC) No 2092/91 (OJ L189, 20.7.2007, p 1).

9 Regulation (EC) No 110/2008 of the European Parliament and of the Council of 15 January 2008 on the definition, description, presentation, labelling and the protection of geographical indications of spirit drinks and repealing Council Regulation (EEC) No 1576/89 (OJ L39, 13.2.2008, p 16).

10 Regulation (EU) No 1151/2012 of the European Parliament and of the Council of 21 November 2012 on quality schemes for agricultural products and foodstuffs (OJ L343, 14.12.2012, p 1).

11 Regulation (EU) No 1308/2013 of the European Parliament and of the Council of 17 December 2013 establishing a common organisation of the markets in agricultural products and repealing Council Regulations (EEC) No 922/72, (EEC) No 234/79, (EC) No 1037/2001 and (EC) No 1234/2007 (OJ L347, 20.12.2013, p 671).

12 Regulation (EU) No 182/2011 of the European Parliament and of the Council of 16 February 2011 laying down the rules and general principles concerning mechanisms for control by Member States of the Commission's exercise of implementing powers (OJ L55, 28.2.2011, p 13).

HAVE ADOPTED THIS REGULATION:

CHAPTER I
SCOPE AND DEFINITIONS

[8.719]
Article 1
Subject matter and scope

1. This Regulation lays down rules on the definition, description, presentation and labelling of aromatised wine products as well as on the protection of geographical indications of aromatised wine products.
2. Regulation (EU) No 1169/2011 shall apply to the presentation and labelling of aromatised wine products, save as otherwise provided for in this Regulation.
3. This Regulation shall apply to all aromatised wine products placed on the market in the Union whether produced in the Member States or in third countries, as well as to those produced in the Union for export.

[8.720]
Article 2
Definitions

For the purpose of this Regulation, the following definitions apply:

(1) 'sales denomination' means the name of any of the aromatised wine products laid down in this Regulation;

(2) 'description' means the list of the specific characteristics of an aromatised wine product;

(3) 'geographical indication' means an indication which identifies an aromatised wine product as originating in a region, a specific place, or a country, where a given quality, reputation or other characteristics of that product is essentially attributable to its geographical origin.

CHAPTER II
DEFINITION, DESCRIPTION, PRESENTATION AND LABELLING OF AROMATISED WINE PRODUCTS

[8.721]
Article 3
Definition and classification of aromatised wine products

1. Aromatised wine products are products obtained from products of the wine sector as referred to in Regulation (EU) No 1308/2013 that have been flavoured. They are classified into the following categories:
   (a) aromatised wines;
   (b) aromatised wine-based drinks;
   (c) aromatised wine-product cocktails.
2. Aromatised wine is a drink:
   (a) obtained from one or more of the grapevine products defined in point 5 of Part IV of Annex II and in points 1 and 3 to 9 of Part II of Annex VII to Regulation (EU) No 1308/2013, with the exception of 'Retsina' wine;
   (b) in which the grapevine products referred to in point (a) represent at least 75% of the total volume;
   (c) to which alcohol may have been added;
   (d) to which colours may have been added;
   (e) to which grape must, partially fermented grape must or both may have been added;
   (f) which may have been sweetened;
   (g) which has an actual alcoholic strength by volume of not less than 14.5% vol and less than 22% vol and a total alcoholic strength by volume of not less than 17.5% vol.
3. Aromatised wine-based drink is a drink:
   (a) obtained from one or more of the grapevine products defined in points 1, 2 and 4 to 9 of Part II of Annex VII to Regulation (EU) No 1308/2013, with the exception of wines produced with the addition of alcohol and 'Retsina' wine;
   (b) in which the grapevine products referred to in point (a) represent at least 50% of the total volume;
   (c) to which no alcohol has been added, except where Annex II provides otherwise;
   (d) to which colours may have been added;
   (e) to which grape must, partially fermented grape must or both may have been added;
   (f) which may have been sweetened;
   (g) which has an actual alcoholic strength by volume of not less than 4.5% vol and less than 14.5% vol.
4. Aromatised wine-product cocktail is a drink:
   (a) obtained from one or more of the grapevine products defined in points 1, 2 and 4 to 11 of Part II of Annex VII to Regulation (EU) No 1308/2013, with the exception of wines produced with the addition of alcohol and 'Retsina' wine;
   (b) in which the grapevine products referred to in point (a) represent at least 50% of the total volume;
   (c) to which no alcohol has been added;
   (d) to which colours may have been added;
   (e) which may have been sweetened;
   (f) which has an actual alcoholic strength by volume of more than 1.2% vol and less than 10% vol.

[8.722]
Article 4
Production processes and methods of analysis for aromatised wine products

1. Aromatised wine products shall be produced in accordance with the requirements, restrictions and descriptions laid down in Annexes I and II.
2. The Commission shall be empowered to adopt delegated acts in accordance with Article 33 concerning the establishment of authorised production processes for obtaining aromatised wine products, taking into account consumers' expectations.

In establishing the authorised production processes referred to in the first subparagraph, the Commission shall take into account the production processes recommended and published by the OIV.

3. The Commission shall, where necessary, adopt, by means of implementing acts, methods of analysis for determining the composition of aromatised wine products. Those methods shall be based on any relevant methods recommended and published by the OIV, unless they would be ineffective or inappropriate in view of the objective pursued. Those implementing acts shall be adopted in accordance with the examination procedure referred to in Article 34(2).

Pending the adoption of such methods by the Commission, the methods to be used shall be those allowed by the Member State concerned.
4. The oenological practices and restrictions laid down in accordance with Articles 74, 75(4) and 80 of Regulation (EU) No 1308/2013 shall apply to the grapevine products used in the production of aromatised wine products.

[8.723]
Article 5
Sales denominations
1. The sales denominations set out in Annex II shall be used for any aromatised wine product placed on the market in the Union, provided that it complies with the requirements for the corresponding sales denomination laid down in that Annex. Sales denominations may be supplemented by a customary name as defined in Article 2(2)(o) of Regulation (EU) No 1169/2011.
2. Where aromatised wine products comply with the requirements of more than one sales denomination, the use of only one of those sales denominations is authorised, except where Annex II provides otherwise.
3. An alcoholic beverage not fulfilling the requirements laid down in this Regulation shall not be described, presented or labelled by associating words or phrases such as 'like', 'type', 'style', 'made', 'flavour' or any other term similar to any of the sales denominations.
4. Sales denominations may be supplemented or replaced by a geographical indication protected under this Regulation.
5. Without prejudice to Article 26, sales denominations shall not be supplemented by protected designations of origin or protected geographical indications allowed for wine products.

[8.724]
Article 6
Additional particulars to the sales denominations
1. The sales denominations referred to in Article 5 may also be supplemented by the following particulars concerning the sugar content of the aromatised wine product:
(a) 'extra-dry': in the case of products with a sugar content of less than 30 grams per litre and, for the category of aromatised wines and by way of derogation from Article 3(2)(g), a minimum total alcoholic strength by volume of 15% vol;
(b) 'dry': in the case of products with a sugar content of less than 50 grams per litre and, for the category of aromatised wines and by way of derogation from Article 3(2)(g), a minimum total alcoholic strength by volume of 16% vol;
(c) 'semi-dry': in the case of products with a sugar content of between 50 and less than 90 grams per litre;
(d) 'semi-sweet': in the case of products with a sugar content of between 90 and less than 130 grams per litre;
(e) 'sweet': in the case of products with a sugar content of 130 grams per litre or more.

The sugar content indicated in points (a) to (e) of the first subparagraph is expressed as invert sugar. The particulars 'semi-sweet' and 'sweet' may be accompanied by an indication of the sugar content, expressed in grams of invert sugar per litre.
2. Where the sales denomination is supplemented by or includes the particular 'sparkling', the quantity of sparkling wine used shall be not less than 95%.
3. Sales denominations may also be supplemented by a reference to the main flavouring used.

[8.725]
Article 7
Indication of provenance
Where the provenance of aromatised wine products is indicated, it shall correspond to the place where the aromatised wine product is produced. The provenance shall be indicated with the words 'produced in (. . .)', or expressed in equivalent terms, supplemented by the name of the corresponding Member State or third country.

[8.726]
Article 8
Use of language in the presentation and labelling of aromatised wine products
1. The sales denominations set out in italics in Annex II shall not be translated on the label or in the presentation of aromatised wine products.
Additional particulars provided for in this Regulation shall, where expressed in words, appear in at least one of the official languages of the Union.
2. The name of the geographical indication protected under this Regulation shall appear on the label in the language or languages in which it is registered, even where the geographical indication replaces the sales denomination in accordance with Article 5(4).
Where the name of a geographical indication protected under this Regulation is written in a non-Latin alphabet, it may also appear in one or more of the official languages of the Union.

[8.727]

Article 9

Stricter rules decided by Member States

In applying a quality policy for aromatised wine products with geographical indications protected under this Regulation which are produced on their own territory or for the establishment of new geographical indications, Member States may lay down rules on production and description which are stricter than those referred to in Article 4 and in Annexes I and II in so far as they are compatible with Union law.

CHAPTER III
GEOGRAPHICAL INDICATIONS

[8.728]

Article 10

Content of applications for protection

1. Applications for the protection of names as geographical indications shall include a technical file containing:
   (a) the name to be protected;
   (b) the name and address of the applicant;
   (c) a product specification as referred to in paragraph 2; and
   (d) a single document summarising the product specification referred to in paragraph 2.

2. To be eligible for a geographical indication protected under this Regulation a product shall comply with the corresponding product specification which shall include at least:
   (a) the name to be protected;
   (b) a description of the product, in particular its principal analytical characteristics as well as an indication of its organoleptic characteristics;
   (c) where applicable, the particular production processes and specifications as well as the relevant restrictions on making the product;
   (d) the demarcation of the geographical area concerned;
   (e) the details bearing out the link referred to in point (3) of Article 2;
   (f) the applicable requirements laid down in Union or national law or, where provided for by Member States, by an organisation which manages the protected geographical indication, having regard to the fact that such requirements shall be objective, and non-discriminatory and compatible with Union law;
   (g) an indication of the main raw material from which the aromatised wine product is obtained;
   (h) the name and address of the authorities or bodies verifying compliance with the provisions of the product specification and their specific tasks.

[8.729]

Article 11

Application for protection relating to a geographical area in a third country

1. Where the application for protection concerns a geographical area in a third country, it shall contain in addition to the elements provided for in Article 10, proof that the name in question is protected in its country of origin.

2. The application for protection shall be sent to the Commission, either directly by the applicant or via the authorities of the third country concerned.

3. The application for protection shall be filed in one of the official languages of the Union or accompanied by a certified translation into one of those languages.

[8.730]

Article 12

Applicants

1. Any interested group of producers, or in exceptional cases a single producer, may lodge an application for protection of a geographical indication. Other interested parties may participate in the application for protection.

2. Producers may lodge an application for protection only for aromatised wine products which they produce.

3. In the case of a name designating a trans-border geographical area, a joint application for protection may be lodged.

[8.731]

Article 13

Preliminary national procedure

1. Applications for protection of a geographical indication of aromatised wine products originating in the Union shall be subject to a preliminary national procedure in accordance with paragraphs 2 to 7 of this Article.

2. The application for protection shall be filed with the Member State in whose territory the geographical indication originates.

3. The Member State shall examine the application for protection in order to verify whether it meets the conditions set out in this Chapter.

The Member State shall, by means of a national procedure, ensure the adequate publication of the application for protection and shall provide for a period of at least two months from the date of publication within which any natural or legal person with a legitimate interest and resident or established on its territory may object to the proposed protection by lodging a duly substantiated statement with the Member State.

4. If the Member State considers that the geographical indication does not meet the relevant requirements or is incompatible with Union law in general, it shall reject the application.

5. If the Member State considers that the relevant requirements are met, it shall:
(a) publish the single document and the product specification at least on the internet; and
(b) forward to the Commission an application for protection containing the following information:
(i) the name and address of the applicant;
(ii) the product specification referred in Article 10(2);
(iii) the single document referred to in Article 10(1)(d);
(iv) a declaration by the Member State that it considers that the application lodged by the applicant meets the conditions required; and
(v) the reference to the publication, as referred to in point (a).

The information referred to in point (b) of the first subparagraph shall be forwarded in one of the official languages of the Union or accompanied by a certified translation into one of those languages.

6. Member States shall adopt the laws, regulations or administrative provisions necessary to comply with this Article by 28 March 2015.

7. Where a Member State has no national legislation concerning the protection of geographical indications, it may, on a transitional basis only, grant protection to the name in accordance with the terms of this Chapter at national level. Such protection shall take effect from the date the application is lodged with the Commission and shall cease on the date on which a decision on registration or refusal under this Chapter is taken.

[8.732]
Article 14
Scrutiny by the Commission

1. The Commission shall make the date of submission of the application for protection public.

2. The Commission shall examine whether the applications for protection referred to in Article 13(5) meet the conditions laid down in this Chapter.

3. Where the Commission considers that the conditions laid down in this Chapter are met, it shall, by means of implementing acts adopted without applying the procedure referred to in Article 34(2), publish in the *Official Journal of the European Union* the single document referred to in Article 10(1)(d) and the reference to the publication of the product specification referred to in Article 13(5)(a).

4. Where the Commission considers that the conditions laid down in this Chapter are not met, it shall, by means of implementing acts, decide to reject the application. Those implementing acts shall be adopted in accordance with the examination procedure referred to in Article 34(2).

[8.733]
Article 15
Objection procedure

Within two months from the date of publication provided for in Article 14(3), any Member State or third country, or any natural or legal person with a legitimate interest, resident or established in a Member State other than that applying for the protection or in a third country, may object to the proposed protection by lodging with the Commission a duly substantiated statement relating to the conditions of eligibility as laid down in this Chapter.

In the case of natural or legal persons resident or established in a third country, such statement shall be lodged, either directly or via the authorities of the third country concerned, within the time limit of two months referred to in the first paragraph.

[8.734]
Article 16
Decision on protection

On the basis of the information available to the Commission upon the completion of the objection procedure referred to in Article 15, the Commission shall, by means of implementing acts, either confer protection on the geographical indication which meets the conditions laid down in this Chapter and is compatible with Union law, or reject the application where those conditions are not met. Those implementing acts shall be adopted in accordance with the examination procedure referred to in Article 34(2).

[8.735]
Article 17
Homonyms

1. A name, for which an application for protection is lodged, and which is wholly or partially homonymous with that of a name already registered under this Regulation, shall be registered with due regard for local and traditional usage and for any risk of confusion.
2. A homonymous name which misleads the consumer into believing that products come from another territory shall not be registered even if the name is accurate as far as the actual territory, region or place of origin of the products in question is concerned.
3. The use of a registered homonymous name shall be subject to there being a sufficient distinction in practice between the homonym registered subsequently and the name already on the register, having regard to the need to treat the producers concerned in an equitable manner and not to mislead the consumer.

[8.736]
Article 18
Grounds for refusal of protection

1. Names that have become generic shall not be protected as a geographical indication.

For the purposes of this Chapter, a 'name that has become generic' means the name of an aromatised wine product which, although relating to the place or the region where this product was originally produced or placed on the market, has become the common name of an aromatised wine product in the Union.

To establish whether or not a name has become generic, account shall be taken of all relevant factors, in particular:

(a) the existing situation in the Union, notably in areas of consumption;
(b) the relevant Union or national law.

2. A name shall not be protected as a geographical indication where, in the light of a trademark's reputation and renown, protection is liable to mislead the consumer as to the true identity of the aromatised wine product.

[8.737]
Article 19
Relationship with trademarks

1. Where a geographical indication is protected under this Regulation, the registration of a trademark the use of which falls under Article 20(2) and relating to an aromatised wine product shall be refused if the application for registration of the trademark is submitted after the date of submission of the application for protection of the geographical indication to the Commission and the geographical indication is subsequently protected.

Trademarks registered in breach of the first subparagraph shall be invalidated.

2. Without prejudice to Article 17(2), a trademark the use of which falls under Article 20(2), which has been applied for, registered or established by use, if that possibility is provided for by the legislation concerned, in the territory of the Union before the date on which the application for protection of the geographical indication is submitted to the Commission, may continue to be used and renewed notwithstanding the protection of a geographical indication, provided that no grounds for the trademark's invalidity or revocation exist as specified by the Directive 2008/95/EC of the European Parliament of the Council[1] or by Council Regulation (EC) No 207/2009.[2]

In such cases the use of the geographical indication shall be permitted alongside the relevant trademarks.

NOTES

[1] Directive 2008/95/EC of the European Parliament of the Council of 22 October 2008 to approximate the laws of the Member States relating to trade marks (OJ L299, 8.11.2008, p 25).

[2] Council Regulation (EC) No 207/2009 of 26 February 2009 on the Community trade mark (OJ L78, 24.3.2009, p 1).

[8.738]
Article 20
Protection

1. Geographical indications protected under this Regulation may be used by any operator marketing an aromatised wine product which has been produced in conformity with the corresponding product specification.
2. Geographical indications protected under this Regulation and the aromatised wine products using those protected names in conformity with the product specification shall be protected against:

(a) any direct or indirect commercial use of a protected name:
  (i) by comparable products not complying with the product specification of the protected name; or
  (ii) in so far as such use exploits the reputation of a geographical indication;

(b) any misuse, imitation or evocation, even if the true origin of the product or service is indicated or if the protected name is translated, transcribed or transliterated or accompanied by an expression such as 'style', 'type', 'method', 'as produced in', 'imitation', 'flavour', 'like' or similar;

(c) any other false or misleading indication as to the provenance, origin, nature or essential qualities of the product, on the inner or outer packaging, advertising material or documents relating to the wine product concerned, and the packing of the product in a container liable to convey a false impression as to its origin;

(d) any other practice liable to mislead the consumer as to the true origin of the product.

3. Geographical indications protected under this Regulation shall not become generic in the Union within the meaning of Article 18(1).

4. Member States shall take the appropriate administrative and judicial measures to prevent or to stop unlawful use of geographical indications protected under this Regulation as referred to in paragraph 2.

[8.739]
Article 21
Register

The Commission shall, by means of implementing acts adopted without applying the procedure referred to in Article 34(2), establish and maintain an electronic register of geographical indications protected under this Regulation for aromatised wine products which shall be publicly accessible.

Geographical indications pertaining to products of third countries that are protected in the Union pursuant to an international agreement to which the Union is a contracting party may be entered in the register referred to in the first paragraph as geographical indications protected under this Regulation.

[8.740]
Article 22
Designation of competent authority

1. Member States shall designate the competent authority or authorities responsible for checks in respect of the obligations established by this Chapter in accordance with the criteria laid down in Article 4 of Regulation (EC) No 882/2004 of the European Parliament and of the Council.[1]

2. Member States shall ensure that any operator complying with this Chapter is entitled to be covered by a system of checks.

3. Member States shall inform the Commission of the competent authority or authorities referred to in paragraph 1. The Commission shall make their names and addresses public and update them periodically.

[8.741]
Article 23
Verification of compliance with specifications

1. In respect of geographical indications protected under this Regulation relating to a geographical area within the Union, annual verification of compliance with the product specification, during the production and during or after conditioning of the aromatised wine product, shall be ensured by:

(a) the competent authority or authorities referred to in Article 22; or

(b) one or more control bodies responsible for the verification within the meaning of point 5 of the second paragraph of Article 2 of Regulation (EC) No 882/2004 operating as a product certification body in accordance with the requirements laid down in Article 5 of that Regulation.

The costs of such verification shall be borne by the operators subject to it.

2. In respect of geographical indications protected under this Regulation relating to a geographical area in a third country, annual verification of compliance with the product specification, during the production and during or after conditioning of the aromatised wine product, shall be ensured by:

(a) one or more public authorities designated by the third country; or

(b) one or more certification bodies.

3. The bodies referred to in point (b) of paragraph 1 and point (b) of paragraph 2 shall comply with, and be accredited in accordance with, the Standard EN ISO/IEC 17065:2012 (Conformity assessments — Requirements for bodies certifying products processes and services).

4. Where the authority or authorities referred to in point (a) of paragraph 1 and point (a) of paragraph 2 verify compliance with the product specification, they shall offer adequate guarantees of objectivity and impartiality, and have at their disposal the qualified staff and resources needed to carry out their tasks.

NOTES

1 Regulation (EC) No 882/2004 of the European Parliament and of the Council of 29 April 2004 on official controls performed to ensure the verification of compliance with feed and food law, animal health and animal welfare rules (OJ L165, 30.4.2004, p 1).

[8.742]
Article 24
Amendments to product specifications
1. An applicant satisfying the conditions of Article 12 may apply for approval of an amendment to the product specification of a geographical indication protected under this Regulation, in particular in order to take account of developments in scientific and technical knowledge or to redefine the geographical area referred to in point (d) of Article 10(2). Applications shall describe and give reasons for the amendments requested.
2. Where the proposed amendment involves one or more changes to the single document referred to in point (d) of Article 10(1), Articles 13 to 16 shall apply *mutatis mutandis* to the application for amendment. However, if the proposed amendment is only minor, the Commission shall, by means of implementing acts, decide whether to approve the application without following the procedure laid down in Article 14(2) and Article 15 and in the case of approval, the Commission shall proceed to the publication of the elements referred to in Article 14(3). Those implementing acts shall be adopted in accordance with the examination procedure referred to in Article 34(2).

[8.743]
Article 25
Cancellation
The Commission may, on its own initiative or at the duly substantiated request of a Member State, of a third country or of a natural or legal person having a legitimate interest, decide, by means of implementing acts, to cancel the protection of a geographical indication if compliance with the corresponding product specification is no longer ensured. Those implementing acts shall be adopted in accordance with the examination procedure referred to in Article 34(2).
Articles 13 to 16 shall apply *mutatis mutandis*.

[8.744]
Article 26
Existing geographical designations
1. Geographical designations of aromatised wine products listed in Annex II to Regulation (EEC) No 1601/91 and any geographical designation submitted to a Member State and approved by that Member State before 27 March 2014, shall automatically be protected as geographical indications under this Regulation. The Commission shall, by means of implementing acts adopted without applying the procedure referred to in Article 34(2) of this Regulation, list them in the register provided for in Article 21 of this Regulation.
2. Member States shall, in respect of existing geographical designations referred to in paragraph 1, transmit to the Commission:
(a) the technical files as provided for in Article 10(1);
(b) the national decisions of approval.
3. Existing geographical designations referred to in paragraph 1, for which the information referred to in paragraph 2 is not submitted by 28 March 2017, shall lose protection under this Regulation. The Commission shall, by means of implementing acts adopted without applying the procedure referred to in Article 34(2), take the corresponding formal step of removing such names from the register provided for in Article 21.
4. Article 25 shall not apply in respect of existing geographical designations referred to in paragraph 1 of this Article.
Until 28 March 2018 the Commission may, by means of implementing acts, on its own initiative, decide to cancel the protection of existing geographical designations referred to in paragraph 1 of this Article if they do not comply with point (3) of Article 2. Those implementing acts shall be adopted in accordance with the examination procedure referred to in Article 34(2).

[8.745]
Article 27
Fees
Member States may charge a fee to cover their costs, including those incurred in examining applications for protection, statements of objections, applications for amendments and requests for cancellations under this Chapter.

[8.746]
Article 28
Delegated powers
1. In order to take account of the specific characteristics of the production in the demarcated geographical area, the Commission shall be empowered to adopt delegated acts in accordance with Article 33 concerning:
(a) criteria for the demarcation of the geographical area; and
(b) rules, restrictions and derogations related to the production in the demarcated geographical area.
2. In order to ensure product quality and traceability, the Commission shall be empowered to adopt delegated acts in accordance with Article 33 in order to establish the conditions under which product specifications may include additional requirements to those referred to in Article 10(2)(f).

3. In order to ensure the rights or legitimate interests of producers or operators, the Commission shall be empowered to adopt delegated acts in accordance with Article 33 in order to:

(a) determine the cases in which a single producer may apply for the protection of a geographical indication;

(b) determine the restrictions governing the type of applicant that may apply for the protection of a geographical indication;

(c) establish the conditions to be followed in respect of an application for the protection of a geographical indication, scrutiny by the Commission, the objection procedure, and procedures for amendment and cancellation of geographical indications;

(d) establish the conditions applicable to transborder applications;

(e) set the date of submission of an application or a request;

(f) set the date from which protection shall run;

(g) establish the conditions under which an amendment is to be considered as minor as referred to in Article 24(2);

(h) set the date on which an amendment shall enter into force;

(i) establish the conditions relating to the applications for, and approval of, amendments to the product specification of a geographical indication protected under this Regulation, where such amendments do not involve any change to the single document referred to in point (d) of Article 10(1).

4. In order to ensure adequate protection, the Commission shall be empowered to adopt delegated acts in accordance with Article 33 concerning the restrictions regarding the protected name.

[8.747]
Article 29
Implementing powers

1. The Commission may, by means of implementing acts, adopt all necessary measures related to this Chapter regarding:

(a) the information to be provided in the product specification with regard to the link referred to in point (3) of Article 2 between the geographical area and the final product;

(b) the means of making the decisions on protection or rejection referred to in Article 16 available to the public;

(c) the submission of trans-border applications;

(d) checks and verification to be carried out by the Member States, including testing.

Those implementing acts shall be adopted in accordance with the examination procedure referred to in Article 34(2).

2. The Commission may, by means of implementing acts, adopt all necessary measures related to this Chapter as regards the procedure, including admissibility, for the examination of applications for protection or for the approval of an amendment of a geographical indication, as well as the procedure, including admissibility, for requests for objection, cancellation, or conversion, and the submission of information relating to existing protected geographical designations, in particular with respect to:

(a) models for documents and the transmission format;

(b) time limits;

(c) the details of the facts, evidence and supporting documents to be submitted in support of the application or request.

Those implementing acts shall be adopted in accordance with the examination procedure referred to in Article 34(2).

[8.748]
Article 30
Inadmissible application or request

Where an application or a request submitted under this Chapter is deemed inadmissible, the Commission shall, by means of implementing acts adopted without applying the procedure referred to in Article 34(2), decide to reject it as inadmissible.

CHAPTER IV
GENERAL, TRANSITIONAL AND FINAL PROVISIONS

[8.749]
Article 31
Checks and verification of aromatised wine products

1. Member States shall be responsible for the checks of aromatised wine products. They shall take the measures necessary to ensure compliance with the provisions of this Regulation and in particular they shall designate the competent authority or authorities responsible for checks in respect of the obligations established by this Regulation in accordance with Regulation (EC) No 882/2004.

2. The Commission shall, when necessary, by means of implementing acts, adopt the rules concerning administrative and physical checks to be conducted by the Member States with regard to the respect of obligations resulting from the application of this Regulation.

Those implementing acts shall be adopted in accordance with the examination procedure referred to in Article 34(2).

[8.750]
Article 32
Exchange of information
1. Member States and the Commission shall notify each other of any information necessary for the application of this Regulation and for complying with the international obligations concerning the aromatised wine products. That information may, where appropriate, be transmitted or made available to the competent authorities of third countries and may be made public.
2. In order to make the notifications referred to in paragraph 1 fast, efficient, accurate, and cost effective, the Commission shall be empowered to adopt delegated acts in accordance with Article 33 to lay down:
(a) the nature and type of the information to be notified;
(b) the methods of notification;
(c) the rules related to the access rights to the information or information systems made available;
(d) the conditions and means of publication of the information.
3. The Commission shall, by means of implementing acts, adopt:
(a) rules on providing the information necessary for the application of this Article;
(b) arrangements for the management of the information to be notified, as well as rules on content, form, timing, frequency and deadlines of the notifications;
(c) arrangements for transmitting or making information and documents available to the Member States, the competent authorities in third countries, or the public.
Those implementing acts shall be adopted in accordance with the examination procedure referred to in Article 34(2).

[8.751]
Article 33
Exercise of the delegation
1. The power to adopt delegated acts is conferred on the Commission subject to the conditions laid down in this Article.
2. The power to adopt delegated acts referred to in Articles 4(2), 28, 32(2) and 36(1) shall be conferred on the Commission for a period of five years from 27 March 2014. The Commission shall draw up a report in respect of the delegation of power not later than nine months before the end of the five-year period. The delegation of power shall be tacitly extended for periods of an identical duration, unless the European Parliament or the Council opposes such extension not later than three months before the end of each period.
3. The delegation of power referred to in Articles 4(2), 28, 32(2) and 36(1) may be revoked at any time by the European Parliament or by the Council. A decision of revocation shall put an end to the delegation of the powers specified in that decision. It shall take effect the day following the publication in the *Official Journal of the European Union* or at a later date specified therein. It shall not affect the validity of the delegated acts already in force.
4. As soon as it adopts a delegated act, the Commission shall notify it simultaneously to the European Parliament and to the Council.
5. A delegated act adopted pursuant to Articles 4(2), 28, 32(2) and 36(1) shall enter into force only if no objection has been expressed either by the European Parliament or the Council within a period of two months of notification of that act or if, before the expiry of that period, the European Parliament and the Council have both informed the Commission that they will not object. That period shall be extended by two months on the initiative of the European Parliament or the Council.

[8.752]
Article 34
Committee procedure
1. The Commission shall be assisted by the Committee on aromatised wine products. That Committee shall be a committee within the meaning of Regulation (EU) No 182/2011.
2. Where reference is made to this paragraph, Article 5 of Regulation (EU) No 182/2011 shall apply.
In the case of implementing acts referred to in the first subparagraph of Article 4(3) and Article 29(1)(b), where the Committee delivers no opinion, the Commission shall not adopt the draft implementing act and the third subparagraph of Article 5(4) of Regulation (EU) No 182/2011 shall apply.

[8.753]
Article 35
Repeal
Regulation (EEC) No 1601/91 is hereby repealed as from 28 March 2015.
References made to the repealed Regulation shall be construed as references to this Regulation and shall be read in accordance with the correlation table set out in Annex III to this Regulation.

[8.754]
Article 36
Transitional measures

1. In order to facilitate the transition from the rules provided for in Regulation (EEC) No 1601/91 to those established by this Regulation, the Commission shall be empowered to adopt, where appropriate, delegated acts in accordance with Article 33 concerning the adoption of measures to amend or derogate from this Regulation, which shall remain in force until 28 March 2018.

2. Aromatised wine products not meeting the requirements of this Regulation but which have been produced in accordance with Regulation (EEC) No 1601/91 prior to 28 March 2015 may be placed on the market until stocks are exhausted.

3. Aromatised wine products which comply with Articles 1 to 6 and Article 9 of this Regulation and which have been produced prior to 28 March 2015 may be placed on the market until stocks are exhausted, provided that such products comply with Regulation (EEC) No 1601/91 in respect of all aspects not regulated by Articles 1 to 6 and Article 9 of this Regulation.

[8.755]
Article 37
Entry into force

This Regulation shall enter into force on the seventh day following that of its publication in the *Official Journal of the European Union*.

It shall apply from 28 March 2015. However, Article 36(1) and (3) shall apply from 27 March 2014.

This Regulation shall be binding in its entirety and directly applicable in all Member States.

ANNEX I
TECHNICAL DEFINITIONS, REQUIREMENTS AND RESTRICTIONS

[8.756]

(1) Flavouring

(a) The following products are authorised for the flavouring of aromatised wines:

(i) natural flavouring substances and/or flavouring preparations as defined in Article 3(2)(c) and (d) of Regulation (EC) No 1334/2008;

(ii) flavourings as defined in Article 3(2)(a) of Regulation (EC) No 1334/2008, which:

— are identical to vanillin,

— smell and/or taste of almonds,

— smell and/or taste of apricots,

— smell and/or taste of eggs; and

(iii) aromatic herbs and/or spices and/or flavouring foodstuffs.

(b) The following products are authorised for the flavouring of aromatised wine-based drinks and aromatised wine-product cocktails:

(i) flavouring substances and/or flavouring preparations as defined in Article 3(2)(b) and (d) of Regulation (EC) No 1334/2008; and

(ii) aromatic herbs and/or spices and/or flavouring foodstuffs.

Addition of such substances confers on the final product organoleptic characteristics other than those of wine.

(2) Sweetening

The following products are authorised for the sweetening of aromatised wine products:

(a) semi-white sugar, white sugar, extra-white sugar, dextrose, fructose, glucose syrup, sugar solution, invert sugar solution, invert sugar syrup, as defined in Council Directive 2001/111/EC;[1]

(b) grape must, concentrated grape must and rectified concentrated grape must, as defined in points 10, 13 and 14 of Part II of Annex VII to Regulation (EU) No 1308/2013;

(c) burned sugar, which is the product obtained exclusively from the controlled heating of sucrose without bases, mineral acids or other chemical additives;

(d) honey as defined in Council Directive 2001/110/EC;[2]

(e) carob syrup;

(f) any other natural carbohydrate substances having a similar effect to those products.

(3) Addition of alcohol

The following products are authorised for the preparation of some aromatised wines and, some aromatised wine-based drinks:

(a) ethyl alcohol of agricultural origin, as defined in Annex I, point 1, to Regulation (EC) No 110/2008, including viticultural origin;

(b) wine alcohol or dried grape alcohol;

(c) wine distillate or dried grape distillate;

(d) distillate of agricultural origin, as defined in Annex I, point 2, to Regulation (EC) No 110/2008;

(e) wine spirit, as defined in Annex II, point 4, to Regulation (EC) No 110/2008;

(f) grape-marc spirit, as defined in Annex II, point 6, to Regulation (EC) No 110/2008;

(g) spirit drinks distilled from fermented dried grapes.

The ethyl alcohol used to dilute or dissolve colorants, flavourings or any other authorised additives used in the preparation of aromatised wine products must be of agricultural origin and must be used in the dose strictly necessary and is not considered as addition of alcohol for the purpose of production of an aromatised wine product.

(4) Additives and colouring

The rules on food additives, including colours, laid down in Regulation (EC) No 1333/2008 apply to aromatised wine products.

(5) Addition of water

For the preparation of aromatised wine products, the addition of water is authorised provided that it is used in the dose necessary:

— to prepare flavouring essence,
— to dissolve colorants and sweeteners,
— to adjust the final composition of the product.

The quality of the water added has to be in conformity with Directive 2009/54/EC of the European Parliament and of the Council[3] and Council Directive 98/83/EC,[4] and it should not change the nature of the product.

This water may be distilled, demineralised, permuted or softened.

(6) For the preparation of aromatised wine products, the addition of carbon dioxide is authorised.

(7) Alcoholic strength

'Alcoholic strength by volume' means the ratio of the volume of pure alcohol contained in the product in question at a temperature of 20 °C to the total volume of that product at the same temperature.

'Actual alcoholic strength by volume' means the number of volumes of pure alcohol contained at a temperature of 20 °C in 100 volumes of the product at that temperature.

'Potential alcoholic strength by volume' means the number of volumes of pure alcohol at a temperature of 20 °C capable of being produced by total fermentation of the sugars contained in 100 volumes of the product at the same temperature.

'Total alcoholic strength by volume' means the sum of the actual and potential alcoholic strengths by volume.

NOTES

1 Council Directive 2001/111/EC of 20 December 2001 relating to certain sugars intended for human consumption (OJ L10, 12.1.2002, p 53).

2 Council Directive 2001/110/EC of 20 December 2001 relating to honey (OJ L10, 12.1.2002, p 47).

3 Directive 2009/54/EC of the European Parliament and of the Council of 18 June 2009 on the exploitation and marketing of natural mineral waters (recast) (OJ L164, 26.6.2009, p 45).

4 Council Directive 98/83/EC of 3 November 1998 on the quality of water intended for human consumption (OJ L330, 5.12.1998, p 32).

ANNEX II
SALES DENOMINATIONS AND DESCRIPTIONS OF AROMATISED WINE PRODUCTS

[8.757]

A. SALES DENOMINATIONS AND DESCRIPTIONS OF AROMATISED WINES

(1) Aromatised wine

Products complying with the definition set out in Article 3(2).

(2) Wine-based aperitif

Aromatised wine to which alcohol may have been added.

The use of the term 'aperitif' in this connection is without prejudice to its use to define products which do not fall within the scope of this Regulation.

(3) Vermouth

Aromatised wine:

— to which alcohol has been added, and
— whose characteristic taste has been obtained by the use of appropriate substances of *Artemisia* species.

(4) Bitter aromatised wine

Aromatised wine with a characteristic bitter flavour to which alcohol has been added.

The sales denomination 'bitter aromatised wine' is followed by the name of the main bitter-flavouring substance.

The sales denomination 'bitter aromatised wine' may be supplemented or replaced by the following terms:

— 'Quinquina wine', whose main flavouring is natural quinine flavouring,
— '*Bitter vino*', whose main flavouring is natural gentian flavouring and which has been coloured with authorised yellow and/or red colour; the use of the word 'bitter' in this connection is without prejudice to its use to define products which do not fall within the scope of this Regulation,
— '*Americano*', where the flavouring is due to the presence of natural flavouring substances derived from wormwood and gentian and which has been coloured with authorised yellow and/or red colours.

(5) Egg-based aromatised wine
Aromatised wine:
— to which alcohol has been added,
— to which good-quality egg yolk or extracts thereof have been added,
— which has a sugar content expressed in terms of invert sugar of more than 200 grams, and
— in the preparation of which the minimum quantity of egg yolk used in the mixture is 10 grams per litre.

The sales denomination 'egg-based aromatised wine' may be accompanied by the term '*cremovo*' where such product contains wine of the protected designation of origin 'Marsala' in a proportion of not less than 80%.
The sales denomination 'egg-based aromatised wine' may be accompanied by the term '*cremovo zabaione*', where such product contains wine of the protected designation of origin 'Marsala' in a proportion of not less than 80% and has an egg yolk content of not less than 60 grams per litre.

(6) *Väkevä viiniglögi/Starkvinsglögg*
An aromatised wine:
— to which alcohol has been added, and
— whose characteristic taste has been obtained by the use of cloves and/or cinnamon.

B. SALES DENOMINATIONS AND DESCRIPTIONS OF AROMATISED WINE BASED DRINKS

(1) Aromatised wine-based drink
Products complying with the definition set out in Article 3(3).

(2) Aromatised fortified wine-based drink
Aromatised wine-based drink
— to which alcohol has been added,
— which has actual alcoholic strength by volume not less than 7% vol,
— which has been sweetened,
— which is obtained from white wine,
— to which dried grape distillate has been added, and
— which has been flavoured exclusively by cardamom extract;

or
— to which alcohol has been added,
— which has actual alcoholic strength by volume not less than 7% vol,
— which has been sweetened,
— which is obtained from red wine, and
— to which flavouring preparations obtained exclusively from spices, ginseng, nuts, citrus fruit essences and aromatic herbs, have been added.

(3) *Sangría/Sangria*
Aromatised wine-based drink
— which is obtained from wine,
— which is aromatised with the addition of natural citrus-fruit extracts or essences, with or without the juice of such fruit,
— to which spices may have been added,
— to which carbon dioxide may have been added,
— which has not been coloured,
— which have an actual alcoholic strength by volume of not less than 4.5% vol, and less than 12% vol, and
— which may contain solid particles of citrus-fruit pulp or peel and its colour must come exclusively from the raw materials used.

'*Sangría*' or '*Sangria*' may be used as a sales denomination only when the product is produced in Spain or Portugal. When the product is produced in other Member States, '*Sangría*' or '*Sangria*' may only be used to supplement the sales denomination 'aromatised wine-based drink', provided that it is accompanied by the words: 'produced in . . . ', followed by the name of the Member State of production or of a more restricted region.

(4) *Clarea*

Aromatised wine-based drink, which is obtained from white wine under the same conditions as for *Sangría/Sangria*.
'*Clarea*' may be used as a sales denomination only when the product is produced in Spain. When the product is produced in other Member States, '*Clarea*' may only be used to supplement the sales denomination 'aromatised wine-based drink', provided that it is accompanied by the words: 'produced in . . . ', followed by the name of the Member State of production or of a more restricted region.

(5) *Zurra*
Aromatised wine-based drink obtained by adding brandy or wine spirit as defined in Regulation (EC) No 110/2008 to *Sangría/Sangria* and *Clarea*, possibly with the addition of pieces of fruit. The actual alcoholic strength by volume must be not less than 9% vol and less than 14% vol.

(6) *Bitter soda*
Aromatised wine-based drink
— which is obtained from '*bitter vino*' the content of which in the finished product must not be less than 50% by volume,
— to which carbon dioxide or carbonated water has been added, and
— which has an actual alcoholic strength by volume of not less than 8% vol, and less than 10.5% vol.

The use of the word 'bitter' in this context shall be without prejudice to its use to define products which do not fall within the scope of this Regulation.

(7) *Kalte Ente*
Aromatised wine-based drink
— which is obtained by mixing wine, semi-sparkling wine or aerated semi-sparkling wine with sparkling wine or aerated sparkling wine,
— to which natural lemon substances or extracts thereof have been added, and
— which has an actual alcoholic strength by volume of not less than 7% vol.

The finished product must contain not less than 25% by volume of the sparkling wine or aerated sparkling wine.

(8) *Glühwein*
Aromatised wine-based drink
— which is obtained exclusively from red or white wine,
— which is flavoured mainly with cinnamon and/or cloves, and
— which has an actual alcoholic strength by volume of not less than 7% vol.

Without prejudice to the quantities of water resulting from the application of Annex I, point 2, the addition of water is forbidden.
Where it has been prepared from white wine, the sales denomination '*Glühwein*' must be supplemented by words indicating white wine, such as the word 'white'.

(9) *Viiniglögi/Vinglögg/Karštas vynas*
Aromatised wine-based drink
— which is obtained exclusively from red or white wine,
— which is flavoured mainly with cinnamon and/or cloves, and
— which has an actual alcoholic strength by volume of not less than 7% vol.

Where it has been prepared from white wine, the sales denomination '*Viiniglögi/Vinglögg/Karštas vynas*' must be supplemented by words indicating white wine, such as the word 'white'.

(10) *Maiwein*
Aromatised wine-based drink
— which is obtained from wine in which *Galium odoratum* (L.) Scop. (*Asperula odorata* L.), plants or extracts thereof has been added so as to ensure a predominant taste of *Galium odoratum* (L.) Scop. (*Asperula odorata* L.), and
— which has an actual alcoholic strength by volume of not less than 7% vol.

(11) *Maitrank*
Aromatised wine-based drink
— which is obtained from white wine in which *Galium odoratum* (L.) Scop. (*Asperula odorata* L.) plants have been macerated or to which extracts thereof have been added with the addition of oranges and/or other fruits, possibly in the form of juice, concentrated or extracts, and with maximum 5% sugar sweetening, and
— which has an actual alcoholic strength by volume of not less than 7% vol.

(12) *Pelin*
Aromatised wine-based drink
— which is obtained from red or white wine and specific mixture of herbs,
— which has an actual alcoholic strength by volume of not less than 8.5% vol, and

— which has a sugar content expressed as invert sugar of 45–50 grams per litre, and a total acidity of not less than 3 grams per litre expressed as tartaric acid.

(13) *Aromatizovaný dezert*
Aromatised wine-based drink
— which is obtained from white or red wine, sugar and dessert spices mixture,
— which has an actual alcoholic strength by volume of not less than 9% vol and less than 12% vol, and
— which has a sugar content expressed as invert sugar of 90–130 grams per litre and a total acidity of at least 2.5 grams per litre expressed as tartaric acid.
'*Aromatizovaný dezert*' may be used as a sales denomination only when the product is produced in the Czech Republic. When the product is produced in other Member States, '*Aromatizovaný dezert*' may only be used to supplement the sales denomination 'aromatised wine-based drink' provided that it is accompanied by the words 'produced in . . . ' followed by the name of the Member State of production or of a more restricted region.

C. Sales Denominations and Descriptions of Aromatised Wine-Product Cocktails

(1) Aromatised wine-product cocktail
Product complying with the definition set out in Article 3(4).
The use of the term 'cocktail' in this connection is without prejudice to its use to define products which do not fall within the scope of this Regulation.

(2) Wine-based cocktail
Aromatised wine-product cocktail
— in which the proportion of concentrated grape must does not exceed 10% of the total volume of the finished product,
— which has an actual alcoholic strength by volume less than 7% vol, and
— in which the sugar content, expressed as invert sugar, is less than 80 grams per litre.

(3) Aromatised semi-sparkling grape-based cocktail
Aromatised wine-product cocktail
— which is obtained exclusively from grape must,
— which has an actual alcoholic strength by volume less than 4% vol, and
— which contains carbon dioxide obtained exclusively from fermentation of the products used.

(4) Sparkling wine cocktail
Aromatised wine-product cocktail, which is mixed with sparkling wine.

ANNEX III
CORRELATION TABLE

[8.758]

Regulation (EEC) No 1601/91	This Regulation
Article 1	Article 1
Article 2(1) to (4)	Article 3 and Annex II
Article 2(5)	Article 6(1)
Article 2(6)	Article 6(2)
Article 2(7)	—
Article 3	Article 4(1) and Annex I
Article 4(1) to (3)	Article 4(1) and Annex I
Article 4(4)	Article 4(3)
Article 5	Article 4(2)
Article 6(1)	Article 5(1) and (2)
Article 6(2)(a)	Article 5(4)
Article 6(2)(b)	Article 20(1)
Article 6(3)	Article 5(5)
Article 6(4)	Article 9
Article 7(1) and (3)	—
Article 7(2)	Article 5(3)
Article 8(1)	—
Article 8(2)	Article 5(1) and (2)
Article 8(3)	Article 6(3)
—	Article 7

Regulation (EEC) No 1601/91	This Regulation
Article 8(4), first and second paragraphs	—
Article 8(4) third paragraph	Annex I, point 3, second paragraph
Article 8(4a)	—
Article 8(5) to (8)	Article 8
Article 8(9)	—
Article 9(1) to (3)	Article 31
Article 9(4)	Article 32
Article 10	Article 11
Article 10a	Article 2, point 3, and Articles 10 to 30
Article 11	Article 1(3)
Articles 12 to 15	Articles 33 and 34
—	Article 35
Article 16	Article 36
Article 17	Article 37
Annex I	Annex I(3)(a)
Annex II	—

COMMISSION IMPLEMENTING REGULATION

(668/2014/EU)

of 13 June 2014

laying down rules for the application of Regulation (EU) No 1151/2012 of the European Parliament and of the Council on quality schemes for agricultural products and foodstuffs

NOTES

Date of publication in OJ: OJ L179, 19.6.2014, p 36.
This Regulation is reproduced as corrected by the corrigendum published in OJ L39, 14.2.2015, p 23.

THE EUROPEAN COMMISSION,

Having regard to the Treaty on the Functioning of the European Union,

Having regard to Regulation (EU) No 1151/2012 of the European Parliament and of the Council of 21 November 2012 on quality schemes for agricultural products and foodstuffs,[1] and in particular the second subparagraph of Article 7(2), Article 11(3), the second subparagraph of Article 12(7), the second subparagraph of Article 19(2), Article 22(2), the second subparagraph of Article 23(4), Article 44(3), the second subparagraph of Article 49(7), the second subparagraph of Article 51(6), the second subparagraph of Article 53(3) and the second subparagraph of Article 54(2) thereof,

Whereas:

(1) Regulation (EU) No 1151/2012 has repealed and replaced Council Regulations (EC) No 509/2006 of 20 March 2006 on agricultural products and foodstuffs as traditional specialities guaranteed[2] and (EC) No 510/2006 of 20 March 2006 on the protection of geographical indications and designations of origin for agricultural products and foodstuffs.[3] Regulation (EU) No 1151/2012 empowers the Commission to adopt delegated and implementing acts. In order to ensure the smooth functioning of the quality schemes for agricultural products and foodstuffs in the new legal framework, certain rules should be adopted by means of such acts. The new rules should replace the implementing rules of Commission Regulations (EC) No 1898/2006 of 14 December 2006 laying down detailed rules of implementation of Council Regulation (EC) No 510/2006 on the protection of geographical indications and designations of origin for agricultural products and foodstuffs[4] and (EC) No 1216/2007 of 18 October 2007 laying down detailed rules for the implementation of Council Regulation (EC) No 509/2006 on agricultural products and foodstuffs as traditional specialities guaranteed.[5] Those Regulations are repealed by Commission Delegated Regulation (EU) No 664/2014 of 18 December 2013 supplementing Regulation (EU) No 1151/2012 of the European Parliament and of the Council with regard to the establishment of the Union symbols for protected designations of origin, protected geographical indications and traditional specialities guaranteed and with regard to certain rules on sourcing, certain procedural rules and certain additional transitional rules.[6]

(2) Specific rules concerning the use of linguistic characters for a protected designation of origin, a protected geographical indication and a traditional speciality guaranteed and the translations

Part 8 Other EU Materials

of the claim accompanying a traditional speciality guaranteed should be laid down in order to ensure that operators and consumers in all Member States are able to read and understand such names and claims.

(3) The geographical area of protected designations of origin and protected geographical indications should be defined in the product specification in a detailed, precise way that presents no ambiguities in order to allow producers, competent authorities and control bodies to operate on certain and reliable bases.

(4) An obligation to include detailed rules on the origin and quality of feed in the product specifications of products of animal origin the names of which are registered as protected designations of origin should be established in order to guarantee uniform quality of the product and to harmonise the way of drafting those rules.

(5) The product specification for protected designations of origin and protected geographical indications should include the measures taken to ensure that the product originates in the defined geographical area, as referred to in point (d) of Article 7(1) of Regulation (EU) No 1151/2012. Those measures should be clear and detailed in order to allow to trace the product, raw materials, feed and other items coming from the defined geographical area.

(6) As regards applications for registration of a name or approval of an amendment covering distinct products it is necessary to define in which cases products bearing the same registered name are considered distinct products. In order to avoid that products not complying with the requirements for designations of origin and geographical indications referred to in Article 5(1) and (2) of Regulation (EU) No 1151/2012 are marketed using a registered name, compliance with the requirements for registration should be demonstrated for each distinct product covered by an application.

(7) Packaging of an agricultural product or a foodstuff or operations concerning its presentation, such as slicing or grating, restricted to a defined geographical area, constitute a restriction on free movement of goods and freedom to provide services. In the light of the case-law of the Court of Justice of the European Union, such restrictions can only be imposed if they are necessary, proportionate and capable of upholding the reputation of the geographical indication or the designation of origin. As referred to in point (e) of Article 7(1) of Regulation (EU) No 1151/2012, product specific justifications for such restrictions shall be provided.

(8) For the smooth functioning of the system, procedures for applications, oppositions, amendments and cancellations should be specified.

(9) To ensure uniform and efficient procedures, forms concerning applications, oppositions, amendments, cancellations as well as forms concerning the publication of single documents for names that were registered prior to 31 March 2006 should be provided.

(10) For the sake of legal certainty, the criteria for the identification of the date of submission of an application for registration and of submission of an amendment application should be clearly specified.

(11) A limit to the length of single documents should be set out in order to have a more streamlined process and for standardisation needs.

(12) Specific rules on the description of the product and the production method should be adopted for standardisation needs. In order to allow easy and quick examination of applications for registration of a name or approval of an amendment, the description of the product and of the production method should contain only relevant and comparable elements. Repetitions, implicit requirements and redundant parts should be avoided.

(13) For the sake of legal certainty, deadlines concerning the opposition procedure should be fixed and criteria for the identification of the starting dates of those deadlines should be established.

(14) For the sake of transparency, the information concerning applications for amendment and requests for cancellation to be published in accordance with Article 50(2) of Regulation (EU) No 1151/2012 should be exhaustive.

(15) For streamlining and simplification purposes, the electronic form should be the only means of communication admitted for the transmission of applications, information and documents.

(16) Rules on the use of symbols and indications on the products marketed under protected designations of origin, protected geographical indications or traditional specialities guaranteed should be set out, including on the appropriate linguistic versions to be used.

(17) The rules on the use of registered names in association with the symbols, indications or corresponding abbreviations, as referred to in Article 12(3) and (6) and Article 23(3) of Regulation (EU) No 1151/2012, should be clarified.

(18) In order to ensure uniform protection of indications, abbreviations and symbols and to raise public awareness about the quality schemes of the Union, rules on the use of indications, abbreviations and symbols in media or advertising supports in connection with products produced in conformity with the respective quality scheme should be established.

(19) Rules on the content and the form of the Register of protected designations of origin,

protected geographical indications and traditional specialities guaranteed should be adopted to ensure transparency and legal certainty.

(20) The measures provided for in this Regulation are in accordance with the opinion of the Agricultural Product Quality Policy Committee,

NOTES

1 OJ L343, 14.12.2012, p 1.

2 OJ L93, 31.3.2006, p 1.

3 OJ L93, 31.3.2006, p 12.

4 OJ L369, 23.12.2006, p 1.

5 OJ L275, 19.10.2007, p 3.

6 See p. 17 of this Official Journal.

HAS ADOPTED THIS REGULATION:

[8.759]
Article 1
Specific rules for a name

1. The name of a protected designation of origin, a protected geographical indication or a traditional speciality guaranteed shall be registered in its original script. Where the original script is not in Latin characters, a transcription in Latin characters shall be registered together with the name in its original script.

2. Where the name of a traditional speciality guaranteed is accompanied by the claim referred to in Article 18(3) of Regulation (EU) No 1151/2012 and that claim is to be translated in the other official languages, such translations shall be included in the product specification.

[8.760]
Article 2
Definition of the geographical area

As regards protected designations of origin and protected geographical indications, the geographical area shall be defined in a precise way that presents no ambiguities, referring as far as possible to physical or administrative boundaries.

[8.761]
Article 3
Specific rules on feed

The product specification of a product of animal origin the name of which is registered as a protected designation of origin shall contain detailed rules on the origin and the quality of feed.

[8.762]
Article 4
Proof of origin

1. The product specification for a protected designation of origin or a protected geographical indication shall identify the procedures which operators must have in place as regards the proof of origin concerning the product, raw materials, feed and other items that, according to the product specification, are required to come from the defined geographical area.

2. Operators shall be able to identify:
   (a) the supplier, quantity and origin of all batches of raw material and/or products received;
   (b) the recipient, quantity and destination of products supplied;
   (c) the correlation between each batch of inputs referred to in point (a) and each batch of outputs referred to in point (b).

[8.763]
Article 5
Description of several distinct products

Where the application for registration of a name or approval of an amendment describes several distinct products which are entitled to use that name, compliance with the requirements for registration shall be shown separately for each such product.

For the purposes of this Article, 'distinct products' mean products that, although using the same registered name, are differentiated when placed on the market or considered as different products by consumers.

[8.764]
Article 6
Procedural requirements for applications for registration

1. The single document of a protected designation of origin or a protected geographical indication referred to in point (c) of Article 8(1) of Regulation (EU) No 1151/2012 shall include the information requested in Annex I to this Regulation. It shall be drawn up in accordance with the form provided for in that Annex. It shall be concise and not exceed 2,500 words, except in duly justified cases.

The reference to the publication of the product specification included in the single document shall lead to the version of the product specification as proposed.

2. The product specification of a traditional speciality guaranteed referred to in Article 19 of Regulation (EU) No 1151/2012 shall include the information requested in Annex II to this Regulation. It shall be drawn up in accordance with the form provided for in that Annex.

3. The date of submission of an application shall be the date on which the application is delivered to the Commission by electronic means. A delivery receipt shall be sent by the Commission.

[8.765]
Article 7
Specific rules for the description of the product and the production method

1. The single document for an application for registration of a protected designation of origin or a protected geographical indication referred to in point (c) of Article 8(1) of Regulation (EU) No 1151/2012 shall identify the product by using definitions and standards commonly used for that product.

The description shall focus on the specificity of the product bearing the name to be registered, using measurement units and common or technical terms of comparison, without including technical characteristics inherent to all products of that type and related mandatory legal requirements applicable to all products of that type.

2. The description of the product for a traditional speciality guaranteed referred to in point (b) of Article 19(1) of Regulation (EU) No 1151/2012 shall only mention the characteristics necessary to identify the product and its specific characteristics. It shall not repeat general obligations and, in particular, technical characteristics inherent to all products of that type and related mandatory legal requirements.

The description of the production method referred to in point (c) of Article 19(1) of Regulation (EU) No 1151/2012 shall only include the production method in force. Historical practices are only to be included if they are still followed. Only the method necessary for obtaining the specific product shall be described and in a way that enables reproduction of the product anywhere.

The key elements proving the product's traditional character shall include the main elements that have remained unchanged, with precise and well established references.

[8.766]
Article 8
Joint applications

A joint application as referred to in Article 49(1) of Regulation (EU) No 1151/2012 shall be submitted to the Commission by a Member State concerned, or by an applicant group in a third country concerned, directly or through the authorities of that third country. It shall include the declaration referred to in point (c) of Article 8(2) or point (b) of Article 20(2) of Regulation (EU) No 1151/2012 from all the Member States concerned. Requirements laid down in Articles 8 and 20 of Regulation (EU) No 1151/2012 shall be fulfilled in all Member States and third countries concerned.

[8.767]
Article 9
Procedural rules for oppositions

1. For the purposes of Article 51(2) of Regulation (EU) No 1151/2012 a reasoned statement of opposition shall be drawn up in accordance with the form set out in Annex III to this Regulation.

2. The period of three months referred to in the first subparagraph of Article 51(3) of Regulation (EU) No 1151/2012 shall start on the date on which the invitation to the interested parties to reach agreement among them is delivered by electronic means.

3. The notification referred to in Article 5 of Delegated Regulation (EU) No 664/2014 and the communication of the information to be provided to the Commission pursuant to the second subparagraph of Article 51(3) of Regulation (EU) No 1151/2012 shall be made within one month from the end of the consultations in accordance with the form set out in Annex IV to this Regulation.

[8.768]
Article 10
Procedural requirements for amendments to a product specification

1. Applications for approval of an amendment to the product specification for protected designations of origin and protected geographical indications which is not minor shall be drawn up in accordance with the form set out in Annex V. Those applications shall be completed in

accordance with the requirements laid down in Article 8 of Regulation (EU) No 1151/2012. The amended single document shall be drawn up in accordance with the form set out in Annex I to this Regulation. The reference to the publication of the product specification in the amended single document shall lead to the updated version of the product specification proposed.

Applications for approval of an amendment to the product specification for traditional specialities guaranteed which is not minor shall be drawn up in accordance with the form set out in Annex VI to this Regulation. Those applications shall be completed in accordance with the requirements laid down in Article 20 of Regulation (EU) No 1151/2012. The amended product specification shall be drawn up in accordance with the form set out in Annex II to this Regulation.

The information to be published in accordance with Article 50(2) of Regulation (EU) No 1151/2012 shall contain the duly completed application as referred to in the first and second subparagraphs of this paragraph.

2. Applications for approval of a minor amendment referred to in the second subparagraph of Article 53(2) of Regulation (EU) No 1151/2012 shall be drawn up in accordance with the form set out in Annex VII to this Regulation.

Applications for approval of a minor amendment concerning protected designations of origin or protected geographical indications shall be accompanied by the updated single document, if amended, which shall be drawn up in accordance with the form set out in Annex I. The reference to the publication of the product specification in the amended single document shall lead to the updated version of the product specification proposed.

For applications originating in the Union, Member States shall include a declaration that they consider that the application meets the conditions of Regulation (EU) No 1151/2012 and of the provisions adopted pursuant thereto and the publication reference of the updated product specification. For applications originating in third countries, the group concerned or the third country's authorities shall enclose the updated product specification. Applications for a minor amendment in cases referred to in the fifth subparagraph of Article 6(2) of Delegated Regulation (EU) No 664/2014 shall include the reference to the publication of the updated product specification, for applications originating in Member States, and the updated product specification, for applications originating in third countries.

Applications for approval of a minor amendment concerning traditional specialities guaranteed shall be accompanied by the updated product specification drawn up in accordance with the form set out in Annex II. Member States shall include a declaration that they consider that the application meets the conditions of Regulation (EU) No 1151/2012 and of the provisions adopted pursuant thereto.

The information to be published in accordance with the second subparagraph of Article 53(2) of Regulation (EU) No 1151/2012 shall contain the duly completed application as referred to in the first subparagraph of this paragraph.

3. The communication to the Commission of a temporary amendment referred to in the second subparagraph of Article 6(3) of Delegated Regulation (EU) No 664/2014 shall be drawn up in accordance with the form set out in Annex VIII to this Regulation. It shall be accompanied by the documents as provided for in the second subparagraph of Article 6(3) of Delegated Regulation (EU) No 664/2014.

4. The date of submission of an amendment application shall be the date on which the application is delivered to the Commission by electronic means. A delivery receipt shall be sent by the Commission.

[8.769]

Article 11

Cancellation

1. A request for cancellation of a registration pursuant to Article 54(1) of Regulation (EU) No 1151/2012 shall be drawn up in accordance with the form set out in Annex IX to this Regulation.

Requests for cancellation shall be accompanied by the declaration referred to in point (c) of Article 8(2) or point (b) of Article 20(2) of Regulation (EU) No 1151/2012.

2. The information to be published pursuant to Article 50(2) of Regulation (EU) No 1151/2012 shall contain the duly completed request for a cancellation as referred to in the first subparagraph of paragraph 1 of this Article.

[8.770]

Article 12

Means of submission

Applications, information and documents submitted to the Commission pursuant to Articles 6, 8, 9, 10, 11, and 15 shall be in electronic form.

[8.771]
Article 13
The use of symbols and indications
1. The Union symbols as referred to in Articles 12(2) and 23(2) of Regulation (EU) No 1151/2012 and established by Article 2 of Delegated Regulation (EU) No 664/2014 shall be reproduced as laid down in Annex X to this Regulation.
2. The indications 'PROTECTED DESIGNATION OF ORIGIN', 'PROTECTED GEOGRAPHICAL INDICATION' and 'TRADITIONAL SPECIALITY GUARANTEED' within the symbol may be used in any of the official languages of the Union as laid down in Annex X to this Regulation.
3. Where the Union symbols, indications or corresponding abbreviations as referred to in Articles 12 and 23 of Regulation (EU) No 1151/2012 appear on the labelling of a product, they shall be accompanied by the registered name.
4. Indications, abbreviations and symbols may be used in accordance with Article 44(1) of Regulation (EU) No 1151/2012 in media or in advertising supports for the purpose of divulgation of the quality scheme or of advertisement of the registered names.
5. Products placed on the market before the entry into force of this Regulation which do not comply with paragraphs 1 and 2 may remain on the market until the stocks are exhausted.

[8.772]
Article 14
Register of protected designations of origin and protected geographical indications and Register of traditional specialities guaranteed
1. Upon the entry into force of a legal instrument registering a protected designation of origin or a protected geographical indication the Commission shall record the following data in the Register of protected designations of origin and protected geographical indications referred to in Article 11(1) of Regulation (EU) No 1151/2012:
- (a) the registered name (or names) of the product;
- (b) the class of the product as referred to in Annex XI to this Regulation;
- (c) reference to the instrument registering the name;
- (d) information that the name is protected as a geographical indication or as a designation of origin;
- (e) indication of the country or countries of origin.

2. Upon the entry into force of a legal instrument registering a traditional speciality guaranteed, the Commission shall record the following data in the Register of traditional specialities guaranteed referred to in Article 22(1) of Regulation (EU) No 1151/2012:
- (a) the registered name (or names) of the product;
- (b) the class of the product as referred to in Annex XI to this Regulation;
- (c) reference to the instrument registering the name;
- (d) indication of the country or countries of the group or groups that made the application;
- (e) information whether the decision on registration provides that the name of the traditional speciality guaranteed is to be accompanied by the claim as referred to in Article 18(3) of Regulation (EU) No 1151/2012;
- (f) only for applications received before the entry into force of Regulation (EU) No 1151/2012, information whether the registration is without reservation of the name.

3. Where the Commission approves an amendment to the product specification that includes a change to the information recorded in the Registers, it shall delete the original data and record the new data with effect from the entry into force of the decision approving the amendment.
4. When a cancellation takes effect, the Commission shall delete the name from the Register concerned.

[8.773]
Article 15
Transitional rules
A request for publication of the single document submitted by a Member State pursuant to Article 8(1) of Delegated Regulation (EU) No 664/2014 in respect of a protected designation of origin or a protected geographical indication registered prior to 31 March 2006 shall be drawn up in accordance with the form set out in Annex I to this Regulation.

[8.774]
Article 16
Entry into force and application
This Regulation shall enter into force on the third day following that of its publication in the *Official Journal of the European Union*.
Article 9(1) shall only apply to opposition procedures for which the three-month period established in the first subparagraph of Article 51(1) of Regulation (EU) No 1151/2012 has not started on the date of entry into force of this Regulation.

Article 9(3) shall only apply to opposition procedures for which the three-month period established in the first subparagraph of Article 51(1) of Regulation (EU) No 1151/2012 has not expired on the date of entry into force of this Regulation.
The first sentence of point 2 of Annex X shall apply from 1 January 2016, without prejudice to products already placed on the market before that date.
This Regulation shall be binding in its entirety and directly applicable in all Member States.

ANNEX I
SINGLE DOCUMENT

[8.775]
[Insert name, as in 1 below:] ' . . . '

EU No: [for EU use only]
[Select one, 'X':] ☐ PDO ☐ PGI

1. **Name(s) [of PDO or PGI]**
[Insert the name proposed for registration or, in the case of an application for approval of an amendment to a product specification or a request for publication pursuant to Article 15 of this Regulation, the registered name]

2. **Member State or Third Country**
. . .

3. **Description of the agricultural product or foodstuff**

3.1. *Type of product [listed in Annex XI]*
. . .

3.2. *Description of the product to which the name in (1) applies*
[Main points referred to in point (b) of Article 7(1) of Regulation (EU) No 1151/2012. To identify the product use definitions and standards commonly used for that product. In the description of the product, focus on its specificity, using measurement units and common or technical terms of comparison, without including technical characteristics inherent to all products of that type and related mandatory legal requirements applicable to all products of that type (Article 7(1) of this Regulation).]

3.3. *Feed (for products of animal origin only) and raw materials (for processed products only)*
[For PDO: give confirmation that feed and raw material are from the area. In case feed or raw material come from outside the area, provide a detailed description of those exceptions and state justifications. Those exceptions must be in line with the rules adopted pursuant to Article 5, paragraph 4, of Regulation (EU) No 1151/2012.
For PGI: State any quality requirements, or restrictions on origin of raw materials. State justifications for any such restrictions. Such restrictions must be in line with the rules adopted pursuant to Article 5, paragraph 4, of Regulation (EU) No 1151/2012 and must be justified in relation to the link referred to in point (f) of Article 7(1) of that Regulation.]
. . .

3.4. *Specific steps in production that must take place in the identified geographical area*
[State justifications for any restrictions or derogations.]
. . .

3.5. *Specific rules concerning slicing, grating, packaging, etc. of the product the registered name refers to*
[If none, leave blank. State product-specific justifications for any restrictions.]
. . .

3.6. *Specific rules concerning labelling of the product the registered name refers to*
[If none, leave blank. State justifications for any restrictions.]
. . .

4. **Concise definition of the geographical area**
[Where appropriate, insert a map of the area]
. . .

5. **Link with the geographical area**
[For PDO: causal link between the quality or characteristics of the product and the geographical environment, with its inherent natural and human factors, including, where appropriate, elements of the product description or production method justifying the link.
For PGI: causal link between the geographical origin and, where appropriate, a given quality, the reputation or other characteristics of the product.

State explicitly on which ones of the given factors (reputation, given quality, other characteristic of the product) the causal link is based and give information only with respect to the relevant factors, including, where appropriate, elements of the product description or production method justifying the link.]

Reference to publication of the product specification

(the second subparagraph of Article 6(1) of this Regulation)

. . .

ANNEX II
PRODUCT SPECIFICATION OF A TRADITIONAL SPECIALITY GUARANTEED

[8.776]
[Insert name, as in 1. below:] ''

EU No: [for EU use only]

Member State or Third Country ''

1. **Name(s) to be registered**
   . . .

2. **Type of product [as in Annex XI]**
   . . .

3. **Grounds for registration**

3.1. *Whether the product:*
☐ results from a mode of production, processing or composition corresponding to traditional practice for that product or foodstuff
☐ is produced from raw materials or ingredients that are those traditionally used.
[Provide explanation]

3.2. *Whether the name:*
☐ has been traditionally used to refer to the specific product
☐ identifies the traditional character or specific character of the product
[Provide explanation]

4. **Description**

4.1. *Description of the product to which the name under point 1 applies, including its main physical, chemical, microbiological or organoleptic characteristics showing the product's specific character (Article 7(2) of this Regulation)*

. . .

4.2. *Description of the production method of the product to which the name under point 1 applies that the producers must follow including, where appropriate, the nature and characteristics of the raw materials or ingredients used, and the method by which the product is prepared (Article 7(2) of this Regulation)*

. . .

4.3. *Description of the key elements establishing the product's traditional character (Article 7(2) of this Regulation)*

. . .

ANNEX III
REASONED STATEMENT OF OPPOSITION

[8.777]
[Select one, 'X':] ☐ PDO ☐ PGI ☐ TSG

1. **Name of product**
   [as given in *Official Journal (OJ)* publication]
   . . .

2. **Official reference**
   [as given in *Official Journal (OJ)* publication]
   Reference number: . . .
   Date of *OJ* publication: . . .

3. **Contact details**

Contact person: Title (Mr, Ms . . .): Name: . . .

. . .

Group/organisation/individual:

Or national authority:

Department: . . .

Address: . . .

Telephone + . . .

e-mail address: . . .

4. **Reason for the opposition:**

For PDO PGI:

☐ Non-compliance with the conditions laid down in Article 5 and 7(1) of Regulation (EU) No 1151/2012

☐ Registration of the name would be contrary to Article 6(2) of Regulation (EU) No 1151/2012 (plant variety or animal breed)

☐ Registration of the name would be contrary to Article 6(3) of Regulation (EU) No 1151/2012 (name wholly or partially homonymous)

☐ Registration of the name would be contrary to Article 6(4) of Regulation (EU) No 1151/2012 (existing trade mark)

☐ Registration would jeopardize the existence of names, trade marks or products as specified in point (c) of Article 10(1) of Regulation (EU) No 1151/2012

☐ The name proposed for registration is generic; details to be provided as set down in point (d) of Article 10(1) of Regulation (EU) No 1151/2012

For TSG:

☐ Non-compliance with the conditions laid down in Article 18 of Regulation (EU) No 1151/2012

☐ Registration of the name would be incompatible with the terms of Regulation (EU) No 1151/2012 (point (a) of Article 21(1) of Regulation (EU) No 1151/2012).

☐ The name proposed for registration is lawful, renowned and economically significant for similar agricultural products or foodstuffs (point (b) of Article 21(1) of Regulation (EU) No 1151/2012).

5. **Detail of opposition**

Provide duly substantiated reasons and justification for the opposition.

Provide also a statement explaining the legitimate interest of the opposition, unless the opposition is lodged by the national authorities, in which case no statement of legitimate interest is required. The statement of opposition should be signed and dated.

ANNEX IV
NOTIFICATION OF END OF CONSULTATIONS FOLLOWING THE OPPOSITION PROCEDURE

[8.778]

[Select one, 'X':] ☐ PDO ☐ PGI ☐ TSG

1. **Name of product**

[as given in *Official Journal (OJ)* publication]

2. **Official reference [as given in *Official Journal (OJ)* publication]**

Reference number:

Date of *OJ* publication:

3. **Result of consultations**

3.1. *Agreement was reached with the following opponent(s):*

[annex copies of letters showing agreement and all the factors that enabled the agreement (Article 5 of Delegated Regulation (EU) No 664/2014]

3.2. *Agreement was not reached with the following opponent(s):*

[annex the information referred to in the last sentence of the second subparagraph of Article 51(3) of Regulation (EU) No 1151/2012]

4. **Product Specification and single document**

4.1. *The product specification has been amended:*

. . . Yes(*) . . . No

(*) If 'Yes', annex description of amendments and the amended product specification

4.2. *The single document has been amended (only for PDO and PGI):*

. . . Yes(*) . . . No

(*) If 'Yes', annex copy of updated document

5. **Dated and signed**

[Name]

[Department/Organisation]

[Address]

[Telephone: +]

[e-mail address:]

ANNEX V
APPLICATION FOR APPROVAL OF AN AMENDMENT TO THE PRODUCT SPECIFICATION OF PROTECTED DESIGNATIONS OF ORIGIN/PROTECTED GEOGRAPHICAL INDICATIONS WHICH IS NOT MINOR

[8.779]

Application for approval of an amendment in accordance with the first subparagraph of Article 53(2), of Regulation (EU) No 1151/2012

[Registered name] ' . . . '

EU No: [for EU use only]

[Select one, 'X':] ☐ PDO ☐ PGI

1. **Applicant group and legitimate interest**

[Provide name, address, telephone and e-mail address of the group proposing the amendment (for third countries applications provide also name and address of the authorities or, if available, bodies verifying compliance with the provision of the product specification). Provide also a statement explaining the legitimate interest of the applicant group]

2. **Member State or third country**

. . .

3. **Heading in the product specification affected by the amendment(s)**

☐ Name of product
☐ Description of product
☐ Geographical area
☐ Proof of origin
☐ Method of production
☐ Link
☐ Labelling
☐ Other [to be specified]

4. **Type of amendment(s)**

☐ Amendment to product specification of a registered PDO or PGI not to be qualified as minor in accordance with the third subparagraph of Article 53(2) of Regulation (EU) No 1151/2012.

☐ Amendment to product specification of registered PDO or PGI for which a Single Document (or equivalent) has not been published not to be qualified as minor in accordance with the third subparagraph of Article 53(2) of Regulation (EU) No 1151/2012

5. **Amendment(s)**

[For each heading checked in section 3 above, provide an exhaustive description and the specific reasons for each amendment. The original product specification and, where relevant, the original single document must be compared in detail with the proposed amended versions for each amendment. The amendment application must be self-sufficient. The information given in this section must be exhaustive (the first and the second subparagraph of Article 6(1) of Delegated Regulation (EU) No 664/2014].

ANNEX VI
APPLICATION FOR APPROVAL OF AN AMENDMENT TO THE PRODUCT SPECIFICATION OF TRADITIONAL SPECIALITIES GUARANTEED WHICH IS NOT MINOR

[8.780]

Application for approval of an amendment in accordance with the first subparagraph of Article 53(2), of Regulation (EU) No 1151/2012

[Registered name] ''

EU No: [for EU use only]

1. **Applicant group and legitimate interest**
   Name of the group
   Address
   Telephone: +
   e-mail address:
   Provide a statement explaining the legitimate interest of the group proposing the amendment.
2. **Member State or third country**
   . . .
3. **Heading in the product specification affected by the amendment(s)**
   ☐ Name of product
   ☐ Description of product
   ☐ Method of production
   ☐ Other [to be specified]
4. **Type of amendment(s)**
   ☐ Amendment to product specification of registered TSG not to be qualified as minor in accordance with the fourth subparagraph of Article 53(2) of Regulation (EU) No 1151/2012.
5. **Amendment(s)**
   [For each heading checked in section 3 above, provide an exhaustive description and the specific reasons for each amendment. The original product specification must be compared in detail with the proposed amended version for each amendment. The amendment application must be self-sufficient. The information given in this section must be exhaustive (the first and the second subparagraph of Article 6(1) of Delegated Regulation (EU) No 664/2014].

ANNEX VII
APPLICATION FOR APPROVAL OF A MINOR AMENDMENT

[8.781]

Application for approval of a minor amendment in accordance with the second subparagraph of Article 53(2), of Regulation (EU) No 1151/2012

[Registered name] ' . . . '

EU No: [for EU use only]

[Select one, 'X':] ☐ PDO ☐ PGI ☐ TSG

1. **Applicant group and legitimate interest**
   [Provide name, address, telephone and e-mail address of the group proposing the amendment (for applications concerning PDO and PGI from third countries provide also name and address of the authorities or, if available, bodies verifying compliance with the provision of the product specification). Provide also a statement explaining the legitimate interest of the applicant group]
2. **Member State or third country**
   . . .
3. **Heading in the product specification affected by the amendment(s)**
   ☐ Description of product
   ☐ Proof of origin
   ☐ Method of production
   ☐ Link
   ☐ Labelling
   ☐ Other [to be specified]
4. **Type of amendment(s)**

☐ Amendment to product specification of registered PDO or PGI to be qualified as minor in accordance with the third subparagraph of Article 53(2) of Regulation (EU) No 1151/2012, that requires no amendment to the published single document
☐ Amendment to product specification of registered PDO or PGI to be qualified as minor in accordance with the third subparagraph of Article 53(2) of Regulation (EU) No 1151/2012, that requires an amendment to the published single document
☐ Amendment to product specification of registered PDO or PGI to be qualified as minor in accordance with the third subparagraph of Article 53(2) of Regulation (EU) No 1151/2012, for which a single document (or equivalent) has not been published.
☐ Amendment to product specification of registered TSG to be qualified as minor in accordance with the fourth subparagraph of Article 53(2) of Regulation (EU) No 1151/2012.

5. **Amendment(s)**
[For each heading checked in section above, provide a description and the summary of reasons for each amendment. The original product specification and, where relevant, the original single document must be compared with the proposed amended versions for each amendment. Provide also a clear reasoning why in accordance with the third and/or the fourth subparagraph of Article 53(2) of Regulation (EU) No 1151/2012, the amendment is to be qualified as minor. The minor amendment application must be self-sufficient (the second subparagraph of Article 6(2) of Delegated Regulation (EU) No 664/2014].

6. **Updated Product Specification (only for PDO and PGI)**
[Only in cases referred to in the fifth subparagraph of Article 6(2) of Delegated Regulation (EU) No 664/2014]:
   a) in case of applications submitted by Member States insert the reference to publication of the updated product specification;
   b) in case of applications from third countries, insert the updated product specification.]

ANNEX VIII
COMMUNICATION OF TEMPORARY AMENDMENT

[8.782]
Communication concerning temporary amendment in accordance with the second subparagraph of Article 6(3) of Delegated Regulation (EU) No 664/2014.
[Registered name] ''

EU No: [for EU use only]
[Select one, 'X':] ☐ PDO ☐ PGI ☐ TSG

1. **Member State or third country**
. . .

2. **Amendment(s)**
[Indicate the heading in the product specification affected by the temporary amendment. Provide a detailed description and the reasons of each approved temporary amendment, including a description and an assessment of the consequences of that amendment on the requirements and criteria that qualify the product under the quality scheme (Article 5(1) and (2) and Article 18(1) and (2) of Regulation (EU) No 1151/2012 for PDO, PGI and TSG respectively). Provide also a detailed description of the measures justifying the temporary amendments (sanitary and phyto-sanitary measures, formal recognition of natural disasters or adverse weather conditions etc.) and the reasons for those measures to be taken. Describe also the relation between those measures and the approved temporary amendment.]

ANNEX IX
CANCELLATION REQUEST

[8.783]
Cancellation request in accordance with Article 54(1) of Regulation (EU) No 1151/2012

[Registered name:] ' . . . '

EU No: [for EU use only]
[Select one, 'X':] ☐ PGI ☐ PDO ☐ TSG

1. **Registered name proposed for cancellation**
. . .

2. **Member State or Third Country**
. . .

3. **Type of product [as in Annex XI]**

   . . .

4. **Person or body making request for cancellation**
   [Provide name, address, telephone and e-mail address of the natural or legal person or of the producers referred to in Article 54(1) of Regulation (EU) No 1151/2012 requesting cancellation (for requests concerning PDO and PGI from third countries provide also name and address of the authorities or, if available, bodies verifying compliance with the provision of the product specification). Provide also a statement explaining the legitimate interest of the natural or legal person requesting cancellation]

   . . .

5. **Type of cancellation and related reasons**
   ☐ In accordance with the first subparagraph of Article 54(1) of Regulation (EU) No 1151/2012
   ☐ point (a)
   [Provide the detailed reasons and, where appropriate, evidence for the cancellation of the registration of the name in accordance with point (a) of first subparagraph of Article 54(1) of Regulation (EU) No 1151/2012.]
   ☐ point (b)
   [Provide the detailed reasons and, where appropriate, evidence for the cancellation of the registration of the name in accordance with point (b) of first subparagraph of Article 54(1) of Regulation (EU) No 1151/2012.]
   ☐ In accordance with the second subparagraph of Article 54(1) of Regulation (EU) No 1151/2012
   [Provide the detailed reasons and, where appropriate, evidence for the cancellation of the registration of the name in accordance with the second subparagraph of Article 54(1) of Regulation (EU) No 1151/2012.]

ANNEX X
REPRODUCTION OF THE UNION SYMBOLS AND INDICATIONS FOR PDO PGI TSG

[8.784]

1. **Union symbols in colour**

(**Editor's Note:** *the colour logos are not reproduced in this work. Please refer to the original.*)

2. **Union symbols in black and white**
   Use of the symbols in black and white is allowed only when black and white are the only ink colours used on the package.

When used in black and white Union symbols are reproduced as follows:

Union symbols in black and white in negative

If the background of the packaging or labelling is dark, the symbols may be used in negative format as follows:

3. **Typography**
   Times Roman capitals must be used for the text.

4. **Reduction**
   The minimum size of the Union symbols is 15 mm in diameter, however, it may be reduced to 10 mm in case of small packages or products.

5. **'Protected Designation of Origin' and its abbreviation in EU languages**
   EU Language | Term | Abbreviation |
   BG | защитено наименование за произход | ЗНП |
   ES | denominación de origen protegida | DOP |
   CS | chráněné označení původu | CHOP |
   DA | beskyttet oprindelsesbetegnelse | BOB |
   DE | geschützte Ursprungsbezeichnung | g.U. |
   ET | kaitstud päritolunimetus | KPN |
   EL | προστατευόμενη ονομασία προέλευσης | ΠΟΠ |
   EN | protected designation of origin | PDO |
   FR | appellation d'origine protégée | AOP |
   GA | bunús ainmníochta cosanta | BAC |

HR | zaštićena oznaka izvornosti | ZOI |
IT | denominazione d'origine protetta | DOP |
LV | aizsargāts cilmes vietas nosaukums | ACVN |
LT | saugoma kilmės vietos nuoroda | SKVN |
HU | oltalom alatt álló eredetmegjelölés | OEM |
MT | denominazzjoni protetta ta' oriġini | DPO |
NL | beschermde oorsprongsbenaming | BOB |
PL | chroniona nazwa pochodzenia | CHNP |
PT | denominação de origem protegida | DOP |
RO | denumire de origine protejată | DOP |
SK | chránené označenie pôvodu | CHOP |
SL | zaščitena označba porekla | ZOP |
FI | suojattu alkuperänimitys | SAN |
SV | skyddad ursprungsbeteckning | SUB |

6. **'Protected Geographical Indication' and its abbreviation in EU languages**
EU Language | Term | Abbreviation |
BG | защитено географско указание | ЗГУ |
ES | indicación geográfica protegida | IGP |
CS | chráněné zeměpisné označení | CHZO |
DA | beskyttet geografisk betegnelse | BGB |
DE | geschützte geografische Angabe | g.g.A. |
ET | kaitstud geograafiline tähis | KGT |
EL | προστατευόμενη γεωγραφική ένδειξη | ΠΓΕ |
EN | protected geographical indication | PGI |
FR | indication géographique protégée | IGP |
GA | sonra geografach cosanta | SGC |
HR | zaštićena oznaka zemljopisnog podrijetla | ZOZP |
IT | indicazione geografica protetta | IGP |
LV | aizsargāta ģeogrāfiskās izcelsmes norāde | AĢIN |
LT | saugoma geografinė nuoroda | SGN |
HU | oltalom alatt álló földrajzi jelzés | OFJ |
MT | indikazzjoni ġeografika protetta | IĠP |
NL | beschermde geografische aanduiding | BGA |
PL | chronione oznaczenie geograficzne | CHOG |
PT | indicação geográfica protegida | IGP |
RO | indicaţie geografică protejată | IGP |
SK | chránené zemepisné označenie | CHZO |
SL | zaščitena geografska označba | ZGO |
FI | suojattu maantieteellinen merkintä | SMM |
SV | skyddad geografisk beteckning | SGB |

7. **'Traditional Speciality Guaranteed' and its abbreviation in EU languages**
EU language | Term | Abbreviation |
BG | храна с традиционно специфичен характер | ХТСХ |
ES | especialidad tradicional garantizada | ETG |
CS | zaručená tradiční specialita | ZTS |
DA | garanteret traditionel specialitet | GTS |
DE | garantiert traditionelle Spezialität | g.t.S. |
ET | garanteeritud traditsiooniline toode | GTT |
EL | εγγυημένο παραδοσιακό ιδιότυπο προϊόν | Ε Π Ι Π |
EN | traditional speciality guaranteed | TSG |
FR | spécialité traditionnelle garantie | STG |
GA | speisialtacht thraidisiúnta ráthaithe | STR |
HR | zajamčeno tradicionalni specijalitet | ZTS |
IT | specialità tradizionale garantita | STG |
LV | garantēta tradicionālā īpatnība | GTI |
LT | garantuotas tradicinis gaminys | GTG |
HU | hagyományos különleges termék | HKT |
MT | speċjalità tradizzjonali garantita | STG |
NL | gegarandeerde traditionele specialiteit | GTS |
PL | gwarantowana tradycyjna specjalność | GTS |
PT | especialidade tradicional garantida | ETG |
RO | specialitate tradiţională garantată | STG |
SK | zaručená tradičná špecialita | ZTŠ |
SL | zajamčena tradicionalna posebnost | ZTP |
FI | aito perinteinen tuote | APT |
SV | garanterad traditionell specialitet | GTS |

ANNEX XI
CLASSIFICATION OF PRODUCTS

[8.785]
1. **Agricultural products intended for the human consumption listed in Annex I to the Treaty**
— Class 1.1. Fresh meat (and offal)
— Class 1.2. Meat products (cooked, salted, smoked, etc.)
— Class 1.3. Cheeses
— Class 1.4. Other products of animal origin (eggs, honey, various dairy products except butter, etc.)
— Class 1.5. Oils and fats (butter, margarine, oil, etc.)
— Class 1.6. Fruit, vegetables and cereals fresh or processed
— Class 1.7. Fresh fish, molluscs, and crustaceans and products derived therefrom
— Class 1.8. other products listed in Annex I to the Treaty (spices etc.)

2. **Agricultural products and foodstuffs referred to in Annex I to Regulation (EU) No 1151/2012**
I. Designations of Origin and Geographical indications
— Class 2.1. beer,
— Class 2.2. chocolate and derived products,
— Class 2.3. bread, pastry, cakes, confectionery, biscuits and other baker's wares
— Class 2.4. beverages made from plant extracts,
— Class 2.5. pasta,
— Class 2.6. salt,
— Class 2.7. natural gums and resins,
— Class 2.8. mustard paste,
— Class 2.9. hay,
— Class 2.10. essential oils,
— Class 2.11. cork,
— Class 2.12. cochineal,
— Class 2.13. flowers and ornamental plants,
— Class 2.14. cotton,
— Class 2.15. wool,
— Class 2.16. wicker,
— Class 2.17. scutched flax,
— Class 2.18. leather,
— Class 2.19. fur,
— Class 2.20. feather.
II. Traditional specialities guaranteed
— Class 2.21. prepared meals,
— Class 2.22. beer,
— Class 2.23. chocolate and derived products,
— Class 2.24. bread, pastry, cakes, confectionery, biscuits and other baker's wares,
— Class 2.25. beverages made from plant extracts,
— Class 2.26. pasta,
— Class 2.27. salt.

REGULATION OF THE EUROPEAN PARLIAMENT AND OF THE COUNCIL

(2015/1843/EU)
of 06 October 2015

laying down Union procedures in the field of the common commercial policy in order to ensure the exercise of the Union's rights under international trade rules, in particular those established under the auspices of the World Trade Organization

(codification)

NOTES
Date of publication in OJ: OJ L272, 16.10.2015, p 1.

THE EUROPEAN PARLIAMENT AND THE COUNCIL OF THE EUROPEAN UNION,
Having regard to the Treaty on the Functioning of the European Union, and in particular Article 207(2) thereof,
Having regard to the proposal from the European Commission,
After transmission of the draft legislative act to the national parliaments,
Having regard to the opinion of the European Economic and Social Committee,[1]

Acting in accordance with the ordinary legislative procedure,[2]

Whereas:

(1) Council Regulation (EC) No 3286/94[3] has been substantially amended several times.[4] In the interests of clarity and rationality, that Regulation should be codified.

(2) It is necessary that the common commercial policy be based on uniform principles, in particular with regard to commercial defence.

(3) It appears necessary to provide for Union procedures to ensure the effective exercise of the rights of the Union under international trade rules.

(4) International trade rules are primarily those established under the auspices of the World Trade Organization ('WTO') and laid down in the Annexes to the WTO Agreement, but they can also include rules laid down in any other agreement to which the Union is a party and which are applicable to trade between the Union and third countries. It is appropriate to give a clear idea of the types of agreements to which the term 'international trade rules' refers.

(5) Union procedures to ensure the effective exercise of the rights of the Union under international trade rules should be based on a legal mechanism under Union law which is fully transparent, and ensures that the decision to invoke the Union's rights under international trade rules is taken on the basis of accurate factual information and legal analysis.

(6) Such a mechanism should aim to provide procedural means for requesting that the Union institutions react to obstacles to trade that are adopted or maintained by third countries and which cause injury or otherwise adverse trade effects, provided that a right of action exists, in respect of such obstacles, under applicable international trade rules.

(7) The right of Member States to resort to such a mechanism should be without prejudice to the possibility for Member States to raise the same or similar matters through other existing Union procedures, and in particular before the committee established by Article 207(3) of the Treaty.

(8) Regard should be paid to the institutional role of the committee established by Article 207(3) of the Treaty in formulating advice for the institutions of the Union on all issues of commercial policy. Therefore, that committee should be kept informed of the development of individual cases, in order to enable it to consider their broader policy implications.

(9) It is appropriate to require that the Union act in compliance with its international obligations and, where such obligations result from agreements, that the Union maintain the balance of rights and obligations which it is the purpose of those agreements to establish.

(10) It is also appropriate to provide that any measures taken under the procedures in question should also be in conformity with the Union's international obligations, as well as being without prejudice to other measures in cases not covered by this Regulation which might be adopted directly pursuant to Article 207 of the Treaty.

(11) The rules of procedure to be followed during the examination procedure provided for in this Regulation should also be laid down, in particular as regards the rights and obligations of the Union authorities and the parties involved, and the conditions under which interested parties may have access to information and may ask to be informed of the essential facts and considerations resulting from the examination procedure.

(12) In acting pursuant to this Regulation, the Union has to bear in mind the need for rapid and effective action through the application of the decision-making procedures provided for in this Regulation.

(13) It is incumbent on the Commission to act in respect of obstacles to trade that are adopted or maintained by third countries, within the framework of the Union's international rights and obligations, only when the interests of the Union call for intervention. When assessing such interests, the Commission should give due consideration to the views of all interested parties in the proceedings.

(14) The implementation of the examination procedures provided for in this Regulation requires uniform conditions for the adoption of decisions on the conduct of those examination procedures and measures resulting therefrom. Those measures should be adopted in accordance with Regulation (EU) No 182/2011 of the European Parliament and of the Council.[5]

(15) The advisory procedure should be used for the suspension of ongoing examinations given the effects of such measures and their sequential logic in relation to the adoption of measures.

(16) The European Parliament and the Council should be kept informed of the developments under this Regulation, in order to enable them to consider their broader policy implications.

(17) Moreover, in cases where an agreement with a third country appears to be the most appropriate means of resolving a dispute arising from an obstacle to trade, negotiations to this end should be conducted in accordance with the procedures established in Article 207 of the Treaty,

NOTES

1 Opinion of 10 December 2014 (not yet published in the Official Journal).

2 Position of the European Parliament of 7 July 2015 (not yet published in the Official Journal) and decision of the Council of 18 September 2015.

3 Council Regulation (EC) No 3286/94 of 22 December 1994 laying down Community procedures in the field of the common commercial policy in order to ensure the exercise of the Community's rights under international trade rules, in particular those established under the auspices of the World Trade Organization (OJ L349, 31.12.1994, p 71).

[4] See Annex I.

[5] Regulation (EU) No 182/2011 of the European Parliament and of the Council of 16 February 2011 laying down the rules and general principles concerning mechanisms for control by Member States of the Commission's exercise of implementing powers (OJ L55, 28.2.2011, p 13).

HAVE ADOPTED THIS REGULATION:

[8.786]
Article 1
Subject matter

This Regulation provides for Union procedures in the field of the common commercial policy in order to ensure the exercise of the Union's rights under international trade rules, in particular those established under the auspices of the World Trade Organization ('WTO') which, subject to compliance with existing international obligations and procedures, aim to:

(a) responding to obstacles to trade that have an effect on the market of the Union, with a view to removing the injury resulting therefrom;

(b) responding to obstacles to trade that have an effect on the market of a third country, with a view to removing the adverse trade effects resulting therefrom.

The procedures referred to in the first paragraph shall be applied in particular to the initiation and subsequent conduct and termination of international dispute settlement procedures in the area of common commercial policy.

[8.787]
Article 2
Definitions

1. For the purposes of this Regulation, the following definitions apply:

(a) 'obstacles to trade' means any trade practice adopted or maintained by a third country in respect of which international trade rules establish a right of action; such a right of action exists when international trade rules either prohibit a practice outright, or give another party affected by the practice a right to seek elimination of the effect of the practice in question;

(b) 'the Union's rights' means the international trade rights of which the Union may avail itself under international trade rules; in this context, 'international trade rules' are primarily those established under the auspices of the WTO and laid down in the Annexes to the WTO Agreement, but they can also be those laid down in any other agreement to which the Union is a party and which sets out rules applicable to trade between the Union and third countries;

(c) 'injury' means any material injury which an obstacle to trade causes or threatens to cause, in respect of a product or service, to a Union industry, on the market of the Union;

(d) 'adverse trade effects' means the adverse effects which an obstacle to trade causes or threatens to cause, in respect of a product or service, to Union enterprises, on the market of any third country, and which have a material impact on the economy of the Union or of a region of the Union, or on a sector of economic activity in the Union; the fact that the complainant suffers from such adverse effects shall not be considered sufficient to justify, on its own, the Union institutions proceeding with any action;

(e) 'Union industry' means either:

(i) all Union producers or providers:

— of products or services identical or similar to the product or service which is the subject of an obstacle to trade;

— of products or services competing directly with that product or service;

or

— who are consumers or processors of the product or consumers or users of the service which is the subject of an obstacle to trade;

or

(ii) all those producers or providers whose combined output constitutes a major proportion of total Union production of the products or services in question; however:

— when producers or providers are related to the exporters or importers or are themselves importers of the product or service alleged to be the subject of obstacles to trade, the term 'Union industry' may be interpreted as referring to the rest of the producers or providers;

— in particular circumstances, the producers or providers within a region of the Union may be regarded as the Union industry if their collective output constitutes the major proportion of the output of the product or service in question in the Member State or Member States within which the region is located provided that the effect of the obstacle to trade is concentrated in that Member State or those Member States;

(f) 'Union enterprise' means a company or firm formed in accordance with the law of a Member State and having its registered office, central administration or principal place of business within the Union, that is directly concerned by the production of goods or the provision of services which are the subject of the obstacle to trade;

(g) 'services' means those services in respect of which international agreements can be concluded by the Union on the basis of Article 207 of the Treaty.

2. For the purposes of this Regulation, the notion of 'providers of services' in the context of both the term 'Union industry' and the term 'Union enterprise' is without prejudice to the non-commercial nature which the provision of any particular service may have according to the legislation or regulation of a Member State.

[8.788]

Article 3

Complaint on behalf of the Union industry

1. Any natural or legal person, or any association not having legal personality, acting on behalf of a Union industry which considers that it has suffered injury as a result of obstacles to trade that have an effect on the market of the Union may lodge a written complaint.

2. The complaint shall contain sufficient evidence of the existence of the obstacles to trade and of the injury resulting therefrom. Evidence of injury shall be given on the basis of the illustrative list of factors set out in Article 11, where applicable.

[8.789]

Article 4

Complaint on behalf of Union enterprises

1. Any Union enterprise, or any association, having or not legal personality, acting on behalf of one or more Union enterprises, which considers that such Union enterprises have suffered adverse trade effects as a result of obstacles to trade that have an effect on the market of a third country may lodge a written complaint.

2. The complaint shall contain sufficient evidence of the existence of the obstacles to trade and of the adverse trade effects resulting therefrom. Evidence of adverse trade effects shall be given on the basis of the illustrative list of factors set out in Article 11, where applicable.

[8.790]

Article 5

Complaint procedures

1. The complaints referred to in Articles 3 and 4 shall be submitted to the Commission, which shall send a copy thereof to the Member States.

2. The complaint may be withdrawn, in which case the procedure may be terminated unless such termination would not be in the interests of the Union.

3. Where it becomes apparent that the complaint does not provide sufficient evidence to justify initiating an investigation, the complainant shall be informed accordingly.

The Commission shall inform the Member States where it decides that the complaint does not provide sufficient evidence to justify initiating an investigation.

4. The Commission shall take a decision as soon as possible on the opening of a Union examination procedure following any complaint made in accordance with Article 3 or 4.

The decision shall be taken within 45 days of the lodging of the complaint. That period may be suspended at the request, or with the agreement, of the complainant, in order to allow for the provision of complementary information which may be needed to fully assess the validity of the complainant's case.

[8.791]

Article 6

Request by a Member State

1. Any Member State may ask the Commission to initiate the procedures referred to in Article 1.

2. The Member State shall supply the Commission with sufficient evidence to support its request, as regards obstacles to trade and of any effects resulting therefrom. Where evidence of injury or of adverse trade effects is appropriate, it shall be given on the basis of the illustrative list of factors set out in Article 11, where applicable.

3. The Commission shall notify the other Member States of the requests without delay.

4. Where it becomes apparent that the request does not provide sufficient evidence to justify initiating an investigation, the Member State shall be informed accordingly.

The Commission shall inform the Member States where it decides that the request does not provide sufficient evidence to justify initiating an investigation.

5. The Commission shall take a decision as soon as possible on the opening of a Union examination procedure following any request by a Member State made in accordance with this Article. The decision shall be taken within 45 days of the request. That period may be suspended at the request, or with the agreement, of the referring Member State, in order to allow for the provision of complementary information which may be needed to fully assess the validity of the case presented by the referring Member State.

[8.792]
Article 7
Committee procedure

1. The Commission shall be assisted by the Trade Barriers Committee ('the Committee'). That Committee shall be a committee within the meaning of Regulation (EU) No 182/2011.
2. Where reference is made to this paragraph, Article 4 of Regulation (EU) No 182/2011 shall apply.
3. Where reference is made to this paragraph, Article 5 of Regulation (EU) No 182/2011 shall apply.

[8.793]
Article 8
Information to the European Parliament and to the Council

The Commission shall refer to the European Parliament and to the Council information provided pursuant to this Regulation, to allow them to consider any wider implications for the common commercial policy.

[8.794]
Article 9
Union examination procedure

1. Where it is apparent to the Commission that there is sufficient evidence to justify initiating an examination procedure and that it is necessary in the interest of the Union, the Commission shall:
   (a) announce the initiation of an examination procedure in the *Official Journal of the European Union;* the announcement shall indicate the product or service and the countries concerned, give a summary of the information received, and provide that all relevant information is to be communicated to the Commission; it shall state the period within which interested parties may apply to be heard orally by the Commission in accordance with paragraph 5;
   (b) officially notify the representatives of the country or countries which are the subject of the procedure and with whom, where appropriate, consultations may be held;
   (c) conduct the examination at Union level, acting in cooperation with the Member States.

The Commission shall inform the Member States where it decides that the complaint provides sufficient evidence to justify initiating an investigation.

2. Where necessary, the Commission shall:
   (a) seek all the information it deems necessary and attempt to check this information with importers, traders, agents, producers, trade associations and organisations, provided that the undertakings or organisations concerned give their consent;
   (b) carry out investigations in the territory of third countries, provided that the governments of those countries have been officially notified and raised no objection within a reasonable time.

The Commission shall be assisted in its investigations by officials of the Member State in whose territory the checks are carried out, provided that the Member State in question so requests.

3. Member States shall supply the Commission, upon request, with all information necessary for the examination, in accordance with the detailed arrangements laid down by the Commission.
4. The complainants and the exporters and importers concerned and the representatives of the country or countries concerned may:
   (a) inspect all information made available to the Commission except for internal documents for the use of the Commission and the administrations, provided that such information is relevant to the protection of their interests and not confidential within the meaning of Article 10 and that it is used by the Commission in its examination procedure; the persons concerned shall address a reasoned request in writing to the Commission, indicating the information required;
   (b) ask to be informed of the principal facts and considerations resulting from the examination procedure.
5. The Commission may hear the parties concerned. It shall hear them if they have, within the period prescribed in the notice published in the *Official Journal of the European Union*, made a written request for a hearing showing that they are a party primarily concerned by the result of the procedure.
6. The Commission shall, on request, give the parties primarily concerned an opportunity to meet, so that opposing views may be presented and any rebuttal argument put forward. In providing this opportunity the Commission shall take account of the wishes of the parties and of the need to preserve confidentiality. There shall be no obligation on any party to attend a meeting and failure to do so shall not be prejudicial to that party's case.
7. Where the information requested by the Commission is not supplied within a reasonable time or where the investigation is significantly impeded, findings may be made on the basis of the facts available.

8. When it has concluded its examination the Commission shall report to the Committee. The report shall be presented within five months of the announcement of initiation of the procedure, unless the complexity of the examination is such that the Commission extends the period to seven months.

[8.795]
Article 10
Confidentiality

1. Information received pursuant to this Regulation shall be used only for the purpose for which it was requested.
2. The Commission and the Member States, including the officials of either, shall not reveal any information of a confidential nature received pursuant to this Regulation, or any information provided on a confidential basis by a party to an examination procedure, without specific permission from the party submitting such information.
Each request for confidential treatment shall indicate why the information is confidential and shall be accompanied by a non-confidential summary of the information or a statement of the reasons why the information is not capable of being summarised.
3. Information shall be considered to be confidential if its disclosure is likely to have a significantly adverse effect upon the supplier or the source of such information.
4. Where it appears that a request for confidentiality is not warranted and if the supplier is unwilling either to make the information public or to authorise its disclosure in generalised or summary form, the information in question may be disregarded.
5. This Article shall not preclude the disclosure of general information by the Union authorities and in particular of the reasons on which decisions taken pursuant to this Regulation are based. Such disclosure shall take into account the legitimate interest of the parties concerned that their business secrets shall not be divulged.

[8.796]
Article 11
Evidence

1. An examination of injury shall involve, where applicable, the following factors:
(a) the volume of Union imports or exports concerned, notably where there has been a significant increase or decrease, either in absolute terms or relative to production or consumption on the market in question;
(b) the prices of the Union industry's competitors, in particular in order to determine whether there has been, either in the Union or on third country markets, significant undercutting of the prices of the Union industry;
(c) the consequent impact on the Union industry and as indicated by trends in certain economic factors such as: production, capacity utilisation, stocks, sales, market share, prices (that is to say depression of prices or prevention of price increases which would normally have occurred), profits, return on capital, investment, employment.
2. Where a threat of injury is alleged, the Commission shall also examine whether it is clearly foreseeable that a particular situation is likely to develop into actual injury. In this regard, account may also be taken of factors such as:
(a) the rate of increase of exports to the market where the competition with Union products is taking place;
(b) export capacity in the country of origin or export, which is already in existence or will be operational in the foreseeable future, and the likelihood that the exports resulting from that capacity will be to the market referred to in point (a).
3. Injury caused by other factors which, either individually or in combination, are also adversely affecting the Union industry shall not be attributed to the practices under consideration.
4. Where adverse trade effects are alleged, the Commission shall examine the impact of such adverse effects on the economy of the Union or of a region of the Union, or on a sector of economic activity therein. To this effect, the Commission may take into account, where relevant, factors of the type listed in paragraphs 1 and 2. Adverse trade effects may arise, *inter alia*, in situations in which trade flows concerning a product or service are prevented, impeded or diverted as a result of any obstacle to trade, or from situations in which obstacles to trade have materially affected the supply or inputs, for example parts and components or raw materials, to Union enterprises. Where a threat of adverse trade effects is alleged, the Commission shall also examine whether it is clearly foreseeable that a particular situation is likely to develop into actual adverse trade effects.
5. The Commission shall also, in examining evidence of adverse trade effects, have regard to the provisions, principles or practice which govern the right of action under relevant international rules referred to in Article 2(1)(a).
6. The Commission shall further examine any other relevant evidence contained in the complaint or in the request. In this respect, the list of factors and the indications given in paragraphs 1 to 5 are not exhaustive, nor can one or several of such factors and indications necessarily give decisive guidance as to the existence of injury or of adverse trade effects.

[8.797]
Article 12
Termination and suspension of the procedure

1. When it is found, as a result of the examination procedure conducted pursuant to Article 9, that the interests of the Union do not require any action to be taken, the procedure shall be terminated by the Commission acting in accordance with the examination procedure referred to in Article 7(3).

2. When, after an examination procedure conducted pursuant to Article 9, the third country or countries concerned take(s) measures which are considered satisfactory, and therefore no action by the Union is required, the procedure may be suspended by the Commission acting in accordance with the advisory procedure referred to in Article 7(2).

The Commission shall supervise the application of those measures, where appropriate on the basis of information supplied at intervals, which it may request from the third countries concerned and check as necessary.

Where the measures taken by the third country or countries concerned have been rescinded, suspended or improperly implemented or where the Commission has grounds for believing this to be the case or, where information requested by the Commission pursuant to the second subparagraph of this paragraph has not been provided, the Commission shall inform the Member States, and where necessary and justified by the results of the investigation and the new facts available, any measures shall be taken in accordance with Article 14(2).

3. Where, either after an examination procedure conducted pursuant to Article 9, or at any time before, during or after an international dispute settlement procedure, it appears that the most appropriate means of resolving a dispute arising from an obstacle to trade is the conclusion of an agreement with the third country or countries concerned which may change the substantive rights of the Union and of the third country or countries concerned, the procedure shall be suspended by the Commission acting in accordance with the advisory procedure referred to in Article 7(2), and negotiations shall be carried out in accordance with the provisions of Article 207 of the Treaty.

[8.798]
Article 13
Adoption of commercial policy measures

1. Where it is found, as a result of the examination procedure conducted pursuant to Article 9, unless the factual and legal situation is such that an examination procedure may not be required, that action is necessary in the interests of the Union in order to ensure the exercise of the Union's rights under international trade rules, with a view to removing the injury or the adverse trade effects resulting from obstacles to trade that are adopted or maintained by third countries, the appropriate measures shall be determined in accordance with the procedure laid down in Article 14.

2. Where the Union's international obligations require the prior discharge of an international procedure for consultation or for the settlement of disputes, the measures referred to in paragraph 3 shall only be determined after that procedure has been terminated, and taking account of the results of the procedure. In particular, where the Union has requested an international dispute settlement body to indicate and authorise the measures which are appropriate for the implementation of the results of an international dispute settlement procedure, the Union commercial policy measures which may be needed in consequence of such authorisation shall be in accordance with the recommendation of such international dispute settlement body.

3. Any commercial policy measures may be taken which are compatible with existing international obligations and procedures, notably:

(a) suspension or withdrawal of any concession resulting from commercial policy negotiations;
(b) the raising of existing customs duties or the introduction of any other charge on imports;
(c) the introduction of quantitative restrictions or any other measures modifying import or export conditions or otherwise affecting trade with the third country concerned.

4. The corresponding decisions shall state the reasons on which they are based and shall be published in the *Official Journal of the European Union*. Publication shall also be deemed to constitute notification to the countries and parties primarily concerned.

[8.799]
Article 14
Decision-making procedures

1. Where the Union, as a result of a complaint pursuant to Article 3 or Article 4, or of a request pursuant to Article 6, follows formal international consultation or dispute settlement procedures, decisions relating to the initiation, conduct or termination of such procedures shall be taken by the Commission.

The Commission shall inform the Member States in the event that it decides to initiate, conduct or terminate formal international consultations or dispute settlement procedures.

2. Where the Union, having acted in accordance with Article 13(2), has to take a decision on the measures of commercial policy to be adopted pursuant to the third subparagraph of Article 12(2) or pursuant to Article 13, it shall act, without delay, in accordance with Article 207 of the Treaty and, as appropriate, Regulation (EU) No 654/2014 of the European Parliament and of the Council[1] or any other applicable procedures.

NOTES

[1] Regulation (EU) No 654/2014 of the European Parliament and of the Council of 15 May 2014 concerning the exercise of the Union's rights for the application and enforcement of international trade rules and amending Council Regulation (EC) No 3286/94 laying down Community procedures in the field of the common commercial policy in order to ensure the exercise of the Community's rights under international trade rules, in particular those established under the auspices of the World Trade Organization (OJ L189, 27.6.2014, p 50).

[8.800]
Article 15
Report

The Commission shall include information on the implementation of this Regulation in its annual report on the application and implementation of trade defence measures presented to the European Parliament and to the Council pursuant to Article 22a of Council Regulation (EC) No 1225/2009.[1]

NOTES

[1] Council Regulation (EC) No 1225/2009 of 30 November 2009 on protection against dumped imports from countries not members of the European Community (OJ L343, 22.12.2009, p 51).

[8.801]
Article 16
General provisions

This Regulation shall not apply in cases covered by other existing rules in the common commercial policy field. It shall operate by way of complement to:

(a) the rules establishing the common organisation of agricultural markets and their implementing provisions; and

(b) the specific rules adopted pursuant to Article 352 of the Treaty, applicable to goods processed from agricultural products.

It shall be without prejudice to other measures which may be taken pursuant to Article 207 of the Treaty, as well as to Union procedures for dealing with matters concerning obstacles to trade raised by Member States in the committee established by Article 207 of the Treaty.

[8.802]
Article 17
Repeal

Regulation (EC) No 3286/94 is repealed.

References to the repealed Regulation shall be construed as references to this Regulation and shall be read in accordance with the correlation table in Annex II.

[8.803]
Article 18
Entry into force

This Regulation shall enter into force on the twentieth day following that of its publication in the *Official Journal of the European Union*.

This Regulation shall be binding in its entirety and directly applicable in all Member States.

Annex I
Repealed Regulation with list of its successive amendments
[8.804]

Council Regulation (EC) No 3286/94 (OJ L 349, 31.12.1994, p. 71)	
Council Regulation (EC) No 356/95 (OJ L 41, 23.2.1995, p. 3)	
Council Regulation (EC) No 125/2008 (OJ L 40, 14.2.2008, p. 1)	
Regulation (EU) No 37/2014 of the European Parliament and of the Council (OJ L 18, 21.1.2014, p. 1)	Only point 4 of the Annex
Regulation (EU) No 654/2014 of the European Parliament and of the Council (OJ L 189, 27.6.2014, p. 50)	Only Article 11

Annex II
Correlation Table
[8.805]

Regulation (EC) No 3286/94	This Regulation
Article 1	Article 1
Article 2(1)	Article 2(1), introductory wording and point (a)
Article 2(2)	Article 2(1)(b)
Article 2(3)	Article 2(1)(c)
Article 2(4)	Article 2(1)(d)
Article 2(5), first subparagraph, first part of the introductory wording	Article 2(1)(e), introductory wording
Article 2(5), first subparagraph, second part of the introductory wording	Article 2(1)(e)(i), introductory wording
Article 2(5), first subparagraph, first indent	Article 2(1)(e)(i), first indent
Article 2(5), first subparagraph, second indent	Article 2(1)(e)(i), second indent
Article 2(5), first subparagraph, third indent	Article 2(1)(e)(i), third indent
Article 2(5), second subparagraph, introductory sentence	Article 2(1)(e)(ii), introductory wording
Article 2(5), second subparagraph, point (a)	Article 2(1)(e)(ii), first indent
Article 2(5), second subparagraph, point (b)	Article 2(1)(e)(ii), second indent
Article 2(6)	Article 2(1)(f)
Article 2(7)	Article 2(2)
Article 2(8)	Article 2(1)(g)
Articles 3 to 6	Articles 3 to 6
Article 7(1)(a)	Article 7(1)
Article 7(1)(b)	Article 7(2)
Article 7(1)(c)	Article 7(3)
Article 7(2)	Article 8
Article 8(1)	Article 9(1)
Article 8(2)(a)	Article 9(2), first subparagraph, introductory wording and point (a)
Article 8(2)(b)	Article 9(2), first subparagraph, introductory wording and point (b)
Article 8(2)(c)	Article 9(2), second subparagraph
Article 8(3)	Article 9(3)
Article 8(4)(a)	Article 9(4), first subparagraph, introductory wording and point (a)
Article 8(4)(b)	Article 9(4), first subparagraph, introductory wording and point (b)
Article 8(5) to (8)	Article 9(5) to (8)
Article 9(1)	Article 10(1)
Article 9(2)(a)	Article 10(2), first subparagraph
Article 9(2)(b)	Article 10(2), second subparagraph
Article 9(3), (4) and (5)	Article 10(3), (4) and (5)
Article 10	Article 11
Article 11(1)	Article 12(1)
Article 11(2)(a)	Article 12(2), first subparagraph
Article 11(2)(b)	Article 12(2), second subparagraph
Article 11(2)(c)	Article 12(2), third subparagraph
Article 11(3)	Article 12(3)
Article 12	Article 13

Regulation (EC) No 3286/94	This Regulation
Article 13	Article 14
Article 13a	Article 15
Article 15(1), first subparagraph, introductory sentences	Article 16, first paragraph, introductory sentences
Article 15(1), first subparagraph, first indent	Article 16, first paragraph, point (a)
Article 15(1), first subparagraph, second indent	Article 16, first paragraph, point (b)
Article 15(1), second subparagraph	Article 16, second paragraph
Article 15(2), first sentence	Article 17, first paragraph
Article 15(2), second sentence	Article 17, second paragraph
Article 16	Article 18
—	Annex I
—	Annex II

DIRECTIVE OF THE EUROPEAN PARLIAMENT AND OF THE COUNCIL

(2016/943/EU)

of 8 June 2016

on the protection of undisclosed know-how and business information (trade secrets) against their unlawful acquisition, use and disclosure

(Text with EEA relevance)

NOTES

Date of publication in OJ: OJ L157, 15.6.2016, p 1.

Domestic implementation of this Directive is required by 9 June 2018 (see Article 19 at **[8.824]**).

THE EUROPEAN PARLIAMENT AND THE COUNCIL OF THE EUROPEAN UNION,

Having regard to the Treaty on the Functioning of the European Union, and in particular Article 114 thereof,

Having regard to the proposal from the European Commission,

After transmission of the draft legislative act to the national parliaments,

Having regard to the opinion of the European Economic and Social Committee,[1]

Acting in accordance with the ordinary legislative procedure,[2]

Whereas:

(1) Businesses and non-commercial research institutions invest in acquiring, developing and applying know-how and information which is the currency of the knowledge economy and provides a competitive advantage. This investment in generating and applying intellectual capital is a determining factor as regards their competitiveness and innovation-related performance in the market and therefore their returns on investment, which is the underlying motivation for business research and development. Businesses have recourse to different means to appropriate the results of their innovation-related activities when openness does not allow for the full exploitation of their investment in research and innovation. Use of intellectual property rights, such as patents, design rights or copyright, is one such means. Another means of appropriating the results of innovation is to protect access to, and exploit, knowledge that is valuable to the entity and not widely known. Such valuable know-how and business information, that is undisclosed and intended to remain confidential, is referred to as a trade secret.

(2) Businesses, irrespective of their size, value trade secrets as much as patents and other forms of intellectual property right. They use confidentiality as a business competitiveness and research innovation management tool, and in relation to a diverse range of information that extends beyond technological knowledge to commercial data such as information on customers and suppliers, business plans, and market research and strategies. Small and medium-sized enterprises (SMEs) value and rely on trade secrets even more. By protecting such a wide range of know-how and business information, whether as a complement or as an alternative to intellectual property rights, trade secrets allow creators and innovators to derive profit from their creation or innovation and, therefore, are particularly important for business competitiveness as well as for research and development, and innovation-related performance.

(3) Open innovation is a catalyst for new ideas which meet the needs of consumers and tackle societal challenges, and allows those ideas to find their way to the market. Such innovation is an important lever for the creation of new knowledge, and underpins the emergence of new and innovative business models based on the use of co-created knowledge. Collaborative research, including cross-border cooperation, is particularly important in increasing the levels of business research and development within the internal market. The dissemination of knowledge and information should be considered as being essential for the purpose of ensuring dynamic, positive and equal business development opportunities, in particular for SMEs. In an internal market in which barriers to cross-border collaboration are minimised and cooperation is not distorted, intellectual creation and innovation should encourage investment in innovative processes, services and products. Such an environment conducive to intellectual creation and innovation, and in which employment mobility is not hindered, is also important for employment growth and for improving the competitiveness of the Union economy. Trade secrets have an important role in protecting the exchange of knowledge between businesses, including in particular SMEs, and research institutions both within and across the borders of the internal market, in the context of research and development, and innovation. Trade secrets are one of the most commonly used forms of protection of intellectual creation and innovative know-how by businesses, yet at the same time they are the least protected by the existing Union legal framework against their unlawful acquisition, use or disclosure by other parties.

(4) Innovative businesses are increasingly exposed to dishonest practices aimed at misappropriating trade secrets, such as theft, unauthorised copying, economic espionage or the breach of confidentiality requirements, whether from within or from outside of the Union. Recent developments, such as globalisation, increased outsourcing, longer supply chains, and the increased use of information and communication technology contribute to increasing the risk of those practices. The unlawful acquisition, use or disclosure of a trade secret compromises legitimate trade secret holders' ability to obtain first-mover returns from their innovation-related efforts. Without effective and comparable legal means for protecting trade secrets across the Union, incentives to engage in innovation-related cross-border activity within the internal market are undermined, and trade secrets are unable to fulfil their potential as drivers of economic growth and jobs. Thus, innovation and creativity are discouraged and investment diminishes, thereby affecting the smooth functioning of the internal market and undermining its growth-enhancing potential.

(5) International efforts made in the framework of the World Trade Organisation to address this problem led to the conclusion of the Agreement on Trade-related Aspects of Intellectual Property Rights (the TRIPS Agreement). The TRIPS Agreement contains, inter alia, provisions on the protection of trade secrets against their unlawful acquisition, use or disclosure by third parties, which are common international standards. All Member States, as well as the Union itself, are bound by this Agreement which was approved by Council Decision 94/800/EC.[3]

(6) Notwithstanding the TRIPS Agreement, there are important differences in the Member States' legislation as regards the protection of trade secrets against their unlawful acquisition, use or disclosure by other persons. For example, not all Member States have adopted national definitions of a trade secret or the unlawful acquisition, use or disclosure of a trade secret, therefore knowledge on the scope of protection is not readily accessible and that scope differs across the Member States. Furthermore, there is no consistency as regards the civil law remedies available in the event of unlawful acquisition, use or disclosure of trade secrets, as cease and desist orders are not always available in all Member States against third parties who are not competitors of the legitimate trade secret holder. Divergences also exist across the Member States with respect to the treatment of a third party who has acquired the trade secret in good faith but subsequently learns, at the time of use, that the acquisition derived from a previous unlawful acquisition by another party.

(7) National rules also differ as to whether legitimate trade secret holders are allowed to seek the destruction of goods produced by third parties who use trade secrets unlawfully, or the return or destruction of any documents, files or materials containing or embodying the unlawfully acquired or used trade secret. Furthermore, applicable national rules on the calculation of damages do not always take account of the intangible nature of trade secrets, which makes it difficult to demonstrate the actual profits lost or the unjust enrichment of the infringer where no market value can be established for the information in question. Only a few Member States allow for the application of abstract rules on the calculation of damages based on the reasonable royalty or fee which could have been due had a licence for the use of the trade secret existed. Additionally, many national rules do not provide for appropriate protection of the confidentiality of a trade secret where the trade secret holder introduces a claim for alleged unlawful acquisition, use or disclosure of the trade secret by a third party, thereby reducing the attractiveness of the existing measures and remedies and weakening the protection offered.

(8) The differences in the legal protection of trade secrets provided for by the Member States imply that trade secrets do not enjoy an equivalent level of protection throughout the Union, thus leading to fragmentation of the internal market in this area and a weakening of the overall deterrent effect of the relevant rules. The internal market is affected in so far as such differences lower the incentives for businesses to undertake innovation-related cross-border economic activity, including research cooperation or production cooperation with partners, outsourcing or investment in other

Member States, which depends on the use of information that enjoys protection as trade secrets. Cross-border network research and development, as well as innovation-related activities, including related production and subsequent cross-border trade, are rendered less attractive and more difficult within the Union, thus also resulting in Union-wide innovation-related inefficiencies.

(9) In addition, there is a higher risk for businesses in Member States with comparatively lower levels of protection, due to the fact that trade secrets may be stolen or otherwise unlawfully acquired more easily. This leads to inefficient allocation of capital to growth-enhancing innovation within the internal market because of the higher expenditure on protective measures to compensate for the insufficient legal protection in some Member States. It also favours the activity of unfair competitors who, subsequent to the unlawful acquisition of trade secrets, could spread goods resulting from such acquisition across the internal market. Differences in legislative regimes also facilitate the importation of goods from third countries into the Union through entry points with weaker protection, when the design, production or marketing of those goods rely on stolen or otherwise unlawfully acquired trade secrets. On the whole, such differences hinder the proper functioning of the internal market.

(10) It is appropriate to provide for rules at Union level to approximate the laws of the Member States so as to ensure that there is a sufficient and consistent level of civil redress in the internal market in the event of unlawful acquisition, use or disclosure of a trade secret. Those rules should be without prejudice to the possibility for Member States of providing for more far-reaching protection against the unlawful acquisition, use or disclosure of trade secrets, as long as the safeguards explicitly provided for in this Directive for protecting the interests of other parties are respected.

(11) This Directive should not affect the application of Union or national rules that require the disclosure of information, including trade secrets, to the public or to public authorities. Nor should it affect the application of rules that allow public authorities to collect information for the performance of their duties, or rules that allow or require any subsequent disclosure by those public authorities of relevant information to the public. Such rules include, in particular, rules on the disclosure by the Union's institutions and bodies or national public authorities of business-related information they hold pursuant to Regulation (EC) No 1049/2001 of the European Parliament and of the Council,[4] Regulation (EC) No 1367/2006 of the European Parliament and of the Council[5] and Directive 2003/4/EC of the European Parliament and of the Council, [6] or pursuant to other rules on public access to documents or on the transparency obligations of national public authorities.

(12) This Directive should not affect the right of social partners to enter into collective agreements, where provided for under labour law, as regards any obligation not to disclose a trade secret or to limit its use, and the consequences of a breach of such an obligation by the party subject to it. This should be on the condition that any such collective agreement does not restrict the exceptions laid down in this Directive when an application for measures, procedures or remedies provided for in this Directive for alleged acquisition, use or disclosure of a trade secret is to be dismissed.

(13) This Directive should not be understood as restricting the freedom of establishment, the free movement of workers or the mobility of workers as provided for in Union law. Nor is it intended to affect the possibility of concluding non-competition agreements between employers and employees, in accordance with applicable law.

(14) It is important to establish a homogenous definition of a trade secret without restricting the subject matter to be protected against misappropriation. Such definition should therefore be constructed so as to cover know-how, business information and technological information where there is both a legitimate interest in keeping them confidential and a legitimate expectation that such confidentiality will be preserved. Furthermore, such know-how or information should have a commercial value, whether actual or potential. Such know-how or information should be considered to have a commercial value, for example, where its unlawful acquisition, use or disclosure is likely to harm the interests of the person lawfully controlling it, in that it undermines that person's scientific and technical potential, business or financial interests, strategic positions or ability to compete. The definition of trade secret excludes trivial information and the experience and skills gained by employees in the normal course of their employment, and also excludes information which is generally known among, or is readily accessible to, persons within the circles that normally deal with the kind of information in question.

(15) It is also important to identify the circumstances in which legal protection of trade secrets is justified. For this reason, it is necessary to establish the conduct and practices which are to be regarded as unlawful acquisition, use or disclosure of a trade secret.

(16) In the interest of innovation and to foster competition, the provisions of this Directive should not create any exclusive right to know-how or information protected as trade secrets. Thus, the independent discovery of the same know-how or information should remain possible. Reverse engineering of a lawfully acquired product should be considered as a lawful means of acquiring information, except when otherwise contractually agreed. The freedom to enter into such contractual arrangements can, however, be limited by law.

(17) In some industry sectors, where creators and innovators cannot benefit from exclusive rights

and where innovation has traditionally relied upon trade secrets, products can nowadays be easily reverse-engineered once in the market. In such cases, those creators and innovators can be victims of practices such as parasitic copying or slavish imitations that free-ride on their reputation and innovation efforts. Some national laws dealing with unfair competition address those practices. While this Directive does not aim to reform or harmonise the law on unfair competition in general, it would be appropriate that the Commission carefully examine the need for Union action in that area.

(18) Furthermore, the acquisition, use or disclosure of trade secrets, whenever imposed or permitted by law, should be treated as lawful for the purposes of this Directive. This concerns, in particular, the acquisition and disclosure of trade secrets in the context of the exercise of the rights of workers' representatives to information, consultation and participation in accordance with Union law and national laws and practices, and the collective defence of the interests of workers and employers, including co-determination, as well as the acquisition or disclosure of a trade secret in the context of statutory audits performed in accordance with Union or national law. However, such treatment of the acquisition of a trade secret as lawful should be without prejudice to any obligation of confidentiality as regards the trade secret or any limitation as to its use that Union or national law imposes on the recipient or acquirer of the information. In particular, this Directive should not release public authorities from the confidentiality obligations to which they are subject in respect of information passed on by trade secret holders, irrespective of whether those obligations are laid down in Union or national law. Such confidentiality obligations include, inter alia, the obligations in respect of information forwarded to contracting authorities in the context of procurement procedures, as laid down, for example, in Directive 2014/23/EU of the European Parliament and of the Council,[7] Directive 2014/24/EU of the European Parliament and of the Council[8] and Directive 2014/25/EU of the European Parliament and of the Council.[9]

(19) While this Directive provides for measures and remedies which can consist of preventing the disclosure of information in order to protect the confidentiality of trade secrets, it is essential that the exercise of the right to freedom of expression and information which encompasses media freedom and pluralism, as reflected in Article 11 of the Charter of Fundamental Rights of the European Union ('the Charter'), not be restricted, in particular with regard to investigative journalism and the protection of journalistic sources.

(20) The measures, procedures and remedies provided for in this Directive should not restrict whistleblowing activity. Therefore, the protection of trade secrets should not extend to cases in which disclosure of a trade secret serves the public interest, insofar as directly relevant misconduct, wrongdoing or illegal activity is revealed. This should not be seen as preventing the competent judicial authorities from allowing an exception to the application of measures, procedures and remedies in a case where the respondent had every reason to believe in good faith that his or her conduct satisfied the appropriate criteria set out in this Directive.

(21) In line with the principle of proportionality, measures, procedures and remedies intended to protect trade secrets should be tailored to meet the objective of a smooth-functioning internal market for research and innovation, in particular by deterring the unlawful acquisition, use and disclosure of a trade secret. Such tailoring of measures, procedures and remedies should not jeopardise or undermine fundamental rights and freedoms or the public interest, such as public safety, consumer protection, public health and environmental protection, and should be without prejudice to the mobility of workers. In this respect, the measures, procedures and remedies provided for in this Directive are aimed at ensuring that competent judicial authorities take into account factors such as the value of a trade secret, the seriousness of the conduct resulting in the unlawful acquisition, use or disclosure of the trade secret and the impact of such conduct. It should also be ensured that the competent judicial authorities have the discretion to weigh up the interests of the parties to the legal proceedings, as well as the interests of third parties including, where appropriate, consumers.

(22) The smooth-functioning of the internal market would be undermined if the measures, procedures and remedies provided for were used to pursue illegitimate intents incompatible with the objectives of this Directive. Therefore, it is important to empower judicial authorities to adopt appropriate measures with regard to applicants who act abusively or in bad faith and submit manifestly unfounded applications with, for example, the aim of unfairly delaying or restricting the respondent's access to the market or otherwise intimidating or harassing the respondent.

(23) In the interest of legal certainty, and considering that legitimate trade secret holders are expected to exercise a duty of care as regards the preservation of the confidentiality of their valuable trade secrets and the monitoring of their use, it is appropriate to restrict substantive claims or the possibility of initiating actions for the protection of trade secrets to a limited period. National law should also specify, in a clear and unambiguous manner, from when that period is to begin to run and under what circumstances that period is to be interrupted or suspended.

(24) The prospect of losing the confidentiality of a trade secret in the course of legal proceedings often deters legitimate trade secret holders from instituting legal proceedings to defend their trade secrets, thus jeopardising the effectiveness of the measures, procedures and remedies provided for. For this reason, it is necessary to establish, subject to appropriate safeguards ensuring the right to an effective remedy and to a fair trial, specific requirements aimed at protecting the confidentiality of

the litigated trade secret in the course of legal proceedings instituted for its defence. Such protection should remain in force after the legal proceedings have ended and for as long as the information constituting the trade secret is not in the public domain.

(25) Such requirements should include, as a minimum, the possibility of restricting the circle of persons entitled to have access to evidence or hearings, bearing in mind that all such persons should be subject to the confidentiality requirements set out in this Directive, and of publishing only the non-confidential elements of judicial decisions. In this context, considering that assessing the nature of the information which is the subject of a dispute is one of the main purposes of legal proceedings, it is particularly important to ensure both the effective protection of the confidentiality of trade secrets and respect for the right of the parties to those proceedings to an effective remedy and to a fair trial. The restricted circle of persons should therefore consist of at least one natural person from each of the parties as well as the respective lawyers of the parties and, where applicable, other representatives appropriately qualified in accordance with national law in order to defend, represent or serve the interests of a party in legal proceedings covered by this Directive, who should all have full access to such evidence or hearings. In the event that one of the parties is a legal person, that party should be able to propose a natural person or natural persons who ought to form part of that circle of persons so as to ensure proper representation of that legal person, subject to appropriate judicial control to prevent the objective of the restriction of access to evidence and hearings from being undermined. Such safeguards should not be understood as requiring the parties to be represented by a lawyer or another representative in the course of legal proceedings where such representation is not required by national law. Nor should they be understood as restricting the competence of the courts to decide, in conformity with the applicable rules and practices of the Member State concerned, whether and to what extent relevant court officials should also have full access to evidence and hearings for the exercise of their duties.

(26) The unlawful acquisition, use or disclosure of a trade secret by a third party could have devastating effects on the legitimate trade secret holder, as once publicly disclosed, it would be impossible for that holder to revert to the situation prior to the loss of the trade secret. As a result, it is essential to provide for fast, effective and accessible provisional measures for the immediate termination of the unlawful acquisition, use or disclosure of a trade secret, including where it is used for the provision of services. It is essential that such relief be available without having to await a decision on the merits of the case, while having due respect for the right of defence and the principle of proportionality, and having regard to the characteristics of the case. In certain instances, it should be possible to permit the alleged infringer, subject to the lodging of one or more guarantees, to continue to use the trade secret, in particular where there is little risk that it will enter the public domain. It should also be possible to require guarantees of a level sufficient to cover the costs and the injury caused to the respondent by an unjustified application, particularly where any delay would cause irreparable harm to the legitimate trade secret holder.

(27) For the same reasons, it is also important to provide for definitive measures to prevent unlawful use or disclosure of a trade secret, including where it is used for the provision of services. For such measures to be effective and proportionate, their duration, when circumstances require a limitation in time, should be sufficient to eliminate any commercial advantage which the third party could have derived from the unlawful acquisition, use or disclosure of the trade secret. In any event, no measure of this type should be enforceable if the information originally covered by the trade secret is in the public domain for reasons that cannot be attributed to the respondent.

(28) It is possible that a trade secret could be used unlawfully to design, produce or market goods, or components thereof, which could be spread across the internal market, thus affecting the commercial interests of the trade secret holder and the functioning of the internal market. In such cases, and when the trade secret in question has a significant impact on the quality, value or price of the goods resulting from that unlawful use or on reducing the cost of, facilitating or speeding up their production or marketing processes, it is important to empower judicial authorities to order effective and appropriate measures with a view to ensuring that those goods are not put on the market or are withdrawn from it. Considering the global nature of trade, it is also necessary that such measures include the prohibition of the importation of those goods into the Union or their storage for the purposes of offering or placing them on the market. Having regard to the principle of proportionality, corrective measures should not necessarily entail the destruction of the goods if other viable options are present, such as depriving the good of its infringing quality or the disposal of the goods outside the market, for example, by means of donations to charitable organisations.

(29) A person could have originally acquired a trade secret in good faith, but only become aware at a later stage, including upon notice served by the original trade secret holder, that that person's knowledge of the trade secret in question derived from sources using or disclosing the relevant trade secret in an unlawful manner. In order to avoid, under those circumstances, the corrective measures or injunctions provided for causing disproportionate harm to that person, Member States should provide for the possibility, in appropriate cases, of pecuniary compensation being awarded to the injured party as an alternative measure. Such compensation should not, however, exceed the amount of royalties or fees which would have been due had that person obtained authorisation to use the trade secret in question, for the period of time for which use of the trade secret could have been prevented by the original trade secret holder. Nevertheless, where the

unlawful use of the trade secret would constitute an infringement of law other than that provided for in this Directive or would be likely to harm consumers, such unlawful use should not be allowed.

(30) In order to avoid a person who knowingly, or with reasonable grounds for knowing, unlawfully acquires, uses or discloses a trade secret being able to benefit from such conduct, and to ensure that the injured trade secret holder, to the extent possible, is placed in the position in which he, she or it would have been had that conduct not taken place, it is necessary to provide for adequate compensation for the prejudice suffered as a result of that unlawful conduct. The amount of damages awarded to the injured trade secret holder should take account of all appropriate factors, such as loss of earnings incurred by the trade secret holder or unfair profits made by the infringer and, where appropriate, any moral prejudice caused to the trade secret holder. As an alternative, for example where, considering the intangible nature of trade secrets, it would be difficult to determine the amount of the actual prejudice suffered, the amount of the damages might be derived from elements such as the royalties or fees which would have been due had the infringer requested authorisation to use the trade secret in question. The aim of that alternative method is not to introduce an obligation to provide for punitive damages, but to ensure compensation based on an objective criterion while taking account of the expenses incurred by the trade secret holder, such as the costs of identification and research. This Directive should not prevent Member States from providing in their national law that the liability for damages of employees is restricted in cases where they have acted without intent.

(31) As a supplementary deterrent to future infringers and to contribute to the awareness of the public at large, it is useful to publicise decisions, including, where appropriate, through prominent advertising, in cases concerning the unlawful acquisition, use or disclosure of trade secrets, on the condition that such publication does not result in the disclosure of the trade secret or disproportionally affect the privacy and reputation of a natural person.

(32) The effectiveness of the measures, procedures and remedies available to trade secret holders could be undermined in the event of non-compliance with the relevant decisions adopted by the competent judicial authorities. For this reason, it is necessary to ensure that those authorities enjoy the appropriate powers of sanction.

(33) In order to facilitate the uniform application of the measures, procedures and remedies provided for in this Directive, it is appropriate to provide for systems of cooperation and the exchange of information as between Member States on the one hand, and between the Member States and the Commission on the other, in particular by creating a network of correspondents designated by Member States. In addition, in order to review whether those measures fulfil their intended objective, the Commission, assisted, as appropriate, by the European Union Intellectual Property Office, should examine the application of this Directive and the effectiveness of the national measures taken.

(34) This Directive respects the fundamental rights and observes the principles recognised in particular by the Charter, notably the right to respect for private and family life, the right to protection of personal data, the freedom of expression and information, the freedom to choose an occupation and right to engage in work, the freedom to conduct a business, the right to property, the right to good administration, and in particular the access to files, while respecting business secrecy, the right to an effective remedy and to a fair trial and the right of defence.

(35) It is important that the rights to respect for private and family life and to protection of personal data of any person whose personal data may be processed by the trade secret holder when taking steps to protect a trade secret, or of any person involved in legal proceedings concerning the unlawful acquisition, use or disclosure of trade secrets under this Directive, and whose personal data are processed, be respected. Directive 95/46/EC of the European Parliament and of the Council[10] governs the processing of personal data carried out in the Member States in the context of this Directive and under the supervision of the Member States' competent authorities, in particular the public independent authorities designated by the Member States. Thus, this Directive should not affect the rights and obligations laid down in Directive 95/46/EC, in particular the rights of the data subject to access his or her personal data being processed and to obtain the rectification, erasure or blocking of the data where it is incomplete or inaccurate and, where appropriate, the obligation to process sensitive data in accordance with Article 8(5) of Directive 95/46/EC.

(36) Since the objective of this Directive, namely to achieve a smooth-functioning internal market by means of the establishment of a sufficient and comparable level of redress across the internal market in the event of the unlawful acquisition, use or disclosure of a trade secret, cannot be sufficiently achieved by Member States but can rather, by reason of its scale and effects, be better achieved at Union level, the Union may adopt measures in accordance with the principle of subsidiarity as set out in Article 5 of the Treaty on European Union. In accordance with the principle of proportionality, as set out in that Article, this Directive does not go beyond what is necessary in order to achieve that objective.

(37) This Directive does not aim to establish harmonised rules for judicial cooperation, jurisdiction, the recognition and enforcement of judgments in civil and commercial matters, or deal with applicable law. Other Union instruments which govern such matters in general terms should, in principle, remain equally applicable to the field covered by this Directive.

(38) This Directive should not affect the application of competition law rules, in particular Articles 101 and 102 of the Treaty on the Functioning of the European Union ('TFEU'). The measures, procedures and remedies provided for in this Directive should not be used to restrict unduly competition in a manner contrary to the TFEU.

(39) This Directive should not affect the application of any other relevant law in other areas, including intellectual property rights and the law of contract. However, where the scope of application of Directive 2004/48/EC of the European Parliament and of the Council and the scope of this Directive[11] overlap, this Directive takes precedence as *lex specialis*.

(40) The European Data Protection Supervisor was consulted in accordance with Article 28(2) of Regulation (EC) No 45/2001 of the European Parliament and of the Council[12] and delivered an opinion on 12 March 2014,

NOTES

1 OJ C226, 16.7.2014, p 48.

2 Position of the European Parliament of 14 April 2016 (not yet published in the Official Journal) and decision of the Council of 27 May 2016.

3 Council Decision 94/800/EC of 22 December 1994 concerning the conclusion on behalf of the European Community, as regards matters within its competence, of the agreements reached in the Uruguay Round multilateral negotiations (1986–1994) (OJ L336, 23.12.1994, p 1).

4 Regulation (EC) No 1049/2001 of the European Parliament and of the Council of 30 May 2001 regarding public access to European Parliament, Council and Commission documents (OJ L145, 31.5.2001, p 43).

5 Regulation (EC) No 1367/2006 of the European Parliament and of the Council of 6 September 2006 on the application of the provisions of the Aarhus Convention on Access to Information, Public Participation in Decision-making and Access to Justice in Environmental Matters to Community institutions and bodies (OJ L264, 25.9.2006, p 13).

6 Directive 2003/4/EC of the European Parliament and of the Council of 28 January 2003 on public access to environmental information and repealing Council Directive 90/313/EEC (OJ L41, 14.2.2003, p 26).

7 Directive 2014/23/EU of the European Parliament and of the Council of 26 February 2014 on the award of concession contracts (OJ L94, 28.3.2014, p 1).

8 Directive 2014/24/EU of the European Parliament and of the Council of 26 February 2014 on public procurement and repealing Directive 2004/18/EC (OJ L94, 28.3.2014, p 65).

9 Directive 2014/25/EU of the European Parliament and of the Council of 26 February 2014 on procurement by entities operating in the water, energy, transport and postal services sectors and repealing Directive 2004/17/EC (OJ L94, 28.3.2014, p 243).

10 Directive 95/46/EC of the European Parliament and of the Council of 24 October 1995 on the protection of individuals with regard to the processing of personal data and on the free movement of such data (OJ L281, 23.11.1995, p 31).

11 Directive 2004/48/EC of the European Parliament and of the Council of 29 April 2004 on the enforcement of intellectual property rights (OJ L157, 30.4.2004, p 45).

12 Regulation (EC) No 45/2001 of the European Parliament and of the Council of 18 December 2000 on the protection of individuals with regard to the processing of personal data by the Community institutions and bodies and on the free movement of such data (OJ L8, 12.1.2001, p 1).

HAVE ADOPTED THIS DIRECTIVE:

CHAPTER I
SUBJECT MATTER AND SCOPE

[8.806]
Article 1
Subject matter and scope

1. This Directive lays down rules on the protection against the unlawful acquisition, use and disclosure of trade secrets.

Member States may, in compliance with the provisions of the TFEU, provide for more far-reaching protection against the unlawful acquisition, use or disclosure of trade secrets than that required by this Directive, provided that compliance with Articles 3, 5, 6, Article 7(1), Article 8, the second subparagraph of Article 9(1), Article 9(3) and (4), Article 10(2), Articles 11, 13 and Article 15(3) is ensured.

2. This Directive shall not affect:

(a) the exercise of the right to freedom of expression and information as set out in the Charter, including respect for the freedom and pluralism of the media;

(b) the application of Union or national rules requiring trade secret holders to disclose, for reasons of public interest, information, including trade secrets, to the public or to administrative or judicial authorities for the performance of the duties of those authorities;

(c) the application of Union or national rules requiring or allowing Union institutions and bodies or national public authorities to disclose information submitted by businesses which those institutions, bodies or authorities hold pursuant to, and in compliance with, the obligations and prerogatives set out in Union or national law;

(d) the autonomy of social partners and their right to enter into collective agreements, in accordance with Union law and national laws and practices.

3. Nothing in this Directive shall be understood to offer any ground for restricting the mobility of employees. In particular, in relation to the exercise of such mobility, this Directive shall not offer any ground for:

(a) limiting employees' use of information that does not constitute a trade secret as defined in point (1) of Article 2;

(b) limiting employees' use of experience and skills honestly acquired in the normal course of their employment;

(c) imposing any additional restrictions on employees in their employment contracts other than restrictions imposed in accordance with Union or national law.

[8.807]
Article 2
Definitions

For the purposes of this Directive, the following definitions apply:

(1) 'trade secret' means information which meets all of the following requirements:

(a) it is secret in the sense that it is not, as a body or in the precise configuration and assembly of its components, generally known among or readily accessible to persons within the circles that normally deal with the kind of information in question;

(b) it has commercial value because it is secret;

(c) it has been subject to reasonable steps under the circumstances, by the person lawfully in control of the information, to keep it secret;

(2) 'trade secret holder' means any natural or legal person lawfully controlling a trade secret;

(3) 'infringer' means any natural or legal person who has unlawfully acquired, used or disclosed a trade secret;

(4) 'infringing goods' means goods, the design, characteristics, functioning, production process or marketing of which significantly benefits from trade secrets unlawfully acquired, used or disclosed.

CHAPTER II
ACQUISITION, USE AND DISCLOSURE OF TRADE SECRETS

[8.808]
Article 3
Lawful acquisition, use and disclosure of trade secrets

1. The acquisition of a trade secret shall be considered lawful when the trade secret is obtained by any of the following means:

(a) independent discovery or creation;

(b) observation, study, disassembly or testing of a product or object that has been made available to the public or that is lawfully in the possession of the acquirer of the information who is free from any legally valid duty to limit the acquisition of the trade secret;

(c) exercise of the right of workers or workers' representatives to information and consultation in accordance with Union law and national laws and practices;

(d) any other practice which, under the circumstances, is in conformity with honest commercial practices.

2. The acquisition, use or disclosure of a trade secret shall be considered lawful to the extent that such acquisition, use or disclosure is required or allowed by Union or national law.

[8.809]
Article 4
Unlawful acquisition, use and disclosure of trade secrets

1. Member States shall ensure that trade secret holders are entitled to apply for the measures, procedures and remedies provided for in this Directive in order to prevent, or obtain redress for, the unlawful acquisition, use or disclosure of their trade secret.

2. The acquisition of a trade secret without the consent of the trade secret holder shall be considered unlawful, whenever carried out by:

(a) unauthorised access to, appropriation of, or copying of any documents, objects, materials, substances or electronic files, lawfully under the control of the trade secret holder, containing the trade secret or from which the trade secret can be deduced;

(b) any other conduct which, under the circumstances, is considered contrary to honest commercial practices.

3. The use or disclosure of a trade secret shall be considered unlawful whenever carried out, without the consent of the trade secret holder, by a person who is found to meet any of the following conditions:

(a) having acquired the trade secret unlawfully;

(b) being in breach of a confidentiality agreement or any other duty not to disclose the trade secret;

(c) being in breach of a contractual or any other duty to limit the use of the trade secret.

4. The acquisition, use or disclosure of a trade secret shall also be considered unlawful whenever a person, at the time of the acquisition, use or disclosure, knew or ought, under the circumstances, to have known that the trade secret had been obtained directly or indirectly from another person who was using or disclosing the trade secret unlawfully within the meaning of paragraph 3.
5. The production, offering or placing on the market of infringing goods, or the importation, export or storage of infringing goods for those purposes, shall also be considered an unlawful use of a trade secret where the person carrying out such activities knew, or ought, under the circumstances, to have known that the trade secret was used unlawfully within the meaning of paragraph 3.

[8.810]
Article 5
Exceptions

Member States shall ensure that an application for the measures, procedures and remedies provided for in this Directive is dismissed where the alleged acquisition, use or disclosure of the trade secret was carried out in any of the following cases:

(a) for exercising the right to freedom of expression and information as set out in the Charter, including respect for the freedom and pluralism of the media;
(b) for revealing misconduct, wrongdoing or illegal activity, provided that the respondent acted for the purpose of protecting the general public interest;
(c) disclosure by workers to their representatives as part of the legitimate exercise by those representatives of their functions in accordance with Union or national law, provided that such disclosure was necessary for that exercise;
(d) for the purpose of protecting a legitimate interest recognised by Union or national law.

CHAPTER III
MEASURES, PROCEDURES AND REMEDIES

SECTION 1
GENERAL PROVISIONS

[8.811]
Article 6
General obligation

1. Member States shall provide for the measures, procedures and remedies necessary to ensure the availability of civil redress against the unlawful acquisition, use and disclosure of trade secrets.
2. The measures, procedures and remedies referred to in paragraph 1 shall:

(a) be fair and equitable;
(b) not be unnecessarily complicated or costly, or entail unreasonable time-limits or unwarranted delays; and
(c) be effective and dissuasive.

[8.812]
Article 7
Proportionality and abuse of process

1. The measures, procedures and remedies provided for in this Directive shall be applied in a manner that:

(a) is proportionate;
(b) avoids the creation of barriers to legitimate trade in the internal market; and
(c) provides for safeguards against their abuse.

2. Member States shall ensure that competent judicial authorities may, upon the request of the respondent, apply appropriate measures as provided for in national law, where an application concerning the unlawful acquisition, use or disclosure of a trade secret is manifestly unfounded and the applicant is found to have initiated the legal proceedings abusively or in bad faith. Such measures may, as appropriate, include awarding damages to the respondent, imposing sanctions on the applicant or ordering the dissemination of information concerning a decision as referred to in Article 15.
Member States may provide that measures as referred to in the first subparagraph are dealt with in separate legal proceedings.

[8.813]
Article 8
Limitation period

1. Member States shall, in accordance with this Article, lay down rules on the limitation periods applicable to substantive claims and actions for the application of the measures, procedures and remedies provided for in this Directive.
The rules referred to in the first subparagraph shall determine when the limitation period begins to run, the duration of the limitation period and the circumstances under which the limitation period is interrupted or suspended.
2. The duration of the limitation period shall not exceed 6 years.

[8.814]
Article 9
Preservation of confidentiality of trade secrets in the course of legal proceedings

1. Member States shall ensure that the parties, their lawyers or other representatives, court officials, witnesses, experts and any other person participating in legal proceedings relating to the unlawful acquisition, use or disclosure of a trade secret, or who has access to documents which form part of those legal proceedings, are not permitted to use or disclose any trade secret or alleged trade secret which the competent judicial authorities have, in response to a duly reasoned application by an interested party, identified as confidential and of which they have become aware as a result of such participation or access. In that regard, Member States may also allow competent judicial authorities to act on their own initiative.

The obligation referred to in the first subparagraph shall remain in force after the legal proceedings have ended. However, such obligation shall cease to exist in any of the following circumstances:

(a) where the alleged trade secret is found, by a final decision, not to meet the requirements set out in point (1) of Article 2; or
(b) where over time, the information in question becomes generally known among or readily accessible to persons within the circles that normally deal with that kind of information.

2. Member States shall also ensure that the competent judicial authorities may, on a duly reasoned application by a party, take specific measures necessary to preserve the confidentiality of any trade secret or alleged trade secret used or referred to in the course of legal proceedings relating to the unlawful acquisition, use or disclosure of a trade secret. Member States may also allow competent judicial authorities to take such measures on their own initiative.

The measures referred to in the first subparagraph shall at least include the possibility:

(a) of restricting access to any document containing trade secrets or alleged trade secrets submitted by the parties or third parties, in whole or in part, to a limited number of persons;
(b) of restricting access to hearings, when trade secrets or alleged trade secrets may be disclosed, and the corresponding record or transcript of those hearings to a limited number of persons;
(c) of making available to any person other than those comprised in the limited number of persons referred to in points (a) and (b) a non-confidential version of any judicial decision, in which the passages containing trade secrets have been removed or redacted.

The number of persons referred to in points (a) and (b) of the second subparagraph shall be no greater than necessary in order to ensure compliance with the right of the parties to the legal proceedings to an effective remedy and to a fair trial, and shall include, at least, one natural person from each party and the respective lawyers or other representatives of those parties to the legal proceedings.

3. When deciding on the measures referred to in paragraph 2 and assessing their proportionality, the competent judicial authorities shall take into account the need to ensure the right to an effective remedy and to a fair trial, the legitimate interests of the parties and, where appropriate, of third parties, and any potential harm for either of the parties, and, where appropriate, for third parties, resulting from the granting or rejection of such measures.

4. Any processing of personal data pursuant to paragraphs 1, 2 or 3 shall be carried out in accordance with Directive 95/46/EC.

SECTION 2
PROVISIONAL AND PRECAUTIONARY MEASURES

[8.815]
Article 10
Provisional and precautionary measures

1. Member States shall ensure that the competent judicial authorities may, at the request of the trade secret holder, order any of the following provisional and precautionary measures against the alleged infringer:

(a) the cessation of or, as the case may be, the prohibition of the use or disclosure of the trade secret on a provisional basis;
(b) the prohibition of the production, offering, placing on the market or use of infringing goods, or the importation, export or storage of infringing goods for those purposes;
(c) the seizure or delivery up of the suspected infringing goods, including imported goods, so as to prevent their entry into, or circulation on, the market.

2. Member States shall ensure that the judicial authorities may, as an alternative to the measures referred to in paragraph 1, make the continuation of the alleged unlawful use of a trade secret subject to the lodging of guarantees intended to ensure the compensation of the trade secret holder. Disclosure of a trade secret in return for the lodging of guarantees shall not be allowed.

[8.816]
Article 11
Conditions of application and safeguards

1. Member States shall ensure that the competent judicial authorities have, in respect of the measures referred to in Article 10, the authority to require the applicant to provide evidence that may reasonably be considered available in order to satisfy themselves with a sufficient degree of certainty that:

(a) a trade secret exists;
(b) the applicant is the trade secret holder; and
(c) the trade secret has been acquired unlawfully, is being unlawfully used or disclosed, or unlawful acquisition, use or disclosure of the trade secret is imminent.

2. Member States shall ensure that in deciding on the granting or rejection of the application and assessing its proportionality, the competent judicial authorities shall be required to take into account the specific circumstances of the case, including, where appropriate:

(a) the value and other specific features of the trade secret;
(b) the measures taken to protect the trade secret;
(c) the conduct of the respondent in acquiring, using or disclosing the trade secret;
(d) the impact of the unlawful use or disclosure of the trade secret;
(e) the legitimate interests of the parties and the impact which the granting or rejection of the measures could have on the parties;
(f) the legitimate interests of third parties;
(g) the public interest; and
(h) the safeguard of fundamental rights.

3. Member States shall ensure that the measures referred to in Article 10 are revoked or otherwise cease to have effect, upon the request of the respondent, if:

(a) the applicant does not institute legal proceedings leading to a decision on the merits of the case before the competent judicial authority, within a reasonable period determined by the judicial authority ordering the measures where the law of a Member State so permits or, in the absence of such determination, within a period not exceeding 20 working days or 31 calendar days, whichever is the longer; or
(b) the information in question no longer meets the requirements of point (1) of Article 2, for reasons that cannot be attributed to the respondent.

4. Member States shall ensure that the competent judicial authorities may make the measures referred to in Article 10 subject to the lodging by the applicant of adequate security or an equivalent assurance intended to ensure compensation for any prejudice suffered by the respondent and, where appropriate, by any other person affected by the measures.

5. Where the measures referred to in Article 10 are revoked on the basis of point (a) of paragraph 3 of this Article, where they lapse due to any act or omission by the applicant, or where it is subsequently found that there has been no unlawful acquisition, use or disclosure of the trade secret or threat of such conduct, the competent judicial authorities shall have the authority to order the applicant, upon the request of the respondent or of an injured third party, to provide the respondent, or the injured third party, appropriate compensation for any injury caused by those measures.

Member States may provide that the request for compensation referred to in the first subparagraph is dealt with in separate legal proceedings.

SECTION 3
MEASURES RESULTING FROM A DECISION ON THE MERITS OF THE CASE

[8.817]
Article 12
Injunctions and corrective measures

1. Member States shall ensure that, where a judicial decision taken on the merits of the case finds that there has been unlawful acquisition, use or disclosure of a trade secret, the competent judicial authorities may, at the request of the applicant, order one or more of the following measures against the infringer:

(a) the cessation of or, as the case may be, the prohibition of the use or disclosure of the trade secret;
(b) the prohibition of the production, offering, placing on the market or use of infringing goods, or the importation, export or storage of infringing goods for those purposes;
(c) the adoption of the appropriate corrective measures with regard to the infringing goods;
(d) the destruction of all or part of any document, object, material, substance or electronic file containing or embodying the trade secret or, where appropriate, the delivery up to the applicant of all or part of those documents, objects, materials, substances or electronic files.

2. The corrective measures referred to in point (c) of paragraph 1 shall include:

(a) recall of the infringing goods from the market;
(b) depriving the infringing goods of their infringing quality;

(c) destruction of the infringing goods or, where appropriate, their withdrawal from the market, provided that the withdrawal does not undermine the protection of the trade secret in question.

3. Member States may provide that, when ordering the withdrawal of the infringing goods from the market, their competent judicial authorities may order, at the request of the trade secret holder, that the goods be delivered up to the holder or to charitable organisations.

4. The competent judicial authorities shall order that the measures referred to in points (c) and (d) of paragraph 1 be carried out at the expense of the infringer, unless there are particular reasons for not doing so. Those measures shall be without prejudice to any damages that may be due to the trade secret holder by reason of the unlawful acquisition, use or disclosure of the trade secret.

[8.818]
Article 13
Conditions of application, safeguards and alternative measures

1. Member States shall ensure that, in considering an application for the adoption of the injunctions and corrective measures provided for in Article 12 and assessing their proportionality, the competent judicial authorities shall be required to take into account the specific circumstances of the case, including, where appropriate:

(a) the value or other specific features of the trade secret;
(b) the measures taken to protect the trade secret;
(c) the conduct of the infringer in acquiring, using or disclosing the trade secret;
(d) the impact of the unlawful use or disclosure of the trade secret;
(e) the legitimate interests of the parties and the impact which the granting or rejection of the measures could have on the parties;
(f) the legitimate interests of third parties;
(g) the public interest; and
(h) the safeguard of fundamental rights.

Where the competent judicial authorities limit the duration of the measures referred to in points (a) and (b) of Article 12(1), such duration shall be sufficient to eliminate any commercial or economic advantage that the infringer could have derived from the unlawful acquisition, use or disclosure of the trade secret.

2. Member States shall ensure that the measures referred to in points (a) and (b) of Article 12(1) are revoked or otherwise cease to have effect, upon the request of the respondent, if the information in question no longer meets the requirements of point (1) of Article 2 for reasons that cannot be attributed directly or indirectly to the respondent.

3. Member States shall provide that, at the request of the person liable to be subject to the measures provided for in Article 12, the competent judicial authority may order pecuniary compensation to be paid to the injured party instead of applying those measures if all the following conditions are met:

(a) the person concerned at the time of use or disclosure neither knew nor ought, under the circumstances, to have known that the trade secret was obtained from another person who was using or disclosing the trade secret unlawfully;
(b) execution of the measures in question would cause that person disproportionate harm; and
(c) pecuniary compensation to the injured party appears reasonably satisfactory.

Where pecuniary compensation is ordered instead of the measures referred to in points (a) and (b) of Article 12(1), it shall not exceed the amount of royalties or fees which would have been due, had that person requested authorisation to use the trade secret in question, for the period of time for which use of the trade secret could have been prohibited.

[8.819]
Article 14
Damages

1. Member States shall ensure that the competent judicial authorities, upon the request of the injured party, order an infringer who knew or ought to have known that he, she or it was engaging in unlawful acquisition, use or disclosure of a trade secret, to pay the trade secret holder damages appropriate to the actual prejudice suffered as a result of the unlawful acquisition, use or disclosure of the trade secret.

Member States may limit the liability for damages of employees towards their employers for the unlawful acquisition, use or disclosure of a trade secret of the employer where they act without intent.

2. When setting the damages referred to in paragraph 1, the competent judicial authorities shall take into account all appropriate factors, such as the negative economic consequences, including lost profits, which the injured party has suffered, any unfair profits made by the infringer and, in appropriate cases, elements other than economic factors, such as the moral prejudice caused to the trade secret holder by the unlawful acquisition, use or disclosure of the trade secret.

Alternatively, the competent judicial authorities may, in appropriate cases, set the damages as a lump sum on the basis of elements such as, at a minimum, the amount of royalties or fees which would have been due had the infringer requested authorisation to use the trade secret in question.

[8.820]
Article 15
Publication of judicial decisions

1. Member States shall ensure that, in legal proceedings instituted for the unlawful acquisition, use or disclosure of a trade secret, the competent judicial authorities may order, at the request of the applicant and at the expense of the infringer, appropriate measures for the dissemination of the information concerning the decision, including publishing it in full or in part.
2. Any measure referred to in paragraph 1 of this Article shall preserve the confidentiality of trade secrets as provided for in Article 9.
3. In deciding whether to order a measure referred to in paragraph 1 and when assessing its proportionality, the competent judicial authorities shall take into account, where appropriate, the value of the trade secret, the conduct of the infringer in acquiring, using or disclosing the trade secret, the impact of the unlawful use or disclosure of the trade secret, and the likelihood of further unlawful use or disclosure of the trade secret by the infringer.

The competent judicial authorities shall also take into account whether the information on the infringer would be such as to allow a natural person to be identified and, if so, whether publication of that information would be justified, in particular in the light of the possible harm that such measure may cause to the privacy and reputation of the infringer.

CHAPTER IV
SANCTIONS, REPORTING AND FINAL PROVISIONS

[8.821]
Article 16
Sanctions for non-compliance with this Directive

Member States shall ensure that the competent judicial authorities may impose sanctions on any person who fails or refuses to comply with any measure adopted pursuant to Articles 9, 10 and 12.

The sanctions provided for shall include the possibility of imposing recurring penalty payments in the event of non-compliance with a measure adopted pursuant to Articles 10 and 12.

The sanctions provided for shall be effective, proportionate and dissuasive.

[8.822]
Article 17
Exchange of information and correspondents

For the purpose of promoting cooperation, including the exchange of information, among Member States and between Member States and the Commission, each Member State shall designate one or more national correspondents for any question relating to the implementation of the measures provided for by this Directive. It shall communicate the details of the national correspondent or correspondents to the other Member States and the Commission.

[8.823]
Article 18
Reports

1. By 9 June 2021, the European Union Intellectual Property Office, in the context of the activities of the European Observatory on Infringements of Intellectual Property Rights, shall prepare an initial report on the litigation trends regarding the unlawful acquisition, use or disclosure of trade secrets pursuant to the application of this Directive.
2. By 9 June 2022, the Commission shall draw up an intermediate report on the application of this Directive, and shall submit it to the European Parliament and to the Council. That report shall take due account of the report referred to in paragraph 1.

The intermediate report shall examine, in particular, the possible effects of the application of this Directive on research and innovation, the mobility of employees and on the exercise of the right to freedom of expression and information.

3. By 9 June 2026, the Commission shall carry out an evaluation of the impact of this Directive and submit a report to the European Parliament and to the Council.

[8.824]
Article 19
Transposition

1. Member States shall bring into force the laws, regulations and administrative provisions necessary to comply with this Directive by 9 June 2018. They shall immediately communicate the text of those measures to the Commission.

When Member States adopt those measures, they shall contain a reference to this Directive or be accompanied by such a reference on the occasion of their official publication. Member States shall determine how such reference is to be made.

2. Member States shall communicate to the Commission the text of the main provisions of national law which they adopt in the field covered by this Directive.

[8.825]
Article 20
Entry into force
This Directive shall enter into force on the twentieth day following that of its publication in the *Official Journal of the European Union*.

[8.826]
Article 21
Addressees
This Directive is addressed to the Member States.

MEMORANDUM OF UNDERSTANDING (ON TAKE-DOWN NOTICES)

21 June 2016, Brussels

NOTES

The original source of this document is ec.europa.eu/DocsRoom/documents/18023/attachments/1/translations/en/renditions/native.

[8.827]

The development of e-commerce offers unprecedented opportunities to increase European consumers' choice and access in the Internal Market. However, even if the vast majority of e-commerce that takes place on the major internet platforms is legitimate, internet platforms can also be abused by some who seek to distribute counterfeit goods. The sale of counterfeit goods over the internet is damaging and harmful to all legitimate stakeholders including internet platforms, intellectual property rights owners and, most importantly, consumers.

The sale of counterfeit goods over the internet presents a threat to all stakeholders, including consumers, rights owners, internet platforms and society in general as: i) consumers are at growing risk of buying inferior and possibly dangerous products, ii) the brand values, reputation and economic interests of rights owners are jeopardized through the sale of counterfeit versions of their branded products, iii) the efforts of internet platforms to be widely regarded as safe places to buy and sell legitimate products are undermined.

The purpose of this Memorandum of Understanding (hereinafter referred to as "MoU") is to establish a code of practice in the fight against the sale of counterfeit goods over the internet and to enhance collaboration between the signatories including and in addition to Notice and Take-Down procedures. The MoU will also set an example for other stakeholders that are not signatories to this MoU.

This MoU is agreed in good faith between the signatories, on the basis that it is a fair and honest representation of their intentions. The signatories recognise that trade associations who have signed this MoU cannot bind their members. However, these associations commit to make their members fully aware of this MoU and encourage them to respect its principles.

This MoU is limited to each signatory to the extent that it provides services in the Member States of the European Union / European Economic Area. It is not legally binding and does not now nor in the future create any contractual or pre-contractual obligations under any law or legal system. Nothing in this MoU shall be construed as creating any liability, rights, waiver of any rights or obligations for any parties or as releasing any parties from their legal obligations. This MoU shall not be construed in any way as replacing or interpreting the existing legal framework. This MoU is not to be used as, or form part of, evidence in any legal proceedings. This MoU concerns counterfeit and pirated goods. In particular, parallel imports of goods, "grey-market" goods, disputes over licensing agreements, or issues relating to the exhaustion of rights and selective distribution are not covered by this MoU.

1. DEFINITIONS AND GENERAL PRINCIPLES

DEFINITIONS

[8.828]
For the sole purpose of this MoU:

1. An **"Internet Platform"** means any information society service provider whose service is used by third parties to initiate online the trading of physical goods, and which is operated by a signatory of the MoU, to the extent so indicated by the service provider.

2. A **"Rights Owner"** means a signatory of the MoU who holds a registered trade mark, design right[1] or copyright (hereinafter referred to as "IPR"), pursuant to applicable Member State or EU law, for goods covered by this MoU, including exclusive licensees of such IPR.

3. **"Counterfeit Goods"** mean non-original physical goods manufactured without the consent of the Rights Owner which infringe IPR, pursuant to applicable Member State or EU law.

4. An **"Offer"** means a specific proposal for the sale of (a) good(s), entered by a seller on the system of an Internet Platform established in the EU/EEA.

5. **"Notice and Take-Down Procedures"** (hereinafter referred to as "NTD") means any procedure, including the associated processes, by an Internet Platform, that enables a Rights Owner to notify efficiently to an Internet Platform any relevant Offer, including closed Offers, of an alleged Counterfeit Good made publicly available using the relevant services of that Internet Platform, in order to allow the Internet Platform to take appropriate action, including making the Offer unavailable to the general public through the Internet Platform.

6. **"pro-active and preventive Measures"** means any measures, technical or procedural, automated or non automated, including the associated procedures and processes, by an Internet Platform or a Rights Owner, aimed at a timely and adequate response to attempts to sell Counterfeit Goods over an Internet Platform, either prior to the Offer being made available to the general public, or as soon as technically and reasonably feasible thereafter, according to respective business models.

GENERAL PRINCIPLES

7. The signatories agree that the primary responsibility for the protection and enforcement of IPR remains with the respective Rights Owners and that it is the primary responsibility of Internet Platforms to enable a safe online environment for consumers. Hence, it is the parties' goal to collaborate in the fight against the sale of Counterfeit Goods over the Internet.

8. To address more effectively the problem of the sale of Counterfeit Goods over the Internet, the signatories have jointly established a number of principles that shall apply to the Offer of Counterfeit Goods over Internet Platforms. The signatories intend that commitment to the principles set out below, and taken as a whole, will result in a safer online trading environment for all.

9. The methods of implementation of the MoU by Internet Platforms and Rights Owners are in all instances governed by commercial reasonableness standards, taking into consideration the respective business models of the signatories.

MORATORIUM ON LITIGATION

10. In order to facilitate an atmosphere of good faith, in which the signatories are willing to cooperate and assist each other in the fight against the sale of Counterfeit Goods over the Internet, the signatories agree not to initiate any new litigation[2] against each other, concerning matters covered by this MoU, following the signing of this MoU and until the end of the period referred to in paragraph 40.

NOTES

[1] Internet Platforms may choose to limit measures related to design rights to Notice and Take Down Procedures, as laid down in Section 2.

[2] The term "new litigation" means the filing or commencement of a lawsuit or legal proceedings which are not pending at the time of signature of this MoU or related in any manner to prior or existing legal actions.

2. NOTICE AND TAKE-DOWN PROCEDURES (NTD)

[8.829]

11. NTD are indispensable measures in the fight against the sale of Counterfeit Goods over Internet Platforms.

12. In addition to item-based NTD, Rights Owners should have the ability to notify Internet Platforms of sellers who they have a good faith belief are generally engaged in the sale of Counterfeit Goods, provided that Rights Owners identify Offers from such sellers, which are alleged to offer Counterfeit Goods. Internet Platforms commit to take this information into consideration as part of their Pro-active and Preventive Measures.

REPORTING SYSTEM

13. Internet Platforms commit to offer efficient and effective NTD, which should be accessible through electronic means. They should be accessible via the website of the Internet Platform, understandable, not excessively burdensome and simple to subscribe to, complete and process. Notifications should be limited to necessary information, such as a clear identification of both the reporting party and the identification of the specific Offer of the Counterfeit Good. They should also contain a clear allegation that the Offer in question concerns a Counterfeit Good.

14. While notifications may be "Offer" based, Internet Platforms commit to allow notifications to contain multiple Offers of the same seller, as long as such notifications provide sufficient information to permit the identification of the relevant Offers.

RIGHTS OWNERS' USE OF NTD SYSTEMS

15. Rights Owners commit to use NTD offered by Internet Platforms for notifications of Offers of Counterfeit Goods and commit to join respective rights protection programs of Internet Platforms

(if such programs exist). Rights Owners commit to take commercially reasonable and available steps to ensure that they notify Internet Platforms in an efficient and comprehensive manner, of the presence of Offers of Counterfeit Goods and commit to ensure that their use of NTD is undertaken in good faith.

16. Rights Owners commit to take commercially reasonable and available steps to notify in a responsible and accurate way and with necessary precision to identify Counterfeit Goods and to avoid unjustified, unfounded and abusive notifications. In cases where it is obvious that notifications are made without exercising appropriate care, Rights Owners may be denied or may have only restricted access to NTD. Rights Owners and Internet Platforms commit to cooperate to minimize potential consequences to sellers in cases of erroneous notifications. Upon a request by the Internet Platform, Rights Owners commit to pay to the Internet Platform the listing fee and the commission fee[3] of any Offers that were deleted as a result of a notification(s) of multiple Offers made without exercising appropriate care. Sellers relisting offers that have been deleted upon unjustified notification should not incur additional costs.

17. Rights Owners commit to limit their notifications of Offers of Counterfeit Goods to those in which they hold the relevant rights.

INTERNET PLATFORMS' RESPONSE

18. Internet Platforms commit to deal with notifications in an efficient and comprehensive manner, without undue delay and to ensure that valid notifications of Offers of Counterfeit Goods lead to a swift removal or disabling of the notified Offer (take-down) and to take deterrent measures in relation to such sellers. In all cases, Internet Platforms commit to assess the completeness and validity of a notification. In cases of doubt, or where the Internet Platform does not have the necessary information to permit the identification of the notified Offer, Internet Platforms may request additional information from the notifying party. Such requests shall be made in good faith and should not lead to an unreasonable or undue delay in taking down notified Offers in response to valid notifications where the Internet Platform can identify the specific Offer at issue.

FEEDBACK ON NTD

19. Internet Platforms and Rights Owners commit to provide each other with feedback on their notifications. Relevant sellers should also be informed where an Offer has been taken down, including the underlying reason, and should be provided with the means to respond including the notifying party's contact details provided by Rights Owners to Internet Platforms for this purpose.

NOTES

3 Where such fee is part of the business model of the relevant internet Platform.

3. PRO-ACTIVE AND PREVENTIVE MEASURES

PRO-ACTIVE AND PREVENTIVE MEASURES BY RIGHTS OWNERS

[8.830]

20. Rights Owners commit to take commercially reasonable and available steps to effectively fight counterfeiting at its source, including at points of manufacture and initial distribution.

21. Rights Owners commit to take commercially reasonable and available steps to actively monitor Offers on the websites of Internet Platforms with the aim of identifying Counterfeit Goods and notifying them, using NTD, to Internet Platforms.

22. Rights Owners commit to take commercially reasonable and available steps to provide and update general information to Internet Platforms giving priority to specific products that Rights Owners contend present a substantial and pervasive Counterfeit Goods problem on that Internet Platform, including those products which are particularly susceptible to constituting Counterfeit Goods (such as products or ranges/measures of products that do not exist in a Rights Owners' product line but have been specifically developed by counterfeiters to attract consumers). The provision of such information shall not constitute actual or implied notice or actual or constructive knowledge.

23. Rights Owners commit to provide to Internet Platforms at their request a list of keywords commonly used by sellers for the purpose of offering for sale obvious Counterfeit Goods[4], to assist Internet Platforms, as appropriate, with their Proactive and Preventive Measures.

PRO-ACTIVE AND PREVENTIVE MEASURES BY INTERNET PLATFORMS

24. Internet Platforms commit to take commercially and technically reasonable steps to request seller contact information and to verify this information, provided by sellers, in specific circumstances that warrant such identification, in order to gain a reasonable assurance of a seller's identity.

25. Internet Platforms commit to take into consideration information not exclusively related to specific Offers, provided by Rights Owners, in their Pro-active and Preventive Measures. Such information shall not constitute actual or implied notice or actual or constructive knowledge.

26. While Rights Owners have agreed to take commercially reasonable and available steps to actively monitor Offers on the websites of Internet Platforms, Internet Platforms commit to take into consideration information received pursuant to paragraphs 22, 23 and 25. Internet Platforms commit to use this information at their discretion. The receipt of such information shall not lead to a general obligation to monitor for Internet Platforms.

27. Internet Platforms commit to take appropriate, commercially reasonable and technically feasible measures, taking into consideration their respective business models, to identify and/or prevent pro- actively the sale of Counterfeit Goods, especially obvious Counterfeit Goods, and to prevent such goods being offered or sold through their services. The measures taken by Internet Platforms shall be at their discretion.

NOTES

[4] Goods expressly offered for sale using language expressly indicating that such goods are counterfeit.

4. COOPERATION, INCLUDING SHARING OF INFORMATION

COOPERATION INCLUDING SHARING OF INFORMATION BY INTERNET PLATFORMS

[8.831]

28. Internet Platforms commit to adopt, publish and enforce IPR policies, which should be clearly communicated and indicated on their sites and reflected in the contracts which they conclude with their sellers.

29. To facilitate legal actions and investigations into the sale of Counterfeit Goods, Internet Platforms commit to disclose, upon request, relevant information including the identity and contact details of alleged infringers and their user names insofar as permitted by applicable data protection laws.[5]

COOPERATION INCLUDING SHARING OF INFORMATION BY RIGHTS OWNERS

30. For the purpose of, or in connection with, legal proceedings or investigations into the sale of Counterfeit Goods, Rights Owners' requests for the disclosure of the identity and contact details of alleged infringers should be made in good faith and in compliance with applicable law, including data protection laws.

NOTES

[5] Signatories recognize that in certain jurisdicrions, authorisation by a designated state agency or court may be requited under local law for disclosure of personal data and that in case of doubt on the admissibility of disclosure, the Internet Platforms may require the Rights Owner to obtain such authorisation.

5. CONSUMER CONFIDENCE, INFORMATION AND PROTECTION

[8.832]

31. Internet Platforms and Rights Owners recognize that consumers can be active parties in the fight against counterfeiting. They jointly recognize that consumers need to be provided with appropriate tools to help them report Offer of Counterfeit Goods and rogue sellers.

32. Internet Platforms and Rights Owners commit to provide appropriate means to consumers to identify and report Offers of Counterfeit Goods, prior to, or after purchase, to Internet Platforms and to Rights Owners.

33. Internet Platforms recognize the importance of consumer confidence and satisfaction. To this end, they commit to assist consumers who unintentionally purchase Counterfeit Goods on their website. Signatories endorse the principle, but need not mandate, that buyers should not return confirmed Counterfeit Goods to sellers.[6]

NOTES

[6] Some Rights Owners and Internet Platforms have in place consumer guarantee schemes.

6. REPEAT INFRINGERS

INTERNET PLATFORMS' POLICIES RELATING TO REPEAT INFRINGERS

[8.833]

34. Internet Platforms and Rights Owners commit to cooperate in the detection of repeat infringers, especially, but not limited to, those selling high volumes, dangerous, pre-release or obvious Counterfeit Goods.

35. Internet Platforms commit to implement and enforce deterrent repeat infringer policies, according to their internal guidelines. These policies should be enforced objectively and include the suspension (temporary or permanent) or restriction of accounts or sellers. Internet Platforms commit to use their best efforts to prevent re-registration of permanently suspended sellers. These policies should take particular account of factors, such as the severity of a violation, the number of alleged infringements (not taking into account the Offers deleted upon unjustified notification[7]), the apparent intent of the alleged infringer and the record of notices and feedback, received from Rights Owners.

NOTES

[7] Paragraph 16.

36. Internet Platforms commit to share, upon request, information on suspension of repeat infringers on an individual and case-by-case basis with the Rights Owners concerned, in so far as permitted under applicable data protection laws and in accordance with Internet Platform's data disclosure agreements.

RIGHTS OWNERS' MONITORING OF REPEAT INFRINGERS

37. Subject to applicable data protection laws, Rights Owners commit to provide information to Internet Platforms concerning those sellers they believe to be repeat infringers and commit to provide feedback to Internet Platforms on the effectiveness of Internet Platforms' policies regarding repeat infringers (e.g. if Rights Owners feel that there has been a failure to take measures against a repeat infringer).

7. COOPERATION WITH CUSTOMS, BORDER AUTHORITIES AND LAW ENFORCEMENT AUTHORITIES

[8.834]

38. The signatories agree on the importance of supporting the work of law enforcement authorities in the fight against the sale of Counterfeit Goods over the Internet. To this end, Rights Owners and Internet Platforms commit to cooperate and assist law enforcement authorities, where appropriate and in accordance with applicable law, in the investigation of the sale of Counterfeit Goods.

8. ASSESSMENT AND FOLLOW-UP

ENTRY INTO FORCE

[8.835]

39. This Memorandum of Understanding will become effective and will enter into force on 21/06/2016.

ASSESSMENT PERIOD

40. The signature of this MoU will be followed by an assessment period of twelve months. During this assessment period, the signatories will meet quarterly under the auspices of the European Commission, to analyze the progress, implementation and functioning of this MoU on the basis of the Key Performance Indicators (KPIs) set out in the annex to this MoU.

41. The signatories, together with the European Commission, will meet at the end of the assessment period to evaluate, on the basis of a report prepared by the European Commission upon consultation of the signatories, the effectiveness of the MoU in reducing the sale of Counterfeit Goods over Internet Platforms, to discuss the continuation of the MoU and, if appropriate, to discuss and propose appropriate follow-up actions.

REVIEW

42. After the assessment period, signatories may prolong this MoU for an indefinite period.

Each year, the European Commission may draw up, upon consultation of the signatories, a report on the functioning and application of this MoU.

The signatories of the MoU will meet biannually or more frequently if serious problems arise with regard to the functioning or the application of the MoU, under the auspices of the European Commission, to review the MoU and to take further steps, if necessary.

SIGNATORIES

43. Additional signatories may adhere after the assessment period.

44. Each signatory may at any time terminate its participation in this MoU by notification to the other signatories and the European Commission.

45. Each signatory may at any time request the European Commission to convene a plenary meeting of all or specific signatories, if it feels that a signatory is not respecting the principles established by this MoU. Signatories, after consultation of the European Commission, may decide to ask such a signatory to withdraw from the MoU.

46. This MoU only applies to its signatories. It shall, however, be open to other parties. Any additional party signing the MoU agrees not to initiate any new litigation against any other signatory of this MoU concerning matters covered by this MoU within twelve months following such signing.

47. Signatories may indicate on their websites or in commercial or other communications that they have signed this MoU.

Parties indicate their agreement to this MoU by their signatures.

Endorsed in Brussels on 21 June 2016

ANNEX
KEY PERFORMANCE INDICATORS (KPI)

[8.836]
Data received under this MoU by any party in the course of verification for the implementation of the KPIs will be treated confidentially.

KPI NO 1

Number of search results that link to an offer of alleged counterfeit goods* (expressed as a percentage of the total) appearing on the first 100 unique listings per platform per country obtained for a limited number of representative categories of products per brand**. The data would be collected every 6 months*** and reported in aggregate form.

NOTES

* criteria to determine that a product is counterfeit will be the same criteria used for NTDs.

** to be agreed in advance by the Internet Platforms and the Rights Owners, and targeting especially vulnerable ("future-proof") product categories, for example: "X Co trainers" - "Y Co football shirts" - "Z Co handbags".

*** As agreed by the parties 15 November - 15 December and 15 May -15 June will be the two monthly windows per year to collect the data for KPI N° 1 ; the data will be verified by the parties on a bilateral basis before being sent to EUIPO for aggregation.

MAIN CATEGORY	SUB CATEGORY
1. SPORTING GOODS	1. Footwear 2. Football jerseys
2. LUXURY BRANDS	1. Clothes, shoes and accessories 2. Jewelry and watches
3. FASHION BRANDS	1. Shirts 2. Polo Shirts 3. Sweaters
4. FMCG	1. Toys 2. Games 3. Hygiene, cosmetics and personal care (deodorants, hair and skin care) 4. Home or household cleaning and laundry products 5. Foodstuffs and non-alcoholic beverages
5. ELECTRONICS	1. Batteries 2. Computers (including tablets) 3. Telecom equipment (mobile phones and related accessories) 4. Gaming portals/devices 5. Video game consoles and accessories

KPI NO 2

(a) Number of listings removed by MoU signatory Internet Platforms as a result of Proactive and Preventive Measures ("PP")* in place (expressed as a percentage of listing removals related to alleged infringements of MOU signatory Rights Owners' IPR).

(b) Number of listings removed by MOU signatory Internet Platforms as a result of MoU signatory Rights Owners' reports (expressed as a percentage of listing removals related to alleged infringements of MoU signatory Rights Owners' IPR).

The data should be collected by category every 6 months**

NOTES

* For the purpose of this KPI we define PP measures as actions taken in absence of a report sent by MOU signatory Rights Owners.

** As agreed by the parties 15 November - 15 December and 15 May -15 June will be the two monthly windows per year to collect the data for KPI N° 2; the data will be verified by the parties on a bilateral basis before being sent to EUIPO for aggregation.

KPI NO 3

Number of permanent and temporary sellers restrictions imposed by MoU signatory Internet Platforms linked to alleged infringements of MoU signatory Rights Owners' IPR expressed as a percentage of total restrictions imposed by platforms linked to any alleged infringements of IPR*.

NOTES

* As agreed by the parties 15 November - 15 December and 15 May - 15 June will be the two monthly windows per year to collect the data for KPI N°3; the data will be verified by the parties on a bilateral basis before being sent to EUIPO for aggregation.

PART 9
INTERNATIONAL

PARIS CONVENTION FOR THE PROTECTION OF INDUSTRIAL PROPERTY

(20 March 1883)

(as revised at Brussels on 14 December 1900, at Washington on 2 June 1911, at the Hague on 6 November 1925, at London on 2 June 1934, at Lisbon on 31 October 1958, and at Stockholm on 14 July 1967, and as amended on 28 September 1979)

NOTES

The original source for this Convention is the World Intellectual Property Organisation (WIPO).

Articles have been given titles to facilitate their identification. There are no titles in the signed (French) text.

[9.1]

Article 1

[Establishment of the Union; Scope of Industrial Property]

(1) The countries to which this Convention applies constitute a Union for the protection of industrial property.

(2) The protection of industrial property has as its object patents, utility models, industrial designs, trademarks, service marks, trade names, indications of source or appellations of origin, and the repression of unfair competition.

(3) Industrial property shall be understood in the broadest sense and shall apply not only to industry and commerce proper, but likewise to agricultural and extractive industries and to all manufactured or natural products, for example, wines, grain, tobacco leaf, fruit, cattle, minerals, mineral waters, beer, flowers, and flour.

(4) Patents shall include the various kinds of industrial patents recognised by the laws of the countries of the Union, such as patents of importation, patents of improvement, patents and certificates of addition, etc.

[9.2]

Article 2

[National Treatment for Nationals of Countries of the Union]

(1) Nationals of any country of the Union shall, as regards the protection of industrial property, enjoy in all the other countries of the Union the advantages that their respective laws now grant, or may hereafter grant, to nationals; all without prejudice to the rights specially provided for by this Convention. Consequently, they shall have the same protection as the latter, and the same legal remedy against any infringement of their rights, provided that the conditions and formalities imposed upon nationals are complied with.

(2) However, no requirement as to domicile or establishment in the country where protection is claimed may be imposed upon nationals of countries of the Union for the enjoyment of any industrial property rights.

(3) The provisions of the laws of each of the countries of the Union relating to judicial and administrative procedure and to jurisdiction, and to the designation of an address for service or the appointment of an agent, which may be required by the laws on industrial property are expressly reserved.

[9.3]

Article 3

[Same Treatment for Certain Categories of Persons as for Nationals of Countries of the Union]

Nationals of countries outside the Union who are domiciled or who have real and effective industrial or commercial establishments in the territory of one of the countries of the Union shall be treated in the same manner as nationals of the countries of the Union.

[9.4]

Article 4

[A to I. Patents, Utility Models, Industrial Designs, Marks, Inventors' Certificates: Right of Priority.—G. Patents: Division of the Application]

A.—(1) Any person who has duly filed an application for a patent, or for the registration of a utility model, or of an industrial design, or of a trademark, in one of the countries of the Union, or his successor in title, shall enjoy, for the purpose of filing in the other countries, a right of priority during the periods hereinafter fixed.

(2) Any filing that is equivalent to a regular national filing under the domestic legislation of any country of the Union or under bilateral or multilateral treaties concluded between countries of the Union shall be recognised as giving rise to the right of priority.

(3) By a regular national filing is meant any filing that is adequate to establish the date on which the application was filed in the country concerned, whatever may be the subsequent fate of the application.

B. Consequently, any subsequent filing in any of the other countries of the Union before the expiration of the periods referred to above shall not be invalidated by reason of any acts accomplished in the interval, in particular, another filing, the publication or exploitation of the invention, the putting on sale of copies of the design, or the use of the mark, and such acts cannot give rise to any third-party right or any right of personal possession. Rights acquired by third parties before the date of the first application that serves as the basis for the right of priority are reserved in accordance with the domestic legislation of each country of the Union.

C.—(1) The periods of priority referred to above shall be twelve months for patents and utility models, and six months for industrial designs and trademarks.

(2) These periods shall start from the date of filing of the first application; the day of filing shall not be included in the period.

(3) If the last day of the period is an official holiday, or a day when the Office is not open for the filing of applications in the country where protection is claimed, the period shall be extended until the first following working day.

(4) A subsequent application concerning the same subject as a previous first application within the meaning of paragraph (2), above, filed in the same country of the Union, shall be considered as the first application, of which the filing date shall be the starting point of the period of priority, if, at the time of filing the subsequent application, the said previous application has been withdrawn, abandoned, or refused, without having been laid open to public inspection and without leaving any rights outstanding, and if it has not yet served as a basis for claiming a right of priority. The previous application may not thereafter serve as a basis for claiming a right of priority.

D.—(1) Any person desiring to take advantage of the priority of a previous filing shall be required to make a declaration indicating the date of such filing and the country in which it was made. Each country shall determine the latest date on which such declaration must be made.

(2) These particulars shall be mentioned in the publications issued by the competent authority, and in particular in the patents and the specifications relating thereto.

(3) The countries of the Union may require any person making a declaration of priority to produce a copy of the application (description, drawings, etc) previously filed. The copy, certified as correct by the authority which received such application, shall not require any authentication, and may in any case be filed, without fee, at any time within three months of the filing of the subsequent application. They may require it to be accompanied by a certificate from the same authority showing the date of filing, and by a translation.

(4) No other formalities may be required for the declaration of priority at the time of filing the application. Each country of the Union shall determine the consequences of failure to comply with the formalities prescribed by this Article, but such consequences shall in no case go beyond the loss of the right of priority.

(5) Subsequently, further proof may be required.

Any person who avails himself of the priority of a previous application shall be required to specify the number of that application; this number shall be published as provided for by paragraph (2), above.

E.—(1) Where an industrial design is filed in a country by virtue of a right of priority based on the filing of a utility model, the period of priority shall be the same as that fixed for industrial designs.

(2) Furthermore, it is permissible to file a utility model in a country by virtue of a right of priority based on the filing of a patent application, and vice versa.

F. No country of the Union may refuse a priority or a patent application on the ground that the applicant claims multiple priorities, even if they originate in different countries, or on the ground that an application claiming one or more priorities contains one or more elements that were not included in the application or applications whose priority is claimed, provided that, in both cases, there is unity of invention within the meaning of the law of the country.

With respect to the elements not included in the application or applications whose priority is claimed, the filing of the subsequent application shall give rise to a right of priority under ordinary conditions.

G.—(1) If the examination reveals that an application for a patent contains more than one invention, the applicant may divide the application into a certain number of divisional applications and preserve as the date of each the date of the initial application and the benefit of the right of priority, if any.

(2) The applicant may also, on his own initiative, divide a patent application and preserve as the date of each divisional application the date of the initial application and the benefit of the right of priority, if any. Each country of the Union shall have the right to determine the conditions under which such division shall be authorised.

H. Priority may not be refused on the ground that certain elements of the invention for which priority is claimed do not appear among the claims formulated in the application in the country of origin, provided that the application documents as a whole specifically disclose such elements.

I.—(1) Applications for inventors' certificates filed in a country in which applicants have the right to apply at their own option either for a patent or for an inventor's certificate shall give rise to the right of priority provided for by this Article, under the same conditions and with the same effects as applications for patents.
(2) In a country in which applicants have the right to apply at their own option either for a patent or for an inventor's certificate, an applicant for an inventor's certificate shall, in accordance with the provisions of this Article relating to patent applications, enjoy a right of priority based on an application for a patent, a utility model, or an inventor's certificate.

[9.5]
Article 4bis
[Patents: Independence of Patents Obtained for the Same Invention in Different Countries]
(1) Patents applied for in the various countries of the Union by nationals of countries of the Union shall be independent of patents obtained for the same invention in other countries, whether members of the Union or not.
(2) The foregoing provision is to be understood in an unrestricted sense, in particular, in the sense that patents applied for during the period of priority are independent, both as regards the grounds for nullity and forfeiture, and as regards their normal duration.
(3) The provision shall apply to all patents existing at the time when it comes into effect.
(4) Similarly, it shall apply, in the case of the accession of new countries, to patents in existence on either side at the time of accession.
(5) Patents obtained with the benefit of priority shall, in the various countries of the Union, have a duration equal to that which they would have, had they been applied for or granted without the benefit of priority.

[9.6]
Article 4ter
[Patents: Mention of the Inventor in the Patent]
The inventor shall have the right to be mentioned as such in the patent.

[9.7]
Article 4quater
[Patents: Patentability in Case of Restrictions of Sale by Law]
The grant of a patent shall not be refused and a patent shall not be invalidated on the ground that the sale of the patented product or of a product obtained by means of a patented process is subject to restrictions or limitations resulting from the domestic law.

[9.8]
Article 5
[A. Patents: Importation of Articles; Failure to Work or Insufficient Working; Compulsory Licenses.—B. Industrial Designs: Failure to Work; Importation of Articles.—C. Marks: Failure to Use; Different Forms; Use by Co-proprietors.— D. Patents, Utility Models, Marks, Industrial Designs: Marking]
A.—(1) Importation by the patentee into the country where the patent has been granted of articles manufactured in any of the countries of the Union shall not entail forfeiture of the patent.
(2) Each country of the Union shall have the right to take legislative measures providing for the grant of compulsory licenses to prevent the abuses which might result from the exercise of the exclusive rights conferred by the patent, for example, failure to work.
(3) Forfeiture of the patent shall not be provided for except in cases where the grant of compulsory licenses would not have been sufficient to prevent the said abuses. No proceedings for the forfeiture or revocation of a patent may be instituted before the expiration of two years from the grant of the first compulsory license.
(4) A compulsory license may not be applied for on the ground of failure to work or insufficient working before the expiration of a period of four years from the date of filing of the patent application or three years from the date of the grant of the patent, whichever period expires last; it shall be refused if the patentee justifies his inaction by legitimate reasons. Such a compulsory license shall be non-exclusive and shall not be transferable, even in the form of the grant of a sub-license, except with that part of the enterprise or goodwill which exploits such license.
(5) The foregoing provisions shall be applicable, *mutatis mutandis*, to utility models.
B. The protection of industrial designs shall not, under any circumstance, be subject to any forfeiture, either by reason of failure to work or by reason of the importation of articles corresponding to those which are protected.
C.—(1) If, in any country, use of the registered mark is compulsory, the registration may be cancelled only after a reasonable period, and then only if the person concerned does not justify his inaction.
(2) Use of a trademark by the proprietor in a form differing in elements which do not alter the distinctive character of the mark in the form in which it was registered in one of the countries of the Union shall not entail invalidation of the registration and shall not diminish the protection granted to the mark.

(3) Concurrent use of the same mark on identical or similar goods by industrial or commercial establishments considered as co-proprietors of the mark according to the provisions of the domestic law of the country where protection is claimed shall not prevent registration or diminish in any way the protection granted to the said mark in any country of the Union, provided that such use does not result in misleading the public and is not contrary to the public interest.

D. No indication or mention of the patent, of the utility model, of the registration of the trademark, or of the deposit of the industrial design, shall be required upon the goods as a condition of recognition of the right to protection.

[9.9]
Article 5bis
[All Industrial Property Rights: Period of Grace for the Payment of Fees for the Maintenance of Rights; Patents: Restoration]

(1) A period of grace of not less than six months shall be allowed for the payment of the fees prescribed for the maintenance of industrial property rights, subject, if the domestic legislation so provides, to the payment of a surcharge.

(2) The countries of the Union shall have the right to provide for the restoration of patents which have lapsed by reason of non-payment of fees.

[9.10]
Article 5ter
[Patents: Patented Devices Forming Part of Vessels, Aircraft, or Land Vehicles]

In any country of the Union the following shall not be considered as infringements of the rights of a patentee—

1. the use on board vessels of other countries of the Union of devices forming the subject of his patent in the body of the vessel, in the machinery, tackle, gear and other accessories, when such vessels temporarily or accidentally enter the waters of the said country, provided that such devices are used there exclusively for the needs of the vessel;
2. the use of devices forming the subject of the patent in the construction or operation of aircraft or land vehicles of other countries of the Union, or of accessories of such aircraft or land vehicles, when those aircraft or land vehicles temporarily or accidentally enter the said country.

[9.11]
Article 5quater
[Patents: Importation of Products Manufactured by a Process Patented in the Importing Country]

When a product is imported into a country of the Union where there exists a patent protecting a process of manufacture of the said product, the patentee shall have all the rights, with regard to the imported product, that are accorded to him by the legislation of the country of importation, on the basis of the process patent, with respect to products manufactured in that country.

[9.12]
Article 5quinquies
[Industrial Designs]

Industrial designs shall be protected in all the countries of the Union.

[9.13]
Article 6
[Marks: Conditions of Registration; Independence of Protection of Same Mark in Different Countries]

(1) The conditions for the filing and registration of trademarks shall be determined in each country of the Union by its domestic legislation.

(2) However, an application for the registration of a mark filed by a national of a country of the Union may not be refused, nor may a registration be invalidated, on the ground that filing, registration, or renewal, has not been effected in the country of origin.

(3) A mark duly registered in a country of the Union shall be regarded as independent of marks registered in the other countries of the Union, including the country of origin.

[9.14]
Article 6bis
[Marks: Well-known Marks]

(1) The countries of the Union undertake, *ex officio* if their legislation so permits, or at the request of an interested party, to refuse or to cancel the registration, and to prohibit the use, of a trademark which constitutes a reproduction, an imitation, or a translation, liable to create confusion, of a mark considered by the competent authority of the country of registration or use to be well known in that country as being already the mark of a person entitled to the benefits of this Convention and used for identical or similar goods. These provisions shall also apply when the essential part of the mark constitutes a reproduction of any such well-known mark or an imitation liable to create confusion therewith.

(2) A period of at least five years from the date of registration shall be allowed for requesting the cancellation of such a mark. The countries of the Union may provide for a period within which the prohibition of use must be requested.
(3) No time limit shall be fixed for requesting the cancellation or the prohibition of the use of marks registered or used in bad faith.

[9.15]
Article 6ter
[Marks: Prohibitions concerning State Emblems, Official Hallmarks, and Emblems of Intergovernmental Organisations]

(1)

(a) The countries of the Union agree to refuse or to invalidate the registration, and to prohibit by appropriate measures the use, without authorisation by the competent authorities, either as trademarks or as elements of trademarks, of armorial bearings, flags, and other State emblems, of the countries of the Union, official signs and hallmarks indicating control and warranty adopted by them, and any imitation from a heraldic point of view.

(b) The provisions of subparagraph (a), above, shall apply equally to armorial bearings, flags, other emblems, abbreviations, and names, of international intergovernmental organisations of which one or more countries of the Union are members, with the exception of armorial bearings, flags, other emblems, abbreviations, and names, that are already the subject of international agreements in force, intended to ensure their protection.

(c) No country of the Union shall be required to apply the provisions of subparagraph (b), above, to the prejudice of the owners of rights acquired in good faith before the entry into force, in that country, of this Convention. The countries of the Union shall not be required to apply the said provisions when the use or registration referred to in subparagraph (a), above, is not of such a nature as to suggest to the public that a connection exists between the organisation concerned and the armorial bearings, flags, emblems, abbreviations, and names, or if such use or registration is probably not of such a nature as to mislead the public as to the existence of a connection between the user and the organisation.

(2) Prohibition of the use of official signs and hallmarks indicating control and warranty shall apply solely in cases where the marks in which they are incorporated are intended to be used on goods of the same or a similar kind.

(3)

(a) For the application of these provisions, the countries of the Union agree to communicate reciprocally, through the intermediary of the International Bureau, the list of State emblems, and official signs and hallmarks indicating control and warranty, which they desire, or may hereafter desire, to place wholly or within certain limits under the protection of this Article, and all subsequent modifications of such list. Each country of the Union shall in due course make available to the public the lists so communicated.

Nevertheless such communication is not obligatory in respect of flags of States.

(b) The provisions of subparagraph (b) of paragraph (1) of this Article shall apply only to such armorial bearings, flags, other emblems, abbreviations, and names, of international intergovernmental organisations as the latter have communicated to the countries of the Union through the intermediary of the International Bureau.

(4) Any country of the Union may, within a period of twelve months from the receipt of the notification, transmit its objections, if any, through the intermediary of the International Bureau, to the country or international intergovernmental organisation concerned.
(5) In the case of State flags, the measures prescribed by paragraph (1), above, shall apply solely to marks registered after 6 November 1925.
(6) In the case of State emblems other than flags, and of official signs and hallmarks of the countries of the Union, and in the case of armorial bearings, flags, other emblems, abbreviations, and names of intergovernmental organisations, these provisions shall apply only to marks registered more than two months after receipt of the communication provided for in paragraph (3), above.
(7) In cases of bad faith, the countries shall have the right to cancel even those marks incorporating State emblems, signs, and hallmarks, which were registered before 6 November 1925.
(8) Nationals of any country who are authorised to make use of the State emblems, signs, and hallmarks, of their country may use them even if they are similar to those of another country.
(9) The countries of the Union undertake to prohibit the unauthorised use in trade of the State armorial bearings of the other countries of the Union, when the use is of such a nature as to be misleading as to the origin of the goods.
(10) The above provisions shall not prevent the countries from exercising the right given in paragraph (3) of Article 6quinqies, Section B, to refuse or to invalidate the registration of marks incorporating, without authorisation, armorial bearings, flags, other State emblems, or official signs and hallmarks adopted by a country of the Union, as well as the distinctive signs of international intergovernmental organisations referred to in paragraph (1), above.

[9.16]
Article 6quater
[Marks: Assignment of Marks]

(1) When, in accordance with the law of a country of the Union, the assignment of a mark is valid only if it takes place at the same time as the transfer of the business or goodwill to which the mark belongs, it shall suffice for the recognition of such validity that the portion of the business or goodwill located in that country be transferred to the assignee, together with the exclusive right to manufacture in the said country, or to sell therein, the goods bearing the mark assigned.

(2) The foregoing provision does not impose upon the countries of the Union any obligation to regard as valid the assignment of any mark the use of which by the assignee would, in fact, be of such a nature as to mislead the public, particularly as regards the origin, nature, or essential qualities, of the goods to which the mark is applied.

[9.17]
Article 6quinquies
[Marks: Protection of Marks Registered in One Country of the Union in the Other Countries of the Union]

A.—(1) Every trademark duly registered in the country of origin shall be accepted for filing and protected as is in the other countries of the Union, subject to the reservations indicated in this Article. Such countries may, before proceeding to final registration, require the production of a certificate of registration in the country of origin, issued by the competent authority. No authentication shall be required for this certificate.

(2) Shall be considered the country of origin the country of the Union where the applicant has a real and effective industrial or commercial establishment, or, if he has no such establishment within the Union, the country of the Union where he has his domicile, or, if he has no domicile within the Union but is a national of a country of the Union, the country of which he is a national.

B. Trademarks covered by this Article may be neither denied registration nor invalidated except in the following cases—

1. when they are of such a nature as to infringe rights acquired by third parties in the country where protection is claimed;
2. when they are devoid of any distinctive character, or consist exclusively of signs or indications which may serve, in trade, to designate the kind, quality, quantity, intended purpose, value, place of origin, of the goods, or the time of production, or have become customary in the current language or in the bona fide and established practices of the trade of the country where protection is claimed;
3. when they are contrary to morality or public order and, in particular, of such a nature as to deceive the public. It is understood that a mark may not be considered contrary to public order for the sole reason that it does not conform to a provision of the legislation on marks, except if such provision itself relates to public order.

This provision is subject, however, to the application of Article 10*bis*.

C.—(1) In determining whether a mark is eligible for protection, all the factual circumstances must be taken into consideration, particularly the length of time the mark has been in use.

(2) No trademark shall be refused in the other countries of the Union for the sole reason that it differs from the mark protected in the country of origin only in respect of elements that do not alter its distinctive character and do not affect its identity in the form in which it has been registered in the said country of origin.

D. No person may benefit from the provisions of this Article if the mark for which he claims protection is not registered in the country of origin.

E. However, in no case shall the renewal of the registration of the mark in the country of origin involve an obligation to renew the registration in the other countries of the Union in which the mark has been registered.

F. The benefit of priority shall remain unaffected for applications for the registration of marks filed within the period fixed by Article 4, even if registration in the country of origin is effected after the expiration of such period.

[9.18]
Article 6sexies
[Marks: Service Marks]

The countries of the Union undertake to protect service marks. They shall not be required to provide for the registration of such marks.

[9.19]
Article 6septies
[Marks: Registration in the Name of the Agent or Representative of the Proprietor Without the Latter's Authorisation]

(1) If the agent or representative of the person who is the proprietor of a mark in one of the countries of the Union applies, without such proprietor's authorisation, for the registration of the mark in his own name, in one or more countries of the Union, the proprietor shall be entitled to

oppose the registration applied for or demand its cancellation or, if the law of the country so allows, the assignment in his favour of the said registration, unless such agent or representative justifies his action.

(2) The proprietor of the mark shall, subject to the provisions of paragraph (1), above, be entitled to oppose the use of his mark by his agent or representative if he has not authorised such use.

(3) Domestic legislation may provide an equitable time limit within which the proprietor of a mark must exercise the rights provided for in this Article.

[9.20]
Article 7
[Marks: Nature of the Goods to which the Mark is Applied]

The nature of the goods to which a trademark is to be applied shall in no case form an obstacle to the registration of the mark.

[9.21]
Article 7bis
[Marks: Collective Marks]

(1) The countries of the Union undertake to accept for filing and to protect collective marks belonging to associations the existence of which is not contrary to the law of the country of origin, even if such associations do not possess an industrial or commercial establishment.

(2) Each country shall be the judge of the particular conditions under which a collective mark shall be protected and may refuse protection if the mark is contrary to the public interest.

(3) Nevertheless, the protection of these marks shall not be refused to any association the existence of which is not contrary to the law of the country of origin, on the ground that such association is not established in the country where protection is sought or is not constituted according to the law of the latter country.

[9.22]
Article 8
[Trade Names]

A trade name shall be protected in all the countries of the Union without the obligation of filing or registration whether or not it forms part of a trademark.

[9.23]
Article 9
[Marks, Trade Names: Seizure, on Importation, etc, of Goods Unlawfully Bearing a Mark or Trade Name]

(1) All goods unlawfully bearing a trademark or trade name shall be seized on importation into those countries of the Union where such mark or trade name is entitled to legal protection.

(2) Seizure shall likewise be effected in the country where the unlawful affixation occurred or in the country into which the goods were imported.

(3) Seizure shall take place at the request of the public prosecutor, or any other competent authority, or any interested party, whether a natural person or a legal entity, in conformity with the domestic legislation of each country.

(4) The authorities shall not be bound to effect seizure of goods in transit.

(5) If the legislation of a country does not permit seizure on importation, seizure shall be replaced by prohibition of importation or by seizure inside the country.

(6) If the legislation of a country permits neither seizure on importation nor prohibition of importation nor seizure inside the country, then, until such time as the legislation is modified accordingly, these measures shall be replaced by the actions and remedies available in such cases to nationals under the law of such country.

[9.24]
Article 10
[False Indications: Seizure, on Importation, etc, of Goods Bearing False Indications as to their Source or the Identity of the Producer]

(1) The provisions of the preceding Article shall apply in cases of direct or indirect use of a false indication of the source of the goods or the identity of the producer, manufacturer, or merchant.

(2) Any producer, manufacturer, or merchant, whether a natural person or a legal entity, engaged in the production or manufacture of or trade in such goods and established either in the locality falsely indicated as the source, or in the region where such locality is situated, or in the country falsely indicated, or in the country where the false indication of source is used, shall in any case be deemed an interested party.

[9.25]
Article 10bis
[Unfair Competition]

(1) The countries of the Union are bound to assure to nationals of such countries effective protection against unfair competition.

(2) Any act of competition contrary to honest practices in industrial or commercial matters constitutes an act of unfair competition.

(3) The following in particular shall be prohibited—

1. all acts of such a nature as to create confusion by any means whatever with the establishment, the goods, or the industrial or commercial activities, of a competitor;
2. false allegations in the course of trade of such a nature as to discredit the establishment, the goods, or the industrial or commercial activities, of a competitor;
3. indications or allegations the use of which in the course of trade is liable to mislead the public as to the nature, the manufacturing process, the characteristics, the suitability for their purpose, or the quantity, of the goods.

[9.26]
Article 10ter
[Marks, Trade Names, False Indications, Unfair Competition: Remedies, Right to Sue]

(1) The countries of the Union undertake to assure to nationals of other countries of the Union appropriate legal remedies effectively to repress all the acts referred to in Articles 9, 10, and 10*bis*.

(2) They undertake, further, to provide measures to permit federations and associations representing interested industrialists, producers, or merchants, provided that the existence of such federations and associations is not contrary to the laws of their countries, to take action in the courts or before the administrative authorities, with a view to the repression of the acts referred to in Articles 9, 10, and 10*bis*, in so far as the law of the country in which protection is claimed allows such action by federations and associations of that country.

[9.27]
Article 11
[Inventions, Utility Models, Industrial Designs, Marks: Temporary Protection at Certain International Exhibitions]

(1) The countries of the Union shall, in conformity with their domestic legislation, grant temporary protection to patentable inventions, utility models, industrial designs, and trademarks, in respect of goods exhibited at official or officially recognised international exhibitions held in the territory of any of them.

(2) Such temporary protection shall not extend the periods provided by Article 4. If, later, the right of priority is invoked, the authorities of any country may provide that the period shall start from the date of introduction of the goods into the exhibition.

(3) Each country may require, as proof of the identity of the article exhibited and of the date of its introduction, such documentary evidence as it considers necessary.

[9.28]
Article 12
[Special National Industrial Property Services]

(1) Each country of the Union undertakes to establish a special industrial property service and a central office for the communication to the public of patents, utility models, industrial designs, and trademarks.

(2) This service shall publish an official periodical journal. It shall publish regularly—

(a) the names of the proprietors of patents granted, with a brief designation of the inventions patented;

(b) the reproductions of registered trademarks.

[9.29]
Article 13
[Assembly of the Union]

(1)

(a) The Union shall have an Assembly consisting of those countries of the Union which are bound by Articles 13 to 17.

(b) The Government of each country shall be represented by one delegate, who may be assisted by alternate delegates, advisors, and experts.

(c) The expenses of each delegation shall be borne by the Government which has appointed it.

(2)

(a) The Assembly shall—

(i) deal with all matters concerning the maintenance and development of the Union and the implementation of this Convention;

(ii) give directions concerning the preparation for conferences of revision to the International Bureau of Intellectual Property (hereinafter designated as "the International Bureau") referred to in the Convention establishing the World Intellectual Property Organisation (hereinafter designated as "the Organisation"), due account being taken of any comments made by those countries of the Union which are not bound by Articles 13 to 17;

(iii) review and approve the reports and activities of the Director-General of the Organisation concerning the Union, and give him all necessary instructions concerning matters within the competence of the Union;

(iv) elect the members of the Executive Committee of the Assembly;
(v) review and approve the reports and activities of its Executive Committee, and give instructions to such Committee;
(vi) determine the program and adopt the triennial budget of the Union, and approve its final accounts;
(vii) adopt the financial regulations of the Union;
(viii) establish such committees of experts and working groups as it deems appropriate to achieve the objectives of the Union;
(ix) determine which countries not members of the Union and which intergovernmental and international nongovernmental organisations shall be admitted to its meetings as observers;
(x) adopt amendments to Articles 13 to 17;
(xi) take any other appropriate action designed to further the objectives of the Union;
(xii) perform such other functions as are appropriate under this Convention;
(xiii) subject to its acceptance, exercise such rights as are given to it in the Convention establishing the Organisation.

(b) With respect to matters which are of interest also to other Unions administered by the Organisation, the Assembly shall make its decisions after having heard the advice of the Coordination Committee of the Organisation.

(3)
(a) Subject to the provisions of subparagraph (b), a delegate may represent one country only.
(b) Countries of the Union grouped under the terms of a special agreement in a common office possessing for each of them the character of a special national service of industrial property as referred to in Article 12 may be jointly represented during discussions by one of their number.

(4)
(a) Each country member of the Assembly shall have one vote.
(b) One-half of the countries members of the Assembly shall constitute a quorum.
(c) Notwithstanding the provisions of subparagraph (b), if, in any session, the number of countries represented is less than one-half but equal to or more than one-third of the countries members of the Assembly, the Assembly may make decisions but, with the exception of decisions concerning its own procedure, all such decisions shall take effect only if the conditions set forth hereinafter are fulfilled. The International Bureau shall communicate the said decisions to the countries members of the Assembly which were not represented and shall invite them to express in writing their vote or abstention within a period of three months from the date of the communication. If, at the expiration of this period, the number of countries having thus expressed their vote or abstention attains the number of countries which was lacking for attaining the quorum in the session itself, such decisions shall take effect provided that at the same time the required majority still obtains.
(d) Subject to the provisions of Article 17(2), the decisions of the Assembly shall require two-thirds of the votes cast.
(e) Abstentions shall not be considered as votes.

(5)
(a) Subject to the provisions of subparagraph (b), a delegate may vote in the name of one country only.
(b) The countries of the Union referred to in paragraph (3)(b) shall, as a general rule, endeavour to send their own delegations to the sessions of the Assembly. If, however, for exceptional reasons, any such country cannot send its own delegation, it may give to the delegation of another such country the power to vote in its name, provided that each delegation may vote by proxy for one country only. Such power to vote shall be granted in a document signed by the Head of State or the competent Minister.

(6) Countries of the Union not members of the Assembly shall be admitted to the meetings of the latter as observers.

(7)
(a) The Assembly shall meet once in every third calendar year in ordinary session upon convocation by the Director-General and, in the absence of exceptional circumstances, during the same period and at the same place as the General Assembly of the Organisation.
(b) The Assembly shall meet in extraordinary session upon convocation by the Director-General, at the request of the Executive Committee or at the request of one-fourth of the countries members of the Assembly.

(8) The Assembly shall adopt its own rules of procedure.

[9.30]
Article 14
[Executive Committee]

(1) The Assembly shall have an Executive Committee.

(2)

(a) The Executive Committee shall consist of countries elected by the Assembly from among countries members of the Assembly. Furthermore, the country on whose territory the Organisation has its headquarters shall, subject to the provisions of Article 16(7)(b), have an *ex officio* seat on the Committee.

(b) The Government of each country member of the Executive Committee shall be represented by one delegate, who may be assisted by alternate delegates, advisors, and experts.

(c) The expenses of each delegation shall be borne by the Government which has appointed it.

(3) The number of countries members of the Executive Committee shall correspond to one-fourth of the number of countries members of the Assembly. In establishing the number of seats to be filled, remainders after division by four shall be disregarded.

(4) In electing the members of the Executive Committee, the Assembly shall have due regard to an equitable geographical distribution and to the need for countries party to the Special Agreements established in relation with the Union to be among the countries constituting the Executive Committee.

(5)

(a) Each member of the Executive Committee shall serve from the close of the session of the Assembly which elected it to the close of the next ordinary session of the Assembly.

(b) Members of the Executive Committee may be re-elected, but only up to a maximum of two-thirds of such members.

(c) The Assembly shall establish the details of the rules governing the election and possible re-election of the members of the Executive Committee.

(6)

(a) The Executive Committee shall—

(i) prepare the draft agenda of the Assembly;

(ii) submit proposals to the Assembly in respect of the draft program and triennial budget of the Union prepared by the Director-General;

(iii) approve, within the limits of the program and the triennial budget, the specific yearly budgets and programs prepared by the Director-General;

(iv) submit, with appropriate comments, to the Assembly the periodical reports of the Director-General and the yearly audit reports on the accounts;

(v) take all necessary measures to ensure the execution of the program of the Union by the Director-General, in accordance with the decisions of the Assembly and having regard to circumstances arising between two ordinary sessions of the Assembly;

(vi) perform such other functions as are allocated to it under this Convention.

(b) With respect to matters which are of interest also to other Unions administered by the Organisation, the Executive Committee shall make its decisions after having heard the advice of the Coordination Committee of the Organisation.

(7)

(a) The Executive Committee shall meet once a year in ordinary session upon convocation by the Director-General, preferably during the same period and at the same place as the Coordination Committee of the Organisation.

(b) The Executive Committee shall meet in extraordinary session upon convocation by the Director-General, either on his own initiative, or at the request of its Chairman or one-fourth of its members.

(8)

(a) Each country member of the Executive Committee shall have one vote.

(b) One-half of the members of the Executive Committee shall constitute a quorum.

(c) Decisions shall be made by a simple majority of the votes cast.

(d) Abstentions shall not be considered as votes.

(e) A delegate may represent, and vote in the name of, one country only.

(9) Countries of the Union not members of the Executive Committee shall be admitted to its meetings as observers.

(10) The Executive Committee shall adopt its own rules of procedure.

[9.31]
Article 15
[International Bureau]

(1)

(a) Administrative tasks concerning the Union shall be performed by the International Bureau, which is a continuation of the Bureau of the Union united with the Bureau of the Union established by the International Convention for the Protection of Literary and Artistic Works.

(b) In particular, the International Bureau shall provide the secretariat of the various organs of the Union.

(c) The Director-General of the Organisation shall be the chief executive of the Union and shall represent the Union.

(2) The International Bureau shall assemble and publish information concerning the protection of industrial property. Each country of the Union shall promptly communicate to the International Bureau all new laws and official texts concerning the protection of industrial property. Furthermore, it shall furnish the International Bureau with all the publications of its industrial property service of direct concern to the protection of industrial property which the International Bureau may find useful in its work.

(3) The International Bureau shall publish a monthly periodical.

(4) The International Bureau shall, on request, furnish any country of the Union with information on matters concerning the protection of industrial property.

(5) The International Bureau shall conduct studies, and shall provide services, designed to facilitate the protection of industrial property.

(6) The Director-General and any staff member designated by him shall participate, without the right to vote, in all meetings of the Assembly, the Executive Committee, and any other committee of experts or working group. The Director-General, or a staff member designated by him, shall be *ex officio* secretary of these bodies.

(7)

(a) The International Bureau shall, in accordance with the directions of the Assembly and in cooperation with the executive Committee, make the preparations for the conferences of revision of the provisions of the Convention other than Articles 13 to 17.

(b) The International Bureau may consult with intergovernmental and international non-governmental organisations concerning preparations for conferences of revision.

(c) The Director-General and persons designated by him shall take part, without the right to vote, in the discussions at these conferences.

(8) The International Bureau shall carry out any other tasks assigned to it.

[9.32]
Article 16
[Finances]

(1)

(a) The Union shall have a budget.

(b) The budget of the Union shall include the income and expenses proper to the Union, its contribution to the budget of expenses common to the Unions, and, where applicable, the sum made available to the budget of the Conference of the Organisation.

(c) Expenses not attributable exclusively to the Union but also to one or more other Unions administered by the Organisation shall be considered as expenses common to the Unions. The share of the Union in such common expenses shall be in proportion to the interest the Union has in them.

(2) The budget of the Union shall be established with due regard to the requirements of coordination with the budgets of the other Unions administered by the Organisation.

(3) The budget of the Union shall be financed from the following sources—

(i) contributions of the countries of the Union;

(ii) fees and charges due for services rendered by the International Bureau in relation to the Union;

(iii) sale of, or royalties on, the publications of the International Bureau concerning the Union:

(iv) gifts, bequests, and subventions;

(v) rents, interests, and other miscellaneous income.

(4)

(a) For the purpose of establishing its contribution towards the budget, each country of the Union shall belong to a class, and shall pay its annual contributions on the basis of a number of units fixed as follows—

Class I	25
Class II	20
Class III	15
Class IV	10
Class V	5
Class VI	3
Class VII	1

(b) Unless it has already done so, each country shall indicate, concurrently with depositing its instrument of ratification or accession, the class to which it wishes to belong. Any country may change class. If it chooses a lower class, the country must announce such change to the Assembly at one of its ordinary sessions. Any such change shall take effect at the beginning of the calendar year following the said session.

(c) The annual contribution of each country shall be an amount in the same proportion to the total sum to be contributed to the budget of the Union by all countries as the number of its units is to the total of the units of all contributing countries.

(d) Contributions shall become due on the first of January of each year.

(e) A country which is in arrears in the payment of its contributions may not exercise its right to vote in any of the organs of the Union of which it is a member if the amount of its arrears equals or exceeds the amount of the contributions due from it for the preceding two full years. However, any organ of the Union may allow such a country to continue to exercise its right to vote in that organ if, and as long as, it is satisfied that the delay in payment is due to exceptional and unavoidable circumstances.

(f) If the budget is not adopted before the beginning of a new financial period, it shall be at the same level as the budget of the previous year, as provided in the financial regulations.

(5) The amount of the fees and charges due for services rendered by the International Bureau in relation to the Union shall be established, and shall be reported to the Assembly and the Executive Committee, by the Director-General.

(6)

(a) the Union shall have a working capital fund which shall be constituted by a single payment made by each country of the Union. If the fund becomes insufficient, the Assembly shall decide to increase it.

(b) The amount of the initial payment of each country to the said fund or of its participation in the increase thereof shall be a proportion of the contribution of that country for the year in which the fund is established or the decision to increase it is made.

(c) The proportion and the terms of payment shall be fixed by the Assembly on the proposal of the Director-General and after it has heard the advice of the Coordination Committee of the Organisation.

(7)

(a) In the headquarters agreement concluded with the country on the territory of which the Organisation has its headquarters, it shall be provided that, whenever the working capital fund is insufficient, such country shall grant advances. The amount of these advances and the conditions on which they are granted shall be the subject of separate agreements, in each case, between such country and the Organisation. As long as it remains under the obligation to grant advances, such country shall have an *ex officio* seat on the Executive Committee.

(b) The country referred to in subparagraph (a) and the Organisation shall each have the right to denounce the obligation to grant advances, by written notification. Denunciation shall take effect three years after the end of the year in which it has been notified.

(8) The auditing of the accounts shall be effected by one or more of the countries of the Union or by external auditors, as provided in the financial regulations. They shall be designated, with their agreement, by the Assembly.

[9.33]
Article 17
[Amendment of Articles 13 to 17]

(1) Proposals for the amendment of Articles 13, 14, 15, 16, and the present Article, may be initiated by any country member of the Assembly, by the Executive Committee, or by the Director-General. Such proposals shall be communicated by the Director-General to the member countries of the Assembly at least six months in advance of their consideration by the Assembly.

(2) Amendments to the Articles referred to in paragraph (1) shall be adopted by the Assembly. Adoption shall require three-fourths of the votes cast, provided that any amendment to Article 13, and to the present paragraph, shall require four-fifths of the votes cast.

(3) Any amendment to the Articles referred to in paragraph (1) shall enter into force one month after written notifications of acceptance, effected in accordance with their respective constitutional processes, have been received by the Director-General from three-fourths of the countries members of the Assembly at the time it adopted the amendment. Any amendment to the said Articles thus accepted shall bind all the countries which are members of the Assembly at the time the amendment enters into force, or which become members thereof at a subsequent date, provided that any amendment increasing the financial obligations of countries of the Union shall bind only those countries which have notified their acceptance of such amendment.

[9.34]
Article 18
[Revision of Articles 1 to 12 and 18 to 30]

(1) This Convention shall be submitted to revision with a view to the introduction of amendments designed to improve the system of the Union.

(2) For that purpose, conferences shall be held successively in one of the countries of the Union among the delegates of the said countries.

(3) Amendments to Articles 13 to 17 are governed by the provisions of Article 17.

[9.35]
Article 19
[Special Agreements]

It is understood that the countries of the Union reserve the right to make separately between themselves special agreements for the protection of industrial property, in so far as these agreements do not contravene the provisions of this Convention.

[9.36]
Article 20
[Ratification or Accession by Countries of the Union; Entry Into Force]

(1)

(a) Any country of the Union which has signed this Act may ratify it, and, if it has not signed it, may accede to it. Instruments of ratification and accession shall be deposited with the Director General.

(b) Any country of the Union may declare in its instrument of ratification or accession that its ratification or accession shall not apply—

(i) to Articles 1 to 12, or

(ii) to Articles 13 to 17.

(c) Any country of the Union which, in accordance with subparagraph (b), has excluded from the effects of its ratification or accession one of the two groups of Articles referred to in that subparagraph may at any later time declare that it extends the effects of its ratification or accession to that group of Articles. Such declaration shall be deposited with the Director General.

(2)

(a) Articles 1 to 12 shall enter into force, with respect to the first ten countries of the Union which have deposited instruments of ratification or accession without making the declaration permitted under paragraph (1)(b)(i), three months after the deposit of the tenth such instrument of ratification or accession.

(b) Articles 13 to 17 shall enter into force, with respect to the first ten countries of the Union which have deposited instruments of ratification or accession without making the declaration permitted under paragraph (1)(b)(ii). three months after the deposit of the tenth such instrument of ratification or accession.

(c) Subject to the initial entry into force, pursuant to the provisions of subparagraphs (a) and (b), of each of the two groups of Articles referred to in paragraph (1)(b)(i) and (ii) and subject to the provisions of paragraph (1)(b), Articles 1 to 17 shall, with respect to any country of the Union, other than those referred to in subparagraphs (a) and (b), which deposits an instrument of ratification or accession or any country of the Union which deposits a declaration pursuant to paragraph (1)(c), enter into force three months after the date of notification by the Director General of such deposit, unless a subsequent date has been indicated in the instrument or declaration deposited. In the latter case, this Act shall enter into force with respect to that country on the date thus indicated.

(3) With respect to any country of the Union which deposits an instrument of ratification or accession, Articles 18 to 30 shall enter into force on the earlier of the dates on which any of the groups of Articles referred to in paragraph (1)(b) enters into force with respect to that country pursuant to paragraph (2)(a), (b), or (c).

[9.37]
Article 21
[Accession by Countries Outside the Union; Entry Into Force]

(1) Any country outside the Union may accede to this Act and thereby become a member of the Union. Instruments of accession shall be deposited with the Director General.

(2)

(a) With respect to any country outside the Union which deposits its instrument of accession one month or more before the date of entry into force of any provisions of the present Act, this Act shall enter into force, unless a subsequent date has been indicated in the instrument of accession, on the date upon which provisions first enter into force pursuant to Article 20(2)(a) or (b); provided that—

(i) if Articles 1 to 12 do not enter into force on that date, such country shall, during the interim period before the entry into force of such provisions, and in substitution therefor, be bound by Articles 1 to 12 of the Lisbon Act,

(ii) if Articles 13 to 17 do not enter into force on that date, such country shall, during the interim period before the entry into force of such provisions, and in substitution therefor, be bound by Articles 13 and 14(3), (4), and (5), of the Lisbon Act.

If a country indicates a subsequent date in its instrument of accession, this Act shall enter into force with respect to that country on the date thus indicated.

(b) With respect to any country outside the Union which deposits its instrument of accession on a date which is subsequent to, or precedes by less than one month, the entry into force of one group of Articles of the present Act, this Act shall, subject to the proviso of subparagraph (a), enter into force three months after the date on which its accession has been notified by the Director General, unless a subsequent date has been indicated in the instrument of accession. In the latter case, this Act shall enter into force with respect to that country on the date thus indicated.

(3) With respect to any country outside the Union which deposits its instrument of accession after the date of entry into force of the present Act in its entirety, or less than one month before such date, this Act shall enter into force three months after the date on which its accession has been notified by the Director General, unless a subsequent date has been indicated in the instrument of accession. In the latter case, this Act shall enter into force with respect to that country on the date thus indicated.

[9.38]
Article 22
[Consequences of Ratification or Accession]

Subject to the possibilities of exceptions provided for in Articles 20(1)(b) and 28(2), ratification or accession shall automatically entail acceptance of all the clauses and admission to all the advantages of this Act.

[9.39]
Article 23
[Accession to Earlier Acts]

After the entry into force of this Act in its entirety, a country may not accede to earlier Acts of this Convention.

[9.40]
Article 24
[Territories]

(1) Any country may declare in its instrument of ratification or accession, or may inform the Director General by written notification any time thereafter, that this Convention shall be applicable to all or part of those territories, designated in the declaration or notification, for the external relations of which it is responsible.

(2) Any country which has made such a declaration or given such a notification may, at any time, notify the Director General that this Convention shall cease to be applicable to all or part of such territories.

(3)

(a) Any declaration made under paragraph (1) shall take effect on the same date as the ratification or accession in the instrument of which it was included, and any notification given under such paragraph shall take effect three months after its notification by the Director General.

(b) Any notification given under paragraph (2) shall take effect twelve months after its receipt by the Director General.

[9.41]
Article 25
[Implementation of the Convention on the Domestic Level]

(1) Any country party to this Convention undertakes to adopt, in accordance with its constitution, the measures necessary to ensure the application of this Convention.

(2) It is understood that, at the time a country deposits its instrument of ratification or accession, it will be in a position under its domestic law to give effect to the provisions of this Convention.

[9.42]
Article 26
[Denunciation]

(1) This Convention shall remain in force without limitation as to time.

(2) Any country may denounce this Act by notification addressed to the Director General. Such denunciation shall constitute also denunciation of all earlier Acts and shall affect only the country making it, the Convention remaining in full force and effect as regards the other countries of the Union.

(3) Denunciation shall take effect one year after the day on which the Director General has received the notification.

(4) The right of denunciation provided by this Article shall not be exercised by any country before the expiration of five years from the date upon which it becomes a member of the Union.

[9.43]
Article 27
[Application of Earlier Acts]

(1) The present Act shall, as regards the relations between the countries to which it applies, and to the extent that it applies, replace the Convention of Paris of March 20, 1883, and the subsequent Acts of revision.

(2)

(a) As regards the countries to which the present Act does not apply, or does not apply in its entirety, but to which the Lisbon Act of October 31, 1958, applies, the latter shall remain in force in its entirety or to the extent that the present Act does not replace it by virtue of paragraph (1).

(b) Similarly, as regards the countries to which neither the present Act, nor portions thereof, nor the Lisbon Act applies, the London Act of June 2, 1934, shall remain in force in its entirety or to the extent that the present Act does not replace it by virtue of paragraph (1).

(c) Similarly, as regards the countries to which neither the present Act, nor portions thereof, nor the Lisbon Act, nor the London Act applies, the Hague Act of November 6, 1925, shall remain in force in its entirety or to the extent that the present Act does not replace it by virtue of paragraph (1).

(3) Countries outside the Union which become party to this Act shall apply it with respect to any country of the Union not party to this Act or which, although party to this Act, has made a declaration pursuant to Article 20(1)(b)(i). Such countries recognise that the said country of the Union may apply, in its relations with them, the provisions of the most recent Act to which it is party.

[9.44]
Article 28
[Disputes]

(1) Any dispute between two or more countries of the Union concerning the interpretation or application of this Convention, not settled by negotiation, may, by any one of the countries concerned, be brought before the International Court of Justice by application in conformity with the Statute of the Court, unless the countries concerned agree on some other method of settlement. The country bringing the dispute before the Court shall inform the International Bureau; the International Bureau shall bring the matter to the attention of the other countries of the Union.

(2) Each country may, at the time it signs this Act or deposits its instrument of ratification or accession, declare that it does not consider itself bound by the provisions of paragraph (1). With regard to any dispute between such country and any other country of the Union, the provisions of paragraph (1) shall not apply.

(3) Any country having made a declaration in accordance with the provisions of paragraph (2) may, at any time, withdraw its declaration by notification addressed to the Director General.

[9.45]
Article 29
[Signature, Languages, Depositary Functions]

(1)

(a) This Act shall be signed in a single copy in the French language and shall be deposited with the Government of Sweden.

(b) Official texts shall be established by the Director General, after consultation with the interested Governments, in the English, German, Italian, Portuguese, Russian and Spanish languages, and such other languages as the Assembly may designate.

(c) In case of differences of opinion on the interpretation of the various texts, the French text shall prevail.

(2) This Act shall remain open for signature at Stockholm until January 13, 1968.

(3) The Director General shall transmit two copies, certified by the Government of Sweden, of the signed text of this Act to the Governments of all countries of the Union and, on request, to the Government of any other country.

(4) The Director General shall register this Act with the Secretariat of the United Nations.

(5) The Director General shall notify the Governments of all countries of the Union of signatures, deposits of instruments of ratification or accession and any declarations included in such instruments or made pursuant to Article 20(1)(c), entry into force of any provisions of this Act, notifications of denunciation, and notifications pursuant to Article 24.

[9.46]
Article 30
[Transitional Provisions]

(1) Until the first Director General assumes office, references in this Act to the International Bureau of the Organisation or to the Director General shall be deemed to be references to the Bureau of the Union or its Director, respectively.

(2) Countries of the Union not bound by Articles 13 to 17 may, until five years after the entry into force of the Convention establishing the Organisation, exercise, if they so desire, the rights provided under Articles 13 to 17 of this Act as if they were bound by those Articles. Any country desiring to exercise such rights shall give written notification to that effect to the Director General; such notification shall be effective from the date of its receipt. Such countries shall be deemed to be members of the Assembly until the expiration of the said period.

(3) As long as all the countries of the Union have not become Members of the Organisation, the International Bureau of the Organisation shall also function as the Bureau of the Union, and the Director General as the Director of the said Bureau.

(4) Once all the countries of the Union have become Members of the Organisation, the rights, obligations, and property, of the Bureau of the Union shall devolve on the International Bureau of the Organisation.

THE HAGUE AGREEMENT CONCERNING THE INTERNATIONAL DEPOSIT OF INDUSTRIAL DESIGNS

of November 6, 1925

The Hague Act of November 28, 1960

NOTES

The original source for this Agreement is the World Intellectual Property Organisation (WIPO).

[9.47]
Article 1

(1) The contracting States constitute a Special Union for the international deposit of industrial designs.

(2) Only States members of the International Union for the Protection of Industrial Property may become party to this Agreement.

[9.48]
Article 2

For the purposes of this Agreement—

'1925 Agreement' shall mean the Hague Agreement concerning the International Deposit of Industrial Designs of November 6, 1925;

'1934 Agreement' shall mean the Hague Agreement concerning the International Deposit of Industrial Designs of November 6, 1925, as revised at London on June 2, 1934;

'this Agreement' or 'the present Agreement' shall mean the Hague Agreement concerning the International Deposit of Industrial Designs as established by the present Act;

'Regulations' shall mean the Regulations for carrying out this Agreement;

'International Bureau' shall mean the Bureau of the International Union for the Protection of Industrial Property;

'international deposit' shall mean a deposit made at the International Bureau;

'national deposit' shall mean a deposit made at the national Office of a contracting State;

'multiple deposit' shall mean a deposit including several designs;

'State of origin of an international deposit' shall mean the contracting State in which the applicant has a real and effective industrial or commercial establishment or, if the applicant has such establishments in several contracting States, the contracting State which he has indicated in his application; if the applicant has no such establishment in any contracting State, the contracting State in which he has his domicile; if he has no domicile in a contracting State, the contracting State of which he is a national;

'State having a novelty examination' shall mean a contracting State the domestic law of which provides for a system which involves a preliminary *ex officio* search and examination by its national Office as to the novelty of each deposited design.

NOTES

International Bureau: references to "the Bureau of the International Union for the Protection of Industrial Property" or to "the International Bureau" are to be construed as references to the International Bureau as defined in Art 1 of the Complementary Act of Stockholm (1967) at **[9.111]**, by virtue of Art 7(1) of that Act.

[9.49]
Article 3

Nationals of contracting States and persons who, without being nationals of any contracting State, are domiciled or have a real and effective industrial or commercial establishment in the territory of a contracting State may deposit designs at the International Bureau.

NOTES

International Bureau: references to "the Bureau of the International Union for the Protection of Industrial Property" or to "the International Bureau" are to be construed as references to the International Bureau as defined in Art 1 of the Complementary Act of Stockholm (1967) at **[9.111]**, by virtue of Art 7(1) of that Act.

[9.50]
Article 4

(1) International deposit may be made at the International Bureau—

1. direct, or
2. through the intermediary of the national Office of a contracting State if the law of that State so permits.

(2) The domestic law of any contracting State may require that international deposits of which it is deemed to be the State of origin shall be made through its national Office. Non-compliance with this requirement shall not prejudice the effects of the international deposit in the other contracting States.

NOTES

International Bureau: references to "the Bureau of the International Union for the Protection of Industrial Property" or to "the International Bureau" are to be construed as references to the International Bureau as defined in Art 1 of the Complementary Act of Stockholm (1967) at **[9.111]**, by virtue of Art 7(1) of that Act.

[9.51]

Article 5

(1) The international deposit shall consist of an application and one or more photographs or other graphic representations of the design, and shall involve payment of the fees prescribed by the Regulations.

(2) The application shall contain—

1. a list of the contracting States in which the applicant requests that the international deposit shall have effect;
2. the designation of the article or articles in which it is intended to incorporate the design;
3. if the applicant wishes to claim the priority provided for in Article 9, an indication of the date, the State, and the number of the deposit giving rise to the right of priority;
4. such other particulars as the Regulations may prescribe.

(3)

(a) In addition, the application may contain—

1. a short description of characteristic features of the design;
2. a declaration as to who is the true creator of the design;
3. a request for deferment of publication as provided in Article 6(4).

(b) The application may be accompanied also by samples or models of the article or articles incorporating the design.

(4) A multiple deposit may include several designs intended to be incorporated in articles included in the same class of the International Design Classification referred to in Article 21(2)4.

[9.52]

Article 6

(1) The International Bureau shall maintain the International Design Register and shall register international deposits therein.

(2) The international deposit shall be deemed to have been made on the date on which the International Bureau received the application in due form, the fees payable with the application, and the photograph or photographs or other graphic representations of the design, or, if the International Bureau received them on different dates, on the last of these dates. The registration shall bear the same date.

(3)

(a) For each international deposit, the International Bureau shall publish in a periodical bulletin—

1. reproductions in black and white or, at the request of the applicant, in colour of the deposited photographs or other graphic representations;
2. the date of the international deposit;
3. the particulars prescribed by the Regulations.

(b) The International Bureau shall send the periodical bulletin to the national Offices as soon as possible.

(4)

(a) The publication referred to in paragraph (3)(a) shall, at the request of the applicant, be deferred for such period as he may request. The said period may not exceed twelve months from the date of the international deposit. However, if priority is claimed, the starting date of such period shall be the priority date.

(b) At any time during the period referred to in subparagraph (a), the applicant may request immediate publication or may withdraw his deposit. Withdrawal of the deposit may be limited to one or a few only of the contracting States and, in the case of a multiple deposit, to some only of the designs included therein.

(c) If the applicant fails to pay within the proper time the fees payable before the expiration of the period referred to in subparagraph (a), the International Bureau shall cancel the deposit and shall not effect the publication referred to in paragraph (3)(a).

(d) Until the expiration of the period referred to in subparagraph (a), the International Bureau shall keep in confidence the registration of deposits made subject to deferred publication, and the public shall have no access to any documents or articles concerning such deposits. These provisions shall apply without limitation as to time if the applicant has withdrawn his deposit before the expiration of the said period.

(5) Except as provided in paragraph (4), the Register and all documents and articles filed with the International Bureau shall be open to inspection by the public.

NOTES

International Bureau: references to "the Bureau of the International Union for the Protection of Industrial Property" or to "the International Bureau" are to be construed as references to the International Bureau as defined in Art 1 of the Complementary Act of Stockholm (1967) at **[9.111]**, by virtue of Art 7(1) of that Act.

[9.53]
Article 7

(1)

(a) A deposit registered at the International Bureau shall have the same effect in each of the contracting States designated by the applicant in his application as if all the formalities required by the domestic law for the grant of protection had been complied with by the applicant and as if all administrative acts required to that end had been accomplished by the Office of such State.

(b) Subject to the provisions of Article 11, the protection of designs the deposit of which has been registered at the International Bureau is governed in each contracting State by those provisions of the domestic law which are applicable in that State to designs for which protection has been claimed on the basis of a national deposit and in respect of which all formalities and administrative acts have been complied with and accomplished.

(2) An international deposit shall have no effect in the State of origin if the laws of that State so provide.

NOTES

International Bureau: references to "the Bureau of the International Union for the Protection of Industrial Property" or to "the International Bureau" are to be construed as references to the International Bureau as defined in Art 1 of the Complementary Act of Stockholm (1967) at **[9.111]**, by virtue of Art 7(1) of that Act.

[9.54]
Article 8

(1) Notwithstanding the provisions of Article 7, the national Office of a contracting State whose domestic law provides that the national Office may, on the basis of an administrative *ex officio* examination or pursuant to an opposition by a third party, refuse protection shall, in case of refusal, notify the International Bureau within six months that the design does not meet the requirements of its domestic law other than the formalities and administrative acts referred to in Article 7(1). If no such refusal is notified within a period of six months the international deposit shall become effective in that State as from the date of that deposit. However, in a contracting State having a novelty examination, the international deposit, while retaining its priority, shall, if no refusal is notified within a period of six months, become effective from the expiration of the said period unless the domestic law provides for an earlier date for deposits made with its national Office.

(2) The period of six months referred to in paragraph (1) shall be computed from the date on which the national Office receives the issue of the periodical bulletin in which the registration of the international deposit has been published. The national Office shall communicate that date to any person so requesting.

(3) The applicant shall have the same remedies against the refusal of the national Office referred to in paragraph (1) as if he had deposited his design in that Office; in any case, the refusal shall be subject to a request for re-examination or appeal. Notification of such refusal shall indicate—

1. the reasons for which it has been found that the design does not meet the requirements of the domestic law;
2. the date referred to in paragraph (2);
3. the time allowed for a request for re-examination or appeal;
4. the authority to which such request or appeal may be addressed.

(4)

(a) The national Office of a contracting State whose domestic law contains provisions of the kind referred to in paragraph (1) requiring a declaration as to who is the true creator of the design or a description of the design may provide that, upon request and within a period of not less than sixty days from the dispatch of such a request by the said Office, the applicant shall file in the language of the application filed with the International Bureau—

1. a declaration as to who is the true creator of the design;
2. a short description emphasizing the essential characteristic features of the design as shown by the photographs or other graphic representations.

(b) No fees shall be charged by a national Office in connection with the filing of such declarations or descriptions, or for their possible publication by that national Office.

(5)

(a) Any contracting State whose domestic law contains provisions of the kind referred to in paragraph (1) shall notify the International Bureau accordingly.

(b) If, under its legislation, a contracting State has several systems for the protection of designs one of which provides for novelty examination, the provisions of this Agreement concerning States having a novelty examination shall apply only to the said system.

NOTES

International Bureau: references to "the Bureau of the International Union for the Protection of Industrial Property" or to "the International Bureau" are to be construed as references to the International Bureau as defined in Art 1 of the Complementary Act of Stockholm (1967) at **[9.111]**, by virtue of Art 7(1) of that Act.

[9.55]
Article 9

If the international deposit of a design is made within six months of the first deposit of the same design in a State member of the International Union for the Protection of Industrial Property, and if priority is claimed for the international deposit, the priority date shall be that of the first deposit.

[9.56]
Article 10

(1) An international deposit may be renewed every five years by payment only, during the last year of each period of five years, of the renewal fees prescribed by the Regulations.
(2) Subject to the payment of a surcharge fixed by the Regulations, a period of grace of six months shall be granted for renewal of the international deposit.
(3) At the time of paying the renewal fees, the international deposit number must be indicated and also, if renewal is not to be effected for all the contracting States for which the deposit is about to expire, those of the contracting States for which the renewal is to be effected.
(4) Renewal may be limited to some only of the designs included in a multiple deposit.
(5) The International Bureau shall record and publish renewals.

NOTES

International Bureau: references to "the Bureau of the International Union for the Protection of Industrial Property" or to "the International Bureau" are to be construed as references to the International Bureau as defined in Art 1 of the Complementary Act of Stockholm (1967) at **[9.111]**, by virtue of Art 7(1) of that Act.

[9.57]
Article 11

(1)
(a) The term of protection granted by a contracting State to designs which have been the subject of an international deposit shall not be less than—
1. ten years from the date of the international deposit if the deposit has been renewed;
2. five years from the date of the international deposit in the absence of renewal.

(b) However, if, under the provisions of the domestic law of a contracting State having a novelty examination, protection commences at a date later than that of the international deposit, the minimum terms provided for in subparagraph (a) shall be computed from the date at which protection commences in that State. The fact that the international deposit is not renewed or is renewed only once shall in no way affect the minimum terms of protection thus defined.

(2) If the domestic law of a contracting State provides, in respect of designs which have been the subject of a national deposit, for protection whose duration, with or without renewal, is longer than ten years, protection of the same duration shall, on the basis of the international deposit and its renewals, be granted in that State to designs which have been the subject of an international deposit.
(3) A contracting State may, under its domestic law, limit the term of protection of designs which have been the subject of an international deposit to the terms provided for in paragraph (1).
(4) Subject to the provisions of paragraph (1)(b), protection in a contracting State shall terminate at the date of expiration of the international deposit, unless the domestic law of that State provides that protection shall continue after the date of expiration of the international deposit.

[9.58]
Article 12

(1) The International Bureau shall record and publish changes affecting ownership of a design which is the subject of an international deposit in force. It is understood that transfer of ownership may be limited to the rights arising from the international deposit in one or a few only of the contracting States and, in the case of a multiple deposit, to some only of the designs included therein.
(2) The recording referred to in paragraph (1) shall have the same effect as if it had been made in the national Offices of the contracting States.

NOTES

International Bureau: references to "the Bureau of the International Union for the Protection of Industrial Property" or to "the International Bureau" are to be construed as references to the International Bureau as defined in Art 1 of the Complementary Act of Stockholm (1967) at **[9.111]**, by virtue of Art 7(1) of that Act.

[9.59]
Article 13
(1) The owner of an international deposit may, by means of a declaration addressed to the International Bureau, renounce his rights in respect of all or some only of the contracting States and, in the case of a multiple deposit, in respect of some only of the designs included therein.
(2) The International Bureau shall record and publish such declaration.

NOTES
International Bureau: references to "the Bureau of the International Union for the Protection of Industrial Property" or to "the International Bureau" are to be construed as references to the International Bureau as defined in Art 1 of the Complementary Act of Stockholm (1967) at **[9.111]**, by virtue of Art 7(1) of that Act.

[9.60]
Article 14
(1) No contracting State may, as a condition of recognition of the right to protection, require that the article incorporating the design bear a sign or notice concerning the deposit of the design.
(2) If the domestic law of a contracting State provides for a notice on the article for any other purpose, such State shall regard such requirement as satisfied if all the articles offered to the public with the authorisation of the owner of the rights in the design, or the tags attached to such articles, bear the international design notice.
(3) The international design notice shall consist of the symbol D accompanied by—
1. the year of the international deposit and the name, or the usual abbreviation of the name, of the depositor, or
2. the number of the international deposit.

(4) The mere appearance of the international design notice on the article or the tags shall in no case be interpreted as implying a waiver of protection by virtue of copyright or on any other grounds, whenever, in the absence of such notice, such protection may be claimed.

[9.61]
Article 15
(1) The fees prescribed by the Regulations shall consist of—
1. fees for the International Bureau;
2. fees for the contracting States designated by the applicant, namely—
   (a) a fee for each contracting State;
   (b) a fee for each contracting State having a novelty examination and requiring the payment of a fee for such examination.

(2) Any fees paid in respect of one and the same deposit for a contracting State under paragraph (1)2(a), shall be deducted from the amount of the fee referred to in paragraph (1)2(b), if the latter fee becomes payable for the same State.

NOTES
International Bureau: references to "the Bureau of the International Union for the Protection of Industrial Property" or to "the International Bureau" are to be construed as references to the International Bureau as defined in Art 1 of the Complementary Act of Stockholm (1967) at **[9.111]**, by virtue of Art 7(1) of that Act.

[9.62]
Article 16
(1) The fees for contracting States referred to in Article 15(1)2, shall be collected by the International Bureau and paid over annually to the contracting States designated by the applicant.
(2)
(a) Any contracting State may notify the International Bureau that it waives its right to the supplementary fees referred to in Article 15(1)2(a), in respect of international deposits of which any other contracting State making a similar waiver is deemed to be the State of origin.
(b) Such State may make a similar waiver in respect of international deposits of which it is itself deemed to be the State of origin.

NOTES
International Bureau: references to "the Bureau of the International Union for the Protection of Industrial Property" or to "the International Bureau" are to be construed as references to the International Bureau as defined in Art 1 of the Complementary Act of Stockholm (1967) at **[9.111]**, by virtue of Art 7(1) of that Act.

[9.63]
Article 17
The Regulations shall govern the details concerning the implementation of this Agreement and in particular—
1. the languages and the number of copies in which the application for deposit must be filed, and the data to be supplied in the application;

2. the amounts and the dates and method of payment of the fees for the International Bureau and for the States, including the limits imposed on the fee for contracting States having a novelty examination;
3. the number, size, and other characteristics, of the photographs or other graphic representations of each design deposited;
4. the length of the description of characteristic features of the design;
5. the limits within which and conditions under which samples or models of the articles incorporating the design may accompany the application;
6. the number of designs that may be included in a multiple deposit and other conditions governing multiple deposits;
7. all matters relating to the publication and distribution of the periodical bulletin referred to in Article 6(3)(a), including the number of copies of the bulletin which shall be given free of charge to the national Offices and the number of copies which may be sold at a reduced price to such Offices;
8. the procedure for notification by contracting States of any refusal provided for under Article 8(1), and the procedure for communication and publication of such refusals by the International Bureau;
9. the conditions for recording and publication by the International Bureau of the changes affecting the ownership of a design referred to in Article 12(1), and for the renunciations referred to in Article 13;
10. the disposal of documents and articles concerning deposits for which the possibility of renewal has ceased to exist.

NOTES

International Bureau: references to "the Bureau of the International Union for the Protection of Industrial Property" or to "the International Bureau" are to be construed as references to the International Bureau as defined in Art 1 of the Complementary Act of Stockholm (1967) at **[9.111]**, by virtue of Art 7(1) of that Act.

[9.64]
Article 18

The provisions of this Agreement shall not preclude the making of a claim to the benefit of any greater protection which may be granted by domestic legislation in a contracting State, nor shall they affect in any way the protection accorded to works of art and works of applied art by international copyright treaties and conventions.

Articles 19–22 (*Repealed by the Complementary Act of Stockholm (1967), Art 7(2).*)

[9.65]
Article 23

(1) This Agreement shall remain open for signature until December 31, 1961.
(2) It shall be ratified and the instruments of ratification shall be deposited with the Government of the Netherlands.

[9.66]
Article 24

(1) States members of the International Union for the Protection of Industrial Property which have not signed this Agreement may accede thereto.
(2) Such accessions shall be notified through diplomatic channels to the Government of the Swiss Confederation, and by the latter to the Governments of all contracting States.

NOTES

Government of the Swiss Confederation: this is to be construed as a reference to the Director General of the World Intellectual Property Organization by virtue of the Complementary Act of Stockholm (1967), Art 7(3).

[9.67]
Article 25

(1) Each contracting State undertakes to provide for the protection of industrial designs and to adopt, in accordance with its constitution, the measures necessary to ensure the application of this Agreement.
(2) At the time a contracting State deposits its instrument of ratification or accession, it must be in a position under its domestic law to give effect to the provisions of this Agreement.

[9.68]
Article 26

(1) This Agreement shall enter into force one month after the date on which the Government of the Swiss Confederation has dispatched a notification to the contracting States of the deposit of ten instruments of ratification or accession, at least four of which are those of States which, at the date of the present Agreement, are not party either to the 1925 Agreement or to the 1934 Agreement.

(2) Thereafter, the deposit of instruments of ratification and accession shall be notified to the contracting States by the Government of the Swiss Confederation. Such ratifications and accessions shall become effective one month after the date of the dispatch of such notification unless, in the case of accession, a later date is indicated in the instrument of accession.

NOTES

Government of the Swiss Confederation: this is to be construed as a reference to the Director General of the World Intellectual Property Organization by virtue of the Complementary Act of Stockholm (1967), Art 7(3).

[9.69]
Article 27

Any contracting State may at any time notify the Government of the Swiss Confederation that this Agreement shall also apply to all or part of those territories for the external relations of which it is responsible. Thereupon, the Government of the Swiss Confederation shall communicate such notification to the contracting States and the Agreement shall apply also to the said territories one month after the dispatch of the communication by the Government of the Swiss Confederation to the contracting States unless a later date is indicated in the notification.

NOTES

Government of the Swiss Confederation: this is to be construed as a reference to the Director General of the World Intellectual Property Organization by virtue of the Complementary Act of Stockholm (1967), Art 7(3).

[9.70]
Article 28

(1) Any contracting State may, by notification addressed to the Government of the Swiss Confederation, denounce this Agreement in its own name and on behalf of all or part of the territories designated in the notification under Article 27. Such notification shall take effect one year after its receipt by the Government of the Swiss Confederation.

(2) Denunciation shall not relieve any contracting State of its obligations under this Agreement in respect of designs deposited at the International Bureau prior to the date on which the denunciation takes effect.

NOTES

International Bureau: references to "the Bureau of the International Union for the Protection of Industrial Property" or to "the International Bureau" are to be construed as references to the International Bureau as defined in Art 1 of the Complementary Act of Stockholm (1967) at **[9.111]**, by virtue of Art 7(1) of that Act.

Government of the Swiss Confederation: this is to be construed as a reference to the Director General of the World Intellectual Property Organization by virtue of the Complementary Act of Stockholm (1967), Art 7(3).

[9.71]
Article 29

(1) This Agreement shall be submitted to . . . revision with a view to the introduction of amendments designed to improve the protection resulting from the international deposit of designs.

(2) Revision conferences shall be called at the request . . . of not less than one-half of the contracting States.

NOTES

Words omitted repealed by the Complementary Act of Stockholm (1967), Art 7(4).

[9.72]
Article 30

(1) Two or more contracting States may at any time notify the Government of the Swiss Confederation that, subject to the conditions indicated in the notification—

1. a common Office shall be substituted for the national Office of each of them;
2. they shall be deemed to be a single State for the purposes of the application of Articles 2 to 17 of this Agreement.

(2) Such notification shall not take effect until six months after the date of dispatch of the communication thereof by the Government of the Swiss Confederation to the other contracting States.

NOTES

Government of the Swiss Confederation: this is to be construed as a reference to the Director General of the World Intellectual Property Organization by virtue of the Complementary Act of Stockholm (1967), Art 7(3).

[9.73]
Article 31

(1) This Agreement alone shall be applicable as regards the mutual relations of States party to both the present Agreement and the 1925 Agreement or the 1934 Agreement. However, such States shall, in their mutual relations, apply the 1925 Agreement or the 1934 Agreement, as the case may be, to designs deposited at the International Bureau prior to the date on which the present Agreement becomes applicable as regards their mutual relations.

(2)

(a) Any State party to both the present Agreement and the 1925 Agreement shall continue to apply the 1925 Agreement in its relations with States party only to the 1925 Agreement, unless the said State has denounced the 1925 Agreement.

(b) Any State party to both the present Agreement and the 1934 Agreement shall continue to apply the 1934 Agreement in its relations with States party only to the 1934 Agreement, unless the said State has denounced the 1934 Agreement.

(3) States party to the present Agreement only shall not be bound to States which, without being party to the present Agreement, are party to the 1925 Agreement or the 1934 Agreement.

NOTES

International Bureau: references to "the Bureau of the International Union for the Protection of Industrial Property" or to "the International Bureau" are to be construed as references to the International Bureau as defined in Art 1 of the Complementary Act of Stockholm (1967) at **[9.111]**, by virtue of Art 7(1) of that Act.

[9.74]
Article 32

(1) Signature and ratification of, or accession to, the present Agreement by a State party, at the date of this Agreement, to the 1925 Agreement or the 1934 Agreement shall be deemed to include signature and ratification of, or accession to, the Protocol annexed to the present Agreement, unless such State makes an express declaration to the contrary at the time of signing or depositing its instrument of accession.

(2) Any contracting State having made the declaration referred to in paragraph (1), or any other contracting State not party to the 1925 Agreement or the 1934 Agreement, may sign or accede to the Protocol annexed to this Agreement. At the time of signing or depositing its instrument of accession, it may declare that it does not consider itself bound by the provisions of paragraphs 1(2)(a) or 1(2)(b) of the Protocol; in such case, the other States party to the Protocol shall be under no obligation to apply, in their relations with that State, the provisions mentioned in such declaration. The provisions of Articles 23 to 28 inclusive shall apply by analogy.

[9.75]
Article 33

This Act shall be signed in a single copy which shall be deposited in the archives of the Government of the Netherlands. A certified copy shall be transmitted by the latter to the Government of each State which has signed or acceded to this Agreement.

PROTOCOL*

[9.76]

States party to this Protocol have agreed as follows—

(1) The provisions of this Protocol shall apply to designs which have been the subject of an international deposit and of which one of the States party to this Protocol is deemed to be the State of origin.

(2) In respect of designs referred to in paragraph (1), above—

(a) the term of protection granted by States party to this Protocol to the designs referred to in paragraph (1) shall not be less than fifteen years from the date provided for in paragraphs 11(1)(a) or 11(1)(b), as the case may be;

(b) the appearance of a notice on the articles incorporating the designs or on the tags attached thereto shall in no case be required by the States party to this Protocol, either for the exercise in their territories of rights arising from the international deposit, or for any other purpose.

NOTES

* This protocol is not yet in force.

INTERNATIONAL CONVENTION FOR THE PROTECTION OF PERFORMERS, PRODUCERS OF PHONOGRAMS AND BROADCASTING ORGANISATIONS ('ROME CONVENTION')

(Rome, 26 October 1961)

NOTES

The original source for this Convention is the World Intellectual Property Organisation (WIPO).

Articles have been given titles to facilitate their identification. There are no titles in the signed text.

[9.77]
Article 1
[Safeguard of copyright proper]
Protection granted under this Convention shall leave intact and shall in no way affect the protection of copyright in literary and artistic works. Consequently, no provision of this Convention may be interpreted as prejudicing such protection.

[9.78]
Article 2
[Protection given by the Convention. Definition of national treatment]
1. For the purposes of this Convention, national treatment shall mean the treatment accorded by the domestic law of the Contracting State in which protection is claimed—
(a) to performers who are its nationals, as regards performance taking place, broadcast, or first fixed, on its territory;
(b) to producers of phonograms who are its nationals, as regards phonograms first fixed or first published on its territory;
(c) to broadcasting organisations which have their headquarters on its territory, as regards broadcasts transmitted from transmitters situated on its territory.
2. National treatment shall be subject to the protection specifically guaranteed, and the limitations specifically provided for, in this Convention.

[9.79]
Article 3
[Definitions: (a) Performers; (b) Phonogram; (c) Producers of Phonograms; (d) Publication; (e) Reproduction; (f) Broadcasting; (g) Rebroadcasting]
For the purposes of this Convention—
(a) "performers" means actors, singers, musicians, dancers, and other persons who act, sing, deliver, declaim, play in, or otherwise perform literary or artistic works;
(b) "phonogram" means any exclusively aural fixation of sounds of a performance or of other sounds;
(c) "producer of phonograms" means the person who, or the legal entity which, first fixes the sounds of a performance or other sounds;
(d) "publication" means the offering of copies of a phonogram to the public in reasonable quantity;
(e) "reproduction" means the making of a copy or copies of a fixation;
(f) "broadcasting" means the transmission by wireless means for public reception of sounds or of images and sounds;
(g) "rebroadcasting" means the simultaneous broadcasting by one broadcasting organisation of the broadcast of another broadcasting organisation.

[9.80]
Article 4
[Performances protected. Points of attachment for performers]
Each Contracting State shall grant national treatment to performers if any of the following conditions is met—
(a) the performance takes place in another Contracting State;
(b) the performance is incorporated in a phonogram which is protected under Article 5 of this Convention;
(c) the performance, not being fixed on a phonogram, is carried by a broadcast which is protected by Article 6 of this Convention.

[9.81]
Article 5
[Protected phonograms: 1. Points of attachment for producers of phonograms; 2. Simultaneous publication; 3. Power to exclude certain criteria]
1. Each Contracting State shall grant national treatment to producers of phonograms if any of the following conditions is met—
(a) the producer of the phonogram is a national of another Contracting State (criterion of nationality);
(b) the first fixation of the sound was made in another Contracting State (criterion of fixation);
(c) the phonogram was first published in another Contracting State (criterion of publication).
2. If a phonogram was first published in a non-Contracting State but if it was also published, within thirty days of its first publication, in a Contracting State (simultaneous publication), it shall be considered as first published in the Contracting State.
3. By means of a notification deposited with the Secretary-General of the United Nations, any Contracting State may declare that it will not apply the criterion of publication or, alternatively, the criterion of fixation. Such notification may be deposited at the time of ratification, acceptance or accession, or at any time thereafter; in one last case, it shall become effective six months after it has been deposited.

[9.82]
Article 6
[Protected broadcasts: 1. Points of attachment for broadcasting organisations; 2. Power to reserve]

1. Each Contracting State shall grant national treatment to broadcasting organisations if either of the following conditions is met—
   (a) the headquarters of the broadcasting organisation is situated in another Contracting State;
   (b) the broadcast was transmitted from a transmitter situated in another Contracting State.

2. By means of a notification deposited with the Secretary-General of the United Nations, any Contracting State may declare that it will protect broadcasts only if the headquarters of the broadcasting organisation is situated in another Contracting State and the broadcast was transmitted from a transmitter situated in the same Contracting State. Such notification may be deposited at the time of ratification, acceptance or accession, or at any time thereafter; in the last case, it shall become effective six months after it has been deposited.

[9.83]
Article 7
[Minimum protection for performers: 1. Particular rights; 2. Relations between performers and broadcasting organisations]

1. The protection provided for performers by this Convention shall include the possibility of preventing—
   (a) the broadcasting and the communication to the public, without their consent, of their performance, except where the performance used in the broadcasting or the public communication is itself already a broadcast performance or is made from a fixation;
   (b) the fixation, without their consent, of their unfixed performance;
   (c) the reproduction, without their consent, of a fixation of their performance—
      (i) if the original fixation itself was made without their consent;
      (ii) if the reproduction is made for purposes different from those for which the performers gave their consent;
      (iii) if the original fixation was made in accordance with the provisions of Article 15, and the reproduction is made for purposes different from those referred to in those provisions.

2.—(1) If broadcasting was consented to by the performers, it shall be a matter for the domestic law of the Contracting State where protection is claimed to regulate the protection against rebroadcasting, fixation for broadcasting purposes and the reproduction of such fixation for broadcasting purposes.

(2) The terms and conditions governing the use by broadcasting organisations of fixations made for broadcasting purposes shall be determined in accordance with the domestic law of the Contracting State where protection is claimed.

(3) However, the domestic law referred to in sub-paragraphs (1) and (2) of this paragraph shall not operate to deprive performers of the ability to control, by contract, their relations with broadcasting organisations.

[9.84]
Article 8
[Performers acting jointly]

Any Contracting State may, by its domestic laws and regulations, specify the manner in which performers will be represented in connection with the exercise of their rights if several of them participate in the same performance.

[9.85]
Article 9
[Variety and circus artists]

Any Contracting State may, by its domestic laws and regulations, extend the protection provided for in this Convention to artists who do not perform literary or artistic works.

[9.86]
Article 10
[Right of reproduction for phonogram producers]

Producers of phonograms shall enjoy the right to authorise or prohibit the direct or indirect reproduction of their phonograms.

[9.87]
Article 11
[Formalities for phonograms]

If, as a condition of protecting the rights of producers of phonograms, or of performers, or both, in relation to phonograms, a Contracting State, under its domestic law, requires compliance with formalities, these shall be considered as fulfilled if all the copies in commerce of the published phonogram or their containers bear a notice consisting of the symbol P, accompanied by the year date of the first publication, placed in such a manner as to give reasonable notice of claim of protection; and if the copies or their containers do not identify the producer or the licensee of the producer (by carrying his name, trade mark or other appropriate designation), the notice shall also include the name of the owner of the rights of the producer; and, furthermore, if the copies or their containers do not identify the principal performers, the notice shall also include the name of the person who, in the country in which the fixation was effected, owns the rights of such performers.

[9.88]
Article 12
[Secondary uses of phonograms]
If a phonogram published for commercial purposes, or a reproduction of such phonogram, is used directly for broadcasting or for any communication to the public, a single equitable remuneration shall be paid by the user to the performers, or to the producers of the phonograms, or to both. Domestic law may, in the absence of agreement between these parties, lay down the conditions as to the sharing of this remuneration.

[9.89]
Article 13
[Minimum rights for broadcasting organisations]
Broadcasting organisations shall enjoy the right to authorise or prohibit—

(a) the rebroadcasting of their broadcasts;
(b) the fixation of their broadcasts;
(c) the reproduction—
  (i) of fixations, made without their consent, of their broadcasts;
  (ii) of fixations, made in accordance with the provisions of Article 15, of their broadcasts, if the reproduction is made for purposes different from those referred to in those provisions;
(d) the communication to the public of their television broadcasts if such communication is made in places accessible to the public against payment of an entrance fee; it shall be a matter for the domestic law of the State where protection of this right is claimed to determine the conditions under which it may be exercised.

[9.90]
Article 14
[Minimum duration of protection]
The term of protection to be granted under this Convention shall last at least until the end of a period of twenty years computed from the end of the year in which—

(a) the fixation was made—for phonograms and for performances incorporated therein;
(b) the performance took place—for performances not incorporated in phonograms;
(c) the broadcast took place—for broadcasts.

[9.91]
Article 15
[Permitted exceptions: 1. Specific limitations; 2. Equivalents with copyright]
1. Any Contracting State may, in its domestic laws and regulations, provide for exceptions to the protection guaranteed by this Convention as regards—

(a) private use;
(b) use of short excerpts in connection with the reporting of current events;
(c) ephemeral fixation by a broadcasting organisation by means of its own facilities and for its own broadcasts;
(d) use solely for the purposes of teaching or scientific research.

2. Irrespective of paragraph 1 of this Article, any Contracting State may, in its domestic laws and regulations, provide for the same kinds of limitations with regard to the protection of performers, producers of phonograms and broadcasting organisations, as it provides for, in its domestic laws and regulations, in connection with the protection of copyright in literary and artistic works. However, compulsory licences may be provided for only to the extent to which they are compatible with this Convention.

[9.92]
Article 16
[Reservations]
1. Any State, upon becoming party to this Convention, shall be bound by all the obligations and shall enjoy all the benefits thereof. However, a State may at any time, in a notification deposited with the Secretary-General of the United Nations, declare that—

(a) as regards Article 12—
  (i) it will not apply the provisions of that Article;
  (ii) it will not apply the provisions of that Article in respect of certain uses;
  (iii) as regards phonograms the producer of which is not a national of another Contracting State, it will not apply that Article;
  (iv) as regards phonograms the producer of which is a national of another Contracting State, it will limit the protection provided for by that Article to

the extent to which, and to the term for which, the latter State grants protection to phonograms first fixed by a national of the State making the declaration; however, the fact that the Contracting State of which the producer is a national does not grant the protection to the same beneficiary or beneficiaries as the State making the declaration shall not be considered as a difference in the extent of the protection;

(b) as regards Article 13, it will not apply item (d) of that Article; if a Contracting State makes such a declaration, the other Contracting States shall not be obliged to grant the right referred to in Article 13, item (d), to broadcasting organisations whose headquarters are in that State.

2. If the notification referred to in paragraph 1 of this Article is made after the date of the deposit of the instrument of ratification, acceptance or accession, the declaration will become effective six months after it has been deposited.

[9.93]
Article 17
[Certain countries applying only the "fixation" criterion]

Any State which, on October 26, 1961, grants protection to producers of phonograms solely on the basis of the criterion of fixation may, by a notification deposited with the Secretary-General of the United Nations at the time of ratification, acceptance or accession, declare that it will apply, for the purposes of Article 5, the criterion of fixation alone and, for the purposes of paragraph 1(a)(iii) and (iv) of Article 16, the criterion of fixation instead of the criterion of nationality.

[9.94]
Article 18
[Withdrawal of reservations]

Any State which has deposited a notification under paragraph 3 of Article 5, paragraph 2 of Article 6, paragraph 1 of Article 16 or Article 17, may, by a further notification deposited with the Secretary-General of the United Nations, reduce its scope or withdraw it.

[9.95]
Article 19
[Performers' rights in films]

Notwithstanding anything in this Convention, once a performer has consented to the incorporation of his performance in a visual or audio-visual fixation, Article 7 shall have no further application.

[9.96]
Article 20
[Non-retroactivity]

1. This Convention shall not prejudice rights acquired in any Contracting State before the date of coming into force of this Convention for that State.

2. No Contracting State shall be bound to apply the provisions of this Convention to performances or broadcasts which took place, or to phonograms which were fixed, before the date of coming into force of this Convention for that State.

[9.97]
Article 21
[Protection by other means]

The protection provided for in this Convention shall not prejudice any protection otherwise secured to performers, producers of phonograms and broadcasting organisations.

[9.98]
Article 22
[Special agreements]

Contracting States reserve the right to enter into special agreements among themselves in so far as such agreements grant to performers, producers of phonograms or broadcasting organisations more extensive rights than those granted by this Convention or contain other provisions not contrary to this Convention.

[9.99]
Article 23
[Signature and deposit]

This Convention shall be deposited with the Secretary-General of the United Nations. It shall be open until June 30, 1962, for signature by any State invited to the Diplomatic Conference on the International Protection of Performers, Producers of Phonograms and Broadcasting Organisations which is a party to the Universal Copyright Convention or a member of the International Union for the Protection of Literary and Artistic Works.

[9.100]
Article 24
[Becoming party to the convention]

1. This Convention shall be subject to ratification or acceptance by the signatory States.

2. This Convention shall be open for accession by any State invited to the Conference referred to in Article 23, and by any State Member of the United Nations, provided that in either case such State is a party to the Universal Copyright Convention or a member of the International Union for the Protection of Literary and Artistic Works.
3. Ratification, acceptance or accession shall be effected by the deposit of an instrument to that effect with the Secretary-General of the United Nations.

[9.101]
Article 25
[Entry into force]
1. This Convention shall come into force three months after the date of deposit of the sixth instrument of ratification, acceptance or accession.
2. Subsequently, this Convention shall come into force in respect of each State three months after the date of deposit of its instrument of ratification, acceptance or accession.

[9.102]
Article 26
[Implementation of the convention by the provision of domestic law]
1. Each Contracting State undertakes to adopt, in accordance with its Constitution, the measures necessary to ensure the application of this Convention.
2. At the time of deposit of its instrument of ratification, acceptance or accession, each State must be in a position under its domestic law to give effect to the terms of this Convention.

[9.103]
Article 27
[Applicability of the convention to certain territories]
1. Any State may, at the time of ratification, acceptance or accession, or at any time thereafter, declare by notification addressed to the Secretary-General of the United Nations that this Convention shall extend to all or any of the territories for whose international relations it is responsible, provided that the Universal Copyright Convention or the International Convention for the Protection of Literary and Artistic Works applies to the territory or territories concerned. This notification shall take effect three months after the date of its receipt.
2. The notifications referred to in paragraph 3 of Article 5, paragraph 2 of Article 6, paragraph 1 of Article 16 and Articles 17 and 18, may be extended to cover all or any of the territories referred to in paragraph 1 of this Article.

[9.104]
Article 28
[Denunciation of the convention]
1. Any Contracting State may denounce this Convention, on its own behalf, or on behalf of all or any of the territories referred to in Article 27.
2. The denunciation shall be effected by a notification addressed to the Secretary-General of the United Nations and shall take effect twelve months after the date of receipt of the notification.
3. The right of denunciation shall not be exercised by a Contracting State before the expiry of a period of five years from the date on which the Convention came into force with respect to that State.
4. A Contracting State shall cease to be a party to this Convention from that time when it is neither a party to the Universal Copyright Convention nor a member of the International Union for the Protection of Literary and Artistic Works.
5. This Convention shall cease to apply to any territory referred to in Article 27 from that time when neither the Universal Copyright Convention nor the International Convention for the Protection of Literary and Artistic Works applies to that territory.

[9.105]
Article 29
[Revision of the convention]
1. After this Convention has been in force for five years, any Contracting State may, by notification addressed to the Secretary-General of the United Nations, request that a conference be convened for the purpose of revising the Convention. The Secretary-General shall notify all Contracting States of this request. If, within a period of six months following the date of notification by the Secretary-General of the United Nations, not less than one half of the Contracting States notify him of their concurrence with the request, the Secretary-General shall inform the Director-General of the International Labour Office, the Director-General of the United Nations Educational, Scientific and Cultural Organisation and the Director of the Bureau of the International Union for the Protection of Literary and Artistic Works, who shall convene a revision conference in co-operation with the Intergovernmental Committee provided for in Article 32.
2. The adoption of any revision of this Convention shall require an affirmative vote by two-thirds of the States attending the revision conference, provided that this majority includes two-thirds of the States which, at the time of the revision conference, are parties to the Convention.

3. In the event of adoption of a Convention revising this Convention in whole or in part, and unless the revising Convention provides otherwise—
   (a) this Convention shall cease to be open to ratification, acceptance or accession as from the date of entry into force of the revising Convention;
   (b) this Convention shall remain in force as regards relations between or with Contracting States which have not become parties to the revising Convention.

[9.106]
Article 30
[Settlement of disputes]
Any dispute which may arise between two or more Contracting States concerning the interpretation or application of this Convention and which is not settled by negotiation shall, at the request of any one of the parties to the dispute, be referred to the International Court of Justice for decision, unless they agree to another mode of settlement.

[9.107]
Article 31
[Limits on reservations]
Without prejudice to the provisions of paragraph 3 of Article 5, paragraph 2 of Article 6, paragraph 1 of Article 16 and Article 17, no reservation may be made to this Convention.

[9.108]
Article 32
[Intergovernmental committee]
1. An Intergovernmental Committee is hereby established with the following duties—
   (a) to study questions concerning the application and operation of this Convention; and
   (b) to collect proposals and to prepare documentation for possible revision of this Convention.
2. The Committee shall consist of representatives of the Contracting States, chosen with due regard to equitable geographical distribution. The number of members shall be six if there are twelve Contracting States or less, nine if there are thirteen to eighteen Contracting States and twelve if there are more than eighteen Contracting States.
3. The Committee shall be constituted twelve months alter the Convention comes into force by an election organised among the Contracting States, each of which shall have one vote, by the Director-General of the International Labour Office, the Director-General of the United Nations Educational, Scientific and Cultural Organisation and the Director of the Bureau of the International Union for the Protection of Literary and Artistic Works, in accordance with rules previously approved by a majority of all Contracting States.
4. The Committee shall elect its Chairman and officers. It shall establish its own rules of procedure. These rules shall in particular provide for the future operation of the Committee and for a method of selecting its members for the future in such a way as to ensure rotation among the various Contracting States.
5. Officials of the International Labour Office, the United Nations Educational, Scientific and Cultural Organisation and the Bureau of the International Union for the Protection of Literary and Artistic Works, designated by the Directors-General and the Director thereof, shall constitute the Secretariat of the Committee.
6. Meetings of the Committee, which shall be convened whenever a majority of its members deems it necessary, shall be held successively at the headquarters of the International Labour Office, the United Nations Educational, Scientific and Cultural Organisation and the Bureau of the International Union for the Protection of Literary and Artistic Works.
7. Expenses of members of the Committee shall be borne by their respective Governments.

[9.109]
Article 33
[Languages]
1. The present Convention is drawn up in English, French and Spanish, the three texts being equally authentic.
2. In addition, official texts of the present Convention shall be drawn up in German, Italian and Portuguese.

[9.110]
Article 34
[Notifications]
1. The Secretary-General of the United Nations shall notify the States invited to the Conference referred to in Article 23 and every State Member of the United Nations, as well as the Director-General of the International Labour Office, the Director-General of the United Nations Educational, Scientific and Cultural Organisation and the Director of the Bureau of the International Union for the Protection of Literary and Artistic Works—
   (a) of the deposit of each instrument of ratification, acceptance or accession;
   (b) of the date of entry into force of the Convention;
   (c) of all notifications, declarations or communications provided for in this Convention;

(d) if any of the situations referred to in paragraphs 4 and 5 of Article 28 arise.

2. The Secretary-General of the United Nations shall also notify the Director-General of the International Labour Office, the Director-General of the United Nations Educational, Scientific and Cultural Organisation and the Director of the Bureau of the International Union for the Protection of Literary and Artistic Works of the requests communicated to him in accordance with Article 29, as well as of any communication received from the Contracting States concerning the revision of the Convention.

IN FAITH WHEREOF, the undersigned, being duly authorised thereto, have signed this Convention.

DONE at Rome, this twenty-sixth day of October 1961, in a single copy in the English, French and Spanish languages. Certified true copies shall be delivered by the Secretary-General of the United Nations to all the States invited to the Conference referred to in Article 23 and to every State Member of the United Nations, as well as to the Director-General of the International Labour Office, the Director-General of the United Nations Educational, Scientific and Cultural Organisation and the Director of the Bureau of the International Union for the Protection of Literary and Artistic Works.

COMPLEMENTARY ACT OF STOCKHOLM

of July 14, 1967

as amended on September 28, 1979

NOTES

The original source for this Agreement is the World Intellectual Property Organisation (WIPO).

[9.111]
Article 1
Definitions

For the purposes of this Complementary Act:

"1934 Act" shall mean the Act signed at London on June 2, 1934, of the Hague Agreement concerning the International Deposit of Industrial Designs;

"1960 Act" shall mean the Act signed at The Hague on November 28, 1960, of the Hague Agreement concerning the International Deposit of Industrial Designs;

"1961 Additional Act" shall mean the Act signed at Monaco on November 18, 1961, additional to the 1934 Act;

"Organization" shall mean the World Intellectual Property Organization;

"International Bureau" shall mean the International Bureau of Intellectual Property;

"Director General" shall mean the Director General of the Organization;

"Special Union" shall mean the Hague Union established by the Hague Agreement of November 6, 1925, concerning the International Deposit of Industrial Designs, and maintained by the 1934 and 1960 Acts, by the 1961 Additional Act, and by this Complementary Act.

[9.112]
Article 2
Assembly

(1)

(a) The Special Union shall have an Assembly consisting of those countries which have ratified or acceded to this Complementary Act.

(b) The Government of each country shall be represented by one delegate, who may be assisted by alternate delegates, advisors, and experts.

(c) The expenses of each delegation shall be borne by the Government which has appointed it.

(2)

(a) The Assembly shall:

(i) deal with all matters concerning the maintenance and development of the Special Union and the implementation of this Agreement;

(ii) give directions to the International Bureau concerning the preparation for conferences of revision, due account being taken of any comments made by those countries of the Special Union which have not ratified or acceded to this Complementary Act;

(iii) modify the Regulations, including the fixation of the amounts of the fees relating to the international deposit of industrial designs;

(iv) review and approve the reports and activities of the Director General concerning the Special Union, and give him all necessary instructions concerning matters within the competence of the Special Union;

(v) determine the program and adopt the biennial budget of the Special Union, and approve its final accounts;

(vi) adopt the financial regulations of the Special Union;

(vii) establish such committees of experts and working groups as it may deem necessary to achieve the objectives of the Special Union;

(viii) determine which countries not members of the Special Union and which intergovernmental and international non-governmental organizations shall be admitted to its meetings as observers;

(ix) adopt amendments to Articles 2 to 5;

(x) take any other appropriate action designed to further the objectives of the Special Union;

(xi) perform such other functions as are appropriate under this Complementary Act.

(b) With respect to matters which are of interest also to other Unions administered by the Organization, the Assembly shall make its decisions after having heard the advice of the Coordination Committee of the Organization.

(3)

(a) Each country member of the Assembly shall have one vote.

(b) One-half of the countries members of the Assembly shall constitute a quorum.

(c) Notwithstanding the provisions of subparagraph (b), if, in any session, the number of countries represented is less than one-half but equal to or more than one-third of the countries members of the Assembly, the Assembly may make decisions but, with the exception of decisions concerning its own procedure, all such decisions shall take effect only if the conditions set forth hereinafter are fulfilled. The International Bureau shall communicate the said decisions to the countries members of the Assembly which were not represented and shall invite them to express in writing their vote or abstention within a period of three months from the date of the communication. If, at the expiration of this period, the number of countries having thus expressed their vote or abstention attains the number of countries which was lacking for attaining the quorum in the session itself, such decisions shall take effect provided that at the same time the required majority still obtains.

(d) Subject to the provisions of Article 5(2), the decisions of the Assembly shall require two-thirds of the votes cast.

(e) Abstentions shall not be considered as votes.

(f) A delegate may represent, and vote in the name of, one country only.

(g) Countries of the Special Union not members of the Assembly shall be admitted to the meetings of the latter as observers.

(4)

(a) The Assembly shall meet once in every second calendar year in ordinary session upon convocation by the Director General and, in the absence of exceptionnal circumstances, during the same period and at the same place as the General Assembly of the Organization.

(b) The Assembly shall meet in extraordinary session upon convocation by the Director General, at the request of one-fourth of the countries members of the Assembly.

(c) The agenda of each session shall be prepared by the Director General.

(5) The Assembly shall adopt its own rules of procedure.

[9.113]
Article 3
International Bureau

(1)

(a) International deposit of industrial designs and related duties, as well as all other administrative tasks concerning the Special Union, shall be performed by the International Bureau.

(b) In particular, the International Bureau shall prepare the meetings and provide the secretariat of the Assembly and of such committees of experts and working groups as may have been established by the Assembly.

(c) The Director General shall be the chief executive of the Special Union and shall represent the Special Union.

(2) The Director General and any staff member designated by him shall participate, without the right to vote, in all meetings of the Assembly and of such committees of experts or working groups as may have been established by the Assembly. The Director General, or a staff member designated by him, shall be ex officio secretary of those bodies.

(3)

(a) The International Bureau shall, in accordance with the directions of the Assembly, make the preparations for the conferences of revision of the provisions of the Agreement.

(b) The International Bureau may consult with intergovernmental and international non-governmental organizations concerning preparations for conferences of revision.

(c) The Director General and persons designated by him shall take part, without the right to vote, in the discussions at those conferences.

(4) The International Bureau shall carry out any other tasks assigned to it.

[9.114]
Article 4
Finances

(1)

(a) The Special Union shall have a budget.

(b) The budget of the Special Union shall include the income and expenses proper to the Special Union, its contribution to the budget of expenses common to the Unions, and, where applicable, the sum made available to the budget of the Conference of the Organization.

(c) Expenses not attributable exclusively to the Special Union but also to one or more other Unions administered by the Organization shall be deemed to be expenses common to the Unions. The share of the Special Union in such common expenses shall be in proportion to the interest the Special Union has in them.

(2) The budget of the Special Union shall be established with due regard to the requirements of coordination with the budgets of the other Unions administered by the Organization.

(3) The budget of the Special Union shall be financed from the following sources:

(i) international deposit fees and other fees and charges due for other services rendered by the International Bureau in relation to the Special Union;

(ii) sale of, or royalties on, the publications of the International Bureau concerning the Special Union;

(iii) gifts, bequests, and subventions;

(iv) rents, interests, and other miscellaneous income.

(4)

(a) The amounts of the fees referred to in paragraph (3)(i) shall be fixed by the Assembly on the proposal of the Director General.

(b) The amounts of such fees shall be so fixed that the revenues of the Special Union from fees and other sources shall be at least sufficient to cover the expenses of the International Bureau concerning the Special Union.

(c) If the budget is not adopted before the beginning of a new financial period, it shall be at the same level as the budget of the previous year, as provided in the financial regulations.

(5) Subject to the provisions of paragraph (4)(a), the amount of the fees and charges due for other services rendered by the International Bureau in relation to the Special Union shall be established, and shall be reported to the Assembly, by the Director General.

(6)

(a) The Special Union shall have a working capital fund which shall be constituted by the excess receipts and, if such excess does not suffice, by a single payment made by each country of the Special Union. If the fund becomes insufficient, the Assembly shall decide to increase it.

(b) The amount of the initial payment of each country to the said fund or of its participation in the increase thereof shall be a proportion of the contribution of that country as a member of the Paris Union for the Protection of Industrial Property to the budget of the said Union for the year in which the fund is established or the decision to increase it is made.

(c) The proportion and the terms of payment shall be fixed by the Assembly on the proposal of the Director General and after it has heard the advice of the Coordination Committee of the Organization.

(7)

(a) In the headquarters agreement concluded with the country on the territory of which the Organization has its headquarters, it shall be provided that, whenever the working capital fund is insufficient, such country shall grant advances. The amount of those advances and the conditions on which they are granted shall be the subject of separate agreements, in each case, between such country and the Organization.

(b) The country referred to in subparagraph (a) and the Organization shall each have the right to denounce the obligation to grant advances, by written notification. Denunciation shall take effect three years after the end of the year in which it has been notified.

(8) The auditing of the accounts shall be effected by one or more of the countries of the Special Union or by external auditors, as provided in the financial regulations. They shall be designated, with their agreement, by the Assembly.

[9.115]
Article 5
Amendment of Articles 2 to 5

(1) Proposals for the amendment of this Complementary Act may be initiated by any country member of the Assembly, or by the Director General. Such proposals shall be communicated by the Director General to the member countries of the Assembly at least six months in advance of their consideration by the Assembly.

(2) Amendments referred to in paragraph (1) shall be adopted by the Assembly. Adoption shall require three-fourths of the votes cast, provided that any amendment to Article 2 and to the present paragraph, shall require four-fifths of the votes cast.

(3) Any amendment referred to in paragraph (1) shall enter into force one month after written notifications of acceptance, effected in accordance with their respective constitutional processes, have been received by the Director General from three-fourths of the countries members of the Assembly at the time it adopted the amendment. Any amendment thus accepted shall bind all the countries which are members of the Assembly at the time the amendment enters into force, or which become members thereof at a subsequent date.

Articles 6, 7 *(Art 6(1) modifies the Act signed at London on June 2, 1934, of the Hague Agreement concerning the International Deposit of Industrial Designs, repeals Art 15 of that Act and amends Art 21 of that Act; Art 6(2) modifies the Act signed at Monaco on November 18, 1961, additional to the 1934 Act, and amends Art 4 of that Act; Art 7(1) and (3) modify the Act signed at The Hague on November 28, 1960, of the Hague Agreement concerning the International Deposit of Industrial Designs at* **[9.47]–[9.75]**; *Art 7(2) repeals Arts 19–22 of that Act; Art 7(4) amends Art 29 of that Act at* **[9.71]**.)

[9.116]
Article 8
Ratification of, and Accession to, the Complementary Act

(1)

(a) Countries which, before January 13, 1968, have ratified the 1934 Act or the 1960 Act, and countries which have acceded to at least one of those Acts, may sign this Complementary Act and ratify it, or may accede to it.

(b) Ratification of, or accession to, this Complementary Act by a country which is bound by the 1934 Act without being bound also by the 1961 Additional Act shall automatically entail ratification of, or accession to, the 1961 Additional Act.

(2) Instruments of ratification and accession shall be deposited with the Director General.

[9.117]
Article 9
Entry Into Force of the Complementary Act

(1) With respect to the first five countries which have deposited their instruments of ratification or accession, this Complementary Act shall enter into force three months after the deposit of the fifth such instrument of ratification or accession.

(2) With respect to any other country, this Complementary Act shall enter into force three months after the date on which its ratification or accession has been notified by the Director General, unless a subsequent date has been indicated in the instrument of ratification or accession. In the latter case, this Complementary Act shall enter into force with respect to that country on the date thus indicated.

[9.118]
Article 10
Automatic Acceptance of Certain Provisions by Certain Countries

(1) Subject to the provisions of Article 8 and the following paragraph, any country which has not ratified or acceded to the 1934 Act shall become bound by the 1961 Additional Act and by Articles 1 to 6 of this Complementary Act from the date on which its accession to the 1934 Act enters into force, provided that, if on the said date this Complementary Act has not yet entered into force pursuant to Article 9(1), then, such country shall become bound by the said Articles of this Complementary Act only from the date of entry into force of the Complementary Act pursuant to Article 9(1).

(2) Subject to the provisions of Article 8 and the foregoing paragraph, any country which has not ratified or acceded to the 1960 Act shall become bound by Articles 1 to 7 of this Complementary Act from the date on which its ratification of, or accession to, the 1960 Act enters into force, provided that, if on the said date this Complementary Act has not yet entered into force pursuant to Article 9(1), then, such country shall become bound by the said Articles of this Complementary Act only from the date of entry into force of the Complementary Act pursuant to Article 9(1).

[9.119]
Article 11
Signature, etc, of the Complementary Act

(1)

(a) This Complementary Act shall be signed in a single copy in the French language and shall be deposited with the Government of Sweden.

(b) Official texts shall be established by the Director General, after consultation with the interested Governments, in such other languages as the Assembly may designate.

(2) This Complementary Act shall remain open for signature at Stockholm until January 13, 1968.

(3) The Director General shall transmit two copies, certified by the Government of Sweden, of the signed text of this Complementary Act to the Governments of all countries of the Special Union and, on request, to the Government of any other country.

(4) The Director General shall register this Complementary Act with the Secretariat of the United Nations.

(5) The Director General shall notify the Governments of all countries of the Special Union of signatures, deposits of instruments of ratification or accession, entry into force, and all other relevant notifications.

[9.120]
Article 12
Transitional Provision

Until the first Director General assumes office, references in this Complementary Act to the International Bureau of the Organization or to the Director General shall be construed as references to the Bureau of the Union established by the Paris Convention for the Protection of Industrial Property or its Director, respectively.

LOCARNO AGREEMENT ESTABLISHING AN INTERNATIONAL CLASSIFICATION FOR INDUSTRIAL DESIGNS

Signed at Locarno on October 8, 1968 as amended on September 28, 1979

NOTES

The original source for this Agreement is the World Intellectual Property Organisation (WIPO).

[9.121]
Article 1
Establishment of a Special Union; Adoption of an International Classification

(1) The countries to which this Agreement applies constitute a Special Union.

(2) They adopt a single classification for industrial designs (hereinafter designated as "the international classification").

(3) The international classification shall comprise:
- (i) a list of classes and subclasses;
- (ii) an alphabetical list of goods in which industrial designs are incorporated, with an indication of the classes and subclasses into which they fall;
- (iii) explanatory notes.

(4) The list of classes and subclasses is the list annexed to the present Agreement, subject to such amendments and additions as the Committee of Experts set up under Article 3 (hereinafter designated as "the Committee of Experts") may make to it.

(5) The alphabetical list of goods and the explanatory notes shall be adopted by the Committee of Experts in accordance with the procedure laid down in Article 3.

(6) The international classification may be amended or supplemented by the Committee of Experts, in accordance with the procedure laid down in Article 3.

(7)
- (a) The international classification shall be established in the English and French languages.
- (b) Official texts of the international classification, in such other languages as the Assembly referred to in Article 5 may designate, shall be established, after consultation with the interested Governments, by the International Bureau of Intellectual Property (hereinafter designated as "the International Bureau") referred to in the Convention Establishing the World Intellectual Property organisation (hereinafter designated as "the organisation").

[9.122]
Article 2
Use and Legal Scope of the International Classification

(1) Subject to the requirements prescribed by this Agreement, the international classification shall be solely of an administrative character. Nevertheless, each country may attribute to it the legal scope which it considers appropriate. In particular, the international classification shall not bind the countries of the Special Union as regards the nature and scope of the protection afforded to the design in those countries.

(2) Each country of the Special Union reserves the right to use the international classification as a principal or as a subsidiary system.

(3) The Offices of the countries of the Special Union shall include in the official documents for the deposit or registration of designs, and, if they are officially published, in the publications in question, the numbers of the classes and subclasses of the international classification into which the goods incorporating the designs belong.

(4) In selecting terms for inclusion in the alphabetical list of goods, the Committee of Experts shall exercise reasonable care to avoid using terms in which exclusive rights may exist. The inclusion of any word in the alphabetical index, however, is not an expression of opinion of the Committee of Experts on whether or not it is subject to exclusive rights.

[9.123]
Article 3
Committee of Experts

(1) A Committee of Experts shall be entrusted with the tasks referred to in Article 1(4) to Article 1(6). Each country of the Special Union shall be represented on the Committee of Experts, which shall be organised according to rules of procedure adopted by a simple majority of the countries represented.

(2) The Committee of Experts shall adopt the alphabetical list and explanatory notes by a simple majority of the votes of the countries of the Special Union.

(3) Proposals for amendments or additions to the international classification may be made by the Office of any country of the Special Union or by the International Bureau. Any proposal emanating from an Office shall be communicated by that Office to the International Bureau. Proposals from Offices and from the International Bureau shall be transmitted by the latter to the members of the Committee of Experts not later than two months before the session of the Committee at which the said proposals are to be considered.

(4) The decisions of the Committee of Experts concerning the adoption of amendments and additions to be made in the international classification shall be by a simple majority of the countries of the Special Union. Nevertheless, if such decisions entail the setting up of a new class or any transfer of goods from one class to another, unanimity shall be required.

(5) Each expert shall have the right to vote by mail.

(6) If a country does not appoint a representative for a given session of the Committee of Experts, or if the expert appointed has not expressed his vote during the session or within a period to be prescribed by the rules of procedure of the Committee of Experts, the country concerned shall be considered to have accepted the decision of the Committee.

[9.124]
Article 4
Notification and Publication of the Classification and of Amendments and Additions Thereto

(1) The alphabetical list of goods and the explanatory notes adopted by the Committee of Experts, as well as any amendment or addition to the international classification decided by the Committee, shall be communicated to the Offices of the countries of the Special Union by the International Bureau. The decisions of the Committee of Experts shall enter into force as soon as the communication is received. Nevertheless, if such decisions entail the setting up of a new class or any transfer of goods from one class to another, they shall enter into force within a period of six months from the date of the said communication.

(2) The International Bureau, as depositary of the international classification, shall incorporate therein the amendments and additions which have entered into force. Announcements of the amendments and additions shall be published in the periodicals to be designated by the Assembly.

[9.125]
Article 5
Assembly of the Special Union

(1)
- (a) The Special Union shall have an Assembly consisting of the countries of the Special Union.
- (b) The Government of each country of the Special Union shall be represented by one delegate, who may be assisted by alternate delegates, advisors, and experts.
- (c) The expenses of each delegation shall be borne by the Government which has appointed it.

(2)
- (a) Subject to the provisions of Article 3, the Assembly shall:
  - (i) deal with all matters concerning the maintenance and development of the Special Union and the implementation of this Agreement;
  - (ii) give directions to the International Bureau concerning the preparation for conferences of revision;
  - (iii) review and approve the reports and activities of the Director General of the organisation (hereinafter designated as "the Director General") concerning the Special Union, and give him all necessary instructions concerning matters within the competence of the Special Union;
  - (iv) determine the program and adopt the biennial budget of the Special Union, and approve its final accounts;
  - (v) adopt the financial regulations of the Special Union;
  - (vi) decide on the establishment of official texts of the international classification in languages other than English and French;
  - (vii) establish, in addition to the Committee of Experts set up under Article 3, such other committees of experts and working groups as it deems appropriate to achieve the objectives of the Special Union;
  - (viii) determine which countries not members of the Special Union and which intergovernmental and international non-governmental organisations shall be admitted to its meetings as observers;

(ix) adopt amendments to Articles 5 to Article 8;
(x) take any other appropriate action designed to further the objectives of the Special Union;
(xi) perform such other functions as are appropriate under this Agreement.

(b) With respect to matters which are of interest also to other Unions administered by the organisation, the Assembly shall make its decisions after having heard the advice of the Coordination Committee of the organisation.

(3)

(a) Each country member of the Assembly shall have one vote.
(b) One-half of the countries members of the Assembly shall constitute a quorum.
(c) Notwithstanding the provisions of Subparagraph b, if, in any session, the number of countries represented is less than one-half but equal to or more than one-third of the countries members of the Assembly, the Assembly may make decisions but, with the exception of decisions concerning its own procedure, all such decisions shall take effect only if the conditions set forth hereinafter are fulfilled. The International Bureau shall communicate the said decisions to the countries members of the Assembly which were not represented and shall invite them to express in writing their vote or abstention within a period of three months from the date of the communication. If, at the expiration of this period, the number of countries having thus expressed their vote or abstention attains the number of countries which was lacking for attaining the quorum in the session itself, such decisions shall take effect provided that at the same time the required majority still obtains.
(d) Subject to the provisions of Article 8(2), the decisions of the Assembly shall require two-thirds of the votes cast.
(e) Abstentions shall not be considered as votes.
(f) A delegate may represent, and vote in the name of, one country only.

(4)

(a) The Assembly shall meet once in every second calendar year in ordinary session upon convocation by the Director General and, in the absence of exceptional circumstances, during the same period and at the same place as the General Assembly of the organisation.
(b) The Assembly shall meet in extraordinary session upon convocation by the Director General, at the request of one-fourth of the countries members of the Assembly.
(c) The agenda of each session shall be prepared by the Director General.

(5) The Assembly shall adopt its own rules of procedure.

[9.126]
Article 6
International Bureau

(1)

(a) Administrative tasks concerning the Special Union shall be performed by the International Bureau.
(b) In particular, the International Bureau shall prepare the meetings and provide the secretariat of the Assembly, the Committee of Experts, and such other committees of experts and working groups as may have been established by the Assembly or the Committee of Experts.
(c) The Director General shall be the chief executive of the Special Union and shall represent the Special Union.

(2) The Director General and any staff member designated by him shall participate, without the right to vote, in all meetings of the Assembly, the Committee of Experts, and such other committees of experts or working groups as may have been established by the Assembly or the Committee of Experts. The Director General, or a staff member designated by him, shall be *ex officio* secretary of those bodies.

(3)

(a) The International Bureau shall, in accordance with the directions of the Assembly, make the preparations for the conferences of revision of the provisions of the Agreement other than Article 5 to Article 8.
(b) The International Bureau may consult with intergovernmental and international non-governmental organisations concerning preparations for conferences of revision.
(c) The Director General and persons designated by him shall take part, without the right to vote, in the discussions at those conferences.

(4) The International Bureau shall carry out any other tasks assigned to it.

[9.127]
Article 7
Finances

(1)

(a) The Special Union shall have a budget.

(b) The budget of the Special Union shall include the income and expenses proper to the Special Union, its contribution to the budget of expenses common to the Unions, and, where applicable, the sum made available to the budget of the Conference of the organisation.

(c) Expenses not attributable exclusively to the Special Union but also to one or more other Unions administered by the organisation shall be considered as expenses common to the Unions. The share of the Special Union in such common expenses shall be in proportion to the interest the Special Union has in them.

(2) The budget of the Special Union shall be established with due regard to the requirements of coordination with the budgets of the other Unions administered by the organisation.

(3) The budget of the Special Union shall be financed from the following sources:

(i) contributions of the countries of the Special Union;

(ii) fees and charges due for services rendered by the International Bureau in relation to the Special Union;

(iii) sale of, or royalties on, the publications of the International Bureau concerning the Special Union;

(iv) gifts, bequests, and subventions;

(v) rents, interests, and other miscellaneous income.

(4)

(a) For the purpose of establishing its contribution referred to in paragraph (3)(i), each country of the Special Union shall belong to the same class as it belongs to in the Paris Union for the Protection of Industrial Property, and shall pay its annual contributions on the basis of the same number of units as is fixed for that class in that Union.

(b) The annual contribution of each country of the Special Union shall be an amount in the same proportion to the total sum to be contributed to the budget of the Special Union by all countries as the number of its units is to the total of the units of all contributing countries.

(c) Contributions shall become due on the first of January of each year.

(d) A country which is in arrears in the payment of its contributions may not exercise its right to vote in any organ of the Special Union if the amount of its arrears equals or exceeds the amount of the contributions due from it for the preceding two full years. However, any organ of the Special Union may allow such a country to continue to exercise its right to vote in that organ if, and as long as, it is satisfied that the delay in payment is due to exceptional and unavoidable circumstances.

(e) If the budget is not adopted before the beginning of a new financial period, it shall be at the same level as the budget of the previous year, as provided in the financial regulations.

(5) The amount of the fees and charges due for services rendered by the International Bureau in relation to the Special Union shall be established, and shall be reported to the Assembly, by the Director General.

(6)

(a) The Special Union shall have a working capital fund which shall be constituted by a single payment made by each country of the Special Union. If the fund becomes insufficient, the Assembly shall decide to increase it.

(b) The amount of the initial payment of each country to the said fund or of its participation in the increase thereof shall be a proportion of the contribution of that country for the year in which the fund is established or the decision to increase it is made.

(c) The proportion and the terms of payment shall be fixed by the Assembly on the proposal of the Director General and after it has heard the advice of the Coordination Committee of the organisation.

(7)

(a) In the headquarters agreement concluded with the country on the territory of which the organisation has its headquarters, it shall be provided that, whenever the working capital fund is insufficient, such country shall grant advances. The amount of those advances and the conditions on which they are granted shall be the subject of separate agreements, in each case, between such country and the organisation.

(b) The country referred to in subparagraph (a) and the organisation shall each have the right to denounce the obligation to grant advances, by written notification. Denunciation shall take effect three years after the end of the year in which it has been notified.

(8) The auditing of the accounts shall be effected by one or more of the countries of the Special Union or by external auditors, as provided in the financial regulations. They shall be designated, with their agreement, by the Assembly.

[9.128]
Article 8
Amendment of Article 5 to Article 7

(1) Proposals for the amendment of Article 5 to Article 7, and the present Article, may be initiated by any country of the Special Union or by the Director General. Such proposals shall be communicated by the Director General to the countries of the Special Union at least six months in advance of their consideration by the Assembly.

(2) Amendments to the Articles referred to in paragraph (1) shall be adopted by the Assembly. Adoption shall require three-fourths of the votes cast, provided that any amendment to Article 5, and to the present paragraph, shall require four-fifths of the votes cast.
(3) Any amendment to the Articles referred to in paragraph (1) shall enter into force one month after written notifications of acceptance, effected in accordance with their respective constitutional processes, have been received by the Director General from three-fourths of the countries members of the Special Union at the time the amendment was adopted. Any amendment to the said Articles thus accepted shall bind all the countries which are members of the Special Union at the time the amendment enters into force, or which become members thereof at a subsequent date, provided that any amendment increasing the financial obligations of countries of the Special Union shall bind only those countries which have notified their acceptance of such amendment.

[9.129]
Article 9
Ratification and Accession; Entry Into Force
(1) Any country party to the Paris Convention for the Protection of Industrial Property which has signed this Agreement may ratify it, and, if it has not signed it, may accede to it.
(2) Instruments of ratification and accession shall be deposited with the Director General.
(3)
- (a) With respect to the first five countries which have deposited their instruments of ratification or accession, this Agreement shall enter into force three months after the deposit of the fifth such instrument.
- (b) With respect to any other country, this Agreement shall enter into force three months after the date on which its ratification or accession has been notified by the Director General, unless a subsequent date has been indicated in the instrument of ratification or accession. In the latter case, this Agreement shall enter into force with respect to that country on the date thus indicated.

(4) Ratification or accession shall automatically entail acceptance of all the clauses and admission to all the advantages of this Agreement.

[9.130]
Article 10
Force and Duration of the Agreement
This Agreement shall have the same force and duration as the Paris Convention for the Protection of Industrial Property.

[9.131]
Article 11
Revision of Article 1 to Article 4 and Article 9 to Article 15
(1) Article 1 to Article 4 and Article 9 to Article 15 of this Agreement may be submitted to revision with a view to the introduction of desired improvements.
(2) Every revision shall be considered at a conference which shall be held among the delegates of the countries of the Special Union.

[9.132]
Article 12
Denunciation
(1) Any country may denounce this Agreement by notification addressed to the Director General. Such denunciation shall affect only the country making it, the Agreement remaining in full force and effect as regards the other countries of the Special Union.
(2) Denunciation shall take effect one year after the day on which the Director General has received the notification.
(3) The right of denunciation provided by this Article shall not be exercised by any country before the expiration of five years from the date upon which it becomes a member of the Special Union.

[9.133]
Article 13
Territories
The provisions of Article 24 of the Paris Convention for the Protection of Industrial Property shall apply to this Agreement.

[9.134]
Article 14
Signature, Languages, Notifications
(1)
- (a) This Agreement shall be signed in a single copy in the English and French languages, both texts being equally authentic, and shall be deposited with the Government of Switzerland.
- (b) This Agreement shall remain open for signature at Berne until June 30, 1969.

(2) Official texts shall be established by the Director General, after consultation with the interested Governments, in such other languages as the Assembly may designate.

(3) The Director General shall transmit two copies, certified by the Government of Switzerland, of the signed text of this Agreement to the Governments of the countries that have signed it and, on request, to the Government of any other country.
(4) The Director General shall register this Agreement with the Secretariat of the United Nations.
(5) The Director General shall notify the Governments of all countries of the Special Union of the date of entry into force of the Agreement, signatures, deposits of instruments of ratification or accession, acceptances of amendments to this Agreement and the dates on which such amendments enter into force, and notifications of denunciation.

[9.135]
Article 15
Transitional Provision

Until the first Director General assumes office, references in this Agreement to the International Bureau of the organisation or to the Director General shall be deemed to be references to the United International Bureaux for the Protection of Intellectual Property (BIRPI) or its Director, respectively.

ANNEX
LIST OF CLASSES AND SUBCLASSES OF THE INTERNATIONAL CLASSIFICATION NINTH EDITION

(as in force from January 1, 2009)

Class 1
Foodstuffs

[9.136]
01 Bakers' products, biscuits, pastry, macaroni and other cereal products, chocolates, confectionery, ices

02 Fruit and vegetables

03 Cheeses, butter and butter substitutes, other dairy produce

04 Butchers' meat (including pork products), fish

05 [vacant]

06 Animal foodstuffs

99 Miscellaneous

Class 2
Articles of Clothing and Haberdashery

01 Undergarments, lingerie, corsets, brassieres, nightwear

02 Garments

03 Headwear

04 Footwear, socks and stockings

05 Neckties, scarves, neckerchiefs and handkerchiefs

06 Gloves

07 Haberdashery and clothing accessories

99 Miscellaneous

Class 3
Travel Goods, Cases, Parasols and Personal Belongings, not Elsewhere Specified

01 Trunks, suitcases, briefcases, handbags, keyholders, cases specially designed for their contents, wallets and similar articles

02 [vacant]

03 Umbrellas, parasols, sunshades and walking sticks

04 Fans

99 Miscellaneous

Class 4
Brushware

01 Brushes and brooms for cleaning

02 Toilet brushes, clothes brushes and shoe brushes

03 Brushes for machines

04 Paintbrushes, brushes for use in cooking

99 Miscellaneous

Class 5
Textile Piecegoods, Artificial and Natural Sheet Material

01 Spun articles

02 Lace

03 Embroidery

04 Ribbons, braids and other decorative trimmings

05 Textile fabrics

06 Artificial or natural sheet material

99 Miscellaneous

Class 6
Furnishing

01 Seats

02 Beds

03 Tables and similar furniture

04 Storage furniture

05 Composite furniture

06 Other furniture and furniture parts

07 Mirrors and frames

08 Clothes hangers

09 Mattresses and cushions

10 Curtains and indoor blinds

11 Carpets, mats and rugs

12 Tapestries

13 Blankets and other covering materials, household linen and napery

99 Miscellaneous

Class 7
Household Goods, not Elsewhere Specified

01 China, glassware, dishes and other articles of a similar nature

02 Cooking appliances, utensils and containers

03 Tables knives, forks and spoons

04 Appliances and utensils, hand-manipulated, for preparing food or drink

05 Flatirons and washing, cleaning and drying equipment

06 Other table utensils

07 Other household receptacles

08 Fireplace implements

99 Miscellaneous

Class 8
Tools and Hardware

01 Tools and implements for drilling, milling or digging

02 Hammers and other similar tools and implements

03 Cutting tools and implements

04 Screwdrivers and other similar tools and implements

05 Other tools and implements

06 Handles, knobs and hinges

07 Locking or closing devices

08 Fastening, supporting or mounting devices not included in other Classes

09 Metal fittings and mountings for doors, windows and furniture, and similar articles

10 Bicycle and motorcycle racks

99 Miscellaneous

Class 9
Packages and Containers for the Transport or Handling of Goods

01 Bottles, flasks, pots, carboys, demijohns, and containers with dynamic dispensing means

02 Storage cans, drums and casks

03 Boxes, cases, containers, (preserve) tins or cans

04 Hampers, crates and baskets

05 Bags, sachets, tubes and capsules

06 Ropes and hooping materials

07 Closing means and attachments

08 Pallets and platforms for forklifts

09 Refuse and trash containers and stands therefor

99 Miscellaneous

Class 10
Clocks and Watches and other Measuring Instruments,
Checking and Signalling Instruments

01 Clocks and alarm clocks

02 Watches and wrist watches

03 Other time-measuring instruments

04 Other measuring instruments, apparatus and devices

05 Instruments, apparatus and devices for checking, security or testing

06 Signalling apparatus and devices

07 Casings, cases, dials, hands and all other parts and accessories of instruments for measuring, checking and signalling

99 Miscellaneous

Class 11
Articles of Adornment

01 Jewellery

02 Trinkets, table, mantel and wall ornaments, flower vases and pots

03 Medals and badges

04 Artificial flowers, fruit and plants

05 Flags, festive decorations

99 Miscellaneous

Class 12
Means of Transport or Hoisting

01 Vehicles drawn by animals

02 Handcarts, wheelbarrows

03 Locomotives and rolling stock for railways and all other rail vehicles

04 Telpher carriers, chair lifts and ski lifts

05 Elevators and hoists for loading or conveying

06 Ships and boats

07 Aircraft and space vehicles

08 Motor cars, buses and lorries

09 Tractors

10 Road vehicle trailers

11 Cycles and motorcycles

12 Perambulators, invalid chairs, stretchers

13 Special-purpose vehicles

14 Other vehicles

15 Tyres and anti-skid chains for vehicles

16 Parts, equipment and accessories for vehicles, not included in other Classes or sub Classes

99 Miscellaneous

Class 13
Equipment for Production, Distribution or Transformation of Electricity

01 Generators and motors

02 Power transformers, rectifiers, batteries and accumulators

03 Equipment for distribution or control of electric power

99 Miscellaneous

Class 14
Recording, Communication or Information Retrieval Equipment

01 Equipment for the recording or reproduction of sounds or pictures

02 Data processing equipment as well as peripheral apparatus and devices

03 Communications equipment, wireless remote controls and radio amplifiers

04 Screen displays and icons

99 Miscellaneous

Class 15
Machines, not Elsewhere Specified

01 Engines

02 Pumps and compressors

03 Agricultural machinery

04 Construction machinery

05 Washing, cleaning and drying machines

06 Textile, sewing, knitting and embroidering machines including their integral parts

07 Refrigeration machinery and apparatus

08 [vacant]

09 Machine tools, abrading and founding machinery

99 Miscellaneous

Class 16
Photographic, Cinematographic and Optical Apparatus

01 Photographic cameras and film cameras

02 Projectors and viewers

03 Photocopying apparatus and enlargers

04 Developing apparatus and equipment

05 Accessories

06 Optical articles

99 Miscellaneous

Class 17
Musical Instruments

01 Keyboard instruments

02 Wind instruments

03 Stringed instruments

04 Percussion instruments

05 Mechanical instruments

99 Miscellaneous

Class 18
Printing and Office Machinery

01 Typewriters and calculating machines

02 Printing machines

03 Type and type faces

04 Bookbinding machines, printers' stapling machines, guillotines and trimmers (for bookbinding)

99 Miscellaneous

Class 19
Stationery and Office Equipment, Artists' and Teaching Materials

01 Writing paper, cards for correspondence and announcements

02 Office equipment

03 Calendars

04 Books and other objects of similar outward appearance

05 [vacant]

06 Materials and instruments for writing by hand, for drawing, for painting, for sculpture, for engraving and for other artistic techniques

07 Teaching materials

08 Other printed matter

99 Miscellaneous

Class 20
Sales and Advertising Equipment, Signs

01 Automatic vending machines

02 Display and sales equipment

03 Signs, signboards and advertising devices

99 Miscellaneous

Class 21
Games, Toys, Tents and Sports Goods

01 Games and toys

02 Gymnastics and sports apparatus and equipment

03 Other amusement and entertainment articles

04 Tents and accessories thereof

99 Miscellaneous

Class 22
Arms, Pyrotechnic Articles, Articles for Hunting, Fishing and Pest Killing

01 Projectile weapons

02 Other weapons

03 Ammunition, rockets and pyrotechnic articles

04 Targets and accessories

05 Hunting and fishing equipment

06 Traps, articles for pest killing

99 Miscellaneous

Class 23
Fluid Distribution Equipment, Sanitary, Heating, Ventilation and Air-conditioning Equipment, Solid Fuel

01 Fluid distribution equipment

02 Sanitary appliances

03 Heating equipment

04 Ventilation and air-conditioning equipment

05 Solid fuel

99 Miscellaneous

Class 24
Medical and Laboratory Equipment

01 Apparatus and equipment for doctors, hospitals and laboratories

02 Medical instruments, instruments and tools for laboratory use

03 Prosthetic articles

04 Materials for dressing wounds, nursing and medical care

99 Miscellaneous

Class 25
Building Units and Construction Elements

01 Building materials

02 Prefabricated or pre-assembled building parts

03 Houses, garages and other buildings

04 Steps, ladders and scaffolds

99 Miscellaneous

Class 26
Lighting Apparatus

01 Candlesticks and candelabra

02 Torches and hand lamps and lanterns

03 Public lighting fixtures

04 Luminous sources, electrical or not

05 Lamps, standard lamps, chandeliers, wall and ceiling fixtures, lampshades, reflectors, photographic and cinematographic projector lamps

06 Luminous devices for vehicles

99 Miscellaneous

Class 27
Tobacco and Smokers' Supplies

01 Tobacco, cigars and cigarettes

02 Pipes, cigar and cigarette holders

03 Ashtrays

04 Matches

05 Lighters

06 Cigar cases, cigarette cases, tobacco jars and pouches

99 Miscellaneous

Class 28
Pharmaceutical and Cosmetic Products, Toilet Articles and Apparatus

01 Pharmaceutical products

02 Cosmetic products

03 Toilet articles and beauty parlour equipment

04 Wigs, false hairpieces

99 Miscellaneous

Class 29
Devices and Equipment Against Fire Hazards, for Accident Prevention and for Rescue

01 Devices and equipment against fire hazards

02 Devices and equipment for accident prevention and for rescue, not elsewhere specified

99 Miscellaneous

Class 30
Articles for the Care and Handling of Animals

01 Animal clothing

02 Pens, cages, kennels and similar shelters

03 Feeders and waterers

04 Saddlery

05 Whips and prods

06 Beds and nests

07 Perches and other cage attachments

08 Markers, marks and shackles

09 Hitching posts

99 Miscellaneous

Class 31
Machines and Appliances for Preparing Food or Drink, Not Elsewhere Specified

00 Machines and appliances for preparing food or drink, not elsewhere specified

Class 32
Graphic Symbols and Logos, Surface Patterns, Ornamentation

00 Graphic symbols and logos, surface patterns, ornamentation

Class 99
Miscellaneous

00 Miscellaneous

UNIVERSAL COPYRIGHT CONVENTION

(As revised at Paris on 24 July 1971)

NOTES

THE CONTRACTING STATES,

Moved by the desire to ensure in all countries copyright protection of literary, scientific and artistic works,

Convinced that a system of copyright protection appropriate to all nations of the world and expressed in a universal convention, additional to, and without impairing international systems already in force, will ensure respect for the rights of the individual and encourage the development of literature, the sciences and the arts,

Persuaded that such a universal copyright system will facilitate a wider dissemination of works of the human mind and increase international understanding,

Have resolved to revise the Universal Copyright Convention as signed at Geneva on 6 September 1952 (hereinafter called "the 1952 Convention"), and consequently,

HAVE AGREED AS FOLLOWS—

[9.137]
Article I
Each Contracting State undertakes to provide for the adequate and effective protection of the rights of authors and other copyright proprietors in literary, scientific and artistic works, including writings, musical, dramatic and cinematographic works, and paintings, engravings and sculpture.

[9.138]
Article II
1. Published works of nationals of any Contracting State and works first published in that State shall enjoy in each other Contracting State the same protection as that other State accords to works of its nationals first published in its own territory, as well as the protection specially granted by this Convention.
2. Unpublished works of nationals of each Contracting State shall enjoy in each other Contracting State the same protection as that other State accords to unpublished works of its own nationals, as well the protection specially granted by this Convention.
3. For the purpose of this Convention any Contracting State may, by domestic legislation, assimilate to its own nationals any person domiciled in that State.

[9.139]
Article III
1. Any Contracting State which, under its domestic law, requires as a condition of copyright, compliance with formalities such as deposit, registration, notice, notarial certificates, payment of fees or manufacture or publication in that Contracting State, shall regard these requirements as satisfied with respect to all works protected in accordance with this Convention and first published outside its territory and the author of which is not one of its nationals, if from the time of the first publication all the copies of the work published with the authority of the author or other copyright proprietor bear the symbol © accompanied by the name of the copyright proprietor and the year of first publication placed in such manner and location as to give reasonable notice of claim of copyright.
2. The provisions of paragraph 1 shall not preclude any Contracting State from requiring formalities or other conditions for the acquisition and enjoyment of copyright in respect of works first published in its territory or works of its nationals wherever published.
3. The provisions of paragraph 1 shall not preclude any Contracting State from providing that a person seeking judicial relief must, in bringing the action, comply with procedural requirements, such as that the complainant must appear through domestic counsel or that the complainant must deposit with the court or an administrative office, or both, a copy of the work involved in the litigation; provided that failure to comply with such requirements shall not affect the validity of the copyright, nor shall any such requirement be imposed upon a national of another Contracting State if such requirement is not imposed on nationals of the State in which protection is claimed.
4. In each Contracting State there shall be legal means of protecting without formalities the unpublished works of nationals of other Contracting States.
5. If a Contracting State grants protection for more than one term of copyright and the first term is for a period longer than one of the minimum periods prescribed in Article IV, such State shall not be required to comply with the provisions of paragraph 1 of this Article in respect of the second or any subsequent term of copyright.

[9.140]
Article IV
1. The duration of protection of a work shall be governed, in accordance with the provisions of Article II and this Article, by the law of the Contracting State in which protection is claimed.
2.—
(a) The term of protection for works protected under this Convention shall not be less than the life of the author and twenty-five years after his death. However, any Contracting State which, on the effective date of this Convention in that State, has limited this term for certain classes of works to a period computed from the first publication of the work, shall be entitled to maintain these exceptions and to extend them to other classes of works. For all these classes the term of protection shall not be less than twenty-five years from the date of first publication.
(b) Any Contracting State which, upon the effective date of this Convention in that State, does not compute the term of protection upon the basis of the life of the author, shall be entitled to compute the term of protection from the date of the first publication of the work or from its registration prior to publication, as the case may be, provided the term of protection shall not be less than twenty-five years from the date of first publication or from its registration prior to publication, as the case may be.
(c) If the legislation of a Contracting State grants two or more successive terms of protection, the duration of the first term shall not be less than one of the minimum periods specified in subparagraphs (a) and (b).

3. The provisions of paragraph 2 shall not apply to photographic works or to works of applied art; provided, however, that the term of protection in those Contracting States which protects photographic works, or works of applied art in so far as they are protected as artistic works, shall not be less than ten years for each of said classes of work.

4.—

(a) No Contracting State shall be obliged to grant protection to a work for a period longer than that fixed for the class of works to which the work in question belongs, in the case of unpublished works by the law of the Contracting State of which the author is a national, and in the case of published works by the law of the Contracting State in which the work has been first published.

(b) For the purposes of the application of subparagraph (a), if the law of any Contracting State grants two or more successive terms of protection the period of protection of that State shall be considered to be the aggregate of those terms. However, if a specified work is not protected by such State during the second or any subsequent term for any reason, the other Contracting States shall not be obliged to protect it during the second or any subsequent term.

5. For the purposes of the application of paragraph 4, the work of a national of a Contracting State, first published in a non-Contracting State, shall be treated as though first published in the Contracting State of which the author is a national.

6. For the purposes of the application of paragraph 4, in case of simultaneous publication in two or more Contracting States, the work shall be treated as though first published in the State which affords the shortest term; any work published in two or more Contracting States within thirty days of its first publication shall be considered as having been published simultaneously in said Contracting States.

[9.141]
Article IVbis

1. The rights referred to in Article I shall include the basic rights ensuring the author's economic interests, including the exclusive rights to authorise reproduction by any means, public performance and broadcasting. The provisions of this Article shall extend to works protected under this Convention either in their original form or in any form recognisably derived from the original.

2. However, any Contracting State may, by its domestic legislation, make exceptions that do not conflict with the spirit and provisions of this Convention, to the rights mentioned in paragraph 1 of this Article. Any State whose legislation so provides, shall nevertheless accord a reasonable degree of effective protection to each of the rights to which exception has been made.

[9.142]
Article V

1. The rights referred to in Article I shall include the exclusive right of the author to make, publish and authorise the making and publication of translations of works protected under this Convention.

2. However, any Contracting State may, by its domestic legislation, restrict the right of translation of writings, but only subject to the following provisions—

(a) If, after the expiration of a period of seven years from the date of the first publication of a writing, a translation of such writing has not been published in a language in general use in the Contracting State, by the owner of the right of translation or with his authorisation, any national of such Contracting State may obtain a non-exclusive licence from the competent authority thereof to translate the work into that language and publish the work so translated.

(b) Such national shall in accordance with the procedure of the State concerned, establish either that he has requested, and been denied, authorisation by the proprietor of the right to make and publish the translation, or that, after due diligence on his part, he was unable to find the owner of the right. A licence may also be granted on the same conditions if all previous editions of a translation in a language in general use in the Contracting State are out of print.

(c) If the owner of the right of translation cannot be found, then the applicant for a licence shall send copies of his application to the publisher whose name appears on the work and, if the nationality of the owner of the right of translation is known, to the diplomatic or consular representative of the State of which such owner is a national, or to the organisation which may have been designated by the government of that State. The licence shall not be granted before the expiration of a period of two months from the date of dispatch of the copies of the application.

(d) Due provision shall be made by domestic legislation to ensure to the owner of the right of translation a compensation which is just and conforms to international standards, to ensure payment and transmittal of such compensation and to ensure a correct translation of the work.

(e) The original title and the name of the author of the work shall be printed on all copies of the published translation. The licence shall be valid only for publication of the translation in the territory of the Contracting State where it has been applied for. Copies so published may be imported and sold in another Contracting State if a language in general use in such other State is the same language as that into which the work has been so translated, and if the domestic law in such other State makes provision for such licences and does not prohibit such importation and sale. Where the foregoing conditions do not exist, the importation and sale of such copies in a Contracting State shall be governed by its domestic law and its agreements. The licence shall not be transferred by the licensee.

(f) The licence shall not be granted when the author has withdrawn from circulation all copies of the work.

[9.143]
Article Vbis

1. Any Contracting State regarded as a developing country in conformity with the established practice of the General Assembly of the United Nations may, by a notification deposited with the Director-General of the United Nations Educational, Scientific and Cultural Organisation (hereinafter called "the Director-General") at the time of its ratification, acceptance or accession or thereafter, avail itself of any or all of the exceptions provided for in Articles V*ter* and V*quater*.

2. Any such notification shall be effective for ten years from the date of coming into force of this Convention, or for such part of that ten-year period as remains at the date of deposit of the notification, and may be renewed in whole or in part for further periods of ten years each, if not more than fifteen or less than three months before the expiration of the relevant ten-year period, the Contracting State deposits a further notification with the Director-General. Initial notifications may also be made during these further periods of ten years in accordance with the provisions of this Article.

3. Notwithstanding the provisions of paragraph 2, a Contracting State that has ceased to be regarded as a developing country as referred to in paragraph 1 shall no longer be entitled to renew its notification made under the provisions of paragraph 1 or 2, and whether or not it formally withdraws the notification such State shall be precluded from availing itself of the exceptions provided for in Articles V*ter* and V*quater* at the end of the current ten-year period, or at the end of the three years after it has ceased to be regarded as developing country, whichever period expires later.

4. Any copies of a work already made under the exceptions provided for in Articles V*ter* and V*quater* may continue to be distributed after the expiration of the period for which notifications under this Article were effective until their stock is exhausted.

5. Any Contracting State that has deposited a notification in accordance with Article XIII with respect to the application of this Convention to a particular country or territory, the situation of which can be regarded as analogous to that of the States referred to in paragraph 1 of this Article, may also deposit notifications and renew them in accordance with the provisions of this Article with respect to any such country or territory. During the effective period of such notifications, the provisions of Articles V*ter* and V*quater* may be applied with respect to such country or territory. The sending of copies from the country or territory to the Contracting States shall be considered as export within the meaning of Articles V*ter* and V*quater*.

[9.144]
Article Vter

1.—

(a) Any Contracting State to which Article V*bis* (1) applies may substitute for the period of seven years provided for in Article V(2) a period of three years or any longer period prescribed by its legislation. However, in the case of a translation into a language not in general use in one or more of the developed countries that are party to this Convention or only the 1952 Convention, the period shall be one year instead of three.

(b) A Contracting State to which Article V*bis* (1) applies may, with the unanimous agreement of the developed countries party to this Convention or only the 1952 Convention and in which the same language is in general use, substitute, in the case of translation into that language, for the period of three years provided for in subparagraph (a) another period as determined by such agreement but not shorter than one year. However, this subparagraph shall not apply where the language in question is English, French or Spanish. Notification of any such agreement shall be made to the Director-General.

(c) The licence may only be granted if the applicant, in accordance with the procedure of the State concerned, establishes either that he has requested, and been denied, authorisation by the owner of the right of translation, or that, after due diligence on his part he was unable to find the owner of the right. At the same time as he makes his request he shall inform either the International Copyright Information Centre established by the United Nations Educational, Scientific and Cultural Organisation or any national or regional information centre which may have been designated in a notification to that effect deposited with the Director-General by the government of the State in which the publisher is believed to have his principal place of business.

(d) If the owner of the right of translation cannot be found, the applicant for a licence shall send, by registered airmail, copies of his application to the publisher whose name appears on the work and to any national or regional information centre as mentioned in subparagraph (c). If no such centre is notified he shall also send a copy to the international copyright information centre established by the United Nations Educational, Scientific and Cultural Organisation.

2.—

(a) Licences obtainable after three years shall not be granted under this Article until a further period of six months has elapsed and licences obtainable after one year until a further period of nine months has elapsed. The further period shall begin either from the date of the request for permission to translate mentioned in paragraph 1(c) or, if the identify or address of the owner of the right of translation is not known, from the date of dispatch of the copies of the application for a licence mentioned in paragraph 1(d).

(b) Licences shall not be granted if a translation has been published by the owner of the right of translation or with his authorisation during the said period of six months or nine months.

3. Any licence under this Article shall be granted only for the purpose of teaching, scholarship or research.

4.—

(a) Any licence granted under this Article shall not extend to the export of copies and shall be valid only for publication in the territory of the Contracting State where it has been applied for.

(b) Any copy published in accordance with a licence granted under this Article shall bear a notice in the appropriate language stating that the copy is available for distribution only in the Contracting State granting the licence. If the writing bears the notice specified in Article III(1) the copies shall bear the same notice.

(c) The prohibition of export provided for in subparagraph (a) shall not apply where a governmental or other public entity of a State which was granted a licence under this Article to translate a work into a language other than English, French or Spanish sends copies of a translation prepared under such licence to another country if—

(i) the recipients are individuals who are nationals of the Contracting State granting the licence, or organisations grouping such individuals;

(ii) the copies are to be used only for the purpose of teaching, scholarship or research;

(iii) the sending of the copies and their subsequent distribution to recipients is without the object of commercial purpose; and

(iv) the country to which the copies have been sent has agreed with the Contracting State to allow the receipt, distribution or both and the Director-General has been notified of such governments which have concluded it.

5. Due provision shall be made at the national level to ensure—

(a) that the licence provides for just compensation that is consistent with standards of royalties normally operating in the case of licences freely negotiated between persons in the two countries concerned; and

(b) payment and transmittal of the compensation; however, should national currency regulations intervene, the competent authority shall make all efforts, by the use of international machinery, to ensure transmittal in internationally convertible currency or its equivalent.

6. Any licence granted by a Contracting State under this Article shall terminate if a translation of the work in the same language with substantially the same content as the edition in respect of which the licence was granted is published in the said State by the owner of the right of translation or with his authorisation, at a price reasonably related to that normally charged in the same State for comparable works. Any copies already made before the licence is terminated may continue to be distributed until their stock is exhausted.

7. For works which are composed mainly of illustrations a licence to translate the text and to reproduce the illustrations may be granted only if the conditions of Article V*quater* are also fulfilled.

8.—

(a) A licence to translate a work protected under this Convention, published in printed or analogous forms of reproduction may also be granted to a broadcasting organisation having its headquarters in a Contracting State to which Article V*bis* (1) applies, upon an application made in that State by the said organisation under the following conditions—

(i) the translation is made from a copy made and acquired in accordance with the laws of the Contracting State;

(ii) the translation is for use only in broadcasts intended exclusively for teaching or for the dissemination of the results of specialised technical or scientific research to experts in a particular profession;

(iii) the translation is used exclusively for the purposes set out in condition (ii), through broadcasts lawfully made which are intended for recipients on the territory of the Contracting State, including broadcasts made through the medium of sound or visual recording lawfully and exclusively made for the purpose of such broadcasts;

(iv) sound or visual recordings of the translation may be exchanged only between broadcasting organisations having their headquarters in the Contracting State granting the licence; and

(v) all uses made of the translation are without any commercial purpose.

(b) Provided all of the criteria and conditions set out in subparagraph (a) are met, a licence may also be granted to a broadcasting organisation to translate any text incorporated in an audio-visual fixation which was itself prepared and published for the sole purpose of being used in connection with systematic instructional activities.

(c) Subject to subparagraphs (a) and (b), the other provisions of this Article shall apply to the grant and exercise of the licence.

9. Subject to the provisions of this Article, any licence granted under this Article shall be governed by the provisions of Article V, and shall continue to be governed by the provisions of Article V and of this Article, even after the seven-year period provided for in Article V(2) has expired. However, after the said period has expired, the licensee shall be free to request that the said licence be replaced by a new licence governed exclusively by the provisions of Article V.

[9.145]
Article Vquater

1. Any Contracting State to which Article V*bis* (1) applies may adopt the following provisions—

(a) If, after the expiration of (i) the relevant period specified in subparagraph (c) commencing from the date of first publication of a particular edition of a literary, scientific or artistic work referred to in paragraph 3, or (ii) any longer period determined by national legislation of the State, copies of such edition have not been distributed in that State to the general public or in connection with systematic instructional activities at a price reasonably related to that normally charged in the State for comparable works, by the owner of the right of reproduction or with his authorisation, any national of such State may obtain a non-exclusive licence from the competent authority to publish such edition at that or a lower price for use in connection with systematic instructional activities. The licence may only be granted if such national, in accordance with the procedure of the State concerned, establishes either that he has requested, and has been denied, authorisation by the proprietor of the right to publish such work, or that, after due diligence on his part, he was unable to find the owner of the right. At the same time as he makes his request he shall inform either the international copyright information centre established by the United Nations Educational, Scientific and Cultural Organisation or any national or regional information centre referred to in subparagraph (d).

(b) A licence may also be granted on the same conditions if, for a period of six months, no authorised copies of the edition in question have been on sale in the State concerned to the general public or in connection with systematic instructional activities at a price reasonably related to that normally charged in the State for comparable works.

(c) The period referred to in subparagraph (a) shall be five years except that—

(i) for works of the natural and physical sciences, including mathematics, and of technology, the period shall be three years;

(ii) for works of fiction, poetry, drama, and music, and for art books, the period shall be seven years.

(d) If the owner of the right of reproduction cannot be found, the applicant for a licence shall send, by registered airmail, copies of his application to the publisher whose name appears on the work and to any national or regional information centre identified as such in a notification deposited with the Director-General by the State in which the publisher is believed to have his principal place of business. In the absence of any such notification, he shall also send a copy to the international copyright information centre established by the United Nations Educational, Scientific and Cultural Organisation. The licence shall not be granted before the expiration of a period of three months from the date of dispatch of the copies of the application.

(e) Licences obtainable after three years shall not be granted under this Article—

(i) until a period of six months has elapsed from the date of the request for permission referred to in subparagraph (a) or, if the identity or address of the owner of the right of reproduction is unknown, from the date of the dispatch of the copies of the application for a licence referred to in subparagraph (d);

(ii) if any such distribution of copies of the edition as is mentioned in subparagraph (a) has taken place during that period.

(f) The name of the author and the title of the particular edition of the work shall be printed on all copies of the published reproduction. The licence shall not extend to the export of copies and shall be valid only for publication in the territory of the Contracting State where it has been applied for. The licence shall not be transferable by the licensee.

(g) Due provision shall be made by domestic legislation to ensure an accurate reproduction of the particular edition in question.

(h) A licence to reproduce and publish a translation of a work shall not be granted under this Article in the following cases—

(i) where the translation was not published by the owner of the right of translation or with his authorisation;

(ii) where the translation is not in a language in general use in the State with power to grant the licence.

2. The exceptions provided for in paragraph 1 are subject to the following additional provisions—

(a) Any copy published in accordance with a licence granted under this Article shall bear a notice in the appropriate language stating that the copy is available for distribution only in the Contracting State to which the said licence applies. If the edition bears the notice specified in Article III(1), the copies shall bear the same notice.

(b) Due provision shall be made at the national level to ensure—

(i) that the licence provides for just compensation that is consistent with standards of royalties normally operating in the case of licences freely negotiated between persons in the two countries concerned; and

(ii) payment and transmittal of the compensation; however, should national currency regulations intervene, the competent authority shall make all efforts, by the use of international machinery, to ensure transmittal in international convertible currency or its equivalent.

(c) Whenever copies of an edition of a work are distributed in the Contracting State to the general public or in connection with systematic instructional activities, by the owner of the right of reproduction or with his authorisation, at a price reasonably related to that normally charged in the State for comparable works, any licence granted under this Article shall terminate if such edition is in the same language and is substantially the same in content as the edition published under licence. Any copies already made before the licence is terminated may continue to be distributed until their stock is exhausted.

(d) No licence shall be granted when the author has withdrawn from circulation all copies of the edition in question.

3.—

(a) Subject to subparagraph (b), the literary, scientific or artistic works to which this Article applies shall be limited to works published in printed or analogous forms of reproduction.

(b) The provisions of this Article shall also apply to reproduction in audio-visual form of lawfully made audio-visual fixations including any protected works incorporated therein and to the translation of any incorporated text into a language in general use in the State with power to rant the licence; always provided that the audio-visual fixations in question were prepared and published for the sole purpose of being used in connection with systematic instructional activities.

[9.146]
Article VI

'Publication', as used in this Convention, means the reproduction in tangible form and the general distribution to the public of copies of a work from which it can be read or otherwise visually perceived.

[9.147]
Article VII

This Convention shall not apply to works or rights in works which, at the effective date of this Convention in a Contracting State where protection is claimed, are permanently in the public domain in the said Contracting State.

[9.148]
Article VIII

1. This Convention, shall bear the date of 24 July 1971, shall be deposited with the Director-General and shall remain open for signature by all States party to the 1952 Convention for a period of 120 days after the date of this Convention. It shall be subject to ratification or acceptance by the signatory States.

2. Any State which has not signed this Convention may accede thereto.

3. Ratification, acceptance or accession shall be effected by the deposit of an instrument to that effect with the Director-General.

[9.149]
Article IX

1. This Convention shall come into force three months after the deposit of twelve instruments of ratification, acceptance or accession.

2. Subsequently, this Convention shall come into force in respect of each State three months after that State has deposited its instrument of ratification, acceptance or accession.

3. Accession to this Convention by a State not party to the 1952 Convention shall also constitute accession to that Convention; however, if its instrument of accession is deposited before this Convention comes into force, such State may make its accession to the 1952 Convention conditional upon the coming into force of this Convention. After the coming into force of this Convention, no State may accede solely to the 1952 Convention.

4. Relations between States party to this Convention and States that are party only to the 1952 Convention, shall be governed by the 1952 Convention. However, any State party only to the 1952 Convention may, by a notification deposited with the Director-General, declare that it will admit the application of the 1971 Convention to works of its nationals or works first published in its territory by all States party to this Convention.

[9.150]
Article X

1. Each Contracting State undertakes to adopt, in accordance with its Constitution, such measures as are necessary to ensure the application of this Convention.
2. It is understood that at the date this Convention comes into force in respect of any State, that State must be in a position under its domestic law to give effect to the terms of this Convention.

[9.151]
Article XI

1. An Intergovernmental Committee is hereby established with the following duties—
   (a) to study the problems concerning the application and operation of the Universal Copyright Convention;
   (b) to make preparation for periodic revisions of this Convention;
   (c) to study any other problems concerning the international protection of copyright, in cooperation with the various interested international organisations, such as the United Nations Educational, Scientific and Cultural Organisation, the International Union for the protection of Literary and Artistic Works and the Organisation of American States;
   (d) to inform States party to the Universal Copyright Convention as to its activities.
2. The Committee shall consist of the representatives of eighteen States party to this Convention or only to the 1952 Convention.
3. The Committee shall be selected with due consideration to a fair balance of national interests on the basis of geographical location, population, languages and stage of development.
4. The Director-General of the United Nations Educational, Scientific and Cultural Organisation, the Director-General of the World Intellectual Property Organisation and the Secretary-General of the Organisation of American States, or their representatives, may attend meetings of the Committee in an advisory capacity.

[9.152]
Article XII

The Intergovernmental Committee shall convene a conference for revision whenever it deems necessary, or at the request of at least ten States party to this Convention.

[9.153]
Article XIII

1. Any Contracting State may, at the time of deposit of its instrument of ratification, acceptance or accession, or at any time thereafter, declare by notification addressed to the Director-General that this Convention shall apply to all or any of the countries or territories for the international relations of which it is responsible and this Convention shall thereupon apply to the countries or territories named in such notification after the expiration of the term of three months provided for in Article IX. In the absence of such notification, this Convention shall not apply to any such country or territory.
2. However, nothing in this Article shall be understood as implying the recognition or tacit acceptance by a Contracting State of the factual situation concerning a country or territory to which this Convention is made applicable by another Contracting State in accordance with the provisions of this Article.

[9.154]
Article XIV

1. Any Contracting State may denounce this Convention in its own name or on behalf of all or any of the countries or territories with respect to which a notification has been given under Article XIII. The denunciation shall be made by notification addressed to the Director-General. Such denunciation shall also constitute denunciation of the 1952 Convention.
2. Such denunciation shall operate only in respect of the State or of the country or territory on whose behalf it was made and shall not take effect until twelve months after the date of receipt of the notification.

[9.155]
Article XV

A dispute between two or more Contracting States concerning the interpretation or application of this Convention, not settled by negotiation, shall, unless the States concerned agree on some other method of settlement, be brought before the International Court of Justice for determination by it.

[9.156]
Article XVI

1. This Convention shall be established in English, French and Spanish. The three texts shall be signed and shall be equally authoritative.
2. Official texts of this Convention shall be established by the Director-General, after consultation with the governments concerned, in Arabic, German, Italian and Portuguese.

3. Any Contracting State or group of Contracting States shall be entitled to have established by the Director-General other texts in the language of its choice by arrangement with the Director-General.
4. All such texts shall be annexed to the signed texts of this Convention.

[9.157]
Article XVII
1. This Convention shall not in any way affect the provisions of the Berne Convention for the Protection of Literary and Artistic Works or membership in the Union created by that Convention.
2. In application of the foregoing paragraph, a declaration has been annexed to the present Article. This declaration is an integral part of this Convention for the States bound by the Berne Convention on 1 January 1951, or which have or may become bound to it at a later date. The signature of this Convention by such States shall also constitute signature of the said declaration, and ratification, acceptance or accession by such States shall include the Declaration, as well as this Convention.

[9.158]
Article XVIII
This Convention shall not abrogate multilateral or bilateral copyright conventions or arrangements that are or may be in effect exclusively between two or more American Republics. In the event of any difference either between the provisions of such existing conventions or arrangements and the provisions of this Convention, or between the provisions of this Convention and those of any new convention or arrangement which may be formulated between two or more American Republics after this Convention comes into force, the convention or arrangement most recently formulated shall prevail between the parties thereto. Rights in works acquired in any Contracting State under existing conventions or arrangements before the date this Convention comes into force in such State shall not be affected.

[9.159]
Article XIX
This Convention shall not abrogate multilateral or bilateral conventions or arrangements in effect between two or more Contracting States. In the event of any difference between the provisions of such existing conventions or arrangements and the provisions of this Convention, the provisions of this Convention shall prevail. Rights in works acquired in any Contracting State under existing conventions or arrangements before the date on which this Convention comes into force in such State shall not be affected. Nothing in this Article shall affect the provisions of Articles XVII and XVIII.

[9.160]
Article XX
Reservations to this Convention shall not be permitted.

[9.161]
Article XXI
1. The Director-General shall send duly certified copies of this Convention to the States interested and to the Secretary-General of the United Nations for registration by him.
2. He shall also inform all interested States of the ratifications, acceptances and accessions which have been deposited, the date on which this Convention comes into force, the notifications under this Convention, and denunciations under Article XIV.

APPENDIX

[9.162]

Declaration relating to Article XVII

The States which are members of the International Union for the Protection of Literary and Artistic Works (hereinafter called 'the Berne Union') and which arc signatories to this Convention,

Desiring to reinforce their mutual relations on the basis of the said Union and to avoid any conflict which might result from the co-existence of the Berne Convention and the Universal Copyright Convention,

Recognising the temporary need of some States to adjust their level of copyright protection in accordance with their stage of culture, social and economic development,

Have, by common agreement, accepted the terms of the following declaration—

(a) Except as provided by paragraph (b), works which, according to the Berne Convention, have as their country of origin a country which has withdrawn from the Berne Union after 1 January 1951, shall not be protected by the Universal Copyright Convention in the countries of the Berne Union;

(b) Where a Contracting State is regarded as a developing country in conformity with the established practice of the General Assembly of the United Nations, and has deposited with the Director-General of the United Nations Educational, Scientific and Cultural

Organisation, at the time of its withdrawal from the Berne Union, a notification to the effect that it regards itself as a developing country, the provisions of paragraph (a) shall not be applicable as long as such State may avail itself of the exceptions provided for by this Convention in accordance with Article V*bis*;

(c) The Universal Copyright Convention shall not be applicable to the relationships among countries of the Berne Union in so far as it relates to the protection of works having as their country of origin, within the meaning of the Berne Convention, a country of the Berne Union.

[9.163]

Resolution concerning Article XI

The Conference for Revision of the Universal Copyright Convention,

Having considered the problems relating to the Intergovernmental Committee provided for in Article XI of this Convention, to which this resolution is annexed,

Resolves that—

1. At its inception, the Committee shall include representatives of the twelve States members of the Intergovernmental Committee established under Article XI of the 1952 Convention and the resolution annexed to it, and, in addition representatives of the following States: Algeria, Australia, Japan, Mexico, Senegal and Yugoslavia.

2. Any States that are not party to the 1952 Convention and have not acceded to this Convention before the first ordinary session of the Committee following the entry into force of this Convention shall be replaced by other States to be selected by the Committee at its first ordinary session in conformity with the provisions of Article XI(2) and (3).

3. As soon as this Convention comes into force the Committee as provided for in paragraph 1 shall be deemed to be constituted in accordance with Article XI of this Convention.

4. A session of the Committee shall take place within one year after the coming into force of this Convention; thereafter the Committee shall meet in ordinary session at intervals of not more than two years.

5. The Committee shall elect its Chairman and two Vice-Chairmen. It shall establish its Rules of Procedure having regard to the following principles—

(a) the normal duration of the term of office of the members represented on the Committee shall be six years with one-third retiring every two years, it being however understood that, of the original terms of office, one-third shall expire at the end of the Committee's second ordinary session which will follow the entry into force of this Convention, a further third at the end of its third ordinary session, and the remaining third at the end of its fourth ordinary session.

(b) The rules governing the procedure whereby the Committee shall fill vacancies, the order in which terms of membership expire, eligibility for re-election, and election procedures, shall be based upon a balancing of the needs for continuity of membership and rotation of representation, as well as the considerations set out in Article XI(3).

Expresses the wish that the United Nations Educational, Scientific and Cultural Organisation provide its Secretariat.

In faith whereof the undersigned, having deposited their respective full powers, have signed this Convention.

Done at Paris, this twenty-fourth day of July 1971, in a single copy.

[9.164]

Protocol 1

Annexed to the Universal Copyright Convention as revised at Paris on 24 July 1971 concerning the application of that Convention to works of Stateless persons and refugees

The States party hereto, being also party to the Universal Copyright Convention as revised at Paris on 24 July 1971 (hereinafter called 'the 1971 Convention'),

Have accepted the following provisions—

1. Stateless persons and refugees who have their habitual residence in a State party to this Protocol shall, for the purposes of the 1971 Convention, be assimilated to the nationals of that State.

2.

(a) This Protocol shall be signed and shall be subject to ratification or acceptance, or may be acceded to, as if the provisions of Article VIII of the 1971 Convention applied hereto.

(b) This Protocol shall enter into force in respect of each State, on the date of deposit of the instrument of ratification, acceptance or accession of the State concerned or on the date of entry into force of the 1971 Convention with respect to such State, whichever is the later.

(c) On the entry into force of this Protocol in respect of a State not party to Protocol 1 annexed to the 1952 Convention, the latter Protocol shall be deemed to enter into force in respect of such State.

In faith whereof the undersigned, being duly authorised thereto, have signed this protocol.

Done at Paris this twenty-fourth day of July 1971, in the English, French and Spanish languages, the three texts being equally authoritative, in a single copy which shall be deposited with the Director-General of the United Nations Educational, Scientific and Cultural Organisation. The Director-General shall send certified copies to the signatory States, and to the Secretary-General of the United Nations for registration.

[9.165]

Protocol 2

Annexed to the Universal Copyright Convention as revised at Paris on 24 July 1971 concerning the application of that Convention to the works of certain international organisations

The States party hereto, being also party to the Universal Copyright Convention as revised at Paris on 24 July 1971 (hereinafter called 'the 1971 Convention'),

Have accepted the following provisions—

1.

(a) The protection provided for in Article II(1) of the 1971 Convention shall apply to works published for the first time by the United Nations, by the Specialised Agencies in relationship therewith, or by the Organisation of American States.

(b) Similarly, Article II(2) of the 1971 Convention shall apply to the said organisation or agencies.

2.

(a) This Protocol shall be signed and shall be subject to ratification or acceptance, or may be acceded to, as if the provisions of Article VIII of the 1971 Convention applied hereto.

(b) This Protocol shall enter into force for each State on the date of deposit of the instrument of ratification, acceptance or accession of the State concerned or on the date of entry into force of the 1971 Convention with respect to such State, whichever is the later.

In faith whereof the undersigned, being duly authorised thereto, have signed this Protocol.

Done at Paris, this twenty-fourth day of July 1971, in the English, French and Spanish languages, the three texts being equally authoritative, in a single copy which shall be deposited with the Director-General of the United Nations Educational, Scientific and Cultural Organisation. The Director-General shall send certified copies to the signatory States, and to the Secretary-General of the United Nations for registration.

BERNE CONVENTION FOR THE PROTECTION OF LITERARY AND ARTISTIC WORKS

(Paris Act, 24 July 1971)

(as amended on 29 September 1979)

NOTES

The original source for this Convention is the World Intellectual Property Organisation (WIPO).

Each Article and the Appendix have been given titles to facilitate their identification. There are no titles in the signed (English) text.

The countries of the Union, being equally animated by the desire to protect, in as effective and uniform a manner as possible, the rights of authors in their literary and artistic works,

Recognising the importance of work of the Revision Conference held at Stockholm in 1967,

Have resolved to revise the Act adopted by the Stockholm Conference, while maintaining without change Articles 1 to 20 and 22 to 26 of that Act.

Consequently, the undersigned Plentipotentaries, having presented their full powers, recognised as in good and due form, have agreed as follows—

[9.166]

Article 1

[Establishment of a Union]

The countries to which this Convention applies constitute a Union for the protection of the rights of authors in their literary and artistic works.

[9.167]

Article 2

[Protected Works: 1. "Literary and artistic works"; 2. Possible requirement of fixation; 3. Derivative works; 4. Official texts; 5. Collections; 6. Obligation to protect; beneficiaries of protection; 7. Works of applied art and industrial designs; 8. News]

(1) The expression "literary and artistic works" shall include every production in the literary, scientific and artistic domain, whatever may be the mode or form of its expression, such as books, pamphlets and other writings; lectures, addresses, sermons and other works of the same nature;

dramatic or dramatico-musical works; choreographic works and entertainments in dumb show; musical compositions with or without words; cinematographic works to which are assimilated works expressed by a process analogous to cinematography; works of drawing, painting, architecture, sculpture, engraving and lithography; photographic works to which are assimilated works expressed by a process analogous to photography; works of applied art; illustrations, maps, plans, sketches and three-dimensional works relative to geography, topography, architecture or science.

(2) It shall, however, be a matter for legislation in the countries of the Union to prescribe that works in general or any specified categories of works shall not be protected unless they have been fixed in some material form.

(3) Translations, adaptations, arrangements of music and other alterations of a literary or artistic work shall be protected as original works without prejudice to the copyright in the original work.

(4) It shall be a matter for legislation in the countries of the Union to determine the protection to be granted to official texts of a legislative, administrative and legal nature, and to official translations of such texts.

(5) Collections of literary or artistic works such as encyclopaedias and anthologies which, by reason of the selection and arrangement of their contents, constitute intellectual creations shall be protected as such, without prejudice to the copyright in each of the works forming part of such collections.

(6) The works mentioned in this Article shall enjoy protection in all countries of the Union. This protection shall operate for the benefit of the author and his successors in title.

(7) Subject to the provisions of Article 7(4) of this Convention, it shall be a matter for legislation in the countries of the Union to determine the extent of the application of their laws to works of applied art and industrial designs and models, as well as the conditions under which such works, designs and models shall be protected. Works protected in the country of origin solely as designs and models shall be entitled in another country of the Union only to such special protection as is granted in that country to designs and models; however, if no such special protection is granted in that country, such works shall be protected as artistic works.

(8) The protection of this Convention shall not apply to news of the day or to miscellaneous facts having the character of mere items of press information.

[9.168]
Article 2bis
[Possible Limitation of Protection of Certain Works: 1. Certain speeches; 2. Certain uses of lectures and addresses; 3. Right to make collections of such works]

(1) It shall be a matter for legislation in the countries of the Union to exclude, wholly or in part, from the protection provided by the preceding Article political speeches and speeches delivered in the course of legal proceedings.

(2) It shall also be a matter for legislation in the countries of the Union to determine the conditions under which lectures, addresses and other works of the same nature which are delivered in public may be reproduced by the press, broadcast, communicated to the public by wire and made the subject of public communication as envisaged in Article 11*bis* (1) of this Convention, when such use is justified by the informatory purpose.

(3) Nevertheless, the author shall enjoy the exclusive right of making a collection of his works mentioned in the preceding paragraphs.

[9.169]
Article 3
[Criteria of Eligibility for Protection: 1. Nationality of author; place of publication of work; 2. Residence of author; 3. "Published" works; 4. "Simultaneously published" works]

(1) The protection of this Convention shall apply to—

(a) authors who are nationals of one of the countries of the Union, for their works, whether published or not;

(b) authors who are not nationals of one of the countries of the Union, for their works first published in one of those countries, or simultaneously in a country outside the Union and in a country of the Union.

(2) Authors who are not nationals of one of the countries of the Union but who have their habitual residence in one of them shall, for the purposes of this Convention, be assimilated to nationals of that country.

(3) The expression "published works" means works published with the consent of their authors, whatever may be the means of manufacture of the copies, provided that the availability of such copies has been such as to satisfy the reasonable requirements of the public, having regard to the nature of the work. The performance of a dramatic, dramatico-musical, cinematographic or musical work, the public recitation of a literary work, the communication by wire or the broadcasting of literary or artistic works, the exhibition of a work of art and the construction of a work of architecture shall not constitute publication.

(4) A work shall be considered as having been published simultaneously in several countries if it has been published in two or more countries within thirty days of its first publication.

[9.170]
Article 4
[Criteria of Eligibility for Protection of Cinematographic Works, Works of Architecture and Certain Artistic Works]

The protection of this Convention shall apply, even if the conditions of Article 3 are not fulfilled, to—

(a) authors of cinematographic works the maker of which has his headquarters or habitual residence in one of the countries of the Union;

(b) authors of works of architecture erected in a country of the Union or of other artistic works incorporated in a building or other structure located in a country of the Union.

[9.171]
Article 5
[Rights Guaranteed: 1. and 2. Outside the country of origin; 3. in the country of origin; 4. "Country of origin"]

(1) Authors shall enjoy, in respect of works for which they are protected under this Convention, in countries of the Union other than the country of origin, the rights which their respective laws do now or may hereafter grant to their nationals, as well as the rights specially granted by this Convention.

(2) The enjoyment and the exercise of these rights shall not be subject to any formality; such enjoyment and such exercise shall be independent of the existence of protection in the country of origin of the work. Consequently, apart from the provisions of this Convention, the extent of protection, as well as the means of redress afforded to the author to protect his rights, shall be governed exclusively by the laws of the country where protection is claimed.

(3) Protection in the country of origin is governed by domestic law. However, when the author is not a national of the country of origin of the work for which he is protected under this Convention, he shall enjoy in that country the same rights as national authors.

(4) The country of origin shall be considered to be—

(a) in the case of works first published in a country of the Union, that country; in the case of works published simultaneously in several countries of the Union which grant different terms of protection, the country whose legislation grants the shortest term of protection;

(b) in the case of works published simultaneously in a country outside the Union and in a country of the Union, the latter country;

(c) in the case of unpublished works or of works first published in a country outside the Union, without simultaneous publication in a country of the Union, the country of the Union of which the author is a national, provided that—

(i) when these are cinematographic works the maker of which has his headquarters or his habitual residence in the country of the Union, the country of origin shall be that country, and

(ii) when these are works of architecture erected in a country of the Union or other artistic works incorporated in a building or other structure located in a country of the Union, the country of origin shall be that country.

[9.172]
Article 6
[Possible Restriction of Protection in Respect of Certain Works of Nationals of Certain Countries Outside the Union: 1. in the country of the first publication and in other countries; 2. No retroactivity; 3. Notice]

(1) Where any country outside the Union fails to protect in an adequate manner the works of authors who are nationals of one of the countries of the Union, the latter country may restrict the protection given to the works of authors who are, at the date of the first publication thereof, nationals of the other country and are not habitually resident in one of the countries of the Union. If the country of first publication avails itself of this right, the other countries of the Union shall not be required to grant to works thus subjected to special treatment a wider protection than that granted to them in the country of first publication.

(2) No restrictions introduced by virtue of the preceding paragraph shall affect the rights which an author may have acquired in respect of a work published in a country of the Union before such restrictions were put into force.

(3) The countries of the Union which restrict the grant of copyright in accordance with this Article shall give notice thereof to the Director-General of the World Intellectual Property Organisation (hereinafter designated as "the Director-General") by a written declaration specifying the countries in regard to which protection is restricted, and the restrictions to which rights of authors who are nationals of those countries are subjected. The Director-General shall immediately communicate this declaration to all the countries of the Union.

[9.173]
Article 6bis
[Moral Rights: 1. to claim authorship; to object to certain modifications and other derogatory actions; 2. After the author's death; 3. Means of redress]

(1) Independently of the author's economic rights, and even after the transfer of the said rights, the author shall have the right to claim authorship of the work and to object to any distortion, mutilation or other modification of, or other derogatory action in relation to, the said work, which would be prejudicial to his honour or reputation.

(2) The rights granted to the author in accordance with the preceding paragraph shall, after his death, be maintained, at least until the expiry of the economic rights, and shall be exercisable by the persons or institutions authorised by the legislation of the country where protection is claimed. However, those countries whose legislation, at the moment of their ratification of or accession to this Act, does not provide for the protection after the death of the author of all the rights set out in the preceding paragraph may provide that some of these rights may, after his death, cease to be maintained.

(3) The means of redress for safeguarding the rights granted by this Article shall be governed by the legislation of the country where protection is claimed.

[9.174]
Article 7
[Term of Protection: 1. Generally; 2. for cinematographic works; 3. for anonymous and pseudonymous works; 4. for photographic works and works of applied art; 5. Starting date of computation; 6. Longer terms; 7. Shorter terms; 8. Applicable law; 'comparison' of terms]

(1) The term of protection granted by this Convention shall be the life of the author and fifty years after his death.

(2) However, in the case of cinematographic works, the countries of the Union may provide that the term of protection shall expire fifty years after the work has been made available to the public with the consent of the author, or, failing such an event within fifty years from the making of such a work, fifty years after the making.

(3) In the case of anonymous or pseudonymous works, the term of protection granted by this Convention shall expire fifty years after the work has been lawfully made available to the public. However, when the pseudonym adopted by the author leaves no doubt as to his identity, the term of protection shall be that provided in paragraph (1). If the author of an anonymous or pseudonymous work discloses his identity during the above-mentioned period, the term of protection applicable shall be that provided in paragraph (1). The countries of the Union shall not be required to protect anonymous or pseudonymous works in respect of which it is reasonable to presume that their author has been dead for fifty years.

(4) It shall be a matter for legislation in the countries of the Union to determine the term of protection of photographic works and that of works of applied art in so far as they are protected as artistic works; however, this term shall last at least until the end of a period of twenty-five years from the making of such a work.

(5) The term of protection subsequent to the death of the author and the terms provided by paragraphs (2), (3) and (4) shall run from the date of death or of the event referred to in those paragraphs, but such terms shall always be deemed to begin on the first of January of the year following the death or such event.

(6) The countries of the Union may grant a term of protection in excess of those provided by the preceding paragraphs.

(7) Those countries of the Union bound by the Rome Act of this Convention which grant, in their national legislation in force at the time of signature of the present Act, shorter terms of protection than those provided for in the preceding paragraphs shall have the right to maintain such terms when ratifying or acceding to the present Act.

(8) In any case, the term shall be governed by the legislation of the country where protection is claimed; however, unless the legislation of that country otherwise provides, the term shall not exceed the term fixed in the country of origin of the work.

[9.175]
Article 7bis
[Term of Protection for Works of Joint Authorship]

The provisions of the preceding Article shall also apply in the case of a work of joint authorship, provided that the terms measured from the death of the author shall be calculated from the death of the last surviving author.

[9.176]
Article 8
[Right of Translation]

Authors of literary and artistic works protected by this Convention shall enjoy the exclusive right of making and of authorising the translation of their works throughout the term of protection of their rights in the original work.

[9.177]
Article 9
[Right of Reproduction: 1. Generally; 2. Possible exceptions; 3. Sound and visual recordings]
(1) Authors of literary and artistic works protected by this Convention shall have the exclusive right of authorising the reproduction of these works, in any manner or form.
(2) It shall be a matter for legislation in the countries of the Union to permit the reproduction of such works in certain special cases, provided that such reproduction does not conflict with a normal exploitation of the work and does not unreasonably prejudice the legitimate interests of the author.
(3) Any sound or visual recording shall be considered as a reproduction for the purposes of this Convention.

[9.178]
Article 10
[Certain Free Uses of Works: 1. Quotations; 2. Illustrations for teaching; 3. Indication of source and author]
(1) It shall be permissible to make quotations from a work which has already been lawfully made available to the public, provided that their making is compatible with fair practice, and their extent does not exceed that justified by the purpose, including quotations from newspaper articles and periodicals in the form of press summaries.
(2) It shall be a matter for legislation in the countries of the Union, and for special agreements existing or to be concluded between them, to permit the utilisation, to the extent justified by the purpose, of literary or artistic works by way of illustration in publications, broadcasts or sound or visual recordings for teaching, provided such utilisation is compatible with fair practice.
(3) Where use is made of works in accordance with the preceding paragraphs of this Article, mention shall be made of the source, and of the name of the author if it appears thereon.

[9.179]
Article 10bis
[Further Possible Free Uses of Works: 1. of certain articles and broadcast works; 2. of works seen or heard in connection with current events]
(1) It shall be a matter for legislation in the countries of the Union to permit the reproduction by the press, the broadcasting or the communication to the public by wire of articles published in newspapers or periodicals on current economic, political or religious topics, and of broadcast works of the same character, in cases in which the reproduction, broadcasting or such communication thereof is not expressly reserved. Nevertheless, the source must always be clearly indicated; the legal consequences of a breach of this obligation shall be determined by the legislation of the country where protection is claimed.
(2) It shall also be a matter for legislation in the countries of the Union to determine the conditions under which, for the purpose of reporting current events by means of photography, cinematography, broadcasting or communication to the public by wire, literary or artistic works seen or heard in the course of the event may, to the extent justified by the informatory purpose, be reproduced and made available to the public.

[9.180]
Article 11
[Certain Rights in Dramatic and Musical Works: 1. Right of public performance and of communication to the public of a performance; 2. in respect of translations]
(1) Authors of dramatic, dramatico-musical and musical works shall enjoy the exclusive right of authorising—
- (i) the public performance of their works, including such public performance by any means or process;
- (ii) any communication to the public of the performance of their works.

(2) Authors of dramatic or dramatico-musical works shall enjoy, during the full term of their rights in the original works, the same rights with respect to translations thereof.

[9.181]
Article 11bis
[Broadcasting and Related Rights: 1. Broadcasting and other wireless communications, public communication of broadcast by wire or rebroadcast, public communication of broadcast by loudspeaker or analogous instruments; 2. Compulsory licences; 3. Recording; ephemeral recordings]
(1) Authors of literary and artistic works shall enjoy the exclusive right of authorising—
- (i) the broadcasting of their works or the communication thereof to the public by any other means of wireless diffusion of signs, sounds or images;
- (ii) any communication to the public by wire or by rebroadcasting of the broadcast of the work, when this communication is made by an organisation other than the original one;
- (iii) the public communication by loudspeaker or any other analogous instrument transmitting, by signs, sounds or images, the broadcast of the work.

(2) It shall be a matter for legislation in the countries of the Union to determine the conditions under which the rights mentioned in the preceding paragraph may be exercised, but these conditions shall apply only in the countries where they have been prescribed. They shall not in any circumstances be prejudicial to the moral rights of the author, nor to his right to obtain equitable remuneration which, in the absence of agreement, shall be fixed by competent authority.
(3) In the absence of any contrary stipulation, permission granted in accordance with paragraph (1) of this Article shall not imply permission to record, by means of instruments recording sounds or images, the work broadcast. It shall, however, be a matter for legislation in the countries of the Union to determine the regulations for ephemeral recordings made by a broadcasting organisation by means of its own facilities and used for its own broadcasts. The preservation of these recordings in official archives may, on the ground of their exceptional documentary character, be authorised by such legislation.

[9.182]
Article 11ter
[Certain Rights in Literary Works: 1. Right of public recitation and of communication to the public of a recitation; 2. in respect of translations]

(1) Authors of literary works shall enjoy the exclusive right of authorising—
- (i) the public recitation of their works, including such public recitation by any means or process;
- (ii) any communication to the public of the recitation of their works.

(2) Authors of literary works shall enjoy, during the full term of their rights in the original works, the same rights with respect to translations thereof.

[9.183]
Article 12
[Right of Adaptation, Arrangement and Other Alteration]

Authors of literary or artistic works shall enjoy the exclusive right of authorising adaptations, arrangements and other alterations of their works.

[9.184]
Article 13
[Possible Limitation of the Right of Recording of Musical Works and Any Words Pertaining Thereto: 1. Compulsory licences; 2. Transitory measures; 3. Seizure on importation of copies made without the author's permission]

(1) Each country of the Union may impose for itself reservations and conditions on the exclusive right granted to the author of a musical work and to the author of any words, the recording of which together with the musical work has already been authorised by the latter, to authorise the sound recording of that musical work, together with such words, if any; but all such reservations and conditions shall apply only in the countries which have imposed them and shall not, in any circumstances, be prejudicial to the rights of these authors to obtain equitable remuneration which, in the absence of agreement, shall be fixed by competent authority.
(2) Recordings of musical works made in a country of the Union in accordance with Article 13(3) of the Conventions signed at Rome on 2 June 1928, and at Brussels on 26 June 1948, may be reproduced in that country without the permission of the author of the musical work until a date two years after that country becomes bound by this Act.
(3) Recordings made in accordance with paragraphs (1) and (2) of this Article and imported without permission from the parties concerned into a country where they are treated as infringing recordings shall be liable to seizure.

[9.185]
Article 14
[Cinematographic and Related Rights: 1. Cinematographic adaptation and reproduction; distribution; public performance and public communication by wire of works thus adapted or reproduced; 2. Adaptation of cinematographic productions; 3. No compulsory licences]

(1) Authors of literary or artistic works shall have the exclusive right of authorising—
- (i) the cinematographic adaptation and reproduction of these works, and the distribution of the works thus adapted or reproduced;
- (ii) the public performance and communication to the public by wire of the works thus adapted or reproduced.

(2) The adaptation into any other artistic form of a cinematographic production derived from literary or artistic works shall, without prejudice to the authorisation of the author of the cinematographic production, remain subject to the authorisation of the authors of the original works.
(3) The provisions of Article 13(1) shall not apply.

[9.186]
Article 14bis
[Special Provisions Concerning Cinematographic Works: 1. Assimilation to "original" works; 2. Ownership; limitation of certain rights of certain contributors; 3. Certain other contributors]

(1) Without prejudice to the copyright in any work which may have been adapted or reproduced a cinematographic work shall be protected as an original work. The owner of copyright in a cinematographic work shall enjoy the same rights as the author of an original work, including the rights referred to in the preceding Article.

(2)

(a) Ownership of copyright in a cinematographic work shall be a matter for legislation in the country where protection is claimed.

(b) However, in the countries of the Union which, by legislation, include among the owners of copyright in a cinematographic work authors who have brought contributions to the making of the work, such authors, if they have undertaken to bring such contributions, may not, in the absence of any contrary or special stipulation, object to the reproduction, distribution, public performance, communication to the public by wire, broadcasting or any other communication to the public, or to the subtitling or dubbing of texts, of the work.

(c) The question whether or not the form of the undertaking referred to above should, for the application of the preceding subparagraph (b), be in a written agreement or a written act of the same effect shall be a matter for the legislation of the country where the maker of the cinematographic work has his headquarters or habitual residence. However, it shall be a matter for the legislation of the country of the Union where protection is claimed to provide that the said undertaking shall be in a written agreement or a written act of the same effect. The countries whose legislation so provides shall notify the Director-General by means of a written declaration, which will be immediately communicated by him to all the other countries of the Union.

(d) By 'contrary or special stipulation' is meant any restrictive condition which is relevant to the aforesaid undertaking.

(3) Unless the national legislation provides to the contrary, the provisions of paragraph (2)(b) above shall not be applicable to authors of scenarios, dialogues and musical works created for the making of the cinematographic work, or to the principal director thereof. However, those countries of the Union whose legislation does not contain rules providing for the application of the said paragraph (2)(b) to such director shall notify the Director-General by means of a written declaration, which will be immediately communicated by him to all the other countries of the Union.

[9.187]
Article 14ter
["Droit de suite" in Works of Art and Manuscripts: 1. Right to an interest in resales; 2. Applicable law; 3. Procedure]

(1) The author, or after his death the persons or institutions authorised by national legislation, shall, with respect to original works of art and original manuscripts of writers and composers, enjoy the inalienable right to an interest in any sale of the work subsequent to the first transfer by the author of the work.

(2) The protection provided by the preceding paragraph may be claimed in a country of the Union only if legislation in the country to which the author belongs so permits, and to the extent permitted by the country where this protection is claimed.

(3) The procedure for collection and the amounts shall be matters for determination by national legislation.

[9.188]
Article 15
[Right to Enforce Protected Rights: 1. Where author's name is indicated or where pseudonym leaves no doubt as to author's identity; 2. in the case of cinematographic works; 3. in the case of anonymous and pseudonymous works; 4. in the case of certain unpublished works of unknown authorship]

(1) In order that the author of a literary or artistic work protected by this Convention shall, in the absence of proof to the contrary, be regarded as such, and consequently be entitled to institute infringement proceedings in the countries of the Union, it shall be sufficient for his name to appear on the work in the usual manner. This paragraph shall be applicable even if this name is a pseudonym, where the pseudonym adopted by the author leaves no doubt as to his identity.

(2) The person or body corporate whose name appears on a cinematographic work in the usual manner shall, in the absence of proof to the contrary, be presumed to be the maker of the said work.

(3) In the case of anonymous and pseudonymous works, other than those referred to in paragraph (1) above, the publisher whose name appears on the work shall, in the absence of proof to the contrary, be deemed to represent the author, and in this capacity he shall be entitled to protect and enforce the author's rights. The provisions of this paragraph shall cease to apply when the author reveals his identity and establishes his claim to authorship of the work.

(4)

(a) In the case of unpublished works where the identity of the author is unknown, but where there is every ground to presume that he is a national of a country of the Union, it shall be a matter for legislation in that country to designate the competent authority which shall represent the author and shall be entitled to protect and enforce his rights in the countries of the Union.

(b) Countries of the Union which make such designation under the terms of this provision shall notify the Director-General by means of a written declaration giving full information concerning the authority thus designated. The Director-General shall at once communicate this declaration to all other countries of the Union.

[9.189]
Article 16
[Infringing Copies: 1. Seizure; 2. Seizure on importation; 3. Applicable law]

(1) Infringing copies of a work shall be liable to seizure in any country of the Union where the work enjoys legal protection.
(2) The provisions of the preceding paragraph shall also apply to reproductions coming from a country where the work is not protected, or has ceased to be protected.
(3) The seizures shall take place in accordance with the legislation of each country.

[9.190]
Article 17
[Possibility of Control of Circulation, Presentation and Exhibition of Works]

The provisions of this Convention cannot in any way affect the right of the Government of each country of the Union to permit, to control, or to prohibit, by legislation or regulation, the circulation, presentation, or exhibition of any work or production in regard to which the competent authority may find it necessary to exercise that right.

[9.191]
Article 18
[Works Existing on Convention's Entry Into Force: 1. Protectable where protection not yet expired in country of origin; 2. Non-protectable where protection already expired in country where it is claimed; 3. Application of these principles; 4. Special cases]

(1) This Convention shall apply to all works which, at the moment of its coming into force, have not yet fallen into the public domain in the country of origin through the expiry of the term of protection.
(2) If, however, through the expiry of the term of protection which was previously granted, a work has fallen into the public domain of the country where protection is claimed, that work shall not be protected anew.
(3) The application of this principle shall be subject to any provisions contained in special conventions to that effect existing or to be concluded between countries of the Union. In the absence of such provisions, the respective countries shall determine, each in so far as it is concerned, the conditions of application of this principle.
(4) The preceding provisions shall also apply in the case of new accessions to the Union and to cases in which protection is extended by the application of Article 7 or by the abandonment of reservations.

[9.192]
Article 19
[Protection Greater than Resulting from Convention]

The provisions of this Convention shall not preclude the making of a claim to the benefit of any greater protection which may be granted by legislation in a country of the Union.

[9.193]
Article 20
[Special Agreements among Countries of the Union]

The Governments of the countries of the Union reserve the right to enter into special agreements among themselves, in so far as such agreements grant to authors more extensive rights than those granted by the Convention, or contain other provisions not contrary to this Convention. The provisions of existing agreements which satisfy these conditions shall remain applicable.

[9.194]
Article 21
[Special Provisions Regarding Developing Countries: 1. Reference to Appendix; 2. Appendix part of Act]

(1) Special provisions regarding developing countries are included in the Appendix.
(2) Subject to the provisions of Article 28(1)(b), the Appendix forms an integral part of this Act.

[9.195]
Article 22
[Assembly: 1. Constitution and composition; 2. Tasks; 3. Quorum, voting, observers; 4. Convocation; 5. Rules of procedure]

(1)

(a) The Union shall have an Assembly consisting of those countries of the Union which are bound by Articles 22 to 26.

(b) The Government of each country shall be represented by one delegate, who may be assisted by alternate delegates, advisors, and experts.

(c) The expenses of each delegation shall be borne by the Government which has appointed it.

(2)

(a) The Assembly shall—

(i) deal with all matters concerning the maintenance and development of the Union and the implementation of this Convention;

(ii) give directions concerning the preparation for conferences of revision to the International Bureau of Intellectual Property (hereinafter designated as "the International Bureau") referred to in the Convention Establishing the World Intellectual Property Organisation (hereinafter designated as "the Organisation"), due account being taken of any comments made by those countries of the Union which are not bound by Articles 22 to 26;

(iii) review and approve the reports and activities of the Director General of the Organisation concerning the Union, and give him all necessary instructions concerning matters within the competence of the Union;

(iv) elect the members of the Executive Committee of the Assembly;

(v) review and approve the reports and activities of its Executive Committee, and give instructions to such Committee;

(vi) determine the program and adopt the biennial budget of the Union, and approve its final accounts;

(vii) adopt the financial regulations of the Union;

(viii) establish such committees of experts and working groups as may be necessary for the work of the Union;

(ix) determine which countries not members of the Union and which intergovernmental and international nongovernmental organisations shall be admitted to its meetings as observers;

(x) adopt amendments to Articles 22 to 26;

(xi) take any other appropriate action designed to further the objectives of the Union;

(xii) exercise such other functions as are appropriate under this Convention;

(xiii) subject to its acceptance, exercise such rights as are given to it in the Convention establishing the Organisation.

(b) With respect to matters which are of interest also to other Unions administered by the Organisation, the Assembly shall make its decisions after having heard the advice of the Coordination Committee of the Organisation.

(3)

(a) Each country member of the Assembly shall have one vote.

(b) One-half of the countries members of the Assembly shall constitute a quorum.

(c) Notwithstanding the provisions of subparagraph (b), if, in any session, the number of countries represented is less than one-half but equal to or more than one-third of the countries members of the Assembly, the Assembly may make decisions but, with the exception of decisions concerning its own procedure, all such decisions shall take effect only if the following conditions are fulfilled. The International Bureau shall communicate the said decisions to the countries members of the Assembly which were not represented and shall invite them to express in writing their vote or abstention within a period of three months from the date of the communication. If, at the expiration of this period, the number of countries having thus expressed their vote or abstention attains the number of countries which was lacking for attaining the quorum in the session itself, such decisions shall take effect provided that at the same time the required majority still obtains.

(d) Subject to the provisions of Article 26(2), the decisions of the Assembly shall require two-thirds of the votes cast.

(e) Abstentions shall not be considered as votes.

(f) A delegate may represent, and vote in the name of, one country only.

(g) Countries of the Union not members of the Assembly shall be admitted to its meetings as observers.

(4)

(a) The Assembly shall meet once in every second calendar year in ordinary session upon convocation by the Director General and, in the absence of exceptional circumstances, during the same period and at the same place as the General Assembly of the Organisation.

(b) The Assembly shall meet in extraordinary session upon convocation by the Director General, at the request of the Executive Committee or at the request of one-fourth of the countries members of the Assembly.

(5) The Assembly shall adopt its own rules of procedure.

[9.196]
Article 23
[Executive Committee: 1. Constitution; 2. Composition; 3. Number of members; 4. Geographical distribution; special agreements; 5. Term, limits of re-eligibility, rules of election; 6. Tasks; 7. Convocation; 8. Quorum, voting; 9. Observers; 10. Rules of Procedure]

(1) The Assembly shall have an Executive Committee.

(2)

(a) The Executive Committee shall consist of countries elected by the Assembly from among countries members of the Assembly. Furthermore, the country on whose territory the Organisation has its headquarters shall, subject to the provisions of Article 25(7)(b), have an *ex officio* seat on the Committee.

(b) The Government of each country member of the Executive Committee shall be represented by one delegate, who may be assisted by alternate delegates, advisors, and experts.

(c) The expenses of each delegation shall be borne by the Government which has appointed it.

(3) The number of countries members of the Executive Committee shall correspond to one-fourth of the number of countries members of the Assembly. In establishing the number of seats to be filled, remainders after division by four shall be disregarded.

(4) In electing the members of the Executive Committee, the Assembly shall have due regard to an equitable geographical distribution and to the need for countries party to the Special Agreements which might be established in relation with the Union to be among the countries constituting the Executive Committee.

(5)

(a) Each member of the Executive Committee shall serve from the close of the session of the Assembly which elected it to the close of the next ordinary session of the Assembly.

(b) Members of the Executive Committee may be re-elected, but not more than two-thirds of them.

(c) The Assembly shall establish the details of the rules governing the election and possible re-election of the members of the Executive Committee.

(6)

(a) The Executive Committee shall—

(i) prepare the draft agenda of the Assembly;

(ii) submit proposals to the Assembly respecting the draft program and biennial budget of the Union prepared by the Director General;

(iii) [deleted]

(iv) submit, with appropriate comments, to the Assembly the periodical reports of the Director General and the yearly audit reports on the accounts;

(v) in accordance with the decisions of the Assembly and having regard to circumstances arising between two ordinary sessions of the Assembly, take all necessary measures to ensure the execution of the program of the Union by the Director General;

(vi) perform such other functions as are allocated to it under this Convention.

(b) With respect to matters which are of interest also to other Unions administered by the Organisation, the Executive Committee shall make its decisions after having heard the advice of the Coordination Committee of the Organisation.

(7)

(a) The Executive Committee shall meet once a year in ordinary session upon convocation by the Director General, preferably during the same period and at the same place as the Coordination Committee of the Organisation.

(b) The Executive Committee shall meet in extraordinary session upon convocation by the Director General, either on his own initiative, or at the request of its Chairman or one-fourth of its members.

(8)

(a) Each country member of the Executive Committee shall have one vote.

(b) One-half of the members of the Executive Committee shall constitute a quorum.

(c) Decisions shall be made by a simple majority of the votes cast.

(d) Abstentions shall not be considered as votes.

(e) A delegate may represent, and vote in the name of, one country only.

(9) Countries of the Union not members of the Executive Committee shall be admitted to its meetings as observers.

(10) The Executive Committee shall adopt its own rules of procedure.

[9.197]
Article 24
[International Bureau: 1. Tasks in general, Director General; 2. General information; 3. Periodical; 4. Information to countries; 5. Studies and services; 6. Participation in meetings; 7. Conferences of revision; 8. Other tasks]

(1)
(a) The administrative tasks with respect to the Union shall be performed by the International Bureau, which is a continuation of the Bureau of the Union united with the Bureau of the Union established by the International Convention for the Protection of Industrial Property.
(b) In particular, the International Bureau shall provide the secretariat of the various organs of the Union.
(c) The Director General of the Organisation shall be the chief executive of the Union and shall represent the Union.

(2) The International Bureau shall assemble and publish information concerning the protection of copyright. Each country of the Union shall promptly communicate to the International Bureau all new laws and official texts concerning the protection of copyright.
(3) The International Bureau shall publish a monthly periodical.
(4) The International Bureau shall, on request, furnish information to any country of the Union on matters concerning the protection of copyright.
(5) The International Bureau shall conduct studies, and shall provide services, designed to facilitate the protection of copyright.
(6) The Director General and any staff member designated by him shall participate, without the right to vote, in all meetings of the Assembly, the Executive Committee and any other committee of experts or working group. The Director General, or a staff member designated by him, shall be *ex officio* secretary of these bodies.
(7)
(a) The International Bureau shall, in accordance with the directions of the Assembly and in cooperation with the Executive Committee, make the preparations for the conferences of revision of the provisions of the Convention other than Articles 22 to 26.
(b) The International Bureau may consult with intergovernmental and international nongovernmental organisations concerning preparations for conferences of revision.
(c) The Director General and persons designated by him shall take part, without the right to vote, in the discussions at these conferences.

(8) The International Bureau shall carry out any other tasks assigned to it.

[9.198]
Article 25
[Finances: 1. Budget; 2. Coordination with other Unions; 3. Resources; 4. Contributions; possible extension of previous budget; 5. Fees and charges; 6. Working capital fund; 7. Advances by host Government; 8. Auditing of accounts]

(1)
(a) The Union shall have a budget.
(b) The budget of the Union shall include the income and expenses proper to the Union, its contribution to the budget of expenses common to the Unions, and, where applicable, the sum made available to the budget of the Conference of the Organisation.
(c) Expenses not attributable exclusively to the Union but also to one or more other Unions administered by the Organisation shall be considered as expenses common to the Unions. The share of the Union in such common expenses shall be in proportion to the interest the Union has in them.

(2) The budget of the Union shall be established with due regard to the requirements of coordination with the budgets of the other Unions administered by the Organisation.
(3) The budget of the Union shall be financed from the following sources—
(i) contributions of the countries of the Union;
(ii) fees and charges due for services performed by the International Bureau in relation to the Union;
(iii) sale of, or royalties on, the publications of the International Bureau concerning the Union;
(iv) gifts, bequests, and subventions;
(v) rents, interests, and other miscellaneous income.

(4)
(a) For the purpose of establishing its contribution towards the budget, each country of the Union shall belong to a class, and shall pay its annual contributions on the basis of a number of units fixed as follows—

Class I	25
Class II	20
Class III	15
Class IV	10
Class V	5

Class VI 3

Class VII 1

(b) Unless it has already done so, each country shall indicate, concurrently with depositing its instrument of ratification or accession, the class to which it wishes to belong. Any country may change class. If it chooses a lower class, the country must announce it to the Assembly at one of its ordinary sessions. Any such change shall take effect at the beginning of the calendar year following the session.

(c) The annual contribution of each country shall be an amount in the same proportion to the total sum to be contributed to the annual budget of the Union by all countries as the number of its units is to the total of the units of all contributing countries.

(d) Contributions shall become due on the first of January of each year.

(e) A country which is in arrears in the payment of its contributions shall have no vote in any of the organs of the Union of which it is a member if the amount of its arrears equals or exceeds the amount of the contributions due from it for the preceding two full years. However, any organ of the Union may allow such a country to continue to exercise its vote in that organ if, and as long as, it is satisfied that the delay in payment is due to exceptional and unavoidable circumstances.

(f) If the budget is not adopted before the beginning of a new financial period, it shall be at the same level as the budget of the previous year, in accordance with the financial regulations.

(5) The amount of the fees and charges due for services rendered by the International Bureau in relation to the Union shall be established, and shall be reported to the Assembly and the Executive Committee, by the Director General.

(6)

(a) The Union shall have a working capital fund which shall be constituted by a single payment made by each country of the Union. If the fund becomes insufficient, an increase shall be decided by the Assembly.

(b) The amount of the initial payment of each country to the said fund or of its participation in the increase thereof shall be a proportion of the contribution of that country for the year in which the fund is established or the increase decided.

(c) The proportion and the terms of payment shall be fixed by the Assembly on the proposal of the Director General and after it has heard the advice of the Coordination Committee of the Organisation.

(7)

(a) In the headquarters agreement concluded with the country on the territory of which the Organisation has its headquarters, it shall be provided that, whenever the working capital fund is insufficient, such country shall grant advances. The amount of these advances and the conditions on which they are granted shall be the subject of separate agreements, in each case, between such country and the Organisation. As long as it remains under the obligation to grant advances, such country shall have an *ex officio* seat on the Executive Committee.

(b) The country referred to in subparagraph (a) and the Organisation shall each have the right to denounce the obligation to grant advances, by written notification. Denunciation shall take effect three years after the end of the year in which it has been notified.

(8) The auditing of the accounts shall be effected by one or more of the countries of the Union or by external auditors, as provided in the financial regulations. They shall be designated, with their agreement, by the Assembly.

[9.199]
Article 26
[Amendments: 1. Provisions susceptible of amendment by the Assembly; proposals; 2. Adoption; 3. Entry into force]

(1) Proposals for the amendment of Articles 22, 23, 24, 25 and the present Article, may be initiated by any country member of the Assembly, by the Executive Committee, or by the Director General. Such proposals shall be communicated by the Director General to the member countries of the Assembly at least six months in advance of their consideration by the Assembly.

(2) Amendments to the Articles referred to in paragraph (1) shall be adopted by the Assembly. Adoption shall require three-fourths of the votes cast, provided that any amendment of Article 22, and of the present paragraph shall require four-fifths of the votes cast.

(3) Any amendment to the Articles referred to in paragraph (1) shall enter into force one month after written notifications of acceptance, effected in accordance with their respective constitutional processes, have been received by the Director General from three-fourths of the countries members of the Assembly at the time it adopted the amendment. Any amendment to the said Articles thus accepted shall bind all the countries which are members of the Assembly at the time the amendment enters into force, or which become members thereof at a subsequent date, provided that any amendment increasing the financial obligations of countries of the Union shall bind only those countries which have notified their acceptance of such amendment.

[9.200]
Article 27
[Revision: 1. Objective; 2. Conferences; 3. Adoption]
(1) This Convention shall be submitted to revision with a view to the introduction of amendments designed to improve the system of the Union.
(2) For this purpose, conferences shall be held successively in one of the countries of the Union among the delegates of the said countries.
(3) Subject to the provisions of Article 26 which apply to the amendment of Articles 22 to 26, any revision of this Act, including the Appendix, shall require the unanimity of the votes cast.

[9.201]
Article 28
[Acceptance and Entry Into Force of Act for Countries of the Union: 1. Ratification, accession; possibility of excluding certain provisions; withdrawal of exclusion; 2. Entry into force of Articles 1 to 21 and Appendix; 3. Entry into force of Articles 22 to 38]
(1)
(a) Any country of the Union which has signed this Act may ratify it, and, if it has not signed it, may accede to it. Instruments of ratification or accession shall be deposited with the Director General.
(b) Any country of the Union may declare in its instrument of ratification or accession that its ratification or accession shall not apply to Articles 1 to 21 and the Appendix, provided that, if such country has previously made a declaration under Article VI(1) of the Appendix, then it may declare in the said instrument only that its ratification or accession shall not apply to Articles 1 to 20.
(c) Any country of the Union which, in accordance with subparagraph (6), has excluded provisions therein referred to from the effects of its ratification or accession may at any later time declare that it extends the effects of its ratification or accession to those provisions. Such declaration shall be deposited with the Director General.
(2)
(a) Articles 1 to 21 and the Appendix shall enter into force three months after both of the following two conditions are fulfilled—
(i) at least five countries of the Union have ratified or acceded to this Act without making a declaration under paragraph (1)(b),
(ii) France, Spain, the United Kingdom of Great Britain and Northern Ireland, and the United States of America, have become bound by the Universal Copyright Convention as revised at Paris on July 24, 1971.
(b) The entry into force referred to in subparagraph (a) shall apply to those countries of the Union which, at least three months before the said entry into force, have deposited instruments of ratification or accession not containing a declaration under paragraph (1)(b).
(c) With respect to any country of the Union not covered by subparagraph (b) and which ratifies or accedes to this Act without making a declaration under paragraph (1)(b), Articles 1 to 21 and the Appendix shall enter into force three months after the date on which the Director General has notified the deposit of the relevant instrument of ratification or accession, unless a subsequent date has been indicated in the instrument deposited. In the latter case, Articles 1 to 21 and the Appendix shall enter into force with respect to that country on the date thus indicated.
(d) The provisions of subparagraphs (a) to (c) do not affect the application of Article VI of the Appendix.
(3) With respect to any country of the Union which ratifies or accedes to this Act with or without a declaration made under paragraph (1)(b), Articles 22 to 38 shall enter into force three months after the date on which the Director General has notified the deposit of the relevant instrument of ratification or accession, unless a subsequent date has been indicated in the instrument deposited. In the latter case, Articles 22 to 38 shall enter into force with respect to that country on the date thus indicated.

[9.202]
Article 29
[Acceptance and Entry Into Force for Countries Outside the Union: 1. Accession; 2. Entry into force]
(1) Any country outside the Union may accede to this Act and thereby become party to this Convention and a member of the Union. Instruments of accession shall be deposited with the Director General.
(2)
(a) Subject to subparagraph (b), this Convention shall enter into force with respect to any country outside the Union three months after the date on which the Director General has notified the deposit of its instrument of accession, unless a subsequent date has been indicated in the instrument deposited. In the latter case, this Convention shall enter into force with respect to that country on the date thus indicated.

(b) If the entry into force according to subparagraph (a) precedes the entry into force of Articles 1 to 21 and the Appendix according to Article 28(2)(a), the said country shall in the meantime, be bound, instead of by Articles 1 to 21 and the Appendix, by Articles 1 to 20 of the Brussels Act of this Convention.

[9.203]
Article 29bis
[Effect of Acceptance of Act for the Purposes of Article 14(2) of the WIPO Convention]
Ratification of or accession to this Act by any country not bound by Articles 22 to 38 of the Stockholm Act of this Convention shall, for the sole purposes of Article 14(2) of the Convention establishing the Organisation, amount to ratification of or accession to the said Stockholm Act with the limitation set forth in Article 28(1)(b)(i) thereof.

[9.204]
Article 30
[Reservations: 1. Limits of possibility of making reservations; 2. Earlier reservations; reservation as to the right of translation; withdrawal of reservation]
(1) Subject to the exceptions permitted by paragraph (2) of this Article, by Article 28(1)(b), by Article 33(2), and by the Appendix, ratification or accession shall automatically entail acceptance of all the provisions and admission to all the advantages of this Convention.
(2)
(a) Any country of the Union ratifying or acceding to this Act may, subject to Article V(2) of the Appendix, retain the benefit of the reservations it has previously formulated on condition that it makes a declaration to that effect at the time of the deposit of its instrument of ratification or accession.
(b) Any country outside the Union may declare, in acceding to this Convention and subject to Article V(2) of the Appendix, that it intends to substitute, temporarily at least, for Article 8 of this Act concerning the right of translation, the provisions of Article 5 of the Union Convention of 1886, as completed at Paris in 1896, on the clear understanding that the said provisions are applicable only to translations into a language in general use in the said country. Subject to Article I(6)(b) of the Appendix, any country has the right to apply, in relation to the right of translation of works whose country of origin is a country availing itself of such a reservation, a protection which is equivalent to the protection granted by the latter country.
(c) Any country may withdraw such reservations at any time by notification addressed to the Director General.

[9.205]
Article 31
[Applicability to Certain Territories: 1. Declaration; 2. Withdrawal of declaration; 3. Effective date; 4. Acceptance of factual situations not implied]
(1) Any country may declare in its instrument of ratification or accession, or may inform the Director General by written notification at any time thereafter, that this Convention shall be applicable to all or part of those territories, designated in the declaration or notification, for the external relations of which it is responsible.
(2) Any country which has made such a declaration or given such a notification may, at any time, notify the Director General that this Convention shall cease to be applicable to all or part of such territories.
(3)
(a) Any declaration made under paragraph (1) shall take effect on the same date as the ratification or accession in which it was included, and any notification given under that paragraph shall take effect three months after its notification by the Director General.
(b) Any notification given under paragraph (2) shall take effect twelve months after its receipt by the Director General.
(4) This Article shall in no way be understood as implying the recognition or tacit acceptance by a country of the Union of the factual situation concerning a territory to which this Convention is made applicable by another country of the Union by virtue of a declaration under paragraph (1).

[9.206]
Article 32
[Applicability of this Act and of Earlier Acts: 1. As between countries already members of the Union; 2. As between a country becoming a member of the Union and other countries members of the Union; 3. Applicability of the Appendix in Certain Relations]
(1) This Act shall, as regards relations between the countries of the Union, and to the extent that it applies, replace the Berne Convention of September 9, 1886, and the subsequent Acts of revision. The Acts previously in force shall continue to be applicable, in their entirety or to the extent that this Act does not replace them by virtue of the preceding sentence, in relations with countries of the Union which do not ratify or accede to this Act.

(2) Countries outside the Union which become party to this Act shall, subject to paragraph (3), apply it with respect to any country of the Union not bound by this Act or which, although bound by this Act, has made a declaration pursuant to Article 28(1)(b). Such countries recognise that the said country of the Union, in its relations with them—

(i) may apply the provisions of the most recent Act by which it is bound, and
(ii) subject to Article I(6) of the Appendix, has the right to adapt the protection to the level provided for by this Act.

(3) Any country which has availed itself of any of the faculties provided for in the Appendix may apply the provisions of the Appendix relating to the faculty or faculties of which it has availed itself in its relations with any other country of the Union which is not bound by this Act, provided that the latter country has accepted the application of the said provisions.

[9.207]
Article 33
[Disputes: 1. Jurisdiction of the International Court of Justice; 2. Reservation as to such jurisdiction; 3. Withdrawal of reservation]

(1) Any dispute between two or more countries of the Union concerning the interpretation or application of this Convention, not settled by negotiation, may, by any one of the countries concerned, be brought before the International Court of Justice by application in conformity with the Statute of the Court, unless the countries concerned agree on some other method of settlement. The country bringing the dispute before the Court shall inform the International Bureau; the International Bureau shall bring the matter to the attention of the other countries of the Union.

(2) Each country may, at the time it signs this Act or deposits its instrument of ratification or accession, declare that it does not consider itself bound by the provisions of paragraph (1). With regard to any dispute between such country and any other country of the Union, the provisions of paragraph (1) shall not apply.

(3) Any country having made a declaration in accordance with the provisions of paragraph (2) may, at any time, withdraw its declaration by notification addressed to the Director General.

[9.208]
Article 34
[Closing of Certain Earlier Provisions: 1. of Earlier Acts; 2. of the Protocol to the Stockholm Act]

(1) Subject to Article 29*bis*, no country may ratify or accede to earlier Acts of this Convention once Articles 1 to 21 and the Appendix have entered into force.

(2) Once Articles 1 to 21 and the Appendix have entered into force, no country may make a declaration under Article 5 of the Protocol Regarding Developing Countries attached to the Stockholm Act.

[9.209]
Article 35
[Duration of the Convention; Denunciation: 1. Unlimited duration; 2. Possibility of denunciation; 3. Effective date of denunciation; 4. Moratorium on denunciation]

(1) This Convention shall remain in force without limitation as to time.

(2) Any country may denounce this Act by notification addressed to the Director General. Such denunciation shall constitute also denunciation of all earlier Acts and shall affect only the country making it, the Convention remaining in full force and effect as regards the other countries of the Union.

(3) Denunciation shall take effect one year after the day on which the Director General has received the notification.

(4) The right of denunciation provided by this Article shall not be exercised by any country before the expiration of five years from the date upon which it becomes a member of the Union.

[9.210]
Article 36
[Application of the Convention: 1. Obligation to adopt the necessary Measures; 2. Time from which obligation exists]

(1) Any country party to this Convention undertakes to adopt, in accordance with its constitution, the measures necessary to ensure the application of this Convention.

(2) It is understood that, at the time a country becomes bound by this Convention, it will be in a position under its domestic law to give effect to the provisions of this Convention.

[9.211]
Article 37
[Final Clauses: 1. Languages of the Act; 2. Signature; 3. Certified copies; 4. Registration; 5. Notifications]

(1)

(a) This Act shall be signed in a single copy in the French and English languages and, subject to paragraph (2), shall be deposited with the Director General.

(b) Official texts shall be established by the Director General, after consultation with the interested Governments, in the Arabic, German, Italian, Portuguese and Spanish languages, and such other languages as the Assembly may designate.

(c) In case of differences of opinion on the interpretation of the various texts, the French text shall prevail.

(2) This Act shall remain open for signature until January 31, 1972. Until that date, the copy referred to in paragraph (1)(a) shall be deposited with the Government of the French Republic.

(3) The Director General shall certify and transmit two copies of the signed text of this Act to the Governments of all countries of the Union and, on request, to the Government of any other country.

(4) The Director General shall register this Act with the Secretariat of the United Nations.

(5) The Director General shall notify the Governments of all countries of the Union of signatures, deposits of instruments of ratification or accession and any declarations included in such instruments or made pursuant to Articles 28(1)(c), 30(2)(a) and (b), and 33(2), entry into force of any provisions of this Act, notifications of denunciation, and notifications pursuant to Articles 30(2)(c), 31(1) and (2), 33(3), and 38(1), as well as the Appendix.

[9.212]
Article 38
[Transitory Provisions: 1. Exercise of the "five-year privilege"; 2. Bureau of the Union, Director of the Bureau; 3. Succession of Bureau of the Union]

(1) Countries of the Union which have not ratified or acceded to this Act and which are not bound by Articles 22 to 26 of the Stockholm Act of this Convention may, until April 26, 1975, exercise, if they so desire, the rights provided under the said Articles as if they were bound by them. Any country desiring to exercise such rights shall give written notification to this effect to the Director General; this notification shall be effective on the date of its receipt. Such countries shall be deemed to be members of the Assembly until the said date.

(2) As long as all the countries of the Union have not become Members of the Organisation, the International Bureau of the Organisation shall also function as the Bureau of the Union, and the Director General as the Director of the said Bureau.

(3) Once all the countries of the Union have become Members of the Organisation, the rights, obligations, and property, of the Bureau of the Union shall devolve on the International Bureau of the Organisation.

APPENDIX
[SPECIAL PROVISIONS REGARDING DEVELOPING COUNTRIES]

[9.213]
Article I [Faculties Open to Developing Countries: 1. Availability of certain faculties; declaration; 2. Duration of effect of declaration; 3. Cessation of developing country status; 4. Existing stocks of copies; 5. Declarations concerning certain territories; 6. Limits of reciprocity]

(1) Any country regarded as a developing country in conformity with the established practice of the General Assembly of the United Nations which ratifies or accedes to this Act, of which this Appendix forms an integral part, and which, having regard to its economic situation and its social or cultural needs, does not consider itself immediately in a position to make provision for the protection of all the rights provided for in this Act, may, by a notification deposited with the Director General at the time of depositing its instrument of ratification or accession or, subject to Article V(I)(c), at any time thereafter, declare that it will avail itself of the faculty provided for in Article II, or of the faculty provided for in Article III, or of both of those faculties. It may, instead of availing itself of the faculty provided for in Article II, make a declaration according to Article V(1)(a).

(2)

(a) Any declaration under paragraph (1) notified before the expiration of the period of ten years from the entry into force of Articles 1 to 21 and this Appendix according to Article 28(2) shall be effective until the expiration of the said period. Any such declaration may be renewed in whole or in part for periods of ten years each by a notification deposited with the Director General not more than fifteen months and not less than three months before the expiration of the ten-year period then running.

(b) Any declaration under paragraph (1) notified after the expiration of the period of ten years from the entry into force of Articles 1 to 21 and this Appendix according to Article 28(2) shall be effective until the expiration of the ten-year period then running. Any such declaration may be renewed as provided for in the second sentence of subparagraph (a).

(3) Any country of the Union which has ceased to be regarded as a developing country as referred to in paragraph (1) shall no longer be entitled to renew its declaration as provided in paragraph (2), and, whether or not it formally withdraws its declaration, such country shall be precluded from availing itself of the faculties referred to in paragraph (1) from the expiration of the ten-year period then running or from the expiration of a period of three years after it has ceased to be regarded as a developing country, whichever period expires later.

(4) Where, at the time when the declaration made under paragraph (1) or (2) ceases to be effective, there are copies in stock which were made under a license granted by virtue of this Appendix, such copies may continue to be distributed until their stock is exhausted.

(5) Any country which is bound by the provisions of this Act and which has deposited a declaration or a notification in accordance with Article 31(1) with respect to the application of this Act to a particular territory, the situation of which can be regarded as analogous to that of the countries referred to in paragraph (1), may, in respect of such territory, make the declaration referred to in paragraph (1) and the notification of renewal referred to in paragraph (2). As long as such declaration or notification remains in effect, the provisions of this Appendix shall be applicable to the territory in respect of which it was made.

(6)

(a) The fact that a country avails itself of any of the facilities referred to in paragraph (1) does not permit another country to give less protection to works of which the country of origin is the former country than it is obliged to grant under Articles 1 to 20.

(b) The right to apply reciprocal treatment provided for in Article 30(2)(b), second sentence, shall not, until the date on which the period applicable under Article I(3) expires, be exercised in respect of works the country of origin of which is a country which has made a declaration according to Article V(1)(a).

[9.214]

Article II [Limitations on the Right of Translation: 1. Licenses grantable by competent authority; 2. to 4. Conditions allowing the grant of such licenses; 5. Purposes for which licenses may be granted; 6. Termination of licenses; 7. Works composed mainly of illustrations; 8. Works withdrawn from circulation; 9. Licenses for broadcasting organisations]

(1) Any country which has declared that it will avail itself of the faculty provided for in this Article shall be entitled, so far as works published in printed or analogous forms of reproduction are concerned, to substitute for the exclusive right of translation provided for in Article 8 a system of non-exclusive and non-transferable licenses, granted by the competent authority under the following conditions and subject to Article IV.

(2)

(a) Subject to paragraph (3), if, after the expiration of a period of three years, or of any longer period determined by the national legislation of the said country, commencing on the date of the first publication of the work, a translation of such work has not been published in a language in general use in that country by the owner of the right of translation, or with his authorisation, any national of such country may obtain a license to make a translation of the work in the said language and publish the translation in printed or analogous forms of reproduction.

(b) A license under the conditions provided for in this Article may also be granted if all the editions of the translation published in the language concerned are out of print.

(3)

(a) In the case of translations into a language which is not in general use in one or more developed countries which are members of the Union, a period of one year shall be substituted for the period of three years referred to in paragraph (2)(a).

(b) Any country referred to in paragraph (1) may, with the unanimous agreement of the developed countries which are members of the Union and in which the same language is in general use, substitute, in the case of translations into that language for the period of three years referred to in paragraph (2)(a) a shorter period as determined by such agreement but not less than one year. However, the provisions of the foregoing sentence shall not apply where the language in question is English, French or Spanish. The Director General shall be notified of any such agreement by the Governments which have concluded it.

(4)

(a) No license obtainable after three years shall be granted under this Article until a further period of six months has elapsed, and no license obtainable after one year shall be granted under this Article until a further period of nine months has elapsed—

(i) from the date on which the applicant complies with the requirements mentioned in Article IV(1), or

(ii) where the identity or the address of the owner of the right of translation is unknown, from the date on which the applicant sends, as provided for in Article IV(2), copies of his application submitted to the authority competent to grant the license.

(b) If, during the said period of six or nine months, a translation in the language in respect of which the application was made is published by the owner of the right of translation or with his authorisation, no license under this Article shall be granted.

(5) Any license under this Article shall be granted only for the purpose of teaching, scholarship or research.

(6) If a translation of a work is published by the owner of the right of translation or with his authorisation at a price reasonably related to that normally charged in the country for comparable works, any license granted under this Article shall terminate if such translation is in the same language and with substantially the same content as the translation published under the license. Any copies already made before the license terminates may continue to be distributed until their stock is exhausted.

(7) For works which are composed mainly of illustrations, a license to make and publish a translation of the text and to reproduce and publish the illustrations may be granted only if the conditions of Article III are also fulfilled.

(8) No license shall be granted under this Article when the author has withdrawn from circulation all copies of his work.

(9)

(a) A license to make a translation of a work which has been published in printed or analogous forms of reproduction may also be granted to any broadcasting organisation having its headquarters in a country referred to in paragraph (1), upon an application made to the competent authority of that country by the said organisation, provided that all of the following conditions are met—

(i) the translation is made from a copy made and acquired in accordance with the laws of the said country;

(ii) the translation is only for use in broadcasts intended exclusively for teaching or for the dissemination of the results of specialised technical or scientific research to experts in a particular profession;

(iii) the translation is used exclusively for the purposes referred to in condition (ii) through broadcasts made lawfully and intended for recipients on the territory of the said country, including broadcasts made through the medium of sound or visual recordings lawfully and exclusively made for the purpose of such broadcasts;

(iv) all uses made of the translation are without any commercial purpose.

(b) Sound or visual recordings of a translation which was made by a broadcasting organisation under a license granted by virtue of this paragraph may, for the purposes and subject to the conditions referred to in subparagraph (a) and with the agreement of that organisation, also be used by any other broadcasting organisation having its headquarters in the country whose competent authority granted the license in question.

(c) Provided that all of the criteria and conditions set out in subparagraph (a) are met, a license may also be granted to a broadcasting organisation to translate any text incorporated in an audio-visual fixation where such fixation was itself prepared and published for the sole purpose of being used in connection with systematic instructional activities.

(d) Subject to subparagraphs (a) to (c), the provisions of the preceding paragraphs shall apply to the grant and exercise of any license granted under this paragraph.

[9.215]

Article III [Limitation on the Right of Reproduction: 1. Licenses grantable by competent authority; 2. to 5. Conditions allowing the grant of such licenses; 6. Termination of licenses. 7. Works to which this Article applies]

(1) Any country which has declared that it will avail itself of the faculty provided for in this Article shall be entitled to substitute for the exclusive right of reproduction provided for in Article 9 a system of non-exclusive and non-transferable licenses, granted by the competent authority under the following conditions and subject to Article IV.

(2)

(a) If, in relation to a work to which this Article applies by virtue of paragraph (7), after the expiration of—

(i) the relevant period specified in paragraph (3), commencing on the date of first publication of a particular edition of the work, or

(ii) any longer period determined by national legislation of the country referred to in paragraph (1), commencing on the same date,

copies of such edition have not been distributed in that country to the general public or in connection with systematic instructional activities, by the owner of the right of reproduction or with his authorisation, at a price reasonably related to that normally charged in the country for comparable works, any national of such country may obtain a license to reproduce and publish such edition at that or a lower price for use in connection with systematic instructional activities.

(b) A license to reproduce and publish an edition which has been distributed as described in subparagraph (d) may also be granted under the conditions provided for in this Article if, after the expiration of the applicable period, no authorised copies of that edition have been on sale for a period of six months in the country concerned to the general public or in connection with systematic instructional activities at a price reasonably related to that normally charged in the country for comparable works.

(3) The period referred to in paragraph (2)(a)(i) shall be five years, except that—

(i) for works of the natural and physical sciences, including mathematics, and of technology, the period shall be three years;

(ii) for works of fiction, poetry, drama and music, and for art books, the period shall be seven years.

(4)

(a) No license obtainable after three years shall be granted under this Article until a period of six months has elapsed—

(i) from the date on which the applicant complies with the requirements mentioned in Article IV(1), or

(ii) where the identity or the address of the owner of the right of reproduction is unknown, from the date on which the applicant sends, as provided for in Article IV(2), copies of his application submitted to the authority competent to grant the license.

(b) Where licenses are obtainable after other periods and Article IV(2) is applicable, no license shall be granted until a period of three months has elapsed from the date of the dispatch of the copies of the application.

(c) If, during the period of six or three months referred to in subparagraphs (a) and (b), a distribution as described in paragraph (2)(a) has taken place, no license shall be granted under this Article.

(d) No license shall be granted if the author has withdrawn from circulation all copies of the edition for the reproduction and publication of which the license has been applied for.

(5) A license to reproduce and publish a translation of a work shall not be granted under this Article in the following cases—

(i) where the translation was not published by the owner of the right of translation or with his authorisation, or

(ii) where the translation is not in a language in general use in the country in which the license is applied for.

(6) If copies of an edition of a work are distributed in the country referred to in paragraph (1) to the general public or in connection with systematic instructional activities, by the owner of the right of reproduction or with his authorisation, at a price reasonably related to that normally charged in the country for comparable works, any license granted under this Article shall terminate if such edition is in the same language and with substantially the same content as the edition which was published under the said license. Any copies already made before the license terminates may continue to be distributed until their stock is exhausted.

(7)

(a) Subject to subparagraph (b), the works to which this Article applies shall be limited to works published in printed or analogous forms of reproduction.

(b) This Article shall also apply to the reproduction in audio-visual form of lawfully made audio-visual fixations including any protected works incorporated therein and to the translation of any incorporated text into a language in general use in the country in which the license is applied for, always provided that the audio-visual fixations in question were prepared and published for the sole purpose of being used in connection with systematic instructional activities.

[9.216]

Article IV [Provisions Common to Licenses Under Articles II and Iii: 1 and 2. Procedure. 3. Indication of author and title of work; 4. Exportation of copies; 5. Notice; 6. Compensation]

(1) A license under Article II or Article III may be granted only if the applicant, in accordance with the procedure of the country concerned, establishes either that he has requested, and has been denied, authorisation by the owner of the right to make and publish the translation or to reproduce and publish the edition, as the case may be, or that, after due diligence on his part, he was unable to find the owner of the right. At the same time as making the request, the applicant shall inform any national or international information centre referred to in paragraph (2).

(2) If the owner of the right cannot be found, the applicant for a license shall send, by registered airmail, copies of his application, submitted to the authority competent to grant the license, to the publisher whose name appears on the work and to any national or international information centre which may have been designated, in a notification to that effect deposited with the Director General, by the Government of the country in which the publisher is believed to have his principal place of business.

(3) The name of the author shall be indicated on all copies of the translation or reproduction published under a license granted under Article II or Article III. The title of the work shall appear on all such copies. In the ease of a translation, the original title of the work shall appear in any case on all the said copies.

(4)

(a) No license granted under Article II or Article III shall extend to the export of copies, and any such license shall be valid only for publication of the translation or of the reproduction, as the case may be, in the territory of the country in which it has been applied for.

(b) For the purposes of subparagraph (a), the notion of export shall include the sending of copies from any territory to the country which, in respect of that territory, has made a declaration under Article I(5).

(c) Where a governmental or other public entity of a country which has granted a license to make a translation under Article II into a language other than English, French or Spanish sends copies of a translation published under such licence to another country, such sending of copies shall not, for the purposes of subparagraph (a), be considered to constitute export if all of the following conditions are met—

(i) the recipients are individuals who are nationals of the country whose competent authority has granted the license, or organisations grouping such individuals;

(ii) the copies are to be used only for the purpose of teaching, scholarship or research;

(iii) the sending of the copies and their subsequent distribution to recipients is without any commercial purpose; and

(iv) the country to which the copies have been sent has agreed with the country whose competent authority has granted the license to allow the receipt, or distribution, or both, and the Director General has been notified of the agreement by the Government of the country in which the license has been granted.

(5) All copies published under a license granted by virtue of Article II or Article III shall bear a notice in the appropriate language stating that the copies are available for distribution only in the country or territory to which the said license applies.

(6)

(a) Due provision shall be made at the national level to ensure—

(i) that the license provides, in favour of the owner of the right of translation or of reproduction, as the case may be, for just compensation that is consistent with standards of royalties normally operating on licenses freely negotiated between persons in the two countries concerned, and

(ii) payment and transmittal of the compensation: should national currency regulations intervene, the competent authority shall make all efforts, by the use of international machinery, to ensure transmittal in internationally convertible currency or its equivalent.

(b) Due provision shall be made by national legislation to ensure a correct translation of the work, or an accurate reproduction of the particular edition, as the case may be.

[9.217]

Article V [Alternative Possibility for Limitation of the Right of Translation: 1. Regime provided for under the 1886 and 1896 Acts; 2. No possibility of change to regime under Article II; 3. Time limit for choosing the alternative possibility]

(1)

(a) Any country entitled to make a declaration that it will avail itself of the faculty provided for in Article II may, instead, at the time of ratifying or acceding to this Act—

(i) if it is a country to which Article 30(2)(a) applies, make a declaration under that provision as far as the right of translation is concerned;

(ii) if it is a country to which Article 30(2)(a) does not apply, and even if it is not a country outside the Union, make a declaration as provided for in Article 30(2)(b), first sentence.

(b) In the case of a country which ceases to be regarded as a developing country as referred to in Article 1(1), a declaration made according to this paragraph shall be effective until the date on which the period applicable under Article 1(3) expires.

(c) Any country which has made a declaration according to this paragraph may not subsequently avail itself of the faculty provided for in Article II even if it withdraws the said declaration.

(2) Subject to paragraph (3), any country which has availed itself of the faculty provided for in Article II may not subsequently make a declaration according to paragraph (1).

(3) Any country which has ceased to be regarded is a developing country as referred to in Article 1(1) may, not later than two years prior to the expiration of the period applicable under Article I(3), make a declaration to the effect provided for in Article 30(2)(b), first sentence, notwithstanding the fact that it is not a country outside the Union. Such declaration shall take effect at the date on which the period applicable under Article I(3) expires.

[9.218]

Article VI [Possibilities of applying or admitting the application of, certain provisions of the Appendix before becoming bound by it: 1. Declaration; 2. Depository and effective date of declaration]

(1) Any country of the Union may declare, as from the date of this Act, and at any time before becoming bound by Articles 1 to 21 and this Appendix—

(i) if it is a country which, were it bound by Articles 1 to 21 and this Appendix, would be entitled to avail itself of the faculties referred to in Article I(1), that it will apply the provisions of Article II or of Article III or of both to works whose country of origin is a country which, pursuant to (ii) below, admits the application of those Articles to such works, or which is bound by Articles 1 to 21 and this Appendix; such declaration may, instead of referring to Article II, refer to Article V;

(ii) that it admits the application of this Appendix to works of which it is the country of origin by countries which have made a declaration under (i) above or a notification under Article I.

(2) Any declaration made under paragraph (1) shall be in writing and shall be deposited with the Director General. The declaration shall become effective from the date of its deposit.

CONVENTION FOR THE PROTECTION OF PRODUCERS OF PHONOGRAMS AGAINST UNAUTHORISED DUPLICATION OF THEIR PHONOGRAMS ('PHONOGRAMS CONVENTION')

Geneva, October 29, 1971

NOTES

The original source for this Convention is the World Intellectual Property Organisation (WIPO).

Entered into force: 18 April 1973.

Articles have been given titles to facilitate their identification. There are no titles in the signed (French) text.

THE CONTRACTING STATES,

concerned at the widespread and increasing unauthorised duplication of phonograms and the damage this is occasioning to the interests of authors, performers and producers of phonograms;

convinced that the protection of producers of phonograms against such acts will also benefit the performers whose performances, and the authors whose works, are recorded on the said phonograms;

recognising the value of the work undertaken in this field by the United Nations Educational, Scientific and Cultural Organisation and the World Intellectual Property Organisation;

anxious not to impair in any way international agreements already in force and in particular in no way to prejudice wider acceptance of the Rome Convention of October 26, 1961, which affords protection to performers and to broadcasting organisations as well as to producers of phonograms;

HAVE AGREED AS FOLLOWS—

[9.219]
Article 1
[Definitions]

For the purposes of this Convention—

(a) "phonogram" means any exclusively aural fixation of sounds of a performance or of other sounds;

(b) "producer of phonograms" means the person who, or the legal entity which, first fixes the sounds of a performance or other sounds;

(c) "duplicate" means an article which contains sounds taken directly or indirectly from a phonogram and which embodies all or a substantial part of the sounds fixed in that phonogram;

(d) "distribution to the public" means any act by which duplicates of a phonogram are offered, directly or indirectly, to the general public or any section thereof.

[9.220]
Article 2
[Obligations of Contracting States; Whom they must protect and against what]

Each Contracting State shall protect producers of phonograms who are nationals of other Contracting States against the making of duplicates without the consent of the producer and against the importation of such duplicates, provided that any such making or importation is for the purpose of distribution to the public, and against the distribution of such duplicates to the public.

[9.221]
Article 3
[Means of Implementation by Contracting States]

The means by which this Convention is implemented shall be a matter for the domestic law of each Contracting State and shall include one or more of the following: protection by means of the grant of a copyright or other specific right; protection by means of the law relating to unfair competition; protection by means of penal sanctions.

[9.222]
Article 4
[Terms of Protection]

The duration of the protection given shall be a matter for the domestic law of each Contracting State. However, if the domestic law prescribes a specific duration for the protection, that duration shall not be less than twenty years from the end either of the year in which the sounds embodied in the phonogram were first fixed or of the year in which the phonogram was first published.

[9.223]
Article 5
[Formalities]

If, as a condition of protecting the producers of phonograms, a Contracting State, under its domestic law, requires compliance with formalities, these shall be considered as fulfilled if all the authorised duplicates of the phonogram distributed to the public or their containers bear a notice consisting of the symbol (P), accompanied by the year date of the first publication, placed in such manner as to give reasonable notice of claim of protection; and, if the duplicates or their containers do not identify the producer, his successor in title or the exclusive licensee (by carrying his name, trademark or other appropriate designation), the notice shall also include the name of the producer, his successor in title or the exclusive licensee.

[9.224]
Article 6
[Limitations on Protection]

Any Contracting State which affords protection by means of copyright or other specific right, or protection by means of penal sanctions, may in its domestic law provide, with regard to the protection of producers of phonograms, the same kinds of limitations as are permitted with respect to the protection of authors of literary and artistic works. However, no compulsory licences may be permitted unless all of the following conditions are met—

(a) the duplication is for use solely for the purpose of teaching or scientific research;
(b) the licence shall be valid for duplication only within the territory of the Contracting State whose competent authority has granted the licence and shall not extend to the export of duplicates;
(c) the duplication made under the licence gives rise to an equitable remuneration fixed by the said authority taking into account, *inter alia,* the number of duplicates which will be made.

[9.225]
Article 7
[Savings: 1. Safeguard of Copyright and Neighbouring Rights; 2. Protection for Performers; 3. Non-retroactivity; 4. Substitution of the Criterion of Fixation]

(1) This Convention shall in no way be interpreted to limit or prejudice the protection otherwise secured to authors, to performers, to producers of phonograms or to broadcasting organisations under any domestic law or international agreement.

(2) It shall be a matter for the domestic law of each Contracting State to determine the extent, if any, to which performers whose performances are fixed in a phonogram are entitled to enjoy protection and the conditions for enjoying any such protection.

(3) No Contracting State shall be required to apply the provisions of this Convention to any phonogram fixed before this Convention entered into force with respect to that State.

(4) Any Contracting State which, on October 29, 1971, affords protection to producers of phonograms solely on the basis of the place of first fixation may, by a notification deposited with the Director General of the World Intellectual Property Organisation, declare that it will apply this criterion instead of the criterion of the nationality of the producer.

[9.226]
Article 8
[Secretariat]

(1) The International Bureau of the World Intellectual Property Organisation shall assemble and publish information concerning the protection of phonograms. Each Contracting State shall promptly communicate to the International Bureau all new laws and official texts on this subject.

(2) The International Bureau shall, on request, furnish information to any Contracting State on matters concerning this Convention, and shall conduct studies and provide services designed to facilitate the protection provided for therein.

(3) The International Bureau shall exercise the functions enumerated in paragraphs (1) and (2) above in co-operation, for matters within their respective competence, with the United Nations Educational, Scientific and Cultural Organisation and the International Labour Organisation.

[9.227]
Article 9
[Joining the Convention: 1. Signature and Deposit; 2. Ratification and Accession; 4. States' Obligations as to their Domestic Law]

(1) This Convention shall be deposited with the Secretary-General of the United Nations. It shall be open until April 30, 1972, for signature by any State that is a member of the United Nations, any of the Specialised Agencies brought into relationship with the United Nations, or the International Atomic Energy Agency, or is a party to the Statute of the International Court of Justice.

(2) This Convention shall be subject to ratification or acceptance by the signatory States. It shall be open for accession by any State referred to in paragraph (1) of this Article.

(3) Instruments of ratification, acceptance or accession shall be deposited with the Secretary-General of the United Nations.

(4) It is understood that, at the time a State becomes bound by this Convention, it will be in a position in accordance with its domestic law to give effect to the provisions of the Convention.

[9.228]
Article 10
[Reservations]

No reservations to this Convention are permitted.

[9.229]
Article 11
[Entry into Force and Applicability: 1 and 2. Entry into Force of the Convention; 3 and 4. Applicability of the Convention to Certain Territories]

(1) This Convention shall enter into force three months after deposit of the fifth instrument of ratification, acceptance or accession.

(2) For each State ratifying, accepting or acceding to this Convention after the deposit of the fifth instrument of ratification, acceptance or accession, the Convention shall enter into force three months after the date on which the Director General of the World Intellectual Property Organisation informs the States, in accordance with Article 13, paragraph (4), of the deposit of its instrument.

(3) Any State may, at the time of ratification, acceptance or accession or at any later date, declare by notification addressed to the Secretary-General of the United Nations that this Convention shall apply to all or any one of the territories for whose international affairs it is responsible. This notification will take effect three months after the date on which it is received.

(4) However, the preceding paragraph may in no way be understood as implying the recognition or tacit acceptance by a Contracting State of the factual situation concerning a territory to which this Convention is made applicable by another Contracting State by virtue of the said paragraph.

[9.230]
Article 12
[Denunciation of the Convention]

(1) Any Contracting State may denounce this Convention, on its own behalf or on behalf of any of the territories referred to in Article 11, paragraph (3), by written notification addressed to the Secretary-General of the United Nations.

(2) Denunciation shall take effect twelve months after the date on which the Secretary-General of the United Nations has received the notification.

[9.231]
Article 13
[Languages and Notifications]

(1) This Convention shall be signed in a single copy in English, French, Russian and Spanish, the four texts being equally authentic.

(2) Official texts shall be established by the Director General of the World Intellectual Property Organisation, after consultation with the interested Governments, in the Arabic, Dutch, German, Italian and Portuguese languages.

(3) The Secretary-General of the United Nations shall notify the Director General of the World Intellectual Property Organisation, the Director-General of the United Nations Educational, Scientific and Cultural Organisation and the Director-General of the International Labour Office of—

- (a) signatures to this Convention;
- (b) the deposit of instruments of ratification, acceptance or accession;
- (c) the date of entry into force of this Convention;
- (d) any declaration notified pursuant to Article 11, paragraph (3);
- (e) the receipt of notifications of denunciation.

(4) The Director General of the World Intellectual Property Organisation shall inform the States referred to in Article 9, paragraph (1), of the notifications received pursuant to the preceding paragraph and of any declarations made under Article 7, paragraph (4). He shall also notify the Director-General of the United Nations Educational, Scientific and Cultural Organisation and the Director-General of the International Labour Office of such declarations.

(5) The Secretary-General of the United Nations shall transmit two certified copies of

this Convention to the States referred to in Article 9, paragraph (1).

CONVENTION RELATING TO THE DISTRIBUTION OF PROGRAMME-CARRYING SIGNALS TRANSMITTED BY SATELLITE ('BRUSSELS CONVENTION')

Brussels, May 21, 1974

NOTES

The original source for this Convention is the World Intellectual Property Organisation (WIPO).

THE CONTRACTING STATES,

Aware that the use of satellites for the distribution of programme-carrying signals is rapidly growing both in volume and geographical coverage;

Concerned that there is no world-wide system to prevent distributors from distributing programme-carrying signals transmitted by satellite which were not intended for those distributors, and that this lack is likely to hamper the use of satellite communications;

Recognising, in this respect, the importance of the interests of authors, performers, producers of phonograms and broadcasting organisations;

Convinced that an international system should be established under which measures would be provided to prevent distributors from distributing programme-carrying signals transmitted by satellite which were not intended for those distributors;

Conscious of the need not to impair in any way international agreements already in force, including the International Telecommunication Convention and the Radio Regulations annexed to that Convention, and in particular in no way to prejudice wider acceptance of the Rome Convention of October 26, 1961, which affords protection to performers, producers of phonograms and broadcasting organisations,

HAVE AGREED AS FOLLOWS—

[9.232]
Article 1

For the purposes of this Convention—

(i) "signal" is an electronically-generated carrier capable of transmitting programmes;
(ii) "programme" is a body of live or recorded material consisting of images, sounds or both, embodied in signals emitted for the purpose of ultimate distribution;
(iii) "satellite" is any device in extraterrestrial space capable of transmitting signals;
(iv) "emitted signal" or "signal emitted" is any programme-carrying signal that goes to or passes through a satellite;
(v) "derived signal" is a signal obtained by modifying the technical characteristics of the emitted signal, whether or not there have been one or more intervening fixations;
(vi) "originating organisation" is the person or legal entity that decides what programme the emitted signals will carry;
(vii) "distributor" is the person or legal entity that decides that the transmission of the derived signals to the general public or any section thereof should take place;
(viii) "distribution" is the operation by which a distributor transmits derived signals to the general public or any section thereof.

[9.233]
Article 2

(1) Each Contracting State undertakes to take adequate measures to prevent the distribution on or from its territory of any programme-carrying signal by any distributor for whom the signal emitted to or passing through the satellite is not intended. This obligation shall apply where the originating organisation is a national of another Contracting State and where the signal distributed is a derived signal.

(2) In any Contracting State in which the application of the measures referred to in paragraph (1) is limited in time, the duration thereof shall be fixed by its domestic law. The Secretary-General of the United Nations shall be notified in writing of such duration at the time of ratification, acceptance or accession, or if the domestic law comes into force or is changed thereafter, within six months of the coming into force of that law or of its modification.

(3) The obligation provided for in paragraph (1) shall not apply to the distribution of derived signals taken from signals which have already been distributed by a distributor for whom the emitted signals were intended.

[9.234]
Article 3

This Convention shall not apply where the signals emitted by or on behalf of the originating organisation are intended for direct reception from the satellite by the general public.

[9.235]
Article 4
No Contracting State shall be required to apply the measures referred to in Article 2(1) where the signal distributed on its territory by a distributor for whom the emitted signal is not intended—
- (i) carries short excerpts of the programme carried by the emitted signal, consisting of reports of current events, but only to the extent justified by the informatory purpose of such excerpts, or
- (ii) carries, as quotations, short excerpts of the programme carried by the emitted signal, provided that such quotations are compatible with fair practice and are justified by the informatory purpose of such quotations, or
- (iii) carries, where the said territory is that of a Contracting State regarded as a developing country in conformity with the established practice of the General Assembly of the United Nations, a programme carried by the emitted signal, provided that the distribution is solely for the purpose of teaching, including teaching in the framework of adult education, or scientific research.

[9.236]
Article 5
No Contracting State shall be required to apply this Convention with respect to any signal emitted before this Convention entered into force for that State.

[9.237]
Article 6
This Convention shall in no way be interpreted to limit or prejudice the protection secured to authors, performers, producers of phonograms, or broadcasting organisations, under any domestic law or international agreement.

[9.238]
Article 7
This Convention shall in no way be interpreted as limiting the right of any Contracting State to apply its domestic law in order to prevent abuses of monopoly.

[9.239]
Article 8
(1) Subject to paragraphs (2) and (3), no reservation to this Convention shall be permitted.
(2) Any Contracting State whose domestic law, on May 21, 1974, so provides may, by a written notification deposited with the Secretary-General of the United Nations, declare that, for its purposes, the words "where the originating organisation is a national of another Contracting State" appearing in Article 2(1) shall be considered as if they were replaced by the words "where the signal is emitted from the territory of another Contracting State."
(3)
- (a) Any Contracting State which, on May 21, 1974, limits or denies protection with respect to the distribution of programme-carrying signals by means of wires, cable or other similar communications channels to subscribing members of the public may, by a written notification deposited with the Secretary-General of the United Nations, declare that, to the extent that and as long as its domestic law limits or denies protection, it will not apply this Convention to such distributions.
- (b) Any State that has deposited a notification in accordance with subparagraph (a) shall notify the Secretary-General of the United Nations in writing, within six months of their coming into force, of any changes in its domestic law whereby the reservation under that subparagraph becomes inapplicable or more limited in scope.

[9.240]
Article 9
(1) This Convention shall be deposited with the Secretary-General of the United Nations. It shall be open until March 31, 1975, for signature by any State that is a member of the United Nations, any of the Specialised Agencies brought into relationship with the United Nations, or the International Atomic Energy Agency, or is a party to the Statute of the International Court of Justice.
(2) This Convention shall be subject to ratification or acceptance by the signatory States. It shall be open for accession by any State referred to in paragraph (1).
(3) Instruments of ratification, acceptance or accession shall be deposited with the Secretary-General of the United Nations.
(4) It is understood that, at the time a State becomes bound by this Convention, it will be in a position in accordance with its domestic law to give effect to the provisions of the Convention.

[9.241]
Article 10
(1) This Convention shall enter into force three months after the deposit of the fifth instrument of ratification, acceptance or accession.

(2) For each State ratifying, accepting or acceding to this Convention after the deposit of the fifth instrument of ratification, acceptance or accession, this Convention shall enter into force three months after the deposit of its instrument.

[9.242]
Article 11
(1) Any Contracting State may denounce this Convention by written notification deposited with the Secretary-General of the United Nations.
(2) Denunciation shall take effect twelve months after the date on which the notification referred to in paragraph (1) is received.

[9.243]
Article 12
(1) This Convention shall be signed in a single copy in English, French, Russian and Spanish, the four texts being equally authentic.
(2) Official texts shall be established by the Director-General of the United Nations Educational, Scientific and Cultural Organisation and the Director General of the World Intellectual Property Organisation, after consultation with the interested Governments, in the Arabic, Dutch, German, Italian and Portuguese languages.
(3) The Secretary-General of the United Nations shall notify the States referred to in Article 9(1), as well as the Director-General of the United Nations Educational, Scientific and Cultural Organisation, the Director General of the World Intellectual Property Organisation, the Director-General of the International Labour Office and the Secretary-General of the International Telecommunication Union, of—
(i) signatures to this Convention;
(ii) the deposit of instruments of ratification, acceptance or accession;
(iii) the date of entry into force of this Convention under Article 10(1);
(iv) the deposit of any notification relating to Article 2(2) or Article 8(2) or (3), together with its text;
(v) the receipt of notifications of denunciation.
(4) The Secretary-General of the United Nations shall transmit two certified copies of this Convention to all States referred to in Article 9(1).

AGREEMENT BETWEEN THE UNITED NATIONS AND THE WORLD INTELLECTUAL PROPERTY ORGANIZATION

This Agreement entered into effect on December 17, 1974[1]

NOTES
The original source for this Agreement is the World Intellectual Property Organisation (WIPO).

[1] A Protocol incorporating the Agreement was signed by Kurt Waldheim, Secretary-General of the United Nations, and Arpad Bogsch, Director General of the World Intellectual Property Organization, on January 21, 1975.

PREAMBLE
In consideration of the provisions of Article 57 of the Charter of the United Nations and of Article 13, paragraph (1), of the Convention Establishing the World Intellectual Property Organization, the United Nations and the World Intellectual Property Organization agree as follows:

[9.244]
Article 1
Recognition
The United Nations recognizes the World Intellectual Property Organization (hereinafter called the "Organization") as a specialized agency and as being responsible for taking appropriate action in accordance with its basic instrument, treaties and agreements administered by it, inter alia, for promoting creative intellectual activity and for facilitating the transfer of technology related to industrial property to the developing countries in order to accelerate economic, social and cultural development, subject to the competence and responsibilities of the United Nations and its organs, particularly the United Nations Conference on Trade and Development, the United Nations Development Programme and the United Nations Industrial Development Organization, as well as of the United Nations Educational, Scientific and Cultural Organization and of other agencies within the United Nations system.

[9.245]
Article 2
Co-ordination and Co-operation
In its relations with the United Nations, its organs and the agencies within the United Nations system, the Organization recognizes the responsibilities for co-ordination of the General Assembly and of the Economic and Social Council under the Charter of the United Nations. Accordingly, the

Organization agrees to co-operate in whatever measures may be necessary to make co-ordination of the policies and activities of the United Nations and those of the organs and agencies within the United Nations system fully effective. The Organization agrees further to participate in the work of any United Nations bodies which have been established or may be established for the purpose of facilitating such co-operation and co-ordination, in particular through membership in the Administrative Committee on Co-ordination.

[9.246]
Article 3
Reciprocal Representation

(a) Representatives of the United Nations shall be invited to attend the sessions of all the bodies of the Organization and all such other meetings convened by the Organization, and to participate, without the right to vote, in the deliberations of such bodies and at such meetings. Written statements presented by the United Nations shall be distributed by the Organization to its members.

(b) Representatives of the Organization shall be invited to attend meetings and to participate, without the right to vote, in the deliberations of the Economic and Social Council, its commissions and committees, of the main committees and the organs of the General Assembly, and of other conferences and meetings of the United Nations, with respect to items on the agenda relating to intellectual property matters within the scope of the activities of the Organization and other matters of mutual interest. Written statements presented by the Organization shall be distributed by the Secretariat of the United Nations to the members of the above-mentioned bodies, in accordance with the rules of procedure.

(c) Representatives of the Organization shall be invited, for purposes of consultation, to attend meetings of the General Assembly of the United Nations when questions as defined in paragraph (b) above are under discussion.

[9.247]
Article 4
Proposal of Agenda Items

Subject to such preliminary consultation as may be necessary, the Organization shall arrange for the inclusion in the provisional agenda of its appropriate bodies of items proposed by the United Nations, and the Economic and Social Council, its commissions and committees shall arrange for the inclusion in their provisional agenda of items proposed by the Organization.

[9.248]
Article 5
Recommendations of the United Nations

(a) The Organization, having regard to the obligation of the United Nations to promote the objectives set forth in Article 55 of the Charter of the United Nations and the function and power of the Economic and Social Council, under Article 62 of the Charter, to make or initiate studies and reports with respect to international economic, social, cultural, educational, health and related matters and to make recommendations concerning these matters to the specialized agencies concerned, and having regard also to the responsibility of the United Nations, under Articles 58 and 63 of the Charter, to make recommendations for the co-ordination of the policies and activities of such specialized agencies, agrees to arrange for the submission, as soon as possible, to the appropriate organ of the Organization, of all formal recommendations which the United Nations may make to it.

(b) The Organization agrees to enter into consultation with the United Nations upon request with respect to such recommendations, and in due course to report to the United Nations on the action taken by the Organization or by its members to give effect to such recommendations, or on the other results of their consideration.

[9.249]
Article 6
Information and Documents

(a) Subject to such arrangements as may be necessary for the safeguarding of confidential material, full and prompt exchange of appropriate information and documents shall be made between the United Nations and the Organization.

(b) The Organization shall submit to the United Nations an annual report on its activities.

[9.250]
Article 7
Statistical Services

(a) The United Nations and the Organization agree to strive for the maximum co-operation, the elimination of all undesirable duplication between them and the most efficient use of their technical personnel in their respective collection, analysis, publication and dissemination of statistical information. They agree to combine their efforts to secure the greatest possible usefulness and utilization of statistical information and to minimize the burden placed upon Governments and other organizations from which such information may be collected.

(b) The Organization recognizes the United Nations as the central agency for the collection, analysis, publication, standardization and improvement of statistics serving the general purposes of international organizations.

(c) The United Nations recognizes the Organization as an appropriate agency for the collection, analysis, publication, standardization and improvement of statistics within its special sphere, without prejudice to the right of the United Nations, its organs and other agencies within the United Nations system to concern themselves with such statistics in so far as they may be essential for their own purposes or for the improvement of statistics throughout the world.

(d) The United Nations shall, in consultation with the Organization and other agencies within the United Nations system, develop administrative instruments and procedures through which effective statistical co-operation may be secured between the United Nations, the Organization and other agencies within the United Nations system brought into relationship with it.

(e) It is recognized as desirable that the collection of statistical information should not be duplicated by the United Nations or any of the agencies within the United Nations system whenever it is practicable for any of them to utilize information or materials which another may have available.

(f) In order to collect statistical information for general use, it is agreed that data supplied to the Organization for incorporation in its basic statistical series or special reports should, so far as practicable, be made available to the United Nations on request.

(g) It is agreed that data supplied to the United Nations for incorporation in its basic statistical series or special reports should, so far as is practicable and appropriate, be made available to the Organization upon request.

[9.251]
Article 8
Assistance to the United Nations

The Organization shall, in accordance with the Charter of the United Nations and the basic instrument of the Organization, treaties and agreements administered by the Organization, co-operate with the United Nations by furnishing to it such information, special reports and studies, and by rendering such assistance to it, as the United Nations may request.

[9.252]
Article 9
Technical Assistance

The United Nations and the Organization undertake to cooperate in the provision of technical assistance for' development in the field of intellectual creation. They also undertake to avoid undesirable duplication of activities and services relating to such technical assistance and agree to take such action as may be necessary to achieve effective co-ordination of their technical assistance activities within the framework of existing co-ordination machinery in the field of technical assistance. To this end, the Organization agrees to give consideration to the common use of available services as far as practicable. The United Nations will make available to the Organization its administrative services in this field for use as requested.

[9.253]
Article 10
Transfer of Technology

The Organization agrees to co-operate within the field of its competence with the United Nations and its organs, particularly the United Nations Conference on Trade and Development, the United Nations Development Programme and the United Nations Industrial Development Organization, as well as the agencies within the United Nations system, in promoting and facilitating the transfer of technology to developing countries in such a manner as to assist these countries in attaining their objectives in the fields of science and technology and trade and development.

[9.254]
Article 11
Trust, Non-Self-Governing and Other Territories

The Organization agrees to co-operate within the field of its competence with the United Nations in giving effect to the principles and obligations set forth in Chapters XI, XII and XIII of the Charter of the United Nations and in the Declaration on the Granting of Independence to Colonial Countries and Peoples, with regard to matters affecting the well-being and development of the peoples of the Trust, Non-Self-Governing and other Territories.

[9.255]
Article 12
International Court of Justice

(a) The Organization agrees to furnish any information which may be requested by the International Court of justice in pursuance of Article 34 of the Statute of the Court.

(b) The General Assembly of the United Nations authorizes the Organization to request advisory opinions of the International Court of Justice on legal questions arising within the scope of its competence other than questions concerning the mutual relationships of the Organization and; the United Nations or other specialized agencies.
(c) Such requests may be addressed to the International Court of Justice by the General Assembly of the Organization, or by the Co-ordination Committee of the Organization acting in pursuance of an authorization by the General Assembly of the Organization.
(d) When requesting the International Court of Justice to give an advisory opinion, the Organization shall inform the Economic and Social Council of the request.

[9.256]
Article 13
Relations with Other International Organizations
Before the conclusion of any formal agreement between the Organization and any other specialized agency, any intergovernmental organization other than a specialized agency or any non-governmental organization, the Organization shall inform the Economic and Social Council of the nature and scope of the proposed agreement; furthermore, the Organization shall inform the Economic and Social Council of any matter of interagency concern within its competence.

[9.257]
Article 14
Administrative Co-operation
(a) The United Nations and the Organization recognize the desirability of co-operation in administrative matters of mutual interest.
(b) Accordingly, the United Nations and the Organization undertake to consult together from time to time concerning these matters, particularly the most efficient use of facilities, staff and services and the appropriate methods of avoiding the establishment and operation of competitive or overlapping facilities and services among the United Nations and the agencies within the United Nations system and the Organization and with a view to securing, within the limits of the Charter of the United Nations and the Convention establishing the Organization, as much uniformity in these matters as shall be found practicable.
(c) The consultations referred to in this article shall be utilized to establish the most equitable manner in which any special services or assistance furnished, on request, by the Organization to the United Nations or by the United Nations to the Organization shall be financed.

[9.258]
Article 15
Personnel Arrangements
(a) The United Nations and the Organization agree to develop, in the interests of uniform standards of international employment and to the extent feasible, common personnel standards, methods and arrangements designed to avoid unjustified differences in terms and conditions of employment, to avoid competition in recruitment of personnel, and to facilitate any mutually desirable and beneficial interchange of personnel.
(b) The United Nations and the Organization agree:
(i) to consult together from time to time concerning matters of mutual interest relating to the terms and conditions of employment of the officers and staff, with a view to securing as much uniformity in these matters as may be feasible;
(ii) to co-operate in the interchange of personnel when desirable, on a temporary or a permanent basis, making due provision for the retention of seniority and pension rights;
(iii) to co-operate, on such terms and conditions as may be agreed, in the operation of a common pension fund;
(iv) to co-operate in the establishment and operation of suitable machinery for the settlement of disputes arising in connexion with the employment of personnel and related matters.
(c) The terms and conditions on which any facilities or services of the Organization or the United Nations in connexion with the matters referred to in this article are to be extended to the other shall, where necessary, be the subject of subsidiary agreements concluded for this purpose after the entry into force of this Agreement.

[9.259]
Article 16
Budgetary and Financial Matters
(a) The Organization recognizes the desirability of establishing close budgetary and financial relationships with the United Nations in order that the administrative operations of the United Nations and the agencies within the United Nations system shall be carried out in the most efficient and economical manner possible, and that the maximum measure of co-ordination and uniformity with respect to these operations shall be secured.
(b) The Organization agrees to conform, as far as may be practicable and appropriate, to standard practices and forms recommended by the United Nations.

(c) In the preparation of the budget of the Organization, the Director General of the Organization shall consult with the Secretary-General of the United Nations with a view to achieving, in so far as is practicable, uniformity in presentation of the budgets of the United Nations and of the agencies within the United Nations system for the purposes of providing a basis for comparison of the several budgets.
(d) The Organization agrees to transmit to the United Nations its draft triennial and annual budgets not later than when the said draft budgets are transmitted to its members so as to give the General Assembly sufficient time to examine the said draft budgets, or budgets, and make such recommendations as it deems desirable.
(e) The United Nations may arrange for studies to be undertaken concerning financial and fiscal questions of interest both to the Organization and to the other agencies within the United Nations system, with a view to the provision of common services and the securing of uniformity in such matters.

[9.260]
Article 17
United Nations Laissez-Passer
Officials of the Organization shall be entitled, in accordance with such special arrangements as may be concluded between the Secretary-General of the United Nations and the Director General of the Organization, to use the laissez-passer of the United Nations.

[9.261]
Article 18
Implementation of the Agreement
The Secretary-General of the United Nations and the Director General of the Organization may enter into such supplementary arrangements for the implementation of this Agreement as may be found desirable.

[9.262]
Article 19
Amendment and Revision
This Agreement may be amended or revised by agreement between the United Nations and the Organization and any such amendment or revision shall come into force on approval by the General Assembly of the United Nations and the General Assembly of the Organization.

[9.263]
Article 20
Entry Into Force
This Agreement shall enter into force on its approval by the General Assembly of the United Nations and the General Assembly of the Organization.

AGREEMENT ON TRADE-RELATED ASPECTS OF INTELLECTUAL PROPERTY RIGHTS ('TRIPS')

NOTES

See the WTO website at www.wto.org/publications.
The TRIPS Agreement is Annex 1C of the Marrakesh Agreement Establishing the World Trade Organisation, signed in Marrakesh, Morocco on 15 April 1994.

MEMBERS,

Desiring to reduce distortions and impediments to international trade, and taking into account the need to promote effective and adequate protection of intellectual property rights, and to ensure that measures and procedures to enforce intellectual property rights do not themselves become barriers to legitimate trade;

Recognising, to this end, the need for new rules and disciplines concerning:

(a) the applicability of the basic principles of the GATT 1994 and of relevant international intellectual property agreements or conventions;
(b) the provision of adequate standards and principles concerning the availability, scope and use of trade-related intellectual property rights;
(c) the provision of effective and appropriate means for the enforcement of trade-related intellectual property rights, taking into account differences in national legal systems;
(d) the provision of effective and expeditious procedures for the multilateral prevention and settlement of disputes between governments; and
(e) transitional arrangements aiming at the fullest participation in the results of the negotiations;

Recognising the need for a multilateral framework of principles, rules and disciplines dealing with international trade in counterfeit goods;

Recognising that intellectual property rights are private rights;

Recognising the underlying public policy objectives of national systems for the protection of intellectual property, including developmental and technological objectives;

Recognising also the special needs of the least-developed country Members in respect of maximum flexibility in the domestic implementation of laws and regulations in order to enable them to create a sound and viable technological base;

Emphasising the importance of reducing tensions by reaching strengthened commitments to resolve disputes on trade-related intellectual property issues through multilateral procedures;

Desiring to establish a mutually supportive relationship between the WTO and the World Intellectual Property Organisation (referred to in this Agreement as "WIPO") as well as other relevant international organisations;

HEREBY AGREE AS FOLLOWS—

PART I
GENERAL PROVISIONS AND BASIC PRINCIPLES

[9.264]
Article 1
Nature and Scope of Obligations

1. Members shall give effect to the provisions of this Agreement. Members may, but shall not be obliged to, implement in their law more extensive protection than is required by this Agreement, provided that such protection does not contravene the provisions of this Agreement. Members shall be free to determine the appropriate method of implementing the provisions of this Agreement within their own legal system and practice.

2. For the purposes of this Agreement, the term "intellectual property" refers to all categories of intellectual property that are the subject of Sections 1 through 7 of Part II.

3. Members shall accord the treatment provided for in this Agreement to the nationals of other Members.[1] In respect of the relevant intellectual property right, the nationals of other Members shall be understood as those natural or legal persons that would meet the criteria for eligibility for protection provided for in the Paris Convention (1967), the Berne Convention (1971), the Rome Convention and the Treaty on Intellectual Property in Respect of Integrated Circuits, were all Members of the WTO members of those Conventions.[2] Any Member availing itself of the possibilities provided in paragraph 3 of Article 5 or paragraph 2 of Article 6 of the Rome Convention shall make a notification as foreseen in those provisions to the Council for Trade-Related Aspects of Intellectual Property Rights (the "Council for TRIPS").

NOTES

1 When "nationals" are referred to in this Agreement, they shall be deemed, in the case of a separate customs territory Member of the WTO, to mean persons, natural or legal, who are domiciled or who have a real and effective industrial or commercial establishment in that customs territory.

2 In this Agreement, "Paris Convention" refers to the Paris Convention for the Protection of Industrial Property: "Paris Convention (1967)" refers to the Stockholm Act of this Convention of 14 July 1967. "Berne Convention" refers to the Berne Convention for the Protection of Literary and Artistic Works: "Berne Convention (1971)" refers to the Paris Act of this Convention of 24 July 1971. "Rome Convention" refers to the International Convention for the Protection of Performers, Producers of Phonograms and Broadcasting Organisations, adopted at Rome on 26 October 1961. "Treaty on Intellectual Property in Respect of Integrated Circuits" (IPC Treaty) refers to the Treaty on Intellectual Property in Respect of Integrated Circuits, adopted at Washington on 26 May 1989. "WTO Agreement" refers to the Agreement Establishing the WTO.

[9.265]
Article 2
Intellectual Property Conventions

1. In respect of Parts II, III and IV of this Agreement, Members shall comply with Articles 1 through 12, and Article 19, of the Paris Convention (1967).

2. Nothing in Parts I to IV of this Agreement shall derogate from existing obligations that Members may have to each other under the Paris Convention, the Berne Convention, the Rome Convention and the Treaty on Intellectual Property in Respect of Integrated Circuits.

[9.266]
Article 3
National Treatment

1. Each Member shall accord to the nationals of other Members treatment no less favourable than that it accords to its own nationals with regard to the protection[1] of intellectual property, subject to the exceptions already provided in, respectively, the Paris Convention (1967), the Berne Convention (1971), the Rome Convention or the Treaty on Intellectual Property in Respect of Integrated Circuits. In respect of performers, producers of phonograms and broadcasting organisations, this obligation only applies in respect of the rights provided under this Agreement.

Any Member availing itself of the possibilities provided in Article 6 of the Berne Convention (1971) or paragraph 1(b) of Article 16 of the Rome Convention shall make a notification as foreseen in those provisions to the Council for TRIPS.

2. Members may avail themselves of the exceptions permitted under paragraph 1 in relation to judicial and administrative procedures, including the designation of an address for service or the appointment of an agent within the jurisdiction of a Member, only where such exceptions are necessary to secure compliance with laws and regulations which are not inconsistent with the provisions of this Agreement and where such practices are not applied in a manner which would constitute a disguised restriction on trade.

NOTES

[1] For the purposes of Articles 3 and 4, "protection" shall include matters affecting the availability, acquisition, scope, maintenance and enforcement of intellectual property rights as well as those matters affecting the use of intellectual property rights specifically addressed in this Agreement.

[9.267]
Article 4
Most-favoured-nation Treatment

With regard to the protection of intellectual property, any advantage, favour, privilege or immunity granted by a Member to the nationals of any other country shall be accorded immediately and unconditionally to the nationals of all other Members. Exempted from this obligation are any advantage, favour, privilege or immunity accorded by a Member—

(a) deriving from international agreements on judicial assistance or law enforcement of a general nature and not particularly confined to the protection of intellectual property;
(b) granted in accordance with the provisions of the Berne Convention (1971) or the Rome Convention authorising that the treatment accorded be a function not of national treatment but of the treatment accorded in another country;
(c) in respect of the rights of performers, producers of phonograms and broadcasting organisations not provided under this Agreement;
(d) deriving from international agreements related to the protection of intellectual property which entered into force prior to the entry into force of the WTO Agreement, provided that such agreements are notified to the Council for TRIPS and do not constitute all arbitrary or unjustifiable discrimination against nationals of other Members.

[9.268]
Article 5
Multilateral Agreements on Acquisition or Maintenance of Protection

The obligations under Articles 3 and 4 do not apply to procedures provided in multilateral agreements concluded under the auspices of WIPO relating to the acquisition or maintenance of intellectual property rights.

[9.269]
Article 6
Exhaustion

For the purposes of dispute settlement under this Agreement, subject to the provisions of Articles 3 and 4 nothing in this Agreement shall be used to address the issue of the exhaustion of intellectual property rights.

[9.270]
Article 7
Objectives

The protection and enforcement of intellectual property rights should contribute to the promotion of technological innovation and to the transfer and dissemination of technology, to the mutual advantage of producers and users of technological knowledge and in a manner conducive to social and economic welfare, and to a balance of rights and obligations.

[9.271]
Article 8
Principles

1. Members may, in formulating or amending their laws and regulations, adopt measures necessary to protect public health and nutrition, and to promote the public interest in sectors of vital importance to their socio-economic and technological development, provided that such measures are consistent with the provisions of this Agreement.

2. Appropriate measures, provided that they are consistent with the provisions of this Agreement, may be needed to prevent the abuse of intellectual property rights by right holders or the resort to practices which unreasonably restrain trade or adversely affect the international transfer of technology.

PART II
STANDARDS CONCERNING THE AVAILABILITY, SCOPE AND USE OF INTELLECTUAL PROPERTY RIGHTS

SECTION 1
COPYRIGHT AND RELATED RIGHTS

[9.272]
Article 9
Relation to the Berne Convention

1. Members shall comply with Articles 1 through 21 of the Berne Convention (1971) and the Appendix thereto. However, Members shall not have rights or obligations under this Agreement in respect of the rights conferred under Article 6*bis* of that Convention or of the rights derived therefrom.
2. Copyright protection shall extend to expressions and not to ideas, procedures, methods of operation or mathematical concepts as such.

[9.273]
Article 10
Computer Programs and Compilations of Data

1. Computer programs, whether in source or object code, shall be protected as literary works under the Berne Convention (1971).
2. Compilations of data or other material, whether in machine readable or other form, which by reason of the selection or arrangement of their contents constitute intellectual creations shall be protected as such. Such protection, which shall not extend to the data or material itself, shall be without prejudice to any copyright subsisting in the data or material itself.

[9.274]
Article 11
Rental Rights

In respect of at least computer programs and cinematographic works, a Member shall provide authors and their successors in title the right to authorise or to prohibit the commercial rental to the public of originals or copies of their copyright works. A Member shall be excepted from this obligation in respect of cinematographic works unless such rental has led to widespread copying of such works which is materially impairing the exclusive right of reproduction conferred in that Member on authors and their successors in title. In respect of computer programs, this obligation does not apply to rentals where the program itself is not the essential object of the rental.

[9.275]
Article 12
Term of Protection

Whenever the term of protection of a work, other than a photographic work or a work of applied art, is calculated on a basis other than the life of a natural person, such term shall be no less than 50 years from the end of the calendar year of authorised publication, or, failing such authorised publication within 50 years from the making of the work, 50 years from the end of the calendar year of making.

[9.276]
Article 13
Limitations and Exceptions

Members shall confine limitations or exceptions to exclusive rights to certain special cases which do not conflict with a normal exploitation of the work and do not unreasonably prejudice the legitimate interests of the right holder.

[9.277]
Article 14
Protection of Performers, Producers of Phonograms (Sound Recordings) and Broadcasting Organisations

1. In respect of a fixation of their performance on a phonogram, performers shall have the possibility of preventing the following acts when undertaken without their authorisation: the fixation of their unfixed performance and the reproduction of such fixation. Performers shall also have the possibility of preventing the following acts when undertaken without their authorisation: the broadcasting by wireless means and the communication to the public of their live performance.
2. Producers of phonograms shall enjoy the right to authorise or prohibit the direct or indirect reproduction of their phonograms.
3. Broadcasting organisations shall have the right to prohibit the following acts when undertaken without their authorisation: the fixation, the reproduction of fixations, and the rebroadcasting by wireless means of broadcasts, as well as the communication to the public of television broadcasts of

the same. Where Members do not grant such rights to broadcasting organisations, they shall provide owners of copyright in the subject matter of broadcasts with the possibility of preventing the above acts, subject to the provisions of the Berne Convention (1971).

4. The provisions of Article 11 in respect of computer programs shall apply *mutatis mutandis* to producers of phonograms and any other right holders in phonograms as determined in a Member's law. If on 15 April 1994 a Member has in force a system of equitable remuneration of right holders in respect of the rental of phonograms, it may maintain such system provided that the commercial rental of phonograms is not giving rise to the material impairment of the exclusive rights of reproduction of right holders.

5. The term of the protection available under this Agreement to performers and producers of phonograms shall last at least until the end of a period of 50 years computed from the end of the calendar year in which the fixation was made or the performance took place. The term of protection granted pursuant to paragraph 3 shall last for at least 20 years from the end of the calendar year in which the broadcast took place.

6. Any Member may, in relation to the rights conferred under paragraphs 1, 2 and 3, provide for conditions, limitations, exceptions and reservations to the extent permitted by the Rome Convention. However, the provisions of Article 18 of the Berne Convention (1971) shall also apply, *mutatis mutandis*, to the rights of performers and producers of phonograms in phonograms.

SECTION 2
TRADEMARKS

[9.278]
Article 15
Protectable Subject Matter

1. Any sign, or any combination of signs, capable of distinguishing the goods or services of one undertaking from those of other undertakings, shall be capable of constituting a trademark. Such signs, in particular words including personal names, letters, numerals, figurative elements and combinations of colours as well as any combination of such signs, shall be eligible for registration as trademarks. Where signs are not inherently capable of distinguishing the relevant goods or services, Members may make registrability depend on distinctiveness acquired through use. Members may require, as a condition of registration, that signs be visually perceptible.

2. Paragraph 1 shall not be understood to prevent a Member from denying registration of a trademark on other grounds, provided that they do not derogate from the provisions of the Paris Convention (1967).

3. Members may make registrability depend on use. However, actual use of a trademark shall not be a condition for filing an application for registration. An application shall not be refused solely on the ground that intended use has not taken place before the expiry of a period of three years from the date of application.

4. The nature of the goods or services to which a trademark is to be applied shall in no case form an obstacle to registration of the trademark.

5. Members shall publish each trademark either before it is registered or promptly after it is registered and shall afford a reasonable opportunity for petitions to cancel the registration. In addition, Members may afford an opportunity for the registration of a trademark to be opposed.

[9.279]
Article 16
Rights Conferred

1. The owner of a registered trademark shall have the exclusive right to prevent all third parties not having the owner's consent from using in the course of trade identical or similar signs for goods or services which are identical or similar to those in respect of which the trademark is registered where such use would result in a likelihood of confusion. In case of the use of an identical sign for identical goods or services, a likelihood of confusion shall be presumed. The rights described above shall not prejudice any existing prior rights, nor shall they affect the possibility of Members making rights available on the basis of use.

2. Article 6*bis* of the Paris Convention (1967) shall apply, *mutatis mutandis*, to services. In determining whether a trademark is well known, Members shall take account of the knowledge of the trademark in the relevant sector of the public, including knowledge in the Member concerned which has been obtained as a result of the promotion of the trademark.

3. Article 6*bis* of the Paris Convention (1967) shall apply, *mutatis mutandis*, to goods or services which are not similar to those in respect of which a trademark is registered, provided that use of that trademark in relation to those goods or services would indicate a connection between those goods or services and the owner of the registered trademark and provided that the interests of the owner of the registered trademark are likely to be damaged by such use.

[9.280]
Article 17
Exceptions

Members may provide limited exceptions to the rights conferred by a trademark, such as fair use of descriptive terms, provided that such exceptions take account of the legitimate interests of the owner of the trademark and of third parties.

[9.281]
Article 18
Term of Protection

Initial registration, and each renewal of registration, of a trademark shall be for a term of no less than seven years. The registration of a trademark shall be renewable indefinitely.

[9.282]
Article 19
Requirement of Use

1. If use is required to maintain a registration, the registration may be cancelled only after an uninterrupted period of at least three years of non-use, unless valid reasons based on the existence of obstacles to such use are shown by the trademark owner. Circumstances arising independently of the will of the owner of the trademark which constitute an obstacle to the use of the trademark, such as import restrictions on or other government requirements for goods or services protected by the trademark, shall be recognised as valid reasons for non-use.

2. When subject to the control of its owner, use of a trademark by another person shall be recognised as use of the trademark for the purpose of maintaining the registration.

[9.283]
Article 20
Other Requirements

The use of a trademark in the course of trade shall not be unjustifiably encumbered by special requirements, such as use with another trademark, use in a special form or use in a manner detrimental to its capability to distinguish the goods or services of one undertaking from those of other undertakings. This will not preclude a requirement prescribing the use of the trademark identifying the undertaking producing the goods or services along with, but without linking it to, the trademark distinguishing the specific goods or services in question of that undertaking.

[9.284]
Article 21
Licensing and Assignment

Members may determine conditions on the licensing and assignment of trademarks, it being understood that the compulsory licensing of trademarks shall not be permitted and that the owner of a registered trademark shall have the right to assign the trademark with or without the transfer of the business to which the trademark belongs.

SECTION 3
GEOGRAPHICAL INDICATIONS

[9.285]
Article 22
Protection of Geographical Indications

1. Geographical indications are, for the purposes of this Agreement, indications which identify a good as originating in the territory of a Member, or a region or locality in that territory, where a given quality, reputation or other characteristic of the good is essentially attributable to its geographical origin.

2. In respect of geographical indications, Members shall provide the legal means for interested parties to prevent—

(a) the use of any means in the designation or presentation of a good that indicates or suggests that the good in question originates in a geographical area other than the true place of origin in a manner which misleads the public as to the geographical origin of the good;

(b) any use which constitutes an act of unfair competition within the meaning of Article 10*bis* of the Paris Convention (1967).

3. A Member shall, *ex officio* if its legislation so permits or at the request of an interested party, refuse or invalidate the registration of a trademark which contains or consists of a geographical indication with respect to goods not originating in the territory indicated, if use of the indication in the trademark for such goods in that Member is of such a nature as to mislead the public as to the true place of origin.

4. The protection under paragraphs 1, 2 and 3 shall be applicable against a geographical indication which, although literally true as to the territory, region or locality in which the goods originate, falsely represents to the public that the goods originate in another territory.

[9.286]
Article 23
Additional Protection for Geographical Indications for Wines and Spirits

1. Each Member shall provide the legal means for interested parties to prevent use of a geographical indication identifying wines for wines not originating in the place indicated by the geographical indication in question or identifying spirits for spirits not originating in the place indicated by the geographical indication in question, even where the true origin of the goods is indicated or the geographical indication is used in translation or accompanied by expressions such as "kind", "type", "style", "imitation" or the like.[1]

2. The registration of a trademark for wines which contains or consists of a geographical indication identifying wines or for spirits which contains or consists of a geographical indication identifying spirits shall be refused or invalidated, *ex officio* if a Member's legislation so permits or at the request of an interested party, with respect to such wines or spirits not having this origin.

3. In the case of homonymous geographical indications for wines, protection shall be accorded to each indication, subject to the provisions of paragraph 4 of Article 22. Each Member shall determine the practical conditions under which the homonymous indications in question will be differentiated from each other, taking into account the need to ensure equitable treatment of the producers concerned and that consumers are not misled.

4. In order to facilitate the protection of geographical indications for wines, negotiations shall be undertaken in the Council for TRIPS concerning the establishment of a multilateral system of notification and registration of geographical indications for wines eligible for protection in those Members participating in the system.

NOTES

[1] Notwithstanding the first sentence of Article 42, Members may, with respect to these obligations, instead provide for enforcement by administrative action.

[9.287]
Article 24
International Negotiations: Exceptions

1. Members agree to enter into negotiations aimed at increasing the protection of individual geographical indications under Article 23. The provisions of paragraphs 4 through 8 below shall not be used by a Member to refuse to conduct negotiations or to conclude bilateral or multilateral agreements. In the context of such negotiations, Members shall be willing to consider the continued applicability of these provisions to individual geographical indications whose use was the subject of such negotiations.

2. The Council for TRIPS shall keep under review the application of the provisions of this Section: the first such review shall take place within two years of the entry into force of the WTO Agreement. Any matter affecting the compliance with the obligations under these provisions may be drawn to the attention of the Council, which, at the request of a Member, shall consult with any Member or Members in respect of such matter in respect of which it has not been possible to find a satisfactory solution through bilateral or plurilateral consultations between the Members concerned. The Council shall take such action as may be agreed to facilitate the operation and further the objectives of this Section.

3. In implementing this Section, a Member shall not diminish the protection of geographical indications that existed in that Member immediately prior to the date of entry into force of the WTO Agreement.

4. Nothing in this Section shall require a Member to prevent continued and similar use of a particular geographical indication of another Member identifying wines or spirits in connection with goods or services by any of its nationals or domiciliaries who have used that geographical indication in a continuous manner with regard to the same or related goods or services in the territory of that Member either (a) for at least 10 years preceding 15 April 1994 or (b) in good faith preceding that date.

5. Where a trademark has been applied for or registered in good faith, or where rights to a trademark have been acquired through use in good faith either—

(a) before the date of application of these provisions in that Member as defined in Part VI; or
(b) before the geographical indication is protected in its country of origin;

measures adopted to implement this Section shall not prejudice eligibility for or the validity of the registration of a trademark, or the right to use a trademark, on the basis that such a trademark is identical with, or similar to, a geographical indication.

6. Nothing in this Section shall require a Member to apply its provisions in respect of a geographical indication of any other Member with respect to goods or services for which the relevant indication is identical with the term customary in common language as the common name for such goods or services in the territory of that Member. Nothing in this Section shall require a Member to apply its provisions in respect of a geographical indication of any other Member with respect to products of the vine for which the relevant indication is identical with the customary name of a grape variety existing in the territory of that Member as of the date of entry into force of the WTO Agreement.

7. A Member may provide that any request made under this Section in connection with the use or registration of a trademark must be presented within five years after the adverse use of the protected indication has become generally known in that Member or after the date of registration of the trademark in that Member provided that the trademark has been published by that date, if such date is earlier than the date on which the adverse use became generally known in that Member, provided that the geographical indication is not used or registered in bad faith.
8. The provisions of this Section shall in no way prejudice the right of any person to use, in the course of trade, that person's name or the name of that person's predecessor in business, except where such name is used in such a manner as to mislead the public.
9. There shall be no obligation under this Agreement to protect geographical indications which are not or cease to be protected in their country of origin, or which have fallen in to disuse in that country.

SECTION 4
INDUSTRIAL DESIGNS

[9.288]
Article 25
Requirements for Protection
1. Members shall provide for the protection of independently created industrial designs that are new or original. Members may provide that designs are not new or original if they do not significantly differ from known designs or combinations of known design features. Members may provide that such protection shall not extend to designs dictated essentially by technical or functional considerations.
2. Each Member shall ensure that requirements for securing protection for textile designs, in particular in regard to any cost, examination or publication, do not unreasonably impair the opportunity to seek and obtain such protection. Members shall be free to meet this obligation through industrial design law or through copyright law.

[9.289]
Article 26
Protection
1. The owner of a protected industrial design shall have the right to prevent third parties not having the owner's consent from making, selling or importing articles bearing or embodying a design which is a copy, or substantially a copy, of the protected design, when such acts are undertaken for commercial purposes.
2. Members may provide limited exceptions to the protection of industrial designs, provided that such exceptions do not unreasonably conflict with the normal exploitation of protected industrial designs and do not unreasonably prejudice the legitimate interests of the owner of the protected design, taking account of the legitimate interests of third parties.
3. The duration of protection available shall amount to at least 10 years.

SECTION 5
PATENTS

[9.290]
Article 27
Patentable Subject Matter
1. Subject to the provisions of paragraphs 2 and 3, patents shall be available for any inventions, whether products or processes, in all fields of technology, provided that they are new, involve an inventive step and are capable of industrial application.[1] Subject to paragraph 4 of Article 65, paragraph 8 of Article 70 and paragraph 3 of this Article, patents shall be available and patent rights enjoyable without discrimination as to the place of invention, the field of technology and whether products are imported or locally produced.
2. Members may exclude from patentability inventions, the prevention within their territory of the commercial exploitation of which is necessary to protect *ordre public* or morality, including to protect human, animal or plant life or health or to avoid serious prejudice to the environment, provided that such exclusion is not made merely because the exploitation is prohibited by their law.
3. Members may also exclude from patentability—
(a) diagnostic, therapeutic and surgical methods for the treatment of humans or animals;
(b) plants and animals other than micro-organisms, and essentially biological processes for the production of plants or animals other than non-biological and microbiological processes. However, Members shall provide for the protection of plant varieties either by patents or by an effective *sui generis* system or by any combination thereof. The provisions of this subparagraph shall be reviewed four years after the date of entry into force of the WTO Agreement.

NOTES

[1] For the purposes of this Article, the terms "inventive step" and "capable of industrial application" may be deemed by a Member to be synonymous with the terms "non-obvious" and "useful" respectively.

[9.291]
Article 28
Rights Conferred

1. A patent shall confer on its owner the following exclusive rights—

(a) where the subject matter of a patent is a product, to prevent third parties not having the owner's consent from the acts of: making, using, offering for sale, selling, or importing[1] for these purposes that product;

(b) where the subject matter of a patent is a process, to prevent third parties not having the owner's consent from the act of using the process, and from the acts of: using, offering for sale, selling, or importing for these purposes at least the product obtained directly by that process.

2. Patent owners shall also have the right to assign, or transfer by succession, the patent and to conclude licensing contracts.

NOTES

[1] This right, like all other rights conferred under this Agreement in respect of the use, sale, importation or other distribution of goods, is subject to the provisions of Article 6.

[9.292]
Article 29
Conditions on Patent Applicants

1. Members shall require that an applicant for a patent shall disclose the invention in a manner sufficiently clear and complete for the invention to be carried out by a person skilled in the art and may require the applicant to indicate the best mode for carrying out the invention known to the inventor at the filing date or, where priority is claimed, at the priority date of the application.

2. Members may require an applicant for a patent to provide information concerning the applicant's corresponding foreign applications and grants.

[9.293]
Article 30
Exceptions to Rights Conferred

Members may provide limited exceptions to the exclusive rights conferred by a patent, provided that such exceptions do not unreasonably conflict with a normal exploitation of the patent and do not unreasonably prejudice the legitimate interests of the patent owner, taking account of the legitimate interests of third parties.

[9.294]
Article 31
Other Use Without Authorisation of the Right Holder

Where the law of a Member allows for other use[1] of the subject matter of a patent without the authorisation of the right holder, including use by the government or third parties authorised by the government, the following provisions shall be respected—

(a) authorisation of such use shall be considered on its individual merits;

(b) such use may only be permitted if, prior to such use, the proposed user has made efforts to obtain authorisation from the right holder on reasonable commercial terms and conditions and that such efforts have not been successful within a reasonable period of time. This requirement may be waived by a Member in the case of a national emergency or other circumstances of extreme urgency or in cases of public non-commercial use. In situations of national emergency or other circumstances of extreme urgency, the right holder shall, nevertheless, be notified as soon as reasonably practicable. In the case of public non-commercial use, where the government or contractor, without making a patent search, knows or has demonstrable grounds to know that a valid patent is or will be used by or for the government, the right holder shall be informed promptly;

(c) the scope and duration of such use shall be limited to the purpose for which it was authorised, and in the case of semi-conductor technology shall only be for public non-commercial use or to remedy a practice determined after judicial or administrative process to be anti-competitive;

(d) such use shall be non-exclusive;

(e) such use shall be non-assignable, except with that part of the enterprise or goodwill which enjoys such use;

(f) any such use shall be authorised predominantly for the supply of the domestic market of the Member authorising such use;

(g) authorisation for such use shall be liable, subject to adequate protection of the legitimate interests of the persons so authorised, to be terminated if and when the circumstances which led to it cease to exist and are unlikely to recur. The competent authority shall have the authority to review, upon motivated request, the continued existence of these circumstances;
(h) the right holder shall be paid adequate remuneration in the circumstances of each case, taking into account the economic value of the authorisation;
(i) the legal validity of any decision relating to the authorisation of such use shall be subject to judicial review or other independent review by a distinct higher authority in that Member;
(j) any decision relating to the remuneration provided in respect of such use shall be subject to judicial review or other independent review by a distinct higher authority in that Member;
(k) Members are not obliged to apply the conditions set forth in subparagraphs (b) and (f) where such use is permitted to remedy a practice determined after judicial or administrative process to be anti-competitive. The need to correct anti-competitive practices may be taken into account in determining the amount of remuneration in such cases. Competent authorities shall have the authority to refuse termination of authorisation if and when the conditions which led to such authorisation are likely to recur;
(l) where such use is authorised to permit the exploitation of a patent ("the second patent") which cannot be exploited without infringing another patent ("the first patent"), the following additional conditions shall apply—
  (i) the invention claimed in the second patent shall involve an important technical advance of considerable economic significance in relation to the invention claimed in the first patent;
  (ii) the owner of the first patent shall be entitled to a cross-licence on reasonable terms to use the invention claimed in the second patent; and
  (iii) the use authorised in respect of the first patent shall be non-assignable except with the assignment of the second patent.

NOTES

[1] "Other use" refers to use other than that allowed under Article 30.

[9.295]
[Article 31bis

1. The obligations of an exporting Member under Article 31(f) shall not apply with respect to the grant by it of a compulsory licence to the extent necessary for the purposes of production of a pharmaceutical product(s) and its export to an eligible importing Member(s) in accordance with the terms set out in paragraph 2 of the Annex to this Agreement.
2. Where a compulsory licence is granted by an exporting Member under the system set out in this Article and the Annex to this Agreement, adequate remuneration pursuant to Article 31(h) shall be paid in that Member taking into account the economic value to the importing Member of the use that has been authorized in the exporting Member. Where a compulsory licence is granted for the same products in the eligible importing Member, the obligation of that Member under Article 31(h) shall not apply in respect of those products for which remuneration in accordance with the first sentence of this paragraph is paid in the exporting Member.
3. With a view to harnessing economies of scale for the purposes of enhancing purchasing power for, and facilitating the local production of, pharmaceutical products: where a developing or least developed country WTO Member is a party to a regional trade agreement within the meaning of Article XXIV of the GATT 1994 and the Decision of 28 November 1979 on Differential and More Favourable Treatment Reciprocity and Fuller Participation of Developing Countries (L/4903), at least half of the current membership of which is made up of countries presently on the United Nations list of least developed countries, the obligation of that Member under Article 31(f) shall not apply to the extent necessary to enable a pharmaceutical product produced or imported under a compulsory licence in that Member to be exported to the markets of those other developing or least developed country parties to the regional trade agreement that share the health problem in question. It is understood that this will not prejudice the territorial nature of the patent rights in question.
4. Members shall not challenge any measures taken in conformity with the provisions of this Article and the Annex to this Agreement under subparagraphs 1(b) and 1(c) of Article XXIII of GATT 1994.
5. This Article and the Annex to this Agreement are without prejudice to the rights, obligations and flexibilities that Members have under the provisions of this Agreement other than paragraphs (f) and (h) of Article 31, including those reaffirmed by the Declaration on the TRIPS Agreement and Public Health (WT/MIN(01)/DEC/2), and to their interpretation. They are also without prejudice to the extent to which pharmaceutical products produced under a compulsory licence can be exported under the provisions of Article 31(f).]

NOTES

Inserted following a Decision of the General Council of the WTO in document WT/L/641 on 6 December 2005. Members had until 31 December 2009 to accept this amendment.

[9.296]
Article 32
Revocation/forfeiture

An opportunity for judicial review of any decision to revoke or forfeit a patent shall be available.

[9.297]
Article 33
Term of Protection

The term of protection available shall not end before the expiration of a period of twenty years counted from the filing date.[1]

NOTES

[1] It is understood that those Members which do not have a system of original grant may provide that the term of protection shall be computed from the filing date in the system of original grant.

[9.298]
Article 34
Process Patents: Burden of Proof

1. For the purposes of civil proceedings in respect of the infringement of the rights of the owner referred to in paragraph 1(b) of Article 28, if the subject matter of a patent is a process for obtaining a product, the judicial authorities shall have the authority to order the defendant to prove that the process to obtain an identical product is different from the patented process. Therefore, Members shall provide, in at least one of the following circumstances, that any identical product when produced without the consent of the patent owner shall, in the absence of proof to the contrary, be deemed to have been obtained by the patented process—

(a) if the product obtained by the patented process is new;

(b) if there is a substantial likelihood that the identical product was made by the process and the owner of the patent has been unable through reasonable efforts to determine the process actually used.

2. Any Member shall be free to provide that the burden of proof indicated in paragraph 1 shall be on the alleged infringer only if the condition referred to in subparagraph (a) is fulfilled or only if the condition referred to in subparagraph (b) is fulfilled.

3. In the adduction of proof to the contrary, the legitimate interests of defendants in protecting their manufacturing and business secrets shall be taken into account.

SECTION 6
LAYOUT-DESIGNS (TOPOGRAPHIES) OF INTEGRATED CIRCUITS

[9.299]
Article 35
Relation to the IPIC Treaty

Members agree to provide protection to the layout-designs (topographies) of integrated circuits (referred to in this Agreement as "layout designs") in accordance with Articles 2 through 7 (other than paragraph 3 of Article 6), Article 12 and paragraph 3 of Article 16 of the Treaty on Intellectual Property in Respect of Integrated Circuits and, in addition, to comply with the following provisions.

[9.300]
Article 36
Scope of the Protection

Subject to the provisions of paragraph 1 of Article 37, Members shall consider unlawful the following acts if performed without the authorisation of the right holder:[1] importing, selling, or otherwise distributing for commercial purposes a protected layout-design, an integrated circuit in which a protected layout-design is incorporated, or an article incorporating such an integrated circuit only in so far as it continues to contain an unlawfully reproduced layout-design.

NOTES

[1] The term "right holder" in this Section shall be understood as having the same meaning as the term "holder of the right" in the IPIC Treaty.

[9.301]
Article 37
Acts Not Requiring the Authorisation of the Right Holder

1. Notwithstanding Article 36, no Member shall consider unlawful the performance of any of the acts referred to in that Article in respect of an integrated circuit incorporating an unlawfully reproduced layout-design or any article incorporating such an integrated circuit where the person performing or ordering such acts did not know and had no reasonable ground to know, when acquiring the integrated circuit or article incorporating such an integrated circuit, that it incorporated an unlawfully reproduced layout-design. Members shall provide that, after the time that such person has received sufficient notice that the layout-design was unlawfully reproduced,

that person may perform any of the acts with respect to the stock on hand or ordered before such time, but shall be liable to pay to the right holder a sum equivalent to a reasonable royalty such as would be payable under a freely negotiated licence in respect of such a layout-design.
2. The conditions set out in subparagraphs (a) through (k) of Article 31 shall apply *mutatis mutandis* in the event of any non-voluntary licensing of a layout-design or of its use by or for the government without the authorisation of the right holder.

[9.302]
Article 38
Term of Protection
1. In Members requiring registration as a condition of protection, the term of protection of layout-designs shall not end before the expiration of a period of 10 years counted from the date of filing an application for registration or from the first commercial exploitation wherever in the world it occurs.
2. In Members not requiring registration as a condition for protection, layout-designs shall be protected for a term of no less than 10 years from the date of the first commercial exploitation wherever in the world it occurs.
3. Notwithstanding paragraphs 1 and 2, a Member may provide that protection shall lapse 15 years after the creation of the layout-design.

SECTION 7
PROTECTION OF UNDISCLOSED INFORMATION

[9.303]
Article 39
1. In the course of ensuring effective protection against unfair competition as provided in Article 10*bis* of the Paris Convention (1967), Members shall protect undisclosed information in accordance with paragraph 2 and data submitted to governments or governmental agencies in accordance with paragraph 3.
2. Natural and legal persons shall havc the possibility of preventing information lawfully within their control from being disclosed to, acquired by, or used by others without their consent in a manner contrary to honest commercial practices[1] so long as such information—
(a) is secret in the sense that it is not, as a body or in the precise configuration and assembly of its components, generally known among or readily accessible to persons within the circles that normally deal with the kind of information in question;
(b) has commercial value because it is secret; and
(c) has been subject to reasonable steps under the circumstances, by the person lawfully in control of the information, to keep it secret.
3. Members, when requiring, as a condition of approving the marketing of pharmaceutical or of agricultural chemical products which utilise new chemical entities, the submission of undisclosed test or other data, the origination of which involves a considerable effort, shall protect such data against unfair commercial use. In addition, Members shall protect such data against disclosure, except where necessary to protect the public, or unless steps are taken to ensure that the data are protected against unfair commercial use.

NOTES

[1] For the purpose of this provision, "a manner contrary to honest commercial practices" shall mean at least practices such as breach of contract, breach of confidence and inducement to breach, and includes the acquisition of undisclosed information by third parties who knew, or were grossly negligent in failing to know, that such practices were involved in the acquisition.

SECTION 8
CONTROL OF ANTI-COMPETITIVE PRACTICES IN CONTRACTUAL LICENCES

[9.304]
Article 40
1. Members agree that some licensing practices or conditions pertaining to intellectual property rights which restrain competition may have adverse effects on trade and may impede the transfer and dissemination of technology.
2. Nothing in this Agreement shall prevent Members from specifying in their legislation licensing practices or conditions that may in particular cases constitute an abuse of intellectual property rights having an adverse effect on competition in the relevant market. As provided above, a Member may adopt, consistently with the other provisions of this Agreement, appropriate measures to prevent or control such practices, which may include for example exclusive grantback conditions, conditions preventing challenges to validity and coercive package licensing, in the light of the relevant laws and regulations of that Member.
3. Each Member shall enter, upon request, into consultations with any other Member which has cause to believe that an intellectual property right owner that is a national or domiciliary of the Member to which the request for consultations has been addressed is undertaking practices in

violation of the requesting Member's laws and regulations on the subject matter of this Section, and which wishes to secure compliance with such legislation, without prejudice to any action under the law and to the full freedom of an ultimate decision of either Member. The Member addressed shall accord full and sympathetic consideration to, and shall afford adequate opportunity for, consultations with the requesting Member, and shall cooperate through supply of publicly available non-confidential information of relevance to the matter in question and of other information available to the Member, subject to domestic law and to the conclusion of mutually satisfactory agreements concerning the safeguarding of its confidentiality by the requesting Member.

4. A Member whose nationals or domiciliaries are subject to proceedings in another Member concerning alleged violation of that other Member's laws and regulations on the subject matter of this Section shall, upon request, be granted an opportunity for consultations by the other Member under the same conditions as those foreseen in paragraph 3.

PART III
ENFORCEMENT OF INTELLECTUAL PROPERTY RIGHTS

SECTION 1
GENERAL OBLIGATIONS

[9.305]
Article 41

1. Members shall ensure that enforcement procedures as specified in this Part are available under their law so as to permit effective action against any act of infringement of intellectual property rights covered by this Agreement, including expeditious remedies to prevent infringements and remedies which constitute a deterrent to further infringements. These procedures shall be applied in such a manner as to avoid the creation of barriers to legitimate trade and to provide for safeguards against their abuse.

2. Procedures concerning the enforcement of intellectual property rights shall be fair and equitable. They shall not be unnecessarily complicated or costly, or entail unreasonable time-limits or unwarranted delays.

3. Decisions on the merits of a case shall preferably be in writing and reasoned. They shall be made available at least to the parties to the proceeding without undue delay. Decisions on the merits of a case shall be based only on evidence in respect of which parties were offered the opportunity to be heard.

4. Parties to a proceeding shall have an opportunity for review by a judicial authority of final administrative decisions and, subject to jurisdictional provisions in a Member's law concerning the importance of a case, of at least the legal aspects of initial judicial decisions on the merits of a case. However, there shall be no obligation to provide an opportunity for review of acquittals in criminal cases.

5. It is understood that this Part does not create any obligation to put in place a judicial system for the enforcement of intellectual property rights distinct from that for the enforcement of law in general, nor does it affect the capacity of Members to enforce their law in general. Nothing in this Part creates any obligation with respect to the distribution of resources as between enforcement of intellectual property rights and the enforcement of law in general.

SECTION 2
CIVIL AND ADMINISTRATIVE PROCEDURES AND REMEDIES

[9.306]
Article 42
Fair and Equitable Procedures

Members shall make available to right holders[1] civil judicial procedures concerning the enforcement of any intellectual property right covered by this Agreement. Defendants shall have the right to written notice which is timely and contains sufficient detail, including the basis of the claims. Parties shall be allowed to be represented by independent legal counsel, and procedures shall not impose overly burdensome requirements concerning mandatory personal appearances. All parties to such procedures shall be duly entitled to substantiate their claims and to present all relevant evidence. The procedure shall provide a means to identify and protect confidential information, unless this would be contrary to existing constitutional requirements.

NOTES

1 For the purpose of this Part, the term "right holder" includes federations and associations having legal standing to assert such rights.

[9.307]
Article 43
Evidence

1. The judicial authorities shall have the authority, where a party has presented reasonably available evidence sufficient to support its claims and has specified evidence relevant to substantiation of its claims which lies in the control of the opposing party, to order that this evidence be produced by the opposing party, subject in appropriate cases to conditions which ensure the protection of confidential information.

2. In cases in which a party to a proceeding voluntarily and without good reason refuses access to, or otherwise does not provide necessary information within a reasonable period, or significantly impedes a procedure relating to an enforcement action, a Member may accord judicial authorities the authority to make preliminary and final determinations, affirmative or negative, on the basis of the information presented to them, including the complaint or the allegation presented by the party adversely affected by the denial of access to information, subject to providing the parties an opportunity to be heard on the allegations or evidence.

[9.308]
Article 44
Injunctions

1. The judicial authorities shall have the authority to order a party to desist from an infringement, *inter alia* to prevent the entry into the channels of commerce in their jurisdiction of imported goods that involve the infringement of an intellectual property right, immediately after customs clearance of such goods. Members are not obliged to accord such authority in respect of protected subject matter acquired or ordered by a person prior to knowing or having reasonable grounds to know that dealing in such subject matter would entail the infringement of an intellectual property right.

2. Notwithstanding the other provisions of this Part and provided that the provisions of Part II specifically addressing use by governments, or by third parties authorised by a government, without the authorisation of the right holder are complied with, Members may limit the remedies available against such use to payment of remuneration in accordance with subparagraph (h) of Article 31. In other cases, the remedies under this Part shall apply or, where these remedies are inconsistent with a Member's law, declaratory judgments and adequate compensation shall be available.

[9.309]
Article 45
Damages

1. The judicial authorities shall have the authority to order the infringer to pay the right holder damages adequate to compensate for the injury the right holder has suffered because of an infringement of that person's intellectual property right by an infringer who knowingly, or with reasonable grounds to know, engaged in infringing activity.

2. The judicial authorities shall also have the authority to order the infringer to pay the right holder expenses, which may include appropriate attorney's fees. In appropriate cases, Members may authorise the judicial authorities to order recovery of profits and/or payment of pre-established damages even where the infringer did not knowingly, or with reasonable grounds to know, engage in infringing activity.

[9.310]
Article 46
Other Remedies

In order to create an effective deterrent to infringement, the judicial authorities shall have the authority to order that goods that they have found to be infringing be, without compensation of any sort, disposed of outside the channels of commerce in such a manner as to avoid any harm caused to the right holder, or, unless this would be contrary to existing constitutional requirements, destroyed. The judicial authorities shall also have the authority to order that materials and implements the predominant use of which has been in the creation of infringing goods be, without compensation of any sort, disposed of outside the channels of commerce in such a manner as to minimise the risks of further infringements. In considering such requests, the need for proportionality between the seriousness of the infringement and the remedies ordered as well as the interests of third parties shall be taken into account. In regard to counterfeit trademark goods, the simple removal of the trademark unlawfully affixed shall not be sufficient, other than in exceptional cases, to permit release of the goods into the channels of commerce.

[9.311]
Article 47
Right of Information

Members may provide that the judicial authorities shall have the authority, unless this would be out of proportion to the seriousness of the infringement, to order the infringer to inform the right holder of the identity of third persons involved in the production and distribution of the infringing goods or services and of their channels of distribution.

[9.312]
Article 48
Indemnification of the Defendant

1. The judicial authorities shall have the authority to order a party at whose request measures were taken and who has abused enforcement procedures to provide to a party wrongfully enjoined or restrained adequate compensation for the injury suffered because of such abuse. The judicial authorities shall also have the authority to order the applicant to pay the defendant expenses, which may include appropriate attorney's fees.

2. In respect of the administration of any law pertaining to the protection or enforcement of intellectual property rights, Members shall only exempt both public authorities and officials from liability to appropriate remedial measures where actions are taken or intended in good faith in the course of the administration of that law.

[9.313]
Article 49
Administrative Procedures

To the extent that any civil remedy can be ordered as a result of administrative procedures on the merits of a case, such procedures shall conform to principles equivalent in substance to those set forth in this Section.

SECTION 3
PROVISIONAL MEASURES

[9.314]
Article 50

1. The judicial authorities shall have the authority to order prompt and effective provisional measures—
   (a) to prevent an infringement of any intellectual property right from occurring, and in particular to prevent the entry into the channels of commerce in their jurisdiction of goods, including imported goods immediately after customs clearance;
   (b) to preserve relevant evidence in regard to the alleged infringement.

2. The judicial authorities shall have the authority to adopt provisional measures *inaudita altera parte* where appropriate, in particular where any delay is likely to cause irreparable harm to the right holder, or where there is a demonstrable risk of evidence being destroyed.

3. The judicial authorities shall have the authority to require the applicant to provide any reasonably available evidence in order to satisfy themselves with a sufficient degree of certainty that the applicant is the right holder and that the applicant's right is being infringed or that such infringement is imminent, and to order the applicant to provide a security or equivalent assurance sufficient to protect the defendant and to prevent abuse.

4. Where provisional measures have been adopted *inaudita altera parte*, the parties affected shall be given notice, without delay after the execution of the measures at the latest. A review, including a right to be heard, shall take place upon request of the defendant with a view to deciding, within a reasonable period after the notification of the measures, whether these measures shall be modified, revoked or confirmed.

5. The applicant may be required to supply other information necessary for the identification of the goods concerned by the authority that will execute the provisional measures.

6. Without prejudice to paragraph 4, provisional measures taken on the basis of paragraphs 1 and 2 shall, upon request by the defendant, be revoked or otherwise cease to have effect, if proceedings leading to a decision on the merits of the case are not initiated within a reasonable period, to be determined by the judicial authority ordering the measures where a Member's law so permits or, in the absence of such a determination, not to exceed 20 working days or 31 calendar days, whichever is the longer.

7. Where the provisional measures are revoked or where they lapse due to any act or omission by the applicant, or where it is subsequently found that there has been no infringement or threat of infringement of an intellectual property right, the judicial authorities shall have the authority to order the applicant, upon request of the defendant, to provide the defendant appropriate compensation for any injury caused by these measures.

8. To the extent that any provisional measure can be ordered as a result of administrative procedures, such procedures shall conform to principles equivalent in substance to those set forth in this Section.

SECTION 4
SPECIAL REQUIREMENTS RELATED TO BORDER MEASURES[1]

NOTES

1 Where a Member has dismantled substantially all controls over movement of goods across its border with another Member with which it forms part of a customs union, it shall not be required to apply the provisions of this Section at that border.

[9.315]
Article 51
Suspension of Release by Customs Authorities

Members shall, in conformity with the provisions set out below, adopt procedures[1] to enable a right holder, who has valid grounds for suspecting that the importation of counterfeit trademark or pirated copyright goods[2] may take place, to lodge an application in writing with competent authorities, administrative or judicial, for the suspension by the customs authorities of the release into free circulation of such goods. Members may enable such an application to be made in respect of goods which involve other infringements of intellectual property rights, provided that the requirements of this Section are met. Members may also provide for corresponding procedures concerning the suspension by the customs authorities of the release of infringing goods destined for exportation from their territories.

NOTES

1 It is understood that there shall be no obligation to apply such procedures to imports of goods put on the market in another country by or with the consent of the right holder, or to goods in transit.

2 For the purposes of this Agreement—

(a) "counterfeit trademark goods" shall mean any goods, including packaging, bearing without authorisation a trademark which is identical to the trademark validly registered in respect of such goods, or which cannot be distinguished in its essential aspects from such a trademark, and which thereby infringes the rights of the owner of the trademark in question under the law of the country of importation;

(b) "pirated copyright goods" shall mean any goods which are copies made without the consent of the right holder or person duly authorised by the right holder in the country of production and which are made directly or indirectly from an article where the making of that copy would have constituted an infringement of a copyright or a related right under the law of the country of importation.

[9.316]
Article 52
Application

Any right holder initiating the procedures under Article 51 shall be required to provide adequate evidence to satisfy the competent authorities that, under the laws of the country of importation, there is *prima facie* an infringement of the right holder's intellectual property right and to supply a sufficiently detailed description of the goods to make them readily recognisable by the customs authorities. The competent authorities shall inform the applicant within a reasonable period whether they have accepted the application and, where determined by the competent authorities, the period for which the customs authorities will take action.

[9.317]
Article 53
Security or Equivalent Assurance

1. The competent authorities shall have the authority to require an applicant to provide a security or equivalent assurance sufficient to protect the defendant and the competent authorities and to prevent abuse. Such security or equivalent assurance shall not unreasonably deter recourse to these procedures.

2. Where pursuant to an application under this Section the release of goods involving industrial designs, patents, layout-designs or undisclosed information into free circulation has been suspended by customs authorities on the basis of a decision other than by a judicial or other independent authority, and the period provided for in Article 55 has expired without the granting of provisional relief by the duly empowered authority, and provided that all other conditions for importation have been complied with, the owner, importer, or consignee of such goods shall be entitled to their release on the posting of a security in an amount sufficient to protect the right holder for any infringement. Payment of such security shall not prejudice any other remedy available to the right holder, it being understood that the security shall be released if the right holder fails to pursue the right of action within a reasonable period of time.

[9.318]
Article 54
Notice of Suspension

The importer and the applicant shall be promptly notified of the suspension of the release of goods according to Article 51.

[9.319]
Article 55
Duration of Suspension

If, within a period not exceeding 10 working days after the applicant has been served notice of the suspension, the customs authorities have not been informed that proceedings leading to a decision on the merits of the case have been initiated by a party other than the defendant, or that the duly empowered authority has taken provisional measures prolonging the suspension of the release of the goods, the goods shall be released, provided that all other conditions for importation or exportation have been complied with: in appropriate cases, this time-limit may be extended by another 10 working days. If proceedings leading to a decision on the merits of the case have been initiated, a review, including a right to be heard, shall take place upon request of the defendant with a view to deciding, within a reasonable period, whether these measures shall be modified, revoked or confirmed. Notwithstanding the above, where the suspension of the release of goods is carried out or continued in accordance with a provisional judicial measure, the provisions of paragraph 6 of Article 50 shall apply.

[9.320]
Article 56
Indemnification of the importer and of the Owner of the Goods
Relevant authorities shall have the authority to order the applicant to pay the importer, the consignee and the owner of the goods appropriate compensation for any injury caused to them through the wrongful detention of goods or through the detention of goods released pursuant to Article 55.

[9.321]
Article 57
Right of inspection and Information
Without prejudice to the protection of confidential information, Members shall provide the competent authorities the authority to give the right holder sufficient opportunity to have any goods detained by the customs authorities inspected in order to substantiate the right holder's claims. The competent authorities shall also have authority to give the importer an equivalent opportunity to have any such goods inspected. Where a positive determination has been made on the merits of a case, Members may provide the competent authorities the authority to inform the right holder of the names and addresses of the consignor, the importer and the consignee and of the quantity of the goods in question.

[9.322]
Article 58
Ex Officio Action
Where Members require competent authorities to act upon their own initiative and to suspend the release of goods in respect of which they have acquired *prima facie* evidence that an intellectual property right is being infringed—

(a) the competent authorities may at any time seek from the right holder any information that may assist them to exercise these powers;
(b) the importer and the right holder shall be promptly notified of the suspension. Where the importer has lodged an appeal against the suspension with the competent authorities, the suspension shall be subject to the conditions, *mutatis mutandis,* set out at Article 55;
(c) Members shall only exempt both public authorities and officials from liability to appropriate remedial measures where actions are taken or intended in good faith.

[9.323]
Article 59
Remedies
Without prejudice to other rights of action open to the right holder and subject to the right of the defendant to seek review by a judicial authority, competent authorities shall have the authority to order the destruction or disposal of infringing goods in accordance with the principles set out in Article 46. In regard to counterfeit trademark goods, the authorities shall not allow the re-exportation of the infringing goods in an unaltered state or subject them to a different customs procedure, other than in exceptional circumstances.

[9.324]
Article 60
De Minimis imports
Members may exclude from the application of the above provisions small quantities of goods of a non-commercial nature contained in travellers' personal luggage or sent in small consignments.

SECTION 5
CRIMINAL PROCEDURES

[9.325]
Article 61
Members shall provide for criminal procedures and penalties to be applied at least in cases of wilful trademark counterfeiting or copyright piracy on a commercial scale. Remedies available shall include imprisonment and/or monetary fines sufficient to provide a deterrent, consistently with the level of penalties applied for crimes of a corresponding gravity. In appropriate cases, remedies available shall also include the seizure, forfeiture and destruction of the infringing goods and of any materials and implements the predominant use of which has been in the commission of the offence.

Members may provide for criminal procedures and penalties to be applied in other cases of infringement of intellectual property rights, in particular where they are committed wilfully and on a commercial scale.

PART IV
ACQUISITION AND MAINTENANCE OF INTELLECTUAL PROPERTY RIGHTS AND RELATED INTER PARTES PROCEDURES

[9.326]
Article 62

1. Members may require, as a condition of the acquisition or maintenance of the intellectual property rights provided for under Sections 2 through 6 of Part II, compliance with reasonable procedures and formalities. Such procedures and formalities shall be consistent with the provisions of this Agreement.
2. Where the acquisition of an intellectual property right is subject to the right being granted or registered, Members shall ensure that the procedures for grant or registration, subject to compliance with the substantive conditions for acquisition of the right, permit the granting or registration of the right within a reasonable period of time so as to avoid unwarranted curtailment of the period of protection.
3. Article 4 of the Paris Convention (1967) shall apply *mutatis mutandis* to service marks.
4. Procedures concerning the acquisition or maintenance of intellectual property rights and, where a Member's law provides for such procedures, administrative revocation and *inter partes* procedures such as opposition, revocation and cancellation, shall be governed by the general principles set out in paragraphs 2 and 3 of Article 41.
5. Final administrative decisions in any of the procedures referred to under paragraph 4 shall be subject to review by a judicial or quasi-judicial authority. However, there shall be no obligation to provide an opportunity for such review of decisions in cases of unsuccessful opposition or administrative revocation, provided that the grounds for such procedures can be the subject of invalidation procedures.

PART V
DISPUTE PREVENTION AND SETTLEMENT

[9.327]
Article 63
Transparency

1. Laws and regulations, and final judicial decisions and administrative rulings of general application, made effective by a Member pertaining to the subject matter of this Agreement (the availability, scope, acquisition, enforcement and prevention of the abuse of intellectual property rights) shall be published, or where such publication is not practicable made publicly available, in a national language, in such a manner as to enable governments and right holders to become acquainted with them. Agreements concerning the subject matter of this Agreement which are in force between the government or a governmental agency of a Member and the government or a governmental agency of another Member shall also be published.
2. Members shall notify the laws and regulations referred to in paragraph 1 to the Council for TRIPS in order to assist that Council in its review of the operation of this Agreement. The Council shall attempt to minimise the burden on Members in carrying out this obligation and may decide to waive the obligation to notify such laws and regulations directly to the Council if consultations with WIPO on the establishment of a common register containing these laws and regulations are successful. The Council shall also consider in this connection any action required regarding notifications pursuant to the obligations under this Agreement stemming from the provisions of Article 6*ter* of the Paris Convention (1967).
3. Each Member shall be prepared to supply, in response to a written request from another Member, information of the sort referred to in paragraph 1. A Member, having reason to believe that a specific judicial decision or administrative ruling or bilateral agreement in the area of intellectual property rights affects its rights under this Agreement, may also request in writing to be given access to or be informed in sufficient detail of such specific judicial decisions or administrative rulings or bilateral agreements.
4. Nothing in paragraphs 1, 2 and 3 shall require Members to disclose confidential information which would impede law enforcement or otherwise be contrary to the public interest or would prejudice the legitimate commercial interests of particular enterprises, public or private.

[9.328]
Article 64
Dispute Settlement

1. The provisions of Articles XXII and XXIII of GATT 1994 as elaborated and applied by the Dispute Settlement Understanding shall apply to consultations and the settlement of disputes under this Agreement except as otherwise specifically provided herein.

2. Subparagraphs 1(b) and 1(c) of Article XXIII of GATT 1994 shall not apply to the settlement of disputes under this Agreement for a period of five years from the date of entry into force of the WTO Agreement.
3. During the time period referred to in paragraph 2, the Council for TRIPS shall examine the scope and modalities for complaints of the type provided for under subparagraphs 1(b) and 1(c) of Article XXIII of GATT 1994 made pursuant to this Agreement, and submit its recommendations to the Ministerial Conference for approval. Any decision of the Ministerial Conference to approve such recommendations or to extend the period in paragraph 2 shall be made only by consensus, and approved recommendations shall be effective for all Members without further formal acceptance process.

PART VI
TRANSITIONAL ARRANGEMENTS

[9.329]
Article 65
Transitional Arrangements

1. Subject to the provisions of paragraphs 2, 3 and 4, no Member shall be obliged to apply the provisions of this Agreement before the expiry of a general period of one year following the date of entry into force of the WTO Agreement.
2. A developing country Member is entitled to delay for a further period of four years the date of application, as defined in paragraph 1, of the provisions of this Agreement other than Articles 3, 4 and 5.
3. Any other Member which is in the process of transformation from a centrally-planned into a market, free-enterprise economy and which is undertaking structural reform of its intellectual property system and facing special problems in the preparation and implementation of intellectual property laws and regulations, may also benefit from a period of delay as foreseen in paragraph 2.
4. To the extent that a developing country Member is obliged by this Agreement to extend product patent protection to areas of technology not so protectable in its territory on the general date of application of this Agreement for that Member, as defined in paragraph 2, it may delay the application of the provisions on product patents of Section 5 of Part II to such areas of technology for an additional period of five years.
5. A Member availing itself of a transitional period under paragraphs 1, 2, 3 or 4 shall ensure that any changes in its laws, regulations and practice made during that period do not result in a lesser degree of consistency with the provisions of this Agreement.

[9.330]
Article 66
Least-developed Country Members

1. In view of the special needs and requirements of least-developed country Members, their economic, financial and administrative constraints, and their need for flexibility to create a viable technological base, such Members shall not be required to apply the provisions of this Agreement, other than Articles 3, 4 and 5, for a period of 10 years from the date of application as defined under paragraph 1 of Article 65. The Council for TRIPS shall, upon duly motivated request by a least-developed country Member, accord extensions of this period.
2. Developed country Members shall provide incentives to enterprises and institutions in their territories for the purpose of promoting and encouraging technology transfer to least-developed country Members in order to enable them to create a sound and viable technological base.

[9.331]
Article 67
Technical Cooperation

In order to facilitate the implementation of this Agreement, developed country Members shall provide, on request and on mutually agreed terms and conditions, technical and financial cooperation in favour of developing and least-developed country Members. Such cooperation shall include assistance in the preparation of laws and regulations on the protection and enforcement of intellectual property rights as well as on the prevention of their abuse, and shall include support regarding the establishment or reinforcement of domestic offices and agencies relevant to these matters, including the training of personnel.

PART VII
INSTITUTIONAL ARRANGEMENTS: FINAL PROVISIONS

[9.332]
Article 68
Council for Trade-related Aspects of Intellectual Property Rights

The Council for TRIPS shall monitor the operation of this Agreement and, in particular, Members' compliance with their obligations hereunder, and shall afford Members the opportunity of consulting on matters relating to the trade-related aspects of intellectual property rights. It shall carry out such other responsibilities as assigned to it by the Members, and it shall, in particular, provide any assistance requested by them in the context of dispute settlement procedures. In carrying out its functions, the Council for TRIPS may consult with and seek information from any source it deems appropriate. In consultation with WIPO, the Council shall seek to establish, within one year of its first meeting, appropriate arrangements for cooperation with bodies of that Organisation.

[9.333]
Article 69
International Cooperation

Members agree to cooperate with each other with a view to eliminating international trade in goods infringing intellectual property rights. For this purpose, they shall establish and notify contact points in their administrations and be ready to exchange information on trade in infringing goods. They shall, in particular, promote the exchange of information and cooperation between customs authorities with regard to trade in counterfeit trademark goods and pirated copyright goods.

[9.334]
Article 70
Protection of Existing Subject Matter

1. This Agreement does not give rise to obligations in respect of acts which occurred before the date of application of the Agreement for the Member in question.
2. Except as otherwise provided for in this Agreement, this Agreement gives rise to obligations in respect of all subject matter existing at the date of application of this Agreement for the Member in question, and which is protected in that Member on the said date, or which meets or comes subsequently to meet the criteria for protection under the terms of this Agreement. In respect of this paragraph and paragraphs 3 and 4, copyright obligations with respect to existing works shall be solely determined under Article 18 of the Berne Convention (1971), and obligations with respect to the rights of producers of phonograms and performers in existing phonograms shall be determined solely under Article 18 of the Berne Convention (1971) as made applicable under paragraph 6 of Article 14 of this Agreement.
3. There shall be no obligation to restore protection to subject matter which on the date of application of this Agreement for the Member in question has fallen into the public domain.
4. In respect of any acts in respect of specific objects embodying protected subject matter which become infringing under the terms of legislation in conformity with this Agreement, and which were commenced, or in respect of which a significant investment was made, before the date of acceptance of the WTO Agreement by that Member, any Member may provide for a limitation of the remedies available to the right holder as to the continued performance of such acts after the date of application of this Agreement for that Member. In such cases the Member shall, however, at least provide for the payment of equitable remuneration.
5. A Member is not obliged to apply the provisions of Article 11 and of paragraph 4 of Article 14 with respect to originals or copies purchased prior to the date of application of this Agreement for that Member.
6. Members shall not be required to apply Article 31, or the requirement in paragraph 1 of Article 27 that patent rights shall be enjoyable without discrimination as to the field of technology, to use without the authorisation of the right holder where authorisation for such use was granted by the government before the date this Agreement became known.
7. In the case of intellectual property rights for which protection is conditional upon registration, applications for protection which are pending on the date of application of this Agreement for the Member in question shall be permitted to be amended to claim any enhanced protection provided under the provisions of this Agreement. Such amendments shall not include new matter.
8. Where a Member does not make available as of the date of entry into force of the WTO Agreement patent protection for pharmaceutical and agricultural chemical products commensurate with its obligations under Article 27, that Member shall—
   (a) notwithstanding the provisions of Part VI, provide as from the date of entry into force of the WTO Agreement a means by which applications for patents for such inventions can be filed;
   (b) apply to these applications, as of the date of application of this Agreement, the criteria for patentability as laid down in this Agreement as if those criteria were being applied on the date of filing in that Member or, where priority is available and claimed, the priority date of the application; and
   (c) provide patent protection in accordance with this Agreement as from the grant of the patent and for the remainder of the patent term, counted from the filing date in accordance with Article 33 of this Agreement, for those of these applications that meet the criteria for protection referred to in subparagraph (b).
9. Where a product is the subject of a patent application in a Member in accordance with paragraph 8(a), exclusive marketing rights shall be granted, notwithstanding the provisions of Part VI, for a period of five years after obtaining marketing approval in that Member or until a product patent is granted or rejected in that Member, whichever period is shorter, provided that,

subsequent to the entry into force of the WTO Agreement, a patent application has been filed and a patent granted for that product in another Member and marketing approval obtained in such other Member.

[9.335]
Article 71
Review and Amendment

1. The Council for TRIPS shall review the implementation of this Agreement after the expiration of the transitional period referred to in paragraph 2 of Article 65. The Council shall, having regard to the experience gained in its implementation, review it two years after that date, and at identical intervals thereafter. The Council may also undertake reviews in the light of any relevant new developments which might warrant modification or amendment of this Agreement.
2. Amendments merely serving the purpose of adjusting to higher levels of protection of intellectual property rights achieved, and in force, in other multilateral agreements and accepted under those agreements by all Members of the WTO may be referred to the Ministerial Conference for action in accordance with paragraph 6 of Article X of the WTO Agreement on the basis of a consensus proposal from the Council for TRIPS.

[9.336]
Article 72
Reservations

Reservations may not be entered in respect of any of the provisions of this Agreement without the consent of the other Members.

[9.337]
Article 73
Security Exceptions

Nothing in this Agreement shall be construed—

(a) to require a Member to furnish any information the disclosure of which it considers contrary to its essential security interests; or
(b) to prevent a Member from taking any action which it considers necessary for the protection of its essential security interests—
  (i) relating to fissionable materials or the materials from which they are derived;
  (ii) relating to the traffic in arms, ammunition and implements of war and to such traffic in other goods and materials as is carried on directly or indirectly for the purpose of supplying a military establishment;
  (iii) taken in time of war or other emergency in international relations; or
(c) to prevent a Member from taking any action in pursuance of its obligations under the United Nations Charter for the maintenance of international peace and security.

[ANNEX

[9.338]

1. For the purposes of Article 31*bis* and this Annex:
(a) "pharmaceutical product" means any patented product, or product manufactured through a patented process, of the pharmaceutical sector needed to address the public health problems as recognized in paragraph 1 of the Declaration on the TRIPS Agreement and Public Health (WT/MIN(01)/DEC/2). It is understood that active ingredients necessary for its manufacture and diagnostic kits needed for its use would be included;[1]
(b) "eligible importing Member" means any least-developed country Member, and any other Member that has made a notification[2] to the Council for TRIPS of its intention to use the system set out in Article 31*bis* and this Annex ("system") as an importer, it being understood that a Member may notify at any time that it will use the system in whole or in a limited way, for example only in the case of a national emergency or other circumstances of extreme urgency or in cases of public non-commercial use. It is noted that some Members will not use the system as importing Members[3] and that some other Members have stated that, if they use the system, it would be in no more than situations of national emergency or other circumstances of extreme urgency;
(c) "exporting Member" means a Member using the system to produce pharmaceutical products for, and export them to, an eligible importing Member.

2. The terms referred to in paragraph 1 of Article 31*bis* are that:
(a) the eligible importing Member(s)[4] has made a notification[2] to the Council for TRIPS, that:
  (i) specifies the names and expected quantities of the product(s) needed;[5]
  (ii) confirms that the eligible importing Member in question, other than a least developed country Member, has established that it has insufficient or no manufacturing capacities in the pharmaceutical sector for the product(s) in question in one of the ways set out in the Appendix to this Annex; and

(iii) confirms that, where a pharmaceutical product is patented in its territory, it has granted or intends to grant a compulsory licence in accordance with Articles 31 and 31*bis* of this Agreement and the provisions of this Annex;[6]

(b) the compulsory licence issued by the exporting Member under the system shall contain the following conditions:

(i) only the amount necessary to meet the needs of the eligible importing Member(s) may be manufactured under the licence and the entirety of this production shall be exported to the Member(s) which has notified its needs to the Council for TRIPS;

(ii) products produced under the licence shall be clearly identified as being produced under the system through specific labelling or marking. Suppliers should distinguish such products through special packaging and/or special colouring/shaping of the products themselves, provided that such distinction is feasible and does not have a significant impact on price; and

(iii) before shipment begins, the licensee shall post on a website[7] the following information:

— the quantities being supplied to each destination as referred to in indent (i) above; and

— the distinguishing features of the product(s) referred to in indent (ii) above;

(c) the exporting Member shall notify[8] the Council for TRIPS of the grant of the licence, including the conditions attached to it.[9] The information provided shall include the name and address of the licensee, the product(s) for which the licence has been granted, the quantity(ies) for which it has been granted, the country(ies) to which the product(s) is (are) to be supplied and the duration of the licence. The notification shall also indicate the address of the website referred to in subparagraph (b)(iii) above.

3. In order to ensure that the products imported under the system are used for the public health purposes underlying their importation, eligible importing Members shall take reasonable measures within their means, proportionate to their administrative capacities and to the risk of trade diversion to prevent re-exportation of the products that have actually been imported into their territories under the system. In the event that an eligible importing Member that is a developing country Member or a least-developed country Member experiences difficulty in implementing this provision, developed country Members shall provide, on request and on mutually agreed terms and conditions, technical and financial cooperation in order to facilitate its implementation.

4. Members shall ensure the availability of effective legal means to prevent the importation into, and sale in, their territories of products produced under the system and diverted to their markets inconsistently with its provisions, using the means already required to be available under this Agreement. If any Member considers that such measures are proving insufficient for this purpose, the matter may be reviewed in the Council for TRIPS at the request of that Member.

5. With a view to harnessing economies of scale for the purposes of enhancing purchasing power for, and facilitating the local production of, pharmaceutical products, it is recognized that the development of systems providing for the grant of regional patents to be applicable in the Members described in paragraph 3 of Article 31*bis* should be promoted. To this end, developed country Members undertake to provide technical cooperation in accordance with Article 67 of this Agreement, including in conjunction with other relevant intergovernmental organisations.

6. Members recognize the desirability of promoting the transfer of technology and capacity building in the pharmaceutical sector in order to overcome the problem faced by Members with insufficient or no manufacturing capacities in the pharmaceutical sector. To this end, eligible importing Members and exporting Members are encouraged to use the system in a way which would promote this objective. Members undertake to cooperate in paying special attention to the transfer of technology and capacity building in the pharmaceutical sector in the work to be undertaken pursuant to Article 66.2 of this Agreement, paragraph 7 of the Declaration on the TRIPS Agreement and Public Health and any other relevant work of the Council for TRIPS.

7. The Council for TRIPS shall review annually the functioning of the system with a view to ensuring its effective operation and shall annually report on its operation to the General Council.

APPENDIX TO THE ANNEX

Assessment of Manufacturing Capacities in the Pharmaceutical Sector

Least-developed country Members are deemed to have insufficient or no manufacturing capacities in the pharmaceutical sector.

For other eligible importing Members insufficient or no manufacturing capacities for the product(s) in question may be established in either of the following ways:

(i) the Member in question has established that it has no manufacturing capacity in the pharmaceutical sector; or

(ii) where the Member has some manufacturing capacity in this sector, it has examined this capacity and found that, excluding any capacity owned or controlled by the patent owner, it is currently insufficient for the purposes of meeting its needs. When it is established that such capacity has become sufficient to meet the Member's needs, the system shall no longer apply.]

NOTES

Inserted following a Decision of the General Council of the WTO in document WT/L/641 on 6 December 2005. Members had until 31 December 2009 to accept this amendment.

1 This subparagraph is without prejudice to subparagraph 1(b).

2 It is understood that this notification does not need to be approved by a WTO body in order to use the system.

3 Australia, Canada, the European Communities with, for the purposes of Article 31*bis* and this Annex, its member States, Iceland, Japan, New Zealand, Norway, Switzerland, and the United States.

4 Joint notifications providing the information required under this subparagraph may be made by the regional organisations referred to in paragraph 3 of Article 31*bis* on behalf of eligible importing Members using the system that are parties to them, with the agreement of those parties.

5 The notification will be made available publicly by the WTO Secretariat through a page on the WTO website dedicated to the system.

6 This subparagraph is without prejudice to Article 66.1 of this Agreement.

7 The licensee may use for this purpose its own website or, with the assistance of the WTO Secretariat, the page on the WTO website dedicated to the system.

8 It is understood that this notification does not need to be approved by a WTO body in order to use the system.

9 The notification will be made available publicly by the WTO Secretariat through a page on the WTO website dedicated to the system.

AGREEMENT BETWEEN THE WORLD INTELLECTUAL PROPERTY ORGANIZATION AND THE WORLD TRADE ORGANIZATION

of December 22, 1995

NOTES

The original source for this Agreement is the World Intellectual Property Organisation (WIPO).

PREAMBLE

The World Intellectual Property Organization (WIPO) and the World Trade Organization (WTO),

Desiring to establish a mutually supportive relationship between them, and with a view to establishing appropriate arrangements for cooperation between them,

Agree as follows:

[9.339]

Article 1

Abbreviated Expressions

For the purposes of this Agreement:

(i) "WIPO" means the World Intellectual Property Organization;

(ii) "WTO" means the World Trade Organization;

(iii) "International Bureau" means the International Bureau of WIPO;

(iv) "WTO Member" means a party to the Agreement Establishing the World Trade Organization;

(v) "the TRIPS Agreement" means the Agreement on Trade-Related Aspects of Intellectual Property Rights, Annex 1C to the Agreement Establishing the World Trade Organization;

(vi) "Paris Convention" means the Paris Convention for the Protection of Industrial Property of March 20, 1883, as revised;

(vii) "Paris Convention (1967)" means the Paris Convention for the Protection of Industrial Property of March 20, 1883, as revised at Stockholm on July 14, 1967;

(viii) "emblem" means, in the case of a WTO Member, any armorial bearing, flag and other State emblem of that WTO Member, or any official sign or hallmark indicating control and warranty adopted by it, and, in the case of an international intergovernmental organization, any armorial bearing, flag, other emblem, abbreviation or name of that organization.

[9.340]
Article 2
Laws and Regulations

(1) [*Accessibility of Laws and Regulations in the WIPO Collection by WTO Members and Their Nationals*] The International Bureau shall, on request, furnish to WTO Members and to nationals of WTO Members copies of laws and regulations, and copies of translations thereof, that exist in its collection, on the same terms as apply to the Member States of WIPO and to nationals of the Member States of WIPO, respectively.

(2) [*Accessibility of the Computerized Database*] WTO Members and nationals of WTO Members shall have access, on the same terms as apply to the Member States of WIPO and to nationals of the Member States of WIPO, respectively, to any computerized database of the International Bureau containing laws and regulations. The WTO Secretariat shall have access, free of any charge by WIPO, to any such database.

(3) [*Accessibility of Laws and Regulations in the WIPO Collection by the WTO Secretariat and the Council for TRIPS*]

(a) Where, on the date of its initial notification of a law or regulation under Article 63.2 of the TRIPS Agreement, a WTO Member has already communicated that law or regulation, or a translation thereof, to the International Bureau and that WTO Member has sent to the WTO Secretariat a statement to that effect, and that law, regulation or translation actually exists in the collection of the International Bureau, the International Bureau shall, on request of the WTO Secretariat, give, free of charge, a copy of the said law, regulation or translation to the WTO Secretariat.

(b) Furthermore, if, for the purposes of carrying out its obligations under Article 68 of the TRIPS Agreement, such as monitoring the operation of the TRIPS Agreement or providing assistance in the context of dispute settlement procedures, the Council for TRIPS of the WTO requires a copy of a law or regulation, or a copy of a translation thereof, which had not previously been given to the WTO Secretariat under subparagraph (a), and which exists in the collection of the International Bureau, the International Bureau shall, upon request of either the Council for TRIPS or the WTO Secretariat, give to the WTO Secretariat, free of charge, the requested copy.

(c) The International Bureau shall, on request, furnish to the WTO Secretariat on the same terms as apply to Member States of WIPO any additional copies of the laws, regulations and translations given under subparagraph (a) or (b), as well as copies of any other laws and regulations, and copies of translations thereof, which exist in the collection of the International Bureau.

(d) The International Bureau shall not put any restriction on the use that the WTO Secretariat may make of the copies of laws, regulations and translations transmitted under subparagraph (a), (b) or (c).

(4) [*Laws and Regulations Received by the WTO Secretariat from WTO Members*]

(a) The WTO Secretariat shall transmit to the International Bureau, free of charge, a copy of the laws and regulations received by the WTO Secretariat from WTO Members under Article 63.2 of the TRIPS Agreement in the language or languages and in the form or forms in which they were received, and the International Bureau shall place such copies in its collection.

(b) The WTO Secretariat shall not put any restriction on the further use that the International Bureau may make of the copies of the laws and regulations transmitted under subparagraph (a).

(5) [*Translation of Laws and Regulations*] The International Bureau shall make available to developing country WTO Members which are not Member States of WIPO the same assistance for translation of laws and regulations for the purposes of Article 63.2 of the TRIPS Agreement as it makes available to Members of WIPO which are developing countries.

[9.341]
Article 3
Implementation of Article 6*ter* of the Paris Convention for the Purposes of the TRIPS Agreement

(1) [*General*]

(a) The procedures relating to communication of emblems and transmittal of objections under the TRIPS Agreement shall be administered by the International Bureau in accordance with the procedures applicable under Article 6*ter* of the Paris Convention (1967).

(b) The International Bureau shall not recommunicate to a State party to the Paris Convention which is a WTO Member an emblem which had already been communicated to it by the International Bureau under Article 6*ter* of the Paris Convention prior to January 1, 1996, or, where that State became a WTO Member after January 1, 1996, prior to the date on which it became a WTO Member, and the International Bureau shall not transmit any objection received from the said WTO Member concerning the said emblem if the objection is received by the International Bureau more than 12 months after receipt of the communication of the said emblem under Article 6*ter* of the Paris Convention by the said State.

(2) [*Objections*] Notwithstanding paragraph (1)(a), any objection received by the International Bureau from a WTO Member which concerns an emblem that had been communicated to the International Bureau by another WTO Member where at least one of the said WTO Members is not party to the Paris Convention, and any objection which concerns an emblem of an international intergovernmental organization and which is received by the International Bureau from a WTO Member not party to the Paris Convention or not bound under the Paris Convention to protect emblems of international intergovernmental organizations, shall be transmitted by the International Bureau to the WTO Member or international intergovernmental organization concerned regardless of the date on which the objection had been received by the International Bureau. The provisions of the preceding sentence shall not affect the time limit of 12 months for the lodging of an objection.
(3) [*Information to Be Provided to the WTO Secretariat*] The International Bureau shall provide to the WTO Secretariat information relating to any emblem communicated by a WTO Member to the International Bureau or communicated by the International Bureau to a WTO Member.

[9.342]
Article 4
Legal-Technical Assistance and Technical Cooperation
(1) [*Availability of Legal-Technical Assistance and Technical Cooperation*] The International Bureau shall make available to developing country WTO Members which are not Member States of WIPO the same legal-technical assistance relating to the TRIPS Agreement as it makes available to Member States of WIPO which are developing countries. The WTO Secretariat shall make available to Member States of WIPO which are developing countries and are not WTO Members the same technical cooperation relating to the TRIPS Agreement as it makes available to developing country WTO Members.
(2) [*Cooperation Between the International Bureau and the WTO Secretariat*] The International Bureau and the WTO Secretariat shall enhance cooperation in their legal-technical assistance and technical cooperation activities relating to the TRIPS Agreement for developing countries, so as to maximize the usefulness of those activities and ensure their mutually supportive nature.
(3) [*Exchange of Information*] For the purposes of paragraphs (1) and (2), the International Bureau and the WTO Secretariat shall keep in regular contact and exchange non-confidential information.

[9.343]
Article 5
Final Clauses
(1) [*Entry into Force of this Agreement*] This Agreement shall enter into force on January 1, 1996.
(2) [*Amendment of this Agreement*] This Agreement may be amended by common agreement of the parties to this Agreement.
(3) [*Termination of this Agreement*] If one of the parties to this Agreement gives the other party written notice to terminate this Agreement, this Agreement shall terminate one year after receipt of the notice by the other party, unless a longer period is specified in the notice or unless both parties agree on a longer or a shorter period.

WIPO COPYRIGHT TREATY

Adopted by the Diplomatic Conference on December 20, 1996

NOTES
The original source for this Treaty is the World Intellectual Property Organisation (WIPO).

PREAMBLE
THE CONTRACTING PARTIES,
Desiring to develop and maintain the protection of the rights of authors in their literary and artistic works in a manner as effective and uniform as possible,
Recognising the need to introduce new international rules and clarify the interpretation of certain existing rules in order to provide adequate solutions to the questions raised by new economic, social, cultural and technological developments,
Recognising the profound impact of the development and convergence of information and communication technologies on the creation and use of literary and artistic works,
Emphasising the outstanding significance of copyright protection as an incentive for literary and artistic creation,
Recognising the need to maintain a balance between the rights of authors and the larger public interest, particularly education, research and access to information, as reflected in the Berne Convention,
HAVE AGREED AS FOLLOWS—

[9.344]
Article 1
Relation to the Berne Convention
(1) This Treaty is a special agreement within the meaning of Article 20 of the Berne Convention for the Protection of Literary and Artistic Works, as regards Contracting Parties that are countries of the Union established by that Convention. This Treaty shall not have any connection with treaties, other than the Berne Convention, nor shall it prejudice any rights and obligations under any other treaties.
(2) Nothing in this Treaty shall derogate from existing obligations that Contracting Parties have to each other under the Berne Convention for the Protection of Literary and Artistic Works.
(3) Hereinafter, "Berne Convention" shall refer to the Paris Act of July 24, 1971 of the Berne Convention for the Protection of Literary and Artistic Works.
(4) Contracting Parties shall comply with Articles 1 to 21 and the Appendix of the Berne Convention.

[9.345]
Article 2
Scope of Copyright Protection
Copyright protection extends to expressions and not to ideas, procedures, methods of operation or mathematical concepts as such.

[9.346]
Article 3
Application of Articles 2 to 6 of the Berne Convention
Contracting Parties shall apply *mutatis mutandis* the provisions of Articles 2 to 6 of the Berne Convention in respect of the protection provided for in this Treaty.

[9.347]
Article 4
Computer Programs
Computer programs are protected as literary works within the meaning of Article 2 of the Berne Convention. Such protection applies to computer programs, whatever may be the mode or form of their expression.

[9.348]
Article 5
Compilations of Data (Databases)
Compilations of data or other material, in any form, which by reason of the selection or arrangement of their contents constitute intellectual creations, arc protected as such. This protection does not extend to the data or the material itself and is without prejudice to any copyright subsisting in the data or material contained in the compilation.

[9.349]
Article 6
Right of Distribution
(1) Authors of literary and artistic works shall enjoy the exclusive right of authorising the making available to the public of the original and copies of their works through sale or other transfer of ownership.
(2) Nothing in this Treaty shall affect the freedom of Contracting Parties to determine the conditions, if any, under which the exhaustion of the right in paragraph (1) applies after the first sale or other transfer of ownership of the original or a copy of the work with the authorisation of the author.

[9.350]
Article 7
Right of Rental
(1) Authors of—
(i) computer programs;
(ii) cinematographic works; and
(iii) works embodied in phonograms as determined in the national law of Contracting Parties,
shall enjoy the exclusive right of authorising commercial rental to the public of the originals or copies of their works.
(2) Paragraph (1) shall not apply—
(i) in the case of computer programs, where the program itself is not the essential object of the rental, and
(ii) in the case of cinematographic works, unless such commercial rental has led to widespread copying of such works materially impairing the exclusive right of reproduction.

(3) Notwithstanding the provisions of paragraph (1), a Contracting Party that, on April 15, 1994, had and continues to have in force a system of equitable remuneration of authors for the rental of copies of their works embodied in phonograms may maintain that system provided that the commercial rental of works embodied in phonograms is not giving rise to the material impairment of the exclusive right of reproduction of authors.

[9.351]
Article 8
Right of Communication to the Public

Without prejudice to the provisions of Articles 11(1)(ii), 11*bis* (1)(i) and (ii), 11*ter* (1)(ii), 14(1)(ii) and 14*bis* (1) of the Berne Convention, authors of literary and artistic works shall enjoy the exclusive right of authorising any communication to the public of their works, by wire or wireless means, including the making available to the public of their works in such a way that members of the public may access these works from a place and at a time individually chosen by them.

[9.352]
Article 9
Duration of the Protection of Photographic Works

In respect of photographic works, the Contracting Parties shall not apply the provisions of Article 7(4) of the Berne Convention.

[9.353]
Article 10
Limitations and Exceptions

(1) Contracting Parties may, in their national legislation, provide for limitations of or exceptions to the rights granted to authors of literary and artistic works under this Treaty in certain special cases that do not conflict with a normal exploitation of the work and do not unreasonably prejudice the legitimate interests of the author.

(2) Contracting Parties shall, when applying the Berne Convention, confine any limitations of or exceptions to rights provided for therein to certain special cases that do not conflict with a normal exploitation of the work and do not unreasonably prejudice the legitimate interests of the author.

[9.354]
Article 11
Obligations Concerning Technological Measures

Contracting Parties shall provide adequate legal protection and effective legal remedies against the circumvention of effective technological measures that are used by authors in connection with the exercise of their rights under this Treaty or the Berne Convention and that restrict acts, in respect of their works, which are not authorised by the authors concerned or permitted by law.

[9.355]
Article 12
Obligations concerning Rights Management Information

(1) Contracting Parties shall provide adequate and effective legal remedies against any person knowingly performing any of the following acts knowing, or with respect to civil remedies having reasonable grounds to know that it will induce, enable, facilitate or conceal an infringement of any right covered by this Treaty or the Berne Convention—

- (i) to remove or alter any electronic rights management information without authority;
- (ii) to distribute, import for distribution, broadcast or communicate to the public, without authority, works or copies of works knowing that electronic rights management information has been removed or altered without authority.

(2) As used in this Article, "rights management information" means information which identifies the work, the author of the work, the owner of any right in the work, or information about the terms and conditions of use of the work, and any numbers or codes that represent such information, when any of these items of information is attached to a copy of a work or appears in connection with the communication of a work to the public.

[9.356]
Article 13
Application in Time

Contracting Parties shall apply the provisions of Article 18 of the Berne Convention to all protection provided for in this Treaty.

[9.357]
Article 14
Provisions on Enforcement of Rights

(1) Contracting Parties undertake to adopt, in accordance with their legal systems, the measures necessary to ensure the application of this Treaty.

(2) Contracting Parties shall ensure that enforcement procedures are available under their law so as to permit effective action against any act of infringement of rights covered by this Treaty, including expeditious remedies to prevent infringements and remedies which constitute a deterrent to further infringements.

[9.358]
Article 15
Assembly

(1)

(a) The Contracting Parties shall have an Assembly.

(b) Each Contracting Party shall be represented by one delegate who may be assisted by alternate delegates, advisors and experts.

(c) The expenses of each delegation shall be borne by the Contracting Party that has appointed the delegation. The Assembly may ask the World Intellectual Property Organisation (hereinafter referred to as "WIPO") to grant financial assistance to facilitate the participation of delegations of Contracting Parties that are regarded as developing countries in conformity with the established practice of the General Assembly of the United Nations or that are countries in transition to a market economy.

(2)

(a) The Assembly shall deal with matters concerning the maintenance and development of this Treaty and the application and operation of this Treaty.

(b) The Assembly shall perform the function allocated to it under Article 17(2) in respect of the admission of certain intergovernmental organisations to become party to this Treaty.

(c) The Assembly shall decide the convocation of any diplomatic conference for the revision of this Treaty and give the necessary instructions to the Director General of WIPO for the preparation of such diplomatic conference.

(3)

(a) Each Contracting Party that is a State shall have one vote and shall vote only in its own name.

(b) Any Contracting Party that is an intergovernmental organisation may participate in the vote, in place of its Member States, with a number of votes equal to the number of its Member States which are party to this Treaty. No such intergovernmental organisation shall participate in the vote if any one of its Member States exercises its right to vote and vice versa.

(4) The Assembly shall meet in ordinary session once every two years upon convocation by the Director General of WIPO.

(5) The Assembly shall establish its own rules of procedure, including the convocation of extraordinary sessions, the requirements of a quorum and, subject to the provisions of this Treaty, the required majority for various kinds of decisions.

[9.359]
Article 16
International Bureau

The International Bureau of WIPO shall perform the administrative tasks concerning the Treaty.

[9.360]
Article 17
Eligibility for Becoming Party to the Treaty

(1) Any Member State of WIPO may become party to this Treaty.

(2) The Assembly may decide to admit any intergovernmental organisation to become party to this Treaty which declares that it is competent in respect of, and has its own legislation binding on all its Member States on, matters covered by this Treaty and that it has been duly authorised, in accordance with its internal procedures, to become party to this Treaty.

(3) The European Community, having made the declaration referred to in the preceding paragraph in the Diplomatic Conference that has adopted this Treaty may become party to this Treaty.

[9.361]
Article 18
Rights and Obligations under the Treaty

Subject to any specific provisions to the contrary in this Treaty, each Contracting Party shall enjoy all of the rights and assume all of the obligations under this Treaty.

[9.362]
Article 19
Signature of the Treaty

This Treaty shall be open for signature until December 31, 1997, by any Member Stare of WIPO and by the European Community.

[9.363]
Article 20
Entry into Force of the Treaty
This Treaty shall enter into force three months after 30 instruments of ratification or accession by States have been deposited with the Director General of WIPO.

[9.364]
Article 21
Effective Date of Becoming Party to the Treaty
This Treaty shall bind—
- (i) the 30 States referred to in Article 20, from the date on which this Treaty has entered into force;
- (ii) each other State from the expiration of three months from the date on which the State has deposited its instrument with the Director General of WIPO;
- (iii) the European Community, from the expiration of three months after the deposit of its instrument of ratification or accession if such instrument has been deposited after the entry into force of this Treaty according to Article 20, or, three months after the entry into force of this Treaty if such instrument has been deposited before the entry into force of this Treaty;
- (iv) any other intergovernmental organisation that is admitted to become party to this Treaty, from the expiration of three months after the deposit of its instrument of accession.

[9.365]
Article 22
No Reservations to the Treaty
No reservation to this Treaty shall be admitted.

[9.366]
Article 23
Denunciation of the Treaty
This Treaty may be denounced by any Contracting Party by notification addressed to the Director General of WIPO. Any denunciation shall take effect one year from the date on which the Director General of WIPO received the notification.

[9.367]
Article 24
Languages of the Treaty
(1) This Treaty is signed in a single original in English, Arabic, Chinese, French, Russian and Spanish languages, the versions in all these languages being equally authentic.
(2) An official text in any language other than those referred to in paragraph (1) shall be established by the Director General of WIPO on the request of an interested party, after consultation with all the interested parties. For the purposes of this paragraph, "interested party" means any Member State of WIPO whose official language, or one of whose official languages, is involved and the European Community, and any other intergovernmental organisation that may become party to this Treaty, if one of its official languages is involved.

[9.368]
Article 25
Depositary
The Director General of WIPO is the depositary of this Treaty.

WIPO PERFORMANCES AND PHONOGRAMS TREATY

Adopted by the Diplomatic Conference on December 20, 1996

NOTES
The original source for this Treaty is the World Intellectual Property Organisation (WIPO).

PREAMBLE
THE CONTRACTING PARTIES,
Desiring to develop and maintain the protection of the rights of performers and producers of phonograms in a manner as effective and uniform as possible,
Recognising the need to introduce new international rules in order to provide adequate solutions to the questions raised by economic, social, cultural and technological developments,
Recognising the profound impact of the development and convergence of information and communication technologies on the production and use of performances and phonograms,

Recognising the need to maintain a balance between the rights of the performers and producers of phonograms and the larger public interest, particularly education, research and access to information,

HAVE AGREED AS FOLLOWS—

CHAPTER I
GENERAL PROVISIONS

[9.369]
Article 1
Relation to Other Conventions

(1) Nothing in this Treaty shall derogate from existing obligations that Contracting Parties have to each other under the International Convention for the Protection of Performers, Producers of Phonograms and Broadcasting Organisations done in Rome, October 26, 1961 (hereinafter the "Rome Convention").

(2) Protection granted under this Treaty shall leave intact and shall in no way affect the protection of copyright in literary and artistic works. Consequently, no provision of this Treaty may be interpreted as prejudicing such protection.

(3) This Treaty shall not have any connection with, nor shall it prejudice any rights and obligations under, any other treaties.

[9.370]
Article 2
Definitions

For the purposes of this Treaty—

(a) "performers" are actors, singers, musicians, dancers, and other persons who act, sing, deliver, declaim, play in, interpret, or otherwise perform literary or artistic works or expressions of folklore;

(b) "phonogram" means the fixation of the sounds of a performance or of other sounds, or of a representation of sounds, other than in the form of a fixation incorporated in a cinematographic or other audiovisual work;

(c) "fixation" means the embodiment of sounds, or of the representations thereof, from which there can be perceived, reproduced or communicated through a device;

(d) "producer of a phonogram" means the person, or the legal entity, who or which takes the initiative and has the responsibility for the first fixation of the sounds of a performance or other sounds, or the representations of sounds;

(e) "publication" of a fixed performance or a phonogram means the offering of copies of the fixed performance or the phonogram to the public, with the consent of the rightholder, and provided that copies are offered to the public in reasonable quantity;

(f) "broadcasting" means the transmission by wireless means for public reception of sounds or of images and sounds or of the representations thereof; such transmission by satellite is also "broadcasting"; transmission of encrypted signals is "broadcasting" where the means for decrypting are provided to the public by the broadcasting organisation or with its consent;

(g) "communication to the public" of a performance or a phonogram means the transmission to the public by any medium, otherwise than by broadcasting, of sounds of a performance or the sounds or the representations of sounds fixed in a phonogram. For the purposes of Article 15, "communication to the public" includes making the sounds or representations of sounds fixed in a phonogram audible to the public.

[9.371]
Article 3
Beneficiaries of Protection under this Treaty

(1) Contracting Parties shall accord the protection provided under this Treaty to the performers and producers of phonograms who are nationals of other Contracting Parties.

(2) The nationals of other Contracting Parties shall be understood to be those performers or producers of phonograms who would meet the criteria for eligibility for protection provided under the Rome Convention, were all the Contracting Parties to this Treaty Contracting States of that Convention. In respect of these criteria of eligibility Contracting Parties shall apply the relevant definitions in Article 2 of this Treaty.

(3) Any Contracting Party availing itself of the possibilities provided in Article 5(3) of the Rome Convention or, for the purposes of Article 5 of the same Convention, Article 17 thereof shall make a notification as foreseen in those provisions to the Director General of the World Intellectual Property Organisation (WIPO).

[9.372]
Article 4
National Treatment

(1) Each Contracting Party shall accord to nationals of other Contracting Parties, as defined in Article 3(2), the treatment it accords to its own nationals with regard to the exclusive rights specifically granted in this Treaty and to the right to equitable remuneration provided for in Article 15 of this Treaty.

(2) The obligation provided for in paragraph (1) does not apply to the extent that another Contracting Party makes use of the reservations permitted by Article 15(3) of this Treaty.

CHAPTER II
RIGHT OF PERFORMERS

[9.373]
Article 5
Moral Rights of Performers

(1) Independently of a performer's economic rights, and even after the transfer of those rights, the performer shall, as regards his live aural performances or performances fixed in phonograms have the right to claim to be identified as the performer of his performances, except where omission is dictated by the manner of the use of the performance, and to object to any distortion, mutilation or other modification of his performances that would be prejudicial to his reputation.

(2) The rights granted to a performer in accordance with paragraph (1) shall, after his death, be maintained, at least until the expiry of the economic rights, and shall be exercisable by the persons or institutions authorised by the legislation of the Contracting Party where protection is claimed. However, those Contracting Parties whose legislation, at the moment of their ratification of or accession to this Treaty, does not provide for protection after the death of the performer of all rights set out in the preceding paragraph may provide that some of these rights will, after his death, cease to be maintained.

(3) The means of redress for safeguarding the rights granted under this Article shall be governed by the legislation of the Contracting Party where protection is claimed.

[9.374]
Article 6
Economic Rights of Performers in their Unfixed Performances

Performers shall enjoy the exclusive right of authorising, as regards their performances—

(i) the broadcasting and communication to the public of their unfixed performances except where the performance is already a broadcast performance; and
(ii) the fixation of their unfixed performance.

[9.375]
Article 7
Right of Reproduction

Performers shall enjoy the exclusive right of authorising the direct or indirect reproduction of their performances fixed in phonograms, in any manner or form.

[9.376]
Article 8
Right of Distribution

(1) Performers shall enjoy the exclusive right of authorising the making available to the public of the original and copies of their performances fixed in phonograms through sale or other transfer of ownership.

(2) Nothing in this Treaty shall affect the freedom of Contracting Parties to determine the conditions, if any, under which the exhaustion of the right in paragraph (1) applies after the first sale or other transfer of ownership of the original or a copy of the fixed performance with the authorisation of the performer.

[9.377]
Article 9
Right of Rental

(1) Performers shall enjoy the exclusive right of authorising the commercial rental to the public of the original and copies of their performances fixed in phonograms as determined in the national law of Contracting Parties, even after distribution of them by, or pursuant to, authorisation by the performer.

(2) Notwithstanding the provisions of paragraph (1), a Contracting Party that, on April 15, 1994, had and continues to have in force a system of equitable remuneration of performers for the rental of copies of their performances fixed in phonograms, may maintain that system provided that the commercial rental of phonograms is not giving rise to the material impairment of the exclusive rights of reproduction of performers.

[9.378]
Article 10
Right of Making Available of Fixed Performances
Performers shall enjoy the exclusive right of authorising the making available to the public of their performances fixed in phonograms, by wire or wireless means, in such a way that members of the public may access them from a place and at a time individually chosen by them.

CHAPTER III
RIGHTS OF PRODUCERS OF PHONOGRAMS

[9.379]
Article 11
Right of Reproduction
Producers of phonograms shall enjoy the exclusive right of authorising the direct or indirect reproduction of their phonograms, in any manner or form.

[9.380]
Article 12
Right of Distribution
(1) Producers of phonograms shall enjoy the exclusive right of authorising the making available to the public of the original and copies of their phonograms through sale or other transfer of ownership.
(2) Nothing in this Treaty shall affect the freedom of Contracting Parties to determine the conditions, if any, under which the exhaustion of the right in paragraph (1) applies after the first sale or transfer of ownership of the original or a copy of the phonogram with the authorisation of the producer of the phonograms.

[9.381]
Article 13
Right of Rental
(1) Producers of phonograms shall enjoy the exclusive right of authorising the commercial rental to the public of the original and copies of their phonograms, even after distribution of them by or pursuant to authorisation by the producer.
(2) Notwithstanding the provisions of paragraph (1), a Contracting Party that, on April 15, 1994, had and continues to have in force a system of equitable remuneration of producers of phonograms for the rental of copies of their phonograms, may maintain that system provided that the commercial rental of phonograms is not giving rise to the material impairment of the exclusive rights of reproduction of producers of phonograms.

[9.382]
Article 14
Right of Making Available of Phonograms
Producers of phonograms shall enjoy the exclusive right of authorising the making available to the public of their phonograms, by wire or wireless means, in such a way that members of the public may access them from a place and at a time individually chosen by them.

CHAPTER IV
COMMON PROVISIONS

[9.383]
Article 15
Right to Remuneration for Broadcasting and Communication to the Public
(1) Performers and producers of phonogram shall enjoy the right to a single equitable remuneration for the direct or indirect use of phonograms published for commercial purposes for broadcasting or for any communication to the public.
(2) Contracting Parties may establish in their national legislation that the single equitable remuneration shall be claimed from the user by the performer or by the producer of a phonogram or by both. Contracting Parties may enact national legislation that in the absence of an agreement between the performer and the producer of a phonogram, sets the terms according to which performers and producers of phonograms shall share the single equitable remuneration.
(3) Any Contracting Party may in a notification deposited with the Director General of WIPO, declare that it will apply the provisions of paragraph (1) only in respect of certain uses, or that it will limit their application in some other way, or that it will not apply these provisions at all.
(4) For the purposes of this Article, phonograms made available to the to the public by wire or wireless means in such a way that members of the public may access them from a place and at a time individually chosen by them shall be considered as if they had been published for commercial purposes.

[9.384]
Article 16
Limitations and Exceptions

(1) Contracting Parties may, in their national legislation, provide for the same kinds of limitations or exceptions with regard to the protection of performers and producers of phonograms as they provide for, in their national legislation, in connection with the protection of copyright in literary and artistic works.

(2) Contracting Parties shall confine any limitations of or exceptions to rights provided for in this Treaty to certain special cases which do not conflict with a normal exploitation of the performance or phonogram and do not unreasonably prejudice the legitimate interests of the performer or of the producer of the phonograms.

[9.385]
Article 17
Term of Protection

(1) The term of protection to be granted to performers under this Treaty shall last, at least, until the end of a period of 50 years computed from the end of the year in which the performance was fixed in a phonogram.

(2) The term of protection to be granted to producers of phonograms under this Treaty shall last, at least, until the end of a period of 50 years computed from the end of the year in which the phonogram was published, or failing such publication within 50 years from fixation of the phonogram, 30 years from the end of the year in which the fixation was made.

[9.386]
Article 18
Obligations concerning Technological Measures

Contracting Parties shall provide adequate legal protection and effective legal remedies against the circumvention of effective technological measures that are used by performers or producers of phonograms in connection with the exercise of their rights under this Treaty and that restrict acts, in respect of their performances or phonograms, which are not authorised by the performers or the producers of phonograms concerned or permitted by law.

[9.387]
Article 19
Obligations concerning Rights Management Information

(1) Contracting Parties shall provide adequate and effective legal remedies against any person knowingly performing any of the following acts knowing, or with respect to civil remedies, having reasonable grounds to know, that it will induce, enable, facilitate or conceal an infringement of any right covered by this Treaty—

(i) to remove or alter any electronic rights management information without authority;

(ii) to distribute, import for distribution, broadcast, communicate or make available to the public, without authority, performances, copies of fixed performances or phonograms knowing that electronic rights management information has been removed or altered without authority.

(2) As used in this Article, "rights management information" means information which identifies the performer, the performance of the performer, the producer of the phonogram, the phonogram, the owner of any right in the performance or phonogram, or information about the terms and conditions of use of the performance or phonogram, and any numbers or codes that represent such information, when any of these items of information is attached to a copy of a fixed performance or a phonogram or appears in connection with the communication or making available of a fixed performance or a phonogram to the public.

[9.388]
Article 20
Formalities

The enjoyment and exercise of the rights provided for in this Treaty shall not be subject to any formality.

[9.389]
Article 21
Reservations

Subject to the provisions of Article 15(3), no reservations to this Treaty shall be permitted.

[9.390]
Article 22
Application in Time

(1) Contracting Parties shall apply the provisions of Article 15(3) of the Berne Convention, *mutatis mutandis,* to the rights of performers and producers of phonograms provided for in this Treaty.

(2) Notwithstanding paragraph (1), a Contracting Party may limit the application of Article 5 of this Treaty to performances which occurred after the entry into force of this Treaty for that Party.

[9.391]
Article 23
Provisions on Enforcement of Rights

(1) Contracting Parties undertake to adopt, in accordance with their legal systems, the measures necessary to ensure the application of this Treaty.

(2) Contracting Parties shall ensure that enforcement procedures are available under their law so as to permit effective action against any act of infringement of rights covered by this Treaty, including expeditious remedies to prevent infringements and remedies which constitute a deterrent to further infringements.

CHAPTER V
ADMINISTRATIVE AND FINAL CLAUSES

[9.392]
Article 24
Assembly

(1)
- (a) The Contracting Parties shall have an Assembly.
- (b) Each Contracting Party shall be represented by one delegate who may be assisted by alternate delegates, advisors and experts.
- (c) The expenses of each delegation shall be borne by the Contracting Party that has appointed the delegation. The Assembly may ask WIPO to grant financial assistance to facilitate the participation of delegations of Contracting Parties that are regarded as developing countries in conformity with the established practice of the General Assembly of the United Nations or that are countries in transition to a market economy.

(2)
- (a) The Assembly shall deal with matters concerning the maintenance and development of this Treaty and the application and operation of this Treaty.
- (b) The Assembly shall perform the function allocated to it under Article 26(2) in respect of the admission of certain intergovernmental organisations to become party to this Treaty.
- (c) The Assembly shall decide the convocation of any diplomatic conference for the revision of this Treaty and give the necessary instructions to the Director General of WIPO for the preparation of such diplomatic conference.

(3)
- (a) Each Contracting Party that is a State shall have one vote and shall vote only in its own name.
- (b) Any Contracting Party that is an intergovernmental organisation may participate in the vote, in place of its Member States, with a number of votes equal to the number of its Member States which are party to this Treaty. No such intergovernmental organisation shall participate in the vote if any one of its Member States exercises its right to vote and vice versa.

(4) The Assembly shall meet in ordinary session once every two years upon convocation by the Director General of WIPO.

(5) The Assembly shall establish its own rules of procedure, including the convocation of extraordinary sessions, the requirements of a quorum and, subject to the provisions of this Treaty, the required majority for various kinds of decisions.

[9.393]
Article 25
International Bureau

The International Bureau of WIPO shall perform the administrative tasks concerning the Treaty.

[9.394]
Article 26
Eligibility for Becoming Party to the Treaty

(1) Any Member State of WIPO may become party to this Treaty.

(2) The Assembly may decide to admit any intergovernmental organisation to become party to this Treaty which declares that it is competent in respect of, and has its own legislation binding on all its Member States on, matters covered by this Treaty and that it has been duly authorised, in accordance with its internal procedures, to become party to this Treaty.

(3) The European Community, having made the declaration referred to in the preceding paragraph in the Diplomatic Conference that has adopted this Treaty may become party to this Treaty.

[9.395]
Article 27
Rights and Obligations under the Treaty

Subject to any specific provisions to the contrary in this Treaty, each Contracting Party shall enjoy all of the rights and assume all of the obligations under this Treaty.

[9.396]
Article 28
Signature of the Treaty

This Treaty shall be open for signature until December 31, 1997, by any Member State of WIPO and by the European Community.

[9.397]
Article 29
Entry into Force of the Treaty

This Treaty shall enter into force three months after 30 instruments of ratification or accession by States have been deposited with the Director General of WIPO.

[9.398]
Article 30
Effective Date of Becoming Party to the Treaty

This Treaty shall bind—

(i) the 30 States referred to in Article 29, from the date on which this Treaty has entered into force;

(ii) each other State from the expiration of three months from the date on which the State has deposited its instrument with the Director General of WIPO;

(iii) the European Community, from the expiration of three months after the deposit of its instrument of ratification or accession if such instrument has been deposited after the entry into force of this Treaty according to Article 29, on three months after the entry into force of this Treaty if such instrument has been deposited before the entry into force of this Treaty;

(iv) any other intergovernmental organisation that is admitted to become party to this Treaty, from the expiration of three months after the deposit of its instrument of accession.

[9.399]
Article 31
Denunciation of the Treaty

This Treaty may be denounced by any Contracting Party by notification addressed to the Director General of WIPO. Any denunciation shall take effect one year from the date on which the Director General of WIPO received the notification.

[9.400]
Article 32
Languages of the Treaty

(1) This Treaty is signed in a single original in English, Arabic, Chinese, French, Russian and Spanish languages, the versions in all these languages being equally authentic.

(2) An official text in any language other than those referred to in paragraph (1) shall be established by the Director General of WIPO on the request of an interested party, after consultation with all the interested parties. For the purposes of this paragraph, "interested party" means any Member State of WIPO whose official language, or one of whose official languages, is involved and the European Community, and any other intergovernmental organisation that may become party to this Treaty if one of its official languages is involved.

[9.401]
Article 33
Depositary

The Director General of WIPO is the depositary of this Treaty.

GENEVA ACT OF THE HAGUE AGREEMENT CONCERNING THE INTERNATIONAL REGISTRATION OF INDUSTRIAL DESIGNS, REGULATIONS UNDER THE GENEVA ACT AND AGREED STATEMENTS BY THE DIPLOMATIC CONFERENCE

Adopted by the Diplomatic Conference on 2 July 1999

NOTES

The original source for this Act is the World Intellectual Property Organisation (WIPO).

INTRODUCTORY PROVISIONS

[9.402]
Article 1
Abbreviated Expressions

For the purposes of this Act:

(i) "the Hague Agreement" means the Hague Agreement Concerning the International Deposit of Industrial Designs, henceforth renamed the Hague Agreement Concerning the International Registration of Industrial Designs;

(ii) "this Act" means the Hague Agreement as established by the present Act;

(iii) "Regulations" means the Regulations under this Act;

(iv) "prescribed" means prescribed in the Regulations;

(v) "Paris Convention" means the Paris Convention for the Protection of Industrial Property, signed at Paris on March 20, 1883, as revised and amended;

(vi) "international registration" means the international registration of an industrial design effected according to this Act;

(vii) "international application" means an application for international registration;

(viii) "International Register" means the official collection of data concerning international registrations maintained by the International Bureau, which data this Act or the Regulations require or permit to be recorded, regardless of the medium in which such data are stored;

(ix) "person" means a natural person or a legal entity;

(x) "applicant" means the person in whose name an international application is filed;

(xi) "holder" means the person in whose name an international registration is recorded in the International Register;

(xii) "intergovernmental organisation" means an intergovernmental organisation eligible to become party to this Act in accordance with Article 27(1)(ii);

(xiii) "Contracting Party" means any State or intergovernmental organisation party to this Act;

(xiv) "applicant's Contracting Party" means the Contracting Party or one of the Contracting Parties from which the applicant derives its entitlement to file an international application by virtue of satisfying, in relation to that Contracting Party, at least one of the conditions specified in Article 3; where there are two or more Contracting Parties from which the applicant may, under Article 3, derive its entitlement to file an international application, "applicant's Contracting Party" means the one which, among those Contracting Parties, is indicated as such in the international application;

(xv) "territory of a Contracting Party" means, where the Contracting Party is a State, the territory of that State and, where the Contracting Party is an intergovernmental organisation, the territory in which the constituent treaty of that intergovernmental organisation applies;

(xvi) "Office" means the agency entrusted by a Contracting Party with the grant of protection for industrial designs with effect in the territory of that Contracting Party;

(xvii) "Examining Office" means an Office which *ex officio* examines applications filed with it for the protection of industrial designs at least to determine whether the industrial designs satisfy the condition of novelty;

(xviii) "designation" means a request that an international registration have effect in a Contracting Party; it also means the recording, in the International Register, of that request;

(xix) "designated Contracting Party" and "designated Office" means the Contracting Party and the Office of the Contracting Party, respectively, to which a designation applies;

(xx) "1934 Act" means the Act signed at London on June 2, 1934, of the Hague Agreement;

(xxi) "1960 Act" means the Act signed at The Hague on November 28, 1960, of the Hague Agreement;

(xxii) "1961 Additional Act" means the Act signed at Monaco on November 18, 1961, additional to the 1934 Act;

(xxiii) "Complementary Act of 1967" means the Complementary Act signed at Stockholm on July 14, 1967, as amended, of the Hague Agreement;

(xxiv) "Union" means the Hague Union established by the Hague Agreement of November 6, 1925, and maintained by the 1934 and 1960 Acts, the 1961 Additional Act, the Complementary Act of 1967 and this Act;

(xxv) "Assembly" means the Assembly referred to in Article 21(1)(a) or any body replacing that Assembly;

(xxvi) "organisation" means the World Intellectual Property organisation;

(xxvii) "Director General" means the Director General of the organisation;

(xxviii) "International Bureau" means the International Bureau of the organisation;

(xxix) "instrument of ratification" shall be construed as including instruments of acceptance or approval.

[9.403]
Article 2
Applicability of Other Protection Accorded by Laws of Contracting Parties and by Certain International Treaties

(1) [*Laws of Contracting Parties and Certain International Treaties*] The provisions of this Act shall not affect the application of any greater protection which may be accorded by the law of a Contracting Party, nor shall they affect in any way the protection accorded to works of art and works of applied art by international copyright treaties and conventions, or the protection accorded to industrial designs under the Agreement on Trade-Related Aspects of Intellectual Property Rights annexed to the Agreement Establishing the World Trade organisation.

(2) [*Obligation to Comply with the Paris Convention*] Each Contracting Party shall comply with the provisions of the Paris Convention which concern industrial designs.

CHAPTER I
INTERNATIONAL APPLICATION AND INTERNATIONAL REGISTRATION

[9.404]
Article 3
Entitlement to File an International Application

Any person that is a national of a State that is a Contracting Party or of a State member of an intergovernmental organisation that is a Contracting Party, or that has a domicile, a habitual residence or a real and effective industrial or commercial establishment in the territory of a Contracting Party, shall be entitled to file an international application.

[9.405]
Article 4
Procedure for Filing the International Application

(1) [*Direct or Indirect Filing*]

(a) The international application may be filed, at the option of the applicant, either directly with the International Bureau or through the Office of the applicant's Contracting Party.

(b) Notwithstanding subparagraph (a), any Contracting Party may, in a declaration, notify the Director General that international applications may not be filed through its Office.

(2) [*Transmittal Fee in Case of Indirect Filing*] The Office of any Contracting Party may require that the applicant pay a transmittal fee to it, for its own benefit, in respect of any international application filed through it.

[9.406]
Article 5
Contents of the International Application

(1) [*Mandatory Contents of the International Application*] The international application shall be in the prescribed language or one of the prescribed languages and shall contain or be accompanied by

(i) a request for international registration under this Act;

(ii) the prescribed data concerning the applicant;

(iii) the prescribed number of copies of a reproduction or, at the choice of the applicant, of several different reproductions of the industrial design that is the subject of the international application, presented in the prescribed manner; however, where the industrial design is two-dimensional and a request for deferment of publication is made in accordance with paragraph (5), the international application may, instead of containing reproductions, be accompanied by the prescribed number of specimens of the industrial design;

(iv) an indication of the product or products which constitute the industrial design or in relation to which the industrial design is to be used, as prescribed;

(v) an indication of the designated Contracting Parties;

(vi) the prescribed fees;

(vii) any other prescribed particulars.

(2) [*Additional Mandatory Contents of the International Application*]

(a) Any Contracting Party whose Office is an Examining Office and whose law, at the time it becomes party to this Act, requires that an application for the grant of protection to an industrial design contain any of the elements specified in subparagraph (b) in order for that application to be accorded a filing date under that law may, in a declaration, notify the Director General of those elements.

(b) The elements that may be notified pursuant to subparagraph (a) are the following:

(i) indications concerning the identity of the creator of the industrial design that is the subject of that application;

(ii) a brief description of the reproduction or of the characteristic features of the industrial design that is the subject of that application;

(iii) a claim.

(c) Where the international application contains the designation of a Contracting Party that has made a notification under subparagraph (a), it shall also contain, in the prescribed manner, any element that was the subject of that notification.

(3) [*Other Possible Contents of the International Application*] The international application may contain or be accompanied by such other elements as are specified in the Regulations.

(4) [*Several Industrial Designs in the Same International Application*] Subject to such conditions as may be prescribed, an international application may include two or more industrial designs.

(5) [*Request for Deferred Publication*] The international application may contain a request for deferment of publication.

[9.407]
Article 6
Priority

(1) [*Claiming of Priority*]

(a) The international application may contain a declaration claiming, under Article 4 of the Paris Convention, the priority of one or more earlier applications filed in or for any country party to that Convention or any Member of the World Trade organisation.

(b) The Regulations may provide that the declaration referred to in subparagraph (a) may be made after the filing of the international application. In such case, the Regulations shall prescribe the latest time by which such declaration may be made.

(2) [*International Application Serving as a Basis for Claiming Priority*] The international application shall, as from its filing date and whatever may be its subsequent fate, be equivalent to a regular filing within the meaning of Article 4 of the Paris Convention.

[9.408]
Article 7
Designation Fees

(1) [*Prescribed Designation Fee*] The prescribed fees shall include, subject to paragraph (2), a designation fee for each designated Contracting Party.

(2) [*Individual Designation Fee*] Any Contracting Party whose Office is an Examining Office and any Contracting Party that is an intergovernmental organisation may, in a declaration, notify the Director General that, in connection with any international application in which it is designated, and in connection with the renewal of any international registration resulting from such an international application, the prescribed designation fee referred to in paragraph (1) shall be replaced by an individual designation fee, whose amount shall be indicated in the declaration and can be changed in further declarations. The said amount may be fixed by the said Contracting Party for the initial term of protection and for each term of renewal or for the maximum period of protection allowed by the Contracting Party concerned. However, it may not be higher than the equivalent of the amount which the Office of that Contracting Party would be entitled to receive from an applicant for a grant of protection for an equivalent period to the same number of industrial designs, that amount being diminished by the savings resulting from the international procedure.

(3) [*Transfer of Designation Fees*] The designation fees referred to in paragraphs (1) and (2) shall be transferred by the International Bureau to the Contracting Parties in respect of which those fees were paid.

[9.409]
Article 8
Correction of Irregularities

(1) [*Examination of the International Application*] If the International Bureau finds that the international application does not, at the time of its receipt by the International Bureau, fulfil the requirements of this Act and the Regulations, it shall invite the applicant to make the required corrections within the prescribed time limit.

(2) [*Irregularities Not Corrected*]

(a) If the applicant does not comply with the invitation within the prescribed time limit, the international application shall, subject to subparagraph (b), be considered abandoned.

(b) In the case of an irregularity which relates to Article 5(2) or to a special requirement notified to the Director General by a Contracting Party in accordance with the Regulations, if the applicant does not comply with the invitation within the prescribed time limit, the international application shall be deemed not to contain the designation of that Contracting Party.

[9.410]
Article 9
Filing Date of the International Application

(1) [*International Application Filed Directly*] Where the international application is filed directly with the International Bureau, the filing date shall, subject to paragraph (3), be the date on which the International Bureau receives the international application.

(2) [*International Application Filed Indirectly*] Where the international application is filed through the Office of the applicant's Contracting Party, the filing date shall be determined as prescribed.

(3) [*International Application with Certain Irregularities*] Where the international application has, on the date on which it is received by the International Bureau, an irregularity which is prescribed as an irregularity entailing a postponement of the filing date of the international application, the filing date shall be the date on which the correction of such irregularity is received by the International Bureau.

[9.411]
Article 10
International Registration, Date of the International Registration, Publication and Confidential Copies of the International Registration

(1) [*International Registration*] The International Bureau shall register each industrial design that is the subject of an international application immediately upon receipt by it of the international application or, where corrections are invited under Article 8, immediately upon receipt of the required corrections. The registration shall be effected whether or not publication is deferred under Article 11.

(2) [*Date of the International Registration*]

(a) Subject to subparagraph (b), the date of the international registration shall be the filing date of the international application.

(b) Where the international application has, on the date on which it is received by the International Bureau, an irregularity which relates to Article 5(2), the date of the international registration shall be the date on which the correction of such irregularity is received by the International Bureau or the filing date of the international application, whichever is the later.

(3) [*Publication*]

(a) The international registration shall be published by the International Bureau. Such publication shall be deemed in all Contracting Parties to be sufficient publicity, and no other publicity may be required of the holder.

(b) The International Bureau shall send a copy of the publication of the international registration to each designated Office.

(4) [*Maintenance of Confidentiality Before Publication*] Subject to paragraph (5) and Article 11(4)(b), the International Bureau shall keep in confidence each international application and each international registration until publication.

(5) [*Confidential Copies*]

(a) The International Bureau shall, immediately after registration has been effected, send a copy of the international registration, along with any relevant statement, document or specimen accompanying the international application, to each Office that has notified the International Bureau that it wishes to receive such a copy and has been designated in the international application.

(b) The Office shall, until publication of the international registration by the International Bureau, keep in confidence each international registration of which a copy has been sent to it by the International Bureau and may use the said copy only for the purpose of the examination of the international registration and of applications for the protection of industrial designs filed in or for the Contracting Party for which the Office is competent. In particular, it may not divulge the contents of any such international registration to any person outside the Office other than the holder of that international registration, except for the purposes of an administrative or legal proceeding involving a conflict over entitlement to file the international application on which the international registration is based. In the case of such an administrative or legal proceeding, the contents of the international registration may only be disclosed in confidence to the parties involved in the proceeding who shall be bound to respect the confidentiality of the disclosure.

[9.412]
Article 11
Deferment of Publication

(1) [*Provisions of Laws of Contracting Parties Concerning Deferment of Publication*]

(a) Where the law of a Contracting Party provides for the deferment of the publication of an industrial design for a period which is less than the prescribed period, that Contracting Party shall, in a declaration, notify the Director General of the allowable period of deferment.

(b) Where the law of a Contracting Party does not provide for the deferment of the publication of an industrial design, the Contracting Party shall, in a declaration, notify the Director General of that fact.

(2) [*Deferment of Publication*] Where the international application contains a request for deferment of publication, the publication shall take place,

(i) where none of the Contracting Parties designated in the international application has made a declaration under paragraph (1), at the expiry of the prescribed period or,

(ii) where any of the Contracting Parties designated in the international application has made a declaration under paragraph (1)(a), at the expiry of the period notified in such declaration or, where there is more than one such designated Contracting Party, at the expiry of the shortest period notified in their declarations.

(3) [*Treatment of Requests for Deferment Where Deferment Is Not Possible Under Applicable Law*] Where deferment of publication has been requested and any of the Contracting Parties designated in the international application has made a declaration under paragraph (1)(b) that deferment of publication is not possible under its law,

(i) subject to item (ii), the International Bureau shall notify the applicant accordingly; if, within the prescribed period, the applicant does not, by notice in writing to the International Bureau, withdraw the designation of the said Contracting Party, the International Bureau shall disregard the request for deferment of publication;

(ii) where, instead of containing reproductions of the industrial design, the international application was accompanied by specimens of the industrial design, the International Bureau shall disregard the designation of the said Contracting Party and shall notify the applicant accordingly.

(4) [*Request for Earlier Publication or for Special Access to the International Registration*]

(a) At any time during the period of deferment applicable under paragraph (2), the holder may request publication of any or all of the industrial designs that are the subject of the international registration, in which case the period of deferment in respect of such industrial design or designs shall be considered to have expired on the date of receipt of such request by the International Bureau.

(b) The holder may also, at any time during the period of deferment applicable under paragraph (2), request the International Bureau to provide a third party specified by the holder with an extract from, or to allow such a party access to, any or all of the industrial designs that are the subject of the international registration.

(5) [*Renunciation and Limitation*]

(a) If, at any time during the period of deferment applicable under paragraph (2), the holder renounces the international registration in respect of all the designated Contracting Parties, the industrial design or designs that are the subject of the international registration shall not be published.

(b) If, at any time during the period of deferment applicable under paragraph (2), the holder limits the international registration, in respect of all of the designated Contracting Parties, to one or some of the industrial designs that are the subject of the international registration, the other industrial design or designs that are the subject of the international registration shall not be published.

(6) [*Publication and Furnishing of Reproductions*]

(a) At the expiration of any period of deferment applicable under the provisions of this Article, the International Bureau shall, subject to the payment of the prescribed fees, publish the international registration. If such fees are not paid as prescribed, the international registration shall be cancelled and publication shall not take place.

(b) Where the international application was accompanied by one or more specimens of the industrial design in accordance with Article 5(1)(iii), the holder shall submit the prescribed number of copies of a reproduction of each industrial design that is the subject of that application to the International Bureau within the prescribed time limit. To the extent that the holder does not do so, the international registration shall be cancelled and publication shall not take place.

[9.413]
Article 12
Refusal

(1) [*Right to Refuse*] The Office of any designated Contracting Party may, where the conditions for the grant of protection under the law of that Contracting Party are not met in respect of any or all of the industrial designs that are the subject of an international registration, refuse the effects, in part or in whole, of the international registration in the territory of the said Contracting Party, provided that no Office may refuse the effects, in part or in whole, of any international registration on the ground that requirements relating to the form or contents of the international application that are provided for in this Act or the Regulations or are additional to, or different from, those requirements have not been satisfied under the law of the Contracting Party concerned.

(2) [*Notification of Refusal*]

(a) The refusal of the effects of an international registration shall be communicated by the Office to the International Bureau in a notification of refusal within the prescribed period.

(b) Any notification of refusal shall state all the grounds on which the refusal is based.

(3) [*Transmission of Notification of Refusal; Remedies*]

(a) The International Bureau shall, without delay, transmit a copy of the notification of refusal to the holder.

(b) The holder shall enjoy the same remedies as if any industrial design that is the subject of the international registration had been the subject of an application for the grant of protection under the law applicable to the Office that communicated the refusal. Such remedies shall at least consist of the possibility of a re-examination or a review of the refusal or an appeal against the refusal.

(4) [*Withdrawal of Refusal*] Any refusal may be withdrawn, in part or in whole, at any time by the Office that communicated it.

[9.414]
Article 13
Special Requirements Concerning Unity of Design

(1) [*Notification of Special Requirements*] Any Contracting Party whose law, at the time it becomes party to this Act, requires that designs that are the subject of the same application conform to a requirement of unity of design, unity of production or unity of use, or belong to the same set or composition of items, or that only one independent and distinct design may be claimed in a single application, may, in a declaration, notify the Director General accordingly. However, no such declaration shall affect the right of an applicant to include two or more industrial designs in an international application in accordance with Article 5(4), even if the application designates the Contracting Party that has made the declaration.

(2) [*Effect of Declaration*] Any such declaration shall enable the Office of the Contracting Party that has made it to refuse the effects of the international registration pursuant to Article 12(1) pending compliance with the requirement notified by that Contracting Party.

(3) [*Further Fees Payable on Division of Registration*] Where, following a notification of refusal in accordance with paragraph (2), an international registration is divided before the Office concerned in order to overcome a ground of refusal stated in the notification, that Office shall be entitled to charge a fee in respect of each additional international application that would have been necessary in order to avoid that ground of refusal.

[9.415]
Article 14
Effects of the International Registration

(1) [*Effect as Application Under Applicable Law*] The international registration shall, from the date of the international registration, have at least the same effect in each designated Contracting Party as a regularly-filed application for the grant of protection of the industrial design under the law of that Contracting Party.

(2) [*Effect as Grant of Protection Under Applicable Law*]

(a) In each designated Contracting Party the Office of which has not communicated a refusal in accordance with Article 12, the international registration shall have the same effect as a grant of protection for the industrial design under the law of that Contracting Party at the latest from the date of expiration of the period allowed for it to communicate a refusal or, where a Contracting Party has made a corresponding declaration under the Regulations, at the latest at the time specified in that declaration.

(b) Where the Office of a designated Contracting Party has communicated a refusal and has subsequently withdrawn, in part or in whole, that refusal, the international registration shall, to the extent that the refusal is withdrawn, have the same effect in that Contracting Party as a grant of protection for the industrial design under the law of the said Contracting Party at the latest from the date on which the refusal was withdrawn.

(c) The effect given to the international registration under this paragraph shall apply to the industrial design or designs that are the subject of that registration as received from the International Bureau by the designated Office or, where applicable, as amended in the procedure before that Office.

(3) [*Declaration Concerning Effect of Designation of Applicant's Contracting Party*]

(a) Any Contracting Party whose Office is an Examining Office may, in a declaration, notify the Director General that, where it is the applicant's Contracting Party, the designation of that Contracting Party in an international registration shall have no effect.

(b) Where a Contracting Party having made the declaration referred to in subparagraph (a) is indicated in an international application both as the applicant's Contracting Party and as a designated Contracting Party, the International Bureau shall disregard the designation of that Contracting Party.

[9.416]
Article 15
Invalidation

(1) [*Requirement of Opportunity of Defence*] Invalidation, by the competent authorities of a designated Contracting Party, of the effects, in part or in whole, in the territory of that Contracting Party, of the international registration may not be pronounced without the holder having, in good time, been afforded the opportunity of defending his rights.

(2) [*Notification of Invalidation*] The Office of the Contracting Party in whose territory the effects of the international registration have been invalidated shall, where it is aware of the invalidation, notify it to the International Bureau.

[9.417]
Article 16
Recording of Changes and Other Matters Concerning International Registrations

(1) [*Recording of Changes and Other Matters*] The International Bureau shall, as prescribed, record in the International Register

(i) any change in ownership of the international registration, in respect of any or all of the designated Contracting Parties and in respect of any or all of the industrial designs that are the subject of the international registration, provided that the new owner is entitled to file an international application under Article 3,

(ii) any change in the name or address of the holder,

(iii) the appointment of a representative of the applicant or holder and any other relevant fact concerning such representative,

(iv) any renunciation, by the holder, of the international registration, in respect of any or all of the designated Contracting Parties,

(v) any limitation, by the holder, of the international registration, in respect of any or all of the designated Contracting Parties, to one or some of the industrial designs that are the subject of the international registration,

(vi) any invalidation, by the competent authorities of a designated Contracting Party, of the effects, in the territory of that Contracting Party, of the international registration in respect of any or all of the industrial designs that are the subject of the international registration,

(vii) any other relevant fact, identified in the Regulations, concerning the rights in any or all of the industrial designs that are the subject of the international registration.

(2) [*Effect of Recording in International Register*] Any recording referred to in items (i), (ii), (iv), (v), (vi) and (vii) of paragraph (1) shall have the same effect as if it had been made in the Register of the Office of each of the Contracting Parties concerned, except that a Contracting Party may, in a declaration, notify the Director General that a recording referred to in item (i) of paragraph (1) shall not have that effect in that Contracting Party until the Office of that Contracting Party has received the statements or documents specified in that declaration.

(3) [*Fees*] Any recording made under paragraph (1) may be subject to the payment of a fee.

(4) [*Publication*] The International Bureau shall publish a notice concerning any recording made under paragraph (1). It shall send a copy of the publication of the notice to the Office of each of the Contracting Parties concerned.

[9.418]
Article 17
Initial Term and Renewal of the International Registration and Duration of Protection

(1) [*Initial Term of the International Registration*] The international registration shall be effected for an initial term of five years counted from the date of the international registration.

(2) [*Renewal of the International Registration*] The international registration may be renewed for additional terms of five years, in accordance with the prescribed procedure and subject to the payment of the prescribed fees.

(3) [*Duration of Protection in Designated Contracting Parties*]

(a) Provided that the international registration is renewed, and subject to subparagraph (b), the duration of protection shall, in each of the designated Contracting Parties, be 15 years counted from the date of the international registration.

(b) Where the law of a designated Contracting Party provides for a duration of protection of more than 15 years for an industrial design for which protection has been granted under that law, the duration of protection shall, provided that the international registration is renewed, be the same as that provided for by the law of that Contracting Party.

(c) Each Contracting Party shall, in a declaration, notify the Director General of the maximum duration of protection provided for by its law.

(4) [*Possibility of Limited Renewal*] The renewal of the international registration may be effected for any or all of the designated Contracting Parties and for any or all of the industrial designs that are the subject of the international registration.

(5) [*Recording and Publication of Renewal*] The International Bureau shall record renewals in the International Register and publish a notice to that effect. It shall send a copy of the publication of the notice to the Office of each of the Contracting Parties concerned.

[9.419]
Article 18
Information Concerning Published International Registrations

(1) [*Access to Information*] The International Bureau shall supply to any person applying therefor, upon the payment of the prescribed fee, extracts from the International Register, or information concerning the contents of the International Register, in respect of any published international registration.

(2) [*Exemption from Legalization*] Extracts from the International Register supplied by the International Bureau shall be exempt from any requirement of legalization in each Contracting Party.

CHAPTER II
ADMINISTRATIVE PROVISIONS

[9.420]
Article 19
Common Office of Several States

(1) [*Notification of Common Office*] If several States intending to become party to this Act have effected, or if several States party to this Act agree to effect, the unification of their domestic legislation on industrial designs, they may notify the Director General

(i) that a common Office shall be substituted for the national Office of each of them, and

(ii) that the whole of their respective territories to which the unified legislation applies shall be deemed to be a single Contracting Party for the purposes of the application of Articles 1, 3 to 18 and 31 of this Act.

(2) [*Time at Which Notification Is to Be Made*] The notification referred to in paragraph (1) shall be made,

(i) in the case of States intending to become party to this Act, at the time of the deposit of the instruments referred to in Article 27(2);

(ii) in the case of States party to this Act, at any time after the unification of their domestic legislation has been effected.

(3) [*Date of Entry into Effect of the Notification*] The notification referred to in paragraphs (1) and (2) shall take effect,

(i) in the case of States intending to become party to this Act, at the time such States become bound by this Act;

(ii) in the case of States party to this Act, three months after the date of the communication thereof by the Director General to the other Contracting Parties or at any later date indicated in the notification.

[9.421]
Article 20
Membership of the Hague Union

The Contracting Parties shall be members of the same Union as the States party to the 1934 Act or the 1960 Act.

[9.422]
Article 21
Assembly

(1) [*Composition*]

(a) The Contracting Parties shall be members of the same Assembly as the States bound by Article 2 of the Complementary Act of 1967.

(b) Each member of the Assembly shall be represented in the Assembly by one delegate, who may be assisted by alternate delegates, advisors and experts, and each delegate may represent only one Contracting Party.

(c) Members of the Union that are not members of the Assembly shall be admitted to the meetings of the Assembly as observers.

(2) [*Tasks*]

(a) The Assembly shall

(i) deal with all matters concerning the maintenance and development of the Union and the implementation of this Act;

(ii) exercise such rights and perform such tasks as are specifically conferred upon it or assigned to it under this Act or the Complementary Act of 1967;

(iii) give directions to the Director General concerning the preparations for conferences of revision and decide the convocation of any such conference;

(iv) amend the Regulations;

(v) review and approve the reports and activities of the Director General concerning the Union, and give the Director General all necessary instructions concerning matters within the competence of the Union;

(vi) determine the program and adopt the biennial budget of the Union, and approve its final accounts;

(vii) adopt the financial regulations of the Union;

(viii) establish such committees and working groups as it deems appropriate to achieve the objectives of the Union;

(ix) subject to paragraph (1)(c), determine which States, intergovernmental organisations and non-governmental organisations shall be admitted to its meetings as observers;

(x) take any other appropriate action to further the objectives of the Union and perform any other functions as are appropriate under this Act.

(b) With respect to matters which are also of interest to other Unions administered by the organisation, the Assembly shall make its decisions after having heard the advice of the Coordination Committee of the organisation.

(3) [*Quorum*]

(a) One-half of the members of the Assembly which are States and have the right to vote on a given matter shall constitute a quorum for the purposes of the vote on that matter.

(b) Notwithstanding the provisions of subparagraph (a), if, in any session, the number of the members of the Assembly which are States, have the right to vote on a given matter and are represented is less than one-half but equal to or more than one-third of the members of the Assembly which are States and have the right to vote on that matter, the Assembly may make decisions but, with the exception of decisions concerning its own procedure, all such decisions shall take effect only if the conditions set forth hereinafter are fulfilled. The International Bureau shall communicate the said decisions to the members of the Assembly which are States, have the right to vote on the said matter and were not represented and shall invite them to express in writing their vote or abstention within a period of three months from the date of the communication. If, at the expiration of this period, the number of such members having thus expressed their vote or abstention attains the number of the members which was lacking for attaining the quorum in the session itself, such decisions shall take effect provided that at the same time the required majority still obtains.

(4) [*Taking Decisions in the Assembly*]

(a) The Assembly shall endeavour to take its decisions by consensus.

(b) Where a decision cannot be arrived at by consensus, the matter at issue shall be decided by voting. In such a case,

(i) each Contracting Party that is a State shall have one vote and shall vote only in its own name, and

(ii) any Contracting Party that is an intergovernmental organisation may vote, in place of its Member States, with a number of votes equal to the number of its Member States which are party to this Act, and no such intergovernmental organisation shall participate in the vote if any one of its Member States exercises its right to vote, and *vice versa*.

(c) On matters concerning only States that are bound by Article 2 of the Complementary Act of 1967, Contracting Parties that are not bound by the said Article shall not have the right to vote, whereas, on matters concerning only Contracting Parties, only the latter shall have the right to vote.

(5) [*Majorities*]

(a) Subject to Articles 24(2) and 26(2), the decisions of the Assembly shall require two-thirds of the votes cast.

(b) Abstentions shall not be considered as votes.

(6) [*Sessions*]

(a) The Assembly shall meet once in every second calendar year in ordinary session upon convocation by the Director General and, in the absence of exceptional circumstances, during the same period and at the same place as the General Assembly of the organisation.

(b) The Assembly shall meet in extraordinary session upon convocation by the Director General, either at the request of one-fourth of the members of the Assembly or on the Director General's own initiative.

(c) The agenda of each session shall be prepared by the Director General.

(7) [*Rules of Procedure*] The Assembly shall adopt its own rules of procedure.

[9.423]
Article 22
International Bureau

(1) [*Administrative Tasks*]

(a) International registration and related duties, as well as all other administrative tasks concerning the Union, shall be performed by the International Bureau.

(b) In particular, the International Bureau shall prepare the meetings and provide the secretariat of the Assembly and of such committees of experts and working groups as may be established by the Assembly.

(2) [*Director General*] The Director General shall be the chief executive of the Union and shall represent the Union.

(3) [*Meetings Other than Sessions of the Assembly*] The Director General shall convene any committee and working group established by the Assembly and all other meetings dealing with matters of concern to the Union.

(4) [*Role of the International Bureau in the Assembly and Other Meetings*]

(a) The Director General and persons designated by the Director General shall participate, without the right to vote, in all meetings of the Assembly, the committees and working groups established by the Assembly, and any other meetings convened by the Director General under the aegis of the Union.

(b) The Director General or a staff member designated by the Director General shall be *ex officio* secretary of the Assembly, and of the committees, working groups and other meetings referred to in subparagraph (a).

(5) [*Conferences*]

(a) The International Bureau shall, in accordance with the directions of the Assembly, make the preparations for any revision conferences.

(b) The International Bureau may consult with intergovernmental organisations and international and national non-governmental organisations concerning the said preparations.

(c) The Director General and persons designated by the Director General shall take part, without the right to vote, in the discussions at revision conferences.

(6) [*Other Tasks*] The International Bureau shall carry out any other tasks assigned to it in relation to this Act.

[9.424]
Article 23
Finances

(1) [*Budget*]

(a) The Union shall have a budget.

(b) The budget of the Union shall include the income and expenses proper to the Union and its contribution to the budget of expenses common to the Unions administered by the organisation.

(c) Expenses not attributable exclusively to the Union but also to one or more other Unions administered by the organisation shall be considered to be expenses common to the Unions. The share of the Union in such common expenses shall be in proportion to the interest the Union has in them.

(2) [*Coordination with Budgets of Other Unions*] The budget of the Union shall be established with due regard to the requirements of coordination with the budgets of the other Unions administered by the organisation.

(3) [*Sources of Financing of the Budget*] The budget of the Union shall be financed from the following sources:

(i) fees relating to international registrations;

(ii) charges due for other services rendered by the International Bureau in relation to the Union;

(iii) sale of, or royalties on, the publications of the International Bureau concerning the Union;

(iv) gifts, bequests and subventions;

(v) rents, interests and other miscellaneous income.

(4) [*Fixing of Fees and Charges; Level of the Budget*]

(a) The amounts of the fees referred to in paragraph (3)(i) shall be fixed by the Assembly on the proposal of the Director General. Charges referred to in paragraph 3(ii) shall be established by the Director General and shall be provisionally applied subject to approval by the Assembly at its next session.

(b) The amounts of the fees referred to in paragraph (3)(i) shall be so fixed that the revenues of the Union from fees and other sources shall be at least sufficient to cover all the expenses of the International Bureau concerning the Union.

(c) If the budget is not adopted before the beginning of a new financial period, it shall be at the same level as the budget of the previous year, as provided in the financial regulations.

(5) [*Working Capital Fund*] The Union shall have a working capital fund which shall be constituted by the excess receipts and, if such excess does not suffice, by a single payment made by each member of the Union. If the fund becomes insufficient, the Assembly shall decide to increase it. The proportion and the terms of payment shall be fixed by the Assembly on the proposal of the Director General.

(6) [*Advances by Host State*]

(a) In the headquarters agreement concluded with the State on the territory of which the organisation has its headquarters, it shall be provided that, whenever the working capital fund is insufficient, such State shall grant advances. The amount of those advances and the conditions on which they are granted shall be the subject of separate agreements, in each case, between such State and the organisation.

(b) The State referred to in subparagraph (a) and the organisation shall each have the right to denounce the obligation to grant advances, by written notification. Denunciation shall take effect three years after the end of the year in which it has been notified.

(7) [*Auditing of Accounts*] The auditing of the accounts shall be effected by one or more of the States members of the Union or by external auditors, as provided in the financial regulations. They shall be designated, with their agreement, by the Assembly.

[9.425]
Article 24
Regulations

(1) [*Subject Matter*] The Regulations shall govern the details of the implementation of this Act. They shall, in particular, include provisions concerning

(i) matters which this Act expressly provides are to be prescribed;

(ii) further details concerning, or any details useful in the implementation of, the provisions of this Act;

(iii) any administrative requirements, matters or procedures.

(2) [*Amendment of Certain Provisions of the Regulations*]

(a) The Regulations may specify that certain provisions of the Regulations may be amended only by unanimity or only by a four-fifths majority.

(b) In order for the requirement of unanimity or a four-fifths majority no longer to apply in the future to the amendment of a provision of the Regulations, unanimity shall be required.

(c) In order for the requirement of unanimity or a four-fifths majority to apply in the future to the amendment of a provision of the Regulations, a four-fifths majority shall be required.

(3) [*Conflict Between This Act and the Regulations*] In the case of conflict between the provisions of this Act and those of the Regulations, the former shall prevail.

CHAPTER III
REVISION AND AMENDMENT

[9.426]
Article 25
Revision of This Act

(1) [*Revision Conferences*] This Act may be revised by a conference of the Contracting Parties.

(2) [*Revision or Amendment of Certain Articles*] Articles 21, 22, 23 and 26 may be amended either by a revision conference or by the Assembly according to the provisions of Article 26.

[9.427]
Article 26
Amendment of Certain Articles by the Assembly

(1) [*Proposals for Amendment*]

(a) Proposals for the amendment by the Assembly of Articles 21, 22, 23 and this Article may be initiated by any Contracting Party or by the Director General.

(b) Such proposals shall be communicated by the Director General to the Contracting Parties at least six months in advance of their consideration by the Assembly.

(2) [*Majorities*] Adoption of any amendment to the Articles referred to in paragraph (1) shall require a three-fourths majority, except that adoption of any amendment to Article 21 or to the present paragraph shall require a four-fifths majority.

(3) [*Entry into Force*]

(a) Except where subparagraph (b) applies, any amendment to the Articles referred to in paragraph (1) shall enter into force one month after written notifications of acceptance, effected in accordance with their respective constitutional processes, have been received by the Director General from three-fourths of those Contracting Parties which, at the time the amendment was adopted, were members of the Assembly and had the right to vote on that amendment.

(b) Any amendment to Article 21(3) or (4) or to this subparagraph shall not enter into force if, within six months of its adoption by the Assembly, any Contracting Party notifies the Director General that it does not accept such amendment.

(c) Any amendment which enters into force in accordance with the provisions of this paragraph shall bind all the States and intergovernmental organisations which are Contracting Parties at the time the amendment enters into force, or which become Contracting Parties at a subsequent date.

CHAPTER IV
FINAL PROVISIONS

[9.428]
Article 27
Becoming Party to This Act

(1) [*Eligibility*] Subject to paragraphs (2) and (3) and Article 28,

(i) any State member of the organisation may sign and become party to this Act;

(ii) any intergovernmental organisation which maintains an Office in which protection of industrial designs may be obtained with effect in the territory in which the constituting treaty of the intergovernmental organisation applies may sign and become party to this Act, provided that at least one of the member States of the intergovernmental organisation is a member of the organisation and provided that such Office is not the subject of a notification under Article 19.

(2) [*Ratification or Accession*] Any State or intergovernmental organisation referred to in paragraph (1) may deposit

(i) an instrument of ratification if it has signed this Act, or

(ii) an instrument of accession if it has not signed this Act.

(3) [*Effective Date of Deposit*]

(a) Subject to subparagraphs (b) to (d), the effective date of the deposit of an instrument of ratification or accession shall be the date on which that instrument is deposited.

(b) The effective date of the deposit of the instrument of ratification or accession of any State in respect of which protection of industrial designs may be obtained only through the Office maintained by an intergovernmental organisation of which that State is a member shall be the date on which the instrument of that intergovernmental organisation is deposited if that date is later than the date on which the instrument of the said State has been deposited.

(c) The effective date of the deposit of any instrument of ratification or accession containing or accompanied by the notification referred to in Article 19 shall be the date on which the last of the instruments of the States members of the group of States having made the said notification is deposited.

(d) Any instrument of ratification or accession of a State may contain or be accompanied by a declaration making it a condition to its being considered as deposited that the instrument of one other State or one intergovernmental organisation, or the instruments of two other States, or the instruments of one other State and one intergovernmental organisation, specified by name and eligible to become party to this Act, is or are also deposited. The instrument containing or accompanied by such a declaration shall be considered to have been deposited on the day on which the condition indicated in the declaration is fulfilled. However, when an instrument specified in the declaration itself contains, or is itself accompanied by, a declaration of the said kind, that instrument shall be considered as deposited on the day on which the condition specified in the latter declaration is fulfilled.

(e) Any declaration made under paragraph (d) may be withdrawn, in its entirety or in part, at any time. Any such withdrawal shall become effective on the date on which the notification of withdrawal is received by the Director General.

[9.429]
Article 28
Effective Date of Ratifications and Accessions

(1) [*Instruments to Be Taken into Consideration*] For the purposes of this Article, only instruments of ratification or accession that are deposited by States or intergovernmental organisations referred to in Article 27(1) and that have an effective date according to Article 27(3) shall be taken into consideration.

(2) [*Entry into Force of This Act*] This Act shall enter into force three months after six States have deposited their instruments of ratification or accession, provided that, according to the most recent annual statistics collected by the International Bureau, at least three of those States fulfil at least one of the following conditions:

(i) at least 3,000 applications for the protection of industrial designs have been filed in or for the State concerned, or

(ii) at least 1,000 applications for the protection of industrial designs have been filed in or for the State concerned by residents of States other than that State.

(3) [*Entry into Force of Ratifications and Accessions*]

(a) Any State or intergovernmental organisation that has deposited its instrument of ratification or accession three months or more before the date of entry into force of this Act shall become bound by this Act on the date of entry into force of this Act.

(b) Any other State or intergovernmental organisation shall become bound by this Act three months after the date on which it has deposited its instrument of ratification or accession or at any later date indicated in that instrument.

[9.430]
Article 29
Prohibition of Reservations

No reservations to this Act are permitted.

[9.431]
Article 30
Declarations Made by Contracting Parties

(1) [*Time at Which Declarations May Be Made*] Any declaration under Articles 4(1)(b), 5(2)(a), 7(2), 11(1), 13(1), 14(3), 16(2) or 17(3)(c) may be made

(i) at the time of the deposit of an instrument referred to in Article 27(2), in which case it shall become effective on the date on which the State or intergovernmental organisation having made the declaration becomes bound by this Act, or

(ii) after the deposit of an instrument referred to in Article 27(2), in which case it shall become effective three months after the date of its receipt by the Director General or at any later date indicated in the declaration but shall apply only in respect of any international registration whose date of international registration is the same as, or is later than, the effective date of the declaration.

(2) [*Declarations by States Having a Common Office*] Notwithstanding paragraph (1), any declaration referred to in that paragraph that has been made by a State which has, with another State or other States, notified the Director General under Article 19(1) of the substitution of a common Office for their national Offices shall become effective only if that other State or those other States makes or make a corresponding declaration or corresponding declarations.

(3) [*Withdrawal of Declarations*] Any declaration referred to in paragraph (1) may be withdrawn at any time by notification addressed to the Director General. Such withdrawal shall take effect three months after the date on which the Director General has received the notification or at any later date indicated in the notification. In the case of a declaration made under Article 7(2), the withdrawal shall not affect international applications filed prior to the coming into effect of the said withdrawal.

[9.432]
Article 31
Applicability of the 1934 and 1960 Acts

(1) [*Relations Between States Party to Both This Act and the 1934 or 1960 Acts*] This Act alone shall be applicable as regards the mutual relations of States party to both this Act and the 1934 Act or the 1960 Act. However, such States shall, in their mutual relations, apply the 1934 Act or the 1960 Act, as the case may be, to industrial designs deposited at the International Bureau prior to the date on which this Act becomes applicable as regards their mutual relations.

(2) [*Relations Between States Party to Both This Act and the 1934 or 1960 Acts and States Party to the 1934 or 1960 Acts Without Being Party to This Act*]

(a) Any State that is party to both this Act and the 1934 Act shall continue to apply the 1934 Act in its relations with States that are party to the 1934 Act without being party to the 1960 Act or this Act.

(b) Any State that is party to both this Act and the 1960 Act shall continue to apply the 1960 Act in its relations with States that are party to the 1960 Act without being party to this Act.

[9.433]
Article 32
Denunciation of This Act

(1) [*Notification*] Any Contracting Party may denounce this Act by notification addressed to the Director General.

(2) [*Effective Date*] Denunciation shall take effect one year after the date on which the Director General has received the notification or at any later date indicated in the notification. It shall not affect the application of this Act to any international application pending and any international registration in force in respect of the denouncing Contracting Party at the time of the coming into effect of the denunciation.

[9.434]
Article 33
Languages of This Act; Signature

(1) [*Original Texts; Official Texts*]

(a) This Act shall be signed in a single original in the English, Arabic, Chinese, French, Russian and Spanish languages, all texts being equally authentic.

(b) Official texts shall be established by the Director General, after consultation with the interested Governments, in such other languages as the Assembly may designate.

(2) [*Time Limit for Signature*] This Act shall remain open for signature at the headquarters of the organisation for one year after its adoption.

[9.435]
Article 34
Depositary

The Director General shall be the depositary of this Act.

REGULATIONS UNDER THE GENEVA ACT OF THE HAGUE AGREEMENT CONCERNING THE INTERNATIONAL REGISTRATION OF INDUSTRIAL DESIGNS

as in force on January 1, 2017

NOTES

The original source of these Regulations is the World Intellectual Property Organisation (WIPO).

CHAPTER 1
GENERAL PROVISIONS

[9.436]
Rule 1
Definitions

(1) *[Abbreviated Expressions]* For the purposes of these Regulations,

(i) "1999 Act" means the Act signed at Geneva on July 2, 1999, of the Hague Agreement;

(ii) "1960 Act" means the Act signed at The Hague on November 28, 1960, of the Hague Agreement;

(iii) an expression which is used in these Regulations and is referred to in Article 1 of the 1999 Act has the same meaning as in that Act;

(iv) "Administrative Instructions" means the Administrative Instructions referred to in Rule 34;

(v) "communication" means any international application or any request, declaration, invitation, notification or information relating to or accompanying an international application or an international registration that is addressed to the Office of a Contracting Party, the International Bureau, the applicant or the holder by means permitted by these Regulations or the Administrative Instructions;

(vi) "official form" means a form established by the International Bureau or any form having the same contents and format;

(vii) "International Classification" means the Classification established under the Locarno Agreement Establishing an International Classification for Industrial Designs;

(viii) "prescribed fee" means the applicable fee set out in the Schedule of Fees;

(ix) "Bulletin" means the periodical bulletin in which the International Bureau effects the publications provided for in the 1999 Act, the 1960 Act or these Regulations, whatever the medium used;

(x) "Contracting Party designated under the 1999 Act" means a designated Contracting Party in respect of which the 1999 Act is applicable, either as the only common Act to which that designated Contracting Party and the applicant's Contracting Party are bound, or by virtue of Article 31(1), first sentence, of the 1999 Act;

(xi) "Contracting Party designated under the 1960 Act" means a designated Contracting Party in respect of which the 1960 Act is applicable, either as the only common Act to which that designated Contracting Party and the State of origin referred to in Article 2 of the 1960 Act are bound, or by virtue of Article 31(1), second sentence, of the 1999 Act;

(xii) "international application governed exclusively by the 1999 Act" means an international application in respect of which all designated Contracting Parties are Contracting Parties designated under the 1999 Act;

(xiii) "international application governed exclusively by the 1960 Act" means an international application in respect of which all designated Contracting Parties are Contracting Parties designated under the 1960 Act;

(xiv) "international application governed by both the 1999 Act and the 1960 Act" means an international application in respect of which

— at least one Contracting Party has been designated under the 1999 Act,

— at least one Contracting Party has been designated under the 1960 Act.

(2) *[Correspondence Between Some Expressions Used in the 1999 Act and the 1960 Act]* For the purposes of these Regulations,

(i) reference to "international application" or "international registration" shall be deemed, where appropriate, to include a reference to "international deposit" as referred to in the 1960 Act;

(ii) reference to "applicant" or "holder" shall be deemed, where appropriate, to include a reference to, respectively, "depositor" or "owner" as referred to in the 1960 Act;

(iii) reference to "Contracting Party" shall be deemed, where appropriate, to include a reference to a State party to the 1960 Act;

(iv) reference to "Contracting Party whose Office is an examining Office" shall be deemed, where appropriate, to include a reference to "State having a novelty examination" as defined in Article 2 of the 1960 Act;

(v) reference to "individual designation fee" shall be deemed, where appropriate, to include a reference to the fee mentioned in Article 15(1)2(b) of the 1960 Act.

[9.437]
Rule 2
Communication with the International Bureau

Communications addressed to the International Bureau shall be effected as specified in the Administrative Instructions.

[9.438]
Rule 3
Representation Before the International Bureau

(1) [*Representative; Number of Representatives*]

(a) The applicant or the holder may have a representative before the International Bureau.

(b) Only one representative may be appointed in respect of a given international application or international registration. Where the appointment indicates several representatives, only the one indicated first shall be considered to be a representative and be recorded as such.

(c) Where a partnership or firm composed of attorneys or patent or trademark agents has been indicated as representative to the International Bureau, it shall be regarded as one representative.

(2) [*Appointment of the Representative*]

(a) The appointment of a representative may be made in the international application, provided that the application is signed by the applicant.

(b) The appointment of a representative may also be made in a separate communication which may relate to one or more specified international applications or international registrations of the same applicant or holder. The said communication shall be signed by the applicant or the holder.

(c) Where the International Bureau considers that the appointment of a representative is irregular, it shall notify accordingly the applicant or holder and the purported representative.

(3) [*Recording and Notification of Appointment of a Representative; Effective Date of Appointment*]

(a) Where the International Bureau finds that the appointment of a representative complies with the applicable requirements, it shall record the fact that the applicant or holder has a representative, as well as the name and address of the representative, in the International Register. In such a case, the effective date of the appointment shall be the date on which the International Bureau received the international application or separate communication in which the representative is appointed.

(b) The International Bureau shall notify the recording referred to in subparagraph (a) to both the applicant or holder and the representative.

(4) [*Effect of Appointment of a Representative*]

(a) Except where these Regulations expressly provide otherwise, the signature of a representative recorded under paragraph (3)(a) shall replace the signature of the applicant or holder.

(b) Except where these Regulations expressly require that a communication be addressed to both the applicant or holder and the representative, the International Bureau shall address to the representative recorded under paragraph (3)(a) any communication which, in the absence of a representative, would have to be sent to the applicant or holder; any communication so addressed to the said representative shall have the same effect as if it had been addressed to the applicant or holder.

(c) Any communication addressed to the International Bureau by the representative recorded under paragraph (3)(a) shall have the same effect as if it had been addressed to the said Bureau by the applicant or holder.

(5) [*Cancellation of Recording; Effective Date of Cancellation*]

(a) Any recording under paragraph (3)(a) shall be cancelled where cancellation is requested in a communication signed by the applicant, holder or representative. The recording shall be cancelled *ex officio* by the International Bureau where a new representative is appointed or where a change in ownership is recorded and no representative is appointed by the new holder of the international registration.

(b) The cancellation shall be effective from the date on which the International Bureau receives the corresponding communication.

(c) The International Bureau shall notify the cancellation and its effective date to the representative whose recording has been cancelled and to the applicant or holder.

[9.439]
Rule 4
Calculation of Time Limits

(1) [*Periods Expressed in Years*] Any period expressed in years shall expire, in the relevant subsequent year, in the month having the same name and on the day having the same number as the month and the day of the event from which the period starts to run, except that, where the event occurred on February 29 and in the relevant subsequent year February ends on the 28th, the period shall expire on February 28.

(2) [*Periods Expressed in Months*] Any period expressed in months shall expire, in the relevant subsequent month, on the day which has the same number as the day of the event from which the period starts to run, except that, where the relevant subsequent month has no day with the same number, the period shall expire on the last day of that month.
(3) [*Periods Expressed in Days*] The calculation of any period expressed in days shall start with the day following the day on which the relevant event occurred and shall expire accordingly.
(4) [*Expiry on a Day on Which the International Bureau or an Office Is Not Open to the Public*] If a period expires on a day on which the International Bureau or the Office concerned is not open to the public, the period shall, notwithstanding paragraphs (1) to (3), expire on the first subsequent day on which the International Bureau or the Office concerned is open to the public.

[9.440]
Rule 5
Excuse of Delay in Meeting Time Limits
(1) [*Communications Sent Through a Postal Service*] Failure by an interested party to meet a time limit for a communication addressed to the International Bureau and mailed through a postal service shall be excused if the interested party submits evidence showing, to the satisfaction of the International Bureau,
- (i) that the communication was mailed at least five days prior to the expiry of the time limit, or, where the postal service was, on any of the ten days preceding the day of expiry of the time limit, interrupted on account of war, revolution, civil disorder, strike, natural calamity, or other like reason, that the communication was mailed not later than five days after postal service was resumed,
- (ii) that the mailing of the communication was registered, or details of the mailing were recorded, by the postal service at the time of mailing, and
- (iii) in cases where not all classes of mail normally reach the International Bureau within two days of mailing, that the communication was mailed by a class of mail which normally reaches the International Bureau within two days of mailing or by airmail.

(2) [*Communications Sent Through a Delivery Service*] Failure by an interested party to meet a time limit for a communication addressed to the International Bureau and sent through a delivery service shall be excused if the interested party submits evidence showing, to the satisfaction of the International Bureau,
- (i) that the communication was sent at least five days prior to the expiry of the time limit, or, where the delivery service was, on any of the ten days preceding the day of expiry of the time limit, interrupted on account of war, revolution, civil disorder, natural calamity, or other like reason, that the communication was sent not later than five days after the delivery service was resumed, and
- (ii) that details of the sending of the communication were recorded by the delivery service at the time of sending.

(3) [*Communication Sent Electronically*] Failure by an interested party to meet a time limit for a communication addressed to the International Bureau and submitted by electronic means shall be excused if the interested party submits evidence showing, to the satisfaction of the International Bureau, that the time limit was not met because of failure in the electronic communication with the International Bureau, or which affects the locality of the interested party owing to extraordinary circumstances beyond the control of the interested party, and that the communication was effected not later than five days after the electronic communication service was resumed.
(4) [*Limitation on Excuse*] Failure to meet a time limit shall be excused under this Rule only if the evidence referred to in paragraph (1), (2) or (3) and the communication or, where applicable, a duplicate thereof are received by the International Bureau not later than six months after the expiry of the time limit.
(3) [*Exception*] This rule shall not apply to the payment of the second part of the individual designation fee through the International Bureau as referred to in Rule 12(3)(c).

[9.441]
Rule 6
Languages
(1) [*International Application*] The international application shall be in English, French or Spanish.
(2) [*Recording and Publication*] The recording in the International Register and the publication in the Bulletin of the international registration and of any data to be both recorded and published under these Regulations in respect of that international registration shall be in English, French and Spanish. The recording and publication of the international registration shall indicate the language in which the international application was received by the International Bureau.
(3) [*Communications*] Any communication concerning an international application or an international registration shall be
- (i) in English, French or Spanish where such communication is addressed to the International Bureau by the applicant or holder or by an Office;

(ii) in the language of the international application where the communication is addressed by the International Bureau to an Office, unless that Office has notified the International Bureau that any such communications are to be in English, or in French or in Spanish;
(iii) in the language of the international application where the communication is addressed by the International Bureau to the applicant or holder unless that applicant or holder has expressed the wish that all such communications be in English, or be in French or be in Spanish.

(4) [*Translation*] The translations needed for the recordings and publications under paragraph (2) shall be made by the International Bureau. The applicant may annex to the international application a proposed translation of any text matter contained in the international application. If the proposed translation is not considered by the International Bureau to be correct, it shall be corrected by the International Bureau after having invited the applicant to make, within one month from the invitation, observations on the proposed corrections.

CHAPTER 2
INTERNATIONAL APPLICATIONS AND INTERNATIONAL REGISTRATIONS

[9.442]
Rule 7
Requirements Concerning the International Application

(1) [*Form and Signature*] The international application shall be presented on the official form. The international application shall be signed by the applicant.

(2) [*Fees*] The prescribed fees applicable to the international application shall be paid as provided for in Rules 27 and 28.

(3) [*Mandatory Contents of the International Application*] The international application shall contain or indicate

(i) the name of the applicant, given in accordance with the Administrative Instructions;
(ii) the address of the applicant, given in accordance with the Administrative Instructions;
(iii) the Contracting Party or Parties in respect of which the applicant fulfils the conditions to be the holder of an international registration;
(iv) the product or products which constitute the industrial design or in relation to which the industrial design is to be used, with an indication whether the product or products constitute the industrial design or are products in relation to which the industrial design is to be used; the product or products shall preferably be identified by using terms appearing in the list of goods of the International Classification;
(v) the number of industrial designs included in the international application, which may not exceed 100, and the number of reproductions or specimens of the industrial designs accompanying the international application in accordance with Rule 9 or 10;
(vi) the designated Contracting Parties;
(vii) the amount of the fees being paid and the method of payment, or instructions to debit the required amount of fees to an account opened with the International Bureau, and the identification of the party effecting the payment or giving the instructions.

(4) [*Additional Mandatory Contents of an International Application*]

(a) With respect to Contracting Parties designated under the 1999 Act in an international application, that application shall contain, in addition to the indications referred to in paragraph (3)(iii), the indication of the applicant's Contracting Party.
(b) Where a Contracting Party designated under the 1999 Act has notified the Director General, in accordance with Article 5(2)(a) of the 1999 Act, that its law requires one or more of the elements referred to in Article 5(2)(b) of the 1999 Act, the international application shall contain such element or elements, as prescribed in Rule 11.
(c) Where Rule 8 applies, the international application shall contain the indications referred to in Rule 8(2) and, where applicable, be accompanied by the statement or document referred to in that Rule.

(5) [*Optional Contents of an International Application*]

(a) An element referred to in item (i) or (ii) of Article 5(2)(b) of the 1999 Act or in Article 8(4)(a) of the 1960 Act may, at the option of the applicant, be included in the international application even where that element is not required in consequence of a notification in accordance with Article 5(2)(a) of the 1999 Act or in consequence of a requirement under Article 8(4)(a) of the 1960 Act.
(b) Where the applicant has a representative, the international application shall state the name and address of the representative, given in accordance with the Administrative Instructions.
(c) Where the applicant wishes, under Article 4 of the Paris Convention, to take advantage of the priority of an earlier filing, the international application shall contain a declaration claiming the priority of that earlier filing, together with an indication of the name of the Office where such filing was made and of the date and, where available, the number of that filing and, where the priority claim relates to less than all the industrial designs contained in the international application, the indication of those industrial designs to which the priority claim relates or does not relate.

(d) Where the applicant wishes to take advantage of Article 11 of the Paris Convention, the international application shall contain a declaration that the product or products which constitute the industrial design or in which the industrial design is incorporated have been shown at an official or officially recognised international exhibition, together with the place where the exhibition was held and the date on which the product or products were first exhibited there and, where less than all the industrial designs contained in the international application are concerned, the indication of those industrial designs to which the declaration relates or does not relate.

(e) Where the applicant wishes that publication of the industrial design be deferred, the international application shall contain a request for deferment of publication.

(f) The international application may also contain any declaration, statement or other relevant indication as may be specified in the Administrative Instructions.

(g) The international application may be accompanied by a statement that identifies information known by the applicant to be material to the eligibility for protection of the industrial design concerned.

(6) [*No Additional Matter*] If the international application contains any matter other than that required or permitted by the 1999 Act, the 1960 Act, these Regulations or the Administrative Instructions, the International Bureau shall delete it *ex officio*. If the international application is accompanied by any document other than those required or permitted, the International Bureau may dispose of the said document.

(7) [*All Products to Be in Same Class*] All the products which constitute the industrial designs to which an international application relates, or in relation to which the industrial designs are to be used, shall belong to the same class of the International Classification.

[9.443]
Rule 8
Special Requirements Concerning the Applicant

(1) [*Notification of Special Requirements Concerning the Applicant and the Creator*]

(a)

(i) Where the law of a Contracting Party bound by the 1999 Act requires that an application for the protection of an industrial design be filed in the name of the creator of the industrial design, that Contracting Party may, in a declaration, notify the Director General of that fact.

(ii) Where the law of a Contracting Party bound by the 1999 Act requires the furnishing of an oath or declaration of the creator, that Contracting Party may, in a declaration, notify the Director General of that fact.

(b) The declaration referred to in subparagraph (a)(i) shall specify the form and mandatory contents of any statement or document required for the purposes of paragraph (2). The declaration referred to in subparagraph (a)(ii) shall specify the form and mandatory contents of the oath or declaration required.

(2) [*Identity of the Creator and Assignment of International Application*] Where an international application contains the designation of a Contracting Party that has made the declaration referred to in paragraph (1)(a)(i),

(i) it shall also contain indications concerning the identity of the creator of the industrial design, together with a statement, complying with the requirements specified in accordance with paragraph (1)(b), that the latter believes himself to be the creator of the industrial design; the person so identified as the creator shall be deemed to be the applicant for the purposes of the designation of that Contracting Party, irrespective of the person named as the applicant in accordance with Rule 7(3)(i);

(ii) where the person identified as the creator is a person other than the person named as the applicant in accordance with Rule 7(3)(i), the international application shall be accompanied by a statement or document, complying with the requirements specified in accordance with paragraph (1)(b), to the effect that it has been assigned by the person identified as the creator to the person named as the applicant. The latter person shall be recorded as the holder of the international registration.

[9.444]
Rule 9
Reproductions of the Industrial Design

(1) [*Form and Number of Reproductions of the Industrial Design*]

(a) Reproductions of the industrial design shall, at the option of the applicant, be in the form of photographs or other graphic representations of the industrial design itself or of the product or products which constitute the industrial design. The same product may be shown from different angles; views from different angles shall be included in different photographs or other graphic representations.

(b) Any reproduction shall be submitted in the number of copies specified in the Administrative Instructions.

(2) [*Requirements Concerning Reproductions*]

(a) Reproductions shall be of a quality permitting all the details of the industrial design to be clearly distinguished and permitting publication.
(b) Matter which is shown in a reproduction but for which protection is not sought may be indicated as provided for in the Administrative Instructions.

(3) [*Views Required*]
(a) Subject to subparagraph (b), any Contracting Party bound by the 1999 Act which requires certain specified views of the product or products which constitute the industrial design or in relation to which the industrial design is to be used shall, in a declaration, so notify the Director General, specifying the views that are required and the circumstances in which they are required.
(b) No Contracting Party may require more than one view where the industrial design or product is two-dimensional, or more than six views where the product is three-dimensional.

(4) [*Refusal on Grounds Relating to the Reproductions of the Industrial Design*] A Contracting Party may not refuse the effects of the international registration on the ground that requirements relating to the form of the reproductions of the industrial design that are additional to, or different from, those notified by that Contracting Party in accordance with paragraph (3)(a) have not been satisfied under its law. A Contracting Party may however refuse the effects of the international registration on the ground that the reproductions contained in the international registration are not sufficient to disclose fully the industrial design.

[9.445]
Rule 10
Specimens of the Industrial Design Where Deferment of Publication Is Requested

(1) [*Number of Specimens*] Where an international application governed exclusively by the 1999 Act contains a request for deferment of publication in respect of a two-dimensional industrial design and, instead of being accompanied by the reproductions referred to in Rule 9, is accompanied by specimens of the industrial design, the following number of specimens shall accompany the international application:
(i) one specimen for the International Bureau, and
(ii) one specimen for each designated Office that has notified the International Bureau under Article 10(5) of the 1999 Act that it wishes to receive copies of international registrations.

(2) [*Specimens*] All the specimens shall be contained in a single package. The specimens may be folded. The maximum dimensions and weight of the package shall be specified in the Administrative Instructions.

[9.446]
Rule 11
Identity of Creator; Description; Claim

(1) [*Identity of Creator*] Where the international application contains indications concerning the identity of the creator of the industrial design, his name and address shall be given in accordance with the Administrative Instructions.

(2) [*Description*] Where the international application contains a description, the latter shall concern those features that appear in the reproductions of the industrial design and may not concern technical features of the operation of the industrial design or its possible utilisation. If the description exceeds 100 words, an additional fee, as set out in the Schedule of Fees, shall be payable.

(3) [*Claim*] A declaration under Article 5(2)(a) of the 1999 Act that the law of a Contracting Party requires a claim in order for an application for the grant of protection to an industrial design to be accorded a filing date under that law shall specify the exact wording of the required claim. Where the international application contains a claim, the wording of that claim shall be as specified in the said declaration.

[9.447]
Rule 12
Fees Concerning the International Application

(1) [*Prescribed Fees*]
(a) The international application shall be subject to the payment of the following fees:
(i) a basic fee;
(ii) a standard designation fee in respect of each designated Contracting Party that has not made a declaration under Article 7(2) of the 1999 Act or under Rule 36(1), the level of which will depend on a declaration made under subparagraph (c);
(iii) an individual designation fee in respect of each designated Contracting Party that has made a declaration under Article 7(2) of the 1999 Act or under Rule 36(1);
(iv) a publication fee.
(b) The level of the standard designation fee referred to in subparagraph (a)(ii) shall be as follows:
(i) for Contracting Parties whose Office does not carry out any examination on substantive grounds: . . . . one

(ii) for Contracting Parties whose Office carries out examination on substantive grounds, other than as to novelty: . . . . two

(iii) for Contracting Parties whose Office carries out examination on substantive grounds, including examination as to novelty either *ex officIo* or following opposition by third parties: . . . . three

(c)

(i) Any Contracting Party whose legislation entitles it to the application of level two or three under subparagraph (b) may, in a declaration, notify the Director General accordingly. A Contracting Party may also, in its declaration, specify that it opts for the application of level two, even if its legislation entitles it to the application of level three.

(ii) Any declaration made under item (i) shall take effect three months after its receipt by the Director General or at any later date indicated in the declaration. It may also be withdrawn at any time by notification addressed to the Director General, in which case such withdrawal shall take effect one month after its receipt by the Director General or at any later date indicated in the notification. In the absence of such a declaration, or where a declaration has been withdrawn, level one will be deemed to be the level applicable to the standard designation fee in respect of that Contracting Party.

(2) [*When Fees to Be Paid*] The fees referred to in paragraph (1) are, subject to paragraph (3), payable at the time of filing the international application, except that, where the international application contains a request for deferment of publication, the publication fee may be paid later, in accordance with Rule 16(3)(a).

(3) [*Individual Designation Fee Payable in Two Parts*]

(a) A declaration under Article 7(2) of the 1999 Act or under Rule 36(1) may also specify that the individual designation fee to be paid in respect of the Contracting Party concerned comprises two parts, the first part to be paid at the time of filing the international application and the second part to be paid at a later date which is determined in accordance with the law of the Contracting Party concerned.

(b) Where subparagraph (a) applies, the reference in paragraph (1)(iii) to an individual designation fee shall be construed as a reference to the first part of the individual designation fee.

(c) The second part of the individual designation fee may be paid either directly to the Office concerned or through the International Bureau, at the option of the holder. Where it is paid directly to the Office concerned, the Office shall notify the International Bureau accordingly and the International Bureau shall record any such notification in the International Register. Where it is paid through the International Bureau, the International Bureau shall record the payment in the International Register and notify the Office concerned accordingly.

(d) Where the second part of the individual designation fee is not paid within the applicable period, the Office concerned shall notify the International Bureau and request the International Bureau to cancel the international registration in the International Register with respect to the Contracting Party concerned. The International Bureau shall proceed accordingly and so notify the holder.

[9.448]
Rule 13
International Application Filed Through an Office

(1) [*Date of Receipt by Office and Transmittal to the International Bureau*] Where an international application governed exclusively by the 1999 Act is filed through the Office of the applicant's Contracting Party, that Office shall notify the applicant of the date on which it received the application. At the same time as it transmits the international application to the International Bureau, the Office shall notify the International Bureau of the date on which it received the application. The Office shall notify the applicant of the fact that it has transmitted the international application to the International Bureau.

(2) [*Transmittal Fee*] An Office that requires a transmittal fee, as provided for in Article 4(2) of the 1999 Act, shall notify the International Bureau of the amount of such fee, which should not exceed the administrative costs of receiving and transmitting the international application, and its due date.

(3) [*Filing Date of International Application Filed Indirectly*] Subject to Rule 14(2), the filing date of an international application filed through an Office shall be

(i) where the international application is governed exclusively by the 1999 Act, the date on which the international application was received by that Office, provided that it is received by the International Bureau within one month of that date;

(ii) in any other case, the date on which the International Bureau receives the international application.

(4) [*Filing Date Where Applicant's Contracting Party Requires a Security Clearance*] Notwithstanding paragraph (3), a Contracting Party whose law, at the time that it becomes party to the 1999 Act, requires security clearance may, in a declaration, notify the Director General that the period of one month referred to in that paragraph shall be replaced by a period of six months.

[9.449]
Rule 14
Examination by the International Bureau

(1) [*Time Limit for Correcting Irregularities*] If the International Bureau finds that the international application does not, at the time of its receipt by the International Bureau, fulfil the applicable requirements, it shall invite the applicant to make the required corrections within three months from the date of the invitation sent by the International Bureau.

(2) [*Irregularities Entailing a Postponement of the Filing Date of the International Application*] Where the international application has, on the date on which it is received by the International Bureau, an irregularity which is prescribed as an irregularity entailing a postponement of the filing date of the international application, the filing date shall be the date on which the correction of such irregularity is received by the International Bureau. The irregularities which are prescribed as entailing a postponement of the filing date of the international application are the following:

(a) the international application is not in one of the prescribed languages;
(b) any of the following elements is missing from the international application:
  (i) an express or implicit indication that international registration under the 1999 Act or the 1960 Act is sought;
  (ii) indications allowing the identity of the applicant to be established;
  (iii) indications sufficient to enable the applicant or its representative, if any, to be contacted;
  (iv) a reproduction, or, in accordance with Article 5(1)(iii) of the 1999 Act, a specimen, of each industrial design that is the subject of the international application;
  (v) the designation of at least one Contracting Party.

(3) [*International Application Considered Abandoned; Reimbursement of Fees*] Where an irregularity, other than an irregularity referred to in Article 8(2)(b) of the 1999 Act, is not remedied within the time limit referred to in paragraph (1), the international application shall be considered abandoned and the International Bureau shall refund any fees paid in respect of that application, after deduction of an amount corresponding to the basic fee.

[9.450]
Rule 15
Registration of the Industrial Design in the International Register

(1) [*Registration of the Industrial Design in the International Register*] Where the International Bureau finds that the international application conforms to the applicable requirements, it shall register the industrial design in the International Register and send a certificate to the holder.

(2) [*Contents of the Registration*] The international registration shall contain

(i) all the data contained in the international application, except any priority claim under Rule 7(5)(c) where the date of the earlier filing is more than six months before the filing date of the international application;
(ii) any reproduction of the industrial design;
(iii) the date of the international registration;
(iv) the number of the international registration;
(v) the relevant class of the International Classification, as determined by the International Bureau.

[9.451]
Rule 16
Deferment of Publication

(1) [*Maximum Period of Deferment*]

(a) The prescribed period for deferment of publication in respect of an international application governed exclusively by the 1999 Act shall be 30 months from the filing date or, where priority is claimed, from the priority date of the application concerned.
(b) The maximum period for deferment of publication in respect of an international application governed exclusively by the 1960 Act or by both the 1999 Act and the 1960 Act shall be 12 months from the filing date or, where priority is claimed, from the priority date of the application concerned.

(2) [*Period for Withdrawal of Designation Where Deferment Is Not Possible Under Applicable Law*] The period referred to in Article 11(3)(i) of the 1999 Act for the applicant to withdraw the designation of a Contracting Party whose law does not allow the deferment of publication shall be one month from the date of the notification sent by the International Bureau.

(3) [*Period for Paying Publication Fee*]

(a) The publication fee referred to in Rule 12(1)(a)(iv) shall be paid not later than three weeks before the period of deferment applicable under Article 11(2) of the 1999 Act or under

Article 6(4)(a) of the 1960 Act expires or not later than three weeks before the period of deferment is considered to have expired in accordance with Article 11(4)(a) of the 1999 Act or with Article 6(4)(b) of the 1960 Act.

(b) Three months before the expiry of the period of deferment of publication referred to in subparagraph (a), the International Bureau shall, by sending an unofficial notice, remind the holder of the international registration, where applicable, of the date by which the publication fee referred to in subparagraph (a) shall be paid.

(4) [*Period for Submitting Reproductions and Registration of Reproductions*]

(a) Where specimens have been submitted instead of reproductions in accordance with Rule 10, those reproductions shall be submitted not later than three months before the expiry of the period for paying the publication fee set under paragraph (3)(a).

(b) The International Bureau shall record in the International Register any reproduction submitted under subparagraph (a), provided that the requirements under Rule 9(1) and (2) are complied with.

(5) [*Requirements Not Complied With*] If the requirements of paragraphs (3) and (4) are not complied with, the international registration shall be canceled and shall not be published.

[9.452]
Rule 17
Publication of the International Registration

(1) [*Timing of Publication*] The international registration shall be published

(i) where the applicant so requests, immediately after the registration,

(ii) where deferment of publication has been requested and the request has not been disregarded, immediately after the date on which the period of deferment expired or is considered to have expired,

(iii) in any other case, six months after the date of the international registration or as soon as possible thereafter.

(2) [*Contents of Publication*] The publication of the international registration in the Bulletin shall contain

(i) the data recorded in the International Register;

(ii) the reproduction or reproductions of the industrial design;

(iii) where publication has been deferred, an indication of the date on which the period of deferment expired or is considered to have expired.

CHAPTER 3
REFUSALS AND INVALIDATIONS

[9.453]
Rule 18
Notification of Refusal

(1) [*Period for Notification of Refusal*]

(a) The prescribed period for the notification of refusal of the effects of an international registration in accordance with Article 12(2) of the 1999 Act or Article 8(1) of the 1960 Act shall be six months from the publication of the international registration as provided for by Rule 26(3).

(b) Notwithstanding subparagraph (a), any Contracting Party whose Office is an Examining Office, or whose law provides for the possibility of opposition to the grant of protection, may, in a declaration, notify the Director General that, where it is designated under the 1999 Act, the period of six months referred to in that subparagraph shall be replaced by a period of 12 months.

(c) The declaration referred to in subparagraph (b) may also state that the international registration shall produce the effect referred to in Article 14(2)(a) of the 1999 Act at the latest

(i) at a time specified in the declaration which may be later than the date referred to in that Article but which shall not be more than six months after the said date or

(ii) at a time at which protection is granted according to the law of the Contracting Party where a decision regarding the grant of protection was unintentionally not communicated within the period applicable under subparagraph (a) or (b); in such a case, the Office of the Contracting Party concerned shall notify the International Bureau accordingly and endeavour to communicate such decision to the holder of the international registration concerned promptly thereafter.

(2) [*Notification of Refusal*]

(a) The notification of any refusal shall relate to one international registration, shall be dated and shall be signed by the Office making the notification.

(b) The notification shall contain or indicate

(i) the Office making the notification,

(ii) the number of the international registration,

(iii) all the grounds on which the refusal is based together with a reference to the corresponding essential provisions of the law,

(iv) where the grounds on which the refusal is based refer to similarity with an industrial design which has been the subject of an earlier national, regional or international application or registration, the filing date and number, the priority date (if any), the registration date and number (if available), a copy of a reproduction of the earlier industrial design (if that reproduction is accessible to the public) and the name and address of the owner of the said industrial design, as provided for in the Administrative Instructions,

(v) where the refusal does not relate to all the industrial designs that are the subject of the international registration, those to which it relates or does not relate,

(vi) whether the refusal may be subject to review or appeal and, if so, the time limit, reasonable under the circumstances, for any request for review of, or appeal against, the refusal and the authority to which such request for review or appeal shall lie, with the indication, where applicable, that the request for review or the appeal has to be filed through the intermediary of a representative whose address is within the territory of the Contracting Party whose Office has pronounced the refusal, and

(vii) the date on which the refusal was pronounced.

(3) [*Notification of Division of International Registration*] Where, following a notification of refusal in accordance with Article 13(2) of the 1999 Act, an international registration is divided before the Office of a designated Contracting Party in order to overcome a ground of refusal stated in that notification, that Office shall notify the International Bureau of such data concerning the division as shall be specified in the Administrative Instructions.

(4) [*Notification of Withdrawal of Refusal*]

(a) The notification of any withdrawal of refusal shall relate to one international registration, shall be dated and shall be signed by the Office making the notification.

(b) The notification shall contain or indicate

(i) the Office making the notification,

(ii) the number of the international registration,

(iii) where the withdrawal does not relate to all the industrial designs to which the refusal applied, those to which it relates or does not relate,

(iv) the date on which the international registration produced the effect as a grant of protection under the applicable law, and

(v) the date on which the refusal was withdrawn.

(c) Where the international registration was amended in a procedure before the Office, the notification shall also contain or indicate all amendments.

(5) [*Recording*] The International Bureau shall record any notification received under paragraph (1)(c)(ii), (2) or (4) in the International Register together with, in the case of a notification of refusal, an indication of the date on which the notification of refusal was sent to the International Bureau.

(6) [*Transmittal of Copies of Notifications*] The International Bureau shall transmit copies of notifications received under paragraph (1)(c)(ii), (2) or (4) to the holder.

[9.454]
Rule 18bis
Statement of Grant of Protection

(1) [*Statement of Grant of Protection Where No Notification of Provisional Refusal Has Been Communicated*]

(a) An Office which has not communicated a notification of refusal may, within the period applicable under Rule 18(1)(a) or (b), send to the International Bureau a statement to the effect that protection is granted to the industrial designs that are the subject of the international registration in the Contracting Party concerned, it being understood that, where Rule 12(3) applies, the grant of protection will be subject to the payment of the second part of the individual designation fee.

(b) The statement shall indicate

(i) the Office making the statement,

(ii) the number of the international registration,

(iii) where the statement does not relate to all the industrial designs that are the subject of the international registration, those to which it relates,

(iv) the date on which the international registration produced or shall produce the effect as a grant of protection under the applicable law, and

(v) the date of the statement.

(c) Where the international registration was amended in a procedure before the Office, the statement shall also contain or indicate all amendments.

(d) Notwithstanding subparagraph (a), where Rule 18(1)(c)(i) or (ii) applies, as the case may be, or where protection is granted to the industrial designs following amendments in a procedure before the Office, the said Office must send to the International Bureau the statement referred to in subparagraph (a).

(e) The applicable period referred to in subparagraph (a) shall be the period allowed pursuant to Rule 18(1)(c)(i) or (ii), as the case may be, to produce the effect as a grant of protection under the applicable law, with respect to a designation of a Contracting Party having made a declaration under either of the aforementioned Rules.

(2) [*Statement of Grant of Protection Following a Refusal*]

(a) An Office which has communicated a notification of refusal and which has decided to either partially or totally withdraw such refusal, may, instead of notifying a withdrawal of refusal in accordance with Rule 18(4)(a), send to the International Bureau a statement to the effect that protection is granted to the industrial designs, or some of the industrial designs, as the case may be, that are the subject of the international registration in the Contracting Party concerned, it being understood that, where Rule 12(3) applies, the grant of protection will be subject to the payment of the second part of the individual designation fee.

(b) The statement shall indicate

(i) the Office making the notification,

(ii) the number of the international registration,

(iii) where the statement does not relate to all the industrial designs that are the subject of the international registration, those to which it relates or does not relate,

(iv) the date on which the international registration produced the effect as a grant of protection under the applicable law, and

(v) the date of the statement.

(c) Where the international registration was amended in a procedure before the Office, the statement shall also contain or indicate all amendments.

(3) [*Recording, Information to the Holder and Transmittal of Copies*] The International Bureau shall record any statement received under this Rule in the International Register, inform the holder accordingly and, where the statement was communicated, or can be reproduced, in the form of a specific document, transmit a copy of that document to the holder.

[9.455]
Rule 19
Irregular Refusals

(1) [*Notification Not Regarded as Such*]

(a) A notification of refusal shall not be regarded as such by the International Bureau and shall not be recorded in the International Register

(i) if it does not indicate the number of the international registration concerned, unless other indications contained in the notification permit the said registration to be identified,

(ii) if it does not indicate any grounds for refusal, or

(iii) if it is sent to the International Bureau after the expiry of the period applicable under Rule 18(1).

(b) Where subparagraph (a) applies, the International Bureau shall, unless it cannot identify the international registration concerned, transmit a copy of the notification to the holder, shall inform, at the same time, the holder and the Office that sent the notification that the notification of refusal is not regarded as such by the International Bureau and has not been recorded in the International Register, and shall indicate the reasons therefor.

(2) [*Irregular Notification*] If the notification of refusal

(i) is not signed on behalf of the Office which communicated the refusal, or does not comply with the requirements established under Rule 2,

(ii) does not comply, where applicable, with the requirements of Rule 18(2)(b)(iv),

(iii) does not indicate, where applicable, the authority to which a request for review or an appeal lies and the applicable time limit, reasonable under the circumstances, for lodging such a request or appeal (Rule 18(2)(b)(vi)),

(iv) does not indicate the date on which the refusal was pronounced (Rule 18(2)(b)(vii)),

the International Bureau shall nevertheless record the refusal in the International Register and transmit a copy of the notification to the holder. If so requested by the holder, the International Bureau shall invite the Office which communicated the refusal to rectify its notification without delay.

[9.456]
Rule 20
Invalidation in Designated Contracting Parties

(1) [*Contents of the Notification of Invalidation*] Where the effects of an international registration are invalidated in a designated Contracting Party and the invalidation is no longer subject to any review or appeal, the Office of the Contracting Party whose competent authority has pronounced the invalidation shall, where it is aware of the invalidation, notify the International Bureau accordingly. The notification shall indicate

(i) the authority which pronounced the invalidation,

(ii) the fact that the invalidation is no longer subject to appeal,

(iii) the number of the international registration,

(iv) where the invalidation does not relate to all the industrial designs that are the subject of the international registration, those to which it relates or does not relate,
(v) the date on which the invalidation was pronounced and its effective date.

(2) [*Recording of the Invalidation*] The International Bureau shall record the invalidation in the International Register, together with the data contained in the notification of invalidation.

CHAPTER 4
CHANGES AND CORRECTIONS

[9.457]
Rule 21
Recording of a Change

(1) [*Presentation of the Request*]

(a) A request for the recording shall be presented to the International Bureau on the relevant official form where the request relates to any of the following:
  (i) a change in the ownership of the international registration in respect of all or some of the industrial designs that are the subject of the international registration;
  (ii) a change in the name or address of the holder;
  (iii) a renunciation of the international registration in respect of any or all of the designated Contracting Parties;
  (iv) a limitation, in respect of any or all of the designated Contracting Parties, to one or some of the industrial designs that are the subject of the international registration.

(b) The request shall be presented by the holder and signed by the holder; however, a request for the recording of a change in ownership may be presented by the new owner, provided that it is
  (i) signed by the holder, or
  (ii) signed by the new owner and accompanied by an attestation from the competent authority of the holder's Contracting Party that the new owner appears to be the successor in title of the holder.

(2) [*Contents of the Request*] The request for the recording of a change shall, in addition to the requested change, contain or indicate
  (i) the number of the international registration concerned,
  (ii) the name of the holder, unless the change relates to the name or address of the representative,
  (iii) in case of a change in the ownership of the international registration, the name and address, given in accordance with the Administrative Instructions, of the new owner of the international registration,
  (iv) in case of a change in the ownership of the international registration, the Contracting Party or Parties in respect of which the new owner fulfils the conditions to be the holder of an international registration,
  (v) in case of a change in the ownership of the international registration that does not relate to all the industrial designs and to all the Contracting Parties, the numbers of the industrial designs and the designated Contracting Parties to which the change in ownership relates, and
  (vi) the amount of the fees being paid and the method of payment, or instruction to debit the required amount of fees to an account opened with the International Bureau, and the identification of the party effecting the payment or giving the instructions.

(3) [*Request Not Admissible*] A change in the ownership of an international registration may not be recorded in respect of a designated Contracting Party if that Contracting Party is not bound by an Act to which the Contracting Party, or one of the Contracting Parties, indicated under paragraph (2)(iv) is bound.

(4) [*Irregular Request*] If the request does not comply with the applicable requirements, the International Bureau shall notify that fact to the holder and, if the request was made by a person claiming to be the new owner, to that person.

(5) [*Time Allowed to Remedy Irregularity*] The irregularity may be remedied within three months from the date of the notification of the irregularity by the International Bureau. If the irregularity is not remedied within the said three months, the request shall be considered abandoned and the International Bureau shall notify accordingly and at the same time the holder and, if the request was presented by a person claiming to be the new owner, that person, and shall refund any fees paid, after deduction of an amount corresponding to one-half of the relevant fees.

(6) [*Recording and Notification of a Change*]

(a) The International Bureau shall, provided that the request is in order, promptly record the change in the International Register and shall inform the holder. In the case of a recording of a change in ownership, the International Bureau will inform both the new holder and the previous holder.

(b) The change shall be recorded as of the date of receipt by the International Bureau of the request complying with the applicable requirements. Where however the request indicates that the change should be recorded after another change, or after renewal of the international registration, the International Bureau shall proceed accordingly.

(7) [*Recording of Partial Change in Ownership*] Assignment or other transfer of the international registration in respect of some only of the industrial designs, or some only of the designated Contracting Parties shall be recorded in the International Register under the number of the international registration of which a part has been assigned or otherwise transferred; any assigned or otherwise transferred part shall be cancelled under the number of the said international registration and recorded as a separate international registration. The separate international registration shall bear the number of the international registration of which a part has been assigned or otherwise transferred, together with a capital letter.

(8) [*Recording of Merger of International Registrations*] Where the same person becomes the holder of two or more international registrations resulting from a partial change in ownership, the registrations shall be merged at the request of the said person and paragraphs (1) to (6) shall apply *mutatis mutandis*. The international registration resulting from the merger shall bear the number of the international registration of which a part had been assigned or otherwise transferred, together, where applicable, with a capital letter.

[9.458]
Rule 21bis
Declaration That a Change in Ownership Has No Effect

(1) [*Declaration and Its Effect*] The Office of a designated Contracting Party may declare that a change in ownership recorded in the International Register has no effect in the said Contracting Party. The effect of such a declaration shall be that, with respect to the said Contracting Party, the international registration concerned shall remain in the name of the transferor.

(2) [*Contents of the Declaration*] The declaration referred to in paragraph (1) shall indicate

(a) the reasons for which the change in ownership has no effect,

(b) the corresponding essential provisions of the law,

(c) where the declaration does not relate to all the industrial designs that are the subject of the change in ownership, those to which it relates, and

(d) whether such declaration may be subject to review or appeal and, if so, the time limit, reasonable under the circumstances, for any request for review of, or appeal against, the declaration and the authority to which such request for review or appeal shall lie, with the indication, where applicable, that the request for review or the appeal has to be filed through the intermediary of a representative whose address is within the territory of the Contracting Party whose Office has pronounced the declaration.

(3) [*Period for Declaration*] The declaration referred to in paragraph (1) shall be sent to the International Bureau within six months from the date of the publication of the said change in ownership or within the applicable refusal period in accordance with Article 12(2) of the 1999 Act or Article 8(1) of the 1960 Act, whichever expires later.

(4) [*Recording and Notification of the Declaration; Consequential Modification of the International Register*] The International Bureau shall record in the International Register any declaration made in accordance with paragraph (3) and shall modify the International Register, whereby that part of the international registration which has been the subject of the said declaration shall be recorded as a separate international registration in the name of the previous holder (transferor). The International Bureau shall notify accordingly the previous holder (transferor) and the new holder (transferee).

(5) [*Withdrawal of Declaration*] Any declaration made in accordance with paragraph (3) may be withdrawn, in part or in whole. The withdrawal of declaration shall be notified to the International Bureau which shall record it in the International Register. The International Bureau shall modify the International Register accordingly, and shall notify accordingly the previous holder (transferor) and the new holder (transferee).

[9.459]
Rule 22
Corrections in the International Register

(1) [*Correction*] Where the International Bureau, acting *ex officio* or at the request of the holder, considers that there is an error concerning an international registration in the International Register, it shall modify the Register and inform the holder accordingly.

(2) [*Refusal of Effects of Correction*] The Office of any designated Contracting Party shall have the right to declare in a notification to the International Bureau that it refuses to recognise the effects of the correction. Rules 18 to 19 shall apply *mutatis mutandis*.

CHAPTER 5
RENEWALS

[9.460]
Rule 23
Unofficial Notice of Expiry
Six months before the expiry of a five-year term, the International Bureau shall send to the holder and the representative, if any, a notice indicating the date of expiry of the international registration. The fact that the said notice is not received shall not constitute an excuse for failure to comply with any time limit under Rule 24.

[9.461]
Rule 24
Details Concerning Renewal
(1) [*Fees*]
(a) The international registration shall be renewed upon payment of the following fees:
(i) a basic fee;
(ii) a standard designation fee in respect of each Contracting Party designated under the 1999 Act that has not made a declaration under Article 7(2) of the 1999 Act, and each Contracting Party designated under the 1960 Act, for which the international registration is to be renewed;
(iii) an individual designation fee for each Contracting Party designated under the 1999 Act that has made a declaration under Article 7(2) of the 1999 Act and for which the international registration is to be renewed.
(b) The amounts of the fees referred to in items (i) and (ii) of subparagraph (a) are set out in the Schedule of Fees.
(c) The payment of the fees referred to in subparagraph (a) shall be made at the latest on the date on which the renewal of the international registration is due. However, it may still be made within six months from the date on which the renewal of the international registration is due, provided that the surcharge specified in the Schedule of Fees is paid at the same time.
(d) If any payment made for the purposes of renewal is received by the International Bureau earlier than three months before the date on which the renewal of the international registration is due, it shall be considered as having been received three months before that date.
(2) [*Further Details*]
(a) Where the holder does not wish to renew the international registration
(i) in respect of a designated Contracting Party, or
(ii) in respect of any of the industrial designs that are the subject of the international registration,
payment of the required fees shall be accompanied by a statement indicating the Contracting Party or the numbers of the industrial designs for which the international registration is not to be renewed.
(b) Where the holder wishes to renew the international registration in respect of a designated Contracting Party notwithstanding the fact that the maximum period of protection for industrial designs in that Contracting Party has expired, payment of the required fees, including the standard designation fee or the individual designation fee, as the case may be, for that Contracting Party, shall be accompanied by a statement that the renewal of the international registration is to be recorded in the International Register in respect of that Contracting Party.
(c) Where the holder wishes to renew the international registration in respect of a designated Contracting Party notwithstanding the fact that a refusal is recorded in the International Register for that Contracting Party in respect of all the industrial designs concerned, payment of the required fees, including the standard designation fee or the individual designation fee, as the case may be, for that Contracting Party, shall be accompanied by a statement specifying that the renewal of the international registration is to be recorded in the International Register in respect of that Contracting Party.
(d) The international registration may not be renewed in respect of any designated Contracting Party in respect of which an invalidation has been recorded for all the industrial designs under Rule 20 or in respect of which a renunciation has been recorded under Rule 21. The international registration may not be renewed in respect of any designated Contracting Party for those industrial designs in respect of which an invalidation in that Contracting Party has been recorded under Rule 20 or in respect of which a limitation has been recorded under Rule 21.
(3) [*Insufficient Fees*]
(a) If the amount of the fees received is less than the amount required for renewal, the International Bureau shall promptly notify at the same time both the holder and the representative, if any, accordingly. The notification shall specify the missing amount.

(b) If the amount of the fees received is, on the expiry of the period of six months referred to in paragraph (1)(c), less than the amount required for renewal, the International Bureau shall not record the renewal, shall refund the amount received and shall notify accordingly the holder and the representative, if any.

[9.462]
Rule 25
Recording of the Renewal; Certificate

(1) [*Recording and Effective Date of the Renewal*] Renewal shall be recorded in the International Register with the date on which renewal was due, even if the fees required for renewal are paid within the period of grace referred to in Rule 24(1)(c).

(2) [*Certificate*] The International Bureau shall send a certificate of renewal to the holder.

CHAPTER 6
PUBLICATION

[9.463]
Rule 26
Publication

(1) [*Information Concerning International Registrations*] The International Bureau shall publish in the Bulletin relevant data concerning

(i) international registrations, in accordance with Rule 17;

(ii) refusals, with an indication as to whether there is a possibility of review or appeal, but without the grounds for refusal, and other communications recorded under Rules 18(5) and 18*bis* (3);

(iii) invalidations recorded under Rule 20(2);

(iv) changes in ownership and mergers, changes of name or address of the holder, renunciations and limitations recorded under Rule 21;

(v) corrections effected under Rule 22;

(vi) renewals recorded under Rule 25(1);

(vii) international registrations which have not been renewed;

(viii) cancellations recorded under Rule 12(3)(d);

(ix) declarations that a change in ownership has no effect and withdrawals of such declarations recorded under Rule 21bis.

(2) [*Information Concerning Declarations; Other Information*] The International Bureau shall publish in the Bulletin any declaration made by a Contracting Party under the 1999 Act, the 1960 Act or these Regulations, as well as a list of the days on which the International Bureau is not scheduled to open to the public during the current and the following calendar year.

(3) [*Mode of Publishing the Bulletin*] The Bulletin shall be published on the website of the Organisation. The publication of each issue of the Bulletin shall be deemed to replace the sending of the Bulletin referred to in Article 10(3)(b) and 16(4) of the 1999 Act and Article 6(3)(b) of the 1960 Act, and, for the purposes of Article 8(2) of the 1960 Act, each issue of the Bulletin shall be deemed to have been received by each Office concerned on the date of its publication on the website of the Organisation.

CHAPTER 7
FEES

[9.464]
Rule 27
Amounts and Payment of Fees

(1) [*Amounts of Fees*] The amounts of fees due under the 1999 Act, the 1960 Act and these Regulations, other than individual designation fees referred to in Rule 12(1)(a)(iii), shall be specified in the Schedule of Fees which is annexed to these Regulations and forms an integral part thereof.

(2) [*Payment*]

(a) Subject to subparagraph (b) and Rule 12(3)(c), the fees shall be paid directly to the International Bureau.

(b) Where the international application is filed through the Office of the applicant's Contracting Party, the fees payable in connection with that application may be paid through that Office if it accepts to collect and forward such fees and the applicant or the holder so wishes. Any Office which accepts to collect and forward such fees shall notify that fact to the Director General.

(3) [*Modes of Payment*] Fees shall be paid to the International Bureau in accordance with the Administrative Instructions.

(4) [*Indications Accompanying the Payment*] At the time of the payment of any fee to the International Bureau, an indication must be given,

(i) before international registration, of the name of the applicant, the industrial design concerned and the purpose of the payment;

(ii) after international registration, of the name of the holder, the number of the international registration concerned and the purpose of the payment.

(5) [*Date of Payment*]

(a) Subject to Rule 24(1)(d) and subparagraph (b), any fee shall be considered to have been paid to the International Bureau on the day on which the International Bureau receives the required amount.

(b) Where the required amount is available in an account opened with the International Bureau and that Bureau has received instructions from the holder of the account to debit it, the fee shall be considered to have been paid to the International Bureau on the day on which the International Bureau receives an international application, a request for the recording of a change, or an instruction to renew an international registration.

(6) [*Change in the Amount of the Fees*]

(a) Where an international application is filed through the Office of the applicant's Contracting Party and the amount of the fees payable in respect of the filing of the international application is changed between, on the one hand, the date on which the international application was received by that Office and, on the other hand, the date of the receipt of the international application by the International Bureau, the fee that was valid on the first date shall be applicable.

(b) Where the amount of the fees payable in respect of the renewal of an international registration is changed between the date of payment and the due date of the renewal, the fee that was valid on the date of payment, or on the date considered to be the date of payment under Rule 24(1)(d), shall be applicable. Where the payment is made after the due date, the fee that was valid on the due date shall be applicable.

(c) Where the amount of any fee other than the fees referred to in subparagraphs (a) and (b) is changed, the amount valid on the date on which the fee was received by the International Bureau shall be applicable.

[9.465]
Rule 28
Currency of Payments

(1) [*Obligation to Use Swiss Currency*] All payments made under these Regulations to the International Bureau shall be in Swiss currency irrespective of the fact that, where the fees are paid through an Office, such Office may have collected those fees in another currency.

(2) [*Establishment of the Amount of Individual Designation Fees in Swiss Currency*]

(a) Where a Contracting Party makes a declaration under Article 7(2) of the 1999 Act or under Rule 36(1) that it wants to receive an individual designation fee, the amount of the fee indicated to the International Bureau shall be expressed in the currency used by its Office.

(b) Where the fee is indicated in the declaration referred to in subparagraph (a) in a currency other than Swiss currency, the Director General shall, after consultation with the Office of the Contracting Party concerned, establish the amount of the fee in Swiss currency on the basis of the official exchange rate of the United Nations.

(c) Where, for more than three consecutive months, the official exchange rate of the United Nations between the Swiss currency and the currency in which the amount of an individual designation fee has been indicated by a Contracting Party is higher or lower by at least 5% than the last exchange rate applied to establish the amount of the fee in Swiss currency, the Office of that Contracting Party may ask the Director General to establish a new amount of the fee in Swiss currency according to the official exchange rate of the United Nations prevailing on the day preceding the day on which the request is made. The Director General shall proceed accordingly. The new amount shall be applicable as from a date which shall be fixed by the Director General, provided that such date is between one and two months after the date of the publication of the said amount on the website of the Organisation.

(d) Where, for more than three consecutive months, the official exchange rate of the United Nations between the Swiss currency and the currency in which the amount of an individual designation fee has been indicated by a Contracting Party is lower by at least 10% than the last exchange rate applied to establish the amount of the fee in Swiss currency, the Director General shall establish a new amount of the fee in Swiss currency according to the current official exchange rate of the United Nations. The new amount shall be applicable as from a date which shall be fixed by the Director General, provided that such date is between one and two months after the date of the publication of the said amount on the website of the Organisation.

[9.466]
Rule 29
Crediting of Fees to the Accounts of the Contracting Parties Concerned

Any standard designation fee or individual designation fee paid to the International Bureau in respect of a Contracting Party shall be credited to the account of that Contracting Party with the International Bureau within the month following the month in the course of which the recording of the international registration or renewal for which that fee has been paid was effected or, as regards the second part of the individual designation fee, immediately upon its receipt by the International Bureau.

CHAPTER 8

Rules 30, 31 [Deleted]

CHAPTER 9
MISCELLANEOUS

[9.467]
Rule 32
Extracts, Copies and Information Concerning Published International Registrations

(1) [*Modalities*] Against payment of a fee whose amount shall be fixed in the Schedule of Fees, any person may obtain from the International Bureau, in respect of any published international registration:
- (i) extracts from the International Register;
- (ii) certified copies of recordings made in the International Register or of items in the file of the international registration;
- (iii) uncertified copies of recordings made in the International Register or of items in the file of the international registration;
- (iv) written information on the contents of the International Register or of the file of the international registration;
- (v) a photograph of a specimen.

(2) [*Exemption from Authentication, Legalisation or any Other Certification*] In respect of a document referred to in paragraph (1)(i) and (ii), bearing the seal of the International Bureau and the signature of the Director General or a person acting on his behalf, no authority of any Contracting Party shall require authentication, legalisation or any other certification of such document, seal or signature, by any other person or authority. The present paragraph applies *mutatis mutandis* to the international registration certificate referred to in Rule 15(1).

[9.468]
Rule 33
Amendment of Certain Rules

(1) [*Requirement of Unanimity*] Amendment of the following provisions of these Regulations shall require unanimity of the Contracting Parties bound by the 1999 Act:
- (i) Rule 13(4);
- (ii) Rule 18(1).

(2) [*Requirement of Four-Fifths Majority*] Amendment of the following provisions of the Regulations and of paragraph (3) of the present Rule shall require a four-fifths majority of the Contracting Parties bound by the 1999 Act:
- (i) Rule 7(7);
- (ii) Rule 9(3)(b);
- (iii) Rule 16(1)(a);
- (iv) Rule 17(1)(iii).

(3) [*Procedure*] Any proposal for amending a provision referred to in paragraph (1) or (2) shall be sent to all Contracting Parties at least two months prior to the opening of the session of the Assembly which is called upon to make a decision on the proposal.

[9.469]
Rule 34
Administrative Instructions

(1) [*Establishment of Administrative Instructions; Matters Governed by Them*]
- (a) The Director General shall establish Administrative Instructions. The Director General may modify them. The Director General shall consult the Offices of the Contracting Parties with respect to the proposed Administrative Instructions or their proposed modification.
- (b) The Administrative Instructions shall deal with matters in respect of which these Regulations expressly refer to such Instructions and with details in respect of the application of these Regulations.

(2) [*Control by the Assembly*] The Assembly may invite the Director General to modify any provision of the Administrative Instructions, and the Director General shall proceed accordingly.

(3) [*Publication and Effective Date*]
- (a) The Administrative Instructions and any modification thereof shall be published on the website of the Organisation.
- (b) Each publication shall specify the date on which the published provisions become effective. The dates may be different for different provisions, provided that no provision may be declared effective prior to its publication on the website of the Organisation.

(4) [*Conflict with the 1999 Act, the 1960 Act or These Regulations*] In the case of conflict between, on the one hand, any provision of the Administrative Instructions and, on the other hand, any provision of the 1999 Act, the 1960 Act or of these Regulations, the latter shall prevail.

[9.470]
Rule 35
Declarations Made by Contracting Parties to the 1999 Act
(1) [*Making and Coming into Effect of Declarations*] Article 30(1) and (2) of the 1999 Act shall apply *mutatis mutandis* to the making of any declaration under Rules 8(1), 9(3)(a), 13(4) or 18(1)(b) and to its coming into effect.
(2) [*Withdrawal of Declarations*] Any declaration referred to in paragraph (1) may be withdrawn at any time by notification addressed to the Director General. Such withdrawal shall take effect upon receipt by the Director General of the notification of withdrawal or at any later date indicated in the notification. In the case of a declaration made under Rule 18(1)(b), the withdrawal shall not affect an international registration whose date is earlier than the coming into effect of the said withdrawal.

[9.471]
Rule 36
Declarations Made by Contracting Parties to the 1960 Act
(1)[1] [*Individual Designation Fee*] For the purpose of Article 15(1)2(b) of the 1960 Act, any Contracting Party to the 1960 Act whose Office is an Examining Office may, in a declaration, notify the Director General that, in connection with any international application in which it is designated under the 1960 Act, the standard designation fee referred to in Rule 12(1)(a)(ii) shall be replaced by an individual designation fee, whose amount shall be indicated in the declaration and can be changed in further declarations. The said amount may not be higher than the equivalent of the amount which the Office of that Contracting Party would be entitled to receive from an applicant for a grant of protection for an equivalent period to the same number of industrial designs, that amount being diminished by the savings resulting from the international procedure.
(2) [*Maximum Duration of Protection*] Each Contracting Party to the 1960 Act shall, in a declaration, notify the Director General of the maximum duration of protection provided for by its law.
(3) [*Time at Which Declarations May Be Made*] Any declaration under paragraphs (1) and (2) may be made
(i) at the time of the deposit of an instrument referred to in Article 26(2) of the 1960 Act, in which case it shall become effective on the date on which the State having made the declaration becomes bound by this Act, or
(ii) after the deposit of an instrument referred to in Article 26(2) of the 1960 Act, in which case it shall become effective one month after the date of its receipt by the Director General or at any later date indicated in the declaration but shall apply only in respect of any international registration whose date of international registration is the same as, or is later than, the effective date of the declaration.

NOTES

[1] [WIPO Note]: Recommendation adopted by the Assembly of the Hague Union:

"Contracting Parties that make, or that have made, a declaration under Article 7(2) of the 1999 Act or under Rule 36(1) of the Common Regulations are encouraged to indicate, in that declaration or in a new declaration, that for international applications filed by applicants whose sole entitlement is a connection with a Least Developed Country, in accordance with the list established by the United Nations, or with an intergovernmental organisation the majority of whose member States are Least Developed Countries, the individual fee payable with respect to their designation is reduced to 10% of the fixed amount (rounded, where appropriate, to the nearest full figure). Those Contracting Parties are further encouraged to indicate that the reduction also applies in respect of an international application filed by an applicant whose entitlement is not solely a connection with such an intergovernmental organisation, provided that any other entitlement of the applicant is a connection with a Contracting Party which is a Least Developed Country or, if not a Least Developed Country, is a member State of that intergovernmental organisation and the international application is governed exclusively by the 1999 Act."

[9.472]
Rule 37
Transitional Provisions
(1) [*Transitional Provision Relating to the 1934 Act*]
(a) For the purpose of this provision,
(i) "1934 Act" means the Act signed at London on June 2, 1934, of the Hague Agreement;
(ii) "Contracting Party designated under the 1934 Act" means a Contracting Party recorded as such in the International Register;
(iii) reference to "international application" or "international registration" shall be deemed, where appropriate, to include a reference to "international deposit" as referred to in the 1934 Act.

(b) The Common Regulations Under the 1999 Act, the 1960 Act and the 1934 Act of the Hague Agreement as in force before January 1, 2010, shall remain applicable to an international application filed before that date and that is still pending on that date, as well as in respect of any Contracting Party designated under the 1934 Act in an international registration resulting from an international application filed before that date.

(2) [*Transitional Provision Concerning Languages*] Rule 6 as in force before April 1, 2010, shall continue to apply to any international application filed before that date and to the international registration resulting therefrom.

SCHEDULE OF FEES

(as in force on January 1, 2015)

[9.473]

				Swiss francs
I. *International Applications*				
1.	Basic fee[1]			
	1.1	For one design		397
	1.2	For each additional design included in the same international application		19
2.	Publication fee[1]			
	2.1	For each reproduction to be published		17
	2.2	For each page, in addition to the first, on which one or more reproductions are shown (where the reproductions are submitted on paper)		150
3.	Additional fee where the description exceeds 100 words per word exceeding 100 words			2
4.	Standard designation fee[2]			
	4.1	Where level one applies:		
		4.1.1	For one design	42
		4.1.2	For each additional design included in the same international application	2
	4.2	Where level two applies:		
		4.2.1	For one design	60
		4.2.2	For each additional design included in the same international application	20
	4.3	Where level three applies:		
		4.3.1	For one design	90
		4.3.2	For each additional design included in the same international application	50
5.	Individual designation fee (the amount of the individual designation fee is fixed by each Contracting Party concerned)[3]			
II. [Deleted]				
6.	[Deleted]			
III. *Renewal of an International Registration Resulting From an International Application Governed Exclusively or Partly by the 1960 Act or by the 1999 Act*				
7.	Basic fee			
	7.1	For one design		200
	7.2	For each additional design included in the same international registration		17
8.	Standard designation fee			
	8.1	For one design		21
	8.2	For each additional design included in the same international registration		1
9.	Individual designation fee (the amount of the individual designation fee is fixed by each Contracting Party concerned)			
10.	Surcharge (period of grace)[4]			
IV. [Deleted]				
11.	[Deleted]			

			Swiss francs
12.	[Deleted]		
V. *Miscellaneous Recordings*			
13.	Change in ownership		144
14.	Change of name and/or address of the holder		
	14.1	For one international registration	144
	14.2	For each additional international registration of the same holder included in the same request	72
15.	Renunciation		144
16.	Limitation		144
VI. *Information Concerning Published International Registrations*			
17.	Supply of an extract from the International Register relating to a published international registration		144
18.	Supply of non-certified copies of the International Register or of items in the file of a published international registration		
	18.1	For the first five pages	26
	18.2	For each additional page after the fifth if the copies are requested at the same time and relate to the same international registration	2
19	Supply of certified copies from the International Register or of items in the file of a published international registration		
	19.1	For the first five pages	46
	19.2	For each additional page after the fifth if the copies are requested at the same time and relate to the same international registration	2
20.	Supply of a photograph of a specimen		57
21.	Supply of written information on the contents of the International Register or of the file of a published international registration		
	21.1	Concerning one international registration	82
	21.2	Concerning any additional international registration of the same holder if the same information is requested at the same time	10
22.	Search in the list of owners of international registrations		
	22.1	Per search by the name of a given person or entity	82
	22.2	For each international registration found beyond the first one	10
23.	Surcharge for the communication of extracts, copies, information or search reports by telefacsimile (per page)		4
VII. *Services Provided by the International Bureau*			
24.	The International Bureau is authorized to collect a fee, whose amount it shall itself fix, for services not covered by this Schedule of Fees.		

NOTES

[1] For international applications filed by applicants whose sole entitlement is a connection with a Least Developed Country (LDC), in accordance with the list established by the United Nations, or with an intergovernmental organization the majority of whose member States are LDCs, the fees intended for the International Bureau are reduced to 10% of the prescribed amounts (rounded to the nearest full figure). The reduction also applies in respect of an international application filed by an applicant whose entitlement is not solely a connection with such an intergovernmental organization, provided that any other entitlement of the applicant is a connection with a Contracting Party which is an LDC or, if not an LDC, is a member State of that intergovernmental organization and the international application is governed exclusively by the 1999 Act. If there are several applicants, each must fulfill the said criteria. Where such fee reduction applies, the basic fee is fixed at 40 Swiss francs (for one design) and 2 Swiss francs (for each additional design included in the same international application), the publication fee is fixed at 2 Swiss francs for each reproduction and 15 Swiss francs for each page, in addition to the first, on which one or more reproductions are shown, and the additional fee where the description exceeds 100 words is fixed at 1 Swiss franc per group of five words exceeding 100 words.

[2] For international applications filed by applicants whose sole entitlement is a connection with a Least Developed Country (LDC), in accordance with the list established by the United Nations, or with an intergovernmental organization the majority of whose member States are LDCs, the standard fees are reduced to 10% of the prescribed amounts (rounded to the nearest full figure). The reduction also applies in respect of an international application filed by an applicant whose entitlement is not solely a connection with such an intergovernmental organization, provided that any other entitlement of the applicant is a connection with a Contracting Party which is an LDC or, if not an LDC, is a member State of that intergovernmental organization and the international application is governed exclusively by the 1999 Act. If there are several applicants, each must fulfill the said criteria.

Where such reduction applies, the standard designation fee is fixed at 4 Swiss francs (for one design) and 1 Swiss franc (for each additional design included in the same international application) under level one, 6 Swiss francs (for one design) and 2 Swiss francs (for each additional design included in the same international application) under level two, and 9 Swiss francs (for one design) and 5 Swiss francs (for each additional design included in the same international application) under level three.

3 [WIPO Note]: Recommendation adopted by the Assembly of the Hague Union: "Contracting Parties that make, or that have made, a declaration under Article 7(2) of the 1999 Act or under Rule 36(1) of the Common Regulations are encouraged to indicate, in that declaration or in a new declaration, that for international applications filed by applicants whose sole entitlement is a connection with a Least Developed Country, in accordance with the list established by the United Nations, or with an intergovernmental organization the majority of whose member States are Least Developed Countries, the individual fee payable with respect to their designation is reduced to 10% of the fixed amount (rounded, where appropriate, to the nearest full figure). Those Contracting Parties are further encouraged to indicate that the reduction also applies in respect of an international application filed by an applicant whose entitlement is not solely a connection with such an intergovernmental organization, provided that any other entitlement of the applicant is a connection with a Contracting Party which is a Least Developed Country or, if not a Least Developed Country, is a member State of that intergovernmental organization and the international application is governed exclusively by the 1999 Act.".

4 50% of the renewal basic fee.

AGREED STATEMENTS BY THE DIPLOMATIC CONFERENCE REGARDING THE GENEVA ACT AND THE REGULATIONS UNDER THE GENEVA ACT

NOTES

The original source of this document is the World Intellectual Property Organisation (WIPO).

[9.474]

1. When adopting Article 12(4), Article 14(2)(b) and Rule 18(4), the Diplomatic Conference understood that a withdrawal of refusal by an Office that has communicated a notification of refusal may take the form of a statement to the effect that the Office concerned has decided to accept the effects of the international registration in respect of the industrial designs, or some of the industrial designs, to which the notification of refusal related. It was also understood that an Office may, within the period allowed for communicating a notification of refusal, send a statement to the effect that it has decided to accept the effects of the international registration even where it has not communicated such a notification of refusal.

2. When adopting Article 10, the Diplomatic Conference understood that nothing in this Article precludes access to the international application or the international registration by the applicant or the holder or a person having the consent of the applicant or the holder.

CONVENTION ON BIOLOGICAL DIVERSITY

Open for signature at Rio de Janeiro from 5 to 14 June 1992 and thereafter at the Headquarters of the United Nations at New York from 15 June 1992 until 4 June 1993

NOTES

The original source of this Convention is the Convention on Biological Diversity website at www.cbd.int.

THE CONTRACTING PARTIES,

Conscious of the intrinsic value of biological diversity and of the ecological, genetic, social, economic, scientific, educational, cultural, recreational and aesthetic values of biological diversity and its components,

Conscious also of the importance of biological diversity for evolution and for maintaining life sustaining systems of the biosphere,

Affirming that the conservation of biological diversity is a common concern of humankind,

Reaffirming that States have sovereign rights over their own biological resources,

Reaffirming also that States are responsible for conserving their biological diversity and for using their biological resources in a sustainable manner,

Concerned that biological diversity is being significantly reduced by certain human activities,

Aware of the general lack of information and knowledge regarding biological diversity and of the urgent need to develop scientific, technical and institutional capacities to provide the basic understanding upon which to plan and implement appropriate measures,

Noting that it is vital to anticipate, prevent and attack the causes of significant reduction or loss of biological diversity at source,

Noting also that where there is a threat of significant reduction or loss of biological diversity, lack of full scientific certainty should not be used as a reason for postponing measures to avoid or minimize such a threat,

Noting further that the fundamental requirement for the conservation of biological diversity is the in-situ conservation of ecosystems and natural habitats and the maintenance and recovery of viable populations of species in their natural surroundings,

Noting further that ex-situ measures, preferably in the country of origin, also have an important role to play,

Recognizing the close and traditional dependence of many indigenous and local communities embodying traditional lifestyles on biological resources, and the desirability of sharing equitably benefits arising from the use of traditional knowledge, innovations and practices relevant to the conservation of biological diversity and the sustainable use of its components,

Recognizing also the vital role that women play in the conservation and sustainable use of biological diversity and affirming the need for the full participation of women at all levels of policy-making and implementation for biological diversity conservation,

Stressing the importance of, and the need to promote, international, regional and global cooperation among States and intergovernmental organisations and the non-governmental sector for the conservation of biological diversity and the sustainable use of its components,

Acknowledging that the provision of new and additional financial resources and appropriate access to relevant technologies can be expected to make a substantial difference in the world's ability to address the loss of biological diversity,

Acknowledging further that special provision is required to meet the needs of developing countries, including the provision of new and additional financial resources and appropriate access to relevant technologies,

Noting in this regard the special conditions of the least developed countries and small island States,

Acknowledging that substantial investments are required to conserve biological diversity and that there is the expectation of a broad range of environmental, economic and social benefits from those investments,

Recognizing that economic and social development and poverty eradication are the first and overriding priorities of developing countries,

Aware that conservation and sustainable use of biological diversity is of critical importance for meeting the food, health and other needs of the growing world population, for which purpose access to and sharing of both genetic resources and technologies are essential,

Noting that, ultimately, the conservation and sustainable use of biological diversity will strengthen friendly relations among States and contribute to peace for humankind,

Desiring to enhance and complement existing international arrangements for the conservation of biological diversity and sustainable use of its components, and

Determined to conserve and sustainably use biological diversity for the benefit of present and future generations,

HAVE AGREED AS FOLLOWS:—

[9.475]
Article 1
Objectives

The objectives of this Convention, to be pursued in accordance with its relevant provisions, are the conservation of biological diversity, the sustainable use of its components and the fair and equitable sharing of the benefits arising out of the utilization of genetic resources, including by appropriate access to genetic resources and by appropriate transfer of relevant technologies, taking into account all rights over those resources and to technologies, and by appropriate funding.

[9.476]
Article 2
Use of Terms

For the purposes of this Convention:—

"Biological diversity" means the variability among living organisms from all sources including, inter alia, terrestrial, marine and other aquatic ecosystems and the ecological complexes of which they are part; this includes diversity within species, between species and of ecosystems;

"Biological resources" includes genetic resources, organisms or parts thereof, populations, or any other biotic component of ecosystems with actual or potential use or value for humanity;

"Biotechnology" means any technological application that uses biological systems, living organisms, or derivatives thereof, to make or modify products or processes for specific use;

"Country of origin of genetic resources" means the country which possesses those genetic resources in in-situ conditions;

"Country providing genetic resources" means the country supplying genetic resources collected from in-situ sources, including populations of both wild and domesticated species, or taken from ex-situ sources, which may or may not have originated in that country;

"Domesticated or cultivated species" means species in which the evolutionary process has been influenced by humans to meet their needs;

"Ecosystem" means a dynamic complex of plant, animal and micro-organism communities and their non-living environment interacting as a functional unit;

"Ex-situ conservation" means the conservation of components of biological diversity outside their natural habitats;

"Genetic material" means any material of plant, animal, microbial or other origin containing functional units of heredity;

"Genetic resources" means genetic material of actual or potential value;

"Habitat" means the place or type of site where an organism or population naturally occurs;

"In-situ conditions" means conditions where genetic resources exist within ecosystems and natural habitats, and, in the case of domesticated or cultivated species, in the surroundings where they have developed their distinctive properties;

"In-situ conservation" means the conservation of ecosystems and natural habitats and the maintenance and recovery of viable populations of species in their natural surroundings and, in the case of domesticated or cultivated species, in the surroundings where they have developed their distinctive properties;

"Protected area" means a geographically defined area which is designated or regulated and managed to achieve specific conservation objectives;

"Regional economic integration organisation" means an organisation constituted by sovereign States of a given region, to which its member States have transferred competence in respect of matters governed by this Convention and which has been duly authorized, in accordance with its internal procedures, to sign, ratify, accept, approve or accede to it;

"Sustainable use" means the use of components of biological diversity in a way and at a rate that does not lead to the long-term decline of biological diversity, thereby maintaining its potential to meet the needs and aspirations of present and future generations;

"Technology" includes biotechnology.

[9.477]
Article 3
Principle

States have, in accordance with the Charter of the United Nations and the principles of international law, the sovereign right to exploit their own resources pursuant to their own environmental policies, and the responsibility to ensure that activities within their jurisdiction or control do not cause damage to the environment of other States or of areas beyond the limits of national jurisdiction.

[9.478]
Article 4
Jurisdictional Scope

Subject to the rights of other States, and except as otherwise expressly provided in this Convention, the provisions of this Convention apply, in relation to each Contracting Party:—

(a) In the case of components of biological diversity, in areas within the limits of its national jurisdiction; and

(b) In the case of processes and activities, regardless of where their effects occur, carried out under its jurisdiction or control, within the area of its national jurisdiction or beyond the limits of national jurisdiction.

[9.479]
Article 5
Cooperation

Each Contracting Party shall, as far as possible and as appropriate, cooperate with other Contracting Parties, directly or, where appropriate, through competent international organisations, in respect of areas beyond national jurisdiction and on other matters of mutual interest, for the conservation and sustainable use of biological diversity.

[9.480]
Article 6
General Measures for Conservation and Sustainable Use

Each Contracting Party shall, in accordance with its particular conditions and capabilities:—

(a) Develop national strategies, plans or programmes for the conservation and sustainable use of biological diversity or adapt for this purpose existing strategies, plans or programmes which shall reflect, inter alia, the measures set out in this Convention relevant to the Contracting Party concerned; and

(b) Integrate, as far as possible and as appropriate, the conservation and sustainable use of biological diversity into relevant sectoral or cross-sectoral plans, programmes and policies.

[9.481]
Article 7
Identification and Monitoring

Each Contracting Party shall, as far as possible and as appropriate, in particular for the purposes of Articles 8 to 10:—

(a) Identify components of biological diversity important for its conservation and sustainable use having regard to the indicative list of categories set down in Annex I;
(b) Monitor, through sampling and other techniques, the components of biological diversity identified pursuant to subparagraph (a) above, paying particular attention to those requiring urgent conservation measures and those which offer the greatest potential for sustainable use;
(c) Identify processes and categories of activities which have or are likely to have significant adverse impacts on the conservation and sustainable use of biological diversity, and monitor their effects through sampling and other techniques; and
(d) Maintain and organise, by any mechanism data, derived from identification and monitoring activities pursuant to subparagraphs (a), (b) and (c) above.

[9.482]
Article 8
In-situ Conservation

Each Contracting Party shall, as far as possible and as appropriate:—

(a) Establish a system of protected areas or areas where special measures need to be taken to conserve biological diversity;
(b) Develop, where necessary, guidelines for the selection, establishment and management of protected areas or areas where special measures need to be taken to conserve biological diversity;
(c) Regulate or manage biological resources important for the conservation of biological diversity whether within or outside protected areas, with a view to ensuring their conservation and sustainable use;
(d) Promote the protection of ecosystems, natural habitats and the maintenance of viable populations of species in natural surroundings;
(e) Promote environmentally sound and sustainable development in areas adjacent to protected areas with a view to furthering protection of these areas;
(f) Rehabilitate and restore degraded ecosystems and promote the recovery of threatened species, inter alia, through the development and implementation of plans or other management strategies;
(g) Establish or maintain means to regulate, manage or control the risks associated with the use and release of living modified organisms resulting from biotechnology which are likely to have adverse environmental impacts that could affect the conservation and sustainable use of biological diversity, taking also into account the risks to human health;
(h) Prevent the introduction of, control or eradicate those alien species which threaten ecosystems, habitats or species;
(i) Endeavour to provide the conditions needed for compatibility between present uses and the conservation of biological diversity and the sustainable use of its components;
(j) Subject to its national legislation, respect, preserve and maintain knowledge, innovations and practices of indigenous and local communities embodying traditional lifestyles relevant for the conservation and sustainable use of biological diversity and promote their wider application with the approval and involvement of the holders of such knowledge, innovations and practices and encourage the equitable sharing of the benefits arising from the utilization of such knowledge, innovations and practices;
(k) Develop or maintain necessary legislation and/or other regulatory provisions for the protection of threatened species and populations;
(l) Where a significant adverse effect on biological diversity has been determined pursuant to Article 7, regulate or manage the relevant processes and categories of activities; and
(m) Cooperate in providing financial and other support for in-situ conservation outlined in subparagraphs (a) to (l) above, particularly to developing countries.

[9.483]
Article 9
Ex-situ Conservation

Each Contracting Party shall, as far as possible and as appropriate, and predominantly for the purpose of complementing in-situ measures:—

(a) Adopt measures for the ex-situ conservation of components of biological diversity, preferably in the country of origin of such components;
(b) Establish and maintain facilities for ex-situ conservation of and research on plants, animals and micro-organisms, preferably in the country of origin of genetic resources;
(c) Adopt measures for the recovery and rehabilitation of threatened species and for their reintroduction into their natural habitats under appropriate conditions;

(d) Regulate and manage collection of biological resources from natural habitats for ex-situ conservation purposes so as not to threaten ecosystems and in-situ populations of species, except where special temporary ex-situ measures are required under subparagraph (c) above; and

(e) Cooperate in providing financial and other support for ex-situ conservation outlined in subparagraphs (a) to (d) above and in the establishment and maintenance of ex-situ conservation facilities in developing countries.

[9.484]
Article 10
Sustainable Use of Components of Biological Diversity

Each Contracting Party shall, as far as possible and as appropriate:—

(a) Integrate consideration of the conservation and sustainable use of biological resources into national decision-making;

(b) Adopt measures relating to the use of biological resources to avoid or minimize adverse impacts on biological diversity;

(c) Protect and encourage customary use of biological resources in accordance with traditional cultural practices that are compatible with conservation or sustainable use requirements;

(d) Support local populations to develop and implement remedial action in degraded areas where biological diversity has been reduced; and

(e) Encourage cooperation between its governmental authorities and its private sector in developing methods for sustainable use of biological resources.

[9.485]
Article 11
Incentive Measures

Each Contracting Party shall, as far as possible and as appropriate, adopt economically and socially sound measures that act as incentives for the conservation and sustainable use of components of biological diversity.

[9.486]
Article 12
Research and Training

The Contracting Parties, taking into account the special needs of developing countries, shall:—

(a) Establish and maintain programmes for scientific and technical education and training in measures for the identification, conservation and sustainable use of biological diversity and its components and provide support for such education and training for the specific needs of developing countries;

(b) Promote and encourage research which contributes to the conservation and sustainable use of biological diversity, particularly in developing countries, inter alia, in accordance with decisions of the Conference of the Parties taken in consequence of recommendations of the Subsidiary Body on Scientific, Technical and Technological Advice; and

(c) In keeping with the provisions of Articles 16, 18 and 20, promote and cooperate in the use of scientific advances in biological diversity research in developing methods for conservation and sustainable use of biological resources.

[9.487]
Article 13
Public Education and Awareness

The Contracting Parties shall:—

(a) Promote and encourage understanding of the importance of, and the measures required for, the conservation of biological diversity, as well as its propagation through media, and the inclusion of these topics in educational programmes; and

(b) Cooperate, as appropriate, with other States and international organisations in developing educational and public awareness programmes, with respect to conservation and sustainable use of biological diversity.

[9.488]
Article 14
Impact Assessment and Minimizing Adverse Impacts

1. Each Contracting Party, as far as possible and as appropriate, shall:—

(a) Introduce appropriate procedures requiring environmental impact assessment of its proposed projects that are likely to have significant adverse effects on biological diversity with a view to avoiding or minimizing such effects and, where appropriate, allow for public participation in such procedures;

(b) Introduce appropriate arrangements to ensure that the environmental consequences of its programmes and policies that are likely to have significant adverse impacts on biological diversity are duly taken into account;

(c) Promote, on the basis of reciprocity, notification, exchange of information and consultation on activities under their jurisdiction or control which are likely to significantly affect adversely the biological diversity of other States or areas beyond the limits of national jurisdiction, by encouraging the conclusion of bilateral, regional or multilateral arrangements, as appropriate;

(d) In the case of imminent or grave danger or damage, originating under its jurisdiction or control, to biological diversity within the area under jurisdiction of other States or in areas beyond the limits of national jurisdiction, notify immediately the potentially affected States of such danger or damage, as well as initiate action to prevent or minimize such danger or damage; and

(e) Promote national arrangements for emergency responses to activities or events, whether caused naturally or otherwise, which present a grave and imminent danger to biological diversity and encourage international cooperation to supplement such national efforts and, where appropriate and agreed by the States or regional economic integration organisations concerned, to establish joint contingency plans.

(2) The Conference of the Parties shall examine, on the basis of studies to be carried out, the issue of liability and redress, including restoration and compensation, for damage to biological diversity, except where such liability is a purely internal matter.

[9.489]
Article 15
Access to Genetic Resources

1. Recognizing the sovereign rights of States over their natural resources, the authority to determine access to genetic resources rests with the national governments and is subject to national legislation.

2. Each Contracting Party shall endeavour to create conditions to facilitate access to genetic resources for environmentally sound uses by other Contracting Parties and not to impose restrictions that run counter to the objectives of this Convention.

3. For the purpose of this Convention, the genetic resources being provided by a Contracting Party, as referred to in this Article and Articles 16 and 19, are only those that are provided by Contracting Parties that are countries of origin of such resources or by the Parties that have acquired the genetic resources in accordance with this Convention.

4. Access, where granted, shall be on mutually agreed terms and subject to the provisions of this Article.

5. Access to genetic resources shall be subject to prior informed consent of the Contracting Party providing such resources, unless otherwise determined by that Party.

6. Each Contracting Party shall endeavour to develop and carry out scientific research based on genetic resources provided by other Contracting Parties with the full participation of, and where possible in, such Contracting Parties.

7. Each Contracting Party shall take legislative, administrative or policy measures, as appropriate, and in accordance with Articles 16 and 19 and, where necessary, through the financial mechanism established by Articles 20 and 21 with the aim of sharing in a fair and equitable way the results of research and development and the benefits arising from the commercial and other utilization of genetic resources with the Contracting Party providing such resources. Such sharing shall be upon mutually agreed terms.

[9.490]
Article 16
Access to and Transfer of Technology

1. Each Contracting Party, recognizing that technology includes biotechnology, and that both access to and transfer of technology among Contracting Parties are essential elements for the attainment of the objectives of this Convention, undertakes subject to the provisions of this Article to provide and/or facilitate access for and transfer to other Contracting Parties of technologies that are relevant to the conservation and sustainable use of biological diversity or make use of genetic resources and do not cause significant damage to the environment.

2. Access to and transfer of technology referred to in paragraph 1 above to developing countries shall be provided and/or facilitated under fair and most favourable terms, including on concessional and preferential terms where mutually agreed, and, where necessary, in accordance with the financial mechanism established by Articles 20 and 21. In the case of technology subject to patents and other intellectual property rights, such access and transfer shall be provided on terms which recognize and are consistent with the adequate and effective protection of intellectual property rights. The application of this paragraph shall be consistent with paragraphs 3, 4 and 5 below.

3. Each Contracting Party shall take legislative, administrative or policy measures, as appropriate, with the aim that Contracting Parties, in particular those that are developing countries, which provide genetic resources are provided access to and transfer of technology which makes use of those resources, on mutually agreed terms, including technology protected by patents and other intellectual property rights, where necessary, through the provisions of Articles 20 and 21 and in accordance with international law and consistent with paragraphs 4 and 5 below.

4. Each Contracting Party shall take legislative, administrative or policy measures, as appropriate, with the aim that the private sector facilitates access to, joint development and transfer of technology referred to in paragraph 1 above for the benefit of both governmental institutions and the private sector of developing countries and in this regard shall abide by the obligations included in paragraphs 1, 2 and 3 above.
5. The Contracting Parties, recognizing that patents and other intellectual property rights may have an influence on the implementation of this Convention, shall cooperate in this regard subject to national legislation and international law in order to ensure that such rights are supportive of and do not run counter to its objectives.

[9.491]
Article 17
Exchange of Information

1. The Contracting Parties shall facilitate the exchange of information, from all publicly available sources, relevant to the conservation and sustainable use of biological diversity, taking into account the special needs of developing countries.
2. Such exchange of information shall include exchange of results of technical, scientific and socio-economic research, as well as information on training and surveying programmes, specialized knowledge, indigenous and traditional knowledge as such and in combination with the technologies referred to in Article 16, paragraph 1. It shall also, where feasible, include repatriation of information.

[9.492]
Article 18
Technical and Scientific Cooperation

1. The Contracting Parties shall promote international technical and scientific cooperation in the field of conservation and sustainable use of biological diversity, where necessary, through the appropriate international and national institutions.
2. Each Contracting Party shall promote technical and scientific cooperation with other Contracting Parties, in particular developing countries, in implementing this Convention, inter alia, through the development and implementation of national policies. In promoting such cooperation, special attention should be given to the development and strengthening of national capabilities, by means of human resources development and institution building.
3. The Conference of the Parties, at its first meeting, shall determine how to establish a clearing-house mechanism to promote and facilitate technical and scientific cooperation.
4. The Contracting Parties shall, in accordance with national legislation and policies, encourage and develop methods of cooperation for the development and use of technologies, including indigenous and traditional technologies, in pursuance of the objectives of this Convention. For this purpose, the Contracting Parties shall also promote cooperation in the training of personnel and exchange of experts.
5. The Contracting Parties shall, subject to mutual agreement, promote the establishment of joint research programmes and joint ventures for the development of technologies relevant to the objectives of this Convention.

[9.493]
Article 19
Handling of Biotechnology and Distribution of its Benefits

1. Each Contracting Party shall take legislative, administrative or policy measures, as appropriate, to provide for the effective participation in biotechnological research activities by those Contracting Parties, especially developing countries, which provide the genetic resources for such research, and where feasible in such Contracting Parties.
2. Each Contracting Party shall take all practicable measures to promote and advance priority access on a fair and equitable basis by Contracting Parties, especially developing countries, to the results and benefits arising from biotechnologies based upon genetic resources provided by those Contracting Parties. Such access shall be on mutually agreed terms.
3. The Parties shall consider the need for and modalities of a protocol setting out appropriate procedures, including, in particular, advance informed agreement, in the field of the safe transfer, handling and use of any living modified organism resulting from biotechnology that may have adverse effect on the conservation and sustainable use of biological diversity.
4. Each Contracting Party shall, directly or by requiring any natural or legal person under its jurisdiction providing the organisms referred to in paragraph 3 above, provide any available information about the use and safety regulations required by that Contracting Party in handling such organisms, as well as any available information on the potential adverse impact of the specific organisms concerned to the Contracting Party into which those organisms are to be introduced.

[9.494]
Article 20
Financial Resources

1. Each Contracting Party undertakes to provide, in accordance with its capabilities, financial support and incentives in respect of those national activities which are intended to achieve the objectives of this Convention, in accordance with its national plans, priorities and programmes.
2. The developed country Parties shall provide new and additional financial resources to enable developing country Parties to meet the agreed full incremental costs to them of implementing measures which fulfil the obligations of this Convention and to benefit from its provisions and which costs are agreed between a developing country Party and the institutional structure referred to in Article 21, in accordance with policy, strategy, programme priorities and eligibility criteria and an indicative list of incremental costs established by the Conference of the Parties. Other Parties, including countries undergoing the process of transition to a market economy, may voluntarily assume the obligations of the developed country Parties. For the purpose of this Article, the Conference of the Parties, shall at its first meeting establish a list of developed country Parties and other Parties which voluntarily assume the obligations of the developed country Parties. The Conference of the Parties shall periodically review and if necessary amend the list. Contributions from other countries and sources on a voluntary basis would also be encouraged. The implementation of these commitments shall take into account the need for adequacy, predictability and timely flow of funds and the importance of burden-sharing among the contributing Parties included in the list.
3. The developed country Parties may also provide, and developing country Parties avail themselves of, financial resources related to the implementation of this Convention through bilateral, regional and other multilateral channels.
4. The extent to which developing country Parties will effectively implement their commitments under this Convention will depend on the effective implementation by developed country Parties of their commitments under this Convention related to financial resources and transfer of technology and will take fully into account the fact that economic and social development and eradication of poverty are the first and overriding priorities of the developing country Parties.
5. The Parties shall take full account of the specific needs and special situation of least developed countries in their actions with regard to funding and transfer of technology.
6. The Contracting Parties shall also take into consideration the special conditions resulting from the dependence on, distribution and location of, biological diversity within developing country Parties, in particular small island States.
7. Consideration shall also be given to the special situation of developing countries, including those that are most environmentally vulnerable, such as those with arid and semi-arid zones, coastal and mountainous areas.

[9.495]
Article 21
Financial Mechanism

1. There shall be a mechanism for the provision of financial resources to developing country Parties for purposes of this Convention on a grant or concessional basis the essential elements of which are described in this Article. The mechanism shall function under the authority and guidance of, and be accountable to, the Conference of the Parties for purposes of this Convention. The operations of the mechanism shall be carried out by such institutional structure as may be decided upon by the Conference of the Parties at its first meeting. For purposes of this Convention, the Conference of the Parties shall determine the policy, strategy, programme priorities and eligibility criteria relating to the access to and utilization of such resources. The contributions shall be such as to take into account the need for predictability, adequacy and timely flow of funds referred to in Article 20 in accordance with the amount of resources needed to be decided periodically by the Conference of the Parties and the importance of burden-sharing among the contributing Parties included in the list referred to in Article 20, paragraph 2. Voluntary contributions may also be made by the developed country Parties and by other countries and sources. The mechanism shall operate within a democratic and transparent system of governance.
2. Pursuant to the objectives of this Convention, the Conference of the Parties shall at its first meeting determine the policy, strategy and programme priorities, as well as detailed criteria and guidelines for eligibility for access to and utilization of the financial resources including monitoring and evaluation on a regular basis of such utilization. The Conference of the Parties shall decide on the arrangements to give effect to paragraph 1 above after consultation with the institutional structure entrusted with the operation of the financial mechanism.
3. The Conference of the Parties shall review the effectiveness of the mechanism established under this Article, including the criteria and guidelines referred to in paragraph 2 above, not less than two years after the entry into force of this Convention and thereafter on a regular basis. Based on such review, it shall take appropriate action to improve the effectiveness of the mechanism if necessary.
4. The Contracting Parties shall consider strengthening existing financial institutions to provide financial resources for the conservation and sustainable use of biological diversity.

[9.496]
Article 22
Relationship with Other International Conventions

1. The provisions of this Convention shall not affect the rights and obligations of any Contracting Party deriving from any existing international agreement, except where the exercise of those rights and obligations would cause a serious damage or threat to biological diversity.
2. Contracting Parties shall implement this Convention with respect to the marine environment consistently with the rights and obligations of States under the law of the sea.

[9.497]
Article 23
Conference of the Parties

1. A Conference of the Parties is hereby established. The first meeting of the Conference of the Parties shall be convened by the Executive Director of the United Nations Environment Programme not later than one year after the entry into force of this Convention. Thereafter, ordinary meetings of the Conference of the Parties shall be held at regular intervals to be determined by the Conference at its first meeting.
2. Extraordinary meetings of the Conference of the Parties shall be held at such other times as may be deemed necessary by the Conference, or at the written request of any Party, provided that, within six months of the request being communicated to them by the Secretariat, it is supported by at least one third of the Parties.
3. The Conference of the Parties shall by consensus agree upon and adopt rules of procedure for itself and for any subsidiary body it may establish, as well as financial rules governing the funding of the Secretariat. At each ordinary meeting, it shall adopt a budget for the financial period until the next ordinary meeting.
4. The Conference of the Parties shall keep under review the implementation of this Convention, and, for this purpose, shall:—
   (a) Establish the form and the intervals for transmitting the information to be submitted in accordance with Article 26 and consider such information as well as reports submitted by any subsidiary body;
   (b) Review scientific, technical and technological advice on biological diversity provided in accordance with Article 25;
   (c) Consider and adopt, as required, protocols in accordance with Article 28;
   (d) Consider and adopt, as required, in accordance with Articles 29 and 30, amendments to this Convention and its annexes;
   (e) Consider amendments to any protocol, as well as to any annexes thereto, and, if so decided, recommend their adoption to the parties to the protocol concerned;
   (f) Consider and adopt, as required, in accordance with Article 30, additional annexes to this Convention;
   (g) Establish such subsidiary bodies, particularly to provide scientific and technical advice, as are deemed necessary for the implementation of this Convention;
   (h) Contact, through the Secretariat, the executive bodies of conventions dealing with matters covered by this Convention with a view to establishing appropriate forms of cooperation with them; and
   (i) Consider and undertake any additional action that may be required for the achievement of the purposes of this Convention in the light of experience gained in its operation.

(5) The United Nations, its specialized agencies and the International Atomic Energy Agency, as well as any State not Party to this Convention, may be represented as observers at meetings of the Conference of the Parties. Any other body or agency, whether governmental or non-governmental, qualified in fields relating to conservation and sustainable use of biological diversity, which has informed the Secretariat of its wish to be represented as an observer at a meeting of the Conference of the Parties, may be admitted unless at least one third of the Parties present object. The admission and participation of observers shall be subject to the rules of procedure adopted by the Conference of the Parties.

[9.498]
Article 24
Secretariat

1. A secretariat is hereby established. Its functions shall be:
   (a) To arrange for and service meetings of the Conference of the Parties provided for in Article 23;
   (b) To perform the functions assigned to it by any protocol;
   (c) To prepare reports on the execution of its functions under this Convention and present them to the Conference of the Parties;
   (d) To coordinate with other relevant international bodies and, in particular to enter into such administrative and contractual arrangements as may be required for the effective discharge of its functions; and
   (e) To perform such other functions as may be determined by the Conference of the Parties.

2. At its first ordinary meeting, the Conference of the Parties shall designate the secretariat from amongst those existing competent international organisations which have signified their willingness to carry out the secretariat functions under this Convention.

[9.499]

Article 25

Subsidiary Body on Scientific, Technical and Technological Advice

1. A subsidiary body for the provision of scientific, technical and technological advice is hereby established to provide the Conference of the Parties and, as appropriate, its other subsidiary bodies with timely advice relating to the implementation of this Convention. This body shall be open to participation by all Parties and shall be multidisciplinary. It shall comprise government representatives competent in the relevant field of expertise. It shall report regularly to the Conference of the Parties on all aspects of its work.

2. Under the authority of and in accordance with guidelines laid down by the Conference of the Parties, and upon its request, this body shall:—

(a) Provide scientific and technical assessments of the status of biological diversity;

(b) Prepare scientific and technical assessments of the effects of types of measures taken in accordance with the provisions of this Convention;

(c) Identify innovative, efficient and state-of-the-art technologies and knowhow relating to the conservation and sustainable use of biological diversity and advise on the ways and means of promoting development and/or transferring such technologies;

(d) Provide advice on scientific programmes and international cooperation in research and development related to conservation and sustainable use of biological diversity; and

(e) Respond to scientific, technical, technological and methodological questions that the Conference of the Parties and its subsidiary bodies may put to the body.

3. The functions, terms of reference, organisation and operation of this body may be further elaborated by the Conference of the Parties.

[9.500]

Article 26

Reports

Each Contracting Party shall, at intervals to be determined by the Conference of the Parties, present to the Conference of the Parties, reports on measures which it has taken for the implementation of the provisions of this Convention and their effectiveness in meeting the objectives of this Convention.

[9.501]

Article 27

Settlement of Disputes

1. In the event of a dispute between Contracting Parties concerning the interpretation or application of this Convention, the parties concerned shall seek solution by negotiation.

2. If the parties concerned cannot reach agreement by negotiation, they may jointly seek the good offices of, or request mediation by, a third party.

3. When ratifying, accepting, approving or acceding to this Convention, or at any time thereafter, a State or regional economic integration organisation may declare in writing to the Depositary that for a dispute not resolved in accordance with paragraph 1 or paragraph 2 above, it accepts one or both of the following means of dispute settlement as compulsory:—

(a) Arbitration in accordance with the procedure laid down in Part 1 of Annex II;

(b) Submission of the dispute to the International Court of Justice.

4. If the parties to the dispute have not, in accordance with paragraph 3 above, accepted the same or any procedure, the dispute shall be submitted to conciliation in accordance with Part 2 of Annex II unless the parties otherwise agree.

5. The provisions of this Article shall apply with respect to any protocol except as otherwise provided in the protocol concerned.

[9.502]

Article 28

Adoption of Protocols

1. The Contracting Parties shall cooperate in the formulation and adoption of protocols to this Convention.

2. Protocols shall be adopted at a meeting of the Conference of the Parties.

3. The text of any proposed protocol shall be communicated to the Contracting Parties by the Secretariat at least six months before such a meeting.

[9.503]

Article 29

Amendment of the Convention or Protocols

1. Amendments to this Convention may be proposed by any Contracting Party. Amendments to any protocol may be proposed by any Party to that protocol.

2. Amendments to this Convention shall be adopted at a meeting of the Conference of the Parties. Amendments to any protocol shall be adopted at a meeting of the Parties to the Protocol in question. The text of any proposed amendment to this Convention or to any protocol, except as may otherwise be provided in such protocol, shall be communicated to the Parties to the instrument in question by the secretariat at least six months before the meeting at which it is proposed for adoption. The secretariat shall also communicate proposed amendments to the signatories to this Convention for information.
3. The Parties shall make every effort to reach agreement on any proposed amendment to this Convention or to any protocol by consensus. If all efforts at consensus have been exhausted, and no agreement reached, the amendment shall as a last resort be adopted by a two-third majority vote of the Parties to the instrument in question present and voting at the meeting, and shall be submitted by the Depositary to all Parties for ratification, acceptance or approval.
4. Ratification, acceptance or approval of amendments shall be notified to the Depositary in writing. Amendments adopted in accordance with paragraph 3 above shall enter into force among Parties having accepted them on the ninetieth day after the deposit of instruments of ratification, acceptance or approval by at least two thirds of the Contracting Parties to this Convention or of the Parties to the protocol concerned, except as may otherwise be provided in such protocol. Thereafter the amendments shall enter into force for any other Party on the ninetieth day after that Party deposits its instrument of ratification, acceptance or approval of the amendments.
5. For the purposes of this Article, "Parties present and voting" means Parties present and casting an affirmative or negative vote.

[9.504]
Article 30
Adoption and Amendment of Annexes

1. The annexes to this Convention or to any protocol shall form an integral part of the Convention or of such protocol, as the case may be, and, unless expressly provided otherwise, a reference to this Convention or its protocols constitutes at the same time a reference to any annexes thereto. Such annexes shall be restricted to procedural, scientific, technical and administrative matters.
2. Except as may be otherwise provided in any protocol with respect to its annexes, the following procedure shall apply to the proposal, adoption and entry into force of additional annexes to this Convention or of annexes to any protocol:—
   (a) Annexes to this Convention or to any protocol shall be proposed and adopted according to the procedure laid down in Article 29;
   (b) Any Party that is unable to approve an additional annex to this Convention or an annex to any protocol to which it is Party shall so notify the Depositary, in writing, within one year from the date of the communication of the adoption by the Depositary. The Depositary shall without delay notify all Parties of any such notification received. A Party may at any time withdraw a previous declaration of objection and the annexes shall thereupon enter into force for that Party subject to subparagraph (c) below;
   (c) On the expiry of one year from the date of the communication of the adoption by the Depositary, the annex shall enter into force for all Parties to this Convention or to any protocol concerned which have not submitted a notification in accordance with the provisions of subparagraph (b) above.
3. The proposal, adoption and entry into force of amendments to annexes to this Convention or to any protocol shall be subject to the same procedure as for the proposal, adoption and entry into force of annexes to the Convention or annexes to any protocol.
4. If an additional annex or an amendment to an annex is related to an amendment to this Convention or to any protocol, the additional annex or amendment shall not enter into force until such time as the amendment to the Convention or to the protocol concerned enters into force.

[9.505]
Article 31
Right to Vote

1. Except as provided for in paragraph 2 below, each Contracting Party to this Convention or to any protocol shall have one vote.
2. Regional economic integration organisations, in matters within their competence, shall exercise their right to vote with a number of votes equal to the number of their member States which are Contracting Parties to this Convention or the relevant protocol. Such organisations shall not exercise their right to vote if their member States exercise theirs, and vice versa.

[9.506]
Article 32
Relationship between this Convention and Its Protocols

1. A State or a regional economic integration organisation may not become a Party to a protocol unless it is, or becomes at the same time, a Contracting Party to this Convention.
2. Decisions under any protocol shall be taken only by the Parties to the protocol concerned. Any Contracting Party that has not ratified, accepted or approved a protocol may participate as an observer in any meeting of the parties to that protocol.

[9.507]
Article 33
Signature
This Convention shall be open for signature at Rio de Janeiro by all States and any regional economic integration organisation from 5 June 1992 until 14 June 1992, and at the United Nations Headquarters in New York from 15 June 1992 to 4 June 1993.

[9.508]
Article 34
Ratification, Acceptance or Approval
1. This Convention and any protocol shall be subject to ratification, acceptance or approval by States and by regional economic integration organisations. Instruments of ratification, acceptance or approval shall be deposited with the Depositary.
2. Any organisation referred to in paragraph 1 above which becomes a Contracting Party to this Convention or any protocol without any of its member States being a Contracting Party shall be bound by all the obligations under the Convention or the protocol, as the case may be. In the case of such organisations, one or more of whose member States is a Contracting Party to this Convention or relevant protocol, the organisation and its member States shall decide on their respective responsibilities for the performance of their obligations under the Convention or protocol, as the case may be. In such cases, the organisation and the member States shall not be entitled to exercise rights under the Convention or relevant protocol concurrently.
3. In their instruments of ratification, acceptance or approval, the organisations referred to in paragraph 1 above shall declare the extent of their competence with respect to the matters governed by the Convention or the relevant protocol. These organisations shall also inform the Depositary of any relevant modification in the extent of their competence.

[9.509]
Article 35
Accession
1. This Convention and any protocol shall be open for accession by States and by regional economic integration organisations from the date on which the Convention or the protocol concerned is closed for signature. The instruments of accession shall be deposited with the Depositary.
2. In their instruments of accession, the organisations referred to in paragraph 1 above shall declare the extent of their competence with respect to the matters governed by the Convention or the relevant protocol. These organisations shall also inform the Depositary of any relevant modification in the extent of their competence.
3. The provisions of Article 34, paragraph 2, shall apply to regional economic integration organisations which accede to this Convention or any protocol.

[9.510]
Article 36
Entry Into Force
1. This Convention shall enter into force on the ninetieth day after the date of deposit of the thirtieth instrument of ratification, acceptance, approval or accession.
2. Any protocol shall enter into force on the ninetieth day after the date of deposit of the number of instruments of ratification, acceptance, approval or accession, specified in that protocol, has been deposited.
3. For each Contracting Party which ratifies, accepts or approves this Convention or accedes thereto after the deposit of the thirtieth instrument of ratification, acceptance, approval or accession, it shall enter into force on the ninetieth day after the date of deposit by such Contracting Party of its instrument of ratification, acceptance, approval or accession.
4. Any protocol, except as otherwise provided in such protocol, shall enter into force for a Contracting Party that ratifies, accepts or approves that protocol or accedes thereto after its entry into force pursuant to paragraph 2 above, on the ninetieth day after the date on which that Contracting Party deposits its instrument of ratification, acceptance, approval or accession, or on the date on which this Convention enters into force for that Contracting Party, whichever shall be the later.
5. For the purposes of paragraphs 1 and 2 above, any instrument deposited by a regional economic integration organisation shall not be counted as additional to those deposited by member States of such organisation.

[9.511]
Article 37
Reservations
No reservations may be made to this Convention.

[9.512]
Article 38
Withdrawals

1. At any time after two years from the date on which this Convention has entered into force for a Contracting Party, that Contracting Party may withdraw from the Convention by giving written notification to the Depositary.
2. Any such withdrawal shall take place upon expiry of one year after the date of its receipt by the Depositary, or on such later date as may be specified in the notification of the withdrawal.
3. Any Contracting Party which withdraws from this Convention shall be considered as also having withdrawn from any protocol to which it is party.

[9.513]
Article 39
Financial Interim Arrangements

Provided that it has been fully restructured in accordance with the requirements of Article 21, the Global Environment Facility of the United Nations Development Programme, the United Nations Environment Programme and the International Bank for Reconstruction and Development shall be the institutional structure referred to in Article 21 on an interim basis, for the period between the entry into force of this Convention and the first meeting of the Conference of the Parties or until the Conference of the Parties decides which institutional structure will be designated in accordance with Article 21.

[9.514]
Article 40
Secretariat Interim Arrangements

The secretariat to be provided by the Executive Director of the United Nations Environment Programme shall be the secretariat referred to in Article 24, paragraph 2, on an interim basis for the period between the entry into force of this Convention and the first meeting of the Conference of the Parties.

[9.515]
Article 41
Depositary

The Secretary-General of the United Nations shall assume the functions of Depositary of this Convention and any protocols.

[9.516]
Article 42
Authentic Texts

The original of this Convention, of which the Arabic, Chinese, English, French, Russian and Spanish texts are equally authentic, shall be deposited with the Secretary-General of the United Nations.

IN WITNESS WHEREOF the undersigned, being duly authorized to that effect, have signed this Convention.

Done at Rio de Janeiro on this fifth day of June, one thousand nine hundred and ninety-two.

ANNEX I
IDENTIFICATION AND MONITORING

[9.517]

1. Ecosystems and habitats: containing high diversity, large numbers of endemic or threatened species, or wilderness; required by migratory species; of social, economic, cultural or scientific importance; or, which are representative, unique or associated with key evolutionary or other biological processes;

2. Species and communities which are: threatened; wild relatives of domesticated or cultivated species; of medicinal, agricultural or other economic value; or social, scientific or cultural importance; or importance for research into the conservation and sustainable use of biological diversity, such as indicator species; and

3. Described genomes and genes of social, scientific or economic importance.

ANNEX II

PART I
ARBITRATION

[9.518]

Article 1 The claimant party shall notify the secretariat that the parties are referring a dispute to arbitration pursuant to Article 27. The notification shall state the subject-matter of arbitration and include, in particular, the articles of the Convention or the protocol, the interpretation or application of which are at issue. If the parties do not agree on the subject matter of the dispute before the President of the tribunal is designated, the arbitral tribunal shall determine the subject matter. The secretariat shall forward the information thus received to all Contracting Parties to this Convention or to the protocol concerned.

Article 2 1. In disputes between two parties, the arbitral tribunal shall consist of three members. Each of the parties to the dispute shall appoint an arbitrator and the two arbitrators so appointed shall designate by common agreement the third arbitrator who shall be the President of the tribunal. The latter shall not be a national of one of the parties to the dispute, nor have his or her usual place of residence in the territory of one of these parties, nor be employed by any of them, nor have dealt with the case in any other capacity.

2. In disputes between more than two parties, parties in the same interest shall appoint one arbitrator jointly by agreement.

3. Any vacancy shall be filled in the manner prescribed for the initial appointment.

Article 3 1. If the President of the arbitral tribunal has not been designated within two months of the appointment of the second arbitrator, the Secretary-General of the United Nations shall, at the request of a party, designate the President within a further two-month period.

2. If one of the parties to the dispute does not appoint an arbitrator within two months of receipt of the request, the other party may inform the Secretary-General who shall make the designation within a further two-month period.

Article 4 The arbitral tribunal shall render its decisions in accordance with the provisions of this Convention, any protocols concerned, and international law.

Article 5 Unless the parties to the dispute otherwise agree, the arbitral tribunal shall determine its own rules of procedure.

Article 6 The arbitral tribunal may, at the request of one of the parties, recommend essential interim measures of protection.

Article 7 The parties to the dispute shall facilitate the work of the arbitral tribunal and, in particular, using all means at their disposal, shall:

(a) Provide it with all relevant documents, information and facilities; and

(b) Enable it, when necessary, to call witnesses or experts and receive their evidence.

Article 8 The parties and the arbitrators are under an obligation to protect the confidentiality of any information they receive in confidence during the proceedings of the arbitral tribunal.

Article 9 Unless the arbitral tribunal determines otherwise because of the particular circumstances of the case, the costs of the tribunal shall be borne by the parties to the dispute in equal shares. The tribunal shall keep a record of all its costs, and shall furnish a final statement thereof to the parties.

Article 10 Any Contracting Party that has an interest of a legal nature in the subject-matter of the dispute which may be affected by the decision in the case, may intervene in the proceedings with the consent of the tribunal.

Article 11 The tribunal may hear and determine counterclaims arising directly out of the subject-matter of the dispute.

Article 12 Decisions both on procedure and substance of the arbitral tribunal shall be taken by a majority vote of its members.

Article 13 If one of the parties to the dispute does not appear before the arbitral tribunal or fails to defend its case, the other party may request the tribunal to continue the proceedings and to make its award. Absence of a party or a failure of a party to defend its case shall not constitute a bar to the proceedings. Before rendering its final decision, the arbitral tribunal must satisfy itself that the claim is well founded in fact and law.

Article 14 The tribunal shall render its final decision within five months of the date on which it is fully constituted unless it finds it necessary to extend the time-limit for a period which should not exceed five more months.

Article 15 The final decision of the arbitral tribunal shall be confined to the subject-matter of the dispute and shall state the reasons on which it is based. It shall contain the names of the members who have participated and the date of the final decision. Any member of the tribunal may attach a separate or dissenting opinion to the final decision.

Article 16 The award shall be binding on the parties to the dispute. It shall be without appeal unless the parties to the dispute have agreed in advance to an appellate procedure.

Article 17 Any controversy which may arise between the parties to the dispute as regards the interpretation or manner of implementation of the final decision may be submitted by either party for decision to the arbitral tribunal which rendered it.

PART 2
CONCILIATION

[9.519]

Article 1 A conciliation commission shall be created upon the request of one of the parties to the dispute. The commission shall, unless the parties otherwise agree, be composed of five members, two appointed by each Party concerned and a President chosen jointly by those members.

Article 2 In disputes between more than two parties, parties in the same interest shall appoint their members of the commission jointly by agreement. Where two or more parties have separate interests or there is a disagreement as to whether they are of the same interest, they shall appoint their members separately.

Article 3 If any appointments by the parties are not made within two months of the date of the request to create a conciliation commission, the Secretary-General of the United Nations shall, if asked to do so by the party that made the request, make those appointments within a further two-month period.

Article 4 If a President of the conciliation commission has not been chosen within two months of the last of the members of the commission being appointed, the Secretary-General of the United Nations shall, if asked to do so by a party, designate a President within a further two-month period.

Article 5 The conciliation commission shall take its decisions by majority vote of its members. It shall, unless the parties to the dispute otherwise agree, determine its own procedure. It shall render a proposal for resolution of the dispute, which the parties shall consider in good faith.

Article 6 A disagreement as to whether the conciliation commission has competence shall be decided by the commission.

UNIFORM DOMAIN NAME DISPUTE RESOLUTION POLICY

(As approved by ICANN on October 24, 1999)

NOTES

The original source for this document is ICANN (Internet Corporation for Assigned Names and Numbers).

1 PURPOSE

[9.520]

This Uniform Domain Name Dispute Resolution Policy (the "Policy") has been adopted by the Internet Corporation for Assigned Names and Numbers ("ICANN"), is incorporated by reference into your Registration Agreement, and sets forth the terms and conditions in connection with a dispute between you and any party other than us (the registrar) over the registration and use of an Internet domain name registered by you. Proceedings under Paragraph 4 of this Policy will be conducted according to the Rules for Uniform Domain Name Dispute Resolution Policy (the "Rules of Procedure"), which are available at www.icann.org/udrp/udrp-rules-24oct99.htm, and the selected administrative-dispute-resolution service provider's supplemental rules.

2 YOUR REPRESENTATIONS

By applying to register a domain name, or by asking us to maintain or renew a domain name registration, you hereby represent and warrant to us that—

(a) the statements that you made in your Registration Agreement are complete and accurate;

(b) to your knowledge, the registration of the domain name will not infringe upon or otherwise violate the rights of any third party;

(c) you are not registering the domain name for an unlawful purpose; and

(d) you will not knowingly use the domain name in violation of any applicable laws or regulations. It is your responsibility to determine whether your domain name registration infringes or violates someone else's rights.

3 CANCELLATIONS, TRANSFERS, AND CHANGES

We will cancel, transfer or otherwise make changes to domain name registrations under the following circumstances—

(a) subject to the provisions of Paragraph 8, our receipt of written or appropriate electronic instructions from you or your authorised agent to take such action;

(b) our receipt of an order from a court or arbitral tribunal, in each case of competent jurisdiction, requiring such action; and/or

(c) our receipt of a decision of an Administrative Panel requiring such action in any administrative proceeding to which you were a party and which was conducted under this Policy or a later version of this Policy adopted by ICANN. (See Paragraph 4(i) and (k) below.)

We may also cancel, transfer or otherwise make changes to a domain name registration in accordance with the terms of your Registration Agreement or other legal requirements.

4 MANDATORY ADMINISTRATIVE PROCEEDING

This Paragraph sets forth the type of disputes for which you are required to submit to a mandatory administrative proceeding. These proceedings will be conducted before one of the administrative-dispute-resolution service providers listed at www.icann.org/udrp/approved-providers.htm (each, a "Provider").

(a) *Applicable Disputes*

You are required to submit to a mandatory administrative proceeding in the event that a third party (a "complainant") asserts to the applicable Provider, in compliance with the Rules of Procedure, that

(i) your domain name is identical or confusingly similar to a trademark or service mark in which the complainant has rights; and

(ii) you have no rights or legitimate interests in respect of the domain name; and

(iii) your domain name has been registered and is being used in bad faith.

In the administrative proceeding, the complainant must prove that each of these three elements are present.

(b) *Evidence of Registration and Use in Bad Faith*

For the purposes of Paragraph 4(a)(iii), the following circumstances, in particular but without limitation, if found by the Panel to be present, shall be evidence of the registration and use of a domain name in bad faith—

(i) circumstances indicating that you have registered or you have acquired the domain name primarily for the purpose of selling, renting, or otherwise transferring the domain name registration to the complainant who is the owner of the trademark or service mark or to a competitor of that complainant, for valuable consideration in excess of your documented out-of-pocket costs directly related to the domain name; or

(ii) you have registered the domain name in order to prevent the owner of the trademark or service mark from reflecting the mark in a corresponding domain name, provided that you have engaged in a pattern of such conduct; or

(iii) you have registered the domain name primarily for the purpose of disrupting the business of a competitor; or

(iv) by using the domain name, you have intentionally attempted to attract, for commercial gain, Internet users to your web site or other on-line location, by creating a likelihood of confusion with the complainant's mark as to the source, sponsorship, affiliation, or endorsement of your web site or location or of a product or service on your web site or location.

(c) *How to Demonstrate Your Rights to and Legitimate Interests in the Domain Name in Responding to a Complaint*

When you receive a complaint, you should refer to Paragraph 5 of the Rules of Procedure in determining how your response should be prepared. Any of the following circumstances, in particular but without limitation, if found by the Panel to be proved based on its evaluation of all evidence presented, shall demonstrate your rights or legitimate interests to the domain name for purposes of Paragraph 4(a)(ii)—

(i) before any notice to you of the dispute, your use of, or demonstrable preparations to use, the domain name or a name corresponding to the domain name in connection with a bona fide offering of goods or services; or

(ii) you (as an individual, business, or other organisation) have been commonly known by the domain name, even if you have acquired no trademark or service mark rights; or

(iii) you are making a legitimate non-commercial or fair use of the domain name, without intent for commercial gain to misleadingly divert consumers or to tarnish the trademark or service mark at issue.

(d) *Selection of Provider*

The complainant shall select the Provider from among those approved by ICANN by submitting the complaint to that Provider. The selected Provider will administer the proceeding, except in cases of consolidation as described in Paragraph 4(f).

(e) *Initiation of Proceeding and Process and Appointment of Administrative Panel*

The Rules of Procedure state the process for initiating and conducting a proceeding and for appointing the panel that will decide the dispute (the "Administrative Panel").

(f) *Consolidation*

In the event of multiple disputes between you and a complainant, either you or the complainant may petition to consolidate the disputes before a single Administrative Panel. This petition shall be made to the first Administrative Panel appointed to hear a pending dispute between the parties. This Administrative Panel may consolidate before it any or all such disputes in its sole discretion, provided that the disputes being consolidated are governed by this Policy or a later version of this Policy adopted by ICANN.

(g) *Fees*

All fees charged by a Provider in connection with any dispute before an Administrative Panel pursuant to this Policy shall be paid by the complainant, except in cases where you elect to expand the Administrative Panel from one to three panelists as provided in Paragraph 5(b)(iv) of the Rules of Procedure, in which case all fees will be split evenly by you and the complainant.

(h) *Our Involvement in Administrative Proceedings*

We do not, and will not, participate in the administration or conduct of any proceeding before an Administrative Panel. In addition, we will not be liable as a result of any decisions rendered by the Administrative Panel.

(i) *Remedies*

The remedies available to a complainant pursuant to any proceeding before an Administrative Panel shall be limited to requiring the cancellation of your domain name or the transfer of your domain name registration to the complainant.

(j) *Notification and Publication*

The Provider shall notify us of any decision made by an Administrative Panel with respect to a domain name you have registered with us. All decisions under this Policy will be published in full over the Internet, except when an Administrative Panel determines in an exceptional case to redact portions of its decision.

(k) *Availability of Court Proceedings*

The mandatory administrative proceeding requirements set forth in Paragraph 4 shall not prevent either you or the complainant from submitting the dispute to a court of competent jurisdiction for independent resolution before such mandatory administrative proceeding is commenced or after such proceeding is concluded. If an Administrative Panel decides that your domain name registration should be cancelled or transferred, we will wait ten (10) business days (as observed in the location of our principal office) after we are informed by the applicable Provider of the Administrative Panel's decision before implementing that decision. We will then implement the decision unless we have received from you during that ten (10) business day period official documentation (such as a copy of a complaint, file-stamped by the clerk of the court) that you have commenced a lawsuit against the complainant in a jurisdiction to which the complainant has submitted under Paragraph 3(b)(xiii) of the Rules of Procedure. (In general, that jurisdiction is either the location of our principal office or of your address as shown in our Whois database. See Paragraphs 1 and 3(b)(xiii) of the Rules of Procedure for details.) If we receive such documentation within the ten (10) business day period, we will not implement the Administrative Panel's decision, and we will take no further action, until we receive (i) evidence satisfactory to us of a resolution between the parties; (ii) evidence satisfactory to us that your lawsuit has been dismissed or withdrawn; or (iii) a copy of an order from such court dismissing your lawsuit or ordering that you do not have the right to continue to use your domain name.

5 ALL OTHER DISPUTES AND LITIGATION

All other disputes between you and any party other than us regarding your domain name registration that are not brought pursuant to the mandatory administrative proceeding provisions of Paragraph 4 shall be resolved between you and such other party through any court, arbitration or other proceeding that may be available.

6 OUR INVOLVEMENT IN DISPUTES

We will not participate in any way in any dispute between you and any party other than us regarding the registration and use of your domain name. You shall not name us as a party or otherwise include us in any such proceeding. In the event that we are named as a party in any such proceeding, we reserve the right to raise any and all defences deemed appropriate, and to take any other action necessary to defend ourselves.

7 MAINTAINING THE STATUS QUO

We will not cancel, transfer, activate, deactivate, or otherwise change the status of any domain name registration under this Policy except as provided in Paragraph 3 above.

8 TRANSFERS DURING A DISPUTE

(a) *Transfers of a Domain Name to a New Holder*

You may not transfer your domain name registration to another holder

(i) during a pending administrative proceeding brought pursuant to Paragraph 4 or for a period of fifteen (15) business days (as observed in the location of our principal place of business) after such proceeding is concluded; or

(ii) during a pending court proceeding or arbitration commenced regarding your domain name unless the party to whom the domain name registration is being transferred agrees, in writing, to be bound by the decision of the court or arbitrator. We reserve the right to cancel any transfer of a domain name registration to another holder that is made in violation of this subparagraph.

(b) *Changing Registrars*
You may not transfer your domain name registration to another registrar during a pending administrative proceeding brought pursuant to Paragraph 4 or for a period of fifteen (15) business days (as observed in the location of our principal place of business) after such proceeding is concluded. You may transfer administration of your domain name registration to another registrar during a pending court action or arbitration, provided that the domain name you have registered with us shall continue to be subject to the proceedings commenced against you in accordance with the terms of this Policy. In the event that you transfer a domain name registration to us during the pendency of a court action or arbitration, such dispute shall remain subject to the domain name dispute policy of the registrar from which the domain name registration was transferred.

9 POLICY MODIFICATIONS

We reserve the right to modify this Policy at any time with the permission of ICANN. We will post our revised Policy at least thirty (30) calendar days before it becomes effective. Unless this Policy has already been invoked by the submission of a complaint to a Provider, in which event the version of the Policy in effect at the time it was invoked will apply to you until the dispute is over, all such changes will be binding upon you with respect to any domain name registration dispute, whether the dispute arose before, on or after the effective date of our change. In the event that you object to a change in this Policy, your sole remedy is to cancel your domain name registration with us, provided that you will not be entitled to a refund of any fees you paid to us. The revised Policy will apply to you until you cancel your domain name registration.

RULES FOR UNIFORM DOMAIN NAME DISPUTE RESOLUTION POLICY (THE "RULES")

(As approved by ICANN on 28 September 2013)

NOTES

The original source for this document is ICANN (Internet Corporation for Assigned Names and Numbers).

Note: these Rules are in effect for all UDRP proceedings in which a complaint is submitted to a provider on or after 31 July 2015. The prior version of the Rules, applicable to all proceedings in which a complaint was submitted to a Provider on or before 30 July 2015, is at www.icann.org/resources/pages/rules-be-2012-02-25-en.. UDRP Providers may elect to adopt the notice procedures set forth in these Rules prior to 31 July 2015.

[9.521]

Administrative proceedings for the resolution of disputes under the Uniform Dispute Resolution Policy adopted by ICANN shall be governed by these Rules and also the Supplemental Rules of the Provider administering the proceedings, as posted on its web site. To the extent that the Supplemental Rules of any Provider conflict with these Rules, these Rules supersede.

1 DEFINITIONS

In these Rules—

"Complainant" means the party initiating a complaint concerning a domain-name registration.

"ICANN" refers to the Internet Corporation for Assigned Names and Numbers.

"Lock" means a set of measures that a registrar applies to a domain name, which prevents at a minimum any modification to the registrant and registrar information by the Respondent, but does not affect the resolution of the domain name or the renewal of the domain name.

"Mutual Jurisdiction" means a court jurisdiction at the location of either

(a) the principal office of the Registrar (provided the domain-name holder has submitted in its Registration Agreement to that jurisdiction for court adjudication of disputes concerning or arising from the use of the domain name) or

(b) the domain-name holder's address as shown for the registration of the domain name in Registrar's Whois database at the time the complaint is submitted to the Provider.

"Panel" means an administrative panel appointed by a Provider to decide a complaint concerning a domain-name registration.

"Panelist" means an individual appointed by a Provider to be a member of a Panel.

"Party" means a Complainant or a Respondent.

"Pendency" means the time period from the moment a UDRP complaint has been submitted by the Complainant to the UDRP Provider to the time the UDRP decision has been implemented or the UDRP complaint has been terminated.

"Policy" means the Uniform Domain Name Dispute Resolution Policy that is incorporated by reference and made a part of the Registration Agreement.

"Provider" means a dispute-resolution service provider approved by ICANN. A list of such Providers appears at www.icann.org/en/dndr/udrp/approved-providers.htm.

"Registrar" means the entity with which the Respondent has registered a domain name that is the subject of a complaint.

"Registration Agreement" means the agreement between a Registrar and a domain-name holder.

"Respondent" means the holder of a domain-name registration against which a complaint is initiated.

"Reverse Domain Name Hijacking" means using the Policy in bad faith to attempt to deprive a registered domain-name holder of a domain name.

"Supplemental Rules" means the rules adopted by the Provider administering a proceeding to supplement these Rules. Supplemental Rules shall not be inconsistent with the Policy or these Rules and shall cover such topics as fees, word and page limits and guidelines, file size and format modalities, the means for communicating with the Provider and the Panel, and the form of cover sheets.

"Written Notice" means hardcopy notification by the Provider to the Respondent of the commencement of an administrative proceeding under the Policy which shall inform the respondent that a complaint has been filed against it, and which shall state that the Provider has electronically transmitted the complaint including any annexes to the Respondent by the means specified herein. Written notice does not include a hardcopy of the complaint itself or of any annexes.

2 COMMUNICATIONS

(a) When forwarding a complaint, including any annexes, electronically to the Respondent, it shall be the Provider's responsibility to employ reasonably available means calculated to achieve actual notice to Respondent. Achieving actual notice, or employing the following measures to do so, shall discharge this responsibility—

(i) sending Written Notice of the complaint to all postal-mail and facsimile addresses (A) shown in the domain name's registration data in Registrar's Whois database for the registered domain-name holder, the technical contact, and the administrative contact and (B) supplied by Registrar to the Provider for the registration's billing contact; and

(ii) sending the complaint, including any annexes, in electronic form (including annexes to the extent available in that form) by e-mail to—

(A) the e-mail addresses for those technical, administrative, and billing contacts;

(B) postmaster@<the contested domain name>; and

(C) if the domain name (or "www." followed by the domain name) resolves to an active web page (other than a generic page the Provider concludes is maintained by a registrar or ISP for parking domain-names registered by multiple domain-name holders), any e-mail address shown or e-mail links on that web page; and

(iii) sending the complaint, including any annexes, to any e-mail address the Respondent has notified the Provider it prefers and, to the extent practicable, to all other addresses provided to the Provider by Complainant under Paragraph 3(b)(v).

(b) Except as provided in Paragraph 2(a), any written communication to Complainant or Respondent provided for under these Rules shall be made by electronically via the Internet (a record of its transmission being available), or by any reasonably requested preferred means stated by the Complainant or Respondent, respectively (see Paragraphs 3(b)(iii) and 5(b)(iii)).

(c) Any communication to the Provider or the Panel shall be made by the means and in the manner (including, where applicable, the number of copies) stated in the Provider's Supplemental Rules.

(d) Communications shall be made in the language prescribed in Paragraph 11.

(e) Either Party may update its contact details by notifying the Provider and the Registrar.

(f) Except as otherwise provided in these Rules, or decided by a Panel, all communications provided for under these Rules shall be deemed to have been made—

(i) if via the Internet, on the date that the communication was transmitted, provided that the date of transmission is verifiable; or, where applicable

(ii) if delivered by telecopy or facsimile transmission, on the date shown on the confirmation of transmission; or

(iii) if by postal or courier service, on the date marked on the receipt.

(g) Except as otherwise provided in these Rules, all time periods calculated under these Rules to begin when a communication is made shall begin to run on the earliest date that the communication is deemed to have been made in accordance with Paragraph 2(f).

(h) Any communication by
(i) a Panel to any Party shall be copied to the Provider and to the other Party,
(ii) the Provider to any Party shall be copied to the other Party; and
(iii) a Party shall be copied to the other Party, the Panel and the Provider, as the case may be.

(i) It shall be the responsibility of the sender to retain records of the fact and circumstances of sending, which shall be available for inspection by affected parties and for reporting purposes. This includes the Provider in sending Written Notice to the Respondent by post and/or facsimile under Paragraph 2(a)(i).

(j) In the event a Party sending a communication receives notification of non-delivery of the communication, the Party shall promptly notify the Panel (or, if no Panel is yet appointed, the Provider) of the circumstances of the notification. Further proceedings concerning the communication and any response shall be as directed by the Panel (or the Provider).

3 THE COMPLAINT

(a) Any person or entity may initiate an administrative proceeding by submitting a complaint in accordance with the Policy and these Rules to any Provider approved by ICANN. (Due to capacity constraints or for other reasons, a Provider's ability to accept complaints may be suspended at times. In that event, the Provider shall refuse the submission. The person or entity may submit the complaint to another Provider.)

(b) The complaint including any annexes shall be submitted in electronic form and shall—
(i) Request that the complaint be submitted for decision in accordance with the Policy and these Rules;
(ii) Provide the name, postal and e-mail addresses, and the telephone and telefax numbers of the Complainant and of any representative authorised to act for the Complainant in the administrative proceeding;
(iii) Specify a preferred method for communications directed to the Complainant in the administrative proceeding (including person to be contacted, medium, and address information) for each of (A) electronic-only material and (B) material including hard copy (where applicable);
(iv) Designate whether Complainant elects to have the dispute decided by a single-member or a three-member Panel and, in the event Complainant elects a three-member Panel, provide the names and contact details of three candidates to serve as one of the Panelists (these candidates may be drawn from any ICANN-approved Provider's list of panelists);
(v) Provide the name of the Respondent (domain-name holder) and all information (including any postal and e-mail addresses and telephone and telefax numbers) known to Complainant regarding how to contact Respondent or any representative of Respondent, including contact information based on pre-complaint dealings, in sufficient detail to allow the Provider to send the complaint as described in Paragraph 2(a);
(vi) Specify the domain name(s) that is/are the subject of the complaint;
(vii) Identify the Registrar(s) with whom the domain name(s) is/are registered at the time the complaint is filed;
(viii) Specify the trademark(s) or service mark(s) on which the complaint is based and, for each mark, describe the goods or services, if any, with which the mark is used (Complainant may also separately describe other goods and services with which it intends, at the time the complaint is submitted, to use the mark in the future.);
(ix) Describe, in accordance with the Policy, the grounds on which the complaint is made including, in particular,
(1) the manner in which the domain name(s) is/are identical or confusingly similar to a trademark or service mark in which the Complainant has rights; and
(2) why the Respondent (domain-name holder) should be considered as having no rights or legitimate interests in respect of the domain name(s) that is/are the subject of the complaint; and
(3) why the domain name(s) should be considered as having been registered and being used in bad faith
(The description should, for elements (2) and (3), discuss any aspects of Paragraphs 4(b) and 4(c) of the Policy that are applicable. The description shall comply with any word or page limit set forth in the Provider's Supplemental Rules.);
(x) Specify, in accordance with the Policy, the remedies sought;
(xi) Identify any other legal proceedings that have been commenced or terminated in connection with or relating to any of the domain name(s) that are the subject of the complaint;
(xii) State that Complainant will submit, with respect to any challenges to a decision in the administrative proceeding canceling or transferring the domain name, to the jurisdiction of the courts in at least one specified Mutual Jurisdiction;

(xiii) Conclude with the following statement followed by the signature (in any electronic format) of the Complainant or its authorized representative—

"Complainant agrees that its claims and remedies concerning the registration of the domain name, the dispute, or the dispute's resolution shall be solely against the domain-name holder and waives all such claims and remedies against (a) the dispute-resolution provider and panelists, except in the case of deliberate wrongdoing, (b) the registrar, (c) the registry administrator, and (d) the Internet Corporation for Assigned Names and Numbers, as well as their directors, officers, employees, and agents."

"Complainant certifies that the information contained in this Complaint is to the best of Complainant's knowledge complete and accurate, that this Complaint is not being presented for any improper purpose, such as to harass, and that the assertions in this Complaint are warranted under these Rules and under applicable law, as it now exists or as it may be extended by a good-faith and reasonable argument."; and

(xiv) Annex any documentary or other evidence, including a copy of the Policy applicable to the domain name(s) in dispute and any trademark or service mark registration upon which the complaint relies, together with a schedule indexing such evidence.

(c) The complaint may relate to more than one domain name, provided that the domain names are registered by the same domain-name holder.

4 NOTIFICATION OF COMPLAINT

(a) The Provider shall submit a verification request to the Registrar. The verification request will include a request to Lock the domain name.

(b) Within two (2) business days of receiving the Provider's verification request, the Registrar shall provide the information requested in the verification request and confirm that a Lock of the domain name has been applied. The Registrar shall not notify the Respondent of the proceeding until the Lock status has been applied. The Lock shall remain in place through the remaining Pendency of the UDRP proceeding. Any updates to the Respondent's data, such as through the result of a request by a privacy or proxy provider to reveal the underlying customer data, must be made before the two (2) business day period concludes or before the Registrar verifies the information requested and confirms the Lock to the UDRP Provider, whichever occurs first. Any modification(s) of the Respondent's data following the two (2) business day period may be addressed by the Panel in its decision.

(c) The Provider shall review the complaint for administrative compliance with the Policy and these Rules and, if in compliance, shall forward the complaint, including any annexes, electronically to the Respondent and Registrar and shall send Written Notice of the complaint (together with the explanatory cover sheet prescribed by the Provider's Supplemental Rules) to the Respondent, in the manner prescribed by Paragraph 2(a), within three (3) calendar days following receipt of the fees to be paid by the Complainant in accordance with Paragraph 19.

(d) If the Provider finds the complaint to be administratively deficient, it shall promptly notify the Complainant and the Respondent of the nature of the deficiencies identified. The Complainant shall have five (5) calendar days within which to correct any such deficiencies, after which the administrative proceeding will be deemed withdrawn without prejudice to submission of a different complaint by Complainant.

(e) If the Provider dismisses the complaint due to an administrative deficiency, or the Complainant voluntarily withdraws its complaint, the Provider shall inform the Registrar that the proceedings have been withdrawn, and the Registrar shall release the Lock within one (1) business day of receiving the dismissal or withdrawal notice from the Provider.

(f) The date of commencement of the administrative proceeding shall be the date on which the Provider completes its responsibilities under Paragraph 2(a) in connection with sending the complaint to the Respondent.

(g) The Provider shall immediately notify the Complainant, the Respondent, the concerned Registrar(s), and ICANN of the date of commencement of the administrative proceeding. The Provider shall inform the Respondent that any corrections to the Respondent's contact information during the remaining Pendency of the UDRP proceedings shall be communicated to the Provider further to Rule 5(c)(ii) and 5(c)(iii).

5 THE RESPONSE

(a) Within twenty (20) days of the date of commencement of the administrative proceeding the Respondent shall submit a response to the Provider.

(b) The Respondent may expressly request an additional four (4) calendar days in which to respond to the complaint, and the Provider shall automatically grant the extension and notify the Parties thereof. This extension does not preclude any additional extensions that may be given further to 5(d) of the Rules.

(c) The response, including any annexes, shall be submitted in electronic form and shall—

(i) Respond specifically to the statements and allegations contained in the complaint and include any and all bases for the Respondent (domain-name holder) to retain registration and use of the disputed domain name (This portion of the response shall comply with any word or page limit set forth in the Provider's Supplemental Rules.);

(ii) Provide the name, postal and e-mail addresses, and the telephone and telefax numbers of the Respondent (domain-name holder) and of any representative authorized to act for the Respondent in the administrative proceeding;

(iii) Specify a preferred method for communications directed to the Respondent in the administrative proceeding (including person to be contacted, medium, and address information) for each of (A) electronic-only material and (B) material including hard copy (where applicable);

(iv) If Complainant has elected a single-member panel in the complaint (see Paragraph 3(b)(iv)), state whether Respondent elects instead to have the dispute decided by a three-member panel;

(v) If either Complainant or Respondent elects a three-member Panel, provide the names and contact details of three candidates to serve as one of the Panelists (these candidates may be drawn from any ICANN-approved Provider's list of panelists);

(vi) Identify any other legal proceedings that have been commenced or terminated in connection with or relating to any of the domain name(s) that are the subject of the complaint;

(vii) State that a copy of the response including any annexes has been sent or transmitted to the Complainant, in accordance with Paragraph 2(b); and

(viii) Conclude with the following statement followed by the signature (in any electronic format) of the Respondent or its authorized representative—

"Respondent certifies that the information contained in this Response is to the best of Respondent's knowledge complete and accurate, that this Response is not being presented for any improper purpose, such as to harass, and that the assertions in this Response are warranted under these Rules and under applicable law, as it now exists or as it may be extended by a good-faith and reasonable argument."; and

(ix) Annex any documentary or other evidence upon which the Respondent relies, together with a schedule indexing such documents.

(d) If Complainant has elected to have the dispute decided by a single-member Panel and Respondent elects a three-member Panel, Respondent shall be required to pay one-half of the applicable fee for a three-member Panel as set forth in the Provider's Supplemental Rules. This payment shall be made together with the submission of the response to the Provider. In the event that the required payment is not made, the dispute shall be decided by a single-member Panel.

(e) At the request of the Respondent, the Provider may, in exceptional cases, extend the period of time for the filing of the response. The period may also be extended by written stipulation between the Parties, provided the stipulation is approved by the Provider.

(f) If a Respondent does not submit a response, in the absence of exceptional circumstances, the Panel shall decide the dispute based upon the complaint.

6 APPOINTMENT OF THE PANEL AND TIMING OF DECISION

(a) Each Provider shall maintain and publish a publicly available list of panelists and their qualifications.

(b) If neither the Complainant nor the Respondent has elected a three-member Panel (Paragraphs 3(b)(iv) and 5(b)(iv)), the Provider shall appoint, within five (5) calendar days following receipt of the response by the Provider, or the lapse of the time period for the submission thereof, a single Panelist from its list of panelists. The fees for a single-member Panel shall be paid entirely by the Complainant.

(c) If either the Complainant or the Respondent elects to have the dispute decided by a three-member Panel, the Provider shall appoint three Panelists in accordance with the procedures identified in Paragraph 6(e). The fees for a three-member Panel shall be paid in their entirety by the Complainant, except where the election for a three-member Panel was made by the Respondent, in which case the applicable fees shall be shared equally between the Parties.

(d) Unless it has already elected a three-member Panel, the Complainant shall submit to the Provider, within five (5) calendar days of communication of a response in which the Respondent elects a three-member Panel, the names and contact details of three candidates to serve as one of the Panelists. These candidates may be drawn from any ICANN-approved Provider's list of panelists.

(e) In the event that either the Complainant or the Respondent elects a three-member Panel, the Provider shall endeavour to appoint one Panelist from the list of candidates provided by each of the Complainant and the Respondent. In the event the Provider is unable within five (5) calendar days to secure the appointment of a Panelist on its customary terms from either Party's list of candidates, the Provider shall make that appointment from its list of panelists. The third Panelist shall be appointed by the Provider from a list of five candidates submitted by the Provider to the Parties, the Provider's selection from among the five being made in a manner that reasonably balances the preferences of both Parties, as they may specify to the Provider within five (5) calendar days of the Provider's submission of the five-candidate list to the Parties.

(f) Once the entire Panel is appointed, the Provider shall notify the Parties of the Panelists appointed and the date by which, absent exceptional circumstances, the Panel shall forward its decision on the complaint to the Provider.

7 IMPARTIALITY AND INDEPENDENCE

A Panelist shall be impartial and independent and shall have, before accepting appointment, disclosed to the Provider any circumstances giving rise to justifiable doubt as to the Panelist's impartiality or independence. If, at any stage during the administrative proceeding, new circumstances arise that could give rise to justifiable doubt as to the impartiality or independence of the Panelist, that Panelist shall promptly disclose such circumstances to the Provider. In such event, the Provider shall have the discretion to appoint a substitute Panelist.

8 COMMUNICATION BETWEEN PARTIES AND THE PANEL

No Party or anyone acting on its behalf may have any unilateral communication with the Panel. All communications between a Party and the Panel or the Provider shall be made to a case administrator appointed by the Provider in the manner prescribed in the Provider's Supplemental Rules.

9 TRANSMISSION OF THE FILE TO THE PANEL

The Provider shall forward the file to the Panel as soon as the Panelist is appointed in the case of a Panel consisting of a single member, or as soon as the last Panelist is appointed in the case of a three-member Panel.

10 GENERAL POWERS OF THE PANEL

(a) The Panel shall conduct the administrative proceeding in such manner as it considers appropriate in accordance with the Policy and these Rules.

(b) In all cases, the Panel shall ensure that the Parties are treated with equality and that each Party is given a fair opportunity to present its case.

(c) The Panel shall ensure that the administrative proceeding takes place with due expedition. It may, at the request of a Party or on its own motion, extend, in exceptional cases, a period of time fixed by these Rules or by the Panel.

(d) The Panel shall determine the admissibility, relevance, materiality and weight of the evidence.

(e) A Panel shall decide a request by a Party to consolidate multiple domain name disputes in accordance with the Policy and these Rules.

11 LANGUAGE OF PROCEEDINGS

(a) Unless otherwise agreed by the Parties, or specified otherwise in the Registration Agreement, the language of the administrative proceeding shall be the language of the Registration Agreement, subject to the authority of the Panel to determine otherwise, having regard to the circumstances of the administrative proceeding.

(b) The Panel may order that any documents submitted in languages other than the language of the administrative proceeding be accompanied by a translation in whole or in part into the language of the administrative proceeding.

12 FURTHER STATEMENTS

In addition to the complaint and the response, the Panel may request, in its sole discretion, further statements or documents from either of the Parties.

13 IN-PERSON HEARINGS

There shall be no in-person hearings (including hearings by teleconference, videoconference, and web conference), unless the Panel determines, in its sole discretion and as an exceptional matter, that such a hearing is necessary for deciding the complaint.

14 DEFAULT

(a) In the event that a Party, in the absence of exceptional circumstances, does not comply with any of the time periods established by these Rules or the Panel, the Panel shall proceed to a decision on the complaint.

(b) If a Party, in the absence of exceptional circumstances, does not comply with any provision of, or requirement under, these Rules or any request from the Panel, the Panel shall draw such inferences therefrom as it considers appropriate.

15 PANEL DECISIONS

(a) A Panel shall decide a complaint on the basis of the statements and documents submitted and in accordance with the Policy, these Rules and any rules and principles of law that it deems applicable.

(b) In the absence of exceptional circumstances, the Panel shall forward its decision on the complaint to the Provider within fourteen (14) days of its appointment pursuant to Paragraph 6.

(c) In the case of a three-member Panel, the Panel's decision shall be made by a majority.

(d) The Panel's decision shall be in writing, provide the reasons on which it is based, indicate the date on which it was rendered and identify the name(s) of the Panelist(s).

(e) Panel decisions and dissenting opinions shall normally comply with the guidelines as to length set forth in the Provider's Supplemental Rules. Any dissenting opinion shall accompany the majority decision. If the Panel concludes that the dispute is not within the scope of Paragraph 4(a) of the Policy, it shall so state. If after considering the submissions the Panel finds that the complaint was brought in bad faith, for example in an attempt at Reverse Domain Name Hijacking or was brought primarily to harass the domain-name holder, the Panel shall declare in its decision that the complaint was brought in bad faith and constitutes an abuse of the administrative proceeding.

16 COMMUNICATION OF DECISION TO PARTIES

(a) Within three (3) business days after receiving the decision from the Panel, the Provider shall communicate the full text of the decision to each Party, the concerned Registrar(s), and ICANN. The concerned Registrar(s) shall within three (3) business days of receiving the decision from the Provider communicate to each Party, the Provider, and ICANN the date for the implementation of the decision in accordance with the Policy.

(b) Except if the Panel determines otherwise (see Paragraph 4(j) of the Policy), the Provider shall publish the full decision and the date of its implementation on a publicly accessible web site. In any event, the portion of any decision determining a complaint to have been brought in bad faith (see Paragraph 15(e) of these Rules) shall be published.

17 SETTLEMENT OR OTHER GROUNDS FOR TERMINATION

(a) If, before the Panel's decision, the Parties agree on a settlement, the Panel shall terminate the administrative proceeding. A settlement shall follow steps 17(a)(i) – 17(a)(vii):

- (i) The Parties provide written notice of a request to suspend the proceedings because the parties are discussing settlement to the Provider.
- (ii) The Provider acknowledges receipt of the request for suspension and informs the Registrar of the suspension request and the expected duration of the suspension.
- (iii) The Parties reach a settlement and provide a standard settlement form to the Provider further to the Provider's supplemental rules and settlement form. The standard settlement form is not intended to be an agreement itself, but only to summarize the essential terms of the Parties' separate settlement agreement. The Provider shall not disclose the completed standard settlement form to any third party.
- (iv) The Provider shall confirm to the Registrar, copying the Parties, the outcome of the settlement as it relates to actions that need to be taken by the Registrar.
- (v) Upon receiving notice from the Provider further to 17(a)(iv), the Registrar shall remove the Lock within two (2) business days.
- (vi) The Complainant shall confirm to the Provider that the settlement as it relates to the domain name(s) has been implemented further to the Provider's supplemental rules.
- (vii) The Provider will dismiss the proceedings without prejudice unless otherwise stipulated in the settlement.

(b) If, before the Panel's decision is made, it becomes unnecessary or impossible to continue the administrative proceeding for any reason, the Panel shall terminate the administrative proceeding, unless a Party raises justifiable grounds for objection within a period of time to be determined by the Panel.

18 EFFECT OF COURT PROCEEDINGS

(a) In the event of any legal proceedings initiated prior to or during an administrative proceeding in respect of a domain-name dispute that is the subject of the complaint, the Panel shall have the discretion to decide whether to suspend or terminate the administrative proceeding, or to proceed to a decision.

(b) In the event that a Party initiates any legal proceedings during the Pendency of an administrative proceeding in respect of a domain-name dispute that is the subject of the complaint, it shall promptly notify the Panel and the Provider. See Paragraph 8 above.

19 FEES

(a) The Complainant shall pay to the Provider an initial fixed fee, in accordance with the Provider's Supplemental Rules, within the time and in the amount required. A Respondent electing under Paragraph 5(b)(iv) to have the dispute decided by a three-member Panel, rather than the single-member Panel elected by the Complainant, shall pay the Provider one-half the fixed fee for a three-member Panel. See Paragraph 5(c). In all other cases, the Complainant shall bear all of the Provider's fees, except as prescribed under Paragraph 19(d). Upon appointment of the Panel, the Provider shall refund the appropriate portion, if any, of the initial fee to the Complainant, as specified in the Provider's Supplemental Rules.

(b) No action shall be taken by the Provider on a complaint until it has received from Complainant the initial fee in accordance with Paragraph 19(a).

(c) If the Provider has not received the fee within ten (10) calendar days of receiving the complaint, the complaint shall be deemed withdrawn and the administrative proceeding terminated.

(d) In exceptional circumstances, for example in the event an in-person hearing is held, the Provider shall request the Parties for the payment of additional fees, which shall be established in agreement with the Parties and the Panel.

20 EXCLUSION OF LIABILITY

Except in the case of deliberate wrongdoing, neither the Provider nor a Panelist shall be liable to a Party for any act or omission in connection with any administrative proceeding under these Rules.

21 AMENDMENTS

The version of these Rules in effect at the time of the submission of the complaint to the Provider shall apply to the administrative proceeding commenced thereby. These Rules may not be amended without the express written approval of ICANN.

CONVENTION FOR THE SAFEGUARDING OF THE INTANGIBLE CULTURAL HERITAGE (UNESCO)

(Paris, 17 October 2003)

NOTES

The Convention entered into force on 20 April 2006, following ratification by 30 States.

The General Conference of the United Nations Educational, Scientific and Cultural organisation hereinafter referred to as UNESCO, meeting in Paris, from 29 September to 17 October 2003, at its 32nd session,

Referring to existing international human rights instruments, in particular to the Universal Declaration on Human Rights of 1948, the International Covenant on Economic, Social and Cultural Rights of 1966, and the International Covenant on Civil and Political Rights of 1966,

Considering the importance of the intangible cultural heritage as a mainspring of cultural diversity and a guarantee of sustainable development, as underscored in the UNESCO Recommendation on the Safeguarding of Traditional Culture and Folklore of 1989, in the UNESCO Universal Declaration on Cultural Diversity of 2001, and in the Istanbul Declaration of 2002 adopted by the Third Round Table of Ministers of Culture,

Considering the deep-seated interdependence between the intangible cultural heritage and the tangible cultural and natural heritage,

Recognizing that the processes of globalization and social transformation, alongside the conditions they create for renewed dialogue among communities, also give rise, as does the phenomenon of intolerance, to grave threats of deterioration, disappearance and destruction of the intangible cultural heritage, in particular owing to a lack of resources for safeguarding such heritage,

Being aware of the universal will and the common concern to safeguard the intangible cultural heritage of humanity,

Recognizing that communities, in particular indigenous communities, groups and, in some cases, individuals, play an important role in the production, safeguarding, maintenance and recreation of the intangible cultural heritage, thus helping to enrich cultural diversity and human creativity,

Noting the far-reaching impact of the activities of UNESCO in establishing normative instruments for the protection of the cultural heritage, in particular the Convention for the Protection of the World Cultural and Natural Heritage of 1972,

Noting further that no binding multilateral instrument as yet exists for the safeguarding of the intangible cultural heritage,

Considering that existing international agreements, recommendations and resolutions concerning the cultural and natural heritage need to be effectively enriched and supplemented by means of new provisions relating to the intangible cultural heritage,

Considering the need to build greater awareness, especially among the younger generations, of the importance of the intangible cultural heritage and of its safeguarding,

Considering that the international community should contribute, together with the States Parties to this Convention, to the safeguarding of such heritage in a spirit of cooperation and mutual assistance,

Recalling UNESCO's programmes relating to the intangible cultural heritage, in particular the Proclamation of Masterpieces of the Oral and Intangible Heritage of Humanity,

Considering the invaluable role of the intangible cultural heritage as a factor in bringing human beings closer together and ensuring exchange and understanding among them,

Adopts this Convention on this seventeenth day of October 2003.

I.
GENERAL PROVISIONS

[9.522]
Article 1
Purposes of the Convention

The purposes of this Convention are:

(a) to safeguard the intangible cultural heritage;
(b) to ensure respect for the intangible cultural heritage of the communities, groups and individuals concerned;
(c) to raise awareness at the local, national and international levels of the importance of the intangible cultural heritage, and of ensuring mutual appreciation thereof;
(d) to provide for international cooperation and assistance.

[9.523]
Article 2
Definitions

For the purposes of this Convention,

1. The "intangible cultural heritage" means the practices, representations, expressions, knowledge, skills—as well as the instruments, objects, artefacts and cultural spaces associated therewith—that communities, groups and, in some cases, individuals recognize as part of their cultural heritage. This intangible cultural heritage, transmitted from generation to generation, is constantly recreated by communities and groups in response to their environment, their interaction with nature and their history, and provides them with a sense of identity and continuity, thus promoting respect for cultural diversity and human creativity. For the purposes of this Convention, consideration will be given solely to such intangible cultural heritage as is compatible with existing international human rights instruments, as well as with the requirements of mutual respect among communities, groups and individuals, and of sustainable development.
2. The "intangible cultural heritage", as defined in paragraph 1 above, is manifested inter alia in the following domains:
   (a) oral traditions and expressions, including language as a vehicle of the intangible cultural heritage;
   (b) performing arts;
   (c) social practices, rituals and festive events;
   (d) knowledge and practices concerning nature and the universe;
   (e) traditional craftsmanship.
3. "Safeguarding" means measures aimed at ensuring the viability of the intangible cultural heritage, including the identification, documentation, research, preservation, protection, promotion, enhancement, transmission, particularly through formal and non-formal education, as well as the revitalization of the various aspects of such heritage.
4. "States Parties" means States which are bound by this Convention and among which this Convention is in force.
5. This Convention applies mutatis mutandis to the territories referred to in Article 33 which become Parties to this Convention in accordance with the conditions set out in that Article. To that extent the expression "States Parties" also refers to such territories.

[9.524]
Article 3
Relationship to other international instruments

Nothing in this Convention may be interpreted as:

(a) altering the status or diminishing the level of protection under the 1972 Convention concerning the Protection of the World Cultural and Natural Heritage of World Heritage properties with which an item of the intangible cultural heritage is directly associated; or
(b) affecting the rights and obligations of States Parties deriving from any international instrument relating to intellectual property rights or to the use of biological and ecological resources to which they are parties.

II.
ORGANS OF THE CONVENTION

[9.525]
Article 4
General Assembly of the States Parties

1. A General Assembly of the States Parties is hereby established, hereinafter referred to as "the General Assembly". The General Assembly is the sovereign body of this Convention.
2. The General Assembly shall meet in ordinary session every two years. It may meet in extraordinary session if it so decides or at the request either of the Intergovernmental Committee for the Safeguarding of the Intangible Cultural Heritage or of at least one-third of the States Parties.
3. The General Assembly shall adopt its own Rules of Procedure.

[9.526]
Article 5
Intergovernmental Committee for the Safeguarding of the Intangible Cultural Heritage
1. An Intergovernmental Committee for the Safeguarding of the Intangible Cultural Heritage, hereinafter referred to as "the Committee", is hereby established within UNESCO. It shall be composed of representatives of 18 States Parties, elected by the States Parties meeting in General Assembly, once this Convention enters into force in accordance with Article 34.
2. The number of States Members of the Committee shall be increased to 24 once the number of the States Parties to the Convention reaches 50.

[9.527]
Article 6
Election and terms of office of States Members of the Committee
1. The election of States Members of the Committee shall obey the principles of equitable geographical representation and rotation.
2. States Members of the Committee shall be elected for a term of four years by States Parties to the Convention meeting in General Assembly.
3. However, the term of office of half of the States Members of the Committee elected at the first election is limited to two years. These States shall be chosen by lot at the first election.
4. Every two years, the General Assembly shall renew half of the States Members of the Committee.
5. It shall also elect as many States Members of the Committee as required to fill vacancies.
6. A State Member of the Committee may not be elected for two consecutive terms.
7. States Members of the Committee shall choose as their representatives persons who are qualified in the various fields of the intangible cultural heritage.

[9.528]
Article 7
Functions of the Committee
Without prejudice to other prerogatives granted to it by this Convention, the functions of the Committee shall be to:
(a) promote the objectives of the Convention, and to encourage and monitor the implementation thereof;
(b) provide guidance on best practices and make recommendations on measures for the safeguarding of the intangible cultural heritage;
(c) prepare and submit to the General Assembly for approval a draft plan for the use of the resources of the Fund, in accordance with Article 25;
(d) seek means of increasing its resources, and to take the necessary measures to this end, in accordance with Article 25;
(e) prepare and submit to the General Assembly for approval operational directives for the implementation of this Convention;
(f) examine, in accordance with Article 29, the reports submitted by States Parties, and to summarize them for the General Assembly;
(g) examine requests submitted by States Parties, and to decide thereon, in accordance with objective selection criteria to be established by the Committee and approved by the General Assembly for:
  (i) inscription on the lists and proposals mentioned under Articles 16, 17 and 18;
  (ii) the granting of international assistance in accordance with Article 22.

[9.529]
Article 8
Working methods of the Committee
1. The Committee shall be answerable to the General Assembly. It shall report to it on all its activities and decisions.
2. The Committee shall adopt its own Rules of Procedure by a two-thirds majority of its Members.
3. The Committee may establish, on a temporary basis, whatever ad hoc consultative bodies it deems necessary to carry out its task.
4. The Committee may invite to its meetings any public or private bodies, as well as private persons, with recognized competence in the various fields of the intangible cultural heritage, in order to consult them on specific matters.

[9.530]
Article 9
Accreditation of advisory organisations
1. The Committee shall propose to the General Assembly the accreditation of nongovernmental organisations with recognized competence in the field of the intangible cultural heritage to act in an advisory capacity to the Committee.
2. The Committee shall also propose to the General Assembly the criteria for and modalities of such accreditation.

[9.531]
Article 10
The Secretariat

1. The Committee shall be assisted by the UNESCO Secretariat.
2. The Secretariat shall prepare the documentation of the General Assembly and of the Committee, as well as the draft agenda of their meetings, and shall ensure the implementation of their decisions.

III.
SAFEGUARDING OF THE INTANGIBLE CULTURAL HERITAGE AT THE NATIONAL LEVEL

[9.532]
Article 11
Role of States Parties

Each State Party shall:

(a) take the necessary measures to ensure the safeguarding of the intangible cultural heritage present in its territory;
(b) among the safeguarding measures referred to in Article 2, paragraph 3, identify and define the various elements of the intangible cultural heritage present in its territory, with the participation of communities, groups and relevant nongovernmental organisations.

[9.533]
Article 12
Inventories

1. To ensure identification with a view to safeguarding, each State Party shall draw up, in a manner geared to its own situation, one or more inventories of the intangible cultural heritage present in its territory. These inventories shall be regularly updated.
2. When each State Party periodically submits its report to the Committee, in accordance with Article 29, it shall provide relevant information on such inventories.

[9.534]
Article 13
Other measures for safeguarding

To ensure the safeguarding, development and promotion of the intangible cultural heritage present in its territory, each State Party shall endeavour to:

(a) adopt a general policy aimed at promoting the function of the intangible cultural heritage in society, and at integrating the safeguarding of such heritage into planning programmes;
(b) designate or establish one or more competent bodies for the safeguarding of the intangible cultural heritage present in its territory;
(c) foster scientific, technical and artistic studies, as well as research methodologies, with a view to effective safeguarding of the intangible cultural heritage, in particular the intangible cultural heritage in danger;
(d) adopt appropriate legal, technical, administrative and financial measures aimed at:
   (i) fostering the creation or strengthening of institutions for training in the management of the intangible cultural heritage and the transmission of such heritage through forums and spaces intended for the performance or expression thereof;
   (ii) ensuring access to the intangible cultural heritage while respecting customary practices governing access to specific aspects of such heritage;
   (iii) establishing documentation institutions for the intangible cultural heritage and facilitating access to them.

[9.535]
Article 14
Education, awareness-raising and capacity-building

Each State Party shall endeavour, by all appropriate means, to:

(a) ensure recognition of, respect for, and enhancement of the intangible cultural heritage in society, in particular through:
   (i) educational, awareness-raising and information programmes, aimed at the general public, in particular young people;
   (ii) specific educational and training programmes within the communities and groups concerned;
   (iii) capacity-building activities for the safeguarding of the intangible cultural heritage, in particular management and scientific research; and
   (iv) non-formal means of transmitting knowledge;
(b) keep the public informed of the dangers threatening such heritage, and of the activities carried out in pursuance of this Convention;
(c) promote education for the protection of natural spaces and places of memory whose existence is necessary for expressing the intangible cultural heritage.

[9.536]
Article 15
Participation of communities, groups and individuals
Within the framework of its safeguarding activities of the intangible cultural heritage, each State Party shall endeavour to ensure the widest possible participation of communities, groups and, where appropriate, individuals that create, maintain and transmit such heritage, and to involve them actively in its management.

IV.
SAFEGUARDING OF THE INTANGIBLE CULTURAL HERITAGE AT THE INTERNATIONAL LEVEL

[9.537]
Article 16
Representative List of the Intangible Cultural Heritage of Humanity
1. In order to ensure better visibility of the intangible cultural heritage and awareness of its significance, and to encourage dialogue which respects cultural diversity, the Committee, upon the proposal of the States Parties concerned, shall establish, keep up to date and publish a Representative List of the Intangible Cultural Heritage of Humanity.
2. The Committee shall draw up and submit to the General Assembly for approval the criteria for the establishment, updating and publication of this Representative List.

[9.538]
Article 17
List of Intangible Cultural Heritage in Need of Urgent Safeguarding
1. With a view to taking appropriate safeguarding measures, the Committee shall establish, keep up to date and publish a List of Intangible Cultural Heritage in Need of Urgent Safeguarding, and shall inscribe such heritage on the List at the request of the State Party concerned.
2. The Committee shall draw up and submit to the General Assembly for approval the criteria for the establishment, updating and publication of this List.
3. In cases of extreme urgency—the objective criteria of which shall be approved by the General Assembly upon the proposal of the Committee—the Committee may inscribe an item of the heritage concerned on the List mentioned in paragraph 1, in consultation with the State Party concerned.

[9.539]
Article 18
Programmes, projects and activities for the safeguarding of the intangible cultural heritage
1. On the basis of proposals submitted by States Parties, and in accordance with criteria to be defined by the Committee and approved by the General Assembly, the Committee shall periodically select and promote national, sub-regional and regional programmes, projects and activities for the safeguarding of the heritage which it considers best reflect the principles and objectives of this Convention, taking into account the special needs of developing countries.
2. To this end, it shall receive, examine and approve requests for international assistance from States Parties for the preparation of such proposals.
3. The Committee shall accompany the implementation of such projects, programmes and activities by disseminating best practices using means to be determined by it.

V.
INTERNATIONAL COOPERATION AND ASSISTANCE

[9.540]
Article 19
Cooperation
1. For the purposes of this Convention, international cooperation includes, inter alia, the exchange of information and experience, joint initiatives, and the establishment of a mechanism of assistance to States Parties in their efforts to safeguard the intangible cultural heritage.
2. Without prejudice to the provisions of their national legislation and customary law and practices, the States Parties recognize that the safeguarding of intangible cultural heritage is of general interest to humanity, and to that end undertake to cooperate at the bilateral, sub-regional, regional and international levels.

[9.541]
Article 20
Purposes of international assistance
International assistance may be granted for the following purposes:
(a) the safeguarding of the heritage inscribed on the List of Intangible Cultural Heritage in Need of Urgent Safeguarding;
(b) the preparation of inventories in the sense of Articles 11 and 12;

(c) support for programmes, projects and activities carried out at the national, sub-regional and regional levels aimed at the safeguarding of the intangible cultural heritage;
(d) any other purpose the Committee may deem necessary.

[9.542]
Article 21
Forms of international assistance

The assistance granted by the Committee to a State Party shall be governed by the operational directives foreseen in Article 7 and by the agreement referred to in Article 24, and may take the following forms:

(a) studies concerning various aspects of safeguarding;
(b) the provision of experts and practitioners;
(c) the training of all necessary staff;
(d) the elaboration of standard-setting and other measures;
(e) the creation and operation of infrastructures;
(f) the supply of equipment and know-how;
(g) other forms of financial and technical assistance, including, where appropriate, the granting of low-interest loans and donations.

[9.543]
Article 22
Conditions governing international assistance

1. The Committee shall establish the procedure for examining requests for international assistance, and shall specify what information shall be included in the requests, such as the measures envisaged and the interventions required, together with an assessment of their cost.
2. In emergencies, requests for assistance shall be examined by the Committee as a matter of priority.
3. In order to reach a decision, the Committee shall undertake such studies and consultations as it deems necessary.

[9.544]
Article 23
Requests for international assistance

1. Each State Party may submit to the Committee a request for international assistance for the safeguarding of the intangible cultural heritage present in its territory.
2. Such a request may also be jointly submitted by two or more States Parties.
3. The request shall include the information stipulated in Article 22, paragraph 1, together with the necessary documentation.

[9.545]
Article 24
Role of beneficiary States Parties

1. In conformity with the provisions of this Convention, the international assistance granted shall be regulated by means of an agreement between the beneficiary State Party and the Committee.
2. As a general rule, the beneficiary State Party shall, within the limits of its resources, share the cost of the safeguarding measures for which international assistance is provided.
3. The beneficiary State Party shall submit to the Committee a report on the use made of the assistance provided for the safeguarding of the intangible cultural heritage.

VI.
INTANGIBLE CULTURAL HERITAGE FUND

[9.546]
Article 25
Nature and resources of the Fund

1. A "Fund for the Safeguarding of the Intangible Cultural Heritage", hereinafter referred to as "the Fund", is hereby established.
2. The Fund shall consist of funds-in-trust established in accordance with the Financial Regulations of UNESCO.
3. The resources of the Fund shall consist of:

(a) contributions made by States Parties;
(b) funds appropriated for this purpose by the General Conference of UNESCO;
(c) contributions, gifts or bequests which may be made by:
 (i) other States;
 (ii) organisations and programmes of the United Nations system, particularly the United Nations Development Programme, as well as other international organisations;
 (iii) public or private bodies or individuals;
(d) any interest due on the resources of the Fund;
(e) funds raised through collections, and receipts from events organised for the benefit of the Fund;

(f) any other resources authorized by the Fund's regulations, to be drawn up by the Committee.

4. The use of resources by the Committee shall be decided on the basis of guidelines laid down by the General Assembly.

5. The Committee may accept contributions and other forms of assistance for general and specific purposes relating to specific projects, provided that those projects have been approved by the Committee.

6. No political, economic or other conditions which are incompatible with the objectives of this Convention may be attached to contributions made to the Fund.

[9.547]
Article 26
Contributions of States Parties to the Fund

1. Without prejudice to any supplementary voluntary contribution, the States Parties to this Convention undertake to pay into the Fund, at least every two years, a contribution, the amount of which, in the form of a uniform percentage applicable to all States, shall be determined by the General Assembly. This decision of the General Assembly shall be taken by a majority of the States Parties present and voting which have not made the declaration referred to in paragraph 2 of this Article. In no case shall the contribution of the State Party exceed 1% of its contribution to the regular budget of UNESCO.

2. However, each State referred to in Article 32 or in Article 33 of this Convention may declare, at the time of the deposit of its instruments of ratification, acceptance, approval or accession, that it shall not be bound by the provisions of paragraph 1 of this Article.

3. A State Party to this Convention which has made the declaration referred to in paragraph 2 of this Article shall endeavour to withdraw the said declaration by notifying the Director-General of UNESCO. However, the withdrawal of the declaration shall not take effect in regard to the contribution due by the State until the date on which the subsequent session of the General Assembly opens.

4. In order to enable the Committee to plan its operations effectively, the contributions of States Parties to this Convention which have made the declaration referred to in paragraph 2 of this Article shall be paid on a regular basis, at least every two years, and should be as close as possible to the contributions they would have owed if they had been bound by the provisions of paragraph 1 of this Article.

5. Any State Party to this Convention which is in arrears with the payment of its compulsory or voluntary contribution for the current year and the calendar year immediately preceding it shall not be eligible as a Member of the Committee; this provision shall not apply to the first election. The term of office of any such State which is already a Member of the Committee shall come to an end at the time of the elections provided for in Article 6 of this Convention.

[9.548]
Article 27
Voluntary supplementary contributions to the Fund

States Parties wishing to provide voluntary contributions in addition to those foreseen under Article 26 shall inform the Committee, as soon as possible, so as to enable it to plan its operations accordingly.

[9.549]
Article 28
International fund-raising campaigns

The States Parties shall, insofar as is possible, lend their support to international fund-raising campaigns organised for the benefit of the Fund under the auspices of UNESCO.

VII.
REPORTS

[9.550]
Article 29
Reports by the States Parties

The States Parties shall submit to the Committee, observing the forms and periodicity to be defined by the Committee, reports on the legislative, regulatory and other measures taken for the implementation of this Convention.

[9.551]
Article 30
Reports by the Committee

1. On the basis of its activities and the reports by States Parties referred to in Article 29, the Committee shall submit a report to the General Assembly at each of its sessions.

2. The report shall be brought to the attention of the General Conference of UNESCO.

VIII.
TRANSITIONAL CLAUSE

[9.552]
Article 31
Relationship to the Proclamation of Masterpieces of the Oral and Intangible Heritage of Humanity

1. The Committee shall incorporate in the Representative List of the Intangible Cultural Heritage of Humanity the items proclaimed "Masterpieces of the Oral and Intangible Heritage of Humanity" before the entry into force of this Convention.
2. The incorporation of these items in the Representative List of the Intangible Cultural Heritage of Humanity shall in no way prejudge the criteria for future inscriptions decided upon in accordance with Article 16, paragraph 2.
3. No further Proclamation will be made after the entry into force of this Convention.

IX.
FINAL CLAUSES

[9.553]
Article 32
Ratification, acceptance or approval

1. This Convention shall be subject to ratification, acceptance or approval by States Members of UNESCO in accordance with their respective constitutional procedures.
2. The instruments of ratification, acceptance or approval shall be deposited with the Director-General of UNESCO.

[9.554]
Article 33
Accession

1. This Convention shall be open to accession by all States not Members of UNESCO that are invited by the General Conference of UNESCO to accede to it.
2. This Convention shall also be open to accession by territories which enjoy full internal self-government recognized as such by the United Nations, but have not attained full independence in accordance with General Assembly resolution 1514 (XV), and which have competence over the matters governed by this Convention, including the competence to enter into treaties in respect of such matters.
3. The instrument of accession shall be deposited with the Director-General of UNESCO.

[9.555]
Article 34
Entry into force

This Convention shall enter into force three months after the date of the deposit of the thirtieth instrument of ratification, acceptance, approval or accession, but only with respect to those States that have deposited their respective instruments of ratification, acceptance, approval, or accession on or before that date. It shall enter into force with respect to any other State Party three months after the deposit of its instrument of ratification, acceptance, approval or accession.

[9.556]
Article 35
Federal or non-unitary constitutional systems

The following provisions shall apply to States Parties which have a federal or non-unitary constitutional system:

(a) with regard to the provisions of this Convention, the implementation of which comes under the legal jurisdiction of the federal or central legislative power, the obligations of the federal or central government shall be the same as for those States Parties which are not federal States;
(b) with regard to the provisions of this Convention, the implementation of which comes under the jurisdiction of individual constituent States, countries, provinces or cantons which are not obliged by the constitutional system of the federation to take legislative measures, the federal government shall inform the competent authorities of such States, countries, provinces or cantons of the said provisions, with its recommendation for their adoption.

[9.557]
Article 36
Denunciation

1. Each State Party may denounce this Convention.
2. The denunciation shall be notified by an instrument in writing, deposited with the Director-General of UNESCO.

3. The denunciation shall take effect twelve months after the receipt of the instrument of denunciation. It shall in no way affect the financial obligations of the denouncing State Party until the date on which the withdrawal takes effect.

[9.558]
Article 37
Depositary functions

The Director-General of UNESCO, as the Depositary of this Convention, shall inform the States Members of the organisation, the States not Members of the organisation referred to in Article 33, as well as the United Nations, of the deposit of all the instruments of ratification, acceptance, approval or accession provided for in Articles 32 and 33, and of the denunciations provided for in Article 36.

[9.559]
Article 38
Amendments

1. A State Party may, by written communication addressed to the Director-General, propose amendments to this Convention. The Director-General shall circulate such communication to all States Parties. If, within six months from the date of the circulation of the communication, not less than one half of the States Parties reply favourably to the request, the Director-General shall present such proposal to the next session of the General Assembly for discussion and possible adoption.
2. Amendments shall be adopted by a two-thirds majority of States Parties present and voting.
3. Once adopted, amendments to this Convention shall be submitted for ratification, acceptance, approval or accession to the States Parties.
4. Amendments shall enter into force, but solely with respect to the States Parties that have ratified, accepted, approved or acceded to them, three months after the deposit of the instruments referred to in paragraph 3 of this Article by two-thirds of the States Parties. Thereafter, for each State Party that ratifies, accepts, approves or accedes to an amendment, the said amendment shall enter into force three months after the date of deposit by that State Party of its instrument of ratification, acceptance, approval or accession.
5. The procedure set out in paragraphs 3 and 4 shall not apply to amendments to Article 5 concerning the number of States Members of the Committee. These amendments shall enter into force at the time they are adopted.
6. A State which becomes a Party to this Convention after the entry into force of amendments in conformity with paragraph 4 of this Article shall, failing an expression of different intention, be considered:
   (a) as a Party to this Convention as so amended; and
   (b) as a Party to the unamended Convention in relation to any State Party not bound by the amendments.

[9.560]
Article 39
Authoritative texts

This Convention has been drawn up in Arabic, Chinese, English, French, Russian and Spanish, the six texts being equally authoritative.

[9.561]
Article 40
Registration

In conformity with Article 102 of the Charter of the United Nations, this Convention shall be registered with the Secretariat of the United Nations at the request of the Director-General of UNESCO.

CONVENTION ON THE PROTECTION AND PROMOTION OF THE DIVERSITY OF CULTURAL EXPRESSIONS (UNESCO)

Paris, 20 October 2005

NOTES

In accordance with Article 29, this Convention entered into force on 18 March 2007, with respect to those States or regional economic integration organisations that have deposited their respective instruments of ratification, acceptance, approval, or accession on or before 18 December 2006. It enters into force with respect to any other Party three months after the deposit of its instrument of ratification, acceptance, approval or accession.

The General Conference of the United Nations Educational, Scientific and Cultural organisation, meeting in Paris from 3 to 21 October 2005 at its 33rd session,

Affirming that cultural diversity is a defining characteristic of humanity,
Conscious that cultural diversity forms a common heritage of humanity and should be cherished and preserved for the benefit of all,
Being aware that cultural diversity creates a rich and varied world, which increases the range of choices and nurtures human capacities and values, and therefore is a mainspring for sustainable development for communities, peoples and nations,
Recalling that cultural diversity, flourishing within a framework of democracy, tolerance, social justice and mutual respect between peoples and cultures, is indispensable for peace and security at the local, national and international levels,
Celebrating the importance of cultural diversity for the full realization of human rights and fundamental freedoms proclaimed in the Universal Declaration of Human Rights and other universally recognized instruments,
Emphasizing the need to incorporate culture as a strategic element in national and international development policies, as well as in international development cooperation, taking into account also the United Nations Millennium Declaration (2000) with its special emphasis on poverty eradication,
Taking into account that culture takes diverse forms across time and space and that this diversity is embodied in the uniqueness and plurality of the identities and cultural expressions of the peoples and societies making up humanity,
Recognizing the importance of traditional knowledge as a source of intangible and material wealth, and in particular the knowledge systems of indigenous peoples, and its positive contribution to sustainable development, as well as the need for its adequate protection and promotion,
Recognizing the need to take measures to protect the diversity of cultural expressions, including their contents, especially in situations where cultural expressions may be threatened by the possibility of extinction or serious impairment,
Emphasizing the importance of culture for social cohesion in general, and in particular its potential for the enhancement of the status and role of women in society,
Being aware that cultural diversity is strengthened by the free flow of ideas, and that it is nurtured by constant exchanges and interaction between cultures,
Reaffirming that freedom of thought, expression and information, as well as diversity of the media, enable cultural expressions to flourish within societies,
Recognizing that the diversity of cultural expressions, including traditional cultural expressions, is an important factor that allows individuals and peoples to express and to share with others their ideas and values,
Recalling that linguistic diversity is a fundamental element of cultural diversity, and *reaffirming* the fundamental role that education plays in the protection and promotion of cultural expressions,
Taking into account the importance of the vitality of cultures, including for persons belonging to minorities and indigenous peoples, as manifested in their freedom to create, disseminate and distribute their traditional cultural expressions and to have access thereto, so as to benefit them for their own development,
Emphasizing the vital role of cultural interaction and creativity, which nurture and renew cultural expressions and enhance the role played by those involved in the development of culture for the progress of society at large,
Recognizing the importance of intellectual property rights in sustaining those involved in cultural creativity,
Being convinced that cultural activities, goods and services have both an economic and a cultural nature, because they convey identities, values and meanings, and must therefore not be treated as solely having commercial value,
Noting that while the processes of globalization, which have been facilitated by the rapid development of information and communication technologies, afford unprecedented conditions for enhanced interaction between cultures, they also represent a challenge for cultural diversity, namely in view of risks of imbalances between rich and poor countries,
Being aware of UNESCO's specific mandate to ensure respect for the diversity of cultures and to recommend such international agreements as may be necessary to promote the free flow of ideas by word and image,
Referring to the provisions of the international instruments adopted by UNESCO relating to cultural diversity and the exercise of cultural rights, and in particular the Universal Declaration on Cultural Diversity of 2001,
Adopts this Convention on 20 October 2005.

I.
OBJECTIVES AND GUIDING PRINCIPLES

[9.562]
Article 1
Objectives

The objectives of this Convention are:

- (a) to protect and promote the diversity of cultural expressions;
- (b) to create the conditions for cultures to flourish and to freely interact in a mutually beneficial manner;
- (c) to encourage dialogue among cultures with a view to ensuring wider and balanced cultural exchanges in the world in favour of intercultural respect and a culture of peace;
- (d) to foster interculturality in order to develop cultural interaction in the spirit of building bridges among peoples;
- (e) to promote respect for the diversity of cultural expressions and raise awareness of its value at the local, national and international levels;
- (f) to reaffirm the importance of the link between culture and development for all countries, particularly for developing countries, and to support actions undertaken nationally and internationally to secure recognition of the true value of this link;
- (g) to give recognition to the distinctive nature of cultural activities, goods and services as vehicles of identity, values and meaning;
- (h) to reaffirm the sovereign rights of States to maintain, adopt and implement policies and measures that they deem appropriate for the protection and promotion of the diversity of cultural expressions on their territory;
- (i) to strengthen international cooperation and solidarity in a spirit of partnership with a view, in particular, to enhancing the capacities of developing countries in order to protect and promote the diversity of cultural expressions.

Article 2
Guiding principles

1. Principle of respect for human rights and fundamental freedoms
Cultural diversity can be protected and promoted only if human rights and fundamental freedoms, such as freedom of expression, information and communication, as well as the ability of individuals to choose cultural expressions, are guaranteed. No one may invoke the provisions of this Convention in order to infringe human rights and fundamental freedoms as enshrined in the Universal Declaration of Human Rights or guaranteed by international law, or to limit the scope thereof.

2. Principle of sovereignty
States have, in accordance with the Charter of the United Nations and the principles of international law, the sovereign right to adopt measures and policies to protect and promote the diversity of cultural expressions within their territory.

3. Principle of equal dignity of and respect for all cultures
The protection and promotion of the diversity of cultural expressions presuppose the recognition of equal dignity of and respect for all cultures, including the cultures of persons belonging to minorities and indigenous peoples.

4. Principle of international solidarity and cooperation
International cooperation and solidarity should be aimed at enabling countries, especially developing countries, to create and strengthen their means of cultural expression, including their cultural industries, whether nascent or established, at the local, national and international levels.

5. Principle of the complementarity of economic and cultural aspects of development
Since culture is one of the mainsprings of development, the cultural aspects of development are as important as its economic aspects, which individuals and peoples have the fundamental right to participate in and enjoy.

6. Principle of sustainable development
Cultural diversity is a rich asset for individuals and societies. The protection, promotion and maintenance of cultural diversity are an essential requirement for sustainable development for the benefit of present and future generations.

7. Principle of equitable access
Equitable access to a rich and diversified range of cultural expressions from all over the world and access of cultures to the means of expressions and dissemination constitute important elements for enhancing cultural diversity and encouraging mutual understanding.

8. Principle of openness and balance
When States adopt measures to support the diversity of cultural expressions, they should seek to promote, in an appropriate manner, openness to other cultures of the world and to ensure that these measures are geared to the objectives pursued under the present Convention.

II.
SCOPE OF APPLICATION

[9.563]
Article 3
Scope of application
This Convention shall apply to the policies and measures adopted by the Parties related to the protection and promotion of the diversity of cultural expressions.

III.
DEFINITIONS

[9.564]
Article 4
Definitions
For the purposes of this Convention, it is understood that:

1. Cultural diversity
"Cultural diversity" refers to the manifold ways in which the cultures of groups and societies find expression. These expressions are passed on within and among groups and societies.
Cultural diversity is made manifest not only through the varied ways in which the cultural heritage of humanity is expressed, augmented and transmitted through the variety of cultural expressions, but also through diverse modes of artistic creation, production, dissemination, distribution and enjoyment, whatever the means and technologies used.

2. Cultural content
"Cultural content" refers to the symbolic meaning, artistic dimension and cultural values that originate from or express cultural identities.

3. Cultural expressions
"Cultural expressions" are those expressions that result from the creativity of individuals, groups and societies, and that have cultural content.

4. Cultural activities, goods and services
"Cultural activities, goods and services" refers to those activities, goods and services, which at the time they are considered as a specific attribute, use or purpose, embody or convey cultural expressions, irrespective of the commercial value they may have. Cultural activities may be an end in themselves, or they may contribute to the production of cultural goods and services.

5. Cultural industries
"Cultural industries" refers to industries producing and distributing cultural goods or services as defined in paragraph 4 above.

6. Cultural policies and measures
"Cultural policies and measures" refers to those policies and measures relating to culture, whether at the local, national, regional or international level that are either focused on culture as such or are designed to have a direct effect on cultural expressions of individuals, groups or societies, including on the creation, production, dissemination, distribution of and access to cultural activities, goods and services.

7. Protection
"Protection" means the adoption of measures aimed at the preservation, safeguarding and enhancement of the diversity of cultural expressions.
"Protect" means to adopt such measures.

8. Interculturality
"Interculturality" refers to the existence and equitable interaction of diverse cultures and the possibility of generating shared cultural expressions through dialogue and mutual respect.

IV.
RIGHTS AND OBLIGATIONS OF PARTIES

[9.565]
Article 5
General rule regarding rights and obligations
1. The Parties, in conformity with the Charter of the United Nations, the principles of international law and universally recognized human rights instruments, reaffirm their sovereign right to formulate and implement their cultural policies and to adopt measures to protect and promote the diversity of cultural expressions and to strengthen international cooperation to achieve the purposes of this Convention.
2. When a Party implements policies and takes measures to protect and promote the diversity of cultural expressions within its territory, its policies and measures shall be consistent with the provisions of this Convention.

Article 6
Rights of parties at the national level

1. Within the framework of its cultural policies and measures as defined in Article 4.6 and taking into account its own particular circumstances and needs, each Party may adopt measures aimed at protecting and promoting the diversity of cultural expressions within its territory.

2. Such measures may include the following:

(a) regulatory measures aimed at protecting and promoting diversity of cultural expressions;

(b) measures that, in an appropriate manner, provide opportunities for domestic cultural activities, goods and services among all those available within the national territory for the creation, production, dissemination, distribution and enjoyment of such domestic cultural activities, goods and services, including provisions relating to the language used for such activities, goods and services;

(c) measures aimed at providing domestic independent cultural industries and activities in the informal sector effective access to the means of production, dissemination and distribution of cultural activities, goods and services;

(d) measures aimed at providing public financial assistance;

(e) measures aimed at encouraging non-profit organisations, as well as public and private institutions and artists and other cultural professionals, to develop and promote the free exchange and circulation of ideas, cultural expressions and cultural activities, goods and services, and to stimulate both the creative and entrepreneurial spirit in their activities;

(f) measures aimed at establishing and supporting public institutions, as appropriate;

(g) measures aimed at nurturing and supporting artists and others involved in the creation of cultural expressions;

(h) measures aimed at enhancing diversity of the media, including through public service broadcasting.

Article 7
Measures to promote cultural expressions

1. Parties shall endeavour to create in their territory an environment which encourages individuals and social groups:

(a) to create, produce, disseminate, distribute and have access to their own cultural expressions, paying due attention to the special circumstances and needs of women as well as various social groups, including persons belonging to minorities and indigenous peoples;

(b) to have access to diverse cultural expressions from within their territory as well as from other countries of the world.

2. Parties shall also endeavour to recognize the important contribution of artists, others involved in the creative process, cultural communities, and organisations that support their work, and their central role in nurturing the diversity of cultural expressions.

Article 8
Measures to protect cultural expressions

1. Without prejudice to the provisions of Articles 5 and 6, a Party may determine the existence of special situations where cultural expressions on its territory are at risk of extinction, under serious threat, or otherwise in need of urgent safeguarding.

2. Parties may take all appropriate measures to protect and preserve cultural expressions in situations referred to in paragraph 1 in a manner consistent with the provisions of this Convention.

3. Parties shall report to the Intergovernmental Committee referred to in Article 23 all measures taken to meet the exigencies of the situation, and the Committee may make appropriate recommendations.

Article 9
Information sharing and transparency

Parties shall:

(a) provide appropriate information in their reports to UNESCO every four years on measures taken to protect and promote the diversity of cultural expressions within their territory and at the international level;

(b) designate a point of contact responsible for information sharing in relation to this Convention;

(c) share and exchange information relating to the protection and promotion of the diversity of cultural expressions.

Article 10
Education and public awareness

Parties shall:

(a) encourage and promote understanding of the importance of the protection and promotion of the diversity of cultural expressions, *inter alia,* through educational and greater public awareness programmes;
(b) cooperate with other Parties and international and regional organisations in achieving the purpose of this article;
(c) endeavour to encourage creativity and strengthen production capacities by setting up educational, training and exchange programmes in the field of cultural industries. These measures should be implemented in a manner which does not have a negative impact on traditional forms of production.

Article 11
Participation of civil society
Parties acknowledge the fundamental role of civil society in protecting and promoting the diversity of cultural expressions. Parties shall encourage the active participation of civil society in their efforts to achieve the objectives of this Convention.

Article 12
Promotion of international cooperation
Parties shall endeavour to strengthen their bilateral, regional and international cooperation for the creation of conditions conducive to the promotion of the diversity of cultural expressions, taking particular account of the situations referred to in Articles 8 and 17, notably in order to:
(a) facilitate dialogue among Parties on cultural policy;
(b) enhance public sector strategic and management capacities in cultural public sector institutions, through professional and international cultural exchanges and sharing of best practices;
(c) reinforce partnerships with and among civil society, non-governmental organisations and the private sector in fostering and promoting the diversity of cultural expressions;
(d) promote the use of new technologies, encourage partnerships to enhance information sharing and cultural understanding, and foster the diversity of cultural expressions;
(e) encourage the conclusion of co-production and co-distribution agreements.

Article 13
Integration of culture in sustainable development
Parties shall endeavour to integrate culture in their development policies at all levels for the creation of conditions conducive to sustainable development and, within this framework, foster aspects relating to the protection and promotion of the diversity of cultural expressions.

Article 14
Cooperation for development
Parties shall endeavour to support cooperation for sustainable development and poverty reduction, especially in relation to the specific needs of developing countries, in order to foster the emergence of a dynamic cultural sector by, *inter alia,* the following means:
(a) the strengthening of the cultural industries in developing countries through:
  (i) creating and strengthening cultural production and distribution capacities in developing countries;
  (ii) facilitating wider access to the global market and international distribution networks for their cultural activities, goods and services;
  (iii) enabling the emergence of viable local and regional markets;
  (iv) adopting, where possible, appropriate measures in developed countries with a view to facilitating access to their territory for the cultural activities, goods and services of developing countries;
  (v) providing support for creative work and facilitating the mobility, to the extent possible, of artists from the developing world;
  (vi) encouraging appropriate collaboration between developed and developing countries in the areas, *inter alia,* of music and film;
(b) capacity-building through the exchange of information, experience and expertise, as well as the training of human resources in developing countries, in the public and private sector relating to, *inter alia,* strategic and management capacities, policy development and implementation, promotion and distribution of cultural expressions, small-, medium- and micro-enterprise development, the use of technology, and skills development and transfer;
(c) technology transfer through the introduction of appropriate incentive measures for the transfer of technology and know-how, especially in the areas of cultural industries and enterprises;
(d) financial support through:
  (i) the establishment of an International Fund for Cultural Diversity as provided in Article 18;

(ii) the provision of official development assistance, as appropriate, including technical assistance, to stimulate and support creativity;

(iii) other forms of financial assistance such as low interest loans, grants and other funding mechanisms.

Article 15

Collaborative arrangements

Parties shall encourage the development of partnerships, between and within the public and private sectors and non-profit organisations, in order to cooperate with developing countries in the enhancement of their capacities in the protection and promotion of the diversity of cultural expressions. These innovative partnerships shall, according to the practical needs of developing countries, emphasize the further development of infrastructure, human resources and policies, as well as the exchange of cultural activities, goods and services.

Article 16

Preferential treatment for developing countries

Developed countries shall facilitate cultural exchanges with developing countries by granting, through the appropriate institutional and legal frameworks, preferential treatment to artists and other cultural professionals and practitioners, as well as cultural goods and services from developing countries.

Article 17

International cooperation in situations of serious threat to cultural expressions

Parties shall cooperate in providing assistance to each other, and, in particular to developing countries, in situations referred to under Article 8.

Article 18

International fund for cultural diversity

1. An International Fund for Cultural Diversity, hereinafter referred to as "the Fund", is hereby established.

2. The Fund shall consist of funds-in-trust established in accordance with the Financial Regulations of UNESCO.

3. The resources of the Fund shall consist of:

(a) voluntary contributions made by Parties;

(b) funds appropriated for this purpose by thc General Conference of UNESCO;

(c) contributions, gifts or bequests by other States; organisations and programmes of the United Nations system, other regional or international organisations; and public or private bodies or individuals;

(d) any interest due on resources of the Fund;

(e) funds raised through collections and receipts from events organised for the benefit of the Fund;

(f) any other resources authorized by the Fund's regulations.

4. The use of resources of the Fund shall be decided by the Intergovernmental Committee on the basis of guidelines determined by the Conference of Parties referred to in Article 22.

5. The Intergovernmental Committee may accept contributions and other forms of assistance for general and specific purposes relating to specific projects, provided that those projects have been approved by it.

6. No political, economic or other conditions that are incompatible with the objectives of this Convention may be attached to contributions made to the Fund.

7. Parties shall endeavour to provide voluntary contributions on a regular basis towards the implementation of this Convention.

Article 19

Exchange, analysis and dissemination of information

1. Parties agree to exchange information and share expertise concerning data collection and statistics on the diversity of cultural expressions as well as on best practices for its protection and promotion.

2. UNESCO shall facilitate, through the use of existing mechanisms within the Secretariat, the collection, analysis and dissemination of all relevant information, statistics and best practices.

3. UNESCO shall also establish and update a data bank on different sectors and governmental, private and non-profit organisations involved in the area of cultural expressions.

4. To facilitate the collection of data, UNESCO shall pay particular attention to capacity-building and the strengthening of expertise for Parties that submit a request for such assistance.

5. The collection of information identified in this Article shall complement the information collected under the provisions of Article 9.

V.
RELATIONSHIP TO OTHER INSTRUMENTS

[9.566]
Article 20
Relationship to other treaties: Mutual supportiveness, complementarity and non-subordination

1. Parties recognize that they shall perform in good faith their obligations under this Convention and all other treaties to which they are parties. Accordingly, without subordinating this Convention to any other treaty,

(a) they shall foster mutual supportiveness between this Convention and the other treaties to which they are parties; and

(b) when interpreting and applying the other treaties to which they are parties or when entering into other international obligations, Parties shall take into account the relevant provisions of this Convention.

2. Nothing in this Convention shall be interpreted as modifying rights and obligations of the Parties under any other treaties to which they are parties.

Article 21
International consultation and coordination

Parties undertake to promote the objectives and principles of this Convention in other international forums. For this purpose, Parties shall consult each other, as appropriate, bearing in mind these objectives and principles.

VI.
ORGANS OF THE CONVENTION

[9.567]
Article 22
Conference of parties

1. A Conference of Parties shall be established. The Conference of Parties shall be the plenary and supreme body of this Convention.

2. The Conference of Parties shall meet in ordinary session every two years, as far as possible, in conjunction with the General Conference of UNESCO. It may meet in extraordinary session if it so decides or if the Intergovernmental Committee receives a request to that effect from at least one-third of the Parties.

3. The Conference of Parties shall adopt its own rules of procedure.

4. The functions of the Conference of Parties shall be, *inter alia:*

(a) to elect the Members of the Intergovernmental Committee;

(b) to receive and examine reports of the Parties to this Convention transmitted by the Intergovernmental Committee;

(c) to approve the operational guidelines prepared upon its request by the Intergovernmental Committee;

(d) to take whatever other measures it may consider necessary to further the objectives of this Convention.

Article 23
Intergovernmental committee

1. An Intergovernmental Committee for the Protection and Promotion of the Diversity of Cultural Expressions, hereinafter referred to as "the Intergovernmental Committee", shall be established within UNESCO. It shall be composed of representatives of 18 States Parties to the Convention, elected for a term of four years by the Conference of Parties upon entry into force of this Convention pursuant to Article 29.

2. The Intergovernmental Committee shall meet annually.

3. The Intergovernmental Committee shall function under the authority and guidance of and be accountable to the Conference of Parties.

4. The Members of the Intergovernmental Committee shall be increased to 24 once the number of Parties to the Convention reaches 50.

5. The election of Members of the Intergovernmental Committee shall be based on the principles of equitable geographical representation as well as rotation.

6. Without prejudice to the other responsibilities conferred upon it by this Convention, the functions of the Intergovernmental Committee shall be:

(a) to promote the objectives of this Convention and to encourage and monitor the implementation thereof;

(b) to prepare and submit for approval by the Conference of Parties, upon its request, the operational guidelines for the implementation and application of the provisions of the Convention;

(c) to transmit to the Conference of Parties reports from Parties to the Convention, together with its comments and a summary of their contents;

(d) to make appropriate recommendations to be taken in situations brought to its attention by Parties to the Convention in accordance with relevant provisions of the Convention, in particular Article 8;

(e) to establish procedures and other mechanisms for consultation aimed at promoting the objectives and principles of this Convention in other international forums;

(f) to perform any other tasks as may be requested by the Conference of Parties.

7. The Intergovernmental Committee, in accordance with its Rules of Procedure, may invite at any time public or private organisations or individuals to participate in its meetings for consultation on specific issues.

8. The Intergovernmental Committee shall prepare and submit to the Conference of Parties, for approval, its own Rules of Procedure.

Article 24
UNESCO Secretariat

1. The organs of the Convention shall be assisted by the UNESCO Secretariat.

2. The Secretariat shall prepare the documentation of the Conference of Parties and the Intergovernmental Committee as well as the agenda of their meetings and shall assist in and report on the implementation of their decisions.

VII.
FINAL CLAUSES

[9.568]
Article 25
Settlement of disputes

1. In the event of a dispute between Parties to this Convention concerning the interpretation or the application of the Convention, the Parties shall seek a solution by negotiation.

2. If the Parties concerned cannot reach agreement by negotiation, they may jointly seek the good offices of, or request mediation by, a third party.

3. If good offices or mediation are not undertaken or if there is no settlement by negotiation, good offices or mediation, a Party may have recourse to conciliation in accordance with the procedure laid down in the Annex of this Convention. The Parties shall consider in good faith the proposal made by the Conciliation Commission for the resolution of the dispute.

4. Each Party may, at the time of ratification, acceptance, approval or accession, declare that it does not recognize the conciliation procedure provided for above. Any Party having made such a declaration may, at anytime, withdraw this declaration by notification to the Director-General of UNESCO.

Article 26
Ratification, acceptance, approval or accession by member states

1. This Convention shall be subject to ratification, acceptance, approval or accession by Member States of UNESCO in accordance with their respective constitutional procedures.

2. The instruments of ratification, acceptance, approval or accession shall be deposited with the Director-General of UNESCO.

Article 27
Accession

1. This Convention shall be open to accession by all States not Members of UNESCO but members of the United Nations, or of any of its specialized agencies, that are invited by the General Conference of UNESCO to accede to it.

2. This Convention shall also be open to accession by territories which enjoy full internal self-government recognized as such by the United Nations, but which have not attained full independence in accordance with General Assembly resolution 1514 (XV), and which have competence over the matters governed by this Convention, including the competence to enter into treaties in respect of such matters.

3. The following provisions apply to regional economic integration organisations:

(a) This Convention shall also be open to accession by any regional economic integration organisation, which shall, except as provided below, be fully bound by the provisions of the Convention in the same manner as States Parties;

(b) In the event that one or more Member States of such an organisation is also Party to this Convention, the organisation and such Member State or States shall decide on their responsibility for the performance of their obligations under this Convention. Such distribution of responsibility shall take effect following completion of the notification procedure described in subparagraph (c). The organisation and the Member States shall not be entitled to exercise rights under this Convention concurrently. In addition, regional economic integration organisations, in matters within their competence, shall exercise their rights to vote with a number of votes equal to the number of their Member States that are Parties to this Convention. Such an organisation shall not exercise its right to vote if any of its Member States exercises its right, and vice-versa;

(c) A regional economic integration organisation and its Member State or States which have agreed on a distribution of responsibilities as provided in subparagraph (b) shall inform the Parties of any such proposed distribution of responsibilities in the following manner:

(i) in their instrument of accession, such organisation shall declare with specificity, the distribution of their responsibilities with respect to matters governed by the Convention;

(ii) in the event of any later modification of their respective responsibilities, the regional economic integration organisation shall inform the depositary of any such proposed modification of their respective responsibilities; the depositary shall in turn inform the Parties of such modification;

(d) Member States of a regional economic integration organisation which become Parties to this Convention shall be presumed to retain competence over all matters in respect of which transfers of competence to the organisation have not been specifically declared or informed to the depositary;

(e) "Regional economic integration organisation" means an organisation constituted by sovereign States, members of the United Nations or of any of its specialized agencies, to which those States have transferred competence in respect of matters governed by this Convention and which has been duly authorized, in accordance with its internal procedures, to become a Party to it.

4. The instrument of accession shall be deposited with the Director-General of UNESCO.

Article 28
Point of contact

Upon becoming Parties to this Convention, each Party shall designate a point of contact as referred to in Article 9.

Article 29
Entry into force

1. This Convention shall enter into force three months after the date of deposit of the thirtieth instrument of ratification, acceptance, approval or accession, but only with respect to those States or regional economic integration organisations that have deposited their respective instruments of ratification, acceptance, approval, or accession on or before that date. It shall enter into force with respect to any other Party three months after the deposit of its instrument of ratification, acceptance, approval or accession.

2. For the purposes of this Article, any instrument deposited by a regional economic integration organisation shall not be counted as additional to those deposited by Member States of the organisation.

Article 30
Federal or non-unitary constitutional systems

Recognizing that international agreements are equally binding on Parties regardless of their constitutional systems, the following provisions shall apply to Parties which have a federal or non-unitary constitutional system:

(a) with regard to the provisions of this Convention, the implementation of which comes under the legal jurisdiction of the federal or central legislative power, the obligations of the federal or central government shall be the same as for those Parties which are not federal States;

(b) with regard to the provisions of the Convention, the implementation of which comes under the jurisdiction of individual constituent units such as States, counties, provinces, or cantons which are not obliged by the constitutional system of the federation to take legislative measures, the federal government shall inform, as necessary, the competent authorities of constituent units such as States, counties, provinces or cantons of the said provisions, with its recommendation for their adoption.

Article 31
Denunciation

1. Any Party to this Convention may denounce this Convention.
2. The denunciation shall be notified by an instrument in writing deposited with the Director-General of UNESCO.
3. The denunciation shall take effect 12 months after the receipt of the instrument of denunciation. It shall in no way affect the financial obligations of the Party denouncing the Convention until the date on which the withdrawal takes effect.

Article 32
Depositary functions
The Director-General of UNESCO, as the depositary of this Convention, shall inform the Member States of the organisation, the States not members of the organisation and regional economic integration organisations referred to in Article 27, as well as the United Nations, of the deposit of all the instruments of ratification, acceptance, approval or accession provided for in Articles 26 and 27, and of the denunciations provided for in Article 31.

Article 33
Amendments
1. A Party to this Convention may, by written communication addressed to the Director-General, propose amendments to this Convention. The Director-General shall circulate such communication to all Parties. If, within six months from the date of dispatch of the communication, no less than one half of the Parties reply favourably to the request, the Director-General shall present such proposal to the next session of the Conference of Parties for discussion and possible adoption.
2. Amendments shall be adopted by a two-thirds majority of Parties present and voting.
3. Once adopted, amendments to this Convention shall be submitted to the Parties for ratification, acceptance, approval or accession.
4. For Parties which have ratified, accepted, approved or acceded to them, amendments to this Convention shall enter into force three months after the deposit of the instruments referred to in paragraph 3 of this Article by two-thirds of the Parties. Thereafter, for each Party that ratifies, accepts, approves or accedes to an amendment, the said amendment shall enter into force three months after the date of deposit by that Party of its instrument of ratification, acceptance, approval or accession.
5. The procedure set out in paragraphs 3 and 4 shall not apply to amendments to Article 23 concerning the number of Members of the Intergovernmental Committee. These amendments shall enter into force at the time they are adopted.
6. A State or a regional economic integration organisation referred to in Article 27 which becomes a Party to this Convention after the entry into force of amendments in conformity with paragraph 4 of this Article shall, failing an expression of different intention, be considered to be:
(a) Party to this Convention as so amended; and
(b) a Party to the unamended Convention in relation to any Party not bound by the amendments.

Article 34
Authoritative texts
This Convention has been drawn up in Arabic, Chinese, English, French, Russian and Spanish, all six texts being equally authoritative.

Article 35
Registration
In conformity with Article 102 of the Charter of the United Nations, this Convention shall be registered with the Secretariat of the United Nations at the request of the Director-General of UNESCO.

ANNEX
CONCILIATION PROCEDURE

[9.569]
Article 1 Conciliation commission
A Conciliation Commission shall be created upon the request of one of the Parties to the dispute. The Commission shall, unless the Parties otherwise agree, be composed of five members, two appointed by each Party concerned and a President chosen jointly by those members.

Article 2 Members of the commission
In disputes between more than two Parties, Parties in the same interest shall appoint their members of the Commission jointly by agreement. Where two or more Parties have separate interests or there is a disagreement as to whether they are of the same interest, they shall appoint their members separately.

Article 3 Appointments
If any appointments by the Parties are not made within two months of the date of the request to create a Conciliation Commission, the Director-General of UNESCO shall, if asked to do so by the Party that made the request, make those appointments within a further two-month period.

Article 4 President of the commission

If a President of the Conciliation Commission has not been chosen within two months of the last of the members of the Commission being appointed, the Director-General of UNESCO shall, if asked to do so by a Party, designate a President within a further two-month period.

Article 5 Decisions

The Conciliation Commission shall take its decisions by majority vote of its members. It shall, unless the Parties to the dispute otherwise agree, determine its own procedure. It shall render a proposal for resolution of the dispute, which the Parties shall consider in good faith.

Article 6 Disagreement

A disagreement as to whether the Conciliation Commission has competence shall be decided by the Commission.

SINGAPORE TREATY ON THE LAW OF TRADEMARKS

Adopted in Singapore on 27 March 2006

NOTES

The original source for this Treaty is the World Intellectual Property Organisation (WIPO).

The Treaty entered into force on March 16, 2009, after the following ten States ratified or acceded to it: Australia, Bulgaria, Denmark, Kyrgyzstan, Latvia, Republic of Moldova, Romania, Singapore, Switzerland, United States of America. For further States that have ratified the Treaty, and for Model International Forms and Resolution by Diplomatic Conference, please see www.wipo.int/treaties/en/ip/singapore.

[9.570]
Article 1
Abbreviated Expressions

For the purposes of this Treaty, unless expressly stated otherwise:

(i) "Office" means the agency entrusted by a Contracting Party with the registration of marks;

(ii) "registration" means the registration of a mark by an Office;

(iii) "application" means an application for registration;

(iv) "communication" means any application, or any request, declaration, correspondence or other information relating to an application or a registration, which is filed with the Office;

(v) references to a "person" shall be construed as references to both a natural person and a legal entity;

(vi) "holder" means the person whom the register of marks shows as the holder of the registration;

(vii) "register of marks" means the collection of data maintained by an Office, which includes the contents of all registrations and all data recorded in respect of all registrations, irrespective of the medium in which such data are stored;

(viii) "procedure before the Office" means any procedure in proceedings before the Office with respect to an application or a registration;

(ix) "Paris Convention" means the Paris Convention for the Protection of Industrial Property, signed at Paris on March 20, 1883, as revised and amended;

(x) "Nice Classification" means the classification established by the Nice Agreement Concerning the International Classification of Goods and Services for the Purposes of the Registration of Marks, signed at Nice on June 15, 1957, as revised and amended;

(xi) "license" means a license for the use of a mark under the law of a Contracting Party;

(xii) "licensee" means the person to whom a license has been granted;

(xiii) "Contracting Party" means any State or intergovernmental organisation party to this Treaty;

(xiv) "Diplomatic Conference" means the convocation of Contracting Parties for the purpose of revising or amending the Treaty;

(xv) "Assembly" means the Assembly referred to in Article 23;

(xvi) references to an "instrument of ratification" shall be construed as including references to instruments of acceptance and approval;

(xvii) "organisation" means the World Intellectual Property organisation;

(xviii) "International Bureau" means the International Bureau of the organisation;

(xix) "Director General" means the Director General of the organisation;

(xx) "Regulations" means the Regulations under this Treaty that are referred to in Article 22;

(xxi) references to an "Article" or to a "paragraph", "subparagraph" or "item" of an Article shall be construed as including references to the corresponding rule(s) under the Regulations;

(xxii) "TLT 1994" means the Trademark Law Treaty done at Geneva on October 27, 1994.

[9.571]
Article 2
Marks to Which the Treaty Applies

(1) [*Nature of Marks*] Any Contracting Party shall apply this Treaty to marks consisting of signs that can be registered as marks under its law.

(2) [*Kinds of Marks*]

(a) This Treaty shall apply to marks relating to goods (trademarks) or services (service marks) or both goods and services.

(b) This Treaty shall not apply to collective marks, certification marks and guarantee marks.

[9.572]
Article 3
Application

(1) [*Indications or Elements Contained in or Accompanying an Application; Fee*]

(a) Any Contracting Party may require that an application contain some or all of the following indications or elements:

(i) a request for registration;

(ii) the name and address of the applicant;

(iii) the name of a State of which the applicant is a national if he/she is the national of any State, the name of a State in which the applicant has his/her domicile, if any, and the name of a State in which the applicant has a real and effective industrial or commercial establishment, if any;

(iv) where the applicant is a legal entity, the legal nature of that legal entity and the State, and, where applicable, the territorial unit within that State, under the law of which the said legal entity has been organised;

(v) where the applicant has a representative, the name and address of that representative;

(vi) where an address for service is required under Article 4(2)(b), such address;

(vii) where the applicant wishes to take advantage of the priority of an earlier application, a declaration claiming the priority of that earlier application, together with indications and evidence in support of the declaration of priority that may be required pursuant to Article 4 of the Paris Convention;

(viii) where the applicant wishes to take advantage of any protection resulting from the display of goods and/or services in an exhibition, a declaration to that effect, together with indications in support of that declaration, as required by the law of the Contracting Party;

(ix) at least one representation of the mark, as prescribed in the Regulations;

(x) where applicable, a statement, as prescribed in the Regulations, indicating the type of mark as well as any specific requirements applicable to that type of mark;

(xi) where applicable, a statement, as prescribed in the Regulations, indicating that the applicant wishes that the mark be registered and published in the standard characters used by the Office;

(xii) where applicable, a statement, as prescribed in the Regulations, indicating that the applicant wishes to claim colour as a distinctive feature of the mark;

(xiii) a transliteration of the mark or of certain parts of the mark;

(xiv) a translation of the mark or of certain parts of the mark;

(xv) the names of the goods and/or services for which the registration is sought, grouped according to the classes of the Nice Classification, each group preceded by the number of the class of that Classification to which that group of goods or services belongs and presented in the order of the classes of the said Classification;

(xvi) a declaration of intention to use the mark, as required by the law of the Contracting Party.

(b) The applicant may file, instead of or in addition to the declaration of intention to use the mark referred to in subparagraph (a)(xvi), a declaration of actual use of the mark and evidence to that effect, as required by the law of the Contracting Party.

(c) Any Contracting Party may require that, in respect of the application, fees be paid to the Office.

(2) [*Single Application for Goods and/or Services in Several Classes*] One and the same application may relate to several goods and/or services, irrespective of whether they belong to one class or to several classes of the Nice Classification.

(3) [*Actual Use*] Any Contracting Party may require that, where a declaration of intention to use has been filed under paragraph (1)(a)(xvi), the applicant furnish to the Office within a time limit fixed in its law, subject to the minimum time limit prescribed in the Regulations, evidence of the actual use of the mark, as required by the said law.

(4) [*Prohibition of Other Requirements*] No Contracting Party may demand that requirements other than those referred to in paragraphs (1) and (3) and in Article 8 be complied with in respect of the application. In particular, the following may not be required in respect of the application throughout its pendency:

(i) the furnishing of any certificate of, or extract from, a register of commerce;

(ii) an indication of the applicant's carrying on of an industrial or commercial activity, as well as the furnishing of evidence to that effect;
(iii) an indication of the applicant's carrying on of an activity corresponding to the goods and/or services listed in the application, as well as the furnishing of evidence to that effect;
(iv) the furnishing of evidence to the effect that the mark has been registered in the register of marks of another Contracting Party or of a State party to the Paris Convention which is not a Contracting Party, except where the applicant claims the application of Article 6 *quinquies* of the Paris Convention.

(5) [*Evidence*] Any Contracting Party may require that evidence be furnished to the Office in the course of the examination of the application where the Office may reasonably doubt the veracity of any indication or element contained in the application.

[9.573]
Article 4
Representation; Address for Service

(1) [*Representatives Admitted to Practice*]
(a) Any Contracting Party may require that a representative appointed for the purposes of any procedure before the Office
(i) have the right, under the applicable law, to practice before the Office in respect of applications and registrations and, where applicable, be admitted to practice before the Office;
(ii) provide, as its address, an address on a territory prescribed by the Contracting Party.
(b) An act, with respect to any procedure before the Office, by or in relation to a representative who complies with the requirements applied by the Contracting Party under subparagraph (a), shall have the effect of an act by or in relation to the applicant, holder or other interested person who appointed that representative.

(2) [*Mandatory Representation; Address for Service*]
(a) Any Contracting Party may require that, for the purposes of any procedure before the Office, an applicant, holder or other interested person who has neither a domicile nor a real and effective industrial or commercial establishment on its territory be represented by a representative.
(b) Any Contracting Party may, to the extent that it does not require representation in accordance with subparagraph (a), require that, for the purposes of any procedure before the Office, an applicant, holder or other interested person who has neither a domicile nor a real and effective industrial or commercial establishment on its territory have an address for service on that territory.

(3) [*Power of Attorney*]
(a) Whenever a Contracting Party allows or requires an applicant, a holder or any other interested person to be represented by a representative before the Office, it may require that the representative be appointed in a separate communication (hereinafter referred to as "power of attorney") indicating the name of the applicant, the holder or the other person, as the case may be.
(b) The power of attorney may relate to one or more applications and/or registrations identified in the power of attorney or, subject to any exception indicated by the appointing person, to all existing and future applications and/or registrations of that person.
(c) The power of attorney may limit the powers of the representative to certain acts. Any Contracting Party may require that any power of attorney under which the representative has the right to withdraw an application or to surrender a registration contain an express indication to that effect.
(d) Where a communication is submitted to the Office by a person who refers to itself in the communication as a representative but where the Office is, at the time of the receipt of the communication, not in possession of the required power of attorney, the Contracting Party may require that the power of attorney be submitted to the Office within the time limit fixed by the Contracting Party, subject to the minimum time limit prescribed in the Regulations. Any Contracting Party may provide that, where the power of attorney has not been submitted to the Office within the time limit fixed by the Contracting Party, the communication by the said person shall have no effect.

(4) [*Reference to Power of Attorney*] Any Contracting Party may require that any communication made to the Office by a representative for the purposes of a procedure before the Office contain a reference to the power of attorney on the basis of which the representative acts.

(5) [*Prohibition of Other Requirements*] No Contracting Party may demand that requirements other than those referred to in paragraphs (3) and (4) and in Article 8 be complied with in respect of the matters dealt with in those paragraphs.

(6) [*Evidence*] Any Contracting Party may require that evidence be furnished to the Office where the Office may reasonably doubt the veracity of any indication contained in any communication referred to in paragraphs (3) and (4).

[9.574]
Article 5
Filing Date

(1) [*Permitted Requirements*]

(a) Subject to subparagraph (b) and paragraph (2), a Contracting Party shall accord as the filing date of an application the date on which the Office received the following indications and elements in the language required under Article 8(2):

(i) an express or implicit indication that the registration of a mark is sought;
(ii) indications allowing the identity of the applicant to be established;
(iii) indications allowing the applicant or its representative, if any, to be contacted by the Office;
(iv) a sufficiently clear representation of the mark whose registration is sought;
(v) the list of the goods and/or services for which the registration is sought;
(vi) where Article 3(1)(a)(xvi) or (b) applies, the declaration referred to in Article 3(1)(a)(xvi) or the declaration and evidence referred to in Article 3(1)(b), respectively, as required by the law of the Contracting Party.

(b) Any Contracting Party may accord as the filing date of the application the date on which the Office received only some, rather than all, of the indications and elements referred to in subparagraph (a) or received them in a language other than the language required under Article 8(2).

(2) [*Permitted Additional Requirement*]

(a) A Contracting Party may provide that no filing date shall be accorded until the required fees are paid.

(b) A Contracting Party may apply the requirement referred to in subparagraph (a) only if it applied such requirement at the time of becoming party to this Treaty.

(3) [*Corrections and Time Limits*] The modalities of, and time limits for, corrections under paragraphs (1) and (2) shall be fixed in the Regulations.

(4) [*Prohibition of Other Requirements*] No Contracting Party may demand that requirements other than those referred to in paragraphs (1) and (2) be complied with in respect of the filing date.

[9.575]
Article 6
Single Registration for Goods and/or Services in Several Classes

Where goods and/or services belonging to several classes of the Nice Classification have been included in one and the same application, such an application shall result in one and the same registration.

[9.576]
Article 7
Division of Application and Registration

(1) [*Division of Application*]

(a) Any application listing several goods and/or services (hereinafter referred to as "initial application") may,

(i) at least until the decision by the Office on the registration of the mark,
(ii) during any opposition proceedings against the decision of the Office to register the mark,
(iii) during any appeal proceedings against the decision on the registration of the mark,

be divided by the applicant or at its request into two or more applications (hereinafter referred to as "divisional applications") by distributing among the latter the goods and/or services listed in the initial application. The divisional applications shall preserve the filing date of the initial application and the benefit of the right of priority, if any.

(b) Any Contracting Party shall, subject to subparagraph (a), be free to establish requirements for the division of an application, including the payment of fees.

(2) [*Division of Registration*] Paragraph (1) shall apply, *mutatis mutandis*, with respect to a division of a registration. Such a division shall be permitted

(i) during any proceedings in which the validity of the registration is challenged before the Office by a third party,
(ii) during any appeal proceedings against a decision taken by the Office during the former proceedings,

provided that a Contracting Party may exclude the possibility of the division of registrations if its law allows third parties to oppose the registration of a mark before the mark is registered.

[9.577]
Article 8
Communications

(1) [*Means of Transmittal and Form of Communications*] Any Contracting Party may choose the means of transmittal of communications and whether it accepts communications on paper, communications in electronic form or any other form of communication.

(2) [*Language of Communications*]

(a) Any Contracting Party may require that any communication be in a language admitted by the Office. Where the Office admits more than one language, the applicant, holder or other interested person may be required to comply with any other language requirement applicable with respect to the Office, provided that no indication or element of the communication may be required to be in more than one language.

(b) No Contracting Party may require the attestation, notarization, authentication, legalization or any other certification of any translation of a communication other than as provided under this Treaty.

(c) Where a Contracting Party does not require a communication to be in a language admitted by its Office, the Office may require that a translation of that communication by an official translator or a representative, into a language admitted by the Office, be supplied within a reasonable time limit.

(3) [*Signature of Communications on Paper*]

(a) Any Contracting Party may require that a communication on paper be signed by the applicant, holder or other interested person. Where a Contracting Party requires a communication on paper to be signed, that Contracting Party shall accept any signature that complies with the requirements prescribed in the Regulations.

(b) No Contracting Party may require the attestation, notarization, authentication, legalization or other certification of any signature except, where the law of the Contracting Party so provides, if the signature concerns the surrender of a registration.

(c) Notwithstanding subparagraph (b), a Contracting Party may require that evidence be filed with the Office where the Office may reasonably doubt the authenticity of any signature of a communication on paper.

(4) [*Communications Filed in Electronic Form or by Electronic Means of Transmittal*] Where a Contracting Party permits the filing of communications in electronic form or by electronic means of transmittal, it may require that any such communications comply with the requirements prescribed in the Regulations.

(5) [*Presentation of a Communication*] Any Contracting Party shall accept the presentation of a communication the content of which corresponds to the relevant Model International Form, if any, provided for in the Regulations.

(6) [*Prohibition of Other Requirements*] No Contracting Party may demand that, in respect of paragraphs (1) to (5), requirements other than those referred to in this Article be complied with.

(7) [*Means of Communication with Representative*] Nothing in this Article regulates the means of communication between an applicant, holder or other interested person and its representative.

[9.578]
Article 9
Classification of Goods and/or Services

(1) [*Indications of Goods and/or Services*] Each registration and any publication effected by an Office which concerns an application or registration and which indicates goods and/or services shall indicate the goods and/or services by their names, grouped according to the classes of the Nice Classification, and each group shall be preceded by the number of the class of that Classification to which that group of goods or services belongs and shall be presented in the order of the classes of the said Classification.

(2) [*Goods or Services in the Same Class or in Different Classes*]

(a) Goods or services may not be considered as being similar to each other on the ground that, in any registration or publication by the Office, they appear in the same class of the Nice Classification.

(b) Goods or services may not be considered as being dissimilar from each other on the ground that, in any registration or publication by the Office, they appear in different classes of the Nice Classification.

[9.579]
Article 10
Changes in Names or Addresses

(1) [*Changes in the Name or Address of the Holder*]

(a) Where there is no change in the person of the holder but there is a change in its name and/or address, each Contracting Party shall accept that a request for the recordal of the change by the Office in its register of marks be made by the holder in a communication indicating the registration number of the registration concerned and the change to be recorded.

(b) Any Contracting Party may require that the request indicate

(i) the name and address of the holder;

(ii) where the holder has a representative, the name and address of that representative;

(iii) where the holder has an address for service, such address.

(c) Any Contracting Party may require that, in respect of the request, a fee be paid to the Office.

(d) A single request shall be sufficient even where the change relates to more than one registration, provided that the registration numbers of all registrations concerned are indicated in the request.

(2) [*Change in the Name or Address of the Applicant*] Paragraph (1) shall apply, *mutatis mutandis*, where the change concerns an application or applications, or both an application or applications and a registration or registrations, provided that, where the application number of any application concerned has not yet been issued or is not known to the applicant or its representative, the request otherwise identifies that application as prescribed in the Regulations.

(3) [*Change in the Name or Address of the Representative or in the Address for Service*] Paragraph (1) shall apply, *mutatis mutandis*, to any change in the name or address of the representative, if any, and to any change relating to the address for service, if any.

(4) [*Prohibition of Other Requirements*] No Contracting Party may demand that requirements other than those referred to in paragraphs (1) to (3) and in Article 8 be complied with in respect of the request referred to in this Article. In particular, the furnishing of any certificate concerning the change may not be required.

(5) [*Evidence*] Any Contracting Party may require that evidence be furnished to the Office where the Office may reasonably doubt the veracity of any indication contained in the request.

[9.580]
Article 11
Change in Ownership

(1) [*Change in the Ownership of a Registration*]

(a) Where there is a change in the person of the holder, each Contracting Party shall accept that a request for the recordal of the change by the Office in its register of marks be made by the holder or by the person who acquired the ownership (hereinafter referred to as "new owner") in a communication indicating the registration number of the registration concerned and the change to be recorded.

(b) Where the change in ownership results from a contract, any Contracting Party may require that the request indicate that fact and be accompanied, at the option of the requesting party, by one of the following:

(i) a copy of the contract, which copy may be required to be certified, by a notary public or any other competent public authority, as being in conformity with the original contract;

(ii) an extract of the contract showing the change in ownership, which extract may be required to be certified, by a notary public or any other competent public authority, as being a true extract of the contract;

(iii) an uncertified certificate of transfer drawn up in the form and with the content as prescribed in the Regulations and signed by both the holder and the new owner;

(iv) an uncertified transfer document drawn up in the form and with the content as prescribed in the Regulations and signed by both the holder and the new owner.

(c) Where the change in ownership results from a merger, any Contracting Party may require that the request indicate that fact and be accompanied by a copy of a document, which document originates from the competent authority and evidences the merger, such as a copy of an extract from a register of commerce, and that that copy be certified by the authority which issued the document or by a notary public or any other competent public authority, as being in conformity with the original document.

(d) Where there is a change in the person of one or more but not all of several co-holders and such change in ownership results from a contract or a merger, any Contracting Party may require that any co-holder in respect of which there is no change in ownership give its express consent to the change in ownership in a document signed by it.

(e) Where the change in ownership does not result from a contract or a merger but from another ground, for example, from operation of law or a court decision, any Contracting Party may require that the request indicate that fact and be accompanied by a copy of a document evidencing the change and that that copy be certified as being in conformity with the original document by the authority which issued the document or by a notary public or any other competent public authority.

(f) Any Contracting Party may require that the request indicate

(i) the name and address of the holder;

(ii) the name and address of the new owner;

(iii) the name of a State of which the new owner is a national if he/she is the national of any State, the name of a State in which the new owner has his/her domicile, if any, and the name of a State in which the new owner has a real and effective industrial or commercial establishment, if any;

(iv) where the new owner is a legal entity, the legal nature of that legal entity and the State, and, where applicable, the territorial unit within that State, under the law of which the said legal entity has been organised;

(v) where the holder has a representative, the name and address of that representative;

(vi) where the holder has an address for service, such address;

(vii) where the new owner has a representative, the name and address of that representative;

(viii) where the new owner is required to have an address for service under Article 4(2)(b), such address.

(g) Any Contracting Party may require that, in respect of the request, a fee be paid to the Office.

(h) A single request shall be sufficient even where the change relates to more than one registration, provided that the holder and the new owner are the same for each registration and that the registration numbers of all registrations concerned are indicated in the request.

(i) Where the change of ownership does not affect all the goods and/or services listed in the holder's registration, and the applicable law allows the recording of such change, the Office shall create a separate registration referring to the goods and/or services in respect of which the ownership has changed.

(2) [*Change in the Ownership of an Application*] Paragraph (1) shall apply, *mutatis mutandis*, where the change in ownership concerns an application or applications, or both an application or applications and a registration or registrations, provided that, where the application number of any application concerned has not yet been issued or is not known to the applicant or its representative, the request otherwise identifies that application as prescribed in the Regulations.

(3) [*Prohibition of Other Requirements*] No Contracting Party may demand that requirements other than those referred to in paragraphs (1) and (2) and in Article 8 be complied with in respect of the request referred to in this Article. In particular, the following may not be required:

(i) subject to paragraph (1)(c), the furnishing of any certificate of, or extract from, a register of commerce;

(ii) an indication of the new owner's carrying on of an industrial or commercial activity, as well as the furnishing of evidence to that effect;

(iii) an indication of the new owner's carrying on of an activity corresponding to the goods and/or services affected by the change in ownership, as well as the furnishing of evidence to either effect;

(iv) an indication that the holder transferred, entirely or in part, its business or the relevant goodwill to the new owner, as well as the furnishing of evidence to either effect.

(4) [*Evidence*] Any Contracting Party may require that evidence, or further evidence where paragraph (1)(c) or (e) applies, be furnished to the Office where that Office may reasonably doubt the veracity of any indication contained in the request or in any document referred to in the present Article.

[9.581]
Article 12
Correction of a Mistake

(1) [*Correction of a Mistake in Respect of a Registration*]

(a) Each Contracting Party shall accept that the request for the correction of a mistake which was made in the application or other request communicated to the Office and which mistake is reflected in its register of marks and/or any publication by the Office be made by the holder in a communication indicating the registration number of the registration concerned, the mistake to be corrected and the correction to be entered.

(b) Any Contracting Party may require that the request indicate

(i) the name and address of the holder;

(ii) where the holder has a representative, the name and address of that representative;

(iii) where the holder has an address for service, such address.

(c) Any Contracting Party may require that, in respect of the request, a fee be paid to the Office.

(d) A single request shall be sufficient even where the correction relates to more than one registration of the same person, provided that the mistake and the requested correction are the same for each registration and that the registration numbers of all registrations concerned are indicated in the request.

(2) [*Correction of a Mistake in Respect of an Application*] Paragraph (1) shall apply, *mutatis mutandis*, where the mistake concerns an application or applications, or both an application or applications and a registration or registrations, provided that, where the application number of any application concerned has not yet been issued or is not known to the applicant or its representative, the request otherwise identifies that application as prescribed in the Regulations.

(3) [*Prohibition of Other Requirements*] No Contracting Party may demand that requirements other than those referred to in paragraphs (1) and (2) and in Article 8 be complied with in respect of the request referred to in this Article.

(4) [*Evidence*] Any Contracting Party may require that evidence be furnished to the Office where the Office may reasonably doubt that the alleged mistake is in fact a mistake.

(5) [*Mistakes Made by the Office*] The Office of a Contracting Party shall correct its own mistakes, *ex officio* or upon request, for no fee.

(6) [*Uncorrectable Mistakes*] No Contracting Party shall be obliged to apply paragraphs (1), (2) and (5) to any mistake which cannot be corrected under its law.

[9.582]
Article 13
Duration and Renewal of Registration

(1) [*Indications or Elements Contained in or Accompanying a Request for Renewal; Fee*]

(a) Any Contracting Party may require that the renewal of a registration be subject to the filing of a request and that such request contain some or all of the following indications:
(i) an indication that renewal is sought;
(ii) the name and address of the holder;
(iii) the registration number of the registration concerned;
(iv) at the option of the Contracting Party, the filing date of the application which resulted in the registration concerned or the registration date of the registration concerned;
(v) where the holder has a representative, the name and address of that representative;
(vi) where the holder has an address for service, such address;
(vii) where the Contracting Party allows the renewal of a registration to be made for some only of the goods and/or services which are recorded in the register of marks and such a renewal is requested, the names of the recorded goods and/or services for which the renewal is requested or the names of the recorded goods and/or services for which the renewal is not requested, grouped according to the classes of the Nice Classification, each group preceded by the number of the class of that Classification to which that group of goods or services belongs and presented in the order of the classes of the said Classification;
(viii) where a Contracting Party allows a request for renewal to be filed by a person other than the holder or its representative and the request is filed by such a person, the name and address of that person.
(b) Any Contracting Party may require that, in respect of the request for renewal, a fee be paid to the Office. Once the fee has been paid in respect of the initial period of the registration or of any renewal period, no further payment may be required for the maintenance of the registration in respect of that period. Fees associated with the furnishing of a declaration and/or evidence of use shall not be regarded, for the purposes of this subparagraph, as payments required for the maintenance of the registration and shall not be affected by this subparagraph.
(c) Any Contracting Party may require that the request for renewal be presented, and the corresponding fee referred to in subparagraph (b) be paid, to the Office within the period fixed by the law of the Contracting Party, subject to the minimum periods prescribed in the Regulations.

(2) [*Prohibition of Other Requirements*] No Contracting Party may demand that requirements other than those referred to in paragraph (1) and in Article 8 be complied with in respect of the request for renewal. In particular, the following may not be required:
(i) any representation or other identification of the mark;
(ii) the furnishing of evidence to the effect that the mark has been registered, or that its registration has been renewed, in any other register of marks;
(iii) the furnishing of a declaration and/or evidence concerning use of the mark.

(3) [*Evidence*] Any Contracting Party may require that evidence be furnished to the Office in the course of the examination of the request for renewal where the Office may reasonably doubt the veracity of any indication or element contained in the request for renewal.

(4) [*Prohibition of Substantive Examination*] No Office of a Contracting Party may, for the purposes of effecting the renewal, examine the registration as to substance.

(5) [*Duration*] The duration of the initial period of the registration, and the duration of each renewal period, shall be 10 years.

[9.583]
Article 14
Relief Measures in Case of Failure to Comply with Time Limits

(1) [*Relief Measure Before the Expiry of a Time Limit*] A Contracting Party may provide for the extension of a time limit for an action in a procedure before the Office in respect of an application or a registration, if a request to that effect is filed with the Office prior to the expiry of the time limit.

(2) [*Relief Measures After the Expiry of a Time Limit*] Where an applicant, holder or other interested person has failed to comply with a time limit ("the time limit concerned") for an action in a procedure before the Office of a Contracting Party in respect of an application or a registration, the Contracting Party shall provide for one or more of the following relief measures, in accordance with the requirements prescribed in the Regulations, if a request to that effect is filed with the Office:
(i) extension of the time limit concerned for the period prescribed in the Regulations;
(ii) continued processing with respect to the application or registration;
(iii) reinstatement of the rights of the applicant, holder or other interested person with respect to the application or registration if the Office finds that the failure to comply with the time limit concerned occurred in spite of due care required by the circumstances having been taken or, at the option of the Contracting Party, that the failure was unintentional.

(3) [*Exceptions*] No Contracting Party shall be required to provide for any of the relief measures referred to in paragraph (2) with respect to the exceptions prescribed in the Regulations.

(4) [*Fee*] Any Contracting Party may require that a fee be paid in respect of any of the relief measures referred to in paragraphs (1) and (2).

(5) [*Prohibition of Other Requirements*] No Contracting Party may demand that requirements other than those referred to in this Article and in Article 8 be complied with in respect of any of the relief measures referred to in paragraph (2).

[9.584]
Article 15
Obligation to Comply with the Paris Convention
Any Contracting Party shall comply with the provisions of the Paris Convention which concern marks.

[9.585]
Article 16
Service Marks
Any Contracting Party shall register service marks and apply to such marks the provisions of the Paris Convention which concern trademarks.

[9.586]
Article 17
Request for Recordal of a License
(1) [*Requirements Concerning the Request for Recordal*] Where the law of a Contracting Party provides for the recordal of a license with its Office, that Contracting Party may require that the request for recordal
  (i) be filed in accordance with the requirements prescribed in the Regulations, and
  (ii) be accompanied by the supporting documents prescribed in the Regulations.

(2) [*Fee*] Any Contracting Party may require that, in respect of the recordal of a license, a fee be paid to the Office.
(3) [*Single Request Relating to Several Registrations*] A single request shall be sufficient even where the license relates to more than one registration, provided that the registration numbers of all registrations concerned are indicated in the request, the holder and the licensee are the same for all registrations, and the request indicates the scope of the license in accordance with the Regulations with respect to all registrations.
(4) [*Prohibition of Other Requirements*]
  (a) No Contracting Party may demand that requirements other than those referred to in paragraphs (1) to (3) and in Article 8 be complied with in respect of the recordal of a license with its Office. In particular, the following may not be required:
    (i) the furnishing of the registration certificate of the mark which is the subject of the license;
    (ii) the furnishing of the license contract or a translation of it;
    (iii) an indication of the financial terms of the license contract.
  (b) Subparagraph (a) is without prejudice to any obligations existing under the law of a Contracting Party concerning the disclosure of information for purposes other than the recording of the license in the register of marks.

(5) [*Evidence*] Any Contracting Party may require that evidence be furnished to the Office where the Office may reasonably doubt the veracity of any indication contained in the request or in any document referred to in the Regulations.
(6) [*Requests Relating to Applications*] Paragraphs (1) to (5) shall apply, *mutatis mutandis,* to requests for recordal of a license for an application, where the law of a Contracting Party provides for such recordal.

[9.587]
Article 18
Request for Amendment or Cancellation of the Recordal of a License
(1) [*Requirements Concerning the Request*] Where the law of a Contracting Party provides for the recordal of a license with its Office, that Contracting Party may require that the request for amendment or cancellation of the recordal of a license
  (i) be filed in accordance with the requirements prescribed in the Regulations, and
  (ii) be accompanied by the supporting documents prescribed in the Regulations.

(2) [*Other Requirements*] Article 17(2) to (6) shall apply, *mutatis mutandis,* to requests for amendment or cancellation of the recordal of a license.

[9.588]
Article 19
Effects of the Non-Recordal of a License
(1) [*Validity of the Registration and Protection of the Mark*] The non-recordal of a license with the Office or with any other authority of the Contracting Party shall not affect the validity of the registration of the mark which is the subject of the license or the protection of that mark.
(2) [*Certain Rights of the Licensee*] A Contracting Party may not require the recordal of a license as a condition for any right that the licensee may have under the law of that Contracting Party to join infringement proceedings initiated by the holder or to obtain, by way of such proceedings, damages resulting from an infringement of the mark which is the subject of the license.

(3) [*Use of a Mark Where License Is Not Recorded*] A Contracting Party may not require the recordal of a license as a condition for the use of a mark by a licensee to be deemed to constitute use by the holder in proceedings relating to the acquisition, maintenance and enforcement of marks.

[9.589]
Article 20
Indication of the License

Where the law of a Contracting Party requires an indication that the mark is used under a license, full or partial non-compliance with that requirement shall not affect the validity of the registration of the mark which is the subject of the license or the protection of that mark, and shall not affect the application of Article 19(3).

[9.590]
Article 21
Observations in Case of Intended Refusal

An application under Article 3 or a request under Articles 7, 10 to 14, 17 and 18 may not be refused totally or in part by an Office without giving the applicant or the requesting party, as the case may be, an opportunity to make observations on the intended refusal within a reasonable time limit. In respect of Article 14, no Office shall be required to give an opportunity to make observations where the person requesting the relief measure has already had an opportunity to present an observation on the facts on which the decision is to be based.

[9.591]
Article 22
Regulations

(1) [*Content*]
- (a) The Regulations annexed to this Treaty provide rules concerning
  - (i) matters which this Treaty expressly provides to be "prescribed in the Regulations";
  - (ii) any details useful in the implementation of the provisions of this Treaty;
  - (iii) any administrative requirements, matters or procedures.
- (b) The Regulations also contain Model International Forms.

(2) [*Amending the Regulations*] Subject to paragraph (3), any amendment of the Regulations shall require three-fourths of the votes cast.

(3) [*Requirement of Unanimity*]
- (a) The Regulations may specify provisions of the Regulations which may be amended only by unanimity.
- (b) Any amendment of the Regulations resulting in the addition of provisions to, or the deletion of provisions from, the provisions specified in the Regulations pursuant to subparagraph (a) shall require unanimity.
- (c) In determining whether unanimity is attained, only votes actually cast shall be taken into consideration. Abstentions shall not be considered as votes.

(4) [*Conflict Between the Treaty and the Regulations*] In the case of conflict between the provisions of this Treaty and those of the Regulations, the former shall prevail.

[9.592]
Article 23
Assembly

(1) [*Composition*]
- (a) The Contracting Parties shall have an Assembly.
- (b) Each Contracting Party shall be represented in the Assembly by one delegate, who may be assisted by alternate delegates, advisors and experts. Each delegate may represent only one Contracting Party.

(2) [*Tasks*] The Assembly shall
- (i) deal with matters concerning the development of this Treaty;
- (ii) amend the Regulations, including the Model International Forms;
- (iii) determine the conditions for the date of application of each amendment referred to in item (ii);
- (iv) perform such other functions as are appropriate to implementing the provisions of this Treaty.

(3) [*Quorum*]
- (a) One-half of the members of the Assembly which are States shall constitute a quorum.
- (b) Notwithstanding subparagraph (a), if, in any session, the number of the members of the Assembly which are States and are represented is less than one-half but equal to or more than one-third of the members of the Assembly which are States, the Assembly may make decisions but, with the exception of decisions concerning its own procedure, all such decisions shall take effect only if the conditions set forth hereinafter are fulfilled. The International Bureau shall communicate the said decisions to the members of the Assembly which are States and were not represented and shall invite them to express in writing their vote or abstention within a period of three months from the date of the communication. If,

at the expiration of this period, the number of such members having thus expressed their vote or abstention attains the number of the members which was lacking for attaining the quorum in the session itself, such decisions shall take effect, provided that at the same time the required majority still obtains.

(4) [*Taking Decisions in the Assembly*]

(a) The Assembly shall endeavour to take its decisions by consensus.

(b) Where a decision cannot be arrived at by consensus, the matter at issue shall be decided by voting. In such a case,

(i) each Contracting Party that is a State shall have one vote and shall vote only in its own name; and

(ii) any Contracting Party that is an intergovernmental organisation may participate in the vote, in place of its Member States, with a number of votes equal to the number of its Member States which are party to this Treaty. No such intergovernmental organisation shall participate in the vote if any one of its Member States exercises its right to vote and vice versa. In addition, no such intergovernmental organisation shall participate in the vote if any one of its Member States party to this Treaty is a Member State of another such intergovernmental organisation and that other intergovernmental organisation participates in that vote.

(5) [*Majorities*]

(a) Subject to Articles 22(2) and (3), the decisions of the Assembly shall require two-thirds of the votes cast.

(b) In determining whether the required majority is attained, only votes actually cast shall be taken into consideration. Abstentions shall not be considered as votes.

(6) [*Sessions*] The Assembly shall meet upon convocation by the Director General and, in the absence of exceptional circumstances, during the same period and at the same place as the General Assembly of the organisation.

(7) [*Rules of Procedure*] The Assembly shall establish its own rules of procedure, including rules for the convocation of extraordinary sessions.

[9.593]
Article 24
International Bureau

(1) [*Administrative Tasks*]

(a) The International Bureau shall perform the administrative tasks concerning this Treaty.

(b) In particular, the International Bureau shall prepare the meetings and provide the secretariat of the Assembly and of such committees of experts and working groups as may be established by the Assembly.

(2) [*Meetings Other than Sessions of the Assembly*] The Director General shall convene any committee and working group established by the Assembly.

(3) [*Role of the International Bureau in the Assembly and Other Meetings*]

(a) The Director General and persons designated by the Director General shall participate, without the right to vote, in all meetings of the Assembly, the committees and working groups established by the Assembly.

(b) The Director General or a staff member designated by the Director General shall be *ex officio* secretary of the Assembly, and of the committees and working groups referred to in subparagraph (a).

(4) [*Conferences*]

(a) The International Bureau shall, in accordance with the directions of the Assembly, make the preparations for any revision conferences.

(b) The International Bureau may consult with Member States of the organisation, intergovernmental organisations and international and national non-governmental organisations concerning the said preparations.

(c) The Director General and persons designated by the Director General shall take part, without the right to vote, in the discussions at revision conferences.

(5) [*Other Tasks*] The International Bureau shall carry out any other tasks assigned to it in relation to this Treaty.

[9.594]
Article 25
Revision or Amendment

This Treaty may only be revised or amended by a diplomatic conference. The convocation of any diplomatic conference shall be decided by the Assembly.

[9.595]
Article 26
Becoming Party to the Treaty

(1) [*Eligibility*] The following entities may sign and, subject to paragraphs (2) and (3) and Article 28(1) and (3), become party to this Treaty:

(i) any State member of the organisation in respect of which marks may be registered with its own Office;

(ii) any intergovernmental organisation which maintains an Office in which marks may be registered with effect in the territory in which the constituting treaty of the intergovernmental organisation applies, in all its Member States or in those of its Member States which are designated for such purpose in the relevant application, provided that all the Member States of the intergovernmental organisation are members of the organisation;

(iii) any State member of the organisation in respect of which marks may be registered only through the Office of another specified State that is a member of the organisation;

(iv) any State member of the organisation in respect of which marks may be registered only through the Office maintained by an intergovernmental organisation of which that State is a member;

(v) any State member of the organisation in respect of which marks may be registered only through an Office common to a group of States members of the organisation.

(2) [*Ratification or Accession*] Any entity referred to in paragraph (1) may deposit

(i) an instrument of ratification, if it has signed this Treaty,

(ii) an instrument of accession, if it has not signed this Treaty.

(3) [*Effective Date of Deposit*] The effective date of the deposit of an instrument of ratification or accession shall be,

(i) in the case of a State referred to in paragraph (1)(i), the date on which the instrument of that State is deposited;

(ii) in the case of an intergovernmental organisation, the date on which the instrument of that intergovernmental organisation is deposited;

(iii) in the case of a State referred to in paragraph (1)(iii), the date on which the following condition is fulfilled: the instrument of that State has been deposited and the instrument of the other, specified State has been deposited;

(iv) in the case of a State referred to in paragraph (1)(iv), the date applicable under item (ii), above;

(v) in the case of a State member of a group of States referred to in paragraph (1)(v), the date on which the instruments of all the States members of the group have been deposited.

[9.596]

Article 27

Application of the TLT 1994 and This Treaty

(1) [*Relations Between Contracting Parties to Both This Treaty and the TLT 1994*] This Treaty alone shall be applicable as regards the mutual relations of Contracting Parties to both this Treaty and the TLT 1994.

(2) [*Relations Between Contracting Parties to This Treaty and Contracting Parties to the TLT 1994 That Are Not Party to This Treaty*] Any Contracting Party to both this Treaty and the TLT 1994 shall continue to apply the TLT 1994 in its relations with Contracting Parties to the TLT 1994 that are not party to this Treaty.

[9.597]

Article 28

Entry into Force; Effective Date of Ratifications and Accessions

(1) [*Instruments to Be Taken into Consideration*] For the purposes of this Article, only instruments of ratification or accession that are deposited by entities referred to in Article 26(1) and that have an effective date according to Article 26(3) shall be taken into consideration.

(2) [*Entry into Force of the Treaty*] This Treaty shall enter into force three months after ten States or intergovernmental organisations referred to in Article 26(1)(ii) have deposited their instruments of ratification or accession.

(3) [*Entry into Force of Ratifications and Accessions Subsequent to the Entry into Force of the Treaty*] Any entity not covered by paragraph (2) shall become bound by this Treaty three months after the date on which it has deposited its instrument of ratification or accession.

[9.598]

Article 29

Reservations

(1) [*Special Kinds of Marks*] Any State or intergovernmental organisation may declare through a reservation that, notwithstanding Article 2(1) and (2)(a), any of the provisions of Articles 3(1), 5, 7, 8(5), 11 and 13 shall not apply to associated marks, defensive marks or derivative marks. Such reservation shall specify those of the aforementioned provisions to which the reservation relates.

(2) [*Multiple-class Registration*] Any State or intergovernmental organisation, whose legislation at the date of adoption of this Treaty provides for a multiple-class registration for goods and for a multiple-class registration for services may, when acceding to this Treaty, declare through a reservation that the provisions of Article 6 shall not apply.

(3) [*Substantive Examination on the Occasion of Renewal*] Any State or intergovernmental organisation may declare through a reservation that, notwithstanding Article 13(4), the Office may, on the occasion of the first renewal of a registration covering services, examine such registration as to substance, provided that such examination shall be limited to the elimination of multiple registrations based on applications filed during a period of six months following the entry into force of the law of such State or organisation that introduced, before the entry into force of this Treaty, the possibility of registering service marks.
(4) [*Certain Rights of the Licensee*] Any State or intergovernmental organisation may declare through a reservation that, notwithstanding Article 19(2), it requires the recordal of a license as a condition for any right that the licensee may have under the law of that State or intergovernmental organisation to join infringement proceedings initiated by the holder or to obtain, by way of such proceedings, damages resulting from an infringement of the mark which is the subject of the license.
(5) [*Modalities*] Any reservation under paragraphs (1), (2), (3) or (4) shall be made in a declaration accompanying the instrument of ratification of, or accession to, this Treaty of the State or intergovernmental organisation making the reservation.
(6) [*Withdrawal*] Any reservation under paragraphs (1), (2), (3) or (4) may be withdrawn at any time.
(7) [*Prohibition of Other Reservations*] No reservation to this Treaty other than the reservations allowed under paragraphs (1), (2), (3) and (4) shall be permitted.

[9.599]
Article 30
Denunciation of the Treaty
(1) [*Notification*] Any Contracting Party may denounce this Treaty by notification addressed to the Director General.
(2) [*Effective Date*] Denunciation shall take effect one year from the date on which the Director General has received the notification. It shall not affect the application of this Treaty to any application pending or any mark registered in respect of the denouncing Contracting Party at the time of the expiration of the said one-year period, provided that the denouncing Contracting Party may, after the expiration of the said one-year period, discontinue applying this Treaty to any registration as from the date on which that registration is due for renewal.

[9.600]
Article 31
Languages of the Treaty; Signature
(1) [*Original Texts; Official Texts*]
- (a) This Treaty shall be signed in a single original in the English, Arabic, Chinese, French, Russian and Spanish languages, all texts being equally authentic.
- (b) An official text in a language not referred to in subparagraph (a) that is an official language of a Contracting Party shall be established by the Director General after consultation with the said Contracting Party and any other interested Contracting Party.

(2) [*Time Limit for Signature*] This Treaty shall remain open for signature at the headquarters of the organisation for one year after its adoption.

[9.601]
Article 32
Depositary
The Director General shall be the depositary of this Treaty.

REGULATIONS UNDER THE SINGAPORE TREATY ON THE LAW OF TRADEMARKS

(as in force on November 1, 2011)

NOTES
The original source for these Regulations is the World Intellectual Property Organisation (WIPO).

[9.602]
Rule 1
Abbreviated Expressions
(1) [*Abbreviated Expressions Defined in the Regulations*] For the purposes of these Regulations, unless expressly stated otherwise:
- (i) "Treaty" means the Singapore Treaty on the Law of Trademarks;
- (ii) "Article" refers to the specified Article of the Treaty;

(iii) "exclusive license" means a license which is only granted to one licensee and which excludes the holder from using the mark and from granting licenses to any other person;

(iv) "sole license" means a license which is only granted to one licensee and which excludes the holder from granting licenses to any other person but does not exclude the holder from using the mark;

(v) "non-exclusive license" means a license which does not exclude the holder from using the mark or from granting licenses to any other person.

(2) [*Abbreviated Expressions Defined in the Treaty*] The abbreviated expressions defined in Article 1 for the purposes of the Treaty shall have the same meaning for the purposes of these Regulations.

[9.603]
Rule 2
Manner of Indicating Names and Addresses

(1) [*Names*]

(a) Where the name of a person is to be indicated, any Contracting Party may require,

(i) where the person is a natural person, that the name to be indicated be the family or principal name and the given or secondary name or names of that person or that the name to be indicated be, at that person's option, the name or names customarily used by the said person;

(ii) where the person is a legal entity, that the name to be indicated be the full official designation of the legal entity.

(b) Where the name of a representative which is a firm or partnership is to be indicated, any Contracting Party shall accept as indication of the name the indication that the firm or partnership customarily uses.

(2) [*Addresses*]

(a) Where the address of a person is to be indicated, any Contracting Party may require that the address be indicated in such a way as to satisfy the customary requirements for prompt postal delivery at the indicated address and, in any case, consist of all the relevant administrative units up to, and including, the house or building number, if any.

(b) Where a communication to the Office of a Contracting Party is in the name of two or more persons with different addresses, that Contracting Party may require that such communication indicate a single address as the address for correspondence.

(c) The indication of an address may contain a telephone number, a telefacsimile number and an e-mail address and, for the purposes of correspondence, an address different from the address indicated under subparagraph (a).

(d) Subparagraphs (a) and (c) shall apply, *mutatis mutandis*, to addresses for service.

(3) [*Other Means of Identification*] Any Contracting Party may require that a communication to the Office indicate the number or other means of identification, if any, with which the applicant, holder, representative or interested person is registered with its Office. No Contracting Party may refuse a communication on grounds of failure to comply with any such requirement, except for applications filed in electronic form.

(4) [*Script to Be Used*] Any Contracting Party may require that any indication referred to in paragraphs (1) to (3) be in the script used by the Office.

[9.604]
Rule 3
Details Concerning the Application

(1) [*Standard Characters*] Where the Office of a Contracting Party uses characters (letters and numbers) that it considers as being standard, and where the application contains a statement to the effect that the applicant wishes that the mark be registered and published in the standard characters used by the Office, the Office shall register and publish that mark in such standard characters.

(2) [*Mark Claiming Color*] Where the application contains a statement to the effect that the applicant wishes to claim color as a distinctive feature of the mark, the Office may require that the application indicate the name or code of the color or colors claimed and an indication, in respect of each color, of the principal parts of the mark which are in that color.

(3) [*Number of Reproductions*]

(a) Where the application does not contain a statement to the effect that the applicant wishes to claim color as a distinctive feature of the mark, a Contracting Party may not require more than

(i) five reproductions of the mark in black and white where the application may not, under the law of that Contracting Party, or does not contain a statement to the effect that the applicant wishes the mark to be registered and published in the standard characters used by the Office of the said Contracting Party;

(ii) one reproduction of the mark in black and white where the application contains a statement to the effect that the applicant wishes the mark to be registered and published in the standard characters used by the Office of that Contracting Party.

(b) Where the application contains a statement to the effect that the applicant wishes to claim color as a distinctive feature of the mark, a Contracting Party may not require more than five reproductions of the mark in black and white and five reproductions of the mark in color.

(4) [*Three-Dimensional Mark*]

(a) Where the application contains a statement to the effect that the mark is a three-dimensional mark, the reproduction of the mark shall consist of a two-dimensional graphic or photographic reproduction.

(b) The reproduction furnished under subparagraph (a) may, at the option of the applicant, consist of one single view of the mark or of several different views of the mark.

(c) Where the Office considers that the reproduction of the mark furnished by the applicant under subparagraph (a) does not sufficiently show the particulars of the three-dimensional mark, it may invite the applicant to furnish, within a reasonable time limit fixed in the invitation, up to six different views of the mark and/or a description by words of that mark.

(d) Where the Office considers that the different views and/or the description of the mark referred to in subparagraph (c) still do not sufficiently show the particulars of the three-dimensional mark, it may invite the applicant to furnish, within a reasonable time limit fixed in the invitation, a specimen of the mark.

(e) Notwithstanding subparagraphs (a) to (d), a sufficiently clear reproduction showing the three-dimensional character of the mark in one view shall be sufficient for the granting of a filing date.

(f) Paragraph (3)(a)(i) and (b) shall apply *mutatis mutandis.*

(5) [*Hologram Mark*] Where the application contains a statement to the effect that the mark is a hologram mark, the representation of the mark shall consist of one or several views of the mark capturing the holographic effect in its entirety. Where the Office considers that the view or views submitted do not capture the holographic effect in its entirety, it may require the furnishing of additional views. The Office may also require the applicant to furnish a description of the hologram mark.

(6) [*Motion Mark*] Where the application contains a statement to the effect that the mark is a motion mark, the representation of the mark shall, at the option of the Office, consist of one image or a series of still or moving images depicting movement. Where the Office considers that the image or images submitted do not depict movement, it may require the furnishing of additional images. The Office may also require that the applicant furnish a description explaining the movement.

(7) [*Color Mark*] Where the application contains a statement to the effect that the mark is a color per se mark or a combination of colors without delineated contours, the reproduction of the mark shall consist of a sample of the color or colors. The Office may require a designation of the color or colors by using their common names. The Office may also require a description on how the color is or the colors are applied to the goods or used in relation to the services. The Office may further require an indication of the color or colors by a recognized color code chosen by the applicant and accepted by the Office.

(8) [*Position Mark*] Where the application contains a statement to the effect that the mark is a position mark, the reproduction of the mark shall consist of a single view of the mark showing its position on the product. The Office may require that matter for which protection is not claimed shall be indicated. The Office may also require a description explaining the position of the mark in relation to the product.

(9) [*Sound Mark*] Where the application contains a statement to the effect that the mark is a sound mark, the representation of the mark shall, at the option of the Office, consist of a musical notation on a stave, or a description of the sound constituting the mark, or an analog or digital recording of that sound, or any combination thereof.

(10) [*Mark Consisting of a Non-Visible Sign Other Than a Sound Mark*] Where the application contains a statement to the effect that the mark consists of a non-visible sign, other than a sound mark, a Contracting Party may require one or more representations of the mark, an indication of the type of mark and details concerning the mark, as prescribed by the law of that Contracting Party.

(11) [*Transliteration of the Mark*] For the purposes of Article 3(1)(a)(xiii), where the mark consists of or contains matter in script other than the script used by the Office or numbers expressed in numerals other than numerals used by the Office, a transliteration of such matter in the script and numerals used by the Office may be required.

(12) [*Translation of the Mark*] For the purposes of Article 3(1)(a)(xiv), where the mark consists of or contains a word or words in a language other than the language, or one of the languages, admitted by the Office, a translation of that word or those words into that language or one of those languages may be required.

(13) [*Time Limit for Furnishing Evidence of Actual Use of the Mark*] The time limit referred to in Article 3(3) shall not be shorter than six months counted from the date of allowance of the application by the Office of the Contracting Party where that application was filed. The applicant or holder shall have the right to an extension of that time limit, subject to the conditions provided for by the law of that Contracting Party, by periods of at least six months each, up to a total extension of at least two years and a half.

[9.605]
Rule 4
Details Concerning Representation and Address for Service
(1) [*Address Where a Representative Is Appointed*] Where a representative is appointed, a Contracting Party shall consider the address of that representative to be the address for service.
(2) [*Address Where No Representative Is Appointed*] Where no representative is appointed and an applicant, holder or other interested person has provided as its address an address on the territory of the Contracting Party, that Contracting Party shall consider that address to be the address for service.
(3) [*Time Limit*] The time limit referred to in Article 4(3)(d) shall be counted from the date of receipt of the communication referred to in that Article by the Office of the Contracting Party concerned and shall not be less than one month where the address of the person on whose behalf the communication is made is on the territory of that Contracting Party and not less than two months where such an address is outside the territory of that Contracting Party.

[9.606]
Rule 5
Details Concerning the Filing Date
(1) [*Procedure in Case of Non-Compliance with Requirements*] If the application does not, at the time of its receipt by the Office, comply with any of the applicable requirements of Article 5(1)(a) or (2)(a), the Office shall promptly invite the applicant to comply with such requirements within a time limit indicated in the invitation, which time limit shall be at least one month from the date of the invitation where the applicant's address is on the territory of the Contracting Party concerned and at least two months where the applicant's address is outside the territory of the Contracting Party concerned. Compliance with the invitation may be subject to the payment of a special fee. Even if the Office fails to send the said invitation, the said requirements remain unaffected.
(2) [*Filing Date in Case of Correction*] If, within the time limit indicated in the invitation, the applicant complies with the invitation referred to in paragraph (1) and pays any required special fee, the filing date shall be the date on which all the required indications and elements referred to in Article 5(1)(a) have been received by the Office and, where applicable, the required fees referred to in Article 5(2)(a) have been paid to the Office. Otherwise, the application shall be treated as if it had not been filed.

[9.607]
Rule 6
Details Concerning Communications
(1) [*Indications Accompanying Signature of Communications on Paper*] Any Contracting Party may require that the signature of the natural person who signs be accompanied by
- (i) an indication in letters of the family or principal name and the given or secondary name or names of that person or, at the option of that person, of the name or names customarily used by the said person;
- (ii) an indication of the capacity in which that person signed, where such capacity is not obvious from reading the communication.

(2) [*Date of Signing*] Any Contracting Party may require that a signature be accompanied by an indication of the date on which the signing was effected. Where that indication is required but is not supplied, the date on which the signing is deemed to have been effected shall be the date on which the communication bearing the signature was received by the Office or, if the Contracting Party so allows, a date earlier than the latter date.
(3) [*Signature of Communications on Paper*] Where a communication to the Office of a Contracting Party is on paper and a signature is required, that Contracting Party
- (i) shall, subject to item (iii), accept a handwritten signature;
- (ii) may permit, instead of a handwritten signature, the use of other forms of signature, such as a printed or stamped signature, or the use of a seal or of a bar-coded label;
- (iii) may, where the natural person who signs the communication is a national of the Contracting Party and such person's address is on its territory, or where the legal entity on behalf of which the communication is signed is organized under its law and has either a domicile or a real and effective industrial or commercial establishment on its territory, require that a seal be used instead of a handwritten signature.

(4) [*Signature of Communications on Paper Filed by Electronic Means of Transmittal*] A Contracting Party that provides for communications on paper to be filed by electronic means of transmittal shall consider any such communication signed if a graphic representation of a signature accepted by that Contracting Party under paragraph (3) appears on the communication as received.
(5) [*Original of a Communication on Paper Filed by Electronic Means of Transmittal*] A Contracting Party that provides for communications on paper to be filed by electronic means of transmittal may require that the original of any such communication be filed
- (i) with the Office accompanied by a letter identifying that earlier transmission and
- (ii) within a time limit which shall be at least one month from the date on which the Office received the communication by electronic means of transmittal.

(6) [*Authentication of Communications in Electronic Form*] A Contracting Party that permits the filing of communications in electronic form may require that any such communication be authenticated through a system of electronic authentication as prescribed by that Contracting Party.
(7) [*Date of Receipt*] Each Contracting Party shall be free to determine the circumstances in which the receipt of a document or the payment of a fee shall be deemed to constitute receipt by or payment to the Office in cases in which the document was actually received by or payment was actually made to

(i) a branch or sub-office of the Office,
(ii) a national Office on behalf of the Office of the Contracting Party, where the Contracting Party is an intergovernmental organization referred to in Article 26(1)(ii),
(iii) an official postal service,
(iv) a delivery service, or an agency, specified by the Contracting Party,
(v) an address other than the nominated addresses of the Office.

(8) [*Electronic Filing*] Subject to paragraph (7), where a Contracting Party provides for the filing of a communication in electronic form or by electronic means of transmittal and the communication is so filed, the date on which the Office of that Contracting Party receives the communication in such form or by such means shall constitute the date of receipt of the communication.

[9.608]
Rule 7
Manner of Identification of an Application Without Its Application Number

(1) [*Manner of Identification*] Where it is required that an application be identified by its application number but where such a number has not yet been issued or is not known to the applicant or its representative, that application shall be considered identified if the following is supplied:

(i) the provisional application number, if any, given by the Office, or
(ii) a copy of the application, or
(iii) a representation of the mark, accompanied by an indication of the date on which, to the best knowledge of the applicant or the representative, the application was received by the Office and an identification number given to the application by the applicant or the representative.

(2) [*Prohibition of Other Requirements*] No Contracting Party may demand that requirements other than those referred to in paragraph (1) be complied with in order for an application to be identified where its application number has not yet been issued or is not known to the applicant or its representative.

[9.609]
Rule 8
Details Concerning Duration and Renewal

For the purposes of Article 13(1)(c), the period during which the request for renewal may be presented and the renewal fee may be paid shall start at least six months before the date on which the renewal is due and shall end at the earliest six months after that date. If the request for renewal is presented and/or the renewal fees are paid after the date on which the renewal is due, any Contracting Party may subject the acceptance of the request for renewal to the payment of a surcharge.

[9.610]
Rule 9
Relief Measures in Case of Failure to Comply with Time Limits

(1) [*Requirements Concerning Extension of Time Limits Under Article 14(2)(i)*] A Contracting Party that provides for the extension of a time limit under Article 14(2)(i) shall extend the time limit for a reasonable period of time from the date of filing the request for extension and may require that the request

(i) contain an identification of the requesting party, the relevant application or registration number and the time limit concerned, and
(ii) be filed within a time limit which shall not be less than two months from the date of expiry of the time limit concerned.

(2) [*Requirements Concerning Continued Processing Under Article 14(2)(ii)*] A Contracting Party may require that the request for continued processing under Article 14(2)(ii)

(i) contain an identification of the requesting party, the relevant application or registration number and the time limit concerned, and
(ii) be filed within a time limit which shall not be less than two months from the date of expiry of the time limit concerned. The omitted act shall be completed within the same period or, where the Contracting Party so provides, together with the request.

(3) [*Requirements Concerning Reinstatement of Rights Under Article 14(2)(iii)*]
(a) A Contracting Party may require that the request for reinstatement of rights under Article 14(2)(iii)

(i) contain an identification of the requesting party, the relevant application or registration number and the time limit concerned, and
(ii) set out the facts and evidence in support of the reasons for the failure to comply with the time limit concerned.

(b) The request for reinstatement of rights shall be filed with the Office within a reasonable time limit, the duration of which shall be determined by the Contracting Party from the date of the removal of the cause of failure to comply with the time limit concerned. The omitted act shall be completed within the same period or, where the Contracting Party so provides, together with the request.

(c) A Contracting Party may provide for a maximum time limit for complying with the requirements under subparagraphs (a) and (b) of not less than six months from the date of expiry of the time limit concerned.

(4) [*Exceptions Under Article 14(3)*] The exceptions referred to in Article 14(3) are the cases of failure to comply with a time limit

(i) for which a relief measure has already been granted under Article 14(2),
(ii) for filing a request for a relief measure under Article 14,
(iii) for payment of a renewal fee,
(iv) for an action before a board of appeal or other review body constituted in the framework of the Office,
(v) for an action in *inter partes* proceedings,
(vi) for filing the declaration referred to in Article 3(1)(a)(vii) or the declaration referred to in Article 3(1)(a)(viii),
(vii) for filing a declaration which, under the law of the Contracting Party, may establish a new filing date for a pending application, and
(viii) for the correction or addition of a priority claim.

[9.611]
Rule 10
Requirements Concerning the Request for Recordal of a License or for Amendment or Cancellation of the Recordal of a License

(1) [*Content of Request*]

(a) A Contracting Party may require that the request for recordal of a license under Article 17(1) contain some or all of the following indications or elements:

(i) the name and address of the holder;
(ii) where the holder has a representative, the name and address of that representative;
(iii) where the holder has an address for service, such address;
(iv) the name and address of the licensee;
(v) where the licensee has a representative, the name and address of that representative;
(vi) where the licensee has an address for service, such address;
(vii) the name of a State of which the licensee is a national if he/she is a national of any State, the name of a State in which the licensee has his/her domicile, if any, and the name of a State in which the licensee has a real and effective industrial or commercial establishment, if any;
(viii) where the holder or the licensee is a legal entity, the legal nature of that legal entity and the State, and, where applicable, the territorial unit within that State, under the law of which the said legal entity has been organized;
(ix) the registration number of the mark which is the subject of the license;
(x) the names of the goods and/or services for which the license is granted, grouped according to the classes of the Nice Classification, each group preceded by the number of the class of that Classification to which that group of goods or services belongs and presented in the order of the classes of the said Classification;
(xi) whether the license is an exclusive license, a non-exclusive license or a sole license;
(xii) where applicable, that the license concerns only a part of the territory covered by the registration, together with an explicit indication of that part of the territory;
(xiii) the duration of the license.

(b) A Contracting Party may require that the request for amendment or cancellation of the recordal of a license under Article 18(1) contain some or all of the following indications or elements:

(i) the indications specified in items (i) to (ix) of subparagraph (a);
(ii) where the amendment or cancellation concerns any of the indications or elements specified under subparagraph (a), the nature and scope of the amendment or cancellation to be recorded.

(2) [*Supporting Documents for Recordal of a License*]

(a) A Contracting Party may require that the request for recordal of a license be accompanied, at the option of the requesting party, by one of the following:

(i) an extract of the license contract indicating the parties and the rights being licensed, certified by a notary public or any other competent public authority as being a true extract of the contract; or

(ii) an uncertified statement of license, the content of which corresponds to the statement of license Form provided for in the Regulations, and signed by both the holder and the licensee.

(b) Any Contracting Party may require that any co-holder who is not a party to the license contract give its express consent to the license in a document signed by it.

(3) [*Supporting Documents for Amendment of Recordal of a License*]

(a) A Contracting Party may require that the request for amendment of the recordal of a license be accompanied, at the option of the requesting party, by one of the following:

(i) documents substantiating the requested amendment of the recordal of the license; or

(ii) an uncertified statement of amendment of license, the content of which corresponds to the statement of amendment of license Form provided for in these Regulations, and signed by both the holder and the licensee.

(b) Any Contracting Party may require that any co-holder who is not a party to the license contract give its express consent to the amendment of the license in a document signed by it.

(4) [*Supporting Documents for Cancellation of Recordal of a License*] A Contracting Party may require that the request for cancellation of the recordal of a license be accompanied, at the option of the requesting party, by one of the following:

(i) documents substantiating the requested cancellation of the recordal of the license; or

(ii) an uncertified statement of cancellation of license, the content of which corresponds to the statement of cancellation of license Form provided for in these Regulations, and signed by both the holder and the licensee.

NAGOYA PROTOCOL ON ACCESS TO GENETIC RESOURCES AND THE FAIR AND EQUITABLE SHARING OF BENEFITS ARISING FROM THEIR UTILISATION TO THE CONVENTION ON BIOLOGICAL DIVERSITY

(Done at Nagoya on 29 October 2010)

NOTES

The original source of this Protocol is the Convention on Biological Diversity website at www.cbd.int

Introduction

The Convention on Biological Diversity was opened for signature on 5 June 1992 at the United Nations Conference on Environment and Development (the Rio "Earth Summit") and entered into force on 29 December 1993. The Convention is the only international instrument comprehensively addressing biological diversity. The Convention's three objectives are the conservation of biological diversity, the sustainable use of its components and the fair and equitable sharing of benefits arising from the utilisation of genetic resources.

To further advance the implementation of the third objective, the World Summit on Sustainable Development (Johannesburg, September 2002) called for the negotiation of an international regime, within the framework of the Convention, to promote and safeguard the fair and equitable sharing of benefits arising from the utilisation of genetic resources. The Convention's Conference of the Parties responded at its seventh meeting, in 2004, by mandating its Ad Hoc Open-ended Working Group on Access and Benefit-sharing to elaborate and negotiate an international regime on access to genetic resources and benefit-sharing in order to effectively implement Articles 15 (Access to Genetic Resources) and 8(j) (Traditional Knowledge) of the Convention and its three objectives.

After six years of negotiation, the Nagoya Protocol on Access to Genetic Resources and the Fair and Equitable Sharing of Benefits Arising from their Utilization to the Convention on Biological Diversity was adopted at the tenth meeting of the Conference of the Parties on 29 October 2010, in Nagoya, Japan.

The Protocol significantly advances the Convention's third objective by providing a strong basis for greater legal certainty and transparency for both providers and users of genetic resources. Specific obligations to support compliance with domestic legislation or regulatory requirements of the Party providing genetic resources and contractual obligations reflected in mutually agreed terms are a signifi cant innovation of the Protocol. These compliance provisions as well as provisions establishing more predictable conditions for access to genetic resources will contribute to ensuring the sharing of benefits when genetic resources leave a Party providing genetic resources. In addition, the Protocol's provisions on access to traditional knowledge held by indigenous and local communities when it is associated with genetic resources will strengthen the ability of these communities to benefit from the use of their knowledge, innovations and practices.

By promoting the use of genetic resources and associated traditional knowledge, and by strengthening the opportunities for fair and equitable sharing of benefits from their use, the Protocol will create incentives to conserve biological diversity, sustainably use its components, and further enhance the contribution of biological diversity to sustainable development and human well-being.

THE PARTIES TO THIS PROTOCOL,

Being Parties to the Convention on Biological Diversity, hereinafter referred to as "the Convention",

Recalling that the fair and equitable sharing of benefits arising from the utilization of genetic resources is one of three core objectives of the Convention, and recognizing that this Protocol pursues the implementation of this objective within the Convention,

Reaffirming the sovereign rights of States over their natural resources and according to the provisions of the Convention,

Recalling further Article 15 of the Convention,

Recognizing the important contribution to sustainable development made by technology transfer and cooperation to build research and innovation capacities for adding value to genetic resources in developing countries, in accordance with Articles 16 and 19 of the Convention,

Recognizing that public awareness of the economic value of ecosystems and biodiversity and the fair and equitable sharing of this economic value with the custodians of biodiversity are key incentives for the conservation of biological diversity and the sustainable use of its components,

Acknowledging the potential role of access and benefit-sharing to contribute to the conservation and sustainable use of biological diversity, poverty eradication and environmental sustainability and thereby contributing to achieving the Millennium Development Goals,

Acknowledging the linkage between access to genetic resources and the fair and equitable sharing of benefits arising from the utilization of such resources, Recognizing the importance of providing legal certainty with respect to access to genetic resources and the fair and equitable sharing of benefits arising from their utilization,

Further recognizing the importance of promoting equity and fairness in negotiation of mutually agreed terms between providers and users of genetic resources,

Recognizing also the vital role that women play in access and benefit-sharing and affirming the need for the full participation of women at all levels of policy-making and implementation for biodiversity conservation,

Determined to further support the effective implementation of the access and benefit-sharing provisions of the Convention,

Recognizing that an innovative solution is required to address the fair and equitable sharing of benefits derived from the utilization of genetic resources and traditional knowledge associated with genetic resources that occur in transboundary situations or for which it is not possible to grant or obtain prior informed consent,

Recognizing the importance of genetic resources to food security, public health, biodiversity conservation, and the mitigation of and adaptation to climate change,

Recognizing the special nature of agricultural biodiversity, its distinctive features and problems needing distinctive solutions,

Recognizing the interdependence of all countries with regard to genetic resources for food and agriculture as well as their special nature and importance for achieving food security worldwide and for sustainable development of agriculture in the context of poverty alleviation and climate change and acknowledging the fundamental role of the International Treaty on Plant Genetic Resources for Food and Agriculture and the FAO Commission on Genetic Resources for Food and Agriculture in this regard,

Mindful of the International Health Regulations (2005) of the World Health organisation and the importance of ensuring access to human pathogens for public health preparedness and response purposes,

Acknowledging ongoing work in other international forums relating to access and benefit-sharing,

Recalling the Multilateral System of Access and Benefit-sharing established under the International Treaty on Plant Genetic Resources for Food and Agriculture developed in harmony with the Convention,

Recognizing that international instruments related to access and benefit-sharing should be mutually supportive with a view to achieving the objectives of the Convention,

Recalling the relevance of Article 8(j) of the Convention as it relates to traditional knowledge associated with genetic resources and the fair and equitable sharing of benefits arising from the utilization of such knowledge,

Noting the interrelationship between genetic resources and traditional knowledge, their inseparable nature for indigenous and local communities, the importance of the traditional knowledge for the conservation of biological diversity and the sustainable use of its components, and for the sustainable livelihoods of these communities,

Recognizing the diversity of circumstances in which traditional knowledge associated with genetic resources is held or owned by indigenous and local communities,

Mindful that it is the right of indigenous and local communities to identify the rightful holders of their traditional knowledge associated with genetic resources, within their communities,

Further recognizing the unique circumstances where traditional knowledge associated with genetic resources is held in countries, which may be oral, documented or in other forms, reflecting a rich cultural heritage relevant for conservation and sustainable use of biological diversity,

Noting the United Nations Declaration on the Rights of Indigenous Peoples, and

Affirming that nothing in this Protocol shall be construed as diminishing or extinguishing the existing rights of indigenous and local communities,

HAVE AGREED AS FOLLOWS:

[9.612]
Article 1
Objective

The objective of this Protocol is the fair and equitable sharing of the benefits arising from the utilization of genetic resources, including by appropriate access to genetic resources and by appropriate transfer of relevant technologies, taking into account all rights over those resources and to technologies, and by appropriate funding, thereby contributing to the conservation of biological diversity and the sustainable use of its components.

[9.613]
Article 2
Use of Terms

The terms defined in Article 2 of the Convention shall apply to this Protocol. In addition, for the purposes of this Protocol:

(a) "Conference of the Parties" means the Conference of the Parties to the Convention;
(b) "Convention" means the Convention on Biological Diversity;
(c) "Utilization of genetic resources" means to conduct research and development on the genetic and/or biochemical composition of genetic resources, including through the application of biotechnology as defined in Article 2 of the Convention;
(d) "Biotechnology" as defined in Article 2 of the Convention means any technological application that uses biological systems, living organisms, or derivatives thereof, to make or modify products or processes for specific use;
(e) "Derivative" means a naturally occurring biochemical compound resulting from the genetic expression or metabolism of biological or genetic resources, even if it does not contain functional units of heredity.

[9.614]
Article 3
Scope

This Protocol shall apply to genetic resources within the scope of Article 15 of the Convention and to the benefits arising from the utilization of such resources. This Protocol shall also apply to traditional knowledge associated with genetic resources within the scope of the Convention and to the benefits arising from the utilization of such knowledge.

[9.615]
Article 4
Relationship with International Agreements and Instruments

1. The provisions of this Protocol shall not affect the rights and obligations of any Party deriving from any existing international agreement, except where the exercise of those rights and obligations would cause a serious damage or threat to biological diversity. This paragraph is not intended to create a hierarchy between this Protocol and other international instruments.
2. Nothing in this Protocol shall prevent the Parties from developing and implementing other relevant international agreements, including other specialized access and benefit-sharing agreements, provided that they are supportive of and do not run counter to the objectives of the Convention and this Protocol.
3. This Protocol shall be implemented in a mutually supportive manner with other international instruments relevant to this Protocol. Due regard should be paid to useful and relevant ongoing work or practices under such international instruments and relevant international organisations, provided that they are supportive of and do not run counter to the objectives of the Convention and this Protocol.
4. This Protocol is the instrument for the implementation of the access and benefit-sharing provisions of the Convention. Where a specialized international access and benefit-sharing instrument applies that is consistent with, and does not run counter to the objectives of the Convention and this Protocol, this Protocol does not apply for the Party or Parties to the specialized instrument in respect of the specific genetic resource covered by and for the purpose of the specialized instrument.

[9.616]
Article 5
Fair and Equitable Benefit-Sharing

1. In accordance with Article 15, paragraphs 3 and 7 of the Convention, benefits arising from the utilization of genetic resources as well as subsequent applications and commercialization shall be shared in a fair and equitable way with the Party providing such resources that is the country of origin of such resources or a Party that has acquired the genetic resources in accordance with the Convention. Such sharing shall be upon mutually agreed terms.
2. Each Party shall take legislative, administrative or policy measures, as appropriate, with the aim of ensuring that benefits arising from the utilization of genetic resources that are held by indigenous and local communities, in accordance with domestic legislation regarding the established rights of these indigenous and local communities over these genetic resources, are shared in a fair and equitable way with the communities concerned, based on mutually agreed terms.
3. To implement paragraph 1 above, each Party shall take legislative, administrative or policy measures, as appropriate.
4. Benefits may include monetary and non-monetary benefits, including but not limited to those listed in the Annex.
5. Each Party shall take legislative, administrative or policy measures, as appropriate, in order that the benefits arising from the utilization of traditional knowledge associated with genetic resources are shared in a fair and equitable way with indigenous and local communities holding such knowledge. Such sharing shall be upon mutually agreed terms.

[9.617]
Article 6
Access to Genetic Resources

1. In the exercise of sovereign rights over natural resources, and subject to domestic access and benefit-sharing legislation or regulatory requirements, access to genetic resources for their utilization shall be subject to the prior informed consent of the Party providing such resources that is the country of origin of such resources or a Party that has acquired the genetic resources in accordance with the Convention, unless otherwise determined by that Party.
2. In accordance with domestic law, each Party shall take measures, as appropriate, with the aim of ensuring that the prior informed consent or approval and involvement of indigenous and local communities is obtained for access to genetic resources where they have the established right to grant access to such resources.
3. Pursuant to paragraph 1 above, each Party requiring prior informed consent shall take the necessary legislative, administrative or policy measures, as appropriate, to:
   (a) Provide for legal certainty, clarity and transparency of their domestic access and benefit-sharing legislation or regulatory requirements;
   (b) Provide for fair and non-arbitrary rules and procedures on accessing genetic resources;
   (c) Provide information on how to apply for prior informed consent;
   (d) Provide for a clear and transparent written decision by a competent national authority, in a cost-effective manner and within a reasonable period of time;
   (e) Provide for the issuance at the time of access of a permit or its equivalent as evidence of the decision to grant prior informed consent and of the establishment of mutually agreed terms, and notify the Access and Benefitsharing Clearing-House accordingly;
   (f) Where applicable, and subject to domestic legislation, set out criteria and/or processes for obtaining prior informed consent or approval and involvement of indigenous and local communities for access to genetic resources; and
   (g) Establish clear rules and procedures for requiring and establishing mutually agreed terms. Such terms shall be set out in writing and may include, *inter alia*:
      (i) A dispute settlement clause;
      (ii) Terms on benefit-sharing, including in relation to intellectual property rights;
      (iii) Terms on subsequent third-party use, if any; and
      (iv) Terms on changes of intent, where applicable.

[9.618]
Article 7
Access to Traditional Knowledge Associated with Genetic Resources

In accordance with domestic law, each Party shall take measures, as appropriate, with the aim of ensuring that traditional knowledge associated with genetic resources that is held by indigenous and local communities is accessed with the prior and informed consent or approval and involvement of these indigenous and local communities, and that mutually agreed terms have been established.

[9.619]
Article 8
Special Considerations

In the development and implementation of its access and benefit-sharing legislation or regulatory requirements, each Party shall:

(a) Create conditions to promote and encourage research which contributes to the conservation and sustainable use of biological diversity, particularly in developing countries, including through simplified measures on access for non-commercial research purposes, taking into account the need to address a change of intent for such research;
(b) Pay due regard to cases of present or imminent emergencies that threaten or damage human, animal or plant health, as determined nationally or internationally. Parties may take into consideration the need for expeditious access to genetic resources and expeditious fair and equitable sharing of benefits arising out of the use of such genetic resources, including access to affordable treatments by those in need, especially in developing countries;
(c) Consider the importance of genetic resources for food and agriculture and their special role for food security.

[9.620]
Article 9
Contribution to Conservation and Sustainable Use

The Parties shall encourage users and providers to direct benefits arising from the utilization of genetic resources towards the conservation of biological diversity and the sustainable use of its components.

[9.621]
Article 10
Global Multilateral Benefit-Sharing Mechanism

Parties shall consider the need for and modalities of a global multilateral benefitsharing mechanism to address the fair and equitable sharing of benefits derived from the utilization of genetic resources and traditional knowledge associated with genetic resources that occur in transboundary situations or for which it is not possible to grant or obtain prior informed consent. The benefits shared by users of genetic resources and traditional knowledge associated with genetic resources through this mechanism shall be used to support the conservation of biological diversity and the sustainable use of its components globally.

[9.622]
Article 11
Transboundary Cooperation

1. In instances where the same genetic resources are found *in situ* within the territory of more than one Party, those Parties shall endeavour to cooperate, as appropriate, with the involvement of indigenous and local communities concerned, where applicable, with a view to implementing this Protocol.
2. Where the same traditional knowledge associated with genetic resources is shared by one or more indigenous and local communities in several Parties, those Parties shall endeavour to cooperate, as appropriate, with the involvement of the indigenous and local communities concerned, with a view to implementing the objective of this Protocol.

[9.623]
Article 12
Traditional Knowledge Associated with Genetic Resources

1. In implementing their obligations under this Protocol, Parties shall in accordance with domestic law take into consideration indigenous and local communities' customary laws, community protocols and procedures, as applicable, with respect to traditional knowledge associated with genetic resources.
2. Parties, with the effective participation of the indigenous and local communities concerned, shall establish mechanisms to inform potential users of traditional knowledge associated with genetic resources about their obligations, including measures as made available through the Access and Benefit-sharing Clearing-House for access to and fair and equitable sharing of benefits arising from the utilization of such knowledge.
3. Parties shall endeavour to support, as appropriate, the development by indigenous and local communities, including women within these communities, of:
(a) Community protocols in relation to access to traditional knowledge associated with genetic resources and the fair and equitable sharing of benefits arising out of the utilization of such knowledge;
(b) Minimum requirements for mutually agreed terms to secure the fair and equitable sharing of benefits arising from the utilization of traditional knowledge associated with genetic resources; and
(c) Model contractual clauses for benefit-sharing arising from the utilization of traditional knowledge associated with genetic resources.
4. Parties, in their implementation of this Protocol, shall, as far as possible, not restrict the customary use and exchange of genetic resources and associated traditional knowledge within and amongst indigenous and local communities in accordance with the objectives of the Convention.

[9.624]
Article 13
National Focal Points and Competent National Authorities

1. Each Party shall designate a national focal point on access and benefit-sharing. The national focal point shall make information available as follows:
   (a) For applicants seeking access to genetic resources, information on procedures for obtaining prior informed consent and establishing mutually agreed terms, including benefit-sharing;
   (b) For applicants seeking access to traditional knowledge associated with genetic resources, where possible, information on procedures for obtaining prior informed consent or approval and involvement, as appropriate, of indigenous and local communities and establishing mutually agreed terms including benefit-sharing; and
   (c) Information on competent national authorities, relevant indigenous and local communities and relevant stakeholders.

The national focal point shall be responsible for liaison with the Secretariat.

2. Each Party shall designate one or more competent national authorities on access and benefit-sharing. Competent national authorities shall, in accordance with applicable national legislative, administrative or policy measures, be responsible for granting access or, as applicable, issuing written evidence that access requirements have been met and be responsible for advising on applicable procedures and requirements for obtaining prior informed consent and entering into mutually agreed terms.

3. A Party may designate a single entity to fulfil the functions of both focal point and competent national authority.

4. Each Party shall, no later than the date of entry into force of this Protocol for it, notify the Secretariat of the contact information of its national focal point and its competent national authority or authorities. Where a Party designates more than one competent national authority, it shall convey to the Secretariat, with its notification thereof, relevant information on the respective responsibilities of those authorities. Where applicable, such information shall, at a minimum, specify which competent authority is responsible for the genetic resources sought. Each Party shall forthwith notify the Secretariat of any changes in the designation of its national focal point or in the contact information or responsibilities of its competent national authority or authorities.

5. The Secretariat shall make information received pursuant to paragraph 4 above available through the Access and Benefit-sharing Clearing-House.

[9.625]
Article 14
The Access and Benefit-Sharing Clearing-House and Information-Sharing

1. An Access and Benefit-sharing Clearing-House is hereby established as part of the clearing-house mechanism under Article 18, paragraph 3, of the Convention. It shall serve as a means for sharing of information related to access and benefitsharing. In particular, it shall provide access to information made available by each Party relevant to the implementation of this Protocol.

2. Without prejudice to the protection of confidential information, each Party shall make available to the Access and Benefit-sharing Clearing-House any information required by this Protocol, as well as information required pursuant to the decisions taken by the Conference of the Parties serving as the meeting of the Parties to this Protocol. The information shall include:
   (a) Legislative, administrative and policy measures on access and benefit-sharing;
   (b) Information on the national focal point and competent national authority or authorities; and
   (c) Permits or their equivalent issued at the time of access as evidence of the decision to grant prior informed consent and of the establishment of mutually agreed terms.

3. Additional information, if available and as appropriate, may include:
   (a) Relevant competent authorities of indigenous and local communities, and information as so decided;
   (b) Model contractual clauses;
   (c) Methods and tools developed to monitor genetic resources; and
   (d) Codes of conduct and best practices.

4. The modalities of the operation of the Access and Benefit-sharing Clearing-House, including reports on its activities, shall be considered and decided upon by the Conference of the Parties serving as the meeting of the Parties to this Protocol at its first meeting, and kept under review thereafter.

[9.626]
Article 15
Compliance with Domestic Legislation or Regulatory Requirements on Access and Benefit-Sharing

1. Each Party shall take appropriate, effective and proportionate legislative, administrative or policy measures to provide that genetic resources utilized within its jurisdiction have been accessed in accordance with prior informed consent and that mutually agreed terms have been established, as required by the domestic access and benefit-sharing legislation or regulatory requirements of the other Party.

2. Parties shall take appropriate, effective and proportionate measures to address situations of non-compliance with measures adopted in accordance with paragraph 1 above.
3. Parties shall, as far as possible and as appropriate, cooperate in cases of alleged violation of domestic access and benefit-sharing legislation or regulatory requirements referred to in paragraph 1 above.

[9.627]
Article 16
Compliance with Domestic Legislation or Regulatory Requirements on Access and Benefitsharing for Traditional Knowledge Associated with Genetic Resources
1. Each Party shall take appropriate, effective and proportionate legislative, administrative or policy measures, as appropriate, to provide that traditional knowledge associated with genetic resources utilized within their jurisdiction has been accessed in accordance with prior informed consent or approval and involvement of indigenous and local communities and that mutually agreed terms have been established, as required by domestic access and benefit-sharing legislation or regulatory requirements of the other Party where such indigenous and local communities are located.
2. Each Party shall take appropriate, effective and proportionate measures to address situations of non-compliance with measures adopted in accordance with paragraph 1 above.
3. Parties shall, as far as possible and as appropriate, cooperate in cases of alleged violation of domestic access and benefit-sharing legislation or regulatory requirements referred to in paragraph 1 above.

[9.628]
Article 17
Monitoring the Utilization of Genetic Resources
1. To support compliance, each Party shall take measures, as appropriate, to monitor and to enhance transparency about the utilization of genetic resources. Such measures shall include:
- (a) The designation of one or more checkpoints, as follows:
  - (i) Designated checkpoints would collect or receive, as appropriate, relevant information related to prior informed consent, to the source of the genetic resource, to the establishment of mutually agreed terms, and/or to the utilization of genetic resources, as appropriate;
  - (ii) Each Party shall, as appropriate and depending on the particular characteristics of a designated checkpoint, require users of genetic resources to provide the information specified in the above paragraph at a designated checkpoint. Each Party shall take appropriate, effective and proportionate measures to address situations of non-compliance;
  - (iii) Such information, including from internationally recognized certificates of compliance where they are available, will, without prejudice to the protection of confidential information, be provided to relevant national authorities, to the Party providing prior informed consent and to the Access and Benefit-sharing Clearing-House, as appropriate;
  - (iv) Checkpoints must be effective and should have functions relevant to implementation of this subparagraph (a) They should be relevant to the utilization of genetic resources, or to the collection of relevant information at, *inter alia*, any stage of research, development, innovation, pre-commercialization or commercialization.
- (b) Encouraging users and providers of genetic resources to include provisions in mutually agreed terms to share information on the implementation of such terms, including through reporting requirements; and
- (c) Encouraging the use of cost-effective communication tools and systems.

2. A permit or its equivalent issued in accordance with Article 6, paragraph 3 (e) and made available to the Access and Benefit-sharing Clearing-House, shall constitute an internationally recognized certificate of compliance.
3. An internationally recognized certificate of compliance shall serve as evidence that the genetic resource which it covers has been accessed in accordance with prior informed consent and that mutually agreed terms have been established, as required by the domestic access and benefit-sharing legislation or regulatory requirements of the Party providing prior informed consent.
4. The internationally recognized certificate of compliance shall contain the following minimum information when it is not confidential:
- (a) Issuing authority;
- (b) Date of issuance;
- (c) The provider;
- (d) Unique identifier of the certificate;
- (e) The person or entity to whom prior informed consent was granted;
- (f) Subject-matter or genetic resources covered by the certificate;
- (g) Confirmation that mutually agreed terms were established;
- (h) Confirmation that prior informed consent was obtained; and
- (i) Commercial and/or non-commercial use.

[9.629]
Article 18
Compliance with Mutually Agreed Terms

1. In the implementation of Article 6, paragraph 3(g)(i) and Article 7, each Party shall encourage providers and users of genetic resources and/or traditional knowledge associated with genetic resources to include provisions in mutually agreed terms to cover, where appropriate, dispute resolution including:

(a) The jurisdiction to which they will subject any dispute resolution processes;
(b) The applicable law; and/or
(c) Options for alternative dispute resolution, such as mediation or arbitration.

2. Each Party shall ensure that an opportunity to seek recourse is available under their legal systems, consistent with applicable jurisdictional requirements, in cases of disputes arising from mutually agreed terms.

3. Each Party shall take effective measures, as appropriate, regarding:

(a) Access to justice; and
(b) The utilization of mechanisms regarding mutual recognition and enforcement of foreign judgments and arbitral awards.

4. The effectiveness of this article shall be reviewed by the Conference of the Parties serving as the meeting of the Parties to this Protocol in accordance with Article 31 of this Protocol.

[9.630]
Article 19
Model Contractual Clauses

1. Each Party shall encourage, as appropriate, the development, update and use of sectoral and cross-sectoral model contractual clauses for mutually agreed terms.

2. The Conference of the Parties serving as the meeting of the Parties to this Protocol shall periodically take stock of the use of sectoral and cross-sectoral model contractual clauses.

[9.631]
Article 20
Codes of Conduct, Guidelines and Best Practices and/or Standards

1. Each Party shall encourage, as appropriate, the development, update and use of voluntary codes of conduct, guidelines and best practices and/or standards in relation to access and benefit-sharing.

2. The Conference of the Parties serving as the meeting of the Parties to this Protocol shall periodically take stock of the use of voluntary codes of conduct, guidelines and best practices and/or standards and consider the adoption of specific codes of conduct, guidelines and best practices and/or standards.

[9.632]
Article 21
Awareness-raising

Each Party shall take measures to raise awareness of the importance of genetic resources and traditional knowledge associated with genetic resources, and related access and benefit-sharing issues. Such measures may include, *inter alia*:

(a) Promotion of this Protocol, including its objective;
(b) organisation of meetings of indigenous and local communities and relevant stakeholders;
(c) Establishment and maintenance of a help desk for indigenous and local communities and relevant stakeholders;
(d) Information dissemination through a national clearing-house;
(e) Promotion of voluntary codes of conduct, guidelines and best practices and/or standards in consultation with indigenous and local communities and relevant stakeholders;
(f) Promotion of, as appropriate, domestic, regional and international exchanges of experience;
(g) Education and training of users and providers of genetic resources and traditional knowledge associated with genetic resources about their access and benefit-sharing obligations;
(h) Involvement of indigenous and local communities and relevant stakeholders in the implementation of this Protocol; and
(i) Awareness-raising of community protocols and procedures of indigenous and local communities.

[9.633]
Article 22
Capacity

1. The Parties shall cooperate in the capacity-building, capacity development and strengthening of human resources and institutional capacities to effectively implement this Protocol in developing country Parties, in particular the least developed countries and small island developing States among them, and Parties with economies in transition, including through existing global, regional,

subregional and national institutions and organisations. In this context, Parties should facilitate the involvement of indigenous and local communities and relevant stakeholders, including non-governmental organisations and the private sector.

2. The need of developing country Parties, in particular the least developed countries and small island developing States among them, and Parties with economies in transition for financial resources in accordance with the relevant provisions of the Convention shall be taken fully into account for capacity-building and development to implement this Protocol.

3. As a basis for appropriate measures in relation to the implementation of this Protocol, developing country Parties, in particular the least developed countries and small island developing States among them, and Parties with economies in transition should identify their national capacity needs and priorities through national capacity self-assessments. In doing so, such Parties should support the capacity needs and priorities of indigenous and local communities and relevant stakeholders, as identified by them, emphasizing the capacity needs and priorities of women.

4. In support of the implementation of this Protocol, capacity-building and development may address, *inter alia,* the following key areas:

(a) Capacity to implement, and to comply with the obligations of, this Protocol;
(b) Capacity to negotiate mutually agreed terms;
(c) Capacity to develop, implement and enforce domestic legislative, administrative or policy measures on access and benefit-sharing; and
(d) Capacity of countries to develop their endogenous research capabilities to add value to their own genetic resources.

5. Measures in accordance with paragraphs 1 to 4 above may include, *inter alia:*

(a) Legal and institutional development;
(b) Promotion of equity and fairness in negotiations, such as training to negotiate mutually agreed terms;
(c) The monitoring and enforcement of compliance;
(d) Employment of best available communication tools and Internet-based systems for access and benefit-sharing activities;
(e) Development and use of valuation methods;
(f) Bioprospecting, associated research and taxonomic studies;
(g) Technology transfer, and infrastructure and technical capacity to make such technology transfer sustainable;
(h) Enhancement of the contribution of access and benefit-sharing activities to the conservation of biological diversity and the sustainable use of its components;
(i) Special measures to increase the capacity of relevant stakeholders in relation to access and benefit-sharing; and
(j) Special measures to increase the capacity of indigenous and local communities with emphasis on enhancing the capacity of women within those communities in relation to access to genetic resources and/or traditional knowledge associated with genetic resources.

6. Information on capacity-building and development initiatives at national, regional and international levels, undertaken in accordance with paragraphs 1 to 5 above, should be provided to the Access and Benefit-sharing Clearing-House with a view to promoting synergy and coordination on capacity-building and development for access and benefit-sharing.

[9.634]
Article 23
Technology Transfer, Collaboration and Cooperation

In accordance with Articles 15, 16, 18 and 19 of the Convention, the Parties shall collaborate and cooperate in technical and scientific research and development programmes, including biotechnological research activities, as a means to achieve the objective of this Protocol. The Parties undertake to promote and encourage access to technology by, and transfer of technology to, developing country Parties, in particular the least developed countries and small island developing States among them, and Parties with economies in transition, in order to enable the development and strengthening of a sound and viable technological and scientific base for the attainment of the objectives of the Convention and this Protocol. Where possible and appropriate such collaborative activities shall take place in and with a Party or the Parties providing genetic resources that is the country or are the countries of origin of such resources or a Party or Parties that have acquired the genetic resources in accordance with the Convention.

[9.635]
Article 24
Non-Parties

The Parties shall encourage non-Parties to adhere to this Protocol and to contribute appropriate information to the Access and Benefit-sharing Clearing-House.

[9.636]
Article 25
Financial Mechanism and Resources

1. In considering financial resources for the implementation of this Protocol, the Parties shall take into account the provisions of Article 20 of the Convention.
2. The financial mechanism of the Convention shall be the financial mechanism for this Protocol.
3. Regarding the capacity-building and development referred to in Article 22 of this Protocol, the Conference of the Parties serving as the meeting of the Parties to this Protocol, in providing guidance with respect to the financial mechanism referred to in paragraph 2 above, for consideration by the Conference of the Parties, shall take into account the need of developing country Parties, in particular the least developed countries and small island developing States among them, and of Parties with economies in transition, for financial resources, as well as the capacity needs and priorities of indigenous and local communities, including women within these communities.
4. In the context of paragraph 1 above, the Parties shall also take into account the needs of the developing country Parties, in particular the least developed countries and small island developing States among them, and of the Parties with economies in transition, in their efforts to identify and implement their capacity-building and development requirements for the purposes of the implementation of this Protocol.
5. The guidance to the financial mechanism of the Convention in relevant decisions of the Conference of the Parties, including those agreed before the adoption of this Protocol, shall apply, *mutatis mutandis*, to the provisions of this Article.
6. The developed country Parties may also provide, and the developing country Parties and the Parties with economies in transition avail themselves of, financial and other resources for the implementation of the provisions of this Protocol through bilateral, regional and multilateral channels.

[9.637]
Article 26
Conference of the Parties Serving as the Meeting of the Parties to this Protocol

1. The Conference of the Parties shall serve as the meeting of the Parties to this Protocol.
2. Parties to the Convention that are not Parties to this Protocol may participate as observers in the proceedings of any meeting of the Conference of the Parties serving as the meeting of the Parties to this Protocol. When the Conference of the Parties serves as the meeting of the Parties to this Protocol, decisions under this Protocol shall be taken only by those that are Parties to it.
3. When the Conference of the Parties serves as the meeting of the Parties to this Protocol, any member of the Bureau of the Conference of the Parties representing a Party to the Convention but, at that time, not a Party to this Protocol, shall be substituted by a member to be elected by and from among the Parties to this Protocol.
4. The Conference of the Parties serving as the meeting of the Parties to this Protocol shall keep under regular review the implementation of this Protocol and shall make, within its mandate, the decisions necessary to promote its effective implementation. It shall perform the functions assigned to it by this Protocol and shall:
   (a) Make recommendations on any matters necessary for the implementation of this Protocol;
   (b) Establish such subsidiary bodies as are deemed necessary for the implementation of this Protocol;
   (c) Seek and utilize, where appropriate, the services and cooperation of, and information provided by, competent international organisations and intergovernmental and non-governmental bodies;
   (d) Establish the form and the intervals for transmitting the information to be submitted in accordance with Article 29 of this Protocol and consider such information as well as reports submitted by any subsidiary body;
   (e) Consider and adopt, as required, amendments to this Protocol and its Annex, as well as any additional annexes to this Protocol, that are deemed necessary for the implementation of this Protocol; and
   (f) Exercise such other functions as may be required for the implementation of this Protocol.
5. The rules of procedure of the Conference of the Parties and financial rules of the Convention shall be applied, *mutatis mutandis*, under this Protocol, except as may be otherwise decided by consensus by the Conference of the Parties serving as the meeting of the Parties to this Protocol.
6. The first meeting of the Conference of the Parties serving as the meeting of the Parties to this Protocol shall be convened by the Secretariat and held concurrently with the first meeting of the Conference of the Parties that is scheduled after the date of the entry into force of this Protocol. Subsequent ordinary meetings of the Conference of the Parties serving as the meeting of the Parties to this Protocol shall be held concurrently with ordinary meetings of the Conference of the Parties, unless otherwise decided by the Conference of the Parties serving as the meeting of the Parties to this Protocol.

7. Extraordinary meetings of the Conference of the Parties serving as the meeting of the Parties to this Protocol shall be held at such other times as may be deemed necessary by the Conference of the Parties serving as the meeting of the Parties to this Protocol, or at the written request of any Party, provided that, within six months of the request being communicated to the Parties by the Secretariat, it is supported by at least one third of the Parties.
8. The United Nations, its specialized agencies and the International Atomic Energy Agency, as well as any State member thereof or observers thereto not party to the Convention, may be represented as observers at meetings of the Conference of the Parties serving as the meeting of the Parties to this Protocol. Any body or agency, whether national or international, governmental or non-governmental, that is qualified in matters covered by this Protocol and that has informed the Secretariat of its wish to be represented at a meeting of the Conference of the Parties serving as a meeting of the Parties to this Protocol as an observer, may be so admitted, unless at least one third of the Parties present object. Except as otherwise provided in this Article, the admission and participation of observers shall be subject to the rules of procedure, as referred to in paragraph 5 above.

[9.638]
Article 27
Subsidiary Bodies

1. Any subsidiary body established by or under the Convention may serve this Protocol, including upon a decision of the Conference of the Parties serving as the meeting of the Parties to this Protocol. Any such decision shall specify the tasks to be undertaken.
2. Parties to the Convention that are not Parties to this Protocol may participate as observers in the proceedings of any meeting of any such subsidiary bodies. When a subsidiary body of the Convention serves as a subsidiary body to this Protocol, decisions under this Protocol shall be taken only by Parties to this Protocol.
3. When a subsidiary body of the Convention exercises its functions with regard to matters concerning this Protocol, any member of the bureau of that subsidiary body representing a Party to the Convention but, at that time, not a Party to this Protocol, shall be substituted by a member to be elected by and from among the Parties to this Protocol.

[9.639]
Article 28
Secretariat

1. The Secretariat established by Article 24 of the Convention shall serve as the secretariat to this Protocol.
2. Article 24, paragraph 1, of the Convention on the functions of the Secretariat shall apply, *mutatis mutandis*, to this Protocol.
3. To the extent that they are distinct, the costs of the secretariat services for this Protocol shall be met by the Parties hereto. The Conference of the Parties serving as the meeting of the Parties to this Protocol shall, at its first meeting, decide on the necessary budgetary arrangements to this end.

[9.640]
Article 29
Monitoring and Reporting

Each Party shall monitor the implementation of its obligations under this Protocol, and shall, at intervals and in the format to be determined by the Conference of the Parties serving as the meeting of the Parties to this Protocol, report to the Conference of the Parties serving as the meeting of the Parties to this Protocol on measures that it has taken to implement this Protocol.

[9.641]
Article 30
Procedures and Mechanisms to Promote Compliance with this Protocol

The Conference of the Parties serving as the meeting of the Parties to this Protocol shall, at its first meeting, consider and approve cooperative procedures and institutional mechanisms to promote compliance with the provisions of this Protocol and to address cases of non-compliance. These procedures and mechanisms shall include provisions to offer advice or assistance, where appropriate. They shall be separate from, and without prejudice to, the dispute settlement procedures and mechanisms under Article 27 of the Convention.

[9.642]
Article 31
Assessment and Review

The Conference of the Parties serving as the meeting of the Parties to this Protocol shall undertake, four years after the entry into force of this Protocol and thereafter at intervals determined by the Conference of the Parties serving as the meeting of the Parties to this Protocol, an evaluation of the effectiveness of this Protocol.

[9.643]
Article 32
Signature
This Protocol shall be open for signature by Parties to the Convention at the United Nations Headquarters in New York, from 2 February 2011 to 1 February 2012.

[9.644]
Article 33
Entry into Force
1. This Protocol shall enter into force on the ninetieth day after the date of deposit of the fiftieth instrument of ratification, acceptance, approval or accession by States or regional economic integration organisations that are Parties to the Convention.
2. This Protocol shall enter into force for a State or regional economic integration organisation that ratifies, accepts or approves this Protocol or accedes thereto after the deposit of the fiftieth instrument as referred to in paragraph 1 above, on the ninetieth day after the date on which that State or regional economic integration organisation deposits its instrument of ratification, acceptance, approval or accession, or on the date on which the Convention enters into force for that State or regional economic integration organisation, whichever shall be the later.
3. For the purposes of paragraphs 1 and 2 above, any instrument deposited by a regional economic integration organisation shall not be counted as additional to those deposited by member States of such organisation.

[9.645]
Article 34
Reservations
No reservations may be made to this Protocol.

[9.646]
Article 35
Withdrawal
1. At any time after two years from the date on which this Protocol has entered into force for a Party, that Party may withdraw from this Protocol by giving written notification to the Depositary.
2. Any such withdrawal shall take place upon expiry of one year after the date of its receipt by the Depositary, or on such later date as may be specified in the notification of the withdrawal.

[9.647]
Article 36
Authentic Texts
The original of this Protocol, of which the Arabic, Chinese, English, French, Russian and Spanish texts are equally authentic, shall be deposited with the Secretary-General of the United Nations.

IN WITNESS WHEREOF the undersigned, being duly authorized to that effect, have signed this Protocol on the dates indicated.

DONE at Nagoya on this twenty-ninth day of October, two thousand and ten.

ANNEX

MONETARY AND NON-MONETARY BENEFITS

[9.648]
1. Monetary benefits may include, but not be limited to:
   (a) Access fees/fee per sample collected or otherwise acquired;
   (b) Up-front payments;
   (c) Milestone payments;
   (d) Payment of royalties;
   (e) Licence fees in case of commercialization;
   (f) Special fees to be paid to trust funds supporting conservation and sustainable use of biodiversity;
   (g) Salaries and preferential terms where mutually agreed;
   (h) Research funding;
   (i) Joint ventures;
   (j) Joint ownership of relevant intellectual property rights.
2. Non-monetary benefits may include, but not be limited to:
   (a) Sharing of research and development results;
   (b) Collaboration, cooperation and contribution in scientific research and development programmes, particularly biotechnological research activities, where possible in the Party providing genetic resources;
   (c) Participation in product development;
   (d) Collaboration, cooperation and contribution in education and training;
   (e) Admittance to *ex situ* facilities of genetic resources and to databases;

(f) Transfer to the provider of the genetic resources of knowledge and technology under fair and most favourable terms, including on concessional and preferential terms where agreed, in particular, knowledge and technology that make use of genetic resources, including biotechnology, or that are relevant to the conservation and sustainable utilization of biological diversity;
(g) Strengthening capacities for technology transfer;
(h) Institutional capacity-building;
(i) Human and material resources to strengthen the capacities for the administration and enforcement of access regulations;
(j) Training related to genetic resources with the full participation of countries providing genetic resources, and where possible, in such countries;
(k) Access to scientific information relevant to conservation and sustainable use of biological diversity, including biological inventories and taxonomic studies;
(l) Contributions to the local economy;
(m) Research directed towards priority needs, such as health and food security, taking into account domestic uses of genetic resources in the Party providing genetic resources;
(n) Institutional and professional relationships that can arise from an access and benefit-sharing agreement and subsequent collaborative activities;
(o) Food and livelihood security benefits;
(p) Social recognition;
(q) Joint ownership of relevant intellectual property rights.

BEIJING TREATY ON AUDIOVISUAL PERFORMANCES

Adopted by the Diplomatic Conference on June 24, 2013

NOTES

The original source of this Treaty is the World Intellectual Property Organisation (WIPO).

This Treaty will enter into force three months after 30 parties ratify the Treaty. See art 26 at **[9.674]**.

THE CONTRACTING PARTIES,

Desiring to develop and maintain the protection of the rights of performers in their audiovisual performances in a manner as effective and uniform as possible,

Recalling the importance of the Development Agenda recommendations, adopted in 2007 by the General Assembly of the Convention Establishing the World Intellectual Property Organization (WIPO), which aim to ensure that development considerations form an integral part of the Organization's work,

Recognizing the need to introduce new international rules in order to provide adequate solutions to the questions raised by economic, social, cultural and technological developments,

Recognizing the profound impact of the development and convergence of information and communication technologies on the production and use of audiovisual performances,

Recognizing the need to maintain a balance between the rights of performers in their audiovisual performances and the larger public interest, particularly education, research and access to information,

Recognizing that the WIPO Performances and Phonograms Treaty (WPPT) done in Geneva on December 20, 1996, does not extend protection to performers in respect of their performances fixed in audiovisual fixations,

Referring to the Resolution concerning Audiovisual Performances adopted by the Diplomatic Conference on Certain Copyright and Neighboring Rights Questions on December 20, 1996,

HAVE AGREED AS FOLLOWS:

[9.649]
Article 1
Relation to Other Conventions and Treaties

(1) Nothing in this Treaty shall derogate from existing obligations that Contracting Parties have to each other under the WPPT or the International Convention for the Protection of Performers, Producers of Phonograms and Broadcasting Organizations done in Rome on October 26, 1961.

(2) Protection granted under this Treaty shall leave intact and shall in no way affect the protection of copyright in literary and artistic works. Consequently, no provision of this Treaty may be interpreted as prejudicing such protection.

(3) This Treaty shall not have any connection with treaties other than the WPPT, nor shall it prejudice any rights and obligations under any other treaties.[1,2]

NOTES

1 Agreed statement concerning Article 1: It is understood that nothing in this Treaty affects any rights or obligations under the WIPO Performances and Phonograms Treaty (WPPT) or their interpretation and it is further understood that

paragraph 3 does not create any obligations for a Contracting Party to this Treaty to ratify or accede to the WPPT or to comply with any of its provisions.

[2] Agreed statement concerning Article 1(3): It is understood that Contracting Parties who are members of the World Trade Organization (WTO) acknowledge all the principles and objectives of the Agreement on Trade-Related Aspects of Intellectual Property Rights (TRIPS Agreement) and understand that nothing in this Treaty affects the provisions of the TRIPS Agreement, including, but not limited to, the provisions relating to anti-competitive practices.

[9.650]
Article 2
Definitions

For the purposes of this Treaty:

(a) "performers" are actors, singers, musicians, dancers, and other persons who act, sing, deliver, declaim, play in, interpret, or otherwise perform literary or artistic works or expressions of folklore;[3]

(b) "audiovisual fixation" means the embodiment of moving images, whether or not accompanied by sounds or by the representations thereof, from which they can be perceived, reproduced or communicated through a device;[4]

(c) "broadcasting" means the transmission by wireless means for public reception of sounds or of images or of images and sounds or of the representations thereof; such transmission by satellite is also "broadcasting"; transmission of encrypted signals is "broadcasting" where the means for decrypting are provided to the public by the broadcasting organization or with its consent;

(d) "communication to the public" of a performance means the transmission to the public by any medium, otherwise than by broadcasting, of an unfixed performance, or of a performance fixed in an audiovisual fixation. For the purposes of Article 11, "communication to the public" includes making a performance fixed in an audiovisual fixation audible or visible or audible and visible to the public.

NOTES

[3] Agreed statement concerning Article 2(a): It is understood that the definition of "performers" includes those who perform a literary or artistic work that is created or first fixed in the course of a performance.

[4] Agreed statement concerning Article 2(b): It is hereby confirmed that the definition of "audiovisual fixation" contained in Article 2(b) is without prejudice to Article 2(c) of the WPPT.

[9.651]
Article 3
Beneficiaries of Protection

(1) Contracting Parties shall accord the protection granted under this Treaty to performers who are nationals of other Contracting Parties.

(2) Performers who are not nationals of one of the Contracting Parties but who have their habitual residence in one of them shall, for the purposes of this Treaty, be assimilated to nationals of that Contracting Party.

[9.652]
Article 4
National Treatment

(1) Each Contracting Party shall accord to nationals of other Contracting Parties the treatment it accords to its own nationals with regard to the exclusive rights specifically granted in this Treaty and the right to equitable remuneration provided for in Article 11 of this Treaty.

(2) A Contracting Party shall be entitled to limit the extent and term of the protection accorded to nationals of another Contracting Party under paragraph (1), with respect to the rights granted in Article 11(1) and 11(2) of this Treaty, to those rights that its own nationals enjoy in that other Contracting Party.

(3) The obligation provided for in paragraph (1) does not apply to a Contracting Party to the extent that another Contracting Party makes use of the reservations permitted by Article 11(3) of this Treaty, nor does it apply to a Contracting Party, to the extent that it has made such reservation.

[9.653]
Article 5
Moral Rights

(1) Independently of a performer's economic rights, and even after the transfer of those rights, the performer shall, as regards his live performances or performances fixed in audiovisual fixations, have the right:

(i) to claim to be identified as the performer of his performances, except where omission is dictated by the manner of the use of the performance; and

(ii) to object to any distortion, mutilation or other modification of his performances that would be prejudicial to his reputation, taking due account of the nature of audiovisual fixations.

(2) The rights granted to a performer in accordance with paragraph (1) shall, after his death, be maintained, at least until the expiry of the economic rights, and shall be exercisable by the persons or institutions authorized by the legislation of the Contracting Party where protection is claimed. However, those Contracting Parties whose legislation, at the moment of their ratification of or accession to this Treaty, does not provide for protection after the death of the performer of all rights set out in the preceding paragraph may provide that some of these rights will, after his death, cease to be maintained.

(3) The means of redress for safeguarding the rights granted under this Article shall be governed by the legislation of the Contracting Party where protection is claimed.[5]

NOTES

[5] Agreed statement concerning Article 5: For the purposes of this Treaty and without prejudice to any other treaty, it is understood that, considering the nature of audiovisual fixations and their production and distribution, modifications of a performance that are made in the normal course of exploitation of the performance, such as editing, compression, dubbing, or formatting, in existing or new media or formats, and that are made in the course of a use authorized by the performer, would not in themselves amount to modifications within the meaning of Article 5(1)(ii). Rights under Article 5(1)(ii) are concerned only with changes that are objectively prejudicial to the performer's reputation in a substantial way. It is also understood that the mere use of new or changed technology or media, as such, does not amount to modification within the meaning of Article 5(1)(ii).

[9.654]
Article 6
Economic Rights of Performers in their Unfixed Performances

Performers shall enjoy the exclusive right of authorizing, as regards their performances:

(i) the broadcasting and communication to the public of their unfixed performances except where the performance is already a broadcast performance; and
(ii) the fixation of their unfixed performances.

[9.655]
Article 7
Right of Reproduction

Performers shall enjoy the exclusive right of authorizing the direct or indirect reproduction of their performances fixed in audiovisual fixations, in any manner or form.[6]

NOTES

[6] Agreed statement concerning Article 7: The reproduction right, as set out in Article 7, and the exceptions permitted thereunder through Article 13, fully apply in the digital environment, in particular to the use of performances in digital form. It is understood that the storage of a protected performance in digital form in an electronic medium constitutes a reproduction within the meaning of this Article.

[9.656]
Article 8
Right of Distribution

(1) Performers shall enjoy the exclusive right of authorizing the making available to the public of the original and copies of their performances fixed in audiovisual fixations through sale or other transfer of ownership.

(2) Nothing in this Treaty shall affect the freedom of Contracting Parties to determine the conditions, if any, under which the exhaustion of the right in paragraph (1) applies after the first sale or other transfer of ownership of the original or a copy of the fixed performance with the authorization of the performer.[7]

NOTES

[7] Agreed statement concerning Articles 8 and 9: As used in these Articles, the expression "original and copies," being subject to the right of distribution and the right of rental under the said Articles, refers exclusively to fixed copies that can be put into circulation as tangible objects.

[9.657]
Article 9
Right of Rental

(1) Performers shall enjoy the exclusive right of authorizing the commercial rental to the public of the original and copies of their performances fixed in audiovisual fixations as determined in the national law of Contracting Parties, even after distribution of them by, or pursuant to, authorization by the performer.

(2) Contracting Parties are exempt from the obligation of paragraph (1) unless the commercial rental has led to widespread copying of such fixations materially impairing the exclusive right of reproduction of performers.[8]

NOTES

[8] Agreed statement concerning Articles 8 and 9: As used in these Articles, the expression "original and copies," being subject to the right of distribution and the right of rental under the said Articles, refers exclusively to fixed copies that

can be put into circulation as tangible objects.

[9.658]
Article 10
Right of Making Available of Fixed Performances

Performers shall enjoy the exclusive right of authorizing the making available to the public of their performances fixed in audiovisual fixations, by wire or wireless means, in such a way that members of the public may access them from a place and at a time individually chosen by them.

[9.659]
Article 11
Right of Broadcasting and Communication to the Public

(1) Performers shall enjoy the exclusive right of authorizing the broadcasting and communication to the public of their performances fixed in audiovisual fixations.

(2) Contracting Parties may in a notification deposited with the Director General of WIPO declare that, instead of the right of authorization provided for in paragraph (1), they will establish a right to equitable remuneration for the direct or indirect use of performances fixed in audiovisual fixations for broadcasting or for communication to the public. Contracting Parties may also declare that they will set conditions in their legislation for the exercise of the right to equitable remuneration.

(3) Any Contracting Party may declare that it will apply the provisions of paragraphs (1) or (2) only in respect of certain uses, or that it will limit their application in some other way, or that it will not apply the provisions of paragraphs (1) and (2) at all.

[9.660]
Article 12
Transfer of Rights

(1) A Contracting Party may provide in its national law that once a performer has consented to fixation of his or her performance in an audiovisual fixation, the exclusive rights of authorization provided for in Articles 7 to 11 of this Treaty shall be owned or exercised by or transferred to the producer of such audiovisual fixation subject to any contract to the contrary between the performer and the producer of the audiovisual fixation as determined by the national law.

(2) A Contracting Party may require with respect to audiovisual fixations produced under its national law that such consent or contract be in writing and signed by both parties to the contract or by their duly authorized representatives.

(3) Independent of the transfer of exclusive rights described above, national laws or individual, collective or other agreements may provide the performer with the right to receive royalties or equitable remuneration for any use of the performance, as provided for under this Treaty including as regards Articles 10 and 11.

[9.661]
Article 13
Limitations and Exceptions

(1) Contracting Parties may, in their national legislation, provide for the same kinds of limitations or exceptions with regard to the protection of performers as they provide for, in their national legislation, in connection with the protection of copyright in literary and artistic works.

(2) Contracting Parties shall confine any limitations of or exceptions to rights provided for in this Treaty to certain special cases which do not conflict with a normal exploitation of the performance and do not unreasonably prejudice the legitimate interests of the performer.[9]

NOTES

[9] Agreed statement concerning Article 13: The Agreed statement concerning Article 10 (on Limitations and Exceptions) of the WIPO Copyright Treaty (WCT) is applicable *mutatis mutandis* also to Article 13 (on Limitations and Exceptions) of the Treaty.

[9.662]
Article 14
Term of Protection

The term of protection to be granted to performers under this Treaty shall last, at least, until the end of a period of 50 years computed from the end of the year in which the performance was fixed.

[9.663]
Article 15
Obligations concerning Technological Measures

Contracting Parties shall provide adequate legal protection and effective legal remedies against the circumvention of effective technological measures that are used by performers in connection with the exercise of their rights under this Treaty and that restrict acts, in respect of their performances, which are not authorized by the performers concerned or permitted by law.[10,11]

NOTES

[10] Agreed statement concerning Article 15 as it relates to Article 13: It is understood that nothing in this Article prevents a Contracting Party from adopting effective and necessary measures to ensure that a beneficiary may enjoy limitations and exceptions provided in that Contracting Party's national law, in accordance with Article 13, where technological measures have been applied to an audiovisual performance and the beneficiary has legal access to that performance, in circumstances such as where appropriate and effective measures have not been taken by rights holders in relation to that performance to enable the beneficiary to enjoy the limitations and exceptions under that Contracting Party's national law. Without prejudice to the legal protection of an audiovisual work in which a performance is fixed, it is further understood that the obligations under Article 15 are not applicable to performances unprotected or no longer protected under the national law giving effect to this Treaty.

[11] Agreed statement concerning Article 15: The expression "technological measures used by performers" should, as this is the case regarding the WPPT, be construed broadly, referring also to those acting on behalf of performers, including their representatives, licensees or assignees, including producers, service providers, and persons engaged in communication or broadcasting using performances on the basis of due authorization.

[9.664]
Article 16
Obligations concerning Rights Management Information

(1) Contracting Parties shall provide adequate and effective legal remedies against any person knowingly performing any of the following acts knowing, or with respect to civil remedies having reasonable grounds to know, that it will induce, enable, facilitate, or conceal an infringement of any right covered by this Treaty:

(i) to remove or alter any electronic rights management information without authority;

(ii) to distribute, import for distribution, broadcast, communicate or make available to the public, without authority, performances or copies of performances fixed in audiovisual fixations knowing that electronic rights management information has been removed or altered without authority.

(2) As used in this Article, "rights management information" means information which identifies the performer, the performance of the performer, or the owner of any right in the performance, or information about the terms and conditions of use of the performance, and any numbers or codes that represent such information, when any of these items of information is attached to a performance fixed in an audiovisual fixation.[12]

NOTES

[12] Agreed statement concerning Article 16: The Agreed statement concerning Article 12 (on Obligations concerning Rights Management Information) of the WCT is applicable *mutatis mutandis* also to Article 16 (on Obligations concerning Rights Management Information) of the Treaty.

[9.665]
Article 17
Formalities

The enjoyment and exercise of the rights provided for in this Treaty shall not be subject to any formality.

[9.666]
Article 18
Reservations and Notifications

(1) Subject to provisions of Article 11(3), no reservations to this Treaty shall be permitted.

(2) Any notification under Article 11(2) or 19(2) may be made in instruments of ratification or accession, and the effective date of the notification shall be the same as the date of entry into force of this Treaty with respect to the Contracting Party having made the notification. Any such notification may also be made later, in which case the notification shall have effect three months after its receipt by the Director General of WIPO or at any later date indicated in the notification.

[9.667]
Article 19
Application in Time

(1) Contracting Parties shall accord the protection granted under this Treaty to fixed performances that exist at the moment of the entry into force of this Treaty and to all performances that occur after the entry into force of this Treaty for each Contracting Party.

(2) Notwithstanding the provisions of paragraph (1), a Contracting Party may declare in a notification deposited with the Director General of WIPO that it will not apply the provisions of Articles 7 to 11 of this Treaty, or any one or more of those, to fixed performances that existed at the moment of the entry into force of this Treaty for each Contracting Party. In respect of such Contracting Party, other Contracting Parties may limit the application of the said Articles to performances that occurred after the entry into force of this Treaty for that Contracting Party.

(3) The protection provided for in this Treaty shall be without prejudice to any acts committed, agreements concluded or rights acquired before the entry into force of this Treaty for each Contracting Party.

(4) Contracting Parties may in their legislation establish transitional provisions under which any person who, prior to the entry into force of this Treaty, engaged in lawful acts with respect to a performance, may undertake with respect to the same performance acts within the scope of the rights provided for in Articles 5 and 7 to 11 after the entry into force of this Treaty for the respective Contracting Parties.

[9.668]
Article 20
Provisions on Enforcement of Rights

(1) Contracting Parties undertake to adopt, in accordance with their legal systems, the measures necessary to ensure the application of this Treaty.
(2) Contracting Parties shall ensure that enforcement procedures are available under their law so as to permit effective action against any act of infringement of rights covered by this Treaty, including expeditious remedies to prevent infringements and remedies which constitute a deterrent to further infringements.

[9.669]
Article 21
Assembly

(1)
(a) The Contracting Parties shall have an Assembly.
(b) Each Contracting Party shall be represented in the Assembly by one delegate who may be assisted by alternate delegates, advisors and experts.
(c) The expenses of each delegation shall be borne by the Contracting Party that has appointed the delegation. The Assembly may ask WIPO to grant financial assistance to facilitate the participation of delegations of Contracting Parties that are regarded as developing countries in conformity with the established practice of the General Assembly of the United Nations or that are countries in transition to a market economy.

(2)
(a) The Assembly shall deal with matters concerning the maintenance and development of this Treaty and the application and operation of this Treaty.
(b) The Assembly shall perform the function allocated to it under Article 23(2) in respect of the admission of certain intergovernmental organizations to become party to this Treaty.
(c) The Assembly shall decide the convocation of any diplomatic conference for the revision of this Treaty and give the necessary instructions to the Director General of WIPO for the preparation of such diplomatic conference.

(3)
(a) Each Contracting Party that is a State shall have one vote and shall vote only in its own name.
(b) Any Contracting Party that is an intergovernmental organization may participate in the vote, in place of its Member States, with a number of votes equal to the number of its Member States which are party to this Treaty. No such intergovernmental organization shall participate in the vote if any one of its Member States exercises its right to vote and vice versa.

(4) The Assembly shall meet upon convocation by the Director General and, in the absence of exceptional circumstances, during the same period and at the same place as the General Assembly of WIPO.
(5) The Assembly shall endeavor to take its decisions by consensus and shall establish its own rules of procedure, including the convocation of extraordinary sessions, the requirements of a quorum and, subject to the provisions of this Treaty, the required majority for various kinds of decisions.

[9.670]
Article 22
International Bureau

The International Bureau of WIPO shall perform the administrative tasks concerning the Treaty.

[9.671]
Article 23
Eligibility for Becoming Party to the Treaty

(1) Any Member State of WIPO may become party to this Treaty.
(2) The Assembly may decide to admit any intergovernmental organization to become party to this Treaty which declares that it is competent in respect of, and has its own legislation binding on all its Member States on, matters covered by this Treaty and that it has been duly authorized, in accordance with its internal procedures, to become party to this Treaty.
(3) The European Union, having made the declaration referred to in the preceding paragraph in the Diplomatic Conference that has adopted this Treaty, may become party to this Treaty.

[9.672]
Article 24
Rights and Obligations under the Treaty

Subject to any specific provisions to the contrary in this Treaty, each Contracting Party shall enjoy all of the rights and assume all of the obligations under this Treaty.

[9.673]
Article 25
Signature of the Treaty

This Treaty shall be open for signature at the headquarters of WIPO by any eligible party for one year after its adoption.

[9.674]
Article 26
Entry into Force of the Treaty

This Treaty shall enter into force three months after 30 eligible parties referred to in Article 23 have deposited their instruments of ratification or accession.

[9.675]
Article 27
Effective Date of Becoming Party to the Treaty

This Treaty shall bind:

(i) the 30 eligible parties referred to in Article 26, from the date on which this Treaty has entered into force;

(ii) each other eligible party referred to in Article 23, from the expiration of three months from the date on which it has deposited its instrument of ratification or accession with the Director General of WIPO.

[9.676]
Article 28
Denunciation of the Treaty

This Treaty may be denounced by any Contracting Party by notification addressed to the Director General of WIPO. Any denunciation shall take effect one year from the date on which the Director General of WIPO received the notification.

[9.677]
Article 29
Languages of the Treaty

(1) This Treaty is signed in a single original in English, Arabic, Chinese, French, Russian and Spanish languages, the versions in all these languages being equally authentic.

(2) An official text in any language other than those referred to in paragraph (1) shall be established by the Director General of WIPO on the request of an interested party, after consultation with all the interested parties. For the purposes of this paragraph, "interested party" means any Member State of WIPO whose official language, or one of whose official languages, is involved and the European Union, and any other intergovernmental organization that may become party to this Treaty, if one of its official languages is involved.

[9.678]
Article 30
Depositary

The Director General of WIPO is the depositary of this Treaty.

MARRAKESH TREATY TO FACILITATE ACCESS TO PUBLISHED WORKS FOR PERSONS WHO ARE BLIND, VISUALLY IMPAIRED, OR OTHERWISE PRINT DISABLED

Adopted by the Diplomatic Conference on June 27, 2013

NOTES

The original source of this Treaty is the World Intellectual Property Organisation (WIPO).

This Treaty will enter into force three months after 20 parties ratify the Treaty. See art 18 at **[9.696]**.

THE CONTRACTING PARTIES,

Recalling the principles of non-discrimination, equal opportunity, accessibility and full and effective participation and inclusion in society, proclaimed in the Universal Declaration of Human Rights and the United Nations Convention on the Rights of Persons with Disabilities,

Mindful of the challenges that are prejudicial to the complete development of persons with visual impairments or with other print disabilities, which limit their freedom of expression, including the freedom to seek, receive and impart information and ideas of all kinds on an equal basis with others, including through all forms of communication of their choice, their enjoyment of the right to education, and the opportunity to conduct research,

Emphasizing the importance of copyright protection as an incentive and reward for literary and artistic creations and of enhancing opportunities for everyone, including persons with visual impairments or with other print disabilities, to participate in the cultural life of the community, to enjoy the arts and to share scientific progress and its benefits,

Aware of the barriers of persons with visual impairments or with other print disabilities to access published works in achieving equal opportunities in society, and the need to both expand the number of works in accessible formats and to improve the circulation of such works,

Taking into account that the majority of persons with visual impairments or with other print disabilities live in developing and least-developed countries,

Recognizing that, despite the differences in national copyright laws, the positive impact of new information and communication technologies on the lives of persons with visual impairments or with other print disabilities may be reinforced by an enhanced legal framework at the international level,

Recognizing that many Member States have established limitations and exceptions in their national copyright laws for persons with visual impairments or with other print disabilities, yet there is a continuing shortage of available works in accessible format copies for such persons, and that considerable resources are required for their effort of making works accessible to these persons, and that the lack of possibilities of cross-border exchange of accessible format copies has necessitated duplication of these efforts,

Recognizing both the importance of rightholders' role in making their works accessible to persons with visual impairments or with other print disabilities and the importance of appropriate limitations and exceptions to make works accessible to these persons, particularly when the market is unable to provide such access,

Recognizing the need to maintain a balance between the effective protection of the rights of authors and the larger public interest, particularly education, research and access to information, and that such a balance must facilitate effective and timely access to works for the benefit of persons with visual impairments or with other print disabilities,

Reaffirming the obligations of Contracting Parties under the existing international treaties on the protection of copyright and the importance and flexibility of the three-step test for limitations and exceptions established in Article 9(2) of the Berne Convention for the Protection of Literary and Artistic Works and other international instruments,

Recalling the importance of the Development Agenda recommendations, adopted in 2007 by the General Assembly of the World Intellectual Property Organization (WIPO), which aim to ensure that development considerations form an integral part of the Organization's work,

Recognizing the importance of the international copyright system and desiring to harmonize limitations and exceptions with a view to facilitating access to and use of works by persons with visual impairments or with other print disabilities.

HAVE AGREED AS FOLLOWS:

[9.679]
Article 1
Relation to other Conventions and Treaties

Nothing in this treaty shall derogate from any obligations that Contracting Parties have to each other under any other treaties, nor shall it prejudice any rights that a Contracting Party has under any other treaties.

[9.680]
Article 2
Definitions

For the purposes of this Treaty:

(a) "works" means literary and artistic works within the meaning of Article 2(1) of the Berne Convention for the Protection of Literary and Artistic Works, in the form of text, notation and/or related illustrations, whether published or otherwise made publicly available in any media;[1]

(b) "accessible format copy" means a copy of a work in an alternative manner or form which gives a beneficiary person access to the work, including to permit the person to have access as feasibly and comfortably as a person without visual impairment or other print disability. The accessible format copy is used exclusively by beneficiary persons and it must respect the integrity of the original work, taking due consideration of the changes needed to make the work accessible in the alternative format and of the accessibility needs of the beneficiary persons;

(c) "authorized entity" means an entity that is authorized or recognized by the government to provide education, instructional training, adaptive reading or information access to beneficiary persons on a non-profit basis. It also includes a government institution or non-profit organization that provides the same services to beneficiary persons as one of its primary activities or institutional obligations.[2]

An authorized entity establishes and follows its own practices:

(i) to establish that the persons it serves are beneficiary persons;

(ii) to limit to beneficiary persons and/or authorized entities its distribution and making available of accessible format copies;

(iii) to discourage the reproduction, distribution and making available of unauthorized copies; and

(iv) to maintain due care in, and records of, its handling of copies of works, while respecting the privacy of beneficiary persons in accordance with Article 8.

NOTES

1 Agreed statement concerning Article 2(a): For the purposes of this Treaty, it is understood that this definition includes such works in audio form, such as audiobooks.

2 Agreed statement concerning Article 2(c): For the purposes of this Treaty, it is understood that "entities recognized by the government" may include entities receiving financial support from the government to provide education, instructional training, adaptive reading or information access to beneficiary persons on a non-profit basis.

[9.681]
Article 3
Beneficiary Persons

A beneficiary person is a person who:

(a) is blind;

(b) has a visual impairment or a perceptual or reading disability which cannot be improved to give visual function substantially equivalent to that of a person who has no such impairment or disability and so is unable to read printed works to substantially the same degree as a person without an impairment or disability; or[3]

(c) is otherwise unable, through physical disability, to hold or manipulate a book or to focus or move the eyes to the extent that would be normally acceptable for reading;

regardless of any other disabilities.

NOTES

3 Agreed statement concerning Article 3(b): Nothing in this language implies that "cannot be improved" requires the use of all possible medical diagnostic procedures and treatments.

[9.682]
Article 4
National Law Limitations and Exceptions Regarding Accessible Format Copies

1.

(a) Contracting Parties shall provide in their national copyright laws for a limitation or exception to the right of reproduction, the right of distribution, and the right of making available to the public as provided by the WIPO Copyright Treaty (WCT), to facilitate the availability of works in accessible format copies for beneficiary persons. The limitation or exception provided in national law should permit changes needed to make the work accessible in the alternative format.

(b) Contracting Parties may also provide a limitation or exception to the right of public performance to facilitate access to works for beneficiary persons.

2. A Contracting Party may fulfill Article 4(1) for all rights identified therein by providing a limitation or exception in its national copyright law such that:

(a) Authorized entities shall be permitted, without the authorization of the copyright rightholder, to make an accessible format copy of a work, obtain from another authorized entity an accessible format copy, and supply those copies to beneficiary persons by any means, including by non-commercial lending or by electronic communication by wire or wireless means, and undertake any intermediate steps to achieve those objectives, when all of the following conditions are met:

(i) the authorized entity wishing to undertake said activity has lawful access to that work or a copy of that work;

(ii) the work is converted to an accessible format copy, which may include any means needed to navigate information in the accessible format, but does not introduce changes other than those needed to make the work accessible to the beneficiary person;

(iii) such accessible format copies are supplied exclusively to be used by beneficiary persons; and

(iv) the activity is undertaken on a non-profit basis;

and

(b) A beneficiary person, or someone acting on his or her behalf including a primary caretaker or caregiver, may make an accessible format copy of a work for the personal use of the beneficiary person or otherwise may assist the beneficiary person to make and use accessible format copies where the beneficiary person has lawful access to that work or a copy of that work.

3. A Contracting Party may fulfill Article 4(1) by providing other limitations or exceptions in its national copyright law pursuant to Articles 10 and 11.[4]
4. A Contracting Party may confine limitations or exceptions under this Article to works which, in the particular accessible format, cannot be obtained commercially under reasonable terms for beneficiary persons in that market. Any Contracting Party availing itself of this possibility shall so declare in a notification deposited with the Director General of WIPO at the time of ratification of, acceptance of or accession to this Treaty or at any time thereafter.[5]
5. It shall be a matter for national law to determine whether limitations or exceptions under this Article are subject to remuneration.

NOTES

4 Agreed Statement concerning Article 4(3): It is understood that this paragraph neither reduces nor extends the scope of applicability of limitations and exceptions permitted under the Berne Convention, as regards the right of translation, with respect to persons with visual impairments or with other print disabilities.

5 Agreed Statement concerning Article 4(4): It is understood that a commercial availability requirement does not prejudge whether or not a limitation or exception under this Article is consistent with the three-step test.

[9.683]
Article 5
Cross-Border Exchange of Accessible Format Copies

1. Contracting Parties shall provide that if an accessible format copy is made under a limitation or exception or pursuant to operation of law, that accessible format copy may be distributed or made available by an authorized entity to a beneficiary person or an authorized entity in another Contracting Party.[6]
2. A Contracting Party may fulfill Article 5(1) by providing a limitation or exception in its national copyright law such that:
   (a) authorized entities shall be permitted, without the authorization of the rightholder, to distribute or make available for the exclusive use of beneficiary persons accessible format copies to an authorized entity in another Contracting Party; and
   (b) authorized entities shall be permitted, without the authorization of the rightholder and pursuant to Article 2, to distribute or make available accessible format copies to a beneficiary person in another Contracting Party;

provided that prior to the distribution or making available the originating authorized entity did not know or have reasonable grounds to know that the accessible format copy would be used for other than beneficiary persons.[7]
3. A Contracting Party may fulfill Article 5(1) by providing other limitations or exceptions in its national copyright law pursuant to Articles 5(4), 10 and 11.
4.
   (a) When an authorized entity in a Contracting Party receives accessible format copies pursuant to Article 5(1) and that Contracting Party does not have obligations under Article 9 of the Berne Convention, it will ensure, consistent with its own legal system and practices, that the accessible format copies are only reproduced, distributed or made available for the benefit of beneficiary persons in that Contracting Party's jurisdiction.
   (b) The distribution and making available of accessible format copies by an authorized entity pursuant to Article 5(1) shall be limited to that jurisdiction unless the Contracting Party is a Party to the WIPO Copyright Treaty or otherwise limits limitations and exceptions implementing this Treaty to the right of distribution and the right of making available to the public to certain special cases which do not conflict with a normal exploitation of the work and do not unreasonably prejudice the legitimate interests of the rightholder.[8, 9]
   (c) Nothing in this Article affects the determination of what constitutes an act of distribution or an act of making available to the public.
5. Nothing in this Treaty shall be used to address the issue of exhaustion of rights.

NOTES

6 Agreed statement concerning Article 5(1): It is further understood that nothing in this Treaty reduces or extends the scope of exclusive rights under any other treaty.

7 Agreed statement concerning Article 5(2): It is understood that, to distribute or make available accessible format copies directly to a beneficiary person in another Contracting Party, it may be appropriate for an authorized entity to apply further measures to confirm that the person it is serving is a beneficiary person and to follow its own practices as described in Article 2.

8 Agreed statement concerning Article 5(4)(b): It is understood that nothing in this Treaty requires or implies that a Contracting Party adopt or apply the three-step test beyond its obligations under this instrument or under other international treaties.

9 Agreed statement concerning Article 5(4)(b): It is understood that nothing in this Treaty creates any obligations for a Contracting Party to ratify or accede to the WCT or to comply with any of its provisions and nothing in this Treaty prejudices any rights, limitations and exceptions contained in the WCT.

[9.684]
Article 6
Importation of Accessible Format Copies

To the extent that the national law of a Contracting Party would permit a beneficiary person, someone acting on his or her behalf, or an authorized entity, to make an accessible format copy of a work, the national law of that Contracting Party shall also permit them to import an accessible format copy for the benefit of beneficiary persons, without the authorization of the rightholder.[10]

NOTES

10 Agreed statement concerning Article 6: It is understood that the Contracting Parties have the same flexibilities set out in Article 4 when implementing their obligations under Article 6.

[9.685]
Article 7
Obligations Concerning Technological Measures

Contracting Parties shall take appropriate measures, as necessary, to ensure that when they provide adequate legal protection and effective legal remedies against the circumvention of effective technological measures, this legal protection does not prevent beneficiary persons from enjoying the limitations and exceptions provided for in this Treaty.[11]

NOTES

11 Agreed statement concerning Article 7: It is understood that authorized entities, in various circumstances, choose to apply technological measures in the making, distribution and making available of accessible format copies and nothing herein disturbs such practices when in accordance with national law.

[9.686]
Article 8
Respect for Privacy

In the implementation of the limitations and exceptions provided for in this Treaty, Contracting Parties shall endeavor to protect the privacy of beneficiary persons on an equal basis with others.

[9.687]
Article 9
Cooperation to Facilitate Cross-Border Exchange

1. Contracting Parties shall endeavor to foster the cross-border exchange of accessible format copies by encouraging the voluntary sharing of information to assist authorized entities in identifying one another. The International Bureau of WIPO shall establish an information access point for this purpose.
2. Contracting Parties undertake to assist their authorized entities engaged in activities under Article 5 to make information available regarding their practices pursuant to Article)2, both through the sharing of information among authorized entities, and through making available information on their policies and practices, including related to cross-border exchange of accessible format copies, to interested parties and members of the public as appropriate.
3. The International Bureau of WIPO is invited to share information, where available, about the functioning of this Treaty.
4. Contracting Parties recognize the importance of international cooperation and its promotion, in support of national efforts for realization of the purpose and objectives of this Treaty.[12]

NOTES

12 Agreed statement concerning Article 9: It is understood that Article 9 does not imply mandatory registration for authorized entities nor does it constitute a precondition for authorized entities to engage in activities recognized under this Treaty; but it provides for a possibility for sharing information to facilitate the cross-border exchange of accessible format copies.

[9.688]
Article 10
General Principles on Implementation

1. Contracting Parties undertake to adopt the measures necessary to ensure the application of this Treaty.
2. Nothing shall prevent Contracting Parties from determining the appropriate method of implementing the provisions of this Treaty within their own legal system and practice.[13]
3. Contracting Parties may fulfill their rights and obligations under this Treaty through limitations or exceptions specifically for the benefit of beneficiary persons, other limitations or exceptions, or a combination thereof, within their national legal system and practice. These may include judicial, administrative or regulatory determinations for the benefit of beneficiary persons as to fair practices, dealings or uses to meet their needs consistent with the Contracting Parties' rights and obligations under the Berne Convention, other international treaties, and Article 11.

NOTES

[13] Agreed Statement concerning Article 10(2): It is understood that when a work qualifies as a work under Article 2, including such works in audio form, the limitations and exceptions provided for by this Treaty apply *mutatis mutandis* to related rights as necessary to make the accessible format copy, to distribute it and to make it available to beneficiary persons.

[9.689]
Article 11
General Obligations on Limitations and Exceptions

In adopting measures necessary to ensure the application of this Treaty, a Contracting Party may exercise the rights and shall comply with the obligations that that Contracting Party has under the Berne Convention, the Agreement on Trade-Related Aspects of Intellectual Property Rights and the WCT, including their interpretative agreements so that:

1. in accordance with Article 9(2) of the Berne Convention, a Contracting Party may permit the reproduction of works in certain special cases provided that such reproduction does not conflict with a normal exploitation of the work and does not unreasonably prejudice the legitimate interests of the author;
2. in accordance with Article 13 of the Agreement on Trade-Related Aspects of Intellectual Property Rights, a Contracting Party shall confine limitations or exceptions to exclusive rights to certain special cases which do not conflict with a normal exploitation of the work and do not unreasonably prejudice the legitimate interests of the rightholder;
3. in accordance with Article 10(1) of the WIPO Copyright Treaty, a Contracting Party may provide for limitations of or exceptions to the rights granted to authors under the WCT in certain special cases, that do not conflict with a normal exploitation of the work and do not unreasonably prejudice the legitimate interests of the author;
4. in accordance with Article 10(2) of the WIPO Copyright Treaty, a Contracting Party shall confine, when applying the Berne Convention, any limitations of or exceptions to rights to certain special cases that do not conflict with a normal exploitation of the work and do not unreasonably prejudice the legitimate interests of the author.

[9.690]
Article 12
Other Limitations and Exceptions

1. Contracting Parties recognize that a Contracting Party may implement in its national law other copyright limitations and exceptions for the benefit of beneficiary persons than are provided by this Treaty having regard to that Contracting Party's economic situation, and its social and cultural needs, in conformity with that Contracting Party's international rights and obligations, and in the case of a least-developed country taking into account its special needs and its particular international rights and obligations and flexibilities thereof.
2. This Treaty is without prejudice to other limitations and exceptions for persons with disabilities provided by national law.

[9.691]
Article 13
Assembly

1

(a) The Contracting Parties shall have an Assembly.
(b) Each Contracting Party shall be represented in the Assembly by one delegate who may be assisted by alternate delegates, advisors and experts.
(c) The expenses of each delegation shall be borne by the Contracting Party that has appointed the delegation. The Assembly may ask WIPO to grant financial assistance to facilitate the participation of delegations of Contracting Parties that are regarded as developing countries in conformity with the established practice of the General Assembly of the United Nations or that are countries in transition to a market economy.

2

(a) The Assembly shall deal with matters concerning the maintenance and development of this Treaty and the application and operation of this Treaty.
(b) The Assembly shall perform the function allocated to it under Article 15 in respect of the admission of certain intergovernmental organizations to become party to this Treaty.
(c) The Assembly shall decide the convocation of any diplomatic conference for the revision of this Treaty and give the necessary instructions to the Director General of WIPO for the preparation of such diplomatic conference.

3

(a) Each Contracting Party that is a State shall have one vote and shall vote only in its own name.
(b) Any Contracting Party that is an intergovernmental organization may participate in the vote, in place of its Member States, with a number of votes equal to the number of its

Member States which are party to this Treaty. No such intergovernmental organization shall participate in the vote if any one of its Member States exercises its right to vote and vice versa.

4 The Assembly shall meet upon convocation by the Director General and, in the absence of exceptional circumstances, during the same period and at the same place as the General Assembly of WIPO.

5 The Assembly shall endeavor to take its decisions by consensus and shall establish its own rules of procedure, including the convocation of extraordinary sessions, the requirements of a quorum and, subject to the provisions of this Treaty, the required majority for various kinds of decisions.

[9.692]
Article 14
International Bureau

The International Bureau of WIPO shall perform the administrative tasks concerning this Treaty.

[9.693]
Article 15
Eligibility for Becoming Party to the Treaty

(1) Any Member State of WIPO may become party to this Treaty.

(2) The Assembly may decide to admit any intergovernmental organization to become party to this Treaty which declares that it is competent in respect of, and has its own legislation binding on all its Member States on, matters covered by this Treaty and that it has been duly authorized, in accordance with its internal procedures, to become party to this Treaty.

(3) The European Union, having made the declaration referred to in the preceding paragraph at the Diplomatic Conference that has adopted this Treaty, may become party to this Treaty.

[9.694]
Article 16
Rights and Obligations under the Treaty

Subject to any specific provisions to the contrary in this Treaty, each Contracting Party shall enjoy all of the rights and assume all of the obligations under this Treaty.

[9.695]
Article 17
Signature of the Treaty

This Treaty shall be open for signature at the Diplomatic Conference in Marrakesh, and thereafter at the headquarters of WIPO by any eligible party for one year after its adoption.

[9.696]
Article 18
Entry into Force of the Treaty

This Treaty shall enter into force three months after 20 eligible parties referred to in Article 15 have deposited their instruments of ratification or accession.

[9.697]
Article 19
Effective Date of Becoming Party to the Treaty

This Treaty shall bind:

(i) the 20 eligible parties referred to in Article 18, from the date on which this Treaty has entered into force;

(ii) each other eligible party referred to in Article 15, from the expiration of three months from the date on which it has deposited its instrument of ratification or accession with the Director General of WIPO.

[9.698]
Article 20
Denunciation of the Treaty

This Treaty may be denounced by any Contracting Party by notification addressed to the Director General of WIPO. Any denunciation shall take effect one year from the date on which the Director General of WIPO received the notification.

[9.699]
Article 21
Languages of the Treaty

(1) This Treaty is signed in a single original in English, Arabic, Chinese, French, Russian and Spanish languages, the versions in all these languages being equally authentic.

(2) An official text in any language other than those referred to in paragraph (1) shall be established by the Director General of WIPO on the request of an interested party, after consultation with all the interested parties. For the purposes of this paragraph, "interested party" means any

Member State of WIPO whose official language, or one of whose official languages, is involved and the European Union, and any other intergovernmental organization that may become party to this Treaty, if one of its official languages is involved.

[9.700]
Article 22
Depositary
The Director General of WIPO is the depositary of this Treaty.

GENEVA ACT OF THE LISBON AGREEMENT ON APPELLATIONS OF ORIGIN AND GEOGRAPHICAL INDICATIONS

(As adopted on May 20, 2015)

NOTES

The original source for this Act is the World Intellectual Property Organisation (WIPO).

CHAPTER I
INTRODUCTORY AND GENERAL PROVISIONS

[9.701]
Article 1
Abbreviated Expressions
For the purposes of this Act, unless expressly stated otherwise:

(i) "Lisbon Agreement" means the Lisbon Agreement for the Protection of Appellations of Origin and their International Registration of October 31, 1958;
(ii) "1967 Act" means the Lisbon Agreement as revised at Stockholm on July 14, 1967, and amended on September 28, 1979;
(iii) "this Act" means the Lisbon Agreement on Appellations of Origin and Geographical Indications, as established by the present Act;
(iv) "Regulations" means the Regulations as referred to in Article 25;
(v) "Paris Convention" means the Paris Convention for the Protection of Industrial Property of March 20, 1883, as revised and amended;
(vi) "appellation of origin" means a denomination as referred to in Article 2(1)(i);
(vii) "geographical indication" means an indication as referred to in Article 2(1)(ii);
(viii) "International Register" means the International Register maintained by the International Bureau in accordance with Article 4 as the official collection of data concerning international registrations of appellations of origin and geographical indications, regardless of the medium in which such data are maintained;
(ix) "international registration" means an international registration recorded in the International Register;
(x) "application" means an application for international registration;
(xi) "registered" means entered in the International Register in accordance with this Act;
(xii) "geographical area of origin" means a geographical area as referred to in Article 2(2);
(xiii) "trans-border geographical area" means a geographical area situated in, or covering, adjacent Contracting Parties;
(xiv) "Contracting Party" means any State or intergovernmental organization party to this Act;
(xv) "Contracting Party of Origin" means the Contracting Party where the geographical area of origin is situated or the Contracting Parties where the trans-border geographical area of origin is situated;
(xvi) "Competent Authority" means an entity designated in accordance with Article 3;
(xvii) "beneficiaries" means the natural persons or legal entities entitled under the law of the Contracting Party of Origin to use an appellation of origin or a geographical indication;
(xviii) "intergovernmental organization" means an intergovernmental organization eligible to become party to this Act in accordance with Article 28(1)(iii);
(xix) "Organization" means the World Intellectual Property Organization;
(xx) "Director General" means the Director General of the Organization;
(xxi) "International Bureau" means the International Bureau of the Organization.

[9.702]
Article 2
Subject-Matter
(1) *[Appellations of Origin and Geographical Indications]* This Act applies in respect of:

(i) any denomination protected in the Contracting Party of Origin consisting of or containing the name of a geographical area, or another denomination known as referring to such area, which serves to designate a good as originating in that geographical area, where the quality or characteristics of the good are due exclusively or essentially to the geographical environment, including natural and human factors, and which has given the good its reputation; as well as

(ii) any indication protected in the Contracting Party of Origin consisting of or containing the name of a geographical area, or another indication known as referring to such area, which identifies a good as originating in that geographical area, where a given quality, reputation or other characteristic of the good is essentially attributable to its geographical origin.

(2) *[Possible Geographical Areas of Origin]* A geographical area of origin as described in paragraph (1) may consist of the entire territory of the Contracting Party of Origin or a region, locality or place in the Contracting Party of Origin. This does not exclude the application of this Act in respect of a geographical area of origin, as described in paragraph (1), consisting of a trans-border geographical area, or a part thereof.

[9.703]
Article 3
Competent Authority

Each Contracting Party shall designate an entity which shall be responsible for the administration of this Act in its territory and for communications with the International Bureau under this Act and the Regulations. The Contracting Party shall notify the name and contact details of such Competent Authority to the International Bureau, as specified in the Regulations.

[9.704]
Article 4
International Register

The International Bureau shall maintain an International Register recording international registrations effected under this Act, under the Lisbon Agreement and the 1967 Act, or under both, and data relating to such international registrations.

CHAPTER II
APPLICATION AND INTERNATIONAL REGISTRATION

[9.705]
Article 5
Application

(1) *[Place of Filing]* Applications shall be filed with the International Bureau.

(2) *[Application Filed by Competent Authority]* Subject to paragraph (3), the application for the international registration of an appellation of origin or a geographical indication shall be filed by the Competent Authority in the name of:

(i) the beneficiaries; or

(ii) a natural person or legal entity having legal standing under the law of the Contracting Party of Origin to assert the rights of the beneficiaries or other rights in the appellation of origin or geographical indication.

(3) *[Application Filed Directly]*

(a) Without prejudice to paragraph (4), if the legislation of the Contracting Party of Origin so permits, the application may be filed by the beneficiaries or by a natural person or legal entity referred to in paragraph (2)(ii).

(b) Subparagraph (a) applies subject to a declaration from the Contracting Party that its legislation so permits. Such declaration may be made by the Contracting Party at the time of deposit of its instrument of ratification or accession or at any later time. Where the declaration is made at the time of the deposit of its instrument of ratification or accession, it shall take effect upon the entry into force of this Act with respect to that Contracting Party. Where the declaration is made after the entry into force of this Act with respect to the Contracting Party, it shall take effect three months after the date on which the Director General has received the declaration.

(4) *[Possible Joint Application in the Case of a Trans-border Geographical Area]* In case of a geographical area of origin consisting of a trans-border geographical area, the adjacent Contracting Parties may, in accordance with their agreement, file an application jointly through a commonly designated Competent Authority.

(5) *[Mandatory Contents]* The Regulations shall specify the mandatory particulars that must be included in the application, in addition to those specified in Article 6(3).

(6) *[Optional Contents]* The Regulations may specify the optional particulars that may be included in the application.

[9.706]
Article 6
International Registration

(1) *[Formal Examination by the International Bureau]* Upon receipt of an application for the international registration of an appellation of origin or a geographical indication in due form, as specified in the Regulations, the International Bureau shall register the appellation of origin, or the geographical indication, in the International Register.

(2) *[Date of International Registration]* Subject to paragraph (3), the date of the international registration shall be the date on which the application was received by the International Bureau.

(3) *[Date of International Registration Where Particulars Missing]* Where the application does not contain all the following particulars:

- (i) the identification of the Competent Authority or, in the case of Article 5(3), the applicant or applicants;
- (ii) the details identifying the beneficiaries and, where applicable, the natural person or legal entity referred to in Article 5(2)(ii);
- (iii) the appellation of origin, or the geographical indication, for which international registration is sought;
- (iv) the good or goods to which the appellation of origin, or the geographical indication, applies;

the date of the international registration shall be the date on which the last of the missing particulars is received by the International Bureau.

(4) *[Publication and Notification of International Registrations]* The International Bureau shall, without delay, publish each international registration and notify the Competent Authority of each Contracting Party of the international registration.

(5) *[Date of Effect of International Registration]*

- (a) Subject to subparagraph (b), a registered appellation of origin or geographical indication shall, in each Contracting Party that has not refused protection in accordance with Article 15, or that has sent to the International Bureau a notification of grant of protection in accordance with Article 18, be protected from the date of the international registration.
- (b) A Contracting Party may, in a declaration, notify the Director General that, in accordance with its national or regional legislation, a registered appellation of origin or geographical indication is protected from a date that is mentioned in the declaration, which date shall however not be later than the date of expiry of the time limit for refusal specified in the Regulations in accordance with Article 15(1)(a).

[9.707]
Article 7
Fees

(1) *[International Registration Fee]* International registration of each appellation of origin, and each geographical indication, shall be subject to payment of the fee specified in the Regulations.

(2) *[Fees for Other Entries in the International Register]* The Regulations shall specify the fees to be paid in respect of other entries in the International Register and for the supply of extracts, attestations, or other information concerning the contents of the international registration.

(3) *[Fee Reductions]* Reduced fees shall be established by the Assembly in respect of certain international registrations of appellations of origin, and in respect of certain international registrations of geographical indications, in particular those in respect of which the Contracting Party of Origin is a developing country or a least-developed country.

(4) *[Individual Fee]*

- (a) Any Contracting Party may, in a declaration, notify the Director General that the protection resulting from international registration shall extend to it only if a fee is paid to cover its cost of substantive examination of the international registration. The amount of such individual fee shall be indicated in the declaration and can be changed in further declarations. The said amount may not be higher than the equivalent of the amount required under the national or regional legislation of the Contracting Party diminished by the savings resulting from the international procedure. Additionally, the Contracting Party may, in a declaration, notify the Director General that it requires an administrative fee relating to the use by the beneficiaries of the appellation of origin or the geographical indication in that Contracting Party.
- (b) Non-payment of an individual fee shall, in accordance with the Regulations, have the effect that protection is renounced in respect of the Contracting Party requiring the fee.

[9.708]
Article 8
Period of Validity of International Registrations

(1) *[Dependency]* International registrations shall be valid indefinitely, on the understanding that the protection of a registered appellation of origin or geographical indication shall no longer be required if the denomination constituting the appellation of origin, or the indication constituting the geographical indication, is no longer protected in the Contracting Party of Origin.

(2) *[Cancellation]*

(a) The Competent Authority of the Contracting Party of Origin, or, in the case of Article 5(3), the beneficiaries or the natural person or legal entity referred to in Article 5(2)(ii) or the Competent Authority of the Contracting Party of Origin, may at any time request the International Bureau to cancel the international registration concerned.

(b) In case the denomination constituting a registered appellation of origin, or the indication constituting a registered geographical indication, is no longer protected in the Contracting Party of Origin, the Competent Authority of the Contracting Party of Origin shall request cancellation of the international registration.

CHAPTER III
PROTECTION

[9.709]
Article 9
Commitment to Protect

Each Contracting Party shall protect registered appellations of origin and geographical indications on its territory, within its own legal system and practice but in accordance with the terms of this Act, subject to any refusal, renunciation, invalidation or cancellation that may become effective with respect to its territory, and on the understanding that Contracting Parties that do not distinguish in their national or regional legislation as between appellations of origin and geographical indications shall not be required to introduce such a distinction into their national or regional legislation.

[9.710]
Article 10
Protection Under Laws of Contracting Parties or Other Instruments

(1) *[Form of Legal Protection]* Each Contracting Party shall be free to choose the type of legislation under which it establishes the protection stipulated in this Act, provided that such legislation meets the substantive requirements of this Act.

(2) *[Protection Under Other Instruments]* The provisions of this Act shall not in any way affect any other protection a Contracting Party may accord in respect of registered appellations of origin or registered geographical indications under its national or regional legislation, or under other international instruments.

(3) *[Relation to Other Instruments]* Nothing in this Act shall derogate from any obligations that Contracting Parties have to each other under any other international instruments, nor shall it prejudice any rights that a Contracting Party has under any other international instruments.

[9.711]
Article 11
Protection in Respect of Registered Appellations of Origin and Geographical Indications

(1) *[Content of Protection]* Subject to the provisions of this Act, in respect of a registered appellation of origin or a registered geographical indication, each Contracting Party shall provide the legal means to prevent:

(a) use of the appellation of origin or the geographical indication

(i) in respect of goods of the same kind as those to which the appellation of origin or the geographical indication applies, not originating in the geographical area of origin or not complying with any other applicable requirements for using the appellation of origin or the geographical indication;

(ii) in respect of goods that are not of the same kind as those to which the appellation of origin or geographical indication applies or services, if such use would indicate or suggest a connection between those goods or services and the beneficiaries of the appellation of origin or the geographical indication, and would be likely to damage their interests, or, where applicable, because of the reputation of the appellation of origin or geographical indication in the Contracting Party concerned, such use would be likely to impair or dilute in an unfair manner, or take unfair advantage of, that reputation;

(b) any other practice liable to mislead consumers as to the true origin, provenance or nature of the goods.

(2) *[Content of Protection in Respect of Certain Uses]* Paragraph (1)(a) shall also apply to use of the appellation of origin or geographical indication amounting to its imitation, even if the true origin of the goods is indicated, or if the appellation of origin or the geographical indication is used in translated form or is accompanied by terms such as "style", "kind", "type", "make", "imitation", "method", "as produced in", "like", "similar" or the like.[1]

(3) *[Use in a Trademark]* Without prejudice to Article 13(1), a Contracting Party shall, *ex officio* if its legislation so permits or at the request of an interested party, refuse or invalidate the registration of a later trademark if use of the trademark would result in one of the situations covered by paragraph (1).

NOTES

[1] Agreed Statement concerning Article 11(2): For the purposes of this Act, it is understood that where certain elements of the denomination or indication constituting the appellation of origin or geographical indication have a generic character in the Contracting Party of Origin, their protection under this subparagraph shall not be required in the other Contracting Parties. For greater certainty, a refusal or invalidation of a trademark, or a finding of infringement, in the Contracting Parties under the terms of Article 11 cannot be based on the component that has a generic character.

[9.712]
Article 12
Protection Against Becoming Generic

Subject to the provisions of this Act, registered appellations of origin and registered geographical indications cannot be considered to have become generic[2] in a Contracting Party.

NOTES

[2] Agreed Statement concerning Article 12: For the purposes of this Act, it is understood that Article 12 is without prejudice to the application of the provisions of this Act concerning prior use, as, prior to international registration, the denomination or indication constituting the appellation of origin or geographical indication may already, in whole or in part, be generic in a Contracting Party other than the Contracting Party of Origin, for example, because the denomination or indication, or part of it, is identical with a term customary in common language as the common name of a good or service in such Contracting Party, or is identical with the customary name of a grape variety in such Contracting Party.

[9.713]
Article 13
Safeguards in Respect of Other Rights

(1) *[Prior Trademark Rights]* The provisions of this Act shall not prejudice a prior trademark applied for or registered in good faith, or acquired through use in good faith, in a Contracting Party. Where the law of a Contracting Party provides a limited exception to the rights conferred by a trademark to the effect that such a prior trademark in certain circumstances may not entitle its owner to prevent a registered appellation of origin or geographical indication from being granted protection or used in that Contracting Party, protection of the registered appellation of origin or geographical indication shall not limit the rights conferred by that trademark in any other way.

(2) *[Personal Name Used in Business]* The provisions of this Act shall not prejudice the right of any person to use, in the course of trade, that person's name or the name of that person's predecessor in business, except where such name is used in such a manner as to mislead the public.

(3) *[Rights Based on a Plant Variety or Animal Breed Denomination]* The provisions of this Act shall not prejudice the right of any person to use a plant variety or animal breed denomination in the course of trade, except where such plant variety or animal breed denomination is used in such a manner as to mislead the public.

(4) *[Safeguards in the Case of Notification of Withdrawal of Refusal or a Grant of Protection]* Where a Contracting Party that has refused the effects of an international registration under Article 15 on the ground of use under a prior trademark or other right, as referred to in this Article, notifies the withdrawal of that refusal under Article 16 or a grant of protection under Article 18, the resulting protection of the appellation of origin or geographical indication shall not prejudice that right or its use, unless the protection was granted following the cancellation, non-renewal, revocation or invalidation of the right.

[9.714]
Article 14
Enforcement Procedures and Remedies

Each Contracting Party shall make available effective legal remedies for the protection of registered appellations of origin and registered geographical indications and provide that legal proceedings for ensuring their protection may be brought by a public authority or by any interested party, whether a natural person or a legal entity and whether public or private, depending on its legal system and practice.

CHAPTER IV
REFUSAL AND OTHER ACTIONS IN RESPECT OF INTERNATIONAL REGISTRATIONS

[9.715]
Article 15
Refusal

(1) *[Refusal of Effects of International Registration]*

(a) Within the time limit specified in the Regulations, the Competent Authority of a Contracting Party may notify the International Bureau of the refusal of the effects of an international registration in its territory. The notification of refusal may be made by the Competent Authority *ex officio*, if its legislation so permits, or at the request of an interested party.

(b) The notification of refusal shall set out the grounds on which the refusal is based.
(2) *[Protection Under Other Instruments]* The notification of a refusal shall not be detrimental to any other protection that may be available, in accordance with Article 10(2), to the denomination or indication concerned in the Contracting Party to which the refusal relates.
(3) *[Obligation to Provide Opportunity for Interested Parties]* Each Contracting Party shall provide a reasonable opportunity, for anyone whose interests would be affected by an international registration, to request the Competent Authority to notify a refusal in respect of the international registration.
(4) *[Registration, Publication and Communication of Refusals]* The International Bureau shall record the refusal and the grounds for the refusal in the International Register. It shall publish the refusal and the grounds for the refusal and shall communicate the notification of refusal to the Competent Authority of the Contracting Party of Origin or, where the application has been filed directly in accordance with Article 5(3), the beneficiaries or the natural person or legal entity referred to in Article 5(2)(ii) as well as the Competent Authority of the Contracting Party of Origin.
(5) *[National Treatment]* Each Contracting Party shall make available to interested parties affected by a refusal the same judicial and administrative remedies that are available to its own nationals in respect of the refusal of protection for an appellation of origin or a geographical indication.

[9.716]
Article 16
Withdrawal of Refusal

A refusal may be withdrawn in accordance with the procedures specified in the Regulations. A withdrawal shall be recorded in the International Register.

[9.717]
Article 17
Transitional Period

(1) *[Option to Grant Transitional Period]* Without prejudice to Article 13, where a Contracting Party has not refused the effects of an international registration on the ground of prior use by a third party or has withdrawn such refusal or has notified a grant of protection, it may, if its legislation so permits, grant a defined period as specified in the Regulations, for terminating such use.
(2) *[Notification of a Transitional Period]* The Contracting Party shall notify the International Bureau of any such period, in accordance with the procedures specified in the Regulations.

[9.718]
Article 18
Notification of Grant of Protection

The Competent Authority of a Contracting Party may notify the International Bureau of the grant of protection to a registered appellation of origin or geographical indication. The International Bureau shall record any such notification in the International Register and publish it.

[9.719]
Article 19
Invalidation

(1) *[Opportunity to Defend Rights]* Invalidation of the effects, in part or in whole, of an international registration in the territory of a Contracting Party may be pronounced only after having given the beneficiaries an opportunity to defend their rights. Such opportunity shall also be given to the natural person or legal entity referred to in Article 5(2)(ii).
(2) *[Notification, Recordal and Publication]* The Contracting Party shall notify the invalidation of the effects of an international registration to the International Bureau, which shall record the invalidation in the International Register and publish it.
(3) *[Protection Under Other Instruments]* Invalidation shall not be detrimental to any other protection that may be available, in accordance with Article 10(2), to the denomination or indication concerned in the Contracting Party that invalidated the effects of the international registration.

[9.720]
Article 20
Modifications and Other Entries in the International Register

Procedures for the modification of international registrations and other entries in the International Register shall be specified in the Regulations.

CHAPTER V
ADMINISTRATIVE PROVISIONS

[9.721]
Article 21
Membership of the Lisbon Union

The Contracting Parties shall be members of the same Special Union as the States party to the Lisbon Agreement or the 1967 Act, whether or not they are party to the Lisbon Agreement or the 1967 Act.

[9.722]
Article 22
Assembly of the Special Union

(1) *[Composition]*

(a) The Contracting Parties shall be members of the same Assembly as the States party to the 1967 Act.

(b) Each Contracting Party shall be represented by one delegate, who may be assisted by alternate delegates, advisors and experts.

(c) Each delegation shall bear its own expenses.

(2) *[Tasks]*

(a) The Assembly shall:

(i) deal with all matters concerning the maintenance and development of the Special Union and the implementation of this Act;

(ii) give directions to the Director General concerning the preparation of revision conferences referred to in Article 26(1), due account being taken of any comments made by those members of the Special Union which have not ratified or acceded to this Act;

(iii) amend the Regulations;

(iv) review and approve the reports and activities of the Director General concerning the Special Union, and give him or her all necessary instructions concerning matters within the competence of the Special Union;

(v) determine the program and adopt the biennial budget of the Special Union, and approve its final accounts;

(vi) adopt the financial Regulations of the Special Union;

(vii) establish such committees and working groups as it deems appropriate to achieve the objectives of the Special Union;

(viii) determine which States, intergovernmental and non-governmental organizations shall be admitted to its meetings as observers;

(ix) adopt amendments to Articles 22 to 24 and 27;

(x) take any other appropriate action to further the objectives of the Special Union and perform any other functions as are appropriate under this Act.

(b) With respect to matters which are of interest also to other Unions administered by the Organization, the Assembly shall make its decisions after having heard the advice of the Coordination Committee of the Organization.

(3) *[Quorum]*

(a) One-half of the members of the Assembly which have the right to vote on a given matter shall constitute a quorum for the purposes of the vote on that matter.

(b) Notwithstanding the provisions of subparagraph (a), if, in any session, the number of the members of the Assembly which are States, have the right to vote on a given matter and are represented is less than one-half but equal to or more than one-third of the members of the Assembly which are States and have the right to vote on that matter, the Assembly may make decisions but, with the exception of decisions concerning its own procedure, all such decisions shall take effect only if the conditions set forth hereinafter are fulfilled. The International Bureau shall communicate the said decisions to the members of the Assembly which are States, have the right to vote on the said matter and were not represented and shall invite them to express in writing their vote or abstention within a period of three months from the date of the communication. If, at the expiration of this period, the number of such members having thus expressed their vote or abstention attains the number of the members which was lacking for attaining the quorum in the session itself, such decisions shall take effect provided that at the same time the required majority still obtains.

(4) *[Taking Decisions in the Assembly]*

(a) The Assembly shall endeavor to take its decisions by consensus.

(b) Where a decision cannot be arrived at by consensus, the matter at issue shall be decided by voting. In such a case,

(i) each Contracting Party that is a State shall have one vote and shall vote only in its own name; and

(ii) any Contracting Party that is an intergovernmental organization may vote, in place of its member States, with a number of votes equal to the number of its member States which are party to this Act. No such intergovernmental organization shall participate in the vote if any one of its member States exercises its right to vote, and *vice versa*.

(c) On matters concerning only States that are bound by the 1967 Act, Contracting Parties that are not bound by the 1967 Act shall not have the right to vote, whereas, on matters concerning only Contracting Parties, only the latter shall have the right to vote.

(5) *[Majorities]*

(a) Subject to Articles 25(2) and 27(2), the decisions of the Assembly shall require two-thirds of the votes cast.

(b) Abstentions shall not be considered as votes.

(6) *[Sessions]*

(a) The Assembly shall meet upon convocation by the Director General and, in the absence of exceptional circumstances, during the same period and at the same place as the General Assembly of the Organization.

(b) The Assembly shall meet in extraordinary session upon convocation by the Director General, either at the request of one-fourth of the members of the Assembly or on the Director General's own initiative.

(c) The agenda of each session shall be prepared by the Director General.

(7) *[Rules of Procedure]* The Assembly shall adopt its own rules of procedure.

[9.723]
Article 23
International Bureau

(1) *[Administrative Tasks]*

(a) International registration and related duties, as well as all other administrative tasks concerning the Special Union, shall be performed by the International Bureau.

(b) In particular, the International Bureau shall prepare the meetings and provide the Secretariat of the Assembly and of such committees and working groups as may have been established by the Assembly.

(c) The Director General shall be the Chief Executive of the Special Union and shall represent the Special Union.

(2) *[Role of the International Bureau in the Assembly and Other Meetings]* The Director General and any staff member designated by him shall participate, without the right to vote, in all meetings of the Assembly, the committees and working groups established by the Assembly. The Director General, or a staff member designated by him, shall be *ex officio* Secretary of such a body.

(3) *[Conferences]*

(a) The International Bureau shall, in accordance with the directions of the Assembly, make the preparations for any revision conferences.

(b) The International Bureau may consult with intergovernmental and international and national non-governmental organizations concerning the said preparations.

(c) The Director General and persons designated by him shall take part, without the right to vote, in the discussions at revision conferences.

(4) *[Other Tasks]* The International Bureau shall carry out any other tasks assigned to it in relation to this Act.

[9.724]
Article 24
Finances

(1) *[Budget]* The income and expenses of the Special Union shall be reflected in the budget of the Organization in a fair and transparent manner.

(2) *[Sources of Financing of the Budget]* The income of the Special Union shall be derived from the following sources:

(i) fees collected under Article 7(1) and (2);

(ii) proceeds from the sale of, or royalties on, the publications of the International Bureau;

(iii) gifts, bequests, and subventions;

(iv) rent, investment revenue, and other, including miscellaneous, income;

(v) special contributions of the Contracting Parties or any alternative source derived from the Contracting Parties or beneficiaries, or both, if and to the extent to which receipts from the sources indicated in items (i) to (iv) do not suffice to cover the expenses, as decided by the Assembly.

(3) *[Fixing of Fees; Level of the Budget]*

(a) The amounts of the fees referred to in paragraph (2) shall be fixed by the Assembly on the proposal of the Director General and shall be so fixed that, together with the income derived form other sources under paragraph (2), the revenue of the Special Union should, under normal circumstances, be sufficient to cover the expenses of the International Bureau for maintaining the international registration service.

(b) If the Program and Budget of the Organization is not adopted before the beginning of a new financial period, the authorization to the Director General to incur obligations and make payments shall be at the same level as it was in the previous financial period.

(4) *[Establishing the Special Contributions Referred to in Paragraph (2)(v)]* For the purpose of establishing its contribution, each Contracting Party shall belong to the same class as it belongs to in the context of the Paris Convention or, if it is not a Contracting Party of the Paris Convention, as it would belong to if it were a Contracting Party of the Paris Convention. Intergovernmental organizations shall be considered to belong to contribution class I (one), unless otherwise unanimously decided by the Assembly. The contribution shall be partially weighted according to the number of registrations originating in the Contracting Party, as decided by the Assembly.

(5) *[Working Capital Fund]* The Special Union shall have a working capital fund, which shall be constituted by payments made by way of advance by each member of the Special Union when the Special Union so decides. If the fund becomes insufficient, the Assembly may decide to increase it. The proportion and the terms of payment shall be fixed by the Assembly on the proposal of the Director General. Should the Special Union record a surplus of income over expenditure in any financial period, the Working Capital Fund advances may be repaid to each member proportionate to their initial payments upon proposal by the Director General and decision by the Assembly..

(6) *[Advances by Host State]*

(a) In the headquarters agreement concluded with the State on the territory of which the Organization has its headquarters, it shall be provided that, whenever the working capital fund is insufficient, such State shall grant advances. The amount of those advances and the conditions on which they are granted shall be the subject of separate agreements, in each case, between such State and the Organization.

(b) The State referred to in subparagraph (a) and the Organization shall each have the right to denounce the obligation to grant advances, by written notification. Denunciation shall take effect three years after the end of the year in which it has been notified.

(7) *[Auditing of Accounts]* The auditing of the accounts shall be effected by one or more of the States members of the Special Union or by external auditors, as provided in the Financial Regulations of the Organization. They shall be designated, with their agreement, by the Assembly.

[9.725]
Article 25
Regulations

(1) *[Subject-Matter]* The details for carrying out this Act shall be established in the Regulations.

(2) *[Amendment of Certain Provisions of the Regulations]*

(a) The Assembly may decide that certain provisions of the Regulations may be amended only by unanimity or only by a three-fourths majority.

(b) In order for the requirement of unanimity or a three-fourths majority no longer to apply in the future to the amendment of a provision of the Regulations, unanimity shall be required.

(c) In order for the requirement of unanimity or a three-fourths majority to apply in the future to the amendment of a provision of the Regulations, a three-fourths majority shall be required.

(3) *[Conflict Between This Act and the Regulations]* In the case of conflict between the provisions of this Act and those of the Regulations, the former shall prevail.

CHAPTER VI
REVISION AND AMENDMENT

[9.726]
Article 26
Revision

(1) *[Revision Conferences]* This Act may be revised by Diplomatic Conferences of the Contracting Parties. The convocation of any Diplomatic Conference shall be decided by the Assembly.

(2) *[Revision or Amendment of Certain Articles]* Articles 22 to 24 and 27 may be amended either by a revision conference or by the Assembly according to the provisions of Article 27.

[9.727]
Article 27
Amendment of Certain Articles by the Assembly

(1) *[Proposals for Amendment]*

(a) Proposals for the amendment of Articles 22 to 24, and the present Article, may be initiated by any Contracting Party or by the Director General.

(b) Such proposals shall be communicated by the Director General to the Contracting Parties at least six months in advance of their consideration by the Assembly.

(2) *[Majorities]* Adoption of any amendment to the Articles referred to in paragraph (1) shall require a three-fourths majority, except that adoption of any amendment to Article 22, and to the present paragraph, shall require a four-fifths majority.

(3) *[Entry into Force]*

(a) Except where subparagraph (b) applies, any amendment to the Articles referred to in paragraph (1) shall enter into force one month after written notifications of acceptance, effected in accordance with their respective constitutional processes, have been received by the Director General from three-fourths of those Contracting Parties which, at the time the amendment was adopted, were members of the Assembly and had the right to vote on that amendment.

(b) Any amendment to Article 22(3) or (4) or to this subparagraph shall not enter into force if, within six months of its adoption by the Assembly, any Contracting Party notifies the Director General that it does not accept such amendment.

(c) Any amendment which enters into force in accordance with the provisions of this paragraph shall bind all the States and intergovernmental organizations which are Contracting Parties at the time the amendment enters into force, or which become Contracting Parties at a subsequent date.

CHAPTER VII
FINAL PROVISIONS

[9.728]
Article 28
Becoming Party to This Act

(1) *[Eligibility]* Subject to Article 29 and paragraphs (2) and (3) of the present Article,

(i) any State which is party to the Paris Convention may sign and become party to this Act;

(ii) any other State member of the Organization may sign and become party to this Act if it declares that its legislation complies with the provisions of the Paris Convention concerning appellations of origin, geographical indications and trademarks;

(iii) any intergovernmental organization may sign and become party to this Act, provided that at least one member State of that intergovernmental organization is party to the Paris Convention and provided that the intergovernmental organization declares that it has been duly authorized, in accordance with its internal procedures, to become party to this Act and that, under the constituting treaty of the intergovernmental organization, legislation applies under which regional titles of protection can be obtained in respect of geographical indications.

(2) *[Ratification or Accession]* Any State or intergovernmental organization referred to in paragraph (1) may deposit

(i) an instrument of ratification, if it has signed this Act; or

(ii) an instrument of accession, if it has not signed this Act.

(3) *[Effective Date of Deposit]*

(a) Subject to subparagraph (b), the effective date of the deposit of an instrument of ratification or accession shall be the date on which that instrument is deposited.

(b) The effective date of the deposit of the instrument of ratification or accession of any State that is a member State of an intergovernmental organization and in respect of which the protection of appellations of origin or geographical indications can only be obtained on the basis of legislation applying between the member States of the intergovernmental organization shall be the date on which the instrument of ratification or accession of that intergovernmental organization is deposited, if that date is later than the date on which the instrument of the said State has been deposited. However, this subparagraph does not apply with regard to States that are party to the Lisbon Agreement or the 1967 Act and shall be without prejudice to the application of Article 31 with regard to such States.

[9.729]
Article 29
Effective Date of Ratifications and Accessions

(1) *[Instruments to Be Taken into Consideration]* For the purposes of this Article, only instruments of ratification or accession that are deposited by States or intergovernmental organizations referred to in Article 28(1) and that have an effective date according to Article 28(3) shall be taken into consideration.

(2) *[Entry into Force of This Act]* This Act shall enter into force three months after five eligible parties referred to in Article 28 have deposited their instruments of ratification or accession.

(3) *[Entry into Force of Ratifications and Accessions]*

(a) Any State or intergovernmental organization that has deposited its instrument of ratification or accession three months or more before the date of entry into force of this Act shall become bound by this Act on the date of the entry into force of this Act.

(b) Any other State or intergovernmental organization shall become bound by this Act three months after the date on which it has deposited its instrument of ratification or accession or at any later date indicated in that instrument.

(4) *[International Registrations Effected Prior to Accession]* In the territory of the acceding State and, where the Contracting Party is an intergovernmental organization, the territory in which the constituting treaty of that intergovernmental organization applies, the provisions of this Act shall apply in respect of appellations of origin and geographical indications already registered under this Act at the time the accession becomes effective, subject to Article 7(4) as well as the provisions of

Chapter IV, which shall apply *mutatis mutandis*. The acceding State or intergovernmental organization may also specify, in a declaration attached to its instrument of ratification or accession, an extension of the time limit referred to in Article 15(1), and the periods referred to in Article 17, in accordance with the procedures specified in the Regulations in that respect.

[9.730]
Article 30
Prohibition of Reservations
No reservations to this Act are permitted.

[9.731]
Article 31
Application of the Lisbon Agreement and the 1967 Act
(1) *[Relations Between States Party to Both This Act and the Lisbon Agreement or the 1967 Act]* This Act alone shall be applicable as regards the mutual relations of States party to both this Act and the Lisbon Agreement or the 1967 Act. However, with regard to international registrations of appellations of origin effective under the Lisbon Agreement or the 1967 Act, the States shall accord no lower protection than is required by the Lisbon Agreement or the 1967 Act.
(2) *[Relations Between States Party to Both This Act and the Lisbon Agreement or the 1967 Act and States Party to the Lisbon Agreement or the 1967 Act Without Being Party to This Act]* Any State party to both this Act and the Lisbon Agreement or the 1967 Act shall continue to apply the Lisbon Agreement or the 1967 Act, as the case may be, in its relations with States party to the Lisbon Agreement or the 1967 Act that are not party to this Act.

[9.732]
Article 32
Denunciation
(1) *[Notification]* Any Contracting Party may denounce this Act by notification addressed to the Director General.
(2) *[Effective Date]* Denunciation shall take effect one year after the date on which the Director General has received the notification or at any later date indicated in the notification. It shall not affect the application of this Act to any application pending and any international registration in force in respect of the denouncing Contracting Party at the time of the coming into effect of the denunciation.

[9.733]
Article 33
Languages of this Act; Signature
(1) *[Original Texts; Official Texts]*
- (a) This Act shall be signed in a single original in the English, Arabic, Chinese, French, Russian and Spanish languages, all texts being equally authentic.
- (b) Official texts shall be established by the Director General, after consultation with the interested Governments, in such other languages as the Assembly may designate.

(2) *[Time Limit for Signature]* This Act shall remain open for signature at the headquarters of the Organization for one year after its adoption.

[9.734]
Article 34
Depositary
The Director General shall be the depositary of this Act.

REGULATIONS UNDER THE GENEVA ACT OF THE LISBON AGREEMENT ON APPELLATIONS OF ORIGIN AND GEOGRAPHICAL INDICATIONS

(As adopted on May 20, 2015)

NOTES

The original source for these Regulations is the World Intellectual Property Organisation (WIPO).

CHAPTER I
INTRODUCTORY AND GENERAL PROVISIONS

[9.735]
Rule 1
Abbreviated Expressions
For the purposes of these Regulations, unless expressly stated otherwise:

(i) abbreviated expressions defined in Article 1 shall have the same meaning in these Regulations;
(ii) "Rule" refers to a rule of these Regulations;
(iii) "Administrative Instructions" means the Administrative Instructions referred to in Rule 24;
(iv) "Official Form" means a form drawn up by the International Bureau.

[9.736]
Rule 2
Calculation of Time Limits

(1) *[Periods Expressed in Years]* A period expressed in years shall expire in the subsequent year on the same day and month as the day and month of the event from which the period starts to run, except that, where the event occurred on February 29, the period shall expire on February 28 of the subsequent year.

(2) *[Periods Expressed in Months]* A period expressed in months shall expire in the relevant subsequent month on the same day as the day of the event from which the period starts to run, except that, where the relevant subsequent month has no day with the same number, the period shall expire on the last day of that month.

(3) *[Expiry on a Day Which Is Not a Working Day for the International Bureau or a Competent Authority]* If the period of a time limit applying to the International Bureau or a Competent Authority expires on a day which is not a working day for the International Bureau or a Competent Authority, the period shall, notwithstanding paragraphs (1) and (2), expire for the International Bureau or the Competent Authority, as the case may be, on the first subsequent working day.

[9.737]
Rule 3
Working Languages

(1) *[Application]* The application shall be in English, French or Spanish.

(2) *[Communications Subsequent to the International Application]* Any communication concerning an application or an international registration shall be in English, French or Spanish, at the choice of the Competent Authority concerned or, in the case of Article 5(3), at the choice of the beneficiaries or the natural person or legal entity referred to in Article 5(2)(ii). Any translation needed for the purposes of these procedures shall be made by the International Bureau.

(3) *[Entries in the International Register and Publication]* Entries in the International Register and publication of such entries by the International Bureau shall be in English, French and Spanish. The translations needed for those purposes shall be made by the International Bureau. However, the International Bureau shall not translate the appellation of origin or the geographical indication.

(4) *[Transliteration of the Appellation of Origin or Geographical Indication]* Where the application contains a transliteration of the appellation of origin or the geographical indication in accordance with Rule 5(2)(b), the International Bureau shall not check whether the transliteration is correct.

[9.738]
Rule 4
Competent Authority

(1) *[Notification to the International Bureau]* Upon accession, each Contracting Party shall notify the International Bureau of the name and contact details of its Competent Authority, i.e. the authority it has designated to present applications and other notifications to, and receive notifications from, the International Bureau. In addition, such Competent Authority shall make available information on the applicable procedures in the Contracting Party for the enforcement of rights in appellations of origin and geographical indications.

(2) *[One Authority or Different Authorities]* The notification referred to in paragraph (1) shall, preferably, indicate a single Competent Authority. When a Contracting Party notifies different Competent Authorities, this notification shall clearly indicate their respective competence in respect of the presentation of applications to, and the receipt of notifications from, the International Bureau.

(3) *[Modifications]* Contracting Parties shall notify the International Bureau of any change in the particulars referred to in paragraph (1). However, the International Bureau may *ex officio* take cognizance of a change in the absence of a notification where it has clear indications that such a change has taken place.

CHAPTER II
APPLICATION AND INTERNATIONAL REGISTRATION

[9.739]
Rule 5
Requirements Concerning the Application

(1) *[Filing]* The application shall be filed with the International Bureau on the Official Form provided to that end and shall be signed by the Competent Authority presenting it or, in the case of Article 5(3), the beneficiaries or the natural person or legal entity referred to in Article 5(2)(ii).

(2) *[Application – Mandatory Contents]*

(a) The application shall indicate:

(i) the Contracting Party of Origin;

(ii) the Competent Authority presenting the application or, in the case of Article 5(3), details identifying the beneficiaries or the natural person or legal entity referred to in Article 5(2)(ii);

(iii) the beneficiaries, designated collectively or, where collective designation is not possible, by name, or the natural person or legal entity having legal standing under the law of the Contracting Party of Origin to assert the rights of the beneficiaries or other rights in the appellation of origin or the geographical indication;

(iv) the appellation of origin or the geographical indication for which registration is sought, in the official language of the Contracting Party of Origin or, where the Contracting Party of Origin has more than one official language, in the official language or languages in which the appellation of origin or the geographical indication is contained in the registration, act or decision, by virtue of which protection is granted in the Contracting Party of Origin;[1]

(v) the good or goods to which the appellation of origin, or the geographical indication, applies, as precisely as possible;

(vi) the geographical area of origin or the geographical area of production of the good or goods;

(vii) the identifying details, including the date of the registration, the legislative or administrative act, or the judicial or administrative decision, by virtue of which protection is granted to the appellation of origin, or to the geographical indication, in the Contracting Party of Origin.

(b) If they are not in Latin characters, the application shall include a transliteration of the names of the beneficiaries or the natural person or legal entity referred to in Article 5(2)(ii), of the geographical area of origin, and of the appellation of origin or the geographical indication for which registration is sought. The transliteration shall use the phonetics of the language of the application.[1]

(c) The application shall be accompanied by the registration fee and any other fees, as specified in Rule 8.

(3) *[Application – Particulars Concerning the Quality, Reputation or Characteristic(s)]*

(a) To the extent that a Contracting Party requires that, for the protection of a registered appellation of origin or geographical indication in its territory, the application further indicate particulars concerning, in the case of an appellation of origin, the quality or characteristics of the good and its connection with the geographical environment of the geographical area of production, and, in the case of a geographical indication, the quality, reputation or other characteristic of the good and its connection with the geographical area of origin, it shall notify that requirement to the Director General.

(b) In order to meet such a requirement, particulars as referred to in subparagraph (a) shall be provided in a working language, but they shall not be translated by the International Bureau.

(c) An application that is not in accordance with a requirement as notified by a Contracting Party under subparagraph (a) shall, subject to Rule 6, have the effect that protection is renounced in respect of that Contracting Party.

(4) *[Application – Signature and/or Intention to Use]*

(a) To the extent that a Contracting Party requires that for protection of a registered appellation of origin or geographical indication the application be signed by a person having legal standing to assert the rights conferred by such protection, it shall notify that requirement to the Director General.

(b) To the extent that a Contracting Party requires that for protection of a registered appellation of origin or geographical indication the application be accompanied by a declaration of intention to use the registered appellation of origin or geographical indication in its territory or a declaration of intention to exercise control over the use by others of the registered appellation of origin or geographical indication in its territory, it shall notify that requirement to the Director General.

(c) An application that is not signed in accordance with subparagraph (a), or that is not accompanied by a declaration indicated in subparagraph (b), shall, subject to Rule 6, have the effect that protection is renounced in respect of the Contracting Party requiring such signature or declaration, as notified under subparagraphs (a) and (b).

(5) *[Application – Protection Not Claimed for Certain Elements of the Appellation of Origin or the Geographical Indication]* The application shall indicate whether or not, to the best knowledge of the applicant, the registration, the legislative or administrative act, or the judicial or administrative decision, by virtue of which protection is granted to the appellation of origin, or to the geographical indication, in the Contracting Party of Origin, specifies that protection is not granted for certain elements of the appellation of origin or the geographical indication. Any such elements shall be indicated in the application in a working language.

(6) *[Application – Optional Contents]* The application may indicate or contain:

(i) the addresses of the beneficiaries;

(ii) a declaration that protection is renounced in one or more Contracting Parties;
(iii) a copy in the original language of the registration, the legislative or administrative act, or the judicial or administrative decision, by virtue of which protection is granted to the appellation of origin or the geographical indication in the Contracting Party of Origin;
(iv) a statement to the effect that protection is not claimed for certain elements, other than those refered to in paragraph (5) of the appellation of origin or the geographical indication.

NOTES

1 The application of Rule 5(2)(a)(iv) and Rule 5(2)(b) is subject to the provisions of Rule 3(3) and (4).

[9.740]
Rule 6
Irregular Applications

(1) *[Examination of the Application and Correction of Irregularities]*
(a) Subject to paragraph (2), if the International Bureau finds that an application does not satisfy the conditions set out in Rule 3(1) or Rule 5, it shall defer registration and invite the Competent Authority or, in the case of Article 5(3), the beneficiaries or the natural person or legal entity referred to in Article 5(2)(ii), to remedy the irregularity found within a period of three months from the date on which the invitation was sent.
(b) If the irregularity found is not corrected within two months of the date of the invitation referred to in subparagraph (a), the International Bureau shall send a reminder of its invitation. The sending of such a reminder shall have no effect on the three-month period referred to in subparagraph (a).
(c) If the correction of the irregularity is not received by the International Bureau within the three-month period referred to in subparagraph (a), the application shall, subject to subparagraph (d), be rejected by the International Bureau, which shall inform the Competent Authority or, in the case of Article 5(3), the beneficiaries or the natural person or legal entity referred to in Article 5(2)(ii) as well as the Competent Authority, accordingly.
(d) In the case of an irregularity with respect to a requirement based on a notification made under Rule 5(3) or (4), or on a declaration made under Article 7(4), if the correction of the irregularity is not received by the International Bureau within the three-month period referred to in subparagraph (a), the protection resulting from the international registration shall be considered to be renounced in the Contracting Party having made the notification or the declaration.
(e) Where, in accordance with subparagraph (c), the application is rejected, the International Bureau shall refund the fees paid in respect of the application, after deduction of an amount corresponding to half the registration fee referred to in Rule 8.

(2) *[Application Not Considered as Such]* If the application is not filed by the Competent Authority of the Contracting Party of Origin or, in the case of Article 5(3), the beneficiaries or the natural person or legal entity referred to in Article 5(2)(ii), it shall not be considered as such by the International Bureau and shall be returned to the sender.

[9.741]
Rule 7
Entry in the International Register

(1) *[Registration]*
(a) Where the International Bureau finds that the application satisfies the conditions set out in Rules 3(1) and 5, it shall enter the appellation of origin or the geographical indication in the International Register.
(b) Where the application is also governed by the Lisbon Agreement or the 1967 Act, the International Bureau shall enter the appellation of origin in the International Register if it finds that the application satisfies the conditions set out in Rules 3(1) and 5 of the Regulations that apply in respect of the Lisbon Agreement or the 1967 Act.
(c) The International Bureau shall indicate per Contracting Party whether the international registration is governed by this Act or by the Lisbon Agreement or the 1967 Act.

(2) *[Contents of the Registration]* The international registration shall contain or indicate:
(i) all the particulars given in the application;
(ii) the language in which the International Bureau received the application;
(iii) the number of the international registration;
(iv) the date of the international registration.

(3) *[Certificate and Notification]* The International Bureau shall:
(i) send a certificate of international registration to the Competent Authority of the Contracting Party of Origin or, in the case of Article 5(3), to the beneficiaries or the natural person or legal entity referred to in Article 5(2)(ii) that requested the registration; and

(ii) notify the International registration to the Competent Authority of each Contracting Party.

(4) *[Implementation of Article 31(1)]*

(a) In case of the ratification of, or accession to, this Act by a State that is party to the Lisbon Agreement or the 1967 Act, Rule 5(2) to (4) shall apply *mutatis mutandis* with regard to international registrations or appellations of origin effective under the Lisbon Agreement or the 1967 Act in respect of that State. The International Bureau shall verify with the Competent Authority concerned any modifications to be made, in view of the requirements of Rules 3(1) and 5(2) to (4), for the purpose of their registration under this Act and notify international registrations thus effected to all other Contracting Parties. Modifications shall be subject to payment of the fee specified in Rule 8(1)(ii).

(b) Any declaration of refusal or notification of invalidation issued by a Contracting Party that is also party to the Lisbon Agreement or the 1967 Act shall remain effective under this Act, unless the Contracting Party notifies a withdrawal of refusal under Article 16 or a grant of protection under Article 18.

(c) Where subparagraph (b) does not apply, any Contracting Party that is also party to the Lisbon Agreement or the 1967 Act shall, upon receipt of a notification under subparagraph (a), continue to protect the appellation of origin concerned thenceforth also under this Act, unless the Contracting Party indicates otherwise. Any period granted under Article 5(6) of the Lisbon Agreement or the 1967 Act and still effective at the time the notification under subparagraph (a) is received shall, for its remainder, be subject to the provisions of Article 17.

[9.742]
Rule 8
Fees

(1) *[Amount of Fees]* The International Bureau shall collect the following fees,[2] payable in Swiss francs:

(i) fee for international registration
(ii) fee for each modification of an international registration
(iii) fee for providing an extract from the International Register
(iv) fee for providing an attestation or any other written information concerning the contents of the International Register
(v) individual fees as referred to in paragraph (2).

(2) *[Establishment of the Amount of Individual Fees]*

(a) Where a Contracting Party makes a declaration as referred to in Article 7(4) that it wants to receive an individual fee, as referred to in that provision, the amount of such fee shall be indicated in the currency used by the Competent Authority.

(b) Where the fee is indicated in the declaration referred to in subparagraph (a) in a currency other than Swiss currency, the Director General shall, after consultation with the Competent Authority of the Contracting Party, establish the amount of the fee in Swiss currency on the basis of the official exchange rate of the United Nations.

(c) Where, for more than three consecutive months, the official exchange rate of the United Nations between the Swiss currency and the currency in which the amount of an individual fee has been indicated by a Contracting Party is higher or lower by at least 5 per cent than the last exchange rate applied to establish the amount of the fee in Swiss currency, the Competent Authority of that Contracting Party may ask the Director General to establish a new amount of the fee in Swiss currency according to the official exchange rate of the United Nations prevailing on the day preceding the day on which the request is made. The Director General shall proceed accordingly. The new amount shall be applicable as from a date which shall be fixed by the Director General, provided that such date is between one and two months after the date of the publication of the said amount on the website of the Organization.

(d) Where, for more than three consecutive months, the official exchange rate of the United Nations between the Swiss currency and the currency in which the amount of an individual fee has been indicated by a Contracting Party is lower by at least 10 per cent than the last exchange rate applied to establish the amount of the fee in Swiss currency, the Director General shall establish a new amount of the fee in Swiss currency according to the current official exchange rate of the United Nations. The new amount shall be applicable as from a date which shall be fixed by the Director General, provided that such date is between one and two months after the date of the publication of the said amount on the web site of the Organization.

(3) *[Crediting of Individual Fees to the Accounts of the Contracting Parties Concerned]* Any individual fee paid to the International Bureau in respect of a Contracting Party shall be credited to the account of that Contracting Party with the International Bureau within the month following the month in the course of which the recording of the international registration for which that fee has been paid was effected.

(4) *[Obligation to Use Swiss Currency]* All payments made under these Regulations to the International Bureau shall be in Swiss currency irrespective of the fact that, where the fees are paid through the Competent Authority, such Competent Authority may have collected those fees in another currency.

(5) *[Payment]*

(a) Subject to subparagraph (b), the fees shall be paid directly to the International Bureau.

(b) The fees payable in connection with an application may be paid through the Competent Authority if the Competent Authority accepts to collect and forward such fees and the beneficiaries so wish. Any Competent Authority which accepts to collect and forward such fees shall notify that fact to the Director General.

(6) *[Modes of Payment]* Fees shall be paid to the International Bureau in accordance with the Administrative Instructions.

(7) *[Indications Accompanying the Payment]* At the time of the payment of any fee to the International Bureau, an indication must be given of the appellation of origin or the geographical indication concerned and the purpose of the payment.

(8) *[Date of Payment]*

(a) Subject to subparagraph (b), any fee shall be considered to have been paid to the International Bureau on the day on which the International Bureau receives the required amount.

(b) Where the required amount is available in an account opened with the International Bureau and that Bureau has received instructions from the holder of the account to debit it, the fee shall be considered to have been paid to the International Bureau on the day on which the International Bureau receives an application or a request for the recording of a modification.

(9) *[Change in the Amount of the Fees]* Where the amount of any fee is changed, the amount valid on the date on which the fee was received by the International Bureau shall be applicable.

NOTES

2 The amounts of the fees are to be decided by the Assembly.

CHAPTER III
REFUSAL AND OTHER ACTIONS IN RESPECT OF INTERNATIONAL REGISTRATION

[9.743]
Rule 9
Refusal

(1) *[Notification to the International Bureau]*

(a) A refusal shall be notified to the International Bureau by the Competent Authority of the concerned Contracting Party and shall be signed by that Competent Authority.

(b) The refusal shall be notified within a period of one year from the receipt of the notification of international registration under Article 6(4). In the case of Article 29(4), this time limit may be extended by another year.

(2) *[Contents of the Notification of Refusal]* A notification of refusal shall indicate or contain:

(i) the Competent Authority notifying the refusal;

(ii) the number of the relevant international registration, preferably accompanied by further information enabling the identity of the international registration to be confirmed, such as the denomination constituting the appellation of origin or the indication constituting the geographical indication;

(iii) the grounds on which the refusal is based;

(iv) where the refusal is based on the existence of a prior right, as referred to in Article 13, the essential particulars of that prior right and, in particular, if it is constituted by a national, regional or international trademark application or registration, the date and number of such application or registration, the priority date (where appropriate), the name and address of the holder, a reproduction of the trademark, together with the list of relevant goods and services given in the trademark application or registration, it being understood that the list may be submitted in the language of the said application or registration;

(v) where the refusal concerns only certain elements of the appellation of origin, or the geographical indication, an indication of the elements that it concerns;

(vi) the judicial or administrative remedies available to contest the refusal, together with the applicable time limits.

(3) *[Entry in the International Register and Notifications by the International Bureau]* Subject to Rule 10(1), the International Bureau shall enter in the International Register any refusal, together with the date on which the notification of refusal was sent to the International Bureau, and shall communicate a copy of the notification of refusal to the Competent Authority of the Contracting Party of Origin or, in the case of Article 5(3), the beneficiaries or the natural person or legal entity referred to in Article 5(2)(ii) as well as the Competent Authority of the Contracting Party of Origin.

[9.744]
Rule 10
Irregular Notification of Refusal

(1) *[Declaration of Refusal Not Considered as Such]*

(a) A notification of refusal shall not be considered as such by the International Bureau:

(i) if it does not indicate the number of the international registration concerned, unless other information given in the declaration enables the registration to be identified without ambiguity;

(ii) if it does not indicate any ground for refusal;

(iii) if it is sent to the International Bureau after the expiry of the relevant time limit referred to in Rule 9(1);

(iv) if it is not notified to the International Bureau by the Competent Authority.

(b) Where subparagraph (a) applies, the International Bureau shall inform the Competent Authority that submitted the notification of refusal that the refusal is not considered as such by the International Bureau and has not been entered in the International Register, shall state the reasons therefore and shall, unless it is unable to identify the international registration concerned, communicate a copy of the notification of refusal to the Competent Authority of the Contracting Party of Origin or, in the case of Article 5(3), the beneficiaries or the natural person or legal entity referred to in Article 5(2)(ii) as well as the Competent Authority of the Contracting Party of Origin.

(2) *[Irregular Declaration]* If the notification of refusal contains an irregularity other than those referred to in paragraph (1), the International Bureau shall nevertheless enter the refusal in the International Register and shall communicate a copy of the notification of refusal to the Competent Authority of the Contracting Party of Origin or, in the case of Article 5(3), the beneficiaries or the natural person or legal entity referred to in Article 5(2)(ii) as well as the Competent Authority of the Contracting party of Origin. At the request of that Competent Authority or, in the case of Article 5(3), the beneficiaries or the natural person or legal entity referred to in Article 5(2)(ii), the International Bureau shall invite the Competent Authority that submitted the notification of refusal to regularize the notification without delay.

[9.745]
Rule 11
Withdrawal of Refusal

(1) *[Notification to the International Bureau]* A refusal may be withdrawn, in part or in whole, at any time by the Competent Authority that notified it. The withdrawal of a refusal shall be notified to the International Bureau by the relevant Competent Authority and shall be signed by such authority.

(2) *[Contents of the Notification]* The notification of withdrawal of a refusal shall indicate:

(i) the number of the international registration concerned, preferably accompanied by other information enabling the identity of the international registration to be confirmed, such as the denomination constituting the appellation of origin or the indication constituting the geographical indication;

(ii) the reason for the withdrawal and, in case of a partial withdrawal, the particulars referred to in Rule 9(2)(v);

(iii) the date on which the refusal was withdrawn.

(3) *[Entry in the International Register and Notifications by the International Bureau]* The International Bureau shall enter in the International Register any withdrawal referred to in paragraph (1) and shall communicate a copy of the notification of withdrawal to the Competent Authority of the Contracting Party of Origin or, in the case of Article 5(3), the beneficiaries or the natural person or legal entity referred to in Article 5(2)(ii) as well as the Competent Authority of the Contracting Party of Origin.

[9.746]
Rule 12
Notification of Grant of Protection

(1) *[Optional Statement of Grant of Protection]*

(a) A Competent Authority of a Contracting Party which does not refuse the effects of an international registration may, within the time limit referred to in Rule 9(1), send to the International Bureau a statement confirming that protection is granted to the appellation of origin, or the geographical indication, that is the subject of an international registration.

(b) The statement shall indicate:

(i) the Competent Authority of the Contracting Party making the statement;

(ii) the number of the international registration concerned, preferably accompanied by other information enabling the identity of the international registration to be confirmed, such as the denomination constituting the appellation of origin, or the indication constituting the geographical indication; and

(iii) the date of the statement.

(2) *[Optional Statement of Grant of Protection Following a Refusal]*

(a) Where a Competent Authority that has previously submitted a notification of refusal wishes to withdraw that refusal, it may, instead of notifying the withdrawal of refusal in accordance with Rule 11(1), send to the International Bureau a statement to the effect that protection is granted to the relevant appellation of origin or geographical indication.

(b) The statement shall indicate:

(i) the Competent Authority of the Contracting Party making the statement;

(ii) the number of the international registration concerned, preferably accompanied by other information enabling the identity of the international registration to be confirmed, such as the denomination constituting the appellation of origin, or the indication constituting the geographical indication;

(iii) the reason for the withdrawal and, in case of a grant of protection that amounts to a partial withdrawal of refusal, the particulars referred to in Rule 9(2)(v); and

(iv) the date on which protection was granted.

(3) *[Entry in the International Register and Notifications by the International Bureau]* The International Bureau shall enter in the International Register any statement referred to in paragraphs (1) or (2) and communicate a copy of such statement to the Competent Authority of the Contracting Party of Origin or, in the case of Article 5(3), the beneficiaries or the natural person or legal entity referred to in Article 5(2)(ii) as well as the Competent Authority of the Contracting Party of Origin.

[9.747]
Rule 13
Notification of Invalidation of the Effects of an International Registration in a Contracting Party

(1) *[Notification of Invalidation to the International Bureau]* Where the effects of an international registration are invalidated in a Contracting Party, in whole or in part, and the invalidation is no longer subject to appeal, the Competent Authority of the concerned Contracting Party shall transmit to the International Bureau a notification of invalidation. The notification shall indicate or contain:

(i) the number of the international registration concerned, preferably accompanied by other information enabling the identity of the international registration to be confirmed, such as the denomination constituting the appellation of origin, or the indication constituting the geographical indication;

(ii) the authority that pronounced the invalidation;

(iii) the date on which the invalidation was pronounced;

(iv) where the invalidation is partial, the particulars referred to in Rule 9(2)(v);

(v) the grounds on the basis of which the invalidation was pronounced;

(vi) a copy of the decision that invalidated the effects of the international registration.

(2) *[Entry in the International Register and Notifications by the International Bureau]* The International Bureau shall enter the invalidation in the International Register together with the particulars referred to in items (i) to (v) of paragraph (1) and shall communicate a copy of the notification to the Competent Authority of the Contracting Party of Origin or, in the case of Article 5(3), the beneficiaries or the natural person or legal entity referred to in Article 5(2)(ii) as well as the Competent Authority of the Contracting Party of Origin.

[9.748]
Rule 14
Notification of Transitional Period Granted to Third Parties

(1) *[Notification to the International Bureau]* Where a third party has been granted a defined period of time in which to terminate the use of a registered appellation of origin, or a registered geographical indication, in a Contracting Party, in accordance with Article 17(1), the Competent Authority of that Contracting Party shall notify the International Bureau accordingly. The notification shall indicate:

(i) the number of the international registration concerned, preferably accompanied by other information enabling the identity of the international registration to be confirmed, such as the denomination constituting the appellation of origin, or the indication constituting the geographical indication;

(ii) the identity of the third party concerned;

(iii) the period granted to the third party, preferably accompanied by information about the scope of the use during the transitional period;

(iv) the date from which the defined period begins, it being understood that the date may not be later than one year and three months from the receipt of the notification of international registration under Article 6(4) or, in the case of Article 29(4), no later than two years and three months from such receipt.

(2) *[Desirable Duration]* The duration of the period granted to a third party shall not be longer than 15 years, it being understood that the period may depend on the specific situation of each case and that a period longer than ten years would be exceptional.

(3) *[Entry in the International Register and Notifications by the International Bureau]* Subject to the notification referred to in paragraph (1) being sent by the Competent Authority to the International Bureau before the date referred to in paragraph (1)(iv), the International Bureau shall

enter such notification in the International Register together with the particulars shown therein and shall communicate a copy of the notification to the Competent Authority of the Contracting Party of Origin or, in the case of Article 5(3), the beneficiaries or the natural person or legal entity referred to in Article 5(2)(ii) as well as the Competent Authority of the Contracting Party of Origin.

[9.749]
Rule 15
Modifications

(1) *[Permissible Modifications]* The following modifications may be recorded in the International Register:

(i) the addition or deletion of a beneficiary or some beneficiaries;
(ii) a modification of the names or addresses of the beneficiaries;
(iii) a modification of the limits of the geographical area of origin of the good or goods to which the appellation of origin, or the geographical indication, applies;
(iv) a modification relating to the legislative or administrative act, the judicial or administrative decision, or the registration referred to in Rule 5(2)(a)(vii);
(v) a modification relating to the Contracting Party of Origin that does not affect the geographical area of origin of the good or goods to which the appellation of origin, or the geographical indication, applies;
(vi) a modification under Rule 16.

(2) *[Procedure]*

(a) A request for entry of a modification referred to in paragraph (1) shall be presented to the International Bureau by the Competent Authority of the Contracting Party of Origin or, in the case of Article 5(3), the beneficiaries or the natural person or legal entity referred to in Article 5(2)(ii), and shall be accompanied by the fee specified in Rule 8.

(b) A request for entry of a modification referred to in paragraph (1) shall, where it concerns a newly established trans-border geographical area of origin, be presented to the International Bureau by the commonly designated Competent Authority.

(3) *[Entry in the International Register and Notification to the Competent Authorities]* The International Bureau shall enter in the International Register any modification requested in accordance with paragraphs (1) and (2) together with the date of receipt of the request by the International Bureau, confirm the entry to the Competent Authority that requested the modification, and communicate such modification to the Competent Authorities of the other Contracting Parties.

(4) *[Optional Alternative]* In the case of Article 5(3), paragraphs (1) to (3) shall apply *mutatis mutandis*, it being understood that a request from the beneficiaries or from the natural person or legal entity referred to in Article 5(2)(ii) must indicate that the change is requested because of a corresponding change to the registration, the legislative or administrative act, or the judicial or administrative decision, on the basis of which the appellation of origin, or the geographical indication, had been granted protection in the Contracting Party of Origin; and that the entry of the modification in the International Register shall be confirmed to the concerned beneficiaries or natural person or legal entity by the International Bureau, which shall also inform the Competent Authority of the Contracting Party of Origin.

[9.750]
Rule 16
Renunciation of Protection

(1) *[Notification to the International Bureau]* The Competent Authority of the Contracting Party of Origin, or, in the case of Article 5(3), the beneficiaries or the natural person or legal entity referred to in Article 5(2)(ii) or the Competent Authority of the Contracting Party of Origin, may at any time notify the International Bureau that protection of the appellation of origin, or the geographical indication, is renounced, in whole or in part, in respect of one or some of the Contracting Parties. The notification of renunciation of protection shall state the number of the international registration concerned, preferably accompanied by other information enabling the identity of the international registration to be confirmed, such as the denomination constituting the appellation of origin, or the indication constituting the geographical indication.

(2) *[Withdrawal of a Renunciation]* Any renunciation, including a renunciation under Rule 6(1)(d), may be withdrawn, in whole or in part, at any time by the Competent Authority or, in the case of Article 5(3), the beneficiaries or the natural person or legal entity referred to in Article 5(2)(ii) or the Competent Authority of the Contracting Party of Origin, subject to payment of the fee for a modification and, in the case of a renunciation under Rule 6(1)(d), the correction of the irregularity.

(3) *[Entry in the International Register and Notification to the Competent Authorities]* The International Bureau shall enter in the International Register any renunciation of protection referred to in paragraph (1), or any withdrawal of a renunciation referred to in paragraph (2), confirm the entry to the Competent Authority of the Contracting Party of Origin and, in the case of Article 5(3), the beneficiaries or the natural person or legal entity, while also informing the Competent Authority of the Contracting Party of Origin, and shall communicate the entry of such modification in the International Register to the Competent Authorities of each Contracting Party to which the renunciation, or the withdrawal of the renunciation, relates.

(4) *[Application of Rules 9 to 12]* The Competent Authority of a Contracting Party that receives a notification of the withdrawal of a renunciation may notify the International Bureau of the refusal of the effects of the international registration in its territory. The declaration shall be addressed to the International Bureau by such Competent Authority within a period of one year from the date of receipt of the notification by the International Bureau of the withdrawal of the renunciation. Rules 9 to 12 shall apply *mutatis mutandis*.

[9.751]
Rule 17
Cancellation of an International Registration

(1) *[Request for Cancellation]* The request for cancellation shall state the number of the international registration concerned, preferably accompanied by other information enabling the identity of the international registration to be confirmed, such as the denomination constituting the appellation of origin or the indication constituting the geographical indication.

(2) *[Entry in the International Register and Notification to the Competent Authorities]* The International Bureau shall enter in the International Register any cancellation together with the particulars given in the request, confirm the entry to the Competent Authority of the Contracting Party of Origin or, in the case of Article 5(3), the beneficiaries or the natural person or legal entity referred to in Article 5(2)(ii), while also informing the Competent Authority of the Contracting Party of Origin, and shall communicate the cancellation to the Competent Authorities of the other Contracting Parties.

[9.752]
Rule 18
Corrections Made to the International Register

(1) *[Procedure]* If the International Bureau, acting *ex officio* or at the request of the Competent Authority of the Contracting Party of Origin, finds that the International Register contains an error with respect to an international registration, it shall correct the Register accordingly.

(2) *[Optional Alternative]* In the case of Article 5(3), a request under paragraph (1) can also be submitted by the beneficiaries or by the natural person or legal entity referred to in Article 5(2)(ii). The beneficiaries or the natural person or legal entity shall be notified by the International Bureau of any correction concerning the international registration.

(3) *[Notification of Corrections to the Competent Authorities]* The International Bureau shall notify any correction of the International Register to the Competent Authorities of all Contracting Parties as well as, in the case of Article 5(3), the beneficiaries or the natural person or legal entity referred to in Article 5(2)(ii).

(4) *[Application of Rules 9 to 12]* Where the correction of an error concerns the appellation of origin or the geographical indication, or the good or goods to which the appellation of origin or the geographical indication applies, the Competent Authority of a Contracting Party has the right to declare that it cannot ensure the protection of the appellation of origin or geographical indication after the correction. The declaration shall be addressed to the International Bureau by such Competent Authority within a period of one year from the date of notification by the International Bureau of the correction. Rules 9 to 12 shall apply *mutatis mutandis*.

CHAPTER IV
MISCELLANEOUS PROVISIONS

[9.753]
Rule 19
Publication

The International Bureau shall publish all entries made in the International Register.

[9.754]
Rule 20
Extracts from the International Register and Other Information Provided by the International Bureau

(1) *[Information on the Contents of the International Register]* Extracts from the International Register or any other information on the contents of the Register shall be provided by the International Bureau to any person so requesting, on payment of the fee specified in Rule 8.

(2) *[Communication of Provisions, Decisions or the Registration Under Which an Appellation of Origin or a Geographical Indication Is Protected]*

(a) Any person may request from the International Bureau a copy in the original language of the provisions, the decisions or the registration referred to in Rule 5(2)(a)(vii), on payment of the fee specified in Rule 8.

(b) Where such documents have already been communicated to the International Bureau, the latter shall transmit without delay a copy to the person who has made the request.

(c) If such a document has never been communicated to the International Bureau, the latter shall request a copy of it from the Competent Authority of the Contracting Party of Origin and shall transmit the document, on receipt, to the person who has made the request.

[9.755]
Rule 21
Signature

Where the signature of a Competent Authority is required under these Regulations, such signature may be printed or replaced by the affixing of a facsimile or an official seal.

[9.756]
Rule 22
Date of Dispatch of Various Communications

Where the notifications referred to in Rules 9(1), 14(1), 16(4) and 18(4) are communicated through a postal service, the date of dispatch shall be determined by the postmark. If the postmark is illegible or missing, the International Bureau shall treat the communication concerned as if it had been sent 20 days before the date on which it was received. Where such notifications are sent through a mail delivery service, the date of dispatch shall be determined by the information provided by such delivery service on the basis of the details of the mailing as recorded by it. Such notifications may also be communicated by facsimile or by electronic means, as provided for in the Administrative Instructions.

[9.757]
Rule 23
Modes of Notification by the International Bureau

(1) *[Notification of the International Registration]* The notification of the international registration, referred to in Rule 7(3)(ii), or the notification of the withdrawal of a renunciation referred to in Rule 16(3), shall be addressed by the International Bureau to the Competent Authority of each Contracting Party concerned by any means enabling the International Bureau to establish the date on which the notification was received, as provided for in the Administrative Instructions.
(2) *[Other Notifications]* Any other notification by the International Bureau referred to in these Regulations shall be addressed to the Competent Authorities by any means enabling the International Bureau to establish that the notification has been received.

[9.758]
Rule 24
Administrative Instructions

(1) *[Establishment of Administrative Instructions; Matters Governed by Them]*
- (a) The Director General shall establish Administrative Instructions and may modify them. Before establishing or modifying the Administrative Instructions, the Director General shall consult the Competent Authorities of the Contracting Parties which have direct interest in the proposed Administrative Instructions or their proposed modification.
- (b) The Administrative Instructions shall deal with matters in respect of which these Regulations expressly refer to such Instructions and with details in respect of the application of these Regulations.

(2) *[Supervision by the Assembly]* The Assembly may invite the Director General to modify any provision of the Administrative Instructions and the Director General shall act upon any such invitation.
(3) *[Publication and Effective Date]*
- (a) The Administrative Instructions and any modification thereof shall be published.
- (b) Each publication shall specify the date on which the published provisions become effective.

(4) *[Conflict with the Act or These Regulations]* In the case of conflict between, on the one hand, any provision of the Administrative Instructions and, on the other hand, any provision of the Act or these Regulations, the latter shall *prevail.*

PART 10
PROCEDURE

CIVIL PROCEDURE RULES 1998

(SI 1998/3132)

NOTES

Made: 10 December 1998.
Authority: Civil Procedure Act 1997, s 2.
Commencement: 26 April 1999.
Only provisions of these Rules relevant to this work are reproduced. Provisions not reproduced are not annotated.

ARRANGEMENT OF RULES

PART 45
FIXED COSTS

Section IV Scale Costs for Claims in the Intellectual Property Enterprise Court

PART 63
INTELLECTUAL PROPERTY CLAIMS

I.
PATENTS AND REGISTERED DESIGNS

II.
REGISTERED TRADE MARKS AND OTHER INTELLECTUAL PROPERTY RIGHTS

III.
SERVICE OF DOCUMENTS AND PARTICIPATION BY THE COMPTROLLER

IV.
APPEALS

V.
INTELLECTUAL PROPERTY ENTERPRISE COURT

[PART 45
FIXED COSTS

SECTION IV
SCALE COSTS FOR CLAIMS IN [THE INTELLECTUAL PROPERTY ENTERPRISE COURT]

[10.1]
45.30 Scope and interpretation

(1) Subject to paragraph (2), this Section applies to proceedings in [the Intellectual Property Enterprise Court].

(2) This Section does not apply where—

(a) the court considers that a party has behaved in a manner which amounts to an abuse of the court's process; or

(b) the claim concerns the infringement or revocation of a patent or registered design [or registered trade mark] the validity of which has been certified by a court [or by the Comptroller-General of Patents, Designs and Trade Marks] in earlier proceedings.

(3) The court will make a summary assessment of the costs of the party in whose favour any order for costs is made. Rules 44.2(8), 44.7(b) and Part 47 do not apply to this Section.

(4) "Scale costs" means the costs set out in Table A and Table B of the Practice Direction supplementing this Part.]

NOTES

Part 45 substituted by the Civil Procedure (Amendment) Rules 2013, SI 2013/262, r 16, Schedule.

Section heading: words in square brackets substituted by the Civil Procedure (Amendment No 7) Rules 2013, SI 2013/1974, r 20(c), subject to transitional provisions in r 30 thereof.

Para (1): words in square brackets substituted by SI 2013/1974, r 20(f)(i), subject to transitional provisions in r 30 thereof.

Para (2): words in first pair of square brackets inserted by the Civil Procedure (Amendment) Rules 2014, SI 2014/407, r 19; words in second pair of square brackets inserted by SI 2013/1974, r 20(f)(ii), subject to transitional provisions in r 30 thereof.

[10.2]
[45.31 Amount of scale costs

(1) Subject to rule 45.32, the court will not order a party to pay total costs of more than—

(a) £50,000 on the final determination of a claim in relation to liability; and

(b) £25,000 on an inquiry as to damages or account of profits.

(2) The amounts in paragraph (1) apply after the court has applied the provision on set off in accordance with rule 44.12(a).

(3) The maximum amount of scale costs that the court will award for each stage of the claim is set out in Practice Direction 45.

(4) The amount of the scale costs awarded by the court in accordance with paragraph (3) will depend on the nature and complexity of the claim.

[(4A) Subject to assessment where appropriate, the following may be recovered in addition to the amount of the scale costs set out in Practice Direction 45—Fixed Costs—

(a) court fees;

(b) costs relating to the enforcement of any court order; and

(c) wasted costs.]

(5) Where appropriate, [VAT] may be recovered in addition to the amount of the scale costs and any reference in this Section to scale costs is a reference to those costs net of any such VAT.]

NOTES

Substituted as noted to r 45.30 at **[10.1]**.

Para (4A): inserted by the Civil Procedure (Amendment No 7) Rules 2013, SI 2013/1974, r 20(g)(i), subject to transitional provisions in r 30 thereof.

Para (5): word in square brackets substituted by SI 2013/1974, r 20(g)(ii), subject to transitional provisions in r 30 thereof.

[10.3]
[45.32 Summary assessment of the costs of an application where a party has behaved unreasonably

Costs awarded to a party under rule 63.26(2) are in addition to the total costs that may be awarded to that party under rule 45.31.]

NOTES

Substituted as noted to r 45.30 at **[10.1]**.

PART 63
INTELLECTUAL PROPERTY CLAIMS

[10.4]

[63.1 Scope of this Part and interpretation

(1) This Part applies to all intellectual property claims including—
- (a) registered intellectual property rights such as—
  - (i) patents;
  - (ii) registered designs; and
  - (iii) registered trade marks; and
- (b) unregistered intellectual property rights such as—
  - (i) copyright;
  - (ii) design right;
  - (iii) the right to prevent passing off; and
  - (iv) the other rights set out in [Practice Direction 63].

(2) In this Part—
- (a) "the 1977 Act" means the Patents Act 1977;
- (b) "the 1988 Act" means the Copyright, Designs and Patents Act 1988;
- (c) "the 1994 Act" means the Trade Marks Act 1994;
- (d) "the Comptroller" means the Comptroller General of Patents, Designs and Trade Marks;
- (e) "patent" means a patent under the 1977 Act or a supplementary protection certificate granted by the Patent Office under Article 10(1) of Council Regulation (EEC) No 1768/92 or of Regulation (EC) No 1610/96 of the European Parliament and the Council and includes any application for a patent or supplementary protection certificate;
- (f) "Patents Court" means the Patents Court of the High Court constituted as part of the Chancery Division by section 6(1) of the Senior Courts Act 1981;
- [(g) "Intellectual Property Enterprise Court" means a specialist list established within the Chancery Division of the High Court;]
- [(h) "enterprise judge" means a judge authorised by the Chancellor of the High Court to sit in the Intellectual Property Enterprise Court,]
- (i) . . .
- (j) "the register" means whichever of the following registers is appropriate—
  - (i) patents maintained by the Comptroller under section 32 of the 1977 Act;
  - (ii) designs maintained by the registrar under section 17 of the Registered Designs Act 1949;
  - (iii) trade marks maintained by the registrar under section 63 of the 1994 Act;
  - (iv) Community trade marks maintained by the Office for Harmonisation in the Internal Market under Article 83 of Council Regulation (EC) No [207/2009];
  - (v) Community designs maintained by the Office for Harmonisation in the Internal Market under Article 72 of Council Regulation (EC) No 6/2002; . . .
  - (vi) plant varieties maintained by the Controller under regulation 12 of the Plant Breeders' Rights Regulations 1998; [and]
  - [(vii) Community plant variety rights maintained by the Community Plant Variety Right Office under Article 87 of Council Regulation (EC) No 2100/94; and]
- (k) "the registrar" means—
  - (i) the registrar of trade marks; or
  - (ii) the registrar of registered designs,

  whichever is appropriate.

(3) [Save as provided in rule 63.27, claims] to which this Part applies are allocated to the multi-track. [Rule 26.3(1) applies save for the modification that the court will send the parties a notice requiring the parties to file proposed directions by the date specified in the notice. For a claim which is allocated to the multi-track by this rule, rule 26.3(1B) and rules 26.4 to 26.10 do not apply.]]

NOTES

This Part (Part 63 (originally rr 63.1–63.4, 63.5–63.17)) inserted by the Civil Procedure (Amendment No 2) Rules 2002, SI 2002/3219, r 8, Schedule; substituted (by new rr 63.1–63.4, 63.5–63.16 and associated headings) by the Civil Procedure (Amendment) Rules 2009, SI 2009/2092, r 12, Sch 1.

Para (1): words in square brackets in sub-para (b)(iv) substituted by the Civil Procedure (Amendment No 2) Rules 2009, SI 2009/3390, r 38(a).

Para (2): sub-para (g), (h) substituted and in sub-para (j) reference in square brackets substituted, word omitted revoked and words in square brackets inserted, by the Civil Procedure (Amendment No 7) Rules 2013, SI 2013/1974, r 26(b), subject to transitional provisions in r 30 thereof; sub-para (i) revoked by SI 2009/3390, r 38(b).

Para (3): words in first pair of square brackets substituted by the Civil Procedure (Amendment No 2) Rules 2012, SI 2012/2208, rr 2, 10(b); words in second pair of square brackets added by SI 2013/1974, r 26(c), subject to transitional provisions in r 30 thereof.

[I
PATENTS AND REGISTERED DESIGNS

[10.5]
63.2 Scope of Section I and allocation

(1) This Section applies to—
(a) any claim under—
(i) the 1977 Act;
(ii) the Registered Designs Act 1949;
(iii) the Defence Contracts Act 1958; and
(b) any claim relating to—
(i) Community registered designs;
(ii) semiconductor topography rights; or
(iii) plant varieties.

(2) Claims to which this Section applies must be started in—
(a) the Patents Court; or
(b) [the Intellectual Property Enterprise Court].]

NOTES

Inserted and substituted as noted to r 63.1 at **[10.4]**.

Para (2): words in square brackets substituted by the Civil Procedure (Amendment No 7) Rules 2013, SI 2013/1974, r 26(d), subject to transitional provisions in r 30 thereof.

[10.6]
[63.3 Specialist list

Claims in the Patents Court [form a specialist list] for the purpose of rule 30.5.]

NOTES

Inserted and substituted as noted to r 63.1 at **[10.4]**.

Words in square brackets substituted by the Civil Procedure (Amendment No 7) Rules 2013, SI 2013/1974, r 26(e), subject to transitional provisions in r 30 thereof.

63.4, 63.4A (*Rule 63.4 inserted and substituted as noted to r 63.1 at* **[10.4]** *and revoked by the Civil Procedure (Amendment No 2) Rules 2010, SI 2010/1953, r 8(b); r 63.4A inserted by the Civil Procedure (Amendment No 3) Rules 2005, SI 2005/2292, r 47 and revoked by virtue of the Civil Procedure (Amendment) Rules 2009, SI 2009/2092, r 12, Sch 1.*)

[10.7]
[63.5 Starting the claim

Claims to which this Section applies must be started—
(a) by a Part 7 claim form; or
(b) in existing proceedings under Part 20.]

NOTES

Inserted and substituted as noted to r 63.1 at **[10.4]**.

[10.8]
[63.6 Claim for infringement or challenge to validity of a patent or registered design

A statement of case in a claim for infringement or a claim in which the validity of a patent or registered design is challenged must contain particulars as set out in [Practice Dirction 63].]

NOTES

Inserted and substituted as noted to r 63.1 at **[10.4]**.

Words in square brackets substituted by the Civil Procedure (Amendment No 2) Rules 2009, SI 2009/3390, r 38(a).

[10.9]
[63.7 Defence and reply

Part 15 applies with the modification—
(a) to rule 15.4(1)(b) that in a claim for infringement under rule 63.6, the period for filing a defence where the defendant files an acknowledgment of service under Part 10 is 42 days after service of the particulars of claim;
(b) that where rule 15.4(2) provides for a longer period to file a defence than in rule 63.7(a), then the period of time in rule 15.4(2) will apply; and
(c) to rule 15.8 that the claimant must—
(i) file any reply to a defence; and
(ii) serve it on all other parties,
within 21 days of service of the defence.]

NOTES

Inserted and substituted as noted to r 63.1 at **[10.4]**.

[10.10]
[63.8 Case Management

(1) Parties do not need to file [a directions questionnaire].

(2) The following provisions only of Part 29 apply—

(a) rule 29.3(2) (legal representatives to attend case management conferences);
(b) rule 29.4 [(the parties must endeavour to agree case management directions)]; and
(c) rule 29.5 (variation of case management timetable) with the exception of paragraph (1)(b) and (c).

(3) As soon as practicable the court will hold a case management conference which must be fixed in accordance with [Practice Direction 63].]

NOTES

Inserted and substituted as noted to r 63.1 at **[10.4]**.

Paras (1), (2): words in square brackets substituted by the Civil Procedure (Amendment No 7) Rules 2013, SI 2013/1974, r 26(f), subject to transitional provisions in r 30 thereof.

Para (3): words in square brackets substituted by the Civil Procedure (Amendment No 2) Rules 2009, SI 2009/3390, r 38(a).

[10.11]
[63.9 Disclosure and inspection

Part 31 is modified to the extent set out in [Practice Direction 63].]

NOTES

Inserted and substituted as noted to r 63.1 at **[10.4]**.

Words in square brackets substituted by the Civil Procedure (Amendment No 2) Rules 2009, SI 2009/3390, r 38(a).

[10.12]
[63.10 Application to amend a patent specification in existing proceedings

(1) An application under section 75 of the 1977 Act for permission to amend the specification of a patent by the proprietor of the patent must be made by application notice.

(2) The application notice must—

(a) give particulars of—
  (i) the proposed amendment sought; and
  (ii) the grounds upon which the amendment is sought;
(b) state whether the applicant will contend that the claims prior to amendment are valid; and
(c) be served by the applicant on all parties and the Comptroller within 7 days of it being filed.

(3) The application notice must, if it is reasonably possible, be served on the Comptroller electronically.

(4) Unless the court otherwise orders, the Comptroller will, as soon as practicable, advertise the application to amend in the journal.

(5) The advertisement will state that any person may apply to the Comptroller for a copy of the application notice.

(6) Within 14 days of the first appearance of the advertisement any person who wishes to oppose the application must file and serve on all parties and the Comptroller a notice opposing the application which must include the grounds relied on.

(7) Within 28 days of the first appearance of the advertisement the applicant must apply to the court for directions.

(8) Unless the court otherwise orders, the applicant must within 7 days serve on the Comptroller any order of the court on the application.

(9) In this rule, "the journal" means the journal published pursuant to rules under section 123(6) of the 1977 Act.]

NOTES

Inserted and substituted as noted to r 63.1 at **[10.4]**.

[10.13]
[63.11 Court's determination of question or application

This rule applies where the Comptroller—

(a) declines to deal with a question under section 8(7), 12(2), 37(8) or 61(5) of the 1977 Act;
(b) declines to deal with an application under section 40(5) of the 1977 Act; or
(c) certifies under section 72(7)(b) of the 1977 Act that the court should determine the question whether a patent should be revoked,

(2) Any person seeking the court's determination of that question or application must start a claim for that purpose within 14 days of receiving notification of the Comptroller's decision.

(3) A person who fails to start a claim within the time prescribed by rule 63.11(2) will be deemed to have abandoned the reference or application.

(4) A party may apply to the Comptroller or the court to extend the period for starting a claim prescribed by rule 63.11(2) even where the application is made after expiration of that period.]

NOTES

Inserted and substituted as noted to r 63.1 at **[10.4]**.

[10.14]
[63.12 Application by employee for compensation

(1) An application by an employee for compensation under section 40(1) or (2) of the 1977 Act must be made—

- (a) in a claim form; and
- (b) within the period prescribed by paragraphs (2), (3) and (4).

(2) The prescribed period begins on the date of the grant of the patent and ends 1 year after the patent has ceased to have effect.

(3) Where the patent has ceased to have effect as a result of failure to pay renewal fees, the prescribed period continues as if the patent has remained continuously in effect provided that—

- (a) the renewal fee and any additional fee are paid in accordance with section 25(4) of the 1977 Act; or
- (b) restoration is ordered by the Comptroller following an application under section 28 of the 1977 Act.

(4) Where restoration is refused by the Comptroller following an application under section 28 of the 1977 Act, the prescribed period will end 1 year after the patent has ceased to have effect or 6 months after the date of refusal, whichever is the later.]

NOTES

Inserted and substituted as noted to r 63.1 at **[10.4]**.

[II
REGISTERED TRADE MARKS AND OTHER INTELLECTUAL PROPERTY RIGHTS

[10.15]
63.13 Allocation

Claims relating to matters arising out of the 1994 Act and other intellectual property rights set out in [Practice Direction 63] must be started in—

- (a) the Chancery Division;
- (b) [the Intellectual Property Enterprise Court]; or
- (c) save as set out in [Practice Direction 63], a [County Court hearing centre] where there is also a Chancery District Registry.]

NOTES

Inserted and substituted as noted to r 63.1 at **[10.4]**.

Words in first pair of square brackets and words in first pair of square brackets in para (c) substituted by the Civil Procedure (Amendment No 2) Rules 2009, SI 2009/3390, r 38(a); words in square brackets in para (b) substituted by the Civil Procedure (Amendment No 7) Rules 2013, SI 2013/1974, r 26(g), subject to transitional provisions in r 30 thereof; words in second pair of square brackets in para (c) substituted by the Civil Procedure (Amendment) Rules 2014, SI 2014/407, r 27(a).

[III
SERVICE OF DOCUMENTS AND PARTICIPATION BY THE COMPTROLLER

[10.16]
63.14 Service of documents

(1) Subject to paragraph (2), Part 6 applies to service of a claim form and any document in any proceedings under this Part.

(2) A claim form relating to a registered right may be served—

- [(a) on a party who has registered the right at the address for service given for that right in the appropriate register at—
  - (i) the United Kingdom Patent Office; or
  - (ii) the Office for Harmonisation in the Internal Market,

  provided the address is within the United Kingdom; or]
- (b) in accordance with rule . . . 6.33(1) or 6.33(2) on a party who has registered the right at the address for service given for that right in the appropriate register at—
  - (i) the United Kingdom Patent Office; or
  - (ii) the Office for Harmonisation in the Internal Market.

(3) Where a party seeks any remedy (whether by claim form, counterclaim or application notice), which would if granted affect an entry in any United Kingdom Patent Office register, that party must serve on the Comptroller or registrar—

(a) the claim form, counterclaim or application notice;

(b) any other statement of case where relevant (including any amended statement of case); and

(c) any accompanying documents.]

NOTES

Inserted and substituted as noted to r 63.1 at **[10.4]**.

Para (2): sub-para (a) substituted and figure omitted from sub-para (b) revoked, by the Civil Procedure (Amendment) Rules 2014, SI 2014/407, r 27(b).

[10.17]
[63.15 Participation by the Comptroller

Where the documents set out in rule 63.14(3) are served, the Comptroller or registrar—

(a) may take part in proceedings; and

(b) need not serve a defence or other statement of case unless the court orders otherwise.]

NOTES

Inserted and substituted as noted to r 63.1 at **[10.4]**.

[IV
APPEALS

[10.18]
63.16 Appeals from decisions of the Comptroller or the registrar

(1) Part 52 applies to appeals from decisions of the Comptroller and the registrar.

(2) Appeals about patents [and registered designs] must be made to the Patents Court, and other appeals to the Chancery Division.

(3) Where Part 52 requires a document to be served, it must also be served on the Comptroller or registrar, as appropriate.]

NOTES

Inserted and substituted as noted to r 63.1 at **[10.4]**.

Para (2): words in square brackets inserted by the Civil Procedure (Amendment) Rules 2017, SI 2017/95, rr 4, 11(2).

[V
[INTELLECTUAL PROPERTY ENTERPRISE COURT]

NOTES

Section heading: words in square brackets substituted by the Civil Procedure (Amendment No 7) Rules 2013, SI 2013/1974, r 26(h), subject to transitional provisions in r 30 thereof.

[10.19]
63.17 Scope of this Section

This Part, as modified by this Section, applies to claims started in or transferred to [the Intellectual Property Enterprise Court].]

NOTES

Inserted, together with preceding heading and rr 63.18–63.26, by the Civil Procedure (Amendment No 2) Rules 2010, SI 2010/1953, r 8(c), Sch 2.

Words in square brackets substituted by the Civil Procedure (Amendment No 7) Rules 2013, SI 2013/1974, r 26(i), subject to transitional provisions in r 30 thereof.

[10.20]
[63.17A

(1) In proceedings in the Intellectual Property Enterprise Court in which a claim is made for damages or an account of profits, the amount or value of that claim shall not exceed £500,000.

(2) In determining the amount or value of a claim for the purpose of paragraph (1), a claim for—

(a) interest, other than interest payable under an agreement; or

(b) costs,

shall be disregarded.

(3) Paragraph (1) shall not apply if the parties agree that the Intellectual Property Enterprise Court shall have jurisdiction to award damages or profits in excess of £500,000.]

NOTES

Commencement: 1 October 2013.

Inserted by the Civil Procedure (Amendment No 7) Rules 2013, SI 2013/1974, r 26(j), subject to transitional provisions in r 30 thereof.

[10.21]
[63.18

(1) Rule 30.5 applies save for the modifications—

(a) a judge sitting in the County Court or the general Chancery Division may order proceedings to be transferred to the Intellectual Property Enterprise Court; and

(b) an application for the transfer of proceedings from the County Court or the general Chancery Division to the Intellectual Property Enterprise Court may be made to a judge sitting in the County Court or the general Chancery Division respectively.

(2) When considering whether to transfer proceedings to or from the Intellectual Property Enterprise Court, the court will have regard to the provisions of Practice Direction 30.]

NOTES

Commencement: 1 October 2013.

Inserted as noted to r 63.17 at **[10.19]** and substituted by the Civil Procedure (Amendment No 7) Rules 2013, SI 2013/1974, r 26(k), subject to transitional provisions in r 30 thereof.

[10.22]
[63.19 [Enterprise judges and district judges]

(1) Subject to paragraph (2), proceedings in [the Intellectual Property Enterprise Court will be dealt with by an enterprise judge.]

[(1A) . . .]

[(2) Unless the court otherwise orders, the following matters will be dealt with by a district judge—

(a) allocation of claims to the small claims track or multi-track in accordance with rule 63.27(3);

(b) claims allocated to the small claims track; and

(c) all proceedings for the enforcement of any financial element of an Intellectual Property Enterprise Court judgment.

(3) For the purposes of the Practice Direction 52A – Appeals: General Provisions, a decision of a district judge shall be treated as a decision by a district judge hearing a . . . claim in the County Court. An appeal from such a decision shall be heard by an enterprise judge.]]

NOTES

Inserted as noted to r 63.17 at **[10.19]**.

Rule heading: substituted by the Civil Procedure (Amendment No 7) Rules 2013, SI 2013/1974, r 26(l)(i), subject to transitional provisions in r 30 thereof.

Para (1): words in square brackets substituted by SI 2013/1974, r 26(l)(ii), subject to transitional provisions in r 30 thereof.

Para (1A): inserted by SI 2013/1974, r 26(l)(iii); revoked by the Civil Procedure (Amendment No 3) Rules 2016, SI 2016/788, rr 4, 12(a).

Paras (2), (3): substituted for original para (2), by SI 2013/1974, r 26(l)(iv), subject to transitional provisions in r 30 thereof; word omitted from para (3) revoked by SI 2016/788, rr 4, 12(b).

[10.23]
[63.20 Statements of case

(1) Part 16 applies with the modification that a statement of case must set out concisely all the facts and arguments upon which the party serving it relies.

(2) The particulars of claim must state whether the claimant has complied with paragraph [6] of the Practice Direction (Pre-Action Conduct).]

NOTES

Inserted as noted to r 63.17 at **[10.19]**.

Para (2): figure in square brackets substituted by the Civil Procedure (Amendment) Rules 2017, SI 2017/95, rr 4, 11(1).

[10.24]
[63.21 Statement of truth

Part 22 applies with the modification that the statement of truth verifying a statement of case must be signed by a person with knowledge of the facts alleged, or if no one person has knowledge of all the facts, by persons who between them have knowledge of all the facts alleged.]

NOTES

Inserted as noted to r 63.17 at **[10.19]**.

[10.25]
[63.22 Defence and reply

(1) Rule 63.7 does not apply and Part 15 applies with the following modifications.

(2) Where the particulars of claim contain a confirmation in accordance with rule 63.20(2), the period for filing a defence [where the defendant files an acknowledgment of service under Part 10] is 42 days after service of the particulars of claim unless rule 15.4(2) provides for a longer period to do so.

(3) Where the particulars of claim do not contain a confirmation in accordance with rule 63.20(2), the period for filing a defence [where the defendant files an acknowledgment of service under Part 10] is 70 days after service of the particulars of claim.

(4) Where the claimant files a reply to a defence it must be filed and served on all other parties within 28 days of service of the defence.

(5) Where the defendant files a reply to a defence to a counterclaim it must be filed and served on all other parties within 14 days of service of the defence to the counterclaim.

(6) The periods in this rule may only be extended by order of the court and for good reason.]

NOTES

Inserted as noted to r 63.17 at **[10.19]**.

Paras (2), (3): words in square brackets inserted by the Civil Procedure (Amendment No 7) Rules 2013, SI 2013/1974, r 26(m), subject to transitional provisions in r 30 thereof.

[10.26]

[63.23 Case management

(1) At the first case management conference after those defendants who intend to file and serve a defence have done so, the court will identify the issues and decide whether to make an order in accordance with paragraph 29.1 of Practice Direction 63.

(2) Save in exceptional circumstances the court will not [permit] a party to submit material in addition to that ordered under paragraph (1).

(3) The court may determine the claim on the papers where all parties consent.]

NOTES

Inserted as noted to r 63.17 at **[10.19]**.

Para (2): word in square brackets substituted by the Civil Procedure (Amendment No 7) Rules 2013, SI 2013/1974, r 26(n), subject to transitional provisions in r 30 thereof.

[10.27]

[63.24 Disclosure and inspection

(1) Rule 63.9 does not apply.

(2) Part 31 applies save that the provisions on standard disclosure do not apply.]

NOTES

Inserted as noted to r 63.17 at **[10.19]**.

[10.28]

[63.25 Applications

(1) Part 23 applies with the modifications set out in this rule.

(2) Except at the case management conference provided for in rule 63.23(1), a respondent to an application must file and serve on all relevant parties a response within 5 days of the service of the application notice.

(3) The court will deal with an application without a hearing unless the court considers it necessary to hold a hearing.

(4) An application to transfer the claim to the [Patents Court or general Chancery Division] or to stay proceedings must be made before or at the case management conference provided for in rule 63.23(1).

(5) The court will consider an application to transfer the claim later in the proceedings only where there are exceptional circumstances.]

NOTES

Inserted as noted to r 63.17 at **[10.19]**.

Para (4): words in square brackets substituted by the Civil Procedure (Amendment No 7) Rules 2013, SI 2013/1974, r 26(o), subject to transitional provisions in r 30 thereof.

[10.29]

[63.26 Costs

(1) Subject to paragraph (2), the court will reserve the costs of an application to the conclusion of the trial when they will be subject to summary assessment.

(2) Where a party has behaved unreasonably the court [may] make an order for costs at the conclusion of the hearing.

(3) Where the court makes a summary assessment of costs, it will do so in accordance with [Section IV] of Part 45.]

NOTES

Inserted as noted to r 63.17 at **[10.19]**.

Paras (2), (3): words in square brackets substituted by the Civil Procedure (Amendment No 7) Rules 2013, SI 2013/1974, r 26(p), subject to transitional provisions in r 30 thereof.

[10.30]

[63.27 Allocation to the small claims track

(1) A claim started in or transferred to [the Intellectual Property Enterprise Court] will be allocated to the small claims track if—

(a) rule 63.13, but not rule 63.2, applies to the claim;

(b) the value of the claim is not more than [£10,000];

(c) it is stated in the particulars of claim that the claimant wishes the claim to be allocated to the small claims track; and

(d) no objection to the claim being allocated to the small claims track is raised by the defendant in the defence.

(2) . . .

(3) If either—

(a) the requirements of rule 63.27(1)(a), (b) and (c) are satisfied, but in the defence the defendant objects to the claim being allocated to the small claims track; or

(b) the requirements of rule 63.27(1)(a) and (b) are satisfied, but not (c), and in the defence the defendant requests that the claim be allocated to the small claims track,

the court will allocate the claim to the small claims track or the multi-track in accordance with Part 26 (case management—preliminary stage). [For that purpose the court will send the parties a directions questionnaire and require them to file completed directions questionnaires and to serve them on all other parties within 14 days.]

(4) Part 27 (small claims track) shall apply to claims allocated to the small claims track in [the Intellectual Property Enterprise Court] with the modification to rule 27.2(1)(a) that Part 25 (interim remedies) shall not apply to such claims at all. [Section IV] of Part 45 (scale costs for claims in [the Intellectual Property Enterprise Court]) shall not apply to claims allocated to the small claims track in [the Intellectual Property Enterprise Court].]

NOTES

Commencement: 1 October 2012.

Inserted, together with r 63.26, by the Civil Procedure (Amendment No 2) Rules 2012, SI 2012/2208, rr 2, 10(c).

Para (1): words in first pair of square brackets substituted by the Civil Procedure (Amendment No 7) Rules 2013, SI 2013/1974, r 26(q)(i), subject to transitional provisions in r 30 thereof; sum in square brackets substituted, except in relation to claims issued before 1 April 2013, by the Civil Procedure (Amendment) Rules 2013, SI 2013/262, rr 19, 22(3)(a).

Para (2): revoked by SI 2013/1974, r 26(q)(ii), subject to transitional provisions in r 30 thereof.

Para (3): words in square brackets added by SI 2013/1974, r 26(q)(iii), subject to transitional provisions in r 30 thereof.

Para (4): words in square brackets substituted by SI 2013/1974, r 26(q)(iv), subject to transitional provisions in r 30 thereof.

[10.31]

[63.28 Extent to which rules in this Part apply to small claims

(1) To the extent provided by this rule, this Part shall apply to a claim allocated to, or requested to be allocated to, the small claims track in [the Intellectual Property Enterprise Court].

(2) Rules 63.1, 63.13, 63.18, 63.20, 63.21, 63.22, 63.25, 63.26(1) and (2), and 63.27 shall apply to the claim.

(3) No other rules in this Part shall apply.]

NOTES

Commencement: 1 October 2012.

Inserted as noted to r 63.27 at **[10.30]**.

Para (1): words in square brackets substituted by the Civil Procedure (Amendment No 7) Rules 2013, SI 2013/1974, r 26(r), subject to transitional provisions in r 30 thereof.

EXTRACTS OF TREATIES

NOTES

This document is available on the General Court section of the Curia website at curia.europa.eu/jcms/jcms/Jo2_7040/en/.

A.
TREATY ON THE EUROPEAN UNION

[10.32]
Article 13

1. The Union shall have an institutional framework which shall aim to promote its values, advance its objectives, serve its interests, those of its citizens and those of the Member States, and ensure the consistency, effectiveness and continuity of its policies and actions.

The Union's institutions shall be:

– the European Parliament,
– the European Council,
– the Council,
– the European Commission (hereinafter referred to as 'the Commission'),
– the Court of Justice of the European Union,
– the European Central Bank,
– the Court of Auditors.

2. Each institution shall act within the limits of the powers conferred on it in the Treaties, and in conformity with the procedures, conditions and objectives set out in them. The institutions shall practice mutual sincere cooperation.

3. The provisions relating to the European Central Bank and the Court of Auditors and detailed provisions on the other institutions are set out in the Treaty on the Functioning of the European Union.

4. The European Parliament, the Council and the Commission shall be assisted by an Economic and Social Committee and a Committee of the Regions acting in an advisory capacity.

[10.33]
Article 19

1. The Court of Justice of the European Union shall include the Court of Justice, the General Court and specialised courts. It shall ensure that in the interpretation and application of the Treaties the law is observed.

Member States shall provide remedies sufficient to ensure effective legal protection in the fields covered by Union law.

2. The Court of Justice shall consist of one judge from each Member State. It shall be assisted by Advocates-General.

The General Court shall include at least one judge per Member State.

The Judges and the Advocates-General of the Court of Justice and the Judges of the General Court shall be chosen from persons whose independence is beyond doubt and who satisfy the conditions set out in Articles 253 and 254 of the Treaty on the Functioning of the European Union. They shall be appointed by common accord of the governments of the Member States for six years. Retiring Judges and Advocates-General may be reappointed.

3. The Court of Justice of the European Union shall, in accordance with the Treaties:

(a) rule on actions brought by a Member State, an institution or a natural or legal person;
(b) give preliminary rulings, at the request of courts or tribunals of the Member States, on the interpretation of Union law or the validity of acts adopted by the institutions;
(c) rule in other cases provided for in the Treaties.

B.
TREATY ON THE FUNCTIONING OF THE EUROPEAN UNION

[10.34]
Article 108
(ex Article 88 TEC)

1. The Commission shall, in cooperation with Member States, keep under constant review all systems of aid existing in those States. It shall propose to the latter any appropriate measures required by the progressive development or by the functioning of the internal market.

2. If, after giving notice to the parties concerned to submit their comments, the Commission finds that aid granted by a State or through State resources is not compatible with the internal market having regard to Article 107, or that such aid is being misused, it shall decide that the State concerned shall abolish or alter such aid within a period of time to be determined by the Commission.

If the State concerned does not comply with this decision within the prescribed time, the Commission or any other interested State may, in derogation from the provisions of Articles 258 and 259, refer the matter to the Court of Justice of the European Union direct.

On application by a Member State, the Council may, acting unanimously, decide that aid which that State is granting or intends to grant shall be considered to be compatible with the internal market, in derogation from the provisions of Article 107 or from the regulations provided for in Article 109, if such a decision is justified by exceptional circumstances. If, as regards the aid in question, the Commission has already initiated the procedure provided for in the first subparagraph of this paragraph, the fact that the State concerned has made its application to the Council shall have the effect of suspending that procedure until the Council has made its attitude known.

If, however, the Council has not made its attitude known within three months of the said application being made, the Commission shall give its decision on the case.

3. The Commission shall be informed, in sufficient time to enable it to submit its comments, of any plans to grant or alter aid. If it considers that any such plan is not compatible with the internal market having regard to Article 107, it shall without delay initiate the procedure provided for in paragraph 2. The Member State concerned shall not put its proposed measures into effect until this procedure has resulted in a final decision.

4. The Commission may adopt regulations relating to the categories of State aid that the Council has, pursuant to Article 109, determined may be exempted from the procedure provided for by paragraph 3 of this Article.

[10.35]
Article 218
(ex Article 300 TEC)

1. Without prejudice to the specific provisions laid down in Article 207, agreements between the Union and third countries or international organisations shall be negotiated and concluded in accordance with the following procedure.

2. The Council shall authorise the opening of negotiations, adopt negotiating directives, authorise the signing of agreements and conclude them.

3. The Commission, or the High Representative of the Union for Foreign Affairs and Security Policy where the agreement envisaged relates exclusively or principally to the common foreign and security policy, shall submit recommendations to the Council, which shall adopt a decision authorising the opening of negotiations and, depending on the subject of the agreement envisaged, nominating the Union negotiator or the head of the Union's negotiating team.

4. The Council may address directives to the negotiator and designate a special committee in consultation with which the negotiations must be conducted.

5. The Council, on a proposal by the negotiator, shall adopt a decision authorising the signing of the agreement and, if necessary, its provisional application before entry into force.

6. The Council, on a proposal by the negotiator, shall adopt a decision concluding the agreement.

Except where agreements relate exclusively to the common foreign and security policy, the Council shall adopt the decision concluding the agreement:

(a) after obtaining the consent of the European Parliament in the following cases:
   (i) association agreements;
   (ii) agreement on Union accession to the European Convention for the Protection of Human Rights and Fundamental Freedoms;
   (iii) agreements establishing a specific institutional framework by organising cooperation procedures;
   (iv) agreements with important budgetary implications for the Union;
   (v) agreements covering fields to which either the ordinary legislative procedure applies, or the special legislative procedure where consent by the European Parliament is required.

   The European Parliament and the Council may, in an urgent situation, agree upon a time-limit for consent.

(b) after consulting the European Parliament in other cases. The European Parliament shall deliver its opinion within a time-limit which the Council may set depending on the urgency of the matter. In the absence of an opinion within that time-limit, the Council may act.

7. When concluding an agreement, the Council may, by way of derogation from paragraphs 5, 6 and 9, authorise the negotiator to approve on the Union's behalf modifications to the agreement where it provides for them to be adopted by a simplified procedure or by a body set up by the agreement. The Council may attach specific conditions to such authorisation.

8. The Council shall act by a qualified majority throughout the procedure.

However, it shall act unanimously when the agreement covers a field for which unanimity is required for the adoption of a Union act as well as for association agreements and the agreements referred to in Article 212 with the States which are candidates for accession. The Council shall also act unanimously for the agreement on accession of the Union to the European Convention for the protection of Human Rights and Fundamental Freedoms; the decision concluding this agreement shall enter into force after it has been approved by the Member States in accordance with their respective constitutional requirements.

9. The Council, on a proposal from the Commission or the High Representative of the Union for Foreign Affairs and Security Policy, shall adopt a decision suspending application of an agreement and establishing the positions to be adopted on the Union's behalf in a body set up by an agreement, when that body is called upon to adopt acts having legal effects, with the exception of acts supplementing or amending the institutional framework of the agreement.
10. The European Parliament shall be immediately and fully informed at all stages of the procedure.
11. A Member State, the European Parliament, the Council or the Commission may obtain the opinion of the Court of Justice as to whether an agreement envisaged is compatible with the Treaties. Where the opinion of the Court is adverse, the agreement envisaged may not enter into force unless it is amended or the Treaties are revised.

[10.36]
Article 251
(ex Article 221 TEC)
The Court of Justice shall sit in chambers or in a Grand Chamber, in accordance with the rules laid down for that purpose in the Statute of the Court of Justice of the European Union.

When provided for in the Statute, the Court of Justice may also sit as a full Court.

[10.37]
Article 252
(ex Article 222 TEC)
The Court of Justice shall be assisted by eight Advocates-General. Should the Court of Justice so request, the Council, acting unanimously, may increase the number of Advocates-General.

It shall be the duty of the Advocate-General, acting with complete impartiality and independence, to make, in open court, reasoned submissions on cases which, in accordance with the Statute of the Court of Justice of the European Union, require his involvement.

[10.38]
Article 253
(ex Article 223 TEC)
The Judges and Advocates-General of the Court of Justice shall be chosen from persons whose independence is beyond doubt and who possess the qualifications required for appointment to the highest judicial offices in their respective countries or who are jurisconsults of recognised competence; they shall be appointed by common accord of the governments of the Member States for a term of six years, after consultation of the panel provided for in Article 255.

Every three years there shall be a partial replacement of the Judges and Advocates-General, in accordance with the conditions laid down in the Statute of the Court of Justice of the European Union.

The Judges shall elect the President of the Court of Justice from among their number for a term of three years. He may be re-elected.

Retiring Judges and Advocates-General may be reappointed.

The Court of Justice shall appoint its Registrar and lay down the rules governing his service.

The Court of Justice shall establish its Rules of Procedure. Those Rules shall require the approval of the Council.

[10.39]
Article 254
(ex Article 224 TEC)
The number of Judges of the General Court shall be determined by the Statute of the Court of Justice of the European Union. The Statute may provide for the General Court to be assisted by Advocates-General.

The members of the General Court shall be chosen from persons whose independence is beyond doubt and who possess the ability required for appointment to high judicial office. They shall be appointed by common accord of the governments of the Member States for a term of six years, after consultation of the panel provided for in Article 255. The membership shall be partially renewed every three years. Retiring members shall be eligible for reappointment.

The Judges shall elect the President of the General Court from among their number for a term of three years. He may be re-elected.

The General Court shall appoint its Registrar and lay down the rules governing his service.

The General Court shall establish its Rules of Procedure in agreement with the Court of Justice. Those Rules shall require the approval of the Council.

Unless the Statute of the Court of Justice of the European Union provides otherwise, the provisions of the Treaties relating to the Court of Justice shall apply to the General Court.

[10.40]
Article 255
A panel shall be set up in order to give an opinion on candidates' suitability to perform the duties of Judge and Advocate-General of the Court of Justice and the General Court before the governments of the Member States make the appointments referred to in Articles 253 and 254.

The panel shall comprise seven persons chosen from among former members of the Court of Justice and the General Court, members of national supreme courts and lawyers of recognised competence, one of whom shall be proposed by the European Parliament. The Council shall adopt a decision establishing the panel's operating rules and a decision appointing its members. It shall act on the initiative of the President of the Court of Justice.

[10.41]
Article 256
(ex Article 225 TEC)

1. The General Court shall have jurisdiction to hear and determine at first instance actions or proceedings referred to in Articles 263, 265, 268, 270 and 272, with the exception of those assigned to a specialised court set up under Article 257 and those reserved in the Statute for the Court of Justice. The Statute may provide for the General Court to have jurisdiction for other classes of action or proceeding.

Decisions given by the General Court under this paragraph may be subject to a right of appeal to the Court of Justice on points of law only, under the conditions and within the limits laid down by the Statute.

2. The General Court shall have jurisdiction to hear and determine actions or proceedings brought against decisions of the specialised courts.

Decisions given by the General Court under this paragraph may exceptionally be subject to review by the Court of Justice, under the conditions and within the limits laid down by the Statute, where there is a serious risk of the unity or consistency of Union law being affected.

3. The General Court shall have jurisdiction to hear and determine questions referred for a preliminary ruling under Article 267, in specific areas laid down by the Statute.

Where the General Court considers that the case requires a decision of principle likely to affect the unity or consistency of Union law, it may refer the case to the Court of Justice for a ruling.

Decisions given by the General Court on questions referred for a preliminary ruling may exceptionally be subject to review by the Court of Justice, under the conditions and within the limits laid down by the Statute, where there is a serious risk of the unity or consistency of Union law being affected.

[10.42]
Article 257
(ex Article 225A TEC)

The European Parliament and the Council, acting in accordance with the ordinary legislative procedure, may establish specialised courts attached to the General Court to hear and determine at first instance certain classes of action or proceeding brought in specific areas. The European Parliament and the Council shall act by means of regulations either on a proposal from the Commission after consultation of the Court of Justice or at the request of the Court of Justice after consultation of the Commission.

The regulation establishing a specialised court shall lay down the rules on the organisation of the court and the extent of the jurisdiction conferred upon it.

Decisions given by specialised courts may be subject to a right of appeal on points of law only or, when provided for in the regulation establishing the specialised court, a right of appeal also on matters of fact, before the General Court.

The members of the specialised courts shall be chosen from persons whose independence is beyond doubt and who possess the ability required for appointment to judicial office. They shall be appointed by the Council, acting unanimously.

The specialised courts shall establish their Rules of Procedure in agreement with the Court of Justice. Those Rules shall require the approval of the Council.

Unless the regulation establishing the specialised court provides otherwise, the provisions of the Treaties relating to the Court of Justice of the European Union and the provisions of the Statute of the Court of Justice of the European Union shall apply to the specialised courts. Title I of the Statute and Article 64 thereof shall in any case apply to the specialised courts.

[10.43]
Article 258
(ex Article 226 TEC)

If the Commission considers that a Member State has failed to fulfil an obligation under the Treaties, it shall deliver a reasoned opinion on the matter after giving the State concerned the opportunity to submit its observations.

If the State concerned does not comply with the opinion within the period laid down by the Commission, the latter may bring the matter before the Court of Justice of the European Union.

[10.44]
Article 259
(ex Article 227 TEC)

A Member State which considers that another Member State has failed to fulfil an obligation under the Treaties may bring the matter before the Court of Justice of the European Union.

Before a Member State brings an action against another Member State for an alleged infringement of an obligation under the Treaties, it shall bring the matter before the Commission.

The Commission shall deliver a reasoned opinion after each of the States concerned has been given the opportunity to submit its own case and its observations on the other party's case both orally and in writing.

If the Commission has not delivered an opinion within three months of the date on which the matter was brought before it, the absence of such opinion shall not prevent the matter from being brought before the Court.

[10.45]
Article 260
(ex Article 228 TEC)

1. If the Court of Justice of the European Union finds that a Member State has failed to fulfil an obligation under the Treaties, the State shall be required to take the necessary measures to comply with the judgment of the Court.

2. If the Commission considers that the Member State concerned has not taken the necessary measures to comply with the judgment of the Court, it may bring the case before the Court after giving that State the opportunity to submit its observations. It shall specify the amount of the lump sum or penalty payment to be paid by the Member State concerned which it considers appropriate in the circumstances.

If the Court finds that the Member State concerned has not complied with its judgment it may impose a lump sum or penalty payment on it.

This procedure shall be without prejudice to Article 259.

3. When the Commission brings a case before the Court pursuant to Article 258 on the grounds that the Member State concerned has failed to fulfil its obligation to notify measures transposing a directive adopted under a legislative procedure, it may, when it deems appropriate, specify the amount of the lump sum or penalty payment to be paid by the Member State concerned which it considers appropriate in the circumstances.

If the Court finds that there is an infringement it may impose a lump sum or penalty payment on the Member State concerned not exceeding the amount specified by the Commission. The payment obligation shall take effect on the date set by the Court in its judgment.

[10.46]
Article 261
(ex Article 229 TEC)

Regulations adopted jointly by the European Parliament and the Council, and by the Council, pursuant to the provisions of the Treaties, may give the Court of Justice of the European Union unlimited jurisdiction with regard to the penalties provided for in such regulations.

[10.47]
Article 262
(ex Article 229 A TEC)

Without prejudice to the other provisions of the Treaties, the Council, acting unanimously in accordance with a special legislative procedure and after consulting the European Parliament, may adopt provisions to confer jurisdiction, to the extent that it shall determine, on the Court of Justice of the European Union in disputes relating to the application of acts adopted on the basis of the Treaties which create European intellectual property rights. These provisions shall enter into force after their approval by the Member States in accordance with their respective constitutional requirements.

[10.48]
Article 263
(ex Article 230 TEC)

The Court of Justice of the European Union shall review the legality of legislative acts, of acts of the Council, of the Commission and of the European Central Bank, other than recommendations and opinions, and of acts of the European Parliament and of the European Council intended to produce legal effects vis-à-vis third parties. It shall also review the legality of acts of bodies, offices or agencies of the Union intended to produce legal effects vis-à-vis third parties.

It shall for this purpose have jurisdiction in actions brought by a Member State, the European Parliament, the Council or the Commission on grounds of lack of competence, infringement of an essential procedural requirement, infringement of the Treaties or of any rule of law relating to their application, or misuse of powers.

The Court shall have jurisdiction under the same conditions in actions brought by the Court of Auditors, by the European Central Bank and by the Committee of the Regions for the purpose of protecting their prerogatives.

Any natural or legal person may, under the conditions laid down in the first and second paragraphs, institute proceedings against an act addressed to that person or which is of direct and individual concern to them, and against a regulatory act which is of direct concern to them and does not entail implementing measures.

Acts setting up bodies, offices and agencies of the Union may lay down specific conditions and arrangements concerning actions brought by natural or legal persons against acts of these bodies, offices or agencies intended to produce legal effects in relation to them.

The proceedings provided for in this Article shall be instituted within two months of the publication of the measure, or of its notification to the plaintiff, or, in the absence thereof, of the day on which it came to the knowledge of the latter, as the case may be.

[10.49]
Article 264
(ex Article 231 TEC)

If the action is well founded, the Court of Justice of the European Union shall declare the act concerned to be void.

However, the Court shall, if it considers this necessary, state which of the effects of the act which it has declared void shall be considered as definitive.

[10.50]
Article 265
(ex Article 232 TEC)

Should the European Parliament, the European Council, the Council, the Commission or the European Central Bank, in infringement of the Treaties, fail to act, the Member States and the other institutions of the Union may bring an action before the Court of Justice of the European Union to have the infringement established. This Article shall apply, under the same conditions, to bodies, offices and agencies of the Union which fail to act.

The action shall be admissible only if the institution, body, office or agency concerned has first been called upon to act. If, within two months of being so called upon, the institution, body, office or agency concerned has not defined its position, the action may be brought within a further period of two months.

Any natural or legal person may, under the conditions laid down in the preceding paragraphs, complain to the Court that an institution, body, office or agency of the Union has failed to address to that person any act other than a recommendation or an opinion.

[10.51]
Article 266
(ex Article 233 TEC)

The institution whose act has been declared void or whose failure to act has been declared contrary to the Treaties shall be required to take the necessary measures to comply with the judgment of the Court of Justice of the European Union.

This obligation shall not affect any obligation which may result from the application of the second paragraph of Article 340.

[10.52]
Article 267
(ex Article 234 TEC)

The Court of Justice of the European Union shall have jurisdiction to give preliminary rulings concerning:

(a) the interpretation of the Treaties;

b) the validity and interpretation of acts of the institutions, bodies, offices or agencies of the Union;

Where such a question is raised before any court or tribunal of a Member State, that court or tribunal may, if it considers that a decision on the question is necessary to enable it to give judgment, request the Court to give a ruling thereon.

Where any such question is raised in a case pending before a court or tribunal of a Member State against whose decisions there is no judicial remedy under national law, that court or tribunal shall bring the matter before the Court.

If such a question is raised in a case pending before a court or tribunal of a Member State with regard to a person in custody, the Court of Justice of the European Union shall act with the minimum of delay.

[10.53]
Article 268
(ex Article 235 TEC)

The Court of Justice of the European Union shall have jurisdiction in disputes relating to compensation for damage provided for in the second and third paragraphs of Article 340.

[10.54]
Article 269

The Court of Justice shall have jurisdiction to decide on the legality of an act adopted by the European Council or by the Council pursuant to Article 7 of the Treaty on European Union solely at the request of the Member State concerned by a determination of the European Council or of the Council and in respect solely of the procedural stipulations contained in that Article.

Such a request must be made within one month from the date of such determination. The Court shall rule within one month from the date of the request.

[10.55]
Article 270
(ex Article 236 TEC)
The Court of Justice of the European Union shall have jurisdiction in any dispute between the Union and its servants within the limits and under the conditions laid down in the Staff Regulations of Officials and the Conditions of Employment of other servants of the Union.

[10.56]
Article 271
(ex Article 237 TEC)
The Court of Justice of the European Union shall, within the limits hereinafter laid down, have jurisdiction in disputes concerning:
(a) the fulfilment by Member States of obligations under the Statute of the European Investment Bank. In this connection, the Board of Directors of the Bank shall enjoy the powers conferred upon the Commission by Article 258;
(b) measures adopted by the Board of Governors of the European Investment Bank. In this connection, any Member State, the Commission or the Board of Directors of the Bank may institute proceedings under the conditions laid down in Article 263;
(c) measures adopted by the Board of Directors of the European Investment Bank. Proceedings against such measures may be instituted only by Member States or by the Commission, under the conditions laid down in Article 263, and solely on the grounds of non-compliance with the procedure provided for in Article 19(2), (5), (6) and (7) of the Statute of the Bank;
(d) the fulfilment by national central banks of obligations under the Treaties and the Statute of the ESCB and of the ECB. In this connection the powers of the Governing Council of the European Central Bank in respect of national central banks shall be the same as those conferred upon the Commission in respect of Member States by Article 258. If the Court finds that a national central bank has failed to fulfil an obligation under the Treaties, that bank shall be required to take the necessary measures to comply with the judgment of the Court.

[10.57]
Article 272
(ex Article 238 TEC)
The Court of Justice of the European Union shall have jurisdiction to give judgment pursuant to any arbitration clause contained in a contract concluded by or on behalf of the Union, whether that contract be governed by public or private law.

[10.58]
Article 273
(ex Article 239 TEC)
The Court of Justice shall have jurisdiction in any dispute between Member States which relates to the subject matter of the Treaties if the dispute is submitted to it under a special agreement between the parties.

[10.59]
Article 274
(ex Article 240 TEC)
Save where jurisdiction is conferred on the Court of Justice of the European Union by the Treaties, disputes to which the Union is a party shall not on that ground be excluded from the jurisdiction of the courts or tribunals of the Member States.

[10.60]
Article 275
The Court of Justice of the European Union shall not have jurisdiction with respect to the provisions relating to the common foreign and security policy nor with respect to acts adopted on the basis of those provisions.

However, the Court shall have jurisdiction to monitor compliance with Article 40 of the Treaty on European Union and to rule on proceedings, brought in accordance with the conditions laid down in the fourth paragraph of Article 263 of this Treaty, reviewing the legality of decisions providing for restrictive measures against natural or legal persons adopted by the Council on the basis of Chapter 2 of Title V of the Treaty on European Union.

[10.61]
Article 276
In exercising its powers regarding the provisions of Chapters 4 and 5 of Title V of Part Three relating to the area of freedom, security and justice, the Court of Justice of the European Union shall have no jurisdiction to review the validity or proportionality of operations carried out by the

police or other law-enforcement services of a Member State or the exercise of the responsibilities incumbent upon Member States with regard to the maintenance of law and order and the safeguarding of internal security.

[10.62]
Article 277
(ex Article 241 TEC)
Notwithstanding the expiry of the period laid down in Article 263, sixth paragraph, any party may, in proceedings in which an act of general application adopted by an institution, body, office or agency of the Union is at issue, plead the grounds specified in Article 263, second paragraph, in order to invoke before the Court of Justice of the European Union the inapplicability of that act.

[10.63]
Article 278
(ex Article 242 TEC)
Actions brought before the Court of Justice of the European Union shall not have suspensory effect. The Court may, however, if it considers that circumstances so require, order that application of the contested act be suspended.

[10.64]
Article 279
(ex Article 243 TEC)
The Court of Justice of the European Union may in any cases before it prescribe any necessary interim measures.

[10.65]
Article 280
(ex Article 244 TEC)
The judgments of the Court of Justice of the European Union shall be enforceable under the conditions laid down in Article 299.

[10.66]
Article 281
(ex Article 245 TEC)
The Statute of the Court of Justice of the European Union shall be laid down in a separate Protocol.

The European Parliament and the Council, acting in accordance with the ordinary legislative procedure, may amend the provisions of the Statute, with the exception of Title I and Article 64. The European Parliament and the Council shall act either at the request of the Court of Justice and after consultation of the Commission, or on a proposal from the Commission and after consultation of the Court of Justice.

[10.67]
Article 299
(ex Article 256 TEC)
Acts of the Council, the Commission or the European Central Bank which impose a pecuniary obligation on persons other than States, shall be enforceable.

Enforcement shall be governed by the rules of civil procedure in force in the State in the territory of which it is carried out. The order for its enforcement shall be appended to the decision, without other formality than verification of the authenticity of the decision, by the national authority which the government of each Member State shall designate for this purpose and shall make known to the Commission and to the Court of Justice of the European Union.

When these formalities have been completed on application by the party concerned, the latter may proceed to enforcement in accordance with the national law, by bringing the matter directly before the competent authority. Enforcement may be suspended only by a decision of the Court. However, the courts of the country concerned shall have jurisdiction over complaints that enforcement is being carried out in an irregular manner.

[10.68]
Article 340
(ex Article 288 TEC)
The contractual liability of the Union shall be governed by the law applicable to the contract in question.

In the case of non-contractual liability, the Union shall, in accordance with the general principles common to the laws of the Member States, make good any damage caused by its institutions or by its servants in the performance of their duties.

Notwithstanding the second paragraph, the European Central Bank shall, in accordance with the general principles common to the laws of the Member States, make good any damage caused by it or by its servants in the performance of their duties.

The personal liability of its servants towards the Union shall be governed by the provisions laid down in their Staff Regulations or in the Conditions of Employment applicable to them.

C.
TREATY ESTABLISHING THE EUROPEAN ATOMIC ENERGY COMMUNITY

[10.69]
Article 12

Member States, persons or undertakings shall have the right, on application to the Commission, to obtain non-exclusive licences under patents, provisionally protected patent rights, utility models or patent applications owned by the Community, where they are able to make effective use of the inventions covered thereby.

Under the same conditions, the Commission shall grant sublicences under patents, provisionally protected patent rights, utility models or patent applications, where the Community holds contractual licences conferring power to do so.

The Commission shall grant such licences or sublicences on terms to be agreed with the licensees and shall furnish all the information required for their use. These terms shall relate in particular to suitable remuneration and, where appropriate, to the right of the licensee to grant sublicences to third parties and to the obligation to treat the information as a trade secret.

Failing agreement on the terms referred to in the third paragraph, the licensees may bring the matter before the Court of Justice of the European Union so that appropriate terms may be fixed.

[10.70]
Article 18

An Arbitration Committee is hereby established for the purposes provided for in this Section. The Council shall appoint the members and lay down the Rules of Procedure of this Committee, acting on a proposal from the Court of Justice of the European Union.

An appeal, having suspensory effect, may be brought by the parties before the Court of Justice of the European Union against a decision of the Arbitration Committee within one month of notification thereof. The Court of Justice of the European Union shall confine its examination to the formal validity of the decision and to the interpretation of the provisions of this Treaty by the Arbitration Committee.

The final decisions of the Arbitration Committee shall have the force of res judicata between the parties concerned. They shall be enforceable as provided in Article 164.

[10.71]
Article 21

If the proprietor does not propose that the matter be referred to the Arbitration Committee, the Commission may call upon the Member State concerned or its appropriate authorities to grant the licence or cause it to be granted.

If, having heard the proprietor's case, the Member State, or its appropriate authorities, considers that the conditions of Article 17 have not been complied with, it shall notify the Commission of its refusal to grant the licence or to cause it to be granted.

If it refuses to grant the licence or to cause it to be granted, or if, within four months of the date of the request, no information is forthcoming with regard to the granting of the licence, the Commission shall have two months in which to bring the matter before the Court of Justice of the European Union.

The proprietor must be heard in the proceedings before the Court of Justice of the European Union.

If the judgment of the Court of Justice of the European Union establishes that the conditions of Article 17 have been complied with, the Member State concerned, or its appropriate authorities, shall take such measures as enforcement of that judgment may require.

[10.72]
Article 81

The Commission may send inspectors into the territories of Member States. Before sending an inspector on his first assignment in the territory of a Member State, the Commission shall consult the State concerned; such consultation shall suffice to cover all future assignments of this inspector.

On presentation of a document establishing their authority, inspectors shall at all times have access to all places and data and to all persons who, by reason of their occupation, deal with materials, equipment or installations subject to the safeguards provided for in this Chapter, to the extent necessary in order to apply such safeguards to ores, source materials and special fissile materials and to ensure compliance with the provisions of Article 77. Should the State concerned so request, inspectors appointed by the Commission shall be accompanied by representatives of the authorities of that State; however, the inspectors shall not thereby be delayed or otherwise impeded in the performance of their duties.

If the carrying out of an inspection is opposed, the Commission shall apply to the President of the Court of Justice of the European Union for an order to ensure that the inspection be carried out compulsorily. The President of the Court of Justice of the European Union shall give a decision within three days.

If there is danger in delay, the Commission may itself issue a written order, in the form of a decision, to proceed with the inspection. This order shall be submitted without delay to the President of the Court of Justice of the European Union for subsequent approval.

After the order or decision has been issued, the authorities of the State concerned shall ensure that the inspectors have access to the places specified in the order or decision.

[10.73]
Article 82
Inspectors shall be recruited by the Commission.

They shall be responsible for obtaining and verifying the records referred to in Article 79. They shall report any infringement to the Commission.

The Commission may issue a directive calling upon the Member State concerned to take, by a time limit set by the Commission, all measures necessary to bring such infringement to an end; it shall inform the Council thereof.

If the Member State does not comply with the Commission directive by the time limit set, the Commission or any Member State concerned may, in derogation from Articles 226 and 227 of the Treaty on the Functioning of the European Union, refer the matter to the Court of Justice of the European Union direct.

[10.74]
Article 83
1. In the event of an infringement on the part of persons or undertakings of the obligations imposed on them by this Chapter, the Commission may impose sanctions on such persons or undertakings.

These sanctions shall be in order of severity:

(a) a warning;
(b) the withdrawal of special benefits such as financial or technical assistance;
(c) the placing of the undertaking for a period not exceeding four months under the administration of a person or board appointed by common accord of the Commission and the State having jurisdiction over the undertaking;
(d) total or partial withdrawal of source materials or special fissile materials.

2. Decisions taken by the Commission in implementation of paragraph 1 and requiring the surrender of materials shall be enforceable. They may be enforced in the territories of Member States in accordance with Article 164.

By way of derogation from Article 157, appeals brought before the Court of Justice of the European Union against decisions of the Commission which impose any of the sanctions provided for in paragraph 1 shall have suspensory effect. The Court of Justice of the European Union may, however, on application by the Commission or by any Member State concerned, order that the decision be enforced forthwith.

There shall be an appropriate legal procedure to ensure the protection of interests that have been prejudiced.

3. The Commission may make any recommendations to Member States concerning laws or regulations which are designed to ensure compliance in their territories with the obligations arising under this Chapter.

4. Member States shall ensure that sanctions are enforced and, where necessary, that the infringements are remedied by those committing them.

[10.75]
Article 103
Member States shall communicate to the Commission draft agreements or contracts with a third State, an international organisation or a national of a third State to the extent that such agreements or contracts concern matters within the purview of this Treaty.

If a draft agreement or contract contains clauses which impede the application of this Treaty, the Commission shall, within one month of receipt of such communication, make its comments known to the State concerned.

The State shall not conclude the proposed agreement or contract until it has satisfied the objections of the Commission or complied with a ruling by the Court of Justice of the European Union, adjudicating urgently upon an application from the State, on the compatibility of the proposed clauses with the provisions of this Treaty. An application may be made to the Court of Justice of the European Union at any time after the State has received the comments of the Commission.

[10.76]
Article 104
No person or undertaking concluding or renewing an agreement or contract with a third State, an international organisation the date of their accession, may invoke that agreement or contract in order to evade the obligations imposed by this Treaty.

Each Member State shall take such measures as it considers necessary in order to communicate to the Commission, at the request of the latter, all information relating to agreements or contracts concluded after the dates referred to in the first paragraph, within the scope of this Treaty, by a person or undertaking with a third State, an international organisation or a national of a third State. The Commission may require such communication only for the purpose of verifying that such agreements or contracts do not contain clauses impeding the implementation of this Treaty.

On application by the Commission, the Court of Justice of the European Union shall give a ruling on the compatibility of such agreements or contracts with the provisions of this Treaty.

[10.77]
Article 105
The provisions of this Treaty shall not be invoked so as to prevent the implementation of agreements or contracts concluded before 1 January 1958 or, for acceding States, before the date of their accession, by a Member State, a person or an undertaking with a third State, an international organisation or a national of a third State where such agreements or contracts have been communicated to the Commission not later than 30 days after the aforesaid dates.

Agreements or contracts concluded between 25 March 1957 and 1 January 1958 or, for acceding States, between the signature of the instrument of accession and the date of their accession, by a person or an undertaking with a third State, an international organisation or a national of a third State shall not, however, be invoked as grounds for failure to implement this Treaty if, in the opinion of the Court of Justice of the European Union, ruling on an application from the Commission, one of the decisive reasons on the part of either of the parties in concluding the agreement or contract was an intention to evade the provisions of this Treaty.

[10.78]
Article 106a
1. Article 7, Articles 9 to 9F, Article 48(2) to (5), and Articles 49 and 49A of the Treaty on European Union, Article 16A, Articles 190 to 201b, Articles 204 to 211a, Article 213, Articles 215 to 236, Articles 238, 239 and 240, Articles 241 to 245, Articles 246 to 262, Articles 268 to 277, Articles 279 to 280 and Articles 283, 290 and 292 of the Treaty on the Functioning of the European Union, and the Protocol on Transitional Provisions, shall apply to this Treaty.
2. Within the framework of this Treaty, the references to the Union, to the 'Treaty on European Union', to the 'Treaty on the Functioning of the European Union' or to the 'Treaties' in the provisions referred to in paragraph 1 and those in the protocols annexed both to those Treaties and to this Treaty shall be taken, respectively, as references to the European Atomic Energy Community and to this Treaty.
3. The provisions of the Treaty on European Union and of the Treaty on the Functioning of the European Union shall not derogate from the provisions of this Treaty.

[10.79]
Article 144
The Court of Justice of the European Union shall have unlimited jurisdiction in:
(a) proceedings instituted under Article 12 to have the appropriate terms fixed for the granting by the Commission of licences or sub licences;
(b) proceedings instituted by persons or undertakings against sanctions imposed on them by the Commission under Article 83.

[10.80]
Article 145
If the Commission considers that a person or undertaking has committed an infringement of this Treaty to which the provisions of Article 83 do not apply, it shall call upon the Member State having jurisdiction over that person or undertaking to cause sanctions to be imposed in respect of the infringement in accordance with its national law.

If the State concerned does not comply with such a request within the period laid down by the Commission, the latter may bring an action before the Court of Justice of the European Union to have the infringement of which the person or undertaking is accused established.

[10.81]
Article 157
Save as otherwise provided in this Treaty, actions brought before the Court of Justice of the European Union shall not have suspensory effect. The Court of Justice of the European Union may, however, if it considers that circumstances so require, order that application of the contested act be suspended.

[10.82]
Article 188
The contractual liability of the Community shall be governed by the law applicable to the contract in question.

In the case of non-contractual liability, the Community shall, in accordance with the general principles common to the laws of the Member States, make good any damage caused by its institutions or by its servants in the performance of their duties.

The personal liability of its servants towards the Community shall be governed by the provisions laid down in the Staff Regulations or in the Conditions of Employment applicable to them.

STATUTE OF THE COURT OF JUSTICE OF THE EUROPEAN UNION (2010) (CONSOLIDATED 2016)

[10.83]

NOTES

Date of original publication in OJ: C83, 30.3.2010, p 210.

A consolidated version was published in September 2016 and is available at curia.europa.eu/jcms/upload/docs/application/pdf/2016-08/tra-doc-en-div-c-0000-2016-201606984-05_00.pdf.

The consolidated version includes the amendments made by: Regulation (EU, Euratom) No 741/2012 of the European Parliament and of the Council of 11 August 2012 (OJ L228, 23.8.2012, p 1), by Article 9 of the Act concerning the conditions of accession to the EU of the Republic of Croatia and the adjustments to the Treaty on European Union, the Treaty on the Functioning of the European Union and the Treaty establishing the European Atomic Energy Community (OJ L112, 24.4.2012, p 21), by Regulation (EU, Euratom) 2015/2422 of the European Parliament and of the Council of 16 December 2015 (OJ L341, 24.12.2015, p 14), and by Regulation (EU, Euratom) 2016/1192 of the European Parliament and of the Council of 6 July 2016 on the transfer to the General Court of jurisdiction at first instance in disputes between the European Union and its servants (OJ L200, 26.7.2016, p 137).

THE HIGH CONTRACTING PARTIES,

DESIRING to lay down the Statute of the Court of Justice of the European Union provided for in Article 281 of the Treaty on the Functioning of the European Union,

HAVE AGREED UPON the following provisions, which shall be annexed to the Treaty on European Union, the Treaty on the Functioning of the European Union and the Treaty establishing the European Atomic Energy Community:

[10.84]

Article 1

The Court of Justice of the European Union shall be constituted and shall function in accordance with the provisions of the Treaties, of the Treaty establishing the European Atomic Energy Community (EAEC Treaty) and of this Statute.

TITLE I
JUDGES AND ADVOCATES-GENERAL

[10.85]

Article 2

Before taking up his duties each Judge shall, before the Court of Justice sitting in open court, take an oath to perform his duties impartially and conscientiously and to preserve the secrecy of the deliberations of the Court.

[10.86]

Article 3

The Judges shall be immune from legal proceedings. After they have ceased to hold office, they shall continue to enjoy immunity in respect of acts performed by them in their official capacity, including words spoken or written.

The Court of Justice, sitting as a full Court, may waive the immunity. If the decision concerns a member of the General Court or of a specialised court, the Court shall decide after consulting the court concerned.

Where immunity has been waived and criminal proceedings are instituted against a Judge, he shall be tried, in any of the Member States, only by the court competent to judge the members of the highest national judiciary.

Articles 11 to 14 and Article 17 of the Protocol on the privileges and immunities of the European Union shall apply to the Judges, Advocates-General, Registrar and Assistant Rapporteurs of the Court of Justice of the European Union, without prejudice to the provisions relating to immunity from legal proceedings of Judges which are set out in the preceding paragraphs.

[10.87]

Article 4

The Judges may not hold any political or administrative office.

They may not engage in any occupation, whether gainful or not, unless exemption is exceptionally granted by the Council, acting by a simple majority.

When taking up their duties, they shall give a solemn undertaking that, both during and after their term of office, they will respect the obligations arising therefrom, in particular the duty to behave with integrity and discretion as regards the acceptance, after they have ceased to hold office, of certain appointments or benefits.

Any doubt on this point shall be settled by decision of the Court of Justice. If the decision concerns a member of the General Court or of a specialised court, the Court shall decide after consulting the court concerned.

[10.88]
Article 5
Apart from normal replacement, or death, the duties of a Judge shall end when he resigns.
Where a Judge resigns, his letter of resignation shall be addressed to the President of the Court of Justice for transmission to the President of the Council. Upon this notification a vacancy shall arise on the bench.
Save where Article 6 applies, a Judge shall continue to hold office until his successor takes up his duties.

[10.89]
Article 6
A Judge may be deprived of his office or of his right to a pension or other benefits in its stead only if, in the unanimous opinion of the Judges and Advocates-General of the Court of Justice, he no longer fulfils the requisite conditions or meets the obligations arising from his office. The Judge concerned shall not take part in any such deliberations. If the person concerned is a member of the General Court or of a specialised court, the Court shall decide after consulting the court concerned.
The Registrar of the Court shall communicate the decision of the Court to the President of the European Parliament and to the President of the Commission and shall notify it to the President of the Council.
In the case of a decision depriving a Judge of his office, a vacancy shall arise on the bench upon this latter notification.

[10.90]
Article 7
A Judge who is to replace a member of the Court whose term of office has not expired shall be appointed for the remainder of his predecessor's term.

[10.91]
Article 8
The provisions of Articles 2 to 7 shall apply to the Advocates-General.

TITLE II
ORGANISATION OF THE COURT OF JUSTICE

[10.92]
[Article 9
When, every three years, the Judges are partially replaced, one half of the number of Judges shall be replaced. If the number of Judges is an uneven number, the number of Judges who shall be replaced shall alternately be the number which is the next above one half of the number of Judges and the number which is next below one half.
The first paragraph shall also apply when the Advocates-General are partially replaced, every three years.]

NOTES
Substituted by Regulation (EU, Euratom) 2015/2422 of the European Parliament and of the Council of 16 December 2015 amending Protocol No 3 on the Statute of the Court of Justice of the European Union, Article 1(1).

[10.93]
[Article 9a
The Judges shall elect the President and the Vice-President of the Court of Justice from among their number for a term of three years. They may be re-elected.
The Vice-President shall assist the President in accordance with the conditions laid down in the Rules of Procedure. He shall take the President's place when the latter is prevented from attending or when the office of President is vacant.]

NOTES
Inserted by Regulation (EU, Euratom) No 741/2012 of the European Parliament and of the Council of 11 August 2012 amending the Protocol on the Statute of the Court of Justice of the European Union and Annex I thereto, Article 1(1). Note that this amendment applies from the first occasion when the Judges are partially replaced, as provided for in the first paragraph of Article 9 (see Article 3 of the 2012 Regulation).

[10.94]
Article 10
The Registrar shall take an oath before the Court of Justice to perform his duties impartially and conscientiously and to preserve the secrecy of the deliberations of the Court of Justice.

[10.95]
Article 11
The Court of Justice shall arrange for replacement of the Registrar on occasions when he is prevented from attending the Court of Justice.

[10.96]
Article 12
Officials and other servants shall be attached to the Court of Justice to enable it to function. They shall be responsible to the Registrar under the authority of the President.

[10.97]
Article 13
At the request of the Court of Justice, the European Parliament and the Council may, acting in accordance with the ordinary legislative procedure, provide for the appointment of Assistant Rapporteurs and lay down the rules governing their service. The Assistant Rapporteurs may be required, under conditions laid down in the Rules of Procedure, to participate in preparatory inquiries in cases pending before the Court and to cooperate with the Judge who acts as Rapporteur.
The Assistant Rapporteurs shall be chosen from persons whose independence is beyond doubt and who possess the necessary legal qualifications; they shall be appointed by the Council, acting by a simple majority. They shall take an oath before the Court to perform their duties impartially and conscientiously and to preserve the secrecy of the deliberations of the Court.

[10.98]
Article 14
The Judges, the Advocates-General and the Registrar shall be required to reside at the place where the Court of Justice has its seat.

[10.99]
Article 15
The Court of Justice shall remain permanently in session. The duration of the judicial vacations shall be determined by the Court with due regard to the needs of its business.

[10.100]
Article 16
The Court of Justice shall form chambers consisting of three and five Judges. The Judges shall elect the Presidents of the chambers from among their number. The Presidents of the chambers of five Judges shall be elected for three years. They may be re-elected once.
[The Grand Chamber shall consist of 15 Judges. It shall be presided over by the President of the Court. The Vice-President of the Court and, in accordance with the conditions laid down in the Rules of Procedure, three of the Presidents of the chambers of five Judges and other Judges shall also form part of the Grand Chamber.]
The Court shall sit in a Grand Chamber when a Member State or an institution of the Union that is party to the proceedings so requests.
The Court shall sit as a full Court where cases are brought before it pursuant to Article 228(2), Article 245(2), Article 247 or Article 286(6) of the Treaty on the Functioning of the European Union.
Moreover, where it considers that a case before it is of exceptional importance, the Court may decide, after hearing the Advocate-General, to refer the case to the full Court.

NOTES
Words in square brackets substituted by Regulation (EU, Euratom) No 741/2012 of the European Parliament and of the Council of 11 August 2012 amending the Protocol on the Statute of the Court of Justice of the European Union and Annex I thereto, Article 1(2). Note that this amendment applies from the first occasion when the Judges are partially replaced, as provided for in the first paragraph of Article 9 (see Article 3 of the 2012 Regulation).

[10.101]
Article 17
Decisions of the Court of Justice shall be valid only when an uneven number of its members is sitting in the deliberations.
Decisions of the chambers consisting of either three or five Judges shall be valid only if they are taken by three Judges.
[Decisions of the Grand Chamber shall be valid only if 11 Judges are sitting.
Decisions of the full Court shall be valid only if 17 Judges are sitting.]
In the event of one of the Judges of a chamber being prevented from attending, a Judge of another chamber may be called upon to sit in accordance with conditions laid down in the Rules of Procedure.

NOTES
Words in square brackets substituted by Regulation (EU, Euratom) No 741/2012 of the European Parliament and of the Council of 11 August 2012 amending the Protocol on the Statute of the Court of Justice of the European Union and Annex I thereto, Article 1(3). Note that this amendment applies from the first occasion when the Judges are partially replaced, as provided for in the first paragraph of Article 9 (see Article 3 of the 2012 Regulation).

[10.102]
Article 18

No Judge or Advocate-General may take part in the disposal of any case in which he has previously taken part as agent or adviser or has acted for one of the parties, or in which he has been called upon to pronounce as a member of a court or tribunal, of a commission of inquiry or in any other capacity.

If, for some special reason, any Judge or Advocate-General considers that he should not take part in the judgment or examination of a particular case, he shall so inform the President. If, for some special reason, the President considers that any Judge or Advocate-General should not sit or make submissions in a particular case, he shall notify him accordingly.

Any difficulty arising as to the application of this Article shall be settled by decision of the Court of Justice.

A party may not apply for a change in the composition of the Court or of one of its chambers on the grounds of either the nationality of a Judge or the absence from the Court or from the chamber of a Judge of the nationality of that party.

TITLE III
PROCEDURE BEFORE THE COURT OF JUSTICE

[10.103]
Article 19

The Member States and the institutions of the Union shall be represented before the Court of Justice by an agent appointed for each case; the agent may be assisted by an adviser or by a lawyer.

The States, other than the Member States, which are parties to the Agreement on the European Economic Area and also the EFTA Surveillance Authority referred to in that Agreement shall be represented in same manner.

Other parties must be represented by a lawyer.

Only a lawyer authorised to practise before a court of a Member State or of another State which is a party to the Agreement on the European Economic Area may represent or assist a party before the Court.

Such agents, advisers and lawyers shall, when they appear before the Court, enjoy the rights and immunities necessary to the independent exercise of their duties, under conditions laid down in the Rules of Procedure.

As regards such advisers and lawyers who appear before it, the Court shall have the powers normally accorded to courts of law, under conditions laid down in the Rules of Procedure.

University teachers being nationals of a Member State whose law accords them a right of audience shall have the same rights before the Court as are accorded by this Article to lawyers.

[10.104]
Article 20

The procedure before the Court of Justice shall consist of two parts: written and oral.

The written procedure shall consist of the communication to the parties and to the institutions of the Union whose decisions are in dispute, of applications, statements of case, defences and observations, and of replies, if any, as well as of all papers and documents in support or of certified copies of them.

Communications shall be made by the Registrar in the order and within the time laid down in the Rules of Procedure.

[The oral procedure shall consist of the hearing by the Court of agents, advisers and lawyers and of the submissions of the Advocate-General, as well as the hearing, if any, of witnesses and experts.]

Where it considers that the case raises no new point of law, the Court may decide, after hearing the Advocate-General, that the case shall be determined without a submission from the Advocate-General.

NOTES

Words in square brackets substituted by Regulation (EU, Euratom) No 741/2012 of the European Parliament and of the Council of 11 August 2012 amending the Protocol on the Statute of the Court of Justice of the European Union and Annex I thereto, Article 1(4).

[10.105]
Article 21

A case shall be brought before the Court of Justice by a written application addressed to the Registrar. The application shall contain the applicant's name and permanent address and the description of the signatory, the name of the party or names of the parties against whom the application is made, the subject-matter of the dispute, the form of order sought and a brief statement of the pleas in law on which the application is based.

The application shall be accompanied, where appropriate, by the measure the annulment of which is sought or, in the circumstances referred to in Article 265 of the Treaty on the Functioning of the European Union, by documentary evidence of the date on which an institution was, in accordance with those Articles, requested to act. If the documents are not submitted with the application, the Registrar shall ask the party concerned to produce them within a reasonable period, but in that event the rights of the party shall not lapse even if such documents are produced after the time limit for bringing proceedings.

[10.106]
Article 22
A case governed by Article 18 of the EAEC Treaty shall be brought before the Court of Justice by an appeal addressed to the Registrar. The appeal shall contain the name and permanent address of the applicant and the description of the signatory, a reference to the decision against which the appeal is brought, the names of the respondents, the subject-matter of the dispute, the submissions and a brief statement of the grounds on which the appeal is based.
The appeal shall be accompanied by a certified copy of the decision of the Arbitration Committee which is contested.
If the Court rejects the appeal, the decision of the Arbitration Committee shall become final.
If the Court annuls the decision of the Arbitration Committee, the matter may be re-opened, where appropriate, on the initiative of one of the parties in the case, before the Arbitration Committee. The latter shall conform to any decisions on points of law given by the Court.

[10.107]
Article 23
In the cases governed by Article 267 of the Treaty on the Functioning of the European Union, the decision of the court or tribunal of a Member State which suspends its proceedings and refers a case to the Court of Justice shall be notified to the Court by the court or tribunal concerned. The decision shall then be notified by the Registrar of the Court to the parties, to the Member States and to the Commission, and to the institution, body, office or agency of the Union which adopted the act the validity or interpretation of which is in dispute.
Within two months of this notification, the parties, the Member States, the Commission and, where appropriate, the institution, body, office or agency which adopted the act the validity or interpretation of which is in dispute, shall be entitled to submit statements of case or written observations to the Court.
In the cases governed by Article 267 of the Treaty on the Functioning of the European Union, the decision of the national court or tribunal shall, moreover, be notified by the Registrar of the Court to the States, other than the Member States, which are parties to the Agreement on the European Economic Area and also to the EFTA Surveillance Authority referred to in that Agreement which may, within two months of notification, where one of the fields of application of that Agreement is concerned, submit statements of case or written observations to the Court.
Where an agreement relating to a specific subject matter, concluded by the Council and one or more non-member States, provides that those States are to be entitled to submit statements of case or written observations where a court or tribunal of a Member State refers to the Court of Justice for a preliminary ruling a question falling within the scope of the agreement, the decision of the national court or tribunal containing that question shall also be notified to the non-member States concerned. Within two months from such notification, those States may lodge at the Court statements of case or written observations.

[10.108]
[Article 23a
The Rules of Procedure may provide for an expedited or accelerated procedure and, for references for a preliminary ruling relating to the area of freedom, security and justice, an urgent procedure.
Those procedures may provide, in respect of the submission of statements of case or written observations, for a shorter period than that provided for by Article 23, and, in derogation from the fourth paragraph of Article 20, for the case to be determined without a submission from the Advocate General.
In addition, the urgent procedure may provide for restriction of the parties and other interested persons mentioned in Article 23, authorised to submit statements of case or written observations and, in cases of extreme urgency, for the written stage of the procedure to be omitted.][1]

NOTES

[1] Article inserted by Decision 2008/79/EC, Euratom (OJ L24, 29.1.2008, p 42).

[10.109]
Article 24
The Court of Justice may require the parties to produce all documents and to supply all information which the Court considers desirable. Formal note shall be taken of any refusal.
The Court may also require the Member States and institutions, bodies, offices and agencies not being parties to the case to supply all information which the Court considers necessary for the proceedings.

[10.110]
Article 25
The Court of Justice may at any time entrust any individual, body, authority, committee or other organisation it chooses with the task of giving an expert opinion.

[10.111]
Article 26
Witnesses may be heard under conditions laid down in the Rules of Procedure.

[10.112]
Article 27
With respect to defaulting witnesses the Court of Justice shall have the powers generally granted to courts and tribunals and may impose pecuniary penalties under conditions laid down in the Rules of Procedure.

[10.113]
Article 28
Witnesses and experts may be heard on oath taken in the form laid down in the Rules of Procedure or in the manner laid down by the law of the country of the witness or expert.

[10.114]
Article 29
The Court of Justice may order that a witness or expert be heard by the judicial authority of his place of permanent residence.
The order shall be sent for implementation to the competent judicial authority under conditions laid down in the Rules of Procedure. The documents drawn up in compliance with the letters rogatory shall be returned to the Court under the same conditions.
The Court shall defray the expenses, without prejudice to the right to charge them, where appropriate, to the parties.

[10.115]
Article 30
A Member State shall treat any violation of an oath by a witness or expert in the same manner as if the offence had been committed before one of its courts with jurisdiction in civil proceedings. At the instance of the Court of Justice, the Member State concerned shall prosecute the offender before its competent court.

[10.116]
Article 31
The hearing in court shall be public, unless the Court of Justice, of its own motion or on application by the parties, decides otherwise for serious reasons.

[10.117]
Article 32
During the hearings the Court of Justice may examine the experts, the witnesses and the parties themselves. The latter, however, may address the Court of Justice only through their representatives.

[10.118]
Article 33
Minutes shall be made of each hearing and signed by the President and the Registrar.

[10.119]
Article 34
The case list shall be established by the President.

[10.120]
Article 35
The deliberations of the Court of Justice shall be and shall remain secret.

[10.121]
Article 36
Judgments shall state the reasons on which they are based. They shall contain the names of the Judges who took part in the deliberations.

[10.122]
Article 37
Judgments shall be signed by the President and the Registrar. They shall be read in open court.

[10.123]
Article 38
The Court of Justice shall adjudicate upon costs.

[10.124]
Article 39
The President of the Court of Justice may, by way of summary procedure, which may, in so far as necessary, differ from some of the rules contained in this Statute and which shall be laid down in the Rules of Procedure, adjudicate upon applications to suspend execution, as provided for in Article 278 of the Treaty on the Functioning of the European Union and Article 157 of the EAEC Treaty, or to prescribe interim measures pursuant to Article 279 of the Treaty on the Functioning of the European Union, or to suspend enforcement in accordance with the fourth paragraph of Article 299 of the Treaty on the Functioning of the European Union or the third paragraph of Article 164 of the EAEC Treaty.
[The powers referred to in the first paragraph may, under the conditions laid down in the Rules of Procedure, be exercised by the Vice-President of the Court of Justice.
Should the President and the Vice-President be prevented from attending, another Judge shall take their place under the conditions laid down in the Rules of Procedure.]
The ruling of the President or of the Judge replacing him shall be provisional and shall in no way prejudice the decision of the Court on the substance of the case.

NOTES
Words in square brackets substituted by Regulation (EU, Euratom) No 741/2012 of the European Parliament and of the Council of 11 August 2012 amending the Protocol on the Statute of the Court of Justice of the European Union and Annex I thereto, Article 1(5). Note that this amendment applies from the first occasion when the Judges are partially replaced, as provided for in the first paragraph of Article 9 (see Article 3 of the 2012 Regulation).

[10.125]
Article 40
Member States and institutions of the Union may intervene in cases before the Court of Justice.
The same right shall be open to the bodies, offices and agencies of the Union and to any other person which can establish an interest in the result of a case submitted to the Court. Natural or legal persons shall not intervene in cases between Member States, between institutions of the Union or between Member States and institutions of the Union.
Without prejudice to the second paragraph, the States, other than the Member States, which are parties to the Agreement on the European Economic Area, and also the EFTA Surveillance Authority referred to in that Agreement, may intervene in cases before the Court where one of the fields of application of that Agreement is concerned.
An application to intervene shall be limited to supporting the form of order sought by one of the parties.

[10.126]
Article 41
Where the defending party, after having been duly summoned, fails to file written submissions in defence, judgment shall be given against that party by default. An objection may be lodged against the judgment within one month of it being notified. The objection shall not have the effect of staying enforcement of the judgment by default unless the Court of Justice decides otherwise.

[10.127]
Article 42
Member States, institutions, bodies, offices and agencies of the Union and any other natural or legal persons may, in cases and under conditions to be determined by the Rules of Procedure, institute third-party proceedings to contest a judgment rendered without their being heard, where the judgment is prejudicial to their rights.

[10.128]
Article 43
If the meaning or scope of a judgment is in doubt, the Court of Justice shall construe it on application by any party or any institution of the Union establishing an interest therein.

[10.129]
Article 44
An application for revision of a judgment may be made to the Court of Justice only on discovery of a fact which is of such a nature as to be a decisive factor, and which, when the judgment was given, was unknown to the Court and to the party claiming the revision.
The revision shall be opened by a judgment of the Court expressly recording the existence of a new fact, recognising that it is of such a character as to lay the case open to revision and declaring the application admissible on this ground.
No application for revision may be made after the lapse of 10 years from the date of the judgment.

[10.130]
Article 45
Periods of grace based on considerations of distance shall be determined by the Rules of Procedure.
No right shall be prejudiced in consequence of the expiry of a time limit if the party concerned proves the existence of unforeseeable circumstances or of *force majeure*.

[10.131]
Article 46

Proceedings against the Union in matters arising from non-contractual liability shall be barred after a period of five years from the occurrence of the event giving rise thereto. The period of limitation shall be interrupted if proceedings are instituted before the Court of Justice or if prior to such proceedings an application is made by the aggrieved party to the relevant institution of the Union. In the latter event the proceedings must be instituted within the period of two months provided for in Article 263 of the Treaty on the Functioning of the European Union; the provisions of the second paragraph of Article 265 of the Treaty on the Functioning of the European Union shall apply where appropriate.

This Article shall also apply to proceedings against the European Central Bank regarding non-contractual liability.

TITLE IV
GENERAL COURT

[10.132]
Article 47

[The first paragraph of Article 9, Article 9a, Articles 14 and 15, the first, second, fourth and fifth paragraphs of Article 17 and Article 18 shall apply to the General Court and its members.]

The fourth paragraph of Article 3 and Articles 10, 11 and 14 shall apply to the Registrar of the General Court *mutatis mutandis*.

NOTES

Words in square brackets substituted by Regulation (EU, Euratom) No 741/2012 of the European Parliament and of the Council of 11 August 2012 amending the Protocol on the Statute of the Court of Justice of the European Union and Annex I thereto, Article 1(6). Note that this amendment applies from the first occasion when the Judges are partially replaced, as provided for in the first paragraph of Article 9 (see Article 3 of the 2012 Regulation).

[10.133]
[Article 48

The General Court shall consist of:

(a) 40 Judges as from 25 December 2015;
(b) 47 Judges as from 1 September 2016;
(c) two Judges per Member State as from 1 September 2019.]

NOTES

Substituted by Regulation (EU, Euratom) 2015/2422 of the European Parliament and of the Council of 16 December 2015 amending Protocol No 3 on the Statute of the Court of Justice of the European Union, Article 1(2).

Article 2 of Regulation (EU, Euratom) 2015/2422 of the European Parliament and of the Council of 16 December 2015 amending Protocol No 3 on the Statute of the Court of Justice of the European Union provides as follows—

"The term of office of the additional Judges of the General Court to be appointed pursuant to Article 48 of Protocol No 3 on the Statute of the Court of Justice of the European Union shall be as follows:

(a) The term of office of six of the twelve additional Judges to be appointed as from 25 December 2015 shall end on 31 August 2016. Those six Judges shall be chosen in such a way that the governments of six Member States nominate two Judges for the partial replacement of the General Court in 2016. The term of office of the other six Judges shall end on 31 August 2019;
(b) The term of office of three of the seven additional Judges to be appointed as from 1 September 2016 shall end on 31 August 2019. Those three Judges shall be chosen in such a way that the governments of three Member States nominate two Judges for the partial replacement of the General Court in 2019. The term of office of the other four Judges shall end on 31 August 2022;
(c) The term of office of four of the nine additional Judges to be appointed as from 1 September 2019 shall end on 31 August 2022. Those four Judges shall be chosen in such a way that the governments of four Member States nominate two Judges for the partial replacement of the General Court in 2022. The term of office of the other five Judges shall end on 31 August 2025.".

Note also that Article 3 of the 2015 Regulation provides that, by 26 December 2020, the Court of Justice shall draw up a report, using an external consultant, for the European Parliament, the Council and the Commission on the functioning of the General Court. In particular, that report shall focus on the efficiency of the General Court, the necessity and effectiveness of the increase to 56 Judges, the use and effectiveness of resources and the further establishment of specialised chambers and/or other structural changes.

[10.134]
Article 49

The Members of the General Court may be called upon to perform the task of an Advocate-General.

It shall be the duty of the Advocate-General, acting with complete impartiality and independence, to make, in open court, reasoned submissions on certain cases brought before the General Court in order to assist the General Court in the performance of its task.

The criteria for selecting such cases, as well as the procedures for designating the Advocates-General, shall be laid down in the Rules of Procedure of the General Court.

A Member called upon to perform the task of Advocate-General in a case may not take part in the judgment of the case.

[10.135]
Article 50
The General Court shall sit in chambers of three or five Judges. The Judges shall elect the Presidents of the chambers from among their number. The Presidents of the chambers of five Judges shall be elected for three years. They may be re-elected once.
The composition of the chambers and the assignment of cases to them shall be governed by the Rules of Procedure. In certain cases governed by the Rules of Procedure, the General Court may sit as a full court or be constituted by a single Judge.
The Rules of Procedure may also provide that the General Court may sit in a Grand Chamber in cases and under the conditions specified therein.

[10.136]
[Article 50a
1. he General Court shall exercise at first instance jurisdiction in disputes between the Union and its servants as referred to in Article 270 of the Treaty on the Functioning of the European Union, including disputes between all institutions, bodies, offices or agencies, on the one hand, and their servants, on the other, in respect of which jurisdiction is conferred on the Court of Justice of the European Union.
2. At all stages of the procedure, including the time when the application is filed, the General Court may examine the possibilities of an amicable settlement of the dispute and may try to facilitate such settlement.]

NOTES
Inserted by Regulation (EU, Euratom) 2016/1192 of the European Parliament and of the Council of 6 July 2016 on the transfer to the General Court of jurisdiction at first instance in disputes between the European Union and its servants, Art 2(1).

[10.137]
Article 51
By way of derogation from the rule laid down in Article 256(1) of the Treaty on the Functioning of the European Union, jurisdiction shall be reserved to the Court of Justice in the actions referred to in Articles 263 and 265 of the Treaty on the Functioning of the European Union when they are brought by a Member State against:
- (a) an act of or failure to act by the European Parliament or the Council, or by those institutions acting jointly, except for:
  - — decisions taken by the Council under the third subparagraph of Article 108(2) of the Treaty on the Functioning of the European Union;
  - — acts of the Council adopted pursuant to a Council regulation concerning measures to protect trade within the meaning of Article 207 of the Treaty on the Functioning of the European Union;
  - — acts of the Council by which the Council exercises implementing powers in accordance with the second paragraph of Article 291 of the Treaty on the Functioning of the European Union;
- (b) against an act of or failure to act by the Commission under the first paragraph of Article 331 of the Treaty on the Functioning of the European Union.

Jurisdiction shall also be reserved to the Court of Justice in the actions referred to in the same Articles when they are brought by an institution of the Union against an act of or failure to act by the European Parliament, the Council, both those institutions acting jointly, or the Commission, or brought by an institution of the Union against an act of or failure to act by the European Central Bank.

[10.138]
Article 52
The President of the Court of Justice and the President of the General Court shall determine, by common accord, the conditions under which officials and other servants attached to the Court of Justice shall render their services to the General Court to enable it to function. Certain officials or other servants shall be responsible to the Registrar of the General Court under the authority of the President of the General Court.

[10.139]
Article 53
The procedure before the General Court shall be governed by Title III.
Such further and more detailed provisions as may be necessary shall be laid down in its Rules of Procedure. The Rules of Procedure may derogate from the fourth paragraph of Article 40 and from Article 41 in order to take account of the specific features of litigation in the field of intellectual property.
Notwithstanding the fourth paragraph of Article 20, the Advocate-General may make his reasoned submissions in writing.

[10.140]
Article 54
Where an application or other procedural document addressed to the General Court is lodged by mistake with the Registrar of the Court of Justice, it shall be transmitted immediately by that Registrar to the Registrar of the General Court; likewise, where an application or other procedural document addressed to the Court of Justice is lodged by mistake with the Registrar of the General Court, it shall be transmitted immediately by that Registrar to the Registrar of the Court of Justice.

Where the General Court finds that it does not have jurisdiction to hear and determine an action in respect of which the Court of Justice has jurisdiction, it shall refer that action to the Court of Justice; likewise, where the Court of Justice finds that an action falls within the jurisdiction of the General Court, it shall refer that action to the General Court, whereupon that Court may not decline jurisdiction.

Where the Court of Justice and the General Court are seised of cases in which the same relief is sought, the same issue of interpretation is raised or the validity of the same act is called in question, the General Court may, after hearing the parties, stay the proceedings before it until such time as the Court of Justice has delivered judgment or, where the action is one brought pursuant to Article 263 of the Treaty on the Functioning of the European Union, may decline jurisdiction so as to allow the Court of Justice to rule on such actions. In the same circumstances, the Court of Justice may also decide to stay the proceedings before it; in that event, the proceedings before the General Court shall continue.

Where a Member State and an institution of the Union are challenging the same act, the General Court shall decline jurisdiction so that the Court of Justice may rule on those applications.

[10.141]
Article 55
Final decisions of the General Court, decisions disposing of the substantive issues in part only or disposing of a procedural issue concerning a plea of lack of competence or inadmissibility, shall be notified by the Registrar of the General Court to all parties as well as all Member States and the institutions of the Union even if they did not intervene in the case before the General Court.

[10.142]
Article 56
An appeal may be brought before the Court of Justice, within two months of the notification of the decision appealed against, against final decisions of the General Court and decisions of that Court disposing of the substantive issues in part only or disposing of a procedural issue concerning a plea of lack of competence or inadmissibility.

Such an appeal may be brought by any party which has been unsuccessful, in whole or in part, in its submissions. However, interveners other than the Member States and the institutions of the Union may bring such an appeal only where the decision of the General Court directly affects them.

With the exception of cases relating to disputes between the Union and its servants, an appeal may also be brought by Member States and institutions of the Union which did not intervene in the proceedings before the General Court. Such Member States and institutions shall be in the same position as Member States or institutions which intervened at first instance.

[10.143]
Article 57
Any person whose application to intervene has been dismissed by the General Court may appeal to the Court of Justice within two weeks from the notification of the decision dismissing the application.

The parties to the proceedings may appeal to the Court of Justice against any decision of the General Court made pursuant to Article 278 or Article 279 or the fourth paragraph of Article 299 of the Treaty on the Functioning of the European Union or Article 157 or the third paragraph of Article 164 of the EAEC Treaty within two months from their notification.

The appeal referred to in the first two paragraphs of this Article shall be heard and determined under the procedure referred to in Article 39.

[10.144]
Article 58
An appeal to the Court of Justice shall be limited to points of law. It shall lie on the grounds of lack of competence of the General Court, a breach of procedure before it which adversely affects the interests of the appellant as well as the infringement of Union law by the General Court.

No appeal shall lie regarding only the amount of the costs or the party ordered to pay them.

[10.145]
Article 59
Where an appeal is brought against a decision of the General Court, the procedure before the Court of Justice shall consist of a written part and an oral part. In accordance with conditions laid down in the Rules of Procedure, the Court of Justice, having heard the Advocate-General and the parties, may dispense with the oral procedure.

[10.146]
Article 60

Without prejudice to Articles 278 and 279 of the Treaty on the Functioning of the European Union or Article 157 of the EAEC Treaty, an appeal shall not have suspensory effect.

By way of derogation from Article 280 of the Treaty on the Functioning of the European Union, decisions of the General Court declaring a regulation to be void shall take effect only as from the date of expiry of the period referred to in the first paragraph of Article 56 of this Statute or, if an appeal shall have been brought within that period, as from the date of dismissal of the appeal, without prejudice, however, to the right of a party to apply to the Court of Justice, pursuant to Articles 278 and 279 of the Treaty on the Functioning of the European Union or Article 157 of the EAEC Treaty, for the suspension of the effects of the regulation which has been declared void or for the prescription of any other interim measure.

[10.147]
Article 61

If the appeal is well founded, the Court of Justice shall quash the decision of the General Court. It may itself give final judgment in the matter, where the state of the proceedings so permits, or refer the case back to the General Court for judgment.

Where a case is referred back to the General Court, that Court shall be bound by the decision of the Court of Justice on points of law.

When an appeal brought by a Member State or an institution of the Union, which did not intervene in the proceedings before the General Court, is well founded, the Court of Justice may, if it considers this necessary, state which of the effects of the decision of the General Court which has been quashed shall be considered as definitive in respect of the parties to the litigation.

[10.148]
Article 62

In the cases provided for in Article 256(2) and (3) of the Treaty on the Functioning of the European Union, where the First Advocate-General considers that there is a serious risk of the unity or consistency of Union law being affected, he may propose that the Court of Justice review the decision of the General Court.

The proposal must be made within one month of delivery of the decision by the General Court. Within one month of receiving the proposal made by the First Advocate-General, the Court of Justice shall decide whether or not the decision should be reviewed.

[10.149]
Article 62a

The Court of Justice shall give a ruling on the questions which are subject to review by means of an urgent procedure on the basis of the file forwarded to it by the General Court.

Those referred to in Article 23 of this Statute and, in the cases provided for in Article 256(2) of the EC Treaty, the parties to the proceedings before the General Court shall be entitled to lodge statements or written observations with the Court of Justice relating to questions which are subject to review within a period prescribed for that purpose.

The Court of Justice may decide to open the oral procedure before giving a ruling.

[10.150]
Article 62b

In the cases provided for in Article 256(2) of the Treaty on the Functioning of the European Union, without prejudice to Articles 278 and 279 of the Treaty on the Functioning of the European Union, proposals for review and decisions to open the review procedure shall not have suspensory effect. If the Court of Justice finds that the decision of the General Court affects the unity or consistency of Union law, it shall refer the case back to the General Court which shall be bound by the points of law decided by the Court of Justice; the Court of Justice may state which of the effects of the decision of the General Court are to be considered as definitive in respect of the parties to the litigation. If, however, having regard to the result of the review, the outcome of the proceedings flows from the findings of fact on which the decision of the General Court was based, the Court of Justice shall give final judgment.

In the cases provided for in Article 256(3) of the Treaty on the Functioning of the European Union, in the absence of proposals for review or decisions to open the review procedure, the answer(s) given by the General Court to the questions submitted to it shall take effect upon expiry of the periods prescribed for that purpose in the second paragraph of Article 62. Should a review procedure be opened, the answer(s) subject to review shall take effect following that procedure, unless the Court of Justice decides otherwise. If the Court of Justice finds that the decision of the General Court affects the unity or consistency of Union law, the answer given by the Court of Justice to the questions subject to review shall be substituted for that given by the General Court.

TITLE IVA
SPECIALISED COURTS

[10.151]
[Article 62c
The provisions relating to the jurisdiction, composition, organisation and procedure of any specialised court established under Article 257 of the Treaty on the Functioning of the European Union shall be contained in an Annex to this Statute.]

NOTES
Substituted by Regulation (EU, Euratom) 2016/1192 of the European Parliament and of the Council of 6 July 2016 on the transfer to the General Court of jurisdiction at first instance in disputes between the European Union and its servants, Art 2(2).

TITLE V
FINAL PROVISIONS

[10.152]
Article 63
The Rules of Procedure of the Court of Justice and of the General Court shall contain any provisions necessary for applying and, where required, supplementing this Statute.

[10.153]
Article 64
The rules governing the language arrangements applicable at the Court of Justice of the European Union shall be laid down by a regulation of the Council acting unanimously. This regulation shall be adopted either at the request of the Court of Justice and after consultation of the Commission and the European Parliament, or on a proposal from the Commission and after consultation of the Court of Justice and of the European Parliament.
Until those rules have been adopted, the provisions of the Rules of Procedure of the Court of Justice and of the Rules of Procedure of the General Court governing language arrangements shall continue to apply. By way of derogation from Articles 253 and 254 of the Treaty on the Functioning of the European Union, those provisions may only be amended or repealed with the unanimous consent of the Council.

ANNEX I
THE EUROPEAN UNION CIVIL SERVICE TRIBUNAL

[10.154]
Article 1
The European Union Civil Service Tribunal (hereafter 'the Civil Service Tribunal') shall exercise at first instance jurisdiction in disputes between the Union and its servants referred to in Article 270 of the Treaty on the Functioning of the European Union, including disputes between all bodies or agencies and their servants in respect of which jurisdiction is conferred on the Court of Justice of the European Union.
Article 2
[1.] The Civil Service Tribunal shall consist of seven judges. Should the Court of Justice so request, the Council, acting by a qualified majority, may increase the number of judges.

The judges shall be appointed for a period of six years. Retiring judges may be reappointed.

Any vacancy shall be filled by the appointment of a new judge for a period of six years.

[2. Temporary Judges shall be appointed, in addition to the Judges referred to in the first subparagraph of paragraph 1, in order to cover the absence of Judges who, while not suffering from disablement deemed to be total, are prevented from participating in the disposal of cases for a lengthy period of time.]
Article 3
1. The judges shall be appointed by the Council, acting in accordance with the fourth paragraph of Article 257 of the Treaty on the Functioning of the European Union, after consulting the committee provided for by this Article. When appointing judges, the Council shall ensure a balanced composition of the Civil Service Tribunal on as broad a geographical basis as possible from among nationals of the Member States and with respect to the national legal systems represented.

2. Any person who is a Union citizen and fulfils the conditions laid down in the fourth paragraph of Article 257 of the Treaty on the Functioning of the European Union may submit an application. The Council, acting on a recommendation from the Court of Justice, shall determine the conditions and the arrangements governing the submission and processing of such applications.

3. A committee shall be set up comprising seven persons chosen from among former members of the Court of Justice and the General Court and lawyers of recognised competence. The committee's membership and operating rules shall be determined by the Council, acting on a recommendation by the President of the Court of Justice.

4. The committee shall give an opinion on candidates' suitability to perform the duties of judge at the Civil Service Tribunal. The committee shall append to its opinion a list of candidates having the most suitable high-level experience. Such list shall contain the names of at least twice as many candidates as there are judges to be appointed by the Council.

Article 4

1. The judges shall elect the President of the Civil Service Tribunal from among their number for a term of three years. He may be re-elected.

2. The Civil Service Tribunal shall sit in chambers of three judges. It may, in certain cases determined by its rules of procedure, sit in full court or in a chamber of five judges or of a single judge.

3. The President of the Civil Service Tribunal shall preside over the full court and the chamber of five judges. The Presidents of the chambers of three judges shall be designated as provided in paragraph 1. If the President of the Civil Service Tribunal is assigned to a chamber of three judges, he shall preside over that chamber.

4. The jurisdiction of and quorum for the full court as well as the composition of the chambers and the assignment of cases to them shall be governed by the rules of procedure.

Article 5

Articles 2 to 6, 14, 15, the first, second and fifth paragraphs of Article 17, and Article 18 of the Statute of the Court of Justice of the European Union shall apply to the Civil Service Tribunal and its members.

The oath referred to in Article 2 of the Statute shall be taken before the Court of Justice, and the decisions referred to in Articles 3, 4 and 6 thereof shall be adopted by the Court of Justice after consulting the Civil Service Tribunal.

Article 6

1. The Civil Service Tribunal shall be supported by the departments of the Court of Justice and of the General Court. The President of the Court of Justice or, in appropriate cases, the President of the General Court, shall determine by common accord with the President of the Civil Service Tribunal the conditions under which officials and other servants attached to the Court of Justice or the General Court shall render their services to the Civil Service Tribunal to enable it to function. Certain officials or other servants shall be responsible to the Registrar of the Civil Service Tribunal under the authority of the President of that Tribunal.

2. The Civil Service Tribunal shall appoint its Registrar and lay down the rules governing his service. The fourth paragraph of Article 3 and Articles 10, 11 and 14 of the Statute of the Court of Justice of the European Union shall apply to the Registrar of the Tribunal.

Article 7

1. The procedure before the Civil Service Tribunal shall be governed by Title III of the Statute of the Court of Justice of the European Union, with the exception of Articles 22 and 23. Such further and more detailed provisions as may be necessary shall be laid down in the rules of procedure.

2. The provisions concerning the General Court's language arrangements shall apply to the Civil Service Tribunal.

3. The written stage of the procedure shall comprise the presentation of the application and of the statement of defence, unless the Civil Service Tribunal decides that a second exchange of written pleadings is necessary. Where there is such second exchange, the Civil Service Tribunal may, with the agreement of the parties, decide to proceed to judgment without an oral procedure.

4. At all stages of the procedure, including the time when the application is filed, the Civil Service Tribunal may examine the possibilities of an amicable settlement of the dispute and may try to facilitate such settlement.

5. The Civil Service Tribunal shall rule on the costs of a case. Subject to the specific provisions of the Rules of Procedure, the unsuccessful party shall be ordered to pay the costs should the court so decide.

Article 8

1. Where an application or other procedural document addressed to the Civil Service Tribunal is lodged by mistake with the Registrar of the Court of Justice or General Court, it shall be transmitted immediately by that Registrar to the Registrar of the Civil Service Tribunal. Likewise, where an application or other procedural document addressed to the Court of Justice or to the General Court is lodged by mistake with the Registrar of the Civil Service Tribunal, it shall be transmitted immediately by that Registrar to the Registrar of the Court of Justice or General Court.

2. Where the Civil Service Tribunal finds that it does not have jurisdiction to hear and determine an action in respect of which the Court of Justice or the General Court has jurisdiction, it shall refer that action to the Court of Justice or to the General Court. Likewise, where the Court of Justice or the General Court finds that an action falls within the jurisdiction of the Civil Service Tribunal, the Court seised shall refer that action to the Civil Service Tribunal, whereupon that Tribunal may not decline jurisdiction.

3. Where the Civil Service Tribunal and the General Court are seised of cases in which the same issue of interpretation is raised or the validity of the same act is called in question, the Civil Service Tribunal, after hearing the parties, may stay the proceedings until the judgment of the General Court has been delivered.

Where the Civil Service Tribunal and the General Court are seised of cases in which the same relief is sought, the Civil Service Tribunal shall decline jurisdiction so that the General Court may act on those cases.

Article 9

An appeal may be brought before the General Court, within two months of notification of the decision appealed against, against final decisions of the Civil Service Tribunal and decisions of that Tribunal disposing of the substantive issues in part only or disposing of a procedural issue concerning a plea of lack of jurisdiction or inadmissibility.

Such an appeal may be brought by any party which has been unsuccessful, in whole or in part, in its submissions. However, interveners other than the Member States and the institutions of the Union may bring such an appeal only where the decision of the Civil Service Tribunal directly affects them.

Article 10

1. Any person whose application to intervene has been dismissed by the Civil Service Tribunal may appeal to the General Court within two weeks of notification of the decision dismissing the application.

2. The parties to the proceedings may appeal to the General Court against any decision of the Civil Service Tribunal made pursuant to Article 278 or Article 279 or the fourth paragraph of Article 299 of the Treaty on the Functioning of the European Union or Article 157 or the third paragraph of Article 164 of the EAEC Treaty within two months of its notification.

3. The President of the General Court may, by way of summary procedure, which may, in so far as necessary, differ from some of the rules contained in this Annex and which shall be laid down in the rules of procedure of the General Court, adjudicate upon appeals brought in accordance with paragraphs 1 and 2.

Article 11

1. An appeal to the General Court shall be limited to points of law. It shall lie on the grounds of lack of jurisdiction of the Civil Service Tribunal, a breach of procedure before it which adversely affects the interests of the appellant, as well as the infringement of Union law by the Tribunal.

2. No appeal shall lie regarding only the amount of the costs or the party ordered to pay them.

Article 12

1. Without prejudice to Articles 278 and 279 of the Treaty on the Functioning of the European Union or Article 157 of the EAEC Treaty, an appeal before the General Court shall not have suspensory effect.

2. Where an appeal is brought against a decision of the Civil Service Tribunal, the procedure before the General Court shall consist of a written part and an oral part. In accordance with conditions laid down in the rules of procedure, the General Court, having heard the parties, may dispense with the oral procedure.

Article 13

1. If the appeal is well founded, the General Court shall quash the decision of the Civil Service Tribunal and itself give judgment in the matter. It shall refer the case back to the Civil Service Tribunal for judgment where the state of the proceedings does not permit a decision by the Court.

2. Where a case is referred back to the Civil Service Tribunal, the Tribunal shall be bound by the decision of the General Court on points of law.

NOTES

Annex I is repealed by Regulation (EU, Euratom) 2016/1192 of the European Parliament and of the Council of 6 July 2016 on the transfer to the General Court of jurisdiction at first instance in disputes between the European Union and its servants, Art 2(3), subject to Art 4 thereof which provides that Articles 9 to 12 of Annex I shall continue to apply to the appeals against decisions of the Civil Service Tribunal of which the General Court is seised as at 31 August 2016 or which are brought after that date. If the General Court sets aside a decision of the Civil Service Tribunal but considers that the state of the proceedings does not permit a decision, it shall refer the case to a chamber other than that which ruled on the appeal.

In Article 2, para 1 numbered as such and para 2 added, by Regulation (EU, Euratom) No 741/2012 of the European Parliament and of the Council of 11 August 2012 amending the Protocol on the Statute of the Court of Justice of the European Union and Annex I thereto, Article 2 (OJ L228, 23.8.2012).

EDITORIAL NOTE: this Protocol does not contain an Annex II even though this Annex is numbered as Annex I.

RULES OF PROCEDURE OF THE COURT OF JUSTICE 2012 (CONSOLIDATED 2016)

[10.155]

NOTES

Date of original publication in OJ: OJ L265, 29.9.2012, p 1.

The consolidated version of these Rules (reproduced here) is also available on the Court of Justice section of the Curia website at curia.europa.eu/jcms/upload/docs/application/pdf/2012-10/rp_en.pdf. It includes the amendments published in OJ L173, 26.6.2013 and in OJ L217, 12.8.2016, p 69.

THE COURT OF JUSTICE

Having regard to the Treaty on European Union, and in particular Article 19 thereof,

Having regard to the Treaty on the Functioning of the European Union, and in particular the sixth paragraph of Article 253 thereof,

Having regard to the Treaty establishing the European Atomic Energy Community, and in particular Article 106a(1) thereof,

Having regard to the Protocol on the Statute of the Court of Justice of the European Union, and in particular Article 63 and the second paragraph of Article 64 thereof,

Whereas:

(1) Despite having been amended on several occasions over the years, the Rules of Procedure of the Court of Justice have remained fundamentally unchanged in structure since their original adoption on 4 March 1953. The Rules of Procedure of 19 June 1991, which are currently in force, still reflect the initial preponderance of direct actions, whereas in fact the majority of such actions now fall within the jurisdiction of the General Court, and references for a preliminary ruling from the courts and tribunals of the Member States represent, quantitatively, the primary category of cases brought before the Court. That fact should be taken into account and the structure and content of the Rules of Procedure of the Court adapted, in consequence, to changes in its caseload.

(2) While references for a preliminary ruling should be given their proper place in the Rules of Procedure, it is also appropriate to draw a clearer distinction between the rules that apply to all types of action and those that are specific to each type, to be contained in separate titles. In the interests of clarification, procedural provisions common to all cases brought before the Court should, therefore, all be contained in an initial title.

(3) In the light of experience gained in the course of implementing the various procedures, it is also necessary to supplement or to clarify, for the benefit of litigants as well as of national courts and tribunals, the rules that apply to each procedure. The rules in question concern, in particular, the concepts of party to the main proceedings, intervener and party to the proceedings before the General Court, or, in preliminary rulings, the rules governing the bringing of matters before the Court and the content of the order for reference. With regard to appeals against decisions of the General Court, a clearer distinction must also be drawn between appeals and cross-appeals in consequence of the service of an appeal on the cross-appellant.

(4) Conversely, the excessive complexity of certain procedures, such as the review procedure, has come to light on their implementation. Accordingly, they should be simplified by providing, inter alia, for a Chamber of five Judges to be designated for a period of one year to be responsible for ruling both on the First Advocate General's proposal to review and on the questions to be reviewed.

(5) Similarly, the procedural arrangements for dealing with requests for Opinions should be eased by aligning them with those that apply to other cases and by providing, in consequence, for a single Advocate General to be involved in dealing with the request for an Opinion. In the interests of making the Rules easier to understand, all the particular procedures currently to be found in a number of separate titles and chapters of the Rules of Procedure should also be brought together in a single title.

(6) In order to maintain the Court's capacity, in the face of an ever-increasing caseload, to dispose within a reasonable period of time of the cases brought before it, it is also necessary to continue the efforts made to reduce the duration of proceedings before the Court, in particular by extending the opportunities for the Court to rule by reasoned order, simplifying the rules relating to the intervention of the States and institutions referred to in the first and third paragraphs of Article 40 of the Statute and providing for the Court to be able to rule without a hearing if it considers that it has sufficient information on the basis of all the written observations lodged in a case.

(7) In the interests of making the Rules applied by the Court easier to understand, lastly, certain rules which are outdated or not applied should be deleted, every paragraph of the present Rules numbered, each article given a specific heading summarising its content and the terminology harmonised.

With the Council's approval given on 24 September 2012.

HAS ADOPTED THESE RULES OF PROCEDURE:

INTRODUCTORY PROVISIONS

[10.156]
Article 1
Definitions

1. In these Rules:
   (a) provisions of the Treaty on European Union are referred to by the number of the article concerned followed by 'TEU',
   (b) provisions of the Treaty on the Functioning of the European Union are referred to by the number of the article concerned followed by 'TFEU',
   (c) provisions of the Treaty establishing the European Atomic Energy Community are referred to by the number of the article concerned followed by 'TEAEC',
   (d) 'Statute' means the Protocol on the Statute of the Court of Justice of the European Union,
   (e) 'EEA Agreement' means the Agreement on the European Economic Area,[1]
   (f) 'Council Regulation No 1' means Council Regulation No 1 of 15 April 1958 determining the languages to be used by the European Economic Community.[2]
2. For the purposes of these Rules:
   (a) 'institutions' means the institutions of the European Union referred to in Article 13(1) TEU and bodies, offices and agencies established by the Treaties, or by an act adopted in implementation thereof, which may be parties before the Court,
   (b) 'EFTA Surveillance Authority' means the surveillance authority referred to in the EEA Agreement,
   (c) 'interested persons referred to in Article 23 of the Statute' means all the parties, States, institutions, bodies, offices and agencies authorised, pursuant to that Article, to submit statements of case or observations in the context of a reference for a preliminary ruling.

NOTES

1 OJ L1, 3.1.1994, p 27.

2 OJ, English Special Edition 1952-1958 (I), p 59.

[10.157]
Article 2
Purport of these Rules

These Rules implement and supplement, so far as necessary, the relevant provisions of the EU, FEU and EAEC Treaties, and the Statute.

TITLE I
ORGANISATION OF THE COURT

CHAPTER 1
JUDGES AND ADVOCATES GENERAL

[10.158]
Article 3
Commencement of the term of office of Judges and Advocates General

The term of office of a Judge or Advocate General shall begin on the date fixed for that purpose in the instrument of appointment. In the absence of any provisions in that instrument regarding the date of commencement of the term of office, that term shall begin on the date of publication of the instrument in the *Official Journal of the European Union*.

[10.159]
Article 4
Taking of the oath

Before taking up his duties, a Judge or Advocate General shall, at the first public sitting of the Court which he attends after his appointment, take the following oath provided for in Article 2 of the Statute:

> 'I swear that I will perform my duties impartially and conscientiously; I swear that I will preserve the secrecy of the deliberations of the Court.'

[10.160]
Article 5
Solemn undertaking

Immediately after taking the oath, a Judge or Advocate General shall sign a declaration by which he gives the solemn undertaking provided for in the third paragraph of Article 4 of the Statute.

[10.161]
Article 6
Depriving a Judge or Advocate General of his office

1. Where the Court is called upon, pursuant to Article 6 of the Statute, to decide whether a Judge or Advocate General no longer fulfils the requisite conditions or no longer meets the obligations arising from his office, the President shall invite the Judge or Advocate General concerned to make representations.
2. The Court shall give a decision in the absence of the Registrar.

[10.162]
Article 7
Order of seniority

1. The seniority of Judges and Advocates General shall be calculated without distinction according to the date on which they took up their duties.
2. Where there is equal seniority on that basis, the order of seniority shall be determined by age.
3. Judges and Advocates General whose terms of office are renewed shall retain their former seniority.

CHAPTER 2
PRESIDENCY OF THE COURT, CONSTITUTION OF THE CHAMBERS AND DESIGNATION OF THE FIRST ADVOCATE GENERAL

[10.163]
Article 8
Election of the President and of the Vice-President of the Court

1. The Judges shall, immediately after the partial replacement provided for in the second paragraph of Article 253 TFEU, elect one of their number as President of the Court for a term of three years.
2. If the office of the President falls vacant before the normal date of expiry of the term thereof, the Court shall elect a successor for the remainder of the term.
3. The elections provided for in this Article shall be by secret ballot. The Judge obtaining the votes of more than half the Judges of the Court shall be elected. If no Judge obtains that majority, further ballots shall be held until that majority is attained.
4. The Judges shall then elect one of their number as Vice-President of the Court for a term of three years, in accordance with the procedures laid down in the preceding paragraph. Paragraph 2 shall apply if the office of the Vice-President of the Court falls vacant before the normal date of expiry of the term thereof.
5. The names of the President and Vice-President elected in accordance with this Article shall be published in the *Official Journal of the European Union*.

[10.164]
Article 9
Responsibilities of the President of the Court

1. The President shall represent the Court.
2. The President shall direct the judicial business of the Court. He shall preside at general meetings of the Members of the Court and at hearings before and deliberations of the full Court and the Grand Chamber.
3. The President shall ensure the proper functioning of the services of the Court.

[10.165]
Article 10
Responsibilities of the Vice-President of the Court

1. The Vice-President shall assist the President of the Court in the performance of his duties and shall take the President's place when the latter is prevented from acting.
2. He shall take the President's place, at his request, in performing the duties referred to in Article 9(1) and (3) of these Rules.
3. The Court shall, by decision, specify the conditions under which the Vice-President shall take the place of the President of the Court in the performance of his judicial duties. That decision shall be published in the *Official Journal of the European Union*.

[10.166]
Article 11
Constitution of Chambers

1. The Court shall set up Chambers of five and three Judges in accordance with Article 16 of the Statute and shall decide which Judges shall be attached to them.
2. The Court shall designate the Chambers of five Judges which, for a period of one year, shall be responsible for cases of the kind referred to in Article 107 and Articles 193 and 194.
3. In respect of cases assigned to a formation of the Court in accordance with Article 60, the word 'Court' in these Rules shall mean that formation.

4. In respect of cases assigned to a Chamber of five or three Judges, the powers of the President of the Court shall be exercised by the President of the Chamber.
5. The composition of the Chambers and the designation of the Chambers responsible for cases of the kind referred to in Article 107 and Articles 193 and 194 shall be published in the *Official Journal of the European Union*.

[10.167]
Article 12
Election of Presidents of Chambers
1. The Judges shall, immediately after the election of the President and Vice-President of the Court, elect the Presidents of the Chambers of five Judges for a term of three years.
2. The Judges shall then elect the Presidents of the Chambers of three Judges for a term of one year.
3. The provisions of Article 8(2) and (3) shall apply.
4. The names of the Presidents of Chambers elected in accordance with this Article shall be published in the *Official Journal of the European Union*.

[10.168]
Article 13
Where the President and Vice-President of the Court are prevented from acting
When the President and the Vice-President of the Court are prevented from acting, the functions of President shall be exercised by one of the Presidents of the Chambers of five Judges or, failing that, by one of the Presidents of the Chambers of three Judges or, failing that, by one of the other Judges, according to the order of seniority laid down in Article 7.

[10.169]
Article 14
Designation of the First Advocate General
1. The Court shall, after hearing the Advocates General, designate a First Advocate General for a period of one year.
2. If the office of the First Advocate General falls vacant before the normal date of expiry of the term thereof, the Court shall designate a successor for the remainder of the term.
3. The name of the First Advocate General designated in accordance with this Article shall be published in the *Official Journal of the European Union*.

CHAPTER 3
ASSIGNMENT OF CASES TO JUDGE-RAPPORTEURS AND ADVOCATES GENERAL

[10.170]
Article 15
Designation of the Judge-Rapporteur
1. As soon as possible after the document initiating proceedings has been lodged, the President of the Court shall designate a Judge to act as Rapporteur in the case.
2. For cases of the kind referred to in Article 107 and Articles 193 and 194, the Judge-Rapporteur shall be selected from among the Judges of the Chamber designated in accordance with Article 11(2), on a proposal from the President of that Chamber. If, pursuant to Article 109, the Chamber decides that the reference is not to be dealt with under the urgent procedure, the President of the Court may reassign the case to a Judge-Rapporteur attached to another Chamber.
3. The President of the Court shall take the necessary steps if a Judge-Rapporteur is prevented from acting.

[10.171]
Article 16
Designation of the Advocate General
1. The First Advocate General shall assign each case to an Advocate General.
2. The First Advocate General shall take the necessary steps if an Advocate General is prevented from acting.

CHAPTER 4
ASSISTANT RAPPORTEURS

[10.172]
Article 17
Assistant Rapporteurs
1. Where the Court is of the opinion that the consideration of and preparatory inquiries in cases before it so require, it shall, pursuant to Article 13 of the Statute, propose the appointment of Assistant Rapporteurs.
2. Assistant Rapporteurs shall in particular:
   (a) assist the President of the Court in interim proceedings and
   (b) assist the Judge-Rapporteurs in their work.

3. In the performance of their duties the Assistant Rapporteurs shall be responsible to the President of the Court, the President of a Chamber or a Judge-Rapporteur, as the case may be.
4. Before taking up his duties, an Assistant Rapporteur shall take before the Court the oath set out in Article 4 of these Rules.

CHAPTER 5
REGISTRY

[10.173]
Article 18
Appointment of the Registrar

1. The Court shall appoint the Registrar.
2. When the post of Registrar is vacant, an advertisement shall be published in the *Official Journal of the European Union*. Interested persons shall be invited to submit their applications within a time-limit of not less than three weeks, accompanied by full details of their nationality, university degrees, knowledge of languages, present and past occupations, and experience, if any, in judicial and international fields.
3. The vote, in which the Judges and the Advocates General shall take part, shall take place in accordance with the procedure laid down in Article 8(3) of these Rules.
4. The Registrar shall be appointed for a term of six years. He may be reappointed. The Court may decide to renew the term of office of the incumbent Registrar without availing itself of the procedure laid down in paragraph 2 of this Article.
5. The Registrar shall take the oath set out in Article 4 and sign the declaration provided for in Article 5.
6. The Registrar may be deprived of his office only if he no longer fulfils the requisite conditions or no longer meets the obligations arising from his office. The Court shall take its decision after giving the Registrar an opportunity to make representations.
7. If the office of Registrar falls vacant before the normal date of expiry of the term thereof, the Court shall appoint a new Registrar for a term of six years.
8. The name of the Registrar elected in accordance with this Article shall be published in the *Official Journal of the European Union*.

[10.174]
Article 19
Deputy Registrar

The Court may, in accordance with the procedure laid down in respect of the Registrar, appoint a Deputy Registrar to assist the Registrar and to take his place if he is prevented from acting.

[10.175]
Article 20
Responsibilities of the Registrar

1. The Registrar shall be responsible, under the authority of the President of the Court, for the acceptance, transmission and custody of all documents and for effecting service as provided for by these Rules.
2. The Registrar shall assist the Members of the Court in all their official functions.
3. The Registrar shall have custody of the seals and shall be responsible for the records. He shall be in charge of the publications of the Court and, in particular, the European Court Reports.
4. The Registrar shall direct the services of the Court under the authority of the President of the Court. He shall be responsible for the management of the staff and the administration, and for the preparation and implementation of the budget.

[10.176]
Article 21
Keeping of the register

1. There shall be kept in the Registry, under the responsibility of the Registrar, a register in which all procedural documents and supporting items and documents lodged shall be entered in the order in which they are submitted.
2. When a document has been registered, the Registrar shall make a note to that effect on the original and, if a party so requests, on any copy submitted for the purpose.
3. Entries in the register and the notes provided for in the preceding paragraph shall be authentic.
4. A notice shall be published in the *Official Journal of the European Union* indicating the date of registration of an application initiating proceedings, the names of the parties, the form of order sought by the applicant and a summary of the pleas in law and of the main supporting arguments or, as the case may be, the date of lodging of a request for a preliminary ruling, the identity of the referring court or tribunal and the parties to the main proceedings, and the questions referred to the Court.

[10.177]
Article 22
Consultation of the register and of judgments and orders

1. Anyone may consult the register at the Registry and may obtain copies or extracts on payment of a charge on a scale fixed by the Court on a proposal from the Registrar.
2. The parties to a case may, on payment of the appropriate charge, obtain certified copies of procedural documents.
3. Anyone may, on payment of the appropriate charge, also obtain certified copies of judgments and orders.

CHAPTER 6
THE WORKING OF THE COURT

[10.178]
Article 23
Location of the sittings of the Court

The Court may choose to hold one or more specific sittings in a place other than that in which it has its seat.

[10.179]
Article 24
Calendar of the Court's judicial business

1. The judicial year shall begin on 7 October of each calendar year and end on 6 October of the following year.
2. The judicial vacations shall be determined by the Court.
3. In a case of urgency, the President may convene the Judges and the Advocates General during the judicial vacations.
4. The Court shall observe the official holidays of the place in which it has its seat.
5. The Court may, in proper circumstances, grant leave of absence to any Judge or Advocate General.
6. The dates of the judicial vacations and the list of official holidays shall be published annually in the *Official Journal of the European Union*.

[10.180]
Article 25
General meeting

Decisions concerning administrative issues or the action to be taken upon the proposals contained in the preliminary report referred to in Article 59 of these Rules shall be taken by the Court at the general meeting in which all the Judges and Advocates General shall take part and have a vote. The Registrar shall be present, unless the Court decides to the contrary.

[10.181]
Article 26
Drawing-up of minutes

Where the Court sits without the Registrar being present it shall, if necessary, instruct the most junior Judge for the purposes of Article 7 of these Rules to draw up minutes, which shall be signed by that Judge and by the President.

CHAPTER 7
FORMATIONS OF THE COURT

SECTION 1.
COMPOSITION OF THE FORMATIONS OF THE COURT

[10.182]
Article 27
Composition of the Grand Chamber

1. The Grand Chamber shall, for each case, be composed of the President and the Vice-President of the Court, three Presidents of Chambers of five Judges, the Judge-Rapporteur and the number of Judges necessary to reach 15. The last-mentioned Judges and the three Presidents of Chambers of five Judges shall be designated from the lists referred to in paragraphs 3 and 4 of this Article, following the order laid down therein. The starting-point on each of those lists, in every case assigned to the Grand Chamber, shall be the name of the Judge immediately following the last Judge designated from the list concerned for the preceding case assigned to that formation of the Court.
2. After the election of the President and the Vice-President of the Court, and then of the Presidents of the Chambers of five Judges, a list of the Presidents of Chambers of five Judges and a list of the other Judges shall be drawn up for the purposes of determining the composition of the Grand Chamber.

3. The list of the Presidents of Chambers of five Judges shall be drawn up according to the order laid down in Article 7 of these Rules.
4. The list of the other Judges shall be drawn up according to the order laid down in Article 7 of these Rules, alternating with the reverse order: the first Judge on that list shall be the first according to the order laid down in that Article, the second Judge shall be the last according to that order, the third Judge shall be the second according to that order, the fourth Judge the penultimate according to that order, and so on.
5. The lists referred to in paragraphs 3 and 4 shall be published in the *Official Journal of the European Union*.
6. In cases which are assigned to the Grand Chamber between the beginning of a calendar year in which there is a partial replacement of Judges and the moment when that replacement has taken place, two substitute Judges may be designated to complete the formation of the Court for so long as the attainment of the quorum referred to in the third paragraph of Article 17 of the Statute is in doubt. Those substitute Judges shall be the two Judges appearing on the list referred to in paragraph 4 immediately after the last Judge designated for the composition of the Grand Chamber in the case.
7. The substitute Judges shall replace, in the order of the list referred to in paragraph 4, such Judges as are unable to take part in the determination of the case.

[10.183]
Article 28
Composition of the Chambers of five and of three Judges
1. The Chambers of five Judges and of three Judges shall, for each case, be composed of the President of the Chamber, the Judge-Rapporteur and the number of Judges required to attain the number of five and three Judges respectively. Those last-mentioned Judges shall be designated from the lists referred to in paragraphs 2 and 3, following the order laid down therein. The starting-point on those lists, in every case assigned to a Chamber, shall be the name of the Judge immediately following the last Judge designated from the list for the preceding case assigned to the Chamber concerned.
2. For the composition of the Chambers of five Judges, after the election of the Presidents of those Chambers lists shall be drawn up including all the Judges attached to the Chamber concerned, with the exception of its President. The lists shall be drawn up in the same way as the list referred to in Article 27(4).
3. For the composition of the Chambers of three Judges, after the election of the Presidents of those Chambers lists shall be drawn up including all the Judges attached to the Chamber concerned, with the exception of its President. The lists shall be drawn up according to the order laid down in Article 7.
4. The lists referred to in paragraphs 2 and 3 shall be published in the *Official Journal of the European Union*.

[10.184]
Article 29
Composition of Chambers where cases are related or referred back
1. Where the Court considers that a number of cases must be heard and determined together by one and the same formation of the Court, the composition of that formation shall be that fixed for the case in respect of which the preliminary report was examined first.
2. Where a Chamber to which a case has been assigned requests the Court, pursuant to Article 60(3) of these Rules, to assign the case to a formation composed of a greater number of Judges, that formation shall include the members of the Chamber which has referred the case back.

[10.185]
Article 30
Where a President of a Chamber is prevented from acting
1. When the President of a Chamber of five Judges is prevented from acting, the functions of President of the Chamber shall be exercised by a President of a Chamber of three Judges, where necessary according to the order laid down in Article 7 of these Rules, or, if that formation of the Court does not include a President of a Chamber of three Judges, by one of the other Judges according to the order laid down in Article 7.
2. When the President of a Chamber of three Judges is prevented from acting, the functions of President of the Chamber shall be exercised by a Judge of that formation of the Court according to the order laid down in Article 7.

[10.186]
Article 31
Where a member of the formation of the Court is prevented from acting
1. When a member of the Grand Chamber is prevented from acting, he shall be replaced by another Judge according to the order of the list referred to in Article 27(4).

2. When a member of a Chamber of five Judges is prevented from acting, he shall be replaced by another Judge of that Chamber, according to the order of the list referred to in Article 28(2). If it is not possible to replace the Judge prevented from acting by a Judge of the same Chamber, the President of that Chamber shall so inform the President of the Court who may designate another Judge to complete the Chamber.

3. When a member of a Chamber of three Judges is prevented from acting, he shall be replaced by another Judge of that Chamber, according to the order of the list referred to in Article 28(3). If it is not possible to replace the Judge prevented from acting by a Judge of the same Chamber, the President of that Chamber shall so inform the President of the Court who may designate another Judge to complete the Chamber.

SECTION 2. DELIBERATIONS

[10.187]

Article 32

Procedures concerning deliberations

1. The deliberations of the Court shall be and shall remain secret.

2. When a hearing has taken place, only those Judges who participated in that hearing and, where relevant, the Assistant Rapporteur responsible for the consideration of the case shall take part in the deliberations.

3. Every Judge taking part in the deliberations shall state his opinion and the reasons for it.

4. The conclusions reached by the majority of the Judges after final discussion shall determine the decision of the Court.

[10.188]

Article 33

Number of Judges taking part in the deliberations

Where, by reason of a Judge being prevented from acting, there is an even number of Judges, the most junior Judge for the purposes of Article 7 of these Rules shall abstain from taking part in the deliberations unless he is the Judge-Rapporteur. In that case the Judge immediately senior to him shall abstain from taking part in the deliberations.

[10.189]

Article 34

Quorum of the Grand Chamber

1. If, for a case assigned to the Grand Chamber, it is not possible to attain the quorum referred to in the third paragraph of Article 17 of the Statute, the President of the Court shall designate one or more other Judges according to the order of the list referred to in Article 27(4) of these Rules.

2. If a hearing has taken place before that designation, the Court shall re-hear oral argument from the parties and the Opinion of the Advocate General.

[10.190]

Article 35

Quorum of the Chambers of five and of three Judges

1. If, for a case assigned to a Chamber of five or of three Judges, it is not possible to attain the quorum referred to in the second paragraph of Article 17 of the Statute, the President of the Court shall designate one or more other Judges according to the order of the list referred to in Article 28(2) or (3), respectively, of these Rules. If it is not possible to replace the Judge prevented from acting by a Judge of the same Chamber, the President of that Chamber shall so inform the President of the Court forthwith who shall designate another Judge to complete the Chamber.

2. Article 34(2) shall apply, *mutatis mutandis*, to the Chambers of five and of three Judges.

CHAPTER 8 LANGUAGES

[10.191]

[Article 36

Language of a case

The language of a case shall be Bulgarian, Croatian, Czech, Danish, Dutch, English, Estonian, Finnish, French, German, Greek, Hungarian, Irish, Italian, Latvian, Lithuanian, Maltese, Polish, Portuguese, Romanian, Slovak, Slovenian, Spanish or Swedish.]

NOTES

Substituted by the Amendment of the Rules of Procedure of the Court of Justice, Article 1 (OJ L173, 26.6.2013, p 65). Note that the substituted text did not provide for an Article heading, but the original heading has been retained here.

[10.192]
Article 37
Determination of the language of a case

1. In direct actions, the language of a case shall be chosen by the applicant, except that:
   (a) where the defendant is a Member State, the language of the case shall be the official language of that State; where that State has more than one official language, the applicant may choose between them;
   (b) at the joint request of the parties, the use of another of the languages mentioned in Article 36 for all or part of the proceedings may be authorised;
   (c) at the request of one of the parties, and after the opposite party and the Advocate General have been heard, the use of another of the languages mentioned in Article 36 may be authorised as the language of the case for all or part of the proceedings by way of derogation from subparagraphs (a) and (b); such a request may not be submitted by one of the institutions of the European Union.

2. Without prejudice to the provisions of paragraph 1(b) and (c), and of Article 38(4) and (5) of these Rules,
   (a) in appeals against decisions of the General Court as referred to in Articles 56 and 57 of the Statute, the language of the case shall be the language of the decision of the General Court against which the appeal is brought;
   (b) where, in accordance with the second paragraph of Article 62 of the Statute, the Court decides to review a decision of the General Court, the language of the case shall be the language of the decision of the General Court which is the subject of review;
   (c) in the case of challenges concerning the costs to be recovered, applications to set aside judgments by default, third-party proceedings and applications for interpretation or revision of a judgment or for the Court to remedy a failure to adjudicate, the language of the case shall be the language of the decision to which those applications or challenges relate.

3. In preliminary ruling proceedings, the language of the case shall be the language of the referring court or tribunal. At the duly substantiated request of one of the parties to the main proceedings, and after the other party to the main proceedings and the Advocate General have been heard, the use of another of the languages mentioned in Article 36 may be authorised for the oral part of the procedure. Where granted, such authorisation shall apply in respect of all the interested persons referred to in Article 23 of the Statute.

4. Requests as above may be decided on by the President; the latter may, and where he wishes to accede to a request without the agreement of all the parties must, refer the request to the Court.

[10.193]
Article 38
Use of the language of the case

1. The language of the case shall in particular be used in the written and oral pleadings of the parties, including the items and documents produced or annexed to them, and also in the minutes and decisions of the Court.

2. Any item or document produced or annexed that is expressed in another language must be accompanied by a translation into the language of the case.

3. However, in the case of substantial items or lengthy documents, translations may be confined to extracts. At any time the Court may, of its own motion or at the request of one of the parties, call for a complete or fuller translation.

4. Notwithstanding the foregoing provisions, a Member State shall be entitled to use its official language when taking part in preliminary ruling proceedings, when intervening in a case before the Court or when bringing a matter before the Court pursuant to Article 259 TFEU. This provision shall apply both to written documents and to oral statements. The Registrar shall arrange in each instance for translation into the language of the case.

5. The States, other than the Member States, which are parties to the EEA Agreement, and also the EFTA Surveillance Authority, may be authorised to use one of the languages mentioned in Article 36, other than the language of the case, when they take part in preliminary ruling proceedings or intervene in a case before the Court. This provision shall apply both to written documents and to oral statements. The Registrar shall arrange in each instance for translation into the language of the case.

6. Non-Member States taking part in preliminary ruling proceedings pursuant to the fourth paragraph of Article 23 of the Statute may be authorised to use one of the languages mentioned in Article 36 other than the language of the case. This provision shall apply both to written documents and to oral statements. The Registrar shall arrange in each instance for translation into the language of the case.

7. Where a witness or expert states that he is unable adequately to express himself in one of the languages referred to in Article 36, the Court may authorise him to give his evidence in another language. The Registrar shall arrange for translation into the language of the case.

8. The President and the Vice-President of the Court and also the Presidents of Chambers in conducting oral proceedings, Judges and Advocates General in putting questions and Advocates General in delivering their Opinions may use one of the languages referred to in Article 36 other than the language of the case. The Registrar shall arrange for translation into the language of the case.

[10.194]
Article 39
Responsibility of the Registrar concerning language arrangements
The Registrar shall, at the request of any Judge, of the Advocate General or of a party, arrange for anything said or written in the course of the proceedings before the Court to be translated into the languages chosen from those referred to in Article 36.

[10.195]
Article 40
Languages of the publications of the Court
Publications of the Court shall be issued in the languages referred to in Article 1 of Council Regulation No 1.

[10.196]
Article 41
Authentic texts
The texts of documents drawn up in the language of the case or, where applicable, in another language authorised pursuant to Articles 37 or 38 of these Rules shall be authentic.

[10.197]
Article 42
Language service of the Court
The Court shall set up a language service staffed by experts with adequate legal training and a thorough knowledge of several official languages of the European Union.

TITLE II
COMMON PROCEDURAL PROVISIONS

CHAPTER 1
RIGHTS AND OBLIGATIONS OF AGENTS, ADVISERS AND LAWYERS

[10.198]
Article 43
Privileges, immunities and facilities
1. Agents, advisers and lawyers who appear before the Court or before any judicial authority to which the Court has addressed letters rogatory shall enjoy immunity in respect of words spoken or written by them concerning the case or the parties.
2. Agents, advisers and lawyers shall also enjoy the following privileges and facilities:
(a) any papers and documents relating to the proceedings shall be exempt from both search and seizure. In the event of a dispute, the customs officials or police may seal those papers and documents; they shall then be immediately forwarded to the Court for inspection in the presence of the Registrar and of the person concerned;
(b) agents, advisers and lawyers shall be entitled to travel in the course of duty without hindrance.

[10.199]
Article 44
Status of the parties' representatives
1. In order to qualify for the privileges, immunities and facilities specified in Article 43, persons entitled to them shall furnish proof of their status as follows:
(a) agents shall produce an official document issued by the party for whom they act, who shall immediately serve a copy thereof on the Registrar;
(b) lawyers shall produce a certificate that they are authorised to practise before a court of a Member State or of another State which is a party to the EEA Agreement, and, where the party which they represent is a legal person governed by private law, an authority to act issued by that person;
(c) advisers shall produce an authority to act issued by the party whom they are assisting.
2. The Registrar of the Court shall issue them with a certificate, as required. The validity of this certificate shall be limited to a specified period, which may be extended or curtailed according to the duration of the proceedings.

[10.200]
Article 45
Waiver of immunity

1. The privileges, immunities and facilities specified in Article 43 of these Rules are granted exclusively in the interests of the proper conduct of proceedings.
2. The Court may waive immunity where it considers that the proper conduct of proceedings will not be hindered thereby.

[10.201]
Article 46
Exclusion from the proceedings

1. If the Court considers that the conduct of an agent, adviser or lawyer before the Court is incompatible with the dignity of the Court or with the requirements of the proper administration of justice, or that such agent, adviser or lawyer is using his rights for purposes other than those for which they were granted, it shall inform the person concerned. If the Court informs the competent authorities to whom the person concerned is answerable, a copy of the letter sent to those authorities shall be forwarded to the person concerned.
2. On the same grounds, the Court may at any time, having heard the person concerned and the Advocate General, decide to exclude an agent, adviser or lawyer from the proceedings by reasoned order. That order shall have immediate effect.
3. Where an agent, adviser or lawyer is excluded from the proceedings, the proceedings shall be suspended for a period fixed by the President in order to allow the party concerned to appoint another agent, adviser or lawyer.
4. Decisions taken under this Article may be rescinded.

[10.202]
Article 47
University teachers and parties to the main proceedings

1. The provisions of this Chapter shall apply to university teachers who have a right of audience before the Court in accordance with Article 19 of the Statute.
2. They shall also apply, in the context of references for a preliminary ruling, to the parties to the main proceedings where, in accordance with the national rules of procedure applicable, those parties are permitted to bring or defend court proceedings without being represented by a lawyer, and to persons authorised under those rules to represent them.

CHAPTER 2
SERVICE

[10.203]
Article 48
Methods of service

1. Where these Rules require that a document be served on a person, the Registrar shall ensure that service is effected at that person's address for service either by the dispatch of a copy of the document by registered post with a form for acknowledgement of receipt or by personal delivery of the copy against a receipt. The Registrar shall prepare and certify the copies of documents to be served, save where the parties themselves supply the copies in accordance with Article 57(2) of these Rules.
2. Where the addressee has agreed that service is to be effected on him by telefax or any other technical means of communication, any procedural document, including a judgment or order of the Court, may be served by the transmission of a copy of the document by such means.
3. Where, for technical reasons or on account of the nature or length of the document, such transmission is impossible or impracticable, the document shall be served, if the addressee has not specified an address for service, at his address in accordance with the procedures laid down in paragraph 1 of this Article. The addressee shall be so informed by telefax or any other technical means of communication. Service shall then be deemed to have been effected on the addressee by registered post on the 10th day following the lodging of the registered letter at the post office of the place in which the Court has its seat, unless it is shown by the acknowledgement of receipt that the letter was received on a different date or the addressee informs the Registrar, within three weeks of being informed by telefax or any other technical means of communication, that the document to be served has not reached him.
4. The Court may, by decision, determine the criteria for a procedural document to be served by electronic means. That decision shall be published in the *Official Journal of the European Union*.

CHAPTER 3
TIME-LIMITS

[10.204]
Article 49
Calculation of time-limits

1. Any procedural time-limit prescribed by the Treaties, the Statute or these Rules shall be calculated as follows:

(a) where a time-limit expressed in days, weeks, months or years is to be calculated from the moment at which an event occurs or an action takes place, the day during which that event occurs or that action takes place shall not be counted as falling within the time-limit in question;

(b) a time-limit expressed in weeks, months or years shall end with the expiry of whichever day in the last week, month or year is the same day of the week, or falls on the same date, as the day during which the event or action from which the time-limit is to be calculated occurred or took place. If, in a time-limit expressed in months or years, the day on which it should expire does not occur in the last month, the time-limit shall end with the expiry of the last day of that month;

(c) where a time-limit is expressed in months and days, it shall first be calculated in whole months, then in days;

(d) time-limits shall include Saturdays, Sundays and the official holidays referred to in Article 24(6) of these Rules;

(e) time-limits shall not be suspended during the judicial vacations.

2. If the time-limit would otherwise end on a Saturday, Sunday or an official holiday, it shall be extended until the end of the first subsequent working day.

[10.205]
Article 50
Proceedings against a measure adopted by an institution

Where the time-limit allowed for initiating proceedings against a measure adopted by an institution runs from the publication of that measure, that time-limit shall be calculated, for the purposes of Article 49(1)(a), from the end of the 14th day after publication of the measure in the *Official Journal of the European Union.*

[10.206]
Article 51
Extension on account of distance

The procedural time-limits shall be extended on account of distance by a single period of 10 days.

[10.207]
Article 52
Setting and extension of time-limits

1. Any time-limit prescribed by the Court pursuant to these Rules may be extended.

2. The President and the Presidents of Chambers may delegate to the Registrar power of signature for the purposes of setting certain time-limits which, pursuant to these Rules, it falls to them to prescribe, or of extending such time-limits.

CHAPTER 4
DIFFERENT PROCEDURES FOR DEALING WITH CASES

[10.208]
Article 53
Procedures for dealing with cases

1. Without prejudice to the special provisions laid down in the Statute or in these Rules, the procedure before the Court shall consist of a written part and an oral part.

2. Where it is clear that the Court has no jurisdiction to hear and determine a case or where a request or an application is manifestly inadmissible, the Court may, after hearing the Advocate General, at any time decide to give a decision by reasoned order without taking further steps in the proceedings.

3. The President may in special circumstances decide that a case be given priority over others.

4. A case may be dealt with under an expedited procedure in accordance with the conditions provided by these Rules.

5. A reference for a preliminary ruling may be dealt with under an urgent procedure in accordance with the conditions provided by these Rules.

[10.209]
Article 54
Joinder

1. Two or more cases of the same type concerning the same subject-matter may at any time be joined, on account of the connection between them, for the purposes of the written or oral part of the procedure or of the judgment which closes the proceedings.
2. A decision on whether cases should be joined shall be taken by the President after hearing the Judge-Rapporteur and the Advocate General, if the cases concerned have already been assigned, and, save in the case of references for a preliminary ruling, after also hearing the parties. The President may refer the decision on this matter to the Court.
3. Joined cases may be disjoined, in accordance with the provisions of paragraph 2.

[10.210]
Article 55
Stay of proceedings

1. The proceedings may be stayed:
(a) in the circumstances specified in the third paragraph of Article 54 of the Statute, by order of the Court, made after hearing the Advocate General;
(b) in all other cases, by decision of the President adopted after hearing the Judge-Rapporteur and the Advocate General and, save in the case of references for a preliminary ruling, the parties.
2. The proceedings may be resumed by order or decision, following the same procedure.
3. The orders or decisions referred to in paragraphs 1 and 2 shall be served on the parties or interested persons referred to in Article 23 of the Statute.
4. The stay of proceedings shall take effect on the date indicated in the order or decision of stay or, in the absence of such indication, on the date of that order or decision.
5. While proceedings are stayed time shall cease to run for the parties or interested persons referred to in Article 23 of the Statute for the purposes of procedural time-limits.
6. Where the order or decision of stay does not fix the length of stay, it shall end on the date indicated in the order or decision of resumption or, in the absence of such indication, on the date of the order or decision of resumption.
7. From the date of resumption of proceedings following a stay, the suspended procedural time-limits shall be replaced by new time-limits and time shall begin to run from the date of that resumption.

[10.211]
Article 56
Deferment of the determination of a case

After hearing the Judge-Rapporteur, the Advocate General and the parties, the President may in special circumstances, either of his own motion or at the request of one of the parties, defer a case to be dealt with at a later date.

CHAPTER 5
WRITTEN PART OF THE PROCEDURE

[10.212]
Article 57
Lodging of procedural documents

1. The original of every procedural document must bear the handwritten signature of the party's agent or lawyer or, in the case of observations submitted in the context of preliminary ruling proceedings, that of the party to the main proceedings or his representative, if the national rules of procedure applicable to those main proceedings so permit.
2. The original, accompanied by all annexes referred to therein, shall be submitted together with five copies for the Court and, in the case of proceedings other than preliminary ruling proceedings, a copy for every other party to the proceedings. Copies shall be certified by the party lodging them.
3. The institutions shall in addition produce, within time-limits laid down by the Court, translations of any procedural document into the other languages provided for by Article 1 of Council Regulation No 1. The preceding paragraph of this Article shall apply.
4. To every procedural document there shall be annexed a file containing the items and documents relied on in support of it, together with a schedule listing them.
5. Where in view of the length of an item or document only extracts from it are annexed to the procedural document, the whole item or document or a full copy of it shall be lodged at the Registry.
6. All procedural documents shall bear a date. In the calculation of procedural time-limits, only the date and time of lodgment of the original at the Registry shall be taken into account.
7. Without prejudice to the provisions of paragraphs 1 to 6, the date on and time at which a copy of the signed original of a procedural document, including the schedule of items and documents referred to in paragraph 4, is received at the Registry by telefax or any other technical means of

communication available to the Court shall be deemed to be the date and time of lodgment for the purposes of compliance with the procedural time-limits, provided that the signed original of the procedural document, accompanied by the annexes and copies referred to in paragraph 2, is lodged at the Registry no later than 10 days thereafter.

8. Without prejudice to paragraphs 3 to 6, the Court may, by decision, determine the criteria for a procedural document sent to the Registry by electronic means to be deemed to be the original of that document. That decision shall be published in the *Official Journal of the European Union*.

[10.213]
Article 58
Length of procedural documents

Without prejudice to any special provisions laid down in these Rules, the Court may, by decision, set the maximum length of written pleadings or observations lodged before it. That decision shall be published in the *Official Journal of the European Union*.

CHAPTER 6
THE PRELIMINARY REPORT AND ASSIGNMENT OF CASES TO FORMATIONS OF THE COURT

[10.214]
Article 59
Preliminary report

1. When the written part of the procedure is closed, the President shall fix a date on which the Judge-Rapporteur is to present a preliminary report to the general meeting of the Court.

2. The preliminary report shall contain proposals as to whether particular measures of organisation of procedure, measures of inquiry or, if appropriate, requests to the referring court or tribunal for clarification should be undertaken, and as to the formation to which the case should be assigned. It shall also contain the Judge-Rapporteur's proposals, if any, as to whether to dispense with a hearing and as to whether to dispense with an Opinion of the Advocate General pursuant to the fifth paragraph of Article 20 of the Statute.

3. The Court shall decide, after hearing the Advocate General, what action to take on the proposals of the Judge-Rapporteur.

[10.215]
Article 60
Assignment of cases to formations of the Court

1. The Court shall assign to the Chambers of five and of three Judges any case brought before it in so far as the difficulty or importance of the case or particular circumstances are not such as to require that it should be assigned to the Grand Chamber, unless a Member State or an institution of the European Union participating in the proceedings has requested that the case be assigned to the Grand Chamber, pursuant to the third paragraph of Article 16 of the Statute.

2. The Court shall sit as a full Court where cases are brought before it pursuant to the provisions referred to in the fourth paragraph of Article 16 of the Statute. It may assign a case to the full Court where, in accordance with the fifth paragraph of Article 16 of the Statute, it considers that the case is of exceptional importance.

3. The formation to which a case has been assigned may, at any stage of the proceedings, request the Court to assign the case to a formation composed of a greater number of Judges.

4. Where the oral part of the procedure is opened without an inquiry, the President of the formation determining the case shall fix the opening date.

CHAPTER 7
MEASURES OF ORGANISATION OF PROCEDURE AND MEASURES OF INQUIRY

SECTION 1.
MEASURES OF ORGANISATION OF PROCEDURE

[10.216]
Article 61
Measures of organisation prescribed by the Court

1. In addition to the measures which may be prescribed in accordance with Article 24 of the Statute, the Court may invite the parties or the interested persons referred to in Article 23 of the Statute to answer certain questions in writing, within the time-limit laid down by the Court, or at the hearing. The written replies shall be communicated to the other parties or the interested persons referred to in Article 23 of the Statute.

2. Where a hearing is organised, the Court shall, in so far as possible, invite the participants in that hearing to concentrate in their oral pleadings on one or more specified issues.

[10.217]
Article 62
Measures of organisation prescribed by the Judge-Rapporteur or the Advocate General
1. The Judge-Rapporteur or the Advocate General may request the parties or the interested persons referred to in Article 23 of the Statute to submit within a specified time-limit all such information relating to the facts, and all such documents or other particulars, as they may consider relevant. The replies and documents provided shall be communicated to the other parties or the interested persons referred to in Article 23 of the Statute.
2. The Judge-Rapporteur or the Advocate General may also send to the parties or the interested persons referred to in Article 23 of the Statute questions to be answered at the hearing.

SECTION 2.
MEASURES OF INQUIRY

[10.218]
Article 63
Decision on measures of inquiry
1. The Court shall decide in its general meeting whether a measure of inquiry is necessary.
2. Where the case has already been assigned to a formation of the Court, the decision shall be taken by that formation.

[10.219]
Article 64
Determination of measures of inquiry
1. The Court, after hearing the Advocate General, shall prescribe the measures of inquiry that it considers appropriate by means of an order setting out the facts to be proved.
2. Without prejudice to Articles 24 and 25 of the Statute, the following measures of inquiry may be adopted:
(a) the personal appearance of the parties;
(b) a request for information and production of documents;
(c) oral testimony;
(d) the commissioning of an expert's report;
(e) an inspection of the place or thing in question.
3. Evidence may be submitted in rebuttal and previous evidence may be amplified.

[10.220]
Article 65
Participation in measures of inquiry
1. Where the formation of the Court does not undertake the inquiry itself, it shall entrust the task of so doing to the Judge-Rapporteur.
2. The Advocate General shall take part in the measures of inquiry.
3. The parties shall be entitled to attend the measures of inquiry.

[10.221]
Article 66
Oral testimony
1. The Court may, either of its own motion or at the request of one of the parties, and after hearing the Advocate General, order that certain facts be proved by witnesses.
2. A request by a party for the examination of a witness shall state precisely about what facts and for what reasons the witness should be examined.
3. The Court shall rule by reasoned order on the request referred to in the preceding paragraph. If the request is granted, the order shall set out the facts to be established and state which witnesses are to be heard in respect of each of those facts.
4. Witnesses shall be summoned by the Court, where appropriate after lodgment of the security provided for in Article 73(1) of these Rules.

[10.222]
Article 67
Examination of witnesses
1. After the identity of the witness has been established, the President shall inform him that he will be required to vouch the truth of his evidence in the manner laid down in these Rules.
2. The witness shall give his evidence to the Court, the parties having been given notice to attend. After the witness has given his evidence the President may, at the request of one of the parties or of his own motion, put questions to him.
3. The other Judges and the Advocate General may do likewise.
4. Subject to the control of the President, questions may be put to witnesses by the representatives of the parties.

[10.223]
Article 68
Witnesses' oath

1. After giving his evidence, the witness shall take the following oath:
'I swear that I have spoken the truth, the whole truth and nothing but the truth.'
2. The Court may, after hearing the parties, exempt a witness from taking the oath.

[10.224]
Article 69
Pecuniary penalties

1. Witnesses who have been duly summoned shall obey the summons and attend for examination.
2. If, without good reason, a witness who has been duly summoned fails to appear before the Court, the Court may impose upon him a pecuniary penalty not exceeding EUR 5,000 and may order that a further summons be served on the witness at his own expense.
3. The same penalty may be imposed upon a witness who, without good reason, refuses to give evidence or to take the oath.

[10.225]
Article 70
Expert's report

1. The Court may order that an expert's report be obtained. The order appointing the expert shall define his task and set a time-limit within which he is to submit his report.
2. After the expert has submitted his report and that report has been served on the parties, the Court may order that the expert be examined, the parties having been given notice to attend. At the request of one of the parties or of his own motion, the President may put questions to the expert.
3. The other Judges and the Advocate General may do likewise.
4. Subject to the control of the President, questions may be put to the expert by the representatives of the parties.

[10.226]
Article 71
Expert's oath

1. After making his report, the expert shall take the following oath:
'I swear that I have conscientiously and impartially carried out my task.'
2. The Court may, after hearing the parties, exempt the expert from taking the oath.

[10.227]
Article 72
Objection to a witness or expert

1. If one of the parties objects to a witness or an expert on the ground that he is not a competent or proper person to act as a witness or expert or for any other reason, or if a witness or expert refuses to give evidence or to take the oath, the matter shall be resolved by the Court.
2. An objection to a witness or an expert shall be raised within two weeks after service of the order summoning the witness or appointing the expert; the statement of objection must set out the grounds of objection and indicate the nature of any evidence offered.

[10.228]
Article 73
Witnesses' and experts' costs

1. Where the Court orders the examination of witnesses or an expert's report, it may request the parties or one of them to lodge security for the witnesses' costs or the costs of the expert's report.
2. Witnesses and experts shall be entitled to reimbursement of their travel and subsistence expenses. The cashier of the Court may make an advance payment towards these expenses.
3. Witnesses shall be entitled to compensation for loss of earnings, and experts to fees for their services. The cashier of the Court shall pay witnesses and experts these sums after they have carried out their respective duties or tasks.

[10.229]
Article 74
Minutes of inquiry hearings

1. The Registrar shall draw up minutes of every inquiry hearing. The minutes shall be signed by the President and by the Registrar. They shall constitute an official record.
2. In the case of the examination of witnesses or experts, the minutes shall be signed by the President or by the Judge-Rapporteur responsible for conducting the examination of the witness or expert, and by the Registrar. Before the minutes are thus signed, the witness or expert must be given an opportunity to check the content of the minutes and to sign them.
3. The minutes shall be served on the parties.

[10.230]
Article 75
Opening of the oral part of the procedure after the inquiry

1. Unless the Court decides to prescribe a time-limit within which the parties may submit written observations, the President shall fix the date for the opening of the oral part of the procedure after the measures of inquiry have been completed.
2. Where a time-limit has been prescribed for the submission of written observations, the President shall fix the date for the opening of the oral part of the procedure after that time-limit has expired.

CHAPTER 8
ORAL PART OF THE PROCEDURE

[10.231]
Article 76
Hearing

1. Any reasoned requests for a hearing shall be submitted within three weeks after service on the parties or the interested persons referred to in Article 23 of the Statute of notification of the close of the written part of the procedure. That time-limit may be extended by the President.
2. On a proposal from the Judge-Rapporteur and after hearing the Advocate General, the Court may decide not to hold a hearing if it considers, on reading the written pleadings or observations lodged during the written part of the procedure, that it has sufficient information to give a ruling.
3. The preceding paragraph shall not apply where a request for a hearing, stating reasons, has been submitted by an interested person referred to in Article 23 of the Statute who did not participate in the written part of the procedure.

[10.232]
Article 77
Joint hearing

If the similarities between two or more cases of the same type so permit, the Court may decide to organise a joint hearing of those cases.

[10.233]
Article 78
Conduct of oral proceedings

Oral proceedings shall be opened and directed by the President, who shall be responsible for the proper conduct of the hearing.

[10.234]
Article 79
Cases heard in camera

1. For serious reasons related, in particular, to the security of the Member States or to the protection of minors, the Court may decide to hear a case *in camera*.
2. The oral proceedings in cases heard *in camera* shall not be published.

[10.235]
Article 80
Questions

The members of the formation of the Court and the Advocate General may in the course of the hearing put questions to the agents, advisers or lawyers of the parties and, in the circumstances referred to in Article 47(2) of these Rules, to the parties to the main proceedings or to their representatives.

[10.236]
Article 81
Close of the hearing

After the parties or the interested persons referred to in Article 23 of the Statute have presented oral argument, the President shall declare the hearing closed.

[10.237]
Article 82
Delivery of the Opinion of the Advocate General

1. Where a hearing takes place, the Opinion of the Advocate General shall be delivered after the close of that hearing.
2. The President shall declare the oral part of the procedure closed after the Advocate General has delivered his Opinion.

[10.238]
Article 83
Opening or reopening of the oral part of the procedure
The Court may at any time, after hearing the Advocate General, order the opening or reopening of the oral part of the procedure, in particular if it considers that it lacks sufficient information or where a party has, after the close of that part of the procedure, submitted a new fact which is of such a nature as to be a decisive factor for the decision of the Court, or where the case must be decided on the basis of an argument which has not been debated between the parties or the interested persons referred to in Article 23 of the Statute.

[10.239]
Article 84
Minutes of hearings
1. The Registrar shall draw up minutes of every hearing. The minutes shall be signed by the President and by the Registrar. They shall constitute an official record.
2. The parties and interested persons referred to in Article 23 of the Statute may inspect the minutes at the Registry and obtain copies.

[10.240]
Article 85
Recording of the hearing
The President may, on a duly substantiated request, authorise a party or an interested person referred to in Article 23 of the Statute who has participated in the written or oral part of the proceedings to listen, on the Court's premises, to the soundtrack of the hearing in the language used by the speaker during that hearing.

CHAPTER 9
JUDGMENTS AND ORDERS

[10.241]
Article 86
Date of delivery of a judgment
The parties or interested persons referred to in Article 23 of the Statute shall be informed of the date of delivery of a judgment.

[10.242]
Article 87
Content of a judgment
A judgment shall contain:
- (a) a statement that it is the judgment of the Court,
- (b) an indication as to the formation of the Court,
- (c) the date of delivery,
- (d) the names of the President and of the Judges who took part in the deliberations, with an indication as to the name of the Judge-Rapporteur,
- (e) the name of the Advocate General,
- (f) the name of the Registrar,
- (g) a description of the parties or of the interested persons referred to in Article 23 of the Statute who participated in the proceedings,
- (h) the names of their representatives,
- (i) in the case of direct actions and appeals, a statement of the forms of order sought by the parties,
- (j) where applicable, the date of the hearing,
- (k) a statement that the Advocate General has been heard and, where applicable, the date of his Opinion,
- (l) a summary of the facts,
- (m) the grounds for the decision,
- (n) the operative part of the judgment, including, where appropriate, the decision as to costs.

[10.243]
Article 88
Delivery and service of the judgment
1. The judgment shall be delivered in open court.
2. The original of the judgment, signed by the President, by the Judges who took part in the deliberations and by the Registrar, shall be sealed and deposited at the Registry; certified copies of the judgment shall be served on the parties and, where applicable, the referring court or tribunal, the interested persons referred to in Article 23 of the Statute and the General Court.

[10.244]
Article 89
Content of an order

1. An order shall contain:
   (a) a statement that it is the order of the Court,
   (b) an indication as to the formation of the Court,
   (c) the date of its adoption,
   (d) an indication as to the legal basis of the order,
   (e) the names of the President and, where applicable, the Judges who took part in the deliberations, with an indication as to the name of the Judge-Rapporteur,
   (f) the name of the Advocate General,
   (g) the name of the Registrar,
   (h) a description of the parties or of the parties to the main proceedings,
   (i) the names of their representatives,
   (j) a statement that the Advocate General has been heard,
   (k) the operative part of the order, including, where appropriate, the decision as to costs.
2. Where, in accordance with these Rules, an order must be reasoned, it shall in addition contain:
   (a) in the case of direct actions and appeals, a statement of the forms of order sought by the parties,
   (b) a summary of the facts,
   (c) the grounds for the decision.

[10.245]
Article 90
Signature and service of the order

The original of the order, signed by the President and by the Registrar, shall be sealed and deposited at the Registry; certified copies of the order shall be served on the parties and, where applicable, the referring court or tribunal, the interested persons referred to in Article 23 of the Statute and the General Court.

[10.246]
Article 91
Binding nature of judgments and orders

1. A judgment shall be binding from the date of its delivery.
2. An order shall be binding from the date of its service.

[10.247]
Article 92
Publication in the Official Journal of the European Union

A notice containing the date and the operative part of the judgment or order of the Court which closes the proceedings shall be published in the *Official Journal of the European Union*.

TITLE III
REFERENCES FOR A PRELIMINARY RULING

CHAPTER 1
GENERAL PROVISIONS

[10.248]
Article 93
Scope

The procedure shall be governed by the provisions of this Title:
   (a) in the cases covered by Article 23 of the Statute,
   (b) as regards references for interpretation which may be provided for by agreements to which the European Union or the Member States are parties.

[10.249]
Article 94
Content of the request for a preliminary ruling

In addition to the text of the questions referred to the Court for a preliminary ruling, the request for a preliminary ruling shall contain:
   (a) a summary of the subject-matter of the dispute and the relevant findings of fact as determined by the referring court or tribunal, or, at least, an account of the facts on which the questions are based;
   (b) the tenor of any national provisions applicable in the case and, where appropriate, the relevant national case-law;
   (c) a statement of the reasons which prompted the referring court or tribunal to inquire about the interpretation or validity of certain provisions of European Union law, and the relationship between those provisions and the national legislation applicable to the main proceedings.

[10.250]
Article 95
Anonymity

1. Where anonymity has been granted by the referring court or tribunal, the Court shall respect that anonymity in the proceedings pending before it.
2. At the request of the referring court or tribunal, at the duly reasoned request of a party to the main proceedings or of its own motion, the Court may also, if it considers it necessary, render anonymous one or more persons or entities concerned by the case.

[10.251]
Article 96
Participation in preliminary ruling proceedings

1. Pursuant to Article 23 of the Statute, the following shall be authorised to submit observations to the Court:
   (a) the parties to the main proceedings,
   (b) the Member States,
   (c) the European Commission,
   (d) the institution which adopted the act the validity or interpretation of which is in dispute,
   (e) the States, other than the Member States, which are parties to the EEA Agreement, and also the EFTA Surveillance Authority, where a question concerning one of the fields of application of that Agreement is referred to the Court for a preliminary ruling,
   (f) non-Member States which are parties to an agreement relating to a specific subject-matter, concluded with the Council, where the agreement so provides and where a court or tribunal of a Member State refers to the Court of Justice for a preliminary ruling a question falling within the scope of that agreement.
2. Non-participation in the written part of the procedure does not preclude participation in the oral part of the procedure.

[10.252]
Article 97
Parties to the main proceedings

1. The parties to the main proceedings are those who are determined as such by the referring court or tribunal in accordance with national rules of procedure.
2. Where the referring court or tribunal informs the Court that a new party has been admitted to the main proceedings, when the proceedings before the Court are already pending, that party must accept the case as he finds it at the time when the Court was so informed. That party shall receive a copy of every procedural document already served on the interested persons referred to in Article 23 of the Statute.
3. As regards the representation and attendance of the parties to the main proceedings, the Court shall take account of the rules of procedure in force before the court or tribunal which made the reference. In the event of any doubt as to whether a person may under national law represent a party to the main proceedings, the Court may obtain information from the referring court or tribunal on the rules of procedure applicable.

[10.253]
Article 98
Translation and service of the request for a preliminary ruling

1. The requests for a preliminary ruling referred to in this Title shall be served on the Member States in the original version, accompanied by a translation into the official language of the State to which they are being addressed. Where appropriate, on account of the length of the request, such translation shall be replaced by the translation into the official language of the State to which it is addressed of a summary of that request, which will serve as a basis for the position to be adopted by that State. The summary shall include the full text of the question or questions referred for a preliminary ruling. That summary shall contain, in particular, in so far as that information appears in the request for a preliminary ruling, the subject-matter of the main proceedings, the essential arguments of the parties to those proceedings, a succinct presentation of the reasons for the reference for a preliminary ruling and the case-law and the provisions of national law and European Union law relied on.
2. In the cases covered by the third paragraph of Article 23 of the Statute, the requests for a preliminary ruling shall be served on the States, other than the Member States, which are parties to the EEA Agreement and also on the EFTA Surveillance Authority in the original version, accompanied by a translation of the request, or where appropriate of a summary, into one of the languages referred to in Article 36, to be chosen by the addressee.
3. Where a non-Member State has the right to take part in preliminary ruling proceedings pursuant to the fourth paragraph of Article 23 of the Statute, the original version of the request for a preliminary ruling shall be served on it accompanied by a translation of the request, or where appropriate of a summary, into one of the languages referred to in Article 36, to be chosen by the non-Member State concerned.

[10.254]
Article 99
Reply by reasoned order
Where a question referred to the Court for a preliminary ruling is identical to a question on which the Court has already ruled, where the reply to such a question may be clearly deduced from existing case-law or where the answer to the question referred for a preliminary ruling admits of no reasonable doubt, the Court may at any time, on a proposal from the Judge-Rapporteur and after hearing the Advocate General, decide to rule by reasoned order.

[10.255]
Article 100
Circumstances in which the Court remains seised
1. The Court shall remain seised of a request for a preliminary ruling for as long as it is not withdrawn by the court or tribunal which made that request to the Court. The withdrawal of a request may be taken into account until notice of the date of delivery of the judgment has been served on the interested persons referred to in Article 23 of the Statute.
2. However, the Court may at any time declare that the conditions of its jurisdiction are no longer fulfilled.

[10.256]
Article 101
Request for clarification
1. Without prejudice to the measures of organisation of procedure and measures of inquiry provided for in these Rules, the Court may, after hearing the Advocate General, request clarification from the referring court or tribunal within a time-limit prescribed by the Court.
2. The reply of the referring court or tribunal to that request shall be served on the interested persons referred to in Article 23 of the Statute.

[10.257]
Article 102
Costs of the preliminary ruling proceedings
It shall be for the referring court or tribunal to decide as to the costs of the preliminary ruling proceedings.

[10.258]
Article 103
Rectification of judgments and orders
1. Clerical mistakes, errors in calculation and obvious inaccuracies affecting judgments or orders may be rectified by the Court, of its own motion or at the request of an interested person referred to in Article 23 of the Statute made within two weeks after delivery of the judgment or service of the order.
2. The Court shall take its decision after hearing the Advocate General.
3. The original of the rectification order shall be annexed to the original of the rectified decision. A note of this order shall be made in the margin of the original of the rectified decision.

[10.259]
Article 104
Interpretation of preliminary rulings
1. Article 158 of these Rules relating to the interpretation of judgments and orders shall not apply to decisions given in reply to a request for a preliminary ruling.
2. It shall be for the national courts or tribunals to assess whether they consider that sufficient guidance is given by a preliminary ruling, or whether it appears to them that a further reference to the Court is required.

CHAPTER 2
EXPEDITED PRELIMINARY RULING PROCEDURE

[10.260]
Article 105
Expedited procedure
1. At the request of the referring court or tribunal or, exceptionally, of his own motion, the President of the Court may, where the nature of the case requires that it be dealt with within a short time, after hearing the Judge-Rapporteur and the Advocate General, decide that a reference for a preliminary ruling is to be determined pursuant to an expedited procedure derogating from the provisions of these Rules.
2. In that event, the President shall immediately fix the date for the hearing, which shall be communicated to the interested persons referred to in Article 23 of the Statute when the request for a preliminary ruling is served.

3. The interested persons referred to in the preceding paragraph may lodge statements of case or written observations within a time-limit prescribed by the President, which shall not be less than 15 days. The President may request those interested persons to restrict the matters addressed in their statement of case or written observations to the essential points of law raised by the request for a preliminary ruling.
4. The statements of case or written observations, if any, shall be communicated to all the interested persons referred to in Article 23 of the Statute prior to the hearing.
5. The Court shall rule after hearing the Advocate General.

[10.261]
Article 106
Transmission of procedural documents
1. The procedural documents referred to in the preceding Article shall be deemed to have been lodged on the transmission to the Registry, by telefax or any other technical means of communication available to the Court, of a copy of the signed original and the items and documents relied on in support of it, together with the schedule referred to in Article 57(4). The original of the document and the annexes referred to above shall be sent to the Registry immediately.
2. Where the preceding Article requires that a document be served on or communicated to a person, such service or communication may be effected by transmission of a copy of the document by telefax or any other technical means of communication available to the Court and the addressee.

CHAPTER 3
URGENT PRELIMINARY RULING PROCEDURE

[10.262]
Article 107
Scope of the urgent preliminary ruling procedure
1. A reference for a preliminary ruling which raises one or more questions in the areas covered by Title V of Part Three of the Treaty on the Functioning of the European Union may, at the request of the referring court or tribunal or, exceptionally, of the Court's own motion, be dealt with under an urgent procedure derogating from the provisions of these Rules.
2. The referring court or tribunal shall set out the matters of fact and law which establish the urgency and justify the application of that exceptional procedure and shall, in so far as possible, indicate the answer that it proposes to the questions referred.
3. If the referring court or tribunal has not submitted a request for the urgent procedure to be applied, the President of the Court may, if the application of that procedure appears, prima facie, to be required, ask the Chamber referred to in Article 108 to consider whether it is necessary to deal with the reference under that procedure.

[10.263]
Article 108
Decision as to urgency
1. The decision to deal with a reference for a preliminary ruling under the urgent procedure shall be taken by the designated Chamber, acting on a proposal from the Judge-Rapporteur and after hearing the Advocate General. The composition of that Chamber shall be determined in accordance with Article 28(2) on the day on which the case is assigned to the Judge-Rapporteur if the application of the urgent procedure is requested by the referring court or tribunal, or, if the application of that procedure is considered at the request of the President of the Court, on the day on which that request is made.
2. If the case is connected with a pending case assigned to a Judge-Rapporteur who is not a member of the designated Chamber, that Chamber may propose to the President of the Court that the case be assigned to that Judge-Rapporteur. Where the case is reassigned to that Judge-Rapporteur, the Chamber of five Judges which includes him shall carry out the duties of the designated Chamber in respect of that case. Article 29(1) shall apply.

[10.264]
Article 109
Written part of the urgent procedure
1. A request for a preliminary ruling shall, where the referring court or tribunal has requested the application of the urgent procedure or where the President has requested the designated Chamber to consider whether it is necessary to deal with the reference under that procedure, be served forthwith by the Registrar on the parties to the main proceedings, on the Member State from which the reference is made, on the European Commission and on the institution which adopted the act the validity or interpretation of which is in dispute.
2. The decision as to whether or not to deal with the reference for a preliminary ruling under the urgent procedure shall be served immediately on the referring court or tribunal and on the parties, Member State and institutions referred to in the preceding paragraph. The decision to deal with the

reference under the urgent procedure shall prescribe the time-limit within which those parties or entities may lodge statements of case or written observations. The decision may specify the matters of law to which such statements of case or written observations must relate and may specify the maximum length of those documents.

3. Where a request for a preliminary ruling refers to an administrative procedure or judicial proceedings conducted in a Member State other than that from which the reference is made, the Court may invite that first Member State to provide all relevant information in writing or at the hearing.

4. As soon as the service referred to in paragraph 1 above has been effected, the request for a preliminary ruling shall also be communicated to the interested persons referred to in Article 23 of the Statute, other than the persons served, and the decision whether or not to deal with the reference for a preliminary ruling under the urgent procedure shall be communicated to those interested persons as soon as the service referred to in paragraph 2 has been effected.

5. The interested persons referred to in Article 23 of the Statute shall be informed as soon as possible of the likely date of the hearing.

6. Where the reference is not to be dealt with under the urgent procedure, the proceedings shall continue in accordance with the provisions of Article 23 of the Statute and the applicable provisions of these Rules.

[10.265]
Article 110
Service and information following the close of the written part of the procedure

1. Where a reference for a preliminary ruling is to be dealt with under the urgent procedure, the request for a preliminary ruling and the statements of case or written observations which have been lodged shall be served on the interested persons referred to in Article 23 of the Statute other than the parties and entities referred to in Article 109(1). The request for a preliminary ruling shall be accompanied by a translation, where appropriate of a summary, in accordance with Article 98.

2. The statements of case or written observations which have been lodged shall also be served on the parties and other interested persons referred to in Article 109(1).

3. The date of the hearing shall be communicated to the interested persons referred to in Article 23 of the Statute at the same time as the documents referred to in the preceding paragraphs are served.

[10.266]
Article 111
Omission of the written part of the procedure

The designated Chamber may, in cases of extreme urgency, decide to omit the written part of the procedure referred to in Article 109(2).

[10.267]
Article 112
Decision on the substance

The designated Chamber shall rule after hearing the Advocate General.

[10.268]
Article 113
Formation of the Court

1. The designated Chamber may decide to sit in a formation of three Judges. In that event, it shall be composed of the President of the designated Chamber, the Judge-Rapporteur and the first Judge or, as the case may be, the first two Judges designated from the list referred to in Article 28(2) on the date on which the composition of the designated Chamber is determined in accordance with Article 108(1).

2. The designated Chamber may also request the Court to assign the case to a formation composed of a greater number of Judges. The urgent procedure shall continue before the new formation of the Court, where necessary after the reopening of the oral part of the procedure.

[10.269]
Article 114
Transmission of procedural documents

Procedural documents shall be transmitted in accordance with Article 106.

CHAPTER 4
LEGAL AID

[10.270]
Article 115
Application for legal aid

1. A party to the main proceedings who is wholly or in part unable to meet the costs of the proceedings before the Court may at any time apply for legal aid.

2. The application shall be accompanied by all information and supporting documents making it possible to assess the applicant's financial situation, such as a certificate issued by a competent national authority attesting to his financial situation.
3. If the applicant has already obtained legal aid before the referring court or tribunal, he shall produce the decision of that court or tribunal and specify what is covered by the sums already granted.

[10.271]
Article 116
Decision on the application for legal aid

1. As soon as the application for legal aid has been lodged it shall be assigned by the President to the Judge-Rapporteur responsible for the case in the context of which the application has been made.
2. The decision to grant legal aid, in full or in part, or to refuse it shall be taken, on a proposal from the Judge-Rapporteur and after hearing the Advocate General, by the Chamber of three Judges to which the Judge-Rapporteur is assigned. The formation of the Court shall, in that event, be composed of the President of that Chamber, the Judge-Rapporteur and the first Judge or, as the case may be, the first two Judges designated from the list referred to in Article 28(3) on the date on which the application for legal aid is brought before that Chamber by the Judge-Rapporteur.
3. If the Judge-Rapporteur is not a member of a Chamber of three Judges, the decision shall be taken, under the same conditions, by the Chamber of five Judges to which he is assigned. In addition to the Judge-Rapporteur, the formation of the Court shall be composed of four Judges designated from the list referred to in Article 28(2) on the date on which the application for legal aid is brought before that Chamber by the Judge-Rapporteur.
4. The formation of the Court shall give its decision by way of order. Where the application for legal aid is refused in whole or in part, the order shall state the reasons for that refusal.

[10.272]
Article 117
Sums to be advanced as legal aid

Where legal aid is granted, the cashier of the Court shall be responsible, where applicable within the limits set by the formation of the Court, for costs involved in the assistance and representation of the applicant before the Court. At the request of the applicant or his representative, an advance on those costs may be paid.

[10.273]
Article 118
Withdrawal of legal aid

The formation of the Court which gave a decision on the application for legal aid may at any time, either of its own motion or on request, withdraw that legal aid if the circumstances which led to its being granted alter during the proceedings.

TITLE IV
DIRECT ACTIONS

CHAPTER 1
REPRESENTATION OF THE PARTIES

[10.274]
Article 119
Obligation to be represented

1. A party may be represented only by his agent or lawyer.
2. Agents and lawyers must lodge at the Registry an official document or an authority to act issued by the party whom they represent.
3. The lawyer acting for a party must also lodge at the Registry a certificate that he is authorised to practise before a court of a Member State or of another State which is a party to the EEA Agreement.
4. If those documents are not lodged, the Registrar shall prescribe a reasonable time-limit within which the party concerned is to produce them. If the applicant fails to produce the required documents within the time-limit prescribed, the Court shall, after hearing the Judge-Rapporteur and the Advocate General, decide whether the non-compliance with that procedural requirement renders the application or written pleading formally inadmissible.

CHAPTER 2
WRITTEN PART OF THE PROCEDURE

[10.275]
Article 120
Content of the application

An application of the kind referred to in Article 21 of the Statute shall state:

(a) the name and address of the applicant;
(b) the name of the party against whom the application is made;
(c) the subject-matter of the proceedings, the pleas in law and arguments relied on and a summary of those pleas in law;
(d) the form of order sought by the applicant;
(e) where appropriate, any evidence produced or offered.

[10.276]
Article 121
Information relating to service

1. For the purpose of the proceedings, the application shall state an address for service. It shall indicate the name of the person who is authorised and has expressed willingness to accept service.
2. In addition to, or instead of, specifying an address for service as referred to in paragraph 1, the application may state that the lawyer or agent agrees that service is to be effected on him by telefax or any other technical means of communication.
3. If the application does not comply with the requirements referred to in paragraphs 1 or 2, all service on the party concerned for the purpose of the proceedings shall be effected, for so long as the defect has not been cured, by registered letter addressed to the agent or lawyer of that party. By way of derogation from Article 48, service shall then be deemed to be duly effected by the lodging of the registered letter at the post office of the place in which the Court has its seat.

[10.277]
Article 122
Annexes to the application

1. The application shall be accompanied, where appropriate, by the documents specified in the second paragraph of Article 21 of the Statute.
2. An application submitted under Article 273 TFEU shall be accompanied by a copy of the special agreement concluded between the Member States concerned.
3. If an application does not comply with the requirements set out in paragraphs 1 or 2 of this Article, the Registrar shall prescribe a reasonable time-limit within which the applicant is to produce the abovementioned documents. If the applicant fails to put the application in order, the Court shall, after hearing the Judge-Rapporteur and the Advocate General, decide whether the non-compliance with these conditions renders the application formally inadmissible.

[10.278]
Article 123
Service of the application

The application shall be served on the defendant. In cases where Article 119(4) or Article 122(3) applies, service shall be effected as soon as the application has been put in order or the Court has declared it admissible notwithstanding the failure to observe the requirements set out in those two Articles.

[10.279]
Article 124
Content of the defence

1. Within two months after service on him of the application, the defendant shall lodge a defence, stating:
   (a) the name and address of the defendant;
   (b) the pleas in law and arguments relied on;
   (c) the form of order sought by the defendant;
   (d) where appropriate, any evidence produced or offered.
2. Article 121 shall apply to the defence.
3. The time-limit laid down in paragraph 1 may exceptionally be extended by the President at the duly reasoned request of the defendant.

[10.280]
Article 125
Transmission of documents

Where the European Parliament, the Council or the European Commission is not a party to a case, the Court shall send to them copies of the application and of the defence, without the annexes thereto, to enable them to assess whether the inapplicability of one of their acts is being invoked under Article 277 TFEU.

[10.281]
Article 126
Reply and rejoinder

1. The application initiating proceedings and the defence may be supplemented by a reply from the applicant and by a rejoinder from the defendant.
2. The President shall prescribe the time-limits within which those procedural documents are to be produced. He may specify the matters to which the reply or the rejoinder should relate.

CHAPTER 3
PLEAS IN LAW AND EVIDENCE

[10.282]
Article 127
New pleas in law

1. No new plea in law may be introduced in the course of proceedings unless it is based on matters of law or of fact which come to light in the course of the procedure.
2. Without prejudice to the decision to be taken on the admissibility of the plea in law, the President may, on a proposal from the Judge-Rapporteur and after hearing the Advocate General, prescribe a time-limit within which the other party may respond to that plea.

[10.283]
Article 128
Evidence produced or offered

1. In reply or rejoinder a party may produce or offer further evidence in support of his arguments. The party must give reasons for the delay in submitting such evidence.
2. The parties may, exceptionally, produce or offer further evidence after the close of the written part of the procedure. They must give reasons for the delay in submitting such evidence. The President may, on a proposal from the Judge-Rapporteur and after hearing the Advocate General, prescribe a time-limit within which the other party may comment on such evidence.

CHAPTER 4
INTERVENTION

[10.284]
Article 129
Object and effects of the intervention

1. The intervention shall be limited to supporting, in whole or in part, the form of order sought by one of the parties. It shall not confer the same procedural rights as those conferred on the parties and, in particular, shall not give rise to any right to request that a hearing be held.
2. The intervention shall be ancillary to the main proceedings. It shall become devoid of purpose if the case is removed from the register of the Court as a result of a party's discontinuance or withdrawal from the proceedings or of an agreement between the parties, or where the application is declared inadmissible.
3. The intervener must accept the case as he finds it at the time of his intervention.
4. Consideration may be given to an application to intervene which is made after the expiry of the time-limit prescribed in Article 130 but before the decision to open the oral part of the procedure provided for in Article 60(4). In that event, if the President allows the intervention, the intervener may submit his observations during the hearing, if it takes place.

[10.285]
Article 130
Application to intervene

1. An application to intervene must be submitted within six weeks of the publication of the notice referred to in Article 21(4).
2. The application to intervene shall contain:
   (a) a description of the case;
   (b) a description of the main parties;
   (c) the name and address of the intervener;
   (d) the form of order sought, in support of which the intervener is applying for leave to intervene;
   (e) a statement of the circumstances establishing the right to intervene, where the application is submitted pursuant to the second or third paragraph of Article 40 of the Statute.
3. The intervener shall be represented in accordance with Article 19 of the Statute.
4. Articles 119, 121 and 122 of these Rules shall apply.

[10.286]
Article 131
Decision on applications to intervene

1. The application to intervene shall be served on the parties in order to obtain any written or oral observations they may wish to make on that application.
2. Where the application is submitted pursuant to the first or third paragraph of Article 40 of the Statute, the intervention shall be allowed by decision of the President and the intervener shall receive a copy of every procedural document served on the parties, provided that those parties have not, within 10 days after the service referred to in paragraph 1 has been effected, put forward observations on the application to intervene or identified secret or confidential items or documents which, if communicated to the intervener, the parties claim would be prejudicial to them.
3. In any other case, the President shall decide on the application to intervene by order or shall refer the application to the Court.

4. If the application to intervene is granted, the intervener shall receive a copy of every procedural document served on the parties, save, where applicable, for the secret or confidential items or documents excluded from such communication pursuant to paragraph 3.

[10.287]
Article 132
Submission of statements
1. The intervener may submit a statement in intervention within one month after communication of the procedural documents referred to in the preceding Article. That time-limit may be extended by the President at the duly reasoned request of the intervener.
2. The statement in intervention shall contain:
(a) the form of order sought by the intervener in support, in whole or in part, of the form of order sought by one of the parties;
(b) the pleas in law and arguments relied on by the intervener;
(c) where appropriate, any evidence produced or offered.
3. After the statement in intervention has been lodged, the President shall, where necessary, prescribe a time-limit within which the parties may reply to that statement.

CHAPTER 5
EXPEDITED PROCEDURE

[10.288]
Article 133
Decision relating to the expedited procedure
1. At the request of the applicant or the defendant, the President of the Court may, where the nature of the case requires that it be dealt with within a short time, after hearing the other party, the Judge-Rapporteur and the Advocate General, decide that a case is to be determined pursuant to an expedited procedure derogating from the provisions of these Rules.
2. The request for a case to be determined pursuant to an expedited procedure must be made by a separate document submitted at the same time as the application initiating proceedings or the defence, as the case may be, is lodged.
3. Exceptionally the President may also take such a decision of his own motion, after hearing the parties, the Judge-Rapporteur and the Advocate General.

[10.289]
Article 134
Written part of the procedure
1. Under the expedited procedure, the application initiating proceedings and the defence may be supplemented by a reply and a rejoinder only if the President, after hearing the Judge-Rapporteur and the Advocate General, considers this to be necessary.
2. An intervener may submit a statement in intervention only if the President, after hearing the Judge-Rapporteur and the Advocate General, considers this to be necessary.

[10.290]
Article 135
Oral part of the procedure
1. Once the defence has been submitted or, if the decision to determine the case pursuant to an expedited procedure is not made until after that pleading has been lodged, once that decision has been taken, the President shall fix a date for the hearing, which shall be communicated forthwith to the parties. He may postpone the date of the hearing where it is necessary to undertake measures of inquiry or where measures of organisation of procedure so require.
2. Without prejudice to Articles 127 and 128, a party may supplement his arguments and produce or offer evidence during the oral part of the procedure. The party must, however, give reasons for the delay in producing such further arguments or evidence.

[10.291]
Article 136
Decision on the substance
The Court shall give its ruling after hearing the Advocate General.

CHAPTER 6
COSTS

[10.292]
Article 137
Decision as to costs
A decision as to costs shall be given in the judgment or order which closes the proceedings.

[10.293]
Article 138
General rules as to allocation of costs

1. The unsuccessful party shall be ordered to pay the costs if they have been applied for in the successful party's pleadings.
2. Where there is more than one unsuccessful party the Court shall decide how the costs are to be shared.
3. Where each party succeeds on some and fails on other heads, the parties shall bear their own costs. However, if it appears justified in the circumstances of the case, the Court may order that one party, in addition to bearing its own costs, pay a proportion of the costs of the other party.

[10.294]
Article 139
Unreasonable or vexatious costs

The Court may order a party, even if successful, to pay costs which the Court considers that party to have unreasonably or vexatiously caused the opposite party to incur.

[10.295]
Article 140
Costs of interveners

1. The Member States and institutions which have intervened in the proceedings shall bear their own costs.
2. The States, other than the Member States, which are parties to the EEA Agreement, and also the EFTA Surveillance Authority, shall similarly bear their own costs if they have intervened in the proceedings.
3. The Court may order an intervener other than those referred to in the preceding paragraphs to bear his own costs.

[10.296]
Article 141
Costs in the event of discontinuance or withdrawal

1. A party who discontinues or withdraws from proceedings shall be ordered to pay the costs if they have been applied for in the other party's observations on the discontinuance.
2. However, at the request of the party who discontinues or withdraws from proceedings, the costs shall be borne by the other party if this appears justified by the conduct of that party.
3. Where the parties have come to an agreement on costs, the decision as to costs shall be in accordance with that agreement.
4. If costs are not claimed, the parties shall bear their own costs.

[10.297]
Article 142
Costs where a case does not proceed to judgment

Where a case does not proceed to judgment the costs shall be in the discretion of the Court.

[10.298]
Article 143
Costs of proceedings

Proceedings before the Court shall be free of charge, except that:

(a) where a party has caused the Court to incur avoidable costs the Court may, after hearing the Advocate General, order that party to refund them;
(b) where copying or translation work is carried out at the request of a party, the cost shall, in so far as the Registrar considers it excessive, be paid for by that party on the Registry's scale of charges referred to in Article 22.

[10.299]
Article 144
Recoverable costs

Without prejudice to the preceding Article, the following shall be regarded as recoverable costs:

(a) sums payable to witnesses and experts under Article 73 of these Rules;
(b) expenses necessarily incurred by the parties for the purpose of the proceedings, in particular the travel and subsistence expenses and the remuneration of agents, advisers or lawyers.

[10.300]
Article 145
Dispute concerning the costs to be recovered

1. If there is a dispute concerning the costs to be recovered, the Chamber of three Judges to which the Judge-Rapporteur who dealt with the case is assigned shall, on application by the party concerned and after hearing the opposite party and the Advocate General, make an order. In that

event, the formation of the Court shall be composed of the President of that Chamber, the Judge-Rapporteur and the first Judge or, as the case may be, the first two Judges designated from the list referred to in Article 28(3) on the date on which the dispute is brought before that Chamber by the Judge-Rapporteur.
2. If the Judge-Rapporteur is not a member of a Chamber of three Judges, the decision shall be taken, under the same conditions, by the Chamber of five Judges to which he is assigned. In addition to the Judge-Rapporteur, the formation of the Court shall be composed of four Judges designated from the list referred to in Article 28(2) on the date on which the dispute is brought before that Chamber by the Judge-Rapporteur.
3. The parties may, for the purposes of enforcement, apply for an authenticated copy of the order.

[10.301]
Article 146
Procedure for payment
1. Sums due from the cashier of the Court and from its debtors shall be paid in euro.
2. Where costs to be recovered have been incurred in a currency other than the euro or where the steps in respect of which payment is due were taken in a country of which the euro is not the currency, the conversion shall be effected at the European Central Bank's official rates of exchange on the day of payment.

CHAPTER 7
AMICABLE SETTLEMENT, DISCONTINUANCE, CASES THAT DO NOT PROCEED TO JUDGMENT AND PRELIMINARY ISSUES

[10.302]
Article 147
Amicable settlement
1. If, before the Court has given its decision, the parties reach a settlement of their dispute and inform the Court of the abandonment of their claims, the President shall order the case to be removed from the register and shall give a decision as to costs in accordance with Article 141, having regard to any proposals made by the parties on the matter.
2. This provision shall not apply to proceedings under Articles 263 TFEU and 265 TFEU.

[10.303]
Article 148
Discontinuance
If the applicant informs the Court in writing or at the hearing that he wishes to discontinue the proceedings, the President shall order the case to be removed from the register and shall give a decision as to costs in accordance with Article 141.

[10.304]
Article 149
Cases that do not proceed to judgment
If the Court declares that the action has become devoid of purpose and that there is no longer any need to adjudicate on it, the Court may at any time of its own motion, on a proposal from the Judge-Rapporteur and after hearing the parties and the Advocate General, decide to rule by reasoned order. It shall give a decision as to costs.

[10.305]
Article 150
Absolute bar to proceeding with a case
On a proposal from the Judge-Rapporteur, the Court may at any time of its own motion, after hearing the parties and the Advocate General, decide to rule by reasoned order on whether there exists any absolute bar to proceeding with a case.

[10.306]
Article 151
Preliminary objections and issues
1. A party applying to the Court for a decision on a preliminary objection or issue not going to the substance of the case shall submit the application by a separate document.
2. The application must state the pleas of law and arguments relied on and the form of order sought by the applicant; any supporting items and documents must be annexed to it.
3. As soon as the application has been submitted, the President shall prescribe a time-limit within which the opposite party may submit in writing his pleas in law and the form of order which he seeks.
4. Unless the Court decides otherwise, the remainder of the proceedings on the application shall be oral.
5. The Court shall, after hearing the Advocate General, decide on the application as soon as possible or, where special circumstances so justify, reserve its decision until it rules on the substance of the case.

6. If the Court refuses the application or reserves its decision, the President shall prescribe new time-limits for the further steps in the proceedings.

CHAPTER 8
JUDGMENTS BY DEFAULT

[10.307]
Article 152
Judgments by default

1. If a defendant on whom an application initiating proceedings has been duly served fails to respond to the application in the proper form and within the time-limit prescribed, the applicant may apply to the Court for judgment by default.
2. The application for judgment by default shall be served on the defendant. The Court may decide to open the oral part of the procedure on the application.
3. Before giving judgment by default the Court shall, after hearing the Advocate General, consider whether the application initiating proceedings is admissible, whether the appropriate formalities have been complied with, and whether the applicant's claims appear well founded. The Court may adopt measures of organisation of procedure or order measures of inquiry.
4. A judgment by default shall be enforceable. The Court may, however, grant a stay of execution until the Court has given its decision on any application under Article 156 to set aside the judgment, or it may make execution subject to the provision of security of an amount and nature to be fixed in the light of the circumstances; this security shall be released if no such application is made or if the application fails.

CHAPTER 9
REQUESTS AND APPLICATIONS RELATING TO JUDGMENTS AND ORDERS

[10.308]
Article 153
Competent formation of the Court

1. With the exception of applications referred to in Article 159, the requests and applications referred to in this Chapter shall be assigned to the Judge-Rapporteur who was responsible for the case to which the request or application relates, and shall be assigned to the formation of the Court which gave a decision in that case.
2. If the Judge-Rapporteur is prevented from acting, the President of the Court shall assign the request or application referred to in this Chapter to a Judge who was a member of the formation of the Court which gave a decision in the case to which that request or application relates.
3. If the quorum referred to in Article 17 of the Statute can no longer be attained, the Court shall, on a proposal from the Judge-Rapporteur and after hearing the Advocate General, assign the request or application to a new formation of the Court.

[10.309]
Article 154
Rectification

1. Without prejudice to the provisions relating to the interpretation of judgments and orders, clerical mistakes, errors in calculation and obvious inaccuracies may be rectified by the Court, of its own motion or at the request of a party made within two weeks after delivery of the judgment or service of the order.
2. Where the request for rectification concerns the operative part or one of the grounds constituting the necessary support for the operative part, the parties, whom the Registrar shall duly inform, may submit written observations within a time-limit prescribed by the President.
3. The Court shall take its decision after hearing the Advocate General.
4. The original of the rectification order shall be annexed to the original of the rectified decision. A note of this order shall be made in the margin of the original of the rectified decision.

[10.310]
Article 155
Failure to adjudicate

1. If the Court has failed to adjudicate on a specific head of claim or on costs, any party wishing to rely on that may, within a month after service of the decision, apply to the Court to supplement its decision.
2. The application shall be served on the opposite party and the President shall prescribe a time-limit within which that party may submit written observations.
3. After these observations have been submitted, the Court shall, after hearing the Advocate General, decide both on the admissibility and on the substance of the application.

[10.311]
Article 156
Application to set aside

1. Application may be made pursuant to Article 41 of the Statute to set aside a judgment delivered by default.
2. The application to set aside the judgment must be made within one month from the date of service of the judgment and must be submitted in the form prescribed by Articles 120 to 122 of these Rules.
3. After the application has been served, the President shall prescribe a time-limit within which the other party may submit his written observations.
4. The proceedings shall be conducted in accordance with Articles 59 to 92 of these Rules.
5. The Court shall decide by way of a judgment which may not be set aside.
6. The original of this judgment shall be annexed to the original of the judgment by default. A note of the judgment on the application to set aside shall be made in the margin of the original of the judgment by default.

[10.312]
Article 157
Third-party proceedings

1. Articles 120 to 122 of these Rules shall apply to an application initiating third-party proceedings made pursuant to Article 42 of the Statute. In addition such an application shall:
   (a) specify the judgment or order contested;
   (b) state how the contested decision is prejudicial to the rights of the third party;
   (c) indicate the reasons for which the third party was unable to take part in the original case.
2. The application must be made against all the parties to the original case.
3. The application must be submitted within two months of publication of the decision in the *Official Journal of the European Union*.
4. The Court may, on application by the third party, order a stay of execution of the contested decision. The provisions of Chapter 10 of this Title shall apply.
5. The contested decision shall be varied on the points on which the submissions of the third party are upheld.
6. The original of the judgment in the third-party proceedings shall be annexed to the original of the contested decision. A note of the judgment in the third-party proceedings shall be made in the margin of the original of the contested decision.

[10.313]
Article 158
Interpretation

1. In accordance with Article 43 of the Statute, if the meaning or scope of a judgment or order is in doubt, the Court shall construe it on application by any party or any institution of the European Union establishing an interest therein.
2. An application for interpretation must be made within two years after the date of delivery of the judgment or service of the order.
3. An application for interpretation shall be made in accordance with Articles 120 to 122 of these Rules. In addition it shall specify:
   (a) the decision in question;
   (b) the passages of which interpretation is sought.
4. The application must be made against all the parties to the case in which the decision of which interpretation is sought was given.
5. The Court shall give its decision after having given the parties an opportunity to submit their observations and after hearing the Advocate General.
6. The original of the interpreting decision shall be annexed to the original of the decision interpreted. A note of the interpreting decision shall be made in the margin of the original of the decision interpreted.

[10.314]
Article 159
Revision

1. In accordance with Article 44 of the Statute, an application for revision of a decision of the Court may be made only on discovery of a fact which is of such a nature as to be a decisive factor and which, when the judgment was delivered or the order served, was unknown to the Court and to the party claiming the revision.
2. Without prejudice to the time-limit of 10 years prescribed in the third paragraph of Article 44 of the Statute, an application for revision shall be made within three months of the date on which the facts on which the application is founded came to the applicant's knowledge.
3. Articles 120 to 122 of these Rules shall apply to an application for revision. In addition such an application shall:
   (a) specify the judgment or order contested;
   (b) indicate the points on which the decision is contested;

(c) set out the facts on which the application is founded;
(d) indicate the nature of the evidence to show that there are facts justifying revision, and that the time-limits laid down in paragraph 2 have been observed.

4. The application for revision must be made against all parties to the case in which the contested decision was given.
5. Without prejudice to its decision on the substance, the Court shall, after hearing the Advocate General, give in the form of an order its decision on the admissibility of the application, having regard to the written observations of the parties.
6. If the Court declares the application admissible, it shall proceed to consider the substance of the application and shall give its decision in the form of a judgment in accordance with these Rules.
7. The original of the revising judgment shall be annexed to the original of the decision revised. A note of the revising judgment shall be made in the margin of the original of the decision revised.

CHAPTER 10
SUSPENSION OF OPERATION OR ENFORCEMENT AND OTHER INTERIM MEASURES

[10.315]
Article 160
Application for suspension or for interim measures

1. An application to suspend the operation of any measure adopted by an institution, made pursuant to Article 278 TFEU or Article 157 TEAEC, shall be admissible only if the applicant has challenged that measure in an action before the Court.
2. An application for the adoption of one of the other interim measures referred to in Article 279 TFEU shall be admissible only if it is made by a party to a case before the Court and relates to that case.
3. An application of a kind referred to in the preceding paragraphs shall state the subject-matter of the proceedings, the circumstances giving rise to urgency and the pleas of fact and law establishing a prima facie case for the interim measure applied for.
4. The application shall be made by a separate document and in accordance with the provisions of Articles 120 to 122 of these Rules.
5. The application shall be served on the opposite party, and the President shall prescribe a short time-limit within which that party may submit written or oral observations.
6. The President may order a preparatory inquiry.
7. The President may grant the application even before the observations of the opposite party have been submitted. This decision may be varied or cancelled even without any application being made by any party.

[10.316]
Article 161
Decision on the application

1. The President shall either decide on the application himself or refer it immediately to the Court.
2. If the President is prevented from acting, Articles 10 and 13 of these Rules shall apply.
3. Where the application is referred to it, the Court shall give a decision immediately, after hearing the Advocate General.

[10.317]
Article 162
Order for suspension of operation or for interim measures

1. The decision on the application shall take the form of a reasoned order, from which no appeal shall lie. The order shall be served on the parties forthwith.
2. The execution of the order may be made conditional on the lodging by the applicant of security, of an amount and nature to be fixed in the light of the circumstances.
3. Unless the order fixes the date on which the interim measure is to lapse, the measure shall lapse when the judgment which closes the proceedings is delivered.
4. The order shall have only an interim effect, and shall be without prejudice to the decision of the Court on the substance of the case.

[10.318]
Article 163
Change in circumstances

On application by a party, the order may at any time be varied or cancelled on account of a change in circumstances.

[10.319]
Article 164
New application

Rejection of an application for an interim measure shall not bar the party who made it from making a further application on the basis of new facts.

[10.320]
Article 165
Applications pursuant to Articles 280 TFEU and 299 TFEU and Article 164 TEAEC
1. The provisions of this Chapter shall apply to applications to suspend the enforcement of a decision of the Court or of any measure adopted by the Council, the European Commission or the European Central Bank, submitted pursuant to Articles 280 TFEU and 299 TFEU or Article 164 TEAEC.
2. The order granting the application shall fix, where appropriate, a date on which the interim measure is to lapse.

[10.321]
Article 166
Application pursuant to Article 81 TEAEC
1. An application of a kind referred to in the third and fourth paragraphs of Article 81 TEAEC shall contain:
(a) the names and addresses of the persons or undertakings to be inspected;
(b) an indication of what is to be inspected and of the purpose of the inspection.
2. The President shall give his decision in the form of an order. Article 162 of these Rules shall apply.
3. If the President is prevented from acting, Articles 10 and 13 of these Rules shall apply.

TITLE V
APPEALS AGAINST DECISIONS OF THE GENERAL COURT

CHAPTER 1
FORM AND CONTENT OF THE APPEAL, AND FORM OF ORDER SOUGHT

[10.322]
Article 167
Lodging of the appeal
1. An appeal shall be brought by lodging an application at the Registry of the Court of Justice or of the General Court.
2. The Registry of the General Court shall forthwith transmit to the Registry of the Court of Justice the file in the case at first instance and, where necessary, the appeal.

[10.323]
Article 168
Content of the appeal
1. An appeal shall contain:
(a) the name and address of the appellant;
(b) a reference to the decision of the General Court appealed against;
(c) the names of the other parties to the relevant case before the General Court;
(d) the pleas in law and legal arguments relied on, and a summary of those pleas in law;
(e) the form of order sought by the appellant.
2. Articles 119, 121 and 122(1) of these Rules shall apply to appeals.
3. The appeal shall state the date on which the decision appealed against was served on the appellant.
4. If an appeal does not comply with paragraphs 1 to 3 of this Article, the Registrar shall prescribe a reasonable time-limit within which the appellant is to put the appeal in order. If the appellant fails to put the appeal in order within the time-limit prescribed, the Court of Justice shall, after hearing the Judge-Rapporteur and the Advocate General, decide whether the non-compliance with that formal requirement renders the appeal formally inadmissible.

[10.324]
Article 169
Form of order sought, pleas in law and arguments of the appeal
1. An appeal shall seek to have set aside, in whole or in part, the decision of the General Court as set out in the operative part of that decision.
2. The pleas in law and legal arguments relied on shall identify precisely those points in the grounds of the decision of the General Court which are contested.

[10.325]
Article 170
Form of order sought in the event that the appeal is allowed
1. An appeal shall seek, in the event that it is declared well founded, the same form of order, in whole or in part, as that sought at first instance and shall not seek a different form of order. The subject-matter of the proceedings before the General Court may not be changed in the appeal.
2. Where the appellant requests that the case be referred back to the General Court if the decision appealed against is set aside, he shall set out the reasons why the state of the proceedings does not permit a decision by the Court of Justice.

CHAPTER 2
RESPONSES, REPLIES AND REJOINDERS

[10.326]
Article 171
Service of the appeal

1. The appeal shall be served on the other parties to the relevant case before the General Court.
2. In a case where Article 168(4) of these Rules applies, service shall be effected as soon as the appeal has been put in order or the Court of Justice has declared it admissible notwithstanding the failure to observe the formal requirements laid down by that Article.

[10.327]
Article 172
Parties authorised to lodge a response

Any party to the relevant case before the General Court having an interest in the appeal being allowed or dismissed may submit a response within two months after service on him of the appeal. The time-limit for submitting a response shall not be extended.

[10.328]
Article 173
Content of the response

1. A response shall contain:
   (a) the name and address of the party submitting it;
   (b) the date on which the appeal was served on him;
   (c) the pleas in law and legal arguments relied on;
   (d) the form of order sought.
2. Articles 119 and 121 of these Rules shall apply to responses.

[10.329]
Article 174
Form of order sought in the response

A response shall seek to have the appeal allowed or dismissed, in whole or in part.

[10.330]
Article 175
Reply and rejoinder

1. The appeal and the response may be supplemented by a reply and a rejoinder only where the President, on a duly reasoned application submitted by the appellant within seven days of service of the response, considers it necessary, after hearing the Judge-Rapporteur and the Advocate General, in particular to enable the appellant to present his views on a plea of inadmissibility or on new matters relied on in the response.
2. The President shall fix the date by which the reply is to be produced and, upon service of that pleading, the date by which the rejoinder is to be produced. He may limit the number of pages and the subject-matter of those pleadings.

CHAPTER 3
FORM AND CONTENT OF THE CROSS-APPEAL, AND FORM OF ORDER SOUGHT

[10.331]
Article 176
Cross-appeal

1. The parties referred to in Article 172 of these Rules may submit a cross-appeal within the same time-limit as that prescribed for the submission of a response.
2. A cross-appeal must be introduced by a document separate from the response.

[10.332]
Article 177
Content of the cross-appeal

1. A cross-appeal shall contain:
   (a) the name and address of the party bringing the cross-appeal;
   (b) the date on which the appeal was served on him;
   (c) the pleas in law and legal arguments relied on;
   (d) the form of order sought.
2. Articles 119, 121 and 122(1) and (3) of these Rules shall apply to cross-appeals.

[10.333]
Article 178
Form of order sought, pleas in law and arguments of the cross-appeal

1. A cross-appeal shall seek to have set aside, in whole or in part, the decision of the General Court.

2. It may also seek to have set aside an express or implied decision relating to the admissibility of the action before the General Court.
3. The pleas in law and legal arguments relied on shall identify precisely those points in the grounds of the decision of the General Court which are contested. The pleas in law and arguments must be separate from those relied on in the response.

CHAPTER 4
PLEADINGS CONSEQUENT ON THE CROSS-APPEAL

[10.334]
Article 179
Response to the cross-appeal
Where a cross-appeal is brought, the applicant at first instance or any other party to the relevant case before the General Court having an interest in the cross-appeal being allowed or dismissed may submit a response, which must be limited to the pleas in law relied on in that cross-appeal, within two months after its being served on him. That time-limit shall not be extended.

[10.335]
Article 180
Reply and rejoinder on a cross-appeal
1. The cross-appeal and the response thereto may be supplemented by a reply and a rejoinder only where the President, on a duly reasoned application submitted by the party who brought the cross-appeal within seven days of service of the response to the cross-appeal, considers it necessary, after hearing the Judge-Rapporteur and the Advocate General, in particular to enable that party to present his views on a plea of inadmissibility or on new matters relied on in the response to the cross-appeal.
2. The President shall fix the date by which that reply is to be produced and, upon service of that pleading, the date by which the rejoinder is to be produced. He may limit the number of pages and the subject-matter of those pleadings.

CHAPTER 5
APPEALS DETERMINED BY ORDER

[10.336]
Article 181
Manifestly inadmissible or manifestly unfounded appeal or cross-appeal
Where the appeal or cross-appeal is, in whole or in part, manifestly inadmissible or manifestly unfounded, the Court may at any time, acting on a proposal from the Judge-Rapporteur and after hearing the Advocate General, decide by reasoned order to dismiss that appeal or cross-appeal in whole or in part.

[10.337]
Article 182
Manifestly well-founded appeal or cross-appeal
Where the Court has already ruled on one or more questions of law identical to those raised by the pleas in law of the appeal or cross-appeal and considers the appeal or cross-appeal to be manifestly well founded, it may, acting on a proposal from the Judge-Rapporteur and after hearing the parties and the Advocate General, decide by reasoned order in which reference is made to the relevant case-law to declare the appeal or cross-appeal manifestly well founded.

CHAPTER 6
EFFECT ON A CROSS-APPEAL OF THE REMOVAL OF THE APPEAL FROM THE REGISTER

[10.338]
Article 183
Effect on a cross-appeal of the discontinuance or manifest inadmissibility of the appeal
A cross-appeal shall be deemed to be devoid of purpose:
(a) if the appellant discontinues his appeal;
(b) if the appeal is declared manifestly inadmissible for non-compliance with the time-limit for lodging an appeal;
(c) if the appeal is declared manifestly inadmissible on the sole ground that it is not directed against a final decision of the General Court or against a decision disposing of the substantive issues in part only or disposing of a procedural issue concerning a plea of lack of competence or inadmissibility within the meaning of the first paragraph of Article 56 of the Statute.

CHAPTER 7
COSTS AND LEGAL AID IN APPEALS

[10.339]
Article 184
Costs in appeals

1. Subject to the following provisions, Articles 137 to 146 of these Rules shall apply, *mutatis mutandis*, to the procedure before the Court of Justice on an appeal against a decision of the General Court.
2. Where the appeal is unfounded or where the appeal is well founded and the Court itself gives final judgment in the case, the Court shall make a decision as to the costs.
3. When an appeal brought by a Member State or an institution of the European Union which did not intervene in the proceedings before the General Court is well founded, the Court of Justice may order that the parties share the costs or that the successful appellant pay the costs which the appeal has caused an unsuccessful party to incur.
4. Where the appeal has not been brought by an intervener at first instance, he may not be ordered to pay costs in the appeal proceedings unless he participated in the written or oral part of the proceedings before the Court of Justice. Where an intervener at first instance takes part in the proceedings, the Court may decide that he shall bear his own costs.

[10.340]
Article 185
Legal aid

1. A party who is wholly or in part unable to meet the costs of the proceedings may at any time apply for legal aid.
2. The application shall be accompanied by all information and supporting documents making it possible to assess the applicant's financial situation, such as a certificate issued by a competent national authority attesting to his financial situation.

[10.341]
Article 186
Prior application for legal aid

1. If the application is made prior to the appeal which the applicant for legal aid intends to commence, it shall briefly state the subject of the appeal.
2. The application for legal aid need not be made through a lawyer.
3. The introduction of an application for legal aid shall, with regard to the person who made that application, suspend the time-limit prescribed for the bringing of the appeal until the date of service of the order making a decision on that application.
4. The President shall assign the application for legal aid, as soon as it is lodged, to a Judge-Rapporteur who shall put forward, promptly, a proposal as to the action to be taken on it.

[10.342]
Article 187
Decision on the application for legal aid

1. The decision to grant legal aid, in whole or in part, or to refuse it shall be taken, on a proposal from the Judge-Rapporteur and after hearing the Advocate General, by the Chamber of three Judges to which the Judge-Rapporteur is assigned. In that event, the formation of the Court shall be composed of the President of that Chamber, the Judge-Rapporteur and the first Judge or, as the case may be, the first two Judges designated from the list referred to in Article 28(3) on the date on which the application for legal aid is brought before that Chamber by the Judge-Rapporteur. It shall consider, if appropriate, whether the appeal is manifestly unfounded.
2. If the Judge-Rapporteur is not a member of a Chamber of three Judges, the decision shall be taken, under the same conditions, by the Chamber of five Judges to which he is assigned. In addition to the Judge-Rapporteur, the formation of the Court shall be composed of four Judges designated from the list referred to in Article 28(2) on the date on which the application for legal aid is brought before that Chamber by the Judge-Rapporteur.
3. The formation of the Court shall give its decision by way of order. Where the application for legal aid is refused in whole or in part, the order shall state the reasons for that refusal.

[10.343]
Article 188
Sums to be advanced as legal aid

1. Where legal aid is granted, the cashier of the Court shall be responsible, where applicable within the limits set by the formation of the Court, for costs involved in the assistance and representation of the applicant before the Court. At the request of the applicant or his representative, an advance on those costs may be paid.
2. In its decision as to costs the Court may order the payment to the cashier of the Court of sums advanced as legal aid.
3. The Registrar shall take steps to obtain the recovery of these sums from the party ordered to pay them.

[10.344]
Article 189
Withdrawal of legal aid
The formation of the Court which gave a decision on the application for legal aid may at any time, either of its own motion or on request, withdraw that legal aid if the circumstances which led to its being granted alter during the proceedings.

CHAPTER 8
OTHER PROVISIONS APPLICABLE TO APPEALS

[10.345]
Article 190
Other provisions applicable to appeals
1. Articles 127, 129 to 136, 147 to 150, 153 to 155 and 157 to 166 of these Rules shall apply to the procedure before the Court of Justice on an appeal against decisions of the General Court.
2. By way of derogation from Article 130(1), an application to intervene shall, however, be made within one month of the publication of the notice referred to in Article 21(4).
3. Article 95 shall apply, *mutatis mutandis*, to the procedure before the Court of Justice on an appeal against decisions of the General Court.

[10.346]
[Article 190a
Treatment of information or material produced before the General Court in accordance with Article 105 of its Rules of Procedure
1. Where an appeal is brought against a decision of the General Court adopted in proceedings in which information or material has been produced by a main party in accordance with Article 105 of the Rules of Procedure of the General Court and has not been communicated to the other main party, the Registry of the General Court shall make that information or material available to the Court of Justice, on the conditions laid down in the decision referred to in paragraph 11 of that Article.
2. The information or material referred to in paragraph 1 shall not be communicated to the parties to the proceedings before the Court of Justice.
3. The Court of Justice shall ensure that the confidential matters contained in the information or material referred to in paragraph 1 are not disclosed in the decision which closes the proceedings or in any Opinion of the Advocate General.
4. The information or material referred to in paragraph 1 shall be returned to the party that produced it before the General Court as soon as the decision closing the proceedings before the Court of Justice has been served, save where the case is referred back to the General Court. In the latter case, the information or material concerned shall again be made available to the General Court, on the conditions laid down in the decision referred to in paragraph 5.
5. The Court of Justice shall adopt, by decision, the security rules for protecting the information or material referred to in paragraph 1. That decision shall be published in the *Official Journal of the European Union*.]

NOTES
Inserted by the Amendment of the Rules of Procedure of the Court of Justice, Article 1 (OJ L217, 12.8.2016, p 69). Note that Article 2 provides that provisions this Article apply only from the entry into force of the decision referred to in Article 190a(5).

TITLE VI
REVIEW OF DECISIONS OF THE GENERAL COURT

[10.347]
Article 191
Reviewing Chamber
A Chamber of five Judges shall be designated for a period of one year for the purpose of deciding, in accordance with Articles 193 and 194 of these Rules, whether a decision of the General Court is to be reviewed in accordance with Article 62 of the Statute.

[10.348]
Article 192
Information and communication of decisions which may be reviewed
1. As soon as the date for the delivery or signature of a decision to be given under Article 256(2) or (3) TFEU is fixed, the Registry of the General Court shall inform the Registry of the Court of Justice.
2. The decision shall be communicated to the Registry of the Court of Justice immediately upon its delivery or signature, as shall the file in the case, which shall be made available forthwith to the First Advocate General.

[10.349]
Article 193
Review of decisions given on appeal

1. The proposal of the First Advocate General to review a decision of the General Court given under Article 256(2) TFEU shall be forwarded to the President of the Court of Justice and to the President of the reviewing Chamber. Notice of that transmission shall be given to the Registrar at the same time.
2. As soon as he is informed of the existence of a proposal, the Registrar shall communicate the file in the case before the General Court to the members of the reviewing Chamber.
3. As soon as the proposal to review has been received, the President of the Court shall designate the Judge-Rapporteur from among the Judges of the reviewing Chamber on a proposal from the President of that Chamber. The composition of the formation of the Court shall be determined in accordance with Article 28(2) of these Rules on the day on which the case is assigned to the Judge-Rapporteur.
4. That Chamber, acting on a proposal from the Judge-Rapporteur, shall decide whether the decision of the General Court is to be reviewed. The decision to review the decision of the General Court shall indicate only the questions which are to be reviewed.
5. The General Court, the parties to the proceedings before it and the other interested persons referred to in the second paragraph of Article 62a of the Statute shall forthwith be informed by the Registrar of the decision of the Court of Justice to review the decision of the General Court.
6. Notice of the date of the decision to review the decision of the General Court and of the questions which are to be reviewed shall be published in the *Official Journal of the European Union*.

[10.350]
Article 194
Review of preliminary rulings

1. The proposal of the First Advocate General to review a decision of the General Court given under Article 256(3) TFEU shall be forwarded to the President of the Court of Justice and to the President of the reviewing Chamber. Notice of that transmission shall be given to the Registrar at the same time.
2. As soon as he is informed of the existence of a proposal, the Registrar shall communicate the file in the case before the General Court to the members of the reviewing Chamber.
3. The Registrar shall also inform the General Court, the referring court or tribunal, the parties to the main proceedings and the other interested persons referred to in the second paragraph of Article 62a of the Statute of the existence of a proposal to review.
4. As soon as the proposal to review has been received, the President of the Court shall designate the Judge-Rapporteur from among the Judges of the reviewing Chamber on a proposal from the President of that Chamber. The composition of the formation of the Court shall be determined in accordance with Article 28(2) of these Rules on the day on which the case is assigned to the Judge-Rapporteur.
5. That Chamber, acting on a proposal from the Judge-Rapporteur, shall decide whether the decision of the General Court is to be reviewed. The decision to review the decision of the General Court shall indicate only the questions which are to be reviewed.
6. The General Court, the referring court or tribunal, the parties to the main proceedings and the other interested persons referred to in the second paragraph of Article 62a of the Statute shall forthwith be informed by the Registrar of the decision of the Court of Justice as to whether or not the decision of the General Court is to be reviewed.
7. Notice of the date of the decision to review the decision of the General Court and of the questions which are to be reviewed shall be published in the *Official Journal of the European Union*.

[10.351]
Article 195
Judgment on the substance of the case after a decision to review

1. The decision to review a decision of the General Court shall be served on the parties and other interested persons referred to in the second paragraph of Article 62a of the Statute. The decision served on the Member States, and the States, other than the Member States, which are parties to the EEA Agreement, as well as the EFTA Surveillance Authority, shall be accompanied by a translation of the decision of the Court of Justice in accordance with the provisions of Article 98 of these Rules. The decision of the Court of Justice shall also be communicated to the General Court and, if applicable, to the referring court or tribunal.
2. Within one month of the date of service referred to in paragraph 1, the parties and other interested persons on whom the decision of the Court of Justice has been served may lodge statements or written observations on the questions which are subject to review.
3. As soon as a decision to review a decision of the General Court has been taken, the First Advocate General shall assign the review to an Advocate General.
4. The reviewing Chamber shall rule on the substance of the case, after hearing the Advocate General.

5. It may, however, request the Court of Justice to assign the case to a formation of the Court composed of a greater number of Judges.
6. Where the decision of the General Court which is subject to review was given under Article 256(2) TFEU, the Court of Justice shall make a decision as to costs.

TITLE VII
OPINIONS

[10.352]
Article 196
Written part of the procedure
1. In accordance with Article 218(11) TFEU, a request for an Opinion may be made by a Member State, by the European Parliament, by the Council or by the European Commission.
2. A request for an Opinion may relate both to whether the envisaged agreement is compatible with the provisions of the Treaties and to whether the European Union or any institution of the European Union has the power to enter into that agreement.
3. It shall be served on the Member States and on the institutions referred to in paragraph 1, and the President shall prescribe a time-limit within which they may submit written observations.

[10.353]
Article 197
Designation of the Judge-Rapporteur and of the Advocate General
As soon as the request for an Opinion has been submitted, the President shall designate a Judge-Rapporteur and the First Advocate General shall assign the case to an Advocate General.

[10.354]
Article 198
Hearing
The Court may decide that the procedure before it shall also include a hearing.

[10.355]
Article 199
Time-limit for delivering the Opinion
The Court shall deliver its Opinion as soon as possible, after hearing the Advocate General.

[10.356]
Article 200
Delivery of the Opinion
The Opinion, signed by the President, the Judges who took part in the deliberations and the Registrar, shall be delivered in open court. It shall be served on all the Member States and on the institutions referred to in Article 196(1).

TITLE VIII
PARTICULAR FORMS OF PROCEDURE

[10.357]
Article 201
Appeals against decisions of the arbitration committee
1. An application initiating an appeal under the second paragraph of Article 18 TEAEC shall state:
(a) the name and permanent address of the applicant;
(b) the description of the signatory;
(c) a reference to the arbitration committee's decision against which the appeal is made;
(d) the names of the respondents;
(e) a summary of the facts;
(f) the grounds on which the appeal is based and arguments relied on, and a brief statement of those grounds;
(g) the form of order sought by the applicant.
2. Articles 119 and 121 of these Rules shall apply to the application.
3. A certified copy of the contested decision shall be annexed to the application.
4. As soon as the application has been lodged, the Registrar of the Court shall request the arbitration committee registry to transmit to the Court the file in the case.
5. Articles 123 and 124 of these Rules shall apply to this procedure. The Court may decide that the procedure before it shall also include a hearing.
6. The Court shall give its decision in the form of a judgment. Where the Court sets aside the decision of the arbitration committee it may refer the case back to the committee.

[10.358]
Article 202
Procedure under Article 103 TEAEC

1. Four certified copies shall be lodged of an application under the third paragraph of Article 103 TEAEC. The application shall be accompanied by the draft of the agreement or contract concerned, by the observations of the European Commission addressed to the State concerned and by all other supporting documents.
2. The application and annexes thereto shall be served on the European Commission, which shall have a time-limit of 10 days from such service to submit its written observations. This time-limit may be extended by the President after the State concerned has been heard.
3. Following the lodging of such observations, which shall be served on the State concerned, the Court shall give its decision promptly, after hearing the Advocate General and, if they so request, the State concerned and the European Commission.

[10.359]
Article 203
Procedures under Articles 104 TEAEC and 105 TEAEC

Applications under the third paragraph of Article 104 TEAEC and the second paragraph of Article 105 TEAEC shall be governed by the provisions of Titles II and IV of these Rules. Such applications shall also be served on the State to which the respondent person or undertaking belongs.

[10.360]
Article 204
Procedure provided for by Article 111(3) of the EEA Agreement

1. In the case governed by Article 111(3) of the EEA Agreement, the matter shall be brought before the Court by a request submitted by the Contracting Parties which are parties to the dispute. The request shall be served on the other Contracting Parties, on the European Commission, on the EFTA Surveillance Authority and, where appropriate, on the other interested persons on whom a request for a preliminary ruling raising the same question of interpretation of European Union legislation would be served.
2. The President shall prescribe a time-limit within which the Contracting Parties and the other interested persons on whom the request has been served may submit written observations.
3. The request shall be made in one of the languages referred to in Article 36 of these Rules. Article 38 shall apply. The provisions of Article 98 shall apply *mutatis mutandis*.
4. As soon as the request referred to in paragraph 1 of this Article has been submitted, the President shall designate a Judge-Rapporteur. The First Advocate General shall, immediately afterwards, assign the request to an Advocate General.
5. The Court shall, after hearing the Advocate General, give a reasoned decision on the request.
6. The decision of the Court, signed by the President, the Judges who took part in the deliberations and the Registrar, shall be served on the Contracting Parties and on the other interested persons referred to in paragraphs 1 and 2.

[10.361]
Article 205
Settlement of the disputes referred to in Article 35 TEU in the version in force before the entry into force of the Treaty of Lisbon

1. In the case of disputes between Member States as referred to in Article 35(7) TEU in the version in force before the entry into force of the Treaty of Lisbon, as maintained in force by Protocol No 36 annexed to the Treaties, the matter shall be brought before the Court by an application by a party to the dispute. The application shall be served on the other Member States and on the European Commission.
2. In the case of disputes between Member States and the European Commission as referred to in Article 35(7) TEU in the version in force before the entry into force of the Treaty of Lisbon, as maintained in force by Protocol No 36 annexed to the Treaties, the matter shall be brought before the Court by an application by a party to the dispute. The application shall be served on the other Member States, the Council and the European Commission if it was submitted by a Member State. The application shall be served on the Member States and on the Council if it was submitted by the European Commission.
3. The President shall prescribe a time-limit within which the institutions and the Member States on which the application has been served may submit written observations.
4. As soon as the application referred to in paragraphs 1 and 2 has been submitted, the President shall designate a Judge-Rapporteur. The First Advocate General shall, immediately afterwards, assign the application to an Advocate General.
5. The Court may decide that the procedure before it shall also include a hearing.
6. The Court shall, after the Advocate General has delivered his Opinion, give its ruling on the dispute by way of judgment.

7. The same procedure as that laid down in the preceding paragraphs shall apply where an agreement concluded between the Member States confers jurisdiction on the Court to rule on a dispute between Member States or between Member States and an institution.

[10.362]
Article 206
Requests under Article 269 TFEU

1. Four certified copies shall be submitted of a request under Article 269 TFEU. The request shall be accompanied by any relevant document and, in particular, any observations and recommendations made pursuant to Article 7 TEU.
2. The request and annexes thereto shall be served on the European Council or on the Council, as appropriate, each of which shall have a time-limit of 10 days from such service to submit its written observations. This time-limit shall not be extended.
3. The request and annexes thereto shall also be communicated to the Member States other than the State in question, to the European Parliament and to the European Commission.
4. Following the lodging of the observations referred to in paragraph 2, which shall be served on the Member State concerned and on the States and institutions referred to in paragraph 3, the Court shall give its decision within a time-limit of one month from the lodging of the request and after hearing the Advocate General. At the request of the Member State concerned, the European Council or the Council, or of its own motion, the Court may decide that the procedure before it shall also include a hearing, which all the States and institutions referred to in this Article shall be given notice to attend.

FINAL PROVISIONS

[10.363]
Article 207
Supplementary rules

Subject to the provisions of Article 253 TFEU and after consultation with the Governments concerned, the Court shall adopt supplementary rules concerning its practice in relation to:

(a) letters rogatory;
(b) applications for legal aid;
(c) reports by the Court of perjury by witnesses or experts, delivered pursuant to Article 30 of the Statute.

[10.364]
Article 208
Implementing rules

The Court may, by a separate act, adopt practice rules for the implementation of these Rules.

[10.365]
Article 209
Repeal

These Rules replace the Rules of Procedure of the Court of Justice of the European Communities adopted on 19 June 1991, as last amended on 24 May 2011 (*Official Journal of the European Union*, L162 of 22 June 2011, p 17).

[10.366]
Article 210
Publication and entry into force of these Rules

These Rules, which are authentic in the languages referred to in Article 36 of these Rules, shall be published in the *Official Journal of the European Union* and shall enter into force on the first day of the second month following their publication.

RULES OF PROCEDURE: SUPPLEMENTARY RULES OF THE COURT OF JUSTICE

[10.367]

NOTES

Date of publication in OJ: OJ L32, 1.2.2014, p 37.

THE COURT OF JUSTICE

Having regard to Article 207 of the Rules of Procedure,[1]

Having regard to Article 46(3) of the act concerning the conditions of accession to the European Union of the Republic of Bulgaria and Romania and the adjustments to the Treaties on which the European Union is founded,[2]

Having regard to Article 45 of the act concerning the conditions of accession to the European Union of the Republic of Croatia and the adjustments to the Treaty on European Union, the Treaty on the Functioning of the European Union and the Treaty establishing the European Atomic Energy Community,[3]

Whereas:

(1) On 25 September 2012 the Court adopted new Rules of Procedure containing various amendments, both of substance and of form, in relation to the previous Rules, which they repealed. Those amendments concern, in particular, the terminology used in the new Rules of Procedure and the procedure followed when legal aid is granted. Those alterations must, therefore, be reflected in the wording of the Supplementary Rules.

(2) In consequence of several Member States' designation of new authorities responsible for the handling of the matters referred to in Articles 2, 4 and 6 of the Supplementary Rules and of the accession to the European Union of the Republic of Bulgaria and Romania on 1 January 2007 and of the Republic of Croatia on 1 July 2013, it would furthermore appear necessary to bring up to date the lists in the three annexes to those Rules.

With the Council's approval given on 17 December 2013,

NOTES

1 OJ L265, 29.9.2012, p 1, as amended on 18 June 2013 (OJ L173, 26.6.2013, p 65).

2 OJ L157, 21.6.2005, p 203.

3 OJ L112, 24.4.2012, p 21.

HAS ADOPTED THESE SUPPLEMENTARY RULES:

CHAPTER I
LETTERS ROGATORY

[10.368]
Article 1

1. Letters rogatory shall be issued in the form of an order which shall contain the names, forenames, description and address of the witness or expert, set out the facts on which the witness or expert is to be examined, name the parties, their agents, lawyers or advisers, indicate their addresses for service and briefly describe the subject-matter of the proceedings.
2. Notice of the order shall be served on the parties by the Registrar.

[10.369]
Article 2

1. The Registrar shall send the order to the competent authority named in Annex I of the Member State in whose territory the witness or expert is to be examined. Where necessary, the order shall be accompanied by a translation into the official languages of the Member State to which it is addressed.
2. The authority named pursuant to paragraph 1 shall pass on the order to the judicial authority which is competent according to its national law.
3. The competent judicial authority shall give effect to the letters rogatory in accordance with its national law. After implementation the competent judicial authority shall transmit to the authority named pursuant to paragraph 1 the order embodying the letters rogatory, any documents arising from the implementation and a detailed statement of costs. These documents shall be sent to the Registrar of the Court.
4. The Registrar shall be responsible for the translation of the documents into the language of the case.

[10.370]
Article 3

The Court shall defray the expenses occasioned by the letters rogatory without prejudice to the right to charge them, where appropriate, to the parties.

CHAPTER II
LEGAL AID

[10.371]
Article 4

1. The Court, by any order by which it decides that a person is entitled to receive legal aid, shall order that a lawyer be appointed to act for him.
2. If the person does not indicate his choice of lawyer, or if the Court considers that his choice is unacceptable, the Registrar shall send a copy of the order and of the application for legal aid to the authority named in Annex II, being the competent authority of the State concerned.
3. The Court, in the light of the suggestions made by that authority, shall of its own motion appoint a lawyer to act for the person concerned.

[10.372]
Article 5
The Court shall adjudicate on the lawyer's expenses and fees; on request, an advance on those expenses and fees may be paid.

CHAPTER III
REPORTS OF PERJURY BY A WITNESS OR EXPERT

[10.373]
Article 6
The Court, after hearing the Advocate General, may decide to report to the competent authority referred to in Annex III of the Member State whose courts have penal jurisdiction any case of perjury on the part of a witness or expert before the Court.

[10.374]
Article 7
The Registrar shall be responsible for communicating the decision of the Court. The decision shall set out the facts and circumstances on which the report is based.

Final provisions

[10.375]
Article 8
These Supplementary Rules replace the Supplementary Rules of 4 December 1974 (OJ L 350, 28.12.1974, p. 29), as most recently amended on 21 February 2006 (OJ L 72, 11.3.2006, p. 1).

[10.376]
Article 9
1. These Rules, which shall be authentic in the languages referred to in Article 36 of the Rules of Procedure, shall be published in the *Official Journal of the European Union*.
2. These Rules shall enter into force on the date of their publication.

ANNEX I
LIST REFERRED TO IN ARTICLE 2(1)

[10.377]
Belgium

Service public fédéral Justice – Federale Overheidsdienst Justitie

Bulgaria

Министър на правосъдието

Czech Republic

Ministr spravedlnosti

Denmark

Justitsministeriet

Germany

Bundesministerium der Justiz

Estonia

Justiitsministeerium

Ireland

Minister for Justice and Equality

Greece

Υπουργείο Δικαιοσύνης, Διαφάνειας και Ανθρωπίνων Δικαιωμάτων

Spain

Ministerio de Justicia

France

Ministère de la justice

Croatia

Ministarstvo pravosuđa

Italy

Ministero della Giustizia

Cyprus

Υπουργός Δικαιοσύνης και Δημόσιας Τάξεως

Latvia

Latvijas Republikas Tieslietu ministrija

Lithuania

Lietuvos Respublikos teisingumo ministerija

Luxembourg

Parquet général

Hungary

Közigazgatási és Igazságügyi Minisztérium

Malta

Avukat Ġenerali

Netherlands

Minister van Veiligheid en Justitie

Austria

Bundesministerium für Justiz

Poland

Ministerstwo Sprawiedliwości

Portugal

Ministro da Justiça

Romania

Ministerul Justiţiei

Slovenia

Ministrstvo za pravosodje

Slovakia

Minister spravodlivosti

Finland

Oikeusministeriö

Sweden

Regeringskansliet Justitiedepartementet

United Kingdom

Secretary of State for the Home Department

ANNEX II
LIST REFERRED TO IN ARTICLE 4(2)

[10.378]
Belgium

Service public fédéral Justice – Federale Overheidsdienst Justitie

Bulgaria

Министър на правосъдието

Czech Republic

Česká advokátní komora

Denmark

Justitsministeriet

Germany

Bundesrechtsanwaltskammer

Estonia

Justiitsministeerium

Ireland

Minister for Justice and Equality

Greece

Υπουργείο Δικαιοσύνης, Διαφάνειας και Ανθρωπίνων Δικαιωμάτων

Spain

Consejo General de la Abogacía Española

France

Ministère de la justice

Croatia

Ministarstvo pravosuđa

Italy

Ministero della Giustizia

Cyprus

Υπουργός Δικαιοσύνης και Δημόσιας Τάξεως

Latvia

Latvijas Republikas Tieslietu ministrija

Lithuania

Lietuvos Respublikos teisingumo ministerija

Luxembourg

Ministère de la justice

Hungary

Közigazgatási és Igazságügyi Minisztérium

Malta

Segretarju Parlamentari għall-Gustizzja

Netherlands

Algemene Raad van de Nederlandse Orde van Advocaten

Austria

Bundesministerium für Justiz

Poland

Ministerstwo Sprawiedliwości

Portugal

Ministro da Justiça

Romania

Uniunea Naţională a Barourilor din România

Slovenia

Ministrstvo za pravosodje

Slovakia

Slovenská advokátska komora

Finland

Oikeusministeriö

Sweden

Sveriges advokatsamfund

United Kingdom

The Law Society, London (for applicants residing in England or Wales)

The Law Society of Scotland, Edinburgh (for applicants residing in Scotland)

The Law Society of Northern Ireland, Belfast (for applicants residing in Northern Ireland)

ANNEX III
LIST REFERRED TO IN ARTICLE 6

[10.379]
Belgium

Service public fédéral Justice – Federale Overheidsdienst Justitie

Bulgaria

Върховна касационна прокуратура на Република България

Czech Republic

Nejvyšší státní zastupitelství

Denmark

Justitsministeriet

Germany

Bundesministerium der Justiz

Estonia

Riigiprokuratuur

Ireland

The Office of the Attorney General

Greece

Υπουργείο Δικαιοσύνης, Διαφάνειας και Ανθρωπίνων Δικαιωμάτων

Spain

Consejo General del Poder Judicial

France

Ministère de la justice

Croatia

Zamjenik Glavnog državnog odvjetnika

Italy

Ministero della Giustizia

Cyprus

Γενικός Εισαγγελέας της Δημοκρατίας

Latvia

Latvijas Republikas Ģenerālprokuratūra

Lithuania

Lietuvos Respublikos generalinė prokuratūra

Luxembourg

Parquet général

Hungary

Közigazgatási és Igazságügyi Minisztérium

Malta

Avukat Ġenerali

Netherlands

Minister van Veiligheid en Justitie

Austria

Bundesministerium für Justiz

Poland

Ministerstwo Sprawiedliwości

Portugal

Ministro da Justiça

Romania

Parchetul de pe lângă Înalta Curte de Casaţie şi Justiţie

Slovenia

Ministrstvo za pravosodje

Slovakia

Minister spravodlivosti

Finland

Keskusrikospoliisi

Sweden

Åklagarmyndigheten

United Kingdom

Her Majesty's Attorney General (for witnesses or experts residing in England or Wales)

Her Majesty's Advocate General (for witnesses or experts residing in Scotland)

Her Majesty's Attorney General (for witnesses or experts residing in Northern Ireland)

RULES OF PROCEDURE OF THE GENERAL COURT 2015 (CONSOLIDATED)

[10.380]

NOTES

Date of original publication in Official Journal: OJ L105, 23.4.2015, p 1.

A consolidated version of these Rules (reproduced here) is also available on the General Court section of the Curia website at curia.europa.eu/jcms/upload/docs/application/pdf/2016-08/rp_en.pdf. It includes the amendments made in August 2016 and published in OJ L217, 12.8.2016, pp 71–73.

THE GENERAL COURT,

Having regard to the Treaty on European Union, and in particular Article 19 thereof,

Having regard to the Treaty on the Functioning of the European Union, and in particular the fifth paragraph of Article 254 thereof,

Having regard to the Treaty establishing the European Atomic Energy Community, and in particular Article 106a(1) thereof,

Having regard to the Protocol on the Statute of the Court of Justice of the European Union, and in particular the sixth paragraph of Article 19, Article 63 and the second paragraph of Article 64 thereof,

Whereas:

(1) The Rules of Procedure of 2 May 1991 have been amended numerous times in order to equip the General Court gradually with provisions enabling it to deal under the best possible conditions with different kinds of cases falling within increasingly varied areas.

(2) Full revision of the text is necessary in order to give this set of rules a new coherence, to promote consistency in the procedural provisions governing proceedings brought before the Courts of the European Union, to preserve the capacity of the General Court to rule on cases within a reasonable time, to clarify parties' rights, to specify the General Court's expectations regarding the parties' representatives and to adjust a certain number of provisions to take account of certain changes, including technological changes, in relation to the lodging and service of procedural documents, and of difficulties encountered in their implementation.

(3) Actions brought in the field of intellectual property and appeals lodged against decisions of the European Union Civil Service Tribunal must, on account of their specific nature, be subject to particular procedural rules set out in special titles, while being otherwise governed by the procedural provisions applicable to direct actions. The rules relating to direct actions, actions in the field of intellectual property and appeals therefore constitute the framework of these Rules.

(4) In the light of experience, it is also necessary to supplement or to clarify for the benefit of litigants the rules that apply to each procedure. The rules in question concern, in particular, the extent of the rights conferred on the main parties and that of the rights afforded to interveners or, in intellectual property cases, the acquisition of the status of intervener and the extent of his rights. Observance of the adversarial principle and the need, in certain situations, to preserve the confidentiality of sensitive information which is relevant to the outcome of the proceedings are the subject of specific provisions. With regard to appeals against decisions of the Civil Service Tribunal, a clearer distinction must in addition be drawn between appeals and cross-appeals following the service of an appeal. A similar distinction must be drawn, with regard to cases in the field of intellectual property, between the original action and the cross-claim brought by an intervener, following service of the application initiating proceedings.

(5) The excessive complexity of certain procedures has come to light on their implementation. It is appropriate, therefore, to simplify them. On that basis, the rules for determining the language of the case in intellectual property cases ensure greater predictability of situations for the benefit of those concerned and a 'light touch' by the General Court. The rules relating to the default procedure are intended to enable cases to be disposed of more promptly, in the interests of the applicant, who, if successful, is exposed to the risk of the defendant applying for the judgment in default to be set aside.

(6) In the interests of making the Rules easier to understand, all requests and applications relating to judgments and orders, currently to be found in a number of separate titles and chapters of the Rules of Procedure, should be brought together in the title relating to direct actions. Similarly, to assist the reader, the procedures following referral by the Court of Justice, either after a decision has been set aside, or after review, are set out in a single title.

(7) Although required to deal with an ever-increasing caseload, the General Court must continue to deliver its rulings within a reasonable time. It is therefore essential to continue the efforts undertaken to reduce the duration of proceedings before the General Court, in particular by providing for the written part of the procedure in intellectual property cases to be limited to a single exchange of pleadings, managing applications to modify the form of order sought in the application, reducing certain legal time limits, simplifying the rules on intervention by removing as a category of intervention those which may be allowed after expiry of the legal time limit following publication in the *Official Journal of the European Union*, making provision for the General Court to be able to rule without an oral part of the procedure in direct actions if none of the main parties has requested a hearing and if it considers that it has sufficient information available to it from the material in the file in the case, and to be able to rule without an oral part of the procedure in appeals, increasing the decision-making powers of the Presidents of Chambers and, lastly, increasing the circumstances in which a ruling is to be given by means of a simple decision.

(8) With the same objective, provisions have been added to the title relating to the organisation of the General Court with a view, in particular, to specifying the circumstances in which a case may be reassigned and extending the powers of a single Judge so as to enable him to hear and determine intellectual property cases.

(9) The fact that proceedings are to be conducted in accordance with the adversarial principle is confirmed by the affirmation of that principle in a specific article and by a strict set of rules governing the circumstances in which preservation of the confidentiality of certain information provided by a main party which is necessary in order for the General Court to rule in the case justifies, exceptionally, the non-communication of that information to the other main party. New provisions also provide the General Court with a formal framework in the event of a Judge's withdrawal from a case or of his being excused. The reform is also intended to elevate to the status of

rules of procedure provisions which were previously contained in practice directions to parties, such as that relating to the length of pleadings, or in instructions to the registrar of the General Court, such as the provision concerning anonymity and that specifying the circumstances in which a third party may be given access to the file in the case.

(10) Lastly, the text has been made easier to read by the removal of certain rules which are outdated or not applied, the numbering of every paragraph of the articles in these Rules, the addition of a specific heading for each article and the harmonisation of terminology,

With the agreement of the Court of Justice,

With the approval of the Council given on 10 February 2015,

HAS ADOPTED THESE RULES OF PROCEDURE:

INTRODUCTORY PROVISIONS

[10.381]

Article 1

Definitions

1. In these Rules:

(a) provisions of the Treaty on European Union are referred to by the number of the article concerned followed by 'TEU';

(b) provisions of the Treaty on the Functioning of the European Union are referred to by the number of the article concerned followed by 'TFEU';

(c) provisions of the Treaty establishing the European Atomic Energy Community are referred to by the number of the article concerned followed by 'TEAEC';

(d) 'Statute' means the Protocol on the Statute of the Court of Justice of the European Union;

(e) 'EEA Agreement' means the Agreement on the European Economic Area;[1]

(f) 'Council Regulation No 1' means Council Regulation No 1 of 15 April 1958 determining the languages to be used by the European Economic Community.[2]

2. For the purposes of these Rules:

(a) 'General Court' means, in cases assigned or referred to a Chamber, that Chamber, and, in cases delegated or assigned to a single Judge, that Judge;

(b) 'President', unless otherwise specified, means:

— in cases not yet assigned to a formation of the Court, the President of the General Court,

— in cases assigned to Chambers, the President of the Chamber to which the case is assigned,

— in cases delegated or assigned to a single Judge, that Judge;

(c) 'party' and 'parties', unless otherwise specified, means any party to the proceedings, including interveners;

(d) 'main party' and 'main parties' means the applicant or the defendant or both of them, as the case may be;

(e) 'representatives of the parties' means the lawyers and agents, the latter assisted, where appropriate, by an adviser or lawyer, representing the parties before the General Court in accordance with Article 19 of the Statute;

(f) 'institution' and 'institutions' means the institutions of the European Union referred to in Article 13(1) TEU and the bodies, offices or agencies established by the Treaties, or by an act adopted in implementation thereof, which may be parties before the General Court;

(g) 'Office' means the [the European Union Intellectual Property Office] or the Community Plant Variety Office, as the case may be;

(h) 'EFTA Surveillance Authority' means the European Free Trade Association surveillance authority referred to in the EEA Agreement;

[(i) 'direct actions' means actions brought on the basis of Articles 263 TFEU, 265 TFEU, 268 TFEU, 270 TFEU and 272 TFEU;]

[(j) 'Staff Regulations' means the Regulation laying down the Staff Regulations of Officials of the European Union and the Conditions of Employment of other servants of the European Union.]

NOTES

The words in square brackets in sub-para 2(g) were substituted by the Amendment to the Rules of Procedure of the General Court, Article 1 (OJ L217, 12.8.2016, p 71).

Sub-para 2(i) was substituted, and sub-para 2(i) was added, by the Amendment to the Rules of Procedure of the General Court, Article 1(1) (OJ L217, 12.8.2016, p 73).

[1] OJ L1, 3.1.1994, p 3.

[2] OJ, English special edition 1952-1958 (I), p 59.

[10.382]
Article 2
Purport of these Rules
These Rules implement and supplement, so far as necessary, the relevant provisions of the EU, FEU and EAEC Treaties, and the Statute.

TITLE I
ORGANISATION OF THE GENERAL COURT

CHAPTER 1
MEMBERS OF THE GENERAL COURT

[10.383]
Article 3
Duties of Judge and Advocate General
1. Every Member of the General Court shall, as a rule, perform the duties of a Judge.
2. Members of the General Court are hereinafter referred to as 'Judges'.
3. Every Judge, with the exception of the President, the Vice-President and the Presidents of Chambers of the General Court, may, in the circumstances defined in Articles 30 and 31, perform the duties of an Advocate General in a particular case.
4. References to the Advocate General in these Rules shall apply only where a Judge has been designated as Advocate General.

[10.384]
Article 4
Commencement of the term of office of Judges
The term of office of a Judge shall begin on the date fixed for that purpose in the instrument of appointment. In the absence of any provision in that instrument regarding the date of commencement of the term of office, that term shall begin on the date of publication of the instrument in the *Official Journal of the European Union*.

[10.385]
Article 5
Taking of the oath
Before taking up his duties, a Judge shall take the following oath before the Court of Justice, provided for in Article 2 of the Statute:

> 'I swear that I will perform my duties impartially and conscientiously; I swear that I will preserve the secrecy of the deliberations of the Court.'

[10.386]
Article 6
Solemn undertaking
Immediately after taking the oath, a Judge shall sign a declaration by which he gives the solemn undertaking provided for in the third paragraph of Article 4 of the Statute.

[10.387]
Article 7
Depriving a Judge of his office
1. Where the Court of Justice is called upon, pursuant to Article 6 of the Statute, to decide, after consulting the General Court, whether a Judge of the General Court no longer fulfils the requisite conditions or no longer meets the obligations arising from his office, the President of the General Court shall invite the Judge concerned to make representations to the General Court, in the absence of the Registrar.
2. The General Court shall state the reasons for its opinion.
3. An opinion to the effect that a Judge of the General Court no longer fulfils the requisite conditions or no longer meets the obligations arising from his office must receive the votes of a majority of the Judges composing the General Court according to Article 48 of the Statute. In that event, particulars of the voting shall be communicated to the Court of Justice.
4. Voting shall be by secret ballot in the absence of the Registrar; the Judge concerned shall not take part in the deliberations.

[10.388]
Article 8
Order of seniority
1. The seniority of Judges shall be calculated according to the date on which they took up their duties.
2. Where there is equal seniority on that basis, the order shall be determined by age.
3. Judges whose terms of office are renewed shall retain their former seniority.

CHAPTER 2
PRESIDENCY OF THE GENERAL COURT

[10.389]
Article 9
Election of the President and of the Vice-President of the General Court
1. The Judges shall, immediately after the partial replacement provided for in the second paragraph of Article 254 TFEU, elect one of their number as President of the General Court for a term of three years.
2. If the office of President of the General Court falls vacant before the normal date of expiry of the term thereof, the General Court shall elect a successor for the remainder of the term.
3. The elections provided for in this Article shall be by secret ballot. The Judge obtaining the votes of more than half the Judges composing the General Court according to Article 48 of the Statute shall be elected. If no Judge obtains that majority, further ballots shall be held until that majority is attained.
4. The Judges shall then elect one of their number as Vice-President of the General Court for a term of three years, in accordance with the procedures laid down in paragraph 3. Paragraph 2 shall apply if the office of the Vice-President of the General Court falls vacant before the normal date of expiry of the term thereof.
5. The names of the President and Vice-President of the General Court elected in accordance with this Article shall be published in the *Official Journal of the European Union*.

[10.390]
Article 10
Responsibilities of the President of the General Court
1. The President of the General Court shall represent the General Court.
2. The President of the General Court shall direct the judicial business and the administration of the General Court.
3. The President of the General Court shall preside at the plenum referred to in Article 42.
4. The President of the General Court shall preside over the Grand Chamber. In that case Article 19 shall apply.
5. If the President of the General Court is attached to a Chamber, he shall preside over that Chamber. In that case Article 19 shall apply.
6. In cases not yet assigned to a formation of the Court, the President of the General Court may adopt the measures of organisation of procedure provided for in Article 89.

[10.391]
Article 11
Responsibilities of the Vice-President of the General Court
1. The Vice-President of the General Court shall assist the President of the General Court in the performance of his duties and shall take the President's place when the latter is prevented from acting.
2. He shall take the President's place, at the latter's request, in performing the duties referred to in Article 10(1) and (2).
3. The General Court shall, by decision, specify the conditions under which the Vice-President of the General Court shall take the place of the President of the General Court in the performance of his judicial duties. That decision shall be published in the *Official Journal of the European Union*.
4. Subject to Article 10(5), if the Vice-President of the General Court is attached to a Chamber, he shall preside over that Chamber. In that case Article 19 shall apply.

[10.392]
Article 12
Where the President and Vice-President of the General Court are prevented from acting
When the President and the Vice-President of the General Court are simultaneously prevented from acting, the functions of President shall be exercised by a President of a Chamber or, failing that, by one of the other Judges, according to the order of seniority laid down in Article 8.

CHAPTER 3
CHAMBERS AND FORMATIONS OF THE COURT

SECTION 1

CONSTITUTION OF THE CHAMBERS AND COMPOSITION OF THE FORMATIONS OF THE COURT

[10.393]
Article 13
Constitution of Chambers
1. The General Court shall set up Chambers sitting with three and with five Judges.
2. The General Court shall decide, on a proposal from the President of the General Court, which Judges shall be attached to the Chambers.

3. The decisions taken in accordance with this Article shall be published in the *Official Journal of the European Union.*

[10.394]
Article 14
Competent formation of the Court

1. Cases before the General Court shall be heard and determined by Chambers sitting with three or with five Judges in accordance with Article 13.
2. Cases may be heard and determined by the Grand Chamber under the conditions laid down in Article 28.
3. Cases may be heard and determined by a single Judge where they are delegated to him under the conditions laid down in Article 29.

[10.395]
Article 15
Composition of the Grand Chamber

1. The Grand Chamber shall be composed of 15 Judges.
2. The General Court shall decide how to designate the Judges composing the Grand Chamber. The decision shall be published in the *Official Journal of the European Union*.

[10.396]
Article 16
Withdrawal and excusing of a Judge

1. Where a Judge considers, in accordance with the first and second paragraphs of Article 18 of the Statute, that he should not take part in the disposal of a case, he shall so inform the President of the General Court who shall exempt him from sitting.
2. Where the President of the General Court considers that a Judge should not, in accordance with the first and second paragraphs of Article 18 of the Statute, take part in the disposal of a case, he shall notify the Judge concerned and shall hear that Judge before giving his decision.
3. In accordance with the third paragraph of Article 18 of the Statute, in the event of any difficulty arising as to the application of this Article, the President of the General Court shall refer the matters referred to in paragraphs 1 and 2 to the plenum. In that case, voting shall be by secret ballot in the absence of the Registrar after the Judge concerned has been heard; the latter shall not take part in the deliberations.

[10.397]
Article 17
Where a member of the formation of the Court is prevented from acting

1. If in the Grand Chamber the number of Judges provided for by Article 15 is not attained as a result of a Judge's being prevented from acting before the deliberations have begun or before the case is pleaded, the President of the General Court shall designate a Judge to complete that Chamber in order to restore the requisite number of Judges.
2. If in a Chamber sitting with three or five Judges the number of Judges provided for is not attained as a result of a Judge's being prevented from acting before the deliberations have begun or before the case is pleaded, the President of that Chamber shall designate another Judge of that Chamber to replace the Judge prevented from acting. If it is not possible to replace the Judge prevented from acting with a Judge of the same Chamber, the President of that Chamber shall notify the President of the General Court, who shall designate, according to the criteria determined by the General Court, another Judge in order to restore the requisite number of Judges. The decision containing those criteria shall be published in the *Official Journal of the European Union*.
3. If the Judge to whom the case has been delegated or assigned as a single Judge is prevented from acting, the President of the General Court shall designate another Judge to replace that Judge.

SECTION 2
PRESIDENTS OF CHAMBERS

[10.398]
Article 18
Election of Presidents of Chambers

1. The Judges shall elect from among their number, in accordance with Article 9(3), the Presidents of the Chambers sitting with three and with five Judges.
2. The Presidents of Chambers sitting with five Judges shall be elected for a term of three years. They may be re-elected once.
3. The Presidents of Chambers sitting with three Judges shall be elected for a defined term.
4. The election of the Presidents of Chambers sitting with five Judges shall take place immediately after the elections of the President and the Vice-President of the General Court provided for in Article 9.
5. If the office of the President of a Chamber falls vacant before the normal date of expiry of the term thereof, the Judges shall elect a successor for the remainder of the term.

6. The names of the Presidents of Chambers elected in accordance with this Article shall be published in the *Official Journal of the European Union.*

[10.399]
Article 19
Powers of the President of a Chamber

1. The President of a Chamber shall exercise the powers conferred on him by these Rules after hearing the Judge-Rapporteur.
2. The President of a Chamber may refer any decision falling within his remit to the Chamber.

[10.400]
Article 20
Where the President of a Chamber is prevented from acting

Without prejudice to Article 10(5) and Article 11(4), when the President of a Chamber is prevented from acting, his functions shall be exercised by a Judge of that formation of the Court according to the order laid down in Article 8.

SECTION 3
DELIBERATIONS

[10.401]
Article 21
Procedures concerning deliberations

1. The deliberations of the General Court shall be and shall remain secret.
2. When a hearing has taken place, only those Judges who participated in that hearing shall take part in the deliberations.
3. Every Judge taking part in the deliberations shall state his opinion and the reasons for it.
4. The conclusions reached by the majority of the Judges after final discussion shall determine the decision of the General Court. Votes shall be cast in reverse order to the order laid down in Article 8, with the exception of the Judge-Rapporteur who shall vote first and the President who shall vote last.

[10.402]
Article 22
Number of Judges taking part in the deliberations

Where, as a result of a Judge's being prevented from acting, there is an even number of Judges, the most junior Judge for the purposes of Article 8 shall abstain from taking part in the deliberations unless he is the President or the Judge-Rapporteur. In the latter case, the Judge immediately senior to him shall abstain from taking part in the deliberations.

[10.403]
Article 23
Quorum of the Grand Chamber

1. Decisions of the Grand Chamber shall be valid only if 11 Judges are sitting.
2. If, as a result of a Judge's being prevented from acting, that quorum has not been attained, the President of the General Court shall designate another Judge in order to attain the quorum of the Grand Chamber.
3. If the quorum is no longer attained but the hearing has taken place, the Judge prevented from acting shall be replaced as provided in paragraph 2 and a new hearing shall be organised at the request of a main party. It may also be organised by the General Court of its own motion. A new hearing must be held if measures of inquiry have been adopted in accordance with Article 91(a) and (d) and Article 96(2). If no new hearing is organised, Article 21(2) shall not apply.

[10.404]
Article 24
Quorum of the Chambers sitting with three or with five Judges

1. Decisions of the Chambers sitting with three or with five Judges shall be valid only if three Judges are sitting.
2. If, as a result of a Judge's being prevented from acting, the quorum has not been attained in a Chamber sitting with three or with five Judges, the President of that Chamber shall designate another Judge of the same Chamber to replace the Judge prevented from acting. If it is not possible to replace the Judge prevented from acting with a Judge of the same Chamber, the President of the Chamber concerned shall notify the President of the General Court, who shall designate, according to the criteria determined by the General Court, another Judge in order to attain the quorum of the Chamber. The decision containing those criteria shall be published in the *Official Journal of the European Union*.
3. If the quorum is no longer attained but the hearing has taken place, the Judge prevented from acting shall be replaced as provided in paragraph 2 and a new hearing shall be organised at the request of a main party. It may also be organised by the General Court of its own motion. A new

hearing must be held if measures of inquiry have been adopted in accordance with Article 91(a) and (d) and Article 96(2). A new hearing must be held if more than one Judge who took part in the original hearing has to be replaced. If no new hearing is organised, Article 21(2) shall not apply.

CHAPTER 4
ASSIGNMENT AND REASSIGNMENT OF CASES, DESIGNATION OF JUDGE-RAPPORTEURS, REFERRAL TO FORMATIONS OF THE COURT AND DELEGATION TO A SINGLE JUDGE

[10.405]
Article 25
Assignment criteria

1. The General Court shall lay down criteria by which cases are to be allocated among the Chambers. The General Court may make one or more Chambers responsible for hearing and determining cases in specific matters.
2. The decision shall be published in the *Official Journal of the European Union*.

[10.406]
Article 26
First assignment of a case and designation of the Judge-Rapporteur

1. As soon as possible after the document initiating proceedings has been lodged, the President of the General Court shall assign the case to a Chamber according to the criteria laid down by the General Court in accordance with Article 25.
2. The President of the Chamber shall propose to the President of the General Court, in respect of each case assigned to the Chamber, the designation of a Judge to act as Rapporteur. The President of the General Court shall decide on the proposal.
3. If in any Chamber sitting with three or with five Judges the number of Judges assigned to that Chamber is higher than three or five respectively, the President of the Chamber shall decide which of the Judges will be called upon to take part in the judgment of the case.

[10.407]
Article 27
Designation of a new Judge-Rapporteur and reassignment of a case

1. If the Judge-Rapporteur is prevented from acting, the President of the competent formation of the Court shall notify the President of the General Court, who shall designate a new Judge-Rapporteur. If the new Judge-Rapporteur is not attached to the Chamber to which the case was first assigned, the case shall be heard and determined by the Chamber in which the new Judge-Rapporteur sits.
2. In order to take account of a connection between cases on the basis of their subject-matter, the President of the General Court may, by reasoned decision and after consulting the Judge-Rapporteurs concerned, reassign the cases to enable the same Judge-Rapporteur to conduct preparatory inquiries in all the cases concerned. If the Judge-Rapporteur to whom the cases have been reassigned does not belong to the Chamber to which the cases were first assigned, the cases shall be heard and determined by the Chamber in which the new Judge-Rapporteur sits.
3. In the interests of the proper administration of justice, and by way of exception, the President of the General Court may, before the presentation of the preliminary report referred to in Article 87, by reasoned decision and after consulting the Judges concerned, designate another Judge-Rapporteur. If that Judge-Rapporteur is not attached to the Chamber to which the case was first assigned, the case shall be heard and determined by the Chamber in which the new Judge-Rapporteur sits.
4. Before designating the Judge-Rapporteur as provided in paragraphs 1 to 3, the President of the General Court shall seek the views of the Presidents of the Chambers concerned.
5. Where the composition of the Chambers has changed as a result of a decision of the General Court on the assignment of Judges to Chambers, a case shall be heard and determined by the Chamber in which the Judge-Rapporteur sits following that decision, unless the deliberations have commenced or the oral part of the procedure has been opened.

[10.408]
Article 28
Referral to a Chamber sitting with a different number of Judges

1. Whenever the legal difficulty or the importance of the case or special circumstances so justify, a case may be referred to the Grand Chamber or to a Chamber sitting with a different number of Judges.
2. The Chamber seised of the case or the President of the General Court may, at any stage in the proceedings, either of its or his own motion or at the request of a main party, propose to the plenum that the case be referred as provided for in paragraph 1.
3. The decision to refer a case to a formation sitting with a greater number of Judges shall be taken by the plenum.
4. The decision to refer a case to a formation sitting with a lesser number of Judges shall be taken by the plenum, after the main parties have been heard.

5. The case shall be heard and determined by a Chamber sitting with at least five Judges where a Member State or an institution of the Union which is a party to the proceedings so requests.

[10.409]

Article 29

Delegation to a single Judge

1. The following cases assigned to a Chamber sitting with three Judges may be heard and determined by the Judge-Rapporteur sitting as a single Judge where, having regard to the lack of difficulty of the questions of law or fact raised, to the limited importance of those cases and to the absence of other special circumstances, they are suitable for being so heard and determined and have been delegated under the conditions laid down in this Article:

(a) cases referred to in Article 171 below;

(b) [cases brought pursuant to the fourth paragraph of Article 263 TFEU, the third paragraph of Article 265 TFEU, Article 268 TFEU and Article 270 TFEU] that raise only questions already clarified by established case-law or that form part of a series of cases in which the same relief is sought and of which one has already been finally decided;

(c) cases brought pursuant to Article 272 TFEU.

2. Delegation to the single Judge shall not be possible:

(a) in an action for annulment against an act of general application or in cases in which a plea of illegality is expressly raised against an act of general application;

[(b) in an action brought pursuant to Article 270 TFEU in which a plea of illegality is expressly raised against an act of general application, unless the Court of Justice or the General Court has already given a ruling on the issues raised by that plea;]

[(c)] in cases concerning the implementation of the rules:

— on competition and on control of concentrations,

— relating to aid granted by States,

— relating to measures to protect trade,

— relating to the common organisation of the agricultural markets, with the exception of cases that form part of a series of cases in which the same relief is sought and of which one has already been finally decided.

3. The decision relating to the delegation of a case to the single Judge shall be taken, after the main parties have been heard, by the Chamber sitting with three Judges before which the case is pending. Where a Member State or an institution of the Union which is a party to the proceedings objects to the case being heard and determined by the single Judge the case shall be maintained before the Chamber to which the Judge-Rapporteur belongs.

4. The single Judge shall refer the case back to the Chamber if he finds that the conditions justifying its delegation are no longer satisfied.

NOTES

The words in square brackets in sub-para 1(b) were substituted, sub-para 2(c) was designated as such (it was formerly sub-para 2(b)), and a new sub-para 2(b) was inserted, by the Amendment to the Rules of Procedure of the General Court, Article 1(2) (OJ L217, 12.8.2016, p 73).

CHAPTER 5
DESIGNATION OF ADVOCATES GENERAL

[10.410]

Article 30

Circumstances in which an Advocate General may be designated

The General Court may be assisted by an Advocate General if it is considered that the legal difficulty or the factual complexity of the case so requires.

[10.411]

Article 31

Procedures concerning the designation of an Advocate General

1. The decision to designate an Advocate General in a particular case shall be taken by the plenum at the request of the Chamber to which the case has been assigned or referred.

2. The President of the General Court shall designate the Judge called upon to perform the function of Advocate General in that case.

3. After being so designated, the Advocate General shall be heard before the decisions provided for in Articles 16, 28, 45, 68, 70, 83, 87, 90, 92, 98, 103, 105, 106, 113, 126 to 132, 144, 151, 165, 168, 169 and 207 to 209 are taken.

CHAPTER 6
REGISTRY

SECTION 1
THE REGISTRAR

[10.412]
Article 32
Appointment of the Registrar

1. The General Court shall appoint the Registrar.
2. When the post of Registrar is vacant, an advertisement shall be published in the *Official Journal of the European Union*. Interested persons shall be invited to submit their applications within a period of not less than three weeks, accompanied by full details of their nationality, university degrees, knowledge of languages, present and past professional activities, and experience, if any, in judicial and international fields.
3. Voting shall take place in accordance with the procedure laid down in Article 9(3).
4. The Registrar shall be appointed for a term of six years. He may be reappointed. The General Court may decide to renew the term of office of the incumbent Registrar without availing itself of the procedure laid down in paragraph 2. In that case paragraph 3 shall apply.
5. The Registrar shall take the oath set out in Article 5 and sign the declaration provided for in Article 6.
6. The Registrar may be deprived of his office only if he no longer fulfils the requisite conditions or no longer meets the obligations arising from his office. The General Court shall take its decision, in the absence of the Registrar, after giving him an opportunity to make representations.
7. If the office of Registrar falls vacant before the normal date of expiry of the term thereof, the General Court shall appoint a new Registrar for a term of six years.
8. The name of the Registrar elected in accordance with this Article shall be published in the *Official Journal of the European Union*.

[10.413]
Article 33
Deputy Registrar

The General Court may, in accordance with the procedure laid down in respect of the Registrar, appoint one or more Deputy Registrars to assist the Registrar and to take his place if he is prevented from acting.

[10.414]
Article 34
Where the Registrar and Deputy Registrar are prevented from acting

Where the Registrar is prevented from acting and, if necessary, where the Deputy Registrar is so prevented, the President of the General Court shall designate an official or servant to carry out the duties of Registrar.

[10.415]
Article 35
Responsibilities of the Registrar

1. The Registrar shall be responsible, under the authority of the President of the General Court, for the acceptance, transmission and custody of all documents and for effecting service as provided for by these Rules.
2. The Registrar shall assist the Members of the General Court in all their official functions.
3. The Registrar shall have custody of the seals and shall be responsible for the records. He shall be in charge of the publications of the General Court, in particular, the European Court Reports, and of the dissemination on the internet of documents concerning the General Court.
4. The Registrar shall be responsible, under the authority of the President of the General Court, for the administration of the General Court, its financial management and its accounts, and shall be assisted in this by the departments of the Court of Justice of the European Union.
5. Save as otherwise provided in these Rules, the Registrar shall attend the sittings of the General Court.

[10.416]
Article 36
Keeping of the register

1. There shall be kept in the Registry, under the responsibility of the Registrar, a register in which all procedural documents shall be entered in the order in which they are lodged.
2. When a document has been registered, the Registrar shall make a note to that effect on the original procedural document or on the version deemed to be the original of that document for the purposes of decisions adopted pursuant to Article 74, and, if a party so requests, on any copy submitted for the purpose.
3. Entries in the register and the notes provided for in paragraph 2 shall be authentic.

[10.417]
Article 37
Consultation of the register

Anyone may consult the register at the Registry and obtain copies or extracts on payment of a charge on a scale fixed by the General Court on a proposal from the Registrar.

[10.418]
Article 38
Access to the file in the case

1. Subject to the provisions of Article 68(4), Articles 103 to 105 and of Article 144(7), any party to the proceedings may have access to the file in the case and, on payment of the appropriate charge referred to in Article 37, may obtain copies of procedural documents and authenticated copies of orders and judgments.
2. No third party, private or public, may have access to the file in a case without the express authorisation of the President of the General Court, once the parties have been heard. That authorisation may be granted, in whole or in part, only upon written request accompanied by a detailed explanation of the third party's legitimate interest in having access to the file.

SECTION 2
OTHER DEPARTMENTS

[10.419]
Article 39
Officials and other servants

1. [The officials and other servants whose task is to assist directly the President, the Judges and the Registrar shall be appointed under the conditions laid down by the Staff Regulations]. They shall be responsible to the Registrar, under the authority of the President of the General Court.
2. They shall take one of the following two oaths before the President of the General Court in the presence of the Registrar:

> 'I swear that I will perform loyally, discreetly and conscientiously the duties assigned to me by the General Court.'

or

> 'I solemnly and sincerely affirm that I will perform loyally, discreetly and conscientiously the duties assigned to me by the General Court.'

NOTES

Para 1: words in square brackets substituted by the Amendment to the Rules of Procedure of the General Court, Article 1(3) (OJ L217, 12.8.2016, p 73).

CHAPTER 7
THE WORKING OF THE GENERAL COURT

[10.420]
Article 40
Location of the sittings of the General Court

The General Court may choose to hold one or more specific sittings in a place other than that in which the General Court has its seat.

[10.421]
Article 41
Calendar of the General Court's judicial business

1. The judicial year shall begin on 1 September of each calendar year and end on 31 August of the following year.
2. The judicial vacations shall be determined by the General Court.
3. In a case of urgency, the President of the General Court and the Presidents of Chambers may convene the Judges and, if necessary, the Advocate General during the judicial vacations.
4. The General Court shall observe the official holidays of the place where it has its seat.
5. The General Court may, in proper circumstances, grant leave of absence to any Judge.
6. The dates of the judicial vacations shall be published annually in the *Official Journal of the European Union*.

[10.422]
Article 42
Plenum

1. Decisions concerning administrative issues and the decisions referred to in Articles 7, 9, 11, 13, 15, 16, 18, 25, 28, 31 to 33, 41, 74 and 224 shall be taken by the General Court at the plenum in which all the Judges shall take part and have a vote, save as otherwise provided in these Rules. The Registrar shall be present, unless the General Court decides to the contrary.

2. If, after the plenum has been convened, it is found that the quorum referred to in the fourth paragraph of Article 17 of the Statute has not been attained, the President of the General Court shall adjourn the sitting until there is a quorum.

[10.423]
Article 43
Drawing-up of minutes
1. Where the General Court sits in the presence of the Registrar, the Registrar shall, if necessary, draw up minutes which shall be signed by the President of the General Court or by the President of the Chamber, as the case may be, and by the Registrar.
2. Where the General Court sits without the Registrar being present it shall, if necessary, instruct the most junior Judge for the purposes of Article 8 to draw up minutes which shall be signed by the President of the General Court or by the President of the Chamber, as the case may be, and by that Judge.

TITLE II
LANGUAGES

[10.424]
Article 44
Language of a case
The language of a case shall be Bulgarian, Croatian, Czech, Danish, Dutch, English, Estonian, Finnish, French, German, Greek, Hungarian, Irish, Italian, Latvian, Lithuanian, Maltese, Polish, Portuguese, Romanian, Slovak, Slovenian, Spanish or Swedish.

[10.425]
Article 45
Determination of the language of a case
1. In direct actions within the meaning of Article 1, the language of a case shall be chosen by the applicant, except that:
- (a) where the defendant is a Member State or a natural or legal person having the nationality of a Member State, the language of the case shall be the official language of that State; where that State has more than one official language, the applicant may choose between them;
- (b) at the joint request of the main parties, the use of another of the languages mentioned in Article 44 for all or part of the proceedings may be authorised;
- (c) at the request of one of the parties, and after the other parties have been heard, the use of another of the languages mentioned in Article 44 as the language of the case for all or part of the proceedings may be authorised by way of derogation from subparagraph (b); such a request may not be submitted by an institution.

2. Requests as above shall be decided on by the President; where the latter proposes to accede to a request without the agreement of all the parties, he must refer the request to the General Court.
3. Without prejudice to the provisions of paragraph 1(b) and (c):
- (a) in appeals against decisions of the Civil Service Tribunal as referred to in Articles 9 and 10 of Annex I to the Statute, the language of the case shall be the language of the decision of the Civil Service Tribunal against which the appeal is brought;
- (b) in the case of applications for rectification, applications for the General Court to remedy a failure to adjudicate or for it to set aside judgments by default, third-party proceedings and applications for interpretation or revision of a judgment or in the case of disputes concerning the costs to be recovered, the language of the case shall be the language of the decision to which those applications or disputes relate.

4. Without prejudice to the provisions in paragraph 1(b) and (c), in proceedings brought against decisions of the Boards of Appeal of the Office, referred to in Article 1, with respect to the application of the rules relating to an intellectual property regime:
- (a) the language of the case shall be chosen by the applicant if the applicant was the only party to the proceedings before the Board of Appeal of the Office;
- (b) the language of the application, chosen by the applicant from among the languages referred to in Article 44, shall be the language of the case if another party to the proceedings before the Board of Appeal of the Office does not object to this within the time limit laid down for that purpose by the Registrar after the application has been lodged;
- (c) in the event of an objection to the language of the application by a party to the proceedings before the Board of Appeal of the Office other than the applicant, the language of the decision that is contested before the General Court shall become the language of the case; in such cases, the Registrar shall ensure the translation of the application into the language of the case.

[10.426]
Article 46
Use of the language of the case

1. The language of the case shall in particular be used in the written and oral pleadings of the parties, including the material annexed to them, and also in the minutes and decisions of the General Court.
2. Any material produced or annexed that is expressed in another language must be accompanied by a translation into the language of the case.
3. However, in the case of substantial material, translations may be confined to extracts. At any time the President may, of his own motion or at the request of one of the parties, call for a complete or fuller translation.
4. Notwithstanding the foregoing provisions, a Member State shall be entitled to use its official language when intervening in a case before the General Court. This provision shall apply both to written documents and to oral statements. The Registrar shall arrange in each instance for translation into the language of the case.
5. The States, other than the Member States, which are parties to the EEA Agreement, and also the EFTA Surveillance Authority, may be authorised to use one of the languages mentioned in Article 44, other than the language of the case, when they intervene in a case before the General Court. This provision shall apply both to written documents and to oral statements. The Registrar shall arrange in each instance for translation into the language of the case.
6. Where a witness or expert states that he is unable adequately to express himself in one of the languages referred to in Article 44, the President may authorise him to give his evidence in another language. The Registrar shall arrange for translation into the language of the case.
7. The President in conducting oral proceedings, Judges and, where appropriate, the Advocate General in putting questions and the Advocate General in delivering his Opinion may use one of the languages referred to in Article 44 other than the language of the case. The Registrar shall arrange for translation into the language of the case.

[10.427]
Article 47
Responsibility of the Registrar concerning language arrangements

The Registrar shall, at the request of any Judge, of the Advocate General or of a party, arrange for anything said or written in the course of the proceedings before the General Court to be translated into the languages chosen from those referred to in Article 44.

[10.428]
Article 48
Languages of the publications of the General Court

Publications of the General Court shall be issued in the languages referred to in Article 1 of Council Regulation No 1.

[10.429]
Article 49
Authentic texts

The texts of documents drawn up in the language of the case or, where applicable, in another language authorised pursuant to Articles 45 and 46 of these Rules shall be authentic.

TITLE III
DIRECT ACTIONS

[10.430]
Article 50
Scope

The provisions of this Title shall apply to direct actions within the meaning of Article 1.

CHAPTER 1
GENERAL PROVISIONS

SECTION 1
REPRESENTATION OF THE PARTIES

[10.431]
Article 51
Obligation to be represented

1. A party must be represented by an agent or a lawyer in accordance with the provisions of Article 19 of the Statute.
2. The lawyer representing or assisting a party must lodge at the Registry a certificate that he is authorised to practise before a court of a Member State or of another State which is a party to the EEA Agreement.

3. Where the party represented by the lawyer is a legal person governed by private law, the lawyer must lodge at the Registry an authority to act given by that person.
4. If the documents referred to in paragraphs 2 and 3 are not lodged, the Registrar shall prescribe a reasonable time limit within which the party concerned is to produce them. If the party concerned fails to produce the required documents within the time limit prescribed, the General Court shall decide whether the non-compliance with that procedural requirement renders the application or written pleadings formally inadmissible.

SECTION 2
RIGHTS AND OBLIGATIONS OF PARTIES' REPRESENTATIVES

[10.432]
Article 52
Privileges, immunities and facilities

1. Agents, advisers and lawyers who appear before the General Court or before any judicial authority to which it has addressed letters rogatory shall enjoy immunity in respect of words spoken or written by them concerning the case or the parties.
2. Agents, advisers and lawyers shall also enjoy the following privileges and facilities:
   (a) any papers and documents relating to the proceedings shall be exempt from both search and seizure; in the event of a dispute, the customs officials or police may seal those papers and documents; they shall then be immediately forwarded to the General Court for inspection in the presence of the Registrar and of the person concerned;
   (b) agents, advisers and lawyers shall be entitled to travel in the course of duty without hindrance.

[10.433]
Article 53
Status of the parties' representatives

1. In order to qualify for the privileges, immunities and facilities specified in Article 52, persons entitled to them shall furnish proof of their status as follows:
   (a) agents shall produce an official document issued by the party for whom they act, who shall immediately serve a copy thereof on the Registrar;
   (b) lawyers shall produce a certificate that they are authorised to practise before a court of a Member State or of another State which is a party to the EEA Agreement, and, where the party which they represent is a legal person governed by private law, an authority to act issued by that person;
   (c) advisers shall produce an authority to act issued by the party whom they are assisting.
2. The Registrar shall issue them with a certificate, as required. The validity of this certificate shall be limited to a specified period, which may be extended or curtailed according to the duration of the proceedings.

[10.434]
Article 54
Waiver of immunity

1. The privileges, immunities and facilities specified in Article 52 are granted exclusively in the interests of the proper conduct of proceedings.
2. The General Court may waive immunity where it considers that the proper conduct of proceedings will not be hindered thereby.

[10.435]
Article 55
Exclusion from the proceedings

1. If the General Court considers that the conduct of an agent, adviser or lawyer before the General Court, the President, a Judge or the Registrar is incompatible with the dignity of the General Court or with the requirements of the proper administration of justice, or that such agent, adviser or lawyer is using his rights for purposes other than those for which they were granted, it shall inform the person concerned. The General Court may inform the competent authorities to whom the person concerned is answerable. A copy of the letter sent to those authorities shall be forwarded to the person concerned.
2. On the same grounds, the General Court may at any time, having heard the person concerned, decide to exclude an agent, adviser or lawyer from the proceedings by reasoned order. That order shall have immediate effect.
3. Where an agent, adviser or lawyer is excluded from the proceedings, the proceedings shall be suspended for a period fixed by the President in order to allow the party concerned to appoint another agent, adviser or lawyer.
4. Decisions taken under this Article may be rescinded.

[10.436]
Article 56
University teachers
The provisions of this Section shall apply to the university teachers referred to in the seventh paragraph of Article 19 of the Statute.

SECTION 3
SERVICE

[10.437]
Article 57
Methods of service
1. Without prejudice to Article 77(2) and Article 80(1), where the Statute or these Rules require a document to be served on a person the Registrar shall ensure that service is effected by the method referred to in paragraph 4 or by telefax.
2. Where, for technical reasons or on account of the nature or size of the document, service of the document in accordance with the procedures laid down in paragraph 1 is impossible or impracticable, the document shall be served at the address of the representative of the party concerned by registered post with a form for acknowledgement of receipt or by personal delivery of the copy against a receipt. The addressee shall be so informed by the method referred to in paragraph 4 or by telefax. Service shall then be deemed to have been effected on the addressee by registered post on the tenth day following the lodging of the registered letter at the post office of the place in which the General Court has its seat, unless it is shown by the acknowledgement of receipt that the letter was received on a different date or the addressee informs the Registrar, within three weeks of being informed by the method referred to in paragraph 4 or by telefax, that the document to be served has not reached him.
3. The Registrar shall prepare and certify the copies of documents to be served pursuant to paragraph 2, save where the parties themselves supply the copies in accordance with Article 73(2).
4. The General Court may, by decision, determine the criteria for a procedural document to be served by electronic means. That decision shall be published in the *Official Journal of the European Union*.

SECTION 4
TIME LIMITS

[10.438]
Article 58
Calculation of time limits
1. Any procedural time limit prescribed by the Treaties, the Statute or these Rules shall be calculated as follows:

(a) where a time limit expressed in days, weeks, months or years is to be calculated from the moment at which an event occurs or an action takes place, the day during which that event occurs or that action takes place shall not be counted as falling within the time limit in question;
(b) a time limit expressed in weeks, months or years shall end with the expiry of whichever day in the last week, month or year is the same day of the week, or falls on the same date, as the day during which the event or action from which the time limit is to be calculated occurred or took place; if, in a time limit expressed in months or years, the day on which it should expire does not occur in the last month, the time limit shall end with the expiry of the last day of that month;
(c) where a time limit is expressed in months and days, it shall first be calculated in whole months, then in days;
(d) timc limits shall include Saturdays, Sundays and official holidays;
(e) time limits shall not be suspended during the judicial vacations.

2. If the time limit would otherwise end on a Saturday, Sunday or an official holiday, it shall be extended until the end of the next working day.
3. The list of official holidays drawn up by the Court of Justice and published in the *Official Journal of the European Union* shall apply to the General Court.

[10.439]
Article 59
Proceedings against a measure adopted by an institution and published in the Official Journal of the European Union
Where the time limit allowed for initiating proceedings against a measure adopted by an institution runs from the publication of that measure in the *Official Journal of the European Union*, that time limit shall be calculated, for the purposes of Article 58(1)(a), from the end of the fourteenth day after such publication.

[10.440]
Article 60
Extension on account of distance

The procedural time limits shall be extended on account of distance by a single period of 10 days.

[10.441]
Article 61
Setting and extension of time limits

1. Any time limit prescribed pursuant to these Rules may be extended by whoever prescribed it.
2. The President may delegate to the Registrar power of signature for the purposes of setting certain time limits which, pursuant to these Rules, it falls to the President to prescribe, or of extending such time limits.

[10.442]
Article 62
Procedural documents lodged out of time

A procedural document lodged at the Registry after expiry of the time limit set by the President or by the Registrar pursuant to these Rules may be accepted only pursuant to a decision of the President to that effect.

SECTION 5
CONDUCT OF THE PROCEEDINGS AND PROCEDURES FOR DEALING WITH CASES

[10.443]
Article 63
Conduct of the proceedings

Without prejudice to the special provisions laid down in the Statute or in these Rules, the procedure before the General Court shall consist of a written part and an oral part.

[10.444]
Article 64
Adversarial nature of the proceedings

Subject to the provisions of Article 68(4), Article 104, Article 105(8) and Article 144(7), the General Court shall take into consideration only those procedural documents and items which have been made available to the representatives of the parties and on which they have been given an opportunity of expressing their views.

[10.445]
Article 65
Service of procedural documents and of decisions taken in the course of proceedings

1. Subject to the provisions of Article 68(4), Articles 103 to 105 and Article 144(7), procedural documents and items included in the file in the case shall be served on the parties.
2. The Registrar shall ensure that decisions taken in the course of the proceedings and included in the file in the case are brought to the attention of the parties.

[10.446]
Article 66
Anonymity and omission of certain information vis-à-vis the public

On a reasoned application by a party, made by a separate document, or of its own motion, the General Court may omit the name of a party to the dispute or of other persons mentioned in connection with the proceedings, or certain information, from those documents relating to a case to which the public has access if there are legitimate reasons for keeping the identity of a person or the information confidential.

[10.447]
Article 67
Order in which cases are dealt with

1. The General Court shall deal with the cases before it in the order in which they become ready for examination.
2. The President may in special circumstances decide that a case be given priority over others.

[10.448]
Article 68
Joinder

1. Two or more cases concerning the same subject-matter may at any time, either of the General Court's own motion or on application by a main party, be joined, on account of the connection between them, for the purposes, alternatively or cumulatively, of the written or oral part of the procedure or of the decision which closes the proceedings.
2. A decision on whether cases should be joined shall be taken by the President. Before taking that decision, the President shall prescribe a time limit within which the main parties may submit their observations on any joinder, if they have not already expressed their views in that regard.

3. Joined cases may be disjoined, in accordance with the provisions of paragraph 2.
4. All the parties to the joined cases may examine the files in the cases concerned at the Registry. The President may, however, on application by a party, order that certain confidential information from the case-file be excluded from that consultation.
5. Without prejudice to paragraph 4, procedural documents included in the files of the cases concerned by the joinder shall be served on the parties to the joined cases, provided that the representatives of those parties request it and have agreed to the method of service referred to in Article 57(4).

[10.449]
Article 69
Circumstances in which proceedings may be stayed
Without prejudice to Article 163, proceedings may be stayed:
- (a) in the circumstances specified in the third paragraph of Article 54 of the Statute;
- (b) where an appeal is brought before the Court of Justice against a decision of the General Court disposing of the substantive issues in part only, disposing of a procedural issue concerning a plea of lack of competence or inadmissibility or dismissing an application to intervene;
- (c) at the request of a main party with the agreement of the other main party;
- (d) in other particular cases where the proper administration of justice so requires.

[10.450]
Article 70
Decisions to stay and to resume proceedings
1. The decision to stay the proceedings shall be taken by the President. Before taking that decision, the President shall prescribe a time limit within which the main parties may submit their observations on any stay of the proceedings, if they have not already expressed their views in that regard.
2. A decision ordering that the proceedings be resumed before the end of the stay, or as referred to in Article 71(3), shall be taken in accordance with the procedures laid down in paragraph 1.

[10.451]
Article 71
Length and effects of a stay
1. The stay of proceedings shall take effect on the date indicated in the decision to stay or, in the absence of such indication, on the date of that decision.
2. During the period in which proceedings are stayed all procedural time limits shall be suspended, except for the time limit prescribed in Article 143(1) for an application to intervene.
3. Where the decision to stay the proceedings does not fix the length of stay, it shall end on the date indicated in the decision to resume the proceedings or, in the absence of such indication, on the date of the latter decision.
4. From the date of the resumption of proceedings following a stay, any suspended procedural time limits shall be replaced by new time limits and time shall begin to run from the date of that resumption.

CHAPTER 2
PROCEDURAL DOCUMENTS

[10.452]
Article 72
Common rules for the lodging of procedural documents
1. A procedural document shall be lodged at the Registry either in paper form, where appropriate after transmission of a copy of the original of that document by telefax in accordance with Article 73(3), or by the method referred to in the decision of the General Court adopted pursuant to Article 74.
2. All procedural documents shall bear a date. In the calculation of procedural time limits, only the date and time in the Grand Duchy of Luxembourg of lodgement at the Registry shall be taken into account.
3. To every procedural document there shall be annexed the material relied on in support of it, together with a schedule listing each item.
4. Where, in view of the length of the material, only extracts from it are annexed to the procedural document, the whole item or a full copy of it shall be lodged at the Registry.
5. The institutions shall produce, within time limits laid down by the President, translations of any procedural document into the other languages provided for by Article 1 of Council Regulation No 1.

[10.453]
Article 73
Lodging at the Registry of a procedural document in paper form

1. The original paper version of a procedural document must bear the handwritten signature of the party's agent or lawyer.

2. The original, accompanied by all annexes referred to therein, shall be submitted together with three copies for the General Court and a copy for every other party to the proceedings. Copies shall be certified by the party lodging them.

3. By way of derogation from the second sentence of Article 72(2), the date on and time at which a full copy of the signed original of a procedural document, including the schedule of items referred to in Article 72(3), is received at the Registry by telefax shall be deemed to be the date and time of lodgement for the purposes of compliance with the procedural time limits, provided that the signed original of the procedural document, accompanied by the annexes and copies referred to in paragraph 2, is lodged at the Registry no later than 10 days thereafter. Article 60 shall not apply to that time limit of 10 days.

[10.454]
Article 74
Electronic lodgement

The General Court may, by decision, determine the criteria for a procedural document sent to the Registry by electronic means to be deemed to be the original of that document. That decision shall be published in the *Official Journal of the European Union*.

[10.455]
Article 75
Length of written pleadings

1. The General Court shall set, in accordance with Article 224, the maximum length of written pleadings lodged pursuant to this Title.

2. Authorisation to exceed the maximum length of written pleadings may be given by the President only in cases involving particularly complex legal or factual issues.

CHAPTER 3
WRITTEN PART OF THE PROCEDURE

[10.456]
Article 76
Content of the application

An application of the kind referred to in Article 21 of the Statute shall contain:

(a) the name and address of the applicant;
(b) particulars of the status and address of the applicant's representative;
(c) the name of the main party against whom the action is brought;
(d) the subject-matter of the proceedings, the pleas in law and arguments relied on and a summary of those pleas in law;
(e) the form of order sought by the applicant;
(f) where appropriate, any evidence produced or offered.

[10.457]
Article 77
Information relating to service

1. For the purposes of the proceedings, the application shall state whether the method of service to which the applicant's representative agrees is that referred to in Article 57(4) or telefax.

2. If the application does not comply with the requirements referred to in paragraph 1, all service on the party concerned for the purposes of the proceedings shall be effected, for so long as the defect has not been cured, by registered letter addressed to the representative of that party. Service shall then be deemed to be duly effected by the lodging of the registered letter at the post office of the place in which the General Court has its seat.

[10.458]
Article 78
Annexes to the application

1. The application shall be accompanied, where appropriate, by the documents specified in the second paragraph of Article 21 of the Statute.

[2. An application submitted pursuant to Article 270 TFEU shall be accompanied, where appropriate, by the complaint within the meaning of Article 90(2) of the Staff Regulations and the decision responding to the complaint, together with an indication of the dates on which the complaint was submitted and the decision notified.]

[3]. An application submitted under Article 272 TFEU pursuant to an arbitration clause in a contract governed by public or private law, entered into by the Union or on its behalf, shall be accompanied by a copy of the contract which contains that clause.

[4]. An application made by a legal person governed by private law shall be accompanied by recent proof of that person's existence in law (extract from the register of companies, firms or associations or any other official document).
[5]. The application shall be accompanied by the documents referred to in Article 51(2) and (3).
[6]. If the application does not comply with the requirements set out in [paragraphs 1 to 5], the Registrar shall prescribe a reasonable time limit within which the applicant is to produce the abovementioned documents. If the applicant fails to put the application in order within the time limit prescribed, the General Court shall decide whether the non-compliance with these conditions renders the application formally inadmissible.

NOTES

The original paras 2–5 were renumbered as paras 3–6, a new para 2 was inserted, and the words in square brackets in para 6 (as so renumbered) were substituted, by the Amendment to the Rules of Procedure of the General Court, Article 1(4) (OJ L217, 12.8.2016, p 73).

[10.459]
Article 79
Notice in the Official Journal of the European Union

A notice shall be published in the *Official Journal of the European Union* indicating the date of lodging of an application initiating proceedings, the names of the main parties, the form of order sought by the applicant and a summary of the pleas in law and of the main supporting arguments.

[10.460]
Article 80
Service of the application

1. The application shall be served on the defendant in the form of a certified copy sent by registered post with a form for acknowledgement of receipt or by personal delivery of the copy against a receipt. Where the defendant has previously agreed to applications being served on him by the method referred to in Article 57(4) or by telefax, service of the application may be effected accordingly.
2. In cases where [Article 78(6)] applies, service shall be effected as soon as the application has been put in order or the General Court has declared it admissible notwithstanding the failure to observe the requirements set out in that Article.

NOTES

Para 2: words in square brackets substituted by the Amendment to the Rules of Procedure of the General Court, Article 1(5) (OJ L217, 12.8.2016, p 73).

[10.461]
Article 81
Defence

1. Within two months after service on him of the application, the defendant shall lodge a defence, containing:
   (a) the name and address of the defendant;
   (b) particulars of the status and address of the applicant's representative;
   (c) the pleas in law and arguments relied on;
   (d) the form of order sought by the defendant;
   (e) where appropriate, any evidence produced or offered.
2. Article 77 and [Article 78(4) to (6)] shall apply to the defence.
3. The time limit laid down in paragraph 1 of this Article may, in exceptional circumstances, be extended by the President at the reasoned request of the defendant.

NOTES

Para 2: words in square brackets substituted by the Amendment to the Rules of Procedure of the General Court, Article 1(6) (OJ L217, 12.8.2016, p 73).

[10.462]
Article 82
Transmission of documents

Where the European Parliament, the Council or the European Commission is not a party to a case, the General Court shall send to them copies of the application and of the defence, without the annexes thereto, to enable them to assess whether the inapplicability of one of their acts is being invoked under Article 277 TFEU.

[10.463]
Article 83
Reply and rejoinder

1. The application initiating proceedings and the defence may be supplemented by a reply from the applicant and by a rejoinder from the defendant unless the General Court decides that a second exchange of pleadings is unnecessary because the contents of the file in the case are sufficiently comprehensive.

2. Where the General Court decides that a second exchange of pleadings is unnecessary it may authorise the main parties to supplement the file in the case if the applicant presents a reasoned request to that effect within two weeks from the service of that decision.

3. The President shall prescribe the time limits within which those procedural documents are to be produced. He may specify the matters to which the reply or the rejoinder should relate.

CHAPTER 4
PLEAS IN LAW, EVIDENCE AND MODIFICATION OF THE APPLICATION

[10.464]
Article 84
New pleas in law

1. No new plea in law may be introduced in the course of proceedings unless it is based on matters of law or of fact which come to light in the course of the procedure.

2. Any new pleas in law shall be introduced in the second exchange of pleadings and identified as such. Where the matters of law or of fact justifying the introduction of new pleas in law are known after the second exchange of pleadings or after it has been decided not to authorise a second exchange of pleadings, the main party concerned shall introduce the new pleas in law as soon as those matters come to his knowledge.

3. Without prejudice to the decision to be taken by the General Court on the admissibility of the new pleas in law, the President shall give the other parties an opportunity to respond to those pleas.

[10.465]
Article 85
Evidence produced or offered

1. Evidence produced or offered shall be submitted in the first exchange of pleadings.

2. In reply or rejoinder a main party may produce or offer further evidence in support of his arguments, provided that the delay in the submission of such evidence is justified.

3. The main parties may, exceptionally, produce or offer further evidence before the oral part of the procedure is closed or before the decision of the General Court to rule without an oral part of the procedure, provided that the delay in the submission of such evidence is justified.

4. Without prejudice to the decision to be taken by the General Court on the admissibility of the evidence produced or offered pursuant to paragraphs 2 and 3, the President shall give the other parties an opportunity to comment on such evidence.

[10.466]
Article 86
Modification of the application

1. Where a measure the annulment of which is sought is replaced or amended by another measure with the same subject-matter, the applicant may, before the oral part of the procedure is closed, or before the decision of the General Court to rule without an oral part of the procedure, modify the application to take account of that new factor.

2. The modification of the application must be made by a separate document within the time limit laid down in the sixth paragraph of Article 263 TFEU within which the annulment of the measure justifying the modification of the application may be sought.

[3. In cases brought pursuant to Article 270 TFEU, the modification of the application must be made by a separate document and, by way of derogation from paragraph 2, within the time limit laid down in Article 91(3) of the Staff Regulations within which the annulment of the measure justifying the modification of the application may be sought.]

[4]. The statement of modification shall contain:

(a) the modified form of order sought;

(b) where appropriate, the modified pleas in law and arguments;

(c) where appropriate, the evidence produced and offered in connection with the modification of the form of order sought.

[5]. The statement of modification must be accompanied by the measure justifying the modification of the application. If that measure is not produced, the Registrar shall prescribe a reasonable time limit within which the applicant is to produce it. If the applicant fails to produce the measure within the time limit prescribed, the General Court shall decide whether the non-compliance with that requirement renders the statement modifying the application inadmissible.

[6]. Without prejudice to the decision to be taken by the General Court on the admissibility of the statement modifying the application, the President shall prescribe a time limit within which the defendant may respond to the statement of modification.

[7]. The President shall, where appropriate, prescribe a time limit within which any interveners may supplement their statements in intervention in the light of the statement modifying the application and the statement in response. Those statements shall be served simultaneously on the interveners for that purpose.

NOTES

The original paras 3–6 were renumbered as paras 4–7, and a new para 3 was inserted, by the Amendment to the Rules of Procedure of the General Court, Article 1(7) (OJ L217, 12.8.2016, p 73).

CHAPTER 5
THE PRELIMINARY REPORT

[10.467]
Article 87
Preliminary report

1. When the written part of the procedure is closed, the President shall fix a date on which the Judge-Rapporteur is to present a preliminary report to the General Court.
2. The preliminary report shall contain an analysis of the relevant issues of fact and of law raised by the action, proposals as to whether measures of organisation of procedure or measures of inquiry should be undertaken, whether there should be an oral part of the procedure and whether the case should be referred to the Grand Chamber or to a Chamber sitting with a different number of Judges, and whether the case should be delegated to a single Judge.
3. The General Court shall decide what action to take on the proposals of the Judge-Rapporteur and, where appropriate, whether to open the oral part of the procedure.

CHAPTER 6
MEASURES OF ORGANISATION OF PROCEDURE AND MEASURES OF INQUIRY

[10.468]
Article 88
General

1. Measures of organisation of procedure and measures of inquiry may be taken or modified at any stage of the proceedings either of the General Court's own motion or on the application of a main party.
2. The application referred to in paragraph 1 must state precisely the purpose of the measures sought and the reasons for them. Where the application is made after the first exchange of pleadings, the party submitting that application must state the reasons for which he was unable to submit it earlier.
3. Where an application for measures of organisation of procedure or for measures of inquiry is made, the President shall give the other parties an opportunity to comment on that application.

SECTION 1
MEASURES OF ORGANISATION OF PROCEDURE

[10.469]
Article 89
Purpose

1. The purpose of measures of organisation of procedure shall be to ensure that cases are prepared for hearing, procedures carried out and disputes resolved under the best possible conditions.
2. Measures of organisation of procedure shall, in particular, have as their purpose:
   (a) to ensure the efficient conduct of the written or oral part of the procedure and to facilitate the taking of evidence;
   (b) to determine the points on which the parties must present further argument or which call for measures of inquiry;
   (c) to clarify the forms of order sought by the parties, their pleas in law and arguments and the points at issue between them;
   (d) to facilitate the amicable settlement of proceedings.
3. Measures of organisation of procedure may, in particular, consist of:
   (a) putting questions to the parties;
   (b) inviting the parties to make written or oral submissions on certain aspects of the proceedings;
   (c) asking the parties or third parties for the information referred to in the second paragraph of Article 24 of the Statute;
   (d) asking the parties to produce any material relating to the case;
   (e) summoning the parties to meetings.
4. Where a hearing is organised, the General Court shall, in so far as possible, invite the parties to concentrate in their oral pleadings on one or more specified issues.

[10.470]
Article 90
Procedure

1. Measures of organisation of procedure shall be prescribed by the General Court.
2. If the General Court decides to adopt measures of organisation of procedure and does not undertake such measures itself, it shall entrust the task of so doing to the Judge-Rapporteur.

SECTION 2
MEASURES OF INQUIRY

[10.471]
Article 91
Purpose

Without prejudice to Articles 24 and 25 of the Statute, the following measures of inquiry may be adopted:

(a) the personal appearance of the parties;
(b) a request to a party for information or for production of any material relating to the case;
(c) a request for production of documents to which access has been denied by an institution in proceedings relating to the legality of that denial;
(d) oral testimony;
(e) the commissioning of an expert's report;
(f) an inspection of the place or thing in question.

[10.472]
Article 92
Procedure

1. The General Court shall prescribe the measures of inquiry that it considers appropriate by means of an order setting out the facts to be proved.
2. Before the General Court decides on the measures of inquiry referred to in Article 91(d) to (f), the parties shall be heard.
3. A measure of inquiry referred to in Article 91(b) may be ordered only where the party concerned by the measure has not complied with a measure of organisation of procedure previously adopted to that end, or where expressly requested by the party concerned by the measure and that party explains the need for such a measure to be in the form of an order for a measure of inquiry. The order prescribing the measure of inquiry may provide that inspection by the parties' representatives of information and material obtained by the General Court in consequence of that order may take place only at the Registry and that no copies may be made.
4. If the General Court orders a preparatory inquiry and does not undertake such an inquiry itself, it shall entrust the task of so doing to the Judge-Rapporteur.
5. The Advocate General shall take part in the measures of inquiry.
6. The parties shall be entitled to attend the measures of inquiry.
7. Evidence may be submitted in rebuttal and previous evidence may be amplified.

[10.473]
Article 93
Summoning of witnesses

1. Witnesses whose examination is deemed necessary shall be summoned by an order, referred to in Article 92(1), containing the following information:
   (a) the name, description and address of the witness;
   (b) the date and place of the examination;
   (c) an indication of the facts to be established and which witnesses are to be heard in respect of each of those facts.
2. Witnesses shall be summoned by the General Court, where appropriate after lodgement of the security provided for in Article 100(1).

[10.474]
Article 94
Examination of witnesses

1. After the identity of the witness has been established, the President shall inform him that he will be required to vouch the truth of his evidence in the manner laid down in paragraph 5 and in Article 97.
2. The witness shall give his evidence to the General Court, the parties having been given notice to attend. After the witness has given his evidence the President may, at the request of one of the parties or of his own motion, put questions to him.
3. The other Judges and the Advocate General may do likewise.
4. Subject to the control of the President, questions may be put to witnesses by the representatives of the parties.
5. Subject to the provisions of Article 97, the witness shall, after giving his evidence, take the following oath:

'I swear that I have spoken the truth, the whole truth and nothing but the truth.'

6. The General Court may, after hearing the main parties, exempt a witness from taking the oath.

[10.475]
Article 95
Duties of witnesses

1. Witnesses who have been duly summoned shall obey the summons and attend for examination.
2. If, without good reason, a witness who has been duly summoned fails to appear before the General Court, the General Court may impose upon him a pecuniary penalty not exceeding EUR 5,000 and may order that a further summons be served on the witness at his own expense.
3. The same penalty may be imposed upon a witness who, without good reason, refuses to give evidence or to take the oath.

[10.476]
Article 96
Expert's report

1. The order appointing the expert shall define his task and set a time limit within which he is to submit his report.
2. After the expert has submitted his report and that report has been served on the parties, the General Court may order that the expert be examined, the parties having been given notice to attend. At the request of one of the parties or of his own motion, the President may put questions to the expert.
3. The other Judges and the Advocate General may do likewise.
4. Subject to the control of the President, questions may be put to the expert by the representatives of the parties.
5. Subject to the provisions of Article 97, the expert shall, after making his report, take the following oath before the General Court:

'I swear that I have conscientiously and impartially carried out my task.'

6. The General Court may, after hearing the main parties, exempt the expert from taking the oath.

[10.477]
Article 97
Witnesses' and experts' oath

1. The President shall instruct any person who is required to take an oath before the General Court, as witness or expert, to tell the truth or to carry out his task conscientiously and impartially, as the case may be, and shall warn him of the criminal liability provided for in his national law in the event of any breach of this duty.
2. Witnesses and experts shall take the oath either in accordance with Article 94(5) and Article 96(5) or in the manner laid down by their national law.

[10.478]
Article 98
Perjury by witnesses or experts

1. The General Court may decide to report to the competent authority referred to in the Rules supplementing the Rules of Procedure of the Court of Justice of the Member State whose courts have penal jurisdiction any case of perjury on the part of a witness or expert before the General Court.
2. The Registrar shall be responsible for communicating the decision of the General Court. The decision shall set out the facts and circumstances on which the report is based.

[10.479]
Article 99
Objection to a witness or expert

1. If one of the parties objects to a witness or an expert on the ground that he is not a competent or proper person to act as a witness or expert or for any other reason, or if a witness or expert refuses to give evidence or to take the oath, the matter shall be resolved by the General Court.
2. An objection to a witness or an expert shall be raised within two weeks after service of the order summoning the witness or appointing the expert; the statement of objection must set out the grounds of objection and indicate the nature of any evidence offered.

[10.480]
Article 100
Witnesses' and experts' costs

1. Where the General Court orders the examination of witnesses or an expert's report, it may request the main parties or one of them to lodge security for the witnesses' costs or the costs of the expert's report.
2. Witnesses and experts shall be entitled to reimbursement of their travel and subsistence expenses. The cashier of the General Court may make an advance payment towards these expenses.
3. Witnesses shall be entitled to compensation for loss of earnings, and experts to fees for their services. The cashier of the General Court shall pay witnesses and experts these sums after they have carried out their respective duties or tasks.

[10.481]
Article 101
Letters rogatory

1. The General Court may, on application by a main party or of its own motion, issue letters rogatory for the examination of witnesses or experts.
2. Letters rogatory shall be issued in the form of an order. The order shall contain the name, description and address of the witness or expert, set out the facts on which the witness or expert is to be examined, name the parties, their representatives, indicate their addresses and briefly describe the subject-matter of the proceedings.
3. The Registrar shall send the order to the competent authority named in the Rules supplementing the Rules of Procedure of the Court of Justice of the Member State in whose territory the witness or expert is to be examined. Where necessary, the order shall be accompanied by a translation into the official language or languages of the Member State to which it is addressed.
4. The authority named pursuant to paragraph 3 shall transmit the order to the judicial authority which is competent according to its national law.
5. The competent judicial authority shall give effect to the letters rogatory in accordance with its national law. After implementation the competent judicial authority shall transmit to the authority named pursuant to paragraph 3 the order embodying the letters rogatory, any documents arising from the implementation and a detailed statement of costs. These documents shall be sent to the Registrar.
6. The Registrar shall be responsible for the translation of the documents into the language of the case.
7. The General Court shall defray thc expenses occasioned by the letters rogatory without prejudice to the right to charge them, where appropriate, to the main parties.

[10.482]
Article 102
Minutes of inquiry hearings

1. The Registrar shall draw up minutes of every inquiry hearing. The minutes shall be signed by the President and by the Registrar. They shall constitute an official record.
2. In the case of the examination of witnesses or experts, the minutes shall be signed by the President or by the Judge-Rapporteur responsible for conducting the examination of the witness or expert, and by the Registrar. Before the minutes are thus signed, the witness or expert must be given an opportunity to check the content of the minutes and to sign them.
3. The minutes shall be served on the parties.

SECTION 3
TREATMENT OF CONFIDENTIAL INFORMATION, ITEMS AND DOCUMENTS PRODUCED IN THE CONTEXT OF MEASURES OF INQUIRY

[10.483]
Article 103
Treatment of confidential information and material

1. Where it is necessary for the General Court to examine, on the basis of the matters of law and of fact relied on by a main party, the confidentiality, vis-à-vis the other main party, of certain information or material produced before the General Court following a measure of inquiry referred to in Article 91(b) that may be relevant in order for the General Court to rule in a case, that information or material shall not be communicated to that other party at the stage of such examination.
2. Where the General Court concludes in the examination provided for in paragraph 1 that certain information or material produced before it is relevant in order for it to rule in the case and is confidential vis-à-vis the other main party, it shall weigh that confidentiality against the requirements linked to the right to effective judicial protection, particularly observance of the adversarial principle.
3. After weighing up the matters referred to in paragraph 2, the General Court may decide to bring the confidential information or material to the attention of the other main party, making its disclosure subject, if necessary, to the giving of specific undertakings, or it may decide not to communicate such information or material, specifying, by reasoned order, the procedures enabling the other main party, to the greatest extent possible, to make his views known, including ordering the production of a non-confidential version or a non-confidential summary of the information or material, containing the essential content thereof.
4. The procedural regime in this Article shall not apply to the cases referred to in Article 105.

[10.484]
Article 104
Documents to which access has been denied by an institution

Where, following a measure of inquiry referred to in Article 91(c), a document to which access has been denied by an institution has been produced before the General Court in proceedings relating to the legality of that denial, that document shall not be communicated to the other parties.

CHAPTER 7
INFORMATION OR MATERIAL PERTAINING TO THE SECURITY OF THE UNION OR THAT OF ONE OR MORE OF ITS MEMBER STATES OR TO THE CONDUCT OF THEIR INTERNATIONAL RELATIONS

[10.485]
Article 105
Treatment of information or material pertaining to the security of the Union or that of one or more of its Member States or to the conduct of their international relations

1. Where, contrary to the adversarial principle set out in Article 64 under which all information and material must be fully communicated between the parties, a main party intends to base his claims on certain information or material but submits that its communication would harm the security of the Union or that of one or more of its Member States or the conduct of their international relations, he shall produce that information or material by a separate document. The information or material thus produced shall be accompanied by an application for confidential treatment thereof, setting out the overriding reasons which, to the extent strictly required by the exigencies of the situation, justify the confidentiality of that information or material being preserved and which militate against its communication to the other main party. The application for confidential treatment shall also be submitted by a separate document and shall not contain anything which is confidential. Where the information or material in respect of which confidential treatment is sought has been transmitted to the main party by one or more Member States, the overriding reasons put forward by the main party to justify the confidential treatment of that information or material may include those provided by the Member State(s) concerned.
2. The production of information or material the confidential nature of which is based on the overriding reasons referred to in paragraph 1 may be requested by the General Court in the form of a measure of inquiry. Formal note shall be taken of any refusal. By way of derogation from Article 103, the procedural regime applicable to such information or material produced following a measure of inquiry shall be that of the present Article.
3. While the information or material produced by a main party in accordance with paragraph 1 or 2 is being examined as to its relevance to the General Court's ruling in the case and as to its confidential nature vis-à-vis the other main party, that information or material shall not be communicated to the other main party.
4. Where the General Court decides, after the examination provided for in paragraph 3, that the information or material produced before it is relevant in order for it to rule in the case and is not confidential for the purposes of the proceedings before the General Court, it shall ask the party concerned to authorise the communication of that information or material to the other main party. If the first party objects to such communication within a period prescribed by the President, or fails to reply by the end of that period, that information or material shall not be taken into account in the determination of the case and shall be returned to that party.
5. Where the General Court decides, after the examination provided for in paragraph 3, that certain information or material produced before it is relevant in order for it to rule in the case and is confidential vis-à-vis the other main party, it shall not communicate that information or material to that main party. It shall then weigh the requirements linked to the right to effective judicial protection, particularly observance of the adversarial principle, against the requirements flowing from the security of the Union or of one or more of its Member States or the conduct of their international relations.
6. After weighing up the matters referred to in paragraph 5, the General Court shall make a reasoned order specifying the procedures to be adopted to accommodate the requirements referred to in paragraph 5, such as the production by the party concerned, for subsequent communication to the other main party, of a non-confidential version or a non-confidential summary of the information or material, containing the essential content thereof and enabling the other main party, to the greatest extent possible, to make its views known.
7. The information or material that is confidential vis-à-vis the other main party may be withdrawn, wholly or in part, by the main party who produced it in accordance with paragraph 1 or 2, within two weeks after service of the decision taken pursuant to paragraph 5. The information or material withdrawn shall not be taken into account in the determination of the case and shall be returned to the main party concerned.
8. Where the General Court considers that information or material which, owing to its confidential nature, has not been communicated to the other main party in accordance with the procedures referred to in paragraph 6 is essential in order for it to rule in the case, it may, by way of derogation from Article 64 and confining itself to what is strictly necessary, base its judgment on such information or material. When assessing that information or material, the General Court shall take account of the fact that a main party has not been able to make his views on it known.
9. The General Court shall ensure that confidential matters contained in the information or material produced by a main party in accordance with paragraph 1 or 2 which have not been communicated to the other main party are not disclosed in the order made pursuant to paragraph 6 or in the decision which closes the proceedings.

[10. The information or material referred to in paragraph 5, which has not been withdrawn pursuant to paragraph 7 by the main party that produced it, shall be returned to the party concerned as soon as the period referred to in the first paragraph of Article 56 of the Statute has expired, unless, within that period, an appeal has been brought against the decision of the General Court. Where such an appeal is brought, the abovementioned information or material shall be made available to the Court of Justice on the conditions laid down in the decision referred to in paragraph 11.]

11. The General Court shall determine, by decision, the security rules for protecting the information or material produced in accordance with paragraph 1 or paragraph 2, as the case may be. That decision shall be published in the *Official Journal of the European Union*.

NOTES

Para 10: substituted by the Amendment to the Rules of Procedure of the General Court, Article 1 (OJ L217, 12.8.2016, p 72).

CHAPTER 8
ORAL PART OF THE PROCEDURE

[10.486]
Article 106
Oral part of the procedure

1. The procedure before the General Court shall include, in the oral part, a hearing arranged either of the General Court's own motion or at the request of a main party.
2. Any request for a hearing made by a main party must state the reasons for which that party wishes to be heard. It must be submitted within three weeks after service on the parties of notification of the close of the written part of the procedure. That time limit may be extended by the President.
3. If there is no request as referred to in paragraph 2, the General Court may, if it considers that it has sufficient information available to it from the material in the file, decide to rule on the action without an oral part of the procedure. In that case, it may nevertheless later decide to open the oral part of the procedure.

[10.487]
Article 107
Date of the hearing

1. If the General Court decides to open the oral part of the procedure, the President shall fix the date of the hearing.
2. The President may, in exceptional circumstances, of his own motion or at the reasoned request of a main party, adjourn the hearing to another date.

[10.488]
Article 108
Absence of the parties from the hearing

1. Where a party informs the General Court that he will not be present at the hearing or where the General Court finds at the hearing that a party who has been duly given notice to attend is absent without excuse, the hearing shall proceed in the absence of the party concerned.
2. Where the main parties indicate to the General Court that they will not be present at the hearing, the President shall decide whether the oral part of the procedure may be closed.

[10.489]
Article 109
Cases heard in camera

1. After hearing the parties, the General Court may, in accordance with Article 31 of the Statute, decide to hear a case *in camera*.
2. The request by a party for a case to be heard *in camera* must include reasons and specify whether it concerns all or part of the hearing.
3. The oral proceedings in cases heard *in camera* shall not be published.

[10.490]
Article 110
Conduct of the hearing

1. The oral proceedings shall be opened and directed by the President, who shall be responsible for the proper conduct of the hearing.
2. A party may address the General Court only through his representative.
3. The members of the formation of the Court and the Advocate General may in the course of the hearing put questions to the representatives of the parties.

[4. In cases brought pursuant to Article 270 TFEU, the members of the formation of the Court and the Advocate General may in the course of the hearing invite the parties themselves to express their views on certain aspects of the case.]

NOTES

Para 4: added by the Amendment to the Rules of Procedure of the General Court, Article 1(8) (OJ L217, 12.8.2016, p 73).

[10.491]
Article 111
Close of the oral part of the procedure

Where an Advocate General has not been designated in a case, the President shall declare the oral part of the procedure closed at the end of the hearing.

[10.492]
Article 112
Delivery of the Opinion of the Advocate General

1. Where an Advocate General has been designated in a case and delivers his Opinion in writing, he shall lodge it at the Registry, which shall communicate it to the parties.
2. The President shall declare the oral part of the procedure closed after the delivery, orally or in writing, of the Opinion of the Advocate General.

[10.493]
Article 113
Reopening of the oral part of the procedure

1. The General Court shall order the reopening of the oral part of the procedure when the conditions set out in Article 23(3) or Article 24(3) are satisfied.
2. The General Court may order the reopening of the oral part of the procedure:
  (a) if it considers that it lacks sufficient information;
  (b) where the case must be decided on the basis of an argument which has not been debated between the parties;
  (c) where requested by a main party who is relying on facts which are of such a nature as to be a decisive factor for the decision of the General Court but which it was unable to put forward before the oral part of the procedure was closed.

[10.494]
Article 114
Minutes of the hearing

1. The Registrar shall draw up minutes of every hearing. The minutes shall be signed by the President and by the Registrar. They shall constitute an official record.
2. The minutes shall be served on the parties.

[10.495]
Article 115
Recording of the hearing

The President of the General Court may, on a duly substantiated request, authorise a party who has participated in the written part or the oral part of the proceedings to listen, on the General Court's premises, to the sound recording of the hearing in the language used by the speakers during that hearing.

CHAPTER 9
JUDGMENTS AND ORDERS

[10.496]
Article 116
Date of delivery of a judgment

The parties shall be informed of the date of delivery of a judgment.

[10.497]
Article 117
Content of a judgment

A judgment shall contain:
  (a) a statement that it is the judgment of the General Court;
  (b) an indication as to the formation of the Court;
  (c) the date of delivery;
  (d) the names of the President and of the Judges who took part in the deliberations, with an indication as to the name of the Judge-Rapporteur;
  (e) the name of the Advocate General, if designated;
  (f) the name of the Registrar;
  (g) a description of the parties;
  (h) the names of their representatives;
  (i) a statement of the forms of order sought by the parties;
  (j) where applicable, the date of the hearing;

(k) a statement, where appropriate, that the Advocate General has been heard and, where applicable, the date of his Opinion;
(l) a summary of the facts;
(m) the grounds for the decision;
(n) the operative part of the judgment, including the decision as to costs.

[10.498]
Article 118
Delivery and service of the judgment

1. The judgment shall be delivered in open court.
2. The original of the judgment, signed by the President, by the Judges who took part in the deliberations and by the Registrar, shall be sealed and deposited at the Registry. A copy of the judgment shall be served on each of the parties.

[10.499]
Article 119
Content of an order

Any order from which an appeal may lie under Article 56 or Article 57 of the Statute shall contain:
(a) a statement that it is the order of the General Court, the President or the Judge hearing applications for interim measures, as the case may be;
(b) where applicable, an indication as to the formation of the Court;
(c) the date of its adoption;
(d) an indication as to the legal basis of the order;
(e) the names of the President and, where applicable, the Judges who took part in the deliberations, with an indication as to the name of the Judge-Rapporteur;
(f) the name of the Advocate General, if designated;
(g) the name of the Registrar;
(h) a description of the parties;
(i) the names of their representatives;
(j) a statement of the forms of order sought by the parties;
(k) a statement, where appropriate, that the Advocate General has been heard;
(l) a summary of the facts;
(m) the grounds for the decision;
(n) the operative part of the order, including, where appropriate, the decision as to costs.

[10.500]
Article 120
Signature and service of the order

The original of every order, signed by the President and by the Registrar, shall be sealed and deposited at the Registry. A copy of the order shall be served on each of the parties and, if necessary, on the Court of Justice . . . .

NOTES

Words omitted repealed by the Amendment to the Rules of Procedure of the General Court, Article 1(9) (OJ L217, 12.8.2016, p 73).

[10.501]
Article 121
Binding nature of judgments and orders

1. Subject to the provisions of Article 60 of the Statute, a judgment shall be binding from the date of its delivery.
2. Subject to the provisions of Article 60 of the Statute, an order shall be binding from the date of its service.

[10.502]
Article 122
Publication in the Official Journal of the European Union

A notice containing the date and the operative part of the judgment or order of the General Court which closes the proceedings shall be published in the *Official Journal of the European Union*, save in the case of decisions adopted before the application has been served on the defendant.

CHAPTER 10
JUDGMENTS BY DEFAULT

[10.503]
Article 123
Judgments by default

1. Where the General Court finds that a defendant on whom an application initiating proceedings has been duly served has failed to respond to the application in the proper form or within the time limit prescribed in Article 81, without prejudice to the application of the provisions of the second paragraph of Article 45 of the Statute, the applicant may, within a time limit prescribed by the President, apply to the General Court for judgment by default.
2. A defendant in default shall not intervene in the default procedure and, with the exception of the decision which closes the proceedings, no procedural document shall be served on him.
3. The General Court shall give judgment in favour of the applicant in the judgment by default, unless it is clear that the General Court has no jurisdiction to hear and determine the action or that the action is manifestly inadmissible or manifestly lacking any foundation in law.
4. A judgment by default shall be enforceable. The General Court may, however, grant a stay of execution until it has given its decision on any application under Article 166 to set aside the judgment, or it may make execution subject to the provision of security of an amount and nature to be fixed in the light of the circumstances. This security shall be released if no such application is made or if the application fails.

CHAPTER 11
AMICABLE SETTLEMENT AND DISCONTINUANCE

[10.504]
Article 124
Amicable settlement

1. [If, before the General Court has given its decision, the main parties reach an out-of-court settlement of their dispute] and inform the General Court of the abandonment of their claims, the President shall order the case to be removed from the register and shall give a decision as to costs in accordance with Articles 136 and 138, having regard to any proposals made by the parties on the matter.
2. This provision shall not apply to proceedings under Articles 263 TFEU and 265 TFEU.

NOTES

Para 1: words in square brackets substituted by the Amendment to the Rules of Procedure of the General Court, Article 1(10) (OJ L217, 12.8.2016, p 73).

[10.505]
Article 125
Discontinuance

If the applicant informs the General Court in writing or at the hearing that he wishes to discontinue the proceedings, the President shall order the case to be removed from the register and shall give a decision as to costs in accordance with Articles 136 and 138.

[CHAPTER 11A
PROCEDURE IN RELATION TO AMICABLE SETTLEMENTS INITIATED BY THE GENERAL COURT IN CASES BROUGHT PURSUANT TO ARTICLE 270 TFEU

[10.506]
Article 125a
Procedure

1. The General Court may, at all stages of the procedure, examine the possibilities of an amicable settlement of all or part of the dispute between the main parties.
2. The General Court shall instruct the Judge-Rapporteur, assisted by the Registrar, to seek the amicable settlement of a dispute.
3. The Judge-Rapporteur may propose one or more solutions capable of putting an end to the dispute, adopt appropriate measures with a view to facilitating its amicable settlement and implement the measures which he has adopted to that end. He may, in particular:
   - (a) invite the main parties to supply information or particulars;
   - (b) invite the main parties to produce documents;
   - (c) invite to meetings the main parties' representatives, the main parties themselves or any official or servant of the institution empowered to negotiate an agreement;
   - (d) on the occasion of the meetings referred to in point (c), have contact with each of the main parties separately, if they consent to that.
4. Paragraphs 1 to 3 shall apply to proceedings for interim measures also.]

NOTES

Chapter 11a (Articles 125a–125d) inserted by the Amendment to the Rules of Procedure of the General Court, Article 1(11) (OJ L217, 12.8.2016, p 73).

[10.507]
[Article 125b
Effect of the main parties' agreement

1. Where the main parties come to an agreement before the Judge-Rapporteur on a solution which brings the dispute to an end, they may request that the terms of that agreement be recorded in a document signed by the Judge-Rapporteur and by the Registrar. That document shall be served on the main parties and shall constitute an official record.
2. The case shall be removed from the register by reasoned order of the President. At the request of a main party with the agreement of the other main party, the terms of the agreement reached by the main parties shall be recorded in the order removing the case from the register.
3. The President shall give a decision as to costs in accordance with the agreement or, failing that, at his discretion. Where appropriate, he shall give a decision as to the costs of an intervener in accordance with Article 138.]

NOTES

Chapter 11a (Articles 125a–125d) inserted by the Amendment to the Rules of Procedure of the General Court, Article 1(11) (OJ L217, 12.8.2016, p 73).

[10.508]
[Article 125c
Specific register and file

1. Material produced in the context of the amicable settlement procedure as provided for in Article 125a:
   - shall be entered in a specific register which shall not be subject to the rules laid down in Articles 36 and 37,
   - shall be placed in a file separate from the case file.
2. Material produced in the context of the amicable settlement procedure as provided for in Article 125a shall be brought to the attention of the main parties, with the exception of material which either of them has communicated to the Judge-Rapporteur in the separate meetings provided for in Article 125a(3)(d).
3. The main parties may have access to the material in the file separate from the case file as referred to in paragraph 1, with the exception of material which either of the main parties has communicated to the Judge-Rapporteur in the separate meetings provided for in Article 125a(3)(d).
4. An intervener may not have access to material in the file separate from the case file as referred to in paragraph 1.
5. The parties may examine the specific register referred to in paragraph 1 at the Registry.]

NOTES

Chapter 11a (Articles 125a–125d) inserted by the Amendment to the Rules of Procedure of the General Court, Article 1(11) (OJ L217, 12.8.2016, p 73).

[10.509]
[Article 125d
Amicable settlement and judicial proceedings

No opinion expressed, suggestion made, proposal put forward, concession made or document drawn up for the purposes of the amicable settlement may be relied upon as evidence by the General Court or the main parties in the judicial proceedings.]

NOTES

Chapter 11a (Articles 125a–125d) inserted by the Amendment to the Rules of Procedure of the General Court, Article 1(11) (OJ L217, 12.8.2016, p 73).

CHAPTER 12
ACTIONS AND ISSUES DETERMINED BY ORDER

[10.510]
Article 126
Action manifestly bound to fail

Where it is clear that the General Court has no jurisdiction to hear and determine an action or where the action is manifestly inadmissible or manifestly lacking any foundation in law, the General Court may, on a proposal from the Judge-Rapporteur, at any time decide to give a decision by reasoned order without taking further steps in the proceedings.

[10.511]
Article 127
[Referral of a case to the Court of Justice]
Decisions referring an action in the circumstances specified in the second paragraph of Article 54 of the Statute . . . shall be made by the General Court by reasoned order on a proposal from the Judge-Rapporteur.

NOTES
Article heading substituted, and words omitted repealed, by the Amendment to the Rules of Procedure of the General Court, Article 1(12) (OJ L217, 12.8.2016, p 73).

[10.512]
Article 128
Declining of jurisdiction
Decisions declining jurisdiction in the circumstances specified in the third paragraph of Article 54 of the Statute shall be made by the General Court by reasoned order on a proposal from the Judge-Rapporteur.

[10.513]
Article 129
Absolute bar to proceeding with a case
On a proposal from the Judge-Rapporteur, the General Court may at any time of its own motion, after hearing the main parties, decide to rule by reasoned order on whether there exists any absolute bar to proceeding with a case.

[10.514]
Article 130
Preliminary objections and issues
1. A defendant applying to the General Court for a decision on inadmissibility or lack of competence without going to the substance of the case shall submit the application by a separate document within the time limit referred to in Article 81.
2. A party applying to the General Court for a declaration that the action has become devoid of purpose and that there is no longer any need to adjudicate on it or for a decision on another preliminary issue shall submit the application by a separate document.
3. The applications referred to in paragraphs 1 and 2 must state the pleas of law and arguments relied on and the form of order sought; any supporting material must be annexed to the applications.
4. As soon as the application referred to in paragraph 1 has been submitted, the President shall prescribe a time limit within which the applicant in the action may submit in writing his pleas in law and the form of order which he seeks.
5. As soon as the application referred to in paragraph 2 has been submitted, the President shall prescribe a time limit within which the other parties may submit in writing their observations on that application.
6. The General Court may decide to open the oral part of the procedure in respect of the applications referred to in paragraphs 1 and 2. Article 106 shall not apply.
7. The General Court shall decide on the application as soon as possible or, where special circumstances so justify, reserve its decision until it rules on the substance of the case. [It shall refer the case to the Court of Justice if the case falls within the latter's jurisdiction].
8. If the General Court refuses the application or reserves its decision, the President shall prescribe new time limits for further steps in the proceedings.

NOTES
Para 7: words in square brackets substituted by the Amendment to the Rules of Procedure of the General Court, Article 1(13) (OJ L217, 12.8.2016, p 73).

[10.515]
Article 131
Cases that, of the General Court's own motion, do not proceed to judgment
1. If the General Court declares that the action has become devoid of purpose and that there is no longer any need to adjudicate on it, it may at any time, of its own motion, on a proposal from the Judge-Rapporteur and after hearing the parties, decide to rule by reasoned order.
2. If the applicant ceases to reply to the General Court's requests, the General Court may, on a proposal from the Judge-Rapporteur and after hearing the parties, declare of its own motion, by reasoned order, that there is no longer any need to adjudicate.

[10.516]
Article 132
Actions that are manifestly well founded

Where the Court of Justice or the General Court has already ruled on one or more questions of law identical to those raised by the pleas in law of the action and the General Court finds that the facts have been established, it may, after the written part of the procedure has been closed, on a proposal from the Judge-Rapporteur and after hearing the parties, decide by reasoned order in which reference is made to the relevant case-law to declare the action manifestly well founded.

CHAPTER 13
COSTS

[10.517]
Article 133
Decision as to costs

A decision as to costs shall be given in the judgment or order which closes the proceedings.

[10.518]
Article 134
General rules as to allocation of costs

1. The unsuccessful party shall be ordered to pay the costs if they have been applied for in the successful party's pleadings.
2. Where there is more than one unsuccessful party the General Court shall decide how the costs are to be shared.
3. Where each party succeeds on some and fails on other heads, the parties shall bear their own costs. However, if it appears justified in the circumstances of the case, the General Court may order that one party, in addition to bearing his own costs, pay a proportion of the costs of the other party.

[10.519]
Article 135
Equity and unreasonable or vexatious costs

1. . . . if equity so requires, the General Court may decide that an unsuccessful party is to pay only a proportion of the costs of the other party in addition to bearing his own, or even that he is not to be ordered to pay any.
2. The General Court may order a party, even if successful, to pay some or all of the costs, if this appears justified by the conduct of that party, including before the proceedings were brought, especially if he has made the opposite party incur costs which the General Court holds to be unreasonable or vexatious.

NOTES

Para 1: word omitted repealed by the Amendment to the Rules of Procedure of the General Court, Article 1(14) (OJ L217, 12.8.2016, p 73).

[10.520]
Article 136
Costs in the event of discontinuance or withdrawal

1. A party who discontinues or withdraws from proceedings shall be ordered to pay the costs if they have been applied for in the other party's observations on the discontinuance.
2. However, at the request of the party who discontinues or withdraws from proceedings, the costs shall be borne by the other party if this appears justified by the conduct of that party.
3. Where the parties have come to an agreement on costs, the decision as to costs shall be in accordance with that agreement.
4. If costs are not claimed, the parties shall bear their own costs.

[10.521]
Article 137
Costs where a case does not proceed to judgment

Where a case does not proceed to judgment, the costs shall be in the discretion of the General Court.

[10.522]
Article 138
Costs of interveners

1. The Member States and institutions which have intervened in the proceedings shall bear their own costs.
2. The States other than the Member States, which are parties to the EEA Agreement, and also the EFTA Surveillance Authority, shall similarly bear their own costs if they have intervened in the proceedings.

3. The General Court may order an intervener other than those referred to in paragraphs 1 and 2 to bear his own costs.

[10.523]
Article 139
Costs of proceedings

Proceedings before the General Court shall be free of charge, except that:

(a) where a party has caused the General Court to incur avoidable costs, in particular where the action is manifestly an abuse of process, the General Court may order that party to refund them;

(b) where copying or translation work is carried out at the request of a party, the cost shall, in so far as the Registrar considers it excessive, be paid for by that party on the Registry's scale of charges referred to in Article 37;

(c) in the event of any repeated failure to comply with the requirements of these Rules or of the practice rules referred to in Article 224, requiring regularisation to be sought, the costs involved in the requisite processing thereof by the General Court shall, at the request of the Registrar, be paid for by the party concerned on the Registry's scale of charges referred to in Article 37.

[10.524]
Article 140
Recoverable costs

Without prejudice to Article 139, the following shall be regarded as recoverable costs:

(a) sums payable to witnesses and experts under Article 100;

(b) expenses necessarily incurred by the parties for the purpose of the proceedings, in particular the travel and subsistence expenses and the remuneration of agents, advisers or lawyers.

[10.525]
Article 141
Procedure for payment

1. Sums due from the cashier of the General Court and from its debtors shall be paid in euros.
2. Where costs to be recovered have been incurred in a currency other than the euro or where the steps in respect of which payment is due were taken in a country of which the euro is not the currency, the conversion shall be effected at the European Central Bank's official rates of exchange on the day of payment.

CHAPTER 14
INTERVENTION

[10.526]
Article 142
Object and effects of the intervention

1. The intervention shall be limited to supporting, in whole or in part, the form of order sought by one of the main parties. It shall not confer the same procedural rights as those conferred on the main parties and, in particular, shall not give rise to any right to request that a hearing be held.
2. The intervention shall be ancillary to the main proceedings. It shall become devoid of purpose if the case is removed from the register of the General Court as a result of a main party's discontinuance or withdrawal from the proceedings or of an agreement between the main parties, or where the application is declared inadmissible.
3. The intervener must accept the case as he finds it at the time of his intervention.

[10.527]
Article 143
Application to intervene

1. An application to intervene must be submitted within six weeks of the publication of the notice referred to in Article 79.
2. The application to intervene shall contain:

(a) a description of the case;

(b) a description of the main parties;

(c) the name and address of the applicant for leave to intervene;

(d) particulars of the status and address of the representative of the applicant for leave to intervene;

(e) the form of order sought in support of which the applicant for leave to intervene is applying for leave to intervene;

(f) a statement of the circumstances establishing the right to intervene, where the application is submitted pursuant to the second or third paragraph of Article 40 of the Statute.

3. The applicant for leave to intervene shall be represented in accordance with Article 19 of the Statute.
4. Article 77, [Article 78(4) to (6)] and Article 139 shall apply to the application to intervene.

NOTES

Para 4: words in square brackets substituted by the Amendment to the Rules of Procedure of the General Court, Article 1(15) (OJ L217, 12.8.2016, p 73).

[10.528]
Article 144
Decision on applications to intervene

1. The application to intervene shall be served on the main parties.
2. The President shall give the main parties an opportunity to submit their written or oral observations on the application to intervene and to apply, if necessary, for certain confidential information in the file in the case not to be communicated to an intervener.
3. Where the defendant lodges a plea of inadmissibility or of lack of competence, as provided in Article 130(1), a decision on the application to intervene shall not be given until after the plea has been rejected or the decision on the plea reserved.
4. Where the application is submitted pursuant to the first paragraph of Article 40 of the Statute and the main parties have not identified information in the file in the case that is confidential and which they claim would be prejudicial to them if communicated to the intervener, the intervention shall be allowed by decision of the President.
5. In any other case the President shall decide on the application to intervene as soon as possible, by order, and, where applicable, on the communication to the intervener of information which it is claimed is confidential.
6. If the application to intervene is refused, the order referred to in paragraph 5 must state the reasons on which it is based and include a decision as to the costs relating to the application to intervene, including the costs of the applicant for leave to intervene, pursuant to Articles 134 and 135.
7. If the application to intervene is granted, the intervener shall receive a copy of every procedural document served on the main parties, save, where applicable, for the confidential information excluded from such communication pursuant to paragraph 5.
8. In the event that the application to intervene is withdrawn, the President shall order that the applicant for leave to intervene be removed from the case and shall give a decision as to costs, including the costs of the applicant for leave to intervene, pursuant to Article 136.
9. In the event that the intervention is withdrawn, the President shall order that the intervener be removed from the case and shall give a decision as to costs pursuant to Articles 136 and 138. 10.If the proceedings in the main case are concluded before the application to intervene has been decided, the applicant for leave to intervene and the main parties shall each bear their own costs relating to the application to intervene. A copy of the order closing the proceedings shall be transmitted to the applicant for leave to intervene.

[10.529]
Article 145
Submission of statements

1. The intervener may submit a statement in intervention within the time limit prescribed by the President.
2. The statement in intervention shall contain:
   (a) the form of order sought by the intervener in support, in whole or in part, of the form of order sought by one of the main parties;
   (b) the pleas in law and arguments relied on by the intervener;
   (c) where appropriate, any evidence produced or offered.
3. After the statement in intervention has been lodged, the President shall prescribe a time limit within which the main parties may reply to that statement.

CHAPTER 15
LEGAL AID

[10.530]
Article 146
General

1. Any person who, because of his financial situation, is wholly or partly unable to meet the costs of the proceedings shall be entitled to legal aid.
2. Legal aid shall be refused if it is clear that the General Court has no jurisdiction to hear and determine the action in respect of which the application for legal aid is made or if that action appears to be manifestly inadmissible or manifestly lacking any foundation in law.

[10.531]
Article 147
Application for legal aid

1. An application for legal aid may be made before the action has been brought or while it is pending.

2. The application for legal aid must be made using a form which is published in the *Official Journal of the European Union* and available on the internet site of the Court of Justice of the European Union. Without prejudice to Article 74, the form must be signed by the applicant for legal aid or, if he is represented, by his lawyer. An application for legal aid submitted without the application form will not be taken into consideration.
3. The application for legal aid must be accompanied by all information and supporting documents making it possible to assess the applicant's financial situation, such as a certificate issued by a competent national authority attesting to his financial situation.
4. If the application for legal aid is made before the action has been brought, the applicant must briefly state the subject-matter of the proposed action, the facts of the case and the arguments in support of the action. The application must be accompanied by supporting documents in that regard.
5. Where applicable, the application for legal aid shall be accompanied by the documents referred to in Article 51(2) and (3) and [Article 78(4)]. In that case Article 51(4) and [Article 78(6)] shall apply.
6. If the applicant for legal aid is represented by a lawyer when the application for legal aid is lodged, Article 77 shall apply.
7. The introduction of an application for legal aid shall, for the person who made it, suspend the time limit prescribed for the bringing of an action until the date of service of the order making a decision on that application or, in the cases referred to in Article 148(6), of the order designating the lawyer instructed to represent the applicant.

NOTES

Para 5: words in square brackets substituted by the Amendment to the Rules of Procedure of the General Court, Article 1(16) (OJ L217, 12.8.2016, p 73).

[10.532]
Article 148
Decision on the application for legal aid

1. Before giving his decision on an application for legal aid, the President shall prescribe a time limit within which the other main party may submit his written observations unless it is already apparent from the information produced that the conditions laid down in Article 146(1) have not been satisfied or that those laid down in Article 146(2) have been satisfied.
2. The decision on the application for legal aid shall be taken by the President by way of an order.
3. An order refusing legal aid shall state the reasons on which it is based.
4. Any order granting legal aid may designate a lawyer to represent the person concerned if that lawyer has been proposed by the applicant in the application for legal aid and has agreed to represent the applicant before the General Court.
5. If the person concerned has not indicated his choice of lawyer in the application for legal aid or following an order granting legal aid or if his choice is unacceptable, the Registrar shall send a copy of the order granting legal aid and a copy of the application to the competent authority of the Member State concerned mentioned in the Rules supplementing the Rules of Procedure of the Court of Justice. If the person concerned is not resident in the Union, the Registrar shall send a copy of the order granting legal aid and a copy of the application to the competent authority of the State in which the Court of Justice of the European Union has its seat.
6. Without prejudice to paragraph 4, the lawyer instructed to represent the applicant shall be designated by way of an order, having regard to the suggestions made by the person concerned or to the suggestions made by the authority referred to in paragraph 5, as the case may be.
7. An order granting legal aid may specify the amount to be paid to the lawyer instructed to represent the person concerned or fix a limit which the lawyer's disbursements and fees may not, in principle, exceed. It may provide for a contribution to be made by the person concerned to the costs referred to in Article 149(1), having regard to his financial situation.
8. No appeal shall lie from orders made under this Article.
9. Without prejudice to Article 147(6), service on the applicant for legal aid and on the other parties shall be effected as provided for in Article 80(1).

[10.533]
Article 149
Advances and responsibility for costs

1. Where legal aid is granted, the cashier of the General Court shall be responsible, where applicable within the limits fixed, for costs involved in the assistance and representation of the applicant before the General Court. At the request of the lawyer designated in accordance with Article 148, the President may decide that an amount by way of advance should be paid to that lawyer.
2. Where, by virtue of the decision closing the proceedings, the recipient of legal aid has to bear his own costs, the President shall fix the lawyer's disbursements and fees which are to be paid by the cashier of the General Court by way of a reasoned order from which no appeal shall lie.
3. Where, in the decision closing the proceedings, the General Court has ordered another party to pay the costs of the recipient of legal aid, that other party shall be required to refund to the cashier of the General Court any sums advanced by way of aid.

4. The Registrar shall take steps to obtain the recovery of the sums referred to in paragraph 3 from the party ordered to pay them.
5. Where the recipient of the legal aid is unsuccessful, the General Court may, in ruling as to costs in the decision closing the proceedings, if equity so requires, order that one or more parties should bear their own costs or that those costs should be borne, in whole or in part, by the cashier of the General Court by way of legal aid.

[10.534]
Article 150
Withdrawal of legal aid
1. If the circumstances which led to the grant of legal aid alter during the proceedings, the President may, of his own motion or on request, withdraw that legal aid, having heard the person concerned.
2. An order withdrawing legal aid shall contain a statement of reasons and no appeal shall lie from it.

CHAPTER 16
URGENT PROCEDURES

SECTION 1
EXPEDITED PROCEDURE

[10.535]
Article 151
Decision relating to the expedited procedure
1. The General Court may, at the request of the applicant or the defendant, after hearing the other main party, decide, having regard to the particular urgency and the circumstances of the case, to adjudicate under an expedited procedure. That decision shall be taken as soon as possible.
2. On a proposal from the Judge-Rapporteur, the General Court may, in exceptional circumstances, of its own motion and after hearing the main parties, decide to adjudicate under an expedited procedure.
3. The decision of the General Court to adjudicate under an expedited procedure may prescribe conditions as to the volume and presentation of the pleadings of the main parties; the subsequent conduct of the proceedings or as to the pleas in law and arguments on which the General Court will be called upon to decide.
4. If one of the main parties does not comply with any one of the conditions referred to in paragraph 3, the decision to adjudicate under an expedited procedure may be revoked. The proceedings shall then continue in accordance with the ordinary procedure.

[10.536]
Article 152
Request for an expedited procedure
1. A request for an expedited procedure shall be made by a separate document lodged at the same time as the application initiating the proceedings or the defence, and shall contain a statement of reasons specifying the particular urgency of the case and any other relevant circumstances.
2. The request for an expedited procedure may state that certain pleas in law or arguments or certain passages of the application initiating the proceedings or the defence are raised only in the event that the case is not decided under an expedited procedure, in particular by enclosing with the request an abridged version of the application initiating the proceedings and a schedule of annexes and only the annexes which are to be taken into consideration if the case is decided under an expedited procedure.

[10.537]
Article 153
Priority treatment
By way of derogation from Article 67(1), cases on which the General Court has decided to adjudicate under an expedited procedure shall be given priority.

[10.538]
Article 154
Written part of the procedure
1. By way of derogation from Article 81(1), where the applicant has requested that the case be decided under an expedited procedure, the period prescribed for the lodging of the defence shall be one month. That period may be extended pursuant to Article 81(3).
2. If the General Court decides not to allow a request for an expedited procedure, the defendant shall be granted an additional period of one month in order to lodge or, as the case may be, supplement the defence.
3. Under the expedited procedure, the pleadings referred to in Articles 83(1) and 145(1) and (3) may be lodged only if the General Court, by way of measures of organisation of procedure adopted in accordance with Articles 88 to 90, so allows.

4. Under the expedited procedure, the President shall take account, when setting the time limits provided for by these Rules, of the particular urgency in adjudicating on the action.

[10.539]
Article 155
Oral part of the procedure

1. Where the General Court has approved an expedited procedure, it shall decide to open the oral part of the procedure as soon as possible after the presentation of the preliminary report by the Judge-Rapporteur. The General Court may nevertheless decide to rule without an oral part of the procedure where the main parties decide not to participate in a hearing and the General Court considers that it has sufficient information available to it from the material in the file in the case.
2. Without prejudice to Articles 84 and 85, the main parties may supplement their arguments and offer further evidence during the oral part of the procedure, provided that the delay in submission is justified.

SECTION 2
SUSPENSION OF OPERATION OR ENFORCEMENT AND OTHER INTERIM MEASURES

[10.540]
Article 156
Application for suspension or other interim measures

1. An application to suspend the operation of any measure adopted by an institution, made pursuant to Article 278 TFEU or Article 157 TEAEC, shall be admissible only if the applicant has challenged that measure in an action before the General Court.
2. An application for the adoption of one of the other interim measures referred to in Article 279 TFEU shall be admissible only if it is made by a main party to a case before the General Court and relates to that case.
[3. In cases brought pursuant to Article 270 TFEU, an application of a kind referred to in paragraphs 1 and 2 may be presented as soon as the complaint under Article 90(2) of the Staff Regulations has been submitted, on the conditions laid down in Article 91(4) of those Regulations.]
[4]. An application of a kind referred to in paragraphs 1 and 2 shall state the subject-matter of the proceedings, the circumstances giving rise to urgency and the pleas of fact and law establishing a prima facie case for the interim measure applied for. It shall contain all the evidence and offers of evidence available to justify the grant of interim measures.
[5]. The application shall be made by a separate document and in accordance with the provisions of Articles 76 to 78.

NOTES

The original paras 3 and 4 were renumbered as paras 4 and 5, and a new para 3 was inserted, by the Amendment to the Rules of Procedure of the General Court, Article 1(17) (OJ L217, 12.8.2016, p 73).

[10.541]
Article 157
Procedure

1. The application shall be served on the opposite party, and the President of the General Court shall prescribe a short time limit within which that party may submit written or oral observations.
2. The President of the General Court may grant the application even before the observations of the opposite party have been submitted. This decision may be varied or cancelled even without any application being made by any party.
3. The President of the General Court shall prescribe, where appropriate, measures of organisation of procedure and measures of inquiry.
4. In the event that the President of the General Court is prevented from acting, Articles 11 and 12 shall apply.

[10.542]
Article 158
Decision on the application

1. The President of the General Court shall decide on the application by way of a reasoned order. The order shall be served on the parties forthwith.
2. The execution of the order may be made conditional on the lodging by the applicant of security, of an amount and nature to be fixed in the light of the circumstances.
3. Unless the order fixes the date on which the interim measure is to lapse, the measure shall lapse upon delivery of the final judgment.
4. The order shall have only an interim effect, and shall be without prejudice to the decision of the General Court on the substance of the case.
5. In the order closing the proceedings for interim relief, costs shall be reserved until the decision of the General Court on the substance of the case. However, if it appears justified in the light of the circumstances of the case, a decision as to the costs relating to the proceedings for interim relief shall be given in the order, pursuant to Articles 134 to 138.

[10.543]
Article 159
Change in circumstances

On application by a party, the order may at any time be varied or cancelled on account of a change in circumstances.

[10.544]
Article 160
New application

Refusal of an application for an interim measure shall not bar the main party who made it from making a further application on the basis of new facts.

[10.545]
Article 161
Applications pursuant to Articles 280 TFEU, 299 TFEU and 164 TEAEC

1. The provisions of this Section shall apply to applications to suspend the enforcement of a decision of the General Court or of any measure adopted by the Council, the European Commission or the European Central Bank, submitted pursuant to Articles 280 TFEU, 299 TFEU or 164 TEAEC.
2. The order granting the application shall fix, where appropriate, a date on which the interim measure is to lapse.

CHAPTER 17
APPLICATIONS RELATING TO JUDGMENTS AND ORDERS

[10.546]
Article 162
Assignment of the application

1. The applications referred to in this Chapter shall be assigned to the formation of the Court which delivered the decision to which the application relates.
2. If the quorum referred to in Articles 23 and 24 can no longer be attained, the application shall be assigned to another formation of the Court sitting with the same number of Judges. If the decision was delivered by a Judge ruling as a single Judge who is prevented from acting, the application shall be assigned to another Judge.

[10.547]
Article 163
Stay of proceedings

Where an appeal before the Court of Justice and one of the applications referred to in this Chapter, with the exception of the applications referred to in Articles 164 and 165, concern the same decision of the General Court, the President, after hearing the parties, may decide to stay the proceedings until the Court of Justice has delivered its ruling on the appeal.

[10.548]
Article 164
Rectification of judgments and orders

1. Without prejudice to the provisions relating to the interpretation of judgments and orders, the General Court may, of its own motion or on application by a party, rectify clerical mistakes, errors in calculation and obvious inaccuracies.
2. The application for rectification shall be made within two weeks after delivery of the judgment or service of the order.
3. Where the rectification concerns the operative part or one of the grounds constituting the necessary support for the operative part, the parties may submit written observations within the time limit prescribed by the President.
4. The General Court shall give its decision by way of an order.
5. The original of the rectification order shall be annexed to the original of the rectified decision. A note of this order shall be made in the margin of the original of the rectified decision.

[10.549]
Article 165
Failure to adjudicate

1. If the General Court has failed to adjudicate on a specific head of claim or on costs, any party wishing to rely on that may apply to the General Court to supplement its decision.
2. The application shall be made within one month after delivery of the judgment or service of the order.
3. The application shall be served on the other parties, who may submit written observations within the time limit prescribed by the President.
4. After giving the parties an opportunity to submit their observations, the General Court shall decide, by way of an order, both on the admissibility and on the substance of the application.

[10.550]
Article 166
Application to set aside a judgment by default

1. Application may be made pursuant to Article 41 of the Statute to set aside a judgment given by default.
2. The application to set aside the judgment must be made by the defendant in default within one month from the date of service of the judgment given by default. It must be submitted in the form prescribed by Articles 76 to 78.
3. After the application has been served, the President shall prescribe a time limit within which the other party may submit his written observations.
4. The proceedings shall be conducted in accordance with the provisions of Title III or of Title IV, as the case may be.
5. The General Court shall decide by way of a judgment which may not be set aside.
6. The original of this judgment shall be annexed to the original of the judgment by default. A note of the judgment on the application to set aside shall be made in the margin of the original of the judgment by default.

[10.551]
Article 167
Third-party proceedings

1. The provisions of Articles 76 to 78 shall apply to an application initiating third-party proceedings made pursuant to Article 42 of the Statute. In addition such an application shall:
   (a) specify the judgment or order contested;
   (b) state how the contested judgment or order is prejudicial to the rights of the third party;
   (c) indicate the reasons for which the third party was unable to take part in the case before the General Court.
2. The application initiating third-party proceedings must be submitted within two months of the publication referred to in Article 122.
3. The General Court may, on application by the third party, order a stay of execution of the contested judgment or order. The provisions of Articles 156 to 161 shall apply.
4. The application shall be served on the parties, who may submit written observations within the time limit prescribed by the President.
5. After giving the parties an opportunity to submit their observations, the General Court shall decide on the application.
6. The contested judgment or order shall be varied on the points on which the submissions of the third party are upheld.
7. The original of the decision in the third-party proceedings shall be annexed to the original of the contested judgment or order. A note of the decision in the third-party proceedings shall be made in the margin of the original of the contested judgment or order.

[10.552]
Article 168
Interpretation of judgments and orders

1. In accordance with Article 43 of the Statute, if the meaning or scope of a judgment or order is in doubt, the General Court shall construe it on application by any party or any institution of the Union establishing an interest therein.
2. An application for interpretation must be submitted within two years after the date of delivery of the judgment or service of the order.
3. An application for interpretation shall be submitted in the form prescribed by Articles 76 to 78. In addition it shall specify:
   (a) the judgment or order in question;
   (b) the passages of which interpretation is sought.
4. The application for interpretation shall be served on the other parties, who may submit written observations within the time limit prescribed by the President.
5. After giving the parties an opportunity to submit their observations, the General Court shall decide on the application.
6. The original of the interpreting decision shall be annexed to the original of the decision interpreted. A note of the interpreting decision shall be made in the margin of the original of the decision interpreted.

[10.553]
Article 169
Revision

1. In accordance with Article 44 of the Statute, an application for revision of a decision of the General Court may be made only on discovery of a fact which is of such a nature as to be a decisive factor and which, when the judgment was delivered or the order served, was unknown to the General Court and to the party claiming revision.

2. Without prejudice to the time limit of 10 years prescribed in the third paragraph of Article 44 of the Statute, an application for revision shall be made within three months of the date on which the facts on which the application is founded came to the applicant's knowledge.
3. Articles 76 to 78 shall apply to an application for revision. In addition the application shall:
   (a) specify the judgment or order contested;
   (b) indicate the points on which the judgment or order is contested;
   (c) set out the facts on which the application is founded;
   (d) indicate the nature of the evidence to show that there are facts justifying revision, and that the time limits laid down in paragraph 2 have been observed.
4. The application for revision shall be served on the other parties, who may submit written observations within the time limit prescribed by the President.
5. After giving the parties an opportunity to submit their observations, the General Court shall, without prejudice to its decision on the substance, give its decision on the admissibility of the application by way of an order.
6. If the General Court declares the application admissible, it shall give its decision on the substance of the case, in accordance with the provisions of these Rules.
7. The original of the revising decision shall be annexed to the original of the decision revised. A note of the revising decision shall be made in the margin of the original of the decision revised.

[10.554]
Article 170
Dispute concerning the costs to be recovered
1. If there is a dispute concerning the costs to be recovered, the party concerned may apply to the General Court to determine the dispute. The application shall be submitted in the form prescribed in Articles 76 to 78.
2. The application shall be served on the party concerned by the application, who may submit written observations within the time limit prescribed by the President.
3. After giving the party concerned by the application an opportunity to submit his observations, the General Court shall give its decision by way of an order from which no appeal shall lie.
4. The parties may, for the purposes of enforcement, request an authenticated copy of the order.

TITLE IV
PROCEEDINGS RELATING TO INTELLECTUAL PROPERTY RIGHTS

[10.555]
Article 171
Scope
The provisions of this Title shall apply to actions brought against decisions of the Boards of Appeal of the Office, as referred to in Article 1, and concerning the application of the rules relating to an intellectual property regime.

CHAPTER 1
THE PARTIES TO THE PROCEEDINGS

[10.556]
Article 172
Defendant
The application shall be made against the Office to which the Board of Appeal which adopted the contested decision belongs, as defendant.

[10.557]
Article 173
Status before the General Court of the other parties to the proceedings before the Board of Appeal
1. A party to the proceedings before the Board of Appeal other than the applicant may participate, as intervener, in the proceedings before the General Court by responding to the application in the manner and within the time limit prescribed.
2. Before the expiry of the time limit prescribed for the lodging of a response, a party to the proceedings before the Board of Appeal other than the applicant shall become a party to the proceedings before the General Court, as intervener, on lodging a procedural document. He shall lose the status of intervener before the General Court if he fails to respond to the application in the manner and within the time limit prescribed. In that case, the intervener shall bear his own costs in relation to the procedural documents lodged by him.
3. The intervener referred to in paragraphs 1 and 2 shall have the same procedural rights as the main parties. He may support the form of order sought by a main party and may apply for a form of order and put forward pleas in law independently of those applied for and put forward by the main parties.
4. A party to the proceedings before the Board of Appeal other than the applicant, who becomes a party before the General Court in accordance with paragraphs 1 and 2, shall be represented in accordance with the provisions of Article 19 of the Statute.

5. Article 77 and [Article 78(4) to (6)] shall apply to the procedural document referred to in paragraph 2.
6. By way of derogation from Article 123, the default procedure shall not apply where an intervener, as referred to in paragraphs 1 and 2, has responded to the application in the manner and within the time limit prescribed.

NOTES

Para 5: words in square brackets substituted by the Amendment to the Rules of Procedure of the General Court, Article 1(18) (OJ L217, 12.8.2016, p 73).

[10.558]
Article 174
Replacement of a party

Where an intellectual property right affected by the proceedings has been transferred to a third party by a party to the proceedings before the Board of Appeal of the Office, the successor to that right may apply to replace the original party in the proceedings before the General Court.

[10.559]
Article 175
Application for replacement of a party

1. An application for replacement shall be made by a separate document. It may be lodged at any stage of the proceedings.
2. The application shall contain:
 (a) a description of the case;
 (b) a description of the parties to the case and of the party whom the applicant for replacement proposes to replace;
 (c) the name and address of the applicant for replacement;
 (d) particulars of the status and address of the representative of the applicant for replacement;
 (e) a statement of the circumstances justifying replacement, together with supporting evidence.
3. The applicant for replacement shall be represented in accordance with the provisions of Article 19 of the Statute.
4. Article 77, [Article 78(4) to (6)] and Article 139 shall apply to the application for replacement.

NOTES

Para 4: words in square brackets substituted by the Amendment to the Rules of Procedure of the General Court, Article 1(19) (OJ L217, 12.8.2016, p 73).

[10.560]
Article 176
Decision on the application for replacement of a party

1. The application for replacement shall be served on the parties.
2. The President shall give the parties an opportunity to submit their written or oral observations on the application for replacement.
3. The decision on the application for replacement shall take the form of a reasoned order of the President or shall be included in the decision closing the proceedings.
4. If the application for replacement is refused, a decision shall be given as to the costs relating to that application, including the costs of the applicant for replacement, pursuant to the provisions of Articles 134 and 135.
5. If the application for replacement is granted, the successor to the party who is replaced must accept the case as he finds it at the time of that replacement. He shall be bound by the procedural documents lodged by the party whom he replaces.

CHAPTER 2
THE APPLICATION AND RESPONSES

[10.561]
Article 177
Application

1. An application shall contain:
 (a) the name and address of the applicant;
 (b) particulars of the status and address of the applicant's representative;
 (c) the name of the Office against which the action is brought;
 (d) the subject-matter of the proceedings, the pleas in law and arguments relied on and a summary of those pleas in law;
 (e) the form of order sought by the applicant.
2. Where the applicant was not the only party to the proceedings before the Board of Appeal of the Office, the application shall also contain the names of all the parties to those proceedings and the addresses which they had given for the purposes of notifications.
3. The contested decision of the Board of Appeal shall be appended to the application. The date on which the applicant was notified of that decision must be indicated.

4. An application made by a legal person governed by private law shall be accompanied by recent proof of that person's existence in law (extract from the register of companies, firms or associations or any other official document).
5. The application shall be accompanied by the documents referred to in Article 51(2) and (3).
6. Article 77 shall apply.
7. If an application does not comply with paragraphs 2 to 5, the Registrar shall prescribe a reasonable time limit within which the applicant is to put the application in order. If the applicant fails to put the application in order within the time limit prescribed, the General Court shall decide whether the non-compliance with that procedural requirement renders the application formally inadmissible.

[10.562]
Article 178
Service of the application

1. The Registrar shall inform the defendant and all the parties to the proceedings before the Board of Appeal of the lodging of the application as provided for in Article 80(1). He shall arrange for service of the application after determining the language of the case in accordance with Article 45(4) and, where appropriate, for service of the translation of the application into the language of the case.
2. The application shall be served on the defendant in the form of a certified copy sent by registered post with a form for acknowledgement of receipt or by personal delivery of the copy against a receipt. Where the defendant has previously agreed to applications being served on him by the method referred to in Article 57(4) or by telefax, service of the application may be effected accordingly.
3. Service of the application on a party to the proceedings before the Board of Appeal shall be effected by the method to which that party agreed when lodging the procedural document referred to in Article 173(2), and, if no such document was lodged, by registered post with a form for acknowledgement of receipt at the address given by the party concerned for the purposes of the notifications to be effected in the course of the proceedings before the Board of Appeal.
4. In cases where Article 177(7) applies, service shall be effected as soon as the application has been put in order or the General Court has declared it admissible notwithstanding the failure to observe the requirements set out in that Article.
5. Once the application has been served, the defendant shall forward to the General Court the file relating to the proceedings before the Board of Appeal.

[10.563]
Article 179
Parties authorised to lodge a response

The defendant and the parties to the proceedings before the Board of Appeal other than the applicant shall submit their responses to the application within a time limit of two months from the service of the application. That time limit may, in exceptional circumstances, be extended by the President at the reasoned request of the party concerned.

[10.564]
Article 180
Response

1. A response shall contain:
   (a) the name and address of the party lodging it;
   (b) particulars of the status and address of the party's representative;
   (c) the pleas in law and arguments relied on;
   (d) the form of order sought by the party lodging it.
2. Article 177(4) to (7) shall apply to the response.

[10.565]
Article 181
Close of the written part of the procedure

Without prejudice to the provisions of Chapter 3, the written part of the procedure shall be closed after the submission of the response of the defendant and, where applicable, of the intervener within the meaning of Article 173.

CHAPTER 3
CROSS-CLAIMS

[10.566]
Article 182
Cross-claim

1. The parties to the proceedings before the Board of Appeal other than the applicant may submit a cross-claim within the same time limit as that prescribed for the submission of a response.
2. A cross-claim must be submitted by a document separate from the response.

[10.567]
Article 183
Content of the cross-claim

A cross-claim shall contain:

(a) the name and address of the party lodging it;
(b) particulars of the status and address of the party's representative;
(c) the pleas in law and arguments relied on;
(d) the form of order sought.

[10.568]
Article 184
Form of order sought, pleas in law and arguments contained in the cross-claim

1. The cross-claim shall seek an order annulling or altering the decision of the Board of Appeal on a point not raised in the application.

2. The pleas in law and arguments relied on shall identify precisely the points in the grounds of the decision being challenged that are contested.

[10.569]
Article 185
Response to the cross-claim

Where a cross-claim is lodged, the other parties may submit a pleading confined to responding to the form of order sought, the pleas in law and arguments relied on in the cross-claim, within two months of its being served on them. That time limit may, in exceptional circumstances, be extended by the President at the reasoned request of the party concerned.

[10.570]
Article 186
Close of the written part of the procedure

When a cross-claim has been lodged, the written part of the procedure shall be closed after the submission of the last response to that cross-claim.

[10.571]
Article 187
Relationship between the main action and the cross-claim

A cross-claim shall be deemed to be devoid of purpose:

(a) if the applicant discontinues the main action;
(b) if the main action is declared manifestly inadmissible.

CHAPTER 4
OTHER ASPECTS OF THE PROCEDURE

[10.572]
Article 188
Subject-matter of the proceedings before the General Court

The pleadings lodged by the parties in proceedings before the General Court may not change the subject-matter of the proceedings before the Board of Appeal.

[10.573]
Article 189
Length of written pleadings

1. The General Court shall set, in accordance with Article 224, the maximum length of written pleadings lodged pursuant to this Title.

2. Authorisation to exceed the maximum length of written pleadings may be given by the President only in cases involving particularly complex legal or factual issues.

[10.574]
Article 190
Provisions relating to costs

1. Where an action against a decision of a Board of Appeal is successful, the General Court may order the defendant to bear only its own costs.

2. Costs necessarily incurred by the parties for the purposes of the proceedings before the Board of Appeal shall be regarded as recoverable costs.

[10.575]
Article 191
Other provisions applicable

Subject to the special provisions of this Title, the provisions of Title III shall apply to the proceedings referred to in this Title.

TITLE V
APPEALS AGAINST DECISIONS OF THE CIVIL SERVICE TRIBUNAL

[10.576]
Article 192
Scope

The provisions of this Title shall apply to appeals against decisions of the Civil Service Tribunal as referred to in Articles 9 and 10 of Annex I to the Statute.

CHAPTER 1
THE APPEAL

[10.577]
Article 193
Lodging of the appeal

. . . An appeal shall be brought by lodging an application at the Registry of the General Court . . .

2. . . .

NOTES

Number and words omitted repealed by the Amendment to the Rules of Procedure of the General Court, Article 1(20) (OJ L217, 12.8.2016, p 73).

[10.578]
Article 194
Content of the appeal

1. An appeal shall contain:
   (a) the name and address of the appellant;
   (b) particulars of the status and address of the appellant's representative;
   (c) a reference to the decision of the Civil Service Tribunal appealed against;
   (d) the names of the other parties to the relevant case before the Civil Service Tribunal;
   (e) the pleas in law and legal arguments relied on, and a summary of those pleas in law;
   (f) the form of order sought by the appellant.
2. The appeal shall state the date on which the decision appealed against was served on the appellant.
3. An appeal brought by a legal person governed by private law shall be accompanied by recent proof of that person's existence in law (extract from the register of companies, firms or associations or any other official document).
4. The appeal shall be accompanied by the documents referred to in Article 51(2) and (3).
5. Article 77 shall apply.
6. If an appeal does not comply with paragraphs 2 to 4, the Registrar shall prescribe a reasonable time limit within which the appellant is to put the appeal in order. If the appellant fails to put the appeal in order within the time limit prescribed, the General Court shall decide whether the non-compliance with that procedural requirement renders the appeal formally inadmissible.

[10.579]
Article 195
Form of order sought, pleas in law and arguments contained in the appeal

1. An appeal shall seek to have set aside, in whole or in part, the decision of the Civil Service Tribunal as set out in the operative part of that decision.
2. The pleas in law and legal arguments relied on shall identify precisely those points in the grounds of the decision of the Civil Service Tribunal that are contested.

[10.580]
Article 196
Form of order sought in the event that the appeal is allowed

1. An appeal shall seek, in the event that it is declared well founded, the same form of order, in whole or in part, as that sought at first instance and shall not seek a different form of order. The subject-matter of the proceedings before the Civil Service Tribunal may not be changed in the appeal.
2. Where the appellant requests that the case be referred back to the [General Court ruling as a court of first instance] in the event of the decision appealed against being set aside, he shall set out the reasons why the state of the proceedings does not permit a decision by the General Court [ruling as a court of appeal].

NOTES

Para 2: words in first pair of square brackets substituted, and words in second pair of square brackets inserted, by the Amendment to the Rules of Procedure of the General Court, Article 1(21) (OJ L217, 12.8.2016, p 73).

CHAPTER 2
THE RESPONSE, THE REPLY AND THE REJOINDER

[10.581]
Article 197
Service of the appeal
1. The appeal shall be served on the other parties to the relevant case before the Civil Service Tribunal. Article 80(1) shall apply.
2. Where Article 194(6) applies, service shall be effected as soon as the appeal has been put in order or the General Court has declared it admissible notwithstanding the failure to observe the formal requirements laid down by that Article.

[10.582]
Article 198
Parties authorised to lodge a response
Any party to the relevant case before the Civil Service Tribunal having an interest in the appeal being allowed or dismissed may submit a response within two months after service on him of the appeal. The time limit for submitting a response shall not be extended.

[10.583]
Article 199
Content of the response
1. A response shall contain:
(a) the name and address of the party submitting it;
(b) particulars of the status and address of that party's representative;
(c) the date on which the appeal was served on him;
(d) the pleas in law and legal arguments relied on;
(e) the form of order sought.
2. Article 194(3) to (6) shall apply to responses.

[10.584]
Article 200
Form of order sought in the response
A response shall seek to have the appeal allowed or dismissed, in whole or in part.

[10.585]
Article 201
Reply and rejoinder
1. The appeal and the response may be supplemented by a reply and a rejoinder only where the President, on a reasoned application submitted by the appellant within seven days of service of the response, considers it necessary, in particular to enable the appellant to present his views on a plea of inadmissibility or on new matters relied on in the response.
2. The President shall fix the date by which the reply is to be produced and, upon service of that pleading, the date by which the rejoinder is to be produced. He may limit the number of pages and the subject-matter of those pleadings.

CHAPTER 3
THE CROSS-APPEAL

[10.586]
Article 202
Cross-appeal
1. The parties referred to in Article 198 may submit a cross-appeal within the same time limit as that prescribed for the submission of a response.
2. A cross-appeal must be introduced by a document separate from the response.

[10.587]
Article 203
Content of the cross-appeal
A cross-appeal shall contain:
(a) the name and address of the party bringing the cross-appeal;
(b) particulars of the status and address of that party's representative;
(c) the date on which the appeal was served on him;
(d) the pleas in law and legal arguments relied on;
(e) the form of order sought.

[10.588]
Article 204
Form of order sought, pleas in law and arguments contained in the cross-appeal
1. A cross-appeal shall seek to have set aside, in whole or in part, the decision of the Civil Service Tribunal.

2. It may also seek to have set aside an express or implied decision relating to the admissibility of the action before the Civil Service Tribunal.
3. The pleas in law and legal arguments relied on shall identify precisely those points in the grounds of the decision of the Civil Service Tribunal which are contested. The pleas in law and arguments must be separate from those relied on in the response.

CHAPTER 4
PLEADINGS CONSEQUENT ON THE CROSS-APPEAL

[10.589]
Article 205
Response to the cross-appeal
Where a cross-appeal is brought, the appellant or any other party to the relevant case before the Civil Service Tribunal having an interest in the cross-appeal being allowed or dismissed may submit a response, which must be limited to the pleas in law relied on in that cross-appeal, within two months after its being served on him. That time limit shall not be extended.

[10.590]
Article 206
Reply and rejoinder following a cross-appeal
1. The cross-appeal and the response thereto may be supplemented by a reply and a rejoinder only where the President, on a reasoned application submitted by the party who brought the cross-appeal within seven days of service of the response to the cross-appeal, considers it necessary, in particular to enable that party to present his views on a plea of inadmissibility or on new matters relied on in the response to the cross-appeal.
2. The President shall fix the date by which that reply is to be produced and, upon service of that pleading, the date by which the rejoinder is to be produced. He may limit the number of pages and the subject-matter of those pleadings.

CHAPTER 5
THE ORAL PART OF THE PROCEDURE

[10.591]
Article 207
Oral part of the procedure
1. The parties to the appeal proceedings may request an opportunity to state their case in a hearing. Any such request must be reasoned and be submitted within three weeks after service on the parties of notification of the close of the written part of the procedure. That time limit may be extended by the President.
2. On a proposal from the Judge-Rapporteur, the General Court may, if it considers that it has sufficient information available to it from the material in the file, decide to rule on the appeal without an oral part of the procedure. It may nevertheless later decide to open the oral part of the procedure.

CHAPTER 6
APPEALS DETERMINED BY ORDER

[10.592]
Article 208
Manifestly inadmissible or manifestly unfounded appeal or cross-appeal
Where the appeal or cross-appeal is, in whole or in part, manifestly inadmissible or manifestly unfounded, the General Court may at any time, acting on a proposal from the Judge-Rapporteur, decide by reasoned order to dismiss that appeal or cross-appeal in whole or in part.

[10.593]
Article 209
Manifestly well-founded appeal or cross-appeal
Where the Court of Justice or the General Court has already ruled on one or more questions of law identical to those raised by the pleas in law of the appeal or cross-appeal, and the General Court considers the appeal or cross-appeal to be manifestly well founded, it may, acting on a proposal from the Judge-Rapporteur and after hearing the parties, decide by reasoned order in which reference is made to the relevant case-law to declare the appeal or cross-appeal manifestly well founded.

CHAPTER 7
EFFECT ON A CROSS-APPEAL OF THE REMOVAL OF THE APPEAL FROM THE REGISTER

[10.594]
Article 210
Effect on a cross-appeal of the discontinuance or manifest inadmissibility of the appeal

A cross-appeal shall be deemed to be devoid of purpose:

(a) if the appellant discontinues his appeal;
(b) if the appeal is declared manifestly inadmissible for non-compliance with the time limit for lodging an appeal;
(c) if the appeal is declared manifestly inadmissible on the sole ground that it is not directed against a final decision of the Civil Service Tribunal or against a decision disposing of the substantive issues in part only or disposing of a procedural issue concerning a plea of lack of jurisdiction or inadmissibility within the meaning of the first paragraph of Article 9 of Annex I to the Statute.

CHAPTER 8
COSTS IN APPEALS

[10.595]
Article 211
Provisions relating to costs in appeals

1. Subject to the following provisions, Articles 133 to 141 shall apply, *mutatis mutandis*, to the procedure before the General Court on appeal from a decision of the Civil Service Tribunal.
2. Where the appeal is unfounded or where the appeal is well founded and the General Court itself gives final judgment in the case, the General Court shall make a decision as to costs.
3. In appeals brought by institutions, the institutions shall bear their own costs, without prejudice to Article 135(2).
4. By way of derogation from Article 134(1) and (2), the General Court may, in appeals brought by officials or other servants of an institution, decide to apportion the costs between the parties where equity so requires.
5. Where he has not brought the appeal, an intervener at first instance may not be ordered to pay costs in the appeal proceedings unless he participated in the written or oral part of the proceedings before the General Court. Where an intervener at first instance takes part in the proceedings, the General Court may decide that he shall bear his own costs.

CHAPTER 9
OTHER PROVISIONS APPLICABLE TO APPEALS

[10.596]
Article 212
Length of written pleadings

1. The General Court shall set, in accordance with Article 224, the maximum length of written pleadings lodged pursuant to this Title.
2. Authorisation to exceed the maximum length of written pleadings may be given by the President only in cases involving particularly complex issues.

[10.597]
Article 213
Other provisions applicable to appeals

1. Articles 51 to 58, 60 to 74, 79, 84, 87, 89, 90, 107 to 122, 124, 125, 129, 131, 142 to 162, 164, 165 and 167 to 170 shall apply to the procedure before the General Court on appeal from a decision of the Civil Service Tribunal.
2. By way of derogation from Article 143(1), an application to intervene must be submitted within one month of the publication of the notice referred to in Article 79.
3. Decisions given pursuant to Article 256(2) TFEU shall be communicated to the Court of Justice . . .

NOTES

Para 3: words omitted repealed by the Amendment to the Rules of Procedure of the General Court, Article 1(22) (OJ L217, 12.8.2016, p 73).

CHAPTER 10
APPEALS AGAINST DECISIONS DISMISSING AN APPLICATION TO INTERVENE AND AGAINST DECISIONS ON INTERIM MEASURES

[10.598]
Article 214
Appeals against decisions dismissing an application to intervene and against decisions on interim measures
By way of derogation from the provisions of this Title, the President of the General Court shall adjudicate upon the appeals referred to in Article 10(1) and (2) of Annex I to the Statute in accordance with the procedure laid down in Article 157(1) and (3) and Article 158(1).

TITLE VI
PROCEDURES AFTER A CASE IS REFERRED BACK TO THE GENERAL COURT

CHAPTER 1
DECISIONS OF THE GENERAL COURT GIVEN AFTER ITS DECISION HAS BEEN SET ASIDE AND THE CASE REFERRED BACK TO IT

[10.599]
Article 215
Setting aside and referral back by the Court of Justice
Where the Court of Justice sets aside a judgment or an order of the General Court and refers the case back to that Court, the latter shall be seised of the case by the decision so referring it.

[10.600]
Article 216
Assignment of the case
1. Where the Court of Justice sets aside a judgment or an order of a Chamber, the President of the General Court may assign the case to another Chamber sitting with the same number of Judges.
2. Where the Court of Justice sets aside a judgment delivered or an order made by the Grand Chamber of the General Court, the case shall be assigned to that Chamber.
3. Where the Court of Justice sets aside a judgment delivered or an order made by a Judge ruling as a single Judge, the President of the General Court may assign the case to a single Judge, without prejudice to the referral of the case by that single Judge to the Chamber in which he sits.

[10.601]
Article 217
Conduct of the proceedings
1. Where the decision later set aside by the Court of Justice was made after the written procedure before the General Court on the substance of the case had been closed, the parties to the proceedings before the General Court may lodge their written observations on the conclusions to be drawn from the decision of the Court of Justice for the outcome of the proceedings within two months of the service on them of the decision of the Court of Justice. This time limit may not be extended.
2. Where the decision later set aside by the Court of Justice was made when the written procedure before the General Court on the substance of the case had not yet been closed, it shall be resumed at the stage which it had reached.
3. The President may, if the circumstances so justify, allow supplementary statements of written observations to be lodged.

[10.602]
Article 218
Rules applicable to the procedure
Subject to the provisions of Article 217, the procedure shall be conducted in accordance with the provisions of Title III or of Title IV, as the case may be.

[10.603]
Article 219
Costs
The General Court shall decide on the costs relating to the proceedings instituted before it and to the proceedings on the appeal before the Court of Justice.

CHAPTER 2
DECISIONS OF THE GENERAL COURT GIVEN AFTER ITS DECISION HAS BEEN REVIEWED AND THE CASE REFERRED BACK TO IT

[10.604]
Article 220
Review and referral back by the Court of Justice
Where the Court of Justice reviews a judgment or an order of the General Court and refers the case back to that Court, the latter shall be seised of the case by the judgment so referring it.

[10.605]
Article 221
Assignment of the case
1. Where the Court of Justice refers back to the General Court a case that was originally heard by a Chamber, the President of the General Court may assign the case to another Chamber sitting with the same number of Judges.
2. Where the Court of Justice refers back to the General Court a case that was originally heard by the Grand Chamber of the General Court, the case shall be assigned to that Chamber.

[10.606]
Article 222
Conduct of the proceedings
1. Within one month of the service of the judgment of the Court of Justice, the parties to the proceedings before the General Court may lodge their written observations on the conclusions to be drawn from that judgment for the outcome of the proceedings. This time limit may not be extended.
2. The General Court may, by way of measures of organisation of procedure, invite the parties to the proceedings before it to lodge written submissions and may decide to hear the parties' submissions in a hearing.

[10.607]
Article 223
Costs
The General Court shall decide on the costs relating to the proceedings instituted before it following the review of its decision by the Court of Justice.

FINAL PROVISIONS

[10.608]
Article 224
Implementing rules
The General Court shall, by a separate act, adopt practice rules for the implementation of these Rules.

[10.609]
Article 225
Enforcement
Penalties imposed and other measures ordered under these Rules shall be enforced in accordance with Articles 280 TFEU, 299 TFEU and 164 TEAEC.

[10.610]
Article 226
Repeal
These Rules replace the Rules of Procedure of the General Court of 2 May 1991, as last amended on 19 June 2013.

[10.611]
Article 227
Publication and entry into force of these Rules
1. These Rules, which are authentic in the languages referred to in Article 44, shall be published in the *Official Journal of the European Union.*
2. These Rules shall enter into force on the first day of the third month following their publication.
3. The provisions of Article 105 shall apply only from the entry into force of the decision referred to in Article 105(11).
4. The provisions of Article 45(4), Article 139(c) and Article 181 shall apply only to actions brought before the General Court after the entry into force of these Rules.
5. The provisions of Articles 106 and 207 shall apply only to cases in which the written part of the procedure has not yet been closed on the date on which these Rules enter into force.
6. The provisions of Article 115(1), Article 116(6), Article 131 and Article 135(2) of the Rules of Procedure of the General Court of 2 May 1991, as last amended on 19 June 2013, shall continue to apply to actions brought before the General Court before the entry into force of these Rules.

7. The provisions of Articles 135a and 146 of the Rules of Procedure of the General Court of 2 May 1991, as last amended on 19 June 2013, shall continue to apply to actions pending before the General Court in which the written part of the procedure was closed before the entry into force of these Rules.

RULES OF PROCEDURE OF THE GENERAL COURT 1991 (CONSOLIDATED: 2013)

of 2 May 1991[1]

[10.612]

NOTES

The text of this version (consolidated 1 July 2013) is available at: curia.europa.eu/jcms/upload/docs/application/pdf/2008-09/txt7_2008-09-25_14-08-6_431.pdf.

This edition consolidates:

The Rules of Procedure of the Court of First Instance of the European Communities of 2 May 1991 (OJ L136 of 30.5.1991, p 1, and OJ L317 of 19.11.1991, p 34 (corrigenda)) and the amendments resulting from the following measures:

(1) Amendments to the Rules of Procedure of the Court of First Instance of the European Communities of 15 September 1994 (OJ L249 of 24.9.1994, p 17),
(2) Amendments to the Rules of Procedure of the Court of First Instance of the European Communities of 17 February 1995 (OJ L44 of 28.2.1995, p 64),
(3) Amendments to the Rules of Procedure of the Court of First Instance of the European Communities of 6 July 1995 (OJ L172 of 22.7.1995, p 3),
(4) Amendments to the Rules of Procedure of the Court of First Instance of the European Communities of 12 March 1997 (OJ L103 of 19.4.1997, p 6, and OJ L351 of 23.12.1997, p 72 (corrigenda)),
(5) Amendments to the Rules of Procedure of the Court of First Instance of the European Communities of 17 May 1999 (OJ L135 of 29.5.1999, p 92),
(6) Amendments to the Rules of Procedure of the Court of First Instance of the European Communities of 6 December 2000 (OJ L322 of 19.12.2000, p 4),
(7) Amendments to the Rules of Procedure of the Court of First Instance of the European Communities of 21 May 2003 (OJ L147 of 14.6.2003, p 22),
(8) Council Decision 2004/406/EC, Euratom of 19 April 2004 amending Article 35(1) and (2) of the Rules of Procedure of the Court of First Instance of the European Communities (OJ L132 of 29.4.2004, p 3),
(9) Amendments to the Rules of Procedure of the Court of First Instance of the European Communities of 21 April 2004 (OJ L127 of 29.4.2004, p 108),
(10) Amendments to the Rules of Procedure of the Court of First Instance of the European Communities of 12 October 2005 (OJ L298 of 15.11.2005, p 1),
(11) Council Decision 2006/956/EC, Euratom of 18 December 2006 amending the Rules of Procedure of the Court of First Instance of the European Communities with regard to languages (OJ L386 of 29.12.2006, p 45),
(12) Amendments to the Rules of Procedure of the Court of First Instance of the European Communities of 12 June 2008 (OJ L179 of 8.7.2008, p 12),
(13) Amendments to the Rules of Procedure of the Court of First Instance of the European Communities of 14 January 2009 (OJ L24 of 28.1.2009, p 9),
(14) Council Decision 2009/170/EC, Euratom of 16 February 2009 amending the Rules of Procedure of the Court of First Instance of the European Communities as regards the language arrangements applicable to appeals against decisions of the European Union Civil Service Tribunal (OJ L60 of 4.3.2009, p 3),
(15) Amendments to the Rules of Procedure of the Court of First Instance of the European Communities of 7 July 2009 (OJ L184 of 16.7.2009, p 10),
(16) Amendments to the Rules of Procedure of the General Court of 26 March 2010 (OJ L92 of 13.4.2010, p 14).
(17) Amendments to the Rules of Procedure of the General Court of 24 May 2011 (OJ L 162 of 22.6.2011, p 18).
(18) Amendments to the Rules of Procedure of the General Court of 19 June 2013 (OJ L 173 of 26.6.2013, p. 66).

This edition has no legal force and the preambles have therefore been omitted.

[1] OJ L 136 of 30.5.1991 and OJ L 317 of 19.11.1991, p 34 (corrigenda), with amendments dated 15 September 1994 (OJ L 249 of 24.9.1994, p 17), 17 February 1995 (OJ L 44 of 28.2.1995, p 64), 6 July 1995 (OJ L 172 of 22.7.1995, p 3), 12 March 1997 (OJ L 103 of 19.4.1997, p 6, and OJ L 351 of 23.12.1997, p 72 (corrigenda), 17 May 1999 (OJ L 135 of 29.5.1999, p 92), 6 December 2000 (OJ L 322 of 19.12.2000, p 4), 21 May 2003 (OJ L 147 of 14.6.2003, p 22), 19 April 2004 (OJ L 132 of 29.4.2004, p 3), 21 April 2004 (OJ L 127 of 29.4.2004, p 108), 12 October 2005 (OJ L 298 of 15.11.2005, p 1), 18 December 2006 (OJ L 386 of 29.12.2006, p 45), 12 June 2008 (OJ L 179 of 8.7.2008, p 12), 14 January 2009 (OJ L 24 of 28.1.2009, p 9), 16 February 2009 (OJ L 60 of 4.3.2009, p 3), 7 July 2009 (OJ L 184 of 16.7.2009, p 10), 26 March 2010 (OJ L 92 of 13.4.2010, p 14), 24 May 2011 (OJ L 162 of 22.6.2011, p 18), and 18 June 2013 (OJ L173, 26.6.2013, p 66).

INTERPRETATION

[10.613]

Article 1

Throughout these Rules:

— provisions of the Treaty on the Functioning of the European Union are referred to by the number of the article concerned followed by 'TFEU';
— provisions of the Treaty establishing the European Atomic Energy Community are referred to by the number of the article followed by 'TEAEC';
— 'Statute' means the Protocol on the Statute of the Court of Justice of the European Union;

— 'EEA Agreement' means the Agreement on the European Economic Area.

For the purposes of these Rules:

— 'institution' or 'institutions' means the institutions of the Union and the bodies, offices and agencies established by the Treaties, or by an act adopted in implementation thereof, and which may be parties before the General Court;

— 'EFTA Surveillance Authority' means the surveillance authority referred to in the EEA Agreement.

TITLE 1
ORGANISATION OF THE GENERAL COURT

CHAPTER 1
PRESIDENT AND MEMBERS OF THE GENERAL COURT

[10.614]
Article 2

1. Every Member of the General Court shall, as a rule, perform the function of Judge.

Members of the General Court are hereinafter referred to as 'Judges'.

2. Every Judge, with the exception of the President, may, in the circumstances specified in Articles 17 to 19, perform the function of Advocate General in a particular case.

References to the Advocate General in these Rules shall apply only where a Judge has been designated as Advocate General.

[10.615]
Article 3

The term of office of a Judge shall begin on the date laid down in his instrument of appointment. In the absence of any provision regarding the date, the term shall begin on the date of the instrument.

[10.616]
Article 4

1. Before taking up his duties, a Judge shall take the following oath before the Court of Justice: 'I swear that I will perform my duties impartially and conscientiously; I swear that I will preserve the secrecy of the deliberations of the Court.'

2. Immediately after taking the oath, a Judge shall sign a declaration by which he solemnly undertakes that, both during and after his term of office, he will respect the obligations arising therefrom, and in particular the duty to behave with integrity and discretion as regards the acceptance, after he has ceased to hold office, of certain appointments and benefits.

[10.617]
Article 5

When the Court of Justice is called upon to decide, after consulting the General Court, whether a Judge of the General Court no longer fulfils the requisite conditions or no longer meets the obligations arising from his office, the President of the General Court shall invite the Judge concerned to make representations to the General Court, in closed session and in the absence of the Registrar.

The General Court shall state the reasons for its opinion.

An opinion to the effect that a Judge of the General Court no longer fulfils the requisite conditions or no longer meets the obligations arising from his office must receive the votes of a majority of the Judges of the General Court. In that event, particulars of the voting shall be communicated to the Court of Justice.

Voting shall be by secret ballot; the Judge concerned shall not take part in the deliberations.

[10.618]
Article 6

With the exception of the President of the General Court and of the Presidents of the Chambers, the Judges shall rank equally in precedence according to their seniority in office.

Where there is equal seniority in office, precedence shall be determined by age.

Retiring Judges who are reappointed shall retain their former precedence.

[10.619]
Article 7

1. The Judges shall, immediately after the partial replacement provided for in Article 254 TFEU, elect one of their number as President of the General Court for a term of three years.

2. If the office of President of the General Court falls vacant before the normal date of expiry thereof, the General Court shall elect a successor for the remainder of the term.

3. The elections provided for in this Article shall be by secret ballot. The Judge obtaining the votes of more than half the Judges composing the Court shall be elected. If no Judge obtains that majority, further ballots shall be held until that majority is attained.

[10.620]
Article 8

The President of the General Court shall direct the judicial business and the administration of the General Court. He shall preside at plenary sittings and deliberations.

The President of the General Court shall preside over the Grand Chamber.

If the President of the General Court is assigned to a Chamber of three or of five Judges, he shall preside over that Chamber.

[10.621]
Article 9

When the President of the General Court is absent or prevented from attending or when the office of President is vacant, the functions of President shall be exercised by a President of a Chamber according to the order of precedence laid down in Article 6.

If the President of the General Court and the Presidents of the Chambers are all absent or prevented from attending at the same time, or their posts are vacant at the same time, the functions of President shall be exercised by one of the other Judges according to the order of precedence laid down in Article 6.

CHAPTER 2
CONSTITUTION OF THE CHAMBERS AND DESIGNATION OF JUDGE-RAPPORTEURS AND ADVOCATES GENERAL

[10.622]
Article 10

1. The General Court shall set up Chambers of three and of five Judges and a Grand Chamber of thirteen Judges and shall decide which Judges shall be attached to them.
2. The decision taken in accordance with this Article shall be published in the *Official Journal of the European Union.*

[10.623]
Article 11

1. Cases before the General Court shall be heard by Chambers composed of three or of five Judges in accordance with Article 10.

Cases may be heard by the General Court sitting in plenary session or by the Grand Chamber under the conditions laid down in Articles 14, 51, 106, 118, 124, 127 and 129.

Cases may be heard by a single Judge where they are delegated to him under the conditions specified in Articles 14 and 51 or assigned to him pursuant to Articles 124, 127(1) or 129(2).

2. In cases coming before a Chamber, the term 'General Court' in these Rules shall designate that Chamber. In cases delegated or assigned to a single Judge the term 'General Court' in these Rules shall designate that Judge.

[10.624]
Article 12

1. The General Court shall lay down criteria by which cases are to be allocated among the Chambers.

The decision shall be published in the *Official Journal of the European Union.*

[10.625]
Article 13

1. As soon as the application initiating proceedings has been lodged, the President of the General Court shall assign the case to one of the Chambers.
2. The President of the Chamber shall propose to the President of the General Court, in respect of each case assigned to the Chamber, the designation of a Judge to act as Rapporteur; the President of the General Court shall decide on the proposal.

[10.626]
Article 14

1. Whenever the legal difficulty or the importance of the case or special circumstances so justify, a case may be referred to the General Court sitting in plenary session, to the Grand Chamber or to a Chamber composed of a different number of Judges.

2. (1) The following cases assigned to a Chamber composed of three Judges may be heard and determined by the Judge-Rapporteur sitting as a single Judge where, having regard to the lack of difficulty of the questions of law or fact raised, to the limited importance of those cases and to the absence of other special circumstances, they are suitable for being so heard and determined and have been delegated under the conditions laid down in Article 51:

(a) cases brought pursuant to Article 270 TFEU;

(b) cases brought pursuant to the fourth paragraph of Article 263 TFEU, the third paragraph of Article 265 TFEU and Article 268 TFEU that raise only questions already clarified by established case-law or that form part of a series of cases in which the same relief is sought and of which one has already been finally decided;

(c) cases brought pursuant to Article 272 TFEU.

(2) Delegation to a single Judge shall not be possible:

(a) in cases which raise issues as to the legality of an act of general application;

(b) in cases concerning the implementation of the rules:

— on competition and on control of concentrations,

— relating to aid granted by States,

— relating to measures to protect trade,

— relating to the common organisation of the agricultural markets, with the exception of cases that form part of a series of cases in which the same relief is sought and of which one has already been finally decided;

(c) in the cases referred to in Article 130(1).

(3) The single Judge shall refer the case back to the Chamber if he finds that the conditions justifying its delegation are no longer satisfied.

3. The decisions to refer or to delegate a case which are provided for in paragraphs 1 and 2 shall be taken under the conditions laid down in Article 51.

[10.627]
Article 15

1. The Judges shall elect from amongst themselves, pursuant to the provisions of Article 7(3), the Presidents of the Chambers composed of three and of five Judges.

2. The Presidents of Chambers of five Judges shall be elected for a term of three years. Their term of office shall be renewable once.

The election of the Presidents of Chambers of five Judges shall take place immediately after the election of the President of the General Court as provided for in Article 7(1).

3. The Presidents of Chambers of three Judges shall be elected for a defined term.

4. If the office of the President of a Chamber falls vacant before the normal date of expiry thereof, a successor shall be elected as President of the Chamber for the remainder of the term.

5. The results of those elections shall be published in the *Official Journal of the European Union*.

[10.628]
Article 16

In cases coming before a Chamber the powers of the President shall be exercised by the President of the Chamber.

In cases delegated or assigned to a single Judge, with the exception of those referred to in Articles 105 and 106, the powers of the President shall be exercised by that Judge.

[10.629]
Article 17

When the General Court sits in plenary session, it shall be assisted by an Advocate General designated by the President of the General Court.

[10.630]
Article 18

A Chamber of the General Court may be assisted by an Advocate General if it is considered that the legal difficulty or the factual complexity of the case so requires.

[10.631]
Article 19

The decision to designate an Advocate General in a particular case shall be taken by the General Court sitting in plenary session at the request of the Chamber before which the case comes.

The President of the General Court shall designate the Judge called upon to perform the function of Advocate General in that case.

CHAPTER 3
REGISTRY

Section 1 — The Registrar

[10.632]
Article 20

1. The General Court shall appoint the Registrar.

Two weeks before the date fixed for making the appointment, the President of the General Court shall inform the Judges of the applications which have been submitted for the post.

2. An application shall be accompanied by full details of the candidate's age, nationality, university degrees, knowledge of any languages, present and past occupations and experience, if any, in judicial and international fields.

3. The appointment shall be made following the procedure laid down in Article 7(3).

4. The Registrar shall be appointed for a term of six years. He may be reappointed.

5. Before he takes up his duties the Registrar shall take the oath before the General Court in accordance with Article 4.

6. The Registrar may be deprived of his office only if he no longer fulfils the requisite conditions or no longer meets the obligations arising from his office; the General Court shall take its decision after giving the Registrar an opportunity to make representations.
7. If the office of Registrar falls vacant before the usual date of expiry of the term thereof, the General Court shall appoint a new Registrar for a term of six years.

[10.633]
Article 21
The General Court may, following the procedure laid down in respect of the Registrar, appoint one or more Assistant Registrars to assist the Registrar and to take his place in so far as the Instructions to the Registrar referred to in Article 23 allow.

[10.634]
Article 22
Where the Registrar is absent or prevented from attending and, if necessary, where the Assistant Registrar is absent or so prevented, or where their posts are vacant, the President of the General Court shall designate an official or servant to carry out the duties of Registrar.

[10.635]
Article 23
Instructions to the Registrar shall be adopted by the General Court acting on a proposal from the President of the General Court.

[10.636]
Article 24
1. There shall be kept in the Registry, under the control of the Registrar, a register in which all pleadings and supporting documents shall be entered in the order in which they are lodged.
2. When a document has been registered, the Registrar shall make a note to that effect on the original and, if a party so requests, on any copy submitted for the purpose.
3. Entries in the register and the notes provided for in the preceding paragraph shall be authentic.
4. Rules for keeping the register shall be prescribed by the Instructions to the Registrar referred to in Article 23.
5. Persons having an interest may consult the register at the Registry and may obtain copies or extracts on payment of a charge on a scale fixed by the General Court on a proposal from the Registrar.

The parties to a case may on payment of the appropriate charge also obtain copies of pleadings and authenticated copies of orders and judgments.
6. Notice shall be given in the *Official Journal of the European Union* of the date of registration of an application initiating proceedings, the names and addresses of the parties, the subject-matter of the proceedings, the form of order sought by the applicant and a summary of the pleas in law and of the main supporting arguments.
7. Where the Council or the European Commission is not a party to a case, the General Court shall send to it copies of the application and of the defence, without the annexes thereto, to enable it to assess whether the inapplicability of one of its acts is being invoked under Article 277 TFEU. Copies of those documents shall likewise be sent to the European Parliament to enable it to assess whether the inapplicability of an act adopted jointly by that institution and by the Council is being invoked under Article 277 TFEU.

[10.637]
Article 25
1. The Registrar shall be responsible, under the authority of the President, for the acceptance, transmission and custody of documents and for effecting service as provided for by these Rules.
2. The Registrar shall assist the General Court, the President and the Judges in all their official functions.

[10.638]
Article 26
The Registrar shall have custody of the seals. He shall be responsible for the records and be in charge of the publications of the General Court.

[10.639]
Article 27
Subject to Articles 5 and 33, the Registrar shall attend the sittings of the General Court.

Section 2 — Other Departments

[10.640]
Article 28
The officials and other servants whose task is to assist directly the President, the Judges and the Registrar shall be appointed in accordance with the Staff Regulations. They shall be responsible to the Registrar, under the authority of the President of the General Court.

[10.641]
Article 29
The officials and other servants referred to in Article 28 shall take the oath provided for in Article 20(2) of the Rules of Procedure of the Court of Justice before the President of the General Court in the presence of the Registrar.

[10.642]
Article 30
The Registrar shall be responsible, under the authority of the President of the General Court, for the administration of the General Court, its financial management and its accounts; he shall be assisted in this by the departments of the Court of Justice.

CHAPTER 4
THE WORKING OF THE GENERAL COURT

[10.643]
Article 31
1. The dates and times of the sittings of the General Court shall be fixed by the President.
2. The General Court may choose to hold one or more sittings in a place other than that in which the General Court has its seat.

[10.644]
Article 32
1. Where, by reason of a Judge being absent or prevented from attending, there is an even number of Judges, the most junior Judge within the meaning of Article 6 shall abstain from taking part in the deliberations unless he is the Judge-Rapporteur. In this case, the Judge immediately senior to him shall abstain from taking part in the deliberations.

Where, following the designation of an Advocate General pursuant to Article 17, there is an even number of Judges in the General Court sitting in plenary session, the President of the Court shall designate, before the hearing and in accordance with a rota established in advance by the General Court and published in the *Official Journal of the European Union*, the Judge who will not take part in the judgment of the case.
2. If after the General Court has been convened in plenary session, it is found that the quorum of nine Judges has not been attained, the President of the General Court shall adjourn the sitting until there is a quorum.
3. If in any Chamber of three or of five Judges, the quorum of three Judges has not been attained, the President of that Chamber shall so inform the President of the General Court who shall designate another Judge to complete the Chamber.

The quorum of the Grand Chamber shall be nine Judges. If that quorum has not been attained, the President of the General Court shall designate another Judge to complete the Chamber.

If in the Grand Chamber or in any Chamber of five Judges the number of Judges provided for by Article 10(1) is not attained by reason of a Judge's being absent or prevented from attending before the date of the opening of the oral procedure, the President of the General Court shall designate a Judge to complete that Chamber in order to restore the number of Judges provided for.
4. If in any Chamber of three or five Judges the number of Judges assigned to that Chamber is higher than three or five respectively, the President of the Chamber shall decide which of the Judges will be called upon to take part in the judgment of the case.
5. If the single Judge to whom the case has been delegated or assigned is absent or prevented from attending, the President of the General Court shall designate another Judge to replace that Judge.

[10.645]
Article 33
1. The General Court shall deliberate in closed session.
2. Only those Judges who were present at the oral proceedings may take part in the deliberations.
3. Every Judge taking part in the deliberations shall state his opinion and the reasons for it.
4. Any Judge may require that any question be formulated in the language of his choice and communicated in writing to the other Judges before being put to the vote.
5. The conclusions reached by the majority of the Judges after final discussion shall determine the decision of the General Court. Votes shall be cast in reverse order to the order of precedence laid down in Article 6.
6. Differences of view on the substance, wording or order of questions, or on the interpretation of a vote shall be settled by decision of the General Court.
7. Where the deliberations of the General Court concern questions of its own administration, the Registrar shall be present, unless the General Court decides to the contrary.
8. Where the General Court sits without the Registrar being present it shall, if necessary, instruct the most junior Judge within the meaning of Article 6 to draw up minutes. The minutes shall be signed by this Judge and by the President.

[10.646]
Article 34

1. Subject to any special decision of the General Court, its vacations shall be as follows:
— from 18 December to 10 January,
— from the Sunday before Easter to the second Sunday after Easter,
— from 15 July to 15 September.

During the vacations, the functions of President shall be exercised at the place where the General Court has its seat either by the President himself, keeping in touch with the Registrar, or by a President of Chamber or other Judge invited by the President to take his place.

2. In a case of urgency, the President may convene the Judges during the vacations.
3. The General Court shall observe the official holidays of the place where it has its seat.
4. The General Court may, in proper circumstances, grant leave of absence to any Judge.

CHAPTER 5
LANGUAGES

[10.647]
Article 35

1. The language of a case shall be Bulgarian, Croatian, Czech, Danish, Dutch, English, Estonian, Finnish, French, German, Greek, Hungarian, Irish, Italian, Latvian, Lithuanian, Maltese, Polish, Portuguese, Romanian, Slovak, Slovene, Spanish or Swedish.
2. The language of the case shall be chosen by the applicant, except that:
(a) where the defendant is a Member State or a natural or legal person having the nationality of a Member State, the language of the case shall be the official language of that State; where that State has more than one official language, the applicant may choose between them;
(b) at the joint request of the parties, the use of another of the languages mentioned in paragraph 1 for all or part of the proceedings may be authorised;
(c) at the request of one of the parties, and after the opposite party and the Advocate General have been heard, the use of another of the languages mentioned in paragraph 1 as the language of the case for all or part of the proceedings may be authorised by way of derogation from subparagraph (b); such a request may not be submitted by an institution.

Requests as above may be decided on by the President; the latter may and, where he proposes to accede to a request without the agreement of all the parties, must refer the request to the General Court.

3. The language of the case shall be used in the written and oral pleadings of the parties and in supporting documents, and also in the minutes and decisions of the General Court.

Any supporting documents expressed in another language must be accompanied by a translation into the language of the case.

In the case of lengthy documents, translations may be confined to extracts. However, the General Court may, of its own motion or at the request of a party, at any time call for a complete or fuller translation.

Notwithstanding the foregoing provisions, a Member State shall be entitled to use its official language when intervening in a case before the General Court. This provision shall apply both to written statements and to oral addresses. The Registrar shall cause any such statement or address to be translated into the language of the case.

The States, other than the Member States, which are parties to the EEA Agreement, and also the EFTA Surveillance Authority, may be authorised to use one of the languages mentioned in paragraph 1, other than the language of the case, when they intervene in a case before the General Court. This provision shall apply both to written statements and oral addresses. The Registrar shall cause any such statement or address to be translated into the language of the case.

4. Where a witness or expert states that he is unable adequately to express himself in one of the languages referred to in paragraph 1 of this Article, the General Court may authorise him to give his evidence in another language. The Registrar shall arrange for translation into the language of the case.
5. The President in conducting oral proceedings, the Judge-Rapporteur both in his preliminary report and in his report for the hearing, Judges and the Advocate General in putting questions and the Advocate General in delivering his opinion may use one of the languages referred to in paragraph 1 of this Article other than the language of the case. The Registrar shall arrange for translation into the language of the case.

[10.648]
Article 36

1. The Registrar shall, at the request of any Judge, of the Advocate General or of a party, arrange for anything said or written in the course of the proceedings before the General Court to be translated into the languages he chooses from those referred to in Article 35(1).
2. Publications of the General Court shall be issued in the languages referred to in Article 1 of Council Regulation No 1.

[10.649]
Article 37
The texts of documents drawn up in the language of the case or in any other language authorised by the General Court pursuant to Article 35 shall be authentic.

CHAPTER 6
RIGHTS AND OBLIGATIONS OF AGENTS, ADVISERS AND LAWYERS

[10.650]
Article 38
1. Agents, advisers and lawyers, appearing before the General Court or before any judicial authority to which it has addressed letters rogatory, shall enjoy immunity in respect of words spoken or written by them concerning the case or the parties.
2. Agents, advisers and lawyers shall enjoy the following further privileges and facilities:
(a) papers and documents relating to the proceedings shall be exempt from both search and seizure; in the event of a dispute the customs officials or police may seal those papers and documents; they shall then be immediately forwarded to the General Court for inspection in the presence of the Registrar and of the person concerned;
(b) agents, advisers and lawyers shall be entitled to such allocation of foreign currency as may be necessary for the performance of their duties;
(c) agents, advisers and lawyers shall be entitled to travel in the course of duty without hindrance.

[10.651]
Article 39
In order to qualify for the privileges, immunities and facilities specified in Article 38, persons entitled to them shall furnish proof of their status as follows:
(a) agents shall produce an official document issued by the party for whom they act and shall forward without delay a copy thereof to the Registrar;
(b) advisers and lawyers shall produce a certificate signed by the Registrar. The validity of this certificate shall be limited to a specified period, which may be extended or curtailed according to the length of the proceedings.

[10.652]
Article 40
The privileges, immunities and facilities specified in Article 38 are granted exclusively in the interests of the proper conduct of proceedings.
The General Court may waive the immunity where it considers that the proper conduct of proceedings will not be hindered thereby.

[10.653]
Article 41
1. If the General Court considers that the conduct of an adviser or lawyer towards the General Court, the President, a Judge or the Registrar is incompatible with the dignity of the General Court or with the requirements of the proper administration of justice, or that such adviser or lawyer uses his rights for purposes other than those for which they were granted, it shall so inform the person concerned. The General Court may inform the competent authorities to whom the person concerned is answerable; a copy of the letter sent to those authorities shall be forwarded to the person concerned.
On the same grounds the General Court may at any time, having heard the person concerned, exclude that person from the proceedings by order. That order shall have immediate effect.
2. Where an adviser or lawyer is excluded from the proceedings, the proceedings shall be suspended for a period fixed by the President in order to allow the party concerned to appoint another adviser or lawyer.
3. Decisions taken under this Article may be rescinded.

[10.654]
Article 42
The provisions of this Chapter shall apply to university teachers who have a right of audience before the General Court in accordance with Article 19 of the Statute.

TITLE 2
PROCEDURE

CHAPTER 1
WRITTEN PROCEDURE

[10.655]
Article 43
1. The original of every pleading must be signed by the party's agent or lawyer.

The original, accompanied by all annexes referred to therein, shall be lodged together with five copies for the General Court and a copy for every other party to the proceedings. Copies shall be certified by the party lodging them.

2. Institutions shall in addition produce, within time-limits laid down by the General Court, translations of all pleadings into the other languages provided for by Article 1 of Council Regulation No 1. The second subparagraph of paragraph 1 of this Article shall apply.

3. All pleadings shall bear a date. In the reckoning of time-limits for taking steps in proceedings only the date of lodgment at the Registry shall be taken into account.

4. To every pleading there shall be annexed a file containing the documents relied on in support of it, together with a schedule listing them.

5. Where in view of the length of a document only extracts from it are annexed to the pleading, the whole document or a full copy of it shall be lodged at the Registry.

6. Without prejudice to the provisions of paragraphs 1 to 5, the date on which a copy of the signed original of a pleading, including the schedule of documents referred to in paragraph 4, is received at the Registry by telefax or other technical means of communication available to the General Court shall be deemed to be the date of lodgment for the purposes of compliance with the time-limits for taking steps in proceedings, provided that the signed original of the pleading, accompanied by the annexes and copies referred to in the second subparagraph of paragraph 1, is lodged at the Registry no later than ten days thereafter. Article 102(2) shall not be applicable to this period of ten days.

7. Without prejudice to the first subparagraph of paragraph 1 or to paragraphs 2 to 5, the General Court may by decision determine the criteria for a procedural document sent to the Registry by electronic means to be deemed to be the original of that document. That decision shall be published in the *Official Journal of the European Union*.

[10.656]
Article 44

1. An application of the kind referred to in Article 21 of the Statute shall state:
   (a) the name and address of the applicant;
   (b) the designation of the party against whom the application is made;
   (c) the subject-matter of the proceedings and a summary of the pleas in law on which the application is based;
   (d) the form of order sought by the applicant;
   (e) where appropriate, the nature of any evidence offered in support.

2. For the purposes of the proceedings, the application shall state an address for service in the place where the General Court has its seat and the name of the person who is authorised and has expressed willingness to accept service.

In addition to or instead of specifying an address for service as referred to in the first subparagraph, the application may state that the lawyer or agent agrees that service is to be effected on him by telefax or other technical means of communication.

If the application does not comply with the requirements referred to in the first and second subparagraphs, all service on the party concerned for the purposes of the proceedings shall be effected, for so long as the defect has not been cured, by registered letter addressed to the agent or lawyer of that party. By way of derogation from the first paragraph of Article 100, service shall then be deemed to have been duly effected by the lodging of the registered letter at the post office of the place where the General Court has its seat.

3. The lawyer acting for a party must lodge at the Registry a certificate that he is authorised to practise before a Court of a Member State or of another State which is a party to the EEA Agreement.

4. The application shall be accompanied, where appropriate, by the documents specified in the second paragraph of Article 21 of the Statute.

5. An application made by a legal person governed by private law shall be accompanied by:
   (a) the instrument or instruments constituting and regulating that legal person or a recent extract from the register of companies, firms or associations or any other proof of its existence in law;
   (b) proof that the authority granted to the applicant's lawyer has been properly conferred on him by someone authorised for the purpose.

5a. An application submitted under Article 272 TFEU pursuant to an arbitration clause contained in a contract governed by public or private law, entered into by the Union or on its behalf, shall be accompanied by a copy of the contract which contains that clause.

6. If an application does not comply with the requirements set out in paragraphs 3 to 5 of this Article, the Registrar shall prescribe a reasonable period within which the applicant is to comply with them whether by putting the application itself in order or by producing any of the above-mentioned documents. If the applicant fails to put the application in order or to produce the required documents within the time prescribed, the General Court shall decide whether the non-compliance with these conditions renders the application formally inadmissible.

[10.657]
Article 45
The application shall be served on the defendant. In a case where Article 44(6) applies, service shall be effected as soon as the application has been put in order or the General Court has declared it admissible notwithstanding the failure to observe the formal requirements set out in that Article.

[10.658]
Article 46
1. Within two months after service on him of the application, the defendant shall lodge a defence, stating:
(a) the name and address of the defendant;
(b) the arguments of fact and law relied on;
(c) the form of order sought by the defendant;
(d) the nature of any evidence offered by him.

The provisions of Article 44(2) to (5) shall apply to the defence.
2. In proceedings between the Union and its servants the defence shall be accompanied by the complaint within the meaning of Article 90(2) of the Staff Regulations of Officials and by the decision rejecting the complaint together with the dates on which the complaint was submitted and the decision notified.
3. The time-limit laid down in paragraph 1 of this Article may, in exceptional circumstances, be extended by the President on a reasoned application by the defendant.

[10.659]
Article 47
1. The application initiating the proceedings and the defence may be supplemented by a reply from the applicant and by a rejoinder from the defendant unless the General Court, after hearing the Advocate General, decides that a second exchange of pleadings is unnecessary because the documents before it are sufficiently comprehensive to enable the parties to elaborate their pleas and arguments in the course of the oral procedure. However, the General Court may authorise the parties to supplement the documents if the applicant presents a reasoned request to that effect within two weeks from the notification of that decision.
2. The President shall fix the time-limits within which these pleadings are to be lodged.

[10.660]
Article 48
1. In reply or rejoinder a party may offer further evidence. The party must, however, give reasons for the delay in offering it.
2. No new plea in law may be introduced in the course of proceedings unless it is based on matters of law or of fact which come to light in the course of the procedure.

If in the course of the procedure one of the parties puts forward a new plea in law which is so based, the President may, even after the expiry of the normal procedural time-limits, acting on a report of the Judge-Rapporteur and after hearing the Advocate General, allow the other party time to answer on that plea.

Consideration of the admissibility of the plea shall be reserved for the final judgment.

[10.661]
Article 49
At any stage of the proceedings the General Court may, after hearing the Advocate General, prescribe any measure of organisation of procedure or any measure of inquiry referred to in Articles 64 and 65 or order that a previous inquiry be repeated or expanded.

[10.662]
Article 50
1. The President may, at any time, after hearing the parties and the Advocate General, order that two or more cases concerning the same subject-matter shall, on account of the connection between them, be joined for the purposes of the written or oral procedure or of the final judgment. The cases may subsequently be disjoined. The President may refer these matters to the General Court.
2. The agents, advisers or lawyers of all the parties to the joined cases, including interveners, may examine at the Registry the pleadings served on the parties in the other cases concerned. The President may, however, on application by a party, without prejudice to Article 67(3), exclude secret or confidential documents from that consultation.

[10.663]
Article 51
1. In the cases specified in Article 14(1), and at any stage in the proceedings, the Chamber hearing the case or the President of the General Court may, either on its or his own initiative or at the request of one of the parties, propose to the General Court sitting in plenary session that the case be referred to the General Court sitting in plenary session, to the Grand Chamber or to a Chamber

composed of a different number of Judges. The decision to refer a case to a formation composed of a greater number of Judges shall be taken by the General Court in plenary session, after hearing the Advocate General.

The case shall be decided by a Chamber composed of at least five Judges where a Member State or an institution of the Union which is a party to the proceedings so requests.

2. The decision to delegate a case to a single Judge in the situations specified in Article 14(2) shall be taken, after the parties have been heard, unanimously by the Chamber composed of three Judges before which the case is pending.

Where a Member State or an institution of the Union which is a party to the proceedings objects to the case being heard by a single Judge the case shall be maintained before or referred to the Chamber to which the Judge-Rapporteur belongs.

[10.664]
Article 52

1. Without prejudice to Article 49, the President shall,
   (a) after the rejoinder has been lodged, or
   (b) where no reply or no rejoinder has been lodged within the time limit fixed in accordance with Article 47(2), or
   (c) where the party concerned has waived his right to lodge a reply or rejoinder, or
   (d) where the General Court has decided that there is no need, in accordance with Article 47(1), to supplement the application and the defence by a reply and a rejoinder, or
   (e) where the General Court has decided that it is appropriate to adjudicate under an expedited procedure in accordance with Article 76a(1),

fix a date on which the Judge-Rapporteur is to present his preliminary report to the General Court.

2. The preliminary report shall contain recommendations as to whether measures of organisation of procedure or measures of inquiry should be undertaken and whether the case should be referred to the General Court sitting in plenary session, to the Grand Chamber or to a Chamber composed of a different number of Judges.

The General Court shall decide, after hearing the Advocate General, what action to take upon the recommendations of the Judge-Rapporteur.

[10.665]
Article 53

Where the General Court decides to open the oral procedure without undertaking measures of organisation of procedure or ordering a preparatory inquiry, the President of the General Court shall fix the opening date.

[10.666]
Article 54

Without prejudice to any measures of organisation of procedure or measures of inquiry which may be arranged at the stage of the oral procedure, where, during the written procedure, measures of organisation of procedure or measures of inquiry have been instituted and completed, the President shall fix the date for the opening of the oral procedure.

CHAPTER 2
ORAL PROCEDURE

[10.667]
Article 55

1. The General Court shall deal with the cases before it in the order in which the preparatory inquiries in them have been completed. Where the preparatory inquiries in several cases are completed simultaneously, the order in which they are to be dealt with shall be determined by the dates of entry in the register of the applications initiating them respectively.

2. The President may in special circumstances order that a case be given priority over others.

The President may in special circumstances, after hearing the parties and the Advocate General, either on his own initiative or at the request of one of the parties, defer a case to be dealt with at a later date. On a joint application by the parties the President may order that a case be deferred.

[10.668]
Article 56

The proceedings shall be opened and directed by the President, who shall be responsible for the proper conduct of the hearing.

[10.669]
Article 57

The oral proceedings in cases heard in camera shall not be published.

[10.670]
Article 58
The President may in the course of the hearing put questions to the agents, advisers or lawyers of the parties.

The other Judges and the Advocate General may do likewise.

[10.671]
Article 59
A party may address the General Court only through his agent, adviser or lawyer.

[10.672]
Article 60
Where an Advocate General has not been designated in a case, the President shall declare the oral procedure closed at the end of the hearing.

[10.673]
Article 61
1. Where the Advocate General delivers his opinion in writing, he shall lodge it at the Registry, which shall communicate it to the parties.
2. After the delivery, orally or in writing, of the opinion of the Advocate General the President shall declare the oral procedure closed.

[10.674]
Article 62
The General Court may, after hearing the Advocate General, order the reopening of the oral procedure.

[10.675]
Article 63
1. The Registrar shall draw up minutes of every hearing. The minutes shall be signed by the President and by the Registrar and shall constitute an official record.
2. The parties may inspect the minutes at the Registry and obtain copies at their own expense.

CHAPTER 3
MEASURES OF ORGANISATION OF PROCEDURE AND MEASURES OF INQUIRY

Section 1 — Measures of organisation of procedure

[10.676]
Article 64
1. The purpose of measures of organisation of procedure shall be to ensure that cases are prepared for hearing, procedures carried out and disputes resolved under the best possible conditions. They shall be prescribed by the General Court, after hearing the Advocate General.
2. Measures of organisation of procedure shall, in particular, have as their purpose:
(a) to ensure efficient conduct of the written and oral procedure and to facilitate the taking of evidence;
(b) to determine the points on which the parties must present further argument or which call for measures of inquiry;
(c) to clarify the forms of order sought by the parties, their pleas in law and arguments and the points at issue between them;
(d) to facilitate the amicable settlement of proceedings.
3. Measures of organisation of procedure may, in particular, consist of:
(a) putting questions to the parties;
(b) inviting the parties to make written or oral submissions on certain aspects of the proceedings;
(c) asking the parties or third parties for information or particulars;
(d) asking for documents or any papers relating to the case to be produced;
(e) summoning the parties' agents or the parties in person to meetings.
4. Each party may, at any stage of the procedure, propose the adoption or modification of measures of organisation of procedure. In that case, the other parties shall be heard before those measures are prescribed.

Where the procedural circumstances so require, the Registrar shall inform the parties of the measures envisaged by the General Court and shall give them an opportunity to submit comments orally or in writing.
5. If the General Court sitting in plenary session or as the Grand Chamber decides to prescribe measures of organisation of procedure and does not undertake such measures itself, it shall entrust the task of so doing to the Chamber to which the case was originally assigned or to the Judge-Rapporteur.

If a Chamber prescribes measures of organisation of procedure and does not undertake such measures itself, it shall entrust the task to the Judge-Rapporteur.

The Advocate General shall take part in measures of organisation of procedure.

Section 2 Measures of inquiry

[10.677]
Article 65

Without prejudice to Articles 24 and 25 of the Statute, the following measures of inquiry may be adopted:

(a) the personal appearance of the parties;
(b) a request for information and production of documents;
(c) oral testimony;
(d) the commissioning of an expert's report;
(e) an inspection of the place or thing in question.

[10.678]
Article 66

1. The General Court, after hearing the Advocate General, shall prescribe the measures of inquiry that it considers appropriate by means of an order setting out the facts to be proved. Before the General Court decides on the measures of inquiry referred to in Article 65(c), (d) and (e) the parties shall be heard.

The order shall be served on the parties.

2. Evidence may be submitted in rebuttal and previous evidence may be amplified.

[10.679]
Article 67

1. Where the General Court sitting in plenary session or as the Grand Chamber orders a preparatory inquiry and does not undertake such an inquiry itself, it shall entrust the task of so doing to the Chamber to which the case was originally assigned or to the Judge-Rapporteur.

Where a Chamber orders a preparatory inquiry and does not undertake such an inquiry itself, it shall entrust the task of so doing to the Judge-Rapporteur.

The Advocate General shall take part in the measures of inquiry.

2. The parties may be present at the measures of inquiry.

3. Subject to the provisions of Article 116(2) and (6), the General Court shall take into consideration only those documents which have been made available to the lawyers and agents of the parties and on which they have been given an opportunity of expressing their views.

Where it is necessary for the General Court to verify the confidentiality, in respect of one or more parties, of a document that may be relevant in order to rule in a case, that document shall not be communicated to the parties at the stage of such verification.

Where a document to which access has been denied by an institution has been produced before the General Court in proceedings relating to the legality of that denial, that document shall not be communicated to the other parties.

Section 3 — The summoning and examination of witnesses and experts

[10.680]
Article 68

1. The General Court may, either of its own motion or on application by a party, and after hearing the Advocate General and the parties, order that certain facts be proved by witnesses. The order shall set out the facts to be established.

The General Court may summon a witness of its own motion or on application by a party or at the instance of the Advocate General.

An application by a party for the examination of a witness shall state precisely about what facts and for what reasons the witness should be examined.

2. The witness shall be summoned by an order containing the following information:

(a) the surname, forenames, description and address of the witness;
(b) an indication of the facts about which the witness is to be examined;
(c) where appropriate, particulars of the arrangements made by the General Court for reimbursement of expenses incurred by the witness, and of the penalties which may be imposed on defaulting witnesses.

The order shall be served on the parties and the witnesses.

3. The General Court may make the summoning of a witness for whose examination a party has applied conditional upon the deposit with the cashier of the General Court of a sum sufficient to cover the taxed costs thereof; the General Court shall fix the amount of the payment.

The cashier of the General Court shall advance the funds necessary in connection with the examination of any witness summoned by the General Court of its own motion.

4. After the identity of the witness has been established, the President shall inform him that he will be required to vouch the truth of his evidence in the manner laid down in paragraph 5 of this Article and in Article 71.

The witness shall give his evidence to the General Court, the parties having been given notice to attend. After the witness has given his main evidence the President may, at the request of a party or of his own motion, put questions to him.

The other Judges and the Advocate General may do likewise.

Subject to the control of the President, questions may be put to witnesses by the representatives of the parties.

5. Subject to the provisions of Article 71, the witness shall, after giving his evidence, take the following oath:

'I swear that I have spoken the truth, the whole truth and nothing but the truth.'

The General Court may, after hearing the parties, exempt a witness from taking the oath.

6. The Registrar shall draw up minutes in which the evidence of each witness is reproduced.

The minutes shall be signed by the President or by the Judge-Rapporteur responsible for conducting the examination of the witness, and by the Registrar. Before the minutes are thus signed, witnesses must be given an opportunity to check the content of the minutes and to sign them.

The minutes shall constitute an official record.

[10.681]
Article 69

1. Witnesses who have been duly summoned shall obey the summons and attend for examination.

2. If a witness who has been duly summoned fails to appear before the General Court, the latter may impose upon him a pecuniary penalty not exceeding EUR 5000 and may order that a further summons be served on the witness at his own expense.

The same penalty may be imposed upon a witness who, without good reason, refuses to give evidence or to take the oath or where appropriate to make a solemn affirmation equivalent thereto.

3. If the witness proffers a valid excuse to the General Court, the pecuniary penalty imposed on him may be cancelled. The pecuniary penalty imposed may be reduced at the request of the witness where he establishes that it is disproportionate to his income.

4. Penalties imposed and other measures ordered under this Article shall be enforced in accordance with Articles 280 TFEU and 299 TFEU and Article 164 TEAEC.

[10.682]
Article 70

1. The General Court may order that an expert's report be obtained. The order appointing the expert shall define his task and set a time-limit within which he is to make his report.

2. The expert shall receive a copy of the order, together with all the documents necessary for carrying out his task. He shall be under the supervision of the Judge-Rapporteur, who may be present during his investigation and who shall be kept informed of his progress in carrying out his task.

The General Court may request the parties or one of them to lodge security for the costs of the expert's report.

3. At the request of the expert, the General Court may order the examination of witnesses. Their examination shall be carried out in accordance with Article 68.

4. The expert may give his opinion only on points which have been expressly referred to him.

5. After the expert has made his report, the General Court may order that he be examined, the parties having been given notice to attend.

Subject to the control of the President, questions may be put to the expert by the representatives of the parties.

6. Subject to the provisions of Article 71, the expert shall, after making his report, take the following oath before the General Court:

'I swear that I have conscientiously and impartially carried out my task.'

The General Court may, after hearing the parties, exempt the expert from taking the oath.

[10.683]
Article 71

1. The President shall instruct any person who is required to take an oath before the General Court, as witness or expert, to tell the truth or to carry out his task conscientiously and impartially, as the case may be, and shall warn him of the criminal liability provided for in his national law in the event of any breach of this duty.

2. Witnesses and experts shall take the oath either in accordance with the first subparagraph of Article 68(5) and the first subparagraph of Article 70(6) or in the manner laid down by their national law.

3. Where the national law provides the opportunity to make, in judicial proceedings, a solemn affirmation equivalent to an oath as well as or instead of taking an oath, the witnesses and experts may make such an affirmation under the conditions and in the form prescribed in their national law.

Where their national law provides neither for taking an oath nor for making a solemn affirmation, the procedure described in the first paragraph of this Article shall be followed.

[10.684]
Article 72

1. The General Court may, after hearing the Advocate General, decide to report to the competent authority referred to in Annex III to the Rules supplementing the Rules of Procedure of the Court of Justice of the Member State whose courts have penal jurisdiction in any case of perjury on the part of a witness or expert before the General Court, account being taken of the provisions of Article 71.

2. The Registrar shall be responsible for communicating the decision of the General Court. The decision shall set out the facts and circumstances on which the report is based.

[10.685]
Article 73
1. If one of the parties objects to a witness or to an expert on the ground that he is not a competent or proper person to act as witness or expert or for any other reason, or if a witness or expert refuses to give evidence, to take the oath or to make a solemn affirmation equivalent thereto, the matter shall be resolved by the General Court.
2. An objection to a witness or to an expert shall be raised within two weeks after service of the order summoning the witness or appointing the expert; the statement of objection must set out the grounds of objection and indicate the nature of any evidence offered.

[10.686]
Article 74
1. Witnesses and experts shall be entitled to reimbursement of their travel and subsistence expenses. The cashier of the General Court may make a payment to them towards these expenses in advance.
2. Witnesses shall be entitled to compensation for loss of earnings, and experts to fees for their services. The cashier of the General Court shall pay witnesses and experts their compensation or fees after they have carried out their respective duties or tasks.

[10.687]
Article 75
1. The General Court may, on application by a party or of its own motion, issue letters rogatory for the examination of witnesses or experts.
2. Letters rogatory shall be issued in the form of an order which shall contain the name, forenames, description and address of the witness or expert, set out the facts on which the witness or expert is to be examined, name the parties, their agents, lawyers or advisers, indicate their addresses for service and briefly describe the subject-matter of the proceedings.

Notice of the order shall be served on the parties by the Registrar.
3. The Registrar shall send the order to the competent authority named in Annex I to the Rules supplementing the Rules of Procedure of the Court of Justice of the Member State in whose territory the witness or expert is to be examined. Where necessary, the order shall be accompanied by a translation into the official language or languages of the Member State to which it is addressed.

The authority named pursuant to the first subparagraph shall pass on the order to the judicial authority which is competent according to its national law.

The competent judicial authority shall give effect to the letters rogatory in accordance with its national law. After implementation the competent judicial authority shall transmit to the authority named pursuant to the first subparagraph the order embodying the letters rogatory, any documents arising from the implementation and a detailed statement of costs. These documents shall be sent to the Registrar.

The Registrar shall be responsible for the translation of the documents into the language of the case.
4. The General Court shall defray the expenses occasioned by the letters rogatory without prejudice to the right to charge them, where appropriate, to the parties.

[10.688]
Article 76
1. The Registrar shall draw up minutes of every hearing. The minutes shall be signed by the President and by the Registrar and shall constitute an official record.
2. The parties may inspect the minutes and any expert's report at the Registry and obtain copies at their own expense.

CHAPTER 3A
EXPEDITED PROCEDURES

[10.689]
Article 76a
1. The General Court may, on application by the applicant or the defendant, after hearing the other parties and the Advocate General, decide, having regard to the particular urgency and the circumstances of the case, to adjudicate under an expedited procedure.

An application for a case to be decided under an expedited procedure shall be made by a separate document lodged at the same time as the application initiating the proceedings or the defence. That application may state that certain pleas in law or arguments or certain passages of the application initiating the proceedings or the defence are raised only in the event that the case is not decided under an expedited procedure, in particular by enclosing with the application an abbreviated version of the application initiating the proceedings and a list of the annexes which are to be taken into consideration only if the case is decided under an expedited procedure.

By way of derogation from Article 55, cases on which the General Court has decided to adjudicate under an expedited procedure shall be given priority.

2. By way of derogation from Article 46(1), where the applicant has requested, in accordance with paragraph 1 of this Article, that the case should be decided under an expedited procedure, the period prescribed for the lodging of the defence shall be one month. If the General Court decides not to allow the request, the defendant shall be granted an additional period of one month in order to lodge or, as the case may be, supplement the defence. The time-limits laid down in this subparagraph may be extended pursuant to Article 46(3).

Under the expedited procedure, the pleadings referred to in Articles 47(1) and 116(4) and (5) may be lodged only if the General Court, by way of measures of organisation of procedure adopted in accordance with Article 64, so allows.

3. Without prejudice to Article 48, the parties may supplement their arguments and offer further evidence in the course of the oral procedure. They must, however, give reasons for the delay in offering such further evidence.

4. The decision of the General Court to adjudicate under an expedited procedure may prescribe conditions as to the volume and presentation of the pleadings of the parties; the subsequent conduct of the proceedings or as to the pleas in law and arguments on which the General Court will be called upon to decide.

If one of the parties does not comply with any one of those conditions, the decision to adjudicate under an expedited procedure may be revoked. The proceedings shall then continue in accordance with the ordinary procedure.

CHAPTER 4
STAY OF PROCEEDINGS AND DECLINING OF JURISDICTION BY THE GENERAL COURT

[10.690]
Article 77

Without prejudice to Article 123(4), Article 128 and Article 129(4), proceedings may be stayed:

(a) in the circumstances specified in the third paragraph of Article 54 of the Statute;
(b) where an appeal is brought before the Court of Justice against a decision of the General Court disposing of the substantive issues in part only, disposing of a procedural issue concerning a plea of lack of competence or inadmissibility or dismissing an application to intervene;
(c) at the joint request of the parties;
(d) in other particular cases where the proper administration of justice so requires.

[10.691]
Article 78

The decision to stay the proceedings shall be made by order of the President after hearing the parties and the Advocate General; the President may refer the matter to the General Court. A decision ordering that the proceedings be resumed shall be adopted in accordance with the same procedure. The orders referred to in this Article shall be served on the parties.

[10.692]
Article 79

1. The stay of proceedings shall take effect on the date indicated in the order of stay or, in the absence of such an indication, on the date of that order.

While proceedings are stayed time shall, except for the purposes of the time-limit prescribed in Article 115(1) for an application to intervene, cease to run for the purposes of prescribed time-limits for all parties.

2. Where the order of stay does not fix the length of the stay, it shall end on the date indicated in the order of resumption or, in the absence of such indication, on the date of the order of resumption.

From the date of resumption time shall begin to run afresh for the purposes of the time-limits.

[10.693]
Article 80

Decisions declining jurisdiction in the circumstances specified in the third paragraph of Article 54 of the Statute shall be made by the General Court by way of an order which shall be served on the parties.

CHAPTER 5
JUDGMENTS

[10.694]
Article 81

The judgment shall contain:

— a statement that it is the judgment of the General Court,
— the date of its delivery,
— the names of the President and of the Judges taking part in it,

— the name of the Advocate General, if designated,
— the name of the Registrar,
— the description of the parties,
— the names of the agents, advisers and lawyers of the parties,
— a statement of the forms of order sought by the parties,
— a statement, where appropriate, that the Advocate General delivered his opinion,
— a summary of the facts,
— the grounds for the decision,
— the operative part of the judgment, including the decision as to costs.

[10.695]
Article 82
1. The judgment shall be delivered in open court; the parties shall be given notice to attend to hear it.
2. The original of the judgment, signed by the President, by the Judges who took part in the deliberations and by the Registrar, shall be sealed and deposited at the Registry; the parties shall be served with certified copies of the judgment.
3. The Registrar shall record on the original of the judgment the date on which it was delivered.

[10.696]
Article 83
Subject to the provisions of the second paragraph of Article 60 of the Statute, the judgment shall be binding from the date of its delivery.

[10.697]
Article 84
1. Without prejudice to the provisions relating to the interpretation of judgments, the General Court may, of its own motion or on application by a party made within two weeks after the delivery of a judgment, rectify clerical mistakes, errors in calculation and obvious slips in it.
2. The parties, whom the Registrar shall duly notify, may lodge written observations within a period prescribed by the President.
3. The General Court shall take its decision in closed session.
4. The original of the rectification order shall be annexed to the original of the rectified judgment. A note of this order shall be made in the margin of the original of the rectified judgment.

[10.698]
Article 85
If the General Court should omit to give a decision on costs, any party may within a month after service of the judgment apply to the General Court to supplement its judgment.

The application shall be served on the opposite party and the President shall prescribe a period within which that party may lodge written observations.

After these observations have been lodged, the General Court shall decide both on the admissibility and on the substance of the application.

[10.699]
Article 86
The Registrar shall arrange for the publication of cases before the General Court.

CHAPTER 6
COSTS

[10.700]
Article 87
1. A decision as to costs shall be given in the final judgment or in the order which closes the proceedings.
2. The unsuccessful party shall be ordered to pay the costs if they have been applied for in the successful party's pleadings.

Where there are several unsuccessful parties the General Court shall decide how the costs are to be shared.

3. Where each party succeeds on some and fails on other heads, or where the circumstances are exceptional, the General Court may order that the costs be shared or that each party bear its own costs.

The General Court may order a party, even if successful, to pay costs which it considers that party to have unreasonably or vexatiously caused the opposite party to incur.

4. The Member States and institutions which intervened in the proceedings shall bear their own costs.

The States, other than the Member States, which are parties to the EEA Agreement, and also the EFTA Surveillance Authority, shall bear their own costs if they intervene in the proceedings.

The General Court may order an intervener other than those mentioned in the preceding subparagraph to bear his own costs.

5. A party who discontinues or withdraws from proceedings shall be ordered to pay the costs if they have been applied for in the observations of the other party on the discontinuance. However, upon application by the party who discontinues or withdraws from proceedings, the costs shall be borne by the other party if this appears justified by the conduct of that party.

Where the parties have come to an agreement on costs, the decision as to costs shall be in accordance with that agreement.

If costs are not applied for, the parties shall bear their own costs.

6. Where a case does not proceed to judgment, the costs shall be in the discretion of the General Court.

[10.701]
Article 88

Without prejudice to the second subparagraph of Article 87(3), in proceedings between the Union and its servants the institutions shall bear their own costs.

[10.702]
Article 89

Costs necessarily incurred by a party in enforcing a judgment or order of the General Court shall be refunded by the opposite party on the scale in force in the State where the enforcement takes place.

[10.703]
Article 90

Proceedings before the General Court shall be free of charge, except that:

(a) where a party has caused the General Court to incur avoidable costs, the General Court may order that party to refund them;
(b) where copying or translation work is carried out at the request of a party, the cost shall, in so far as the Registrar considers it excessive, be paid for by that party on the scale of charges referred to in Article 24(5).

[10.704]
Article 91

Without prejudice to the preceding Article, the following shall be regarded as recoverable costs:

(a) sums payable to witnesses and experts under Article 74;
(b) expenses necessarily incurred by the parties for the purpose of the proceedings, in particular the travel and subsistence expenses and the remuneration of agents, advisers or lawyers.

[10.705]
Article 92

1. If there is a dispute concerning the costs to be recovered, the General Court hearing the case shall, on application by the party concerned and after hearing the opposite party, make an order, from which no appeal shall lie.

2. The parties may, for the purposes of enforcement, apply for an authenticated copy of the order.

[10.706]
Article 93

1. Sums due from the cashier of the General Court and from debtors of the General Court shall be paid in euro.

2. Where expenses to be refunded have been incurred in a currency other than the euro or where the steps in respect of which payment is due were taken in a country of which the euro is not the currency, conversions of currency shall be made at the official rates of exchange of the European Central Bank on the day of payment.

CHAPTER 7
LEGAL AID

[10.707]
Article 94

1. In order to ensure effective access to justice, legal aid shall be granted for proceedings before the General Court in accordance with the following rules.

Legal aid shall cover, in whole or in part, the costs involved in legal assistance and representation by a lawyer in proceedings before the General Court. The cashier of the General Court shall be responsible for those costs.

2. Any natural person who, because of his economic situation, is wholly or partly unable to meet the costs referred to in paragraph 1 shall be entitled to legal aid.

The economic situation shall be assessed, taking into account objective factors such as income, capital and the family situation.

3. Legal aid shall be refused if the action in respect of which the application is made appears to be manifestly inadmissible or manifestly unfounded.

[10.708]
Article 95

1. An application for legal aid may be made before or after the action has been brought.

The application need not be made through a lawyer.

2. The application for legal aid must be accompanied by all information and supporting documents making it possible to assess the applicant's economic situation, such as a certificate issued by the competent national authority attesting to his economic situation.

If the application is made before the action has been brought, the applicant must briefly state the subject-matter of the proposed action, the facts of the case and the arguments in support of the action. The application must be accompanied by supporting documents in that regard.

3. The General Court may provide, in accordance with Article 150, for the compulsory use of a form in making an application for legal aid.

[10.709]
Article 96

1. Before giving its decision on an application for legal aid, the General Court shall invite the other party to submit its written observations unless it is already apparent from the information produced that the conditions laid down in Article 94(2) have not been satisfied or that those laid down in Article 94(3) have been satisfied.

2. The decision on the application for legal aid shall be taken by the President by way of an order. He may refer the matter to the General Court.

An order refusing legal aid shall state the reasons on which it is based.

3. In any order granting legal aid a lawyer shall be designated to represent the person concerned.

If the person has not indicated his choice of lawyer or if his choice is unacceptable, the Registrar shall send a copy of the order granting legal aid and a copy of the application to the competent authority of the Member State concerned mentioned in Annex II to the Rules supplementing the Rules of Procedure of the Court of Justice. The lawyer instructed to represent the applicant shall be designated having regard to the suggestions made by that authority.

An order granting legal aid may specify an amount to be paid to the lawyer instructed to represent the person concerned or fix a limit which the lawyer's disbursements and fees may not, in principle, exceed. It may provide for a contribution to be made by the person concerned to the costs referred to in Article 94(1), having regard to his economic situation.

4. The introduction of an application for legal aid shall suspend the period prescribed for the bringing of the action until the date of notification of the order making a decision on that application or, in the cases referred to in the second subparagraph of paragraph 3, of the order designating the lawyer instructed to represent the applicant.

5. If the circumstances which led to the grant of legal aid should alter during the proceedings, the President may at any time, on his own motion or on application, withdraw legal aid, having heard the person concerned. He may refer the matter to the General Court.

An order withdrawing legal aid shall contain a statement of reasons.

6. No appeal shall lie from orders made under this article.

[10.710]
Article 97

1. Where legal aid is granted, the President may, on application by the lawyer of the person concerned, decide that an amount by way of advance should be paid to the lawyer.

2. Where, by virtue of the decision closing the proceedings, the recipient of legal aid has to bear his own costs, the President shall fix the lawyer's disbursements and fees which are to be paid by the cashier of the General Court by way of a reasoned order from which no appeal shall lie. He may refer the matter to the General Court.

3. Where, in the decision closing the proceedings, the General Court has ordered another party to pay the costs of the recipient of legal aid, that other party shall be required to refund to the cashier of the General Court any sums advanced by way of aid.

In the event of challenge or if the party does not comply with a demand by the Registrar to refund those sums, the President shall rule by way of reasoned order from which no appeal shall lie. The President may refer the matter to the General Court.

4. Where the recipient of the aid is unsuccessful, the General Court may, in its decision, as to costs, closing the proceedings, if equity so requires, order that one or more parties should bear their own costs or that those costs should be borne, in whole or in part, by the cashier of the General Court by way of legal aid.

CHAPTER 8
DISCONTINUANCE

[10.711]
Article 98
If, before the General Court has given its decision, the parties reach a settlement of their dispute and intimate to the General Court the abandonment of their claims, the President shall order the case to be removed from the register and shall give a decision as to costs in accordance with Article 87(5) having regard to any proposals made by the parties on the matter.
This provision shall not apply to proceedings under Articles 263 TFEU and 265 TFEU.

[10.712]
Article 99
If the applicant informs the General Court in writing that he wishes to discontinue the proceedings, the President shall order the case to be removed from the register and shall give a decision as to costs in accordance with Article 87(5).

CHAPTER 9
SERVICE

[10.713]
Article 100
1. Where these Rules require that a document be served on a person, the Registrar shall ensure that service is effected at that person's address for service either by the dispatch of a copy of the document by registered post with a form for acknowledgement of receipt or by personal delivery of the copy against a receipt.
The Registrar shall prepare and certify the copies of documents to be served, save where the parties themselves supply the copies in accordance with Article 43(1).
2. Where, in accordance with the second subparagraph of Article 44(2), the addressee has agreed that service is to be effected on him by telefax or other technical means of communication, any procedural document including a judgment or order of the General Court may be served by the transmission of a copy of the document by such means.
Judgments and orders notified pursuant to Article 55 of the Statute to the Member States and institutions which were not parties to the proceedings shall be sent to them by telefax or any other technical means of communication.
Where, for technical reasons or on account of the length of the document, such transmission is impossible or impracticable, the document shall be served, if the addressee has failed to state an address for service, at his address in accordance with the procedures laid down in paragraph 1. The addressee shall be so advised by telefax or other technical means of communication. Service shall then be deemed to have been effected on the addressee by registered post on the tenth day following the lodging of the registered letter at the post office of the place where the General Court has its seat, unless it is shown by the acknowledgement of receipt that the letter was received on a different date or the addressee informs the Registrar, within three weeks of being advised by telefax or other technical means of communication, that the document to be served has not reached him.
3. The General Court may by decision determine the criteria for a procedural document to be served by electronic means. That decision shall be published in the *Official Journal of the European Union*.

CHAPTER 10
TIME-LIMITS

[10.714]
Article 101
1. Any period of time prescribed by the Treaties, the Statute or these Rules for the taking of any procedural step shall be reckoned as follows:
(a) Where a period expressed in days, weeks, months or years is to be calculated from the moment at which an event occurs or an action takes place, the day during which that event occurs or that action takes place shall not be counted as falling within the period in question;
(b) A period expressed in weeks, months or in years shall end with the expiry of whichever day in the last week, month or year is the same day of the week, or falls on the same date, as the day during which the event or action from which the period is to be calculated occurred or took place. If, in a period expressed in months or in years, the day on which it should expire does not occur in the last month, the period shall end with the expiry of the last day of that month;
(c) Where a period is expressed in months and days, it shall first be reckoned in whole months, then in days;
(d) Periods shall include official holidays, Sundays and Saturdays;
(e) Periods shall not be suspended during the judicial vacations.

2. If the period would otherwise end on a Saturday, Sunday or official holiday, it shall be extended until the end of the first following working day.

The list of official holidays drawn up by the Court of Justice and published in the *Official Journal of the European Union* shall apply to the General Court.

[10.715]
Article 102

1. Where the period of time allowed for commencing proceedings against a measure adopted by an institution runs from the publication of that measure, that period shall be calculated, for the purposes of Article 101(1)(a), from the end of the 14th day after publication thereof in the *Official Journal of the European Union.*

2. The prescribed time-limits shall be extended on account of distance by a single period of ten days.

[10.716]
Article 103

1. Any time-limit prescribed pursuant to these Rules may be extended by whoever prescribed it.

2. The President may delegate power of signature to the Registrar for the purpose of fixing time-limits which, pursuant to these Rules, it falls to the President to prescribe, or of extending such time-limits.

TITLE 3
SPECIAL FORMS OF PROCEDURE

CHAPTER 1
SUSPENSION OF OPERATION OR ENFORCEMENT AND OTHER INTERIM MEASURES

[10.717]
Article 104

1. An application to suspend the operation of any measure adopted by an institution, made pursuant to Article 278 TFEU and Article 157 TEAEC, shall be admissible only if the applicant is challenging that measure in proceedings before the General Court.

An application for the adoption of any other interim measure referred to in Article 279 TFEU shall be admissible only if it is made by a party to a case before the General Court and relates to that case.

2. An application of a kind referred to in paragraph 1 of this Article shall state the subject-matter of the proceedings, the circumstances giving rise to urgency and the pleas of fact and law establishing a prima facie case for the interim measures applied for.

3. The application shall be made by a separate document and in accordance with the provisions of Articles 43 and 44.

[10.718]
Article 105

1. The application shall be served on the opposite party, and the President of the General Court shall prescribe a short period within which that party may submit written or oral observations.

2. The President of the General Court may order a preparatory inquiry.

The President of the General Court may grant the application even before the observations of the opposite party have been submitted. This decision may be varied or cancelled even without any application being made by any party.

[10.719]
Article 106

A Judge, designated for the purpose in the decision adopted by the General Court in accordance with Article 10, shall replace the President of the General Court in deciding an application in the event that the President is absent or prevented from dealing with it.

[10.720]
Article 107

1. The decision on the application shall take the form of a reasoned order. The order shall be served on the parties forthwith.

2. The enforcement of the order may be made conditional on the lodging by the applicant of security, of an amount and nature to be fixed in the light of the circumstances.

3. Unless the order fixes the date on which the interim measure is to lapse, the measure shall lapse when final judgment is delivered.

4. The order shall have only an interim effect, and shall be without prejudice to the decision on the substance of the case by the General Court.

[10.721]
Article 108
On application by a party, the order may at any time be varied or cancelled on account of a change in circumstances.

[10.722]
Article 109
Rejection of an application for an interim measure shall not bar the party who made it from making a further application on the basis of new facts.

[10.723]
Article 110
The provisions of this Chapter shall apply to applications to suspend the enforcement of a decision of the General Court or of any measure adopted by another institution, submitted pursuant to Articles 280 TFEU and 299 TFEU and Article 164 TEAEC.

The order granting the application shall fix, where appropriate, a date on which the interim measure is to lapse.

CHAPTER 2
PRELIMINARY ISSUES

[10.724]
Article 111
Where it is clear that the General Court has no jurisdiction to take cognisance of an action or where the action is manifestly inadmissible or manifestly lacking any foundation in law, the General Court may, by reasoned order, after hearing the Advocate General and without taking further steps in the proceedings, give a decision on the action.

[10.725]
Article 112
The decision to refer an action to the Court of Justice, pursuant to the second paragraph of Article 54 of the Statute, shall, in the case of manifest lack of competence, be made by reasoned order and without taking any further steps in the proceedings.

[10.726]
Article 113
The General Court may at any time, of its own motion, after hearing the parties, decide whether there exists any absolute bar to proceeding with an action or declare that the action has become devoid of purpose and that there is no need to adjudicate on it; it shall give its decision in accordance with Article 114(3) and (4).

[10.727]
Article 114
1. A party applying to the General Court for a decision on admissibility, on lack of competence or other preliminary plea not going to the substance of the case shall make the application by a separate document.

The application must contain the pleas of fact and law relied on and the form of order sought by the applicant; any supporting documents must be annexed to it.

2. As soon as the application has been lodged, the President shall prescribe a period within which the opposite party may lodge a document containing the form of order sought and the arguments of fact and law relied on.
3. Unless the General Court otherwise decides, the remainder of the proceedings shall be oral.
4. The General Court shall, after hearing the Advocate General, decide on the application or reserve its decision for the final judgment. It shall refer the case to the Court of Justice if the case falls within the jurisdiction of that Court.

If the General Court refuses the application or reserves its decision, the President shall prescribe new time-limits for further steps in the proceedings.

CHAPTER 3
INTERVENTION

[10.728]
Article 115
1. An application to intervene must be made either within six weeks of the publication of the notice referred to in Article 24(6) or, subject to Article 116(6), before the decision to open the oral procedure as provided for in Article 53.
2. The application shall contain:
   (a) the description of the case;
   (b) the description of the parties;
   (c) the name and address of the intervener;
   (d) the intervener's address for service at the place where the General Court has its seat;

(e) the form of order sought, by one or more of the parties, in support of which the intervener is applying for leave to intervene;

(f) a statement of the circumstances establishing the right to intervene, where the application is submitted pursuant to the second or third paragraph of Article 40 of the Statute.

Articles 43 and 44 shall apply.

3. The intervener shall be represented in accordance with Article 19 of the Statute.

[10.729]
Article 116

1. The application shall be served on the parties.

The President shall give the parties an opportunity to submit their written or oral observations before deciding on the application.

The President shall decide on the application by order or shall refer the decision to the General Court. The order must be reasoned if the application is dismissed.

2. If an intervention for which application has been made within the period of six weeks prescribed in Article 115(1) is allowed, the intervener shall receive a copy of every document served on the parties. The President may, however, on application by one of the parties, omit secret or confidential documents.

3. The intervener must accept the case as he finds it at the time of his intervention.

4. In the cases referred to in paragraph 2 above, the President shall prescribe a period within which the intervener may submit a statement in intervention.

The statement in intervention shall contain:

(a) a statement of the form of order sought by the intervener in support of or opposing, in whole or in part, the form of order sought by one of the parties;

(b) the pleas in law and arguments relied on by the intervener;

(c) where appropriate, the nature of any evidence offered.

5. After the statement in intervention has been lodged, the President shall, where necessary, prescribe a time-limit within which the parties may reply to that statement.

6. Where the application to intervene is made after the expiry of the period of six weeks prescribed in Article 115(1), the intervener may, on the basis of the Report for the Hearing communicated to him, submit his observations during the oral procedure.

CHAPTER 4
JUDGMENTS OF THE GENERAL COURT DELIVERED AFTER ITS DECISION HAS BEEN SET ASIDE AND THE CASE REFERRED BACK TO IT

[10.730]
Article 117

Where the Court of Justice sets aside a judgment or an order of the General Court and refers the case back to that Court, the latter shall be seised of the case by the judgment so referring it.

[10.731]
Article 118

1. Where the Court of Justice sets aside a judgment or an order of a Chamber, the President of the General Court may assign the case to another Chamber composed of the same number of Judges.

2. Where the Court of Justice sets aside a judgment delivered or an order made by the General Court sitting in plenary session or by the Grand Chamber, the case shall be assigned to that Court or that Chamber as the case may be.

2a. Where the Court of Justice sets aside a judgment delivered or an order made by a single Judge, the President of the General Court shall assign the case to a Chamber composed of three Judges of which that Judge is not a member.

3. In the cases provided for in paragraphs 1, 2 and 2a of this Article, Articles 13(2), 14(1) and 51 shall apply.

[10.732]
Article 119

1. Where the written procedure before the General Court has been completed when the judgment referring the case back to it is delivered, the course of the procedure shall be as follows:

(a) Within two months from the service upon him of the judgment of the Court of Justice the applicant may lodge a statement of written observations;

(b) In the month following the communication to him of that statement, the defendant may lodge a statement of written observations. The time allowed to the defendant for lodging it may in no case be less than two months from the service upon him of the judgment of the Court of Justice;

(c) In the month following the simultaneous communication to the intervener of the observations of the applicant and the defendant, the intervener may lodge a statement of written observations. The time allowed to the intervener for lodging it may in no case be less than two months from the service upon him of the judgment of the Court of Justice.

2. Where the written procedure before the General Court had not been completed when the judgment referring the case back to the General Court was delivered, it shall be resumed, at the stage which it had reached, by means of measures of organisation of procedure adopted by the General Court.
3. The General Court may, if the circumstances so justify, allow supplementary statements of written observations to be lodged.

[10.733]
Article 120
The procedure shall be conducted in accordance with the provisions of Title 2 of these Rules.

[10.734]
Article 121
The General Court shall decide on the costs relating to the proceedings instituted before it and to the proceedings on the appeal before the Court of Justice.

CHAPTER 4A
DECISIONS OF THE GENERAL COURT GIVEN AFTER ITS DECISION HAS BEEN REVIEWED AND THE CASE REFERRED BACK TO IT

[10.735]
Article 121a
Where the Court of Justice reviews a judgment or an order of the General Court and refers the case back to that Court, the latter shall be seised of the case by the judgment so referring it.

[10.736]
Article 121b
1. Where the Court of Justice refers back to the General Court a case which was originally heard by a Chamber, the President of the General Court may assign the case to another Chamber composed of the same number of Judges.
2. Where the Court of Justice refers back to the General Court a case which was originally heard by the General Court sitting in plenary session or by the Grand Chamber, the case shall be assigned to that Court or that Chamber as the case may be.
3. In the cases provided for in paragraphs 1 and 2 of this Article, Articles 13(2), 14(1) and 51(1) shall apply.

[10.737]
Article 121c
1. Within one month of the service of the judgment of the Court of Justice, the parties to the proceedings before the General Court may lodge their observations on the conclusions to be drawn from that judgment for the outcome of the proceedings. This time-limit may not be extended.
2. The General Court may, by way of measures of organisation of procedure, invite the parties to the proceedings before it to lodge written submissions and may decide to hear the parties in an oral procedure.

[10.738]
Article 121d
The General Court shall decide on the costs relating to the proceedings instituted before it following the review of its decision by the Court of Justice.

CHAPTER 5
JUDGMENTS BY DEFAULT AND APPLICATIONS TO SET THEM ASIDE

[10.739]
Article 122
1. If a defendant on whom an application initiating proceedings has been duly served fails to lodge a defence to the application in the proper form within the time prescribed, the applicant may apply to the General Court for judgment by default.

The application shall be served on the defendant. The General Court may decide to open the oral procedure on the application.
2. Before giving judgment by default the General Court shall consider whether the application initiating proceedings is admissible, whether the appropriate formalities have been complied with, and whether the application appears well founded. It may order a preparatory inquiry.
3. A judgment by default shall be enforceable. The General Court may, however, grant a stay of execution until it has given its decision on any application under paragraph 4 of this Article to set aside the judgment, or it may make execution subject to the provision of security of an amount and nature to be fixed in the light of the circumstances; this security shall be released if no such application is made or if the application fails.
4. Application may be made to set aside a judgment by default.

The application to set aside the judgment must be made within one month from the date of service of the judgment and must be lodged in the form prescribed by Articles 43 and 44.

5. After the application has been served, the President shall prescribe a period within which the other party may submit his written observations.

The proceedings shall be conducted in accordance with the provisions of Title 2 of these Rules.

6. The General Court shall decide by way of a judgment which may not be set aside. The original of this judgment shall be annexed to the original of the judgment by default. A note of the judgment on the application to set aside shall be made in the margin of the original of the judgment by default.

CHAPTER 6
EXCEPTIONAL REVIEW PROCEDURES

Section 1 — Third-party proceedings

[10.740]
Article 123

1. Articles 43 and 44 shall apply to an application initiating third-party proceedings. In addition such an application shall:
   (a) specify the judgment contested;
   (b) state how that judgment is prejudicial to the rights of the third party;
   (c) indicate the reasons for which the third party was unable to take part in the original case before the General Court.

The application must be made against all the parties to the original case.

Where the judgment has been published in the Official Journal of the European Union, the application must be lodged within two months of the publication.

2. The General Court may, on application by the third party, order a stay of execution of the judgment. The provisions of Title 3, Chapter 1, shall apply.

3. The contested judgment shall be varied on the points on which the submissions of the third party are upheld.

The original of the judgment in the third-party proceedings shall be annexed to the original of the contested judgment. A note of the judgment in the third-party proceedings shall be made in the margin of the original of the contested judgment.

4. Where an appeal before the Court of Justice and an application initiating third-party proceedings before the General Court contest the same judgment of the General Court, the General Court may, after hearing the parties, stay the proceedings until the Court of Justice has delivered its judgment.

[10.741]
Article 124

The application initiating third-party proceedings shall be assigned to the Chamber which delivered the judgment which is the subject of the application; if the General Court sitting in plenary session or the Grand Chamber of the General Court delivered the judgment, the application shall be assigned to it. If the judgment has been delivered by a single Judge, the application initiating third-party proceedings shall be assigned to that Judge.

Section 2 — Revision

[10.742]
Article 125

Without prejudice to the period of ten years prescribed in the third paragraph of Article 44 of the Statute, an application for revision of a judgment shall be made within three months of the date on which the facts on which the application is based came to the applicant's knowledge.

[10.743]
Article 126

1. Articles 43 and 44 shall apply to an application for revision. In addition such an application shall:
   (a) specify the judgment contested;
   (b) indicate the points on which the application is based;
   (c) set out the facts on which the application is based;
   (d) indicate the nature of the evidence to show that there are facts justifying revision of the judgment, and that the time-limits laid down in Article 125 have been observed.

2. The application must be made against all parties to the case in which the contested judgment was given.

[10.744]
Article 127
1. The application for revision shall be assigned to the Chamber which delivered the judgment which is the subject of the application; if the General Court sitting in plenary session or the Grand Chamber of the General Court delivered the judgment, the application shall be assigned to it. If the judgment has been delivered by a single Judge, the application for revision shall be assigned to that Judge.
2. Without prejudice to its decision on the substance, the General Court shall, after hearing the Advocate General, having regard to the written observations of the parties, give its decision on the admissibility of the application.
3. If the General Court finds the application admissible, it shall proceed to consider the substance of the application and shall give its decision in the form of a judgment in accordance with these Rules.
4. The original of the revising judgment shall be annexed to the original of the judgment revised. A note of the revising judgment shall be made in the margin of the original of the judgment revised.

[10.745]
Article 128
Where an appeal before the Court of Justice and an application for revision before the General Court concern the same judgment of the General Court, the General Court may, after hearing the parties, stay the proceedings until the Court of Justice has delivered its judgment.

Section 3 — Interpretation of judgments

[10.746]
Article 129
1. An application for interpretation of a judgment shall be made in accordance with Articles 43 and 44. In addition it shall specify:
(a) the judgment in question;
(b) the passages of which interpretation is sought.

The application must be made against all the parties to the case in which the judgment was given.
2. The application for interpretation shall be assigned to the Chamber which delivered the judgment which is the subject of the application; if the General Court sitting in plenary session or the Grand Chamber of the General Court delivered the judgment, the application shall be assigned to it. If the judgment has been delivered by a single Judge, the application for interpretation shall be assigned to that Judge.
3. The General Court shall give its decision in the form of a judgment after having given the parties an opportunity to submit their observations and after hearing the Advocate General.

The original of the interpreting judgment shall be annexed to the original of the judgment interpreted. A note of the interpreting judgment shall be made in the margin of the original of the judgment interpreted.
4. Where an appeal before the Court of Justice and an application for interpretation before the General Court concern the same judgment of the General Court, the General Court may, after hearing the parties, stay the proceedings until the Court of Justice has delivered its judgment.

TITLE 4
PROCEEDINGS RELATING TO INTELLECTUAL PROPERTY RIGHTS

[10.747]
Article 130
1. Subject to the special provisions of this Title, the provisions of these Rules of Procedure shall apply to proceedings brought against the Office for Harmonisation in the Internal Market (Trade Marks and Designs) and against the Community Plant Variety Office (both hereinafter referred to as 'the Office'), and concerning the application of the rules relating to an intellectual property regime.
2. The provisions of this Title shall not apply to actions brought directly against the Office without prior proceedings before a Board of Appeal.

[10.748]
Article 131
1. The application shall be drafted in one of the languages described in Article 35(1), according to the applicant's choice.
2. The language in which the application is drafted shall become the language of the case if the applicant was the only party to the proceedings before the Board of Appeal or if another party to those proceedings does not object to this within a period laid down for that purpose by the Registrar after the application has been lodged.

If, within that period, the parties to the proceedings before the Board of Appeal inform the Registrar of their agreement on the choice, as the language of the case, of one of the languages referred to in Article 35(1), that language shall become the language of the case before the General Court.

In the event of an objection to the choice of the language of the case made by the applicant within the period referred to above and in the absence of an agreement on the matter between the parties to the proceedings before the Board of Appeal, the language in which the application for registration in question was filed at the Office shall become the language of the case. If, however, on a reasoned request by any party and after hearing the other parties, the President finds that the use of that language would not enable all parties to the proceedings before the Board of Appeal to follow the proceedings and defend their interests and that only the use of another language from among those mentioned in Article 35(1) makes it possible to remedy that situation, he may designate that other language as the language of the case; the President may refer the matter to the General Court.

3. In the pleadings and other documents addressed to the General Court and during the oral procedure, the applicant may use the language chosen by him in accordance with paragraph 1 and each of the other parties may use a language chosen by that party from those mentioned in Article 35(1).

4. If, by virtue of paragraph 2, a language other than that in which the application is drafted becomes the language of the case, the Registrar shall cause the application to be translated into the language of the case.

Each party shall be required, within a reasonable period to be prescribed for that purpose by the Registrar, to produce a translation into the language of the case of the pleadings or documents other than the application that are lodged by that party in a language other than the language of the case pursuant to paragraph 3. The party producing the translation, which shall be authentic within the meaning of Article 37, shall certify its accuracy. If the translation is not produced within the period prescribed, the pleading or the procedural document in question shall be removed from the file.

The Registrar shall cause everything said during the oral procedure to be translated into the language of the case and, at the request of any party, into the language used by that party in accordance with paragraph 3.

[10.749]
Article 132

1. Without prejudice to Article 44, the application shall contain the names of all the parties to the proceedings before the Board of Appeal and the addresses which they had given for the purposes of the notifications to be effected in the course of those proceedings.

The contested decision of the Board of Appeal shall be appended to the application. The date on which the applicant was notified of that decision must be indicated.

2. If the application does not comply with paragraph 1, Article 44(6) shall apply.

[10.750]
Article 133

1. The Registrar shall inform the Office and all the parties to the proceedings before the Board of Appeal of the lodging of the application. He shall arrange for service of the application after determining the language of the case in accordance with Article 131(2).

2. The application shall be served on the Office, as defendant, and on the parties to the proceedings before the Board of Appeal other than the applicant. Service shall be effected in the language of the case.

Service of the application on a party to the proceedings before the Board of Appeal shall be effected by registered post with a form of acknowledgment of receipt at the address given by the party concerned for the purposes of the notifications to be effected in the course of the proceedings before the Board of Appeal.

3. Once the application has been served, the Office shall forward to the General Court the file relating to the proceedings before the Board of Appeal.

[10.751]
Article 134

1. The parties to the proceedings before the Board of Appeal other than the applicant may participate, as interveners, in the proceedings before the General Court by responding to the application in the manner and within the period prescribed.

2. The interveners referred to in paragraph 1 shall have the same procedural rights as the main parties.

They may support the form of order sought by a main party and they may apply for a form of order and put forward pleas in law independently of those applied for and put forward by the main parties.

3. An intervener, as referred to in paragraph 1, may, in his response lodged in accordance with Article 135(1), seek an order annulling or altering the decision of the Board of Appeal on a point not raised in the application and put forward pleas in law not raised in the application.

Such submissions seeking orders or putting forward pleas in law in the intervener's response shall cease to have effect should the applicant discontinue the proceedings.

4. In derogation from Article 122, the default procedure shall not apply where an intervener, as referred to in paragraph 1 of this Article, has responded to the application in the manner and within the period prescribed.

[10.752]
Article 135
1. The Office and the parties to the proceedings before the Board of Appeal other than the applicant shall lodge their responses to the application within a period of two months from the service of the application.

Article 46 shall apply to the responses.

2. The application and the responses may be supplemented by replies and rejoinders by the parties, including the interveners referred to in Article 134(1), where the President, on a reasoned application made within two weeks of service of the responses or replies, considers such further pleading necessary and allows it in order to enable the party concerned to put forward its point of view.

The President shall prescribe the period within which such pleadings are to be submitted.

3. Without prejudice to the foregoing, in the cases referred to in Article 134(3), the other parties may, within a period of two months of service upon them of the response, submit a pleading confined to responding to the form of order sought and the pleas in law submitted for the first time in the response of an intervener. That period may be extended by the President on a reasoned application from the party concerned.

4. The parties' pleadings may not change the subject-matter of the proceedings before the Board of Appeal.

[10.753]
Article 135a
After the submission of pleadings as provided for in Article 135(1) and, if applicable, Article 135(2) and (3), the General Court, acting upon a report of the Judge-Rapporteur and after hearing the Advocate General and the parties, may decide to rule on the action without an oral procedure unless one of the parties submits an application setting out the reasons for which he wishes to be heard. The application shall be submitted within a period of one month from notification to the party of closure of the written procedure. That period may be extended by the President.

[10.754]
Article 136
1. Where an action against a decision of a Board of Appeal is successful, the General Court may order the Office to bear only its own costs.

2. Costs necessarily incurred by the parties for the purposes of the proceedings before the Board of Appeal and costs incurred for the purposes of the production, prescribed by the second subparagraph of Article 131(4), of translations of pleadings or other documents into the language of the case shall be regarded as recoverable costs.

In the event of inaccurate translations being produced, the second subparagraph of Article 87(3) shall apply.

TITLE 5
APPEALS AGAINST DECISIONS OF THE EUROPEAN UNION CIVIL SERVICE TRIBUNAL

[10.755]
Article 136a
Without prejudice to the arrangements laid down in Article 35(2)(b) and (c) and the fourth subparagraph of Article 35(3) of these Rules, in appeals against decisions of the Civil Service Tribunal as referred to in Articles 9 and 10 of the Annex to the Statute, the language of the case shall be the language of the decision of the Civil Service Tribunal against which the appeal is brought.

[10.756]
Article 137
1. An appeal shall be brought by lodging a notice of appeal at the Registry of the General Court or of the Civil Service Tribunal.

2. The Registry of the Civil Service Tribunal shall immediately transmit to the Registry of the General Court the papers in the case at first instance and, where necessary, the appeal.

[10.757]
Article 138
1. The notice of appeal shall contain:

(a) the name and address of the appellant;
(b) the names of the other parties to the proceedings before the Civil Service Tribunal;
(c) the pleas in law and legal arguments relied on;
(d) the form of order sought by the appellant.

Article 43 and Article 44(2) and (3) shall apply to appeals.

2. The decision of the Civil Service Tribunal appealed against shall be attached to the notice. The notice shall state the date on which the decision appealed against was notified to the appellant.

3. If a notice of appeal does not comply with Article 44(3) or with paragraph (2) of this Article, Article 44(6) shall apply.

[10.758]
Article 139
1. An appeal may seek:
(a) to set aside, in whole or in part, the decision of the Civil Service Tribunal;
(b) the same form of order, in whole or in part, as that sought at first instance and shall not seek a different form of order.
2. The subject-matter of the proceedings before the Civil Service Tribunal may not be changed in the appeal.

[10.759]
Article 140
The notice of appeal shall be served on all the parties to the proceedings before the Civil Service Tribunal. Article 45 shall apply.

[10.760]
Article 141
1. Any party to the proceedings before the Civil Service Tribunal may lodge a response within two months after service on him of the notice of appeal. The time-limit for lodging a response shall not be extended.
2. A response shall contain:
(a) the name and address of the respondent;
(b) the date on which notice of the appeal was served on the respondent;
(c) the pleas in law and legal arguments relied on;
(d) the form of order sought by the respondent.
Article 43 and Article 44(2) and (3) shall apply.

[10.761]
Article 142
1. A response may seek:
(a) to dismiss, in whole or in part, the appeal or to set aside, in whole or in part, the decision of the Civil Service Tribunal;
(b) the same form of order, in whole or in part, as that sought at first instance and shall not seek a different form of order.
2. The subject-matter of the proceedings before the Civil Service Tribunal may not be changed in the response.

[10.762]
Article 143
1. The notice of appeal and the response may be supplemented by a reply and a rejoinder where the President, on application made by the appellant within seven days of service of the response, considers such further pleading necessary and expressly allows the submission of a reply in order to enable the appellant to put forward his point of view or in order to provide a basis for the decision on the appeal. The President shall prescribe the date by which the reply is to be submitted and, upon service of that pleading, the date by which the rejoinder is to be submitted.
2. Where the response seeks to set aside, in whole or in part, the decision of the Civil Service Tribunal on a plea in law which was not raised in the appeal, the appellant or any other party may submit a reply on that plea alone within two months of the service of the response in question. Paragraph 1 shall apply to any further pleading following such a reply.

[10.763]
Article 144
Subject to the provisions of Articles 144 to 149 inclusive, Articles 48(2) and Articles 49, 50, 51(1), 52, 55 to 64, 76a to 110, 115(2) and (3), 116, 123 to 127 and 129 shall apply to the procedure before the General Court on appeal from a decision of the Civil Service Tribunal.

[10.764]
Article 145
Where the appeal is, in whole or in part, clearly inadmissible or clearly unfounded, the General Court may at any time, acting on a report from the Judge-Rapporteur and after hearing the Advocate General, by reasoned order dismiss the appeal in whole or in part.

[10.765]
Article 146
After the submission of pleadings as provided for in Article 141(1) and, if applicable, Article 143(1) and (2), the General Court, acting on a report from the Judge-Rapporteur and after hearing the Advocate General and the parties, may decide to rule on the appeal without an oral procedure

unless one of the parties submits an application setting out the reasons for which he wishes to be heard. The application shall be submitted within a period of one month from notification to the party of the closure of the written procedure. That period may be extended by the President.

[10.766]
Article 147
The preliminary report referred to in Article 52 shall be presented to the General Court after the pleadings provided for in Article 141(1) and where appropriate Article 143(1) and (2) have been lodged. Where no such pleadings are lodged, the same procedure shall apply after the expiry of the period prescribed for lodging them.

[10.767]
Article 148
Where the appeal is unfounded or where the appeal is well founded and the General Court itself gives judgment in the case, the General Court shall make a decision as to costs.

Article 88 shall apply only to appeals brought by institutions;

By way of derogation from Article 87(2), the General Court may, in appeals brought by officials or other servants of an institution, decide to apportion the costs between the parties where equity so requires.

If the appeal is withdrawn Article 87(5) shall apply.

[10.768]
Article 149
An application to intervene made to the Court in appeal proceedings shall be lodged before the expiry of a period of one month running from the date of the publication of the notice referred to in Article 24(6).

FINAL PROVISIONS

[10.769]
Article 150
The General Court may issue practice directions relating, in particular, to the preparations for and conduct of hearings before it and to the lodging of written pleadings or observations.

[10.770]
Article 151
These Rules, which are authentic in the languages mentioned in Article 35(1), shall be published in the *Official Journal of the European Union*. They shall enter into force on the first day of the second month from the date of their publication.

PRACTICE RULES FOR THE IMPLEMENTATION OF THE RULES OF PROCEDURE OF THE GENERAL COURT

[10.771]

NOTES

Date of publication in Official Journal: OJ L152, 18.6.2015, p 1.

The consolidated version of these Rules (reproduced here) is also available on the Curia website at curia.europa.eu/jcms/upload/docs/application/pdf/2016-08/dpe_vc_en.pdf. It includes the corrigendum (OJ 2016 L196, p 56) and the amendments adopted on 13 July 2016 (OJ 2016 L217, p 78).

THE GENERAL COURT,

[10.772]
Having regard to Article 224 of its Rules of Procedure;[1]

Whereas in the interests of transparency, legal certainty and the proper implementation of the Rules of Procedure, implementing rules must be laid down in respect of the responsibilities of the Registrar, in particular those relating to the maintenance of the register and case-files, the regularisation and service of procedural documents and items and the Registry's scale of charges;

Whereas in accordance with Article 37 of the Rules of Procedure, it is appropriate to fix the Registry's scale of charges;

Whereas in the interests of the proper administration of justice, parties' representatives, whether lawyers or agents within the meaning of Article 19 of the Protocol on the Statute of the Court of Justice of the European Union ('the Statute'), should be given practice directions on the presentation of procedural documents and items and as to how best to prepare for hearings before the General Court;

Whereas these Practice Rules explain, detail and supplement certain provisions of the Rules of Procedure and are intended to enable the parties' representatives to take account of matters which the General Court must take into consideration, particularly those relating to the lodging of procedural documents and items, to their presentation and translation and to interpretation at hearings;

Whereas there are particular features relating to the confidential treatment of procedural documents and items;

Whereas the Registrar is required to ensure that procedural documents and items placed on the case-file are in conformity with the provisions of the Statute, the Rules of Procedure and these Practice Rules;

Whereas the lodging of procedural documents and items that do not comply with the provisions of the Statute, the Rules of Procedure or these Practice Rules contributes, sometimes significantly, to an increase in the duration of proceedings and in the costs;

Whereas by complying with these Practice Rules, the parties' representatives, acting in their capacity as officers of the court, contribute through their adherence to procedural fairness to the efficiency of justice by enabling the General Court to deal effectively with the procedural documents and items which they lodge, thereby avoiding the risk of Article 139(a) of the Rules of Procedure being applied with regard to the points covered in these Practice Rules;

Whereas any repeated failure to comply with the requirements of the Rules of Procedure or of these Practice Rules, requiring regularisation to be sought, may result in the costs involved in the requisite processing thereof by the General Court having to be repaid pursuant to Article 139(c) of the Rules of Procedure;

Whereas the treatment of information or material produced pursuant to Article 105(1) or (2) of the Rules of Procedure is to be governed by the decision adopted by the General Court under Article 105(11) of the Rules of Procedure;

After consulting the agents of the Member States, the institutions intervening in proceedings before the General Court, the Office for Harmonisation in the Internal Market (Trade Marks and Designs) (OHIM) and the Council of Bars and Law Societies of Europe (CCBE);

NOTES

1 Rules of Procedure of the General Court (OJ L105, 23.4.2015, p 1).

HAS ADOPTED THESE PRACTICE RULES:

I.
THE REGISTRY

A.
TASKS OF THE REGISTRAR

[10.773]

1. The Registrar shall be responsible for the maintenance of the register of the General Court ('the Court') and the files of pending cases, for the acceptance, transmission, service and custody of documents, for correspondence with the parties, applicants for leave to intervene and applicants for legal aid, and for the custody of the seals of the Court. He shall ensure that Registry charges are collected and that sums due to the cashier of the Court are recovered. He shall be in charge of the publications of the Court and of the dissemination on the internet site of the Court of Justice of the European Union of documents concerning the Court.

2. In carrying out the duties specified in point 1 above, the Registrar shall be assisted by one or more Deputy Registrars. If the Registrar is prevented from acting, those duties shall be performed by one of the Deputy Registrars, according to seniority, who shall take the decisions reserved to the Registrar by the Rules of Procedure of the General Court or these Practice Rules, or delegated to him pursuant to these Practice Rules.

B.
OPENING HOURS OF THE REGISTRY

3. The offices of the Registry shall be open every working day. All days other than Saturdays, Sundays and the official holidays on the list referred to in Article 58(3) of the Rules of Procedure shall be working days.

4. If a working day as referred to in point 3 above is a holiday for the officials and servants of the institution, arrangements shall be made for a skeleton staff to be on duty at the Registry during the hours in which it is normally open.

5. The Registry shall be open at the following times:

— in the morning, from Monday to Friday, from 9.30 a.m. to 12 noon,

— in the afternoon, from Monday to Thursday, from 2.30 p.m. to 5.30 p.m. and on Fridays from 2.30 p.m. to 4.30 p.m.

6. The Registry shall be open half an hour before the commencement of a hearing to the representatives of the parties who have been given notice to attend that hearing.

7. Outside the Registry's opening hours, procedural documents may be validly lodged with the janitor at the entrances to the buildings of the Court of Justice of the European Union at any time of the day or night. The janitor shall make a record, which shall constitute good evidence, of the date and time of such lodgement and shall issue a receipt upon request.

C.
REGISTER

8. All documents placed on the file in cases brought before the Court shall be entered in the register.

9. Information or material produced pursuant to Article 105(1) or (2) of the Rules of Procedure, the treatment of which shall be governed by the decision adopted by the Court under Article 105(11) of the Rules of Procedure, shall also be entered in the register.

10. Entries in the register shall be numbered consecutively. They shall be made in the language of the case and contain the information necessary for identifying the document, in particular the date of lodgement, the date of registration, the number of the case and the nature of the document.

11. The register kept in electronic form shall be set up and maintained in such a way that no registration can be deleted therefrom and that following any amendment the original entry is preserved.

12. The registration number of every document issued by the Court shall be noted on its first page.

13. The note of the registration, including the registration number, the date of lodgement and the date of entry in the register, shall be made on the original of the procedural document lodged by the parties or on the version deemed to be the original of that document,[1] as well as on every copy which is served on them. This note shall be made in the language of the case.

14. For the purposes of establishing the date of lodgement referred to in point 13 above, the following dates shall be taken into account, depending on the circumstances: the date on which the procedural document was received by the Registry, the date referred to in Article 5 of the decision of the Court of 14 September 2011, the date referred to in point 7 above or, [in the cases provided for in the first paragraph of Article 54 of the Statute, the date on which the procedural document was lodged with the Registrar of the Court of Justice].

NOTES

Words in square brackets substituted by Amendments of the Practice Rules for the Implementation of the Rules of Procedure of the General Court, Article 1(1) (OJ L217 12.8.2016, p 78).

[14a. In accordance with Article 125c of the Rules of Procedure, material produced in the context of the amicable settlement procedure referred to in Articles 125a to 125d of the Rules of Procedure shall be entered in a specific register which shall not be subject to the rules set out in Articles 36 and 37 of those Rules.]

NOTES

Inserted by Amendments of the Practice Rules for the Implementation of the Rules of Procedure of the General Court, Article 1(2) (OJ L217 12.8.2016, p 78).

D.
CASE NUMBER

15. When an application initiating proceedings is registered, the case shall be given a serial number preceded by 'T-' and followed by an indication of the year. In the case of an appeal against a decision of the European Union Civil Service Tribunal, that number shall be followed by a specific reference.

16. Applications for interim measures, applications to intervene, applications for rectification or interpretation, applications for the Court to remedy a failure to adjudicate, applications for revision, applications for the Court to set aside judgments by default or initiating third-party proceedings, applications for the taxation of costs and applications for legal aid relating to pending cases shall be given the same serial number as the principal action, followed by a reference to indicate that the proceedings concerned are separate special forms of procedure.

17. An application for legal aid made with a view to bringing an action shall be given a serial number preceded by 'T-', followed by an indication of the year and a specific reference.

18. An action which is preceded by an application for legal aid in connection therewith shall be given the same case number as the latter.

19. Where the Court of Justice refers a case back to the Court following the setting aside or review of a decision, that case shall be given the number previously allocated to it when it was before the Court, followed by a specific reference.

20. The serial number of the case together with the names of the parties shall be indicated on the procedural documents, in correspondence relating to the case and, without prejudice to Article 66 of the Rules of Procedure, in the publications of the Court and in the documents of the Court on the internet site of the Court of Justice of the European Union.

E.
CASE-FILE AND INSPECTION OF THE CASE-FILE

E.1.
MAINTENANCE OF THE CASE-FILE

21. The case-file shall contain: the procedural documents (where applicable together with the annexes thereto) which will be taken into account in the determination of the case, bearing the note referred to in point 13 above, signed by the Registrar; the correspondence with the parties; where applicable, the report for the hearing, minutes of the hearing and minutes of the inquiry hearing, and the decisions taken in the case.

22. The documents placed on the case-file shall be given a serial number.

23. The confidential and non-confidential versions of procedural documents and of the annexes thereto shall be filed separately in the case-file.

24. Documents relating to the special forms of procedure referred to in point 16 above shall be filed separately in the case-file.

[24a. Material produced in the context of the amicable settlement procedure as provided for in Article 125a of the Rules of Procedure shall be placed in a file separate from the case-file.]

NOTES

Inserted by Amendments of the Practice Rules for the Implementation of the Rules of Procedure of the General Court, Article 1(3) (OJ L217 12.8.2016, p 78).

25. A procedural document and annexes thereto which are produced in a case and placed on the file of that case may not be taken into account for the purpose of preparing another case for hearing.

26. [At the close of the proceedings before the Court, the Registry shall arrange for the case-file and the file referred to in Article 125c(1) of the Rules of Procedure to be closed and archived.] The closed file shall contain a list of all the documents on the case-file, an indication of their number, and a cover page showing the serial number of the case, the parties and the date on which the case was closed.

NOTES

Words in square brackets substituted by Amendments of the Practice Rules for the Implementation of the Rules of Procedure of the General Court, Article 1(4) (OJ L217 12.8.2016, p 78).

27. The treatment of information or material produced pursuant to Article 105(1) or (2) of the Rules of Procedure shall be governed by the decision adopted by the Court under Article 105(11) of the Rules of Procedure.

E.2.
INSPECTION OF THE CASE-FILE

28. The representatives of the main parties to a case before the Court may inspect the case-file, including administrative files produced before the Court, at the Registry and may request copies of procedural documents or extracts of the case-file and of the register.

29. The representatives of the parties granted leave to intervene pursuant to Article 144 of the Rules of Procedure shall have the same right of inspection of the case-file as the main parties, subject to Article 144(5) and (7) of the Rules of Procedure.

30. In joined cases, the representatives of all parties shall have the right to inspect the files in the cases concerned by the joinder, subject to Article 68(4) of the Rules of Procedure.

31. Any person having made an application for legal aid pursuant to Article 147 of the Rules of Procedure without the assistance of a lawyer shall have the right to inspect the file relating to the legal aid.

32. Authorisation to inspect the confidential version of procedural documents and of any annexes thereto shall be granted only to the parties in respect of whom no confidential treatment has been ordered.

33. As regards information or material produced pursuant to Article 105(1) or (2) of the Rules of Procedure, reference is made to point 27 above.

[33a. The requirements of points 28 to 33 above do not apply to access to the file referred to in Article 125c(1) of the Rules of Procedure. Access to that specific file is governed by Article 125c of the Rules of Procedure.]

NOTES

Inserted by Amendments of the Practice Rules for the Implementation of the Rules of Procedure of the General Court, Article 1(5) (OJ L217 12.8.2016, p 78).

F.
ORIGINALS OF JUDGMENTS AND ORDERS

34. Originals of judgments and orders of the Court shall be kept in chronological order in the archives of the Registry. A certified copy shall be placed on the case-file.

35. At the parties' request, the Registrar shall supply them with a copy of the original of a judgment or of an order, if necessary in a non-confidential version.

36. The Registrar may supply uncertified copies of judgments and orders to third parties who so request, provided that those decisions are not already publicly accessible and do not contain confidential information.

37. Orders rectifying a judgment or an order, judgments or orders interpreting a judgment or an order, judgments given on applications to set aside judgments by default, judgments given and orders made in third-party proceedings or on applications for revision and judgments or orders of the Court of Justice in appeals or in reviews of decisions shall be mentioned in the margin of the judgment or order concerned. The original or a certified copy shall be appended to the original of the judgment or order.

G.
TRANSLATIONS

38. The Registrar shall, in accordance with Article 47 of the Rules of Procedure, arrange for everything said or written in the course of the proceedings to be translated, at the request of a Judge, an Advocate General or a party, into the language of the case or, where necessary, into another language as provided for in Article 45(1) of the Rules of Procedure. Where, for the purposes of the efficient conduct of the proceedings, a translation into another language, as provided for in Article 44 of the Rules of Procedure, is necessary, the Registrar shall also arrange for such a translation to be made.

H.
WITNESSES AND EXPERTS

39. The Registrar shall take the measures necessary for giving effect to orders requiring the taking of expert opinion or the examination of witnesses.

40. The Registrar shall obtain from witnesses evidence of their expenses and loss of earnings and from experts a fee note accounting for their expenses and services.

41. The Registrar shall cause sums due to witnesses and experts under the Rules of Procedure to be paid by the cashier of the Court. In the event of a dispute concerning such sums, the Registrar shall refer the matter to the President in order for a decision to be taken.

I.
REGISTRY'S SCALE OF CHARGES

42. Where an extract from the register is supplied in accordance with Article 37 of the Rules of Procedure, the Registrar shall impose a Registry charge of EUR 3.50 per page for a certified copy and EUR 2.50 per page for an uncertified copy.

43. Where a copy of a procedural document or an extract from the case-file is supplied to a party on paper at his request in accordance with Article 38(1) of the Rules of Procedure, the Registrar shall impose a Registry charge of EUR 3.50 per page for a certified copy and EUR 2.50 per page for an uncertified copy.

44. Where an authenticated copy of an order or of a judgment is, for the purposes of enforcement, supplied to a party at his request in accordance with Article 38(1) or Article 170 of the Rules of Procedure, the Registrar shall impose a Registry charge of EUR 3.50 per page.

45. Where an uncertified copy of a judgment or of an order is supplied in accordance with point 36 above to a third party at his request, the Registrar shall impose a Registry charge of EUR 2.50 per page.

46. Where, at the request of a party, the Registrar arranges for a procedural document or an extract from the case-file to be translated, the size of which is considered in accordance with Article 139(b) of the Rules of Procedure to be excessive, a Registry charge of EUR 1.25 per line shall be imposed.

47. Where a party or an applicant for leave to intervene has repeatedly failed to comply with the requirements of the Rules of Procedure or of these Practice Rules, the Registrar shall impose a Registry charge, in accordance with Article 139(c) of the Rules of Procedure, which may not exceed EUR 7,000 (2,000 times the charge of EUR 3.50 referred to in points 42 to 44 above).

J.
RECOVERY OF SUMS

48. Where sums paid out by way of legal aid, sums paid to witnesses or experts, or avoidable costs, within the meaning of Article 139(a) of the Rules of Procedure, incurred by the Court are recoverable by the cashier of the Court, the Registrar shall demand payment of those sums from the party who is to bear them.

49. If the sums referred to in point 48 above are not paid within the period prescribed by the Registrar, he may request the Court to make an enforceable order and, if necessary, require its enforcement.

50. Where Registry charges are recoverable by the cashier of the Court, the Registrar shall demand payment of those sums from the party or the third party who is to bear them.

51. If the sums referred to in point 50 above are not paid within the period prescribed by the Registrar, he may adopt an enforceable decision under Article 35(4) of the Rules of Procedure and, if necessary, require its enforcement.

K.
PUBLICATIONS AND POSTING OF DOCUMENTS ON THE INTERNET

52. The Registrar shall cause to be published in the *Official Journal of the European Union* the names of the President and of the Vice-President of the Court and of the Presidents of Chambers who have been elected by the Court, the composition of the Chambers and the criteria applied in the allocation of cases to them, the criteria applied in order to complete the formation of the Court or to attain the quorum, as the case may be, where a member of the formation of the Court is prevented from acting, the name of the Registrar and of any Deputy Registrar(s) elected by the Court, and the dates of the judicial vacations.

53. The Registrar shall cause to be published in the *Official Journal of the European Union* the decisions referred to in Article 11(3), Article 57(4), Article 74 and Article 105(11) of the Rules of Procedure.

54. The Registrar shall cause to be published in the *Official Journal of the European Union* the legal aid form.

55. The Registrar shall cause to be published in the *Official Journal of the European Union* notices of proceedings brought and of decisions closing proceedings, save in the case of decisions closing proceedings adopted before the application has been served on the defendant.

56. The Registrar shall ensure that the case-law of the Court is made public in accordance with arrangements adopted by the Court. Information concerning those arrangements shall be available on the internet site of the Court of Justice of the European Union.

NOTES

[1] In accordance with Article 3 of the decision of the General Court of 14 September 2011 on the lodging and service of procedural documents by means of e-Curia (OJ C289, 1.10.2011, p 9) ('the decision of the Court of 14 September 2011').

II.
GENERAL PROVISIONS ON PROCEDURES FOR DEALING WITH CASES

A.
SERVICE

[10.774]

57. Service shall be effected by the Registry in accordance with Article 57 of the Rules of Procedure.

58. The copy of the document to be served shall be accompanied by a letter specifying the case number, the register number and a brief indication of the nature of the document.

59. Where a document is served in accordance with Article 57(2) of the Rules of Procedure, the addressee shall be informed of such service by the transmission by e-Curia or by fax of a copy of the letter accompanying the document to be served and drawing his attention to the provisions of Article 57(2) of the Rules of Procedure.

60. The proof of service shall be kept on the case-file.

61. Where, owing to its size, only one copy of the full version of an annex to a procedural document is produced in accordance with Article 72(4) of the Rules of Procedure, the Registrar shall inform the parties accordingly and indicate to them that the item is available to them at the Registry for inspection.

62. If service of the application on the defendant is attempted unsuccessfully, the Registrar shall prescribe a time limit within which the applicant is to supply additional information for service or to ask whether the applicant will agree to use, at his own expense, the services of a judicial officer for the purpose of re-serving the application.

B.
TIME LIMITS

63. As regards Article 58(1)(a) and (b) of the Rules of Procedure, where a time limit is expressed in weeks, months or years, it shall expire at the end of the day which, in the last week, month or year indicated in the time limit, is the same day of the week, or falls on the same date, as the day on which the time limit began to run, that is the day on which the event which started time running occurred, or the action which started time running took place, and not the following day.

64. The Registrar shall prescribe the time limits provided for in the Rules of Procedure, in accordance with the authority accorded to him by the President.

65. In accordance with Article 62 of the Rules of Procedure, procedural documents or items received at the Registry after the time limit prescribed for their lodgement has expired may be accepted only with the authorisation of the President.

66. The Registrar may extend the time limits prescribed, in accordance with the authority accorded to him by the President. When necessary, he shall submit to the President proposals for the extension of time limits. Applications for extensions of time limits must be duly reasoned and be submitted in good time before the expiry of the time limit prescribed.

67. A time limit may not be extended more than once save for exceptional reasons.

C.
ANONYMITY

68. Where a party considers that his identity should not be made public in a case brought before the Court, he may request, pursuant to Article 66 of the Rules of Procedure, that the Court 'anonymise' the relevant case, in whole or in part.

69. The application for anonymity must be made by a separate document stating appropriate reasons.

70. In order to ensure that anonymity is preserved, it is recommended that the application be made at the outset of the proceedings. On account of the dissemination of information concerning the case on the internet, granting anonymity becomes much more difficult if the notice of the case concerned has already been published in the *Official Journal of the European Union*.

D.
OMISSION OF INFORMATION VIS-À-VIS THE PUBLIC

71. In accordance with Article 66 of the Rules of Procedure, a party may submit an application for the identity of third parties mentioned in connection with the proceedings or certain confidential information to be omitted from those documents relating to the case to which the public has access.

72. The application for omission must be made by a separate document. It must accurately identify the information concerned and state the reasons for which each item of information is regarded as confidential.

73. In order to ensure that the information concerned is not disclosed to the public, it is recommended that the application be made at the outset of the proceedings, or when lodging the procedural document containing the information concerned, or immediately after becoming aware of that procedural document, as the case may be. On account of the dissemination of information concerning the case on the internet, omitting information vis-à-vis the public becomes much more

difficult if the notice of the case concerned has already been published in the *Official Journal of the European Union*, or where the decision of the Court taken in the course of proceedings or closing them has been made available on the internet site of the Court of Justice of the European Union.

III.
PROCEDURAL DOCUMENTS AND THE ANNEXES THERETO

A.
LODGING OF PROCEDURAL DOCUMENTS AND ANNEXES

A.1.
BY E-CURIA

[10.775]

74. The lodging of procedural documents by exclusively electronic means shall be permitted using the e-Curia application (https://curia.europa.eu/e-Curia) in compliance with the decision of the Court of 14 September 2011 and the Conditions of use of the e-Curia application. Those documents shall be available on the internet site of the Court of Justice of the European Union.

75. If the e-Curia application is used, a paper version of the procedural document and certified copies of that document should not be sent to the Court by post.

76. Annexes to a procedural document, mentioned in the body of that document, which by their nature cannot be lodged by e-Curia, may be sent separately in accordance with Article 73(2) of the Rules of Procedure, provided that they are mentioned in the schedule of annexes to the document lodged by e-Curia. The schedule of annexes must identify which annexes are to be lodged separately. Those annexes must reach the Registry no later than 10 days after the lodging of the procedural document by e-Curia.

77. Without prejudice to specific rules, these Practice Rules shall be applicable to procedural documents lodged by means of the e-Curia application.

A.2.
BY FAX

78. A full copy of the original of a procedural document bearing the handwritten signature of the representative, including the schedule of annexes, may be transmitted to the Registry in accordance with Article 73(3) of the Rules of Procedure by fax to fax number +352 43032100.

79. The date on which a procedural document is lodged by fax shall be deemed to be the date of lodgement for the purposes of compliance with a time limit only if the original document bearing the handwritten signature of the representative that was transmitted by fax is lodged at the Registry no later than 10 days thereafter, as prescribed under Article 73(3) of the Rules of Procedure.

80. The original document bearing the handwritten signature of the representative must be sent without delay, immediately after its dispatch by fax, without any corrections or amendments, even of a minor nature, being made thereto.

81. In the event of any discrepancy between the original document bearing the handwritten signature of the representative and the copy previously received at the Registry by fax, the date on which that original signed document is lodged shall be deemed to be the date of receipt.

82. In accordance with Article 73(2) of the Rules of Procedure, the original of every procedural document bearing the handwritten signature of the representative must be accompanied by the adequate number of certified copies.

83. Where, in accordance with Article 77(1) of the Rules of Procedure, a party consents to being served by fax, the statement to that effect must specify the fax number for the purpose of service by the Registry. A single fax number must be stated, failing which regularisation will be required.

A.3.
BY POST

84. Procedural documents may be lodged by post at the following address:
Registry of the General Court of the European Union
Rue du Fort Niedergrünewald
L-2925 Luxembourg

85. In accordance with Article 73(2) of the Rules of Procedure, the original of every procedural document bearing the handwritten signature of the representative must be accompanied by the adequate number of certified copies.

B.
NON-ACCEPTANCE OF PROCEDURAL DOCUMENTS AND ITEMS

86. The Registrar shall refuse to enter in the register and to place on the case-file procedural documents and, where appropriate, items which are not provided for by the Rules of Procedure. If in doubt the Registrar shall refer the matter to the President in order for a decision to be taken.

87. Without prejudice to Article 73(3) of the Rules of Procedure and to Article 3 of the decision of the Court of 14 September 2011, the Registrar shall accept only procedural documents bearing the original handwritten signature of the lawyer or agent of the party concerned.

88. The Registrar may request the lodgement of a lawyer's or agent's specimen handwritten signature, if necessary certified as a true specimen, in order to enable him to verify that Article 73(1) of the Rules of Procedure has been complied with.

89. Save in the cases expressly provided for by the Rules of Procedure and subject to points 108 and 109 below, the Registrar shall refuse to enter in the register and to place on the case-file procedural documents or items drawn up in a language other than the language of the case.

90. Where a party challenges the Registrar's refusal to enter a procedural document or an item in the register and to place it on the case-file, the Registrar shall submit that issue to the President for a decision on whether the document or item in question is to be accepted.

C.
PRESENTATION OF PROCEDURAL DOCUMENTS AND ANNEXES

C.1.
PROCEDURAL DOCUMENTS

91. The following information must appear on the first page of each procedural document:
(a) the case number (T- . / .), where it has already been notified by the Registry;
(b) the title of the procedural document (application, defence, response, reply, rejoinder, application to intervene, statement in intervention, plea of inadmissibility, observations on . . . , replies to questions, etc.);
(c) the names of the applicant, of the defendant, of the intervener, if any, and of any other party to the proceedings in intellectual property cases and appeals against decisions of the Civil Service Tribunal;
(d) the name of the party on whose behalf the procedural document is lodged.

92. Each paragraph of the procedural document must be numbered consecutively.

93. Subject to Article 3 of the decision of the Court of 14 September 2011, each procedural document shall be required to bear a handwritten signature for the purposes of authenticating the author of the procedural document. The handwritten signature is also intended to ensure that the signatory accepts responsibility for the content of that procedural document. For those reasons, in procedural documents not lodged by means of the e-Curia application,
— the handwritten signature of the party's representative must appear at the end of the procedural document,
— the handwritten signature must not appear on its own on the last page of the procedural document,
— procedural documents signed *per procurationem* or in the name of a firm of lawyers cannot be accepted.

94. Where more than one representative is acting for the party concerned, the handwritten signature of the procedural document by one representative shall be sufficient.

95. The first page of each copy of the original of every procedural document bearing the handwritten signature of the representative of the party concerned that is not lodged by means of the e-Curia application and that is required to be produced by the parties pursuant to Article 73(2) of the Rules of Procedure must be endorsed with the words 'certified copy', initialled underneath by the representative.

96. Procedural documents must be submitted in such a way as to enable them to be processed electronically by the Court and, in particular, enabling their digitisation and character recognition. Accordingly, the following requirements must be complied with:
(a) the text, in A4 format, must be easily legible and appear on one side of the page only;
(b) documents produced in paper format must be assembled in such a way as to be easily separable (not bound together or permanently attached by other means, such as glue or staples);
(c) the text must be in a commonly-used font (such as Times New Roman, Courier or Arial) in at least 12 point in the body of the text and at least 10 point in the footnotes, with single line spacing, and upper, lower, left and right margins of at least 2.5 cm;

(d) the pages of each procedural document must be numbered consecutively.

C.2.

SCHEDULE OF ANNEXES

97. The schedule of annexes must appear at the end of the procedural document. Annexes submitted without a schedule of annexes will not be accepted.

98. The schedule of annexes must indicate, for each item annexed:

(a) the number of the annex (by reference to the procedural document to which the items are annexed, using a letter and a number: for example, Annex A.1, A.2, . . . for annexes to the application; B.1, B.2, . . . for annexes to the defence or to the response; C.1, C.2, . . . for annexes to the reply; D.1, D.2, . . . for annexes to the rejoinder);

(b) a short description of the annex (for example: 'letter', followed by its date, author and addressee and the number of pages);

(c) the page numbers of the first and last pages of each annex, according to the consecutive page numbering of the annexes (for example: pages 43 to 49 of the annexes);

(d) the page reference and paragraph number in the procedural document where that item is mentioned and its relevance is described.

99. In order to ensure optimal handling by the Registry, it is recommended that any annexes that are in colour be clearly indicated as such in the schedule of annexes.

C.3.

ANNEXES

100. Only those items mentioned in the actual text of a procedural document which are referred to in the schedule of annexes and which are necessary in order to prove or illustrate its contents may be submitted as annexes to a procedural document.

101. Items annexed to a procedural document must be submitted in such a way as to enable them to be processed electronically by the Court and to avoid any possibility of confusion. Accordingly, the following requirements must be complied with:

(a) each annex must be numbered in accordance with point 98(a) above;

(b) the use of dividers must be avoided, but it is recommended that each annex be introduced by means of a specific cover page in simple A4 paper format;

(c) where annexes are documents which themselves contain annexes, they must be arranged and numbered in such a way as to avoid any possibility of confusion;

(d) items annexed to a procedural document must be paginated in the top right-hand corner, in ascending order. Those items must be paginated consecutively but separately from the procedural document to which they are annexed;

(e) the annexes must be easily legible.

102. Each reference to an item lodged must state the relevant annex number as given in the schedule of annexes and indicate the procedural document with which the annex has been lodged (for example: Annex A.1 to the application).

D.

PRESENTATION OF FILES LODGED BY E-CURIA

103. Procedural documents and annexes thereto lodged by means of the e-Curia application shall be presented in the form of files. In order to assist the Registry in handling them, it is recommended to follow the practical guidance given in the e-Curia User Manual available online on the internet site of the Court of Justice of the European Union, namely:

— files must include names identifying the procedural document (Pleading, Annexes Part 1, Annexes Part 2, Covering letter, etc.),
— the text of the procedural document can be saved in PDF directly from the word-processing software without the need for scanning,
— the procedural document must include the schedule of annexes,
— the annexes must be contained in one or more files separate from the file containing the procedural document. A file may contain several annexes. It is not obligatory to create one file per annex. It is recommended that annexes be added in ascending order when they are lodged, and that they be sufficiently clearly named (for example: Annexes 1 to 3, Annexes 4 to 6, etc.).

E.
REGULARISATION OF PROCEDURAL DOCUMENTS AND ANNEXES

E.1.
GENERAL

104. The Registrar shall ensure that procedural documents placed on the case-file and the annexes thereto are in conformity with the provisions of the Statute and the Rules of Procedure, and with these Practice Rules.

105. If necessary, he shall allow the parties a period of time for making good any formal irregularities in the procedural documents lodged.

106. In the event of any repeated failure to comply with the requirements of the Rules of Procedure or of these Practice Rules, requiring regularisation to be sought, the Registrar will request the party or applicant for leave to intervene to pay the costs involved in the requisite processing thereof by the Court, in accordance with Article 139(c) of the Rules of Procedure.

107. Where annexes are still not submitted in accordance with the provisions of the Rules of Procedure or of these Practice Rules despite requests for regularisation, the Registrar shall refer the matter to the President for a decision on whether to refuse to accept those annexes.

108. Where material annexed to a procedural document is not accompanied by a translation into the language of the case, the Registrar shall require the party concerned to make good the irregularity if such a translation appears necessary for the purposes of the efficient conduct of the proceedings. If the irregularity is not made good, the annexes in question shall be removed from the case-file.

109. Where an application to intervene originating from a third party other than a Member State is not drawn up in the language of the case, the Registrar shall require the application to be put in order before it is served on the parties. If a version of such an application drawn up in the language of the case is lodged within the time limit prescribed for this purpose by the Registrar, the date on which the first version, not in the language of the case, was lodged shall be taken as the date on which the procedural document was lodged.

E.2.
REGULARISATION OF APPLICATIONS

110. If an application does not comply with the requirements specified in Annex 1 to these Practice Rules, the Registry shall not serve it and a reasonable time limit shall be prescribed for the purposes of putting it in order. Failure to put the application in order may result in the action being dismissed as inadmissible, in accordance with [Article 78(6)], Article 177(7) and Article 194(6) of the Rules of Procedure.

NOTES

Words in square brackets substituted by Amendments of the Practice Rules for the Implementation of the Rules of Procedure of the General Court, Article 1(6) (OJ L217 12.8.2016, p 78).

111. If an application does not comply with the procedural rules specified in Annex 2 to these Practice Rules, service of the application shall be delayed and a reasonable time limit shall be prescribed for the purposes of putting the application in order.

112. If an application does not comply with the procedural rules specified in Annex 3 to these Practice Rules, the application shall be served and a reasonable time limit shall be prescribed for the purposes of putting it in order.

E.3.
REGULARISATION OF OTHER PROCEDURAL DOCUMENTS

113. The instances of regularisation referred to in points 110 to 112 above shall apply as necessary to procedural documents other than the application.

IV.
THE WRITTEN PART OF THE PROCEDURE

A.
LENGTH OF WRITTEN PLEADINGS

A.1.
DIRECT ACTIONS

[10.776]
[114. In direct actions within the meaning of Article 1 of the Rules of Procedure, the maximum number of pages[1] shall be as follows:

In direct actions other than those brought pursuant to Article 270 TFEU:

— 50 pages for the application and for the defence,
— 25 pages for the reply and for the rejoinder,
— 20 pages for a plea of inadmissibility and for observations thereon,
— 20 pages for a statement in intervention and 15 pages for observations thereon.

In direct actions brought pursuant to Article 270 TFEU:

— 30 pages for the application and for the defence,
— 15 pages for the reply and for the rejoinder,
— 10 pages for a plea of inadmissibility and for observations thereon,
— 10 pages for a statement in intervention and 5 pages for observations thereon.]

NOTES

Substituted by Amendments of the Practice Rules for the Implementation of the Rules of Procedure of the General Court, Article 1(7) (OJ L217 12.8.2016, p 78).

115. Authorisation to exceed those maximum lengths will be given only in cases involving particularly complex legal or factual issues.

A.2.
INTELLECTUAL PROPERTY CASES

116. In intellectual property cases, the maximum number of pages[1] shall be as follows:

— 20 pages for the application and for responses,
— 15 pages for the cross-claim and for responses thereto,
— 10 pages for a plea of inadmissibility and for observations thereon,
— 10 pages for a statement in intervention and 5 pages for observations thereon.

117. Authorisation to exceed those maximum lengths will be given only in cases involving particularly complex legal or factual issues.

A.3.
APPEALS

118. In appeal cases, the maximum number of pages[1] shall be as follows:

— 15 pages for the appeal and for the response,
— 10 pages for the reply and for the rejoinder,
— 15 pages for the cross-appeal and for responses thereto,
— 10 pages for the reply and for the rejoinder following a cross-appeal,
— 10 pages for a statement in intervention and 5 pages for observations thereon.

119. Authorisation to exceed those maximum lengths will be given only in cases involving particularly complex legal or factual issues.

A.4.
REGULARISATION OF EXCESSIVELY LONG PLEADINGS

120. A pleading comprising a number of pages which exceeds by 40% or more the maximum number of pages prescribed in points 114, 116 or 118 above, as the case may be, shall require regularisation, unless otherwise directed by the President.

121. A pleading comprising a number of pages which exceeds by less than 40% the maximum number of pages prescribed in points 114, 116 or 118 above, as the case may be, may require regularisation if so directed by the President.

122. Where a party is requested to put his pleading in order on account of its excessive length, service of the pleading which requires regularisation on account of its length shall be delayed.

B.
STRUCTURE AND CONTENT OF WRITTEN PLEADINGS

B.1.
DIRECT ACTIONS

1.
Application initiating proceedings

123. The mandatory information to be included in the application initiating proceedings is prescribed by Article 76 of the Rules of Procedure.

124. The application must also contain the statement referred to in Article 77(1) of the Rules of Procedure.

125. The introductory part of the application should be followed by a brief account of the facts giving rise to the dispute.

126. The precise wording of the form of order sought by the applicant must be stated either at the beginning or at the end of the application.

127. Legal arguments should be set out and grouped by reference to the particular pleas in law to which they relate. Each argument or group of arguments should generally be preceded by a summary statement of the relevant plea. In addition, the pleas in law put forward should ideally each be given a heading to enable them to be identified easily.

128. The documents referred to in Article 51(2) and (3) and Article 78 of the Rules of Procedure must be produced together with the application.

129. For the purposes of the production of the document required by Article 51(2) of the Rules of Procedure certifying that the lawyer representing a party or assisting the party's agent is authorised to practise before a court of a Member State or of another State which is a party to the Agreement on the European Economic Area, reference may be made to a document previously lodged at the Registry of the Court.

130. Each application must be accompanied by a summary of the pleas in law and main arguments relied on, designed to facilitate the drafting of the notice prescribed by Article 79 of the Rules of Procedure. Since the notice is required to be published in the *Official Journal of the European Union* in all the official languages, it is requested that the summary not exceed two pages and that it be prepared in the language of the case in accordance with the model available online on the internet site of the Court of Justice of the European Union.

131. The summary of the pleas in law and main arguments relied on must be produced separately from the body of the application and the annexes mentioned in the application.

132. The summary of the pleas in law and main arguments relied on must, if not lodged by means of the e-Curia application, be sent by e-mail, as an ordinary electronic file produced using word-processing software, to GC.Registry@curia.europa.eu, indicating the case to which it relates.

133. If the application is lodged after the submission of an application for legal aid, the effect of which, under Article 147(7) of the Rules of Procedure, is to suspend the time limit prescribed for the bringing of an action, this must be stated at the beginning of the application initiating proceedings.

134. If the application is lodged after service of the order making a decision on an application for legal aid or, where no lawyer is designated in that order to represent the applicant for legal aid, after service of the order designating the lawyer instructed to represent the applicant for legal aid, reference must also be made in the application to the date on which the order was served on the applicant.

135. In order to facilitate formal preparation of the application, the parties' representatives are invited to consult the following documents, available on the internet site of the Court of Justice of the European Union: 'Aide-mémoire: Application lodged in paper format' and 'Aide-mémoire: Application lodged by means of e-Curia'.

2.
Defence

136. The mandatory information to be included in the defence is prescribed by Article 81(1) of the Rules of Procedure.

137. The precise wording of the form of order sought by the defendant must be stated either at the beginning or at the end of the defence.

138. Any fact alleged by the applicant which is contested must be specified and the basis on which it is contested expressly stated.

139. Since the legal framework of the proceedings is fixed by the application, the legal arguments developed in the defence must, so far as is possible, be set out and grouped by reference to the pleas in law or complaints put forward in the application.

140. Points 124, 128 and 129 above shall apply to the defence.

[140a. In cases brought pursuant to Article 270 TFEU, the institutions should preferably annex to the defence any acts of general application cited which have not been published in the Official Journal of the European Union, together with details of the dates of their adoption, their entry into force and, where applicable, their repeal.]

NOTES

Inserted by Amendments of the Practice Rules for the Implementation of the Rules of Procedure of the General Court, Article 1(8) (OJ L217 12.8.2016, p 78).

3.
Reply and rejoinder

141. Where there is a second exchange of pleadings, the main parties may supplement their legal arguments with a reply or a rejoinder, as the case may be.

142. The framework and the pleas in law or complaints at the heart of the dispute having been set out (or disputed) in depth in the application and the defence, the purpose of the reply and the rejoinder shall be to allow the applicant and the defendant to make clear their position or to refine their arguments on an important issue, and to respond to new matters raised in the defence and in the reply. The President may also, pursuant to Article 83(3) of the Rules of Procedure, himself specify the matters to which those procedural documents should relate.

B.2.
INTELLECTUAL PROPERTY CASES

1.
Application initiating proceedings

143. The mandatory information to be included in the application initiating proceedings is prescribed by Article 177(1) of the Rules of Procedure.

144. The application must also contain the statement referred to in Article 77(1) of the Rules of Procedure and the information referred to in Article 177(2) and (3) of the Rules of Procedure.

145. The documents referred to Article 177(3) to (5) of the Rules of Procedure must be produced together with the application.

146. Points 125 to 127, 129 and 133 to 135 above shall apply to applications in intellectual property cases.

2.
Response

147. The mandatory information to be included in the response is prescribed by Article 180(1) of the Rules of Procedure.

148. The response must also contain the statement referred to in Article 77(1) of the Rules of Procedure.

149. The precise wording of the form of order sought by the defendant or by the intervener must be stated either at the beginning or at the end of the response.

150. The documents referred to Article 177(4) and (5) of the Rules of Procedure must be produced together with the response lodged by the intervener, in so far as those documents have not already been lodged in accordance with Article 173(5) of the Rules of Procedure.

151. Points 129, 138 and 139 above shall apply to the response.

3.
Cross-claim and responses to the cross-claim

152. If, when the application has been served on him, a party to the proceedings before the Board of Appeal other than the applicant intends to challenge the contested decision on a point not raised in the application, that party must introduce a cross-claim when lodging his response. That cross-claim must be introduced by a separate document and meet the requirements set out in Articles 183 and 184 of the Rules of Procedure.

153. Where such a cross-claim is made, the other parties to the proceedings may submit a pleading in response confined to the form of order sought, the pleas in law and the arguments relied on in the cross-claim.

B.3.
APPEALS

1.
Appeal

154. The appeal must contain the information prescribed by Article 194(1) of the Rules of Procedure.

155. The appeal must also contain the information referred to in Article 77(1) and Article 194(2) of the Rules of Procedure.

156. The precise wording of the form of order sought by the appellant must be stated either at the beginning or at the end of the appeal. In accordance with Article 195(1) of the Rules of Procedure, the form of order sought must necessarily seek the setting aside, in whole or in part, of the decision of the Civil Service Tribunal as set out in the operative part of that decision.

157. It will not generally be necessary to describe the background or subject-matter of the proceedings. A reference to the decision of the Civil Service Tribunal shall be sufficient.

158. It is recommended that the pleas in law be summarised at the beginning of the appeal. Legal arguments should be set out and grouped by reference to the particular grounds of appeal to which they relate, in particular the errors of law relied on.

159. The pleas in law and legal arguments relied on in the appeal must identify the grounds of the decision of the Civil Service Tribunal that are contested by specifying the points at issue in that decision, and set out in detail the reasons for which that decision is alleged to be vitiated by an error of law.

160. The documents referred to in Article 194(3) and (4) of the Rules of Procedure must, where applicable, be produced together with the appeal.

161. Each appeal must be accompanied by a summary of the pleas in law and main arguments relied on, designed to facilitate the drafting of the notice for publication prescribed by Article 79 of the Rules of Procedure. Since the notice is required to be published in the *Official Journal of the European Union* in all the official languages, it is requested that the summary not exceed two pages and that it be prepared in the language of the case in accordance with the model available online on the internet site of the Court of Justice of the European Union.

162. The summary of the pleas in law and main arguments relied on must be produced separately from the body of the appeal and the annexes mentioned in the appeal.

163. The summary of the pleas in law and main arguments relied on must, if not lodged by means of the e-Curia application, be sent by e-mail, as an ordinary electronic file produced using word-processing software, to GC.Registry@curia.europa.eu, indicating the case to which it relates.

164. Point 129 above shall apply to appeals in appeal cases.

2.
Response

165. The response must contain the information prescribed by Article 199(1) of the Rules of Procedure.

166. The response must also contain the information referred to in Article 77(1) of the Rules of Procedure.

167. The precise wording of the form of order sought by the party submitting the response must be stated either at the beginning or at the end of the response. In accordance with Article 200 of the Rules of Procedure, the form of order sought must seek to have the appeal allowed or dismissed, in whole or in part.

168. Legal arguments must, so far as is possible, be set out and grouped by reference to the pleas in law put forward by the appellant.

169. Since the factual and legal background will already be included in the judgment or order under appeal, it should be repeated in the response only in truly exceptional circumstances, in so far as its presentation in the appeal is contested or requires clarification. The contested matter of fact or of law must be identified and the basis of that contest clearly stated.

170. Any challenge to the admissibility, in whole or in part, of the appeal must be included in the actual body of the response, since the possibility — provided for in Article 130 of the Rules of Procedure — of raising a plea of inadmissibility in relation to the proceedings by a separate document is not applicable to appeals.

171. The documents referred to in Article 194(3) and (4) of the Rules of Procedure must, where applicable, be produced together with the response.

172. Point 129 above shall apply to responses lodged in appeal cases.

3.
Cross-appeal and responses to the cross-appeal

173. If, when the appeal has been served on him, one of the parties to the relevant case before the Civil Service Tribunal intends to challenge the Civil Service Tribunal's decision on an aspect not mentioned in the appeal, that party must bring a cross-appeal against the Civil Service Tribunal's decision. That cross-appeal must be introduced by a separate document and meet the requirements set out in Articles 203 and 204 of the Rules of Procedure. The pleas in law and legal arguments which it contains must be separate from those relied on in the response.

174. Where such a cross-appeal is brought, the appellant, or any other party to the relevant case before the Civil Service Tribunal having an interest in the cross-appeal being allowed or dismissed, may submit a response, which must be limited to the pleas in law relied on in that cross-appeal.

4.
Reply and rejoinder

175. Whether in the case of a main appeal or a cross-appeal, the appeal and the response may be supplemented by a reply and a rejoinder, in particular in order to allow the parties to present their views on a plea of inadmissibility or on new matters relied on in the response.

176. In accordance with Article 201(1) and Article 206(1) of the Rules of Procedure, that possibility is subject to the express authorisation of the President on application by the appellant or the party who brought the cross-appeal.

177. Save in exceptional circumstances, such an application must not exceed 2 pages and must be confined to summarising the precise reasons for which a reply is necessary. The request must be intelligible in itself, without necessitating reference to the appeal or to the response.

178. Due to the special nature of appeals, which are restricted to the examination of questions of law, the President may, if he grants the application to lodge a reply, limit the number of pages and the subject-matter of that reply and of the rejoinder submitted subsequently. The observance of those instructions is an essential condition for the efficient conduct of the proceedings.

NOTES

[1] The text must be presented in accordance with the requirements set out in point 96(c) of these Practice Rules.

V.
THE ORAL PART OF THE PROCEDURE

A.
REQUESTS FOR A HEARING

A.1.
REQUESTS FOR A HEARING IN DIRECT ACTIONS AND IN INTELLECTUAL PROPERTY CASES

[10.777]

179. As is apparent from Article 106 of the Rules of Procedure, the Court shall arrange a hearing either of its own motion or at the request of a main party.

180. A main party who wishes to present oral argument must submit a reasoned request for a hearing, within three weeks after service on the parties of notification of the close of the written part of the procedure. That reasoning — which is not to be confused with written pleadings or observations and should not exceed three pages — must be based on a real assessment of the benefit

of a hearing to the party in question and must indicate the elements of the case-file or arguments which that party considers it necessary to develop or refute more fully at a hearing. In order better to ensure that the arguments remain focused at the hearing, the statement of reasons should preferably not be in general terms merely referring, for example, to the importance of the case.

181. If no reasoned request is submitted by a main party within the prescribed time limit, the Court may decide to rule on the action without an oral part of the procedure.

A.2.
REQUESTS FOR A HEARING IN APPEAL PROCEEDINGS

182. As is apparent from Article 12(2) of Annex I to the Statute and Article 207(1) of the Rules of Procedure, a party to the appeal proceedings who wishes to present oral argument must submit a reasoned request for a hearing, within three weeks after service on the parties of notification of the close of the written part of the procedure. That reasoning — which is not to be confused with written pleadings or observations and should not exceed three pages — must be based on a real assessment of the benefit of a hearing to the party in question and must indicate the elements of the case-file or arguments which that party considers it necessary to develop or refute more fully at a hearing. In order better to ensure that the arguments remain focused at the hearing, the statement of reasons should preferably not be in general terms merely referring, for example, to the importance of the case.

183. However, the Court may, if it considers that it has sufficient information available to it from the material in the file, decide to rule on the appeal without an oral part of the procedure. In appeal cases, the Court may proceed without arranging a hearing notwithstanding the submission of a reasoned request by a party to the appeal proceedings.

B.
PREPARATION FOR THE HEARING

184. The parties shall be given notice to attend the hearing by the Registry at least one month before it takes place, provided always that, where the circumstances so require, a shorter period of notice may apply.

185. In accordance with Article 107(2) of the Rules of Procedure, requests for an adjournment of the hearing shall be granted only in exceptional circumstances. Such requests may be lodged only by the main parties, must state adequate reasons, be accompanied by appropriate supporting documents, and be submitted to the Court as soon as possible after notice to attend has been given.

186. If the representative of a party intends not to be present at the hearing, he is requested to inform the Court as soon as possible after notice to attend has been given.

187. The Court will make every effort to ensure that the parties' representatives receive a summary report for the hearing three weeks before the hearing. The purpose of the summary report for the hearing is to enable the parties to prepare for the hearing.

188. The summary report for the hearing, drawn up by the Judge-Rapporteur, shall be confined to setting out the pleas in law and a succinct summary of the parties' arguments.

189. Any observations the parties may wish to make on the summary report for the hearing may be made at the hearing. In such cases, a reference to such observations shall be recorded in the minutes of the hearing.

190. The summary report for the hearing shall be made available to the public outside the courtroom on the day of the hearing, unless the case is to be heard in camera.

191. Before every public hearing the Registrar shall cause the following information to be displayed outside the courtroom in the language of the case: the date and time of the hearing, the competent formation of the Court, the case(s) which will be called and the names of the parties.

192. A request to use particular technical means for the purposes of a presentation must be made at least two weeks before the date of the hearing. Arrangements for such use of technology should be made with the Registry, so that any technical or practical constraints can be taken into account. Supporting material for such presentations shall not be placed on the case-file, unless the President otherwise decides.

193. In view of the security measures in place to control access to the buildings of the Court of Justice of the European Union, it is recommended that the parties' representatives take the necessary steps to ensure that they are present in the courtroom at least 15 minutes before the hearing is due to start, as the members of the formation of the Court will normally wish to discuss the organisation of the hearing with them.

194. In order to prepare for their participation in a hearing, the parties' representatives are invited to consult the following document, which is available on the internet site of the Court of Justice of the European Union: 'Aide-mémoire: Hearing of oral argument'.

C.
CONDUCT OF THE HEARING

195. The parties' representatives shall be required to appear before the Court in their gowns.

196. The purpose of the hearing shall be:

— where necessary, to reiterate in condensed form the position taken by the parties, emphasising the key submissions advanced in writing,

— to clarify, if necessary, certain arguments advanced during the written part of the procedure and to submit any new material arising from events occurring after the close of the written part of the procedure and which therefore could not have been set out in the pleadings,

— to reply to any questions put by the Court.

197. It will be for each party to assess, in the light of the purpose of the hearing, as defined in point 196 above, whether oral argument is really necessary or whether it would be sufficient simply to refer to the written observations or pleadings. The hearing can then concentrate on the replies to questions put by the Court. If the representative does consider it necessary to address the Court, he may always confine himself to making specific points and referring to the pleadings in relation to other points.

198. Where, before the hearing, the Court has invited the parties, in accordance with Article 89(4) of the Rules of Procedure, to concentrate in their oral pleadings on one or more specified issues, those issues must be addressed as a matter of priority in the oral submissions.

199. If a party refrains from presenting oral argument, this shall not constitute acquiescence in the oral argument presented by another party where the arguments in question have already been refuted in writing. Such silence shall not preclude that party from responding to the other party's submission.

200. In the interests of clarity and in order to enable the Members of the Court to understand oral submissions better, it will generally be preferable for Counsel to speak freely on the basis of notes rather than to read out a written text. The parties' representatives are also requested to simplify their presentation of the case as far as possible and to use short sentences. It would also assist the Court if representatives could structure their oral argument and indicate, before developing it, the structure they intend to adopt.

201. The time taken in presenting oral submissions may vary, depending on the complexity of the case and on whether or not new facts have arisen. Each of the main parties will be allowed 15 minutes and each intervener will be allowed 10 minutes to present oral submissions (in joined cases, each of the main parties will be allowed 15 minutes for each case and each intervener will be allowed 10 minutes for each case), unless the Registry has indicated otherwise. These limitations shall apply only to the oral submissions themselves and not to the time required to answer questions put at the hearing or for final replies.

202. If circumstances so require, a request for leave to exceed the speaking time normally allowed, giving reasons and indicating the speaking time considered necessary, may be made to the Registry at least two weeks (or less, in duly substantiated exceptional circumstances) before the date fixed for the hearing. When such requests are made, representatives will be informed of the time which they will have for presenting their oral submissions.

203. When several representatives act for a party, only two of them may normally present oral argument, and their combined speaking time must not exceed the time limits indicated in point 201 above. However, representatives other than those who addressed the Court may answer questions from Members of the Court and make final replies.

204. Where two or more parties are advancing the same argument before the Court (a situation which may arise where, in particular, there are interventions or where cases are joined), their representatives are requested to confer with each other before the hearing in order to avoid any repetition.

205. When citing a decision of the Court of Justice, the General Court or the Civil Service Tribunal, representatives are requested to refer to it by the usual name of the case and the case number, and, where relevant, to specify the relevant paragraph(s).

206. In accordance with Article 85(3) of the Rules of Procedure, the main parties may, exceptionally, produce further evidence at the hearing. In such cases, the other parties will be heard on the admissibility and content thereof. It would be prudent to bring sufficient copies where appropriate.

D.
INTERPRETATION

207. In order to facilitate interpretation, parties' representatives are requested to send any text or written notes for their submissions to the Interpretation Directorate in advance by e-mail (interpret@curia.europa.eu).

208. Any notes for submissions thus transmitted will be treated in the strictest confidence. In order to avoid any misunderstanding, the name of the party must be stated. Notes for submissions will not be placed on the case-file.

209. Representatives are reminded that, depending on the case being heard, only some of the Members of the bench may be following the oral argument in the language in which it is being presented; the other Members will be listening to the simultaneous interpretation. In the interests of the better conduct of the hearing and of maintaining the quality of the simultaneous interpretation, representatives are strongly advised to speak slowly and directly into the microphone.

210. Where representatives intend to cite verbatim passages from certain texts or documents, particularly passages not appearing in the case-file, it would be helpful if they would indicate the passages concerned to the interpreters before the hearing. Similarly, it may be helpful to draw the interpreters' attention to any terms which may be difficult to translate.

E.
MINUTES OF THE HEARING

211. The Registrar shall draw up in the respective language of each case the minutes of every hearing. Those minutes shall contain: an indication of the case; the date, time and place of the hearing; an indication, where applicable, that the case was heard in camera; the names of the Judges and the Registrar present; the names and status of the parties' representatives present; a reference to any observations on the summary report for the hearing; the surnames, forenames, status and permanent addresses of any witnesses or experts examined; an indication, where applicable, of the procedural documents or items produced at the hearing; and, in so far as is necessary, the statements made at the hearing and the decisions pronounced at the hearing by the Court or the President.

VI.
CONFIDENTIAL TREATMENT

A.
GENERAL

[10.778]
212. In accordance with Article 64 and subject to the provisions of Article 68(4), Article 104, Article 105(8) and Article 144(7) of the Rules of Procedure, the Court shall take into consideration only those procedural documents and items which have been made available to the representatives of the parties and on which they have been given an opportunity of expressing their views.

213. It follows that, without prejudice to the provisions of Articles 103 to 105 of the Rules of Procedure, no consideration may be given to an application by the applicant for certain information on the case-file to be treated as confidential in relation to the defendant. Likewise, no such application may be made by the defendant in relation to the applicant.

214. Nevertheless, a main party may apply for certain confidential information on the case-file to be excluded from the documents to be communicated to an intervener in accordance with Article 144(7) of the Rules of Procedure.

215. Each party may also apply for certain information in the files concerned by the joinder to be excluded from the files to be examined by a party to the joined cases in accordance with Article 68(4) of the Rules of Procedure.

B.
CONFIDENTIAL TREATMENT WHERE AN APPLICATION TO INTERVENE HAS BEEN MADE

216. Where an application to intervene is made in a case, the main parties are requested to state, within the time limit prescribed by the Registrar to that effect, whether they wish to seek confidential treatment in respect of certain information included in the procedural documents already placed on the case-file.

217. The main parties must submit simultaneously with any procedural document or item that they may lodge subsequently any application for confidential treatment that may be required in respect of the procedural document or item concerned. In the absence of such an application, the procedural documents and items lodged will be communicated to the intervener.

218. Any application for confidential treatment must be made by a separate document. It may not be lodged as a confidential version and must not, therefore, contain confidential information.

219. An application for confidential treatment must specify the party in relation to whom confidentiality is requested.

220. An application for confidential treatment must be limited to what is strictly necessary and may not in any event cover the entirety of a procedural document; only exceptionally may it extend to the entirety of an annexed document. It should usually be possible to furnish a non-confidential version of a procedural document and items in which certain passages, words or figures have been deleted without affecting the interests it is sought to protect.

221. An application for confidential treatment must accurately identify the particulars or passages to be excluded and state the reasons for which each of those particulars or passages is regarded as confidential. Failure to provide such information may result in the application being refused by the Court.

222. On lodging an application for confidential treatment in respect of one or more procedural documents, a party must produce a full non-confidential version of each procedural document and item concerned, with the confidential particulars or passages removed.

223. Where an application for confidential treatment does not comply with points 218, 219 and 222 above, the Registrar shall request the party concerned to put the application in order. If, despite such a request, the application for confidential treatment is not made to comply with the requirements of these Practice Rules, it will not be possible for it to be properly processed, and a copy of every procedural document and item concerned will be communicated to the intervener.

C.
CONFIDENTIAL TREATMENT WHERE CASES ARE JOINED

224. Where it is envisaged that several cases will be joined, the parties are requested to state, within the time limit prescribed by the Registrar to that effect, whether they wish to seek confidential treatment in respect of certain information included in the procedural documents and material already placed on the files of the cases concerned by the joinder.

225. The parties must submit simultaneously with any procedural document or item that they may lodge subsequently any application for confidential treatment that may be required in respect of the procedural document or item concerned. In the absence of such an application, the procedural documents and items lodged will be made available to the other parties in the joined cases.

226. Points 218 to 223 above shall apply to applications for confidential treatment submitted where cases are joined.

D.
CONFIDENTIAL TREATMENT UNDER ARTICLE 103 OF THE RULES OF PROCEDURE

227. The Court may, pursuant to the measures of inquiry referred to in Article 91 of the Rules of Procedure, order a party to produce information or material relating to the case. In accordance with Article 92(3) of the Rules of Procedure, such production may be ordered only where the party concerned has not complied with a measure of organisation of procedure previously adopted to that end, or where expressly requested by the party concerned by the measure and that party explains the need for such a measure to be in the form of an order for a measure of inquiry.

228. Where a main party submits in his response to an application for a measure of organisation of procedure that certain information or material is confidential and he therefore objects to its transmission or proposes that a measure of inquiry be adopted, the Court shall, if it considers that that information or material may be relevant in order for it to rule in the case, order its production by means of an order for a measure of inquiry under Article 91(b) of the Rules of Procedure. The treatment of confidential information or material thus produced before the Court shall be governed by Article 103 of the Rules of Procedure. The regime in question does not provide for any derogation from the principle of the adversarial nature of the proceedings, but lays down the rules for the implementation of that principle.

229. In accordance with that provision, the Court shall examine the relevance of the information or material to the outcome of the proceedings and verify the confidential nature of that information or material. If it considers that the information concerned is both relevant to the outcome of the proceedings and confidential, the Court shall weigh that confidentiality against the requirements linked to the right to effective judicial protection, particularly observance of the adversarial principle, and, after weighing up those matters, will have two options.

230. The Court may decide that the information or material must be brought to the attention of the other main party, notwithstanding its confidential nature. In that respect, the Court may, by way of a measure of organisation of procedure, request the representatives of the parties other than the

party who produced the confidential information to give an undertaking to preserve the confidentiality of the document or item by not communicating to their respective clients or to a third party the information that is to be disclosed to them. Any breach of that undertaking may result in Article 55 of the Rules of Procedure being applied.

231. Alternatively, the Court may decide not to communicate the confidential information, whilst nevertheless ensuring that the other main party is provided with non-confidential information so that he can, to the greatest extent possible, make his views known in compliance with the adversarial principle. The Court shall then order the main party who produced the confidential information to communicate certain particulars in such a way as to enable the preservation of the confidentiality of the information to be reconciled with the adversarial nature of the proceedings. It will, for example, be possible for the information to be transmitted in summarised form. If the Court considers that the other main party cannot properly exercise his rights of defence, it may make one or more orders, until it considers that the proceedings can properly be continued on an adversarial basis.

232. Where the Court considers that the communication of information to the other main party in accordance with the procedures prescribed by the order made under Article 103(3) of the Rules of Procedure has enabled that party to present his views effectively, the confidential information or material which has not been brought to the attention of that party shall not be taken into consideration by the Court and shall be returned to the main party who produced it.

E. CONFIDENTIAL TREATMENT UNDER ARTICLE 104 OF THE RULES OF PROCEDURE

233. In the context of its review of the legality of a measure adopted by an institution denying access to a document, the Court may, by way of a measure of inquiry under Article 91(c) of the Rules of Procedure, order that the document be produced.

234. The document produced by the institution shall not be communicated to the other parties, as the action would otherwise be devoid of purpose.

F. CONFIDENTIAL TREATMENT UNDER ARTICLE 105 OF THE RULES OF PROCEDURE

235. In accordance with Article 105(1) and (2) of the Rules of Procedure, a main party to the proceedings may, on his own initiative or following a measure of inquiry ordered by the Court, produce information or material pertaining to the security of the European Union or to that of one or more of its Member States or to the conduct of their international relations. Article 105(3) to (10) lays down the procedural rules applicable to such information or material.

236. In view of the sensitive, confidential nature of information or material pertaining to the security of the Union or to that of one or more of its Member States or to the conduct of their international relations, the application of the body of rules established by Article 105 of the Rules of Procedure requires a suitable security framework to be set up in order to ensure a high level of protection for that information or material. That framework shall be documented in the decision of the Court taken under Article 105(11) of the Rules of Procedure.

237. According to Article 227(3) of the Rules of Procedure, the provisions of Article 105 shall apply only from the entry into force of the decision referred to in Article 105(11).

VII. LEGAL AID

[10.779]
238. In accordance with Article 147(2) of the Rules of Procedure, the use of a form in making an application for legal aid shall be compulsory. The form is available on the internet site of the Court of Justice of the European Union.

239. An applicant for legal aid who is not represented by a lawyer when the legal aid form is lodged may lodge the duly completed and signed paper form at the Registry by post or by hand, where appropriate after transmission of a copy of the original of that form by fax In the event of transmission by fax, points 78 to 81 above shall apply.

240. Where the applicant for legal aid is represented by a lawyer when the legal aid form is lodged, the form shall be lodged in accordance with Article 72(1) of the Rules of Procedure, taking into account the requirements of points 74 to 85 above.

241. The legal aid form is intended to provide the Court, in accordance with Article 147(3) and (4) of the Rules of Procedure, with the information required to give an effective decision on the application for legal aid. The information required concerns:

— the legal aid applicant's financial situation,

and

— where the action has not yet been brought, the subject-matter of that action, the facts of the case and the arguments relating thereto.

242. The legal aid applicant shall be required to produce, together with the legal aid form, documentary evidence to support the information referred to in point 241 above.

243. Where applicable, the documents referred to in Article 51(2) and (3) and [Article 78(4)] of the Rules of Procedure must be produced together with the legal aid form.

NOTES

Words in square brackets substituted by Amendments of the Practice Rules for the Implementation of the Rules of Procedure of the General Court, Article 1(9) (OJ L217 12.8.2016, p 78).

244. Where the applicant for legal aid is represented by a lawyer when the legal aid form is lodged, the form must also contain the statement referred to in Article 77(1) of the Rules of Procedure.

245. The duly completed legal aid form and supporting documents must be intelligible in themselves.

246. Without prejudice to the Court's power to request information or the production of further documents under Articles 89 and 90 of the Rules of Procedure, the application for legal aid may not be supplemented by the subsequent filing of additional material. Such material shall be rejected, unless it has been lodged at the request of the Court. In exceptional cases, supporting documents intended to establish the applicant's lack of means may nevertheless be accepted subsequently, subject to the delay in their production being adequately explained.

247. Under Article 147(7) of the Rules of Procedure, the introduction of an application for legal aid shall suspend the time limit prescribed for the bringing of the action to which the application refers until the date of service of the order making a decision on that application or, where no lawyer is designated in that order to represent the applicant for legal aid, until the date of service of the order designating the lawyer instructed to represent him.

248. Since the lodging of an application for legal aid has the effect of suspending the time limit prescribed for bringing an action until service of the order referred to in point 247 above, the remaining period within which the application initiating proceedings may be lodged may be very short. Recipients of legal aid who are duly represented by a lawyer are therefore advised to pay particular attention to compliance with the legal time limit.

VIII.
URGENT PROCEDURES

A.
EXPEDITED PROCEDURE

A.1.
REQUEST FOR AN EXPEDITED PROCEDURE

[10.780]

249. In accordance with Article 152(1) of the Rules of Procedure, a request for an expedited procedure must be made by a separate document lodged simultaneously with the application initiating the proceedings or the defence, as the case may be, and contain a statement of reasons specifying the particular urgency of the case and any other relevant circumstances.

250. In order to facilitate immediate processing by the Registry, the request for an expedited procedure must state on the first page that it is lodged under Articles 151 and 152 of the Rules of Procedure.

251. The application in respect of which the expedited procedure is requested must not in principle exceed 25 pages. Such an application must be submitted in accordance with the requirements set out in points 123 to 134 above.

252. It is recommended that the party applying for the expedited procedure specify in his request the pleas in law, arguments or passages of the pleading in question (application or defence) which are put forward only in the event that the case is not decided under the expedited procedure. That information, referred to in Article 152(2) of the Rules of Procedure, must be clearly specified in the request, indicating the numbers of the paragraphs concerned.

A.2.
Abridged version

253. It is recommended that an abridged version of the relevant pleading be annexed to any request for an expedited procedure which contains the information referred to in point 252 above.

254. Where an abridged version is annexed, it must comply with the following directions:
(a) the abridged version shall be in the same format as the original version of the pleading in question, with omitted passages being identified by the word 'omissis' in square brackets;
(b) paragraphs which are retained in the abridged version shall keep the same numbering as in the original version of the pleading in question;
(c) if the abridged version does not refer to all the annexes to the original version of the pleading in question, the schedule of annexes accompanying the abridged version shall identify each annex omitted by the word 'omissis';
(d) annexes which are retained in the abridged version must keep the same numbering as in the schedule of annexes in the original version of the pleading in question;
(e) the annexes referred to in the schedule accompanying the abridged version must be attached to that version.

255. In order to ensure that it is dealt with as expeditiously as possible, the abridged version must comply with the above directions.

256. Where the production of an abridged version of the pleading is requested by the Court under Article 151(3) of the Rules of Procedure, the abridged version must be prepared in accordance with the above directions, unless otherwise specified.

A.3.
Defence

257. If the applicant has not specified in his request for an expedited procedure the pleas in law, arguments or passages of the application initiating the proceedings which are to be taken into consideration only in the event that the case is not decided under the expedited procedure, the defendant must respond to the application initiating the proceedings within a period of one month.

258. If the applicant has specified in his request for an expedited procedure the pleas in law, arguments or passages of the application initiating the proceedings which are to be taken into consideration only in the event that the case is not decided under the expedited procedure, the defendant must respond, within a period of one month, to the pleas in law and arguments advanced in the application, in the light of the information provided in the request for the expedited procedure.

259. If the applicant has attached an abridged version of the application initiating proceedings to his request for an expedited procedure, the defendant must respond, within a period of one month, to the pleas in law and arguments contained in that abridged version of the application.

260. If the Court decides to refuse the request for an expedited procedure before the defendant has lodged his defence, the period of one month for the lodging of the defence prescribed by Article 154(1) of the Rules of Procedure shall be extended by a further month.

261. If the Court decides to refuse the request for an expedited procedure after the defendant has lodged his defence within the period of one month prescribed by Article 154(1) of the Rules of Procedure, the defendant shall be allowed a further period of one month from the date of service of the decision refusing the request for an expedited procedure, in order to supplement his defence.

A.4.
Oral part of the procedure

262. Under the expedited procedure, since the written part of the procedure is in principle limited to one exchange of pleadings, the emphasis shall be on the oral part of the procedure and a hearing shall be organised promptly after the written part of the procedure has been closed. The Court may nevertheless decide to rule without an oral part of the procedure where the main parties indicate, within a period prescribed by the President, that they have decided not to participate in a hearing and the Court considers that it has sufficient information available to it from the material in the file in the case.

263. Where the Court has not authorised the lodging of a statement in intervention, the intervener may submit his observations only orally, if a hearing is organised.

B.
SUSPENSION OF OPERATION OR ENFORCEMENT AND OTHER INTERIM MEASURES

264. In accordance with [Article 156(5)] of the Rules of Procedure, an application for suspension of operation or enforcement or other interim measures must be made by a separate document. It must be intelligible in itself, without necessitating reference to the application lodged in the main proceedings, including the annexes thereto.

NOTES

Words in square brackets substituted by Amendments of the Practice Rules for the Implementation of the Rules of Procedure of the General Court, Article 1(10) (OJ L217 12.8.2016, p 78).

265. In order to facilitate immediate processing by the Registry, the application for suspension of operation or enforcement or other interim measures must state on the first page that it is lodged under Article 156 of the Rules of Procedure. In addition, it is recommended that such an application be lodged by means of the e-Curia application or, if transmitted by fax, that it be accompanied by all the annexes, including the documents referred to in Article 78 of the Rules of Procedure.

266. The application for suspension of operation or enforcement or other interim measures must state, with the utmost concision, the subject-matter of the proceedings, the pleas of fact and of law on which the main action is based (establishing a prima facie case on the merits in that action) and the circumstances giving rise to urgency. It must specify the measure(s) applied for. It must also contain all the evidence and offers of evidence available to justify the grant of interim measures.

267. Since an application for interim measures requires the existence of a prima facie case to be assessed for the purposes of a summary procedure, it need not set out in full the text of the application in the main proceedings.

268. In order that an application for interim measures may be dealt with urgently, the number of pages it contains must not in principle (depending on the subject-matter and the circumstances of the case) exceed a maximum of 25 pages.

IX.
ENTRY INTO FORCE OF THESE PRACTICE RULES

[10.781]

269. The Instructions to the Registrar of 5 July 2007 (OJ L232, 4.9.2007, p 1), as amended on 17 May 2010 (OJ L170, 6.7.2010, p 53) and on 24 January 2012 (OJ L68, 7.3.2012, p 20), and the Practice Directions to parties before the General Court of 24 January 2012 (OJ L68, 7.3.2012, p 23) are hereby repealed and replaced by these Practice Rules.

270. These Practice Rules shall be published in the *Official Journal of the European Union*. They shall enter into force on the first day of the first month following their publication.

Done at Luxembourg, on 20 May 2015.

Registrar	*President*
E. COULON	M. JAEGER

ANNEX 1
REQUIREMENTS NON-COMPLIANCE WITH WHICH IS GROUNDS FOR NOT SERVING THE APPLICATION (POINT 110 OF THESE PRACTICE RULES)

[10.782]

Failure to put the following points in order may result in the action being dismissed as inadmissible, in accordance with [Article 78(6)], Article 177(7) and Article 194(6) of the Rules of Procedure.

	Direct actions	Intellectual property cases	Appeals
a)	production of the certificate of the lawyer's authorisation to practise (Article 51(2) of the Rules of Procedure)	production of the certificate of the lawyer's authorisation to practise (Article 51(2) of the Rules of Procedure)	production of the certificate of the lawyer's authorisation to practise (Article 51(2) of the Rules of Procedure)
b)	production of proof of the existence in law of a legal person governed by private law ([Article 78(4)] of the Rules of Procedure)	production of proof of the existence in law of a legal person governed by private law (Article 177(4) of the Rules of Procedure)	production of proof of the existence in law of a legal person governed by private law (Article 194(3) of the Rules of Procedure)

	Direct actions	Intellectual property cases	Appeals
c)	production of authority to act if the party represented is a legal person governed by private law (Article 51(3) of the Rules of Procedure)	production of authority to act if the party represented is a legal person governed by private law (Article 51(3) of the Rules of Procedure)	production of authority to act if the party represented is a legal person governed by private law (Article 51(3) of the Rules of Procedure)
d)	production of the contested measure (action for annulment) or of the documentary evidence of the date on which the institution was requested to act (action for failure to act) (second paragraph of Article 21 of the Statute; Article 78(1) of the Rules of Procedure)	production of the contested decision of the Board of Appeal (Article 177(3) of the Rules of Procedure)	
[e)	production of the complaint within the meaning of Article 90(2) of the Staff Regulations and the decision responding to the complaint (Article 78(2) of the Rules of Procedure)]		
[f])	production of a copy of the contract containing the arbitration clause ([Article 78(3)] of the Rules of Procedure)		
[g])		indication of the name of the party/ parties to the proceedings before the Board of Appeal and the address which they had given for the purposes of the notifications to be effected in the course of those proceedings (Article 177(2) of the Rules of Procedure)	
[h])		indication of the date on which the decision of the Board of Appeal was notified (Article 177(3) of the Rules of Procedure)	indication of the date of service of the decision of the Civil Service Tribunal that is the subject of the appeal (Article 194(2) of the Rules of Procedure)
[i)	indication of the dates on which the complaint within the meaning of Article 90(2) of the Staff Regulations was submitted and the decision responding to the complaint notified (Article 78(2) of the Rules of Procedure).]		

NOTES

All amendments to this Annex were made by Amendments of the Practice Rules for the Implementation of the Rules of Procedure of the General Court, Article 1(11) (OJ L217 12.8.2016, p 78). Note that point i) above was actually inserted as a second point h). It is assumed that this is an error as the original points e) to g) were renumbered points f) to h).

ANNEX 2
PROCEDURAL RULES NON-COMPLIANCE WITH WHICH JUSTIFIES DELAYING SERVICE (POINT 111 OF THESE PRACTICE RULES)

[10.783]

	Application lodged in paper format (after prior dispatch by fax, where applicable)	Application lodged by e-Curia
a)	indication of the applicant's permanent address (first paragraph of Article 21 of the Statute; Article 76(a), Article 177(1)(a) and Article 194(1)(a) of the Rules of Procedure)	indication of the applicant's permanent address (first paragraph of Article 21 of the Statute; Article 76(a), Article 177(1)(a) and Article 194(1)(a) of the Rules of Procedure)
b)	indication of the address of the applicant's representative (Article 76(b), Article 177(1)(b) and Article 194(1)(b) of the Rules of Procedure)	indication of the address of the applicant's representative (Article 76(b), Article 177(1)(b) and Article 194(1)(b) of the Rules of Procedure)
c)	new original of the application the length of which will have been reduced (points 120 and 121 of these Practice Rules)	new original of the application the length of which will have been reduced (points 120 and 121 of these Practice Rules)
d)	new original of the application with identical content but with numbered paragraphs (point 92 of these Practice Rules)	new original of the application with identical content but with numbered paragraphs (point 92 of these Practice Rules)
e)	new, paginated original of the application with identical content (point 96(d) of these Practice Rules)	new, paginated original of the application with identical content (point 96(d) of these Practice Rules)
f)	new original of the application with identical content, in which the representative's handwritten signature appears at the end (point 93 of these Practice Rules)	
g)	production of a schedule of annexes containing the mandatory information (Article 72(3) of the Rules of Procedure; point 98 of these Practice Rules)	production of a schedule of annexes containing the mandatory information (Article 72(3) of the Rules of Procedure; point 98 of these Practice Rules)
h)	production of a sufficient number of copies of the schedule of annexes containing the mandatory information (Article 73(2) of the Rules of Procedure)	
i)	production of the annexes mentioned in the application but not produced (Article 72(3) of the Rules of Procedure)	production of the annexes mentioned in the application but not produced (Article 72(3) of the Rules of Procedure)
j)	production of a sufficient number of copies of the annexes mentioned in the application (Article 73(2) of the Rules of Procedure)	
k)	production of paginated annexes (point 101(d) of these Practice Rules)	production of paginated annexes (point 101(d) of these Practice Rules)
l)	production of numbered annexes (point 101(a) of these Practice Rules)	production of numbered annexes (point 101(a) of these Practice Rules)
m)	production of a sufficient number of certified copies of the application (Article 73(2) of the Rules of Procedure, points 82, 85 and 95 of these Practice Rules)	

ANNEX 3
PROCEDURAL RULES NON-COMPLIANCE WITH WHICH DOES NOT PREVENT SERVICE (POINT 112 OF THESE PRACTICE RULES)

[10.784]

a)	choice of methods of service, namely acceptance of service by e-Curia or by fax (stating a single fax number) (Article 77(1) of the Rules of Procedure; point 83 of these Practice Rules)
b)	production of the certificate of any additional lawyer's authorisation to practise (Article 51(2) of the Rules of Procedure)
c)	in cases other than intellectual property cases, production of the summary of pleas in law and main arguments (points 130 to 132 and 161 to 163 of these Practice Rules)

d)	production of a translation into the language of the case of material drawn up in a language other than the language of the case (Article 46(2) of the Rules of Procedure; point 108 of these Practice Rules)

DECISION OF THE COURT OF JUSTICE

(2016/2386/EU)

of 20 September 2016

concerning the security rules applicable to information or material produced before the General Court in accordance with Article 105 of its Rules of Procedure

NOTES

Date of publication in Official Journal: OJ L355, 24.12.2016, p 5.

THE COURT

Having regard to the Rules of Procedure, and in particular Article 190a(5) thereof,

Whereas:

(1) In accordance with Article 105(1) and (2) of the Rules of Procedure of the General Court, a main party to the proceedings may, on his own initiative or following a measure of inquiry ordered by the General Court, produce information or material pertaining to the security of the European Union or to that of one or more of its Member States or to the conduct of their international relations. Article 105(3) to (10) of those Rules lays down the procedural rules applicable to such information or material.

(2) In view of the sensitive, confidential nature of the information or material concerned, the application of the body of rules established by Article 105 of the Rules of Procedure of the General Court requires a suitable security framework to be set up in order to ensure a high level of protection for that information or material.

(3) To this end, the security framework must be applied to all information or material produced in accordance with Article 105(1) or (2) of those Rules if it is European Union classified information or if the main party producing it has indicated that to communicate it to the other main party would harm the security of the Union or of its Member States or the conduct of their international relations, even when that information or material is not European Union classified information.

(4) In order to guarantee a high level of protection for that information or for that material, the fundamental principles and minimum security rules for the protection of that information or material are based on those applicable for the protection of SECRET UE/EU SECRET classified information according to the rules of the EU institutions on the protection of European Union classified information (EUCI), in particular those adopted by the Council of the European Union, the European Parliament and the European Commission.

(5) Information or material produced in accordance with Article 105(1) or (2) of the Rules of Procedure of the General Court shall be given a mark specific to the Court of Justice of the European Union, called 'FIDUCIA', which is to determine the security rules applicable to it throughout proceedings before the General Court and, in the event of an appeal, before the Court of Justice. The affixing and removing of this marking shall have no consequences for the classification of information communicated to the General Court.

(6) Access to FIDUCIA information shall be provided in accordance with the need-to-know principle,

HAS DECIDED:

[10.785]

Article 1

Definitions

For the purposes of this decision, the following definitions shall apply:

(a) 'security authority' means the authority responsible for the security of the Court of Justice of the European Union designated by the latter, which may delegate, in whole or in part, the performance of the tasks provided for by this decision;

(b) 'FIDUCIA office' means the office of the Court of Justice of the European Union responsible for the management of FIDUCIA information;

(c) 'holder' means a duly authorised person who, on the basis of an established need to know, is in possession of FIDUCIA information and who is, in consequence, required to ensure its protection;

(d) 'document' means any information, whatever its physical form or characteristics;

(e) 'information' means any written or oral information, whatever its medium or author;

(f) 'European Union classified information' (EUCI) means any information or any material identified as such according to the security classification of the European Union under the rules applicable in that respect within the EU institutions, covered by one of the following levels of classification:
— TRÈS SECRET UE/EU TOP SECRET;
— SECRET UE/EU SECRET;
— CONFIDENTIEL UE/EU CONFIDENTIAL;
— RESTREINT UE/EU RESTRICTED;

(g) 'FIDUCIA information' means any information bearing the FIDUCIA mark;

(h) 'handling' of FIDUCIA information means all treatment which FIDUCIA information could undergo during the proceedings before the Court of Justice. Its registration, consultation, creation, copying, storage, return and destruction are accordingly covered.

[10.786]
Article 2
Purpose and scope

1. This decision shall define the fundamental principles and minimum security rules for the protection of FIDUCIA information in proceedings before the Court of Justice.
2. Those fundamental principles and minimum security rules shall apply to all FIDUCIA information, and to any use of it, written or oral, and to any copies of it that may be made in accordance with the security rules laid down in this decision.

[10.787]
Article 3
Rules governing lodging and return

For the purpose of setting up the security framework provided for by this decision:

— the main party shall inform the General Court Registry of the day on which the information or material is lodged in accordance with Article 105(1) or (2) of the Rules of Procedure of the General Court;

— the main party, accompanied by a representative of the General Court Registry, shall be required to lodge the information or material provided pursuant to Article 105(1) or (2) of those Rules with the FIDUCIA office during the hours the Registry is open to the public;

— the main party producing the information or material in accordance with Article 105(1) or (2) of the Rules of Procedure of the General Court shall be required to remove it from the FIDUCIA office in the presence of a representative of the General Court Registry if that party does not authorise its disclosure in accordance with Article 105(4) of those Rules, as soon as it is withdrawn in accordance with Article 105(7) of those Rules or as soon as the period referred to in the first paragraph of Article 56 of the Statute of the Court of Justice of the European Union has expired, unless an appeal has been brought within that period;

— if, within the period referred to in the first paragraph of Article 56 of the Statute of the Court of Justice of the European Union, an appeal is brought against the decision of the General Court, the information or material produced in that case in accordance with Article 105(1) or (2) of the Rules of Procedure of the General Court shall be made available to the Court of Justice. To that end, as soon as the Registrar of the General Court is informed of the existence of that appeal, he shall send a letter to the Registrar of the Court of Justice, informing him of the fact that the information or material concerned is available to the Court of Justice. The Registrar of the General Court shall simultaneously notify the security authority of the fact that the information or material concerned must be made available to the Court of Justice, without that information or material being physically moved. That notification shall be registered by the FIDUCIA office. The main party that produced that information or that material shall be required to remove it from the FIDUCIA office, in the presence of a representative of the Registry of the Court of Justice, as soon as the decision disposing of the appeal has been served, save where the case is referred back to the General Court for a ruling;

— in the event that the case is referred back to the General Court, the Court of Justice shall make the information or material concerned available to the General Court as soon as the decision disposing of the appeal has been served. To that end, the Registrar of the Court of Justice shall send a letter to the Registrar of the General Court informing him of the fact that the information or material concerned is available to the General Court. The Registrar of the Court of Justice shall simultaneously notify the security authority of the fact that the information or material concerned must be made available to the General Court, without that information or material being physically moved. That notification shall be registered by the FIDUCIA office. The main party that produced that information or that material shall be required to remove it from the FIDUCIA office, in the presence of a representative of the Registry of the General Court, as soon as the period referred to in the first paragraph of Article 56 of the Statute of the Court of Justice of the European Union has expired, unless an appeal has been brought within that period.

[10.788]
Article 4
FIDUCIA marking

1. All information or material produced in accordance with Article 105(1) or (2) of the Rules of Procedure of the General Court shall be given a FIDUCIA mark by the FIDUCIA office.
2. Any information reproducing, in whole or in part, the content of information or material produced in accordance with Article 105(1) or (2) of those Rules, and every copy of such information or material, shall likewise be given a FIDUCIA mark by the FIDUCIA office.
3. Documents and registers drawn up by the FIDUCIA office in accordance with this decision whose unauthorised disclosure could harm the security of the Union or that of one or more of its Member States or the conduct of their international relations shall also be given a FIDUCIA mark by the FIDUCIA office.
4. The FIDUCIA mark shall be placed visibly on all FIDUCIA information pages and media.
5. The affixing and removing of the FIDUCIA mark, on the conditions set out in Annex III, shall have no consequences for the classification of information communicated to the General Court.

[10.789]
Article 5
Protection of FIDUCIA information

1. The protection of FIDUCIA information shall be equivalent to that given to SECRET EU/EU SECRET EUCI in accordance with the rules on the protection of EUCI applicable within the EU institutions.
2. The holder of any FIDUCIA information shall be responsible for protecting it in accordance with this decision.

[10.790]
Article 6
Security risk management

1. The risks threatening FIDUCIA information shall be managed as a process of risk analysis aimed at determining known security risks, defining security measures making it possible to reduce those risks to an acceptable level in accordance with the fundamental principles and minimum standards set out in this decision, and applying those measures. The effectiveness of such measures shall be continuously evaluated by the security authority.
2. Security measures for protecting FIDUCIA information throughout the proceedings before the Court of Justice shall be commensurate with, in particular, the form in which the information or material concerned is presented and its volume, the environment and structure of the FIDUCIA office premises and the locally assessed threat of malicious and/ or criminal activities, including espionage, sabotage and terrorism.
3. The internal contingency plan of the Court of Justice of the European Union shall take account of the necessity of protecting FIDUCIA information in the event of emergency in order to prevent unauthorised access or disclosure or loss of integrity or availability.
4. Preventative and recovery measures to minimise the impact of major failures or incidents on the handling and storage of FIDUCIA information shall be included in the internal contingency plan of the Court of Justice of the European Union.

[10.791]
Article 7
Personnel security measures

1. Access to FIDUCIA information may be granted only to persons who:
— have a need to know it,
— subject to paragraph 2 of this Article, have been authorised to have access to FIDUCIA information, and
— have been briefed on their responsibilities.
2. The Judges and Advocates General of the Court of Justice shall, by reason of their office, be deemed authorised to have access to FIDUCIA information.
3. The procedure designed to determine whether an official or other servant of the Court of Justice of the European Union, having regard to his loyalty, trustworthiness and reliability, may be authorised to have access to FIDUCIA information is laid down in Annex I.
4. Before being given access to FIDUCIA information and thereafter at regular intervals, all the persons concerned shall be briefed on their responsibilities as regards the protection of FIDUCIA information in accordance with this decision and shall acknowledge their responsibilities in writing.

[10.792]
Article 8
Physical security

1. 'Physical security' means the application of physical and technical protective measures to prevent unauthorised access to FIDUCIA information.

2. Physical security measures shall be designed to prevent surreptitious or forced entry into the FIDUCIA office premises by an intruder, to deter, impede and detect unauthorised acts and to enable a distinction to be drawn between persons with and without authority to have access to FIDUCIA information in accordance with the need-to-know principle. Such measures shall be determined on the basis of a risk management process.
3. Physical security measures shall be put in place for the FIDUCIA office premises in which FIDUCIA information is handled and stored. These measures shall be designed to ensure protection equivalent to that afforded to SECRET UE/EU SECRET EUCI in accordance with the rules on the protection of EUCI applicable within the EU institutions. No FIDUCIA information may be stored or consulted outside the FIDUCIA office premises created for that purpose within an area that has itself been secured.
4. Only approved equipment or devices in conformity with the rules on the protection of EUCI applicable within the EU institutions shall be used for protecting FIDUCIA information.
5. Provisions for implementing this Article are set out in Annex II.

[10.793]
Article 9
Management of FIDUCIA information
1. 'Management of FIDUCIA information' means the application of administrative measures designed to protect FIDUCIA information throughout the proceedings before the Court of Justice, and to control it in order to help deter and detect deliberate or accidental compromise or loss of such information.
2. Measures for the management of FIDUCIA information relate to, in particular, the registration, consultation, creation, copying, storage, return and destruction of FIDUCIA information.
3. On reception, and before any handling, FIDUCIA information shall be registered by the FIDUCIA office.
4. The FIDUCIA office premises shall be subject to regular inspection by the security authority.
5. Provisions for implementing this Article are set out in Annex III.

[10.794]
Article 10
Protection of FIDUCIA information handled electronically
1. The communication and information systems (computers and peripheral devices) used in the handling of FIDUCIA information shall be situated in the FIDUCIA office premises. They shall be isolated from any computerised network.
2. Security measures shall be implemented in order to protect the information technology equipment used for the handling of FIDUCIA information against the compromise of that information by unintentional electromagnetic emanations (security measures equivalent to those in place for SECRET UE/EU SECRET EUCI in accordance with the rules on the protection of EUCI applicable within the EU institutions).
3. The communication and information systems shall be subject to accreditation issued by the security authority which shall satisfy itself that they comply with the rules on the protection of EUCI applicable within the EU institutions.
4. Provisions for implementing this Article are set out in Annex IV.

[10.795]
Article 11
Security in the event of external action
1. 'Security in the event of external action' means the application of measures designed to ensure the protection of FIDUCIA information by contractors required to carry out work in connection with the maintenance of communication and information systems isolated from the computerised network or when action has to be taken that entails the urgent removal of FIDUCIA information to a place of safety.
2. The security authority may entrust the performance of tasks involving or entailing, under the contract, access to FIDUCIA information to contractors registered in a Member State.
3. The security authority shall ensure that the minimum security standards laid down in this decision and mentioned in the contract are observed when contracts are granted.
4. Members of a contractor's staff may have access to FIDUCIA information only if they have been authorised for that purpose by the security authority on the basis of personnel security clearance issued by the National Security Authority or any other competent security authority in accordance with national laws and regulations.
5. Provisions for implementing this Article are set out in Annex V.

[10.796]
Article 12
No digital transmission, communication or exchange of FIDUCIA information
1. FIDUCIA information shall in no circumstances be transmitted digitally.
2. The Court of Justice shall not send FIDUCIA information to the institutions, bodies, offices or agencies of the Union, or to the Member States, or to the other parties to the proceedings or to any third party.

[10.797]
Article 13
Breaches of security and compromise of FIDUCIA information

1. A breach of security is an act or omission by an individual that is contrary to the security rules laid down in this decision.
2. Compromise occurs when, as a result of a breach of security, FIDUCIA information has been disclosed in whole or in part to persons who are not, or are not deemed to be, authorised persons.
3. Any breach or suspected breach of security shall be reported forthwith to the security authority.
4. Where it is established, or where there are reasonable grounds to assume, that FIDUCIA information has been compromised or lost, the security authority, liaising closely with the President and the Registrar of the Court of Justice, shall take all appropriate measures in accordance with the applicable provisions in order to:
(a) inform the main party that produced the information or material concerned;
(b) request the competent authority to commence an administrative investigation;
(c) assess the potential damage caused to the security of the Union or to that of one or more of its Member States or to the conduct of their international relations;
(d) prevent any recurrence; and
(e) inform the competent authorities of the steps taken.
5. Any person responsible for a breach of the security rules laid down in this decision shall be liable to disciplinary action in accordance with the applicable provisions. Any person responsible for compromise or loss of FIDUCIA information shall be liable to disciplinary and/or legal action in accordance with the applicable provisions.

[10.798]
Article 14
Organisation of security within the Court of Justice

1. The FIDUCIA office shall put in hand the protection of FIDUCIA information in accordance with this decision.
2. The security authority shall be responsible for the proper application of this decision. For that purpose, the security authority shall:
(a) apply the security policy of the Court of Justice of the European Union and review it at regular intervals;
(b) supervise the implementation of this decision by the FIDUCIA office;
(c) where appropriate, cause an investigation to be carried out, on the conditions laid down in Article 13, of any compromise or loss, or suspected compromise or loss, of FIDUCIA information;
(d) periodically inspect the security arrangements intended to ensure the protection of FIDUCIA information on FIDUCIA office premises.

[10.799]
Article 15
Practice rules for implementation

Practice rules for the implementation of this decision shall be laid down by the security authority in agreement with the Registrar of the Court of Justice.

[10.800]
Article 16
Entry into force

This decision shall enter into force on the day following that of its publication in the *Official Journal of the European Union*.

ANNEX I
PERSONNEL SECURITY MEASURES

[10.801]

1. This Annex sets out provisions for implementing Article 7 of this decision.
2. The Registrar of the Court of Justice shall be responsible for identifying, so far as concerns him and in so far as strictly necessary, the posts necessitating access to FIDUCIA information and therefore requiring the officials or other servants occupying the posts concerned to be authorised to have access to FIDUCIA information.

3. With a view to the grant of authority to have access to FIDUCIA information, the FIDUCIA office shall send the security questionnaire, filled in by the official or other servant concerned, to the National Security Authority of the Member State of which the person concerned is a national or to any other competent national authority, identified in the rules on the protection of EUCI applicable within the EU institutions ('the competent NSA'), and request a security investigation for a SECRET UE/EU SECRET level of classification.

4. At the end of the security investigation, acting in accordance with the laws and regulations in force in the Member State concerned, the competent NSA shall notify the FIDUCIA office of the conclusions of the investigation in question.

5. When the result of the security investigation is that the competent NSA is certain that nothing adverse is known that would call into question the loyalty, trustworthiness or reliability of the person concerned, the competent appointing authority ('the appointing authority') may authorise that person to have access to FIDUCIA information.

6. When the completed security investigation does not lead to the certainty referred to in paragraph 5, the appointing authority shall inform the person concerned. In such a case, the FIDUCIA office, acting on the instructions of the appointing authority, may ask the competent NSA for any further clarification it is in a position to offer in accordance with its national laws and regulations. If the outcome of the security investigation is confirmed, authorisation shall not be granted for access to FIDUCIA information.

7. Authorisation of access to FIDUCIA information shall be valid for a period of five years. It shall be withdrawn when the person concerned leaves the post necessitating access to FIDUCIA information or if the appointing authority considers that there are grounds for withdrawal of authorisation.

8. Authorisation of access to FIDUCIA information may be renewed in accordance with the procedure set out in paragraphs 3 to 5.

9. The FIDUCIA office shall keep a record of authorisations of access to FIDUCIA information.

10. If it is brought to the FIDUCIA office's knowledge that a risk to security is posed by a person holding authorisation for access to FIDUCIA information, the FIDUCIA office shall give notice of this to the competent NSA and the appointing authority may suspend access to FIDUCIA information or withdraw the authorisation of access to that information.

11. In an emergency, the appointing authority may, after consulting the competent NSA and subject to the results of preliminary checks to ascertain that no adverse information is known, grant temporary authorisation of access to FIDUCIA information to the officials and other servants concerned. Such temporary authorisation shall be valid until the end of the procedure referred to in paragraphs 3 to 5, but may not, however, exceed a period of six months from the date on which the request for a security investigation is made to the competent NSA.

12. Before being granted access to FIDUCIA information, the persons holding that authorisation shall follow a training programme in order to enable them to discharge their responsibility for handling FIDUCIA information. Authorisation of access to FIDUCIA information shall not become effective until that training has been completed and responsibility has been acknowledged in writing.

ANNEX II
PHYSICAL SECURITY

[10.802]

I. Introduction

1. This Annex sets out provisions for implementing Article 8 of the decision. It lays down minimum requirements for the physical protection of the FIDUCIA office premises in which FIDUCIA information is handled and stored.

2. Physical security measures shall be designed to prevent unauthorised access to FIDUCIA information by:

(a) ensuring that FIDUCIA information is properly handled and stored;
(b) enabling a distinction to be drawn between persons with and without authorisation to have access to FIDUCIA information, in accordance with the need-to-know principle;
(c) deterrence, by preventing and detecting unauthorised acts; and
(d) preventing or delaying surreptitious or forced entry into the FIDUCIA office premises.

3. Physical security measures shall be chosen in the light of an appraisal of the threats posed to FIDUCIA information. These measures shall take into consideration the environment and structure of the FIDUCIA office premises. The security authority shall determine the degree of security to be attained for every one of the following physical measures:

(a) a perimeter barrier defending the boundaries of the area to be protected;
(b) an intrusion detection system connected to the security command post of the Court of Justice of the European Union;
(c) an access control system exercised by electronic or electro-mechanical means, and operated by a member of the security staff;
(d) security staff trained, supervised and holding authorisation to have access to FIDUCIA information;

(e) closed-circuit video-surveillance system operated by security staff and connected to the intrusion detection and access control systems;
(f) security lighting allowing effective surveillance directly, or indirectly through a video-surveillance system;
(g) any other appropriate physical measures designed to deter unauthorised access or to detect it, or to prevent consultation or loss of, or damage to, FIDUCIA information.

II. Premises in Which FIDUCIA Information is Stored and Consulted

Creation of physically protected premises for storage and consultation

4. Secured premises shall be created for the purpose of storage and consulting FIDUCIA information. FIDUCIA information may be stored and consulted only in FIDUCIA office premises which comply in all respects with the rules on the protection of EUCI applicable within the EU institutions.

5. Within those premises, FIDUCIA information shall be kept in security containers also complying in all respects with the rules on the protection of EUCI applicable within the EU institutions.

6. No communications system (telephone or other electronic device) may be brought into the FIDUCIA office premises.

7. The FIDUCIA office meeting room shall be protected against eavesdropping. Electronic security inspections of them shall be carried out at regular intervals.

Access to storage and consultation premises

8. Access to the FIDUCIA office premises shall be controlled by an identification security door under video surveillance.

9. Persons who have been authorised to have access to FIDUCIA information and persons deemed to be so authorised may gain access to the FIDUCIA office premises in order to consult FIDUCIA information on the conditions laid down in Article 7(1) and (2) of this decision.

10. The security authority may in exceptional cases issue access authorisation to persons without FIDUCIA authorisation if it is essential that they should enter the FIDUCIA office premises, provided that access to those premises does not involve access to FIDUCIA information which is to remain protected from sight in security containers. Those persons may gain access only if they are accompanied, and continuously watched, by a member of the FIDUCIA office with authorisation for access to FIDUCIA information.

11. All access to FIDUCIA office premises shall be recorded in an access logbook. This logbook shall be kept at a work station in those premises. The communication and information system used for this purpose shall be compatible with the security requirements laid down in Article 10 of, and Annex IV to, this decision.

12. The protection measures governing the written use of FIDUCIA information shall apply in the case of oral use of that information.

III. Control of Keys and Combinations Used to Protect FIDUCIA Information

13. The security authority shall define procedures for managing keys and combination settings for the FIDUCIA office premises and security containers. Such procedures shall protect against unauthorised access.

14. Combination settings shall be committed to memory by the smallest possible number of persons needing to know them. Combination settings for security containers storing FIDUCIA information shall be changed;
(a) on receipt of a new container;
(b) when there is a change in personnel knowing the combination;
(c) when compromise has occurred or is suspected;
(d) when a lock has undergone maintenance or repair;
(e) at least every 12 months.

15. Technical equipment intended for the physical protection of FIDUCIA information shall comply with the rules on the protection of EUCI applicable within the EU institutions. The security authority shall be responsible for the observance of these rules.

16. Technical equipment shall be periodically inspected and maintained at regular intervals. Maintenance shall take account of the inspection results in order that the best possible operation of the equipment may be guaranteed.

17. At every inspection the efficiency of the various security measures and of the security system as a whole is to be reappraised.

ANNEX III
MANAGEMENT OF FIDUCIA INFORMATION

[10.803]

I. Introduction

1. This Annex sets out provisions for implementing Article 9 of the decision. It lays down the administrative measures designed to protect FIDUCIA information throughout the proceedings before the Court of Justice, and to control it in order to help deter and detect deliberate or accidental compromise or loss of such information.

II. Register of FIDUCIA Information

2. A register of FIDUCIA information shall be created. This register shall be kept, by the FIDUCIA office, at a work station situated in the FIDUCIA office premises. The communication and information system used to keep this register shall be compatible with the security requirements laid down in Article 10 of, and Annex IV to, this decision.

III. Registration of FIDUCIA Information

3. For the purposes of this decision, registration for security purposes ('registration') means the application of procedures keeping track of the life-cycle of FIDUCIA information, including its destruction.

4. Registration of FIDUCIA information shall be the responsibility of the FIDUCIA office.

5. The FIDUCIA office shall automatically give a FIDUCIA mark to information or material produced in accordance with Article 105(1) or (2) of the Rules of Procedure of the General Court. The FIDUCIA office shall register FIDUCIA information in the FIDUCIA information register.

6. The FIDUCIA office shall draw up a report annexed to the FIDUCIA information register, specifying the circumstances in which information is received. The information shall then be handled according to the rules laid down in the previous paragraph.

7. FIDUCIA information shall be registered, in accordance with paragraphs 5 and 6 above, in the FIDUCIA information register without prejudice to the procedural registration performed by persons within the Registry authorised to have access to FIDUCIA information.

IV. Management of FIDUCIA Information

Marking

8. When EUCI or any other information, in respect of which it has been indicated that its communication would harm the security of the Union or that of one or more of its Member States or the conduct of their international relations, is produced under Article 105(1) or (2) of the Rules of Procedure of the General Court, it shall be given the FIDUCIA mark by the FIDUCIA office.

9. The FIDUCIA mark shall be clearly and correctly indicated in every part of the document, irrespective of the form in which the information is presented, whether the format is paper, audio, electronic or other.

Creation of FIDUCIA information

10. Only a person authorised to have access to FIDUCIA information or a person deemed to be so authorised may create FIDUCIA information, as specified in Article 4(2) to (3) of this decision.

11. All FIDUCIA information created shall be registered by the FIDUCIA office in the FIDUCIA information register.

12. All FIDUCIA information created shall be subject to all the rules on the handling of FIDUCIA information as laid down in this decision and in the annexes thereto.

Removal of the FIDUCIA mark

13. FIDUCIA information shall lose its mark in two cases:

(a) when the main party that produced the FIDUCIA information authorises its communication to the other main party, the information originally communicated and all information created on the basis thereof shall lose its FIDUCIA mark;

(b) when FIDUCIA information is returned to the main party that produced it.

14. The FIDUCIA office shall remove the FIDUCIA mark and record that removal in the FIDUCIA information register.

15. Removal of the FIDUCIA mark shall not mean that EUCI has been declassified.

V. Copies of FIDUCIA Information

16. FIDUCIA information shall not be copied unless this is essential. In that case, copies shall be made by the FIDUCIA office which shall number and register them.

17. Copies shall be subject to all the security rules laid down in this decision and in the annexes thereto.

VI. Destruction of FIDUCIA Information

18. When information or material produced in accordance with Article 105(1) or (2) of the Rules of Procedure of the General Court is returned to the main party that produced it, all information reproducing, in whole or in part, the content of that information or material, and any copies made, shall be destroyed.

19. The destruction of FIDUCIA information referred to in paragraph 18 shall be carried out by the FIDUCIA office, using methods complying with the rules on the protection of EUCI applicable within the EU institutions, in order to prevent that information being reconstructed in whole or in part.

20. The destruction of FIDUCIA information referred to in paragraph 18 shall be performed in the presence of a witness authorised to have access to FIDUCIA information.

21. The FIDUCIA office shall draw up a destruction certificate.

22. The destruction certificate shall be annexed to the FIDUCIA information register. A copy shall be sent to the main party that produced the document concerned.

ANNEX IV
PROTECTION OF FIDUCIA INFORMATION HANDLED ELECTRONICALLY

[10.804]

1. This Annex sets out provisions for implementing Article 10.

2. FIDUCIA information may be handled only on electronic equipment (work stations, printers, photocopiers) that is not connected to the computerised network and is placed in the FIDUCIA office premises.

3. All electronic equipment used in the handling of FIDUCIA information shall comply with the rules on the protection of EUCI applicable within the EU institutions. The security of this equipment shall be ensured throughout its life-cycle.

4. All possible connections to the internet and to other tools (LAN, WLAN, Bluetooth etc.) shall be permanently deactivated.

5. Work stations shall be equipped with appropriate anti-virus protection. Anti-virus updates shall be performed using a dedicated CD-ROM or USB stick.

6. The memories of printers and photocopiers shall be erased before any maintenance operation.

7. Only cryptographic products approved in accordance with the rules on the protection of EUCI applicable within the EU institutions shall be used to handle the requests for investigations referred to in Annex I.

ANNEX V
SECURITY IN THE EVENT OF EXTERNAL ACTION

[10.805]

1. This Annex sets out provisions for implementing Article 11.

2. Contractors may gain access to FIDUCIA information only in connection with the maintenance of the communication and information systems isolated from the computerised network or when action has to be taken that entails the urgent removal of FIDUCIA information to a place of safety.

3. The security authority shall draw up guidelines for external action covering, in particular, security clearances for the contractors' staff, and also the content of the contracts referred to in this Annex.

4. Documents relating to the tendering procedures and maintenance contracts for the communication and information systems isolated from the computerised network shall be given the FIDUCIA mark when they contain information whose unauthorised disclosure could harm the security of the Union or that of one or more of its Member States or the conduct of their international relations. The security aspects letter annexed to the contract shall contain provisions requiring the contractor to comply with the minimum standards laid down in this decision. Failure to comply with those minimum standards may constitute sufficient grounds for termination of the contract.

5. The contract involving action having to be taken that entails the urgent removal of FIDUCIA information to a place of safety shall include the number of security guards who are to have personnel security clearance. It shall be silent with regard to the procedures to be put in hand. This contract shall not be given the FIDUCIA mark.

6. The contractor may not sub-contract the activities defined in the call for tenders and in the contract involving or entailing access to FIDUCIA information.

DECISION OF THE COURT OF JUSTICE
of 13 September 2011

on the lodging and service of procedural documents by means of e-Curia

[10.806]

NOTES

Date of publication in OJ: OJ C289, 1.10.2011, p 7.

This Decision is available on the Court of Justice section of the Curia website at curia.europa.eu/jcms/jcms/Jo2_7031/en/.

THE COURT OF JUSTICE,

Having regard to the Rules of Procedure and, in particular, Articles 37(7) and 79(3) thereof,

Whereas:

(1) In order to take account of developments in communication technology, an information technology application has been developed to allow the lodging and service of procedural documents by electronic means.

(2) This application, which is based on an electronic authentication system using a combination of a user identification and a password, meets the requirements of authenticity, integrity and confidentiality of documents exchanged,

HAS DECIDED AS FOLLOWS:

Article 1

The information technology application known as 'e-Curia', common to the three constituent courts of the Court of Justice of the European Union, allows the lodging and service of procedural documents by electronic means under the conditions laid down by this Decision.

Article 2

Use of this application shall require a personal user identification and password.

Article 3

A procedural document lodged by means of e-Curia shall be deemed to be the original of that document for the purposes of the first subparagraph of Article 37(1) of the Rules of Procedure where the representative's user identification and password have been used to effect that lodgment. Such identification shall constitute the signature of the document concerned.

Article 4

A document lodged by means of e-Curia must be accompanied by the Annexes referred to therein and a schedule listing such Annexes.

It shall not be necessary to lodge certified copies of a document lodged by means of e-Curia or of any Annexes thereto.

Article 5

A procedural document shall be deemed to have been lodged for the purposes of Article 37(3) of the Rules of Procedure at the time of the representative's validation of lodgment of that document.

The relevant time shall be the time in the Grand Duchy of Luxembourg.

Article 6

Procedural documents, including judgments and orders, shall be served on the parties' representatives by means of e-Curia where they have expressly accepted this method of service or, in the context of a case, where they have consented to this method of service by lodging a procedural document by means of e-Curia.

Procedural documents shall also be served by means of e-Curia on Member States, other States which are parties to the Agreement on the European Economic Area and institutions, bodies, offices or agencies of the Union that have accepted this method of service.

Article 7
The intended recipients of the documents served referred to in Article 6 shall be notified by e-mail of any document served on them by means of e-Curia.

A procedural document shall be served at the time when the intended recipient (representative or his assistant) requests access to that document. In the absence of any request for access, the document shall be deemed to have been served on the expiry of the seventh day following the day on which the notification e-mail was sent.

Where a party is represented by more than one agent or lawyer, the time to be taken into account in the reckoning of time-limits shall be the time when the first request for access was made.

The relevant time shall be the time in the Grand Duchy of Luxembourg.

Article 8
The Registrar shall draw up the conditions of use of e-Curia and ensure that they are observed. Any use of e-Curia contrary to those conditions may result in the deactivation of the access account concerned.

The Court shall take the necessary steps to protect e-Curia from any abuse or malicious use.

Users shall be notified by e-mail of any action taken pursuant to this Article that prevents them from using their access account.

Article 9
This decision shall enter into force on the day following that of its publication in the *Official Journal of the European Union*.

E-CURIA: CONDITIONS OF USE APPLICABLE TO PARTIES' REPRESENTATIVES

NOTES
This document is available on the General Court section of the Curia website at curia.europa.eu/jcms/upload/docs/application/pdf/2011-10/en08602.pdf.

[10.807]
1. e-Curia is an information technology application which allows procedural documents to be lodged and served electronically. It also allows such documents to be consulted on-line.

2. Users are asked to read the following information carefully and to indicate their acceptance of the undertakings set out at the end of this document.

3. Every e-Curia page contains precise information on the steps to be followed and an on-line Help facility which is accessible via the (?) icon.

ACCESS TO E-CURIA

4. Access to e-Curia is free of charge.

5. e-Curia is common to the three constituent courts of the Court of Justice of the European Union. An access account opened by the Registry of one of those courts is equally valid as regards the Registries of the other two courts.

6. Without prejudice to compliance with the provisions of Article 19 of the Protocol on the Statute of the Court of Justice of the European Union and those relating to the admissibility of actions, agents and lawyers authorised to practise before a court of a Member State or of another State party to the Agreement on the European Economic Area may apply for an account to be opened giving them access to all the functionalities of e-Curia. Once such an account has been opened, they may use e-Curia in every case in which they have been appointed as a representative.

7. The application form for the opening of an account, which is available on the website of the Court of Justice via the e-Curia login page, must be completed, printed, dated and signed, and then sent by post to the Registry of one of the three courts, accompanied by the necessary supporting documents. The transmission of those documents does not relieve representatives of the obligation to lodge in each case the supporting documents required by the procedural rules applicable to the proceedings concerned.

8. Once the application has been validated by the Registry of the Court/Tribunal concerned, two separate e-mails will be sent to the user. The first informs the user of his user identification and the second, of his personal password. The user must change that password when he first logs on to e-Curia and, thereafter, at least once every six months.

9. In addition, representatives may also apply for an account to be opened for every assistant designated by name. This account allows the assistant to receive documents served, to consult procedural documents lodged or served by means of e-Curia and to prepare the lodgment of a document, which lodgment, once prepared, must be validated by the representative. The representative is responsible for the use of this account and is required regularly to update the list of his assistants and, in particular, in the event of a change in professional responsibilities or termination of activity to cancel any account that he assigned to his assistant(s).

10. An access account which remains unused for a period of three years will be deactivated automatically. In that event, a fresh application for the opening of an account will be required.

E-CURIA FUNCTIONALITIES

LODGING OF PROCEDURAL DOCUMENTS

11. e-Curia allows representatives to lodge procedural documents (together with any annexes) electronically, without the need for such lodging to be confirmed by post. As a rule, the lodging of a procedural document by means of e-Curia means that the representative will lodge subsequent documents in the same case in the same way. However, the lodging of a procedural document by means of e-Curia in a case does not preclude a document from being lodged subsequently in the same case by any other means of transmission provided for by the procedural rules applicable, if so required by the nature of the document concerned.

12. An assistant holding an access account may also prepare the lodgment of a document on behalf of a representative. In that case, the representative will be required to enter his password personally in order to validate lodgment.

13. Procedural documents lodged by means of e-Curia must be transmitted in PDF format (image and text).

14. Documents transmitted to the Courts of the European Union are checked to ensure that transmission is secure. If such checks reveal an anomaly, lodgment will be refused.

15. In the event of any malfunction during the transmission of a procedural document, the user is invited to inform the Registry of the Court/Tribunal concerned immediately. To avoid any delay in lodging the procedural document concerned, the document will, if necessary, have to be lodged by one of the other means of transmission provided for, following the procedural rules applicable.

16. Confirmation of lodgment stating, inter alia, the date and time of lodgment will be sent to the user. The point in time taken into account for the lodging of a procedural document is that of the representative's validation of lodgment of that document. The relevant time is that in the Grand Duchy of Luxembourg. That time is displayed on all e-Curia pages.

17. Since the length of time involved in the operations of preparing lodgment of documents and uploading files can vary, users are advised not to wait until the very last minute before expiry of a time-limit before starting to prepare the lodgment of a document.

18. Confirmation of lodgment is without prejudice to the procedural admissibility of the documents transmitted.

19. The transmission of procedural documents is automatically encrypted. Every procedural document lodged is given a digital signature unique to that document, in accordance with a standard hashing procedure (SHA-512). That digital signature appears in the confirmation of lodging which users are advised to retain in electronic format for the duration of the case. It is possible at any time to check that a procedural document has not been altered or amended; any change to that document will result in the allocation of a new digital signature.

SERVICE OF PROCEDURAL DOCUMENTS

20. e-Curia allows the constituent courts of the Court of Justice of the European Union to serve procedural documents electronically.

21. Where a representative has lodged a document in a case by means of e-Curia, any documents to be served in connection with that case will, as a rule, be sent to him by means of e-Curia. Irrespective of the representative's chosen method of lodgment, service of documents will also be effected by means of e-Curia where, in accordance with the requirements of the Rules of Procedure applicable, the representative has expressly agreed to accept service of documents by electronic means for the purpose of a particular case.

22. The user is notified by e-mail when a procedural document awaiting service is available in e-Curia. The same notice appears as soon as the user logs on to e-Curia.

23. Where a party is represented by more than one representative holding an access account, an e-mail confirming that a procedural document is awaiting service is sent to each representative and, if applicable, to any assistants designated by them. The same notice will appear when logging on to e-Curia.

24. The user is advised to consult and print as soon as possible the procedural document of which he is the intended recipient. The date and time of service is the point in time at which the user requests access to the procedural document. The relevant time is that in the Grand Duchy of Luxembourg. Where a party is represented by more than one agent or lawyer, the point in time taken into account in the reckoning of time-limits is that when the first request for access was made.

25. A procedural document is, however, deemed to have been served on the expiry of the seventh day following the day on which an e-mail was sent to the user notifying him of the availability of the document in e-Curia. Users are advised to log on to e-Curia at least once a week.

26. The date of actual or presumed service of a procedural document is stated in e-Curia. In the event of presumed service, a further e-mail is sent to the user to notify him of the date of service.

27. If any difficulties arise in relation to access to a procedural document, users are invited to inform the Registry of the Court or Tribunal concerned immediately.

CONSULTATION OF PROCEDURAL DOCUMENTS

28. e-Curia also allows the user to consult the documents which he has lodged or which have been served on him by means of e-Curia in respect of all the cases in which he is involved.

29. The procedural documents in a case may be consulted until the expiry of a period of three months from the date of the decision closing that case in the Court/Tribunal concerned.

UNDERTAKINGS TO BE GIVEN BY THE REPRESENTATIVE

You are requested to indicate your acceptance of the following undertakings, breach of which may result in deactivation of your access account:

I have taken note of how e-Curia operates, as described above, and I expressly undertake:

- Not to inform third parties of my user identification and password; any process carried out using that user identification and password will be deemed to have been carried out by me;
- To give notice immediately of any change of my e-mail address, the termination of my professional activity or a change in my responsibilities;
- To accept service by means of e-Curia of procedural documents relating to a case if I have lodged a procedural document by means of e-Curia in that case;
- To log on regularly to e-Curia and to consult the procedural documents awaiting service of which I am the intended recipient; I accept that, in the event of my failure to consult any such document, it will be deemed to have been served on me on the expiry of the seventh day following the day on which an e-mail was sent to notify me of the availability of that document in e-Curia;
- To update regularly the list of any assistants I may have and, in particular, in the event of a change in professional responsibilities or termination of activity to cancel any accounts that I have assigned to them.

Done at Luxembourg, on 11 October 2011.

E-CURIA: CONDITIONS OF USE APPLICABLE TO ASSISTANTS

NOTES

This document is available on the General Court section of the Curia website at curia.europa.eu/jcms/upload/docs/application/pdf/2011-10/en08603.pdf.

[10.808]

1. e-Curia is an information technology application which allows procedural documents to be lodged and served electronically. It also allows such documents to be consulted on-line.

2. Users are asked to read the following information carefully and to indicate their acceptance of the undertakings set out at the end of this document.

3. Every e-Curia page contains precise information on the steps to be followed and an on-line Help facility which is accessible via the (?) icon.

ACCESS TO E-CURIA

4. Access to e-Curia is free of charge.

5. e-Curia is common to the three constituent courts of the Court of Justice of the European Union. An access account opened by the Registry of one of those courts is equally valid as regards the Registries of the other two courts.

6. Without prejudice to compliance with the provisions of Article 19 of the Protocol on the Statute of the Court of Justice of the European Union and those relating to the admissibility of actions, agents and lawyers authorised to practise before a court of a Member State or of another State party to the Agreement on the European Economic Area may apply for an account to be opened giving them access to all the functionalities of e-Curia. Once such an account has been opened, they may use e-Curia in every case in which they have been appointed as a representative.

7. The application form for the opening of an account, which is available on the website of the Court of Justice via the e-Curia login page, must be completed, printed, dated and signed, and then sent by post to the Registry of one of the three courts, accompanied by the necessary supporting documents. The transmission of those documents does not relieve representatives of the obligation to lodge in each case the supporting documents required by the procedural rules applicable to the proceedings concerned.

8. Once the application has been validated by the Registry of the Court/Tribunal concerned, two separate e-mails will be sent to the user. The first informs the user of his user identification and the second, of his personal password. The user must change that password when he first logs on to e-Curia and, thereafter, at least once every six months.

9. In addition, representatives may also apply for an account to be opened for every assistant designated by name. This account allows the assistant to receive documents served, to consult procedural documents lodged or served by means of e-Curia and to prepare the lodgment of a document, which lodgment, once prepared, must be validated by the representative. The representative is responsible for the use of this account and is required regularly to update the list of his assistants and, in particular, in the event of a change in professional responsibilities or termination of activity to cancel any account that he assigned to his assistant(s).

10. An access account which remains unused for a period of three years will be deactivated automatically. In that event, a fresh application for the opening of an account will be required.

E-CURIA FUNCTIONALITIES

LODGING OF PROCEDURAL DOCUMENTS

11. e-Curia allows representatives to lodge procedural documents (together with any annexes) electronically, without the need for such lodging to be confirmed by post. As a rule, the lodging of a procedural document by means of e-Curia means that the representative will lodge subsequent documents in the same case in the same way. However, the lodging of a procedural document by means of e-Curia in a case does not preclude a document from being lodged subsequently in the same case by any other means of transmission provided for by the procedural rules applicable, if so required by the nature of the document concerned.

12. An assistant holding an access account may also prepare the lodgment of a document on behalf of a representative. In that case, the representative will be required to enter his password personally in order to validate lodgment.

13. Procedural documents lodged by means of e-Curia must be transmitted in PDF format (image and text).

14. Documents transmitted to the Courts of the European Union are checked to ensure that transmission is secure. If such checks reveal an anomaly, lodgment will be refused.

15. In the event of any malfunction during the transmission of a procedural document, the user is invited to inform the Registry of the Court/Tribunal concerned immediately. To avoid any delay in lodging the procedural document concerned, the document will, if necessary, have to be lodged by one of the other means of transmission provided for, following the procedural rules applicable.

16. Confirmation of lodgment stating, inter alia, the date and time of lodgment will be sent to the user. The point in time taken into account for the lodging of a procedural document is that of the representative's validation of lodgment of that document. The relevant time is that in the Grand Duchy of Luxembourg. That time is displayed on all e-Curia pages.

17. Since the length of time involved in the operations of preparing lodgment of documents and uploading files can vary, users are advised not to wait until the very last minute before expiry of a time-limit before starting to prepare the lodgment of a document.

18. Confirmation of lodgment is without prejudice to the procedural admissibility of the documents transmitted.

19. The transmission of procedural documents is automatically encrypted. Every procedural document lodged is given a digital signature unique to that document, in accordance with a standard hashing procedure (SHA-512). That digital signature appears in the confirmation of lodging which users are advised to retain in electronic format for the duration of the case. It is possible at any time to check that a procedural document has not been altered or amended; any change to that document will result in the allocation of a new digital signature.

SERVICE OF PROCEDURAL DOCUMENTS

20. e-Curia allows the constituent courts of the Court of Justice of the European Union to serve procedural documents electronically.

21. Where a representative has lodged a document in a case by means of e-Curia, any documents to be served in connection with that case will, as a rule, be sent to him by means of e-Curia. Irrespective of the representative's chosen method of lodgment, service of documents will also be effected by means of e-Curia where, in accordance with the requirements of the Rules of Procedure applicable, the representative has expressly agreed to accept service of documents by electronic means for the purpose of a particular case.

22. The user is notified by e-mail when a procedural document awaiting service is available in e-Curia. The same notice appears as soon as the user logs on to e-Curia.

23. Where a party is represented by more than one representative holding an access account, an e-mail confirming that a procedural document is awaiting service is sent to each representative and, if applicable, to any assistants designated by them. The same notice will appear when logging on to e-Curia.

24. The user is advised to consult and print as soon as possible the procedural document of which he is the intended recipient. The date and time of service is the point in time at which the user requests access to the procedural document. The relevant time is that in the Grand Duchy of Luxembourg. Where a party is represented by more than one agent or lawyer, the point in time taken into account in the reckoning of time-limits is that when the first request for access was made.

25. A procedural document is, however, deemed to have been served on the expiry of the seventh day following the day on which an e-mail was sent to the user notifying him of the availability of the document in e-Curia. Users are advised to log on to e-Curia at least once a week.

26. The date of actual or presumed service of a procedural document is stated in e-Curia. In the event of presumed service, a further e-mail is sent to the user to notify him of the date of service.

27. If any difficulties arise in relation to access to a procedural document, users are invited to inform the Registry of the Court or Tribunal concerned immediately.

CONSULTATION OF PROCEDURAL DOCUMENTS

28. e-Curia also allows the user to consult the documents which he has lodged or which have been served on him by means of e-Curia in respect of all the cases in which he is involved.

29. The procedural documents in a case may be consulted until the expiry of a period of three months from the date of the decision closing that case in the Court/Tribunal concerned.

UNDERTAKING TO BE GIVEN BY THE ASSISTANT

You are requested to indicate your acceptance of the following undertaking, breach of which may result in deactivation of your access account:

I have taken note of how e-Curia operates, as described above, and I expressly undertake:

• Not to inform third parties of my user identification and password; any process carried out using that user identification and password will be deemed to have been carried out by me.

COURT OF JUSTICE OF THE EUROPEAN UNION RECOMMENDATIONS

(2016/C 439/01)

to national courts and tribunals, in relation to the initiation of preliminary ruling proceedings

NOTES

Date of publication in OJ: OJ C439, 25.11.2016, p 1.

[10.809]
This text updates the recommendations to national courts and tribunals adopted following the entry into force on 1 November 2012 of the new Rules of Procedure of the Court of Justice (OJ C338, 6.11.2012, p 1). Based on experience gained in implementing those rules, and on the latest case-law, the present recommendations serve as a reminder of the essential characteristics of the preliminary ruling procedure and to provide courts and tribunals making references to the Court for a preliminary ruling with all the practical information required in order for the Court to be in a position to give a useful reply to the questions referred.

INTRODUCTION

[10.810]
1. The reference for a preliminary ruling, provided for in Article 19(3)(b) of the Treaty on European Union ('TEU') and Article 267 of the Treaty on the Functioning of the European Union ('TFEU'), is a fundamental mechanism of EU law. It is designed to ensure the uniform interpretation and application of that law within the European Union, by offering the courts and tribunals of the Member States a means of bringing before the Court of Justice of the European Union ('the Court') for a preliminary ruling questions concerning the interpretation of EU law or the validity of acts adopted by the institutions, bodies, offices or agencies of the Union.

2. The preliminary ruling procedure is based on close cooperation between the Court and the courts and tribunals of the Member States. In order to ensure that that procedure is fully effective, it is necessary to recall its essential characteristics and to provide further information to clarify the provisions of the rules of procedure relating, in particular, to the originator and scope of a request for a preliminary ruling, as well as to the form and content of such a request. That information — which applies to all requests for a preliminary ruling (I) — is supplemented by the provisions that apply to requests for a preliminary ruling requiring particularly expeditious handling (II) and by an annex which summarises the essential elements of any request for a preliminary ruling.

I.
PROVISIONS WHICH APPLY TO ALL REQUESTS FOR A PRELIMINARY RULING

THE ORIGINATOR OF THE REQUEST FOR A PRELIMINARY RULING

[10.811]
3. The jurisdiction of the Court to give a preliminary ruling on the interpretation or validity of EU law is exercised exclusively on the initiative of the national courts and tribunals, whether or not the parties to the main proceedings have expressed the wish that a question be referred to the Court. In so far as it is called upon to assume responsibility for the subsequent judicial decision, it is for the national court or tribunal before which a dispute has been brought — and for that court or tribunal alone — to determine, in the light of the particular circumstances of each case, both the need for a request for a preliminary ruling in order to enable it to deliver judgment and the relevance of the questions which it submits to the Court.

4. Status as a court or tribunal is interpreted by the Court as a self-standing concept of EU law, the Court taking account of a number of factors such as whether the body making the reference is established by law, whether it is permanent, whether its jurisdiction is compulsory, whether its procedure is *inter partes*, whether it applies rules of law and whether it is independent.

5. The courts and tribunals of the Member States may refer a question to the Court on the interpretation or validity of EU law where they consider that a decision of the Court on the question is necessary to enable them to give judgment (see second paragraph of Article 267 TFEU). A reference for a preliminary ruling may, inter alia, prove particularly useful when a question of interpretation is raised before the national court or tribunal that is new and of general interest for the uniform application of EU law, or where the existing case-law does not appear to provide the necessary guidance in a new legal context or set of facts.

6. Where a question is raised in the context of a case that is pending before a court or tribunal against whose decisions there is no judicial remedy under national law, that court or tribunal is nonetheless required to bring a request for a preliminary ruling before the Court (see third paragraph of Article 267 TFEU), unless there is already well-established case-law on the point or unless the correct interpretation of the rule of law in question admits of no reasonable doubt.

7. It follows, moreover, from settled case-law that although national courts and tribunals may reject pleas raised before them challenging the validity of acts of an institution, body, office or agency of the Union, the Court has exclusive jurisdiction to declare such acts invalid. When it has doubts about the validity of such an act, a court or tribunal of a Member State must therefore refer the matter to the Court, stating the reasons for which it considers that the act is invalid.

THE SUBJECT MATTER AND SCOPE OF THE REQUEST FOR A PRELIMINARY RULING

8. A request for a preliminary ruling must concern the interpretation or validity of EU law, not the interpretation of rules of national law or issues of fact raised in the main proceedings.

9. The Court can give a preliminary ruling only if EU law applies to the case in the main proceedings. It is essential, in that respect, that the referring court or tribunal set out all the relevant matters of fact and of law that have prompted it to consider that any provisions of EU law may be applicable in the case.

10. With regard to references for a preliminary ruling concerning the interpretation of the Charter of Fundamental Rights of the European Union, it must be noted that, under Article 51(1) of the Charter, the provisions of the Charter are addressed to the Member States only when they are implementing EU law. While the circumstances of such implementation can vary, it must nevertheless be clearly and unequivocally apparent from the request for a preliminary ruling that a rule of EU law other than the Charter is applicable to the case in the main proceedings. Since the Court has no jurisdiction to give a preliminary ruling where a legal situation does not come within the scope of EU law, any provisions of the Charter that may be relied upon by the referring court or tribunal cannot, of themselves, form the basis for such jurisdiction.

11. Lastly, although, in order to deliver its decision, the Court necessarily takes into account the legal and factual context of the dispute in the main proceedings, as defined by the referring court or tribunal in its request for a preliminary ruling, it does not itself apply EU law to that dispute. When ruling on the interpretation or validity of EU law, the Court makes every effort to give a reply which will be of assistance in resolving the dispute in the main proceedings, but it is for the referring court or tribunal to draw case-specific conclusions, if necessary by disapplying the rule of national law held incompatible with EU law.

THE APPROPRIATE STAGE AT WHICH TO MAKE A REFERENCE FOR A PRELIMINARY RULING

12. A national court or tribunal may submit a request for a preliminary ruling to the Court as soon as it finds that a ruling on the interpretation or validity of EU law is necessary to enable it to give judgment. It is that court or tribunal which is in fact in the best position to decide at what stage of the proceedings such a request should be made.

13. Since, however, that request will serve as the basis of the proceedings before the Court and the Court must therefore have available to it all the information that will enable it both to assess whether it has jurisdiction to give a reply to the questions raised and, if so, to give a useful reply to those questions, it is necessary that a decision to make a reference for a preliminary ruling be taken when the national proceedings have reached a stage at which the referring court or tribunal is able to define, in sufficient detail, the legal and factual context of the case in the main proceedings, and the legal issues which it raises. In the interests of the proper administration of justice, it may also be desirable for the reference to be made only after both sides have been heard.

THE FORM AND CONTENT OF THE REQUEST FOR A PRELIMINARY RULING

14. The request for a preliminary ruling may be in any form allowed by national law in respect of procedural issues, but it should be borne in mind that that request serves as the basis of the proceedings before the Court and is served on all the interested persons referred to in Article 23 of the Statute of the Court ('the Statute') and, in particular, on all the Member States, with a view to obtaining any observations they may wish to make. Owing to the consequential need to translate it into all the official languages of the European Union, the request for a preliminary ruling should therefore be drafted simply, clearly and precisely by the referring court or tribunal, avoiding superfluous detail. As experience has shown, about 10 pages are often sufficient to set out adequately the legal and factual context of a request for a preliminary ruling.

15. The content of any request for a preliminary ruling is prescribed by Article 94 of the Rules of Procedure of the Court and is summarised in the annex hereto. In addition to the text of the questions referred to the Court for a preliminary ruling, the request for a preliminary ruling must contain:

— a summary of the subject matter of the dispute and the relevant findings of fact as determined by the referring court or tribunal, or, at the very least, an account of the facts on which the questions referred are based,

— the tenor of any national provisions applicable in the case and, where appropriate, the relevant national case-law, and

— a statement of the reasons which prompted the referring court or tribunal to inquire about the interpretation or validity of certain provisions of EU law, and the relationship between those provisions and the national legislation applicable to the main proceedings.

In the absence of one or more of the above, the Court may have to decline jurisdiction to give a preliminary ruling on the questions referred or dismiss the request for a preliminary ruling as inadmissible.

16. In its request for a preliminary ruling, the referring court or tribunal must provide precise references for the national provisions applicable to the facts of the dispute in the main proceedings, and accurately identify the provisions of EU law whose interpretation is sought or whose validity is challenged. The request should include, if need be, a brief summary of the relevant arguments of the parties to the main proceedings. It is helpful to bear in mind in that context that it is only the request for a preliminary ruling that will be translated, not any annexes to that request.

17. The referring court or tribunal may also briefly state its view on the answer to be given to the questions referred for a preliminary ruling. That information may be useful to the Court, particularly where it is called upon to give a preliminary ruling in an expedited or urgent procedure.

18. Lastly, the questions referred to the Court for a preliminary ruling must appear in a separate and clearly identified section of the order for reference, preferably at the beginning or the end. It must be possible to understand them on their own terms, without it being necessary to refer to the statement of the grounds for the request.

19. In order to make the request for a preliminary ruling easier to read, it is essential that the Court receive it in typewritten form and that the pages and paragraphs of the order for reference be numbered.

20. The request for a preliminary ruling must be dated and signed, then sent, by registered post, to the Court Registry at the following address: Rue du Fort Niedergrünewald, 2925 Luxembourg, LUXEMBOURG. The request must be accompanied by any relevant documents and, in particular, precise contact details for the parties to the main proceedings and their representatives, if any, as well as the file of the case in the main proceedings or a copy of it. The file (or copy file) will be retained at the Registry throughout the proceedings where, unless otherwise indicated by the referring court or tribunal, it may be consulted by the interested persons referred to in Article 23 of the Statute.

21. Under the preliminary ruling procedure, the Court will, as a rule, use the information contained in the order for reference, including nominative or personal data. It is therefore for the referring court or tribunal itself, if it considers it necessary, to redact certain details in its request for a preliminary ruling or to render anonymous one or more persons or entities concerned by the dispute in the main proceedings.

22. After the request for a preliminary ruling has been lodged, the Court may also render such persons or entities anonymous of its own motion, or at the request of the referring court or tribunal or of a party to the main proceedings. In order to maintain its effectiveness, such a request for anonymity must, however, be made at the earliest possible stage of the proceedings, and in any event prior to publication in the *Official Journal of the European Union* of the notice relating to the case concerned, and to service of the request for a preliminary ruling on the interested persons referred to in Article 23 of the Statute, which generally takes place about one month after the request for a preliminary ruling has been lodged. Given the increasing use of new information and communication technologies, any anonymisation after such publication and service would be devoid of practical purpose.

INTERACTION BETWEEN THE REFERENCE FOR A PRELIMINARY RULING AND THE NATIONAL PROCEEDINGS

23. Although the referring court or tribunal may still order protective measures, particularly in connection with a reference on determination of validity, the lodging of a request for a preliminary ruling nevertheless calls for the national proceedings to be stayed until the Court has given its ruling.

24. While the Court, in principle, remains seised of a request for a preliminary ruling for so long as that request is not withdrawn, it must nevertheless be borne in mind that the Court's role in the preliminary ruling procedure is to contribute to the effective administration of justice in the Member States and not to give opinions on general or hypothetical questions. Since the preliminary ruling procedure is predicated on there being proceedings actually pending before the referring court or tribunal, it is incumbent on that court or tribunal to inform the Court of any procedural step that may affect the referral and, in particular, of any discontinuance or withdrawal, amicable settlement or other event leading to the termination of the proceedings. The referring court or tribunal must also inform the Court of any decision delivered in the context of an appeal against the order for reference and of the consequences of that decision for the request for a preliminary ruling.

25. In the interests of the proper conduct of the preliminary ruling proceedings before the Court and in order to maintain their effectiveness, it is important, however, that such information is communicated to the Court with the minimum of delay. The national courts and tribunals should also note that the withdrawal of a request for a preliminary ruling may have an impact on the management of similar cases (or of a series of cases) by the referring court or tribunal. Where the outcome of a number of cases pending before the referring court or tribunal depends on the reply to

be given by the Court to the questions submitted by that court or tribunal, it may be appropriate for that court or tribunal to join those cases in the request for a preliminary ruling in order to enable the Court to reply to the questions referred notwithstanding any withdrawal of one or more cases.

COSTS AND LEGAL AID

26. Preliminary ruling proceedings before the Court are free of charge and the Court does not rule on the costs of the parties to the proceedings pending before the referring court or tribunal; it is for the referring court or tribunal to rule on those costs.

27. If a party to the main proceedings has insufficient means and where it is possible under national rules, the referring court or tribunal may grant that party legal aid to cover the costs, including those of lawyers' fees, which it incurs before the Court. The Court itself may also grant legal aid where the party in question is not already in receipt of aid under national rules or to the extent to which that aid does not cover, or covers only partly, costs incurred before the Court.

COMMUNICATION BETWEEN THE COURT AND THE NATIONAL COURT OR TRIBUNAL

28. The Court Registry will remain in contact with the referring court or tribunal throughout the proceedings, and will send it copies of all procedural documents and any requests for information or clarification deemed necessary in order for a useful reply to be given to the questions referred by that court or tribunal.

29. At the end of the proceedings, the Registry will send the Court's decision to the referring court or tribunal, which is invited to inform the Court of the action taken upon that decision in the case in the main proceedings and to communicate to the Court its final decision in that case.

II.
PROVISIONS APPLICABLE TO REQUESTS FOR A PRELIMINARY RULING REQUIRING PARTICULARLY EXPEDITIOUS HANDLING

[10.812]

30. As provided in Article 23a of the Statute and Articles 105 to 114 of the Rules of Procedure, a reference for a preliminary ruling may, in certain circumstances, be determined pursuant to an expedited procedure or an urgent procedure. The Court will decide whether these procedures are to be applied, either on submission by the referring court or tribunal of a duly reasoned request setting out the matters of fact or of law which justify the application of such procedure(s), or, exceptionally, of its own motion, where that appears to be required by the nature or the particular circumstances of the case.

CONDITIONS FOR THE APPLICATION OF THE EXPEDITED AND URGENT PROCEDURES

31. Article 105 of the Rules of Procedure provides that a reference for a preliminary ruling may thus be determined pursuant to an expedited procedure derogating from the provisions of those rules where the nature of the case requires that it be dealt with within a short time. Since that procedure imposes significant constraints on all those involved in it, and, in particular, on all the Member States called upon to lodge observations, whether written or oral, within much shorter time limits than would ordinarily apply, its application must be sought only in particular circumstances that warrant the Court giving its ruling quickly on the questions referred. According to settled case-law, the large number of persons or legal situations potentially affected by the decision that the referring court or tribunal has to deliver after bringing the matter before the Court for a preliminary ruling does not, in itself, constitute an exceptional circumstance that would justify the use of the expedited procedure.

32. The same applies *a fortiori* to the urgent preliminary ruling procedure, provided for in Article 107 of the Rules of Procedure. That procedure, which applies only in the areas covered by Title V of Part Three of the TFEU, relating to the area of freedom, security and justice, imposes even greater constraints on those concerned, since it limits the number of parties authorised to lodge written observations and, in cases of extreme urgency, allows the written part of the procedure before the Court to be omitted altogether. The application of the urgent procedure must therefore be requested only where it is absolutely necessary for the Court to give its ruling very quickly on the questions submitted by the referring court or tribunal.

33. Although it is not possible to provide an exhaustive list of such circumstances, particularly because of the varied and evolving nature of the rules of EU law governing the area of freedom, security and justice, a national court or tribunal may, for example, consider submitting a request for the urgent preliminary ruling procedure to be applied in the case, referred to in the fourth paragraph of Article 267 TFEU, of a person in custody or deprived of his liberty, where the answer to the

question raised is decisive as to the assessment of that person's legal situation, or in proceedings concerning parental authority or custody of young children, where the identity of the court having jurisdiction under EU law depends on the answer to the question referred for a preliminary ruling.

THE REQUEST FOR APPLICATION OF THE EXPEDITED PROCEDURE OR THE URGENT PROCEDURE

34. To enable the Court to decide quickly whether the expedited procedure or the urgent preliminary ruling procedure should be applied, the request must set out precisely the matters of fact and law which establish the urgency and, in particular, the risks involved in following the ordinary procedure. In so far as it is possible to do so, the referring court or tribunal must also briefly state its view on the answer to be given to the questions referred. Such a statement makes it easier for the parties to the main proceedings and the other interested persons participating in the procedure to define their positions, and therefore contributes to the rapidity of the procedure.

35. The request for the application of the expedited procedure or the urgent procedure must in any event be submitted in an unambiguous form that enables the Registry to establish immediately that the file has to be dealt with in a particular way. Accordingly, the referring court or tribunal is requested to specify which of the two procedures is required in the particular case, and to mention in its request the relevant article of the Rules of Procedure (Article 105 for the expedited procedure or Article 107 for the urgent procedure). That mention must be included in a clearly identifiable place in its order for reference (for example, at the head of the page or in a separate judicial document). Where appropriate, it may be helpful for a covering letter from the referring court or tribunal to refer to that request.

36. As regards the order for reference itself, it is particularly important that it should be concise where the matter is urgent, as this will help to ensure the rapidity of the procedure.

COMMUNICATION BETWEEN THE COURT, THE REFERRING COURT OR TRIBUNAL AND THE PARTIES TO THE MAIN PROCEEDINGS

37. In order to expedite and facilitate communication with the referring court or tribunal and the parties to the main proceedings, a court or tribunal submitting a request for the expedited procedure or the urgent procedure to be applied is requested to state the email address and any fax number which may be used by the Court, together with the email addresses and any fax numbers of the representatives of the parties to the proceedings.

38. A copy of the signed order for reference together with a request for the expedited procedure or the urgent procedure to be applied can initially be sent to the Court by email (ECJ-Registry@curia.europa.eu) or by fax (+352 433766). Processing of the reference and of the request can then begin upon receipt of the emailed or faxed copy. The originals of those documents must, however, be sent to the Court Registry as soon as possible.

ANNEX

THE ESSENTIAL ELEMENTS OF A REQUEST FOR A PRELIMINARY RULING

1. THE REFERRING COURT OR TRIBUNAL

[10.813]
A request for a preliminary ruling must specify the referring court or tribunal and, where appropriate, the chamber or formation of the court or tribunal making the reference, and must include full contact details for that court or tribunal, in order to facilitate subsequent contact between that court or tribunal and the Court of Justice.

2. THE PARTIES TO THE MAIN PROCEEDINGS AND THEIR REPRESENTATIVES

After specifying the referring court or tribunal, the request for a preliminary ruling should state the names of the parties to the main proceedings and anyone representing them before that court or tribunal. Those particulars must be as comprehensive as possible and must notably include, in the order for reference or in the covering letter, the exact postal address of the persons concerned, their telephone or fax number and, in so far as they have one, their email address.

The attention of the national courts and tribunals is here drawn to Article 95 of the Rules of Procedure of the Court, and to points 21 and 22 of these recommendations. If the referring court or tribunal considers it necessary, it must itself redact certain names or details in its request for a preliminary ruling, or send an anonymised version of that request in addition to the full request for a preliminary ruling, which will serve as the basis of the proceedings before the Court.

3.
THE SUBJECT MATTER OF THE DISPUTE IN THE MAIN PROCEEDINGS AND THE RELEVANT FACTS

The referring court or tribunal must briefly describe the subject matter of the dispute in the main proceedings and the relevant findings of fact, as determined by that court or tribunal.

4.
THE RELEVANT LEGAL PROVISIONS

The request for a preliminary ruling must contain precise references to the national provisions applicable to the facts of the dispute in the main proceedings, including any relevant case-law, and the provisions of EU law whose interpretation is sought or whose validity is challenged. Those references must be comprehensive and must include the precise title of and citations for the provisions concerned, as well as their publication references. As far as possible, case-law citations, whether national or European, should also include the ECLI number ('European Case Law Identifier') of the decision concerned.

5.
THE GROUNDS FOR THE REFERENCE

The Court can rule on the request for a preliminary ruling only if EU law is applicable to the case in the main proceedings. The referring court or tribunal must therefore set out the reasons which prompted it to inquire about the interpretation or validity of provisions of EU law, and the relationship between those provisions and the national legislation applicable to the main proceedings. If it considers it helpful for the purposes of understanding the case, the referring court or tribunal may set out here the arguments of the parties in that regard.

6.
THE QUESTIONS REFERRED FOR A PRELIMINARY RULING

The referring court or tribunal should set out, clearly and distinctly, the questions it is submitting to the Court for a preliminary ruling. It must be possible to understand those questions on their own terms, without the need to refer to the statement of the grounds for the request for a preliminary ruling.

In so far as it is able to do so, the referring court or tribunal should also briefly state its view on the answer to be given to the questions referred for a preliminary ruling.

7.
POSSIBLE NEED FOR SPECIFIC TREATMENT

Lastly, where the referring court or tribunal considers that the request it is submitting to the Court has to be dealt with in a particular way, both as regards the need to preserve the anonymity of the persons concerned by the dispute in the main proceedings and as regards the rapidity with which the request may have to be dealt with by the Court, the reasons for such treatment must be set out in detail in the request for a preliminary ruling and in any covering letter.

FORMAL ASPECTS OF THE REQUEST FOR A PRELIMINARY RULING

Requests for a preliminary ruling must be submitted in a form that facilitates electronic processing by the Court and, in particular, that enables them to be scanned and optical character recognition to be applied. To that end:

— the request should be typed on white, unlined, A4-size paper,

— the text should be in a commonly used font (such as Times New Roman, Courier or Arial), in at least 12 point in the body of the text and at least 10 point in any footnotes, with 1,5 line spacing and horizontal and vertical margins of at least 2,5 cm (above, below, at the left and at the right of the page), and

— all the pages of the request, and the paragraphs they contain, should be numbered consecutively.

The request for a preliminary ruling must be dated and signed. It should be sent by registered post, together with the file of the case in the main proceedings, to the Registry of the Court of Justice, Rue du Fort Niedergrünewald, 2925 Luxembourg, LUXEMBOURG.

In the event of a request for the expedited procedure or the urgent procedure to be applied, it is recommended that a signed copy of the request for a preliminary ruling is first sent by email (ECJ-Registry@curia.europa.eu) or by fax (+352 433766), and that the original of that request is then sent by post.

RULES OF PROCEDURE: PRACTICE DIRECTIONS TO PARTIES CONCERNING CASES BROUGHT BEFORE THE COURT

NOTES

Date of publication in Official Journal: OJ L31, 31.1.2014, p 1.

THE COURT OF JUSTICE,

Having regard to the Rules of Procedure of 25 September 2012[1] and, in particular, Article 208 thereof,

Whereas:

(1) On 25 September 2012, the Court of Justice, with the approval of the Council, adopted new Rules of Procedure repealing the Rules of Procedure of 19 June 1991, as last amended on 24 May 2011. The new Rules entered into force on 1 November 2012 and are intended, inter alia, to ensure that the structure and content of the Rules of Procedure of the Court are adapted to changes in its caseload and, in particular, to the increasing number of references for a preliminary ruling made by the courts and tribunals of the Member States of the European Union, while at the same time supplementing and clarifying, in several important respects, the rules applicable to the conduct of proceedings before the Court.

(2) In the interests of the proper administration of justice and of making the Rules easier to understand, it is appropriate, therefore, to replace the practice directions relating to direct actions and appeals, adopted on the basis of the earlier Rules of Procedure, and to give the parties and their representatives practice directions based on the new Rules of Procedure that take into account, in particular, the experience gained in the course of their implementation.

(3) These new directions, which apply to all categories of cases brought before the Court, are not intended to replace the relevant provisions of the Statute and of the Rules of Procedure. Their purpose is to afford the parties and their representatives a better understanding of the implications of those provisions and to outline in greater detail the conduct of proceedings before the Court and, in particular, the constraints on the Court, particularly those associated with the processing and translation of procedural documents or the simultaneous interpretation of the observations submitted in the course of a hearing. In a context notable, on the one hand, for a constant increase in the number of cases brought before the Court and, on the other hand, for the growing complexity of their subject-matter, observing and taking into account these directions constitutes, both for the parties and for the Court, the best guarantee that the latter will be able to deal with cases with the greatest efficiency.

(4) In the interests of clarification, it is also necessary to incorporate into these new directions certain provisions of a rather more practical nature — which have until now been included in the Notes for the guidance of Counsel, the Instructions to the Registrar of the Court or letters of notice to attend a hearing — relating to the lodging and service of procedural documents and to the actual conduct of the oral part of the procedure,

NOTES

1 OJ L265, 29.9.2012, p 1, as amended on 18 June 2013 (OJ L173, 26.6.2013, p 65).

HEREBY ADOPTS THE FOLLOWING PRACTICE DIRECTIONS:

I. GENERAL PROVISIONS

THE STAGES IN THE PROCEDURE BEFORE THE COURT AND THEIR ESSENTIAL CHARACTERISTICS

[10.814]

1. Subject to special provisions laid down in the Protocol on the Statute of the Court of Justice of the European Union ('the Statute') or in the Rules of Procedure, the procedure before the Court is to consist, as a general rule, of a written part and an oral part. The purpose of the written part of the procedure is to put before the Court the claims, pleas and arguments of the parties to the proceedings or, in preliminary rulings, the observations which the interested persons referred to in Article 23 of the Statute intend to submit concerning the questions put by the courts and tribunals of the Member States of the European Union. The oral part, which follows it, is intended for its part to allow the Court to complete its knowledge of the case by the possible hearing of submissions from those parties or interested persons at a hearing and, if appropriate, by hearing the Opinion of the Advocate General.

REPRESENTATION OF THE PARTIES BEFORE THE COURT

2. In accordance with Article 19 of the Statute, parties to proceedings before the Court must be represented by a person who is duly authorised to represent them. With the exception of the Member States, other States which are parties to the Agreement on the European Economic Area ('the EEA Agreement'), the European Free Trade Association ('EFTA') Surveillance Authority and the institutions of the European Union, which are to be represented by an agent appointed for each case, other parties to the proceedings must be represented by a lawyer authorised to practise before a court of a Member State or of another State which is a party to the EEA Agreement. The evidence of that capacity must be capable of being produced, on request, at any stage of the proceedings. University teachers who are nationals of a Member State whose law accords them a right of audience are treated as lawyers by virtue of the seventh paragraph of Article 19 of the Statute.

3. In preliminary ruling proceedings, the Court is to take account, so far as concerns the representation of the parties to the main proceedings, of the procedural rules applicable in the court or tribunal which made the reference. Any person empowered to represent a party before that court or tribunal may therefore also represent him before the Court of Justice and, if the national procedural rules do not require parties to be represented, the parties to the main proceedings are entitled to submit their own written and oral observations. In the event of uncertainty in this respect, the Court may, at any time, request those parties, their representatives or the court or tribunal which made the reference to provide the relevant information.

4. The persons called upon to present oral argument before the Court, irrespective of their qualifications or the capacity in which they are called upon, are required to wear gowns. Where a hearing is organised, agents and lawyers taking part in that hearing are therefore requested to provide their own gowns; the Court has a number of plain gowns available for parties or representatives who have none.

COSTS OF PROCEEDINGS BEFORE THE COURT AND LEGAL AID

5. Subject to the provisions set out in Article 143 of the Rules of Procedure, proceedings before the Court are to be free of charge, no charge or tax being payable to that latter on account of the initiation of proceedings or the lodging of a procedural document. The costs referred to in Article 137 et seq. of the Rules of Procedure include only 'recoverable' costs, that is, any sums payable to witnesses and experts, and expenses necessarily incurred by the parties for the purpose of the proceedings before the Court, in connection with the remuneration of their representative and the expenses of his travel to and subsistence in Luxembourg, if a hearing is organised. The Court rules on the amount of those costs and the party ordered to pay them in the judgment or order which closes the proceedings, whereas in preliminary rulings it is for the referring court or tribunal to rule on the costs of the proceedings.

6. A party or, in preliminary ruling proceedings, a party to the main proceedings who is wholly or partly unable to meet the costs of the proceedings before the Court may, at any time, apply for legal aid under the conditions provided for, respectively, in Articles 115 to 118 and 185 to 189 of the Rules of Procedure. In order for it to be possible for such applications to be considered, they must however be accompanied by all the information and supporting documents necessary to enable the Court to assess the legal aid applicant's true financial situation. Since, in preliminary rulings, the Court gives its ruling at the request of a court or tribunal of a Member State, the parties to the main proceedings must, first of all, apply for any legal aid from that court or tribunal or the competent authorities of the Member State concerned, the aid granted by the Court being only subsidiary to the aid granted at national level.

7. It is worth noting that, where it grants the application for legal aid, the Court is responsible, where applicable within the limits set by the formation of the Court, solely for costs involved in the assistance and representation before the Court of the applicant for legal aid. In accordance with the rules set out in the Rules of Procedure, those costs can be recovered subsequently by the Court in the decision ending the proceedings and ruling on costs, and the formation of the Court which gave a decision on the application for legal aid may, moreover, withdraw that legal aid at any time if the circumstances which led to its being granted alter during the proceedings.

ANONYMITY

8. Where a party considers it necessary that its identity or certain information concerning it should not be disclosed in a case brought before the Court, it may request that the Court 'anonymise' the relevant case, in whole or in part. To be effective, such an application must, however, be made as early as possible. On account of the increasing use of new information and communication technologies, granting anonymity becomes much more difficult if the notice of the case concerned has already been published in the *Official Journal of the European Union* or, in preliminary ruling proceedings, if the request for a preliminary ruling has already been served on the interested persons referred to in Article 23 of the Statute, about one month after the request has been lodged at the Court.

II.
THE WRITTEN PART OF THE PROCEDURE

THE PURPOSE OF THE WRITTEN PART OF THE PROCEDURE

[10.815]
9. The written part of the procedure plays an essential role in the Court's understanding of the case in so far as it must allow the Court, by reading the written pleadings or observations lodged, to acquire a detailed and accurate idea of the subject-matter of the case before it and the issues raised by that case. Although this is the Court's objective when dealing with any case brought before it, the conduct and the pattern of the written part of the procedure differ depending on the nature of the action. Whereas in direct actions or appeals the parties are requested to adopt a position on the written pleadings lodged by the other parties to the proceedings, the written part of the procedure in preliminary rulings is characterised by the absence of adversarial proceedings, the interested persons referred to in Article 23 of the Statute being merely requested to submit any observations they may make on the questions referred by a national court or tribunal, without as a general rule knowing the position adopted by the other interested persons on those questions. This gives rise to different requirements as regards both the form and length of those observations and also the subsequent conduct of the procedure.

THE WRITTEN PART OF THE PROCEDURE IN REFERENCES FOR A PRELIMINARY RULING

10. On account of the non-adversarial nature of preliminary ruling proceedings, the lodging of written observations by the interested persons referred to in Article 23 of the Statute does not involve any specific formalities. Where a request for a preliminary ruling is served on them by the Court, those persons may thus submit, if they wish, written observations in which they set out their point of view on the request made by the referring court or tribunal. The purpose of those observations — which must be lodged within a time-limit of two months from service of the request for a preliminary ruling (extended on account of distance by a single period of 10 days) that cannot otherwise be extended — is to help clarify for the Court the scope of that request, and above all the answers to be provided to the questions referred by the referring court or tribunal.

11. Although the statement must be complete and include, in particular, the arguments on which the Court may base its answer to the questions referred, it is not necessary, on the other hand, to repeat the factual and legal background of the dispute set out in the order for reference, unless it requires further comment. Subject to special circumstances or specific provisions of the Rules of Procedure providing for a restriction of the length of the documents because of the urgency of the case, written observations lodged in a preliminary ruling should not exceed 20 pages.

THE WRITTEN PART OF THE PROCEDURE IN DIRECT ACTIONS

THE APPLICATION

12. On account of its adversarial nature, the written part of the procedure in direct actions follows stricter rules. These are set out in Article 119 et seq. (Title IV) of the Rules of Procedure and concern both the obligation for the parties to be represented by an agent or lawyer and the formal requirements linked to the content and the submission of written pleadings. It is apparent, in particular, from Article 120 of the Rules of Procedure, that the application initiating proceedings must, in addition to stating the name and address of the applicant and the name of the party against whom the application is made, state accurately the subject-matter of the proceedings, the pleas in law and arguments relied upon supported, as appropriate, by any evidence produced or offered, and the form of order sought by the applicant. Failure to comply with those requirements renders the application inadmissible. Unless there are special circumstances, the application should not exceed 30 pages.

13. As is apparent from Article 120(c) of the Rules of Procedure, the application must also include a summary of the pleas in law relied upon. That summary — which must not exceed two pages — is intended to facilitate the drafting of the notice, on each case brought before the Court, which must be published in the *Official Journal of the European Union* in accordance with Article 21(4) of the Rules of Procedure.

THE DEFENCE

14. The defence, to which Article 124 of the Rules of Procedure relates, is essentially subject to the same formal requirements as the application and must be lodged within two months of service of that latter. That time-limit — extended on account of distance by a single period of 10 days — may otherwise be extended only exceptionally and where a duly reasoned request setting out the circumstances capable of justifying such an extension has been submitted within the prescribed time-limit.

15. Since the legal framework of the proceedings is fixed by the application, the structure of the legal argument developed in the defence must, so far as is possible, reflect that of the pleas in law or complaints put forward in the application. No new plea in law may be introduced in the course of the proceedings unless it is based on matters of law or of fact which come to light in the course of the procedure. The factual and legal background is to be recapitulated in the defence only in so far as its presentation in the application is disputed or calls for further particulars. As in the case of the application, unless there are special circumstances the defence should not exceed 30 pages.

The reply and rejoinder

16. If they consider it necessary, the applicant and the defendant may supplement their arguments, the former by a reply and the latter by a rejoinder. Those written pleadings are subject to the same formal rules as the application and the defence but, since they are optional and supplementary, they are necessarily shorter than those documents. The framework and the pleas in law or claims at the heart of the dispute having been set out (or disputed) in depth in the application and the defence, the only purpose of the reply and the rejoinder is to allow the applicant and the defendant to make clear their position or to refine their arguments on an important issue, the President also being able, pursuant to Article 126 of the Rules of Procedure, to specify himself the matters to which those documents should relate. Except in special circumstances, a reply or a rejoinder should therefore be no more than approximately 10 pages long. Those documents must be lodged with the Registry within the time-limits set by the Court, an extension of those time-limits being granted by the President only in exceptional circumstances and on a duly reasoned request.

Request for an expedited procedure

17. Where the nature of the case requires it to be dealt with within a short time, the applicant or defendant may request the Court to deal with the case under an expedited procedure derogating from the provisions of the Rules of Procedure. Provided for in Article 133 of those Rules, that possibility is nevertheless subject to the lodging, by a separate document, of an express request to that effect setting out in detail the circumstances capable of justifying the use of such a procedure and involves, where such a request is granted, an adjustment to the written part of the procedure. The ordinary time-limits for the lodging of written pleadings are reduced, as is the length of those pleadings and, pursuant to Article 134 of the Rules of Procedure, a reply, a rejoinder or a statement in intervention can be submitted only if the President considers this to be necessary.

Application for suspension of operation or for interim measures (Interim proceedings)

18. A direct action may also be accompanied by an application for suspension of operation of a measure or by an application for interim measures, as referred to in Articles 278 and 279 respectively of the Treaty on the Functioning of the European Union ('TFEU'). In accordance with the provisions of Article 160 of the Rules of Procedure, such an application is however admissible only if it is made by the applicant having challenged the measure at issue before the Court or another party to the case before the Court and it must be made by a separate document stating the subject-matter of the proceedings and the circumstances giving rise to urgency as well as the pleas of fact and law establishing a prima facie case for the measure applied for. As a general rule, the application is then served on the opposite party, and the President is to prescribe a short period within which that party may submit written or oral observations. In cases of extreme urgency, the President may grant the application provisionally even before such observations have been submitted. In such a case, the decision closing the interim proceedings can, however, be adopted only after that party has been heard.

THE WRITTEN PART OF THE PROCEDURE IN APPEALS

19. The written part of the procedure in an appeal is similar in many respects to the conduct of that part of the procedure in direct actions. The relevant rules are in Article 167 et seq. (Title V) of the Rules of Procedure, which state both the mandatory content of the appeal and of the response and the scope of the forms of order sought.

The appeal

20. As is apparent from Articles 168 and 169 of the Rules of Procedure (which supplement, in this respect, Articles 56 to 58 of the Statute), an appeal is not brought against a measure of an institution, a body or an office or agency of the European Union, but against the decision of the General Court ruling on an action brought at first instance. It is apparent from that information that the form of order sought in the appeal must necessarily seek to have set aside, in whole or in part, the decision of the General Court as set out in the operative part of that decision, and not the annulment of the measure challenged before the General Court. If they are not to be held inadmissible, the pleas in law and legal arguments relied upon in the appeal — which, unless there are special circumstances, should not exceed 25 pages — must moreover identify precisely those points in the grounds of that decision that are contested and set out in detail the reasons for which that decision is alleged to be vitiated by an error of law.

21. In order to facilitate the drawing up of the notice published in the *Official Journal of the European Union*, in accordance with Article 21(4) of the Rules of Procedure, the appellant must also attach to his appeal a summary of those pleas in law, no more than two pages long, and lodge at the Registry the necessary items and documents attesting that the requirements set out in Article 19 of the Statute and reiterated in Article 119 of the Rules of Procedure are met.

THE RESPONSE

22. Within a time-limit of two months from the service upon him of the appeal (extended on account of distance by a single period of 10 days), which may not otherwise be extended, any party to the case at issue before the General Court may submit a response. The content of the written pleadings is subject to the requirements fixed in Article 173 of the Rules of Procedure and, in accordance with Article 174 of those Rules, the form of order must seek to have the appeal allowed or dismissed, in whole or in part. The structure of the legal arguments in the response must, so far as is possible, reflect the pleas in law put forward by the appellant but it is not necessary to reiterate in those pleadings the factual and legal background to the proceedings, unless its presentation in the appeal is disputed or calls for further particulars. On the other hand, any challenge to the admissibility, in whole or in part, of that appeal must be included in the actual body of the response, since the possibility — provided for in Article 151 of the Rules of Procedure — of raising a plea of inadmissibility in relation to the proceedings by a separate document is not applicable to appeals. Like the appeal, and subject to special circumstances, the response should not exceed 25 pages.

THE CROSS-APPEAL

23. If, when the appeal has been served on him, one of the parties to the relevant case before the General Court intends to dispute that court's decision on an aspect which was not mentioned in the appeal, that party must bring a cross-appeal against the General Court's decision. That appeal must be introduced by a separate document, within the same time-limit, which may not be extended, as the time-limit for submission of the response and meet the requirements set out in Articles 177 and 178 of the Rules of Procedure. The pleas in law and legal arguments which it contains must be separate from those relied on in the response.

THE RESPONSE TO THE CROSS-APPEAL

24. Where such a cross-appeal is brought, the applicant, or any other party to the relevant case before the General Court having an interest in the cross-appeal being allowed or dismissed, may submit a response, which must be limited to the pleas in law relied on in that cross-appeal. In accordance with Article 179 of the Rules of Procedure, those written pleadings must be submitted within a time-limit, which may not be extended, of two months from service of the cross-appeal (extended on account of distance by a single period of 10 days).

THE REPLY AND REJOINDER

25. Whether in the case of a main appeal or a cross-appeal, the appeal and the response may be supplemented by a reply and a rejoinder, in particular in order to allow the parties to adopt a position on a plea of inadmissibility or new matters raised in the response. Unlike the rules applicable to direct actions, that possibility is however made subject to the express authorisation of the President of the Court. To that effect, the appellant (or the party having brought the cross-appeal) is requested to submit, within a time-limit of seven days from service of the response (or of the response to the cross-appeal), extended on account of distance by a single period of 10 days, a duly reasoned application setting out the reasons for which, in that party's opinion, a reply is necessary. That application — which should not exceed three pages — must be intelligible in itself, without necessitating reference to the appeal or to the response.

26. Due to the special nature of appeals, which are restricted to the examination of questions of law, the President may also, if he grants the application to lodge a reply, limit the number of pages and the subject-matter of that reply and of the rejoinder submitted subsequently. The observance of those instructions is an essential condition for the proper conduct of the procedure, and exceeding the number of pages authorised or referring to other questions in the reply or the rejoinder will lead to the pleadings being sent back to their author.

APPEALS BROUGHT UNDER ARTICLE 57 OF THE STATUTE

27. The rules set out in points 19 to 26 of these directions are nevertheless not applicable in their entirety to appeals brought against decisions of the General Court dismissing an application to intervene or adopted following an application for interim measures submitted under Articles 278 or 279 TFEU. Pursuant to the third paragraph of Article 57 of the Statute, such appeals are subject to the same procedure as an application for interim measures made directly to the Court. The parties are therefore set a short period for the submission of any observations on the appeal and the Court rules on that appeal without any additional written part of the procedure, or even without an oral part of the procedure.

INTERVENTION IN DIRECT ACTIONS AND APPEALS

THE APPLICATION TO INTERVENE

28. In accordance with Article 40 of the Statute, the Member States and institutions of the European Union, on the one hand, and, in the circumstances provided for in the second and third paragraphs of that article, non-Member States party to the Agreement on the EEA, the EFTA Surveillance Authority, the bodies, offices and agencies of the European Union and any other natural or legal person, on the other hand, may intervene in cases before the Court for the purposes of supporting, in whole or in part, the form of order sought by one of the parties. To be taken into account, the application to intervene must be submitted within the time-limit referred to in Article 130(1) (direct actions), or Article 190(2) (appeals) of the Rules of Procedure and meet the conditions set in Article 130(2) to (4) of those Rules.

THE STATEMENT IN INTERVENTION

29. If the application to intervene is granted, the intervener receives a copy of every procedural document served on the parties save, where applicable, secret or confidential items or documents, and he has one month from receipt of those documents to submit a statement in intervention. Although that statement must meet the requirements in Article 132(2) of the Rules of Procedure, its content is, however, necessarily more succinct than the written pleadings of the party supported and its length should not exceed 10 pages. Since the intervention is ancillary to the main proceedings, the intervener must refrain from repeating in his statement the pleas in law and arguments in the written pleadings of the party which he is supporting and must set out only additional pleas in law or arguments which bear out that party's submissions. Recapitulation of the factual or legal background to the case is not necessary, except in so far as its presentation in the written pleadings of the main parties is disputed or, exceptionally, calls for further particulars.

OBSERVATIONS ON THE STATEMENT IN INTERVENTION

30. After the statement in intervention has been lodged, the President may, if he considers this necessary, prescribe a time-limit for the submission of brief observations on that statement. The lodging of those observations, the length of which should not exceed five pages, is nevertheless optional. The purpose of such observations is merely to enable the main parties to respond to inaccurate claims or to adopt a position on new pleas in law or arguments raised by the intervener. Where there are no such matters, it is recommended that the parties desist from lodging those observations in order to avoid unnecessarily prolonging the written part of the procedure.

APPLICATIONS TO INTERVENE MADE OUT OF TIME

31. In so far as it meets the conditions set out in Article 130(2) to (4) of the Rules of Procedure, the Court may also give consideration to an application to intervene made after the passing of the time-limit prescribed in Article 130(1) or 190(2) of the Rules of Procedure, provided, however, that that application reaches it before the decision to open the oral part of the procedure provided for in Article 60(4) of those Rules is adopted. In that case, the intervener will be able to submit his observations, if any, during the hearing, if it takes place.

INTERVENTION IN THE CONTEXT OF AN APPLICATION FOR INTERIM MEASURES OR AN EXPEDITED PROCEDURE

32. The same is true in general in the context of an application for interim measures or where a case is to be dealt with under an expedited procedure. If there are no special circumstances warranting the lodging of written observations, the person or entity authorised to intervene in the context of such a procedure may submit his observations only orally, if a hearing is organised.

NO INTERVENTION IN PRELIMINARY RULINGS

33. The above rules on intervention are, in contrast, not applicable to references for a preliminary ruling. Due to the non-adversarial nature of that category of cases and the special function of the Court when it is called upon to give a preliminary ruling on the interpretation or validity of European Union law, only the interested persons referred to in Article 23 of the Statute are authorised to submit observations, written or oral, on the questions submitted to the Court by the courts or tribunals of the Member States.

THE FORM AND STRUCTURE OF PROCEDURAL DOCUMENTS

34. Irrespective of the foregoing matters and the prerequisites relating to the content of procedural documents resulting from the provisions of the Statute and the Rules of Procedure, the written pleadings and observations lodged before the Court must meet certain additional requirements intended to facilitate the reading and processing of those documents by the Court, in particular by electronic means. Those requirements concern the form and the presentation of procedural documents as well as their length or structure.

35. As to the formal conditions, first of all, it is essential that the written pleadings or observations lodged by the parties are presented in a form in which they can be processed electronically by the Court and that, in particular, documents can be scanned and character recognition used. To that end, the following requirements must be taken into account:

— the written pleadings or observations are to be drafted on white, unlined and A4-size paper, with text on one side of the page only (recto), and not on both sides of the page (recto-verso),
— the text is to be in a commonly-used font (such as Times New Roman, Courier or Arial), in at least 12 point in the body of the text and at least 10 point in the footnotes, with 1,5 line spacing and horizontal and vertical margins of at least 2,5 cm (above, below, at the left and at the right of the page),
— all the paragraphs of the written pleadings or observations are to be numbered consecutively,
— the same is true for the pages of the written pleadings or observations, including any annexes to them and their schedule, which are to be numbered consecutively, at the top right-hand corner,
— lastly, where they are not sent to the Court by electronic means, pages of written pleadings or observations are to be assembled in such a way as to be easily separable and not permanently attached by means such as glue or staples.

36. In addition to these formal requirements, the procedural documents lodged before the Court must be drafted in a form which allows their structure and scope to be grasped from the first few pages. Besides stating, on the first page of the written pleadings or observations concerned, the title of the document, the case number (if it has already been notified by the Registry) and the parties concerned (parties to the dispute in the main proceedings, the applicant (appellant) and the defendant (respondent) or parties to the case at issue before the General Court), the written pleadings or observations lodged are to begin with a brief summary of the schema adopted by the author or by a table of contents. Those written pleadings or those observations must end with the forms of order sought by the author or, in preliminary ruling proceedings, by the answers which the author proposes to the questions of the referring court or tribunal.

37. Although the documents which are sent to the Court are not subject, as regards their content, to any requirement other than those resulting from the Statute and the Rules of Procedure, it must nevertheless be borne in mind that such documents constitute the basis for the Court's study of the file and that they must, as a general rule, be translated by the Court or the institution which produced them. In the interests of the proper conduct of the procedure as in the interests of the parties themselves, the written pleadings or observations must therefore be drafted in clear, concise language, without use of technical terms specific to a national legal system. Repetition must be avoided and short sentences must, as far as possible, be used in preference to long and complex sentences which include parenthetical and subordinate clauses.

38. When, in their written pleadings or observations, the parties refer to a specific text or piece of legislation, of national or European Union law, references to that text or legislation must be accurately cited, both so far as concerns the date of adoption and, where possible, the date of publication of that document and so far as concerns its temporal applicability. Likewise, when they cite an extract or a passage of a judgment or of an Opinion of an Advocate General, the parties are requested to specify both the name and number of the case concerned and the exact references of the extract or the passage at issue.

39. Lastly, it must be pointed out that legal argument of the parties or the interested persons referred to in Article 23 of the Statute must appear in the written pleadings or observations, and not in any attached annexes, which are not as a general rule translated. Only documents mentioned in the actual body of written pleadings or observations and necessary in order to prove or illustrate its contents may be submitted as annexes. Annexes are furthermore not accepted, pursuant to Article 57(4) of the Rules of Procedure, unless they are accompanied by a schedule of annexes. That schedule is to indicate, for each document annexed, the number of the annex, a short description of the document and the page or paragraph of the written pleadings or observations in which the document is cited and which justifies its production.

THE LODGING AND TRANSMISSION OF PROCEDURAL DOCUMENTS

40. Only the documents expressly provided for by the procedural rules may be lodged at the Registry. Those documents must be lodged within the prescribed time-limits and observing the requirements set out in Article 57 of the Rules of Procedure. Documents may be lodged electronically or by post, or delivered in person to the Court Registry or, outside the opening hours of the Registry, to the reception of the Court buildings (rue du Fort Niedergrünewald) where the janitor will acknowledge receipt of that document by recording on it the date and time of lodgement.

41. The most reliable, quickest way to lodge a procedural document is by using the *e-Curia application*. That application, common to the three constituent courts of the Court of Justice of the European Union, was introduced in 2011. It allows the lodging and service of procedural documents by exclusively electronic means, without it being necessary to provide certified copies of the document transmitted to the Court or to duplicate that transmission by sending the document by post. The procedure for access to the e-Curia application and its conditions of use are described in detail in the Decision of the Court of 13 September 2011 on the lodging and service of procedural documents by means of e-Curia and in the conditions of use to which that decision refers. Those documents are available on the Court's internet site (under 'Court of Justice — Procedure').

42. If it is not transmitted to the Court by means of the abovementioned application, a procedural document may also be sent to the Court *by post*. The envelope containing that document must be addressed to the Court Registry at the following address: Rue du Fort Niedergrünewald — L-2925 Luxembourg. In this connection, it is appropriate to mention that pursuant to Article 57(7) of the Rules of Procedure, only the date and time of lodgement of the original at the Registry are taken into consideration in the calculation of procedural time-limits. To prevent any time-barring, it is therefore strongly recommended that it be sent by registered post or by express delivery, several days before the passing of the time-limit prescribed for lodgement of the document.

43. At the present time, a copy of the signed original of a procedural document may also be transmitted to the Registry *by fax* ((+ 352 433766) or as an attachment to an *electronic mail* (ecj.registry@curia.europa.eu). However, a document lodged by either of these methods will be treated as complying with the relevant time-limit only if the signed original itself, together with the annexes and copies referred to in Article 57(2) of the Rules of Procedure, reaches the Registry at the latest 10 days after that electronic mail or telefax was sent. That original must therefore be sent without delay, immediately after the dispatch of the copy, without any corrections or amendments, even of a minor nature. In the event of any discrepancy between the signed original and the copy previously transmitted, only the date on which the signed original was lodged will be taken into consideration.

III.
THE ORAL PART OF THE PROCEDURE

[10.816]
44. As is apparent from the fourth paragraph of Article 20 of the Statute, the oral part of the procedure essentially consists of two distinct stages: the hearing of the parties or interested persons referred to in Article 23 of the Statute and the presentation of the Advocate General's Opinion. Under the fifth paragraph of Article 20 of the Statute, the Court may nevertheless decide, where it considers that the case raises no new point of law, that the case is to be determined without hearing the Advocate General's Opinion. A hearing will not automatically be arranged.

THE PURPOSE OF THE HEARING

45. Having regard to the importance of the written part of the procedure in cases brought before the Court and subject to the application of Article 76(3) of the Rules of Procedure, the decisive criterion for holding a hearing is not so much whether an express request has been made to that effect as the assessment made by the Court itself as to the potential contribution of that hearing to the outcome of the dispute or to determining the answers which it could provide to the questions referred by a court or tribunal of a Member State. A hearing is therefore arranged by the Court whenever it is likely to contribute to a better understanding of the case and the issues raised by it, whether or not a request to that effect has been made by the parties or the interested persons referred to in Article 23 of the Statute.

THE REQUEST FOR A HEARING

46. Where those parties or interested persons consider that a hearing must be arranged in a case, the onus is on them, in any event, as soon as they have received notification of the end of the written part of the procedure, to inform the Court by letter why they wish be heard. That reasoning — which is not to be confused with written pleadings or observations and should not exceed three pages — must be based on a real assessment of the benefit of a hearing to the party in question and must indicate the documentary elements or arguments which that party considers it necessary to develop or disprove more fully at the hearing. It is not in itself sufficient to provide a general statement of reasons referring, for example, to the importance of the case or of the questions to be decided by the Court.

THE NOTICE TO ATTEND THE HEARING AND THE NEED FOR A RAPID ANSWER TO THAT NOTICE

47. When the Court decides to arrange a hearing in a particular case, it fixes the exact date and time and the parties or interested persons referred to in Article 23 of the Statute are immediately sent a letter of notice to attend by the Registry, which also notifies them of the composition of the formation to which the Court has assigned the case, of any measures of organisation of procedure

decided on by the Court and, where applicable, that there is to be no Advocate General's Opinion. In order to enable the Court to arrange that hearing in the best possible conditions, the parties or abovementioned interested persons are requested to reply to the Registry's letter within a short period stating, in particular, whether they intend actually to attend the hearing and the name of the lawyer or agent who will represent them at it. A late reply to the Registry's letter of notice to attend is likely to jeopardise the proper organisation of the hearing, both from the point of view of the speaking time allocated by the Court to the party concerned and with regard to the constraints on the operation of the interpretation service.

THE STEPS TO BE TAKEN WITH A VIEW TO THE HEARING

48. On account both of the sometimes difficult traffic conditions in Luxembourg and of the security measures applicable to access to the Court buildings, it is advisable to take the steps necessary to be present in the room where the hearing will take place on the day of the hearing well before it is due to start. Before the hearing begins, the members of the formation of the Court usually hold a short meeting with the representatives of the parties or interested persons referred to in Article 23 of the Statute about the organisation of the hearing. At that meeting the Judge-Rapporteur and the Advocate General may invite those representatives to provide, at the hearing, further information on certain questions or to develop one or more specific aspects of the case at issue.

THE NORMAL PROCEDURE AT A HEARING

49. While the procedure at a hearing before the Court may vary depending on the circumstances of each case, in general it consists of three separate parts: the oral submissions proper, questions from the members of the Court and replies.

THE FIRST STAGE OF THE HEARING: ORAL SUBMISSIONS

THE PURPOSE OF THE ORAL SUBMISSIONS

50. Subject to any special circumstances, the hearing usually starts with the *oral submissions* of the parties or the interested persons referred to in Article 23 of the Statute. The aim of those submissions is, firstly, to respond to any requests to concentrate on specified issues in the submissions and to answer the questions that the Court might have put to the parties or interested persons before the hearing, under Articles 61 or 62 of the Rules of Procedure, and, if applicable, then to draw attention to the points which the person presenting oral argument considers to be particularly important for the Court's decision, in particular, in preliminary ruling proceedings, having regard to the written observations submitted by the other participants in the proceedings.

51. In the light of the knowledge which the Court already has of the case following the written part of the procedure, it is not necessary, at the hearing, to recall the content of the written pleadings or observations lodged or, in particular, the factual or legal background to the case. Only the decisive points for the purposes of the Court's decision must be brought to its attention. It must none the less be stated that where, before the hearing, the Court has requested the parties or the abovementioned interested persons to concentrate in their submissions on a question or a particular aspect of the case, in general only that question or that aspect should be addressed during those submissions. As far as possible, participants in the hearing who are advocating the same line of argument or adopting the same position must also liaise before the hearing to avoid repeating arguments which have already been submitted.

SPEAKING TIME AND ITS POSSIBLE EXTENSION

52. The speaking time is fixed by the President of the formation of the Court, after consulting the Judge-Rapporteur and, if applicable, the Advocate General responsible for the case. As a general rule, the speaking time is fixed at 15 minutes, irrespective of the formation of the Court to which the case has been assigned. However, that duration may be made longer or shorter depending on the nature or the specific complexity of the case, the number and procedural status of the participants in the hearing and any measures of organisation of procedure. An extension of the speaking time allocated may, exceptionally, be granted by the President of the formation of the Court on the duly reasoned application of a party or one of the interested persons referred to in Article 23 of the Statute. To be taken into account, such an application must nevertheless be made by the party or interested person concerned in his reply to the letter of notice to attend and, in any event, reach the Court at least two weeks before the actual date of the hearing.

THE NUMBER OF PERSONS PRESENTING ORAL ARGUMENT

53. For reasons connected with the proper conduct of the hearing, the oral submissions of the parties or the interested persons present at the hearing must, as regards each of them, be made by a single person. In exceptional circumstances, a second person may nevertheless be authorised to present oral argument where the nature or specific complexity of the case warrants this, provided a duly reasoned application to this effect has been submitted in the reply of the party or interested

person concerned to the letter of notice to attend the hearing and, in any event, at least two weeks before the actual date of the hearing. If it is granted, that authorisation does not however include any extension of the speaking time, and the two persons presenting oral argument must share the speaking time allocated to the party concerned.

THE SECOND STAGE OF THE HEARING: QUESTIONS FROM MEMBERS OF THE COURT

54. Without prejudice to the questions which may be asked or the clarifications which may be sought by the members of the Court during the oral submissions, the persons presenting oral argument may be requested, at the end of the oral submissions, to answer *additional questions from the members of the Court*. The purpose of those questions is to supplement the members' knowledge of the file and to allow the persons presenting oral argument to explain or elaborate on certain points on which additional information may be required following the written part of the procedure and the oral submissions.

THE THIRD STAGE OF THE HEARING: REPLIES

55. After that exchange, the representatives of the parties or the interested persons referred to in Article 23 of the Staff Regulations finally have the opportunity, if they consider it necessary, of replying briefly. Those *replies*, of a maximum duration of five minutes each, do not constitute a second round of oral submissions. They are designed only to enable the persons presenting oral argument to react succinctly to observations made or questions put during the hearing by the other participants or by the members of the Court. If two persons have been authorised to speak for a party, only one of them is authorised to reply.

THE IMPLICATIONS AND CONSTRAINTS OF SIMULTANEOUS INTERPRETATION

56. Whether in their oral submissions, their replies or their responses to questions from the Court, the persons presenting oral argument must bear in mind that very frequently the members of the formation of the Court will listen to their argument by means of simultaneous interpretation. In the interests of the proper conduct of the hearing and in order to guarantee the quality of the interpretation provided, the representatives of the parties or the interested persons referred to in Article 23 of the Statute are therefore requested, if they have a text available, however short, of notes for the oral submissions or an outline of their argument, to send it in advance to the interpretation directorate, either by fax ((+ 352 43033697), or by electronic mail (interpret@curia.europa.eu). That text or those notes for the oral submissions is intended solely for the interpreters and is neither transmitted to the members of the formation of the Court and the Advocate General responsible for the case nor included in the case file.

57. At the hearing itself, it is however inadvisable to read out a text. To facilitate interpretation, it is recommended to speak freely on the basis of properly structured notes. In any event, it is essential to speak directly into the microphone, at a natural pace and not too quickly, stating in advance the outline of the argument made and using short and simple sentences as a matter of course.

THE PROCEDURE FOLLOWING THE HEARING

58. The active participation of the parties or interested persons referred to in Article 23 of the Statute comes to an end at the end of the hearing. Subject to the exceptional situation in which the oral part of the procedure is reopened, pursuant to Article 83 of the Rules of Procedure, the parties or abovementioned interested persons are no longer authorised to put forward written or oral observations, in particular in response to the Advocate General's Opinion, once the President of the formation of the Court has declared the hearing closed.

IV.
FINAL PROVISIONS

[10.817]
59. The practice directions relating to direct actions and appeals of 15 October 2004 (OJ L361, p 15), as amended on 27 January 2009 (OJ L29, p 51), are hereby revoked and replaced by these Practice Directions.

60. These Practice Directions shall be published in the *Official Journal of the European Union*. They shall enter into force on the day following their publication.

Adopted at Luxembourg, 25 November 2013.

DECISION OF THE GENERAL COURT

(2016/C 111/02)

of 27 January 2016

on judicial vacations

[10.818]

NOTES

Date of publication in Official Journal: OJ C111, 29.3.2016, p 2.

THE GENERAL COURT

Having regard to Article 41(2) of the Rules of Procedure,

HAS ADOPTED THIS DECISION:

Article 1

For the judicial year beginning on 1 September 2016, the dates of the judicial vacations within the meaning of Article 41(2) and (6) of the Rules of Procedure are as follows:

— Christmas 2016: from Monday 19 December 2016 to Sunday 8 January 2017 inclusive,
— Easter 2017: from Monday 10 April 2017 to Sunday 23 April 2017 inclusive,
— Summer 2017: from Friday 21 July 2017 to Sunday 3 September 2017 inclusive.

Article 2

This Decision shall enter into force on the day of its publication in the *Official Journal of the European Union.*

Luxembourg, 27 January 2016.

DECISION OF THE COURT OF JUSTICE

(2016/C 145/02)

of 09 March 2016

on official holidays and judicial vacations

[10.819]

NOTES

Date of publication in Official Journal: OJ C145, 25.4.2016, p 2.

THE COURT

having regard to Article 24(2), (4) and (6) of the Rules of Procedure,

whereas it is necessary, in accordance with that provision, to establish the list of official holidays and to set the dates of the judicial vacations,

HAS ADOPTED THIS DECISION:

Article 1

The list of official holidays within the meaning of Article 24(4) and (6) of the Rules of Procedure is established as follows:

— New Year's Day,
— Easter Monday,
— 1 May,
— Ascension,
— Whit Monday,
— 23 June,
— 15 August,
— 1 November,
— 25 December,
— 26 December.

Article 2

For the period from 1 November 2016 to 31 October 2017, the dates of the judicial vacations within the meaning of Article 24(2) and (6) of the Rules of Procedure are as follows:

— Christmas 2016: from Monday 19 December 2016 to Sunday 8 January 2017 inclusive,

— Easter 2017: from Monday 10 April 2017 to Sunday 23 April 2017 inclusive,
— Summer 2017: from Friday 21 July 2017 to Sunday 3 September 2017 inclusive.

Article 3
This Decision shall enter into force on the day of its publication in the *Official Journal of the European Union*.

ANONYMITY IN JUDICIAL PROCEEDINGS BEFORE THE COURT OF JUSTICE

NOTES
This document is available on the Curia website at curia.europa.eu/jcms/upload/docs/application/pdf/2015-11/tra-doc-en-div-c-0000-2015-201508723-05_00.pdf.

[10.820]
Where anonymity has been granted by the referring court or tribunal, the Court of Justice will respect that anonymity in the preliminary ruling proceedings pending before it. At the request of the referring court or tribunal, at the duly reasoned request of a party to the main proceedings or of its own motion, the Court may also, if it considers it necessary, render anonymous one or more persons or entities concerned by the case.[1] These provisions apply, *mutatis mutandis*, to the procedure before the Court of Justice on an appeal against decisions of the General Court.[2]

Under the preliminary ruling procedure, the Court of Justice will, as a rule, use the information contained in the order for reference, including nominative or personal data. It is therefore for the referring court or tribunal itself, if it considers it necessary, to delete certain details in its request for a preliminary ruling or to render anonymous one or more persons or entities concerned by the dispute in the main proceedings.[3] After the request for a preliminary ruling has been lodged, the Court may also render such persons or entities anonymous of its own motion, or at the request of the referring court or tribunal or of a party to the main proceedings. In order to maintain its effectiveness, such a request for anonymity must, however, be made at the earliest possible stage of the proceedings.[4]

Where a party considers it necessary that its identity or certain information concerning it should not be disclosed in a case brought before the Court of Justice, it may request that the Court 'anonymise' the relevant case, in whole or in part. To be effective, such an application must, however, be made as early as possible. On account of the increasing use of new information and communication technologies, granting anonymity becomes much more difficult if the notice of the case concerned has already been published in the *Official Journal of the European Union* or, in preliminary ruling proceedings, if the request for a preliminary ruling has already been served on the interested persons referred to in Article 23 of the Statute, about one month after the request has been lodged at the Court.[5]

NOTES
1 Article 95 of the Rules of Procedure of the Court of Justice.
2 Article 190(3) of the Rules of Procedure of the Court of Justice.
3 Point 27 of the Recommendations to national courts and tribunals in relation to the initiation of preliminary ruling proceedings.
4 Point 28 of the Recommendations to national courts and tribunals in relation to the initiation of preliminary ruling proceedings.
5 Point 8 of the Practice Directions to parties concerning cases brought before the Court.

ADVICE TO COUNSEL APPEARING BEFORE THE COURT

NOTES
This document is available on the Court of Justice section of the Curia website at curia.europa.eu/jcms/jcms/Jo2_7031/en/.

[10.821]
The task of simultaneous interpreters in the multilingual environment of the Court of Justice of the European Union is to help you to communicate easily and fluently with the Judges and the other participants in the hearing. The interpreters prepare in advance for every hearing by studying the case-file in depth. However, it may be helpful to bear the following points in mind when pleading:
— Reading out a written text at speed makes simultaneous interpretation into another language particularly difficult. The interpreters will be able to work much more effectively if you speak freely, at a natural and calm pace.

— If you do decide to read out a written text which you have prepared, please send it if possible in advance to the Interpretation Directorate[1] by email. This will help the interpreters to prepare for the hearing. It goes without saying that:
  — your text will be used only by the interpreters and will not be communicated or disclosed to anyone else;
  — at the hearing, only what you actually say when addressing the Court will be interpreted.
— Even handwritten notes with references are helpful. You can always give a copy to the interpreters just before the hearing.
— Please remember to quote citations, references, figures, names and acronyms clearly and slowly.
— Before you speak, please remove your earphone, lower the volume, and place it away from the microphone in order to avoid any interference.
— Turn off your mobile phone / PDA completely.

For more information please see the Practice directions to parties, available on the Court of Justice's 'Procedure' page.

NOTES

1 Interpretation Directorate: Email: interpret@curia.europa.eu Fax: +352/4303-3697 Telephone: +352/4303-1

REPORT ON THE USE OF THE URGENT PRELIMINARY RULING PROCEDURE BY THE COURT OF JUSTICE[1]

NOTES

This document is available on the Court of Justice section of the Curia website at curia.europa.eu/jcms/upload/docs/application/pdf/2012-07/en_rapport.pdf.

[10.822]

As of 1 March 2008, a reference for a preliminary ruling which raises one or more questions concerning the area of freedom, security and justice may, at the request of the national court or tribunal or, exceptionally, of the Court's own motion, be dealt with under an urgent procedure.[2] This report on the Court's application of that procedure is its first review and covers the period 1 March 2008 to 6 October 2011 ('the reference period'), which includes three full judicial years.

It may be recalled that that procedure was introduced in response to the Presidency Conclusions of the European Council inviting the Commission to bring forward, after consultation of the Court of Justice, a proposal to '*enable the Court to respond quickly*' by creating a solution '*for the speedy and appropriate handling of requests for preliminary rulings concerning the area of freedom, security and justice*'.[3] The Commission considered that it was necessary to '*trust in the proper functioning of the Court of Justice*' and stated that '*where necessary, special rules allowing immediate treatment of particularly urgent cases might be inserted in the Statute of the Court of Justice . . . and in its Rules of Procedure.*'[4]

In the proposal ultimately drawn up by the Court, as endorsed by the Council, the Court opted for the introduction of an urgent preliminary ruling procedure which has, in essence, three specific features distinguishing it from the ordinary preliminary ruling procedure (and, therefore, from the accelerated procedure, which reproduces in all respects the procedural rules of an ordinary procedure, while significantly accelerating it). First, only the parties to the main proceedings, the Member State of the referring court or tribunal, the Commission, and the other institutions if one of their measures is at issue, may participate in the written procedure. Since these have a command of the language of the case, the written procedure can be initiated immediately, without any need to await the translation of the reference for a preliminary ruling into all the official languages. Second, cases that may be dealt with under an urgent procedure are referred to a Chamber specifically designated for that purpose, which gives its ruling without first going through the General Meeting of the Court. Third, communications in the urgent procedure (both internal and those involving the parties and interested persons) are, as far as possible, entirely electronic. These measures were expected to achieve substantial savings in terms of the duration of proceedings.

[10.823]

1.

Average duration of proceedings in cases dealt with under the urgent preliminary ruling procedure

The cases dealt with under the urgent preliminary ruling procedure were completed, on average, within 66 days (see Table 1 annexed). In no case did proceedings exceed three months. The Court's principal intended and declared objective – to dispose of that type of case speedily, in approximately two to four months, with possible variations depending on the level of urgency – has thus been fully achieved.

[10.824]
2.
Volume and nature of litigation affected by the urgent preliminary ruling procedure

Before the entry into force of the Treaty of Lisbon, the urgent preliminary ruling procedure was applicable in the areas covered by Title VI of the Union Treaty or Title IV of Part Three of the EC Treaty. Since 1 December 2009, the procedure has been applicable in the areas covered by Title V of Part Three of the Treaty on the Functioning of the European Union, which brought together the previous provisions.[5] In particular, since the entry into force of the Treaty of Lisbon, the Court's jurisdiction has been substantially extended by virtue of the number of national courts and tribunals which may now refer questions to the Court in the areas concerned.

During the reference period, the Court received **126** requests for a preliminary ruling relating to the area of freedom, security and justice which were thus capable of being dealt with under the urgent procedure. That figure represents **11.64%** of all references for a preliminary ruling made during that period, that is 1 082.

It is interesting to note that after the introduction of the urgent preliminary ruling procedure, but before the entry into force of the Treaty of Lisbon, only 4.85% of references for a preliminary ruling concerned the area of freedom, security and justice.[6]

Of the 126 cases falling within the scope of the urgent preliminary ruling procedure, more than half (68 cases, or 54%) concerned judicial cooperation in civil matters, of which two thirds (42 cases) related to Regulation No 44/2001.[7] Ten of those cases concerned the interpretation of Regulations No 1347/2000 and No 2201/2003.[8]

One third of the 126 cases capable of being dealt with under the urgent preliminary ruling procedure concerned the area of 'visas, asylum and immigration' (43 cases, or 34%), of which 22 related specifically to Directive 2008/115/EC[9] and 14 to Directive 2004/83/EC.[10]

Lastly, 18 of those 126 cases (that is 14%) related to cooperation in criminal matters, of which 10 related to Framework Decision 2002/584/JHA.[11]

Of those 126 cases, 21 were accompanied by a request for application of the urgent preliminary ruling procedure from the national court or tribunal, and in one case, exceptionally, that procedure was applied of the Court's own motion, following a request by the President of the Court.[12]

Thus, during the reference period, almost **one fifth** (17.5%) **of cases capable of being dealt with under the urgent preliminary ruling procedure were the subject of a request to that effect. Of those 22 requests, 12 were granted**, including that of the President of the Court, **that is more than half** (around 55%). 8 were refused (see Table 2 annexed) and 2 did not proceed.[13]

Half of the 12 cases dealt with under the urgent preliminary ruling procedure concerned the jurisdiction and the recognition and enforcement of judgments in matrimonial matters and in matters of parental responsibility.[14] One quarter related to the European arrest warrant.[15] The remaining cases fell within the area of 'visas, asylum and immigration' and concerned, in particular, the interpretation of Directive 2008/115/EC.[16]

Two main conclusions can be drawn from these figures.

First, although in absolute terms the number of requests has remained modest,[17] the proportion of those requests in comparison with cases that could potentially fall within the scope of the urgent preliminary ruling procedure (almost one fifth) is not negligible.

Second, the reasons which the national courts and tribunals put forward in support of their requests for application of the urgent procedure were for the most part valid, since more than half of those requests were successful.

[10.825]
3.
Conduct of the written and oral procedure

The Court has never availed itself of the possibility afforded by Article 104b(4) of the Rules of Procedure of omitting the written procedure in cases of extreme urgency.

On average, the duration of the written procedure in cases dealt with under the urgent preliminary ruling procedure was more than 16 days[18] (see Table 3 annexed). The Court has thus ensured that the Member States are allowed the time necessary for drafting written observations, the Court having been called upon by the Council not to reduce the time allowed to less than 10 working days.[19]

The same concern has governed the fixing of the date for the hearing, which has been held, on average, a little over 16 days after written observations lodged, together with their translations, have been communicated to the parties and interested persons (see Table 3 annexed).

Participation in the hearing of Member States other than the Member State of the referring court or tribunal has been comparatively high: on average, three Member States have attended to submit oral observations (see Table 4 annexed), whereas, based on a representative sample of hearings held in preliminary ruling proceedings,[20] on average, just one Member State (over and above that of the referring court or tribunal) takes part in the hearing.

Views of the Advocate General in urgent preliminary ruling procedures have been delivered on average in a little over three days after the hearing (see Table 3), and, with just one exception,[21] have all been published.[22]

[10.826]
4.
Designation of the Chamber responsible for cases in which the urgent preliminary ruling procedure is requested

Pursuant to the second and third subparagraphs of Article 9(1) of the Rules of Procedure, the Court has designated the Chambers responsible for cases in which the urgent preliminary ruling procedure is requested. It has never designated more than one Chamber of five Judges for that purpose.

During the reference period, the four Chambers of five Judges currently within the Court have each been designated in turn.[23] Thus, the great majority of Judges of the Court have had occasion to sit in a case in which the urgent preliminary ruling procedure has been requested.

Successive designated Chambers have always sat with five Judges.[24] Only once has the designated Chamber decided to refer the case back to the Court in order for it to be assigned to a formation composed of a greater number of Judges.[25]

While the number of requests for application of the urgent preliminary ruling procedure – which have largely been consecutive and have only rarely needed to be dealt with concurrently by the designated Chamber – has not justified the designation of several Chambers ruling simultaneously, the management of cases dealt with under the urgent procedure has proved to be particularly demanding for the Chamber concerned.

[10.827]
5.
The Court's practice with regard to decisions as to whether or not to initiate the urgent procedure

Owing to the extreme urgency with which the designated Chamber is obliged to rule on requests for application of the urgent preliminary ruling procedure – which, during the reference period, it did in a little more than an average of 8 days[26] (see Table 3 annexed) – decisions as to whether or not to initiate the urgent procedure do not include a statement of reasons.

However, it is possible, on the basis of an analysis of the circumstances of fact and of law in which the urgent preliminary ruling procedure has been approved, to isolate two types of situation which have resulted in the Court delivering a ruling in the shortest possible time:

- where there is a risk of an irreparable change for the worse in the parent/child relationship, for example, where what is at stake is the return of a child who has been deprived of contact with one of its parents (C-195/08 PPU *Rinau*; C-403/09 PPU *Detiček*; C-211/10 PPU *Povse*; C-400/10 PPU *McB*; C-491/10 PPU *Aguirre Zarraga*; C-497/10 PPU *Mercredi*) or family reunification (C-155/11 PPU *Imran*);
- where a person is being detained and further detention depends on the answer to be given by the Court (C-296/08 PPU *Santesteban Goicoechea*; C-388/08 PPU *Leymann and Pustovarov*; C-357/09 PPU *Kadzoev*; C-105/10 PPU *Gataev and Gataeva*; C-61/11 PPU *El Dridi Hassen*).

This practice is consistent with the scenarios envisaged by the Court in its Information note on references from national courts for a preliminary ruling[27] and with the Council's request that the urgent preliminary ruling procedure be applied in situations involving deprivation of liberty,[28] which has been enshrined in the fourth paragraph of Article 267 of the Treaty on the Functioning of the European Union.

[10.828]
6.
Method of communication

Documents have been communicated, both internally and with the parties and interested persons, electronically, by virtue of the creation of 'functional mailboxes' specifically dedicated to communication in relation to the urgent preliminary ruling procedure.

Since the establishment in the Court of a general system of lodging and service of procedural documents by electronic means,[29] the relative advantage of these 'functional mailboxes' has been reduced, as regards the anticipated acceleration of the transmission of information. Nevertheless, they have enabled communications in relation to an urgent preliminary ruling procedure to be put on a separate track that is subject to special and continuous monitoring, thereby helping to ensure that all involved are kept on standby.

The reference period has been a good running-in period for the application of the urgent preliminary ruling procedure by the Court. The modest flow of requests has facilitated its smooth application, while at the same time providing an opportunity to gauge the constraints associated with the procedure, which weigh not only on the designated Chamber but also on the Court's services, in particular the translation, Registry and interpreting services. With the same resources, considerable efforts would be required to maintain the objectives set, in the event of an appreciable increase in reasoned requests, and would probably have an impact on the handling of other cases.

[10.829]

Table 1 Duration of proceedings in cases dealt with under the urgent preliminary ruling procedure

Case	Duration (in days)
1. **C-195/08 PPU Rinau** ***Referring court or tribunal:*** *Lietuvos Aukščiausiasis Teismas, Lithuania* ***Re:*** *Jurisdiction, recognition and enforcement of judgments in matrimonial matters and matters of parental responsibility*	58[30]
2. **C-296/08 PPU Santesteban Goicoechea** ***Referring court or tribunal:*** *Cour d'appel de Montpellier, France* ***Re:*** *European arrest warrant*	40
3. **C-388/08 PPU Leymann and Pustovarov** ***Referring court or tribunal:*** *Korkein oikeus, Finland* ***Re:*** *European arrest warrant*	87
4. **C-357/09 PPU Kadzoev**[31] ***Referring court or tribunal:*** *Administrativen sad Sofia-grad, Bulgaria* ***Re:*** *Return of illegally staying third-country nationals*	84
5. **C-403/09 PPU Detiček** ***Referring court or tribunal:*** *Višje sodišče v Mariboru, Slovenia* ***Re:*** *Jurisdiction, recognition and enforcement of judgments in matrimonial matters and matters of parental responsibility*	64
6. **C-105/10 PPU Gataev and Gataeva**[32] ***Referring court or tribunal:*** *Korkein oikeus, Finland* ***Re:*** *European arrest warrant and refugee status*	/
7. **C-211/10 PPU Povse** ***Referring court or tribunal:*** *Oberster Gerichtshof, Austria* ***Re:*** *Jurisdiction, recognition and enforcement of judgments in matrimonial matters and matters of parental responsibility*	59
8. **C-400/10 PPU McB.** ***Referring court or tribunal:*** *Supreme Court, Ireland* ***Re:*** *Jurisdiction, recognition and enforcement of judgments in matrimonial matters and matters of parental responsibility*	60
9. **C-491/10 PPU Aguirre Zarraga** ***Referring court or tribunal:*** *Oberlandesgericht Celle, Germany* ***Re:*** *Jurisdiction, recognition and enforcement of judgments in matrimonial matters and matters of parental responsibility*	68
10. **C-497/10 PPU Mercredi** ***Referring court or tribunal:*** *Court of Appeal (England & Wales) (Civil Division), United Kingdom* ***Re:*** *Jurisdiction, recognition and enforcement of judgments in matrimonial matters and matters of parental responsibility*	65
11. **C-61/11 PPU El Dridi Hassen** ***Referring court or tribunal:*** *Corte di Appello di Trento, Italy* ***Re:*** *Return of illegally staying third-country nationals*	77
12. C-155/11 PPU Imran[33] ***Referring court or tribunal:*** *Rechtbank's-Gravenhage, zittinghoudende te Zwolle-Lelystad, Netherlands* ***Re:*** *Right to family reunification*	/
Average	**66.2**

[10.830]

Table 2 List of cases in which the request for an urgent preliminary ruling procedure was refused

	Traitement procédural ultérieur
1. **C-123/08 Wolzenburg** ***Referring court or tribunal:*** *Rechtbank Amsterdam, Netherlands* ***Re:*** *European arrest warrant*	/
2. **C-261/08 Zurita García** ***Referring court or tribunal:*** *Tribunal Superior de Justicia de Murcia, Spain* ***Re:*** *Schengen Borders Code*	/
3. **C-375/08 Pontini** ***Referring court or tribunal:*** *Tribunale di Treviso, Italy* ***Re:*** *does not fall within the area covered by the urgent preliminary ruling procedure*	/
4. **C-261/09 Mantello** ***Referring court or tribunal:*** *Oberlandesgericht Stuttgart, Germany* ***Re:*** *European arrest warrant*	/
5. **C-264/10 Kita**[34] ***Referring court or tribunal:*** *Inalta Curte de Casaţie şi Justiţie, Roumanie* ***Re:*** *European arrest warrant*	/
6. **C-175/11 HID and BA** ***Referring court or tribunal:*** *High Court of Ireland, Ireland* ***Re:*** *Refugee status*	/
7. **C-277/11 MM**[35] ***Referring court or tribunal:*** *High Court of Ireland, Ireland* ***Re:*** *Refugee status*	Priority treatment
8. **C-329/11 Achughbabian** ***Referring court or tribunal:*** *Cour d'appel de Paris, France* ***Re:*** *Return of illegally staying third-country nationals*	Accelerated procedure[36]

[10.831]

Table 3 Duration of particular stages of the procedure

Case	**Time between the submission of the request and the decision (days)**	**Duration of the written procedure (days)**	**Time between service of pleadings and the hearing (days)**	**Time between the hearing and the Advocate General's View (days)**
1. C-123/08 Wolzenburg	12			
2. **C-195/08 PPU Rinau**	1	17	10	5
3. C-261/08 Zurita García	6			
4. **C-296/08 PPU Santesteban Goicoechea**	4	15	13	0
5. C-375/08 Pontini	3			
6. **C-388/08 PPU Leymann and Pustovarov**	6	19	33	0
7. C-261/09 Mantello	6			
8. **C-357/09 PPU Kadzoev**	15	15	18	14
9. **C-403/09 PPU Detiček**	7	16	21	2
10. ***C-105/10 PPU Gataev and Gataeva***	5	15		
11. **C-211/10 PPU Povse**	8	15	11	2
12. C-264/10 Kita	11			

Case	Time between the submission of the request and the decision (days)	Duration of the written procedure (days)	Time between service of pleadings and the hearing (days)	Time between the hearing and the Advocate General's View (days)
13. **C-400/10 PPU McB.**	5	16	19	2
14. **C-491/10 PPU Aguirre Zarraga**	9	18	17	1
15. **C-497/10 PPU Mercredi**	10	17	8	5
16. **C-61/11 PPU El Dridi Hassen**	7	17	15	2
17. *C-155/11 PPU Imran*	3	21		
18. C-175/11 HID and BA	19			
19. C-277/11 MM	16 (10[37])			
20. C-329/11 Achughbabian	12			
Average	**8.3**	**16.75**	**16.5**	**3.3**

[10.832]

Table 4 Participation of Member States (other than the Member State of the referring court or tribunal) in the oral procedure in cases dealt with under the urgent preliminary ruling procedure

Case
1. **C-195/08 PPU Rinau** ***Germany, France, Latvia, Netherlands, United Kingdom***
2. **C-296/08 PPU Santesteban Goicoechea** ***Spain***
3. **C-388/08 PPU Leymann and Pustovarov** ***Spain, Netherlands***
4. **C-357/09 PPU Kadzoev** ***Lithuania***
5. **C-403/09 PPU Detiček** ***Czech Republic, Germany, France, Italy, Latvia, Poland***
6. *C-105/10 PPU Gataev and Gataeva*[38]
7. **C-211/10 PPU Povse** ***Czech Republic, Germany, France, Italy, Latvia, Slovenia, United Kingdom***
8. **C-400/10 PPU McB.** ***Germany***
9. **C-491/10 PPU Aguirre Zarraga** ***Greece, Spain, France, Latvia***
10. **C-497/10 PPU Mercredi** ***Germany, Ireland, France***
11. **C-61/11 PPU El Dridi Hassen** /
12. *C-155/11 PPU Imran*[39]

NOTES

1 Report delivered to the Council in accordance with the statement annexed to its decision of 20 December 2007 (OJ L 24 of 29 January 2008, p. 44).

2 Council Decision of 20 December 2007 amending the Protocol on the Statute of the Court of Justice, OJ L 24 of 29 January 2008, p. 42; Amendments to the Rules of Procedure of the Court of Justice, OJ L 24 of 29 January 2008, p. 39, and OJ L 92 of 13 April 2010, p. 12.

3 Presidency Conclusions, Brussels European Council, 4 and 5 November 2004, 14292/1/04, paragraph 3.1.

4 Communication from the Commission to the European Parliament, the Council, the European Economic and Social Committee, the Committee of the Regions and the Court of Justice of the European Communities Adaptation of the provisions of Title IV of the Treaty establishing the European Community relating to the jurisdiction of the Court of Justice with a view to ensuring more effective judicial protection, 28 June 2006, COM(2006) 346 final.

5 Amendments to the Rules of Procedure of the Court of Justice, OJ L 92 of 13 April 2010, p. 12.

6 25 cases out of a total of 515 references for a preliminary ruling made between 1 March 2008 and 30 November 2009.

7 Council Regulation (EC) No 44/2001 of 22 December 2000 on jurisdiction and the recognition and enforcement of judgments in civil and commercial matters, OJ L 12 of 16 January 2001, p. 1.

8 Council Regulation (EC) No 1347/2000 of 29 May 2000 on jurisdiction and the recognition and enforcement of judgments in matrimonial matters and in matters of parental responsibility for children of both spouses, OJ L 160 of 30 June 2000, p. 19, and Council Regulation (EC) No 2201/2003 of 27 November 2003 concerning jurisdiction and the recognition and enforcement of judgments in matrimonial matters and the matters of parental responsibility, repealing Regulation (EC) No 1347/2000, OJ L 338 of 23 December 2003, p. 1.

9 Directive 2008/115/EC of the European Parliament and of the Council of 16 December 2008 on common standards and procedures in Member States for returning illegally staying third-country nationals, OJ L 348 of 24 December 2008, p. 98.

10 Council Directive 2004/83/EC of 29 April 2004 on minimum standards for the qualification and status of third country nationals or stateless persons as refugees or as persons who otherwise need international protection and the content of the protection granted, OJ L 304 of 30 September 2004, p. 2 or 12.

11 Council Framework Decision 2002/584/JHA of 13 June 2002 on the European arrest warrant and the surrender procedures between Member States, OJ L 190 of 18 July 2002, p. 1.

12 The first and third subparagraphs of Article 104b(1) of the Rules of Procedure allow the Court, exceptionally, of its own motion to deal with a reference for a preliminary ruling under the urgent procedure. It is for the President of the Court to ask the designated Chamber to consider whether it is necessary to deal with the reference under the urgent preliminary ruling procedure, if the application of that procedure appears, prima facie, to be required, even though it has not been requested by the national court or tribunal. That provision has been used only once, in Case C-491/10 *Aguirre Zarraga.*

13 The cases in question are Cases C-140/11 *Ngagne* and C-156/11 *Music*, in which the references were withdrawn by the referring courts after delivery of the judgment in related Case C-61/11 PPU *El Dridi Hassen*, and which were removed from the register before the designated Chamber had determined the request for application of the urgent preliminary ruling procedure.

14 See footnote 8.

15 See footnote 11.

16 See footnote 9.

17 It is unlikely that the relative restraint on the part of national courts and tribunals can be attributed to any lack of awareness of the procedure established, since the requests submitted during the reference period were made by courts at various levels of the court hierarchy, in various locations throughout a number of Member States.

18 The second subparagraph of Article 104b(2) of the Rules of Procedure provides that the decision to deal with the reference under the urgent procedure is to prescribe the period within which the parties and interested persons entitled to participate in the written procedure may lodge statements of case or written observations.

19 Statement of the Council, annexed to its decision of 20 December 2007, OJ L 24 of 29 January 2008, p. 44.

20 That is all hearings held, before any and all formations of the Court, in the month of October 2011.

21 In Case C-388/08 PPU *Leymann and Pustovarov.*

22 In accordance with the Court's practice, Views, where presented in writing, are published unless the formation of the Court decides otherwise after hearing the Advocate General.

23 The Third Chamber for the period 1 March 2008 to 6 October 2008; the Second Chamber for the period 7 October 2008 to 6 October 2009; the new Third Chamber (former Fourth Chamber) for the period 7 October 2009 to 6 October 2010; the First Chamber for the period 7 October 2010 to 6 October 2011.

24 Under Article 104b(5) of the Rules of Procedure, the designated Chamber may decide to sit in a formation of three Judges.

25 In Case C-357/09 PPU *Kadzoev*, which the Court referred to the Grand Chamber.

26 This period includes the necessary time for translation of the request before it is dealt with.

27 OJ C 160 of 28 May 2011, p. 1, point 37: ' . . . *a national court or tribunal might, for example, consider submitting a request for the urgent preliminary ruling procedure to be applied in the following situations: in the case, referred to in the fourth paragraph of Article 267 TFEU, of a person in custody or deprived of his liberty, where the answer to the question raised is decisive as to the assessment of that person's legal situation or, in proceedings concerning parental authority or custody of children, where the identity of the court having jurisdiction under European Union law depends on the answer to the question referred for a preliminary ruling.*'

28 Statement of the Council, annexed to its decision of 20 December 2007, OJ L 24 of 29 January 2008, p. 44.

29 Decision of the Court of Justice of 13 September 2011 on the lodging and service of procedural documents by means of e-Curia, OJ C 289 of 1 October 2011, p. 7.

30 50 days from the request for the case to be dealt with under the urgent preliminary ruling procedure.

31 This case was referred to the Grand Chamber.

32 In this case the reference was withdrawn by the referring court and the case was removed from the register by order of 3 April 2010.

33 This case was concluded by order of 10 June 2011 declaring that there was no need to adjudicate.

34 This case was removed from the register as a result of the referring court's withdrawal of the reference.

35 In this case, the referring court twice submitted a request for the urgent preliminary ruling procedure; in each case it was refused.

36 See order of the President of the Court of 30 September 2011 (in particular, paragraphs 9 to 12).

37 On the second request for application of the urgent preliminary ruling procedure.

[38] The referring court's withdrawal of the reference reached the Court before the hearing was held.

[39] No hearing was held in this case which was concluded by an order declaring that there was no need to adjudicate.

TABLE OF CORRESPONDENCE

NOTES

Date of publication in Official Journal: OJ C337, 6.11.2012, p 43.

This document is available on the Court of Justice section of the Curia website at eur-lex.europa.eu/LexUriServ/LexUriServ.do?uri=OJ:C:2012:337:0043:0060:EN:PDF.

[10.833]

The following table shows in relation to each Article, paragraph or subparagraph of the Rules of Procedure of 19 June 1991, as last amended on 24 May 2011, the Article and, where relevant, the corresponding paragraph of the Rules of Procedure of 25 September 2012, which entered into force on 1 November 2012.

Where appropriate, reference is also made in brackets to the Articles of the 1991 Rules of Procedure that have been substantively amended in the new Rules of Procedure, excluding purely formal or terminological amendments.

Rules of Procedure of 19 June 1991	Rules of Procedure of 25 September 2012
INTERPRETATION	
Article 1, first paragraph (amended)	Article 1(1)
Article 1, second paragraph (amended)	Article 1(2)
TITLE I - ORGANISATION OF THE COURT	
Chapter 1: JUDGES AND ADVOCATES GENERAL	
Article 2 (amended)	Article 3
Article 3(1) (amended)	Article 4
Article 3(2) (amended)	Article 5
Article 4 (amended)	Article 6
Article 5	See Articles 3 to 6
Article 6 (amended)	Article 7
Chapter 2: PRESIDENCY OF THE COURT AND CONSTITUTION OF THE CHAMBERS	
Article 7(1)	Article 8(1)
Article 7(2)	Article 8(2)
Article 7(3)	Article 8(3)
Article 8 (amended)	Article 9
Article 9(1), first subparagraph	Article 11(1)
Article 9(1), second subparagraph (amended)	Article 11(2)
Article 9(1), third subparagraph (amended)	Article 11(5)
Article 9(2), first subparagraph (amended)	Article 15(1)
Article 9(2), second subparagraph (amended)	Article 15(2)
Article 9(2), third subparagraph	Article 15(3)
Article 9(3)	Article 11(3)
Article 9(4)	Article 11(4)
Article 10(1), first subparagraph (amended)	Article 12(1)
Article 10(1), second subparagraph (amended)	Article 12(2)
Article 10(1), third subparagraph (amended)	Article 14(1)
Article 10(1), fourth subparagraph	Article 12(3)
Article 10(1), fifth subparagraph (amended)	Articles 8(5), 12(4) and 14(3)
Article 10(2) (amended)	Article 16
Article 11 (amended)	Article 13
Chapter 2a: FORMATIONS OF THE COURT	

Rules of Procedure of 19 June 1991	Rules of Procedure of 25 September 2012
Article 11a	Repealed
Article 11b(1) (amended)	Article 27(1)
Article 11b(2), first subparagraph (amended)	Article 27(2) to (4)
Article 11b(2), second subparagraph (amended)	Article 27(5)
Article 11b(3), first subparagraph (amended)	Article 27(6)
Article 11b(3), second subparagraph	Article 27(7)
Article 11c(1)	Article 28(1)
Article 11c(2), first subparagraph	Article 28(2)
Article 11c(2), second subparagraph	Article 28(3)
Article 11c(2), third subparagraph	Article 28(4)
Article 11d(1)	Article 29(1)
Article 11d(2)	Article 29(2)
Article 11e, first paragraph (amended)	Article 31
Article 11e, second paragraph (amended)	Article 13
Article 11e, third paragraph	Article 30(1)
Article 11e, fourth paragraph	Article 30(2)
Chapter 3: REGISTRY	
Section 1 – The Registrar and Assistant Registrars	
Article 12(1), first subparagraph	Article 18(1)
Article 12(1), second subparagraph	Repealed
Article 12(2) (amended)	Article 18(2)
Article 12(3) (amended)	Article 18(3)
Article 12(4) (amended)	Article 18(4)
Article 12(5) (amended)	Article 18(5)
Article 12(6)	Article 18(6)
Article 12(7)	Article 18(7)
Article 13 (amended)	Article 19
Article 14	Repealed
Article 15	See Article 208
Article 16(1) (amended)	Article 21(1)
Article 16(2)	Article 21(2)
Article 16(3)	Article 21(3)
Article 16(4)	Repealed
Article 16(5), first subparagraph (amended)	Article 22(1)
Article 16(5), second subparagraph (amended)	Article 22(2) and (3)
Article 16(6) (amended)	Article 21(4)
Article 16(7) (amended)	Article 125
Article 17(1)	Article 20(1)
Article 17(2) (amended)	Article 20(2)
Article 18 (amended)	Article 20(3)
Article 19	Repealed
Section 2 – Other departments	
Article 20	Repealed
Article 21	Repealed
Article 22	Article 42
Article 23 (amended)	Article 20(4)
Chapter 4: ASSISTANT RAPPORTEURS	
Article 24	Article 17
Chapter 5: THE WORKING OF THE COURT	
Article 25(1)	Repealed

Rules of Procedure of 19 June 1991	Rules of Procedure of 25 September 2012
Article 25(2)	Repealed
Article 25(3)	Article 23
Article 26(1)	Article 33
Article 26(2)	Repealed
Article 26(3)	Article 35(1)
Article 27(1) (amended)	Article 32(1)
Article 27(2) (amended)	Article 32(2)
Article 27(3)	Article 32(3)
Article 27(4)	Repealed
Article 27(5) (amended)	Article 32(4)
Article 27(6)	Repealed
Article 27(7) (amended)	Article 25
Article 27(8)	Article 26
Article 28(1), first subparagraph (amended)	Article 24(2)
Article 28(1), second subparagraph	Repealed
Article 28(2)	Article 24(3)
Article 28(3)	Article 24(4)
Article 28(4)	Article 24(5)
Chapter 6: LANGUAGES	
Article 29(1)	Article 36
Article 29(2), first subparagraph (amended)	Article 37(1)
Article 29(2), second subparagraph (amended)	Article 37(3)
Article 29(2), third subparagraph	Article 37(4)
Article 29(3), first subparagraph	Article 38(1)
Article 29(3), second subparagraph	Article 38(2)
Article 29(3), third subparagraph	Article 38(3)
Article 29(3), fourth subparagraph (amended)	Article 38(4)
Article 29(3), fifth subparagraph	Article 38(5)
Article 29(3), sixth subparagraph	Article 38(6)
Article 29(4)	Article 38(7)
Article 29(5) (amended)	Article 38(8)
Article 30(1)	Article 39
Article 30(2)	Article 40
Article 31	Article 41
Chapter 7: RIGHTS AND OBLIGATIONS OF AGENTS, ADVISERS AND LAWYERS	
Article 32(1)	Article 43(1)
Article 32(2) (amended)	Article 43(2)
Article 33 (amended)	Article 44
Article 34, first paragraph	Article 45(1)
Article 34, second paragraph	Article 45(2)
Article 35(1), first subparagraph (amended)	Article 46(1)
Article 35(1), second subparagraph (amended)	Article 46(2)
Article 35(2) (amended)	Article 46(3)
Article 35(3)	Article 46(4)
Article 36	Article 47(1)
TITLE II - PROCEDURE	
Chapter 1: WRITTEN PROCEDURE	
Article 37(1), first subparagraph (amended)	Article 57(1)
Article 37(1), second subparagraph (amended)	Article 57(2)
Article 37(2)	Article 57(3)
Article 37(3) (amended)	Article 57(6)

Rules of Procedure of 19 June 1991	**Rules of Procedure of 25 September 2012**
Article 37(4)	Article 57(4)
Article 37(5)	Article 57(5)
Article 37(6) (amended)	Article 57(7)
Article 37(7) (amended)	Article 57(8)
Article 38(1) (amended)	Article 120
Article 38(2), first subparagraph (amended)	Article 121(1)
Article 38(2), second subparagraph	Article 121(2)
Article 38(2), third subparagraph (amended)	Article 121(3)
Article 38(3)	Article 119(3)
Article 38(4)	Article 122(1)
Article 38(5)	Repealed
Article 38(6)	Article 122(2)
Article 38(7) (amended)	Articles 119(4) and 122(3)
Article 39	Article 123
Article 40(1), first subparagraph (amended)	Article 124(1)
Article 40(1), second subparagraph (amended)	Article 124(2)
Article 40(2) (amended)	Article 124(3)
Article 41(1)	Article 126(1)
Article 41(2) (amended)	Article 126(2)
Article 42(1) (amended)	Article 128(1)
Article 42(2), first subparagraph	Article 127(1)
Article 42(2), second subparagraph (amended)	Article 127(2)
Article 42(2), third subparagraph (amended)	Article 127(2)
Article 43 (amended)	Article 54
Chapter 1a: THE PRELIMINARY REPORT AND ASSIGNMENT OF CASES TO FORMATIONS	
Article 44(1) (amended)	Article 59(1)
Article 44(2), first subparagraph (amended)	Article 59(2)
Article 44(2), second subparagraph	Article 59(3)
Article 44(3), first subparagraph (amended)	Article 60(1)
Article 44(3), second subparagraph (amended)	Article 60(1)
Article 44(3), third subparagraph	Article 60(2)
Article 44(4)	Article 60(3)
Article 44(5), first subparagraph	Article 65(1)
Article 44(5), second subparagraph	Article 60(4)
Article 44a (amended)	Article 76
Chapter 2: PREPARATORY INQUIRIES AND OTHER PREPARATORY MEASURES	
Section 1 – Measures of inquiry	
Article 45(1), first subparagraph (amended)	Article 64(1)
Article 45(1), second subparagraph	See Article 90
Article 45(2)	Article 64(2)
Article 45(3)	Article 65(2)
Article 45(4)	Article 64(3)
Article 46	Article 65(3)
Section 2 – The summoning and examination of witnesses and experts	
Article 47(1), first subparagraph (amended)	Article 66(1)
Article 47(1), second subparagraph (amended)	Article 66(4)
Article 47(1), third subparagraph	Article 66(2)
Article 47(2), first subparagraph (amended)	Articles 64(1) and 66(3)

Rules of Procedure of 19 June 1991	Rules of Procedure of 25 September 2012
Article 47(2), second subparagraph	See Article 90
Article 47(3), first subparagraph (amended)	Article 73(1)
Article 47(3), second subparagraph	Repealed
Article 47(4), first subparagraph	Article 67(1)
Article 47(4), second subparagraph	Article 67(2)
Article 47(4), third subparagraph	Article 67(3)
Article 47(4), fourth subparagraph	Article 67(4)
Article 47(5), first subparagraph	Article 68(1)
Article 47(5), second subparagraph	Article 68(2)
Article 47(6), first subparagraph (amended)	Article 74(1)
Article 47(6), second subparagraph	Article 74(2)
Article 47(6), third subparagraph	Article 74(1)
Article 48(1)	Article 69(1)
Article 48(2), first subparagraph (amended)	Article 69(2)
Article 48(2), second subparagraph (amended)	Article 69(3)
Article 48(3) (amended)	Article 69(2)
Article 48(4)	Repealed
Article 49(1)	Article 70(1)
Article 49(2), first subparagraph	Repealed
Article 49(2), second subparagraph	Article 73(1)
Article 49(3)	Repealed
Article 49(4)	Repealed
Article 49(5), first subparagraph (amended)	Article 70(2)
Article 49(5), second subparagraph	Article 70(4)
Article 49(6), first subparagraph	Article 71(1)
Article 49(6), second subparagraph	Article 71(2)
Article 50(1) (amended)	Article 72(1)
Article 50(2)	Article 72(2)
Article 51(1)	Article 73(2)
Article 51(2)	Article 73(3)
Article 52	Repealed
Article 53(1)	Article 74(1)
Article 53(2) (amended)	Articles 70(2) and 74(3)
Section 3 – Closure of the preparatory inquiry	
Article 54, first paragraph	Article 75(1)
Article 54, second paragraph	Article 75(2)
Section 4 – Preparatory measures	
Article 54a	Article 62(1)
Chapter 3: ORAL PROCEDURE	
Article 55(1)	Repealed
Article 55(2), first subparagraph	Article 53(3)
Article 55(2), second subparagraph (amended)	Article 56
Article 56(1)	Article 78
Article 56(2)	Article 79(2)
Article 57, first paragraph (amended)	Article 80
Article 57, second paragraph (amended)	Article 80
Article 58	Articles 47 and 119(1)
Article 59(1) (amended)	Article 82(1)
Article 59(2)	Article 82(2)
Article 60 (amended)	Articles 63 and 65(1)
Article 61 (amended)	Article 83

Rules of Procedure of 19 June 1991	Rules of Procedure of 25 September 2012
Article 62(1)	Article 84(1)
Article 62(2) (amended)	Article 84(2)
Chapter 3a: EXPEDITED PROCEDURES	
Article 62a(1), first subparagraph (amended)	Article 133(1)
Article 62a(1), second subparagraph	Article 133(2)
Article 62a(2), first subparagraph (amended)	Article 134(1)
Article 62a(2), second subparagraph (amended)	Article 134(2)
Article 62a(3), first subparagraph	Article 135(1)
Article 62a(3), second subparagraph	Article 135(2)
Article 62a(4)	Article 136
Chapter 4: JUDGMENTS	
Article 63 (amended)	Article 87
Article 64(1) (amended)	Articles 86 and 88(1)
Article 64(2)	Article 88(2)
Article 64(3)	Repealed
Article 65	Article 91(1)
Article 66(1)	Articles 103(1) and 154(1)
Article 66(2) (amended)	Article 154(2)
Article 66(3)	Articles 103(2) and 154(3)
Article 66(4)	Articles 103(3) and 154(4)
Article 67, first paragraph	Article 155(1)
Article 67, second paragraph	Article 155(2)
Article 67, third paragraph	Article 155(3)
Article 68	Article 20(3)
Chapter 5: COSTS	
Article 69(1)	Article 137
Article 69(2), first subparagraph	Article 138(1)
Article 69(2), second subparagraph	Article 138(2)
Article 69(3), first subparagraph (amended)	Article 138(3)
Article 69(3), second subparagraph	Article 139
Article 69(4), first subparagraph	Article 140(1)
Article 69(4), second subparagraph	Article 140(2)
Article 69(4), third subparagraph	Article 140(3)
Article 69(5), first subparagraph	Article 141(1) and (2)
Article 69(5), second subparagraph	Article 141(3)
Article 69(5), third subparagraph	Article 141(4)
Article 69(6)	Article 142
Article 70	Repealed
Article 71	Repealed
Article 72	Article 143
Article 73	Article 144
Article 74(1) (amended)	Article 145(1) and (2)
Article 74(2)	Article 145(3)
Article 75(1)	Article 146(1)
Article 75(2)	Article 146(2)
Chapter 6: LEGAL AID	
Article 76(1), first subparagraph	Articles 115(1) and 185(1)
Article 76(1), second subparagraph (amended)	Articles 115(2) and 185(2)
Article 76(2), first subparagraph (amended)	Article 186(1)
Article 76(2), second subparagraph	Article 186(2)

Rules of Procedure of 19 June 1991	Rules of Procedure of 25 September 2012
Article 76(3), first subparagraph (amended)	Article 116(1) to (3), Article 186(4) and Article 187(1) and (2)
Article 76(3), second subparagraph	Articles 116(4) and 187(3)
Article 76(4)	Articles 118 and 189
Article 76(5), first subparagraph (amended)	Articles 117 and 188(1)
Article 76(5), second subparagraph	Article 188(2)
Article 76(5), third subparagraph	Article 188(3)
Chapter 7: DISCONTINUANCE	
Article 77, first paragraph	Article 147(1)
Article 77, second paragraph	Article 147(2)
Article 78 (amended)	Article 148
Chapter 8: SERVICE	
Article 79(1), first subparagraph	Article 48(1)
Article 79(1), second subparagraph	Article 48(1)
Article 79(2), first subparagraph	Article 48(2)
Article 79(2), second subparagraph	Article 48(3)
Article 79(3)	Article 48(4)
Chapter 9: TIME-LIMITS	
Article 80(1) (amended)	Article 49(1)
Article 80(2), first subparagraph	Article 49(2)
Article 80(2), second subparagraph (amended)	Article 24(6)
Article 81(1)	Article 50
Article 81(2)	Article 51
Article 82, first paragraph	Article 52(1)
Article 82, second paragraph	Article 52(2)
Chapter 10: STAY OF PROCEEDINGS	
Article 82a(1), first subparagraph (amended)	Article 55(1)
Article 82a(1), second subparagraph	Article 55(2)
Article 82a(1), third subparagraph	Article 55(3)
Article 82a(2), first subparagraph	Article 55(4)
Article 82a(2), second subparagraph	Article 55(5)
Article 82a(3), first subparagraph	Article 55(6)
Article 82a(3), second subparagraph (amended)	Article 55(7)
TITLE III - SPECIAL FORMS OF PROCEDURE	
Chapter 1: SUSPENSION OF OPERATION OR ENFORCEMENT AND OTHER INTERIM MEASURES	
Article 83(1), first subparagraph	Article 160(1)
Article 83(1), second subparagraph	Article 160(2)
Article 83(2)	Article 160(3)
Article 83(3)	Article 160(4)
Article 84(1)	Article 160(5)
Article 84(2), first subparagraph	Article 160(6)
Article 84(2), second subparagraph	Article 160(7)
Article 85, first paragraph (amended)	Article 161(1)
Article 85, second paragraph (amended)	Article 161(2)
Article 85, third paragraph (amended)	Article 161(3)
Article 86(1)	Article 162(1)
Article 86(2)	Article 162(2)
Article 86(3)	Article 162(3)
Article 86(4)	Article 162(4)

Rules of Procedure of 19 June 1991	Rules of Procedure of 25 September 2012
Article 87	Article 163
Article 88	Article 164
Article 89, first paragraph	Article 165(1)
Article 89, second paragraph	Article 165(2)
Article 90(1)	Article 166(1)
Article 90(2), first subparagraph	Article 166(2)
Article 90(2), second subparagraph (amended)	Article 166(3)
Chapter 2: PRELIMINARY ISSUES	
Article 91(1), first subparagraph	Article 151(1)
Article 91(1), second subparagraph (amended)	Article 151(2)
Article 91(2)	Article 151(3)
Article 91(3)	Article 151(4)
Article 91(4), first subparagraph (amended)	Article 151(5)
Article 91(4), second subparagraph	Article 151(6)
Article 92(1) (amended)	Article 53(2)
Article 92(2) (amended)	Articles 149 and 150
Chapter 3: INTERVENTION	
Article 93(1), first subparagraph	Article 130(1)
Article 93(1), second subparagraph (amended)	Article 130(2)
Article 93(1), third subparagraph	Article 130(3)
Article 93(1), fourth subparagraph	Article 130(4)
Article 93(2), first subparagraph	Article 131(1)
Article 93(2), second subparagraph	Article 131(1)
Article 93(2), third subparagraph (amended)	Article 131(2) and (3)
Article 93(3)	Article 131(4)
Article 93(4)	Article 129(3)
Article 93(5), first subparagraph (amended)	Article 132(1)
Article 93(5), second subparagraph (amended)	Article 132(2)
Article 93(6)	Article 132(3)
Article 93(7)	Article 129(4)
Chapter 4: JUDGMENTS BY DEFAULT AND APPLICATIONS TO SET THEM ASIDE	
Article 94(1), first subparagraph	Article 152(1)
Article 94(1), second subparagraph	Article 152(2)
Article 94(2) (amended)	Article 152(3)
Article 94(3)	Article 152(4)
Article 94(4), first subparagraph	Article 156(1)
Article 94(4), second subparagraph	Article 156(2)
Article 94(5), first subparagraph	Article 156(3)
Article 94(5), second subparagraph	Article 156(4)
Article 94(6), first subparagraph	Article 156(5)
Article 94(6), second subparagraph	Article 156(6)
Chapter 5	
Article 95 (repealed)	
Article 96 (repealed)	
Chapter 6: EXCEPTIONAL REVIEW PROCEDURES	
Section 1 – Third-party proceedings	
Article 97(1), first subparagraph	Article 157(1)
Article 97(1), second subparagraph	Article 157(2)
Article 97(1), third subparagraph (amended)	Article 157(3)

Rules of Procedure of 19 June 1991	Rules of Procedure of 25 September 2012
Article 97(2)	Article 157(4)
Article 97(3), first subparagraph	Article 157(5)
Article 97(3), second subparagraph	Article 157(6)
Section 2 – Revision	
Article 98 (amended)	Article 159(2)
Article 99(1)	Article 159(3)
Article 99(2)	Article 159(4)
Article 100(1) (amended)	Article 159(5)
Article 100(2)	Article 159(6)
Article 100(3)	Article 159(7)
Chapter 7: APPEALS AGAINST DECISIONS OF THE ARBITRATION COMMITTEE	
Article 101(1) (amended)	Article 201(1)
Article 101(2), first subparagraph (amended)	Article 201(2)
Article 101(2), second subparagraph	Article 201(3)
Article 101(3)	Article 201(4)
Article 101(4) (amended)	Article 201(5)
Article 101(5)	Article 201(6)
Chapter 8: INTERPRETATION OF JUDGMENTS	
Article 102(1), first subparagraph	Article 158(3)
Article 102(1), second subparagraph	Article 158(4)
Article 102(2), first subparagraph (amended)	Article 158(5)
Article 102(2), second subparagraph	Article 158(6)
Chapter 9: PRELIMINARY RULINGS AND OTHER REFERENCES FOR INTERPRETATION	
Article 103(1) (amended)	Article 93(a)
Article 103(2), first subparagraph (amended)	Article 93(b)
Article 103(2), second subparagraph (amended)	Article 93(b)
Article 104(1), first subparagraph	Article 98(1)
Article 104(1), second subparagraph	Article 98(2)
Article 104(1), third subparagraph	Article 98(3)
Article 104(2) (amended)	Article 97(3)
Article 104(3), first subparagraph	Article 99
Article 104(3), second subparagraph (amended)	Article 99
Article 104(4) (amended)	Article 76
Article 104(5) (amended)	Article 101
Article 104(6), first subparagraph	Article 102
Article 104(6), second subparagraph (amended)	Articles 115 to 118
Article 104a, first paragraph (amended)	Article 105(1)
Article 104a, second paragraph	Article 105(2)
Article 104a, third paragraph	Article 105(3)
Article 104a, fourth paragraph	Article 105(4)
Article 104a, fifth paragraph	Article 105(5)
Article 104b(1), first subparagraph	Article 107(1)
Article 104b(1), second subparagraph	Article 107(2)
Article 104b(1), third subparagraph	Article 107(3)
Article 104b(1), fourth subparagraph	Article 108(1)
Article 104b(2), first subparagraph	Article 109(1)

Rules of Procedure of 19 June 1991	Rules of Procedure of 25 September 2012
Article 104b(2), second subparagraph	Article 109(2)
Article 104b(2), third subparagraph	Article 109(4)
Article 104b(2), fourth subparagraph	Article 109(5)
Article 104b(2), fifth subparagraph	Article 109(6)
Article 104b(3), first subparagraph	Article 110(1)
Article 104b(3), second subparagraph	Article 110(2)
Article 104b(3), third subparagraph	Article 110(3)
Article 104b(4)	Article 111
Article 104b(5), first subparagraph	Article 112
Article 104b(5), second subparagraph	Article 113(1)
Article 104b(5), third subparagraph	Article 113(2)
Article 104b(6), first subparagraph (amended)	Articles 106(1) and 114
Article 104b(6), second subparagraph	Articles 106(2) and 114
Chapter 10: SPECIAL PROCEDURES UNDER ARTICLES 103 TEAEC TO 105 TEAEC	
Article 105(1)	Article 202(1) and (2)
Article 105(2), first subparagraph	Article 202(1)
Article 105(2), second subparagraph	Article 202(2)
Article 105(2), third subparagraph	Article 202(3)
Article 105(3)	See Articles 15(1) and 16(1)
Article 105(4), first subparagraph (amended)	Article 202(3)
Article 105(4), second subparagraph	Article 202(3)
Article 106(1)	Article 203
Article 106(2)	Article 203
Chapter 11: OPINIONS	
Article 107(1), first subparagraph (amended)	Article 196(1) and (3)
Article 107(1), second subparagraph	Article 196(3)
Article 107(2)	Article 196(2)
Article 108(1) (amended)	Article 197
Article 108(2) (amended)	Article 199
Article 108(3) (amended)	Article 200
Article 109 (repealed)	
Chapter 12: REQUESTS FOR INTERPRETATION UNDER ARTICLE 68 OF THE EC TREATY	
Article 109a (repealed)	
Chapter 13: SETTLEMENT OF THE DISPUTES REFERRED TO IN ARTICLE 35 OF THE UNION TREATY IN THE VERSION IN FORCE BEFORE THE ENTRY INTO FORCE OF THE TREATY OF LISBON	
Article 109b(1), first subparagraph	Article 205(1)
Article 109b(1), second subparagraph	Article 205(2)
Article 109b(1), third subparagraph	Article 205(3)
Article 109b(2)	Article 205(4)
Article 109b(3), first subparagraph	Article 205(6)
Article 109b(3), second subparagraph (amended)	Article 205(5)
Article 109b(4)	Article 205(7)
TITLE IV – APPEALS AGAINST DECISIONS OF THE GENERAL COURT	
Article 110	Article 37(2)(a)
Article 111(1)	Article 167(1)

Rules of Procedure of 19 June 1991	Rules of Procedure of 25 September 2012
Article 111(2)	Article 167(2)
Article 112(1), first subparagraph (amended)	Article 168(1)
Article 112(1), second subparagraph	Article 168(2)
Article 112(2) (amended)	Article 168(3)
Article 112(3) (amended)	Article 168(4)
Article 113(1) (amended)	Articles 169(1) and 170(1)
Article 113(2)	Article 170(1)
Article 114 (amended)	Article 171
Article 115(1) (amended)	Article 172
Article 115(2), first subparagraph	Article 173(1)
Article 115(2), second subparagraph	Article 173(2)
Article 116(1) (amended)	Articles 174 and 178(1)
Article 116(2)	Repealed
Article 117(1) (amended)	Article 175
Article 117(2) (amended)	Articles 179 and 180
Article 118	Articles 184(1) and 190(1)
Article 119	Article 181
Article 120 (amended)	Article 76
Article 121	See Article 59(1)
Article 122, first paragraph	Article 184(2)
Article 122, second paragraph	Repealed
Article 122, third paragraph (amended)	Article 184(1)
Article 122, fourth paragraph	Article 184(3)
Article 123	Article 190(2)
TITLE IV A – REVIEW OF DECISIONS OF THE GENERAL COURT	
Article 123a	Article 37(2)(b)
Article 123b, first paragraph (amended)	Article 191
Article 123b, second paragraph (amended)	Articles 193(3) and 194(4)
Article 123c (amended)	Article 192
Article 123d, first paragraph (amended)	Articles 193(1) and 194(1) and (3)
Article 123d, second paragraph (amended)	Articles 193(3) and 194(4)
Article 123d, third paragraph (amended)	Articles 193(4) and 194(5)
Article 123d, fourth paragraph	Article 193(5)
Article 123d, fifth paragraph (amended)	Article 194(6) and (7)
Article 123e, first paragraph	Article 195(1)
Article 123e, second paragraph	Article 195(2)
Article 123e, third paragraph	Article 195(3)
Article 123e, fourth paragraph	See Article 59
Article 123e, fifth paragraph	Article 195(6)
TITLE V – PROCEDURES PROVIDED FOR BY THE EEA AGREEMENT	
Article 123f(1), first subparagraph	Article 204(1)
Article 123f(1), second subparagraph	Article 204(2)
Article 123f(1), third subparagraph	Article 204(3)
Article 123f(2), first subparagraph	Article 204(4)
Article 123f(2), second subparagraph	Article 204(5)
Article 123f(3)	Article 204(6)
Article 123g	Repealed
MISCELLANEOUS PROVISIONS	
Article 124	Repealed
Article 125	Article 207

Rules of Procedure of 19 June 1991	Rules of Procedure of 25 September 2012
Article 125a (amended)	Article 208
Article 126 (amended)	Article 209
Article 127	Article 210
ANNEX: DECISION ON OFFICIAL HOLIDAYS	Repealed (see Article 24(4) and (6))

ANONYMITY IN JUDICIAL PROCEEDINGS BEFORE THE GENERAL COURT OF THE EUROPEAN UNION

of 30 September 2015

NOTES

This document is available on the General Court section of the Curia website at curia.europa.eu/jcms/upload/docs/application/pdf/2015-11/tra-doc-en-div-c-0000-2015-201508724-05_00.pdf.

[10.834]

Under the Rules of Procedure of the General Court, parties are afforded the possibility of being granted anonymity.

Article 66 of the Rules of Procedure of the General Court provides that, '[o]n a reasoned application by a party, made by a separate document, or of its own motion, the General Court may omit the name of a party to the dispute or of other persons mentioned in connection with the proceedings, or certain information, from those documents relating to a case to which the public has access if there are legitimate reasons for keeping the identity of a person or the information confidential'.

Points 68 to 70 of the Practice Rules for the implementation of the Rules of Procedure of the General Court define the scope of that article as regards anonymity and provide as follows:

'68. Where a party considers that his identity should not be made public in a case brought before the Court, he may request, pursuant to Article 66 of the Rules of Procedure, that the Court "anonymise" the relevant case, in whole or in part.

69. The application for anonymity must be made by a separate document stating appropriate reasons.

70. In order to ensure that anonymity is preserved, it is recommended that the application be made at the outset of the proceedings. On account of the dissemination of information concerning the case on the internet, granting anonymity becomes much more difficult if the notice of the case concerned has already been published in the *Official Journal of the European Union*.'

In view of the development of search engines on the internet and the fact that anyone can now freely access information contained in publications relating to court proceedings, the Registrar of the General Court consistently draws the attention of representatives of parties before the General Court to Article 35(3) and Articles 79 and 122 of the Rules of Procedure of the General Court concerning the publication and the dissemination on the internet of documents relating to cases brought before the General Court, as well as to Article 66 of the aforementioned Rules of Procedure. The party's representative will accordingly be invited to consider whether there are in his case legitimate reasons for keeping a person's identity confidential, and, if so, to make a reasoned application for anonymity, by a separate document.

In order to be effective, any such application must be submitted to the Registry prior to the publication or the dissemination on the internet of the documents concerned.

AIDE-MÉMOIRE – APPLICATION LODGED IN PAPER FORMAT[1]

NOTES

This document is available on the General Court section of the Curia website at curia.europa.eu/jcms/upload/docs/application/pdf/2009-07/en_aide_memoire_requete.pdf.

[1] This aide-mémoire is a practical guide and is not exhaustive. For further information, please refer to the Rules of Procedure of the General Court and the Practice Rules for the Implementation of the Rules of Procedure of the General Court.

[10.835]

General Information

- **Address** for any postal communication or lodging of documents: Registry of the General Court of the European Union, Rue du Fort Niedergrünewald, L-2925 Luxembourg.
- **In the case of prior transmission by fax:** a full copy of the original of the application bearing the handwritten signature of the representative, including the schedule of annexes, may be transmitted to the Registry by fax to fax number (+352) 43 03 21 00. The date on which the application is lodged by fax shall then be deemed to be the date of lodgement for the purposes of compliance with the time-limit for bringing an action only if the original document bearing the handwritten signature of the representative that was transmitted by fax is lodged at the Registry no later than 10 days thereafter.
- **certified copies:** the first page of each set of copies must be endorsed with the words 'certified copy', initialled underneath by the applicant's representative.
- **Requisite number of certified copies:**
  – for all cases, save as set out below, **four** complete sets of the pleading, schedule and annexes referred to in the schedule;
  – for intellectual property cases involving another party to the proceedings before the Board of Appeal: **five** complete sets of the pleading, schedule and annexes referred to in the schedule.

Presentation of the Application

☐ **Medium:** A4 paper on one side of the page only, **not bound, glued or stapled**

☐ **Text:** in a commonly-used font (such as Times New Roman, Courier or Arial) in at least 12 point in the body of the text and at least 10 point in the footnotes, with single line spacing, and upper, lower, left and right margins of at least 2.5 cm

☐ **Page numbering:** the pages of the application must be numbered consecutively

☐ **Paragraph numbering:** paragraphs must be numbered consecutively

☐ **Maximum number of pages: 50** pages for the application in a direct action other than an action brought pursuant to Article 270 TFEU; **30** pages for the application in an action brought pursuant to Article 270 TFEU; **20** pages for the application in an intellectual property case; **15** pages for an appeal

Content of the Application

☐ **Title** of the pleading

☐ **Identity of the applicant:** name(s) and address(es) of the applicant(s)

☐ **Identity of the representative(s):** name – status – address

☐ **Identity of the defendant:**

For direct actions: specify the defendant institution, body, office or agency or, if the action is based on an arbitration clause, the natural or legal person, as the case may be

☐ *For intellectual property cases: specify the defendant **Office** and the name(s) of **any other party** to the proceedings before the Board of Appeal, as well as (1) the address(es) given by them for the purposes of notifications before the Office, and (2) the **date of notification** of the decision of the Board of Appeal*

☐ *For appeals: specify the **other party/parties** to the proceedings before the European Union Civil Service Tribunal and the **date of service** of the decision under appeal (order or judgment)*

☐ **Indication of the method of service chosen:**

- acceptance of service by means of the e-Curia application;
- acceptance of service by fax (stating a single fax number)

Structure of the Application

☐ **Subject-matter of the dispute:** type of action, basis, brief account of the facts and legal context

☐ **Legal arguments** set out and grouped by reference to the pleas in law to which they relate (admissibility and substance) **with a heading for each plea in law put forward**

☐ **Form of order sought:** precise wording thereof (at the beginning or at the end of the application)

☐ **Handwritten signature of the party's representative at the end of the application** (no stamp, photocopy, electronic or scanned signature, signature *per procurationem* or signature in the name of a firm of lawyers). The handwritten signature must not appear on its own on the last page of the application. where more than one representative is acting for the party concerned, the handwritten signature of one representative is sufficient.

Presentation of Annexes

The parties should be rigorous in their selection of relevant documents for the purposes of the proceedings. Case-law of the Courts of the European Union and acts published in the *Official Journal of the European Union* that are cited in the procedural documents should not be produced.

☐ **Schedule of annexes** at the end of the application indicating (i) the number of the annex, (ii) a short description of the annex, (iii) the page numbers of the first and last pages of the annex, according to the consecutive page numbering, and (iv) the page reference and paragraph number where the item is mentioned

☐ **Numbering of annexes:** by reference to the procedural document to which the items are annexed, using a letter and a number. For example, for annexes to the application: Annex A.1, A.2,

Pagination of annexes: in the top right-hand corner of each page, in ascending order and consecutively, but separately from the application

☐ **Annexes in the language of the case** (a translation may be requested if not supplied)

MANDATORY ANNEXES

☐ **Any lawyer representing a party or assisting an agent** must produce a certificate that he is authorised to practise before a court of a Member State or of another State which is a party to the Agreement on the European Economic Area (reference may be made to a document previously lodged at the Registry of the Court)

☐ **If the applicant is a legal person governed by private law, the lawyer must in addition produce:**

- recent proof of the existence in law of that legal person (extract from the register of companies, firms or associations or any other official document)

and

- an authority to act

☐ **Save in the case of an appeal against a decision of the European Union Civil Service Tribunal, the representative must produce one of the following, as appropriate:**

- **the measure the annulment of which is sought** (action for annulment)

or

- **documentary evidence of the date on which the institution was requested to act** (action for failure to act)

or

- **the complaint within the meaning of Article 90(2) of the Staff Regulations** and the **decision responding** to that complaint (action brought pursuant to Article 270 TFEU)

or

- **the contract** containing the arbitration clause establishing the Court's jurisdiction (action brought under an arbitration clause)

SUMMARY OF THE PLEAS IN LAW AND MAIN ARGUMENTS

☐ For all cases, except for intellectual property cases, the representative must lodge a **summary of the pleas in law and main arguments** to facilitate the drafting of the notice in the *Official Journal of the European Union.* That summary must:

- consist of no more than 2 pages;
- be prepared in the language of the case;
- accord with the model available online on the website of the Court of Justice of the European Union under 'General Court/Procedure';
- be produced separately from the body of the application and the annexes mentioned therein;
- be sent by e-mail, as an ordinary electronic file produced using word-processing software, to GC.Registry@curia.europa.eu, indicating the case to which it relates.

AIDE-MÉMOIRE: APPLICATION LODGED BY MEANS OF E-CURIA[1]

NOTES

This document is available on the General Court section of the Curia website at curia.europa.eu/jcms/upload/docs/application/pdf/2012-06/02451_en.pdf.

[1] This aide-mémoire is a practical guide and is not exhaustive. For further information, please refer to the Rules of Procedure of the General Court and the Practice Rules for the Implementation of the Rules of Procedure of the General Court.

[10.836]

GENERAL INFORMATION

- **Address of the e-Curia application:** https://curia.europa.eu/e-Curia
- **Preparation of the application:** the text of the application, including the schedule of annexes, can be saved in PDF format directly from word-processing software, without the need for scanning. It is not necessary for the application to bear a handwritten signature.

- **Preparation of the annexes:** the annexes must be contained in one or more files separate from the file containing the text of the application and the schedule of annexes. A file may contain several annexes. It is not obligatory to create one file per annex. It is recommended that annexes be added in ascending order when they are lodged, and that they be sufficiently clearly named (for example: Annexes A.1 to A.3, Annexes A.4 to A.6, etc.).
- The files being lodged must include names identifying the procedural document (Application, Annexes Part 1, Annexes Part 2, Covering letter, etc.)

PRESENTATION OF THE APPLICATION

☐ **Presentation of pages:** A4 format

☐ **Text:** in a commonly-used font (such as Times New Roman, Courier or Arial) in at least 12 point in the body of the text and at least 10 point in the footnotes, with single line spacing, and upper, lower, left and right margins of at least 2.5 cm

☐ **Page numbering:** the pages of the application must be numbered consecutively

☐ **Paragraph numbering:** paragraphs must be numbered consecutively

☐ **Maximum number of pages: 50** pages for the application in a direct action other than an action brought pursuant to Article 270 TFEU; **30** pages for the application in an action brought pursuant to Article 270 TFEU; **20** pages for the application in an intellectual property case; **15** pages for an appeal

CONTENT OF THE APPLICATION

☐ **Title** of the pleading

☐ **Identity of the applicant:** name(s) and address(es) of the applicant(s)

☐ **Identity of the representative(s):** name – status – address

☐ **Identity of the defendant:**

For direct actions: specify the defendant institution, body, office or agency or, if the action is based on an arbitration clause, the natural or legal person, as the case may be

☐ *For intellectual property cases*: specify the defendant **Office** and the name(s) of **any other party** to the proceedings before the Board of Appeal, as well as (1) the address(es) given by them for the purposes of notifications before the Office, and (2) the **date of notification** of the decision of the Board of Appeal

☐ *For appeals*: specify the **other party/parties** to the proceedings before the European Union Civil Service Tribunal and the **date of service** of the decision under appeal (order or judgment)

☐ **Where appropriate, indication of consent to fax (single fax number)** being used as another method of service in addition to the e-Curia application

STRUCTURE OF THE APPLICATION

☐ **Subject-matter of the dispute:** type of action, basis, brief account of the facts and legal context

☐ **Legal arguments** set out and grouped by reference to the pleas in law to which they relate (admissibility and substance) **with a heading for each plea in law put forward**

☐ **Form of order sought:** precise wording thereof (at the beginning or at the end of the application)

PRESENTATION OF ANNEXES

The parties should be rigorous in their selection of relevant documents for the purposes of the proceedings. Case-law of the Courts of the European Union and acts published in the *Official Journal of the European Union* that are cited in the procedural documents should not be produced.

☐ **Schedule of annexes** at the end of the application indicating (i) the number of the annex, (ii) a short description of the annex, (iii) the page numbers of the first and last pages of the annex, according to the consecutive page numbering, and (iv) the page reference and paragraph number where the item is mentioned

☐ **Numbering of annexes:** by reference to the procedural document to which the items are annexed, using a letter and a number. For example, for annexes to the application: Annex A.1, A.2, …

☐ **Pagination of annexes:** in the top right-hand corner of each page, in ascending order and consecutively, but separately from the application

☐ **Annexes in the language of the case** (a translation may be requested if not supplied)

MANDATORY ANNEXES

☐ **Any lawyer representing a party or assisting an agent** must produce a certificate that he is authorised to practise before a court of a Member State or of another State which is a party to the Agreement on the European Economic Area (reference may be made to a document previously lodged at the Registry of the Court)

☐ **If the applicant is a legal person governed by private law, the lawyer must in addition produce:**

- recent proof of the existence in law of that legal person (extract from the register of companies, firms or associations or any other official document)

and

- an authority to act

Save in the case of an appeal against a decision of the European Union Civil Service Tribunal, the representative must produce one of the following, as appropriate:

- **the measure the annulment of which is sought** (action for annulment)

or

- **documentary evidence of the date on which the institution was requested to act** (action for failure to act)

or

- **the complaint within the meaning of Article 90(2) of the Staff Regulations** and the **decision responding** to that complaint (action brought pursuant to Article 270 TFEU)

or

- **the contract** containing the arbitration clause establishing the Court's jurisdiction (action brought under an arbitration clause)

SUMMARY OF THE PLEAS IN LAW AND MAIN ARGUMENTS

☐ For all cases, except for intellectual property cases, the representative must lodge a **summary of the pleas in law and main arguments** to facilitate the drafting of the notice in the *Official Journal of the European Union*. That summary must:

- consist of no more than 2 pages;
- be prepared in the language of the case;
- accord with the model available online on the website of the Court of Justice of the European Union under 'General Court/Procedure';
- be produced separately from the body of the application and the annexes mentioned therein.

AIDE-MÉMOIRE: HEARING OF ORAL ARGUMENT[1]

NOTES

This document is available on the General Court section of the Curia website at curia.europa.eu/jcms/upload/docs/application/pdf/2009-07/en_aide_memoire_audience_de_plaidoiries.pdf.

[1] This aide-mémoire is a practical guide and is not exhaustive. For further information, please refer to the Rules of Procedure of the General Court and the Practice Rules for the Implementation of the Rules of Procedure of the General Court.

[10.837]

Before the hearing

- **General calendar of hearings before the General Court:** available on the website http://curia.europa.eu under 'Calendar'.
- **Notice to attend the hearing:** without prejudice to special circumstances, the parties will be given notice to attend the hearing by the Registry at least one month before it takes place (please take note of the time of the hearing).
- **Dispatch of the summary report for the hearing:** the Court will make every effort to ensure that the parties' representatives receive a summary report for the hearing three weeks before the hearing.
- **Participation in the hearing:** any party who will not be present at the hearing must inform the Court. It is also necessary to **warn** the Registry of any possible **delay** or difficulty concerning the attendance of a party's representative or of other persons summoned to the hearing (telephone: (+352) 43 03 1; fax: (+352) 43 03 21 00; e-mail: GC.Registry@curia.europa.eu). Please ensure that the Registry has **appropriate telephone numbers** to enable it to contact the parties' representatives. If a representative does not arrive on time for a hearing, it will proceed in his absence.
- **Interpretation:** in order to facilitate interpretation, parties' representatives are requested to send any text or written notes for their submissions to the Interpretation Directorate of the Court of Justice of the European Union in advance by e-mail (interpret@curia.europa.eu). Notes for submissions will not be forwarded to the Judges or placed on the case-file.
- **Request for the use of technical facilities:** any request to use technical facilities for the purposes of a presentation must be made as soon as possible and at least two weeks before the date of the hearing.
- **Location of the hearing:** depending on the case, hearings are held in the courtrooms of the 'C', Erasmus or Thomas More buildings (entrance in Rue du Fort Niedergrünewald or Boulevard Konrad Adenauer, L-2925 Luxembourg). The courtroom will be confirmed to parties' representatives on arrival by the reception staff of the Court of Justice of the European Union.
- **Map of Court buildings:** available on the website http://curia.europa.eu under 'The Institution/Visiting the Court/Access map'.

• **Parking:** for security reasons, parties' representatives and anyone accompanying them may not park in the car parks of the Court and must therefore use external parking facilities.
• **Entry into Court buildings: an identity document** must be presented to security staff. In view of the security measures in place to control access to the buildings of the Court of Justice of the European Union, it is recommended that the parties' representatives take the necessary steps to ensure that they are present in the courtroom in good time.

Your arrival in the courtroom
• **At least 15 minutes** before the hearing is due to start.
• **Contact the court usher** so that he may:
– record attendance;
– be informed of any change of or additional representative and as to the representative(s) who will be making oral submissions;
– be informed, if applicable, of the attendance of persons accompanying the representative(s).
• **The Judges** meet the parties' representatives, wearing court dress, 5 to 10 minutes before the hearing begins (follow the court usher's directions).

Conduct of the hearing
• The parties' representatives are required to **present oral argument in court dress, standing behind the lectern provided for that purpose**. Each representative must bring his own gown.
• The parties are seated as follows, seen from the audience:
– table on the right: applicant's representative(s);
– table on the left: defendant's representative(s);
– the representative(s) of the intervener(s) will generally be seated behind the representative of the party in whose support the intervention is made (depending on the courtroom).
• Speakers standing behind the lectern must always use the **microphone**; it can be switched on and off using the button at the base of the microphone. For the purpose of providing simultaneous interpretation, speakers are advised to **speak slowly**.
• The use of electronic recording equipment is prohibited.
• **Mobile telephones**: mobile telephones must be switched off ('silent' mode does not prevent interference with the systems used for the purpose of providing interpretation)
• **Order of events** (save in special cases):
√ the President opens the hearing;
√ if appropriate, delivery of judgments in other cases;
√ the case in question is called by the Registrar;
√ opening argument of the applicant's representative(s);
√ if appropriate, opening argument of the representative(s) of the intervener(s) in support of the applicant;
√ opening argument of the defendant's representative(s);
√ if appropriate, opening argument of the representative(s) of the intervener(s) in support of the defendant;
√ if appropriate, replies to the Judges' questions;
√ closing submissions of the applicant's representative(s);
√ closing submissions of the representative(s) of the intervener(s) in support of the applicant;
√ closing submissions of the defendant's representative(s);
√ closing submissions of the representative(s) of the intervener(s) in support of the defendant;
√ the President closes the hearing.
• **Time allowed for oral argument:** do not exceed the time allowed for opening argument as indicated in the letter of notice to attend the hearing. In principle, in cases other than intellectual property cases, each main party will be allowed 15 minutes and each intervener will be allowed 10 minutes to present oral submissions. In intellectual property cases, each party will be allowed 15 minutes, except for interveners admitted under Article 144 of the Rules of Procedure.
• **Lodging of documents:** if, exceptionally, a main party proposes to produce evidence at the hearing, he should ideally bring sufficient photocopies for the Judges sitting in the case, the Registry, the other parties, the interpreters and the Judge-Rapporteur's legal secretary.
• **Interpretation:** the lectern from behind which the representatives speak is equipped with a simultaneous interpretation system.
• **Sound recording:** the oral proceedings are recorded on audiotape.

LEGAL AID FORM: GENERAL COURT

NOTES

Date of publication in Official Journal: OJ L152, 18.6.2015, p 31.

LEGAL AID FORM: GENERAL COURT

[10.838]

1)

Legal context

The provisions concerning legal aid are contained in the Rules of Procedure of the General Court (Articles 146 to 150) and in the Practice Rules for the Implementation of the Rules of Procedure of the General Court (points 16 to 18, 31, 48, 54, 133, 134 and 238 to 248).

The Rules of Procedure of the General Court and the Practice Rules for the Implementation of the Rules of Procedure of the General Court are available on the website of the Court of Justice of the European Union (http://curia.europa.eu) under 'General Court'/'Procedure'.

2)

Rules of representation before the General Court

In order to bring an action before the General Court, any natural or legal person must be represented by a lawyer authorised to practise before a court of a Member State or of another State which is a party to the Agreement on the European Economic Area (Article 51 of the Rules of Procedure). This rule lays down the principle of the mandatory representation of an applicant by a lawyer.

If, because of his financial situation, that person is wholly or partly unable to meet the costs of the proceedings, the Rules of Procedure provide that he is to be entitled to legal aid (Article 146(1) of the Rules of Procedure). Unlike an action, which must be lodged by a lawyer representing the applicant, an application for legal aid may be submitted with or without the assistance of a lawyer.

3)

Jurisdiction of the General Court and admissibility criteria

Legal aid cannot be granted by the General Court if the Court has no jurisdiction to hear and determine the action in respect of which the application for legal aid is made (Article 146(2) of the Rules of Procedure).

Under the Treaties and the Protocol on the Statute of the Court of Justice of the European Union, the General Court has jurisdiction in:

- direct actions brought by individuals and by Member States[1] seeking annulment of acts of the institutions, bodies, offices and agencies of the Union, a declaration that those institutions, bodies, offices or agencies have unlawfully failed to act or compensation for damage sustained, and actions based on arbitration clauses,
- actions for annulment of decisions taken by the Boards of Appeal of the Office for Harmonisation in the Internal Market (Trade Marks and Designs) (OHIM) and of the Community Plant Variety Office (CPVO),
- appeals brought against decisions of the European Union Civil Service Tribunal.

Thus, an application for legal aid will be refused on the grounds of the General Court's lack of jurisdiction in the action if that action is brought for the purpose of:

- contesting the lawfulness of an act adopted by national authorities (whether administrative or judicial),
- contesting a decision taken by an international body which is not within the institutional system of the European Union (for example, the European Court of Human Rights).

Nor can legal aid be granted if the action in respect of which the application for legal aid is made appears to be manifestly inadmissible or manifestly lacking any foundation in law (Article 146(2) of the Rules of Procedure).

Thus, an application for legal aid made before the action to which it relates is brought, but after the time limit for bringing that action has expired, will be refused, since the action would be dismissed as inadmissible on the ground of delay.

NOTES

[1] With the exception of those reserved to the Court of Justice by the Statute and of those falling within the jurisdiction of the European Union Civil Service Tribunal.

4)

Mandatory legal aid form

The legal aid form, published in the *Official Journal of the European Union*, is available on the website of the Court of Justice of the European Union under 'General Court'/'Procedure'.

The use of that form is mandatory when applying for legal aid, both before an action is brought and while a case is ongoing. An application for legal aid submitted without the application form will not be taken into consideration (Article 147 of the Rules of Procedure and point 238 of the Practice Rules for the Implementation of the Rules of Procedure of the General Court).
An application for legal aid made after the General Court has delivered its decision ruling on the action in respect of which that application is made will not be taken into consideration.

5)
Content of the application for legal aid and supporting documents
The legal aid form is intended to provide the General Court, in accordance with Article 147(3) and (4) of the Rules of Procedure, with the information required to give an effective decision on the application for legal aid. The information required concerns:

— the legal aid applicant's financial situation, and
— where the action has not yet been brought, the subject-matter of that action, the facts of the case and the arguments relating thereto (point 241 of the Practice Rules for the Implementation of the Rules of Procedure of the General Court).

a) Financial situation of the applicant

The application for legal aid must be accompanied by all information and supporting documents making it possible to assess the applicant's financial situation, such as a certificate issued by a competent national authority attesting to his financial situation (Article 147(3) of the Rules of Procedure).
The applicant's financial capacity is assessed on the basis of evidence proving his lack of means:

— a natural person cannot therefore confine himself to providing the Court with information relating to his income but must also produce, for example, tax returns, proof of salary, certificates issued by social security or unemployment benefit authorities, bank statements and information making it possible to assess his capital (value of movable or immovable property),
— a legal person cannot simply rely on its inability to pay but must provide information concerning the legal form of the entity, whether it is for-profit or not-for-profit, the financial capacity of its partner(s) or shareholders, and produce, for example, financial statements or any other document evidencing its accounts, and any evidence supporting a claim that it is insolvent, in receivership or administration, unable to meet its financial obligations or in liquidation.

Sworn statements made and signed by the applicant himself are not sufficient proof of lack of means.
The information given on the form concerning the applicant's financial situation and the documents lodged in support of the information provided should give a complete picture of the applicant's financial situation.
Applications which do not establish to the requisite legal standard the applicant's inability to meet the costs of the proceedings will be rejected.

b) Subject-matter of the proposed action

If the application for legal aid is lodged before the action to which it relates has been brought, the applicant must briefly state the subject-matter of that action, the facts of the case and the arguments he proposes to put forward in support of the action. A section for that purpose is included in the legal aid form.
A copy of any supporting document that is relevant for the purposes of assessing whether the proposed action is admissible and well founded must be attached — for example, correspondence with the prospective defendant or, in the case of an action for annulment, the decision which is to be contested as to its lawfulness.
The duly completed legal aid form and supporting documents must be intelligible in themselves.

c) Supplementary material

The application for legal aid may not be supplemented by the subsequent filing of additional material. Such material will be rejected, unless it has been lodged at the request of the Court. It is essential, therefore, to include all the necessary information on the form and to attach copies of any documentary proof of the information provided.
In exceptional cases, however, supporting documents intended to establish the applicant's lack of means may be accepted subsequently, subject to the delay in their production being adequately explained (point 246 of the Practice Rules for the Implementation of the Rules of Procedure of the General Court).

6)
Lodging of the application

a) By the applicant himself

An applicant for legal aid who is not represented by a lawyer must send to or lodge at the Registry of the General Court the duly completed and signed paper version of the form, together with any supporting documents referred to. The Registry's address is as follows:

Registry of the General Court of the European Union

Rue du Fort Niedergrünewald

L-2925 Luxembourg

The dispatch or the delivery by hand of the paper version of the duly completed and signed form may be preceded by the transmission of that document by fax to fax number +352 43032100.

Where the duly completed and signed form is sent by fax:

— it will not be processed until the original is received at the Registry,

— the date of lodgement by fax will be deemed to be the date of lodgement of the form, provided that the original, bearing a handwritten signature, that was transmitted by fax reaches the Registry no later than 10 days after such transmission; if that original is not lodged within that period of 10 days, the date of lodgement will be the date on which the original is actually received by the Registry,

— it must be sent without delay, immediately after its dispatch by fax, without any corrections or amendments, even of a minor nature, being made thereto,

— in the event of any discrepancy between the original form bearing the handwritten signature and the copy previously received at the Registry by fax, the date of lodgement will be the date on which the original signed form is lodged.

b) By the applicant's lawyer

Where the applicant for legal aid is represented by a lawyer when the legal aid form is lodged, the lawyer may lodge the form at the Court Registry either in a paper version, which may have previously been sent by fax, or by means of the e-Curia application, in compliance with the requirements contained in the Conditions of use of the e-Curia application (point 240 of the Practice Rules for the Implementation of the Rules of Procedure of the General Court).

Where the duly completed and signed form is transmitted by fax, the information set out at point a) above is applicable.

c) Signing of the form

Without prejudice to the lodging of the form by a lawyer by means of the e-Curia application, the form must be signed by hand by the applicant if lodged by the applicant himself, or, if the applicant is represented, by his lawyer. Forms not bearing a handwritten signature will not be processed.

7)
Suspension and resumption of the time limit for bringing an action

The introduction of an application for legal aid suspends, for the person who made it, the time limit prescribed for the bringing of the action until the date of service of the order making a decision on that application or, where no lawyer is designated in that order to represent the applicant for legal aid, until the date of service of the order designating the lawyer instructed to represent the applicant (Article 147(7) of the Rules of Procedure).

The time limit for bringing an action does not run, therefore, while the application for legal aid is being examined by the Court.

After the order making a decision on the application for legal aid has been served or, if that order did not designate a lawyer to represent the applicant for legal aid, after the order designating the lawyer instructed to represent that applicant has been served, the remaining period within which the application initiating proceedings may be lodged may be very short. Recipients of legal aid who are duly represented by a lawyer are therefore advised to pay particular attention to compliance with the legal time limit (point 248 of the Practice Rules for the Implementation of the Rules of Procedure of the General Court).

8)
Additional information

Any originals of supporting documents lodged will not be returned. It is therefore advisable to submit photocopies of supporting documents.

Index

A

B

N

W